FOR REFERENCE
Do Not Take From This Room

W9-APY-323

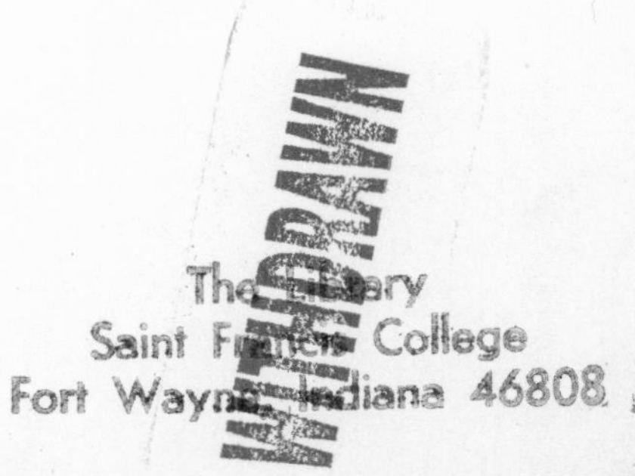

THE HARVARD CONCORDANCE TO SHAKESPEARE

Ref
PR 2892
S62

THE HARVARD CONCORDANCE TO SHAKESPEARE

by Marvin Spevack

BELKNAP PRESS OF HARVARD UNIVERSITY PRESS CAMBRIDGE, MASSACHUSETTS

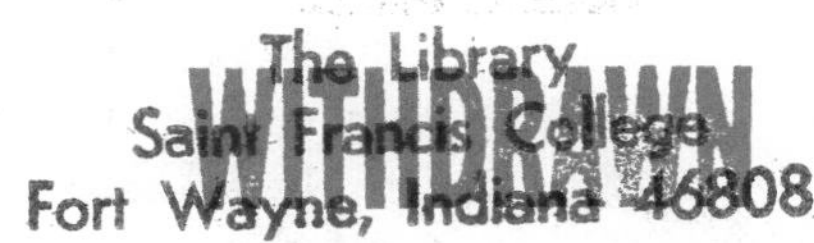
The Library
Saint Francis College
Fort Wayne, Indiana 46808
WITHDRAWN
76-542

© Copyright 1969, 1970 by Georg Olms, Hildesheim / © Copyright 1973 by Marvin Spevack / All rights reserved / Library of Congress Catalog Card Number 73-76385 / ISBN 0-674-37475-4 / Printed in the United States of America / Second Printing, 1974

Preface

The Harvard Concordance to Shakespeare is the first complete and reliable one-volume concordance to all the plays and poems of Shakespeare. Based on the most advanced Shakespeare scholarship and produced by means of computer technology, this concordance is able not only to fulfill the general requirements of thoroughness and accuracy but also to present supplementary information and special features, not normally available in concordances, which reflect the findings of modern research and attempt to meet the needs of those interested in Shakespeare and in the English language.

The concordance lists alphabetically all words exactly as they appear in Shakespeare. None are subsumed: inflected forms, contractions, and the like are given separately. Each different word (or linguistic type)—a word is defined as a graphic unit—is followed by a line of statistical information: its absolute frequency (FR), its relative frequency (REL FR), the number of occurrences in verse passages (V), and the number of occurrences in prose (P). There follows, for all but forty-three words, a specially determined context for each occurrence of a word, along with its location in Shakespeare. The letter P following the act-scene-line reference indicates a prose context; the simple reference, a verse context.

In order to fit the entire vocabulary into one volume it has been necessary to compress the entries for forty-three of the total of 29,066 different words. These relatively few words are listed with full statistical information but without context. The decision as to which entries were to be compressed was not simple, for it is well nigh impossible, linguistically or otherwise, to arrive at a satisfactory distinction between "significant" and "insignificant" words, especially when the variegated interests of *all* the users of a reference work of this kind are considered. The soundest principle—the clearest and most objective—seemed the quantitative. Accordingly—this is the only substantive difference between this one-volume concordance and volumes IV–VI of my *Complete and Systematic Concordance to the Works of Shakespeare* (Georg Olms, Hildesheim, 1968–1970)—contexts have been omitted for the first forty-three words in order of frequency in Shakespeare: *the, and, I, to, of, a, you, my, that, in, is, not, me, for, it, with, be, his, this, your, he, but, have, as, thou, so, him, will, what, her, thy, no, all, by, do, shall, if, are, we, thee, our, on, now.* Stage directions and indications of speakers, as well as significant variants, will be treated in supplementary volumes.

The concordance utilizes the modern-spelling text of *The Riverside Shakespeare*, published by Houghton Mifflin Company in 1974. This text, edited by Gwynne Blakemore Evans, is based on a fresh collation of the early substantive editions of Shakespeare and a consultation of all the major edited texts of the last three centuries; making full use of the important investigations of twentieth-century textual criticism, it exemplifies the latest thinking on what may be called the "true text" of Shakespeare. The concordance has benefited from the extensive textual apparatus and other traits of the edition (described by Professor Evans in his introduction). In addition, the cooperation between textual editor and concordance maker during the production of both works has made possible an unusual degree of precision and consistency in each. A few changes made too late for inclusion are noted on the last page of this volume.

Although the references are keyed to the *Riverside* edition, the concordance may be used with other editions which also employ the traditional act-scene divisions. Slight differences in line-numbering may occur in prose passages, where the lineation is often dependent upon the width of the column or page in a particular edition.

Special Features

In order to broaden the scope and sharpen the focus of this work, special features not usually found in concordances are included.

Prose-Verse Distinctions. For the first time a distinction has been made, for each occurrence of each word, between prose and verse contexts. The identification of a context as prose or verse stems from the edition used, which conveniently gives changes from the copy-texts in the textual notes. In the case of short lines, a consultation of previous editions, metrical studies, and where necessary an attempt, admittedly intuitive, to grasp the logic of a given context governed the decision.

Statistics. The total and relative frequency of every word in Shakespeare, as well as its total frequency in verse and in prose contexts, has been provided. (In the relative frequencies, 1 percent appears as 1.0000.) Although these counts are based on the edition used, they nevertheless offer a more detailed statistical description of Shakespeare's vocabulary than any hitherto available.

The following totals may be of interest: in the complete works, there are 884,647 words, of which 680,755 occur in verse passages, 203,892 in prose; the number of lines is 118,406, of which 91,464 are verse (both less 5,572 split lines), 26,942 prose. The plays contain 31,959 speeches, 21,726 in verse, 10,062 in prose, 171 in verse and prose.

Departures from the Basic Copy-Texts. In the edition used, emendations and additions to the declared copy-texts are placed in square brackets, with the original readings and the source for the new ones recorded in the textual notes. They are marked in the concordance as they are in the text, with a slash replacing the square brackets, to direct the reader to the textual notes for editorial clarification.

Homographs. To add further precision and detail, the homographs in Shakespeare are indicated for the first time. They have been selected and marked with an asterisk to alert the reader to their presence and to the list of more than seven hundred examples in Shakespeare that appears in Appendix II.

Defining and identifying homographs are not easy matters, given the limitations of current lexicographical works and the lack of agreement on schemata, not to mention the differences in interpretation. In order to keep the lid on what could be a Pandora's box, strong emphasis has been placed on differences of etymology, with separate catchwords in *The Oxford English Dictionary* as a requisite. The semantic shadings of the same word, however, or its appearance as different parts of speech have not been included. Similarly, the forms of a word which may otherwise constitute a homograph but which do not actually occur in Shakespeare are not marked, nor is the obvious distinction between *'s* (and at times *s'*) in the possessive and the contraction. Malapropisms, puns, and very disputed readings of particular words are as a rule excluded. When practicality seemed more important than pedantry, exceptions have been made for a very small number of words —like *affection* meaning *affectation*, *ought* meaning *owed* —but only when they are given separate catchwords in *The Oxford English Dictionary* and offer a rather common Shakespearean usage now generally obsolete, and also for a relatively small group of words—like *corporal*, *palm*, *season*—whose forms, though etymologically related, are widely differentiated in Shakespeare. Furthermore, three groups of homographs (in addition to all inflected forms) not to be found in *The Oxford English Dictionary* are included when they are different in meaning and origin: dialect forms, proper nouns, and foreign words.

Cross-References. The text upon which this concordance is based, although fundamentally in modern spelling, has retained, in its strict adherence to the declared copy-texts and its sensitivity to the range and variety of Shakespeare's vocabulary, a number of distinctive Elizabethan forms (especially in proper nouns, such as *Birnan*, *Callice*, *Roan*), as well as typical variant spellings (like *ambassador-embassador*, *jealous-jealious*, *precedent-president*). Since these special and variant forms are interesting for a number of obvious reasons, not the least of which is a grasp of the whole vocabulary, an attempt has been made to make them easily accessible by means of cross-references. It must be underlined that the 1745 select insertions were assembled with no help from the computer. As was the case with the homographs and the prose-verse distinctions, they are "handmade"—the result of a long process of examining and evaluating each word in the complete canon as well as consulting the relevant reference and other works. Since the process of selection is complex, they are included, like the homographs and prose-verse distinctions, not so much with a pretension to absolute authority as, in alerting the user to the phenomenon, with the hope they may prove useful. They also serve to guide the reader to words that may be spelled differently in another edition.

In order to assure both an uncluttered and linguistically sound presentation, certain guidelines were employed. For one thing, included are only forms which do not appear in the normal or expected (that is, modern) alphabetical order: there is no singling out of a word like *jaundies*, for example, because it comes exactly where *jaundice* would, were it in the text. Further, variants which appear one after another—like *random* and *randon*—are in general not cross-referenced since they are easily seen. In fact, in order to keep the whole network from getting too intricate and thus needlessly complicating the entries, cross-references are not given for all the inflected forms of a word since they tend to be listed in an alphabetical cluster anyway: for example, there are no cross-references for such obvious forms as *learn'd*, *learned*, *learnt*. And, in much the same vein, there are no cross-references to words which are spelled differently because of the predictable presence or absence of the vowel *e* before *n* (as in *fallen-fall'n*), before *r* (as in *flower-flow'r*), and in the endings *'d*, *'st*, *'dst* (as in *believed-believ'd*, *followest-follow'st*, *lovedst-lov'dst*). Exceptions are made, of course, for cases which may not be easily anticipated, especially when they are not in each other's immediate vicinity.

On the whole, the determination of what constitutes a variant is based most heavily on *The Oxford English Dictionary*: cross-references are given, as a rule, for forms which appear therein as catchwords or which, in some instances, may not appear at all, as well as for words which are labelled in such a variety of ways as "obsolete," "archaic," "variant," "formerly spelt," "now vulgar," or the like, and for those for which the variant form is followed by an equal sign and then the more customary spelling but with no extended definition. Also included are words labelled aphetic, as well as two categories not normally listed in *The Oxford English Dictionary*: proper names and the vocabulary of those figures who are characterized by their peculiar dialect (like Evans in *The Merry Wives of Windsor* or Fluellen in *Henry V*; Pistol, incidentally, is not included, his vocabulary being too often a matter of conjecture). *Not* cross-referenced because they are linguistically too problematic or unclear are contractions of two words into one (*and't* or *h'as*) or the reverse situation (*by'r* to *by* and *our*); nor, on the whole, are words which are considered perversions, corruptions, blunders, malapropisms, and the like; foreign words; puns; and, naturally, disputed readings or editorial conjectures.

As far as the mechanics are concerned, there are basically two kinds of entries. The first, which uses the word *see*, points to a special form, often a proper name, which has not been modernized in the text: thus, WRECK (*see wrack*). The second, and more prevalent, uses *also*, and refers to alternate spellings: thus PEERING (*also piring*), and later PIRING (*also peering*). In some cases, there may even be more than two spellings, in which case the entry will read, for example, ALEVEN (*also eleven*, *'leven*)—with the appropriate adjustment when the indexed word is changed—or, in the event that more than one inflection of a word within an alphabetical cluster is affected, the cross-reference will read HECKFER (*also heifer*, *etc.*). Entries containing homographs (marked with an asterisk) must, naturally, be read with some care since it may be that only one of the meanings is involved in the cross-reference. Finally, to keep from inventing forms which do not actually occur in Shakespeare, cross-references are given only for the forms which exist: in one instance, the entry is SHEAL'D (*also shell*)—that is, the parallel *shell'd* is not manufactured.

Appendices

Appendix I: Hyphenated Words. In order to make available all the elements of hyphenated words (hyphens often the work of the editor of Shakespeare), three lists are given, in each of which a different element is isolated. In HYPHENATED WORDS 1, the words are alphabetized according to the first element; in HYPHENATED WORDS 2, according to the second element; in HYPHENATED WORDS 3, according to the third element (the number of words with more than three elements is so small they can be easily identified in this list).

Appendix II: Homographs. The complete list of the words marked with asterisks in the concordance is not intended to be a glossary but rather provides briefly only the most essential semantic or grammatical distinctions, to be used along with the contexts and relevant reference works.

Appendix III: A Conversion Table to Through Line Numbering. For the convenience of those working with the Through Line Numbering system, a table giving corresponding act-scene-line references, for every twenty lines and beginning anew at the head of every act and scene, has been provided.

The Context

The context for each word was determined by the computer. The task was not without problems. These, of course, are to be expected when one is dealing with almost a million words in a myriad of configurations and is confronted with the drastic fact, albeit not widely enough appreciated, that the computer is first of all a machine, a precariously balanced mechanical system: the more it has to perform, even of the same function, the greater the likelihood of errors resulting not merely from human failings but also from mechanical failures leading to errors, often in the smallest details, which are not easily detectable, if at all. This may be why most works of this kind choose perhaps the simplest, least complicated of methods: they present as context the typographical line (often the contents of one punch-card) in which the indexed word or lemma appears. In most instances, this method will do. In Shakespeare, however, it will hardly suffice because of the frequency of enjambment, of sentence breaks within the typographical line, and especially of prose (which accounts for almost one-third of all Shakespeare). Thus, for example, in the lines

> Nay, 'twill be this hour ere I have done
> weeping; all the kind of the Launces have this very
> fault (TGV 2.3.1—3)

the context for *weeping* would be identical with the second line itself—and obviously of limited use. Be that as it may, it was decided to attempt, for the first time in a work of this nature and size, a more meaningful mechanically determined context—that is, one based on at least an acknowledgment of the syntactical integrity of the lemma and the words surrounding it, and so aiming at the ideal of contexts worked out individually for each word. What this meant was the achieving of some sort of reasonable and viable equilibrium of three main pressures: the fact that it is impossible to anticipate all the forms and situations likely to appear in an edited text which is in general lightly pointed, or to be certain that the limited samples (with which perforce the attempt was made) are indeed representative, since the whole of Shakespeare has not heretofore been approached this way; the fact that no context, however long, can ever replace the text itself; and the fact that space was not, perhaps should not be, unlimited. In short, this meant programming a flexible and useful context for each unit of a vast and unwieldy body of material, using at a maximum the but forty-eight spaces (including those for blanks and punctuation) which the format allowed. A brief, simplified description of the process may be in order not merely for itself alone but also for such other information as an understanding of it may make accessible. The main principles of this program were contributed by Dr. Jürgen Schäfer expressly for this concordance.

The system is essentially one based on a hierarchy of punctuation marks and, to a certain extent, patterns of versification. In the beginning, with the speech as the absolute limit of a context (speeches of fewer than forty-eight spaces are given in their entirety), the lemma was placed in the middle of the available forty-eight spaces. The computer first read left and then right, allotting roughly equal space to both sides (but taking into account complete words only). For example, if *n* is the number of spaces for the lemma, *n1* the number for the movement left, and *n2* the number for the movement right, the process would look like this for the word *weeping* (from the lines quoted above):

. . . this hour ere I have done weeping; all the kind of the. . .

|—n1 $\left(=\frac{48-n}{2}\right)$ —|n (=7)| n2 (= 48 − n1 − n)|

This simple system provides a reasonable context for a large percentage of the words and is certainly an improvement, most notably in prose passages, over giving merely a typographical line: it has been adopted in those instances in which no punctuation marks exist within the allotted space. The system was refined to take into account punctuation marks (including, later, verse line endings) arranged according to their relative value. After much experimentation with samples of the various Shakespearean and editorial "styles," the punctuation marks were classified as follows: as "full stops"—the period, question mark, exclamation mark, semicolon, colon; as "half stops"—the comma, dash, and parenthesis. Quotation marks were not included. Following the same procedure of reading first left and then right, the computer was instructed to stop as soon as a full stop was reached in one direction and then fill in the remaining blanks in the other direction until another full stop was found or there was no space left. For example, the thus adjusted process for the lemma *kind* (from the lines quoted above) would look like this:

. . . weeping; all the kind of the Launces have this very fault

n1 n n2

If, however, a half stop were encountered first, the computer would stop temporarily, then swing to the other direction, searching for another signal: if (1) it came next upon a full stop, it would stop, reverse direction, and continue until it reached another full stop or the space was exhausted; if (2) it came next upon a half stop, it would stop temporarily, reverse direction, and continue beyond the first encountered half stop until such a point as it found another signal to stop completely or reverse direction again. In the following lines

. . . What's
the matter? Why weep'st thou, man? Away, ass, you'll
lose the tide, if you tarry any longer (TGV 2.3.34–36)

the lemma *man* illustrates the first procedure:

. . . the matter? Why weep'st thou, man ? Away, ass. . .

n3 n1 n n2

The second occurs with the lemma *ass*:

. . . man? Away, ass , you'll lose the tide, if you tarry. . .

n3 n1 n n2 n4

And so forth, in alternating movements, until either there were full stops on both sides of the lemma or the forty-eight spaces were filled.

One last major adjustment was spurred by an analysis of certain patterns of versification in Shakespeare, which showed that quite often the verse line itself operates much like a syntactical unit. Consequently, the verse line ending without punctuation was, at the outset at least, considered a half stop, and the combination of punctuation mark and verse line ending was considered a full stop. Finally, all the elements were judged together and incorporated into a hierarchy of signals which, in descending order, is as follows: (1) full stop; (2) combination of half stop and verse line ending; (3) half stop; (4) verse line ending without punctuation.

This is, in essence, the way a context was mechanically determined for each of the 884,647 words. The system is, admittedly, not able to tailor the contexts down to the very last detail in every single instance. For one thing, certain features of the text itself are by nature difficult to deal with. A text which is very lightly pointed—commas, for example, being used where modern English would require semicolons or periods—tends to yield a larger context than may be necessary (as may also be the case when, in the absence of full stops, the outer limits of a context are automatically filled out, left or right, by words that fit); but, on the other hand, experience has shown that this extra bit is, more often than not, useful. Also, where there is little or no punctuation, shorter words tend to receive more of a context than longer ones; happily, contexts which are not long enough are almost nonexistent since only a thimbleful of words have more than, say, a dozen letters. Further, much consideration was given to the extending of contexts consisting only of the lemma itself (those occurring when the lemma makes up a whole speech or when it is preceded and followed by full stops), but was ultimately discarded as not being practical because relatively few words were involved, not enough contexts were noticeably improved, and a word framed by full stops is a defined and legitimate entity in itself. The system, in short, is not perfect (indeed no context can ever replace the text itself). But all things considered, it seems to work: it does appear to produce clear, coherent, and useful contexts.

And an understanding, however superficial, of the way it was devised may be helpful for the clues it provides to information other than the identification of a word. If, for example, the indexed word appears at the beginning of a line of context, then (except perhaps when there is no following punctuation) it may be assumed on the whole that it begins a speech or clause—a situation which may be of interest to those studying word order or usage. Obviously, other stylistic and linguistic features—contained, ordered, and predictable in a context so determined—are easily scannable and otherwise made available.

Conventions

Type and Symbols. When the corpus of Shakespeare was put into computerized form some years ago, the print-chain had only capital letters. These have been retained in catchwords, play abbreviations, and statistical information. In order to make possible a readable three-column format, contexts have been converted by technical means to lower case. As in the larger work, italics and accent marks are omitted; a vertical stroke inserted in a context separates verse lines. Two symbols are of special importance: the asterisk and the slash. A word followed by an asterisk is a homograph. A slash preceding a word represents square brackets enclosing the word—in *The Riverside Shakespeare* the indication of an editorial alteration of the basic copy-texts. In the case of hyphenated compounds, two slashes indicate that the two (or more) parts are in square brackets in the text. If only one part is in square brackets, then a single slash precedes only that part.

Alphabetical Order. Since certain punctuation marks present problems for a computer, the normal alphabetical order is modified in one small instance. For all practical purposes, the troublesome apostrophe is, as it were, not read: for example, DAR'D precedes DARE. However, if two units have identical letters, but one has an apostrophe, it comes first: for example, MASTERS' precedes MASTERS.

If both such units contain an apostrophe, then the one with the earlier apostrophe comes first: for example, 'A precedes A'. Words with slashes are listed immediately preceding the same words without slashes.

Acknowledgments

My debt and thanks to the institutions, students, colleagues, and friends who helped in the production of the six-volume concordance must be renewed, since the present work is based on the same magnetic tapes. To that list I am pleased to add, with special gratitude, Hermann Kamp and Bernfried Neukäter, who with admirable skill and devotion programmed this work for the IBM 360/50 computer and the Linotron 505 phototypesetting system.

I dedicate this work to my mother and father.

Marvin Spevack

Cambridge, Massachusetts
August 1973

THE HARVARD CONCORDANCE TO SHAKESPEARE

Symbols and Abbreviations

The slash represents square brackets; the asterisk indicates a homograph. In the contexts a vertical line separates verse lines. The letter P after an act-scene-line reference indicates a prose context (the simple reference, a verse context).

The standard abbreviations of Shakespeare's works, in the customary Folio order of citation, have been adopted:

TMP	*The Tempest*
TGV	*The Two Gentlemen of Verona*
WIV	*The Merry Wives of Windsor*
MM	*Measure for Measure*
ERR	*The Comedy of Errors*
ADO	*Much Ado About Nothing*
LLL	*Love's Labor's Lost*
MND	*A Midsummer Night's Dream*
MV	*The Merchant of Venice*
AYL	*As You Like It*
SHR	*The Taming of the Shrew*
AWW	*All's Well That Ends Well*
TN	*Twelfth Night*
WT	*The Winter's Tale*
JN	*King John*
R2	*King Richard The Second*
1H4	*The First Part of King Henry The Fourth*
2H4	*The Second Part of King Henry The Fourth*
H5	*King Henry The Fifth*
1H6	*The First Part of King Henry The Sixth*
2H6	*The Second Part of King Henry The Sixth*
3H6	*The Third Part of King Henry The Sixth*
R3	*King Richard The Third*
H8	*King Henry The Eighth*
TRO	*Troilus and Cressida*
COR	*Coriolanus*
TIT	*Titus Andronicus*
ROM	*Romeo and Juliet*
TIM	*Timon of Athens*
JC	*Julius Caesar*
MAC	*Macbeth*
HAM	*Hamlet*
LR	*King Lear*
OTH	*Othello*
ANT	*Antony and Cleopatra*
CYM	*Cymbeline*
PER	*Pericles*
TNK	*The Two Noble Kinsmen*
STM	*Sir Thomas More*
VEN	*Venus and Adonis*
LUC	*The Rape of Lucrece*
PP	*The Passionate Pilgrim*
PHT	*The Phoenix and Turtle*
SON	*The Sonnets*
LC	*A Lover's Complaint*

'**A**' *(also ave, ha', have)*
'**A**' 7 FR 0.0008 REL FR 4 V 3 P
she might 'a' been /a grandam ere she died. LLL 5.02. 17
a good pantler, 'a would 'a' chipp'd bread well. 2H4 2.04.238 P
had been a man's tailor, he'd 'a' prick'd you. 3.02.153 P
if i could 'a' rememb'red a gilt counterfeit, TRO 2.03. 25 P
this | i should 'a' fatted all the region kites HAM 2.02.579
"'so would i 'a' done, by yonder sun, | and thou 4.05. 65
we cast away moan, | god 'a' mercy on his soul!" 4.05.199
'**A** *(also he*)*
/'**A** 5 FR 0.0005 REL FR 2 V 3 P
if /'a be in debt and theft, and a sergeant in ERR 4.02. 61
ancient /swagger, /'a comes not in my doors. 2H4 2.04. 84 P
/'a gives us note | the force of his own merit H8 1.01. 63
catch, and /'a knock /out either of your brains; TRO 2.01.100 P
/'a does well to commend it himself, there are HAM 5.02.183 P
'**A** 178 FR 0.0201 REL FR 39 V 139 P
"the humor of it," quoth 'a! WIV 2.01.138 P
meet a sergeant, 'a turns back for very fear. ERR 4.02. 56
will cost him a thousand pound ere 'a be cur'd. ADO 1.01. 90 P
in the world, if 'a could get her good will. 2.01. 16 P
tell benedick of it, and hear what 'a will say. 2.03.171 P
he do fear god, 'a must necessarily keep peace; 2.03.193 P
'a brushes his hat a' mornings; 3.02. 41 P
nay, 'a rubs himself with civet. 3.02. 50 P
how if 'a will not stand? 3.03. 27 P
nay, by'r lady, that i think 'a cannot. 3.03. 77 P
'a has been a vile thief this seven year; 3.03.125 P
'a goes up and down like a gentleman. 3.03.126 P
how giddily 'a turns about all the hot–bloods 3.03.131 P
i know him, 'a wears a lock. 3.03.170 P
is 'a not approv'd in the height a villain, that 4.01.301 P
'a shall wear nothing handsome about him. 5.04.103 P
no penance, but 'a must fast three days a week. LLL 1.02.129 P
whoe'er 'a was, 'a show'd a mounting mind. 4.01. 4
whoe'er 'a was, 'a show'd a mounting mind. 4.01. 4
indeed 'a must shoot nearer, or he'll ne'er hit 4.01.134
and how most sweetly 'a will swear! 4.01.146
be friends with him, 'a kill'd your sister. 5.02. 13
'a can carve too, and lisp; 5.02.323
'a speaks not like a man of god his making. 5.02.526 P
if 'a have no more man's blood in his belly than 5.02.691 P
and that 'a wears next his heart for a favor. 5.02.714 P
yea, mock the lion when 'a roars for prey, | to MV 2.01. 30
let his father be what 'a will, we talk of young 2.02. 54 P
'a will make the man mad, to make /a woman of SHR 4.05. 35 P
i believe 'a means to cozen somebody in this 5.01. 38 P
'a has a little gall'd me, i confess; 5.02. 60
one in ten, quoth 'a? AWW 1.03. 86 P
a man may draw his heart out ere 'a pluck one. 1.03. 88 P
'a will betray us all unto ourselves: 4.01. 92
nothing of me, has 'a? 4.03.112 P
'a was a botcher's prentice in paris, from 4.03.185 P
sir, 'a has an english /name, but his fisnomy is 4.05. 39 P
so 'a is. 4.05. 64 P
'a will be here to–morrow, or i am deceiv'd by 4.05. 81 P
'a pops me out | at least from fair five hundred JN 1.01. 68
you, | and 'a may catch your hide and you alone. 2.01.136
i look'd 'a should have sent me two and twenty 2H4 1.02. 43 P
and covetousness than 'a can part young limbs 1.02.229 P
will 'a stand to't? 2.01. 4 P
'a cares not what mischief he does, if his 2.01. 14 P
him once, and 'a come but within my /vice — 2.01. 21 P
'a comes /continuantly to pie–corner (saving 2.01. 26 P
'a had him from me christian, and look if the 2.02. 70 P
'a calls me /e'en /now, my lord, through a red 2.02. 79 P
now 'a said so, i can tell whereupon. 2.04. 90 P
nay, and 'a do nothing but speak nothing, 'a 2.04.193 P
but speak nothing, 'a shall be nothing here. 2.04.193 P
methought 'a made a shrewd thrust at your belly. 2.04.210 P
'a would have made a good pantler, 'a would 'a' 2.04.237 P
a good pantler, 'a would 'a' chipp'd bread well. 2.04.238 P
both of a bigness, and 'a plays at quoits well, 2.04.244 P
and such other gambol faculties 'a has, that 2.04.251 P
'a must then to the inns a' court shortly. 3.02. 13 P
court–gate, when 'a was a crack not thus high; 3.02. 30 P
'a drew a good bow, and dead! 3.02. 43 P
'a shot a fine shoot. 3.02. 44 P
'a would have clapp'd i' th' clout at twelve 3.02. 46 P
a man is being whereby 'a may be thought to be 3.02. 79 P
'a shall charge you and discharge you with the 3.02.261 P
fellow, and 'a would manage you his piece thus, 3.02.281 P
his piece thus, and 'a would about and about, 3.02.282 P
tah, tah," would 'a say, "bounce," would 'a say, 3.02.284 P
"bounce," would 'a say, and away again would 'a 3.02.284 P
would 'a say, and away again would 'a go, and 3.02.285 P
away again would 'a go, and again would 'a come. 3.02.285 P
when 'a was naked, he was for all the world like 3.02.310 P
'a was so forlorn, that his dimensions to any 3.02.312 P
'a was the very genius of famine, yet lecherous 3.02.313 P
'a came /ever in the rearward of the fashion, 3.02.315 P
and i'll be sworn 'a ne'er saw him but once in 3.02.321 P
'a shall answer it. 5.01. 26 P
and 'a shall laugh without intervallums. 5.01. 81 P
sirrah, quoth 'a, we shall "do nothing but eat, 5.03. 16 P
i can assure thee that 'a will not out, 'a. 5.03. 66 P
i can assure thee that 'a will not out, 'a. 5.03. 67 P
by'r lady, i think 'a be, but goodman puff of 5.03. 89 P
i will leer upon him as 'a comes by, and do but 5.05. 6 P
unless already 'a be kill'd with your hard ep 31 P
'a made a finer end, and went away and it had H5 2.03. 10 P
'a parted ev'n just between twelve and one, ev'n 2.03. 12 P
sharp as a pen, and 'a /babbl'd of green fields. 2.03. 16 P
so 'a cried out, "god, god, god!" 2.03. 18 P
comfort him, bid him 'a should not think of god; 2.03. 20 P
so 'a bade me lay more clothes on his feet. 2.03. 22 P
ay, that 'a did. 2.03. 28 P
nay, that 'a did not. 2.03. 30 P
yes, that 'a did, and said they were dev'ls 2.03. 31 P
'a could never abide carnation — 'twas a color 2.03. 33 P
'a said once, the dev'l would have him about 2.03. 35 P
'a did in some sort, indeed, handle women; 2.03. 37 P
'a saw a flea stick upon bardolph's nose, and 'a 2.03. 40 P
and 'a said it was a black soul burning in hell? 2.03. 41 P
by the means whereof 'a faces it out, but fights 3.02. 33 P
by the means whereof 'a breaks words, and keeps 3.02. 35 P
his prayers, lest 'a should be thought a coward; 3.02. 38 P
for 'a never broke any man's head but his own, 3.02. 40 P
by cheshu, i think 'a will plow up all, if there 3.02. 63 P
here 'a comes, and the scots captain, captain 3.02. 74 P
he hath stol'n a pax, and hanged must 'a be — 3.06. 40
'a utt'red as prave words at the pridge as you 3.06. 63 P
here 'a comes, methinks, and the queen with him. 2H6 1.03. 6 P
'a must needs, for beggary is valiant. 4.02. 54 P
he is but a knight, is 'a? 4.02.117 P
would 'a were himself! TRO 1.02. 76 P
is 'a not? 1.02.204 P
'a were as good crack a fusty nut with no kernel 2.01.101 P
'a should not bear it so, 'a should eat swords 2.03.217 P
not bear it so, 'a should eat swords first. 2.03.217 P
'a would have ten shares. 2.03.220 P
why, 'a stalks up and down like a peacock — a 3.03.251 P
"sweet," quoth 'a! 5.01. 75 P
will 'a swagger himself out on 's own eyes? 5.02.136 P
brings 'a victory in his pocket? COR 2.01.122 P
bred i' th' wars | since 'a could draw a sword, 3.01.319
'a shall not tread on me; 5.03.127
'a was a merry man — took up the child. ROM 1.03. 40
tickling a parson's nose as 'a lies asleep, 1.04. 80
alone, | 'a bears him like a portly gentleman; 1.05. 66
"for himself to mar," quoth 'a! 2.04.118 P
and 'a speak any thing against me, i'll take him 2.04.150 P
take him down, and 'a were lustier than he is, 2.04.151 P
and hereabouts 'a dwells — which late i noted 5.01. 38
looks 'a not like the king? mark it, horatio. HAM 1.01. 43
i saw him once, 'a was a goodly king. 1.02.186
'a was a man, take him for all in all, | i shall 1.02.187
and then, sir, does 'a this — 'a does — what 2.01. 49
does 'a this — 'a does — what was i about to 2.01. 49
there was 'a gaming, there o'ertook in 's rouse, 2.01. 56
such perusal of my face | as 'a would draw it. 2.01. 88
me not at first, 'a said i was a fishmonger. 2.02.188 P
'a is far gone. 2.02.189 P
if 'a do blench, | i know my course. 2.02.597
but from what cause 'a will by no means speak. 3.01. 6
if 'a steal aught the whilst this play is 3.02. 88
by'r lady, 'a must build churches then, or else 3.02.133 P
then, or else shall 'a suffer not thinking on, 3.02.134 P
will 'a tell us what this show meant? 3.02.143 P
'a poisons him i' th' garden for his estate. 3.02.261 P
now might i do it /pat, now 'a is a–praying; 3.03. 73
and now i'll do't — and so 'a goes to heaven, 3.03. 74
'a took my father grossly, full of bread, | with 3.03. 80
'a will come straight. 3.04. 1
'a weeps for what is done. 4.01. 27
not where he eats, but where 'a is eaten; 4.03. 19 P
'a will stay till you come. 4.03. 39 P
they say 'a made a good end — "for bonny sweet 4.05.185 P
"and will 'a not come again? 4.05.190
and will 'a not come again? 4.05.191
'a shall, sir, and/'t please him. 4.06. 9 P
'a was the first that ever bore arms. 5.01. 33 P
'a sings in grave–making. 5.01. 66 P
such–a–one's horse, when 'a /meant to beg it, 5.01. 85 P
why, because 'a was mad. 5.01.150 P
'a shall recover his wits there, or, if 'a do 5.01.150 P
or, if 'a do not, 'tis no great matter there. 5.01.151 P
faith, if 'a be not rotten before 'a die — as 5.01.165 P
if 'a be not rotten before 'a die — as we have 5.01.165 P
'a will last you some eight year or nine year. 5.01.167 P
with his trade that 'a will keep out water a 5.01.171 P
'a pour'd a flagon of rhenish on my head once. 5.01.179 P
alexander, till 'a find it stopping a bunghole? 5.01.204 P
me signify to you that 'a has laid a great wager 5.02.102 P
'a did /comply, sir, with his dug before 'a 5.02.187 P
/comply, sir, with his dug before 'a suck'd it. 5.02.187 P
'a bears the third part of the world, man; ANT 2.07. 90 P
hoo, says 'a. there's my cap. 2.07.134
we sent our schoolmaster, | is 'a come back? 3.11. 72
cried he? and begg'd 'a pardon? 3.13.132
'a plays and tumbles, driving the poor fry PER 2.01. 30 P
die, keth 'a? 2.01. 78 P
'a keeps a plentiful shrievaltry, and 'a made my STM II.C 42 P
and 'a made my brother arthur watchins sergeant II.C 42 P
faith, 'a says true. II.C 141 P
A'* *(also at, in, o'*, of, on)*
/**A**'* 6 FR 0.0006 REL FR 5 V 1 P
armado /a' /th' /one side — o, a most dainty LLL 4.01.144
temple hall | at two /a' clock in the afternoon; 1H4 3.03.200
/ay, /what's /a' /clock? R3 4.02.109
/well, /but /what's /a' /clock? 4.02.111
/whose /lungs /are /tickle /a' /th' /sere, and HAM 2.02.324 P
you are pictures out /a' /doors, | bells in your OTH 2.01.109
A'* 189 FR 0.0213 REL FR 98 V 91 P
by seven a' clock i'll get you such a ladder. TGV 3.01.126
let him be sent for to–morrow, eight a' clock, WIV 3.03.198 P
it hath strook ten a' clock. 5.02. 10 P
but till 'tis one a' clock, | our dance of 5.05. 74
what's a' clock, think you? MM 2.01.276 P
block and your axe to–morrow, four a' clock. 4.02. 53 P
soon at five a' clock, | please you, i'll meet ERR 1.02. 26
sixpence that i had a' we'nsday last | to pay 1.02. 55
sure, luciana, it is two a' clock. 2.01. 3
because their business still lies out a' door. 2.01. 11
would that alone a' love he would detain, | so 2.01.107
at five a' clock | i shall receive the money for 4.01. 10
but keep your way a' god's name, i have done. ADO 1.01.143 P
would the cook were a' my mind! 1.03. 73 P
for, out a' question, you were born in a merry 2.01.332 P
'a brushes his hat a' mornings; 3.02. 42 P
cloth a' gold and cuts, and lac'd with silver, 3.04. 19 P
clap 's into "light a' love"; 3.04. 44 P
ye light a' love with your heels! 3.04. 47 P
'tis almost five a' clock, cousin, 'tis time you 3.04. 52 P
what time a' day? LLL 2.01.121
one a' these maids' girdles for your waist 4.01. 50
wide a' the bow–hand! 4.01.133
and his page a' t'other side, that handful of 4.01.147
well prov'd again a' my side! 4.03. 7 P
well, she hath one a' my sonnets already: 4.03. 15 P
we are much out a' th' way. 4.03. 74
writ a' both sides the leaf, margent and all, 5.02. 8
monday last at six a' clock i' th' morning, MV 2.05. 25 P
'tis nine a' clock — our friends all stay for 2.06. 63
luck stirring but what lights a' my shoulders, 3.01. 95 P
a' my shoulders, no sighs but a' my breathing, 3.01. 96 P
a' my breathing, no tears but a' my shedding. 3.01. 96 P
therefore be a' good cheer, for truly i think 3.05. 5 P
eye, | says very wisely, "it is ten a' clock. AYL 2.07. 22
i pray you, what is't a' clock? 3.02.299 P
by two a' clock i will be with thee again. 4.01.181 P
two a' clock is your hour? 4.01.186 P
is it not past two a' clock? 4.03. 1 P
a' my word, and she knew him as well as i do, SHR 1.02.108 P
but if you have a stomach, to't a' god's name; 1.02.194
and kiss me, kate, we will be married a' sunday. 2.01.324
why, what a' devil's name, tailor, call'st thou 4.03. 92
let's see, i think 'tis now some seven a' clock, 4.03.187
i do, | it shall be what a' clock i say it is. 4.03.195
come on a' god's name! 4.05. 1
faith, i'll see the church a' your back, and 5.01. 4 P
blessing of god till i have issue a' my body; AWW 1.03. 25 P
i am out a' friends, madam, and i hope to have 1.03. 39 P
in ten, madam, which is a purifying a' th' song. 1.03. 83 P
thou hast to pull at a smack a' th' contrary. 2.03.225 P
dost thou garter up thy arms a' this fashion? 2.03.250 P
you will take your instant leave a' th' king, 2.04. 48
/ling and our isbels a' th' country are nothing 3.02. 13 P
like your old ling and your isbels a' th' court. 3.02. 14 P
ten a' clock: 4.01. 24 P
no more a' that. 4.02. 13
me this other day to turn him out a' th' band. 4.03.200 P
e'en a crow a' th' same nest; 4.03.286 P
all that | he gave it to a commoner a' th' camp, 5.03.194
with all the spots a' th' world tax'd and 5.03.206
sir toby, you must come in earlier a' nights. TN 1.03. 5 P
what dish a' poison has she dress'd him! 2.05.112 P
and furbish new the name of john a' gaunt, R2 1.03. 76
but what, a' god's name, doth become of this? 2.01.251
a' god's name let it go. 3.03.146
to–morrow morning by four a' clock early, at 1H4 1.02.125 P
good morrow, carriers, what's a' clock? 2.01. 32 P
i think it be two a' clock. 2.01. 33 P
and when i am a' horseback, i will swear | i 2.03.101
or, francis, a' thursday; 2.04. 66 P
age of this present twelve a' clock at midnight. 2.04. 94 P
what's a' clock, francis? 2.04. 96 P
that runs a' horseback up a hill perpendicular 2.04.343 P

a' horseback, ye cuckoo, but afoot he will not 2.04.353 P
indeed, my lord, i think it be two a' clock. 2.04.525
he that died a' wednesday. 5.01.136 P
or i will ride thee a' nights like the mare. 2H4 2.01. 77 P
a' my word, captain, there's none such here. 2.04.176 P
have you turn'd him out a' doors? 2.04.212 P
wilt thou leave fighting a' days and foining a' 2.04.232 P
leave fighting a' days and foining a' nights, 2.04.232 P
i shall receive money a' thursday, shalt have a 2.04.275 P
till thy return — well, hearken a' th' end. 2.04.280 P
no abuse, hal, a' mine honor, no abuse. 2.04.313 P
'tis one a' clock, and past. 3.01. 34
'a must then to the inns a' court shortly. 3.02. 13 P
swingebucklers in all the inns a' court again; 3.02. 22 P
john a' gaunt lov'd him well, and betted much 3.02. 44 P
as familiarly of john a' gaunt as if he had been 3.02.320 P
it, and told john a' gaunt he beat his own name, 3.02.324 P
of woncote against clement perkes a' th' hill. 5.01. 39 P
be merry, now comes in the sweet a' th' night. 5.03. 51 P
'twill be two a' clock ere they come from the 5.05. 3 P
is it four a' clock? H5 1.01. 93
be a' good cheer." 2.03. 18 P
and knobs, and flames a' fire, and his lips 3.06.103 P
it is now two a' clock; 3.07.156
will stand a' tiptoe when this day is named, 4.03. 42
i have sworn to take him a box a' th' ear; 4.07.128 P
favor | may haply purchase him a box a' th' ear. 4.07.173
then come a' god's name, i fear no woman. 1H6 1.02.102
a' god's name see the lists and all things fit; 2H6 2.03. 54
sirs, what's a' clock? 2.04. 5
under his tongue, he speaks not a' god's name. 4.07.108 P
what is't a' clock? R3 3.02. 4
and towards three or four a' clock | look for 3.05.101
what is't a' clock? 5.03. 47
supper–time, my lord, | it's /nine a' clock. 5.03. 48
lead on a' god's name. H8 2.01. 78
it's one a' clock, boy, is't not? 5.01. 1
body a' me, where is it? 5.02. 22
she would be as fair a' friday as helen is on TRO 1.01. 76 P
a red murrion a' thy jade's tricks! 2.01. 19 P
but she'll bereave you a' th' deeds too, if she 3.02. 56 P
you fillip me a' th' head. 4.05. 45
/catarrhs, loads a' gravel in the back, 5.01. 19 P
that i shall leave you one a' th's days; 5.03.104 P
a' th' t' other side, the policy of those crafty 5.04. 9 P
the other side a' th' city is risen; COR 1.01. 47 P
a gulf it did remain | i' th' midst a' th' body, 1.01. 99
be restrain'd, | who is the sink a' th' body — 1.01.122
rightly | touching the weal a' th' common, you 1.01.151
they would hang them on the horns a' th' moon, 1.01.213
a' my word, the father's son. 1.03. 57 P
a' my troth, i look'd upon him a' we'nsday half 1.03. 58 P
i look'd upon him a' we'nsday half an hour 1.03. 58 P
turn thy solemnness out a' door, and go along 1.03.108 P
call thither all the officers a' th' town, 1.05. 27
are you lords a' th' field? 1.06. 47
the city, i mean of us a' th' right–hand file? 2.01. 22 P
masters a' th' people, | we do request your 2.02. 51
be at once to all the points a' th' compass. 2.03. 24 P
well then, i pray, your price a' th' consulship? 2.03. 73 P
you speak a' th' people | as if you were a god, 3.01. 80
give forth | the corn a' th' store–house gratis, 3.01.114
in time | break ope the locks a' th' senate, and 3.01.138
and suffer it | a brand to th' end a' th' world. 3.01.302
the violent fit a' th' time craves it as physic 3.02. 33
so | i' th' right and strength a' th' commons," 3.03. 14
and power i' th' truth a' th' cause. 3.03. 18
doth distribute it — in the name a' th' people, 3.03. 99
breath i hate | as reek a' th' rotten fens, 3.03.121
the hoarded plague a' th' gods | requite your 4.02. 11
till he had forg'd himself a name a' th' fire 5.01. 14
to tear with thunder the wide cheeks a' th' air, 5.03.151
see you yond coign a' th' capitol, yond 5.04. 1 P
go tell the lords a' th' city i am here. 5.06. 1
together with the seal a' th' senate, what | we 5.06. 82
you lords and heads a' th' state, perfidiously 5.06. 90
silk, never admitting | counsel a' th' war; 5.06. 96
help, three a' th' chiefest soldiers; 5.06.148
time out a' mind the fairies' coachmakers. ROM 1.04. 61
what a' clock to–morrow | shall i send to thee? 2.02.167
my back a' t' other side — ah, my back, my back 2.05. 50
a plague a' both houses! 3.01. 91
a plague a' both your houses! 3.01. 99 P
a plague a' both your houses! 3.01.106
a' thursday let it be — a' thursday, tell her, 3.04. 20
a' thursday let it be — a' thursday, tell her, 3.04. 20
well, get you gone, a' thursday be it then. 3.04. 30
get thee to church a' thursday, | or never after 3.05.161
the curfew–bell hath rung, 'tis three a' clock. 4.04. 4
the maid is fair, a' th' youngest for a bride, TIM 1.01.123
what time a' day is't, apemantus? 1.01.256
i will fly, like a dog, the heels a' th' ass. 1.01.272 P
where liest a' nights, timon? 4.03.292
where feed'st thou a' days, apemantus? 4.03.293 P
what is't a' clock? JC 2.02.114
what is't a' clock? 2.04. 23
'tis three a' clock, and, romans, yet ere night 5.03.109
for out a' doors he went without their helps, HAM 2.01. 96
sir, a' monday morning, 'twas then indeed. 2.02.387 P
we may call it herb of grace a' sundays. 4.05.183 P
i have a speech a' fire that fain would blaze, 4.07.190
should have been buried out a' christian burial. 5.01. 25 P
think alexander look'd a' this fashion i' th' 5.01.197 P
your grace has laid the odds a' th' weaker side. 5.02.261
thy drink and thy whore, | and keep in a' door, LR 1.04.125
us staunch from edge to edge | a' th' world, i ANT 2.02.116
and scald rhymers | ballad 's out a' tune. 5.02.216
i am advis'd to give her music a' mornings; CYM 2.03. 12 P
such whales have i heard on a' th' land, who PER 2.01. 33 P
come, queen a' th' feast — | for, daughter, so 2.03. 17
bring your grace e'en to the edge a' th' shore, 3.03. 35
true, there's two unwholesome, a' conscience. 4.02. 22 P
to equal any single crown a' th' earth | i' th' 4.03. 8
being proud, swallowed some part a' th' earth. 4.04. 39
and gallops to the /tune of "light a' love." TNK 5.02. 54
A* *(also ah)*
/A* 146 FR 0.0165 REL FR 110 V 36 P
A* 14675 FR 1.6588 REL FR 9794 V 4881 P

AARON 24 FR 0.0027 REL FR 24 V 0 P
then, aaron, arm thy heart, and fit thy thoughts TIT 2.01. 12
aaron, a thousand deaths | would i propose to 2.01. 79
aaron, thou hast hit it. 2.01. 97
my lovely aaron, wherefore look'st thou sad, 2.03. 10
under their sweet shade, aaron, let us sit, 2.03. 16
this is the hole where aaron bid us hide him. 2.03.186
heart, | aaron and thou look down into this den, 2.03.215
aaron is gone, and my compassionate heart | will 2.03.217
o gentle aaron! 3.01.157
good aaron, wilt thou help to chop it off? 3.01.161
come hither, aaron. 3.01.186
good aaron, give his majesty my hand. 3.01.193
aaron will have his soul black like his face. 3.01.205
o, tell me, did you see aaron the moor? 4.02. 52
all, | here aaron is, and what with aaron now? 4.02. 54
all, | here aaron is, and what with aaron now? 4.02. 54
o gentle aaron, we are all undone! 4.02. 55
aaron, it must, the mother wills it so. 4.02. 82
aaron, what shall i say unto the empress? 4.02.128
advise thee, aaron, what is to be done, | and we 4.02.129
the ocean swells not so as aaron storms. 4.02.139
what mean'st thou, aaron? 4.02.147
aaron, i see thou wilt not trust the air | with 4.02.169
thy life–blood out, if aaron now be wise, | then 4.04. 37
AARON'S 1 FR 0.0001 REL FR 1 V 0 P
and faster bound to aaron's charming eyes | than TIT 2.01. 16
A,B 1 FR 0.0001 REL FR 0 V 1 P
what is a,b, spell'd backward, with the horn on LLL 5.01. 47 P
ABAISSEZ 1 FR 0.0001 REL FR 0 V 1 P
veux point que vous abaissez votre /grandeur en H5 5.02.254 P
ABANDON 4 FR 0.0004 REL FR 2 V 2 P
you clown, abandon — which is in the vulgar AYL 5.01. 47 P
together is, abandon the society of this female, 5.01. 50 P
but where one villain is, then him abandon. TIM 5.01.111
abandon all remorse; OTH 3.03.369
ABANDON'D 6 FR 0.0006 REL FR 5 V 1 P
have | i'll stay to know at your abandon'd cave. AYL 5.04.196
being all this time abandon'd from your bed. SHR in.2. 115
he hath abandon'd his physicians, madam, under AWW 1.01. 13 P
if she be so abandon'd to her sorrow | as it is TN 1.04. 19
or live in peace abandon'd and despis'd! 3H6 1.01.188
i have abandon'd troy, left my possession, TRO 3.03. 5
ABANDONED 2 FR 0.0002 REL FR 2 V 0 P
left and abandoned of his velvet /friends: AYL 2.01. 50
who hath abandoned her holy groves | to see the TIT 2.03. 58
ABANDONER 1 FR 0.0001 REL FR 1 V 0 P
abandoner of revels, mute, contemplative, TNK 5.01.138
ABASE 2 FR 0.0002 REL FR 2 V 0 P
and never more abase our sight so low | as to 2H6 1.02. 15
and will she yet abase her eyes on me, | that R3 1.02.246
ABASH'D 1 FR 0.0001 REL FR 1 V 0 P
do you with cheeks abash'd behold our works, TRO 1.03. 18
ABATE *(also bate*, etc.)*
ABATE 15 FR 0.0017 REL FR 14 V 1 P
abate throw at novum, and the whole world again LLL 5.02.544
o long and tedious night, | abate thy hours! MND 3.02.432
you would abate the strength of your displeasure MV 5.01.198
presence | may well abate the over–merry spleen, SHR in.1. 137
an oath of mickle might, and fury shall abate. H5 2.01. 66
abate thy rage, abate thy manly rage, | abate 3.02. 23
abate thy rage, abate thy manly rage, | abate 3.02. 23
thy manly rage, | abate thy rage, great duke! 3.02. 24
tell him my fury shall abate, and i | the crowns 4.04. 47
abate the edge of traitors, gracious lord, R3 5.05. 35
that you withdraw you, and abate your strength, TIT 1.01. 43
fear, | abate thy valor in the acting it. ROM 4.01.120
a kind of week or snuff that will abate it, HAM 4.07.115
as i was in france, i would abate her nothing, CYM 1.04. 68 P
desire, | as air and water do abate the fire. VEN 654
ABATED 3 FR 0.0003 REL FR 3 V 0 P
which once in him abated, all the rest | turn'd 2H4 1.01.117
you as most | abated captives to some nation COR 3.03.132
she hath abated me of half my train; LR 2.04.159
ABATEMENT 4 FR 0.0004 REL FR 3 V 1 P
but falls into abatement and low price | even in TN 1.01. 13
there's a great abatement of kindness appears as LR 1.04. 60 P
letting them thrive again | on their abatement. CYM 5.04. 21
feast, of which i pray you | make no abatement. TNK 1.01.225
ABATEMENTS 1 FR 0.0001 REL FR 1 V 0 P
and hath abatements and delays as many | as HAM 4.07.120
ABATES 1 FR 0.0001 REL FR 1 V 0 P
upon my heart | abates the ardor of my liver. TMP 4.01. 56
A–BATFOWLING 1 FR 0.0001 REL FR 0 V 1 P
we would so, and then go a–batfowling. TMP 2.01.185 P
ABBESS 5 FR 0.0005 REL FR 5 V 0 P
and take perforce my husband from the abbess. ERR 5.01.117
justice, most sacred duke, against the abbess! 5.01.133
and here the abbess shuts the gates on us, | and 5.01.156
and bid the lady abbess come to me: 5.01.166
go call the abbess hither. 5.01.281
ABBEY 13 FR 0.0014 REL FR 13 V 0 P
out at the postern by the abbey wall; TGV 5.01. 9
behind the ditches of the abbey here. ERR 5.01.122
kneel to the duke before he pass the abbey. 5.01.129
then they fled | into this abbey, whither we 5.01.155
even now we hous'd him in the abbey here, | and 5.01.188
and then you fled into this abbey here, | from 5.01.264
i never came within these abbey walls, | nor 5.01.266
saw'st thou him enter at the abbey here? 5.01.279
the pains | to go with us into the abbey here, 5.01.395
tell him toward swinstead, to the abbey there. JN 5.03. 8
among the crowd i' th' abbey, where a finger H8 4.01. 57
he came to leicester, | lodg'd in the abbey; 4.02. 18
behind the abbey wall | within this hour my man ROM 2.04.187
ABBEY–GATE 1 FR 0.0001 REL FR 1 V 0 P
go, some of you, knock at the abbey–gate, | and ERR 5.01.165
ABBEYS 1 FR 0.0001 REL FR 1 V 0 P
our abbeys and our priories shall pay | this JN 1.01. 48
ABBOMINABLE *(also abhominable, abominable)*
ABBOMINABLE 1 FR 0.0001 REL FR 0 V 1 P
which he would call "abbominable"; LLL 5.01. 24 P
ABBOT 4 FR 0.0004 REL FR 4 V 0 P
but for our trusty brother–in–law and the abbot, R2 5.03.137
the grand conspirator, abbot of westminster, 5.06. 19
where the reverend abbot | with all his covent H8 4.02. 18
"o father abbot, | an old man, broken with the 4.02. 20

ABBOTS 1 FR 0.0001 REL FR 1 V 0 P
see thou shake the bags | of hoarding abbots, JN 3.03. 8
ABBREVIATED 1 FR 0.0001 REL FR 0 V 1 P
neigh abbreviated "ne." LLL 5.01. 23 P
ABC *(also absey)*
ABC 1 FR 0.0001 REL FR 0 V 1 P
to sigh, like a schoolboy that had lost his abc; TGV 2.01. 23 P
A–BED 10 FR 0.0011 REL FR 9 V 1 P
saw her a–bed, and in the morning early | they AYL 2.02. 6
and this was it i gave him, being a–bed. AWW 5.03.228
not to be a–bed after midnight is to be up TN 2.03. 1 P
and gentlemen in england, now a–bed, | shall H5 4.03. 64
i would they were a–bed! COR 3.01.260
i mean she is brought a–bed. TIT 4.02. 62
company, | i would have been a–bed an hour ago. ROM 3.04. 7
the king's a–bed. MAC 2.01. 12
you have not been a–bed then? OTH 3.01. 31
it is | a cell of ignorance, travelling a–bed, CYM 3.03. 33
A–BEGGING 1 FR 0.0001 REL FR 1 V 0 P
maim your honor | (for now i am set a–begging, TNK 3.06.238
ABEL 1 FR 0.0001 REL FR 1 V 0 P
cain, | to slay thy brother abel, if thou wilt. 1H6 1.03. 40
ABEL'S 1 FR 0.0001 REL FR 1 V 0 P
which blood, like sacrificing abel's, cries, R2 1.01.104
ABERGAVENNY *(see aburga'ny)*
ABET 1 FR 0.0001 REL FR 1 V 0 P
and you that do abet him in this kind | cherish R2 2.03.146
ABETTING 1 FR 0.0001 REL FR 1 V 0 P
slave, | abetting him to thwart me in my mood! ERR 2.02.170
ABETTOR 1 FR 0.0001 REL FR 1 V 0 P
troth, | thou foul abettor, thou notorious bawd! LUC 886
ABHOMINABLE *(also abbominable, abominable)*
ABHOMINABLE 1 FR 0.0001 REL FR 0 V 1 P
this is abhominable — which he would call LLL 5.01. 24 P
ABHOR 23 FR 0.0026 REL FR 19 V 4 P
was shelvy and shallow — a death that i abhor; WIV 3.05. 16 P
there is a vice that most i do abhor, | and most MM 2.02. 29
time | that i should do what i abhor to name, 3.01.101
husband, even my soul | doth for a wife abhor. ERR 3.02.159
in all outward behaviors seem'd ever to abhor. ADO 2.03. 97 P
i abhor such fanatical phantasimes, such LLL 5.01. 17 P
abhor it, fear it, do not enter it. AYL 2.03. 28
all you whose souls abhor | th' uncleanly savors JN 4.03.111
i utterly abhor, yea, from my soul | refuse you H8 2.04. 81
i abhor | this dilatory sloth and tricks of rome 2.04.237
not afric owns a serpent i abhor | more than thy COR 1.08. 3
few things loves better | than to abhor himself; TIM 1.01. 60
eat, timon, and abhor /them. 4.03.397
ever i did dream of such a matter, | abhor me. OTH 1.01. 6
heave the gorge, disrelish and abhor the moor; 2.01.233 P
it does abhor me now i speak the word; 4.02.162
for nature doth abhor to make his bed | with the CYM 4.02.357
but having no defects, why dost abhor me? VEN 138
let fair humanity abhor the deed | that spots LUC 195
the powers to whom i pray abhor this fact, | how 349
age, i do abhor thee, youth, i do adore thee: PP 12. 9
o, though i love what others do abhor, | with SON 150.11
with others thou shouldst not abhor my state: 150.12
/ABHORR'D 1 FR 0.0001 REL FR 1 V 0 P
/shunn'd /my /abhorr'd /society, /but /then, LR 5.03.211
ABHORR'D 11 FR 0.0012 REL FR 9 V 2 P
to act her earthy and abhorr'd commands, TMP 1.02.273
her body stoop | to such abhorr'd pollution. MM 2.04.183
till they attain to their abhorr'd ends; AWW 4.03. 23 P
present | th' abhorr'd ingredient to his eye, WT 2.01. 43
but taking note of thy abhorr'd aspect, JN 4.02.224
more abhorr'd | than spotted livers in the TRO 5.03. 17
that you may be abhorr'd | farther than seen, COR 1.04. 32
his name remains | to th' ensuing age abhorr'd." 5.03.148
therefore be abhorr'd | all feasts, societies, TIM 4.03. 20
and now how abhorr'd in my imagination it is! HAM 5.01.187 P
was wife to your place, | abhorr'd your person. CYM 5.05. 40
ABHORR'DST 1 FR 0.0001 REL FR 1 V 0 P
though thou abhorr'dst in us our human griefs, TIM 5.04. 75
ABHORRED 8 FR 0.0009 REL FR 7 V 1 P
abhorred slave, | which any print of goodness TMP 1.02.351
and when they show'd me this abhorred pit, TIT 2.03. 98
and that the lean abhorred monster keeps | thee ROM 5.03.104
with all th' abhorred births below crisp heaven TIM 4.03.183
whose thankless natures (o abhorred spirits!) 5.01. 60
thou liest, abhorred tyrant, with my sword MAC 5.07. 10
abhorred villain! LR 1.02. 76 P
that all th' abhorred things o' th' earth amend CYM 5.05.216
ABHORRING 2 FR 0.0002 REL FR 2 V 0 P
words to thee will flatter | beneath abhorring. COR 1.01.168
let the water–flies | blow me into abhorring! ANT 5.02. 60
/ABHORS 1 FR 0.0001 REL FR 1 V 0 P
marry | vain thurio, whom my very soul /abhors. TGV 4.03. 17
ABHORS 3 FR 0.0003 REL FR 2 V 1 P
and 'tis a color she abhors, and cross–garter'd, TN 2.05.199 P
mayst move | that heart, which now abhors, to 3.01.164
o, how my heart abhors | to hear him nam'd, and ROM 3.05. 99
ABHORSON 3 FR 0.0003 REL FR 0 V 3 P
what ho, abhorson! where's abhorson, there? MM 4.02. 19 P
what ho, abhorson! where's abhorson, there? 4.02. 19 P
how now, abhorson? what's the news with you? 4.03. 39 P
ABIDE* *(also aby)*
/ABIDE* 1 FR 0.0001 REL FR 1 V 0 P
/to /abide /a /field | /where /nothing /but /the 2H4 2.03. 36
ABIDE* 40 FR 0.0045 REL FR 28 V 12 P
which good natures | could not abide to be with; TMP 1.02.360
brother, and yours, abide all three distracted, 5.01. 12
i cannot abide the smell of hot meat since. WIV 1.01.286 P
women, indeed, cannot abide 'em, they are very 1.01.298 P
he cannot abide the old woman of brainford. 4.02. 85 P
the deputy cannot abide a whoremaster. MM 3.02. 35 P
by the year, and let him abide here with you; 4.02. 24 P
shall entreat you to abide here till he come and 5.01.265 P
which the ladies cannot abide. MND 3.01. 12 P
abide me, if thou dar'st; 3.02.422
two miles off, | and there we will abide. MV 3.04. 32
be rend'red | why he cannot abide a gaping pig; 4.01. 54
and yet it will no more but abide. WT 4.03. 93 P
to abide | thy kingly doom and sentence of his R2 5.06. 22
i cannot abide swagg'rers. 2H4 2.04.109 P
always say she could not abide master shallow. 3.02.203 P
'a could never abide carnation — 'twas a color H5 2.03. 33 P
which before would not abide looking on. 5.02.311 P

i am your butt, and i abide your shot. 3H6 1.04. 29
dens, | poor harmless lambs abide their enmity. 2.05. 75
what fates impose, that men must needs abide; 4.03. 58
wilt thou not, beast, abide? TRO 5.06. 30
what say you, boys, will you abide with him, TIT 5.02.137
do so, and let no man abide this deed, | but we JC 3.01. 94
if it be found so, some will dear abide it. 3.02.114
abide within. MAC 3.01.139
i dare abide no longer. 4.02. 73
make yourself my guest | whilst you abide here. ANT 2.02.244
shall i abide | in this dull world, which in thy 4.15. 60
and i shall here abide the hourly shot | of CYM 1.01. 89
but abide the change of time, | quake in the 2.04. 4
to, and will abide it with | a prince's courage. 3.04.183
go you to hunting, i'll abide with him. 4.02. 6
where you may abide till your date expire. PER 3.04. 14
where thou with patience must my will abide — LUC 486
lights are soon blown out, huge fires abide, 647
and blood untainted still doth red abide, 1749
for then my thoughts (from far where i abide) SON 27. 5
fire, | are both with thee, where ever i abide; 45. 2
and when in his fair parts she did abide, | she LC 83
ABIDES 8 FR 0.0009 REL FR 7 V 1 P
your provost knows the place where he abides, MM 5.01.252
me, sorrow abides and happiness takes his leave. ADO 1.01.102 P
a rotten case abides no handling. 2H4 4.01.159
comfort go with thee, | for none abides with me. 2H6 2.04. 88
to richmond, in the parts where he abides. R3 4.02. 49
yet much less spirit to curse | abides in me; 4.04.198
the place, it cannot be far | where he abides. TIM 5.01. 2
our separation so abides and flies, | that thou, ANT 1.03.102
ABILIMENTS *(also habiliments)*
ABILIMENTS 1 FR 0.0001 REL FR 1 V 0 P
she | in th' abiliments of the goddess isis ANT 3.06. 17
ABILITIES 5 FR 0.0005 REL FR 4 V 1 P
of my desires, | yet fill'd with my abilities. H8 3.02.171
all our abilities, gifts, natures, shapes, TRO 1.03.179
your abilities are too infant-like for doing COR 2.01. 37 P
but altogether lacks th' abilities | that rhodes OTH 1.03. 25
i will do | all my abilities in thy behalf. 3.03. 2
/ABILITY 1 FR 0.0001 REL FR 1 V 0 P
/which /if /we /find /outweighs /ability, 2H4 1.03. 45
ABILITY 8 FR 0.0009 REL FR 6 V 2 P
ability in means, and choice of friends, | to ADO 4.01.199
and have ability enough to make such knaveries AWW 1.03. 11 P
out of my lean and low ability | i'll lend you TN 3.04.344
that my ability may undergo | and nobleness WT 2.03.164
hath something seiz'd | his wish'd ability, he 5.01.143
able, and yet reserve an ability that they never TRO 3.02. 85 P
had it th' ability of life to thank you. HAM 5.02.373
for sure he fills it up with great ability — OTH 3.03.247
ABILITY'S 1 FR 0.0001 REL FR 1 V 0 P
what poor ability's in me | to do him good? MM 1.04. 75
A-BILLING 1 FR 0.0001 REL FR 1 V 0 P
showed like two silver doves that sit a-billing. VEN 366
A-BIRDING 4 FR 0.0004 REL FR 0 V 4 P
after, we'll a-birding together. WIV 3.03.230 P
her husband goes this morning a-birding; 3.05. 45 P
her husband is this morning gone a-birding. 3.05.128 P
he's a-birding, sweet sir john. 4.02. 8 P
/ABJECT 2 FR 0.0002 REL FR 2 V 0 P
what things there are | most /abject in regard, TRO 3.03.128
/there /for /pavement /to /the /abject /rear, 3.03.162
ABJECT 9 FR 0.0010 REL FR 9 V 0 P
pack | to make a loathsome abject scorn of me; ERR 4.04.103
mules, | you use in abject and in slavish parts, MV 4.01. 92
and banish hence these abject lowly dreams. SHR in.2. 32
came like itself, in base and abject routs, 2H4 4.01. 33
that he should be so abject, base, and poor, 1H6 5.05. 49
abrook | the abject people gazing on thy face, 2H6 2.04. 11
upon these paltry, servile, abject drudges! 4.01.105
flint, | i am so angry at these abject terms; 5.01. 25
and his eye revil'd | me as his abject object; H8 1.01.127
ABJECTLY 1 FR 0.0001 REL FR 1 V 0 P
let him that thinks of me so abjectly | know TIT 2.03. 4
ABJECTS 1 FR 0.0001 REL FR 1 V 0 P
we are the queen's abjects, and must obey. R3 1.01.106
ABJUR'D 2 FR 0.0002 REL FR 2 V 0 P
checks | as ovid be an outcast quite abjur'd. SHR 1.01. 33
she hath abjur'd the /company | and /sight of TN 1.02. 40
ABJURE 4 FR 0.0004 REL FR 4 V 0 P
but this rough magic | i here abjure; TMP 5.01. 51
or to abjure | for ever the society of men. MND 1.01. 65
here abjure | the taints and blames i laid upon MAC 4.03.123
no, rather i abjure all roofs, and choose | to LR 2.04.208
/ABLE* 1 FR 0.0001 REL FR 1 V 0 P
/how /able /such /a /work /to /undergo, | /to 2H4 1.03. 54
ABLE* 64 FR 0.0072 REL FR 34 V 30 P
were dry, i am able to fill it with my tears; TGV 2.03. 52 P
when she is able to overtake seventeen years old WIV 1.01. 53 P
of man's disposition is able to bear. 4.05.109 P
till thou art able to woo her in good english. 5.05.134 P
i am not able to answer the welsh flannel; 5.05.162 P
to your sufficiency as your worth is able, | and MM 1.01. 8
not being able to buy out his life | according ERR 1.02. 5
hath not seen, man's hand is not able to taste, MND 4.01.212 P
a man in all athens able to discharge pyramus 4.02. 8 P
swore he would pay him again when he was able. MV 1.02. 81 P
is he not able to discharge the money? 4.01.208
my fortunes were more able to relieve her; AYL 2.04. 77
thank my good father, i am able to maintain it. SHR 5.01. 76 P
be able for thine enemy | rather in power than AWW 1.01. 65
that's able to breathe life into a stone, 2.01. 73
why, he's able to lead her a coranto. 2.03. 43 P
of as able body as when he number'd thirty. 4.05. 81 P
(not able to produce more accusation | than your WT 2.03.118
that ballad-makers cannot be able to express it. 5.02. 25 P
his face, | not able to endure the sight of day, R2 3.02. 52
and art indeed able to corrupt a saint. 1H4 1.02. 91 P
with that he gave his able horse the head, | and 2H4 1.01. 43
is not able to invent any thing that intends to 1.02. 8 P
that show a weak mind and an able body, for the 2.04.252 P
sir, is able to speak for himself, when a knave 5.01. 46 P
would i were able to load him with his desert! H5 3.07. 79 P
or am not able | verbatim to rehearse the method 1H6 3.01. 12
persuade | than i am able to instruct or teach; 4.01.159
lines, | able to ravish any dull conceit; 5.05. 15
henry is able to enrich his queen, | and not to 5.05. 51
i shall never be able to fight a blow. 2H6 1.03.215 P
alas, master, i am not able to stand alone; 2.01.142
i am not able to stand. 2.01.149 P
god, for i am never able to deal with my master, 2.03. 77 P
late, not able to travel with her furr'd pack, 4.02. 47 P
i am able to endure much. 4.02. 56 P
them about matters they were not able to answer. 4.07. 42 P
is able with the change to kill and cure. 5.01.101
queen, | you have a father able to maintain you, 3H6 3.03.154
in field | should not be able to encounter mine. 4.08. 36
and as prone to mischief | as able to perform't) H8 1.01.161
not able to maintain | the many to them 'longing 1.02. 31
would it not grieve an able man to leave | so 2.02.141
i am able now, methinks | (out of a fortitude of 3.02.387
as well as i am able. 4.01. 62
to have given me longer life | and able means, 4.02.153
their dear brothers, are able to endure. 5.03. 63 P
swear more performance than they are able, and TRO 3.02. 85 P
but is | able to bear against the great aufidius COR 1.06. 79
he is able to pierce a corslet with his eye, 5.04. 20 P
i am as able and as fit as thou | to serve, and TIT 2.01. 33
me they shall feel while i am able to stand, and ROM 1.01. 28 P
i am the greatest, able to do least, | yet most 5.03.223
it him, it foals me straight | and able horses. TIM 2.01. 10
now before the gods, i am not able to do (the 3.02. 49 P
now or whensoever, provided i be so able as now. HAM 5.02.202 P
does offend, none, i say none, i'll able 'em. LR 4.06.168
both what by sea and land i can be able | to ANT 1.04. 78
upon her, she's able to freeze the god priapus, PER 4.06. 3 P
able to lock jove from a synod, shall | by TNK 1.01.176
what thou feel'st being able | to make mars 1.01.181
able once again | to out-dure danger. 3.06. 9
he lisps in 's neighing able to entice | a 5.02. 66
"amen" | to every hymn that able spirit affords SON 85. 7
A-BLEEDING 2 FR 0.0002 REL FR 1 V 1 P
that my nose fell a-bleeding on black monday MV 2.05. 24 P
blood for your rude brawls doth lie a-bleeding; ROM 3.01.189
ABLER 1 FR 0.0001 REL FR 1 V 0 P
abler than yourself | to make conditions. JC 4.03. 31
ABLEST 1 FR 0.0001 REL FR 1 V 0 P
and do my ablest service | to such a well-found TNK 2.05. 26
ABOARD 36 FR 0.0040 REL FR 27 V 9 P
good, yet remember whom thou hast aboard. TMP 1.01. 19 P
in few, they hurried us aboard a bark, | bore us 1.02.144
wrack, | which cannot perish having thee aboard, TGV 1.01.149
aboard! 2.03. 33 P
too soon | we came aboard. ERR 1.01. 61
that stays but till her owner comes aboard, 4.01. 86
i have convey'd aboard, and i have bought | the 4.01. 88
i long that we were safe and sound aboard, 4.04.150
therefore away, to get our stuff aboard. 4.04.158
come about, | bassanio presently will go aboard. MV 2.06. 65
he, as if | he had been aboard, carousing to his SHR 3.02.171
go get aboard; WT 3.03. 7
well may i get aboard! 3.03. 57
he is gone aboard a new ship to purge melancholy 4.04.763 P
i'll bring you where he is aboard, tender your 4.04.796 P
these two moles, these blind ones, aboard him. 4.04.837 P
the old man and his son aboard the prince; 5.02.115 P
now sits the wind fair, and we will aboard. H5 2.02. 12
and uncle exeter, | we will aboard to-night. 2.02. 71
i lost mine eye in laying the prize aboard, 2H6 4.01. 25
one paris, that would fain lay knife aboard; ROM 2.04.202 P
aboard, aboard, for shame! HAM 1.03. 55
aboard, aboard, for shame! 1.03. 55
follow him at foot, tempt him with speed aboard. 4.03. 54
myself will straight aboard, and to the state OTH 5.02.370
aboard my galley i invite you all. ANT 2.06. 80
come, sir, will you aboard? 2.06.133 P
you shall, at least, | go see my lord aboard. CYM 1.01.178
i must aboard to-morrow. 1.06.199
convey thy deity | aboard our dancing boat, make PER 3.01. 13
come, let's have her aboard suddenly. 4.01. 95 P
themselves upon her, | not carry her aboard. 4.01.101
the governor, | who craves to come aboard. 5.01. 5
there is some of worth would come aboard; 5.01. 9
riding, her fortunes brought the maid aboard us, 5.03. 11
clap her aboard to-morrow night and stow her, TNK 2.03. 32
ABODE 10 FR 0.0011 REL FR 8 V 2 P
to mantua, where i hear he makes abode; TGV 4.03. 23
sweet friends, your patience for my long abode; MV 2.06. 21
sweet, | whither away, or /where is thy abode? SHR 4.05. 38
beams | upon the country where you make abode; 1H6 5.04. 88
than death can yield me here by my abode. R3 1.03.168
shall our abode | make with you by due turn. LR 1.01.134
unless his abode be ling'red here by some OTH 4.02.226 P
cleopatra's, which wholly depends on your abode. ANT 1.02.175 P
desire my man's abode where i did leave him: CYM 1.06. 53
would not afford you an abode on earth, | whet STM II.C 133
ABODED *(also boded, etc.)*
ABODED 1 FR 0.0001 REL FR 1 V 0 P
of this peace, aboded | the sudden breach on't. H8 1.01. 93
ABODEMENTS 1 FR 0.0001 REL FR 1 V 0 P
tush, man, abodements must not now affright us. 3H6 4.07. 13
ABODING 1 FR 0.0001 REL FR 1 V 0 P
the night-crow cried, aboding luckless time; 3H6 5.06. 45
ABOMINABLE *(also abbominable, abhominable)*
ABOMINABLE 15 FR 0.0017 REL FR 6 V 9 P
an abominable monster! TMP 2.02.159 P
stand under the adoption of abominable terms, WIV 2.02.295 P
from their abominable and beastly touches | i MM 3.02. 24
in extremity of either are abominable fellows, AYL 4.01. 6 P
that villainous abominable misleader of youth, 1H4 2.04.462 P
thou abominable damn'd cheater, art thou not 2H4 2.04.140 P
abominable gloucester, guard thy head, | for i 1H6 1.03. 87
and such abominable words as no christian ear 2H6 4.07. 40 P
the want thereof makes thee abominable. 3H6 1.04.133
that dissembling abominable varlet, diomed, has TRO 5.04. 2 P
you /vile abominable tents, | thus proudly 5.10. 23
body's hue, | spotted, detested, and abominable. TIT 2.03. 74
acts of black night, abominable deeds, 5.01. 64
abominable villain! LR 1.02. 78 P
o abominable! PER 4.06.134 P
ABOMINABLY 1 FR 0.0001 REL FR 0 V 1 P
them well, they imitated humanity so abominably. HAM 3.02. 35 P
ABOMINATION 2 FR 0.0002 REL FR 2 V 0 P
receipt | ere he can see his own abomination. LUC 704
and shift, | guilty of incest, that abomination; 921
ABOMINATIONS 2 FR 0.0002 REL FR 2 V 0 P
most large | in his abominations, turns you off, ANT 3.06. 94
that they will suffer these abominations LUC 1832
ABORN *(also abram*, auburn)*
ABORN 1 FR 0.0001 REL FR 1 V 0 P
but such a manly color | next to an aborn; TNK 4.02.125
ABORTIVE 4 FR 0.0004 REL FR 4 V 0 P
why should i joy in any abortive birth? LLL 1.01.104
ay, and allay this thy abortive pride: 2H6 4.01. 60
if ever he have child, abortive be it, R3 1.02. 21
thou elvish-mark'd, abortive, rooting hog! 1.03.227
ABORTIVES 1 FR 0.0001 REL FR 1 V 0 P
abortives, presages, and tongues of heaven, JN 3.04.158
ABOUND 7 FR 0.0008 REL FR 7 V 0 P
the air, | that rheumatic diseases do abound. MND 2.01.105
prison, then abound in tears | as i come out; WT 2.01.120
for humors do abound: H5 3.02. 7
so cares and joys abound, as seasons fleet. 2H6 2.04. 4
that never | they shall abound as formerly. H8 1.01. 83
though perils did | abound, as thick as thought 3.02.195
but abound | in the division of each several MAC 4.03. 95
ABOUNDING 1 FR 0.0001 REL FR 1 V 0 P
mark then abounding valor in our english: H5 4.03.104
ABOUND'ST 1 FR 0.0001 REL FR 1 V 0 P
wit, | which, like a usurer, abound'st in all, ROM 3.03.123
ABOUT *(also 'bout)*
/ABOUT 4 FR 0.0004 REL FR 2 V 2 P
/has /been /much /throwing /about /of /brains. HAM 2.02.358 P
/remembers | /what /we /are /come /about, /and LR 4.03. 40
/'tis /time /to /look /about, /the /powers /of 4.07. 92 P
rout, | no din but snores /the /house /about, PER 3.ch. 2
ABOUT 414 FR 0.0468 REL FR 281 V 133 P
lord, how it looks about! TMP 1.02.411
his fellows, | and strays about to find 'em. 1.02.418
prithee do not turn me about, my stomach is not 2.02.114 P
instruments | will hum about mine ears, and 3.02.138
blessings | of a glad father compass thee about! 5.01.180
a while, | we have some secrets to confer about. TGV 3.01. 2
about it, gentlemen! 3.02. 94
even now about it! i will pardon you. 3.02. 97
stand, sir, and throw us that you have about ye. 4.01. 3
about my stature; 4.04.158
therefore i know she is about my height. 4.04.164
and now it is about the very hour | that silvia 5.01. 2
you have not the book of riddles about you, have WIV 1.01.202 P
my honest lads, i will tell you what i am about. 1.03. 39 P
indeed i am in the waist two yards about; 1.03. 42 P
but i am now about no waste; 1.03. 42 P
i am about thrift. 1.03. 43 P
at a word, hang no more about me, i am no gibbet 2.02. 17 P
i will about it; 2.02.312 P
and i will bring the doctor about by the fields. 2.03. 78 P
go about the fields with me through frogmore, i 2.03. 85 P
will knog his urinals about his knave's costard 3.01. 14 P
knog your /urinals about your knave's cogscomb 3.01. 89 P
we have linger'd about a match between anne page 3.02. 57 P
very courageous mad about his throwing into the 4.01. 4 P
walk round about an oak, with great ragg'd horns 4.04. 31
then let them all encircle him about, | and, 4.04. 57
let us about it. 4.04. 80 P
'tis painted about with the story of the 4.05. 7 P
i spake with the old woman about it. 4.05. 34 P
they were nothing but about mistress anne page, 4.05. 46 P
that you cannot see a white spot about her. 4.05.113 P
be you in the park about midnight, at herne's 5.01. 11 P
about, about; 5.05. 55
about, about; 5.05. 55
round about the oak | of herne the hunter, let 5.05. 75
be, | to guide our measure round about the tree. 5.05. 79
about him, fairies, sing a scornful rhyme, | and 5.05. 91
pinch him, and burn him, and turn him about, 5.05.101
i will about it straight; MM 1.04. 85
a book, his face is the worst thing about him. 2.01.156 P
if his face be the worst thing about him, how 2.01.157 P
and your bum is the greatest thing about you, so 2.01.218 P
and be blown with restless violence round about 3.01.124
and see how he goes about to abuse me! 3.02.203 P
whose persuasion is | i come about my brother. 4.01. 47
proclaim it, provost, round about the city, | if 5.01.508
what, will you walk with me about the town, ERR 1.02. 22
and about evening come yourself alone | to know 3.01. 96
told me what privy marks i had about me, as, the 3.02.142 P
well, sir, i will. have you the chain about you? 4.01. 42
and that self chain about his neck, | which he 5.01. 10
witness you, | that he is borne about invisible: 5.01.187
these people saw the chain about his neck. 5.01.259
he is very busy about it. ADO 1.02. 3 P
goest about to apply a moral medicine to a 1.03. 11 P
lady, will you walk about with your friend? 2.01. 86 P
withdrawn her father to break with him about it. 2.01.157 P
to the next willow, about your own business, 2.01.187 P
about your neck, like an usurer's chain? 2.01.189 P
for my life, to break with him about beatrice. 3.02. 74 P
i pray you watch about signior leonato's door, 3.03. 92 P
how giddily 'a turns about all the hot-bloods 3.03.131 P
that have gone about | to link my dear friend to 4.01. 64
about thy thoughts and counsels of thy heart! 4.01.102
happy hour, i was about to protest i lov'd you. 4.01.284 P
i assure you, but i will go about with him. 4.02. 26 P
two gowns, and every thing handsome about him. 4.02. 86 P
songs of woe, | round about her tomb they go. 5.03. 15
round about | dapples the drowsy east with spots 5.03. 26
'a shall wear nothing handsome about him. 5.04.104 P
about surrender up of aquitaine | to her LLL 1.01.137
about the sixt hour; 1.01.235 P
all about the breast! 4.03.171
to make one, and i will whip about your infamy, 5.01. 69 P
a lady wall'd about with diamonds! 5.02. 3
signs | have brought about the annual reckoning. 5.02.798
i'll put a girdle round about the earth | in MND 2.01.175
or some loam, or some rough-cast about him, to 3.01. 69 P
i'll follow you, i'll lead you about a round, 3.01.106
what night-rule now about this haunted grove? 3.02. 5
about the wood go swifter than the wind, | and 3.02. 94

methinks i am marvail's hairy about the face; 4.01. 25 P
an ass, if he go about /t' expound this dream. 4.01.207 P
time | to wind about my love with circumstance, MV 1.01.154
have rated me | about my moneys and my usances. 1.03.108
conscience, hanging about the neck of my heart, 2.02. 14 P
pray you let's have no more fooling about it, 2.02. 83 P
ay, marry, i'll be gone about it straight. 2.04. 24
no masque to-night, the wind is come about, 2.06. 64
for who shall go about | to cozen fortune, and 2.09. 37
she doth stray about | by holy crosses, where 5.01. 30
about a hoop of gold, a paltry ring | that she 5.01.147
kindle the boy thither, which now i'll go about. AYL 1.01.173 P
son) | of him i was about to call his father — 2.03. 21
as yet to question you about your fortunes. 2.07.172
and a chain, that you once wore, about his neck. 3.02.181 P
and every thing about you demonstrating a 3.02.380 P
a sheep-cote fenc'd about with olive-trees? 4.03. 77
about his neck | a green and gilded snake had 4.03.107
master, master, look about you! SHR 1.02.140 P
about a schoolmaster for the fair bianca, | and 1.02.166
she hung about my neck, and kiss on kiss | she 2.01.308
he took the bride about the neck | and kiss'd 3.02.177
fault | i'll find about the making of the bed, 4.01.200
you might have heard it else proclaim'd about. 4.02. 87
they are busied about a counterfeit assurance. 4.04. 92 P
hap what hap may, i'll roundly go about her; 4.04.107
go not about; AWW 1.03.188
and the bannerets about thee did manifoldly 2.03.204 P
i'll about it this evening, and i will presently 3.06. 74 P
to acquaint his grace you are gone about it? 3.06. 79 P
but let's about it. 3.07. 48
little harm, save to his bed-clothes about him; 4.03.257 P
so, look about you. 4.03.312 P
and i was about to tell you, since i heard of 4.05. 69 P
shall we /set about some revels? TN 1.03.135 P
he is about the house. 2.04. 12 P
about your years, my lord. 2.04. 28
o' favor with my lady about a bear-baiting here. 2.05. 8 P
calling my officers about me, in my branch'd 2.05. 47 P
sir, does walk about the orb like the sun, it 3.01. 38 P
go about it. 3.02. 48 P
about it. 3.02. 50 P
ladyship were best to have some guard about you, 3.04. 12 P
certain, or forswear to wear iron about you. 3.04.252 P
her like her medal hanging | about his neck, WT 1.02.308
if i | had servants true about me, that bare 1.02.309
bear the boy hence, he shall not come about her. 2.01. 59
be but about | to say she is a goodly lady, and 2.01. 65
about some gossips for your highness. 2.03. 41
charg'd thee that she should not come about me: 2.03. 43
good, so were i | a man, the worst about you. 2.03. 62
i have known to go about with troll-my-dames. 4.03. 86 P
sleeve-hand and the work about the square on't. 4.04.210 P
ay, good brother, or go about to think. 4.04.217 P
sir, for i have about me many parcels of charge. 4.04.257 P
for once or twice | i was about to speak, and 4.04.443
the prince himself is about a piece of iniquity: 4.04.678 P
show those things you found about her, those 4.04.696 P
to go about to make me the king's brother-in-law 4.04.701 P
sir — about his son, that should have married a 4.04.766 P
her jewel about the neck of it; 5.02. 33 P
that think it is unlawful business | i am about, 5.03. 97
she hangs about his neck. 5.03.112
something about, a little from the right, | in JN 1.01.170
stones, | that as a waist doth girdle you about, 2.01.217
the yearly course that brings this day about 3.01. 81
side, | or as a little snow, tumbled about, 3.04.176
i knit my handkercher about your brows | (the 4.01. 42
it makes the course of thoughts to fetch about, 4.02. 24
and the fift did whirl about | the other four in 4.02.183
that neptune's arms, who clippeth thee about, 5.02. 34
breath | already smokes about the burning crest 5.04. 34
them, | and they are all about his majesty. 5.06. 36
change their moons and bring their times about, R2 1.03.220
of poor bullingbrook | about his marriage, nor 2.01.168
with signs of war about his aged neck. 2.02. 74
as if this flesh which walls about our life 3.02.167
rated me the other day in the street about you, 1H4 1.02. 85 P
the devil and thee about thy soul that thou 1.02.114 P
you were about to speak. 1.03. 22
my brother mortimer doth stir | about his title, 2.03. 82
me see — about michaelmas next i shall be — 2.04. 54 P
when i was about thy years, hal, i was not an 2.04.329 P
my skin hangs about me like an old lady's loose 3.03. 3 P
should, how would thy guts fall about thy knees! 3.03.153 P
boys | seek percy and thyself about the field, 5.04. 32
said master dommelton about the satin for my 2H4 1.02. 29 P
the prince for striking him about bardolph. 1.02. 56 P
and every part about you blasted with antiquity? 1.02.184 P
lord, i was born about three of the clock in the 1.02.187 P
about it, you know where to find me. 1.02.242 P
there is a good angel about him, but the devil 2.04.335 P
cousin, that comes hither anon about soldiers? 3.02. 28 P
nobody to do any thing about her when i am gone, 3.02.231 P
his piece thus, and 'a would about and about, 3.02.282 P
and 'a would about and about, and come you in 3.02.283 P
the feats he hath done about turnbull street, 3.02.306 P
and some about him have too lavishly | wrested 4.02. 57
wages, about the sack he lost at /hinckley fair? 5.01. 24 P
well conceited, davy. about thy business, davy. 5.01. 36 P
look about, davy. 5.01. 53 P
bardolph, and to all the cabileros about london. 5.03. 59 P
there hath been a man or two kill'd about her. 5.04. 6 P
may have their throats about them at that time, H5 2.01. 21 P
said once, the dev'l would have him about women. 2.03. 35 P
for i would fain be about the ears of the 3.07. 84 P
come, shall we about it? 3.07.155 P
tell him i'll knock his leek about his pate 4.01. 54
cap that day, lest he knock that about yours. 4.01. 57 P
that is by his father sent about merchandise do 4.01.147 P
you may as well go about to turn the sun to ice 4.01.200 P
action swarm | about our squares of battle, were 4.02. 28
a new-married wife about her husband's neck, 5.02.180 P
you'll question this gentlewoman about me; 5.02.199 P
the voice nor the heart of flattery about me, i 5.02.288 P
take my leave, | to go about my preparation. 1H6 1.01.166
come, let's away about it. 1.02.149
i had | that walk'd about me every minute while; 1.04. 54
to and fro, | about relieving of the sentinels. 2.01. 70
he, | no one, but he, should be about the king; 3.01. 38
tongue, | upbraided me about the rose i wear, 4.01. 91
the truth | about a certain question in the law 4.01. 95
iron | and hemm'd about with grim destruction. 4.03. 21
talbot, | who, ring'd about with bold adversity, 4.04. 14
alanson, /reignier, compass him about, | and 4.04. 27
approacheth, to confer about some matter. 5.04.101
with walking once about the quadrangle, | i come 2H6 1.03.153
you go about to torture me in vain. 2.01.143
that he should come about your royal person, 3.01. 26
him with his pen and inkhorn about his neck. 4.02.110 P
that thou hast men about thee that usually talk 4.07. 38 P
poor men before them about matters they were not 4.07. 42 P
lest they consult about the giving up of some 4.07.132 P
be hang'd with your pardons about your necks? 4.08. 22 P
about what? 3H6 1.02. 7
about that which concerns your grace and us: 1.02. 8
i saw him in the battle range about, | and 2.01. 11
but sound the trumpets, and about our task. 2.01.200
complete, | how many hours brings about the day, 2.05. 27
him | about the marriage of the lady bona. 4.01. 31
his soldiers lurking in the town about, | and 4.02. 15
his chief followers lodge in towns about him, 4.03. 13
that if about this hour he make this way, 4.05. 10
come therefore, let's about it speedily. 4.06.102
this hand, fast wound about thy coal-black hair, 5.01. 54
or shall we beat the stones about thine ears? 5.01.108
clarence closely be mew'd up | about a prophecy, R3 1.01. 39
spider | whose deadly web ensnareth thee about? 1.03.242
well thought upon, i have it here about me. 1.03.343
i like you, lads, about your business straight. 1.03.353
to the tower | to sit about the coronation. 3.01.173
about it, for it stands me much upon | to stop 4.02. 58
hover about me with your aery wings | and hear 4.04. 13
hover about her; 4.04. 15
thus hath the course of justice whirl'd about, 4.04.105
what need'st thou run so many miles about, 4.04.460
much about cock-shut time, from troop to troop 5.03. 70
about the mid of night come to my tent | and 5.03. 77
your choler question | what 'tis you go about: H8 1.01.131
reprov'd the duke | about sir william /bulmer — 1.02.190
or some about him near, have out of malice | to 2.01.157
has hung twenty years | about his neck, yet 2.02. 32
there ye shall meet about this weighty business. 2.02.139
sir, | i am about to weep; 2.04. 70
there be moe wasps that buzz about his nose 3.02. 55
about the giving-back the great seal to us, 3.02.347
the voice is now | only about her coronation. 3.02.406
alter'd that the old name | is fresh about me. 4.01. 99
about the hour of eight, which he himself 4.02. 26
this is about that which the bishop spake. 5.01. 84
all that stand about him are under the line, 5.03. 42 P
royal infant — heaven still move about her! 5.04. 17
and those about her | from her shall read the 5.04. 36
his branches | to all the plains about him. 5.04. 54
i was about to tell thee — when my heart, | as TRO 1.01. 34
he'll lay about him to-day, i can tell them that 1.02. 56 P
the first sword was drawn about this question, 2.02. 18
no, pandarus, i stalk about her door, | like to 3.02. 8
farewell, the gods with safety stand about thee! 5.03. 94
come here about me, you my myrmidons, | mark 5.07. 1
empale him with your weapons round about, | in 5.07. 5
till then i'll sweat and seek about for eases, 5.10. 55
y' are long about it. COR 1.01.127
was forc'd to wheel | three or four miles about, 1.06. 20
as with a man busied about decrees: 1.06. 34
for once we stood up about the corn, he himself 2.03. 15 P
what is about to be? 3.01.188
let them pull all about mine ears, present me 3.02. 1
prithee now, say you will, and go about it. 3.02. 98
go about it. 3.03. 24
let me twine | mine arms about that body, where 4.05.107
he turn'd me about with his finger and his thumb 4.05.152 P
and going | about their functions friendly. 4.06. 9
than when these fellows ran about the streets, 4.06. 28
he'll shake | your rome about your ears. 4.06. 99
gods sit in hourly synod about thy particular 5.02. 69 P
and thou, and i, sit round about some fountain, TIT 3.01.123
you heavy people, circle me about, | that i may 3.01.276
a scroll, and written round about. 4.02. 18
and sends them weapons wrapp'd about with lines 4.02. 27
sweet scrolls to fly about the streets of rome! 4.04. 16
and whirl along with thee about the globes. 5.02. 49
look round about the wicked streets of rome, 5.02. 98
now will i hence about thy business, | and take 5.02.132
he swung about his head and cut the winds, | who ROM 1.01.111
sirrah, trudge about | through fair verona, find 1.02. 34
she could have run and waddled all about; 1.03. 37
to see now how a jest shall come about! 1.03. 45
i am so vex'd that every part about me quivers. 2.04.162 P
beshrew your heart for sending me about | to 2.05. 51
lest mine be about your ears ere it be out. 3.01. 81 P
the day is broke, be wary, look about. 3.05. 40
tush, i will stir about, | and all things shall 4.02. 39
and about his shelves | a beggarly account of 5.01. 44
ground is bloody, search about the churchyard. 5.03.172
true; for he bears it not about him, 'tis hid. TIM 4.03.406 P
i never had honest men about me, i; 4.03.477
why dost thou lead these men about the streets? JC 1.01. 28
i'll about, | and drive away the vulgar from the 1.01. 69
and peep about | to find ourselves dishonorable 1.02.137
let me have men about me that are fat, 1.02.192
for my part, i have walk'd about the streets, 1.03. 46
sir, their hats are pluck'd about their ears, 2.01. 73
at supper | you suddenly arose and walk'd about, 2.01.239
ghosts did shriek and squeal about the streets. 2.02. 24
if thou beest not immortal, look about you; 2.03. 7 P
about the ninth hour, lady. 2.04. 23
run hence, proclaim, cry it about the streets. 3.01. 79
not have any hand at all | about his funeral. 3.01.249
then make a ring about the corpse of caesar, 3.02.158
about! 3.02.204 P
the stake, | and bay'd about with many enemies, 4.01. 49
now sit we close about this taper here, | and 4.03.164
and tell me what thou not'st about the field. 5.03. 22
titinius is enclosed round about | with horsemen 5.03. 28
i will proclaim my name about the field. 5.04. 3
thus do go, about, about, | thrice to thine, and MAC 1.03. 34
of the sea and land, | thus do go, about, about, 1.03. 34
were such things here as we do speak about? 1.03. 83
he is about it: 2.02. 4
that death and nature do contend about them, 2.02. 7
have napkins enow about you, here you'll sweat 2.03. 6 P
his horses go about. 3.03. 11
round about the cauldron go; 4.01. 4
and now about the cauldron sing, | like elves 4.01. 41
hanging a golden stamp about their necks, | put 4.03.153
and sundry blessings hang about his throne 4.03.158
does he feel his title | hang loose about him, 5.02. 21
it was about to speak, when the cock crew. HAM 1.01.147
mine, | and a most instant tetter bark'd about, 1.05. 71
'a this — 'a does — what was i about to say? 2.01. 49
by the mass, i was about to say something. 2.01. 50
then you live about her waist, or in the middle 2.02.232 P
about her lank and all o'er-teemed loins, | a 2.02.508
about, my brains! 2.02.588
they are here about the court, | and, as i think 3.01. 19
about the world have times twelve thirties been, 3.02.158
why do you go about to recover the wind of me, 3.02.346 P
for we will fetters put about this fear, | which 3.03. 25
or about some act | that has no relish of 3.03. 91
cudgel thy brains no more about it, for your 5.01. 56 P
and knock'd about the /mazzard with a sexton's 5.01. 89 P
now to knock him about the sconce with a dirty 5.01.102 P
my sea-gown scarf'd about me, in the dark 5.02. 13
not think how ill all's here about my heart — 5.02.212 P
unknowing world | how these things came about. 5.02.380
father's curse | pierce every sense about thee! LR 1.04.301
thy asses are gone about 'em. 1.05. 34 P
having more man than wit about me, drew. 2.04. 42
for many miles about | there's scarce a bush. 2.04.301
see what breeds about her heart. 3.06. 77 P
thou dost bear | with something rich about me. 4.01. 77
father, | it is thy business that i go about; 4.04. 24
and give the letters which thou find'st about me 4.06.248
about it, and write happy when th' hast done. 5.03. 35
i have charg'd thee not to haunt about my doors. OTH 1.01. 96
the senate hath sent about three several quests 1.02. 46
whose messengers are here about my side, | upon 1.02. 89
i am about it, but indeed my invention | comes 2.01.125
down, | /then take thy auld cloak about thee." 2.03. 96
iago, look with care about the town, | and 2.03.255
that she reserves it evermore about her | to 3.03.295
above, | you elements that clip us round about, 3.03.464
i have it not about me. 3.04. 53
rub him about the temples. 4.01. 52
/by /this /hand, falls me thus about my neck — 4.01.135 P
about it. 4.02.243 P
blow me about in winds! 5.02.279
about the mount misena. ANT 2.02.160
is shorter, | my purposes do draw me much about. 2.04. 8
the hangman thank | for being yare about him. 3.13.131
heard you of nothing strange about the streets? 4.03. 3
them home | with clouts about their heads. 4.07. 6
none about caesar trust but proculeius. 4.15. 48
and my hands i'll trust, | none about caesar. 4.15. 50
i'll fetch a turn about the garden, pitying CYM 1.01. 81
about some half hour hence, | pray you speak 1.01.176
that others do | (i was about to say) enjoy your 1.06. 91
ah, but some natural notes about her body, 2.02. 28
i know her women are about her; 2.03. 66
render to me some corporal sign about her, 2.04.119
the king, he rages, none | dare come about him. 3.05. 68
the noise is round about us. 4.04. 1
were clipt about | with this most tender air. 5.05.451
had princes sit like stars about his throne, PER 2.03. 39
you shall like diamonds sit about his crown. 2.04. 53
having | rich tire about you, should at these 3.02. 22
and we shall tack about | and something do to TNK pr 26
prorogue this business we are going about, and 1.01.196
your heart, about that neck | which is my fee, 1.01.197
with mind assur'd | 'tis bad he goes about? 1.02. 98
then but beginning | to swell about the blossom) 1.03. 68
up with a course or two, and tack about, boys! 3.04. 10
"there was three fools fell out about an howlet: 3.05. 67
about this hour my cousin gave his faith | to 3.06. 1
live, | and have the agony of love about 'em, 3.06.219
every day | they'ld fight about you; 3.06.221
about her stuck | thousand fresh water-flowers 4.01. 84
tack about! 4.01.152
about his head he wears the winner's oak, | and 4.02.137
show | bravely about the titles of two kingdoms. 4.02.145
what broken piece of matter soe'er she's about, 4.03. 6 P
his testy master goeth about to take him, | when VEN 319
some twin'd about her thigh to make her stay. 873
the curtains being close, about he walks, LUC 367
who like a foul usurper went about | from this 412
knit poisonous clouds about his golden head. 777
about him were a press of gaping faces, | which 1408
she throws her eyes about the painting round, 1499
and round about her tear-distained eye | blue 1586
about the mourning and congealed face | of that 1744
and that which governs me to go about | doth SON 113. 2

ABOVE *(also 'bove)*

/ABOVE 2 FR 0.0002 REL FR 2 V 0 P
and more /above, hath his solicitings, | as they HAM 2.02.126
/the /stars /above /us, /govern /our /conditions LR 4.03. 33

ABOVE 134 FR 0.0151 REL FR 108 V 26 P
the wills above be done! TMP 1.01. 67 P
with volumes that | i prize above my dukedom. 1.02.168
i hear it now above me. 1.02.408
lest it should burn above the bounds of reason. TGV 2.07. 23
therefore, above the rest, we parley to you: 4.01. 58
troth, sir, all is in his hands above. WIV 1.04.144 P
have not your worship a wart above your eye? 1.04.147 P
i'll be sure to keep him above deck. 2.01. 91 P
the fat woman of brainford, has a gown above. 4.02. 76 P
over and above that you have suffer'd, i think 5.05.168 P
one that, above all other strifes, contended MM 3.02.232 P
then, o you blessed ministers above, | keep me 5.01.115
husband, i'll dine above with you to-day, | and ERR 2.02.207
"the god of love, | that sits above, | and knows ADO 5.02. 27
above their functions and their offices. LLL 4.03.329
above the sense of sense, so sensible | seemeth 5.02.259
eyesight, and did value me | above this world; 5.02.446

have discontinued school | above a twelvemonth. MV 3.04. 76
but mercy is above this sceptred sway, | it is 4.01.193
are not with me esteem'd above thy life. 4.01.285
and stand indebted, over and above, | in love 4.01.413
with thy chaste eye, from thy pale sphere above, AYL 3.02. 3
hast hawks will soar | above the morning lark. SHR in.2. 44
and slept above some fifteen year or more. in.2. 113
star | and think to wed it, he is so above me. AWW 1.01. 87
love make your fortunes twenty times above | her 2.03. 82
whom i serve above is my master. 2.03.246 P
she'll not match above her degree, neither in TN 1.03.110 P
one draught above heat makes him a fool, the 1.05.132 P
above my fortunes, yet my state is well: 1.05.278
"above my fortunes, yet my state is well: 1.05.290
in my stars i am above thee, but be not afraid 2.05.144 P
feign, you witnesses above | punish my life for 5.01.137
forty thousand fadom above water, and sung this WT 4.04.277 P
time doth boast itself | above a better gone, so 5.01. 97
nobleness which nature shows above her breeding; 5.02. 37 P
now, by the sky that hangs above our heads, | i JN 2.01.397
and tempt us not to bear above our power! 5.06. 38
lift me up | to reach at victory above my head, R2 1.03. 72
so high above his limits swells the rage | of 3.02.109
thee behind the arras, the rest walk up above. 1H4 2.04.501 P
swore little, dic'd not above seven times — a 3.03. 16 P
to a bawdy-house not above once in a quarter — 3.03. 17 P
the sun begins to peer | above yon bulky hill! 5.01. 2
where valiant talbot above human thought 1H6 1.01.121
love, | for my profession's sacred from above. 1.02.114
virtuous and holy, chosen from above, | by 5.04. 39
above the reach or compass of thy thought? 2H6 1.02. 46
and what a pitch she flew above the rest! 2.01. 6
and bears his thoughts above his falcon's pitch. 2.01. 12
i thought as much, he would be above the clouds. 2.01. 15
above the felon or what trespass else. 3.01.132
here on my knee i vow to god above | i'll never 3H6 2.03. 29
woe above woe! 2.05. 94
i'll stay above the hill, so both may shoot. 3.01. 5
his car | above the border of this horizon, 4.07. 81
which pleaseth god above | and all good men of R3 3.07.109
single, but now married | to one above itself. H8 1.01. 16
given a president of wisdom | above all princes, 2.02. 86
not (so much i am happy | above a number) if my 3.01. 34
heaven is above all yet; 3.01.100
what can happen | to me above this wretchedness? 3.01.123
think | his contemplation were above the earth, 3.02.131
within me | a peace above all earthly dignities, 3.02.379
'tis well there's one above 'em yet. 5.02. 27
well, the gods are above, time must friend or TRO 1.02. 77 P
she prais'd his complexion above paris. 1.02. 98 P
if she prais'd him above, his complexion is 1.02.102 P
they pass by, but mark troilus above the rest. 1.02.183 P
price hath launch'd above a thousand ships, 2.02. 82
sweet, above thought i love /thee! 3.01.159
that dwells with gods above. 3.02.157
i were as deep under the earth as i am above! 4.02. 83 P
above an hour, my lord. COR 1.06. 15
while i remain above the ground, you shall 4.01. 51
musty chaff, and you are smelt | above the moon. 5.01. 32
rome, | lov'd me above the measure of a father, 5.03. 10
advanc'd above pale envy's threat'ning reach. TIT 2.01. 4
and soar with them above a common bound. ROM 1.04. 18
bound | i cannot bound a pitch above dull woe; 1.04. 21
soul | is but a little way above our heads, 3.01.127
the vaulty heaven so high above our heads. 3.05. 22
which she hath prais'd him with above compare 3.05.238
seeing she is advanc'd | above the clouds, as 4.05. 74
lifts me above the ground with cheerful thoughts 5.01. 5
mean eyes have seen | the foot above the head. TIM 1.01. 94
no meed but he repays | sevenfold above itself; 1.01.278
to dispense, | for policy sits above conscience. 3.02. 87
sum | your master's confidence was above mine, 3.04. 31
hath to the marbled mansion all above | never 4.03.191
under that's above me. 4.03.292
ingratitude with loves | above their quantity. 5.04. 18
who else would soar above the view of men, | and JC 1.01. 74
that this foul deed shall smell above the earth 3.01.274
of these (with him above | to ratify the work) MAC 3.06. 32
but god above | deal between thee and me! 4.03.120
and the pow'rs above | put on their instruments. 4.03.238
this above all: HAM 1.03. 78
was never acted, or, if it was, not above once; 2.02.435 P
but 'tis not so above: 3.03. 60
above the rest, be gone. LR 4.01. 48
this shows you are above, | you /justicers, that 4.02. 78
this is above all strangeness. 4.06. 66
nature's above art in that respect. 4.06. 86 P
they are centaurs, | though women all above; 4.06.125
well, /god's above all; OTH 2.03.102 P
witness, you ever-burning lights above, | you 3.03.463
when thou wast here above the ground, i was | a ANT 1.05. 30
they show'd his back above | the element they 5.02. 89
the fiery orbs above and the twinn'd stones CYM 1.06. 35
above ten thousand meaner moveables | would 2.02. 29
in my respect than all the hairs above thee, 2.03.135
and cydnus swell'd above the banks, or for | the 2.04. 71
o, above measure false! 2.04.113
when you above perceive me like a crow, | that 3.03. 12
the advantage of the time, above him in birth, 4.01. 12 P
the fingers of the pow'rs above do tune | the 5.05.466
thunder above, and deeps below, | makes such PER 2.ch. 30
for who hates honor hates the gods above. 2.03. 22
princes in this should live like gods above, 2.03. 59
she hath not been | entranc'd above five hours. 3.02. 94
we cannot but obey | the powers above us. 3.03. 10
if not above him, for | thou, being but mortal, TNK 1.01.228
they stand a grise above the reach of report. 2.01. 28 P
i'll cut my green coat a foot above my knee, 3.04. 19
their swelling incense | to those above us. 5.01. 5
you leave dispute | that are above our question. 5.04.136
is the provision of the power above | fitted and STM III 3
"the field's chief flower, sweet above compare, VEN 8
spirits taught to write | above a mortal pitch, SON 86. 6
wherein it finds a joy above the rest, | but 91. 6
but, by all above, | these blenches gave my 110. 6
which shall above that idle rank remain | beyond 122. 3
which like a cherubin above them hover'd. LC 319

ABRAHAM 4 FR 0.0004 REL FR 2 V 2 P
between master abraham and mistress anne page. WIV 1.01. 56 P
cousin abraham slender, can you love her? 1.01.232 P
sweet soul to the bosom | of good old abraham! R2 4.01.104
young abraham cupid, he that shot so /trim, ROM 2.01. 13

ABRAHAM'S 1 FR 0.0001 REL FR 1 V 0 P
the sons of edward sleep in abraham's bosom, R3 4.03. 38

ABRAM* *(also aborn, auburn)*

ABRAM* 3 FR 0.0003 REL FR 2 V 1 P
this jacob from our holy abram was | (as his MV 1.03. 72
o father abram, what these christians are, 1.03.160
some brown, some black, some abram, some bald, COR 2.03. 19 P

ABREAST 3 FR 0.0003 REL FR 3 V 0 P
tarry, sweet soul, for mine, then fly abreast, H5 4.06. 17
lord clifford, and lord stafford, all abreast, 3H6 1.01. 7
strait so narrow, | where one but goes abreast. TRO 3.03.155

A-BREEDING 1 FR 0.0001 REL FR 1 V 0 P
spring is near when green geese are a-breeding. LLL 1.01. 97

A-BREWING 1 FR 0.0001 REL FR 1 V 0 P
there is some ill a-brewing towards my rest, MV 2.05. 17

ABRIDG'D 2 FR 0.0002 REL FR 2 V 0 P
nor do i now make moan to be abridg'd | from MV 1.01.126
that have abridg'd | his time of fearing death. JC 3.01.104

ABRIDGE 2 FR 0.0002 REL FR 2 V 0 P
besides, thy staying will abridge thy life. TGV 3.01.247
death rock me asleep, abridge my doleful days! 2H4 2.04.197

ABRIDGMENT 5 FR 0.0005 REL FR 4 V 1 P
say, what abridgment have you for this evening? MND 5.01. 39
then brook abridgment, and your eyes advance H5 5.pr. 44
you more, for look where my abridgment comes. HAM 2.02.420 P
this fierce abridgment | hath to it CYM 5.05.382
"this brief abridgment of my will i make: LUC 1198

ABROACH 3 FR 0.0003 REL FR 3 V 0 P
what mischiefs might he set abroach | in shadow 2H4 4.02. 14
the secret mischiefs that i set abroach | i lay R3 1.03.324
who set this ancient quarrel new abroach? ROM 1.01.104

ABROAD 66 FR 0.0074 REL FR 53 V 13 P
how features are abroad | i am skilless of; TMP 3.01. 52
i few attendants, | and subjects none abroad. 5.01.167
to see the wonders of the world abroad, | than TGV 1.01. 6
what news abroad, friar? MM 3.02. 83 P
what news abroad i' th' world? 3.02.221 P
there's villainy abroad. LLL 1.01.188 P
all-telling fame | doth noise abroad, navarre 2.01. 22
my affections would | be with my hopes abroad. MV 1.01. 17
and other ventures he hath, squand'red abroad. 1.03. 21 P
fond | to come abroad with him at his request. 3.03. 10
home, | and so am come abroad to see the world. SHR 1.02. 58
i have for the most part been air'd abroad, i WT 4.02. 5 P
sir, there are cozeners abroad, therefore it 4.04.253 P
why should i carry lies abroad? 4.04.271 P
james, | there's toys abroad; JN 1.01.232
hear'st thou the news abroad, who are arriv'd? 4.02.160
come, come; sans compliment, what news abroad? 5.06. 16
then thieves and robbers range abroad unseen R2 3.02. 39
there's villainous news abroad. 1H4 2.04.333 P
is | to noise abroad that harry monmouth fell 2H4 in 29
i am glad to see your lordship abroad. 1.02. 94 P
i hope your lordship goes abroad by advice. 1.02. 96 P
how now, rain within doors, and none abroad? 4.05. 9
while that the armed hand doth fight abroad, H5 1.02.178
others, like merchants, venter trade abroad; 1.02.192
so much fear'd abroad | that with his name the 1H6 2.03. 16
his hands abroad display'd, as one that grasp'd 2H6 3.02.172
what news abroad? 3H6 2.01. 95
unless abroad they purchase great alliance? 3.03. 70
(as i will meet thee, if thou stir abroad), | to 5.01. 96
for i will buzz abroad such prophecies | that 5.06. 86
what news abroad? R3 1.01.134
no news so bad abroad as this at home: 1.01.135
hear you the news abroad? 2.03. 3
rumor it abroad | that anne, my wife, is very 4.02. 50
bevy, has brought with her | one care abroad. H8 1.04. 5
is he ready | to come abroad? 3.02. 83
what news abroad? 3.02.391
but to the sport abroad — are you bound thither TRO 1.01.115
life, | and set abroad new business for you all? TIT 1.01.192
blow these sands like sibyl's leaves abroad, 4.01.105
east, | a troubled mind drive me to walk abroad, ROM 1.01.120
the day is hot, the capels /are abroad, | and if 3.01. 2
what should it be that is so /shrik'd abroad? 5.03.190
valor in the bearing, what make we | abroad? TIM 3.05. 47
to walk abroad and recreate yourselves. JC 3.02.251
thy spirit walks abroad, and turns our swords 5.03. 95
foul whisp'rings are abroad. MAC 5.01. 71
as calling home our exil'd friends abroad | that 5.09. 32
and then they say no spirit dare stir abroad, HAM 1.01.161
if you do stir abroad, go arm'd. LR 1.02.170 P
you have heard of the news abroad, i mean the 2.01. 7 P
and it is thought abroad that 'twixt my sheets OTH 1.03.387
or heard him say — as knaves be such abroad, 4.01. 25
shalt thou have report | how 'tis abroad. ANT 1.04. 36
what you shall know mean time | of stirs abroad, 1.04. 82
there's none abroad so wholesome as that you CYM 1.02. 4 P
your means abroad — | you have me, rich, and i 3.04.177
no company's abroad? 4.02.101
what company | discover you abroad? 4.02.130
what a misery | it is to live abroad, and every TNK 2.02. 98
remember, cousin, | else there be tales abroad. 3.03. 38
is blown abroad, help me, thy poor well-willer, 3.05.116
do, very /rearly, i must be abroad else, | to 4.01.110
the goodly objects which abroad they find | of LC 137
"'all my offenses that abroad you see | are 183

ABROGATE 1 FR 0.0001 REL FR 0 V 1 P
so it shall please you to abrogate squirility. LLL 4.02. 54 P

ABROOK *(also brook*)*

ABROOK 1 FR 0.0001 REL FR 1 V 0 P
nell, ill can thy noble mind abrook | the abject 2H6 2.04. 10

ABRUPT 1 FR 0.0001 REL FR 1 V 0 P
to know the cause of your abrupt departure. 1H6 2.03. 30

ABRUPTION 1 FR 0.0001 REL FR 0 V 1 P
what makes this pretty abruption? TRO 3.02. 65 P

ABRUPTLY 1 FR 0.0001 REL FR 1 V 0 P
if thou hast not broke from company | abruptly, AYL 2.04. 41

ABSENCE 57 FR 0.0064 REL FR 46 V 11 P
else | betideth here in absence of thy friend; TGV 1.01. 59
i will not be absence at the grace. WIV 1.01.264 P
that her husband will be absence from his house 2.02. 84 P
to take an ill advantage of his absence. 3.03.109 P
soul | elected him our absence to supply, | lent MM 1.01. 18
lord angelo dukes it well in his absence; 3.02. 94 P
you at the prison, in the absence of the duke. 5.01.328 P
from whom my absence was not six months old ERR 1.01. 44
your absence only. LLL 5.02.225
which death, or absence, soon shall remedy. MND 3.02.244
one among them but i dote on his very absence, MV 1.02.110 P
in bearing thus the absence of your lord. 3.04. 4
if you would walk in absence of the sun. 5.01.128
by reason of his absence, there is nothing AYL 2.04. 85
my lady will hang thee for thy absence. TN 1.05. 4 P
of what may chance | or breed upon our absence, WT 1.02. 12
thinks she has been sluic'd in 's absence, | and 1.02.194
what you have underta'en to do in 's absence. 3.02. 78
and with my best endeavors, in your absence, 4.04.531
our absence makes us unthrifty to our knowledge. 5.02.111 P
th' advantage of his absence took the king, JN 1.01.102
thy grief is but thy absence for a time. R2 1.03.258
and we create, in absence of ourself, | our 2.01.219
this absence of your father's draws a curtain 1H4 4.01. 73
i rather of his absence make this use: 4.01. 76
and what with owen glendower's absence thence, 4.04. 16
our substitutes in absence well invested, | and 2H4 4.04. 6
eggs, | playing the mouse in absence of the cat, H5 1.02.172
my lord, your nobles, jealous of your absence, 4.01.285
trust | my absence doth neglect no great design, R3 3.04. 24
and we forgetful | in our long absence. H8 2.03.106
had she no lover there | that wails her absence? TRO 4.05.289
rejoice in that absence wherein he won honor COR 1.03. 3 P
yarn she spun in ulysses' absence did but fill 1.03. 83 P
or defend yourself | by calmness or by absence. 3.02. 95
doth ever cool | i' th' absence of the needer. 4.01. 44
safety were remotion and thy defense absence. TIM 4.03.343 P
impatient of my absence, | and grief that young JC 4.03.152
whose absence is no less material to me | than MAC 3.01.135
his absence, sir, | lays blame upon his promise. 3.04. 42
interim shall support | by his dear absence. OTH 1.03.259
time, | strike off this score of absence. 3.04.179
to the felt absence now i feel a cause. 3.04.182
in the state | cannot endure my absence. ANT 1.02.172
which in thy absence is | no better than a sty? 4.15. 61
i pray his absence | proceed by swallowing that; CYM 3.05. 57
as i'ld give to him | (after long absence), such 3.06. 73
a fever with the absence of her son; 4.03. 2
but failing of her end by his strange absence, 5.05. 57
but should he wrong my liberties in my absence? PER 1.02.112
you | to forbear the absence of your king; 2.04. 46
o absence, what a torment wouldst thou prove, SON 39. 9
you, | nor think the bitterness of absence sour, 57. 7
beck) | th' imprison'd absence of your liberty, 58. 6
how like a winter hath my absence been | from 97. 1
though absence seem'd my flame to qualify! 109. 2
and makes her absence valiant, not her might. LC 245

ABSENT 34 FR 0.0038 REL FR 27 V 7 P
and much please the absent duke, if peradventure MM 3.01.203 P
would the duke that is absent have done this? 3.02.116 P
i never heard the absent duke much detected for 3.02.121 P
how came it that the absent duke had not either 4.02.132 P
combined by a sacred vow, | and shall be absent. 4.03.145
fashion the matter that hero shall be absent — ADO 2.02. 47 P
no note at all of our being absent hence — MV 5.01.120
when i am absent, then lie with my wife. 5.01.285
if he be absent, bring his brother to me; AYL 2.02. 18
i should not seek an absent argument | of my 3.01. 3
that i should yet absent me from your bed. SHR in.2. 123
of my thoughts | happily been absent then. AWW 1.03.235
the coming space, | expecting absent friends. 2.03.182
fill the time, | herself most chastely absent. 3.07. 34
yet you will be hang'd for being so long absent, TN 1.05. 17 P
they have seem'd to be together, though absent; WT 1.01. 29 P
twenty-three days | they have been absent. 2.03.199
grief fills the room up of my absent child, JN 3.04. 93
joy absent, grief is present for that time. R2 1.03.259
you on | to take advantage of the absent time, 2.03. 79
of all the favorites that the absent king | in 1H4 4.03. 86
what with our help, what with the absent king, 5.01. 49
the queen hath best success when you are absent. 3H6 2.02. 74
the queen being absent, 'tis a needful fitness H8 2.04.232
and, her attendants absent, swallow'd fire. JC 4.03.156
things, | whose hearts are absent too. MAC 5.04. 14
thy heart, | absent thee from felicity a while, HAM 5.02.347
that, i being absent and my place supplied, | my OTH 3.03. 17
and lovers' absent hours, | more tedious than 3.04.174
the perturb'd court | for my being absent? CYM 3.04.106
bird melodious, or bird fair, | is absent hence! TNK 1.01. 18
when i am sometime absent from thy heart, | thy SON 41. 2
be absent from thy walks, and in my tongue | thy 89. 9
from you have i been absent in the spring, 98. 1

ABSEY *(also abc)*

ABSEY 1 FR 0.0001 REL FR 1 V 0 P
and then comes answer like an absey book: JN 1.01.196

ABSOLUTE 34 FR 0.0038 REL FR 28 V 6 P
it for, he needs will be | absolute milan — me TMP 1.02.109
thou wouldst make an absolute courtier, and the WIV 3.03. 62 P
my absolute power and place here in vienna, MM 1.03. 13
be absolute for death: 3.01. 5
shy, as grave, as just, as absolute | as angelo. 5.01. 54
and pardon absolute for yourself and these 1H4 4.03. 50
upon such large terms and so absolute | as our 2H4 4.01.184
lord, it is a most absolute and excellent horse. H5 3.07. 25 P
mark you | his absolute "shall"? COR 3.01. 90
though there the people had more absolute pow'r, 3.01.116
you are too absolute, | though therein you can 3.02. 39
therefore, most absolute sir, if thou wilt have 4.05.136
allow'd with absolute power, and thy good name TIM 5.01.162
a gentleman on whom i built | an absolute trust. MAC 1.04. 14
and with an absolute "sir, not i," | the cloudy 3.06. 40
i speak not as in absolute fear of you. 4.03. 38
how absolute the knave is! HAM 5.01.137 P
believe me, an absolute /gentleman, full of most 5.02.107 P
this old majesty, | to him our absolute power. LR 5.03.301
my soul hath her content so absolute | that not OTH 2.01.191
not out of absolute lust (though peradventure 2.01.292
any thing alexas, almost most absolute alexas, ANT 1.02. 2 P
but by sea | he is an absolute master. 2.02.163
of lower syria, cyprus, lydia, | absolute queen. 3.06. 11

the absolute soldiership you have by land, 3.07. 42
i have an absolute hope | our landmen will stand 4.03. 10
most absolute lord, | my mistress cleopatra sent 4.14.117
levy, he commands | his absolute commission. CYM 3.07. 10
i am absolute | 'twas very cloten. 4.02.106
not | absolute madness could so far have rav'd 4.02.135
nay, how absolute she's in't, | not minding PER 2.05. 19
contends in skill | with absolute marina: 4.ch. 31
they are fam'd to be a pair of absolute men. TNK 2.01. 26 P
but no perfection is so absolute, | that some LUC 853

ABSOLUTELY 2 FR 0.0002 REL FR 1 V 1 P
amaz'd, but this shall absolutely resolve you. MM 4.02.209 P
to hear and absolutely to determine | of what 2H4 4.01.162

ABSOLUTION 1 FR 0.0001 REL FR 1 V 0 P
the blackest sin is clear'd with absolution; LUC 354

ABSOLV'D 3 FR 0.0003 REL FR 3 V 0 P
ever yet committed | may be absolv'd in english. H8 3.01. 50
out of holy pity, | absolv'd him with an axe. 3.02.264
cell, | to make confession and to be absolv'd. ROM 3.05.233

ABSTAINING 2 FR 0.0002 REL FR 2 V 0 P
think, | did i not by th' abstaining of my joy, TNK 1.01.189
weak–built hopes persuade him to abstaining: LUC 130

ABSTAINS 1 FR 0.0001 REL FR 1 V 0 P
and who abstains from meat that is not gaunt? R2 2.01. 76

ABSTENIOUS 1 FR 0.0001 REL FR 1 V 0 P
be more abstenious, | or else good night your TMP 4.01. 53

ABSTINENCE 5 FR 0.0005 REL FR 5 V 0 P
(a man of stricture and firm abstinence) | my MM 1.03. 12
he doth with holy abstinence subdue | that in 4.02. 81
too young, | and abstinence engenders maladies. LLL 4.03.291
a kind of easiness | to the next abstinence, the HAM 3.04.167
and here to keep in abstinence we shame | as in TNK 1.02. 6

/ABSTRACT 1 FR 0.0001 REL FR 1 V 0 P
there | a man who is th' /abstract of all faults ANT 1.04. 9

ABSTRACT 6 FR 0.0006 REL FR 3 V 3 P
but he hath an abstract for the remembrance of WIV 4.02. 62 P
length a–piece, by an abstract of success. AWW 4.03. 86 P
this little abstract doth contain that large JN 2.01.101
brief abstract and record of tedious days, R3 4.04. 28
for they are the abstract and brief chronicles HAM 2.02.524 P
being an abstract 'tween his lust and him. ANT 3.06. 61

ABSURD 4 FR 0.0004 REL FR 4 V 0 P
this proffer is absurd and reasonless. 1H6 5.04.137
to reason most absurd, whose common theme | is HAM 1.02.103
no, let the candied tongue lick absurd pomp, 3.02. 60
and to conquer | their most absurd intents. ANT 5.02.226

ABSYRTUS 1 FR 0.0001 REL FR 1 V 0 P
i cut it | as wild medea young absyrtus did; 2H6 5.02. 59

ABUNDANCE 14 FR 0.0015 REL FR 8 V 6 P
of it own kind, all foison, all abundance, | to TMP 2.01.164
were in the same abundance as your good fortunes
MV 1.02. 4 P
than lack it where there is such abundance. AWW 1.01. 10 P
with this abundance of superfluous breath? JN 2.01.148
one that hath abundance of charge too — god 1H4 2.01. 58 P
for he hath the horn of abundance, and the 2H4 1.02. 46 P
rich, | that have abundance and enjoy it not. 4.04.108
an inventory to particularize their abundance; COR 1.01. 21 P
poor in, that you two have not in abundance? 2.01. 17 P
although they gave their creatures in abundance, PER 1.04. 36
fuel, | making a famine where abundance lies, SON 1. 7
whose strength's abundance weakens his own heart 23. 4
give, | that i in thy abundance am suffic'd, 37.11
still, | and in abundance addeth to his store, 135.10

ABUNDANT 4 FR 0.0004 REL FR 3 V 1 P
to breathe the abundant dolor of the heart. R2 1.03.257
and thy abundant goodness shall excuse | this 5.03. 65
ignorance itself knows is so abundant scarce, it TRO 2.03. 15 P
yet this abundant issue seem'd to me | but hope SON 97. 9

ABUNDANTLY 1 FR 0.0001 REL FR 1 V 0 P
for though abundantly they lack discretion, COR 1.01.202

ABURGA'NY 2 FR 0.0002 REL FR 2 V 0 P
o my lord aburga'ny, fare you well! H8 1.01.211
lord aburga'ny, to whom by oath he menac'd 1.02.137

/ABUS'D 1 FR 0.0001 REL FR 1 V 0 P
/as /flatteries, /when /they /are /seen /abus'd. LR 1.03. 20

ABUS'D 40 FR 0.0045 REL FR 31 V 9 P
my bed shall be abus'd, my coffers ransack'd, my WIV 2.02.292 P
lord, and i have heard | your royal ear abus'd. MM 5.01.139
the prince and claudio mightily abus'd, and don ADO 5.02. 98 P
should of another therefore be abus'd! MND 2.02.134
see, | none could be so abus'd in sight as he. AYL 3.05. 79
thus strangers may be hal'd and abus'd. SHR 5.01.108 P
lord, | who hath abus'd me, as he knows himself, AWW 5.03.298
and i say there was never man thus abus'd. TN 4.02. 47 P
fool, there was never man so notoriously abus'd; 4.02. 88 P
of myself, and by my friends i am abus'd; 5.01. 20 P
he hath been most notoriously abus'd. 5.01.379
you are abus'd, and by some putter–on | that WT 2.01.141
of the french upbraided or abus'd in disdainful H5 3.06.111 P
but thus his simple truth must be abus'd | with R3 1.03. 52
to hear the city | abus'd extremely, and to cry, H8 ep 6
the people are abus'd, set on. COR 3.01. 58
the highest degree | he hath abus'd your powers. 5.06. 85
poor soul, thy face is much abus'd with tears. ROM 4.01. 29
by a forged process of my death | rankly abus'd; HAM 1.05. 38
much more worse | to have her gentleman abus'd, LR 2.02.149
being apt | to have his ear abus'd, wisdom bids 2.04.307
then edgar was abus'd. 3.07. 91
i am mightily abus'd; 4.07. 52
property of youth and maidhood | may be abus'd?
OTH 1.01.173
abus'd her delicate youth with drugs or minerals 1.02. 74
she is abus'd, stol'n from me, and corrupted 1.03. 60
her delicate tenderness will find itself abus'd, 2.01.232 P
noble nature, | out of self–bounty, be abus'd; 3.03.200
i am abus'd, and my relief | must be to loathe 3.03.267
i swear 'tis better to be much abus'd | than but 3.03.336
the moor's abus'd by some most villainous knave, 4.02.139
too cruel, | that he his high authority abus'd, ANT 3.06. 33
you are abus'd | beyond the mark of thought; 3.06. 86
to be abus'd | by one that looks on feeders? 3.13.108
you are a great deal abus'd in too bold a CYM 1.04.114 P
you have abus'd me. | "his meanest garment"! 2.03.149
why hast thou abus'd | so many miles with a 3.04.102
it cannot be | but that my master is abus'd. 3.04.120
saying, some shape in sinon's was abus'd: LUC 1529
where cheeks need blood, in thee it is abus'd. SON 82.14

/ABUSE 1 FR 0.0001 REL FR 1 V 0 P
/would /turn /their /own /perfection /to /abuse 2H4 2.03. 27

ABUSE 54 FR 0.0061 REL FR 43 V 11 P
or some enchanted trifle to abuse me | (as late TMP 5.01.112
falstaffs, he shall not abuse robert shallow, WIV 1.01. 3 P
so much at the abuse of falstaff as he will 5.03. 7 P
and see how he goes about to abuse me! MM 3.02.203 P
this is a strange abuse. let's see thy face. 5.01.205
him your kind pains | to find out this abuse, 5.01.247
she does abuse our ears. to prison with her! AWW 5.03.294
so did i abuse | myself, my servant, and, i fear TN 3.01.113
if your lass | interpretation should abuse, and WT 4.04.353
drive you then to confess the willful abuse, and 2H4 2.04.312 P
no abuse, hal, a' mine honor, no abuse. 2.04.313 P
no abuse, hal, a' mine honor, no abuse. 2.04.313 P
no abuse, hal. 2.04.316 P
no abuse? 2.04.317 P
no abuse, ned, i' th' world, honest ned, none. 2.04.318 P
no abuse, hal; 2.04.323 P
would he abuse the countenance of the king, 4.02. 13
on, and we'll digest | th' abuse of distance; H5 2.pr. 32
it was ourself thou didst abuse. 4.08. 49
victorious talbot, pardon my abuse. 1H6 2.03. 67
him, | and give him chastisement for this abuse. 4.01. 69
yes, your renowned name. shall flight abuse it? 4.05. 41
matter, | in thine own person answer thy abuse. 2H6 2.01. 40
with me, | knowing how hardly i can brook abuse? 5.01. 92
or wherefore dost abuse it if thou hast it? 5.01.172
did i let pass th' abuse done to my niece? 3H6 3.03.188
that they'll take no offense at our abuse. 4.01. 13
revolts from true birth, stumbling on abuse. ROM 2.03. 20
hang him, he'll abuse us. TIM 2.02. 48 P
th' abuse of greatness is when it disjoins JC 2.01. 18
the sufferance of our souls, the time's abuse — 2.01.115
and wicked dreams abuse | the curtain'd sleep; MAC 2.01. 50
or is it some abuse, and no such thing? HAM 4.07. 50
do not abuse me. LR 4.07. 76
time, to abuse othello's /ear | that he is too OTH 1.03.395
abuse him to the moor in the /rank garb | (for i 2.01.306
it doth abuse your bosom. 4.02. 14
that there be women do abuse their husbands | in 4.03. 62
of life as honest | as you that thus abuse me. 5.01.123
do not abuse my master's bounty by | th' undoing ANT 5.02. 43
that both mine ears | must not in haste abuse), CYM 1.06.131
portends | (unless my sins abuse my divination) 4.02.351
so bad | as with foul incest to abuse your soul; PER 1.01.126
they do abuse the king that flatter him, | for 1.02. 38
his hoarse throat, | abuse young lays of love. TNK 5.01. 89
things growing to themselves are growth's abuse. VEN 166
when reason is the bawd to lust's abuse. 792
who in their pride do presently abuse it; LUC 864
body spread, | and who cannot abuse a body dead? 1267
lest he should hold it her own gross abuse, 1315
my gross blood be stain'd with this abuse, 1655
why dost thou abuse | the bounteous largess SON 4. 5
and for my sake even so doth she abuse me, 42. 7
sake, | so him i lose through my unkind abuse. 134.12

ABUSED 6 FR 0.0006 REL FR 6 V 0 P
that hath abused and dishonored me, | even in ERR 5.01.199
navarre and his book–men, for here 'tis abused. LLL 2.01.227
the noble duke hath been too much abused. R2 2.03.137
long, | good king, to be so mightily abused. TIT 2.03. 87
edgar, | the food of thy abused father's wrath! LR 4.01. 22
cure this great breach in his abused nature, 4.07. 14

ABUSER 1 FR 0.0001 REL FR 1 V 0 P
and do attach thee | for an abuser of the world, OTH 1.02. 78

/ABUSES 1 FR 0.0001 REL FR 1 V 0 P
/that /thought /abuses /you. LR 5.01. 11

ABUSES 13 FR 0.0014 REL FR 8 V 5 P
nothing but use their abuses in common houses, i MM 2.01. 43 P
would close now, after his treasonable abuses! 5.01.343 P
that abuses our young plants with carving AYL 3.02.360 P
blind rascally boy that abuses every one's eyes 4.01.213 P
for the poor abuses of the time want countenance 1H4 1.02.156 P
cries out upon abuses, seems to weep | over his 4.03. 81
nor tears nor prayers shall purchase out abuses: ROM 3.01.193
with such spirits, | abuses me to damn me. HAM 2.02.603
it is my nature's plague | to spy into abuses, OTH 3.03.147
poor wretches have remorse in poor abuses, LUC 269
to hide the truth of this false night's abuses. 1075
that they are so fulfill'd | with men's abuses: 1259
that level | at my abuses reckon up their own; SON 121.10

ABUSING 4 FR 0.0004 REL FR 3 V 1 P
here will be an old abusing of god's patience WIV 1.04. 5 P
from the corruption of abusing times | unto a R3 3.07.199
abusing better men than they can be | out of a H8 1.03. 28
have time to wail th' abusing of his time. LUC 994

ABUTS 1 FR 0.0001 REL FR 1 V 0 P
the leavy shelter that abuts against | the PER 5.01. 51

ABUTTING 1 FR 0.0001 REL FR 1 V 0 P
and abutting fronts | the perilous narrow ocean H5 pr 21

ABY *(also abide*)*

ABY 2 FR 0.0002 REL FR 2 V 0 P
know, | lest, to thy peril, thou aby it dear. MND 3.02.175
little show of love to her, | thou shalt aby it. 3.02.335

ABYSM 3 FR 0.0003 REL FR 3 V 0 P
else | in the dark backward and abysm of time? TMP 1.02. 50
and shot their fires | into th' abysm of hell. ANT 3.13.147
in so profound abysm i throw all care | of SON 112. 9

ACADEME 1 FR 0.0001 REL FR 1 V 0 P
our court shall be a little academe, | still and LLL 1.01. 13

ACADEMES 2 FR 0.0002 REL FR 2 V 0 P
they are the ground, the books, the academes, LLL 4.03.299
they are the books, the arts, the academes, 4.03.349

A–CAP'RING 1 FR 0.0001 REL FR 0 V 1 P
a throstle sing, he falls straight a–cap'ring. MV 1.02. 61 P

ACCENT 17 FR 0.0019 REL FR 10 V 7 P
not the apostraphas, and so miss the accent. LLL 4.02.120 P
action and accent did they teach him there: 5.02. 99
throttle their practic'd accent in their fears, MND 5.01. 97
your accent is something finer than you could AYL 3.02.341 P
with a swaggering accent sharply twang'd off, TN 3.04.180 P
face, | the accent of his tongue affecteth him. JN 1.01. 86
me | that any accent breaking from thy tongue 5.06. 14
the heavy accent of thy moving tongue, | and in R2 5.01. 47
your mock | in second accent of his ordinance. H5 2.04.126
that cannot brook the accent of reproof. R3 4.04.159
and with an accent tun'd in self–same key TRO 1.03. 53
/phantasimes, these new tuners of accent! ROM 2.04. 29 P
spoken, with good accent and good discretion. HAM 2.02.467 P
neither having th' accent of christians nor the 3.02. 31 P
you in a plain accent was a plain knave, which LR 2.02.111 P
do, with like timorous accent and dire yell | as OTH 1.01. 75
and midst the sentence so her accent breaks, LUC 566

/ACCENTS 2 FR 0.0002 REL FR 2 V 0 P
/became /the /accents /of /the /valiant; 2H4 2.03. 25
his rougher /accents for malicious sounds, | but COR 3.03. 55

ACCENTS 6 FR 0.0006 REL FR 6 V 0 P
and breathe short–winded accents of new broils 1H4 1.01. 3
in /states unborn and accents yet unknown! JC 3.01.113
death, | and prophesying, with accents terrible, MAC 2.03. 57
if but as /well i other accents borrow, | that LR 1.04. 1
not speak, | till after many accents and delays, LUC 1719
in other accents do this praise confound | by SON 69. 7

ACCEPT 33 FR 0.0037 REL FR 30 V 3 P
will, if you should refuse to accept him. MV 1.02. 94 P
his ring i do accept most thankfully, | and so i 4.02. 9
so please your lordship to accept our duty. SHR in.1. 82
accept of him, or else you do me wrong. 2.01. 59
pray accept his service. 2.01. 83 P
if you accept them, then their worth is great. 2.01.101
if this be court'sy, sir, accept of it. 4.02.112
please you t' accept it — that the queen is WT 2.01.131
an offer, uncle, that we will accept, | but we R2 2.03.162
i would you would accept of grace and love. 1H4 4.03.112
pass our accept and peremptory answer. H5 5.02. 82
accept this scroll, most gracious sovereign, 1H6 3.01.148
and, lords, accept this hearty kind embrace. 3.03. 82
there is my pledge, accept it, somerset. 4.01.120
wilt thou accept of ransom, yea or no? 5.03. 80
either accept the title thou usurp'st, | of 5.04.151
and i accept the combat willingly. 2H6 1.03.212
humphrey of buckingham, i accept thy greeting. 5.01. 15
yes, i accept her, for she well deserves it, 3H6 3.03.249
yet know, whe'er you accept our suit or no, R3 3.07.214
call him again, sweet prince, accept their suit. 3.07.221
therefore accept such kindness as i can. 4.04.310
accept distracted thanks. TRO 5.02.189
which they did refuse | and cannot now accept, COR 5.03. 15
next, | accept my thankfulness. 5.04. 59
rome, | the people will accept whom he admits. TIT 1.01.222
which i do beseech | your lordship to accept. TIM 1.01.156
accept it and wear it, | kind my lord. 1.02.170
i shall accept them fairly; 1.02.184
t' accept my grief, and whilst this poor wealth 4.03.488
times, | when wit's more ripe, accept my rhymes, PER 1.ch. 12
which welcome we'll accept; 1.04.107
we accept of the king's mercy, but we will show STM II.C 19 P

ACCEPTABLE 1 FR 0.0001 REL FR 1 V 0 P
gone, | what acceptable audit canst thou leave? SON 4.12

ACCEPTANCE 9 FR 0.0010 REL FR 6 V 3 P
i leave him to your gracious acceptance, whose MV 4.01.164 P
treasury and have pour'd it | to her acceptance; WT 4.04.351
with good acceptance of his majesty; H5 1.01. 83
in your fair minds let this acceptance take. ep 14
must also tell him our noble acceptance of them. COR 2.03. 9 P
with vain thanks, but with acceptance bounteous, OTH 3.03.470
petition of grace and acceptance into her favor. TNK 4.03. 89 P
and in my will no fair acceptance shine? SON 135. 8
their kind acceptance weepingly beseech'd, LC 207

ACCEPTED 3 FR 0.0003 REL FR 3 V 0 P
when nought would be accepted but the ring, MV 5.01.197
it will not be accepted, on my life. 1H4 5.01.115
service i have done, | in most accepted pain. TRO 3.03. 30

ACCEPTS 1 FR 0.0001 REL FR 1 V 0 P
ay, my good lord, and she accepts of it. TIM 1.01.135

/ACCESS 1 FR 0.0001 REL FR 1 V 0 P
/we /are /denied /access /unto /his /person 2H4 4.01. 78

ACCESS 22 FR 0.0024 REL FR 18 V 4 P
of men, | that no man hath access by day to her. TGV 3.01.109
upon this warrant shall you have access | where 3.02. 60
him, | i have access my own love to prefer — 4.02. 4
of the man condemn'd | desires access to you. MM 2.02. 19
one isabel, a sister, desires access to you. 2.04. 18
here at the door, and importunes access to you. AYL 1.01. 92 P
may yet again have access to our fair mistress SHR 1.01.116 P
that none shall have access unto bianca | till 1.02.127
her father keeps from all access of suitors, 1.02.259
set the younger free | for our access — whose 1.02.267
woo, | and free access and favor as the rest; 2.01. 97
be not denied access, stand at her doors, | and TN 1.04. 16
and honor from th' access of gentle visitors. WT 2.02. 10
beheld), desires access | to your high presence. 5.01. 87
would be thence that has the benefit of access? 5.02.110 P
if you cannot | bar his access to th' king, H8 3.02. 17
who like a block hath denied my access to thee. COR 5.02. 78 P
he may not have access | to breathe such vows as ROM 2.pr. 9
stop up th' access and passage to remorse, MAC 1.05. 44
his letters, and denied | his access to me. HAM 2.01.107
to virtuous desdemona | procure me some access. OTH 3.01. 36
may we not get access to her, my lord? PER 2.05. 7

ACCESSARY 5 FR 0.0005 REL FR 5 V 0 P
i am your accessary, and so farewell. AWW 2.01. 35
to both their deaths shalt thou be accessary. R3 1.02.191
an accessary by thine inclination | to all sins LUC 922
never was inclin'd | to accessary yieldings, but 1658
that i an accessary needs must be | to that SON 35.13

ACCESSIBLE 1 FR 0.0001 REL FR 1 V 0 P
accessible is none but milford way. CYM 3.02. 82

ACCIDENCE 1 FR 0.0001 REL FR 0 V 1 P
you ask him some questions in his accidence. WIV 4.01. 16 P

ACCIDENT 23 FR 0.0026 REL FR 22 V 1 P
by accident most strange, bountiful fortune TMP 1.02.178
o, 'tis an accident that heaven provides! MM 4.03. 77
this is an accident of hourly proof, | which i ADO 2.01.181
you shall not know by what strange accident | i MV 5.01.278
yet doth this accident and flood of fortune | so TN 4.03. 11
to think your father, by some accident, | should WT 4.04. 19
but as th' unthought–on accident is guilty | to 4.04.538
fram'd, but forc'd | by need and accident. 5.01. 92
dismay not, princes, at this accident, | nor 1H6 3.03. 1
age, | but by some unlook'd accident cut off! R3 1.03.213
favor — | prizes of accident as oft as merit, TRO 3.03. 83
alone | till accident or purpose bring you to't. 4.05.262
john, | was stayed by accident, and yesternight ROM 5.03.251
that he, as 'twere by accident, may here HAM 3.01. 30

grief /joys, joy grieves, on slender accident. 3.02.199
uncharge the practice, | and call it accident. 4.07. 68
this accident is not unlike my dream, | belief OTH 1.01.142
virtue | the shot of accident nor dart of chance 4.01.267
his abode be ling'red here by some accident; 4.02.226 P
chance of war, the day | was yours by accident. CYM 5.05. 76
by accident | i had a feigned letter of my 5.05.278
no, it was builded far from accident; SON 124. 5
the accident which brought me to her eye | upon LC 247
ACCIDENTAL 4 FR 0.0004 REL FR 4 V 0 P
thy sin's not accidental, but a trade. MM 3.01.148
no use, | if you give place to accidental evils. JC 4.03.146
of accidental judgments, casual slaughters, | of HAM 5.02.382
him, | he takes for accidental things of trial; LUC 326
ACCIDENTALLY 3 FR 0.0003 REL FR 1 V 2 P
children, | which accidentally are met together. ERR 5.01.362
of the stranger queen's, which accidentally, or LLL 4.02.139 P
fortunate thus accidentally to encounter you. COR 4.03. 38 P
ACCIDENTS 14 FR 0.0015 REL FR 14 V 0 P
probable) of every | these happen'd accidents; TMP 5.01.250
and the particular accidents gone by | since i 5.01.306
and think no more of this night's accidents MND 4.01. 68
come, | and nothing pleaseth but rare accidents. 1H4 1.02.207
me | and give me signs of future accidents. 1H6 5.03. 4
romeo | hath had no notice of these accidents; ROM 5.02. 27
as there are tongues, are hands, are accidents, HAM 4.07.121
of moving accidents by flood and field, | of OTH 1.03.135
these bloody accidents must excuse my manners 5.01. 94
services are all | but accidents unpurpos'd. ANT 4.14. 84
which shackles accidents and bolts up change, 5.02. 6
solemn things | should answer solemn accidents. CYM 4.02.192
be not with mortal accidents oppress'd, | no 5.04. 99
whose million'd accidents | creep in 'twixt vows SON 115. 5
ACCITE 2 FR 0.0002 REL FR 2 V 0 P
our coronation done, we will accite | (as i 2H4 5.02.141
which might accite thee to embrace and hug them,
STM III 16
ACCITED 1 FR 0.0001 REL FR 1 V 0 P
he by the senate is accited home | from weary TIT 1.01. 27
ACCITES 1 FR 0.0001 REL FR 0 V 1 P
and what accites your most worshipful thought to 2H4 2.02. 60 P
ACCLAMATIONS 1 FR 0.0001 REL FR 1 V 0 P
/shout me forth | in acclamations hyperbolical, COR 1.09. 51
ACCOMMODATE 1 FR 0.0001 REL FR 1 V 0 P
the safer sense will ne'er accommodate | his LR 4.06. 81
/ACCOMMODATED 1 FR 0.0001 REL FR 0 V 1 P
soldier is better /accommodated than with a wife 2H4 3.02. 66 P
ACCOMMODATED 6 FR 0.0006 REL FR 1 V 5 P
better accommodated! 2H4 3.02. 69 P
accommodated! 3.02. 71 P
accommodated: 3.02. 77 P
is, as they say, accommodated, or when a man is 3.02. 78 P
whereby 'a may be thought to be accommodated — 3.02. 79 P
accommodated by the place, more charming | with
CYM 5.03. 32
ACCOMMODATION 1 FR 0.0001 REL FR 1 V 0 P
with such accommodation and besort | as levels OTH 1.03.238
ACCOMMODATIONS 1 FR 0.0001 REL FR 1 V 0 P
for all th' accommodations that thou bear'st MM 3.01. 14
ACCOMMODO 1 FR 0.0001 REL FR 0 V 1 P
it comes of accommodo, very good, a good phrase.
2H4 3.02. 72 P
ACCOMPANIED 8 FR 0.0009 REL FR 7 V 1 P
thy time, but also how thou art accompanied; 1H4 2.04.399 P
and how accompanied? 2H4 4.04. 15
and how accompanied? /canst /thou /tell /that? 4.04. 52
where you shall find me well accompanied | with R3 3.05. 99
accompanied with other | learned and reverend H8 4.01. 25
how accompanied? COR 3.03. 6
plot, | accompanied but with a barbarous moor, TIT 2.03. 78
month, accompanied | with three fair knights, TNK 3.06.291
ACCOMPANY 8 FR 0.0009 REL FR 6 V 2 P
and fresh days of love | accompany your hearts! MND 5.01. 30
unless you will accompany me thither. SHR 1.02.106
thou shalt accompany us to the place, where we WT 4.02. 47 P
to, | accompany the greatness of thy blood, 1H4 3.02. 16
business, and i will merrily accompany you home. COR 4.03. 39 P
accompany | your noble emperor and his lovely TIT 1.01.333
and shall, or him we will accompany. 1.01.358
leaf, | and that which should accompany old age, MAC 5.03. 24
ACCOMPANYING 1 FR 0.0001 REL FR 1 V 0 P
down, | not one accompanying his declining foot. TIM 1.01. 88
ACCOMPLICES *(also complices)*
ACCOMPLICES 1 FR 0.0001 REL FR 1 V 0 P
general, | and happiness to his accomplices! 1H6 5.02. 9
ACCOMPLISH 3 FR 0.0003 REL FR 3 V 0 P
than to accomplish twenty golden crowns! 3H6 3.02.152
out of my files, his projects to accomplish, COR 5.06. 33
you must perforce accomplish as you may. TIT 2.01.107
ACCOMPLISH'D 9 FR 0.0010 REL FR 5 V 4 P
valiant, wise, remorseful, well accomplish'd: TGV 4.03. 13
with most austere sanctimony she accomplish'd; AWW 4.03. 50 P
most excellent accomplish'd lady, the heavens TN 3.01. 84 P
accomplish'd with /the number of thy hours; R2 2.01.177
shall be accomplish'd without contradiction. 3.03.124
a (that way) accomplish'd courtier, would hazard CYM 1.04. 92 P
contains none so accomplish'd a courtier to 1.04. 94 P
battle, at this instant | is full accomplish'd: 5.05.470
accomplish'd in himself, not in his case; LC 116
ACCOMPLISHED 2 FR 0.0002 REL FR 2 V 0 P
that they shall think we are accomplished | with MV 3.04. 61
ladies | unto their lords, by them accomplished; SHR in.1. 112
ACCOMPLISHING 1 FR 0.0001 REL FR 1 V 0 P
tents | the armorers, accomplishing the knights, H5 4.pr. 12
ACCOMPLISHMENT 2 FR 0.0002 REL FR 2 V 0 P
turning th' accomplishment of many years | into H5 pr 30
rome, | who this accomplishment so hotly chased, LUC 716
ACCOMPT *(also account, etc.)*
/ACCOMPT 1 FR 0.0001 REL FR 1 V 0 P
/and /summ'd /the /accompt /of /chance /before 2H4 1.01.167
ACCOMPT 10 FR 0.0011 REL FR 8 V 2 P
sins | stand more for number than for accompt. MM 2.04. 58
that we may do it still without accompt. LLL 5.02.200
sir, their speed | hath been beyond accompt. WT 2.03.198
o, when the last accompt 'twixt heaven and earth JN 4.02.216
and let us, ciphers to this great accompt, | on H5 pr 17
he can write and read and cast accompt. 2H6 4.02. 86 P
'tis th' accompt | of all that world of wealth i H8 3.02.210
takes no accompt | how things go from him, nor TIM 2.02. 3
it, when none can call our pow'r to accompt? MAC 5.01. 39 P
but though they jump not on a just accompt | (as OTH 1.03. 5
ACCOMPTANT 1 FR 0.0001 REL FR 1 V 0 P
i stand accomptant for as great a sin), | but OTH 2.01.293
ACCOMPTS 1 FR 0.0001 REL FR 1 V 0 P
lord, | at many times i brought in my accompts, TIM 2.02.133
ACCORD 10 FR 0.0011 REL FR 9 V 1 P
for your father's remembrance, be at accord. AYL 1.01. 64 P
you to his love must accord, | or have a woman 5.04.133
"gamouth i am, the ground of all accord: SHR 3.01. 73
on mine own accord i'll off, | but first i'll do WT 2.03. 64
you know how apt our love was to accord | to H5 2.02. 86
with full accord to all our just demands, 5.02. 71
plant neighborhood and christian–like accord 5.02.353
joints, true swords, and, great jove's accord, TRO 1.03.238
talk, | wanting a hand to give/'t that accord? TIT 5.02. 18
this gentle and unforc'd accord of hamlet | sits HAM 1.02.123
ACCORDANT 1 FR 0.0001 REL FR 0 V 1 P
and if he found her accordant, he meant to take ADO 1.02. 14 P
ACCORDED 1 FR 0.0001 REL FR 1 V 0 P
my spirits t' attend this double voice accorded, LC 3
ACCORDETH 1 FR 0.0001 REL FR 1 V 0 P
but that my heart accordeth with my tongue, 2H6 3.01.269
ACCORDING 45 FR 0.0050 REL FR 33 V 12 P
my mind | according to my shallow simple skill. TGV 1.02. 8
welcome him then according to his worth — 2.04. 83
according to our proclamation, gone? 3.02. 12
according to your ladyship's impose, | i am thus 4.03. 8
the ort is (according to our meaning) WIV 1.01.254 P
done, | and sent according to command, whiles i MM 4.03. 80
this world, | and squar'st thy life according. 5.01.482
my lord, i spoke it but according to the trick. 5.01.504 P
his life | according to the statute of the town, ERR 1.02. 6
according to our law | immediately provided in MND 1.01. 44
generally, man by man, according to the scrip. 1.02. 3 P
and so every one according to his cue. 3.01. 75 P
and according to my description level at my MV 1.02. 37 P
gentleman, according to fates and destinies, and 2.02. 62 P
when it is paid according to the tenure. 4.01.235
according as marriage binds and blood breaks. AYL 5.04. 56 P
according to the fool's bolt, sir, and such 5.04. 64 P
according to the measure of their states. 5.04.175
well, | according to the fashion and the time. SHR 4.03. 95
our celebration keep | according to my birth. TN 4.03. 31
of my poor babe, according to thine oath, WT 3.03. 30
according to the fair play of the world, | let JN 5.02.118
hast thou, according to thy oath and band, R2 1.01. 2
of war, | and formally, according to our law, 1.03. 29
right | according to our threefold order ta'en? 1H4 3.01. 70
will, according to your strengths and qualities, 2H4 5.05. 69
merit, | according to the weight and worthiness. H5 2.02. 35
the mines is not according to the disciplines of 3.02. 59 P
all, | according to their firm proposed natures. 5.02.334
madam, | according as your ladyship desir'd, 1H6 2.03. 12
man, | there to be us'd according to your state. 2H6 2.04. 95
according to that state you shall be us'd. 2.04. 99
things well, | according as i gave directions? 3.02. 12
and had he match'd according to his state, | he 3H6 2.02.152
not according to the prayer of the people, for COR 2.01. 4 P
lies my consent and fair according voice. ROM 1.02. 19
according as he pleas'd and displeas'd them, as JC 1.02.259 P
according to the which thou shalt discourse | to 3.01.295
according to his virtue let us use him, | with 5.05. 76
according to the gift which bounteous nature MAC 3.01. 97
else remains to do, | according to our order. 5.06. 6
according to the phrase or the addition | of man HAM 2.01. 47
lord, i will use them according to their desert. 2.02.527 P
i love your majesty | according to my bond, no LR 1.01. 93
him | according to the honor of his sender, CYM 2.03. 58
ACCORDINGLY 9 FR 0.0010 REL FR 5 V 4 P
that i may minister | to them accordingly. MM 2.03. 8
seen more, and heard more, proceed accordingly. ADO 3.02.122 P
great in knowledge, and accordingly valiant. AWW 2.05. 9 P
which trust accordingly, kind citizens, | and JN 2.01.231
for accordingly | you tread upon my patience; 1H4 1.03. 3
i do, my lord, and mean accordingly. 1H6 2.02. 60
isis, keep decorum, and fortune him accordingly! ANT 1.02. 74 P
the ships behold, | and so proceed accordingly. 3.09. 4
reflect upon him accordingly, as you value your CYM 1.06. 24 P
ACCORDS 3 FR 0.0003 REL FR 3 V 0 P
my heart accords thereto, | and yet a thousand TGV 1.03. 90
then let your will attend on their accords. ERR 2.01. 25
accords not with the sadness of my suit. 3H6 3.02. 77
ACCOST 6 FR 0.0006 REL FR 0 V 6 P
accost, sir andrew, accost. TN 1.03. 49 P
accost, sir andrew, accost. 1.03. 49 P
good mistress accost, i desire better 1.03. 52 P
good mistress mary accost — 1.03. 55 P
"accost" is front her, board her, woo her, 1.03. 56 P
is that the meaning of "accost"? 1.03. 59 P
ACCOSTED 1 FR 0.0001 REL FR 0 V 1 P
you should have accosted her, and with some
TN 3.02. 21 P
ACCOUNT *(also accompt, etc.)*
ACCOUNT 39 FR 0.0044 REL FR 30 V 9 P
how esteem'st thou me? i account of her beauty. TGV 2.01. 61 P
to make an account of her life to a clod of ADO 2.01. 62 P
hand, claudio shall render me a dear account. 4.01.333 P
rich, | that only to stand high in your account, MV 3.02.155
beauties, livings, friends, | exceed account. 3.02.157
and therein do account myself well paid. 4.01.417
beverage, | account me not your servant. WT 1.02.347
bouget, | then my account i well may give, | and 4.03. 21
in my debt, | upon remainder of a dear account, R2 1.01.130
and i will call him to so strict account | that 1H4 3.02.149
by which account, | our business valued, some 3.02.176
when yet you were in place and in account 5.01. 37
and so i hear he doth account me too; 5.01. 95
and his achievements of no less account; 1H6 2.03. 8
by this account then, margaret may win him, 3H6 3.01. 35
whiles i live, t' account this world but hell, 3.02.169
the princes both make high account of you — R3 3.02. 69
for they account his head upon the bridge. 3.02. 70
why, our battalia trebles that account; 5.03. 11
o thou whose captain i account myself, | look on 5.03.108
help in his nature, you account a vice in him. COR 1.01. 42 P
you should account me the more virtuous that i 2.03. 94 P
'tis a condition they account gentle. 2.03. 97 P
when he shall come to his account, he knows not 4.07. 18
hazard mine, | when e'er we come to our account. 4.07. 26
say i account of them | as jewels purchas'd at TIT 3.01.197
o dear account! ROM 1.05.118
his shelves | a beggarly account of empty boxes, 5.01. 45
that we may account thee a whoremaster and a TIM 2.02.104 P
are crown'd, | that i account them blessings; 2.02.182
from this time | such i account thy love. MAC 1.07. 39
made, but sent to my account | with all my HAM 1.05. 78
than this, who yet is no dearer in my account. LR 1.01. 21 P
in you, which i account his, beyond all talents. CYM 1.06. 80
and would account i had a great penn'worth on'i TNK 4.03. 66 P
o'er | the sad account of fore–bemoaned moan, SON 30.11
or at your hand th' account of hours to crave, 58. 3
no shape so true, no truth of such account, 62. 6
though in thy store's account i one must be, 136.10
ACCOUNTANT 1 FR 0.0001 REL FR 1 V 0 P
appears, | accountant to the law upon that pain. MM 2.04. 86
ACCOUNT'D 1 FR 0.0001 REL FR 1 V 0 P
did begin | was with long use account'd no sin. PER 1.ch. 30
ACCOUNTED 8 FR 0.0009 REL FR 4 V 4 P
to me, your honor is accounted a merciful man. MM 3.02.192 P
kill, | and shooting well is then accounted ill. LLL 4.01. 25
me, was yet of many accounted beautiful; TN 2.01. 26 P
york, | i will not live to be accounted warwick. 1H6 2.04.120
we are accounted poor citizens, the patricians COR 1.01. 15 P
to do good sometime | accounted dangerous folly. MAC 4.02. 77
did i, my lord, and was accounted a good actor. HAM 3.02.100 P
ill, | no more than wax shall be accounted evil, LUC 1245
ACCOUNTEDST 1 FR 0.0001 REL FR 1 V 0 P
if thou accountedst it shame, lay it on me, SHR 4.03.181
ACCOUNTS 3 FR 0.0003 REL FR 3 V 0 P
lost | in this which he accounts so clearly won. JN 3.04.122
and he that otherwise accounts of me, | this PER 2.05. 63
and casts himself th' accounts | of all his hay TNK 5.02. 58
ACCOUSTREMENT 1 FR 0.0001 REL FR 0 V 1 P
office of love, but in all the accoustrement, WIV 4.02. 5 P
ACCOUSTREMENTS 1 FR 0.0001 REL FR 0 V 1 P
are rather point–device in your accoustrements, AYL 3.02.383 P
ACCOUTERED 1 FR 0.0001 REL FR 1 V 0 P
when we are both accoutered like young men, MV 3.04. 63
ACCOUTRED 1 FR 0.0001 REL FR 1 V 0 P
accoutred as i was, i plunged in | and bade him JC 1.02.105
ACCOUTREMENT 1 FR 0.0001 REL FR 1 V 0 P
device, | exterior form, outward accoutrement, JN 1.01.211
ACCOUTREMENTS 1 FR 0.0001 REL FR 1 V 0 P
me, | as i can change these poor accoutrements, SHR 3.02.119
ACCRUE 1 FR 0.0001 REL FR 1 V 0 P
be | unto the camp, and profits will accrue. H5 2.01.112
ACCUMULATE 2 FR 0.0002 REL FR 2 V 0 P
on horror's head horrors accumulate; OTH 3.03.370
down, | and on just proof surmise accumulate; SON 117.10
ACCUMULATED 1 FR 0.0001 REL FR 1 V 0 P
what piles of wealth hath he accumulated | to H8 3.02.107
ACCUMULATION 1 FR 0.0001 REL FR 1 V 0 P
lieutenant, | for quick accumulation of renown, ANT 3.01. 19
/ACCURS'D 1 FR 0.0001 REL FR 1 V 0 P
/o /thoughts /of /men /accurs'd! 2H4 1.03.107
ACCURS'D 18 FR 0.0020 REL FR 16 V 2 P
security enough to make fellowships accurs'd. MM 3.02.228 P
how accurs'd | in being so blest! WT 2.01. 38
and most accurs'd am i | to be by oath enjoin'd 3.03. 52
i am accurs'd to rob in that thieve's company. 1H4 2.02. 10 P
think themselves accurs'd they were not here; H5 4.03. 65
of all base passions, fear is most accurs'd. 1H6 5.02. 18
accurs'd be he that seeks to make them foes! 3H6 1.01.205
thou wast the cause, and most accurs'd effect. R3 1.02.120
quoth i, "accurs'd | for making me, so young, so 4.01. 71
accurs'd the offspring of so foul a fiend! TIT 4.02. 79
accurs'd, unhappy, wretched, hateful day! ROM 4.05. 43
my dearest lord, blest to be most accurs'd, TIM 4.02. 42
knit and break religions, bless th' accurs'd, 4.03. 35
our suffering country | under a hand accurs'd! MAC 3.06. 49
in second husband let me be accurs'd! HAM 3.02.179
it was in rome — accurs'd | the mansion where! CYM 5.05.154
horror, who does stand accurs'd | of many mortal TNK 5.03. 23
my youth with his, the more am i accurs'd." VEN 1120
ACCURSED 16 FR 0.0018 REL FR 16 V 0 P
accursed tower! 1H6 1.04. 76
accursed fatal hand | that hath contriv'd this 1.04. 76
to ashes, | thou foul accursed minister of hell! 5.04. 93
as for the brat of this accursed duke, | whose 3H6 1.03. 4
and till i root out their accursed line, | and 1.03. 32
accursed and unquiet wrangling days, | how many R3 2.04. 55
o my accursed womb, the bed of death! 4.01. 53
thee, | by strangling thee in her accursed womb, 4.04.138
that this fell fault of my accursed sons — TIT 2.03.290
accursed, if the /fault be prov'd in them — 2.03.291
what accursed hand | hath made thee handless in 3.01. 66
this ravenous tiger, this accursed devil; 5.03. 5
die, frantic wretch, for this accursed deed! 5.03. 64
the most accursed thou, that still omit'st it. TIM 1.01.259
hour | stand aye accursed in the calendar! MAC 4.01.134
accursed be that tongue that tells me so, | for 5.08. 17
ACCURST 1 FR 0.0001 REL FR 1 V 0 P
o time most accurst! TGV 5.04. 71
ACCUSATION 13 FR 0.0014 REL FR 8 V 5 P
th' state, | will so your accusation overweigh, MM 2.04.157
now stands, he will avoid your accusation: 3.01.196 P
be you constant in the accusation, and my ADO 2.02. 54 P
no, though he thought his accusation true. 4.01.233
and then, with public accusation, uncover'd 4.01.305 P
dead upon mine and my master's false accusation; 5.01.242 P
(not able to produce more accusation | than your WT 2.03.118
be but that | which contradicts my accusation, 3.02. 23
innocence shall make | false accusation blush, 3.02. 31
come current for an accusation | betwixt my love 1H4 1.03. 68
away an honest man for a villain's accusation. 2H6 1.03.202 P
we come not by the way of accusation | to taint H8 3.01. 54
th' accusation | which they have often made COR 3.01.127
/ACCUSATIONS 1 FR 0.0001 REL FR 1 V 0 P
/but /that /you /read | /these /accusations, R2 4.01.223
ACCUSATIONS 5 FR 0.0005 REL FR 4 V 1 P
and makes him roar these accusations forth. 1H6 3.01. 40
where to his accusations | he pleaded still not H8 2.01. 12
i must not, i need not be barren of accusations; COR 1.01. 44 P
for they are prepar'd | with accusations, as i 3.02.140

it, and have now receiv'd | his accusations. ANT 3.06. 23
ACCUSATIVE 1 FR 0.0001 REL FR 0 V 1 P
well, what is your accusative case? WIV 4.01. 43 P
ACCUSATIVO 2 FR 0.0002 REL FR 0 V 2 P
accusativo, hinc. WIV 4.01. 45 P
accusativo, /hung, hang, hog. 4.01. 47 P
ACCUS'D 21 FR 0.0023 REL FR 16 V 5 P
given, might have been accus'd in fornication, MM 2.01. 80 P
woman | most wrongfully accus'd your substitute, 5.01.140
nobleman, | so vulgarly and personally accus'd, 5.01.160
lady, what man is he you are accus'd of? ADO 4.01.176
upon the instant that she was accus'd, | shall 4.01.215
hero was in this manner accus'd, in this very 4.02. 62 P
prov'd my lady hero hath been falsely accus'd, 5.02. 97 P
who accus'd her | upon the error that you heard 5.04. 2
and for thy life let justice be accus'd. MV 4.01.129
wherefore hast thou accus'd him all this while? AWW 5.03.288
as she hath | been publicly accus'd, so shall WT 2.03.204
for polixenes | (with whom i am accus'd), i do 3.02. 62
my witness, i am falsely accus'd by the villain. 2H6 1.03.189 P
who being accus'd a crafty murtherer, | his 3.01.254
or, if she be accus'd on true report, | bear R3 1.03. 27
than some that have accus'd them wear their hats 3.02. 93
all these accus'd him strongly, which he fain H8 2.01. 24
wondrous malicious, | or be accus'd of folly. COR 1.01. 89
thus accus'd it: 1.01. 97
when peradventure thou wert accus'd by the ass; TIM 4.03.331 P
throne | by his own interdiction stands accus'd, MAC 4.03.107
/ACCUSE 1 FR 0.0001 REL FR 1 V 0 P
by circumstance /t' /accuse thy cursed self. R3 1.02. 80
ACCUSE 38 FR 0.0043 REL FR 33 V 5 P
but these that accuse him in his intent towards WIV 2.01.174 P
the head of angelo | accuse him home and home. MM 4.03.143
i would say the truth, but to accuse him so, 4.06. 2
in self–same manner doth accuse my husband, 5.01.196
villain's mouth | which here you come to accuse. 5.01.303
these women | to accuse this worthy man, but, in 5.01.307
they know that do accuse me, i know none. ADO 4.01.177
you in the prince's name accuse these men. 4.02. 38 P
the part of virginity is to accuse your mothers, AWW 1.01.137 P
they cannot praise us, as little accuse us. WT 1.01. 16 P
you — i mean, | in this which you accuse her. 2.01.133
let not my cold words here accuse my zeal. R2 1.01. 47
and beg thy pardon ere he do accuse thee. 5.02.113
humphrey of gloucester, if thou canst accuse, 1H6 3.01. 3
well | (there were so many) whom she may accuse. 5.04. 81
doth any one accuse york for a traitor? 2H6 1.03.179
that doth accuse his master of high treason. 1.03.182
who can accuse me? 3.01.103
back, | by false accuse doth level at my life. 3.01.160
by such despair i should accuse myself. R3 1.02. 85
where is the evidence that doth accuse me? 1.04.183
stubborn to justice, apt to accuse it, and H8 2.04.122
and, by that virtue, no man dare accuse you. 5.02. 85
you shall know many dare accuse you boldly, 5.02. 91
let them accuse me by invention; COR 3.02.143
him i accuse | the city ports by this hath 5.06. 5
accuse some innocent, and forswear myself, | set TIT 5.01.130
but yet i could accuse me of such things that it HAM 3.01.122 P
from my chin | will quicken, and accuse thee. LR 3.07. 39
who does he accuse? ANT 3.06. 23
of which i do accuse myself so sorely | that i 4.06. 18
lack of charity | to accuse myself i hate you; CYM 2.03.110
write you not | what monsters her accuse? 3.02. 2
thou didst accuse him of incontinency; 3.04. 47
how dare you ghosts | accuse the thunderer, 5.04. 95
i accuse them not. PER 4.02. 71
accuse me thus: SON 117. 1
but why of two oaths' breach do i accuse thee, 152. 5
ACCUSED 4 FR 0.0004 REL FR 3 V 1 P
liver, | and wish he had not so accused her — ADO 4.01.232
thou art here accused and arraigned of high WT 3.02. 13 P
hear | the accuser and the accused freely speak. R2 1.01. 17
because here is a man accused of treason. 2H6 1.03.177
ACCUSER 2 FR 0.0002 REL FR 1 V 1 P
hear | the accuser and the accused freely speak. R2 1.01. 17
my accuser is my prentice, and when i did 2H6 1.03.198 P
ACCUSER'S 1 FR 0.0001 REL FR 1 V 0 P
who have the power | to seal th' accuser's lips. LR 4.06.170
ACCUSERS 6 FR 0.0006 REL FR 5 V 1 P
call forth the watch that are their accusers. ADO 4.02. 35 P
the envious slanders of her false accusers; R3 1.03. 26
yet i am richer than my base accusers, | that H8 2.01.104
to bring together | yourself and your accusers, 5.01.120
that, in this case of justice, my accusers, | be 5.02. 81
not rash like his accuse., and thus answered: COR 1.01.129
ACCUSES 2 FR 0.0002 REL FR 1 V 1 P
she that accuses him of fornication, | in MM 5.01.195
accuses him of letters he had formerly wrote to ANT 3.05. 10 P
ACCUSETH 1 FR 0.0001 REL FR 0 V 1 P
a man cannot steal, but it accuseth him; R3 1.04.135 P
ACCUSING 3 FR 0.0003 REL FR 2 V 1 P
ducats of don john for accusing the lady hero ADO 4.02. 48 P
accusing it, i put it on my head, | to try with 2H4 4.05.165
each check | without accusing you of injury. SON 58. 8
ACCUSTOM'D 6 FR 0.0006 REL FR 4 V 2 P
bate one breath of her accustom'd crossness. ADO 2.03.177 P
whose heart th' accustom'd sight of death makes AYL 3.05. 4
proof | of your accustom'd diligence to me. 1H6 5.03. 9
will soon recover his accustom'd health. R3 1.03. 2
this night i hold an old accustom'd feast, ROM 1.02. 20
it is an accustom'd action with her, to seem MAC 5.01. 28 P
ACE 3 FR 0.0003 REL FR 0 V 3 P
no die, but an ace, for him; for he is but one. MND 5.01.307 P
less than an ace, man; 5.01.308 P
loss, the most coldest that ever turn'd up ace. CYM 2.03. 2 P
/ACERB 1 FR 0.0001 REL FR 0 V 1 P
be to him shortly as /acerb as /the coloquintida OTH 1.03.349 P
ACHE 13 FR 0.0014 REL FR 10 V 3 P
and most loathed worldly life | that age, ache, MM 3.01.129
let him knock till it ache. ERR 3.01. 58
charm ache with air, and agony with words. ADO 5.01. 26
when your head did but ache, | i knit my JN 4.01. 41
fellow that never had the ache in his shoulders! 2H4 5.01. 83 P
stand close up, or i'll make your head ache. H8 5.03. 88
eyes too, and such an ache in my bones that, TRO 5.03.105 P
fie, how my bones ache! ROM 2.05. 26
my wounds ache at you. TIM 3.05. 95
mine ache to think on't. HAM 5.01. 93 P
for let our finger ache, and it endues | our OTH 3.04.146
like a milch doe, whose swelling dugs do ache, VEN 875
to see the salve doth make the wound ache more, LUC 1116
ACHERON 3 FR 0.0003 REL FR 3 V 0 P
anon | with drooping fog as black as acheron, MND 3.02.357
and pull her out of acheron by the heels. TIT 4.03. 45
and at the pit of acheron | meet me i' th' MAC 3.05. 15
ACHES 7 FR 0.0008 REL FR 7 V 0 P
fill all thy bones with aches, make thee roar TMP 1.02.370
i can go no further, sir, | my old bones aches. 3.03. 2
and my soul aches | to know, when two COR 3.01.108
lord, how my head aches! ROM 2.05. 48
aches contract and starve your supple joints! TIM 1.01.248
their fears of hostile strokes, their aches, 5.01.199
so sweet | that the sense aches at thee, would OTH 4.02. 69
/ACHIEV'D 1 FR 0.0001 REL FR 1 V 0 P
/with /all /pleas'd, /that /hast /all /achiev'd! R2 4.01.217
ACHIEV'D 11 FR 0.0012 REL FR 10 V 1 P
experience is by industry achiev'd, | and TGV 1.03. 22
that your fortune | achiev'd her mistress. MV 3.02.208
happiness | by virtue specially to be achiev'd. SHR 1.01. 20
no certain life achiev'd by others' death. JN 4.02.105
which his noble ancestors achiev'd with blows. R2 2.01.254
have no sooner achiev'd but we'll set upon them. 1H4 1.02.173 P
the treasure in this field achiev'd and city, COR 1.09. 33
he hath achiev'd a maid | that paragons OTH 2.01. 61
which he achiev'd by th' minute, lost his favor. ANT 3.01. 20
and how achiev'd you these endowments which PER 5.01.116
and i know your office | unjustly is achiev'd. TNK 3.01.112
/ACHIEVE 1 FR 0.0001 REL FR 0 V 1 P
some are /born great, some /achieve greatness, TN 2.05.145 P
ACHIEVE 13 FR 0.0014 REL FR 11 V 2 P
if i achieve not this young modest girl. SHR 1.01.156
maid, | bend thoughts and wits to achieve her. 1.01.179
t' achieve that maid | whose sudden sight hath 1.01.219
achieve the elder, set the younger free | for 1.02.266
"some achieve greatness" — TN 3.04. 43 P
"some are born great, some achieve greatness, 5.01.370 P
bid them achieve me, and then sell my bones. H5 4.03. 91
and to achieve | the silver livery of advised 2H6 5.02. 46
and does achieve as soon | as draw his sword; COR 4.07. 23
would i propose to achieve her whom i love. TIT 2.01. 80
to achieve her how? 2.01. 81
that what you cannot as you would achieve, | you 2.01.106
that sin by him advantage should achieve, | and SON 67. 3
ACHIEVED 1 FR 0.0001 REL FR 1 V 0 P
by which the world's best garden he achieved, H5 ep 7
ACHIEVEMENT 3 FR 0.0003 REL FR 3 V 0 P
for all the soil of the achievement goes | with 2H4 4.05.189
fear, | and for achievement offer us his ransom. H5 3.05. 60
achievement is command; TRO 1.02.293
ACHIEVEMENTS 4 FR 0.0004 REL FR 4 V 0 P
and his achievements of no less account; 1H6 2.03. 8
achievements, plots, orders, preventions, TRO 1.03.181
how my achievements mock me! 4.02. 69
and indeed it takes | from our achievements, HAM 1.04. 21
ACHIEVER 1 FR 0.0001 REL FR 0 V 1 P
twice itself when the achiever brings home full ADO 1.01. 8 P
ACHIEVES 1 FR 0.0001 REL FR 0 V 1 P
derives her honesty and achieves her goodness. AWW 1.01. 45 P
ACHILLES' 8 FR 0.0009 REL FR 6 V 2 P
whose smile and frown, like to achilles' spear, 2H6 5.01.100
and achilles' horse | makes many thetis' sons. TRO 1.03.211
with surety stronger than achilles' arm, | 'fore 1.03.220
ajax employ'd plucks down achilles' plumes. 1.03.385
hold my peace when achilles' /brach bids me, 2.01.114 P
his merit, | as amply /titled as achilles' is, 2.03.193
thou art said to be achilles' male varlot. 5.01. 15 P
that for achilles' image stood his spear, LUC 1424
/ACHILLES 1 FR 0.0001 REL FR 0 V 1 P
/agamemnon /is /a /fool, /achilles /is /a /fool, TRO 2.03. 58 P
ACHILLES 71 FR 0.0080 REL FR 50 V 21 P
hide thy head, achilles — here comes hector in LLL 5.02.632 P
there is amongst the greeks achilles, a better TRO 1.02.247 P
achilles! a drayman, a porter, a very camel. 1.02.249 P
the great achilles, whom opinion crowns | the 1.03.142
at this fusty stuff | the large achilles, on his 1.03.162
yet god achilles still cries, "excellent! 1.03.169
in full as proud a place | as broad achilles; 1.03.190
achilles shall have word of this intent, | so 1.03.306
up | in rank achilles must or now be cropp'd 1.03.318
name, | relates in purpose only to achilles. 1.03.323
make no strain | but that achilles, were his 1.03.327
bring those honors off, | if not achilles? 1.03.335
therefore 'tis meet achilles meet not hector. 1.03.357
consent | that ever hector and achilles meet, 1.03.362
what glory our achilles shares from hector, 1.03.366
grumblest and railest every hour on achilles, 2.01. 33 P
this lord, achilles, ajax, who wears his wit in 2.01. 72 P
yes, good sooth. to achilles, to ajax, to — 2.01.109 P
then there's achilles, a rare enginer! 2.03. 7 P
my lord achilles! 2.03. 22 P
where's achilles? 2.03. 34 P
thy commander, achilles. 2.03. 44 P
then tell me, patroclus, what's achilles? 2.03. 45 P
agamemnon commands achilles, achilles is my lord 2.03. 53 P
commands achilles, achilles is my lord, i am 2.03. 53 P
is a fool to offer to command achilles, achilles 2.03. 63 P
achilles, achilles is a fool to be commanded /of 2.03. 63 P
where is achilles? 2.03. 76
achilles hath inveigled his fool from him. 2.03. 91 P
is his argument that has his argument, achilles. 2.03. 97 P
no achilles with him. 2.03.104 P
achilles bids me say, he is much sorry | if any 2.03.107
achilles will not to the field to–morrow. 2.03.162
parts | kingdom'd achilles in commotion rages, 2.03.175
that ajax makes | when they go from achilles. 2.03.184
/titled as achilles' is, | by going to achilles. 2.03.194
and say in thunder, "achilles go to him." 2.03.199
you must prepare to fight without achilles. 2.03.227
he is not emulous, as achilles is. 2.03.231
the hart achilles | keeps thicket. 2.03.258
let achilles sleep: 2.03.265
achilles stands i' th' entrance of his tent. 3.03. 38
what says achilles? would he aught with us? 3.03. 57
what mean these fellows? know they not achilles? 3.03. 70
to send their smiles before them to achilles, 3.03. 72
'tis known, achilles, that you are in love 3.03.193
and better would it fit achilles much | to throw 3.03.207
sing, | "great hector's sister did achilles win, 3.03.212
to this effect, achilles, have i mov'd you. 3.03.216
i come from the worthy achilles — 3.03.282 P
though the great bulk achilles be thy guard, 4.04.128
achilles bids you welcome. 4.05. 25
if not achilles, sir, | what is your name? 4.05. 75
if not achilles, nothing. 4.05. 76
therefore achilles, but what e'er, know this: 4.05. 77
and great achilles | doth long to see unarm'd 4.05.152
but for achilles, my own searching eyes | shall 4.05.161
is this achilles? 4.05.233
i am achilles. 4.05.234
and you, achilles, let these threats alone 4.05.261
against that dog of as bad a kind, achilles; 5.04. 14 P
is the cur ajax prouder than the cur achilles, 5.04. 15 P
go bear patroclus' body to achilles, | and bid 5.05. 17
great achilles | is arming, weeping, cursing, 5.05. 30
face, | know what it is to meet achilles angry. 5.05. 46
"achilles hath the mighty hector slain!" 5.08. 14
achilles! achilles! hector's slain! achilles! 5.09. 3
achilles! achilles! hector's slain! achilles! 5.09. 3
achilles! achilles! hector's slain! achilles! 5.09. 3
the bruit is, hector's slain, and by achilles. 5.09. 4
be sent | to pray achilles see us at our tent. 5.09. 8
ACHING 3 FR 0.0003 REL FR 2 V 1 P
a goodly medicine for my aching bones! TRO 5.10. 35 P
though not for me, yet for /your aching bones. 5.10. 50
is this the poultice for my aching bones? ROM 2.05. 63
ACHITOPHEL 1 FR 0.0001 REL FR 0 V 1 P
a whoreson achitophel! 2H4 1.02. 35 P
/ACKNOWLEDG'D 1 FR 0.0001 REL FR 1 V 0 P
thou art too base | to be /acknowledg'd. WT 4.04.419
ACKNOWLEDG'D 3 FR 0.0003 REL FR 2 V 1 P
making, and the whoreson must be acknowledg'd. LR 1.01. 24 P
to be acknowledg'd, madam, is o'erpaid. 4.07. 4
what you have reserv'd, nor what acknowledg'd, ANT 5.02.180
ACKNOWLEDGE 20 FR 0.0022 REL FR 14 V 6 P
this thing of darkness i | acknowledge mine. TMP 5.01.276
if the encounter acknowledge itself hereafter, MM 3.01.251 P
son, | thou sham'st to acknowledge me in misery. ERR 5.01.323
and meant to acknowledge it this night in a ADO 1.02. 13 P
and will acknowledge you and jessica | in place MV 3.04. 38
spirit that will not acknowledge it to be the — AWW 2.03. 30 P
as your due, time claims, he does acknowledge, 2.04. 42
the parts of man | which honor does acknowledge, WT 1.02.401
name of fault, i must not | at all acknowledge. 3.02. 61
acknowledge then the king, and let me in. JN 2.01.269
all the kingdoms that acknowledge christ. 1H4 3.02.111
complexion of my greatness to acknowledge it. 2H4 2.02. 5 P
if ever thou dar'st acknowledge it, i will make H5 4.01.209 P
for, by my soul, i'll ne'er acknowledge thee, ROM 3.05.193
best senses | acknowledge thee their patron, and TIM 1.02.124
i have so often blush'd to acknowledge him, that LR 1.01. 10 P
nature is asham'd | almost t' acknowledge hers. 1.01.213
tributaries | that do acknowledge caesar, should ANT 3.13. 97
acknowledge to the gods | our thanks that you TNK 5.04.100
i may not evermore acknowledge thee, | lest my SON 36. 9
ACKNOWLEDGMENT 1 FR 0.0001 REL FR 1 V 0 P
but with this acknowledgment, | that god fought H5 4.08.119
ACKNOWN 1 FR 0.0001 REL FR 1 V 0 P
be not acknown on't; OTH 3.03.319
A–COLD 5 FR 0.0005 REL FR 1 V 4 P
tom's a–cold — o, do de, do de, do de. LR 3.04. 58 P
tom's a–cold. 3.04. 83 P
poor tom's a–cold. 3.04.147 P
tom's a–cold. 3.04.173 P
poor tom's a–cold. i cannot daub it further. 4.01. 52
A–COMING 1 FR 0.0001 REL FR 0 V 1 P
but there are worthies a–coming will speak their LLL 5.02.585 P
ACONITUM 1 FR 0.0001 REL FR 1 V 0 P
work as strong | as aconitum or rash gunpowder. 2H4 4.04. 48
ACORDO 1 FR 0.0001 REL FR 1 V 0 P
acordo linta. AWW 4.01. 87
ACORN 3 FR 0.0003 REL FR 2 V 1 P
roots, and husks | wherein the acorn cradled. TMP 1.02.465
you bead, you acorn. MND 3.02.330
i found him under a tree, like a dropp'd acorn. AYL 3.02.235 P
ACORN–CUPS 1 FR 0.0001 REL FR 1 V 0 P
creep into acorn–cups and hide them there. MND 2.01. 31
ACQUAINT 22 FR 0.0024 REL FR 14 V 8 P
acquaint her with the danger of my state; MM 1.02.179
but i will acquaint my daughter withal, that she ADO 1.02. 21 P
they did entreat me to acquaint her of it, | but 3.01. 40
and i came to acquaint you with a matter. AYL 1.01.122 P
to you, i came hither to acquaint you withal, 1.01.132 P
i held my duty speedily to acquaint you withal, AWW 1.03.119 P
house, | acquaint my mother with my hate to her, 2.03.287
may i be bold to acquaint his grace you are gone 3.06. 78 P
acquaint the queen of your most noble offer, WT 2.02. 46
i not acquaint | my father of this business. 4.04.412
a piece of honesty to acquaint the king withal, 4.04.680 P
and broke out | to acquaint you with this evil, JN 5.06. 25
i must acquaint you that i have receiv'd 2H4 4.01. 7
i will acquaint his majesty | of those gross R3 1.03.104
that i'll acquaint our duteous citizens | with 3.05. 65
acquaint the princess | with the sweet silent 4.04.329
will we acquaint withal what we intend, | and TIT 2.01.122
bed, | acquaint her here of my son paris' love, ROM 3.04. 16
acquaint you with the perfect spy o' th' time, MAC 3.01.129
do you consent we shall acquaint him with it, HAM 1.01.172
as i shall find means, and acquaint you withal. LR 1.02.102 P
acquaint my daughter no further with any thing 1.05. 2 P
/ACQUAINTANCE 1 FR 0.0001 REL FR 1 V 0 P
/not /grieve | /lending /me /this /acquaintance. LR 4.03. 54
ACQUAINTANCE 39 FR 0.0044 REL FR 22 V 17 P
your eld'st acquaintance cannot be three hours. TMP 5.01.186
heaven may decrease it upon better acquaintance, WIV 1.01.247 P
that altogether's acquaintance with mistress 1.02. 8 P
/brook, i desire more acquaintance of you. 2.02.162 P
i am blest in your acquaintance. 2.02.268 P
how her acquaintance grew with this lewd fellow. ADO 5.01.332
i shall desire you of more acquaintance, good MND 3.01.182 P
i shall desire you of more acquaintance too. 3.01.189 P

i desire you /of more acquaintance, good master 3.01.195 P
feast to–night | my best esteem'd acquaintance. MV 2.02.172
or have acquaintance with mine own desires; AYL 1.03. 48
that on so little acquaintance you should like 5.02. 1 P
the poverty of her, the small acquaintance, my 5.02. 6 P
balk logic with acquaintance that you have, SHR 1.01. 34
have a desire to hold my acquaintance with thee, AWW 2.03.228 P
i saw him hold acquaintance with the waves | so TN 1.02. 16
mistress accost, i desire better acquaintance. 1.03. 53 P
i will wash off gross acquaintance, i will be 2.05.163 P
taught him to face me out of his acquaintance, 5.01. 88
should scape the true acquaintance of mine ear. JN 5.06. 15
and be no more oppos'd | against acquaintance, 1H4 1.01. 16
what, old acquaintance! 5.04.102
to see how many of my old acquaintance are dead! 2H4 3.02. 34 P
our house, let our old acquaintance be renew'd. 3.02.294 P
and yet must | perforce be their acquaintance. H8 1.02. 47
utterly | grow from the king's acquaintance, by 3.01.161
from me all | that time, acquaintance, custom, TRO 3.03. 9
i urg'd our old acquaintance, and the drops COR 5.01. 10
what sorrow craves acquaintance at my hand, ROM 3.03. 5
how does my old acquaintance of this isle? OTH 2.01.203
and comforts of sudden respect and acquaintance, 4.02.190 P
how creeps acquaintance? CYM 1.04. 25 P
faith, my acquaintance lies little amongst them. PER 4.06.195 P
we are father, friends, acquaintance; TNK 2.02. 81
us, envy of ill men | crave our acquaintance; 2.02. 91
both stood like old acquaintance in a trance, LUC 1595
brain, | to take a new acquaintance of thy mind. SON 77.12
i will acquaintance strangle and look strange, 89. 8
wrong, | and haply of our old acquaintance tell. 89.12

ACQUAINTED 41 FR 0.0046 REL FR 23 V 18 P
i, having been acquainted with the smell before, TGV 4.04. 23 P
myself like one that i am not acquainted withal; WIV 2.01. 86 P
and page's wife acquainted each other how they 2.02.109 P
fain speak with you, and be acquainted with you; 2.02.145 P
as desire to make myself acquainted with you. 2.02.183 P
as you would desires to be acquainted withal. 3.01. 67 P
from time to time i have acquainted you | with 4.06. 8
i would not have you acquainted with tapsters; MM 2.01.204 P
i pray you be acquainted with this maid, | she 4.01. 50
i am as well acquainted here as i was in our 4.03. 1 P
what need she be acquainted? ERR 3.02. 15
belike his wife, acquainted with his fits, | on 4.03. 90
as it were, i have acquainted you withal, to the LLL 5.01.115 P
they have acquainted me with their MV 1.02.101 P
i acquainted him with the cause in controversy 4.01.154 P
are you acquainted with the difference | that 4.01.171
have you not been acquainted with goldsmiths' AYL 3.02.271 P
youth, let me /be better acquainted with thee. 4.01. 2 P
that you must kiss, and be acquainted with. SHR 4.01.152
made me acquainted with a weighty cause | of 4.04. 26
nothing acquainted with these businesses, | and AWW 3.07. 5
art not acquainted with him? 4.01. 8 P
that you are well acquainted with yourself, 5.03.106
acquainted me with interest to this land, | yea, JN 5.02. 89
john, i am well acquainted with your manner of 2H4 2.01.109 P
well, i'll be acquainted with him if i return, 3.02.328 P
be | as things acquainted and familiar to us, 5.02.139
as one being best acquainted with her humor. R3 4.04.269
the queen shall be acquainted | forthwith for H8 2.02.107
and to be | acquainted with this stranger. 5.01.168
we are too well acquainted with these answers, TRO 2.03.113
that were ne'er acquainted with their wards TIM 3.03. 37
make me acquainted with your cause of grief. JC 2.01.256
i did not think he had been acquainted with her. OTH 3.03. 99
for war, acquainted | my grieved ear withal; ANT 3.06. 58
was born, and i pray you be better acquainted. CYM 1.04.122 P
the king my father shall be made acquainted | of 1.06.149
i will make them acquainted with your purpose, PER 4.06.198 P
i was acquainted | once with a time when i TNK 1.03. 49
but not acquainted | with shifting change, as is SON 20. 3
with mine own weakness being best acquainted, 88. 5

ACQUAINTS 1 FR 0.0001 REL FR 0 V 1 P
misery acquaints a man with strange bedfellows; TMP 2.02. 39 P

ACQUIR'D 2 FR 0.0002 REL FR 1 V 1 P
his valor hath here acquir'd for him shall at AWW 4.03. 69 P
shall not so /stale his palm, nobly acquir'd, TRO 2.03.191

ACQUIRE 4 FR 0.0004 REL FR 3 V 1 P
bitter than | 'tis sweet at first t' acquire — H8 2.03. 9
you must acquire and beget a temperance that may HAM 3.02. 7 P
acquire too high a fame when him we serve's away ANT 3.01. 15
shall acquire no honor | demuring upon me. 4.15. 28

ACQUISITION 1 FR 0.0001 REL FR 1 V 0 P
and thine own acquisition | worthily purchas'd, TMP 4.01. 13

ACQUIT 10 FR 0.0011 REL FR 7 V 3 P
i am glad i am so acquit of this tinderbox; WIV 1.03. 24 P
without some broken limb shall acquit him well. AYL 1.01.128 P
i will acquit you. TN 3.04.215
if my tongue cannot entreat you to acquit me, 2H4 ep 18 P
law, | and god acquit them of their practices! H5 2.02.144
pray god he may acquit him of suspicion! 2H6 3.02. 25
me leave | by circumstance but to acquit myself. R3 1.02. 77
courageous richmond, well hast thou acquit thee. 5.05. 3
till life to death acquit my forc'd offense. LUC 1071
may any terms acquit me from this chance? 1706

ACQUITTANCE 3 FR 0.0003 REL FR 2 V 1 P
your mere enforcement shall acquittance me R3 3.07.233
now must your conscience my acquittance seal, HAM 4.07. 1
so the acquittance follows. CYM 5.04.170 P

ACQUITTANCES 1 FR 0.0001 REL FR 1 V 0 P
you can produce acquittances | for such a sum LLL 2.01.160

ACQUITTED 3 FR 0.0003 REL FR 3 V 0 P
have by your wisdom been this day acquitted | of MV 4.01.409
no more than i am well acquitted of. 5.01.138
action | acquitted by a true substantial form 2H4 4.01.171

ACRE 3 FR 0.0003 REL FR 2 V 1 P
furlongs of sea for an acre of barren ground, TMP 1.01. 66 P
furlongs ere | with spur we heat an acre. WT 1.02. 96
search every acre in the high–grown field, | and LR 4.04. 7

ACRES 4 FR 0.0004 REL FR 4 V 0 P
crown | my bosky acres and my unshrubb'd down, TMP 4.01. 81
between the acres of the rye, | with a hey, and AYL 5.03. 22
over whose acres walk'd those blessed feet 1H4 1.01. 25
let them throw | millions of acres on us, till HAM 5.01.281

ACROSS *(also 'cross)*

ACROSS 7 FR 0.0008 REL FR 6 V 1 P
back, slave, or i will break thy pate across. ERR 2.01. 78
good faith, across! AWW 2.01. 67
h'as broke my head across and has given sir toby TN 5.01.175 P
when my good falcon made her flight across | thy WT 4.04. 15
musing and sighing, with your arms across; JC 2.01.240
who calls me villain, breaks my pate across, HAM 2.02.572
with sad set eyes, and wretched arms across, LUC 1662

ACT 134 FR 0.0151 REL FR 118 V 16 P
to act her earthy and abhorr'd commands, TMP 1.02.273
to perform an act | whereof what's past is 2.01.252
thy brother was a furtherer in the act. 5.01. 73
i will consent to act any villainy against him, WIV 2.01. 98 P
i warrant thee, if i do not act it, hiss me. 3.03. 38 P
we do not act that often jest and laugh; 4.02.106
now puts the drowsy and neglected act | freshly MM 1.02.170
law, | as mice by lions) hath pick'd out an act, 1.04. 64
one foul wrong, | lives not to act another. 2.02.104
so then it seems your most offenseful act | was 2.03. 26
condemn'd upon the act of fornication | to lose 5.01. 70
his act did not o'ertake his bad intent, | and 5.01.451
was | between these woolly breeders in the act, MV 1.03. 83
fashion of thy malice | to the last hour of act, 4.01. 19
thyself shalt see the act; 4.01.314
haggish age steal on, | and wore us out of act. AWW 1.02. 30
the help of heaven we count the act of men. 2.01.152
not put my reputation now | in any staining act. 3.07. 7
deed, | and lawful meaning in a lawful act, 3.07. 46
sir, so should i be a great deal of his act. 4.03. 46 P
it shall become thee well to act my woes. TN 1.04. 26
that they may fairly note this act of mine! 4.03. 35
he finished indeed his mortal act | that day 5.01.247
(for in an act of this importance 'twere | most WT 2.01.181
honor, or in act or will | that way inclining, 3.02. 51
the dignity of this act was worth the audience 5.02. 79 P
the better act of purposes mistook | is to JN 3.01.274
though that my death were adjunct to my act, 3.03. 57
this act so evilly borne shall cool the hearts 3.04.149
done, | this act is as an ancient tale new told, 4.02. 18
and consequently thy rude hand to act | the deed 4.02.240
thou didst but consent | to this most cruel act, 4.03.126
if i in act, consent, or sin of thought | be 4.03.135
be great in act, as you have been in thought. 5.01. 45
and future ages groan for this foul act. R2 4.01.138
a stage | to feed contention in a ling'ring act; 2H4 1.01.156
sack commences it and sets it in act and use. 4.03.116 P
a kingdom for a stage, princes to act, | and H5 pr 3
teach | the act of order to a peopled kingdom. 1.02.189
doing the execution and the act | for which we 2.02. 17
up, | and with the same to act controlling laws. 2H6 5.01.103
him off, | persuaded him from any further act: 5.03. 10
before i would have granted to that act. 3H6 1.01.245
bed, | until that act of parliament be repeal'd 1.01.249
have caus'd him, by new act of parliament, | to 2.02. 91
what scene of death hath roscius now to act? 5.06. 10
to make an act of tragic violence. R3 2.02. 39
the tyrannous and bloody act is done, | the most 4.03. 1
grosser quality, is cried up | for our best act. H8 1.02. 85
the part my father meant to act upon | th' 1.02.195
the honor of it | does pay the act of it, as i' 3.02.182
to take their ease, | and sleep an act or two; ep 3
and esteem no act | but that of hand. TRO 1.03.199
and choice (being mutual act of all our souls) 1.03.348
we may not think the justness of each act | such 2.02.119
is boundless and the act a slave to limit. 3.02. 83 P
have the voice of lions and the act of hares, 3.02. 88 P
an act that very chance doth throw upon him — 3.03.131
daily any wholesome act establish'd against the COR 1.01. 83 P
that could be brought to bodily act ere rome 1.02. 5
his good will | hath overta'en mine act. 1.09. 19
when he might act the woman in the scene, | he 2.02. 96
so smile the heavens upon this holy act, | that ROM 2.06. 1
my dismal scene i needs must act alone. 4.03. 19
performance is ever the duller for his act, TIM 5.01. 24
do, | stir up their servants to an act of rage, JC 2.01.176
as by our hands and this our present act | you 3.01.166
as happy prologues to the swelling act | of the MAC 1.03.128
to be the same in thine own act and valor | as 1.07. 40
seest the heavens, as troubled with man's act, 2.04. 5
that doth guide his valor | to act in safety. 3.01. 53
almost to jelly with the act of fear, | stand HAM 1.02.205
as he in his particular act and place | may give 1.03. 26
nor any unproportion'd thought his act. 1.03. 60
but, howsomever thou pursues this act, | taint 1.05. 84
to give them shape, or time to act them in. 3.01.126 P
i prithee, when thou seest that act afoot, 3.02. 78
or about some act | that has no relish of 3.03. 91
such an act | that blurs the grace and blush of 3.04. 40
is thought–sick at the act. 3.04. 51
ay me, what act, | that roars so loud and 3.04. 51
if i drown myself wittingly, it argues an act, 5.01. 11 P
argues an act, and an act hath three branches — 5.01. 11 P
and an act hath three branches — it is to act, 5.01. 12 P
that are but mutes or audience to this act, 5.02.335
thing, of a queasy question, | which i must act. LR 2.01. 18
this act persuades me | that this remotion of 2.04.113
heart and did the act of darkness with her; 3.04. 87 P
the sparks of nature, | to quit this horrid act. 3.07. 87
oppos'd against the act, bending his sword | to 4.02. 74
the native act and figure of my heart | in OTH 1.01. 62
wars | (which even now stands in act) that, for 1.01.151
daughters' minds | by what you see them act. 1.01.171
the blood is made dull with the act of sport, 2.01.227 P
though i am bound to every act of duty, | i am 3.03.134
but with a little act upon the blood | burn like 3.03.328
to do the act that might the addition earn, 4.02.163
o monstrous act! 5.02.190
i know this act shows horrible and grim. 5.02.203
that she with cassio hath the act of shame | a 5.02.211
state | this heavy act with heavy heart relate. 5.02.371
which commits some loving act upon her, she hath ANT 1.02.144 P
my brother never | did urge me in his act. 2.02. 46
me have thy hand | further this act of grace; 2.02.146
e'er thy tongue | hath so betray'd thine act. 2.07. 78
place, note well, | may make too great an act. 3.01. 13
see him rouse himself | to praise my noble act. 5.02.285
to see perform'd the dreaded act which thou | so 5.02.331
and apply | allayments to their act, and by them CYM 1.05. 22
than that horrid act | of the divorce he'ld make 2.01. 61
art thou a feodary for this act, and look'st 3.02. 21
a sland'rous epitaph | as record of fair act; 3.03. 53
pisanio, must act for me, if thy faith be not 3.04. 26 P
hereafter find | it is no act of common passage, 3.04. 91
three thousand confident, in act as many — 5.03. 29
what, mak'st thou me a dullard in this act? 5.05.265
few love to hear the sins they love to act; PER 1.01. 92
since he's so great can make his will his act, 1.02. 18
graves, and smiling | extremity out of act. 5.01.139
whilst we dispatch | this grand act of our life, TNK 1.01.164
other instruments | to his own nerves and act; 1.02. 69
as well | speak this, and act it in your glass, 3.01. 70
if i priz'd life so much | as to deny my act; 3.02. 24
of her holy altar | with sacred act advances: 5.01.165
nature now | shall make and act the story, the 5.03. 14
i did but act, he's author of thy slander. VEN 1006
o impious act, including all foul harms! LUC 199
fact, | how can they then assist me in the act? 350
you did fulfill | the loathsome act of lust, and 1636
this act will be | my fame and thy perpetual 1637
may my pure mind with the foul act dispense, 1704
for his foul act by whom thy fair wife bleeds? 1824
and with her lips on his did act the seizure: PP 11.10
in act thy bed–vow broke, and new faith torn SON 152. 3

ACTAEON 2 FR 0.0002 REL FR 1 V 1 P
or go thou | like sir actaeon he, with ringwood WIV 2.01.118
page himself for a secure and willful actaeon; 3.02. 43 P

ACTAEON'S 1 FR 0.0001 REL FR 1 V 0 P
presently | with horns, as was actaeon's, and TIT 2.03. 63

ACTED 7 FR 0.0008 REL FR 5 V 2 P
which i so lively acted with my tears | that my TGV 4.04.169
of kings and princes, for by such was it acted. WT 5.02. 81 P
bold, | think true love acted simple modesty. ROM 3.02. 16
shall this our lofty scene be acted over | in JC 3.01.112
which must be acted ere they may be scann'd. MAC 3.04.139
speak me a speech once, but it was never acted, HAM 2.02.435 P
let the world see | his nobleness well acted, ANT 5.02. 45

ACTING 8 FR 0.0009 REL FR 8 V 0 P
or that the resolute acting of /your blood MM 2.01. 12
and, acting this in an obedient hope, | why have TN 5.01.340
hath been but as a scene | acting that argument. 2H4 4.05.198
it is a part | that i shall blush in acting, and COR 2.02.145
fear, | abate thy valor in the acting it. ROM 4.01.120
between the acting of a dreadful thing | and the JC 2.01. 63
of each several crime, | acting it many ways. MAC 4.03. 97
by | th' important acting of your dread command? HAM 3.04.108

/ACTION 5 FR 0.0005 REL FR 5 V 0 P
/could /restrain | /the //stiff–borne /action. 2H4 1.01.177
/the /action /of /their /bodies /from /their 1.01.195
/indeed /the /instant /action, /a /cause /on 1.03. 37
passage and whole /carriage /of /this /action TRO 2.03.131
/in /thy /dumb /action /will /i /be /as /perfect TIT 3.02. 40

ACTION 115 FR 0.0130 REL FR 84 V 31 P
the rarer action is | in virtue than in TMP 5.01. 27
what dangerous action, stood it next to death, TGV 5.04. 41
i can construe the action of her familiar style, WIV 1.03. 46 P
my counterfeiting the action of an old woman, 4.05.118 P
moe reasons for this action | at our more MM 1.03. 48
being one) | in hand, and hope of action; 1.04. 52
or i'll have mine action of batt'ry on thee. 2.01.179 P
ear, you might have your action of slander too. 2.01.181 P
in action all of precept, he did show me | the 4.01. 39
how many gentlemen have you lost in this action? ADO 1.01. 6 P
when you went onward on this ended action, | i 1.01.297
as motion and long–during action tires | the LLL 4.03.303
action and accent did they teach him there: 5.02. 99
and we will do it in action as we will do it MND 3.01. 5 P
do not fret yourself too much in the action, 4.01. 14 P
by the stern brow and waspish action | which she AYL 4.03. 9
love, | he bear himself with honorable action, SHR in.1. 110
voice, gait, and action of a gentlewoman. in.1. 132
i'll bring mine action on the proudest he | that 3.02.234
i knew in what particular action to try him. AWW 3.06. 17 P
so he that in this action contrives against his 4.03. 24 P
i'll have an action of battery against him, if TN 4.01. 34 P
he upon some action | is now in durance, at 5.01.275
this action i now go on | is for my better grace WT 2.01.121
forewearied in this action of swift speed, JN 2.01.233
or heard | of any kindred action like to this? 3.04. 14
whilst he that hears makes fearful action | with 4.02.191
work, | the graceless action of a heavy hand — 4.03. 58
what munition sent, | to underprop this action? 5.02. 99
the plot and the general course of the action. 1H4 2.03. 22 P
a dish of skim–milk with so honorable an action! 2.03. 34 P
honor that thou wert not with me in this action. 2.04. 21 P
i not fall'n away vilely since this last action? 3.03. 2 P
time for your quiet o'erposting that action. 2H4 1.02.151 P
is not a dangerous action can peep out his head 1.02.212 P
master fang, have you ent'red the action? 2.01. 1 P
go wash thy face, and draw the action. 2.01.150 P
may sleep when the man of action is call'd on. 2.04.376 P
that are ensinewed to this action | acquitted by 4.01.170
shall to the king taste of this action, | that, 4.01.190
the manner how this action hath been borne 4.04. 88
minds | with foreign quarrels, that action, 4.05.214
by, | all out of work and cold for action! H5 1.02.114
that this fair action may on foot be brought. 1.02.310
ears, | then imitate the action of the tiger; 3.01. 6
who in unnecessary action swarm | about our 4.02. 27
i cannot give due action to my words, | except a 2H6 5.01. 8
my soul and body on the action both! 5.02. 26
that in your outward action shows itself R3 1.03. 66
and becoming | the action of good women. H8 2.03. 55
sith /every action that hath gone before, TRO 1.03. 13
and with ridiculous and /awkward action, | which 1.03.149
shall be oddly pois'd | in this vild action, for 1.03.340
as smiles upon the forehead of this action | for 2.02.205
"bring action hither, this cannot go to war." 2.03.136
than an effeminate man | in time of action. 3.03.219
but he in heat of action | is more vindicative 4.05.106
they are in action. 4.05.113
singularity, he goes | upon this present action. COR 1.01.279

than one voluptuously surfeit out of action. 1.03. 25 P
choice of those | that best can aid your action. 1.06. 66
he hath in this action outdone his former deeds 2.01.136 P
holding them, | in human action and capacity, 2.01.249
(for in such business | action is eloquence, and 3.02. 76
and by my body's action teach my mind | a most 3.02.122
i think, that shall set them in present action. 4.03. 47 P
and you are dark'ned in this action, sir, | even 4.07. 5
but either | have borne the action of yourself, 4.07. 15
my partner in this action, | you must report to 5.03. 2
sold the blood and labor | of our great action; 5.06. 47
a full third part | the charges of the action. 5.06. 78
and vice sometime by action dignified. ROM 2.03. 22
in personal action, yet prodigious grown, | and JC 1.03. 77
action, nor utterance, nor the power of speech 3.02.222
it is an accustom'd action with her, to seem MAC 5.01. 28 P
look with what courteous action | it waves you HAM 1.04. 60
how express and admirable in action! 2.02.306 P
visage | and pious action we do sugar o'er | the 3.01. 47
turn awry, | and lose the name of action. 3.01. 87
suit the action to the word, the word to the 3.02. 17 P
the action to the word, the word to the action, 3.02. 18 P
there the action lies | in his true nature, and 3.03. 61
lest with this piteous action you convert | my 3.04.128
and will not tell him of his action of battery? 5.01.103 P
no unchaste action, or dishonored step, | that LR 1.01.228
for when my outward action doth demonstrate OTH 1.01. 61
though our proper son | stood in your action. 1.03. 70
us'd | their dearest action in the tented field; 1.03. 85
am i to put our cassio in some action | that may 2.03. 60
it were an honest action to say | so to the moor 2.03.141
and would in action glorious i had lost | those 2.03.186
pleasure and action make the hours seem short. 2.03.379
great, and let not | a leaner action rend us. ANT 2.02. 19
not let him partake in the glory of the action. 3.05. 9 P
but his whole action grows | not in the power 3.07. 68
i never saw an action of such shame; 3.10. 21
and what thou think'st his very action speaks 3.12. 35
the violence of action hath made you reek as a CYM 1.02. 2 P
than in my every action to be guided by others' 1.04. 45 P
if you will make't an action, call witness to't. 2.03.151
her pretty action did outsell her gift, | and 2.04.102
mine action? 3.04.104
that since the common men are now in action 3.07. 2
in life, to lock it | from action and adventure? 4.04. 3
the action of my life is like it, which | i'll 5.04.149
action may | conveniently the rest convey, PER 3.ch. 55
they with continual action are even as good as 4.02. 8 P
where what is done in action, more, if might, 5.ch. 23
i had as lief trace this good action with you TNK 1.01.102
words, till action might become them better. LUC 1323
fight, | making such sober action with his hand, 1403
and to their hope they such odd action yield, 1433
whose action is no stronger than a flower? SON 65. 4
spirit in a waste of shame | is lust in action, 129. 2
of shame | is lust in action, and till action, 129. 2

ACTION'S 2 FR 0.0002 REL FR 2 V 0 P
some life, | which action's self was tongue to. H8 1.01. 42
when that his action's dregg'd with mind assur'd TNK 1.02. 97

ACTIONS 29 FR 0.0032 REL FR 24 V 5 P
his actions show much like to madness, pray MM 4.04. 4 P
how many actions most ridiculous | hast thou AYL 2.04. 30
a woman's thought runs before her actions. 4.01.141 P
thy limbs, actions, and spirit | do give thee TN 1.05.292
if pow'rs divine | behold our human actions (as WT 3.02. 29
your actions are my dreams. 3.02. 82
her actions shall be holy, as | you hear my 5.03.104
strong reasons makes strange actions. JN 3.04.182
and on our actions set the name of right | with 5.02. 67
which is four terms, or two actions, and 'a 2H4 5.01. 80 P
so may a thousand actions, once afoot, | end in H5 1.02.211
not stint | our necessary actions in the fear H8 1.02. 77
if my actions | were tried by ev'ry tongue, 3.01. 34
no other speaker of my living actions | to keep 4.02. 70
grow in the veins of actions highest rear'd, TRO 1.03. 6
or else your actions would grow wondrous single; COR 2.01. 36 P
their eyes and his actions in their hearts that 2.02. 29 P
when our actions do not, | our fears do make us MAC 4.02. 3
for they are actions that a man might play, HAM 1.02. 84
that to the use of actions fair and good | he 3.04.163
for if such actions may have passage free, OTH 1.02. 98
that though his actions were not visible, yet CYM 3.04.149
blush not in actions blacker than the night PER 1.01.135
and our mind partakes her private actions | to 1.01.152
nor never did my actions yet commence | a deed 2.05. 53
my actions are as noble as my thoughts, | that 2.05. 59
your premeditating | more than their actions; TNK 1.01.137
but, o jove, your actions, | soon as they /move, 1.01.137
me | than all the actions that i have foregone 1.01.173

ACTION-TAKING 1 FR 0.0001 REL FR 0 V 1 P
a lily-liver'd, action-taking, whoreson, LR 2.02. 18 P

/ACTIUM 1 FR 0.0001 REL FR 1 V 0 P
from th' head of /actium | beat th' approaching ANT 3.07. 51

ACTIVE 8 FR 0.0009 REL FR 6 V 2 P
despite his nice fence and his active practice, ADO 5.01. 75
more active, valiant, or more valiant, young, 1H4 5.01. 90
i were simply the most active fellow in europe. 2H4 4.03. 21 P
is simply the most active gentleman of france. H5 3.07. 97 P
the people liberal, valiant, active, wealthy, 2H6 4.07. 63
that 'twixt his mental and his active parts TRO 2.03.174
and nimble set, | which shows an active soul; TNK 4.02.126
to see his active child do deeds of youth, | so SON 37. 2

ACTIVELY 1 FR 0.0001 REL FR 1 V 0 P
since frost itself as actively doth burn, | and HAM 3.04. 87

ACTIVITY 3 FR 0.0003 REL FR 1 V 2 P
doing is activity, and he will still be doing. H5 3.07. 99 P
too, if she call your activity in question. TRO 3.02. 57 P
that your activity may defeat and quell | the TIM 4.03.163

ACTOR 12 FR 0.0013 REL FR 9 V 3 P
condemn the fault, and not the actor of it? MM 2.02. 37
stands in record, | and let go by the actor. 2.02. 41
auditor, | an actor too perhaps, if i see cause. MND 3.01. 80
say | i'll prove a busy actor in their play. AYL 3.04. 59
of a heavenly effect in an earthly actor." AWW 2.03. 24 P
after a well-graced actor leaves the stage, R2 5.02. 24
like a dull actor now | i have forgot my part, COR 5.03. 40
when roscius was an actor in rome — HAM 2.02.391 P
"then came each actor on his ass" — 2.02.395
did i, my lord, and was accounted a good actor. 3.02.101 P
come too short, | the actor may plead pardon. ANT 2.05. 9
as an unperfect actor on the stage, | who with SON 23. 1

/ACTOR'S 1 FR 0.0001 REL FR 1 V 0 P
/of /author's /pen /or /actor's /voice, /but TRO pr 24

ACTORS 11 FR 0.0012 REL FR 5 V 6 P
these our actors | (as i foretold you) were all TMP 4.01.148
sir, the parties themselves, the actors, sir, LLL 5.02.500 P
then read the names of the actors; MND 1.02. 9 P
quince, call forth your actors by the scroll. 1.02. 15 P
and, most dear actors, eat no onions nor garlic, 4.02. 42 P
here repent you, | the actors are at hand; 5.01.116
were play'd in jest by counterfeiting actors? 3H6 2.03. 28
purposes, | but bear it as our roman actors do, JC 2.01.226
the actors are come hither, my lord. HAM 2.02.392 P
the best actors in the world, either for tragedy 2.02.396 P
thing | from vassal actors can be wip'd away; LUC 608

/ACTS 2 FR 0.0002 REL FR 2 V 0 P
/my /acts, /decrees, /and /statutes /i /deny; R2 4.01.213
meet for rebellion /and /such /acts /as /yours. 2H4 4.02.117

ACTS 23 FR 0.0026 REL FR 23 V 0 P
plays many parts, | his acts being seven ages. AYL 2.07.143
when rather from our acts we them derive | than AWW 2.03.136
present deeds, | that all your acts are queens. WT 4.04.146
at your industrious scenes and acts of death. JN 2.01.376
the acts commenced on this ball of earth. 2H4 in 5
the chevalry of england move | to do brave acts. 2.03. 21
with full mouth | speak freely of our acts, or H5 1.02.231
for his acts | so much applauded through the 1H6 2.02. 35
and, brother york, thy acts in ireland, | in 2H6 1.01.194
his father's acts commenc'd in burning troy! 3.02.118
o'er-wrested seeming | he acts thy greatness in; TRO 1.03.158
i have been | the book of his good acts, whence COR 5.02. 15
acts of black night, abominable deeds, TIT 5.01. 64
thy wild acts /denote | the unreasonable fury of ROM 3.03.110
to crown my thoughts with acts, be it thought MAC 4.01.149
to what it would, | acts little of his will. HAM 4.05.126
hear | of carnal, bloody, and unnatural acts, 5.02.381
our conditions | so diff'ring in their acts. ANT 2.02.114
to this great fairy i'll commend thy acts, 4.08. 12
which writ his honor in the acts it did | hath, 5.01. 22
puts himself in posture | that acts my words. CYM 3.03. 95
gives heaven countless eyes to view men's acts, PER 1.01. 73
and all this dumb play had his acts made plain VEN 359

ACTUAL 2 FR 0.0002 REL FR 1 V 1 P
her walking and other actual performances, what, MAC 5.01. 12 P
either in discourse of thought or actual deed, OTH 4.02.153

ACTURE 1 FR 0.0001 REL FR 1 V 0 P
love made them not, with acture they may be, LC 185

A-CURSING 1 FR 0.0001 REL FR 1 V 0 P
and fall a-cursing, like a very drab, | a HAM 2.02.586

ACUTE 2 FR 0.0002 REL FR 1 V 1 P
a most acute juvenal, volable and free of grace! LLL 3.01. 66
the gift is good in those /in whom it is acute, 4.02. 71 P

ACUTELY 1 FR 0.0001 REL FR 0 V 1 P
of businesses, i cannot answer thee acutely. AWW 1.01.207 P

'AD *(also had)*

'AD 1 FR 0.0001 REL FR 1 V 0 P
't 'ad been a kindness | becoming well thy /fact PER 4.03. 11

AD 6 FR 0.0006 REL FR 4 V 2 P
go to, thou hast it ad dunghill, at the fingers' LLL 5.01. 77 P
of her, cum privilegio ad imprimendum solum; SHR 4.04. 93 P
a pile | ad /manes fratrum sacrifice his flesh TIT 1.01. 98
"ad jovem," that's for you; 4.03. 54
here, "ad apollinem"; 4.03. 54
"ad martem," that's for myself; 4.03. 55

ADAGE 2 FR 0.0002 REL FR 2 V 0 P
queen, | unless the adage must be verified, 3H6 1.04.126
"i would," | like the poor cat i' th' adage? MAC 1.07. 45

ADALLAS 1 FR 0.0001 REL FR 1 V 0 P
the thracian king, adallas; ANT 3.06. 71

/ADAM 1 FR 0.0001 REL FR 0 V 1 P
/the /scripture /says /adam /digg'd; HAM 5.01. 36 P

ADAM 20 FR 0.0022 REL FR 7 V 13 P
you got the picture of old adam new apparell'd? ERR 4.03. 13 P
what gold is this? what adam dost thou mean? 4.03. 15 P
not that adam that kept the paradise, but that 4.03. 17 P
paradise, but that adam that keeps the prison; 4.03. 18 P
him be clapp'd on the shoulder, and call'd adam. ADO 1.01.259 P
endow'd with all that adam had left him before 2.01.252 P
the moon was a month old when adam was no more. LLL 4.02. 39
had he been adam, he had tempted eve. 5.02.322
as i remember, adam, it was upon this fashion AYL 1.01. 1 P
this is it, adam, that grieves me, and the 1.01. 22 P
go apart, adam, and thou shalt hear how he will 1.01. 27 P
here feel we not the penalty of adam, | the 2.01. 5
why, whither, adam, wouldst thou have me go? 2.03. 29
why, how now, adam? 2.06. 4 P
cheerly, good adam! 2.06. 18 P
there were none fine but adam, rafe, and gregory SHR 4.01.136
the old days of goodman adam to the pupil age of 1H4 2.04. 94 P
knowest in the state of innocency adam fell, and 3.03.165 P
came | and whipt th' offending adam out of him, H5 1.01. 29
and adam was a gardener. 2H6 4.02.134

ADAMANT 3 FR 0.0003 REL FR 3 V 0 P
you draw me, you hard-hearted adamant; MND 2.01.195
steel, | and spurn in pieces posts of adamant; 1H6 1.04. 52
as iron to adamant, as earth to th' centre, TRO 3.02.179

ADAM'S 3 FR 0.0003 REL FR 1 V 2 P
adam's sons are my brethren, and truly i hold it ADO 2.01. 63 P
thou old adam's likeness, set to dress this R2 3.04. 73
they hold up adam's profession. HAM 5.01. 31 P

ADD 51 FR 0.0057 REL FR 47 V 4 P
a great disguiser, and you may add to it. MM 4.02.175 P
left | is that she will not add to her damnation ADO 4.01.172
i will add the l'envoy. say the moral again. LLL 3.01. 87 P
now, to our perjury to add more terror, | we are 5.02.470
if i could add a lie unto a fault, | i would MV 5.01.186
love concerneth us to add | her father's liking, SHR 3.02.128
won, and i will add | unto their losses twenty 5.02.112
her, i'll add three thousand crowns | to what is AWW 3.07. 35
they that add, moreov'r, he's drunk nightly in TN 1.03. 36 P
life i gave him, and did thereto add | my love, 5.01. 80
the justice of your hearts will thereto add WT 2.01. 67
we bear, | or add a royal number to the dead, JN 2.01.347
from the mouth of england | add thus much more, 3.01.153
the ice, or add another hue | unto the rainbow, 4.02. 13
good hap, | add an immortal title to your crown! R2 1.01. 24
add proof unto mine armor with thy prayers, 1.03. 73
and to thy worth will add right worthy gains. 5.06. 12
and these unseasoned hours perforce must add 2H4 3.01.105
that may with reasonable swiftness add | more H5 1.02.306
to this add defiance; 3.06.133 P
my gracious lords, to add to your laments, 1H6 1.01.103
him, | thou wilt but add increase unto my wrath. 2H6 3.02.292
the words would add more anguish than the wounds 3H6 2.01. 99
and now, to add more measure to your woes, | i 2.01.105
i can add colors to the chameleon, | change 3.02.191
lad, | with tearful eyes add water to the sea, 5.04. 8
i need not add more fuel to your fire, | for 5.04. 70
yet will i add an honor — a great patience. H8 3.01.137
and, to add greater honors to his age | than man 4.02. 67
that nothing canst but cry, | add to my clamors! TRO 2.02.106
go tell him this, and add, | that if he overhold 2.03.132
and add more coals to cancer when he burns 2.03.196
doth add more grief to too much of mine own. ROM 1.01.189
may these add to the number that may scald thee! TIM 3.01. 51
and unpurged air | to add unto his sickness? JC 2.01.267
add thereto a tiger's chawdron, | for th' MAC 4.01. 33
these murther'd deer | to add the death of you. 4.03.207
and thereto add such reasons of your own | as LR 1.04.338
for nothing canst thou to damnation add OTH 3.03.372
add more, | from thine invention, offers. ANT 3.12. 28
heir of his reward, which i will add | to you, CYM 5.05. 13
true nor modest, | unless i add, we are honest. 5.05. 19
nor come we to add sorrow to your tears, | but PER 1.04. 90
this day i'll rise, or else add ill to ill. 2.01.166
and to add ampler majesty to this | he hath not STM II.C 101
spring, | to add a more rejoicing to the prime, LUC 332
with their fresh falls' haste | add to his flow, 651
to thy fair flower add the rank smell of weeds: SON 69.12
you to your beauteous blessings add a curse, 84.13
and to the most of praise add something more, 85.10
in will, add to thy will | one will of mine, to 135.11

ADDED 20 FR 0.0022 REL FR 17 V 3 P
to have it added to the faults of mine, | and MM 2.04. 72
ba, pueritia, with a horn added. LLL 5.01. 49 P
added to their familiarity | (which was as gross WT 2.01.175
hours | and added years to his short banishment, R2 1.04. 17
happiness | added to that that i am to deliver! 2H4 4.04. 82
added to these, | of knights, esquires, and H5 4.08. 83
a thought of added honor torn from hector. TRO 4.05.145
what fool hath added water to the sea? TIT 3.01. 68
which, added to the goose, proves thee far and ROM 2.04. 86 P
you have added worth unto't and lustre, | and TIM 1.02.149
have added slaughter to the sword of traitors. JC 5.01. 55
each new day a gash | is added to her wounds. MAC 4.03. 41
from my heart all love, | and added to the gall. LR 1.04.270
no, i rather added | a lustre to it. CYM 1.01.142
enough of your own, but he added to your having, 1.02. 18 P
proceeding | who ever but his approbation added, PER 4.03. 26
rain added to a river that is rank | perforce VEN 71
soon, | but now are minutes added to the hours; PP 14.26
have added feathers to the learned's wing, | and SON 78. 7
than when it hath my added praise beside. 103. 4

ADDER 13 FR 0.0014 REL FR 13 V 0 P
could not a worm, an adder, do so much? MND 3.02. 71
an adder did it! 3.02. 72
than thine, thou serpent, never adder stung. 3.02. 73
or is the adder better than the eel, | because SHR 4.03.177
guard it, i pray thee, with a lurking adder, R2 3.02. 20
art thou like the adder waxen deaf? 2H6 3.02. 76
even as an adder when she doth unroll | to do TIT 2.03. 35
engenders the black toad and adder blue, | the TIM 4.03.181
is the bright day that brings forth the adder, JC 2.01. 14
of the other, as the stung | are of the adder. LR 5.01. 57
were it toad, or adder, spider, | 'twould move CYM 4.02. 90
whereat she starts like one that spies an adder VEN 878
the adder hisses where the sweet birds sing, LUC 871

ADDER'S 3 FR 0.0003 REL FR 3 V 0 P
tongue more poisons than the adder's tooth! 3H6 1.04.112
of dog, | adder's fork and blind-worm's sting, MAC 4.01. 16
voices, that my adder's sense | to critic and to SON 112.10

ADDERS' 1 FR 0.0001 REL FR 0 V 1 P
and how she long'd to eat adders' heads, and WT 4.04.264 P

ADDERS 3 FR 0.0003 REL FR 3 V 0 P
sometime am i | all wound with adders, who with TMP 2.02. 13
have ears more deaf than adders to the voice TRO 2.02.172
whom i will trust as i will adders fang'd, HAM 3.04.203

ADDETH 1 FR 0.0001 REL FR 1 V 0 P
still, | and in abundance addeth to his store, SON 135.10

ADDICT 2 FR 0.0002 REL FR 1 V 1 P
thin potations and to addict themselves to sack. 2H4 4.03.124 P
if he be addict to vice, | quickly him they will PP 20.41

ADDICTED 2 FR 0.0002 REL FR 1 V 1 P
being addicted to a melancholy as she is, that TN 2.05.202 P
addicted so and so," and there put on him | what HAM 2.01. 19

/ADDICTION 1 FR 0.0001 REL FR 0 V 1 P
what sport and revels his /addiction leads him; OTH 2.02. 6 P

ADDICTION 1 FR 0.0001 REL FR 1 V 0 P
it, | since his addiction was to courses vain, H5 1.01. 54

ADDING 9 FR 0.0010 REL FR 9 V 0 P
by adding a tongue which i know will not lie. LLL 2.01.253
of door, | and stayed the odds by adding four. 3.01. 92
out of door, | staying the odds by adding four. 3.01. 98
sore i an hundred make by adding but one more l. 4.02. 61
adding thereto, moreover, | that he would wed me 5.02.446
adding withal, how blest this land would be | in R2 4.01. 18
adding further | that, had the king in his last H8 1.02.183
adding to clouds more clouds with his deep sighs ROM 1.01.133
by adding one thing to my purpose nothing. SON 20.12

ADDITION 30 FR 0.0034 REL FR 23 V 7 P
drop again, | without addition or diminishing, ERR 2.02.128
by my troth, it is no addition to her wit, nor ADO 2.03.233 P
titled goddess, | and worth it, with addition! AWW 4.02. 3
with her to thee, and this addition more, | full JN 2.01.529
"you are welcome," with this shrill addition, 1H4 2.04. 26 P
highness in this form, and with this addition, H5 5.02.339 P
bull-bearing milo his addition yield | to sinowy TRO 2.03.247
and, being born, his addition shall be humble. 3.02. 94 P
hence | a great addition earned in thy death. 4.05.141
bear | th' addition nobly ever! COR 1.09. 66

to undercrest your good addition | to th' 1.09. 72
with what addition? JC 4.03.172
in which addition, hail, most worthy thane, MAC 1.03.106
whereby he does receive | particular addition, 3.01. 99
and with swinish phrase | soil our addition, and HAM 1.04. 20
according to the phrase or the addition | of man 2.01. 47
truly to speak, and with no addition, | we go to 4.04. 17
the name, and all th' addition to a king; LR 1.01.136
thou deni'st the least syllable of thy addition. 2.02. 24 P
piece out the comfort with what addition i can. 3.06. 3 P
exalt himself, | more than in your addition. 5.03. 68
and such addition as your honors | have more 5.03.302
and think it no addition, nor my wish, | to have OTH 3.04.194
the worser that you give me the addition | whose 4.01.104
to do the act that might the addition earn, 4.02.163
sum of my disgraces by | addition of his envy! ANT 5.02.164
of, and thereto make an addition of some other TNK 4.03. 84 P
sound | when there is no addition but a rebel STM II.C 118
a–doting, | and by addition me of thee defeated, SON 20.11
still, | to thy sweet will making addition thus. 135. 4

ADDITIONS 4 FR 0.0004 REL FR 2 V 2 P
yet they are devils' additions, the names of WIV 2.02.298 P
where great additions swell 's, and virtue none, AWW 2.03.127
many beasts of their particular additions: TRO 1.02. 20 P
/came for additions, yet their purpos'd trim LC 118

ADDLE 3 FR 0.0003 REL FR 0 V 3 P
esteems her no more than i esteem an addle egg. TRO 1.02.132 P
if you love an addle egg as well as you love an 1.02.133 P
thy head hath been beaten as addle as an egg for ROM 3.01. 24 P

/ADDRESS 1 FR 0.0001 REL FR 1 V 0 P
/let /us /address /to /tend /on /hector's /heels TRO 4.04.146

ADDRESS 10 FR 0.0011 REL FR 8 V 2 P
i will then address me to my appointment. WIV 3.05.133 P
address your love and might | to honor helen and MND 2.02.143
that so seriously he does address himself unto? AWW 3.06. 95 P
good youth, address thy gait unto her, | be not TN 1.04. 15
address yourself to entertain them sprightly, WT 4.04. 53
unto your grace do i in chief address | the 2H4 4.01. 31
a dreadful lay! address thee instantly! 2H6 5.02. 27
that gods and men | address their dangers in. TRO 5.10. 14
it lifted up it head and did address | itself to HAM 1.02.216
we first address toward you, who with this king LR 1.01.190

ADDRESS'D 11 FR 0.0012 REL FR 11 V 0 P
in oath | were all address'd to meet you, gentle LLL 2.01. 83
toward that shade i might behold address'd | the 5.02. 92
so please your grace, the prologue is address'd. MND 5.01.106
and so have i address'd me. MV 2.09. 19
address'd a mighty power, which were on foot AYL 5.04.156
our navy is address'd, our power collected, 2H4 4.04. 5
to–morrow for the march are we address'd. H5 3.03. 58
he is address'd; press near and second him. JC 3.01. 29
prayers, and address'd them | again to sleep. MAC 2.02. 22
even in your armors, as you are address'd, PER 2.03. 94
at length address'd to answer his desire, | she LUC 1606

ADDS 7 FR 0.0008 REL FR 6 V 1 P
it adds a precious seeing to the eye: LLL 4.03.330
she adds, moreover, that you should put your TN 2.02. 7 P
over that art | which you say adds to nature, is WT 4.04. 91
had, | it adds more sorrow to my want of joy; R2 3.04. 16
annual support, | out of his grace he adds. H8 2.03. 65
now she adds honors to his hateful name; VEN 994
mixed, | which to her oratory adds more grace. LUC 564

ADD'ST 1 FR 0.0001 REL FR 1 V 0 P
to phoebus thou | add'st flames, hotter than his TNK 5.01. 91

ADHERE 2 FR 0.0002 REL FR 1 V 1 P
but they do no more adhere and keep place WIV 2.01. 62 P
did then adhere, and yet you would make both: MAC 1.07. 52

ADHERES 4 FR 0.0004 REL FR 3 V 1 P
why, every thing adheres together, that no dram TN 3.04. 78 P
and what to her adheres, which follows after, WT 4.01. 28
there is not living | to whom he more adheres. HAM 2.02. 21
nay, any where that not adheres to england, STM II.C 129

/ADIEU 1 FR 0.0001 REL FR 1 V 0 P
fo, fo, /adieu, you palter. TRO 5.02. 48

ADIEU 104 FR 0.0117 REL FR 75 V 29 P
sweet valentine, adieu! TGV 1.01. 11
once more adieu. 1.01. 53
adieu, my lord, sir valentine is coming. 3.01. 50
go, adieu. WIV 1.03. 18 P
adieu. 2.01.135 P
adieu. 2.01.137 P
adieu, good master doctor. 2.03. 81 P
adieu. 3.05.136 P
adieu, good sir hugh. 4.01. 84 P
adieu. 4.05. 89 P
i know vat i have to do. adieu. 5.03. 5 P
good sir, adieu. MM 1.04. 90
adieu, trusty pompey. 3.02. 77 P
contempt, farewell, and maiden pride, adieu! ADO 3.01.109
adieu! 3.03. 94 P
well, sit you out; go home, berowne; adieu. LLL 1.01.110
adieu, valor, rust, rapier, be still, drum, for 1.02.181 P
o, you are welcome, sir, adieu. 2.01.213
like the sequel, i. signior costard, adieu. 3.01.134
adieu. 4.02.143 P
and so, adieu — | twice to your visor, and half 5.02.226
seventh sweet, adieu. 5.02.234
you, | as much in private, and i'll bid adieu. 5.02.241
and so adieu, sweet jude! 5.02.626
helena, adieu: MND 1.01.224
adieu. 1.02.109 P
adieu, adieu, adieu. 5.01.347
adieu, adieu, adieu. 5.01.347
adieu, adieu, adieu. 5.01.347
if he will take it, so, if not, adieu; MV 1.03.169
adieu! 2.03. 10 P
but adieu, these foolish drops do something 2.03. 13 P
adieu! 2.03. 14 P
portia, adieu. 2.07. 76
sweet, adieu. 2.09. 77
adieu, good monsieur melancholy. AYL 3.02.293 P
so adieu. 4.01.198 P
adieu. 4.01.200 P
and shape be true, | why then my love adieu! 5.04.121
father, and wife, and gentlemen, adieu. SHR 2.01.321
adieu, good neighbor. 2.01.399
and so adieu, sir; 4.04.102 P
yourself within the list of too cold an adieu. AWW 2.01. 52 P

adieu till then, then fail not. 4.02. 64
with the duke, done my adieu with his nearest; 4.03. 87 P
and so adieu, good madam, never more | will i my TN 3.01.161
adieu, goodman devil. 4.02.131
adieu, my lord. WT 2.01.122
adieu, sir. 4.04.659
brother, adieu, good fortune come to thee! JN 1.01.180
fair day, adieu! 3.01.326
adieu. 4.01.126
england's ground, farewell, sweet soil, adieu; R2 1.03.306
once more, adieu, the rest let sorrow say. 5.01.102
uncle, farewell, and, cousin, adieu! 5.03.144
uncle, adieu! 1H4 1.03.301
adieu, and take thy praise with thee to heaven! 5.04. 99
but adieu. H5 2.03. 61 P
farewell; adieu. 2.03. 63 P
and my kind kinsman, warriors all, adieu! 4.03. 10
if he be dead, brave talbot, then adieu! 1H6 4.04. 45
soldiers, adieu! 4.07. 31
and thus i seal my truth, and bid adieu. 3H6 4.08. 29
were for myself — and so, my lord, adieu. R3 3.05. 97
poor heart, adieu, i pity thy complaining. 4.01. 87
adieu, poor soul, that tak'st thy leave of it! 4.01. 90
once more, adieu! 5.03.102
adieu, uncle. TRO 1.02.277 P
to them, | he fumbles up into a loose adieu; 4.04. 46
my courteous lord, adieu. 5.02.185
i have your alms, adieu. COR 2.03. 81 P
cominius, | droop not, adieu. 4.01. 20
dear love, adieu! ROM 2.02.136
adieu, adieu! 3.05. 59
adieu, adieu! 3.05. 59
till then adieu, and keep this holy kiss. 4.01. 43
adieu, | lest our old robes sit easier than our MAC 2.04. 37
adieu, | till you return at night. 3.01. 34
adieu, adieu, adieu! HAM 1.05. 91
adieu, adieu, adieu! 1.05. 91
adieu, adieu, adieu! 1.05. 91
it is "adieu, adieu! 1.05.111
it is "adieu, adieu! 1.05.111
adieu. 2.02.122 P
adieu, my lord, | i have a speech a' fire that 4.07.189
wretched queen, adieu! 5.02.333
thus kent, o princes, bids you all adieu, LR 1.01.186
adieu, brave moor, use desdemona well. OTH 1.03.291
adieu. 1.03.372 P
adieu. 2.01.285 P
emilia, | give me my nightly wearing, and adieu. 4.03. 16
then bid adieu to me, and say the tears | belong ANT 1.03. 77
adieu, noble agrippa. 3.02. 21
adieu, be happy! 3.02. 64
adieu. 4.04. 34
you, | that we remain your friend, and so adieu. 5.02.189
not so. adieu. 5.02.190
adieu, good queen, i must attend on caesar. 5.02.206
adieu! CYM 1.01.108
thaliard, adieu! PER 1.01.168
so adieu, | and heaven's good eyes look on you! TNK 1.04. 12
adieu; 5.04. 37
and, ere he says "adieu," | the honey fee of VEN 537
when you have bid your servant once adieu. SON 57. 8

ADIEUS 2 FR 0.0002 REL FR 2 V 0 P
twenty adieus, my frozen muscovits. LLL 5.02.265
(i will subscribe) gentle adieus and greetings; ANT 4.05. 14

ADJACENT 2 FR 0.0002 REL FR 2 V 0 P
and the demesnes that there adjacent lie, | that ROM 2.01. 20
perfume hits the sense | of the adjacent wharfs. ANT 2.02.213

ADJOIN'D 1 FR 0.0001 REL FR 1 V 0 P
lesser things | are mortis'd and adjoin'd, which HAM 3.03. 20

ADJOINING 1 FR 0.0001 REL FR 1 V 0 P
our foot | upon the hills adjoining to the city ANT 4.10. 5

ADJOURN 1 FR 0.0001 REL FR 1 V 0 P
that we adjourn this court till further day. H8 2.04.233

ADJOURN'D 1 FR 0.0001 REL FR 1 V 0 P
why hast thou thus adjourn'd | the graces for CYM 5.04. 78

/ADJUDG'D 1 FR 0.0001 REL FR 1 V 0 P
to be /adjudg'd some direful slaught'ring death, TIT 5.03.144

ADJUDG'D 3 FR 0.0003 REL FR 3 V 0 P
but as he adjudg'd your brother — | being MM 5.01.403
such as by god's book are adjudg'd to death. 2H6 2.03. 4
adjudg'd an olive branch and laurel crown, | as 3H6 4.06. 34

ADJUDGED 1 FR 0.0001 REL FR 1 V 0 P
but, though thou art adjudged to the death, ERR 1.01.146

ADJUNCT 5 FR 0.0005 REL FR 5 V 0 P
learning is but an adjunct to ourself, | and LLL 4.03.310
though that my death were adjunct to my act, JN 3.03. 57
though death be adjunct, there's no death LUC 133
and every humor hath his adjunct pleasure, SON 91. 5
to keep an adjunct to remember thee | were to 122.13

ADMINISTER 1 FR 0.0001 REL FR 1 V 0 P
to keep the oath that we administer: R2 1.03.182

ADMINISTRATION 1 FR 0.0001 REL FR 1 V 0 P
in me, | and, in th' administration of his law, 2H4 5.02. 75

ADMIRABLE 15 FR 0.0017 REL FR 3 V 12 P
of excellent breeding, admirable discourse, of WIV 2.02.226 P
it is admirable pleasures and fery honest 4.04. 80 P
but that my admirable dexterity of wit, my 4.05.117 P
but, howsoever, strange and admirable. MND 5.01. 27
most admirable! i have seen those wars. AWW 2.01. 26
beshrew me, the knight's in admirable fooling. TN 2.03. 80 P
o, 'twill be admirable! 2.03.171 P
thou talkest of an admirable conceited fellow. WT 4.04.202 P
o admirable youth! TRO 1.02.234 P
o admirable man! 1.02.237 P
admirable! TIM 1.01. 30
how express and admirable in action! HAM 2.02.305 P
an admirable evasion of whoremaster man, to lay LR 1.02.126 P
an admirable musician! OTH 4.01.188 P
sweet air, with admirable rich words to it — CYM 2.03. 18 P

ADMIRAL 5 FR 0.0005 REL FR 4 V 1 P
thou art our admiral, thou bearest the lantern 1H4 3.03. 25 P
jacques of chatillion, admiral of france, | the H5 4.08. 93
and thou, lord bourbon, our high admiral, 3H6 3.03.252
'tis thought that richmond is their admiral; R3 4.04.437
th' antoniad, the egyptian admiral, | with all ANT 3.10. 2

ADMIRATION 14 FR 0.0015 REL FR 9 V 5 P
admir'd miranda, | indeed the top of admiration! TMP 3.01. 38
bring in the admiration, that we with thee | may AWW 2.01. 88
king and camillo were very notes of admiration. WT 5.02. 11 P
cause | that admiration did not hoop at them; H5 2.02.108
it is the greatest admiration in the universal 4.01. 66 P
heir | as great in admiration as herself, | so H8 5.04. 42
season your admiration for a while | with an HAM 1.02.192
hath strook her into amazement and admiration. 3.02.327 P
sequel at the heels of this mother's admiration? 3.02.330 P
this admiration, sir, is much o' th' savor | of LR 1.04.237
look'd on him without the help of admiration, CYM 1.04. 5 P
what makes your admiration? 1.06. 38
and not protract with admiration what | is now 4.02.232
with more than admiration he admired | her azure LUC 418

ADMIR'D 11 FR 0.0012 REL FR 10 V 1 P
admir'd miranda, | indeed the top of admiration! TMP 3.01. 37
on the trees, wherein rosalind is so admir'd? AYL 3.02.393 P
that all the court admir'd him for submission; 2H6 3.01. 12
'tis virtue that doth make them most admir'd, 3H6 1.04.130
the good meeting, | with most admir'd disorder. MAC 3.04.109
to make itself, in thee, fair and admir'd! ANT 1.01. 51
sister by the mother's side, | admir'd octavia. 2.02.119
celerity is never more admir'd | than by the 3.07. 24
whom | he serv'd with glory and admir'd success: CYM 1.01. 32
chaucer (of all admir'd) the story gives; TNK pr 13
lies, | to be admir'd of lewd unhallowed eyes. LUC 392

ADMIRE 9 FR 0.0010 REL FR 7 V 2 P
at this encounter do so much admire | that they TMP 5.01.154
is to me some praise that i thy parts admire. LLL 4.02.114
while we do admire | this virtue and this moral SHR 1.01. 29
"wonder not, nor admire not in thy mind, why i TN 3.04.150 P
see his weakness, and admire our sufferance. H5 3.06.125 P
shall attend and shrug, | i' th' end admire; COR 1.09. 5
i admire him; TNK 2.05. 17
is to me some praise, that i thy parts admire. PP 5.10
and therefore we admire | what thou dost foist SON 123. 5

/ADMIRED 1 FR 0.0001 REL FR 1 V 0 P
/after /th' /admired /heels /of /bullingbrook, 2H4 1.03.105

ADMIRED 7 FR 0.0008 REL FR 7 V 0 P
grace did lend her, | that she might admired be. TGV 4.02. 43
or vainly comes th' admired princess hither. LLL 1.01.140
with all the admired beauties of verona. ROM 1.02. 84
foam, | settlest admired reverence in a slave. TIM 5.01. 51
dances | as goddess–like to her admired lays. PER 5.ch. 4
with more than admiration he admired | her azure LUC 418
his wit, | making his style admired every where. SON 84.12

ADMIRER 1 FR 0.0001 REL FR 1 V 0 P
and ever since a fresh admirer | of what i saw H8 1.01. 3

ADMIRING 6 FR 0.0006 REL FR 5 V 1 P
eyes, | so i, admiring of his qualities. MND 1.01.231
my sir's song, and admiring the nothing of it. WT 4.04.613 P
from thy admiring daughter took the spirits, 5.03. 41
when it shines seldom in admiring eyes; 1H4 3.02. 80
of auvergne, | with modesty admiring thy renown, 1H6 2.02. 39
to subjects worse have given admiring praise. SON 59.14

ADMIRINGLY 2 FR 0.0002 REL FR 1 V 1 P
lately spoke of him admiringly and mourningly. AWW 1.01. 29 P
admiringly, my liege. 5.03. 44

ADMIT 24 FR 0.0027 REL FR 22 V 2 P
for no kind of traffic | would i admit; TMP 2.01.150
my haste may not admit it, | nor need you, on MM 1.01. 62
admit no other way to save his life | (as i 2.04. 88
to admit no traffic to our adverse towns: ERR 1.01. 15
evil that they will not admit any good part to ADO 5.02. 63 P
to know your answer, whether you'll admit him. MV 4.01.146
because she will admit no kind of suit, | no, TN 1.02. 45
as it is spoke, she never will admit me. 1.04. 20
let us hear them speak | whose title they admit, JN 2.01.200
whose party do the townsmen yet admit? 2.01.361
well, by my will we shall admit no parley. 2H4 4.01.157
argument | is all too heavy to admit much talk. 5.02. 24
which supply, | admit me chorus to this history; H5 pr 32
and therefore we must needs admit the means 1.01. 68
although i did admit it as a motive | the sooner 2.02.156
this is the latest parle we will admit; 3.03. 2
i humbly pray them to admit th' excuse | of time 5.pr. 3
if sorrow can admit society, | /tell /over /your R3 4.04. 38
admit him entrance, griffith; H8 4.02.107
the people do admit you and are summon'd | to COR 2.03.143
admit no messengers, receive no tokens. HAM 2.02.144
/your /honesty should admit no discourse to your 3.01.107 P
admit him, sir. ANT 3.13. 40
the marriage of true minds | admit impediments; SON 116. 2

ADMITS 8 FR 0.0009 REL FR 6 V 2 P
precisian, he admits him not for his counsellor. WIV 2.01. 5 P
able body, for the which the prince admits him. 2H4 2.04.252 P
my love admits no qualifying dross, | no more my TRO 4.04. 9
admits no orifex for a point as subtle | as 5.02.151
and my pretext to strike at him admits | a good COR 5.06. 19
there was a yielding — this admits no excuse. 5.06. 68
rome, | the people will accept whom he admits. TIT 1.01.222
his ear her prayers admits, but his heart LUC 558

ADMITTANCE 10 FR 0.0011 REL FR 6 V 4 P
admirable discourse, of great admittance, WIV 2.02.226 P
or any tire of venetian admittance. 3.03. 58 P
now, what admittance, lord? LLL 2.01. 80
to give admittance to a thought of fear. 2H4 4.01.151
england | do crave admittance to your majesty. H5 2.04. 66
are certain ladies most desirous of admittance. TIM 1.02.117 P
welcome all, let 'em have kind admittance. 1.02.128
give first admittance to th' embassadors; HAM 2.02. 51
even to the yielding, had i admittance, and CYM 1.04.105 P
'tis gold | which buys admittance (oft it doth), 2.03. 68

/ADMITTED 1 FR 0.0001 REL FR 1 V 0 P
/of /aids /incertain /should /not /be /admitted. 2H4 1.03. 24

ADMITTED 13 FR 0.0014 REL FR 10 V 3 P
let her be admitted. MM 2.02. 22
you shall not be admitted to his sight. 4.03.120
with what manners i might safely be admitted. AWW 4.05. 89 P
so please my lord, i might not be admitted, TN 1.01. 23
excuses shall not be admitted, there is no 2H4 5.01. 5 P
or be admitted to your highness' council. 2H6 3.01. 27
warrant, | that we may be admitted where he is. R3 1.03.342
never admitted | a private whisper, no, not with COR 5.03. 6
rome | desires to be admitted to your presence. TIT 5.01.153
i pray let them be admitted. TIM 1.02.121 P
sir, | he fell upon me, ere admitted, then; ANT 2.02. 75

exactly valued, | not petty things admitted. 5.02.140
and will, thy soul knows, is admitted there; SON 136. 3
ADMITTING 1 FR 0.0001 REL FR 1 V 0 P
silk, never admitting | counsel a' th' war; COR 5.06. 95
ADMONISH 1 FR 0.0001 REL FR 1 V 0 P
and ye choice spirits that admonish me | and 1H6 5.03. 3
ADMONISHING 1 FR 0.0001 REL FR 1 V 0 P
admonishing | that we should dress us fairly for H5 4.01. 9
ADMONISHMENT 1 FR 0.0001 REL FR 1 V 0 P
to stop his ears against admonishment? TRO 5.03. 2
ADMONISHMENTS 1 FR 0.0001 REL FR 1 V 0 P
thy grave admonishments prevail with me. 1H6 2.05. 98
ADMONITION 2 FR 0.0002 REL FR 1 V 1 P
double and treble admonition, and still forfeit MM 3.02.193 P
darest with thy frozen admonition | make pale R2 2.01.117
ADO 19 FR 0.0021 REL FR 15 V 4 P
he makes me no more ado, but whips me out of the
TGV 4.04. 28 P
hearts, what ado here is to bring you together! WIV 4.05.124 P
of me, | that i have much ado to know myself. MV 1.01. 7
let's follow, to see the end of this ado. SHR 5.01.142
you had much ado to make his anchor hold, | when
WT 1.02.213
here's ado, to lock up honesty | and honor from 2.02. 9
here's such ado to make no stain a stain | as 2.02. 17
to the outside of his hand, and no more ado. 4.04.804 P
with much ado (at length) have gotten leave | to R2 5.05. 74
i made me no more ado but took all their seven 1H4 2.04.201 P
and now no more ado, brave burgundy, | but 1H6 3.02.101
come then, away, let's ha' no more ado. 3H6 4.05. 27
make me no more ado, but all embrace him. H8 5.02.193
then should not we be tir'd with this ado. TIT 2.01. 98
4.03.102
sirrah, come hither, make no more ado, | but
we'll keep no great ado — a friend or two, ROM 3.04. 23
madam, with much ado; LR 4.05. 2
no father, nor no more ado | with that harsh, CYM 3.04.131
with much ado the cold fault cleanly out; VEN 694
A–DOING 2 FR 0.0002 REL FR 2 V 0 P
the precedent was full as long a–doing, | and R3 3.06. 7
after it is done | than when it was a–doing. COR 4.02. 5
ADON 2 FR 0.0002 REL FR 2 V 0 P
"nay then," quoth adon, "you will fall again VEN 769
a brook where adon us'd to cool his spleen. PP 6. 6
ADONIS' 5 FR 0.0005 REL FR 5 V 0 P
thy promises are like adonis' garden, | that one 1H6 1.06. 6
proud, | adonis' trampling courser doth espy; VEN 261
because adonis' heart hath made mine hard." 378
rejoice, | and flatters her it is adonis' voice. 978
to smell, | comparing it to her adonis' breath, 1172
ADONIS 19 FR 0.0021 REL FR 19 V 0 P
straight | adonis painted by a running brook, SHR in.2. 50
rose–cheek'd adonis hied him to the chase; VEN 3
in a net, | so fast'ned in her arms adonis lies; 68
them, | wishing adonis had his team to guide, 179
and now adonis, with a lazy sprite, | and with a 181
at this adonis smiles as in disdain, | that in 241
with her the horse, and left adonis there. 322
all swoll'n with chafing, down adonis sits, 325
adonis lives, and death is not to blame; 992
thus hoping that adonis is alive, | her rash 1009
but when adonis liv'd, sun and sharp air 1085
then would adonis weep; 1090
"'tis true, 'tis true, thus was adonis slain: 1111
sitting by a brook | with young adonis, lovely, PP 4. 2
a longing tarriance for adonis made | under an 6. 4
anon adonis comes with horn and hounds; 9. 6
venus, with adonis sitting by her, | under a 11. 1
me," | and then she clipt adonis in her arms; 11. 6
describe adonis, and the counterfeit | is poorly SON 53. 5
ADON'S 1 FR 0.0001 REL FR 1 V 0 P
for adon's sake, a youngster proud and wild, PP 9. 4
ADONS 1 FR 0.0001 REL FR 1 V 0 P
and yet," quoth she, "behold two adons dead! VEN 1070
ADOPT 4 FR 0.0004 REL FR 4 V 0 P
tell me, may not a king adopt an heir? 3H6 1.01.135
you adopt your policy, how is it less or worse COR 3.02. 48
i had rather to adopt a child than get it. OTH 1.03.191
the stage of death, | whom i adopt my friends. TNK 5.04.124
ADOPTED 6 FR 0.0006 REL FR 6 V 0 P
that calling | to be adopted heir to frederick. AYL 1.02.234
of blood, | and an adopted name of privilege, 1H4 5.02. 18
chair, | and this is he was his adopted heir. 3H6 1.04. 98
i was adopted heir by his consent. 2.02. 88
in rome, | a roman now adopted happily, | and TIT 1.01.463
she owes, | unfriended, new adopted to our hate, LR 1.01.203
ADOPTEDLY 1 FR 0.0001 REL FR 1 V 0 P
adoptedly, as school–maids change their names MM 1.04. 47
ADOPTION 4 FR 0.0004 REL FR 3 V 1 P
but stand under the adoption of abominable terms
WIV 2.02.295 P
'tis often seen | adoption strives with nature, AWW 1.03.145
friends thou hast, and their adoption tried, HAM 1.03. 62
work | her son into th' adoption of the crown; CYM 5.05. 56
ADOPTIOUS 1 FR 0.0001 REL FR 1 V 0 P
adoptious christendoms | that blinking cupid AWW 1.01.174
ADOPTS 1 FR 0.0001 REL FR 1 V 0 P
who with willing soul | adopts /thee heir, and R2 4.01.109
/ADORATION 1 FR 0.0001 REL FR 1 V 0 P
what is thy soul of /adoration? H5 4.01.245
ADORATION 1 FR 0.0001 REL FR 1 V 0 P
all adoration, duty, and observance, | all AYL 5.02. 96
ADORATIONS 1 FR 0.0001 REL FR 1 V 0 P
with adorations, fertile tears, | with groans TN 1.05.255
ADOR'D 4 FR 0.0004 REL FR 3 V 1 P
shalt be worshipp'd, kiss'd, lov'd, and ador'd; TGV 4.04.199
i was ador'd once too. TN 2.03.181 P
make the hoar leprosy ador'd, place thieves, TIM 4.03. 36
that all those eyes ador'd them ere their fall PER 2.04. 11
ADORE 16 FR 0.0018 REL FR 14 V 2 P
i have seen thee in her, and i do adore thee. TMP 2.02.140
at first i did adore a twinkling star, | but now TGV 2.06. 9
to worship shadows and adore false shapes, 4.02.130
i do adore thy sweet grace's slipper. LLL 5.02.667 P
religious in mine error, i adore | the sun, that AWW 1.03.205
may, i do adore thee so | that danger shall seem TN 2.01. 47
"i may command where i adore, | but silence, 2.05.104
"i may command where i adore." 2.05.115 P
right, | whom you pretend to honor and adore, TIT 1.01. 42
now, by the gods that warlike goths adore, 2.01. 61
now, gods that we adore, whereof comes this? LR 1.04.290
make us | adore our errors, laugh at 's while we ANT 3.13.114
gate | instructs you how t' adore the heavens, CYM 3.03. 3
"now by the capitol that we adore, | and by this LUC 1835
age, i do abhor thee, youth, i do adore thee: PP 12. 9
age, | yet mortal looks adore his beauty still, SON 7. 7
ADORED 1 FR 0.0001 REL FR 1 V 0 P
this earthly saint, adored by this devil, LUC 85
ADORER 1 FR 0.0001 REL FR 0 V 1 P
though i profess myself her adorer, not her CYM 1.04. 69 P
ADORES 2 FR 0.0002 REL FR 1 V 1 P
a beagle, true–bred, and one that adores me. TN 2.03.180 P
nay, but how dearly he adores mark antony! ANT 3.02. 8
ADOREST 1 FR 0.0001 REL FR 1 V 0 P
it be | that thou adorest and hast in reverence, TIT 5.01. 83
ADORETH 1 FR 0.0001 REL FR 1 V 0 P
and let the soul forth that adoreth thee, | i R3 1.02.176
ADORN 4 FR 0.0004 REL FR 4 V 0 P
adorn his temples with a coronet, | and yet, in 1H6 5.04.134
of tailors | to study fashions to adorn my body: R3 1.02.257
till we with trophies do adorn thy tomb. TIT 1.01.388
lay, | till they might open to adorn the day. LUC 399
ADORN'D 1 FR 0.0001 REL FR 1 V 0 P
whose men and dames so jetted and adorn'd, PER 1.04. 26
ADORNED 1 FR 0.0001 REL FR 1 V 0 P
pomp | she came adorned hither like sweet may, R2 5.01. 79
ADORNINGS 1 FR 0.0001 REL FR 1 V 0 P
i' th' eyes, | and made their bends adornings. ANT 2.02.208
ADORNMENT 2 FR 0.0002 REL FR 1 V 1 P
such | th' adornment of her bed; CYM 2.02. 26
together with the adornment of my qualities. 3.05.136 P
ADORNS 1 FR 0.0001 REL FR 1 V 0 P
which no less adorns | our gentry than our WT 1.02.392
A–DOTING 1 FR 0.0001 REL FR 1 V 0 P
till nature, as she wrought thee, fell a–doting, SON 20.10
A–DOWN 2 FR 0.0002 REL FR 0 V 2 P
you must sing, "a–down, a–down," and you call HAM 4.05.171 P
"a–down, a–down," and you call him a–down–a. 4.05.171 P
ADOWN–A 1 FR 0.0001 REL FR 1 V 0 P
and down, down, adown–a, etc. WIV 1.04. 43
A–DOWN–A 1 FR 0.0001 REL FR 0 V 1 P
"a–down, a–down," and you call him a–down–a. HAM 4.05.172 P
ADRAMADIO *(also armado)*
ADRAMADIO 2 FR 0.0002 REL FR 2 V 0 P
of dun adramadio, dun adramadio. LLL 4.03.195
of dun adramadio, dun adramadio. 4.03.195
ADRIAN 2 FR 0.0002 REL FR 0 V 2 P
which, of he or adrian, for a good wager, first TMP 2.01. 28 P
your name, i think, is adrian. COR 4.03. 2 P
ADRIANA 3 FR 0.0003 REL FR 3 V 0 P
i am not adriana, nor thy wife. ERR 2.02.112
to adriana, villain, hie thee straight: 4.01.102
to adriana! 4.01.109
ADRIANO 3 FR 0.0003 REL FR 0 V 3 P
heat of duty, don adriano de armado." LLL 1.01.278 P
design of industry, don adriano de armado. 4.01. 87 P
nominated, or called, don adriano de armado. 5.01. 8 P
ADRIATIC 1 FR 0.0001 REL FR 1 V 0 P
is as rough | as are the swelling adriatic seas, SHR 1.02. 74
ADSUM 1 FR 0.0001 REL FR 1 V 0 P
adsum. 2H6 1.04. 23
A–DUCKING 1 FR 0.0001 REL FR 1 V 0 P
egyptians | and the phoenicians go a–ducking; ANT 3.07. 64
ADULATION 1 FR 0.0001 REL FR 1 V 0 P
will go out | with titles blown from adulation? H5 4.01.254
ADULTERATE 6 FR 0.0006 REL FR 6 V 0 P
i am possess'd with an adulterate blot; ERR 2.02.140
th' adulterate hastings, rivers, vaughan, grey, R3 4.04. 69
ay, that incestuous, that adulterate beast, HAM 1.05. 42
th' adulterate death of lucrece and her groom. LUC 1645
for why should others' false adulterate eyes SON 121. 5
and bastards of his foul adulterate heart. LC 175
ADULTERATES 1 FR 0.0001 REL FR 1 V 0 P
sh' adulterates hourly with thine uncle john, JN 3.01. 56
ADULTERERS 1 FR 0.0001 REL FR 0 V 1 P
and adulterers by an enforc'd obedience of LR 1.02.124 P
ADULTERESS 1 FR 0.0001 REL FR 1 V 0 P
and then they call'd me foul adulteress, TIT 2.03.109
ADULTERIES 1 FR 0.0001 REL FR 1 V 0 P
that thy adulteries | rates and revenges. CYM 5.04. 33
ADULTEROUS 2 FR 0.0002 REL FR 2 V 0 P
that angelo is an adulterous thief, | an MM 5.01. 40
only th' adulterous antony, most large | in his ANT 3.06. 93
ADULTERY 7 FR 0.0008 REL FR 4 V 3 P
have been accus'd in fornication, adultery, and MM 2.01. 81 P
treason, in committing adultery with polixenes, WT 3.02. 14 P
shall see willful adultery and murther committed H5 2.01. 37 P
adultery? LR 4.06.110
die for adultery? 4.06.111
of adultery? CYM 3.02. 1
and win this ring | by hers and mine adultery. 5.05.186
ADULT'RESS 1 FR 0.0001 REL FR 1 V 0 P
thy /mother's tomb, | sepulchring an adult'ress. LR 2.04.132
ADULTRESS 3 FR 0.0003 REL FR 3 V 0 P
to grieve it should be) | she's an adultress. WT 2.01. 78
i have said | she's an adultress, i have said 2.01. 88
being — part o' th' cause, | she the adultress; 2.03. 4
ADVANC'D 16 FR 0.0018 REL FR 13 V 3 P
advanc'd their eyelids, lifted up their noses TMP 4.01.177
at home, more advanc'd by the king than by that AWW 4.05. 6 P
you, cesario, you are like to be much advanc'd; TN 1.04. 2 P
how he jets under his advanc'd plumes! 2.05. 31 P
by whose fell working i was first advanc'd, 2H4 4.05.206
filling the air with swords advanc'd and darts, COR 1.06. 61
which, being advanc'd, declines, and then men 2.01.161
of goths | is of a sudden thus advanc'd in rome? TIT 1.01.393
advanc'd above pale envy's threat'ning reach. 2.01. 4
and how by this their child shall be advanc'd, 4.02.157
for 'twas your heaven she should be advanc'd, ROM 4.05. 72
now, seeing she is advanc'd | above the clouds, 4.05. 73
the poor advanc'd makes friends of enemies. HAM 3.02.205
one step i have advanc'd thee, if thou dost | as LR 5.03. 28
advanc'd in time to great and high estate. PER 4.04. 16
our hands advanc'd before our hearts, what will TNK 1.02.112
ADVANCE 34 FR 0.0038 REL FR 34 V 0 P
how to deny them, who t' advance, and who | to TMP 1.02. 80
the fringed curtains of thine eye advance | and 1.02.409
manners, | i must advance the colors of my love, WIV 3.04. 81
that advance their pride | against that power ADO 3.01. 10
advance your standards, and upon them, lords; LLL 4.03.364
and every one his love–feat will advance | unto 5.02.123
you do advance your cunning more and more; MND 3.02.128
how in our means we should advance ourselves 2H4 1.03. 7
the signs of war advance! H5 2.02.192
and your eyes advance | after your thoughts, 5.pr. 44
that never war advance | his bleeding sword 5.02.354
advance our waving colors on the walls, 1H6 1.06. 1
and here advance it in the market–place, | the 2.02. 5
or how haps it i seek not to advance | or raise 3.01. 31
hopeful colors | advance our half–fac'd sun, 2H6 4.01. 98
advance thy halberd higher than my breast, | or, R3 1.02. 40
advance your standards, draw your willing swords 5.03.264
advance our standards, set upon our foes. 5.03.348
he will advance thee. H8 3.02.416
advance, brave titus! COR 1.04. 25
inclinable to honor and advance | the theme of 2.02. 56
to advance | thy name and honorable family, TIT 1.01.238
if saturnine advance the queen of goths, | she 1.01.330
but to your wishes' height advance you both. 2.01.125
now, ere the sun advance his burning eye, | the ROM 2.03. 5
you honor me so much | as to advance this jewel; TIM 1.02.170
must arbitrate, | towards which advance the war. MAC 5.04. 21
and for your faithfulness | we will advance you, PER 1.01.154
require him he advance it o'er our heads; TNK 1.01. 93
say "ay," and all shall presently advance. 3.05.134
that to thy laud | i may advance my streamer, 5.01. 59
dispense, | my low–declined honor to advance? LUC 1705
and dost advance | as high as learning my rude SON 78.13
"'o, then advance of yours that phraseless hand, LC 225
ADVANCED 4 FR 0.0004 REL FR 4 V 0 P
that are advanced here | before the eye and JN 2.01.207
thou hast hung /thy advanced sword i' th' air, TRO 4.05.188
so, | captives, to be advanced to this height? TIT 4.02. 34
and death's pale flag is not advanced there. ROM 5.03. 96
ADVANCEMENT 9 FR 0.0010 REL FR 7 V 2 P
what a sleep were this | for your advancement! TMP 2.01.268
knows how that may turn back to my advancement?
WT 4.04.835 P
strengths and qualities, | give you advancement. 2H4 5.05. 70
endeavor'd my advancement to the throne. 1H6 2.05. 69
you envy my advancement and my friends'. R3 1.03. 74
th' advancement of your children, gentle lady. 4.04.242
for what advancement may i hope from thee | that
HAM 3.02. 57
sir, i lack advancement. 3.02.340 P
own disorders | deserv'd much less advancement. LR 2.04.200
ADVANCEMENTS 1 FR 0.0001 REL FR 0 V 1 P
fear not your advancements, i will be the man 2H4 5.05. 79 P
ADVANCES 1 FR 0.0001 REL FR 1 V 0 P
of her holy altar | with sacred act advances: TNK 5.01.165
ADVANTAG'D 1 FR 0.0001 REL FR 0 V 1 P
honor untainted, the poor mariana advantag'd, MM 3.01.254 P
/ADVANTAGE 1 FR 0.0001 REL FR 1 V 0 P
there, at your meet'st /advantage of the time, R3 3.05. 74
ADVANTAGE 77 FR 0.0087 REL FR 59 V 18 P
our cable, for our own doth little advantage. TMP 1.01. 32 P
the next advantage | will we take throughly. 3.03. 13
name) | made use and fair advantage of his days; TGV 2.04. 68
where your good word cannot advantage him, 3.02. 42
he gives her folly motion and advantage; WIV 3.02. 35 P
to take an ill advantage of his absence. 3.03.109 P
i hate, | for his advantage that i dearly love. MM 2.04.120
only refer yourself to this advantage: 3.01.246 P
upon you anon for some advantage to yourself. 4.01. 23 P
when i did him at this advantage take, | an MND 3.02. 16
you neither lend nor borrow | upon advantage. MV 1.03. 70
and finds no other advantage in the process but AWW 1.01. 15 P
that's for advantage. 1.01.201 P
and she herself, without other advantage, may 1.03.102 P
it shall advantage thee more than ever the TN 4.02.111 P
th' advantage of his absence took the king, JN 1.01.102
for our advantage — therefore hear us first: 2.01.206
speed then to take advantage of the field. 2.01.297
till this advantage, this vile–drawing bias, 2.01.577
and with advantage means to pay thy love; 3.03. 22
that none so small advantage shall step forth 3.04.151
his youth | the rich advantage of good exercise. 4.02. 60
of my pow'r, | as i upon advantage did remove, 5.07. 62
for their advantage and your highness' loss. R2 1.04. 41
you on | to take advantage of the absent time, 2.03. 79
if not, i'll use the advantage of my power, 3.03. 42
nail'd | for our advantage on the bitter cross. 1H4 1.01. 27
keep close, we'll read it at more advantage. 2.04.542 P
money shall be paid back again with advantage. 2.04.548 P
me up | with like advantage on the other side, 3.01.108
away, | advantage feeds him fat while men delay. 3.02.180
you give him then advantage. 4.03. 2
nor lose the good advantage of his grace | by 2H4 4.04. 28
advantage is a better soldier than rashness. H5 3.06.120 P
and dying so, death is to him advantage; 4.01.180 P
and thence discover how with most advantage 1H6 1.04. 12
or make my will th' advantage of my good. 2.05.129
and, in advantage ling'ring, looks for rescue, 4.04. 19
on that advantage, bought with such a shame, 4.06. 44
and, when i spy advantage, claim the crown, 2H6 1.01.242
and his advantage following your decease, | that 3.01. 25
take all the swift advantage of the hours. R3 4.01. 48
with best advantage will deceive the time, | and 5.03. 92
as he pleases, | and for his own advantage. H8 1.01.193
not lose | so rich advantage of a promis'd glory TRO 2.02.204
th' advantage of the time prompts me aloud | to 3.03. 2
do not give advantage | to stubborn critics, apt 5.02.130
should have ta'en th' advantage of his choler, COR 2.03.198
and lose advantage, which doth ever cool | i' 4.01. 43
that highly may advantage thee to hear. TIT 5.01. 56
it shall advantage more than do us wrong. JC 3.01.242
from which advantage shall we cut him off | if 4.03.210
early, | who, having some advantage on octavius, 5.03. 6
for where there is advantage to be given, | both MAC 5.04. 11
co–leagued with this dream of his advantage, HAM 1.02. 21
you have now the good advantage of the night. LR 2.01. 22
and bring them after in the best advantage. OTH 1.03.297
though true advantage never present itself; 2.01.244 P
give me advantage of some brief discourse | with 3.01. 52
and, to th' advantage, i, being here, took't up. 3.03.312

suppliest me with the least advantage of hope. 4.02.178 P
and our advantage serves | for a fair victory. ANT 4.07. 11
to the vales, | and hold our best advantage. 4.11. 4
with no more advantage than the opportunity of a
CYM 1.04.129 P
beyond him in the advantage of the time, above 4.01. 11 P
we have th' advantage of the ground, | the lane 5.02. 11
which gave advantage to an ancient soldier | (an 5.03. 15
nation, | taking advantage of our misery, PER 1.04. 66
or i will make th' advantage of this hour | mine TNK 3.06.123
choose but much advantage the poor handicrafts STM II.C 71 P
make use of time, let not advantage slip, VEN 129
thee, | to take advantage on presented joy; 405
what may a heavy groan advantage thee? 950
gain | advantage on the kingdom of the shore, SON 64. 6
that sin by him advantage should achieve, | and 67. 3
a maid of dian's this advantage found, | and his 153. 2
for his advantage still did wake and sleep. LC 123
ADVANTAGEABLE 1 FR 0.0001 REL FR 1 V 0 P
best | shall see advantageable for our dignity, H5 5.02. 88
ADVANTAGEOUS 2 FR 0.0002 REL FR 1 V 1 P
here is every thing advantageous to life. TMP 2.01. 50 P
but advantageous care | withdrew me from the TRO 5.04. 21
ADVANTAGES 11 FR 0.0012 REL FR 9 V 2 P
hazard all | do it in hope of fair advantages; MV 2.07. 19
to cull the plots of best advantages. JN 2.01. 40
and from this swarm of fair advantages | you 1H4 5.01. 55
of other, | turning past evils to advantages. 2H4 4.04. 78
will make road upon us | with all advantages. H5 1.02.139
whose hours the peasant best advantages. 4.01.284
but he'll remember with advantages | what feats 4.03. 50
change shapes with proteus for advantages, | and 3H6 3.02.192
intelligent party to the advantages of france. LR 3.05. 12 P
an eye can stamp and counterfeit advantages, OTH 2.01.243 P
sharp | to spy advantages, and where he finds TNK 4.02.133
ADVANTAGING 1 FR 0.0001 REL FR 1 V 0 P
advantaging their love with interest | of ten R3 4.04.323
ADVENG'D *(also aveng'd)*
ADVENG'D 1 FR 0.0001 REL FR 1 V 0 P
fields, | and be adveng'd on cursed tamora. TIT 5.01. 16
ADVENTEROUS 2 FR 0.0002 REL FR 1 V 1 P
as full of peril and adventerous spirit | as to 1H4 1.03.191
the adventerous knight shall use his foil and HAM 2.02.320 P
ADVENT'ROUS 2 FR 0.0002 REL FR 2 V 0 P
sheathing the steel in my advent'rous body. TIT 5.03.112
drawn by report, advent'rous by desire, | tell PER 1.01. 35
ADVENTUR'D 1 FR 0.0001 REL FR 1 V 0 P
that i have adventur'd | to try your taking of a CYM 1.06.172
ADVENTURE 25 FR 0.0028 REL FR 20 V 5 P
i will not adventure my discretion so weakly. TMP 2.01.187 P
tow'r, | so bold leander would adventure it. TGV 3.01.120
the fear of your adventure would counsel you to AYL 1.02.177 P
i have by hard adventure found mine own. 2.04. 45
yet of your royal presence i'll adventure | the WT 1.02. 38
what will you adventure | to save this brat's 2.03.162
and wouldst adventure | to mingle faith with him 4.04.459
pains, much less | th' adventure of her person? 5.01.156
as i, | to try the fair adventure of to-morrow. JN 5.05. 22
which he in this adventure hath surpris'd | to 1H4 1.01. 93
reasons for this adventure that he shall go. 1.02.151 P
and then will they adventure upon the exploit 1.02.171 P
withal | in the adventure of this perilous day. 5.02. 95
by this unheedful, desperate, wild adventure. 1H6 4.04. 7
well assur'd, | adventure to be banished myself; 2H6 3.02.350
our scouts have found the adventure very easy; 3H6 4.02. 18
i dare adventure to be sent to th' tow'r. R3 1.03.115
sea, | i should adventure for such merchandise. ROM 2.02. 84
here in the churchyard, yet i will adventure. 5.03. 11
if you fall in the adventure, our crows shall CYM 3.01. 81 P
my modesty, not death on't, | i would adventure. 3.04.153
in life, to lock it | from action and adventure? 4.04. 3
yon celestial tree | (or die in th' adventure), PER 1.01. 22
air, or at adventure humm'd /one | from musical TNK 1.03. 75
off | this great adventure to a second trial. 3.06.119
ADVENTURES 4 FR 0.0004 REL FR 3 V 1 P
so, | and in this mist at all adventures go. ERR 2.02.216
and i by him, at all adventures, so we were quit H5 4.01.116 P
to desperate adventures and assur'd destruction. R3 5.03.319
who, looking for adventures in the world, | was PER 2.03. 83
ADVENTURING 1 FR 0.0001 REL FR 1 V 0 P
and by adventuring both | i oft found both. MV 1.01.143
ADVENTUROUS 1 FR 0.0001 REL FR 1 V 0 P
and in your search spend your adventurous worth;
PER 2.04. 51
ADVENTUROUSLY 1 FR 0.0001 REL FR 0 V 1 P
be, if he durst steal any thing adventurously. H5 4.04. 74 P
ADVERSARIES 11 FR 0.0012 REL FR 9 V 2 P
health, | and do as adversaries do in law, SHR 1.02.276
is carried into the leaguer of the adversaries, AWW 3.06. 26 P
death, | suggest his soon-believing adversaries, R2 1.01.101
aspect | as cloudy men use to their adversaries, 1H4 3.02. 83
deeds | even in the bosom of our adversaries. 5.05. 31
to fright the souls of fearful adversaries, | he R3 1.01. 11
a weeder-out of his proud adversaries, | a 1.03.122
his ancient knot of dangerous adversaries 3.01.182
because they have been still my adversaries. 3.02. 52
fall | the usurping helmets of our adversaries; 5.03.112
all tending to the good of their adversaries. COR 4.03. 42 P
ADVERSARY *(also athversary)*
ADVERSARY 6 FR 0.0006 REL FR 5 V 1 P
which i will be thy adversary toward anne page. WIV 2.03. 94 P
thou art come to answer | a stony adversary, an MV 4.01. 4
this feast of battle with mine adversary. R2 1.03. 92
here were the servants of your adversary, | and ROM 1.01.106
yet am i noble as the adversary | i come to cope LR 5.03.123
which is that adversary? 5.03.124
ADVERSARY'S 3 FR 0.0003 REL FR 2 V 1 P
of strangers i' th' adversary's entertainment. AWW 4.01. 15 P
the lists | by reason of his adversary's odds. 1H6 5.05. 33
thy adversary's wife doth pray for thee. R3 5.03.166
ADVERSE 12 FR 0.0013 REL FR 11 V 1 P
he speak against me on the adverse side, | i MM 4.06. 6
to admit no traffic to our adverse towns: ERR 1.01. 15
grow this to what adverse issue it can, i will ADO 2.02. 51 P
though time seem so adverse and means unfit. AWW 5.01. 26
love) | into the danger of this adverse town, TN 5.01. 84
the adverse winds, | whose leisure i have stay'd JN 2.01. 57
when adverse foreigners affright my towns | with 4.02.172
on the casque | of thy adverse pernicious enemy. R2 1.03. 82
combat with adverse planets in the heavens! 1H6 1.01. 54
my prayers on the adverse party fight, | and R3 4.04.191
which they upon the adverse faction want. 5.03. 13
sense — | thy adverse party is thy advocate — SON 35.10
ADVERSELY 1 FR 0.0001 REL FR 0 V 1 P
the drink you give me touch my palate adversely, COR 2.01. 56 P
/ADVERSITIES 1 FR 0.0001 REL FR 1 V 0 P
let me embrace /thee, sour /adversities, | for 3H6 3.01. 24
ADVERSITIES 1 FR 0.0001 REL FR 1 V 0 P
and all indign and base adversities | make head OTH 1.03.273
ADVERSITY 7 FR 0.0008 REL FR 4 V 3 P
a man i am cross'd with adversity; TGV 4.01. 12
a wretched soul, bruis'd with adversity, | we ERR 2.01. 34
i am in adversity. 4.04. 20 P
sweet are the uses of adversity, | which, like AYL 2.01. 12
talbot, | who, ring'd about with bold adversity, 1H6 4.04. 14
well said, adversity! TRO 5.01. 12 P
have patience to make any adversity asham'd. TNK 2.01. 24 P
ADVERSITY'S 1 FR 0.0001 REL FR 1 V 0 P
adversity's sweet milk, philosophy, | to comfort ROM 3.03. 55
ADVERTIS'D 4 FR 0.0004 REL FR 4 V 0 P
i have advertis'd him by secret means | that if 3H6 4.05. 9
we are advertis'd by our loving friends | that 5.03. 18
i was advertis'd their great general slept, TRO 2.02.211
you have been well advertis'd | how much i dare; TNK 3.01. 58
ADVERTISE 2 FR 0.0002 REL FR 2 V 0 P
to one that can my part in him advertise. MM 1.01. 41
wherein he might the king his lord advertise H8 2.04.179
ADVERTISED 3 FR 0.0003 REL FR 3 V 0 P
please it your grace to be advertised | the duke 2H6 4.09. 23
for by my scouts i was advertised | that she was 3H6 2.01.116
as i by friends am well advertised, | sir edward R3 4.04.499
ADVERTISEMENT 4 FR 0.0004 REL FR 3 V 1 P
my griefs cry louder than advertisement. ADO 5.01. 32
that is an advertisement to a proper maid in AWW 4.03.213 P
for this advertisement is five days old. 1H4 3.02.172
yet doth he give us bold advertisement | that 4.01. 36
ADVERTISING 1 FR 0.0001 REL FR 1 V 0 P
then | advertising and holy to your business, MM 5.01.383
ADVICE 50 FR 0.0056 REL FR 46 V 4 P
when i could not ask my father | for his advice, TMP 5.01.191
how shall i dote on her with more advice, | that TGV 2.04.207
that thus without advice begin to love her? 2.04.208
upon advice, hath drawn my love from her, | and, 3.01. 73
and thy advice this night i'll put in practice: 3.02. 88
the turn | to give the onset to thy good advice. 3.02. 93
the lists of all advice | my strength can give MM 1.01. 6
whose advice | hath often still'd my brawling 4.01. 8
he wants advice. 4.02.146 P
and say by whose advice | thou cam'st here to 5.01.113
it not, | yet did repent me, after more advice, 5.01.464
my lord bassanio upon more advice | hath sent MV 4.02. 6
know now, upon advice, it toucheth us both, that SHR 1.01.115 P
and understand what advice shall thrust upon AWW 1.01.210 P
share the advice betwixt you. 2.01. 3
you did never lack advice so much | as letting 3.04. 19
yourselves | we need no more of your advice. WT 2.01.168
i would your spirit were easier for advice, | or 4.04.505
so hot a speed with such advice dispos'd, | such JN 3.04. 11
thy son is banish'd upon good advice, | whereto R2 1.03.233
i hope your lordship goes abroad by advice. 2H4 1.02. 96 P
restored | with good advice and little medicine. 3.01. 43
him on, | and on his more advice we pardon him. H5 2.02. 43
but, by the grace of god and hume's advice, 2H6 1.02. 72
perform'd, | but with advice and silent secrecy. 2.02. 68
thus high, by thy advice | and thy assistance, R3 4.02. 3
now, ulysses, i begin to relish thy advice, TRO 1.03.386
then, if you will elect by my advice, | crown TIT 1.01.228
the greeks upon advice did bury ajax | that slew 1.01.379
by my advice, all humbled on your knees, | you 1.01.472
and she shall file our engines with advice, 2.01.123
that we will prosecute by good advice | mortal 4.01. 92
done, | and we will all subscribe to thy advice: 4.02.130
we should have else desir'd your good advice MAC 3.01. 20
if you will take a homely man's advice, | be not 4.02. 68
break we our watch up, and, by my advice, | let HAM 1.01.168
so by my former lecture and advice, | shall you 2.01. 64
which done, she took the fruits of my advice; 2.02.145
wherein we must have use of your advice. LR 2.01.121
when this advice is free i give, and honest, OTH 2.03.337
are, or cease, | as you shall give th' advice. ANT 1.03. 68
yourself some comfort | out of your best advice. CYM 1.01.156
scorning advice, read the conclusion then; PER 1.01. 56
nor ask advice of any other thought | but 1.01. 62
your advice | is cried up with example. TNK 1.02. 12
me use my sword | against th' advice of fear. 3.01. 60
has this advice i told you done any good upon 5.02. 1
advice is sporting while infection breeds. LUC 907
which seem'd to swallow up his sound advice, 1409
advice is often seen | by blunting us to make LC 160
ADVIS'D *(also avis'd)*
/ADVIS'D 1 FR 0.0001 REL FR 1 V 0 P
/you /were /advis'd /his /flesh /was /capable 2H4 1.01.172
ADVIS'D 31 FR 0.0035 REL FR 28 V 3 P
well hast thou advis'd; TGV 1.03. 34
and advis'd him for th' entertainment of death. MM 3.02.213 P
yet i am advis'd to do it, | he says, to veil 4.06. 3
but be first advis'd, | in conflict that you get LLL 4.03.365
good madam, if by me you'll be advis'd, | let's 5.02.300
and were you well advis'd? 5.02.434
be advis'd, fair maid. MND 1.01. 46
therefore be advis'd. MV 2.01. 42
therefore be well advis'd | how you do leave me 5.01.234
but art thou not advis'd, he took some care | to SHR 1.01.186
i will seem friendly, as thou hast advis'd me. WT 1.02.350
be advis'd. 4.04.481
be well advis'd, tell o'er thy tale again. JN 3.01. 5
frowns | more upon humor than advis'd respect. 4.02.214
good cousin, be advis'd, stir not to-night. 1H4 4.03. 5
as i was then advis'd by my learned counsel in 2H4 1.02.134 P
much of your youth, | and bids you be advis'd: H5 1.02.251
advis'd by good intelligence | of this most 2.pr. 12
are ye advis'd? the east side of the grove. 2H6 2.01. 47
so do i ever — being well advis'd; R3 1.03.317
kneel'd /at my feet and bid me be advis'd? 2.01.108
be advis'd; H8 1.01.139
be advis'd; 1.01.145
till i may | be by my friends in spain advis'd, 2.04. 55
my grandsire, well advis'd, hath sent by me TIT 4.02. 10
or whether since he is advis'd by aught | to LR 5.01. 2
general, be advis'd, | he comes to bad intent. OTH 1.02. 55
i am advis'd to give her music a' mornings; CYM 2.03. 11 P
to her | what i shall be advis'd she likes. TNK 1.03. 16
o, be advis'd, thou know'st not what it is VEN 615
sum, | call'd to that audit by advis'd respects; SON 49. 4
ADVISE 40 FR 0.0045 REL FR 29 V 11 P
advise me where i may have such a ladder. TGV 3.01.122
i advise you let me not find you before me again MM 2.01.245 P
we shall advise this wrong'd maid to stead up 3.01.249 P
enterprise upon her, father, | if you advise it. 4.01. 66
him a present shrift and advise him for a better 4.02.208 P
you are to depart, i am come to advise you, 4.03. 51 P
friar, advise him, | i leave him to your hand. 5.01.485
signior leonato, let the friar advise you, | and ADO 4.01.244
gramercies, tranio, well dost thou advise. SHR 1.01. 41
i advise | you use your manners discreetly in 1.01.241
sirrah, be gone, or talk not, i advise you. 1.02. 44
this will i do, and this i will advise you. 4.02. 92
now do your duty throughly, i advise you. 4.04. 11
good my lord, | advise him. AWW 1.01. 72
go with me to my chamber, and advise me. 2.03.294
i hope i need not to advise you further, but i 3.05. 25 P
advise you what you say; TN 4.02. 94 P
thou dost advise me | even so as i mine own WT 1.02.339
go bid thy master well advise himself. H5 3.06.159
i advise you | (and take it from a heart that H8 1.01.102
comes that rock | that i advise your shunning. 1.01.114
not a man in england | can advise me like you; 1.01.135
i shall anon advise you | further in the 1.02.107
good sir, | what peace you'll make, advise me. COR 5.03.197
and must advise the emperor for his good. TIT 1.01.464
advise thee, aaron, what is to be done, | and we 4.02.129
thursday is near, lay hand on heart, advise. ROM 3.05.190
i will advise you where to plant yourselves, MAC 3.01.128
and that well might | advise him to a caution, 3.06. 44
brother, i advise you to the best; LR 1.02.172 P
advise your fellows so. 1.03. 23
advise yourself. 2.01. 27
advise the duke, where you are going, to a most 3.07. 9 P
therefore i do advise you take this note: 4.05. 29
you advise me well. OTH 2.03.326 P
you shall advise me in all for cleopatra. ANT 5.02.137
sir, i would advise you to shift a shirt; CYM 1.02. 1 P
what your own love will out of this advise you, 3.02. 45 P
and with dead cheeks advise thee to desist | for PER 1.01. 39
flies, | but yet i know you'll do as i advise. 4.03. 51
ADVISED 7 FR 0.0008 REL FR 7 V 0 P
my liege, i am advised what i say, | neither ERR 5.01.214
the self-same way with more advised watch | to MV 1.01.142
nor never by advised purpose meet | to plot, R2 1.03.188
th' advised head defends itself at home; H5 1.02.179
laugh, | and bid me be advised how i tread. 2H6 2.04. 36
to achieve | the silver livery of advised age, 5.02. 47
when they had sworn to this advised doom, | they LUC 1849
ADVISEDLY 6 FR 0.0006 REL FR 6 V 0 P
lord | will never more break faith advisedly. MV 5.01.253
we offer fair, take it advisedly. 1H4 5.01.114
this ill presage advisedly she marketh: VEN 457
and to the flame thus speaks advisedly: LUC 180
this picture she advisedly perus'd, | and chid 1527
and arm'd his long-hid wits advisedly, | to 1816
ADVISEMENTS *(see vizaments)*
ADVISES 2 FR 0.0002 REL FR 0 V 2 P
she thus advises thee that sighs for thee. TN 2.05.152 P
the malice of mankind that he thus advises us, TIM 4.03.453 P
ADVISINGS 1 FR 0.0001 REL FR 0 V 1 P
therefore fasten your ear on my advisings: MM 3.01.198 P
ADVOCATE 9 FR 0.0010 REL FR 8 V 1 P
what, | an advocate for an impostor? TMP 1.02.478
my soul should sue as advocate for thee: ERR 1.01.145
undertake to be | her advocate to th' loud'st. WT 2.02. 37
what advocate hast thou to him? 4.04.740 P
of such affections, | step forth mine advocate. 5.01.221
been | an earnest advocate to plead for him. R3 1.03. 86
offended king, | i will be known your advocate. CYM 1.01. 76
be advocate | for us and our distresses! TNK 1.01. 31
sense — | thy adverse party is thy advocate — SON 35.10
ADVOCATE'S 1 FR 0.0001 REL FR 0 V 1 P
advocate's the court-word for a pheasant. WT 4.04.742 P
ADVOCATION 1 FR 0.0001 REL FR 1 V 0 P
cassio, | my advocation is not now in tune. OTH 3.04.123
A-DYING 1 FR 0.0001 REL FR 1 V 0 P
thou, now a-dying, sayest thou flatterest me. R2 2.01. 90
AEACIDA 1 FR 0.0001 REL FR 1 V 0 P
why, this is just | "aio /te, aeacida, romanos 2H6 1.04. 62
AEACIDES 1 FR 0.0001 REL FR 1 V 0 P
mistrust it not, for sure aeacides | was ajax, SHR 3.01. 52
AEDILES 4 FR 0.0004 REL FR 4 V 0 P
the aediles ho! let him be apprehended. COR 3.01.172
seize him, aediles! 3.01.182
aediles, seize him! 3.01.213
our aediles smote, ourselves resisted? 3.01.317
AEGEON *(see egeon)*
/AEGLES 1 FR 0.0001 REL FR 1 V 0 P
and make him with fair /aegles break his faith, MND 2.01. 79
A,E,I 1 FR 0.0001 REL FR 0 V 1 P
i will repeat them — a,e,i — LLL 5.01. 55 P
AEMILIA 3 FR 0.0003 REL FR 3 V 0 P
the man | that hadst a wife once call'd aemilia, ERR 5.01.343
egeon, speak, | and speak unto the same aemilia! 5.01.346
if i dream not, thou art aemilia. 5.01.347
AEMILIUS 4 FR 0.0004 REL FR 4 V 0 P
what news with thee, aemilius? TIT 4.04. 61
aemilius, do this message honorably, | and if he 4.04.104
welcome, aemilius, what's the news from rome? 5.01.155
aemilius, let the emperor give his pledges 5.01.163
AENEAS' 1 FR 0.0001 REL FR 0 V 1 P
i chiefly lov'd, 'twas aeneas' /tale to dido, HAM 2.02.446 P
/AENEAS 1 FR 0.0001 REL FR 1 V 0 P
/to /bid /aeneas /tell /the /tale /twice /o'er TIT 3.02. 27
AENEAS 26 FR 0.0029 REL FR 23 V 3 P
what if he had said "widower aeneas" too? TMP 2.01. 80 P
as did aeneas old anchises bear, | so bear i 2H6 5.02. 62
but then aeneas bare a living load — | nothing 5.02. 64
what news, aeneas, from the field to-day? TRO 1.01.108

by whom, aeneas? 1.01.110
that's aeneas; 1.02.186 P
but peace, aeneas, | peace, troyan, lay thy 1.03.239
sir, you of troy, call you yourself aeneas? 1.03.245
this shall be told our lovers, lord aeneas. 1.03.284
fair lord aeneas, let me touch your hand; 1.03.304
it is the lord aeneas. 4.01. 2
that's my mind too. good morrow, lord aeneas. 4.01. 7
a valiant greek, aeneas, take his hand, 4.01. 8
jove, let aeneas live, | if to my sword his fate 4.01. 26
my lord aeneas! 4.02. 45
and, my lord aeneas, | we met by chance, you did 4.02. 70
and bring aeneas and the grecian with you. 4.04.100
as you and lord aeneas | consent upon the order 4.05. 89
thus says aeneas, one that knows the youth 4.05.110
aeneas, call my brother troilus to me, | and 4.05.154
aeneas is a–field, | and i do stand engag'd to 5.03. 67
ajax hath ta'en aeneas! 5.06. 22
i, as aeneas, our great ancestor, | did from the JC 1.02.112
dido and her aeneas shall want troops, | and all ANT 4.14. 53
true honest men being heard, like false aeneas, CYM 3.04. 58
and then will she be out of love with aeneas. TNK 4.03. 16 P
AEOLUS 1 FR 0.0001 REL FR 1 V 0 P
yet aeolus would not be a murtherer, | but left 2H6 3.02. 92
AER 2 FR 0.0002 REL FR 2 V 0 P
which we call mollis aer, and mollis aer | we CYM 5.05.447
mollis aer, and mollis aer | we term it mulier; 5.05.447
AERIAL 1 FR 0.0001 REL FR 1 V 0 P
even till we make the main and th' aerial blue OTH 2.01. 39
AERY* *(also airy)*
/AERY* 1 FR 0.0001 REL FR 0 V 1 P
/sir, /an /aery /of /children, /little /eyases, HAM 2.02.339 P
AERY* 9 FR 0.0010 REL FR 9 V 0 P
silence, you aery toys! WIV 5.05. 42
so, | that thou shalt like an aery spirit go. MND 3.01.161
turns them to shapes and gives to aery nothing 5.01. 16
some aery devil hovers in the sky | and pours JN 3.02. 2
arms, | and like an eagle o'er his aery tow'rs, 5.02.149
our aery buildeth in the cedar's top | and R3 1.03.263
your aery buildeth in our aery's nest: 1.03.269
hover about me with your aery wings | and hear 4.04. 13
woes, | aery succeeders of /intestate joys, 4.04.128
AERY'S 1 FR 0.0001 REL FR 1 V 0 P
your aery buildeth in our aery's nest: R3 1.03.269
AESCULAPIUS 2 FR 0.0002 REL FR 1 V 1 P
what says my aesculapius? WIV 2.03. 29 P
and aesculapius guide us! PER 3.02.110
AESON 1 FR 0.0001 REL FR 1 V 0 P
the enchanted herbs | that did renew old aeson. MV 5.01. 14
AESOP 1 FR 0.0001 REL FR 1 V 0 P
let aesop fable in a winter's night, | his 3H6 5.05. 25
AETNA 2 FR 0.0002 REL FR 2 V 0 P
now let hot aetna cool in sicily, | and be my TIT 3.01.241
so vanisheth | as smoke from aetna, that in air LUC 1042
AFAR 6 FR 0.0006 REL FR 4 V 2 P
kind of tender, made afar off by sir hugh here. WIV 1.01.208 P
john, saw afar off in the orchard this amiable ADO 3.03.151 P
he who shall speak for her is afar off guilty WT 2.01.104
broils | to be commenc'd in stronds afar remote. 1H4 1.01. 4
face, | and tarquin's eye may read the mot afar, LUC 830
whilst i, thy babe, chase thee afar behind, SON 143.10
AFEARD 33 FR 0.0037 REL FR 21 V 12 P
drowning to be afeard now of your four legs; TMP 2.02. 59 P
for i am trinculo — be not afeard — thy good 2.02.101 P
i afeard of him? 2.02.145 P
art thou afeard? 3.02.133
be not afeard. 3.02.135
i care not for that, but that i am afeard. WIV 3.04. 28 P
my daughter is sometime afeard she will do a ADO 2.03.152 P
a conqueror, and afeard to speak! LLL 5.02.579 P
will not the ladies be afeard of the lion? MND 3.01. 27 P
this is a knavery of them to make me afeard. 3.01.113 P
i am much afeard my lady his mother play'd false MV 1.02. 43 P
and yet to be afeard of my deserving | were but 2.07. 29
i am half afeard | thou wilt say anon he is some 2.09. 96
then never trust me if i be afeard. SHR 5.02. 17
i mean hortensio is afeard of you. 5.02. 19
i am afeard the life of helen, lady, | was AWW 5.03.153
i was not much afeard; WT 4.04.442
i am but sorry, not afeard; 4.04.463
but if you be afeard to hear the worst, | then JN 4.02.135
but tell me, hal, art not thou horrible afeard? 1H4 2.04.366 P
i am afeard there are few die well that die in a H5 4.01.141 P
a phoenix that shall make all france afeard. 1H6 4.07. 93
death, at whose name i oft have been afeard, 2H6 2.04. 89
you call a virtuous sin) | makes me afeard. TRO 4.04. 82
i am afeard, | being in night, all this is but a ROM 2.02.139
to be afeard to tell greybeards the truth? JC 2.02. 67
nothing afeard of what thyself didst make MAC 1.03. 96
art thou afeard | to be the same in thine own 1.07. 39
fie, my lord, fie, a soldier, and afeard? 5.01. 37 P
he is afeard to come. ANT 2.05. 81
half afeard to come. 3.03. 1
art not afeard? CYM 4.02. 94
and wast afeard to scratch her wicked foe, LUC 1035
A–FEASTING 1 FR 0.0001 REL FR 0 V 1 P
anne page is, at a farm–house a–feasting; WIV 2.03. 88 P
AFFABILITY 3 FR 0.0003 REL FR 2 V 1 P
her wit, | her affability and bashful modesty, SHR 2.01. 49
use me with that affability as in discretion you H5 3.02.127 P
hide it in smiles and affability; JC 2.01. 82
AFFABLE 6 FR 0.0006 REL FR 6 V 0 P
minola, | an affable and courteous gentleman. SHR 1.02. 98
with gentle conference, soft, and affable. 2.01.251
and wondrous affable, and as bountiful | as 1H4 3.01.166
we know the time since he was mild and affable, 2H6 3.01. 9
courteous destroyers, affable wolves, meek bears TIM 3.06. 95
nor that affable familiar ghost | which nightly SON 86. 9
AFFAIR 11 FR 0.0012 REL FR 8 V 3 P
but to give the mother | notice of my affair. MM 1.04. 87
whiles i in this affair do thee employ, | i'll MND 3.02.374
constellation is right apt | for this affair. TN 1.04. 36
whereupon i command thee to open thy affair. WT 4.04.738 P
we have lost | best half of our affair. MAC 3.03. 21
which have freely gone | with this affair along. HAM 1.02. 16
but what is your affair in elsinore? 1.02.174
frame, and /start not so wildly from my affair. 3.02.309 P
seal'd and done | that else leans on th' affair. 4.03. 57
th' affair cries haste, | and speed must answer OTH 1.03.276
i have dealt most directly in thy affair. 4.02.208 P
AFFAIRE 1 FR 0.0001 REL FR 0 V 1 P
/je /m'en vois a la cour — la grande affaire. WIV 1.04. 52 P
/AFFAIRS 1 FR 0.0001 REL FR 1 V 0 P
assaulted, | /for /following /her /affairs. LR 2.02.150
AFFAIRS 67 FR 0.0075 REL FR 57 V 10 P
i'll leave you to confer of home affairs; TGV 2.04.119
in these affairs to aid me with thy counsel. 2.04.185
i am to break with thee of some affairs | that 3.01. 59
hope is a curtal dog in some affairs. WIV 2.01.110
lord angelo, having affairs to heaven, | intends MM 3.01. 56
my stay must be stolen out of other affairs; 3.01.158 P
things | save in the office and affairs of love; ADO 2.01.176
not i, but my affairs, have made you wait. MV 2.06. 22
this fruit | till i and my affairs are answered. AYL 2.07. 99
part of a minute in the affairs of love, it may 4.01. 47 P
madam, | in that and all your worthiest affairs. AWW 3.02. 96
one, | to wear your gentle limbs in my affairs, 5.01. 4
be never so hardy to come again in his affairs, TN 2.02. 10 P
take and give back affairs and their dispatch 4.03. 18
my affairs | do even drag me homeward; WT 1.02. 23
in your affairs, my lord, | if ever i were 1.02.254
what his happier affairs may be, are to me 4.02. 30 P
and for the ord'ring your affairs, | to sing 4.04.139
father grown incapable | of reasonable affairs? 4.04.398
your affairs there? 4.04.717 P
to treat of high affairs touching that time. JN 1.01.101
why may not i demand | of thine affairs, as well 5.06. 5
shall furnish us | for our affairs in hand. R2 1.04. 47
and, for these great affairs do ask some charge, 2.01.159
i | know how or which way to order these affairs 2.02.109
look big | upon the maidenhead of our affairs. 1H4 4.01. 59
upon hasty employment in the king's affairs. 2H4 2.01.128 P
daughter, | give even way unto my rough affairs; 2.03. 2
soul, | who like a brother toil'd in my affairs, 3.01. 62
in the king's affairs upon his coronation–day, 3.02.182 P
god prosper your affairs! 3.02.293 P
my friends and brethren in these great affairs, 4.01. 6
else, putting all affairs else in oblivion, as 5.05. 26 P
hear him debate of commonwealth affairs, | you H5 1.01. 41
it rest, | other affairs must now be managed. 1H6 4.01.181
i come to talk of commonwealth affairs. 2H6 1.03.154
henry my lord is cold in great affairs, | too 3.01.224
whiles i take order for mine own affairs. 3.01.320
but, with the first of all your chief affairs, 3H6 4.06. 58
king, | i was a pack–horse in his great affairs: R3 1.03.121
so thrive i in my dangerous affairs | of hostile 4.04.398
look into these affairs see this main end, | the H8 2.02. 40
is this an hour for temporal affairs? 2.02. 72
should be good men, their affairs as righteous. 3.01. 22
affairs that walk | (as they say spirits do) at 5.01. 13
from your affairs | i hinder you too long. 5.01. 53
what's your affairs, i pray you? TRO 1.03.247
bear the great sway of his affairs with reason, 2.02. 35
is such a wrest in their affairs | that their 3.03. 23
my affairs | are servanted to others; COR 5.02. 82
the fortunes and affairs of noble brutus JC 3.01.135
there is a tide in the affairs of men | which, 4.03.218
but since the affairs of men rests still 5.01. 95
with macbeth | in riddles and affairs of death; MAC 3.05. 5
and our affairs from england come too late. HAM 5.02.368
your special mandate for the state affairs OTH 1.03. 72
but still the house affairs would draw her 1.03.147
please it your grace, on to the state affairs. 1.03.190
beseech you proceed to th' affairs of state. 1.03.220
let's to our affairs. 2.03.111 P
that in their sleeps will mutter their affairs; 3.03.417
him, | and his affairs come to me on the wind. ANT 3.06. 63
and went to jewry on | affairs of antony, there 4.06. 12
if one of mean affairs | may plod it in a week, CYM 3.02. 50
his honor, his affairs, his friends, his state, LUC 45
where you may be, or your affairs suppose, | but SON 57.10
be, | to stand in thy affairs, fall by thy side. 151.12
AFFECT 25 FR 0.0028 REL FR 20 V 5 P
there is a lady in /milano here | whom i affect; TGV 3.01. 82
would seem in me t' affect speech and discourse, MM 1.01. 4
man of safe discretion | that does affect it. 1.01. 72
dost thou affect her, claudio? ADO 1.01.296
i do affect the very ground (which is base) LLL 1.02.167 P
i will something affect the letter, for it 4.02. 55
in brief, sir, study what you most affect. SHR 1.01. 40
if you affect him, sister, here i swear | i'll 2.01. 14
rather thought you affect a sorrow than to have AWW 1.01. 53 P
i do affect a sorrow indeed, but i have it too. 1.01. 54 P
maria once told me she did affect me, and i have TN 2.05. 24 P
if i affect it more | than as your honor and as 2H4 4.05.144
how doth your grace affect their motion? 1H6 5.01. 7
how they affect the house and claim of york. 2H6 3.01.375
as i belong to worship and affect | in honor H8 1.01. 39
mock not /that /i affect th' untraded /oath, TRO 4.05.178
to seem to affect the malice and displeasure of COR 2.02. 21 P
policy and stratagem must do | that you affect, TIT 2.01.105
himself, | for he does neither affect company, TIM 1.02. 31
man | can justly praise but what he does affect. 1.02.215
meer report | thou dost affect my manners, and 4.03.199
for bluntness, doth affect | a saucy roughness, LR 2.02. 96
not to affect many proposed matches | of her own OTH 3.03.229
what need i | affect another's gait, which is TNK 1.02. 45
'tis odds | he never will affect me. 2.04. 2
AFFECTATIONS *(also affection*)*
AFFECTATIONS 1 FR 0.0001 REL FR 0 V 1 P
why, it is affectations. WIV 1.01.150 P
AFFECTED 20 FR 0.0022 REL FR 14 V 6 P
and how stand you affected to his wish? TGV 1.03. 60
in conclusion, i stand affected to her. 2.01. 84 P
you, | and as i find her, so am i affected. WIV 3.04. 91
he surely affected her for her wit. LLL 1.02. 88 P
with that which we lovers entitle "affected." 2.01.232
men that most are affected to these. 3.01. 25 P
too spruce, too affected, too odd as it were, 5.01. 13 P
i am, in all affected as yourself, | glad that SHR 1.01. 26
have i affected wealth or honor? 2H6 4.07. 98
how he doth stand affected to our purpose, | and R3 3.01.171
which ever yet | affected eminence, wealth, H8 2.03. 29
without some image of th' affected merit. TRO 2.02. 60
were it not glory that we more affected | than 2.02.195
thou hast affected the /fine strains of honor, COR 5.03.149
and may, for aught thou knowest, affected be. TIT 2.01. 28
the king had more affected the duke of albany LR 1.01. 1 P
no marvel then, though he were ill affected: 2.01. 98
only | affected greatness got by you, not you; CYM 5.05. 38
you she ever affected any man ere she beheld TNK 4.03. 62 P
"is thine own heart to thine own face affected? VEN 157
AFFECTEDLY 1 FR 0.0001 REL FR 1 V 0 P
blood, | with sleided silk feat and affectedly LC 48
AFFECTETH 1 FR 0.0001 REL FR 1 V 0 P
face, | the accent of his tongue affecteth him. JN 1.01. 86
AFFECTING 3 FR 0.0003 REL FR 1 V 2 P
i never heard such a drawling, affecting rogue. WIV 2.01.141 P
and affecting one sole throne, | without COR 4.06. 32
lisping, affecting /phantasimes, these new ROM 2.04. 28 P
AFFECTION* *(also affectations)*
AFFECTION* 83 FR 0.0093 REL FR 55 V 28 P
and your affection not gone forth, i'll make you TMP 1.02.449
were't not affection chains thy tender days | to TGV 1.01. 3
you were set, so your affection would cease. 2.01. 85 P
but can you affection the oman? WIV 1.01.227 P
apply well to the vehemency of your affection, 2.02.239 P
who mutually hath answer'd my affection | (so 4.06. 10
their names | by vain though apt affection. MM 1.04. 48
or, by the affection that now guides me most, 2.04.168
thou hast neither heat, affection, limb, nor 3.01. 37
in her the continuance of her first affection; 3.01.240 P
eye | stray'd his affection in unlawful love — ERR 5.01. 51
i heard him swear his affection. ADO 2.01.168 P
into a mountain of affection th' one with th' 2.01.367 P
comes athwart his affection ranges evenly with 2.02. 6 P
that she loves him with an enrag'd affection; 2.03.100 P
invincible against all assaults of affection. 2.03.115 P
hath she made her affection known to benedick? 2.03.123 P
will rather die than give any sign of affection. 2.03.228 P
benedick, | to wish him wrastle with affection, 3.01. 42
nor take no shape nor project of affection, 3.01. 55
containing her affection unto benedick. 5.04. 90
the humor of affection would deliver me from the LLL 1.02. 60 P
without scurrility, witty without affection, 5.01. 4 P
sweet pleasure and affection to congratulate the 5.01. 88 P
three–pil'd hyperboles, spruce affection, 5.02.407
o that my prayers could such affection move! MND 1.01.197
his soul) | and tender me (forsooth) affection, 3.02.230
is there in your affection towards any of these MV 1.02. 34 P
to my description level at my affection. 1.02. 38 P
comer i have look'd on yet | for my affection. 2.01. 22
and with affection wondrous sensible | he wrung 2.08. 48
for affection, | /mistress of passion, sways it 4.01. 50
perforce, i will render thee again in affection. AYL 1.02. 21 P
my affection hath an unknown bottom, like the 4.01.207 P
that as fast as you pour affection in, /it runs 4.01.210 P
now, | affection is not rated from the heart. SHR 1.01.160
lord, | c fa ut, that loves with all affection. 3.01. 76
heard | of your entire affection to bianca, 4.02. 23
disclose | the state of your affection, for your AWW 1.03.190
or thy affection cannot hold the bent; TN 2.04. 37
rooted betwixt them then such an affection, WT 1.01. 24 P
affection! 1.02.138
this shows a sound affection. 4.04.379
wipe me, father, i | am heir to my affection. 4.04.481
the affection of nobleness which nature shows 5.02. 36 P
with all greediness of affection are they gone, 5.02.103 P
thou hast a better place in his affection | than 2H4 4.04. 22
did with the least affection of a welcome | give 4.05.172
it shows my earnestness of affection — 5.05. 16 P
bear her this jewel, pledge of my affection. 1H6 5.01. 47
my king is tangled in affection to | a creature H8 3.02. 35
law | of nature be corrupted through affection, TRO 2.02.177
unto the appetite and affection common | of the COR 1.01.104
but out, affection, | all bond and privilege of 5.03. 24
lie, | and young affection gapes to be his heir; ROM 2.pr. 2
affection makes him false, he speaks not true. 3.01.177
i weigh my friend's affection with mine own. TIM 1.02.216
ground | do stand but in a forc'd affection, JC 4.03.205
in my most ill–compos'd affection such | a MAC 4.03. 77
and keep you in the rear of your affection, HAM 1.03. 34
late made many tenders | of his affection to me. 1.03.100
affection, puh! 1.03.101
that might indict the author of affection, but 2.02.443 P
who, dipping all his faults in their affection, 4.07. 19
or your fore–vouch'd affection | fall into taint LR 1.01.220
writ this to feel my affection to your honor, 1.02. 87 P
that ceremonious affection as you were wont. 1.04. 59 P
preferment goes by letter and affection, | and OTH 1.01. 36
of his salt and most hidden loose affection? 2.01.241 P
and doth affection breed it? 4.03. 98
antony will use his affection where it is; ANT 2.06.130 P
and that | my sword, made weak by my affection, 3.11. 67
the itch of his affection should not then | have 3.13. 7
bed, | and will continue fast to your affection, CYM 1.06.138
at once subduing | thy force and thy affection; TNK 1.01. 85
what 'twere to filch affection from another! 2.02.210
and love | with all the justice of affection, 3.06. 51
yet i'll preserve | the honor of affection, and 3.06.269
affection is a coal that must be cool'd, | else, VEN 387
affection faints not like a pale–fac'd coward, 569
affection is my captain, and he leadeth; LUC 271
i will not wrong thy true affection so, | to 1060
or my affection put to th' smallest teen, | or LC 192
AFFECTIONATE 1 FR 0.0001 REL FR 0 V 1 P
so i would say) affectionate servant, goneril." LR 4.06.269 P
AFFECTIONATELY 1 FR 0.0001 REL FR 0 V 1 P
commends himself most affectionately to you — TRO 3.01. 67 P
AFFECTION'D 1 FR 0.0001 REL FR 0 V 1 P
but a time–pleaser, an affection'd ass, that TN 2.03.148 P
AFFECTION'S 4 FR 0.0004 REL FR 4 V 0 P
have at you then, affection's men–at–arms. LLL 4.03.286
not removes, at least, | affection's edge in me. SHR 1.02. 73
doth call himself affection's sentinel, | gives VEN 650
but nothing can affection's course control, | or LUC 500
AFFECTIONS' 1 FR 0.0001 REL FR 1 V 0 P
but he, /his own affections' counsellor, | is to ROM 1.01.147
/AFFECTIONS 1 FR 0.0001 REL FR 1 V 0 P
/in /diet, /in /affections /of /delight, | /in 2H4 2.03. 29
AFFECTIONS 43 FR 0.0048 REL FR 38 V 5 P
my affections | are then most humble; TMP 1.02.482
fair encounter | of two most rare affections! 3.01. 75

them, your affections | would become tender. 5.01. 18
that, in the working of your own affections, MM 2.01. 10
has he affections in him, | that thus can make 3.01.107
do their gay vestments his affections bait? ERR 2.01. 94
it seems her affections have their full bent. ADO 2.03.223 P
that war against your own affections | and the LLL 1.01. 9
the better part of my affections would | be with MV 1.01. 16
dimensions, senses, affections, passions; 3.01. 60 P
as night, | and his affections dark as /erebus: 5.01. 87
come, come, wrastle with thy affections. AYL 1.03. 21 P
or both dissemble deeply their affections; SHR 4.04. 42
hath kill'd the flock of all affections else TN 1.01. 35
with thought of such affections, | step forth WT 5.01.220
and great affections wrastling in thy bosom JN 5.02. 41
at thy affections, which do hold a wing | quite 1H4 3.02. 30
o, with what wings shall his affections fly 2H4 4.04. 65
for in his tomb lie my affections, | and with 5.02.124
and though his affections are higher mounted H5 4.01.106 P
you do not love it, nor your affections, and 5.01. 25 P
have i with all my full affections | still met H8 3.01.129
if i could temporize with my affections, | or TRO 4.04. 6
and your affections are | a sick man's appetite, COR 1.01.177
than as guided | by your own true affections, 2.03.231
i, measuring his affections by my own, | which ROM 1.01.126
had she affections and warm youthful blood, 2.05. 12
i have not known when his affections sway'd JC 2.01. 20
his affections do not that way tend, | nor what HAM 3.01.162
subdue and poison this young maid's affections? OTH 1.03.112
and have not we affections, | desires for sport, 4.03.100
hast thou affections? ANT 1.05. 12
yet have i fierce affections, and think | what 1.05. 17
pitying | the pangs of barr'd affections, though CYM 1.01. 82
bestow your love and your affections | upon a PER 2.05. 77
makest affections bend | to godlike honors; TNK 1.01.229
those best affections that the heavens infuse 1.03. 9
no toy | but was her pattern, her affections 1.03. 72
am not i liable to those affections, | those 2.02.187
dear, | made old offenses of affections new; SON 110. 4
and nice affections wavering stood in doubt | if LC 97
art, | threw my affections in his charmed power, 146
"'lo all these trophies of affections hot, | of 218
AFFECTS 11 FR 0.0012 REL FR 11 V 0 P
sir john affects thy wife. WIV 2.01.111
and he my husband best of all affects. 4.04. 87
for every man with his affects is born, | not by LLL 1.01.151
heir, | that thus affects a sheep–hook! WT 4.04.420
as 'twere to banish their affects with him. R2 1.04. 30
not whom we will, but whom his grace affects, 1H6 5.05. 57
and therefore, lords, since he affects her most, 5.05. 59
to what infectiously itself affects, | without TRO 2.02. 59
him home, that he affects | tyrannical power. COR 3.03. 1
with heat (the young affects | in /me defunct) OTH 1.03.263
servant, making peace or war | as thou affects. ANT 1.03. 71
AFFEER'D 1 FR 0.0001 REL FR 1 V 0 P
wear thou thy wrongs, | the title is affeer'd! MAC 4.03. 34
AFFIANC'D 2 FR 0.0002 REL FR 1 V 1 P
was affianc'd to her /by oath, and the nuptial MM 3.01.214 P
i am affianc'd this man's wife as strongly | as 5.01.227
AFFIANCE 3 FR 0.0003 REL FR 3 V 0 P
jealousy infected | the sweetness of affiance! H5 2.02.127
what's more dangerous than this fond affiance! 2H6 3.01. 74
i have spoke this to know if your affiance CYM 1.06.163
AFFIED 1 FR 0.0001 REL FR 1 V 0 P
best | we be affied and such assurance ta'en SHR 4.04. 49
AFFIN'D 3 FR 0.0003 REL FR 3 V 0 P
the hard and soft, seem all affin'd and kin; TRO 1.03. 25
whether i in any just term am affin'd | to love OTH 1.01. 39
if partially affin'd, or /leagu'd in office, 2.03.218
AFFINITY 1 FR 0.0001 REL FR 1 V 0 P
of great fame in cyprus, | and great affinity; OTH 3.01. 46
AFFIRM 4 FR 0.0004 REL FR 3 V 1 P
yet their own authors faithfully affirm | that H5 1.02. 43
katherine, and i must not blush to affirm it. 5.02.114 P
/renege, affirm, and turn their halcyon beaks LR 2.02. 78
in man, but i affirm | it is the woman's part: CYM 2.05. 21
AFFIRMATION 1 FR 0.0001 REL FR 0 V 1 P
(and upon warrant of bloody affirmation) his to CYM 1.04. 59 P
AFFIRMATIVES 1 FR 0.0001 REL FR 0 V 1 P
your four negatives make your two affirmatives, TN 5.01. 22 P
AFFLICT 14 FR 0.0015 REL FR 13 V 1 P
habitation where thou keep'st | hourly afflict. MM 3.01. 11
afflict me with thy mocks, pity me not, | as AYL 3.05. 33
but | i could afflict you farther. WT 5.03. 75
o, how this discord doth afflict my soul! 1H6 3.01.106
ambitious churchman, leave to afflict my heart. 2H6 2.01.178
scorning what e'er you can afflict me with. 3H6 1.04. 38
o coward conscience, how dost thou afflict me! R3 5.03.179
nor with sour looks afflict his gentle heart. TIT 1.01.441
we will afflict the emperor in his pride. 4.03. 63
thy greediness would afflict thee, and oft thou TIM 4.03.334 P
under heaven | that does afflict our natures. HAM 2.01.103
never afflict yourself to know more of it, | but LR 1.04.291
two friends | that does afflict each other! ANT 3.06. 78
afflict him in his bed with bedred groans; LUC 975
AFFLICTED 8 FR 0.0009 REL FR 6 V 2 P
fat knight shall be any further afflicted, we WIV 4.02.218 P
i come to visit the afflicted spirits | here in MM 2.03. 4
will, | in the vild prison of afflicted breath. JN 3.04. 19
how sad he looks! sure he is much afflicted. H8 2.02. 62
shall we be thus afflicted in his wreaks, | his TIT 4.04. 11
we should be thus afflicted with these strange ROM 2.04. 32 P
dishonestly afflicted, but yet honest. CYM 4.02. 40
towards this afflicted fancy fastly drew, | and, LC 61
AFFLICTION 20 FR 0.0022 REL FR 16 V 4 P
th' affliction of my mind amends, with which | i TMP 5.01.115
to repay that money will be a biting affliction. WIV 5.05.169 P
affliction may one day smile again, and till LLL 1.01.314 P
do not receive affliction | at my petition; WT 3.02.223
and whose heart together | affliction alters. 4.04.575
i think affliction may subdue the cheek, | but 4.04.576
for this affliction has a taste as sweet | as 5.03. 76
o fair affliction, peace! JN 3.04. 36
heart's discontent and sour affliction | be 2H6 3.02.301
affliction is enamor'd of thy parts, | and thou ROM 3.03. 2
that whoso please | to stop affliction, let him TIM 5.01.210
in the affliction of these terrible dreams MAC 3.02. 18
if't be th' affliction of his love or no | that HAM 3.01. 35
your mother, in most great affliction of spirit, 3.02.312 P
cannot carry | th' affliction nor the fear. LR 3.02. 49
shake patiently my great affliction off. 4.06. 36
i'll bear | affliction till it do cry out itself 4.06. 76
it pleas'd heaven | to try me with affliction, OTH 4.02. 48
and happier much by his affliction made. CYM 5.04.108
their mirth, and affliction a toy to jest at. TNK 2.01. 35 P
AFFLICTIONS 6 FR 0.0006 REL FR 5 V 1 P
a feeling | of their afflictions, and shall not TMP 5.01. 22
they that must weigh out my afflictions, | they H8 3.01. 88
i count it one of my greatest afflictions, say, TIM 3.02. 56 P
great fortunes | are made thy chief afflictions. 4.02. 44
thought and afflictions, passion, hell itself, HAM 4.05.188
that have afflictions on them, knowing 'tis | a CYM 3.06. 10
AFFLICTS 2 FR 0.0002 REL FR 1 V 1 P
the leanness that afflicts us, the object of our COR 1.01. 20 P
whether aught, to us unknown, afflicts him thus, HAM 2.02. 17
AFFORD 23 FR 0.0026 REL FR 21 V 2 P
only this commendation i can afford her, that ADO 1.01.174 P
and praise we may afford | to any lady that LLL 4.01. 39
we can afford no more at such a price. 5.02.223
and would afford my speechless vizard half. 5.02.246
we cannot afford you so. AWW 4.01. 48 P
now jove afford you cause! WT 4.04. 16
the purest treasure mortal times afford | is R2 1.01.177
with community, | afford no extraordinary gaze, 1H4 3.02. 78
what other pleasure can the world afford? 3H6 3.02.147
the spacious world cannot again afford. R3 1.02.245
can this dark monarchy afford false clarence?" 1.04. 51
that thou wouldst as soon afford a grave | as 4.04. 31
all comfort that the dark night can afford | be 5.03. 80
as easy as a down–bed would afford it. H8 1.04. 18
rome could afford no tribunes like to these. TIT 3.01. 44
could not all hell afford you such a devil? 5.02. 86
the love i bear thee can afford | no better term ROM 3.01. 60
these times of woe afford no times to woo. 3.04. 8
and strength shall help afford. 4.01.125
of his) | what charitable men afford to beggars. TIM 3.02. 75
would not afford you an abode on earth, | whet STM II.C 133
next, vouchsafe t' afford | (if ever, love, thy LUC 1305
he can afford | no praise to thee but what in SON 79.11
AFFORDETH 1 FR 0.0001 REL FR 1 V 0 P
such fair question | as soul to soul affordeth? OTH 1.03.114
AFFORDS 16 FR 0.0018 REL FR 16 V 0 P
that every churl affords. ERR 3.01. 24
let them want nothing that my house affords. SHR in.1. 104
padua affords this kindness, son petruchio. 5.02. 13
padua affords nothing but what is kind. 5.02. 14
and i will see what physic the tavern affords. 1H6 3.01.147
such as my wit affords | and overjoy of heart 2H6 1.01. 30
such pity as my rapier's point affords. 3H6 1.03. 37
since this earth affords no joy to me | but to 3.02.165
look for the news that the guildhall affords. R3 3.05.102
and rome affords no prey | but me and mine. TIT 3.01. 55
the world affords no law to make thee rich; ROM 5.01. 73
the sweet degrees that this brief world affords TIM 4.03.253
humane grace | affords them dust and shadow. TNK 1.01.145
sometime 'tis mad and too much talk affords. LUC 1106
to every hymn that able spirit affords | in SON 85. 7
themes in one, which wondrous scope affords. 105.12
AFFRAY 1 FR 0.0001 REL FR 1 V 0 P
since arm from arm that voice doth us affray, ROM 3.05. 33
AFFRIGHT 12 FR 0.0013 REL FR 11 V 1 P
night, | did scare away, or rather did affright; MND 5.01.141
when adverse foreigners affright my towns | with JN 4.02.172
that did affright the air at agincourt? H5 pr 14
what, doth death affright? 2H6 4.01. 32
even to affright thee with the view thereof. 5.01.207
tush, man, abodements must not now affright us. 3H6 4.07. 13
let not our babbling dreams affright our souls; R3 5.03.308
think upon these gone, | let them affright thee. ROM 5.03. 61
offenseless dog to affright an imperious lion. OTH 2.03.275 P
for death–like dragons here affright thee hard. PER 1.01. 29
let ghastly shadows his lewd eyes affright, LUC 971
will fix a sharp knife to affright mine eye, 1138
AFFRIGHTED 6 FR 0.0006 REL FR 6 V 0 P
affrighted much, | i did in time collect myself WT 3.03. 37
who then, affrighted with their bloody looks, 1H4 1.03.104
no marvel, lord, though it affrighted you; R3 1.04. 64
people and senators, be not affrighted; JC 3.01. 82
o, my lord, my lord, i have been so affrighted! HAM 2.01. 72
and that th' affrighted globe | did yawn at OTH 5.02.100
AFFRIGHTS 5 FR 0.0005 REL FR 5 V 0 P
the scarecrow that affrights our children so. 1H6 1.04. 43
their touch affrights me as a serpent's sting. 2H6 3.02. 47
thy name affrights me, in whose sound is death. 4.01. 33
affrights thee with a hell of ugly devils! R3 1.03.226
the one affrights you, | the other makes you COR 1.01.169
AFFRONT 4 FR 0.0004 REL FR 4 V 0 P
hermione as is her picture, | affront his eye. WT 5.01. 75
'twere by accident, may here | affront ophelia. HAM 3.01. 31
your preparation can affront no less | than what CYM 4.03. 29
silly habit, | that gave th' affront with them. 5.03. 87
AFFRONTED 1 FR 0.0001 REL FR 1 V 0 P
might be affronted with the match and weight TRO 3.02.166
AFFY 2 FR 0.0002 REL FR 2 V 0 P
for daring to affy a mighty lord | unto the 2H6 4.01. 80
so i do affy | in thy uprightness and integrity, TIT 1.01. 47
A–FIELD 4 FR 0.0004 REL FR 3 V 1 P
or else, when thou didst keep my lambs a–field, 1H6 5.04. 30
how now, prince troilus, wherefore not a–field? TRO 1.01.105
sweet lord, who's a–field to–day? 3.01.133 P
aeneas is a–field, | and i do stand engag'd to 5.03. 67
AFIRE 4 FR 0.0004 REL FR 4 V 0 P
then all afire with me, the king's son, TMP 1.02.212
i am hush'd until our city be afire, | and then COR 5.03.181
flask, | is set afire by thine own ignorance, ROM 3.03.133
another wanton ganymede | set /jove afire with, TNK 4.02. 16
AFLOAT 2 FR 0.0002 REL FR 2 V 0 P
on such a full sea are we now afloat, | and we JC 4.03.222
your shallowest help will hold me up afloat, SON 80. 9
/AFOOT 1 FR 0.0001 REL FR 1 V 0 P
/'tis /so, /they /are /afoot. LR 4.03. 49
AFOOT 26 FR 0.0029 REL FR 18 V 8 P
the matter being afoot, keep your instruction, MM 4.05. 3
have walk'd ten mile afoot to see a good armor, ADO 2.03. 16 P
of him, of what strength they are afoot." AWW 4.03.159 P
were i tied to run afoot | even to the frozen R2 1.01. 63
before the game is afoot thou still let'st slip. 1H4 1.03.278
but four foot by the squier further afoot, i 2.02. 13 P
is threescore and ten miles afoot with me, and 2.02. 26 P
my own flesh so far afoot again for all the coin 2.02. 36 P
when a jest is so forward, and afoot too! 2.02. 47 P
we'll walk afoot a while, and ease our legs. 2.02. 79 P
so far afoot, i shall be weary, love. 2.03. 84
ye cuckoo, but afoot he will not budge a foot. 2.04.353 P
and pause us, till these rebels, now afoot, 2H4 4.04. 9
so may a thousand actions, once afoot, | /end in H5 1.02.211
the game's afoot! 3.01. 32
what, all afoot? 2H6 5.02. 8
went all afoot in summer's scalding heat, | that 3H6 5.07. 18
anon he's there afoot, | and there they fly or TRO 5.05. 21
ere (almost) rome | should know we were afoot. COR 1.02. 25
but were our witty empress well afoot, | she TIT 4.02. 29
mischief, thou art afoot, | take thou what JC 3.02.260
for that i saw the tyrant's power afoot. MAC 4.03.185
i prithee, when thou seest that act afoot, HAM 3.02. 78
pension beg | to keep base life afoot. LR 2.04.215
is't said this war's afoot? TNK 1.02.104
emily, i hope | he shall not go afoot. 2.05. 53
AFORE *(also before, 'fore, tofore)*
/AFORE 1 FR 0.0001 REL FR 0 V 1 P
/afore /god, a mad host. WIV 3.01.112 P
AFORE 16 FR 0.0018 REL FR 7 V 9 P
if he have never drunk wine afore, it will go TMP 2.02. 75 P
here, afore heaven, | i ratify this my rich gift 4.01. 7
last, a fortnight afore michaelmas? WIV 1.01.205 P
now, afore god — god forbid i say true! R2 2.01.200
now, afore god, 'tis shame such wrongs are borne 2.01.238
all thy subjects afore thee like a flock of wild 1H4 2.04.138 P
keeping house afore i'll be in these tirrits and 2H4 2.04.205 P
is painted blind, with a muffler afore his eyes, H5 3.06. 31 P
now, afore god, i am so vex'd that every part ROM 2.04.161 P
afore me, it is so very late that we | may call 3.04. 34
now, afore god, this reverend holy friar, | all 4.02. 31
be not speedy, i shall be there afore you. LR 1.05. 5 P
will you go on afore? OTH 5.01.128
now, afore me, a handsome fellow! PER 2.01. 80 P
as it were to stink afore the face of the gods. 4.06.136 P
and hang | your shield afore your heart, about TNK 1.01.197
AFOREHAND *(also beforehand, 'forehand)*
AFOREHAND 1 FR 0.0001 REL FR 1 V 0 P
a consent, | knowing aforehand of our merriment, LLL 5.02.461
AFORESAID *(also foresaid)*
/AFORESAID 1 FR 0.0001 REL FR 0 V 1 P
/and, /as /aforesaid, /patroclus /is /a /fool. TRO 2.03. 59 P
AFORESAID 2 FR 0.0002 REL FR 0 V 2 P
which i apprehended with the aforesaid swain, i LLL 1.01.273 P
or, as aforesaid, "honest launcelot /gobbo, do MV 2.02. 8 P
/AFORE'T 1 FR 0.0001 REL FR 1 V 0 P
something's /afore't. CYM 3.04. 79
/AFRAID 1 FR 0.0001 REL FR 0 V 1 P
/rapiers /are /afraid /of //goose–quills /and HAM 2.02.343 P
AFRAID 42 FR 0.0047 REL FR 28 V 14 P
we are less afraid to be drown'd than thou art. TMP 1.01. 44 P
of her society | be not afraid. 4.01. 92
i am afraid | he will chastise me. 5.01.262
you are afraid if you see the bear loose, are WIV 1.01.292 P
i am half afraid he will have need of washing, 3.03.182 P
answer your master, be not afraid. 4.01. 20 P
i see these witches are afraid of swords. ERR 4.04.147
will sing, that they shall hear i am not afraid. MND 3.01.124 P
be not afraid; she shall not harm thee, helena. 3.02.321
i am afraid, sir, | do what you can, yours will SHR 5.02. 88
be not afraid that i your hand should take, AWW 2.03. 89
not that i am afraid to die, but that, my 4.03.241 P
i am above thee, but be not afraid of greatness. TN 2.05.144 P
be not afraid, good youth, i will not have you, 3.01.131
"be not afraid of greatness": 'twas well writ. 3.04. 39 P
i am afraid this great lubber, the world, will 4.01. 14 P
he is afraid of me and i of him. JN 4.01. 21
i am afraid, and yet i'll venture it. 4.03. 5
art thou not horribly afraid? 1H4 2.04.370 P
i am afraid my daughter will run mad, | so much 3.01.143
i am afraid of this gunpowder percy though he be 5.04.121 P
my faith, i am afraid he would prove the better 5.04.123 P
conjurers and sorcerers, that, afraid of him, 1H6 1.01. 26
or more afraid to fight, than is the appellant, 2H6 2.03. 57
here, peter, i drink to thee, and be not afraid. 2.03. 69 P
are you all afraid? R3 1.02. 43
i am afraid, methinks, to hear you tell it. 1.04. 65
what? art thou afraid? 1.04.109 P
nay, good my lord, be not afraid of shadows. 5.03.215
but i am afraid | his thinkings are below the H8 3.02.133
i am almost afraid to stand alone | here in the ROM 5.03. 10
shall they not whisper, | "lo caesar is afraid"? JC 2.02.101
alack, i am afraid they have awak'd, | and 'tis MAC 2.02. 9
i am afraid to think what i have done; 2.02. 48
poor country, | almost afraid to know itself! 4.03.165
i will not be afraid of death and bane, | till 5.03. 59
thou'lt be afraid to hear it. 5.07. 5
be not afraid though you do see me weapon'd; OTH 5.02.266
spirit | is all afraid to govern thee near him; ANT 2.03. 30
and childish error that they are afraid; VEN 898
play'd, | plays not at all, but seems afraid; PP 17.20
pity | and be not of my holy vows afraid. LC 179
AFRESH 5 FR 0.0005 REL FR 3 V 2 P
free for a husband, and then have to't afresh. SHR 1.01.139 P
and children are even now to be afresh lamented. WT 4.02. 25 P
wrongs i have done thee stir | afresh within me, 5.01.149
open their congeal'd mouths and bleed afresh! R3 1.02. 56
and weep afresh love's long since cancell'd woe, SON 30. 7
AFRIC 4 FR 0.0004 REL FR 3 V 1 P
as fresh as when we put them on first in afric, TMP 2.01. 70 P
and it were better parch in afric sun | than in TRO 1.03.369
not afric owns a serpent i abhor | more than thy COR 1.08. 3
i would they were in afric both together, CYM 1.01.167
AFRICA 1 FR 0.0001 REL FR 1 V 0 P
i speak of africa and golden joys. 2H4 5.03.100
AFRICAN 1 FR 0.0001 REL FR 1 V 0 P
daughter, | but rather loose her to an african, TMP 2.01.126
AFRONT 1 FR 0.0001 REL FR 0 V 1 P
these four came all afront, and mainly thrust at 1H4 2.04.200 P
/AFTER 5 FR 0.0005 REL FR 4 V 1 P
/after /th' /admired /heels /of /bullingbrook, 2H4 1.03.105
/not /live /long /after /i /saw /richmond. R3 4.02.107
/faintly /spoke | /after /the /prompter, /for ROM 1.04. 8

/hide /fox, /and /all /after. HAM 4.02. 31 P
/of /itself | /after /the /thing /it /loves. 4.05.164
AFTER 405 FR 0.0457 REL FR 304 V 101 P
but omit, my fortunes | will ever after droop. TMP 1.02.184
and after two days | i will discharge thee. 1.02.298
that mow and chatter at me, | and after bite me; 2.02. 10
his fit now, and does not talk after the wisest. 2.02. 73 P
after a little time | i'll beat him too. 3.02. 85
that, if i then had wak'd after long sleep, 3.02.139
let's follow it, and after do our work. 3.02.149 P
(like poison given to work a great time after) 3.03.105
the bat's back i do fly | after summer merrily. 5.01. 92
he after honor hunts, i after love: TGV 1.01. 63
he after honor hunts, i after love: 1.01. 63
look what thou want'st shall be sent after thee. 1.03. 74
when you fasted, it was presently after dinner; 2.01. 29 P
shipp'd, and thou art to post after with oars. 2.03. 34 P
is gone with her along, and i must after, | for 2.04.176
marry, after they clos'd in earnest, they parted 2.05. 12 P
as after much turmoil | a blessed soul doth in 2.07. 37
i'll after, to rejoice in the boy's correction. 3.01.384 P
after your dire-lamenting elegies, | visit by 3.02. 81
we'll wait upon your grace till after supper, 3.02. 95
i'll after, more to be reveng'd on eglamour 5.02. 51
and all his ancestors (that come after him) may. WIV 1.01. 15 P
rapier, and come after my heel to the court. 1.04. 59 P
i warrant you, coach after coach, letter after 2.02. 65 P
coach after coach, letter after letter, gift 2.02. 65 P
coach, letter after letter, gift after gift; 2.02. 66 P
will they yet look after thee? 2.02.140 P
wilt thou, after the expense of so much money, 2.02.140 P
after, we'll a-birding together. 3.03.230 P
instant of our encounter, after we had embrac'd, 3.05. 73 P
but, whilst i live, forget to drink after thee. MM 1.02. 39 P
but, after all this fooling, i would not have it 1.02. 70 P
is lechery so look'd after? 1.02.144
send after the duke and appeal to him. 1.02.174 P
the fairest house in it after threepence a bay. 2.01.241 P
i have seen | when, after execution, judgment 2.02. 11
which a dismiss'd offense would after gall, 2.02.102
shifts to strange effects, | after the moon. 3.01. 25
made by man and woman after this downright way 3.02.105 P
you have not been inquir'd after. 4.01. 19 P
after him, fellows, bring him to the block. 4.03. 65
and, after much debatement, | my sisterly 5.01. 99
first, let her show /her face, and after speak. 5.01.168
would close now, after his treasonable abuses! 5.01.342 P
it not, | yet did repent me, after more advice, 5.01.464
whipt first, sir, and hang'd after. 5.01.507
years became inquisitive | after his brother; ERR 1.01.126
straight after did i meet him with a chain. 4.04.140
him, | after you first forswore it on the mart, 5.01.262
with me — | after so long grief, such nativity! 5.01.407
or would you have me speak after my custom, as ADO 1.01.168 P
would you buy her, that you inquire after her? 1.01.179 P
then after to her father will i break, | and the 1.01.326
can see him but i am heart-burn'd an hour after. 2.01. 4 P
after he hath laugh'd at such shallow follies in 2.03. 9 P
come what plague could have come after it. 2.03. 83 P
hearken after their offense, my lord. 5.01.212 P
when after that the holy rites are ended, | i'll 5.04. 68
let fame, that all hunt after in their lives, LLL 1.01. 1
simplicity of man to hearken after the flesh. 1.01.218 P
fair weather after you! 1.02.144 P
your pocket like a man after the old painting; 3.01. 20 P
his inclination, after his undressed, unpolished 4.02. 16 P
of mercury are harsh after the songs of apollo. 5.02.930 P
perchance till after theseus' wedding-day. MND 2.01.139
in silence sad | trip we after night's shade. 4.01. 96
as bird from brier, | and this ditty, after me, 5.01.395
a while, | i'll end my exhortation after dinner. MV 1.01.104
after dinner | your hazard shall be made. 2.01. 44
do as i bid you, shut doors after you; 2.05. 53
after some oration fairly spoke | by a beloved 3.02.178
send the deed after me, | and i will sign it. 4.01.396
i was enforc'd to send it after him, | i was 5.01.216
after his death, of all he dies possess'd of. 5.01.293
you mean to mock me after; AYL 1.02.208 P
pursuit that will be made | after my flight. 1.03.137
and after one hour more 'twill be eleven, | and 2.07. 25
dry as the remainder biscuit | after a voyage, 2.07. 40
who after me hath many a weary step | limp'd in 2.07.130
if the cat will after kind, | so be sure will 3.02.103
and yet again wonderful, and after that, out of 3.02.192 P
after the shepherd that complain'd of love, 3.04. 48
no, faith, proud mistress, hope not after it. 3.05. 45
to glean the broken ears after the man | that 3.05.102
you would have her after you have possess'd her. 4.01.144 P
and after some small space, being strong at 4.03.151
that will i, should i die the hour after. 5.04. 12
after some question with him, was converted 5.04.161
and after, every of this happy number, | that 5.04.172
i, faith, boy, to have the next wish after, SHR 1.01.239
and then i know after who comes by the worst. 1.02. 14
after my death the one half of my lands, | and 2.01.121
of man | after his studies or his usual pain? 3.01. 12
i'll after him, and see the event of this. 3.02.127
but after many ceremonies done, | he calls for 3.02.169
carousing to his mates | after a storm, quaff'd 3.02.172
and after me, i know, the rout is coming. 3.02.181
let us entreat you stay till after dinner. 3.02.198
a fire, and they are coming after to warm them. 4.01. 5 P
our stomachs up | after our great good cheer. 5.02. 10
"after my flame lacks oil, to be the snuff | of AWW 1.02. 59
i, after him, do after him wish too, | since i 1.02. 64
i, after him, do after him wish too, | since i 1.02. 64
after well-ent'red soldiers, to return | and 2.01. 6
after them, and take a more dilated farewell. 2.01. 56 P
much blood let forth | and more thirsts after. 3.01. 4
and, after some dispatch in hand at court, 3.02. 54
when you find him out, you have him ever after. 3.06. 93 P
not seem too dear, | howe'er repented after. 3.07. 28
after, | to marry her, i'll add three thousand 3.07. 34
not till after midnight; 4.03. 29 P
how now, my lord, is't not after midnight? 4.03. 84 P
after he scores, he never pays the score. 4.03.224
i'll after them. 4.03.340
i will come after you with what good speed | our 5.01. 34
sirrah, inquire further after me. 5.02. 52 P
destroy our friends and after weep their dust; 5.03. 64
assure yourself, after our ship did split, TN 1.02. 9
go look after him. 1.05.136 P
run after that same peevish messenger, | the 1.05.300
not to be a-bed after midnight is to be up 2.03. 2 P
to be up after midnight and to go to bed then, 2.03. 7 P
so that to go to bed after midnight is to go to 2.03. 8 P
and after a demure travel of regard — telling 2.05. 53 P
send, | after the last enchantment you did here, 3.01.112
i have sent after him; 3.04. 1
not "malvolio," nor after my degree, but "fellow 3.04. 77 P
way till he take leave, and presently after him. 3.04.198 P
'slid, i'll after him again and beat him. 3.04.391 P
a good report — after fourteen years' purchase. 4.01. 23 P
fulsome to mine ear | as howling after music. 5.01.110
after him i love | more than i love these eyes, 5.01.134
struck anointed kings | and flourish'd after, WT 1.02.359
and what to her adheres, which follows after, 4.01. 28
would never dance again after a tabor and pipe; 4.04.182 P
come bring away thy pack after me. 4.04.312 P
more than man | and after that trust to thee. 4.04.536
hope is i shall so prevail | to force him after; 4.04.665
after i have done what i promis'd? 4.04.810 P
whereupon, after a little amazedness, we were 5.02. 5 P
thus, after greeting, speaks the king of france JN 1.01. 2
your father's wife did after wedlock bear him; 1.01.117
then after fight who shall be king of it? 2.01.400
nay, after that, consume away in rust, | but for 4.01. 65
go after him; 4.02.178
again | after they heard young arthur was alive? 5.01. 38
wherein we step after a stranger, march | upon 5.02. 27
after young arthur, claim this land for mine, 5.02. 94
maids | like amazons come tripping after drums, 5.02.155
after such bloody toil, we bid good night, | and 5.05. 6
after our sentence plaining comes too late. R2 1.03.175
gold, | and send them after to supply our wants, 1.04. 51
apish nation | limps after in base imitation. 2.01. 23
a while to work, and after holiday. 3.01. 44
after your late tossing on the breaking seas? 3.02. 3
after a well-graced actor leaves the stage, 5.02. 24
after, aumerle! 5.02.111
march sadly after, grace my mournings here, | in 5.06. 51
here, | in weeping after this untimely bier. 5.06. 52
and unbuttoning thee after supper, and sleeping 1H4 1.02. 3 P
and sleeping upon benches after noon, that thou 1.02. 4 P
set forth before or after them and appoint them 1.02.169 P
our vizards we will change after we leave them; 1.02.178 P
i will after straight | and tell him so, for i 1.03.126
who strook this heat up after i was gone? 1.03.139
he, and answers, "some fourteen," an hour after; 2.04.108 P
item, anchoves and sack after supper ... 2s.6d.. 2.04.538 P
jack, whose fellows are these that come after? 4.02. 62 P
in short time after, he depos'd the king, | soon 4.03. 90
soon after that, depriv'd him of his life, | and 4.03. 91
i sent | on tuesday last to listen after news. 2H4 1.01. 29
after him came spurring hard | a gentleman, 1.01. 36
his tongue | sounds ever after as a sullen bell, 1.01.102
ill it follows, after you have labor'd so hard, 2.02. 28 P
good wenches, how men of merit are sought after. 2.04.375 P
and in two year after | were they at wars. 3.01. 59
like a man made after supper of a cheese-paring. 3.02.309 P
this had been cheerful after victory. 4.02. 88
mayst effect | of mediation, after i am dead, 4.04. 25
thou hast stol'n that which after some few hours 4.05.101
dead, | and tell him who hath sent me after him. 5.02. 41
after this cold considerance, sentence me, | and 5.02. 98
who hath writ me down | after my seeming. 5.02.129
years | after defunction of king pharamond, H5 1.02. 58
him life | after the taste of much correction. 2.02. 51
for after i saw him fumble with the sheets, and 2.03. 13 P
ay, or more than we should seek after; 4.01.130 P
to see it, i will never trust his word after. 4.01.196 P
you'll never trust his word after! 4.01.202 P
ever thou come to me and say, after to-morrow, 4.01.214 P
next day after dawn, | doth rise and help 4.01.274
since that my penitence comes after all, 4.01.304
horses provender, | and after fight with them? 4.02. 59
life is come after it indifferent well, for 4.07. 32 P
and your eyes advance | after your thoughts, 5.pr. 45
royally, | after this golden day of victory. 1H6 1.06. 31
after that things are set in order here, | we'll 2.02. 32
long after this, when henry the fift 2.05. 82
and all the troops of english after him. 3.03. 32
and after meet you, sooner than you would. 3.04. 45
after some respite, will return to callice; 4.01.170
after the slaughter of so many peers, | so many 5.04.103
and listen after humphrey, how he proceeds. 2H6 1.03.149
who after edward the third's death reign'd as 2.02. 20
shall, after three days' open penance done, 2.03. 11
and after summer evermore succeeds | barren 2.04. 2
and with dimm'd eyes | look after him, and 3.01.219
and after all this fearful homage done, | give 3.02.224
if after three days' space thou here be'st found 3.02.295
the rascal people, thirsting after prey, | join 4.04. 51
shall we after them? 5.03. 27
after them! 5.03. 28
enjoy the kingdom after my decease. 3H6 1.01.175
come, we'll after them. 1.01.256
and after many scorns, many foul taunts, | they 2.01. 64
after the bloody fray at wakefield fought, 2.01.107
expostulate, make speed, | or else come after. 2.05.136
and after john of gaunt, henry the fourth, 3.03. 83
and after that wise prince, henry the fift, 3.03. 85
conceive, when, after many moody thoughts, | at 4.06. 13
but, warwick, after god, thou set'st me free, 4.06. 16
ay, and for much more slaughter after this. 5.06. 59
he hearkens after prophecies and dreams, | and R3 1.01. 54
(after i have solemnly interr'd | at chertsey 1.02.213
and, after many length'ned hours of grief, | die 1.03.207
no, no, my dream was lengthen'd after life. 1.04. 43
and for a season after | could not believe but 1.04. 61
after he once fell in with mistress shore. 3.05. 51
go after, after, cousin buckingham. 3.05. 72
go after, after, cousin buckingham. 3.05. 72
after the battle let george stanley die. 5.03.346
after the hideous storm that follow'd, was | a H8 1.01. 90
whom after under the /confession's seal | he 1.02.164
after your highness had reprov'd the duke 1.02.189
after "the duke his father," with the "knife," 1.02.203
their clothes are after such a pagan cut to't, 1.03. 14
after all this, how did he bear himself? 2.01. 30
now after | so many courses of the sun enthroned 2.03. 5
sweet at first t' acquire — after this process, 2.03. 9
or shortly after | this world had air'd them. 2.04.193
brings his physic | after his patient's death. 3.02. 41
and, after, this, and then to breakfast with 3.02.202
for after the stout earl northumberland 4.02. 12
pursu'd him still, and three nights after this, 4.02. 25
after my death i wish no other herald, | no 4.02. 69
too late, | 'tis like a pardon after execution. 4.02.121
porridge after meat! TRO 1.02.242 P
that after seven years' siege yet troy walls 1.03. 12
after so many hours, lives, speeches spent, 2.02. 1
after this, the vengeance on the whole camp! 2.03. 17 P
falling in, after falling out, may make them 3.01.103 P
/yet, after all comparisons of truth | (as 3.02.180
be call'd to the world's end after my name; 3.02.201 P
t' invite the troyan lords after the combat | to 3.03.236
after the general, i beseech you next | to feast 4.05.228
so much, | after we part from agamemnon's tent, 4.05.285
i'll after — nothing but lechery! 5.01. 97 P
thou take the river styx, | i would swim after. 5.04. 20
i saw him run after a gilded butterfly, and when COR 1.03. 60 P
he let it go again, and after it again, and over 1.03. 61 P
other's slave, | and the gods doom him after! 1.08. 6
we do request your kindest ears, and after, 2.02. 52
after the inveterate hate he bears you. 2.03.226
him | more after our commandment than as guided 2.03.230
son, | who after great hostilius here was king; 2.03.240
let us seem humbler after it is done | than when 4.02. 4
out of their burrows, like conies after rain, 4.05.212 P
rome, after the measure | as you intended well. 5.01. 46
what he would do | he sent in writing after me; 5.01. 68
i would not speak with him till after dinner. 5.02. 35 P
after your way his tale pronounc'd shall bury 5.06. 57
under a tree, | and never after to inherit it. TIT 2.03. 3
and after conflict such as was suppos'd | the 2.03. 21
thrash the corn, then after burn the straw. 2.03.123
guide, if thou canst, | this after me. 4.01. 70
the jest may remain, after the wearing, soly ROM 2.04. 63 P
thursday, | or never after look me in the face. 3.05.162
and left no friendly drop | to help me after? 5.03.164
which labor'd after him to the mountain's top TIM 1.01. 86
help the feeble up, | but to support him after. 1.01.108
your importunacy cease till after dinner, | that 2.02. 41
after distasteful looks, and these hard 2.02.211
if after two days' shine athens contain thee, 3.05.100
and thee after, when thou hast conquer'd! 4.03.105
know unthrift that was belov'd after his means? 4.03.311 P
men and hug them hard, | and after scandal them; JC 1.02. 76
and he will (after his sour fashion) tell you 1.02.180
and after that, he came thus sad away? 1.02.276
and after this let caesar seat him sure, | for 1.02.321
but men may construe things after their fashion, 1.03. 34
for it is after midnight, and ere day | we will 1.03.163
an act of rage, | and after seem to chide 'em. 2.01.177
whereto i am going, | after my speech is ended. 3.01.251
the evil that men do lives after them, | the 3.02. 75
let's after him, | whose care is gone before to MAC 1.04. 56
deeds must not be thought | after these ways; 2.02. 31
after life's fitful fever he sleeps well. 3.02. 23
that, sir, which i will not report after her. 5.01. 14 P
look after her, | remove from her the means of 5.01. 75
bring it after me. 5.03. 58
have after. to what issue will this come? HAM 1.04. 89
so, after pyrrhus' pause, | a roused vengeance 2.02.487
after your death you were better have a bad 2.02.525 P
use every man after his desert, and who shall 2.02.530 P
use them after your own honor and dignity — the 2.02.531 P
but that the dread of something after death, 3.01. 77
after the play | let his queen-mother all alone 3.01.181
and after we will both our judgments join | in 3.02. 86
looks raw and red | after the danish sword, and 4.03. 61
looking before and after, gave us not | that 4.04. 37
sir — after what flourish your nature will. 5.02.180 P
frame the business after your own wisdom. LR 1.02. 98 P
if i like thee no worse after dinner, i will not 1.04. 41 P
after i have cut the egg i' th' middle and eat 1.04.158 P
sir, more knave than fool, after your master. 1.04.314
would buy a halter, | so the fool follows after. 1.04.321
pursue him, ho! go after. by no means what? 2.01. 43
one that goes upward, let him draw thee after. 2.04. 74 P
which even but now, demanding after you, 3.02. 65
hot questrists after him, met him at gate, | who 3.07. 17
stroke which since | hath pluck'd him after. 4.02. 78
i must needs after him, madam, with my letter. 4.05. 15
go after her; she's desperate, govern her. 5.03.162
poison'd for my sake, | and after slew herself. 5.03.242
'tis not long after | but i will wear my heart OTH 1.01. 63
rouse him, make after him, poison his delight, 1.01. 68
have there injointed them with an after fleet. 1.03. 35
in the bitter letter | after your own sense; 1.03. 69
good grace shall think | to be sent after me. 1.03.287
and bring them after in the best advantage. 1.03.297
if thou dost, i shall never love thee after. 1.03.306 P
after some time, to abuse othello's /ear | that 1.03.395
if after every tempest come such calms, | may 2.01.185
in him that folly and green minds look after; 2.01.247 P
i pray you, after the lieutenant, go. 2.03.137
and his spirits should hunt | after new fancies. 3.04. 63
after her, after her. 4.01.162 P
after her, after her. 4.01.162 P
do but go after, | and mark how he continues. 4.01.280
and i will kill thee | and love thee after. 5.02. 19
i'll after that same villain, | for 'tis a 5.02.242
but now he spake | (after long seeming dead) 5.02.328
most gracious pardon, | i sing but after you. ANT 1.05. 73
to other and all loves to both | draw after her. 2.02.136
pray you hasten | your generals after. 2.04. 2
leaving the fight in heighth, flies after her. 3.10. 20
th' strings, | and thou shouldst /tow me after. 3.11. 58
outward | do draw the inward quality after them, 3.13. 33
go, eros, send his treasure after; 4.05. 12
antony | hath after thee sent all thy treasure, 4.06. 20

i'll halt after. 4.07. 16
let's do't after the high roman fashion, | and 4.15. 87
the gods give men | to excuse their after wrath. 5.02.287
after the slander of most stepmothers, CYM 1.01. 71
if after this command thou fraught the court 1.01.126
you have done | not after our command. 1.01.152
and which she after, | except she bend her humor 1.05. 80
first the lamb, | longs after for the garbage. 1.06. 50
not every man patient after the noble temper of 2.03. 4 P
after, a wonderful sweet air, with admirable 2.03. 17 P
go, look after. 3.05. 55
as i'ld give to him | (after long absence), such 3.06. 73
in the cave, | we'll come to you after hunting. 4.02. 2
son to the queen (after his own report), | who 4.02.119
after your will, have cross'd the sea, attending 4.02.334
revolts | during their use, and slay us after. 4.04. 7
being dead many years, shall after revive, be 5.04.142 P
after this strange starting from your orbs, 5.05.371
being dead many years, shall after revive, be 5.05.439 P
as thou | wilt live, fly after, and like an PER 1.01.161
out of the calendar, and nobody look after it. 2.01. 55 P
fortune, yet, that, after all /thy crosses, 2.01.121
and after shipwrack driven upon this shore. 2.03. 85
than to be thirsty after tottering honor, | or 3.02. 40
we wept after her hearse, | and yet we mourn. 4.03. 41
she would serve after a long voyage at sea. 4.06. 44 P
that, after holy tie and first night's stir, TNK pr 6
have sod their infants in (and after eat them) 1.03. 21
and after death our spirits shall be led | to 2.02.116
i lov'd my lips the better ten days after. 2.04. 26
o lady fortune | (next after emily my sovereign) 3.01. 16
after, | when you shall stretch yourself, and 3.01. 86
the /brake i meant, is gone | after his fancy. 3.02. 2
i'll tell you | after a draught or two more. 3.03. 19
after you, coz. 3.03. 30
his red lips, after fights, are fit for ladies. 4.02.111
"love comforteth like sunshine after rain, | but VEN 799
rain, | but lust's effect is tempest after sun; 800
which after him she darts, as one on shore 817
and would say after her, if she said "no." 852
sit, | long after fearing to creep forth again; 1036
for after supper long he questioned | with LUC 122
(and there she stay'd | till after a deep groan) 1276
story | the credulous old priam after slew; 1522
not speak, | till after many accents and delays, 1719
were | /yourself again after yourself's decease, SON 13. 7
after a thousand victories once foil'd, | is 25.10
the counterfeit | is poorly imitated after you; 53. 6
moan, | and mock you with me after i am gone. 71.14
in me that you should love | after my death, 72. 3
such day | as after sunset fadeth in the west, 73. 6
like widowed wombs after their lords' decease: 97. 8
drawn after you, you pattern of all those. 98.12
so run'st thou after that which flies from thee, 143. 9
in vowing new hate after new love bearing. 152. 4
AFTER-AGES 1 FR 0.0001 REL FR 1 V 0 P
will bear the curses else of after-ages | for TNK 3.06.187
AFTER-DEBTS 1 FR 0.0001 REL FR 1 V 0 P
he ne'er pays after-debts, take it before, | and AWW 4.03.226
AFTER-DINNER'S 2 FR 0.0002 REL FR 2 V 0 P
age, | but as it were an after-dinner's sleep, MM 3.01. 33
disgestion sake, | an after-dinner's breath. TRO 2.03.112
AFTER-EYE 1 FR 0.0001 REL FR 1 V 0 P
as a crow, or less, ere left | to after-eye him. CYM 1.03. 16
AFTER-HOURS 2 FR 0.0002 REL FR 2 V 0 P
which after-hours gives leisure to repent. R3 4.04.293
that after-hours with sorrow chide us not! ROM 2.06. 2
AFTER-INQUIRY 1 FR 0.0001 REL FR 0 V 1 P
or jump the after-inquiry on your own peril; CYM 5.04.182 P
AFTER-LOSS 1 FR 0.0001 REL FR 1 V 0 P
me bow, | and do not drop in for an after-loss. SON 90. 4
AFTER-LOVE 2 FR 0.0002 REL FR 2 V 0 P
for scorn at first makes after-love the more. TGV 3.01. 95
it be, | to win thy after-love i pardon thee. R2 5.03. 35
AFTER-MEETING 1 FR 0.0001 REL FR 1 V 0 P
as the main point of this our after-meeting, COR 2.02. 39
AFTERNOON 28 FR 0.0031 REL FR 15 V 13 P
a custom with him | i' th' afternoon to sleep. TMP 3.02. 88
of the clock, and in the afternoon barnardine. MM 4.02.122 P
who is to be executed in th' afternoon? 4.02.129 P
but barnardine must die this afternoon; 4.03. 83
but till this afternoon his passion | ne'er ERR 5.01. 47
o, this afternoon. LLL 3.01.155 P
it must be done this afternoon. 3.01.162 P
in the afternoon | we will with some strange 4.03.373
which the rude multitude call the afternoon. 5.01. 90 P
congruent, and measurable for the afternoon. 5.01. 92 P
and most vildly in the afternoon, when he is MV 1.02. 87 P
on ash we'nsday was four year in th' afternoon. 2.05. 27 P
please ye we may contrive this afternoon | and SHR 1.02.274
wench married in an afternoon as she went to the 4.04.100 P
while shameful hate sleeps out the afternoon. AWW 5.03. 66
this afternoon will post | to consummate this JN 5.07. 94
temple hall | at two /a' clock in the afternoon; 1H4 3.03.200
born about three of the clock in the afternoon, 2H4 1.02.188 P
son, | born to eclipse thy life this afternoon. 1H6 4.05. 53
widow, | even in the afternoon of her best days, R3 3.07.186
play the idle huswife with me this afternoon. COR 1.03. 70 P
shall have the drum strook up this afternoon. 4.05.215 P
me, | and, montague, come you this afternoon, ROM 1.01.100
some means to come to shrift this afternoon, 2.04.180
this afternoon, sir? well, she shall be there. 2.04.185 P
ride you this afternoon? MAC 3.01. 19
my orchard, | my custom always of the afternoon, HAM 1.05. 60
must needs entreat you | this afternoon to ride, TNK 2.05. 46
AFTER-NOURISHMENT 1 FR 0.0001 REL FR 1 V 0 P
have after-nourishment and life by care; PER 1.02. 13
AFTER-SUPPER 2 FR 0.0002 REL FR 2 V 0 P
hours | between /our after-supper and bed-time? MND 5.01. 34
come to me, tyrrel, soon, /at after-supper, R3 4.03. 31
AFTER-TIMES 1 FR 0.0001 REL FR 1 V 0 P
to sound the bottom of the after-times. 2H4 4.02. 51
/AFTERWARD 1 FR 0.0001 REL FR 0 V 1 P
/me /drunk, /and /afterward /pick'd /my /pocket. WIV 1.01.126 P
AFTERWARD 9 FR 0.0010 REL FR 7 V 2 P
and afterward determine our proceedings. TGV 3.02. 96
blood | and lack of temper'd judgment afterward. MM 5.01.473
mart, | and afterward consort you till bed-time: ERR 1.02. 28
we'll have dancing afterward. ADO 5.04.120 P
never to speak to lady afterward | in way of MV 2.01. 41
rescue in the first assault or ransom afterward. AWW 1.03.116 P
and afterward by substitute betroth'd | to bona, R3 3.07.181
on cats and dogs, | then afterward up higher; CYM 1.05. 39
and hang for't afterward! TNK 2.02.264
/AFTERWARDS 1 FR 0.0001 REL FR 0 V 1 P
/will /they /not /say /afterwards, /if /they HAM 2.02.348 P
AFTERWARDS 14 FR 0.0015 REL FR 6 V 8 P
and we will afterwards ork upon the cause with WIV 1.01.145 P
and the devil guide his cudgel afterwards! 4.02. 89 P
till you are executed, and sleep afterwards. MM 4.03. 33 P
you must hang it first, and draw it afterwards. ADO 3.02. 24 P
recount their particular duties afterwards. 4.01. 3 P
say "pardon" first, and afterwards "stand up." R2 5.03.112
that afterwards | we may digest our complots in R3 3.01.199
i shall speak as much as thou afterwards. TRO 2.01.112 P
afterwards, | as hector's leisure and your 4.05.272
like wrath in death and envy afterwards; JC 2.01.164
read it, afterwards seal it, and again return to MAC 5.01. 7 P
i should have found it afterwards well done, ANT 2.07. 79
if you seek us afterwards in other terms, you CYM 3.01. 79 P
most full flame should afterwards burn clearer. SON 115. 4
/AGAIN 6 FR 0.0006 REL FR 5 V 1 P
once /again crown'd, | and look'd upon, i hope, JN 4.02. 1
/say /that /again. R2 4.01.293
/now, "/o /earth, /yield /us /that /king /again, 2H4 1.03.106
/over /your /woes /again /by /viewing /mine: R3 4.04. 39
/old /fools /are /babes /again, /and /must /be LR 1.03. 19
/again to inflame it and to give satiety a fresh OTH 2.01.228 P
AGAIN 816 FR 0.0922 REL FR 643 V 173 P
yet again? TMP 1.01. 38 P
set her two courses off to sea again! 1.01. 50 P
how i cried out then, | will cry it o'er again. 1.02.134
to th' winds, whose pity, sighing back again, 1.02.150
they all have met again | and are upon the 1.02.233
damn'd, which sycorax | could not again undo. 1.02.291
weeping again the king my father's wrack, | this 1.02.391
no, it begins again. 1.02.396
thy nerves are in their infancy again | and have 1.02.485
italy removed | i ne'er again shall see her. 2.01.112
all were sea-swallow'd, though some cast again, 2.01.251
alas, the storm is come again! 2.02. 37 P
and it shall be said so again while stephano 2.02. 62 P
open your chaps again. 2.02. 86 P
fellow trinculo, we'll fill him by and by again. 2.02.177 P
lo, lo, again! bite him to death, i prithee. 3.02. 34 P
to hearken once again to the suit i made to thee 3.02. 39 P
after long sleep, | will make me sleep again; 3.02.140
me, that when i wak'd | i cried to dream again. 3.02.143
who once again | i tender to thy hand. 4.01. 4
in vain, | mars's hot minion is return'd again; 4.01. 98
say again, where didst thou leave these varlots? 4.01.170
my dukedom since you have given me again, | i 5.01.168
it were a shame to call her back again, | and TGV 1.02. 51
and yet take this again — and yet i thank you 2.01.118
writ, | but (since unwillingly) take them again. 2.01.123
for want of idle time, could not again reply; 2.01.166
and with your tears | moist it again, and frame 3.02. 75
here have i brought him back again. 4.04. 53 P
go, get thee hence, and find my dog again, | or 4.04. 59
again, | or ne'er return again into my sight. 4.04. 60
i pray thee let me look on that again. 4.04.125
and once again i do receive thee honest. 5.04. 78
if once again, | /milan shall not hold thee. 5.04.128
cancel all grudge, repeal thee home again, 5.04.143
o' my life, if i were young again, the sword WIV 1.01. 40 P
never come in mine own great chamber again else, 1.01.154 P
i'll ne'er be drunk whilst i live again, but in 1.01.181 P
come under my hatches, i'll never to sea again. 2.01. 93 P
woman, your husband is in his old lines again. 4.02. 22 P
shall i put him into the basket again? 4.02. 48 P
i'll appoint my men to carry the basket again, 4.02. 95 P
sirs, take the basket again on your shoulders. 4.02.108 P
pray heaven it be not full of knight again. 4.02.112 P
page, have you any way then to unfool me again? 4.02.115 P
why may not he be there again? 4.02.147 P
upon no trail, never trust me when i open again. 4.02.198 P
i think, in the way of waste, attempt us again. 4.02.212 P
let our wives | yet once again (to make us 4.04. 13
nay, i'll to him again in name of /brook; 4.04. 76
i will never take you for my love again, but i 5.05.118 P
i will never mistrust my wife again, till thou 5.05.133 P
what (but to speak of) would offend aain. MM 1.02.136
he calls again; 1.04. 14
froth, i could not give you threepence again. 2.01.104 P
not find you before me again upon any complaint 2.01.246 P
why dost thou ask again? 2.02. 9
to him again, entreat him, | kneel down before 2.02. 43
i, that do speak a word, | may call it again. 2.02. 58
i will bethink me. come again to-morrow. 2.02.144
her, | that i desire to hear her speak again? 2.02.177
dear sir, ere long i'll visit you again. 3.01. 46
you'll forswear this again. 3.02.167 P
i would the duke we talk of were return'd again. 3.02.173 P
the duke (i say to thee again) would eat mutton 3.02.181 P
but my kisses bring again, bring again, | seals 4.01. 5
but my kisses bring again, bring again, | seals 4.01. 5
mended again. the matter; proceed. 5.01. 91
call that same isabel here once again, i would 5.01.269 P
which consummate, | return him here again. 5.01.379
again, if any syracusian born | come to the bay ERR 1.01. 18
if i should pay your worship those again, 1.02. 85
till he come home again, i would forbear. 2.01. 31
go back again, thou slave, and fetch him home. 2.01. 75
go back again, and be new beaten home? 2.01. 76
as you love strokes, so jest with me again. 2.02. 8
and take unmingled thence that drop again, 2.02.127
here you must not, come again when you may. 3.01. 41
then, gentle brother, get you in again; 3.02. 25
establish him in his true sense again, | and i 4.04. 48
god, for thy mercy! they are loose again. 4.04.144
let's call more help | to have them bound again. 4.04.146
till i have brought him to his wits again, | or 5.01. 96
prayers, | to make of him a formal man again: 5.01.105
yet once again proclaim it publicly, | if any 5.01.130
met us again, and madly bent on us | chas'd us 5.01.152
of more aid, | we came again to bind them. 5.01.154
i never see a bachelor of threescore again? ADO 1.01.200 P
with love than i will get again with drinking, 1.01.251 P
but i would have thee hence, and here again. 2.03. 7 P
come, balthasar, we'll hear that song again. 2.03. 43
and send her home again without a husband. 3.03.163 P
nothing, unless you render her again. 4.01. 29
there, leonato, take her back again. 4.01. 31
hath drops too few to wash her clean again, 4.01.141
affliction may one day smile again, and till LLL 1.01.314 P
"fair" i give you back again, and "welcome" i 2.01. 91 P
breast, | and go well satisfied to france again. 2.01.152
to-morrow shall we visit you again. 2.01.176
i will add the l'envoy. say the moral again. 3.01. 88 P
first praise me, and again say no? 4.01. 14
to insert again my haud credo for a deer. 4.02. 19 P
i will look again on the intellect of the letter 4.02.133 P
well prov'd again a' my side! 4.03. 7 P
immediately they will again be here | in their 5.02.287
and utters it again when god doth please. 5.02.316
but take it, sir, again. 5.02.453
will you have me, or your pearl again? 5.02.458
we are again forsworn, in will and error. 5.02.471
and the whole world again | cannot pick out five 5.02.544
i bepray you let me borrow my arms again. 5.02.696 P
yet swear not, lest ye be forsworn again. 5.02.832
that fair again unsay. MND 1.01.181
to have his sight thither and back again. 1.01.251
i will make the duke say, "let him roar again; 1.02. 72 P
let him roar again." 1.02. 73 P
land | to fetch me trifles, and return again, 2.01.133
and be thou here again | ere the leviathan can 2.01.173
see a noise that he heard, and is to come again. 3.01. 92 P
i pray thee, gentle mortal, sing again. 3.01.137
"lower"? hark again. 3.02.305
"little" again? 3.02.326
lysander, speak again! 3.02.404
the man shall have his mare again, and all shall 3.02.463
other do, | may all to athens back again repair, 4.01. 67
methinks, being sensible, should curse again. 5.01.183 P
both | or bring your latter hazard back again, MV 1.01.151
swore he would pay him again when he was able. 1.02. 81 P
i am as like to call thee so again, | to spet on 1.03.130
to spet on thee again, to spurn thee too. 1.03.131
where is the horse that doth untread again | his 2.06. 10
i will survey th' inscriptions back again. 2.07. 14
i shall never see my gold again. 3.01.111 P
for, wooing here until i sweat again, | and 3.02.203
but, till i come again, | no bed shall e'er be 3.02.325
so fare you well till we shall meet again. 3.04. 40
i pray you know me when we meet again; 4.01.419
and waft her love | to come again to carthage. 5.01. 12
nor i in yours | till i again see mine! 5.01.192
i dare be bound again, | my soul upon the 5.01.251
if ever he go alone again, i'll never wrastle AYL 1.01.161 P
perforce, i will render thee again in affection. 1.02. 21 P
a pure blush thou mayst in honor come off again. 1.02. 29 P
quail | to bring again these foolish runaways. 2.02. 21
whom i took two cods and, giving her them again, 2.04. 53 P
turning again toward childish treble, pipes 2.07.162
shallow again. 3.02. 61 P
and yet again wonderful, and after that, out of 3.02.192 P
and when shalt thou see him again? 3.02.224 P
i marvel why i answer'd not again. 3.05.132
by two a' clock i will be with thee again. 4.01.181 P
he left a promise to return again | within an 4.03. 99
if i sent him word again, it was not well cut, 5.04. 73 P
if again, it was not well cut, he disabled my 5.04. 75 P
if again, it was not well cut, he would answer i 5.04. 77 P
if again, it was not well cut, he would say i 5.04. 79 P
and all their lands restor'd to /them again 5.04.164
them all, | to-morrow i intend to hunt again. SHR in.1. 29
and once again a pot o' th' smallest ale. in.2. 75
i would be loath to fall into my dreams again. in.2. 127 P
that we may yet again have access to our fair 1.01.116 P
nay, come again, | good kate; 2.01.218
i swear i'll cuff you, if you strike again. 2.01.220
spit in the hole, man, and tune again. 3.01. 40
book, | and as he stoop'd again to take it up, 3.02.162
what said the wench when he rose again? 3.02.166
sleeves should be cut out, and sew'd up again, 4.03.147 P
go on, and fetch our horses back again. 4.05. 9
why then let's home again. 5.01.147
but not frighted me, therefore i'll sleep again. 5.02. 43
marry, in blowing him down again, with the AWW 1.01.125 P
what, pale again? 1.03.169
thoughts | a modest one, to bear me back again. 2.01.128
to be young again, if we could, i will be a fool 2.02. 38 P
o lord, sir! — why, there't serves well again. 2.02. 62 P
haste you again. 2.02. 71 P
cheek for ever, | we'll ne'er come there again." 2.03. 72
when i lose thee again, i care not; 2.03.206 P
beat him, and if i could but meet him again. 2.03.241 P
and out of it you'll run again, rather than 2.05. 38 P
in hand at court, | thither we bend again. 3.02. 55
then hast thou all again. 3.02.102
read it again. 3.04. 3
hearing so much, will speed her foot again, 3.04. 37
let's return again and suffice ourselves with 3.05. 10 P
this instrument of honor again into his native 3.06. 66 P
which i will over-pay and pay again | when i 3.07. 16
linsey-woolsey hast thou to speak to us again? 4.01. 12 P
when back again this ring shall be deliver'd; 4.02. 60
he travel higher, or return again into france? 4.03. 42 P
never trust a man again for keeping his sword 4.03.144 P
i pray you, sir, put it up again. 4.03.216 P
we must to horse again. 5.01. 37
the time is fair again. 5.03. 36
and would never | receive the ring again. 5.03.101
go speedily and bring again the count. 5.03.152
i will return it home, | and give me mine again. 5.03.224
that strain again, it had a dying fall; TN 1.01. 4
would thou mightst never draw sword again. 1.03. 62 P
i would i might never draw sword again. 1.03. 64 P
bade take away the fool, therefore i say again, 1.05. 53 P
you come to me again | to tell me how he takes 1.05.281
i seem to drown her remembrance again with more. 2.01. 31 P
be never so hardy to come again in his affairs, 2.02. 10 P

to anger him we'll have the bear again, and we 2.05. 9 P
i bade you never speak again of him; 3.01.107
why then methinks 'tis time to smile again. 3.01.126
yet come again; 3.01.163
and i beseech you come again to–morrow. 3.04.210
well, come again to–morrow. 3.04.216
i will return again into the house and desire 3.04.241 P
'slid, i'll after him again and beat him. 3.04.391 P
now, sir, have i met you again? there's for you. 4.01. 24 P
sir, | and anon, sir, | i'll be with you again; 4.02.122
a dog and in recompense desire my dog again. 5.01. 7 P
sir, lullaby to your bounty till i come again. 5.01. 46 P
time as long again | would be fill'd up, my WT 1.02. 3
will take again your queen as yours at first, 1.02.336
come, sir, now | i am for you again. 2.01. 22
beseech your highness call the queen again. 2.01.126
a moi'ty of my rest | might come to me again. 2.03. 9
the love i bore your queen — lo, fool again! 3.02.228
the spirits o' th' dead | may walk again. 3.03. 17
you would never dance again after a tabor and 4.04.182 P
more, which will shame you to give him again. 4.04.241 P
and again does nothing | but what he did being 4.04.401
purchase the sight again of dear sicilia | and 4.04.511
then recover'd again with aqua–vitae or some 4.04.786 P
if he think it fit to shore them again, and that 4.04.837 P
you are one of those | would have him wed again. 5.01. 24
to bless the bed of majesty again | with a sweet 5.01. 33
to break his grave | and come again to me; 5.01. 43
her sainted spirit | again possess her corpse, 5.01. 58
be when your first queen's again in breath; 5.01. 83
know'st | he dies to me again when talk'd of. 5.01.120
then again worries he his daughter with clipping 5.02. 53 P
do not shun her | until you see her die again, 5.03.106
there | my mate, that's never to be found again, 5.03.134
now, by this light, were i to get again, | madam JN 1.01.259
we will bear home that lusty blood again | which 2.01.255
and part your mingled colors once again, | turn 2.01.389
and she again wants nothing, to name want, | if 2.01.435
cool and congeal again to what it was. 2.01.479
be well advis'd, tell o'er thy tale again. 3.01. 5
then speak again, not all thy former tale, | but 3.01. 25
that faith would live again by death of need. 3.01.214
as now again to snatch our palm from palm, 3.01.244
act of purposes mistook | is to mistake again; 3.01.275
and will again commit them to their bonds, 3.04. 74
if that be true, i shall see my boy again; 3.04. 78
and, rising so again, | when i shall meet him in 3.04. 86
it me) | and i did never ask it you again; 4.01. 44
here once again we sit; 4.02. 1
this "once again" (but that your highness 4.02. 3
but now i breathe again | aloft the flood, and 4.02.138
i have a way to win their loves again. 4.02.168
and fly, like thought, from them to me again. 4.02.175
and didst in signs again parley with sin, | yea, 4.02.238
your sword is bright, sir, put it up again. 4.03. 79
take again | from this my hand, as holding of 5.01. 2
my tongue shall hush again this storm of war, 5.01. 20
would not my lords return to me again | after 5.01. 37
return the president to these lords again, 5.02. 3
up once again! 5.04. 2
and welcome home again discarded faith. 5.04. 12
i say again, if lewis do win the day, | he is 5.04. 30
lords | by his persuasion are again fall'n off, 5.05. 11
and instantly return with me again | to push 5.07. 76
now these her princes are come home again, 5.07.115
obedience bids i should not bid again. R2 1.01.163
and both return back to their chairs again. 1.03.120
return again, and take an oath with thee. 1.03.178
that speaks thy words again to do thee harm! 2.01.231
yet again methinks | some unborn sorrow, ripe in 2.02. 9
t' other again | is my kinsman, whom the king 2.02.113
we three here part that ne'er shall meet again. 2.02.143
well, we may meet again. 2.02.149
for joy | to stand upon my kingdom once again. 3.02. 5
and, till so much blood thither come again, 3.02. 78
again uncurse their souls, their peace is made 3.02.137
let no man speak again | to alter this, for 3.02.213
and lands restor'd again be freely granted. 3.03. 41
on yon proud man should take it off again | with 3.03.135
restor'd again | to all his lands and signories. 4.01. 88
and wash him fresh again with true–love tears. 5.01. 10
to plant unrightful kings, wilt know again, 5.01. 63
give me mine own again, 'twere no good part | to 5.01. 97
so, now i have mine own again, be gone, | that i 5.01. 99
yet am i sick for fear, speak it again, | twice 5.03.133
"come, little ones," and then again, | "it is as 5.05. 15
then am i king'd again, and by and by | think 5.05. 36
but come yourself with speed to us again, | for 1H4 1.01.105
that, when he please again to be himself, 1.02.200
anon | he gave his nose and took't away again, 1.03. 39
and when i urg'd the ransom once again | of my 1.03.141
into the good thoughts of the world again; 1.03.182
nay, if you have not, to it again, | we will 1.03.257
have you any levers to lift me up again, being 2.02. 34 P
flesh so far afoot again for all the coin in thy 2.02. 36 P
i say unto you again, you are a shallow, 2.03. 15 P
breathe a while, and then to it again, and when 2.04.249 P
royal man, and send him back again to my mother. 2.04.291 P
three such enemies again as that fiend douglas, 2.04.368 P
money shall be paid back again with advantage. 2.04.547 P
leave | to tell you once again that at my birth 3.01. 36
the money is paid back again. 3.03.178 P
impawn'd | some surety for a safe return again, 4.03.109
i must go write again | to other friends, and so 4.04. 40
will you again unknit | this churlish knot of 5.01. 15
and move in that obedient orb again | where you 5.01. 17
every man | shall be my friend again, and i'll 5.01.108
or thou art like | never to hold it up again! 5.04. 40
again. 2H4 1.01. 48
and since we are o'erset, venture again. 1.01.185
and send you back again to your master for a 1.02. 18 P
what, to york? call him back again. 1.02. 64 P
bottle, i would i might never spit white again. 1.02.212 P
but i will have some of it out again, or i will 2.01. 76 P
and whether i shall ever see thee again or no, 2.04. 67 P
sent away post, i will see you again ere i go. 2.04.378 P
swingebucklers in all the inns a' court again; 3.02. 22 P
come prick bullcalf till he roar again. 3.02.176 P
would 'a say, and away again would 'a go, and 3.02.285 P
away again would 'a go, and again would 'a come. 3.02.285 P
we come within our aweful banks again, | and 4.01.174
i never thought to hear you speak again. 4.05. 91
o, thou wilt be a wilderness again, | peopled 4.05.136
well might lodge a fear | to be again displac'd; 4.05.208
and again, sir, shall we sow the hade land with 5.01. 14 P
it do, you shall have a dozen of cushions again; 5.04. 15 P
i /thee /defy again. H5 2.01. 72
me best, | if i begin the batt'ry once again, 3.03. 7
how shall i know thee again? 4.01.207 P
thou wilt once more come again for a ransom. 4.03.128 P
back again! 4.05. 11
thrice up again, and fighting; 4.06. 5
com'st thou again for ransom? 4.07. 70
till harry's back–return again to france. 5.pr. 41
your thoughts, straight back again to france. 5.pr. 45
to wear it in my cap till i see him once again, 5.01. 12 P
they do always reason themselves out again. 5.02.158 P
if henry were recall'd to life again, | these 1H6 1.01. 66
talbot, my life, my joy, again return'd? 1.04. 23
again, in pity of my hard distress, | levied an 2.05. 87
and once again we'll sleep secure in roan. 3.02. 19
fast | before he'll buy again at such a rate. 3.02. 43
damsel, i'll have a bout with you again, | or 3.02. 56
france, | either to get the town again, or die: 3.02. 79
we are like to have the overthrow again. 3.02.106
lost, and recovered in a day again! 3.02.115
done like a frenchman — turn and turn again! 3.03. 85
are not the speedy scouts return'd again | that 4.03. 1
he that flies so will ne'er return again. 4.05. 19
and turn again unto the warlike french. 5.02. 3
go, and be free again, as suffolk's friend. 5.03. 59
and i again, in henry's royal name, | as deputy 5.03.160
but, madam, i must trouble you again, | no 5.03.180
for, were there hope to conquer them again, | my 2H6 1.01.117
wounds | deliver'd up again with peaceful words? 1.01.122
nay, be not angry, i am pleas'd again. 1.02. 55
lays, | and never mount to trouble you again. 1.03. 91
could restore this cripple to his legs again? 2.01.131
to–morrow toward london back again, | to look 2.01.197
you four, from hence to prison back again; 2.03. 5
the world may laugh again, | and i may live to 2.04. 82
the enemy, | and undiscover'd come to me again, 3.01.369
he doth revive again. madam, be patient. 3.02. 36
bank | drove back again unto my native clime? 3.02. 84
to blush and beautify the cheek again. 3.02.167
alive again? 3.03. 12
who in contempt shall hiss at thee again; 4.01. 78
the lent shall be as long again as it is, and 4.03. 6 P
but stay, i'll read it over once again. 4.04. 14
and so farewell, for i must hence again. 4.05. 12
o' th' ear, and that will make 'em red again. 4.07. 87 P
now part them again, lest they consult about the 4.07.132 P
we are thy sovereign, clifford, kneel again; 5.01.127
you were best to go to bed and dream again, | to 5.01.196
then let my father's blood open it again, | he 3H6 1.03. 23
with this we charg'd again; 1.04. 18
we bodg'd again, as i have seen a swan | with 1.04. 19
o clifford, but bethink thee once again, | and 1.04. 44
for never henceforth shall i joy again, | never, 2.01. 77
you were, | making another head to fight again. 2.01.141
and once again bestride our foaming steeds, 2.01.183
foaming steeds, | and once again cry "charge!" 2.01.184
foes, | but never once again turn back and fly. 2.01.185
i vow to god above | i'll never pause again, 2.03. 30
now, lords, take leave until we meet again, 2.03. 42
the scatt'red foe that hopes to rise again; 2.06. 93
my face, | and as the air blows it to me again, 3.01. 85
so would you be again to henry, | if he were 3.01. 95
and i'll be chief to bring him down again; 3.03.263
then fare you well, for i will hence again, | i 4.07. 48
let's levy men, and beat him back again. 4.08. 6
and once again proclaim us king of england. 4.08. 53
and, weakling, warwick takes his gift again, 5.01. 37
doubt | will issue out again and bid us battle. 5.01. 63
we are, | we might recover all our loss again. 5.02. 30
famous grandfather | doth live again in thee. 5.04. 53
take up the sword again, or take up me. R3 1.02.183
speak it again, and even with the word | this 1.02.188
the spacious world cannot again afford. 1.02.245
what if it come to thee again? 1.04.133 P
i shall be reconcil'd to him again. 1.04.179
if you are hir'd for meed, go back again, | and 1.04.228
i'll win our ancient right in france again, | or 3.01. 92
farewell, until we meet again in heaven. 3.03. 26
and then again begin, and stop again, | as if 3.05. 3
a word, | and then again begin, and stop again, 3.05. 3
then he was urg'd to tell my tale again: 3.07. 31
here catesby comes again. 3.07. 82
call him again, sweet prince, accept their suit. 3.07.221
call them again. 3.07.224
come, let us to our holy work again. 3.07.246
lo, ere i can repeat this curse again, | within 4.01. 77
i say again, give out | that anne, my queen, is 4.02. 56
for i shall never speak to thee again. 4.04.182
perish | and never more behold thy face again. 4.04.187
again shall you be mother to a king; 4.04.317
of tears that you have shed | shall come again, 4.04.322
sail, and made his course again for britain. 4.04.527
let's whip these stragglers o'er the seas again; 5.03.327
that would reduce these bloody days again, | and 5.05. 36
now civil wounds are stopp'd, peace lives again; 5.05. 40
i say again, there is no english soul | more H8 1.01.146
treasons of his master | he shall again relate. 1.02. 8
travel, | and understand again like honest men, 1.03. 32
and a measure | to lead 'em once again, and then 1.04.107
when he was brought again to th' bar, to hear 2.01. 31
but he fell to himself again, and sweetly | in 2.01. 35
never found again | but where they mean to sink 2.01.130
for it grows again | fresher than e'er it was, 2.01.154
alas, poor lady! | she's a stranger now again. 2.03. 17
i swear again, i would not be a queen | for all 2.03. 45
therefore i say again, | i utterly abhor, yea, 2.04. 80
that again | i do refuse you for my judge, and 2.04.117
call her again. 2.04.125
again, there is sprung up | an heretic, an 3.02.101
springs out into fast gait, then stops again, 3.02.116
'tis well said again, | and 'tis a kind of good 3.02.152
in spite of fortune | will bring me off again. 3.02.220
he falls like lucifer, | never to hope again. 3.02.372
or gild again the noble troops that waited 3.02.411
y' are well met once again. 4.01. 1
then rose again and bow'd her to the people; 4.01. 85
and with the same full state pac'd back again 4.01. 93
he gave his honors to the world again, | his 4.02. 29
but this fellow | let me ne'er see again. 4.02.108
tower, | where, being but a private man again, 5.02. 90
win straying souls with modesty again, | cast 5.02. 99
let me ne'er hope to see a chine again, | and 5.03. 26
call here my varlet, i'll unarm again. TRO 1.01. 1
in brass, and such again | as venerable nestor, 1.03. 64
thus once again says nestor from the greeks: 2.02. 2
you shall make it whole again — you shall piece 3.01. 51 P
what, are you gone again? 3.02. 43 P
what, billing again? 3.02. 57 P
and they retort that heat again | to the first 3.03.101
like an arch, reverb'rate | the voice again, or, 3.03.121
what things again most dear in the esteem, | and 3.03.129
and still it might, and yet it may again, | if 3.03.185
the fountain of your mind were clear again, that 3.03.311 P
my lord, come you again into my chamber. 4.02. 36
where he answers again, "because thou canst not 4.04. 18 P
when shall we see again? 4.04. 57
o heavens, "be true" again? 4.04. 74
me a kiss | when helen is a maid again and his. 4.05. 50
i am not warm yet, let us fight again. 4.05.118
stand again. 4.05.248
tetter, take and take again such preposterous 5.01. 23 P
in faith, i do not. come hither once again. 5.02. 49
give't me again. 5.02. 70
it is no matter now i ha't again. 5.02. 72
farewell, | thou never shalt mock diomed again. 5.02. 99
now, | but thou anon shalt hear of me again; 5.06. 18
and when he caught it, he let it go again, and COR 1.03. 61 P
he let it go again, and after it again, and over 1.03. 62 P
again, and over and over he comes, and up again; 1.03. 62 P
catch'd it again: 1.03. 63 P
believe me, sirs, | we shall be charg'd again. 1.06. 4
if e'er again i meet him beard to beard, | he's 1.10. 11
i had rather have my wounds to heal again | than 2.02. 69
and 'twere to give again — but 'tis no matter. 2.03. 83 P
and, knowing myself again, | repair to th' 2.03.147
and now again, | of him that did not ask but 2.03.206
shall prompt them, to make road | upon 's again. 3.01. 6
in our ages see | their banners wave again. 3.01. 8
this was my speech, and i will speak't again — 3.01. 62
i say again, | in soothing them we nourish 3.01. 68
he cannot | be rein'd again to temperance; 3.03. 28
that the very hour | you take it off again? 3.03. 61
but a small thing would make it flame again; 4.03. 21 P
sir, his crest up again and the man in blood, 4.05.211 P
why then we shall have a stirring world again. 4.05.219 P
thrusts forth his horns again into the world, 4.06. 44
weaker sort may wish | good martius home again. 4.06. 71
but i fear | they'll roar him in again. 4.06.124
you know the way home again. 5.02. 97 P
or capitulate | again with rome's mechanics. 5.03. 83
i will not loose again, | till thou art here TIT 2.03.243
till all these mischiefs be return'd again, 3.01.273
farewell, proud rome, till lucius come again; 3.01.290
but say again, how many saw the child? 4.02.140
he says that he hath taken them down again, for 4.03. 82 P
and now, sweet emperor, be blithe again, | and 4.04.111
this will i do, and soon return again. 5.02.131
me, | or else i'll call my brother back again, 5.02.135
fair, | and tarry with him till i turn again. 5.02.141
o, let me teach you how to knit again | this 5.03. 70
sheaf, | these broken limbs again into one body. 5.03. 72
would i were dead, so you did live again! 5.03.173
if ever you disturb our streets again | your ROM 1.01. 96
nurse, come back again, | i have rememb'red me, 1.03. 8
swears a prayer or two, | and sleeps again. 1.04. 88
give me my sin again. 1.05.110
now romeo is belov'd and loves again, | alike 2.pr. 5
o, speak again, bright angel, for thou art | as 2.02. 26
and yet i would it were to give again. 2.02.129
but to be frank and give it thee again, | and 2.02.131
stay but a little, i will come again. 2.02.138
voice, | to lure this tassel–gentle back again! 2.02.159
and with a silken thread plucks it back again, 2.02.180
i'll tell thee ere thou ask it me again. 2.03. 48
here comes the furious tybalt back again. 3.01.121
take the "villain" back again | that late thou 3.01.125
o, thou wilt speak again of banishment. 3.03. 53
on romeo cries, | and then down falls again. 3.03.102
be much in years | ere i again behold my romeo! 3.05. 47
o, think'st thou we shall ever meet again? 3.05. 51
how shall that faith return again to earth, 3.05.206
god knows when we shall meet again. 4.03. 14
i'll call them back again to comfort me. 4.03. 17
dress'd, and in your clothes, and down again? 4.05. 12
that i ask again, | for nothing can be ill if 5.01. 15
i could not send it — here it is again — | nor 5.02. 14
but i will write again to mantua, | and keep her 5.02. 28
from this /palace of dim night | depart again. 5.03.108
men | upon whose age we void it up again | with TIM 1.02.138
so soon as dinner's done, we'll forth again, 2.02. 14
and nature, as it grows again toward earth, | is 2.02.218
and come again to supper to him of purpose to 3.01. 24 P
go, bid all my friends again, | lucius, lucullus 3.04.110
who then dares to be half so kind again? 4.02. 40
is it | that makes the wappen'd widow wed again; 4.03. 39
embalms and spices | to th' april day again. 4.03. 42
heart, | for showing me again the eyes of man! 4.03. 51
then the rot returns | to thine own lips again. 4.03. 66
if i thrive well, i'll visit thee again. 4.03.170
hadst thou wealth again, | rascals should have't 4.03.217
thou'dst courtier be again, | wert thou not 4.03.241
i know not what else to do, i'll see thee again. 4.03.354 P
you shall see him a palm in athens again, and 5.01. 10
i like this well, he will return again. 5.01.204
come not to me again, but say to athens, | timon 5.01.214
bid every noise be still; peace yet again! JC 1.02. 14
what say'st thou to me now? speak once again. 1.02. 22
then he offer'd it to him again; 1.02.241 P

then he put it by again; 1.02.241 P
when he came to himself again, he said, if he 1.02.269 P
you that, i'll ne'er look you i' th' face again. 1.02.282 P
get you to bed again, it is not day. 2.01. 39
i would have had thee there and here again | ere 2.04. 4
come to me again, | and bring me word what he 2.04. 45
now mark him, he begins again to speak. 3.02.117
a hasty spark, | and straight is cold again. 4.03.113
it was well done, and thou shalt sleep again; 4.03.264
well; then i shall see thee again? 4.03.284
sleep again, lucius. 4.03.299
when think you that the sword goes up again? 5.01. 52
and whether we shall meet again i know not; 5.01.114
if we do meet again, why, we shall smile; 5.01.117
if we do meet again, we'll smile indeed; 5.01.120
thee up to yonder troops | and here again, that 5.03. 17
i will be here again, even with a thought. 5.03. 19
when shall we three meet again? MAC 1.01. 1
to mine, | and thrice again, to make up nine. 1.03. 36
prayers, and address'd them | again to sleep. 2.02. 23
look on't again i dare not. 2.02. 49
ay, madam, but returns again to-night. 3.02. 2
then comes my fit again. 3.04. 20
to-morrow | we'll hear ourselves again. 3.04. 31
upon a thought | he will again be well. 3.04. 55
but now they rise again | with twenty mortal 3.04. 79
or be alive again, | and dare me to the desert 3.04.102
being gone, | i am a man again. 3.04.107
let's make haste, she'll soon be back again. 3.05. 36
work) we may again | give to our tables meat, 3.06. 33
'shall not be long but i'll be here again. 4.02. 23
then you'll buy 'em to sell again. 4.02. 41
when shalt thou see thy wholesome days again, 4.03.105
it, afterwards seal it, and again return to bed; 5.01. 7 P
i tell you yet again, banquo's buried; 5.01. 63 P
to the very echo, | that should applaud again. 5.03. 54
profit again should hardly draw me here. 5.03. 62
an unbattered edge | i sheathe again undeeded. 5.07. 20
what, has this thing appear'd again to-night? HAM 1.01. 21
night, | that, if again this apparition come, 1.01. 28
while, | and let us once again assail your ears, 1.01. 31
look where it comes again! 1.01. 40
lo where it comes again! 1.01.126
my thoughts and wishes bend again toward france, 1.02. 55
the king's rouse the heaven shall bruit again, 1.02.127
in all, | i shall not look upon his like again. 1.02.188
watch to-night, | perchance 'twill walk again. 1.02.242
and marble jaws | to cast thee up again. 1.04. 51
again in complete steel | revisits thus the 1.04. 52
it waves me forth again, i'll follow it. 1.04. 68
and lay your hands again upon my sword. 1.05.158
i'll speak to him again. 2.02.191 P
will bring him to his wonted way again, | to 3.01. 40
take these again, for to the noble mind | rich 3.01. 99
make us again count o'er ere love be done! 3.02.162
so, again, good night. 3.04.177
let the bloat king tempt you again to bed, 3.04.182
you, and, spunge, you shall be dry again. 4.02. 21 P
"and will 'a not come again? 4.05.190
and will 'a not come again? 4.05.191
go to thy death-bed, | he never will come again. 4.05.194
/a /wind, | would have reverted to my bow again, 4.07. 23
whose worth, if praises may go back again, 4.07. 27
now fear i this will give it start again, 4.07.193
to't again, come. 5.01. 49 P
lie, sir, 'twill away again from me to you. 5.01.128 P
and in fine withdrew | to mine own room again, 5.02. 16
well, again. 5.02.281
nay, come again. 5.02.303
lo here i lie, | never to rise again. 5.02.319
been out nine years, and away he shall again. LR 1.01. 33 P
nothing will come of nothing, speak again. 1.01. 90
nor shall ever see | that face of hers again. 1.01.264
if you will measure your lubber's length again, 1.04. 91 P
beweep this cause again, i'll pluck ye out, 1.04.302
to take't again perforce! monster ingratitude! 1.05. 39 P
he dies that strikes again. 2.02. 49
of this /dread exploit, | drew on me here again. 2.02.124
gives thee better counsel, give me mine again, i 2.04. 76 P
and speak't again, my lord, no more with me. 2.04.255
and there — and there again — and there. 3.04. 62 P
thee in my touch, | i'ld say i had eyes again. 4.01. 24
no, my good lord, i met him back again. 4.02. 90
speak yet again. 4.06. 55
let not my worser spirit tempt me again | to die 4.06.218
let but the herald cry, | and i'll appear again. 5.01. 49
if ever i return to you again, | i'll bring you 5.02. 3
what, in ill thoughts again? 5.02. 9
again! | again! 5.03.116
again! | again! 5.03.117
i say again, hath made a gross revolt, | tying OTH 1.01.134
and let ourselves again but understand | that, 1.03. 21
i therefore vouch again | that with some 1.03.103
she'ld come again, and with a greedy ear 1.03.149
at nine i' th' morning here we'll meet again. 1.03.279
thee often, and i retell thee again and again, i 1.03.365 P
and i retell thee again and again, i hate the 1.03.366 P
which now again you are most apt to play the sir 2.01.174 P
yet again, your fingers to your lips? 2.01.176 P
and duck again as low | as hell's from heaven! 2.01.188
into no true taste again but by the displanting 2.01.276 P
will you hear't again? 2.03.100 P
even as again they were | when you yourself did 2.03.238
are more ways to recover the general again. 2.03.272 P
sue to him again, and he's yours. 2.03.276 P
i will ask him for my place again, he shall tell 2.03.303 P
her help to put you in your place again. 2.03.319 P
and indeed the course | to win the moor again? 2.03.339
and a little more wit, return again to venice. 2.03.368 P
any music that may not be heard, to't again; 3.01. 16 P
/by /the /front | to bring you in again. 3.01. 50
but i will have my lord and you again | as 3.03. 6
and when i love thee not, | chaos is come again. 3.03. 92
/faith, that's with watching, 'twill away again. 3.03.285
for some purpose of import, | give't me again. 3.03.317
pray you let cassio be receiv'd again. 3.04. 88
that by your virtuous means i may again | exist, 3.04.111
futurity, | can ransom me into his love again, 3.04.118
when | he hath, and is again to cope your wife. 4.01. 86
her body and beauty unprovide my mind again. 4.01.206 P
and yet go on | and turn again; 4.01.254
iago, | what shall i do to win my lord again? 4.02.149
othello and desdemona return again to venice. 4.02.223 P
i can again thy former light restore, | should i 5.02. 9
thy rose, | i cannot give it vital growth again, 5.02. 14
i think she stirs again. 5.02. 95
o lady, speak again! 5.02.120
often hurl from us, | we wish it ours again. ANT 1.02.124
if thou with caesar paragon again | my man of 1.05. 71
hear no more words of pompey, return it again. 2.02.105 P
our hearts, and never | fly off our loves again! 2.02.152
but yet hie you to egypt again. 2.03. 15
i say again, thy spirit | is all afraid to 2.03. 29
call the slave again, | though i am mad, i will 2.05. 79
thee worser than i do, | if thou again say yes. 2.05. 91
if he do, sure he cannot weep't back again. 2.06.106 P
he will to his egyptian dish again. 2.06.126 P
i will employ thee back again; 3.03. 36
to him again, tell him he wears the rose | of 3.13. 20
being whipt, | bring him again; 3.13.103
our sever'd navy too | have knit again, and 3.13.171
but since my lord | is antony again, i will be 3.13.186
honor in the blood | shall make it live again. 4.02. 7
hie thee again. 5.02.194
i am again for cydnus | to meet mark antony. 5.02.228
never be beheld | of eyes again so royal! 5.02.318
this jewel in the world | that i may see again. CYM 1.01. 92
o the gods! | when shall we see again? 1.01.124
they were again together; 1.01.151
to th' trunk again, and shut the spring of it. 2.02. 47
and now 'tis up again. 2.04. 97
and take your ring again, 'tis not yet won. 2.04.114
and it gave me present hunger | to feed again, 2.04.138
had to take from 's, to resume | we have again. 3.01. 16
honor, | which he to seek of me again, perforce, 3.01. 71
madam, | i thought you would not back again. 3.04.116
or, by jupiter, | i will not ask again. 3.05. 85
safe mayst thou wander, safe return again! 3.05.105
court i'll knock her back, foot her home again. 3.05.144 P
the ground that gave them first has them again: 4.02.289
again; 4.03. 1
i have resum'd again | the part i came in. 5.03. 75
which neither here i'll keep nor bear again, 5.03. 82
letting them thrive again | on their abatement. 5.04. 20
all offices of nature should again | do their 5.05.257
you are upon a rock, and now | throw me again. 5.05.263
prithee, valiant youth, | deny't again. 5.05.290
here are your sons again, and i must lose | two 5.05.348
i am down again; 5.05.412
should again unite | his favor with the radiant 5.05.474
bells, steeple, church, and parish up again. PER 2.01. 43 P
it in rage, though calm'd have given't again. 2.01.132
but fortune, mov'd, | varies again; 3.ch. 47
and yet the fire of life kindle again | the 3.02. 83
how she gins | to blow into life's flower again! 3.02. 95
my wedded lord, i ne'er shall see again, | a 3.04. 9
walk, and be cheerful once again, reserve | that 4.01. 39
ay, to eleven, and brought them down again. 4.02. 16 P
i think you'll turn a child again. 4.03. 4
is now again thwarting /the wayward seas, 4.04. 10
leaves tharsus and again embarks. 4.04. 27
take me home again | and prostitute me to the 4.06.189
and to her father turn our thoughts again, 5.ch. 12
buried at tharsus, | and found at sea again! 5.01.197
descend again into their throats and have not TNK 1.02. 82
joy seize on you again! 1.05. 12
our arms again, and feel our fiery horses | like 2.02. 19
she locks her beauties in her bud again, | and 2.02.142
i say again, i love, and, in loving her, 2.02.178
and so fair, | let honest men ne'er love again. 2.02.231
he shall see thebes again and call to arms | the 2.02.248
night and stow her, | and all's made up again. 2.03. 33
and there i'll be, for our town, and here again, 2.03. 48
for our town, and here again, | and there again. 2.03. 49
do, maids will not so easily | trust men again. 2.06. 21
again betake you to your hawthorn house. 3.01. 82
i say again, | that sigh was breath'd for emily. 3.03. 43
i'll come again some two hours hence and bring 3.03. 49
if we can get her dance, we are made again. 3.05. 74
but a tree or twain | for a maypole, and again, 3.05.145
now to our sports again. 3.05.153
my cousin gave his faith | to visit me again, 3.06. 2
able once again | to out-dure danger. 3.06. 9
and safely presently | into your bush again, sir 3.06.111
decider of all injuries, | say, "fight again!" 3.06.154
let it not fall again, sir. 3.06.272
it, | and, by mine honor, once again it stands, 3.06.289
three fair knights, appear again in this place, 3.06.292
arcite, | i am friends again till that hour. 3.06.300
come shake hands again then, | and take heed, as 3.06.302
and then she wept, and sung again, and sigh'd, 4.01. 92
may return and settle again to execute their 4.03. 72 P
this i shall never do again. 5.01. 32
if she entreat again, do any thing, | lie with 5.02. 17
and ill lodging, | but i'll kiss him up again. 5.02. 98
three or four days | i'll make her right again. 5.02.105
higher, | anon the other, then again the first, 5.03.126
to fan and blow them dry again she seeks. VEN 52
then wink again, | and i will wink, so shall the 121
give me one kiss, i'll give it thee again, | and 209
the air, and forth again | as from a furnace, 273
and once made perfect, never lost again." 408
till his breath breatheth life in her again. 474
"o, thou didst kill me, kill me once again. 499
adon, "you will fall again | into your idle 769
she treads the path that she untreads again; 908
and sighing it again, exclaims on death. 930
and with his strong course opens them again. 960
sighs dry her cheeks, tears make them wet again. 966
and, beauty dead, black chaos comes again. 1020
sit, | long after fearing to creep forth again; 1036
and never wound the heart with looks again, 1042
who did not whet his teeth at him again, | but 1113
return again in haste, | thou seest our LUC 321
then collatine again by lucrece' side | in his 381
and he hath won what he would lose again; 688
night's black bosom should not peep again. 788
but long she thinks till he return again, | and 1359
and than | retire again, till meeting greater 1441
what he breathes out his breath drinks up again. 1666
the poisoned fountain clears itself again, | and 1707
lucrece, live again and see | thy father die, 1770
he doth again repeat, and that they swore. 1848
quoth she, "and come again to-morrow." PP 14. 5
't may be again, to make me wander thither: 14.10
were | /yourself again after yourself's decease, SON 13. 7
thou gav'st me thine not to give back again. 22.14
who even but now come back again, assured | of 45.11
i send them back again and straight grow sad. 45.14
to-morrow see again, and do not kill | the 56. 7
new, | spending again what is already spent: 76.12
he robs thee of, and pays it thee again. 79. 8
and so my patent back again is swerving. 87. 8
comes home again, on better judgment making. 87.12
rang'd, | like him that travels i return again, 109. 6
when he again desires her, being sat, | her LC 66
make | what i should do again for such a sake. 322
would yet again betray the fore-betray'd, | and 328

AGAINST *(also 'gainst)*

/AGAINST 6 FR 0.0006 REL FR 4 V 2 P
/against /the /state /and /profit /of /this R2 4.01.225
/undergo, | /to /weigh /against /his /opposite; 2H4 1.03. 55
/and /just /against /thy /heart /make /thou /a TIT 3.02. 17
/them /exclaim /against /their /own /succession? HAM 2.02.351 P
/and /maledictions /against /king /and /nobles, LR 1.02.147 P
/to /stand /against /the /deep //dread-bolted 4.07. 32

AGAINST 613 FR 0.0693 REL FR 484 V 129 P
though every drop of water swear against it, TMP 1.01. 59
o, the cry did knock | against my very heart. 1.02. 9
stomach, to bear up | against what should ensue. 1.02.158
you cram these words into mine ears against 2.01.107
good will is to it, | and yours it is against. 3.01. 31
yea, all the creatures, | against your peace. 3.03. 75
i do believe it | against an oracle. 4.01. 12
caliban and his confederates | against my life. 4.01.141
if i should take a displeasure against you, look 4.01.202 P
to whisper and conspire against my youth? TGV 1.02. 43
i throw thy name against the bruising stones, 1.02.108
excuse | hath he excepted most against my love. 1.03. 83
any, | except thou wilt except against my love. 2.04.155
and manage it against despairing thoughts. 3.01.249
ignorant | how she opposes her against my will? 3.02. 26
gentleman, | especially against his very friend. 3.02. 41
up my leg and make water against a gentlewoman's 4.04. 38 P
what matter have you against me? WIV 1.01.122 P
sir, i have matter in my head against you, and 1.01.124 P
you, and against your cony-catching rascals, 1.01.124 P
i will consent to act any villainy against him, 2.01. 99 P
consult together against this greasy knight. 2.01.107 P
hast thou no suit against my knight, my 2.01.212 P
she is too bright to be look'd against. 2.02.245 P
now are too too strongly embattled against me. 2.02.251 P
you go against the hair of your professions. 2.03. 40 P
do, | perforce, against all checks, rebukes, and 3.04. 80
so rails against all married mankind; 4.02. 23 P
knot, a /ging, a pack, a conspiracy against me. 4.02.118 P
(even strong against that match | and firm for 4.06. 27
against such lewdsters and their lechery | those 5.03. 21
upon your tongue | against my brother's life. MM 2.02.141
for i can speak | against the thing i say. 2.04. 60
my vouch against you, and my place i' th' state, 2.04.156
this is one lucio's information against me. 3.02.199 P
craft against vice i must apply. 3.02.277
i profess, i will plead against it with my life. 4.02.180 P
pardon me, good father, it is against my oath. 4.02.181 P
shall then have no power to stand against us. 4.04. 14 P
eminent body that enforc'd | the law against it! 4.04. 23
will not proclaim against her maiden loss, | how 4.04. 24
he speak against me on the adverse side, | i 4.06. 6
or else thou art suborn'd against his honor | in 5.01.106
for certain words he spake against your grace 5.01.129
words against me? 5.01.131
wretched woman here | against our substitute! 5.01.133
were testimonies against his worth and credit 5.01.244
here till he come and enforce them against him. 5.01.266 P
what can you vouch | against him, signior lucio? 5.01.324
against all sense you do importune her. 5.01.433
now trust me, were it not against our laws, ERR 1.01.142
against my crown, my oath, my dignity, | which 1.01.143
herein you war against your reputation, | and 3.01. 86
why at this time the doors are made against you. 3.01. 93
rout | against your yet ungalled estimation, 3.01.102
against my soul's pure truth, why labor you, 3.02. 37
arm'd and reverted, making war against her heir. 3.02.124 P
i'll stop mine ears against the mermaid's song. 3.02.164
thither i must, although against my will, | for 4.01.112
his own doors being shut against his entrance. 4.03. 89
on purpose shut the doors against his way. 4.03. 91
honor and mine honesty | against thee presently, 5.01. 31
against the laws and statutes of this town, 5.01.126
justice, most sacred duke, against the abbess! 5.01.133
justice, sweet prince, against that woman there! 5.01.197
you have of late stood out against your brother, ADO 1.03. 21 P
against whose charms faith melteth into blood. 2.01.180
had been invincible against all assaults of 2.03.115 P
it had, my lord, especially against benedick. 2.03.117 P
because i have rail'd so long against marriage; 2.03.237 P
against my will i am sent to bid you come in to 2.03.247 P
"against my will i am sent to bid you come in to 2.03.257 P
their pride | against that power that bred it. 3.01. 11
and counsel him to fight against his passion, 3.01. 83
it is an offense to stay a man against his will. 3.03. 82 P
i will write against it: 4.01. 56
these princes hold | against her maiden truth. 4.01.164
wisdom thus to second grief | against yourself. 5.01. 3
wit in the career, and you charge it against me. 5.01.136 P
love indeed, for i love thee against my will. 5.02. 67 P
although against her will, as it appears | in 5.04. 5
here's our own hands against our hearts. 5.04. 91 P
any purpose that the world can say against it, 5.04.106 P
flout at me for what i have said against it; 5.04.108 P
that war against your own affections | and the LLL 1.01. 9
how well he's read, to reason against reading! 1.01. 94
a dangerous law against gentility. 1.01.128

if drawing my sword against the humor of 1.02. 59 P
master, against the reason of white and red. 1.02.107 P
hard | against the steep–up rising of the hill? 4.01. 2
encounters mounted are | against your peace. 5.02. 83
are they | that charge their breath against us? 5.02. 88
give it the rein, for it runs against hector. 5.02.658 P
with complaint | against my child, my daughter MND 1.01. 23
you in some business | against our nuptial, and 1.01.125
and when she drinks, against her lips i bob, 2.01. 49
i'll charm his eyes against she do appear. 3.02. 99
are bent | to set against me for your merriment. 3.02.146
with this same play, against your nuptial. 5.01. 75
i'll have my bond, speak not against my bond, MV 3.03. 4
that i follow thus | a losing suit against him. 4.01. 62
of venice, | if it be proved against an alien, 4.01.349
thou hast contrived against the very life | of 4.01.360
me, begins to mutiny against this servitude. AYL 1.01. 23 P
to come in disguis'd against me to try a fall. 1.01.125 P
his own search, and altogether against my will. 1.01.135 P
and villainous contriver against me his natural 1.01.145 P
thee, he will practice against thee by poison, 1.01.150 P
mine own wit till i break my shins against it. 2.04. 59 P
i'll rail against all the first–born of egypt. 2.05. 61 P
brother's mouth | of what we think against thee. 3.01. 12
plenty in it, it goes much against my stomach. 3.02. 21 P
and we two will rail against our mistress the 3.02.278 P
but myself, against whom i know most faults. 3.02.281 P
i have heard him read many lectures against it, 3.02.347 P
more clamorous than a parrot against rain, more 4.01.152 P
the howling of irish wolves against the moon. 5.02.110 P
to give my hand oppos'd against my heart | unto SHR 3.02. 9
i'll buckler thee against a million. 3.02.239
be ready to come against you come with your 4.04.103 P
run, | and not unluckily against the bias. 4.05. 25
if knowledge could be set up against mortality. AWW 1.01. 31 P
how may we barricado it against him? 1.01.113 P
be said in't, 'tis against the rule of nature. 1.01.135 P
limit, as a desperate offendress against nature. 1.01.141 P
against the proclamation of thy passion, | to 1.03.174
i know i love in vain, strive against hope; 1.03.201
proclaim | myself against the level of mine aim, 2.01.156
i have then sinn'd against his experience and 2.05. 10 P
experience and transgress'd against his valor, 2.05. 11 P
at my hand, but we must do good against evil. 2.05. 48 P
shut his bosom | against our borrowing prayers. 3.01. 9
the king had married him | against his liking. 3.05. 54
all the intelligence in his power against you, 3.06. 31 P
i prithee do not strive against my vows. 4.02. 14
protest to love | that i will work against him; 4.02. 29
honor on my part, | against your vain assault. 4.02. 51
action contrives against his own nobility in his 4.03. 24 P
displeasure he hath conceiv'd against your son, 4.05. 76 P
stop my nose, or against any man's metaphor. 5.02. 13 P
he's fortified against any denial. TN 1.05.145 P
i know the knight is incens'd against you, even 3.04.260 P
i do assure you, 'tis against my will. 3.04.311 P
i'll have an action of battery against him, if 4.01. 34 P
uncivil and unjust extent | against thy peace. 4.01. 54
him, | so much against the mettle of your sex, 5.01.322
toby | set this device against malvolio here, 5.01.360
parts | we had conceiv'd against him. 5.01.362
gates open'd, | as mine, against their will. WT 1.02.198
did cry out | against the non–performance, 'twas 1.02.261
there is a plot against my life, my crown; 2.01. 47
against this cruelty fight thy side, | poor 2.03.191
since fate (against thy better disposition) 3.03. 28
i was promis'd them against the feast, but they 4.04.235 P
and sung this ballad against the hard hearts of 4.04.278 P
in with a whoobub against his daughter and the 4.04.616 P
shall he be set against a brick–wall, the sun 4.04.789 P
for i am proof against that title and what shame 4.04.840 P
be contrary, | oppose against their wills. 5.01. 46
a graceful gentleman, against whose person | (so 5.01.171
come those i have done good to against my will, 5.02.124 P
then you'll think | (which i protest against) i 5.03. 90
against whose fury and unmatched force | the JN 1.01.265
bent | against the brows of this resisting town. 2.01. 38
and stir them up against a mightier task. 2.01. 55
against th' /invulnerable clouds of heaven, 2.01.252
which here we came to spout against your town, 2.01.256
have we ramm'd up our gates against the world. 2.01.272
as we will ours, against these saucy walls, 2.01.404
arm, you heavens, against these perjur'd kings! 3.01.107
demand | why thou against the church, our holy 3.01.141
alone do me oppose | against the pope, and count 3.01.171
oath to oath, | thy tongue against thy tongue. 3.01.265
since thou swor'st is sworn against thyself, 3.01.268
kept, | but thou hast sworn against religion, 3.01.280
by what thou swear'st against the thing thou 3.01.281
oath the surety for thy truth | against an oath; 3.01.283
therefore thy later vows, against thy first, 3.01.288
parts | against these giddy loose suggestions; 3.01.292
against the blood that thou hast married? 3.01.301
knee i beg, go not to arms | against mine uncle. 3.01.309
holding th' eternal spirit, against her will, 3.04. 18
hand and seal | witness against us to damnation! 4.02.218
arm you against your other enemies, | i'll make 4.02.249
defend | my innocent life against an emperor. 4.03. 89
in, | that so stood out against the holy church, 5.02. 71
and his siege is now | against the /mind, the 5.07. 17
and against this fire | do i shrink up. 5.07. 33
against the duke of norfolk, thomas mowbray? R2 1.01. 6
dost thou object | against the duke of norfolk, 1.01. 29
will i make good against thee, arm to arm, 1.01. 76
to stir against the butchers of his life! 1.02. 3
never lift | an angry arm against his minister. 1.02. 41
against what man thou com'st, and what thy 1.03. 13
against the duke of herford that appeals me, 1.03. 21
against whom /com'st thou? 1.03. 33
as is the falcon's flight | against a bird, do i 1.03. 62
of "never to return" | breathe i against thee, 1.03.153
against my will to do myself this wrong. 1.03.246
which then blew bitterly against our faces, 1.04. 7
herself | against infection and the hand of war, 2.01. 44
house, | against the envy of less happier lands; 2.01. 49
but when he frowned it was against the french, 2.01.178
the french, | and not against his friends. 2.01.179
time, | in braving arms against thy sovereign. 2.03.112
to lift shrewd steel against our golden crown, 3.02. 59
thin and hairless scalps | against thy majesty; 3.02.113
in stiff unwieldy arms against thy crown; 3.02.115
bows | of double–fatal yew against thy state; 3.02.117
manage rusty bills | against thy seat: 3.02.119
and so your follies fight against yourself. 3.02.182
and oppose not myself | against their will. 3.03. 19
is mann'd, my lord, | against thy entrance. 3.03. 22
that lift your vassal hands against my head, 3.03. 89
and that my fortune runs against the bias. 3.04. 5
state, for every one doth so | against a change; 3.04. 28
against aumerle we will enforce his trial. 4.01. 90
of the christian cross | against black pagans, 4.01. 95
o, if you raise this house against this house, 4.01.145
child, child's children, cry against you "woe!" 4.01.149
against them both my true joints bended be. 5.03. 98
that sets the word itself against the word! 5.03.122
and do set the word itself | against the word, 5.05. 14
and be no more oppos'd | against acquaintance, 1H4 1.01. 16
against the irregular and wild glendower, | was 1.01. 40
up | the crest of youth against your dignity. 1.01. 99
did lead to fight | against that great magician, 1.03. 83
so i do, against my will. 2.02. 49 P
henry bullingbrook made head | against my power; 3.01. 64
and gave his countenance, against his name, | to 3.02. 65
turns head against the lion's armed jaws, | and, 3.02.102
honor hath he got | against renowmed douglas! 3.02.107
mortimer, | capitulate against us, and are up. 3.02.120
spleen, | to fight against me under percy's pay, 3.02.126
can make a head | to push against a kingdom, 4.01. 81
against the bosom of the prince of wales. 4.01.121
quality, | but stand against us like an enemy. 4.03. 37
true rule | you stand against anointed majesty. 4.03. 40
and 'tis but wisdom to make strong against him. 4.04. 39
as you yourself have forg'd against yourself 5.01. 68
considerations infinite | do make against it. 5.01.103
are confident against the world in arms. 5.01.117
against the panting sides of his poor jade | up 2H4 1.01. 45
there were matters against you for your life, to 1.02.133 P
john of lancaster against the archbishop and the 1.02.204 P
i can get no remedy against this consumption of 1.02.236 P
one power against the french, | and one against 1.03. 71
against the french, | and one against glendower; 1.03. 72
and come against us in full puissance, | need 1.03. 77
against the welsh, himself and harry monmouth; 1.03. 83
but who is substituted against the french, | i 1.03. 84
i beseech you i may have redress against them. 2.01.108 P
against northumberland and the archbishop. 2.01.175
grace says that which his flesh rebels against. 2.04.351 P
and both against the peace of heaven and him 4.02. 29
i am not here against your father's peace, | but 4.02. 31
against ill chances men are ever merry, | but 4.02. 81
and, when they stand against you, may they fall 4.04. 95
visor of woncote against clement perkes a' th' 5.01. 39 P
is many complaints, davy, against that visor. 5.01. 40 P
quarter bear out a knave against an honest man, 5.01. 49 P
which swims against your stream of quality. 5.02. 34
was like, and had indeed against us pass'd, H5 1.01. 3
if it pass against us, | we lose the better half 1.01. 7
than'cherishing th' exhibiters against us; 1.01. 74
to make against your highness' claim to france 1.02. 36
our proportions to defend | against the scot, 1.02.138
yesterday, | that rail'd against our person. 2.02. 41
you have conspir'd against our royal person, 2.02.167
render fair return, | it is against my will; 2.04.128
and that was against a post when he was drunk. 3.02. 41 P
which makes much against my manhood, if i should 3.02. 49 P
their villainy goes against my weak stomach, and 3.02. 52 P
who to disobey were against all proportion of 4.01.146 P
a private displeasure can do against a monarch! 4.01.199 P
'tis positive against all exceptions, lords, 4.02. 25
'tis expressly against the law of arms. 4.07. 2 P
against the french that met them in their bent 5.02. 16
than midday sun fierce bent against their faces. 1H6 1.01. 14
go'st | except it be to pray against thy foes. 1.01. 43
in arms this day against god's peace and the 1.03. 75 P
the other yet may rise against their force. 2.01. 32
red, | and fall on my side so against your will. 2.04. 51
this blot that they object against your house 2.04.116
thee, | against proud somerset and william pole, 2.04.122
first, lean thine aged back against mine arm, 2.05. 43
stoop then and set your knee against my foot, 3.01.168
that grudge one thought against your majesty! 3.01.175
then, thou fight'st against thy countrymen | and 3.03. 74
tongue | against my lord the duke of somerset. 3.04. 34
pretend | malicious practices against his state. 4.01. 7
provokes the mightiest hulk against the tide, 5.05. 6
when i imagine ill | against my king and nephew, 2H6 1.02. 20
and't please your grace, against john goodman, 1.03. 16 P
"against the duke of suffolk, for enclosing the 1.03. 20 P
against my master, thomas horner, for saying 1.03. 25 P
sweet aunt, be quiet, 'twas against her will. 1.03.143
against her will, good king? 1.03.144
the spite of man prevaileth against me. 1.03.214 P
against this proud protector with my sword! 2.01. 36
have practic'd dangerously against your state, 2.01.167
my use, | be brought against me at my trial day! 3.01.114
some, | and try your hap against the irishmen? 3.01.314
cade | oppose himself against a troop of kerns, 3.01.361
against the senseless winds shall grin in vain, 4.01. 77
let ten thousand devils come against me, and 4.10. 61 P
against thy oath and true allegiance sworn, 5.01. 20
and fight against that monstrous rebel cade, 5.01. 62
makes him oppose himself against his king. 5.01.133
so let it help me now against thy sword, | as i 5.02. 24
'twas by rebellion against his king. 3H6 1.01.133
he rose against him, being his sovereign, | and 1.01.141
art thou against us, duke of exeter? 1.01.147
with bootless labor swim against the tide, | and 1.04. 20
now in his life, against your holy oath? 1.04.105
and stood against them, as the hope of troy 2.01. 51
against the greeks that would have ent'red troy. 2.01. 52
may make against the house of lancaster. 2.01.176
warwick, canst thou speak against thy liege, 3.03. 95
more incens'd against your majesty | than all 4.01.108
yet am i arm'd against the worst can happen; 4.01.128
loss of some pitch'd battle against warwick? 4.04. 4
or did he make the jest against his will? 5.01. 30
war | against his brother and his lawful king? 5.01. 88
king | in deadly hate the one against the other; R3 1.01. 35
which thou once didst bend against her breast, 1.02. 95
god, her conscience, and these bars against me, 1.02.234
action shows itself | against my children, 1.03. 67
his majesty | against the duke of clarence, but 1.03. 85
bitterness of soul | denounc'd against thee, are 1.03.179
have you breath'd your curse against yourself. 1.03.239
that stir the king against the duke my brother. 1.03.330
(that now give evidence against my soul) | for 1.04. 67
you have been factious one against the other. 2.01. 20
i'll join with black despair against my soul, 2.02. 36
to brother, | blood to blood, self against self. 2.04. 63
that he will not be won to aught against him. 3.01.166
or that we would, against the form of law, 3.05. 42
something against our meanings, have prevented; 3.05. 55
albeit against my conscience and my soul. 3.07.226
men, | to fight against this guilty homicide. 5.02. 18
those whom we fight against | had rather have us 5.03.243
then if you fight against god's enemy, | god 5.03.253
if you do fight against your country's foes, 5.03.257
i read in 's looks | matter against me, and his H8 1.01.126
by my life, | this is against our pleasure. 1.02. 68
at which appear'd against him his surveyor, 2.01. 19
then my guiltless blood must cry against 'em. 2.01. 68
any malice in your heart | were hid against me, 2.01. 81
who first rais'd head against usurping richard, 2.01.108
and prove it too, against mine honor aught — 2.04. 39
against your sacred person — in god's name 2.04. 41
i have no spleen against you, nor injustice 2.04. 89
for no dislike i' th' world against the person 2.04.224
(i would be all) against the worst may happen. 3.01. 25
'em, | envy and base opinion set against 'em, 3.01. 36
the way of our profession is against it; 3.01.157
found | matter against him that for ever mars 3.02. 21
and anon he casts | his eye against the moon. 3.02.118
as doth a rock against the chiding flood, 3.02.197
packets | you writ to th' pope against the king. 3.02.287
but that i am bound in charity against it! 3.02.298
that therefore such a writ be sued against you, 3.02.341
and who dare speak | one syllable against him? 5.01. 39
or else no witness | would come against you. 5.01.108
i fear nothing | what can be said against me. 5.01.126
knaves as corrupt | to swear against you? 5.01.133
a man that more detests, more stirs against, 5.02. 74
face to face, | and freely urge against me. 5.02. 83
tales and informations | against this man, whose 5.02.146
we may as well push against powle's as stir 'em. 5.03. 16
three times was his nose discharg'd against me; 5.03. 45 P
as she is stubborn–chaste against all suit. TRO 1.01. 97
without cause, and merry against the hair; 1.02. 27 P
up in his tears an' 'twere a nettle against may. 1.02.176 P
it were no match, your nail against his horn. 4.05. 46
be menelaus, i would conspire against destiny. 5.01. 63 P
that cause sets up, with and against itself, 5.02.143
to stop his ears against admonishment? 5.03. 2
cur, ajax, against that dog of as bad a kind, 5.04. 13 P
you proceed especially against caius martius? COR 1.01. 26 P
against him first; 1.01. 28 P
staves as lift them | against the roman state, 1.01. 69
any wholesome act establish'd against the rich, 1.01. 83 P
the body's members | rebell'd against the belly; 1.01. 97
of the city | you cry against the noble senate, 1.01.186
against whom cominius the general is gone, with 1.03. 96 P
one infect another | against the wind a mile! 1.04. 34
set me against aufidius and his antiates, | and 1.06. 59
but is | able to bear against the great aufidius 1.06. 79
shall say against their hearts, "we thank the 1.09. 8
against the hospitable canon, would i | wash my 1.10. 26
set up the bloody flag against all patience, and 2.01. 75 P
ever spake against | your liberties and the 2.03.179
to cry | against the rectorship of judgment? 2.03.205
made you against the grain | to voice him consul 2.03.233
against the volsces for they had so vildly 3.01. 10
in authority, | against all noble sufferance. 3.01. 24
the people are incens'd against him. 3.01. 32
words till their decay against those measles 3.01. 78
against a graver bench | than ever frown'd in 3.01.106
which they have often made against the senate, 3.01.128
when it stands | against a falling fabric. 3.01.246
should grind it | and throw't against the wind. 3.02.104
from time to time | envied against the people, 3.03. 95
and my services are, as you are, against 'em. 4.03. 5 P
the people against the senators, patricians, and 4.03. 14 P
against my cank'red country with the spleen | of 4.05. 91
where against | my grained ash an hundred times 4.05.107
strength i did | contend against thy valor. 4.05.113
me, | who am prepar'd against your territories, 4.05.134
whether to knock against the gates of rome, | or 4.05.141
him | against us brats with no less confidence 4.06. 93
and defense | that rome can make against them. 4.06.128
to his banishment, yet it was against our will. 4.06.145 P
he knows not | what i can urge against him. 4.07. 19
mine ears against your suits are stronger than 5.02. 88
are stronger than | your gates against my force. 5.02. 89
stopp'd your ears against | the general suit of 5.03. 5
from weary wars against the barbarous goths, TIT 1.01. 28
you were as good to shoot against the wind. 4.03. 58
against the willful sons | of old andronicus. 4.04. 8
what's this but libelling against the senate, 4.04. 17
and see them ready against their mother comes. 5.02.205
your lady's love against some other maid | that ROM 1.02. 97
sweet, | and i am proof against their enmity. 2.02. 73
desirest me to stop in my tale against the hair. 2.04. 95 P
and 'a speak any thing against me, i'll take him 2.04.150 P
prepare her, wife, against this wedding–day. 3.04. 32
in the mean time, against thou shalt awake, 4.01.113
paris, to prepare up him | against to–morrow. 4.02. 46
for i come hither arm'd against myself. 5.03. 65
what further woe conspires against mine age? 5.03.212
as the time and place | doth make against me, of 5.03.225
bowing his head against the steepy mount | to TIM 1.01. 75
men shut their doors against a setting sun. 1.02.145
of long since due debts, | against my honor? 2.02. 39
i to disfurnish myself against such a good time, 3.02. 45 P
it is against my heart. 3.04. 21
such may rail against great buildings. 3.04. 65 P
what, are my doors oppos'd against my passage? 3.04. 79

swear against objects, | put armor on thine ears 4.03.123
that /scolds against the quality of flesh | and 4.03.156
a satire against the softness of prosperity, 5.01. 35
then do we sin against our own estate, | when we 5.01. 41
threat'ning sword | against the walls of athens. 5.01.167
his fellowship i' th' cause against your city, 5.02. 12
against our rampir'd gates and they shall ope, 5.04. 47
my sword — | against the capitol i met a lion, JC 1.03. 20
since cassius first did whet me against caesar, 2.01. 61
we all stand up against the spirit of caesar, 2.01.167
in all these men, and it is bent against caesar. 2.03. 6 P
friend demand why brutus rose against caesar, 3.02. 21 P
of caesar might | have stood against the world; 3.02.119
look, | i draw a sword against conspirators; 5.01. 51
be thou my witness that against my will | (as 5.01. 73
point against point, rebellious arm 'gainst arm, MAC 1.02. 56
knock at my ribs, | against the use of nature? 1.03.137
against those honors deep and broad wherewith 1.06. 17
and his subject, | strong both against the deed; 1.07. 14
who should against his murtherer shut the door, 1.07. 15
against | the deep damnation of his taking–off; 1.07. 19
swear in both the scales against either scale, 2.03. 9 P
thence | against the undivulg'd pretense i fight 2.03.131
his being thrusts | against my near'st of life; 3.01.117
and let them fight | against the churches; 4.01. 53
to high dunsinane hill | shall come against him. 4.01. 94
her young ones in her nest, against the owl. 4.02. 11
where the flight | so runs against all reason. 4.02. 14
quarrels unjust against the good and loyal, 4.03. 83
ears, | that are so fortified against our story, HAM 1.01. 32
against the which, a moi'ty competent | was 1.01. 90
a fault against the dead, a fault to nature, 1.02.102
truster of your own report | against yourself. 1.02.173
thy soul contrive | against thy mother aught. 1.05. 86
he truly found | it was against your highness. 2.02. 65
to give th' assay of arms against your majesty. 2.02. 71
so levied, as before, against the polack, | with 2.02. 75
but, as we often see, against some storm, | a 2.02.483
or to take arms against a sea of troubles, | and 3.01. 58
so | that it be proof and bulwark against sense. 3.04. 38
wag thy tongue | in noise so rude against me? 3.04. 40
mass, | with heated visage, as against the doom; 3.04. 50
against some part of poland. 4.04. 12
goes it against the main of poland, sir, | or 4.04. 15
how all occasions do inform against me, | and 4.04. 32
me | why you /proceeded not against these feats, 4.07. 6
i have seen myself, and serv'd against, the 4.07. 83
singeing his pate against the burning zone, 5.01.282
horses, against the which he has impawn'd, as i 5.02.148 P
six barb'ry horses against six french swords, 5.02.161 P
that's the french bet against the danish. 5.02.163 P
and yet it is almost against my conscience. 5.02.296
but as /a pawn | to wage against thine enemies, LR 1.01.156
your indignation against my brother till you can 1.02. 80 P
if you violently proceed against him, mistaking 1.02. 83 P
there's son against father: 1.02.110 P
there's father against child. 1.02.111 P
and did the third a blessing against his will; 1.04.103 P
if i would stand against thee, would the reposal 2.01. 68
you come with letters against the king, and take 2.02. 36 P
the puppet's part against the royalty of her 2.02. 37 P
against the grace and person of my master, 2.02.131
display'd so saucily against your highness — 2.04. 41
to oppose the bolt | against my coming in. 2.04.177
choose | to wage against the enmity o' th' air, 2.04.209
these daughters' hearts | against their father, 2.04.275
of them hath borne | against the old kind king; 3.01. 28
i am a man | more sinn'd against than sinning. 3.02. 60
oppos'd against the act, bending his sword | to 4.02. 74
'twas he inform'd against him, | and quit the 4.02. 92
he arrives he moves | all hearts against us. 4.05. 11
face | to be oppos'd against the /warring winds? 4.07. 31
should have stood that night | against my fire, 4.07. 37
(as, if i stay, i shall) | against the moor; OTH 1.01.147
scurvy and provoking terms | against your honor 1.02. 8
employ you | against the general enemy ottoman. 1.03. 49
so could err | against all rules of nature, and 1.03.101
of modern seeming do prefer against him. 1.03.109
this present wars against the ottomites. 1.03.234
adversities | make head against my estimation! 1.03.274
us be conjunctive in our revenge against him. 1.03.368 P
heavens | give him defense against the elements, 2.01. 45
exclaim no more against it. 2.03.310 P
and, my fortunes against any lay worth naming, 2.03.324 P
though other things grow fair against the sun, 2.03.376
thou dost conspire against thy friend, iago, 3.03.142
it speaks against her with the other proofs. 3.03.441
it is hypocrisy against the devil. 4.01. 6
thou hast taken against me a most just exception 4.02.207 P
all, all, cry shame against me, yet i'll speak. 5.02.222
man but a rush against othello's breast, | and 5.02.270
against my brother lucius? ANT 1.02. 89
did famine follow, whom thou fought'st against 1.04. 59
were't not that we stand up against them all, 2.01. 44
and make the wars alike against my stomach, 2.02. 50
regiment to a trull | that noises it against us. 3.06. 96
if not denounc'd against us, why should not we 3.07. 5
and their tongues rot | that speak against us! 3.07. 16
speak not against it, | i will not stay behind. 3.07. 18
though my reason | sits in the wind against me. 3.10. 36
and answer me declin'd, sword against sword, 3.13. 27
and be stag'd to th' show | against a sworder! 3.13. 31
against the blown rose may they stop their nose 3.13. 39
i fight against thee? 4.06. 36
against the flint and hardness of my fault, 4.09. 16
why is my lord enrag'd against his love? 4.12. 31
his honor | against the romans with cassibelan, CYM 1.01. 30
i make my wager rather against your confidence 1.04.110 P
i durst attempt it against any lady in the world 1.04.112 P
i will wage against your gold, gold to it. 1.04.132 P
you sin against | obedience, which you owe your 2.03.111
the present wrath | he hath against himself. 2.04.152
i'll write against them, | detest them, curse 2.05. 32
against all color here | did put the yoke upon 3.01. 50
against self–slaughter | there is a prohibition 3.04. 76
full weak to undertake our wars against | the 3.07. 5
which he did wave against my throat, i have 4.02.150
and to fight | against my lady's kingdom. 5.01. 19
so i'll fight | against the part i come with; 5.01. 25
shining synod of the rest | against thy deity. 5.04. 90
some of them too that die against their wills. 5.04.202 P
i speak against my present profit, but my wish 5.04.205 P
against the face of death | i sought the PER 1.02. 71
i trod upon a worm against my will, | but i wept 4.01. 78
the leavy shelter that abuts against | the 5.01. 51
he broke his whipstock and exclaim'd against TNK 1.02. 86
i am not | against your faith, yet i continue 1.03. 97
teach 'em | boldly to gaze against bright arms, 2.02. 35
do we all hold against the maying? 2.03. 36
me use my sword | against th' advice of fear. 3.01. 60
like a nightingale, | to put my breast against! 3.04. 26
against /thy own edict, follows thy sister, 3.06.145
as thou art just, thy noble ear against us; 3.06.174
were't one eye | against another, arm oppress'd 5.01. 22
have never been foul–mouth'd against thy law, 5.01. 98
and will perfume me finely against the wedding. 5.02. 89
if he will | against his conscience, let him ep 8
that you like rebels lift against the peace STM II.C 109
whet their detested knives against your throats, II.C 134
and all in vain you strive against the stream, VEN 772
against the welkin volleys out his voice; 921
dew | against the golden splendor of the sun! LUC 25
against love's fire fear's frost hath 355
thou back'st reproach against long–living laud, 622
for now against himself he sounds this doom, 717
here she exclaims against repose and rest, | and 757
her spite | against the unseen secrecy of night: 763
make war against proportion'd course of time; 774
let him have time against himself to rave, | let 982
"and whiles against a thorn thou bear'st thy 1135
against my heart | will fix a sharp knife to 1137
no man inveigh against the withered flow'r, 1254
and then against my heart he set his sword, 1640
against this coming end you should prepare, SON 13. 3
against the stormy gusts of winter's day | and 13.11
in me | worthy perusal stand against thy sight, 38. 6
against that time (if ever that time come) 49. 1
against that time when thou shalt strangely pass 49. 5
against that time do i insconce me here | within 49. 9
and this my hand against myself uprear, | to 49.11
against my love shall be as i am now | with 63. 1
fortify | against confounding age's cruel knife, 63.10
against the wrackful siege of batt'ring days, 65. 6
upon those boughs which shake against the cold, 73. 3
upon thy side against myself i'll fight, | and 88. 3
halt, | against thy reasons making no defense. 89. 4
for thee, against myself i'll vow debate, | for 89.13
not, | when i against myself with thee partake? 149. 2
or made them swear against the thing they see; 152.12
eye, | to swear against the truth so foul a lie! 152.14
against strange maladies a sovereign cure. 153. 8
against the thing he sought he would exclaim: LC 313

/AGAMEMNON 2 FR 0.0002 REL FR 0 V 2 P

/agamemnon /is /a /fool, /achilles /is /a /fool, TRO 2.03. 58 P
is a fool to be commanded /of /agamemnon, 2.03. 64 P

AGAMEMNON 25 FR 0.0028 REL FR 13 V 12 P

as hector of troy, worth five of agamemnon, and 2H4 2.04.220 P
duke of exeter is as maganimous as agamemnon, H5 3.06. 7 P
a man as troilus than agamemnon and all greece. TRO 1.02.245 P
great agamemnon, nestor shall apply | thy latest 1.03. 32
agamemnon, | thou great commander, nerves and 1.03. 54
were such | as agamemnon and the hand of greece 1.03. 63
great agamemnon, | this chaos, when degree is 1.03.124
sometime, great agamemnon, | thy topless 1.03.151
'tis agamemnon right! 1.03.164
one voice | call agamemnon head and general. 1.03.222
which is the high and mighty agamemnon? 1.03.232
we have, great agamemnon, here in troy | a 1.03.260
give a taste thereof forthwith | to agamemnon. 1.03.388
agamemnon, how if he had biles — full, all over 2.01. 2 P
come, what's agamemnon? 2.03. 43 P
agamemnon commands achilles, achilles is my lord 2.03. 52 P
agamemnon is a fool to offer to command achilles 2.03. 62 P
o agamemnon, let it not be so! 2.03.182
and he replies, "thanks, agamemnon." 3.03.261 P
captain–general of the army, agamemnon, /et 3.03.278 P
and to procure safe–conduct from agamemnon. 3.03.287 P
agamemnon? 3.03.289 P
great agamemnon comes to meet us here. 4.05.159
i thank thee, most imperious agamemnon. 4.05.172
here's agamemnon, an honest fellow enough, and 5.01. 51 P

AGAMEMNON'S 6 FR 0.0006 REL FR 6 V 0 P

and ne'er was agamemnon's brother wrong'd | by 3H6 2.02.148
is this great agamemnon's tent, i pray you? TRO 1.03.216
sir, pardon, 'tis for agamemnon's ears. 1.03.248
the wind, | it is not agamemnon's sleeping hour. 1.03.254
'tis agamemnon's wish, and great achilles | doth 4.05.152
so much, | after we part from agamemnon's tent, 4.05.285

AGATE–RING *(also agot, etc.)*

AGATE–RING 1 FR 0.0001 REL FR 0 V 1 P

not–pated, agate–ring, puke–stocking, 1H4 2.04. 70 P

AGAZ'D 1 FR 0.0001 REL FR 1 V 0 P

all the whole army stood agaz'd on him. 1H6 1.01.126

AG'D 4 FR 0.0004 REL FR 3 V 1 P

as dangerous to be ag'd in any kind of course, MM 3.02.225 P
ag'd sir, hands off. COR 3.01.177
an ag'd interpreter, though young in days. TIM 5.03. 8
love, dear love, and our ag'd father's right. LR 4.04. 28

AGE 224 FR 0.0253 REL FR 191 V 33 P

who with age and envy | was grown into a hoop? TMP 1.02.258
govern, sir, | t' excel the golden age. 2.01.169
and as with age his body uglier grows, | so his 4.01.191
let me embrace thine age, whose honor cannot 5.01.121
which would be great impeachment to his age, TGV 1.03. 15
to clothe mine age with angel–like perfection, 2.04. 66
you, | it would be much vexation to your age. 3.01. 16
where i thought the remnant of mine age | should 3.01. 74
falstaff will learn the /humor of the age, WIV 1.03. 83
worn to pieces with age to show himself a young 2.01. 22 P
receiv'd and did deliver to our age | this tale 4.04. 37
thou hast nor youth nor age, | but as it were an MM 3.01. 32
and most loathed worldly life | that age, ache, 3.01.129
hath homely age th' alluring beauty took | from ERR 2.01. 89
i see thy age and dangers make thee dote. 5.01.330
borne himself beyond the promise of his age, ADO 1.01. 14 P
in his youth that he cannot endure in his age. 2.03.240 P
as they say, "when the age is in, the wit is out 3.05. 34 P
trust not my age, | my reverence, calling, nor 4.01.167
blood of mine, | nor age so eat up my invention, 4.01.194
if it should give your age such cause of fear. 5.01. 56
as under privilege of age to brag | what i have 5.01. 60
man do not erect in this age his own tomb ere he 5.02. 78 P
beauty doth varnish age, as if new born, | and LLL 4.03.240
to wear away this long age of three hours MND 5.01. 33
the boy was the very staff of my age, my very MV 2.02. 67 P
eye and wrinkled brow | an age of poverty; 4.01.271
lame, | and unregarded age in corners thrown. AYL 2.03. 42
caters for the sparrow, | be comfort to my age! 2.03. 45
therefore my age is as a lusty winter, | frosty, 2.03. 52
oppress'd with two weak evils, age and hunger, 2.07.132
the sixt age shifts | into the lean and 2.07.157
of a span | buckles in his sum of age; 3.02.132
foolish chroniclers of that age found it was — 4.01.105 P
whose boughs were moss'd with age | and high top 4.03.104
a ripe age. is thy name william? 5.01. 20 P
beautiful | than any woman in this waning age. SHR in.2. 63
'tis age that nourisheth. 2.01.339
and in his waning age | set foot under thy table 2.01.401
and now by law, as well as reverent age, | i may 4.05. 60
long, | but on us both did haggish age steal on, AWW 1.02. 29
to which title age cannot bring thee. 2.03.199 P
by thee, in what motion age will give me leave. 2.03.234 P
no more pity of his age than i would have of — 2.03.240 P
my heart is heavy, and mine age is weak; 3.04. 41
whose age and honor | both suffer under this 5.03.162
with the innocence of love, | like the old age. TN 2.04. 48
to see this age! 3.01. 11 P
either thou art most ignorant by age, | or thou WT 2.01.173
i would there were no age between ten and 3.03. 59 P
i think they are given | to men of middle age. 4.04.108
is he not stupid | with age and alt'ring rheums? 4.04.399
strength indeed | than most have of his age. 4.04.404
age, thou hast lost thy labor. 4.04.760 P
now, in age, | is she become the suitor? 5.03.108
ah, none but in this iron age would do it! JN 4.01. 60
to be a make–peace shall become my age. R2 1.01.160
shall be extinct with age and endless /night; 1.03.222
thou canst help time to furrow me with age, 1.03.229
have, | and thy unkindness be like crooked age, 2.01.133
and let them die that age and sullens have, 2.01.139
words | to wayward sickliness and age in him. 2.01.142
who, weak with age, cannot support myself. 2.02. 83
the time shall not be many hours of age | more 5.01. 57
and wilt thou pluck my fair son from mine age, 5.02. 92
"look when his infant fortune came to age" | and 1H4 1.03.253
adam to the pupil age of this present twelve a' 2.04. 94 P
and, as i think, his age some fifty, or, by'r 2.04.424 P
of the age of two and twenty or threereabouts! 3.03.189 P
in this fine age were not thought flattery, 4.01. 2
to grace this latter age with noble deeds. 5.01. 92
as the malice of /this age shapes /them, /are 2H4 1.02.172 P
written down old with all the characters of age? 1.02.180 P
can no more separate age and covetousness than 1.02.229 P
(as, force perforce, the age will pour it in), 4.04. 46
and weak age | of indigent faint souls past H5 1.01. 15
you must learn to know such slanders of the age, 3.06. 80 P
he that shall see this day, and live old age, 4.03. 44
my comfort is, that old age, that ill layer–up 5.02.230 P
kind keepers of my weak decaying age, | let 1H6 2.05. 1
of death, | nestor–like aged, in an age of care, 2.05. 6
might but redeem the passage of your age! 2.05.108
becomes it thee to taunt his valiant age, | and 3.02. 54
place, | fitter for sickness and for crazy age. 3.02. 89
when sapless age and weak unable limbs | should 4.05. 4
my age was never tainted with such shame. 4.05. 46
then leaden age, | quicken'd with youthful 4.06. 12
rage, | to–morrow i shall die with mickle age. 4.06. 35
hell, | an age of discord and continual strife? 5.05. 63
he being of age to govern of himself? 2H6 1.01.166
warwick, my son, the comfort of my age, | thy 1.01.190
this dishonor in thine age | will bring thy head 2.03. 18
sorrow would solace, and mine age would ease. 2.03. 21
o miserable age! 4.02. 10 P
became a bricklayer when he came to age. 4.02.145
war, | and shame thine honorable age with blood? 5.01.170
me | that bows unto the grave with mickle age. 5.01.174
to achieve | the silver livery of advised age, 5.02. 47
york | shall be eterniz'd in all age to come. 5.03. 31
king, | had slipp'd our claim until another age. 3H6 2.02.162
o, pity, god, this miserable age! 2.05. 88
that none of you may live his natural age, | but R3 1.03.212
weigh it but with the grossness of this age, 3.01. 46
or else reported | successively from age to age, 3.01. 73
or else reported | successively from age to age, 3.01. 73
methinks the truth should live from age to age, 3.01. 76
methinks the truth should live from age to age, 3.01. 76
thee | that ever wretched age hath look'd upon. 3.04.105
thy age confirm'd, proud, subtle, sly, and 4.04.172
or i with grief and extreme age shall perish 4.04.186
but mine shall be a comfort to your age. 4.04.306
ungovern'd youth, to wail it /in their age; 4.04.392
old barren plants, to wail it with their age. 4.04.394
your children's children quits it in your age. 5.03.262
he would not in mine age | have left me naked to H8 3.02.456
and, to add greater honors to his age | than man 4.02. 67
prerogative of age, crowns, sceptres, laurels, TRO 1.03.107
the faint defects of age | must be the scene of 1.03.172
his pupil age | man–ent'red thus, he waxed like COR 2.02. 98
examples of the like hath been | within my age. 4.06. 52
and your misery increase with your age! 5.02.107 P
his name remains | to th' ensuing age abhorr'd." 5.03.148
in me, | nor wrong mine age with this indignity. TIT 1.01. 8
the cordial of mine age to glad my heart! 1.01.166
than his that shakes for age and feebleness. 1.01.188
give me a staff of honor for mine age, | but not 1.01.198
for pity of mine age, whose youth was spent | in 3.01. 2
i bring consuming sorrow to thine age. 3.01. 61
empress from me, i am of age | to keep mine own, 4.02.104
calm thee, and bear the faults of titus' age, 4.04. 29
hair, | nor age nor honor shall shape privilege; 4.04. 57
but if my frosty signs and chaps of age, | grave 5.03. 77
thou knowest my daughter's of a pretty age. ROM 1.03. 10
faith, i can tell her age unto an hour. 1.03. 11

were of an age. 1.03. 19
thou wilt fall backward when thou comest to age, 1.03. 56
a bell | that warns my old age to a sepulchre. 5.03.207
what further woe conspires against mine age? 5.03.212
pleas'd the gods to remember my father's age, TIM 1.02. 2
those men | upon whose age we void it up again 1.02.138
i cannot think but your age has forgot me, | it 3.05. 92
pity not honor'd age for his white beard, | he 4.03.112
age, thou art sham'd! JC 1.02.150
when went there by an age since the great flood 1.02.152
rushing on us, should do your age some mischief. 3.01. 93
the choice and master spirits of this age. 3.01.163
may, | lovers in peace, lead on our days to age! 5.01. 94
that of an hour's age doth hiss the speaker; MAC 4.03.175
leaf, | and that which should accompany old age, 5.03. 24
by heaven it is as proper to our age | to cast HAM 2.01.111
that so his sickness, age, and impotence | was 2.02. 66
and the very age and body of the time his form 3.02. 23 P
for at your age | the heyday in the blood is 3.04. 68
stood challenger on mount of all the age | for 4.07. 28
than settled age his sables and his weeds, 4.07. 80
"but age with his stealing steps | hath clawed 5.01. 71
the age is grown so pick'd that the toe of the 5.01.139 P
same breed that i know the drossy age dotes on, 5.02.189 P
to shake all cares and business from our age, LR 1.01. 39
the argument of your praise, balm of your age, 1.01.215
you see how full of changes his age is; 1.01.288 P
'tis the infirmity of his age, yet he hath ever 1.01.293 P
must we look from his age to receive not alone 1.01.296 P
and reverence of age makes the world bitter to 1.02. 46 P
that, sons at perfect age and fathers declin'd, 1.02. 72 P
depend, | to be such men as may besort your age, 1.04.251
age is unnecessary. 2.04.155
as full of grief as age, wretched in both. 2.04.273
us hate thee, | life would not yield to age. 4.01. 12
whose age had charms in it, whose title more, 5.03. 48
it /yet hath felt no age nor known no sorrow. OTH 3.04. 37
though age from folly could not give me freedom, ANT 1.03. 57
age cannot wither her, nor custom stale | her 2.02.234
my youth, thou heap'st | a year's age on me. CYM 1.01.133
well corresponding | with your stiff age; 3.03. 32
have skipp'd from sixteen years of age to sixty, 4.02.199
he it is that hath | assum'd this age: 5.05.319
height, her age, with warrant of her virginity, PER 4.02. 58 P
and you, to outlive the age i am, | and die as i 5.01. 15
/ravish'd our sides, like age, must run to rust, TNK 2.02. 22
her age must find us, | and which is heaviest, 2.02. 28
ourselves shall we ev'r see | to glad our age, 2.02. 34
his age some five and twenty. 4.02.116
his age some six and thirty. 4.02.139
we prevent | the loathsome misery of age, 5.04. 7
thy mark is feeble age, but thy false dart VEN 941
teaching decrepit age to tread the measures; 1148
which virtue gave the golden age to gild | their LUC 60
with honor, wealth, and ease, in waning age; 142
respect and reason, wait on wrinkled age! 275
"how will thy shame be seeded in thine age, 603
one poor retiring minute in an age | would 962
even so this pattern of the worn-out age 1350
in thy sweet semblance my old age new born, 1759
and age in love, loves not to have years told. PP 1.12
crabbed age and youth cannot live together: 12. 1
youth is full of pleasance, age is full of care, 12. 2
youth like summer morn, age like winter weather, 12. 3
youth like summer brave, age like winter bare. 12. 4
breath is short, | youth is nimble, age is lame, 12. 6
youth is hot and bold, age is weak and cold, 12. 7
weak and cold, | youth is wild, and age is tame. 12. 8
age, i do abhor thee, youth, i do adore thee: 12. 9
age, i do defy thee. 12.11
then, | when time with age shall them attaint. 18.46
so thou through windows of thine age shalt see, SON 3.11
resembling strong youth in his middle age, | yet 7. 6
car, | like feeble age he reeleth from the day, 7.10
without this, folly, age, and cold decay. 11. 6
the age to come would say, "this poet lies, 17. 7
so should my papers (yellowed with their age) 17. 9
my friend's muse grown with this growing age, 32.10
painting my age with beauty of thy days. 62.14
the rich proud cost of outworn buried age; 64. 2
anon | doubting the filching age will steal his 75. 6
for fear of which, hear this, thou age unbred: 104.13
and peace proclaims olives of endless age. 107. 8
case | weighs not the dust and injury of age, 108.10
in the old age black was not counted fair, | or 127. 1
and age in love loves not t' have years told. 138.12
beauty peep'd through lettice of sear'd age. LC 14
and, privileg'd by age, desires to know | in 62
assuage, | 'tis promis'd in the charity of age. 70
old, | not age, but sorrow, over me hath power; 74

/AGED 1 FR 0.0001 REL FR 1 V 0 P
/a /father, /and /a /gracious /aged /man, LR 4.02. 41

AGED 29 FR 0.0032 REL FR 28 V 1 P
shorten up their sinews | with aged cramps, and TMP 4.01.260
and coy, | and nought esteems my aged eloquence. TGV 3.01. 83
for all thy blessed youth | becomes as aged, and MM 3.01. 35
words | that aged ears play truant at his tales, LLL 2.01. 74
whose aged honor cites a virtuous youth, | did AWW 1.03.210
much wrinkled, nothing | so aged as this seems. WT 5.03. 29
what comfort, man? how is't with aged gaunt? R2 2.01. 72
with signs of war about his aged neck. 2.02. 74
nestor-like aged, in an age of care, | argue the 1H6 2.05. 6
first, lean thine aged back against mine arm, 2.05. 43
forgets | aged contusions and all brush of time, 2H6 5.03. 3
hath dimm'd your infant morn to aged night. R3 4.04. 16
to the happiness of england, | an aged princess; H8 5.04. 57
"aged custom, | but by your voices, will not so COR 2.03.168
see | filling the aged wrinkles in my cheeks, TIT 3.01. 7
o gentle, aged men! 3.01. 23
titus, prepare thy aged eyes to weep, | or, if 3.01. 59
for i can smooth and fill his aged ears | with 4.04. 96
let him, | as he regards his aged father's life. 5.02.130
and take our goodly aged men by th' beards, TIM 5.01.172
speaks it, | in pity of our aged and our youth, 5.01.176
fond bondage in the oppression of aged tyranny, LR 1.02. 50 P
a drop of blood a day, and, being aged, | die of CYM 1.01.157
i shall with aged patience bear your yoke. PER 2.04. 48
that shook the aged forest with their echoes, TNK 2.02. 47
the aged cramp | had screw'd his square foot 5.01.110
not /one of you should live an aged man, | for STM II.C 83
"the aged man that coffers up his gold | is LUC 855
to stamp the seal of time in aged things, | to 941

AGENOR 1 FR 0.0001 REL FR 1 V 0 P
her face, | such as the daughter of agenor had, SHR 1.01.168

AGENT 10 FR 0.0011 REL FR 8 V 2 P
here is her hand, the agent of her heart; TGV 1.03. 46
this ungenitur'd agent will unpeople the MM 3.02.174 P
eye negotiate for itself, | and trust no agent; ADO 2.01.179
fertile bosom, | and well become the agent; WT 1.02.114
whiles we, god's wrathful agent, do correct JN 2.01. 87
tongue | (the agent of thy foul inconstancy) 2H6 3.02.115
and | is posted, as the agent of our cardinal, H8 3.02. 59
thus is the poor agent despis'd! TRO 5.10. 36 P
up | each corporal agent to this terrible feat. MAC 1.07. 80
the agent for his master, | and the remembrancer CYM 1.05. 76

AGENTS 5 FR 0.0005 REL FR 5 V 0 P
being the agents or base second means, | the 1H4 1.03.165
the former agents, if they did complain, | what COR 1.01.123
whiles night's black agents to their preys do MAC 3.02. 53
to themselves | been death's most horrid agents, TNK 1.01.144
fed, | his other agents aim at like delight? VEN 400

AGE'S 6 FR 0.0006 REL FR 5 V 1 P
word too great for any mouth of this age's size. AYL 3.02.227 P
sweet, sweet, sweet poison for the age's tooth, JN 1.01.213
and groaning underneath this age's yoke, | have JC 1.02. 61
youth is full of sport, age's breath is short, PP 12. 5
morn | hath travell'd on to age's steepy night, SON 63. 5
fortify | against confounding age's cruel knife, 63.10

AGES 13 FR 0.0014 REL FR 11 V 2 P
all sects, all ages smack of this vice, and he MM 2.02. 5
guilty of such a ballet some three ages since, LLL 1.02.112 P
plays many parts, | his acts being seven ages. AYL 2.07.143
well you fit our ages | with flow'rs of winter. WT 4.04. 78
your ages? 4.04.719 P
and future ages groan for this foul act. R2 4.01.138
/thee tales | of woeful ages long ago betid; 5.01. 42
and that hereafter ages may behold | what ruin 1H6 2.02. 10
which, since, succeeding ages have re-edified. R3 3.01. 71
that we shall hardly in our ages see | their COR 3.01. 7
for i know your reverend ages love | security, TIM 3.05. 79
how many ages hence | shall this our lofty scene JC 3.01.111
tomb, | and to be prais'd of ages yet to be. SON 101.12

AGGRAVATE 5 FR 0.0005 REL FR 2 V 3 P
ford's a knave, and i will aggravate his style; WIV 2.02.284 P
but i will aggravate my voice so that i will MND 1.02. 81 P
once more, the more to aggravate the note, R2 1.01. 43
i beseek you now, aggravate your choler. 2H4 2.04.162 P
and let that pine to aggravate thy store; SON 146.10

AGGRIEF'D 1 FR 0.0001 REL FR 0 V 1 P
that shall find himself aggrief'd at this glove; H5 4.07.163 P

AGHAST 1 FR 0.0001 REL FR 1 V 0 P
with prey, | make lanes in troops aghast. TNK 1.04. 19

/AGILE 1 FR 0.0001 REL FR 1 V 0 P
his /agile arm beats down their fatal points, ROM 3.01.166

AGINCOURT 4 FR 0.0004 REL FR 4 V 0 P
that did affright the air at agincourt? H5 pr 14
in brawl ridiculous) | the name of agincourt. 4.pr. 52
they call it agincourt. 4.07. 89
then call we this the field of agincourt, 4.07. 90

AGITATION 2 FR 0.0002 REL FR 0 V 2 P
and so now i speak my agitation of the matter; MV 3.05. 4 P
in this slumb'ry agitation, besides her walking MAC 5.01. 11 P

AGLET-BABY 1 FR 0.0001 REL FR 0 V 1 P
and marry him to a puppet or an aglet-baby, or SHR 1.02. 79 P

AGLETS 1 FR 0.0001 REL FR 1 V 0 P
the little stars and all, that look like aglets. TNK 3.04. 2

AGNIZE 1 FR 0.0001 REL FR 1 V 0 P
i do agnize | a natural and prompt alacrity | i OTH 1.03.231

AGO 29 FR 0.0032 REL FR 21 V 8 P
four days ago. LLL 1.01.122
'tis but an hour ago since it was nine, | and AYL 2.07. 24
why, i am past my gamouth long ago. SHR 3.01. 71
remember me | near twenty years ago in genoa, 4.04. 4
for but a month ago i went from hence, | and TN 1.02. 31
he might have took his answer long ago. 1.05.263
the vows | we made each other but so late ago. 5.01.215
a great while ago the world begun, | /with hey 5.01.405
did expect my hence departure | two days ago. WT 1.02.451
we had the tune on't a month ago. 4.04.294 P
are wrack'd three nights ago on goodwin sands; JN 5.03. 11
/thee tales | of woeful ages long ago betid; R2 5.01. 42
which fourteen hundred years ago were nail'd 1H4 1.01. 26
he is, my lord, an hour ago. 2.03. 66
thou stolest a cup of sack eighteen years ago, 2.04.315 P
my sweet creature of bumbast, how long is't ago, 2.04.327 P
to me — 'twas no longer ago than wed'sday last, 2H4 2.04. 86 P
that's fifty-five year ago. 3.02.210 P
ten days ago i drown'd these news in tears; 3H6 2.01.104
he should have brav'd the east an hour ago. R3 5.03.279
me his bed already, | his love, too long ago! H8 3.01.120
it well, | i read it in the grammar long ago. TIT 4.02. 23
his son was but a ward two years ago. ROM 1.05. 40
company, | i would have been a-bed an hour ago. 3.04. 7
that not long ago one of his men was with the TIM 3.02. 11 P
o heavens, die two months ago, and not forgotten HAM 3.02.131 P
how, how oft, how long ago, and when | he hath, OTH 4.01. 85
how long is this ago? CYM 1.01. 61
overroasted rather; ready long ago. 5.04.152 P

A-GOING 1 FR 0.0001 REL FR 1 V 0 P
sir thomas, | whither were you a-going? H8 1.03. 50

AGONE 2 FR 0.0002 REL FR 1 V 1 P
tutor | (for long agone i have forgot to court; TGV 3.01. 85
o, he's drunk, sir toby, an hour agone; TN 5.01.198 P

AGONY 7 FR 0.0008 REL FR 7 V 0 P
charm ache with air, and agony with words. ADO 5.01. 26
mirth cannot move a soul in agony. LLL 5.02.857
sprawl'st thou? take that, to end thy agony. 3H6 5.05. 39
awak'd you not in this sore agony? R3 1.04. 42
for thee, | god knows, in torment and in agony. 4.04.164
stirr'd | with such an agony he sweat extremely, H8 2.01. 33
live, | and have the agony of love about 'em, TNK 3.06.219

AGOOD 1 FR 0.0001 REL FR 1 V 0 P
and at that time i made her weep agood, | for i TGV 4.04.165

AGOT *(also agate-ring)*

AGOT 3 FR 0.0003 REL FR 2 V 1 P
if low, an agot very vildly cut; ADO 3.01. 65
his heart, like an agot, with your print LLL 2.01.236
i was never mann'd with an agot till now, but i 2H4 1.02. 16 P

AGOT-STONE 1 FR 0.0001 REL FR 1 V 0 P
in shape no bigger than an agot-stone | on the ROM 1.04. 55

AGREE *(also 'gree, etc.)*

AGREE 21 FR 0.0023 REL FR 14 V 7 P
obedience, agree with his demands to the point; MM 3.01.244 P
good wits will be jangling, but, gentles, agree: LLL 2.01.225
how dost thou and thy master agree? MV 2.02.100 P
at last, though long, our jarring notes agree, SHR 5.02. 1
should well agree with our external parts? 5.02.168
i very well agree with you in the hopes of him; WT 1.01. 37 P
the gentlemen do not agree with the gentlewomen, 2H4 ep 24 P
and your disgestions doo's not agree with it, i H5 5.01. 26 P
how can these contrarieties agree? 1H6 2.03. 59
agree to any covenants, and procure | that lady 5.05. 88
one livery, that they may agree like brothers, 2H6 4.02. 74 P
that if our queen and this young prince agree, 3H6 3.03.241
yes, i agree, and thank you for your motion. 3.03.244
a show or two, and so agree | the play may pass, H8 pr 10
agree these deeds with that proud brag of thine, TIT 1.01.306
nay, come, agree whose hand shall go along, 3.01.174
agree between you, i will spare my hand. 3.01.183
meat cool ere we can agree upon the first place; TIM 3.06. 68 P
therein our letters do not well agree; JC 4.03.176
well, agree then. TNK 2.02.152
if music and sweet poetry agree, | as they must PP 8. 1

/AGREED 1 FR 0.0001 REL FR 0 V 1 P
item, /it /is /further /agreed /between /them, 2H6 1.01. 50 P

AGREED 19 FR 0.0021 REL FR 13 V 6 P
welcome, how agreed? MM 4.01. 64
are you agreed? 4.02. 48 P
unwilling i agreed. ERR 1.01. 60
and there heard it agreed upon that the prince ADO 1.03. 61 P
i am agreed, and would i had given him the best SHR 1.01.142 P
forget, forgive, conclude and be agreed, | our R2 1.01.156
the sum is paid, the traitors are agreed, | the H5 2.pr. 33
agreed. i'll to yond corner. 1H6 2.01. 33
it is thus agreed | that peaceful truce shall be 5.04.116
it is agreed between the french king charles, 2H6 1.01. 43 P
"item, it is further agreed between them, that 1.01. 57 P
the peers agreed, and henry was well pleas'd 1.01.218
then thus for you, my lord, it stands agreed, H8 5.02.122
are you all agreed, lords? 5.02.126
agreed. COR 1.04. 2
and, she agreed, within her scope of choice ROM 1.02. 18
thus we are agreed. ANT 2.06. 57
agreed. CYM 1.04.169 P
what, are you both agreed? PER 2.05. 90

AGREEING 3 FR 0.0003 REL FR 2 V 1 P
but most of all agreeing with the proclamation. MM 1.02. 79 P
all agreeing | in earnestness to see him. COR 2.01.212
black, hands apt, drugs fit, and time agreeing, HAM 3.02.255

AGREEMENT 4 FR 0.0004 REL FR 4 V 0 P
i met, | upon agreement from us to his liking, SHR 1.02.182
i, upon some agreement | me shall you find ready 4.04. 33
as shall with either part's agreement stand? 4.04. 50
upon agreement, of swift severn's flood, | who 1H4 1.03.103

AGREES 8 FR 0.0009 REL FR 6 V 2 P
it agrees well, passant. WIV 1.01. 20 P
how ill agrees it with your gravity | to ERR 2.02.168
how agrees the devil and thee about thy soul 1H4 1.02.114 P
agrees not with the leanness of his purse. 2H6 1.01.112
if love be blind, | it best agrees with night. ROM 3.02. 10
well, mistress, your choice agrees with mine; PER 2.05. 18
for nothing else with his proud sight agrees. VEN 288
who wayward once, his mood with nought agrees. LUC 1095

AGRIPPA 11 FR 0.0012 REL FR 9 V 2 P
worthy menenius agrippa, one that hath always COR 1.01. 51 P
i do not know, | maecenas, ask agrippa. ANT 2.02. 17
speak, agrippa. 2.02.117
say not /so, agrippa. 2.02.120
let me hear agrippa further speak. 2.02.123
what power is in agrippa, | if i would say, 2.02.140
if i would say, "agrippa, be it so," | to make 2.02.141
my honorable friend, agrippa! 2.02.173 P
adieu, noble agrippa. 3.02. 21
go forth, agrippa, and begin the fight. 4.06. 1
go charge agrippa | plant those that have 4.06. 7

AGROUND 1 FR 0.0001 REL FR 0 V 1 P
fall to't, yarely, or we run ourselves aground. TMP 1.01. 4 P

A-GROWING 1 FR 0.0001 REL FR 1 V 0 P
so long a-growing and so leisurely | that, if R3 2.04. 19

AGUE 10 FR 0.0011 REL FR 6 V 4 P
four legs, who hath got, as i take it, an ague. TMP 2.02. 66 P
bottle will recover him, i will help his ague. 2.02. 93 P
how does thine ague? 2.02.136 P
broth | would blow me to an ague when i thought MV 1.01. 23
this ague fit of fear is overblown, | an easy R2 3.02.190
have yet some smack of an ague in you, some 2H4 1.02. 98 P
an untimely ague | stay'd me a prisoner in my H8 1.01. 4
and danger, like an ague, subtly taints | even TRO 3.03.232
as that same ague which hath made you lean. JC 2.02.113
them lie | till famine and the ague eat them up. MAC 5.05. 4

AGUECHEEK 3 FR 0.0003 REL FR 0 V 3 P
who, sir andrew aguecheek? TN 1.03. 18 P
him, and thy sworn enemy, andrew aguecheek." 3.04.170 P
set upon aguecheek a notable report of valor, 3.04.191 P

AGUED 1 FR 0.0001 REL FR 1 V 0 P
and faces pale | with flight and agued fear! COR 1.04. 38

AGUEFACE 1 FR 0.0001 REL FR 0 V 1 P
for here comes sir andrew agueface. TN 1.03. 43 P

AGUE-PROOF 1 FR 0.0001 REL FR 0 V 1 P
'tis a lie, i am not ague-proof. LR 4.06.105 P

AGUE'S 2 FR 0.0002 REL FR 2 V 0 P
a ghost, | as dim and meagre as an ague's fit, JN 3.04. 85
fool, | presuming on an ague's privilege, R2 2.01.116

AGUES 4 FR 0.0004 REL FR 4 V 0 P
how scapes he agues, in the devil's name? 1H4 3.01. 68
sun in march, | this praise doth nourish agues. 4.01.112
into strong shudders and to heavenly agues | th' TIM 4.03.138
"as burning fevers, agues pale and faint, VEN 739

AH *(also a*)*

/AH 3 FR 0.0003 REL FR 2 V 1 P

here, here, here he comes. /ah, sweet ducks! TRO 4.04. 11 P
/ah, /wherefore /dost /thou /urge /the /name /of TIT 3.02. 26
/ah, /sirrah! 3.02. 75
AH 187 FR 0.0211 REL FR 155 V 32 P
decks a thing divine — | ah, silvia, silvia! TGV 2.01. 5
ah, ha! WIV 2.02.152 P
ah, sweet anne page! 3.01. 40 P
in quest of them (unhappy), ah, lose myself. ERR 1.02. 40
ah, do not tear away thyself from me; 2.02.124
ah, luciana, did he tempt thee so? 4.02. 1
ah, but i think him better than i say, | and yet 4.02. 25
ha, ah ha! ADO 3.03. 84 P
all thy tediousness on me, ah? 3.05. 23 P
why then, some be of laughing, as, ah, ha, he! 4.01. 22 P
ah, how much might the man deserve of me that 4.01.261 P
ah, heavens, it is /a most pathetical nit! LLL 4.01.148
ah, good old mantuan! 4.02. 94 P
ah, never faith could hold, if not to beauty 4.02.106
ah, good my liege, i pray thee pardon me! 4.03.150
ah, you whoreson loggerhead! 4.03.200
ah pyramus, my lover dear! MND 1.02. 53 P
ah, good demetrius, wilt thou give him me? 3.02. 63
ah, sirrah, a body would think this was well AYL 4.03.165 P
ah, tranio, what a cruel father's he! SHR 1.01.185
ah, what sharp stings are in her mildest words! AWW 3.04. 18
ah, rogue! TN 2.05. 36 P
ah ha, does she so? 3.04. 94 P
in his rage and his wrath, | cries, ah, ha! 4.02.128
but, ah, i will not! JN 3.03. 54
ah, none but in this iron age would do it! 4.01. 60
ah, foul shrewd news! 5.05. 14
ah, gaunt, his blood was thine! R2 1.02. 22
bid him — ah, what? 1.02. 65
ah, would the scandal vanish with my life, | how 2.01. 67
ah, how long | shall tender duty make me suffer 2.01.163
ah, madam! 2.02. 52
ah, richard! 2.04. 18
ah, thou, the model where old troy did stand, 5.01. 11
ah, my sour husband, my hard–hearted lord, 5.03.121
ah, whoreson caterpillars! 1H4 2.02. 84 P
ah, no more of that, hal, and thou lovest me! 2.04.283 P
ah, thou honeysuckle villain! 2H4 2.01. 50 P
ah, thou honeyseed rogue! 2.01. 52 P
ah, you whoreson little valiant villain, you! 2.04.209 P
ah, you sweet little rogue, you! 2.04.216 P
ah, rogue! 2.04.218 P
ah, villain! 2.04.221 P
ah, rascally slave! 2.04.222 P
ah, sirrah, quoth 'a, we shall "do nothing but 5.03. 16 P
ah, poor heart! H5 2.01.118 P
ah, thou shalt find us ready for thee still; 1H6 2.04.104
ah, joan, this kills thy father's heart outright 5.04. 2
ah, joan, sweet daughter joan, i'll die with 5.04. 6
ah, humphrey, this dishonor in thine age | will 2H6 2.03. 18
ah, gloucester, hide thee from their hateful 2.04. 23
ah, gloucester, teach me to forget myself! 2.04. 27
ah, humphrey, can i bear this shameful yoke? 2.04. 37
ah, nell, forbear! 2.04. 58
ah, what's more dangerous than this fond 3.01. 74
ah, gracious lord, these days are dangerous: 3.01.142
ah, thus king henry throws away his crutch 3.01.189
ah, that my fear were false, ah, that it were! 3.01.193
ah, that my fear were false, ah, that it were! 3.01.193
ah, uncle humphrey, in thy face i see | the map 3.01.202
ah, york, no man alive so fain as i! 3.01.244
ah, woe is me for gloucester, wretched man! 3.02. 72
ah, what a sign it is of evil life, | where 3.03. 5
ah, barbarous villains! 4.04. 15
ah, were the duke of suffolk now alive, | these 4.04. 41
ah, thou say, thou serge, nay, thou buckram lord 4.07. 25 P
ah, countrymen! 4.07.114
ah, villain, thou wilt betray me, and get a 4.10. 26 P
ah, sancta majestas! 5.01. 5
ah, know you not the city favors them, | and 3H6 1.01. 67
ah, exeter! 1.01.191
ah, wretched man, would i had died a maid | and 1.01.216
ah, timorous wretch, | thou hast undone thyself, 1.01.231
ah, whither shall i fly to scape their hands? 1.03. 1
ah, tutor, look where bloody clifford comes! 1.03. 2
ah, clifford, murther not this innocent child, 1.03. 8
ah, gentle clifford, kill me with thy sword 1.03. 16
ah, let me live in prison all my days, | and 1.03. 43
ah, hark, the fatal followers do pursue, | and i 1.04. 22
ah, one that was a woeful looker–on | when as 2.01. 45
ah, would she break from hence, that this my 2.01. 75
ah, what a shame were this! 2.02. 39
ah, cousin york, would thy best friends did know 2.02. 54
ah, warwick, why hast thou withdrawn thyself? 2.03. 14
ah! 2.05. 41
ah, no, no, no, it is mine only son! 2.05. 83
ah, boy, if any life be left in thee, | throw up 2.05. 84
ah, simple men, you know not what you swear! 3.01. 83
ah, froward clarence, how evil it beseems thee 4.07. 84
ah, who is nigh? 5.02. 5
ah, warwick, warwick, wert thou as we are, | we 5.02. 29
ah, couldst thou fly! 5.02. 32
ah, montague, | if thou be there, sweet brother, 5.02. 33
ah, warwick! 5.02. 40
ah, what a shame, ah, what a fault were this! 5.04. 12
ah, what a shame, ah, what a fault were this! 5.04. 12
ah, that thy father had been so resolv'd! 5.05. 22
ah, kill me with thy weapon, not with words! 5.06. 26
ah! R3 1.03. 11
ah, gentle villain, do not turn away! 1.03.162
ah, keeper, keeper, i have done these things 1.04. 66
ah, poor clarence! 2.01.134
ah! 2.02. 27
ah! 2.02. 34
ah, so much interest have /i in thy sorrow | as 2.02. 47
ah, aunt! 2.02. 62
ah for my husband, for my dear lord edward! 2.02. 71
ah for our father, for our dear lord clarence! 2.02. 72
ah ha, my lord, this prince is not an edward! 3.07. 71
ah, cut my lace asunder, | that my pent heart 4.01. 33
ah, buckingham, now do i play the touch, | to 4.02. 8
ah, my poor princes! 4.04. 9
ah, my tender babes! 4.04. 9
ah, that thou wouldst as soon afford a grave 4.04. 31
ah, who hath any cause to mourn but we? 4.04. 34
ah ha, | there's mischief in this man. H8 1.02.186
ah, my good lord, i grieve at what i speak, 5.01. 95
ah, my good lord of winchester — i thank you, 5.02. 93
ah, ah! TRO 4.02. 79 P
ah, ah! 4.02. 79 P
ah, sir, there's many a greek and troyan dead 4.05.214
ah, how the poor world is pest'red with such 5.01. 33 P
ah, poor our sex! 5.02.109
ah, my dear, | such eyes the widows in corioles COR 2.01.177
ah, my sweet moor, sweeter to me than life! TIT 2.03. 51
ah, beastly creature, | the blot and enemy to 2.03.182
ah, now thou turn'st away thy face for shame! 2.04. 28
ah, lucius, for thy brothers let me plead. 3.01. 30
ah, son lucius, look on her! 3.01.110
ah, marcus, marcus! 3.01.139
ah, my lavinia, i will wipe thy cheeks. 3.01.142
ah, that this sight should make so deep a wound, 3.01.246
ah, now no more will i control thy griefs. 3.01.259
ah, boy, cornelia never with more care | read to 4.01. 12
ah, rome! 4.03. 18
ah, why should wrath be mute and fury dumb? 5.03.184
ah, my mistresses, which of you all | will now ROM 1.05. 18
ah, sirrah, this unlook'd–for sport comes well. 1.05. 29
ah, sirrah, by my fay, it waxes late, | i'll to 1.05.126
ah, the immortal passado, the punto reverso, the 2.04. 25 P
ah, mocker, that's the /dog's name. 2.04.209 P
my back a' t' other side — ah, my back, my back 2.05. 50
ah, juliet, if the measure of thy joy | be 2.06. 24
ah, weraday, he's dead, he's dead, he's dead! 3.02. 37
ah, where's my man? 3.02. 88
ah, poor my lord, what tongue shall smooth thy 3.02. 98
ah sir, ah sir, death's the end of all! 3.03. 92
ah sir, ah sir, death's the end of all! 3.03. 92
honest good fellows, ah, put up, put up, | for 4.05. 98
ah me, how sweet is love itself possess'd, 5.01. 10
ah, dear juliet, | why art thou yet so fair? 5.03.101
ah, what an unkind hour | is guilty of this 5.03.145
ah, when the means are gone that buy this praise TIM 2.02.169
ah, my good friend, what cheer? 3.06. 40 P
fie on't, ah fie! HAM 1.02.135
ah, rosencrantz! 2.02.225 P
"but who, ah woe, had seen the mobled queen" — 2.02.502
ah, ha! 3.02.291 P
ah, mine own lord, what have i seen to–night! 4.01. 5
where i found, horatio — | ah, royal knavery! 5.02. 19
ah, that good kent! LR 3.04.163
ah, desdemon! away, away, away! OTH 4.02. 41
them every one an antony, | and say, "ah, ha! ANT 2.05. 15
ah, this thou shouldst have done, | and not have 2.07. 73
ah, stand by. 3.11. 41
ah, you kite! 3.13. 89
ah, dear, if i be so, | from my cold heart let 3.13.158
ah, let be, let be! 4.04. 6
ah, thou spell! 4.12. 30
ah, women, women! 4.15. 84
ah, women, women! 4.15. 90
ah, soldier! 5.02.328
ah, but some natural notes about her body, CYM 2.02. 28
ah, you precious pandar! 3.05. 81
ah ha, my friend, my friend! TNK 5.04. 23
he rose and ran away, ah, fool too froward! PP 4.14
ah, that i had my lady at this bay: 11.13
ah, neither be my share! 14. 1
ah, thought i, thou mourn'st in vain! 20.19
ah! SON 9. 3
ah, but those tears are pearl which thy love 34.13
but ah, thought kills me that i am not thought, 44. 9
ah, wherefore with infection should he live, 67. 1
ah, do not, when my heart hath scap'd this 90. 5
ah, yet doth beauty, like a dial hand, | steal 104. 9
ah, my love well knows | her pretty looks have 139. 9
"but, ah, who ever shunn'd by precedent | the LC 155
A–HANGING 1 FR 0.0001 REL FR 1 V 0 P
i kill'd the slave that was a–hanging thee. LR 5.03.275
A–HEIGHT 1 FR 0.0001 REL FR 1 V 0 P
look up a–height, the shrill–gorg'd lark so far LR 4.06. 58
A–HIGH 1 FR 0.0001 REL FR 1 V 0 P
one heav'd a–high, to be hurl'd down below; R3 4.04. 86
A–HOLD 2 FR 0.0002 REL FR 0 V 2 P
lay her a–hold, a–hold! TMP 1.01. 49 P
lay her a–hold, a–hold! 1.01. 49 P
A–HOOTING 1 FR 0.0001 REL FR 1 V 0 P
the people fall a–hooting. LLL 4.02. 59
A–HUNGRY *(also an–hungry)*
A–HUNGRY 2 FR 0.0002 REL FR 0 V 2 P
i am not a–hungry, i thank you, forsooth. WIV 1.01.270 P
good a deed as to drink when a man's a–hungry, TN 2.03.127 P
A–HUNTING 2 FR 0.0002 REL FR 2 V 0 P
was a time | when young men went a–hunting, and TNK 3.03. 40
this is the duke, a–hunting as i told you. 3.06.108
AI 1 FR 0.0001 REL FR 0 V 1 P
vous deja oublie ce que je vous ai enseigne? H5 3.04. 42 P
AID 64 FR 0.0072 REL FR 61 V 3 P
by whose aid | (weak masters though ye be) i TMP 5.01. 40
for the like loss i have her sovereign aid, 5.01.143
in these affairs to aid me with thy counsel. TGV 2.04.185
lest the devil that guides him should aid him, i WIV 3.05.148 P
till, raising of more aid, | we came again to ERR 5.01.153
the florentine will move us | for speedy aid; AWW 1.02. 7
helen, | if you should tender your supposed aid, 1.03.236
by the good aid that i of you shall borrow, 3.07. 11
and aid me with that store of power you have 5.01. 20
for i can guess that by thy honest aid | thou 5.03.329
and be my aid | for such disguise as haply shall TN 1.02. 53
of a true subject, didst counsel and aid them, WT 3.02. 20 P
omit | nothing may give us aid. 4.04.625
hath drawn him from his own determin'd aid, JN 2.01.584
we all have strongly sworn to give him aid; R2 2.03.150
to this we swore our aid. 1H4 5.01. 46
in aid whereof we of the spiritualty | will H5 1.02.132
whilst such a worthy leader, wanting aid, | unto 1H6 1.01.143
her aid she promis'd, and assur'd success; 1.02. 82
renowned talbot doth expect my aid, | and i am 4.03. 12
can, | but curse the cause i cannot aid the man. 4.03. 44
set from our o'ermatch'd forces forth for aid. 4.04. 11
the levied succors that should lend him aid, 4.04. 23
york set him on, york should have sent him aid. 4.04. 29
within six hours they will be at his aid. 4.04. 41
north, | appear, and aid me in this enterprise. 5.03. 7
the lord mayor craves aid of your honor from the 2H6 4.05. 4 P
such aid as i can spare you shall command, | but 4.05. 6
with aid of soldiers to this needful war. 3H6 2.01.147
i'll aid thee tear for tear, | and let our 2.05. 76
my queen and son are gone to france for aid; 3.01. 28
she, on his left side, craving aid for henry; 3.01. 43
am come to crave thy just and lawful aid; 3.03. 32
from giving aid which late i promised. 3.03.148
last, i firmly am resolv'd | you shall have aid. 3.03.220
how can we aid you with our kindred tears? R3 2.02. 63
expecting but the aid | of buckingham to welcome 4.04.438
the fear of that holds off my present aid. 4.05. 5
and aid thee in this doubtful shock of arms; 5.03. 93
i died for hope ere i could lend thee aid, | but 5.03.173
and never seek for aid out of himself. H8 1.02.114
choice of those | that best can aid your action. COR 1.06. 66
do send, dispatch | those centuries to our aid; 1.07. 3
if you refuse your aid | in this so never–needed 5.01. 33
tell him it is for justice and for aid, | and TIT 4.03. 15
feeling in itself | a lack of timon's aid, hath TIM 5.01.147
of it own fall, restraining aid to timon, | and 5.01.148
not to their mould | but with the aid of use. MAC 1.03.146
which fate and metaphysical aid doth seem | to 1.05. 29
king, upon his aid | to wake northumberland and 3.06. 30
friends both, go join you with some further aid: HAM 4.01. 33
to lend me arms and aid when i requir'd them, ANT 2.02. 88
a conqueror that will pray in aid for kindness 5.02. 27
lucina lent not me her aid, | but took me in my CYM 5.04. 43
to me and to my aid the blest infusions | that PER 3.02. 35
diana aid my purpose! 4.02.148
i' th' aid o' th' current were almost to sink, TNK 1.02. 8
give me your aid | and bend your spirits towards 5.01. 47
by whose swift aid | their mistress mounted VEN 1190
a thousand crosses keep them from thy aid: LUC 912
each present lord began to promise aid, | as 1696
words, so thick come in his poor heart's aid, 1784
whilst i alone did call upon thy aid, | my verse SON 79. 1
nor his compeers by night | giving him aid, my 86. 8
AIDANCE 2 FR 0.0002 REL FR 2 V 0 P
attracts the same for aidance 'gainst the enemy, 2H6 3.02.165
when it is barr'd the aidance of the tongue. VEN 330
AIDANT 1 FR 0.0001 REL FR 1 V 0 P
be aidant and remediate | in the good man's LR 4.04. 17
AIDED 1 FR 0.0001 REL FR 0 V 1 P
the instruments which aided to expose the child WT 5.02. 71 P
AIDING 2 FR 0.0002 REL FR 2 V 0 P
my husband hies him home, where, heaven aiding, AWW 4.04. 12
and then deny her aiding hand therein | and lay R3 1.03. 95
AIDLESS 1 FR 0.0001 REL FR 1 V 0 P
aidless came off, | and with a sudden COR 2.02.112
/AIDS 1 FR 0.0001 REL FR 1 V 0 P
/of /aids /incertain /should /not /be /admitted. 2H4 1.03. 24
AIDS 1 FR 0.0001 REL FR 1 V 0 P
all aids, themselves made fairer by their place, LC 117
AIL 2 FR 0.0002 REL FR 1 V 1 P
what does she ail that she's not very well? AWW 2.04. 6 P
hold? | what should ail us? TNK 2.03. 37
AIL'ST 1 FR 0.0001 REL FR 0 V 1 P
what ail'st thou, man? WT 3.03. 82 P
AIM 41 FR 0.0046 REL FR 38 V 3 P
but, fearing lest my jealous aim might err, TGV 3.01. 28
behold her that gave aim to all thy oaths, | and 5.04.101
proceedings all my neighbors shall cry aim. WIV 3.02. 44 P
the very riches of thyself | that now i aim at. 3.04. 18
my food, my fortune, and my sweet hope's aim, ERR 3.02. 63
and aim better at me by that i now will manifest ADO 3.02. 96 P
but if all aim but this be levell'd false, | the 4.01.237
a certain aim he took | at a fair vestal throned MND 2.01.157
as i will watch the aim, or to find both | or MV 1.01.150
that from the hunter's aim had ta'en a hurt, AYL 2.01. 34
proclaim | myself against the level of mine aim, AWW 2.01.156
fly with false aim, move the still–peering air 3.02.110
it ill beseems this presence to cry aim | to JN 2.01.196
that arrows fled not swifter toward their aim 2H4 1.01.123
princes, flesh'd with conquest, aim to hit. 1.01.149
with a near aim, of the main chance of things 3.01. 83
may with as great aim level at the edge of a 3.02.267 P
to which is fixed, as an aim or butt, H5 1.02.186
at them, | howe'er unfortunate i miss'd my aim. 1H6 1.04. 4
here stand we both and aim we at the best; 3H6 3.01. 8
your highness aims at, if i aim aright. 3.02. 68
to tell thee plain, i aim to lie with thee. 3.02. 69
my thoughts aim at a further matter: 4.01.125
but canst thou guess that he doth aim at it? R3 3.02. 45
flag | to be the aim of every dangerous shot; 4.04. 89
madam, you wander from the good we aim at. H8 3.01.138
makes the church | the chief aim of his honor, 5.02.153
not answering the aim | and that unbodied figure TRO 1.03. 15
discovery | we shall be short'ned in our aim, COR 1.02. 23
but, gentle people, give me aim a while, | for TIT 5.03.149
what you would work me to, i have some aim. JC 1.02.163
myself | even in the aim and very flash of it. 1.03. 52
and our safest way | is to avoid the aim. MAC 2.03.143
(as in these cases where the aim reports, | 'tis OTH 1.03. 6
darts, | though enemy, lost aim and could not? ANT 4.14. 71
fed, | his other agents aim at like delight? VEN 400
mistakes that aim and cleaves an infant's heart. 942
the aim of all is but to nurse the life | with LUC 141
and in this aim there is such thwarting strife 143
end thy ill aim before thy shoot be ended; 579
could scape the hail of his all–hurting aim, LC 310
/AIM'D 1 FR 0.0001 REL FR 1 V 0 P
my lord, i /aim'd a mile beyond the moon, | your TIT 4.03. 66
AIM'D 8 FR 0.0009 REL FR 8 V 0 P
well aim'd of such a young one. SHR 2.01.235
this bird you aim'd at, though you hit her not; 5.02. 50
danger seen in him | aim'd at your highness, no R2 1.01. 14
in faith, it is exceedingly well aim'd. 1H4 1.03.282
i aim'd so near when i suppos'd you lov'd. ROM 1.01.205
my bow again, | but not where i have aim'd them. HAM 4.07. 24
such vild success | which my thoughts aim'd not. OTH 3.03.223
that never aim'd so high to love your daughter, PER 2.05. 47
AIMED 1 FR 0.0001 REL FR 1 V 0 P
cunningly | that my discovery be not aimed at: TGV 3.01. 45

AIMEST 1 FR 0.0001 REL FR 1 V 0 P
thou aimest all awry. 2H6 2.04. 58
AIMING 4 FR 0.0004 REL FR 4 V 0 P
enemy, | aiming at silvia as a sweeter friend. TGV 2.06. 30
than did our soldiers, aiming at their safety, 2H4 1.01.124
aiming, belike, at your interior hatred, | that R3 1.03. 65
as when his virtues, aiming upon others, | heat TRO 3.03.100
AIMS 4 FR 0.0004 REL FR 4 V 0 P
more grave and wrinkled than the aims and ends MM 1.03. 5
grant what i perceive | your highness aims at, 3H6 3.02. 68
for i know the britain richmond aims | at young R3 4.03. 40
fame, at the which he aims, | in whom already COR 1.01.263
AIM'ST 1 FR 0.0001 REL FR 1 V 0 P
all the ends thou aim'st at be thy country's, H8 3.02.447
AINSI 2 FR 0.0002 REL FR 0 V 2 P
ainsi dis–je; H5 3.04. 49 P
oui, vraiment, sauf votre grace, ainsi dit–il. 5.02.112 P
AIO 1 FR 0.0001 REL FR 1 V 0 P
why, this is just | "aio /te, aeacida, romanos 2H6 1.04. 62
/AIR 2 FR 0.0002 REL FR 2 V 0 P
/the /emptier /ever /dancing /in /the /air, R2 4.01.186
/and /buzz /lamenting /doings /in /the /air! TIT 3.02. 62
AIR 204 FR 0.0230 REL FR 175 V 29 P
whom i left cooling of the air with sighs, | in TMP 1.02.222
i' th' air, or th' earth? 1.02.388
their fury and my passion | with its sweet air; 1.02.394
the air breathes upon us here most sweetly. 2.01. 47 P
where thou thyself dost air — the queen o' th' 4.01. 70
and | are melted into air, into thin air, | and, 4.01.150
and | are melted into air, into thin air, | and, 4.01.150
so full of valor that they smote the air | for 4.01.172
end, and thou | shalt have the air at freedom. 4.01.265
hast thou, which art but air, a touch, a feeling 5.01. 21
a solemn air, and the best comforter | to an 5.01. 58
i drink the air before me, and return | or ere 5.01.102
though the chameleon love can feed on the air, i TGV 2.01.173 P
to feed on your blood than live in your air. 2.04. 28 P
the air hath starv'd the roses in her cheeks, 4.04.154
an idle plume, | which the air beats for vain. MM 2.04. 12
and so stop the air | by which he should revive; 2.04. 25
now, divine air! ADO 2.03. 58 P
if i should speak, | she would mock me into air; 3.01. 75
charm ache with air, and agony with words. 5.01. 26
most wholesome physic of thy health–giving air; LLL 1.01.234 P
sweet air! 3.01. 4 P
passing fair | playing in the wanton air: 4.03.102
air, quoth he, thy cheeks may blow; 4.03.107
air, would i might triumph so! 4.03.108
blow like sweet roses in this summer air. 5.02.293
and your tongue's sweet air | more tuneable than MND 1.01.183
floods, | pale in her anger, washes all the air, 2.01.104
and, in the spiced indian air, by night, | full 2.01.124
how all the other passions fleet to air, | as MV 3.02.108
hand, | and bring your music forth into the air. 5.01. 53
sound, | or any air of music touch their ears, 5.01. 76
yet thou liest in the bleak air. AYL 2.06. 15 P
and with her breath she did perfume the air. SHR 1.01.175
move the still–peering air | that sings with AWW 3.02.110
although | the air of paradise did fan the house 3.02.125
methought she purg'd the air of pestilence! TN 1.01. 19
and make the babbling gossip of the air | cry 1.05.273
rest | between the elements of air and earth, 1.05.275
him now, lest the device take air and taint. 3.04.132 P
this is the air, that is the glorious sun, 4.03. 1
the climate's delicate, the air most sweet, WT 3.01. 1
hurried | here to this place, i' th' open air, 3.02.105
and so, with shrieks, | she melted into air. 3.03. 37
seest thou not the air of the court in these 4.04.731 P
a new ship to purge melancholy and air himself; 4.04.763 P
father's image is so hit in you | (his very air) 5.01.128
purge all infection from our air whilest you 5.01.169
still methinks | there is an air comes from her. 5.03. 78
leave them as naked as the vulgar air. JN 2.01.387
mocking the air with colors idlely spread, | and 5.01. 72
belief | that, being brought into the open air, 5.07. 7
a maim | as to be cast forth in the common air, R2 1.03.157
us, | one of our souls had wand'red in the air, 1.03.195
suppose | devouring pestilence hangs in our air, 1.03.284
how brooks your grace the air | after your late 3.02. 2
as high in the air as this unthankful king, | as 1H4 1.03.136
hang in the air a thousand leagues from hence, 3.01.224
air. 5.01.135 P
hope, | eating the air, and promise of supply, 2H4 1.03. 28
stand from him, give him air, he'll straight be 4.04.116
marry, good air. 5.03. 8 P
that did affright the air at agincourt? H5 pr 14
the air, a charter'd libertine, is still, | and 1.01. 48
for now sits expectation in the air, | and hides 2.pr. 8
up in the air, crown'd with the golden sun, 2.04. 58
this your air of france | hath blown that vice 3.06.151
he trots the air; 3.07. 16 P
he is pure air and fire; 3.07. 21 P
and our air shakes them passing scornfully. 4.02. 42
they would but stink, and putrefy the air. 1H6 4.07. 90
whose sweet smell the air shall be perfum'd, 2H6 1.01.255
he shall not breathe infection in this air | but 3.02.287
makes him gasp, and stare, and catch the air, 3.02.371
here could i breathe my soul into the air, | as 3.02.391
breathe foul contagious darkness in the air. 4.01. 7
hast, | and if mine arm be heaved in the air, 4.10. 51
and dead men's cries do fill the empty air, 5.02. 4
for what doth cherish weeds but gentle air? 3H6 2.06. 21
the air hath got into my deadly wounds, | and 2.06. 27
my face, | and as the air blows it to me again, 3.01. 85
not knowing how to find the open air | but 3.02.177
well are you welcome to /the open air. R3 1.01.124
the lips of those that breathe them in the air. 1.03.285
to find the empty, vast, and wand'ring air, 1.04. 39
who builds his hope in air of your good looks 3.04. 98
if yet your gentle souls fly in the air | and be 4.04. 11
root, thus hack'd, | the air will drink the sap. H8 1.02. 98
there's fresher air, my lord, | in the next 1.04.101
should with a bond of air, strong as the TRO 1.03. 66
untent his person and share th' air with us? 2.03.168
build there, carpenter, the air is sweet. 3.02. 51 P
when th' have said as false | as air, as water, 3.02.192
dewdrop from the lion's mane, | be shook to air. 3.03.225
that the appalled air | may pierce the head of 4.05. 4
thou hast hung /thy advanced sword i' th' air, 4.05.188
filling the air with swords advanc'd and darts, COR 1.06. 61
of unburied men | that do corrupt my air — i 3.03.123
you are they | that made the air unwholesome, 4.06.130
to tear with thunder the wide cheeks a' th' air, 5.03.151
but he returns | splitting the air with noise. 5.06. 51
i see thou wilt not trust the air | with secrets TIT 4.02.169
ere he can spread his sweet leaves to the air ROM 1.01.152
which is as thin of substance as the air, | and 1.04. 99
clouds, | and sails upon the bosom of the air. 2.02. 32
gossamers | that idles in the wanton summer air, 2.06. 19
sweeten with thy breath | this neighbor air, and 2.06. 27
whose foul mouth no healthsome air breathes in, 4.03. 34
stirrup, and through him | drink the free air. TIM 1.01. 83
his poor self, | a dedicated beggar to the air, 4.02. 13
we must all part | into this sea of air. 4.02. 22
below thy sister's orb | infect the air! 4.03. 3
city hang his poison | in the sick air. 4.03.111
think'st | that the bleak air, thy boisterous 4.03.222
promising is the very air o' th' time; 5.01. 22
fearful scouring | doth choke the air with dust. 5.02. 16
of opening my lips and receiving the bad air. JC 1.02.250 P
the exhalations whizzing in the air | give so 2.01. 44
and tempt the rheumy and unpurged air | to add 2.01.266
the noise of battle hurtled in the air; 2.02. 22
is fair, | hover through the fog and filthy air. MAC 1.01. 12
into the air; 1.03. 81
question them further, they made themselves air, 1.05. 5 P
the air | nimbly and sweetly recommends itself 1.06. 1
haunt, i have observ'd | the air is delicate. 1.06. 10
hors'd | upon the sightless couriers of the air, 1.07. 23
and, as they say, | lamentings heard i' th' air; 2.03. 56
rock, | as broad and general as the casing air; 3.04. 22
i am for th' air; 3.05. 20
i'll charm the air to give a sound, | while you 4.01.129
infected be the air whereon they ride, | and 4.01.138
and shrieks that rent the air | are made, not 4.03.168
that would be howl'd out in the desert air, 4.03.194
as easy mayst thou the intrenchant air | with 5.08. 9
for it is, as the air, invulnerable, | and our HAM 1.01.145
whether in sea or fire, in earth or air, | th' 1.01.153
the air bites shrowdly, it is very cold. 1.04. 1
it is /a nipping and an eager air. 1.04. 2
but soft, methinks i scent the morning air, 1.05. 58
will you walk out of the air, my lord? 2.02.206 P
indeed that's out of the air. 2.02.208 P
this most excellent canopy, the air, look you, 2.02.300 P
of reverent priam, seem'd i' th' air to stick. 2.02.479
nor do not saw the air too much with your hand, 3.02. 4 P
faith — of the chameleon's dish, i eat the air, 3.02. 94 P
and with th' incorporal air do hold discourse? 3.04.118
may miss our name, | and hit the woundless air. 4.01. 44
choose | to wage against the enmity o' th' air, LR 2.04.209
now all the plagues that in the pendulous air 3.04. 67
here is better than the open air, take it 3.06. 1 P
then, | thou unsubstantial air that i embrace: 4.01. 7
would stretch thy spirits up into the air. 4.02. 23
the crows and choughs that wing the midway air 4.06. 13
goss'mer, feathers, air | (so many fathom down 4.06. 49
the first time that we smell the air | we wawl 4.06.179
go, vanish into air, away! OTH 3.01. 20 P
trifles light as air | are to the jealious 3.03.322
when it hath blown his ranks into the air, | and 3.04.135
o, bear him /out o' th' air. 5.01.104
whistling to th' air, which, but for vacancy, ANT 2.02.216
music i' th' air. 4.03. 13
i would they'ld fight i' th' fire or i' th' air; 4.10. 3
nod unto the world | and mock our eyes with air. 4.14. 7
i am fire and air; 5.02.289
as sweet as balm, as soft as air, as gentle — 5.02.311
as we do air, fast as 'twas minist'red, | and in CYM 1.01. 45
were you but riding forth to air yourself, 1.01.110
where air comes out, air comes in; 1.02. 3 P
where air comes out, air comes in; 1.02. 3 P
melted from | the smallness of a gnat to air, 1.03. 21
after, a wonderful sweet air, with admirable 2.03. 18 P
be pale, i beg but leave to air this jewel. 2.04. 96
and the air on't | revengingly enfeebles me, or 5.02. 3
find, and be embrac'd by a piece of tender air; 5.04.140 P
find, and be embrac'd by a piece of tender air; 5.05.437 P
the piece of tender air, thy virtuous daughter, 5.05.446
were clipt about | with this most tender air. 5.05.452
see clear | to stop the air would hurt them. PER 1.01.100
that i should open to the list'ning air | how 1.02. 87
sorrows to sound deep our woes | into the air, 1.04. 14
and air | were all too little to content and 1.04. 34
thou hast as chiding a nativity | as fire, air, 3.01. 33
i pray you give her air. 3.02. 91
walk with leonine, the air is quick there, | and 4.01. 27
the meanest bird | that flies i' th' purer air! 4.06.102
not an /angel of the air, | bird melodious, or TNK 1.01. 16
had mine ear | stol'n some new air, or at 1.03. 75
bear 'em speedily | from our kind air, to them 1.04. 38
and clamors through the wild air flying! 1.05. 6
by this air, | i could for each word give a cuff 3.01.103
and calls it heavenly moisture, air of grace, VEN 64
his nostrils drink the air, and forth again | as 273
desire, | as air and water do abate the fire. 654
sun and sharp air | lurk'd like two thieves, to 1085
"with rotten damps ravish the morning air; LUC 778
as smoke from aetna, that in air consumes, | or 1042
with clamors fill'd | the dispers'd air, who, 1805
passing fair, | playing in the wanton air. PP 16. 4
"air," quoth he, "thy cheeks may blow, | air, 16. 9
may blow, | air, would i might triumph so! 16.10
that heaven's air in this huge rondure hems. SON 21. 8
as those gold candles fix'd in heaven's air: 21.12
the other two, slight air and purging fire, 45. 1
a crow that flies in heaven's sweetest air. 70. 4
AIR–BRAVING 1 FR 0.0001 REL FR 1 V 0 P
shall lay your stately and air–braving towers, 1H6 4.02. 13
AIR'D 2 FR 0.0002 REL FR 1 V 1 P
i have for the most part been air'd abroad, i WT 4.02. 5 P
or shortly after | this world had air'd them. H8 2.04.194
AIR–DRAWN 1 FR 0.0001 REL FR 1 V 0 P
this is the air–drawn dagger which you said MAC 3.04. 61
/AIRE 1 FR 0.0001 REL FR 1 V 0 P
his new–come champion, virtuous joan of /aire, 1H6 2.02. 20
AIRE 1 FR 0.0001 REL FR 1 V 0 P
joan of aire hath been | a virgin from her 1H6 5.04. 49
AIRLESS 1 FR 0.0001 REL FR 1 V 0 P
nor airless dungeon, nor strong links of iron, JC 1.03. 94
AIR'S 1 FR 0.0001 REL FR 1 V 0 P
th' nest, nor /know not | what air's from home. CYM 3.03. 29
AIRS 5 FR 0.0005 REL FR 5 V 0 P
sure, the goddess | on whom these airs attend! TMP 1.02.423
sounds, and sweet airs, that give delight and 3.02.136
more than light airs and recollected terms | of TN 2.04. 5
bring with thee airs from heaven, or blasts from HAM 1.04. 41
young bones, | you taking airs, with lameness! LR 2.04.164
AIRY *(also aery*)*
/AIRY 1 FR 0.0001 REL FR 0 V 1 P
/ambition /of /so /airy /and /light /a /quality HAM 2.02.261 P
AIRY 6 FR 0.0006 REL FR 6 V 0 P
upon their senses that | this airy charm is for, TMP 5.01. 54
host, | having his ear full of his airy fame, TRO 1.03.144
three civil brawls, bred of an airy word, | by ROM 1.01. 89
would through the airy region stream so bright 2.02. 21
and make her airy tongue more hoarse than /mine, 2.02.162
white weighs down the airy scale of praise, LC 226
AJAX' 3 FR 0.0003 REL FR 3 V 0 P
were your days | as green as ajax', and your TRO 2.03.254
thersites' body is as good as ajax', | when CYM 4.02.252
in ajax' eyes blunt rage and rigor roll'd, | but LUC 1398
/AJAX 1 FR 0.0001 REL FR 0 V 1 P
your mind is the clearer, /ajax, and your TRO 2.03.153 P
AJAX 59 FR 0.0066 REL FR 40 V 19 P
by the lord, this love is as mad as ajax. LLL 4.03. 6 P
sitting on a close–stool, will be given to ajax; 5.02.578 P
for sure aeacides | was ajax, call'd so from his SHR 3.01. 53
and now, like ajax telamonius, | on sheep or 2H6 5.01. 26
blood, nephew to hector, | they call him ajax. TRO 1.02. 14
ajax is grown self–will'd, and bears his head 1.03.188
and by device let blockish ajax draw | the sort 1.03.374
if the dull brainless ajax come safe off, 1.03.380
ajax employ'd plucks down achilles' plumes. 1.03.385
why, how now, ajax, wherefore do ye thus? 2.01. 55
for, whosomever you take him to be, he is ajax. 2.01. 64 P
achilles, ajax, who wears his wit in his belly 2.01. 73 P
i say, this ajax — 2.01. 76 P
nay, good ajax. 2.01. 77 P
ajax was here the voluntary, and you as under an 2.01. 96 P
yes, good sooth. to achilles, to ajax, to — 2.01.109 P
shall the elephant ajax carry it thus? 2.03. 2 P
what moves ajax thus to bay at him? 2.03. 90 P
then will ajax lack matter, if he have lost his 2.03. 94 P
no, noble ajax, you are as strong, as valiant, 2.03.148 P
let ajax go to him. 2.03.178
we'll consecrate the steps that ajax makes 2.03.183
what a vice were it in ajax now — 2.03.235
milo his addition yield | to sinowy ajax. 2.03.248
not have the eminence of him, | but be as ajax. 2.03.256
be rul'd by him, lord ajax. 2.03.257
/cull their flower, ajax shall cope the best. 2.03.264
ajax is ready. 3.03. 35
good morrow, ajax. 3.03. 66
apprehended here immediately | th' unknown ajax. 3.03.125
chance doth throw upon him — | ajax renown'd! 3.03.132
they clap the lubber ajax on the shoulder, | as 3.03.139
that all the greeks begin to worship ajax; 3.03.182
but our great ajax bravely beat down him." 3.03.213
shall ajax fight with hector? 3.03.225
i'll send the fool to ajax and desire him | t' 3.03.235
ajax goes up and down the field, asking for 3.03.244 P
i said, "good morrow, ajax"; 3.03.261 P
you shall see the pageant of ajax. 3.03.272 P
desire the valiant ajax to invite the /most 3.03.274 P
jove bless great ajax! 3.03.280 P
thou dreadful ajax, that the appalled air | may 4.05. 4
this ajax is half made of hector's blood, | in 4.05. 83
go, gentle knight, | stand by our ajax. 4.05. 89
now, ajax, hold thine own! 4.05.114
his blows are well dispos'd. there, ajax! 4.05.116
let me embrace thee, ajax. 4.05.135
ajax, farewell. 4.05.148
ajax commands the guard to tend on you. 5.01. 72
ajax, your guard, stays to conduct you home. 5.02.184
that mongril cur, ajax, against that dog of as 5.04. 13 P
and now is the cur ajax prouder than the cur 5.04. 14 P
and bid the snail–pac'd ajax arm for shame. 5.05. 18
ajax hath lost a friend, | and foams at mouth, 5.05. 35
ajax hath ta'en aeneas! 5.06. 22
the greeks upon advice did bury ajax | that slew TIT 1.01.379
rogues and cowards | but ajax is their fool. LR 2.02.125
the sevenfold shield of ajax cannot keep | the ANT 4.14. 38
in ajax and ulysses, o, what art | of LUC 1394
A–KILLING 1 FR 0.0001 REL FR 0 V 1 P
i would have him nine years a–killing. OTH 4.01.178 P
AKIN 1 FR 0.0001 REL FR 1 V 0 P
new plays and maidenheads are near akin — TNK pr 1
ALABLASTER 5 FR 0.0005 REL FR 5 V 0 P
sit like his grandsire cut in alablaster? MV 1.01. 84
another | within their alablaster innocent arms. R3 4.03. 11
snow, | and smooth as monumental alablaster. OTH 5.02. 5
jail of snow, | or ivory in an alablaster band, VEN 363
admired | her azure veins, her alablaster skin, LUC 419
ALACK *(also 'lack)*
/ALACK 5 FR 0.0005 REL FR 5 V 0 P
/alack, /why /am /i /sent /for /to /a /king R2 4.01.162
/alack /the /heavy /day, | /that /i /have /worn 4.01.257
/alack, /what /noise /is /this? HAM 4.05. 96
/and /cries, | "/alack, /why /does /he /so?" LR 4.02. 59
/alack, /poor /gentleman! 4.03. 47
ALACK 82 FR 0.0092 REL FR 75 V 7 P
alack, for pity! TMP 1.02.132
alack, what trouble | was i then to you! 1.02.151
alack, for mercy! 1.02.437
alack, how may i do it, having the hour limited, MM 4.02.165 P
alack, when once our grace we have forgot, 4.04. 33
alack, let it blood. LLL 2.01.186
alack for woe! 4.01. 15
"on a day — alack the day! 4.03. 99
but, alack, my hand is sworn | ne'er to pluck 4.03.109
vow, alack, for youth unmeet, | youth so apt to 4.03.111
alack, where are you? MND 2.02.153
alack, alack, alack, | i fear my thisby's 5.01.172

alack, alack, alack, | i fear my thisby's 5.01.172
alack, alack, alack, | i fear my thisby's 5.01.172
alack the day, i know you not, young gentleman, MV 2.02. 70 P
alack, sir, i am sand–blind, i know you not. 2.02. 74 P
alack, what heinous sin is it in me | to be 2.03. 16
alack, in me what strange effect | would they AYL 4.03. 52
alack, for lesser knowledge! WT 2.01. 38
alack, poor soul, thou hast need of more rags to 4.03. 54 P
alack, thou dost usurp authority. JN 2.01.118
ay, alack, how new | is "husband" in my mouth! 3.01.305
alack, and what shall good old york there see R2 1.02. 67
alack the heavy day | when such a sacred king 3.03. 8
alack, alack for woe, | that any harm should 3.03. 70
alack, alack for woe, | that any harm should 3.03. 70
alack, poor richard, where rode he the whilst? 5.02. 22
alack, what mischiefs might he set abroach | in 2H4 4.02. 14
but health, alack, with youthful wings is flown 4.05.228
alack, my lord, that fault is none of yours; R3 1.01. 47
alack, i love myself. 5.03.187
alack, | you are transported by calamity COR 1.01. 74
alack, or we must lose | the country, our dear 5.03.109
alack, there lies more peril in thine eye | than ROM 2.02. 71
alack the day, he's gone, he's kill'd, he's dead 3.02. 39
alack, alack, that heaven should practice 3.05.209
alack, alack, that heaven should practice 3.05.209
alack, alack, is it not like that i, | so early 4.03. 45
alack, alack, is it not like that i, | so early 4.03. 45
she's dead, deceas'd, she's dead, alack the day! 4.05. 23
alack the day, she's dead, she's dead, she's 4.05. 24
alack, my child is dead, | and with my child my 4.05. 63
alack, alack, what blood is this, which stains 5.03.140
alack, alack, what blood is this, which stains 5.03.140
alack, my fellows, what should i say to you? TIM 4.02. 3
alack, i am afraid they have awak'd, | and 'tis MAC 2.02. 9
alack, | i had forgot. 'tis so concluded on. HAM 3.04.200
by saint charity, | alack, and fie for shame! 4.05. 59
alack, the night comes on, and the /bleak winds LR 2.04.300
alack, bare–headed? 3.02. 60
alack, alack, edmund, i like not this unnatural 3.03. 1 P
alack, alack, edmund, i like not this unnatural 3.03. 1 P
alack, sir, he is mad. 4.01. 45
alack, 'tis he! 4.04. 1
alack, i have no eyes. 4.06. 60
alack, alack the day! 4.06.181
alack, alack the day! 4.06.181
alack, alack, | 'tis wonder that thy life and 4.07. 39
alack, alack, | 'tis wonder that thy life and 4.07. 39
but his flaw'd heart | (alack, too weak the 5.03.198
alack, why thus? 5.03.240
alack, my lord, what may you mean by that? OTH 5.02. 29
alack, sir, no, her passions are made of nothing ANT 1.02.146 P
alack, alack! 3.10. 23
alack, alack! 3.10. 23
alack, our terrene moon | is now eclips'd, and 3.13.153
(i mean, that married her, alack, good man! CYM 1.01. 18
alack, the king! 1.01.124
alack, no remedy!) 3.04.162
but alack, | you snatch some hence for little 5.01. 11
no, no, alack, | there's other work in hand. 5.05.102
but, alack, | that monster envy, oft the wrack PER 4.ch. 11
alack that leonine was so slack, so slow! 4.02. 64
lady, lady, alack! TNK 1.01.113
now, alack, weak sister, | i must no more 1.03. 86
kill myself," quoth she, "alack, what were it, LUC 1156
bright orient pearl, alack, too timely shaded! PP 10. 3
on a day (alack the day!) 16. 1
vow, alack, for youth unmeet, | youth, so apt to 16.13
but out, alack, he was but one hour mine, | the SON 33.11
where, alack, | shall time's best jewel from 65. 9
alack, what poverty my muse brings forth, | that 103. 1

/ALACRITY 1 FR 0.0001 REL FR 1 V 0 P
/with /a /bridegroom's /fresh /alacrity | /let TRO 4.04.145

ALACRITY 4 FR 0.0004 REL FR 3 V 1 P
size that i have a kind of alacrity in sinking; WIV 3.05. 12 P
i have not that alacrity of spirit | nor cheer R3 5.03. 73
a natural and prompt alacrity | i find in OTH 1.03.232
still temper, | no stirring in him, no alacrity, TNK 4.02. 29

A–LAND 2 FR 0.0002 REL FR 1 V 1 P
why, as men do a–land; PER 2.01. 28 P
understand, | if e'er this coffin drives a–land, 3.02. 69

ALANSON 17 FR 0.0019 REL FR 13 V 4 P
the heir of alanson, /katherine her name. LLL 2.01.195
alanson, brabant, bar, and burgundy, | jacques H5 3.05. 42
when alanson and myself were down together, i 4.07.154 P
man challenge this, he is a friend to alanson, 4.07.157 P
majesty is take out of the helmet of alanson. 4.08. 27 P
this is the glove of alanson that your majesty 4.08. 37 P
john duke of alanson, anthony duke of brabant, 4.08. 96
the duke of alanson flieth to his side. 1H6 1.01. 95
duke of alanson, this was your default, | that, 2.01. 60
hecate, | but unto thee, alanson, and the rest. 3.02. 65
with charles, alanson, and that traitorous rout. 4.01.173
alanson, /reignier, compass him about, | and 4.04. 27
beat down alanson, orleance, burgundy, | and 4.06. 14
of his, | it was alanson that enjoy'd my love. 5.04. 73
alanson, that notorious machevile? 5.04. 74
of orleance, calaber, bretagne, and alanson, 2H6 1.01. 7
it shall be to the duchess of alanson, | the H8 3.02. 85

ALANSON'S 2 FR 0.0002 REL FR 1 V 1 P
i saw him at the duke alanson's once, | and much LLL 2.01. 61
him, he's a friend of the duke alanson's. H5 4.08. 18 P

ALARBUS' 1 FR 0.0001 REL FR 1 V 0 P
alarbus' limbs are lopp'd, | and entrails feed TIT 1.01.143

ALARBUS 1 FR 0.0001 REL FR 1 V 0 P
alarbus goes to rest, and we survive | to TIT 1.01.133

ALARM *(also alarum, etc., 'larum, etc.)*

ALARM 6 FR 0.0006 REL FR 6 V 0 P
patroclus, | arming to answer in a night alarm." TRO 1.03.171
would to the bleeding and the grim alarm MAC 5.02. 4
a blanket, in the alarm of fear caught up — HAM 2.02.509
and, as the sleeping soldiers in th' alarm, 3.04.120
mars's drum | and turn th' alarm to whispers; TNK 5.01. 81
chin, | the reason of this rash alarm to know, LUC 473

ALARMS 3 FR 0.0003 REL FR 3 V 0 P
be ready to direct these home alarms. R2 1.01.205
to love's alarms it will not ope the gate; VEN 424
gives false alarms, suggesteth mutiny, | and in 651

ALARUM *(also 'larum, etc.)*

ALARUM 9 FR 0.0010 REL FR 8 V 1 P
but hark, what new alarum is this same? H5 4.06. 35
sound, sound alarum! 1H6 1.02. 18
whence cometh this alarum, and the noise? 1.04. 99
sound, trumpets, alarum to the combatants! 2H6 2.03. 92
now, when the angry trumpet sounds alarum, | and 5.02. 3
strike alarum, drums! R3 4.04.149
sun | when the alarum were struck than idly sit COR 2.02. 76
when she speaks, is it not an alarum to love? OTH 2.03. 26 P
anon his beating heart, alarum striking, | gives LUC 433

ALARUM–BELL 2 FR 0.0002 REL FR 2 V 0 P
ring the alarum–bell! MAC 2.03. 74
ring the alarum–bell! 5.05. 50

ALARUM'D 2 FR 0.0002 REL FR 2 V 0 P
alarum'd by his sentinel, the wolf, | whose MAC 2.01. 53
and when he saw my best alarum'd spirits, | bold LR 2.01. 53

ALARUMS 5 FR 0.0005 REL FR 4 V 1 P
patience and mine to endure her loud alarums, SHR 1.01.127 P
beds, | hearing alarums at our chamber–doors. 1H6 2.01. 42
such fierce alarums both of hope and fear, | as 5.05. 85
our stern alarums chang'd to merry meetings, R3 1.01. 7
anon their loud alarums he doth hear, | and now VEN 700

/ALAS 3 FR 0.0003 REL FR 3 V 0 P
/alas, /the /tender /boy, /in /passion /mov'd, TIT 3.02. 48
/alas, /my /lord, /i /have /but /kill'd /a /fly. 3.02. 59
/alas, /poor /man, /grief /has /so /wrought /on 3.02. 79

ALAS 255 FR 0.0288 REL FR 195 V 60 P
and bend | the dukedom yet unbow'd (alas, poor TMP 1.02.115
alas, the storm is come again! 2.02. 37 P
alas, now pray you | work not so hard. 3.01. 15
alas! TGV 2.02. 20
alas, the way is wearisome and long. 2.07. 8
alas! 4.04. 76
why dost thou cry "alas"? 4.04. 77
and thinking on it makes me cry "alas!" 4.04. 84
alas, poor proteus, thou hast entertain'd | a 4.04. 91
alas, poor fool, why do i pity him | that with 4.04. 93
alas, poor lady, desolate and left! 4.04.174
alas, how love can trifle with itself! 4.04.183
out alas! here comes my master. WIV 1.04. 36 P
alas! he speaks but for his friend. 1.04.114 P
alas, the sweet woman leads an ill life with him 2.02. 88 P
alas, sir, i cannot fence. 2.03. 15 P
alas, i should be a pitiful lady! 3.03. 52 P
why, alas, what's the matter? 3.03.105 P
alas, how then? 3.04. 3
alas, i had rather be set quick i' th' earth, 3.04. 86
alas the day! 3.05. 38 P
alas! 4.02. 51 P
alas the day, i know not! 4.02. 69 P
out, alas, sir, cozenage! mere cozenage. 4.05. 63 P
alas, what noise? 5.05. 30 P
alas! MM 1.04. 75
my power? alas, i doubt — 1.04. 77
alas, this gentleman, | whom i would save, had a 2.01. 6
alas, it hath been great pains to you. 2.01.265 P
alas, | he hath but as offended in a dream! 2.02. 3
alas, alas! 2.02. 72
alas, alas! 2.02. 72
alas, alas! 3.01.132
alas, alas! 3.01.132
alas! ERR 1.01. 60
alas, poor women! 3.02. 21
alas, how fiery, and how sharp, he looks! 4.04. 50
alas, i sent you money to redeem you, | by 4.04. 83
alas, he gets nothing by that. ADO 1.01. 65 P
alas, poor hurt fowl! 2.01.202 P
all men are not alike, alas, good neighbor! 3.05. 40 P
alas, poor heart, if you spite it for my sake, i 5.02. 68 P
but, for alisander — alas, you see how 'tis — LLL 5.02.583 P
alas, poor machabeus, how hath he been baited! 5.02.631 P
but, alas, who can converse with a dumb show? MV 1.02. 72 P
but alas the while! 2.01. 31
alas, fifteen wives is nothing! 2.02.161 P
this ring, good sir, alas, it is a trifle! 4.01.430
alas! AYL 1.02.133 P
alas, he is too young! 1.02.153 P
alas, what danger will it be to us, | maids as 1.03.108
alas, poor shepherd! 2.04. 44
alas the day, what shall i do with my doublet 3.02.219 P
alas, dear love, i cannot lack thee two hours! 4.01.179 P
alas, poor shepherd! 4.03. 65
alas, good kate, i will not burthen thee, | for SHR 2.01.202
alas, sir, it is worse for me than so! 4.02. 88
alas! AWW 3.04. 1
alas, poor lady! 3.05. 63
alas, i took great pains to study it, and 'tis TN 1.05.194 P
alas the day! 2.01. 24 P
alas, /our frailty is the cause, not we! 2.02. 31
as i am woman (now alas the day!), 2.02. 38
alas, that they are so! 2.04. 40
alas, their love may be call'd appetite, | no 2.04. 97
"alas, why is she so?" 4.02. 77
alas, sir, how fell you besides your five wits? 4.02. 86 P
alas, sir, be patient. 4.02.103 P
alas, it is the baseness of thy fear | that 5.01.146
and yet, alas, now i remember me, | they say, 5.01.279
alas, malvolio, this is not my writing, | though 5.01.345
alas, poor fool, how have they baffled thee! 5.01.369
but when i came, alas, to wive, | with hey ho, 5.01.397
fear you his tyrannous passion more, alas, WT 2.03. 28
alas, i have show'd too much | the rashness of a 3.02.220
alas, poor man, a million of beating may come to 4.03. 59 P
alas, poor soul! 4.03. 71 P
out, alas! 4.04.110
alas, | i lost a couple, that 'twixt heaven and 5.01.131
of dolor to another, she did (with an "alas!"), 5.02. 88 P
alas, what need you be so boist'rous–rough? JN 4.01. 75
alas, i then have chid away my friend! 4.01. 86
alas, the part i had in woodstock's blood | doth R2 1.02. 1
where then, alas, may i complain myself? 1.02. 42
alas, i look'd when some of you should say | i 1.03.243
alas, poor duke, the task he undertakes | is 2.02.145
he? alas, he is poor, he hath nothing. 1H4 3.03. 76 P
alas the day, take heed of him! 2H4 2.01. 13 P
alas, sweet wife, my honor is at pawn, | and, 2.03. 7
alas, alas, put up your naked weapons, put up 2.04.206 P
alas, alas, put up your naked weapons, put up 2.04.206 P
alas, poor ape, how thou sweat'st! 2.04.216 P
alas, a black woosel, cousin shallow! 3.02. 8 P
alas, your too much love and care of me | are H5 2.02. 52
alas, poor harry of england! 3.07.130 P
alas, she hath from france too long been chas'd, 5.02. 38
alas, this is a child, a silly dwarf! 1H6 2.03. 22
alas, what joy shall noble talbot have | to bid 4.03. 39
alas, my years are young; 5.01. 21
alas, sir, i am but a poor petitioner of our 2H6 1.03. 23 P
alas, my lord, hang me if ever i spake the words 1.03.197 P
alas, my lord, i cannot fight; 1.03.213 P
alas, good master, my wife desired some damsons, 2.01.100
alas, master, i know not. 2.01.116
alas, master, i am not able to stand alone; 2.01.142
alas, master, what shall i do? 2.01.149 P
alas, sir, we did it for pure need. 2.01.154
alas, he hath no home, no place to fly to; 4.08. 38
but out, alas, | we bodg'd again, as i have seen 3H6 1.04. 18
alas, poor york, but that i hate thee deadly, 1.04. 84
tears, | and say, "alas, it was a piteous deed!" 1.04.163
alas, you know, 'tis far from hence to france; 4.01. 4
alas, poor clarence! 4.01. 59
alas, how should you govern any kingdom, | that 4.03. 35
alas, that warwick had no more forecast, | but, 5.01. 42
alas, i am not coop'd here for defense! 5.01.109
say you can swim, alas, 'tis but a while; 5.04. 29
alas, i blame you not, for you are mortal, | and R3 1.02. 44
and turns the sun to shade — alas, alas! 1.03.265
and turns the sun to shade — alas, alas! 1.03.265
alas! 1.04.211
alas for both, both mine, edward and clarence! 2.02. 73
alas! 2.02. 80
alas! 2.02. 86
alas, why would you heap this care on me? 3.07.204
alas, i rather hate myself | for hateful deeds 5.03.189
alas, poor lady! | she's a stranger now again. H8 2.03. 16
alas, sir! 2.04. 18
alas, i am a woman, friendless, hopeless! 3.01. 80
alas, h'as banish'd me his bed already, | his 3.01.119
alas, poor wenches, where are now your fortunes? 3.01.148
alas, our places, | the way of our profession is 3.01.156
alas, good lady! 4.01. 35
alas, poor man! 4.02. 16
alas, good lady! 5.01. 69
alas, i know not, how gets the tide in? 5.03. 18
let him to field, troilus, alas, hath none. TRO 1.01. 5
himself? alas, poor troilus, i would he were! 1.02. 72 P
alas, poor chin! many a wart is richer. 1.02.141 P
for what, alas, can these my single arms? 2.02.135
alas the day, how loath you are to offend 3.02. 47 P
but alas, | i am as true as truth's simplicity, 3.02.168
alas, poor wretch! 4.02. 31 P
alas, a kind of godly jealousy | (which i 4.04. 80
alas, it is my vice, my fault: 4.04.102
for how can we, | alas! COR 5.03.107
but out alas, here have we found him dead. TIT 2.03.258
alas, a crimson river of warm blood, | like to a 2.04. 22
alas, poor heart, that kiss is comfortless | as 3.01.250
alas, sweet aunt, i know not what you mean. 4.01. 4
alas, sir, i know not jubiter, i never drank 4.03. 85 P
alas, sir, i never came there. 4.03. 90 P
alas, you know i am no vaunter, i; 5.03.113
alas that love, so gentle in his view, | should ROM 1.01.169
alas that love, whose view is muffled still, 1.01.171
alas, poor romeo, he is already dead, stabb'd 2.04. 13 P
it did, it did, alas the day, it did! 3.02. 72
alas, alas! 4.05. 14
alas, alas! 4.05. 14
out, alas, she's cold, | her blood is settled, 4.05. 25
alas, my liege, my wife is dead to–night; 5.03.210
alas, good lord! TIM 3.01. 22 P
alas, my lord — 3.04. 91 P
alas, kind lord, | he's flung in rage from this 4.02. 44
in whose breast | doubt and suspect, alas, are 4.03.512
alas, it cried, "give me some drink, titinius," JC 1.02.127
where i stood, cried, "alas, good soul!" 1.02.272 P
but, alas, | caesar must bleed for it! 2.01.170
alas, good cassius, do not think of him. 2.01.185
alas, my lord, | your wisdom is consum'd in 2.02. 48
gentlemen all — alas, what shall i say? 3.01.190
what private griefs they have, alas, i know not, 3.02.213
alas, you know not! 3.02.237
alas, thou hast misconstrued every thing! 5.03. 84
woe, alas! | what, in our house? MAC 2.03. 87
alas the day, | what good could they pretend? 2.04. 23
why then, alas, | do i put up that womanly 4.02. 77
alas, poor country, | almost afraid to know 4.03.164
alas, poor ghost! HAM 1.05. 4
alas, he's mad! 3.04.105
alas, how is't with you, | that you do bend your 3.04.116
alas, how shall this bloody deed be answer'd? 4.01. 16
alas, alas! 4.03. 26 P
alas, alas! 4.03. 26 P
alas, sweet lady, what imports this song? 4.05. 27
alas, look here, my lord. 4.05. 37
alas, then she is drown'd? 4.07.183
alas, poor yorick, i knew him, horatio, a fellow 5.01.184 P
but yet, alas, stood i within his grace, | i LR 1.01.273
alas, sir, are you here? 3.02. 42
alas! she has no speech. OTH 2.01.102
alas, thrice–gentle cassio, | my advocation is 3.04.122
alas the day, i never gave him cause. 3.04.158
alas, poor caitiff! 4.01.108
alas, poor rogue, i think, /i' /faith, she loves 4.01.111
alas, alas! 4.01.276
alas, alas! 4.01.276
alas the heavy day! 4.02. 42
but, alas, to make me | the fixed figure for the 4.02. 53
alas, what ignorant sin have i committed? 4.02. 70
alas, what does this gentleman conceive? 4.02. 95
alas, iago, my lord hath so bewhor'd her, 4.02.115
do not weep, do not weep. alas the day! 4.02.124
alas, iago, | what shall i do to win my lord 4.02.148
alas, he faints! o cassio, cassio, cassio! 5.01. 84
alas, my friend and my dear countryman 5.01. 89
alas, what is the matter? 5.01.111
alas, good gentleman! alas, good cassio! 5.01.115
alas, good gentleman! alas, good cassio! 5.01.115

alas, why gnaw you so your nether lip? 5.02. 43
alas, he is betray'd and i undone! 5.02. 76
out, and alas, that was my lady's voice. 5.02.119
alas! who knows? 5.02.126
no, alas, i found it, | and i did give't my 5.02.230
so speaking as i think, alas, i die. 5.02.251
alas, and woe! ANT 4.14.107
alas, poor princess, | thou divine imogen, what CYM 2.01. 56
alas, good lady! 3.04. 45
alas, my lord, | how can she be with him? 3.05. 89
o posthumus, alas, | where is thy head? 4.02.320
alas, | there is no more such masters. 4.02.370
but, alas, i swerve. 5.04.129
alas, sir! PER 1.02. 95
alas, the seas hath cast me on the rocks, 2.01. 5
alas, poor souls, it griev'd my heart to hear 2.01. 20 P
alas, my father, it befits not me | unto a 2.03. 66
but alas, | being a natural sister of our sex, TNK 1.01.124
but, alas, | our hands advanc'd before our 1.02.111
alas, the prison i keep, though it be for great 2.01. 2 P
alas, alas, | poor cousin palamon, poor prisoner 3.01. 22
alas, alas, | poor cousin palamon, poor prisoner 3.01. 22
alas, | dissolve, my life! 3.02. 28
alas, no; 3.04. 4
alas, the pity! 3.06.185
alas, sir, where's your daughter? 4.01. 32
alas, what pity it is! 4.01. 94
now, come ask me, brother — | alas, i know not! 4.02. 51
alas, 'tis a sore life they have i' th' tother 4.03. 31 P
alas, what then? 4.03. 61 P
alas, | i have no voice, sir, to confirm her 5.02. 14
alas, that's nothing. 5.02. 57
alas, poor chicken! 5.02. 96
alas, poor palamon! 5.03.104
alas, poor things, what is it you have got, STM II.C 68
alas, alas, say now the king, | as he is clement II.C 122
alas, alas, say now the king, | as he is clement II.C 122
"alas, he nought esteems that face of thine, VEN 631
"alas, poor world, what treasure hast thou lost! 1075
alas, how many bear such shameful blows, | which LUC 832
me, | from that, alas, thy lucrece is not free. 1624
to put in practice either, alas, it was a spite PP 15. 7
alas, she could not help it! 15.12
but, alas, my hand hath sworn | ne'er to pluck 16.11
alas, 'tis true i have gone here and there, SON 110. 1
alas, why, fearing of time's tyranny, | might i 115. 9
ALBAN *(see albon, etc.)*
ALBANY 6 FR 0.0006 REL FR 4 V 2 P
more affected the duke of albany than cornwall. LR 1.01. 2 P
and you, our no less loving son of albany, | we 1.01. 42
cornwall and albany, | with my two daughters' 1.01.127
toward, 'twixt the dukes of cornwall and albany? 2.01. 11 P
upon his party 'gainst the duke of albany? 2.01. 26
with mutual cunning) 'twixt albany and cornwall; 3.01. 21
/ALBANY'S 1 FR 0.0001 REL FR 1 V 0 P
/of /albany's /and /cornwall's /powers /you LR 4.03. 48
ALBANY'S 1 FR 0.0001 REL FR 1 V 0 P
to thine and albany's /issue | be this perpetual LR 1.01. 66
ALBEIT 16 FR 0.0018 REL FR 14 V 2 P
albeit i will confess thy father's wealth | was WIV 3.04. 13
albeit my wrongs might make one wiser mad. ERR 5.01.217
albeit i neither lend nor borrow | by taking nor MV 1.03. 61
albeit i'll swear that i do know your tongue. 2.06. 27
albeit i confess your coming before me is nearer AYL 1.01. 50 P
albeit you have deserv'd | high commendation, 1.02.262
albeit the quality of the time and quarrel TN 3.03. 31
albeit we swear | a voluntary zeal and an JN 5.02. 9
my heart, | albeit i make a hazard of my head. 1H4 1.03.128
albeit considerations infinite | do make against 5.01.102
father is sick, albeit i could tell to thee — 2H4 2.02. 40 P
albeit against my conscience and my soul. R3 3.07.226
albeit they were flesh'd villains, bloody dogs, 4.03. 6
and shall, albeit sweet music issues thence. TRO 3.02.134
eyes, | albeit unused to the melting mood, OTH 5.02.349
fellow, | albeit he comes on angry purpose now; CYM 2.03. 56
ALBION 3 FR 0.0003 REL FR 3 V 0 P
farm | in that nook–shotten isle of albion. H5 3.05. 14
from worthy edward, king of albion, | my lord 3H6 3.03. 49
then shall the realm of albion | come to great LR 3.02. 85
ALBION'S 3 FR 0.0003 REL FR 3 V 0 P
isle, | and this the royalty of albion's king? 2H6 1.03. 45
for losing ken of albion's wished coast. 3.02.113
great albion's queen in former golden days; 3H6 3.03. 7
ALBON 3 FR 0.0003 REL FR 2 V 1 P
by good saint albon, who said, "simon, come; 2H6 2.01. 89
clear as day, i thank god and saint albon. 2.01.106 P
my lords, saint albon here hath done a miracle; 2.01.129
ALBON'S 1 FR 0.0001 REL FR 1 V 0 P
forsooth, a blind man at saint albon's shrine, 2H6 2.01. 61
ALBONS 13 FR 0.0014 REL FR 11 V 2 P
stol'n from my host at saint albons, or the 1H4 4.02. 46 P
as the way between saint albons and london. 2H4 2.02.168 P
you do prepare to ride unto saint albons, 2H6 1.02. 57
when from saint albons we do make return, 1.02. 83
king is now in progress towards saint albons, 1.04. 72
my masters of saint albons, have you not 2.01.133
the castle in saint albons, somerset | hath made 5.02. 68
saint albons battle won by famous york | shall 5.03. 30
march'd toward saint albons to intercept the 3H6 2.01.114
short tale to make, we at saint albons met, 2.01.120
when you and i met at saint albons last, | your 2.02.103
at saint albons field | this lady's husband, sir 3.02. 1
in margaret's battle at saint albons slain? R3 1.03.129
AL'CE *(also alice)*
AL'CE 1 FR 0.0001 REL FR 1 V 0 P
al'ce madam, or joan madam? SHR in.2. 110
ALCHEMIST *(see alchymist, alcumist)*
ALCHEMY *(see alchymy, alcumy)*
ALCHYMIST 1 FR 0.0001 REL FR 1 V 0 P
stays in his course and plays the alchymist, JN 3.01. 78
ALCHYMY 1 FR 0.0001 REL FR 1 V 0 P
in us, | his countenance, like richest alchymy, JC 1.03.159
ALCIBIADES' 1 FR 0.0001 REL FR 1 V 0 P
teach them to prevent wild alcibiades' wrath. TIM 5.01.203
ALCIBIADES 13 FR 0.0014 REL FR 9 V 4 P
'tis alcibiades, and some twenty horse, | all of TIM 1.01.241
captain alcibiades, your heart's in the field 1.02. 73 P
alcibiades, | thou art a soldier, therefore 1.02.221
done, we'll forth again, | my alcibiades. 2.02. 15
this is to lord timon, this to alcibiades. 2.02. 84 P
alcibiades is banish'd: hear you of it? 3.06. 53 P
alcibiades banish'd? 3.06. 54 P
alcibiades reports it; 5.01. 4
drive back | of alcibiades th' approaches wild, 5.01.164
if alcibiades kill my countrymen, | let 5.01.169
countrymen, | let alcibiades know this of timon, 5.01.170
be alcibiades your plague, you his, | and last 5.01.189
man was riding | from alcibiades to timon's cave 5.02. 10
ALCIDES' 2 FR 0.0002 REL FR 2 V 0 P
and let it be more than alcides' twelve. SHR 1.02.256
of him | as great alcides' /shows upon an ass. JN 2.01.144
ALCIDES 6 FR 0.0006 REL FR 6 V 0 P
so is alcides beaten by his /page, | and so may MV 2.01. 35
than young alcides, when he did redeem | the 3.02. 55
but where's the great alcides of the field, 1H6 4.07. 60
nor great alcides, nor the god of war, | shall TIT 4.02. 95
me, | alcides, thou mine ancestor, thy rage. ANT 4.12. 44
so charm'd me that methought alcides was | to TNK 5.03.119
ALCUMIST *(also alchymist)*
ALCUMIST 1 FR 0.0001 REL FR 1 V 0 P
you are an alcumist, make gold of that. TIM 5.01.114
ALCUMY *(also alchymy)*
ALCUMY 2 FR 0.0002 REL FR 2 V 0 P
gilding pale streams with heavenly alcumy; SON 33. 4
and that your love taught it this alcumy, | to 114. 4
ALDER–LIEFEST 1 FR 0.0001 REL FR 1 V 0 P
beads, | with you, mine alder–liefest sovereign, 2H6 1.01. 28
ALDERMAN 1 FR 0.0001 REL FR 1 V 0 P
agot–stone | on the forefinger of an alderman, ROM 1.04. 56
ALDERMAN'S 1 FR 0.0001 REL FR 0 V 1 P
could have crept into any alderman's thumb–ring. 1H4 2.04.331 P
ALDERMEN 1 FR 0.0001 REL FR 1 V 0 P
tell him, myself, the mayor and aldermen, | in R3 3.07. 66
ALE 13 FR 0.0014 REL FR 5 V 8 P
in thee as to go to the ale with a christian. TGV 2.05. 58 P
"item, she brews good ale." 3.01.303 P
"blessing of your heart, you brew good ale." 3.01.305 P
bob, | and on her withered dewlop pour the ale. MND 2.01. 50
were he not warm'd with ale, | this were a bed SHR in.1. 32
for god's sake, a pot of small ale. in.2. 1 P
not fourteen pence on the score for sheer ale, in.2. 23 P
and once again a pot o' th' smallest ale. in.2. 75
virtuous, there shall be no more cakes and ale? TN 2.03.116 P
edge, | for a quart of ale is a dish for a king. WT 4.03. 8
i would have him poisoned with a pot of ale. 1H4 1.03.233
give all my fame for a pot of ale and safety. H5 3.02. 13 P
do you look for ale and cakes here, you rude H8 5.03. 10 P
ALECTO'S 1 FR 0.0001 REL FR 1 V 0 P
revenge from ebon den with fell alecto's snake, 2H4 5.05. 37
ALEHOUSE' 1 FR 0.0001 REL FR 1 V 0 P
for underneath an alehouse' paltry sign, | the 2H6 5.02. 67
ALEHOUSE 8 FR 0.0009 REL FR 3 V 5 P
madcap, i'll to the alehouse with you presently; TGV 2.05. 8 P
if thou wilt, go with me to the alehouse; 2.05. 54 P
do ye make an alehouse of my lady's house, that TN 2.03. 89 P
when triumph is become an alehouse guest? R2 5.01. 15
would i were in an alehouse in london, i would H5 3.02. 12 P
it, | and make my image but an alehouse sign. 2H6 3.02. 81
ye alehouse painted signs! TIT 4.02. 98
paradoxes to make fools laugh i' th' alehouse. OTH 2.01.139 P
ALEHOUSES 1 FR 0.0001 REL FR 0 V 1 P
you are to call at all the alehouses, and bid ADO 3.03. 42 P
ALEMBIC *(see limbeck, etc.)*
ALENCON *(see alanson, etc.)*
ALEPPO 2 FR 0.0002 REL FR 2 V 0 P
her husband's to aleppo gone, master o' th' MAC 1.03. 7
and say besides, that in aleppo once, | where a OTH 5.02.352
ALES 2 FR 0.0002 REL FR 0 V 2 P
did, in his ales and his angers, look you, kill H5 4.07. 38 P
friend clytus, being in his ales and his cups; 4.07. 46 P
ALEVEN *(also eleven, 'leven)*
ALEVEN 6 FR 0.0006 REL FR 4 V 2 P
aleven widows and nine maids is a simple MV 2.02.162 P
by aleven of the clock it will go one way or TRO 3.03.295 P
'tis since the earthquake now aleven years, ROM 1.03. 23
and since that time it is aleven years, | for 1.03. 35
upon the platform 'twixt aleven and twelf | i'll HAM 1.02.251
at parting) when our count | was each aleven. TNK 1.03. 54
ALEVENPENCE 1 FR 0.0001 REL FR 0 V 1 P
at a harry groat, butter at alevenpence a pound, STM II.C 2 P
ALEVEN–PENCE–FARTHING 1 FR 0.0001 REL FR 0 V 1 P
than remuneration, aleven–pence–farthing better; LLL 3.01.171 P
ALE–WASH'D 1 FR 0.0001 REL FR 0 V 1 P
do among foaming bottles and ale–wash'd wits, is H5 3.06. 78 P
ALE–WIFE 1 FR 0.0001 REL FR 0 V 1 P
ask marian hacket, the fat ale–wife of wincot, SHR in.2. 22 P
ALE–WIVE'S 1 FR 0.0001 REL FR 0 V 1 P
two holes in the ale–wive's petticoat and so 2H4 2.02. 82 P
ALEXANDER *(also alisander)*
ALEXANDER 19 FR 0.0021 REL FR 5 V 14 P
the parish curate, alexander; LLL 5.02.535 P
proceed, good alexander. 5.02.567
great alexander | left his to th' worthiest; WT 5.01. 47
town's name where alexander the pig was born? H5 4.07. 13 P
alexander the great. 4.07. 14 P
i think alexander the great was born in macedon. 4.07. 19 P
think it is in macedon where alexander is porn. 4.07. 22 P
alexander, god knows, and you know, in his rages 4.07. 34 P
as alexander kill'd his friend clytus, being in 4.07. 45 P
that alexander iden, an esquire of kent, | took 2H6 4.10. 43
alexander iden, that's my name, | a poor esquire 5.01. 74
good morrow, alexander. TRO 1.02. 44 P
in his state, as a thing made for alexander. COR 5.04. 22 P
dost thou think alexander look'd a' this fashion HAM 5.01.197 P
imagination trace the noble dust of alexander, 5.01.204 P
alexander died, alexander was buried, alexander 5.01.208 P
alexander died, alexander was buried, alexander 5.01.209 P
was buried, alexander returneth to dust, the 5.01.209 P
parthia, and armenia | he gave to alexander; ANT 3.06. 15
ALEXANDER'S 1 FR 0.0001 REL FR 0 V 1 P
if you mark alexander's life well, harry of H5 4.07. 31 P
ALEXANDERS 1 FR 0.0001 REL FR 1 V 0 P
fathers that, like so many alexanders, | have in H5 3.01. 19
ALEXANDRIA 5 FR 0.0005 REL FR 5 V 0 P
from alexandria | this is the news: ANT 1.04. 3
when rioting in alexandria you | did pocket up 2.02. 72
he has done all this and more | in alexandria. 3.06. 2
caesar sets down in alexandria, where | i will 3.13.168
through alexandria make a jolly march, | bear 4.08. 30
ALEXANDRIAN 2 FR 0.0002 REL FR 2 V 0 P
this is not yet an alexandrian feast. ANT 2.07. 96
stage us, and present | our alexandrian revels: 5.02.218
ALEXAS 10 FR 0.0011 REL FR 5 V 5 P
lord alexas, sweet alexas, most any thing alexas ANT 1.02. 1 P
lord alexas, sweet alexas, most any thing alexas 1.02. 1 P
sweet alexas, most any thing alexas, almost most 1.02. 2 P
alexas, almost most absolute alexas, where's the 1.02. 2 P
alexas — come, his fortune, his fortune! 1.02. 62 P
seek him, and bring him hither. where's alexas? 1.02. 85
welcome, my good alexas. 1.05. 66
go to the fellow, good alexas, bid him | report 2.05.111
bid you alexas | bring me word how tall she is. 2.05.117
alexas did revolt, and went to jewry on 4.06. 11
ALGIERS *(see argier)*
ALIAS 3 FR 0.0003 REL FR 0 V 3 P
sir, alias the prince of darkness, alias the AWW 4.05. 42 P
alias the prince of darkness, alias the devil. 4.05. 43 P
testy magistrates (alias fools) as any in rome. COR 2.01. 44 P
ALICE *(also al'ce)*
ALICE 4 FR 0.0004 REL FR 0 V 4 P
why, did you not lend it to alice shortcake upon WIV 1.01.204 P
sir alice ford! 2.01. 51 P
alice, tu as ete en angleterre, et tu bien H5 3.04. 1 P
excusez–moi, alice; 3.04. 28 P
ALIEN 3 FR 0.0003 REL FR 3 V 0 P
of venice, | if it be proved against an alien, MV 4.01.349
and art almost an alien to the hearts | of all 1H4 3.02. 34
my verse | as every alien pen hath got my use, SON 78. 3
ALIENA 6 FR 0.0006 REL FR 1 V 5 P
no longer celia, but aliena. AYL 1.03.128
therefore courage, good aliena. 2.04. 8 P
i'll tell thee, aliena, i cannot be out of the 4.01.215 P
but say with me, i love aliena; 5.02. 8 P
go you and prepare aliena; 5.02. 15 P
out, when your brother marries aliena, shall you 5.02. 63 P
A–LIFE 1 FR 0.0001 REL FR 0 V 1 P
i love a ballet in print, a–life, for then we WT 4.04.261 P
ALIGHT 2 FR 0.0002 REL FR 2 V 0 P
bid her alight, | and her troth plight, | and LR 3.04.122
"vouchsafe, thou wonder, to alight thy steed, VEN 13
ALIGHTED 3 FR 0.0003 REL FR 2 V 1 P
madam, there is alighted at your gate | a young MV 2.09. 86
e'en at hand, alighted by this; SHR 4.01.117 P
certain nobles of the senate | newly alighted, TIM 1.02.175
ALIIS 1 FR 0.0001 REL FR 1 V 0 P
long tool, | cum multis aliis that make a dance. TNK 3.05.133
ALIKE 42 FR 0.0047 REL FR 36 V 6 P
of us, 'twere all alike | as if we had them not. MM 1.01. 34
of such a burthen male, twins both alike. ERR 1.01. 55
fortune had left to both of us alike | what to 1.01.105
all men are not alike, alas, good neighbor! ADO 3.05. 40 P
for none offend where all alike do dote. LLL 4.03.124
eyes | to see alike mine honor as their profits WT 1.02.310
visage from our cottage, but | looks on alike. 4.04.446
the odds for high and low's alike. 5.01.207
both are alike, and both alike we like. JN 2.01.331
both are alike, and both alike we like. 2.01.331
that the situations, look you, is both alike. H5 4.07. 26 P
one, 'tis alike as my fingers is to my fingers, 4.07. 30 P
at all times will you have my power alike? 1H6 2.01. 55
"good gloucester" and "good devil" were alike, 3H6 5.06. 4
you that are blam'd for it alike with us, | know H8 1.02. 39
but you frame | things that are known alike, 1.02. 45
his curses and his blessings | touch me alike; 2.02. 53
both alike. TRO 4.01. 55
had i a dozen sons, each in my love alike, and COR 1.03. 23 P
let's fetch him off, or make remain alike. 1.04. 62
we hate alike: 1.08. 2
that when the sea was calm all boats alike 4.01. 6
fair lords, your fortunes are alike in all, TIT 1.01.174
yet every mother breeds not sons alike — | do 2.03.146
two households, both alike in dignity, | in fair ROM pr 1
in penalty alike, and 'tis not hard, i think, 1.02. 2
again, | alike bewitched by the charm of looks; 2.pr. 6
your diet shall be in all places alike. TIM 3.06. 67 P
we are fellows still, | serving alike in sorrow. 4.02. 19
at all times alike | men are not still the same; 5.01.121
from the bill | that writes them all alike: MAC 3.01.100
our dungy earth alike | feeds beast as man; ANT 1.01. 35
your fortunes are alike. 1.02. 55
and make the wars alike against my stomach, 2.02. 50
against my stomach, | having alike your cause? 2.02. 51
quality after them, | to suffer all alike. 3.13. 34
a lady that disdains | thee and the devil alike. CYM 1.06.148
and men in dangerous bonds pray not alike; 3.02. 37
in birth, alike conversant in general services, 4.01. 12 P
differs in dignity, | whose dust is both alike. 4.02. 5
creatures may be alike; 5.05.125
since all alike my songs and praises be | to one SON 105. 3
ALISANDER *(also alexander)*
ALISANDER 6 FR 0.0006 REL FR 2 V 4 P
scutcheon plain declares that i am alisander" — LLL 5.02.564
most true, 'tis right; you were so, alisander. 5.02.569
take away the conqueror, take away alisander. 5.02.572 P
you have overthrown alisander the conqueror! 5.02.575 P
run away for shame, alisander. 5.02.579 P
but, for alisander — alas, you see how 'tis — 5.02.583 P
ALIT 1 FR 0.0001 REL FR 1 V 0 P
"qui me alit, me extinguit." PER 2.02. 33
ALIVE 97 FR 0.0109 REL FR 77 V 20 P
i not doubt | he came alive to land. TMP 2.01.123
professes to persuade) the king his son's alive, 2.01.236
dead or alive? 2.02. 25 P
i will forget that julia is alive, | rememb'ring TGV 2.06. 27
foster'd, illumin'd, cherish'd, kept alive. 3.01.184
now i dare not say | i have one friend alive; 5.04. 66
is scarce truth enough alive to make societies MM 3.02.227 P
danger that might come | if he were known alive? 4.03. 86
order else have died, | i have reserv'd alive. 5.01.467
if i know more of any man alive | than that ADO 4.01.178

me, is my boy, god rest his soul, alive or dead? MV 2.02. 72 P
there be fools alive, iwis, | silver'd o'er, and 2.09. 68
of all the men alive | i never yet beheld that SHR 2.01. 10
there's place and means for every man alive. AWW 4.03.339
daughter–in–law had been alive at this hour, and 4.05. 5 P
you are the cruell'st she alive | if you will TN 1.05.241
tell me what blessings i have here alive, | that WT 3.02.107
o that he were alive, and here beholding | his 3.02.120
i had not left a purse alive in the whole army. 4.04.618 P
he has a son, who shall be flay'd alive; 4.04.783 P
remember "ston'd," and "flay'd alive." 4.04.805 P
young arthur is alive. JN 4.02.251
again | after they heard young arthur was alive? 5.01. 38
and when i mount, alive may i not light, | if i R2 1.01. 82
for methinks in you | i see old gaunt alive. 2.03.118
that man is not alive | might so have tempted 1H4 3.01.171
is now alive | to grace this latter age with 5.01. 91
not three of my hundred and fifty left alive, 5.03. 37 P
hal, if percy be alive, thou gets not my sword, 5.03. 50 P
well, if percy be alive, i'll pierce him. 5.03. 56 P
dead | bears not alive so stout a gentleman. 5.04. 93
art thou alive? 5.04.134
if the man were alive and would deny it, 'zounds 5.04.152 P
many a creature else | had been alive this hour, 5.05. 8
dead, | not he which says the dead is not alive. 2H4 1.01. 99
and is jane nightwork alive? 3.02.199 P
honor, | i am the most offending soul alive. H5 4.03. 29
'tis certain there's not a boy left alive, and 4.07. 5 P
one that i should fight withal, if he be alive. 4.07.123 P
if alive and ever dare to challenge this glove, 4.07.126 P
as he was a soldier, he would wear if alive, i 4.07.130 P
heaven, be thou gracious to none alive, | if 1H6 1.04. 85
ah, york, no man alive so fain as i! 2H6 3.01.244
sighs, | and all to have the noble duke alive. 3.02. 64
alive again? 3.03. 12
and the bricks are alive at this day to testify 4.02.149 P
ah, were the duke of suffolk now alive, | these 4.04. 41
for they lov'd well when they were alive. 4.07.131 P
may that ground gape, and swallow me alive, 3H6 1.01.161
line, | and leave not one alive, i live in hell. 1.03. 33
why then he is alive. R3 1.02. 91
i do not know that englishman alive | with whom 2.01. 70
if that our noble father were alive? 2.02. 7
save that, for reverence to some alive, | i give 3.07.193
what heir of york is there alive but we? 4.04.471
the greatest monarch now alive may glory | in H8 5.02.198
if thou wouldst not entomb thyself alive | and TRO 3.03.186
no man alive can love in such a sort | the thing 4.01. 24
had, | behold the poor remains, alive and dead! TIT 1.01. 81
whom your goths beheld | alive and dead, and for 1.01.123
we know not where you left them all alive, | but 2.03.257
will send thee hither both thy sons alive, | and 3.01.155
the villain is alive in titus' house, | and as 5.03.123
thy juliet is alive, | for whose dear sake thou ROM 3.03.135
so much differ, | and we alive that lived? TIM 3.01. 47
thou art the cap of all the fools alive. 4.03.358
choler does kill me that thou art alive; 4.03.367
i, timon, who, alive, all living men did hate; 5.04. 72
ay, if i be alive, and your mind hold, and your JC 1.02.291 P
well, to our work alive. 4.03.196
enemy | shall ever take alive the noble brutus; 5.04. 22
when you do find him, or alive or dead, | he 5.04. 24
go on, | and see whe'er brutus be alive or dead, 5.04. 30
or be alive again, | and dare me to the desert MAC 3.04.102
for 'twould have anger'd any heart alive | to 3.06. 15
upon the next tree shall thou hang alive, | till 5.05. 38
to the eels when she put 'em i' th' paste alive; LR 2.04.123 P
alive or dead? 4.06. 45
neither can be enjoy'd | if both remain alive: 5.01. 59
i carry out my side, | her husband being alive. 5.01. 62
produce the bodies, be they alive or dead. 5.03.231
let me hear thee say | that cassio's not alive. OTH 3.03.473
there's millions now alive | that nightly lie in 4.01. 67
our will is antony be took alive; ANT 4.06. 2
nor cymbeline dreams that they are alive. CYM 3.03. 81
is as good as ajax', | when neither are alive. 4.02.253
he's alive, my lord. 4.02.359
the same dead thing alive. 5.05.123
he strive | to killen bad, keep good alive, PER 2.ch. 20
she is alive; 3.02. 97
there's many a man alive that hath outliv'd TNK 5.04. 1
in that thy likeness still is left alive." VEN 174
thus hoping that adonis is alive, | her rash 1009
what face remains alive that's worth the viewing 1076
and leave the falt'ring feeble souls alive? LUC 1768
but were some child of yours alive that time, SON 17.13
none else to me, nor i to none alive, | that my 112. 7
/ALL 40 FR 0.0045 REL FR 34 V 6 P
ALL 3997 FR 0.4518 REL FR 3309 V 688 P
ALLA 2 FR 0.0002 REL FR 1 V 1 P
alla nostra casa ben venuto, molto honorato SHR 1.02. 25 P
alla stoccato carries it away. ROM 3.01. 74
ALL–ABHORRED 1 FR 0.0001 REL FR 1 V 0 P
unknit | this churlish knot of all–abhorred war? 1H4 5.01. 16
ALL–ADMIRING 1 FR 0.0001 REL FR 1 V 0 P
and, all–admiring, with an inward wish | you H5 1.01. 39
ALLAY 13 FR 0.0014 REL FR 10 V 3 P
put the wild waters in this roar, allay them. TMP 1.02. 2
pain | to allay with some cold drops of modesty MV 2.02.186
o love, be moderate, allay thy ecstasy, | in 3.02.111
gift of a coward to allay the gust he hath in TN 1.03. 31 P
to whose feeling sorrows i might be some allay WT 4.02. 8 P
that nothing can allay, nothing but blood, | the JN 3.01.342
it would allay the burning quality | of that 5.07. 8
ay, and allay this thy abortive pride: 2H6 4.01. 60
quench, | or but allay, the fire of passion. H8 1.01.149
and allay those tongues | that durst disperse it 2.01.152
desire not | t' allay my rages and revenges with COR 5.03. 85
mischief of your person it would scarcely allay. LR 1.02.164 P
"but yet," it does allay | the good precedence; ANT 2.05. 50
ALLAY'D 2 FR 0.0002 REL FR 2 V 0 P
my mildness hath allay'd their swelling griefs, 3H6 4.08. 42
which but to–day by feeding is allay'd, SON 56. 3
ALLAYING 2 FR 0.0002 REL FR 1 V 1 P
allaying both their fury and my passion | with TMP 1.02.393
hot wine with not a drop of allaying tiber in't; COR 2.01. 49 P
ALLAYMENT 1 FR 0.0001 REL FR 1 V 0 P
the like allayment could i give my grief: TRO 4.04. 8
ALLAYMENTS 1 FR 0.0001 REL FR 1 V 0 P
and apply | allayments to their act, and by them CYM 1.05. 22
ALLAYS 1 FR 0.0001 REL FR 1 V 0 P
and when the rage allays, the rain begins. 3H6 1.04.146
ALL–/BINDING 1 FR 0.0001 REL FR 1 V 0 P
from the manacles | of the all–/binding law; MM 2.04. 94
ALL–CHANGING 1 FR 0.0001 REL FR 1 V 0 P
this bawd, this broker, this all–changing word, JN 2.01.582
ALL–CHEERING 1 FR 0.0001 REL FR 1 V 0 P
but all so soon as the all–cheering sun | should ROM 1.01.134
ALL–DISGRACED 1 FR 0.0001 REL FR 1 V 0 P
she | from egypt drive her all–disgraced friend, ANT 3.12. 22
ALL–DREADED 1 FR 0.0001 REL FR 1 V 0 P
nor th' all–dreaded thunder–stone. CYM 4.02.271
ALL–EATING 1 FR 0.0001 REL FR 1 V 0 P
own deep–sunken eyes | were an all–eating shame, SON 2. 8
ALLEGATION 1 FR 0.0001 REL FR 1 V 0 P
and york, | reprove my allegation if you can, 2H6 3.01. 40
ALLEGATIONS 1 FR 0.0001 REL FR 1 V 0 P
false allegations to o'erthrow his state? 2H6 3.01.181
ALLEGE *(also 'leges)*
ALLEGE 2 FR 0.0002 REL FR 2 V 0 P
the reasons you allege do more conduce | to the TRO 2.02.168
laws, | since why to love i can allege no cause. SON 49.14
ALLEGED 2 FR 0.0002 REL FR 2 V 0 P
and alleged | many sharp reasons to defeat the H8 2.01. 13
the sharp thorny points | of my alleged reasons, 2.04.226
ALLEGIANCE 26 FR 0.0029 REL FR 21 V 5 P
i charge thee on thy allegiance. ADO 1.01.208 P
but on my allegiance, mark you this, on my 1.01.211 P
mark you this, on my allegiance, he is in love. 1.01.211 P
if they should have any allegiance in them, 3.03. 5 P
on your allegiance, | out of the chamber with WT 2.03.121
to the faith and allegiance of a true subject, 3.02. 19 P
doth revolt | from his allegiance to an heretic, JN 3.01.175
swearing allegiance and the love of soul | to 5.01. 10
which honor and allegiance cannot think. R2 2.01.208
and sends allegiance and true faith of heart 3.03. 37
that i did pluck allegiance from men's hearts, 1H4 3.02. 52
as if allegiance in their bosoms sate | crowned H5 2.02. 4
we charge you, on allegiance to ourself, | to 1H6 3.01. 86
then swear allegiance to his majesty, | as thou 5.04.169
peace, | and keep the frenchmen in allegiance. 5.05. 43
against thy oath and true allegiance sworn, 2H6 5.01. 20
hast thou not sworn allegiance unto me? 5.01.179
and we his subjects, sworn in all allegiance, 3H6 3.01. 70
for now we owe allegiance unto henry. 4.07. 19
and thou a kingdom — all of you allegiance. R3 1.03.170
and cold hearts freeze | allegiance in them; H8 1.02. 62
never find a heart | with less allegiance in it! 5.02. 78
keep | my bosom franchis'd and allegiance clear, MAC 2.01. 28
to hell, allegiance! HAM 4.05.132
me, recreant, | on thine allegiance, hear me! LR 1.01.167
endure | to follow with allegiance a fall'n lord ANT 3.13. 44
ALLEGIANT 1 FR 0.0001 REL FR 1 V 0 P
i | can nothing render but allegiant thanks, H8 3.02.176
ALL–ENDING 1 FR 0.0001 REL FR 1 V 0 P
posterity, | even to the general all–ending day. R3 3.01. 78
ALLEY 2 FR 0.0002 REL FR 1 V 1 P
in a thick–pleach'd alley in mine orchard, were ADO 1.02. 10 P
come, | as we do trace this alley up and down, 3.01. 16
ALLEYS 2 FR 0.0002 REL FR 2 V 0 P
one that countermands | the passages of alleys, ERR 4.02. 38
the natural gates and alleys of the body, | and HAM 1.05. 67
ALL–FEAR'D 1 FR 0.0001 REL FR 1 V 0 P
the all–fear'd gods, bow down your stubborn TNK 5.01. 13
ALL–HAIL 2 FR 0.0002 REL FR 2 V 0 P
each in either side | give the all–hail to thee, COR 5.03.139
greater than both, by the all–hail hereafter! MAC 1.05. 55
ALL–HAIL'D 1 FR 0.0001 REL FR 0 V 1 P
the king, who all–hail'd me 'thane of cawdor,' MAC 1.05. 7 P
ALL–HALLOND 1 FR 0.0001 REL FR 0 V 1 P
all–hallond eve. MM 2.01.126 P
ALL–HALLOWMAS 1 FR 0.0001 REL FR 0 V 1 P
it to alice shortcake upon all–hallowmas last, a WIV 1.01.204 P
ALL–HALLOWN 1 FR 0.0001 REL FR 0 V 1 P
farewell, all–hallown summer! 1H4 1.02.158 P
ALL–HATING 1 FR 0.0001 REL FR 1 V 0 P
is a strange brooch in this all–hating world. R2 5.05. 66
ALL–HIDING 1 FR 0.0001 REL FR 1 V 0 P
which underneath thy black all–hiding cloak LUC 801
ALL–HONOR'D 1 FR 0.0001 REL FR 1 V 0 P
and what | made all–honor'd, honest, roman ANT 2.06. 16
ALL–HURTING 1 FR 0.0001 REL FR 1 V 0 P
could scape the hail of his all–hurting aim, LC 310
ALLIANCE 17 FR 0.0019 REL FR 16 V 1 P
good lord, for alliance! ADO 2.01.318 P
one day shall crown th' alliance on't, so please TN 5.01.318
too mighty, | and in his parties, his alliance. WT 2.03. 21
i pray you then, in love and dear alliance, H5 5.02.345
and for alliance sake, declare the cause | my 1H6 2.05. 53
that in alliance, amity, and oaths, | there 4.01. 62
france | as his alliance will confirm our peace, 5.05. 42
unless abroad they purchase great alliance? 3H6 3.03. 70
device | by this alliance to make void my suit. 3.03.142
is this th' alliance that he seeks with france? 3.03.177
yet, to have join'd with france in such alliance 4.01. 36
are near to warwick by blood and by alliance: 4.01.136
this fair alliance quickly shall call home | to R3 4.04.313
infer fair england's peace by this alliance. 4.04.343
for this alliance may so happy prove | to turn ROM 2.03. 91
therefore let our alliance be combin'd, | our JC 4.01. 43
o miserable end of our alliance! TNK 5.04. 86
ALLICHOLY *(also allycholly, mallicholy, melancholy)*
ALLICHOLY 1 FR 0.0001 REL FR 0 V 1 P
she is given too much to allicholy and musing; WIV 1.04.154 P
ALLIED 5 FR 0.0005 REL FR 3 V 2 P
/an heir, and /near allied unto the duke. TGV 4.01. 47
it is well allied; MM 3.02.102 P
kinsman, she's nothing allied to your disorders. TN 2.03. 97 P
courts and kingdoms | known and allied to yours. WT 1.02.339
crown, neither allied | to eminent assistants, H8 1.01. 61
ALLIES 6 FR 0.0006 REL FR 6 V 0 P
you to your land, and love, and great allies; AYL 5.04.189
against acquaintance, kindred, and allies. 1H4 1.01. 16
and tell them 'tis the queen and her allies R3 1.03.329
with thy embracements to my wive's allies, | and 2.01. 30
by the suggestion of the queen's allies; 3.02.101
false to his children and his wive's allies; 5.01. 15
ALLIGANT *(also elegancy)*
ALLIGANT 1 FR 0.0001 REL FR 0 V 1 P
in silk and gold, and in such alligant terms, WIV 2.02. 68 P
ALLIGATOR 1 FR 0.0001 REL FR 1 V 0 P
an alligator stuff'd, and other skins | of ROM 5.01. 43
ALL–LICENS'D 1 FR 0.0001 REL FR 1 V 0 P
not only, sir, this your all–licens'd fool, LR 1.04.201
ALL–NOBLE 2 FR 0.0002 REL FR 2 V 0 P
them more | than thee, all–noble martius. COR 4.05.106
me from the arm | of the all–noble theseus, for TNK 1.03. 93
ALL–OBEYING 1 FR 0.0001 REL FR 1 V 0 P
from his all–obeying breath i hear | the doom of ANT 3.13. 77
ALL–OBLIVIOUS 1 FR 0.0001 REL FR 1 V 0 P
'gainst death and all–oblivious enmity | shall SON 55. 9
/ALLONS 3 FR 0.0003 REL FR 2 V 1 P
/allons! LLL 4.03.380
/allons! 4.03.380
/allons! we will employ thee. 5.01.152 P
ALLONS–NOUS 1 FR 0.0001 REL FR 0 V 1 P
c'est assez pour une fois: allons–nous a diner. H5 3.04. 61 P
ALLOT 1 FR 0.0001 REL FR 1 V 0 P
five days we do allot thee, for provision | to LR 1.01.173
ALLOTS 1 FR 0.0001 REL FR 1 V 0 P
stars | allots thee for his lovely bedfellow! SHR 4.05. 41
ALLOTTED 2 FR 0.0002 REL FR 2 V 0 P
miracle, | thou art allotted to be ta'en by me; 1H6 5.03. 55
and undeserv'd reproach to him allotted | that LUC 824
ALLOTTERY 1 FR 0.0001 REL FR 0 V 1 P
or give me the poor allottery my father left me AYL 1.01. 73 P
/ALLOW 1 FR 0.0001 REL FR 1 V 0 P
/which, /if /convenience /will /not /allow, LR 3.06. 99
ALLOW 28 FR 0.0031 REL FR 19 V 9 P
if the law would allow it, sir. MM 2.01.227 P
but the law will not allow it, pompey; 2.01.228 P
therefore allow me such exercises as may become AYL 1.01. 72 P
prithee allow the wind. AWW 5.02. 8 P
that will allow me very worth his service. TN 1.02. 59
of pythagoras ere i will allow of thy wits, and 4.02. 59 P
have it as it ought to be, you must allow vox. 5.01.295 P
of this allow, | if ever you have spent time WT 4.01. 29
at this time | he will allow no speech (which i 4.04.468
which to maintain i would allow him odds | and R2 1.01. 62
free speech and fearless i to thee allow. 1.01.123
now, | whose state and honor i for aye allow. 5.02. 40
why, they will allow us ne'er a jordan, and then 1H4 2.01. 19 P
i well allow the occasion of our arms, | but 2H4 1.03. 5
i do allow this wen to be as familiar with me as 2.02.106 P
i like them all, and do allow them well, | and 4.02. 54
for competence of life i will allow you, | that 5.05. 66
us as we are tasted, allow us as we prove. TRO 3.02. 91 P
allow their officers, and are content | to COR 3.03. 45
doth grace for grace and love for love allow; ROM 2.03. 86
the scope | of these delated articles allow. HAM 1.02. 38
if your sweet sway | allow obedience, if you LR 2.04.191
allow not nature more than nature needs, | man's 2.04.266
the time will not allow the compliment | which 5.03.234
best, and wrastle, | that these times can allow. TNK 2.05. 4
who, wond'ring at him, did his words allow. LUC 1845
him in thy course untainted do allow | for SON 19.11
ill, | so you o'er–green my bad, my good allow? 112. 4
ALLOWANCE 11 FR 0.0012 REL FR 10 V 1 P
the king's will or the state's allowance, | a H8 3.02.322
give him allowance for the better man, | for TRO 1.03.376
a stirring dwarf we do allowance give | before a 2.03.137
of no allowance to your bosom's truth. COR 3.02. 57
on such regards of safety and allowance | as HAM 2.02. 79
censure of which one must, in your allowance, 3.02. 27 P
this course and put it on | by your allowance; LR 1.04.209
under th' allowance of your great aspect, 2.02.106
if this be known to you, and your allowance, OTH 1.01.127
pilot | of very expert and approv'd allowance; 2.01. 49
which superstition | here finds allowance — on TNK 5.04. 54
ALLOW'D 20 FR 0.0022 REL FR 12 V 8 P
generally allow'd for your many war–like, WIV 2.02.227 P
nor it shall not be allow'd in vienna. MM 2.01.229 P
and the worser allow'd by order of law a furr'd 3.02. 7 P
she is allow'd for the dey–woman. LLL 1.02.131 P
go, you are allow'd; 5.02.478
there is no slander in an allow'd fool, though TN 1.05. 94 P
and allow'd your approach rather to wonder at 1.05.198 P
are such allow'd infirmities that honesty | is WT 1.02.263
for once allow'd the skillful pilot's charge? 3H6 5.04. 20
a full hot horse, who being allow'd his way, H8 1.01.133
(once weak ones) is | not ours, or not allow'd; 1.02. 83
scholars allow'd freely to argue for her. 2.02.112
read, | and on all sides th' authority allow'd; 2.04. 4
weep for me, | almost no grave allow'd me. 3.01.151
allow'd with absolute power, and thy good name TIM 5.01.162
antony | (by our permission) is allow'd to make. JC 3.02. 59
yet here she is allow'd her virgin crants, | her HAM 5.01.232
to sudden death, | not shriving time allow'd. 5.02. 47
there a substitute of most allow'd sufficiency, OTH 1.03.224 P
as since he hath been allow'd the name of. CYM 1.04. 3 P
ALLOWED 2 FR 0.0002 REL FR 2 V 0 P
and though it be allowed in meaner parties CYM 2.03.116
service, so being done, | but being so allowed. 3.03. 17
ALLOWING 3 FR 0.0003 REL FR 3 V 0 P
boldness of a wife | to her allowing husband! WT 1.02.185
your patience this allowing, | i turn my glass, 4.01. 15
allowing him a breath, a little scene, | to R2 3.02.164
/ALLOWS 1 FR 0.0001 REL FR 1 V 0 P
/madness | /allows /itself /to /any /thing. LR 3.07.105
ALLOWS 3 FR 0.0003 REL FR 2 V 1 P
the law allows it, and the court awards it. MV 4.01.303
the courtesy of nations allows you my better, in AYL 1.01. 46 P
and this is all a liberal course allows: TIM 3.03. 40
ALLOW'ST 1 FR 0.0001 REL FR 1 V 0 P
allow'st no more blood than will make a blush, TNK 5.01.141
ALL–PRAISED 1 FR 0.0001 REL FR 1 V 0 P
this gallant hotspur, this all–praised knight, 1H4 3.02.140
ALL–ROYAL 1 FR 0.0001 REL FR 1 V 0 P
remember me | to our all–royal brother, for TNK 1.03. 12
ALL'S 39 FR 0.0044 REL FR 34 V 5 P
speak softly, | all's hush'd as midnight yet. TMP 4.01.207
well, a horn for my money, when all's done. ADO 2.03. 61 P
but all's brave that youth mounts and folly AYL 3.04. 45 P

all's one to him. AWW 4.03.138 P
all's well that ends well! 4.04. 35
all's well that ends well yet, | though time 5.01. 25
all's true that is mistrusted. WT 2.01. 48
all's done, all's won, here breathless lies the 1H4 5.03. 16
all's done, all's won, here breathless lies the 5.03. 16
i hope, my lord, all's well. 2H4 2.01.170 P
but all's not done — yet keep the french the H5 4.06. 2
which, | or somerset or york, all's one to me. 2H6 1.03.102
i hope all's for the best. 3H6 3.03.170
well, all's one for that. R3 5.03. 8
all's now done but the ceremony | of bringing H8 2.01. 4
all's not well. 5.01. 88
all's done, my lord. TRO 5.02.115
now all's his, | when by and by the din of war COR 2.02.114
all's in anger. 3.02. 95
all's well; 4.06. 16
when all's spent, he'ld be cross'd then, and he TIM 1.02.162
all's obliquy; 4.03. 18
stay not, all's in vain. 5.01.184
but all's too weak; MAC 1.02. 15
all's well. 2.01. 19
nought's had, all's spent, | where our desire is 3.02. 4
when all's done, | you look but on a stool. 3.04. 66
not think how ill all's here about my heart — HAM 5.02.212 P
all's not offense that indiscretion finds | and LR 2.04.196
all's cheerless, dark, and deadly. 5.03.291
all's well /now, sweeting; OTH 2.03.252
all's one. 4.03. 23
all's but naught: ANT 4.15. 78
approach ho, all's not well; caesar's beguil'd. 5.02.323
all's well, sir. CYM 1.06.179
our courtiers say all's savage but at court. 4.02. 33
a willing man dies sleeping, and all's done. TNK 2.02. 68
night and stow her, | and all's made up again. 2.03. 33
all's char'd when he is gone. 3.02. 21
ALL–SEEING 2 FR 0.0002 REL FR 2 V 0 P
all–seeing heaven, what a world is this! R3 2.01. 83
the all–seeing sun | ne'er saw her match since ROM 1.02. 92
ALL–SEER 1 FR 0.0001 REL FR 1 V 0 P
that high all–seer, which i dallied with, | hath R3 5.01. 20
ALL–SHAKING 1 FR 0.0001 REL FR 1 V 0 P
and thou, all–shaking thunder, | strike flat the LR 3.02. 6
ALL–SHUNN'D 1 FR 0.0001 REL FR 1 V 0 P
air, | with his disease of all–shunn'd poverty, TIM 4.02. 14
ALL–SOULS' 3 FR 0.0003 REL FR 3 V 0 P
this is all–souls' day, fellow, is it not? R3 5.01. 10
why then all–souls' day is my body's doomsday. 5.01. 12
this, this all–souls' day to my fearful soul, 5.01. 18
ALL–TELLING 1 FR 0.0001 REL FR 1 V 0 P
ignorant, all–telling fame | doth noise abroad, LLL 2.01. 21
ALL–THING 1 FR 0.0001 REL FR 1 V 0 P
in our great feast, | and all–thing unbecoming. MAC 3.01. 13
ALL–TOO–PRECIOUS 1 FR 0.0001 REL FR 1 V 0 P
bound for the prize of all–too–precious you, SON 86. 2
ALL–TRIUMPHANT 1 FR 0.0001 REL FR 1 V 0 P
shine | with all–triumphant splendor on my brow, SON 33.10
ALL–UNABLE 1 FR 0.0001 REL FR 1 V 0 P
thus far, with rough and all–unable pen, | our H5 ep 1
ALLUR'D 1 FR 0.0001 REL FR 1 V 0 P
vomit emptiness, | not so allur'd to feed. CYM 1.06. 46
ALLURE 4 FR 0.0004 REL FR 4 V 0 P
be strong in whore, allure him, burn him up, TIM 4.03.142
look thorough a casement to allure false hearts, CYM 2.04. 34
would allure | and make a batt'ry through his PER 5.01. 46
she show'd him favors to allure his eye; PP 4. 6
ALLUREMENT 1 FR 0.0001 REL FR 0 V 1 P
to take heed of the allurement of one count AWW 4.03.214 P
ALLURING 1 FR 0.0001 REL FR 1 V 0 P
hath homely age th' alluring beauty took | from ERR 2.01. 89
ALLUSION 2 FR 0.0002 REL FR 0 V 2 P
th' allusion holds in the exchange. LLL 4.02. 41 P
i say, th' allusion holds in the exchange. 4.02. 44 P
ALL–WATCHED 1 FR 0.0001 REL FR 1 V 0 P
of color | unto the weary and all–watched night; H5 4.pr. 38
ALL–WORTHY 2 FR 0.0002 REL FR 2 V 0 P
o, my all–worthy lord! CYM 3.05. 94
all–worthy villain! 3.05. 94
ALLY 1 FR 0.0001 REL FR 1 V 0 P
this gentleman, the prince's near ally, | my ROM 3.01.109
ALLYCHOLLY *(also allicholy, mallicholy, melancholy)*
ALLYCHOLLY 1 FR 0.0001 REL FR 0 V 1 P
now, my young guest, methinks you're allycholly; TGV 4.02. 27 P
ALMAIN 1 FR 0.0001 REL FR 0 V 1 P
he sweats not to overthrow your almain; OTH 2.03. 83 P
ALMANAC 3 FR 0.0003 REL FR 1 V 2 P
here comes the almanac of my true date: ERR 1.02. 41
look in the almanac! MND 3.01. 53 P
what says th' almanac to that? 2H4 2.04.264 P
ALMANACS 1 FR 0.0001 REL FR 0 V 1 P
storms and tempests than almanacs can report. ANT 1.02.149 P
ALMIGHTY 8 FR 0.0009 REL FR 8 V 0 P
neglect | of his almighty dreadful little might. LLL 3.01.203
"the armipotent mars, of lances the almighty, 5.02.644
"the armipotent mars, of lances the almighty, 5.02.651
he wills you, in the name of god almighty, H5 2.04. 77
god almighty! 4.01. 3
ay, god almighty help me! 2H6 2.01. 93
call, | constring'd in mass by the almighty sun, TRO 5.02.173
she conjures him by high almighty jove, | by LUC 568
ALMOND 1 FR 0.0001 REL FR 0 V 1 P
will not do more for an almond than he for a TRO 5.02.193 P
/ALMOST 1 FR 0.0001 REL FR 1 V 0 P
(/which /is, /almost, /to /pluck /a /kingdom 2H4 1.03. 49
ALMOST 174 FR 0.0196 REL FR 138 V 36 P
uninhabitable, and almost inaccessible — TMP 2.01. 38 P
it is — which is indeed almost beyond credit — 2.01. 60 P
when he is earth'd, hath here almost persuaded 2.01.234
thy eyes are almost set in thy head. 3.02. 9 P
you shall find | many, nay, almost any. 3.03. 34
the minute of their plot | is almost come. 4.01.142
trust me, i think 'tis almost day. TGV 4.02.138 P
almost as well as i do know myself. 4.04.143
well, sirs, i am almost out at heels. WIV 1.03. 31 P
it makes me almost ready to wrangle with mine 2.01. 84 P
have worn your eyes almost out in the service, MM 1.02.110 P
for, as i take it, it is almost day. 4.02.106 P
come away, it is almost clear dawn. 4.02.210 P
head — | as like almost to claudio as himself. 5.01.489
herself (almost at fainting under | the pleasing ERR 1.01. 45
hath almost made me traitor to myself; 3.02.162
i have not breath'd almost since i did see it. 5.01.181
i have almost matter enough in me for such an ADO 1.01.279 P
'tis almost five a' clock, cousin, 'tis time you 3.04. 52 P
you are almost come to part almost a fray. 5.01.113 P
you are almost come to part almost a fray. 5.01.114 P
almost the copy of my child that's dead, | and 5.01.289
they swore that you were almost sick for me. 5.04. 80
almost i had. LLL 3.01. 34 P
i swoon almost with fear. MND 2.02.154
lovers, to bed, 'tis almost fairy time. 5.01.364
speak, would almost damn those ears | which, MV 1.01. 98
his hour is almost past. 2.06. 2
thou almost mak'st me waver in my faith | to 4.01.130
it is almost morning, | and yet i am sure you 5.01.295
i assure thee (and almost with tears i speak it) AYL 1.01.153 P
stretch his leathern coat | almost to bursting, 2.01. 38
from /seventeen years till now almost fourscore 2.03. 71
i faint almost to death. 2.04. 66
i almost die for food, and let me have it. 2.07.104
and almost chide god for making you that 4.01. 36 P
the poor world is almost six thousand years old, 4.01. 95 P
master and mistress are almost frozen to death. SHR 4.01. 37 P
i dare assure you, sir, 'tis almost two, | and 4.03.189
whose skill was almost as great as his honesty; AWW 1.01. 19 P
but we have almost emboss'd him, you shall see 3.06. 99 P
reading it he chang'd almost into another man. 4.03. 5 P
dear almost as his life, which gratitude 4.04. 6
he hath indeed, almost natural; TN 1.03. 29 P
peascod, or a codling when 'tis almost an apple. 1.05.158 P
"his eyes do show his days are almost done." 2.03.104
i'll tell thee, i am almost sick for one — 3.01. 46 P
yet they say we are | almost as like as eggs; WT 1.02.130
camillo, | may this (almost a miracle) be done? 4.04.534
the one i have almost forgot — your pardon — 5.01.104
they seem'd almost, with staring on one another, 5.02. 11 P
my lord's almost so far transported that | he'll 5.03. 69
i am almost asham'd | to say what good respect i JN 3.03. 27
or do you almost think, although you see, | that 4.03. 43
up, | last in the field, and almost lords of it! 5.05. 8
i left him almost speechless, and broke out | to 5.06. 24
and art almost an alien to the hearts | of all 1H4 3.02. 34
the king is almost wounded to the death, | and, 2H4 1.01. 14
hard | a gentleman, almost forespent with speed, 1.01. 37
keep his own grace, but he's almost out of mine, 1.02. 28 P
and dead almost, my liege, to think you were, 4.05.156
o'er france and all her almost kingly dukedoms, H5 1.02.227
that (almost) mightst have coin'd me into gold, 2.02. 98
i have | almost no better than so many french; 3.06.147
that the fix'd sentinels almost receive | the 4.pr. 6
and made me almost yield upon my knees. 1H6 3.03. 80
and that the french were almost ten to one, 4.01. 21
vexation almost stops my breath, | that sund'red 4.03. 41
and so break off, the day is almost spent; 2H6 3.01.325
were almost like a sharp–quill'd porpentine; 3.01.363
ay, almost slain, for he is taken prisoner, 3H6 4.04. 7
bulk, | who almost burst to belch it in the sea. R3 1.04. 41
when we both lay in the field | frozen (almost) 2.01.116
you cannot reason (almost) with a man | that 2.03. 39
york | has almost overta'en him in his growth. 2.04. 7
/mayor, | would you imagine, or almost believe, 3.05. 35
and almost should'red in the swallowing gulf 3.07.128
/once," quoth forrest, "almost chang'd my mind; 4.03. 15
did almost sweat to bear | the pride upon them, H8 1.01. 24
loyalty, and almost appears | in loud rebellion. 1.02. 28
not almost appears, | it doth appear; 1.02. 29
almost with ravish'd list'ning, could not find 1.02.120
almost forgot my pray'rs to content him? 3.01.132
weep for me, | almost no grave allow'd me. 3.01.151
all famous colleges | almost in christendom. 3.02. 67
her suff'rance made | almost each pang a death. 5.01. 69
and they will almost | give us a prince of blood TRO 3.03. 25
knows almost every /grain /of /pluto's /gold, 3.03.197
keeps place with thought and almost, like the 3.03.199
in hector, | the one almost as infinite as all, 4.05. 80
nay, these are almost thoroughly persuaded; COR 1.01.201
which was | to take in many towns ere (almost) 1.02. 24
come, come, they are almost here. 2.02. 1 P
almost all | repent in their election. 2.03.254
and is almost mature for the violent breaking 4.03. 25 P
and in his praise | have (almost) stamp'd the 5.02. 22
almost at point to enter. 5.04. 61
upon a gath'red lily almost withered. TIT 3.01.113
were his heart | almost impregnable, his old 4.04. 98
and almost broke my heart with extreme laughter. 5.01.113
sport, | she sounded almost at my pleasing tale, 5.01.119
even when their sorrows almost was forgot, | and 5.01.137
'tis almost morning, i would have thee gone — ROM 2.02.176
that almost freezes up the heat of life. 4.03. 16
i am almost afraid to stand alone | here in the 5.03. 10
the painting is almost the natural man; TIM 1.01.157
h'as almost charm'd me from my profession, by 4.03.450 P
it almost turns my dangerous nature wild. 4.03.492
the crown, that it had, almost, chok'd caesar, JC 1.02.248 P
will crowd a feeble man almost to death. 2.04. 36
now they are almost on him. 5.03. 30
tongue | hath almost ended his live's history. 5.05. 40
who, almost dead for breath, had scarcely more MAC 1.05. 36
he has almost supp'd. 1.07. 29
timely on him, | i have almost slipp'd the hour. 2.03. 47
almost a mile; 3.03. 12
almost at odds with morning, which is which. 3.04.126
poor country, | almost afraid to know itself! 4.03.165
i have almost forgot the taste of fears. 5.05. 9
war, | the day almost itself professes yours, 5.07. 27
was sick almost to doomsday with eclipse. HAM 1.01.120
almost to jelly with the act of fear, | stand 1.02.205
lord, | with almost all the holy vows of heaven. 1.03.114
my hour is almost come, | when i to sulph'rous 1.05. 2
yonder cloud that's almost in shape of a camel? 3.02.376 P
almost as bad, good mother, | as kill a king, 3.04. 28
is but to whet thy almost blunted purpose. 3.04.111
for use almost can change the stamp of nature, 3.04.168
queen his mother | lives almost by his looks, 4.07. 12
and yet it is almost against my conscience. 5.02.296
nature is asham'd | almost t' acknowledge hers. LR 1.01.213
nothing almost sees miracles | but misery. 2.02.165
'tis hard, almost impossible. 2.04.242
tell thee, friend, | i am almost mad myself. 3.04.166
her cock, a buoy | almost too small for sight. 4.06. 20
hold it in, | for i am almost ready to dissolve, 5.03.204
(a fellow almost damn'd in a fair wife), | that OTH 1.01. 21
whom love hath turn'd almost the wrong side out, 2.03. 52
my money is almost spent; 2.03.365 P
is not almost a fault | t' incur a private check 3.03. 66
and could almost read | the thoughts of people. 3.04. 57
have rubb'd this young quat almost to the sense, 5.01. 11
he's almost slain, and roderigo quite dead. 5.01.114
that dost almost persuade | justice to break her 5.02. 16
any thing alexas, almost most absolute alexas, ANT 1.02. 2 P
that truth should be silent i had almost forgot. 2.02.108 P
the wild disguise hath almost | antick'd us all. 2.07.124
caesar dead, | he cried almost to roaring; 3.02. 55
overbuys me | almost the sum he pays. CYM 1.01.147
almost, sir: 1.01.148
i had almost forgot | t' entreat your grace but 1.06.180
almost midnight, madam. 2.02. 2
it's almost morning, is't not? 2.03. 9 P
which swell'd so much that it did almost stretch 3.01. 49
i see into thy end and am almost | a man already 3.04.166
to whom being going, almost spent with hunger, 3.06. 62
'tis almost night, you shall have better cheer 3.06. 66
endur'd a sea | that almost burst the deck. PER 4.01. 56
i have cried her almost to the number of her 4.02. 94 P
her monument | is almost finished, and her 4.03. 43
now our sands are almost run, | more a little, 5.02. 1
and almost breathless swim | in this deep water. TNK pr 24
i' th' aid o' th' current were almost to sink, 1.02. 8
which rips my bosom | almost to th' heart's — 1.02. 62
almost puts | faith in a fever, and deifies 1.02. 65
arcite) almost wanton | with my captivity. 2.02. 96
my death was noble, | dying almost a martyr. 2.06. 17
almost all men, and yet i yielded, theseus — 3.06.207
his globy eyes | had almost drawn their spheres, 5.01.114
fear | is almost chok'd by unresisted lust. LUC 282
the scalps of many, almost hid behind, | to jump 1413
yet in these thoughts myself almost despising, SON 29. 9
that every word doth almost /tell my name, 76. 7
and almost thence my nature is subdu'd | to what 111. 6
ALMS 13 FR 0.0014 REL FR 11 V 2 P
as aged, and doth beg the alms | of palsied eld; MM 3.01. 35
and he should, it were an alms to hang him. ADO 2.03.158 P
door | upon entreaty have a present alms, | if SHR 4.03. 5
so give alms; WT 4.04.138
his back, | wherein he puts alms for oblivion, TRO 3.03.146
i have your alms, adieu. COR 2.03. 81 P
bend like his | that hath receiv'd an alms! 3.02.120
so | as with a man by his own alms empoison'd, 5.06. 10
that have their alms out of the empress' chest. TIT 2.03. 9
lord, who hath receiv'd you | at fortune's alms. LR 1.01.278
up in some other course, | to fortune's alms. OTH 3.04.122
one bred of alms and foster'd with cold dishes, CYM 2.03.114
and time to see one that by alms doth live LUC 986
ALMS–BASKET 1 FR 0.0001 REL FR 0 V 1 P
have liv'd long on the alms–basket of words. LLL 5.01. 38 P
ALMS–DEED 1 FR 0.0001 REL FR 1 V 0 P
murther is thy alms–deed; 3H6 5.05. 79
ALMS–DRINK 1 FR 0.0001 REL FR 0 V 1 P
they have made him drink alms–drink. ANT 2.07. 5 P
ALMSHOUSES 1 FR 0.0001 REL FR 1 V 0 P
a hundred almshouses right well supplied; H5 1.01. 17
ALMSMAN'S 1 FR 0.0001 REL FR 1 V 0 P
my gay apparel for an almsman's gown, | my R2 3.03.149
ALOES 1 FR 0.0001 REL FR 1 V 0 P
the aloes of all forces, shocks, and fears. LC 273
ALOFT 13 FR 0.0014 REL FR 12 V 1 P
her chamber is aloft, far from the ground, | and TGV 3.01.114
but now i breathe again | aloft the flood, and JN 4.02.139
then will i raise aloft the milk–white rose, 2H6 1.01.254
master hume, that you be by her aloft, while we 1.04. 8 P
they know their master loves to be aloft, | and 2.01. 11
staff, | this day i'll wear aloft my burgonet, 5.01.204
safe out of fortune's shot, and sits aloft, TIT 2.01. 2
to mount aloft with thy imperial mistress, | and 2.01. 13
again, | till thou art here aloft or i below. 2.03.244
rome, | and rear'd aloft the bloody battle–axe, 3.01.168
from south to west on wing soaring aloft, CYM 5.05.471
this said, he shakes aloft his roman blade, LUC 505
to sing, | and heavy ignorance aloft to fly, SON 78. 6
/ALONE 3 FR 0.0003 REL FR 3 V 0 P
/let /them /alone. 2H4 2.03. 41
/who /alone /suffers, /suffers /most /i' /th' LR 3.06.104
/she /started | /to /deal /with /grief /alone. 4.03. 32
ALONE 240 FR 0.0271 REL FR 201 V 39 P
let it alone, thou fool, it is but trash. TMP 4.01.224
let/'t alone | and do the murther first. 4.01.231
but say, lucetta, now we are alone, | wouldst TGV 1.02. 1
to walk alone, like one that had the pestilence; 2.01. 21 P
she is alone. 2.04.167
then let her alone. 2.04.167
for why, the fools are mad, if left alone. 3.01. 99
i will go to her alone. 3.01.127
to thee, | that i may venture to depart alone. 4.03. 36
here can i sit alone, unseen of any, | and to 5.04. 4
go tell thy master i am alone. WIV 3.03. 36 P
are you not asham'd? let the clothes alone. 4.02.139 P
none, | and some condemned for a fault alone. MM 2.01. 40
would that alone a' love he would detain, | so ERR 2.01.107
and about evening come yourself alone | to know 3.01. 96
alone, it was the subject of my theme; 5.01. 65
to draw don pedro and the count claudio alone, ADO 2.02. 34 P
bear thee well in it, and leave us alone. 3.01. 13
why then let them alone till they are sober. 3.03. 45 P
yea, even i alone. 5.01.264
dead, | and she alone is heir to both of us. 5.01.290
as i for praise alone now seek to spill | the LLL 4.01. 34
eyes, | lives not alone immured in the brain, 4.03.325
then how can it be said i am alone, | when all MND 2.01.225
stay, on thy peril; i alone will go. 2.02. 87
that must needs be sport alone. 3.02.119
you for it, | though i alone do feel the injury. 3.02.219
let her alone; 3.02.332
let your epilogue alone. 5.01.362 P
though for myself alone | i would not be MV 3.02.150

let him alone, | i'll follow him no more with 3.03. 19
like argus, | if you do not, if i be left alone, 5.01.231
if ever he go alone again, i'll never wrastle AYL 1.01.161 P
leave me alone to woo him. 1.03.133
then, being there alone, | left and abandoned of 2.01. 49
thou seest we are not all alone unhappy: 2.07.136
faith, i had as lief have been myself alone. 3.02.254 P
poor men alone? 3.03. 57 P
servants, leave me and her alone. SHR in.2. 116
when i am alone, why then i am tranio; 1.01.243
one, | though paris came in hope to speed alone. 1.02.245
'tis bargain'd 'twixt us twain, being alone, 2.01.304
to see | how tame, when men and women are alone, 2.01.312
take /in your love, and then let me alone. 4.02. 71
sirs, let't alone, | i will not go to–day, and 4.03.193
and show what we alone must think, which never AWW 1.01.185
alone she was, and did communicate to herself 1.03.107 P
use to be made than alone the recov'ry of the 2.03. 36 P
good alone | is good, without a name; 2.03.128
let thy curtsies alone, they are scurvy ones. 5.03.323 P
is fancy | that it alone is high fantastical. TN 1.01. 15
it alone concerns your ear. 1.05.208 P
give us the place alone, we will hear this 1.05.218 P
you your leave, that i may bear my evils alone. 2.01. 6 P
for monsieur malvolio, let me alone with him. 2.03.134 P
none | shall mistress be of it, save i alone. 3.01.160
let me alone. 3.04. 96 P
let me alone with him. 3.04.109 P
nay, let me alone for swearing. 3.04.183 P
nay, let him alone. 4.01. 33 P
not he alone shall suffer what wit can make WT 4.04.772 P
let't alone. 5.03. 73
and not alone in habit and device, | exterior JN 1.01.210
you, | and 'a may catch your hide and you alone. 2.01.136
and leave those woes alone which i alone | am 3.01. 64
and leave those woes alone which i alone | am 3.01. 64
we will alone uphold | without th' assistance of 3.01.157
yet i alone, alone do me oppose | against the 3.01.170
i alone, alone do me oppose | against the pope, 3.01.170
reply | without a tongue, using conceit alone, 3.03. 50
go stand within; let me alone with him. 4.01. 84
in spite of spite, alone upholds the day. 5.04. 5
to have some conference with your grace alone. R2 5.03. 27
withdraw yourselves, and leave us here alone. 5.03. 28
this let alone will all the rest confound. 5.03. 86
i prithee leave the prince and me alone, i will 1H4 1.02.150 P
a jest to execute that i cannot manage alone. 1.02.162 P
he durst as well have met the devil alone | as 1.03.116
o my good lord, why are you thus alone? 2.03. 37
and start so often when thou sit'st alone? 2.03. 43
let them alone awhile, and then open the door. 2.04. 84 P
prithee let him alone, we shall have more anon. 2.04.207 P
prithee let her alone, and list to me. 3.03. 95 P
i might have let alone | the insulting hand of 5.04. 53
let it alone, i'll make other shift. 2H4 2.01.156 P
enough before, and you could have let me alone. 3.02.112 P
why did you leave me here alone, my lords? 4.05. 50
depart the chamber, leave us here alone. 4.05. 90
then i would he were here alone; H5 4.01.121 P
you love him not so ill to wish him here alone, 4.01.125 P
god's will, my liege, would you and i alone, 4.03. 74
and not to us, but to thy arm alone, | ascribe 4.08.107
by my consent, we'll even let them alone. 1H6 1.02. 44
well then, alone (since there's no remedy) | i 2.02. 57
not that alone | but all the whole inheritance i 3.01.162
the quarrel toucheth none but us alone, 4.01.118
but when my angry guardant stood alone, 4.07. 9
man, | we are alone, here's none but thee and i. 2H6 1.02. 69
alas, master, i am not able to stand alone; 2.01.142
let me alone. 4.02.102 P
will i stay | and live alone as secret as i may. 4.04. 48
now, clifford, i have singled thee alone: 3H6 2.04. 1
now, richard, i am with thee here alone: 2.04. 5
as being well content with that alone. 4.07. 24
i am myself alone. 5.06. 83
one) | were best to do it secretly alone. R3 1.01.100
misdeeds, | yet execute thy wrath in me alone! 1.04. 71
scatter'd, | and he himself wand'red away alone, 4.04.512
for my little cure, | let me alone. H8 1.04. 34
nay, sir nicholas, | let it alone; 2.01.101
thou art alone | (if thy rare qualities, sweet 2.04.137
have not alone | employ'd you where high profits 3.02.157
leave me alone, | for i must think of that which 5.01. 74
let 'em alone, and draw the curtain close; 5.02. 34
say he is a very man per se and stands alone. TRO 1.02. 16 P
pride alone | must /tarre the mastiffs on, as 1.03.389
were i alone to pass the difficulties, | and had 2.02.139
let these threats alone | till accident or 4.05.261
i'll fight with him alone. stand, diomed. 5.06. 9
to your bands, | let us alone to guard corioles. COR 1.02. 27
let her alone, lady; 1.03.104 P
he is himself alone, | to answer all the city. 1.04. 51
let him alone, | he did inform the truth. 1.06. 41
let him alone, or so many so minded, | wave thus 1.06. 73
o, me alone! 1.06. 76
tullus, | alone i fought in your corioles walls, 1.08. 8
we do it not alone, sir. 2.01. 34 P
i know you can do very little alone, for your 2.01. 35 P
are too infant–like for doing much alone. 2.01. 38 P
rome, that all alone martius did fight | within 2.01.162
alone he ent'red | the mortal gate of th' city, 2.02.110
believe't not lightly — though i go alone, 4.01. 29
alone i did it. 5.06.116
titus, when wert thou wont to walk alone, TIT 1.01.339
and then let me alone, | i'll find a day to 1.01.449
you are a young huntsman, marcus, let alone; 4.01.101
i warrant you, sir, let me alone. 4.03.114 P
content thee, gentle coz, let him alone, | 'a ROM 1.05. 65
as maids call medlars, when they laugh alone. 2.01. 36
you shall not stay alone | till holy church 2.06. 36
alone, in company, still my care hath been | to 3.05.177
which, too much minded by herself alone, | may 4.01. 13
my lord, we must entreat the time alone. 4.01. 40
to–morrow night look that thou lie alone, | let 4.01. 91
let me alone, | i'll play the huswife for this 4.02. 42
so please you, let me now be left alone, | and 4.03. 9
my dismal scene i needs must act alone. 4.03. 19
now must i to the monument alone, | within this 5.02. 24
i am almost afraid to stand alone | here in the 5.03. 10
stay then, i'll go alone. 5.03.135
then all alone, | at the prefixed hour of her 5.03.252
poverty, | walks, like contempt, alone. TIM 4.02. 15
i had rather be alone. 4.03.100
be crown'd with plagues, that thee alone obey! 5.01. 53
each man apart, all single and alone, | yet an 5.01.107
of the majestic world | and bear the palm alone. JC 1.02.131
is he alone? 2.01. 71
good countrymen, let me depart alone, | and, for 3.02. 55
depart, | save i alone, till antony have spoke. 3.02. 61
come, | revenge yourselves alone on cassius, 4.03. 94
'tis not meet | they be alone. 4.03.126
we will keep ourself | till supper–time alone; MAC 3.01. 43
how now, my lord, why do you keep alone, | of 3.02. 8
though the main part | pertains to you alone. 4.03.199
'tis not alone my inky cloak, /good mother, HAM 1.02. 77
for nature crescent does not grow alone | in 1.03. 11
if it some impartment did desire | to you alone. 1.04. 60
and thy commandement all alone shall live 1.05.102
now i am alone. 2.02.549
let his queen–mother all alone entreat him | to 3.01.182
the cess of majesty | dies not alone, but, like 3.03. 16
never alone | did the king sigh, but /with a 3.03. 22
of our ship, so i alone became their prisoner. 4.06. 20 P
and in a postscript here, he says, "alone." 4.07. 52
and find i am alone felicitate | in your dear LR 1.01. 75
age to receive not alone the imperfections of 1.01.297 P
let me alone. 3.04. 3
he's scarce awake, let him alone a while. 4.07. 50
we two alone will sing like birds i' th' cage; 5.03. 9
of some brief discourse | with desdemon alone. OTH 3.01. 53
let it alone. 3.03.288
how now? what do you here alone? 3.03.300
leave procreants alone, and shut the door; 4.02. 28
no messenger but thine, and all alone, ANT 1.01. 52
for not alone | the death of fulvia, with more 1.02.179
enthron'd i' th' market–place, did sit alone, 2.02.215
let it alone, let's to billards. come, charmian. 2.05. 3
three, | the senators alone of this great world, 2.06. 9
he alone | dealt on lieutenantry, and no 3.11. 38
sword against sword, | ourselves alone. 3.13. 28
and it portends alone | the fall of antony! 3.13.154
i am alone the villain of the earth, | and feel 4.06. 29
let him alone; 5.01. 71
she is alone th' arabian bird, and i | have lost CYM 1.06. 17
pray you away, | let me alone with him. 4.02. 70
so far have rav'd | to bring him here alone; 4.02.136
yet is't not probable | to come alone, either he 4.02.142
so the revenge alone pursu'd me. 4.02.157
she alone knew this; 5.05. 40
dian had hot dreams, | and she alone were cold; 5.05.181
let his arms alone, | they were not born for 5.05.305
how now, marina, why do you keep alone? PER 4.01. 21
care not for me, | i can go home alone. 4.01. 42
being gone, | not royal in their smells alone, TNK 1.01. 2
in a fever, and deifies alone | voluble chance; 1.02. 66
so unlike a noble kinsman, | to love alone? 2.02.191
let us alone, sir. 3.05. 31
him, but i laugh at 'em | and let 'em all alone. 4.01.127
for the tackling | let me alone. 4.01.146
palamon, thou art alone | and only beautiful, 4.02. 37
a virgin flow'r, | must grow alone, unpluck'd. 5.01.168
and dead, | statue contenting but the eye alone, VEN 213
i pray you hence, and leave me here alone, | for 382
but soundly sleeps, while now it sleeps alone. 786
infamy, | but i alone, alone must sit and pine, LUC 795
infamy, | but i alone, alone must sit and pine, 795
let sin, alone committed, light alone | upon his 1480
committed, light alone | upon his head that hath 1480
and blushing fled, and left her all alone. PP 9.14
poor corydon must live alone, | other help for 17.35
did banish moan, | save the nightingale alone. 20. 8
for having traffic with thyself alone, | thou of SON 4. 9
eyes, | i all alone beweep my outcast state, 29. 2
that due of many, now is thine alone. 31.12
without thy help, by me be borne alone. 36. 4
that due to thee which thou deserv'st alone. 39. 8
then she loves but me alone. 42.14
of four, with two alone | sinks down to death, 45. 7
gone, | save that to die, i leave my love alone. 66.14
then thou alone kingdoms of hearts shouldst owe. 70.14
now counting best to be with you alone, | then 75. 7
whilst i alone did call upon thy aid, | my verse 79. 1
aid, | my verse alone had all thy gentle grace, 79. 2
than this rich praise, that you alone are you, 84. 2
wretched in this alone, that thou mayst take 91.13
"kind," and "true" have often liv'd alone, 105.13
hours, | but all alone stands hugely politic, 124.11
so bold, | although i swear it to myself alone. 131. 8
is't not enough to torture me alone, | but slave 133. 3
invited | to any sensual feast with thee alone; 141. 8

ALONG *(also long*)*

/ALONG 1 FR 0.0001 REL FR 1 V 0 P
/i /pray /you /go | /along /with /me. LR 4.03. 55

ALONG 117 FR 0.0132 REL FR 105 V 12 P
i told your ladyship | had come along with me, TGV 2.04. 88
is gone with her along, and i must after, | for 2.04.176
but in what habit will you go along? 2.07. 39
thyself) | regard thy danger, and along with me. 3.01.258
plac'd, | i give consent to go along with you, 4.03. 39
and, as we walk along, i dare be bold | with our 5.04.162
please you, i'll tell you as we pass along, 5.04.168
boy, go along with this woman. WIV 2.02.132 P
both, my good host, to go along with me. 4.06. 47
i am in haste, go along with me, i'll tell you 5.01. 23 P
him know | i have a servant comes with me along, MM 4.01. 45
nay, tarry, i'll go along with thee. 4.03.165 P
come go along, my wife is coming yonder. ERR 4.04. 40
along with them | they brought one pinch, a 5.01.237
did point you to buy them, along as you pass'd; LLL 2.01.245
madam, came nothing else along with that? 5.02. 5
and travelling along this coast, i here am come 5.02.554
demetrius and egeus, go along; MND 1.01.123
under sail, | with him is gratiano gone along; MV 2.08. 2
past all saying nay, | to come with him along. 3.02.230
when it is paid, bring your true friend along. 3.02.308
else had she with her father rang'd along. AYL 1.03. 68
say what thou canst, i'll go along with thee. 1.03.105
so shall we pass along | and never stir 1.03.113
he'll go along o'er the wide world with me; 1.03.132
did steal behind him as he lay along | under an 2.01. 30
upon the brook that brawls along this wood, | to 2.01. 32
jumps along by him | and never stays to greet 2.01. 53
but come thy ways, we'll go along together, 2.03. 66
there lay he, stretch'd along, like a wounded 3.02.240 P
and bring along these rascal knaves with thee? SHR 4.01.131
which way thou travellest — if along with us, 4.05. 51
come go along and see the truth hereof, | for 4.05. 75
had it, save that he comes not along with her. AWW 3.02. 2 P
more i'll entreat you | written to bear along. 3.02. 95
your brother he shall go along with me. 3.06.108
to speak with her, and bring her along with you, TN 5.01. 43 P
trunk which you | shall bear along impawn'd, WT 1.02.436
let's along. 5.02.112 P
with him along is come the mother–queen, | an JN 2.01. 62
go, bear not along | the clogging burthen of a R2 1.03.199
will you go along with us? 2.02.140
and thus still doing, thus he pass'd along. 5.02. 21
they will along with company, for they have 1H4 2.01. 45 P
and lards the lean earth as he walks along. 2.02.109
under whose government come they along? 4.01. 19
i learn'd in worcester, as i rode along, | he 4.01.125
new wound in your thigh, come you along with me. 5.04.129 P
come, go along with me, good master gower. 2H4 2.01.179
and as i came along | i met and overtook a dozen 2.04.357
will't please your grace to go along with us? 4.05. 19
take all his company along with him. 5.05. 92
if they march along | unfought withal, but i H5 3.05. 11
and like a peacock sweep along his tail; 1H6 3.03. 6
as he march'd along, | by your espials were 4.03. 5
land, | methinks i should not thus be led along, 2H6 2.04. 30
mischance and sorrow go along with you! 3.02.300
and still proclaimeth, as he comes along, | his 4.09. 28
queen, | bearing the king in my behalf along; 3H6 2.01.115
proclaim'd | in every borough as we pass along, 2.01.195
and in the towns, as they do march along, 2.02. 70
for vengeance comes along with them. 2.05.134
and you must be contented | to go along with us; 3.01. 68
widow, go you along. 3.02.123
huntsman, what say'st thou? wilt thou go along? 4.05. 25
and lo, where george of clarence sweeps along, 5.01. 76
be augmented | in every county as we go along. 5.03. 23
tressel and berkeley, go along with me. R3 1.02.221
as we pac'd along | upon the giddy footing of 1.04. 16
my lord, will't please you pass along? 3.01.136
he is, and see, he brings the mayor along. 3.05. 13
you, and i'll go along | by your prescription; H8 1.01.150
your lordship shall along. 1.03. 64
thy approach, i know, | my comfort comes along. 2.04.241
as he pass'd along, | how earnestly he cast his 5.02. 11
put on | a form of strangeness as we pass along. TRO 3.03. 51
tail, | along the field i will the troyan trail. 5.08. 22
march patiently along; 5.09. 7
let's along. COR 1.01.279
solemnness out a' door, and go along with us. 1.03.108 P
i'll keep you company. will you along? 2.03.149
come, sir, along with us. 3.01.236
take this along, i writ it for thy sake, | and 5.02. 90
when he lies along, | after your way his tale 5.06. 56
place | i lead espous'd my bride along with me. TIT 1.01.328
along with me! 2.03.246
nay, come, agree whose hand shall go along, 3.01.174
and whirl along with thee about the globes. 5.02. 49
business, | and take my ministers along with me. 5.02.133
you, capulet, shall go along with me, | and, ROM 1.01. 99
soft, i will go along; 1.01.195
i'll go along no such sight to be shown, | but 1.02.100
under yond /yew trees lay thee all along, 5.03. 3
take the bonds along with you, | and have the TIM 2.01. 34
his fortune by the arm, | and go along with him. 4.02. 8
know i these men that come along with you? JC 2.01. 89
now, good metellus, go along by him. 2.01.218
here will i stand till caesar pass along, | and 2.03. 11
there | speak to great caesar as he comes along. 2.04. 38
that now on pompey's basis /lies along | no 3.01.115
stand ho! speak the word along. 4.02. 33
the enemy, marching along by them, | by them 4.03.207
we'll along ourselves, and meet them at philippi 4.03.225
therefore i have entreated him along | with us HAM 1.01. 26
which have freely gone | with this affair along. 1.02. 16
and he to england shall along with you. 3.03. 4
sirrah, come on; go along with us. LR 3.04.179 P
please | to get good guard and go along with me. OTH 1.01.179
stand not amaz'd at it, but go along with me; 4.02.239 P
on, there, pass along! ANT 3.01. 37
gallus, go you along. 5.01. 69
along to go. PER 3.ch. 41
old helicanus goes along. 4.04. 13
thou wilt not go along? TNK 2.03. 68
may fairly carry | our swords and cause along; 3.06.260
so soon was she along as he was down, | each VEN 43
"to see his face the lion walk'd along | behind 1093

ALONSO 2 FR 0.0002 REL FR 2 V 0 P
thee of thy son, alonso, | they have bereft; TMP 3.03. 75
most cruelly | didst thou, alonso, use me and my 5.01. 72

/ALOOF 1 FR 0.0001 REL FR 0 V 1 P
and so stand /aloof for more serious wooing. PER 4.06. 87 P

ALOOF 18 FR 0.0020 REL FR 18 V 0 P
one aloof stand sentinel. MND 2.02. 26
nerissa and the rest, stand all aloof. MV 3.02. 42
the rest aloof are the dardanian wives, | with 3.02. 58
stand you awhile aloof. TN 1.04. 12
side | must keep aloof from strict arbitrement, 1H4 4.01. 70
and make the cowards stand aloof at bay. 1H6 4.02. 52
keep off aloof with worthless emulation. 4.04. 21
stand'st thou aloof upon comparison? 5.04.150
and shakes his head, and trembling stands aloof, 2H6 1.01.227
cry, | the rest stand all aloof and bark at him. 3H6 2.01. 17
stand all aloof, but, uncle, draw you near | to TIT 5.03.151
hence, and stand aloof. ROM 5.03. 1
e'er thou hearest or seest, stand all aloof, 5.03. 26
grave, | and bid me stand aloof, and so i did. 5.03.282
but with a crafty madness keeps aloof | when we HAM 3.01. 8
but in my terms of honor | i stand aloof, and 5.02.247
that stands | aloof from th' entire point. LR 1.01.240

o appetite, from judgment stand aloof! LC 166
ALOUD 26 FR 0.0029 REL FR 23 V 3 P
an outstretch'd throat i'll tell the world aloud MM 2.04.153
i say my prayers aloud. ADO 2.01.104 P
when all aloud the wind doth blow | and coughing LLL 5.02.921
spirit of humors intimate reading aloud to him! TN 2.05. 85 P
i tore them from their bonds, and cried aloud, JN 3.04. 70
he cries aloud, "tarry, my cousin suffolk! H5 4.06. 15
but i will tell thee aloud, "england is thine, 5.02.239 P
not out the bells aloud throughout the town? 1H6 1.06. 11
majesty | that even now he cries aloud for him. 2H6 3.02.378
ring bells aloud, burn bonfires clear and bright 5.01. 3
who spake aloud, "what scourge for perjury | can R3 1.04. 50
dabbled in blood, and he shriek'd out aloud, 1.04. 54
what troy means fairly shall be spoke aloud. TRO 1.03.259
of nature and of nations speak aloud | to have 2.02.185
th' advantage of the time prompts me aloud | to 3.03. 2
bondage is hoarse, and may not speak aloud, ROM 2.02.160
romeo he cries aloud, | "hold, friends! 3.01.164
whose voices i desire aloud with mine: MAC 5.09. 24
now | as mad as the vex'd sea, singing aloud, LR 4.04. 2
here is her father's house, i'll call aloud. OTH 1.01. 74
methinks the wind hath spoke aloud at land, | a 2.01. 5
cringe his face, | and whine aloud for mercy. ANT 3.13.101
so far i read aloud — | but even the very CYM 1.06. 26
stand thou by our side, | make thy demand aloud. 5.05.130
and forth she rushes, snorts, and neighs aloud. VEN 262
place, | where fearfully the dogs exclaim aloud: 886
ALOW *(also hallow*, etc., holla, hollo, hollow*, etc.,'loo, loo)*
ALOW 3 FR 0.0003 REL FR 1 V 2 P
pillicock sat on pillicock–hill, alow! LR 3.04. 76 P
alow, loo, loo! 3.04. 76 P
"the george alow came from the south, | from the TNK 3.05. 59
/ALPHABET 1 FR 0.0001 REL FR 1 V 0 P
/but /i, /of /these, /will /wrest /an /alphabet, TIT 3.02. 44
ALPHABETICAL 1 FR 0.0001 REL FR 0 V 1 P
what should that alphabetical position portend? TN 2.05.119 P
ALPHONSO 1 FR 0.0001 REL FR 1 V 0 P
you, don alphonso | with other gentlemen of good TGV 1.03. 39
ALPS 4 FR 0.0004 REL FR 4 V 0 P
and talking of the alps and apennines, | the JN 1.01.202
afoot | even to the frozen ridges of the alps, R2 1.01. 64
the alps doth spit and void his rheum upon. H5 3.05. 52
on the alps | it is reported thou didst eat ANT 1.04. 66
/ALREADY 3 FR 0.0003 REL FR 3 V 0 P
/they /are /oppos'd /already. TRO 4.05. 94
/has /sorrow /made /thee /dote /already? TIT 3.02. 23
/into /this /scattered /kingdom, /who /already, LR 3.01. 31
ALREADY 146 FR 0.0165 REL FR 96 V 50 P
twenty to one then he is shipp'd already, | and TGV 1.01. 72
so much of bad already hath possess'd them. 3.01.207
o, i have fed upon this woe already, | and now 3.01.221
you are already love's firm votary | and cannot 3.02. 58
already have i been false to valentine, | and 4.02. 1
jack rugby, he is dead already, if he be come. WIV 2.03. 8 P
'tis past eight already, sir. 3.05.132 P
is he at master ford's already, think'st thou? 4.01. 1 P
h'as censur'd him | already, and, as i hear, the MM 1.04. 73
to be shortly of a sisterhood, | if not already. 2.02. 22
hath from nature stol'n | a man already made, as 2.04. 44
the image of it gives me content already, and i 3.01.259 P
already he hath carried | notice to escalus and 4.03.129
you have told me too many of him already, sir, 4.03.167 P
i have already deliver'd him letters, and there ADO 1.01. 20 P
i am here already, sir. 2.03. 5 P
of his cheek hath already stuff'd tennis–balls. 3.02. 47 P
it is prov'd already that you are little better 4.02. 21 P
so much, dear liege, i have already sworn, LLL 1.01. 34
well, she hath one a' my sonnets already: 4.03. 15 P
quick, the child brags in her belly already. 5.02.677 P
burial, | already to their wormy beds are gone. MND 3.02.384
for, you see, it is already in snuff. 5.01.250 P
she hath spied him already with those sweet eyes 5.01.321 P
of these princely suitors that are already come? MV 1.02. 35 P
my people do already know my mind, | and will 3.04. 37
a quarrel ho already! what's the matter? 5.01.146
they say he is already in the forest of arden, AYL 1.01.114 P
please it your majesty, i have done already. AWW 2.03. 68
i have known thee already. 2.03.101 P
great saint jaques bound, | already at my house. 3.05. 96
thousand crowns | to what is pass'd already. 3.07. 36
i have told your lordship already: 4.03.105 P
thou hast spoken all already, unless thou canst 5.03.267 P
but three days, and already you are no stranger. TN 1.04. 3 P
look you now, he's out of his guard already. 1.05. 86 P
she is drown'd already, sir, with salt water, 2.01. 30 P
my niece is already in the belief that he's mad. 3.04.136 P
gone already! WT 1.02.185
they're here with me already, whisp'ring, 1.02.217
here has been too much homely foolery already. 4.04.333 P
up in my heart, which i have given already, 4.04.359
the gentleman is half /flea'd already. 4.04.641 P
and already appearing in the blossoms of their 5.02.125 P
would i were dead but that methinks already — 5.03. 62
if that young arthur be not gone already, | even JN 3.04.163
breath | already smokes about the burning crest 5.04. 34
nay, 'tis in a manner done already, | for many 5.07. 89
that blood already, like the pelican, | hast R2 2.01.126
the earl of wiltshire is already there. 2.02.136
depress'd he is already, and depos'd | 'tis 3.04. 68
thou judgest false already. 1H4 1.02. 66 P
rob those men that we have already waylaid; 1.02.163 P
and see already how he doth begin | to make us 1.03.289
they are up already, and call for eggs and 2.01. 59 P
are they not some of them set forward already? 2.03. 29 P
they take it already upon their salvation, that 2.04. 9 P
so, two more already. 2.04.213 P
your honor had already been at shrewsbury. 4.02. 53 P
and you too, but my powers are there already. 4.02. 56 P
for thy theft hath already made thee butter. 4.02. 61 P
make haste, percy is already in the field. 4.02. 75 P
for one of them, she's in hell already, and 2H4 2.04.338 P
the powers that you already have sent forth 3.01.100
we have sent forth already. 4.01. 5
my lord, our army is dispers'd already: 4.02.102
i have him already temp'ring between my finger 4.03.130 P
unless already 'a be kill'd with your hard ep 31 P
for he is footed in this land already. H5 2.04.143
thoughts, | wherewith already france is overrun. 1H6 1.01.102
your ships already are in readiness. 3.01.185
'tis known already that i am possess'd | with 5.04.138
my master, he hath learnt so much fence already. 2H6 2.03. 78 P
methinks already in this civil broil | i see 4.08. 44
air, | thy grave is digg'd already in the earth. 4.10. 52
thou hast spoke too much already; get thee gone. 3H6 1.01.258
is he dead already? 1.03. 10
each one already blazing by our meeds, | should 2.01. 36
they are already or quickly will be landed. 4.01.132
i have already. R3 1.02.187
you, | imagine i have said farewell already. 1.02.224
hath she forgot already that brave prince, 1.02.239
my life is spann'd already. H8 1.01.223
it hath already publicly been read, | and on all 2.04. 3
alas, h'as banish'd me his bed already, | his 3.01.119
moe new disgraces | with these you bear already. 3.02. 6
the king already | hath married the fair lady. 3.02. 41
house, | and one, already, of the privy council. 4.01.112
th' are come already from the christening. 5.03. 83
but he already is too insolent; TRO 1.03.368
even already | they clap the lubber ajax on the 3.03.138
nay, i have done already. 4.05.236
we cannot, sir, we are undone already. COR 1.01. 64
aims, | in whom already he's well grac'd, cannot 1.01.264
some parcels of their power are forth already, 1.02. 32
billeted, already in th' entertainment, and to 4.03. 44 P
and have already | o'erborne their way, consum'd 4.06. 77
else to ask but that | which you deny already. 5.03. 89
ladies of esteem, | are made already mothers. ROM 1.03. 71
who is already sick and pale with grief | that 2.02. 5
poor romeo, he is already dead, stabb'd with a 2.04. 13 P
o juliet, i already know thy grief, | it strains 4.01. 46
make haste, the bridegroom he is come already, 4.04. 27
i am so far already in your gifts — TIM 1.02.172
there's the fool hangs on your back already. 2.02. 55 P
and what a beast art thou already, that seest 4.03.344 P
i have mov'd already | some certain of the JC 1.03.121
three parts of him | is ours already, and the 1.03.155
sir, octavius is already come to rome. 3.02.262
i have slept, my lord, already. 4.03.263
he is already nam'd, and gone to scone | to be MAC 2.04. 31
note of expectation | already are i' th' court. 3.03. 11
ten thousand warlike men | already at a point, 4.03.135
too much charg'd | with blood of thine already. 5.08. 6
we have sworn, my lord, already. HAM 1.05.147
they have already order | this night to play 3.01. 20
those that are married already (all but one) 3.01.148 P
yes, it is already garrison'd. 4.04. 24
what to this was sequent | thou knowest already. 5.02. 55
his purse is empty already: 5.02.130 P
there is part of a power already footed: LR 3.03. 13 P
says he, | "i have already chose my officer." OTH 1.01. 17
my dream, | belief of it oppresses me already. 1.01.143
rais'd and met, | are at the duke's already. 1.02. 44
all my heart | which, but thou hast already, 1.03.194
knave, and the woman hath found him already. 2.01.248 P
with that which he hath drunk to–night already, 2.03. 49
'fore /god, they have given me a rouse already. 2.03. 65 P
the moor already changes with my poison: 3.03.325
look how he laughs already! 4.01.109
to put up in peace what already i have foolishly 4.02.179 P
antony is touch'd | with what is spoke already. ANT 2.02.140
some o' their plants are ill rooted already, the 2.07. 2 P
queasy with his insolence | already, will their 3.06. 21
'tis done already, and the messenger gone. 3.06. 31
he is already | traduc'd for levity, and 'tis 3.07. 12
six kings already | show me the way of yielding. 3.10. 33
i have spoke already, and it is provided; 5.02.195
sword, the paper | hath cut her throat already! CYM 3.04. 33
see into thy end and am almost | a man already. 3.04.167
forethinking this, i have already fit | ('tis in 3.04.168
lucius hath wrote already to the emperor | how 3.05. 21
the pow'rs that he already hath in gallia | will 3.05. 24
to beat us down, the which are down already, PER 1.04. 68
foretell new storms to those already spent; LUC 1589
new, | spending again what is already spent: SON 76.12
ALSO 36 FR 0.0040 REL FR 13 V 23 P
and also, i think, thou art not ignorant | how TGV 3.02. 25
and there is also another device in my prain, WIV 1.01. 43 P
desire you you will also look that way. 3.01. 9 P
and i will be like a jack–an–apes also, to burn 4.04. 68 P
beam, because i know also life is a shuttle. 5.01. 23 P
you were also, jupiter, a swan for the love of 5.05. 6 P
sir, i will detest myself also, as well as she, MM 2.01. 75 P
you shall also make no noise in the streets; ADO 3.03. 34 P
and also, the watch heard them talk of one 5.01.307 P
your grace was wont to laugh, is also missing. AYL 2.02. 9
his son, her brother, | who shortly also died; TN 1.02. 39
it will also be the bondage of certain ribbons WT 4.04.233 P
a good nose is requisite also, to smell out work 4.04.672 P
but also to effect | what ever i shall happen to R2 4.01.329
thy time, but also how thou art accompanied; 1H4 2.04.399 P
not in words only, but in woes also. 2.04.417 P
deep, with erebus and tortures vile also. 2H4 2.04.158 P
let vultures vile seize on his lungs also! 5.03.139
hugh capet also, who usurp'd the crown | of H5 1.02. 69
also, king lewis the tenth, | who was sole heir 1.02. 77
and she is painted also with a wheel, to signify 3.06. 32 P
meet, think you, that we should also, look you, 4.01. 78 P
this will i also wear in my cap. 4.01.213 P
wounds) | the noble earl of suffolk also lies. 4.06. 10
and there is also moreover a river at monmouth. 4.07. 27 P
and also being a little intoxicates in his 4.07. 37 P
so also harry monmouth, being in his right wits 4.07. 46 P
den it sall also content me. 5.02.250 P
we must also tell him our noble acceptance of COR 2.03. 8 P
a word, i also am | longer to live most weary, 4.05. 94
i also wish it to you. TIM 3.06. 2 P
that must we also. JC 2.01.329
but i must also feel it as a man: MAC 4.03.221
of that i shall have also cause to speak, | and HAM 5.02.391
general dependants as in the duke himself also, LR 1.04. 62 P
yea, the speed also — to go on, i mean, | else TNK 5.01. 41
/ALTAR 1 FR 0.0001 REL FR 1 V 0 P
the mailed mars shall on his /altar sit | up to 1H4 4.01.116
ALTAR 18 FR 0.0020 REL FR 17 V 1 P
say that upon the altar of her beauty | you TGV 3.02. 72
the cudgel hallow'd and hung o'er the altar; WIV 4.02.205 P
or on diana's altar to protest | for aye MND 1.01. 89
now, dian, from thy altar do i fly, | and to AWW 2.03. 74
with me, | upon the altar at saint edmundsbury, JN 5.04. 18
even on that altar where we swore to you | dear 5.04. 19
let's to the altar. 1H6 1.01. 45
and with modest paces | came to the altar, where H8 4.01. 83
think it an altar, and thy brother troilus | a TRO 4.03. 8
thither, | and do upon mine altar sacrifice. PER 5.01.241
sir, | if you have told diana's altar true, 5.03. 17
is with me, i met your groom | by mars's altar. TNK 1.01. 62
then shall offer | to mars's so scorn'd altar? 1.02. 20
be made the altar where the lives of lovers — 4.02. 61
thy priest, | am humbled 'fore thine altar. 5.01.143
out from the bowels of her holy altar | with 5.01.164
the powerful venus well hath grac'd her altar, 5.04.105
be, | since i their altar, you enpatron me. LC 224
ALTARS 6 FR 0.0006 REL FR 6 V 0 P
to whose ingrate and unauspicious altars | my TN 5.01.113
humbly as they us'd to creep | to holy altars. TRO 3.03. 74
climb to their nostrils | from our blest altars. CYM 5.05.478
and the altars | in hallowed clouds commend TNK 5.01. 3
before the holy altars of your helpers, | the 5.01. 12
"over my altars hath he hung his lance, | his VEN 103
ALTER 19 FR 0.0021 REL FR 13 V 6 P
so thou shouldst not alter the article of thy WIV 2.01. 53 P
let me be that i am, and seek not to alter me. ADO 1.03. 37 P
but doth not the appetite alter? 2.03.238 P
this distemperature we see | the seasons alter: MND 2.01.107
thy love ne'er alter till thy sweet life end! 2.02. 61
in venice | can alter a decree established. MV 4.01.219
is no power in the tongue of man | to alter me: 4.01.242
she that would alter services with thee, the TN 2.05.158 P
the world either malice or matter to alter it. WT 1.01. 34 P
alter not the doom | forethought by heaven! JN 3.01.311
let no man speak again | to alter this, for R2 3.02.214
augment, or alter, as your wisdoms best | shall H5 5.02. 87
that he would please to alter the king's course, H8 1.01.189
so short a time can alter the condition of a man COR 5.04. 9 P
to alter favor ever is to fear. MAC 1.05. 72
gentle mariner, | alter thy course for tyre. PER 3.01. 75
add to his flow, but alter not his taste." LUC 651
to blot old books and alter their contents, | to 948
which though it alter not love's sole effect, SON 36. 7
ALTERATION 9 FR 0.0010 REL FR 8 V 1 P
for i must be | a party in this alteration, WT 1.02.383
and settled project | may suffer alteration. 4.04.525
and changes fill the cup of alteration | with 2H4 3.01. 52
pretend some alteration in good will? 1H6 4.01. 54
here's a strange alteration! COR 4.05.148 P
what an alteration of honor has desp'rate want TIM 4.03.462
he's full of alteration | and self–reproving — LR 5.01. 3
th' affrighted globe | did yawn at alteration. OTH 5.02.101
love | which alters when it alteration finds, SON 116. 3
ALTER'D 16 FR 0.0018 REL FR 13 V 3 P
ay, proteus, but that life is alter'd now: TGV 2.04.128
my brother angelo will not be alter'd, claudio MM 3.02.208 P
how now, sir, is your merry humor alter'd? ERR 2.02. 7
sir, alter'd that, for some hour before you took TN 2.01. 21 P
the numbers alter'd! 2.05.101 P
finding | myself thus alter'd with't. WT 1.02.384
the strangeness of his alter'd countenance? 2H6 3.01. 5
ay, but the case is alter'd. 3H6 4.03. 31
but 'tis so lately alter'd that the old name H8 4.01. 98
how much her grace is alter'd on the sudden? 4.02. 96
the times and titles now are alter'd strangely 4.02.112
methinks thy voice is alter'd, and thou speak'st LR 4.06. 7
know him | were he in favor as in humor alter'd. OTH 3.04.125
nature did) | hath alter'd that good picture? CYM 4.02.365
may still seem love to me, though alter'd new: SON 93. 3
"i hate" she alter'd with an end | that follow'd 145. 9
ALTERED 1 FR 0.0001 REL FR 1 V 0 P
a corrupted mind, | thy speech had altered it. PER 4.06.105
ALTERS 4 FR 0.0004 REL FR 4 V 0 P
and whose heart together | affliction alters. WT 4.04.575
so, but alters to | the quality of his thoughts; TNK 5.03. 47
love | which alters when it alteration finds, SON 116. 3
love alters not with his brief hours and weeks, 116.11
ALTHAEA 2 FR 0.0002 REL FR 1 V 1 P
althaea dreamt she was deliver'd of a fire–brand 2H4 2.02. 89 P
as did the fatal brand althaea burnt | unto the 2H6 1.01.234
ALTHAEA'S 1 FR 0.0001 REL FR 0 V 1 P
away, you rascally althaea's dream, away! 2H4 2.02. 87 P
/ALTHOUGH 1 FR 0.0001 REL FR 1 V 0 P
/although /i /be /not /he, | /and /yet /amen, R2 4.01.174
ALTHOUGH 86 FR 0.0097 REL FR 84 V 2 P
although this lord of weak remembrance, this TMP 2.01.232
(although they want the use of tongue) a kind 3.03. 38
although my last, no matter, since i feel | the 3.03. 50
i see things too, although you judge i wink. TGV 1.02.136
although by /confiscation they are ours, | we do MM 5.01.423
thither i must, although against my will, | for ERR 4.01.112
no, truly, not, although, until last night, | i ADO 4.01.148
although against her will, as it appears | in 5.04. 5
but i believe, although i seem so loath, | i am LLL 1.01.159
us, | although not valued to the money's worth. 2.01.136
although i hate her, i'll not harm her so. MND 3.02.270
madam, although i speak it in your presence, MV 3.04. 1
hit | doth very foolishly, although he smart, AYL 2.07. 54
art not seen, | although thy breath be rude. 2.07.179
he, | although i think 'twas in another sense — SHR 1.01.215
although before the solemn priest i have sworn, AWW 2.03.269
although | the air of paradise did fan the house 3.02.124
although the sheet were big enough for the bed TN 3.02. 47 P
request, although | 'twere needful i denied it. WT 1.02. 22
although the print be little, the whole matter 2.03. 99
good lords, although my will to give is living, JN 4.02. 83
or do you almost think, although you see, | that 4.03. 43
not sick, although i have to do with death, R2 1.03. 65
speak sweetly, man, although thy looks be sour. 3.02.193
thus high at least, although your knee be low. 3.03.195
hear, | although apparent guilt be seen in them, 4.01.124
forgive, | although my body pay the price of it. H5 2.02.154
although i did admit it as a motive | the sooner 2.02.156
although in writing i preferr'd | the manner of 1H6 3.01. 10
womb, | although ye hale me to a violent death. 5.04. 64
although you break it when your pleasure serves. 5.04.164

an earl, | although in glorious titles he excel. 5.05. 38
although we fancy not the cardinal, | yet must 2H6 1.03. 94
although by his sight his sin be multiplied. 2.01. 69
although thou hast been conduct of my shame. 2.04.101
although the duke was enemy to him, | yet he 3.02. 57
although the kite soar with unbloodied beak? 3.02.193
thou, | although thy husband may be menelaus; 3H6 2.02.147
warwick, although my head still wear the crown, 4.06. 23
upon my life, she finds (although i cannot) R3 1.02.253
and supper too, although thou know'st it not. 3.02.122
wherein, although, | my good lord cardinal, they H8 1.02. 22
although the king have mercies | more than i 2.01. 70
although there 'long'd | no more to th' crown 2.03. 48
to love, although i knew | he were mine enemy? 2.04. 30
although not there | at once and fully satisfied 2.04.148
although unqueen'd, yet like | a queen, and 4.02.171
although particular, shall give a scantling | of TRO 1.03.341
(although small pricks | to their subsequent 1.03.343
(although my will distaste what it elected) 2.02. 66
although i know thou hadst rather | follow thine COR 3.02. 90
although it seems, | and so he thinks, and is no 4.07. 19
why, boy, although our mother, unadvis'd, | gave TIT 2.01. 38
although, my lord, i know my noble aunt | loves 4.01. 22
although i know | there is enough written upon 4.01. 83
although she lave them hourly in the flood. 4.02.103
side, | although my seal be stamped in his face. 4.02.127
although the cheer be poor, | 'twill fill your 5.03. 28
my scars can witness, dumb although they are, 5.03.114
although i joy in thee, | i have no joy of this ROM 2.02.116
know'st well enough (although thou com'st to me) TIM 3.01. 41 P
although i know you'll swear, terribly swear 4.03.137
although our last and least, to whose young love LR 1.01. 83
(although as yet the face of it is cover'd 3.01. 20
although 'tis fit that cassio have his place — OTH 3.03.246
him, although i think | not mov'd by antony. ANT 2.01. 41
although they wear their faces to the bent | of CYM 1.01. 13
although perhaps | it may be heard at court that 4.02.136
although the victor, we submit to caesar, | and 5.05.460
i shall not be hang'd now, although i would; PER 1.03. 26
although they gave their creatures in abundance, 1.04. 36
although assail'd with fortune fierce and keen, 5.03. 88
so content | to punish, although not done, but 5.03.100
thebes, | and therein wretched, although free. TNK 3.01. 27
although we grant you get the thing you seek? STM II.C 69
he will not manage her, although he mount her, VEN 598
although i know my years be past the best, | i PP 1. 6
twain, | although our undivided loves are one: SON 36. 2
although thou steal thee all my poverty; 40.10
no matter then although my foot did stand | upon 44. 5
although to–day thou fill | thy hungry eyes even 56. 5
their thoughts (although their eyes were kind) 69.11
although in me each part will be forgotten. 81. 4
worth's unknown, although his highth be taken. 116. 8
so bold, | although i swear it to myself alone. 131. 8
although she knows my days are past the best, 138. 6

ALTITUDE 3 FR 0.0003 REL FR 1 V 2 P
which he is, even to the altitude of his virtue. COR 1.01. 40 P
i saw you last, by the altitude of a chopine. HAM 2.02.426 P
ten masts at each make not the altitude | which LR 4.06. 53

/ALTOGETHER 1 FR 0.0001 REL FR 0 V 1 P
/this /is /not /altogether /fool, /my /lord. LR 1.04.151 P

ALTOGETHER 24 FR 0.0027 REL FR 7 V 17 P
made me drunk, yet i am not altogether an ass. WIV 1.01.172 P
my wife, master doctor, is for you altogether. 3.02. 63 P
his own search, and altogether against my will. AYL 1.01.135 P
best know him, that i am altogether mispris'd. 1.01.170 P
demand, you are not altogether of his counsel. AWW 4.03. 44 P
not altogether so great as the first in goodness 4.03.286 P
in masques and revels sometimes altogether. TN 1.03.114 P
this your request | is altogether just; WT 3.02.117
for if of joy, being altogether wanting, | it R2 3.04. 13
or if of grief, being altogether had, | it adds 3.04. 15
for you are altogether govern'd by humors. 1H4 3.01.233 P
but thou art altogether given over, and wert 3.03. 36 P
is given, is altogether directed by an irishman, H5 3.02. 66 P
thereof, | for i am she, and altogether joyless. R3 1.03.155
much more gentle, and altogether more tractable. TRO 2.03.150 P
thou art not altogether a fool. TIM 2.02.115 P
nor thou altogether a wise man; 2.02.116 P
o, reform it altogether. HAM 3.02. 38 P
not altogether so, | i look'd not for you yet, LR 2.04.231
it was not altogether your brother's evil 3.05. 5 P
but altogether lacks th' abilities | that rhodes OTH 1.03. 25
is mended) my quarrel was not altogether slight. CYM 1.04. 47 P
sleeps little, altogether without appetite, save TNK 4.03. 4 P
or altogether balk | the prey wherein by nature LUC 696

ALTOGETHER'S 1 FR 0.0001 REL FR 0 V 1 P
it is a oman that altogether's acquaintance with WIV 1.02. 8 P

ALTON 1 FR 0.0001 REL FR 1 V 0 P
lord strange of blackmere, lord verdon of alton, 1H6 4.07. 65

ALT'RED 4 FR 0.0004 REL FR 4 V 0 P
delay'd, | but nothing alt'red. WT 4.04.464
our scene is alt'red from a serious thing, | and R2 5.03. 79
i'll not have it alt'red. 1H4 3.01.115
he alt'red much upon the hearing it. 2H4 4.05. 13

ALT'RING 2 FR 0.0002 REL FR 2 V 0 P
is he not stupid | with age and alt'ring rheums? WT 4.04.399
strong minds to th' course of alt'ring things: SON 115. 8

ALWAY 2 FR 0.0002 REL FR 1 V 1 P
but it was alway yet the trick of our english 2H4 1.02.214 P
may such purple tears be alway shed | from those 3H6 5.06. 64

ALWAYS 63 FR 0.0071 REL FR 33 V 30 P
lungs that they always use to laugh at nothing. TMP 2.01.174 P
yet always bending | towards their project. 4.01.174
you always end ere you begin. TGV 2.04. 31 P
i reckon this always, that a man is never undone 2.05. 4 P
you would have them always play but one thing? 4.02. 70 P
i would always have one play but one thing. 4.02. 72
and i thank you always with my heart, la! WIV 1.01. 84 P
there they always use to discharge their 4.02. 57 P
love again, but i will always count you my deer. 5.05.118 P
always obedient to your grace's will, | i come MM 1.01. 25
thou art always figuring diseases in me; 1.02. 53 P
which sorrow is always toward ourselves, not 2.03. 32
i am always bound to you. 4.01. 25 P
that thinks a man always going to bed and says, ERR 4.03. 32 P
you always end with a jade's trick, i know you ADO 1.01.144 P
man of italy, | always excepted my dear claudio. 3.01. 93
you have been always call'd a merciful man, 3.03. 61 P
but always hath been just and virtuous | in any 5.01.302
why, shall i always keep below stairs? 5.02. 10 P
and justice always whirls in equal measure: LLL 4.03.381
by jove, i always took three threes for nine. 5.02.495 P
i was always plain with you, and so now i speak MV 3.05. 3 P
for always the dullness of the fool is the AYL 1.02. 54 P
he would always say — | methinks i hear him now AWW 1.02. 52
sir, that always lov'd a great fire, and the 4.05. 47 P
for that's it that always makes a good voyage of TN 2.04. 78 P
we have always truly serv'd you, and beseech' WT 2.03.148
the open ear of youth doth always listen; R2 2.01. 20
for he is just and always loved us well. 2.01.221
the king will always think him in our debt, 1H4 1.03.286
she would always say she could not abide master 2H4 3.02.202 P
o, give me always a little, lean, old, chopp'd, 3.02.275 P
they do always reason themselves out again. H5 5.02.157 P
for soldiers' stomachs always serve them well. 1H6 2.03. 80
but always resolute in most extremes. 4.01. 38
for i always thought | it was both impious and 5.01. 11
justice with favor have i always done; 2H6 4.07. 67
and happy always was it for that son | whose 3H6 2.02. 47
blows, | commanded always by the greater gust, 3.01. 88
edward will always bear himself as king. 4.03. 45
suspicion always haunts the guilty mind; 5.06. 11
the benefit thereof is always granted | to those R3 3.01. 48
i know your majesty has always lov'd her | so H8 2.02.109
i thank you, | you are always my good friend; 5.02. 94
agrippa, one that hath always lov'd the people. COR 1.01. 52 P
and those senators | that always favor'd him. 3.03. 8
general," but he was always good enough for him. 4.05.182 P
always factionary on the party of your general. 5.02. 29 P
my lord, we always have confess'd it. TIM 1.02. 21
i do not always follow lover, elder brother, and 2.02.121 P
flaminius, i have noted thee always wise. 3.01. 31 P
i have observ'd thee always for a towardly 3.01. 34 P
always a villain's office, or a fool's. 4.03.237
for always i am caesar. JC 1.02.212
always thought | that i require a clearness: MAC 3.01.131
my orchard, | my custom always of the afternoon, HAM 1.05. 60
it did always seem so to us; LR 1.01. 3 P
he always lov'd our sister most, and with what 1.01.290 P
but nothing | (always reserv'd my holy duty) CYM 1.01. 87
sir, as i told you always: 1.02. 29 P
love's gentle spring doth always fresh remain, VEN 801
serve always with assured trust, | and in thy PP 18.19
o, know, sweet love, i always write of you, SON 76. 9

ALWAYS–WIND–OBEYING 1 FR 0.0001 REL FR 1 V 0 P
we sail'd | before the always–wind–obeying deep ERR 1.01. 63

/AM 18 FR 0.0020 REL FR 16 V 2 P
/why /am /i /sent /for /to /a /king | /before /i R2 4.01.162
/am /i /both /priest /and /clerk? 4.01.173
/to /do /what /service /am /i /sent /for /hither 4.01.176
/bucket /down /and /full /of /tears /am /i, 4.01.188
/my /crown /i /am, /but /still /my /griefs /are 4.01.191
/still /am /i /king /of /those. 4.01.193
/i /am /greater /than /a /king; 4.01.305
/i /am /thus /bold /to /put /your /grace /in R3 4.02.110
/i /am /not /in /the /giving /vein //to–day. 4.02.116
that is, i /am i. 5.03.183
/all /on /hazard — /and /hither /am /i /come, TRO pr 22
/man, /i /am /most /dreadfully /attended. HAM 2.02.269 P
/but /i /am /very /sorry, /good /horatio, 5.02. 75
/i /am /a /gentleman /of /blood /and /breeding, LR 3.01. 40
/when /i /am /known /aright, /you /shall /not 4.03. 53
/i /am /doubtful /that /you /have /been 5.01. 12
/i /am /chang'd. OTH 1.03.379 P
who /am no more but as the tops of trees, PER 1.02. 30

AM 2284 FR 0.2581 REL FR 1593 V 691 P
i am out of patience. TMP 1.01. 55
nought knowing | of whence i am, nor that i am 1.02. 19
i am, nor that i am more better | than prospero, 1.02. 19
you have often | begun to tell me what i am, but 1.02. 34
i am ready now, | approach, my ariel. 1.02.187
for i am all the subjects that you have, | which 1.02.341
i am the best of them that speak this speech, 1.02.430
a single thing, as i am now, that wonders | to 1.02.433
myself am naples, | who with mine eyes (never 1.02.435
no, as i am a man. 1.02.457
nor this man's threats | to whom i am subdu'd; 1.02.490
this kind of merry fooling, am nothing to you; 2.01.177 P
will you laugh me asleep, for i am very heavy? 2.01.189 P
i am more serious than my custom; 2.01.219
well — i am standing water. 2.01.221
sometime am i | all wound with adders, who with 2.02. 12
for i am trinculo — be not afeard — thy good 2.02.101 P
how features are abroad | i am skilless of; 3.01. 53
i am, in my condition, | a prince, miranda; 3.01. 59
and for your sake | am i this patient log–man. 3.01. 67
i am a fool | to weep at what i am glad of. 3.01. 73
i am a fool | to weep at what i am glad of. 3.01. 74
i am your wife, if you will marry me; 3.01. 83
monster, i am in case to justle a constable. 3.02. 25 P
as i told thee before, i am subject to a tyrant, 3.02. 42
for without them | he's but a sot, as i am; 3.02. 93
i am sorry i beat thee; 3.02.111 P
i am full of pleasure, | let us be jocund. 3.02.116
who am myself attach'd with weariness | to th' 3.03. 5
i am right glad that he's so out of hope. 3.03. 11
what would my potent master? here i am. 4.01. 34
th' sky, | whose wat'ry arch and messenger am i, 4.01. 71
sir, i am vex'd; 4.01.158
go unrewarded while i am king of this country. 4.01.242 P
with their high wrongs i am strook to th' quick, 5.01. 25
i am woe for't, sir. 5.01.139
certain | that i am prospero and that very duke 5.01.159
i am hers. 5.01.196
i am afraid | he will chastise me. 5.01.262
o, touch me not, i am not stephano, but a cramp. 5.01.286 P
'tis love you cavil at; i am not love. TGV 1.01. 38
therefore i am no sheep. 1.01. 88 P
a passing shame | that i (unworthy body as i am) 1.02. 18
what 'fool is she, that knows i am a maid, | and 1.02. 53
i am resolv'd that thou shalt spend some time 1.03. 66
to go — | excuse it not, for i am peremptory. 1.03. 71
and drench'd me in the sea, where i am drown'd. 1.03. 79
why, how know you that i am in love? 2.01. 17 P
air, i am one that am nourish'd by my victuals, 2.01.173 P
air, i am one that am nourish'd by my victuals, 2.01.173 P
and am going with sir proteus to the imperial's 2.03. 4 P
i am the dog — no, the dog is himself, and i am 2.03. 21 P
no, the dog is himself, and i am the dog — o! 2.03. 22 P
the dog is me, and i am myself; 2.03. 23 P
were dry, i am able to fill it with my tears; 2.03. 52 P
what seem i that i am not? 2.04. 14 P
not thyself, sweet youth, for i am not welcome. 2.05. 4 P
i to myself am dearer than a friend, | for love 2.06. 23
it presently, | i am impatient of my tarriance. 2.07. 90
favors | done to me (undeserving as i am), | my 3.01. 7
myself am one made privy to the plot. 3.01. 12
to my friends, | and i am going to deliver them. 3.01. 54
i am to break with thee of some affairs | that 3.01. 59
i now am full resolv'd to take a wife | and turn 3.01. 76
doth silvia know that i am banished? 3.01.223
i am but a fool, look you, and yet i have the 3.01.263 P
that knows me to be in love, yet i am in love, 3.01.266 P
at me, | that i am desperate of obtaining her. 3.02. 5
a man i am cross'd with adversity; 4.01. 12
think'st thou i am so shallow, so conceitless, 4.02. 96
swear), | i am so far from granting thy request, 4.02.101
for i am sure she is not buried. 4.02.107
to whom, thyself art witness, | i am betroth'd; 4.02.110
and so suppose am i; 4.02.113
self | is else devoted, i am but a shadow; 4.02.124
deceive it, | and make it but a shadow, as i am. 4.02.127
i am very loath to be your idol, sir; 4.02.128
i am thus early come to know what service | it 4.03. 9
and now am i, unhappy messenger, | to plead for 4.04. 99
i am my master's true confirmed love; 4.04.103
to hear me speak the message i am sent on. 4.04.112
i fear i am attended by some spies. 5.01. 10
and less than this, i am sure you cannot give. 5.04. 25
o miserable, unhappy that i am! 5.04. 28
i am sorry i must never trust thee more, | but 5.04. 69
then i am paid; 5.04. 77
disparagements unto you, i am of the church, and WIV 1.01. 32 P
i am glad to see your worships well. 1.01. 79 P
master page, i am glad to see you. 1.01. 81 P
i am glad to see you, good master slender. 1.01. 88 P
made me drunk, yet i am not altogether an ass. 1.01.172 P
that i am freely dissolv'd, and dissolutely. 1.01.251 P
i am very well. 1.01.267 P
i am not a–hungry, i thank you, forsooth. 1.01.270 P
i am at a word; 1.03. 14 P
i am glad i am so acquit of this tinderbox; 1.03. 24 P
i am glad i am so acquit of this tinderbox; 1.03. 24 P
well, sirs, i am almost out at heels. 1.03. 31 P
my honest lads, i will tell you what i am about. 1.03. 38 P
indeed i am in the waist two yards about; 1.03. 41 P
but i am now about no waste; 1.03. 42 P
i am about thrift. 1.03. 43 P
rightly) is, "i am sir john falstaff's." 1.03. 48 P
i am glad he went not in himself; 1.04. 49 P
i am glad he is so quiet. 1.04. 89 P
well, farewell, i am in great haste now. 1.04.161 P
of my beauty, and am i now a subject for them? 2.01. 2 P
you are not young, no more am i; 2.01. 7 P
you are merry, so am i; 2.01. 8 P
myself like one that i am not acquainted withal; 2.01. 86 P
far from jealousy as i am from giving him cause, 2.01.103 P
i am not melancholy. 2.01.152 P
i am damn'd in hell for swearing to gentlemen my 2.02. 10 P
hang no more about me, i am no gibbet for you. 2.02. 17 P
mine honor in my necessity, am fain to shuffle, 2.02. 25 P
there's my purse, i am yet thy debtor. 2.02.132 P
sir, i am a gentleman that have spent much. 2.02.160 P
my means, meed, i am sure, i have receiv'd none, 2.02.203 P
and last, as i am a gentleman, you shall, /and 2.02.254 P
i am blest in your acquaintance. 2.02.268 P
doctor caius, i am come to fetch you home. 2.03. 52 P
i am sworn of the peace. 2.03. 52 P
how full of chollors i am and trempling of mind! 3.01. 12 P
how melancholies i am! 3.01. 13 P
as i am a christians–soul, now look you; 3.01. 94 P
am i politic? 3.01.101 P
am i subtle? 3.01.101 P
am i a machivel? 3.01.101 P
by your leave, sir. i am sick till i see her. 3.02. 28 P
go tell thy master i am alone. 3.03. 36 P
how am i mistook in you! 3.03.104 P
you know yourself clear, why, i am glad of it; 3.03.116 P
i am half afraid he will have need of washing, 3.03.182 P
he doth object i am too great of birth, | and 3.04. 4
i care not for that, but that i am afeard. 3.04. 28 P
i am not such a sickly creature, i give heaven 3.04. 59 P
you, | and as i find her, so am i affected. 3.04. 91
what a beast am i to slack it! 3.04.111 P
of that — that am as subject to heat as butter; 3.05.115 P
i am sorry that for my sake you have suffer'd 3.05.123 P
well, i will proclaim myself what i am. 3.05.144 P
though what i am i cannot avoid, yet to be what 3.05.149 P
truly, i am so glad you have nobody here. 4.02. 18 P
i am glad the fat knight is not here. 4.02. 28 P
but i am glad the knight is not here. 4.02. 36 P
i am undone! the knight is here. 4.02. 41 P
master page, as i am a man, there was one 4.02.145 P
in my house i am sure he is. 4.02.148 P
assist me, knight, i am undone! 4.05. 91 P
i am undone! 4.05. 91 P
and, as i am a gentleman, i'll give thee | a 4.06. 4
i am in haste, go along with me, i'll tell you 5.01. 23 P
for me, i am here a windsor stag, and the 5.05. 12 P
am i a woodman, ha? 5.05. 27 P
as i am a true spirit, welcome! 5.05. 29 P
i do begin to perceive that i am made an ass. 5.05.119 P
am i ridden with a welsh goat too? 5.05.137 P
well, i am your theme. 5.05.161 P
you have the start of me, i am dejected. 5.05.162 P
i am not able to answer the welsh flannel; 5.05.162 P
by gar, i am cozen'd. 5.05.204 P
by gar, i am cozen'd. 5.05.207 P
i am glad, though you have ta'en a special stand 5.05.234 P

since i am put to know that your own science MM 1.01. 5
strength and nature | i am not yet instructed. 1.01. 80
but thou art full of error — i am sound. 1.02. 54 P
i am too sure of it; 1.02. 72 P
and what with poverty, i am custom–shrunk. 1.02. 84 P
bear me to prison, where i am committed. 1.02.117
you know | i am that isabella and his sister. 1.04. 23
your honor, i am the poor duke's constable, and 2.01. 47 P
precise villains they are, that i am sure of, 2.01. 54 P
into any room in a tap–house, but i am drawn in. 2.01.209 P
truly, sir, i am a poor fellow that would live. 2.01.223 P
i am a woeful suitor to your honor, | please but 2.02. 27
but that i am | at war 'twixt will and will not. 2.02. 32
for i am that way going to temptation, | where 2.02.158
i am the provost. what's your will, good friar? 2.03. 2
and i am going with instruction to him. 2.03. 38
i am come to know your pleasure. 2.04. 31
good, | but graciously to know i am no better. 2.04. 77
i have hope to live, and am prepar'd to die. 3.01. 4
i am confessor to angelo, and i know this to be 3.01.166 P
i am so out of love with life that i will sue to 3.01.171 P
i am now going to resolve him. 3.01.189 P
i am bound to call upon you, and i pray you your 3.02.157 P
i am a brother | of gracious order, late come 3.02.218
i am made to understand that you have lent him 3.02.240 P
i am going to visit the prisoner. fare you well. 3.02.258 P
i am always bound to you. 4.01. 25 P
i am as well acquainted here as i was in our 4.03. 1 P
away, you rogue, away! i am sleepy. 4.03. 28 P
been drinking all night, i am not fitted for't. 4.03. 44 P
you are to depart, i am come to advise you, 4.03. 51 P
i am your free dependant. 4.03. 91
shall witness to him i am near at home; 4.03. 95
and that by great injunctions i am bound | to 4.03. 96
i am directed by you. 4.03.136
my poor self, | i am combined by a sacred vow, 4.03.144
i am pale at mine heart to see thine eyes so red 4.03.151 P
i am fain to dine and sup with water and bran; 4.03.152 P
nay, friar, i am a kind of bur, i shall stick. 4.03.179 P
to speak so indirectly i am loath. 4.06. 1
yet i am advis'd to do it, | he says, to veil 4.06. 3
that opinion | that i am touch'd with madness. 5.01. 51
i am the sister of one claudio, | condemn'd upon 5.01. 69
married, | and i confess besides i am no maid. 5.01.185
i am affianc'd this man's wife as strongly | as 5.01.227
his subject am i not, | nor here provincial. 5.01.315
i am more amaz'd at his dishonor | than at the 5.01.380
habit, i am still | attorney'd at your service. 5.01.384
i am sorry, one so learned and so wise | as you, 5.01.470
i am sorry that such sorrow i procure, | and so 5.01.474
i am not partial to infringe our laws; ERR 1.01. 4
for with long travel i am stiff and weary. 1.02. 15
oft, | when i am dull with care and melancholy, 1.02. 20
i am invited, sir, to certain merchants, | of 1.02. 24
i to the world am like a drop of water, | that 1.02. 35
i am not in a sportive humor now: 1.02. 58
now, as i am a christian, answer me, | in what 1.02. 77
that stands on tricks when i am undispos'd: 1.02. 80
am i so round with you, as you with me, | that 2.01. 82
poor i am but his stale. 2.01.101
i am glad to see you in this merry vein. 2.02. 20
but i pray, sir, why am i beaten? 2.02. 39 P
nothing, sir, but that i am beaten. 2.02. 41 P
i am not adriana, nor thy wife. 2.02.112
am better than thy dear self's better part. 2.02.123
i am possess'd with an adulterate blot; 2.02.140
in ephesus i am but two hours old, | as strange 2.02.148
i am transformed, master, am /not /i? 2.02.195
i am transformed, master, am /not /i? 2.02.195
i think thou art in mind, and so am i. 2.02.196
no, i am an ape. 2.02.198
'tis so, i am an ass, else it could never be 2.02.201
am i in earth, in heaven, or in hell? 2.02.212
but if that i am i, then well i know | your 3.02. 41
call thyself sister, sweet, for i am thee: 3.02. 66
am i dromio? 3.02. 73 P
am i your man? 3.02. 74 P
am i myself? 3.02. 74 P
i am an ass, i am a woman's man, and besides 3.02. 77 P
i am an ass, i am a woman's man, and besides 3.02. 77 P
marry, sir, besides myself, i am due to a woman: 3.02. 81 P
now i had not, but that i am bound | to persia, 4.01. 3
i am not furnish'd with the present money: 4.01. 34
tell her i am arrested in the street, | and that 4.01.106
come, sister, i am press'd down with conceit — 4.02. 65
the fellow is distract, and so am i, | and here 4.03. 42
money, | to warrant thee, as i am 'rested for. 4.04. 3
rope's end, sir, and to that end am i return'd. 4.04. 16
i am in adversity. 4.04. 19 P
i am an ass indeed; 4.04. 29 P
when i am cold, he heats me with beating; 4.04. 32 P
when i am warm, he cools me with beating. 4.04. 33 P
i am wak'd with it when i sleep, rais'd with it 4.04. 34 P
peace, doting wizard, peace! i am not mad. 4.04. 58
and i am witness with her that she did. 4.04. 89
thou jailer, thou, | i am thy prisoner. 4.04.110
master, i am here ent'red in bond for you. 4.04.125
i am sorry, sir, that i have hind'red you, | but 5.01. 1
i am sorry now that i did draw on him. 5.01. 43
my liege, i am advised what i say, | neither 5.01.214
now am i dromio, and his man, unbound. 5.01.291
i am sure you both of you remember me. 5.01.292
i am sure thou dost! 5.01.304
sir, but i am sure i do not — and whatsoever a 5.01.305 P
i, sir, am dromio, command him away. 5.01.336
i, sir, am dromio, pray let me stay. 5.01.337
i am your master, dromio. 5.01.412
i see by you i am a sweet–fac'd youth. 5.01.419
but it is certain i am lov'd of all ladies, only ADO 1.01.125 P
and my cold blood, i am of your humor for that: 1.01.130 P
i am not of many words, but i thank you. 1.01.157 P
thou thinkest i am in sport. 1.01.177 P
but now i am return'd, and that war–thoughts 1.01.301
disguise, | and tell fair hero i am claudio, 1.01.322
i cannot hide what i am. 1.03. 13 P
sleep when i am drowsy, and tend on no man's 1.03. 16 P
laugh when i am merry, and claw no man in his 1.03. 17 P
not be denied but i am a plain–dealing villain. 1.03. 32 P

i am trusted with a muzzle and enfranchis'd with 1.03. 32 P
in the mean time let me be that i am, and seek 1.03. 36 P
their cheer is the greater that i am subdu'd. 1.03. 72 P
can see him but i am heart–burn'd an hour after. 2.01. 4 P
for the which blessing i am at him upon my knees 2.01. 28 P
he that is less than a man, i am not for him; 2.01. 39 P
and say nothing, i am yours for the walk, and 2.01. 89 P
at a word, i am not. 2.01.114 P
at a word, i am not. 2.01.120 P
i am sure you know him well enough. 2.01.133 P
i am sure he is in the fleet; 2.01.142 P
you know me well, i am he. 2.01.162 P
may be i go under that title because i am merry. 2.01.205 P
yea, but so i am apt to do myself wrong. 2.01.206 P
i am not so reputed. 2.01.207 P
lady, as you are mine, i am yours. 2.01.308 P
every one to the world but i, and i am sunburnt. 2.01.319 P
my lord, i am for you, though it cost me ten 2.01.371 P
i am sick in displeasure to him, and whatsoever 2.02. 5 P
since, how much i am in the favor of margaret, 2.02. 13 P
i am here already, sir. 2.03. 5 P
one woman is fair, yet i am well; 2.03. 27 P
another is wise, yet i am well; 2.03. 27 P
another virtuous, yet i am well; 2.03. 28 P
i am sorry for her, as i have just cause, being 2.03.165 P
well, i am sorry for your niece. 2.03.198 P
i hear how i am censur'd; 2.03.225 P
against my will i am sent to bid you come in to 2.03.247 P
"against my will i am sent to bid you come in to 2.03.257 P
if i do not take pity of her, i am a villain; 2.03.262 P
if i do not love her, i am a jew. 2.03.263 P
gallants, i am not as i have been. 3.02. 15 P
here, man, i am at thy elbow. 3.03. 98 P
i am out of all other tune, methinks. 3.04. 43 P
by my troth, i am exceeding ill. 3.04. 53 P
i am stuff'd, cousin, i cannot smell. 3.04. 64 P
by my troth, i am sick. 3.04. 72 P
lady, i am not such a fool to think what i list, 3.04. 82 P
i thank god i am as honest as any man living 3.05. 13 P
i be but a poor man, i am glad to hear it. 3.05. 27 P
and so am i. 3.05. 28 P
i am now in great haste, as it may appear unto 3.05. 50 P
i'll wait upon them, i am ready. 3.05. 56 P
o, god defend me, how am i beset! 4.01. 77
leonato, | i am sorry you must hear. 4.01. 88
lady, | i am sorry for thy much misgovernment. 4.01. 99
for my part, i am so attir'd in wonder, | i know 4.01.144
i am sorry for my cousin. 4.01.272 P
i am gone, though i am here; 4.01.293 P
i am gone, though i am here; 4.01.293 P
enough, i am engag'd, i will challenge him. 4.01.331 P
marry, that am i and my partner. 4.02. 4 P
i am a gentleman, sir, and my name is conrade. 4.02. 13 P
but, masters, remember that i am an ass; 4.02. 77 P
written down, yet forget not that i am an ass. 4.02. 78 P
i am a wise fellow, and, which is more, an 4.02. 80 P
me | that i am forc'd to lay my reverence by, 5.01. 64
fence, | nay, as i am a gentleman, i will. 5.01. 85
as i am an honest man, he looks pale. 5.01.130 P
time and place shall serve, that i am an ass. 5.01.256 P
trumpet of his own virtues, as i am to myself. 5.02. 86 P
upon the tomb, | praising her when i am /dumb. 5.03. 10
well, i am glad that all things sorts so well. 5.04. 7
and so am i, being else by faith enforc'd | to 5.04. 8
friar — | i am your husband if you like of me. 5.04. 59
i do live, | and surely as i live, i am a maid. 5.04. 64
come, cousin, i am sure you love the gentleman. 5.04. 84
i am resolved, 'tis but a three years' fast: LLL 1.01. 24
so, | to know the thing i am forbid to know: 1.01. 60
dine, | when i to /feast expressly am forbid; 1.01. 62
well, say i am, why should proud summer boast 1.01.102
i am forsworn "on mere necessity." 1.01.154
i am the last that will last keep his oath. 1.01.160
his own person, for i am his grace's farborough; 1.01.183 P
and, as i am a gentleman, betook myself to walk: 1.01.234 P
me, an't shall please you: i am anthony dull. 1.01.270 P
i am answer'd, sir. 1.02. 31 P
i am ill at reck'ning, it fitteth the spirit of 1.02. 40 P
then i am sure you know how much the gross sum 1.02. 45 P
i will hereupon confess i am in love; 1.02. 57 P
to love, so am i in love with a base wench. 1.02. 58 P
i am in love too. 1.02. 75 P
i am more bound to you than your fellows, for 1.02.151 P
god of rhyme, for i am sure i shall turn sonnet. 1.02.183 P
write, pen, for i am for whole volumes in folio. 1.02.185 P
i am less proud to hear you tell my worth | than 2.01. 17
but pardon me, i am too sudden bold; 2.01.107
i am all these three. 3.01. 46 P
i thank my beauty, i am fair that shoot, | and 4.01. 11
i am bound to serve. 4.01. 56
i am the king, for so stands the comparison; 4.01. 78 P
i am much deceived but i remember the style. 4.01. 96
well then i am the shooter. 4.01.114
/in whom it is acute, and i am thankful for it. 4.02. 71 P
i am coursing myself. 4.03. 1 P
i am toiling in a pitch — pitch that defiles — 4.03. 2 P
ay me, i am forsworn! 4.03. 45
am i the first that have been perjur'd so? 4.03. 49
it sin in me, | that i am forsworn for thee; 4.03.114
i that am honest, i that hold it sin | to break 4.03.175
hold it sin | to break the vow i am engaged in. 4.03.176
i am betrayed by keeping company | with men like 4.03.177
i am compar'd to twenty thousand fairs. 5.02. 37
o, i am /stabb'd with laughter! 5.02. 80
i am best pleas'd with that. 5.02.229
i am a fool, and full of poverty. 5.02.380
o, i am yours, and all that i possess! 5.02.383
bear with me, i am sick. 5.02.417
for mine own part, i am, as /they say, but to 5.02.501 P
degree of the worthy, but i am to stand for him. 5.02.507 P
"i pompey am" — 5.02.547
"i pompey am" — 5.02.548
"i pompey am, pompey surnam'd the big" — 5.02.550
along this coast, i here am come by chance, 5.02.554
scutcheon plain declares that i am alisander" — 5.02.564
"judas i am" — 5.02.595
"judas i am, ycliped machabeus." 5.02.598
"judas i am" — 5.02.601

i am that flower" — 5.02.655
i am sorry, madam, for the news i bring | is 5.02.718
please, | without the which i am not to be won, 5.02.849
i am a votary; 5.02.883 P
i know not by what power i am made bold, | nor MND 1.01. 59
i am, my lord, as well deriv'd as he, | as well 1.01. 99
can be) | i am belov'd of beauteous hermia. 1.01.104
through athens i am thought as fair as she. 1.01.227
ready. name what part i am for, and proceed. 1.02. 18 P
if it be, give it me, for i am slow of study. 1.02. 67 P
here are your parts, and i am to entreat you, 1.02. 99 P
i am that merry wanderer of the night. 2.01. 43
tarry, rash wanton! am not i thy lord? 2.01. 63
i am invisible, | and i will overhear their 2.01.186
and here am i, and wode within this wood, 2.01.192
i am your spaniel; 2.01.203
me leave, | unworthy as i am, to follow you. 2.01.207
spirit, | for i am sick when i do look on thee. 2.01.212
and i am sick when i look not on you. 2.01.213
face, | therefore i think i am not in the night, 2.01.222
then how can it be said i am alone, | when all 2.01.225
so awake when i am gone, | for i must now to 2.02. 82
o, i am out of breath in this fond chase! 2.02. 88
i am as ugly as a bear; 2.02. 94
tell them that i pyramus am not pyramus, but 3.01. 20 P
i am no such thing; 3.01. 43 P
i am a man as other men are"; 3.01. 43 P
will sing, that they shall hear i am not afraid. 3.01.123 P
i am a spirit of no common rate; 3.01.154
i am not guilty of lysander's blood; 3.02. 75
when i am sure you hate me with your hearts. 3.02.154
i am amazed at your /passionate words. 3.02.220
am not i hermia? 3.02.273
i am as fair now as i was erewhile. 3.02.274
esteem, | because i am so dwarfish and so low? 3.02.295
how low am i, thou painted maypole? 3.02.296
how low am i? 3.02.297
i am not yet so low | but that my nails can 3.02.297
i am a right maid for my cowardice. 3.02.302
you see how simple and how fond i am. 3.02.317
i am amaz'd, and know not what to say. 3.02.344
and so far am i glad it so did sort, | as this 3.02.352
i am fear'd in field and town. 3.02.398
did fly, | that fallen am i in dark uneven way, 3.02.417
come hither; i am here. 3.02.425
for methinks i am marvail's hairy about the face 4.01. 24 P
and i am such a tender ass, if my hair do but 4.01. 25 P
masters, i am to discourse wonders; 4.02. 29 P
for if i tell you, i am /no true athenian. 4.02. 30 P
this stone doth show | that i am that same wall; 5.01.162
enter now, and i am to spy her through the wall. 5.01.186 P
think what thou wilt, i am thy lover's grace; 5.01.195
and, like limander, am i trusty still. 5.01.196
then know that i as snug the joiner am | a lion 5.01.223
his discretion, i am sure, cannot carry his 5.01.235 P
i am a–weary of this moon. 5.01.251 P
now am i dead, | now am i fled; 5.01.301
now am i dead, | now am i fled; 5.01.302
i am sent with broom before, | to sweep the dust 5.01.389
and, as i am an honest puck, | if we have 5.01.431
in sooth, i know not why i am so sad; MV 1.01. 1
made of, whereof it is born, | i am to learn; 1.01. 5
conceit, | as who should say, "i am sir oracle, 1.01. 93
when, i am very sure, | if they should speak, 1.01. 97
may by me be done, | and i am prest unto it; 1.01.160
i am much afeard my lady his mother play'd false 1.02. 43 P
i am glad this parcel of wooers are so 1.02.108 P
i am debating of my present store, | and, by the 1.03. 53
i am as like to call thee so again, | to spet on 1.03.130
sun, | to whom i am a neighbor and near bred. 2.01. 3
in terms of choice i am not soly led | by nice 2.01. 13
alack, sir, i am sand–blind, i know you not. 2.02. 74 P
i am sure you are not launcelot, my boy. 2.02. 81 P
i am launcelot, your boy that was, your son that 2.02. 84 P
but i am launcelot, the jew's man, and i am sure 2.02. 89 P
and i am sure margery your wife is my mother. 2.02. 89 P
i am sure he had more hair of his tail than i 2.02. 97 P
i am famish'd in his service; 2.02.106 P
father, i am glad you are come; 2.02.107 P
for i am a jew if i serve the jew any longer. 2.02.112 P
i am sorry thou wilt leave my father so. 2.03. 1
play the knave and get thee, i am much deceiv'd. 2.03. 12 P
but though i am a daughter to his blood, | i am 2.03. 18
to his blood, | i am not to his manners. 2.03. 19
i am provided of a torch–bearer. 2.04. 23
i am bid forth to supper, jessica. 2.05. 11
i am not bid for love, they flatter me, | but 2.05. 13
i am right loath to go; 2.05. 16
knows | but you, lorenzo, whether i am yours? 2.06. 31
i am glad 'tis night, you do not look on me, 2.06. 34
on me, | for i am much asham'd of my exchange. 2.06. 35
i am glad on't. 2.06. 67
if you choose that, then i am yours withal. 2.07. 12
and if my form lie there, | then i am yours. 2.07. 62
and in their ship i am sure lorenzo is not. 2.08. 3
if you choose that wherein i am contain'd, 2.09. 5
i am enjoin'd by oath to observe three things: 2.09. 9
i am half afeard | thou wilt say anon he is some 2.09. 96
why, i am sure, if he forfeit, thou wilt not 3.01. 51 P
i am a jew. 3.01. 58 P
i am very glad of it. 3.01.116 P
i am glad of it. 3.01.117 P
how to choose right, but then i am forsworn. 3.02. 11
me choose, | for as i am, i live upon the rack. 3.02. 25
i am lock'd in one of them; 3.02. 40
lord bassanio, where i stand, | such as i am. 3.02.150
for i am sure you can wish none from me; 3.02.191
with leave, bassanio, i am half yourself, | and 3.02.248
cause, | but, since i am a dog, beware my fangs. 3.03. 7
i am sure the duke | will never grant this 3.03. 24
and am well pleas'd | to wish it back on you. 3.04. 43
all my whole device | when i am in my coach, 3.04. 82
for me in heaven because i am a jew's daughter; 3.05. 33 P
i am sorry for thee. 4.01. 3
patience to his fury, and am arm'd | to suffer, 4.01. 11
i am not bound to please thee with my answers. 4.01. 65
i am a tainted wether of the flock, | meetest 4.01.114
at the receipt of your letter i am very sick, 4.01.151 P

i am informed throughly of the cause. 4.01.173
i am arm'd and well prepar'd. 4.01.264
grieve not that i am fall'n to this for you; 4.01.266
i am married to a wife | which is as dear to me 4.01.282
fine for one half of his goods, | i am content; 4.01.382
i am content. 4.01.394
give me leave to go from hence, | i am not well. 4.01.396
i am sorry that your leisure serves you not. 4.01.405
and i, delivering you, am satisfied, | and 4.01.416
i am never merry when i hear sweet music. 5.01. 69
the voice, | or i am much deceiv'd, of portia. 5.01.111
is antonio, | to whom i am so infinitely bound. 5.01.135
no more than i am well acquitted of. 5.01.138
know him i shall, i am well sure of it. 5.01.229
i am th' unhappy subject of these quarrels. 5.01.238
i am dumb. 5.01.279
when i am absent, then lie with my wife. 5.01.285
and yet i am sure you are not satisfied | of 5.01.296
nothing. i am not taught to make any thing. AYL 1.01. 30 P
i am helping you to mar that which god made, a 1.01. 32 P
ay, better than him i am before knows me. 1.01. 43 P
i am no villain; 1.01. 56 P
i am the youngest son of sir rowland de boys. 1.01. 56 P
i am given, sir, secretly to understand that 1.01.123 P
i am heartily glad i came hither to you. 1.01.159 P
best know him, that i am altogether mispris'd. 1.01.170 P
i show more mirth than i am mistress of, and 1.02. 3 P
and swear by your beards that i am a knave. 1.02. 72 P
beseech your grace, i am not yet well breath'd. 1.02.217 P
i am more proud to be sir rowland's son, | his 1.02.232
or be not frantic | (as i do trust i am not), 1.03. 50
if she be a traitor, | why so am i. 1.03. 73
charge thee be not thou more griev'd than i am. 1.03. 92
which teacheth thee that thou and i am one. 1.03. 97
because that i am more than common tall, | that 1.03.115
that feelingly persuade me what i am." 2.01. 11
though i look old, yet i am strong and lusty; 2.03. 47
ay, now am i in arden, the more fool i. 2.04. 16 P
but i am shepherd to another man, | and do not 2.04. 78
i am ambitious for a motley coat. 2.07. 43
that grows rank in them | that i am wise. 2.07. 47
yet am i inland bred | and know some nurture. 2.07. 96
i am the duke | that lov'd your father. 2.07.195
sir, i am a true laborer: 3.02. 73 P
thou think, though i am caparison'd like a man, 3.02.195 P
but doth he know that i am in this forest and in 3.02.229 P
do you not know i am a woman? 3.02.249 P
i am weary of you. 3.02.284 P
i am glad of your departure. 3.02.293 P
against it, and i thank god i am not a woman, to 3.02.348 P
i am he that is so love–shak'd, i pray you tell 3.02.367 P
in which cage of rushes i am sure you /are not 3.02.371 P
by the white hand of rosalind, i am that he, 3.02.395 P
am i the man yet? 3.03. 2 P
i am here with thee and thy goats, as the most 3.03. 7 P
well, i am not fair, and therefore i pray the 3.03. 33 P
i am not a slut, though i thank the gods i am 3.03. 38 P
not a slut, though i thank the gods i am foul. 3.03. 39 P
i am very glad to see you. 3.03. 75 P
i am not in the mind; 3.03. 90 P
nor i am sure there is no force in eyes | that 3.05. 26
me, | for i am falser than vows made in wine. 3.05. 73
why, i am sorry for thee, gentle silvius. 3.05. 85
and, now i am rememb'red, scorn'd at me. 3.05.131
i am so; i do love it better than laughing. 4.01. 4 P
and i am your rosalind. 4.01. 65 P
for now i am in a holiday humor, and like enough 4.01. 68 P
am not i your rosalind? 4.01. 88 P
didst know how many fathom deep i am in love! 4.01.206 P
are out, let him be judge how deep i am in love. 4.01.215 P
pardon me, | i am but as a guiltless messenger. 4.03. 12
she says i am not fair, that i lack manners; 4.03. 15
i am. what must we understand by this? 4.03. 94
if you will know of me | what man i am, and how, 4.03. 96
so sweetly tastes, being the thing i am. 4.03.137
at heart, | he sent me hither, stranger as i am, 4.03.152
now, you are not ipse, for i am he. 5.01. 44 P
i tender dearly, though i say i am a magician. 5.02. 71 P
of sighs and tears, | and so am i for phebe. 5.02. 85
of faith and service, | and so am i for phebe. 5.02. 90
and so am i for phebe. 5.02. 99
and so am i for ganymed. 5.02.100
and so am i for rosalind. 5.02.101
and so am i for no woman. 5.02.102
to you i give myself, for i am yours. 5.04.116
to you i give myself, for i am yours. 5.04.117
i am the second son of old sir rowland, | that 5.04.152
i am for other than for dancing measures. 5.04.193
what a case am i in then, that am neither a good ep 7 P
am i in then, that am neither a good epilogue, ep 8 P
i am not furnish'd like a beggar, therefore to ep 9 P
and i am sure, as many as have good beards, or ep 20 P
but i am doubtful of your modesties, | lest, SHR in.1. 94
i am christophero sly, call not me honor nor in.2. 5 P
am not i christopher sly, old sly's son of in.2. 17 P
if she say i am not fourteen pence on the score in.2. 23 P
i am not bestraught. in.2. 25 P
am i a lord, and have i such a lady? in.2. 68
life, i am a lord indeed | and not a tinker nor in.2. 72
i am your goodman. in.2. 105
and husband, | i am your wife in all obedience. in.2. 107
of arts, | i am arriv'd for fruitful lombardy, 1.01. 3
and by my father's love and leave am arm'd 1.01. 5
for i have pisa left | and am to padua come, as 1.01. 22
i am, in all affected as yourself, | glad that 1.01. 26
for how i firmly am resolv'd you know: 1.01. 49
sorry am i that our good will effects | bianca's 1.01. 86
i am resolv'd. 1.01. 90
i am agreed, and would i had given him the best 1.01.142 P
ay, marry, am i, sir; and now 'tis plotted. 1.01.188
i am tied to be obedient — 1.01.212
pleasure is, | and i am tied to be obedient — 1.01.212
another sense — | i am content to be lucentio, 1.01.216
when i am alone, why then i am tranio; 1.01.243
when i am alone, why then i am tranio; 1.01.243
why, sir, what am i, sir, that i should knock 1.02. 9 P
petruchio, patience, i am grumio's pledge. 1.02. 45
home, | and so am come abroad to see the world. 1.02. 58
trow you whither i am going? 1.02.164
i am a gentleman of verona, sir, | that, hearing 2.01. 47
am bold to show myself a forward guest | within 2.01. 51
this is a gift very grateful, i am sure of it. 2.01. 76 P
i am as peremptory as she proud–minded; 2.01.131
me, | for i am rough, and woo not like a babe. 2.01.137
myself am mov'd to woo thee for my wife. 2.01.194
i am a gentleman — 2.01.219
now, by saint george, i am too young for you. 2.01.236
am i not wise? 2.01.265
now, kate, i am a husband for your turn, | for 2.01.272
for i am he am born to tame you, kate, | and 2.01.276
for i am he am born to tame you, kate, | and 2.01.276
i am your neighbor, and was suitor first. 2.01.334
and i am one that love bianca more | than words 2.01.335
myself am strook in years, i must confess, | and 2.01.360
i am my father's heir and only son. 2.01.364
well, gentlemen, | i am thus resolv'd: 2.01.393
i am no breeching scholar in the schools, | i'll 3.01. 18
you'll leave his lecture when i am in tune? 3.01. 24
you before, "simois," i am lucentio, "hic est," 3.01. 32 P
why, i am past my gamouth long ago. 3.01. 71
"gamouth i am, the ground of all accord: 3.01. 73
i am not so nice | to /change true rules for 3.01. 80
when he stands where i am and sees you there. 3.02. 40 P
i am glad he's come, howsoe'er he comes. 3.02. 74 P
hear — | sufficeth i am come to keep my word, 3.02.106
but what a fool am i to chat with you, | when i 3.02.121
i am to get a man — what e'er he be, | it 3.02.131
i am content. 3.02.201
i am content you shall entreat me stay, | but 3.02.202
i am sent before to make a fire, and they are 4.01. 4 P
away, you three–inch fool! i am no beast. 4.01. 26 P
am i but three inches? 4.01. 27 P
horn is a foot, and so long am i at the least. 4.01. 28 P
away, | and i expressly am forbid to touch it; 4.01.171
mistake no more, i am not litio, | nor a 4.02. 16
know, sir, that i am call'd hortensio. 4.02. 21
i have watch'd so long | that i am dog–weary, 4.02. 60
am starv'd for meat, giddy for lack of sleep, 4.03. 9
thou seest how diligent i am | to dress thy meat 4.03. 39
i am sure, sweet kate, this kindness merits 4.03. 41
i am no child, no babe; 4.03. 74
i am for thee straight. 4.03.151 P
i am content, in a good father's care, | to have 4.04. 31
and bound i am to padua, there to visit | a son 4.05. 56
what am i, sir? 5.01. 65 P
o, i am undone! 5.01. 68 P
i am undone! 5.01. 68 P
thank my good father, i am able to maintain it. 5.01. 76 P
then thou wert best say that i am not lucentio. 5.01.103 P
and i am mean indeed, respecting you. 5.02. 32
am i your bird? 5.02. 46
i am afraid, sir, | do what you can, yours will 5.02. 88
i am asham'd that women are so simple | to offer 5.02.161
his majesty's command, to whom i am now in ward, AWW 1.01. 5 P
i am undone! 1.01. 84
i am so full of businesses, i cannot answer thee 1.01.206 P
not unknown to you, madam, i am a poor fellow. 1.03. 13 P
'tis not so well that i am poor, though many of 1.03. 16 P
i am driven on by the flesh, and he must needs 1.03. 28 P
i am out a' friends, madam, and i hope to have 1.03. 39 P
come to do that for me which i am a–weary of. 1.03. 43 P
of her i am to speak. 1.03. 67 P
i am going, forsooth. 1.03. 95 P
you know, helen, | i am a mother to you. 1.03.138
i say i am your mother, | and put you in the 1.03.142
does it curd thy blood | to say i am thy mother? 1.03.150
that i am not. 1.03.153
i say i am your mother. 1.03.154
i am from humble, he from honored name; 1.03.156
i am commanded here, and kept a coil with | "too 2.01. 27
i am your accessary, and so farewell. 2.01. 35
i am cressid's uncle, | that dare leave two 2.01. 97
i am not an imposture that proclaim | myself 2.01.155
ask me if i am a courtier: 2.02. 36 P
sir, i am a poor friend of yours that loves you. 2.02. 43 P
most fruitfully, i am there before my legs. 2.02. 70 P
i am a simple maid, and therein wealthiest 2.03. 66
wealthiest | that i protest i simply am a maid. 2.03. 67
i am sure thy father drunk wine — but if thou 2.03. 99 P
thou be'st not an ass, i am a youth of fourteen. 2.03.100 P
for doing i am past, as i will by thee, in what 2.03.233 P
with my hate to her, | and wherefore i am fled; 2.03.288
therefore am i found | so much unsettled. 2.05. 62
say, | but that i am your most obedient servant. 2.05. 72
i am not worthy of the wealth i owe, | nor dare 2.05. 79
but i am sure the younger of our nature, | that 3.01. 17
you shall hear i am run away; 3.02. 22 P
child begotten of thy body that i am father to, 3.02. 59 P
i am the caitiff that do hold him to't; 3.02.114
not, i am the cause | his death was so effected. 3.02.115
"i am saint jaques' pilgrim, thither gone. 3.04. 4
do you think i am so far deceiv'd in him? 3.06. 6 P
whom i am sure he knows not from the enemy. 3.06. 23 P
if you misdoubt me that i am not she, | i know 3.07. 1
therefore i'll lie with him | when i am buried. 4.02. 73
spoken it, 'tis dead, and i am the grave of it. 4.03. 13 P
i am heartily sorry that he'll be glad of this. 4.03. 63 P
for her, writ to my lady mother i am returning, 4.03. 89 P
not that i am afraid to die, but that, my 4.03.241 P
what honor i can, but of this i am not certain. 4.03.271 P
i am for france. 4.03.318 P
fare ye well, sir, i am for france too. 4.03.329 P
yet am i thankful. 4.03.330
simply the thing i am | shall make me live. 4.03.333
i duly am inform'd | his grace is at marsellis, 4.04. 8
you must know | i am supposed dead. 4.04. 11
i am yours | upon your will to suffer. 4.04. 29
i am no great nebuchadnezzar, sir, i have not 4.05. 20 P
i am a woodland fellow, sir, that always lov'd a 4.05. 47 P
i am for the house with the narrow gate, which i 4.05. 50 P
to–morrow, or i am deceiv'd by him that in such 4.05. 82 P
i take it, to rossillion, | whither i am going. 5.01. 29
but i am now, sir, muddied in fortune's mood, 5.02. 4 P
i am a man whom fortune hath cruelly scratch'd. 5.02. 26 P
i am for other business. 5.02. 34 P
i am not a day of season, | for thou mayst see a 5.03. 32
i am sure i saw her wear it. 5.03. 91
i am wrapp'd in dismal thinkings. 5.03.128
i am afeard the life of helen, lady, | was 5.03.153
i am, my lord, a wretched florentine, | derived 5.03.158
i am her mother, sir, whose age and honor | both 5.03.162
for i by vow am so embodied yours, | that she 5.03.173
but loath am to produce | so bad an instrument. 5.03.201
am i or that or this for what he'll utter, 5.03.208
i am a poor man, and at your majesty's command. 5.03.251 P
he knows i am no maid, and he'll swear to't; 5.03.290
i'll swear i am a maid, and he knows not. 5.03.291
great king, i am no strumpet, by my life; 5.03.292
i am either maid, or else this old man's wife. 5.03.293
conceal me what i am, and be my aid | for such TN 1.02. 53
i am sure care's an enemy to life. 1.03. 2 P
i'll confine myself no finer than i am. 1.03. 11 P
i am not such an ass but i can keep my hand dry. 1.03. 74 P
marry, now i let go your hand, i am barren. 1.03. 79 P
but i am a great eater of beef and i believe 1.03. 85 P
i am a fellow o' th' strangest mind i' th' world 1.03.112 P
for i myself am best | when least in company. 1.04. 37
so, neither, but i am resolv'd on two points — 1.05. 22 P
and i, that am sure i lack thee, may pass for a 1.05. 34 P
sir toby will be sworn that i am no fox, but he 1.05. 80 P
if it be a suit from the count, i am sick, or 1.05.108 P
i am very comptible, even to the least sinister 1.05.175 P
fangs of malice i swear) i am not that i play. 1.05.184 P
if i do not usurp myself, i am. 1.05.186 P
good swabber, i am to hull here a little longer. 1.05.203 P
tell me your mind — i am a messenger. 1.05.205 P
what i am, and what i would, are as secret as 1.05.215 P
i am a gentleman. 1.05.279
i am no fee'd post, lady; 1.05.284
i am a gentleman." 1.05.291
i am not for him. 1.05.304
not extort from me what i am willing to keep in; 2.01. 14 P
and i am yet so near the manners of my mother, 2.01. 40 P
i am bound to the count orsino's court. 2.01. 42 P
i am the man! 2.02. 25
as i am man, | my state is desperate for my 2.02. 36
as i am woman (now alas the day!), 2.02. 38
a mellifluous voice, as i am true knight. 2.03. 53 P
i am dog at a catch. 2.03. 60 P
am not i consanguineous? 2.03. 77 P
am i not of her blood? 2.03. 77 P
cannot recover your niece, i am a foul way out. 2.03.184 P
for such as i am, all true lovers are, | unstaid 2.04. 17
away, breath, | i am slain by a fair cruel maid. 2.04. 54
i am all the daughters of my father's house, 2.04.120
in my stars i am above thee, but be not afraid 2.05.144 P
i thank my stars, i am happy. 2.05.170 P
"thou canst not choose but know who i am. 2.05.175 P
so false, i am loath to prove reason with them. 3.01. 24 P
i am indeed not her fool, but her corrupter of 3.01. 35 P
i'll tell thee, i am almost sick for one — 3.01. 46 P
i hope, sir, you are, and i am yours. 3.01. 73 P
i am bound to your niece, sir; 3.01. 76 P
then think you right: i am not what i am. 3.01.141
then think you right: i am not what i am. 3.01.141
would it be better, madam, than i am? 3.01.143
i wish it might, for now i am your fool. 3.01.144
i am not weary, and 'tis long to night; 3.03. 21
i am as mad as he, | if sad and merry madness 3.04. 14
am i made? 3.04. 54 P
idle shallow things, i am not of your element. 3.04.124 P
you mistake, sir, i am sure; 3.04.226 P
i am no fighter. 3.04.242 P
i am one that had rather go with sir priest than 3.04.270 P
nay, if you be an undertaker, i am for you. 3.04.318 P
you make me believe that i am not sent for you? 4.01. 1 P
know you, nor i am not sent to you by my lady, 4.01. 6 P
i am afraid this great lubber, the world, will 4.01. 14 P
or i am mad, or else this is a dream. 4.01. 61
i am not tall enough to become the function well 4.02. 6 P
so i, being master parson, am master parson; 4.02. 15 P
good sir topas, do not think i am mad; 4.02. 29 P
for i am one of those gentle ones that will use 4.02. 32 P
i am not mad, sir topas, i say to you this house 4.02. 40 P
i am no more mad than you are; 4.02. 47 P
nay, i am for all waters. 4.02. 63 P
for i am now so far in offense with my niece 4.02. 69 P
as i am a gentleman, i will live to be thankful 4.02. 82 P
i am as well in my wits, fool, as thou art. 4.02. 88 P
i am shent for speaking to you. 4.02.104 P
i tell thee i am as well in my wits as any man 4.02.106 P
by this hand, i am. 4.02.109 P
believe me, i am not, i tell thee true. 4.02.115 P
i am gone, sir, | and anon, sir, | i'll be with 4.02.120
that i am ready to distrust mine eyes | and 4.03. 13
to any other trust but that i am mad | or else 4.03. 15
now my foes tell me plainly i am an ass; 5.01. 18 P
of myself, and by my friends i am abus'd; 5.01. 20 P
let your lady know i am here to speak with her, 5.01. 42 P
ay me, detested! how am i beguil'd! 5.01.139
i am sorry, madam, i have hurt your kinsman, 5.01.209
a spirit i am indeed, | but am in that dimension 5.01.236
but am in that dimension grossly clad | which 5.01.237
do cohere and jump | that i am viola — which to 5.01.253
madam, i am most apt t' embrace your offer. 5.01.320
"by the lord, fool, i am not mad." 5.01.373 P
i am question'd by my fears of what may chance WT 1.02. 11
then didst thou utter, | "i am yours for ever." 1.02.105
i am angling now, | though you perceive me not 1.02.180
there have been | (or i am much deceiv'd) 1.02.191
i am like you, /they say. 1.02.208
how i am gall'd — mightst bespice a cup, | to 1.02.316
dost think i am so muddy, so unsettled, | to 1.02.325
i am his cupbearer: 1.02.345
since i am charg'd in honor and by him | that i 1.02.407
i am appointed him to murther you. 1.02.412
but i am sure 'tis safer to | avoid what's grown 1.02.432
come, sir, now | i am for you again. 2.01. 22
how blest am i | in my just censure! 2.01. 36
i am glad you did not nurse him. 2.01. 56
brands | that calumny doth use — o, i am out — 2.01. 72
i am not prone to weeping, as our sex | commonly 2.01.108
though i am satisfied and need no more | than 2.01.189
let him have knowledge who i am. 2.02. 2

Line	Play	Ref
"my poor prisoner, | i am innocent as you."		2.02. 27
i am as ignorant in that, as you | in so		2.03. 70
i am none, by this good light.		2.03. 83
i am a feather for each wind that blows.		2.03.154
since what i am to say must be but that | which		3.02. 22
as chaste, as true, | as i am now unhappy;		3.02. 35
for polixenes | (with whom i am accus'd), i do		3.02. 62
body, from his presence | i am barr'd, like one		3.02. 98
i am sorry for't.		3.02.218
i am glad at heart | to be so rid o' th'		3.03. 14
and most accurs'd am i | to be by oath enjoin'd		3.03. 52
i am gone for ever.		3.03. 58
though i am not bookish, yet i can read		3.03. 72 P
but i am not to say it is a sea, for it is now		3.03. 84 P
let me pass | the same i am, ere ancient'st		4.01. 10
wore three-pile, but now i am out of service.		4.03. 14 P
who being, as i am, litter'd under mercury, was		4.03. 25 P
what am i to buy for our sheep-shearing feast?		4.03. 37 P
i am robb'd, sir, and beaten;		4.03. 61 P
i must confess to you, sir, i am no fighter.		4.03.107 P
i am false of heart that way, and that he knew,		4.03.108 P
to this i am most constant, | though destiny say		4.04. 45
but being enthrall'd as i am, it will also be		4.04.233 P
i am sorry that by hanging thee i can | but		4.04.421
i am but sorry, not afeard;		4.04.463
what i was, i am:		4.04.464
wipe me, father, i | am heir to my affection.		4.04.481
i am — and by my fancy.		4.04.482
i am put to sea | with her who here i cannot		4.04.498
i am so fraught with curious business that | i		4.04.514
i am bound to you. | there is some sap in this.		4.04.564
i am a poor fellow, sir.		4.04.630 P
i am a poor fellow, sir. i know ye well enough.		4.04.638 P
and therein am i constant to my profession.		4.04.682 P
though i am not naturally honest, i am so		4.04.712 P
naturally honest, i am so sometimes by chance.		4.04.713 P
whether it like me or no, i am a courtier.		4.04.730 P
thee thy business, i am therefore no courtier?		4.04.735 P
i am courtier cap-a-pe, and one that will either		4.04.736 P
i am courted now with a double occasion — gold		4.04.833 P
for i am proof against that title and what shame		4.04.840 P
i am sorry, | most sorry, you have broken from		5.01.211
by your desires, | i am friend to them and you.		5.01.231
for i am sure my heart wept blood.		5.02. 89 P
boy, i am past moe children, but thy sons and		5.02.126 P
and try whether i am not now a gentleman born.		5.02.133 P
not swear it, now i am a gentleman?		5.02.159 P
i am asham'd;		5.03. 37
i am sorry, sir, i have thus far stirr'd you;		5.03. 74
against) i am assisted | by wicked powers.		5.03. 90
you can make her do, | i am content to look on;		5.03. 92
what to speak, | i am content to hear;		5.03. 93
that think it is unlawful business | i am about,		5.03. 97
to be found again, | lament till i am lost.		5.03.135
but that i am as well begot, my liege | (fair	JN	1.01. 77
i am a soldier, and now bound to france.		1.01.150
i am thy grandame, richard, call me so.		1.01.168
well shot, | and i am i, howe'er i was begot.		1.01.175
and so am i, whether i smack or no;		1.01.209
to whom am i beholding for these limbs?		1.01.239
what, i am dubb'd!		1.01.245
but, mother, i am not sir robert's son, | i have		1.01.246
i am not worth this coil that's made for me.		2.01.165
for i am well assur'd | that i did so when i was		2.01.534
well, whiles i am a beggar, i will rail, | and		2.01.593
me, | for i am sick and capable of fears,		3.01. 12
alone which i alone | am bound to underbear.		3.01. 65
i am perplex'd, and know not what to say.		3.01.221
i am with both, each army hath a hand, | and in		3.01.328
france, i am burn'd up with inflaming wrath, | a		3.01.340
i am almost asham'd | to say what good respect i		3.03. 27
i am much bounden to your majesty.		3.03. 29
art /not holy to belie me so, | i am not mad.		3.04. 45
i am not mad, i would to heaven i were!		3.04. 48
i am not mad;		3.04. 59
i am best pleas'd to be from such a deed.		4.01. 85
yet am i sworn, and i did purpose, boy, | with		4.01.123
i, as one that am the tongue of these | to sound		4.02. 47
i am afraid, and yet i'll venture it.		4.03. 5
lords, i am hot with haste in seeking you.		4.03. 74
i am no villain.		4.03. 78
yet i am none.		4.03. 91
lord bigot, i am none.		4.03.103
for i am stifled with this smell of sin.		4.03.113
i am amaz'd, methinks, and lose my way | among		4.03.140
i am not glad that such a sore of time | should		5.02. 12
i am too high-born to be propertied, | to be a		5.02. 79
am i rome's slave?		5.02. 97
i am sent to speak:		5.02.119
weakness possesseth me, and i am faint.		5.03. 17
i am no woman, i'll not swound at it.		5.06. 22
i am the /cygnet to this pale faint swan | who		5.07. 21
i am a scribbled form, drawn with a pen | upon a		5.07. 32
i am scalded with my violent motion | and spleen		5.07. 49
i am disgrac'd, impeach'd, and baffled here,	R2	1.01.170
and derby | am i, who ready here do stand in		1.03. 36
i am too old to fawn upon a nurse, | too far in		1.03.170
methinks i am a prophet new inspir'd, | and thus		2.01. 31
gaunt am i for the grave, gaunt as a grave,		2.01. 82
i am in health, i breathe, and see thee ill.		2.01. 92
i am the last of noble edward's sons, | of whom		2.01.171
pleas'd | not to be pardoned, am content withal.		2.01.188
here am i left to underprop his land, | who,		2.02. 82
lord, | i am a stranger here in gloucestershire.		2.03. 3
and i am come to seek that name in england,		2.03. 71
i am no traitor's uncle, and that word "grace"		2.03. 88
it must be granted i am duke of lancaster.		2.03.124
i am denied to sue my livery here, | and yet my		2.03.129
i am a subject, | and i challenge law.		2.03.133
for i am loath to break our country's laws.		2.03.169
blood, | to show the world i am a gentleman.		3.01. 27
i had forgot myself, am i not king?		3.02. 83
glad am i that your highness is so arm'd | to		3.02.104
thus, | how can you say to me i am a king?		3.02.177
just, | and, as i am a gentleman, i credit him.		3.03.120
your own is yours, and i am yours, and all.		3.03.197
cousin, i am too young to be your father,		3.03.204
i am press'd to death through want of speaking!		3.04. 72
belong to me, | and am i last that knows it?		3.04. 94
i am sworn brother, sweet, | to grim necessity,		5.01. 20
think i am dead, and that even here thou takest,		5.01. 38
i am in parliament pledge for his truth | and		5.02. 44
yet am i sick for fear, speak it again, | twice		5.03.133
i am the king's friend, and will rid his foe.		5.04. 11
sometimes am i king;		5.05. 32
make me wish myself a beggar, | and so i am.		5.05. 34
then am i king'd again, and by and by | think		5.05. 36
by | think that i am unking'd by bullingbrook,		5.05. 37
by bullingbrook, | and straight am nothing.		5.05. 38
patience is stale, and i am weary of it.		5.05.103
i am as melancholy as a gib cat or a lugg'd bear	1H4	1.02. 73 P
i knew nothing, and now am i, if a man should		1.02. 93 P
and i do not, i am a villain, i'll be damn'd for		1.02. 96 P
by how much better than my word i am, | by so		1.02.210
look you, i am /whipt and scourg'd with rods,		1.03.239
i am stung like a tench.		2.01. 15 P
to break the pate on thee, i am a very villain.		2.01. 30 P
i am join'd with no foot land-rakers, no		2.01. 73 P
a share in our purchase, as i am a true man.		2.01. 92 P
i am accurs'd to rob in that thieve's company.		2.02. 10 P
and yet i am bewitch'd with the rogue's company.		2.02. 17 P
i am the veriest varlet that ever chew'd with a		2.02. 23 P
indeed i am not john of gaunt, your grandfather,		2.02. 67 P
and when i am a' horseback, i will swear | i		2.03.101
i am sworn brother to a leash of drawers, and		2.04. 6 P
prince of wales, yet i am the king of courtesy,		2.04. 10 P
and tell me flatly i am no proud jack like		2.04. 11 P
and when i am king of england i shall command		2.04. 13 P
i am so good a proficient in one quarter of an		2.04. 17 P
i am now of all humors that have show'd		2.04. 92 P
i am not yet of percy's mind, the hotspur of the		2.04.101 P
face of the earth, then am i a shotten herring.		2.04.129 P
i am a rogue if i drunk to-day.		2.04.152 P
i am a rogue if i were not at half-sword with a		2.04.164 P
i am eight times thrust through the doublet,		2.04.166 P
every man of them, or i am a jew else, an ebrew		2.04.179 P
not with fifty of them, i am a bunch of radish.		2.04.186 P
poor old jack, then am i no two-legg'd creature.		2.04.188 P
two i am sure i have paid, two rogues in buckrom		2.04.192 P
seven, by these hilts, or i am a villain else.		2.04.206 P
why, thou knowest i am as valiant as hercules;		2.04.270 P
by the lord, lads, i am glad you have the money.		2.04.275 P
well, here i am set.		2.04.438 P
do show | i am not in the roll of common men.		3.01. 42
marry, | and i am glad of it with all my heart.		3.01.126
i am afraid my daughter will run mad, | so much		3.01.143
well, i am school'd:		3.01.188
these swelling heavens | i am too perfect in,		3.01.200
o, i am ignorance itself in this!		3.01.210
excuse | as well as i am doubtless i can purge		3.02. 20
can purge | myself of many i am charg'd withal;		3.02. 21
day | be bold to tell you that i am your son,		3.02.134
am i not fall'n away vilely since this last		3.03. 1 P
i am wither'd like an old apple-john.		3.03. 4 P
and that suddenly, while i am in some liking.		3.03. 5 P
of a church is made of, i am a peppercorn, a		3.03. 8 P
now, as i am a true woman, holland of eight		3.03. 71 P
i am no thing to thank god on, i would thou		3.03.118 P
i am an honest man's wife, and, setting thy		3.03.119 P
any other injuries but these, i am a villain.		3.03.161 P
thou seest i am pacified still.		3.03.173 P
i am good friends with my father and may do any		3.03.181 P
i am heinously unprovided.		3.03.189 P
i am on fire | to hear this rich reprisal is so		4.01.117
i am out of fear | of death or death's hand for		4.01.135
asham'd of my soldiers, i am a sous'd gurnet.		4.02. 11 P
me, i am as vigilant as a cat to steal cream.		4.02. 58 P
i am sure they never learn'd that of me.		4.02. 71 P
shrewsbury, | as i am truly given to understand,		4.04. 11
i am content that he shall take the odds | of		5.01. 97
i am as hot as molten lead, and as heavy too.		5.03. 33 P
i am the douglas, fatal to all those | that wear		5.04. 26
but mine i am sure thou art, whoe'er thou be,		5.04. 37
i am the prince of wales, and think not, percy,		5.04. 63
i lie, i am no counterfeit.		5.04.115 P
i am afraid of this gunpowder percy though he be		5.04.121 P
my faith, i am afraid he would prove the better		5.04.123 P
no, that's certain, i am not a double man;		5.04.138 P
but if i be not jack falstaff, then am i a jack.		5.04.139 P
i am sorry i should force you to believe | that	2H4	1.01.105
i am not only witty in myself, but the cause		1.02. 9 P
twenty yards of satin (as i am a true knight),		1.02. 44 P
boy, tell him i am deaf.		1.02. 66 P
i am sure he is, to the hearing of any thing		1.02. 68 P
throat if you say i am any other than an honest		1.02. 85 P
i am glad to see your lordship abroad.		1.02. 94 P
of not marking, that i am troubled withal.		1.02.122 P
i am as poor as job, my lord, but not so patient		1.02.126 P
i am the fellow with the great belly, and he my		1.02.145 P
well, i am loath to gall a new-heal'd wound.		1.02.147 P
is, i am only old in judgment and understanding;		1.02.191 P
can peep out his head but i am thrust upon it.		1.02.213 P
if ye will needs say i am an old man, you should		1.02.216 P
i am undone by his going, i warrant you, he's an		2.01. 23 P
your grace, i am a poor widow of eastcheap, and		2.01. 70 P
i think i am as like to ride the mare, if i have		2.01. 78 P
john, i am well acquainted with your manner of		2.01.109 P
as i am a gentleman!		2.01.136 P
as i am a gentleman! come, no more words of it.		2.01.138 P
i' faith, i am loath to pawn my plate, so god		2.01.154 P
before god, i am exceeding weary.		2.02. 1 P
by this light, i am well spoke on, i can hear it		2.02. 65 P
can say of me is that i am a second brother, and		2.02. 67 P
and that i am a proper fellow of my hands, and		2.02. 67 P
a /borrower's cap, "i am the king's poor cousin,		2.02.116 P
i am your shadow, my lord, i'll follow you.		2.02.159 P
word to your master that i am yet come to town.		2.02.161 P
there am i, | till time and vantage crave my		2.03. 67
i am in good name and fame with the very best.		2.04. 75 P
i am the worse when one says swagger.		2.04.104 P
i am meat for your master.		2.04.125 P
i am old, i am old.		2.04.271 P
i am old, i am old.		2.04.271 P
thou't forget me when i am gone.		2.04.277 P
i am a gentleman, thou art a drawer.		2.04.287 P
i am robert shallow, sir, a poor esquire of this		3.02. 57 P
i am glad to see you well, good master robert		3.02. 85 P
i am bound to thee, reverend feeble.		3.02.170 P
o lord, sir, i am a diseas'd man.		3.02.179 P
i am glad to see you, by my troth, master		3.02.192 P
care, but rather, because i am unwilling, and,		3.02.224 P
nobody to do any thing about her when i am gone,		3.02.231 P
i am not here against your father's peace, | but		4.02. 31
i am glad of it.		4.02. 77
season, | for i am on the sudden something ill.		4.02. 80
believe me, i am passing light in spirit.		4.02. 85
i am a knight, sir, and my name is colevile of		4.03. 3 P
as good a man as he, sir, whoe'er i am.		4.03. 11 P
posts, and here, travel-tainted as i am, have,		4.03. 37 P
i am, my lord, but as my betters are | that led		4.03. 65
mayst effect | of mediation, after i am dead,		4.04. 25
upon, | when i am sleeping with my ancestors.		4.04. 61
happiness | added to that that i am to deliver!		4.04. 82
fall | as those that i am come to tell you of!		4.04. 96
come near me, now i am much ill.		4.04.111
i am here, brother, full of heaviness.		4.05. 8
ear | that thou art crowned, not that i am dead.		4.05.112
i am glad to see your worship.		5.01. 56 P
i am the sorrier, would 'twere otherwise!		5.02. 32
i am assur'd, if i be measur'd rightly, | your		5.02. 65
"happy am i, that have a man so bold, | that		5.02.108
sir john, i am thy pistol and thy friend, | and		5.03. 93
i am, sir, under the king, in some authority.		5.03.111 P
be what thou wilt, i am fortune's steward — get		5.03.130 P
jest, | presume not that i am the thing i was,		5.05. 56
when thou dost hear i am as i have been,		5.05. 60
tell you the dolphin i am coming on | to venge	H5	1.02.291
i am not barbason, you cannot conjure me.		2.01. 54 P
i'll run him up to the hilts, as i am a soldier.		2.01. 65 P
as young as i am, i have observ'd these three		3.02. 28 P
i am boy to them all three, but all they three,		3.02. 29 P
for, as i am a soldier, | a name that in my		3.03. 5
sorry am i his numbers are so few, | his		3.05. 56
for i am sure, when he shall see our army,		3.05. 58
go therefore tell thy master here i am;		3.06.153
when i bestride him, i soar, i am a hawk;		3.07. 15 P
i am a gentleman of a company.		4.01. 39 P
no, i am a welshman.		4.01. 51 P
to you, i think the king is but a man, as i am.		4.01.102 P
i am afeard there are few die well that die in a		4.01.141 P
i am a king that find thee;		4.01.259
by jove, i am not covetous for gold, | nor care		4.03. 24
honor, | i am the most offending soul alive.		4.03. 29
for i am welsh, you know, good countryman.		4.07.105
by jeshu, i am your majesty's countryman, i care		4.07.111 P
i am no traitor.		4.08. 15 P
i am qualmish at the smell of leek.		5.01. 21
i am glad thou canst speak no better english,		5.02.123 P
when france is mine and i am yours, then yours		5.02.175 P
which i am sure will hang upon my tongue like a		5.02.179 P
hand, and say, "harry of england, i am thine";		5.02.237 P
i am content, so the maiden cities you talk of		5.02.326 P
me they concern, regent i am of france.	1H6	1.01. 84
bonfires in france forthwith i am to make, | to		1.01.153
i am left out;		1.01.174
dolphin, i am by birth a shepherd's daughter,		1.02. 72
that beauty am i blest with which you may see.		1.02. 86
i am prepar'd;		1.02. 98
assign'd am i to be the english scourge.		1.02.129
now am i like that proud insulting ship | which		1.02.138
i am come to survey the tower this day;		1.03. 1
am i dar'd and bearded to my face?		1.03. 45
chief master gunner am i of this town,		1.04. 6
as who should say, "when i am dead and gone,		1.04. 93
wheel, | i know not where i am, nor what i do.		1.05. 20
appear | how much in duty i am bound to both.		2.01. 37
am sure i scar'd the dolphin and his trull,		2.02. 28
i am indeed.		2.03. 48
no, no, i am but shadow of myself.		2.03. 50
for i am sorry that with reverence | i did not		2.03. 71
the law, | good faith, i am no wiser than a daw.		2.04. 18
and keep me on the side where still i am.		2.04. 54
how i am brav'd, and must perforce endure it!		2.04.115
i am bound to you | that you on my behalf would		2.04.128
that was, | for i am ignorant and cannot guess.		2.05. 60
for by my mother i derived am | from lionel duke		2.05. 74
or am not able | verbatim to rehearse the method		3.01. 12
as he will have me, how am i so poor?		3.01. 30
but he shall know i am as good —		3.01. 41
am i not protector, saucy priest?		3.01. 45
and am not i a prelate of the church?		3.01. 46
how joyful am i made by this contract!		3.01.143
for i am marching hence.		3.03. 39
i am vanquished.		3.03. 78
when i was young (as yet i am not old), | i do		3.04. 17
but that i am prevented, | i should have begg'd		4.01. 71
persuade | than i am able to instruct or teach;		4.01.159
and i am louted by a traitor villain | and		4.03. 13
and am i your son?		4.05. 12
o, twice my father, twice am i thy son!		4.06. 6
fly, to revenge my death when i am dead;		4.06. 30
have won, | and if i fly, i am not talbot's son.		4.06. 51
an earl i am, and suffolk am i call'd.		5.03. 53
an earl i am, and suffolk am i call'd.		5.03. 53
for i perceive i am thy prisoner.		5.03. 74
i am unworthy to be henry's wife.		5.03.122
i unworthy am | to woo so fair a dame to be his		5.03.123
and if my father please, i am content.		5.03.127
i am a soldier and unapt to weep | or to exclaim		5.03.133
i am descended of a gentler blood.		5.04. 8
i am with child, ye bloody homicides!		5.04. 62
'tis known already that i am possess'd | with		5.04.138
tide, | so am i driven by breath of her renown,		5.05. 7
but this i am assur'd, | i feel such sharp		5.05. 83
as i am sick with working of my thoughts.		5.05. 86
lordings, farewell, and say, when i am gone, | i	2H6	1.01.145
nay, be not angry, i am pleas'd again.		1.02. 55
what say'st thou? majesty? i am but grace.		1.02. 71
yet am i suffolk and the cardinal's broker.		1.02.101
i am but a poor petitioner of our whole township		1.03. 23 P
am i a queen in title and in style, | and must		1.03. 48
to me, | for i am bold to counsel you in this.		1.03. 93
madam, i am protector of the realm, | and at his		1.03.120
i'll tell thee, suffolk, why i am unmeet:		1.03.165

my witness, i am falsely accus'd by the villain. 1.03.188 P
cardinal, i am with you. 2.01. 48
alas, master, i am not able to stand alone; 2.01.142
i am not able to stand. 2.01.149 P
and, vanquish'd as i am, i yield to thee, | or 2.01.180
sorry i am to hear what i have heard. 2.01.189
son | succeed before the younger, i am king. 2.02. 52
but i am not your king | till i be crown'd, and 2.02. 64
when i am dead and gone, | may honorable peace 2.03. 37
god, for i am never able to deal with my master, 2.03. 77 P
masters, i am come hither, as it were, upon my 2.03. 85 P
for whilest i think i am thy married wife | and 2.04. 28
sometime i'll say, i am duke humphrey's wife, 2.04. 42
procure me any scathe | so long as i am loyal, 2.04. 63
so am i given in charge, may't please your grace 2.04. 80
that's bad enough, for i am but reproach; 2.04. 96
as i am clear from treason to my sovereign. 3.01.102
wherein am i guilty? 3.01.103
great lords, from ireland am i come amain, | to 3.01.282
i am content. 3.01.319
i am no loathsome leper, look on me. 3.02. 75
am i not witch'd like her? 3.02.119
that i am faulty in duke humphrey's death. 3.02.202
i swear, | whose far–unworthy deputy i am, | he 3.02.286
be'st found | on any ground that i am ruler of, 3.02.296
now, by the ground that i am banish'd from, 3.02.334
and banished i am, if but from thee. 3.02.351
and i am sent to tell his majesty | that even 3.02.377
look on my george, i am a gentleman: 4.01. 29
and so am i; 4.01. 31
therefore am i of an honorable house. 4.02. 49 P
valiant i am. 4.02. 53 P
i am able to endure much. 4.02. 56 P
and when i am king, as king i will be — 4.02. 69 P
i am sorry for't. 4.02. 95 P
here i am, thou particular fellow. 4.02.112 P
reign, | for i am rightful heir unto the crown. 4.02.131
his son am i, deny it if you can. 4.02.146
i am content he shall reign, but i'll be 4.02.158 P
and therefore am i bold and resolute. 4.04. 60
but i am troubled here with them myself; 4.05. 7
that i am the besom that must sweep the court 4.07. 31 P
too, as myself, for example, that am a butcher. 4.07. 53 P
that have a sword, and yet am ready to famish! 4.10. 2 P
but now am i so hungry that, if i might have a 4.10. 4 P
o, i am slain! 4.10. 60 P
and hang thee o'er my tomb when i am dead. 4.10. 68
that never fear'd any, am vanquish'd by famine, 4.10. 75 P
or why thou, being a subject as i am, | against 5.01. 19
flint, | i am so angry at these abject terms; 5.01. 25
i am far better born than is the king; 5.01. 28
i am thy king, and thou a false–heart traitor. 5.01.143
hast, | i am resolv'd for death /or dignity. 5.01.194
i am resolv'd to bear a greater storm | than any 5.01.198
i am thy sovereign. 3H6 1.01. 76
i am thine. 1.01. 76
i am the son of henry the fift, | who made the 1.01.107
and if he may, then am i lawful king; 1.01.137
whose heir my father was, and i am his. 1.01.140
i am content: 1.01.174
had i been there, which am a silly woman, | the 1.01.243
i am too mean a subject for thy wrath, | be thou 1.03. 19
and i am faint, and cannot fly their fury; 1.04. 23
i am your butt, and i abide your shot. 1.04. 29
i am his king, and he should bow his knee. 2.02. 87
tongue, | i am a king, and privileg'd to speak. 2.02.120
i am resolv'd | that clifford's manhood lies 2.02.124
now, richard, i am with thee here alone: 2.04. 5
they prosper best of all when i am thence. 2.05. 18
thou didst love york, and i am son to york. 2.06. 73
from scotland am i stol'n, even of pure love, 3.01. 13
why, so i am — in mind, and that's enough. 3.01. 60
am i dead? 3.01. 82
that's soon perform'd, because i am a subject. 3.02. 54
i am a subject fit to jest withal, | but far 3.02. 91
i know i am too mean to be your queen, | and yet 3.02. 97
and am i then a man to be belov'd? 3.02.163
am come to crave thy just and lawful aid; 3.03. 32
in our king's behalf | i am commanded, with your 3.03. 60
that i am clear from this misdeed of edward's; 3.03.183
and am i guerdon'd at the last with shame? 3.03.191
pass, | and henceforth i am thy true servitor. 3.03.196
last, i firmly am resolv'd | you shall have aid. 3.03.219
laid aside, | and i am ready to put armor on. 3.03.230
they are but lewis and warwick, i am edward, 4.01. 15
are done, | and i am ready to put armor on." 4.01.105
yet am i arm'd against the worst can happen; 4.01.128
then am i sure of victory. 4.01.147
i am inform'd that he comes towards london | to 4.04. 26
i am so sorry for my trespass made | that, to 5.01. 92
alas, i am not coop'd here for defense! 5.01.109
come quickly, montague, or i am dead. 5.02. 39
suppose that i am now my father's mouth: 5.05. 18
i tell ye all | i am your better, traitors as ye 5.05. 36
think'st thou i am an executioner? 5.06. 30
a persecutor i am sure thou art. 5.06. 31
i have no brother, i am like no brother; 5.06. 80
i am myself alone. 5.06. 83
laid, | for yet i am not look'd on in the world. 5.07. 22
now am i seated as my soul delights, | having my 5.07. 35
but i, that am not shap'd for sportive tricks, R3 1.01. 14
i, that am rudely stamp'd, and want love's 1.01. 16
i, that am curtail'd of this fair proportion, 1.01. 18
i am determined to prove a villain | and hate 1.01. 30
edward be as true and just | as i am subtle, 1.01. 37
g, | it follows in his thought that i am he. 1.01. 59
him | than i am made by my young lord and thee! 1.02. 28
but i know none, and therefore am no beast. 1.02. 72
on me, that halts and am misshapen thus? 1.02.250
since i am crept in favor with myself, | i will 1.02.258
that i, forsooth, am stern, and love them not? 1.03. 44
withal, what i have been, and what i am. 1.03.132
i am too childish–foolish for this world. 1.03.141
thereof, | for i am she, and altogether joyless. 1.03.155
if not, that i am queen, you bow like subjects, 1.03.160
that, as i am a christian faithful man, | i 1.04. 4
i am afraid, methinks, to hear you tell it. 1.04. 65
i am in this commanded to deliver | the noble 1.04. 91
so i am — to let him live. 1.04.114 P
i am strong–fram'd, he cannot prevail with me. 1.04.150 P
but not, as i am, royal. 1.04.165
i am his brother and i love him well. 1.04.227
son, | being pent from liberty, as i am now, 1.04.258
/god, | when i am cold in love to you or yours. 2.01. 40
i am not barren to bring forth complaints. 2.02. 67
i am the mother of these griefs: 2.02. 80
i am your sorrow's nurse, | and i will pamper it 2.02. 87
because that i am little, like an ape, | he 3.01.130
and look when i am king, claim thou of me | the 3.01.194
indeed i am no mourner for that news, | because 3.02. 51
secure, | i would be so triumphant as i am? 3.02. 82
well met, my lord, i am glad to see your honor. 3.02.108
i am in your debt for your last exercise; 3.02.110
for i myself am not so well provided | as else i 3.04. 44
look how i am bewitch'd; 3.04. 68
sorry i am my noble cousin should | suspect me 3.07. 88
i am unfit for state and majesty. 3.07.205
i am not made of stones, | but penetrable to 3.07.224
see, | how far i am from the desire of this. 3.07.236
i am their mother, who shall bar me from them? 4.01. 21
i am their father's mother, i will see them. 4.01. 22
their aunt i am in law, in love their mother; 4.01. 23
i am bound by oath, and therefore pardon me. 4.01. 27
ha? am i king? 'tis so — but edward lives. 4.02. 14
but i am in | so far in blood that sin will 4.02. 63
thou troublest me, i am not in the vein. 4.02.118
kind tyrrel, am i happy in thy news? 4.03. 24
a dire induction am i witness to, | and will to 4.04. 5
i am hungry for revenge, | and now i cloy me 4.04. 61
and brief, good mother, for i am in haste. 4.04.162
say i, her sovereign, am her subject low. 4.04.355
as i by friends am well advertised, | sir edward 4.04.499
much | (which well i am assur'd i have not done) 5.03. 36
so, i am satisfied. 5.03. 72
yes, i am. 5.03.184
i am a villain; 5.03.191
yet i lie, i am not. 5.03.191
i am thankful to you, and i'll go along | by H8 1.01.150
for i am sure the emperor | paid ere he promis'd 1.01.185
i am sorry | to hear this of him; 1.01.193
i am sorry, | to see you ta'en from liberty, to 1.01.204
i am the shadow of poor buckingham, | whose 1.01.224
nay, we must longer kneel; i am a suitor. 1.02. 9
i am solicited, not by a few, | and those of 1.02. 18
i am much too venturous | in tempting of your 1.02. 54
but am bold'ned | under your promis'd pardon. 1.02. 55
if i am | traduc'd by ignorant tongues, which 1.02. 71
i am sorry that the duke of buckingham | is run 1.02.109
i am glad they are going, | for sure there's no 1.03. 42
now | an honest country lord, as i am, beaten 1.03. 44
i am your lordship's. 1.03. 67
my lord sands, | i am beholding to you; 1.04. 41
i am glad | your grace is grown so pleasant. 1.04. 89
i am sorry for't. 2.01. 9
yet i am richer than my base accusers, | that 2.01.104
i am confident; 2.01.146
as i am made without him, so i'll stand, | if 2.02. 51
who am i? 2.02. 66
bow'd would hire me, | old as i am, to queen it. 2.03. 37
years in court | (am yet a courtier beggarly) 2.03. 83
for | i am a most poor woman, and a stranger, 2.04. 15
sir, | i am about to weep; 2.04. 70
if he know | that i am free of your report, he 2.04. 99
your report, he knows | i am not of your wrong. 2.04.100
i am a simple woman, much too weak | t' oppose 2.04.106
these ears (for, where i am robb'd and bound, 2.04.147
i care not (so much i am happy | above a number) 3.01. 33
seek me out, and that way i am wife in, | out 3.01. 38
i am not such a truant since my coming, | as not 3.01. 43
i am sorry my integrity should breed | (and 3.01. 51
alas, i am a woman, friendless, hopeless! 3.01. 80
i am old, my lords, | and all the fellowship i 3.01.120
and am i thus rewarded? 3.01.133
i am the most unhappy woman living. 3.01.147
you know i am a woman, lacking wit | to make a 3.01.177
i am joyful | to meet the least occasion that 3.02. 6
but i am afraid | his thinkings are below the 3.02.133
and am /glad | to have you therein my companion. 3.02.142
that am, have, and will be | (though all the 3.02.192
but that i am bound in charity against it! 3.02.298
nay, and you weep | i am fall'n indeed. 3.02.376
i am glad your grace has made that right use of 3.02.386
i am able now, methinks | (out of a fortitude of 3.02.387
i am a poor fall'n man, unworthy now | to be thy 3.02.413
and when i am forgotten, as i shall be, | and 3.02.432
i am sure have shown at full their royal minds 4.01. 8
i am stifled | with the mere rankness of their 4.01. 58
as well as i am able. 4.01. 62
which i feel | i am not worthy yet to wear. 4.02. 92
i am most joyful, madam, such good dreams 4.02. 93
but now i am past all comforts here but prayers. 4.02.123
when i am dead, good wench, | let me be us'd 4.02.167
i am happily come hither. 5.01. 85
i am fearful; 5.01. 87
and am right sorry to repeat what follows. 5.01. 96
and am right glad to catch this good occasion 5.01.109
i hope i am not too late, and yet the gentleman 5.02. 1
i am glad | i came this way so happily; 5.02. 8
i | am for his love and service so to him. 5.02.192
it, | that am a poor and humble subject to you? 5.02.200
i am not sampson, nor sir guy, nor colbrand, 5.03. 22
me | that when i am in heaven i shall desire 5.04. 67
and you, good brethren, i am much beholding; 5.04. 70
valiant, | but i am weaker than a woman's tear, TRO 1.01. 9
i tell thee i am mad | in cressid's love; 1.01. 51
say as i say, for i am sure he is not hector. 1.02. 67 P
nay, i am sure she does. 1.02.110 P
if none else, i am he. 1.03.290
i am no more touch'd than all priam's sons; 2.02.126
i am yours, | you valiant offspring of great 2.02.206
achilles is my lord, i am patroclus' knower, and 2.03. 53 P
why am i a fool? 2.03. 66 P
think he thinks himself a better man than i am? 2.03.145 P
friend, know me better, i am the lord pandarus. 3.01. 11 P
i am too courtly and thou too cunning. 3.01. 27 P
i am giddy; 3.02. 18
i am asham'd. 3.02.138
but alas, | i am as true as truth's simplicity, 3.02.169
you service, am become | as new into the world, 3.03. 11
and 'tis a burthen | which i am proud to bear. 3.03. 37
what, am i poor of late? 3.03. 74
longing, | an appetite that i am sick withal, 3.03.238
but i am sure none, unless the fiddler apollo 3.03.303 P
i were as deep under the earth as i am above! 4.02. 82 P
when i am hence, | i'll answer to my lust, and 4.04.131
i am your debtor, claim it when 'tis due. 4.05. 51
i am not warm yet, let us fight again. 4.05.118
most reverend nestor, i am glad to clasp thee. 4.05.204
i am achilles. 4.05.234
i am thwarted quite | from my great purpose in 5.01. 37
i am all patience. 5.02. 64
youth, | i am to–day i' th' vein of chivalry. 5.03. 32
and i myself | am like a prophet suddenly enrapt 5.03. 65
andromache, i am offended with you, | upon the 5.03. 77
no, no, i am a rascal, a scurvy railing knave, a 5.04. 28 P
amorous troyan, | and am her knight by proof. 5.05. 5
i am a bastard too, i love bastards. 5.07. 16 P
i am bastard begot, bastard instructed, bastard 5.07. 16 P
i am unarm'd, forgo this vantage, greek. 5.08. 9
because i am the store–house and the shop | of COR 1.01.133
i am glad on't, then we shall ha' means to vent 1.01.225
and were i any thing but what i am, | i would 1.01.231
he is a lion | that i am proud to hunt. 1.01.236
sir, it is, | and i am constant. 1.01.239
i am glad to see your ladyship. 1.03. 50 P
gifts, am bound to beg | of my lord general. 1.09. 80
i am weary, yea, my memory is tir'd. 1.09. 91
for i cannot, | being a volsce, be that i am. 1.10. 5
him beard to beard, | he's mine, or i am his. 1.10. 12
i am attended at the cypress grove. 1.10. 30
i am known to be a humorous patrician, and one 2.01. 47 P
follows it that i am known well enough too? 2.01. 63 P
i am light, and heavy. 2.01.184
i am half through: 2.03.123
why, so he did, i am sure. 2.03.165
i am out of breath, | confusion's near, i cannot 3.01.188
rather say, i play | the man i am. 3.02. 16
i am in this | your wife, your son, these 3.02. 64
mother, i am going to the market–place; 3.02.131
look, i am going. 3.02.134
i am content. 3.03. 47
i am so dishonor'd that the very hour | you take 3.03. 60
i shall be lov'd when i am lack'd. 4.01. 15
when i am forth, | bid me farewell, and smile. 4.01. 49
i am a roman, and my services are, as you are, 4.03. 4 P
i am most fortunate thus accidentally to 4.03. 37 P
i am joyful to hear of their readiness, and am 4.03. 46 P
to hear of their readiness, and am the man, i 4.03. 46 P
true, so i am. 4.05. 28 P
dost not | think me for the man i am, necessity 4.05. 56
a word, i also am | longer to live most weary, 4.05. 94
me, | who am prepar'd against your territories, 4.05.134
i am one of those; 5.01. 29
i am an officer of state, and come | to speak 5.02. 3
as you say you have, i am one that, telling true 5.02. 32 P
i am, as thy general is. 5.02. 37 P
you shall know now that i am in estimation; 5.02. 61 P
and am not | of stronger earth than others. 5.03. 28
actor now | i have forgot my part, and i am out, 5.03. 41
i'll run away till i am bigger, but then i'll 5.03.128
i am hush'd until our city be afire, | and then 5.03.181
i am glad thou hast set thy mercy and thy honor 5.03.200
go tell the lords a' th' city i am here. 5.06. 1
i am return'd your soldier; 5.06. 70
my rage is gone, | and i am struck with sorrow. 5.06.147
i am his first–born son, that was the last TIT 1.01. 5
unto me | as i am confident and kind to thee. 1.01. 61
how proud i am of thee and of thy gifts | rome 1.01.254
i am not bid to wait upon this bride. 1.01.338
mean while am i possess'd of that is mine. 1.01.408
titus, i am incorporate in rome, | a roman now 1.01.462
and manners, to intrude where i am grac'd, | and 2.01. 27
i am as able and as fit as thou | to serve, and 2.01. 33
for that i am prepar'd and full resolv'd, 2.01. 57
this is a witness that i am thy son. 2.03.116
offended me, | even for his sake am i pitiless. 2.03.162
i am surprised with an uncouth fear, | a 2.03.211
i am the sea; 3.01.225
empress from me, i am of age | to keep mine own, 4.02.104
as who should say, "old lad, i am thine own." 4.02.121
when we join in league | i am a lamb, but if you 4.02.137
i am going with my pigeons to the tribunal plebs 4.03. 92 P
empress i am, but yonder sits the emperor. 4.04. 41
"let not your sorrow die, though i am dead." 5.01.140
and say i am revenge, sent from below | to join 5.02. 3
titus, i am come to talk with thee. 5.02. 16
i am not mad, i know thee well enough. 5.02. 21
know, thou sad man, i am not tamora; 5.02. 28
i am revenge, sent from th' infernal kingdom 5.02. 30
i am, therefore come down and welcome me. 5.02. 43
a rape, | and i am sent to be reveng'd on him. 5.02. 95
mind | that i repair to rome, i am content. 5.03. 2
i am as woeful as virginius was, | and have a 5.03. 50
i am the turned forth, be it known to you, 5.03.109
alas, you know i am no vaunter, i; 5.03.113
i am no baby, i, that with base prayers | i 5.03.185
me they shall feel while i am able to stand, and ROM 1.01. 28 P
and 'tis known i am a pretty piece of flesh. 1.01. 29 P
but if you do, sir, i am for you. 1.01. 54 P
right glad i am he was not at this fray. 1.01.117
out of her favor where i am in love. 1.01.168
tut, i have lost myself, i am not here: 1.01.197
but i am sent to find those persons whose names 1.02. 41 P
madam, i am here, | what is your will? 1.03. 5
give me a torch, i am not for this ambling; 1.04. 11
i am too sore enpierced with his shaft | to soar 1.04. 19
for i am proverb'd with a grandsire phrase, 1.04. 37
the game was ne'er so fair, and i am /done. 1.04. 39
am i come near ye now? 1.05. 20
am i the master here, or you? 1.05. 78
speak but one rhyme, and i am satisfied; 2.01. 9
i am too bold, 'tis not to me she speaks. 2.02. 14
a name | i know not how to tell thee who i am. 2.02. 54
sweet, | and i am proof against their enmity. 2.02. 73

i am no pilot, yet, wert thou as far | as that 2.02. 82
or if thou thinkest i am too quickly won, | i'll 2.02. 95
in truth, fair montague, i am too fond, | and 2.02. 98
i am afeard, | being in night, all this is but a 2.02.139
nay, i am the very pink of courtesy. 2.04. 57 P
if our wits run the wild-goose chase, i am done; 2.04. 72 P
wild goose in one of thy wits than, i am sure, i 2.04. 73 P
i am the youngest of that name, for fault of a 2.04.122 P
scurvy knave, i am none of his flirt-gills, i am 2.04.153 P
his flirt-gills, i am none of his skains-mates. 2.04.153 P
i am so vex'd that every part about me quivers. 2.04.161 P
i am a-weary, give me leave a while. 2.05. 25
do you not see that i am out of breath? 2.05. 30
i' faith, i am sorry that thou art not well. 2.05. 53
i am the drudge, and toil in your delight; 2.05. 75
am i like such a fellow? 3.01. 10 P
villain am i none; 3.01. 64
i am for you. 3.01. 83 P
i am hurt. 3.01. 90
i am sped. 3.01. 91
i am pepper'd, i warrant, for this world. 3.01. 99 P
o, i am fortune's fool! 3.01.136
but not possess'd it, and, though i am sold, 3.02. 27
i am not i, if there be such an ay; 3.02. 48
they are free men, but i am banished: 3.03. 42
death, | i am content, so thou wilt have it so. 3.05. 18
madam, i am not well. 3.05. 68
i am too young, i pray you pardon me." 3.05.186
go in, and tell my lady i am gone, | having 3.05.231
so, | and i am nothing slow to slack his haste. 4.01. 3
so will ye, i am sure, that you love me. 4.01. 26
and am enjoin'd | by holy lawrence to fall 4.02. 19
henceforward i am ever rul'd by you. 4.02. 22
why, i am glad on't, this is well, stand up. 4.02. 28
for i am sure you have your hands full all, | in 4.03. 11
how if, when i am laid into the tomb, | i wake 4.03. 30
i am almost afraid to stand alone | here in the 5.03. 10
o, i am slain! 5.03. 72
or am i mad, hearing him talk of juliet, | to 5.03. 80
my master knows not but i am gone hence, | and 5.03.132
well where i should be, | and there i am. 5.03.150
i am the greatest, able to do least, | yet most 5.03.223
i am glad y' are well. TIM 1.01. 1
i am not of that feather to shake off | my 1.01.100
i am a man | that from my first have been 1.01.117
of nothing so much as that i am not like timon. 1.01.189 P
i am joyful of your sights. 1.01.246
as in grateful virtue i am bound | to your free 1.02. 5
i am to thank you for't. 1.02.151
i am so far already in your gifts — 1.02.172
and so | am i to you. 1.02.227
once, i am sworn not to give regard to you. 1.02.245 P
and i am sent expressly to your lordship. 2.02. 32
that i am thus encount'red | with clamorous 2.02. 36
answer not, i am gone. 2.02. 87 P
my mistress is one, and i am her fool. 2.02. 99 P
i am wealthy in my friends. 2.02.184
and i am proud, say, that my occasions have 2.02.191 P
heads, and i am here | no richer in return. 2.02.202
i am right glad that his health is well, sir; 3.01. 13 P
now, before the gods, i am asham'd on't. 3.02. 18 P
i am so much endear'd to that lord; 3.02. 31 P
now before the gods, i am not able to do (the 3.02. 49 P
i am of your fear for that. 3.04. 16
i am an humble suitor to your virtues; 3.05. 7
i am sorry, when he sent to borrow of me, that 3.06. 15 P
i am sick of that grief too, as i understand how 3.06. 17 P
honorable lord, i am e'en sick of shame that, 3.06. 41 P
by the righteous gods, | i am as poor as you. 4.02. 5
no, gods, i am no idle votarist; 4.03. 27
i am misanthropos, and hate mankind. 4.03. 54
but in thy fortunes am unlearn'd and strange. 4.03. 57
i am thy friend, and pity thee, dear timon. 4.03. 98
ay, that i am not thee. 4.03.277
i, that i am one now. 4.03.278
i am sorry i shall lose a stone by thee. 4.03.370
i am sick of this false world, and will love 4.03.375
but not till i am dead. 4.03.393
long live so, and so die. i am quit. 4.03.396
i am thinking | what i shall say i have provided 5.01. 32
i am rapt and cannot cover | the monstrous bulk 5.01. 64
heard that i have gold, | i am sure you have. 5.01. 77
and am not | one that rejoices in the common 5.01.191
in respect of a fine workman, i am but, as you JC 1.01. 10 P
but withal i am indeed, sir, a surgeon to old 1.01. 23 P
i am not gamesome; 1.02. 28
vexed i am | of late with passions of some 1.02. 39
that you do love me, i am nothing jealous; 1.02.162
i am glad that my weak words | have struck but 1.02.176
for always i am caesar. 1.02.212
mean by that, but i am sure caesar fell down. 1.02.257 P
do the players in the theatre, i am no true man. 1.02.261 P
no, i am promis'd forth. 1.02.289 P
but i am arm'd, | and dangers are to me 1.03.114
am i not stay'd for, cinna? 1.03.136
i am glad on't. 1.03.137
am i not stay'd for? tell me. 1.03.139
and i am sure | it did not lie there when i went 2.01. 37
am i entreated | to speak and strike? 2.01. 55
but if these | (as i am sure they do) bear fire 2.01.120
i am not well in health, and that is all. 2.01.257
am i yourself | but, as it were, in sort or 2.01.282
i grant i am a woman; 2.01.292
i grant i am a woman; 2.01.294
think you i am no stronger than my sex, | being 2.01.296
i am not sick, if brutus have in hand | any 2.01.316
mark antony shall say i am not well, | and, for 2.02. 55
i am ashamed i did yield to them. 2.02.106
i am to blame to be thus waited for. 2.02.119
and commend me to my lord, | say i am merry. 2.04. 45
but i am constant as the northern star, | of 3.01. 60
and that i am he, | let me a little show it, 3.01. 70
friends am i with you all, and love you all, 3.01.220
and am, moreover, suitor that i may | produce 3.01.227
speak | in the same pulpit whereto i am going, 3.01.250
that i am meek and gentle with these butchers! 3.01.255
for brutus' sake, i am beholding to you. 3.02. 65
spoke, | but here i am to speak what i do know. 3.02.101
i am no orator, as brutus is; 3.02.217
whither am i going? 3.03. 13 P
am i a married man or a bachelor? 3.03. 14 P
wisely i say, i am a bachelor. 3.03. 16 P
directly, i am going to caesar's funeral. 3.03. 20 P
i am cinna the poet, i am cinna the poet. 3.03. 29 P
i am cinna the poet, i am cinna the poet. 3.03. 29 P
i am not cinna the conspirator. 3.03. 32 P
i am a soldier, i, | older in practice, abler 4.03. 30
i am. 4.03. 33
for i am arm'd so strong in honesty | that they 4.03. 67
o cassius, i am sick of many griefs. 4.03.144
bear with me, good boy, i am much forgetful. 4.03.255
tut, i am in their bosoms, and i know 5.01. 7
am i compell'd to set | upon one battle all our 5.01. 74
for i am fresh of spirit, and resolv'd | to meet 5.01. 90
o, coward that i am, to live so long, | to see 5.03. 34
so, i am free; 5.03. 47
i am the son of marcus cato, ho! 5.04. 4
i am the son of marcus cato, ho! 5.04. 6
and i am brutus, marcus brutus, i, | brutus, my 5.04. 7
nay, i am sure it is, volumnius. 5.05. 21
but i am faint, my gashes cry for help. MAC 1.02. 42
by sinel's death i know i am thane of glamis, 1.03. 71
i am thane of cawdor. 1.03.133
so valiant, | and in his commendations i am fed; 1.04. 55
first, as i am his kinsman and his subject, 1.07. 13
i am settled, and bend up | each corporal agent 1.07. 79
alack, i am afraid they have awak'd, | and 'tis 2.02. 9
i am afraid to think what i have done; 2.02. 48
i am one, my liege, | whom the vile blows and 3.01.107
hath so incens'd that i am reckless what | i do 3.01.109
but now i am cabin'd, cribb'd, confin'd, bound 3.04. 23
being gone, | i am a man again. 3.04.107
for now i am bent to know, | by the worst means, 3.04.133
i am in blood | stepp'd in so far that, should i 3.04.135
i am for th' air; 3.05. 20
hark, i am call'd; 3.05. 34
i am so much a fool, should i stay longer, | it 4.02. 28
i am not to you known, | though in your state of 4.02. 65
though in your state of honor i am perfect. 4.02. 66
to fright you thus methinks i am too savage; 4.02. 70
i remember now | i am in this earthly world — 4.02. 75
i am young, but something | you may discern of 4.03. 14
i am not treacherous. 4.03. 18
i am as i have spoken. 4.03.102
i am yet | unknown to woman, never was forsworn, 4.03.125
what i am truly | is thine and my poor country's 4.03.131
naught that i am, | not for their own demerits, 4.03.225
spoke what she should not, i am sure of that; 5.01. 48 P
i am sick at heart | when i behold — seyton, i 5.03. 19
such a one | am i to fear, or none. 5.07. 4
'tis bitter cold, | and i am sick at heart. HAM 1.01. 9
not so, my lord, i am too much in the sun. 1.02. 67
i am glad to see you well. 1.02.160
i am very glad to see you. 1.02.167
though i am native here | and to the manner born 1.04. 14
still am i call'd. 1.04. 84
speak, i am bound to hear. 1.05. 6
i am thy father's spirit, | doom'd for a certain 1.05. 9
but that i am forbid | to tell the secrets of my 1.05. 13
at least i am sure it may be so in denmark. 1.05.109
i am sorry they offend you, heartily, | yes, 1.05.134
i am sorry — | what, have you given him any 2.01.103
i am sorry that with better heed and judgment 2.01.108
and sure i am two men there is not living | to 2.02. 20
o dear ophelia, i am ill at these numbers. 2.02.120 P
sir, shall grow old as i am, if like a crab you 2.02.203 P
beggar that i am, i am /even poor in thanks — 2.02.272 P
beggar that i am, i am /even poor in thanks — 2.02.272 P
i am but mad north-north-west. 2.02.378 P
am i not i' th' right, old jephthah? 2.02.410 P
i am glad to see thee well. 2.02.421 P
now i am alone. 2.02.549
o, what a rogue and peasant slave am i! 2.02.550
am i a coward? 2.02.571
for it cannot be | but i am pigeon-liver'd, and 2.02.577
why, what an ass am i! 2.02.582
i am myself indifferent honest, but yet i could 3.01.121 P
i am very proud, revengeful, ambitious, with 3.01.123 P
i am tame, sir. pronounce. 3.02.310 P
do you think i am easier to be play'd on than a 3.02.369 P
since i am still possess'd | of those effects 3.03. 53
so 'a goes to heaven, | and so am i reveng'd. 3.03. 75
and am i then revenged, | to take him in the 3.03. 84
o, i am slain. 3.04. 25
out, | that i essentially am not in madness, 3.04.187
i am glad of it, a knavish speech sleeps in a 4.02. 23 P
that i am guiltless of your father's death, 4.05.150
death, | and am most sensibly in grief for it, 4.05.151
your name be horatio, as i am let to know it is. 4.06. 12 P
i am to do a /good turn for them. 4.06. 22 P
these good fellows will bring thee where i am. 4.06. 27 P
you shall know i am set naked on your kingdom. 4.07. 43 P
i am lost in it, my lord. 4.07. 54
for though i am not splenitive /and rash, | yet 5.01.261
i am constant to my purposes, they follow the 5.02.200 P
how i am punish'd | with a sore distraction. 5.02.229
i am satisfied in nature, | whose motive, in 5.02.244
i am sure you make a wanton of me. 5.02.299
i am justly kill'd with mine own treachery. 5.02.307
i am pois'ned. 5.02.310
o, yet defend me, friends, i am but hurt. 5.02.324
i am dead, horatio. 5.02.333
horatio, i am dead, | thou livest. 5.02.338
i am more an antique roman than a dane. 5.02.341
to acknowledge him, that now i am braz'd to't. LR 1.01. 11 P
i am made of that self metal as my sister, | and 1.01. 69
and find i am alone felicitate | in your dear 1.01. 75
since i am sure my love's | more ponderous than 1.01. 77
unhappy that i am, i cannot heave | my heart 1.01. 91
even for want of that for which i am richer — 1.01.230
and such a tongue | that i am glad i have not, 1.01.232
nothing. i have sworn, i am firm. 1.01.245
i am sorry then you have so lost a father | that 1.01.246
and like a sister am most loath to call | your 1.01.270
for that i am some twelve or fourteen moonshines 1.02. 5
so that it follows, i am rough and lecherous. 1.02.131 P
/fut, i should have been that i am, had the 1.02.132 P
i am thinking, brother, of a prediction i read 1.02.140 P
i am no honest man if there be any good meaning 1.02.172 P
say i am sick. 1.03. 8
ordinary men are fit for, i am qualified in, and 1.04. 34 P
who am i, sir? 1.04. 78 P
i am none of these, my lord, i beseech your 1.04. 82 P
and sometimes i am whipt for holding my peace. 1.04.184 P
i am better than thou art now, i am a fool, thou 1.04.193 P
i am better than thou art now, i am a fool, thou 1.04.193 P
who is it that can tell me who i am? 1.04.230
i am guiltless as i am ignorant | of what hath 1.04.273
i am guiltless as i am ignorant | of what hath 1.04.273
i am asham'd | that thou hast power to shake my 1.04.296
who i am sure is kind and comfortable. 1.04.306
i am sure on't, not a word. 2.01. 27
i am scarce in breath, my lord. 2.02. 52 P
i know, sir, i am no flatterer. 2.02.110 P
sir, i am too old to learn. 2.02.127
i am sorry for thee, friend, 'tis the /duke's 2.02.152
and am bethought | to take the basest and most 2.03. 6
edgar i nothing am. 2.03. 21
and am fallen out with my more headier will, 2.04.110
i am glad to see your highness. 2.04.128
"dear daughter, i confess that i am old; 2.04.154
i am now from home, and out of that provision 2.04.205
you yet, nor am provided | for your fit welcome. 2.04.232
so am i purpos'd. 2.04.293
for confirmation that i am much more | than my 3.01. 44
i am a man | more sinn'd against than sinning. 3.02. 59
i am cold myself. 3.02. 69
if he ask for me, i am ill and gone to bed. 3.03. 17 P
tell thee, friend, | i am almost mad myself. 3.04.166
i am your host, | with robber's hands my 3.07. 39
i am tied to th' stake, and i must stand the 3.07. 54
o, i am slain! 3.07. 81
who is't can say, "i am at the worst"? 4.01. 25
i am worse than e'er i was. 4.01. 26
that i am wretched | makes thee the happier; 4.01. 65
does not love her husband, | i am sure of that; 4.05. 24
in nothing am i chang'd | but in my garments. 4.06. 9
i am the king himself. 4.06. 83 P
'tis a lie, i am not ague-proof. 4.06.105 P
i am even | the natural fool of fortune. 4.06.190
let me have surgeons, | i am cut to th' brains. 4.06.193
come, come, i am a king, | masters, know you 4.06.199
and feeling sorrows, | am pregnant to good pity. 4.06.223
i am only sorry | he had no other deathsman. 4.06.257
then am i the prisoner, and his bed my jail; 4.06.266 P
in bliss, but i am bound | upon a wheel of fire, 4.07. 45
where am i? 4.07. 51
i am mightily abus'd; 4.07. 52
i am a very foolish fond old man, | fourscore 4.07. 59
plainly, | i fear i am not in my perfect mind. 4.07. 62
you, and know this man, | yet i am doubtful: 4.07. 64
for i am mainly ignorant | what place this is, 4.07. 64
for (as i am a man) i think this lady | to be my 4.07. 68
and so i am; i am. 4.07. 69
and so i am; i am. 4.07. 69
am i in france? 4.07. 75
i am old and foolish. 4.07. 83
for thee, oppressed king, i am cast down, 5.03. 5
lady, i am not well, else i should answer | from 5.03. 73
yet am i noble as the adversary | i come to cope 5.03.123
'tis past, and so am i. 5.03.165
i am no less in blood than thou art, edmund; 5.03.168
the wheel is come full circle, i am here. 5.03.175
hold it in, | for i am almost ready to dissolve, 5.03.204
i am come | to bid my king and master aye good 5.03.235
i am old now, | and these same crosses spoil me. 5.03.278
no, my good lord, i am the very man — 5.03.287
i know my price, i am worth no worse a place. OTH 1.01. 11
whether i in any just term am affin'd | to love 1.01. 39
i am not what i am. 1.01. 65
i am not what i am. 1.01. 65
i am one, sir, that comes to tell you your 1.01.115 P
'tis well i am found by you. 1.02. 47
you, roderigo! come, sir, i am for you. 1.02. 58
and your noble self | i am sure is sent for. 1.02. 93
rude am i in my speech, | and little bless'd 1.03. 81
(for such proceeding i am charg'd withal) | i 1.03. 93
to you i am bound for life and education; 1.03.182
i am hitherto your daughter. 1.03.185
i am glad at soul i have no other child, | for 1.03.196
i am glad on't; 'tis a worthy governor. 2.01. 30
nay, it is true, or else i am a turk: 2.01.114
put me to't, | for i am nothing if not critical. 2.01.119
i am not merry; 2.01.122
beguile | the thing i am by seeming otherwise. 2.01.123
i am about it, but indeed my invention | comes 2.01.125
pegs that make this music, | as honest as i am. 2.01.201
content my soul | till i am even'd with him, 2.01.299
i am infortunate in the infirmity, and dare not 2.03. 41 P
am i to put our cassio in some action | that may 2.03. 60
not past a pint, as i am a soldier. 2.03. 67 P
i am for it, lieutenant; 2.03. 87 P
do not think, gentlemen, i am drunk: 2.03.113 P
i am not drunk now; 2.03.115 P
you must not think then that i am drunk. 2.03.119 P
i bleed still, | i am hurt to th' death. 2.03.165
worthy othello, i am hurt to danger. 2.03.197
as i am an honest man, i had thought you had 2.03.266 P
place again, he shall tell me i am a drunkard! 2.03.304 P
i am desperate of my fortunes if they check me 2.03.331 P
how am i then a villain, | to counsel cassio to 2.03.348
i am sorry | for your displeasure; 3.01. 41
i am much bound to you. 3.01. 55
i am very ill at ease, | unfit for mine own 3.03. 32
what e'er you be, i am obedient. 3.03. 89
though i am bound to every act of duty, | i am 3.03.134
i am not bound to that all slaves are free /to. 3.03.135
though i perchance am vicious in my guess | (as 3.03.145
i am glad of this, for now i shall have reason 3.03.193
therefore, as i am bound, | receive it from me. 3.03.195
'twas witchcraft — but i am much to blame. 3.03.211
i am bound to thee for ever. 3.03.213
i am to pray you not to strain my speech | to 3.03.218
my fears | (as worthy cause i have to fear i am) 3.03.254

haply, for i am black, | and have not those soft 3.03.263
or for i am declin'd | into the vale of years 3.03.265
i am abus'd, and my relief | must be to loathe 3.03.267
i am to blame. 3.03.282
i am very sorry that you are not well. 3.03.289
i am glad i have found this napkin; 3.03.290
i am sorry to hear this. 3.03.344
but, sith i am ent'red in this cause so far 3.03.411
a handkerchief | (i am sure it was your wive's) 3.03.438
i am your own for ever. 3.03.480
i am most unhappy in the loss of it. 3.04.102
emilia, | i was (unhandsome warrior as i am) 3.04.151
and knowing what i am, i know what she shall be. 4.01. 73
i am a very villain else. 4.01.125 P
i am very glad to see you, signior; 4.01.220
/by /my /troth, i am glad on't. 4.01.238
i am glad to see you mad. 4.01.239
i am commanded home. 4.01.258
i am sorry that i am deceiv'd in him. 4.01.282
i am sorry that i am deceiv'd in him. 4.01.282
to whom, my lord? with whom? how am i false? 4.02. 40
am i the motive of these tears, my lord? 4.02. 43
no, as i am a christian. 4.02. 82
touch | be not to be a strumpet, i am none. 4.02. 85
for, in good faith, | i am a child to chiding. 4.02.114
am i that name, iago? 4.02.118
i do not know; i am sure i am none such. 4.02.123
i do not know; i am sure i am none such. 4.02.123
nor am i yet persuaded to put up in peace what 4.02.179 P
o, i am slain. 5.01. 26
i am maim'd for ever. help ho! murther, murther! 5.01. 27
o, villain that i am! 5.01. 29
o, i am spoil'd, undone by villains! 5.01. 54
i am sorry to find you thus; 5.01. 81
i am glad to see you. 5.01. 95
i am no strumpet, but of life as honest | as you 5.01.122
i that am cruel am yet merciful, | i would not 5.02. 87
i that am cruel am yet merciful, | i would not 5.02. 87
i am bound to speak. 5.02.184
i am glad thy father's dead. 5.02.204
i am not valiant neither, | but every puny 5.02.243
me, | or, naked as i am, i will assault thee. 5.02.258
that's he that was othello; here i am. 5.02.284
i am not sorry neither, i'ld have thee live; 5.02.289
unlucky deeds relate, | speak of me as i am; 5.02.342
as i am egypt's queen, | thou blushest, antony, ANT 1.01. 29
i'll seem the fool i am not. 1.01. 42
i am full sorry | that he approves the common 1.01. 59
am i not an inch of fortune better than she? 1.02. 58 P
if you find him sad, | say i am dancing; 1.03. 4
if in mirth, report | that i am sudden sick. 1.03. 5
i am sick and sullen. 1.03. 13
i am sorry to give breathing to my purpose — 1.03. 14
i am quickly ill, and well, | so antony loves. 1.03. 72
is a very antony, | and i am all forgotten. 1.03. 91
that am with phoebus' amorous pinches black, 1.05. 28
i know you could not lack, i am certain on't, 2.02. 57
i am not married, caesar; 2.02.122
i am pale, charmian. 2.05. 59
again, | though i am mad, i will not bite him. 2.05. 80
i am paid for't now. 2.05.108
and am well studied for a liberal thanks, 2.06. 47
and well am like to do, for i perceive | four 2.06. 72
my part, i am sorry it is turn'd to a drinking. 2.06.103 P
i am not so well as i should be; 2.07. 30 P
i am the man | will give thee all the world. 2.07. 64
by hercules, i think i am i' th' right. 3.07. 67
i am so lated in the world, that i | have lost 3.11. 3
love, i am full of lead. 3.11. 72
such as i am, i come from antony. 3.12. 7
him, i am prompt | to lay my crown at 's feet, 3.13. 75
i am | antony yet. 3.13. 92
for i am sure, | though you can guess what 3.13.120
proud and disdainful, harping on what i am, 3.13.142
i am satisfied. 3.13.167
look, they weep, | and i, an ass, am onion–ey'd. 4.02. 35
from caesar's camp | say "i am none of thine." 4.05. 9
i am alone the villain of the earth, | and feel 4.06. 29
villain of the earth, | and feel i am so most. 4.06. 30
for when i am reveng'd upon my charm, | i have 4.12. 16
betray'd i am. 4.12. 24
here i am antony, | yet cannot hold this visible 4.14. 13
our caesar tells, | "i am conqueror of myself." 4.14. 62
sent | me to proclaim the truth, and i am come, 4.14.126
i am dying, egypt, dying; 4.15. 18
i am safe: 4.15. 26
o, quick, or i am gone. 4.15. 31
i am dying, egypt, dying. 4.15. 41
i am call'd decretas; 5.01. 5
pray you tell him | i am his fortune's vassal, 5.02. 29
i am loath to tell you what i would you knew. 5.02.107
of money, plate, and jewels | i am possess'd of; 5.02.139
for i am sure mine nails | are stronger than 5.02.223
i am again for cydnus | to meet mark antony. 5.02.228
now from head to foot | i am marble–constant; 5.02.240
you must not think i am so simple but i know the 5.02.272 P
i am fire and air; 5.02.289
i am gone. CYM 1.01.130
your vexation, | i am senseless of your wrath; 1.01.135
i am very glad on't. 1.01.164
with orisons, for then | i am in heaven for him; 1.03. 33
i am the master of my speeches, and would 1.04.140 P
you have prevail'd, i am no further your enemy; 1.04.159 P
desert, am bound | to load thy merit richly. 1.05. 73
to whose kindnesses i am most infinitely tied. 1.06. 23 P
whilst i am bound to wonder, i am bound | to 1.06. 81
i am bound to wonder, i am bound | to pity too. 1.06. 81
am i one, sir? 1.06. 83
and i am something curious, being strange, | to 1.06.191
i am not vex'd more at any thing in th' earth; 2.01. 17 P
i had rather not be so noble as i am. 2.01. 18 P
i am advis'd to give her music a' mornings; 2.03. 11 P
i am glad i was up so late, for that's the 2.03. 33 P
give | is telling you that i am poor of thanks, 2.03. 89
as i am mad, i do. 2.03.102
i am much sorry, sir, | you put me to forget a 2.03.104
and am so near the lack of charity | to accuse 2.03.109
i am sprited with a fool, | frighted, and 2.03.139
confident i am. 2.03.145
so sure | to win the king as i am bold her honor 2.04. 2
i do believe | (statist though i am none, nor 2.04. 16
i am sure | she would not lose it. 2.04.123
i do not say i am one; 3.01. 41 P
i am sorry, cymbeline, | that i am to pronounce 3.01. 61
that i am to pronounce augustus caesar | (caesar 3.01. 62
i am perfect | that the pannonians and 3.01. 72
i am ignorant in what i am commanded. 3.02. 23
i am ignorant in what i am commanded. 3.02. 23
take notice that i am in cambria, at 3.02. 43 P
myself, belarius, that am morgan call'd, | they 3.03.106
poor i am stale, a garment out of fashion, | and 3.04. 51
and, for i am richer than to hang by th' walls, 3.04. 52
i have heard i am a strumpet, and mine ear, 3.04.113
what comfort, when i am | dead to my husband? 3.04.129
i am most glad | you think of other place. 3.04.140
i see into thy end and am almost | a man already 3.04.166
this attempt | i am soldier to, and will abide 3.04.183
and am right sorry that i must report ye | my 3.05. 3
i am throughly weary. 3.06. 36
i am weak with toil, yet strong in appetite. 3.06. 37
with hunger, | i am fall'n in this offense. 3.06. 63
i am near to th' place where they should meet, 4.01. 1 P
i am very sick. 4.02. 5
so sick i am not, yet i am not well; 4.02. 7
so sick i am not, yet i am not well; 4.02. 7
i am ill, but your being by me | cannot amend me 4.02. 11
i am not very sick, | since i can reason of it. 4.02. 13
i am sick still, heart–sick. 4.02. 37
well or ill, | i am bound to you. 4.02. 46
i am faint. 4.02. 63
thou art some fool, | i am loath to beat thee. 4.02. 86
thou shalt know | i am son to th' queen. 4.02. 93
i am sorry for't; 4.02. 93
i am absolute | 'twas very cloten. 4.02.106
i am perfect what: 4.02.118
i am nothing; 4.02.367
i am amaz'd with matter. 4.03. 28
wherein i am false, i am honest; 4.03. 42
wherein i am false, i am honest; 4.03. 42
o, i am known | of many in the army. 4.04. 21
i am asham'd | to look upon the holy sun, to 4.04. 40
i am brought hither | among th' italian gentry, 5.01. 17
yet am i better | than one that's sick o' th' 5.04. 4
is't enough i am sorry? 5.04. 11
and so i am awake. 5.04.127
so am i, | that have this golden chance and know 5.04.131
i am merrier to die than thou art to live. 5.04.171 P
yourself that which i am sure you do not know, 5.04.181 P
want eyes to direct them the way i am going, but 5.04.186 P
i am sure hanging's the way of winking. 5.04.190 P
bring'st good news, i am call'd to be made free. 5.04.193 P
to my grief, i am | the heir of his reward, 5.05. 12
being born your vassal, | am something nearer. 5.05.114
he, i am sure | he would have spoke to us. 5.05.125
i am glad to be constrain'd to utter that 5.05.141
i am posthumus, | that kill'd thy daughter — 5.05.217
i am sorry for't, my lord. 5.05.270
and am right glad he is not standing here | to 5.05.296
i am sorrow for thee; 5.05.297
i am too blunt and saucy: 5.05.325
am that belarius whom you sometime banish'd. 5.05.333
o, what, am i | a mother to the birth of three? 5.05.368
never say hereafter | but i am truest speaker. 5.05.376
i am, sir, | the soldier that did company these 5.05.407
i am down again; 5.05.412
helps, | as i am son and servant to your will, PER 1.01. 23
i am no viper, yet i feed | on mother's flesh 1.01. 64
'gainst whom i am too little to contend, | since 1.02. 17
if i do it not, i am sure to be hang'd at home. 1.03. 2 P
i am thinking of the poor men that were cast 2.01. 18 P
but what i am, want teaches me to think on: 2.01. 72
which if you shall refuse, when i am dead, | for 2.01. 76
for that i am a man, pray you see me buried. 2.01. 77
by your furtherance i am cloth'd in steel, | and 2.01.154
i yet am unprovided | of a pair of bases. 2.01.160
i am at your grace's pleasure. 2.03.111
i am beholding to you | for your sweet music 2.05. 25
i am unworthy for her schoolmaster. 2.05. 40
i am glad on't with all my heart. 2.05. 74
it had conceit, would die, as i | am like to do. 3.01. 17
o dear diana, | where am i? 3.02.105
i am resolv'd. 4.01. 12
ear, and i am sworn | to do my work with haste. 4.01. 69
i am sworn, | and will dispatch. 4.01. 90
that i am pretty. 4.02. 69
come, i am for no more bawdy–houses. 4.05. 6 P
but i am out of the road of rutting for ever. 4.05. 9 P
i am glad to see your honor in good health. 4.06. 22 P
of this country, and a man whom i am bound to. 4.06. 54 P
your principal made known unto you who i am? 4.06. 83 P
that am a maid, though most ungentle fortune 4.06. 96
and you, to outlive the age i am, | and die as i 5.01. 15
i am the governor of this place you lie before. 5.01. 21
recount it to you, | but see, i am prevented. 5.01. 64
i am a maid, | my lord, that ne'er before 5.01. 84
brought forth, and am | no other than i appear. 5.01.104
i am great with woe, and shall deliver weeping. 5.01.106
where i am but a stranger. 5.01.114
o, i am mock'd, | and thou by some incensed god 5.01.142
i am the daughter to king pericles, | if good 5.01.178
i am pericles of tyre; 5.01.204
i am wild in my beholding. 5.01.222
cleon, but i am | for other service first. 5.01.253
that thaisa am i, supposed dead | and drown'd. 5.03. 35
for i am sure | it has a noble breeder and a TNK pr 9
troubled i am. 1.01. 77
action with you | as that whereto i am going, 1.01.103
ladies, | this is a service, whereto i am going, 1.01.171
i am entreating of myself to do | that which you 1.01.206
why am i bound | by any generous bond to follow 1.02. 49
either i am | the forehorse in the team, or i am 1.02. 58
or i am none | that draw i' th' sequent trace. 1.02. 59
i am sure i shall not. 1.03. 85
i am not | against your faith, yet i continue 1.03. 96
i am given out to be better lin'd than it can 2.01. 5 P
i would i were really that i am deliver'd to be. 2.01. 7 P
i am your heir, and you are mine; 2.02. 83
here, | i am sure, a more content, and all those 2.02.100
and am sufficient | to tell the world 'tis but a 2.02.102
i am wondrous merry–hearted, i could laugh now. 2.02.150
i could lie down, i am sure. 2.02.151
maintain | i am as worthy and as free a lover, 2.02.179
am not i | part of /your blood, part of your 2.02.184
am not i liable to those affections, | those 2.02.187
i am ready, keeper. 2.02.222
and then i am sure she would love me. 2.02.243
then i am resolv'd, i will not go. 2.02.269
i am resolv'd: 2.03. 21
either way, i am happy: 2.03. 22
i am sure | to have my wife as jealous as a 2.03. 29
i am base, | my father the mean keeper of his 2.04. 2
i am proud to please you. 2.05. 4
i care not, i am desperate. 2.06. 13
i am then | kissing the man they look for. 2.06. 36
i am in plight," there shall be at your choice 3.01. 88
i am persuaded this question, sick between 's, 3.01.113
i am a suitor | that to your sword you will 3.01.114
i am mop'd: 3.02. 25
i am glad | you have so good a stomach. 3.03. 20
i am gladder | i have so good meat to't. 3.03. 21
i am very cold, and all the stars are out too, 3.04. 1
where am i now? 3.04. 4
i am very hungry: 3.04. 11
and i, that am the rectifier of all, | by title 3.05.109
day discourse you into health, | as i am spar'd. 3.06. 39
your person i am friends with, | and i could 3.06. 39
i am well and lusty, choose your arms. 3.06. 45
you are deceived, for, as i am a soldier, | i 3.06. 48
then as i am an honest man, and love | with all 3.06. 50
i am indifferent. 3.06. 60
faith, so am i. 3.06. 61
am i fall'n much away? 3.06. 66
now i am perfect. 3.06. 88
i am palamon, | that cannot love thee, he that 3.06.138
bequeathing of the soul to) justly | i am, and, 3.06.149
"traitor," | i am a villain fit to lie unburied. 3.06.171
yours, | of more authority, i am sure more love, 3.06.231
maim your honor | (for now i am set a–begging, 3.06.238
sir, i am deaf | to all but your compassion), 3.06.238
me, | till i am nothing but the scorn of women. 3.06.250
arcite, | i am friends again till that hour. 3.06.300
i am a fool, my reason is lost in me; 4.02. 34
i am sotted, | utterly lost. 4.02. 45
i am in labor | to push your name, your ancient 5.01. 25
brief, i am | to those that prate and have done, 5.01.118
such a one i am, | and vow that lover never yet 5.01.124
thy priest, | am humbled 'fore thine altar. 5.01.143
i am bride–habited, | but maiden–hearted. 5.01.150
his success, but i | am guiltless of election. 5.01.154
have half persuaded her that i am palamon. 5.02. 3
i am of your mind, doctor. 5.02. 39
a kind gentleman, and i am much bound to him. 5.02. 44
i am content, | if we shall keep our wedding 5.02. 75
and i am glad my cousin palamon | has made so 5.02. 91
i am extinct, | there is but envy in that light 5.03. 20
i am like to know your husband 'fore yourself 5.03. 37
it is much better | i am not there. 5.03. 65
by my short life, | i am most glad on't. 5.04. 29
i am palamon, | one that yet loves thee dying. 5.04. 89
and am now as glad | as for him sorry. 5.04.130
i am cruel fearful. ep 3
i am not bold, | we have no such cause. ep 11
it is in heaven that i am thus and thus, | and STM III 1
"what am i, that thou shouldst contemn me this? VEN 205
then be my deer, since i am such a park, | no 239
would thou wert as i am, and i a man, | my heart 369
gone, | and 'tis your fault i am bereft him so. 381
"o, where am i?" 493
"i am," quoth he, "expected of my friends, | and 718
my youth with his, the more am i accurs'd." 1120
under that color am i come to scale | thy LUC 481
"yet am i guilty of thy honor's wrack, | yet for 841
so am i now — o no, that cannot be! 1049
for me, i am the mistress of my fate, | and with 1069
and wherefore say not i that i am old? PP 1.10
and i in deep delight am chiefly drown'd | when 8.11
my glass shall not persuade me i am old, | so SON 22. 1
i, that love and am beloved | where i may not 25.13
plight | that am debarr'd the benefit of rest? 28. 2
so then i am not lame, poor, nor despis'd, 37. 9
give, | that i in thy abundance am suffic'd, 37.11
when i am sometime absent from thy heart, | thy 41. 2
but ah, thought kills me that i am not thought, 44. 9
and i am still with them, and they with thee; 47.12
so am i as the rich whose blessed key | can 52. 1
i am to wait, though waiting so be hell, | not 58.13
sure i am the wits of former days | to subjects 59.13
against my love shall be as i am now | with 63. 1
no longer mourn for me when i am dead | than you 71. 1
give warning to the world that i am fled | from 71. 3
when i (perhaps) compounded am with clay, | do 71.10
moan, | and mock you with me after i am gone. 71.14
for i am sham'd by that which i bring forth, 72.13
or (being wrack'd) i am a worthless boat, | he 80.11
or you survive when i in earth am rotten, | from 81. 2
of faults conceal'd, wherein i am attainted, 88. 7
friend, | a god in love, to whom i am confin'd. 110.12
no, i am that i am, and they that level | at my 121. 9
no, i am that i am, and they that level | at my 121. 9
of him, myself, and thee i am forsaken, | a 133. 7
perforce am thine, and all that is in me. 133.14
thine, | and i myself am mortgag'd to thy will, 134. 2
me, | he pays the whole, and yet am i not free. 134.14
more than enough am i that vex thee still, | to 135. 3
and wherefore say not i that i am old? 138.10
yet do not so, but since i am near slain, | kill 139.13
past cure i am, now reason is past care, | and 147. 9
not think on thee when i forgot | am of myself, 149. 4
those that can see thou lov'st, and i am blind. 149.14
in loving thee thou know'st i am forsworn, | but 152. 1
i am perjur'd most, | for all my vows are oaths 152. 6
hour, | let it not tell your judgment i am old, LC 73

AMAIMON *(also amamon)*

AMAIMON 1 FR 0.0001 REL FR 0 V 1 P

amaimon sounds well; WIV 2.02.297 P
AMAIN 14 FR 0.0015 REL FR 14 V 0 P
/her peacocks fly amain. TMP 4.01. 74
two ships from far, making amain to us, | of ERR 1.01. 92
ship is under sail, and here she comes amain. LLL 5.02.546
cried out amain, | and rush'd into the bowels of 1H6 1.01.128
great lords, from ireland am i come amain, | to 2H6 3.01.282
call hither clifford, bid him come amain, | to 5.01.114
foreslow no longer, make we hence amain. 3H6 2.03. 56
mount you, my lord, towards berwick post amain. 2.05.128
are at our backs, and therefore hence amain. 2.05.133
and with his troops doth march amain to london, 4.08. 4
brave warriors, march amain towards coventry. 4.08. 64
on, myrmidons, and cry you all amain, TRO 5.08. 13
they hither march amain, under conduct | of TIT 4.04. 65
sick–thoughted venus makes amain unto him, | and
VEN 5
A–MAKING 2 FR 0.0002 REL FR 2 V 0 P
that is not often vouch'd, while 'tis a–making, MAC 3.04. 33
both | even in their promise, as it is a–making, HAM 1.03.119
AMAMON *(also amaimon)*
AMAMON 1 FR 0.0001 REL FR 0 V 1 P
of wales that gave amamon the bastinado and made
1H4 2.04.336 P
AMAZ'D *(also maz'd)*
/AMAZ'D 1 FR 0.0001 REL FR 1 V 0 P
/stand /you /not /so /amaz'd. LR 3.06. 33
AMAZ'D 35 FR 0.0039 REL FR 29 V 6 P
be not amaz'd, call all your senses to you, WIV 3.03.118 P
if he be not amaz'd, he will be mock'd; 5.03. 18 P
if he be amaz'd, he will every way be mock'd. 5.03. 19 P
stand not amaz'd; 5.05.231
yet you are amaz'd, but this shall absolutely MM 4.02.208 P
i am more amaz'd at his dishonor | than at the 5.01.380
arm, that i, amaz'd, ran from her as a witch. ERR 3.02.144 P
amaz'd, my lord? why looks your highness sad? LLL 5.02.391
i am amaz'd, and know not what to say. MND 3.02.344
speak not so grossly, you are all amaz'd. MV 5.01.266
that, all amaz'd, the priest let fall the book, SHR 3.02.161
that with your strange encounter much amaz'd me, 4.05. 54
hath amaz'd me more | than i dare blame my AWW 2.01. 84
you stand amaz'd, | but be of comfort. TN 3.04.337
be not amaz'd, right noble is his blood. 5.01.264
behold, the french amaz'd vouchsafe a parle, JN 2.01.226
me, cousin, for i was amaz'd | under the tide; 4.02.137
i am amaz'd, methinks, and lose my way | among 4.03.140
and makes me more amaz'd | than had i seen the 5.02. 51
we are amaz'd, and thus long have we stood | to R2 3.03. 72
poor boy, thou art amaz'd. 5.02. 85
be not amaz'd, there's nothing hid from me; 1H6 1.02. 68
what, amaz'd | at my misfortunes? H8 3.02.373
you are amaz'd, my liege, at her exclaim. TRO 5.03. 91
beast in seeming both, | thou hast amaz'd me! ROM 3.03.114
fled to his house amaz'd. JC 3.01. 96
who can be wise, amaz'd, temp'rate, and furious, MAC 2.03.108
my mind she has mated, and amaz'd my sight. 5.01. 78
it would have much amaz'd you. HAM 1.02.235
do deeds to make heaven weep, all earth amaz'd; OTH 3.03.371
come, stand not amaz'd at it, but go along with 4.02.239 P
i am amaz'd with matter. CYM 4.03. 28
and all amaz'd, brake off his late intent, | for VEN 469
whereat amaz'd as one that unaware | hath 823
she much amaz'd breaks ope her lock'd–up eyes, LUC 446
AMAZE 11 FR 0.0012 REL FR 8 V 3 P
that cannot choose but amaze him. WIV 5.03. 17 P
you do amaze her. 5.05.220
you amaze me, i would have thought her spirit ADO 2.03.113 P
you amaze me, ladies. AYL 1.02.109 P
lest your retirement do amaze your friends. 1H4 5.04. 6
here, | it would amaze the proudest of you all. 1H6 4.07. 84
amaze the welkin with your broken staves! R3 5.03.341
it doth amaze me | a man of such a feeble temper JC 1.02.128
and amaze indeed | the very faculties of eyes HAM 2.02.565
men | be like a beacon fir'd t' amaze your eyes. PER 1.04. 87
goes | are like a labyrinth to amaze his foes. VEN 684
AMAZED 6 FR 0.0006 REL FR 6 V 0 P
i am amazed at your /passionate words. MND 3.02.220
way, | and there i stood amazed for a while, SHR 2.01.155
why stand these royal fronts amazed thus? JN 2.01.356
stand not amazed, the prince will doom thee ROM 3.01.134
look how the world's poor people are amazed | at VEN 925
her earnest eye did make him more amazed. LUC 1356
AMAZEDLY 4 FR 0.0004 REL FR 4 V 0 P
my lord, i shall reply amazedly, | half sleep, MND 4.01.146
i speak amazedly, and it becomes | my marvel and
WT 5.01.187
but why | stands macbeth thus amazedly? MAC 4.01.126
saw, | amazedly in her sad face he stares: LUC 1591
AMAZEDNESS 2 FR 0.0002 REL FR 1 V 1 P
sight, | we two in great amazedness will fly; WIV 4.04. 56
whereupon, after a little amazedness, we were WT 5.02. 5 P
AMAZEMENT 13 FR 0.0014 REL FR 11 V 2 P
be collected, | no more amazement. TMP 1.02. 14
the deck, in every cabin, | i flam'd amazement. 1.02.198
trouble, wonder, and amazement | inhabits here. 5.01.104
put not yourself into amazement how these things
MM 4.02.204 P
all this amazement can i qualify, | when after ADO 5.04. 67
the chapel, or resolve you | for more amazement. WT 5.03. 87
and wild amazement hurries up and down | the JN 5.01. 35
will /strike amazement to their drowsy spirits. TRO 2.02.210
behold, /distraction, frenzy, and amazement, 5.03. 85
to th' amazement of mine eyes | that look'd MAC 2.04. 19
hath strook her into amazement and admiration. HAM 3.02.327 P
but look, amazement on thy mother sits, | o, 3.04.112
amazement shall drive courage from the state, PER 1.02. 26
AMAZES 2 FR 0.0002 REL FR 2 V 0 P
his face's own margent did cote such amazes LLL 2.01.246
whose full perfection all the world amazes, VEN 634
AMAZETH 1 FR 0.0001 REL FR 1 V 0 P
steals men's eyes and women's souls amazeth. SON 20. 8
AMAZING 1 FR 0.0001 REL FR 1 V 0 P
fall like amazing thunder on the casque | of thy R2 1.03. 81
AMAZON 3 FR 0.0003 REL FR 3 V 0 P
but that, forsooth, the bouncing amazon, | your MND 2.01. 70
thou art an amazon, | and fightest with the 1H6 1.02.104
belike she minds to play the amazon. 3H6 4.01.106
AMAZONIAN 3 FR 0.0003 REL FR 3 V 0 P
to triumph like an amazonian trull | upon their 3H6 1.04.114
when with his amazonian /chin he drove | the COR 2.02. 91
most dreaded amazonian, that hast slain | the TNK 1.01. 78
AMAZONS 1 FR 0.0001 REL FR 1 V 0 P
maids | like amazons come tripping after drums, JN 5.02.155
AMBASSADE *(see embassade)*
AMBASSADOR *(also embassador, etc.)*
AMBASSADOR 12 FR 0.0013 REL FR 10 V 2 P
heaven, | intends you for his swift ambassador, MM 3.01. 57
shall we call in th' ambassador, my liege? H5 1.02. 3
no, lord ambassador, i'll rather keep | that 1H6 5.04.144
suffolk, ambassador for henry king of england, 2H6 1.01. 45 P
my lord ambassador, these letters are for you, 3H6 3.03.163
i came from edward as ambassador, | but i return 3.03.256
is it therefore | th' ambassador is silenc'd? H8 1.01. 97
when you went | ambassador to the emperor, you 3.02.318
you should be lord ambassador from the emperor, 4.02.109
thou must be my ambassador /to /him, thersites. TRO 3.03.266 P
go thou before, to be our ambassador. TIT 4.04.100
th' ambassador, | lucius the roman, comes to CYM 3.04.141
AMBASSADORS 4 FR 0.0004 REL FR 4 V 0 P
my lords ambassadors, your several suits | have 1H6 5.01. 34
we come ambassadors from the king | unto the 2H6 4.08. 7
hear the ambassadors. ANT 1.01. 48
so like you, sir, ambassadors from rome; CYM 2.03. 54
AMBASSAGE *(also embassage)*
AMBASSAGE 1 FR 0.0001 REL FR 1 V 0 P
to thee i send this written ambassage | to SON 26. 3
AMBASSY *(also embassy)*
AMBASSY 1 FR 0.0001 REL FR 0 V 1 P
receiv'd from her another ambassy of meeting. WIV 3.05.129 P
AMBER 7 FR 0.0008 REL FR 6 V 1 P
her amber hairs for foul hath amber coted. LLL 4.03. 85
her amber hairs for foul hath amber coted. 4.03. 85
with amber bracelets, beads, and all this SHR 4.03. 58
bugle–bracelet, necklace amber, | perfume for a WT 4.04.222
eyes purging thick amber and plum–tree gum, and
HAM 2.02.198 P
ivy buds, | with coral clasps and amber studs: PP 19.14
of amber, crystal, and of beaded jet, | which LC 37
AMBER–COLOR'D 1 FR 0.0001 REL FR 1 V 0 P
an amber–color'd raven was well noted. LLL 4.03. 86
AMBIGUITIES 2 FR 0.0002 REL FR 1 V 1 P
doubt and out of question too, and ambiguities. H5 5.01. 46 P
a while, | till we can clear these ambiguities, ROM 5.03.217
AMBIGUOUS 1 FR 0.0001 REL FR 1 V 0 P
or such ambiguous giving out, to note | that you HAM 1.05.178
/AMBITION 3 FR 0.0003 REL FR 0 V 3 P
/why /then /your /ambition /makes /it /one. HAM 2.02.252 P
/which /dreams /indeed /are /ambition, /for /the 2.02.257 P
/and /i /hold /ambition /of /so /airy /and 2.02.261 P
AMBITION 44 FR 0.0049 REL FR 37 V 7 P
hence his ambition growing — | dost thou hear? TMP 1.02.105
i have no ambition | to see a goodlier man. 1.02.483
even | ambition cannot pierce a wink beyond, 2.01.242
you, brother mine, that /entertain'd ambition, 5.01. 75
this is the period of my ambition. WIV 3.03. 45 P
young fellow of france, full of ambition, an AYL 1.01.143 P
who doth ambition shun, | and loves to live i' 2.05. 38
th' ambition in my love thus plagues itself: AWW 1.01. 90
his humble ambition, proud humility; 1.01.171
their souls | are capable of this ambition, JN 2.01.476
thoughts tending to ambition, they do plot R2 5.05. 18
ill–weav'd ambition, how much art thou shrunk! 1H4 5.04. 88
now beshrew my father's ambition! H5 5.02.225 P
go forward, and be chok'd with thy ambition! 1H6 2.04.112
chok'd with ambition of the meaner sort; 2.05.123
pride went before, ambition follows him. 2H6 1.01.180
with somerset's and buckingham's ambition; 1.01.202
and thy ambition, gloucester. 2.01. 32
at beauford's pride, at somerset's ambition, 2.02. 71
virtue is chok'd with foul ambition, | and 3.01.143
you might haply think | tongue–tied ambition, R3 3.07.145
thy ambition, | thou scarlet sin, robb'd this H8 3.02.254
that, out of mere ambition, you have caus'd 3.02.324
cromwell, i charge thee, fling away ambition! 3.02.440
lord, | become a churchman better than ambition; 5.02. 98
pour in, pour /in, his ambition is dry. TRO 2.03.224 P
a beastly ambition, which the gods grant thee t' TIM 4.03.327 P
this, | whose fall the mark of his ambition is. 5.03. 10
caesar's ambition shall be glanced at. JC 1.02.320
and death for his ambition. 3.02. 29 P
ambition should be made of sterner stuff: 3.02. 92
was this ambition? 3.02. 97
art not without ambition, but without | the MAC 1.05. 19
but only | vaulting ambition, which o'erleaps 1.07. 27
thriftless ambition, that will ravin up | thine 2.04. 28
a most pitiful ambition in the fool that uses it HAM 3.02. 44 P
my crown, mine own ambition, and my queen. 3.03. 55
whose spirit with divine ambition puff'd | makes 4.04. 49
no blown ambition doth our arms incite, | but LR 4.04. 27
and the big wars | that makes ambition virtue! OTH 3.03.350
and ambition | (the soldier's virtue) rather ANT 3.01. 22
caesar's ambition, | which swell'd so much that CYM 3.01. 48
yet their ambition makes them still to fight, LUC 68
these worlds in tarquin new ambition bred, | who 411
AMBITION'S 2 FR 0.0002 REL FR 2 V 0 P
that lowliness is young ambition's ladder, JC 2.01. 22
ambition's debt is paid. 3.01. 83
AMBITIONS 2 FR 0.0002 REL FR 1 V 1 P
fie on ambitions! 2H6 4.10. 1 P
ambitions, covetings, change of prides, disdain, CYM 2.05. 25
/AMBITIOUS 1 FR 0.0001 REL FR 0 V 1 P
/of /the /ambitious /is /merely /the /shadow /of HAM 2.02.258 P
AMBITIOUS 38 FR 0.0043 REL FR 33 V 5 P
his tongue filed, his eye ambitious, his gait LLL 5.01. 11 P
whose ambitious head | spets in the face of MV 2.07. 44
alone | i would not be ambitious in my wish | to 3.02.151
i am ambitious for a motley coat. AYL 2.07. 43
nor the soldier's, which is ambitious; 4.01. 13 P
ambitious love hath so in me offended | that AWW 3.04. 5
how that ambitious constance would not cease JN 1.01. 32
if love ambitious sought a match of birth, 2.01.430
pride | of sky–aspiring and ambitious thoughts, R2 1.03.130
how now, ambitious /humphrey, what means this?
1H6 1.03. 29
farewell, ambitious richard. 2.04.114
if i were covetous, ambitious, or perverse, | as 3.01. 29
lord, | banish the canker of ambitious thoughts! 2H6 1.02. 18
ambitious warwick, let thy betters speak. 1.03.109
ambitious churchman, leave to afflict my heart. 2.01.178
thou great grown | and, like ambitious sylla, 4.01. 84
a bedlam and ambitious humor | makes him oppose 5.01.132
ambitious york did level at thy crown, | thou 3H6 2.02. 19
while proud ambitious edward, duke of york, 3.03. 27
speak like a subject, proud ambitious york! 5.05. 17
man's pie is freed | from his ambitious finger. H8 1.01. 53
you are ambitious for poor knaves' caps and legs COR 2.01. 68 P
thy love | as ever in ambitious strength i did 4.05.112
with pride, ambitious past all thinking, 4.06. 31
oppose not scythia to ambitious rome; TIT 1.01.132
proud and ambitious tribune, canst thou tell? 1.01.202
and i have seen | th' ambitious ocean swell, and JC 1.03. 7
but, as he was ambitious, i slew him. 3.02. 27 P
brutus | hath told you caesar was ambitious; 3.02. 78
but brutus says he was ambitious, | and brutus 3.02. 86
did this in caesar seem ambitious? 3.02. 90
yet brutus says he was ambitious, | and brutus 3.02. 93
yet brutus says he was ambitious, | and sure he 3.02. 98
therefore 'tis certain he was not ambitious. 3.02.113
had on | when he the ambitious norway combated.
HAM 1.01. 61
revengeful, ambitious, with more offenses at my 3.01.124 P
and too ambitious, to aspire to him, | weak as TNK pr 23
and this ambitious foul infirmity, | in having LUC 150
AMBITIOUSLY 2 FR 0.0002 REL FR 2 V 0 P
it | as others would ambitiously receive it. 2H6 2.03. 36
by friends | ambitiously for rule and empery, TIT 1.01. 19
AMBLE 1 FR 0.0001 REL FR 0 V 1 P
you jig and amble, and you /lisp, you nickname HAM 3.01.144 P
AMBLED 1 FR 0.0001 REL FR 1 V 0 P
the skipping king, he ambled up and down, | with 1H4 3.02. 60
AMBLES 4 FR 0.0004 REL FR 0 V 4 P
sir, your wit ambles well, it goes easily. ADO 5.01.158 P
i'll tell you who time ambles withal, who time AYL 3.02.310 P
who ambles time withal? 3.02.318 P
these time ambles withal. 3.02.325 P
AMBLING 3 FR 0.0003 REL FR 2 V 1 P
or a thief to walk my ambling gelding, than my WIV 2.02.305 P
to strut before a wanton ambling nymph; R3 1.01. 17
give me a torch, i am not for this ambling; ROM 1.04. 11
AMBS–ACE *(see ames–ace)*
AMBUSCADOES 1 FR 0.0001 REL FR 1 V 0 P
of breaches, ambuscadoes, spanish blades, | of ROM 1.04. 84
AMBUSH 8 FR 0.0009 REL FR 7 V 1 P
who may, in th' ambush of my name, strike home,
MM 1.03. 41
have suspected an ambush where i was taken? AWW 4.03.302 P
foe, | once did i lay an ambush for your life, R2 1.01.137
him | in secret ambush on the forest side, | and 3H6 4.06. 83
and see the ambush of our friends be strong, | i TIT 5.03. 9
i fear some ambush. CYM 4.02. 65
or sire, | or lain in ambush to betray my life, LUC 233
thou hast pass'd by the ambush of young days, SON 70. 9
/AMEN 3 FR 0.0003 REL FR 3 V 0 P
/will /no /man /say /amen? R2 4.01.172
/well /then, /amen. 4.01.173
/and /yet /amen, /if /heaven /do /think /him /me 4.01.175
AMEN 82 FR 0.0092 REL FR 62 V 20 P
amen! TMP 2.02. 94 P
i say amen, gonzalo! 5.01.204
be it so, amen! 5.01.215
amen, amen! TGV 5.01. 8
amen, amen! 5.01. 8
amen! WIV 3.03.206 P
amen. MM 1.02. 6 P
amen! 2.02.157
amen, if you love her, for the lady is very well ADO 1.01.221 P
i love you the better; the hearers may cry amen. 2.01.106 P
amen. 2.01.108 P
made the match, and all grace say amen to it. 2.01.304 P
amen, so you be none. LLL 2.01.126
amen, so i had mine. is not that a good word? 4.03. 92
amen, amen, to that fair prayer, say i — | and MND 2.02. 62
amen, amen, to that fair prayer, say i — | and 2.02. 62
eyes | thus with my hat, and sigh and say amen, MV 2.02.194
let me say amen betimes, lest the devil cross my 3.01. 19 P
amen. AYL 3.03. 48 P
amen. SHR in.2. 98
amen, say we. we will be witnesses. 2.01.320
marry, amen. TN 4.02.101 P
amen, amen! mount, chevaliers! to arms! JN 2.01.287
amen, amen! mount, chevaliers! to arms! 2.01.287
cardinal, cry thou amen | to my keen curses; 3.01.181
strong as a tower in hope, i cry amen. R2 1.03.102
amen. 1.04. 65
marry and amen! 1H4 2.04.115 P
to cry amen to that, thus we appear. H5 5.02. 21
amen! 5.02.356
god speak this amen! 5.02.368
amen! 5.02.369
to your good prayer will scarcely say amen. R3 1.03. 21
amen! 2.02.109
amen! 3.07.241
i say amen to her. 4.04.198
great god of heaven, say amen to all! 5.05. 8
what traitor hears me, and says not amen? 5.05. 22
that she may long live here, god say amen! 5.05. 41
now i pray god, amen!. H8 2.03. 56
my amen to't! 3.02. 45
marry, amen! 3.02. 54
methinks i could | cry the amen, and yet my 5.01. 24
amen. 5.04. 11
amen. TRO 1.03.303
i have said my prayers, and devil envy say amen. 2.03. 21 P
amen. 2.03. 33 P
amen. 2.03. 37 P
say, amen. 3.02.204 P
amen. 3.02.205
amen. 3.02.206
amen. 3.02.207 P
amen, amen. god save thee, noble consul! COR 2.03.136 P
amen, amen. god save thee, noble consul! 2.03.136 P
amen, sir. 2.03.158
amen, amen. 3.03. 37
amen, amen. 3.03. 37

here lacks but your mother for to say amen. TIT 4.02. 44
amen, amen! ROM 2.06. 3
amen, amen! 2.06. 3
amen! 3.05.228
marry and amen! 4.05. 8
amen. TIM 1.02. 70
amen. 4.01. 41
amen. 4.03.449
and "amen!" MAC 2.02. 24
list'ning their fear, i could not say "amen," 2.02. 26
but wherefore could not i pronounce "amen"? 2.02. 28
of blessing, and "amen" | stuck in my throat. 2.02. 29
sir, amen. 4.03.163
ay, amen! HAM 2.02. 39
amen to that, sweet powers! OTH 2.01.195
lady, amen. 3.04.164
amen, with all my heart! 5.02. 34
i say, amen. 5.02. 57
amen. ANT 1.02. 70 P
amen. 1.02. 75 P
happily, amen! 2.02.152
amen! i thank thee. CYM 3.04.193
so say i, amen. 4.04. 47
may | be wish'd upon thy head, i cry amen to't! TNK 1.04. 3
still cry "amen" | to every hymn that able SON 85. 6
AMEND 18 FR 0.0020 REL FR 9 V 9 P
god amend us, god amend! LLL 4.03. 74
god amend us, god amend! 4.03. 74
do you amend it then; MND 2.01.118
worst are no worse, if imagination amend them. 5.01.212 P
madonna, that drink and good counsel will amend; TN 1.05. 44 P
"you must amend your drunkenness." 2.05. 73 P
thou wilt amend thy life? WT 5.02.154 P
you must needs learn, lord, to amend this fault; 1H4 3.01.178
do thou amend thy face, and i'll amend my life. 3.03. 24 P
do thou amend thy face, and i'll amend my life. 3.03. 24 P
by the heels would amend the attention of your 2H4 1.02.123 P
grace, | on our entreaties, to amend your fault! R3 3.07.115
heaven given his hand, | they presently amend. MAC 4.03.145
so fond, but it is not in my virtue to amend it. OTH 1.03.318 P
of unpav'd eunuch to boot, can never amend. CYM 2.03. 31 P
am ill, but your being by me | cannot amend me; 4.02. 12
that all th' abhorred things o' th' earth amend 5.05.216
weak sights their sickly radiance do amend; LC 214
AMENDED 5 FR 0.0005 REL FR 4 V 1 P
with sainted vow my faults to have amended. AWW 3.04. 7
look what is done cannot be now amended: R3 4.04.291
and i must excuse | what cannot be amended. COR 4.07. 12
ay, /by my troth, the case may be amended. ROM 4.05.101 P
mar not the thing that cannot be amended. LUC 578
A–MENDING 1 FR 0.0001 REL FR 1 V 0 P
'tis like a chime a–mending, with terms TRO 1.03.159
AMENDING 1 FR 0.0001 REL FR 1 V 0 P
where no excuse can give the fault amending. LUC 1614
AMENDMENT 4 FR 0.0004 REL FR 2 V 2 P
your honor's players, hearing your amendment, SHR in.2. 129
what hope is there of his majesty's amendment? AWW 1.01. 11 P
i see a good amendment of life in thee, from 1H4 1.02.102 P
what likelihood of his amendment, lords? R3 1.03. 33
AMENDS 25 FR 0.0028 REL FR 18 V 7 P
your compensation makes amends, for i | have TMP 4.01. 2
th' affliction of my mind amends, with which | i 5.01.115
i'll kiss each several paper for amends. TGV 1.02.105
that makes amends for her sour breath. 3.01.328 P
return, return, and make thy love amends. 4.02. 99
that is, he will make thee amends. WIV 2.03. 67 P
and i will one way or other make you amends. 3.01. 88 P
for to–morrow, eight a' clock, to have amends. 3.03.198 P
she'll make you amends, i warrant you. 3.05. 47 P
i'll make you amends next, to give you nothing ERR 2.02. 53 P
tongue, | we will make amends ere long; MND 5.01.434
we be friends, | and robin shall restore amends. 5.01.438
now lord be thanked for my good amends! SHR in.2. 97
and sin that amends is but patch'd with virtue. TN 1.05. 49 P
and for amends to his posterity, | at our JN 2.01. 6
rest, | yet thus far fortune maketh us amends, 3H6 4.07. 2
pardon me, edward, i will make amends; 5.01.100
the readiest way to make the wench amends | is R3 1.01.155
to make amends i'll give it to your daughter; 4.04.295
i cannot make you what amends i would, 4.04.309
but make amends now. MAC 3.05. 14
'tis very much, | make her amends; OTH 4.01.244
you make amends. CYM 1.06.168
unless thou couldst return to make amends? LUC 961
what shall be thy amends | for thy neglect of SON 101. 1
AMERCE 1 FR 0.0001 REL FR 1 V 0 P
but i'll amerce you with so strong a fine | that ROM 3.01.190
AMERICA 1 FR 0.0001 REL FR 0 V 1 P
where america, the indies? ERR 3.02.133 P
AMES–ACE 1 FR 0.0001 REL FR 0 V 1 P
in this choice than throw ames–ace for my life. AWW 2.03. 79 P
AMIABLE 7 FR 0.0008 REL FR 5 V 2 P
it, as to lay an amiable siege to the honesty of WIV 2.02.234 P
afar off in the orchard this amiable encounter. ADO 3.03.151 P
bull jove, sir, had an amiable low, | and some 5.04. 48
bed, | while i thy amiable cheeks do coy, | and MND 4.01. 2
fair buds, | and in no sense is meet or amiable. SHR 5.02.141
o amiable lovely death! JN 3.04. 25
'twould make her amiable, and subdue my father OTH 3.04. 59
AMID 2 FR 0.0002 REL FR 2 V 0 P
and amid this hurly i intend | that all is done SHR 4.01.203
but rather famish them amid their plenty, VEN 20
AMIDST 1 FR 0.0001 REL FR 1 V 0 P
enthron'd and spher'd | amidst the other; TRO 1.03. 91
AMIENS 1 FR 0.0001 REL FR 1 V 0 P
to–day my lord of amiens and myself | did steal AYL 2.01. 29
AMISS 41 FR 0.0046 REL FR 29 V 12 P
that shall not be much amiss; MM 3.01.195 P
why, 'tis not amiss, pompey. 3.02. 63 P
what error drives our eyes and ears amiss? ERR 2.02.184
yet it had not been amiss the rod had been made, ADO 2.01.227 P
for never any thing can be amiss, | when MND 5.01. 82
that judgment is, | that did never choose amiss. MV 2.09. 65
why, nothing comes amiss, so money comes withal. SHR 1.02. 82 P
it were impossible i should speed amiss. 2.01.283
that talk'd of her, have talk'd amiss of her. 2.01.291
i like him well, 'tis not amiss. AWW 4.05. 68 P
thou'st him some thrice, it shall not be amiss; TN 3.02. 46 P
for that which thou hast sworn to do amiss | is JN 3.01.270
do amiss | is not amiss when it is truly done; 3.01.271
and these, and all, are all amiss employed. R2 2.03.132
it when he will, 'tis not a hair amiss yet. 2H4 1.02. 24 P
then judge, great lords, if i have done amiss; 1H6 4.01. 27
gold cannot come amiss, were she a devil. 2H6 1.02. 92
which is not amiss to cool a man's stomach this 4.10. 9 P
'twere not amiss | he were created knight for 5.01. 76
i do beseech you take it not amiss, | i cannot R3 3.07.206
have we done aught amiss, show us wherein, | and TIT 5.03.129
something hath been amiss — a noble nature TIM 2.02.208
common /lag of people — what is amiss in them, 3.06. 81 P
'tis not amiss | we tender our loves to him in 5.01. 11
what is amiss, plague and infection mend! 5.01.221
said, if he had done or said any thing amiss, he JC 1.02.270 P
this dream is all amiss interpreted, | it was a 2.02. 83
what is now amiss | that caesar and his senate 3.01. 31
what is amiss? MAC 2.03. 97
each toy seems prologue to some great amiss, HAM 4.05. 18
becomes the field, but here shows much amiss. 5.02.402
by me that's said or done amiss this night, OTH 2.03.201
that's not amiss, | but yet keep time in all. 4.01. 91
is not | amiss to tumble on the bed of ptolomy, ANT 1.04. 17
what's amiss, | may it be gently heard. 2.02. 19
'twere not amiss to keep our door hatch'd. PER 4.02. 33 P
how prettily she's amiss! TNK 4.03. 28 P
breed not, | my rams speed not, all is amiss; PP 17. 2
compare, | myself corrupting, salving thy amiss, SON 35. 7
which laboring for invention bear amiss | the 59. 3
then, gentle cheater, urge not my amiss, | lest 151. 3
/AMITIES 1 FR 0.0001 REL FR 0 V 1 P
/dissolutions /of /ancient /amities, /divisions LR 1.02.146 P
AMITIES 1 FR 0.0001 REL FR 1 V 0 P
wear | and stand a comma 'tween their amities, HAM 5.02. 42
AMITY 23 FR 0.0026 REL FR 19 V 4 P
now thou and i are new in amity, | and will MND 4.01. 87
there may as well be amity and life | 'tween MV 3.02. 30
a noble and a true conceit | of godlike amity, 3.04. 3
you make us friends, i will pursue the amity. AWW 2.05. 14 P
amity too, of your brave father, whom | (though WT 5.01.136
gates, | let in that amity which you have made, JN 2.01.537
of war | is cold in amity and painted peace, 3.01.105
peace, amity, true love | between our kingdoms 3.01.231
swore to you | dear amity and everlasting love. 5.04. 20
condition | and the division of our amity. 2H4 3.01. 79
tokens home | of our restored love and amity. 4.02. 65
to join your hearts in love and amity. 1H6 3.01. 68
that in alliance, amity, and oaths, | there 4.01. 62
to effect | and surer bind this knot of amity, 5.01. 16
person, | and then to crave a league of amity, 3H6 3.03. 53
to confirm that amity | with nuptial knot, if 3.03. 54
hand | in sign of league and amity with thee. R3 1.03.280
england and france might through their amity H8 1.01.181
the amity that wisdom knits not, folly may TRO 2.03.101 P
many people under two commands | hold amity? LR 2.04.242
to hold you in perpetual amity, | to make you ANT 2.02.124
will be the very strangler of their amity. 2.06.122 P
is the strength of their amity shall prove the 2.06.129 P
AMONG *(also 'mong, etc.)*
AMONG 95 FR 0.0107 REL FR 69 V 26 P
o villain, that set this down among her vices! TGV 3.01.333 P
is he among these? 4.02. 37 P
and carry it among the whitsters in datchet–mead WIV 3.03. 14 P
a omans as i will desires among five thousand, 3.03.220 P
i bestow | among my wife and /her confederates, ERR 4.01. 17
you have among you kill'd a sweet and innocent ADO 5.01.191 P
not one wise man among twenty that will praise 5.02. 74 P
and, among three, to love the worst of all, | a LLL 3.01.195
and among other /importunate and most serious 5.01. 99 P
dost thou infamonize me among potentates? 5.02.678 P
a lion among ladies, is a most dreadful thing; MND 3.01. 31 P
henceforth be never numb'red among men! 3.02. 67
for there is not one among them but i dote on MV 1.02.109 P
to make me blest or cursed'st among men. 2.01. 46
how now, shylock, what news among the merchants? 3.01. 22 P
appear | among the buzzing pleased multitude, 3.02.180
you have among you many a purchas'd slave, 4.01. 90
poet, honest ovid, was among the goths. AYL 3.03. 8 P
execute — | to make one among these wooers. SHR 1.01.247
among them know you one vincentio? 4.02. 96
my cake is dough, but i'll in among the rest, 5.01.140
"among nine bad if one be good, | among nine bad AWW 1.03. 77
if one be good, | among nine bad if one be good, 1.03. 78
to understand him, unless some one among us, 4.01. 5 P
'tis thought among the prudent he would quickly TN 1.03. 32 P
fear, | among the infinite doings of the world, WT 1.02.253
is there no manners left among maids? 4.04.242 P
not have relish'd among my other discredits. 5.02.122 P
be set | among the high tides in the calendar? JN 3.01. 86
how i have sped among the clergymen | the sums i 4.02.141
among the thorns and dangers of this world. 4.03.141
ran fearfully among the trembling reeds, | and 1H4 1.03.105
body to anatomize | among my household? 2H4 in 22
it shall serve among wits of no higher breeding 2.02. 35 P
and you do not make him hang'd among you, the 2.02. 96 P
no, by my faith, i must live among my neighbors; 2.04. 74 P
his head for crowding among the marshal's men. 3.02.323 P
so merrily, | and ever among so merrily." 5.03. 22
of the camp will do among foaming bottles and H5 3.06. 78 P
among which terms he us'd his lavish tongue 1H6 2.05. 47
should reign among professors of one faith. 5.01. 14
charge, | among the people gather up a tenth. 5.05. 93
are you drawn forth among a world of men | to R3 1.04.181
among this princely heap, if any here | by false 2.01. 54
have been commissions | sent down among 'em, H8 1.02. 21
all in uproar, | and danger serves among them. 1.02. 37
demand | what was the speech among the londoners 1.02.154
the spavin | /and springhalt reign'd among 'em. 1.03. 13
i was set at work | among my maids, full little, 3.01. 75
a woman lost among ye, laugh'd at, scorn'd? 3.01.107
among the crowd i' th' abbey, where a finger 4.01. 57
is come to lay his weary bones among ye; 4.02. 22
they had parted so much honesty among 'em — 5.02. 28
go break among the press, and find a way out 5.03. 84
there is among the greeks | a lord of troyan TRO 1.02. 12
if there be one among the fair'st of greece 1.03.265
among ourselves | give him allowance for the 1.03.375
thou art bought and sold among those of any wit, 2.01. 46 P
from false to false, among false maids in love, 3.02.190
flamens | do press among the popular throngs, COR 2.01.214
why, had your bodies | no heart among you? 2.03.204
there's some among you have beheld me fighting; 3.01.223
plant love among 's! 3.03. 35
home to rome, | and die among our neighbors. 5.03.173
reward | among the nettles at the elder–tree, TIT 2.03.272
perhaps, she cull'd it from among the rest. 4.01. 44
thou shalt inquire him out among the goths: 5.02.123
out | to beg relief among rome's enemies, | who 5.03.106
art thou drawn among these heartless hinds? ROM 1.01. 66
love, and you, among the store | one more, most 1.02. 22
among fresh fennel buds shall you this night 1.02. 29
my soul, | you'll make a mutiny among my guests! 1.05. 80
he hath hid himself among these trees | to be 2.01. 30
of thee | among a sisterhood of holy nuns. 5.03.157
that puts odds | among the rout of nations, i TIM 4.03. 44
good friends be griev'd | (among which number, JC 1.02. 44
i would i might go to hell among the rogues. 1.02.268 P
be bright and jovial among your guests to–night. MAC 3.02. 28
like some ore | among a mineral of metals base, HAM 4.01. 26
and let his knights have colder looks among you; LR 1.03. 22
should play bo–peep, | and go the /fools among." 1.04.178
there's not a nose among twenty but can smell 2.04. 70 P
we have yet many among us can gripe as hard as CYM 3.01. 40 P
not muster'd | among the bands) may drive us to 4.04. 11
i am brought hither | among th' italian gentry, 5.01. 18
he hath been search'd among the dead and living; 5.05. 11
tediosity and disensanity | is here among ye! TNK 3.05. 3
and still among intermingle your petition of 4.03. 88 P
even by the rule you have among yourselves, STM II.C 46
"sometime he runs among a flock of sheep, | to VEN 685
that thou among the wastes of time must go, SON 12.10
weeds among weeds, or flowers with flowers 124. 4
we prove | among a number one is reckon'd none: 136. 8
"'among the many that mine eyes have seen, | not LC 190
my well, | and mine i pour your ocean all among: 256
AMONGEST 1 FR 0.0001 REL FR 1 V 0 P
be small love amongest these sweet knaves, | and TIM 1.01.249
AMONGST 40 FR 0.0045 REL FR 31 V 9 P
him the most unnatural | that liv'd amongst men. AYL 4.03.123
amongst the rest of the country copulatives, to 5.04. 55 P
to make a stale of me amongst these mates? SHR 1.01. 58
must stead us all, and me amongst the rest; 1.02.264
amongst the rest, | there is a remedy, approv'd, AWW 1.03.227
what wisdom stirs amongst you? WT 2.01. 21
but one puritan amongst them, and he sings 4.03. 44 P
amongst much other talk, that very time, | i R2 4.01. 14
amongst a grove the very straightest plant, 1H4 1.01. 82
amongst the rest demanded | my prisoners in your 1.03. 47
or four loggerheads amongst three or four score 2.04. 4 P
is dead that you and pistol beat amongst you. 2H4 5.04. 17 P
amongst the soldiers this is muttered, | that 1H6 1.01. 70
they did amongst the troops of armed men | leap 2.02. 24
amongst his subjects and his loyal friends, | as 3.01.181
in france, amongst a fickle, wavering nation. 4.01.138
were but his picture left amongst you here, | it 4.07. 83
peace be amongst them if they turn to us, | else 5.02. 6
amongst the loving welshmen canst procure, 3H6 2.01.180
for this, amongst the rest, was i ordain'd. 5.06. 58
there should be one amongst 'em, by his person H8 1.04. 78
i, her frail son, amongst my brethren mortal, 3.02.148
the devil was amongst 'em, i think, surely. 5.03. 58 P
there is amongst the greeks achilles, a better TRO 1.02.247 P
and jove forbid there should be done amongst us 2.02.127
i have a roisting challenge sent amongst | the 2.02.208
what work he makes | amongst your cloven army. COR 1.04. 21
not one amongst us, save yourself, but says | he 2.03.162
home, | with burial amongst their ancestors. TIT 1.01. 84
amongst the fair–fac'd breeders of our clime. 4.02. 68
amongst them all, | whose eyes are on this TIM 1.01. 67
the latest of my wealth i'll share amongst you. 4.02. 23
flew on him, and amongst them fell'd him dead, LR 4.02. 76
cyprus, | i have found great love amongst them. OTH 2.01.205
him be so entertain'd amongst you as suits with CYM 1.04. 29 P
best of all | amongst the rar'st of good ones), 5.05.160
but amongst honest /women. PER 4.06.194
faith, my acquaintance lies little amongst them. 4.06.195 P
then start amongst 'em | and, as an east wind, TNK 2.02. 12
grease, amongst a whole million of cutpurses, 4.03. 37 P
AMOROUS 23 FR 0.0026 REL FR 22 V 1 P
force | and strong encounter of my amorous tale; ADO 1.01.325
sure my brother is amorous on hero and hath 2.01.155 P
of corn and versing love | to amorous phillida. MND 2.01. 68
seen together | lorenzo and his amorous jessica. MV 2.08. 9
a proper stripling, and an amorous! SHR 1.02.143
deceiv'd, | our fine musician groweth amorous. 3.01. 63
minola, | the quaint musician, amorous litio, 3.02.147
may be the amorous count solicits her | in the AWW 3.05. 69
send forth your amorous token for fair maudlin. 5.03. 68
nor made to court an amorous looking–glass; R3 1.01. 15
shall from your neck unloose his amorous fold, TRO 3.03.223
but gives all gaze and bent of amorous view | on 4.05.282
tell her i have chastis'd the amorous troyan, 5.05. 4
hast prisoner held, fett'red in amorous chains, TIT 2.01. 15
lovers can see to do their amorous rites | by ROM 3.02. 8
i believe | that unsubstantial death is amorous, 5.03.103
in our court have made their amorous sojourn, LR 1.01. 47
and she did gratify his amorous works | with OTH 5.02.213
that am with phoebus' amorous pinches black, ANT 1.05. 28
this amorous surfeiter would have donn'd his 2.01. 33
to follow faster, | as amorous of their strokes. 2.02.197
wide difference | 'twixt amorous and villainous. CYM 5.05.195
of this false jewel, and his amorous spoil. LC 154
AMOROUSLY 1 FR 0.0001 REL FR 1 V 0 P
hair, | with twisted metal amorously impleach'd, LC 205
AMORT 2 FR 0.0002 REL FR 2 V 0 P
how fares my kate? what, sweeting, all amort? SHR 4.03. 36
what, all amort? 1H6 3.02.124
AMOUNT 7 FR 0.0008 REL FR 3 V 4 P
rate, | cannot amount unto a hundred marks, ERR 1.01. 24
which doth amount to three odd ducats more 4.01. 30
it doth amount to one more than two. LLL 1.02. 47 P

sir, we know whereuntil it doth amount. 5.02.494 P
sir, will show whereuntil it doth amount. 5.02.500 P
indeed three such antics do not amount to a man. H5 3.02. 31 P
will but amount to five and twenty thousand, 3H6 2.01.181
AMOUNTS 3 FR 0.0003 REL FR 1 V 2 P
how much the gross sum of deuce–ace amounts to. LLL 1.02. 46 P
my land amounts not to so much in all. SHR 2.01.373
my life, amounts not to fifteen thousand pole, AWW 4.03.167 P
AMPHIMACHUS 1 FR 0.0001 REL FR 1 V 0 P
is slain, | amphimachus and thoas deadly hurt, TRO 5.05. 12
/AMPLE 1 FR 0.0001 REL FR 1 V 0 P
/now /and /then /an /ample /tear /trill'd /down LR 4.03. 12
AMPLE 15 FR 0.0017 REL FR 14 V 1 P
worth | to undergo such ample grace and honor, MM 1.01. 23
whom i beseech | to give me ample satisfaction ERR 5.01.253
think i know your hostess | as ample as myself. AWW 3.05. 43
at home be encount'red with a shame as ample. 4.03. 70 P
heat, | shall not behold her face at ample view; TN 1.01. 26
be glorified | as to my ample hope was promised JN 5.02.112
in very ample virtue of his father, | to hear 2H4 4.01.161
with ample and brim fullness of his force, H5 1.02.150
ruling in large and ample empery | o'er france 1.02.226
love | and ample interchange of sweet discourse R3 5.03. 99
the ample proposition that hope makes | in all TRO 1.03. 3
and had as ample power as i have will, | paris 2.02.140
enjoy | at ample point all that i did possess, 3.03. 89
you see, my lord, how ample y' are belov'd. TIM 1.02.130
remain this ample third of our fair kingdom, LR 1.01. 80
AMPLER 2 FR 0.0002 REL FR 2 V 0 P
and ampler strength indeed | than most have of WT 4.04.403
and to add ampler majesty to this | he hath not STM II.C 101
AMPLEST 2 FR 0.0002 REL FR 2 V 0 P
your majesty, may plead | for amplest credence. AWW 1.02. 11
embrace and hug | with amplest entertainment. TIM 1.01. 45
AMPLIFIED 1 FR 0.0001 REL FR 1 V 0 P
read | his fame unparallel'd, happily amplified; COR 5.02. 16
/AMPLIFY 1 FR 0.0001 REL FR 1 V 0 P
/to /amplify /too /much, /would /make /much LR 5.03.207
AMPLIFY 2 FR 0.0002 REL FR 2 V 0 P
not meet | that i did amplify my judgment in CYM 1.05. 17
and deep–brain'd sonnets that did amplify | each LC 209
AMPLY 3 FR 0.0003 REL FR 3 V 0 P
that can prate | as amply and unnecessarily | as TMP 2.01.264
a net | than amply to imbar their crooked titles H5 1.02. 94
his merit, | as amply /titled as achilles' is, TRO 2.03.193
AMPTHILL 1 FR 0.0001 REL FR 1 V 0 P
six miles off | from ampthill, where the H8 4.01. 28
AMURATH 2 FR 0.0002 REL FR 2 V 0 P
court, | not amurath an amurath succeeds, | but 2H4 5.02. 48
court, | not amurath an amurath succeeds, | but 5.02. 48
AMYNTAS 1 FR 0.0001 REL FR 1 V 0 P
polemon and amyntas, | the kings of mede and ANT 3.06. 74
AN' *(also and)*
/AN' 4 FR 0.0004 REL FR 2 V 2 P
/an' you'll come to supper to–night, you may; OTH 4.01.159 P
/an' you will not, come when you are next 4.01.160 P
nay, /an' you stare, we shall hear more anon. 5.01.107
nay, /an' you strive — 5.02. 81
AN' 14 FR 0.0015 REL FR 10 V 4 P
come, sir, it wants a twelvemonth an' a day, LLL 5.02.877
on his grace's cure | by such a day an' hour. AWW 1.03.249
an' never will i rise up from the ground | till R2 5.02.116
an' he shall spend mine honor with his shame, 5.03. 68
i'll make one, an' i do not, call me villain and 1H4 1.02.101 P
an' it be not four by the day, i'll be hang'd. 2.01. 1 P
he will weep you an' 'twere a man born in april. TRO 1.02.173 P
i'll spring up in his tears an' 'twere a nettle 1.02.175 P
eye, | my silence, an' my cloudy melancholy, TIT 2.03. 33
an' a courteous, and a kind, and a handsome, ROM 2.05. 56
he come, an' he and i | will watch thy /waking, 4.01.115
i said, | "an' if a man did need a poison now, 5.01. 50
an' his whole function suiting | with forms to HAM 2.02.556
an' can you by no drift of conference | get from 3.01. 1
AN* *(also on)*
/AN* 29 FR 0.0032 REL FR 23 V 6 P
/an heir, and /near allied unto the duke. TGV 4.01. 47
oath on it, till he have made /an oyster of me, ADO 2.03. 25 P
/an end, sir, to your business! AWW 2.02. 63
/and /soon /lie /richard /in /an /earthy /pit! R2 4.01.219
/cracking /the /strong /warrant /of /an /oath, 4.01.235
/showing /an /outward /pity, /yet /you /pilates 4.01.240
/it /is, /crack'd /in /an /hundred /shivers. 4.01.289
/knew /he /walk'd /o'er /perils, /on /an /edge, 2H4 1.01.170
/as /in /an /early /spring | /we /see /th' 1.03. 38
/an /habitation /giddy /and /unsure.| /hath /he 1.03. 89
/nor /do /i /as /an /enemy /to /peace | /troop 4.01. 61
/you /should /have /an /inch /of /any /ground 4.01.107
or like /an /idle thresher with a flail, | fell 3H6 2.01.131
with whom /an upright zeal to right prevails 5.01. 78
/i /for /an /edward /weep, so do not they. R3 2.02. 85
and when /mine oratory drew /to /an end, | i bid 3.07. 20
let me but meet you, ladies, /an hour hence, 4.01. 28
/but /i, /of /these, /will /wrest /an /alphabet, TIT 3.02. 44
(/an honor in him which buys out his fault), TIM 3.05. 17
/to /speak /to /you /like /an /honest /man, /i HAM 2.02.268 P
/sir, /an /aery /of /children, /little /eyases, 2.02.339 P
/an anchor's cheer in prison be my scope! 3.02.219
he keeps them, like /an /ape an apple, in the 4.02. 18 P
should be as mortal as /an /old man's life? 4.05.161
/which /they /will /make /an /obedient /father. LR 1.04.235 P
/what /store /her /heart /is /made /an. 3.06. 54
/and /now /and /then /an /ample /tear /trill'd 4.03. 12
/an excellent /courtesy! OTH 2.01.175 P
truly, /an obedient lady: 4.01.248
AN* 1543 FR 0.1744 REL FR 1001 V 542 P
a nutshell and as leaky as an unstanch'd wench. TMP 1.01. 48 P
furlongs of sea for an acre of barren ground, 1.01. 66 P
not so much perdition as an hair | betid to any 1.02. 30
and rather like a dream than an assurance | that 1.02. 45
in my false brother | awak'd an evil nature, and 1.02. 93
of naples, being an enemy | to me inveterate, 1.02.121
which rais'd in me | an undergoing stomach, to 1.02.157
in an odd angle of the isle, and sitting, | his 1.02.223
i will rend an oak | and peg thee in his knotty 1.02.294
what, | an advocate for an impostor? 1.02.478
what, | an advocate for an impostor? 1.02.478
with an eye of green in't. 2.01. 56 P
in his pocket, and give it his son for an apple. 2.01. 92 P
daughter, | but rather loose her to an african, 2.01.126
to perform an act | whereof what's past is 2.01.252
fright a monster's ear, | to make an earthquake! 2.01.315
this is no fish, but an islander, that hath 2.02. 36 P
four legs, who hath got, as i take it, an ague. 2.02. 66 P
an abominable monster! 2.02.158 P
and now farewell | till half an hour hence. 3.01. 91
i do believe it | against an oracle. 4.01. 12
dishonor in that, monster, but an infinite loss. 4.01.210 P
by line and level" is an excellent pass of pate; 4.01.243 P
and the best comforter | to an unsettled fancy, 5.01. 59
swear'st grace o'erboard, not an oath on shore? 5.01.219
now, trust me, 'tis an office of great worth, TGV 1.02. 44
worth, | and you an officer fit for the place. 1.02. 45
for what i will, i will, and there an end. 1.03. 65
the uncertain glory of an april day, | which now 1.03. 85
shine through you like the water in an urinal, 2.01. 39 P
that not an eye that sees you but is a physician 2.01. 40 P
she gave me none, except an angry word. 2.01.158 P
letter hath she deliver'd, and there an end. 2.01.162 P
you have an exchequer of words and, i think, no 2.04. 43 P
and though myself have been an idle truant, 2.04. 64
he is as worthy for an empress' love | as meet 2.04. 76
love | as meet to be an emperor's counsellor. 2.04. 77
they say that love hath not an eye at all. 2.04. 96
no; but she is an earthly paragon. 2.04.146
what an ass art thou! i understand thee not. 2.05. 24 P
if not, thou art an hebrew, a jew, and not worth 2.05. 54 P
and valentine i'll hold an enemy, | aiming at 2.06. 29
a thousand oaths, an ocean of his tears, | and 2.07. 69
i nightly lodge her in an upper tow'r, | the key 3.01. 35
and here an engine fit for my proceeding! 3.01.138
for reading my letter — an unmannerly slave, 3.01.383 P
which with an hour's heat | dissolves to water, 3.02. 7
'tis an ill office for a gentleman, | especially 3.02. 40
it's an honorable kind of thievery. 4.01. 39
a slave, that still an end turns me to shame! 4.04. 62
that such an ass should owe them. 5.02. 28
he bears an honorable mind, | and will not use a 5.03. 13
uncivil touch, | thou friend of an ill fashion! 5.04. 61
have took upon me | such an immodest raiment — 5.04.106
and think thee worthy of an empress' love. 5.04.141
it is an old coat. WIV 1.01. 18 P
dozen white louses do become an old coat well; 1.01. 19 P
is the fresh fish, the salt fish is an old coat. 1.01. 23 P
made me drunk, yet i am not altogether an ass. 1.01.172 P
i will make an end of my dinner; 1.02. 12 P
thou'rt an emperor — caesar, keiser, and 1.03. 9 P
an old cloak makes a new jerkin; 1.03. 17 P
his filching was like an unskillful singer, he 1.03. 25 P
here will be an old abusing of god's patience 1.04. 5 P
an honest, willing, kind fellow as ever servant 1.04. 10 P
the young man is an honest man. 1.04. 72 P
he came of an errand to me from parson hugh. 1.04. 76 P
i detest, an honest maid as ever broke bread. 1.04.150 P
we had an hour's talk of that wart. 1.04.151 P
truly, an honest gentleman; 1.04.163 P
what an unweigh'd behavior hath this flemish 2.01. 23 P
but go to hell for an eternal moment or so, i 2.01. 49 P
as long as i have an eye to make difference of 2.01. 56 P
and that, i hope, is an unmeasurable distance. 2.01.104 P
we have an hour's talk with you. 2.01.166 P
you, they could never get an eye–wink of her. 2.02. 71 P
the sweet woman leads an ill life with him. 2.02. 89 P
and truly master page is an honest man. 2.02.116 P
know how easy it is to be such an offender. 2.02.189 P
that i have purchas'd at an infinite rate, and 2.02.205 P
it, as to lay an amiable siege to the honesty of 2.02.234 P
page is an ass, a secure ass; 2.02.300 P
cheese, an irishman with my aqua–vitae bottle, 2.02.303 P
thou wouldst make an absolute courtier, and the 3.03. 62 P
of thy foot would give an excellent motion to 3.03. 63 P
ford, having an honest man to your husband, to 3.03.100 P
to take an ill advantage of his absence. 3.03.109 P
by gar, i see 'tis an honest woman. 3.03.222 P
first, an intolerable fright, to be detected 3.05.108 P
but he hath an abstract for the remembrance of 4.02. 62 P
a witch, a quean, an old cozening quean! 4.02.172 P
he send you both these letters at an instant? 4.04. 4 P
within a quarter of an hour. 4.04. 5 P
stand, | in him that was of late an heretic, 4.04. 9
and has been grievously peaten as an old oman. 4.04. 21 P
there is an old tale goes, that herne the hunter 4.04. 28
walk round about an oak, with great ragg'd horns 4.04. 31
that slender, though well landed, is an idiot; 4.04. 86
he'll speak like an anthropophaginian unto thee. 4.05. 9 P
there's an old woman, a fat woman, gone up into 4.05. 11 P
mine host, an old fat woman even now with me, 4.05. 24 P
my counterfeiting the action of an old woman, 4.05.118 P
i do begin to perceive that i am made an ass. 5.05.119 P
ay, and an ox too; both the proofs are extant. 5.05.120 P
had as lief be a list of an english kersey as be MM 1.02. 33 P
if i could speak so wisely under an arrest, i 1.02.131 P
slip, | even like an o'ergrown lion in a cave, 1.03. 22
by your renouncement an immortal spirit, | and 1.04. 35
his /givings–out were of an infinite distance 1.04. 54
law, | as mice by lions) hath pick'd out an act, 1.04. 64
rigor of the statute, | to make him an example. 1.04. 68
ay, sir; whom i thank heaven is an honest woman. 2.01. 72 P
because it is an open room and good for winter. 2.01.131 P
like an angry ape | plays such fantastic tricks 2.02.120
i do repent me as it is an evil, | and take the 2.03. 35
could i, with boot, change for an idle plume, 2.04. 11
proclaim an enshield beauty ten times louder 2.04. 80
or with an outstretch'd throat i'll tell the 2.04.153
for, like an ass whose back with ingots bows, 3.01. 26
age, | but as it were an after–dinner's sleep, 3.01. 33
where you shall be an everlasting leiger; 3.01. 58
only he hath made an assay of her virtue to 3.01.162 P
hath (like an impediment in the current) made it 3.01.242 P
your powder'd bawd, an unshunn'd consequence; 3.02. 60 P
sir, i was an inward of his. 3.02.130 P
or you imagine me too unhurtful an opposite. 3.02.165 P
exacting, | and perform an old contracting. 3.02.282
and your deliverance with an unpitied whipping, 4.02. 13 P
i have been an unlawful bawd time out of mind, 4.02. 15 P
of lord angelo, came not to an undoubtful proof. 4.02.137 P
having the hour limited, and an express command, 4.02.166 P
o, 'tis an accident that heaven provides! 4.03. 77
we proclaim it in an hour before his ent'ring, 4.04. 8 P
and by an eminent body that enforc'd | the law 4.04. 22
that angelo is an adulterous thief, | an 5.01. 40
an hypocrite, a virgin–violator, | is it not 5.01. 41
caracts, titles, forms, | be an arch–villain. 5.01. 57
an officer! 5.01.120
your sheep–biting face, and be hang'd an hour! 5.01.354 P
"an angelo for claudio, death for death!" 5.01.409
and must be buried but as an intent | that 5.01.452
it claudio was beheaded | at an unusual hour? 5.01.458
i find an apt remission in myself; 5.01.498
one all of luxury, an ass, a madman, | wherein 5.01.501
even now, even here, not half an hour since. ERR 2.02. 14
being, as it is, so plentiful an excrement? 2.02. 78 P
i am possess'd with an adulterate blot; 2.02.140
thou art an elm, my husband, i a vine, | whose 2.02.174
no, i am an ape. 2.02.198
if thou art chang'd to aught, 'tis to an ass. 2.02.199
'tis so, i am an ass, else it could never be 2.02.201
i think thou art an ass. 3.01. 15
would keep from my heels, and beware of an ass. 3.01. 18
thy face for a name, or thy name for an ass. 3.01. 47
go, get thee gone, fetch me an iron crow. 3.01. 84
ill deeds is doubled with an evil word. 3.02. 20
you, | to make it wander in an unknown field? 3.02. 38
i am an ass, i am a woman's man, and besides 3.02. 77 P
quarters, that's an ell and three quarters, will 3.02.110 P
that would refuse so fair an offer'd chain. 3.02.181
you know i gave it you half an hour since. 4.01. 65
with words that in an honest suit might move. 4.02. 14
a devil in an everlasting garment hath him; 4.02. 33
he not reason to turn back an hour in a day? 4.02. 62
sir, like an evil angel, and bid you forsake 4.03. 20 P
what, thou mean'st an officer? 4.03. 29 P
i brought you word an hour since that the bark 4.03. 37 P
angels of light, light is an effect of fire, and 4.03. 56 P
sensible in nothing but blows, and so is an ass. 4.04. 28 P
i am an ass indeed; 4.04. 29 P
the which | he did arrest me with an officer. 5.01.230
why, what an intricate impeach is this! 5.01.270
he hath an uncle here in messina will be very ADO 1.01. 18 P
trencherman, he hath an excellent stomach. 1.01. 52 P
lady, for you are like an honorable father. 1.01.112 P
do you question me, as an honest man should do, 1.01.166 P
thou wast ever an obstinate heretic in the 1.01.234 P
or hang my bugle in an invisible baldrick, all 1.01.241 P
i look for an earthquake too then. 1.01.273 P
matter enough in me for such an embassage, and 1.01.280 P
she may be the better prepar'd for an answer, if 1.02. 22 P
give you intelligence of an intended marriage. 1.03. 44 P
can see him but i am heart–burn'd an hour after. 2.01. 4 P
he were an excellent man that were made just in 2.01. 6 P
the one is too like an image and says nothing, 2.01. 8 P
the devil meet me like an old cuckold with horns 2.01. 44 P
to make an account of her life to a clod of 2.01. 62 P
graces will appear, and there's an end. 2.01.124 P
you may do the part of an honest man in it. 2.01.166 P
this is an accident of hourly proof, | which i 2.01.181
about your neck, like an usurer's chain? 2.01.189 P
why, that's spoken like an honest drovier; 2.01.194 P
an oak but with one green leaf on it would have 2.01.240 P
but civil count, civil as an orange, and 2.01.294 P
she were an excellent wife for benedick. 2.01.351 P
if we can do this, cupid is no longer an archer; 2.01.385 P
the purpose (like an honest man and a soldier), 2.03. 19 P
be sworn but love may transform me to an oyster, 2.03. 24 P
noble, or not i for an angel; 2.03. 33 P
of good discourse, an excellent musician, and 2.03. 34 P
and an ill singer, my lord. 2.03. 76 P
that she loves him with an enrag'd affection; 2.03.100 P
and he should, it were an alms to hang him. 2.03.158 P
she's an excellent sweet lady, and (out of all 2.03.159 P
be, when they hold one an opinion of another's 2.03.216 P
if black, why, nature, drawing of an antic, 3.01. 63
if low, an agot very vildly cut; 3.01. 65
know | how much an ill word may empoison liking. 3.01. 86
indeed he hath an excellent good name. 3.01. 98
why, you speak like an ancient and most quiet 3.03. 39 P
and it is an offense to stay a man against his 3.03. 81 P
i will owe thee an answer for that, and now 3.03.101 P
count sent me — they are an excellent perfume. 3.04. 63 P
an old man, sir, and his wits are not so blunt 3.05. 10 P
as any man living that is an old man and no 3.05. 14 P
an honest soul, i' faith, sir, by my troth he is 3.05. 38 P
not to knit my soul to an approved wanton. 4.01. 44
away, you are an ass, you are an ass. 4.02. 73 P
away, you are an ass, you are an ass. 4.02. 73 P
but, masters, remember that i am an ass; 4.02. 77 P
written down, yet forget not that i am an ass. 4.02. 78 P
and, which is more, an officer, and, which is 4.02. 80 P
o that i had been writ down an ass! 4.02. 87 P
as i am an honest man, he looks pale. 5.01.130 P
thus did she an hour together trans–shape thy 5.01.170 P
he is then a giant to an ape, but then is an ape 5.01.201 P
ape, but then is an ape a doctor to such a man. 5.01.202 P
time and place shall serve, that i am an ass. 5.01.256 P
invention, | hang her an epitaph upon her tomb, 5.01.284
i leave an arrant knave with your worship, which 5.01.321 P
rhyme to "lady" but "baby," an innocent rhyme; 5.02. 37 P
an old, an old instance, beatrice, that liv'd in 5.02. 76 P
an old, an old instance, beatrice, that liv'd in 5.02. 76 P
why, an hour in clamor and a quarter in rheum; 5.02. 82 P
your niece regards me with an eye of favor. 5.04. 22
and i do with an eye of love requite her. 5.04. 24
i'll hold my mind were she an ethiope. 5.04. 38
bull jove, sir, had an amiable low, | and some 5.04. 48
thou think i care for a satire or an epigram? 5.04.102 P
berowne is like an envious sneaping frost | that LLL 1.01.100
as we would hear an oracle. 1.01.216 P
these oaths and laws will prove an idle scorn. 1.01.309
and i tough signior as an appertinent title to 1.02. 16 P
i will praise an eel with the same praise. 1.02. 26 P
what? that an eel is ingenious? 1.02. 27 P
that an eel is quick. 1.02. 28 P
you may do it in an hour, sir. 1.02. 37 P
so tempted, and he had an excellent strength; 1.02.174 P

for he hath wit to make an ill shape good, | and 2.01. 59
mirth, | i never spent an hour's talk withal. 2.01. 68
hear me, dear lady: i have sworn an oath. 2.01. 97
being but the one half of an entire sum 2.01.130
not offended, | she is an heir of falconbridge. 2.01.205
his heart, like an agot, with your print 2.01.236
thou art an old love–monger and speakest 2.01.254
a horse to be embassador for an ass. 3.01. 52 P
page, it is an epilogue or discourse, to make 3.01. 81
for fame's sake, for praise, an outward part, 4.01. 32
shall i come upon thee with an old saying, that 4.01.119 P
he is only an animal, only sensible in the 4.02. 26 P
omne bene, say i, being of an old father's mind: 4.02. 32
will you hear an extemporal epitaph on the death 4.02. 50 P
of one sore i an hundred make by adding but one 4.02. 61
heaven's praise with such an earthly tongue." 4.02.118
so wise | to lose an oath to win a paradise?" 4.03. 71
"all hid, all hid," an old infant play. 4.03. 76
an amber–color'd raven was well noted. 4.03. 86
whom jove would swear | juno but an ethiop were, 4.03.116
and jove for your love would infringe an oath. 4.03.142
i | will praise a hand, a foot, a face, an eye, 4.03.182
young blood doth not obey an old decree. 4.03.213
she (an attending star) scarce seen a light. 4.03.227
o, who can give an oath? 4.03.246
learning is but an adjunct to ourself, | and 4.03.310
a lover's eyes will gaze an eagle blind. 4.03.331
offer'd by a child to an old man: 5.01. 62 P
thou disputes like an infant; go whip thy gig. 5.01. 66 P
and i will have an apology for that purpose. 5.01.135 P
an excellent device! 5.01.137 P
that is the way to make an offense gracious, 5.01.140 P
we will have, if this fadge not, an antic. 5.01.147 P
i thought to close mine eyes some half an hour; 5.02. 90
"for," quoth the king, "an angel shalt thou see; 5.02.103
the boy replied, "an angel is not evil; 5.02.105
take all and wean it, it may prove an ox. 5.02.250
here they stay'd an hour, | and talk'd apace; 5.02.368
speak for yourselves, my wit is at an end. 5.02.430
troth, | i never swore this lady such an oath. 5.02.451
there's an eye | wounds like a leaden sword. 5.02.480
a foolish mild man, an honest man, look you, and 5.02.581 P
well follow'd: judas was hang'd on an elder. 5.02.606 P
the face of an old roman coin, scarce seen. 5.02.613 P
therefore as he is, an ass, let him go. 5.02.625
i'll jest a twelvemonth in an hospital. 5.02.871
our wooing doth not end like an old play: 5.02.874
cross'd, | it stands as an edict in destiny. MND 1.01.151
hath | a lovely boy stolen from an indian king; 2.01. 22
crown | an odorous chaplet of sweet summer buds 2.01.110
two bosoms interchained with an oath, | so then 2.02. 49
i'll be an auditor, | an actor too perhaps, | if i 3.01. 79
auditor, | an actor too perhaps, if i see cause. 3.01. 80
you see an ass–head of your own, do you? 3.01.116 P
this is to make an ass of me, to fright me, if 3.01.120 P
so, | that thou shalt like an aery spirit go. 3.01.161
take, | an ass's nole i fixed on his head. 3.02. 17
titania wak'd, and straightway lov'd an ass. 3.02. 34
could not a worm, an adder, do so much? 3.02. 71
an adder did it! 3.02. 72
seeming parted, | but yet an union in partition, 3.02.210
you would not make me such an argument. 3.02.242
that i have 'nointed an athenian's eyes; 3.02.351
i have an exposition of sleep come upon me. 4.01. 39 P
methought i was enamor'd of an ass. 4.01. 77
as the remembrance of an idle gaud | which in my 4.01.167
man is but an ass, if he go about /t' expound 4.01.206 P
to be sung | by an athenian eunuch to the harp." 5.01. 45
that is an old device; 5.01. 50
no die, but an ace, for him; for he is but one. 5.01.307 P
less than an ace, man; 5.01.308 P
he might yet recover, and yet prove an ass. 5.01.311 P
and, as i am an honest puck, | if we have 5.01.431
broth | would blow me to an ague when i thought MV 1.01. 23
with purpose to be dress'd in an opinion | of 1.01. 91
gratiano speaks an infinite deal of nothing, 1.01.114 P
he hath an argosy bound to tripolis, another to 1.03. 18 P
an evil soul producing holy witness | is like a 1.03. 99
the forfeit | be nominated for an equal pound 1.03.149
in the fearful guard | of an unthrifty knave, 1.03.176
friend launcelot, being an honest man's son" — 2.02. 15 P
man's son" — or rather an honest woman's son, 2.02. 16 P
i say't, is an honest exceeding poor man and, 2.02. 52 P
i hope, an old man, shall frutify unto you — 2.02.134 P
us at my lodging, and return | all in an hour. 2.04. 3
why, 'tis an office of discovery, love, | and i 2.06. 43
and weigh thy value with an even hand. 2.07. 25
a coin that bears the figure of an angel 2.07. 56
but here an angel in a golden bed | lies all 2.07. 58
none presume | to wear an undeserved dignity. 2.09. 40
have not seen | so likely an embassador of love. 2.09. 92
if my gossip report be an honest woman of her 3.01. 7 P
hath an argosy cast away, coming from tripolis. 3.01.100 P
go, tubal, fee me an officer; 3.01.126 P
the beauteous scarf | veiling an indian beauty; 3.02. 99
is an unlesson'd girl, unschool'd, unpractic'd, 3.02.159
you lie by portia's side | with an unquiet soul. 3.02.306
i have sworn an oath that i will have my bond. 3.03. 5
whose souls do bear an egall yoke of love, 3.04. 13
but if she be less than an honest woman, she is 3.05. 41 P
show the whole wealth of thy wit in an instant? 3.05. 56 P
planted in his memory | an army of good words, 3.05. 67
meet | the lord bassanio live an upright life, 3.05. 74
answer | a stony adversary, an inhuman wretch, 4.01. 4
glancing an eye of pity on his losses, | that 4.01. 27
of kings, | it is an attribute to god himself; 4.01.195
and many an error by the same example | will 4.01.221
an oath, an oath, i have an oath in heaven! 4.01.228
an oath, an oath, i have an oath in heaven! 4.01.228
an oath, an oath, i have an oath in heaven! 4.01.228
eye and wrinkled brow | an age of poverty; 4.01.271
the wish would make else an unquiet house. 4.01.294
o jew! an upright judge, a learned judge! 4.01.323
of venice, | if it be proved against an alien, 4.01.349
and with an unthrift love did run from venice, 5.01. 16
but in his motion like an angel sings, | still 5.01. 61
as doth an inland brook | into the main of 5.01. 96
double self, | and there's an oath of credit. 5.01.246
i never more will break an oath with thee. 5.01.248
that differs not from the stalling of an ox? AYL 1.01. 10 P
an envious emulator of every man's good parts, a 1.01.143 P
i hope i shall see an end of him; 1.01.164 P
there comes an old man and his three sons — 1.02.118 P
i could match this beginning with an old tale. 1.02.120 P
rose at an instant, learn'd, play'd, eat 1.03. 74
under an oak whose antique root peeps out | upon 2.01. 31
here, a young man and an old in solemn talk. 2.04. 20 P
'tis but an hour ago since it was nine, | and 2.07. 24
laugh sans intermission | an hour by his dial. 2.07. 33
there is an old poor man, | who after me hath 2.07.129
i should not seek an absent argument | of my 3.01. 3
make an extent upon his house and lands. 3.01. 17
damn'd, like an ill–roasted egg all on one side. 3.02. 37 P
shepherd, let us make an honorable retreat, 3.02.160 P
since pythagoras' time, that i was an irish rat, 3.02.177 P
heels, and your heart, both in an instant. 3.02.213 P
but indeed an old religious uncle of mine taught 3.02.343 P
me to speak, who was in his youth an inland man, 3.02.345 P
an unquestionable spirit, which you have not; 3.02.374 P
slut were to put good meat into an unclean dish. 3.03. 36 P
an excellent color. 3.04. 11 P
rosalind, i come within an hour of my promise. 4.01. 42 P
break an hour's promise in love! 4.01. 44 P
more new–fangled than an ape, more giddy in my 4.01.152 P
my affection hath an unknown bottom, like the 4.01.208 P
was writing of it, | it bears an angry tenure. 4.03. 11
what, to make thee an instrument, and play false 4.03. 68 P
if that an eye may profit by a tongue, | then 4.03. 83
left a promise to return again | within an hour, 4.03.100
object did present itself | under an old oak, 4.03.104
a poor virgin, sir, an ill–favor'd thing, sir, 5.04. 57 P
and you may avoid that too, with an if. 5.04. 98 P
one of them thought but of an if, as, "if you 5.04.101 P
where, meeting with an old religious man, 5.04.160
i'll not budge an inch, boy; SHR in.1. 14 P
tears, | an onion will do well for such a shift, in.1. 126
checks | as ovid be an outcast quite abjur'd. 1.01. 33
and marry him to a puppet or an aglet–baby, or 1.02. 79 P
or an old trot with ne'er a tooth in her head, 1.02. 79 P
minola, | an affable and courteous gentleman. 1.02. 98
a proper stripling, and an amorous! 1.02.143
o this woodcock, what an ass it is! 1.02.160
i know she is an irksome brawling scold. 1.02.187
rage like an angry boar chafed with sweat? 1.02.202
and, for an entrance to my entertainment, | i do 2.01. 54
have, besides an argosy | that now is lying in 2.01.374
what, have i chok'd you with an argosy? 2.01.376
an old italian fox is not so kind, my boy. 2.01.403
and when in music we have spent an hour, | your 3.01. 7
for such an injury would vex a very saint, 3.02. 28
is coming in a new hat and an old jerkin; 3.02. 44 P
an old rusty sword ta'en out of the town armory, 3.02. 46 P
with an old mothy saddle and stirrups of no 3.02. 49 P
an old hat, and the humor of forty fancies 3.02. 68 P
estate, | an eye–sore to our solemn festival! 3.02.101
and their garters of an indifferent knit; 4.01. 92 P
i spied | an ancient angel coming down the hill, 4.02. 61
as much as an apple doth an oyster, and all one. 4.02.101 P
as much as an apple doth an oyster, and all one. 4.02.101 P
what, up and down carv'd like an apple–tart? 4.03. 89
a wench married in an afternoon as she went to 4.04.100 P
call forth an officer. 5.01. 91 P
spoke like an officer. ha' to thee, lad! 5.02. 37
an hasty–witted body | would say your head and 5.02. 40
is that an answer? 5.02. 83
the fouler fortune mine, and there an end. 5.02. 98
life, | an aweful rule, and right supremacy; 5.02.109
for where an unclean mind carries virtuous AWW 1.01. 41 P
my lord, | 'tis an unseason'd courtier; 1.01. 71
virginity, like an old courtier, wears her cap 1.01.156 P
a friend, | a phoenix, captain, and an enemy, 1.01.168
lend me an arm. 1.02. 73
but for every blazing star or at an earthquake, 1.03. 87 P
had you not lately an intent — speak truly — 1.03.218
/with his cicatrice, an emblem of war, here on 2.01. 43 P
yourself within the list of too cold an adieu. 2.01. 52 P
of heaven, not me, make an experiment. 2.01.154
i am not an imposture that proclaim | myself 2.01.155
speak | his powerful sound within an organ weak; 2.01.176
but for me, i have an answer will serve all men. 2.02. 13 P
as ten groats is for the hand of an attorney, as 2.02. 21 P
an answer of such fitness for all questions? 2.02. 28 P
it must be an answer of most monstrous size that 2.02. 32 P
we should submit ourselves to an unknown fear. 2.03. 5 P
of a heavenly effect in an earthly actor." 2.03. 24 P
but if thou be'st not an ass, i am a youth of 2.03.100 P
an idle lord, i swear. 2.05. 49 P
but like a common and an outward man | that the 3.01. 11
and i begin to love, as an old man loves money, 3.02. 16 P
notable coward, an infinite and endless liar, an 3.06. 9 P
and endless liar, an hourly promise–breaker, the 3.06. 10 P
but return with an invention and clap upon you 3.06. 97 P
appoints him an encounter; 3.07. 32
us, whom we must produce for an interpreter. 4.01. 6 P
it is an honor 'longing to our house, 4.02. 42
remain there but an hour, nor speak to me. 4.02. 58
i have deliv'red it an hour since. 4.03. 3 P
i hear there is an overture of peace. 4.03. 39 P
length a–piece, by an abstract of success. 4.03. 86 P
that is an advertisement to a proper maid in 4.03.212 P
he will steal, sir, an egg out of a cloister. 4.03.250 P
he has every thing that an honest man should not 4.03.259 P
what an honest man should have, he has nothing. 4.03.260 P
would have suspected an ambush where i was taken 4.03.302 P
much shame, you might begin an impudent nation. 4.03.328 P
that every braggart shall be found an ass. 4.03.336
sir, 'a has an english /name, but his fisnomy is 4.05. 39 P
a shrewd knave and an unhappy. 4.05. 63 P
looks in her | with an importing visage, and she 5.03.136
but loath am to produce | so bad an instrument. 5.03.202
my master hath been an honorable gentleman. 5.03.239 P
what an equivocal companion is this! 5.03.250 P
this woman's an easy glove, my lord, she goes 5.03.277 P
thou shalt present me as an eunuch to him, | it TN 1.02. 56
i am sure care's an enemy to life. 1.03. 2 P
i am not such an ass but i can keep my hand dry. 1.03. 74 P
wit than a christian or an ordinary man has; 1.03. 84 P
then hadst thou had an excellent head of hair. 1.03. 95 P
and yet i will not compare with an old man. 1.03.119 P
the other day with an ordinary fool that has no 1.05. 85 P
there is no slander in an allow'd fool, though 1.05. 94 P
peascod, or a codling when 'tis almost an apple. 1.05.158 P
with an invisible and subtle stealth | to creep 1.05.297
him myself and a sister, both born in an hour. 2.01. 19 P
i hate it as an unfill'd can. 2.03. 6 P
by my troth, the fool has an excellent breast. 2.03. 19 P
do ye make an alehouse of my lady's house, that 2.03. 88 P
if i do not gull him into an ayword, and make 2.03.135 P
but a time–pleaser, an affection'd ass, that 2.03.148 P
and your horse now would make him an ass. 2.03.168 P
still the woman take | an elder than herself, so 2.04. 30
here's an overweening rogue! 2.05. 29 P
seven of my people, with an obedient start, make 2.05. 58 P
my familiar smile with an austere regard of 2.05. 66 P
'slight! will you make an ass o' me? 3.02. 13 P
you will hang like an icicle on a dutchman's 3.02. 27 P
and by all means stir on the youth to an answer. 3.02. 59 P
your purse–bearer and leave you | for an hour. 3.03. 48
consider, he's an enemy to mankind. 3.04. 98 P
i could condemn it as an improbable fiction. 3.04.128 P
nay, if you be an undertaker, i am for you. 3.04.318 P
but o, how vild an idol proves this god! 3.04.365
by my troth, thou hast an open hand. 4.01. 21 P
i'll have an action of battery against him, if 4.01. 34 P
nay then i must have an ounce or two of this 4.01. 43 P
but to be said an honest man and a good 4.02. 8 P
sir, they praise me and make an ass of me. 5.01. 17 P
now my foes tell me plainly i am an ass; 5.01. 18 P
to his use | not half an hour before. 5.01. 92
o, he's drunk, sir toby, an hour agone; 5.01.198 P
an ass–head and a coxcomb and a knave, a 5.01.206 P
an apple, cleft in two, is not more twin | than 5.01.223
and, acting this in an obedient hope, | why have 5.01.340
rooted betwixt them then such an affection, WT 1.01. 23 P
you have an unspeakable comfort of your young 1.01. 34 P
furlongs ere | with spur we heat an acre. 1.02. 96
it has an elder sister, | or i mistake you. 1.02. 98
go play, mamillius, thou'rt an honest man. 1.02.211
as he had seen't or been an instrument | to vice 1.02.415
my best blood turn | to an infected jelly, and 1.02.418
to grieve it should be) | she's an adultress. 2.01. 78
i have said | she's an adultress, i have said 2.01. 88
heavens look | with an aspect more favorable. 2.01.107
(for in an act of this importance 'twere | most 2.01.181
it is an heretic that makes the fire, | not she 2.03.115
you sent to th' oracle are come | an hour since. 2.03.195
even since it could speak, from an infant, 3.02. 70
know of it | is that camillo was an honest man; 3.02. 74
and the king shall live without an heir, if that 3.02.135 P
but to make an end of the ship, to see how the 3.03. 97 P
neighbors, is grown into an unspeakable estate. 4.02. 40 P
doth set my pugging tooth an edge, | for a quart 4.03. 7
he hath been since an ape–bearer, then a 4.03. 95 P
there is an art which in their piedness shares 4.04. 87
adds to nature, is an art | that nature makes. 4.04. 91
this is an art | which does mend nature — 4.04. 95
do plainly give you out an unstain'd shepherd, 4.04.149
thou talkest of an admirable conceited fellow. 4.04.202 P
we'll make an instrument of this; 4.04.624
outside of thy poverty we must make an exchange; 4.04.633 P
to have an open ear, a quick eye, and a nimble 4.04.671 P
what an exchange had this been, without boot! 4.04.674 P
had been the dearer by i know how much an ounce. 4.04.705 P
an old sheep–whistling rogue, a ram–tender, to 4.04.776 P
hang him, he'll be made an example. 4.04.817 P
that king leontes shall not have an heir | till 5.01. 39
not for issue, | the crown will find an heir. 5.01. 47
though fortune, visible an enemy, | should chase 5.01.216
which is call'd true, is so like an old tale, 5.02. 28 P
like an old tale still, which will have matter 5.02. 61 P
though credit be asleep and not an ear open: 5.02. 62 P
of dolor to another, she did (with an "alas!"), 5.02. 88 P
every wink of an eye some new grace will be born 5.02.110 P
still methinks | there is an air comes from her. 5.03. 78
be magic, let it be an art | lawful as eating. 5.03.110
you, should be hooted at | like an old tale; 5.03.117
i, an old turtle, | will wing me to some 5.03.132
his mind) to find thee | an honorable husband. 5.03.143
an honorable conduct let him have. JN 1.01. 29
and once dispatch'd him in an embassy | to 1.01. 99
and then comes answer like an absey book: 1.01.196
stay for an answer to your embassy, | lest 2.01. 44
an /ate, stirring him to blood and strife; 2.01. 63
of him | as great alcides' /shows upon an ass. 2.01.144
i would set an ox–head to your lion's hide, 2.01.292
much work for tears in many an english mother, 2.01.303
to charge me to an answer, as the pope. 3.01.151
doth revolt | from his allegiance to an heretic, 3.01.175
so mak'st thou faith an enemy to faith, | and 3.01.263
and mak'st an oath the surety for thy truth 3.01.282
oath the surety for thy truth | against an oath; 3.01.283
pains | will bring this labor to an happy end. 3.02. 10
a ghost, | as dim and meagre as an ague's fit, 3.04. 85
the misplac'd john should entertain an hour, 3.04.133
a sceptre snatch'd with an unruly hand | must be 3.04.135
and if an angel should have come to me | and 4.01. 68
done, | this act is as an ancient tale new told, 4.02. 18
that such an army could be drawn in france, 4.02.118
or turn'd an eye of doubt upon my face, | as bid 4.02.233
of mine | is yet a maiden and an innocent hand, 4.02.252
mind | than to be butcher of an innocent child. 4.02.259
defend | my innocent life against an emperor. 4.03. 89
'tis not an hour since i left him well. 4.03.104
an empty casket, where the jewel of life | by 5.01. 40
we swear | a voluntary zeal and an unurg'd faith 5.02. 10
/were born to see so sad an hour as this, 5.02. 26
thy bosom | doth make an earthquake of nobility. 5.02. 42
a lady's tears, | being an ordinary inundation; 5.02. 48
and even there, methinks an angel spake. 5.02. 64
crow, | thinking this voice an armed englishman; 5.02.145
arms, | and like an eagle o'er his aery tow'rs, 5.02.149
but start | an echo with the clamor of thy drum, 5.02.168
for that my grandsire was an englishman, 5.04. 42
said | king john did fly an hour or two before 5.05. 17

you breathe these dead news in as dead an ear. 5.07. 65
who half an hour since came from the dolphin, 5.07. 83
good hap, | add an immortal title to your crown! R2 1.01. 24
foe, | once did i lay an ambush for your life, 1.01.137
never lift | an angry arm against his minister. 1.02. 41
me no more | than an unstringed viol or a harp, 1.03.162
return again, and take an oath with thee. 1.03.178
it so, | which finds it an enforced pilgrimage. 1.03.264
off goes his bonnet to an oyster–wench, | a 1.04. 31
fool, | presuming on an ague's privilege, 2.01.116
did not the one deserve to have an heir? 2.01.193
and driven into despair an enemy's hope, | who 2.02. 47
an hour before i came, the duchess died. 2.02. 97
"grace" | in an ungracious mouth is but profane. 2.03. 89
look on my wrongs with an indifferent eye. 2.03.116
an offer, uncle, that we will accept, | but we 2.03.162
can wash the balm off from an anointed king; 3.02. 55
like an unseasonable stormy day, | which makes 3.02.106
overblown, | an easy task it is to win our own. 3.02.191
my gay apparel for an almsman's gown, | my 3.03.149
a little little grave, an obscure grave — | or 3.03.154
and like an executioner | cut off the heads of 3.04. 33
refuse | the offer of an hundred thousand crowns 4.01. 16
when triumph is become an alehouse guest? 5.01. 15
my guilt be on my head, and there an end. 5.01. 69
had not an ear to hear my true time broke. 5.05. 48
a horse, | and yet i bear a burthen like an ass, 5.05. 93
the edge of war, like an ill–sheathed knife, 1H4 1.01. 17
and is not this an honorable spoil? 1.01. 74
will serve to be prologue to an egg and butter. 1.02. 21 P
now in as low an ebb as the foot of the ladder, 1.02. 37 P
or an old lion, or a lover's lute. 1.02. 75 P
an old lord of the council rated me the other 1.02. 83 P
on earth | was parmaciti for an inward bruise, 1.03. 58
not his report | come current for an accusation 1.03. 68
he did confound the best part of an hour | in 1.03.100
devil alone | as owen glendower for an enemy. 1.03.117
and on my face he turn'd an eye of death, 1.03.143
power | did gage them both in an unjust behalf 1.03.173
by heaven, methinks it were an easy leap, | to 1.03.201
hast thou never an eye in thy head? 2.01. 28 P
each takes his fellow for an officer. 2.02.107
for the counterpoise of so great an opposition." 2.03. 13 P
an excellent plot, very good friends. 2.03. 19 P
an infidel! 2.03. 29 P
a dish of skim–milk with so honorable an action! 2.03. 33 P
he is, my lord, an hour ago. 2.03. 66
not an inch further. 2.03.114
so good a proficient in one quarter of an hour, 2.04. 18 P
even now into my hand by an under–skinker, one 2.04. 24 P
he, and answers, "some fourteen," an hour after; 2.04.108 P
man of them, or i am a jew else, an ebrew jew. 2.04.179 P
an old man. 2.04.293 P
hal, i was not an eagle's talent in the waist, i 2.04.330 P
if thou love me, practice an answer. 2.04.375 P
haunts thee in the likeness of an old fat man, a 2.04.448 P
then many an old host that i know is damn'd. 2.04.472 P
to the harp | many an english ditty lovely well, 3.01.122
and that would set my teeth nothing an edge, 3.01.131
and art almost an alien to the hearts | of all 3.02. 34
not an eye | but is a–weary of thy common sight, 3.02. 87
hangs about me like an old lady's loose gown; 3.03. 3 P
i am wither'd like an old apple–john. 3.03. 4 P
not above once in a quarter — of an hour, paid 3.03. 17 P
think thou hadst been an ignis fatuus or a ball 3.03. 39 P
perpetual triumph, an everlasting bonfire light! 3.03. 41 P
a true woman, holland of eight shillings an ell. 3.03. 72 P
i love him well, he is an honest man. 3.03. 93 P
i am an honest man's wife, and, setting thy 3.03.119 P
what beast? why, an otter. 3.03.125 P
an otter, sir john, why an otter? 3.03.126 P
an otter, sir john, why an otter? 3.03.126 P
thou art an unjust man in saying so. 3.03.129 P
charge an honest woman with picking thy pocket! 3.03.155 P
and think how such an apprehension | may turn 4.01. 66
as if an angel /dropp'd down from the clouds 4.01.108
this bottle makes an angel. 4.02. 6 P
dishonorable ragged than an old feaz'd ancient: 4.02. 31 P
quality, | but stand against us like an enemy. 4.03. 37
weak | to wage an instant trial with the king. 4.04. 20
light, | and be no more an exhal'd meteor, | a 5.01. 19
or an arm? 5.01.132 P
of blood, | and an adopted name of privilege, 5.02. 18
point, | still ending at the arrival of an hour. 5.02. 84
honor comes unlook'd for, and there's an end. 5.03. 61 P
i did look for | of such an ungrown warrior. 5.04. 23
but we rose both at an instant and fought a long 5.04.147 P
morton, | tell thou an earl his divination lies. 2H4 1.01. 88
i was never mann'd with an agot till now, but i 1.02. 16 P
why, sir, did i say you were an honest man? 1.02. 80 P
if you say i am any other than an honest man. 1.02. 86 P
have yet some smack of an ague in you, some 1.02. 98 P
beard, a decreasing leg, an increasing belly? 1.02.182 P
if ye will needs say i am an old man, you should 1.02.216 P
bosom burns | with an incensed fire of injuries. 1.03. 14
like /one that draws the model of an house 1.03. 58
you, he's an infinitive thing upon my score. 2.01. 24 P
a woman should be made an ass and a beast, to 2.01. 37 P
marry, if thou wert an honest man, thyself and 2.01. 85 P
faith, and let it be an excellent good thing. 2.02. 33 P
every man would think me an hypocrite indeed. 2.02. 59 P
knowest sir john cannot endure an apple–john. 2.04. 2 P
be old utis, it will be an excellent stratagem. 2.04. 20 P
now you are in an excellent good temperality. 2.04. 23 P
civil, for," said he, "you are in an ill name." 2.04. 90 P
says he, "you are an honest woman, and well 2.04. 92 P
in very truth, do i, and 'twere an aspen leaf. 2.04.108 P
which was an excellent good word before it was 2.04.149 P
that show a weak mind and an able body, for the 2.04.251 P
but an honester and truer–hearted man — well, 2.04.383 P
to the wet //sea–boy in an hour so rude, | and 3.01. 27
an early stirrer, by the rood! 3.02. 2 P
be accommodated — which is an excellent thing. 3.02. 80 P
make as many holes in an enemy's battle as thou 3.02.154 P
thrust him and all his apparel into an eel–skin. 3.02.326 P
let time shape, and there an end. 3.02.332 P
his friends | that, plucking to unfix an enemy, 4.01.206
like an offensive wife | that hath enrag'd him 4.01.208
text | /than now to see you here an iron man, 4.02. 8
do you think me a swallow, an arrow, or a bullet 4.03. 32 P
heart | to stab at half an hour of my life. 4.05.108
what, canst thou not forbear me half an hour? 4.05.109
it, as with an enemy | that had before my face 4.05.166
but as an honor snatch'd with boist'rous hand, 4.05.191
that visor is an arrant knave, on my knowledge. 5.01. 41 P
an honest man, sir, is able to speak for himself 5.01. 45 P
quarter bear out a knave against an honest man, 5.01. 49 P
court, | not amurath an amurath succeeds, | but 5.02. 48
whereon (as an offender to your father) | i gave 5.02. 81
where, in an arbor, we will eat a last year's 5.03. 1 P
why then say an old man can do somewhat. 5.03. 78 P
which if like an ill venture it come unluckily ep 11 P
which was never seen in such an assembly. ep 25 P
scaffold to bring forth | so great an object. H5 pr 11
of many years | into an hour–glass: pr 31
consideration like an angel came | and whipt th' 1.01. 28
with an inward wish | you would desire the king 1.01. 39
for i have made an offer to his majesty, | upon 1.01. 75
to which is fixed, as an aim or butt, 1.02.186
or lay these bones in an unworthy urn, 1.02.228
and there's an end. 2.01. 10 P
i have an humor to knock you indifferently well. 2.01. 55 P
an oath of mickle might, and fury shall abate. 2.01. 66
sword is an oath, and oaths must have their 2.01.101
join'd with an enemy proclaim'd, and from his 2.02.168
he'll call you to so hot an answer of it | that 2.04.123
would i were in an alehouse in london, i would 3.02. 12 P
is altogether directed by an irishman, a very 3.02. 66 P
by cheshu, he is an ass, as in the world; 3.02. 70 P
up the town, so chrish save me law, in an hour! 3.02. 92 P
and there is an end. 3.02.141 P
our expectation hath this day an end. 3.03. 44
there is an aunchient lieutenant there at the 3.06. 12 P
fortune is an excellent moral. 3.06. 38 P
why, this is an arrant counterfeit rascal, i 3.06. 61 P
not good to bruise an injury till it were full 3.06.122 P
so much | unto an enemy of craft and vantage, 3.06.144
you have an excellent armor; 3.07. 3 P
no note | how dread an army hath enrounded him; 4.pr. 36
heart of gold, | a lad of life, an imp of fame, 4.01. 45
if the enemy is an ass and a fool, and a prating 4.01. 77 P
look you, be an ass and a fool, and a prating 4.01. 79 P
sin to think that, making god so free an offer, 4.01.183 P
that's a perilous shot out of an elder–gun, that 4.01.198 P
i would not lose so great an honor | as one man 4.03. 31
know, to this hour is an honorable badge of the 4.07.101 P
god, so long as your majesty is an honest man. 4.07.114 P
an englishman? 4.07.124 P
a friend to alanson, and an enemy to our person. 4.07.157 P
gunpowder, | and quickly will return an injury. 4.07.181
an arrant traitor as any's in the universal 4.08. 9 P
saving your majesty's manhood, what an arrant, 4.08. 34 P
and wear it for an honor in thy cap | till i do 4.08. 59
will you mock at an ancient tradition, /begun 5.01. 70 P
tradition, /begun upon an honorable respect, and 5.01. 71 P
he could not therefore handle an english cudgel. 5.01. 77 P
an angel is like you, kate, and you are like an 5.02.109 P
is like you, kate, and you are like an angel. 5.02.110 P
with a stubborn outside, with an aspect of iron, 5.02.227 P
of your heart with the looks of an empress, take 5.02.236 P
none do you like but an effeminate prince, 1H6 1.01. 35
an army have i muster'd in my thoughts, 1.01.101
thou art an amazon, | and fightest with the 1.02.104
thou with an eagle art inspired then. 1.02.141
in an urn more precious | than the rich–jewell'd 1.06. 24
of death, | nestor–like aged, in an age of care, 2.05. 6
levied an army, weening to redeem | and have 2.05. 88
as an outlaw in a castle keeps | and useth it to 3.01. 47
an uproar, i dare warrant, | begun through 3.01. 74
to be disgraced by an inkhorn mate, | we and our 3.01. 99
france, | and not have title of an earldom here. 3.03. 26
man, | of an invincible unconquer'd spirit! 4.02. 32
an earl i am, and suffolk am i call'd. 5.03. 53
her father is no better than an earl, | although 5.05. 37
hell, | an age of discord and continual strife? 5.05. 63
nay more, an enemy unto you all, | and no great 2H6 1.01.149
had henry got an empire by his marriage, | and 1.01.153
this was nothing but an argument | that he that 1.02. 32
that he was, and that the king was an usurper. 1.03. 31 P
more like an empress than duke humphrey's wife. 1.03. 78
crown | and that your majesty was an usurper. 1.03.185
do not cast away an honest man for a villain's 1.03.202 P
reported to be a woman of an invincible spirit; 1.04. 7 P
beldam, i think we watch'd you at an inch. 1.04. 42
but william of hatfield died without an heir. 2.02. 33
to prove him a knave and myself an honest man; 2.03. 87 P
day, | he knits his brow and shows an angry eye, 3.01. 15
for i should melt at an offender's tears, | and 3.01.126
an empty eagle were set | to guard the chicken 3.01.248
a fox, | by nature prov'd an enemy to the flock, 3.01.258
done, | to send me packing with an host of men: 3.01.342
it, | and make my image but an alehouse sign. 3.02. 81
like an angry hive of bees | that want their 3.02.125
to drain | upon his face an ocean of salt tears, 3.02.143
friend, | and 'tis well seen he found an enemy. 3.02.185
fresh, | and sees fast by a butcher with an axe, 3.02.189
nor cease to be an arrogant controller, | though 3.02.205
an answer from the king, my lord of salisbury! 3.02.270
to show how quaint an orator you are; 3.02.274
an answer from the king, or we will all break in 3.02.278
mine hair be fix'd an end, as one distract; 3.02.318
or like an overcharged gun, recoil, | and turns 3.02.331
but wherefore grieve i at an hour's poor loss, 3.02.381
i'll have an iris that shall find thee out. 3.02.407
then is sin struck down like an ox, and 4.02. 26 P
he was an honest man, and a good bricklayer. 4.02. 40 P
therefore am i of an honorable house. 4.02. 49 P
that of the skin of an innocent lamb should be 4.02. 79 P
gelded the commonwealth, and made it an eunuch; 4.02.166 P
with the tongue of an enemy be a good counsellor 4.02.171 P
there's an army gather'd together in smithfield. 4.06. 11 P
the fift hales them to an hundred mischiefs, and 4.08. 57 P
was ever king that joy'd an earthly throne | and 4.09. 1
but i'll make thee eat iron like an ostridge, 4.10. 28 P
that alexander iden, an esquire of kent, | took 4.10. 43
,and not to grace an aweful princely sceptre. 5.01. 98
nay, do not fright us with an angry look. 5.01.126
thou dispense with heaven for such an oath? 5.01.181
meet i an infant of the house of york, | into as 5.02. 57
for underneath an alehouse' paltry sign, | the 5.02. 67
tell me, may not a king adopt an heir? 3H6 1.01.135
conditionally that here thou take an oath | to 1.01.196
and like an empty eagle | tire on the flesh of 1.01.268
i took an oath that he should quietly reign. 1.02. 15
an oath is of no moment, being not took | before 1.02. 22
a sceptre, or an earthly sepulchre!" 1.04. 17
and made an evening at the noontide prick. 1.04. 34
in thy sex | to triumph like an amazonian trull 1.04.114
yet not so wealthy as an english yeoman. 1.04.123
for i have bought it with an hundred blows. 2.05. 81
gust, | command an argosy to stem the waves. 2.06. 36
what, not an oath? 2.06. 77
when clifford cannot spare his friends an oath. 2.06. 78
but did you never swear and break an oath? 3.01. 72
no, never such an oath, nor will not now. 3.01. 73
an easy task, 'tis but to love a king. 3.02. 53
then no, my lord. my suit is at an end. 3.02. 81
shrub, | to make an envious mountain on my back, 3.02.157
to shape my legs of an unequal size, | to 3.02.159
or an unlick'd bear–whelp | that carries no 3.02.161
that this his love was an /eternal plant, 3.03.124
hath pawn'd an open hand in sign of love; 4.02. 9
but if an humble prayer may prevail, | i then 4.06. 7
adjudg'd an olive branch and laurel crown, | as 4.06. 34
thus far our fortune keeps an upward course, 5.03. 1
the thief doth fear each bush an officer. 5.06. 12
think'st thou i am an executioner? 5.06. 30
executing, | why then thou art an executioner. 5.06. 33
and many an old man's sigh and many a widow's, 5.06. 39
and many an orphan's water–standing eye — | men 5.06. 40
the owl shriek'd at thy birth, an evil sign; 5.06. 44
hope, | to wit, an indigested and deformed lump, 5.06. 51
nor made to court an amorous looking–glass; R3 1.01. 15
heard you not what an humble suppliant | lord 1.01. 74
o, he hath kept an evil diet long, | and 1.01.139
time | my manly eyes did scorn an humble tear; 1.02.164
been | an earnest advocate to plead for him. 1.03. 86
my hair doth stand an end to hear her curses. 1.03.303
then came wand'ring by | a shadow like an angel, 1.04. 53
glories, | an outward honor for an inward toil, 1.04. 79
glories, | an outward honor for an inward toil, 1.04. 79
i every day expect an embassage | from my 2.01. 3
my soul, | and to myself become an enemy. 2.02. 37
to make an act of tragic violence. 2.02. 39
she for an edward weeps, and so do i; 2.02. 82
what an indirect and peevish course | is this of 3.01. 31
because that i am little, like an ape, | he 3.01.130
is it not an easy matter | to make william lord 3.01.161
ah ha, my lord, this prince is not an edward! 3.07. 71
i had an edward, till a richard kill'd him; 4.04. 40
thou hadst an edward, till a richard kill'd him; 4.04. 42
an honest tale speeds best being plainly told. 4.04.358
if thou didst fear to break an oath with him, 4.04.378
if thou hadst fear'd to break an oath by him, 4.04.381
he should have brav'd the east an hour ago. 5.03.279
a man, | daring an opposite to every danger. 5.04. 3
will leave us never an understanding friend. H8 pr 22
an untimely ague | stay'd me a prisoner in my 1.01. 4
or else you suffer | too hard an exclamation. 1.02. 52
as a performance | does an irresolute purpose. 1.02.209
to think an english courtier may be wise | and 1.03. 22
now | an honest country lord, as i am, beaten 1.03. 44
his plain–song | and have an hour of hearing, 1.03. 46
and entreat | an hour of revels with 'em. 1.04. 72
stirr'd | with such an agony he sweat extremely, 2.01. 33
heaven has an end in all; 2.01.124
yet i can give you inkling | of an ensuing evil, 2.01.141
is this an hour for temporal affairs? 2.02. 72
i would your grace would give us but an hour 2.02. 79
believe me, there's an ill opinion spread then, 2.02.124
would it not grieve an able man to leave | so 2.02.141
little england | you'ld venture an emballing. 2.03. 47
there was a lady once ('tis an old story) | that 2.03. 90
of an excellent | and unmatch'd wit and judgment 2.04. 46
mean while must be an earnest motion | made to 2.04.234
but how to make ye suddenly an answer | in such 3.01. 70
yet will i add an honor — a great patience. 3.01.137
and we shall see him | for it an archbishop. 3.02. 74
there is sprung up | an heretic, an arch–one, 3.02.102
there is sprung up | an heretic, an arch–one, 3.02.102
forsooth, an inventory, thus importing | the 3.02.124
sure in that | i deem you an ill husband, and am 3.02.142
out of holy pity, | absolv'd him with an axe. 3.02.264
there take an inventory of all i have, | to the 3.02.451
sir, as i have a soul, she is an angel; 4.01. 44
down | to rest a while, some half an hour or so, 4.01. 66
an old man, broken with the storms of state, 4.02. 21
he was a man | of an unbounded stomach, ever 4.02. 34
though from an humble stock, undoubtedly | was 4.02. 49
but such an honest chronicler as griffith. 4.02. 72
how pale she looks, | and of an earthy cold! 4.02. 98
to the gladding of | your highness with an heir! 5.01. 72
give her an hundred marks. i'll to the queen. 5.01.170
an hundred marks? 5.01.171
an ordinary groom is for such payment. 5.01.172
and has done half an hour, to know your 5.02. 41
monarch now alive may glory |'in such an honor; 5.02.199
an army cannot rule 'em. 5.03. 77
to the happiness of england, | an aged princess; 5.04. 57
to take their ease, | and sleep an act or two; ep 3
will leave all as i found it, and there an end. TRO 1.01. 88 P
nor any man an attaint but he carries some stain 1.02. 25 P
esteems her no more than i esteem an addle egg. 1.02.132 P
if you love an addle egg as well as you love an 1.02.133 P
an addle egg as well as you love an idle head, 1.02.133 P
here, here's an excellent place, here we may see 1.02.181 P
helen, to change, would give an eye to boot. 1.02.239 P
and with an accent tun'd in self–same key 1.03. 53
and appetite, an universal wolf | (so doubly 1.03.121
power), | must make perforce an universal prey, 1.03.123
grows to an envious fever | of pale and 1.03.133
opinion crowns | with an imperial voice — many 1.03.187
bold as an oracle, and sets thersites, | a slave 1.03.192
horse will sooner con an oration without book 2.01. 17 P

have in mine elbows, an asinico may tutor thee. 2.01. 44 P
here the voluntary, and you as under an impress. 2.01. 97 P
you know an enemy intends you harm; 2.02. 39
and for an old aunt whom the greeks held captive 2.02. 77
disgestion sake, | an after-dinner's breath. 2.03.112
yea, like fair fruit in an unwholesome dish, 2.03.120
and underwrite in an observing kind | his 2.03.128
but let him, like an engine | not portable, lie 2.03.134
of that we hold an idol more than he? 2.03.189
come, give me an instrument. 3.01. 95 P
able, and yet reserve an ability that they never 3.02. 85 P
but an unkind self, that itself will leave | to 3.02.149
who, like an arch, reverb'rate | the voice again 3.03.120
an act that very chance doth throw upon him — 3.03.131
like to an ent'red tide, they all rush by | and 3.03.159
which hath an operation more divine | than 3.03.203
is not more loath'd than an effeminate man | in 3.03.218
and danger, like an ague, subtly taints | even 3.03.232
longing, | an appetite that i am sick withal, 3.03.238
so prophetically proud of an heroical cudgelling 3.03.248 P
ruminates like an hostess that hath no 3.03.252 P
clear again, that i might water an ass at it! 3.03.311 P
think it an altar, and thy brother troilus | a 4.03. 8
you are an odd man, give even or give none. 4.05. 41
an odd man, lady? every man is odd. 4.05. 42
nor dignifies an impare thought with breath; 4.05.103
as to one | that would be rid of such an enemy. 4.05.164
/hemm'd thee in, | like an olympian wrastling. 4.05.194
o, let an old man embrace thee, | and, worthy 4.05.199
wert thou an oracle to tell me so, | i'd not 4.05.252
gaging me to keep | an oath that i have sworn. 5.01. 42
here's agamemnon, an honest fellow enough, and 5.01. 51 P
to an ass, were nothing, he is both ass and ox; 5.01. 59 P
to an ox, were nothing, /he /is both ox and ass. 5.01. 59 P
a toad, a lezard, an owl, a puttock, or a 5.01. 61 P
diomed, | keep hector company an hour or two. 5.01. 81
my heart, | an esperance so obstinately strong, 5.02.121
will not do more for an almond than he for a 5.02.193 P
eyes too, and such an ache in my bones that, 5.03.105 P
barbarism, and policy grows into an ill opinion. 5.04. 17 P
is as an inventory to particularize their COR 1.01. 21 P
it was an answer. how apply you this? 1.01.147
should not sell him an hour from her beholding; 1.03. 9 P
upon him a' we'nsday half an hour together; 1.03. 59 P
the volsces have an army forth; 1.03. 96 P
above an hour, my lord. 1.06. 15
how couldst thou in a mile confound an hour, 1.06. 17
i, sir, | half an hour since brought my report. 1.06. 21
fear | /lesser his person than an ill report; 1.06. 70
let him be made an overture for th' wars! 1.09. 46
i thought to crush him in an equal force, | true 1.10. 14
necks and make but an interior survey of your 2.01. 40 P
in hearing a cause between an orange-wife and a 2.01. 70 P
or to be entomb'd in an ass's pack-saddle. 2.01. 89 P
it gives me an estate of seven years' health, in 2.01.114 P
every gash was an enemy's grave. 2.01.155 P
out | to him, or our authorities, for an end. 2.01.244
he bestrid | an o'erpress'd roman, and i' th' 2.02. 93
thus | given hydra here to choose an officer, 3.01. 93
like an unnatural dam | should now eat up her 3.01.291
by many an ounce) he dropp'd it for his country; 3.01.299
into a pipe | small as an eunuch, or the virgin 3.02.114
bend like his | that hath receiv'd an alms! 3.02.120
ay, as an hostler, that /for /th' poorest piece 3.03. 32
what then? | he'ld make an end of thy posterity. 4.02. 26
have you an army ready, say you? 4.03. 42 P
and to be on foot at an hour's warning. 4.03. 45 P
many an heir | of these fair edifices 'fore my 4.04. 2
some trick not worth an egg, shall grow dear 4.04. 21
what an ass it is! 4.05. 43 P
'tis an honester service than to meddle with thy 4.05. 47 P
my grained ash an hundred times hath broke, 4.05.108
and more a friend than e'er an enemy; 4.05.146
what an arm he has! 4.05.152 P
ay, and for an assault too. 4.05.171 P
you stood, confin'd | into an auger's bore. 4.06. 87
bound with an oath to yield to his conditions; 5.01. 69
i am an officer of state, and come | to speak 5.02. 3
i'll say an arrant for you. 5.02. 60 P
young boy | hath an aspect of intercession which 5.03. 32
we must find | an evident calamity, though we 5.03.112
with a bolt | that should but rive an oak. 5.03.153
an end, | this is the last. 5.03.171
his mother now than an eight-year-old horse. 5.04. 17 P
when he walks, he moves like an engine, and the 5.04. 19 P
ne'er through an arch so hurried the blown tide, 5.04. 47
'tis there | that, like an eagle in a dove-cote, 5.06.114
and for an onset, titus, to advance | thy name TIT 1.01.238
now, madam, are you prisoner to an emperor; 1.01.258
even as an adder when she doth unroll | to do 2.03. 35
steed, | and wand'red hither to an obscure plot, 2.03. 77
and if she do, i would i were an eunuch. 2.03.128
i am surprised with an uncouth fear, | a 2.03.211
'tis not an hour since i left them there. 2.03.256
me down, | that i may slumber an eternal sleep! 2.04. 15
sorrow concealed, like an oven stopp'd, | doth 2.04. 36
then i'll go fetch an axe. 3.01.184
and that you'll say ere half an hour pass. 3.01.191
of them | as jewels purchas'd at an easy price, 3.01.198
sicily, | and be my heart an ever-burning hell! 3.01.242
when will this fearful slumber have an end? 3.01.252
besides, this sorrow is an enemy, | and would 3.01.267
thou art an exile, and thou must not stay. 3.01.284
hie to the goths and raise an army there, | and 3.01.285
now, what a thing it is to be an ass! 4.02. 25
can you deliver an oration to the emperor with a 4.03. 98 P
for /then hast made it like an humble suppliant. 4.03.117
ever seen | an emperor in rome thus overborne, 4.04. 2
villain, thou mightst have been an emperor. 5.01. 30
that granted, how canst thou believe an oath? 5.01. 72
i know | an idiot holds his bauble for a god, 5.01. 79
oft have you heard me wish for such an hour, 5.02.159
titus | hath ordain'd to an honorable end, | for 5.03. 22
delivered, | the issue of an irreligious moor, 5.03.121
three civil brawls, bred of an airy word, | by ROM 1.01. 89
an hour before the worshipp'd sun | peer'd forth 1.01.118
out, | and makes himself an artificial night. 1.01.140
as is the bud bit with an envious worm, | ere he 1.01.151
this night i hold an old accustom'd feast, 1.02. 20
faith, i can tell her age unto an hour. 1.03. 11
were of an age. 1.03. 19
it is an /honor that i dream not of. 1.03. 66
an /honor! 1.03. 67
in shape no bigger than an agot-stone | on the 1.04. 55
agot-stone | on the forefinger of an alderman, 1.04. 56
her chariot is an empty hazel-nut, | made by the 1.04. 59
which are the children of an idle brain, | begot 1.04. 97
of night | as a rich jewel in an ethiop's ear — 1.05. 46
slave | come hither, cover'd with an antic face, 1.05. 56
an ill-beseeming semblance for a feast. 1.05. 74
o that she were | an open/-arse, thou a pop'rin 2.01. 38
to myself, | because it is an enemy to thee; 2.02. 56
sit | of an old tear that is not wash'd off yet. 2.03. 76
that stretches from an inch narrow to an ell 2.04. 84 P
stretches from an inch narrow to an ell broad! 2.04. 84 P
an old hare hoar, | and an old hare hoar, | is 2.04.134
an old hare hoar, | and an old hare hoar, | is 2.04.135
truly it were an ill thing to be off'red to any 2.04.169 P
ay, nurse, what of that? both with an r. 2.04.208 P
in half an hour she promised to return. 2.05. 2
your love says, like an honest gentleman, | an' 2.05. 55
"your love says, like an honest gentleman, 2.05. 60
what eye but such an eye would spy out such a 3.01. 21 P
as full of quarrels as an egg is full of meat, 3.01. 22 P
been beaten as addle as an egg for quarrelling. 3.01. 24 P
fee-simple of my life for an hour and a quarter. 3.01. 32 P
tybalt, that an hour | hath been my cousin! 3.01.112
arm | an envious thrust from tybalt hit the life 3.01.168
i have an interest in your heart's proceeding; 3.01.188
to an impatient child that hath new robes | and 3.02. 30
i am not i, if there be such an ay; 3.02. 48
a /damned saint, an honorable villain! 3.02. 79
an hour but married, tybalt murdered, | doting 3.03. 66
do now, | taking the measure of an unmade grave. 3.03. 70
why should you fall into so deep an o? 3.03. 90
doth not she think me an old murtherer, | now i 3.03. 94
company, | i would have been a-bed an hour ago. 3.04. 7
some half a dozen friends, | and there an end. 3.04. 28
o god, i have an ill-divining soul! 3.05. 54
shall give him such an unaccustom'd dram | that 3.05. 90
an eagle, madam, | hath not so green, so quick, 3.05.219
green, so quick, so fair an eye | as paris hath. 3.05.220
which craves as desperate an execution | as that 4.01. 69
to live an unstain'd wife to my sweet love. 4.01. 88
sir, 'tis an ill cook that cannot lick his own 4.02. 6 P
place — | as in a vault, an ancient receptacle, 4.03. 39
death lies on her like an untimely frost | upon 4.05. 28
i will dry-beat you with an iron wit, and put up 4.05.124 P
and all this day an unaccustom'd spirit | lifts 5.01. 4
in my lips | that i reviv'd and was an emperor. 5.01. 9
i do remember an apothecary — | and hereabouts 5.01. 37
an alligator stuff'd, and other skins | of 5.01. 43
get me an iron crow, and bring it straight 5.02. 21
full half an hour. 5.03.130
ah, what an unkind hour | is guilty of this 5.03.145
were, | to an untirable and continuate goodness; TIM 1.01. 11
but flies an eagle flight, bold, and forth on, 1.01. 49
and my estate deserves an heir more rais'd 1.01.119
if she be mated with an equal husband? 1.01.140
to knock out an honest athenian's brains. 1.01.192 P
th' art an athenian, therefore welcome. 1.02. 35 P
ladies, there is an idle banquet attends you, 1.02.155
great gifts, | and all out of an empty coffer; 1.02.193
faith, nothing but an empty box, sir, which, in 3.01. 16 P
my very good friend, and an honorable gentleman. 3.02. 2 P
i cannot pleasure such an honorable gentleman. 3.02. 56 P
man | when he looks out in an ungrateful shape! 3.02. 73
so it may prove an argument of laughter | to th' 3.03. 20
believe't, my lord and i have made an end! 3.04. 55
now | (like all mankind) show me an iron heart? 3.04. 83
i am an humble suitor to your virtues; 3.05. 7
spent, | as if he had but prov'd an argument. 3.05. 23
striving to make an ugly deed look fair. 3.05. 25
he hath sent me an earnest inviting, which many 3.06. 9 P
lordship that i return'd you an empty messenger. 3.06. 37 P
age for his white beard, | he is an usurer. 4.03.113
the moon's an arrant thief, | and her pale fire 4.03.437
i'll believe him as an enemy, and give over my 4.03.454 P
what an alteration of honor has desp'rate want 4.03.462
an honest poor servant of yours. 4.03.475
suspect still comes where an estate is least. 4.03.514
only i will promise him an excellent piece. 5.01. 19
tell him of an intent | that's coming toward him 5.01. 20
alone, | yet an arch-villain keeps him company. 5.01.108
you are an alcumist, make gold of that. 5.01.114
an ag'd interpreter, though young in days. 5.03. 8
appear, | have you not made an universal shout, JC 1.01. 44
wing | will make him fly an ordinary pitch, 1.01. 73
when went there by an age since the great flood 1.02.152
romans | to undergo with me an enterprise | of 1.03.123
suffers then | the nature of an insurrection. 2.01. 69
no, not an oath! 2.01.114
our cause or our performance | did need an oath; 2.01.136
do, | stir up their servants to an act of rage, 2.01.176
but with an angry wafter of your hand | gave 2.01.246
withal | hoping it was but an effect of humor, 2.01.250
such an exploit have i in hand, ligarius, | had 2.01.318
thou, like an exorcist, hast conjur'd up | my 2.01.323
plucking the entrails of an offering forth, 2.02. 39
which, like a fountain with an hundred spouts, 2.02. 77
i have an hour's talk in store for you; 2.02.121
have an eye to cinna; 2.03. 2 P
cimber throws before thy seat | an humble heart. 3.01. 35
may | have an immediate freedom of repeal. 3.01. 54
and the rest | (for brutus is an honorable man, 3.02. 82
was ambitious, | and brutus is an honorable man. 3.02. 87
was ambitious, | and brutus is an honorable man. 3.02. 94
ambitious, | and sure he is an honorable man. 3.02. 99
there were an antony | would ruffle up your 3.02.227
as a friend or an enemy? 3.03. 21 P
and decay | it useth an enforced ceremony. 4.02. 21
are much condemn'd to have an itching palm, | to 4.03. 10
i, an itching palm? 4.03. 12
i said an elder soldier, not a better. 4.03. 56
lepidus | have put to death an hundred senators. 4.03.175
this was an ill beginning of the night. 4.03.234
that's not an office for a friend, my lord. 5.05. 29
and for an earnest of a greater honor, | he bade MAC 1.03.104
a gentleman on whom i built | an absolute trust. 1.04. 14
yet when we can entreat an hour to serve, | we 2.01. 22
going, | and such an instrument i was to use. 2.01. 43
faith, here's an equivocator, that could swear 2.03. 8 P
faith, here's an english tailor come hither for 2.03. 13 P
may be said to be an equivocator with lechery: 2.03. 31 P
had i but died an hour before this chance, | i 2.03. 91
hid in an auger-hole, may rush and seize us? 2.03.122
to show an unfelt sorrow is an office | which 2.03.136
to show an unfelt sorrow is an office | which 2.03.136
thence to be wrench'd with an unlineal hand, 3.01. 62
were out, the man would die, | and there an end; 3.04. 79
and with an absolute "sir, not i," | the cloudy 3.06. 40
me this, | and an eternal curse fall on you! 4.01.105
poor, innocent lamb | t' appease an angry god. 4.03. 17
nature may recoil | in an imperial charge. 4.03. 20
better macbeth | than such an one to reign. 4.03. 66
with an untitled tyrant bloody-sceptred, | when 4.03.104
that of an hour's age doth hiss the speaker; 4.03.175
an older and a better soldier none | that 4.03.191
it is an accustom'd action with her, to seem 5.01. 28 P
known her continue in this a quarter of an hour. 5.01. 30 P
it is a tale | told by an idiot, full of sound 5.05. 27
or else my sword with an unbattered edge | i 5.07. 19
that ever scotland | in such an honor nam'd. 5.09. 30
so frown'd he once, when, in an angry parle, HAM 1.01. 62
with an auspicious, and a dropping eye, | with 1.02. 11
an understanding simple and unschool'd: 1.02. 97
'tis an unweeded garden | that grows to seed, 1.02.135
admiration for a while | with an attent ear, 1.02.193
give it an understanding, but no tongue. 1.02.249
it is /a nipping and an eager air. 1.04. 2
and each particular hair to stand an end, | like 1.05. 19
effect | holds such an enmity with blood of man 1.05. 65
in all denmark — | but he's an arrant knave. 1.05.124
it is an honest ghost, that let me tell you. 1.05.138
think meet | to put an antic disposition on — 1.05.172
with an entreaty, herein further shown, | that 2.02. 76
beautified ophelia" — that's an ill phrase, a 2.02.111 P
be you and i behind an arras then, | mark the 2.02.163
nay then i have an eye of you! 2.02.290 P
how like an angel in apprehension! 2.02.306 P
them, for they say an old man is twice a child. 2.02.385 P
when roscius was an actor in rome — 2.02.391 P
cried in the top of mine — an excellent play, 2.02.439 P
of affection, but call'd it an honest method, as 2.02.444 P
why, what an ass am i! 2.02.582
that show of such an exercise may color | your 3.01. 44
come, come, you answer with an idle tongue. 3.04. 11
such an act | that blurs the grace and blush of 3.04. 40
from the fair forehead of an innocent love | and 3.04. 43
an eye like mars, to threaten and command, | a 3.04. 57
to live | in the rank sweat of an enseamed bed, 3.04. 92
life in excrements, | start up and stand an end. 3.04.122
come, sir, to draw toward an end with you. 3.04.216
he keeps them, like /an /ape an apple, in the 4.02. 18 P
death, and danger dare, | even for an egg-shell. 4.04. 53
indeed without an oath i'll make an end on't. 4.05. 57 P
indeed without an oath i'll make an end on't. 4.05. 57 P
i will work him | to an exploit, now ripe in my 4.07. 64
i bought an unction of a mountebank, | so mortal 4.07.141
clamb'ring to hang, an envious sliver broke, 4.07.173
if i drown myself wittingly, it argues an act, 5.01. 11 P
argues an act, and an act hath three branches — 5.01. 11 P
and tell her, let her paint an inch thick, to 5.01.193 P
what is he whose grief | bears such an emphasis, 5.01.255
an hour of quiet /shortly shall we see, | till 5.01.298
an exact command, | larded with many several 5.02. 19
an earnest conjuration from the king, | as 5.02. 38
believe me, an absolute /gentleman, full of most 5.02.106 P
of the time and, out of an habit of encounter, a 5.02.190 P
and in the cup an /union shall he throw, 5.02.272
in thee there is not half an hour's life. 5.02.315
i am more an antique roman than a dane. 5.02.341
i profess | myself an enemy to all other joys LR 1.01. 73
with reservation of an hundred knights | by you 1.01.133
he wrote this but as an essay or taste of my 1.02. 45 P
i begin to find an idle and fond bondage in the 1.02. 49 P
of this, and by an auricular assurance have your 1.02. 91 P
and adulterers by an enforc'd obedience of 1.02.124 P
an admirable evasion of whoremaster man, to lay 1.02.126 P
then 'tis like the breath of an unfee'd lawyer, 1.04.129 P
nuncle, give me an egg, and i'll give thee two 1.04.156 P
frowning, now thou art an o without a figure. 1.04.192 P
may not an ass know when the cart draws the 1.04.223 P
which, like an engine, wrench'd my frame of 1.04.268
she's as like this as a crab's like an apple, 1.05. 15 P
canst tell how an oyster makes his shell? 1.05. 25 P
a knave, a rascal, an eater of broken meats; 2.02. 15 P
an honest mind and plain, he must speak truth! 2.02. 99
we'll set thee to school to an ant, to teach 2.04. 67 P
thy /mother's tomb, | sepulchring an adult'ress. 2.04.132
in a wild field were like an old lecher's heart, 3.04.112 P
which approves him an intelligent party to the 3.05. 11 P
and tells me nero is an angler in the lake of 3.06. 6 P
if thou shouldst dally half an hour, his life, 3.06. 93
not feel wrongs | which tie him to an answer. 4.02. 14
who hast not in thy brows an eye discerning 4.02. 52
precipitating), | thou'dst shiver'd like an egg: 4.06. 51
give me an ounce of civet; 4.06.130
fourscore and upward, not an hour more nor less; 4.07. 60
your business of the world hath so an end, | and 5.01. 45
an enterlude! 5.03. 89
wast not bound to answer | an unknown opposite. 5.03.154
all three | now marry in an instant. 5.03.230
gentle, and low, an excellent thing in woman. 5.03.274
an old black ram | is tupping your white ewe. OTH 1.01. 88
in an extravagant and wheeling stranger | of 1.01.136
it is too true an evil; 1.01.160
which, when i know that boasting is an honor, 1.02. 20
and do attach thee | for an abuser of the world, 1.02. 78
mine's not an idle cause. 1.02. 95
neglecting an attempt of ease and gain | to wake 1.03. 29
have there injointed them with an after fleet. 1.03. 35
desdemona, i have but an hour | of love, of 1.03.298
distinguish betwixt a benefit and an injury, i 1.03.313 P

defeat thy favor with an usurp'd beard. 1.03.341 P
and thou shalt see an answerable sequestration 1.03.345 P
a frail vow betwixt an erring barbarian and /a 1.03.355 P
main and th' aerial blue | an indistinct regard. 2.01. 40
for even her folly help'd her to an heir. 2.01.137
that /has an eye can stamp and counterfeit 2.01.243 P
an index and obscure prologue to the history of 2.01.257 P
reward me, | for making him egregiously an ass, 2.01.309
what an eye she has! 2.03. 22 P
an inviting eye; and yet methinks right modest. 2.03. 24 P
when she speaks, is it not an alarum to love? 2.03. 26 P
'fore /god, an excellent song. 2.03. 75 P
own second | with one of an ingraft infirmity; 2.03.140
it were an honest action to say | so to the moor 2.03.141
i'll make thee an example. 2.03.251
as i am an honest man, i had thought you had 2.03.266 P
reputation is an idle and most false imposition; 2.03.268 P
offenseless dog to affright an imperious lion. 2.03.275 P
so drunken, and so indiscreet an officer. 2.03.279 P
that men should put an enemy in their mouths to 2.03.290 P
as hydra, such an answer would stop them all. 2.03.305 P
o, that's an honest fellow. 3.03. 5
cunning, | i have no judgment in an honest face. 3.03. 50
why then i think cassio's an honest man. 3.03.129
did an egyptian to my mother give; 3.04. 56
an unauthoriz'd kiss! 4.01. 2
or to be naked with her friend in bed | an hour, 4.01. 4
her honor is an essence that's not seen; 4.01. 16
my lord is fall'n into an epilepsy. 4.01. 50
she might lie by an emperor's side and command 4.01.184 P
an admirable musician! 4.01.188 P
between him and my lord | an unkind breach; 4.01.225
an instrument of this your calling back, | lay 4.02. 45
an old thing 'twas, but it express'd her fortune 4.03. 29
but half an hour! 5.02. 82
an honest man he is, and hates the slime | that 5.02.148
you told a lie, an odious, damned lie; 5.02.180
an antique token | my father gave my mother. 5.02.216
an honorable murderer, if you will; 5.02.294
nay, if an oily palm be not a fruitful ANT 1.02. 52 P
am i not an inch of fortune better than she? 1.02. 58 P
if you were but an inch of fortune better than i 1.02. 59 P
the man from sicyon — is there such an one? 1.02.114
we see how mortal an unkindness is to them; 1.02.134 P
the tears live in an onion that should water 1.02.169 P
to his love, which stands | an honorable trial. 1.03. 75
i take no pleasure | in aught an eunuch has. 1.05. 10
great egypt sends | this treasure of an oyster; 1.05. 44
and soberly did mount an arm–gaunt steed, | who 1.05. 48
to knit your hearts | with an unslipping knot, 2.02.126
but by sea | he is an absolute master. 2.02.163
this was but as a fly by an eagle; 2.02.181 P
as well a woman with an eunuch play'd | as with 2.05. 5
them up, | i'll think them every one an antony, 2.05. 14
th' art an honest man. 2.05. 47
give to a gracious message | an host of tongues, 2.05. 87
this is not yet an alexandrian feast. 2.07. 96
place, note well, | may make too great an act. 3.01. 13
of antony | should have an army for an usher, 3.06. 44
of antony | should have an army for an usher, 3.06. 44
every stage | with an augmented greeting. 3.06. 55
being an abstract 'tween his lust and him. 3.06. 61
in rome | that photinus an eunuch and your maids 3.07. 14
i never saw an action of such shame; 3.10. 21
an argument that he is pluck'd, when hither | he 3.12. 3
a lion's whelp | than with an old one dying. 3.13. 95
of caesar's shall | bear us an arrant to him. 3.13.104
all of you clapp'd up together in | an antony, 4.02. 18
look, they weep, | and i, an ass, am onion–ey'd. 4.02. 35
i have an absolute hope | our landmen will stand 4.03. 10
that was like a t, | but now 'tis made an h. 4.07. 8
i'll give thee, friend, | an armor all of gold; 4.08. 27
false–play'd my glory | unto an enemy's triumph. 4.14. 20
o, make an end | of what i have begun. 4.14.105
i dreamt there was an emperor antony. 5.02. 76
an /autumn it was | that grew the more by 5.02. 87
an antony were nature's piece 'gainst fancy, 5.02. 99
thou, an egyptian puppet, shall be shown | in 5.02.208
what poor an instrument | may do a noble deed! 5.02.236
this is most falliable, the worm's an odd worm. 5.02.258 P
o, sir, you are too sure an augurer; 5.02.334
this is an aspic's trail, and these fig leaves 5.02.351
think | so fair an outward and such stuff within CYM 1.01. 23
i chose an eagle, | and did avoid a puttock. 1.01.139
he takes his part | to draw upon an exile. 1.01.166
unless it had been the fall of an ass, which is 1.02. 37 P
which else an easy battery might lay flat, for 1.04. 22 P
it was much like an argument that fell out last 1.04. 56 P
it is an earnest of a farther good | that i mean 1.05. 65
one | an eminent monsieur that, it seems, much 1.06. 65
but | it is an office of the gods to venge it, 1.06. 92
then by–peeping in an eye | base and illustrious 1.06.108
fair, and fasten'd to an empery | would make the 1.06.120
not | for such an end thou seek'st — as base as 1.06.144
when i kiss'd the jack upon an up–cast, to be 2.01. 2 P
there's an italian come, and, 'tis thought, one 2.01. 37 P
if you will make't an action, call witness to't. 2.03.151
this yellow jachimo, in an hour — was't not? 2.05. 14
and there's an end. 3.01. 82 P
and truly, i would think thee an honest man. 3.05.113 P
by jupiter, an angel! 3.06. 42
or, if not, | an earthly paragon! 3.06. 43
have not i | an arm as big as thine? 4.02. 77
this cloten was a fool, an empty purse, | there 4.02.113
to let an arrogant piece of flesh threat us, 4.02.127
that an invisible instinct should frame them 4.02.177
which gave advantage to an ancient soldier | (5.03. 15
to an ancient soldier | (an honest one, i 5.03. 16
a narrow lane, an old man, and two boys! 5.03. 52
"two boys, an old man (twice a boy), a lane, 5.03. 57
being an ugly monster, | 'tis strange he hides 5.03. 70
what an infinite mock is this, that a man should 5.04.188 P
and that to hear an old man sing | may to your PER 1.ch. 13
life, | for that's an article within our law, 1.01. 88
sin, | when what is done is like an hypocrite, 1.01.122
and she an eater of her mother's flesh | by the 1.01.130
and like an arrow shot | from a well–experienc'd 1.01.161
/be /my so us'd a guest as not an hour | in the 1.02. 3
an angry brow, dread lord. 1.02. 52
from whence an issue i might propagate, | are 1.02. 73
one sorrow never comes but brings an heir | that 1.04. 63
an armor, friends? 2.01.120
is an armed knight that's conquered by a lady; 2.02. 26
the fift, an hand environed with clouds, 2.02. 36
to an honor'd triumph strangely furnished. 2.02. 53
in framing an artist, art hath thus decreed, 2.03. 15
he may my proffer take for an offense, | since 2.03. 68
seated in a chariot | of an inestimable value, 2.04. 8
i heard of an egyptian | that had nine hours 3.02. 84
walk half an hour, leonine, at the least. 4.01. 45
an honest woman, or not a woman. 4.02. 85
innocent | and for an honest attribute cry out, 4.03. 18
find | it greets me as an enterprise of kindness 4.03. 38
i would have you note, this is an honorable man. 4.06. 50 P
and chances | into an honest house, our story 5.ch. 2
her stature to an inch, as wand–like straight, 5.01.109
it may be | you think me an imposture. 5.01.177
tyre, | i left behind an ancient substitute. 5.03. 51
for, to say truth, it were an endless thing, TNK pr 22
not an /angel of the air, | bird melodious, or 1.01. 16
keep the feast full, bate not an hour on't. 1.01.220
'twould bring us to an eddy | where we should 1.02. 10
such most | that, sweating in an honorable toil, 1.02. 33
court hurry is over, we will have an end of it. 2.01. 18 P
then start amongst 'em | and, as an east wind, 2.02. 13
we are an endless mine to one another; 2.02. 79
this is an offer'd opportunity | i durst not 2.03. 74
to hear him | sing in an evening, what a heaven 2.04. 19
you must guess | i have an office there. 3.01.110
the point is this — | an end, and that is all. 3.02. 38
she met him in an arbor: 3.03. 33
clip my yellow locks an inch below mine e'e. 3.04. 20
an eel and woman, | a learned poet says, unless 3.05. 48
"there was three fools fell out about an howlet: 3.05. 67
the one said it was an owl, | the other he said 3.05. 68
'twas an excellent dance, and for a preface, | i 3.05.150
thou art so brave an enemy | that no man but thy 3.06. 43
then as i am an honest man, and love | with all 3.06. 50
a fool, | an innocent, and i was very angry. 4.01. 41
and all we'll dance an antic 'fore the duke, 4.01. 75
gone — she's done, | and undone in an hour. 4.01.125
what an eye, | of what a fiery sparkle and quick 4.02. 12
of an eye as heavy | as if he had lost his 4.02. 27
but such a manly color | next to an aborn; 4.02.125
and nimble set, | which shows an active soul; 4.02.126
'tis not an engraff'd madness, but a most thick 4.03. 48 P
of, and thereto make an addition of some other 4.03. 84 P
lay by your anger for an hour, and dove–like, 5.01. 11
even with an eye–glance, to choke mars's drum 5.01. 80
he'll dance the morris twenty mile an hour, 5.02. 51
yet his eye | is like an engine bent, or a sharp 5.03. 42
might | omit a ward, or forfeit an offense, 5.03. 63
arcite's body | within an inch o' th' pyramid, 5.03. 80
for whom an hour, | but one hour since, i was as 5.04.128
not /one of you should live an aged man, | for STM II.C 83
would not afford you an abode on earth, | whet II.C 133
god, | that i from such an humble bench of birth III 6
a summer's day will seem an hour but short, VEN 23
even as an empty eagle, sharp by fast, | tires 55
an oven that is stopp'd, or river stay'd, 331
jail of snow, | or ivory in an alablaster band, 363
but, like an earthquake, shakes thee on my 648
mine eye | the picture of an angry chafing boar, 662
on his back doth lie | an image like thyself, 664
there lives a son that suck'd an earthly mother, 863
whereat she starts like one that spies an adder 878
mistakes that aim and cleaves an infant's heart. 942
yet sometimes falls an orient drop beside, 981
there shall not be one minute in an hour 1187
an expir'd date, cancell'd ere well begun: LUC 26
persuade | the eyes of men without an orator; 30
survive, | and be an eye–sore in my golden coat; 205
whose crime will bear an ever–during blame. 224
who fears a sentence or an old man's saw | shall 244
white | show'd like an april daisy on the grass, 395
(rude ram, to batter such an ivory wall!), 464
only he hath an eye to gaze on beauty, | and 496
soft pity enters at an iron gate. 595
when wilt thou sort an hour great strifes to end 899
an accessary by thine inclination | to all sins 922
one poor retiring minute in an age | would 962
for who so base would such an office have | as 1000
so, | to flatter thee with an infringed oath; 1061
like an unpractic'd swimmer plunging still, 1098
these means, as frets upon an instrument, 1140
conceit and grief an eager combat fight, | what 1298
stood his spear, | grip'd in an armed hand; 1425
and give the harmless show | an humble gait, 1508
as through an arch the violent roaring tide 1667
what fool is not so wise | to break an oath, to PP 3.14
heaven's praise with such an earthly tongue. 5.14
adonis made | under an osier growing by a brook, 6. 5
lost, vaded, broken, dead within an hour. 13. 6
till looking on an englishman, the fairest that 15. 3
jove would swear | juno but an ethiope were, 16.16
women work, | dissembled with an outward show, 18.38
own deep–sunken eyes | were an all–eating shame, SON 2. 8
look what an unthrift in the world doth spend 9. 9
but beauty's waste hath in the world an end, 9.11
rage, | and stretched metre of an antique song: 17.12
an eye more bright than theirs, less false in 20. 5
as an unperfect actor on the stage, | who with 23. 1
then can i drown an eye (unus'd to flow) | for 30. 5
that i an accessary needs must be | to that 35.13
now proud as an enjoyer, and anon | doubting the 75. 5
me bow, | and do not drop in for an after–loss. 90. 4
praise, | naming thy name blesses an ill report. 95. 8
idolatry, | nor my beloved as an idol show, 105. 2
grind | on newer proof, to try an older friend, 110.11
o no, it is an ever–fixed mark | that looks on 116. 5
to keep an adjunct to remember thee | were to 122.13
"i hate" she alter'd with an end | that follow'd 145. 9
"for lo his passion, but an art of craft, | even LC 295

ANATOMIZ'D 3 FR 0.0003 REL FR 2 V 1 P
the wise man's folly is anatomiz'd | even by the AYL 2.07. 56
gladly have him see his company anatomiz'd, that AWW 4.03. 32 P
in her the painter had anatomiz'd | time's ruin, LUC 1450

ANATOMIZE 3 FR 0.0003 REL FR 1 V 2 P
but should i anatomize him to thee as he is, i AYL 1.01.156 P
my well–known body to anatomize | among my 2H4 in 21
then let them anatomize regan; LR 3.06. 76 P

ANATOMY 5 FR 0.0005 REL FR 4 V 1 P
a mere anatomy, a mountebank, | a threadbare ERR 5.01.239
of a flea, i'll eat the rest of th' anatomy. TN 3.02. 63 P
and rouse from sleep that fell anatomy | which JN 3.04. 40
in what vile part of this anatomy | doth my name ROM 3.03.106
this anatomy | had by his young fair fere a boy, TNK 5.01.115

ANCESTOR 5 FR 0.0005 REL FR 5 V 0 P
twice being censor, | was his great ancestor. COR 2.03.245
speak, rome's dear friend, as erst our ancestor, TIT 5.03. 80
i, as aeneas, our great ancestor, | did from the JC 1.02.112
me, | alcides, thou mine ancestor, thy rage. ANT 4.12. 44
our ancestor was that mulmutius which | ordain'd CYM 3.01. 54

ANCESTORS 21 FR 0.0023 REL FR 20 V 1 P
and all his ancestors (that come after him) may. WIV 1.01. 15 P
and she lies buried with her ancestors — | o, ADO 5.01. 69
house, | bequeathed down from many ancestors, AWW 4.02. 43
house, | bequeathed down from many ancestors, 4.02. 47
of six preceding ancestors, that gem, 5.03.196
which his noble ancestors achiev'd with blows. R2 2.01.254
quite from the flight of all thy ancestors. 1H4 3.02. 31
up, | will have a wild trick of his ancestors. 5.02. 11
upon, | when i am sleeping with my ancestors. 2H4 4.04. 61
flag, | look back into your mighty ancestors; H5 1.02.102
at one time | bring in to any of your ancestors. 1.02.135
from his most fam'd of famous ancestors, 2.04. 92
the sceptred office of your ancestors, | your R3 3.07.119
home, | with burial amongst their ancestors. TIT 1.01. 84
bones | of all my buried ancestors are pack'd, ROM 4.03. 41
have thews and limbs like to their ancestors; JC 1.03. 81
my ancestors did from the streets of rome | the 2.01. 53
give him a statue with his ancestors. 3.02. 50
the kings your ancestors, together with | the CYM 3.01. 17
appears he hath had | good ancestors. 4.02. 48
my derivation was from ancestors | who stood PER 5.01. 90

ANCESTRY 4 FR 0.0004 REL FR 4 V 0 P
now, by the honor of my ancestry, | i do applaud TGV 5.04.139
yet to draw forth your noble ancestry | from the R3 3.07.198
for, being not propp'd by ancestry, whose grace H8 1.01. 59
great nature, like his ancestry, | moulded the CYM 5.04. 48

ANCHISES' 1 FR 0.0001 REL FR 1 V 0 P
now, by anchises' life, | welcome indeed! TRO 4.01. 22

ANCHISES 2 FR 0.0002 REL FR 2 V 0 P
as did aeneas old anchises bear, | so bear i 2H6 5.02. 62
troy upon his shoulder | the old anchises bear, JC 1.02.114

ANCHOR 7 FR 0.0008 REL FR 6 V 1 P
the anchor is deep. will that humor pass? WIV 1.03. 51 P
you had much ado to make his anchor hold, | when WT 1.02.213
say warwick was our anchor; 3H6 5.04. 13
why, is not oxford here another anchor? 5.04. 16
then is all safe, the anchor in the port. TIT 4.04. 38
there would he anchor his aspect, and die | with ANT 1.05. 33
and on this coast | suppose him now at anchor. PER 5.ch. 16

ANCHORAGE 1 FR 0.0001 REL FR 1 V 0 P
from whence at first she weigh'd her anchorage, TIT 1.01. 73

ANCHOR'D 2 FR 0.0002 REL FR 2 V 0 P
till that my nails were anchor'd in thine eyes; R3 4.04.232
be anchor'd in the bay where all men ride, | why SON 137. 6

ANCHORING 2 FR 0.0002 REL FR 2 V 0 P
to cast up, with a pair of anchoring hooks, TGV 3.01.118
and yond tall anchoring bark, | diminish'd to LR 4.06. 18

ANCHOR'S 1 FR 0.0001 REL FR 1 V 0 P
/an anchor's cheer in prison be my scope! HAM 3.02.219

ANCHORS 5 FR 0.0005 REL FR 5 V 0 P
hearing not my tongue, | anchors on isabel; MM 2.04. 4
nothing so certain as your anchors, who | do WT 4.04.570
for, whilst our pinnace anchors in the downs, 2H6 4.01. 9
wedges of gold, great anchors, heaps of pearl, R3 1.04. 26
see, | posthumus anchors upon imogen; CYM 5.05.393

ANCHOVES 1 FR 0.0001 REL FR 0 V 1 P
item, anchoves and sack after supper ... 2s.6d.. 1H4 2.04.538 P

ANCIENT* *(also aunchiant, aunchient, ensign)*

/ANCIENT* 1 FR 0.0001 REL FR 0 V 1 P
/dearth, /dissolutions /of /ancient /amities, LR 1.02.145 P

ANCIENT* 81 FR 0.0091 REL FR 60 V 21 P
wink for aye might put | this ancient morsel, TMP 2.01.286
a very ancient and fish–like smell; 2.02. 26 P
read it not truly, my ancient skill beguiles me; MM 4.02.155 P
why, you speak like an ancient and most quiet ADO 3.03. 39 P
i beg the ancient privilege of athens: MND 1.01. 41
and will you rent our ancient love asunder, | to 3.02.215
i will feed fat the ancient grudge i bear him. MV 1.03. 47
the ancient saying is no heresy, | hanging and 2.09. 82
in whom | the ancient roman honor more appears 3.02.295
call home thy ancient thoughts from banishment, SHR in.2. 31
your ancient, trusty, pleasant servant grumio. 1.02. 47
i spied | an ancient angel coming down the hill, 4.02. 61
you seem a sober ancient gentleman by your habit 5.01. 73 P
florentine, | derived from the ancient capilet. AWW 5.03.159
sir, the year growing ancient, | not yet on WT 4.04. 79
me breathe my life | before this ancient sir, 4.04.361
done, | this act is as an ancient tale new told, JN 4.02. 18
him, | if he appeal the duke on ancient malice, R2 1.01. 9
the nobles hath he fin'd | for ancient quarrels, 2.01.248
go to the rude ribs of that ancient castle; 3.03. 32
this pitch (as ancient writers do report) doth 1H4 2.04.413 P
leads ancient lords and reverend bishops on | to 3.02.104
dishonorable ragged than an old feaz'd ancient: 4.02. 31 P
from me | with new lamenting ancient oversights, 2H4 2.03. 47
sir, ancient pistol's below, and would speak 2.04. 69 P
dost thou hear? it is mine ancient. 2.04. 82 P
and your ancient /swagger, /'a comes not in my 2.04. 84 P
welcome, ancient pistol. 2.04.111 P
pray thee go down, good ancient. 2.04.151 P
be gone, good ancient. 2.04.172 P
what, are ancient pistol and you friends yet? H5 2.01. 3 P
here comes ancient pistol and his wife. 2.01. 26 P
will you mock at an ancient tradition, /begun 5.01. 70 P
corrupted, and exempt from ancient gentry? 1H6 2.04. 93
my ancient incantations are too weak, | and hell 5.03. 27
so, in the famous ancient city tours, | in 2H6 1.01. 5
stay, | we shall begin our ancient bickerings. 1.01.144

the ancient proverb will be well effected: 3.01.170
till you had recover'd your ancient freedom. 4.08. 27 P
i'll win our ancient right in france again, | or R3 3.01. 92
his ancient knot of dangerous adversaries 3.01.182
pity, you ancient stones, those tender babes 4.01. 98
if ancient sorrow be most reverent, | give mine 4.04. 35
our ancient word of courage, fair saint george, 5.03.349
but they | upon their ancient malice will forget COR 2.01.228
nay, mother, | where is your ancient courage? 4.01. 3
and they | stand in their ancient strength. 4.02. 7
my throat to thee and to thy ancient malice; 4.05. 96
weeded from my heart | a root of ancient envy. 4.05.103
that shall distill from these two ancient /urns, TIT 3.01. 17
from ancient grudge break to new mutiny, | where ROM pr 3
and made verona's ancient citizens | cast by 1.01. 92
who set this ancient quarrel new abroach? 1.01.104
at this same ancient feast of capulet's | sups 1.02. 82
thy old groans yet ringing in mine ancient ears; 2.03. 74
farewell, ancient lady, farewell, "lady, lady, 2.04.143 P
ancient damnation! 3.05.235
thou shall be borne to that same ancient vault 4.01.111
place — | as in a vault, an ancient receptacle, 4.03. 39
i met a courier, one mine ancient friend, | whom TIM 5.02. 6
there is no ancient gentlemen but gard'ners, HAM 5.01. 29 P
this ancient ruffian, sir, whose life i have LR 2.02. 62 P
you stubborn ancient knave, you reverent 2.02.126
i' th' way toward dover, do it for ancient love, 4.01. 43
with th' ancient of war on our proceeding. 5.01. 32
his moorship's ancient. OTH 1.01. 33
ancient, what makes he here? 1.02. 49
ancient, conduct them; 1.03.121
so please your grace, my ancient; 1.03.283
'tis one iago, ancient to the general. 2.01. 66
good ancient, you are welcome. 2.01. 96
lieutenant is to be sav'd before the ancient. 2.03.110 P
this is my ancient, this is my right hand, and 2.03.114 P
this is othello's ancient, as i take it. 5.01. 51
which gave advantage to an ancient soldier | (an CYM 5.03. 15
was sung, | from ashes ancient gower is come, PER 1.ch. 2
tyre, | i left behind an ancient substitute. 5.03. 51
juno would | resume her ancient fit of jealousy TNK 1.02. 22
us not, | having our ancient reputation with us, 3.03. 11
in labor | to push your name, your ancient love, 5.01. 26
to pluck the quills from ancient ravens' wings, LUC 949
ANCIENTRY 2 FR 0.0002 REL FR 0 V 2 P
as a measure, full of state and ancientry; ADO 2.01. 77 P
wenches with child, wronging the ancientry, WT 3.03. 62 P
ANCIENTS 1 FR 0.0001 REL FR 0 V 1 P
and now my whole charge consists of ancients, 1H4 4.02. 24 P
ANCIENT'ST 1 FR 0.0001 REL FR 1 V 0 P
pass | the same i am, ere ancient'st order was, WT 4.01. 10
ANCUS 1 FR 0.0001 REL FR 1 V 0 P
from whence came | that ancus martius, numa's COR 2.03.239
AND *(also an')*
/AND 275 FR 0.0310 REL FR 231 V 44 P
AND 26285 FR 2.9712 REL FR 21011 V 5274 P
AND-A 1 FR 0.0001 REL FR 1 V 0 P
"king stephen was and-a worthy peer, | his OTH 2.03. 89
ANDIRONS 1 FR 0.0001 REL FR 1 V 0 P
her andirons | (i had forgot them) were two CYM 2.04. 88
ANDREN 1 FR 0.0001 REL FR 1 V 0 P
two lights of men, | met in the vale of andren. H8 1.01. 7
ANDREW 16 FR 0.0018 REL FR 1 V 15 P
and see my wealthy andrew /dock'd in sand, MV 1.01. 27
who, sir andrew aguecheek? TN 1.03. 18 P
for here comes sir andrew agueface. 1.03. 43 P
sweet sir andrew! 1.03. 46 P
accost, sir andrew, accost. 1.03. 49 P
and thou let part so, sir andrew, would thou 1.03. 61 P
approach, sir andrew. 2.03. 1 P
him black and blue, shall we not, sir andrew? 2.05. 11 P
"one sir andrew" — 2.05. 80 P
you must needs yield your reason, sir andrew. 3.02. 4 P
there is no way but this, sir andrew. 3.02. 39 P
for andrew, if he were open'd and you find so 3.02. 60 P
him, and thy sworn enemy, andrew aguecheek." 3.04.170 P
go, sir andrew, scout me for him at the corner 3.04.176 P
come, sir andrew, there's no remedy, the 3.04.305 P
who has done this, sir andrew? 5.01.179 P
ANDROMACHE 3 FR 0.0003 REL FR 3 V 0 P
he chid andromache and strook his armorer, | and TRO 1.02. 6
andromache, i am offended with you, | upon the 5.03. 77
how poor andromache shrills her dolors forth! 5.03. 84
ANDRONICI 3 FR 0.0003 REL FR 3 V 0 P
indeed | till all the andronici be made away. TIT 2.03.189
the poor remainder of andronici | will hand in 5.03.131
you sad andronici, have done with woes. 5.03.176
ANDRONICUS' 1 FR 0.0001 REL FR 1 V 0 P
afoot, | she would applaud andronicus' conceit, TIT 4.02. 30
ANDRONICUS 44 FR 0.0049 REL FR 44 V 0 P
chosen andronicus, surnamed pius | for many good TIT 1.01. 23
spoils, | returns the good andronicus to rome, 1.01. 37
marcus andronicus, so i do affy | in thy 1.01. 47
the good andronicus, | patron of virtue, rome's 1.01. 64
cometh andronicus, bound with laurel boughs, 1.01. 74
andronicus, stain not thy tomb with blood! 1.01.116
be so, and let andronicus | make this his latest 1.01.148
titus andronicus, the people of rome, | whose 1.01.179
andronicus, would thou were shipp'd to hell, 1.01.206
andronicus, i do not flatter thee, | but honor 1.01.212
will ye bestow them friendly on andronicus? 1.01.219
to gratify the good andronicus, | and gratulate 1.01.220
titus andronicus, for thy favors done | to us in 1.01.234
tell me, andronicus, doth this motion please 1.01.243
full well, andronicus, | agree these deeds with 1.01.305
come, come, sweet emperor — come, andronicus — 1.01.456
this day all quarrels die, andronicus. 1.01.465
but fierce andronicus would not relent. 2.03.165
the unhappy sons of old andronicus, | brought 2.03.250
andronicus himself did take it up. 2.03.294
andronicus, i will entreat the king. 2.03.304
titus andronicus, my lord the emperor | sends 3.01.150
i go, andronicus, and for thy hand | look by and 3.01.200
worthy andronicus, ill art thou repaid | for 3.01.234
die, andronicus. 3.01.253
farewell, andronicus, my noble father, | the 3.01.288
revenge the heavens for old andronicus! 4.01.129
i may, | i greet your honors from andronicus — 4.02. 5
aid, | and that it comes from old andronicus, 4.03. 16
against the willful sons | of old andronicus. 4.04. 9
conduct | of lucius, son to old andronicus, 4.04. 66
i will enchant the old andronicus | with words 4.04. 89
even at his father's house, the old andronicus. 4.04.103
now will i to that old andronicus, | and temper 4.04.108
brave slip, sprung from the great andronicus, 5.01. 9
devil | that robb'd andronicus of his good hand; 5.01. 41
habiliment, | i will encounter with andronicus, 5.02. 2
what wouldst thou have us do, andronicus? 5.02. 92
but would it please thee, good andronicus, | to 5.02.111
what says andronicus to this device? 5.02.120
farewell, andronicus, revenge now goes | to lay 5.02.146
why art thou thus attir'd, andronicus? 5.03. 30
we are beholding to you, good andronicus. 5.03. 33
it was, andronicus. 5.03. 39
AND/'T 1 FR 0.0001 REL FR 0 V 1 P
'a shall, sir, and/'t please him. HAM 4.06. 9 P
AND'T 41 FR 0.0046 REL FR 13 V 28 P
steal by line and level, and't like your grace. TMP 4.01.239 P
not so, and't please your worship. WIV 2.02. 35 P
yes, and't please you, sir. MM 2.01.196 P
that's i, and't like your grace. 5.01. 74
wit, and't be thy will, put me into good fooling TN 1.05. 32 P
and't be any way, it must be with valor, for 3.02. 30 P
good luck, and't be thy will! WT 3.03. 68 P
are you a courtier, and't like you, sir? 4.04.729 P
i know not, and't like you. 4.04.741 P
a son, sir, do you hear, and't like you, sir? 4.04.782 P
and't please you, sir, to undertake the business 4.04.806 P
falstaff, and't please your lordship. 2H4 1.02. 59 P
and't please your lordship, i hear his majesty 1.02.103 P
a kind of lethargy, and't please your lordship, 1.02.112 P
rather, and't please you, it is the disease of 1.02.121 P
most worshipful lord, and't please your grace, i 2.01. 69 P
here, and't please you. 3.02.101 P
yea, and't please you. 3.02.105 P
and't be my dest'ny, so; 3.02.236 P
and't be not, so. 3.02.236 P
return, and't shall go hard but i'll make him a 3.02.329 P
gaultree forest, and't shall please your grace. 4.01. 2
and't please your worship, there's one pistol 5.03. 80 P
and't please your majesty, 'tis the gage of one H5 4.07.122 P
and't please your majesty, a rascal that 4.07.125 P
and a villain else, and't please your majesty, 4.07.133 P
mine is, and't please your grace, against john 2H6 1.03. 16 P
and't shall please your majesty, i never said 1.03.187 P
born blind, and't please your grace. 2.01. 75
his wife, and't like your worship. 2.01. 78
at berwick in the north, and't like your grace. 2.01. 81
and't please your grace, here my commission 2.04. 76
it's long, and't may be said | it reaches far, H8 1.01.110
and't please your grace, the two great cardinals 3.01. 16
and't like your grace — 4.02.100
and't please your honor, | we are but men; 5.03. 74
and't had been a green hair, i should have TRO 1.02.152 P
but, and't please you, deliver. COR 1.01. 94 P
key | (as, and't please heaven, he shall not), MAC 3.06. 19
but first, and't please the gods, | i'll hide my CYM 4.02.387
excess and overflow of power, and't might be, TNK 1.03. 4
/ANEW 1 FR 0.0001 REL FR 1 V 0 P
/what /do /we /then /but /draw /anew /the /model 2H4 1.03. 46
ANEW 10 FR 0.0011 REL FR 9 V 1 P
going, madam, weep o'er my father's death anew; AWW 1.01. 4 P
grace, | begin your suits anew, and sue to him. 2H6 1.03. 39
hue | that i would choose were i to choose anew. TIT 1.01.262
face, | for i will make him tell the tale anew: OTH 4.01. 84
and retain anew | her charitable heart, now hard TNK 1.02. 24
chin, | and where she ends, she doth anew begin. VEN 60
prove unjust, | press never thou to choose anew. PP 18.22
and therefore art enforc'd to seek anew | some SON 82. 7
and ruin'd love, when it is built anew, | grows 119.11
gentle doom, | and taught it thus anew to greet: 145. 8
/ANGEL 2 FR 0.0002 REL FR 1 V 1 P
/croak /not, /black /angel, /i /have /no /food LR 3.06. 31 P
not an /angel of the air, | bird melodious, or TNK 1.01. 16
ANGEL 56 FR 0.0063 REL FR 44 V 12 P
let's write "good angel" on the devil's horn, MM 2.04. 16
him hide, | though angel on the outward side! 3.02.272
sir, like an evil angel, and bid you forsake ERR 4.03. 20 P
noble, or not i for an angel; ADO 2.03. 33 P
in angel whiteness beat away those blushes, 4.01.161
than for that angel knowledge you can say, | yet LLL 1.01.113
there is no evil angel but love. 1.02.173 P
"for," quoth the king, "an angel shalt thou see; 5.02.103
the boy replied, "an angel is not evil; 5.02.105
what angel wakes me from my flow'ry bed? MND 3.01.129
a coin that bears the figure of an angel MV 2.07. 56
but here an angel in a golden bed | lies all 2.07. 58
but in his motion like an angel sings, | still 5.01. 61
i spied | an ancient angel coming down the hill, SHR 4.02. 61
what angel shall | bless this unworthy husband? AWW 3.04. 25
and if an angel should have come to me | and JN 4.01. 68
and even there, methinks an angel spake. 5.02. 64
richard hath in heavenly pay | a glorious angel; R2 3.02. 61
should be "by this fire, that/'s god's angel." 1H4 3.03. 35 P
sweet beef, i must still be good angel to thee. 3.03.178 P
as if an angel /dropp'd down from the clouds 4.01.108
this bottle makes an angel. 4.02. 6 P
young prince up and down, like his ill angel. 2H4 1.02.164 P
your ill angel is light, but i hope he that 1.02.165 P
for the boy, there is a good angel about him, 2.04.335 P
consideration like an angel came | and whipt th' H5 1.01. 28
an angel is like you, kate, and you are like an 5.02.109 P
is like you, kate, and you are like an angel. 5.02.110 P
then came wand'ring by | a shadow like an angel, R3 1.04. 53
which issued from my other angel husband, | and 4.01. 68
sir, as i have a soul, she is an angel; H8 4.01. 44
o, speak again, bright angel, for thou art | as ROM 2.02. 26
for brutus, as you know, was caesar's angel. JC 3.02.181
art thou some god, some angel, or some devil, 4.03.279
some holy angel | fly to the court of england, MAC 3.06. 45
and let the angel whom thou still hast serv'd 5.08. 14
so /lust, though to a radiant angel link'd, HAM 1.05. 55
how like an angel in apprehension! 2.02.306 P
eat, | of habits devil, is angel yet in this, 3.04.162
a minist'ring angel shall my sister be | when 5.01.241
o, the more angel she, | and you the blacker OTH 5.02.130
yea, curse his better angel from his side, | and 5.02.208
near him, thy angel | becomes a fear, as being ANT 2.03. 22
though this a heavenly angel, hell is here. CYM 2.02. 50
by jupiter, an angel! 3.06. 42
yet reverence | (that angel of the world) doth 4.02.248
my better angel is a man (right fair), | my PP 2. 3
evil | tempteth my better angel from my side; 2. 6
and whether that my angel be turn'd fiend, 2. 9
friend, | i guess one angel in another's hell: 2.12
doubt, | till my bad angel fire my good one out. 2.14
the better angel is a man right fair, | the SON 144. 3
evil | tempteth my better angel from my /side, 144. 6
and whether that my angel be turn'd fiend 144. 9
friend, | i guess one angel in another's hell. 144.12
doubt, | till my bad angel fire my good one out. 144.14
ANGELICA 1 FR 0.0001 REL FR 1 V 0 P
look to the bak'd meats, good angelica, | spare ROM 4.04. 5
ANGELICAL 1 FR 0.0001 REL FR 1 V 0 P
fiend angelical! ROM 3.02. 75
ANGEL-LIKE 2 FR 0.0002 REL FR 2 V 0 P
to clothe mine age with angel-like perfection, TGV 2.04. 66
how angel-like he sings! CYM 4.02. 48
ANGELO 75 FR 0.0084 REL FR 53 V 22 P
call hither, | i say, bid come before us angelo. MM 1.01. 15
such ample grace and honor, | it is lord angelo. 1.01. 24
angelo — | there is a kind of character in thy 1.01. 26
hold therefore, angelo: 1.01. 42
but from lord angelo by special charge. 1.02.119
i have deliver'd to lord angelo | (a man of 1.03. 11
would have seem'd | than in lord angelo. 1.03. 34
father, | i have on angelo impos'd the office, 1.03. 40
lord angelo is precise; 1.03. 50
governs lord angelo, a man whose blood | is very 1.04. 57
grace by your fair prayer | to soften angelo. 1.04. 70
go to lord angelo, | and let him learn to know, 1.04. 79
lord angelo is severe. 2.01.282
or what art thou, angelo? 2.02.172
i will proclaim thee, angelo, look for't! 2.04.151
so then you hope of pardon from lord angelo? 3.01. 1
lord angelo, having affairs to heaven, | intends 3.01. 56
the prenzie angelo? 3.01. 93
angelo had never the purpose to corrupt her; 3.01.161 P
i am confessor to angelo, and i know this to be 3.01.166 P
the assault that angelo hath made to you, 3.01.184 P
for his falling, i should wonder at angelo. 3.01.187 P
o, how much is the good duke deceiv'd in angelo! 3.01.192 P
she should this angelo have married; 3.01.213 P
her combinate-husband, this well-seeming angelo. 3.01.223 P
can this be so? did angelo so leave her? 3.01.224 P
go you to angelo, answer his requiring with a 3.01.243 P
haste you speedily to angelo; 3.01.262 P
place call upon me, and dispatch with angelo, 3.01.266 P
lord angelo dukes it well in his absence; 3.02. 94 P
they say this angelo was not made by man and 3.02.104 P
provost, my brother angelo will not be alter'd, 3.02.207 P
twice treble shame on angelo, | to weed my vice 3.02.269
with angelo to-night shall lie | his old 3.02.278
of justice | lord angelo hath to the public ear 4.02. 99
lord angelo, belike, thinking me remiss in mine 4.02.115 P
till now in the government of lord angelo, came 4.02.137 P
to the law than angelo who hath sentenc'd him. 4.02.158 P
to deliver his head in the view of angelo? 4.02.167 P
morning executed, and his head borne to angelo. 4.02.171 P
angelo hath seen them both, and will discover 4.02.172 P
this is a thing that angelo knows not, for he 4.02.199 P
the hour draws on | prefix'd by angelo. 4.03. 79
quick, dispatch, and send the head to angelo. 4.03. 92
now will i write letters to angelo | (the 4.03. 93
form, | we shall proceed with angelo. 4.03.101
the world, | his head is off and sent to angelo. 4.03.116
most damned angelo! 4.03.122
he hath carried | notice to escalus and angelo, 4.03.130
and to the head of angelo | accuse him home and 4.03.142
here is lord angelo shall give you justice; 5.01. 27
that angelo is an adulterous thief, | an 5.01. 40
it is not truer he is angelo | than this is all 5.01. 43
shy, as grave, as just, as absolute | as angelo. 5.01. 55
even so may angelo, | in all his dressings, 5.01. 55
to lose his head, condemn'd by angelo. 5.01. 71
to try her gracious fortune with lord angelo, 5.01. 76
was complaint | intended 'gainst lord angelo, 5.01.154
do you not smile at this, lord angelo? 5.01.163
come, cousin angelo, | in this i'll be impartial 5.01.165
this is no witness for lord angelo. 5.01.193
why, just, my lord, and that is angelo, | who 5.01.202
this is that face, thou cruel angelo, | which 5.01.207
you set these women on to slander lord angelo? 5.01.289 P
"an angelo for claudio, death for death!" 5.01.409
then, angelo, thy fault's thus manifested; 5.01.412
for angelo, | his act did not o'ertake his bad 5.01.450
so learned and so wise | as you, lord angelo, 5.01.471
by this lord angelo perceives he's safe; 5.01.494
well, angelo, your evil quits you well. 5.01.496
love her, angelo! 5.01.526
forgive him, angelo, that brought you home | the 5.01.532
good signior angelo, you must excuse us all, ERR 3.01. 1
one angelo, a goldsmith. do you know him? 4.04.132
report here to the state | by signior angelo. OTH 1.03. 16
ANGELO'S 3 FR 0.0003 REL FR 3 V 0 P
i'll tell him yet of angelo's request, | and fit MM 2.04.186
that angelo's forsworn, is it not strange? 5.01. 38
that angelo's a murtherer, is't not strange? 5.01. 39
ANGEL'S 1 FR 0.0001 REL FR 1 V 0 P
which, to betray, dost, with thine angel's face, PER 4.03. 47
ANGELS' 2 FR 0.0002 REL FR 2 V 0 P
ne'er so black, say they have angels' faces. TGV 3.01.103
ye have angels' faces, but heaven knows your H8 3.01.145
ANGELS 35 FR 0.0039 REL FR 29 V 6 P
this is a caliban, | and they to him are angels. TMP 1.02.482
now, good angels | preserve the king! 2.01.306
he hath a /legion of angels. WIV 1.03. 53 P
humor me the angels. 1.03. 57 P
i had myself twenty angels given me this morning 2.02. 72 P

given me this morning, but i defy all angels (in 2.02. 73 P
before high heaven | as makes the angels weep; MM 2.02.122
here are the angels that you sent for to deliver ERR 4.03. 40 P
they appear to men like angels of light, light 4.03. 55 P
are angels /vailing clouds, or roses blown. LLL 5.02.297
did fan the house | and angels offic'd all. AWW 3.02.126
when his fair angels would salute my palm, | but JN 2.01.590
abbots, imprisoned angels | set at liberty. 3.03. 8
then if angels fight, | weak men must fall, for R2 3.02. 61
god and his angels guard your sacred throne, H5 1.02. 7
more wonderful, when angels are so angry. R3 1.02. 74
go thou to richard, and good angels tend thee! 4.01. 92
good angels guard thy battle! 5.03.138
good angels guard thee from the boar's annoy! 5.03.151
god and good angels fight on richmond's side, 5.03.175
dying, | go with me like good angels to my end, H8 2.01. 75
good angels keep it from us! 2.01.142
excellence | that angels love good men with; 2.02. 34
by that sin fell the angels; 3.02.441
now good angels | fly o'er thy royal head, and 5.01.159
few are angels; 5.02. 47
women are angels, wooing: TRO 1.02.286
free, as debonair, unarm'd, | as bending angels; 1.03.236
and her immortal part with angels lives. ROM 5.01. 19
that his virtues | will plead like angels, MAC 1.07. 19
angels are bright still, though the brightest 4.03. 22
angels and ministers of grace defend us! HAM 1.04. 39
help, angels! 3.03. 69
and flights of angels sing thee to thy rest! 5.02.360
thought the old man and his sons were angels. CYM 5.03. 85

ANGER 66 FR 0.0074 REL FR 56 V 10 P
till this day | saw i him touch'd with anger, so TMP 4.01.145
of it, but i fear'd | lest i might anger thee. 4.01.169
you would be fing'ring them, to anger me. TGV 1.02. 98
urge not my father's anger, eglamour, | but 4.03. 27
with anger, with sickness, or with hunger, my ADO 1.01.249 P
which, not to anger bent, is music and sweet LLL 4.02.116
pale in her anger, washes all the air, | that MND 2.01.104
with his eyes full of anger. AYL 1.03. 40 P
foulness, and she'll fall in love with my anger. 3.05. 67 P
for it engenders choler, planteth anger, | and SHR 4.01.172
my tongue will tell the anger of my heart, | or 4.03. 77
do not plunge thyself too far in anger, lest AWW 2.03.211 P
to anger him we'll have the bear again, and we TN 2.05. 9 P
in the contempt and anger of his lip! 3.01.146
and never to my red–look'd anger be | the WT 2.02. 32
not a party to | the anger of the king, nor 2.02. 60
to be done | than out of anger can be uttered. 1H4 1.01.107
give it him | to keep his anger still in motion. 1.03.226
by the mass, i could anger her to th' heart. 2H4 3.02.204 P
free from gross passion, or of mirth or anger, H5 2.02.132
'tis not for fear, but anger, that thy cheeks 1H6 2.04. 65
my heart for anger burns, i cannot brook it. 3H6 1.01. 60
comes the queen, whose looks bewray her anger. 1.01.211
anger is like | a full hot horse, who being H8 1.01.132
out of anger | he sent command to the lord mayor 2.01.150
mine | that had to him deriv'd your anger did i 2.04. 32
by some of these | the queen is put in anger. 2.04.162
he hears the king | does whet his anger to him. 3.02. 92
i fear, the story of his anger. 3.02.209
what was his cause of anger? TRO 1.02. 11
that were we talking of, and of his anger. 1.02. 52 P
nay, but you part in anger. 5.02. 45
observe and answer | the vantage of his anger. COR 2.03.260
but yet a brain that leads my use of anger | to 3.02. 30
all's in anger. 3.02. 95
and lament as i do, | in anger, juno–like. 4.02. 53
and if he hear thee, thou wilt anger him. ROM 2.01. 22
this cannot anger him; 2.01. 23
'twould anger him | to raise a spirit in his 2.01. 23
i anger her sometimes and tell her that paris is 2.04.203 P
and thou shouldst, thou'dst anger ladies. TIM 1.01.205 P
and unnoted passion | he did behoove his anger, 3.05. 22
to be in anger is impiety; 3.05. 56
do you dare our anger? 3.05. 95
that carries anger as the flint bears fire, JC 4.03.111
of your sword, let grief | convert to anger; MAC 4.03.229
a countenance more | in sorrow than in anger. HAM 1.02.232
yes, sir, but anger hath a privilege. LR 2.02. 70
touch me with noble anger, | and let not women's 2.04.276
nay then come on, and take the chance of anger. 3.07. 79
do you find some occasion to anger cassio, OTH 2.01.267 P
never anger | made good guard for itself. ANT 4.01. 9
play'd than fought | and had no help of anger. CYM 1.01.163
how durst thy tongue move anger to our face? PER 1.02. 54
while, | till that his rage and anger be forgot, 1.02.107
and pitch between her arms to anger thee. TNK 2.02.217
content and anger | in me have but one face. 3.01.107
no more anger, | as you love any thing that's 3.06. 26
sister, | i find no anger to 'em, nor no ruin: 3.06.189
that oath was rashly made, and in your anger, 3.06.227
lay by your anger for an hour, and dove–like, 5.01. 11
and with our patience anger tott'ring fortune, 5.04. 20
'twixt crimson shame and anger ashy–pale. VEN 76
that even for anger makes the lily pale | and LUC 478
which, not to anger bent, is music and sweet PP 5.12
on | that sometimes anger thrusts into his hide, SON 50.10

ANGER'D 3 FR 0.0003 REL FR 3 V 0 P
and, being anger'd, puffs away from thence, ROM 1.04.102
for 'twould have anger'd any heart alive | to MAC 3.06. 15
at whose burthen | the anger'd ocean foams, with ANT 2.06. 21

ANGERLY 3 FR 0.0003 REL FR 3 V 0 P
how angerly i taught my brow to frown, | when TGV 1.02. 62
speak a word, | nor look upon the iron angerly. JN 4.01. 81
why, how now, hecat? you look angerly. MAC 3.05. 1

ANGER'S 2 FR 0.0002 REL FR 2 V 0 P
what sudden anger's this? H8 3.02.204
anger's my meat; COR 4.02. 50

ANGERS 5 FR 0.0005 REL FR 3 V 2 P
for he both pleases men and angers them, and ADO 2.01.141 P
sometime he angers me | with telling me of the 1H4 3.01.146
this is the deadly spite that angers me: 3.01.190
did, in his ales and his angers, look you, kill H5 4.07. 38 P
those joys, griefs, angers, fears, my friend TNK 2.02.188

ANGES 1 FR 0.0001 REL FR 0 V 1 P
que dit–il? que je suis semblable a les anges? H5 5.02.111 P

ANGIERS 13 FR 0.0014 REL FR 13 V 0 P
before angiers well met, brave austria. JN 2.01. 1
welcome before the gates of angiers, duke. 2.01. 17
to my home i will no more return | till angiers, 2.01. 22
hither to the walls | these men of angiers; 2.01.199
you men of angiers, and my loving subjects — 2.01.203
you loving men of angiers, arthur's subjects, 2.01.204
you men of angiers, open wide your gates, | and 2.01.300
rejoice, you men of angiers, ring your bells, 2.01.312
lord of our presence, angiers, and of you. 2.01.367
by heaven, these scroyles of angiers flout you, 2.01.373
and lay this angiers even with the ground, 2.01.399
now, citizens of angiers, ope your gates, | let 2.01.536
is not angiers lost? 3.04. 6

ANGLAIS *(see anglois)*

ANGLE* 9 FR 0.0010 REL FR 8 V 1 P
in an odd angle of the isle, and sitting, | his TMP 1.02.223
so angle we for beatrice, who even now | is ADO 3.01. 29
she knew her distance and did angle for me, AWW 5.03.212
i fear, the angle that plucks our son thither. WT 4.02. 46 P
win | the hearts of all that he did angle for; 1H4 4.03. 84
to angle for your thoughts, but you are wise, TRO 3.02.155
thrown out his angle for my proper life, | and HAM 5.02. 66
give me mine angle, we'll to th' river; ANT 2.05. 10
i then left my angle | to his own skill, came TNK 4.01. 59

ANGLED 1 FR 0.0001 REL FR 0 V 1 P
of all, and that which angled for mine eyes WT 5.02. 83 P

ANGLER 1 FR 0.0001 REL FR 0 V 1 P
and tells me nero is an angler in the lake of LR 3.06. 7 P

ANGLETERRE 1 FR 0.0001 REL FR 0 V 1 P
alice, tu as ete en angleterre, et tu bien H5 3.04. 1 P

ANGLIAE 1 FR 0.0001 REL FR 0 V 1 P
filius noster henricus, rex angliae, et heres H5 5.02.341 P

ANGLING 4 FR 0.0004 REL FR 4 V 0 P
the pleasant'st angling is to see the fish | cut ADO 3.01. 26
i am angling now, | though you perceive me not WT 1.02.180
'twas merry when | you wager'd on your angling; ANT 2.05. 16
as i late was angling | in the great lake that TNK 4.01. 52

ANGLISH *(also english)*

ANGLISH 1 FR 0.0001 REL FR 0 V 1 P
i cannot tell wat is /baiser en anglish. H5 5.02.262 P

ANGLOIS 2 FR 0.0002 REL FR 0 V 2 P
comment appelez–vous la main en anglois? H5 3.04. 6 P
c'est bien dit, madame, il est fort bon anglois. 3.04. 20 P

ANG'RED 5 FR 0.0005 REL FR 4 V 1 P
pleas'd | to be so ang'red with another letter. TGV 1.02.100
nay, would i were so ang'red with the same. 1.02.101
it ang'red him to the heart, but he hath forgot 2H4 2.04. 8 P
she that being ang'red, her revenge being nigh, OTH 2.01.152
with a fool, | frighted, and ang'red worse. CYM 2.03.140

ANGRILY *(see angerly)*

ANG'RING 1 FR 0.0001 REL FR 1 V 0 P
fool to sorrow, | ang'ring itself and others. LR 4.01. 39

ANGRY 107 FR 0.0121 REL FR 92 V 15 P
nay, good my lord, be not angry. TMP 2.01.186 P
she gave me none, except an angry word. TGV 2.01.158 P
what, angry, sir thurio? do you change color? 2.04. 23 P
must needs go in, | her father will be angry. WIV 3.04. 93
good george, be not angry. 5.05.200 P
like an angry ape | plays such fantastic tricks MM 2.02.120
redeem your brother from the angry law; 3.01.201 P
i pray you be not angry with me, madam, ADO 3.01. 94
art thou sick, or angry? 5.01.131 P
i think he be angry indeed. 5.01.141 P
the childing autumn, angry winter, change MND 2.01.112
o, when she is angry, she is keen and shrewd! 3.02.323
was writing of it, | it bears an angry tenure. AYL 4.03. 11
rage like an angry boar chafed with sweat? SHR 1.02.202
come, you wasp, i' faith you are too angry. 2.01.209
nor bite the lip, as angry wenches will, | nor 2.01.248
o kate, content thee, prithee be not angry. 3.02.215
i will be angry; 3.02.216
apollo's angry, and the heavens themselves | do WT 3.02.146
the heavens with that we have in hand are angry, 3.03. 5
sin, | for which the heavens, taking angry note, 5.01.173
the angry lords with all expedient haste. JN 4.02.268
doth dogged war bristle his angry crest, | and 4.03.149
never lift | an angry arm against his minister. R2 1.02. 41
who therewith angry, when it next came there, 1H4 1.03. 40
something too round, i should be angry with you, H5 4.01.204 P
i was not angry since i came to france | until 4.07. 55
and, by my soul, this pale and angry rose, | as 1H6 2.04.107
and digest | your angry choler on your enemies. 4.01.168
but when my angry guardant stood alone, 4.07. 9
nay, be not angry, i am pleas'd again. 2H6 1.02. 55
day, | he knits his brow and shows an angry eye, 3.01. 15
like an angry hive of bees | that want their 3.02.125
but angry, wrathful, and inclin'd to blood, | if 4.02.126
flint, | i am so angry at these abject terms; 5.01. 25
nay, do not fright us with an angry look. 5.01.126
now, when the angry trumpet sounds alarum, | and 5.02. 3
whom angry heavens do make their minister, 5.02. 34
thou smiling while he knit his angry brows: 3H6 2.02. 20
more wonderful, when angels are so angry. R3 1.02. 74
since, | stabb'd in my angry mood at tewksbury? 1.02.241
good madam, be not angry with the child. 2.04. 36
marry, my uncle clarence' angry ghost. 3.01.144
the king is angry, see, he gnaws his lip. 4.02. 27
so in the lethe of thy angry soul | thou drown 4.04.251
pray god he be not angry. H8 2.02. 63
who can be angry now? 2.02. 88
what, art thou angry, pandarus? what, with me? TRO 1.01. 73
man, that makes me smile, make hector angry? 1.02. 32 P
was he angry? 1.02. 53 P
what, is he angry too? 1.02. 59 P
that the blest gods, as angry with my fancy, 4.04. 25
face, | know what it is to meet achilles angry. 5.05. 46
you talk of pride now — will you not be angry? COR 2.01. 26 P
the reins and be angry at your pleasures; 2.01. 31 P
and, being angry, does forget that ever | he 3.01.258
and so would do, | were he more angry at it. 4.06. 15
heart | that dies in tempest of thy angry frown. TIT 1.01.458
the angry northen wind | will blow these sands 4.01.104
and on them shalt thou ease thy angry heart. 5.02.119
which oft the angry mab with blisters plagues, ROM 1.04. 75
that i had no angry wit to be a lord. TIM 1.01.234 P
furor brevis est," | but yond man is very angry. 1.02. 29
h'as much disgrac'd me in't, i'm angry at him, 3.03. 13
but who is man that is not angry? 3.05. 57
now | leap in with me into this angry flood, JC 1.02.103
the angry spot doth glow on caesar's brow, | and 1.02.183
but with an angry wafter of your hand | gave 2.01.246
be angry when you will, it shall have scope; 4.03.108
i did not think you could have been so angry. 4.03.143
poor, innocent lamb | t' appease an angry god. MAC 4.03. 17
so frown'd he once, when, in an angry parle, HAM 1.01. 62
why art thou angry? LR 2.02. 71
is my lord angry? OTH 3.04.132
can he be angry? 3.04.134
arm | puff'd his own brother — and is he angry? 3.04.137
there's matter in't indeed, if he be angry. 3.04.139
what, is he angry? 4.01.235
quat almost to the sense, | and he grows angry. 5.01. 12
fulvia perchance is angry; ANT 1.01. 20
look thou say | he makes me angry with him; 3.13.141
he makes me angry, | and at this time most easy 3.13.143
poor venomous fool, | be angry, and dispatch. 5.02.306
here abide the hourly shot | of angry eyes, not CYM 1.01. 90
be not angry, | most mighty princess, that i 1.06.171
fellow, | albeit he comes on angry purpose now; 2.03. 56
our good deed, | though rome be therefore angry. 3.01. 58
trims, wherein | you made great juno angry. 3.04.165
i see you're angry. 3.06. 55
be a little angry for my so rough usage; 4.01. 20 P
nay, be not angry, sir. 5.03. 59
farewell, you're angry. 5.03. 63
an angry brow, dread lord. PER 1.02. 52
yet cease your ire, you angry stars of heaven! 2.01. 1
resolve your angry father if my tongue | did 2.05. 68
whilst the angry swine | flies like a parthian TNK 2.02. 49
a fool, | an innocent, and i was very angry. 4.01. 41
and when he's angry, then a settled valor | (not 4.02.100
which bred more beauty in his angry eyes: VEN 70
what recketh he his rider's angry stir, | his 283
and with his bonnet hides his angry brow, 339
mine eye | the picture of an angry chafing boar, 662
who, therefore angry, seems to part in sunder, LUC 388
who, angry that the eyes fly from their lights, 461
it seem'd they would debate with angry swords. 1421
and with my knife scratch out the angry eyes 1469
angry that his prescriptions are not kept, SON 147. 6

ANGUISH 6 FR 0.0006 REL FR 6 V 0 P
play | to ease the anguish of a torturing hour? MND 5.01. 37
words would add more anguish than the wounds. 3H6 2.01. 99
/one pain is less'ned by another's anguish; ROM 1.02. 46
whose power | will close the eye of anguish. LR 4.04. 15
senses grow imperfect | by your eyes' anguish. 4.06. 6
more fell than anguish, hunger, or the sea! OTH 5.02.362

ANGUS 1 FR 0.0001 REL FR 1 V 0 P
earl of athol, | of murray, angus, and menteith. 1H4 1.01. 73

AN–HEIRES 1 FR 0.0001 REL FR 0 V 1 P
will you go, an–heires? WIV 2.01.220 P

AN–HUNGRY *(also a–hungry)*

AN–HUNGRY 1 FR 0.0001 REL FR 1 V 0 P
they said they were an–hungry; COR 1.01.205

A–NIGHT 1 FR 0.0001 REL FR 0 V 1 P
him take that for coming a–night to jane smile; AYL 2.04. 48 P

A–NIGHTS 2 FR 0.0002 REL FR 2 V 0 P
sleek–headed men and such as sleep a–nights. JC 1.02.193
see, antony, that revels long a–nights, | is 2.02.116

ANIMAL 3 FR 0.0003 REL FR 1 V 2 P
he is only an animal, only sensible in the LLL 4.02. 27 P
the wretched animal heav'd forth such groans AYL 2.01. 36
such a poor, bare, fork'd animal as thou art. LR 3.04.108 P

ANIMALS 5 FR 0.0005 REL FR 3 V 2 P
or those pamp'red animals | that rage in savage ADO 4.01. 60
that souls of animals infuse themselves | into MV 4.01.132
for the which his animals on his dunghills are AYL 1.01. 15 P
to fright the animals and to kill them up | in 2.01. 62
the paragon of animals! HAM 2.02.307 P

ANIMIS 1 FR 0.0001 REL FR 1 V 0 P
tantaene animis caelestibus irae? 2H6 2.01. 24

/ANJOU 2 FR 0.0002 REL FR 2 V 0 P
england and ireland, /anjou, touraine, maine, JN 2.01.152
for /anjou and fair touraine, maine, poictiers, 2.01.487

ANJOU 13 FR 0.0014 REL FR 11 V 2 P
to ireland, poictiers, anjou, touraine, maine, JN 1.01. 11
poictiers, and anjou, these five provinces, 2.01.528
/reignier, duke of anjou, doth take his part; 1H6 1.01. 94
duke of anjou and maine, yet is he poor, | and 5.03. 95
command in anjou what your honor pleases. 5.03.147
enjoy mine own, the country maine and anjou, 5.03.154
that the duchy of anjou and the county of maine 2H6 1.01. 51 P
that the /duchy of anjou and /the /county /of 1.01. 58 P
hath given the duchy of anjou, and maine, | unto 1.01.110
anjou and maine? 1.01.119
anjou and maine are given to the french, | paris 1.01.214
anjou and maine both given unto the french! 1.01.236
by thee anjou and maine were sold to france. 4.01. 86

ANKLE 1 FR 0.0001 REL FR 1 V 0 P
ungart'red, and down–gyved to his ankle, | pale HAM 2.01. 77

ANNA 1 FR 0.0001 REL FR 1 V 0 P
as dear | as anna to the queen of carthage was: SHR 1.01.154

ANNALS 1 FR 0.0001 REL FR 1 V 0 P
if you have writ your annals true, 'tis there COR 5.06.113

ANNE 64 FR 0.0072 REL FR 17 V 47 P
there is anne page, which is daughter to master WIV 1.01. 45 P
mistress anne page? 1.01. 47 P
between master abraham and mistress anne page. 1.01. 56 P
o heaven! this is mistress anne page. 1.01.190 P
the very point of it — to mistress anne page. 1.01.224 P
here comes fair mistress anne. 1.01.259 P
would i were young for your sake, mistress anne! 1.01.260 P
i will wait on him, fair mistress anne. 1.01.263 P
mistress anne, yourself shall go first. 1.01.307 P
acquaintance with mistress anne page; 1.02. 9 P
your master's desires to mistress anne page. 1.02. 11 P
well, heaven send anne page no worse fortune! 1.04. 32 P
anne is a good girl, and i wish — 1.04. 34 P
good word to mistress anne page for my master in 1.04. 83 P
himself is in love with mistress anne page; 1.04.104 P
tell–a me dat i shall have anne page for myself? 1.04.116 P
by gar, i will myself have anne page. 1.04.119 P
by gar, if i have not anne page, i shall turn 1.04.124 P
you shall have anne — fool's–head of your own. 1.04.126 P
what news? how does pretty mistress anne? 1.04.138 P
but anne loves him not; 1.04.163 P
you are come to see my daughter anne? 2.01.163 P

and i pray, how does good mistress anne? 2.01.165 P
for he speak for a jack–an–ape to anne page. 2.03. 83 P
i will bring thee where mistress anne page is, 2.03. 87 P
which i will be thy adversary toward anne page. 2.03. 95 P
ah, sweet anne page! 3.01. 40 P
o sweet anne page! 3.01. 70 P
o sweet anne page! 3.01.114 P
he promise to bring me where is anne page; 3.01.123 P
we have appointed to dine with mistress anne, 3.02. 55 P
about a match between anne page and my cousin 3.02. 58 P
was the first motive that i woo'd thee, anne; 3.04. 14
i had a father, mistress anne; 3.04. 38 P
tell mistress anne the jest how my father stole 3.04. 40 P
mistress anne, my cousin loves you. 3.04. 42 P
now, good mistress anne — 3.04. 55 P
love him, daughter anne. 3.04. 67
but yet i would my master had mistress anne; 3.04.105 P
they were nothing but about mistress anne page, 4.05. 47 P
with the dear love i bear to fair anne page, 4.06. 9
if anne page be my daughter, she is, by this, 5.05.174 P
came yonder at eton to marry mistress anne page, 5.05.184 P
if i did not think it had been anne page, would 5.05.187 P
she cried "budget," as anne and i had appointed, 5.05.198 P
and i had appointed, and yet it was not anne, 5.05.199 P
it is not anne page. 5.05.206 P
this is strange. who hath got the right anne? 5.05.212 P
yes, by saint anne, do i. SHR 1.01.250 P
yes, by saint anne, and ginger shall be hot i' TN 2.03.117 P
roger had issue, edmund, anne, and eleanor. 2H6 2.02. 38
his eldest sister, anne, | my mother, being heir 2.02. 43
ghost | to hear the lamentations of poor anne, R3 1.02. 9
but, gentle lady anne, | to leave this keen 1.02.114
rumor it abroad | that anne, my wife, is very 4.02. 51
i say again, give out | that anne, my queen, is 4.02. 57
and anne my wife hath bid this world good night. 4.03. 39
mad'st quick conveyance with her good aunt anne. 4.04.283
richard, thy wife, that wretched anne thy wife, 5.03.159
a creature of the queen's, lady anne bullen." H8 3.02. 36
anne bullen? 3.02. 87
i'll no anne bullens for him, | there's more 3.02. 87
last, that the lady anne, | whom the king hath 3.02.402
behold | the lady anne pass from her coronation? 4.01. 3

ANNE'S 4 FR 0.0004 REL FR 0 V 4 P
but notwithstanding that, i know anne's mind — WIV 1.04.105 P
no, i know anne's mind for that. 1.04.127 P
in windsor knows more of anne's mind than i do, 1.04.128 P
for i know anne's mind as well as another does. 1.04.164 P

ANNEX'D 2 FR 0.0002 REL FR 2 V 0 P
which whilst it was mine had annex'd unto't | a ANT 4.14. 17
and to his robb'ry had annex'd thy breath, | but SON 99.11

ANNEXIONS 1 FR 0.0001 REL FR 1 V 0 P
with th' annexions of fair gems enrich'd, | and LC 208

ANNEXMENT 1 FR 0.0001 REL FR 1 V 0 P
each small annexment, petty consequence, HAM 3.03. 21

ANNOTHANIZE 1 FR 0.0001 REL FR 0 V 1 P
which to annothanize in the vulgar — o base and LLL 4.01. 68 P

ANNOY 12 FR 0.0013 REL FR 12 V 0 P
one spark of evil | that might annoy my finger? H5 2.02.102
to mow down thorns that would annoy our foot 2H6 3.01. 67
farewell sour annoy! 3H6 5.07. 45
good angels guard thee from the boar's annoy! R3 5.03.151
and rape, i fear, was root of thy annoy. TIT 4.01. 49
may well stretch so far | as to annoy us all; JC 2.01.160
we fear not | what can from italy annoy us, but CYM 4.03. 34
but now i liv'd, and life was death's annoy, VEN 497
her, | that worse than tantalus' is her annoy, 599
for mirth doth search the bottom of annoy, | sad LUC 1109
threat'ning cloud–kissing ilion with annoy, 1370
or else receiv'st with pleasure thine annoy? SON 8. 4

ANNOYANCE *(also noyance)*

ANNOYANCE 5 FR 0.0005 REL FR 5 V 0 P
hair, | any annoyance in that precious sense! JN 4.01. 93
to souse annoyance that comes near his nest; 5.02.150
way, | doing annoyance to the treacherous feet, R2 3.02. 16
the herd hath more annoyance by the breeze TRO 1.03. 48
remove from her the means of all annoyance, MAC 5.01. 76

ANNOY'D 1 FR 0.0001 REL FR 1 V 0 P
because she will not be annoy'd with suitors. SHR 1.01.184

ANNOYING 1 FR 0.0001 REL FR 1 V 0 P
me, and went surly by, | without annoying me. JC 1.03. 22

ANNUAL 5 FR 0.0005 REL FR 5 V 0 P
th' king of naples | to give him annual tribute, TMP 1.02.113
signs | have brought about the annual reckoning. LLL 5.02.798
title | a thousand pound a year, annual support, H8 2.03. 64
him threescore thousand crowns in annual fee, HAM 2.02. 73
striv'd | god neptune's annual feast to keep, PER 5.ch. 17

ANOINT 2 FR 0.0002 REL FR 2 V 0 P
anoint his eyes, | but do it when the next thing MND 2.01.261
and, for /that purpose, i'll anoint my sword. HAM 4.07.140

ANOINTED *(also 'nointed)*

ANOINTED 19 FR 0.0021 REL FR 18 V 1 P
th' anointed sovereign of sighs and groans, LLL 3.01.182
anointed, i implore so much expense of thy royal 5.02.522 P
of thousands that had struck anointed kings WT 1.02.358
hail, you anointed deputies of heaven! JN 3.01.136
substitute, | his deputy anointed in his sight, R2 1.02. 38
commit'st thy anointed body to the cure | of 2.01. 98
com'st thou because the anointed king is hence? 2.03. 96
can wash the balm off from an anointed king; 3.02. 55
anointed, crowned, planted many years, | be 4.01.127
true rule | you stand against anointed majesty. 1H4 4.03. 40
stoop'd his anointed head as low as death. 2H4 in 32
king henry's faithful and anointed queen. 1H6 5.05. 91
thy balm wash'd off wherewith thou was anointed. 3H6 3.01. 17
i was anointed king at nine months old, | my 3.01. 76
anointed let me be with deadly venom, | and die R3 4.01. 61
tell–tale women | rail on the lord's anointed. 4.04.151
my anointed body | by thee was punched full of 5.03.124
hath broke ope | the lord's anointed temple, and MAC 2.03. 68
in his anointed flesh /rash boarish fangs. LR 3.07. 58

ANON 137 FR 0.0154 REL FR 76 V 61 P
thou wilt anon, i know it by thy trembling. TMP 2.02. 80 P
i will furnish it anon with new contents. 2.02.143 P
go home, john rugby, i come anon. WIV 3.02. 86 P
up, gentlemen, you shall see sport anon. 3.03.169 P
hard by, at street end; he will be here anon. 4.02. 40 P
i shall find you anon. 4.02.140 P
i will call upon you anon for some advantage to MM 4.01. 23 P
more of him anon. 4.02.153 P
you shall anon over–read it at your pleasure; 4.02.197 P
other of our friends | will greet us here anon. 4.05. 13
for the friar and you | must have a word anon. 5.01.359
anon i'm sure the duke himself in person | comes ERR 5.01.119
anon, i wot not by what strong escape, | he 5.01.148
come go with us, we'll look to that anon. 5.01.413
and anon falleth like a crab on the face of LLL 4.02. 6 P
and ever and anon they made a doubt | presence 5.02.101
our queen and all her elves come here anon. MND 2.01. 17
anon his thisby must be answered, | and forth my 3.02. 18
the starry welkin cover thou anon | with 3.02.356
of this discourse we more will hear anon. 4.01.178
anon comes pyramus, sweet youth and tall, | and 5.01.144
and desire gratiano to come anon to my lodging. MV 2.02.117 P
thou wilt say anon he is some kin to thee, 2.09. 97
i will anon, first let us go to dinner. 3.05. 86
anon a careless herd, | full of the pasture, AYL 2.01. 52
anon i'll give thee more instructions. SHR in.1. 130
get you gone, sir, i'll talk with you more anon. AWW 1.03. 65 P
i will speak with you further anon. 1.03.127 P
you shall hear one anon. 4.01. 63 P
we shall hear of your /lordship anon. 4.03.196 P
mine eyes smell onions, i shall weep anon. 5.03.320
i'll be with you anon. TN 3.04.320 P
sir, | and anon, sir, | i'll be with you again; 4.02.121
your bounty take a nap, i will awake it anon. 5.01. 49 P
hath tended upon me, | but more of that anon. 5.01.100
the fury spent, anon | did this break from her: WT 3.03. 26
and anon swallow'd with yest and froth, as 3.03. 92 P
we'll buy the other things anon. 4.04.274 P
we'll have this song out anon by ourselves. 4.04.309 P
on't, lest your fancy | may think anon it moves. 5.03. 61
transported that | he'll think anon it lives. 5.03. 70
anon i'll tell thee more. JN 1.01.232
snow, tumbled about, | anon becomes a mountain. 3.04.177
still and anon cheer'd up the heavy time, 4.01. 47
which ever and anon | he gave his nose and 1H4 1.03. 38
anon, anon. 2.01. 4 P
anon, anon. 2.01. 4 P
with this shrill addition, "anon, anon, sir! 2.04. 27 P
with this shrill addition, "anon, anon, sir! 2.04. 27 P
that his tale to me may be nothing but "anon." 2.04. 33 P
anon, anon, sir. 2.04. 37 P
anon, anon, sir. 2.04. 37 P
anon, anon, sir. 2.04. 44 P
anon, anon, sir. 2.04. 44 P
anon, sir. 2.04. 52 P
anon, sir. pray stay a little, my lord. 2.04. 57 P
anon, anon. 2.04. 64 P
anon, anon. 2.04. 64 P
anon, francis? 2.04. 65 P
anon, anon, sir. 2.04. 86 P
anon, anon, sir. 2.04. 86 P
anon, anon, sir. 2.04. 97 P
anon, anon, sir. 2.04. 97 P
prithee let him alone, we shall have more anon. 2.04.208 P
here will be the prince and master poins anon, 2H4 2.04. 16 P
this will grow to a brawl anon. 2.04.173 P
anon, anon, sir. 2.04.282 P
anon, anon, sir. 2.04.282 P
cousin, that comes hither anon about soldiers? 3.02. 27 P
silence, i'll give you a health for that anon. 5.03. 24 P
sir, sit, i'll be with you anon, most sweet sir, 5.03. 26 P
them, and anon | desire them all to my pavilion. H5 4.01. 26
anon, from thy insulting tyranny, | coupled in 1H6 4.07. 19
nay, we shall heat you thoroughly anon. 2H6 5.01.159
for through this laund anon the deer will come, 3H6 3.01. 2
you shall have wine enough, my lord, anon. R3 1.04.162
win the duke of york, | anon expect him here; 3.01. 39
i shall anon advise you | further in the H8 1.02.107
i told your grace they would talk anon. 1.04. 49
and anon he casts | his eye against the moon. 3.02.117
we shall hear more anon. 5.02. 35
you'll leave your noise anon, ye rascals; 5.03. 1 P
you shall see anon. TRO 1.02.188 P
i'll show you troilus anon. 1.02.194 P
you shall see troilus anon. 1.02.217 P
and anon behold | the strong–ribb'd bark through 1.03. 39
bid them have patience, she shall come anon. 4.04. 52
anon he's there afoot, | and there they fly or 5.05. 21
now, | but thou anon shalt hear of me again; 5.06. 18
marks invested, you | anon do meet the senate. COR 2.03.141
do admit you and are summon'd | to meet anon, 2.03.144
i'll have you talk'd with anon. 4.05. 18 P
to that which thou shalt hear of me anon. TIT 5.01. 90
and then anon | drums in his ear, at which he ROM 1.04. 85
anon, anon! 1.05.143
anon, anon! 1.05.143
anon, good nurse! 2.02.137
i come, anon. 2.02.150
anon! 2.04.105 P
anon! 2.04.216 P
anon comes one with light to ope the tomb, | and 5.03.283
i thank you, you shall hear from me anon. TIM 1.01.153
pray you walk near, i'll speak with you anon. 2.02.123
i'll tell you more anon. 3.06. 59 P
anon! MAC 1.01. 10
anon, anon! 2.03. 20 P
anon, anon! 2.03. 20 P
yourselves apart, | i'll come to you anon. 3.01.138
anon we'll drink a measure | the table round. 3.04. 11
well, more anon. 4.03.140
and anon methought | the wood began to move. 5.05. 33
"anon he finds him | striking too short at HAM 2.02.468
anon the dreadful thunder | doth rend the region 2.02.486
you shall see anon. 3.02.240 P
you shall see anon how the murtherer gets the 3.02.263 P
anon, as patient as the female dove, | when that 5.01.286
shall i hear from you anon? LR 1.02.177 P
bade him anon return and here speak with me, OTH 4.01. 80
i'll send for you anon. 4.01.259
he'll come anon — "sing all a green willow must 4.03. 50 P
nay, /an' you stare, we shall hear more anon. 5.01.107
forbear me till anon. ANT 2.07. 39
to ask him one thing, i'll remember't anon.) CYM 3.05.131 P
anon | a rout, confusion thick. 5.03. 40
i'll speak anon. TNK 1.01.106
but anon | th' assistants made a brave 5.03. 81
anon the other, then again the first, | and by 5.03.126
anon he rears upright, curvets, and leaps, | as VEN 279
anon he starts at stirring of a feather; 302
anon their loud alarums he doth hear, | and now 700
anon she hears them chaunt it lustily, | and all 869
anon his beating heart, alarum striking, | gives LUC 433
anon he comes, and throws his mantle by, | and PP 6. 9
anon adonis comes with horn and hounds; 9. 6
anon permit the basest clouds to ride | with SON 33. 5
and anon | doubting the filching age will steal 75. 5
anon their gazes lend | to every place at once, LC 26

/ANOTHER 4 FR 0.0004 REL FR 4 V 0 P
/owes /two /buckets, /filling /one /another, R2 4.01.185
/a /kingdom /down | /and /set /another /up), 2H4 1.03. 50
/and /here's /another, /whose /warp'd /looks LR 3.06. 53
/to /such /as /love /not /sorrow, /but /another, 5.03.206

ANOTHER 367 FR 0.0414 REL FR 234 V 133 P
way, is | another way so high a hope that even TMP 2.01.241
and another storm brewing, i hear it sing i' th' 2.02. 19 P
as you like this, give me the lie another time. 3.02. 77 P
and i must use you | in such another trick. 4.01. 37
there's another garment for't. 4.01.244 P
it shall go hard but i'll prove it by another. TGV 1.01. 85 P
such another proof will make me cry "baa." 1.01. 93 P
pleas'd | to be so ang'red with another letter. 1.02.100
thus will i fold them one upon another; 1.02.125
and yet you will; and yet another "yet." 2.01.120
please you, i'll write your ladyship another. 2.01.129
even as one heat another heat expels, | or as 2.04.192
or as one nail by strength drives out another, 2.04.193
send her another; 3.01. 94
would serve to scale another hero's tow'r, | so 3.01.119
i'll get me one of such another length. 3.01.133
now, of another thing she may, and that cannot i 3.01.351 P
says another. 4.04. 21 P
and there is also another device in my prain, WIV 1.01. 43 P
that peradventures shall tell you another tale, 1.01. 77 P
and have more occasion to know one another. 1.01.249 P
and here another to page's wife, who even now 1.03. 59 P
here's another letter to her. 1.03. 68 P
good faith, it is such another nan; 1.04.150 P
for i know anne's mind as well as another does. 1.04.164 P
both young and old, one with another, ford. 2.01.114
but i have another messenger to your worship. 2.02. 94 P
turn another into the register of your own, that 2.02.187 P
like a fair house built on another man's ground, 2.02.215 P
master shallow, and another gentleman — from 3.01. 32 P
let the court of france show me such another. 3.03. 54 P
into the water, and give him another hope, to 3.03.195 P
hope, to betray him to another punishment? 3.03.196 P
i must of another errand to sir john falstaff 3.04.109 P
/and i be serv'd such another trick, i'll have 3.05. 7 P
receiv'd from her another ambassy of meeting. 3.05.129 P
to make another experiment of his suspicion. 4.02. 35 P
and we have a nay–word how to know one another. 5.02. 5 P
and by that we know one another. 5.02. 7 P
and then another fault in the semblance of a 5.05. 10 P
to be tempted, escalus, | another thing to fall. MM 2.01. 18
one foul wrong, | lives not to act another. 2.02.104
young man | more fit to do another such offense 2.03. 14
rather rejoicing to see another merry, than 3.02.235 P
there is another comfort than this world, | that 5.01. 49
there is another friar that set them on, | let 5.01.248
i have bethought me of another fault. 5.01.456
this is another prisoner that i sav'd, | who 5.01.487
at length, another ship had seiz'd on us, | and, ERR 1.01.112
water, | that in the ocean seeks another drop, 1.02. 36
choleric, and purchase me another dry basting. 2.02. 63 P
and recover the lost hair of another man. 2.02. 76 P
have at you with another, that's — when? 3.01. 52
let's go hand in hand, not one before another. 5.01.426
fellow, or else make another cur'sy and say, ADO 2.01. 55 P
unless i might have another for working–days. 2.01.327 P
seeing how much another man is a fool when he 2.03. 8 P
another is wise, yet i am well; 2.03. 27 P
another virtuous, yet i am well; 2.03. 28 P
bears will not bite one another when they meet. 3.02. 78 P
my cousin's a fool, and thou art another. 3.04. 11 P
yet benedick was such another, and now is he 3.04. 87 P
i pray you choose another subject. 5.01.136 P
nay then give him another staff, this last was 5.01.138 P
that when i note another man like him | i may 5.01.260
another hero! 5.04. 62
and here's another | writ in my cousin's hand, 5.04. 88
god i have as little patience as another man, LLL 1.02.165 P
another of these students at that time | was 2.01. 64
put up this — 'twill be thine another day. 4.01.107
cannot, cannot, | and i cannot, another can. 4.01.128
one drunkard loves another of the name. 4.03. 48
another, with his finger and his thumb, | cried, 5.02.111
four happy days bring in | another moon; MND 1.01. 3
but i will wed thee in another key, | with pomp, 1.01. 18
sight | (as i can take it with another herb), 2.01.184
should of another therefore be abus'd! 2.02.134
therefore another prologue must tell he is not a 3.01. 34 P
then, there is another thing: 3.01. 62 P
but we are spirits of another sort. 3.02.388
i'll tell thee more of this another time; MV 1.01.100
please | to shoot another arrow that self way 1.01.148
became his surety and seal'd under for another. 1.02. 83 P
gate upon one wooer, another knocks at the door. 1.02.133
argosy bound to tripolis, another to the indies; 1.03. 18 P
me such a day, another time | you call'd me dog; 1.03.127
there i have another bad match. 3.01. 44 P
here comes another of the tribe; 3.01. 77 P
e'en as many as could well live one by another. 3.05. 23 P
jew, | the law hath yet another hold on you. 4.01.347
is there yet another dotes upon rib–breaking? AYL 1.02.142 P
deed | hadst thou descended from another house. 1.02.228
i would thou hadst told me of another father. 1.02.230
no, let my father seek another heir. 1.03. 99
cours'd one another down his innocent nose | in 2.01. 39
but i am shepherd to another man, | and do not 2.04. 78
come, more, another stanzo. 2.05. 18 P
that is another simple sin in you, to bring the 3.02. 78 P
they were all like one another as halfpence are, 3.02.354 P

better to be married of him than of another, for 3.03. 91 P
and you serve me such another trick, never come 4.01. 40 P
sigh'd but they ask'd one another the reason; 5.02. 35 P
look into happiness through another man's eyes! 5.02. 44 P
there is sure another flood toward, and these 5.04. 35 P
another bear the ewer, the third a diaper, | and SHR in.1. 57
another tell him of his hounds and horse, | and in.1. 61
he, | although i think 'twas in another sense — 1.01.215
hath promis'd me to help /me to another, | a 1.02.172
been candle–cases, one buckled, another lac'd; 3.02. 46 P
another way i have to man my haggard, | to make 4.01.193
this way the coverlet, another way the sheets. 4.01.202
knavery, to take upon you another man's name. 5.01. 36 P
crowns, | another dowry to another daughter, 5.02.114
crowns, | another dowry to another daughter, 5.02.114
him | he us'd as creatures of another place, AWW 1.02. 42
slay | in common sense, sense saves another way. 2.01.178
count's master is of another style. 2.03.195 P
you are not worth another word, else i'd call 2.03.263 P
thither they send one another. 3.05. 32 P
i would have that drum or another, or hic jacet. 3.06. 62 P
fancy, not to know what we speak one to another; 4.01. 18 P
mouth and buy myself another of bajazeth's mule, 4.01. 42 P
finger in the night i'll put | another ring, 4.02. 62
reading it he chang'd almost into another man. 4.03. 5 P
sallets ere we light on such another herb. 4.05. 15 P
and pleasure will be paid, one time or another. TN 2.04. 71 P
no other dowry with her but such another jest. 2.05.185 P
but, would you undertake another suit, | i had 3.01.108
that they will kill one another by the look, 3.04.196 P
i'll go another way to work with him; 4.01. 33 P
"she loves another" — who calls, ha? 4.02. 79 P
good master fabian, grant me another request. 5.01. 2 P
sir, i would you could make it another. 5.01. 30 P
there's another. 5.01. 35 P
sometimes her head on one side, some another —
WT 3.03. 20
so), which is another spur to my departure. 4.02. 9 P
if i make not this cheat bring out another, and 4.03.121 P
half a kiss to choose | who loves another best. 4.04.176
here's another ballad, of a fish that appear'd 4.04.275 P
lay it by too. another. 4.04.285 P
you, | but as you shake off one to take another; 4.04.569
house these seven years | be born another such. 4.04.579
unless another, | as like hermione as is her 5.01. 73
with staring on one another, to tear the cases 5.02. 12 P
might you have beheld one joy crown another, so 5.02. 44 P
i never heard of such another encounter, which 5.02. 57 P
another elevated that the oracle was fulfill'd. 5.02. 75 P
till, from one sign of dolor to another, she did 5.02. 88 P
which we, god knows, have turn'd another way, JN 2.01.549
the ice, or add another hue | unto the rainbow, 4.02. 13
heads, | and whisper one another in the ear; 4.02.189
another lean unwash'd artificer | cuts off his 4.02.201
without this object, | form such another? 4.03. 45
sound but another, and another shall | (as loud 5.02.171
sound but another, and another shall | (as loud 5.02.171
of yours | behold another day break in the east; 5.04. 32
stay yet another day, thou trusty welshman. R2 2.04. 5
another way | to pluck him headlong from the 5.01. 64
go thou and fill another room in hell. 5.05.107
it when thieves cannot be true one to another! 1H4 2.02. 28 P
if i become not a cart as well as another man, a 2.04.497 P
as soon be strangled with a halter as another. 2.04.499 P
thou seest i have more flesh than another man, 3.03.167 P
another king? 5.04. 25
i fear thou art another counterfeit, | and yet, 5.04. 35
sway, | meeting the check of such another day, 5.05. 42
as, one for superfluity, and another for use! 2H4 2.02. 18 P
there, | or it will seek me in another place, 2.03. 49
for the prince himself is such another, the 2.04.253 P
marry, there is another indictment upon thee, 2.04.343 P
is caught, as men take diseases, one of another; 5.01. 77 P
and let another half stand laughing by, | all H5 1.02.113
it will endure cold as another man's sword will; 2.01. 9 P
thine, methinks, is like | another fall of man. 2.02.142
though france himself and such another neighbor 3.06.157
here's my glove; give me another of thine. 4.01.211 P
take it, or i have another leek in my pocket, 5.01. 62 P
another would fly swift, but wanteth wings; 1H6 1.01. 75
say | this quarrel will drink blood another day. 2.04.133
o, turn the edged sword another way, | strike 3.03. 52
streams, | twinkling another counterfeited beam, 5.03. 63
is betroth'd | unto another lady of esteem. 5.05. 27
yet have i gold flies from another coast — | i 2H6 1.02. 93
enough to purchase such another island, | so 3.03. 3
let them kiss one another, for they lov'd well 4.07.131 P
i can eat grass, or pick a sallet another while, 4.10. 8 P
you were, | making another head to fight again. 3H6 2.01.141
king, | had slipp'd our claim until another age. 2.02.162
now one the better, then another best; 2.05. 10
blow, | and yielding to another when it blows, 3.01. 87
ay, but, i fear me, in another sense. 3.02. 60
could, | and, like a sinon, take another troy. 3.02.190
why, is not oxford here another anchor? 5.04. 16
and somerset another goodly mast? 5.04. 17
lest in our need he might infect another, | and 5.04. 46
divine, | be resident in men like one another, 5.06. 82
i'll throw thy body in another room, | and 5.06. 92
intent, | clarence hath not another day to live: R3 1.01.150
for love | as for another secret close intent 1.01.158
and see another, as i see thee now, | deck'd in 1.03.204
o, but remember this another day, | when he 1.03.298
i would not spend another such a night | though 1.04. 5
"girdling one another | within their alablaster 4.03. 10
give me another horse! 5.03.177
his mind and place | infecting one another, yea, H8 1.01.162
another spread on 's breast, mounting his eyes, 1.02.205
conscience | has crept too near another lady. 2.02. 18
i another. 2.02. 84
is this the honor they do one another? 5.02. 26
her ashes new create another heir | as great in 5.04. 41
you shall tell me another tale when th' other's TRO 1.02. 85 P
you are such another! 1.02.271 P
incursions, thou strikest as slow as another. 2.01. 30 P
what is he more than another? 2.03.142 P
friend, we understand not one another; 3.01. 27 P
if ever you prove false one to another, since i 3.02.199 P
doth one pluck down another, and together | die 3.03. 86
let me bear another to his horse, for that's the 3.03.306 P
and with another knot, /five–finger–tied, | the 5.02.157
like witless antics, one another meet, | and all 5.03. 86
and what one thing, what another, that i shall 5.03.103 P
th' effect doth operate another way. 5.03.109
she feeds, | but edifies another with her deeds. 5.03.112
now they are clapper–clawing one another; 5.04. 1 P
i think they have swallow'd one another. 5.04. 34 P
one bear will not bite another, and wherefore 5.07. 19 P
in awe, which else | would feed on one another? COR 1.01.188
you would be another penelope: 1.03. 82 P
and one infect another | against the wind a mile 1.04. 33
the state hath another, his wife another, and, i 2.01.109 P
the state hath another, his wife another, and, i 2.01.109 P
wit will not so soon out as another man's will; 2.03. 28 P
one time will owe another. 3.01.241
ay, and it makes men hate one another. 4.05.230 P
because they then less need one another. 4.05.232 P
another word, menenius, | i will not hear thee 5.02. 91
to die by himself fears it not from another. 5.02.105 P
but i'll deceive you in another sort, | and that TIT 3.01.190
why, i have not another tear to shed. 3.01.266
no, boy, not so, i'll teach thee another course. 4.01.119
coal–black is better than another hue, | in that 4.02. 99
hue, | in that it scorns to bear another hue; 4.02.100
here's a young lad fram'd of another leer: 4.02.119
thy hap | to find another that is like to thee, 5.02.102
and see how one another lends content; ROM 1.03. 84
asleep, | then he dreams of another benefice. 1.04. 81
a grave, | to lay one in, another out to have. 2.03. 84
i dare draw as soon as another man, if i see 2.04.159 P
hie you to church, i must another way, | to 2.05. 72
with another for tying his new shoes with old 3.01. 28 P
seal'd, | shall be the label to another deed, 4.01. 57
heart with treacherous revolt | turn to another, 4.01. 59
thee, youth, | put not another sin upon my head, 5.03. 62
here, | i dreamt my master and another fought, 5.03.138
why then another time i'll hear thee. TIM 1.02.178
he forfeits his own blood that spills another. 3.05. 87
man enough, that one need not lend to another; 3.06. 74 P
love not yourselves, away, | rob one another. 4.03.445
thou mightst have sooner got another service; 4.03.504
another general shout! JC 1.02.132
those that understood him smil'd at one another, 1.02.283 P
say, | "break up the senate till another time, 2.02. 98
when comes such another? 3.02.252
hack'd one another in the sides of caesar. 5.01. 40
or till another caesar | have added slaughter to 5.01. 54
reeking wounds, | or memorize another golgotha, MAC 1.02. 40
and i another. 1.03. 13
and i another, | so weary with disasters, tugg'd 3.01.110
here's another, | more potent than the first. 4.01. 75
another yet? 4.01.118
you must not put another scandal on him, | that HAM 2.01. 29
you one face, and you make yourselves another. 3.01.144 P
should i your true–love know | from another one? 4.05. 24
i'll put another question to thee. 5.01. 37 P
there's another. 5.01. 98 P
why he more than another? 5.01.169 P
not possible to understand in another tongue? 5.02.125 P
this is too heavy; let me see another. 5.02.264
another hit; 5.02.285
there's mine, beg another of thy daughters. LR 1.04.108 P
i have another daughter, | who i am sure is kind 1.04.305
we'll no more meet, no more see one another. 2.04.220
one side will mock another; th' other too. 3.07. 71
another way, | the news is not so tart. 4.02. 86
here, friend, 's another purse; 4.06. 28
should ev'n die with pity | to see another thus. 4.07. 53
another of his fadom they have none | to lead OTH 1.01.152
some one way, some another. 1.01.176
here comes another troop to seek for you. 1.02. 54
scale of reason to poise another of sensuality, 1.03.327 P
absolute | that not another comfort like to this 2.01.192
one unperfectness shows me another, to make me 2.03.298 P
'tis such another fitchew! 4.01.146 P
come, mistress, you must tell 's another tale. 5.01.125
if heaven would make me such another world | of 5.02.144
i have another weapon in this chamber; 5.02.252
of the slain roderigo, | and here another. 5.02.310
now here's another discontented paper, | found 5.02.314
be chok'd with such another emphasis! ANT 1.05. 68
i would you had her spirit in such another; 2.02. 62
as they pinch one another by the disposition, he 2.07. 6 P
to–morrow | you'll serve another master. 4.02. 28
o, such another sleep, that i might see | but 5.02. 77
sleep, that i might see | but such another man! 5.02. 78
as she would catch another antony | in her 5.02.347
heart, | but keep it till you woo another wife, CYM 1.01.113
another? 1.01.114
being | is to exchange one misery with another, 1.05. 55
and he's another, whatsoever he be. 2.01. 39 P
the cutter | was as another nature, dumb; 2.04. 84
love, | where there's another man. 2.04.110
and it doth confirm | another stain, as big as 2.04.140
be many caesars, | ere such another julius. 3.01. 12
never | find such another master. 4.02.374
one sand another | not more resembles that sweet 5.05.120
one sin, i know, another doth provoke: PER 1.01.137
we must take another course with you! 4.06.121 P
and /cas'd as richly, in pace another juno; 5.01.111
and another /life | to pericles thy father. 5.01.207
when you come ashore, | i have another /suit. 5.01.261
in his hand, another | directing in his head, TNK 1.03. 31
operance, our souls | did so to one another. 1.03. 64
she would long | till she had such another, and 1.03. 69
we shall know nothing here but one another, 2.02. 41
we are an endless mine to one another; 2.02. 79
we are, in one another, families: 2.02. 82
because another | first sees the enemy, shall i 2.02.193
what 'twere to filch affection from another! 2.02.210
another shape shall make me, | or end my 2.03. 21
of another | you would not hear me doubted, but 3.01. 60
maypole, and again, | ere another year run out, 3.05.146
by that you would have pity in another, | by 3.06.198
of love about 'em, | and not kill one another? 3.06.220
better they fall by th' law than one another. 3.06.225
beside, i have another oath 'gainst yours, | of 3.06.230
shall travel, ever strangers | to one another. 3.06.256
good by me | as by another that less loves her. 4.01. 44
just such another wanton ganymede | set /jove 4.02. 15
there's another, | a little man, but of a tough 4.02.116
dreaming of another world and a better; 4.03. 5 P
were't one eye | against another, arm oppress'd 5.01. 22
ravenous fishes | would feed on /one another. STM II.C 87
pay, | he winks, and turns his lips another way. VEN 90
as if another chase were in the skies. 696
and there another licking of his wound, 915
and here she meets another sadly scowling, | to 917
another flap–mouth'd mourner, black and grim, 920
another, and another, answer him, | clapping 922
another, and another, answer him, | clapping 922
puffs forth another wind that fires the torch. LUC 315
were | to view thy present trespass in another. 632
the branches of another root are rotted, | and 823
and as one shifts, another straight ensues: 1104
another, smother'd, seems to pelt and swear, 1418
i should not live to speak another word; 1642
thy sorrow to my sorrow lendeth | another power; 1677
the joys in bed, | one woman would another wed. PP 18.48
now is the time that face should form another, SON 3. 2
that's for thyself to breed another thee, | or 6. 7
are | from his low tract and look another way: 7.12
mark how one string, sweet husband to another, 8. 9
make thee another self for love of me, | that 10.13
another time mine eye is my heart's guest, | and 47. 7
ere beauty's dead fleece made another gay: 68. 8
and my sick muse doth give another place. 79. 4
/one blushing shame, another white despair; 99. 9
these blenches gave my heart another youth, 110. 7

ANOTHER'S 31 FR 0.0035 REL FR 24 V 7 P

that you may know one another's mind, and the WIV 2.02.127 P
they hold one an opinion of another's dotage, ADO 2.03.216 P
o hell! to choose love by another's eyes. MND 1.01.140
astray | as one come not within another's way. 3.02.359
no! i'll not rear | another's issue. WT 2.03.193
you cannot one bear with another's confirmities. 2H4 2.04. 58 P
we keep knives to cut one another's throats? H5 2.01. 92 P
i should take from another's pocket to put into 3.02. 50 P
i pray, | but one imperious in another's throne? 1H6 3.01. 44
do pelt so fast at one another's pate | that 3.01. 82
or lowly factor for another's gain; R3 3.07.134
sacrifice, | he offers in another's enterprise, TRO 1.02.283
that itself will leave | to be another's fool. 3.02.150
how one man eats into another's pride, | while 3.03.136
wife, | that is another's lawful promis'd love. TIT 1.01.298
tut, man, one fire burns out another's burning, ROM 1.02. 45
/one pain is less'ned by another's anguish; 1.02. 46
desperate grief cures with another's languish: 1.02. 48
like brothers commanding one another's fortunes!
TIM 1.02.105 P
one woe doth tread upon another's heel, | so HAM 4.07.163
this very night at one another's heels; OTH 1.02. 42
if you borrow one another's love for the instant ANT 2.02.103 P
like one another's glass to trim them by; PER 1.04. 27
what need i | affect another's gait, which is TNK 1.02. 45
or to be fond upon | another's way of speech, 1.02. 47
we are one another's wife, ever begetting | new 2.02. 80
here one man's hand lean'd on another's head, LUC 1415
friend, | i guess one angel in another's hell: PP 2.12
and true, | making no summer of another's green, SON 68.11
one on another's neck, do witness bear | thy 131.11
friend, | i guess one angel in another's hell. 144.12

ANSELME 1 FR 0.0001 REL FR 0 V 1 P

county anselme and his beauteous sisters; ROM 1.02. 65 P

/ANSWER 1 FR 0.0001 REL FR 1 V 0 P

/your /sureties /for /your /days /of /answer. R2 4.01.159

ANSWER 387 FR 0.0437 REL FR 267 V 120 P

i come | to answer thy best pleasure; TMP 1.02.190
my slave, who never | yields us kind answer. 1.02.309
quick, thou'rt best, | to answer other business. 1.02.367
and on this green land | answer your summons; 4.01.131
a silly answer, and fitting well a sheep. TGV 1.01. 81 P
answer not; 2.02. 13
come, answer not, but to it presently, | i am 2.07. 89
i will answer it straight: WIV 1.01.115 P
it is a fery discretion answer, save the fall is 1.01.253 P
slender, and this day we shall have our answer. 3.02. 59 P
answer your master, be not afraid. 4.01. 20 P
i am not able to answer the welsh flannel; 5.05.162 P
i pray you answer him. MM 1.04. 14
some run from brakes of ice and answer none, 2.01. 39
answer to this: 2.04. 60
faults of mine, | and nothing of your answer. 2.04. 73
answer me to–morrow, | or, by the affection that 2.04.167
answer his requiring with a plausible obedience, 3.01.243 P
and the place answer to convenience. 3.01.248 P
me desire you to make your answer before him. 3.02.156 P
if his own life answer the straitness of his 3.02.255 P
me your snatches, and yield me a direct answer. 4.02. 7 P
office, as you will answer it at your peril." 4.02.126 P
well; you'll answer this one day. fare ye well. 4.03.163 P
now, as i am a christian, answer me, | in what ERR 1.02. 77
mad, | that thus so madly thou didst answer me? 2.02. 12
what answer, sir? when spake i such a word? 2.02. 13
may answer my good will and your good welcome 3.01. 20
good sir, say whe'r you'll answer me or no: 4.01. 60
i answer you? what should i answer you? 4.01. 62
i answer you? what should i answer you? 4.01. 62
as all the metal in your shop will answer. 4.01. 82
brings any man to answer it that breaks his band 4.03. 31 P
why bear you these rebukes, and answer not? 5.01. 89
mark how short his answer is: ADO 1.01.213 P
she may be the better prepar'd for an answer, if 1.02. 22 P
solicit you in that kind, you know your answer. 2.01. 68 P
in every thing, and so dance out the answer. 2.01. 72 P
answer, clerk. 2.01.110 P
thus answer i in name of benedick, | but hear 2.01.172
if their singing answer your saying, by my faith 2.01.234 P
brief, too, to have all things answer my mind. 2.01.361 P
i knew it would be your answer. 3.03. 18 P
if they make you not then the better answer, you 3.03. 47 P
it baes will never answer a calf when he bleats. 3.03. 71 P
i will owe thee an answer for that, and now 3.03.101 P
i dare make his answer, none. 4.01. 18 P

that you have in her, bid her answer truly. 4.01. 75
to make you answer truly to your name. 4.01. 79
now, if you are a maid, answer to this. 4.01. 85
how answer you for yourselves? 4.02. 23 P
and let it answer every strain for strain, | as 5.01. 12
win me and wear me, let him answer me. 5.01. 82
that dare as well answer a man indeed | as i 5.01. 89
masters, that you are thus bound to your answer? 5.01.227 P
prince, let me go no farther to mine answer: 5.01.231 P
your answer, sir, is enigmatical, | but, for my 5.04. 27
i answer to that name. what is your will? 5.04. 73
so i may answer thee with one as old, that was a LLL 4.01.122 P
they will not answer to that epithet; 5.02.171
what humble suit attends thy answer there. 5.02.839
answer as i call you. nick bottom, the weaver. MND 1.02. 16 P
how answer you that? 3.01. 12 P
that you answer to pyramus. 3.01. 99 P
a man doth mark, | and dares not answer nay — 3.01.133
that hermia should give answer of her choice? 4.01.136
when my cue comes, call me, and i will answer. 4.01.201 P
shall i know your answer? MV 1.03. 8 P
your answer to that. 1.03. 11 P
old, | your answer had not been inscroll'd. 2.07. 72
i shall answer that better to the commonwealth 3.05. 37 P
thou art come to answer | a stony adversary, an 4.01. 3
we all expect a gentle answer, jew! 4.01. 34
i'll not answer that; 4.01. 42
now for your answer: 4.01. 52
this is no answer, thou unfeeling man, | to 4.01. 63
you will answer, | "the slaves are ours." 4.01. 97
so do i answer you: 4.01. 98
answer — shall i have it? 4.01.103
he attendeth here hard by | to know your answer, 4.01.146
and we will answer all things faithfully. 5.01.299
what color, madam? how shall i answer you? AYL 1.02.102 P
answer me in one word. 3.02.224 P
is more than to answer in a catechism. 3.02.228 P
but i answer you right painted cloth, from 3.02.273 P
you shall never take her without her answer, 4.01.172 P
for i must bear answer back | how you excuse my 4.03.179
we that have good wits have much to answer for; 5.01. 12 P
"thank god" — a good answer. art rich? 5.01. 25 P
not well cut, he would answer i spake not true: 5.04. 78 P
fourth, or fift borough, i'll answer him by law. SHR in.1. 13 P
thy hounds shall make the welkin answer them in.2. 45
is that an answer? 5.02. 83
i know her answer. 5.02. 97
answer the time of request. AWW 1.01.155 P
of businesses, i cannot answer thee acutely. 1.01.206 P
he hath arm'd our answer, | and florence is 1.02. 11
but for me, i have an answer will serve all men. 2.02. 13 P
marry, that's a bountiful answer that fits all 2.02. 15 P
will your answer serve fit to all questions? 2.02. 20 P
an answer of such fitness for all questions? 2.02. 28 P
it must be an answer of most monstrous size that 2.02. 32 P
question, hoping to be the wiser by your answer. 2.02. 39 P
you would answer very well to a whipping, if you 2.02. 55 P
this, | and urge her to a present answer back. 2.02. 64
to bring me down | must answer for your raising? 2.03.113
speak, thine answer. 2.03.166
but to answer you as you would be understood, he 4.03.106 P
our general bids you answer to what i shall ask 4.03.127 P
shall i set down your answer so? 4.03.135 P
i beseech you let me answer to the particular of 4.03.182 P
bosom would peep forth | and answer thanks. 4.04. 8
i could not answer in that course of honor | as 5.03. 98
but from her handmaid do return this answer: TN 1.01. 24
a good lenten answer. 1.05. 9 P
good my mouse of virtue, answer me. 1.05. 63 P
speak to me, i shall answer for her. your will? 1.05.168 P
to answer by the method, in the first of his 1.05.226 P
he might have took his answer long ago. 1.05.263
i will answer you with gait and entrance — but 3.01. 82 P
and by all means stir on the youth to an answer. 3.02. 59 P
i can no other answer make but thanks, | and 3.03. 14
at your request! yes, nightingales answer daws. 3.04. 35 P
which with as much safety you might answer him; 3.04.250 P
and on the answer, he pays you as surely as your 3.04.277 P
but there's no remedy, i shall answer it. 3.04.333
th' offenses we have made you do we'll answer, WT 1.02. 83
i may not answer. 1.02.397
this is not, no, | laid to thy answer: 3.02.199
the matter, he makes the maid to answer, "whoop, 4.04.198 P
would speak to her and stand in hope of answer. 5.02.102 P
grace, which never | my life may last to answer. 5.03. 8
and answer to his part | perform'd in this wide 5.03.153
so answer france. JN 1.01. 20
and then comes answer like an absey book: 1.01.196
"o sir," says answer, "at your best command, 1.01.197
and so, ere answer knows what question would, 1.01.200
stay for an answer to your embassy, | lest 2.01. 44
france, | to draw my answer from thy articles? 2.01.111
let me make answer: thy usurping son. 2.01.121
when i have said, make answer to us both. 2.01.235
why answer not the double majesties | this 2.01.480
to charge me to an answer, as the pope. 3.01.151
o, be remov'd from him, and answer well! 3.01.218
o, answer not! 4.02.267
and, as you answer, i do know the scope | and 5.02.122
where /god he knows how we shall answer him; 5.07. 60
earth, | or my divine soul answer it in heaven. R2 1.01. 38
i'll answer thee in any fair degree | or 1.01. 80
be ready, as your lives shall answer it, | at 1.01.198
my lord, my answer is to lancaster, | and i am 2.03. 70
what answer shall i make to this base man? 4.01. 20
breast, | to answer twenty thousand such as you. 4.01. 59
it is no more | than my poor life must answer. 5.02. 83
thy life answer? 5.02. 83
his answer was, he would unto the stews, | and 5.03. 16
but i have sent for him to answer this; 1H4 1.01.100
night | to answer all the debt he owes to you 1.03.185
answer me | directly unto this question that i 2.03. 85
answer me to that. 2.04.142 P
shall i give him his answer? 2.04.295 P
if thou love me, practice an answer. 2.04.375 P
to-morrow dinner-time | send him to answer thee, 2.04.516
shame, | in such a parley should i answer thee. 3.01.201
twenty, take them all, i'll answer the coinage. 4.02. 8 P
shall i return this answer to the king? 4.03.106
for, on their answer, will we set on them, | and 5.01.119
but at the gate, | and he himself will answer. 2H4 1.01. 6
the world, let him be brought in to his answer. 2.01. 32 P
but answer in th' effect of your reputation, and 2.01.130 P
the answer is as ready as a /borrower's cap, "i 2.02.115 P
answer, thou dead elm, answer. 2.04.331 P
answer, thou dead elm, answer. 2.04.331 P
pleaseth your grace to answer them directly 4.02. 52
'a shall answer it. 5.01. 26 P
in answer of which claim, the prince our master H5 1.02.249
open, | arrest them to the answer of the law, 2.02.143
us concerns | to answer royally in our defenses. 2.04. 3
he'll call you to so hot an answer of it | that 2.04.123
pause, | to answer matters of this consequence. 2.04.146
the sum of all our answer is but this: 3.06.163
the king is not bound to answer the particular 4.01.155 P
upon his own head, the king is not to answer it. 4.01.187 P
i do not desire he should answer for me, and yet 4.01.188 P
i pray thee bear my former answer back: 4.03. 90
great sort, quite from the answer of his degree. 4.07.136 P
please your majesty, let his neck answer for it, 4.08. 43 P
to the which, as yet, | there is no answer made. 5.02. 75
which you before so urg'd, lies in his answer. 5.02. 76
pass our accept and peremptory answer. 5.02. 82
give me your answer, i' faith, do, and so clap 5.02.129 P
how answer you, la plus belle katherine du monde 5.02.216 P
come, your answer in broken music; 5.02.243 P
frankness of my mirth, if i answer you for that. 5.02.292 P
possible, | and i will answer unpremeditated; 1H6 1.02. 88
villains, answer you so the lord protector? 1.03. 8
so we answer him. 1.03. 9
thou wilt answer this before the pope. 1.03. 52
i will not answer thee with words, but blows. 1.03. 69
dare no man answer in a case of truth? 2.04. 2
and answer was return'd that he will come. 2.05. 20
purpose to answer what thou canst object. 3.01. 7
first let me know, and then i'll answer you. 4.01. 88
and yet i would that you would answer me. 5.03. 87
to give thee answer of thy just demand. 5.03.144
what answer makes your grace unto my suit? 5.03.150
seen) i will answer our hope in issue of a king; 5.05. 72
that shall make answer to such questions | as by 2H6 1.02. 80
thou tremblest at, answer that i shall ask; 1.04. 26
matter, | in thine own person answer thy abuse. 2.01. 40
an answer from the king, my lord of salisbury! 3.02.270
an answer from the king, or we will all break in 3.02.278
nay, answer if you can. 4.02.169 P
what answer makes your grace to the rebels' 4.04. 7 P
what canst thou answer to my majesty for giving 4.07. 27 P
them about matters they were not able to answer. 4.07. 43 P
that i have given no answer all this while; 5.01. 33
why whisper you, my lords, and answer not? 3H6 1.01.149
ay, crook-back, here i stand to answer thee, 2.02. 96
answer no more, for thou shalt be my queen. 3.02.106
bona, hear me speak | before you answer warwick. 3.03. 66
yet, ere thou go, but answer me one doubt: 3.03.238
me, | but dreadful war shall answer his demand. 3.03.259
what answer makes king lewis unto our letters? 4.01. 91
and tell what answer | lewis and the lady bona 4.03. 55
and, gallant warwick, do but answer this: 5.01. 40
which, traitor, thou wouldst have me answer to. 5.05. 21
let hell make crook'd my mind to answer it. 5.06. 79
should all but answer for that peevish brat? R3 1.03.193
his answer was, the people were not used | to be 3.07. 29
play the maid's part, still answer nay, and take 3.07. 51
if not to answer, you might haply think 3.07.144
the last — | definitively thus i answer you: 3.07.153
letters to richmond, you shall answer it. 4.02. 93
but how to make ye suddenly an answer | in such H8 3.01. 70
wit | to make a seemly answer to such persons. 3.01.178
lay upon my credit, | i answer is most false. 3.02.266
for your stubborn answer | about the giving-back 3.02.346
as a man sorely tainted, to his answer, | he 4.02. 14
those charges | which will require your answer, 5.01.104
you must be godfather, and answer for her. 5.02.197
this woman's answer sorts, | for womanish it is TRO 1.01.106
not so much at the hair as at his pretty answer. 1.02.155 P
what was his answer? 1.02.156 P
patroclus, | arming to answer in a night alarm." 1.03.171
hath no spark of fire | to answer for his love, 1.03.295
and wake him to the answer, think you? 1.03.332
farewell. who shall answer him? 2.01.127
i shall, and bring his answer presently. 2.03.139
why, he'll answer nobody; 3.03.268 P
your answer, sir. 3.03.294 P
your answer, sir. 3.03.298 P
i'll answer to my lust, and know you, lord, 4.04.132
we'll answer it: 4.05.147
who must we answer? 4.05.176
answer me, heavens! 4.05.246
gods, proud man, | to answer such a question. 4.05.248
well, sir, what answer made the belly? COR 1.01.106
your belly's answer — what? 1.01.114
did complain, | what could the belly answer? 1.01.124
patience awhile, you'st hear the belly's answer. 1.01.126
it was an answer. how apply you this? 1.01.147
made doubt but rome was ready | to answer us. 1.02. 19
he is himself alone, | to answer all the city. 1.04. 52
both observe and answer | the vantage of his 2.03.259
a traitor, and shall answer | as traitors do. 3.01.162
i charge thee, | and follow to thine answer. 3.01.176
undertake to bring him | where he shall answer, 3.01.323
arm yourself | to answer mildly; 3.02.139
i | will answer in mine honor. 3.02.144
answer to us. 3.03. 61
coriolanus | he would not answer to; 5.01. 12
his answer to me was, | he could not stay to 5.01. 24
may, | answer i must, and shall do with my life; TIT 1.01.412
to answer their suspicion with their lives. 2.03.298
who, though they cannot answer my distress, 3.01. 38
her eye discourses, i will answer it. ROM 2.02. 13
romeo will answer it. 2.04. 9 P
any man that can write may answer a letter. 2.04. 10 P
nay, he will answer the letter's master, how he 2.04. 11 P
answer to that. 2.05. 35
or those eyes /shut, that makes thee answer ay, 3.02. 49
speak not, reply not, do not answer me! 3.05.163
to answer, "i'll not wed, i cannot love; 3.05.185
to answer that, i should confess to you. 4.01. 23
answer me like men: 4.05.125 P
my mouth, that i might answer thee profitably. TIM 2.02. 77 P
answer not, i am gone. 2.02. 87 P
that answer might have become apemantus. 2.02.118 P
they answer, in a joint and corporate voice, 2.02.204
and with their faint reply this answer join: 3.03. 25
ay, but this answer will not serve. 3.04. 57
now we shall know some answer. 3.04. 67 P
we cannot take this for answer, sir. 3.04. 77
elements expos'd, | answer mere nature; 4.03.231
care not, | while you have throats to answer. 5.01.179
no answer? 5.03. 2
to your public laws | at heaviest answer. 5.04. 63
but what trade art thou? answer me directly. JC 1.01. 12
both meet to hear and answer such high things. 1.02.170
then i know | my answer must be made. 1.03.114
stay not to answer me, but get thee gone. 2.04. 2
brutus rose against caesar, this is my answer: 3.02. 21 P
and will no doubt with reasons answer you. 3.02.215
answer every man directly. 3.03. 9 P
then to answer every man directly and briefly, 3.03. 15 P
he was but a fool that brought | my answer back. 4.03. 85
no, caesar, we will answer on their charge. 5.01. 24
stand not to answer; 5.03. 43
rue the time | that clogs me with this answer." MAC 3.06. 43
(how e'er you come to know it), answer me: 4.01. 51
answer me | to what i ask you. 4.01. 60
we'll answer. 4.01. 61
would i could answer | this comfort with the 4.03.192
nay, answer me. stand and unfold yourself. HAM 1.01. 2
'tis gone, and will not answer. 1.01. 52
my lord, i did, | but answer made it none. 1.02.215
o, answer me! 1.04. 45
read, | answer, and think upon this business. 2.02. 82
i have nothing with this answer, hamlet, these 3.02. 96 P
shall please you to make me a wholesome answer, 3.02.316 P
make you a wholesome answer — my wit's diseas'd 3.02.321 P
but, sir, such answer as i can make, you shall 3.02.322 P
come, come, you answer with an idle tongue. 3.04. 11
and will answer well | the death i gave him. 3.04.176
if your lordship would vouchsafe the answer. 5.02.169 P
how if i answer no? 5.02.170 P
hit, | or quit in answer of the third exchange, 5.02.269
answer my life my judgment, | thy youngest LR 1.01.151
i know no answer. 1.01.201
the fault of it i'll answer. 1.03. 10
best /thought it fit | to answer from our home; 2.01.124
i'll answer that. 2.02.147
and attend | the leisure of their answer, gave 2.04. 37
fetch me a better answer. 2.04. 91
in a grave than to answer with thy uncover'd 3.04.101 P
wherefore to dover? let him answer that. 3.07. 53
his answer was, "the worse." 4.02. 6
not feel wrongs | which tie him to an answer. 4.02. 14
this letter, madam, craves a speedy answer; 4.02. 82
i'll read, and answer. 4.02. 87
well, else i should answer | from a full-flowing 5.03. 73
and why you answer | this present summons? 5.03.120
by th' law of war thou wast not bound to answer 5.03.153
this thou shalt answer; i know thee, roderigo. OTH 1.01.119
sir, i will answer any thing. 1.01.120
will you that i go | to answer this your charge? 1.02. 85
course of direct session | call thee to answer. 1.02. 87
affair cries haste, | and speed must answer it. 1.03.277
give me answer to it. 2.03.196
as hydra, such an answer would stop them all. 2.03.305 P
been born a dog | than answer my wak'd wrath! 3.03.363
that is, make questions, and by them answer. 3.04. 17 P
i shall entreat him | to answer like himself. ANT 2.02. 4
possess it, i'll make answer. 2.07.101
for thy pains, which we | will answer as a law. 3.12. 33
is that his answer? 3.13. 13
and answer me declin'd, sword against sword, 3.13. 27
the full caesar will | answer his emptiness! 3.13. 36
lives he? | wilt thou not answer, man? 4.14.115
we fall, | we answer others' merits in our name, 5.02.178
only, thus far you shall answer: CYM 1.04.157 P
chastity, you shall answer me with your sword. 1.04.163 P
this is no answer. 2.03. 93
i hope the briefness of your answer made | the 2.04. 30
doublet, hat, hose, all | that answer to them. 3.04.170
and there's no answer | that will be given to 3.05. 43
no answer? 3.06. 24
thus did he answer me; 4.02. 41
seek us through | and put us to our answer. 4.02.161
solemn things | should answer solemn accidents. 4.02.192
whose answer would be death | drawn on with 4.04. 13
great the answer be | britains must take. 5.03. 79
give answer to this boy, and do it freely, | or, 5.05.131
can draw him but to answer thee in aught, | thy PER 5.01. 73
friends, | if this but answer to my just belief, 5.01.238
blazon, holds me to | this gentleness of answer: TNK 3.01. 48
most trusty lover, | i call'd him now to answer. 3.06.151
woe, | and still the choir of echoes answer so. VEN 840
she says, "'tis so," they answer all, "'tis so," 851
another, and another, answer him, | clapping 922
who nothing wants to answer her but cries, | and LUC 1459
at length address'd to answer his desire, | she 1606
blow | the grief away that stops his answer so; 1664
if thou couldst answer, "this fair child of mine SON 2.10
grow, | if thy sweet virtue answer not thy show! 93.14
make answer, muse: 101. 5

ANSWERABLE 3 FR 0.0003 REL FR 2 V 1 P
and all things answerable to this portion. SHR 2.01.359
men, | he shall be answerable, and so farewell. 1H4 2.04.522
thou shalt see an answerable sequestration — OTH 1.03.345 P

ANSWER'D 47 FR 0.0053 REL FR 36 V 11 P
tut, a pin! this shall be answer'd. WIV 1.01.114 P
that is now answer'd. 1.01.116 P
who mutually hath answer'd my affection | (so 4.06. 10
th' edict infringe | had answer'd for his deed. MM 2.02. 93
duke yet would have dark deeds darkly answer'd, 3.02.177 P
luce — luce, thou hast answer'd him well. ERR 3.01. 53
no more words; the clerk is answer'd. ADO 2.01.111 P
one green leaf on it would have answer'd her. 2.01.241 P
i am answer'd, sir. LLL 1.02. 31 P

but say it is my humor, is it answer'd? MV 4.01. 43
what, are you answer'd yet? 4.01. 46
you teach me how a beggar should be answer'd. 4.01.440
and you will not be answer'd with reason, i must AYL 2.07.100 P
i marvel why i answer'd not again. 3.05.132
you have answer'd to his reputation with the AWW 4.03.248 P
/i cannot be so answer'd. TN 2.04. 88
must she not then be answer'd? 2.04. 92
were i ta'en here, it would scarce be answer'd. 3.03. 28
it might have since been answer'd in repaying 3.03. 33
blood, we should have answer'd heaven | boldly, WT 1.02. 73
i must be answer'd. 1.02.399
bought blood, and blows have answer'd blows; JN 2.01.329
this must be answer'd either here or hence. 4.02. 89
grief and my impatience | answer'd neglectingly, 1H4 1.03. 52
for the robbery, lad, how is that answer'd? 3.03.176 P
proud majestical high scorn | he answer'd thus: 1H6 4.07. 40
lord, these faults are easy, quickly answer'd; 2H6 3.01.133
who answer'd him, they came from buckingham R3 4.04.525
he answer'd, "tush, | it can do me no damage"; H8 1.02.182
fairly answer'd. 3.02.179
the belly answer'd — COR 1.01.105
vented their complainings, which being answer'd, 1.01.209
yet i insisted, yet you answer'd not, | but with JC 2.01.245
fault, | and grievously hath caesar answer'd it. 3.02. 80
that matter is answer'd directly. 3.03. 23 P
should i have answer'd caius cassius so? 4.03. 78
alas, how shall this bloody deed be answer'd? HAM 4.01. 16
amorous sojourn, | and here are to be answer'd. LR 1.01. 48
sir, he answer'd me in the roundest manner, he 1.04. 54 P
but jealious souls will not be answer'd so; OTH 3.04.159
sir, this should be answer'd. ANT 3.06. 30
how | can her contempt be answer'd? CYM 3.05. 42
whose rudeness | answer'd my steps too loud. 4.02.215
drooping here, if seconds | had answer'd him. 5.03. 91
if he not answer'd, i should call a wolf, | and TNK 3.02. 10
life, | answer'd their cries, "my daughter!" LUC 1806
her audit (though delay'd) answer'd must be, SON 126.11
ANSWERED 12 FR 0.0013 REL FR 12 V 0 P
anon his thisby must be answered, | and forth my MND 3.02. 18
he answered, "do not so, | /slubber not business MV 2.08. 38
are you answered? 4.01. 62
this fruit | till i and my affairs are answered. AYL 2.07. 99
i answered indirectly, as i said, | and i 1H4 1.03. 66
fears | thou seest with peril i have answered; 2H4 4.05.196
measure for measure must be answered. 3H6 2.06. 55
will to–morrow | be answered in this challenge: TRO 3.03. 35
not rash like his accusers, and thus answered: COR 1.01.129
disclos'd, | and open perils surest answered. JC 4.01. 47
now, antony, our hopes are answered. 5.01. 1
and she answered me | so far from what she was, TNK 4.01. 38
ANSWEREST 1 FR 0.0001 REL FR 0 V 1 P
if thou answerest me not to the purpose, confess HAM 5.01. 38 P
ANSWERING 10 FR 0.0011 REL FR 9 V 1 P
and do him right that, answering one foul wrong, MM 2.02.103
not answering the aim | and that unbodied figure TRO 1.03. 15
he professes not answering. 3.03.269 P
our levies, answering us | with our own charge, COR 5.06. 66
here, | answering before we do demand of them. JC 5.01. 6
and you bear it | as answering to the weight. ANT 5.02.102
more slavish did i ne'er than answering | a CYM 4.02. 73
even now, | answering the letter of the oracle, 5.05.450
tyre, | fame answering the most strange inquire, PER 3.ch. 22
shrill–tongu'd tapsters answering every call, VEN 849
ANSWERS 25 FR 0.0028 REL FR 20 V 5 P
and yet a thousand times it answers "no." TGV 1.03. 91
still pays haste, and leisure answers leisure; MM 5.01.410
i do say thou art quick in answers; LLL 1.02. 29 P
tear | impatient answers from my gentle tongue? MND 3.02.287
doth teach me answers for deliverance! MV 3.02. 38
i am not bound to please thee with my answers. 4.01. 65
you are full of pretty answers; AYL 3.02.270 P
as fast as she answers thee with frowning looks, 3.05. 68 P
the king is mov'd, and answers not to this. JN 3.01.217
drench," says he, and answers, "some fourteen," 1H4 2.04.107 P
fire answers fire, and through their paly flames H5 4.pr. 8
so let them have their answers every one. 1H6 5.01. 25
and call these foul offenders to their answers, 2H6 2.01.199
as for words, whose greatness answers words, 4.10. 53
what answers clarence to his sovereign's will? 3H6 4.06. 45
we are too well acquainted with these answers, TRO 2.03.113
where he answers again, "because thou canst not 4.04. 18 P
no trumpet answers. 4.05. 12
(he answers.) HAM 4.05. 64
nor answers have i none | but what should go by OTH 4.02.103
no more light answers. ANT 1.02.176
deliver with more openness your answers | to my CYM 1.06. 88
her, | she answers him, as if she knew his mind; VEN 308
owe | enchanted tarquin answers with surmise, LUC 83
hide, | which heavily he answers with a groan, SON 50.11
ANSWER'ST 2 FR 0.0002 REL FR 2 V 0 P
why prat'st thou to thyself, and answer'st not? ERR 2.02.193
thou answer'st she is fair, | pourest in the TRO 1.01. 52
AN'T* *(also on't)*
/AN'T* 1 FR 0.0001 REL FR 0 V 1 P
/monopoly /out, /they /would /have /part /an't. LR 1.04.153 P
AN'T* 13 FR 0.0014 REL FR 7 V 6 P
me, an't shall please you: i am anthony dull. LLL 1.01.270 P
i see the trick an't; 5.02.460
there, an't shall please you, a foolish mild man 5.02.580 P
of launcelot, an't please your mastership. MV 2.02. 59 P
an't please your honor, players | that offer SHR in.1. 77
of famous memory, an't please your majesty, and H5 4.07. 92 P
an't like your lordly lord's protectorship. 2H6 2.01. 30
i was, an't like your majesty. 5.01. 72
an't please your grace, sir thomas bullen's H8 1.04. 92
ay, my lord, an't please you. JC 4.03.258
an't shall go hard | but i will delve one yard HAM 3.04.207
will you ha' the truth an't? 5.01. 23 P
d' ye take it, and the gods give thee good an't! PER 2.01.147 P
ANT 2 FR 0.0002 REL FR 1 V 1 P
with telling me of the moldwarp and the ant, 1H4 3.01.147
we'll set thee to school to an ant, to teach LR 2.04. 67 P
ANTENOR 11 FR 0.0012 REL FR 5 V 6 P
that's antenor. TRO 1.02.190 P
helenus, antenor, and all the gallantry of troy. 3.01.135 P
you have a troyan prisoner call'd antenor, 3.03. 18
whom troy hath still denied, but this antenor, 3.03. 22
for the enfreed antenor, the fair cressid. 4.01. 39
diomed, and our antenor | deliver'd to /us; 4.02. 62
the devil take antenor! 4.02. 75 P
a plague upon antenor! 4.02. 76 P
a plague upon antenor! 4.02. 87 P
thou art chang'd for antenor. 4.02. 91 P
is the lady | which for antenor we deliver you. 4.04.110
/ANTENORIDES 1 FR 0.0001 REL FR 1 V 0 P
/and /antenorides, /with /massy /staples | /and TRO pr 17
ANTHEM 3 FR 0.0003 REL FR 3 V 0 P
ear, | as ending anthem of my endless dolor. TGV 3.01.242
her heavy anthem still concludes in woe, | and VEN 839
here the anthem doth commence: PHT 21
ANTHEMS 1 FR 0.0001 REL FR 0 V 1 P
lost it with hallowing and singing of anthems. 2H4 1.02.190 P
ANTHONY 7 FR 0.0008 REL FR 4 V 3 P
brother anthony — ADO 5.01. 91
but, brother anthony — 5.01.100
by thy sweet grace's officer, anthony dull, a LLL 1.01.267 P
me, an't shall please you: i am anthony dull. 1.01.270 P
john duke of alanson, anthony duke of brabant, H5 4.08. 96
anthony woodvile, her brother there, | that made R3 1.01. 67
anthony and potpan! ROM 1.05. 10 P
ANTHROPOPHAGI 1 FR 0.0001 REL FR 1 V 0 P
the anthropophagi, and men whose heads | /do OTH 1.03.144
ANTHROPOPHAGINIAN
1 FR 0.0001 REL FR 0 V 1 P
he'll speak like an anthropophaginian unto thee. WIV 4.05. 9 P
/ANTIATES 1 FR 0.0001 REL FR 1 V 0 P
their bands i' th' vaward are the /antiates, COR 1.06. 53
ANTIATES 3 FR 0.0003 REL FR 3 V 0 P
set me against aufidius and his antiates, | and COR 1.06. 59
and that the spoil got on the antiates | was 3.03. 4
with no less honor to the antiates | than shame 5.06. 79
ANTIC 13 FR 0.0014 REL FR 9 V 4 P
if black, why, nature, drawing of an antic, ADO 3.01. 63
or show, or pageant, or antic, or firework. LLL 5.01.112 P
we will have, if this fadge not, an antic. 5.01.147 P
i never may believe | these antic fables, nor MND 5.01. 3
were he the veriest antic in the world. SHR in.1. 101
keeps death his court, and there the antic sits, R2 3.02.162
with the rusty curb of old father antic the law? 1H4 1.02. 61 P
thou antic death, which laugh'st us here to 1H6 4.07. 18
slave | come hither, cover'd with an antic face, ROM 1.05. 56
the pox of such antic, lisping, affecting 2.04. 28 P
a sound, | while you perform your antic round; MAC 4.01.130
think meet | to put an antic disposition on — HAM 1.05.172
and all we'll dance an antic 'fore the duke, TNK 4.01. 75
ANTICIPATE 1 FR 0.0001 REL FR 1 V 0 P
in love, t' anticipate | the ills that were not, SON 118. 9
ANTICIPATES 1 FR 0.0001 REL FR 1 V 0 P
whose footing here anticipates our thoughts | a OTH 2.01. 76
ANTICIPATING 1 FR 0.0001 REL FR 1 V 0 P
appointment fresh and fair, | anticipating time. TRO 4.05. 2
ANTICIPATION 1 FR 0.0001 REL FR 0 V 1 P
so shall my anticipation prevent your discovery, HAM 2.02.293 P
ANTICIPAT'ST 1 FR 0.0001 REL FR 1 V 0 P
time, thou anticipat'st my dread exploits: MAC 4.01.144
ANTICK'D 1 FR 0.0001 REL FR 1 V 0 P
the wild disguise hath almost | antick'd us all. ANT 2.07.125
ANTICLY 1 FR 0.0001 REL FR 1 V 0 P
go anticly, and show outward hideousness, | and ADO 5.01. 96
ANTICS 3 FR 0.0003 REL FR 2 V 1 P
indeed three such antics do not amount to a man. H5 3.02. 31 P
like witless antics, one another meet, | and all TRO 5.03. 86
there appears | quick–shifting antics, ugly in LUC 459
ANTIDOTE 1 FR 0.0001 REL FR 1 V 0 P
and with some sweet oblivious antidote | cleanse MAC 5.03. 43
ANTIDOTES 1 FR 0.0001 REL FR 1 V 0 P
his antidotes are poison, and he slays | moe TIM 4.03.432
ANTIGONUS 6 FR 0.0006 REL FR 3 V 3 P
antigonus, | i charg'd thee that she should not WT 2.03. 42
"good antigonus, | since fate (against thy 3.03. 27
to me for help and said his name was antigonus, 3.03. 97 P
reason | as my antigonus to break his grave 5.01. 42
the letters of antigonus found with it, which 5.02. 34 P
pray you, became of antigonus, that carried 5.02. 59 P
ANTIOCH 8 FR 0.0009 REL FR 8 V 0 P
this' antioch, then; PER 1.ch. 17
antioch, farewell, for wisdom sees those men 1.01.134
and danger, which i fear'd, is at antioch, 1.02. 7
i went to antioch, | where, as thou know'st, 1.02. 70
being at antioch — 1.03. 18
what from antioch? 1.03. 18
as friends to antioch, we may feast in tyre. 1.03. 39
the third, of antioch; 2.02. 28
ANTIOCHUS 13 FR 0.0014 REL FR 13 V 0 P
antiochus the great | built up this city for his PER 1.ch. 17
i have, antiochus, and, with a soul | embold'ned 1.01. 3
that would be son to great antiochus. 1.01. 26
antiochus, i thank thee, who hath taught | my 1.01. 41
or death, | i wait the sharpest blow, antiochus. 1.01. 55
nor tell the world antiochus doth sin | in such 1.01.146
the great antiochus, | 'gainst whom i am too 1.02. 16
antiochus you fear, | and justly too, i think, 1.02.102
royal antiochus, on what cause i know not, 1.03. 19
lord thaliard from antiochus is welcome. 1.03. 30
of me, | antiochus from incest lived not free; 2.04. 2
antiochus and his daughter dead, | the men of 3.ch. 25
in antiochus and his daughter you have heard 5.03. 85
ANTIOPA 1 FR 0.0001 REL FR 1 V 0 P
break his faith, | with ariadne, and antiopa? MND 2.01. 80
ANTIPATHY 1 FR 0.0001 REL FR 1 V 0 P
no contraries hold more antipathy | than i and LR 2.02. 87
ANTIPHOLUS' 1 FR 0.0001 REL FR 1 V 0 P
these two antipholus', these two so like, | and ERR 5.01.358
ANTIPHOLUS 14 FR 0.0015 REL FR 14 V 0 P
ay, ay, antipholus, look strange and frown, ERR 2.02.110
come, come, antipholus, we dine too late. 2.02.219
shall, antipholus, | even in the spring of love, 3.02. 2
master antipholus — 3.02.165
do owe to you | is growing to me by antipholus, 4.01. 8
well met, well met, master antipholus. 4.03. 45
now, out of doubt antipholus is mad, | else 4.03. 81
signior antipholus, i wonder much | that you 5.01. 13
may it please your grace, antipholus, my husband 5.01.136
me dote, | i see my son antipholus and dromio. 5.01.196
is not your name, sir, call'd antipholus? 5.01.287
err — | tell me thou art my son antipholus. 5.01.319
twenty years | have i been patron to antipholus, 5.01.328
antipholus, thou cam'st from corinth first? 5.01.363
ANTIPODES 5 FR 0.0005 REL FR 4 V 1 P
arrand now to the antipodes that you can devise ADO 2.01.265 P
her brother's noontide with th' antipodes. MND 3.02. 55
we should hold day with the antipodes, | if you MV 5.01.127
whilst we were wand'ring with the antipodes, R2 3.02. 49
to every good | as the antipodes are unto us, 3H6 1.04.135
ANTIQUARY 1 FR 0.0001 REL FR 1 V 0 P
nestor, | instructed by the antiquary times; TRO 2.03.251
ANTIQUE 14 FR 0.0015 REL FR 14 V 0 P
under an oak whose antique root peeps out | upon AYL 2.01. 31
the constant service of the antique world, 2.03. 57
that old and antique song we heard last night; TN 2.04. 3
in this the antique and well–noted face | of JN 4.02. 21
like to the senators of th' antique rome, | with H5 5.pr. 26
the dust on antique time would lie unswept, COR 2.03.119
his antique sword, | rebellious to his arm, lies HAM 2.02.469
i am more an antique roman than a dane. 5.02.341
an antique token | my father gave my mother. OTH 5.02.216
rage, | and stretched metre of an antique song: SON 17.12
nor draw no lines there with thine antique pen; 19.10
sun, | show me your image in some antique book, 59. 7
in him those holy antique hours are seen, 68. 9
i see their antique pen would have express'd 106. 7
ANTIQUITIES 1 FR 0.0001 REL FR 1 V 0 P
to spoil antiquities of hammer'd steel, | and LUC 951
ANTIQUITY 7 FR 0.0008 REL FR 4 V 3 P
bawd is he doubtless, and of antiquity too; MM 3.02. 68 P
with age | and high top bald with dry antiquity: AYL 4.03.105
thou not the privilege of antiquity upon thee — AWW 2.03.209 P
and every part about you blasted with antiquity? 2H4 1.02.184 P
antiquity forgot, custom not known, | the HAM 4.05.105
beated and chopp'd with tann'd antiquity, | mine SON 62.10
place, | but makes antiquity for aye his page, 108.12
ANTIQUIUS 1 FR 0.0001 REL FR 1 V 0 P
glorious, | et bonum quo antiquius, eo melius. PER 1.ch. 10
ANTIUM 5 FR 0.0005 REL FR 5 V 0 P
he is retired to antium. COR 3.01. 11
at antium lives he? 3.01. 17
at antium. 3.01. 18
a goodly city is this antium. 4.04. 1
is he in antium? 4.04. 8
ANTONIAD 1 FR 0.0001 REL FR 1 V 0 P
th' antoniad, the egyptian admiral, | with all ANT 3.10. 2
ANTONIO 65 FR 0.0073 REL FR 47 V 18 P
my brother and thy uncle, call'd antonio — | i TMP 1.02. 66
purpose, did antonio open | the gates of milan, 1.02.129
what things are these, my lord antonio? 5.01.264
know ye don antonio, your countryman? TGV 2.04. 54
i know you well enough, you are signior antonio. ADO 2.01.113 P
i know antonio | is sad to think upon his MV 1.01. 39
my lord bassanio, since you have found antonio, 1.01. 69
you look not well, signior antonio, | you have 1.01. 73
i tell thee what, antonio — | i love thee, and 1.01. 86
o my antonio, i do know of these | that 1.01. 95
'tis not unknown to you, antonio, | how much i 1.01.122
to you, antonio, | i owe the most, in money and 1.01.130
o my antonio, had i but the means | to hold a 1.01.173
which, as i told you, antonio shall be bound. 1.03. 4 P
antonio shall become bound — well. 1.03. 6 P
ducats for three months, and antonio bound. 1.03. 10 P
antonio is a good man. 1.03. 12 P
may i speak with antonio? 1.03. 31 P
this is signior antonio. 1.03. 40 P
signior antonio, many a time and oft | in the 1.03.106
signior antonio! 2.06. 61
antonio certified the duke | they were not with 2.08. 10
let good antonio look he keep his day, | or he 2.08. 25
i thought upon antonio when he told me, | and 2.08. 31
you were best to tell antonio what you hear, 2.08. 33
i saw bassanio and antonio part: 2.08. 36
there uncheck'd that antonio hath a ship of rich 3.01. 2 P
plain highway of talk, that the good antonio, 3.01. 12 P
that the good antonio, the honest antonio — o 3.01. 13 P
do you hear whether antonio have had any loss at 3.01. 42 P
my master antonio is at his house and desires to 3.01. 74 P
antonio, as i heard in genoa — 3.01. 97 P
but antonio is certainly undone. 3.01.124 P
signior antonio | commends him to you. 3.02.231
how doth that royal merchant, good antonio? 3.02.239
deny not, | it will go hard with poor antonio. 3.02.290
which makes me think that this antonio, | being 3.04. 16
what, is antonio here? 4.01. 1
hate and a certain loathing | i bear antonio, 4.01. 61
good cheer, antonio! 4.01.111
between the jew and antonio the merchant. 4.01.156 P
antonio and old shylock, both stand forth. 4.01.175
antonio, i am married to a wife | which is as 4.01.282
ay, for the state, not for antonio. 4.01.373
what mercy can you render him, antonio? 4.01.378
antonio, gratify this gentleman, | for in my 4.01.406
come, antonio. 4.01.457
this is the man, this is antonio, | to whom i am 5.01.134
antonio, you are welcome, | and i have better 5.01.273
antonio, my father, is deceas'd, | and i have SHR 1.02. 54
that is antonio, the duke's eldest son, | that, AWW 3.05. 76
you must know of me then, antonio, my name is TN 2.01. 16 P
o good antonio, forgive me your trouble. 2.01. 34 P
my kind antonio, | i can no other answer make 3.03. 13
antonio, i arrest thee at the suit of count 3.04.326 P
where's antonio then? 4.03. 4
this is that antonio | that took the phoenix and 5.01. 60
antonio never yet was thief or pirate, | though 5.01. 74
antonio, o my dear antonio! 5.01.218
antonio, o my dear antonio! 5.01.218
fear'st thou that, antonio? 5.01.221
antonio! JC 1.02. 4
forget not, in your speed, antonio, | to touch 1.02. 6
antonio! 1.02.190
for he did bid antonio | send word to you he 1.03. 37
/ANTONIO'S 1 FR 0.0001 REL FR 1 V 0 P
born in verona, old /antonio's son. SHR 1.02.190
ANTONIO'S 9 FR 0.0010 REL FR 8 V 1 P
came divers of antonio's creditors in my company MV 3.01.113 P
that he would rather have antonio's flesh | than 3.02.286

wife, | tell her the process of antonio's end, 4.01.274
for half thy wealth, it is antonio's; 4.01.370
him, if thou canst, | unto antonio's house. 4.01.454
petruchio is my name, antonio's son, | a man SHR 2.01. 68
stand you directly in antonio's way | when he JC 1.02. 3
jupiter, | were i the wearer of antonio's beard, ANT 2.02. 7
antonio's dead! 2.05. 26

ANTONIUS 3 FR 0.0003 REL FR 2 V 1 P
is caesar with antonius priz'd so slight? ANT 1.01. 56
but she is now the wife of marcus antonius. 2.06.112 P
i could do more to do antonius good, | but 3.01. 25

ANTONY 198 FR 0.0223 REL FR 185 V 13 P
he is as valiant a man as mark antony, and he is H5 3.06. 14 P
part | of that quick spirit that is in antony. JC 1.02. 29
he loves no plays, | as thou dost, antony; 1.02.204
why, antony. 1.02.233 P
i saw mark antony offer him a crown — yet 'twas 1.02.237 P
mark antony, so well belov'd of caesar, | should 2.01.156
prevent, | let antony and caesar fall together. 2.01.161
for antony is but a limb of caesar. 2.01.165
and for mark antony, think not of him; 2.01.181
we'll send mark antony to the senate–house, 2.02. 52
mark antony shall say i am not well, | and, for 2.02. 55
see, antony, that revels long a–nights, | is 2.02.116
good morrow, antony. 2.02.117
brutus, | he draws mark antony out of the way. 3.01. 26
where is antony? 3.01. 96
thus did mark antony bid me fall down; 3.01.124
if brutus will vouchsafe that antony | may 3.01.130
mark antony shall not love caesar dead | so well 3.01.133
so says my master antony. 3.01.137
but here comes antony. welcome, mark antony! 3.01.147
but here comes antony. welcome, mark antony! 3.01.147
o antony! 3.01.164
you our swords have leaden points, mark antony; 3.01.173
thy death, | to see thy antony making his peace, 3.01.197
mark antony — 3.01.211
so full of good regard | that were you, antony, 3.01.225
you shall, mark antony. 3.01.231
not consent | that antony speak in his funeral. 3.01.233
what antony shall speak, i will protest | he 3.01.238
mark antony, here take you caesar's body. 3.01.244
i do, mark antony. 3.01.277
here comes his body, mourn'd by mark antony, who 3.02. 41 P
and, for my sake, stay here with antony. 3.02. 56
tending to caesar's glories, which mark antony 3.02. 58
depart, | save i alone, till antony have spoke. 3.02. 61
stay ho, and let us hear mark antony. 3.02. 62
noble antony, go up. 3.02. 64
peace, let us hear what antony can say. 3.02. 71
there's not a nobler man in rome than antony. 3.02.116
we'll hear the will. read it, mark antony. 3.02.138
read the will, we'll hear it, antony. 3.02.147
room for antony, most noble antony. 3.02.166 P
room for antony, most noble antony. 3.02.166 P
peace there, hear the noble antony. 3.02.207 P
and brutus antony, there were an antony | would 3.02.227
there were an antony | would ruffle up your 3.02.227
peace ho, hear antony, most noble antony! 3.02.234 P
peace ho, hear antony, most noble antony! 3.02.234 P
prick him down, antony. 4.01. 3
live, | who is your sister's son, mark antony. 4.01. 5
come, antony, and young octavius, come, 4.03. 93
and grief that young octavius with mark antony 4.03.153
that young octavius and mark antony | come down 4.03.168
octavius, antony, and lepidus | have put to 4.03.174
now, antony, our hopes are answered. 5.01. 1
mark antony, shall we give sign of battle? 5.01. 23
antony, | the posture of your blows are yet 5.01. 32
for you have stol'n their buzzing, antony, | and 5.01. 37
come, antony; 5.01. 63
spoil, | whilst we by antony are all enclos'd. 5.03. 8
mark antony is in your tents, my lord; 5.03. 10
power, | as cassius' legions are by antony. 5.03. 53
room ho! tell antony, brutus is ta'en. 5.04. 16
safe, antony, brutus is safe enough. 5.04. 20
more than octavius and mark antony | by this 5.05. 37
nay, hear them, antony. ANT 1.01. 19
is come from caesar, therefore hear it, antony. 1.01. 27
thou blushest, antony, and that blood of thine 1.01. 30
antony | will be himself. 1.01. 42
sir, sometimes when he is not antony, | he comes 1.01. 57
property | which still should go with antony. 1.01. 59
hush, here comes antony. 1.02. 79
antony, thou wouldst say — 1.02.104
but here comes antony. 1.03. 13
i am quickly ill, and well, | so antony loves. 1.03. 73
is i would — | o, my oblivion is a very antony, 1.03. 90
yet must antony | no way excuse his foils, when 1.04. 23
antony, | leave thy lascivious /wassails. 1.04. 55
out this great gap of time | my antony is away. 1.05. 6
o happy horse, to bear the weight of antony! 1.05. 21
how much unlike art thou mark antony! 1.05. 35
how goes it with my brave mark antony? 1.05. 38
born that day | when i forget to send to antony, 1.05. 64
say "the brave antony." 1.05. 69
mark antony | in egypt sits at dinner, and will 2.01. 11
they are in rome together, | looking for antony. 2.01. 20
mark antony is every hour in rome | expected. 2.01. 29
widow pluck | the /ne'er–lust–wearied antony. 2.01. 38
caesar and antony shall well greet together: 2.01. 39
him, although i think | not mov'd by antony. 2.01. 42
let antony look over caesar's head | and speak 2.02. 5
here comes | the noble antony. 2.02. 14
great mark antony | is now a widower. 2.02.119
knot, take antony | octavia to his wife; 2.02.126
not till he hears how antony is touch'd | with 2.02.139
noble antony, | not sickness should detain me. 2.02.169
when she first met mark antony, she purs'd up 2.02.186 P
o, rare for antony! 2.02.205
and antony | enthron'd i' th' market–place, did 2.02.214
upon her landing, antony sent to her, | invited 2.02.219
our courteous antony, | whom ne'er the word of 2.02.222
now antony | must leave her utterly. 2.02.232
can settle | the heart of antony, octavia is | a 2.02.241
therefore, o antony, stay not by his side. 2.03. 19
sir, mark antony | will e'en but kiss octavia, 2.04. 2
them up, | i'll think them every one an antony, 2.05. 14
thy face, if antony | be free and healthful — 2.05. 37
yet, if thou say antony lives, 'tis well, | or 2.05. 43
in praising antony i have disprais'd caesar. 2.05.107
but mark antony | put me to some impatience. 2.06. 41
no, antony, take the lot; 2.06. 62
we look'd not for mark antony here. 2.06.108 P
which is mark antony. 2.06.126 P
antony will use his affection where it is; 2.06.130 P
good antony, your hand. 2.07.126
o antony, | you have my /father's house — but 2.07.127
so thy grand captain, antony, | shall set thee 3.01. 9
caesar and antony have ever won | more in their 3.01. 16
thou wilt write to antony? 3.01. 29
nay, but how dearly he adores mark antony! 3.02. 8
what's antony? the god of jupiter. 3.02. 10
o antony! o thou arabian bird! 3.02. 12
but he loves caesar best, yet he loves antony. 3.02. 15
his love to antony. 3.02. 18
most noble antony, | let not the piece of virtue 3.02. 27
when antony found julius caesar dead, | he cried 3.02. 54
but how, when antony is gone, | through whom i 3.03. 5
her led | between her brother and mark antony. 3.03. 10
where's antony? 3.05. 15
bring me to antony. 3.05. 23
the wife of antony | should have an army for an 3.06. 43
my lord, mark antony, | hearing that you 3.06. 57
only th' adulterous antony, most large | in his 3.06. 93
your presence needs must puzzle antony, | take 3.07. 10
loof'd, | the noble ruin of her magic, antony, 3.10. 18
i'll yet follow | the wounded chance of antony, 3.10. 35
let him appear that's come from antony. 3.12. 1
such as i am, i come from antony. 3.12. 7
for antony, | i have no ears to his request. 3.12. 19
from antony win cleopatra, promise, | and in our 3.12. 27
observe how antony becomes his flaw, | and what 3.12. 34
is antony or we in fault for this? 3.13. 2
antony only, that would make his will | lord of 3.13. 3
so haply are they friends to antony. 3.13. 48
he knows that you embrace not antony | as you 3.13. 56
to be sure of that, | i will ask antony. 3.13. 63
spirits | to hear from me you had left antony, 3.13. 70
i am | antony yet. 3.13. 93
mark antony — 3.13.102
and it portends alone | the fall of antony! 3.13.155
but since my lord | is antony again, i will be 3.13.186
dares me to personal combat, | caesar to antony. 4.01. 4
of those that serv'd mark antony but late, 4.01. 13
poor antony! 4.01. 16
all of you clapp'd up together in | an antony, 4.02. 18
'tis the god hercules, whom antony lov'd, | now 4.03. 16
then, antony — but now — well, on. 4.04. 38
the gods make this a happy day to antony! 4.05. 1
our will is antony be took alive; 4.06. 2
antony | is come into the field. 4.06. 6
that antony may seem to spend his fury | upon 4.06. 9
and went to jewry on | affairs of antony, there 4.06. 12
himself to caesar | and leave his master antony; 4.06. 14
antony | hath after thee sent all thy treasure, 4.06. 19
o antony, | thou mine of bounty, how wouldst 4.06. 30
o antony, | nobler than my revolt is infamous, 4.09. 18
o antony! 4.09. 23
o antony! 4.09. 23
antony | is valiant, and dejected, and by starts 4.12. 6
fortune and antony part here, even here | do we 4.12. 19
say that the last i spoke was "antony," | and 4.13. 8
here i am antony, | yet cannot hold this visible 4.14. 13
no, antony, | my mistress lov'd thee, and her 4.14. 23
the last she spake | was "antony, most noble 4.14. 30
she spake | was "antony, most noble antony!" 4.14. 30
a tearing groan did break | the name of antony; 4.14. 32
where's antony? 4.14.114
o antony, | antony, antony! 4.15. 11
o antony, | antony, antony! 4.15. 12
o antony, | antony, antony! 4.15. 12
not caesar's valor hath o'erthrown antony, | but 4.15. 14
that none but antony | should conquer antony, 4.15. 16
that none but antony | should conquer antony, 4.15. 17
but come, come, antony — | help me, my women — 4.15. 29
mark antony i serv'd, who best was worthy | best 5.01. 6
i say, o caesar, antony is dead. 5.01. 13
the death of antony | is not a single doom, in 5.01. 17
o antony, | i have followed thee to this; 5.01. 35
antony | did tell me of you, bade me trust you, 5.02. 12
i dreamt there was an emperor antony. 5.02. 76
an antony were nature's piece 'gainst fancy, 5.02. 99
antony | shall be brought drunken forth, and i 5.02.218
i am again for cydnus | to meet mark antony. 5.02.229
methinks i hear | antony call; 5.02.284
if she first meet the curled antony, | he'll 5.02.301
balm, as soft as air, as gentle — | o antony! 5.02.312
as she would catch another antony | in her 5.02.347
she shall be buried by her antony; 5.02.358

ANTONY'S 5 FR 0.0005 REL FR 5 V 0 P
soft, who comes here? a friend of antony's. JC 3.01.122
as it is said | mark antony's was by caesar. MAC 3.01. 56
thus i do escape the sorrow | of antony's death. ANT 4.14. 95
antony, | but antony's hath triumph'd on itself. 4.15. 15
by taking | antony's course, you shall bereave 5.02.130

ANTRES 1 FR 0.0001 REL FR 1 V 0 P
wherein of antres vast and deserts idle, | rough OTH 1.03.140

ANVIL 2 FR 0.0002 REL FR 2 V 0 P
the whilst his iron did on the anvil cool, JN 4.02.194
here i cleep | the anvil of my sword, and do COR 4.05.110

/ANY 4 FR 0.0004 REL FR 3 V 1 P
/you /should /have /an /inch /of /any /ground 2H4 4.01.107
/nor /any /other /part | belonging to a man. ROM 2.02. 41
/madness | /allows /itself /to /any /thing. LR 3.07.105
/the /queen /to /any /demonstration /of /grief? 4.03. 9 P

ANY 884 FR 0.0999 REL FR 491 V 393 P
ground, long heath, brown /furze, any thing. TMP 1.01. 67 P
had i been any god of power, i would | have sunk 1.02. 10
as an hair | betid to any creature in the vessel 1.02. 31
by any other house, or person? 1.02. 42
of any thing the image, tell me, that | hath 1.02. 43
which any print of goodness wilt not take, 1.02.352
sword, pike, knife, gun, or need of any engine, 2.01.162
they'll tell the clock to any business that | we 2.01.289
bush nor shrub to bear off any weather at all. 2.02. 18 P
any strange beast there makes a man. 2.02. 31 P
he's a present for any emperor that ever trod on 2.02. 70 P
if any be trinculo's legs, these are they. 2.02.104 P
o stephano, hast any more of this? 2.02.133 P
now lead the way without any more talking. 2.02.173 P
never any | with so full soul but some defect in 3.01. 43
not wish | any companion in the world but you; 3.01. 55
if you trouble him any more in 's tale, by this 3.02. 48 P
request, monster, i will do reason, any reason. 3.02.119 P
you shall find | many, nay, almost any. 3.03. 34
(worse than any death | can be at once) shall 3.03. 77
for any or for all these exercises | he said TGV 1.03. 11
you'll lose the tide, if you tarry any longer. 2.03. 36 P
it is the unkindest tied that ever any man tied. 2.03. 38 P
thankful | to any happy messenger from thence. 2.04. 53
sweet, except not any, | except thou wilt except 2.04.154
know | that i had any light from thee of this. 3.01. 49
bear it | under a cloak that is of any length. 3.01.130
why, any cloak will serve the turn, my lord. 3.01.134
tell us this: have you any thing to take to? 4.01. 40
here can i sit alone, unseen of any, | and to 5.04. 4
who writes himself armigero, in any bill, WIV 1.01. 10 P
and have done any time these three hundred years 1.01. 12 P
i will marry her upon any reasonable demands. 1.01.225 P
that, upon your request, cousin, in any reason. 1.01.241 P
as soon quarrel at it as any man in england. 1.01.291 P
i' faith, and find any body in the house, here 1.04. 4 P
a man of his hands as any is between this and 1.04. 26 P
shall i do any good, think'st thou? 1.04.142 P
by day or night, | or any kind of light, | with 2.01. 16
i will consent to act any villainy against him, 2.01. 98 P
fairest, that would have won any woman's heart; 2.02. 70 P
but i defy all angels (in any such sort, as they 2.02. 73 P
nor evening prayer, as any is in windsor, 2.02. 99 P
and in any case have a nay–word, that you may 2.02.126 P
and the boy never need to understand any thing; 2.02.128 P
good that children should know any wickedness. 2.02.129 P
if any man may, you may as soon as any. 2.02.236 P
if any man may, you may as soon as any. 2.02.237 P
i come to her with any detection in my hand, my 2.02.246 P
would any man have thought this? 2.02.291 P
has page any brains? 3.02. 30 P
hath he any eyes? 3.02. 30 P
hath he any thinking? 3.02. 31 P
and (without any pause or staggering) take this 3.03. 12 P
or any tire of venetian admittance. 3.03. 57 P
if he be of any reasonable stature, he may creep 3.03.129 P
if there be any pody in the house, and in the 3.03.210 P
any thing. 3.03.233 P
as well as i love any woman in gloucestershire. 3.04. 43 P
that any madness i ever yet beheld seem'd but 4.02. 26 P
any extremity rather than a mischief. 4.02. 73 P
page, have you any way then to unfool me again? 4.02.115 P
you are not to go loose any longer, you must be 4.02.123 P
do, /and if you suspect me in any dishonesty. 4.02.134 P
conscience, pursue him with any further revenge? 4.02.208 P
fat knight shall be any further afflicted, we 4.02.218 P
as art and practice hath enriched any | that we MM 1.01. 12
if any in vienna be of worth | to undergo such 1.01. 22
on mine honor, have to do | with any scruple. 1.01. 64
i never heard any soldier dislike it. 1.02. 17 P
in any proportion, or in any language. 1.02. 22 P
in any proportion, or in any language. 1.02. 22 P
i think, or in any religion. 1.02. 23 P
if they'll do you any good. 1.02.143
doth your honor see any harm in his face? 2.01.153 P
master froth do the constable's wife any harm? 2.01.158 P
is a more respected person than any of us all. 2.01.166 P
hath she had any more than one husband? 2.01.201 P
part, i never come into any room in a tap–house, 2.01.209 P
before me again upon any complaint whatsoever; 2.01.246 P
faith, sir, few of any wit in such matters. 2.01.268 P
at any time 'fore noon. 2.02.160
life | (as i subscribe not that, nor any other, 2.04. 89
but is there any? 3.01. 62
i have spirit to do any thing that appears not 3.01.206 P
i know none. can you tell me of any? 3.02. 87 P
as dangerous to be ag'd in any kind of course, 3.02.225 P
is virtuous to be constant in any undertaking. 3.02.226 P
than merry at any thing which profess'd to make 3.02.236 P
me, hath any body inquir'd for me here to–day? 4.01. 16 P
if any thing fall to you upon this, more than 4.02.177 P
i will not die to–day for any man's persuasion. 4.03. 59 P
if you have any thing to say to me, come to my 4.03. 62 P
that if any crave redress of injustice, they 4.04. 9 P
your eye | by throwing it on any other object, 5.01. 23
as seems you best, | in any chastisement. 5.01.257
as any in vienna, on my word. 5.01.268 P
if any woman wrong'd by this lewd fellow | (as i 5.01.509
more, if any born at ephesus be seen | at any ERR 1.01. 16
be seen | at any syracusian marts and fairs; 1.01. 17
if any syracusian born | come to the bay of 1.01. 18
deep | gave any tragic instance of our harm: 1.01. 64
or that, or any place that harbors men. 1.01.136
was there ever any man thus beaten out of season 2.02. 47
sirrah, if any ask you for your master, | say he 2.02.209
break any breaking here, and i'll break your 3.01. 74
road, | and if the wind blow any way from shore, 3.02.148
if any bark put forth, come to the mart, | where 3.02.150
if any ship put out, then straight away. 3.02.185
yes, if any hour meet a sergeant, 'a turns back 4.02. 56
he that brings any man to answer it that breaks 4.03. 31 P
is there any ships puts forth to–night? 4.03. 35 P
his word might bear my wealth at any time. 5.01. 8
liv'st | to walk where any honest men resort. 5.01. 28
if any friend will pay the sum for him, | he 5.01.131
rings, jewels, any thing his rage did like. 5.01.144
but few of any sort, and none of name. ADO 1.01. 7 P
there was none such in the army of any sort. 1.01. 33 P
i will not do them the wrong to mistrust any, i 1.01.244 P
ere you flout old ends any further, examine your 1.01.288 P
learn | any hard lesson that may do thee good. 1.01.293
hath leonato any son, my lord? 1.01.294
hath the fellow any wit that told you this? 1.02. 17 P
than to fashion a carriage to rob love from any. 1.03. 30 P
will it serve for any model to build mischief on 1.03. 46 P
if i can cross him any way, i bless myself every 1.03. 68 P
such a man would win any woman in the world, if 2.01. 16 P

The Library
Saint Francis College
Fort Wayne, Indiana 46808

nay, if they lead to any ill, i will leave them 2.01.153 P
your grace command me any service to the world's 2.01.263 P
beard, do you any embassage to the pigmies, 2.01.269 P
i will do any modest office, my lord, to help my 2.01.375 P
any bar, any cross, any impediment will be 2.02. 4 P
any bar, any cross, any impediment will be 2.02. 4 P
cross, any impediment will be med'cinable to me. 2.02. 4 P
i can, at any unseasonable instant of the night, 2.02. 16 P
look you for any other issue? 2.02. 30 P
only to despite them, i will endeavor any thing. 2.02. 32 P
a voice | to slander music any more than once. 2.03. 45
never think that lady would have lov'd any man. 2.03. 94 P
will rather die than give any sign of affection. 2.03.227 P
"any pains that i take for you is as easy as 2.03.261 P
hath any man seen him at the barber's? 3.02. 43 P
if there be any impediment, i pray you discover 3.02. 93 P
if i see any thing to–night why i should not 3.02.123 P
if they should have any allegiance in them, 3.03. 5 P
you are to bid any man stand, in the prince's 3.03. 26 P
much more a man who hath any honesty in him. 3.03. 64 P
one on't, with any man that knows the /statues, 3.03. 78 P
and there be any matter of weight chances, call 3.03. 85 P
is it possible that any villainy should be so 3.03.110 P
if it were possible any villainy should be so 3.03.113 P
which did confirm any slander that don john had 3.03.158 P
is there any harm in "the heavier for a husband" 3.04. 34 P
god i am as honest as any man living that is an 3.05. 13 P
on your worship as of any man in the city, and 3.05. 26 P
a couple of as arrant knaves as any in messina. 3.05. 32 P
if either of you know any inward impediment why 4.01. 12 P
know you any, hero? 4.01. 15 P
know you any, count? 4.01. 17 P
who can blot that name | with any just reproach? 4.01. 81
if i know more of any man alive | than that 4.01.178
prove you that any man with me convers'd | at 4.01.181
the change of words with any creature, | refuse 4.01.183
is there any way to show such friendship? 4.01.263 P
come, bid me do any thing for thee. 4.01.288 P
or that i had any friend would be a man for my 4.01.318 P
as pretty a piece of flesh as any is in messina, 4.02. 82 P
never any did so, though very many have been 5.01.127 P
i would bend under any heavy weight | that he'll 5.01.277
virtuous | in any thing that i do know by her. 5.01.303
they will not admit any good part to intermingle 5.02. 63 P
will think nothing to any purpose that the world 5.04.106 P
boast | before the birds have any cause to sing? LLL 1.01.103
why should i joy in any abortive birth? 1.01.104
if any man be seen to talk with a woman within 1.01.129 P
i'll lay my head to any good man's hat, | these 1.01.308
and ransom him to any french courtier for a new 1.02. 62 P
if virtue's gloss will stain with any soil, | is 2.01. 48
we may afford | to any lady that subdues a lord. 4.01. 40
for where is any author in the world | teaches 4.03.308
so, if any of the audience hiss, you may cry, 5.01.137 P
any thing like? 5.02. 39
majesty | command me any service to her thither? 5.02.312
can any face of brass hold longer out? 5.02.395
sound, | swift as a shadow, short as any dream, MND 1.01.144
nor hath love's mind of any judgment taste; 1.01.236
that i will do any man's heart good to hear me. 1.02. 71 P
i will roar you as gently as any sucking dove; 1.02. 82 P
i will roar you and 'twere any nightingale. 1.02. 83 P
if you have any pity, grace, or manners, | you 3.02.241
simply the best wit of any handicraft man in 4.02. 9 P
in any case, let thisby have clean linen; 4.02. 39 P
for never any thing can be amiss, | when 5.01. 82
it is that — any thing now! MV 1.01.113
of nothing, more than any man in all venice. 1.01.115 P
never be chosen by any rightly but one who you 1.02. 32 P
in your affection towards any of these princely 1.02. 34 P
i will do any thing, nerissa, ere i will be 1.02. 98 P
not fear, lady, the having any of these lords. 1.02.100 P
have you heard any imputation to the contrary? 1.03. 13 P
as fair | as any comer i have look'd on yet 2.01. 21
him, i will run as far as god has any ground. 2.02.110 P
for i am a jew if i serve the jew any longer. 2.02.112 P
if any man in italy have a fairer table, which 2.02.158 P
never to unfold to any one | which casket 'twas 2.09. 10
without any slips of prolixity or crossing the 3.01. 11 P
whether antonio have had any loss at sea or no? 3.01. 43 P
rack, | where men enforced do speak any thing. 3.02. 33
so much the constitution | of any constant man. 3.02.247
and i must freely have the half of any thing 3.02.249
appears | than any that draws breath in italy. 3.02.296
i'll hold thee any wager, | when we are both 3.04. 62
is but one hope in it that can do you any good, 3.05. 7 P
pity, void and empty | from any dram of mercy. 4.01. 6
hates any man the thing he would not kill? 4.01. 67
you may as well do any thing most hard, | as 4.01. 78
you, merchant, have you any thing to say? 4.01.263
would any of the stock of barrabas | had been 4.01.296
attempts | he seek the life of any citizen, 4.01.351
sound, | or any air of music touch their ears, 5.01. 76
to have defended it | with any terms of zeal, 5.01.205
as you, | i'll not deny him any thing i have, 5.01.227
nothing. i am not taught to make any thing. AYL 1.01. 30 P
for if thou dost him any slight disgrace, or if 1.01.148 P
me how to remember any extraordinary pleasure. 1.02. 7 P
swearing by his honor, for he never had any; 1.02. 78 P
but is there any else longs to see this broken 1.02.141 P
to deny so fair and excellent ladies any thing. 1.02.185 P
with reasons and the other mad without any. 1.03. 9 P
i cannot hear of any that did see her. 2.02. 4
yond man | if he for gold will give us any food; 2.04. 65
that little cares for buying any thing. 2.04. 90
well then, if ever i thank any man, i'll thank 2.05. 25 P
if it do come to pass | that any man turn ass, 2.05. 51
if this uncouth forest yield any thing savage, i 2.06. 6 P
a dinner if there live any thing in this desert. 2.06. 17 P
pride | that can therein tax any private party? 2.07. 71
like a wild goose flies, | unclaim'd of any man. 2.07. 87
he dies that touches any of this fruit | till i 2.07. 98
church, | if ever sat at any good man's feast, 2.07.115
hast any philosophy in thee, shepherd? 3.02. 21 P
a word too great for any mouth of this age's 3.02.226 P
can you remember any of the principal evils that 3.02.351 P
yourself, than seeming the lover of any other. 3.02.384 P
did you ever cure any so? 3.02.406 P

something and for no passion truly any thing, as 3.02.414 P
i will not take her on gift of any man. 3.03. 68 P
than any of her lineaments can show her. 3.05. 56
this time there was not any man died in his own 4.01. 96 P
there was never any thing so sudden but the 5.02. 30 P
human as she is, and without any danger. 5.02. 67 P
if any man doubt that, let him put me to my 5.04. 43 P
he's as good at any thing, and yet a fool. 5.04.105 P
and if you give me any conserves, give me SHR in.2. 7 P
beautiful | than any woman in this waning age. in.2. 63
there, there, hortensio, will you any wife? 1.01. 56
or, signior gremio, you, know any such, | prefer 1.01. 96
if i can by any means light on a fit man to 1.01.110 P
any man is so very a fool to be married to hell? 1.01.124 P
we have not yet been seen in any house, | nor 1.01.199
comes there any more of it? 1.01.251 P
is there any man has rebus'd your worship? 1.02. 7 P
all books of love, see that at any hand — | and 1.02.146
not her that chides, sir, at any hand, i pray. 1.02.225
and if i be, sir, is it any offense? 1.02.229
suitors, | and will not promise her to any man, 1.02.260
face | which i could fancy more than any other. 2.01. 12
have been more kindly beholding to you than any, 2.01. 78 P
as any one | old signior gremio has in padua, 2.01.367
than hath been taught by any of my trade; 3.01. 69
"now take them up," quoth he, "if any list." 3.02.165
barn, | my horse, my ox, my ass, my any thing; 3.02.232
bianca | doth fancy any other but lucentio? 4.02. 2
'tis death for any one in mantua | to come to 4.02. 81
then both or one, or any thing thou wilt. 4.03. 29
well, and hold your own in any case | with such 4.04. 6
may beseem | the spouse of any noble gentleman. 4.05. 67
will you any thing with it? AWW 1.01.164 P
jowl horns together like any deer i' th' herd. 1.03. 54 P
for her, they touch'd not any stranger sense. 1.03.109 P
him not | by any token of presumptuous suit, 1.03.198
with any branch or image of thy state; 2.01.198
if god have lent a man any manners, he may 2.02. 8 P
the brawn–buttock, or any buttock. 2.02. 19 P
your constable, it will fit any question. 2.02. 31 P
to any count, to all counts: to what is man. 2.03.193 P
if i can meet him with any convenience, and he 2.03.238 P
is there any unkindness between my lord and you, 2.05. 32 P
mine own direct knowledge, without any malice, 3.06. 8 P
upon oath, never trust my judgment in any thing. 3.06. 33 P
let him fetch off his drum in any hand. 3.06. 43 P
not put my reputation now | in any staining act. 3.07. 7
i would i had any drum of the enemy's. 4.01. 61 P
if the business be of any difficulty, and this 4.03. 93 P
i could endure any thing before but a cat, and 4.03.237 P
my life, sir, in any case! 4.03.241 P
i' th' stocks, or any where, so i may live. 4.03.244 P
in a retreat he outruns any lackey; 4.03.290 P
know you any here? 4.03.313 P
my horses be well look'd to, without any tricks. 4.05. 59 P
if i put any tricks upon 'em, sir, they shall be 4.05. 60 P
stop my nose, or against any man's metaphor. 5.02. 13 P
what he'll utter, | that will speak any thing? 5.03.209
and i had that which any inferior might | at 5.03.218
as any man in illyria, whatsoever he be, under TN 1.03.117 P
simply as strong as any man in illyria. 1.03.124 P
witty a piece of eve's flesh as any in illyria. 1.05. 28 P
any thing that's mended is but patch'd; 1.05. 47 P
he's fortified against any denial. 1.05.145 P
to any other's, profanation. 1.05.217 P
have you any commission from your lord to 1.05.231 P
for your love, to lay any of them on you. 2.01. 7 P
catches without any mitigation or remorse of 2.03. 90 P
art any more than a steward? 2.03.114 P
my lady's favor at any thing more than contempt, 2.03.122 P
is, or any thing constantly but a time–pleaser, 2.03.147 P
exalted respect than any one else that follows 2.05. 27 P
why, this is evident to any formal capacity, 2.05.117 P
ay, and you had any eye behind you, you might 2.05.136 P
and't be any way, it must be with valor, for 3.02. 30 P
no man hath any quarrel to me. 3.04.226 P
free and clear from any image of offense done to 3.04.228 P
clear from any image of offense done to any man. 3.04.228 P
if you hold your life at any price, betake you 3.04.230 P
possibly have found in any part of illyria. 3.04.268 P
none, | nor know i you by voice or any feature. 3.04.353
or any taint of vice whose strong corruption 3.04.356
i dare lay any money 'twill be nothing yet. 3.04.396 P
against him, if there be any law in illyria. 4.01. 35 P
make the trial of it in any constant question. 4.02. 48 P
i cannot pursue with any safety this sport /t' 4.02. 70 P
i am as well in my wits as any man in illyria. 4.02.106 P
me | to any other trust but that i am mad | or 4.03. 15
any thing. 5.01. 4 P
of ill–doing, nor dream'd | that any did. WT 1.02. 71
and that you slipp'd not | with any but with us. 1.02. 86
women say so — | that will say any thing. 1.02.131
taken | by any understanding pate but thine? 1.02.223
a name | as rank as any flax–wench that puts to 1.02.277
any of them? 2.02. 12
my red–look'd anger be | the trumpet any more. 2.02. 33
nor guilty of | (if any be) the trespass of the 2.02. 61
nor i, nor any | but one that's here — and 2.03. 83
any thing, my lord, | that my ability may 2.03.163
to save the innocent — any thing possible. 2.03.167
the fail | of any point in't shall not only be 2.03.171
yet | that any of these bolder vices wanted 3.02. 55
would any but these boil'd–brains of nineteen 3.03. 63 P
if any where i have them, 'tis by the sea–side, 3.03. 67 P
if there be any of him left, i'll bury it. 3.03.131 P
'tis a sickness denying thee any thing; 4.02. 2 P
dost lack any money? 4.03. 77 P
i shall there have money, or any thing i want. 4.03. 82 P
i cannot be | mine own, nor any thing to any, if 4.04. 44
i cannot be | mine own, nor any thing to any, if 4.04. 44
strangle such thoughts as these with any thing 4.04. 47
so she does any thing, though i report it | that 4.04.177
has he any unbraided wares? 4.04.203 P
will you buy any tape, | or lace for your cape, 4.04.315
any silk, any thread, | any toys for your head 4.04.318
any silk, any thread, | any toys for your head 4.04.318
any toys for your head | of the new'st and 4.04.319
i mean not | to see him any more) cast your good 4.04.495

not any yet: 4.04.537
at us, and we may do any thing extempore. 4.04.677 P
and any thing that is fitting to be known — 4.04.720 P
that she is a woman | more worth than any man; 5.01.111
ay, and have been so any time these four hours. 5.02.136 P
as honest a true fellow as any is in bohemia. 5.02.157 P
ay, by any means prove a tall fellow. 5.02.170 P
scarce any joy | did ever so long live; 5.03. 51
has a taste as sweet | as any cordial comfort. 5.03. 77
it would not be sir nob in any case. JN 1.01.147
well, now can i make any joan a lady. 1.01.184
thoughts | in any /breast of strong authority, 2.01.113
there stuck no plume in any english crest | that 2.01.317
holds hand with any princess of the world. 2.01.494
that any thing he sees, which moves his liking, 2.01.512
judge, | that i can find should merit any hate. 2.01.520
that takes away by any secret course | thy 3.01.178
or heard | of any kindred action like to this? 3.04. 14
hair, | any annoyance in that precious sense! 4.01. 93
with any long'd–for change or better state. 4.02. 8
never such a pow'r | for any foreign preparation 4.02.111
and can give audience | to any tongue, speak it 4.02.140
hand — | if that it be the work of any hand. 4.03. 59
if that it be the work of any hand? 4.03. 60
to any sovereign state throughout the world. 5.02. 82
me | that any accent breaking from thy tongue 5.06. 14
or any other ground inhabitable | where ever R2 1.01. 65
i'll answer thee in any fair degree | or 1.01. 80
contrive, or complot any ill | 'gainst us, our 1.03.189
inform, | merely in hate, 'gainst any of us all, 2.01.243
dogs, easily won to fawn on any man! 3.02.130
that bids me be of comfort any more. 3.02.208
that any harm should stain so fair a show! 3.03. 71
do me good, | and never borrow any tear of thee. 3.04. 23
would god that any in this noble presence | were 4.01.117
have any resting for her true king's queen. 5.01. 6
man may be, | not like to me, or any of my kin, 5.02.109
if any plague hang over us, 'tis he. 5.03. 3
ill mayst thou thrive if thou grant any grace! 5.03. 99
e'er i be, | nor i, nor any man that but man is, 5.05. 39
take horse, | uncertain of the issue any way. 1H4 1.01. 61
never rise | to do him wrong or any way impeach 1.03. 75
his company hourly any time this two and twenty 2.02. 16 P
have you any levers to lift me up again, being 2.02. 34 P
that i can drink with any tinker in his own 2.04. 19 P
a weaver, i could sing psalms, or any thing. 2.04.134 P
could have crept into any alderman's thumb–ring. 2.04.331 P
send him to answer thee, or any man, | for any 2.04.516
man, | for any thing he shall be charg'd withal, 2.04.517
why, so can i, or so can any man, | but will 3.01. 53
so much land | to any well–deserving friend; 3.01.136
talk to me | in any summer house in christendom. 3.01.162
if thou wert any way given to virtue, i would 3.03. 33 P
of yours with fire any time this two and thirty 3.03. 47 P
thou or any man knows where to have me, thou 3.03.130 P
if there were any thing in thy pocket but 3.03.157 P
were enrich'd with any other injuries but these, 3.03.161 P
shalt find me tractable to any honest reason; 3.03.173 P
friends with my father and may do any thing. 3.03.182 P
and dear a trust | on any soul remov'd, but on 4.01. 35
you, my lord, or any scot that this day lives. 4.03. 12
king | have any way your good deserts forgot, 4.03. 46
know, | in any case, the offer of the king. 5.02. 25
did you beg any? god forbid! 5.02. 35
did i hear | of any prince so wild a liberty. 5.02. 71
percy, | to share with me in glory any more. 5.04. 64
if your father will do me any honor, so; 5.04.141 P
is not able to invent any thing that intends to 2H4 1.02. 8 P
into my service for any other reason than to set 1.02. 13 P
am sure he is, to the hearing of any thing good. 1.02. 68 P
though it be a shame to be on any side but one, 1.02. 75 P
throat if you say i am any other than an honest 1.02. 85 P
if thou get'st any leave of me, hang me; 1.02. 88 P
hot day, and i brandish any thing but a bottle, 1.02.211 P
a good wit will make use of any thing. 1.02.248 P
he will foin like any devil, he will spare 2.01. 16 P
mare, if i have any vantage of ground to get up. 2.01. 79 P
sup any women with him? 2.02.151 P
i warrant you, is as red as any rose, in good 2.04. 25 P
feathers turn back in any show of resistance. 2.04.100 P
by the mass, i was call'd any thing, and i would 3.02. 17 P
and i would have done any thing indeed too, and 3.02. 18 P
she has nobody to do any thing about her when i 3.02.231 P
that his dimensions to any thick sight were 3.02.313 P
arms, | not to break peace, or any branch of it, 4.01. 85
there is no need of any such redress, | or if 4.01. 95
of them all speaks any other word but my name. 4.03. 19 P
and i had but a belly of any indifferency, i 4.03. 20 P
none of these demure boys come to any proof, for 4.03. 91 P
up with this retinue, doth any deed of courage; 4.03.112 P
or swell my thoughts to any strain of pride, 4.05.170
if any rebel or vain spirit of mine | did with 4.05.171
doth any name particular belong | unto the 4.05.232
sir, do you mean to stop any of william's wages, 5.01. 23 P
of mutton, and any pretty little tiny kickshaws, 5.01. 27 P
if thou want'st any thing, and wilt not call, 5.03. 56 P
let us take any man's horses, the laws of 5.03.136 P
conscience will make any possible satisfaction, ep 21 P
where (for any thing i know) falstaff shall die ep 29 P
turn him to any cause of policy, | the gordian H5 1.01. 45
and never noted in him any study, | any 1.01. 57
any retirement, any sequestration | from open 1.01. 58
any sequestration | from open haunts and 1.01. 58
at one time | bring in to any of your ancestors. 1.02.135
and when i cannot live any longer, i will do as 2.01. 15 P
went away and it had been any christom child. 2.03. 11 P
to trouble himself with any such thoughts yet. 2.03. 21 P
felt them, and they were as cold as any stone; 2.03. 24 P
and up'ard, and all was as cold as any stone. 2.03. 25 P
and any thing that may not misbecome | the 2.04.118
for 'a never broke any man's head but his own, 3.02. 40 P
they will steal any thing, and call it purchase. 3.02. 42 P
his argument as well as any military man in the 3.02. 80 P
any hurt in the world, but keeps the bridge most 3.06. 10 P
provided of both as any prince in the world. 3.07. 9 P
change my horse with any that treads but on four 3.07. 12 P
thou mak'st use of any thing. 3.07. 66 P
or any such proverb so little kin to the purpose 3.07. 68 P

if the english had any apprehension, they would 3.07.135 P
for if their heads had any intellectual armor, 3.07.137 P
should possess him with any appearance of fear, 4.01.111 P
would not wish himself any where but where he is 4.01.119 P
i could not die any where so contented as in the 4.01.126 P
how can they charitably dispose of any thing, 4.01.143 P
give me any gage of thine, and i will wear it in 4.01.208 P
and hold their manhoods cheap whiles any speaks 4.03. 66
thou never shalt hear herald any more. 4.03.127
be, if he durst steal any thing adventurously. 4.04. 73 P
throngs, | if any order might be thought upon. 4.05. 21
he never kill'd any of his friends. 4.07. 41 P
if any man challenge this, he is a friend to 4.07.156 P
if thou encounter any such, apprehend him, and 4.07.158 P
it, if there is any martial law in the world. 4.08. 44 P
never came any from mine that might offend your 4.08. 47 P
if i owe you any thing, i will pay you in 5.01. 64 P
dare not avouch in your deeds any of your words? 5.01. 73 P
dignity, | any thing in or out of our demands, 5.02. 89
his glass for love of any thing he sees there, 5.02.148 P
can any of your neighbors tell, kate? 5.02.196 P
having any occasion to write for matter of grant 5.02.337 P
what towns of any moment but we have? 1H6 1.02. 5
daughter, | my wit untrain'd in any kind of art. 1.02. 73
i must not yield to any rites of love, | for my 1.02.113
not to wear, handle, or use any sword, weapon, 1.03. 78 P
if thou spy'st any, run and bring me word, | and 1.04. 19
whilst any trump did sound, or drum struck up, 1.04. 80
sir thomas gargrave, hast thou any life? 1.04. 88
if any noise or soldier you perceive | near to 2.01. 2
of /aire, | nor any of his false confederates. 2.02. 21
my side | that any purblind eye may find it out. 2.04. 21
my words | on any plot of ground in christendom. 2.04. 89
men, | forbidden late to carry any weapon, 3.01. 79
was infamous | and ill beseeming any common man, 4.01. 31
that any one should therefore be suspicious | i 4.01.153
i shall be well content with any choice | tends 5.01. 26
a knight, | and will not any way dishonor me. 5.03.102
our king, | and not of any challenge of desert, 5.04.153
no interest | in any of our towns of garrison. 5.04.168
lines, | able to ravish any dull conceit; 5.05. 15
attaint | with any passion of inflaming /love, 5.05. 82
agree to any covenants, and procure | that lady 5.05. 88
cost and charges, without having any dowry." 2H6 1.01. 61 P
how now, fellow? wouldst any thing with me? 1.03. 10 P
force, | that york is most unmeet of any man. 1.03.164
doth any one accuse york for a traitor? 1.03.179
i never said nor thought any such matter. 1.03.188 P
i will take my death, i never meant him any ill, 2.03. 88 P
all these could not procure me any scathe | so 2.04. 62
the king, | or any groat i hoarded to my use, 3.01.113
god forbid any malice should prevail, | that 3.02. 23
be'st found | on any ground that i am ruler of, 3.02.296
stoop to the block than these knees bow to any 4.01.125
it shall be treason for any that calls me other 4.06. 5 P
dare any be so bold to sound retreat or parley 4.08. 4 P
in any case, be not too rough in terms, | for he 4.09. 44
for i, that never fear'd any, am vanquish'd by 4.10. 75 P
armor, any thing i have | is his to use, so 5.01. 52
who can be bound by any solemn vow | to do a 5.01.184
storm | than any thou canst conjure up to–day; 5.01.199
that keeps his leaves in spite of any storm, 5.01.206
him off, | persuaded him from any further act: 5.03. 10
but for a kingdom any oath may be broken: 3H6 1.02. 16
my drift, | nor any of the house of lancaster? 1.02. 47
the sight of any of the house of york | is as a 1.03. 30
keep | than in possession any jot of pleasure. 2.02. 53
thee, | or any he the proudest of thy sort. 2.02. 97
defy thee, | not willing any longer conference, 2.02.171
give me thy gold — if thou hast any gold — 2.05. 80
ah, boy, if any life be left in thee, | throw up 2.05. 84
foreign storms than any home–bred marriage. 4.01. 38
alas, how should you govern any kingdom, | that 4.03. 35
provide | a salve for any sore that may betide. 4.06. 88
i speak not this as doubting any here; 5.04. 43
if any such be here — as god forbid! 5.04. 48
if any spark of life be yet remaining, | down, 5.06. 66
you may partake of any thing we say: R3 1.01. 89
or any creeping venom'd thing that lives! 1.02. 20
and thou unfit for any place, but hell. 1.02.109
or any of your faction? 1.03. 57
(and not provok'd by any suitor else), | aiming, 1.03. 64
if heaven have any grievous plague in store 1.03.216
i never did her any to my knowledge. 1.03.308
it beggars any man that keeps it. 1.04.141 P
if any here | by false intelligence or wrong 2.01. 54
that is hardly borne | /by any in this presence, 2.01. 59
if ever any grudge were lodg'd between us; 2.01. 66
alive | with whom my soul is any jot at odds 2.01. 71
i do not like the tower, of any place. 3.01. 68
his gracious pleasure any way therein. 3.04. 17
his face | by any livelihood he show'd to–day? 3.04. 55
offices | at any time to grace my stratagems. 3.05. 11
have any time recourse unto the princes. 3.05.109
and be thy wife — if any be so mad — | more 4.01. 74
know'st thou not any whom corrupting gold | will 4.02. 34
and will, no doubt, tempt him to any thing. 4.02. 39
ah, who hath any cause to mourn but we? 4.04. 34
honor, | canst thou demise to any child of mine? 4.04.248
hath any well–advised friend proclaim'd | reward 4.04.515
for any good | that i myself have done unto 5.03.187
to see if any mean to shrink from me. 5.03.222
i believe, not any. H8 1.02. 92
hast thou heard him | at any time speak aught? 1.02.146
if ever any malice in your heart | were hid 2.01. 80
must now confess, if they have any goodness, 2.02. 90
too early and too late | for any suit of pounds; 2.03. 85
against you, nor injustice | for you or any. 2.04. 90
my appearance make | in any of their courts. 2.04.134
or | laid any scruple in your way which might 2.04.151
nor to betray you any way to sorrow — | you 3.01. 56
that any englishman dare give me counsel? 3.01. 84
would you have me | (if you have any justice, 3.01.116
have me | (if you have any justice, any pity, 3.01.116
if ye be any thing but churchmen's habits) | put 3.01.117
the stamp of nobleness in any person | out of 3.02. 12
to th' king, never attempt | any thing on him; 3.02. 18
more | on you than any, so your hand and heart, 3.02.186
be more | to me, your friend, than any. 3.02.190
i was | from any private malice in his end, 3.02.268
but if i spar'd any | that had a head to hit, 5.03. 23
before | this happy child, did i get any thing. 5.04. 65
than ever i saw her look, or any woman else. TRO 1.01. 33 P
nor any man an attaint but he carries some stain 1.02. 25 P
becomes him better than any man in all phrygia. 1.02.122 P
any thing, he cares not; 1.02.210 P
why, have you any discretion? 1.02.251 P
have you any eyes? 1.02.252 P
if any come, hector shall honor him; 1.03.280
thou art bought and sold among those of any wit, 2.01. 47 P
clatpoles ere i come any more to your tents. 2.01.118 P
than adders to the voice | of any true decision. 2.02.173
sworn upon't she never shrouded any but lazars. 2.03. 33 P
if any thing more than your sport and pleasure 2.03.108
dispose | without observance or respect of any, 2.03.165
than for us to undergo any difficulty impos'd. 3.02. 80 P
hath any honor, but honor for those honors 3.03. 81
proves | that no man is the lord of any thing, 3.03.115
seek her, | not making any scruple of her soil, 4.01. 57
be divided | by any voice or order of the field? 4.05. 70
that any /drop thou borrow'dst from thy mother, 4.05.133
she will sing any man at first sight. 5.02. 9
and any man may sing her, if he can take her 5.02. 10 P
bid me do any thing but that, sweet greek. 5.02. 27
patroclus will give me any thing for the 5.02.192 P
before we proceed any further, hear me speak. COR 1.01. 1 P
repeal daily any wholesome act establish'd 1.01. 82 P
and were i any thing but what i am, | i would 1.01.231
if any such be here | (as it were sin to doubt) 1.06. 67
if any fear | /lesser his person than an ill 1.06. 69
if any think brave death outweighs bad life, 1.06. 71
testy magistrates (alias fools) as any in rome. 2.01. 45 P
you know neither me, yourselves, nor any thing. 2.01. 67 P
without any further deed to have them at all 2.02. 27 P
you must think, if we give you any thing, we 2.03. 71 P
and cannot go without any honest man's voice. 2.03.133 P
not poison any further. 3.01. 88
this must be patch'd | with cloth of any color. 3.01.252
that's worthily | as any ear can hear. 4.01. 54
no question ask'd him by any of the senators but 4.05.193 P
he's as like to do't as any man i can imagine. 4.05.203 P
i can scarce think there's any, y' are so slight 5.02.103 P
you have said you will not grant us any thing; 5.03. 87
thy life | show'd thy dear mother any courtesy, 5.03.161
nor thou, nor he, are any sons of mine, | my TIT 1.01.294
not, | nor her, nor thee, nor any of thy stock. 1.01.300
he that would vouch it in any place but here. 1.01.360
as any mortal body hearing it | should straight 2.03.103
or any one of you, chop off your hand | and send 3.01.153
if any power pities wretched tears, | to that i 3.01.208
my name, | without the help of any hand at all. 4.01. 71
have you any letters? 4.03. 79
and wherein rome hath done you any scath, | let 5.01. 7
or more than any living man could bear. 5.03.127
if any one relieves or pities him, | for the 5.03.181
i will take the wall of any man or maid of ROM 1.01. 12 P
have you importun'd him by any means? 1.01.145
o any thing, of nothing first /create! 1.01.177
but, i pray, can you read any thing you see? 1.02. 60 P
much less | to meet her new–beloved any where. 2.pr. 12
a rose | by any other word would smell as sweet; 2.02. 44
thou art, | if any of my kinsmen find thee here. 2.02. 65
forget, | forgetting any other home but this. 2.02.175
any man that can write may answer a letter. 2.04. 10 P
wast never with me for any thing when thou wast 2.04. 75 P
can any of you tell me where i may find the 2.04.118 P
and 'a speak any thing against me, i'll take him 2.04.150 P
an ill thing to be off'red to any gentlewoman, 2.04.169 P
so, she looks as pale as any clout in the versal 2.04.206 P
though his face be better than any man's, yet 2.05. 40 P
they'll be in scarlet straight at any news. 2.05. 71
art as hot a jack in thy mood as any in italy, 3.01. 12 P
any man should buy the fee–simple of my life for 3.01. 31 P
paris, | from off the battlements of any tower, 4.01. 78
law | is death to any he that utters them. 5.01. 67
put this in any liquid thing you will | and 5.01. 77
think i, what need we have any friends, if we TIM 1.02. 95 P
paid for, be of any power | to expel sickness, 3.01. 62
nor came any of his bounties over me | to mark 3.02. 78
my lords, if not for any parts in him — 3.05. 75
believe't that we'll do any thing for gold. 4.03.150
lord, | for any benefit that points to me, 4.03.519
of this ingratitude | with any size of words. 5.01. 66
thy glove, | or any token of thine honor else, 5.04. 50
you one), | nor construe any further my neglect, JC 1.02. 45
i might entreat you) | be any further mov'd. 1.02.167
that could be mov'd to smile at any thing. 1.02.207
and i had been a man of any occupation, if i 1.02.266 P
said, if he had done or said any thing amiss, he 1.02.270 P
did cicero say any thing? 1.02.278
in execution | of any bold or noble enterprise, 1.02.298
why, saw you any thing more wonderful? 1.03. 14
i may discover them | by any mark of favor. 2.01. 76
what need we any spur but our own cause | to 2.01.123
of any promise that hath pass'd from him. 2.01.140
for he will never follow any thing | that other 2.01.151
in hand | any exploit worthy the name of honor. 2.01.317
know'st thou any harm's intended towards him? 2.04. 31
your voice shall be as strong as any man's | in 3.01.177
else shall you not have any hand at all | about 3.01.248
if there be any in this assembly, any dear 3.02. 18 P
in this assembly, any dear friend of caesar's, 3.02. 18 P
if any, speak, for him have i offended. 3.02. 30 P
if any, speak, for him have i offended. 3.02. 31 P
if any, speak, for him have i offended. 3.02. 33 P
pluck down forms, windows, any thing. 3.02.259 P
and in this mood will give us any thing. 3.02.267
peasants their vile trash | by any indirection. 4.03. 75
art thou any thing? 4.03.278
yes, that thou didst. didst thou see any thing? 4.03.297
ay. saw you any thing? 4.03.304
too cruel any where. MAC 2.03. 88
that i would set my life on any chance, | to 3.01.112
take any shape but that, and my firm nerves 3.04.101
for 'twould have anger'd any heart alive | to 3.06. 15
why, i can buy me twenty at any market. 4.02. 40
what, at any time, have you heard her say? 5.01. 12 P
neither to you nor any one, having no witness to 5.01. 17 P
thyself a hotter name | than any is in hell. 5.07. 7
if thou hast any sound, or use of voice, | speak HAM 1.01.128
if there be any good thing to be done | that may 1.01.130
common | as any the most vulgar thing to sense, 1.02. 99
nor any unproportion'd thought his act. 1.03. 60
day, | thou canst not then be false to any man. 1.03. 80
have you so slander any moment leisure | as to 1.03.133
as oft as any passions under heaven | that does 2.01.102
what, have you given him any hard words of late? 2.01.104
cannot take from me any thing that i will not 2.02.215 P
any thing, but to th' purpose. 2.02.278 P
/french falc'ners — fly at any thing we see; 2.02.430 P
did you assay him | to any pastime? 3.01. 15
for any thing so o'erdone is from the purpose of 3.02. 19 P
ay, or any show that you will show him. 3.02.144 P
have you any further trade with us? 3.02.334 P
cannot i command to any utt'rance of harmony. 3.02.361 P
if your mind dislike any thing, obey it. 5.02.217 P
and that without any further delay than this LR 1.02. 93 P
honest man if there be any good meaning toward 1.02.173 P
nor so old to dote on her for any thing. 1.04. 38 P
i had rather be any kind o' thing than a fool, 1.04.185 P
does any here know me? 1.04.226
no further with any thing you know than comes 1.05. 2 P
thee, would the reposal | of any trust, virtue, 2.01. 69
my time | than stands on any shoulder that i see 2.02. 94
i never gave him any. 2.02.115
that will house | before the head has any, | the 3.02. 28
of him, entreat for him, or any way sustain him. 3.03. 5 P
who gives any thing to poor tom? 3.04. 51 P
is there any cause in nature that make these 3.06. 77 P
you shall have any thing. 4.06.193
"if any man of quality or degree within the 5.03.110 P
thou worse than any name, read thine own evil. 5.03.157
yourself | whether i in any just term am affin'd OTH 1.01. 39
sir, i will answer any thing. 1.01.120
himself, | or any of my brothers of the state, 1.02. 96
do this, if you can bring it to any opportunity. 2.01.281 P
and dare not task my weakness with any more. 2.03. 42 P
to the general, nor any man of quality — i hope 2.03.107 P
speak | any beginning to this peevish odds; 2.03.185
you, or any man living, may be drunk at a time, 2.03.313 P
and, my fortunes against any lay worth naming, 2.03.324 P
desdemona to subdue | in any honest suit; 2.03.341
if you have any music that may not be heard, 3.01. 15 P
he's never any thing but your true servant. 3.03. 9
if i have any grace or power to move you, | his 3.03. 46
with any strong or vehement importunity; 3.03.251
if it be that, or any /that was hers, | it 3.03.440
i dare not say he lies any where. 3.04. 3 P
can any thing be made of this? 3.04. 10 P
in bed | an hour, or more, not meaning any harm? 4.01. 4
hers, | she may, i think, bestow't on any man. 4.01. 13
hath he said any thing? 4.01. 29
if any wretch have put this in your head, | let 4.02. 15
for my lord | from any other foul unlawful touch 4.02. 84
if any such there be, heaven pardon him! 4.02.135
or any sense | delighted them /in any other form 4.02.154
any sense | delighted them /in any other form; 4.02.155
petticoats, nor caps, nor any petty exhibition; 4.03. 74 P
i do not think there is any such woman. 4.03. 83
if you bethink yourself of any crime 5.02. 26
why, any thing: 5.02.293
if there be any cunning cruelty | that can 5.02.333
sweet alexas, most any thing alexas, almost most ANT 1.02. 1 P
of rest, would purge | by any desperate change. 1.03. 54
if thou dost play with him at any game, | thou 2.03. 26
i will praise any man that will praise me, 2.06. 88 P
nor any one. 4.14.110
remember'st thou any that have died on't? 5.02.249
playfellow, and he is | a man worth any woman; CYM 1.01.146
and less attemptable than any the rarest of our 1.04. 61 P
too fair and too good for any lady in brittany. 1.04. 72 P
durst attempt it against any lady in the world. 1.04.112 P
move the king | to any shape of thy preferment, 1.05. 71
it is not for any standers–by to curtal his 2.01. 11 P
i am not vex'd more at any thing in th' earth; 2.01. 17 P
it would make any man cold to lose. 2.03. 3 P
winning will put any man into courage. 2.03. 7 P
lose it for a revenue | of any king's in europe! 2.03.144
not any; 2.04. 4
than have tidings | of any penny tribute paid. 2.04. 20
hast any of thy late master's garments in thy 3.05.123 P
if any thing that's civil, speak; 3.06. 23
at the things you hear | than to work any. 5.03. 55
any thing | that's due to all the villains past, 5.05.211
nor ask advice of any other thought | but PER 1.01. 62
your rule direct to any; 1.02.109
the which when any shall not gratify, | or pay 1.04.101
canst thou catch any fishes then? 2.01. 66 P
till the rough seas, that spares not any man, 2.01.131
show | can any way speak in his just commend; 2.02. 49
to any syllable that made love to you. 2.05. 70
word, nor did ill turn | to any living creature. 4.01. 76
wherein my death might yield her any profit, 4.01. 80
any profit, | or my life imply her any danger? 4.01. 81
neither is our profession any trade, it's no 4.02. 38 P
boult, has she any qualities? 4.02. 46 P
to equal any single crown a' th' earth | i' th' 4.03. 8
i'll do any thing now that is virtuous, but i am 4.05. 8 P
pray you, without any more virginal fencing, 4.06. 57 P
do any thing but this thou doest. 4.06.174
any of these ways are yet better than this; 4.06.177
this three months hath not spoken | to any one, 5.01. 25
he will not speak | to any. 5.01. 34
no, nor of any /shores, | yet i was mortally 5.01.103
perch or sing, | or with them any discord bring, TNK 1.01. 23
key — like such a woman | as any of us three; 1.01. 95
whereto i am going, | greater than any /war. 1.01.172
henceforth i'll not dare | to ask you any thing, 1.01.204
omit not any thing | in the pretended 1.01.209
am i bound | by any generous bond to follow him 1.02. 50
success i dare not | make any timorous question; 1.03. 3
the maid flavina) | love any that's call'd man. 1.03. 85
have patience to make any adversity asham'd. 2.01. 23 P
is there record of any two that lov'd | better 2.02.112

a maid, if she have any honor, would be loath 2.02.145
as any palamon or any living | that is a man's 2.02.181
as any palamon or any living | that is a man's 2.02.181
by any means; 2.03. 51
let's rehearse by any means | before the ladies 2.03. 56
and so would any young wench, o' my conscience, 2.04. 12
and what | you want at any time, let me but know 2.05. 55
yea | (we challenge too), the bank of any nymph, 3.01. 8
the circuit of my breast any gross stuff | to 3.01. 46
the whole week's not fair | if any day it rain. 3.01. 66
dares any | so noble bear a guilty business? 3.01. 89
ay, ay, by any means, dear domine. 3.05.135
anger, | as you love any thing that's honorable. 3.06. 27
by any means. 3.06. 58
that you would nev'r deny me any thing | fit for 3.06.234
shall any thing that loves me perish for me? 3.06.241
kill this cousin, | on any piece the earth has. 3.06.263
any death thou canst invent, duke. 3.06.281
bring 'em in | quickly, by any means, i long to 4.02. 65
but of a tough soul, seeming | as great as any. 4.02.118
you she ever affected any man ere she beheld 4.03. 62 P
this advice i told you done any good upon her? 5.02. 1
if she entreat again, do any thing, | lie with 5.02. 17
the best hobby–horse | (if i have any skill) in 5.02. 53
wish their office | to any of their enemies. 5.03. 36
value's shortness, | to any lady breathing. 5.03. 89
which he frets at rather | than any jot obeys; 5.04. 71
(for 'tis no other) any way content ye | (for to ep 13
to any german province, spain or portigal, | nay STM II.C 128
nay, any where that not adheres to england, II.C 129
as apt as new–fall'n snow takes any dint. VEN 354
if springing things be any jot diminish'd, 417
"fair queen," quoth he, "if any love you owe me, 523
many, | and, being low, never reliev'd by any. 708
of things long since, or any thing ensuing? 1078
day, | as shaming any eye should thee behold, LUC 1143
may any terms acquit me from this chance? 1706
for shame deny that thou bear'st love to any, SON 10. 1
me, my love is as fair | as any mother's child, 21.11
or any of these all, or all, or more, | entitled 37. 6
thee have i not lock'd up in any chest, | save 48. 9
that in your will | (though you do any thing) he 57.14
i was not sick of any fear from thence: 86.12
in hue, | could make me any summer's story tell, 98. 7
survey, | if time have any wrinkle graven there; 100.10
if any, be a satire to decay, | and make time's 100.11
as rare | as any she belied with false compare. 130.14
invited | to any sensual feast with thee alone; 141. 8
teen, | or any of my leisures ever charmed. LC 193
ANYBODY 2 FR 0.0002 REL FR 1 V 1 P
never anybody saw it but his lackey. H5 3.07.110 P
cough, or cry "hem," if anybody come. OTH 4.02. 29
ANY'S 2 FR 0.0002 REL FR 0 V 2 P
he's as tall a man as any's in illyria. TN 1.03. 20 P
an arrant traitor as any's in the universal H5 4.08. 9 P
AP 1 FR 0.0001 REL FR 1 V 0 P
and rice ap thomas, with a valiant crew, | and R3 4.05. 15
/APACE 1 FR 0.0001 REL FR 0 V 1 P
/the /powers /of /the /kingdom /approach /apace. LR 4.07. 92 P
APACE 27 FR 0.0030 REL FR 21 V 6 P
the charm dissolves apace, | and as the morning TMP 5.01. 64
you are pleasant, sir, and speak apace. MM 3.02.113 P
here they stay'd an hour, | and talk'd apace; LLL 5.02.369
hippolyta, our nuptial hour | draws on apace. MND 1.01. 2
tell me who is it quickly, and speak apace. AYL 3.02.198 P
come apace, good audrey; 3.03. 1 P
i will to venice, sunday comes apace. SHR 2.01.322
kate, eat apace. 4.03. 52
that approaches apace. AWW 4.03. 31 P
hark ye, | the queen your mother rounds apace: WT 2.01. 16
look where the holy legate comes apace, | to JN 5.02. 65
my lord, prepare, the king comes on apace. 1H4 5.02. 89
i beseech you now, come apace to the king. H5 4.08. 3 P
herbs have grace, great weeds do grow apace." R3 2.04. 13
before, and apace. ROM 2.04.217 P
gallop apace, you fiery–footed steeds, | towards 3.02. 1
the future comes apace; TIM 2.02.148
brutus, come apace, | and see how i regarded JC 5.03. 87
now spurs the lated traveller apace | to gain MAC 3.03. 6
regan, i bleed apace, | untimely comes this hurt LR 3.07. 97
creeps apace | into the hearts of such as have ANT 1.03. 50
thou bleed'st apace. 4.07. 6
apace, eros, apace. 4.14. 41
apace, eros, apace. 4.14. 41
o, come apace, dispatch! 5.02.322
and homeward through the dark laund runs apace, VEN 813
with brinish current downward flow'd apace: LC 284
APAID 1 FR 0.0001 REL FR 1 V 0 P
fee, | he gratis comes, and thou art well apaid, LUC 914
APART 26 FR 0.0029 REL FR 24 V 2 P
stay, stand apart, i know not which is which. ERR 5.01.365
go apart, adam, and thou shalt hear how he will AYL 1.01. 27 P
"why, thy godhead laid apart, | warr'st thou 4.03. 44
to put apart these your attendants, i | shall WT 2.02. 13
therefore i keep it | /lonely, apart. 5.03. 18
all reverence set apart | to him and his usurp'd JN 3.01.159
stand all apart, | and show fair duty to his R2 3.03.187
and lay apart | the borrowed glories that by H5 2.04. 78
to lay apart their particular functions and 3.07. 38 P
in private will i talk with thee apart. 1H6 1.02. 69
be, | and henry put apart, the next for me. 2H6 3.01.383
sirs, stand apart, the king shall know your mind 3.02.242
stand all apart. cousin of buckingham — R3 4.02. 1
hand, | and when i had it, drew myself apart, TIT 5.01.112
each man apart, all single and alone, | yet an TIM 5.01.107
get thee apart and weep. JC 3.01.282
resolve yourselves apart, | i'll come to you MAC 3.01.137
to draw apart the body he hath kill'd, | o'er HAM 4.01. 24
go but apart, | make choice of whom your wisest 4.05.204
on — | myself a while to draw the moor apart, OTH 2.03.385
come go with me apart, i will withdraw | to 3.03.477
stand you a while apart, | confine yourself but 4.01. 74
therefore | to lay his gay comparisons apart, ANT 3.13. 26
hear it apart. 3.13. 47
some nobler token i have kept apart | for livia 5.02.168
come on, away, apart upon our knees. CYM 4.02.288

/APE 1 FR 0.0001 REL FR 0 V 1 P
he keeps them, like /an /ape an apple, in the HAM 4.02. 18 P
APE 20 FR 0.0022 REL FR 12 V 8 P
gar, you are de coward, de jack dog, john ape. WIV 3.01. 84 P
like an angry ape | plays such fantastic tricks MM 2.02.120
no, i am an ape. ERR 2.02.198
he is then a giant to an ape, but then is an ape ADO 5.01.201 P
ape, but then is an ape a doctor to such a man. 5.01.202 P
the fox, the ape, and the humble–bee, | were LLL 3.01. 84
the fox, the ape, and the humble–bee, | were 3.01. 89
the fox, the ape, and the humble–bee, | were 3.01. 95
doth the hound his master, the ape his keeper, 4.02.126 P
this is the ape of form, monsieur the nice, 5.02.325
on meddling monkey, or on busy ape), | she shall MND 2.01.181
more new–fangled than an ape, more giddy in my AYL 4.01.152 P
of her custom, so perfectly he is her ape. WT 5.02.100 P
out, you mad–headed ape! 1H4 2.03. 77
if the fat villain have not transform'd him ape. 2H4 2.02. 72 P
alas, poor ape, how thou sweat'st! 2.04.217 P
because that i am little, like an ape, | he R3 3.01.130
not, | the ape is dead, and i must conjure him. ROM 2.01. 16
let the birds fly, and like the famous ape, | to HAM 3.04.194
o sleep, thou ape of death, lie dull upon her, CYM 2.02. 31
APE–BEARER 1 FR 0.0001 REL FR 0 V 1 P
he hath been since an ape–bearer, then a WT 4.03. 95 P
APEMANTUS 23 FR 0.0026 REL FR 5 V 18 P
from the glass–fac'd flatterer | to apemantus, TIM 1.01. 59
good morrow to thee, gentle apemantus! 1.01.178
you know me, apemantus? 1.01.185 P
thou art proud, apemantus. 1.01.188 P
how lik'st thou this picture, apemantus? 1.01.195 P
wilt dine with me, apemantus? 1.01.203 P
how dost thou like this jewel, apemantus? 1.01.210 P
what wouldst do then, apemantus? 1.01.228 P
e'en as apemantus does now: 1.01.229 P
ay, apemantus. 1.01.236 P
what time a' day is't, apemantus? 1.01.256
why, apemantus? 1.01.264 P
o, apemantus, you are welcome. 1.02. 23
much good dich thy good heart, apemantus! 1.02. 72 P
now, apemantus (if thou wert not sullen), | i 1.02.236
here comes the fool with apemantus, let's ha' 2.02. 47 P
what are we, apemantus? 2.02. 61 P
how dost thou, apemantus? 2.02. 75 P
prithee, apemantus, read me the superscription 2.02. 78 P
that answer might have become apemantus. 2.02.118 P
where feed'st thou a' days, apemantus? 4.03.293 P
what wouldst thou do with the world, apemantus, 4.03.322 P
i had rather be a beggar's dog than apemantus. 4.03.357 P
APENNINES 1 FR 0.0001 REL FR 1 V 0 P
and talking of the alps and apennines, | the JN 1.01.202
APES 12 FR 0.0013 REL FR 10 V 2 P
sometime like apes that mow and chatter at me, TMP 2.02. 9
or to apes | with foreheads villainous low. 4.01.248
of the berrord, and lead his apes into hell. ADO 2.01. 41 P
so deliver i up my apes, and away to saint peter 2.01. 47 P
boys, apes, braggarts, jacks, milksops! 5.01. 91
and for your love to her lead apes in hell. SHR 2.01. 34
now, | from every region, apes of idleness! 2H4 4.05.122
have you run | from slaves that apes would beat! COR 1.04. 36
you show'd your /teeth like apes, and fawn'd JC 5.01. 41
for apes and monkeys | 'twixt two such shes CYM 1.06. 39
toys, | is jollity for apes, and grief for boys. 4.02.194
power | (unless we fear that apes can tutor 's) TNK 1.02. 43
APEX 1 FR 0.0001 REL FR 1 V 0 P
"me /pompae provexit apex." PER 2.02. 30
A–PIECE 4 FR 0.0004 REL FR 0 V 4 P
shilling and two pence a–piece of yead miller — WIV 1.01.157 P
sixteen businesses, a month's length a–piece, by AWW 4.03. 86 P
three or four bonds of forty pound a–piece, and 1H4 3.03.102 P
a hundred ducats a–piece for his picture in HAM 2.02.366 P
A–PIECES 2 FR 0.0002 REL FR 2 V 0 P
may do, | not being torn a–pieces, we have done. H8 5.03. 76
i'll be cut a–pieces | before i take this oath. TNK 3.06.256
APISH 5 FR 0.0005 REL FR 4 V 1 P
proud, fantastical, apish, shallow, inconstant, AYL 3.02.412 P
should — | this apish and unmannerly approach, JN 5.02.131
apish nation | limps after in base imitation. R2 2.01. 22
cog, | duck with french nods and apish courtesy, R3 1.03. 49
wits to wear, | their manners are so apish." LR 1.04.169
APOLLINEM 1 FR 0.0001 REL FR 1 V 0 P
here, "ad apollinem"; TIT 4.03. 54
APOLLO 21 FR 0.0023 REL FR 19 V 2 P
of mercury are harsh after the songs of apollo. LLL 5.02.931 P
apollo flies, and daphne holds the chase; MND 2.01.231
hark, apollo plays, | and twenty caged SHR in.2. 35
and at that sight shall sad apollo weep, | so in.2. 59
foretells | the great apollo suddenly will have WT 2.03.200
great apollo | turn all to th' best! 3.01. 14
apollo be my judge! 3.02.116
now blessed be the great apollo! 3.02.137
apollo, pardon | my great profaneness 'gainst 3.02.153
and that | apollo would (this being indeed the 3.03. 43
golden apollo, a poor humble swain, | as i seem 4.04. 30
for has not the divine apollo said, | is't not 5.01. 37
tell me, apollo, for thy daphne's love, | what TRO 1.01. 98
as banks of libya (though, apollo knows, | 'tis 1.03.328
unless the fiddler apollo get his sinews to make 3.03.304 P
apollo, pallas, jove, or mercury, | inspire me, TIT 4.01. 66
this to apollo, this to the god of war: 4.04. 15
now, by apollo — LR 1.01.160
now, by apollo, king, | thou swear'st thy gods 1.01.160
apollo, perfect me in the characters! PER 3.02. 67
with his crutch, and cure him | before apollo; TNK 5.01. 83
APOLLODORUS 1 FR 0.0001 REL FR 1 V 0 P
and i have heard, apollodorus carried — ANT 2.06. 68
APOLLO'S 8 FR 0.0009 REL FR 8 V 0 P
as sweet and musical | as bright apollo's lute, LLL 4.03.340
in post | to sacred delphos, to apollo's temple, WT 2.01.183
(thus by apollo's great divine seal'd up) 3.01. 19
bring forth, | and in apollo's name, his oracle. 3.02.118
the hand deliver'd | of great apollo's priest; 3.02.128
apollo's angry, and the heavens themselves | do 3.02.146
whose youth and freshness | wrinkles apollo's, TRO 2.02. 79
and great apollo's mercy, all our best | their TNK 1.04. 46
APOLOGY 6 FR 0.0006 REL FR 5 V 1 P
and i will have an apology for that purpose. LLL 5.01.135 P

in minority, | ergo i come with this apology." 5.02.593
strength'ned with what apology you think | may AWW 2.04. 50
my lord, there needs no such apology. R3 3.07.104
or shall we on without apology? ROM 1.04. 2
what needeth then apology be made | to set forth LUC 31
APOPLEX'D 1 FR 0.0001 REL FR 1 V 0 P
but sure that sense | is apoplex'd, for madness HAM 3.04. 73
APOPLEXY 4 FR 0.0004 REL FR 1 V 3 P
is fall'n into this same whoreson apoplexy. 2H4 1.02.108 P
this apoplexy, as i take it, is a kind of 1.02.111 P
this apoplexy will certain be his end. 4.04.130
peace is a very apoplexy, lethargy, mull'd, deaf COR 4.05.223 P
APORN *(also apron)*
APORN 1 FR 0.0001 REL FR 0 V 1 P
here, robin, and if i die, i give thee my aporn; 2H6 2.03. 75 P
APOSTLE 2 FR 0.0002 REL FR 2 V 0 P
by the apostle paul, shadows to–night | have R3 5.03.216
sin | which oft th' apostle did forewarn us of, STM II.C 94
APOSTLES 1 FR 0.0001 REL FR 1 V 0 P
his champions are the prophets and apostles, 2H6 1.03. 57
APOSTRAPHAS 1 FR 0.0001 REL FR 0 V 1 P
you find not the apostraphas, and so miss the LLL 4.02.119 P
APOTHECARY *(also pothecary)*
APOTHECARY 5 FR 0.0005 REL FR 5 V 0 P
and bid the apothecary | bring the strong poison 2H6 3.03. 17
i do remember an apothecary — | and hereabouts ROM 5.01. 37
what ho, apothecary! 5.01. 57
o true apothecary! 5.03.119
good apothecary, | sweeten my imagination. LR 4.06.130
APPAL'D 1 FR 0.0001 REL FR 1 V 0 P
methinks your looks are sad, your cheer appal'd. 1H6 1.02. 48
APPALL 2 FR 0.0002 REL FR 2 V 0 P
look on that | which might appall the devil. MAC 3.04. 59
make mad the guilty, and appall the free, HAM 2.02.564
APPALLED 2 FR 0.0002 REL FR 2 V 0 P
that the appalled air | may pierce the head of TRO 4.05. 4
property was thus appalled, | that the self was PHT 37
APPALLS 4 FR 0.0004 REL FR 4 V 0 P
the dreadful sagittary | appalls our numbers. TRO 5.05. 15
how is't with me, when every noise appalls me? MAC 2.02. 55
theseus (who where he threats appalls) hath sent TNK 1.02. 90
appalls her senses and her spirit confounds. VEN 882
APPAREL *(also 'parel)*
APPAREL 36 FR 0.0040 REL FR 14 V 22 P
that come like women in men's apparel, and smell WIV 3.03. 72 P
(for all he was in woman's apparel) i would not 5.05.192 P
every true man's apparel fits your thief. MM 4.02. 43 P
so every true man's apparel fits your thief. 4.02. 47 P
apparel vice like virtue's harbinger; ERR 3.02. 12
dress him in my apparel and make him my ADO 2.01. 35 P
shall find her the infernal ate in good apparel. 2.01.256 P
yes, it is apparel. 3.03.120 P
the fashion wears out more apparel than the man. 3.03.140 P
i beseech thee apparel thy head; LLL 5.01. 98 P
for briers and thorns at their apparel snatch; MND 3.02. 29
get your apparel together, good strings to your 4.02. 35 P
and sleep and snore, and rend apparel out — MV 2.05. 5
to disgrace my man's apparel and to cry like a AYL 2.04. 5 P
that i am in this forest and in man's apparel? 3.02.230 P
not out of your apparel, and yet out of your 4.01. 87 P
suit, | and ask him what apparel he will wear; SHR in.1. 60
life, | puts my apparel and my count'nance on, 1.01.229
venice | to buy apparel 'gainst the wedding–day. 2.01.315
costly apparel, tents, and canopies, | fine 2.01.352
a monster, a very monster in apparel, and not 3.02. 70 P
i know not what, but formal in apparel, | in 4.02. 64
thing in him by wearing his apparel neatly. AWW 4.03.146 P
my money and apparel ta'en from me, and these WT 4.03. 62 P
that's the rogue that put me into this apparel. 4.03.104 P
my gay apparel for an almsman's gown, | my R2 3.03.149
into | for gay apparel 'gainst the triumph day. 5.02. 66
neither in gold nor silver, but in vile apparel, 2H4 1.02. 18 P
for /'s apparel is built upon his back, and the 3.02.143 P
thrust him and all his apparel into an eel–skin. 3.02.325 P
and i will apparel them all in one livery, that 2H6 4.02. 74 P
is my apparel sumptuous to behold? 4.07.100
what dost thou with thy best apparel on? JC 1.01. 8
gaudy, | for the apparel oft proclaims the man, HAM 1.03. 72
bring this apparel to my chamber. CYM 3.05.151 P
and puts apparel on my tottered loving, | to SON 26.11
APPARELL'D 6 FR 0.0006 REL FR 5 V 1 P
you got the picture of old adam new apparell'd? ERR 4.03. 14 P
shall come apparell'd in more precious habit, ADO 4.01.227
and are apparell'd thus, | like muscovites or LLL 5.02.120
yet oftentimes he goes but mean apparell'd. SHR 3.02. 73
not so well apparell'd | as i wish you were. 3.02. 89
and on my side it is so well apparell'd, | so 1H6 2.04. 22
APPARELLED 1 FR 0.0001 REL FR 1 V 0 P
see where she comes, apparelled like the spring, PER 1.01. 12
APPARENT 22 FR 0.0024 REL FR 18 V 4 P
climb it | without apparent hazard of his life. TGV 3.01.116
it is now apparent? MM 4.02.138 P
strange | than is thy strange apparent cruelty; MV 4.01. 21
and my young rover, he's | apparent to my heart. WT 1.02.177
(for to a vision so apparent rumor | cannot be 1.02.270
it is apparent foul play and 'tis shame | that JN 4.02. 93
on some apparent danger seen in him | aim'd at R2 1.01. 13
hear, | although apparent guilt be seen in them, 4.01.124
were it not here apparent that thou art heir 1H4 1.02. 58 P
not here apparent that thou art heir apparent — 1.02. 58 P
to hide thee from this open and apparent shame? 2.04.264 P
by some apparent sign | let us have knowledge at 1H6 2.01. 3
but death doth front thee with apparent spoil, 4.02. 26
if death be so apparent, then both fly. 4.05. 44
leave, | i'll draw it as apparent to the crown, 3H6 2.02. 64
as well the fear of harm, as harm apparent, | in R3 2.02.130
be put | to no apparent likelihood of breach, 2.02.136
that, his apparent open guilt omitted — | i 3.05. 30
and is no less apparent | to th' vulgar eye, COR 4.07. 20
you see it is apparent. TIT 2.03.292
it may be these apparent prodigies, | the JC 2.01.198
if you can make't apparent | that you have CYM 2.04. 56
APPARENTLY 1 FR 0.0001 REL FR 1 V 0 P
case, | if he should scorn me so apparently. ERR 4.01. 78
APPARITION 4 FR 0.0004 REL FR 4 V 0 P
fine apparition! TMP 1.02.317

eyes | that shapes this monstrous apparition. JC 4.03.277
night, | that, if again this apparition come, HAM 1.01. 28
word made true and good, | the apparition comes. 1.02.211
APPARITIONS 2 FR 0.0002 REL FR 2 V 0 P
a thousand blushing apparitions | to start into ADO 4.01.159
world's poor people are amazed | at apparitions, VEN 926
APPEACH 2 FR 0.0002 REL FR 2 V 0 P
life, by my troth, | i will appeach the villain. R2 5.02. 79
he twenty times my son, | i would appeach him. 5.02.102
APPEACH'D 1 FR 0.0001 REL FR 1 V 0 P
for your passions | have to the full appeach'd. AWW 1.03.191
APPEAL 20 FR 0.0022 REL FR 18 V 2 P
send after the duke and appeal to him. MM 1.02.174 P
unjust | thus to retort your manifest appeal, 5.01.301
i appeal | to your own conscience, sir, before WT 3.02. 45
here to make good the boist'rous late appeal, R2 1.01. 4
him, | if he appeal the duke on ancient malice, 1.01. 9
namely, to appeal each other of high treason. 1.01. 27
as true | in this appeal as thou art all unjust, 4.01. 45
world, | aumerle is guilty of my true appeal; 4.01. 79
when ever yet was your appeal denied? 2H4 4.01. 88
to whom i do appeal, and in whose name | tell H5 1.02.290
to which we all appeal. 2.02. 78
madam, for myself, to heaven i do appeal, | how 2H6 2.01.186
here, | before you all, appeal unto the pope, H8 2.04.119
made to the queen to call back her appeal | she 2.04.235
and your appeal to us | there make before them. 5.01.151
upon his own appeal, seizes him. ANT 3.05. 11 P
help, jupiter, or we appeal, | and from thy CYM 5.04. 91
but with a pure appeal seeks to the heart, LUC 293
"to thee, to thee, my heav'd-up hands appeal, 638
since my appeal says i did strive to prove | the SON 117.13
APPEAL'D 1 FR 0.0001 REL FR 1 V 0 P
as for the rest appeal'd, | it issues from the R2 1.01.142
APPEALS 1 FR 0.0001 REL FR 1 V 0 P
against the duke of herford that appeals me, R2 1.03. 21
APPEAR *(also 'pear)*
/APPEAR 1 FR 0.0001 REL FR 1 V 0 P
/and /bitter /fool | /will /presently /appear: LR 1.04.145
APPEAR 141 FR 0.0159 REL FR 110 V 31 P
appear, and pertly! TMP 4.01. 58
and, that my love may appear plain and free, TGV 5.04. 82
some say that, though she appear honest to me, WIV 2.02.221 P
buck, and of the season too, it shall appear. 3.03.159 P
their untaught love | must needs appear offense. MM 2.04. 30
thus wisdom wishes to appear most bright | when 2.04. 78
cast, he would appear | a pond as deep as hell. 3.01. 92
and he shall appear to the envious a scholar, a 3.02.145 P
to make the truth appear where it seems hid, 5.01. 66
one | whom he begot with child), let her appear, 5.01.511
so it doth appear | by the wrongs i suffer, and ERR 3.01. 15
they appear to men like angels of light, light 4.03. 55 P
will hold it as a dream till it appear itself; ADO 1.02. 21 P
graces will appear, and there's an end. 2.01.123 P
covertly that no dishonesty shall appear in me. 2.02. 10 P
and there shall appear such seeming truth of 2.02. 48 P
for fancy, as you would have it appear he is. 3.02. 39 P
let that appear hereafter, and aim better at me 3.02. 96 P
let that appear when there is no need of such 3.03. 21 P
now in great haste, as it may appear unto you. 3.05. 50 P
hero, now thy image doth appear | in the rare 5.01.251
now, in thy likeness, one more fool appear! LLL 4.03. 44
when wheat is green, when hawthorn buds appear. MND 1.01.185
in thy eye that shall appear | when thou wak'st, 2.02. 32
a while, | and by and by i will to thee appear." 3.01. 87
i'll charm his eyes against she do appear. 3.02. 99
slumb'red here | while these visions did appear. 5.01.426
and in such eyes as ours appear not faults. MV 2.02.183
still more fool i shall appear | by the time i 2.09. 73
there doth appear | among the buzzing pleased 3.02.179
besides, it should appear, that if he had | the 3.02.272
it must appear | that malice bears down truth. 4.01.213
it doth appear you are a worthy judge; 4.01.236
it must appear in other ways than words, 5.01.140
to me, if it appear not inconvenient to you, to AYL 5.02. 66 P
if it appear not plain and prove untrue, AWW 5.03.317
to be, cast thy humble slough and appear fresh. TN 2.05.149 P
my love, let it appear in thy smiling; 2.05.175 P
why appear you with this ridiculous boldness 3.04. 37 P
on purpose, that i may appear stubborn to him; 3.04. 67 P
yet that dares | less appear so, in comforting WT 2.03. 56
suddenly will have | the truth of this appear. 2.03.201
that the queen | appear in person here in court. 3.02. 10
so uncurrent i | have strain'd t' appear thus; 3.02. 50
them shall | the causes of their death appear 3.02.237
bohemia's son, | nor shall appear in sicilia. 4.04.589
(where we offenders now) appear soul-vex'd, 5.01. 59
see, see, king richard doth himself appear, | as R2 3.03. 62
the manner of their taking may appear | at large 5.06. 9
let them appear as i call; 2H4 3.02. 99 P
it shall appear that your demands are just, 4.01.142
appear more wise and modest to the world. 5.05.101
then doth it well appear the salique law | was H5 1.02. 54
all appear | to hold in right and title of the 1.02. 88
swallow'd, and digested, | appear before us? 2.02. 57
let huswifery appear. 2.03. 62
elements of earth and water never appear in him, 3.07. 22 P
though it appear a little out of fashion, 4.01. 83
to cry amen to that, thus we appear. 5.02. 21
the elder i wax, the better i shall appear. 5.02.229 P
her, that he will appear in his true likeness. 5.02.289 P
true likeness, he must appear naked and blind. 5.02.294 P
cheeks, | god's mother deigned to appear to me, 1H6 1.02. 78
shall this night appear | how much in duty i am 2.01. 36
fury, | as by his smoothed brows it doth appear. 3.01.124
north, | appear, and aid me in this enterprise. 5.03. 7
weak, | as may appear by edward's good success, 3H6 3.03.146
in that very shape | he shall appear in proof. H8 1.01.197
not almost appears, | it doth appear; 1.02. 30
make 'em, and | appear in forms more horrid), 3.02.196
ye appear in every thing may bring my ruin! 3.02.242
this morning see | you do appear before them. 5.01.145
nothing of that shall from mine eyes appear. TRO 1.02.295
appear it to /your mind | that, through the 3.03. 3
of valor, to appear | this morning to them. 5.03. 69
than can ever | appear in your impediment. COR 1.01. 72
to aufidius thus | i will appear, and fight. 1.05. 20
yonder, | that does appear as he were flea'd? 1.06. 22
never would he | appear i' th' market-place, nor 2.01.233
he doth appear. 2.02.131
here | to beg of hob and dick, that does appear, 2.03.116
tullus aufidius /will appear well in these wars, 4.03. 34 P
smells well, but i | appear not like a guest. 4.05. 6
and | intends t' appear before the people, 5.06. 7
appear thou in the likeness of a sigh! ROM 2.01. 8
lie, | that in thy likeness thou appear to us! 2.01. 21
stiff and stark and cold, appear like death, 4.01.103
how fairly this lord strives to appear foul! TIM 3.03. 31 P
me beyond them, and i must needs appear. 3.06. 12 P
and when you saw his chariot but appear, | have JC 1.01. 43
and that which would appear offense in us, | his 1.03.158
our youths and wildness shall no whit appear, 2.01.148
though now we must appear bloody and cruel, | as 3.01.165
but that my noble master will appear | such as 4.02. 11
that you have wrong'd me doth appear in this: 4.03. 1
let it appear so; 4.03. 52
though they do appear | as huge as high olympus. 4.03. 91
if this which he avouches does appear, | there MAC 5.05. 46
tush, tush, 'twill not appear. HAM 1.01. 30
other, | as it doth well appear unto our state, 1.01.101
should more appear like entertainment than yours 2.02.374 P
sith thus thou wilt appear, | freedom lives LR 1.01.180
that /walk upon the beach, | appear like mice; 4.06. 18
tatter'd clothes /small vices do appear; 4.06.164
let but the herald cry, | and i'll appear again. 5.01. 49
t' appear | where you shall hold your session. 5.03. 53
if none appear to prove upon thy person | thy 5.03. 91
let him appear by the third sound of the trumpet 5.03.113 P
let him appear. ANT 1.02.115
thy face, to me | thou wouldst appear most ugly. 2.05. 97
's will permit, | we shall appear before him. 3.01. 37
tell of her approach, | long ere she did appear; 3.06. 46
of my kingdom, will | appear there for a man. 3.07. 18
let him appear that's come from antony. 3.12. 1
to kiss these lips, i will appear in blood; 3.13.174
what art thou that dar'st | appear thus to us? 5.01. 5
poison, 'twould appear | by external swelling; 5.02.345
worthy he is i will leave to appear hereafter, CYM 1.04. 33 P
unseduc'd, you not making it appear otherwise, 1.04.161 P
and but disguise | that which, t' appear itself, 3.04.145
than they, must needs | appear unkinglike. 3.05. 7
court, | where with it i may appear a gentleman; PER 2.01.141
diamonds | of a most praised water doth appear, 3.02.101
dionyza does appear, | with leonine, a murtherer 4.ch. 51
brought forth, and am | no other than i appear. 5.01.105
art, may yet appear | worth two hours' travail. TNK pr 28
lin'd than it can appear to me report is a true 2.01. 6 P
i first appear, though rude, and raw, and muddy, 3.05.122
three fair knights, appear again in this place, 3.06.292
their fame has fir'd me so — till they appear. 4.02.153
palamon in their mouths and appear with tokens, 4.03. 92 P
doth yet in his fair welkin once appear, | till LUC 116
men's faults do seldom to themselves appear, 633
and from the tow'rs of troy there would appear 1382
that through their light joy seemed to appear 1434
dead, which now appear | but things remov'd that SON 31. 7
show, | the other as your bounty doth appear, 53.11
his) | on your broad main doth willfully appear. 80. 8
i love not less, though less the show appear; 102. 2
his phoenix down began but to appear | like LC 93
appear to him, as he to me appears, | all 299
APPEARANCE 13 FR 0.0014 REL FR 9 V 4 P
there is no appearance of fancy in him, unless ADO 3.02. 31 P
three times slain th' appearance of the king, 2H4 1.01.128
wart, you see what a ragged appearance it is. 3.02.261 P
and chas'd your blood | out of appearance? H5 2.02. 76
should possess him with any appearance of fear, 4.01.111 P
if she deny the appearance of a naked blind boy 5.02.297 P
this speedy and quick appearance argues proof 1H6 5.03. 8
upon this business my appearance make | in any H8 2.04.133
for not appearance and | the king's late scruple 4.01. 30
thou hast a grim appearance, and thy face COR 4.05. 60
he requires your haste-post-haste appearance, OTH 1.02. 37
bearing with frank appearance | their purposes 1.03. 38
and says in him /thy fair appearance lies. SON 46. 8
/APPEAR'D 1 FR 0.0001 REL FR 1 V 0 P
if damn'd commotion so /appear'd | in his true, 2H4 4.01. 36
APPEAR'D 26 FR 0.0029 REL FR 16 V 10 P
wise | as you, lord angelo, have still appear'd, MM 5.01.471
and in her eye there hath appear'd a fire | to ADO 4.01.162
is our whole dissembly appear'd? 4.02. 1 P
rudeness that hath appear'd in me have i learn'd TN 1.05.214 P
be, thy mother | appear'd to me last night; WT 3.03. 18
exercises than formerly he hath appear'd. 4.02. 33 P
of a fish that appear'd upon the coast on 4.04.275 P
a notable passion of wonder appear'd in them; 5.02. 16 P
and in thy face strange motions have appear'd, 1H4 2.03. 60
you appear'd to me but as a common man; H5 4.08. 51 P
at which appear'd against him his surveyor, H8 2.01. 19
she was often cited by them, but appear'd not; 4.01. 29
in the hatching, | it seem'd, appear'd to rome. COR 1.02. 22
but your favor is well appear'd by your tongue. 4.03. 9 P
the ghost of caesar hath appear'd to me | two JC 5.05. 17
what, has this thing appear'd again to-night? HAM 1.01. 21
king, | whose image even but now appear'd to us, 1.01. 81
which to him appear'd | to be a preparation 2.02. 62
it hath not appear'd. OTH 4.02.209 P
i grant indeed it hath not appear'd; 4.02.210 P
there she appear'd indeed; ANT 2.02.188 P
of the goddess isis | that day appear'd, and oft 3.06. 18
when vantage like a pair of twins appear'd, 3.10. 12
she hath not appear'd | before the roman, nor to CYM 3.05. 30
appear'd to me, with other spritely shows | of 5.05.428
that methought she appear'd like the fair nymph TNK 4.01. 86
APPEARED 1 FR 0.0001 REL FR 1 V 0 P
which well appeared in his lineaments, | being R3 3.05. 91
APPEARER 1 FR 0.0001 REL FR 1 V 0 P
reverent appearer, no, | i threw her overboard PER 5.03. 18
APPEARETH 3 FR 0.0003 REL FR 2 V 1 P
which here appeareth due upon the bond. MV 4.01.249
us, | as well appeareth by the cause you come: R2 1.01. 26
why, it appeareth nothing to me but a foul and HAM 2.02.302 P
/APPEARING 1 FR 0.0001 REL FR 1 V 0 P
/early /spring | /we /see /th' /appearing /buds, 2H4 1.03. 39
APPEARING 5 FR 0.0005 REL FR 3 V 2 P
where we will (not appearing what we are) have WT 4.02. 48 P
and already appearing in the blossoms of their 5.02.125 P
written on the earth | with yet appearing blood, 2H4 4.01. 82
chin is but enrich'd | with one appearing hair, H5 3.pr. 23
which so appearing to the common eyes, | we JC 2.01.179
/APPEARS 1 FR 0.0001 REL FR 1 V 0 P
/for /your /part, /it /not /appears /to /me, 2H4 4.01.105
APPEARS 58 FR 0.0065 REL FR 42 V 16 P
better nature, sir, | than he appears by speech. TMP 1.02.498
for it appears by their bare liveries that they TGV 2.04. 45 P
it appears so by his weapons. WIV 3.01. 71 P
and his offense is so, as it appears, MM 2.04. 85
to do any thing that appears not foul in the 3.01.206 P
him letters, and there appears much joy in him, ADO 1.01. 21 P
a fancy to this foolery, as it appears he hath, 3.02. 38 P
excuse | that which appears in proper nakedness? 4.01.175
it appears not in this confession; 5.02. 73 P
as it appears | in the true course of all the 5.04. 5
there is no certain princess that appears; LLL 4.03.154
that in this spleen ridiculous appears, | to 5.02.117
so born, | in their nativity all truth appears. MND 3.02.125
it appears, by his small light of discretion, 5.01.253 P
well then, it now appears you need my help. MV 1.03.114
the ancient roman honor more appears | than any 3.02.295
which appears most strongly | in bearing thus 3.04. 3
for it appears, by manifest proceeding, | that 4.01.358
how well in thee appears | the constant service AYL 2.03. 56
the more my wrong, the more his spite appears. SHR 4.03. 2
his dishonesty appears in leaving his friend TN 3.04.386 P
but it appears she lives, | though yet she speak WT 5.03.117
it appears so by the story. 1H4 3.03.169 P
you have, as it appears to me, practic'd upon 2H4 2.01.114 P
sorrow so royally in you appears | that i will 5.02. 51
for so appears this fleet majestical, | holding H5 3.pr. 16
'tis a hooded valor, and when it appears, it 3.07.112 P
laid by, in his nakedness he appears but a man; 4.01.105 P
the truth appears so naked on my side | that any 1H6 2.04. 20
so it appears by that i have to say: R3 3.02. 7
loyalty, and almost appears | in loud rebellion. H8 1.02. 28
not almost appears, | it doth appear; 1.02. 29
wherein he appears | as i would wish mine enemy. 3.02. 27
sometime't appears like a lord, sometime like a TIM 2.02.109 P
and yet the eight appears, who bears a glass MAC 4.01.119
appears before them, and with solemn march HAM 1.02.201
it well appears. 4.07. 5
it appears not which of the dukes he values most LR 1.01. 4 P
he hath now cast her off appears too grossly. 1.01.291 P
of kindness appears as well in the general 1.04. 60 P
why he appears | upon this call o' th' trumpet. 5.03.118
prizes the virtue that appears in cassio, | and OTH 2.03.134
and it appears he is belov'd of those | that ANT 1.04. 37
when it appears to you where this begins, | turn 3.04. 33
how appears the fight? 3.10. 8
appears he hath had | good ancestors. CYM 4.02. 47
for by his rusty outside he appears | to have PER 2.02. 50
the seas-toss'd pericles appears to speak. 3.ch. 60
in reverend cerimon there well appears | the 5.03. 93
the duke appears; TNK 3.05. 13
in 's face appears | all the fair hopes of what 4.02. 98
face | the livery of the warlike maid appears, 4.02.106
lo he appears. 5.04. 85
that in each cheek appears a pretty dimple; VEN 242
and in the breach appears | green-dropping sap, 1175
winking, there appears | quick-shifting antics, LUC 458
and there appears a face | that overgoes my SON 103. 6
appear to him, as he to me appears, | all LC 299
APPEAS'D 5 FR 0.0005 REL FR 5 V 0 P
by penitence th' eternal's wrath's appeas'd: TGV 5.04. 81
these kentish rebels would be soon appeas'd! 2H6 4.04. 42
what if both lewis and warwick be appeas'd | by 3H6 4.01. 34
only be patient till we have appeas'd | the JC 3.01.179
their good souls may be appeas'd with slaughter CYM 5.05. 72
APPEASE 4 FR 0.0004 REL FR 4 V 0 P
if my deep pray'rs cannot appease thee, | but R3 1.04. 69
t' appease their groaning shadows that are gone. TIT 1.01.126
poor, innocent lamb | t' appease an angry god. MAC 4.03. 17
so children temporal fathers do appease; CYM 5.04. 12
APPELE 1 FR 0.0001 REL FR 0 V 1 P
ecoutez: comment etes-vous appele? H5 4.04. 25 P
APPELEE 1 FR 0.0001 REL FR 0 V 1 P
la main? elle est appelee de hand. H5 3.04. 7 P
APPELES 1 FR 0.0001 REL FR 0 V 1 P
je pense qu'ils sont appeles de fingres, oui, de H5 3.04. 11 P
APPELEZ-VOUS 4 FR 0.0004 REL FR 0 V 4 P
comment appelez-vous la main en anglois? H5 3.04. 5 P
comment appelez-vous les ongles? 3.04. 14 P
comment appelez-vous le col? 3.04. 32 P
comment appelez-vous le pied et la robe? 3.04. 50 P
APPELLANT 4 FR 0.0004 REL FR 4 V 0 P
come i appellant to this princely presence. R2 1.01. 34
the appellant in all duty greets your highness, 1.03. 52
and ready are the appellant and defendant, | the 2H6 2.03. 49
or more afraid to fight, than is the appellant, 2.03. 57
APPELLANT'S 1 FR 0.0001 REL FR 1 V 0 P
but the summons of the appellant's trumpet. R2 1.03. 4
APPELLANTS 1 FR 0.0001 REL FR 1 V 0 P
lords appellants, | your differences shall all R2 4.01.104
APPELONS 1 FR 0.0001 REL FR 0 V 1 P
les ongles? /nous les appelons de nailes. H5 3.04. 16 P
APPENDIX 1 FR 0.0001 REL FR 0 V 1 P
to come against you come with your appendix. SHR 4.04.104 P
APPERIL *(also peril)*
APPERIL 1 FR 0.0001 REL FR 1 V 0 P
let me stay at thine apperil, timon. TIM 1.02. 33
APPERTAIN 2 FR 0.0002 REL FR 2 V 0 P
and do all rites | that appertain unto a burial. ADO 4.01.208
should know no secrets | that appertain to you? JC 2.01.282
APPERTAINING 3 FR 0.0003 REL FR 2 V 1 P
must i perform | much business appertaining. TMP 3.01. 96
epitheton appertaining to thy young days, which LLL 1.02. 14 P
doth much excuse the appertaining rage | to such ROM 3.01. 63
APPERTAININGS 2 FR 0.0002 REL FR 2 V 0 P
and we lay by | our appertainings, visiting of TRO 2.03. 80
and grace | to appertainings and to ornament, LC 115
APPERTAINS 1 FR 0.0001 REL FR 0 V 1 P
say of what most nearly appertains to us both. LR 1.01.284 P
APPERTINENT 2 FR 0.0002 REL FR 0 V 2 P
signior as an appertinent title to your old time LLL 1.02. 16 P

all the other gifts appertinent to man, as the 2H4 1.02.171 P
APPERTINENTS *(also appurtenance)*
APPERTINENTS 1 FR 0.0001 REL FR 1 V 0 P
accord | to furnish /him with all appertinents H5 2.02. 87
APPETITE 43 FR 0.0048 REL FR 37 V 6 P
that the appetite of her eye did seem to scorch WIV 1.03. 66 P
or that his appetite | is more to bread than MM 1.03. 52
fit thy consent to my sharp appetite, | lay by 2.04.161
hooking both right and wrong to th' appetite, 2.04.176
but doth not the appetite alter? ADO 2.03.238 P
with that keen appetite that he sits down? MV 2.06. 9
the appetite may sicken, and so die. TN 1.01. 3
malvolio, and taste with a distemper'd appetite. 1.05. 91 P
alas, their love may be call'd appetite, | no 2.04. 97
threw off his spirit, his appetite, his sleep, WT 2.03. 16
or cloy the hungry edge of appetite | by bare R2 1.03.296
belike then my appetite was not princely got, 2H4 2.02. 9 P
luxury | and bestial appetite in change of lust, R3 3.05. 81
then to breakfast with | what appetite you have. H8 3.02.203
in power, | power into will, will into appetite, TRO 1.03.120
and appetite, an universal wolf | (so doubly 1.03.121
longing, | an appetite that i am sick withal, 3.03.238
dexterity so obeying appetite | that what he 5.05. 27
unto the appetite and affection common | of the COR 1.01.104
and your affections are | a sick man's appetite, 1.01.178
let my tears staunch the earth's dry appetite, TIT 3.01. 14
and in the taste confounds the appetite. ROM 2.06. 13
to disgest his words | with better appetite. JC 1.02.302
now good digestion wait on appetite, | and MAC 3.04. 37
on him | as if increase of appetite had grown HAM 1.02.144
his generation messes | to gorge his appetite, LR 1.01.118
horse goes to't | with a more riotous appetite. 4.06.123
it not | to please the palate of my appetite, OTH 1.03.262
inflame it and to give satiety a fresh appetite, 2.01.229 P
even as her appetite shall play the god | with 2.03.347
sharpen with cloyless sauce his appetite, | that ANT 2.01. 25
nor i' th' appetite: CYM 1.06. 43
i am weak with toil, yet strong in appetite. 3.06. 37
thyself) | than i will trust a sickly appetite, TNK 1.03. 89
altogether without appetite, save often drinking 4.03. 4 P
please her appetite, | and do it home; 5.02. 36
disdain, | with leaden appetite, unapt to toy; VEN 34
set | this bateless edge on his keen appetite; LUC 9
right, | nor aught obeys but his foul appetite. 546
said | thy edge should blunter be than appetite, SON 56. 2
mine appetite i never more will grind | on newer 110.10
ill, | th' uncertain sickly appetite to please. 147. 4
o appetite, from judgment stand aloof! LC 166
APPETITES 5 FR 0.0005 REL FR 4 V 1 P
and your appetites and your digestions doo's H5 5.01. 25 P
to curb those raging appetites that are | most TRO 2.02.181
creatures ours, | and not their appetites! OTH 3.03.270
other women cloy | the appetites they feed, but ANT 2.02.236
like as to make our appetites more keen, | with SON 118. 1
APPLAUD 12 FR 0.0013 REL FR 12 V 0 P
o, that our fathers would applaud our loves, TGV 1.03. 48
i do applaud thy spirit, valentine, | and think 5.04.140
fields, and blows, and groans applaud our sport! 1H4 1.03.302
applaud the name of henry with your leader. 3H6 4.02. 27
whose fortunes rome's best citizens applaud! TIT 1.01.164
queen of goths, dost thou applaud my choice? 1.01.321
afoot, | she would applaud andronicus' conceit, 4.02. 30
dearest chuck, | till thou applaud the deed. MAC 3.02. 46
health, | i would applaud thee to the very echo, 5.03. 53
to the very echo, | that should applaud again. 5.03. 54
hands, and tongues applaud it to the clouds, HAM 4.05.108
now, by the gods, i do applaud his courage. PER 2.05. 58
APPLAUDED 1 FR 0.0001 REL FR 1 V 0 P
so much applauded through the realm of france? 1H6 2.02. 36
APPLAUDING 2 FR 0.0002 REL FR 2 V 0 P
great triumphers | in their applauding gates. TIM 5.01.197
sounds together, | applauding our approach. ANT 4.08. 39
/APPLAUSE 1 FR 0.0001 REL FR 1 V 0 P
/with /what /loud /applause | /didst /thou /beat 2H4 1.03. 91
APPLAUSE 12 FR 0.0013 REL FR 11 V 1 P
well | their loud applause and aves vehement; MM 1.01. 70
eyes, | hearing applause and universal shout, MV 3.02.143
deserv'd | high commendation, true applause, and AYL 1.02.263
i, | "this general applause and cheerful shout R3 3.07. 39
besides th' applause and approbation | the which TRO 1.03. 59
from his deep chest laughs out a loud applause, 1.03.163
who broils in loud applause, and make him fall 1.03.378
and how his silence drinks up his applause! 2.03.201
till he behold them formed in th' applause 3.03.119
with all th' applause and clamor of the host, COR 1.09. 64
with voices and applause of every sort, TIT 1.01.230
revel, and applause, transform ourselves into OTH 2.03.292 P
APPLAUSES 1 FR 0.0001 REL FR 1 V 0 P
i do believe that these applauses are | for some JC 1.02.133
APPLE 10 FR 0.0011 REL FR 5 V 5 P
in his pocket, and give it his son for an apple. TMP 2.01. 92 P
squier, | and laugh upon the apple of her eye? LLL 5.02.475
cupid's archery, | sink in apple of his eye. MND 3.02.104
cheek, | a goodly apple rotten at the heart. MV 1.03.101
as much as an apple doth an oyster, and all one. SHR 4.02.101 P
peascod, or a codling when 'tis almost an apple. TN 1.05.158 P
an apple, cleft in two, is not more twin | than 5.01.223
he keeps them, like /an /ape an apple, in the HAM 4.02. 18 P
she's as like this as a crab's like an apple, LR 1.05. 16 P
how like eve's apple doth thy beauty grow, | if SON 93.13
APPLE-JOHN 2 FR 0.0002 REL FR 0 V 2 P
i am wither'd like an old apple-john. 1H4 3.03. 4 P
knowest sir john cannot endure an apple-john. 2H4 2.04. 3 P
APPLE-JOHNS 2 FR 0.0002 REL FR 0 V 2 P
apple-johns? 2H4 2.04. 2 P
once set a dish of apple-johns before him, and 2.04. 5 P
APPLES 3 FR 0.0003 REL FR 0 V 3 P
you say, there's small choice in rotten apples. SHR 1.01.135 P
and have their heads crush'd like rotten apples! H5 3.07.145 P
at a playhouse and fight for bitten apples, that H8 5.03. 61 P
APPLE-TART 1 FR 0.0001 REL FR 1 V 0 P
what, up and down carv'd like an apple-tart? SHR 4.03. 89
APPLIANCE 5 FR 0.0005 REL FR 4 V 1 P
power, | i come to tender it, and my appliance, AWW 2.01.113
that's th' appliance only | which your disease H8 1.01.124
grown | by desperate appliance are reliev'd, HAM 4.03. 10
dead, | who was by good appliance recovered. PER 3.02. 86
of this project, come in with my appliance. TNK 4.03. 99 P
APPLIANCES 2 FR 0.0002 REL FR 2 V 0 P
noble to conserve a life | in base appliances. MM 3.01. 88
night, | with all appliances and means to boot, 2H4 3.01. 29
APPLICATIONS 1 FR 0.0001 REL FR 1 V 0 P
have worn me out | with several applications. AWW 1.02. 74
APPLIED 6 FR 0.0006 REL FR 6 V 0 P
corrosive, | it is applied to a deathful wound. 2H6 3.02.404
to a gentle bath | and balms applied to you, yet COR 1.06. 64
to this great decay may come | shall be applied. LR 5.03.299
being so applied, | his venom in effect is LUC 531
if that from him there may be aught applied LC 68
applied to cautels, all strange forms receives, 303
APPLIES 1 FR 0.0001 REL FR 0 V 1 P
of some great man and now applies it to a fool. TN 4.01. 13 P
/APPLY 1 FR 0.0001 REL FR 1 V 0 P
/of /eggs | /to /apply /to /his /bleeding /face. LR 3.07.107
APPLY 14 FR 0.0015 REL FR 12 V 2 P
would it apply well to the vehemency of your WIV 2.02.238 P
craft against vice i must apply. MM 3.02.277
goest about to apply a moral medicine to a ADO 1.03. 12 P
since all the power thereof it doth apply | to LLL 5.02. 77
i'll apply | /to your eye, | gentle lover, MND 3.02.450
for in my youth i never did apply | hot and AYL 2.03. 48
will i apply that treats of happiness | by SHR 1.01. 19
beseech you tenderly apply to her | some WT 3.02.152
nestor shall apply | thy latest words. TRO 1.03. 32
it was an answer. how apply you this? COR 1.01.147
and these does she apply for warnings and JC 2.02. 80
let your remembrance apply to banquo, | present MAC 3.02. 30
if you apply yourself to our intents, | which ANT 5.02.126
of them, and apply | allayments to their act, CYM 1.05. 21
APPLYING 3 FR 0.0003 REL FR 3 V 0 P
applying this to that, and so to so, | for love VEN 713
applying fears to hopes, and hopes to fears, SON 119. 3
she was set, | like usury, applying wet to wet, LC 40
APPOINT *(also 'point, etc.)*
APPOINT 12 FR 0.0013 REL FR 7 V 5 P
let's appoint him a meeting, give him a show of WIV 2.01. 94 P
have i not, at de place i did appoint? 3.01. 93 P
for i'll appoint my men to carry the basket 4.02. 94 P
appoint a meeting with this old fat fellow, 4.04. 14
the night, appoint her to look out at her lady's ADO 2.02. 17 P
to appoint myself in this vexation, sully | the WT 1.02.326
before or after them and appoint them a place of 1H4 1.02.170 P
to appoint some of your council presently | to H5 5.02. 79
th' king) t' appoint | who should attend on him? H8 1.01. 74
and appoint the meeting | even at his father's TIT 4.04.102
for that | i do appoint him store of provender. JC 4.01. 30
he does; he did appoint so. MAC 2.03. 53
/APPOINTED 2 FR 0.0002 REL FR 2 V 0 P
/and /very /well /appointed, /as /i /thought, 3H6 2.01.113
king | to some retention /and /appointed /guard, LR 5.03. 47
APPOINTED 30 FR 0.0034 REL FR 18 V 12 P
who being then appointed | master of this design TMP 1.02.162
and i have appointed mine host of de jarteer to WIV 1.04.117 P
i think, hath appointed them contrary places; 2.01.208 P
this is the place appointed. 3.01. 95 P
we have appointed to dine with mistress anne, 3.02. 54 P
i was at her house the hour she appointed me. 3.05. 65 P
hath appointed | that he shall likewise shuffle 4.06. 28
sir, as you told me you had appointed? 5.01. 14 P
as anne and i had appointed, and yet it was not 5.05.198 P
to her /by oath, and the nuptial appointed; MM 3.01.214 P
meet her as he was appointed next morning at the ADO 3.03.160 P
in that same place thou hast appointed me MND 1.01.177
here is the place appointed for the wrastling, AYL 1.02.145 P
what, shall i be appointed hours, as though, SHR 1.01.103
my master hath appointed me to go to saint 4.04.102 P
i am appointed him to murther you. WT 1.02.412
be so my care | to have you royally appointed, 4.04.592
appointed to direct these fair designs. R2 1.03. 45
power, | as is appointed us, at shrewsbury. 1H4 3.01. 85
if thou retire, the dolphin, well appointed, 1H6 4.02. 21
next, if i be appointed for the place, | my lord 2H6 1.03.167
and let these have a day appointed them | for 1.03.207
this is the day appointed for the combat, | and 2.03. 48
ten is the hour that was appointed me | to watch 2.04. 6
and sir john stanley is appointed now | to take 2.04. 77
thou hast appointed justices of peace, to call 4.07. 41 P
hath appointed | this conduct to convey me to R3 1.01. 44
need, | you may be armed and appointed well: TIT 4.02. 16
my lords, you are appointed for that office; CYM 3.05. 10
are making battle, thus like knights appointed, TNK 3.06.134
APPOINTMENT 12 FR 0.0013 REL FR 7 V 5 P
her (i may tell you) by her own appointment; WIV 2.02.262 P
i will then address me to my appointment. 3.05.133 P
therefore your best appointment make with speed, MM 3.01. 59
this wrong'd maid to stead up your appointment, 3.01.250 P
forth | in best appointment all our regiments. JN 2.01.296
and by every other appointment to be ourselves. 1H4 1.02.175 P
if i command him, follows my appointment; H8 2.02.133
here art thou in appointment fresh and fair, TRO 4.05. 1
of very warlike appointment gave us chase. HAM 4.06. 16 P
where their appointment we may best discover, ANT 4.10. 8
as may be judg'd | by their appointment. TNK 1.04. 15
with these hands | void of appointment, that 3.01. 40
/APPOINTMENTS 1 FR 0.0001 REL FR 0 V 1 P
/missing /your /meetings /and /appointments. WIV 3.01. 90 P
APPOINTMENTS 2 FR 0.0002 REL FR 2 V 0 P
seem, | and my appointments have in them a need AWW 2.05. 67
our fair appointments may be well perus'd. R2 3.03. 53
APPOINTS 1 FR 0.0001 REL FR 1 V 0 P
appoints him an encounter; AWW 3.07. 32
APPREHEND 17 FR 0.0019 REL FR 12 V 5 P
cousin, you apprehend passing shrewdly. ADO 2.01. 81 P
that apprehend | more than cool reason ever MND 5.01. 5
that, if it would but apprehend some joy, | it 5.01. 19
in private brabble did we apprehend him. TN 5.01. 65
apprehend | nothing but jollity. WT 4.04. 24
if thou encounter any such, apprehend him, and H5 4.07.158 P
charge you in his majesty's name, apprehend him, 4.08. 17 P
allegiance, | will apprehend you as his enemy. 3H6 3.01. 71
o, let my lady apprehend no fear. TRO 3.02. 74 P
i will apprehend him. ROM 5.03. 53
condemned villain, i do apprehend thee. 5.03. 56
and apprehend thee for a felon here. 5.03. 69
i'll apprehend him. LR 1.02. 78 P
this hurt you see, striving to apprehend him. 2.01.108
know | where we may apprehend her and the moor? OTH 1.01.177
i therefore apprehend and do attach thee | for 1.02. 77
to apprehend thus | draws us a profit from all CYM 3.03. 17
/APPREHENDED 1 FR 0.0001 REL FR 1 V 0 P
/this | (/though /strongly /apprehended) /could 2H4 1.01.176
APPREHENDED 8 FR 0.0009 REL FR 6 V 2 P
i was like to be apprehended for the witch of WIV 4.05.116 P
merchant | is apprehended for /arrival here; ERR 1.02. 4
which i apprehended with the aforesaid swain, i LLL 1.01.273 P
where being apprehended, his false cunning TN 5.01. 86
they shall be apprehended by and by. H5 2.02. 2
whom we have apprehended in the fact, | raising 2H6 2.01.169
and apprehended here immediately | th' unknown TRO 3.03.124
the aediles ho! let him be apprehended. COR 3.01.172
APPREHENDS 3 FR 0.0003 REL FR 2 V 1 P
a man that apprehends death no more dreadfully MM 4.02.142 P
that apprehends no further than this world, 5.01.481
he apprehends a world of figures here, | but not 1H4 1.03.209
APPREHEND'ST 1 FR 0.0001 REL FR 0 V 1 P
so thou apprehend'st it, take it for thy labor. TIM 1.01.209 P
APPREHENSION 15 FR 0.0017 REL FR 10 V 5 P
the sense of death is most in apprehension, MM 3.01. 77
me, how long have you profess'd apprehension? ADO 3.04. 68 P
the ear more quick of apprehension makes; MND 3.02.178
no, the apprehension of the good | gives but the R2 1.03.300
and think how such an apprehension | may turn 1H4 4.01. 66
if the english had any apprehension, they would H5 3.07.135 P
memory, | to scourge you for this apprehension. 1H6 2.04.102
took him, | to question of his apprehension. 3H6 3.02.122
you | th' apprehension of his present portance, COR 2.03.224
that's a lascivious apprehension. TIM 1.01.208 P
how like an angel in apprehension! HAM 2.02.306 P
and in this brainish apprehension kills | the 4.01. 11
is, that he may be ready for our apprehension. LR 3.05. 19 P
he had not apprehension | of roaring terrors; CYM 4.02.110
expels the seeds of fear and th' apprehension TNK 5.01. 36
APPREHENSIONS 3 FR 0.0003 REL FR 2 V 1 P
shapes, objects, ideas, apprehensions, motions, LLL 4.02. 67 P
with scorn, | cannot outfly our apprehensions. TRO 2.03.115
/but /some uncleanly apprehensions | keep leets OTH 3.03.139
APPREHENSIVE 3 FR 0.0003 REL FR 2 V 1 P
whose apprehensive senses | all but new things AWW 1.02. 60
vapors which environ it, makes it apprehensive, 2H4 4.03. 99 P
and men are flesh and blood, and apprehensive; JC 3.01. 67
APPRENTICE *(see prentice, etc.)*
APPRENTICEHOOD 1 FR 0.0001 REL FR 1 V 0 P
must i not serve a long apprenticehood | to R2 1.03.271
APPRIS 1 FR 0.0001 REL FR 0 V 1 P
les mots que vous m'avez appris des a present. H5 3.04. 26 P
/APPROACH 1 FR 0.0001 REL FR 0 V 1 P
/the /powers /of /the /kingdom /approach /apace. LR 4.07. 92 P
APPROACH 73 FR 0.0082 REL FR 60 V 13 P
i am ready now, | approach, my ariel. TMP 1.02.188
do not approach | till thou dost hear me call. 4.01. 49
approach, rich ceres, her to entertain. 4.01. 75
by thy approach thou mak'st me most unhappy. TGV 5.04. 31
let her approach. WIV 2.02. 32 P
gives intelligence of ford's approach; 3.05. 85 P
years, | no woman may approach his silent court; LLL 2.01. 24
navarre had notice of your fair approach, | and 2.01. 81
love doth approach disguis'd, | armed in 5.02. 83
let them not approach. 5.02.511
approach. 5.02.890 P
beetles black, approach not near; MND 2.02. 22
at whose approach, ghosts, wand'ring here and 3.02.381
by day's approach look to be visited. 3.02.430
let him approach. 5.01.107
approach, ye furies fell! 5.01.284
four farewell, i should be glad of his approach. MV 1.02.129 P
approach, | here dwells my father jew. 2.06. 24
he saves my labor by his own approach. AYL 2.07. 8
orlando did approach the man | and found it was 4.03.119
come, for if they do approach the city, we shall AWW 3.05. 1 P
let him approach | a stranger, no offender; 5.03. 25
let him approach. call in my gentlewoman. TN 1.05.163 P
and allow'd your approach rather to wonder at 1.05.198 P
approach, sir andrew. 2.03. 1 P
sport, mark his first approach before my lady. 2.05.198 P
where i arrive, and my approach be shunn'd, WT 1.02.422
she did approach | my cabin where i lay; 3.03. 23
see, your guests approach, | address yourself to 4.04. 52
bring him in, and let him approach singing. 4.04.211 P
his approach, | so out of circumstance and 5.01. 89
approach; 5.03. 99
let them approach. JN 1.01. 47
and but for our approach those sleeping stones, 2.01.216
john, your king and england's, doth approach, 2.01.313
o sir, when he shall hear of your approach, | if 3.04.162
should — | this apish and unmannerly approach, 5.02.131
stay | for nothing but his majesty's approach. R2 1.03. 6
and approach | the ragged'st hour that time and 2H4 1.01.150
approach me, and thou shalt be as thou wast, 5.05. 61
no great cause to desire the approach of day. H5 4.01. 88 P
for our approach shall so much dare the field, 4.02. 36
by whose approach the regions of artois, 1H6 2.01. 9
and death approach not ere my tale be done. 2.05. 62
where death's approach is seen so terrible! 2H6 3.03. 6
with thy approach, i know, | my comfort comes H8 2.04.240
should the approach of this wild river break, 3.02.198
rouse him and give him note of our approach, TRO 4.01. 44
and suffer not dishonor to approach | the TIT 1.01. 13
to him, at the first approach you must kneel, 4.03.110 P
ay, now begins our sorrows to approach. 4.04. 72
and yours, close fighting ere i did approach. ROM 1.01.107
as signal that thou hearest something approach. 5.03. 8
the boy gives warning, something doth approach. 5.03. 18
to borrow of your masters, they approach sadly, TIM 2.02.100 P
his expedition promises | present approach. 5.02. 4
and lascivious town | our terrible approach. 5.04. 2
approach the fold and cull th' infected forth, 5.04. 43
the hearing of my wife with your approach; MAC 1.04. 46
approach the chamber, and destroy your sight 2.03. 71

approach thou like the rugged russian bear, 3.04. 99
i doubt some danger does approach you nearly. 4.02. 67
approach, thou beacon to this under globe, LR 2.02.163
he that dares approach: 5.03. 99
former fortune | than that which is to approach. ANT 1.02. 34
the neighs of horse to tell of her approach, 3.06. 45
approach and speak. 3.12. 6
approach there! 3.13. 89
sounds together, | applauding our approach. 4.08. 39
approach ho, all's not well; caesar's beguil'd. 5.02.323
let him approach. TNK 1.02. 93
welcomes the warm approach of sweet desire; VEN 386
for his approach that often there had been. PP 6. 8

APPROACH'D 4 FR 0.0004 REL FR 3 V 1 P
rather approach'd too late: ERR 1.02. 43
don pedro is approach'd. ADO 1.01. 95 P
who with her head nimble in threats approach'd AYL 4.03.109
he was expected then, | but not approach'd. CYM 2.04. 39

APPROACHERS 2 FR 0.0002 REL FR 2 V 0 P
bade welcome) | to knaves and all approachers. TIM 4.03.216
that in lag hours attend | for grey approachers; TNK 5.04. 9

APPROACHES 14 FR 0.0015 REL FR 10 V 4 P
but make haste, | the vaporous night approaches. MM 4.01. 57
of her father never approaches her heart but the AWW 1.01. 49 P
that approaches apace. 4.03. 31 P
toby approaches; TN 2.05. 61 P
for england his approaches makes as fierce | as H5 2.04. 9
honorable menenius, my boy martius approaches.
COR 2.01.100 P
he approaches, you shall hear him. 5.06. 69
drive back | of alcibiades th' approaches wild, TIM 5.01.164
and near approaches | the subject of our watch. MAC 3.03. 7
the time approaches | that will with due 5.04. 16
here, at your service. my lord approaches. ANT 1.02. 86
makes his approaches to the port of rome; 1.03. 46
most noble sir, arise, the queen approaches. 3.11. 46
floats but for | the surge that next approaches. TNK 5.04. 84

APPROACHETH 4 FR 0.0004 REL FR 4 V 0 P
and me, when he approacheth to your presence. TGV 5.04. 32
the period of thy tyranny approacheth. 1H6 4.02. 17
at hand the dolphin and his train | approacheth, 5.04.101
what's he approacheth boldly to our presence? 3H6 3.03. 44

APPROACHING 5 FR 0.0005 REL FR 5 V 0 P
and the approaching tide | will shortly fill the TMP 5.01. 80
for this new-married man approaching here, MM 5.01.400
before | to signify th' approaching of his lord, MV 2.09. 88
approaching near these eyes, would drink my JN 4.01. 62
head of /actium | beat th' approaching caesar. ANT 3.07. 52

APPROBATION 14 FR 0.0015 REL FR 10 V 4 P
enter, | and there receive her approbation. MM 1.02.178
worth and credit | that's seal'd in approbation? 5.01.245
gives manhood more approbation than ever proof
TN 3.04.181 P
only, nought for approbation | but only seeing, WT 2.01.177
shall drop their blood in approbation | of what H5 1.02. 19
me but | by learned approbation of the judges. H8 1.02. 71
besides th' applause and approbation | the which TRO 1.03. 59
menenius, and with most prosperous approbation.
COR 2.01.104 P
summon'd | to meet anon, upon your approbation. 2.03.144
enemy, and revoke | your sudden approbation. 2.03.251
and approbation | with senators on the bench. TIM 4.03. 37
ay, and the approbation of those that weep this CYM 1.04. 19 P
my neighbor's on th' approbation of what i have 1.04.124 P
proceeding | who ever but his approbation added, PER 4.03. 26

APPROOF 4 FR 0.0004 REL FR 3 V 1 P
tongue, | either of condemnation or approof, MM 2.04.174
so in approof lives not his epitaph | as in your AWW 1.02. 50
yes, my lord, and of very valiant approof. 2.05. 3 P
as my farthest band | shall pass on thy approof. ANT 3.02. 27

APPROPRIATE 1 FR 0.0001 REL FR 1 V 0 P
were not all appropriate to your comforts, | but STM II.C 137

APPROPRIATION 1 FR 0.0001 REL FR 0 V 1 P
makes it a great appropriation to his own good MV 1.02. 41 P

APPROV'D 14 FR 0.0015 REL FR 9 V 5 P
o, 'tis the curse in love, and still approv'd, TGV 5.04. 43
he is of a noble strain, of approv'd valor, and ADO 2.01.379 P
is 'a not approv'd in the height a villain, that 4.01.301 P
my trusty servant, well approv'd in all, | here SHR 1.01. 7
approv'd so to your majesty, may plead | for AWW 1.02. 10
there is a remedy, approv'd, set down, | to cure 1.03.228
them when they have approv'd their virtues. WT 4.02. 28 P
esteem | he be approv'd in practice culpable. 2H6 3.02. 22
my very noble and approv'd good masters: OTH 1.03. 77
pilot | of very expert and approv'd allowance; 2.01. 49
and he that is approv'd in this offense, 2.03.211
i have well approv'd it, sir. i drunk! 2.03.312 P
what she lik'd | was then of me approv'd, what TNK 1.03. 65
i have seen it approv'd, how many times i know 4.03. 97 P

APPROVE 28 FR 0.0031 REL FR 24 V 4 P
on whose eyes i might approve | this flower's MND 2.02. 68
will bless it, and approve it with a text, MV 3.02. 79
of the soul, and no way approve his opinion. TN 4.02. 55 P
both to defend himself and to approve | henry of R2 1.03.112
nay, task me to my word, approve me, lord. 1H4 4.01. 9
say of wax, my growth would approve the truth. 2H4 1.02.159 P
to approve my youth further, i will not. 1.02.190 P
i shall not fail t' approve the fair conceit H8 2.03. 74
world to come | approve their truth by troilus. TRO 3.02.174
i muse my mother | does not approve me further, COR 3.02. 8
and that my sword upon thee shall approve, | and TIT 2.01. 35
the temple-haunting /marlet does approve, | by MAC 1.06. 4
come, | he may approve our eyes and speak to it. HAM 1.01. 29
faith, if you did, it would not much approve me. 5.02.135 P
and your large speeches may your deeds approve,
LR 1.01.184
good king, that must approve the common saw, 2.02.160
but the main article i do approve | in fearful OTH 1.03. 11
/this warlike isle, | that so approve the moor! 2.01. 44
if consequence do but approve my dream, | my 2.03. 62
my love doth so approve him, | that even his 4.03. 19
let nobody blame him, his scorn i approve" — 4.03. 52
cleopatra, i approve | your wisdom in the deed. ANT 5.02.149
thou dost approve thyself the very same; CYM 4.02.380
confess'd, | which must approve thee honest. 5.05.245
all that may men approve or men detect! PER 2.01. 51
suff'ring my friend for my sake to approve her. SON 42. 8
good, slander doth but approve | /thy worth the 70. 5
and i desperate now approve | desire is death, 147. 7

APPROVED 6 FR 0.0006 REL FR 6 V 0 P
till i have us'd the approved means i have, ERR 5.01.103
not to knit my soul to an approved wanton. ADO 4.01. 44
of all | my best beloved and approved friend, SHR 1.02. 3
confirm | to more approved service and desert. R2 2.03. 44
that ever-valiant and approved scot, | at 1H4 1.01. 54
approved warriors, and my faithful friends, | i TIT 5.01. 1

APPROVERS 1 FR 0.0001 REL FR 1 V 0 P
known | to their approvers they are people such CYM 2.04. 25

APPROVES 5 FR 0.0005 REL FR 4 V 1 P
for you have show'd me that which well approves AWW 3.07. 13
approves her fit for none but for a king. 1H6 5.05. 69
this approves her letter, | that she would soon LR 2.04.183
which approves him an intelligent party to the 3.05. 11 P
full sorry | that he approves the common liar, ANT 1.01. 60

APPURTENANCE *(also appertinents)*

APPURTENANCE 1 FR 0.0001 REL FR 0 V 1 P
then, th' appurtenance of welcome is fashion and HAM 2.02.371 P

APPURTENANT *(see appertinent)*

A-PRAYING 1 FR 0.0001 REL FR 1 V 0 P
now might i do it /pat, now 'a is a-praying; HAM 3.03. 73

APRICOCK 1 FR 0.0001 REL FR 1 V 0 P
yon little tree, yon blooming apricock! TNK 2.02.236

APRICOCKS 2 FR 0.0002 REL FR 2 V 0 P
feed him with apricocks and dewberries, | with MND 3.01.166
go bind thou up young dangling apricocks, R2 3.04. 29

APRIL 16 FR 0.0018 REL FR 12 V 4 P
brims, | which spungy april at thy hest betrims, TMP 4.01. 65
the uncertain glory of an april day, | which now TGV 1.03. 85
he speaks holiday, he smells april and may — he WIV 3.02. 68 P
a day in april never came so sweet, | to show MV 2.09. 93
orlando, men are april when they woo, december AYL 4.01.147 P
the coast on we'nsday the fourscore of april, WT 4.04.276 P
the first of april died | your noble mother; JN 4.02.120
he will weep you an' 'twere a man born in april. TRO 1.02.174 P
than youthful april shall with all his show'rs. TIT 3.01. 18
when well-apparell'd april on the heel | of ROM 1.02. 27
embalms and spices | to th' april day again. TIM 4.03. 42
white | show'd like an april daisy on the grass, LUC 395
thee | calls back the lovely april of her prime, SON 3.10
when proud-pied april (dress'd in all his trim) 98. 2
three april perfumes in three hot junes burn'd, 104. 7
a storm | as oft 'twixt may and april is to see, LC 102

APRIL'S 3 FR 0.0003 REL FR 3 V 0 P
but flora, | peering in april's front. WT 4.04. 3
the april's in her eyes, it is love's spring, ANT 3.02. 43
with april's first-born flowers, and all things SON 21. 7

APRON *(also aporn)*

APRON 2 FR 0.0002 REL FR 1 V 1 P
where is thy leather apron and thy rule? JC 1.01. 7
he will line your apron with gold. PER 4.06. 58 P

APRON-MEN 1 FR 0.0001 REL FR 1 V 0 P
have made good work, | you and your apron-men;
COR 4.06. 96

APRONS 5 FR 0.0005 REL FR 2 V 3 P
put on two leathern jerkins and aprons, and wait 2H4 2.02.171 P
they will put on two of our jerkins and aprons, 2.04. 17 P
nobility think scorn to go in leather aprons. 2H6 4.02. 13 P
hold up, you sluts, | your aprons mountant. TIM 4.03.136
mechanic slaves | with greasy aprons, rules, and ANT 5.02.210

/APT 1 FR 0.0001 REL FR 1 V 0 P
/they /are /apt /enough /to /dislocate /and LR 4.02. 65

APT 43 FR 0.0048 REL FR 29 V 14 P
their names | by vain though apt affection. MM 1.04. 48
i find an apt remission in myself; 5.01.498
and thou shalt see how apt it is to learn | any ADO 1.01.292
yea, but so i am apt to do myself wrong. 2.01.206 P
pretty and apt. LLL 1.02. 18 P
i pretty, and my saying apt? 1.02. 20 P
or i apt, and my saying pretty? 1.02. 20 P
little pretty, because little. wherefore apt? 1.02. 22 P
and therefore apt, because quick. 1.02. 23 P
delivers in such apt and gracious words | that 2.01. 73
youth unmeet, | youth so apt to pluck a sweet. 4.03.112
chose, sweet, and apt, i do assure you, sir, i 5.01. 93 P
for in all the play | there is not one word apt, MND 5.01. 65
she's apt to learn and thankful for good turns. SHR 2.01.165
i know thy constellation is right apt | for this TN 1.04. 35
apt, in good faith, very apt. 1.05. 26 P
apt, in good faith, very apt. 1.05. 26 P
o world, how apt the poor are to be proud! 3.01.127
and i, most jocund, apt, and willingly, | to do 5.01.132
madam, i am most apt t' embrace your offer. 5.01.320
apt, liable to be employ'd in danger, | i JN 4.02.226
you know how apt our love was to accord | to H5 2.02. 86
is she not apt? 5.02.285 P
stubborn to justice, apt to accuse it, and H8 2.04.122
not give advantage | to stubborn critics, apt, TRO 5.02.131
i have a heart as little apt as yours, | but yet COR 3.02. 29
and i were so apt to quarrel as thou art, any ROM 3.01. 31 P
you shall find me apt enough to that, sir, and 3.01. 41 P
bed, | which heavy sorrow makes them apt unto. 3.03.157
she is young and apt. TIM 1.01.132
it were a mock | apt to be render'd, for some JC 2.02. 97
years, | i shall not find myself so apt to die; 3.01.160
why dost thou show to the apt thoughts of men 5.03. 68
i find thee apt, | and duller shouldst thou be HAM 1.05. 31
thoughts black, hands apt, drugs fit, and time 3.02.255
him to, being apt | to have his ear abus'd, LR 2.04.306
now again you are most apt to play the sir in. OTH 2.01.174 P
she loves him, 'tis apt and of great credit. 2.01.287
free, so kind, so apt, so bless'd a disposition, 2.03.320 P
than what he found himself was apt and true. 5.02.177
the fit and apt construction of thy name, CYM 5.05.444
as apt as new-fall'n snow takes any dint. VEN 354
youth unmeet, | youth, so apt to pluck a sweet. PP 16.14

APTER 3 FR 0.0003 REL FR 2 V 1 P
i warrant she is apter to do than to confess she AYL 3.02.389 P
is apter than thy tongue to tell thy arrand. 2H4 1.01. 69
for, and so apter | to make this cause his own. TNK 4.02. 97

APTEST 1 FR 0.0001 REL FR 1 V 0 P
man | the aptest way for safety and revenge. 2H4 1.01.213

APTLY 9 FR 0.0010 REL FR 8 V 1 P
part | was aptly fitted and naturally perform'd. SHR in.1. 87
(as i know his youth will aptly receive it) into TN 3.04.193 P
uncle, | he prettily and aptly taunts himself: R3 3.01.134
that happy verse | which aptly sings the good." TIM 1.01. 17
gives a frock or livery, | that aptly is put on. HAM 3.04.165
that you aptly will suppose | what pageantry, PER 5.02. 5
he, | "leave me, and then the story aptly ends; VEN 716
what's sweet to do, to do will aptly find: LC 88
aptly understood | in bloodless white and the 200

APTNESS 3 FR 0.0003 REL FR 2 V 1 P
they are in a ripe aptness to take all power COR 4.03. 23 P
and be friended | with aptness of the season; CYM 2.03. 48
in either's aptness, as it best deceives, | to LC 306

AQUA-VITAE 6 FR 0.0006 REL FR 3 V 3 P
an irishman with my aqua-vitae bottle, or a WIV 2.02.304 P
bought | the oil, the balsamum, and aqua-vitae. ERR 4.01. 89
like aqua-vitae with a midwife. TN 2.05.196 P
again with aqua-vitae or some other hot infusion WT 4.04.786 P
give me some aqua-vitae; ROM 3.02. 88
some aqua-vitae ho! 4.05. 16

AQUILON 1 FR 0.0001 REL FR 1 V 0 P
cheek | outswell the colic of puff'd aquilon; TRO 4.05. 9

AQUITAINE 8 FR 0.0009 REL FR 8 V 0 P
about surrender up of aquitaine | to her LLL 1.01.137
the plea of no less weight | than aquitaine, a 2.01. 8
which | one part of aquitaine is bound to us, 2.01.135
we will give up our right in aquitaine, | and 2.01.139
crowns, | to have his title live in aquitaine; 2.01.145
lent, | than aquitaine, so gelded as it is. 2.01.148
it, i'll repay it back, | or yield up aquitaine. 2.01.159
i'll give you aquitaine and all that is his, 2.01.248

ARABIA 5 FR 0.0005 REL FR 4 V 1 P
that in arabia | there is one tree, the phoenix' TMP 3.03. 22
wilds | of wide arabia are as throughfares now MV 2.07. 42
i would my son | were in arabia, and thy tribe COR 4.02. 24
all the perfumes of arabia will not sweeten this MAC 5.01. 51 P
king manchus of arabia; ANT 3.06. 72

ARABIAN 4 FR 0.0004 REL FR 4 V 0 P
drops tears as fast as the arabian trees | their OTH 5.02.350
o antony! o thou arabian bird! ANT 3.02. 12
she is alone th' arabian bird, and i | have lost CYM 1.06. 17
bird of loudest lay, | on the sole arabian tree, PHT 2

ARAGON *(see arragon)*

ARAISE 1 FR 0.0001 REL FR 1 V 0 P
touch | is powerful to araise king pippen, nay, AWW 2.01. 76

/ARBITERMENT 1 FR 0.0001 REL FR 0 V 1 P
/the /arbiterment /is /like /to /be /bloody. LR 4.07. 93 P

ARBITERMENT 1 FR 0.0001 REL FR 0 V 1 P
yes, to be put to the arbiterment of swords, and CYM 1.04. 49 P

ARBITRATE 5 FR 0.0005 REL FR 5 V 0 P
that which long process could not arbitrate. LLL 5.02.743
must | with fearful bloody issue arbitrate. JN 1.01. 38
can arbitrate this cause betwixt us twain; R2 1.01. 50
there shall your swords and lances arbitrate 1.01.200
but certain issue strokes must arbitrate, MAC 5.04. 20

ARBITRATING 1 FR 0.0001 REL FR 1 V 0 P
arbitrating that | which the commission of thy ROM 4.01. 63

ARBITRATOR 3 FR 0.0003 REL FR 3 V 0 P
but now, the arbitrator of despairs, | just 1H6 2.05. 28
and that old common arbitrator, time, | will one TRO 4.05.225
that never-erring arbitrator, tell us | when we TNK 1.02.114

ARBITRATORS 1 FR 0.0001 REL FR 1 V 0 P
unprofitable sounds, weak arbitrators! LUC 1017

ARBITREMENT 5 FR 0.0005 REL FR 3 V 2 P
against you, even to a mortal arbitrement, but TN 3.04.261 P
side | must keep aloof from strict arbitrement, 1H4 4.01. 70
if it come to the arbitrement of swords, can try H5 4.01.160 P
and put thy fortune to the arbitrement | of R3 5.03. 89
the gods by their divine arbitrement | have TNK 5.03.107

ARBOR 3 FR 0.0003 REL FR 1 V 2 P
i will hide me in the arbor. ADO 2.03. 36 P
where, in an arbor, we will eat a last year's 2H4 5.03. 2 P
she met him in an arbor: TNK 3.03. 33

ARBORS 1 FR 0.0001 REL FR 1 V 0 P
his private arbors and new-planted orchards, JC 3.02.248

ARC *(see aire)*

ARCAS 2 FR 0.0002 REL FR 2 V 0 P
arcas will be there. TNK 2.03. 37
and she fail me once — you can tell, arcas, 3.05. 46

ARCH* 8 FR 0.0009 REL FR 8 V 0 P
th' sky, | whose wat'ry arch and messenger am i, TMP 4.01. 71
the most arch deed of piteous massacre | that R3 4.03. 2
who, like an arch, reverb'rate | the voice again TRO 3.03.120
ne'er through an arch so hurried the blown tide, COR 5.04. 47
my worthy arch and patron, comes to-night. LR 2.01. 59
and the wide arch | of the rang'd empire fall! ANT 1.01. 33
to see this vaulted arch and the rich crop | of CYM 1.06. 33
as through an arch the violent roaring tide LUC 1667

/ARCHBISHOP 2 FR 0.0002 REL FR 2 V 0 P
/the /gentle /archbishop /of /york /is /up 2H4 1.01.189
/marshal /and /the /archbishop /are /strong. 2.03. 42

ARCHBISHOP 20 FR 0.0022 REL FR 19 V 1 P
langton, chosen archbishop | of canterbury, from JN 3.01.143
his brother, archbishop late of canterbury, R2 2.01.282
noble prelate well belov'd, | the archbishop. 1H4 1.03.268
lancaster against the archbishop and the earl of 2H4 1.02.205 P
against northumberland and the archbishop. 2.01.175
fain would i go to meet the archbishop, | but 2.03. 65
you, lord archbishop, | whose see is by a civil 4.01. 41
good day to you, gentle lord archbishop, | and 4.02. 2
and you, lord archbishop, and you, lord mowbray, 4.02.108
convey'd | unto my brother, archbishop of york. 3H6 4.03. 53
and we shall see him | for it an archbishop. H8 3.02. 74
install'd lord archbishop of canterbury. 3.02.401
the archbishop | of canterbury, accompanied with 4.01. 24
when by the archbishop of canterbury | she had 4.01. 86
th' archbishop | is the king's hand and tongue, 5.01. 37
sir, i have brought my lord the archbishop, | as 5.01. 80
my lord archbishop; 5.02. 40
my good lord archbishop, i'm very sorry | to sit 5.02. 43
thank you, good lord archbishop. 5.04. 8
o lord archbishop, | thou hast made me now a man 5.04. 63

ARCHBISHOPRIC 1 FR 0.0001 REL FR 1 V 0 P
him at his asking | the archbishopric of toledo, H8 2.01.164

ARCHBISHOP'S 2 FR 0.0002 REL FR 2 V 0 P
the archbishop's grace of york, douglas, 1H4 3.02.119
is held no great good lover of the archbishop's, H8 4.01.104

ARCH'D 3 FR 0.0003 REL FR 2 V 1 P
thou hast the right arch'd beauty of the brow WIV 3.03. 56 P
are arch'd so high that giants may jet through CYM 3.03. 5
arch'd like the great-ey'd juno's, but far TNK 4.02. 20

ARCHDEACON 1 FR 0.0001 REL FR 1 V 0 P

the archdeacon hath divided it | into three 1H4 3.01. 71
ARCHED 1 FR 0.0001 REL FR 1 V 0 P
to sit and draw | his arched brows, his hawking AWW 1.01. 94
ARCHELAUS 1 FR 0.0001 REL FR 1 V 0 P
archelaus | of cappadocia; ANT 3.06. 69
ARCH–ENEMY 1 FR 0.0001 REL FR 1 V 0 P
yonder's the head of that arch–enemy | that 3H6 2.02. 2
ARCHER 3 FR 0.0003 REL FR 2 V 1 P
if we can do this, cupid is no longer an archer; ADO 2.01.385 P
you are a good archer, marcus; TIT 4.03. 53
from a well–experienc'd archer hits the mark PER 1.01.162
ARCHERS 3 FR 0.0003 REL FR 3 V 0 P
he wanted pikes to set before his archers; 1H6 1.01.116
our archers shall be placed in the midst; R3 5.03.295
draw, archers, draw your arrows to the head! 5.03.339
ARCHERY 2 FR 0.0002 REL FR 2 V 0 P
of this purple dye, | hit with cupid's archery, MND 3.02.103
sir boy, let me see your archery. TIT 4.03. 2
ARCH–HERETIC 2 FR 0.0002 REL FR 2 V 0 P
a curse, | let go the hand of that arch–heretic, JN 3.01.192
a most arch–heretic, a pestilence | that does H8 5.01. 45
ARCHIBALD 1 FR 0.0001 REL FR 1 V 0 P
there, | young harry percy, and brave archibald, 1H4 1.01. 53
ARCHITECT 1 FR 0.0001 REL FR 1 V 0 P
chief architect and plotter of these woes. TIT 5.03.122
ARCH–MOCK 1 FR 0.0001 REL FR 1 V 0 P
'tis the spite of hell, the fiend's arch–mock, OTH 4.01. 70
ARCH–ONE 1 FR 0.0001 REL FR 1 V 0 P
there is sprung up | an heretic, an arch–one, H8 3.02.102
ARCH–VILLAIN 2 FR 0.0002 REL FR 2 V 0 P
caracts, titles, forms, | be an arch–villain. MM 5.01. 57
alone, | yet an arch–villain keeps him company. TIM 5.01.108
ARCITE 55 FR 0.0062 REL FR 53 V 2 P
/wi' leave, they're called | arcite and palamon. TNK 1.04. 23
that's arcite looks out. 2.01. 48 P
arcite is the lower of the twain; 2.01. 49 P
o cousin arcite, | where is thebes now? 2.02. 6
like lazy clouds, whilst palamon and arcite, 2.02. 14
'tis too true, arcite. 2.02. 46
me | (i thank you, cousin arcite) almost wanton 2.02. 96
cousin arcite, | had not the loving gods found 2.02.107
any two that lov'd | better than we do, arcite? 2.02.113
never till now i was in prison, arcite. 2.02.132
do reverence; | she is a goddess, arcite! 2.02.135
thou art a traitor, arcite, and a fellow | false 2.02.171
me | that i was palamon, and you were arcite. 2.02.186
till thou art worthy, arcite, it concerns me, 2.02.201
lord arcite, you must presently to th' duke; 2.02.221
where's arcite? 2.02.244
arcite shall have a fortune, | if he dare make 2.02.250
her, | if he be noble arcite — thousand ways! 2.02.255
cozener arcite — give me language such | as 3.01. 44
that thou durst, arcite! 3.01. 57
shall stretch yourself, and say but, "arcite, 3.01. 87
none | but only arcite; 3.01. 91
therefore none but arcite | in this kind is so 3.01. 91
arcite? 3.03. 2
nor none so honest, arcite. 3.03. 4
arcite, thou mightst now poison me. 3.03. 8
here, arcite, to the wenches | we have known in 3.03. 28
and i have heard some call him arcite, and — 3.03. 32
i thank thee, arcite, | thou art yet a fair foe; 3.06. 7
arcite, thou art so brave an enemy | that no man 3.06. 43
thank you, arcite. 3.06. 65
methinks this armor's very like that, arcite, 3.06. 70
farewell, arcite. 3.06.106
look to thine own well, arcite. 3.06.131
and this is arcite, | a bolder traitor never 3.06.140
will you, arcite, | take these conditions? 3.06.263
here, cousin arcite, | i am friends again till 3.06.299
good heaven, | what a sweet face has arcite! 4.02. 7
lie there, arcite! 4.02. 43
me | whether i lov'd, i had run mad for arcite; 4.02. 48
that stands | in the /first place with arcite, 4.02. 76
is not this your cousin arcite? 5.02. 90
arcite is gently visag'd; 5.03. 41
arcite may win me, | and yet may palamon wound 5.03. 57
me, | and yet may palamon wound arcite to | the 5.03. 58
nay, now the sound is "arcite." 5.03. 90
the cry is | "arcite!" 5.03. 93
hark, "arcite! 5.03. 93
half–sights saw | that arcite was no babe. 5.03. 96
i have spoke, your arcite | did not lose by't; 5.03.121
on this horse is arcite | trotting the stones of 5.04. 54
the gods are mighty, arcite. 5.04. 87
and to arcite gave | the grace of the contention 5.04.107
and give grace unto | the funeral of arcite, in 5.04.126
i was as dearly sorry | as glad of arcite; 5.04.130
ARCITE'S 3 FR 0.0003 REL FR 3 V 0 P
so does arcite's mirth, | but palamon's sadness TNK 5.03. 50
they said that palamon had arcite's body 5.03. 79
that arcite's legs, being higher than his head, 5.04. 78
ARCU 1 FR 0.0001 REL FR 1 V 0 P
purus, | non eget mauri jaculis, nec arcu." TIT 4.02. 21
ARDE 1 FR 0.0001 REL FR 1 V 0 P
'twixt guynes and arde — | i was then present, H8 1.01. 7
ARDEA 2 FR 0.0002 REL FR 2 V 0 P
from the besieged ardea all in post, | borne by LUC 1
"at ardea to my lord with more than haste." 1332
ARDEN 4 FR 0.0004 REL FR 1 V 3 P
they say he is already in the forest of arden, AYL 1.01.114 P
to seek my uncle in the forest of arden. 1.03.107
well, this is the forest of arden. 2.04. 15 P
ay, now am i in arden, the more fool i. 2.04. 16 P
ARDENT 1 FR 0.0001 REL FR 0 V 1 P
those that under hot ardent zeal would set whole TIM 3.03. 33 P
ARDENTLY 1 FR 0.0001 REL FR 1 V 0 P
your sorrow beats so ardently upon me | that it TNK 1.01.126
ARDOR 1 FR 0.0001 REL FR 1 V 0 P
upon my heart | abates the ardor of my liver. TMP 4.01. 56
ARDURE 1 FR 0.0001 REL FR 1 V 0 P
when the compulsive ardure gives the charge, HAM 3.04. 86
/ARE 55 FR 0.0062 REL FR 43 V 12 P
ARE 3691 FR 0.4172 REL FR 2756 V 935 P
A–REPAIRING 1 FR 0.0001 REL FR 1 V 0 P
still a–repairing, ever out of frame, | and LLL 3.01.191
ARGAL *(also argo, ergo)*
/ARGAL 1 FR 0.0001 REL FR 0 V 1 P
/argal, she drown'd herself wittingly. HAM 5.01. 12 P
ARGAL 2 FR 0.0002 REL FR 0 V 2 P
argal, he that is not guilty of his own death HAM 5.01. 19 P
argal, the gallows may do well to thee. 5.01. 48 P
ARGENTINE 1 FR 0.0001 REL FR 1 V 0 P
celestial dian, goddess argentine, | i will obey PER 5.01.250
ARGIER 2 FR 0.0002 REL FR 2 V 0 P
sir, in argier. TMP 1.02.261
terrible | to enter human hearing, from argier, 1.02.265
ARGO *(also argal, ergo)*
ARGO 2 FR 0.0002 REL FR 0 V 2 P
argo, their thread of life is spun. 2H6 4.02. 29 P
argo they eat more in our country than they do STM II.C 5 P
ARGOSIES 3 FR 0.0003 REL FR 3 V 0 P
there where your argosies with portly sail MV 1.01. 9
there you shall find three of your argosies 5.01.276
father hath no less | than three great argosies, SHR 2.01.378
ARGOSY 5 FR 0.0005 REL FR 3 V 2 P
he hath an argosy bound to tripolis, another to MV 1.03. 18 P
hath an argosy cast away, coming from tripolis. 3.01.100 P
have, besides an argosy | that now is lying in SHR 2.01.374
what, have i chok'd you with an argosy? 2.01.376
gust, | command an argosy to stem the waves. 3H6 2.06. 36
ARGU'D 1 FR 0.0001 REL FR 1 V 0 P
law | argu'd betwixt the duke of york and him; 1H6 4.01. 96
ARGUE 6 FR 0.0006 REL FR 6 V 0 P
you would have bid me argue like a father. R2 1.03.238
age of care, | argue the end of edmund mortimer. 1H6 2.05. 7
her looks doth argue her replete with modesty, 3H6 3.02. 84
we are too open here to argue this; H8 2.01.168
scholars allow'd freely to argue for her. 2.02.112
that's no matter, | we'll argue that hereafter. TNK 3.03. 5
ARGUED 3 FR 0.0003 REL FR 3 V 0 P
well have you argued, sir, and, for your pains, R2 4.01.150
him, | which argued thee a most unloving father. 3H6 2.02. 25
argued by beauty's red and virtue's white; LUC 65
ARGUES 11 FR 0.0012 REL FR 10 V 1 P
affect the letter, for it argues facility. LLL 4.02. 55
that argues but the shame of your offense: 2H4 4.01.158
this speedy and quick appearance argues proof 1H6 5.03. 8
this argues what her kind of life hath been, 5.04. 15
so bad a death argues a monstrous life. 2H6 3.03. 30
argues your /wisdoms and your love to richard" R3 3.07. 40
my lord, this argues conscience in your grace, 3.07.174
it argues a distempered head | so soon to bid ROM 2.03. 33
which argues a great sickness in his judgment TIM 5.01. 29
if i drown myself wittingly, it argues an act, HAM 5.01. 11 P
this argues fruitfulness and liberal heart; OTH 3.04. 38
ARGUING 3 FR 0.0003 REL FR 3 V 0 P
i should be arguing still upon that doubt. SHR 3.01. 55
greater themes | for insurrection's arguing. COR 1.01.221
if arguing make us sweat, | the proof of it will JC 5.01. 48
/ARGUMENT 2 FR 0.0002 REL FR 1 V 1 P
/in /like /conditions /as /our /argument, | /to TRO pr 25
/for /a /while /no /money /bid /for /argument, HAM 2.02.355 P
ARGUMENT 68 FR 0.0076 REL FR 45 V 23 P
had instance and argument to commend themselves. WIV 2.02.247 P
this faith, thou wilt prove a notable argument. ADO 1.01.256 P
become the argument of his own scorn by falling 2.03. 11 P
come, | or, if thou wilt hold longer argument, 2.03. 53
to her wit, nor no great argument of her folly, 2.03.234 P
for shape, for bearing, argument, and valor, 3.01. 96
(which is a great argument of falsehood) if i LLL 1.02.170 P
how did this argument begin? 3.01.105
thus came your argument in; 3.01.108
'gainst whom the world cannot hold argument, 4.03. 59
verbosity finer than the staple of his argument. 5.01. 17 P
therefore i'll darkly end the argument. 5.02. 23
yet, since love's argument was first on foot, 5.02.747
you would not make me such an argument. MND 3.02.242
sent in this fool to cut off the argument? AYL 1.02. 47 P
grounded upon no other argument | but that the 1.02.279
i should not seek an absent argument | of my 3.01. 3
'tis the rarest argument of wonder that hath AWW 2.03. 7 P
in argument of praise, or to the worth | of the 3.05. 59
this was a great argument of love in her toward TN 3.02. 11 P
might well have given us bloody argument. 3.03. 32
which follows after, | is th' argument of time. WT 4.01. 29
to break into this dangerous argument: JN 4.02. 54
as near as i could sift him on that argument, R2 1.01. 12
to london, it would be argument for a week, 1H4 2.02. 95 P
and the argument shall be thy running away. 2.04.281 P
hath been but as a scene | acting that argument. 2H4 4.05.198
but our argument | is all too heavy to admit 5.02. 23
and sheath'd their swords for lack of argument. H5 3.01. 21
he will maintain his argument as well as any 3.02. 80 P
the roman wars, in the way of argument, look you 3.02. 97 P
tongues, and my horse is argument for them all. 3.07. 35 P
of any thing, when blood is their argument? 4.01.143 P
good argument, i hope, we will not fly — | and 4.03.113
false, | the argument you held was wrong in you; 1H6 2.04. 57
now, somerset, where is your argument? 2.04. 59
this day, in argument upon a case, | some words 2.05. 45
in argument and proof of which contract, | bear 5.01. 46
this was nothing but an argument | that he that 2H6 1.02. 32
and yet we have but trivial argument, | more 3.01.241
i cannot fight upon this argument; TRO 1.01. 92
all the argument is a whore and a cuckold, a 2.03. 72 P
ajax lack matter, if he have lost his argument. 2.03. 95 P
you see he is his argument that has his argument 2.03. 96 P
see he is his argument that has his argument, 2.03. 97 P
i had good argument for kissing once. 4.05. 26
but that's no argument for kissing now, | for 4.05. 27
and parted thus you and your argument. 4.05. 29
meant indeed to occupy the argument no longer. ROM 2.04.100 P
and try the argument of hearts by borrowing, TIM 2.02.178
so it may prove an argument of laughter | to th' 3.03. 20
spent, | as if he had but prov'd an argument. 3.05. 23
that most may claim this argument for ours? MAC 2.03.120
this show imports the argument of the play. HAM 3.02.139 P
have you heard the argument? 3.02.232 P
great | is not to stir without great argument, 4.04. 54
the argument of your praise, balm of your age, LR 1.01.215
an argument that he is pluck'd, when hither | he ANT 3.12. 3
it was much like an argument that fell out last CYM 1.04. 56 P
our argument is love, | which if the goddess of TNK 5.01. 70
for me, i force not argument a straw, | since LUC 1021
'gainst whom the world could not hold argument, PP 3. 2
into my verse | thine own sweet argument, too SON 38. 3
you, | and you and love are still my argument; 76.10
thy lovely argument | deserves the travail of a 79. 5
and gives thy pen both skill and argument. 100. 8
the argument all bare is of more worth | than 103. 3
"fair," "kind," and "true" is all my argument, 105. 9
ARGUMENTS 11 FR 0.0012 REL FR 8 V 3 P
armed in arguments — you'll be surpris'd. LLL 5.02. 84
let thy tongue tang arguments of state; TN 2.05.151 P
love, | the rather by these arguments of fear, 3.03. 12
let thy tongue /tang with arguments of state; 3.04. 70 P
made whole | with very easy arguments of love, JN 1.01. 36
orator, | inferring arguments of mighty force. 3H6 2.02. 44
wrong, | inferreth arguments of mighty strength, 3.01. 49
with lies well steel'd with weighty arguments, R3 1.01.148
their arguments | be now produc'd and heard. H8 2.04. 67
for they are yet but ear–/bussing arguments? LR 2.01. 8 P
all kind of arguments and question deep, | all LC 121
ARGUS 3 FR 0.0003 REL FR 2 V 1 P
though argus were her eunuch and her guard. LLL 3.01.199
watch me like argus, | if you do not, if i be MV 5.01.230
many hands and no use, or purblind argus, all TRO 1.02. 29 P
ARIACHNE'S 1 FR 0.0001 REL FR 1 V 0 P
as subtle | as ariachne's broken woof to enter. TRO 5.02.152
ARIADNE 2 FR 0.0002 REL FR 2 V 0 P
'twas ariadne passioning | for theseus' perjury TGV 4.04.167
break his faith, | with ariadne, and antiopa? MND 2.01. 80
ARIEL 17 FR 0.0019 REL FR 17 V 0 P
i am ready now, | approach, my ariel. TMP 1.02.188
bidding, task | ariel, and all his quality. 1.02.193
but are they, ariel, safe? 1.02.217
ariel, thy charge | exactly is perform'd; 1.02.237
my quaint ariel, | hark in thine ear. 1.02.317
delicate ariel, | i'll set thee free for this. 1.02.442
thou hast done well, fine ariel! 1.02.495
of this harpy hast thou | perform'd, my ariel; 3.03. 84
what, ariel! 4.01. 33
my industrious servant, ariel! 4.01. 33
dearly, my delicate ariel. 4.01. 49
now come, my ariel! 4.01. 57
come with a thought. i thank thee. ariel! come. 4.01.164
go, release them, ariel. 5.01. 30
ariel, | fetch me the hat and rapier in my cell. 5.01. 83
why, that's my dainty ariel! 5.01. 95
my ariel, chick, | that is thy charge. 5.01.317
ARIES 1 FR 0.0001 REL FR 1 V 0 P
gave aries such a knock | that down fell both TIT 4.03. 72
/ARIGHT 1 FR 0.0001 REL FR 1 V 0 P
/when /i /am /known /aright, /you /shall /not LR 4.03. 53
ARIGHT 8 FR 0.0009 REL FR 8 V 0 P
and never going aright, being a watch, | but LLL 3.01.192
thou speakest aright; MND 2.01. 42
your highness aims at, if i aim aright. 3H6 3.02. 68
and, would you represent our queen aright, | it TIT 5.02. 89
thou hast harp'd my fear aright. MAC 4.01. 74
report me and my cause aright | to the HAM 5.02.339
beseech you | to understand my purposes aright, LR 1.04.239
that censures falsely what they see aright? SON 148. 4
/ARION 1 FR 0.0001 REL FR 1 V 0 P
where, like /arion on the dolphin's back, | i TN 1.02. 15
A–RIPENING 1 FR 0.0001 REL FR 1 V 0 P
full surely | his greatness is a–ripening, nips H8 3.02.357
ARISE 41 FR 0.0046 REL FR 40 V 1 P
now i arise. TMP 1.02.169
arise, and say how thou cam'st here. 5.01.181
stay until the officer | arise to let him in; MM 4.02. 91
eyes, | to have my love to bed and to arise; MND 3.01.171
o pyramus, arise! 5.01.326
great, | arise sir richard, and plantagenet. JN 1.01.162
arise forth from the couch of lasting night, 3.04. 27
word, | some sudden mischief may arise of it; H5 4.07.178
a cause | such factious emulations shall arise! 1H6 4.01.113
beside, what infamy will there arise, | when 4.01.143
suffolk, arise. 2H6 1.01. 17
edward plantagenet, arise a knight, | and learn 3H6 2.02. 61
see, see what show'rs arise, | blown with the 2.05. 85
day, | if he arise, be mock'd and wond'red at. 5.04. 57
arise, dissembler! R3 1.02.184
arise, and take place by us. H8 1.02. 10
and spotless shall mine innocence arise | when 3.02.301
pray you arise, | my good and gracious lord of 5.01. 91
faint–hearted boy, arise and look upon her. TIT 3.01. 65
arise, fair sun, and kill the envious moon, ROM 2.02. 4
arise, one knocks. good romeo, hide thyself. 3.03. 71
romeo, arise, | thou wilt be taken. 3.03. 74
come, sir, arise, away! LR 1.04. 89 P
arise, arise! OTH 1.01. 89
arise, arise! 1.01. 89
arise, i say! 1.01. 92
arise, black vengeance, from the hollow hell! 3.03.447
most noble sir, arise, the queen approaches. ANT 3.11. 46
arise, you shall not kneel. 5.02.114
heaven's gate sings, | and phoebus gins arise, CYM 2.03. 21
thing that pretty is, my lady sweet, arise: 2.03. 25
arise, arise! 2.03. 26
arise, arise! 2.03. 26
some falls are means the happier to arise. 4.02.403
arise my knights o' th' battle. 5.05. 20
ere i arise, i will prefer my sons; 5.05.326
arise, i pray you, rise. PER 1.04. 98
arise, great sir, and give the tidings ear TNK 5.04. 46
what following sorrow may on this arise. LUC 186
"thou wronged lord of rome," quoth he, "arise, 1818
so, till the judgment that yourself arise, | you SON 55.13
ARISES 1 FR 0.0001 REL FR 1 V 0 P
here, as i point my sword, the sun arises, JC 2.01.106
ARISETH 2 FR 0.0002 REL FR 2 V 0 P
from whence ariseth this? OTH 2.03.169
silver breast | the sun ariseth in his majesty, VEN 856
ARISING 1 FR 0.0001 REL FR 1 V 0 P
(like to the lark at break of day arising | from SON 29.11
ARISTOTLE 1 FR 0.0001 REL FR 1 V 0 P
whom aristotle thought | unfit to hear moral TRO 2.02.166
ARISTOTLE'S 1 FR 0.0001 REL FR 1 V 0 P
or so devote to aristotle's checks | as ovid be SHR 1.01. 32
ARITHMETIC 6 FR 0.0006 REL FR 2 V 4 P
indeed a tapster's arithmetic may soon bring his TRO 1.02.113 P

that hath no arithmetic but her brain to set 3.03.253 P
but now 'tis odds beyond arithmetic, | and COR 3.01.244
villain, that fights by the book of arithmetic! ROM 3.01.102 P
would dozy th' arithmetic of memory, and yet but HAM 5.02.114 P
spare your arithmetic, never count the turns. CYM 2.04.142
ARITHMETICIAN 1 FR 0.0001 REL FR 1 V 0 P
forsooth, a great arithmetician, | one michael OTH 1.01. 19
ARK 1 FR 0.0001 REL FR 0 V 1 P
toward, and these couples are coming to the ark. AYL 5.04. 36 P
/ARM* 1 FR 0.0001 REL FR 1 V 0 P
conscience, | /to /quit /him /with /this /arm? HAM 5.02. 68
ARM* 147 FR 0.0166 REL FR 136 V 11 P
though others have the arm, show us the sleeve: ERR 3.02. 23
my neck, the great wart on my left arm, that i, 3.02.144 P
or under your arm, like a lieutenant's scarf? ADO 2.01.190 P
arm, wenches, arm! LLL 5.02. 82
arm, wenches, arm! 5.02. 82
look you arm yourself | to fit your fancies to MND 1.01.117
support him by the arm. AYL 2.07.199
and here upon his arm | the lioness had torn 4.03.146
i pray you, will you take him by the arm? 4.03.162
it is my arm. 5.02. 21 P
lend me an arm. AWW 1.02. 73
while i speak this) holds his wife by th' arm, WT 1.02.193
for the harlot king | is quite beyond mine arm, 2.03. 5
arm, arm, you heavens, against these perjur'd JN 3.01.107
arm, arm, you heavens, against these perjur'd 3.01.107
than arm thy constant and thy nobler parts 3.01.291
arm you against your other enemies, | i'll make 4.02.249
my arm shall give thee help to bear thee hence, 5.04. 58
might | the better arm you to the sudden time 5.06. 26
will i make good against thee, arm to arm, R2 1.01. 76
will i make good against thee, arm to arm, 1.01. 76
this arm shall do it, or this life be spent. 1.01.108
never lift | an angry arm against his minister. 1.02. 41
and by the grace of god, and this mine arm, | to 1.03. 22
o, then how quickly should this arm of mine, 2.03.103
off, my gracious lord, | than this weak arm. 3.02. 65
arm, arm, my name! 3.02. 86
arm, arm, my name! 3.02. 86
i heard you say, "is not my arm of length, 4.01. 11
is danger | that we may arm us to encounter it. 5.03. 48
or an arm? 1H4 5.01.132 P
arm, gentlemen, to arms! 5.02. 41
i will embrace him with a soldier's arm | that 5.02. 73
arm, arm with speed! 5.02. 75
arm, arm with speed! 5.02. 75
and knit our powers to the arm of peace. 2H4 4.01.175
and hangs resolv'd correction in the arm | that 4.01.211
man, to arm, and then the vital commoners and 4.03.109 P
the world's whole strength | into one giant arm, 4.05. 45
and do arm myself | to welcome the condition of 5.02. 10
and with your puissant arm renew their feats. H5 1.02.116
we must not only arm t' invade the french, | but 1.02.136
it is most meet we arm us 'gainst the foe; 2.04. 15
and, princes, look you strongly arm to meet him. 2.04. 49
'tis midnight, i'll go arm myself. 3.07. 89 P
now is it time to arm. 3.07.155 P
god's arm strike with us! 4.03. 5
over suffolk's neck | he threw his wounded arm, 4.06. 25
o god, thy arm was here; 4.08.106
and not to us, but to thy arm alone, | ascribe 4.08.107
arm, arm! the enemy doth make assault! 1H6 2.01. 38
arm, arm! the enemy doth make assault! 2.01. 38
when arm in arm they both came swiftly running, 2.02. 29
when arm in arm they both came swiftly running, 2.02. 29
first, lean thine aged back against mine arm, 2.05. 43
in sign whereof, this arm, that hath reclaim'd 3.04. 5
whose overweening arm i have pluck'd back, | by 2H6 3.01.159
hast, | and if mine arm be heaved in the air, 4.10. 51
us | that thus he marcheth with thee arm in arm? 5.01. 57
us | that thus he marcheth with thee arm in arm? 5.01. 57
call buckingham, and bid him arm himself. 5.01.192
ay, to such mercy as his ruthless arm | with 3H6 1.04. 31
but only slaught'red by the ireful arm | of 2.01. 57
suppose this arm is for the duke of york, | and 2.04. 2
to shrink mine arm up like a wither'd shrub, 3.02.156
while life upholds this arm, | this arm upholds 3.03.106
arm, | this arm upholds the house of lancaster. 3.03.107
well, i will arm me, being thus forewarn'd. 4.01.113
which his hell-govern'd arm hath butchered! R3 1.02. 67
take not the quarrel from his pow'rful arm; 1.04.217
blest his three sons with his victorious arm, 1.04.236
behold, mine arm | is like a blasted sapling, 3.04. 68
and when this arm of mine hath chastised | the 4.04.331
of night come to my tent | and help to arm me. 5.03. 78
arm, fight, and conquer for fair england's sake! 5.03.158
why, then 'tis time to arm and give direction. 5.03.236
arm, arm, my lord, the foe vaunts in the field. 5.03.288
arm, arm, my lord, the foe vaunts in the field. 5.03.288
with surety stronger than achilles' arm, | 'fore TRO 1.03.220
i come to lose my arm, or win my sleeve. 5.03. 96
than the cur achilles, and will not arm to-day; 5.04. 15 P
and bid the snail-pac'd ajax arm for shame. 5.05. 18
the counsellor heart, the arm our soldier, | our COR 1.01.116
i' th' shoulder and i' th' left arm. 2.01.147 P
that dark spirit, in 's nervy arm doth lie, 2.01.160
arm yourself | to answer mildly; 3.02.138
target from thy brawn, | or lose mine arm for't. 4.05.121
what an arm he has! 4.05.152 P
aaron, arm thy heart, and fit thy thoughts, | to TIT 2.01. 12
and arm the minds of infants to exclaims. 4.01. 86
arm, my lords! 4.04. 62
foot, | nor arm nor face, /nor /any /other /part ROM 2.02. 41
i was hurt under your arm. 3.01.103 P
his /agile arm beats down their fatal points, 3.01.166
underneath whose arm | an envious thrust from 3.01.167
since arm from arm that voice doth us affray, 3.05. 33
since arm from arm that voice doth us affray, 3.05. 33
though his right arm might purchase his own time TIM 3.05. 76
not | one friend to take his fortune by the arm, 4.02. 7
whom fortune's tender arm | with favor never 4.03.250
for he can do no more than caesar's arm | when JC 2.01.182
have i in conquest stretch'd mine arm so far, 2.02. 66
point against point, rebellious arm 'gainst arm, MAC 1.02. 56
point against point, rebellious arm 'gainst arm, 1.02. 56
arm, arm, and out! 5.05. 45
arm, arm, and out! 5.05. 45
then goes he to the length of all his arm, | and HAM 2.01. 85
at last, a little shaking of mine arm, | and 2.01. 89
rebellious to his arm, lies where it falls, 2.02.470
arm you, i pray you, to this speedy viage, | for 3.03. 24
home | my unprovided body, latch'd mine arm; LR 2.01. 52
give me your arm. 3.07. 98
give me thy arm; | poor tom shall lead thee. 4.01. 78
give me your arm. 4.06. 64
arm it in rags, a pigmy's straw does pierce it. 4.06.167
let go his arm. 4.06.234
a noble heart, | thy arm may do thee justice; 5.03.128
this sword, this arm, and my best spirits are 5.03.140
or do but lift this arm, the best of you | shall OTH 2.03.208
from his very arm | puff'd his own brother — 3.04.136
that, with this little arm and this good sword, 5.02.262
of this earth, the arm | and burgonet of men. ANT 1.05. 23
my arm is sore, best play with mardian. 2.05. 4
the arm of mine own body, and the heart | where 5.01. 45
the ocean, his rear'd arm | crested the world, 5.02. 82
the like is on her arm. 5.02.350
arm me, audacity, from head to foot, | or, like CYM 1.06. 19
a jewel that too casually | hath left mine arm. 2.03.142
last night 'twas on mine arm; 2.03.146
she stripp'd it from her arm. 2.04.101
by jupiter, i had it from her arm. 2.04.121
have not i | an arm as big as thine? 4.02. 77
come, arm him. 4.02.400
whose arm seems far too short to hit me here. PER 1.02. 8
sea, | this jewel holds his building on my arm. 2.01.156
leonine, take her by the arm, walk with her. 4.01. 29
sir, lend me your arm. 5.01.263
that with thy arm, as strong | as it is white, TNK 1.01. 79
have said enough to shake me from the arm | of 1.03. 92
will't please you arm, sir? 3.06. 35
that's mine then. | i'll arm you first. 3.06. 53
his body, | and guides his arm to brave things. 4.02.102
one eye | against another, arm oppress'd by arm, 5.01. 22
one eye | against another, arm oppress'd by arm, 5.01. 22
arm your prize, | i know you will not loose her. 5.03.135
over one arm the lusty courser's rein, | under VEN 31
bed, | throwing his mantle rudely o'er his arm, LUC 170
ARMA 4 FR 0.0004 REL FR 0 V 4 P
de arma, madame. H5 3.04. 22 P
hand, de fingre, de nailes, d' arma, de bilbow. 3.04. 29 P
de nailes, de arma, de ilbow. 3.04. 47 P
de fingre, de nailes, d' arma, d' elbow, de nick 3.04. 58 P
ARMADO *(also adramadio)*
ARMADO 12 FR 0.0013 REL FR 5 V 7 P
this child of fancy, that armado hight, | for LLL 1.01.170
armado is a most illustrious wight, | a man of 1.01.177
a letter from the magnificent armado. 1.01.191 P
heat of duty, don adriano de armado." 1.01.278 P
and don armado shall be your keeper. 1.01.304 P
design of industry, don adriano de armado. 4.01. 87 P
this armado is a spaniard that keeps here in 4.01. 98
armado /a' /th' /one side — o, a most dainty 4.01.144
me by costard, and sent me from don armado. 4.02. 92 P
nominated, or called, don adriano de armado. 5.01. 8 P
it pleaseth his greatness to impart to armado, a 5.01.107 P
a whole armado of convicted sail | is scattered JN 3.04. 2
ARMADOES 1 FR 0.0001 REL FR 0 V 1 P
spain, who sent whole armadoes of carrects to be ERR 3.02.137 P
ARMADO'S 2 FR 0.0002 REL FR 1 V 1 P
heart, | that put armado's page out of his part! LLL 5.02.336
armado's page, hercules; 5.02.536 P
ARMAGNAC *(see arminack)*
/ARM'D* 1 FR 0.0001 REL FR 1 V 0 P
/a /prologue /arm'd, /but /not /in /confidence TRO pr 23
ARM'D* 42 FR 0.0047 REL FR 35 V 7 P
in her forehead, arm'd and reverted, making war ERR 3.02.123 P
if you are arm'd to do, as sworn to do, LLL 1.01. 22
the cold moon and the earth, | cupid all arm'd. MND 2.01.157
patience to his fury, and am arm'd | to suffer, MV 4.01. 11
i am arm'd and well prepar'd. 4.01.264
but he comes arm'd in his fortune, and prevents AYL 4.01. 61 P
and by my father's love and leave am arm'd SHR 1.01. 5
but be thou arm'd for some unhappy words. 2.01.139
though thy little finger be arm'd in a thimble. 4.03.148 P
he hath arm'd our answer, | and florence is AWW 1.02. 11
but she is arm'd for him and keeps her guard 3.05. 73
my lord aumerle, is harry herford arm'd? R2 1.03. 1
glad am i that your highness is so arm'd | to 3.02.104
white-beards have arm'd their thin and hairless 3.02.112
on, | his cushes on his thighs, gallantly arm'd, 1H4 4.01.105
thrice is he arm'd that hath his quarrel just; 2H6 3.02.233
arm'd as we are, let's stay within this house. 3H6 1.01. 38
yet am i arm'd against the worst can happen; 4.01.128
was hector arm'd and gone ere ye came to ilium? TRO 1.02. 48 P
i would fain have arm'd to-day, but my nell 3.01.136 P
but when i meet you arm'd, as black defiance 4.01. 13
here, sister, arm'd, and bloody in intent. 5.03. 8
and foams at mouth, and he is arm'd and at it, 5.05. 36
make motion through my lips, and my arm'd knees, COR 3.02.118
the self-same gods that arm'd the queen of troy TIT 1.01.136
and, in strong proof of chastity well arm'd, ROM 1.01.210
for i come hither arm'd against myself. 5.03. 65
but i am arm'd, | and dangers are to me JC 1.03.114
for i am arm'd so strong in honesty | that they 4.03. 67
no sooner justice had, with valor arm'd, MAC 1.02. 29
the arm'd rhinoceros, or th' hyrcan tiger, 3.04.100
arm'd, say you? HAM 1.02.226
arm'd, my lord. 1.02.227
if you do stir abroad, go arm'd. LR 1.02.170 P
arm'd, brother? 1.02.171 P
until some half hour past, when i was arm'd. 5.03.194
with the arm'd rest, courtiers of beauteous ANT 2.06. 17
chain mine arm'd neck, leap thou, attire and all 4.08. 14
loaden with kisses, arm'd with thousand cupids, TNK 2.02. 31
when we are arm'd | and both upon our guards, 3.06. 28
arm'd long and round, and on his thigh a sword 4.02. 85
and arm'd his long-hid wits advisedly, | to LUC 1816
ARME 2 FR 0.0002 REL FR 0 V 2 P
signior arme — arme — commends you. LLL 1.01.187 P
signior arme — arme — commends you. 1.01.187 P
/ARMED 1 FR 0.0001 REL FR 1 V 0 P
/their /armed /staves /in /charge, /their 2H4 4.01.118
ARMED 28 FR 0.0031 REL FR 28 V 0 P
and brought with armed men back to messina. ADO 5.04.126
armed in arguments — you'll be surpris'd. LLL 5.02. 84
set armed discord 'twixt these perjur'd kings! JN 3.01.111
crow, | thinking this voice an armed englishman; 5.02.145
their thimbles into armed gauntlets change, 5.02.156
and these stones | prove armed soldiers, ere her R2 3.02. 25
nor bruise her flow'rets with the armed hoofs 1H4 1.01. 8
turns head against the lion's armed jaws, | and, 3.02.102
and bending forward strook his armed heels 2H4 1.01. 44
till that the nobles and the armed commons 2.03. 51
while that the armed hand doth fight abroad, H5 1.02.178
others, like soldiers, armed in their stings, 1.02.193
yerk out their armed heels at their dead masters 4.07. 80
they did amongst the troops of armed men | leap 1H6 2.02. 24
york, | or i will fill the house with armed men, 3H6 1.01.167
what means this armed guard | that waits upon R3 1.01. 42
armed in proof and led by shallow richmond. 5.03.219
with my armed fist | i'll /pash him o'er the TRO 2.03.202
and being once subdu'd in armed tail, | sweet 5.10. 43
need, | you may be armed and appointed well: TIT 4.02. 16
figure | comes armed through our watch, so like HAM 1.01.110
armed at point exactly, cap-a-pe, | appears 1.02.200
thou art armed, gloucester, let the trumpet LR 5.03. 90
is an armed knight that's conquered by a lady; PER 2.02. 26
"his brawny sides, with hairy bristles armed, VEN 625
for know, my heart stands armed in mine ear, 779
stood his spear, | grip'd in an armed hand; LUC 1425
to me came tarquin armed to beguild | with 1544
ARMENIA 2 FR 0.0002 REL FR 2 V 0 P
parthia, and armenia | he gave to alexander; ANT 3.06. 14
in his armenia | and other of his conquer'd 3.06. 35
ARM-GAUNT 1 FR 0.0001 REL FR 1 V 0 P
and soberly did mount an arm-gaunt steed, | who ANT 1.05. 48
ARMIES 14 FR 0.0015 REL FR 13 V 1 P
the onset and retire | of both your armies, JN 2.01.327
where these two christian armies might combine 5.02. 37
his clouds on our behalf | armies of pestilence, R2 3.03. 87
in both your armies there is many a soul | shall 1H4 5.01. 83
borne | betwixt our armies true intelligence. 5.05. 10
at home, that our armies join not in a hot day! 2H4 1.02.208 P
meet his grace just distance 'tween our armies. 4.01.224
ours, and here between the armies | let's drink 4.02. 62
and, stickler-like, the armies separates. TRO 5.08. 18
how far off lie these armies? COR 1.04. 8
before the eyes of both our armies here | (which JC 4.02. 43
were we before our armies, and to fight, | i ANT 2.02. 26
like lightning, | to blast whole armies, more! TNK 2.02. 25
to those two armies that would let him go, LUC 76
ARMIGERO 2 FR 0.0002 REL FR 0 V 2 P
who writes himself armigero, in any bill, WIV 1.01. 10 P
warrant, quittance, or obligation, armigero. 1.01. 11 P
ARMINACK 3 FR 0.0003 REL FR 3 V 0 P
pope, | the emperor, and the earl of arminack? 1H6 5.01. 2
the earl of arminack, near knit to charles, | a 5.01. 17
and so the earl of arminack may do, | because he 5.05. 44
ARMING 5 FR 0.0005 REL FR 4 V 1 P
from point, to the full arming of the verity. AWW 4.03. 62 P
patroclus, | arming to answer in a night alarm." TRO 1.03.171
hector, by this, is arming him in troy; 5.02.183
great achilles | is arming, weeping, cursing, 5.05. 31
arming myself with patience | to stay the JC 5.01.105
ARMIPOTENT 4 FR 0.0004 REL FR 3 V 1 P
"the armipotent mars, of lances the almighty, LLL 5.02.644
"the armipotent mars, of lances the almighty, 5.02.651
manifold linguist and the armipotent soldier. AWW 4.03.236 P
with hand armipotent from forth blue clouds TNK 5.01. 54
ARMOR 47 FR 0.0053 REL FR 38 V 9 P
penalties | which have, like unscour'd armor, MM 1.02.167
have walk'd ten mile afoot to see a good armor, ADO 2.03. 16 P
sake | with burden of our armor here we sweat. JN 2.01. 92
and france, whose armor conscience buckled on, 2.01.564
add proof unto mine armor with thy prayers, R2 1.03. 73
carts, | and bring away the armor that is there. 2.02.107
our armor all as strong, our cause the best; 2H4 4.01.154
sit | like a rich armor worn in heat of day, 4.05. 30
tut, i have the best armor of the world. H5 3.07. 1 P
you have an excellent armor; 3.07. 3 P
high constable, you talk of horse and armor? 3.07. 8 P
the armor that i saw in your tent to-night, are 3.07. 69 P
for if their heads had any intellectual armor, 3.07.138 P
the sun doth gild our armor, up, my lords! 4.02. 1
vauting into my saddle with my armor on my back, 5.02.137 P
and would have armor here out of the tower, | to 1H6 1.03. 67
a woman clad in armor chaseth them. 1.05. 3
the french | she carry armor as she hath begun. 2.01. 24
as we were scouring my lord of york's armor. 2H6 1.03.192 P
horse, armor, any thing i have | is his to use, 5.01. 52
head, | for york in justice puts his armor on. 3H6 2.02.130
laid aside, | and i am ready to put armor on. 3.03.230
are done, | and i am ready to put armor on." 4.01.105
than all the complete armor that thou wear'st! R3 4.04.190
and all my armor laid into my tent? 5.03. 51
your friends are up and buckle on their armor. 5.03.211
i like thy armor well; TRO 5.06. 28
thy goodly armor thus hath cost thy life. 5.08. 2
for the whole state, i would put mine armor on, COR 3.02. 34
i'll give thee armor to keep off that word: ROM 3.03. 54
put armor on thine ears and on thine eyes, TIM 4.03.124
give me my armor. MAC 5.03. 33
give me mine armor. 5.03. 36
come, put mine armor on; 5.03. 48
such was the very armor he had on | when he the HAM 1.01. 60
fall | on mars's armor forg'd for proof eterne 2.02.490
with all the strength and armor of the mind | to 3.03. 12
eros, mine armor, eros! ANT 4.04. 1
eros, come, mine armor, eros! 4.04. 2
i'll give thee, friend, | an armor all of gold; 4.08. 27
come at last, and 'tis turn'd to a rusty armor. PER 2.01.119 P
an armor, friends? 2.01.120
and on set purpose let his armor rust | until 2.02. 54
shall be at your choice | both sword and armor. TNK 3.01. 89
a sword and armor. 3.03. 50
me, cousin, | where got'st thou this good armor? 3.06. 54
his naked armor of still-slaughtered lust, | and LUC 188
ARMORER 4 FR 0.0004 REL FR 4 V 0 P
the armorer and his man, to enter the lists, 2H6 2.03. 50
the servant of this armorer, my lords. 2.03. 58

he chid andromache and strook his armorer, | and TRO 1.02. 6
thou art | the armorer of my heart. ANT 4.04. 7
ARMORERS 2 FR 0.0002 REL FR 2 V 0 P
now thrive the armorers, and honor's thought H5 2.pr. 3
and from the tents | the armorers, accomplishing 4.pr. 12
ARMOR'S 1 FR 0.0001 REL FR 1 V 0 P
methinks this armor's very like that, arcite, TNK 3.06. 70
ARMORS 5 FR 0.0005 REL FR 5 V 0 P
their armors, that march'd hence so JN 2.01.315
have in our armors watch'd the winter's night, 3H6 5.07. 17
and when we have our armors buckled on, | the TRO 5.03. 46
even in your armors, as you are address'd, PER 2.03. 94
with him bring | two swords and two good armors. TNK 3.06. 3
ARMORY 3 FR 0.0003 REL FR 2 V 1 P
an old rusty sword ta'en out of the town armory, SHR 3.02. 47 P
come go with me into mine armory; TIT 4.01.113
the goodliest weapons of his armory | to gratify 4.02. 11
ARM'S 3 FR 0.0003 REL FR 2 V 1 P
hold death a while at the arm's end. AYL 2.06. 10 P
fame, | despairing of his own arm's fortitude, 1H6 2.01. 17
and, if one arm's embracement will content thee, TIT 5.02. 68
ARMS' 1 FR 0.0001 REL FR 1 V 0 P
i'll woo you like a soldier, at arms' end, | and TGV 5.04. 57
/ARMS* 7 FR 0.0008 REL FR 6 V 1 P
/and /publish /the /occasion /of /our /arms. 2H4 1.03. 86
/weigh'd | /what /wrongs /our /arms /may /do, 4.01. 68
/our /tenfold /grief | /with /folded /arms. TIT 3.02. 7
/could /he /dig /without /arms? HAM 5.01. 37 P
/arms, /arms, /sword, /fire! LR 3.06. 55
/arms, /arms, /sword, /fire! 3.06. 55
/with /his /strong /arms | /he /fastened /on /my 5.03.212
ARMS* 269 FR 0.0304 REL FR 250 V 19 P
isle, and sitting, | his arms in this sad knot. TMP 1.02.224
himself with his good arms in lusty stroke | to 2.01.120
and his fins like arms! 2.02. 34 P
like sir proteus, to wreathe your arms, like a TGV 2.01. 19 P
give me my gown, or else keep it in your arms. WIV 3.01. 35 P
pinch them, arms, legs, backs, shoulders, sides, 5.05. 54
darkness as a bride, | and hug it in mine arms. MM 3.01. 84
when i'll depose i had him in mine arms | with 5.01.198
well fitted in arts, glorious in arms; LLL 2.01. 45
with your arms cross'd on your thin/–bellied 3.01. 18 P
regent of love–rhymes, lord of folded arms, 3.01.181
nor never lay his wreathed arms athwart | his 4.03.133
and lay my arms before the legs of this sweet 5.02.555
your head, achilles — here comes hector in arms. 5.02.633 P
i bepray you let me borrow my arms again. 5.02.696 P
sleep thou, and i will wind thee in my arms. MND 4.01. 40
mewling and puking in the nurse's arms. AYL 2.07.144
so may you lose your arms. SHR 2.01.221
and if no gentleman, why then no arms. 2.01.223
dost thou garter up thy arms a' this fashion? AWW 2.03.250 P
home, | spending his manly marrow in her arms, 2.03.281
and arms her with the boldness of a wife | to WT 1.02.184
not to be buried, | but quick and in mine arms. 4.04.132
leontes opening his free arms and weeping | his 4.04.548
it should take joy | to see her in your arms. 5.01. 81
my arms such eel–skins stuff'd, my face so thin JN 1.01.141
will i not think of home, but follow arms. 2.01. 31
your just demands, | hath put himself in arms. 2.01. 57
wilt thou resign them and lay down thy arms? 2.01.154
and then our arms, like to a muzzled bear, 2.01.249
amen, amen! mount, chevaliers! to arms! 2.01.287
before we will lay down our just–borne arms 2.01.345
put thee down, 'gainst whom these arms we bear, 2.01.346
you came in arms to spill mine enemies' blood, 3.01.102
but now in arms you strengthen it with yours. 3.01.103
therefore to arms! 3.01.255
father, to arms! 3.01.300
knee i beg, go not to arms | against mine uncle. 3.01.308
no more than he that threats. to arms let's hie! 3.01.347
if but a dozen french | were there in arms, they 3.04.174
or crest unto the crest, | of murther's arms. 4.03. 47
go, bear him in thine arms. 4.03.139
go i to make the french lay down their arms. 5.01. 24
parley, and base truce | to arms invasive? 5.01. 69
let us, my liege, to arms. 5.01. 73
that neptune's arms, who clippeth thee about, 5.02. 34
he flatly says he'll not lay down his arms. 5.02.126
to whip this dwarfish war, this pigmy arms, 5.02.135
know the gallant monarch is in arms, | and like 5.02.148
come the three corners of the world in arms, 5.07.116
the cause of his arrival here in arms; R2 1.03. 8
and why thou comest thus knightly clad in arms, 1.03. 12
marshal, ask yonder knight in arms, | both who 1.03. 26
i, who ready here do stand in arms | to prove by 1.03. 36
we will descend and fold him in our arms. 1.03. 54
bray, | and grating shock of wrathful iron arms, 1.03.136
and with uplifted arms is safe arriv'd | at 2.02. 50
fright our native peace with self–borne arms. 2.03. 80
with war | and ostentation of despised arms? 2.03. 95
time, | in braving arms against thy sovereign. 2.03.112
and royalties | pluck'd from my arms perforce — 2.03.121
but in this kind to come, in braving arms, | be 2.03.143
well, well, i see the issue of these arms. 2.03.152
king | shall falter under foul rebellion's arms. 3.02. 26
in stiff unwieldy arms against thy crown; 3.02.115
and all your southern gentlemen in arms | upon 3.02.202
even at his feet to lay my arms and power, 3.03. 39
should so with civil and uncivil arms | be 3.03.102
his glittering arms he will commend to rust, 3.03.116
whose arms were moulded in their mother's womb, 1H4 1.01. 23
longer than he sees reason, i'll forswear arms. 1.02.186 P
to bear our fortunes in our own strong arms, 1.03.298
letters to meet me in arms by the ninth of the 2.03. 27 P
on | to bloody battles and to bruising arms. 3.02.105
whose hot incursions and great name in arms, 3.02.108
all furnish'd, all in arms; 4.01. 97
dear men | of estimation and command in arms. 4.04. 32
are confident against the world in arms. 5.01.117
with haughty arms this hateful name in us. 5.02. 40
arm, gentlemen, to arms! 5.02. 41
dare | to gentle exercise and proof of arms. 5.02. 54
the arms are fair | when the intent of bearing 5.02. 87
did such deeds in arms as i have done this day. 5.03. 45 P
on, | and rebels' arms triumph in massacres! 5.04. 14
valiant shirley, stafford, blunt are in my arms. 5.04. 41
thy name in arms were now as great as mine! 5.04. 70
scroop, | who, as we hear, are busily in arms. 5.05. 38
breaks like a fire | out of his keeper's arms, 2H4 1.01.143
i well allow the occasion of our arms, | but 1.03. 5
now) | hath put us in these ill–beseeming arms, 4.01. 84
our men more perfect in the use of arms, | our 4.01.153
most shallowly did you these arms commence, 4.02.118
yoke–fellows in arms, | let us to france, like H5 2.03. 54
make, when all those legs, and arms, and heads, 4.01.136 P
'tis expressly against the law of arms. 4.07. 2 P
his arms spread wider than a dragon's wings; 1H6 1.01. 11
in stead of gold, we'll offer up our arms, 1.01. 46
since arms avail not now that henry's dead. 1.01. 47
cropp'd are the flower–de–luces in your arms, 1.01. 80
the french exclaim'd, the devil was in arms; 1.01.125
some odd gimmors or device | their arms are set, 1.02. 42
of men assembled here in arms this day against 1.03. 74 P
but with a baser man of arms by far | once in 1.04. 30
and from my shoulders crack my arms asunder, 1.05. 11
of all exploits since first i follow'd arms, 2.01. 43
and i will chain these legs and arms of thine, 2.03. 39
are his substance, sinews, arms, and strength, 2.03. 63
and pithless arms, like to a withered vine 2.05. 11
reign, | before whose glory i was great in arms, 2.05. 24
direct mine arms i may embrace his neck, | and 2.05. 37
and dare not take up arms like gentlemen. 3.02. 70
and the rest will take thee in their arms. 3.03. 77
thou knowest the law of arms is such | that 3.04. 38
i crave the benefit of law of arms. 4.01.100
servant in arms to harry king of england, | and 4.02. 4
come, come, and lay him in his father's arms, 4.07. 29
now my old arms are young john talbot's grave. 4.07. 32
see where he lies inhearsed in the arms | of the 4.07. 45
created, for his rare success in arms, | great 4.07. 62
those provinces these arms of mine did conquer, 2H6 1.01.120
and in my standard bear the arms of york, | to 1.01.256
th' uncivil kerns of ireland are in arms, | and 3.01.310
will make him say i mov'd him to those arms. 3.01.378
broke be my sword, my arms torn and defac'd, 4.01. 42
vain, | as hating thee, /are rising up in arms; 4.01. 93
the commons here in kent are up in arms, | and 4.01.100
have given out these arms till you had recover'd 4.08. 26 P
his arms are only to remove from thee | the duke 4.09. 29
and now is york in arms to second him. 4.09. 35
and ask him what's the reason of these arms. 4.09. 37
to know the reason of these arms in peace; 5.01. 18
but if thy arms be to no other end, | the king 5.01. 39
and so to arms, victorious father, | to quell 5.01.211
warwick is hoarse with calling thee to arms. 5.02. 7
good brother, as thou lov'st and honorest arms, 3H6 1.01.116
therefore to arms! 1.02. 28
that raught at mountains with outstretched arms, 1.04. 68
foes | tell our devotion with revengeful arms? 2.01.164
warwick, | let me embrace thee in my weary arms. 2.03. 45
these arms of mine shall be thy winding–sheet; 2.05.114
welcome, sir john! but why come you in arms? 4.07. 42
away with scrupulous wit! now arms must rule. 4.07. 61
whose arms gave shelter to the princely eagle, 5.02. 12
and make him, naked, foil a man at arms. 5.04. 42
satisfaction canst thou make | for bearing arms, 5.05. 15
our bruised arms hung up for monuments, | our R3 1.01. 6
and hugg'd me in his arms, and swore with sobs 1.04.245
but death hath snatch'd my husband from my arms, 2.02. 57
and from her jealous arms pluck him perforce. 3.01. 36
another | within their alablaster innocent arms. 4.03. 11
i in my dangerous affairs | of hostile arms! 4.04.399
with many moe confederates, are in arms. 4.04.502
in kent, my liege, the guilfords are in arms, 4.04.503
'tis said, my liege, in yorkshire are in arms. 4.04.519
march on, march on, since we are up in arms, 4.04.528
fellows in arms, and my most loving friends, 5.02. 1
and aid thee in this doubtful shock of arms; 5.03. 93
that he was never trained up in arms. 5.03.272
our strong arms be our conscience, swords our 5.03.311
god and your arms be prais'd, victorious friends 5.05. 1
heralds challeng'd | the noble spirits to arms, H8 1.01. 35
and once more in mine arms i bid him welcome, 2.02. 98
when the brown wench | lay kissing in your arms, 3.02.296
our king has all the indies in his arms, | and 4.01. 45
good arms, strong joints, true swords, and, TRO 1.03.238
and her worth | in other arms than hers — to 1.03.272
truer, | than ever greek did couple in his arms, 1.03.276
to–morrow morning call some knight to arms 2.01.124
for what, alas, can these my single arms? 2.02.135
but he that disciplin'd thine arms to fight, 2.03.244
and with his arms outstretch'd as he would fly 3.03.167
he wears his tongue in 's arms. 3.03.270 P
by him that thunders, thou hast lusty arms! 4.05.136
worthy all arms! 4.05.163
i would my arms could match thee in contention, 4.05.205
be happy that my arms are out of use; 5.06. 16
about, | in fellest manner execute your arms. 5.07. 6
they shall know we have strong arms too. COR 1.01. 61 P
and | your knees to them (not arms) must help. 1.01. 74
the news is, sir, the volsces are in arms. 1.01.224
have lately told us, | the volsces are in arms. 1.01.228
me clip ye | in arms as sound as when i woo'd, 1.06. 30
one seven years | from these old arms and legs, 4.01. 56
let me twine | mine arms about that body, where 4.05.107
the swords | in italy, and her confederate arms, 5.03.208
defend the justice of my cause with arms; TIT 1.01. 2
hath yok'd a nation strong, train'd up in arms. 1.01. 30
and chastised with arms | our enemies' pride; 1.01. 32
to rome, | renowned titus, flourishing in arms. 1.01. 38
knighted in field, slain manfully in arms, | in 1.01.196
we may, each wreathed in the other's arms | (our 2.03. 25
why lifts she up her arms in sequence thus? 4.01. 37
what dost thou wrap and fumble in thy arms? 4.02. 58
there to dispose this treasure in mine arms, 4.02.173
me, | and, for he understands you are in arms, 5.01.158
and op'd their arms to embrace me as a friend. 5.03.108
leap to these arms untalk'd of and unseen! ROM 3.02. 7
arms, take your last embrace! 5.03.113
power | have wander'd with our travers'd arms, TIM 5.04. 7
your infants in your arms, and there have sate JC 1.01. 40
musing and sighing, with your arms across; 2.01.240
our arms in strength of malice, and our hearts 3.01.174
ingratitude, more strong than traitors' arms, 3.02.185
with furbish'd arms and new supplies of men, MAC 1.02. 32
whose arms | are hir'd to bear their staves; 5.07. 17
my father's spirit — in arms! HAM 1.02.254
with arms encumb'red thus, or this headshake, 1.05.174
to give th' assay of arms against your majesty. 2.02. 71
"the rugged pyrrhus, he whose sable arms, 2.02.452
or to take arms against a sea of troubles, | and 3.01. 58
to his good friends thus wide i'll ope my arms, 4.05.146
'a was the first that ever bore arms. 5.01. 33 P
till i have caught her once more in mine arms. 5.01.250
weapons? arms? what's the matter here? LR 2.02. 47 P
strike in their numb'd and mortified arms | pins 2.03. 15
good friend, i prithee take him in thy arms; 3.06. 88
bind fast his corky arms. 3.07. 29
no blown ambition doth our arms incite, | but 4.04. 27
for since these arms of mine had seven years' OTH 1.03. 83
make love's quick pants in desdemona's arms, 2.01. 80
to lend me arms and aid when i requir'd them, ANT 2.02. 88
ere we put ourselves in arms, dispatch we | the 2.02.165
and see | thy master thus with pleach'd arms, 4.14. 73
noses, but to owe such straight arms, none. CYM 3.01. 38 P
for | their liberties are now in arms, a 3.01. 74
and brings the dire occasion in his arms | of 4.02.196
his arms thus leagu'd. 4.02.213
whose rags sham'd gilded arms, whose naked 5.05. 4
let his arms alone, | they were not born for 5.05.305
are arms to princes and bring joys to subjects. PER 1.02. 74
lop that doubt, he'll fill this land with arms, 1.02. 90
i'll show the virtue i have borne in arms. 2.01.145
deeds, | as in a title–page, your worth in arms, 2.03. 4
pericles, | my education been in arts and arms; 2.03. 82
since they love men in arms as well as beds. 2.03. 98
take in your arms this piece | of your dead 3.01. 17
i threw her overboard with these very arms. 5.03. 19
be buried | a second time within these arms. 5.03. 44
when her arms, | able to lock jove from a synod, TNK 1.01.175
our arms again, and feel our fiery horses | like 2.02. 19
teach 'em | boldly to gaze against bright arms, 2.02. 35
and pitch between her arms to anger thee. 2.02.217
and fling my wanton arms | in at her window! 2.02.237
he shall see thebes again and call to arms | the 2.02.248
i am well and lusty, choose your arms. 3.06. 45
without my leave and officers of arms? 3.06.135
his arms are brawny, | lin'd with strong sinews; 4.02.126
never fainting | under the weight of arms; 4.02.130
arms in assurance | my body to this business. 5.01.134
if i told you all you were in arms 'gainst god. STM II.C 95
in a net, | so fast'ned in her arms adonis lies; VEN 68
making my arms his field, his tent my bed. 108
sometime her arms infold him like a band: 225
she would, he will not in her arms be bound; 226
and from her twining arms doth urge releasing. 256
her arms do lend his neck a sweet embrace; 539
and on his neck her yoking arms she throws. 592
of those fair arms which bound him to her breast 812
honor and beauty, in the owner's arms, | are LUC 27
with bruised arms and wreaths of victory. 110
"o shame to knighthood and to shining arms! 197
and in thy dead arms do i mean to place him, 517
to cross their arms and hang their heads with 793
with sad set eyes, and wretched arms across, 1662
to chase injustice with revengeful arms: 1693
by our strong arms from forth her fair streets 1834
me," | and then she clipt adonis in her arms; PP 11. 6
thus art with arms contending was victor of the 15.13
love's arms are peace, 'gainst rule, 'gainst LC 271
ARMY 74 FR 0.0083 REL FR 62 V 12 P
a treacherous army levied, one midnight | fated TMP 1.02.128
there was none such in the army of any sort. ADO 1.01. 33 P
man at a mark, with a whole army shooting at me. 2.01.247 P
and the huge army of the world's desires — LLL 1.01. 10
planted in his memory | an army of good words, MV 3.05. 67
be whipt through the army with this rhyme in 's AWW 4.03.233 P
the secrets of your army and made such 4.03.305 P
the army breaking, | my husband hies him home, 4.04. 11
i had not left a purse alive in the whole army. WT 4.04.618 P
i am with both, each army hath a hand, | and in JN 3.01.328
that such an army could be drawn in france, 4.02.118
for lo, within a ken our army lies: 2H4 4.01.149
and deliver to the army | this news of peace. 4.02. 69
my lord, | and let our army be discharged too. 4.02. 92
now, cousin, wherefore stands our army still? 4.02. 98
my lord, our army is dispers'd already: 4.02.102
the army is discharged all and gone. 4.03.127
for i am sure, when he shall see our army, H5 3.05. 58
my army but a weak and sickly guard; 3.06.155
night, | the hum of either army stilly sounds, 4.pr. 5
no note | how dread an army hath enrounded him; 4.pr. 36
he, by showing it, should dishearten his army. 4.01.112 P
an army have i muster'd in my thoughts, 1H6 1.01.101
all the whole army stood agaz'd on him. 1.01.126
the english army is grown weak and faint; 1.01.158
levied an army, weening to redeem | and have 2.05. 88
that dogg'd the mighty army of the dolphin? 4.03. 2
the english army, that divided was | into two 5.02. 11
so, now dismiss your army when ye please; 5.04.173
assail them with the army of the king. 2H6 4.02.175
his army is a ragged multitude | of hinds and 4.04. 32
there's an army gather'd together in smithfield. 4.06. 11 P
thither, | until his army be dismiss'd from him. 4.09. 40
the cause why i have brought this army hither 5.01. 35
cheer'd up the drooping army, and himself, 3H6 1.01. 6
our army is ready; 1.01.256
the army of the queen mean to besiege us. 1.02. 64
the army of the queen hath got the field. 1.04. 1
my lord, the army of great buckingham — R3 4.04.506
buckingham's army is dispers'd and scatter'd, 4.04.511
from troop to troop | went through the army, 5.03. 71
the sky doth frown and low'r upon our army. 5.03.283
an army cannot rule 'em. H8 5.03. 77
slept, | whilst emulation in the army crept: TRO 2.02.212
captain–general of the army, agamemnon, /et 3.03.278 P
before 's, for the remove | bring up your army; COR 1.02. 29
the volsces have an army forth; 1.03. 96 P
what work he makes | amongst your cloven army. 1.04. 21
what you have done, before our army hear me. 1.09. 27

have you an army ready, say you? 4.03. 42 P
a fearful army, led by caius martius 4.06. 75
more than the instant army we can make, | might 5.01. 37
the army marvell'd at it, and, in the last, 5.06. 41
hie to the goths and raise an army there, | and TIT 3.01.285
comes his army on? JC 4.02. 27
under which | our army lies, ready to give up 5.01. 88
witness this army of such mass and charge | led HAM 4.04. 47
the army of france is landed. LR 3.07. 2 P
i told him of the army that was landed; 4.02. 4
but, by your favor, | how near's the other army? 4.06.212
special cause is here, | her army is mov'd on. 4.06.216
the lists of the army will maintain upon edmund, 5.03.111 P
bear the king's son's body | before our army. ANT 3.01. 4
of antony | should have an army for an usher, 3.06. 44
distract your army, which doth most consist | of 3.07. 43
see it done, | and feast the army; 4.01. 15
'tis a brave army, | and full of purpose. 4.03. 11
our army shall | in solemn show attend this 5.02.363
o, i am known | of many in the army. CYM 4.04. 22
pray, sir, to th' army. 4.04. 31
of his wings destitute, the army broken, | and 5.03. 5
and his army full | of bread and sloth. TNK 1.01.158
our hearts | are in his army, in his tent. 1.03. 17
we will post | to athens /'fore our army. 1.04. 49

ARMY'S 1 FR 0.0001 REL FR 1 V 0 P
our army's in the field. COR 1.02. 17

AROINT 3 FR 0.0003 REL FR 3 V 0 P
"aroint thee, witch!" MAC 1.03. 6
plight, | and aroint thee, witch, aroint thee!" LR 3.04.124
plight, | and aroint thee, witch, aroint thee!" 3.04.124

A–ROLLING 1 FR 0.0001 REL FR 1 V 0 P
we first put this dangerous stone a–rolling, H8 5.02.139

AROSE 3 FR 0.0003 REL FR 3 V 0 P
for me, | and thereupon these errors are arose. ERR 5.01.389
such a noise arose | as the shrouds make at sea H8 4.01. 71
at supper | you suddenly arose and walk'd about, JC 2.01.239

AROUSE 2 FR 0.0002 REL FR 2 V 0 P
and now loud–howling wolves arouse the jades 2H6 4.01. 3
perceive you none that do arouse your pity, TNK 1.02. 30

A–ROW 1 FR 0.0001 REL FR 1 V 0 P
beaten the maids a–row, and bound the doctor, ERR 5.01.170

ARRAGON 3 FR 0.0003 REL FR 1 V 2 P
that don /pedro of arragon comes this night to ADO 1.01. 2 P
be consummate, and then go i toward arragon. 3.02. 2 P
the prince of arragon hath ta'en his oath, | and MV 2.09. 2

/ARRAIGN 2 FR 0.0002 REL FR 1 V 1 P
/be /done, /i /will /arraign /them /straight. LR 3.06. 20
/arraign /her /first, /'tis /goneril. 3.06. 46 P

ARRAIGN 4 FR 0.0004 REL FR 4 V 0 P
teach you how you shall arraign your conscience, MM 2.03. 21
that we may arraign | our most disloyal lady; WT 2.03.202
will nothing stick our person to arraign | in HAM 4.05. 93
who can arraign me for't? LR 5.03.160

ARRAIGNED 1 FR 0.0001 REL FR 0 V 1 P
art here accused and arraigned of high treason, WT 3.02. 14 P

ARRAIGNING 1 FR 0.0001 REL FR 1 V 0 P
i am) | arraigning his unkindness with my soul; OTH 3.04.152

ARRAIGNMENT 1 FR 0.0001 REL FR 1 V 0 P
what not, condemn'd, | no more arraignment. TNK 1.03. 66

ARRAND *(also arrant*, errand, errant*)*

ARRAND 2 FR 0.0002 REL FR 1 V 1 P
go on the slightest arrand now to the antipodes ADO 2.01.264 P
is apter than thy tongue to tell thy arrand. 2H4 1.01. 69

ARRANT* *(also arrand, errand, errant*)*

ARRANT* 20 FR 0.0022 REL FR 5 V 15 P
so that my arrant, due unto my tongue, | i thank ERR 2.01. 72
ha' ta'en a couple of as arrant knaves as any in ADO 3.05. 32 P
i leave an arrant knave with your worship, which 5.01.321 P
the prince and poins be not two arrant cowards, 1H4 2.02.100 P
he comes, and that arrant malmsey–nose knave, 2H4 2.01. 39 P
well, davy, for they are arrant knaves, and will 5.01. 32 P
that visor is an arrant knave, on my knowledge. 5.01. 41 P
no, thou arrant knave, i would to god that i 5.04. 1 P
why, this is an arrant counterfeit rascal, i H5 3.06. 61 P
'tis as arrant a piece of knavery, mark you now, 4.07. 2 P
his reputation is as arrant a villain and a jack 4.07.141 P
an arrant traitor as any's in the universal 4.08. 9 P
saving your majesty's manhood, what an arrant, 4.08. 34 P
luxurious drab, of a sleeveless arrant. TRO 5.04. 9 P
i'll say an arrant for you. COR 5.02. 60 P
the moon's an arrant thief, | and her pale fire TIM 4.03.437
in all denmark — | but he's an arrant knave. HAM 1.05.124
we are arrant knaves, believe none of us. 3.01.128 P
fortune, that arrant whore, | ne'er turns the LR 2.04. 52
of caesar's shall | bear us an arrant to him. ANT 3.13.104

ARRAS 12 FR 0.0013 REL FR 6 V 6 P
not see me, i will ensconce me behind the arras. WIV 3.03. 90 P
i whipt me behind the arras, and there heard it ADO 1.03. 61 P
in cypress chests my arras counterpoints, SHR 2.01.351
hot, and look thou stand | within the arras. JN 4.01. 2
go hide thee behind the arras, the rest walk up 1H4 2.04.500 P
fast asleep behind the arras, and snorting like 2.04.528 P
here behind the arras and had my pocket pick'd. 3.03. 98 P
be you and i behind an arras then, | mark the HAM 2.02.163
behind the arras i'll convey myself | to hear 3.03. 28
fit, | behind the arras hearing something stir, 4.01. 9
the arras, figures, | why, such and such; CYM 2.02. 26
cries, "o, that ever i did it behind the arras!" TNK 4.03. 55 P

/ARRAY 1 FR 0.0001 REL FR 1 V 0 P
i drink, i eat, /array myself, and live. MM 3.02. 25

ARRAY 13 FR 0.0014 REL FR 11 V 2 P
who gave me fresh array and entertainment, AYL 4.03.143
therefore put you in your best array, bid your 5.02. 72 P
we will have rings and things, and fine array; SHR 2.01.323
worse | for this poor furniture and mean array. 4.03.180
in which array, brave soldier, doth he lie, H5 4.06. 7
i'll chase hence, thou wolf in sheep's array. 1H6 1.03. 55
kerns | is marching hitherward in proud array, 2H6 4.09. 27
stand we in good array; 3H6 5.01. 62
back, | happiness courts thee in her best array, ROM 3.03.142
is, | and in her best array, bear her to church; 4.05. 81
spouse, set not thy sweet heart on proud array. LR 3.04. 83 P
when in his fresh array | he cheers the morn, VEN 483
/... these rebel pow'rs that thee array, | why SON 146. 2

ARRAY'D 1 FR 0.0001 REL FR 1 V 0 P
is he array'd? LR 4.07. 19

ARRAYED 1 FR 0.0001 REL FR 1 V 0 P
arrayed in flames like to the prince of fiends, H5 3.03. 16

ARREARAGES 1 FR 0.0001 REL FR 1 V 0 P
he'll grant the tribute, send th' arrearages, CYM 2.04. 13

/ARREST 1 FR 0.0001 REL FR 1 V 0 P
/you /that /here /are /under /our /arrest, R2 4.01.158

ARREST 27 FR 0.0030 REL FR 20 V 7 P
if i could speak so wisely under an arrest, i MM 1.02.131 P
i do arrest your words. 2.04.134
well, officer, arrest him at my suit. ERR 4.01. 69
arrest me, foolish fellow, if thou dar'st. 4.01. 75
here is thy fee, arrest him, officer. 4.01. 76
i do arrest you, sir: you hear the suit. 4.01. 79
thou hast suborn'd the goldsmith to arrest me. 4.04. 82
the which | he did arrest me with an officer. 5.01.230
we arrest your word. LLL 2.01.159
i arrest thee at the suit of count orsino. TN 3.04.326 P
pains, | of capital treason we arrest you here. R2 4.01.151
snare, we must arrest sir john falstaff. 2H4 2.01. 8 P
i arrest you at the suit of mistress quickly. 2.01. 45 P
for the which | i do arrest thee, traitor, of 4.02.107
open, | arrest them to the answer of the law, H5 2.02.143
i arrest thee of high treason, by the name of 2.02.145 P
i arrest thee of high treason, by the name of 2.02.147 P
i arrest thee of high treason, by the name of 2.02.149 P
i do arrest thee of high treason here. 2H6 3.01. 97
nor change my countenance for this arrest; 3.01. 99
i do arrest you in his highness' name, | and 3.01.136
i arrest thee, york, | of capital treason 5.01.106
i | arrest thee of high treason, in the name H8 1.01.201
is strict in his arrest — o, i could tell you HAM 5.02.337
edmund, i arrest thee | on capital treason, and, LR 5.03. 82
hath serv'd a dumb arrest upon his tongue, | who LUC 1780
when that fell arrest | without all bail shall SON 74. 1

ARRESTED *(also 'rested, etc.)*

ARRESTED 12 FR 0.0013 REL FR 8 V 4 P
his horses are arrested for it, master /brook. WIV 5.05.115 P
there's one yonder arrested and carried to MM 1.02. 60 P
i saw him arrested; 1.02. 68 P
tell her i am arrested in the street, | and that ERR 4.01.106
what, is he arrested? tell me at whose suit. 4.02. 43
i know not at whose suit he is arrested well; 4.02. 44
tell me, was he arrested on a band? 4.02. 49
say now, whose suit is he arrested at? 4.04.131
and you, sir, for this chain arrested me. 5.01.380
of eastcheap, and he is arrested at my suit. 2H4 2.01. 71 P
he is arrested, but will not obey. 2H6 5.01.136
earl northumberland | arrested him at york, and H8 4.02. 13

ARRESTS 2 FR 0.0002 REL FR 2 V 0 P
he arrests him on it, | and follows close the MM 1.04. 66
in hand, sends out arrests | on fortinbras, HAM 2.02. 67

/ARRIVAL 1 FR 0.0001 REL FR 1 V 0 P
merchant | is apprehended for /arrival here; ERR 1.02. 4

ARRIVAL 5 FR 0.0005 REL FR 5 V 0 P
son, | who will of thy arrival be full joyous. SHR 4.05. 70
but my arrival, and my wife's, in safety | here, WT 5.01.167
the cause of his arrival here in arms; R2 1.03. 8
point, | still ending at the arrival of an hour. 1H4 5.02. 84
peers, | hearing of your arrival in this realm, 1H6 3.04. 2

/ARRIVANCE 1 FR 0.0001 REL FR 1 V 0 P
every minute is expectancy | of more /arrivance. OTH 2.01. 42

ARRIV'D 24 FR 0.0027 REL FR 22 V 2 P
here in this island we arriv'd, and here | have TMP 1.02.171
when i arriv'd and heard thee, that made gape 1.02.292
of arts, | i am arriv'd for fruitful lombardy, SHR 1.01. 3
this gentleman is happily arriv'd, | my mind 1.02.212
lucentio's father is arriv'd in padua, | and how 4.04. 65
my lord, there's one arriv'd, | if you will see AWW 2.01. 79
a moderate pace i have since arriv'd but hither. TN 2.02. 4 P
being well arriv'd from delphos, are both landed WT 2.03.196
thy wish | our messenger chatillion is arriv'd! JN 2.01. 51
the tidings comes that they are all arriv'd. 4.02.115
hear'st thou the news abroad, who are arriv'd? 4.02.160
and with uplifted arms is safe arriv'd | at R2 2.02. 50
either past or not arriv'd to pith and puissance H5 3.pr. 21
where ne'er from france arriv'd more happy men. 4.08.126
we being thus arriv'd | from ravenspurgh haven 3H6 4.07. 7
hath rais'd in gallia have arriv'd our coast, 5.03. 8
cardinal campeius is arriv'd, and lately, | as H8 2.01.160
hark, he is arriv'd. JC 4.02. 30
i would the friends we miss were safe arriv'd. MAC 5.09. 1
and give us truth who 'tis that is arriv'd. OTH 2.01. 58
he is not yet arriv'd, nor know i aught | but 2.01. 89
that upon certain tidings now arriv'd, importing 2.02. 2 P
imagine pericles arriv'd at tyre, | welcom'd and PER 4.ch. 1
he is arriv'd | here where his daughter dwells, 5.ch. 14

ARRIVE 6 FR 0.0006 REL FR 6 V 0 P
may strike the dullest nostril | where i arrive, WT 1.02.422
this means being there | so soon as you arrive, 4.04.620
or arrive | where i may have fruition of her 1H6 5.05. 8
for many so arrive at second masters, | upon TIM 4.03.505
but ere we could arrive the point propos'd, JC 1.02.110
fair, | ere he arrive his weary noontide prick, LUC 781

ARRIVED 4 FR 0.0004 REL FR 4 V 0 P
me, | and soon, and safe, arrived where i was. ERR 1.01. 48
and happily i have arrived at the last | unto SHR 5.01.127
are here arrived, give order that these bodies HAM 5.02.377
when at collatium this false lord arrived, LUC 50

ARRIVES 2 FR 0.0002 REL FR 2 V 0 P
too swift arrives as tardy as too slow. ROM 2.06. 15
where he arrives he moves | all hearts against LR 4.05. 10

ARRIVING 1 FR 0.0001 REL FR 1 V 0 P
arriving | a place of potency and sway o' th' COR 2.03.181

ARROGANCE 6 FR 0.0006 REL FR 6 V 0 P
o monstrous arrogance! SHR 4.03.107
exempted be from me the arrogance | to choose AWW 2.01.195
i hate not you for her proud arrogance. R3 1.03. 24
lords, | can ye endure to hear this arrogance? H8 3.02.278
that bastes his arrogance with his own seam, TRO 2.03.185
feed arrogance and are the proud man's fees. 3.03. 49

ARROGANCY 1 FR 0.0001 REL FR 1 V 0 P
but your heart | is cramm'd with arrogancy, H8 2.04.110

ARROGANT 4 FR 0.0004 REL FR 4 V 0 P
arrogant winchester, that haughty prelate, 1H6 1.03. 23
nor cease to be an arrogant controller, | though 2H6 3.02.205
whereof thy proud child, arrogant man, is puff'd TIM 4.03.180
to let an arrogant piece of flesh threat us, CYM 4.02.127

ARROUSE 1 FR 0.0001 REL FR 1 V 0 P
the blissful dew of heaven does arrouse you. TNK 5.04.104

ARROW 10 FR 0.0011 REL FR 8 V 2 P
to strike at me, that your arrow hath glanc'd. WIV 5.05.235 P
matter | is little cupid's crafty arrow made, ADO 3.01. 22
bow, | by his best arrow with the golden head, MND 1.01.170
go, | swifter than arrow from the tartar's bow. 3.02.101
please | to shoot another arrow that self way MV 1.01.148
do you think me a swallow, an arrow, or a bullet 2H4 4.03. 33 P
she'll not be hit | with cupid's arrow, she hath ROM 1.01.209
that i have shot my arrow o'er the house | and HAM 5.02.243
and like an arrow shot | from a well–experienc'd PER 1.01.161
love's golden arrow at him should have fled, VEN 947

ARROWS 10 FR 0.0011 REL FR 9 V 1 P
her waspish–headed son has broke his arrows, TMP 4.01. 99
some cupid kills with arrows, some with traps. ADO 3.01.106
their conceits have wings | fleeter than arrows, LLL 5.02.261
wounds invisible | that love's keen arrows make. AYL 3.05. 31
ta'en his bow and arrows and is gone forth — to 4.03. 4 P
that arrows fled not swifter toward their aim 2H4 1.01.123
as many arrows loosed several ways | come to one H5 1.02.207
draw, archers, draw your arrows to the head! R3 5.03.339
the slings and arrows of outrageous fortune, HAM 3.01. 57
convert his gyves to graces, so that my arrows, 4.07. 21

/ART* 8 FR 0.0009 REL FR 6 V 2 P
thou /art clerkly, thou art clerkly, sir john. WIV 4.05. 57 P
come on, thou /art granted space. AWW 4.01. 88
/beastly /feeder, /art /so /full /of /him, 2H4 1.03. 95
/tender /sapling, /thou /art /made /of /tears, TIT 3.02. 50
/i /see /thou /art /not /for /my /company. 3.02. 58
thou /art fled to brutish beasts, | and men have JC 3.02.104
/what, /art /a /heathen? HAM 5.01. 35 P
/howe'er /thou /art /a /fiend, | /a /woman's LR 4.02. 66

ART* 1003 FR 0.1133 REL FR 758 V 245 P
we are less afraid to be drown'd than thou art. TMP 1.01. 45 P
if by your art, my dearest father, you have 1.02. 1
who | art ignorant of what thou art, nought 1.02. 18
who | art ignorant of what thou art, nought 1.02. 18
so, | lie there, my art. 1.02. 25
i have with such provision in mine art | so 1.02. 28
thou art inclin'd to sleep; 1.02.185
it was mine art, | when i arriv'd and heard thee 1.02.291
i have us'd thee | (filth as thou art) with 1.02.346
his art is of such pow'r, | it would control my 1.02.372
what? art thou waking? 2.01.209
wink'st | whiles thou art waking. 2.01.217
my master through his art foresees the danger 2.01.297
thou art very trinculo indeed! 2.02.105 P
but art thou not drown'd, stephano? 2.02.109 P
i hope now thou art not drown'd. 2.02.110 P
and art thou living, stephano? 2.02.112 P
swim like a duck, thou art made like a goose. 2.02.131 P
poor worm, thou art infected! 3.01. 31
art thou afeard? 3.02.133
of this young couple | some vanity of mine art. 4.01. 41
which by mine art | i have from their confines 4.01.120
hast thou, which art but air, a touch, a feeling 5.01. 21
as they, be kindlier mov'd than thou art? 5.01. 24
op'd, and let 'em forth | by my so potent art. 5.01. 50
thou art pinch'd for't now, sebastian. 5.01. 74
i do forgive thee, | unnatural though thou art. 5.01. 79
to the king's ship, invisible as thou art; 5.01. 97
now i want | spirits to enforce, art to enchant, ep 14
counsel thee | that art a votary to fond desire? TGV 1.01. 52
therefore thou art a sheep. 1.01. 92 P
shipp'd, and thou art to post after with oars. 2.03. 34 P
what an ass art thou! i understand thee not. 2.05. 24 P
what a block art thou, that thou canst not! 2.05. 26 P
if not, thou art an hebrew, a jew, and not worth 2.05. 54 P
who art the table wherein all my thoughts | are 2.07. 3
now, as thou art a gentleman of blood, | advise 3.01.121
why, phaeton (for thou art merops' son), | wilt 3.01.153
that thou art banish'd — o, that's the news! 3.01.219
thy letters may be here, though thou art hence, 3.01.250
ay, who art thou? 3.01.375 P
thou art not ignorant | how she opposes her 3.02. 25
friend | survives, to whom, thyself art witness, 4.02.109
and art thou not asham'd | to wrong him with thy 4.02.110
o eglamour, thou art a gentleman — | think not 4.03. 11
thou art not ignorant what dear good will | i 4.03. 14
the more degenerate and base art thou | to make 5.04.136
thou art a gentleman and well deriv'd, | take 5.04.146
thou art the mars of malecontents. WIV 1.03.104 P
how now, sweet frank, why art thou melancholy? 2.01.150 P
use your art of wooing; 2.02.235 P
thou art a castalion–king–urinal! 2.03. 33 P
boys of art, i have deceiv'd you both; 3.01.107 P
/by /the /lord, thou art a tyrant to say so. 3.03. 61 P
i cannot cog and say thou art this and that, 3.03. 70 P
oman, art thou /lunatics? 4.01. 69 P
thou art as foolish christian creatures as i 4.01. 71 P
art thou there? 4.05. 17 P
thou /art clerkly, thou art clerkly, sir john. 4.05. 57 P
sir john? art thou there, my deer? my male deer? 5.05. 16 P
till thou art able to woo her in good english. 5.05.134 P
in | as art and practice hath enriched any MM 1.01. 12
for example, thou thyself art a wicked villain, 1.02. 25 P
thou art the list. 1.02. 30 P
and thou the velvet — thou art good velvet; 1.02. 31 P
english kersey as be pil'd, as thou art pil'd, 1.02. 34 P
whether thou art tainted or free. 1.02. 42 P
thou art always figuring diseases in me; 1.02. 53 P
but thou art full of error — i am sound. 1.02. 54 P
art thou sure of this? 1.02. 71 P
she hath prosperous art | when she will play 1.02.184
thou art to continue now, thou varlet, thou art 2.01.191 P
continue now, thou varlet, thou art to continue. 2.01.191 P
art avis'd o' that? more on't. 2.02.132
or what art thou, angelo? 2.02.172
with all her double vigor, art and nature, 2.02.183
blood, thou art blood. 2.04. 15
i'll tell the world aloud | what man thou art. 2.04.154
a breath thou art, | servile to all the skyey 3.01. 8
merely, thou art death's fool, | for him thou 3.01. 11
thou art not noble, | for all th' accommodations 3.01. 13
thou art not thyself, | for thou exists on many 3.01. 19
happy thou art not, | for what thou hast not, 3.01. 21
thou art not certain, | for thy complexion 3.01. 23
if thou art rich, thou'rt poor, | for, like an 3.01. 25

and when thou art old and rich, | thou hast		3.01. 36
thou art too noble to conserve a life | in base		3.01. 87
art thou led in triumph?		3.02. 44 P
art going to prison, pompey?		3.02. 60 P
thou art deceiv'd in me, friar.		3.02.168 P
or else thou art suborn'd against his honor | in		5.01.106
thou art the first knave that e'er mad'st a duke		5.01.356
thou art said to have a stubborn soul | that		5.01.480
therefore by law thou art condemn'd to die.	ERR	1.01. 25
but, though thou art adjudged to the death,		1.01.146
if no, then thou art doom'd to die.		1.01.154
how chance thou art return'd so soon?		1.02. 42
it, | that thou art then estranged from thyself?		2.02.120
thou art an elm, my husband, i a vine, | whose		2.02.174
i think thou art in mind, and so am i.		2.02.196
if thou art chang'd to aught, 'tis to an ass.		2.02.199
i think thou art an ass.		3.01. 15
what art thou that keep'st me out from the house		3.01. 42
thou art dromio, thou art my man, thou art		3.02. 75 P
thou art dromio, thou art my man, thou art		3.02. 75 P
art dromio, thou art my man, thou art thyself.		3.02. 76 P
thou art, as you are all, a sorceress:		4.03. 66
thou art sensible in nothing but blows, and so		4.04. 27 P
dissembling harlot, thou art false in all, | and		4.04.101
and art confederate with a damned pack | to make		4.04.102
thou art a villain to impeach me thus:		5.01. 29
err — | tell me thou art my son antipholus.		5.01.319
egeon art thou not? or else his ghost?		5.01.338
if i dream not, thou art aemilia.		5.01.347
if thou art she, tell me, where is that son		5.01.348
thou (being, as thou say'st thou art, born under	ADO	1.03. 11 P
that shows thou art unconfirm'd.		3.03.117 P
but art not thou thyself giddy with the fashion		3.03.140 P
my cousin's a fool, and thou art another.		3.04. 11 P
fie upon thee, art not asham'd?		3.04. 28 P
i charge thee do so, as thou art my child.		4.01. 76
thou villain, thou art full of piety, as shall		4.02. 78 P
art thou sick, or angry?		5.01.131 P
art thou the slave that with thy breath hast		5.01.263
but in that thou art like to be my kinsman, live		5.04.110 P
prince, thou art sad, get thee a wife, get thee		5.04.122 P
still and contemplative in living art.	LLL	1.01. 14
i do say thou art quick in answers;		1.02. 29 P
thou art an old love–monger and speakest		2.01.254
"by heaven, that thou art fair, is most		4.01. 60 P
true, that thou art beauteous;		4.01. 61 P
truth itself, that thou art lovely.		4.01. 62 P
if thou strive, poor soul, what art thou then?		4.01. 92
those pleasures live that art would comprehend.		4.02.110
celestial as thou art, o, pardon love this wrong		4.02.117
these worms for loving, that art most in love?		4.03.152
a word, for thou art not so long by the head as		5.01. 40 P
thou art easier swallow'd than a flap–dragon.		5.01. 41 P
go, sickness as thou art!		5.02.280
and what art thou now?		5.02.338
art thou one of the worthies?		5.02.504 P
a kissing traitor. how art thou prov'd judas?		5.02.600 P
look, and with what art | you sway the motion of	MND	1.01.192
why art thou here | come from the farthest steep		2.01. 68
transparent helena, nature shows art, | that		2.02.104
o bottom, thou art chang'd!		3.01.114 P
thou art translated.		3.01.118 P
thou art as wise as thou art beautiful.		3.01.148
thou art as wise as thou art beautiful.		3.01.148
thou art not by mine eye, lysander, found;		3.02.181
where art thou, proud demetrius? speak thou now.		3.02.401
here, villain, drawn and ready. where art thou?		3.02.402
thou runaway, thou coward, art thou fled?		3.02.405
thou coward, art thou bragging to the stars,		3.02.407
yea, art thou there?		3.02.411
where art thou now?		3.02.425
o night, which ever art when day is not!		5.01.171
my love thou art, my love i think.		5.01.194
be launcelot, thou art mine own flesh and blood.	MV	2.02. 92 P
lord, how art thou chang'd!		2.02. 99 P
thou art too wild, too rude, and bold of voice		2.02.181
but where thou art not known, why, there they		2.02.184
and thy thoughts are witness that thou art.		2.06. 32
what, art thou come?		2.06. 58
how much unlike art thou to portia!		2.09. 56
that thou art so fond | to come abroad with him		3.03. 9
thou art come to answer | a stony adversary, an		4.01. 3
how much more elder art thou than thy looks!		4.01.251
art thou contented, jew? what dost thou say?		4.01.393
by our beards (if we had them) thou art.	AYL	1.02. 74 P
but fare thee well, thou art a gallant youth.		1.02.229
thou art overthrown, | or charles, or something		1.02.259
thou art thy father's daughter, there's enough.		1.03. 58
thou art a fool;		1.03. 80
what shall i call thee when thou art a man?		1.03.123
thou art not for the fashion of these times,		2.03. 59
thou speak'st wiser than thou art ware of.		2.04. 57 P
before i come, thou art a mocker of my labor.		2.06. 13 P
art thou thus bolden'd, man, by thy distress?		2.07. 91
thou art not so unkind | as man's ingratitude;		2.07.175
is not so keen, | because thou art not seen,		2.07.178
man, | thou art right welcome as thy /master is.		2.07.198
no wit by nature nor art may complain of good		3.02. 29 P
then thou art damn'd.		3.02. 35 P
truly, thou art damn'd, like an ill–roasted egg		3.02. 37 P
thou art in a parlous state, shepherd.		3.02. 44 P
thou art raw.		3.02. 72 P
for thou swear'st to me thou art honest.		3.03. 26 P
than thine own gladness that thou art employ'd.		3.05. 98
hyen, and that when thou art inclin'd to sleep.		4.01.156 P
"art thou god to shepherd turn'd, | that a		4.03. 40
"thank god" — a good answer. art rich?		5.01. 25 P
art thou wise?		5.01. 28 P
give me your hand. art thou learned?		5.01. 38 P
with a magician, most profound in his art, and		5.02. 61 P
o my dear niece, welcome thou art to me!		5.04.147
i will not eat my word, now thou art mine, | thy		5.04.149
thou art a fool;	SHR	in.1. 26
thou art a lord, and nothing but a lord.		in.2. 61
that art to me as secret and as dear | as anna		1.01.153
but art thou not advis'd, he took some care | to		1.01.186
but th' art too much my friend, | and i'll not		1.02. 63
for thou art pleasant, gamesome, passing		2.01.245
fingering, | i must begin with rudiments of art,		3.01. 66
i read that i profess, the art to love.		4.02. 8
and may you prove, sir, master of your art!		4.02. 9
neither art thou the worse | for this poor		4.03.179
th' art a tall fellow;		4.04. 17
why, how now, kate, i hope thou art not mad.		4.05. 42
now i perceive thou art a reverent father.		4.05. 48
art thou his father?		5.01. 32 P
what, art thou asham'd of me?		5.01.145
that laboring art can never ransom nature | from	AWW	2.01.118
no part, | i knowing all my peril, thou no art.		2.01.133
my art is not past power, nor you past cure.		2.01.158
art thou so confident?		2.01.159
yet art thou good for nothing but taking up, and		2.03.207 P
with all my heart, and thou art worthy of it.		2.03.218 P
methink'st thou art a general offense, and every		2.03.254 P
will this capriccio hold in thee, art sure?		2.03.293
away, th' art a knave.		2.04. 28 P
sir, "before a knave th' art a knave," that's		2.04. 30 P
a knave," that's "before me th' art a knave."		2.04. 30 P
go to, thou art a witty fool, i have found thee.		2.04. 32 P
out of my blood, | and thou art all my child.		3.02. 68
the general of our horse thou art, and we,		3.03. 1
i know th' art valiant, and to the possibility		3.06. 82 P
art not acquainted with him?		4.01. 8 P
and, hoodwink'd as thou art, will lead thee on		4.01. 81
say thou art mine, and ever | my love, as it		4.02. 36
for thee, thou art both knave and fool.		4.05. 32 P
if it should prove | that thou art so inhuman —		5.03.116
as thou art a knave, and no knave.		5.03.249 P
but thou art too fine in thy evidence, therefore		5.03.268 P
o spirit of love, how quick and fresh art thou,	TN	1.01. 9
art thou good at these kickshawses, knight?		1.03.115 P
thy happy years, | that say thou art a man.		1.04. 31
i'll be sworn thou art;		1.05.291
i see thou art a wickedness | wherein the		2.02. 27
th' art a scholar;		2.03. 13 P
art any more than a steward?		2.03.114 P
dost thou think, because thou art virtuous,		2.03.115 P
th' art i' th' right.		2.03.119 P
my life upon't, young though thou art, thine eye		2.04. 23
to inure thyself to what thou art like to be,		2.05.148 P
go to, thou art made if thou desir'st to be so;		2.05.155 P
art thou a churchman?		3.01. 4 P
i warrant thou art a merry fellow and car'st for		3.01. 26 P
art not thou the lady olivia's fool?		3.01. 31 P
practice | as full of labor as a wise man's art;		3.01. 66
"go to, thou art made, if thou desir'st to be		3.04. 52 P
"youth, whatsoever thou art, thou art but a		3.04.148 P
thou art, thou art but a scurvy fellow."		3.04.148 P
go to, go to, thou art a foolish fellow, | let		4.01. 3
shall i vent to her that thou art coming?		4.01. 17 P
make him believe thou art sir topas the curate,		4.02. 2 P
in which thou art more puzzled than the		4.02. 43 P
i am as well in my wits, fool, as thou art.		4.02. 88 P
be that thou know'st thou art, and then thou art		5.01.149
art, and then thou art | as great as that thou		5.01.149
how now, art thou mad?		5.01.293 P
mamillius, | art thou my boy?	WT	1.02.120
how now, you wanton calf, | art thou my calf?		1.02.127
with what's unreal thou co–active art, | and		1.02.141
thou art not honest;		1.02.242
if thou inclin'st that way, thou art a coward,		1.02.243
either thou art most ignorant by age, | or thou		2.01.173
bastard, | thou dotard, thou art woman–tir'd;		2.03. 75
and, lozel, thou art worthy to be hang'd, | that		2.03.109
as thou art liegeman to us, that thou carry		2.03.174
thou art here accused and arraigned of high		3.02. 13 P
thou art perfect then, our ship hath touch'd		3.03. 1
that for thy mother's fault art thus expos'd		3.03. 50
art so near?		3.03. 80 P
thing to talk on when thou art dead and rotten,		3.03. 81 P
there is an art which in their piedness shares		4.04. 87
over that art | which you say adds to nature, is		4.04. 90
adds to nature, is an art | that nature makes.		4.04. 91
this is an art | which does mend nature —		4.04. 95
but | the art itself is nature.		4.04. 97
thou art too base | to be /acknowledg'd.		4.04.418
as cruel for thee | as thou art tender to't.		4.04.441
to the prince thou art as honest a true fellow		5.02.157 P
to the prince thou art a tall fellow of thy		5.02.164 P
but i know thou art no tall fellow of thy hands		5.02.165 P
that i may say indeed | thou art hermione;		5.03. 25
or rather, thou art she | in thy not chiding;		5.03. 25
has motion in't, | as we are mock'd with art.		5.03. 68
be magic, let it be an art | lawful as eating.		5.03.110
what art thou?	JN	1.01. 55
is that the elder, and art thou the heir?		1.01. 57
he is sir robert's son, and so art thou.		1.01.229
charge | that art the issue of my dear offense,		1.01.257
but thou from loving england art so far | that		2.01. 94
how comes it then that thou art call'd a king,		2.01.107
what the devil art thou?		2.01.134
o boy, then where art thou?		3.01. 34
but thou art fair, and at thy birth, dear boy,		3.01. 51
thou art perjur'd too, | and sooth'st up		3.01.120
what a fool art thou, | a ramping fool, to brag		3.01.121
the truth thou art unsure | to swear, swears		3.01.283
look to thyself, thou art in jeopardy.		3.01.346
thou art his keeper.		3.03. 64
thou art /not holy to belie me so, | i am not		3.04. 44
presented thee more hideous than thou art.		4.02.266
thou art a murtherer.		4.03. 90
this deed of death, | art thou damn'd, hubert.		4.03.119
thou art more deep damn'd than prince lucifer.		4.03.122
a friend. what art thou?		5.06. 2
thou art my friend that know'st my tongue so		5.06. 8
who art thou?		5.06. 9
o cousin, thou art come to set mine eye.		5.07. 51
art thou gone so?		5.07. 70
thou art a traitor and a miscreant, | too good	R2	1.01. 39
so art thou.		1.01.122
edward's seven sons, whereof thyself art one,		1.02. 11
and breathest, | yet art thou slain in him.		1.02. 25
say who thou art | and why thou comest thus		1.03. 11
but what thou art, god, thou, and i do know,		1.03.204
esteem as foil wherein thou art to set | the		1.03.266
air, | and thou art flying to a fresher clime.		1.03.285
and thou, too careless patient as thou art,		2.01. 97
which art possess'd now to depose thyself.		2.01.108
landlord of england art thou now, not king,		2.01.113
for how art thou a king | but by fair sequence		2.01.198
so, green, thou art the midwife to my woe, | and		2.02. 62
thou art a banish'd man, and here art come		2.03.110
and here art come | before the expiration of thy		2.03.110
nimble mischance, that art so light of foot,		3.04. 92
fitzwater, thou art damn'd to hell for this.		4.01. 43
as true | in this appeal as thou art all unjust,		4.01. 45
and that thou art so, there i throw my gage,		4.01. 46
which art a lion and the king of beasts?		5.01. 34
wife, thou art a fool.		5.02. 68
poor boy, thou art amaz'd.		5.02. 85
a god on earth thou art.		5.03.136
what art thou?		5.05. 69
taste of it first, as thou art wont to do.		5.05. 99
thou art so fat–witted with drinking of old sack	1H4	1.02. 2 P
i prithee, sweet wag, when thou art a king, as,		1.02. 16 P
sweet wag, when thou art king, let not us that		1.02. 23 P
not here apparent that thou art heir apparent —		1.02. 58 P
gallows standing in england when thou art king?		1.02. 60 P
do not thou, when thou art king, hang a thief.		1.02. 62 P
most unsavory /similes and art indeed the most		1.02. 80 P
and art indeed able to corrupt a saint.		1.02. 90 P
then art thou damn'd for keeping thy word with		1.02.120 P
i'll be a traitor then, when thou art king.		1.02.147 P
art thou not asham'd?		1.03.118
fool | art thou to break into this woman's mood,		1.03.237
thou liest, thou art not colted, thou art		2.02. 38 P
liest, thou art not colted, thou art uncolted.		2.02. 38 P
thou art perfect.		2.04. 35 P
how old art thou, francis?		2.04. 53 P
what, art thou mad?		2.04.229 P
art thou mad?		2.04.229 P
what a slave art thou to hack thy sword as thou		2.04.261 P
why, what a rascal art thou then, to praise him		2.04.351 P
but tell me, hal, art not thou horrible afeard?		2.04.366 P
art thou not horribly afraid?		2.04.369 P
thy time, but also how thou art accompanied;		2.04.399 P
that thou art my son i have partly thy mother's		2.04.402 P
why, being son to me, art thou so pointed at?		2.04.407 P
thou art violently carried away from grace,		2.04.446 P
thou art essentially made, without seeming so.		2.04.492 P
son | can trace me in the tedious ways of art,		3.01. 47
come, kate, thou art perfect in lying down.		3.01.226 P
swear me, kate, like a lady as thou art, | a		3.01.253
make me believe that thou art only mark'd | for		3.02. 9
as thou art match'd withal and grafted to,		3.02. 15
and art almost an alien to the hearts | of all		3.02. 34
as thou art to this hour was richard then | when		3.02. 94
foes, | which art my nearest and dearest enemy?		3.02.123
thou that art like enough, through vassal fear,		3.02.124
frowns, | to show how much thou art degenerate.		3.02.128
thou art our admiral, thou bearest the lantern		3.03. 25 P
thou art the knight of the burning lamp.		3.03. 26 P
but thou art altogether given over, and wert		3.03. 36 P
o, thou art a perpetual triumph, an everlasting		3.03. 41 P
aside, thou art a knave to call me so.		3.03.120 P
aside, thou art a beast to say otherwise.		3.03.122 P
thou art an unjust man in saying so.		3.03.129 P
thou knowest, as thou art but man, i dare, but		3.03.145 P
i dare, but as thou art prince, i fear thee as i		3.03.146 P
art thou not asham'd?		3.03.163 P
thou art the king of honor.		4.01. 10
i think thou art enamored | on his follies.		5.02. 69
because some tell me that thou art a king.		5.03. 5
what art thou | that counterfeit'st the person		5.04. 27
i fear thou art another counterfeit, | and yet,		5.04. 35
but mine i am sure thou art, whoe'er thou be,		5.04. 37
or thou art like | never to hold it up again!		5.04. 39
if i mistake not, thou art harry monmouth.		5.04. 59
no, percy, thou art dust, | and food for —		5.04. 85
ill–weav'd ambition, how much art thou shrunk!		5.04. 88
art thou alive?		5.04.134
thou art not what thou seem'st.		5.04.137
that art a guard too wanton for the head | which	2H4	1.01.148
thou art fitter to be worn in my cap than to		1.02. 15 P
thou art a honeyseed, a man–queller, and a		2.01. 52 P
thou art a great fool.		2.01.194 P
vile company as thou art hath in reason taken		2.02. 49 P
and thou art a blessed fellow to think as every		2.02. 57 P
that he swears thou art to marry his sister nell		2.02.128 P
thou art going to the wars, and whether i shall		2.04. 66 P
art thou not asham'd to be call'd captain?		2.04.140 P
thou art as valorous as hector of troy, worth		2.04.219 P
and art not thou poins his brother?		2.04.283 P
i am a gentleman, thou art a drawer.		2.04.287 P
light flesh and corrupt blood, thou art welcome.		2.04.295 P
no, i think thou art not, i think thou art quit		2.04.342 P
thou art not, i think thou art quit for that.		2.04.342 P
shadow, whose son art thou?		3.02.126 P
thou art a very ragged wart.		3.02.141 P
what trade art thou, feeble?		3.02.149 P
what, dost thou roar before thou art prick'd?		3.02.178 P
well said, th' art a good fellow.		3.02.239 P
well said, i' faith, wart, th' art a good scab.		3.02.276 P
a famous rebel art thou, colevile.		4.03. 63
how chance thou art not with the prince thy		4.04. 20
why art thou not at windsor with him, thomas?		4.04. 50
o westmerland, thou art a summer bird, | which		4.04. 91
bells ring to thine ear | that thou art crowned,		4.05.112
therefore thou best of gold art /worst /of gold.		4.05.160
thou art not firm enough, since griefs are green		4.05.203
thou art now one of the greatest men in this		5.03. 87 P
so that the art and practic part of life | must	H5	1.01. 51
discuss unto me, art thou officer, | or art thou		4.01. 37
or art thou base, common, and popular?		4.01. 38
art thou of cornish crew?		4.01. 50
art thou his friend?		4.01. 58
and what art thou, thou idol ceremony?		4.01.240
what kind of god art thou, that suffer'st more		4.01.241
art thou aught else but place, degree, and form,		4.01.246
wherein thou art less happy, being fear'd,		4.01.248
for thou art fram'd of the firm truth of valor.		4.03. 14
for certainly thou art so near the gulf, | thou		4.03. 82
art thou a gentleman?		4.04. 4 P
ha, art thou bedlam?		5.01. 19

what e'er we like, thou art protector, | and	1H6	1.01. 37
daughter, | my wit untrain'd in any kind of art.		1.02. 73
thou art an amazon, | and fightest with the		1.02.104
thou with an eagle art inspired then.		1.02.141
thou art no friend to god or to the king.		1.03. 25
blood will i draw on thee — thou art a witch —		1.05. 6
deceit | contriv'd by art and baleful sorcery.		2.01. 15
if thou be he, then art thou prisoner.		2.03. 33
why? art not thou the man?		2.03. 48
i find thou art no less than fame hath bruited,		2.03. 68
i did not entertain thee as thou art.		2.03. 72
and, till thou be restor'd, thou art a yeoman.		2.04. 95
thou art my heir;		2.05. 96
thou art a most pernicious usurer, | froward by		3.01. 17
thou art reverent | touching thy spiritual		3.01. 49
now thou art come unto a feast of death, | a		4.05. 7
art thou not weary, john?		4.06. 27
fly, | now thou art seal'd the son of chivalry?		4.06. 29
on what submissive message art thou sent?		4.07. 53
be what thou wilt, thou art my prisoner.		5.03. 45
who art thou?		5.03. 50
king, | the king of naples, whosoe'er thou art.		5.03. 52
miracle, | thou art allotted to be ta'en by me;		5.03. 55
/and natural graces that extinguish art;		5.03.192
thou art no father nor no friend of mine.		5.04. 9
god knows thou art a collop of my flesh, | and		5.04. 18
as thou art knight, never to disobey | nor be		5.04.170
art thou not second woman in the realm?	2H6	1.02. 43
what, art thou lame?		2.01. 93
art thou gone too?		2.04. 87
only convey me where thou art commanded.		2.04. 93
gloucester, know that thou art come too soon,		3.01. 95
unless thou wert more loyal than thou art.		3.01. 96
to be, or what thou art | resign to death;		3.01.333
art thou like the adder waxen deaf?		3.02. 76
whose fruit thou art | and never of the nevils'		3.02.214
unworthy though thou art, i'll cope with thee,		3.02.230
'tis but surmis'd whiles thou art standing by,		3.02.347
for where thou art, there is the world itself,		3.02.362
and where thou art not, desolation.		3.02.364
if thou be found by me, thou art but dead.		3.02.387
for wheresoe'er thou art in this world's globe,		3.02.406
and thou that art his mate, make boot of this;		4.01. 13
base slave, thy words are blunt and so art thou.		4.01. 67
by devilish policy art thou grown great | and,		4.01. 83
and thou thyself a shearman, art thou not?		4.02.133
now art thou within point-blank of our		4.07. 26 P
sweep the court clean of such filth as thou art.		4.07. 32 P
set limb to limb, and thou art far the lesser;		4.10. 47
art thou a messenger, or come of pleasure?		5.01. 16
great god, how just art thou!		5.01. 68
me, my friend, art thou the man that slew him?		5.01. 71
how art thou call'd? and what is thy degree?		5.01. 73
thou art not king;		5.01. 93
why art thou old, and want'st experience?		5.01.171
in love, | but that thou art so fast mine enemy.		5.02. 21
war hath given thee peace, for thou art still.		5.02. 29
exeter, thou art a traitor to the crown, | in	3H6	1.01. 80
/thy father was, as thou art, duke of york,		1.01.105
art thou against us, duke of exeter?		1.01.147
thou art deceiv'd.		1.01.155
art thou king, and wilt be forc'd?		1.01.230
why art thou patient, man?		1.04. 89
thou art as opposite to every good | as the		1.04.134
but what art thou, whose heavy looks foretell		2.01. 43
now thou art gone we have no staff, no stay.		2.01. 69
but thou art neither like thy sire nor dam,		2.02.135
thou not, knowing whence thou art extraught,		2.02.142
art then forsaken, as thou went'st forlorn!		3.01. 54
say, what art thou talk'st of kings and queens?		3.01. 55
thou art a widow, and thou hast some children,		3.02.102
and thou no more art prince than she is queen.		3.03. 80
is it for a wife | that thou art malecontent?		4.01. 60
yea, brother of clarence, art thou here too?		4.03. 41
thee, | for thou art fortunate in all thy deeds.		4.06. 25
no, warwick, thou art worthy of the sway, | to		4.06. 32
thou art no atlas for so great a weight;		5.01. 36
untutor'd lad, thou art too malapert.		5.05. 32
richard, where art thou?		5.05. 78
thou art not here.		5.05. 79
a persecutor i am sure thou art.		5.06. 31
executing, | why then thou art an executioner.		5.06. 33
not thyself, fair creature — thou art both.	R3	1.02.132
a murth'rous villain, and so still thou art.		1.03.133
in thy rights as thou art stall'd in mine!		1.03.205
what? art thou afraid?		1.04.109 P
where art thou, keeper? give me a cup of wine.		1.04.161
in god's name, what art thou?		1.04.163
go, coward as thou art.		1.04.279
thou art a widow;		2.02. 55
yet thou art a mother, | and hast the comfort of		2.02. 55
thou art sworn as deeply to effect what we		3.01.158
thou art a traitor.		3.04. 75
tut, thou art all ice, thy kindness freezes.		4.02. 22
art thou indeed?		4.02. 68
edward plantagenet, why art thou dead?		4.04. 19
decline all this, and see what now thou art:		4.04. 97
to torture thee the more, being what thou art.		4.04.108
art thou my son?		4.04.155
art thou so hasty?		4.04.163
bloody thou art, bloody will be thy end;		4.04.195
conscience, | thou art a cure fit for a king.	H8	2.02. 75
thou art alone | (if thy rare qualities, sweet		2.04.137
in sweet music is such art, | killing care and		3.01. 12
thou art a proud traitor, priest.		3.02.252
i have told him | what, and how true, thou art;		3.02.416
so excellent in art, and still so rising, | that		4.02. 62
what, art thou angry, pandarus? what, with me?	TRO	1.01. 73
thou art proclaim'd fool, i think.		2.01. 25 P
when thou art forth in the incursions, thou		2.01. 29 P
and thou art as full of envy at his greatness as		2.01. 33 P
thou art here but to thrash troyans, and thou		2.01. 45 P
and thou art bought and sold among those of any		2.01. 46 P
at thy heel, and tell what thou art by inches,		2.01. 48 P
of olympus, forget that thou art jove, the king		2.03. 11 P
that lays thee out says thou art a fair corse,		2.03. 32 P
what, art thou devout? wast thou in prayer?		2.03. 35 P
art thou come?		2.03. 40 P
then tell me, patroclus, what art thou?		2.03. 49 P
demand of the prover, it suffices me thou art.		2.03. 68 P
the heavens, lord, thou art of sweet composure.		2.03.240
thou art chang'd for antenor.		4.02. 91 P
here art thou in appointment fresh and fair,		4.05. 1
thou art, great lord, my father's sister's son,		4.05.120
thou art too gentle and too free a man.		4.05.139
thou art too brief.		4.05.237
thou art said to be achilles' male varlot.		5.01. 15 P
why art thou then exasperate, thou idle		5.01. 30 P
what art /thou, greek?		5.04. 26
art thou for hector's match?		5.04. 26
art thou of blood and honor?		5.04. 27
ha, art thou there?		5.06. 8
stand, thou greek, thou art a goodly mark.		5.06. 27
what art thou?		5.07. 14 P
thou rascal, that art worst in blood to run,	COR	1.01.159
what, art thou stiff?		1.01.241
thou art left, martius — | a carbuncle entire,		1.04. 54
a carbuncle entire, as big as thou art, | were		1.04. 55
thou art their soldier, and, being bred in		3.02. 81
and thou art too full | of the wars' surfeits to		4.01. 45
now th' art troublesome.		4.05. 16 P
and that to prove more fortunes | th' art tir'd,		4.05. 94
to rome but that | thou art thence banish'd, we		4.05.128
as best thou art experienc'd, since thou know'st		4.05.139
caius, rome is thine, | thou art poor'st of all;		4.07. 57
then shortly art thou mine.		4.07. 57
thou art preparing fire for us;		5.02. 71 P
thou art my warrior, | i /holp to frame thee.		5.03. 62
thou art not honest, and the gods will plague		5.03.166
friend, | art thou certain this is true?		5.04. 44
thou art a roman, be not barbarous:	TIT	1.01.378
limbs, | unmannerly intruder as thou art!		2.03. 65
what, art thou fallen?		2.03.198
again, | till thou art here aloft or i below.		2.03.244
who art thou that lately didst descend | into		2.03.248
how happy art thou then, | from these devourers		3.01. 56
ill art thou repaid | for that good hand thou		3.01.234
now is a time to storm, why art thou still?		3.01.263
thou art an exile, and thou must not stay.		3.01.284
but thou art deeper read, and better skill'd;		4.01. 33
why, villain, art not thou the carrier?		4.03. 87
and temper him with all the art i have, | to		4.04.109
did not thy hue bewray whose brat thou art,		5.01. 28
who, when he knows thou art the empress' babe,		5.01. 35
i do not, | yet, for i know thou art religious,		5.01. 74
art thou not sorry for these heinous deeds?		5.01.123
art thou revenge?		5.02. 41
and art thou sent to me, | to be a torment to		5.02. 41
now give some surance that thou art revenge —		5.02. 46
fie, publius, fie, thou art too much deceiv'd.		5.02.155
why art thou thus attir'd, andronicus?		5.03. 30
but thou art not quickly mov'd to strike.	ROM	1.01. 7 P
therefore, if thou art mov'd, thou run'st away.		1.01. 10 P
'tis well thou art not fish;		1.01. 30 P
art thou drawn among these heartless hinds?		1.01. 66
why, romeo, art thou mad?		1.02. 53
if thou art dun, we'll draw thee from the mire		1.04. 41
that thou, her maid, art far more fair than she.		2.02. 6
angel, for thou art | as glorious to this night,		2.02. 26
o romeo, romeo, wherefore art thou romeo?		2.02. 33
thou art thyself, though not a montague.		2.02. 39
what man art thou that thus bescreen'd in night		2.02. 52
art thou not romeo, and a montague?		2.02. 60
and the place death, considering who thou art,		2.02. 64
thou art up-rous'd with some distemp'rature;		2.03. 40
and art thou chang'd?		2.03. 79
o flesh, flesh, how art thou fishified!		2.04. 38 P
now art thou sociable, now art thou romeo;		2.04. 89 P
now art thou sociable, now art thou romeo;		2.04. 89 P
now art thou what thou art, by art as well as by		2.04. 90 P
now art thou what thou art, by art as well as by		2.04. 90 P
thou what thou art, by art as well as by nature,		2.04. 90 P
o, thou art deceiv'd;		2.04. 98 P
how art thou out of breath, when thou hast		2.05. 31
to say to me that thou art out of breath?		2.05. 32
i' faith, i am sorry that thou art not well.		2.05. 53
thou art like one of these fellows that, when he		3.01. 5 P
thou art as hot a jack in thy mood as any in		3.01. 11 P
and i were so apt to quarrel as thou art, any		3.01. 31 P
thou art a villain.		3.01. 61
what, art thou hurt?		3.01. 92
prince will doom thee death | if thou art taken.		3.01.135
prince, as thou art true, | for blood of ours,		3.01.148
what devil art thou that dost torment me thus?		3.02. 43
of thy parts, | and thou art wedded to calamity.		3.03. 3
here from verona art thou banished.		3.03. 15
to comfort thee though thou art banished.		3.03. 56
art thou a man?		3.03.109
thy form cries out thou art;		3.03.109
there art thou happy.		3.03.137
there art thou happy.		3.03.138
there art thou happy.		3.03.140
art thou gone so, love — lord, ay, husband,		3.05. 43
methinks i see thee now, thou art so low, | as		3.05. 55
if thou art fickle, what dost thou with him		3.05. 61
that | which the commission of thy years and art		4.01. 64
to rouse thee from thy bed, there art thou dead.		4.01.108
dead art thou!		4.05. 63
tush, thou art deceiv'd.		5.01. 29
thou art swift | to enter in the thoughts of		5.01. 35
i see that thou art poor.		5.01. 58
art thou so bare and full of wretchedness, | and		5.01. 68
thou art not conquer'd, beauty's ensign yet | is		5.03. 94
ah, dear juliet, | why art thou yet so fair?		5.03.102
for thou art early up | to see thy son and heir		5.03.208
then gave i her (so tutor'd by my art) | a		5.03.243
when thou art timon's dog, and these knaves	TIM	1.01.180
thou art proud, apemantus.		1.01.188 P
whither art going?		1.01.191 P
art not one?		1.01.217 P
art not a poet?		1.01.220 P
art not thou a merchant?		1.01.235 P
thou art going to lord timon's feast?		1.01.260
thou art a fool to bid me farewell twice.		1.01.263
fie, th' art a churl.		1.02. 26
th' art an athenian, therefore welcome.		1.02. 35 P
thou art a soldier, therefore seldom rich, | it		1.02.222
thou stand'st single, th' art not on him yet.		2.02. 56 P
learning die then that day thou art hang'd.		2.02. 83 P
thou art not altogether a fool.		2.02.115 P
(prithee be not sad, | thou art true and honest;		2.02.221
lord's a bountiful gentleman, but thou art wise,		3.01. 40 P
now i see thou art a fool, and fit for thy		3.01. 49 P
th' art quick, | but yet i'll bury thee;		4.03. 45
what art thou there? speak.		4.03. 49
a beast, as thou art.		4.03. 50
so hateful to thee, | that art thyself a man?		4.03. 53
the gods plague thee, for thou art a man!		4.03. 75 P
dost perform, confound thee, for thou art a man!		4.03. 76 P
art thou timandra?		4.03. 82
i flatter not, but say thou art a caitiff.		4.03.235
thou art a slave, whom fortune's tender arm		4.03.250
art thou proud yet?		4.03.276
know'st none, but art despis'd for the contrary.		4.03.303 P
and what a beast art thou already, that seest		4.03.344 P
broke the wall, that thou art out of the city?		4.03.350 P
thou art the cap of all the fools alive.		4.03.358
a plague on thee, thou art too bad to curse!		4.03.360
choler does kill me that thou art alive;		4.03.367
away! what art thou?		4.03.472
if thou /grant'st th' art a man, i have forgot		4.03.474
because thou art a woman, and disclaim'st		4.03.483
methinks thou art more honest now than wise;		4.03.502
fly, whilst thou art blest and free.		4.03.535
th' art indeed the best, | thou counterfeit'st		5.01. 81
that thou art even natural in thine art.		5.01. 85
that thou art even natural in thine art.		5.01. 85
if where thou art two villains shall not be,		5.01.109
speak, what trade art thou?	JC	1.01. 5
but what trade art thou? answer me directly.		1.01. 12
thou art a cobbler, art thou?		1.01. 20
thou art a cobbler, art thou?		1.01. 20
but wherefore art not in thy shop to-day?		1.01. 27
age, thou art sham'd!		1.02.150
well, brutus, thou art noble;		1.02.308
art thou here yet?		2.04. 10
thou art the ruins of the noblest man | that		3.01.256
mischief, thou art afoot, | take thou what		3.02.260
portia, art thou gone?		4.03.166
i have as much of this in art as you, | but yet		4.03.194
knave, i blame thee not, thou art o'erwatch'd.		4.03.241
i trouble thee too much, but thou art willing.		4.03.259
art thou any thing?		4.03.278
art thou some god, some angel, or some devil,		4.03.279
speak to me what thou art.		4.03.281
caesar, thou art reveng'd, | even with the sword		5.03. 45
what, pindarus? where art thou, pindarus?		5.03. 72
o julius caesar, thou art mighty yet!		5.03. 94
o young and noble cato, art thou down?		5.04. 9
thou art a fellow of a good respect;		5.05. 45
that do cling together | and choke their art.	MAC	1.02. 9
th' art kind.		1.03. 12
there's no art | to find the mind's construction		1.04. 11
thou art so far before, | that swiftest wing of		1.04. 16
glamis thou art, and cawdor, and shalt be | what		1.05. 15
cawdor, and shalt be | what thou art promis'd.		1.05. 16
art not without ambition, but without | the		1.05. 19
art thou afeard | to be the same in thine own		1.07. 39
thine own act and valor | as thou art in desire?		1.07. 41
art thou not, fatal vision, sensible | to		2.01. 36
or art thou but | a dagger of the mind, a false		2.01. 37
thou art the best o' th' cut-throats, | yet he's		3.04. 16
if thou didst it, thou art the nonpareil.		3.04. 18
to bear my part, | or show the glory of our art?		3.05. 9
what e'er thou art, for thy good caution, thanks		4.01. 73
tell me, if your art | can tell so much, shall		4.01.101
thou art too like the spirit of banquo;		4.01.112
their malady convinces | the great assay of art;		4.03.143
for so thou art.		5.09. 20
thou art a scholar, speak to it, horatio.	HAM	1.01. 42
what art thou that usurp'st this time of night,		1.01. 46
as thou art to thyself.		1.01. 59
if thou art privy to thy country's fate, | which		1.01.133
so art thou to revenge, when thou shalt hear.		1.05. 7
art thou there, truepenny?		1.05.150
more matter, with less art.		2.02. 95
madam, i swear i use no art at all.		2.02. 96
but farewell it, for i will use no art.		2.02. 99
i have not art to reckon my groans, but that i		2.02.121 P
harlot's cheek, beautied with plast'ring art,		3.01. 50
thou art e'en as just a man | as e'er my		3.02. 54
that, struggling to be free, | art more engag'd;		3.03. 69
tell me, laertes, | why thou art thus incens'd.		4.05.127
report | for art and exercise in your defense,		4.07. 97
/hamlet, thou art slain.		5.02.313
as th' art a man, | give me the cup.		5.02.342
if for i want that glib and oily art | to speak	LR	1.01.224
fairest cordelia, that art most rich being poor,		1.01.250
nature, art my goddess, to thy law | my services		1.02. 1
how now, what art thou?		1.04. 9 P
what art thou?		1.04. 18 P
as he's for a king, /th' art poor enough.		1.04. 22 P
how old art thou?		1.04. 36 P
frowning, now thou art an o without a figure.		1.04.192 P
i am better than thou art now, i am a fool, thou		1.04.193 P
thou art now, i am a fool, thou art nothing.		1.04.194 P
good dawning to thee, friend. art of this house?		2.02. 1 P
and art nothing but the composition of a knave,		2.02. 20 P
what a monstrous fellow art thou, thus to rail		2.02. 25 P
what a brazen-fac'd varlet art thou, to deny		2.02. 28 P
thou art a strange fellow. a tailor make a man?		2.02. 56 P
why art thou angry?		2.02. 71
what, art thou mad, old fellow?		2.02. 85
art not asham'd to look upon this beard?		2.04.193
but yet thou art my flesh, my blood, my daughter		2.04.221
thou art a bile, | a plague-sore, or embossed		2.04.223
five and twenty, | and thou art twice her love.		2.04.260
thou art a lady;		2.04.267
thou simular of virtue | that art incestuous!		3.02. 55
art cold?		3.02. 68
the art of our necessities is strange | and can		3.02. 70
what art thou that dost grumble there i' th'		3.04. 44 P
and art thou come to this?		3.04. 50 P
thou art the thing itself:		3.04.106 P

such a poor, bare, fork'd animal as thou art. 3.04.108 P
substance, bleed'st not, speak'st, art sound. 4.06. 52
nature's above art in that respect. 4.06. 86 P
what, art mad? 4.06.150 P
who, by the art of known and feeling sorrows, 4.06.222
thou art a soul in bliss, but i am bound | upon 4.07. 45
thou art armed, gloucester, let the trumpet 5.03. 90
thou art in nothing less | than i have here 5.03. 94
thy valor, and thy heart, thou art a traitor; 5.03.134
thou art not vanquish'd, | but cozen'd and 5.03.154
but what art thou | that hast this fortune on me 5.03.165
i am no less in blood than thou art, edmund; 5.03.168
what profane wretch art thou? OTH 1.01.114
thou art a villain. 1.01.118
damn'd as thou art, thou hast enchanted her, 1.02. 63
thou art sure of me — go make money. 1.03.364 P
high renown, | and thou art but of low degree. 2.03. 94
more or less than truth, | thou art no soldier. 2.03.220
retire thee, go where thou art billeted. 2.03.380
i think that thou art just, and think thou art 3.03.385
that thou art just, and think thou art not. 3.03.385
now art thou my lieutenant. 3.03.479
o, thou art wise; 'tis certain. 4.01. 74
why? what art thou? 4.02. 34
swear thou art honest. 4.02. 38
heaven truly knows that thou art false as hell. 4.02. 39
who art so lovely fair and smell'st so sweet 4.02. 68
be thus when thou art dead, and i will kill thee 5.02. 18
take heed of perjury, thou art on thy death-bed. 5.02. 51
thou art to die. 5.02. 56
where art thou? 5.02.105
thou dost belie her, and thou art a devil. 5.02.133
thou art rash as fire to say | that she was 5.02.134
of the world, | art turn'd the greatest liar. ANT 1.03. 39
how much unlike art thou mark antony! 1.05. 35
thou art a soldier only, speak no more. 2.02.107
with him at any game, | thou art sure to lose; 2.03. 27
be it art or hap, | he hath spoken true. 2.03. 33
th' art an honest man. 2.05. 47
of thee, | that art not what th' art sure of. 2.05.103
of thee, | that art not what th' art sure of. 2.05.103
i think th' art mad. the matter? 2.07. 56
thou art, if thou dar'st be, the earthly jove. 2.07. 67
now, darting parthia, art thou strook, and now 3.01. 1
soldier, thou art; 3.07. 68
thou art so leaky | that we must leave thee to 3.13. 63
what art thou, fellow? 3.13. 86
and thou art honest too. 4.02. 15
thou art | the armorer of my heart. 4.04. 6
'tis well th' art gone, | if it be well to live; 4.12. 39
thou art sworn, eros, | that when the exigent 4.14. 62
art thou there, diomed? 4.14.116
and what art thou that dar'st | appear thus to 5.01. 4
o cleopatra! thou art taken, queen. 5.02. 38
where art thou, death? 5.02. 46
thyself art coming | to see perform'd the 5.02.330
what? art thou mad? CYM 1.01.147
i'll tell thee on the instant thou art then | as 1.05. 50
and no more | but what thou art besides, thou 2.03.126
thou art welcome, caius. 3.01. 68
art thou a feodary for this act, and look'st 3.02. 21
the art o' th' court, | as hard to leave as keep 3.03. 46
thou art the pander to her dishonor and equally 3.04. 30 P
thy hand, thou art | no servant of thy master's. 3.04. 75
thou art too slow to do thy master's bidding 3.04. 97
ay, and singular in his art, hath done you both 3.04.121
thou art all the comfort | the gods will diet me 3.04.179
or else | thou art straightway with the fiends. 3.05. 83
my dear lord, | thou art one o' th' false ones. 3.06. 15
what slave art thou? 4.02. 72
thou art a robber, | a law-breaker, a villain. 4.02. 74
what art thou? 4.02. 76
say what thou art; 4.02. 79
thou art some fool, | i am loath to beat thee. 4.02. 85
art not afeard? 4.02. 94
hast done, | home art gone, and ta'en thy wages. 4.02.261
th' great, | thou art past the tyrant's stroke; 4.02.265
what art thou? 4.02.367
for thou art a way, | i think, to liberty; 5.04. 3
thou art fetter'd | more than my shanks and 5.04. 8
then (as men report | thou orphans' father art) 5.04. 40
i am merrier to die than thou art to live. 5.04.171 P
thyself into my grace, | and art mine own. 5.05. 95
by thine own tongue thou art condemn'd, and must 5.05.298
wilt thou undo the worth thou art unpaid for, 5.05.307
thou art my brother, so we'll hold thee ever. 5.05.399
thou, leonatus, art the lion's whelp; 5.05.443
yet neither pleasure's art can joy my spirits, PER 1.02. 9
thou art | no flatterer. 1.02. 60
which love to all, of which thyself art one, 1.02. 94
in framing an artist, art hath thus decreed, 2.03. 15
bewitch'd my daughter, and thou art | a villain. 2.05. 49
thou art the rudeliest welcome to this world 3.01. 30
through which secret art, | by turning o'er 3.02. 32
thou art resolv'd? 4.01. 12
thou art like the harpy, | which, to betray, 4.03. 46
fare thee well, thou art a piece of virtue, and 4.06.111
neither of these are so bad as thou art, | since 4.06.161
thou art the damned door-keeper to every 4.06.165
that even her art sisters the natural roses; 5.ch. 7
thousand part | of my endurance, thou art a man, 5.01.136
thou art a grave and noble counsellor, | most 5.01.182
rise, th' art my child. 5.01.213
you shall hear | scenes, though below his art, TNK pr 28
thou art wanton. 2.02.146
we'll see how near art can come near their 2.02.149
thou art a traitor, arcite, and a fellow | false 2.02.171
till thou art worthy, arcite, it concerns me, 2.02.201
thou art baser in it than a cutpurse. 2.02.211
not, fool, thou canst not, thou art feeble. 2.02.214
news continually, | thou art not worthy life. 2.02.267
o love, | what a stout-hearted child thou art! 2.06. 9
that thou li'st, and art | a very thief in love, 3.01. 40
but this — | that thou art brave and noble. 3.01. 81
i thank thee, arcite, | thou art yet a fair foe; 3.06. 8
thou art so brave an enemy | that no man but thy 3.06. 43
thou art mine aunt's son, | and that blood we 3.06. 94
as thou art spoken, great and virtuous, | the 3.06.152
as thou art just, thy noble ear against us; 3.06.174
as thou art valiant, for thy cousin's soul, 3.06.175
palamon, thou art alone | and only beautiful, 4.02. 37
thou art a changeling to him, a mere gipsy, 4.02. 44
they show | great and fine art in nature. 4.02.123
glory in a life | that thou art yet to lead. 5.04. 44
his head, | seem'd with strange art to hang. 5.04. 79
thou art a right good man, and while i live, 5.04. 97
th' art a good house-keeper and i thank thy good STM II.C 58 P
boy, | 'tis but a kiss i beg, why art thou coy? VEN 96
"art thou asham'd to kiss? 121
by law of nature thou art bound to breed, | that 171
that thine may live, when thou thyself art dead; 172
"art thou obdurate, flinty, hard as steel? 199
art thou a woman's son and canst not feel | what 201
thou art no man; 215
his art with nature's workmanship at strife, 291
"so in thyself thyself art made away, | a 763
thou art as full of fear | as one with treasure 1021
"since thou art dead, lo here i prophesy, 1135
thou art the next of blood, and 'tis thy right. 1184
thyself art mighty, for thine own sake leave me; LUC 583
o, if no harder than a stone thou art, | melt at 593
thou art not what thou seem'st, and if the same, 600
thou seem'st not what thou art, a god, a king; 601
what dar'st thou not when once thou art a king? 606
"thou art," quoth she, "a sea, a sovereign king, 652
since thou art guilty of my cureless crime, 772
fee, | he gratis comes, and thou art well apaid, 914
"guilty thou art of murther and of theft, 918
that thou art doting father of his fruit. 1064
in scorn of nature, art gave liveless life: 1374
o, what art | of physiognomy might one behold! 1394
priam, why art thou old, and yet not wise? 1550
why art thou thus attir'd in discontent? 1601
those pleasures live that art can comprehend. PP 5. 6
celestial as thou art, o, do not love that wrong 5.13
thus art with arms contending was victor of the 15.13
thou that art now the world's fresh ornament, SON 1. 9
this were to be new made when thou art old, 2.13
thou art thy mother's glass, and she in thee 3. 9
ten times thyself were happier than thou art, 6. 9
for thou art much too fair | to be death's 6.13
to any, | who for thyself art so unprovident. 10. 2
grant, if thou wilt, thou art belov'd of many, 10. 3
for thou art so possess'd with murd'rous hate, 10. 5
in them i read such art | as truth and beauty 14.10
thou art more lovely and more temperate: 18. 2
how can i then be elder than thou art? 22. 8
and perspective it is best painter's art. 24. 4
yet eyes this cunning want to grace their art, 24.13
i tell the day, to please him, thou art bright, 28. 9
desiring this man's art, and that man's scope, 29. 7
thou art the grave where buried love doth live, 31. 9
sing, | when thou art all the better part of me? 39. 2
for still temptation follows where thou art. 41. 4
gentle thou art, and therefore to be won, 41. 5
beauteous thou art, therefore to be assailed; 41. 6
where thou art forc'd to break a twofold truth: 41.12
leap large lengths of miles when thou art gone, 44.10
care, | art left the prey of every vulgar thief. 48. 8
save where thou art not, though i feel thou art, 48.10
save where thou art not, though i feel thou art, 48.10
from where thou art, why should i haste me 51. 3
on helen's cheek all art of beauty set, | and 53. 7
and art made tongue-tied by authority, | and 66. 9
to show false art what beauty was of yore. 68.14
but thou art all my art, and dost advance | as 78.13
but thou art all my art, and dost advance | as 78.13
thou art as fair in knowledge as in hue, 82. 5
and therefore art enforc'd to seek anew | some 82. 7
farewell, thou art too dear for my possessing, 87. 1
prove thee virtuous, though thou art forsworn. 88. 4
away, | for term of life thou art assured mine, 92. 2
so shall i live, supposing thou art true, | like 93. 1
where art thou, muse, that thou forget'st so 100. 1
save thou, my rose, in it thou art my all. 109.14
which is not mix'd with seconds, knows no art, 125.11
thou art as tyrannous, so as thou art, | as 131. 1
thou art as tyrannous, so as thou art, | as 131. 1
thou art the fairest and most precious jewel. 131. 4
in nothing art thou black save in thy deeds, 131.13
free, | for thou art covetous, and he is kind; 134. 6
use power with power and slay me not by art. 139. 4
be wise as thou art cruel, do not press | my 140. 1
who art as black as hell, as dark as night. 147.14
but thou art twice forsworn, to me love swearing 152. 2
what with his art in youth and youth in art, LC 145
what with his art in youth and youth in art, 145
thought characters and words merely but art, 174
for thou art all, and all things else are thine. 266
"for lo his passion, but an art of craft, | even 295

ARTEMIDORUS 1 FR 0.0001 REL FR 0 V 1 P
thy lover, artemidorus." JC 2.03. 10 P

ARTERE 1 FR 0.0001 REL FR 1 V 0 P
and makes each petty artere in this body | as HAM 1.04. 82

ARTERIES 1 FR 0.0001 REL FR 1 V 0 P
poisons up | the nimble spirits in the arteries, LLL 4.03.302

ARTESIUS 1 FR 0.0001 REL FR 1 V 0 P
artesius, that best knowest | how to draw out, TNK 1.01.159

ARTHUR 30 FR 0.0034 REL FR 27 V 3 P
arthur plantagenet, lays most lawful claim | to JN 1.01. 9
arthur, that great forerunner of thy blood, 2.01. 2
maine, | in right of arthur do i claim of thee. 2.01.153
arthur of britain, yield thee to my hand, | and 2.01.156
and let young arthur, duke of britain, in, | who 2.01.301
arthur of britain england's king and yours. 2.01.311
for we'll create young arthur duke of britain 2.01.551
arthur ta'en prisoner? 3.04. 7
wife, | young arthur is my son, and he is lost. 3.04. 47
never | must i behold my pretty arthur more. 3.04. 89
o lord, my boy, my arthur, my fair son! 3.04.103
are not you griev'd that arthur is his prisoner? 3.04.123
john hath seiz'd arthur, and it cannot be | that 3.04.131
john may stand, then arthur needs must fall: 3.04.139
may then make all the claim that arthur did. 3.04.143
and lose it, life and all, as arthur did. 3.04.144
if that young arthur be not gone already, | even 3.04.163
read here, young arthur. 4.01. 33
request | th' enfranchisement of arthur, whose 4.02. 52
he tells us arthur is deceas'd to-night. 4.02. 85
going to seek the grave | of arthur, whom they 4.02.165
young arthur is alive. 4.02.251
doth arthur live? 4.02.260
arthur doth live, the king hath sent for you. 4.03. 75
again | after they heard young arthur was alive? 5.01. 38
after young arthur, claim this land for mine, 5.02. 94
"when arthur first in court" — empty the jordan 2H4 2.04. 33 P
princess dowager | and widow to prince arthur. H8 3.02. 71
and 'a made my brother arthur watchins sergeant STM II.C 43 P
thy good worship for my brother arthur watchins. II.C 59 P

ARTHUR'S 13 FR 0.0014 REL FR 10 V 3 P
and put the same into young arthur's hand, | thy JN 1.01. 14
whose title they admit, arthur's or john's. 2.01.200
you loving men of angiers, arthur's subjects, 2.01.204
john, to stop arthur's title in the whole, 2.01.562
but what shall i gain by young arthur's fall? 3.04.141
may be he will not touch young arthur's life, 3.04.160
young arthur's death is common in their mouths, 4.02.187
cuts off his tale and talks of arthur's death. 4.02.202
why urgest thou so oft young arthur's death? 4.02.204
i faintly broke with thee of arthur's death; 4.02.227
i was then sir dagonet in arthur's show — there 2H4 3.02.280 P
he's in arthur's bosom, if ever man went to H5 2.03. 9 P
bosom, if ever man went to arthur's bosom. 2.03. 10 P

/ARTICLE 1 FR 0.0001 REL FR 1 V 0 P
/shouldst /thou /find /one /heinous /article, R2 4.01.233

ARTICLE 18 FR 0.0020 REL FR 14 V 4 P
to every article. TMP 1.02.195
not mine twice or thrice in that last article. TGV 3.01.356 P
shouldst not alter the article of thy gentry. WIV 2.01. 53 P
you swerve not from the smallest article of it, MM 4.02.104 P
this article, my liege, yourself must break, LLL 1.01.133
therefore this article is made in vain, | or 1.01.139
each several article herein redress'd, | all 2H4 4.01.168
the king hath granted every article: H5 5.02.332
let that one article rank with the rest, | and 5.02.346
which easily endures not article | tying him to COR 2.03.196
comart | and carriage of the article /design'd, HAM 1.01. 94
i take him to be a soul of great article, and 5.02.117 P
in the error | but the main article i do approve OTH 1.03. 11
i'll perform it | to the last article. 3.03. 22
for to deny each article with oath | cannot 5.02. 54
you have broken | the article of your oath, ANT 2.02. 82
but on, caesar, | the article of my oath. 2.02. 87
life, | for that's an article within our law, PER 1.01. 88

/ARTICLES 2 FR 0.0002 REL FR 2 V 0 P
/lord, /dispatch, /read /o'er /these /articles. R2 4.01.243
/time /shall /serve) /to /show /in /articles; 2H4 4.01. 74

ARTICLES 17 FR 0.0019 REL FR 14 V 3 P
what is he, william, that does lend articles? WIV 4.01. 39 P
articles are borrow'd of the pronoun, and be 4.01. 40 P
france, | to draw my answer from thy articles? JN 2.01.111
how far forth you do like their articles. 2H4 4.02. 53
a /cursitory eye | o'erglanc'd the articles. H5 5.02. 78
when articles too nicely urg'd be stood on. 5.02. 94
within the fore-rank of our articles. 5.02. 97
here are the articles of contracted peace 2H6 1.01. 40
suffolk concluded on the articles, | the peers 1.01.217
i cannot stay to hear these articles. 3H6 1.01.180
and now forthwith shall articles be drawn 3.03.135
cardinal | the articles o' th' combination drew H8 1.01.169
sins, the articles | collected from his life. 3.02.293
those articles, my lord, are in the king's hand: 3.02.299
i yet remember | some of these articles, and out 3.02.304
the scope | of these delated articles allow. HAM 1.02. 38
conditions, let us have articles betwixt us. CYM 1.04.156 P

ARTICULATE 2 FR 0.0002 REL FR 2 V 0 P
these things indeed you have articulate, 1H4 5.01. 72
with whom we may articulate | for their own good COR 1.09. 77

ARTIFICER 1 FR 0.0001 REL FR 1 V 0 P
another lean unwash'd artificer | cuts off his JN 4.02.201

ARTIFICIAL 7 FR 0.0008 REL FR 6 V 1 P
we, hermia, like two artificial gods, | have MND 3.02.203
and wet my cheeks with artificial tears, | and 3H6 3.02.184
out, | and makes himself an artificial night. ROM 1.01.140
artificial strife | lives in these touches, TIM 1.01. 37
with two stones moe than 's artificial one. 2.02.111 P
shall raise such artificial sprites | as by the MAC 3.05. 27
if that thy prosperous and artificial /feat PER 5.01. 72

ARTILLERY 5 FR 0.0005 REL FR 5 V 0 P
and heaven's artillery thunder in the skies? SHR 1.02.204
town, | turn thou the mouth of thy artillery, JN 2.01.403
as by discharge of their artillery | and shape 1H4 1.01. 57
i can, | to view th' artillery and munition, 1H6 1.01.168
to rive their dangerous artillery | upon no 4.02. 29

ARTIST 2 FR 0.0002 REL FR 2 V 0 P
the wise and fool, the artist and unread, | the TRO 1.03. 24
in framing an artist, art hath thus decreed, PER 2.03. 15

ARTISTS 1 FR 0.0001 REL FR 0 V 1 P
to be relinquish'd of the artists — AWW 2.03. 10 P

ARTLESS 1 FR 0.0001 REL FR 1 V 0 P
amiss, | so full of artless jealousy is guilt, HAM 4.05. 19

ARTOIS 1 FR 0.0001 REL FR 1 V 0 P
by whose approach the regions of artois, 1H6 2.01. 9

ART'S 1 FR 0.0001 REL FR 1 V 0 P
fairing the foul with art's false borrow'd face, SON 127. 6

ARTS 14 FR 0.0015 REL FR 13 V 1 P
and for the liberal arts | without a parallel; TMP 1.02. 73
well fitted in arts, glorious in arms; LLL 2.01. 45
other slow arts entirely keep the brain; 4.03.321
they are the books, the arts, the academes, 4.03.349
i had | to see fair padua, nursery of arts, | i SHR 1.01. 2
o, had i but follow'd the arts! TN 1.03. 94 P
their sons with arts and martial exercises; 2H4 4.05. 73
dear nurse of arts, plenties, and joyful births, H5 5.02. 35
and swelling o'er with arts and exercise. TRO 4.04. 78
one that feeds | on objects, arts, and JC 4.01. 37
of arts inhibited and out of warrant. OTH 1.02. 79
those arts they have as i | could put into them. CYM 5.05.338
pericles, | my education been in arts and arms; PER 2.03. 82
and arts with thy sweet graces graced be; SON 78.12

ARTS-MAN 1 FR 0.0001 REL FR 0 V 1 P
arts-man, preambulate, we will be singuled from LLL 5.01. 81 P

ARTUS 1 FR 0.0001 REL FR 1 V 0 P

/pene gelidus timor occupat artus: 2H6 4.01.117
/ARUNDEL 1 FR 0.0001 REL FR 1 V 0 P
/son /and /heir /to /th' /earl /of /arundel, R2 2.01.280
ARVIRAGUS 2 FR 0.0002 REL FR 2 V 0 P
once arviragus, in as like a figure, | strikes CYM 3.03. 96
this gentleman, my cadwal, arviragus, | your 5.05.359
/'A'S 1 FR 0.0001 REL FR 1 V 0 P
but /'a's in a suit of buff which 'rested him, ERR 4.02. 45
'AS *(also has)*
'AS 3 FR 0.0003 REL FR 2 V 1 P
't 'as been prov'd. TIM 1.02. 49 P
't 'as been done; 1.02.144
't 'as been a turbulent and stormy night. PER 3.02. 4
AS* *(also asse, 's*)*
/AS* 44 FR 0.0049 REL FR 37 V 7 P
AS* 6090 FR 0.6884 REL FR 4633 V 1457 P
ASCANIUS 1 FR 0.0001 REL FR 1 V 0 P
as ascanius did | when he to madding dido would 2H6 3.02.116
ASCEND 11 FR 0.0012 REL FR 10 V 1 P
a mean | how he her chamber–window will ascend,
TGV 3.01. 39
ascend my chambers, search, seek, find out. WIV 3.03.162 P
not, bleed france, and peace ascend to heaven, JN 2.01. 86
ascend his throne, descending now from him, R2 4.01.111
in god's name i'll ascend the regal throne. 4.01.113
that would ascend | the brightest heaven of H5 pr 1
ascend, brave talbot, we will follow thee. 1H6 2.01. 28
i will not think but they ascend the sky, | and R3 1.03.286
ascend, fair queen, pantheon. TIT 1.01.333
ascend her chamber, hence and comfort her. ROM 3.03.147
the base degrees | by which he did ascend. JC 2.01. 27
ASCENDED 2 FR 0.0002 REL FR 2 V 0 P
the noble brutus is ascended; silence! JC 3.02. 11
should have ascended to the roof of heaven, ANT 3.06. 49
ASCENDS 3 FR 0.0003 REL FR 2 V 1 P
the mounting bullingbrook ascends my throne, R2 5.01. 56
my cousin bullingbrook ascends my throne" 2H4 3.01. 71
it ascends me into the brain, dries me there all 4.03. 97 P
ASCENSION 1 FR 0.0001 REL FR 1 V 0 P
his ascension is | more sweet than our blest CYM 5.04.116
ASCENSION–DAY 4 FR 0.0004 REL FR 4 V 0 P
that, ere the next ascension–day at noon, | your JN 4.02.151
on this ascension–day, remember well, | upon 5.01. 22
is this ascension–day? 5.01. 25
prophet | say that before ascension–day at noon 5.01. 26
ASCENT 1 FR 0.0001 REL FR 0 V 1 P
and his ascent is not by such easy degrees as COR 2.02. 25 P
A–SCORN 1 FR 0.0001 REL FR 1 V 0 P
i have (as when the sun doth light a–scorn) TRO 1.01. 37
ASCRIBE 3 FR 0.0003 REL FR 3 V 0 P
ourselves do lie, | which we ascribe to heaven. AWW 1.01.217
to us, but to thy arm alone, | ascribe we all! H5 4.08.108
and much the reason | why we ascribe it to him; TRO 2.03.117
ASCRIBES 1 FR 0.0001 REL FR 1 V 0 P
heart | ascribes the glory of his conquest got 1H6 3.04. 11
ASH 2 FR 0.0002 REL FR 1 V 1 P
out that year on ash we'nsday was four year in MV 2.05. 26 P
my grained ash an hundred times hath broke, COR 4.05.108
A–SHAKING 1 FR 0.0001 REL FR 1 V 0 P
whose grim aspect sets every joint a–shaking; LUC 452
ASHAM'D 34 FR 0.0038 REL FR 22 V 12 P
and art thou not asham'd | to wrong him with thy TGV 4.02.110
be thou asham'd that i have took upon me | such 5.04.105
fie, fie, master ford, are you not asham'd? WIV 3.03.214 P
are you not asham'd? let the clothes alone. 4.02.138 P
are you not asham'd? 4.02.187 P
perchance, publicly, she'll be asham'd. MM 5.01.277 P
fie upon thee, art not asham'd? ADO 3.04. 28 P
but are you not asham'd? LLL 4.03.157
on me, | for i am much asham'd of my exchange. MV 2.06. 35
what, art thou asham'd of me? SHR 5.01.145
no, sir, god forbid, but asham'd to kiss. 5.01.146
i am asham'd that women are so simple | to offer 5.02.161
invention is asham'd, | against the proclamation AWW 1.03.173
i am asham'd; WT 5.03. 37
i am almost asham'd | to say what good respect i JN 3.03. 27
art thou not asham'd? 1H4 1.03.118
art thou not asham'd? 3.03.163 P
if i be not asham'd of my soldiers, i am a 4.02. 11 P
are you not asham'd to enforce a poor widow to 2H4 2.01. 82 P
art thou not asham'd to be call'd captain? 2.04.141 P
are you not asham'd | with this immodest 1H6 4.01.125
i am asham'd. TRO 3.02.138
upon his brow shame is asham'd to sit; ROM 3.02. 92
now, before the gods, i am asham'd on't. TIM 3.02. 18 P
be not you asham'd to show, he'll not shame to HAM 3.02.145 P
than on a wretch whom nature is asham'd | almost
LR 1.01.212
i am asham'd | that thou hast power to shake my 1.04.296
art not asham'd to look upon this beard? 2.04.193
you'll be asham'd for ever. OTH 2.03.163
no more upon't, | it is asham'd to bear me. ANT 3.11. 2
i am asham'd | to look upon the holy sun, to CYM 4.04. 40
have patience to make any adversity asham'd. TNK 2.01. 24 P
"art thou asham'd to kiss? VEN 121
like stars asham'd of day, themselves withdrew. 1032
ASHAMED 3 FR 0.0003 REL FR 2 V 1 P
in me | to be ashamed to be my father's child! MV 2.03. 17
i need not to be ashamed of your majesty, H5 4.07.113 P
i am ashamed i did yield to them. JC 2.02.106
ASHER–HOUSE 1 FR 0.0001 REL FR 1 V 0 P
and to confine yourself | to asher–house, my H8 3.02.231
ASHES 24 FR 0.0027 REL FR 23 V 1 P
and thou shalt turn | to ashes, ere our blood JN 3.01.345
out, | and strew'd repentant ashes on his head. 4.01.110
and some will mourn in ashes, some coal–black, R2 5.01. 49
marry, not in ashes and sackcloth, but in new 2H4 1.02.198 P
harflew | till in her ashes she lies buried. H5 3.03. 9
her ashes, in an urn more precious | than the 1H6 1.06. 24
burns under feigned ashes of forg'd love, | and 3.01.189
but from their ashes shall be rear'd | a phoenix 4.07. 92
break thou in pieces and consume to ashes, 5.04. 92
the witch in smithfield shall be burnt to ashes, 2H6 2.03. 7
my ashes, as the phoenix, may bring forth | a 3H6 1.04. 35
king, | pale ashes of the house of lancaster, R3 1.02. 6
truth and modesty, | now in his ashes honor. H8 4.02. 75
her ashes new create another heir | as great in 5.04. 41
who from the sacred ashes of her honor | shall 5.04. 45
pale, pale as ashes, all bedaub'd in blood, ROM 3.02. 55
lips and cheeks shall fade | to /wanny ashes, 4.01.100
of my spirits | through th' ashes of my chance. ANT 5.02.174
was sung, | from ashes ancient gower is come, PER 1.ch. 2
to urn their ashes, nor to take th' offense | of TNK 1.01. 44
and lovers yet unborn shall bless my ashes. 3.06.283
following the dead–cold ashes of their sons, 4.02. 5
so of shame's ashes shall my fame be bred, | for LUC 1188
fire | that on the ashes of his youth doth lie, SON 73.10
ASHFORD 2 FR 0.0002 REL FR 1 V 1 P
a headstrong kentishman, | john cade of ashford, 2H6 3.01.357
where's dick, the butcher of ashford? 4.03. 1 P
ASHORE 13 FR 0.0014 REL FR 9 V 4 P
how came we ashore? TMP 1.02.158
here shall i die ashore —" | this is a very 2.02. 43
with mine own hands since i was cast ashore. 2.02.124 P
swom ashore, man, like a duck. 2.02.128 P
tuns of oil in his belly) ashore at windsor? WIV 2.01. 65 P
if, biondello, thou wert come ashore, | we could SHR 1.01. 42
for in a quarrel since i came ashore | i kill'd 1.01.231
send precepts to the leviathan | to come ashore. H5 3.03. 27
the aid | of buckingham to welcome them ashore. R3 4.04.439
i must fetch his necessaries ashore. OTH 2.01.284 P
bear him ashore. i'll pledge it for him, pompey. ANT 2.07. 85
doing bad, | threw him ashore, to give him glad. PER 2.ch. 38
with all my heart, and, when you come ashore, 5.01.260
A–SHOUTING 1 FR 0.0001 REL FR 0 V 1 P
hand thus, and then the people fell a–shouting. JC 1.02.223 P
ASHY 3 FR 0.0003 REL FR 3 V 0 P
of ashy semblance, meagre, pale, and bloodless, 2H6 3.02.162
and dying eyes gleam'd forth their ashy lights, LUC 1378
nor ashy pale the fear that false hearts have. 1512
ASHY–PALE 1 FR 0.0001 REL FR 1 V 0 P
'twixt crimson shame and anger ashy–pale. VEN 76
ASIA 4 FR 0.0004 REL FR 3 V 1 P
roaming clean through the bounds of asia, | and, ERR 1.01.133
toothpicker now from the furthest inch of asia, ADO 2.01.267 P
pack–horses | and hollow pamper'd jades of asia, 2H4 2.04.164
hath with his parthian force | extended asia; ANT 1.02.101
ASIDE 61 FR 0.0069 REL FR 39 V 22 P
whose enmity he flung aside, and breasted | the TMP 2.01.117
peace, stand aside, the company parts. TGV 4.02. 81
setting the attraction of my good parts aside, i WIV 2.02.106 P
will't please you walk aside? MM 4.01. 58
old signior, walk aside with me, i have studied ADO 3.02. 71 P
well, stand aside. 4.02. 30 P
stand aside, good bearer. LLL 4.01. 55
walk aside the true folk, and let the traitors 4.03.209
stand aside, good pompey. 5.02.587 P
stand aside. MND 3.02.116
worn, | our purpos'd hunting shall be set aside. 4.01.183
go, draw aside the curtains and discover | the MV 2.07. 1
here comes my sister reading, stand aside. AYL 3.02.124
he threw his eye aside, | and mark what object 4.03.102
bianca, stand aside. SHR 2.01. 24
and therefore, setting all this chat aside, 2.01.268
kate, let's stand aside and see the end of this 5.01. 61 P
too fine in thy evidence, therefore stand aside. AWW 5.03.269 P
take him aside. TN 5.01.100
casting their savageness aside, have done | like WT 2.03.188
business, and lay aside the thoughts of sicilia. 4.02. 51 P
aside, aside, here is more matter for a hot 4.04.684 P
aside, aside, here is more matter for a hot 4.04.684 P
desiring thee to lay aside the sword | which JN 1.01. 12
setting aside his high blood's royalty, | and R2 1.01. 58
king, | and lay aside my high blood's royalty, 1.01. 71
to lay aside life–harming heaviness | and 2.02. 3
step aside, and i'll show thee a /president. 1H4 2.04. 33 P
and here is my speech. stand aside, nobility. 2.04.389 P
setting thy knighthood aside, thou art a knave 3.03.120 P
setting thy womanhood aside, thou art a beast to 3.03.122 P
that daff'd the world aside | and bid it pass? 4.01. 96
setting my knighthood and my soldiership aside, 2H4 1.02. 81 P
set your knighthood and your soldiership aside, 1.02. 84 P
i lay aside that which grows to me? 1.02. 87 P
peace, stand aside, know you where you are? 3.02.119 P
go to, stand aside. 3.02.228 P
go to, stand aside. 3.02.233 P
broil, | and set this unaccustom'd fight aside. 1H6 3.01. 93
lenity | and harmful pity must be laid aside. 3H6 2.02. 10
vouchsafe, at our request, to stand aside, 3.03.110
all dissembling set aside, | tell me for truth 3.03.119
tell him, my mourning weeds are laid aside, 3.03.229
setting your scorns and your mislike aside, 4.01. 24
but that thy brothers beat aside the point. R3 1.02. 96
or /hedge aside from the direct forthright, TRO 3.03.158
would the nobility lay aside their ruth | and COR 1.01.197
come, lay aside your stitchery, i must have you 1.03. 69 P
so please you step aside, | i'll know his ROM 1.01.156
with one hand beats | cold death aside, and with 3.01.162
taking thy part, hath rush'd aside the law, 3.03. 26
aside, aside, here comes lord timon. TIM 2.02.119 P
aside, aside, here comes lord timon. 2.02.119 P
he is a man (setting his fate aside) | of comely 3.05. 14
throwing it aside | and stemming it with hearts JC 1.02.108
boy, stand aside. 2.01.312
in their newest gloss, | not cast aside so soon. MAC 1.07. 35
i prithee turn aside, and weep for her, | then ANT 1.03. 76
who sees the lurking serpent steps aside; LUC 362
why with the time do i not glance aside | to SON 76. 3
dear heart, forbear to glance thine eye aside; 139. 6
ASINICO 1 FR 0.0001 REL FR 0 V 1 P
have in mine elbows, an asinico may tutor thee. TRO 2.01. 44 P
/ASK 1 FR 0.0001 REL FR 1 V 0 P
/yet /ask. R2 4.01.310
ASK 179 FR 0.0202 REL FR 129 V 50 P
i chose her when i could not ask my father | for TMP 5.01.190
it sound that i | must ask my child forgiveness! 5.01.198
and you ask me if she did nod, and i say, "ay." TGV 1.01.114 P
back | and ask remission for my folly past. 1.02. 65
ask my dog. 2.05. 35 P
to grant one boon that i shall ask of you. 5.04.150
and ask of doctor caius' house which is the way; WIV 1.02. 1 P
better that it pleases your good worship to ask. 1.04.136 P
"ask me no reason why i love you, for though 2.01. 4 P
you may ask your father, here he comes. 3.04. 66 P
i pray you ask him some questions in his 4.01. 16 P
and ask him why, that hour of fairy revel, | in 4.04. 59
let me ask, | the rather for i now must make you MM 1.04. 21
you, sir, ask him what this man did to my wife. 2.01.143 P
i beseech your honor, ask me. 2.01.145 P
why dost thou ask again? 2.02. 9
and ask your heart what it doth know | that's 2.02.137
let me ask my sister pardon. 3.01.171 P
your bawd — he doth oft'ner ask forgiveness. 4.02. 51 P
sirrah, if any ask you for your master, | say he ERR 2.02.209
some devils ask but the parings of one's nail, 4.03. 71
what is he that you ask for, niece? ADO 1.01. 34 P
thou shouldst rather ask if it were possible any 3.03.112 P
ask my lady beatrice else, here she comes. 3.04. 37 P
first, i ask thee what they have done; 5.01.220 P
thirdly, i ask thee what's their offense; 5.01.221 P
how needless was it then | to ask the question? LLL 2.01.117
the hour that fools should ask. 2.01.122
ask for her, | and to her white hand see thou do 3.01.167
ask them how many inches | is in one mile: 5.02.188
i know the reason, lady, why you ask. 5.02.243
why ask you? 5.02.525 P
that will ask some tears in the true performing MND 1.02. 25 P
i then did ask of her her changeling child; 4.01. 59
but ask me not what; 4.02. 30 P
nay, but ask my opinion too of that. MV 3.05. 85
you'll ask me why i rather choose to have | a 4.01. 40
i pardon thee thy life before thou ask it. 4.01.369
with my fortunes, | i'll ask him what he would. AYL 1.02.253
did he ask for me? 3.02.222 P
you should ask me what time o' day; 3.02.300 P
think not i love him, though i ask for him; 3.05.109
and ask me what you will, i will grant it. 4.01.113 P
i might ask you for your commission, but i do 4.01.138 P
suit, | and ask him what apparel he will wear; SHR in.1. 60
ne'er ask me what raiment i'll wear, for i have in.2. 8 P
ask marian hacket, the fat ale–wife of wincot, in.2. 21 P
if thou ask me why, | sufficeth my reasons are 1.01.247
sir, let me be so bold as ask you, | did you yet 1.02.249
i'll crave the day | when i shall ask the banes, 2.01.180
should ask if katherine should be his wife, 3.02.159
and seem'd to ask him sops as he was drinking. 3.02.176
let me ask a question. AWW 1.01.112 P
would you had kneel'd, my lord, to ask me mercy, 2.01. 64
whom i know | is free for me to ask, thee to 2.01.200
ask me if i am a courtier: 2.02. 36 P
and rather muse than ask why i entreat you, 2.05. 65
mend the ruff and sing, ask questions and sing, 3.02. 7 P
answer to what i shall ask you out of a note. 4.03.127 P
i need not to ask you if gold will corrupt him 4.03.277 P
why does he ask him of me? 4.03.284 P
let him not ask our pardon, | the nature of his 5.03. 22
ask him upon his oath, if he does think | he had 5.03.185
do theirs — to ask for my kinsman toby — TN 2.05. 54 P
and ask no other dowry with her but such another 2.05.184 P
what shall you ask of me that i'll deny, | that 3.04.211
my necessity | makes me to ask you for my purse? 3.04.335
and for his cowardship, ask fabian. 3.04.388 P
nay, ask me if i can refrain from love, | for i JN 2.01.525
it me) | and i did never ask it you again; 4.01. 44
mean time but ask | what you would have reform'd 4.02. 43
our suit | that you have bid us ask his liberty, 4.02. 63
which for our goods we do no further ask | than 4.02. 64
i do not ask you much, | i beg cold comfort; 5.07. 41
ask him his name, and orderly proceed | to swear R2 1.03. 9
marshal, ask yonder knight in arms, | both who 1.03. 26
and, for these great affairs do ask some charge, 2.01.159
whose tongue shall ask me for one penny cost 1H4 1.03. 91
me | directly unto this question that i ask. 2.03. 86
ask me when thou wilt, and thou shalt have it. 2.04. 62 P
may i ask how my lady his wife doth? 2H4 3.02. 65 P
your highness bade me ask for it to–day. H5 2.02. 63
ask me this slave in french | what is his name. 4.04. 23
i'll ask them. 5.02.197 P
ask me what question thou canst possible, | and 1H6 1.02. 87
what means he now? go ask him whither he goes. 2.03. 28
thou tremblest at, answer that i shall ask; 2H6 1.04. 26
ask what thou wilt. that i had said, and done! 1.04. 28
go to then, i ask but this: 4.02.170 P
and ask him what's the reason of these arms. 4.09. 37
first let me ask of /these | if they can brook i 5.01.109
clifford, ask mercy and obtain no grace. 3H6 2.06. 69
france, | and ask the lady bona for thy queen. 2.06. 90
ay, but thou canst do what i mean to ask. 3.02. 48
why ask i that? 5.02. 7
the better that your lordship please to ask. R3 3.02. 97
to ask those on the banks | if they were his 4.04.523
ask god for temp'rance, that's th' appliance H8 1.01.124
the other moi'ty ere you ask is given; 1.02. 12
that | a woman of less place might ask by law: 2.02.111
that seal | you ask with such a violence, the 3.02.246
may i be bold to ask what that contains, | that 4.01. 13
i ask, that i might waken reverence, | and bid TRO 1.03.227
hector bade ask. 4.05. 71
ask me /not what i would be if i were not 5.01. 64 P
tell me one thing that i shall ask you. COR 2.01. 13 P
the price is, to ask it kindly. 2.03. 75 P
of him that did not ask but mock, bestow | your 2.03.207
who shall ask it? 4.06.108
or, if you'ld ask, remember this before: 5.03. 79
for we have nothing else to ask but that | which 5.03. 88
yet we will ask, | that, if you fail in our 5.03. 89
slain | religiously they ask a sacrifice: TIT 1.01.124
titus, thou shalt obtain and ask the empery. 1.01.201
here, | i ask your voices and your suffrages: 1.01.218
knees, | you shall ask pardon of his majesty. 1.01.473
but what says jupiter, i ask thee? 4.03. 84
why, may one ask? ROM 1.04. 49
go ask his name. 1.05.134
i'll tell thee ere thou ask it me again. 2.03. 48
ask for me to–morrow, and you shall find me a 3.01. 97 P
that i ask again, | for nothing can be ill if 5.01. 15
ask nothing, give it him, it foals me straight TIM 2.01. 9
that you ask me what you are, and do not know 2.02. 64 P
what do ye ask of me, my friend? 3.04. 45
why dost ask that? 4.03.473
i should not then ask casca what had chanc'd. JC 1.02.220
why ask you? hear you aught of her in yours? 4.03.185
answer me | to what i ask you. MAC 4.01. 61
of this, but when they ask you what it means, HAM 4.05. 47 P

why ask you this? 4.07.109
ask her forgiveness? LR 2.04.152
good nuncle, in, ask thy daughters blessing. 3.02. 12 P
if he ask for me, i am ill and gone to bed. 3.03. 16 P
let me ask you one word in private. 3.04.160
when thou dost ask me blessing, i'll kneel down 5.03. 10
i'll kneel down | and ask of thee forgiveness. 5.03. 11
ask him his purposes, why he appears | upon this 5.03.118
in wisdom i should ask thy name, | but, since 5.03.142
ask me not what i know. 5.03.161
why? wherefore ask you this? OTH 1.01. 85
i will ask him for my place again, he shall tell 2.03.303 P
soul | what you would ask me that i should deny, 3.03. 69
he did, from first to last. why dost thou ask? 3.03. 96
send for the man, and ask him. 5.02. 50
ask thy husband else. 5.02.136
i do believe it, and i ask your pardon. 5.02.300
i do not know, | maecenas, ask agrippa. ANT 2.02. 17
do | so far ask pardon as befits mine honor | to 2.02. 97
i have one thing more to ask him yet, good 3.03. 45
to be sure of that, | i will ask antony. 3.13. 63
he did ask favor. 3.13.133
tend me to–night two hours, i ask no more, | and 4.02. 32
we, with manners, ask what was the difference? CYM 1.04. 52 P
without offense | (my conscience bids me ask), 1.05. 7
or, by jupiter, | i will not ask again. 3.05. 85
(i forgot to ask him one thing, i'll remember't 3.05.130 P
to be i' th' field, and ask "what news?" 5.03. 65
'tis now the time | to ask of whence you are. 5.05. 16
and ask of cymbeline what boon thou wilt, 5.05. 97
think more and more | what's best to ask. 5.05.110
nor ask advice of any other thought | but PER 1.01. 62
it fits thee not | to ask the reason why, 1.01.157
take thy word for faith, not ask thine oath: 1.02.120
being bid to ask what he would of the king, 1.03. 5 P
to give my tongue that heat to ask your help; 2.01. 75
let me ask you one thing: 2.05. 32
henceforth i'll not dare | to ask you any thing, TNK 1.01.204
it but hold, i ask no more | for all my hopes. 3.06. 91
duke, ask that lady | why she is fair, and why 3.06.168
why do you ask? 4.01. 32
on my knees | i ask thy pardon: 4.02. 37
now, come ask me, brother — | alas, i know not! 4.02. 50
ask me now, sweet sister — | i may go look! 4.02. 51
do any thing, | lie with her, if she ask you. 5.02. 18
i would now ask ye how ye like the play, | but, ep 1
to ask the spotted princess how she fares. LUC 721
but durst not ask of her audaciously | why her 1223
he hath no power to ask her how she fares. 1594
ASKANCE 1 FR 0.0001 REL FR 1 V 0 P
nigh, | for all askance he holds her in his eye. VEN 342
ASKAUNCE 3 FR 0.0003 REL FR 3 V 0 P
canst not frown, thou canst not look askaunce, SHR 2.01.247
from their own misdeeds askaunce their eyes! LUC 637
i have look'd on truth | askaunce and strangely: SON 110. 6
ASKAUNT 1 FR 0.0001 REL FR 1 V 0 P
there is a willow grows askaunt the brook, HAM 4.07.166
ASK'D 38 FR 0.0043 REL FR 24 V 14 P
music and see the gentleman that you ask'd for. TGV 4.02. 32 P
in when your husband ask'd who was in the basket
WIV 3.03.181 P
who ask'd them once or twice what they had in 3.05.102 P
he ask'd me for a /thousand marks in gold: ERR 2.01. 61
i thought to have ask'd you. 3.01. 55
were you in doubt, sir, that you ask'd her? ADO 1.01.106 P
he ask'd me of what parentage i was. AYL 3.04. 36 P
it is no boast, being ask'd, to say we are. 4.03. 90
sigh'd but they ask'd one another the reason; 5.02. 35 P
broke thy pate, | and ask'd thee mercy for't. AWW 2.01. 67
a question not to be ask'd. 1H4 2.04.409 P
a question to be ask'd. 2.04.410 P
such as had been ask'd twice on the banes, such 4.02. 17 P
he ask'd the way to chester, and of him | i did 2H4 1.01. 39
and my consent ne'er ask'd herein before? 2H6 2.04. 72
garrisons, | and never ask'd for restitution. 3.01.118
and ask'd the mayor what meant this willful R3 3.07. 28
his suit was granted | ere it was ask'd — but H8 1.01.187
for they have pardons, being ask'd, as free | as COR 3.02. 88
no question ask'd him by any of the senators but 4.05.193 P
indeed i should have ask'd /thee that before. ROM 1.02. 77
you call'd, my young lady ask'd for, the nurse 1.03.101 P
for and call'd for, ask'd for and sought for, in 1.05. 12 P
he last ask'd the question. TIM 2.02. 59 P
and when i ask'd you what the matter was, | you JC 2.01.241
hath he ask'd for me? MAC 1.07. 30
man's knell | is there scarce ask'd for who, and 4.03.171
and, when you are ask'd this question next, say HAM 5.01. 58 P
i ask'd his blessing, and from first to last LR 5.03.196
which was as much | as to have ask'd him pardon. ANT 2.02. 79
men in awe, | that whoso ask'd her for his wife, PER 1.ch. 37
so, this was well ask'd, 'twas so well perform'd 2.03. 99
but this very day | i ask'd her questions, and TNK 4.01. 38
for, if my brother but even now had ask'd me 4.02. 47
and have hotly ask'd them | if they had mothers; 5.01.105
smiling to me | and ask'd me what i would eat, 5.02. 5
then being ask'd where all thy beauty lies, SON 2. 5
ask'd their own wills, and made their wills obey LC 133
ASKER 1 FR 0.0001 REL FR 1 V 0 P
have you | ere now denied the asker; COR 2.03.206
ASKETH 2 FR 0.0002 REL FR 2 V 0 P
signior baptista, my business asketh haste, SHR 2.01.114
the business asketh silent secrecy. 2H6 1.02. 90
ASKING 12 FR 0.0013 REL FR 8 V 4 P
married my daughter without asking my good will?
SHR 5.01.134 P
deny, | that honor, sav'd, may upon asking give? TN 3.04.212
and asking every one for sir john falstaff. 2H4 2.04.360
he, on his right, asking a wife for edward. 3H6 3.01. 44
for not bestowing on him at his asking | the H8 2.01.163
it values not your asking. 2.03. 52
goes up and down the field, asking for himself. TRO 3.03.244 P
to you, yet dare i never | deny your asking. COR 1.06. 65
in asking their good loves, but thou wilt frame 3.02. 84
now i'll tell you without asking. ROM 1.02. 78 P
that shall not be my offer, not thy asking? HAM 1.02. 46
when i shall, first asking you pardon thereunto, 4.07. 45 P
ASKS 4 FR 0.0004 REL FR 3 V 1 P
asks thee there, son, forgiveness, | as 'twere WT 4.04.549
then asks bohemia forgiveness; 5.02. 52 P
he asks of you that never us'd to beg. PER 2.01. 62
and asks the weary caitiff for his master, | and VEN 914
ASK'ST 2 FR 0.0002 REL FR 2 V 0 P
for prisoners ask'st thou? 1H6 4.07. 58
doctor, | thou ask'st me such a question. CYM 1.05. 11
ASLEEP 55 FR 0.0062 REL FR 42 V 13 P
to their suff'red labor, | i have left asleep; TMP 1.02.232
will you laugh me asleep, for i am very heavy? 2.01.188 P
what, all so soon asleep! 2.01.191
repose, to be asleep | with eyes wide open — 2.01.213
speaking, moving — | and yet so fast asleep. 2.01.215
when 's god's asleep, he'll rob his bottle. 2.02.151 P
i'll yield him thee asleep, | where thou mayst 3.02. 60
within this half hour will he be asleep. 3.02.113
there shalt thou find the mariners asleep 5.01. 98
haply when they have judg'd me fast asleep, TGV 3.01. 25
by my halidom, i was fast asleep. 4.02.135 P
how if the nurse be asleep and will not hear us? ADO 3.03. 67 P
juice, | i'll watch titania when she is asleep, MND 2.01.177
sing me now asleep; 2.02. 7
dead, or asleep? 2.02.101
my lord, this' my daughter here asleep, | and 4.01.128
god's my life, stol'n hence, and left me asleep! 4.01.204 P
asleep, my love? 5.01.324
i told him you were asleep; TN 1.05.142 P
though credit be asleep and not an ear open: WT 5.02. 62 P
but i will find him when he lies asleep, | and 1H4 1.03.221
fast asleep behind the arras, and snorting like 2.04.528 P
other night i fell asleep here behind the arras 3.03. 97 P
and now their pride and mettle is asleep, 4.03. 22
then death rock me asleep, abridge my doleful 2H4 2.04.197
my poorest subjects | are at this hour asleep! 3.01. 5
whose dangerous eyes may well be charm'd asleep 4.02. 39
found some months asleep and leapt them over. 4.04.124
i think her old familiar is asleep. 1H6 3.02.122
watch thou, and wake when others be asleep, | to 2H6 1.01.249
there lies the duke asleep, and there the keys. R3 1.04. 95
killing care and grief of heart | fall asleep, H8 3.01. 14
she is asleep. 4.02. 81
or the virgin voice | that babies lull asleep! COR 3.02.115
i think our fellows are asleep. 4.05. 2 P
song | of lullaby to bring her babe asleep. TIT 2.03. 29
pit | where i espied the panther fast asleep. 2.03.194
would have dropp'd his knife, and fell asleep, 2.04. 50
sung thee asleep, his loving breast thy pillow; 5.03.163
in bed asleep, while they do dream things true. ROM 1.04. 52
atomi | over men's noses as they lie asleep. 1.04. 58
tickling a parson's nose as 'a lies asleep, 1.04. 80
thy dog that hath lain asleep in the sun. 3.01. 26 P
how sound is she asleep! 4.05. 8
fast asleep? JC 2.01.229
strato, thou hast been all this while asleep; 5.05. 32
when duncan is asleep | (whereto the rather MAC 1.07. 61
her very guise, and, upon my life, fast asleep. 5.01. 20 P
when he is drunk asleep, or in his rage, | or in HAM 3.03. 89
tribe of fops, | got 'tween asleep and wake? LR 1.02. 15
i think the world's asleep. 1.04. 48 P
faith, half asleep. OTH 4.02. 97
at my breast, | that sucks the nurse asleep? ANT 5.02.310
cupid laid by his brand and fell asleep: SON 153. 1
the little love–god, lying once asleep, | laid 154. 1
A–SLEEPING 1 FR 0.0001 REL FR 1 V 0 P
her weeping, | or a dog that seems a–sleeping, TIM 1.02. 67
ASMATH 1 FR 0.0001 REL FR 1 V 0 P
asmath, | by the eternal god, whose name and 2H6 1.04. 24
ASPECT 28 FR 0.0031 REL FR 26 V 2 P
if you will jest with me, know my aspect, | and ERR 2.02. 32
declining their rich aspect to the hot breath of 3.02.136 P
hair | should ravish doters with a false aspect: LLL 4.03.256
and other of such vinegar aspect | that they'll MV 1.01. 54
this aspect of mine | hath fear'd the valiant; 2.01. 8
strange effect | would they work in mild aspect? AYL 4.03. 53
youth | than in a nuntio's of more grave aspect. TN 1.04. 28
heavens look | with an aspect more favorable. WT 2.01.107
save in aspect, hath all offense seal'd up; JN 2.01.250
that close aspect of his | /doth show the mood 4.02. 72
but taking note of thy abhorr'd aspect, 4.02.224
and for our eyes do hate the dire aspect | of R2 1.03.127
thy sad aspect | hath from the number of his 1.03.209
slept in his face and rend'red such aspect | as 1H4 3.02. 82
then lend the eye a terrible aspect; H5 3.01. 9
with a stubborn outside, with an aspect of iron, 5.02.227 P
for his grim aspect | and large proportion of 1H6 2.03. 20
whose ugly and unnatural aspect | may fright the R3 1.02. 23
that sweet aspect of princes, and their ruin, H8 3.02.369
'tis his aspect of terror. 5.01. 88
young boy | hath an aspect of intercession which COR 5.03. 32
you gone, | put on a most importunate aspect, TIM 2.01. 28
tears in his eyes, distraction in his aspect, HAM 2.02.555
under th' allowance of your great aspect, LR 2.02.106
there would he anchor his aspect, and die | with ANT 1.05. 33
palamon | has a most menacing aspect, his brow TNK 5.03. 45
whose grim aspect sets every joint a–shaking; LUC 452
points on me graciously with fair aspect, | and SON 26.10
/ASPECTS 1 FR 0.0001 REL FR 1 V 0 P
corrects the /ill /aspects /of /planets /evil, TRO 1.03. 92
ASPECTS 4 FR 0.0004 REL FR 4 V 0 P
some other mistress hath thy sweet aspects: ERR 2.02.111
worcester, | malevolent to you in all aspects, 1H4 1.01. 97
sham'd their aspects with store of childish R3 1.02.154
with pure aspects did him peculiar duties. LUC 14
ASPEN 2 FR 0.0002 REL FR 1 V 1 P
in very truth, do i, and 'twere an aspen leaf. 2H4 2.04.109 P
hands | tremble like aspen leaves upon a lute, TIT 2.04. 45
ASPERSION 1 FR 0.0001 REL FR 1 V 0 P
no sweet aspersion shall the heavens let fall TMP 4.01. 18
ASPIC 2 FR 0.0002 REL FR 2 V 0 P
have i the aspic in my lips? ANT 5.02.293
such as th' aspic leaves | upon the caves of 5.02.352
ASPICIOUS 1 FR 0.0001 REL FR 0 V 1 P
have indeed comprehended two aspicious persons,
ADO 3.05. 46 P
ASPIC'S 1 FR 0.0001 REL FR 1 V 0 P
this is an aspic's trail, and these fig leaves ANT 5.02.351
ASPICS' 1 FR 0.0001 REL FR 1 V 0 P
with thy fraught, | for 'tis of aspics' tongues! OTH 3.03.450
ASPIRATION 1 FR 0.0001 REL FR 1 V 0 P
of his | in aspiration lifts him from the earth. TRO 4.05. 16
ASPIR'D 2 FR 0.0002 REL FR 2 V 0 P
pomp, | that hath aspir'd to solon's happiness, TIT 1.01.177
that gallant spirit hath aspir'd the clouds, ROM 3.01.117
ASPIRE 8 FR 0.0009 REL FR 8 V 0 P
wilt thou aspire to guide the heavenly car, TGV 3.01.154
desire, | fed in heart, whose flames aspire, WIV 5.05. 97
to aspire unto the crown and reign as king. 3H6 1.01. 53
there is, betwixt that smile we would aspire to, H8 3.02.368
it, | for who digs hills because they do aspire PER 1.04. 5
thing, | and too ambitious, to aspire to him, TNK pr 23
not gross to sink, but light, and will aspire. VEN 150
hid, lurks to aspire | and girdle with embracing LUC 5
ASPIRING 7 FR 0.0008 REL FR 7 V 0 P
show boldness and aspiring confidence. JN 5.01. 56
which his aspiring rider seem'd to know, | with R2 5.02. 9
betwixt our nation and the aspiring french; 1H6 5.04. 99
they, knowing dame eleanor's aspiring humor, 2H6 1.02. 97
will the aspiring blood of lancaster | sink in 3H6 5.06. 61
put in her tender heart th' aspiring flame | of R3 4.04.328
in his dim mist th' aspiring mountains hiding, LUC 548
ASPRAY 1 FR 0.0001 REL FR 1 V 0 P
he'll be to rome | as is the aspray to the fish, COR 4.07. 34
ASPRAYS 1 FR 0.0001 REL FR 1 V 0 P
soon as they /move, as asprays do the fish, TNK 1.01.138
A–SQUINT 1 FR 0.0001 REL FR 1 V 0 P
that eye that told you so look'd but a–squint. LR 5.03. 72
/AS'S 1 FR 0.0001 REL FR 1 V 0 P
and many such–like /as's of great charge, | that HAM 5.02. 43
ASS 88 FR 0.0099 REL FR 32 V 56 P
what a thrice–double ass | was i to take this TMP 5.01.296
away, ass, you'll lose the tide, if you tarry TGV 2.03. 35 P
what an ass art thou! i understand thee not. 2.05. 24 P
why, thou whoreson ass, thou mistak'st me. 2.05. 47 P
that such an ass should owe them. 5.02. 28
made me drunk, yet i am not altogether an ass. WIV 1.01.172 P
page is an ass, a secure ass; 2.02.300 P
page is an ass, a secure ass; 2.02.301 P
i do begin to perceive that i am made an ass. 5.05.119 P
for, like an ass whose back with ingots bows, MM 3.01. 26
one all of luxury, an ass, a madman, | wherein 5.01.501
if thou art chang'd to aught, 'tis to an ass. ERR 2.02.199
'tis so, i am an ass, else it could never be 2.02.201
i think thou art an ass. 3.01. 15
would keep from my heels, and beware of an ass. 3.01. 18
thy face for a name, or thy name for an ass. 3.01. 47
i am an ass, i am a woman's man, and besides 3.02. 77 P
sensible in nothing but blows, and so is an ass. 4.04. 28 P
i am an ass indeed; 4.04. 29 P
away, you are an ass, you are an ass. ADO 4.02. 73 P
away, you are an ass, you are an ass. 4.02. 73 P
o that he were here to write me down as ass! 4.02. 76 P
but, masters, remember that i am an ass; 4.02. 77 P
written down, yet forget not that i am an ass. 4.02. 78 P
o that i had been writ down an ass! 4.02. 87 P
time and place shall serve, that i am an ass. 5.01.256 P
plaintiff here, the offender, did call me ass. 5.01.306 P
a horse to be embassador for an ass. LLL 3.01. 52 P
sir, you must send the ass upon the horse, for 3.01. 54 P
therefore as he is, an ass, let him go. 5.02.625
for the ass to the jude; 5.02.628
this is to make an ass of me, to fright me, if MND 3.01.120 P
titania wak'd, and straightway lov'd an ass. 3.02. 34
and i am such a tender ass, if my hair do but 4.01. 25 P
methought i was enamor'd of an ass. 4.01. 77
man is but an ass, if he go about /t' expound 4.01.206 P
he might yet recover, and yet prove an ass. 5.01.311 P
if it do come to pass | that any man turn ass, AYL 2.05. 51
o this woodcock, what an ass it is! SHR 1.02.160
preposterous ass, that never read so far | to 3.01. 9
barn, | my horse, my ox, my ass, my any thing; 3.02.232
away, away, mad ass! 5.01. 84 P
but if thou be'st not an ass, i am a youth of AWW 2.03.100 P
that every braggart shall be found an ass. 4.03.336
i am not such an ass but i can keep my hand dry. TN 1.03. 74 P
welcome, ass. now let's have a catch. 2.03. 18 P
but a time–pleaser, an affection'd ass, that 2.03.148 P
and your horse now would make him an ass. 2.03.169 P
ass, i doubt not. 2.03.170 P
'slight! will you make an ass o' me? 3.02. 13 P
sir, they praise me and make an ass of me. 5.01. 17 P
now my foes tell me plainly i am an ass; 5.01. 18 P
of him | as great alcides' /shows upon an ass. JN 2.01.144
but, ass, i'll take that burthen from your back, 2.01.145
a horse, | and yet i bear a burthen like an ass, R2 5.05. 93
a woman should be made an ass and a beast, to 2H4 2.01. 37 P
come, you virtuous ass, you bashful fool, must 2.02. 75 P
by cheshu, he is an ass, as in the world; H5 3.02. 70 P
if the enemy is an ass and a fool, and a prating 4.01. 77 P
look you, be an ass and a fool, and a prating 4.01. 79 P
you scurvy valiant ass! TRO 2.01. 45 P
clear again, that i might water an ass at it! 3.03.311 P
to an ass, were nothing, he is both ass and ox; 5.01. 59 P
to an ass, were nothing, he is both ass and ox; 5.01. 59 P
to an ox, were nothing, /he /is both ox and ass. 5.01. 60 P
that that same young troyan ass, that loves the 5.04. 6 P
when i find the ass in compound with the major COR 2.01. 58 P
what an ass it is! 4.05. 44 P
now, what a thing it is to be an ass! TIT 4.02. 25
i will fly, like a dog, the heels a' th' ass. TIM 1.01.272 P
and the ass more captain than the lion, the 3.05. 49
when peradventure thou wert accus'd by the ass; 4.03.331 P
if thou wert the ass, thy dullness would torment 4.03.332 P
how has the ass broke the wall, that thou art 4.03.349 P
he shall but bear them as the ass bears gold, JC 4.01. 21
and turn him off | (like to the empty ass) to 4.01. 26
"then came each actor on his ass" — HAM 2.02.395
why, what an ass am i! 2.02.582
for your dull ass will not mend his pace with 5.01. 57 P
of a politician, which this ass now o'erreaches, 5.01. 78 P
thou bor'st thine ass on thy back o'er the dirt. LR 1.04.161 P
may not an ass know when the cart draws the 1.04.223 P
wears out his time, much like his master's ass, OTH 1.01. 47
reward me, | for making him egregiously an ass, 2.01.309
look, they weep, | and i, an ass, am onion–ey'd. ANT 4.02. 35
that i might hear thee call great caesar ass 5.02.307
unless it had been the fall of an ass, which is CYM 1.02. 37 P
is his mother | should yield the world this ass! 2.01. 53

ASSAIL 6 FR 0.0006 REL FR 4 V 2 P
is front her, board her, woo her, assail her. TN 1.03. 57 P
assail them with the army of the king. 2H6 4.02.175
parliament | let us assail the family of york. 3H6 1.01. 65
while, | and let us once again assail your ears, HAM 1.01. 31
what lady would you choose to assail? CYM 1.04.125 P
believ'd her eyes when they t' assail begun, LC 262
ASSAILABLE 1 FR 0.0001 REL FR 1 V 0 P
there's comfort yet, they are assailable. MAC 3.02. 39
ASSAILANT 1 FR 0.0001 REL FR 0 V 1 P
in thy preparation, for thy assailant is quick, TN 3.04.225 P
ASSAILANTS 1 FR 0.0001 REL FR 1 V 0 P
shall we pass along | and never stir assailants. AYL 1.03.114
ASSAIL'D 7 FR 0.0008 REL FR 5 V 2 P
of money, be assail'd by robbers and die in many H5 4.01.152 P
alone, | tend'ring my ruin and assail'd of none, 1H6 4.07. 10
i have assail'd her with musics, but she CYM 2.03. 39 P
although assail'd with fortune fierce and keen, PER 5.03. 88
when shame assail'd, the red should fence the LUC 63
assail'd by night with circumstances strong | of 1262
either not assail'd, or victor being charg'd, SON 70.10
ASSAILED 2 FR 0.0002 REL FR 2 V 0 P
my mother is assailed in our tent, | and ta'en, JN 3.02. 6
beauteous thou art, therefore to be assailed; SON 41. 6
ASSAILETH 1 FR 0.0001 REL FR 1 V 0 P
of that fell poison which assaileth him. JN 5.07. 9
ASSAILING 2 FR 0.0002 REL FR 2 V 0 P
to beat assailing death from his weak /legions; 1H6 4.04. 16
nor bide th' encounter of assailing eyes, | nor ROM 1.01.213
ASSAILS 3 FR 0.0003 REL FR 2 V 1 P
but he assails, and our virginity, though AWW 1.01.115 P
it be a sin | when violence assails us. OTH 2.03.204
such passion her assails | that patience is LUC 1562
ASSASSINATION 1 FR 0.0001 REL FR 1 V 0 P
if th' assassination | could trammel up the MAC 1.07. 2
ASSAULT 17 FR 0.0019 REL FR 12 V 5 P
the assault that angelo hath made to you, MM 3.01.184 P
rescue in the first assault or ransom afterward. AWW 1.03.116 P
honor on my part, | against your vain assault. 4.02. 51
let it be so. say, where will you assault? JN 2.01.408
how now, what means death in this rude assault? R2 5.05.105
they may vex us with shot or with assault. 1H6 1.04. 13
arm, arm! the enemy doth make assault! 2.01. 38
in which assault we lost twelve hundred men; 4.01. 24
i will make a complimental assault upon him, for TRO 3.01. 39 P
ay, and for an assault too. COR 4.05.171 P
march to assault thy country than to tread 5.03.123
new supplies of men, | began a fresh assault. MAC 1.02. 33
in unreclaimed blood, | of general assault. HAM 2.01. 35
me, | or, naked as i am, i will assault thee. OTH 5.02.258
ill opinion and th' assault you have made to her CYM 1.04.162 P
shall be made acquainted | of thy assault. 1.06.150
in me, | from me by strong assault it is bereft: LUC 835
ASSAULTED 1 FR 0.0001 REL FR 1 V 0 P
worse | to have her gentleman abus'd, assaulted, LR 2.02.149
ASSAULTS 3 FR 0.0003 REL FR 2 V 1 P
pierces so, that it assaults | mercy itself, and TMP ep 17
invincible against all assaults of affection. ADO 2.03.115 P
such assaults | as would take in some virtue. CYM 3.02. 8
ASSAY 15 FR 0.0017 REL FR 12 V 3 P
that he dares in this manner assay me? WIV 2.01. 25 P
bid herself assay him. MM 1.02.181
assay the pow'r you have. 1.04. 76
only he hath made an assay of her virtue to 3.01.162 P
why then to–night | let us assay our plot, which AWW 3.07. 44
i will assay thee, and defend thyself. 1H4 5.04. 34
i would assay, proud queen, to make thee blush. 3H6 1.04.118
let us make the assay upon him. TIM 4.03.403 P
their malady convinces | the great assay of art; MAC 4.03.143
to give th' assay of arms against your majesty. HAM 2.02. 71
did you assay him | to any pastime? 3.01. 14
make assay, | bow, stubborn knees, and heart, 3.03. 69
this cannot be | by no assay of reason; OTH 1.03. 18
come on, assay. 2.01.120
the destin'd ill she must herself assay? LC 156
ASSAY'D *(also 'say'd)*
ASSAY'D 4 FR 0.0004 REL FR 4 V 0 P
what if we assay'd to steal | the clownish fool AYL 1.03.129
the rebels have assay'd to win the tower. 2H6 4.05. 8
bad performance, | 'twere better not assay'd; HAM 4.07.152
she hath assay'd as much as may be prov'd. VEN 608
ASSAYING 1 FR 0.0001 REL FR 1 V 0 P
wits again, | or lose my labor in assaying it. ERR 5.01. 97
ASSAYS 4 FR 0.0004 REL FR 4 V 0 P
galling the gleaned land with hot assays, H5 1.02.151
with windlasses and with assays of bias, | by HAM 2.01. 62
best judgment collied, | assays to lead the way. OTH 2.03.207
untimely breathings, sick and short assays, LUC 1720
ASSE *(also as*, 's*)*
ASSE 1 FR 0.0001 REL FR 0 V 1 P
i will tell you asse my friend, captain gower: H5 5.01. 4 P
ASSEMBLANCE 1 FR 0.0001 REL FR 0 V 1 P
the stature, bulk, and big assemblance of a man? 2H4 3.02.259 P
ASSEMBLE 7 FR 0.0008 REL FR 7 V 0 P
state of my great grief | let kings assemble; JN 3.01. 71
and to the english court assemble now, | from 2H4 4.05.121
let them assemble; COR 2.03.217
assemble presently the people hither; 3.03. 12
fault | assemble all the poor men of your sort; JC 1.01. 57
to that end | assemble /we immediate council. ANT 1.04. 75
best | as fast as objects to his beams assemble? SON 114. 8
ASSEMBLED 10 FR 0.0011 REL FR 9 V 1 P
and all that are assembled in this place | that ERR 5.01.397
when that your flock, assembled by the bell, 2H4 4.02. 5
act | for which we have in head assembled them? H5 2.02. 18
should be maintain'd, assembled, and collected, 2.04. 19
into our former favor | you are assembled; 5.02. 64
all france with their chief assembled strength 1H6 1.01.139
all manner of men assembled here in arms this 1.03. 74 P
he wonders to what end you have assembled | such
R3 3.07. 84
land, who are assembled | to plead your cause. H8 2.04. 60
he hath assembled | bocchus, the king of libya; ANT 3.06. 68
ASSEMBLIES 2 FR 0.0002 REL FR 2 V 0 P
and held in idle price to haunt assemblies MM 1.03. 9
and in assemblies too. ERR 5.01. 60
/ASSEMBLY 1 FR 0.0001 REL FR 0 V 1 P
/my /oath /before /this /honorable /assembly, LR 3.06. 47 P

ASSEMBLY 14 FR 0.0015 REL FR 9 V 5 P
to disgrace hero before the whole assembly, and ADO 4.02. 55 P
good morrow to this fair assembly. 5.04. 34
but the wood, no assembly but horn–beasts. AYL 3.03. 50 P
that bring these tidings to this fair assembly. 5.04.153
is your assembly so? 2H4 4.02.111
which was never seen in such an assembly. ep 25 P
by whom this great assembly is contriv'd, | we H5 5.02. 6
of this so noble and so fair assembly | this H8 1.04. 67
you hold a fair assembly; 1.04. 87
think, | you, the great toe of this assembly? COR 1.01.155
honor and advance | the theme of our assembly. 2.02. 57
a fair assembly. ROM 1.02. 71
let no assembly of twenty be without a score of TIM 3.06. 77 P
if there be any in this assembly, any dear JC 3.02. 18 P
ASSENT 2 FR 0.0002 REL FR 2 V 0 P
that, without the king's assent or knowledge, H8 3.02.310
by the main assent | of all these learned men 4.01. 31
ASSES 9 FR 0.0010 REL FR 4 V 5 P
there's none but asses will be bridled so. ERR 2.01. 14
one lion may, when many asses do. MND 5.01.154 P
which, like your asses, and your dogs and mules, MV 4.01. 91
asses are made to bear, and so are you. SHR 2.01.199
send ministers to me, asses, and do all they can TN 4.02. 92 P
asses, fools, dolts! TRO 1.02.241 P
asses. TIM 2.02. 62 P
thy asses are gone about 'em. LR 1.05. 34 P
as tenderly be led by th' nose | as asses are. OTH 1.03.402
ASSEZ 1 FR 0.0001 REL FR 0 V 1 P
c'est assez pour une fois: allons–nous a diner. H5 3.04. 61 P
ASS–HEAD 2 FR 0.0002 REL FR 0 V 2 P
you see an ass–head of your own, do you? MND 3.01.116 P
an ass–head and a coxcomb and a knave, a TN 5.01.206 P
ASSIGN 3 FR 0.0003 REL FR 3 V 0 P
i pray | your highness to assign our trial day. R2 1.01.151
gage | till we assign you to your days of trial. 4.01.106
to his conveyance i assign my wife, | with what OTH 1.03.285
ASSIGN'D 5 FR 0.0005 REL FR 5 V 0 P
in their assign'd and native dwelling–place. AYL 2.01. 63
by south and east is to my part assign'd; 1H4 3.01. 74
assign'd am i to be the english scourge. 1H6 1.02.129
to ptolomy he assign'd | syria, cilicia, and ANT 3.06. 15
lands and mansions, theirs in thought assign'd, LC 138
ASSIGNS 2 FR 0.0002 REL FR 0 V 2 P
french rapiers and poniards, with their assigns, HAM 5.02.150 P
horses against six french swords, their assigns, 5.02.162 P
ASSIST 22 FR 0.0024 REL FR 15 V 7 P
you do assist the storm. TMP 1.01. 14 P
let's assist them, | for our case is as theirs. 1.01. 54
gentle girl, assist me; TGV 2.07. 1
assist me, knight, i am undone! WIV 4.05. 90 P
assist me in my purpose, | and, as i am a 4.06. 3
now the hot–bloodied gods assist me! 5.05. 2 P
if you will take it on you to assist him, it MM 4.02. 10 P
you are both sure, and will assist me? ADO 1.03. 69 P
midnight, assist our moan, | help us to sigh and 5.03. 16
father's wit and my mother's tongue assist me! LLL 1.02. 96 P
assist me, some extemporal god of rhyme, for i 1.02.183 P
hand, | wherein your cunning can assist me much. SHR in.1. 92
assist me, tranio, for i know thou wilt. 1.01.158
assist me then, sweet warwick, and i will, | for 3H6 1.01. 28
we'll all assist you; he that flies shall die. 1.01. 30
the gods assist you! COR 1.02. 36
assist. 5.06.154
charter in your voice | t' assist my simpleness. OTH 1.03.246
they shall assist | the deeds of justest men. ANT 2.01. 1
assist, good friends. 4.15. 31
patience, good sir, do not assist the storm. PER 3.01. 19
fact, | how can they then assist me in the act? LUC 350
/ASSISTANCE 2 FR 0.0002 REL FR 1 V 1 P
to be /rend'red by our /assistance, the king's LLL 5.01.120 P
/till /we /had /his /assistance /by /the /hand. 2H4 1.03. 21
ASSISTANCE 12 FR 0.0013 REL FR 9 V 3 P
but minister such assistance as i shall give you ADO 2.01.369 P
you withal, to the end to crave your assistance. LLL 5.01.116 P
without th' assistance of a mortal hand. JN 3.01.158
if lewis by your assistance win the day. 5.04. 39
towards our assistance we do seize to us | the R2 2.01.160
swore him assistance, and perform'd it too. 1H4 4.03. 65
by the heavens' assistance and your strength, 3H6 5.04. 68
by thy advice | and thy assistance, is king R3 4.02. 4
affecting one sole throne, | without assistance. COR 4.06. 33
doubting your present assistance therein. TIM 3.01. 20 P
it is | that i to your assistance do make love, MAC 3.01.123
and found such fair assistance in my verse | as SON 78. 2
ASSISTANCES 1 FR 0.0001 REL FR 1 V 0 P
to upbraid | my gain of it by their assistances, 2H4 4.05.193
ASSISTANT 4 FR 0.0004 REL FR 3 V 1 P
me, her assistant or go–between parted from me. WIV 2.02.263 P
with me, | in one respect i'll thy assistant be; ROM 2.03. 90
winds give benefit | and convey /is assistant, HAM 1.03. 3
thereon, | let me be no assistant for a state, 2.02.166
ASSISTANTS 3 FR 0.0003 REL FR 3 V 0 P
on the banks | if they were his assistants, yea R3 4.04.524
neither allied | to eminent assistants, but H8 1.01. 62
anon | th' assistants made a brave redemption, TNK 5.03. 82
ASSISTED 3 FR 0.0003 REL FR 3 V 0 P
yourself, assisted with your honor'd friends, WT 5.01.113
against) i am assisted | by wicked powers. 5.03. 90
assisted by that most disloyal traitor, | the MAC 1.02. 52
ASSISTING 1 FR 0.0001 REL FR 1 V 0 P
you shall have me assisting you in all. SHR 1.02.195
ASSOCIATE 1 FR 0.0001 REL FR 1 V 0 P
out, | one of our order, to associate me, | here ROM 5.02. 6
ASSOCIATED 1 FR 0.0001 REL FR 1 V 0 P
led by caius martius | associated with aufidius, COR 4.06. 76
ASSOCIATES 1 FR 0.0001 REL FR 1 V 0 P
th' associates tend, and every thing is bent HAM 4.03. 45
ASS'S 2 FR 0.0002 REL FR 1 V 1 P
take, | an ass's nole i fixed on his head. MND 3.02. 17
or to be entomb'd in an ass's pack–saddle. COR 2.01. 89 P
ASSUAG'D 1 FR 0.0001 REL FR 1 V 0 P
grew kinder, and his fury was assuag'd. VEN 318
ASSUAGE 4 FR 0.0004 REL FR 3 V 1 P
the good gods assuage thy wrath, and turn the COR 5.02. 76 P
free vent of words love's fire doth assuage, VEN 334
pain, | and fellowship in woe doth woe assuage, LUC 790
which may her suffering ecstasy assuage, | 'tis LC 69

ASSUBJUGATE 1 FR 0.0001 REL FR 1 V 0 P
nor, by my will, assubjugate his merit, | as TRO 2.03.192
ASSUM'D 1 FR 0.0001 REL FR 1 V 0 P
he it is that hath | assum'd this age: CYM 5.05.319
ASSUME 14 FR 0.0015 REL FR 13 V 1 P
i will assume thy part in some disguise, | and ADO 1.01.321
very visor began to assume life and scold with 2.01.241 P
i will assume desert. MV 2.09. 51
and these assume but valor's excrement | to 3.02. 87
if spirits can assume both form and suit, | you TN 5.01.235
assume the port of mars, and at his heels H5 pr 6
and loss assume all reason | without revolt. TRO 5.02.145
do not assume my likeness. TIM 4.03.218
if it assume my noble father's person, | i'll HAM 1.02.243
and there assume some other horrible form, 1.04. 72
/dev'l hath power | t' assume a pleasing shape, 2.02.600
bed — | assume a virtue, if you have it not. 3.04.160
t' assume a semblance | that very dogs disdain'd LR 5.03.188
like a bold champion i assume the lists, | nor PER 1.01. 61
ASSUMES 2 FR 0.0002 REL FR 2 V 0 P
there is no /vice so simple but assumes | some MV 3.02. 81
our project's life this shape of sense assumes: TRO 1.03.384
ASSUMING 1 FR 0.0001 REL FR 1 V 0 P
gower is come, | assuming man's infirmities, PER 1.ch. 3
ASSURANCE *(also surance)*
/ASSURANCE 1 FR 0.0001 REL FR 1 V 0 P
/from /some /knowledge /and /assurance, /offer LR 3.01. 41
ASSURANCE 30 FR 0.0034 REL FR 20 V 10 P
and rather like a dream than an assurance | that TMP 1.02. 45
for more assurance that a living prince | does 5.01.108
me my cue, and my assurance bids me search — WIV 3.02. 46 P
that jealousy shall be call'd assurance, and all ADO 2.02. 49 P
for the more better assurance, tell them that i MND 3.01. 20 P
and let your father make her the assurance, SHR 2.01.387
be bride to you, if you make this assurance; 2.01.396
and make assurance here in padua | of greater 3.02.134
and give assurance to baptista minola, | as if 4.02. 69
day, | to pass assurance of a dow'r in marriage 4.02.118
we be affied and such assurance ta'en | as shall 4.04. 49
they are busied about a counterfeit assurance. 4.04. 92 P
take you assurance of her, cum privilegio ad 4.04. 92 P
and therefore /for assurance | let's each one 5.02. 65
give me modest assurance if you be the lady of TN 1.05.180 P
into a desperate assurance she will none of him. 2.02. 8 P
plight me the full assurance of your faith, 4.03. 26
tie | thy now unsur'd assurance to the crown, JN 2.01.471
procure him better assurance than bardolph. 2H4 1.02. 32 P
give me assurance with some friendly vow, | that 3H6 4.01.141
or else his head's assurance is but frail. R3 4.04.496
nor no more assurance | of equal friendship and H8 2.04. 17
assurance bless your thoughts! TIM 2.02.180
but yet i'll make assurance double sure, | and MAC 4.01. 83
his seal | to give the world assurance of a man. HAM 3.04. 62
and calves which seek out assurance in that. 5.01.117 P
of this, and by an auricular assurance have your LR 1.02. 92 P
quite forgo | the way which promises assurance, ANT 3.07. 46
in and kneel, with great assurance | that we, TNK 1.03. 94
arms in assurance | my body to this business. 5.01.134
ASSUR'D 46 FR 0.0052 REL FR 40 V 6 P
most ignorant of what he's most assur'd | (his MM 2.02.119
call'd me dromio, swore i was assur'd to her, ERR 3.02.141 P
within the eye of honor, be assur'd | my purse, MV 1.01.137
be assur'd you may. 1.03. 28 P
i will be assur'd i may; 1.03. 29 P
and, that i may be assur'd, i will bethink me. 1.03. 30 P
be assur'd | thou shalt have justice more than 4.01.315
you | as for my patron, stand you so assur'd, SHR 1.02.155
right, as 'twere a man assur'd of a — AWW 2.03. 17 P
for i am well assur'd | that i did so when i was JN 2.01.534
that i did so when i was first assur'd. 2.01.535
written, be assur'd | i will easily be granted. 1H4 1.03.263
and therefore be assur'd, my good lord marshal, 2H4 4.01.218
not, | and thou wilt have me die assur'd of it. 4.05.105
though no man be assur'd what grace to find, 5.02. 30
for me, by heaven (i bid you be assur'd), | i'll 5.02. 56
you are, i think, assur'd i love you not. 5.02. 64
i am assur'd, if i be measur'd rightly, | your 5.02. 65
and, be assur'd, you'll find a difference, | as H5 2.04.134
her aid she promis'd, and assur'd success; 1H6 1.02. 82
but this i am assur'd, | i feel such sharp 5.05. 83
yet be well assur'd | you put sharp weapons in a 2H6 3.01.346
i will repeal thee, or, be well assur'd, 3.02.349
be well assur'd | her faction will be full as 3H6 5.03. 16
assur'd | i hate not you for her proud arrogance R3 1.03. 23
be assur'd; 1.03.350
much | (which well i am assur'd i have not done) 5.03. 36
to desperate adventures and assur'd destruction. 5.03.319
resting well assur'd | they ne'er did service COR 3.01.121
but being assur'd none but myself could move 5.02. 73 P
yet remain assur'd | that he's a made–up villain TIM 5.01. 97
that i may rest assur'd | whether yond troops JC 5.03. 17
guilty, be assur'd | he closes with you in this HAM 2.01. 44
be thou assur'd, if words be made of breath, 3.04.197
would i were assur'd | of my condition! LR 4.07. 55
be assur'd of this, | that the magnifico is much OTH 1.02. 11
be thou assur'd, good cassio, i will do | all my 3.03. 1
him long, and be you well assur'd | he shall in 3.03. 11
he hath, my lord, but be you well assur'd, | no 4.01. 30
no, be assur'd you shall not find me, daughter, CYM 1.01. 70
be assur'd, madam, | with his next vantage. 1.03. 23
her humor, shall be assur'd | to taste of too. 1.05. 81
thy most perfect goodness | her assur'd credit. 1.06.159
were i well assur'd | came of a gentle kind and PER 5.01. 67
when that his action's dregg'd with mind assur'd TNK 1.02. 97
incertainties now crown themselves assur'd, SON 107. 7
ASSURE 57 FR 0.0064 REL FR 30 V 27 P
i assure you, carthage. TMP 2.01. 86 P
out o' th' moon, i do assure thee. 2.02.138 P
/his grave | assure thyself my love is buried. TGV 4.02.114
not i, i assure thee. WIV 2.02.105 P
as hector, i assure you, and in the managing of ADO 2.03.189 P
a marvellous witty fellow, i assure you, but i 4.02. 25 P
i assure ye it was a buck of the first head. LLL 4.02. 10 P
sweet, and apt, i do assure you, sir, i do 5.01. 94 P
and apt, i do assure you, sir, i do assure. 5.01. 94 P
and my familiar, i do assure ye, very good 5.01. 96 P
you cannot beg us, sir, i can assure you, sir, 5.02.490
a very good piece of work, i assure you, and a MND 1.02. 13 P

no, i assure you, the wall is down that parted 5.01.351 P
for i assure thee (and almost with tears i speak AYL 1.01.153 P
counterfeit, i assure you. 4.03.172 P
that dowry, i'll assure her of | her widowhood, SHR 2.01.123
that can assure my daughter greatest dower 2.01.343
say, signior gremio, what can you assure her? 2.01.345
these i will assure her, | and twice as much, 2.01.379
i dare assure you, sir, 'tis almost two, | and 4.03.189
i do assure thee, father, so it is. 4.05. 74
i do assure you, my lord, he is very great in AWW 2.05. 8 P
i know not how i shall assure you further | but 3.07. 2
nay, i assure you a peace concluded. 4.03. 40 P
assure yourself, after our ship did split, TN 1.02. 9
niece shall take note of it, and assure thyself, 3.02. 36 P
you'll find it otherwise, i assure you; 3.04.229 P
i do assure you, 'tis against my will. 3.04.311 P
the man, i do assure you, is not here, | for i 1H4 2.04.512
to be either earl or duke, i can assure you. 5.04.142 P
but he's almost out of mine, i can assure him. 2H4 1.02. 28 P
by thee, i can assure thee that 'a will not out, 5.03. 66 P
i assure you, there is very excellent services H5 3.06. 3 P
i'll assure you, 'a utt'red as prave words at 3.06. 63 P
and, nevil, this i do assure myself, | richard 2H6 2.02. 80
assure yourselves, will never be unkind. 4.09. 19
this shall assure my constant loyalty, | that if 3H6 3.03.240
the beauty of this kingdom, i'll assure you. H8 1.03. 54
i do assure you | the king cried "ha!" 3.02. 60
nor, i'll assure you, better taken, sir. 4.01. 12
that i assure you. TRO 4.01. 46
why, assure thee, lucius, | 'twill vex thy soul TIT 5.01. 61
therefore thy earliness doth me assure | thou ROM 2.03. 39
i dare assure thee that no enemy | shall ever JC 5.04. 21
this is not brutus, friend, but, i assure you, 5.04. 26
i assure my good liege | i hold my duty as i HAM 2.02. 43
nor i, assure thee, regan. LR 2.01.104
assure thee, | if i do vow a friendship, i'll OTH 3.03. 20
assure yourself i will seek satisfaction of you. 4.02.199 P
the stalk, never pluck'd yet, i can assure you. PER 4.06. 42 P
i will assure upon my daughter at the day of my TNK 2.01. 8 P
i dare assure you | you'll find a loving 2.05. 56
to her marriage, | a large one, i'll assure you. 4.01. 24
a leprous witch to be rid on't, i'll assure you. 4.03. 47 P
for there, i will assure you, we shall find 5.02. 77
for one sweet look thy help i would assure thee, VEN 371
and i assure ye | even that your pity is enough SON 111.13

ASSURED 11 FR 0.0012 REL FR 11 V 0 P
assured loss before the match be play'd. JN 3.01.336
as well assured richard their king is dead. R2 2.04. 17
compound, | before thy most assured overthrow; H5 4.03. 81
friend, | and most assured that he is a friend, R3 2.01. 37
offer to defend him, | and stand in assured loss. LR 3.06. 95
's free hours languish for | assured bondage?" CYM 1.06. 73
and villainy assured | beyond its power there's TNK 1.02. 64
serve always with assured trust, | and in thy PP 18.19
come back again, assured | of /thy fair health, SON 45.11
away, | for term of life thou art assured mine, 92. 2
the ills that were not, grew to faults assured, 118.10

ASSUREDLY 4 FR 0.0004 REL FR 4 V 0 P
assuredly the thing is to be sold. AYL 2.04. 96
this night the siege assuredly i'll raise: 1H6 1.02.130
i shall, assuredly. H8 4.02. 92
assuredly you know me. ANT 5.02. 72

ASSURES 1 FR 0.0001 REL FR 1 V 0 P
my heart assures me that the earl of warwick 2H6 2.02. 78

ASSYRIAN 2 FR 0.0002 REL FR 2 V 0 P
o base assyrian knight, what is thy news? 2H4 5.03.101
stones | enforced from the old assyrian slings; H5 4.07. 62

AS'T 4 FR 0.0004 REL FR 4 V 0 P
as't please your lordship. i'll leave you. AWW 3.06.109
serve your will as't please | yourself pronounce H8 2.04.114
this is as't should be. ROM 4.02. 29
cause, but as't had been | each man's like mine; ANT 4.08. 6

ASTONISH *(also stonish, etc.)*

ASTONISH 3 FR 0.0003 REL FR 3 V 0 P
a wife | whose beauty did astonish the survey AWW 5.03. 16
they may astonish these fell–lurking curs. 2H6 5.01.146
send | such dreadful heralds to astonish us. JC 1.03. 56

ASTONISH'D 4 FR 0.0004 REL FR 3 V 1 P
enough, captain, you have astonish'd him. H5 5.01. 39 P
thou hast astonish'd me with thy high terms. 1H6 1.02. 93
of beauteous margaret hath astonish'd me. 5.05. 2
stone–still, astonish'd with this deadly deed, LUC 1730

ASTONISHED 1 FR 0.0001 REL FR 1 V 0 P
by night | giving him aid, my verse astonished. SON 86. 8

ASTRAEA 1 FR 0.0001 REL FR 1 V 0 P
terras astraea reliquit; TIT 4.03. 4

ASTRAEA'S 1 FR 0.0001 REL FR 1 V 0 P
divinest creature, astraea's daughter, | how 1H6 1.06. 4

ASTRAY 2 FR 0.0002 REL FR 1 V 1 P
nay, in that you are astray; TGV 1.01.103 P
and lead these testy rivals so astray | as one MND 3.02.358

ASTRONOMER 1 FR 0.0001 REL FR 1 V 0 P
learn'd indeed were that astronomer | that knew CYM 3.02. 27

ASTRONOMERS 1 FR 0.0001 REL FR 0 V 1 P
but when he performs, astronomers foretell it: TRO 5.01. 92 P

/ASTRONOMICAL 1 FR 0.0001 REL FR 0 V 1 P
/have /you /been /a /sectary /astronomical? LR 1.02.150 P

ASTRONOMY 1 FR 0.0001 REL FR 1 V 0 P
pluck, | and yet methinks i have astronomy, SON 14. 2

ASUNDER 17 FR 0.0019 REL FR 16 V 1 P
keep them asunder; WIV 3.01. 72 P
and will you rent our ancient love asunder, | to MND 3.02.215
of both, | they whirl asunder and dismember me. JN 3.01.330
the perilous narrow ocean parts asunder. H5 pr 22
and from my shoulders crack my arms asunder, 1H6 1.05. 11
that could not live asunder day or night. 2.02. 31
hew them to pieces, hack their bones asunder, 4.07. 47
them be clapp'd up close, | and kept asunder. 2H6 1.04. 51
and so he comes, to rend his limbs asunder. 3H6 1.03. 15
ah, cut my lace asunder, | that my pent heart R3 4.01. 33
where my chaff | and corn shall fly asunder; H8 5.01.111
of more strong link asunder than can ever COR 1.01. 71
villain and he be many miles asunder. ROM 3.05. 81
pluck them asunder. HAM 5.01.264
content — yet not | that we two are asunder; CYM 3.02. 32
and now his woven girths he breaks asunder; VEN 266
hearts remote, yet not asunder; PHT 29

A–SWEARING 1 FR 0.0001 REL FR 1 V 0 P
at game, a–swearing, or about some act | that HAM 3.03. 91

AT' 2 FR 0.0002 REL FR 0 V 2 P
so again while stephano breathes at' nostrils. TMP 2.02. 63 P
pray heartily he be at' palace. WT 4.04.711 P

AT *(also a'*)*

/AT 23 FR 0.0026 REL FR 19 V 4 P
/little /look'd /for /at /your /helping /hands. R2 4.01.161
/not /that /name /was /given /me /at /the /font, 4.01.256
/follies, | /that /was /at /last //out–fac'd /by 4.01.286
/or /at /least /desist | /to /build /at /all? 2H4 1.03. 47
/or /at /least /desist | /to /build /at /all? 1.03. 48
/shillings /i /won /from /you /at /betting? H5 2.01.106 P
and i no friends to back my suit /at /all | but R3 1.02.235
kneel'd /at my feet and bid me be advis'd? 2.01.108
/the /prophet /could /not /at /that /time 4.02.100
/when /last /i /was /at /exeter, | /the /mayor 4.02.103
/it //rouge–mount, /at /which /name /i /started, 4.02.105
come to me, tyrrel, soon, /at after–supper, 4.03. 31
no marvel though you bite so sharp /at reasons, TRO 2.02. 33
good night and welcome, both /at /once, to those 5.01. 77
/what /dost /thou /strike /at, /marcus, /with TIT 3.02. 52
/at /that /that /i /have /kill'd, /my /lord — 3.02. 53
/deserv'd /at /the /hands /of /fortune, /that HAM 2.02.240 P
/and /are /at /point | /to /show /their /open LR 3.01. 33
/want'st /thou /eyes /at /trial, /madam? 3.06. 24 P
/fiends /have /been /in /poor /tom /at /once: 4.01. 59 P
/have /seen | /sunshine /and /rain /at /once; 4.03. 18
/shall /attend /you /presently /at /your /tent. 5.01. 33
/at /this /time | /we /sweat /and /bleed: 5.03. 54

AT 2574 FR 0.2909 REL FR 1932 V 642 P
the king and prince at prayers! TMP 1.01. 54
against it, | and gape at wid'st to glut him. 1.01. 60
as at that time | through all the signories it 1.02. 70
thou call'dst me up at midnight to fetch dew 1.02.228
at least two glasses. 1.02.240
roar | that beasts shall tremble at thy din. 1.02.371
who with mine eyes (never since at ebb) beheld 1.02.436
at the first sight | they have chang'd eyes. 1.02.441
at the marriage of the king's fair daughter 2.01. 70 P
fresh as when we were at tunis at the marriage 2.01. 98 P
as when we were at tunis at the marriage of your 2.01. 98 P
when i wore it at your daughter's marriage? 2.01.106 P
where she, at least, is banish'd from your eye, 2.01.127
at | which end o' th' beam should bow. 2.01.131
lungs that they always use to laugh at nothing. 2.01.175 P
'twas you we laugh'd at. 2.01.176 P
so you may continue, and laugh at nothing still. 2.01.178 P
sometime like apes that mow and chatter at me, 2.02. 9
way, and mount | their pricks at my footfall; 2.02. 12
bush nor shrub to bear off any weather at all. 2.02. 19 P
a very scurvy tune to sing at a man's funeral. 2.02. 44 P
shall laugh myself to death at this puppy–headed 2.02.154 P
for fish, | nor fetch in firing | at requiring, 2.02.182
my father | is hard at study; 3.01. 20
morning with me | when you are by at night. 3.01. 34
i am a fool | to weep at what i am glad of. 3.01. 74
at mine unworthiness, that dare not offer | what 3.01. 77
but my rejoicing | at nothing can be more. 3.01. 94
at thy request, monster, i will do reason, any 3.02.119 P
one phoenix | at this hour reigning there. 3.03. 24
did lie, | though fools at home condemn 'em. 3.03. 27
whose throats had hanging at 'em | wallets of 3.03. 45
(worse than any death | can be at once) shall 3.03. 78
but one fiend at a time, | i'll fight their 3.03.102
do not smile at me that i boast her /off, | for 4.01. 9
brims, | which spungy april at thy hest betrims, 4.01. 65
spring come to you at the farthest | in the very 4.01.114
at which, like unback'd colts, they prick'd 4.01.176
at last i left them | i' th' filthy–mantled pool 4.01.181
at which my nose is in great indignation. 4.01.199 P
at this hour | lies at my mercy all mine enemies 4.01.262
this hour | lies at my mercy all mine enemies. 4.01.263
end, and thou | shalt have the air at freedom. 4.01.265
on the sixt hour, at which time, my lord, | you 5.01. 4
graves at my command | have wak'd their sleepers 5.01. 48
this must crave | (and if this be at all) a most 5.01.117
at this time | i will tell no tales. 5.01.128
lords | at this encounter do so much admire 5.01.154
at least bring forth a wonder, to content ye 5.01.170
what is this maid with whom thou wast at play? 5.01.185
voyage | did claribel her husband find at tunis, 5.01.209
straightway, at liberty; 5.01.235
at pick'd leisure, | which shall be shortly, 5.01.247
than (living dully sluggardiz'd at home) | wear TGV 1.01. 7
'tis love you cavil at; i am not love. 1.01. 38
my father at the road | expects my coming, there 1.01. 53
as much to you at home; and so farewell. 1.01. 62
war with good counsel, set the world at nought; 1.01. 68
and the matter may be both at once deliver'd. 1.01.130 P
sir, i could perceive nothing at all from her; 1.01.136 P
how now? what means this passion at his name? 1.02. 16
would suffer him to spend his youth at home, 1.03. 5
you | to let him spend his time no more at home, 1.03. 14
to speak puling, like a beggar at hallowmas. 2.01. 26 P
she that you gaze on so as she sits at supper? 2.01. 43 P
to have when you chid at sir proteus for going 2.01. 72 P
it goes, | i writ at random, very doubtfully. 2.01.111
you writ them, sir, at my request, | but i will 2.01.126
look you, wept herself blind at my parting. 2.03. 13 P
they say that love hath not an eye at all. 2.04. 96
at thy service. 2.05. 59 P
at first i did adore a twinkling star, | but now 2.06. 9
enemy, | aiming at silvia as a sweeter friend. 2.06. 30
if you think so, then stay at home and go not. 2.07. 62
all that is mine i leave at thy dispose, | my 2.07. 86
cunningly | that my discovery be not aimed at: 3.01. 45
my health and happy being at your court. 3.01. 57
for scorn at first makes after–love the more. 3.01. 95
what lets but one may enter at her window? 3.01.113
those at her father's churlish feet she tender'd 3.01.227
confer at large | of all that may concern thy 3.01.255
him make haste and meet me at the north–gate. 3.01.260
with my /master's /ship? why, it is at sea. 3.01.282 P
close at the heels of her virtues. 3.01.322 P
thy master stays for thee at the north–gate. 3.01.373 P
most, | forsworn my company, and rail'd at me, 3.02. 4
where you with silvia may confer at large — 3.02. 61
which, with ourselves, all rest at thy dispose. 4.01. 74
at saint gregory's well. 4.02. 84
or, at the least, in hers sepulchre thine. 4.02.117
marry, at my house. 4.02.137 P
at friar patrick's cell, | where i intend holy 4.03. 43
indeed, to be, as it were, a dog at all things. 4.04. 13 P
times | his julia gave it him at his departure: 4.04.135
for at pentecost, | when all our pageants of 4.04.158
and at that time i made her weep agood, | for i 4.04.165
that silvia at friar patrick's cell should meet 5.01. 3
out at the postern by the abbey wall; 5.01. 9
and yet she takes exceptions at your person. 5.02. 3
intend confession | at patrick's cell this even, 5.02. 42
i'll woo you like a soldier, at arms' end, | and 5.04. 57
at my depart | i gave this unto julia. 5.04. 96
wrong'd me, indeed he hath, at a word he hath. WIV 1.01.106 P
you'll be laugh'd at. 1.01.119 P
i will marry her, sir, at your request; 1.01.245 P
i will not be absence at the grace. 1.01.265 P
other day with playing at sword and dagger with 1.01.283 P
but i shall as soon quarrel at it as any man in 1.01.291 P
the women have so cried and shriek'd at it, that 1.01.297 P
i sit at ten pounds a week. 1.03. 8 P
i am at a word; 1.03. 14 P
the good humor is to steal at a minute's rest. 1.03. 27 P
well, sirs, i am almost out at heels. 1.03. 31 P
and we'll have a posset for't soon at night, in 1.04. 8 P
in faith, at the latter end of a sea–coal fire. 1.04. 9 P
he shall not have a stone to throw at his dog. 1.04.113 P
mistress page — at the least, if the love of a 2.01. 11 P
tuns of oil in his belly) ashore at windsor? 2.01. 65 P
sir actaeon he, with ringwood at thy heels — 2.01.118
does he lie at the garter? 2.01.180 P
she was in his company at page's house; 2.01.235 P
at a word, hang no more about me, i am no gibbet 2.02. 16 P
of them all (when the court lay at windsor) 2.02. 62 P
that i have purchas'd at an infinite rate, and 2.02.205 P
no promise of satisfaction at her hands? 2.02.210 P
for at that time the jealious rascally knave her 2.02.265 P
come you to me at night, you shall know how i 2.02.266 P
come to me soon at night. 2.02.283 P
come to me soon at night. 2.02.286 P
my coffers ransack'd, my reputation gnawn at, 2.02.293 P
be reveng'd on falstaff, and laugh at page. 2.02.311 P
anne page is, at a farm–house a–feasting; 2.03. 87 P
come at my heels, jack rugby. 2.03. 98 P
person, is at most odds with his own gravity and 3.01. 53 P
have i not, at de place i did appoint? 3.01. 93 P
truly, sir, to see your wife. is she at home? 3.02. 11 P
is your wife at home indeed? 3.02. 26 P
i have good cheer at home, and i pray you all go 3.02. 52 P
we shall have the freer wooing at master page's. 3.02. 85 P
sir john, is come in at your back door, mistress 3.03. 24 P
here's mistress page at the door, sweating, and 3.03. 86 P
coming, with half windsor at his heels, to 3.03.114 P
your husband's here at hand, bethink you of some 3.03.127 P
without cause, why then make sport at me, then 3.03.150 P
heaven forgive my sins at the day of judgment! 3.03.212 P
the very riches of thyself | that now i aim at. 3.04. 18
i was at her house the hour she appointed me. 3.05. 65 P
and at his heels a rabble of his companions, 3.05. 75 P
come to me at your convenient leisure, and you 3.05.134 P
he is at my house. 3.05.145 P
is he at master ford's already, think'st thou? 4.01. 1 P
my son profits nothing in the world at his book. 4.01. 15 P
who's at home besides yourself? 4.02. 12 P
hard by, at street end; he will be here anon. 4.02. 39 P
basket again, to meet him at the door with it, 4.02. 95 P
your master is hard at door. 4.02.109 P
the duke himself will be to–morrow at court, and 4.03. 3 P
they have had my /house a week at command. 4.03. 10 P
he send you both these letters at an instant? 4.04. 3 P
word they'll meet him in the park at midnight? 4.04. 18 P
doth all the winter–time, at still midnight, 4.04. 30
that falstaff at that oak shall meet with us, 4.04. 42
let them from forth a sawpit rush at once | with 4.04. 54
steal my nan away, | and marry her at eton. 4.04. 75
well money'd, and his friends | potent at court. 4.04. 89
prosper'd since i forswore myself at primero. 4.05.101 P
and i will (at the least) keep your counsel. 4.06. 7 P
her | of such contents as you will wonder at; 4.06. 13
image of the jest | i'll show you here at large. 4.06. 18
to–night at herne's oak, just 'twixt twelve and 4.06. 19
and with him at eton | immediately to marry. 4.06. 24
and at the dean'ry, where a priest attends, 4.06. 31
procure the vicar | to stay for me at church, 4.06. 49
you in the park about midnight, at herne's oak, 5.01. 11 P
not rejoice so much at the abuse of falstaff as 5.03. 7 P
as he will chafe at the doctor's marrying my 5.03. 8 P
which, at the very instant of falstaff's and our 5.03. 14 P
meeting, they will at once display to the night. 5.03. 15 P
have i liv'd to stand at the taunt of one that 5.05.143 P
thou shalt eat a posset to–night at my house, 5.05.171 P
where i will desire thee to laugh at my wife, 5.05.172 P
to laugh at my wife, that now laughs at thee. 5.05.172 P
i came yonder at eton to marry mistress anne 5.05.183 P
she is now with the doctor at the dean'ry, and 5.05.202 P
you have ta'en a special stand to strike at me, 5.05.235 P
in our remove be thou at full ourself. MM 1.01. 43
no? a dozen times at least. 1.02. 20 P
be thus foolishly lost at a game of tick–tack. 1.02.190 P
action | at our more leisure shall i render you; 1.03. 49
stands at a guard with envy; 1.03. 51
soon at night | i'll send him certain word of my 1.04. 88
he cannot, sir; he's out at elbow. 2.01. 61 P
house, which at that very distant time stood, as 2.01. 91 P
whose father died at hallowmas. 2.01.124 P
was't not at hallowmas, master froth? 2.01.124 P
but that i am | at war 'twixt will and will not. 2.02. 33
and neither heaven nor man grieve at the mercy. 2.02. 50
that shall be up at heaven and enter there | ere 2.02.152
at what hour to–morrow | shall i attend your 2.02.159
at any time 'fore noon. 2.02.160
to my soul, | it is no sin at all, but charity. 2.04. 66
pleas'd you to do't at peril of your soul, 2.04. 67
better it were a brother died at once, | than 2.04.106
for his falling, i should wonder at angelo. 3.01.187 P
the great soldier who miscarried at sea? 3.01.210 P
her brother frederick was wrack'd at sea, having 3.01.216 P

there, at the moated grange, resides this		3.01.264 P
at that place call upon me, and dispatch with		3.01.265 P
what, at the wheels of caesar?		3.02. 43 P
than merry at any thing which profess'd to make		3.02.236 P
nor, gentle daughter, fear you not at all.		4.01. 70
office, as you will answer it at your peril."		4.02.126 P
it hath not mov'd him at all.		4.02.152 P
you shall anon over–read it at your pleasure;		4.02.197 P
at the suit of master three–pile the mercer, for		4.03. 9 P
shall witness to him i am near at home;		4.03. 95
desire | to meet me at the consecrated fount,		4.03. 98
who do prepare to meet him at the gates, | there		4.03.131
his company | at mariana's house to–night.		4.03.140
i am pale at mine heart to see thine eyes so red		4.03.151 P
duke of dark corners had been at home, he had		4.03.157 P
and why meet him at the gates, and /redeliver		4.04. 5 P
i'll call you at your house.		4.04. 16 P
these letters at fit time deliver me.		4.05. 1
go call at flavio's house, | and tell him where		4.05. 6
she and that friar, | i saw them at the prison.		5.01.135
but at this instant he is sick, my lord, | of a		5.01.151
do you not smile at this, lord angelo?		5.01.163
and did supply thee at thy garden–house | in her		5.01.212
that's the way; for women are light at midnight.		5.01.279 P
boldly, at least.		5.01.297
i met you at the prison, in the absence of the		5.01.328 P
i am more amaz'd at his dishonor | than at the		5.01.380
at his dishonor | than at the strangeness of it.		5.01.381
habit, i am still | attorney'd at your service.		5.01.385
your brother's death i know sits at your heart;		5.01.389
it claudio was beheaded | at an unusual hour?		5.01.458
more, if any born at ephesus be seen | at any	ERR	1.01. 16
be seen | at any syracusian marts and fairs;		1.01. 17
thy substance, valued at the highest rate,		1.01. 23
and /the great care of goods at randon left,		1.01. 42
herself (almost at fainting under | the pleasing		1.01. 45
fast'ned ourselves at either end the mast, | and		1.01. 85
at length the sun, gazing upon the earth,		1.01. 88
at length, another ship had seiz'd on us, | and,		1.01.112
do me the favor to dilate at full | what have		1.01.122
at eighteen years became inquisitive | after his		1.01.125
many a man would take you at your word, | and go		1.02. 17
soon at five a' clock, | please you, i'll meet		1.02. 26
i pray you jest, sir, as you sit at dinner.		1.02. 62
your worship's wife, my mistress at the phoenix;		1.02. 88
are their males' subjects and at their controls:		2.01. 19
say, is your tardy master now at hand?		2.01. 44
nay, he's at two hands with me, and that my two		2.01. 45 P
whilst i at home starve for a merry look:		2.01. 88
gave to dromio is laid up | safe at the centaur,		2.02. 2
i could not speak with dromio since at first | i		2.02. 5
my house was at the phoenix?		2.02. 11
that at dinner they should not drop in his		2.02. 98 P
wouldst thou not spit at me, and spurn at me,		2.02.134
wouldst thou not spit at me, and spurn at me,		2.02.134
so, | and in this mist at all adventures go.		2.02.216
master, shall i be porter at the gate?		2.02.217
say that i linger'd with you at your shop | to		3.01. 3
that you beat me at the mart, i have your hand		3.01. 12
kick, being kick'd, and, being at that pass,		3.01. 17
o, signior balthazar, either at flesh or fish,		3.01. 22
thee from the door, or sit down at the hatch:		3.01. 33
who are those at the gate?		3.01. 48
have at you with a proverb — shall i set in my		3.01. 51
have at you with another, that's — when?		3.01. 52
who is that at the door that keeps all this		3.01. 61
they stand at the door, master, bid them welcome		3.01. 68
why at this time the doors are made against you.		3.01. 93
i'll meet you at that place some hour hence.		3.01.122
and let her read it in thy looks at board:		3.02. 18
armadoes of carrects to be ballast at her nose.		3.02.137 P
i thought to have ta'en you at the porpentine;		3.02.167
and soon at supper–time i'll visit you, | and		3.02.174
at five a' clock | i shall receive the money for		4.01. 10
well, officer, arrest him at my suit.		4.01. 69
they stay for nought at all | but for their		4.01. 91
i will debate this matter at more leisure, | and		4.01.100
what, is he arrested? tell me at whose suit.		4.02. 43
i know not at whose suit he is arrested well;		4.02. 44
this i wonder at, | /that he, unknown to me,		4.02. 47
give me the ring of mine you had at dinner, | or		4.03. 68
rage, | is a mad tale he told to–day at dinner,		4.03. 88
i'll serve you, sir, five hundred at the rate.		4.04. 14
and have nothing at his hands for my service but		4.04. 31 P
face | revel and feast it at my house to–day,		4.04. 62
o husband, god doth know you din'd at home,		4.04. 65
din'd at home? thou villain, what sayest thou?		4.04. 68
sir, sooth to say, you did not dine at home.		4.04. 69
say now, whose suit is he arrested at?		4.04.131
is, | i long to know the truth hereof at large.		4.04.143
his word might bear my wealth at any time.		5.01. 8
at board he fed not for my urging it;		5.01. 64
and at her heels a huge infectious troop | of		5.01. 81
i will fall prostrate at his feet, | and never		5.01.114
by this i think the dial points at five.		5.01.118
at your important letters — this ill day | a		5.01.138
go, some of you, knock at the abbey–gate, | and		5.01.165
and in a dark and dankish vault at home | there		5.01.248
that he din'd not at home, but was lock'd out.		5.01.256
you say he din'd at home;		5.01.274
sir, he din'd with her there, at the porpentine.		5.01.276
saw'st thou him enter at the abbey here?		5.01.279
that bore thee at a burthen two fair sons.		5.01.344
besides her urging of her wrack at sea —		5.01.360
and hear at large discoursed all our fortunes;		5.01.396
with all my heart, i'll gossip at this feast.		5.01.408
your goods that lay at host, sir, in the centaur		5.01.411
there is a fat friend at your master's house,		5.01.415
that kitchen'd me for you to–day at dinner:		5.01.416
much better is it to weep at joy than to joy at	ADO	1.01. 28 P
is it to weep at joy than to joy at weeping!		1.01. 28 P
in messina, and challeng'd cupid at the flight,		1.01. 40 P
for cupid, and challeng'd him at the burbolt.		1.01. 42 P
hear my dog bark at a crow than a man swear he		1.01.131 P
him we shall stay here at the least a month, and		1.01.149 P
i will die in it at the stake.		1.01.233 P
pen and hang me up at the door of a		1.01.253 P
hang me in a bottle like a cat, and shoot at me,		1.01.258 P
and tell him i will not fail him at supper, for		1.01.277 P
a present remedy, at least a patient sufferance.		1.03. 8 P
when i have cause, and smile at no man's jests;		1.03. 14 P
was not count john here at supper?		2.01. 1 P
which blessing i am at him upon my knees every		2.01. 28 P
at a word, i am not.		2.01.114 P
at a word, i am not.		2.01.120 P
them, and then they laugh at him and beat him.		2.01.142 P
not mark'd, or not laugh'd at, strikes him into		2.01.148 P
any ill, i will leave them at the next turning.		2.01.154 P
upon me that i stood like a man at a mark, with		2.01.246 P
man at a mark, with a whole army shooting at me.		2.01.247 P
come, you shake the head at so long a breathing,		2.01.362 P
i can, at any unseasonable instant of the night,		2.02. 16 P
her to look out at her lady's chamber–window.		2.02. 17 P
likelihood than to see me at her chamber–window,		2.02. 43 P
after he hath laugh'd at such shallow follies in		2.03. 10 P
night we would have it at the lady hero'i		2.03. 86 P
rail'd at herself, that she should be so		2.03.141 P
she knew his love, lest she'll make sport at it.		3.01. 58
and the little hangman dare not shoot at him.		3.02. 12 P
or in the shape of two countries at once, as a		3.02. 35 P
hath any man seen him at the barber's?		3.02. 43 P
and aim better at me by that i now will manifest		3.02. 96 P
well, you are to call at all the alehouses, and		3.03. 42 P
here, man, i am at thy elbow.		3.03. 98 P
i wonder at it.		3.03.116 P
she leans me out at her mistress' chamber–window		3.03.146 P
as he was appointed next morning at the temple,		3.03.161 P
our excommunication, and meet me at the jail.		3.05. 64 P
out at your window betwixt twelve and one?		4.01. 84
i talk'd with no man at that hour, my lord.		4.01. 86
at that hour last night | talk with a ruffian at		4.01. 90
talk with a ruffian at her chamber–window, | who		4.01. 91
rearward of reproaches, | strike at thy life.		4.01.127
chid i for that at frugal nature's frame?		4.01.128
hand | took up a beggar's issue at my gates,		4.01.132
any man with me convers'd | at hours unmeet, or		4.01.182
talk with a man out at a window!		4.01.309 P
and made a push at chance and sufferance.		5.01. 38
tush, tush, man, never fleer and jest at me;		5.01. 58
virtues, yet at last she concluded with a sigh,		5.01.171 P
deserve well at my hands by helping me to the		5.02. 2 P
come to your uncle, yonder's old coil at home.		5.02. 96 P
gold, | and all europa shall rejoice at thee,		5.04. 45
at thee, | as once europa did at lusty jove,		5.04. 46
therefore never flout at me for what i have said		5.04.107 P
at christmas i no more desire a rose | than wish	LLL	1.01.105
so to the laws at large i write my name, | and		1.01.155
and shall, at the least of thy sweet notice,		1.01.275 P
i am ill at reck'ning, it fitteth the spirit of		1.02. 40 P
for this damsel, i must keep her at the park;		1.02.130 P
i will visit thee at the lodge.		1.02.135 P
at a marriage–feast, | between lord perigort and		2.01. 40
i saw him at the duke alanson's once, | and much		2.01. 61
another of these students at that time | was		2.01. 64
words | that aged ears play truant at his tales,		2.01. 74
at which interview | all liberal reason i will		2.01.166
mean time receive such welcome at my hand | as		2.01.168
sick at the heart.		2.01.185
it was well done of you to take him at his word.		2.01.217
but to jig off a tune at the tongue's end,		3.01. 12 P
times as much more — and yet nothing at all.		3.01. 48 P
i shoot thee at the swain.		3.01. 65
were still at odds, being but three.		3.01. 85
were still at odds, being but three.		3.01. 90
were still at odds, being but three.		3.01. 96
my sweet soul, i mean setting thee at liberty,		3.01.123 P
with her, boyet, and she strikes at the brow.		4.01.117
let the mark have a prick in't, to mete at, if		4.01.132
she's too hard for you at pricks, sir, challenge		4.01.138
are sweetly varied, like a scholar at the least;		4.02. 9 P
your wit | what was a month old at cain's birth,		4.02. 35
i do dine to–day at the father's of a certain		4.02.153 P
away, the gentles are at their game, and we will		4.02.166 P
you chide at him, offending twice as much.		4.03.130
how will he triumph, leap, and laugh at it!		4.03.146
and nestor play at push–pin with the boys, | and		4.03.167
the boys, | and critic timon laugh at idle toys!		4.03.168
at the first op'ning of the gorgeous east,		4.03.219
the cull'd sovereignty | do meet, as at a fair,		4.03.231
have at you then, affection's men–at–arms.		4.03.286
else none at all in aught proves excellent.		4.03.351
your reasons at dinner have been sharp and		5.01. 2 P
they have been at a great feast of languages,		5.01. 36 P
thou hast it ad dunghill, at the fingers' ends,		5.01. 78 P
you not educate youth at the charge–house on the		5.01. 82 P
at your sweet pleasure, for the mountain.		5.01. 85 P
the princess at her pavilion in the posteriors		5.01. 88 P
sweet self are good at such eruptions and sudden		5.01.114 P
you took the moon at full, but now she's changed		5.02.214
we can afford no more at such a price.		5.02.223
are these the breed of wits so wondered at?		5.02.266
dumaine was at my service, and his sword:		5.02.276
should be presented at our tent to us.		5.02.307
ladies, withdraw; the gallants are at hand.		5.02.308
and retails his wares | at wakes and wassails,		5.02.318
that, when he plays at tables, chides the dice		5.02.326
here stand i, lady, dart thy skill at me,		5.02.396
speak for yourselves, my wit is at an end.		5.02.430
abate throw at novum, and the whole world again		5.02.544
and often, at his very loose, decides | that		5.02.742
as to rejoice at friends but newly found.		5.02.751
in our maiden council rated them | at courtship,		5.02.780
now, at the latest minute of the hour, | grant		5.02.787
then, at the expiration of the year, | come		5.02.804
at the twelvemonth's end | i'll change my black		5.02.833
thou hast by moonlight at her window sung | with	MND	1.01. 30
and the duchess, on his wedding–day at night.		1.02. 7 P
some of your french crowns have no hair at all;		1.02. 98 P
at the duke's oak we meet.		1.02.110 P
mislead night–wanderers, laughing at their harm?		2.01. 39
titania, | glance at my credit with hippolyta,		2.01. 75
set your heart at rest;		2.01.121
that the rude sea grew civil at her song, | and		2.01.152
he took | at a fair vestal throned by /the west,		2.01.158
hoots and wonders | at our quaint spirits.		2.02. 7
when at your hands did i deserve this scorn?		2.02.124
away, | and you sat smiling at his cruel prey.		2.02.150
open, and the moon may shine in at the casement.		3.01. 58 P
i'll meet thee, pyramus, at ninny's tomb."		3.01. 97
you speak all your part at once, cues and all.		3.01.100 P
horse, hound, hog, bear, fire, at every turn.		3.01.111
and light them at the fiery glow–worm's eyes,		3.01.170
when i did him at this advantage take, | an		3.02. 16
sort, | rising and cawing at the gun's report,		3.02. 22
sky, | so, at his sight, away his fellows fly;		3.02. 24
and, at our stamp, here o'er and o'er one falls;		3.02. 25
for briers and thorns at their apparel snatch;		3.02. 29
of our fairy band, | helena is here at hand,		3.02.111
then will two at once woo one;		3.02.118
i am amazed at your /passionate words.		3.02.220
wink each at other, hold the sweet jest up;		3.02.239
i have no gift at all in shrewishness;		3.02.301
at whose approach, ghosts, wand'ring here and		3.02.381
when i had at my pleasure taunted her, | and she		4.01. 57
the more gracious, i shall sing it at her death.		4.01.219 P
meet presently at the palace;		4.02. 37 P
here repent you, | the actors are at hand;		5.01.116
gentles, perchance you wonder at this show;		5.01.127
at the which let no man wonder.		5.01.134
lovers think no scorn | to meet at ninus' tomb,		5.01.138
and lovers twain | at large discourse, while		5.01.151
i kiss the wall's hole, not your lips at all.		5.01.201
wilt thou at ninny's tomb meet me straightway?		5.01.202
the very best at a beast, my lord, that e'er i		5.01.229 P
what harm a wind too great might do at sea.	MV	1.01. 24
eyes, | and laugh like parrots at a bagpiper;		1.01. 53
but at dinner–time | i pray you have in mind		1.01. 70
thou know'st that all my fortunes are at sea,		1.01.177
virtuous, and holy men at their death have good		1.02. 28 P
to my description level at my affection.		1.02. 38 P
gate upon one wooer, another knocks at the door.		1.02.133
upon the rialto, he hath a third at mexico, a		1.03. 20 P
cheek, | a goodly apple rotten at the heart.		1.03.101
then meet me forthwith at the notary's;		1.03.172
if hercules and lichas play at dice | which is		2.01. 32
and either not attempt to choose at all, | or		2.01. 39
the fiend is at mine elbow and tempts me, saying		2.02. 2 P
my heels are at your commandement, i will run.		2.02. 31 P
turn up on your right hand at the next turning,		2.02. 41 P
next turning, but at the next turning of all, on		2.02. 42 P
marry, at the very next turning, turn of no hand		2.02. 43 P
that supper be ready at the farthest by five of		2.02.115 P
rest, | but we will visit you at supper–time.		2.02.206
soon at supper shalt thou see | lorenzo, who is		2.03. 5
disguise us at my lodging, and return | all in		2.04. 2
at gratiano's lodging some hour hence.		2.04. 26
on black monday last at six a' clock i' th'		2.05. 25 P
mistress, look out at window, for all this —		2.05. 40 P
but come at once, | for the close night doth		2.06. 46
and we are stay'd for at bassanio's feast.		2.06. 48
madam, there is alighted at your gate | a young		2.09. 86
sweet, | to show how costly summer was at hand,		2.09. 94
rebels it at these years?		3.01. 35 P
whether antonio have had any loss at sea or no?		3.01. 43 P
me half a million, laugh'd at my losses, mock'd		3.01. 55 P
laugh'd at my losses, mock'd at my gains,		3.01. 56 P
my master antonio is at his house and desires to		3.01. 74 P
i would my daughter were dead at my foot, and		3.01. 88 P
would she were hears'd at my foot, and the		3.01. 89 P
fourscore ducats at a sitting!		3.01.111 P
go, tubal, and meet me at our synagogue;		3.01.129 P
go, good tubal, at our synagogue, tubal.		3.01.130 P
you | even at that time i may be married too.		3.02.194
/roof was dry | with oaths of love, at last, if		3.02.205
no, we shall ne'er win at that sport, and stake		3.02.216 P
rating myself at nothing, you shall see | how		3.02.257
he plies the duke at morning and at night, | and		3.02.277
he plies the duke at morning and at night, | and		3.02.277
you and i, if i might but see you at my death.		3.02.320 P
fond | to come abroad with him at his request.		3.03. 10
many that have at times made moan to me;		3.03. 23
my coach, which stays for us | at the park–gate;		3.04. 83
he is ready at the door; he comes, my lord.		4.01. 15
every offense is not a hate at first.		4.01. 68
shall understand that at the receipt of your		4.01.150 P
comes with him, at my importunity, to fill up		4.01.160 P
forfeiture, | to be so taken at thy peril, jew.		4.01.344
thou must be hang'd at the state's charge.		4.01.367
ring, and doth entreat | your company at dinner.		4.02. 8
before the break of day | be here at belmont.		5.01. 30
within the house, your mistress is at hand,		5.01. 52
no note at all of our being absent hence —		5.01.120
your husband is at hand, i hear his trumpet.		5.01.122
since you do take it, love, so much at heart.		5.01.145
and 'twere to me i should be mad at it.		5.01.176
here is a letter, read it at your leisure.		5.01.267
you are not satisfied | of these events at full.		5.01.297
my brother jaques he keeps at school, and report	AYL	1.01. 5 P
for my part, he keeps me rustically at home, or,		1.01. 7 P
more properly, stays me here at home unkept;		1.01. 8 P
for your father's remembrance, be at accord.		1.01. 64 P
so please you, he is here at the door, and		1.01. 91 P
charles, what's the new news at the new court?		1.01. 97 P
there's no news at the court, sir, but the old		1.01. 98 P
she is at the court, and no less belov'd of her		1.01.110 P
nature hath given us wit to flout at fortune,		1.02. 45 P
and envious disposition | sticks me at heart.		1.02.242
of the duke, | that here was at the wrastling?		1.02.270
not one to throw at a dog.		1.03. 3 P
cast away upon curs, throw some of them at me.		1.03. 5 P
rose at an instant, learn'd, play'd, eat		1.03. 74
for, by this heaven, now at our sorrows pale,		1.03.104
lord, | the melancholy jaques grieves at that,		2.01. 26
at whom so oft | your grace was wont to laugh,		2.02. 8
at seventeen years many their fortunes seek,		2.03. 73
seek, | but at fourscore it is too late a week;		2.03. 74
when i was at home, i was in a better place, but		2.04. 17 P
are now on sale, and at our sheep–cote now, | by		2.04. 84
more at your request than to please myself.		2.05. 23 P
hold death a while at the arm's end.		2.06. 10 P
you touch'd my vein at first.		2.07. 94
church, | if ever sat at any good man's feast,		2.07.115
and sat at good men's feasts, and wip'd our eyes		2.07.122
at first the infant, | mewling and puking in the		2.07.143

the more one sickens the worse at ease he is;		3.02. 24 P
for not being at court? your reason.		3.02. 39 P
why, if thou never wast at court, thou never		3.02. 40 P
those that are good manners at the court are as		3.02. 46 P
of the country is most mockable at the court.		3.02. 48 P
told me you salute not at the court but you kiss		3.02. 49 P
the fairest boughs, | or at every sentence end,		3.02.136
narrow–mouth'd bottle, either too much at once,		3.02.201 P
bottle, either too much at once, or none at all.		3.02.201 P
at which time would i, being but a moonish youth		3.02.409 P
now weep for him, then spit at him;		3.02.417 P
which i have darted at thee, hurt thee not,		3.05. 25
that you insult, exult, and all at once, | over		3.05. 36
'tis at the tuft of olives here hard by.		3.05. 75
"who ever lov'd that lov'd not at first sight?"		3.05. 82
if you do sorrow at my grief in love, | by		3.05. 87
him, | for what had he to do to chide at me?		3.05.129
and, now i am rememb'red, scorn'd at me.		3.05.131
a woman's wit, and it will out at the casement;		4.01.162 P
shut that, and 'twill out at the key–hole;		4.01.163 P
'twill fly with the smoke out at the chimney.		4.01.164 P
i must attend the duke at dinner.		4.01.180 P
patience herself would startle at this letter,		4.03. 13
but at this hour the house doth keep itself,		4.03. 81
after some small space, being strong at heart,		4.03.151
i would i were at home.		4.03.161
the more shall i to–morrow be at the height of		5.02. 46 P
he's as good at any thing, and yet a fool.		5.04.105 P
and to the other | a land itself at large, a		5.04.169
have | i'll stay to know at your abandon'd cave.		5.04.196
how silver made it good | at the hedge–corner,	SHR	in.1. 20
he cried upon it at the merest loss, | and twice		in.1. 23
and that his lady mourns at his disease.		in.1. 62
on thee, | each in his office ready at thy beck.		in.2. 34
and at that sight shall sad apollo weep, | so		in.2. 59
and say you would present her at the leet,		in.2. 87
ashore, | we could at once put us in readiness,		1.01. 43
shall you have to court her at your pleasure.		1.01. 54
to be whipt at the high cross every morning.		1.01.132 P
master, your love must live a maid at home,		1.01.182
tranio, at once | uncase thee;		1.01.206
for so your father charg'd me at our parting;		1.01.213
villain, i say, knock me at this gate, | and rap		1.02. 11
how do you all at verona?		1.02. 22 P
whom would to god i had well knock'd at first,		1.02. 34
knock at the gate?		1.02. 39 P
and come you now with "knocking at the gate"?		1.02. 42 P
to seek their fortunes farther than at home,		1.02. 51
crowns in my purse i have, and goods at home,		1.02. 57
she moves me not, or not removes, at least,		1.02. 72
you | to give you over at this first encounter,		1.02.105
at least | have leave and leisure to make love		1.02.135
all books of love, see that at any hand — | and		1.02.146
not her that chides, sir, at any hand, i pray.		1.02.225
that hath been long studying at rheims, as		2.01. 80 P
i knew you at the first | you were a moveable.		2.01.196
then at my farm | i have a hundred milch–kine to		2.01.356
who woo'd in haste, and means to wed at leisure.		3.02. 11
now must the world point at poor katherine,		3.02. 18
come, where be these gallants? who's at home?		3.02. 87
which at more leisure i will so excuse | as you		3.02.108
the morning wears, 'tis time we were at church.		3.02.111
that at the parting all the church did echo.		3.02.179
that take it on you at the first so roundly.		3.02.214
they shall go forward, kate, at thy command.		3.02.222
wants | for to supply the places at the table,		3.02.247
you know there wants no junkets at the feast.		3.02.248
horn is a foot, and so long am i at the least.		4.01. 28 P
whose hand (she being now at hand) thou shalt		4.01. 30 P
and this cuff was but to knock at your ear, and		4.01. 65 P
e'en at hand, alighted by this;		4.01.117 P
no man at door | to hold my stirrup nor to take		4.01.120
but at last i spied | an ancient angel coming		4.02. 60
travel you far on, or are you at the farthest?		4.02. 73
sir, at the farthest for a week or two, | but		4.02. 74
your ships are stay'd at venice, and the duke,		4.02. 83
first, tell me, have you ever been at pisa?		4.02. 93
to feast and sport us at thy father's house.		4.03.183
genoa, | where we were lodgers at the pegasus.		4.04. 5
i told him that your father was at venice, | and		4.04. 15
then at my lodging, and it like you.		4.04. 55
the worst is this, that, at so slender warning,		4.04. 60
of saint luke's church is at your command at all		4.04. 88 P
luke's church is at your command at all hours.		4.04. 89 P
but they may chance to need thee at home,		5.01. 3 P
pisa, and is here at the door to speak with him.		5.01. 28 P
from padua and here looking out at the window.		5.01. 31 P
while i play the good husband at home, my son		5.01. 69 P
son and my servant spend all at the university.		5.01. 70 P
and happily i have arrived at the last | unto		5.01.127
at last, though long, our jarring notes agree,		5.02. 1
to smile at scapes and perils overblown.		5.02. 3
have at you for a /bitter jest or two!		5.02. 45
this bird you aim'd at, though you hit her not;		5.02. 50
'tis thought your deer does hold you at a bay.		5.02. 56
to come at first when he doth send for her,		5.02. 68
whilst thou li'st warm at home, secure and safe;		5.02.151
and craves no other tribute at thy hands | but		5.02.152
that so generally is at all times good must of	AWW	1.01. 7 P
remember thee, i will think of thee at court.		1.01.189 P
and at this time | his tongue obey'd his hand.		1.02. 40
since the physician at your father's died?		1.02. 70
and sickness | debate it at their leisure.		1.02. 75
but /or every blazing star or at an earthquake,		1.03. 87 P
that man should be at woman's command, and yet		1.03. 92 P
what's in "mother," | that you start at it?		1.03.142
i'll stay at home | and pray god's blessing into		1.03.253
health, at your bidding, serve your majesty!		2.01. 18
and that at my bidding you could so stand up.		2.01. 65
that done, laugh well at me.		2.01. 87
but what at full i know, thou know'st no part,		2.01.132
any manners, he may easily put it off at court.		2.02. 9 P
at your whipping, and "spare not me"?		2.02. 52 P
of noble bachelors stand at my bestowing, | o'er		2.03. 53
she had her breeding at my father's charge —		2.03.114
my honor's at the stake, which to defeat, | i		2.03.149
for thou hast to pull at a smack a' th' contrary		2.03.225 P
that hugs his kicky–wicky here at home,		2.03.280
traveller is something at the latter end of a		2.05. 28 P
do so ever, though i took him at 's prayers.		2.05. 41 P
you than you have or will to deserve at my hand,		2.05. 48 P
you must not marvel, helen, at my course,		2.05. 58
greater than shows itself at the first view | to		2.05. 68
i have no mind to isbel since i was at court.		3.02. 12 P
and, after some dispatch in hand at court,		3.02. 54
where thou | wast shot at with fair eyes, to be		3.02.107
whoever shoots at him, i set him there;		3.02.112
miseries which nature owes | were mine at once.		3.02.120
bless him at home in peace, whilst i from far		3.04. 10
madam, | if i had given you this at overnight,		3.04. 23
i know she will lie at my house;		3.05. 31 P
at the saint francis here beside the port.		3.05. 36
he's shrewdly vex'd at something.		3.05. 89 P
great saint jaques bound, | already at my house.		3.05. 96
he might at some great and trusty business in a		3.06. 14 P
be but your lordship present at his examination,		3.06. 28 P
he will make no deed at all of this that so		3.06. 94 P
have of late knock'd too often at my door.		4.01. 28 P
faith, for seventeen poniards are at my bosom.		4.01. 76 P
nay, i'll speak that | which you will wonder at.		4.01. 86
but unseal'd — | at least in my opinion.		4.02. 31
when midnight comes, knock at my chamber–window;		4.02. 54
acquir'd for him shall at home be encount'red		4.03. 69 P
honor to be the officer at a place there call'd		4.03.269 P
his qualities being at this poor price, i need		4.03.276 P
if my heart were great, | 'twould burst at this.		4.03.331
i duly am inform'd | his grace is at marsellis,		4.04. 9
daughter–in–law had been alive at this hour, and		4.05. 5 P
alive at this hour, and your son here at home,		4.05. 5 P
sir, at a woman's service, and a knave at a		4.05. 24 P
at a woman's service, and a knave at a man's.		4.05. 25 P
so you were a knave at his service indeed.		4.05. 29 P
at your service.		4.05. 34 P
which bow the head, and nod at every man.		4.05.106 P
dost thou put upon me at once both the office of		5.02. 49 P
mayst see a sunshine and a hail | in me at once.		5.03. 34
at first | i stuck my choice upon her, ere my		5.03. 44
the last that e'er i took her leave at court,		5.03. 79
it, and she reckon'd it | at her live's rate.		5.03. 91
so, | he might have bought me at a common price.		5.03.190
inferior might | at market–price have bought.		5.03.219
i am a poor man, and at your majesty's command.		5.03.251 P
that credit with them at that time that i knew		5.03.262 P
glove, my lord, she goes off and on at pleasure.		5.03.278 P
and at that time he got his wife with child.		5.03.301
heat, | shall not behold her face at ample view;	TN	1.01. 26
ay, sir, i have them at my fingers' ends.		1.03. 78 P
art thou good at these kickshawses, knight?		1.03.115 P
her, | be not denied access, stand at her doors,		1.04. 16
wise men that crow so at these set kind of fools		1.05. 88 P
there is at the gate a young gentleman much		1.05. 99 P
i am sick, or not at home — what you will, to		1.05.109 P
what is he at the gate, cousin?		1.05.116 P
there's one at the gate.		1.05.125 P
and he says he'll stand at your door like a		1.05.147 P
i heard you were saucy at my gates, and allow'd		1.05.197 P
rather to wonder at you than to hear you.		1.05.198 P
make me a willow cabin at your gate, | and call		1.05.268
and subtle stealth | to creep in at mine eyes.		1.05.298
here, madam, at your service.		1.05.299
fare ye well at once;		2.01. 39 P
i am dog at a catch.		2.03. 60 P
to gabble like tinkers at this time of night?		2.03. 88 P
priz'd my lady's favor at any thing more than		2.03.122 P
like patience on a monument, | smiling at grief.		2.04.115
and with what wing the /staniel checks at it!		2.05.114 P
o ay, make up that. he is now at a cold scent.		2.05.121 P
the cur is excellent at faults.		2.05.128 P
see more detraction at your heels than fortunes		2.05.137 P
shall i play my freedom at tray–trip, and become		2.05.190 P
for i do live at my house, and my house doth		3.01. 6 P
i saw thee late at the count orsino's.		3.01. 37 P
check at every feather | that comes before his		3.01. 64
have you not set mine honor at the stake, | and		3.01.118
this was look'd for at your hand, and this was		3.02. 24 P
we'll call thee at the cubiculo. go.		3.02. 52 P
i can hardly forbear hurling things at him.		3.02. 81 P
in the south suburbs at the elephant | is best		3.03. 39
at your request! yes, nightingales answer daws.		3.04. 35 P
ill of the devil, how he takes it at heart!		3.04.101 P
for gravity to play at cherry–pit with sathan.		3.04.116 P
at which time we will bring the device to the		3.04.139 P
scout me for him at the corner of the orchard		3.04.176 P
as the hunter, attends thee at the orchard–end.		3.04.223 P
if you hold your life at any price, betake you		3.04.230 P
three, and his incensement at this moment is so		3.04.238 P
and looks pale, as if a bear were at his heels.		3.04.295 P
i arrest thee at the suit of count orsino.		3.04.326 P
up, that thou thereby | mayst smile at this.		4.01. 57
as ever thou wilt deserve well at my hand, help		4.02. 80 P
i could not find him at the elephant, | yet		4.03. 5
and too doubtful soul | may live at peace.		4.03. 28
can fool no more money out of me at this throw.		5.01. 41 P
like to th' egyptian thief at point of death,		5.01.118
i had rather than forty pound i were at home.		5.01.177 P
his eyes were set at eight i' th' morning.		5.01.199 P
action | is now in durance, at malvolio's suit,		5.01.276
he holds belzebub at the stave's end as well as		5.01.284 P
you, | here at my house and at my proper cost.		5.01.319
you, | here at my house and at my proper cost.		5.01.319
this present hour, | which i have wond'red at.		5.01.358
the letter at sir toby's great importance, | in		5.01.363
"madam, why laugh you at such a barren rascal?		5.01.375 P
that may blow | no sneaping winds at home, to	WT	1.02. 13
when at bohemia | you take my lord, i'll give		1.02. 39
i' th' sun, | and bleat the one at th' other.		1.02. 68
at my request he would not.		1.02. 87
if at home, sir, | he's all my exercise, my		1.02.165
and many a man there is (even at this present,		1.02.192
he would not stay at your petitions, made | his		1.02.215
at the good queen's entreaty.		1.02.220
at the queen's be't;		1.02.221
canst with thine eyes at once see good and evil,		1.02.303
will take again your queen as yours at first,		1.02.336
as clear | as friendship wears at feasts, keep		1.02.344
and will by twos and threes at several posterns		1.02.438
you're pow'rful at it.		2.01. 28
yea, a very trick | for them to play at will.		2.01. 52
madam, i must | be present at your conference.		2.02. 16
how he may soften at the sight o' th' child:		2.02. 38
camillo and polixenes | laugh at me;		2.03. 24
make their pastime at my sorrow:		2.03. 24
to–night, commanded | none should come at him.		2.03. 32
him and do sigh | at each his needless heavings,		2.03. 35
at least thus much:		2.03.165
blush, and tyranny | tremble at patience.		3.02. 32
name of fault, i must not | at all acknowledge.		3.02. 61
have | been both at delphos, and from thence		3.02.126
there is no truth at all i' th' oracle.		3.02.140
heavens themselves | do strike at my injustice.		3.02.147
do not receive affliction | at my petition;		3.02.224
i am glad at heart | to be so rid o' th'		3.03. 14
he's at it now.		3.03.106 P
if you had but look'd big and spit at him, he'ld		4.03.106 P
i'll be with you at your sheep–shearing too.		4.03.119 P
to chide at your extremes it not becomes me.		4.04. 6
at upper end o' th' table, now i' th' middle;		4.04. 59
if you did but hear the pedlar at the door, you		4.04.181 P
to bed of twenty money–bags at a burthen, and		4.04.264 P
five justices' hands at it, and witnesses more		4.04.283 P
have at it with you.		4.04.296 P
why, they stay at door, sir.		4.04.342 P
at least if you make a care | of happy holding		4.04.355
a father | is at the nuptial of his son a guest		4.04.395
not need to grieve | at knowing of thy choice.		4.04.416
at this time | he will allow no speech (which i		4.04.467
the which shall point you forth at every sitting		4.04.561
there shall not at your father's house these		4.04.578
sure the gods do this year connive at us, and we		4.04.677 P
away from his father with his clog at his heels.		4.04.679 P
the king is not at the palace.		4.04.762 P
whose miseries are to be smil'd at, their		4.04.792 P
at the last | do as the heavens have done,		5.01. 4
not at all, good lady.		5.01. 20
give you all greetings that a king, at friend,		5.01.140
to th' fearful usage | (at least ungentle) of		5.01.154
at your request | my father will grant precious		5.01.221
you, sir, were you present at this relation?		5.02. 1 P
i was by at the opening of the farthel, heard		5.02. 3 P
was when, at the relation of the queen's death		5.02. 84 P
but he at that time, overfond of the shepherd's		5.02.117 P
you, should be hooted at | like an old tale;		5.03.116
at least from fair five hundred pound a year.	JN	1.01. 69
and in the mean time sojourn'd at my father's;		1.01.103
in at the window, or else o'er the hatch.		1.01.171
he and his toothpick at my worship's mess, | and		1.01.190
"o sir," says answer, "at your best command,		1.01.197
at your employment, at your service, sir."		1.01.198
at your employment, at your service, sir."		1.01.198
sir," says question, "i, sweet sir, at yours";		1.01.199
why scorn'st thou at sir robert?		1.01.228
needs must you lay your heart at his dispose,		1.01.263
at our importance hither is he come | to spread		2.01. 7
have sold their fortunes at their native homes,		2.01. 69
they are at hand, | to parley or to fight,		2.01. 77
sits on 's horseback at mine hostess' door,		2.01.289
sirrah, were i at home, | at your den, sirrah,		2.01.290
at your den, sirrah, with your lioness, | i		2.01.291
so, and at the other hill | command the rest to		2.01.298
who are at hand, triumphantly displayed, | to		2.01.309
at your industrious scenes and acts of death.		2.01.376
for at this match, | with swifter spleen than		2.01.447
for at saint mary's chapel presently | the rites		2.01.538
is sad and passionate at your highness' tent.		2.01.544
but thou art fair, and at thy birth, dear boy,		3.01. 51
abbots, imprisoned angels | set at liberty.		3.03. 9
but now i envy at their liberty, | and will		3.04. 73
not gone already, | even at that news he dies;		3.04.164
out at mine eyes in tender womanish tears.		4.01. 36
and with my hand at midnight held your head;		4.01. 45
but you at your sick service had a prince.		4.01. 52
snatch at his master that doth tarre him on.		4.01.116
being urged at a time unseasonable.		4.02. 20
doth make a stand at what your highness will.		4.02. 39
that, ere the next ascension–day at noon, | your		4.02.151
and on that day at noon, whereon he says | i		4.02.156
even at my gates, with ranks of foreign pow'rs;		4.02.244
lords, i will meet him at saint edmundsbury.		4.03. 11
o, he is bold, and blushes not at death.		4.03. 76
now powers from home and discontents at home		4.03.151
say that before ascension–day at noon | my crown		5.01. 26
or if he do, let it at least be said, | they saw		5.01. 75
my heart hath melted at a lady's tears, | being		5.02. 47
nor met with fortune other than at feasts,		5.02. 58
war, | that, like a lion fostered up at hand,		5.02. 75
hand, | it may lie gently at the foot of peace,		5.02. 76
be propertied, | to be a secondary at control,		5.02. 80
the king doth smile at, and is well prepar'd		5.02.134
hand which had the strength, even at your door,		5.02.137
even at the crying of your nation's crow,		5.02.144
and even at hand a drum is ready brac'd | that		5.02.169
for at hand | (not trusting to this halting		5.02.173
with me, | upon the altar at saint edmundsbury,		5.04. 18
i am no woman, i'll not swound at it.		5.06. 22
time | than if you had at leisure known of this.		5.06. 27
at whose request the king hath pardon'd them,		5.06. 35
it would not out at windows nor at doors.		5.07. 29
it would not out at windows nor at doors.		5.07. 29
the dolphin rages at our very heels.		5.07. 80
the cardinal pandulph is within at rest, | who		5.07. 82
at worcester must his body be interr'd, | for so		5.07. 99
shall, | lie at the proud foot of a conqueror,		5.07.113
danger seen in him | aim'd at your highness, no	R2	1.01. 14
as to be hush'd and nought at all to say.		1.01. 53
to my liege, | i do defy him, and i spit at him,		1.01. 60
myself i throw, dread sovereign, at thy foot,		1.01.165
it, | at coventry upon saint lambert's day.		1.01.199
with all good speed at plashy visit me.		1.02. 66
yea, at all points, and longs to enter in.		1.03. 2
lo, as at english feasts, so i regreet | the		1.03. 67
lift me up | to reach at victory above my head,		1.03. 72
air, | have i deserved at your highness' hands.		1.03.158
why at our justice seem'st thou then to low'r?		1.03.235
the man that mocks at it and sets it light.		1.03.293

our substitutes at home shall have blank 1.04. 48
at ely house. 1.04. 58
the setting sun, and music at the close, | as 2.01. 12
to crop at once a too long withered flower. 2.01.134
no good at all that i can do for him, | unless 2.01.235
at some thing it grieves, | more than with 2.02. 12
uplifted arms is safe arriv'd | at ravenspurgh. 2.02. 51
despair, and be at enmity | with cozening hope. 2.02. 68
whilst others come to make him lose at home. 2.02. 81
comes rushing on this woeful land at once! 2.02. 99
your men, | and meet me presently at berkeley. 2.02.119
and every thing is left at six and seven. 2.02.122
farewell at once, for once, for all, and ever. 2.02.148
uncle, you say the queen is at your house, | for 3.01. 36
with letters of your love to her at large. 3.01. 41
barkloughly castle call they this at hand? 3.02. 1
stand bare and naked, trembling at themselves? 3.02. 46
day, | but, self-affrighted, tremble at his sin. 3.02. 53
a puny subject strikes | at thy great glory. 3.02. 87
ay, all of them at bristow lost their heads. 3.02.142
scoffing his state and grinning at his pomp, 3.02.163
comes at the last and with a little pin | bores 3.02.169
even at his feet to lay my arms and power, 3.03. 39
at meeting tears the cloudy cheeks of heaven. 3.03. 57
i see | i talk but idlely, and you laugh at me. 3.03.171
to come at traitors' calls and do them grace. 3.03.181
thus high at least, although your knee be low. 3.03.195
madam, we'll play at bowls. 3.04. 3
/we at time of year | do wound the bark, the 3.04. 57
meet at london london's king in woe. 3.04. 97
by heaven, i'll throw at all! 4.01. 57
thy men | to execute the noble duke at callice. 4.01. 82
and there at venice gave | his body to that 4.01. 97
at that sad stop, my lord, | where rude 5.02. 4
walls | with painted imagery had said at once, 5.02. 16
down their hands, | to kill the king at oxford. 5.02. 99
inquire at london, 'mongst the taverns there, 5.03. 5
and told him of those triumphs held at oxford. 5.03. 14
straight shall dog them at the heels. 5.03.139
from my heart" — | meaning the king at pomfret. 5.04. 10
with much ado (at length) have gotten leave | to 5.05. 74
appear | at large discoursed in this paper here. 5.06. 10
that sought at oxford thy dire overthrow. 5.06. 16
and approved scot, | at holmedon met, | where 1H4 1.01. 55
next our council we | will hold at windsor, so 1.01.104
morning by four a' clock early, at gadshill, 1.02.125 P
if you will not, tarry at home and be hang'd. 1.02.132 P
ye, yedward, if i tarry at home and go not, i'll 1.02.134 P
well, come what will, i'll tarry at home. 1.02.145 P
meeting, wherein it is at our pleasure to fail; 1.02.170 P
fat rogue will tell us when we meet at supper, 1.02.188 P
at supper, how thirty at least he fought with, 1.02.188 P
he may be more wond'red at | by breaking through 1.02.201
temperate, | unapt to stir at these indignities, 1.03. 2
which harry percy here at holmedon took, | were, 1.03. 24
show'd like a stubble-land at harvest-home. 1.03. 35
at such a time, with all the rest retold, | may 1.03. 73
that we at our own charge shall ransom straight 1.03. 79
death, | trembling even at the name of mortimer. 1.03.144
at berkeley castle. 1.03.249
who bears hard | his brother's death at bristow, 1.03.271
where you and douglas and our powers at once, 1.03.296
arms, | which now we hold at much uncertainty. 1.03.299
at hand, quoth pick-purse. 2.01. 48 P
that's even as fair as — at hand, quoth the 2.01. 49 P
it to one of his company last night at supper, a 2.01. 57 P
thy spirit within thee hath been so at war, 2.03. 56
sir john with half a dozen more are at the door, 2.04. 82 P
and the rest of the thieves are at the door; 2.04. 88 P
age of this present twelve a' clock at midnight. 2.04. 95 P
some six or seven dozen of scots at a breakfast, 2.04.103 P
that melted at the sweet tale of the sun's? 2.04.121 P
a rogue if i were not at half-sword with a dozen 2.04.164 P
sixteen at least, my lord. 2.04.175 P
four rogues in buckrom let drive at me — 2.04.196 P
four came all afront, and mainly thrust at me. 2.04.201 P
in kendal green came at my back and let drive at 2.04.222 P
green came at my back and let drive at me, for 2.04.223 P
'zounds, and i were at the strappado, or all the 2.04.237 P
a nobleman of the court at door would speak with 2.04.288 P
what doth gravity out of his bed at midnight? 2.04.294 P
he that rides at high speed and with his pistol 2.04.345 P
doth not thy blood thrill at it? 2.04.370 P
why, being son to me, art thou so pointed at? 2.04.407 P
with a most monstrous watch is at the door. 2.04.483 P
the sheriff and all the watch are at the door, 2.04.489 P
for i myself at this time have employ'd him. 2.04.513
keep close, we'll read it at more advantage. 2.04.542 P
at my nativity | the front of heaven was full of 3.01. 13
and at my birth | the frame and huge foundation 3.01. 15
at the same season if your mother's cat had 3.01. 18
at your birth | our grandam earth, having this 3.01. 32
to tell you once again that at my birth | the 3.01. 36
power, | as is appointed us, at shrewsbury. 3.01. 85
he held me last night at least nine hours | in 3.01.154
some private conference, but be near at hand, 3.02. 2
at thy affections, which do hold a wing | quite 3.02. 30
not stir | but like a comet i was wond'red at, 3.02. 47
ne'er seen but wond'red at, and so my state, 3.02. 57
to laugh at gibing boys, and stand the push | of 3.02. 66
when i from france set foot at ravenspurgh, 3.02. 95
to dog his heels and curtsy at his frowns, | to 3.02.127
met | the eleventh of this month at shrewsbury. 3.02.166
our general forces at bridgenorth shall meet. 3.02.178
lights as good cheap at the dearest chandler's 3.03. 45 P
hal, to the news at court for the robbery, lad, 3.03.175 P
temple hall | at two /a' clock in the afternoon; 3.03.200
and at the time of my departure thence | he was 4.01. 23
wealth of all our states | all at one cast? 4.01. 47
of may, | and gorgeous as the sun at midsummer; 4.01.102
bid my lieutenant peto meet me at town's end. 4.02. 9 P
the truth, stol'n from my host at saint albons, 4.02. 46 P
your honor had already been at shrewsbury. 4.02. 53 P
know the king | knows at what time to promise, 4.03. 53
him | even at the heels in golden multitudes. 4.03. 73
was poor, | upon the naked shore at ravenspurgh, 4.03. 77
for, sir, at shrewsbury, | as i am truly given 4.04. 10
the day looks pale | at his distemp'rature. 5.01. 3
us, | and you did swear that oath at doncaster, 5.01. 42
hand, | forgot your oath to us at doncaster, 5.01. 58
proclaim'd at market-crosses, read in churches, 5.01. 73
which gape and rub the elbow at the news | of 5.01. 77
looks, | and we shall feed like oxen at a stall, 5.02. 14
point, | still ending at the arrival of an hour. 5.02. 84
o douglas, hadst thou fought at holmedon thus, 5.03. 14
though i could scape shot-free at london, i fear 5.03. 30 P
i saw him hold lord percy at the point, | with 5.04. 21
grieves at heart | so many of his shadows thou 5.04. 29
but we rose both at an instant and fought a long 5.04.147 P
at my tent | the douglas is; 5.05. 22
but what mean i | to speak so true at first? 2H4 in 28
please it your honor knock but at the gate, 1.01. 5
rode on, and, upon my life, | spoke at a venter. 1.01. 59
than did our soldiers, aiming at their safety, 1.01.124
this is the news at full. 1.01.135
men of all sorts take a pride to gird at me. 1.02. 6 P
to be worn in my cap than to wait at my heels. 1.02. 16 P
he may keep it still at a face royal, for a 1.02. 24 P
shoes, and bunches of keys at their girdles, and 1.02. 39 P
he hath since done good service at shrewsbury, 1.02. 62 P
your day's service at shrewsbury hath a little 1.02.148 P
let him lend me the money, and have at him! 1.02.194 P
all you that kiss my lady peace at home, that 1.02.207 P
it was young hotspur's cause at shrewsbury. 1.03. 26
back unarm'd, | they baying him at the heels. 1.03. 80
no, nor i neither, i'll be at your elbow. 2.01. 20 P
i arrest you at the suit of mistress quickly. 2.01. 45 P
of eastcheap, and he is arrested at my suit. 2.01. 71 P
chamber, at the round table by a sea-coal fire, 2.01. 87 P
and harry prince of wales | are near at hand. 2.01.135
will you have doll tearsheet meet you at supper? 2.01.163 P
at /basingstoke, my lord. 2.01.169
fathers being so sick as yours at this time is. 2.02. 31 P
at last i spied his eyes, and methought he had 2.02. 81 P
repent at idle times as thou mayst and so 2.02.129 P
at the old place, my lord, in eastcheap. 2.02.148 P
shall we steal upon them, ned, at supper? 2.02.158 P
and wait upon him at his table as drawers. 2.02.172 P
alas, sweet wife, my honor is at pawn, | and, 2.03. 7
who then persuaded you to stay at home? 2.03. 15
methought 'a made a shrewd thrust at your belly. 2.04.211 P
both of a bigness, and 'a plays at quoits well, 2.04.245 P
you knew i was at your back, and spoke it on 2.04.307 P
who knocks so loud at door? 2.04.352 P
the king your father is at westminster, | and 2.04.355
bare-headed, sweating, knocking at the taverns, 2.04.359
more knocking at the door! 2.04.369 P
a dozen captains stay at door for you. 2.04.372
my poorest subjects | are at this hour asleep! 3.01. 5
and in two year after | were they at wars. 3.01. 60
he is at oxford still, is he not? 3.02. 10 P
and had the best of them all at commandement. 3.02. 24 P
see him break scoggin's head at the court-gate, 3.02. 30 P
how a good yoke of bullocks at /stamford fair? 3.02. 38 P
would have clapp'd i' th' clout at twelve score, 3.02. 46 P
we have heard the chimes at midnight, master 3.02.214 P
mouldy, stay at home till you are past service; 3.02.251 P
as great aim level at the edge of a penknife. 3.02.267 P
i remember at mile-end green, when i lay at 3.02.279 P
mile-end green, when i lay at clement's inn — i 3.02.279 P
at your return visit our house, let our old 3.02.293 P
go to, i have spoke at a word. god keep you! 3.02.297 P
i do remember him at clement's inn, like a man 3.02.308 P
in the law of nature but i may snap at him: 3.02.332 P
the prince is here at hand. 4.01.223
end | to this debate that bleedeth at our doors, 4.04. 2
i think he's gone to hunt, my lord, at windsor. 4.04. 14
why art thou not at windsor with him, thomas? 4.04. 50
here at more leisure may your highness read, 4.04. 89
this packet, please it you, contains at large. 4.04.101
i should rejoice now at this happy news, | and 4.04.109
and at my death | thou hast seal'd up my 4.05.102
heart | to stab at half an hour of my life. 4.05.108
for now a time is come to mock at form. 4.05.118
wages, about the sack he lost at /hinckley fair? 5.01. 24 P
have some countenance at his friend's request. 5.01. 45 P
to have a son set your decrees at nought? 5.02. 85
nay more, to spurn at your most royal image, 5.02. 89
or peace, or both at once, may be | as things 5.02.138
the mass, i have drunk too much sack at supper. 5.03. 14 P
look who's at door there ho! 5.03. 70 P
the laws of england are at my commandement. 5.03.136 P
do not you grieve at this, i shall be sent for 5.05. 77 P
i shall be sent for soon at night. 5.05. 90 P
assume the port of mars, and at his heels H5 pr 6
that did affright the air at agincourt? pr 14
yea, at that very moment, | consideration like 1.01. 27
so soon did lose his seat (and all at once) | as 1.01. 36
which i have open'd to his grace at large, | as 1.01. 78
sum | than ever at one time the clergy yet | did 1.01. 80
sala, | is at this day in germany call'd meisen. 1.02. 53
as never did the clergy at one time | bring in 1.02.134
hath shook and trembled at th' ill neighborhood. 1.02.154
it follows then the cat must stay at home, | yet 1.02.174
th' advised head defends itself at home; 1.02.179
where some, like magistrates, correct at home; 1.02.191
in | their heavy burthens at his narrow gate, 1.02.201
if we, with thrice such powers left at home, 1.02.217
when thousands weep more than did laugh at it. 1.02.296
we hope to make the sender blush at it. 1.02.299
we'll chide this dolphin at his father's door. 1.02.308
may have their throats about them at that time, 2.01. 22 P
me the eight shillings i won of you at betting? 2.01. 95 P
shall not be wink'd at, how shall we stretch our 2.02. 55
cause | that admiration did not hoop at them; 2.02.108
at the discovery of most dangerous treason 2.02.162
than i do at this hour joy o'er myself, 2.02.163
twelve and one, ev'n at the turning o' th' tide; 2.03. 13 P
the mighty sender, doth he prize you at. 2.04.119
do not, in grant of all demands at large, 2.04.121
to-morrow shall you know our mind at full. 2.04.140
seen | the well-appointed king at /hampton pier 3.pr. 4
jewry | at herod's bloody-hunting slaughter-men. 3.03. 41
our madams mock at us, and plainly say | our 3.05. 28
very excellent services committed at the bridge. 3.06. 4 P
is an aunchient lieutenant there at the pridge, 3.06. 12 P
god, and i have merited some love at his hands. 3.06. 24 P
aunchient, it is not a thing to rejoice at; 3.06. 54 P
'a utt'red as prave words at the pridge as you 3.06. 63 P
to grace himself at his return into london under 3.06. 68 P
services were done — at such and such a sconce, 3.06. 72 P
at such and such a sconce, at such a breach, at 3.06. 72 P
a sconce, at such a breach, at such a convoy; 3.06. 73 P
flames a' fire, and his lips blows at his nose, 3.06.104 P
tell him we could have rebuk'd him at harflew, 3.06.121 P
own person kneeling at our feet but a weak and 3.06.132 P
their particular functions and wonder at him. 3.07. 39 P
have at the very eye of that proverb with "a pox 3.07.119 P
you are the better at proverbs, by how much "a 3.07.121 P
french | do the low-rated english play at dice; 4.pr. 19
and i by him, at all adventures, so we were quit 4.01.116 P
shall join together at the latter day and cry 4.01.137 P
day and cry all, "we died at such a place" — 4.01.138 P
knight, | collect them all together at my tent. 4.01.287
named, | and rouse him at the name of crispian. 4.03. 43
/or i will fetch thy rim out at thy throat | in 4.04. 14
these the wretches that we play'd at dice for? 4.05. 8
ay, he was porn at monmouth, captain gower. 4.07. 11 P
and there is also moreover a river at monmouth. 4.07. 27 P
it is call'd wye at monmouth; 4.07. 28 P
tell you there is good men porn at monmouth. 4.07. 53 P
out their armed heels at their dead masters, 4.07. 80
that shall find himself aggrief'd at this glove; 4.07.163 P
follow fluellen closely at the heels. 4.07.171
with the plebeians swarming at their heels, | go 5.pr. 27
invites the king of england's stay at home; 5.pr. 37
i am qualmish at the smell of leek. 5.01. 21
lousy knave, at my desires, and my requests, and 5.01. 23 P
to see leeks hereafter, i pray you mock at 'em, 5.01. 56 P
will you mock at an ancient tradition, /begun 5.01. 70 P
gleeking and galling at this gentleman twice or 5.01. 74 P
terms, | such as will enter at a lady's ear, 5.02.100
your majesty shall mock at me, i cannot speak 5.02.102 P
if i could win a lady at leap-frog, or by 5.02.136 P
thee in french, unless it be to laugh at me. 5.02.187 P
must needs be granted to be much at one. 5.02.192 P
and at night, when you come into your closet, 5.02.197 P
thou hast me, if thou hast me, at the worst; 5.02.232 P
warm kept, are like flies at bartholomew-tide, 5.02.308 P
when at their mothers' moist'ned eyes babes 1H6 1.01. 49
a third thinks, without expense at all, | by 1.01. 76
the circumstance i'll tell you more at large. 1.01.109
and sit at chiefest stern of public weal. 1.01.177
at pleasure here we lie near orleance; 1.02. 6
be not dismay'd, for succor is at hand: 1.02. 50
she takes upon her bravely at first dash. 1.02. 71
the which at touraine, in saint katherine's 1.02.100
my heart and hands thou hast at once subdu'd. 1.02.109
which caesar and his fortune bare at once. 1.02.139
but we shall meet, and break our minds at large. 1.03. 81
father, i know, and oft have shot at them, 1.04. 3
and thou shalt find me at the governor's. 1.04. 20
ground | to hurl at the beholders of my shame. 1.04. 46
i think at the north gate, for there stands 1.04. 66
and i here, at the bulwark of the bridge. 1.04. 67
at least, if thou canst, speak. 1.04. 73
alive, | if salisbury wants mercy at thy hands! 1.04. 86
transported shall be at high festivals | before 1.06. 26
let us have knowledge at the court of guard. 2.01. 4
beds, | hearing alarums at our chamber-doors. 2.01. 42
didst thou at first, to flatter us withal, 2.01. 51
at all times will you have my power alike? 2.01. 55
there hath at least five frenchmen died to-night 2.02. 9
but since your ladyship is not at leisure, 2.03. 26
then say at once if i maintain'd the truth; 2.04. 5
discover more at large what cause that was, 2.05. 59
as well at london bridge as at the tower. 3.01. 23
as well at london bridge as at the tower. 3.01. 23
else would i have a fling at winchester. 3.01. 64
do pelt so fast at one another's pate | that 3.01. 82
then be at peace, except ye thirst for blood. 3.01.117
occasions | at eltam place i told your majesty. 3.01.155
love, | and will at last break out into a flame: 3.01.190
that henry born at monmouth should win all, 3.01.197
win all, | and henry born at windsor lose all: 3.01.198
fast | before he'll buy again at such a rate. 3.02. 43
lance, | and run a-tilt at death within a chair? 3.02. 51
dismay not, princes, at this accident, | nor 3.03. 1
now, sir, to you, that were so hot at sea, 3.04. 28
this dastard, at the battle of poictiers, | when 4.01. 19
and he first took exceptions at this badge, 4.01.105
quiet yourselves, i pray, and be at peace. 4.01.115
nay, let it rest where it began at first. 4.01.121
and make the cowards stand aloof at bay. 4.02. 52
within six hours they will be at his aid. 4.04. 41
if son to talbot, die at talbot's foot. 4.06. 53
young talbot's valor makes me smile at thee. 4.07. 4
stinking and fly-blown lies here at our feet. 4.07. 76
that i in rage might shoot them at your faces! 4.07. 80
i have inform'd his highness so at large, | as, 5.01. 42
wilt thou be daunted at a woman's sight? 5.03. 69
he talks at randon; sure the man is mad. 5.03. 85
hear ye, captain? are you not at leisure? 5.03. 97
at your father's castle walls | we'll crave a 5.03.129
that, when thou com'st to kneel at henry's feet, 5.03.194
will cry for vengeance at the gates of heaven. 5.04. 53
and here at hand the dolphin and his train 5.04.100
shall we at last conclude effeminate peace? 5.04.107
mind | she is content to be at your command — 5.05. 19
or one that at a triumph, having vow'd | to try 5.05. 31
ay, grief, i fear me, both at first and last. 5.05.102
i had in charge at my depart for france, | as 2H6 1.01. 2
my dreams, | in courtly company, or at my beads, 1.01. 27
some sudden qualm hath struck me at the heart, 1.01. 54
there's reason he should be displeas'd at it. 1.01.155
and humphrey with the peers be fall'n at jars: 1.01.253
hanging the head at ceres' plenteous load? 1.02. 2
brows, | as frowning at the favors of the world? 1.02. 4
put forth thy hand, reach at the glorious gold. 1.02. 11
hast thou not worldly pleasure at command 1.02. 45
at last | hume's knavery will be the duchess' 1.02.104
so one by one we'll weed them all at last, | and 1.03. 99
and at his pleasure will resign my place. 1.03.121
whose name and power | thou tremblest at, answer 1.04. 26

beldam, i think we watch'd you at an inch.		1.04. 42
true, madam, none at all.		1.04. 49
at your pleasure, my good lord.		1.04. 78
believe me, lords, for flying at the brook, | i		2.01. 1
forsooth, a blind man at saint albon's shrine,		2.01. 61
at berwick in the north, and't like your grace.		2.01. 81
come offer at my shrine, and i will help thee."		2.01. 90
as more at large your grace shall understand.		2.01.173
means | your lady is forthcoming yet at london.		2.01.175
my lord, i long to hear it at full.		2.02. 6
wink at the duke of suffolk's insolence, | at		2.02. 70
at beauford's pride, at somerset's ambition,		2.02. 71
at beauford's pride, at somerset's ambition,		2.02. 71
at buckingham, and all the crew of them, | till		2.02. 72
we know your mind at full.		2.02. 77
and even as willingly at thy feet i leave it		2.03. 35
two pulls at once — | his lady banish'd, and a		2.03. 41
peter, have at thee with a downright blow!		2.03. 89 P
with envious looks laughing at thy shame, | that		2.04. 12
but be thou mild, and blush not at my shame,		2.04. 48
nor stir at nothing, till the axe of death		2.04. 49
holden at bury the first of this next month.		2.04. 71
death, at whose name i oft have been afeard,		2.04. 89
my lords, at once:		3.01. 66
my use, | be brought against me at my trial day!		3.01.114
for i should melt at an offender's tears, | and		3.01.126
and dogged york, that reaches at the moon,		3.01.158
back, | by false accuse doth level at my life.		3.01.160
rage | be thus upbraided, chid, and rated at,		3.01.175
fourteen days | at bristow i expect my soldiers,		3.01.328
the king and all the peers are here at hand.		3.02. 10
that cardinal beauford is at point of death;		3.02.369
but wherefore grieve i at an hour's poor loss,		3.02.381
rate me at what thou wilt, thou shalt be paid.		4.01. 30
how often hast thou waited at my cup, | fed from		4.01. 56
fed from my trencher, kneel'd down at the board,		4.01. 57
and thou that smil'dst at good duke humphrey's		4.01. 76
who in contempt shall hiss at thee again;		4.01. 78
her furr'd pack, she washes bucks here at home.		4.02. 48 P
now have at him!		4.02.121 P
by her he had two children at one birth.		4.02.139
the bricks are alive at this day to testify it;		4.02.149 P
be hang'd up for example at their doors.		4.02.180
shall be dragg'd at my horse heels till i do		4.03. 12 P
when have i aught exacted at your hands, | /but		4.07. 69
nay, he nods at us, as who should say, i'll be		4.07. 94 P
the streets, and at every corner have them kiss.		4.07.136 P
quake, | shake he his weapon at us and pass by.		4.08. 18
that you should leave me at the white hart in		4.08. 24 P
were't not a shame that, whilst you live at jar,		4.08. 41
but i was made a king, at nine months old.		4.09. 4
flint, | i am so angry at these abject terms;		5.01. 25
is somerset at liberty?		5.01. 87
even at this sight | my heart is turn'd to stone		5.02. 49
and they have troops of soldiers at their beck?	3H6	1.01. 68
and kneel for grace and mercy at my feet:		1.01. 75
why, how now, sons and brother, at a strife?		1.02. 4
and made an evening at the noontide prick.		1.04. 34
that raught at mountains with outstretched arms,		1.04. 68
the contrary doth make thee wond'red at.		1.04.131
to thee | as now i reap at thy too cruel hand!		1.04.166
cry, | the rest stand all aloof and bark at him.		2.01. 17
and at each word's deliverance | stab poniards		2.01. 97
after the bloody fray at wakefield fought,		2.01.107
short tale to make, we at saint albons met,		2.01.120
ambitious york did level at thy crown, | thou		2.02. 19
for all the rest is held at such a rate | as		2.02. 51
darraign your battle, for they are at hand.		2.02. 72
when you and i met at saint albons last, | your		2.02.103
and heap'd sedition on his crown at home.		2.02.158
rewards | as victors wear at the olympian games.		2.03. 53
the like upon thyself — | and so have at thee!		2.04. 11
and i, who at his hands receiv'd my life, | have		2.05. 67
are at our backs, and therefore hence amain.		2.05.133
for at their hands i have deserv'd no pity.		2.06. 26
that i, in all despite, might rail at him,		2.06. 81
here stand we both and aim we at the best;		3.01. 8
a man at least, for less i should not be;		3.01. 57
i was anointed king at nine months old, | my		3.01. 76
at saint albons field | this lady's husband, sir		3.02. 1
grant what i perceive | your highness aims at,		3.02. 68
then no, my lord. my suit is at an end.		3.02. 81
that would be ten days' wonder at the least.		3.02.113
where fame, late ent'ring at his heedful ears,		3.03. 63
these peers of france should smile at that.		3.03. 91
vouchsafe, at our request, to stand aside,		3.03.110
yet shall you have all kindness at my hand		3.03.149
henry now lives in scotland at his ease;		3.03.151
fair queen and mistress | smiles at her news,		3.03.168
smiles at her news, while warwick frowns at his.		3.03.168
and am i guerdon'd at the last with shame?		3.03.191
therefore, at last, i firmly am resolv'd | you		3.03.219
let me give humble thanks for all at once.		3.03.221
that they'll take no offense at our abuse.		4.01. 13
too, | unless they seek for hatred at my hands;		4.01. 80
at my depart, these were his very words:		4.01. 92
my thoughts aim at a further matter:		4.01.125
we may surprise and take him at our pleasure?		4.02. 17
at unawares may beat down edward's guard, | and		4.02. 23
my lord of somerset, at my request, | see that		4.03. 51
his guard | or by his foe surpris'd at unawares;		4.04. 9
to save, at least, the heir of edward's right;		4.04. 32
at whose hands | he hath good usage and great		4.05. 5
your horse stands ready at the park–corner.		4.05. 19
at our enlargement what are thy due fees?		4.06. 5
at last by notes of household harmony | they		4.06. 14
for many men that stumble at the threshold | are		4.07. 11
yet edward, at the least, is duke of york.		4.07. 21
and all at once, once more a happy farewell.		4.08. 31
farewell, sweet lords, let's meet at coventry.		4.08. 32
here at the palace will i rest a while.		4.08. 33
by this at dunsmore, marching hitherward.		5.01. 3
by this at daintry, with a puissant troop.		5.01. 6
at southam i did leave him with his forces,		5.01. 9
then clarence is at hand, i hear his drum.		5.01. 11
they are at hand, and you shall quickly know.		5.01. 15
call edward king and at his hands beg mercy?		5.01. 23
i thought, at least, he would have said the king		5.01. 29
you left poor henry at the bishop's palace,		5.01. 45
i had rather chop this hand off at a blow, | and		5.01. 50
blow, | and with the other fling it at thy face,		5.01. 51
look here, i throw my infamy at thee.		5.01. 82
that, to deserve well at my brother's hands, | i		5.01. 93
but at last | i well might hear, delivered with		5.02. 45
we, having now the best at barnet field, | will		5.03. 20
and make him, naked, foil a man at arms.		5.04. 42
day, | if he arise, be mock'd and wond'red at.		5.04. 57
prepare you, lords, for edward is at hand,		5.04. 60
they that stabb'd caesar shed no blood at all,		5.05. 53
good day, my lord. what, at your book so hard?		5.06. 1
the owl shriek'd at thy birth, an evil sign;		5.06. 44
spurr'd their coursers at the trumpet's sound;		5.07. 9
that dogs bark at me as i halt by them — | why,	R3	1.01. 23
if heaven will take the present at our hands.		1.01.120
whiles kites and buzzards /prey at liberty.		1.01.133
no news so bad abroad as this at home:		1.01.135
may fright the hopeful mother at the view, | and		1.02. 24
here. why dost thou spit at me?		1.02.144
i would they were, that i might die at once;		1.02.151
black–fac'd clifford shook his sword at him;		1.02.158
may | but beg one favor at thy gracious hand,		1.02.207
at chertsey monast'ry this noble king, | and wet		1.02.214
since, | stabb'd in my angry mood at tewksbury?		1.02.241
i'll be at charges for a looking–glass, | and		1.02.255
i fear our happiness is at the height.		1.03. 41
aiming, belike, at your interior hatred, | that		1.03. 65
to be so baited, scorn'd, and stormed at.		1.03.108
tower, | and edward, my poor son, at tewksbury.		1.03.119
in margaret's battle at saint albons slain?		1.03.129
and so doth mine. i muse why she's at liberty.		1.03.304
/'zounds, 'tis even now at my elbow, persuading		1.04.145 P
will you then | spurn at his edict, and fulfill		1.04.198
since i have made my friends at peace on earth.		2.01. 6
'tis death to me to be at enmity;		2.01. 61
with whom my soul is any jot at odds | more than		2.01. 71
then say at once what is it thou requests.		2.01. 99
who told me, in the field at tewksbury, | when		2.01.112
for god sake let not us two stay at home;		2.02.147
was crown'd in paris but at nine months old.		2.03. 17
or by his father there were none at all;		2.03. 24
when great leaves fall, then winter is at hand;		2.03. 33
night, i /hear, they lay at stony–stratford,		2.04. 1
and at northampton they do rest to–night.		2.04. 2
grandam, one night as we did sit at supper, | my		2.04. 10
that he could gnaw a crust at two hours old;		2.04. 28
your highness shall repose you at the tower;		3.01. 65
her | to meet you at the tower and welcome you.		3.01.139
i shall not sleep in quiet at the tower.		3.01.142
to–morrow are let blood at pomfret castle, | and		3.01.183
at crosby house, there shall you find us both.		3.01.190
i'll claim that promise at your grace's hand.		3.01.197
and that may be determin'd at the one | which		3.02. 13
which may make you and him to rue at th' other.		3.02. 14
his honor and myself are at the one, | and at		3.02. 21
and at the other is my good friend catesby;		3.02. 22
but canst thou guess that he doth aim at it?		3.02. 45
the kindred of the queen, must die at pomfret.		3.02. 50
but i shall laugh at this a twelvemonth hence,		3.02. 57
the lords at pomfret, when they rode from london		3.02. 83
your friends at pomfret, they do need the priest		3.02.114
to–day at pomfret bloodily were butcher'd; | and		3.04. 90
come, dispatch, the duke would be at dinner.		3.04. 94
they smile at me who shortly shall be dead.		3.04.107
side, | tremble and start at wagging of a straw;		3.05. 7
ghastly looks | are at my service, like enforced		3.05. 9
offices | at any time to grace my stratagems.		3.05. 11
i never look'd for better at his hands | after		3.05. 50
there, at your meet'st /advantage of the time,		3.05. 74
meet me within this hour at baynard's castle.		3.05.105
untainted, unexamin'd, free, at liberty.		3.06. 9
at lower end of the hall, hurl'd up their caps,		3.07. 35
the mayor is here at hand.		3.07. 45
lewd love–bed, | but on his knees at meditation;		3.07. 73
and devout religious men | are at their beads,		3.07. 93
death and destruction dogs thee at thy heels;		4.01. 39
the britain richmond aims | at young elizabeth,		4.03. 41
but at hand, at hand, | ensues his piteous and		4.04. 73
but at hand, at hand, | ensues his piteous and		4.04. 73
for she that scorn'd at me, now scorn'd of me;		4.04.102
and came i not at last to comfort you?		4.04.165
lo at their birth good stars were opposite.		4.04.216
that at her hands which the king's king forbids.		4.04.346
can make, | and meet me suddenly at salisbury.		4.04.451
may it please you, shall i do at salisbury?		4.04.453
yet to beat down these rebels here at home.		4.04.530
is with a mighty power landed at milford | is		4.04.533
at pembroke or at /ha'rford–west in wales.		4.05. 10
at pembroke or at /ha'rford–west in wales.		4.05. 10
his regiment lies half a mile at least | south		5.03. 37
stab'st me in my prime of youth | at tewksbury.		5.03.120
soul to–morrow, | rivers, that died at pomfret!		5.03.140
devis'd at first to keep the strong in awe:		5.03.310
long kept in britain at our mother's cost?		5.03.324
i do know | kinsmen of mine, three at the least,	H8	1.01. 81
attach'd | our merchants' goods at burdeaux.		1.01. 96
a peace, and purchas'd | at a superfluous rate!		1.01. 99
at this instant | he bores me with some trick.		1.01.127
climb steep hills | requires slow pace at first.		1.01.132
by violent swiftness that which we run at, | and		1.01.142
his pomp as well in france | as here at home,		1.01.164
in fear our motion will be mock'd or carp'd at,		1.02. 86
hast thou heard him | at any time speak aught?		1.02.146
the duke being at the rose, within the parish		1.02.152
being at greenwich, | after your highness had		1.02.188
th' usurper richard, who, being at salisbury,		1.02.196
the lag end of their lewdness and be laugh'd at.		1.03. 35
of beauty | shall shine at full upon them.		1.04. 60
at which appear'd against him his surveyor,		2.01. 19
the cause | he may a little grieve at.		2.01. 39
at his return | no doubt he will requite it.		2.01. 45
at one stroke has taken | for ever from the		2.01.117
held for certain | the king will venture at it.		2.01.156
for not bestowing on him at his asking | the		2.01.163
if it do, | i'll venture one; have at him!		2.02. 84
bitter than | 'tis sweet at first t' acquire —		2.03. 9
wife, | at all times to your will conformable;		2.04. 24
foe, and think not | at all a friend to truth.		2.04. 84
not there | at once and fully satisfied),		2.04.149
the question did at first so stagger me,		2.04.213
i was set at work | among my maids, full little,		3.01. 74
a woman lost among ye, laugh'd at, scorn'd?		3.01.107
lest at once | the burthen of my sorrows fall		3.01.110
madam, you wander from the good we aim at.		3.01.138
gone by him, or at least | strangely neglected?		3.02. 10
at this.		3.02. 61
he's vex'd at something.		3.02.104
which | i find at such proud rate, that it		3.02.127
have at you!		3.02.309
my high–blown pride | at length broke under me,		3.02.362
what, amaz'd | at my misfortunes?		3.02.374
all the ends thou aim'st at be thy country's,		3.02.447
at our last encounter, | the duke of buckingham		4.01. 4
i am sure have shown at full their royal minds		4.01. 8
held a late court at dunstable — six miles off		4.01. 27
as the shrouds make at sea in a stiff tempest,		4.01. 72
at length her grace rose, and with modest paces		4.01. 82
earl northumberland | arrested him at york, and		4.02. 13
at last, with easy roads, he came to leicester,		4.02. 17
and left him at primero | with the duke of		5.01. 7
(as they say spirits do) at midnight, have | in		5.01. 14
ah, my good lord, i grieve at what i speak,		5.01. 95
at what ease | might corrupt minds procure		5.01.131
they would shame to make me | wait else at door,		5.02. 17
who holds his state at door 'mongst pursuivants,		5.02. 24
at least good manners — as not thus to suffer		5.02. 29
and at the door too, like a post with packets.		5.02. 32
i'm very sorry | to sit here at this present,		5.02. 44
the devil | and his disciples only envy at, | ye		5.02.147
now have at ye!		5.02.148
you were ever good at sudden commendations,		5.02.157
he, that dares most, but wag his finger at thee.		5.02.166
wait like a lousy footboy | at chamber–door?		5.02.175
bless me, what a fry of fornication is at door!		5.03. 36 P
at length they came to th' broom–staff to me, i		5.03. 54 P
youths that thunder at a playhouse and fight for		5.03. 60 P
day, no man think | h'as business at his house;		5.04. 75
are like to hear | for this play at this time,		ep 9
doth lesser blench at suff'rance than i do.	TRO	1.01. 28
at priam's royal table do i sit, | and when fair		1.01. 29
better at home, if "would i might" were "may."		1.01.114
when were you at ilium?		1.02. 45 P
at what was all this laughing?		1.02.149 P
at the white hair that helen spied on troilus'		1.02.150 P
laugh'd not so much at the hair as at his pretty		1.02.154 P
not so much at the hair as at his pretty answer.		1.02.154 P
at your pleasure.		1.02.180 P
if he see me, you shall see him nod at me.		1.02.195 P
a woman, a man knows not at what ward you lie.		1.02.258 P
and at all these wards i lie, at a thousand		1.02.263 P
at all these wards i lie, at a thousand watches.		1.02.263 P
at your own house, there he unarms him.		1.02.274 P
puffing at all, winnows the light away, | and		1.03. 28
at this fusty stuff | the large achilles, on his		1.03.161
and at this sport | sir valor dies;		1.03.175
soul in such a kind, | we left them all at home.		1.03.286
of the giant mass | of things to come at large.		1.03.346
art as full of envy at his greatness as cerberus		2.01. 33 P
greatness as cerberus is at proserpina's beauty,		2.01. 34 P
beauty, ay, that thou bark'st at him.		2.01. 35 P
thou use to beat me, i will begin at thy heel,		2.01. 48 P
so to be valiant, is no praise at all.		2.02.145
he beats me, and i rail at him.		2.03. 3 P
that i could beat him, whilst he rail'd at me.		2.03. 5 P
we saw him at the opening of his tent, | he is		2.03. 84
what moves ajax thus to bay at him?		2.03. 90 P
but with a pride | that quarrels at self–breath.		2.03.172
be led | at your request a little from himself.		2.03.181
at whose pleasure, friend?		3.01. 23 P
at mine, sir, and theirs that love music.		3.01. 24 P
at whose request do these men play?		3.01. 28 P
sir, at the request of paris my lord, who is		3.01. 30 P
that if the king call for him at supper, you		3.01. 77 P
he hangs the lip at something.		3.01.139 P
at my cousin cressida's?		3.02. 1 P
like vassalage at /unawares encount'ring | the		3.02. 38
enjoy | at ample point all that i did possess,		3.03. 89
this is not strange at all.		3.03.111
i do not strain at the position — | it is		3.03.112
it is familiar — but at the author's drift,		3.03.113
time hath, my lord, a wallet at his back,		3.03.145
but it must grieve young pyrrhus now at home		3.03.209
i see my reputation is at stake, | my fame is		3.03.227
clear again, that i might water an ass at it!		3.03.311 P
who's that at door?		4.02. 35
there is at hand | paris your brother, and		4.02. 60
they are at hand and ready to effect it.		4.02. 68
nor play at subtile games — fair virtues all,		4.04. 87
at the port, lord, i'll give her to thy hand,		4.04.111
if e'er thou stand at mercy of my sword, | name		4.04.114
out | at every joint and motive of her body.		4.05. 57
in love whereof, half hector stays at home;		4.05. 84
next | to feast with me and see me at my tent.		4.05.229
at menelaus' tent, most princely troilus.		4.05.279
in a chain, /hanging at his /brother's leg — to		5.01. 56 P
she will sing any man at first sight.		5.02. 9
you shake, my lord, at something;		5.02. 50
nothing at all, unless that this were she.		5.02.135
look how thy wounds do bleed at many vents!		5.03. 82
you are amaz'd, my liege, at her exclaim.		5.03. 91
deeds worth praise, and tell you them at night.		5.03. 93
they are at it, hark!		5.03. 95
have at thee!		5.04. 23
i would laugh at that miracle — yet, in a sort,		5.04. 34 P
and foams at mouth, and he is arm'd and at it,		5.05. 36
and foams at mouth, and he is arm'd and at it,		5.05. 36
come both you cogging greeks, have at you both!		5.06. 11
now do i see thee, ha! have at thee, hector!		5.06. 13
the cuckold and the cuckold–maker are at it.		5.07. 9 P
how ugly night comes breathing at his heels;		5.08. 6
be sent | to pray achilles see us at our tent.		5.09. 8
he's dead, and at the murtherer's horse's tail,		5.10. 4
sit, gods, upon your thrones, and smile at troy!		5.10. 7
i say, at once, let your brief plagues be mercy,		5.10. 8
your eyes, half out, weep out at pandar's fall;		5.10. 48

and at that time bequeath you my diseases. 5.10. 56
kill him, and we'll have corn at our own price. COR 1.01. 10 P
strike at the heaven with your staves as lift 1.01. 68
he, \| "that i receive the general food at first 1.01.131
and though that all at once" — \| you, my good 1.01.140
"though all at once cannot \| see what i do 1.01.142
rome and her rats are at the point of battle, 1.01.162
for corn at their own rates, whereof they say 1.01.189
shalt see me once more strike at tullus' face. 1.01.240
the shadow \| which he treads on at noon. 1.01.261
fame, at the which he aims, \| in whom already 1.01.263
sprang not more in joy at first hearing he was a 1.03. 16 P
when it spit forth blood \| at grecian sword, 1.03. 43
no, at a word, madam; 1.03.109 P
o, they are at it! 1.04. 21
following the fliers at the very heels, \| with 1.04. 49
do prize their hours \| at a crack'd drachme! 1.05. 5
in the leash, \| to let him slip at will. 1.06. 39
we have at disadvantage fought, and did \| retire 1.06. 49
the common distribution, at \| your only choice. 1.09. 35
and at all times \| to undercrest your good 1.09. 71
lay here in corioles \| at a poor man's house; 1.09. 83
a treaty find \| i' th' part that is at mercy? 1.10. 7
true sword to sword, i'll potch at him some way, 1.10. 15
him, were it \| at home, upon my brother's guard, 1.10. 25
i am attended at the cypress grove. 1.10. 30
the reins and be angry at your pleasures; 2.01. 31 P
at the least, if you take it as a pleasure to 2.01. 31 P
palate adversely, i make a crooked face at it. 2.01. 57 P
and, i think, there's one at home for you. 2.01.109 P
which time i will make a lip at the physician. 2.01.115 P
a curse begin at very root on 's heart, \| that 2.01.185
some old crab–trees here at home that will not 2.01.188
at some time when his soaring insolence \| shall 2.01.254
deed to have them at all into their estimation 2.02. 27 P
the people than \| he hath hereto priz'd them at. 2.02. 60
at sixteen years, \| when tarquin made a head for 2.02. 87
whom with all praise i point at, saw him fight, 2.02. 90
our spoils he kick'd at, \| and look'd upon 2.02.124
direct way should be at once to all the points 2.03. 23 P
but if it were at liberty, 'twould sure 2.03. 29 P
where? at the senate–house? 2.03.145
by his looks, methinks, \| 'tis warm at 's heart. 2.03.152
so then the volsces stand but as at first, 3.01. 4
at antium lives he? 3.01. 17
at antium. 3.01. 18
at once pluck out \| the multitudinous tongue; 3.01.155
you are at point to lose your liberties. 3.01.193
the public power, \| which he so sets at nought. 3.01.269
death on the wheel, or at wild horses' heels, 3.02. 2
this no more dishonors you at all \| than to take 3.02. 58
my fortunes and my friends at stake requir'd \| i 3.02. 63
at thy choice then. 3.02.123
for i mock at death \| with as big heart as thou. 3.02.127
buy \| their mercy at the price of one fair word, 3.03. 91
power, as now at last \| given hostile strokes, 3.03. 96
your defenders, till at length \| your ignorance 3.03.128
go see him out at gates, and follow him, \| as he 3.03.138
come, come, let's see him out at gates, come. 3.03.142
inevitable strokes, \| as 'tis to laugh at 'em. 4.01. 27
bring me but out at gate. 4.01. 47
and to be on foot at an hour's warning. 4.03. 45 P
nobles of the state \| at his house this night. 4.04. 10
set at upper end o' th' table; 4.05.192 P
and so would do, \| were he more angry at it. 4.06. 15
cast \| your stinking greasy caps in hooting at 4.06.131
their talk at table, and their thanks at end; 4.07. 4
their talk at table, and their thanks at end; 4.07. 4
to hear cominius speak, i'll keep at home. 5.01. 7
lip \| and hum at good cominius much unhearts me. 5.01. 49
down, and this unnatural scene \| they laugh at. 5.03.185
thy mercy and thy honor \| at difference in thee. 5.03.201
almost at point to enter. 5.04. 61
and my pretext to strike at him admits \| a good 5.06. 19
till at the last \| i seem'd his follower, not 5.06. 37
the army marvell'd at it, and, in the last, 5.06. 41
at a few drops of women's rheum, which are \| as 5.06. 45
therefore at your vantage, \| ere he express 5.06. 53
but at his nurse's tears \| he whin'd and roar'd 5.06. 96
that pages blush'd at him, and men of heart 5.06. 98
men of heart \| look'd wond'ring each at others. 5.06. 99
and now at last, laden with honor's spoils, TIT 1.01. 36
from whence at first she weigh'd her anchorage, 1.01. 73
lo at this tomb my tributary tears \| i render 1.01.159
and at thy feet i kneel, with tears of joy 1.01.161
owe, \| mine honor's ensigns humbled at thy feet. 1.01.252
that saidst i begg'd the empire at thy hands. 1.01.307
and at my suit, sweet, pardon what is past. 1.01.431
then at my suit look graciously on him; 1.01.439
my lord, be rul'd by me, be won at last, 1.01.442
to be a heinous sin, \| yield at entreats; 1.01.449
here, \| and at my lovely tamora's entreats, \| i 1.01.483
and virtue stoops and trembles at her frown; 2.01. 11
this way, or not at all, stand you in hope. 2.01.119
horns, \| as if a double hunt were heard at once, 2.03. 19
they told me, here, at dead time of the night, 2.03. 99
even at thy teat thou hadst thy tyranny; 2.03.145
he and his lady both are at the lodge, \| upon 2.03.254
reward \| among the nettles at the elder–tree, 2.03.272
they shall be ready at your highness' will, \| to 2.03.297
that i might rail at him to ease my mind! 2.04. 35
as cerberus at the thracian poet's feet. 2.04. 51
weep, they humbly at my feet \| receive my tears, 3.01. 41
my grief was at the height before thou cam'st, 3.01. 70
man, \| and here my brother, weeping at my woes; 3.01.100
to make us wonder'd at in time to come. 3.01.135
for at your grief \| see how my wretched sister 3.01.136
of them \| as jewels purchas'd at an easy price, 3.01.198
deal, \| but sorrow flouted at is double death. 3.01.245
saturnine and his emperess \| beg at the gates, 3.01.298
my name, \| without the help of any hand at all. 4.01. 71
and here display at last \| what god will have 4.01. 73
lucius and i'll go brave it at the court. 4.01.121
we had a thousand roman dames \| at such a bay, 4.02. 42
well, more or less, or ne'er a whit at all, 4.02. 53
now talk at pleasure of your safety. 4.02.134
yet there's as little justice as at land. 4.03. 9
by me thou shalt have justice at his hands. 4.03.104

to him, at the first approach you must kneel, 4.03.110 P
i'll be at hand, sir, see you do it bravely. 4.03.112 P
knock at my door, and tell me what he says. 4.03.119
wings \| he can at pleasure stint their melody; 4.04. 86
the meeting \| even at his father's house, the 4.04.103
of me, \| as true a dog as ever fought at head. 5.01.102
sport, \| she sounded almost at my pleasing tale, 5.01.119
and set them upright at their dear friends' door 5.01.136
he craves a parley at your father's house, 5.01.159
knock at his study, where they say he keeps \| to 5.02. 5
and whilst i at a banket hold him sure, \| i'll 5.02. 76
goths, \| or at the least make them his enemies. 5.02. 79
and bid him come and banquet at thy house, 5.02.114
when he is here, even at thy solemn feast, \| i 5.02.115
and at thy mercy shall they stoop and kneel, 5.02.118
emperor and the empress too \| feast at my house, 5.02.128
madam, depart at pleasure, leave us here. 5.02.145
the trumpets show the emperor is at hand. 5.03. 16
i will bite my thumb at them, which is disgrace ROM 1.01. 42 P
do you bite your thumb at us, sir? 1.01. 44 P
do you bite your thumb at us, sir? 1.01. 46 P
sir, i do not bite my thumb at you, sir, but i 1.01. 50 P
have at thee, coward! 1.01. 72
right glad i am he was not at this fray. 1.01.117
good heart, at what? 1.01.184
at thy good heart's oppression. 1.01.184
both, \| and pity 'tis you liv'd at odds so long. 1.02. 5
at my poor house look to behold this night 1.02. 24
buds shall you this night \| inherit at my house; 1.02. 30
at this same ancient feast of capulet's \| sups 1.02. 82
that i will show you shining at this feast, 1.02. 98
now, by my maidenhead at twelve year old, \| i 1.03. 2
come lammas–eve at night shall she be fourteen. 1.03. 17
on lammas–eve at night shall she be fourteen, 1.03. 21
my lord and you were then at mantua — \| nay, i 1.03. 28
this night you shall behold him at our feast; 1.03. 80
drums in his ear, at which he starts and wakes, 1.04. 86
face, \| to fleer and scorn at our solemnity? 1.05. 57
in spite \| to scorn at our solemnity this night. 1.05. 63
away, be gone, the sport is at the best. 1.05.119
he jests at scars that never felt a wound. 2.02. 1
shall i hear more, or shall i speak at this? 2.02. 37
i take thee at thy word. 2.02. 49
at lovers' perjuries, \| they say, jove laughs. 2.02. 92
do not swear at all; 2.02.112
and all my fortunes at thy foot i'll lay, \| and 2.02.147
that they cannot sit at ease on the old bench? 2.04. 34 P
suffer every knave to use me at his pleasure! 2.04.156 P
i saw no man use you at his pleasure; 2.04.157 P
and there she shall at friar lawrence' cell \| be 2.04.181
peter, stay at the gate. 2.05. 20 P
what, have you din'd at home? 2.05. 45 P
they'll be in scarlet straight at any news. 2.05. 71
but you shall bear the burthen soon at night. 2.05. 76
with piercing steel at bold mercutio's breast, 3.01.159
i sounded at the sight. 3.02. 56
break, my heart, poor bankrout, break at once! 3.02. 57
o, what a beast was i to chide at him! 3.02. 95
hark ye, your romeo will be here at night. 3.02.140
i'll to him, he is hid at lawrence' cell. 3.02.141
what sorrow craves acquaintance at my hand, 3.03. 5
all three do meet \| in thee at once, which thou 3.03.121
thee at once, which thou at once wouldst lose. 3.03.121
the county paris, at saint peter's church, 3.05.114
i wonder at this haste, that i must wed \| ere he 3.05.118
and see how he will take it at your hands. 3.05.125
are you at leisure, holy father, now, \| or shall 4.01. 37
now, \| or shall i come to you at evening mass? 4.01. 38
i met the youthful lord at lawrence' cell, \| and 4.02. 25
what if this mixture do not work at all? 4.03. 21
at some hours in the night spirits resort — 4.03. 44
then have at you with my wit! 4.05.123 P
my dreams presage some joyful news at hand. 5.01. 2
and keep her at my cell till romeo come — 5.02. 29
wilt thou provoke me? then have at thee, boy! 5.03. 70
how oft when men are at the point of death 5.03. 88
now at once run on \| the dashing rocks thy 5.03.117
to–night \| have my old feet stumbled at graves! 5.03.122
then say at once what thou dost know in this. 5.03.228
all alone, \| at the prefixed hour of her waking, 5.03.253
vault, \| meaning to keep her closely at my cell, 5.03.255
and i for winking at your discords too \| have 5.03.294
there shall no figure at such rate be set \| as 5.03.301
here, at your lordship's service. TIM 1.01.115
and i have bred her at my dearest cost \| in 1.01.124
no, i will do nothing at thy bidding; 1.01.268 P
if our betters play at that game, we must not 1.02. 12
ceremony was but devis'd at first \| to set a 1.02. 15
let me stay at thine apperil, timon. 1.02. 33
man, i should fear to drink at meals, lest they 1.02. 50 P
my heart is ever at your service, my lord. 1.02. 75 P
you had rather be at a breakfast of enemies than 1.02. 76 P
i could wish my best friend at such a feast. 1.02. 79 P
and at that instant like a babe sprung up. 1.02.111
my lord, you take us even at the best. 1.02.152
no porter at his gate, \| but rather one that 2.01. 10
would we could see you at corinth! 2.02. 70 P
if timon stay at home. 2.02. 91 P
at many leisures i /propos'd. 2.02.128
lord, \| at many times i brought in my accompts, 2.02.133
and at length \| how goes our reck'ning? 2.02.149
to a wasteful cock \| and set mine eyes at flow. 2.02.163
that now they are at fall, want treasure, cannot 2.02.205
good boy, wink at me, and say thou saw'st me not 3.01. 44 P
religion groans at it. 3.02. 76
h'as much disgrac'd me in't, i'm angry at him, 3.03. 13
good day at once. 3.04. 7
i wonder on't, he was wont to shine at seven. 3.04. 10
our masters may throw their caps at their money. 3.04.101 P
women are more valiant \| that stay at home, if 3.05. 48
his service done \| at lacedaemon and byzantium 3.05. 60
my wounds ache at you. 3.05. 95
spleen and fury, \| that i may strike at athens. 3.05.113
'tis honor with most lands to be at odds; 3.05.115
ever at the best, hearing well of your lordship. 3.06. 27 P
if there sit twelve women at the table, let a 3.06. 78 P
and ulcerous sores \| would cast the gorge at, 4.03. 41
through the window/–bars bore at men's eyes, 4.03.117

the other, at high wish. 4.03.245
and hearts of men \| at duty, more than i could 4.03.262
that death in me at others' lives may laugh. 4.03.380
for many so arrive at second masters, \| upon 4.03.505
nothing at this time but my visitation; 5.01. 18
i'll meet you at the turn. 5.01. 47
at all times alike \| men are not still the same; 5.01.121
and let him take't at worst — for their knives 5.01.178
camp \| but i do prize it at my love before \| the 5.01.181
to your public laws \| at heaviest answer. 5.04. 63
than that poor brutus, with himself at war, JC 1.02. 46
men at some time are masters of their fates; 1.02.139
now in the names of all the gods at once, \| upon 1.02.148
that could be mov'd to smile at any thing. 1.02.207
such men as he be never at heart's ease \| whiles 1.02.208
and at every putting–by mine honest neighbors 1.02.230 P
caesar, for he swounded, and fell down at it; 1.02.249 P
down in the market–place, and foam'd at mouth, 1.02.253 P
if i would not have taken him at a word, i would 1.02.267 P
those that understood him smil'd at one another, 1.02.283 P
in several hands, in at his windows throw, \| as 1.02.316
caesar's ambition shall be glanced at. 1.02.320
sit \| even at noon–day upon the market–place, 1.03. 27
that i do bear \| i can shake off at pleasure. 1.03.100
and throw this \| in at his window; 1.03.145
and he's gone \| to seek you at your house. 1.03.150
i will yet, ere day, \| see brutus at his house. 1.03.154
i know no personal cause to spurn at him, \| but 2.01. 11
in him \| that at his will he may do danger with. 2.01. 17
thy full petition at the hand of brutus! 2.01. 58
sir, 'tis your brother cassius at the door, 2.01. 70
for he will live, and laugh at this hereafter. 2.01.191
and yesternight at supper \| you suddenly arose 2.01.238
to keep with you at meals, comfort your bed, 2.01.284
heaven nor earth have been at peace to–night. 2.02. 1
if he should stay at home to–day for fear. 2.02. 43
well, \| and, for thy humor, i will stay at home. 2.02. 56
lest i be laugh'd at when i tell them so. 2.02. 70
calphurnia here, my wife, stays me at home: 2.02. 75
hath begg'd that i will stay at home to–day. 2.02. 82
at mine own house, good lady. 2.04. 22
the throng that follows caesar at the heels, 2.04. 34
desire you to o'er–read \| (at your best leisure) 3.01. 5
else shall you not have any hand at all \| about 3.01.248
as he was fortunate, i rejoice at it; 3.02. 26 P
even at the base of pompey's statue \| (which all 3.02.188
he and lepidus are at caesar's house. 3.02.264
or here or at the capitol. 4.01. 11
for we are at the stake, \| and bay'd about with 4.01. 48
he is at hand, and pindarus is come \| to do you 4.02. 4
but if he be at hand \| i shall be satisfied. 4.02. 9
but hollow men, like horses hot at hand, \| make 4.02. 23
strike as thou didst at caesar; 4.03.105
him off \| if at philippi we do face him there, 4.03.211
do face him there, \| these people at our back. 4.03.212
we, at the height, are ready to decline. 4.03.217
the affairs of men \| which, taken at the flood, 4.03.219
along ourselves, and meet them at philippi. 4.03.225
to tell thee thou shalt see me at philippi. 4.03.283
ay, at philippi. 4.03.285
why, i will see thee at philippi then. 4.03.286
he thinks he still is at his instrument. 4.03.292
their battles are at hand; 5.01. 4
they mean to warn us at philippi here, 5.01. 5
let them set on at once; 5.02. 3
of grief, \| that it runs over even at his eyes. 5.05. 14
at sardis once, \| and, this last night, here in 5.05. 18
so fare you well at once, for brutus' tongue 5.05. 39
men \| till he disbursed at saint colme's inch MAC 1.02. 61
by each at once her choppy finger laying \| upon 1.03. 44
and make my seated heart knock at my ribs, 1.03.136
and at more time, \| the interim having weigh'd 1.03.153
the eye wink at the hand; 1.04. 52
we cours'd him at the heels, and had a purpose 1.06. 21
to make their audit at your highness' pleasure, 1.06. 27
so green and pale \| at what it did so freely? 1.07. 38
and she goes down at twelve. 2.01. 3
what, sir, not yet at rest? 2.01. 12
at your kind'st leisure. 2.01. 24
i hear a knocking \| at the south entry. 2.02. 63
never at quiet! 2.03. 16 P
was by a mousing owl hawk'd at, and kill'd. 2.04. 13
adieu, \| till you return at night. 3.01. 35
man be master of his time \| till seven at night. 3.01. 41
within this hour, at most, \| i will advise you 3.01.127
thou marvel'st at my words, but hold thee still: 3.02. 54
at first \| and last, the hearty welcome. 3.04. 1
to feed were best at home; 3.04. 34
never shake \| thy gory locks at me. 3.04. 50
become \| a woman's story at a winter's fire, 3.04. 64
do not muse at me, my most worthy friends, \| i 3.04. 84
at once, good night. 3.04.117
upon the order of your going, \| but go at once. 3.04.119
almost at odds with morning, which is which. 3.04.126
denies his person \| at our great bidding? 3.04.128
and at the pit of acheron \| meet me i' th' 3.05. 15
he fail'd \| his presence at the tyrant's feast, 3.06. 22
smiles upon me, \| and points at them for his. 4.01.124
things at the worst will cease, or else climb 4.02. 24
i take my leave at once. 4.02. 30
why, i can buy me twenty at any market. 4.02. 40
at no time broke my faith, would not betray 4.03.128
ten thousand warlike men \| already at a point, 4.03.135
such welcome and unwelcome things at once \| 'tis 4.03.138
but at his touch, \| such sanctity hath heaven 4.03.143
the tyrant has not batter'd at their peace? 4.03.178
they were well at peace when i did leave 'em. 4.03.179
humh! i guess at it. 4.03.203
chickens, and their dam, \| at one fell swoop? 4.03.219
to receive at once the benefit of sleep and do 5.01. 9 P
what, at any time, have you heard her say? 5.01. 12 P
there's knocking at the gate. 5.01. 66 P
i am sick at heart \| when i behold — seyton, i 5.03. 19
i hope the days are near at hand \| that chambers 5.04. 1
hair \| would at a dismal treatise rouse and stir 5.05. 12
at least we'll die with harness on our back. 5.05. 51
but swords i smile at, weapons laugh to scorn, 5.07. 12
i cannot strike at wretched kerns, whose arms 5.07. 17

	so thanks to all at once and to each one, | whom	5.09. 40
	whom we invite to see us crown'd at scone.	5.09. 41
HAM	'tis bitter cold, | and i am sick at heart.	1.01. 9
	thus twice before, and jump at this dead hour,	1.01. 65
	at least, the whisper goes so.	1.01. 80
	awake the god of day, and at his warning,	1.01.152
	and at last | upon his will i seal'd my hard	1.02. 59
	and thy best graces spend it at thy will!	1.02. 63
	armed at point exactly, cap–a–pe, | appears	1.02.200
	and at the sound it shrunk in haste away | and	1.02.219
	set your entreatments at a higher rate | than a	1.03.122
	our achievements, though perform'd at height,	1.04. 21
	i do not set my life at a pin's fee, | and for	1.04. 65
	of life, of crown, of queen, at once dispatch'd,	1.05. 75
	fare thee well at once!	1.05. 88
	at least i am sure it may be so in denmark.	1.05.109
	and so, without more circumstance at all, | i	1.05.127
	that you, at such times seeing me, never shall,	1.05.173
	so grace and mercy at your most need help you.	1.05.180
	they keep, | what company, at what expense;	2.01. 9
	at "closes in the consequence."	2.01. 51
	at "closes in the consequence," ay, marry.	2.01. 52
	in 's rouse, | there falling out at tennis";	2.01. 57
	at last, a little shaking of mine arm, | and	2.01. 89
	bent, | to lay our service freely at your feet,	2.02. 31
	and at our more considered time we'll read,	2.02. 81
	go to your rest, at night we'll feast together.	2.02. 84
	madam, i swear i use no art at all.	2.02. 96
	o dear ophelia, i am ill at these numbers.	2.02.120 P
	at such a time i'll loose my daughter to him.	2.02.162
	yet he knew me not at first, 'a said i was a	2.02.188 P
	way of friendship, what make you at elsinore?	2.02.270 P
	that would make mouths at him while my father	2.02.364 P
	and you too — at each ear a hearer — that	2.02.382 P
	/french falc'ners — fly at any thing we see;	2.02.430 P
	if it live in your memory, begin at this line —	2.02.448 P
	he finds him | striking too short at greeks.	2.02.469
	pyrrhus at priam drives, in rage strikes wide,	2.02.472
	unless things mortal move them not at all,	2.02.516
	that guilty creatures sitting at a play | have	2.02.589
	with more offenses at my beck than i have	3.01.124 P
	at home, my lord.	3.01.130 P
	whose end, both at the first and now, was and is	3.02. 21 P
	here, sweet lord, at your service.	3.02. 53
	but is there no sequel at the heels of this	3.02.329 P
	at game, a–swearing, or about some act | that	3.03. 91
	trip him, that his heels may kick at heaven,	3.03. 93
	is thought–sick at the act.	3.04. 51
	for at your age | the heyday in the blood is	3.04. 68
	that thus hath cozen'd you at hoodman–blind?	3.04. 77
	forth at your eyes your spirits wildly peep,	3.04.119
	nothing at all, yet all that is i see.	3.04.132
	look where he goes, even now, out at the portal!	3.04.136
	below their mines, | and blow them at the moon.	3.04.209
	appliance are reliev'd, | or not at all.	4.03. 11
	at supper.	4.03. 17 P
	at supper? where?	4.03. 18 P
	convocation of politic worms are e'en at him.	4.03. 20 P
	the bark is ready, and the wind at help, | th'	4.03. 44
	follow him at foot, tempt him with speed aboard.	4.03. 54
	england, if my love thou hold'st at aught —	4.03. 58
	our sovereign process, which imports at full,	4.03. 63
	puff'd | makes mouths at the invisible event,	4.04. 50
	quarrel in a straw | when honor's at the stake.	4.04. 56
	spurns enviously at straws, speaks things in	4.05. 6
	they yawn at it | and botch the words up fit to	4.05. 9
	dead and gone, | at his head a grass–green turf,	4.05. 31
	a grass–green turf, | at his heels a stone."	4.05. 32
	god be at your table!	4.05. 44 P
	morning betime, | and i a maid at your window,	4.05. 50
	ere we were two days old at sea, a pirate of	4.06. 16 P
	as /checking at his voyage, and that he means	4.07. 62
	it, | and nothing is at a like goodness still,	4.07.116
	the breeding, but to play at loggats with them?	5.01. 92 P
	my gorge rises at it.	5.01.188 P
	make her laugh at that.	5.01.195 P
	here's the commission, read it at more leisure.	5.02. 26
	and his crib shall stand at the king's mess.	5.02. 86 P
	lord, if your lordship were at leisure, i should	5.02. 89 P
	i shall win at the odds.	5.02.211 P
	have at you now!	5.02.302
	you that look pale, and tremble at this chance,	5.02.334
	cell, | that thou so many princes at a shot | so	5.02.366
LR	his breeding, sir, hath been at my charge.	1.01. 9 P
	mother fair, there was good sport at his making,	1.01. 23 P
	metal as my sister, | and prize me at her worth.	1.01. 70
	lord, who hath receiv'd you | at fortune's alms.	1.01.278
	who covers faults, at last with shame derides.	1.01.281
	i found it thrown in at the casement of my	1.02. 60 P
	that, sons at perfect age and fathers declin'd,	1.02. 72 P
	none at all.	1.02.158 P
	and at my entreaty forbear his presence until	1.02.160 P
	which at this instant so rageth in him, that	1.02.162 P
	gross crime or other | that sets us all at odds.	1.03. 5
	beat at this gate, that let thy folly in | and	1.04.271
	what, fifty of my followers at a clap?	1.04.294
	to let him keep | at point a hundred knights;	1.04.324
	that's a maid now, and laughs at my departure,	1.05. 51
	that if they come to sojourn at my house, | i'll	2.01.103
	life i have spar'd at suit of his grey beard —	2.02. 63 P
	shoulder that i see | before me at this instant.	2.02. 95
	the king his master very late | to strike at me,	2.02.117
	a good man's fortune may grow out at heels.	2.02.157
	when a /man's overlusty at legs, then he wears	2.04. 10 P
	my lord, when at their home | i did commend your	2.04. 27
	or at their chamber–door i'll beat the drum	2.04.118
	at your choice, sir.	2.04.217
	mend when thou canst, be better at thy leisure,	2.04.229
	moulds, all germains spill at once | that makes	3.02. 8
	he begins at curfew, and walks /till /the first	3.04.116 P
	blanch, and sweetheart, see, they bark at me.	3.06. 63
	tom will throw his head at them.	3.06. 64 P
	and i'll go to bed at noon.	3.06. 85 P
	hot questrists after him, met him at gate, | who	3.07. 17
	wast thou not charg'd at peril —	3.07. 52
	if wolves had at thy gate howl'd that /dearn	3.07. 63
	go thrust him out at gates, and let him smell	3.07. 93
	gone, | thy comforts can do me no good at all;	4.01. 16
	who is't can say, "i am at the worst"?	4.01. 25
	he smil'd at it.	4.02. 5
	i must change names at home, and give the	4.02. 17
	lord edmund spake not with your lord at home?	4.05. 4
	and at her late being here | she gave strange	4.05. 24
	ten masts at each make not the altitude | which	4.06. 53
	when the thunder would not peace at my bidding,	4.06.102 P
	dost thou squiny at me?	4.06.137 P
	it is, | and my heart breaks at it.	4.06.142
	thou hast seen a farmer's dog bark at a beggar?	4.06.155 P
	'tis wonder that thy life and wits at once | had	4.07. 40
	do not laugh at me, | for (as i am a man) i	4.07. 67
	and laugh | at gilded butterflies, and hear poor	5.03. 13
	they are ready | to–morrow, or at further space,	5.03. 53
	would hourly die | rather than die at once!),	5.03.187
	a rat, have life, | and thou no breath at all?	5.03.308
OTH	of whom his eyes had seen the proof | at rhodes,	1.01. 29
	eyes had seen the proof | at rhodes, at cyprus,	1.01. 29
	my heart upon my sleeve | for daws to peck at:	1.01. 65
	at this odd–even and dull watch o' th' night,	1.01.123
	at every house i'll call | (i may command at	1.01.180
	every house i'll call | (i may command at most).	1.01.181
	this very night at one another's heels;	1.02. 42
	rais'd and met, | are at the duke's already.	1.02. 44
	when, being not at your lodging to be found,	1.02. 45
	him, if he do resist | subdue him at his peril.	1.02. 81
	and quiet that her motion | blush'd at herself;	1.03. 96
	take up this mangled matter at the best;	1.03.173
	i am glad at soul i have no other child, | for	1.03.196
	/if /you /please, | /be't at her father's.	1.03.240
	at nine i' th' morning here we'll meet again.	1.03.279
	at my lodging.	1.03.374 P
	what from the cape can you discern at sea?	2.01. 1
	nothing at all, it is a high–wrought flood.	2.01. 2
	methinks the wind hath spoke aloud at land, | a	2.01. 5
	the moor himself at sea, | and is in full	2.01. 28
	our friends at least.	2.01. 57
	had tongue at will, and yet was never loud,	2.01.149
	desdemona, | once more, well met at cyprus.	2.01.212
	do thou meet me presently at the harbor.	2.01.214 P
	hard at hand comes the master and main exercise,	2.01.261 P
	and happily may strike at you — provoke him,	2.01.273 P
	meet me by and by at the citadel.	2.01.283 P
	the moor | at least into a jealousy so strong	2.01.301
	here, at the door; i pray you call them in.	2.03. 46 P
	swords out, and tilting one at other's /breast,	2.03.183
	though he had twinn'd with me, both at a birth,	2.03.212
	found them close together | at blow and thrust,	2.03.238
	you have lost no reputation at all, unless you	2.03.270 P
	or any man living, may be drunk at a time, man.	2.03.313 P
	they do suggest at first with heavenly shows,	2.03.352
	so, with no money at all and a little more wit,	2.03.368 P
	i am very ill at ease, | unfit for mine own	3.03. 32
	shall't be to–night at supper?	3.03. 57
	i shall not dine at home;	3.03. 58
	i meet the captains at the citadel.	3.03. 59
	this — | away at once with love or jealousy!	3.03.192
	and let her down the wind | to prey at fortune.	3.03.263
	which at the first are scarce found to distaste,	3.03.327
	let him not know't, and he's not robb'd at all.	3.03.343
	or, at the least, so prove it | that the	3.03.364
	'tis done at your request.	3.03.474
	and say if i shall see you soon at night.	3.04.198
	i tremble at it.	4.01. 39 P
	if not, he foams at mouth, and by and by	4.01. 54
	did you perceive how he laugh'd at his vice?	4.01.171 P
	lay down my soul at stake.	4.02. 13
	scorn | to point his slow /unmoving finger at!	4.02. 55
	so sweet | that the sense aches at thee, would	4.02. 69
	heaven stops the nose at it, and the moon winks;	4.02. 77
	and one), you may take him at your pleasure.	4.02.237 P
	come, stand not amaz'd at it, but go along with	4.02.239 P
	but to go hang my head all at one side | and	4.03. 32
	i'll be at thy elbow.	5.01. 3
	be near at hand, i may miscarry in't.	5.01. 6
	here, at thy hand; be bold, and take thy stand.	5.01. 7
	what, do you shake at that?	5.01.118
	he supp'd at my house, but i therefore shake not	5.01.119
	th' affrighted globe | did yawn at alteration.	5.02.101
	when we shall meet at compt, | this look of	5.02.273
	from heaven, | and fiends will snatch at it.	5.02.275
ANT	common liar, who | thus speaks of him at rome;	1.01. 61
	let me have a child at fifty, to whom herod of	1.02. 28 P
	here, at your service. my lord approaches.	1.02. 86
	at your noble pleasure.	1.02.112
	friends in rome | petition us at home.	1.02.183
	yet at the first | i saw the treasons planted.	1.03. 25
	and at thy sovereign leisure read | the garboils	1.03. 60
	at the last, best, | see when and where she died	1.03. 61
	to reel the streets at noon, and stand the	1.04. 20
	pompey is strong at sea, | and it appears he is	1.04. 36
	consuls, at thy heel | did famine follow, whom	1.04. 58
	the gilded puddle | which beasts would cough at;	1.04. 63
	at whose foot, | to mend the petty present, i	1.05. 44
	mark antony | in egypt sits at dinner, and will	2.01. 12
	i must be laugh'd at | if, or for nothing or a	2.02. 30
	more laugh'd at, that i should | once name you	2.02. 33
	no more than my residing here at rome | might be	2.02. 37
	you may be pleas'd to catch at mine intent | by	2.02. 41
	at heel of that, defy him.	2.02.157
	eight wild–boars roasted whole at a breakfast,	2.02.179 P
	at the helm | a seeming mermaid steers;	2.02.208
	if thou dost play with him at any game, | thou	2.03. 26
	his quails ever | beat mine, inhoop'd, at odds.	2.03. 39
	the journey, be at /the mount | before you,	2.04. 6
	who at philippi the good brutus ghosted, | there	2.06. 13
	at whose burthen | the anger'd ocean foams, with	2.06. 20
	we'll speak with thee at sea.	2.06. 25
	at land, thou know'st | how much we do	2.06. 25
	at land indeed | thou dost o'er–count me of my	2.06. 26
	when caesar and your brother were at blows,	2.06. 44
	at sea, i think.	2.06. 84 P
	our graver business | frowns at this levity.	2.07.121
	that stands upon the swell at the full of tide,	3.02. 49
	wept | when at philippi he found brutus slain.	3.02. 56
	guess at her years, i prithee.	3.03. 26
	no midway | 'twixt these extremes at all.	3.04. 20
	at the feet sat | caesarion, whom they call my	3.06. 5
	the best of men, | to taunt at slackness.	3.07. 27
	ay, and to wage this battle at pharsalia,	3.07. 31
	shall fall you for refusing him at sea, | being	3.07. 39
	i'll fight at sea.	3.07. 48
	but if we fail, | we then can do't at land.	3.07. 53
	provoke not battle | till we have done at sea.	3.08. 4
	mine eyes did sicken at the sight and could not	3.10. 16
	he at philippi kept | his sword e'en like a	3.11. 35
	have nick'd his captainship, at such a point,	3.13. 8
	i am prompt | to lay my crown at 's feet, and	3.13. 76
	laugh at 's while we strut | to our confusion.	3.13.114
	and at this time most easy 'tis to do't:	3.13.144
	whom | he may at pleasure whip, or hang, or	3.13.150
	mean time | laugh at his challenge.	4.01. 6
	let's to–night | be bounteous at our meal.	4.02. 10
	queen's a squire | more tight at this than thou;	4.04. 15
	riveted trim, | and at the port expect you.	4.04. 23
	had once prevail'd | to make me fight at land!	4.05. 3
	and at thy tent is now | unloading of his mules.	4.06. 22
	had we done so at first, we had droven them home	4.07. 5
	the hearts | that /spannell'd me at heels, to	4.12. 21
	hath at fast and loose | beguil'd me to the very	4.12. 28
	do it at once, | or thy precedent services are	4.14. 82
	then let it do at once | the thing why thou hast	4.14. 88
	and time is at his period.	4.14.107
	the miserable change now at my end | lament nor	4.15. 51
	change now at my end | lament nor sorrow at;	4.15. 52
	me | to throw my sceptre at the injurious gods,	4.15. 76
	but i will tell you at some meeter season.	5.01. 49
	will not wait pinion'd at your master's court,	5.02. 53
	a grief that /smites | my very heart at root.	5.02.105
	yours, | bestow it at your pleasure, and believe	5.02.182
	saucy lictors | will catch at us like strumpets,	5.02.215
	this knot intrinsicate | of life at once untie.	5.02.305
	dost thou not see my baby at my breast, | that	5.02.309
	bravest at the last, | she levell'd at our	5.02.335
	she levell'd at our purposes, and, being royal,	5.02.336
CYM	i think the king | be touch'd at very heart.	1.01. 10
	that is not | glad at the thing they scowl at.	1.01. 15
	that is not | glad at the thing they scowl at.	1.01. 15
	mark it), the eldest of them at three years old,	1.01. 58
	or that the negligence may well be laugh'd at,	1.01. 66
	my residence in rome at one /philario's, | who	1.01. 97
	they were parted | by gentlemen at hand.	1.01.164
	you shall, at least, | go see my lord aboard.	1.01.177
	how i would think on him at certain hours | such	1.03. 27
	at the sixt hour of morn, at noon, at midnight,	1.03. 31
	at the sixt hour of morn, at noon, at midnight,	1.03. 31
	at the sixt hour of morn, at noon, at midnight,	1.03. 31
	this gentleman at that time vouching (and upon	1.04. 58 P
	what do you esteem it at?	1.04. 78 P
	we are familiar at first.	1.04.102 P
	if you buy ladies' flesh at a million a dram,	1.04.135 P
	lie speechless, and his name | is at last gasp.	1.05. 53
	it seems, much loves | a gallian girl at home.	1.06. 66
	that all the plagues of hell should at one time	1.06.111
	for and a daughter who | he not respects at all.	1.06.155
	of him and might not spend them at my pleasure.	2.01. 5 P
	i am not vex'd more at any thing in th' earth;	2.01. 17 P
	i have lost to–day at bowls i'll win to–night of	2.01. 49 P
	hark, hark, the lark at heaven's gate sings,	2.03. 20
	his steeds to water at those springs | on	2.03. 22
	julius caesar | smil'd at their lack of skill,	2.04. 22
	found their courage | worthy his frowning at.	2.04. 23
	or less — at first?	2.05. 15
	the fam'd cassibelan, who was once at point | (o	3.01. 30
	kingdom is stronger than it was at that time;	3.01. 35 P
	perforce, | behooves me keep at utterance.	3.01. 72
	notice that i am in cambria, at milford–haven;	3.02. 44 P
	he is at milford–haven.	3.02. 49
	what's worse, | must curtsy at the censure.	3.03. 55
	where i have liv'd at honest freedom, paid	3.03. 71
	at three and two years old, i stole these babes,	3.03.101
	came from horse, the place | was near at hand.	3.04. 2
	outcrafties him, | and he's at some hard point.	3.04. 16
	i shall give thee opportunity at milford–haven.	3.04. 28 P
	you shall be miss'd at court, | and that will	3.04.126
	if not at court, | then not in britain must you	3.04.134
	so nigh, at least, | that though his actions	3.04.148
	if you are sick at sea, | or stomach–qualm'd at	3.04.189
	or stomach–qualm'd at land, a dram of this	3.04.190
	discover where thy mistress is, at once, | at	3.05. 95
	thy mistress is, at once, | at the next word.	3.05. 96
	my lord, at my lodging, the same suit he wore	3.05.125 P
	meet thee at milford–haven!	3.05.130 P
	my revenge is now at milford;	3.05.155 P
	even before, i was | at point to sink for food.	3.06. 17
	he embark'd at milford;	3.06. 61
	he wrings at some distress.	3.06. 78
	the bier at door, | and a demand who is't shall	4.02. 22
	our courtiers say all's savage but at court.	4.02. 33
	to commix | with winds that sailors rail at.	4.02. 56
	villain, be thy name, | i cannot tremble at it.	4.02. 90
	at fools i laugh, not fear them.	4.02. 96
	it may be heard at court that such as we | cave	4.02.137
	is he at home?	4.02.189
	slumber, | not as death's dart being laugh'd at;	4.02.211
	'twas but a bolt of nothing, shot at nothing,	4.02.300
	pisanio might have kill'd thee at the heart	4.02.322
	you here at milford–haven with your ships.	4.02.335
	heavens, | how deeply you at once do touch me!	4.03. 4
	and in a time | when fearful wars point at me;	4.03. 7
	life is yours, | i humbly set it at your will;	4.03. 13
	italy annoy us, but | we grieve at chances here.	4.03. 35
	nay, do not wonder at it;	5.03. 53
	made | rather to wonder at the things you hear	5.03. 54
	our jovial star reign'd at his birth, and in	5.04.105
	'twas at a feast — o, would | our viands had	5.05.155
	or at least | those which i heav'd to head!	5.05.156
	remember me at court, where i was taught | of	5.05.193
	me | with his sword drawn, foam'd at the mouth,	5.05.276
	have at it then, by leave.	5.05.315
	and at first meeting lov'd, | continu'd so,	5.05.379
	battle, at this instant | is full accomplish'd:	5.05.469
PER	it hath been sung at festivals, | on ember–eves	1.ch. 5
	you have at large received | the danger of the	1.01. 1
	at whose conception, till lucina reigned,	1.01. 8
	gripe not at earthly joys as erst they did;	1.01. 49

time, | hell only danceth at so harsh a chime. 1.01. 85
archer hits the mark | his eye doth level at, so 1.01.163
and danger, which i fear'd, is at antioch, 1.02. 7
if i do it not, i am sure to be hang'd at home. 1.03. 3 P
being at antioch — 1.03. 18
took some displeasure at him, at least he judg'd 1.03. 20
some displeasure at him, at least he judg'd so; 1.03. 20
he scap'd the land to perish at the sea. 1.03. 28
that were to blow at fire in hope to quench it, 1.04. 4
and strangers ne'er beheld but wond'red at; 1.04. 25
is still at tharsus, where each man | thinks all 2.ch. 11
good helicane, that stay'd at home, | not to eat 2.ch. 17
him, and at last devour them all at a mouthful. 2.01. 31 P
him, and at last devour them all at a mouthful. 2.01. 32 P
peace be at your labor, honest fishermen. 2.01. 52
bots on't, 'tis come at last, and 'tis turn'd to 2.01.118 P
gat | for men to see, and seeing wonder at. 2.02. 7
shield | is a black ethiope reaching at the sun; 2.02. 20
a withered branch, that's only green at top; 2.02. 43
which make a sound, but kill'd are wond'red at. 2.03. 63
i am at your grace's pleasure. 2.03.111
love, | and that's the mark i know you level at. 2.03.113
and now at length they overflow their banks. 2.04. 24
who takes offense | at that would make me glad? 2.05. 72
and /crickets sing at the oven's mouth, | are 3.ch. 7
at last from tyre, | fame answering the most 3.ch. 21
even at the first | thy loss is more than can 3.01. 34
with us at sea it hath been still observ'd, and 3.01. 51 P
there i'll leave it | at careful nursing. 3.01. 80
you, should at these early hours | shake off the 3.02. 22
for she was born at sea, i have nam'd so, here 3.03. 13
you in your coffer, which are | at your command. 3.04. 3
that i was shipp'd at sea i well remember, 3.04. 5
imagine pericles arriv'd at tyre, | welcom'd and 4.ch. 1
his woeful queen we leave at ephesus, | unto 4.ch. 3
our fast–growing scene must find | at tharsus, 4.ch. 7
walk half an hour, leonine, at the least. 4.01. 45
he offer'd to cut a caper at the proclamation, 4.02.107 P
at the proclamation, but he made a groan at it, 4.02.108 P
she died at night; 4.03. 16
whilest ours was blurted at and held a mawkin 4.03. 34
and care in us | at whose expense 'tis done. 4.03. 46
marina was she call'd, and at her birth, 4.04. 38
she would serve after a long voyage at sea. 4.06. 44 P
one, how long have you been at this trade? 4.06. 66 P
were you a gamester at five, or at seven? 4.06. 75 P
were you a gamester at five, or at seven? 4.06. 75 P
boult, take her away, use her at thy pleasure. 4.06.141 P
and on this coast | suppose him now at anchor. 5.ch. 16
let me entreat to know at large the cause | of 5.01. 62
sent hither | to make the world to laugh at me. 5.01.144
call'd marina | for i was born at sea. 5.01.156
at sea! what mother? 5.01.156
thou that wast born at sea, buried at tharsus, 5.01.196
thou that wast born at sea, buried at tharsus, 5.01.196
buried at tharsus, | and found at sea again! 5.01.197
she is not dead at tharsus, as she should have 5.01.215
reveal how thou at sea didst lose thy wife. 5.01.244
at ephesus the temple see, | our king and all 5.02. 17
did wed | at pentapolis the fair thaisa. 5.03. 4
at sea in child–bed died she, but brought forth 5.03. 5
she at tharsus | was nurs'd with cleon, who at 5.03. 7
who at fourteen years | he sought to murder, but 5.03. 8
thy burden at the sea, and call'd marina | for 5.03. 47
your daughter, | shall marry her at pentapolis. 5.03. 72
led on by heaven, and crown'd with joy at last. 5.03. 90
you, at such a season | as now it is with me, i TNK 1.01. 60
fortune at you | dimpled her cheek with smiles. 1.01. 65
at once subduing | thy force and thy affection; 1.01. 84
showing the sun his teeth, grinning at the moon, 1.01.100
him lead his line | to catch one at my heart. 1.01.117
and at the banks of /aulis meet us with | the 1.01.212
sir, | i'll follow you at heels; 1.01.221
at least to frustrate striving, and to follow 1.02. 9
who is at hand to seal | the promise of his 1.02. 92
eat them) | the brine they wept at killing 'em. 1.03. 22
you were at wars when she the grave enrich'd, 1.03. 51
(which then look'd pale at parting) when our 1.03. 53
air, or at adventure humm'd /one | from musical 1.03. 75
in their morning state | (sound and at liberty), 1.04. 35
assure upon my daughter at the day of my death. 2.01. 9 P
their mirth, and affliction a toy to jest at. 2.01. 35 P
so chid, or at least a sigher to be comforted. 2.01. 44 P
strong enough to laugh at misery | and bear the 2.02. 2
were we at liberty, | a wife might part us 2.02. 88
you shall not love at all. 2.02.165
not love at all! who shall deny me? 2.02.166
fortune | to be one hour at liberty and grasp 2.02.208
and fling my wanton arms | in at her window! 2.02.238
were i at liberty, i would do things | of such a 2.02.256
and what | you want at any time, let me but know 2.05. 55
and all the devils roar, | he is at liberty! 2.06. 2
me thou deem'st at thebes, | and therein 3.01. 26
there shall be at your choice | both sword and 3.01. 88
at length | i fling my cap up; 3.05. 16
here, my mad boys, have at ye! 3.05. 24
at whose great feet i offer up my penner. 3.05.124
i perceive | you would fain be at that fight. 3.06. 60
have at thy life! 3.06.131
let 's die together, at one instant, duke. 3.06.177
which you'll hear of | at better time. 4.01. 30
him, but i laugh at 'em | and let 'em all alone. 4.01.126
there is at least two hundred now with child by 4.01.129
and at ten years old | they must be all gelt for 4.01.132
her distraction is more at some time of the moon 4.03. 1 P
at some time of the moon than at other some, is 4.03. 2 P
state that both she and i at this present stood 4.03. 68 P
thy flame — at seventy thou canst catch, | and 5.01. 87
i never at great feasts | sought to betray a 5.01.102
but have blush'd | at simp'ring sirs that did. 5.01.104
i think he might be brought to play at tennis. 5.02. 56
why, play at stoolball: 5.02. 74
will grow too, finely, | now he's at liberty. 5.02. 96
go to dinner, | and then we'll play at cards. 5.02.108
i had rather see a wren hawk at a fly | than 5.03. 2
knights must kindle | their valor at your eye. 5.03. 30
well, well then, at your pleasure. 5.03. 34
and | the two bold titlers at this instant are 5.03. 83
at this instant are | hand to hand at it. 5.03. 84
he is a good one | as ever strook at head. 5.03.109
fortune, | who, at her certain'st, reels. 5.04. 21
took toy at this, and fell to what disorder 5.04. 66
pig–like he whines | at the sharp rowel, which 5.04. 70
which he frets at rather | than any jot obeys; 5.04. 70
have at the worst can come, then! ep 10
we, and all our might, | rest at your service. ep 18
will not see a red herring at a harry groat, STM II.C 1 P
at a harry groat, butter at alevenpence a pound, II.C 2 P
a pound, meal at nine shillings a bushel, and II.C 2 P
a bushel, and beef at four nobles a stone, list II.C 3 P
their babies at their backs, with their poor II.C 75
nature that made thee with herself at strife, VEN 11
more than flint, for stone at rain relenteth. 200
at this adonis smiles as in disdain, | that in 241
struck dead at first, what needs a second 250
to love a cheek that smiles at thee in scorn! 252
his art with nature's workmanship at strife, 291
anon he starts at stirring of a feather; 302
spurns at his love, and scorns the heat he feels 311
fed, | his other agents aim at like delight? 400
and at his look she flatly falleth down, | for 463
me, | and pay them at thy leisure, one by one. 518
and yields at last to every light impression? 566
love breaks through, and picks them all at last. 576
she trembles at his tale, | and on his neck her 591
but having thee at vantage (wondrous dread!) 635
knocks at my heart, and whispers in mine ear, 659
so indeed, | that tremble at th' imagination? 668
by me, | uncouple at the timorous flying hare, 674
hare, | or at the fox which lives by subtilty, 675
or at the roe which no encounter dare; 676
by this she hears the hounds are at a bay, 877
full of respects, yet nought at all respecting, 911
hand with all things, nought at all effecting. 912
world's poor people are amazed | at apparitions, 926
so she at these sad signs draws up her breath, 929
seeing his beauty, thou shouldst strike at it: 938
to see, | but hatefully at randon dost thou hit. 940
love's golden arrow at him should have fled, 947
even at this word she hears a merry horn, 1025
so at his bloody view her eyes are fled | into 1037
heavy heart's lead, melt at mine eyes' red fire! 1073
who did not whet his teeth at him again, | but 1113
reck'ning his fortune at such high proud rate LUC 19
when at collatium this false lord arrived, 50
the merchant fears, ere rich at home he lands." 336
thing, | lies at the mercy of his mortal sting. 364
and the red rose blush at her own disgrace, 479
thy kinsmen hang their heads at this disdain, 521
beat at thy rocky and wrack–threat'ning heart, 590
art, | melt at my tears and be compassionate! 594
soft pity enters at an iron gate. 595
but low shrubs wither at the cedar's root. 665
may set at noon and make perpetual night. 784
'tis thou that spurn'st at right, at law, at 880
'tis thou that spurn'st at right, at law, at 880
thou that spurn'st at right, at law, at reason, 880
foes, | and merry fools to mock at him resort; 989
at his own shadow let the thief run mad, 997
"in vain i rail at opportunity, | at time, at 1023
at time, at tarquin, and uncheerful night, | in 1024
at time, at tarquin, and uncheerful night, | in 1024
in vain i spurn at my confirm'd despite: 1026
"poor hand, why quiver'st thou at this decree? 1030
to clear this spot by death, at least, i give 1053
"nor shall he smile at thee in secret thought, 1065
nor laugh with his companions at thy state, 1066
grief grieves most at that would do it good; 1117
as the dank earth weeps at thy languishment, 1130
so i at each sad strain will strain a tear, 1131
as the poor frighted deer that stands at gaze, 1149
grieving themselves to guess at others' smarts, 1238
much like a press of people at a door, | throng 1301
at last she thus begins: 1303
"at ardea to my lord with more than haste." 1332
at last she calls to mind where hangs a piece 1366
join, and shoot their foam at simois' banks. 1442
at last she sees a wretched image bound, | that 1501
at last she smilingly with this gives o'er; 1567
at last he takes her by the bloodless hand, 1597
at length address'd to answer his desire, | she 1606
or (at the least) this refuge let me find: 1654
at this request, with noble disposition | each 1695
with this they all at once began to say, | her 1709
abide, | blushing at that which is so putrefied. 1750
at last it rains, and busy winds give o'er: 1790
who, wond'ring at him, did his words allow. 1845
but smile and jest at every gentle offer. PP 4.12
ah, that i had my lady at this bay: 11.13
yet at my parting sweetly did she smile, | in 14. 7
't may be she joy'd to jest at my exile, | 't 14. 9
play'd, | plays not at all, but seems afraid; 17.20
her feeble force will yield at length, | when 18.33
women he be bent, | they have at commandement. 20.44
or to thyself at least kind–hearted prove: SON 10.12
vaunt in their youthful sap, at height decrease, 15. 7
spread | but as the marigold at the sun's eye, 25. 6
for at a frown they in their glory die. 25. 8
(like to the lark at break of day arising | from 29.11
from sullen earth) sings hymns at heaven's gate, 29.12
then can i grieve at grievances foregone, | and 30. 9
no more be griev'd at that which thou hast done: 35. 1
mine eye and heart are at a mortal war, | how to 46. 1
from whence at pleasure thou mayst come and part 48.12
i have no precious time at all to spend, | nor 57. 3
or at your hand th' account of hours to crave, 58. 3
o, let me suffer (being at your beck) | th' 58. 5
since mind at first in character was done! 59. 8
at first the very worst of fortune's might; 90.12
nor did i wonder at the lily's white, | nor 98. 9
but shoot not at me in your wakened hate: 117.12
grows fairer than at first, more strong, far 119.12
that level | at my abuses reckon up their own; 121.10
or, at the least, so long as brain and heart 122. 5
not wond'ring at the present, nor the past, 123.10
and they mourners seem | at such who, not born 127.11
at the wood's boldness by thee blushing stand. 128. 8
at randon from the truth vainly express'd; 147.12
but, rising at thy name, doth point out thee 151. 9
but at my mistress' eye love's brand new fired, 153. 9
anon their gazes lend | to every place at once, LC 27
to blush at speeches rank, to weep at woes, | or 307
to blush at speeches rank, to weep at woes, | or 307
or to turn white and sound at tragic shows; 308

ATALANTA'S 2 FR 0.0002 REL FR 1 V 1 P
cleopatra's majesty, | atalanta's better part, AYL 3.02.147
i think 'twas made of atalanta's heels. 3.02.277 P

A–TALKING 1 FR 0.0001 REL FR 0 V 1 P
(for she has been too long a–talking of), the ADO 3.02.103 P

/ATE 1 FR 0.0001 REL FR 1 V 0 P
an /ate, stirring him to blood and strife; JN 2.01. 63

ATE 2 FR 0.0002 REL FR 1 V 1 P
shall find her the infernal ate in good apparel. ADO 2.01.256 P
with ate by his side come hot from hell, | shall JC 3.01.271

ATES 2 FR 0.0002 REL FR 0 V 2 P
more ates, more ates! LLL 5.02.688 P
more ates, more ates! 5.02.688 P

/ATHENIAN 1 FR 0.0001 REL FR 1 V 0 P
/from /th' /athenian /bay | /put /forth /toward TRO pr 6

ATHENIAN 19 FR 0.0021 REL FR 17 V 2 P
stir up the athenian youth to merriments, MND 1.01. 12
and to that place the sharp athenian law 1.01.162
a sweet athenian lady is in love | with a 2.01.260
the man | by the athenian garments he hath on. 2.01.264
forest have i gone, | but athenian found i none, 2.02. 67
my master said, | despised the athenian maid; 2.02. 73
that work for bread upon athenian stalls, | were 3.02. 10
too — | and the athenian woman by his side; 3.02. 39
stand close; this is the same athenian. 3.02. 41
the man | by the athenian garments he had on? 3.02.349
from off the head of this athenian swain, | that 4.01. 65
without the peril of the athenian law — 4.01.153
for if i tell you, i am /no true athenian. 4.02. 31 P
to be sung | by an athenian eunuch to the harp." 5.01. 45
th' art an athenian, therefore welcome. TIM 1.02. 35 P
sow all th' athenian bosoms, and their crop | be 4.01. 29
is this th' athenian minion, whom the world 4.03. 81
spare thy athenian cradle and those kin | which 5.04. 40
come, good athenian. LR 3.04.180

ATHENIAN'S 3 FR 0.0003 REL FR 2 V 1 P
but hast thou yet latch'd the athenian's eyes MND 3.02. 36
that i have 'nointed an athenian's eyes; 3.02.351
to knock out an honest athenian's brains. TIM 1.01.192 P

ATHENIANS 5 FR 0.0005 REL FR 4 V 1 P
are they not athenians? TIM 1.01.182 P
th' athenians both within and out that wall! 4.01. 38
it is our part and promise to th' athenians | to 5.01.120
th' athenians, | by two of their most reverend 5.01.128
may, and the athenians pay it | to th' heart of TNK 3.01. 3

/ATHENS 1 FR 0.0001 REL FR 1 V 0 P
/to /the /port /of /athens /sent /their /ships TRO pr 3

ATHENS 58 FR 0.0065 REL FR 49 V 9 P
i beg the ancient privilege of athens: MND 1.01. 41
or else the law of athens yields you up | (which 1.01.119
from athens is her house remote seven leagues; 1.01.159
see, | seem'd athens as a paradise to me; 1.01.205
through athens gates have we devis'd to steal. 1.01.213
and thence from athens turn away our eyes, | to 1.01.218
through athens i am thought as fair as she. 1.01.227
which is thought fit, through all athens, to 1.02. 5 P
weeds of athens he doth wear: 2.02. 71
he murther cries, and help from athens calls. 3.02. 26
the wind, | and helena of athens look thou find. 3.02. 95
quiet go, | to athens will i bear my folly back, 3.02.315
and back to athens shall the lovers wend | with 3.02.372
east, | that i may back to athens by daylight, 3.02.433
other do, | may all to athens back again repair, 4.01. 67
our intent | was to be gone from athens, where 4.01.152
away with us to athens. 4.01.184
have not a man in all athens able to discharge 4.02. 8 P
the best wit of any handicraft man in athens. 4.02. 10 P
hard–handed men that work in athens here, 5.01. 72
the senators of athens, happy men! TIM 1.01. 40
of athens here, my lord. 2.02. 17
free–hearted gentleman of athens, thy very 3.01. 10 P
but i would not, for the wealth of athens, i had 3.02. 52 P
if after two days' shine athens contain thee, 3.05.100
spleen and fury, | that i may strike at athens. 3.05.113
o gods — the senators of athens, together with 3.06. 80 P
sink, athens! 3.06.104
dive in the earth, | and fence not athens! 4.01. 3
potent and infectious fevers heap | on athens, 4.01. 23
how cursed athens, mindless of thy worth, 4.03. 94
when i have laid proud athens on a heap — 4.03.102
warr'st thou 'gainst athens? 4.03.103
strike up the drum towards athens! 4.03.169
that the whole life of athens were in this! 4.03.281
what wouldst thou have to athens? 4.03.287
the commonwealth of athens is become a forest of 4.03.348 P
to athens go, | break open shops; 4.03.446
let us first see peace in athens. 4.03.456 P
you shall see him a palm in athens again, and 5.01. 10
thou draw'st a counterfeit | best in all athens; 5.01. 81
the senators of athens greet thee, timon. 5.01.136
consent of love | entreat thee back to athens, 5.01.141
and of our athens, thine and ours, to take | the 5.01.160
threat'ning sword | against the walls of athens. 5.01.167
but if he sack fair athens, | and take our 5.01.171
love before | the /reverend'st throat in athens. 5.01.182
tell athens, in the sequence of degree, | from 5.01.208
come not to me again, but say to athens, | timon 5.01.214
before proud athens he's set down by this, 5.03. 9
he purposeth to athens, whither, with what haste ANT 3.01. 35
my lord, in athens. 3.06. 64
heavens and earth, | a private man in athens: 3.12. 15
cousin, i charge you | boudge not from athens. TNK 1.01.223
we will post | to athens /'fore our army. 1.04. 49
of their captivity than i of ruling athens. 2.01. 38 P
all the boys in athens | blow wind i' th' breech 2.03. 46
horse is arcite | trotting the stones of athens, 5.04. 55

ATHOL 1 FR 0.0001 REL FR 1 V 0 P
son | to beaten douglas, and the earl of athol, 1H4 1.01. 72

ATHVERSARY *(also adversary)*

ATHVERSARY 3 FR 0.0003 REL FR 0 V 3 P

for look you, th' athversary — you may discuss H5 3.02. 61 P
th' athversary was have possession of the pridge 3.06. 93 P
perdition of th' athversary hath been very great 3.06. 98 P
ATHWART 7 FR 0.0008 REL FR 5 V 2 P
the nurse, and quite athwart | goes all decorum. MM 1.03. 30
him, and whatsoever comes athwart his affection ADO 2.02. 6 P
nor never lay his wreathed arms athwart | his LLL 4.03.133
quite traverse, athwart the heart of his lover, AYL 3.04. 42 P
when all athwart there came | a post from wales 1H4 1.01. 36
upon your winged thoughts | athwart the sea. H5 5.pr. 9
athwart the lane, | he, with two striplings CYM 5.03. 18
A–TILT 2 FR 0.0002 REL FR 2 V 0 P
lance, | and run a–tilt at death within a chair? 1H6 3.02. 51
tours | thou ran'st a–tilt in honor of my love 2H6 1.03. 51
ATLAS 1 FR 0.0001 REL FR 1 V 0 P
thou art no atlas for so great a weight; 3H6 5.01. 36
ATOMI 1 FR 0.0001 REL FR 1 V 0 P
drawn with a team of little atomi | over men's ROM 1.04. 57
ATOMIES 2 FR 0.0002 REL FR 1 V 1 P
it is as easy to count atomies as to resolve the AYL 3.02.232 P
who shut their coward gates on atomies, | should 3.05. 13
ATOMY 1 FR 0.0001 REL FR 0 V 1 P
thou atomy, thou! 2H4 5.04. 29 P
ATONE 7 FR 0.0008 REL FR 6 V 1 P
when earthly things made even | atone together. AYL 5.04.110
since we cannot atone you, we shall see R2 1.01.202
can | no more atone than violent'st contrariety. COR 4.06. 73
to atone your fears | with my more noble meaning TIM 5.04. 58
i would do much | t' atone them, for the love i OTH 4.01.233
that the present need | speaks to atone you. ANT 2.02.102
i was glad i did atone my countryman and you. CYM 1.04. 39 P
ATONEMENT 2 FR 0.0002 REL FR 2 V 0 P
marshal, | if we do now make our atonement well, 2H4 4.01.219
he desires to make atonement | between the duke R3 1.03. 36
ATONEMENTS 1 FR 0.0001 REL FR 0 V 1 P
to make atonements and compremises between you. WIV 1.01. 33 P
ATROPOS 1 FR 0.0001 REL FR 1 V 0 P
come, atropos, i say! 2H4 2.04.199
ATTACH 10 FR 0.0011 REL FR 10 V 0 P
or i'll attach you by this officer. ERR 4.01. 6
sum for me | or i attach you by this officer. 4.01. 73
then homeward every man attach the hand | of his LLL 4.03.372
desires you to attach his son, who has | (his WT 5.01.182
i would attach you all, and make you stoop R2 2.03.156
mowbray, | of capital treason i attach you both. 2H4 4.02.109
from | the king t' attach lord montacute, and H8 1.01.217
myself | attach thee as a traitorous innovator, COR 3.01.174
go, some of you, whoe'er you find attach. ROM 5.03.173
i therefore apprehend and do attach thee | for OTH 1.02. 77
ATTACH'D 5 FR 0.0005 REL FR 4 V 1 P
who am myself attach'd with weariness | to th' TMP 3.03. 5
that i should be attach'd in ephesus; ERR 4.04. 6
durst not have attach'd one of so high blood. 2H4 2.02. 3 P
and hath attach'd | our merchants' goods at H8 1.01. 95
he is attach'd, | call him to present trial. 1.02.210
ATTACHED 2 FR 0.0002 REL FR 2 V 0 P
my father was attached, not attainted, 1H6 2.04. 96
may worthy troilus be half attached | with that TRO 5.02.161
ATTACHMENT 1 FR 0.0001 REL FR 1 V 0 P
and give as soft attachment to thy senses | as TRO 4.02. 5
ATTAIN 9 FR 0.0010 REL FR 7 V 2 P
and humblest suit | cannot attain it, why then WIV 3.04. 21
me, | miss that which one unworthier may attain, MV 2.01. 37
till they attain to their abhorr'd ends; AWW 4.03. 23 P
and far surmounts our labor to attain it. R2 2.03. 64
sun, | ere he attain his easeful western bed: 3H6 5.03. 6
which the gods grant thee t' attain to! TIM 4.03.328 P
by this vile conquest shall attain unto. JC 5.05. 38
that have but labor'd to attain this hour. 5.05. 42
to attain | in suit the place of 's bed and win CYM 5.05.184
ATTAIN'D 5 FR 0.0005 REL FR 5 V 0 P
could have attain'd th' effect of your own MM 2.01. 13
hath rotted ere his youth attain'd a beard. MND 2.01. 95
be look'd upon and learnt, which once attain'd, 2H4 4.04. 71
these oracles | are hardly attain'd, and hardly 2H6 1.04. 71
better be held nor more attain'd than by | a COR 1.01.265
ATTAINDER *(also attendure)*
ATTAINDER 3 FR 0.0003 REL FR 3 V 0 P
degree | stands in attainder of eternal shame. LLL 1.01.157
with the attainder of his slanderous lips. R2 4.01. 24
he liv'd from all attainder of suspects. R3 3.05. 32
ATTAINS 1 FR 0.0001 REL FR 1 V 0 P
but when he once attains the upmost round, | he JC 2.01. 24
/ATTAINT 2 FR 0.0002 REL FR 2 V 0 P
what simple thief brags of his own /attaint? ERR 3.02. 16
thee | on capital treason, and, in thy /attaint, LR 5.03. 83
ATTAINT 9 FR 0.0010 REL FR 8 V 1 P
you are attaint with faults and perjury: LLL 5.02.819
and overbears attaint | with cheerful semblance H5 4.pr. 39
my tender youth was never yet attaint | with any 1H6 5.05. 81
nor any man an attaint but he carries some stain TRO 1.02. 25 P
whose attaint | disorder breeds by heating of VEN 741
that is as clear from this attaint of mine | as LUC 825
"i will not poison thee with my attaint, | nor 1072
then, | when time with age shall them attaint. PP 18.46
and therefore mayest without attaint o'erlook SON 82. 2
ATTAINTED 4 FR 0.0004 REL FR 4 V 0 P
by his treason, stand'st not thou attainted, 1H6 2.04. 92
my father was attached, not attainted, 2.04. 96
i must offend before i be attainted; 2H6 2.04. 59
of faults conceal'd, wherein i am attainted, SON 88. 7
ATTAINTURE 1 FR 0.0001 REL FR 1 V 0 P
and her attainture will be humphrey's fall. 2H6 1.02.106
ATTAME *(see 'tame)*
/ATTAX'D 1 FR 0.0001 REL FR 1 V 0 P
/you are much more /attax'd for want of wisdom LR 1.04.343
ATTEMPT 36 FR 0.0040 REL FR 23 V 13 P
i think, in the way of waste, attempt us again. WIV 4.02.212 P
good we oft might win, | by fearing to attempt. MM 1.04. 79
maid will i frame and make fit for his attempt. 3.01.256 P
nor persuasion can with ease attempt you, i will 4.02.190 P
and either not attempt to choose at all, | or MV 2.01. 39
dear sir, of force i must attempt you further. 4.01.421
your own safety, and give over this attempt. AYL 1.02.179 P
of a fearful heart, stagger in this attempt; 3.03. 49 P
home | and pray god's blessing into thy attempt. AWW 1.03.254
i will grace the attempt for a worthy exploit. 3.06. 68 P
success will be, my lord, but the attempt i vow. 3.06. 81 P
it by some laudable attempt either of valor or TN 3.02. 29 P
return | till my attempt so much be glorified JN 5.02.111
the quality and hair of our attempt | brooks no 1H4 4.01. 61
down, | we have supplies to second our attempt; 2H4 4.02. 45
as in this haughty great attempt | they labored 1H6 2.05. 79
you that will follow me to this attempt, 3H6 4.02. 26
the ransom of my bold attempt | shall be this R3 5.03.265
the gain of my attempt | the least of you shall 5.03.267
to th' king, never attempt | any thing on him; H8 3.02. 17
but with his last attempt he wip'd it out, COR 5.03.146
for which attempt the judges have pronounc'd TIT 3.01. 50
and what love can do, that dares love attempt; ROM 2.02. 68
i did bid thee do, | thou shouldst attempt it. JC 5.03. 40
th' attempt, and not the deed, | confounds us. MAC 2.02. 10
king that he | prepares for some attempt of war. 3.06. 39
neglecting an attempt of ease and gain | to wake OTH 1.03. 29
wit, and therefore i will attempt the doing it. 3.04. 22 P
i will be near to second your attempt, and he 4.02.238 P
if thou attempt it, it will cost thee dear: 5.02.255
i durst attempt it against any lady in the world CYM 1.04.112 P
sustain what y' are worthy of by your attempt. 1.04.116 P
a repulse, though your attempt (as you call it) 1.04.118 P
this attempt | i am soldier to, and will abide 3.04.182
and having wooed | a villain to attempt it, who PER 5.01.173
"i see what crosses my attempt will bring, | i LUC 491
ATTEMPTABLE 1 FR 0.0001 REL FR 0 V 1 P
and less attemptable than any the rarest of our CYM 1.04. 60 P
ATTEMPTED 2 FR 0.0002 REL FR 1 V 1 P
that be true love, which is falsely attempted? LLL 1.02.172 P
to know | that prosperously i have attempted, COR 5.06. 74
ATTEMPTING 2 FR 0.0002 REL FR 2 V 0 P
thy death, | or die renowned by attempting it. 3H6 2.01. 88
king | for him attempting who was self–subdued, LR 2.02.122
ATTEMPTS 7 FR 0.0008 REL FR 7 V 0 P
that by direct or indirect attempts | he seek MV 4.01.350
impossible be strange attempts to those | that AWW 1.01.224
poor, such bare, such lewd, such mean attempts, 1H4 3.02. 13
that your attempts may overlive the hazard | and 2H4 4.01. 15
to warn false traitors from the like attempts. R3 3.05. 49
this man of thine | attempts her love. TIM 1.01.126
it is casca, one incorporate | to our attempts. JC 1.03.136
ATTEND *(also tend*, etc.)*
/ATTEND 2 FR 0.0002 REL FR 2 V 0 P
/lear, | /and /leave /you /to /attend /him. LR 4.03. 51
/i /shall /attend /you /presently /at /your 5.01. 33
ATTEND 126 FR 0.0142 REL FR 115 V 11 P
thy false uncle — | dost thou attend me? TMP 1.02. 78
sure, the goddess | on whom these airs attend! 1.02.423
i charge thee | that thou attend me. 1.02.454
shall step by step attend | you and your ways, 3.03. 78
as thou dost know, | do now attend the queen? 4.01. 88
we'll both attend upon your ladyship. TGV 2.04.121
must use, | and then i'll presently attend you. 2.04.189
tarry i here, i but attend on death, | but, fly 3.01.186
destiny, | attend your office and your quality. WIV 5.05. 40
hour to–morrow | shall i attend your lordship? MM 2.02.160
but i will attend you a while. 3.01.158 P
i shall attend your leisure, but make haste, 4.01. 56
i bought, and brought up to attend my sons. ERR 1.01. 57
then let your will attend on their accords. 2.01. 25
i will attend my husband, be his nurse, | diet 5.01. 98
we here attend you. ADO 5.04. 36
haste, signify so much, while we attend, | like LLL 2.01. 33
we attend. 5.01.146 P
i'll give thee fairies to attend on thee; MND 3.01.157
fairy king, attend and mark; 4.01. 93
we'll make our leisures to attend on yours. MV 1.01. 68
fair thoughts and happy hours attend on you! 3.04. 41
i attend them with all respect and duty. AYL 1.02.167 P
i must attend the duke at dinner. 4.01.180 P
trip, audrey, trip, audrey! i attend, i attend. 5.01. 62 P
trip, audrey, trip, audrey! i attend, i attend. 5.01. 63 P
let one attend him with a silver basin | full of SHR in.1. 55
look how thy servants do attend on thee, | each in.2. 33
i'll attend her here, | and woo her with some 2.01.168
obey the bride, you that attend on her. 3.02.223
but i must attend his majesty's command, to whom AWW 1.01. 4 P
want the best | that shall attend his love. 1.01. 73
feast | shall more attend upon the coming space, 2.03.181
you presently | attend his further pleasure. 2.04. 53
she will attend it better in thy youth | than in TN 1.04. 27
some four or five attend him — | all, if you 1.04. 36
grace and good disposition attend your ladyship! 3.01.135
shall 's attend you there? WT 1.02.178
be your man, attend on you | with all true duty. JN 3.03. 72
which (as they say) attend | the steps of wrong, 4.02. 56
nor attend the foot | that leaves the print of 4.03. 25
we will attend to neither. 5.02.163
ignorance | is made my jailer to attend on me. R2 1.03.169
in the base court he doth attend | to speak with 3.03.176
but not the form of what he should attend. 1H4 1.03.210
to you | when you are better temper'd to attend. 1.03.235
sit and attend. 3.01.225
that the lord bardolph doth attend him here. 2H4 1.01. 3
not wish | success and conquest to attend on us. H5 2.02. 24
shall i attend your grace? 4.01. 29
upon a wooden coffin we attend, | and death's 1H6 1.01. 19
each hath his place and function to attend: 1.01.173
thanks, | and in submission will attend on her. 2.02. 52
i will attend upon your lordship's leisure. 5.01. 55
gone, | may honorable peace attend thy throne! 2H6 2.03. 38
and will that thou henceforth attend on us. 5.01. 80
attend me, lords: 3H6 2.01.168
to white–friars, there attend my coming. R3 1.02.226
on him, | and all their ministers attend on him. 1.03.293
reproach | attend the sequel of your imposition, 3.07.232
to–morrow then we will attend your grace, | and 3.07.244
shame serves thy life and doth thy death attend. 4.04.196
th' king) t' appoint | who should attend on him? H8 1.01. 75
attend. 1.01.158
some attend him. 1.04. 60
you he bade | attend him here this morning. 3.02. 82
is my duty | t' attend your highness' pleasure. 5.01. 91
must be fulfill'd, and i attend with patience. 5.02. 19
is, | with all the virtues that attend the good, 5.04. 27
attend me where i wheel; TRO 5.07. 2
martius, | attend upon cominius to these wars. COR 1.01.237
where i know | our greatest friends attend us. 1.01.245
where great patricians shall attend and shrug, 1.09. 4
i know they do attend us. 2.02.160
we'll attend you there; 3.01.330
away, the tribunes do attend you. 3.02.138
let a guard | attend us through the city. 3.03.141
to attend the emperor's person carefully. TIT 2.02. 8
i will most willingly attend your ladyship. 4.01. 28
marcus, attend him in his ecstasy, | that hath 4.01.125
by day and night t' attend him carefully, | and 4.03. 28
cannot induce you to attend my words. 5.03. 79
time | when it should move ye to attend me most, 5.03. 92
the which if you with patient ears attend, ROM pr 13
bear hence this body and attend our will; 3.01.196
betossed soul | did not attend him as we rode? 5.03. 77
spirits thy power | hath conjur'd to attend. TIM 1.01. 7
we attend his lordship; pray signify so much. 3.04. 37 P
contain thee, | attend our weightier judgment. 3.05.101
but without | the illness should attend it. MAC 1.05. 20
attend those men | our pleasure? 3.01. 44
i would attend his leisure | for a few words. 3.02. 3
night, and better health | attend his majesty! 3.04.120
let our just censures | attend the true event, 5.04. 15
attend! HAM 4.05. 97
back to him that you attend him in the hall. 5.02.197 P
attend the lords of france and burgundy, LR 1.01. 34
several messengers | from hence attend dispatch. 2.01.125
unusual vigilance | does not attend my taking. 2.03. 5
and attend | the leisure of their answer, gave 2.04. 36
i prithee, let thy wife attend on her, | and OTH 1.03.296
by you invited, do attend your presence. 3.03.281
i do attend here on the general, | and think it 3.04.193
way that i can bring you, | for i attend here; 3.04.200
could not with graceful eyes attend those wars ANT 2.02. 60
and there i will attend | what further comes. 3.10. 31
i must attend mine office, | or would have 4.06. 26
adieu, good queen, i must attend on caesar. 5.02.206
army shall | in solemn show attend this funeral, 5.02.364
i'll attend your lordship. CYM 1.02. 39 P
get them dispatch'd, | i will attend the queen. 1.03. 40
i'll attend your lordship. 2.01. 51 P
attend you here the door of our stern daughter? 2.03. 37
to your mistress, | attend the queen and us; 2.03. 62
that did attend themselves and had the virtue 3.06. 83
attend me then: PER 1.02. 70
go tell their general we attend him here, | to 1.04. 79
o, attend, my daughter: 2.03. 58
a niece of mine | shall there attend you. 3.04. 16
that in lag hours attend | for grey approachers; TNK 5.04. 8
sorrow on love hereafter shall attend; VEN 1136
"so, so," quoth he, "these lets attend the time, LUC 330
will tie the hearers to attend each line, | how 818
for she that was thy lucrece, now attend me: 1682
i must attend time's leisure with my moan, SON 44.12
my spirits t' attend this double voice accorded, LC 3
ATTENDANCE 8 FR 0.0009 REL FR 8 V 0 P
no attendance? SHR 4.01.126
on your attendance, my lord, here. TN 1.04. 11
i danc'd attendance on his will | till paris was 2H6 1.03.171
i dance attendance here; R3 3.07. 56
favor, | to dance attendance on their lordships' H8 5.02. 31
wait attendance | till you hear further from me. TIM 1.01.161
receive attendance | from those that she calls LR 2.04.243
sir, your attendance | cannot please heaven, and TNK 3.01.110
ATTENDANT 5 FR 0.0005 REL FR 4 V 1 P
and importun'd me | that his attendant — so his ERR 1.01.127
him, | and with his mad attendant and himself, 5.01.150
because that she as her attendant hath | a MND 2.01. 21
lately attendant on the duke of norfolk. R3 2.01.102
dismiss your attendant there. OTH 4.03. 8 P
ATTENDANTS 9 FR 0.0010 REL FR 9 V 0 P
here have i few attendants, | and subjects none TMP 5.01.166
the ladies, her attendants of her chamber, | saw AYL 2.02. 5
and brave attendants near him when he wakes, SHR in.1. 40
means and attendants, and my loving greetings AWW 1.03.252
to put apart these your attendants, i | shall WT 2.02. 13
you tempt the fury of my three attendants, 1H6 4.02. 10
and, her attendants absent, swallow'd fire. JC 4.03.156
her attendants are | all sworn and honorable. CYM 2.04.124
all safe reason | he must have some attendants. 4.02.132
/ATTENDED 1 FR 0.0001 REL FR 0 V 1 P
/man, /i /am /most /dreadfully /attended. HAM 2.02.269 P
ATTENDED 19 FR 0.0021 REL FR 18 V 1 P
i fear i am attended by some spies. TGV 5.01. 10
contemplation, | only attended by nerissa here, MV 3.04. 29
sweetly as the lark | when neither is attended; 5.01.103
'tis a fair young man, and well attended. TN 1.05.103 P
day, | attended with the pleasures of the world, JN 3.03. 35
it is the curse of kings to be attended | by 4.02.208
attended him on bridges, stood in lanes, | laid 1H4 4.03. 70
about, | and but attended by a simple guard, 3H6 4.02. 16
and, often but attended with weak guard, 4.05. 7
who attended him | in secret ambush on the 4.06. 82
your grace attended to their sug'red words, R3 3.01. 13
i am attended at the cypress grove. COR 1.10. 30
court | there is a queen, attended by a moor; TIT 5.02.105
he is attended with a desperate train, | and LR 2.04.305
mine ears that have | so long attended thee. CYM 1.06.142
they are in a trunk, | attended by my men. 1.06.197
seas, | attended on by many a lord and knight, PER 4.04. 11
mine ears, that to your wanton talk attended, VEN 809
is me, too early i attended | a youthful suit — LC 78
ATTENDETH 2 FR 0.0002 REL FR 2 V 0 P
he attendeth here hard by | to know your answer, MV 4.01.145
which speechless woe of his poor she attendeth, LUC 1674
ATTENDING 14 FR 0.0015 REL FR 14 V 0 P
she (an attending star) scarce seen a light. LLL 4.03.227
who by this i know | is here attending. AWW 5.03.135
desire, | attending but the signal to begin. R2 1.03.116
off | all fears attending on so dire a project. TRO 2.02.134
to love–sick dido's sad attending ear | the TIT 5.03. 82
night, | like softest music to attending ears! ROM 2.02.166
keep yet their hearts attending on themselves, OTH 1.01. 51
life | is nobler than attending for a check; CYM 3.03. 22

attending | you here at milford–haven with your 4.02.334
in the womb he stay'd | attending nature's law; 5.04. 38
so, on your patience evermore attending, | new PER 5.03.101
sedges, | as patiently i was attending sport, TNK 4.01. 55
still, | attending on his golden pilgrimage: SON 7. 8
and captive good attending captain ill: 66.12
ATTENDS 22 FR 0.0024 REL FR 17 V 5 P
attends the emperor in his royal court. TGV 1.03. 27
one that attends your ladyship's command. 4.03. 5
the dinner attends you, sir. WIV 1.01.269 P
and at the dean'ry, where a priest attends, 4.06. 31
what humble suit attends thy answer there. LLL 5.02.839
he attends here in the forest on the duke your AYL 3.04. 33 P
to want the bridegroom when the priest attends SHR 3.02. 5
promis'd gift, | which but attends thy naming. AWW 2.03. 51
he attends your ladyship's pleasure. TN 3.04. 59 P
as the hunter, attends thee at the orchard–end. 3.04.223 P
humorous youth, | that fear attends her not. H5 2.04. 29
he attends your highness' pleasure. H8 5.01. 83
by calamity | thither where more attends you, COR 1.01. 76
howling attends it. ROM 3.03. 48
attends he here, or no? lucilius! TIM 1.01.114
ladies, there is an idle banquet attends you, 1.02.155
consequence, | attends the boist'rous /ruin. HAM 3.03. 22
if the gentlewoman that attends the /general's OTH 3.01. 24 P
which attends | in place of greater state. CYM 3.03. 77
who attends us there? PER 1.01.150
but immortality attends the former, | making a 3.02. 30
the post attends, and she delivers it, LUC 1333
ATTEND'ST 1 FR 0.0001 REL FR 1 V 0 P
thou attend'st not! TMP 1.02. 87
ATTENDURE *(also attainder)*
ATTENDURE 1 FR 0.0001 REL FR 1 V 0 P
first, kildare's attendure, | then deputy of H8 2.01. 41
ATTENT 2 FR 0.0002 REL FR 2 V 0 P
admiration for a while | with an attent ear, HAM 1.02.193
be attent, | and time that is so briefly spent PER 3.ch. 11
ATTENTION 9 FR 0.0010 REL FR 6 V 3 P
will you hear this letter with attention? LLL 1.01.215 P
dying men | enforce attention like deep harmony. R2 2.01. 6
heels would amend the attention of your ears, 2H4 1.02.124 P
i will be bold with time and your attention: H8 2.04.169
with all my heart, | and lend my best attention. CYM 5.05.117
this will catch her attention, for this her mind TNK 4.03. 78 P
i prithee lay attention to the cry; 5.03. 91
that it beguil'd attention, charm'd the sight. LUC 1404
with sad attention long to hear her words. 1610
ATTENTIVE 6 FR 0.0006 REL FR 5 V 1 P
obey, and be attentive. TMP 1.02. 38
the reason is, your spirits are attentive; MV 5.01. 70
lords, | and be you silent and attentive too, 3H6 1.01.122
ear, | to set his /sense on /the attentive bent, TRO 1.03.252
vex not his prescience, be attentive. ANT 1.02. 21 P
and attentive | i gave my ear, when i might well TNK 4.01. 56
ATTENTIVENESS 1 FR 0.0001 REL FR 0 V 1 P
how attentiveness wounded his daughter, till, WT 5.02. 86 P
ATTEST 4 FR 0.0004 REL FR 4 V 0 P
figure may | attest in little place a million, H5 pr 16
now attest | that those whom you call'd fathers 3.01. 22
but i attest the gods, your full consent | gave TRO 2.02.132
that doth invert th' attest of eyes and ears, 5.02.122
ATTESTED 1 FR 0.0001 REL FR 1 V 0 P
hands, | attested by the holy close of lips, TN 5.01.158
ATTIR'D 4 FR 0.0004 REL FR 4 V 0 P
for my part, i am so attir'd in wonder, | i know ADO 4.01.144
i should blush | to see you so attir'd — sworn, WT 4.04. 13
why art thou thus attir'd, andronicus? TIT 5.03. 30
why art thou thus attir'd in discontent? LUC 1601
ATTIRE *(also tire*, etc.)*
ATTIRE 10 FR 0.0011 REL FR 10 V 0 P
i'll put myself in poor and mean attire, | and AYL 1.03.111
he hath some meaning in his mad attire. SHR 3.02.124
both | but this my masculine usurp'd attire, TN 5.01.250
to swearing and stern looks, defus'd attire, H5 5.02. 61
thy sumptuous buildings and thy wive's attire 2H6 1.03.130
and go we to attire you for our journey. 2.04.106
robes, | and show itself, attire me how i can. 2.04.109
and do you now put on your best attire? JC 1.01. 48
these | so wither'd and so wild in their attire, MAC 1.03. 40
mine arm'd neck, leap thou, attire and all, ANT 4.08. 14
ATTIRED 2 FR 0.0002 REL FR 2 V 0 P
fairies, | finely attired in a robe of white. WIV 4.04. 72
me, | and, were they but attired in grave weeds, TIT 3.01. 43
ATTIRES 3 FR 0.0003 REL FR 3 V 0 P
in, | i'll show thee some attires, and have thy ADO 3.01.102
ay, those attires are best, but, gentle nurse, ROM 4.03. 1
go fetch | my best attires. ANT 5.02.228
ATTORNEY* 8 FR 0.0009 REL FR 6 V 2 P
office, | and will have no attorney but myself, ERR 5.01.100
no, faith, die by attorney. AYL 4.01. 94 P
as ten groats is for the hand of an attorney, as AWW 2.02. 21 P
content | to be mine own attorney in this case. 1H6 5.03.166
you so — | be the attorney of my love to her. R3 4.04.413
i, by attorney, bless thee from thy mother, 5.03. 83
the king's attorney on the contrary | urg'd on H8 2.01. 15
but when the heart's attorney once is mute, VEN 335
ATTORNEY'D 2 FR 0.0002 REL FR 1 V 1 P
habit, i am still | attorney'd at your service. MM 5.01.385
hath been royally attorney'd with interchange of WT 1.01. 27 P
ATTORNEYS 2 FR 0.0002 REL FR 2 V 0 P
attorneys are denied me, | and therefore R2 2.03.134
windy attorneys to their client's woes, | aery R3 4.04.127
ATTORNEYS–GENERAL
1 FR 0.0001 REL FR 1 V 0 P
that he hath | by his attorneys–general to sue R2 2.01.203
ATTORNEYSHIP 1 FR 0.0001 REL FR 1 V 0 P
worth | than to be dealt in by attorneyship. 1H6 5.05. 56
ATTRACT 1 FR 0.0001 REL FR 1 V 0 P
shall show more goodly and attract more eyes 1H4 1.02.214
ATTRACTION 2 FR 0.0002 REL FR 1 V 1 P
setting the attraction of my good parts aside, i WIV 2.02.105 P
and with his great attraction | robs the vast TIM 4.03.436
ATTRACTIONS 1 FR 0.0001 REL FR 1 V 0 P
and other chosen attractions, would allure | and PER 5.01. 46
ATTRACTIVE 2 FR 0.0002 REL FR 1 V 1 P
for she hath blessed and attractive eyes. MND 2.02. 91
no, good mother, here's metal more attractive. HAM 3.02.109 P
ATTRACTS 2 FR 0.0002 REL FR 2 V 0 P
that nature pranks her in attracts my soul. TN 2.04. 86
attracts the same for aidance 'gainst the enemy, 2H6 3.02.165
ATTRIBUTE 5 FR 0.0005 REL FR 5 V 0 P
power, | the attribute to awe and majesty, MV 4.01.191
of kings, | it is an attribute to god himself; 4.01.195
much attribute he hath, and much the reason TRO 2.03.116
height, | the pith and marrow of our attribute. HAM 1.04. 22
innocent | and for an honest attribute cry out, PER 4.03. 18
ATTRIBUTED 1 FR 0.0001 REL FR 0 V 1 P
of service is seldom attributed to the true and AWW 3.06. 61 P
ATTRIBUTES 3 FR 0.0003 REL FR 2 V 1 P
if i should swear by jove's great attributes | i AWW 4.02. 25
could not you find out that by her attributes? TRO 3.01. 36 P
who only attributes | the faculties of other TNK 1.02. 67
ATTRIBUTION 1 FR 0.0001 REL FR 1 V 0 P
such attribution should the douglas have | as 1H4 4.01. 3
ATTRIBUTIVE 1 FR 0.0001 REL FR 1 V 0 P
and the will dotes that is attributive | to what TRO 2.02. 58
A–TURNING 2 FR 0.0002 REL FR 2 V 0 P
she bade love last, and yet she fell a–turning. PP 7.16
that eye could see, | her fancy fell a–turning. 15. 4
A–TWAIN 2 FR 0.0002 REL FR 2 V 0 P
oft bite the holy cords a–twain | which are t' LR 2.02. 74
tearing of papers, breaking rings a–twain, LC 6
AU 2 FR 0.0002 REL FR 0 V 2 P
oui, mette le au mon pocket; WIV 1.04. 54 P
vomissement, et la /truie lavee au bourbier." H5 3.07. 65 P
AUBREY 1 FR 0.0001 REL FR 1 V 0 P
doom | my elder brother, the lord aubrey vere, 3H6 3.03.102
AUBURN *(also aborn, abram*)*
AUBURN 1 FR 0.0001 REL FR 1 V 0 P
her hair is auburn, mine is perfect yellow: TGV 4.04.189
AUCUN 1 FR 0.0001 REL FR 0 V 1 P
son jurement de pardonner aucun prisonnier; H5 4.04. 51 P
AUDACIOUS 7 FR 0.0008 REL FR 6 V 1 P
without affection, audacious without impudency, LLL 5.01. 4 P
tongue | of saucy and audacious eloquence. MND 5.01.103
away with that audacious lady! WT 2.03. 42
teaching his duteous land | audacious cruelty. 1H4 4.03. 45
no, prelate, such is thy audacious wickedness, 1H6 3.01. 14
and perish ye, with your audacious prate! 4.01.124
obey, audacious traitor, kneel for grace. 2H6 5.01.108
AUDACIOUSLY 2 FR 0.0002 REL FR 2 V 0 P
yet fear not thou, but speak audaciously." LLL 5.02.104
but durst not ask of her audaciously | why her LUC 1223
AUDACITY 4 FR 0.0004 REL FR 4 V 0 P
suppose | they had such courage and audacity? 1H6 1.02. 36
arm me, audacity, from head to foot, | or, like CYM 1.06. 19
be sure | you tumble with audacity and manhood, TNK 3.05. 36
was defect | of spirit, life, and bold audacity. LUC 1346
AUDIBLE 2 FR 0.0002 REL FR 1 V 1 P
very mercy of the law cries out | most audible, MM 5.01.408
sprightly, /waking, audible, and full of vent. COR 4.05.223 P
/AUDIENCE 2 FR 0.0002 REL FR 2 V 0 P
/and /might /by /no /suit /gain /our /audience. 2H4 4.01. 76
/sir, /in /this /audience, | let my disclaiming HAM 5.02.240
AUDIENCE 33 FR 0.0037 REL FR 26 V 7 P
o, dismiss this audience, and i shall tell you LLL 4.03.206
shall i have audience? 5.01.133 P
so, if any of the audience hiss, you may cry, 5.01.138 P
that she vouchsafe me audience for one word. 5.02.313
if i do it, let the audience look to their eyes. MND 1.02. 26 P
give me audience, good madam. AYL 3.02.238 P
let me have audience for a word or two. 5.04.151
fixed foot shall grow | till thou have audience. TN 1.04. 18
act was worth the audience of kings and princes, WT 5.02. 80 P
and too full of gawds | to give me audience. JN 3.03. 37
flood, and can give audience | to any tongue, 4.02.139
fair play of the world, | let me have audience. 5.02.119
good cousin, give me audience for a while. 1H4 1.03.211
from his grace | that he will give you audience, 2H4 4.01.141
embassador upon that instant | crav'd audience; H5 1.01. 92
we'll give them present audience. 2.04. 67
apples, that no audience but the tribulation of H8 5.03. 61 P
of threepence to a second day of audience. COR 2.01. 72 P
list to your tribunes. audience! peace, i say! 3.03. 40
then follow me, and give me audience, friends. JC 3.02. 2
your griefs, | and i will give you audience. 4.02. 47
have of your audience been most free and HAM 1.03. 93
'tis meet that some more audience than a mother, 3.03. 31
that are but mutes or audience to this act, 5.02.335
hear it, | and call the noblest to the audience. 5.02.387
hardly gave audience, or | /vouchsaf'd to think ANT 1.04. 7
taunts | did gibe my missive out of audience. 2.02. 74
that day appear'd, and oft before gave audience, 3.06. 18
the queen | of audience nor desire shall fail, 3.12. 21
throats and have not | due audience of the gods. TNK 1.02. 83
have among yourselves, | command still audience. STM II.C 47
end without audience and are never done. VEN 846
lending soft audience to my sweet design, | and LC 278
AUDIS 1 FR 0.0001 REL FR 1 V 0 P
dominator poli, | tam lentus audis scelera? TIT 4.01. 82
AUDIT 9 FR 0.0010 REL FR 9 V 0 P
a brief span | to keep your earthly audit; H8 3.02.141
yet i can make my audit up, that all | from me COR 1.01.144
to make their audit at your highness' pleasure, MAC 1.06. 27
and how his audit stands who knows save heaven?
HAM 3.03. 82
if you will take this audit, take this life, CYM 5.04. 27
gone, | what acceptable audit canst thou leave? SON 4.12
sum, | call'd to that audit by advis'd respects; 49. 4
her audit (though delay'd) answer'd must be, 126.11
and to your audit comes | their distract parcels LC 230
AUDITOR 2 FR 0.0002 REL FR 1 V 1 P
i'll be an auditor, | an actor too perhaps, if i MND 3.01. 79
company last night at supper, a kind of auditor, 1H4 2.01. 57 P
AUDITORS 1 FR 0.0001 REL FR 1 V 0 P
call me before th' exactest auditors, | and set TIM 2.02.156
AUDITORY 1 FR 0.0001 REL FR 1 V 0 P
then, gracious auditory, be it known to you TIT 5.03. 96
AUDREY 14 FR 0.0015 REL FR 1 V 13 P
come apace, good audrey; AYL 3.03. 1 P
i will fetch up your goats, audrey. 3.03. 2 P
and how, audrey? 3.03. 2 P
come, sweet audrey, | we must be married, or we 3.03. 96
we shall find a time, audrey, patience, gentle 5.01. 1 P
find a time, audrey, patience, gentle audrey. 5.01. 2 P
a most wicked sir oliver, audrey, a most vile 5.01. 5 P
but, audrey, there is a youth here in the forest 5.01. 6 P
good ev'n, audrey. 5.01. 13 P
trip, audrey, trip, audrey! i attend, i attend. 5.01. 62 P
trip, audrey, trip, audrey! i attend, i attend. 5.01. 62 P
to–morrow is the joyful day, audrey, to–morrow 5.03. 1 P
come, audrey. 5.03. 41 P
remov'd (bear your body more seeming, audrey), 5.04. 69 P
AUFIDIUS' 1 FR 0.0001 REL FR 1 V 0 P
he'll beat aufidius' head below his knee, | and COR 1.03. 46
AUFIDIUS 32 FR 0.0036 REL FR 29 V 3 P
tullus aufidius, that will put you to't. COR 1.01.229
so, your opinion is, aufidius, | that they of 1.02. 1
noble aufidius, | take your commission, hie you 1.02. 25
see him pluck aufidius down by th' hair; 1.03. 30
heavens bless my lord from fell aufidius! 1.03. 45
tullus aufidius, is he within your walls? 1.04. 13
there is aufidius. 1.04. 20
there is the man of my soul's hate, aufidius, 1.05. 10
to aufidius thus | i will appear, and fight. 1.05. 19
o'er them aufidius, | their very heart of hope. 1.06. 54
set me against aufidius and his antiates, | and 1.06. 59
is | able to bear against the great aufidius | a 1.06. 79
but then aufidius was within my view, | and 1.09. 85
has he disciplin'd aufidius soundly? 2.01.126 P
they fought together, but aufidius got off. 2.01.128 P
tullus aufidius then had made new head? 3.01. 1
saw you aufidius? 3.01. 8
your noble tullus aufidius /will appear well in 4.03. 34 P
if it be your will, | where great aufidius lies. 4.04. 8
'tis aufidius, | who, hearing of our martius' 4.06. 42
join'd with aufidius, leads a power 'gainst rome 4.06. 67
he and aufidius can | no more atone than 4.06. 72
led by caius martius | associated with aufidius, 4.06. 76
tullus aufidius, | the second name of men, obeys 4.06.124
and is aufidius with him? 4.06.129
this man, aufidius, | was my belov'd in rome; 5.02. 92
aufidius, and you volsces, mark, for we'll 5.03. 92
aufidius, though i cannot make true wars, | i'll 5.03.190
now, good aufidius, | were you in my stead, 5.03.191
or granted less, aufidius? 5.03.193
stand, aufidius, | and trouble not the peace. 5.06.126
takes from aufidius a great part of blame. 5.06.145
AUFIDIUSES 1 FR 0.0001 REL FR 1 V 0 P
with six aufidiuses, or more, his tribe, | to COR 5.06.128
AUGER–HOLE 1 FR 0.0001 REL FR 1 V 0 P
hid in an auger–hole, may rush and seize us? MAC 2.03.122
AUGER'S 1 FR 0.0001 REL FR 1 V 0 P
you stood, confin'd | into an auger's bore. COR 4.06. 87
AUGHT 83 FR 0.0093 REL FR 79 V 4 P
if thou rememb'rest aught ere thou cam'st here, TMP 1.02. 51
it | by aught that i can speak in his dispraise, TGV 3.02. 47
(though you respect not aught your servant doth) 5.04. 20
if aught possess thee from me, it is dross, ERR 2.02.177
if thou art chang'd to aught, 'tis to an ass. 2.02.199
if your love | can labor aught in sad invention, ADO 5.01.283
else none at all in aught proves excellent. LLL 4.03.351
you will do aught, this shall you do for me: 5.02.793
for aught that i could ever read, | could ever MND 1.01.132
nor is he dead, for aught that i can tell. 3.02. 76
and yet, for aught i see, they are as sick that MV 1.02. 5 P
gramercy! wouldst thou aught with me? 2.02.121 P
i'll then nor give nor hazard aught for lead. 2.07. 21
rather threaten'st than dost promise aught, 3.02.105
and neither man nor master would take aught 5.01.183
being perhaps (for aught i see) two and thirty, SHR 1.02. 33 P
it might be yours or hers, for aught i know. AWW 5.03.280
if it be aught to the old tune, my lord, | it is TN 5.01.108
if you know aught which does behove my knowledge
WT 1.02.395
if he see aught in you that makes him like, JN 2.01.511
so, on my soul, he did, for aught he knew. 5.01. 43
tongue, | before i make reply to aught you say. R2 2.03. 73
a king of beasts indeed — if aught but beasts, 5.01. 35
for aught i know, my lord, they do. 5.02. 53
art thou aught else but place, degree, and form, H5 4.01.246
for aught i see, this city must be famish'd, 1H6 1.04. 68
in spite of us, or aught that we could do. 1.05. 37
to think that you have aught but talbot's shadow 2.03. 46
or aught intend'st to lay unto my charge, | do 3.01. 4
when have i aught exacted at your hands, | /but 2H6 4.07. 69
that never dream'st on aught but butcheries. R3 1.02.100
have aught committed that is hardly borne | /by 2.01. 58
that he will not be won to aught against him. 3.01.166
i know but of a single part in aught | pertains H8 1.02. 41
hast thou heard him | at any time speak aught? 1.02.146
and prove it too, against mine honor aught — 2.04. 39
what's aught but as 'tis valued? TRO 2.02. 52
what says achilles? would he aught with us? 3.03. 57
would you, my lord, aught with the general? 3.03. 58
nor doth he of himself know them for aught, 3.03.118
honors, though indeed | in aught he merit not. COR 1.01.276
easily endures not article | tying him to aught; 2.03.197
and never of me aught | but what is like me 4.01. 52
and may, for aught thou knowest, affected be. TIT 2.01. 28
have we done aught amiss, show us wherein, | and 5.03.129
nor aught so good but, strain'd from that fair ROM 2.03. 19
and if aught in this | miscarried by my fault, 5.03.266
if it be aught toward the general good, | set JC 1.02. 85
why ask you? hear you aught of her in yours? 4.03.185
or are you aught | that man may question? MAC 1.03. 42
thy soul contrive | against thy mother aught. HAM 1.05. 86
to note | that you know aught of me — this do 1.05.179
whether aught, to us unknown, afflicts him thus, 2.02. 17
no, not i, | i never gave you aught. 3.01. 95
if 'a steal aught the whilst this play is 3.02. 88
quantity, | in neither aught, or in extremity. 3.02.168
england, if my love thou hold'st at aught — 4.03. 58
if that his majesty would aught with us, | we 4.04. 5
since no man, of aught he leaves, knows what 5.02.223 P
if aught of woe or wonder, cease your search. 5.02.363
if aught within that little seeming substance, LR 1.01.198
hadst thou been aught but goss'mer, feathers, 4.06. 49
do you hear aught, sir, of a battle toward? 4.06.209
or whether since he is advis'd by aught | to 5.01. 2
neither my place, nor aught i heard of business, OTH 1.03. 53
nor know i aught | but that he's well and will 2.01. 89
nor know i aught | by me that's said or done 2.03.200
discern'st thou aught in that? 3.03.102

my lord, for aught i know. 3.03.104
extenuate, | nor set down aught in malice. 5.02.343
i take no pleasure | in aught an eunuch has. ANT 1.05. 10
gone to tell my lord | that i kiss aught but he. CYM 2.03.148
hath my poor boy done aught but well, | whose 5.04. 35
man, of pelf, | ne aught escapend but himself; PER 2.ch. 36
who, for aught i know, | may be (nor can i think 2.05. 78
this is the man that can, in aught you would, 5.01. 12
can draw him but to answer thee in aught, | thy 5.01. 73
and me my love! is there aught else to say? TNK 3.06. 93
were there aught in me which strove to show 5.01. 20
right, | nor aught obeys but his foul appetite. LUC 546
give thyself the thanks if aught in me | worthy SON 38. 5
were't aught to me i bore the canopy, | with my 125. 1
if that from him there may be aught applied LC 68
AUGMENT 4 FR 0.0004 REL FR 4 V 0 P
augment, or alter, as your wisdoms best | shall H5 5.02. 87
me, | nor store of treasons to augment my guilt. 2H6 3.01.169
run o'er | in seeming to augment it wastes it? H8 1.01.145
so i lose none | in seeking to augment it, but MAC 2.01. 27
AUGMENTATION 1 FR 0.0001 REL FR 0 V 1 P
new map, with the augmentation of the indies; TN 3.02. 80 P
AUGMENTED 3 FR 0.0003 REL FR 3 V 0 P
our strength will be augmented | in every county 3H6 5.03. 22
that what he is, augmented, | would run to these JC 2.01. 30
every stage | with an augmented greeting. ANT 3.06. 55
AUGMENTING 3 FR 0.0003 REL FR 3 V 0 P
of the swift brook, | augmenting it with tears. AYL 2.01. 43
with tears augmenting the fresh morning's dew, ROM 1.01.132
wit, | make something nothing by augmenting it. LUC 154
AUGUR 1 FR 0.0001 REL FR 1 V 0 P
of the fiend, | augur of the fever's end, | to PHT 7
AUGURER 2 FR 0.0002 REL FR 1 V 1 P
the augurer tells me we shall have news to–night COR 2.01. 1 P
o, sir, you are too sure an augurer; ANT 5.02.334
AUGURERS 2 FR 0.0002 REL FR 2 V 0 P
and the persuasion of his augurers | may hold JC 2.01.200
what say the augurers? 2.02. 37
AUGURES 1 FR 0.0001 REL FR 1 V 0 P
augures and understood relations have | by MAC 3.04.123
AUGURIES 1 FR 0.0001 REL FR 1 V 0 P
the auguries | say they know not, they cannot ANT 4.12. 4
AUGURING 1 FR 0.0001 REL FR 1 V 0 P
and my auguring hope | says it will come to th' ANT 2.01. 10
AUGURS 1 FR 0.0001 REL FR 1 V 0 P
and the sad augurs mock their own presage, SON 107. 6
AUGURY 2 FR 0.0002 REL FR 1 V 1 P
behavior, | which, if my augury deceive me not, TGV 4.04. 68
not a whit, we defy augury. HAM 5.02.219 P
AUGUST 2 FR 0.0002 REL FR 2 V 0 P
you sunburn'd sicklemen, of august weary, | come TMP 4.01.134
the tenth of august last this dreadful lord, 1H6 1.01.110
AUGUSTUS' 1 FR 0.0001 REL FR 1 V 0 P
i will pursue her | even to augustus' throne. CYM 3.05.101
AUGUSTUS 4 FR 0.0004 REL FR 4 V 0 P
this, your king | hath heard of great augustus. CYM 2.04. 11
now say, what would augustus caesar with us? 3.01. 1
that i am to pronounce augustus caesar | (caesar 3.01. 62
augustus lives to think on't; 5.05. 82
AULD *(also old)*
AULD 1 FR 0.0001 REL FR 1 V 0 P
down, | /then take thy auld cloak about thee." OTH 2.03. 96
/AULIS 1 FR 0.0001 REL FR 1 V 0 P
and at the banks of /aulis meet us with | the TNK 1.01.212
AUMERLE 20 FR 0.0022 REL FR 20 V 0 P
my lord aumerle, is harry herford arm'd? R2 1.03. 1
of you, my noble cousin, lord aumerle; 1.03. 64
cousin aumerle, | how far brought you high 1.04. 1
you have a son, aumerle, my noble cousin, | had 2.03.125
stone, | and with him are the lord aumerle, lord 3.03. 27
aumerle, thou weep'st, my tender–hearted cousin! 3.03.160
then set before my face the lord aumerle. 4.01. 6
my lord aumerle, i know your daring tongue 4.01. 8
there is my gage, aumerle, in gage to thine. 4.01. 34
aumerle, thou liest, his honor is as true | in 4.01. 44
i task the earth to the like, forsworn aumerle, 4.01. 52
well | the very time aumerle and you did talk. 4.01. 61
world, | aumerle is guilty of my true appeal; 4.01. 79
the banished norfolk say | that thou, aumerle, 4.01. 81
against aumerle we will enforce his trial. 4.01. 90
here comes my son aumerle. 5.02. 41
aumerle that was, | but that is lost for being 5.02. 41
i will not peace. what is the matter, aumerle? 5.02. 81
strike him, aumerle. 5.02. 85
after, aumerle! 5.02.111
AUNCHIANT *(also ancient*, aunchient, ensign)*
AUNCHIANT 1 FR 0.0001 REL FR 0 V 1 P
expedition and knowledge in th' aunchiant wars, H5 3.02. 78 P
AUNCHIENT 7 FR 0.0008 REL FR 0 V 7 P
there is an aunchient lieutenant there at the H5 3.06. 12 P
he is call'd aunchient pistol. 3.06. 18 P
by your patience, aunchient pistol: 3.06. 30 P
aunchient pistol, i do partly understand your 3.06. 50 P
certainly, aunchient, it is not a thing to 3.06. 53 P
when the true and aunchient prerogatifes and 4.01. 67 P
god pless you, aunchient pistol! 5.01. 17 P
/AUNT 1 FR 0.0001 REL FR 1 V 0 P
/make /my /aunt /merry /with /some /pleasing TIT 3.02. 47
AUNT 24 FR 0.0027 REL FR 22 V 2 P
my maid's aunt, the fat woman of brainford, has WIV 4.02. 75 P
why, it is my maid's aunt of brainford. 4.02.170 P
i have a widow aunt, a dowager, | of great MND 1.01.157
the wisest aunt, telling the saddest tale, 2.01. 51
a woman, and thy aunt, great king, 'tis i. R2 5.03. 76
rise up, good aunt. 5.03. 92
good aunt, stand up. 5.03.111
good aunt, stand up. 5.03.129
tell her that she and my aunt percy | shall 1H4 3.01.194
sweet aunt, be quiet, 'twas against her will. 2H6 1.03.143
he was lately sent | from your kind aunt, 3H6 2.01.146
ah, aunt! R3 2.02. 62
led in the hand of her kind aunt of gloucester? 4.01. 2
their aunt i am in law, in love their mother; 4.01. 23
mad'st quick conveyance with her good aunt anne. 4.04.283
under pretense to see the queen his aunt | (for H8 1.01.177
and for an old aunt whom the greeks held captive TRO 2.02. 77
the grecians keep our aunt. 2.02. 80
my sacred aunt, should by my mortal sword | be 4.05.134
my aunt lavinia | follows me every where, i know TIT 4.01. 1
alas, sweet aunt, i know not what you mean. 4.01. 4
stand by me, lucius, do not fear thine aunt. 4.01. 5
i know my noble aunt | loves me as dear as e'er 4.01. 22
but pardon me, sweet aunt, | and, madam, if my 4.01. 26
AUNT–MOTHER 1 FR 0.0001 REL FR 0 V 1 P
my uncle–father and aunt–mother are deceiv'd. HAM 2.02.376 P
AUNT'S 1 FR 0.0001 REL FR 1 V 0 P
thou art mine aunt's son, | and that blood we TNK 3.06. 94
AUNTS 1 FR 0.0001 REL FR 1 V 0 P
are summer songs for me and my aunts, | while we
WT 4.03. 11
AURICULAR 1 FR 0.0001 REL FR 0 V 1 P
of this, and by an auricular assurance have your LR 1.02. 92 P
AURORA'S 2 FR 0.0002 REL FR 2 V 0 P
fast, | and yonder shines aurora's harbinger, MND 3.02.380
to draw | the shady curtains from aurora's bed, ROM 1.01.136
AUSPICIOUS 7 FR 0.0008 REL FR 7 V 0 P
doth depend upon | a most auspicious star, whose TMP 1.02.182
and promise you calm seas, auspicious gales, 5.01.315
prosperous helm | as thy auspicious mistress! AWW 3.03. 8
o lady fortune, | stand you auspicious! WT 4.04. 52
with an auspicious, and a dropping eye, | with HAM 1.02. 11
the moon | to stand /'s auspicious mistress. LR 2.01. 40
and they would stand auspicious to the hour, LUC 347
AUSPICIOUSLY 1 FR 0.0001 REL FR 1 V 0 P
i do take | thy signs auspiciously, and in thy TNK 5.01. 67
AUSSI 2 FR 0.0002 REL FR 0 V 2 P
et vous aussi; votre serviteur. TN 3.01. 72 P
prononcez les mots aussi droit que les natifs H5 3.04. 38 P
AUSTERE 4 FR 0.0004 REL FR 2 V 2 P
if this austere insociable life | change not LLL 5.02.799
with most austere sanctimony she accomplish'd; AWW 4.03. 50 P
smile with an austere regard of control — TN 2.05. 66 P
creatures as | of grave and austere quality, TIM 1.01. 54
AUSTERELY 2 FR 0.0002 REL FR 2 V 0 P
if i have too austerely punish'd you, | your TMP 4.01. 1
mightst thou perceive austerely in his eye ERR 4.02. 2
AUSTERENESS 1 FR 0.0001 REL FR 1 V 0 P
my unsoil'd name, th' austereness of my life, MM 2.04.155
AUSTERITY 3 FR 0.0003 REL FR 3 V 0 P
to protest | for aye austerity and single life. MND 1.01. 90
with such austerity as 'longeth to a father. SHR 4.04. 7
even with the same austerity and garb | as he COR 4.07. 44
AUSTRIA 4 FR 0.0004 REL FR 4 V 0 P
a certainty, vouch'd from our cousin austria, AWW 1.02. 5
before angiers well met, brave austria. JN 2.01. 1
austria and france shoot in each other's mouth. 2.01.414
o lymoges, o austria! 3.01.114
AUSTRIA'S 1 FR 0.0001 REL FR 1 V 0 P
austria's head lie there, | while philip JN 3.02. 3
AUT 1 FR 0.0001 REL FR 1 V 0 P
sit fas aut nefas, till i find the stream | to TIT 2.01.133
AUTHENTIC 4 FR 0.0004 REL FR 2 V 2 P
admittance, authentic in your place and person, WIV 2.02.226 P
of all the learned and authentic fellows — AWW 2.03. 12 P
but by degree, stand in authentic place? TRO 1.03.108
(as truth's authentic author to be cited), | "as 3.02.181
AUTHOR 15 FR 0.0017 REL FR 10 V 5 P
and don john is the author of all, who is fled ADO 5.02. 99 P
for where is any author in the world | teaches LLL 4.03.308
o thou, the earthly author of my blood, | whose R2 1.03. 69
meat, our humble author will continue the story, 2H4 ep 27 P
of the master the author of the servant's H5 4.01.154 P
our bending author hath pursu'd the story, | in ep 2
he was the author, thou the instrument. 3H6 4.06. 18
(as truth's authentic author to be cited), | "as TRO 3.02.181
but stand | as if a man were author of himself, COR 5.03. 36
forfend | i should be author to dishonor you! TIT 1.01.435
that might indict the author of affection, but HAM 2.02.443 P
and he most violent author | of his own just 4.05. 80
prove the immediate author of their variance. ANT 2.06.129 P
i did but act, he's author of thy slander. VEN 1006
and thou, the author of their obloquy, | shalt LUC 523
/AUTHORITIES 1 FR 0.0001 REL FR 1 V 0 P
/that /still /would /manage /those /authorities LR 1.03. 17
AUTHORITIES 5 FR 0.0005 REL FR 3 V 2 P
the gates, and /redeliver our authorities there? MM 4.04. 6 P
it must fall out | to him, or our authorities, COR 2.01.244
aches | to know, when two authorities are up, 3.01.109
countenance, his rewards, his authorities. HAM 4.02. 16 P
by turning o'er authorities, i have, | together PER 3.02. 33
AUTHORITY 60 FR 0.0067 REL FR 45 V 15 P
use your authority. TMP 1.01. 23 P
thus can the demigod, authority, | make us pay MM 1.02.120
place, | and with full line of his authority, 1.04. 56
man, | dress'd in a little brief authority, 2.02.118
because authority, though it err like others, 2.02.134
thieves for their robbery have authority | when 2.02.175
celerity, | when it is borne in high authority. 4.02.111
no, | for my authority bears of a credent bulk, 4.04. 26
what authority and show of truth | can cunning ADO 4.01. 35
won, | save base authority from others' books. LLL 1.01. 87
more authority, dear boy, name more; 1.02. 67 P
o, some authority how to proceed; 4.03.283
if law, authority, and power deny not, | it will MV 3.02.289
you | wrest once the law to your authority: 4.01.215
be patient, there is no fettering of authority. AWW 2.03.237 P
by his authority he remains here, which he 4.05. 65 P
hope, | whereto thy speech serves for authority, TN 1.02. 20
it is in mine authority to command | the keys of WT 1.02.463
by his great authority, | which often hath no 2.01. 53
he seems to be of great authority. 4.04.800 P
and though authority be a stubborn bear, yet he 4.04.801 P
thoughts | in any /breast of strong authority, JN 2.01.113
alack, thou dost usurp authority. 2.01.118
set apart | to him and his usurp'd authority. 3.01.160
and on the winking of authority | to understand 4.02.211
pope, | your sovereign greatness and authority. 5.01. 4
lavishly | wrested his meaning and authority. 2H4 4.02. 58
your father) | i gave bold way to my authority, 5.02. 82
i am, sir, under the king, in some authority. 5.03.112 P
charles, | a man of great authority in france, 1H6 5.01. 18
that neither in birth, or for authority, | the 5.01. 59
coronet, | and yet, in substance and authority, 5.04.135
and of such great authority in france | as his 5.05. 41
why, our authority is his consent, | and what we 2H6 3.01.316
that hath authority over him that swears. 3H6 1.02. 24
read, | and on all sides th' authority allow'd; H8 2.04. 4
words cannot carry | authority so weighty. 3.02.234
and the strong course of my authority | might go 5.02. 70
bi–fold authority, where reason can revolt TRO 5.02.144
what authority surfeits /on would relieve us. COR 1.01. 16 P
for they do prank them in authority, | against 3.01. 23
or let us stand to our authority, | or let us 3.01.207
yea, 'gainst th' authority of manners, pray'd TIM 2.02.138
power, and thy good name | live with authority; 5.01.163
if our father carry authority with such LR 1.01.304 P
authority. 1.04. 30 P
by his authority i will proclaim it, | that he 2.01. 60
mightst behold the great image of authority: 4.06.158 P
and corrigible authority of this lies in our OTH 1.03.326 P
one that, in the authority of her merit, did 2.01.145 P
not rather | discredit my authority with yours, ANT 2.02. 49
if our eyes had authority, here they might take 2.06. 95 P
too cruel, | that he his high authority abus'd, 3.06. 33
authority melts from me. 3.13. 90
pretty one, my authority shall not see thee, or PER 4.06. 89 P
of more authority, i am sure more love, | not TNK 3.06.231
authority quite silenc'd by your brawl, | and STM II.C 78
forewarn us of, urging obedience to authority, II.C 94
wherein it shall discern | authority for sin, LUC 620
and art made tongue–tied by authority, | and SON 66. 9
AUTHORIZ'D 2 FR 0.0002 REL FR 2 V 0 P
at a winter's fire, | authoriz'd by her grandam. MAC 3.04. 65
his rudeness so with his authoriz'd youth | did LC 104
AUTHORIZING 1 FR 0.0001 REL FR 1 V 0 P
this, | authorizing thy trespass with compare, SON 35. 6
/AUTHOR'S 1 FR 0.0001 REL FR 1 V 0 P
/of /author's /pen /or /actor's /voice, /but TRO pr 24
AUTHOR'S 1 FR 0.0001 REL FR 1 V 0 P
it is familiar — but at the author's drift, TRO 3.03.113
/AUTHORS 1 FR 0.0001 REL FR 1 V 0 P
or for men's sake, the /authors of these women, LLL 4.03.356
AUTHORS 7 FR 0.0008 REL FR 6 V 1 P
i will read politic authors, i will baffle sir TN 2.05.161 P
but when we know the grounds and authors of it, 5.01.353
yet their own authors faithfully affirm | that H5 1.02. 43
curses on their heads | that were the authors. H8 2.01.139
all syria — | i tell you what mine authors say. PER 1.ch. 20
we have, as learned authors utter, wash'd a tile TNK 3.05. 40
then call them not the authors of their ill, LUC 1244
AUTOLYCUS 2 FR 0.0002 REL FR 0 V 2 P
my father nam'd me autolycus, who being, as i am
WT 4.03. 24 P
some call him autolycus. 4.03.100 P
AUTRE 1 FR 0.0001 REL FR 0 V 1 P
je reciterai une autre fois ma lecon ensemble: H5 3.04. 57 P
/AUTUMN 1 FR 0.0001 REL FR 1 V 0 P
an /autumn it was | that grew the more by ANT 5.02. 87
AUTUMN 6 FR 0.0006 REL FR 5 V 1 P
the childing autumn, angry winter, change MND 2.01.112
rank, | in end of autumn turned to the rams, MV 1.03. 81
as thunder when the clouds in autumn crack. SHR 1.02. 96
o yes, and 'twere a cloud in autumn. TRO 1.02.126 P
the teeming autumn, big with rich increase, SON 97. 6
three beauteous springs to yellow autumn turn'd 104. 5
/AUTUMN'S 1 FR 0.0001 REL FR 1 V 0 P
water–pots, | /ay, /and /laying /autumn's /dust. LR 4.06.197
AUTUMN'S 1 FR 0.0001 REL FR 1 V 0 P
what valiant foemen, like to autumn's corn, 3H6 5.07. 3
AUVERGNE 1 FR 0.0001 REL FR 1 V 0 P
the virtuous lady, countess of auvergne, | with 1H6 2.02. 38
AVAIL 4 FR 0.0004 REL FR 3 V 1 P
but how out of this can she avail? MM 3.01.234 P
as heaven shall work in me for thine avail, | to AWW 1.03.184
since arms avail not now that henry's dead. 1H6 1.01. 47
now will it best avail your majesty | to cross 3.01.178
AVAILS 3 FR 0.0003 REL FR 3 V 0 P
when better fall, for your avails they fell. AWW 3.01. 22
which to deny concerns more than avails; WT 3.02. 86
know, gentle wench, it small avails my mood; LUC 1273
AVARICE 2 FR 0.0002 REL FR 2 V 0 P
affection such | a stanchless avarice that, were MAC 4.03. 78
this avarice | sticks deeper, grows with more 4.03. 84
AVARICIOUS 1 FR 0.0001 REL FR 1 V 0 P
luxurious, avaricious, false, deceitful, MAC 4.03. 58
AVAUNT 17 FR 0.0019 REL FR 14 V 3 P
rogues, hence, avaunt, vanish like hailstones; WIV 1.03. 81
avaunt, thou witch! come, dromio, let us go. ERR 4.03. 79
avaunt, perplexity! LLL 5.02.298
avaunt, thou hateful villain, get thee gone! JN 4.03. 77
you hunt counter, hence, avaunt! 2H4 1.02. 90 P
avaunt, you cullions! H5 3.02. 20 P
peasant, avaunt! 1H6 5.04. 21
avaunt, thou dreadful minister of hell! R3 1.02. 46
to give her the avaunt, it is a pity | would H8 2.03. 10
traitors, avaunt! TIT 1.01.283
avaunt, and quit my sight! MAC 3.04. 92
avaunt, you curs! LR 3.06. 64 P
avaunt, be gone! OTH 3.03.335
hence, avaunt! 4.01.260
avaunt! ANT 4.12. 30
avaunt, thou damned door–keeper! PER 4.06.118
"then childish fear, avaunt, debating, die! LUC 274
AVE *(also 'a', ha', have)*
AVE 1 FR 0.0001 REL FR 0 V 1 P
your majestee ave fausse french enough to H5 5.02.218 P
AVE–MARIES 2 FR 0.0002 REL FR 2 V 0 P
holiness, | to number ave–maries on his beads; 2H6 1.03. 56
numb'ring our ave–maries with our beads? 3H6 2.01.162
AVENG'D *(also adveng'd)*
AVENG'D 3 FR 0.0003 REL FR 3 V 0 P
shall i not live to be aveng'd on her? 2H6 1.03. 82
thee, | but thou wilt be aveng'd on my misdeeds, R3 1.04. 70
three and thirty wounds | be well aveng'd; JC 5.01. 54
AVENGE 1 FR 0.0001 REL FR 1 V 0 P
gone, | remember to avenge me on the french." 1H6 1.04. 94
AVENGED 1 FR 0.0001 REL FR 1 V 0 P
if god will be avenged for the deed, | o, know R3 1.04.215
AVERRING 1 FR 0.0001 REL FR 1 V 0 P
averring notes | of chamber–hanging, pictures, CYM 5.05.203
AVERT 1 FR 0.0001 REL FR 1 V 0 P
you | t' avert your liking a more worthier way LR 1.01.211
AVES 1 FR 0.0001 REL FR 1 V 0 P
well | their loud applause and aves vehement; MM 1.01. 70

AVEZ 1 FR 0.0001 REL FR 0 V 1 P
et quand vous avez le possession de moi — let H5 5.02.182 P
AVIS'D *(also advis'd)*
AVIS'D 3 FR 0.0003 REL FR 1 V 2 P
be avis'd, sir, and pass good humors. WIV 1.01.166 P
are you avis'd o' that? 1.04.100 P
art avis'd o' that? more on't. MM 2.02.132
AVOID 38 FR 0.0043 REL FR 26 V 12 P
avoid. TMP 4.01.142
sir, that you might avoid him if you saw him. WIV 2.02.277 P
though what i am i cannot avoid, yet to be what 3.05.149 P
now stands, he will avoid your accusation: MM 3.01.196 P
sathan, avoid! i charge thee tempt me not. ERR 4.03. 48
avoid then, fiend! 4.03. 65
the fashion of the world is to avoid cost, and ADO 1.01. 98 P
i note another man like him | i may avoid him. 5.01.261
and therefore red, that would avoid dispraise, LLL 4.03.260
yet i know no wise remedy how to avoid it. AYL 1.01. 25 P
and i have been all this day to avoid him. 2.05. 34 P
all these you may avoid but the lie direct; 5.04. 97 P
and you may avoid that too, with an if. 5.04. 98 P
he cannot by the duello avoid it; TN 3.04.307 P
avoid what's grown than question how 'tis born. WT 1.02.433
let us avoid. 1.02.462
yet, to avoid deceit, i mean to learn; JN 1.01.215
a partial slander sought i to avoid, | and in R2 1.03.241
sing, | yet seek no shelter to avoid the storm; 2.01.264
which to avoid, | i cut them off, and had a 2H4 4.05.208
will you yield, and this avoid? H5 3.03. 42
false fiend, avoid! 2H6 1.04. 40
because he would avoid such bitter taunts 3H6 2.06. 66
t' avoid the censures of the carping world. R3 3.05. 68
therefore — to speak, and to avoid the first, 3.07.151
avoid the gallery. H8 5.01. 86
how may i avoid | (although my will distaste TRO 2.02. 65
pray you avoid the house. COR 4.05. 23 P
pray you avoid. 4.05. 30 P
i do not know the man i should avoid | so soon JC 1.02.200
and our safest way | is to avoid the aim. MAC 2.03.143
fate, | which, happily, foreknowing may avoid, HAM 1.01.134
pray you avoid it. 3.02. 14 P
repent what's past, avoid what is to come, | and 3.04.150
hence, and avoid my sight! LR 1.01.124
avoid, and leave him. ANT 5.02.242
thou basest thing, avoid hence, from my sight! CYM 1.01.125
i chose an eagle, | and did avoid a puttock. 1.01.140
AVOIDED *(also 'voided)*
AVOIDED 8 FR 0.0009 REL FR 8 V 0 P
since not to be avoided it falls on me. 1H4 5.05. 13
mark'd by the destinies to be avoided, | as 3H6 2.02.137
what cannot be avoided | 'twere childish 5.04. 37
true — when avoided grace makes destiny: R3 4.04.219
it cannot be avoided but by this; 4.04.410
it will not be avoided but by this. 4.04.411
what can be avoided | whose end is purpos'd by JC 2.02. 26
of all men else i have avoided thee. MAC 5.08. 4
AVOIDING 1 FR 0.0001 REL FR 1 V 0 P
by spying and avoiding fortune's malice, | for 3H6 4.06. 28
AVOIDS 1 FR 0.0001 REL FR 0 V 1 P
for either he avoids them with great discretion, ADO 2.03.191 P
AVOIRDUPOIS *(see haberdepois)*
AVOUCH 10 FR 0.0011 REL FR 6 V 4 P
i speak and i avouch; WIV 2.01.134 P
if the duke avouch the justice of your dealing? MM 4.02.186 P
demetrius, i'll avouch it to his head, | made MND 1.01.106
i well may give, | and in the stocks avouch it. WT 4.03. 22
and dare not avouch in your deeds any of your H5 5.01. 73 P
avouch the thoughts of your heart with the looks 5.02.235 P
if you'll avouch 'twas wisdom paris went — | as TRO 2.02. 84
and bid my will avouch it, yet i must not, | for MAC 3.01.119
without the sensible and true avouch | of mine HAM 1.01. 57
i dare avouch it, sir. LR 2.04.237
AVOUCHED 1 FR 0.0001 REL FR 1 V 0 P
that will prove | what is avouched there. LR 5.01. 44
AVOUCHES 2 FR 0.0002 REL FR 1 V 1 P
this avouches the shepherd's son, who has not WT 5.02. 64 P
if this which he avouches does appear, | there MAC 5.05. 46
AVOUCHMENT 1 FR 0.0001 REL FR 0 V 1 P
me testimony and witness, and will avouchment, H5 4.08. 36 P
AVOUCH'T 1 FR 0.0001 REL FR 1 V 0 P
i will avouch't in presence of the king. R3 1.03.114
AVOW 2 FR 0.0002 REL FR 2 V 0 P
of which there is not one, i dare avow | (and H8 4.02.142
and dare avow her beauty and her worth | in TRO 1.03.271
AWAIT 1 FR 0.0001 REL FR 1 V 0 P
posterity, await for wretched years, | when at 1H6 1.01. 48
/AWAITS 1 FR 0.0001 REL FR 1 V 0 P
/me what /fate /awaits the duke of suffolk?" 2H6 1.04. 32
AWAITS 1 FR 0.0001 REL FR 1 V 0 P
"tell me what fate awaits the duke of suffolk?" 2H6 1.04. 64
AWAK'D 16 FR 0.0018 REL FR 15 V 1 P
in my false brother | awak'd an evil nature, and TMP 1.02. 93
of sounds, all horrible, | we were awak'd; 5.01.235
we have very oft awak'd him, as if to carry him MM 4.02.150 P
but they shall find, awak'd in such a kind, ADO 4.01.197
i wonder if titania be awak'd; MND 3.02. 1
sleeps with endymion | and would not be awak'd. MV 5.01.110
his equal had awak'd them, and his honor, AWW 1.02. 38
awak'd the sleeping rheum, and so by chance R2 1.04. 8
from which awak'd, the truth of what we are 5.01. 19
but, being awak'd, i do despise my dream. 2H4 5.05. 51
awak'd you not in this sore agony? R3 1.04. 42
but with his timorous dreams was still awak'd. 4.01. 84
my master is awak'd by great occasion | to call TIM 2.02. 21
alack, i am afraid they have awak'd, | and 'tis MAC 2.02. 9
our knocking has awak'd him; 2.03. 43
leisure read | the garboils she awak'd: ANT 1.03. 61
AWAKE 82 FR 0.0092 REL FR 72 V 10 P
awake, dear heart, awake! TMP 1.02.305
awake, dear heart, awake! 1.02.305
thou hast slept well, | awake! 1.02.306
awake, awake! 2.01.305
awake, awake! 2.01.305
awake? 2.01.308
(and that a strange one too) which did awake me. 2.01.318
if he awake, | from toe to crown he'll fill our 4.01.232
the master and the boatswain | being awake, 5.01.100
if i did think, sir, i were well awake, | i'ld 5.01.229
master ford, awake! WIV 3.05.140 P
awake, master ford! 3.05.140 P
now 'tis awake, | takes note of what is done, MM 2.02. 93
tell him he must awake, and that quickly too. 4.03. 30 P
master barnardine, awake till you are executed, 4.03. 32 P
he lie ten nights awake carving the fashion of a ADO 2.03. 17 P
awake the pert and nimble spirit of mirth, MND 1.01. 13
so awake when i am gone, | for i must now to 2.02. 82
lysander, if you live, good sir, awake. 2.02.102
durst thou have look'd upon him being awake? 3.02. 69
noise they make | will cause demetrius to awake. 3.02.117
are you sure | that we are awake? 4.01.193
why then, we are awake. 4.01.198
i pray, awake, sir; SHR 1.01.178
and with the clamor keep her still awake. 4.01.207
to exasperate you, to awake your dormouse valor, TN 3.02. 19 P
along with you, it may awake my bounty further. 5.01. 44 P
your bounty take a nap, i will awake it anon. 5.01. 48 P
sleeping else | but what your jealousies awake), WT 3.02.113
being now awake, i'll queen it no inch farther, 4.04.449
it is requir'd | you do awake your faith. 5.03. 95
awake her! 5.03. 98
by so much | we must awake endeavor for defense, JN 2.01. 81
his innocent prate | he will awake my mercy, 4.01. 26
awake, thou coward majesty! R2 3.02. 84
how you awake our sleeping sword of war — | we H5 1.02. 22
awake remembrance of these valiant dead, | and 1.02.115
awake, awake, english nobility! 1H6 1.01. 78
awake, awake, english nobility! 1.01. 78
and there awake god's gentle–sleeping peace. R3 1.03.287
awake and think our wrongs in richard's bosom 5.03.144
awake and win the day! 5.03.145
bloody and guilty, guiltily awake, | and in a 5.03.154
quiet untroubled soul, awake, awake! 5.03.157
quiet untroubled soul, awake, awake! 5.03.157
i bring a trumpet to awake his ear, | to set his TRO 1.03.251
that thou shalt know, troyan, he is awake, | he 1.03.255
hector, thou sleep'st, | awake thee! 4.05.115
if none, awake | your dangerous lenity. COR 3.01. 98
i have been broad awake two hours and more. TIT 2.02. 17
he'll so awake as he in fury shall | cut off the 4.04. 25
and then awake as from a pleasant sleep. ROM 4.01.106
in the mean time, against thou shalt awake, 4.01.113
ere day | we will awake him and be sure of him. JC 1.03.164
awake, i say! 2.01. 5
awake, and see thyself! 2.01. 46
awake!" 2.01. 48
i have been up this hour, awake all night. 2.01. 88
me in your wisdom, and awake your senses, that 3.02. 16 P
sirs, awake! 4.03.289
lucius, awake! 4.03.293
fellow thou, awake! 4.03.300
awake, awake! MAC 2.03. 73
awake, awake! 2.03. 73
malcolm, awake! 2.03. 75
shrill–sounding throat | awake the god of day, HAM 1.01.152
and exception | roughly awake, i here proclaim 5.02.232
be by, good madam, when we do awake him, | i LR 4.07. 22
he's scarce awake, let him alone a while. 4.07. 50
awake! OTH 1.01. 79
awake the snorting citizens with the bell, | or 1.01. 90
awake, sir, awake, speak to us. ANT 4.09. 28
awake, sir, awake, speak to us. 4.09. 28
and if thou canst awake by four o' th' clock, CYM 2.02. 6
a fearful dream of him, | and cry myself awake? 3.04. 44
and so i am awake. 5.04.127
they may awake their helpers to comfort them. PER 1.04. 17
and will awake him from his melancholy. 2.03. 91
thunder shall not so awake the beds of eels as 4.02.143 P
awake, and tell thy dream. 5.01.249
and softly cried, 'awake, thou roman dame, | and LUC 1628
it is my love that keeps mine eye awake, | mine SON 61.10
AWAKED 1 FR 0.0001 REL FR 1 V 0 P
hurtling | from miserable slumber i awaked. AYL 4.03.132
AWAKEN 1 FR 0.0001 REL FR 1 V 0 P
i offered to awaken his regard | for 's private COR 5.01. 23
AWAKENED 1 FR 0.0001 REL FR 1 V 0 P
ay, mistress bride, hath that awakened you? SHR 5.02. 42
AWAKENING 1 FR 0.0001 REL FR 1 V 0 P
some minute ere the time | of her awakening, ROM 5.03.258
AWAKENS 1 FR 0.0001 REL FR 0 V 1 P
awakens me with this unwonted putting–on, MM 4.02.116 P
AWAKES 5 FR 0.0005 REL FR 5 V 0 P
governor | awakes me all the enrolled penalties MM 1.02.166
awakes my conscience to confess all this. JN 5.04. 43
that, with the hurly, death itself awakes? 2H4 3.01. 25
nature awakes, | a warmth /breathes out of her. PER 3.02. 92
awakes my heart to heart's and eye's delight. SON 47.14
AWAKETH 1 FR 0.0001 REL FR 1 V 0 P
and his untimely frenzy thus awaketh: LUC 1675
AWAKING 2 FR 0.0002 REL FR 2 V 0 P
swain, | that he awaking when the other do, MND 4.01. 66
such as you | nourish the cause of his awaking. WT 2.03. 36
AWARD 1 FR 0.0001 REL FR 1 V 0 P
kings | confound your hidden falsehood and award R3 2.01. 14
AWARDS 3 FR 0.0003 REL FR 3 V 0 P
the court awards it, and the law doth give it. MV 4.01.300
the law allows it, and the court awards it. 4.01.303
that she that makes me sin awards me pain. SON 141.14
/AWAY 16 FR 0.0018 REL FR 14 V 2 P
/cares /i /give /i /have, /though /given /away, R2 4.01.198
/mine /own /tears /i /wash /away /my /balm, 4.01.207
/mine /own /hands /i /give /away /my /crown, 4.01.208
/and /water /cannot /wash /away /your /sin. 4.01.242
/to /melt /myself /away /in //water–drops! 4.01.262
/starting /thence /away | /to /what /may /be TRO pr 28
/but, /march /away. 5.10. 21
/tears /will /quickly /melt /thy /life /away. TIT 3.02. 51
/come, /take /away. 3.02. 81
/do /the /boys /carry /it /away? HAM 2.02.360 P
/authorities | /that /he /hath /given /away! LR 1.03. 18
/counsell'd /thee | /to /give /away /thy /land, 1.04.141
/thy /other /titles /thou /hast /given /away, 1.04.149 P
/tom, /away! 3.06.110
/then /away /she /started | /to /deal /with 4.03. 31
but, he /away, 'tis noble. ANT 2.03. 31
AWAY 876 FR 0.0990 REL FR 644 V 232 P
come away, servant, come; TMP 1.02.187
till | thou hast howl'd away twelve winters. 1.02.296
lead away. 2.01.325
the sound is going away. 3.02.148 P
into lust, to take away | the edge of that day's 4.01. 28
lime upon your fingers, and away with the rest. 4.01.246 P
help to bear this away where my hogshead of wine 4.01.251 P
go to, away! 5.01.298
shall make it | go quick away — the story of my 5.01.305
stray, | and if the shepherd be awhile away. TGV 1.01. 75
ay — if you thought your love not cast away. 1.02. 26
blow not a word away | till i have found each 1.02.115
to the sweet julia" — that i'll tear away — 1.02.122
some to discover islands far away; 1.03. 9
the sun, | and by and by a cloud takes all away. 1.03. 87
launce, away, away! 2.03. 33 P
launce, away, away! 2.03. 33 P
away, ass, you'll lose the tide, if you tarry 2.03. 35 P
come; come away, man — i was sent to call thee. 2.03. 55 P
this night intends to steal away your daughter; 3.01. 11
and should she thus be stol'n away from you, 3.01. 15
and thence she cannot be convey'd away. 3.01. 37
sir valentine, whither away so fast? 3.01. 51
for "get you gone," she doth not mean "away!" 3.01.101
death, | but, fly i hence, i fly away from life. 3.01.187
banished | for practicing to steal away a lady, 4.01. 46
away, i say! 4.04. 61
and threw her sun–expelling mask away, | the air 4.04.153
come, bring her away. 5.03. 5
host, i must turn away some of my followers. WIV 1.03. 4 P
plod away i' th' hoof! 1.03. 82
away, sir corporal nym! 2.01.124
for he swears he'll turn me away. 3.03. 32 P
help me away. 3.03.141 P
i, "will you cast away your child on a fool, and 3.04. 96 P
take away these chalices. 3.05. 28 P
for a search, and away went i for foul clothes. 3.05.106 P
away with him, away with him! 4.02. 44 P
away with him, away with him! 4.02. 44 P
otherwise you might slip away ere he came. 4.02. 53 P
come away. 4.02.142 P
i have turn'd away my other guests; 4.03. 10 P
time | shall master slender steal my nan away, 4.04. 74
run away with the cozeners; 4.05. 66 P
and set spurs and away, like three german devils 4.05. 69 P
hath commanded her to slip | away with slender, 4.06. 24
that he shall likewise shuffle her away, | while 4.06. 29
away, go. 5.01. 3 P
away! 5.01. 4 P
away, i say, time wears, hold up your head and 5.01. 7 P
let's away; 5.02. 14 P
her by the hand, away with her to the deanery, 5.03. 3 P
away, away! 5.05. 33 P
away, away! 5.05. 33 P
away, disperse! 5.05. 74
give me your hand, | i'll privily away. MM 1.01. 67
saw him carried away; 1.02. 68 P
away! let's go learn the truth of it. 1.02. 81 P
away, sir, you must go. 1.02.141
come, officer, away! 1.02.193
holy father, throw away that thought; 1.03. 1
come, bring them away. 2.01. 41 P
bring them away. 2.01. 44 P
go to; 'tis well. away! 2.02.156
as easy | falsely to take away a life true made 2.04. 47
of a codpiece to take away the life of a man! 3.02.115 P
go, away with her to prison. 3.02.190 P
away with her to prison! 3.02.205 P
take, o, take those lips away, | that so sweetly 4.01. 1
break off thy song, and haste thee quick away. 4.01. 7
come away, it is almost clear dawn. 4.02.209 P
away, you rogue, away! i am sleepy. 4.03. 28 P
away, you rogue, away! i am sleepy. 4.03. 28 P
therefore hence away! 4.06. 15
away with her! 5.01. 46
the body | that took away the match from isabel, 5.01.211
slander to th' state! | away with him to prison. 5.01.323
away with him to prison! 5.01.345 P
away with him to prison! 5.01.346 P
away with those giglets too, and with the other 5.01.347 P
sneak not away, sir, for the friar and you 5.01.358
away with him! 5.01.416
away with him to death! 5.01.429
get thee away. ERR 1.02. 16
i'll weep what's left away, and weeping die. 2.01.115
ah, do not tear away thyself from me; 2.02.124
if any ship put out, then straight away. 3.02.185
comes aboard, | and then, sir, she bears away. 4.01. 87
far from her nest the lapwing cries away; 4.02. 27
into my house, and took perforce | my ring away. 4.03. 95
fear me not, man, i will not break away; 4.04. 1
came to my house, and took away my ring — | the 4.04.138
away, they'll kill us. 4.04.146
therefore away, to get our stuff aboard. 4.04.158
some get within him, take his sword away: 5.01. 34
us again, and madly bent on us | chas'd us away; 5.01.153
i, sir, am dromio, command him away. 5.01.336
wear the print of it, and sigh away sundays. ADO 1.01.202 P
deliver i up my apes, and away to saint peter. 2.01. 47 P
for the walk, and especially when i walk away. 2.01. 90 P
i give away myself for you, and dote upon the 2.01.308 P
fire, | consume away in sighs, waste inwardly. 3.01. 78
don john had made, away went claudio enrag'd; 3.03.159 P
take not away thy heavy hand, | death is the 4.01.115
in angel whiteness beat away those blushes, 4.01.161
presently away, | for to strange sores strangely 4.01.251
john is this morning secretly stol'n away. 4.02. 61 P
away, you are an ass, you are an ass. 4.02. 73 P
bring him away. 4.02. 86 P
away, i will not have to do with you. 5.01. 77
no? come, brother, away! i will be heard. 5.01.108
melancholy and would fain have it beaten away. 5.01.124 P
come, bring away the plaintiffs. 5.01.253 P
your oath is pass'd to pass away from these. LLL 1.01. 49
come, jaquenetta, away. 1.02.145 P
take away this villain, shut him up. 1.02.153 P

come, you transgressing slave, away. 1.02.154 P
you will the sooner, that i were away, | for 2.01.112
not too long in one tune, but a snip and away: 3.01. 22 P
the way is but short, away! 3.01. 56 P
come, lords, away. 4.01.106
away, the gentles are at their game, and we will 4.02.165 P
soft, whither away so fast? 4.03.184
the treason and you go in peace away together. 4.03.190
hence, sirs, away! 4.03.208
for fear their colors should be wash'd away. 4.03.267
away, away, no time shall be omitted | that will 4.03.378
away, away, no time shall be omitted | that will 4.03.378
most dull, honest dull! to our sport; away! 5.01.155
but while 'tis spoke each turn away /her face. 5.02.148
and they, well mock'd, depart away with shame. 5.02.156
is he | that kiss'd his hand away in courtesy; 5.02.324
take away the conqueror, take away alisander. 5.02.572 P
take away the conqueror, take away alisander. 5.02.572 P
run away for shame, alisander. 5.02.579 P
jud–as, away! 5.02.628
the honest troyan, the poor wench is cast away. 5.02.676 P
worthies, away! the scene begins to cloud. 5.02.721
boyet, prepare, i will away to–night. 5.02.727
but if they will not, throw away that spirit, 5.02.867
four nights will quickly dream away the time; MND 1.01. 8
god speed fair helena! whither away? 1.01.180
and thence from athens turn away our eyes, | to 1.01.218
when thou hast stolen away from fairy land, 2.01. 65
fairies, away! 2.01.144
hence, away! 2.02. 25
for beasts that meet me run away for fear. 2.02. 95
methought a serpent eat my heart away, | and you 2.02.149
why do they run away? 3.01.112 P
sky, | so, at his sight, away his fellows fly; 3.02. 24
would he have stolen away | from sleeping hermia 3.02. 51
away, you ethiop! 3.02.257
my legs are longer though, to run away. 3.02.343
fairies, be gone, and be /all /ways away. 4.01. 41
with ears that sweep away the morning dew; 4.01.121
they would have stol'n away, they would, 4.01.156
away with us to athens. 4.01.184
away, go, away! 4.02. 45 P
away, go, away! 4.02. 45 P
to wear away this long age of three hours 5.01. 33
night, | did scare away, or rather did affright; 5.01.141
and, being done, thus wall away doth go. 5.01.205
trip away; 5.01.421
use your legs, take the start, run away." MV 2.02. 6 P
"away!" 2.02. 11 P
and, to run away from the jew, i should be rul'd 2.02. 25 P
as i have set up my rest to run away, so i will 2.02.103 P
nay, we will slink away in supper–time, 2.04. 1
on, /gentlemen, away! 2.06. 58
head i came to woo, | but i go away with two. 2.09. 76
hath an argosy cast away, coming from tripolis. 3.01.100 P
away then! 3.02. 40
which when you part from, lose, or give away, 3.02.172
wife, | and then away to venice to your friend; 3.02.304
come away! 3.02.310
since i have your good leave to go away, | i 3.02.324
and therefore haste away, | for we must measure 3.04. 83
pardon, | i must away this night toward padua, 4.01.403
away, make haste. 4.01.454
we'll away to–night, | and be a day before our 4.02. 2
that they did give the rings away to men; 4.02. 16
away, make haste. 4.02. 18
shadow ere himself, | and ran dismayed away. 5.01. 9
my lord bassanio gave his ring away | unto the 5.01.179
him, | and suffer'd him to go displeas'd away — 5.01.213
but the same tradition takes not away my blood, AYL 1.01. 48 P
what he hath taken away from thy father perforce 1.02. 20 P
mistress, you must come away to your father. 1.02. 57 P
he had sworn it away before ever he saw those 1.02. 79 P
bear him away. what is thy name, young man? 1.02.221
are too precious to be cast away upon curs, 1.03. 5 P
hem them away. 1.03. 18 P
let's away, | and get our jewels and our wealth 1.03.133
i will not cast away my physic but on those that 3.02.358 P
and to cast away honesty upon a foul slut were 3.03. 35 P
but — wind away, | be gone, i say, | i will not 3.03.103
'tis but one cast away, and so, come death! 4.01.185 P
and with indented glides did slip away | into a 4.03.112
his arm | the lioness had torn some flesh away, 4.03.147
i kill thee, make thee away, translate thy life 5.01. 53 P
come, away, away! 5.01. 61 P
come, away, away! 5.01. 61 P
i love no chiders, sir. biondello, let's away. SHR 1.02.226
is't possible you will away to–night? 3.02.189
i must away to–day, before night come. 3.02.190
that have beheld me give away myself | to this 3.02.194
away, you three–inch fool! i am no beast. 4.01. 26 P
how i cried, how the horses ran away, how her 4.01. 80 P
i tell thee, kate, 'twas burnt and dried away, 4.01.170
away, away, for he is coming hither. 4.01.187
away, away, for he is coming hither. 4.01.187
here, take away this dish. 4.03. 44
away with it! 4.03. 68
away, thou rag, thou quantity, thou remnant, 4.03.111
away, i say, commend me to thy master. 4.03.168
good morrow, gentle mistress, where away? 4.05. 27
sweet, | whither away, or /where is thy abode? 4.05. 38
away, away, mad ass! 5.01. 84 P
away, away, mad ass! 5.01. 84 P
away with the dotard! to the jail with him! 5.01.106 P
come, sirrah, let's away. 5.01.147
and, as the jest did glance away from me, | 'tis 5.02. 61
away, i say, and bring them hither straight. 5.02.105
there is no living, none, | if bertram be away. AWW 1.01. 85
away with't! 1.01.132 P
away with't! 1.01.149 P
so is running away, when fear proposes the 1.01.202 P
and thine ignorance makes thee away. 1.01.212 P
thy mind stand to't, boy, steal away bravely. 2.01. 29
by heaven, i'll steal away. 2.01. 33
i'll send her straight away. 2.03.295
therefore away, and leave her bravely; 2.03.299
away, th' art a knave. 2.04. 28 P
madam, my lord will go away to–night, | a very 2.04. 39
will she away to–night? 2.05. 22 P
away, and for our flight. 2.05. 92
you shall hear i am run away; 3.02. 22 P
say i, madam, if he run away, as i hear he does. 3.02. 40 P
for my part, i only hear your son was run away. 3.02. 44 P
for with the dark, poor thief, i'll steal away. 3.02.129
with what it loathes for that which is away — 4.04. 25
we must away: 4.04. 33
foh, prithee stand away. 5.02. 16 P
strikes some scores away | from the great compt; 5.03. 56
take him away. 5.03.120
away with him! 5.03.123
you give away this hand, and that is mine; 5.03.170
you give away heaven's vows, and those are mine; 5.03.171
you give away myself, which is known mine; 5.03.172
take her away, i do not like her now, | to 5.03.281
and away with him. 5.03.282
take her away. 5.03.285
away before me to sweet beds of flow'rs, TN 1.01. 39
being so long absent, or to be turn'd away — is 1.05. 17 P
and for turning away, let summer bear it out. 1.05. 20 P
take the fool away. 1.05. 38 P
do you not hear, fellows? take away the lady. 1.05. 39 P
the lady bade take away the fool, therefore i 1.05. 52 P
the fool, therefore i say again, take her away. 1.05. 53 P
sir, i bade them take away you. 1.05. 54 P
take away the fool, gentlemen. 1.05. 71 P
i would be loath to cast away my speech; 1.05.173 P
me my pains, to have taken it away yourself. 2.02. 6 P
come away, come away, death, | and in sad 2.04. 51
come away, come away, death, | and in sad 2.04. 51
/fly away, /fly away, breath, | i am slain by a 2.04. 53
/fly away, /fly away, breath, | i am slain by a 2.04. 53
and when she went away now, "let this fellow be 3.04. 76 P
away! 3.04.182 P
take him away, he knows i know him well. 3.04.331
come, sir, away. 3.04.339
what's that to us? the time goes by; away! 3.04.364
the man grows mad, away with him! 3.04.371
come, away! 5.01.142
away with him! 5.01.202 P
you | shall bear along impawn'd, away to–night! WT 1.02.436
come, sir, away. 1.02.465
away with him! 2.01. 60
away with her, to prison! 2.01.103
away with that audacious lady! 2.03. 42
away with her! 2.03.124
away with't! 2.03.132
with camillo to take away the life of our 3.02. 16 P
for their better safety, to fly away by night." 3.02. 21 P
go thou away, | i'll follow instantly. 3.03. 13
they have scar'd away two of my best sheep, 3.03. 65 P
or take away with thee the very services thou 4.02. 16 P
come bring away thy pack after me. 4.04.311 P
away! 4.04.332 P
stealing away from his father with his clog at 4.04.679 P
on, | which sixteen winters cannot blow away, 5.03. 50
nay, come away; 5.03.101
hastily lead away. 5.03.155
or day | when i was got, sir robert was away! JN 1.01.166
france, hast thou yet more blood to cast away? 2.01.334
come, away, away! 2.01.415
come, away, away! 2.01.415
that takes away by any secret course | thy 3.01.178
cousin, away for england! 3.03. 6
i prithee, lady, go away with me. 3.04. 20
but they will pluck away his natural cause | and 3.04.156
nay, after that, consume away in rust, | but for 4.01. 65
nay, hear me, hubert, drive these men away, 4.01. 78
thrust but these men away, and i'll forgive you, 4.01. 82
alas, i then have chid away my friend! 4.01. 86
hubert, away with him; 4.02.155
i'll find a thousand shifts to get away. 4.03. 7
away with me, all you whose souls abhor | th' 4.03.111
away toward bury, to the dolphin there! 4.03.114
bear away that child, | and follow me with speed 4.03.156
by some damn'd hand was robb'd and ta'en away. 5.01. 41
away, and glister like the god of war | when he 5.01. 54
away then with good courage! 5.01. 78
and with a great heart heave away this storm. 5.02. 55
life, | which bleeds away even as a form of wax 5.04. 24
away, my friends! 5.04. 60
are cast away, and sunk on goodwin sands. 5.05. 13
away before; 5.06. 43
o, let my sovereign turn away his face, | and R2 1.01.111
that away, | men are but gilded loam or painted 1.01.178
of his banish'd years | pluck'd four away. 1.03.211
say | i was too strict to make mine own away; 1.03.244
what reverence he did throw away on slaves, 1.04. 27
take herford's rights away, and take from time 2.01.195
itself, | away with me in post to ravenspurgh; 2.01.296
carts, | and bring away the armor that is there. 2.02.107
and given away | to upstart unthrifts? 2.03.121
which i have sworn to weed and pluck away. 2.03.167
come, lords, away, | to fight with glendower and 3.01. 42
with solemn reverence, throw away respect, 3.02.172
go to flint castle, there i'll pine away — | a 3.02.209
discharge my followers, let them hence away, 3.02.217
to drive away the heavy thought of care? 3.04. 2
i will go root away | the noisome weeds which 3.04. 37
superfluous branches | we lop away, that bearing 3.04. 64
with all swift speed you must away to france. 5.01. 54
away, fond woman, were he twenty times my son, 5.02.101
away, be gone! 5.02.117
if thou love me, 'tis time thou wert away. 5.05. 96
anon | he gave his nose and took't away again, 1H4 1.03. 39
you start away, | and lend no ear unto my 1.03.216
come away and be hang'd! 2.01. 22 P
come away. 2.01. 23 P
they will away presently. 2.01. 60 P
away, good ned. 2.02.108
what is it carries you away? 2.03. 75
away, | away, you trifler! 2.03. 89
away, | away, you trifler! 2.03. 90
ned, to drive away the time till falstaff come, 2.04. 28 P
away, you rogue, dost thou not hear them call? 2.04. 78 P
you carried your guts away as nimbly, with as 2.04.259 P
and the argument shall be thy running away. 2.04.282 P
you are lions too, you ran away upon instinct, 2.04.300 P
and sword on thy side, and yet thou ran'st away; 2.04.317 P
worcester is stol'n away to–night. 2.04.358 P
thou art violently carried away from grace, 2.04.446 P
the moon shines fair, you may away by night. 3.01.140
be drawn, i'll away within these two hours, and 3.01.261 P
your majesty's good thoughts away from me! 3.02.131
which, wash'd away, shall scour my shame with it 3.02.137
our hands are full of business, let's away, 3.02.179
am i not fall'n away vilely since this last 3.03. 1 P
i have given them away to bakers' wives, they 3.03. 70 P
by some that know not why he is away | that 4.01. 63
my father and glendower being both away, | the 4.01.131
you, looks for us all, we must away all night. 4.02. 57 P
or take away the grief of a wound? 5.01.132 P
up and away! 5.03. 28
courtesy, | which i shall give away immediately. 5.05. 33
thou hast a sigh to blow away this praise, 2H4 1.01. 80
took fire and heat away | from the best–temper'd 1.01.114
away, varlets! 2.01. 46 P
away, you scullion! 2.01. 59 P
away, you whoreson upright /rabbit, away! 2.02. 85 P
away, you whoreson upright /rabbit, away! 2.02. 86 P
away, you rascally althaea's dream, away! 2.02. 87 P
away, you rascally althaea's dream, away! 2.02. 87 P
away, you mouldy rogue, away! 2.04.125 P
away, you mouldy rogue, away! 2.04.125 P
away, you cutpurse rascal! 2.04.128 P
you filthy bung, away! 2.04.129 P
away, you bottle–ale rascal! 2.04.131 P
me, as you did when you ran away by gadshill. 2.04.307 P
you must away to court, sir, presently, | a 2.04.371
good wenches, if i be not sent away post, i will 2.04.378 P
we will have away thy cold, and i will take such 3.02.185 P
she never could away with me. 3.02.201 P
would 'a say, and away again would 'a go, and 3.02.285 P
on, bardolph, lead the men away. 3.02.300 P
like a kind fellow, gavest thyself away gratis, 4.03. 69 P
come away. 4.03.132 P
or else a feast | and takes away the stomach — 4.04.107
but wherefore did he take away the crown? 4.05. 88
cock and pie, sir, you shall not away to–night. 5.01. 1 P
how now, my lord chief justice, whither away? 5.02. 1
away, bardolph! 5.03.122 P
away, bardolph! 5.03.132 P
that i have turn'd away my former self; 5.05. 58
take them away. 5.05. 95
away, you rogue! H5 2.01. 86 P
and went away and it had been any christom child 2.03. 11 P
come, let's away. 2.03. 47
and on to–morrow bid them march away. 3.06.172
and 'twere more honor some were away. 3.07. 75 P
had any apprehension, they would run away. 3.07.136 P
and ugly witch doth limp | so tediously away. 4.pr. 22
fear'd the death, they have borne life away; 4.01.172 P
and your fair show shall suck away their souls, 4.02. 17
come, come away! 4.02. 62
now, soldiers, march away, | and how thou 4.03.132
do not run away. 4.05. 6
have burn'd and carried away all that was in the 4.07. 8 P
turn'd away the fat knight with the great belly 4.07. 47 P
and make them skirr away, as swift as stones 4.07. 61
stand away, captain gower, i will give treason 4.08. 13 P
seen, | heave him away upon your winged thoughts 5.pr. 8
nay, pray you throw none away, the skin is good 5.01. 54 P
arms, | of england's coat one half is cut away. 1H6 1.01. 81
away with these disgraceful wailing robes! 1.01. 86
come, let's away about it. 1.02.149
i'll call for clubs, if you will not away. 1.03. 84
are from their hives and houses driven away. 1.05. 24
dogs, | now, like to whelps, we crying run away. 1.05. 26
away, away, good william de la pole! 2.04. 80
away, away, good william de la pole! 2.04. 80
away, my masters, trouble us no more, | but join 3.01.144
till bones and flesh and sinews fall away, | so 3.01.192
away, captains, let's get us from the walls, 3.02. 71
whither away, sir john falstaff, in such haste? 3.02.104
whither away? 3.02.105
we'll pull his plumes and take away his train, 3.03. 7
and wash away thy country's stained spots. 3.03. 57
given, | like to a trusty squire did run away; 4.01. 23
away! 4.03. 41
blois, poictiers, and tours, are won away, 4.03. 45
let not your private discord keep away | the 4.04. 22
stay, | if the first hour i shrink and run away. 4.05. 31
all these are sav'd if thou wilt fly away. 4.06. 41
take her away, for she hath liv'd too long, | to 5.04. 34
ay, ay; away with her to execution! 5.04. 54
wives, | and our king henry gives away his own, 2H6 1.01.130
then let's make haste away, and look unto the 1.01.208
'tis thine they give away, and not their own. 1.01.221
while all is shar'd and all is borne away, 1.01.228
away from me, and let me hear no more! 1.02. 50
away, base cullions! 1.03. 40
and stol'st away the ladies' hearts of france, 1.03. 52
do not cast away an honest man for a villain's 1.03.202 P
away with them to prison; 1.03.218 P
come, somerset, we'll see thee sent away. 1.03.220 P
away with them, let them be clapp'd up close, 1.04. 50
all, away! 1.04. 54
away! 1.04. 80
whipping, leap me over this stool and run away. 2.01.141 P
follow the knave, and take this drab away. 2.01.153
true; made the lame to leap and fly away. 2.01.158
take away his weapon. 2.03. 95 P
why, yet thy scandal were not wip'd away, | but 2.04. 65
the bud, | and caterpillars eat my leaves away; 3.01. 90
and all to make away my guiltless life. 3.01.167
sirs, take away the duke, and guard him sure. 3.01.188
thus king henry throws away his crutch | before 3.01.189
and as the butcher takes away the calf | and 3.01.210
away, be gone. 3.02. 14
can chase away the first–conceived sound? 3.02. 44
yet do not go away. 3.02. 52
it may be judg'd i made the duke away, | so 3.02. 67
what, dost thou turn away and hide thy face? 3.02. 74
away even now, or i will drag thee hence. 3.02.229
well could i curse away a winter's night, 3.02.335

this place | to wash away my woeful monuments.		3.02.342
away!		3.02.403
o, beat away the busy meddling fiend | that lays		3.03. 21
but with our sword we wip'd away the blot;		4.01. 40
away, convey him hence.		4.01.103
hale him away, and let him talk no more.		4.01.131
away with him!		4.02.107 P
away with him, i say!		4.02.109 P
to nurse, | was by a beggar–woman stol'n away,		4.02.143
herald, away, and throughout every town		4.02.176
thee, | therefore away with us to killingworth.		4.04. 44
then linger not, my lord, away, take horse.		4.04. 54
come, let's away.		4.06. 15 P
away, burn all the records of the realm, my		4.07. 13 P
away with him, away with him! he speaks latin.		4.07. 57 P
away with him, away with him! he speaks latin.		4.07. 57 P
take him away, and behead him.		4.07. 96 P
away with him, he has a familiar under his		4.07.107 P
go, take him away, i say, and strike off his		4.07.109 P
away with him, and do as i command ye.		4.07.118 P
away!		4.07.136 P
and chop away that factious pate of his.		5.01.135
away, my lord! you are slow, for shame, away!		5.02. 72
away, my lord! you are slow, for shame, away!		5.02. 72
away, for your relief!		5.02. 88
away, my lord, away!		5.02. 90
away, my lord, away!		5.02. 90
north, | he slily stole away and left his men;	3H6	1.01. 3
i'll steal away.		1.01.212
come, son, let's away.		1.01.255
come, son, away, we may not linger thus.		1.01.263
chaplain, away, thy priesthood saves thy life.		1.03. 3
soldiers, away with him!		1.03. 7
when he might spurn him with his foot away?		1.04. 58
boy, | and i with tears do wash the blood away.		1.04.158
or whether he be scap'd away or no | from		2.01. 2
shall we go throw away our coats of steel, | and		2.01.160
why then it sorts, brave warriors. let's away.		2.01.209
got, | my careless father fondly gave away"?		2.02. 38
away, away! once more, sweet lords, farewell.		2.03. 48
away, away! once more, sweet lords, farewell.		2.03. 48
my tears shall wipe away these bloody marks;		2.05. 71
away!		2.05.127
away!		2.05.134
i'll away before.		2.05.136
forward, away!		2.05.139
come then, away, let's ha' no more ado.		4.05. 27
drummer, strike up, and let us march away.		4.07. 50
away with scrupulous wit! now arms must rule.		4.07. 61
away betimes, before his forces join, | and take		4.08. 62
i will away towards barnet presently, | and bid		5.01.110
away, away, to meet the queen's great power!		5.02. 50
away, away, to meet the queen's great power!		5.02. 50
and away.		5.03. 24
man, | he should have leave to go away betimes,		5.04. 45
away with oxford to hames castle straight;		5.05. 2
for god's sake, take away this captive scold.		5.05. 29
nay, take away this scolding crook–back, rather.		5.05. 30
away with her, go bear her hence perforce.		5.05. 68
away, i say, i charge ye bear her hence.		5.05. 81
and let's away to london | and see our gentle		5.05. 88
away with her, and waft her hence to france.		5.07. 41
peace, | have no delight to pass away the time,	R3	1.01. 25
ah, gentle villain, do not turn away!		1.03.162
and when i have my meed, i will away, | for this		1.04.282
good morrow, neighbor, whither away so fast?		2.03. 1
whither away?		2.03. 45
but come, my lord, let's away.		3.02. 94
and even here brake off, and came away.		3.07. 41
first, if all obstacles were cut away, | and		3.07.156
as much to you, good sister! whither away?		4.01. 7
tell her thou mad'st away her uncle clarence,		4.04.281
scatter'd, | and he himself wand'red away alone,		4.04.512
away towards salisbury!		4.04.535
i'll undertake may see away their shilling	H8	pr 12
"/oui" away | the lag end of their lewdness and		1.03. 34
you, if these fair ladies | pass away frowning.		1.04. 33
whither away so fast?		2.01. 1
your fortunes, fall away | like water from ye,		2.01.129
sacred person — in god's name | turn me away;		2.04. 42
she's going away.		2.04.124
law o'ertake ye, | you'll part away disgrac'd.		3.01. 97
cardinal campeius | is stol'n away to rome, hath		3.02. 57
cromwell, i charge thee, fling away ambition!		3.02.440
that letter | i caus'd you write yet sent away?		4.02.128
souls with modesty again, | cast none away.		5.02.100
come, lords, we trifle time away;		5.02.212
fan, | puffing at all, winnows the light away,	TRO	1.03. 28
take but degree away, untune that string, | and		1.03.109
away!		3.02.209 P
let us cast away nothing, for we may live to		4.04. 21 P
away, patroclus!		5.01. 47
away, away!		5.03. 88
away, away!		5.03. 88
away, away!	COR	1.01. 12 P
away, away!		1.01. 13 P
away, you fool!		1.03. 39
away!		1.05. 28
their trenches driven, | and then i came away.		1.06. 13
being three parts melted away with rotten dews,		2.03. 32 P
be gone, away!		3.01.229
nay, come away.		3.01.252
he's a disease that must be cut away.		3.01.293
away, my disposition, and possess me | some		3.02.111
away, the tribunes do attend you.		3.02.138
seeking means | to pluck away their power, as		3.03. 96
let him away!		3.03.106
the beast | with many heads butts me away.		4.01. 2
away!		4.05. 14 P
away? get you away.		4.05. 15 P
away? get you away.		4.05. 15 P
come, let's away.		4.07. 56
away!		5.02. 80 P
how? away?		5.02. 81 P
i say to you, as i was said to, "away!"		5.02.108 P
i'll run away till i am bigger, but then i'll		5.03.128
he turns away.		5.03.168
and give away | the benefit of our levies,		5.06. 65
tears | he whin'd and roar'd away your victory,		5.06. 97
away with him, and make a fire straight, | and	TIT	1.01.127
bear his betroth'd from all the world away.		1.01.286
brothers, help to convey her hence away, | and		1.01.287
traitors, away, he rests not in this tomb.		1.01.349
away, and talk not, trouble us no more.		1.01.478
away with slavish weeds and servile thoughts!		2.01. 18
away, i say!		2.01. 60
i will not hear her speak, away with her!		2.03.137
to have his princely paws par'd all away.		2.03.152
i know not what it means, away with her!		2.03.157
therefore away with her, and use her as you will		2.03.166
away, for thou hast stay'd us here too long.		2.03.181
indeed | till all the andronici be made away.		2.03.189
how these were they that made away his brother.		2.03.208
my niece, that flies away so fast?		2.04. 11
ah, now thou turn'st away thy face for shame!		2.04. 28
thou hast no hands to wipe away thy tears, | nor		3.01.106
or shall we cut away our hands like thine?		3.01.130
two may keep counsel when the third's away.		4.02.144
the midwife and the nurse well made away, | then		4.02.167
go take him away and hang him presently.		4.04. 45
march away.		5.01.165
the door | that so my sad decrees may fly away,		5.02. 11
jet, | to hale thy vengeful waggon swift away,		5.02. 51
away, inhuman dog, unhallowed slave!		5.03. 14
they ravish'd her, and cut away her tongue,		5.03. 57
to heal rome's harms, and wipe away her woe!		5.03.148
therefore, if thou art mov'd, thou run'st away.	ROM	1.01. 10 P
for this time all the rest depart away.		1.01. 98
bed, | away from light steals home my heavy son,		1.01.137
come, madam, let's away.		1.01.159
and, being anger'd, puffs away from thence,		1.04.102
where's potpan, that he helps not to take away?		1.05. 2 P
away with the join–stools, remove the		1.05. 6 P
away, be gone, the sport is at the best.		1.05.119
come let's away, the strangers all are gone.		1.05.144
how much salt water thrown away in waste, | to		2.03. 71
say, | "two may keep counsel, putting one away"*		2.04.197
send thy man away.		2.05. 19
alla stoccato carries it away.		3.01. 74
away to heaven, respective lenity, | and		3.01.123
romeo, away, be gone!		3.01.132
hence be gone, away!		3.01.135
hie hence, be gone, away!		3.05. 26
o sweet my mother, cast me not away!		3.05.198
a thing like death to chide away this shame,		4.01. 74
say | a madman's mercy bid thee run away.		5.03. 67
come, come away.		5.03.154
go get thee hence, for i will not away.		5.03.160
on him, | and then i ran away to call the watch.		5.03.285
go not away.	TIM	1.01.154
away, unpeaceable dog, or i'll spurn thee hence!		1.01.270 P
o, joy's e'en made away ere't can be born!		1.02.106 P
thou wilt give away thyself in paper shortly.		1.02.241 P
no, 'tis to thyself. come away.		2.02. 53 P
masters, they approach sadly, and go away merry;		2.02.101 P
my master's house merrily, and go away sadly.		2.02.102 P
he goes away in a cloud;		3.04. 42
to his buried fortunes | slink all away, leave		4.02. 11
take the bridge quite away | of him that, his		4.03.158
get thee away, and take | thy beagles with thee.		4.03.174
were i like thee, i'd throw away myself.		4.03.219
thou hast cast away thyself, being like thyself,		4.03.220
first mend /my company, take away thyself.		4.03.283
away, thou issue of a mangy dog!		4.03.366
away, thou tedious rogue!		4.03.369
love not yourselves, away, | rob one another.		4.03.444
away! what art thou?		4.03.472
which | with wax i brought away, whose soft		5.04. 68
and drive away the vulgar from the streets;	JC	1.01. 70
and after that, he came thus sad away?		1.02.276
ay, every man away.		3.01.119
and as he pluck'd his cursed steel away, | mark		3.02.177
i come not, friends, to steal away your hearts.		3.02.216
away then, come, seek the conspirators.		3.02.232
come, away, away!		3.02.253
come, away, away!		3.02.253
away, go!		3.03. 38 P
bid them move away;		4.02. 45
away, slight man!		4.03. 37
away, away, be gone!		4.03.138
away, away, be gone!		4.03.138
away!		5.01. 63
this morning are they fled away and gone, | and		5.01. 83
come ho, away!		5.01.125
hold then my sword, and turn away thy face,		5.05. 47
so call the field to rest, and let's away, | to		5.05. 80
to throw away the dearest thing he ow'd, | as	MAC	1.04. 10
away, and mock the time with fairest show:		1.07. 81
the desire, but it takes away the performance.		2.03. 30 P
let's away, | our tears are not yet brew'd.		2.03.123
not be dainty of leave–taking, | but shift away.		2.03.145
are stol'n away and fled, which puts upon them		2.04. 26
well, let's away, and say how much is done.		3.03. 22
run away, i pray you!		4.02. 85
were i from dunsinane away and clear, | profit		5.03. 61
see, it stalks away!	HAM	1.01. 50
come away.		1.02.128
and at the sound it shrunk in haste away | and		1.02.219
it beckons you to go away with it, | as if it		1.04. 58
i say, away!		1.04. 86
my days of nature | are burnt and purg'd away.		1.05. 13
i'll wipe away all trivial fond records, | all		1.05. 99
away, i do beseech you, both away.		2.02.169
away, i do beseech you, both away.		2.02.169
gods, | in general synod take away her power!		2.02.494
give me some light. away!		3.02.269 P
some must sleep, | thus runs the world away.		3.02.274
look how it steals away!		3.04.134
o, throw away the worser part of it, | and /live		3.04.157
o gertrude, come away!		4.01. 28
o, come away!		4.01. 44
even, | this sudden sending him away must seem		4.03. 8
away!		4.03. 56
he is gone, he is gone, | and we cast away moan,		4.05.198
lie, sir, 'twill away again from me to you.		5.01.128 P
clay, | might stop a hole to keep the wind away.		5.01.214
this lapwing runs away with the shell on his		5.02.185 P
if hamlet from himself be ta'en away, | and when		5.02.234
been out nine years, and away he shall again.	LR	1.01. 32 P
away!		1.01.178
upon, | be it lawful i take up what's cast away.		1.01.253
pray you away.		1.02.176 P
into france, sir, the fool hath much pin'd away.		1.04. 74 P
come, sir, arise, away!		1.04. 89 P
away, away!		1.04. 90 P
away, away!		1.04. 90 P
but away!		1.04. 91 P
/crown i' th' middle and gav'st away both parts,		1.04.161 P
bald crown when thou gav'st thy golden one away.		1.04.163 P
and put away | these dispositions which of late		1.04.220
away, away!		1.04.289
away, away!		1.04.289
let me still take away the harms i fear, | not		1.04.329
take you some company, and away to horse.		1.04.336
head in, not to give it away to his daughters,		1.05. 30 P
away, i have nothing to do with thee.		2.02. 34 P
come, bring away the stocks!		2.02.139
come, my /good lord, away.		2.02.151
the knave turns fool that runs away, | the fool		2.04. 84
away, the foul fiend follows me!		3.04. 46 P
come, come, away.		3.06.101
away, get thee away!		4.01. 15
away, get thee away!		4.01. 15
/then, /prithee, get thee away.		4.01. 41
away, and let me die.		4.06. 48
away, old man, give me thy hand, away!		5.02. 5
away, old man, give me thy hand, away!		5.02. 5
some officers take them away.		5.03. 1
come let's away to prison:		5.03. 8
take them away.		5.03. 19
prithee away.		5.03.269
bring him away;	OTH	1.02. 94
that i have ta'en away this old man's daughter,		1.03. 78
not only take away, but let your sentence | even		1.03.119
you must away to–night.		1.03.277
away, i say;		2.03.157
come away to bed.		2.03.253
in their mouths to steal away their brains!		2.03.291 P
away, i say, thou shalt know more hereafter.		2.03.381
put up your pipes in your bag, for i'll away.		3.01. 20 P
go, vanish into air, away!		3.01. 20 P
shall rather die | than give thy cause away.		3.03. 28
it,| that he would steal away so guilty–like,		3.03. 39
this — | away at once with love or jealousy!		3.03.192
/faith, that's with watching, 'twill away again.		3.03.285
for 'twas that hand that gave away my heart.		3.04. 45
to lose't or give't away were such perdition		3.04. 67
keep a week away?		3.04.173
i shifted him away, | and laid good 'scuses upon		4.01. 78
get you away;		4.01.258
ah, desdemon! away, away, away!		4.02. 41
ah, desdemon! away, away, away!		4.02. 41
ah, desdemon! away, away, away!		4.02. 41
mauritania and taketh away with him the fair		4.02.225 P
of them is hereabout, | and cannot make away.		5.01. 58
come, bring away.		5.02.337
threw a pearl away | richer than all his tribe;		5.02.347
it were pity to cast them away for nothing,	ANT	1.02.138 P
help me away, dear charmian, i shall fall.		1.03. 15
away!		1.03.105
out this great gap of time | my antony is away.		1.05. 6
but come, away, | get me ink and paper.		1.05. 75
pompey doth this day laugh away his fortune.		2.06.104 P
come, let's away.		2.06.136 P
away!		2.07. 53
too high a fame when him we serve's away.		3.01. 15
sir, you therein throw away | the absolute		3.07. 41
we'll to our ship, | away, my thetis!		3.07. 60
well, well, away!		3.07. 66
we have kiss'd away | kingdoms and provinces.		3.10. 7
tug him away.		3.13.102
i turn you not away, but, like a master		4.02. 30
the rest | that fell away have entertainment,		4.06. 16
come, away, | this case of that huge spirit now		4.15. 88
away!	CYM	1.01.127
away with her, | and pen her up.		1.01.152
lawful counsel, and straight away for britain,		1.04.166 P
away, i do condemn mine ears that have | so long		1.06.141
but not away to–morrow!		1.06.204
kiss'd the jack upon an up–cast, to be hit away!		2.01. 2 P
take not away the taper, leave it burning;		2.02. 5
away, i prithee, | do as i bid thee.		3.02. 80
shall we discourse | the freezing hours away?		3.03. 39
let thine own hands take away her life.		3.04. 27 P
away, away, | corrupters of my faith!		3.04. 82
away, away, | corrupters of my faith!		3.04. 82
prithee away, | there's more to be consider'd;		3.04.180
away, i prithee.		3.04.184
a dram of this | will drive away distemper.		3.04.191
we'll not be long away.		4.02. 44
it is great morning. come away! — who's there?		4.02. 61
pray you away, | let me alone with him.		4.02. 69
come on, away, apart upon our knees.		4.02.288
away!		4.03. 35
away, boy, from the troops, and save thyself;		5.02. 14
his full fortune doth confine, | and so away!		5.04.111
away, and, to be blest, | let us with care		5.04.121
away to britain | post i in this design.		5.05.191
away he posts | with unchaste purpose, and with		5.05.283
or private treason | will take away your life.	PER	1.02.105
ha, come and bring away the nets!		2.01. 13 P
come away, or i'll fetch th' with a wanton.		2.01. 16 P
poor men that were cast away before us even now.		2.01. 19 P
goodly gifts | and snatch them straight away?		3.01. 24
away!		4.06.120
we'll have no more gentlemen driven away.		4.06.129 P
and she sent him away as cold as a snowball,		4.06.139 P
boult, take her away, use her at thy pleasure.		4.06.141 P
she conjures, away with her!		4.06.147 P
urns and odors bring away, | vapors, sighs,	TNK	1.05. 1
away, boys, and hold!		2.03. 59
had i a sword, | and these house–clogs away —		3.01. 43
fool, | away with this strain'd mirth!		3.03. 43
it was a hawk, | and her bells were cut away."		3.05. 71

away, boys! 3.05. 92
am i fall'n much away? 3.06. 66
when presently | she slipp'd away, and to the 4.01. 97
she stay'd, | and fell, scarce to be got away. 4.01.102
say, began to throw | her bow away, and sigh. 5.01. 94
nev'r cast your child away for honesty. 5.02. 21
i'll away straight. 5.02.101
that cuts away | a life more worthy from him 5.03.142
the time is spent, her object will away, | and VEN 255
away he springs, and hasteth to his horse. 258
"so in thyself thyself art made away, | a 763
green, | therefore, in sadness, now i will away; 807
as falcons to the lure, away she flies, | the 1027
my sighs are blown away, my salt tears gone, 1071
thus weary of the world, away she hies, | and 1189
retire, | beaten away by brain–sick rude desire. LUC 175
lay, | then white as lawn, the roses took away. 259
away he steals with open list'ning ear, | full 283
thing | from vassal actors can be wip'd away; 608
bearing away the wound that nothing healeth, 731
mire | and unperceiv'd fly with the filth away, 1010
poor helpless help, the treasure stol'n away, 1056
so must my soul, her bark being pill'd away. 1169
of day, | and ere i rose was tarquin gone away. 1281
blow | the grief away that stops his answer so; 1664
while with a joyless smile she turns away | the 1711
"do not take away | my sorrow's interest, let no 1796
he rose and ran away, ah, fool too froward! PP 4.14
and as she fetched breath, away he skips, | and 11.11
to kiss and clip me till i run away! 11.14
she bade good night that kept my rest away, 14. 2
ditty, | and drives away dark dreaming night. 14.20
by a gift of learning did bear the maid away: 15.14
it be day, | that which with scorn she put away. 18.30
and threescore year would make the world away. SON 11. 8
to give away yourself keeps yourself still, 16.13
love, | thyself away are present still with me, 47.10
stealing away the treasure of his spring; 63. 8
that time will come and take my love away. 64.12
the right of sepulchres, were shorn away, | to 68. 6
which by and by black night doth take away, 73. 7
arrest | without all bail shall carry me away, 74. 2
day by day, | or gluttoning on all, or all away. 75.14
then if he thrive and i be cast away, | the 80.13
that thou mayst take | all this away, and me 91.14
but do thy worst to steal thyself away, | for 92. 1
how many gazers mightst thou lead away, | if 96.11
thee, | and, thou away, the very birds are mute; 97.12
yet seem'd it winter still, and, you away, | as 98.13
one of her feathered creatures broke away, 143. 2
a fiend | from heaven to hell is flown away: 145.12
"i hate" from hate away she threw, | and sav'd 145.13

AW'D 2 FR 0.0002 REL FR 2 V 0 P
thee, | since thou, created to be aw'd by man, R2 5.05. 91
pure shame and aw'd resistance made him fret, VEN 69

AWE 20 FR 0.0022 REL FR 18 V 2 P
i will awe him with my cudgel; WIV 2.02.279 P
wrench awe from fools and tie the wiser souls MM 2.04. 14
bullets of the brain awe a man from the career ADO 2.03.241 P
power, | the attribute to awe and majesty, MV 4.01.191
son, | now by /my sceptre's awe i make a vow, R2 1.01.118
is | that doth with awe and terror kneel to it! 2H4 4.05.176
france being ours, we'll bend it to our awe, H5 1.02.224
and form, | creating awe and fear in other men? 4.01.247
thy wife is proud, she holdeth thee in awe, 1H6 1.01. 39
how france and frenchmen might be kept in awe, 2H6 1.01. 92
devis'd at first to keep the strong in awe: R3 5.03.310
(under the gods) keep you in awe, which else COR 1.01.187
domestic awe, night–rest, and neighborhood, TIM 4.01. 17
live to be | in awe of such a thing as i myself. JC 1.02. 96
and that same eye whose bend doth awe the world 1.02.123
shall rome stand under one man's awe? 2.01. 52
sword, and thy free awe | pays homage to us — HAM 4.03. 61
o, that that earth which kept the world in awe 5.01.215
made a law, | to keep her still and men in awe, PER 1.ch. 36
saw | shall by a painted cloth be kept in awe." LUC 245

A–WEARY 9 FR 0.0010 REL FR 5 V 4 P
i am a–weary of this moon. MND 5.01.251 P
my little body is a–weary of this great world. MV 1.02. 2 P
come to do that for me which i am a–weary of. AWW 1.03. 43 P
go thy ways, i begin to be a–weary of thee, and 4.05. 56 P
not an eye | but is a–weary of thy common sight, 1H4 3.02. 88
are you a–weary of me? TRO 4.02. 7
i am a–weary, give me leave a while. ROM 2.05. 25
cassius, | for cassius is a–weary of the world; JC 4.03. 95
i gin to be a–weary of the sun, | and wish th' MAC 5.05. 48

A–WEEPING 1 FR 0.0001 REL FR 0 V 1 P
thou't set me a–weeping and thou say'st so. 2H4 2.04.278 P

AWEFUL 8 FR 0.0009 REL FR 8 V 0 P
youth | thrust from the company of aweful men. TGV 4.01. 44
life, | an aweful rule, and right supremacy; SHR 5.02.109
to pay their aweful duty to our presence? R2 3.03. 76
we come within our aweful banks again, | and 2H4 4.01.174
to pluck down justice from your aweful bench? 5.02. 86
and not to grace an aweful princely sceptre. 2H6 5.01. 98
and wring the aweful sceptre from his fist, 3H6 2.01.154
that will prove aweful both in deed and word. PER 2.ch. 4

AWELESS 2 FR 0.0002 REL FR 2 V 0 P
the aweless lion could not wage the fight, | nor JN 1.01.266
to jut | upon the innocent and aweless throne. R3 2.04. 52

AWFUL *(see aweful)*

/AWHILE 1 FR 0.0001 REL FR 1 V 0 P
/will /in /concealment /wrap /me /up /awhile; LR 4.03. 52

AWHILE 40 FR 0.0045 REL FR 36 V 4 P
stray, | and if the shepherd be awhile away. TGV 1.01. 75
my lord, he lent it me awhile, and i gave him ADO 2.01.278 P
pause awhile, | and let my counsel sway you in 4.01.200
for dead, | let her awhile be secretly kept in, 4.01.203
good, very good, let it be conceal'd awhile. AWW 2.03.266 P
stand you awhile aloof. TN 1.04. 12
soft, swain, awhile, beseech you. WT 4.04.391
be friends awhile, and both conjointly bend JN 2.01.379
vouchsafe awhile to stay, | and i shall show you 2.01.416
let them alone awhile, and then open the door. 1H4 2.04. 84 P
then, york, be still awhile, till time do serve. 2H6 1.01.248
and spite of spite needs must i rest awhile. 3H6 2.03. 5
forbear awhile, we'll hear a little more. 3.01. 27
now for awhile farewell, good duke of york. 4.03. 57
whilst i awhile obsequiously lament | th' R3 1.02. 3
keeper, i prithee sit by me awhile. 1.04. 73
o thou well skill'd in curses, stay awhile, 4.04.116
patience awhile, you'st hear the belly's answer. COR 1.01.126
feast your ears with the music awhile, if they TIM 3.06. 34 P
yet stay awhile, | thou shalt not back till i JC 3.01.290
will you stay awhile? 3.02.149
canst thou hold up thy heavy eyes awhile, | and 4.03.256
good madam, stay awhile. HAM 2.02.115
and, mermaid–like, awhile they bore her up, 4.07.176
but soft, but soft awhile! 5.01.217
now, good my lord, lie here and rest awhile. LR 3.06. 82
the gods defend her! bear him hence awhile. 5.03.257
yet, if you please to /hold him off awhile, OTH 3.03.248
you must awhile be patient. 3.04.129
patience awhile, good cassio. 5.01. 87
fare thee well awhile. ANT 1.02.111
of time commands | our services awhile; 1.03. 43
from me awhile. 4.14. 43
only | i here importune death awhile, until | of 4.15. 19
pray walk awhile. CYM 1.01.176
has | will stupefy and dull the sense awhile, 1.05. 37
be pleas'd awhile: 5.05.356
feast here awhile, | until our stars that frown PER 1.04.107
yet pause awhile, | yon knight doth sit too 2.03. 53
i must awhile bereave you | of your fair TNK 2.02.223

/AWKWARD 1 FR 0.0001 REL FR 1 V 0 P
and with ridiculous and /awkward action, | which TRO 1.03.149

AWKWARD 3 FR 0.0003 REL FR 3 V 0 P
know | 'tis no sinister nor no awkward claim, H5 2.04. 85
and twice by awkward wind from england's bank 2H6 3.02. 83
and to the world and awkward casualties | bound PER 5.01. 93

AWL 1 FR 0.0001 REL FR 0 V 1 P
truly, sir, all that i live by is with the awl: JC 1.01. 21 P

A–WOOING 2 FR 0.0002 REL FR 1 V 1 P
and that lucentio that comes a–wooing, "priami," SHR 3.01. 34 P
that came a–wooing with you, and so many a time, OTH 3.03. 71

A–WORK 5 FR 0.0005 REL FR 2 V 3 P
nothing without sack (for that sets it a–work) 2H4 4.03.114 P
how earnestly are you set a–work, and how ill TRO 5.10. 38 P
pause, | a roused vengeance sets him new a–work, HAM 2.02.488
set a–work by a reprovable badness in himself. LR 3.05. 7 P
so lucrece, set a–work, sad tales doth tell | to LUC 1496

/AWRY 1 FR 0.0001 REL FR 1 V 0 P
your crown's /awry, | i'll mend it, and then ANT 5.02.318

AWRY 6 FR 0.0006 REL FR 6 V 0 P
you pluck my foot awry. SHR 4.01.147
ey'd awry | distinguish form; R2 2.02. 19
looking awry upon your lord's departure, | find 2.02. 21
thou aimest all awry. 2H6 2.04. 58
merely awry. COR 3.01.303
with this regard their currents turn awry, | and HAM 3.01. 86

AXE 20 FR 0.0022 REL FR 18 V 2 P
provide your block and your axe to–morrow, four MM 4.02. 52 P
is the axe upon the block, sirrah? 4.03. 37 P
can, | no, not the hangman's axe, bear half the MV 4.01.125
falls not the axe upon the humbled neck | but AYL 3.05. 5
faded, | by envy's hand and murder's bloody axe. R2 1.02. 21
nothing, till the axe of death | hang over thee, 2H6 2.04. 49
fresh, | and sees fast by a butcher with an axe, 3.02.189
and many strokes, though with a little axe, 3H6 2.01. 54
increase, | we set the axe to thy usurping root; 2.02.165
myself, | or hew my way out with a bloody axe. 3.02.181
even as the axe falls, if i be not faithful! H8 2.01. 61
out of holy pity, | absolv'd him with an axe. 3.02.264
then i'll go fetch an axe. TIT 3.01.184
but i will use the axe. 3.01.185
thou cut'st my head off with a golden axe, | and ROM 3.03. 22
come hither, ere my tree hath felt the axe, TIM 5.01.211
where th' offense is, let the great axe fall. HAM 4.05.219
no, not to stay the grinding of the axe, | my 5.02. 24
i have ground the axe myself, | do but you PER 1.02. 58
he wears a well–steel'd axe, the staff of gold. TNK 4.02.115

AXE'S 1 FR 0.0001 REL FR 1 V 0 P
thus yields the cedar to the axe's edge, | whose 3H6 5.02. 11

AXLE–TREE 2 FR 0.0002 REL FR 2 V 0 P
turn'd, | or a dry wheel grate on the axle–tree, 1H4 3.01.130
strong as the axle–tree | on which heaven rides, TRO 1.03. 66

/AY* 9 FR 0.0010 REL FR 7 V 2 P
/ay, /no, /no /ay; R2 4.01.201
/ay, /no, /no /ay; 4.01.201
/ay, /but /my /deeds /shall /stay /thy /fury 2H6 4.01.113
/ay, /what's /a' /clock? R3 4.02.109
/ay, /that /they /do, /my /lord — /hercules HAM 2.02.361 P
/ay, /my /lord. 3.02.115 P
(as this i would, /ay, though thou didst produce LR 2.01. 71
/ay, /sir, /she /took /them, /read /them /in /my 4.03. 11
water–pots, | /ay, /and /laying /autumn's /dust. 4.06.197

AY* 785 FR 0.0887 REL FR 517 V 268 P
ay, sir. TMP 1.02.268
ay, and a subtle, as he most learnedly deliver'd 2.01. 45 P
ay, or very falsely pocket up his report. 2.01. 68 P
ay. 2.01. 95 P
o, widow dido? ay, widow dido. 2.01.102 P
ay, sir; 2.01.276
ay, with a heart as willing | as bondage e'er of 3.01. 88
ay, lord, she will become thy bed, i warrant, 3.02.104
ay, on mine honor. 3.02.114
ay, with a twink. 4.01. 43
ay, my commander. 4.01.167
ay, but to lose our bottles in the pool — 4.01.208 P
ay, and this. 4.01.254 P
ay, that i will; 5.01.295
ay, sir; TGV 1.01. 96 P
ay. 1.01.111 P
and you ask me if she did nod, and i say, "ay." 1.01.114 P
ay, madam, so you stumble not unheedfully. 1.02. 3
ay — if you thought your love not cast away. 1.02. 26
they would have the profferer construe "ay." 1.02. 56
ay; and melodious were it, would you sing it. 1.02. 83
ay, madam, you may say what sights you see; 1.02.135
ay, give it me, it's mine: 2.01. 3
ay, ay; 2.01.126
ay, ay; 2.01.126
ay, but hearken, sir; 2.01.172 P
ay, so true love should do: 2.02. 17
ay, so, so. 2.03. 23 P
ay, boy, it's for love. 2.04. 4 P
ay, sir, and done too — for this time. 2.04. 30 P
ay, my good lord, i know the gentleman | to be 2.04. 55
ay, my good lord, a son that well deserves | the 2.04. 59
ay, proteus, but that life is alter'd now: 2.04.128
ay, and we are betroth'd: 2.04.179
ay, and what i do too. 2.05. 29 P
if he say ay, it will; 2.05. 35 P
ay, but the doors be lock'd and the keys kept 3.01.111
ay, my good lord. 3.01.132
ay, ay; 3.01.224
ay, ay; 3.01.224
ay, that she can. 3.01.302 P
ay, who art thou? 3.01.375 P
ay, and perversely she persevers so. 3.02. 28
ay, but she'll think that it is spoke in hate. 3.02. 34
ay, if his enemy deliver it; 3.02. 35
ay, much is the force of heaven–bred poesy. 3.02. 71
ay, by my beard, will we, for he is a proper man 4.01. 10
say "ay" and be the captain of us all: 4.01. 63
ay, gentle thurio, for you know that love | will 4.02. 19
ay, but i hope, sir, that you love not here. 4.02. 21
ay, silvia — for your sake. 4.02. 23
ay, that you shall. 4.02. 34 P
ay; but peace, let's hear 'em. 4.02. 38 P
ay, i would i were deaf; 4.02. 64 P
ay; that change is the spite. 4.02. 69 P
"ay, marry, do i," quoth he. 4.04. 26 P
ay, sir, the other squirrel was stol'n from me 4.04. 55 P
ay, madam. 4.04.116
ay, but her forehead's low, and mine's as high. 4.04.193
o, ay; and pities them. 5.02. 26
ay, cousin slender, and custa–lorum. WIV 1.01. 7 P
ay, and rato–lorum too; 1.01. 8 P
ay, that i do, and have done any time these 1.01. 12 P
ay, and her father is make her a petter penny. 1.01. 60 P
ay, it is no matter. 1.01.129 P
ay, it is no matter. 1.01.131 P
ay, by these gloves, did he, or i would i might 1.01.153 P
ay, you spake in latin then too: 1.01.180 P
ay, sir, you shall find me reasonable. 1.01.210 P
ay, there's the point, sir. 1.01.222 P
ay — i think my cousin meant well. 1.01.257 P
ay, or else i would i might be hang'd, la! 1.01.258 P
ay indeed, sir. 1.01.293 P
ay, for fault of a better. 1.04. 17 P
ay, forsooth. 1.04. 19 P
ay, forsooth; 1.04. 25 P
ay, forsooth, i'll fetch it you. 1.04. 48 P
ay me, he'll find the young man there, and be 1.04. 65 P
ay, forsooth; to desire her to — 1.04. 79 P
ay, forsooth; 2.01.164 P
ay, marry, does he. 2.01.181 P
ay, forsooth; 2.02. 86 P
ay, sir. 2.02.149 P
ay, dat is very good, excellant. 3.01. 99 P
ay, and as idle as she may hang together, for 3.02. 13 P
ay, be–gar, and de maid is love–a me. 3.02. 64 P
ay, i'll be sworn. 3.03. 29 P
ay, buck! 3.03.158 P
ay, i do so. 3.03.203 P
ay, ay; i must bear it. 3.03.209 P
ay, ay; i must bear it. 3.03.209 P
ay, that i do — as well as i love any woman in 3.04. 43 P
ay, that i will, come cut and long–tail, under 3.04. 46 P
ay. 4.01. 60 P
ay, in good sadness, is he, and talks of the 4.02. 91 P
ay, but if it prove true, master page, have you 4.02.114 P
ay, sir; i'll call /them to you. 4.03. 7 P
ay, marry, was it, mussel–shell, what would you 4.05. 28 P
ay; come; quick. 4.05. 43 P
ay, sir; like who more bold? 4.05. 54 P
ay, that there was, mine host, one that hath 4.05. 59 P
ay, forsooth, i have spoke with her, and we have 5.02. 4 P
ay, and an ox too; both the proofs are extant. 5.05.120 P
ay, be–gar, and 'tis a boy. 5.05.209 P
ay, that he raz'd. MM 1.02. 11 P
ay, why not? 1.02. 24 P
ay, and more. 1.02. 51 P
ay, but yet | let us be keen, and rather cut a 2.01. 4
ay, sir; whom i thank heaven is an honest woman. 2.01. 72 P
ay, sir, by mistress overdone's means; 2.01. 83 P
ay, so i did indeed. 2.01.108 P
ay, sir, very well. 2.01.150 P
ay, my good lord, a very virtuous maid, | and to 2.02. 20
ay, touch him; there's the vein. 2.02. 70
ay, well said. 2.02. 89
ay, with such gifts that heaven shall share with 2.02.147
ay, as the glasses where they view themselves, 2.04.125
ay, just, perpetual durance — a restraint, 3.01. 67
ay, but to die, and go we know not where; 3.01.117
ay, sir, a mystery. 4.02. 35 P
ay, with my heart, | and punish them to your 5.01.239
ay, ay, he told his mind upon mine ear. ERR 2.01. 48
ay, ay, he told his mind upon mine ear. 2.01. 48
ay, sir, and wherefore; 2.02. 43 P
ay, ay, antipholus, look strange and frown, 2.02.110
ay, ay, antipholus, look strange and frown, 2.02.110
ay, and let none enter, lest i break your pate. 2.02.218
ay, to a niggardly host and more sparing guest: 3.01. 27
ay, and break it in your face, so he break it 3.01. 76
ay, when fowls have no feathers, and fish have 3.01. 79
ay, such a one as a man may not speak of without 3.02. 90 P
ay, that's my name. 3.02.165
ay, sir, the sergeant of the band: 4.03. 30 P
ay me, poor man, how pale and wan he looks! 4.04.108
ay, but not rough enough. 5.01. 58
ay, but not enough. 5.01. 61
ay me, it is my husband! 5.01.186
ay, sir, but i am sure i do not — and 5.01.305 P
o, ay, stalk on, stalk on, the fowl sits. ADO 2.03. 92 P
ay, that is study's godlike recompense. LLL 1.01. 58
ay, that there is. 1.01.162
ay, the best for the worst. 1.01.281 P
my physic says ay. 2.01.188
ay, our way to be gone. 2.01.258

a fat l'envoy — ay, that's a fat goose. 3.01.104
ay, and, by heaven, one that will do the deed 3.01.198
ay, my continent of beauty. 4.01.109
ay, sir, and very learned. 4.02.103 P
ay, sir, from one monsieur berowne, one of the 4.02.129 P
ay me! 4.03. 21
ay me, i am forsworn! 4.03. 45
ay, as some days, but then no sun must shine. 4.03. 89
"ay me!" 4.03.139
ay marry, there — some flattery for this evil. 4.03.282
ay, and a shrowd unhappy gallows too. 5.02. 12
ay, or i would these hands might never part. 5.02. 57
ay, in truth, my lord; 5.02.362
ay, and in a brooch of lead. 5.02.617 P
ay, and worn in the cap of a tooth–drawer. 5.02.618 P
ay, and hector's a greyhound. 5.02.659 P
ay, if 'a have no more man's blood in his belly 5.02.691 P
ay, sweet my lord, and so i take my leave. 5.02.872
ay me! MND 1.01.132
ay, in the temple, in the town, the field, | you 2.01.238
ay, there it is. 2.01.248
ay me, for pity! 2.02.147
ay; 3.01. 59 P
ay, marry, must you; 3.01. 90 P
ay, do! 3.02.237
ay, by my life; 3.02.277
ay, that way goes the game. 3.02.289
ay, that left pap, | where heart doth hop. 5.01.298
ay, and wall too. 5.01.350 P
ay, that's a colt indeed, for he doth nothing MV 1.02. 40 P
ay, sir, for three months. 1.03. 2 P
ay, ay, three thousand ducats. 1.03. 65
ay, ay, three thousand ducats. 1.03. 65
ay, he was the third — 1.03. 74
ay, marry, i'll be gone about it straight. 2.04. 24
ay, but i fear you speak upon the rack, | where 3.02. 32
ay, so he says. 4.01.181
ay, his breast, | so says the bond, doth it not, 4.01.252
i would lose all, ay, sacrifice them all | here 4.01.286
ay, for the state, not for antonio. 4.01.373
ay, if a woman live to be a man. 5.01.160
ay, but the clerk that never means to do it, 5.01.282
ay, and i'll give them him without a fee. 5.01.290
ay, better than him i am before knows me. AYL 1.01. 43 P
ay, marry, now unmuzzle your wisdom. 1.02. 70 P
ay, my liege, so please you give us leave. 1.02.157 P
ay. fare you well, fair gentleman. 1.02.248
ay, celia, we stay'd her for your sake, | else 1.03. 67
"ay," quoth jaques, | "sweep on, you fat and 2.01. 54
ay, now am i in arden, the more fool i. 2.04. 16 P
ay, be so, good touchstone. 2.04. 19 P
ay, but the feet were lame and could not bear 3.02.169 P
to say ay and no to these particulars is more 3.02.227 P
ay, of a snail; 4.01. 54 P
ay, and twenty such. 4.01.119 P
ay, but when? 4.01.133 P
ay, go your ways, go your ways; 4.01.182 P
ay, sweet rosalind. 4.01.187 P
ay, i know who 'tis; 5.01. 8 P
ay, sir, i thank god. 5.01. 24 P
ay, sir, i have a pretty wit. 5.01. 29 P
ay, and greater wonders than that. 5.02. 28 P
ay, fleeter than the roe. SHR in.2. 48
ay, the woman's maid of the house. in.2. 90
ay, and the time seems thirty unto me, | being in.2. 114
ay, it stands so that i may hardly tarry so long in.2. 125 P
ay, marry, am i, sir; and now 'tis plotted. 1.01.188
ay, sir! — ne'er a whit. 1.01.235
will he woo her? ay — or i'll hang her. 1.02.197
ay, when the special thing is well obtain'd, 2.01.128
ay, to the proof, as mountains are for winds, 2.01.140
ay, for a turtle, as he takes a buzzard. 2.01.208
ay, if the fool could find it where it lies. 2.01.212
ay, that petruchio came. 3.02. 78 P
"ay, by gogs–wouns," quoth he, and swore so loud 3.02.160
ay, sir, they be ready; 3.02.205 P
ay, marry, sir, now it begins to work. 3.02.218
o, ay, curtis, ay, and therefore fire, fire; 4.01. 19 P
o, ay, curtis, ay, and therefore fire, fire; 4.01. 19 P
ay, and that thou and the proudest of you all 4.01. 87 P
ay. 4.01.160
ay, and amid this hurly i intend | that all is 4.01.203
ay, and he'll tame her. 4.02. 53
ay, mistress, and petruchio is the master, 4.02. 56
ay, sir, in pisa have i often been, | pisa 4.02. 94
ay, but the mustard is too hot a little. 4.03. 25
why, ay. 4.03. 86
ay, there's the villainy. 4.03.144 P
ay, what else? 4.04. 2
ay, sir, so his mother says, if i may believe 5.01. 33 P
ay, mistress bride, hath that awakened you? 5.02. 42
ay, but not frighted me, therefore i'll sleep 5.02. 43
ay, and a kind one too. 5.02. 83
ay. AWW 1.01.111 P
ay, madam, knowingly. 1.03.250
ay, my good lord. 2.01.100
ay, by my sceptre and my hopes of /heaven. 2.01.192
ay, so i say. 2.03. 32 P
ay; is it not a language i speak? 2.03.189 P
ay, with all my heart, and thou art worthy of it 2.03.218 P
ay, sir. 2.03.248 P
ay, that would be known. 2.03.278
ay, madam, | and for the contents' sake are 3.02. 62
ay, madam. 3.02. 69
ay, madam, with the swiftest wing of speed. 3.02. 73
ay, madam. 3.02. 76
ay, my good lady, he. 3.02. 86
ay, marry, is't. 3.05. 38
ay, surely, mere the truth, i know his lady. 3.05. 55
ay, so you serve us | till we serve you; 4.02. 17
ay, and the particular confirmations, point from 4.03. 61 P
ay, and the captain of his horse, count 4.03.294 P
ay, my lord. 5.03.233
ay, my good lord. 5.03.270
ay, madam, well, for i was bred and born | not TN 1.02. 22
ay, but you must confine yourself within the 1.03. 8 P
ay, he. 1.03. 19 P
ay, but he'll have but a year in all these 1.03. 23 P
ay, sir, i have them at my fingers' ends. 1.03. 78 P
ay, 'tis strong; 1.03.134 P
ay, marry, what is he? 1.05.127 P
ay, ay. i care not for good life. 2.03. 38 P
ay, ay. i care not for good life. 2.03. 38 P
ay, he does well enough if he be dispos'd, and 2.03. 81 P
ay, prithee sing. 2.04. 50
ay, but i know — 2.04.103
ay, that's the theme, | to her in haste. 2.04.122
o ay, make up that. he is now at a cold scent. 2.05.121 P
ay, or i'll cudgel him, and make him cry o! 2.05.133 P
ay, and you had any eye behind you, you might 2.05.136 P
to bed? ay, sweet heart, and i'll come to thee. 3.04. 30 P
ay, biddy, come with me. 3.04.115 P
ay, is't! i warrant him. do but read. 3.04.146 P
ay, but he will not now be pacified. 3.04.281 P
ay, good fool. 4.02. 85 P
ay, sir, we are some of her trappings. 5.01. 9 P
ay me, detested! how am i beguil'd! 5.01.139
ay, husband. can he that deny? 5.01.144
ay, madam. 5.01.313 P
ay, my lord, this same. | how now, malvolio? 5.01.327
ay, my good lord. WT 1.02.120
ay, my good lord. 1.02.210
ay, but why? 1.02.231
ay, and thou, | his cupbearer — whom i from 1.02.312
ay, and privy | to this their late escape. 2.01. 94
ay, every dram of woman's flesh is false, | if 2.01.138
ay, my lord, even so | as it is here set down. 3.02.138
ay, my lord, and fear | we have landed in ill 3.03. 2
ay, good brother, or go about to think. 4.04.217 P
ay, sir. 4.04.811 P
ay; 5.01. 94
ay, and have been so any time these four hours. 5.02.136 P
ay; 5.02.147 P
ay, and it like your good worship. 5.02.155 P
ay, by any means prove a tall fellow. 5.02.170 P
ay, and make it manifest where she has liv'd, 5.03.114
ay, thou unreverend boy, | sir robert's son! JN 1.01.227
ay, my mother, | with all my heart i thank thee 1.01.269
ay, with these crystal beads heaven shall be 2.01.171
ay, who doubts that? 2.01.193
ay, alack, how new | is "husband" in my mouth! 3.01.305
if you say ay, the king will not say no. 3.04.183
ay me, this tyrant fever burns me up, | and will 5.03. 14
ay, marry, now my soul hath elbow–room; 5.07. 28
ay, all of them at bristow lost their heads. R2 3.02.142
you make a leg, and bullingbrook says ay. 3.03.175
ay, hand from hand, my love, and heart from 5.01. 82
ay, when, canst tell? 1H4 2.01. 39 P
ay, ay, he said four. 2.04.199 P
ay, ay, he said four. 2.04.199 P
ay, four, in buckrom suits. 2.04.205 P
ay, and mark thee too, jack. 2.04.210 P
ay, by my faith, that bears a frosty sound. 4.01.128
ay, but, sir john, methinks they are exceeding 4.02. 68 P
ay, hal, 'tis hot, 'tis hot. 5.03. 53 P
o lord, ay! good master snare. 2H4 2.01. 6 P
ay, come, you starv'd bloodhound. 5.04. 27 P
ay, that 'a did. H5 2.03. 28 P
ay, or go to death; 3.02.116 P
ay, i praise god, and i have merited some love 3.06. 23 P
ay, so please your majesty. 3.06. 90 P
ay, but these english are shrowdly out of beef. 3.07.152 P
ay, or more than we should seek after; 4.01.130 P
ay, he said so, to make us fight cheerfully; 4.01.192 P
ay; 4.01.307
ay, he was porn at monmouth, captain gower. 4.07. 11 P
ay, leeks is good. 5.01. 58 P
unready? ay, and glad we scap'd so well. 1H6 2.01. 40
ay, sharp and piercing, to maintain his truth, 2.04. 70
ay, noble uncle, thus ignobly us'd, | your 2.05. 35
ay, lordly sir; 3.01. 43
ay, /so the bishop be not overborne. 3.01. 53
ay, and the very parings of our nails | shall 3.01.102
ay, but, i fear me, with a hollow heart. 3.01.136
ay, we may march in england, or in france, | not 3.01.186
ay, | all the talbots in the world, to save my 3.02.107
ay, marry, sweeting, if we could do that, 3.03. 21
ay, rather than i'll shame my mother's womb. 4.05. 35
ay, marry, uncle, for i always thought | it was 5.01. 11
ay; 5.03. 70
ay, ay; away with her to execution! 5.04. 54
ay, ay; away with her to execution! 5.04. 54
ay, grief, i fear me, both at first and last. 5.05.102
ay, uncle, we will keep it, if we can; 2H6 1.01.107
ay, what else? fear you not her courage. 1.04. 5 P
ay, my lord cardinal, how think you by that? 2.01. 16
ay, where thou dar'st not peep. 2.01. 41
ay indeed was he. 2.01. 76
ay, god almighty help me! 2.01. 93
ay, good my lord; 2.03. 52
ay, ay, farewell, thy office is discharg'd. 2.04.103
ay, ay, farewell, thy office is discharg'd. 2.04.103
ay, night by night, in studying good for england 3.01.111
ay, all of you have laid your heads together — 3.01.165
ay, margaret; 3.01.198
ay, my good lord, he's dead. 3.02. 7
ay me, unhappy, | to be a queen, and crown'd 3.02. 70
ay me, i can no more! 3.02.120
ay, every joint should seem to curse and ban; 3.02.319
ay me! 3.02.380
ay, but these rags are no part of the duke; 4.01. 47
ay, and allay this thy abortive pride: 4.01. 60
ay, kennel, puddle, sink, whose filth and dirt 4.01. 71
ay, by my faith, the field is honorable, and 4.02. 50 P
ay, sir. 4.02.138
ay, there's the question; 4.02.141
ay, marry, will we; therefore get ye gone. 4.02.153
ay, but i hope your highness shall have his. 4.04. 20
ay, here they be that dare and will disturb thee 4.08. 6
ay, by the best blood that ever was broach'd, 4.10. 37 P
ay, clifford, a bedlam and ambitious humor 5.01.132
ay, noble father, if our words will serve. 5.01.139
ay, and their colors, often borne in france, 3H6 1.01.127
ay, to be murther'd by his enemies. 1.01.260
ay, with my sword. 1.02. 53
ay, with five hundred, father, for a need. 1.02. 67
ay, to such mercy as his ruthless arm | with 1.04. 31
ay, ay, so strives the woodcock with the gin. 1.04. 61
ay, ay, so strives the woodcock with the gin. 1.04. 61
ay, marry, sir, now looks he like a king! 1.04. 96
ay, this is he that took king henry's chair, 1.04. 97
if for the last, say ay, and to it, lords. 2.01.165
ay, now methinks i hear great warwick speak. 2.01.186
ay, as the rocks cheer them that fear their 2.02. 5
ay, good my lord, and leave us to our fortune. 2.02. 75
ay, crook–back, here i stand to answer thee, 2.02. 96
ay, and old york, and yet not satisfied. 2.02. 99
ay, like a dastard and a treacherous coward, 2.02.114
ay, here it dies, | which, whiles it lasted, 2.06. 1
ay, but he's dead. 2.06. 85
ay, here's a deer whose skin's a keeper's fee: 3.01. 22
ay, but she's come to beg; 3.01. 42
ay, but thou talk'st as if thou wert a king. 3.01. 59
ay, widow? 3.02. 21
ay, good leave have you, for you will have leave 3.02. 34
ay, full as dearly as i love myself. 3.02. 37
ay, but thou canst do what i mean to ask. 3.02. 48
ay, but, i fear me, in another sense. 3.02. 60
please you dismiss me, either with ay or no. 3.02. 78
ay, if thou wilt say ay to my request; 3.02. 79
ay, if thou wilt say ay to my request; 3.02. 79
ay, edward will use women honorably. 3.02.124
ay, now begins a second storm to rise, | for 3.03. 47
so much his friend, ay, his unfeigned friend, 3.03.202
ay, and 'twere pity | to sunder them that yoke 4.01. 22
ay, what of that? 4.01. 49
ay, gracious sovereign, they are so link'd in 4.01.116
ay, in despite of all that shall withstand you. 4.01.146
ay, but give me worship and quietness, | i like 4.03. 16
ay; 4.03. 21
ay, but the case is alter'd. 4.03. 31
ay, that's the first thing that we have to do, 4.03. 62
ay, almost slain, for he is taken prisoner, 4.04. 7
ay, ay, for this i draw in many a tear, | and 4.04. 21
ay, ay, for this i draw in many a tear, | and 4.04. 21
ay, such a pleasure as incaged birds | conceive, 4.06. 12
ay, therein clarence shall not want his part. 4.06. 57
ay; 4.06. 99
ay, say you so? the gates shall then be opened. 4.07. 29
ay, now my sovereign speaketh like himself, 4.07. 67
ay, by my faith, for a poor earl to give. 5.01. 32
ay, thou wast born to be a plague to men. 5.05. 28
ay, but thou usest to forswear thyself. 5.05. 75
ay, my good lord — my lord, i should say rather 5.06. 2
ay, and for much more slaughter after this. 5.06. 59
ay, madam, he desires to make atonement R3 1.03. 36
what may she not, she may, ay, marry, may she. 1.03. 97
ere you were queen, ay, or your husband king, 1.03.120
ay, and much better blood than his or thine. 1.03.125
ay, and forswore himself — which jesu pardon! 1.03.135
ay, and much more; 1.03.262
ay, ay. 1.04.174
ay, ay. 1.04.174
ay, so we will. 1.04.234
ay, millstones, as he lesson'd us to weep. 1.04.240
ay, my good lord, and no man in the presence 2.01. 85
he is my son — ay, and therein my shame, | yet 2.02. 29
ay, boy. 2.02. 32
ay, sir, it is too true, god help the while! 2.03. 8
ay, mother, but i would not have it so. 2.04. 8
"ay," quoth my uncle gloucester, | "small herbs 2.04. 12
ay me! 2.04. 49
ay, brother, to our grief, as it is yours. 3.01. 98
ay, gentle cousin, were it light enough. 3.01.117
ay, my good lord. 3.02. 42
ay, on my life, and hopes to find you forward 3.02. 46
ay, i thank god, my father, and yourself. 4.04.156
even all i have — ay, and myself and all — 4.04.249
her uncle rivers, ay (and for her sake!), 4.04.282
ay, if the devil tempt you to do good. 4.04.419
ay, if yourself's remembrance wrong yourself. 4.04.421
ay, thou wouldst be gone to join with richmond; 4.04.490
ay, please your grace. H8 1.01.117
ay, marry, | there will be woe indeed, lords; 1.03. 38
ay, and the best she shall have; 2.02.113
how you may hurt yourself — ay, utterly | grow 3.01.160
ay, my good lord. 5.01. 82
say ay, and of a boy. 5.01.163
ay, ay, my liege, | and of a lovely boy. 5.01.163
ay, ay, my liege, | and of a lovely boy. 5.01.163
ay, the grinding; TRO 1.01. 17 P
ay, the bolting; 1.01. 20 P
ay, to the leavening, but here's yet in the word 1.01. 23 P
ay, if i ever saw him before and knew him. 1.02. 65 P
ay, a minc'd man, and then to be bak'd with no 1.02.256 P
ay, a token from troilus. 1.02.280 P
ay, | i ask, that i might waken reverence, | and 1.03.226
ay, greek, that is my name. 1.03.246
ay, with celerity, find hector's purpose 1.03.330
as cerberus is at proserpina's beauty, ay, that 2.01. 34 P
ay, do! 2.01. 42 P
ay, what's the matter? 2.01. 58 P
ay, but that fool knows not himself. 2.01. 66 P
ay, the heavens hear me! 2.03. 36 P
ay, or surly borne — 2.03.238
ay, my good son. 2.03.257
ay, sir, when he goes before me. 3.01. 3 P
ay, good my lord. 3.01. 91 P
ay, ay, prithee now. 3.01.107 P
ay, ay, prithee now. 3.01.107 P
ay, you may, you may. 3.01.109 P
love? ay, that it shall, i' faith. 3.01.112 P
ay, good now, love, love, nothing but love. 3.01.113 P
ay, and good next day too. 3.03. 69
ay, and perhaps receive much honor by him. 3.03.226
ay, my lord. 3.03.290 P
ay, ay, ay, ay, 'tis too plain a case. 4.04. 29 P
ay, ay, ay, ay, 'tis too plain a case. 4.04. 29 P
ay, ay, ay, ay, 'tis too plain a case. 4.04. 29 P
ay, ay, ay, ay, 'tis too plain a case. 4.04. 29 P
ay, that. 5.02. 76
ay, come — o jove! 5.02.105
ay, greek, and that shall be divulged well | in 5.02.163
ay, but thou shalt not go. 5.03. 70

ay, there, there. 5.05. 43
ay, sir, well, well. COR 1.01.142
ay, if you come not in the blood of others, 1.06. 28
ay, to devour him, as the hungry plebeians would 2.01. 9 P
ay, worthy menenius, and with most prosperous 2.01.103 P
ay, i warrant you, and not without his true 2.01.139 P
ay, /not mine own desire. 2.03. 67 P
ay, spare us not. 2.03.235
ay, and burn too. 3.02. 24
ay, but mildly. 3.02.144
ay, as an hostler, that /for /th' poorest piece 3.03. 32
ay, fool, is that a shame? 4.02. 17
ay. 4.05. 40 P
ay, 'tis an honester service than to meddle with 4.05. 47 P
ay, and for an assault too. 4.05.171 P
ay, and it makes men hate one another. 4.05.230 P
ay, and you'll look pale | before you find it 4.06.101
o, ay, what else? 4.06.148
ay, and on mine, | that brought you forth this 5.03.125
ay, by and by; 5.03.202
ay, traitor, martius! 5.06. 86
ay, martius, caius martius! 5.06. 87
ay, noble titus, and resolv'd withal | to do TIT 1.01.278
ay, boy, grow ye so brave? 2.01. 45
ay, and as good as saturninus may. 2.01. 90
ay, so the turn were served. 2.01. 96
ay, for these slips have made him noted long, 2.03. 86
ay, come, semiramis, nay, barbarous tamora, 2.03.118
ay me, this object kills me! 3.01. 64
ay, when my father was in rome she did. 4.01. 7
ay, more there was; 4.01. 39
ay, such a place there is where we did hunt | (o 4.01. 55
ay, that's my boy! 4.01.110
ay, with my dagger in their bosoms, grandsire. 4.01.118
ay, marry, will we, sir, and we'll be waited on. 4.01.122
ay, some mad message from his mad grandfather. 4.02. 3
ay, just — a verse in horace, right, you have 4.02. 24
ay, of my pigeons, sir, nothing else. 4.03. 88 P
ay, sir. 4.03.108 P
ay, now begins our sorrows to approach. 4.04. 72
ay, but the citizens favor lucius, | and will 4.04. 79
ay, like a black dog, as the saying is. 5.01.122
ay, that i had not done a thousand more. 5.01.124
ay, while you live, draw your neck out of collar ROM 1.01. 4 P
ay, the heads of the maids, or their maidenheads 1.01. 25 P
is the law of our side if i say ay? 1.01. 48 P
ay me, sad hours seem long. 1.01.161
ay, mine own fortune in my misery. 1.02. 58
ay, if i know the letters and the language. 1.02. 61
the pretty wretch left crying and said, "ay." 1.03. 44
and, pretty fool, it stinted and said, "ay." 1.03. 48
to think it should leave crying and say, "ay." 1.03. 51
it stinted and said, "ay." 1.03. 57
ay, boy, ready. 1.05. 11 P
ay, pilgrim, lips that they must use in pray'r. 1.05.102
ay, so i fear, the more is my unrest. 1.05.120
cry but "ay me!" 2.01. 10
ay me! 2.02. 25
i know thou wilt say "ay," | and i will take thy 2.02. 90
ay, nurse, what of that? both with an r. 2.04.208 P
ay, a thousand times. peter! 2.04.214 P
ay, ay, a scratch, a scratch, marry, 'tis enough 3.01. 93
ay, ay, a scratch, a scratch, marry, 'tis enough 3.01. 93
ay, ay, the cords. 3.02. 35
ay, ay, the cords. 3.02. 35
ay me, what news? why dost thou wring thy hands? 3.02. 36
say thou but ay, | and that bare vowel i shall 3.02. 45
i am not i, if there be such an ay; 3.02. 48
or those eyes /shut, that makes thee answer ay, 3.02. 49
ay, | if he be slain, say ay, or if not, no. 3.02. 50
thou gone so, love — lord, ay, husband, friend! 3.05. 43
ay, madam, from the reach of these my hands. 3.05. 85
ay, sir, but she will none, she /gives you 3.05.139
ay forsooth. 4.02. 12
ay, marry, go, i say, and fetch him hither. 4.02. 30
ay, those attires are best, but, gentle nurse, 4.03. 1
ay, you have been a mouse–hunt in your time, 4.04. 11
ay, let the county take you in your bed, | he'll 4.05. 10
ay, /by my troth, the case may be amended. 4.05.100 P
ay, that's well known; TIM 1.01. 3
ay, marry, what of these? 1.01. 83
ay, my good lord, five talents is his debt, 1.01. 95
ay, my good lord, and she accepts of it. 1.01.135
ay. 1.01.232 P
ay, apemantus. 1.01.236 P
ay, to see meat fill knaves, and wine heat fools 1.01.261
ay, defil'd land, my lord. 1.02.225
ay, go, sir; 2.01. 34
ay, would they serv'd us! 2.02. 93 P
ay, fool. 2.02. 97 P
ay, too well. 3.02. 63
ay, and i think | one business does command us 3.04. 3
ay, but the days are wax'd shorter with him. 3.04. 11
ay, | if money were as certain as your waiting, 3.04. 46
ay, but this answer will not serve. 3.04. 57
ay, timon, and have cause. 4.03.103
ay. 4.03.238
ay, that i am not thee. 4.03.277
ay, though it look like thee. 4.03.308 P
ay, timon. 4.03.326 P
ay. 4.03.394
ay, you are honest /men. 5.01. 71
ay, and you hear him cog, see him dissemble, 5.01. 95
ay, even such heaps and sums of love and wealth 5.01.152
ay, do you fear it? JC 1.02. 80
ay, and that tongue of his that bade the romans 1.02.125
ay, casca, tell us what hath chanc'd to–day 1.02.217
ay, marry, was't, and he put it by thrice, every 1.02.229 P
ay. 1.02.277 P
ay, he spoke greek. 1.02.279 P
ay, if i be alive, and your mind hold, and your 1.02.291 P
ay me! 2.04. 39
ay, caesar, but not gone. 3.01. 2
ay, every man away. 3.01.119
ay, and briefly. 3.03. 10 P
ay, and wisely. 3.03. 11 P
ay, and truly, you were best. 3.03. 12 P
ay, more. 4.03. 42

ay, my lord, an't please you. 4.03.258
ay, at philippi. 4.03.285
ay. saw you any thing? 4.03.304
ay, if messala will prefer me to you. 5.05. 62
ay. MAC 2.02. 17
ay, my good lord. 3.01. 19
ay, my good lord. our time does call upon 's. 3.01. 36
ay, in the catalogue ye go for men, | as hounds 3.01. 91
ay, madam, but returns again to–night. 3.02. 2
ay, my good lord; 3.04. 25
ay, and a bold one, that dare look on that 3.04. 58
ay, and since too, murthers have been perform'd 3.04. 76
ay, and wisely too; 3.06. 14
ay, sir, all this is so. 4.01.125
ay, my good lord. 4.01.143
ay, that he was. 4.02. 45 P
ay, sir; 4.03.141
ay, but their sense are shut. 5.01. 25 P
ay, my good lord; 5.03. 57
ay, and brought off the field. 5.09. 10
ay, on the front. 5.09. 13
ay, madam, it is common. HAM 1.02. 74
ay, fashion you may call it. go to, go to. 1.03.112
ay, springes to catch woodcocks. 1.03.115
ay, marry, is't, | but to my mind, though i am 1.04. 13
ay, that incestuous, that adulterate beast, 1.05. 42
ay, thou poor ghost, whiles memory holds a seat 1.05. 96
ay, by heaven, /my /lord. 1.05.122
ay, very well, my lord. 2.01. 16
ay, or drinking, fencing, swearing, quarrelling, 2.01. 25
ay, my lord, | i would know that. 2.01. 36
at "closes in the consequence," ay, marry. 2.01. 52
ay, amen! 2.02. 39
ay, sir, to be honest, as this world goes, is to 2.02.178 P
ay, my lord. 2.02.539 P
ay, my lord. 2.02.544 P
ay, so god buy to you! 2.02.549
ay, there's the rub, | for in that sleep of 3.01. 64
ay, truly, for the power of beauty will sooner 3.01.110 P
ay, my lord. 3.02. 51 P
and i will wear him | in my heart's core, ay, in 3.02. 73
ay, my lord, they stay upon your patience. 3.02.107 P
ay, my lord. 3.02.124 P
ay, or any show that you will show him. 3.02.144 P
ay, sir, what of him? 3.02.300 P
ay, sir, but "while the grass grows" — the 3.02.343 P
ay, lady, it was my word. 3.04. 30
ay me, what act, | that roars so loud and 3.04. 51
ay, sir, that soaks up the king's countenance, 4.02. 15 P
ay, hamlet. 4.03. 46
ay, my lord, | so you will not o'errule me to a 4.07. 59
ay, marry, is't — crowner's quest law. 5.01. 22 P
ay, tell me that, and unyoke. 5.01. 52 P
ay, my lord. 5.01. 87 P
ay, my lord, and of calves'–skins too. 5.01.115 P
ay, marry, why was he sent into england? 5.01.149 P
ay, good my lord. 5.02. 37
ay, my good lord. 5.02.266
ay, my good lord. LR 1.01.105
ay, two hours together. 1.02.155 P
ay, madam. 1.03. 2
ay, madam. 1.04.335
ay, boy. 1.05. 10 P
ay, my good lord. 2.01.109
ay. 2.02. 3 P
by juno, i swear ay. 2.04. 22
ay, my good lord. 2.04.100
ay, my lord. 4.01. 40
ay, master. 4.01. 72
ay, my good lord; 4.02. 92
ay, madam. 4.05. 1
to say "ay" and "no" to every thing that i said! 4.06. 99 P
"ay," and "no" too, was no good divinity. 4.06. 99 P
ay, every inch a king! 4.06.107
ay, sir. 4.06.156
ay, madam; 4.07. 20
ay, so i think. 5.03.293
ay, so i thought. how many, as you guess? OTH 1.03. 36
ay, to me: 1.03. 59
ay, madam. 2.01.121
ay, well said, whisper. 2.01.167 P
ay, smile upon her, do; 2.01.169 P
ay; 2.03.109 P
ay, past all surgery. 2.03.260 P
ay, that's the way; 2.03.387
ay, marry, are they, sir. 3.01. 7 P
ay, but, lady, | that policy may either last so 3.03. 13
ay, indeed. 3.03.102
honest? ay, honest. 3.03.104
ay, there's the point; 3.03.228
ay; what of that? 4.01. 23
ay, let her rot, and perish, and be damn'd 4.01.181 P
ay, too gentle. 4.01.194 P
ay, you did wish that i would make her turn. 4.01.252
cherubin — | ay, here, look grim as hell! 4.02. 64
o, ay, as summer flies are in the shambles, 4.02. 66
ay, you! 4.02. 92
ay; 4.02.202 P
ay; 4.02.232 P
know him? ay. 5.01. 92
ay, desdemona. 5.02. 23
ay, my lord. 5.02. 25
ay, i do. 5.02. 33
ay, and for that thou diest. 5.02. 41
ay, but not yet to die. 5.02. 52
ay. 5.02. 70
ay, with cassio. 5.02.143
ay, 'twas he that told me on her first. 5.02.147
ay, ay! o, lay me by my mistress' side. 5.02.237
ay, ay! o, lay me by my mistress' side. 5.02.237
ay. 5.02.298
ay; ANT 1.02. 90
ay, madam, twenty several messengers. 1.05. 62
ay, sir, we did sleep day out of countenance, 2.02.177 P
ay, lepidus. 2.07. 25 P
ay, dread queen. 3.03. 8
ay me, most wretched, | that have my heart 3.06. 76
ay, and to wage this battle at pharsalia, 3.07. 31

ay, are you thereabouts? 3.10. 28
ay, my lord. 3.13. 14
ay, is't not strange? 4.03. 19
ay, noble lord. 4.14. 1
ay, my lord. 4.14. 8
ay, ay, farewell. 5.02.264
ay, ay, farewell. 5.02.264
ay, and the approbation of those that weep this CYM 1.04. 19 P
pleaseth your highness, ay. 1.05. 5
ay, madam, with his eyes in flood with laughter. 1.06. 74
ay, it is fit for your lordship only. 2.01. 30 P
ay, | to keep her chamber. 2.03. 81
ay, i said so, sir; 2.03.150
ay, and it doth confirm | another stain, as big 2.04.139
ay, and singular in his art, hath done you both 3.04.121
ay, my noble lord. 3.05.147 P
ay. 3.07. 11
his /humor | was nothing but mutation, ay, and 4.02.133
ay me! 4.02.321
ay, good youth, | and rather father thee than 4.02.394
ay, or a stomach. 5.04. 2
ay, with all my heart, | and lend my best 5.05.116
ay, so thou dost, | italian fiend! 5.05.209
ay me, most credulous fool, | egregious 5.05.210
ay, my good lord. 5.05.379
sin, | ay, and the targets to put off the shame; PER 1.01.140
ay, sir, and he deserves so to be call'd for his 2.01.102 P
ay, but hark you, my friend, 'twas we that made 2.01.148 P
ay, so well, that you must be her master, | and 2.05. 38
ay, traitor. 2.05. 55
ay me! 4.01. 17
ay, to eleven, and brought them down again. 4.02. 16 P
ay, she quickly poop'd him, she made him 4.02. 24 P
ay, and better too; 4.02. 37 P
ay, and you shall live in pleasure. 4.02. 76 P
ay, he, he offer'd to cut a caper at the 4.02.107 P
ay, by my faith, they shall not be chang'd yet. 4.02.135 P
ay, do but put | a fescue in her fist, and you TNK 2.03. 33
say "ay," and all shall presently advance. 3.05.134
ay, ay, by any means, dear domine. 3.05.135
ay, ay, by any means, dear domine. 3.05.135
ay, and twenty. 5.02.109
ay, by th' mass, will we, more. STM II.C 58 P
"ay me," quoth venus, "young, and so unkind, VEN 187
"ay me!" 833
ay, if the fact be known; LUC 239
ay me, the bark pill'd from the lofty pine, 1167
ay me, but yet thou mightst my seat forbear, SON 41. 9
ay, fill it full with wills, and my will one. 136. 6
/nun, | who, disciplin'd, ay, dieted in grace, LC 261
ay me, i fell, and yet do question make | what i 321

/AYE 1 FR 0.0001 REL FR 1 V 0 P
to feed for /aye her lamp and flames of love, TRO 3.02.160

AYE 17 FR 0.0019 REL FR 17 V 0 P
to the perpetual wink for aye might put | this TMP 2.01.285
and i, thy caliban, | for aye thy foot–licker. 4.01.219
a nun, | for aye to be in shady cloister mew'd, MND 1.01. 71
to protest | for aye austerity and single life. 1.01. 90
and must for aye consort with black–brow'd night 3.02.387
now, | whose state and honor i for aye allow. R2 5.02. 40
let him that will a scritch–owl aye be call'd TRO 5.10. 16
pursue thy life, and live aye with thy name! 5.10. 34
and thy saints for aye | be crown'd with plagues TIM 5.01. 52
taught thee to make vast neptune weep for aye 5.04. 78
hour | stand aye accursed in the calendar! MAC 4.01.134
this world is not for aye, nor 'tis not strange HAM 3.02.200
come | to bid my king and master aye good night. LR 5.03.236
aye hopeless | to have the courtesy your cradle CYM 4.04. 27
the worth that learned charity aye wears. PER 5.03. 94
force, | or sentencing for aye their vigor dumb, TNK 1.01.195
place, | but makes antiquity for aye his page, SON 108.12

AYEZ 1 FR 0.0001 REL FR 0 V 1 P
o, prenez misericorde! ayez pitie de moi! H5 4.04. 12 P

AY'LL *(also i'll)*

AY'LL 1 FR 0.0001 REL FR 0 V 1 P
themselves to slomber, ay'll de gud service, or H5 3.02.115 P

AYWORD *(also nay–word)*

AYWORD 1 FR 0.0001 REL FR 0 V 1 P
if i do not gull him into an ayword, and make TN 2.03.135 P

AZUR'D 2 FR 0.0002 REL FR 2 V 0 P
and 'twixt the green sea and the azur'd vault TMP 5.01. 43
nor | the azur'd harebell, like thy veins; CYM 4.02.222

AZURE 2 FR 0.0002 REL FR 2 V 0 P
white and azure lac'd | with blue of heaven's CYM 2.02. 22
than admiration he admired | her azure veins, LUC 419

B 2 FR 0.0002 REL FR 2 V 0 P
fair as a text b in a copy–book. LLL 5.02. 42
b mi, bianca, take him for thy lord, | c fa ut, SHR 3.01. 75

BA 2 FR 0.0002 REL FR 0 V 2 P
ba, pueritia, with a horn added. LLL 5.01. 49 P
ba, most silly sheep, with a horn. 5.01. 50 P

BAA 1 FR 0.0001 REL FR 0 V 1 P
such another proof will make me cry "baa." TGV 1.01. 93 P

/BABBL'D 1 FR 0.0001 REL FR 0 V 1 P
sharp as a pen, and 'a /babbl'd of green fields. H5 2.03. 17 P

BABBLE 4 FR 0.0004 REL FR 1 V 3 P
this babble shall not henceforth trouble me. TGV 1.02. 95
for, for the watch to babble and to talk, is ADO 3.03. 35 P
to sleep, and leave thy vain bibble babble. TN 4.02. 97 P
taddle nor pibble babble in pompey's camp. H5 4.01. 71 P

BABBLING 6 FR 0.0006 REL FR 5 V 1 P
for "school," "fool," a babbling rhyme: ADO 5.02. 39 P
and make the babbling gossip of the air | cry TN 1.05.273
than lying, vainness, babbling, drunkenness, 3.04.355
let not our babbling dreams affright our souls; R3 5.03.308
and whilst the babbling echo mocks the hounds, TIT 2.03. 17
guilt of ours, | a long–tongu'd babbling gossip? 4.02.150

BABE 45 FR 0.0050 REL FR 43 V 2 P
that, like a testy babe, will scratch the nurse TGV 1.02. 58
and when he was a babe, a child, a shrimp, LLL 5.02.590
me, | for i am rough, and woo not like a babe. SHR 2.01.137
i am no child, no babe; 4.03. 74
a daughter, and a goodly babe, | lusty and like WT 2.02. 24
if she dares trust me with her little babe, 2.02. 35
madam, if't please the queen to send the babe, 2.02. 54
look to your babe, my lord, 'tis yours. 2.03.126
come on, poor babe. 2.03.185
tyrant, his innocent babe truly begotten, and 3.02.134 P

come, poor babe. 3.03. 15
person for the thrower–out | of my poor babe, 3.03. 30
and, for the babe | is counted lost for ever, 3.03. 32
son, | or madly think a babe of clouts were he. JN 3.04. 58
fift | was in the mouth of every sucking babe, 1H6 3.01.196
as looks the mother on her lowly babe | when 3.03. 47
i seal upon the lips of this sweet babe. 3H6 5.07. 29
o, 'twas the foulest deed to slay that babe, R3 1.03.182
song | of lullaby to bring her babe asleep. TIT 2.03. 29
here is the babe, as loathsome as a toad 4.02. 67
the crying babe controll'd with this discourse: 5.01. 26
even thus he rates the babe — | "for i must 5.01. 33
who, when he knows thou art the empress' babe, 5.01. 35
thou wast the prettiest babe that e'er i nurs'd. ROM 1.03. 60
and at that instant like a babe sprung up. TIM 1.02.111
ho, ho! i laugh to think that babe a bastard. 1.02.112 P
spare not the babe, | whose dimpled smiles from 4.03.119
and pity, like a naked new–born babe, | striding MAC 1.07. 21
how tender 'tis to love the babe that milks me; 1.07. 55
finger of birth–strangled babe | ditch–deliver'd 4.01. 30
steel, | be soft as sinews of the new–born babe! HAM 3.03. 71
body never spring | a babe to honor her! LR 1.04.281
the king he takes the babe | to his protection, CYM 1.01. 40
by the loss of maidenhead, | a babe is moulded. PER 3.ch. 11
for a more blusterous birth had never babe. 3.01. 28
lay the babe | upon the pillow. 3.01. 67
cleon, for the babe | cannot hold out to tyrus. 3.01. 78
my gentle babe marina, whom, | for she was born 3.03. 12
half–sights saw | that arcite was no babe. TNK 5.03. 96
a nurse's song ne'er pleas'd her babe so well. VEN 974
and fright her crying babe with tarquin's name; LUC 814
as tender nurse her babe from faring ill. SON 22.12
love is a babe, then might i not say so, | to 115.13
sets down her babe and makes all swift dispatch 143. 3
whilst i, thy babe, chase thee afar behind, 143.10
BABE'S 1 FR 0.0001 REL FR 1 V 0 P
his hopeful son's, his babe's, betrays to WT 2.03. 86
/BABES 1 FR 0.0001 REL FR 1 V 0 P
/old /fools /are /babes /again, /and /must /be LR 1.03. 19
BABES 25 FR 0.0028 REL FR 25 V 0 P
and piteous plainings of the pretty babes, ERR 1.01. 72
so holy writ in babes hath judgment shown, AWW 2.01.138
judgment shown, | when judges have been babes; 2.01.139
their mothers' moist'ned eyes babes shall suck, 1H6 1.01. 49
with his name the mothers still their babes? 2.03. 17
no more will i their babes. 2H6 5.02. 52
tears then for babes; 3H6 2.01. 86
these babes for clarence weep, /and /so /do /i; R3 2.02. 84
those tender babes | whom envy hath immur'd 4.01. 98
thus," quoth dighton, "lay the gentle babes." 4.03. 9
ah, my tender babes! 4.04. 9
a mother only mock'd with two fair babes; 4.04. 87
think that thy babes were sweeter than they were 4.04.120
my babes were destin'd to a fairer death, | if 4.04.220
proof nor yells of mothers, maids, nor babes, TIM 4.03.125
to th' edge o' th' sword | his wife, his babes, MAC 4.01.152
to leave his wife, to leave his babes, | his 4.02. 6
your wife, and babes, | savagely slaughter'd. 4.03.204
those that do teach young babes | do it with OTH 4.02.111
and take a queen | worth many babes and beggars! ANT 5.02. 48
at three and two years old, i stole these babes, CYM 3.03.101
those mothers who, to nousle up their babes, PER 1.04. 42
or tell of babes broach'd on the lance, or women TNK 1.03. 20
there such fellows liv'd when you were babes, STM II.C 63
conclusion | who, having two sweet babes, when LUC 1161
BABIES 4 FR 0.0004 REL FR 4 V 0 P
guarded with grandsires, babies, and old women, H5 3.pr. 20
for tender princes — use my babies well! R3 4.01.102
or the virgin voice | that babies lull asleep! COR 3.02.115
their babies at their backs, with their poor STM II.C 75
BABION *(see bavian)*
BABLE *(also bauble)*
/BABLE 1 FR 0.0001 REL FR 1 V 0 P
richer than doing nothing for a /bable; CYM 3.03. 23
BABLE 2 FR 0.0002 REL FR 1 V 1 P
off with that bable, throw it under–foot. SHR 5.02.122
lolling up and down to hide his bable in a hole. ROM 2.04. 93 P
BABOON 4 FR 0.0004 REL FR 2 V 2 P
hang him, baboon! 2H4 2.04.240 P
of man's bred out | into baboon and monkey. TIM 1.01.251
hen, i would change my humanity with a baboon. OTH 1.03.316 P
for what thou professest, a baboon, could he PER 4.06.178
BABOON'S 1 FR 0.0001 REL FR 1 V 0 P
cool it with a baboon's blood, | then the charm MAC 4.01. 37
BABOONS 1 FR 0.0001 REL FR 0 V 1 P
through the grate, like a geminy of baboons. WIV 2.02. 9 P
BABY 13 FR 0.0014 REL FR 10 V 3 P
the baby beats the nurse, and quite athwart MM 1.03. 30
i can find out no rhyme to "lady" but "baby," an ADO 5.02. 37 P
and speak to me as if | i were a baby still. WT 2.01. 6
commend these waters to those baby eyes | that JN 5.02. 56
she'll hamper thee, and dandle thee like a baby. 2H6 1.03.145
is seen | the baby figure of the giant mass | of TRO 1.03.345
shame's a baby. 3.02. 41 P
into a rapture lets her baby cry | while she COR 2.01.207
i am no baby, i, that with base prayers | i TIT 5.03.185
i inhabit then, protest me | the baby of a girl. MAC 3.04.105
think yourself a baby | that you have ta'en HAM 1.03.105
that great baby you see there is not yet out of 2.02.382 P
dost thou not see my baby at my breast, | that ANT 5.02.309
BABY–BROW 1 FR 0.0001 REL FR 1 V 0 P
and wears upon his baby–brow the round | and top MAC 4.01. 88
BABY–DAUGHTER 1 FR 0.0001 REL FR 1 V 0 P
the casting forth to crows thy baby–daughter WT 3.02.191
BABYLON *(also pabylon)*
BABYLON 2 FR 0.0002 REL FR 0 V 2 P
"there dwelt a man in babylon, lady, lady!" TN 2.03. 79 P
rheumatic, and talk'd of the whore of babylon. H5 2.03. 39 P
BABY'S 1 FR 0.0001 REL FR 1 V 0 P
a knack, a toy, a trick, a baby's cap. SHR 4.03. 67
BACCHANALS 2 FR 0.0002 REL FR 2 V 0 P
"the riot of the tipsy bacchanals, | tearing the MND 5.01. 48
shall we dance now the egyptian bacchanals | and ANT 2.07.104
BACCHUS 2 FR 0.0002 REL FR 2 V 0 P
tongue proves dainty bacchus gross in taste. LLL 4.03.336
of the vine, | plumpy bacchus with pink eyne! ANT 2.07.114

BACHELOR 20 FR 0.0022 REL FR 9 V 11 P
whose shadow the dismissed bachelor loves, TMP 4.01. 67
if the man be a bachelor, sir, i can; MM 4.02. 3 P
shall i never see a bachelor of threescore again ADO 1.01.199 P
i may go the finer), i will live a bachelor. 1.01.246 P
when i said i would die a bachelor, i did not 2.03.243 P
said | becomes a virtuous bachelor and a maid, MND 2.02. 59
turkis, i had it of leah when i was a bachelor. MV 3.01.122 P
more honorable than the bare brow of a bachelor; AYL 3.03. 61 P
he was a bachelor then. TN 1.02. 29
writ man ever since his father was a bachelor. 2H4 1.02. 27 P
moi'ty, take the word of a king and a bachelor. H5 5.02.216 P
and, by god's mother, i, being but a bachelor, 3H6 3.02.103
a bachelor, and a handsome stripling too: R3 1.03.100
i would not part a bachelor from the priest. TIT 1.01.488
marry, bachelor, | her mother is the lady of the ROM 1.05.112
are you a married man or a bachelor? JC 3.03. 8 P
am i a married man or a bachelor? 3.03. 14 P
wisely i say, i am a bachelor. 3.03. 16 P
the poll'd bachelor — | whose youth, like TNK 5.01. 85
surely the gods | would have him die a bachelor, 5.03.117
BACHELORS 3 FR 0.0003 REL FR 1 V 2 P
he shows me where the bachelors sit, and there ADO 2.01. 48 P
of noble bachelors stand at my bestowing, | o'er AWW 2.03. 53
inquire me out contracted bachelors, such as had 1H4 4.02. 16 P
BACH'LORSHIP 1 FR 0.0001 REL FR 1 V 0 P
she was the first fruit of my bach'lorship. 1H6 5.04. 13
/BACK 3 FR 0.0003 REL FR 1 V 2 P
/the /foul /fiend /bites /my /back. LR 3.06. 17 P
/king /of /france /is /so /suddenly /gone /back, 4.03. 2 P
all sleeping, | nymphs /back peeping fearfully. PP 17.28
BACK 343 FR 0.0387 REL FR 282 V 61 P
to th' winds, whose pity, sighing back again, TMP 1.02.150
shall that claribel | measure us back to naples? 2.01.259
i had rather crack my sinews, break my back, 3.01. 26
neptune, and do fly him | when he comes back; 5.01. 36
on the bat's back i do fly | after summer 5.01. 91
it were a shame to call her back again, | and TGV 1.02. 51
to call lucetta back | and ask remission for my 1.02. 64
here have i brought him back again. 4.04. 53 P
thurio, give back, or else embrace thy death; 5.04.126
sir john, is come in at your back door, mistress WIV 3.03. 25 P
the flame will back descend | and turn him to no 5.05. 85
lead forth and bring you back in happiness! MM 1.01. 74
gentle my lord, turn back. 2.02.143
good my lord, turn back. 2.02.145
for, like an ass whose back with ingots bows, 3.01. 26
what 'tis to cram a maw or clothe a back | from 3.02. 22
go back again, thou slave, and fetch him home. ERR 2.01. 75
go back again, and be new beaten home? 2.01. 76
back, slave, or i will break thy pate across. 2.01. 78
the hours come back! that did i never /hear. 4.02. 55
meet a sergeant, 'a turns back for very fear. 4.02. 56
he not reason to turn back an hour in a day? 4.02. 62
no glory lives behind the back of such. ADO 3.01.110
and what have i to give you back whose worth 4.01. 27
there, leonato, take her back again. 4.01. 31
and brought with armed men back to messina. 5.04.126
the town gates on his back like a porter; LLL 1.02. 72 P
"fair" i give you back again, and "welcome" i 2.01. 91 P
and, if you prove it, i'll repay it back, | or 2.01.158
and stand between her back, sir, and the fire, 5.02.476
to have his sight thither and back again. MND 1.01.251
and heard a mermaid on a dolphin's back 2.01.150
coats, and some keep back | the clamorous owl, 2.02. 5
make mouths upon me when i turn my back, | wink 3.02.238
quiet go, | to athens will i bear my folly back, 3.02.315
nay, go not back. 3.02.340
and back to athens shall the lovers wend | with 3.02.372
east, | that i may back to athens by daylight, 3.02.433
other do, | may all to athens back again repair, 4.01. 67
before thisby comes back and finds her lover? 5.01.313 P
both | or bring your latter hazard back again, MV 1.01.151
i will survey th' inscriptions back again. 2.07. 14
and am well pleas'd | to wish it back on you. 3.04. 44
that have of late so huddled on his back, | enow 4.01. 28
'tis well you offer it behind her back, | the 4.01.293
do not draw back your hand, i'll take no more, 4.01.428
he calls us back. AYL 1.02.252
back, friends! 3.02.158 P
o'ergrown with hair, | lay sleeping on his back; 4.03.107
twice did he turn his back, and purpos'd so; 4.03.127
for i must bear answer back | how you excuse my 4.03.179
skipper, stand back! SHR 2.01.339
bots, /sway'd in the back and shoulder–shotten, 3.02. 55 P
i say his horse comes, with him on his back. 3.02. 80 P
go on, and fetch our horses back again. 4.05. 9
i'll see the church a' your back, and then come 5.01. 4 P
and then come back to my /master's as soon as i 5.01. 5 P
thoughts | a modest one, to bear me back again. AWW 2.01.128
this, | and urge her to a present answer back. 2.02. 64
when back again this ring shall be deliver'd; 4.02. 60
where, like /arion on the dolphin's back, | i TN 1.02. 15
i could hardly entreat him back. 3.04. 58 P
back you shall not to the house, unless you 3.04.248 P
take and give back affairs and their dispatch 4.03. 18
more straining on for plucking back, not WT 4.04.465
either push on or pluck back thy business there; 4.04.737 P
he shall feel, will break the back of man, the 4.04.770 P
knows how that may turn back to my advancement? 4.04.835 P
whose foot spurns back the ocean's roaring tides JN 2.01. 24
it lies as sightly on the back of him | as great 2.01.143
but, ass, i'll take that burthen from your back, 2.01.145
back to the stained field, | you equal potents, 2.01.357
bell, book, and candle shall not drive me back, 3.03. 12
let him come back, that his compassion may 4.01. 88
stand back, lord salisbury, stand back, i say; 4.03. 81
stand back, lord salisbury, stand back, i say; 4.03. 81
your grace shall pardon me, i will not back. 5.02. 78
must i back | because that john hath made his 5.02. 95
the lords are all come back, | and brought 5.06. 33
that they may break his foaming courser's back, R2 1.02. 51
and both return back to their chairs again. 1.03.120
save back to england, all the world's my way. 1.03.207
whose rocky shore beats back the envious siege 2.01. 62
as york thrives to beat back bullingbrook. 2.02.144
o, call back yesterday, bid time return, | and 3.02. 69

shall we call back northumberland, and send 3.03.129
northumberland comes back from bullingbrook. 3.03.142
sent back like hollowmas or short'st of day. 5.01. 80
bearing their own misfortunes on the back | of 5.05. 29
so proud that bullingbrook was on his back! 5.05. 84
of that proud man that did usurp his back? 5.05. 89
to be as true–bred cowards as ever turn'd back; 1H4 1.02.184 P
when you and he came back from ravenspurgh — 1.03.248
well, i will back him straight. 2.03. 71
the shoulders, you care not who sees your back. 2.04.150 P
green came at my back and let drive at me, for 2.04.222 P
royal man, and send him back again to my mother. 2.04.291 P
money shall be paid back again with advantage. 2.04.547 P
him | bootless home and weather–beaten back. 3.01. 66
i bought you a dozen of shirts to your back. 3.03. 68 P
the money is paid back again. 3.03.178 P
o, i do not like that paying back, 'tis a double 3.03.179 P
not what impediments | drag back our expedition. 4.03. 19
come bring your luggage nobly on your back. 5.04.156
sir john umfrevile turn'd me back | with joyful 2H4 1.01. 34
and send you back again to your master for a 1.02. 18 P
what, to york? call him back again. 1.02. 64 P
/to french and welsh he leaves his back unarm'd, 1.03. 79
come all his forces back? 2.01.172
comes the king back from wales, my noble lord? 2.01.176 P
but many thousand reasons hold me back. 2.03. 66
hen, if her feathers turn back in any show of 2.04.100 P
you knew i was at your back, and spoke it on 2.04.308 P
for /'s apparel is built upon his back, and the 3.02.144 P
one time or other break some gallows' back. 4.03. 29
now doth it turn and ebb back to the sea, 5.02.131
flag, | look back into your mighty ancestors; H5 1.02.102
and bring you back, charming the narrow seas 2.pr. 38
world, | he might return to vasty tartar back, 2.02.123
full intent | back to our brother of england. 2.04.115
th' embassador from the french comes back, 3.pr. 28
turn thee back, | and tell thy king i do not 3.06.139
your mistress shrewdly shook your back. 3.07. 49 P
i pray thee bear my former answer back: 4.03. 90
back again! 4.05. 11
your thoughts, straight back again to france. 5.pr. 45
vauting into my saddle with my armor on my back, 5.02.138 P
good leg will fall, a straight back will stoop, 5.02.159 P
more dazzled and drove back his enemies | than 1H6 1.01. 13
thrust talbot with a spear into the back, | whom 1.01.138
me, | when he sees me go back one foot or fly. 1.02. 21
stand back, you lords, and give us leave a while 1.02. 70
stand back, thou manifest conspirator, | thou 1.03. 33
nay, stand thou back, i will not budge a foot: 1.03. 38
i will not slay thee, but i'll drive thee back. 1.03. 41
drives back our troops and conquers as she lists 1.05. 22
first, lean thine aged back against mine arm, 2.05. 43
and keep not back your powers in dalliance. 5.02. 5
come back, fool. 2H6 1.03. 8 P
she bears a duke's revenues on her back, | and 1.03. 80
to–morrow toward london back again, | to look 2.01.197
you four, from hence to prison back again; 2.03. 5
mail'd up in shame, with papers on my back, 2.04. 31
whose overweening arm i have pluck'd back, | by 3.01.159
bank | drove back again unto my native clime? 3.02. 84
when from thy shore the tempest beat us back, 3.02.102
but now is cade driven back, his men dispers'd, 4.09. 34
seen a hot o'erweening cur | run back and bite, 5.01.152
followers to the eager foe | turn back and fly, 3H6 1.04. 4
where are your mess of sons to back you now, 1.04. 73
foes, | but never once again turn back and fly. 2.01.185
not he that sets his foot upon her back. 2.02. 16
shrub, | to make an envious mountain on my back, 3.02.157
to keep them back that come to succor you. 4.07. 56
let's levy men, and beat him back again. 4.08. 6
petitioners for blood thou ne'er put'st back. 5.05. 80
heave it shall some weight, or break my back: 5.07. 24
my lord, stand back, and let the coffin pass. R3 1.02. 38
and i no friends to back my suit /at /all | but 1.02.235
i'll back to the duke of gloucester and tell him 1.04.115 P
if you are hir'd for meed, go back again, | and 1.04.228
speak and look back, and pry on every side, 3.05. 6
look back, defend thee, here are enemies! 3.05. 19
men, | since you will buckle fortune on my back, 3.07.228
stay, yet look back with me unto the tower. 4.01. 97
unarm'd, and unresolv'd to beat them back. 4.04.436
where is thy power then, to beat him back? 4.04.479
bear 'em, | the back is sacrifice to th' load. H8 1.02. 50
the ceremony | of bringing back the prisoner. 2.01. 5
if your back | cannot vouchsafe this burthen, 2.03. 42
time | i know your back will bear a duchess. 2.03. 99
madam, you are call'd back. 2.04.128
made to the queen to call back her appeal | she 2.04.235
and with the same full state pac'd back again 4.01. 93
come back! what mean you? 5.01.157
i'll not come back, the tidings that i bring 5.01.158
when they pass back from the christening. 5.03. 74
upon my back, to defend my belly, upon my wit, TRO 1.02.260 P
we turn not back the silks upon the merchant, 2.02. 69
nations speak aloud | to have her back return'd. 2.02.186
receives and renders back | his figure and his 3.03.122
time hath, my lord, a wallet at his back, 3.03.145
where injury of chance | puts back leave–taking, 4.04. 34
loads a' gravel in the back, lethargies, cold 5.01. 19 P
come, hector, come, go back. 5.03. 62
therefore come back. 5.03. 67
villain with the sleeve back to the dissembling 5.04. 8 P
all | from me do back receive the flour of all, COR 1.01.145
you, titus lartius, | must to corioles back. 1.09. 76
'twill be deliver'd back on good condition. 1.10. 2
for you, the city, thus i turn my back; 3.03.134
stand, and go back. 5.02. 1
be it so, go back. 5.02. 12
therefore go back. 5.02. 27 P
therefore go back. 5.02. 33 P
therefore back to rome, and prepare for your 5.02. 47 P
back, i say, go; 5.02. 55 P
back, that's the utmost of your having, back! 5.02. 56 P
back, that's the utmost of your having, back! 5.02. 57 P
we are shent for keeping your greatness back? 5.02. 99 P
say my request's unjust, | and spurn me back; 5.03.165
i'll not to rome, i'll back with you, and pray 5.03.198
shall bear | a better witness back than words, 5.03.204

follow, my lord, and i'll soon bring her back. TIT 1.01.289
sweet heart, look back. 1.01.481
i'll go fetch thy sons | to back thy quarrels, 2.03. 54
do not draw back, for we will mourn with thee. 2.04. 56
here's thy hand, in scorn to thee sent back — 3.01.237
and lulls him whilst she playeth on her back, 4.01. 99
but metal, marcus, steel to the very back, | yet 4.03. 48
me, | or else i'll call my brother back again, 5.02.135
quarrel, i will back thee. ROM 1.01. 34 P
how, turn thy back and run? 1.01. 35 P
nurse, come back again, | i have rememb'red me, 1.03. 8
turn back, dull earth, and find thy centre out. 2.01. 2
eyes | of mortals that fall back to gaze on him, 2.02. 30
voice, | to lure this tassel-gentle back again! 2.02.159
i have forgot why i did call thee back. 2.02.170
and with a silken thread plucks it back again, 2.02.180
driving back shadows over low'ring hills; 2.05. 6
my back a' t' other side — ah, my back, my back 2.05. 50
back a' t' other side — ah, my back, my back! 2.05. 50
back a' t' other side — ah, my back, my back! 2.05. 50
here comes the furious tybalt back again. 3.01.121
take the "villain" back again | that late thou 3.01.125
and with the other sends | it back to tybalt, 3.01.163
but by and by comes back to romeo, | who had but 3.01.170
whiter than new snow upon a raven's back. 3.02. 19
back, foolish tears, back to your native spring, 3.02.102
back, foolish tears, back to your native spring, 3.02.102
a pack of blessings light upon thy back, 3.03.141
prince, and call thee back | with twenty hundred 3.03.152
wilt not keep him long, | but send him back. 3.05. 64
that he dares ne'er come back to challenge you; 3.05.214
being spoke behind your back, than to your face. 4.01. 28
i'll call them back again to comfort me. 4.03. 17
contempt and beggary hangs upon thy back; 5.01. 71
lo his house | is empty on the back of montague, 5.03.204
and yesternight | return'd my letter back. 5.03.252
but must not break my back to heal his finger. TIM 2.01. 24
there's the fool hangs on your back already. 2.02. 55 P
you took, | when my indisposition put you back, 2.02.130
i have kept back their foes, | while they have 3.05.105
let me look back upon thee. 4.01. 1
rather than render back, out with your knives, 4.01. 9
thy back, i prithee. 4.03.395
thank them, and would send them back the plague, 5.01.137
consent of love | entreat thee back to athens, 5.01.141
so soon we shall drive back | of alcibiades th' 5.01.163
he put it by with the back of his hand thus, and JC 1.02.222 P
round, | he then unto the ladder turns his back, 2.01. 25
threaten'd me | ne'er look'd but on my back; 2.02. 11
cassius or caesar never shall turn back, | for i 3.01. 21
post back with speed, and tell him what hath 3.01.287
thou shalt not back till i have borne this corse 3.01.291
and i must pause till it come back to me. 3.02.107
stand back; room, bear back! 3.02.168 P
stand back; room, bear back! 3.02.168 P
he was but a fool that brought | my answer back. 4.03. 85
do face him there, | these people at our back. 4.03.212
this ensign here of mine was turning back; 5.03. 3
torchlight, but, my lord, | he came not back. 5.05. 3
my liege, | they are not yet come back. MAC 1.04. 3
our graves must send | those that we bury back, 3.04. 71
let's make haste, she'll soon be back again. 3.05. 36
i," | the cloudy messenger turns me his back, 3.06. 41
at least we'll die with harness on our back. 5.05. 51
but get thee back, my soul is too much charg'd 5.08. 5
intent | in going back to school in wittenberg, HAM 1.02.113
whose worth, if praises may go back again, 4.07. 27
are all the rest come back? 4.07. 49
hamlet comes back. 4.07.124
this project | should have a back or second, 4.07.153
he hath bore me on his back a thousand times. 5.01.186 P
your lordship is right welcome back to denmark. 5.02. 81
who brings back to him that you attend him in 5.02.196 P
i | return those duties back as are right fit, LR 1.01. 97
and on the sixt to turn thy hated back | upon 1.01.175
i have years on my back forty-eight. 1.04. 39 P
call the clotpole back. 1.04. 47 P
came not the slave back to me when i call'd him? 1.04. 52 P
thou bor'st thine ass on thy back o'er the dirt. 1.04.162 P
from home, | and not send back my /messenger. 2.04. 2
who hath /had three suits to his back, six 3.04.136 P
back, edmund, to my brother, | hasten his 4.02. 15
no, my good lord, i met him back again. 4.02. 90
strip thy own back, | thou hotly lusts to use 4.06.161
back do i toss these treasons to thy head, 5.03.147
when i came back | (for this was brief), i found OTH 2.03.236
i prithee call him back. 3.03. 51
good love, call him back. 3.03. 54
shall nev'r look back, nev'r ebb to humble love, 3.03.458
i do beseech your lordship call her back. 4.01.249
an instrument of this your calling back, | lay 4.02. 45
do you go back dismay'd? 5.02.269
hand could pluck her back that shov'd her on. ANT 1.02.127
goes to and back, /lackeying the varying tide, 1.04. 46
and carry back to sicily much tall youth | that 2.06. 7
to part with unhack'd edges and bear back | our 2.06. 38
if he do, sure he cannot weep't back again. 2.06.106 P
i will employ thee back again; 3.03. 36
eyes | by looking back what i have left behind 3.11. 53
we sent our schoolmaster, | is 'a come back? 3.11. 72
get thee back to caesar, | tell him thy 3.13.139
and o'er green neptune's back | with ships made 4.14. 58
they show'd his back above | the element they 5.02. 89
what have i kept back? 5.02.147
what, goest thou back? 5.02.155
thou shalt | go back, i warrant thee; 5.02.156
make her go back, even to the yielding, had i CYM 1.04.105 P
back my ring! 2.04.118
madam, | i thought you would not back again. 3.04.116
if you'll back to th' court — 3.04.130
with that suit upon my back will i ravish her; 3.05.137 P
to the court i'll knock her back, foot her home 3.05.144 P
and may save | but to look back in frown. 5.03. 28
having found the back door open | of the 5.03. 45
thou not /say, when i did push thee back — PER 5.01.126
lack, | save a proud rider on so proud a back. VEN 300
enfranchising his mouth, his back, his breast. 396
planting oblivion, beating reason back, 557
neck, | he on her belly falls, she on her back. 594
under whose sharp fangs on his back doth lie 663
leaves love upon her back, deeply distress'd. 814
but back retires to rate the boar for murther. 906
coming from thee, i could not put him back, LUC 843
dread night, wouldst thou one hour come back, 965
here one being throng'd bears back, all boll'n 1417
but now the mindful messenger, come back, 1583
back to the strait that forc'd him on so fast 1670
to push grief on, and back the same grief draw. 1673
held back his sorrow's tide, to make it more; 1789
then fell she on her back, fair queen, and PP 4.13
slack | to proffer, though she put thee back. 18.24
thee | calls back the lovely april of her prime, SON 3.10
thou gav'st me thine not to give back again. 22.14
who even but now come back again, assured | of 45.11
i send them back again and straight grow sad. 45.14
what strong hand can hold his swift foot back? 65.11
and so my patent back again is swerving. 87. 8
thou goest onwards, still will pluck thee back, 126. 6
but if thou catch thy hope, turn back to me, 143.11
if thou turn back and my loud crying still. 143.14

/BACKARE 1 FR 0.0001 REL FR 1 V 0 P
/backare! SHR 2.01. 73

BACKBITE 1 FR 0.0001 REL FR 0 V 1 P
for they are arrant knaves, and will backbite. 2H4 5.01. 33 P

BACKBITTEN 1 FR 0.0001 REL FR 0 V 1 P
no worse than they are backbitten, sir, for they 2H4 5.01. 34 P

BACK'D 10 FR 0.0011 REL FR 9 V 1 P
whose western side is with a vineyard back'd; MM 4.01. 29
back'd by the power of warwick, that false peer, 3H6 1.01. 52
but the safer when 'tis back'd with france. 4.01. 41
let us be back'd with god, and with the seas, 4.01. 43
and buckingham, back'd with the hardy welshmen, R3 4.03. 47
it is back'd like a weasel. HAM 3.02.380 P
great jupiter, upon his eagle back'd, | appear'd CYM 5.05.427
might well | be by a pair of kings back'd, in a TNK 3.01. 21
the colt that's back'd and burthen'd being young VEN 419
my will is back'd with resolution. LUC 352

BACK-FRIEND 1 FR 0.0001 REL FR 1 V 0 P
a back-friend, a shoulder-clapper, one that ERR 4.02. 37

BACKING 3 FR 0.0003 REL FR 1 V 2 P
call you that backing of your friends? 1H4 2.04.150 P
a plague upon such backing! 2.04.151 P
comes warwick, backing of the duke of york, 3H6 2.02. 69

BACK-RETURN 1 FR 0.0001 REL FR 1 V 0 P
till harry's back-return again to france. H5 5.pr. 41

BACKS 21 FR 0.0023 REL FR 17 V 4 P
surges under him, | and ride upon their backs. TMP 2.01.116
when gods have hot backs, what shall poor men do WIV 5.05. 11 P
pinch them, arms, legs, backs, shoulders, sides, 5.05. 54
dames | that ever turn'd their — backs — to LLL 5.02.161
for i have no more doublets than backs, no more SHR in.2. 9 P
their birthrights proudly on their backs, | to JN 2.01. 70
of night being pluck'd from off their backs, R2 3.02. 45
the shame | of those that turn'd their backs, 2H4 1.01.130
let them break your backs with burthens, take 2H6 4.08. 29 P
are at our backs, and therefore hence amain. 3H6 2.05.133
so other foes may set upon our backs. 5.01. 61
have broke their backs with laying manors on 'em H8 1.01. 84
backs red, and faces pale | with flight and COR 1.04. 37
wrung with wrongs more than our backs can bear. TIT 4.03. 49
this is the hag, when maids lie on their backs, ROM 1.04. 92
as we do turn our backs | from our companion TIM 4.02. 8
and so i do commend you to their backs. MAC 3.01. 38
moor are /now making the beast with two backs. OTH 1.01.117 P
let us score their backs, | and snatch 'em up, ANT 4.07. 12
and but the backs of britains seen, all flying CYM 5.03. 6
their babies at their backs, with their poor STM II.C 75

BACKSIDE 1 FR 0.0001 REL FR 0 V 1 P
was in deed, it went o' th' backside the town. CYM 1.02. 13 P

BACK'ST 1 FR 0.0001 REL FR 1 V 0 P
thou back'st reproach against long-living laud, LUC 622

BACKSWORD 1 FR 0.0001 REL FR 0 V 1 P
i knew him a good backsword man. 2H4 3.02. 64 P

BACK-TRICK 1 FR 0.0001 REL FR 0 V 1 P
i think i have the back-trick simply as strong TN 1.03.123 P

BACKWARD 24 FR 0.0027 REL FR 18 V 6 P
else | in the dark backward and abysm of time? TMP 1.02. 50
his backward voice is to utter foul speeches and 2.02. 91 P
featur'd, | but she would spell him backward. ADO 3.01. 61
what is a,b, spell'd backward, with the horn on LLL 5.01. 47 P
seem then that dobbin's tail grows backward. MV 2.02. 97 P
you go so much backward when you fight. AWW 1.01.200 P
only doth backward pull | our slow designs when 1.01.218
would demonstrate them now | but goers backward. 1.02. 48
when english measure backward their own ground JN 5.05. 3
perish the man whose mind is backward now! H5 4.03. 72
that by a pace goes backward with a purpose | it TRO 1.03.128
and you draw backward, we'll put you i' th' 3.02. 45 P
a lion that will fly | with his face backward. 4.01. 21
turn giddy, and be holp by backward turning; ROM 1.02. 47
thou wilt fall backward when thou hast more wit, 1.03. 42
thou wilt fall backward when thou comest to age, 1.03. 56
beard to beard, | and beat them backward home. MAC 5.05. 7
as i am, if like a crab you could go backward. HAM 2.02.204 P
and now they do restem | their backward course, OTH 1.03. 38
and presently | backward the jade comes o'er, TNK 5.04. 81
backward she push'd him, as she would be thrust, VEN 41
and backward drew | the heavenly moisture, that 541
shrinks backward in his shelly cave with pain, 1034
o, that record could with a backward look, SON 59. 5

BACKWARDLY 1 FR 0.0001 REL FR 1 V 0 P
and does he think so backwardly of me now, TIM 3.03. 18

BACKWARDS 1 FR 0.0001 REL FR 1 V 0 P
to darkness fleet souls that fly backwards. CYM 5.03. 25

BACK-WOUNDING 1 FR 0.0001 REL FR 1 V 0 P
back-wounding calumny | the whitest virtue MM 3.02.186

BACON 3 FR 0.0003 REL FR 0 V 3 P
"hang-hog" is latin for bacon, i warrant you. WIV 4.01. 48 P
i have a gammon of bacon and two razes of ginger 1H4 2.01. 24 P
boil like a gammon of bacon that will never be TNK 4.03. 38 P

BACON-FED 1 FR 0.0001 REL FR 0 V 1 P
bacon-fed knaves! 1H4 2.02. 84 P

BACONS 1 FR 0.0001 REL FR 0 V 1 P
on, bacons, on! 1H4 2.02. 90 P

BAD *(also pad)*

/BAD 3 FR 0.0003 REL FR 1 V 2 P
/now /good /or /bad, /'tis /but /the /chance /of TRO pr 31
/for /there /is /nothing /either /good /or /bad, HAM 2.02.250 P
/were /it /not /that /i /have /bad /dreams. 2.02.256 P

BAD 130 FR 0.0147 REL FR 105 V 25 P
good wombs have borne bad sons. TMP 1.02.120
to learn his wit t' exchange the bad for better. TGV 2.06. 13
fie, fie, unreverend tongue, to call her bad, 2.06. 14
so much of bad already hath possess'd them. 3.01.207
mine, | for they are harsh, untuneable, and bad. 3.01.209
one that serves a bad woman; MM 2.01. 64 P
music oft hath such a charm | to make bad good, 4.01. 15
much more the better | for being a little bad; 5.01.441
his act did not o'ertake his bad intent, | and 5.01.451
for me, | and by me, had not our hap been bad: ERR 1.01. 38
still did i tell him it was vild and bad. 5.01. 67
and with his bad legs falls into the cinquepace ADO 2.01. 78 P
tax not so bad a voice | to slander music any 2.03. 44
and i pray god his bad voice bode no mischief. 2.03. 81 P
mocks, | which is as bad as die with tickling. 3.01. 80
and bad thinking do not wrest true speaking, 3.04. 33 P
nor my bad life reft me so much of friends, 4.01.196
for which of my bad parts didst thou first fall 5.02. 60 P
else your memory is bad, going o'er it erewhile. LLL 4.01. 97
a better bad habit of frowning than the count MV 1.02. 59 P
there i have another bad match. 3.01. 44 P
blind man knows the cuckoo, | by the bad voice! 5.01.113
truly, the tree yields bad fruit. AYL 3.02.116 P
which are the only prologues to a bad voice? 5.03. 13 P
"among nine bad if one be good, | among nine bad AWW 1.03. 77
if one be good, | among nine bad if one be good, 1.03. 78
but loath am to produce | so bad an instrument. 5.03.202
many a good hanging prevents a bad marriage; TN 1.05. 19 P
it were a bad recompense for your love, to lay 2.01. 7 P
pardon me, sir, your bad entertainment. 2.01. 33 P
even as bad as those | that vulgars give bold'st WT 2.01. 93
all, both joy and terror | of good and bad, that 4.01. 2
bad world the while! JN 4.02.100
too good to be so, and too bad to live, | since R2 1.01. 40
upon his bad life to make all this good, | that 1.01. 99
but by bad courses may be understood | that 2.01.213
bad men, you violate | a twofold marriage — 5.01. 71
thy overflow of good converts to bad, | and thy 5.03. 64
a bad world, i say. 1H4 2.04.132 P
he told me that rebellion had bad luck, | and 2H4 1.01. 41
to wake a wolf is as bad as smell a fox. 1.02.155 P
as chaff, | and good from bad find no partition. 4.01.194
the king hath run bad humors on the knight, H5 2.01.121 P
your honor wins bad humors. 3.02. 26 P
but his few bad words are match'd with as few 3.02. 39 P
for our bad neighbor makes us early stirrers, 4.01. 6
and with them scourge the bad revolting stars 1H6 1.01. 4
lords, view these letters full of bad mischance. 1.01. 89
not half so bad as thine to england's king, 2H6 1.04. 47
becomes | so good a quarrel and so bad a peer. 2.01. 28
that's bad enough, for i am but reproach; 2.04. 96
so bad a death argues a monstrous life. 3.03. 30
hear | that things ill got had ever bad success? 3H6 2.02. 46
rest, | counting myself but bad till i be best. 5.06. 91
no news so bad abroad as this at home: R3 1.01.135
now, by saint john, that news is bad indeed! 1.01.138
which renders good for bad, blessings for curses 1.02. 69
the world is grown so bad | that wrens make prey 1.03. 69
bad is the world, and all will come to nought, 3.06. 13
good or bad news, that thou com'st in so bluntly 4.03. 45
bad news, my lord. 4.03. 46
bett'ring thy loss makes the bad causer worse; 4.04.122
nor none so bad but well may be reported. 4.04.458
neither good nor bad! 4.04.459
so long have slept upon | this bold bad man. H8 2.02. 43
of a king, | sans check, to good and bad. TRO 1.03. 94
a scantling | of good or bad unto the general, 1.03.342
nor fear of bad success in a bad cause, | can 2.02.117
nor fear of bad success in a bad cause, | can 2.02.117
against that dog of as bad a kind, achilles; 5.04. 13 P
if any think brave death outweighs bad life, COR 1.06. 71
good or bad? 2.01. 3 P
of the people is as bad as that which he 2.02. 22 P
in a bad quarrel slain a virtuous son. TIT 1.01.342
is thy news good or bad? ROM 2.05. 35
let me be satisfied, is't good or bad? 2.05. 37
for it was bad enough before their spite. 4.01. 31
a plague on thee, thou art too bad to curse! TIM 4.03.360
canst not paint a man | so bad as is thyself. 5.01. 32
which is indeed, sir, a mender of bad soles. JC 1.01. 14 P
of opening my lips and receiving the bad air. 1.02.250 P
unto bad causes swear | such creatures as men 2.01.131
that one of two bad ways you must conceit me, 3.01.192
tear him for his bad verses, tear him for his 3.03. 30 P
for his bad verses, tear him for his bad verses. 3.03. 31 P
good words are better than bad strokes, octavius 5.01. 29
in your bad strokes, brutus, you give good words 5.01. 30
and with those | that would make good of bad, MAC 2.04. 41
things bad begun make strong themselves by ill. 3.02. 55
you were better have a bad epitaph than their HAM 2.02.525 P
almost as bad, good mother, | as kill a king, 3.04. 28
this bad begins and worse remains behind. 3.04.179
that our drift look through our bad performance, 4.07.151
i know not, madam. 'tis too bad, too bad. LR 2.01. 96
i know not, madam. 'tis too bad, too bad. 2.01. 96
bad is the trade that must play fool to sorrow, 4.01. 38
general, be advis'd, | he comes to bad intent. OTH 1.02. 56
destruction on my head if my bad blame | light 1.03.177
not to pick bad from bad, but by bad mend. 4.03.105
not to pick bad from bad, but by bad mend. 4.03.105
not to pick bad from bad, but by bad mend. 4.03.105
the nature of bad news infects the teller. ANT 1.02. 95
matter to mine ear, | the good and bad together: 2.05. 55
be honest, it is never good | to bring bad news. 2.05. 86
for so bad a prayer as his | was never yet for 4.09. 26
princess is a thing | too bad for bad report; CYM 1.01. 17
princess is a thing | too bad for bad report; 1.01. 17

so slipp'ry that | the fear's as bad as falling; 3.03. 49
but to win time | to lose so bad employment, in 3.04.110
ay, and that | from one bad thing to worse, not 4.02.134
is living, let the time run on | to good or bad. 5.05.129
bad child, worse father, to entice his own | to PER 1.ch. 27
then were it certain you were not so bad | as 1.01.125
for though he strive | to killen bad, keep good 2.ch. 20
till fortune, tir'd with doing bad, | threw him 2.ch. 37
i never spake bad word, nor did ill turn | to 4.01. 75
neither of these are so bad as thou art, | since 4.06.161
with mind assur'd | 'tis bad he goes about? TNK 1.02. 98
being so bad, such numbers seek for thee? LUC 896
lending him wit that to bad debtors lends: 964
"o time, thou tutor both to good and bad, 995
doubt, | till my bad angel fire my good one out. PP 2.14
bad in the best, though excellent in neither. 7.18
in days long since, before these last so bad. SON 67.14
ill, | so you o'er-green my bad, my good allow? 112. 4
creating every bad a perfect best | as fast as 114. 7
in their wills count bad what i think good? 121. 8
all men are bad and in their badness reign. 121.14
now this ill-wresting world is grown so bad, 140.11
doubt, | till my bad angel fire my good one out. 144.14
BADE 47 FR 0.0053 REL FR 38 V 9 P
perform'd to point the tempest that i bade thee? TMP 1.02.194
why, sir, who bade you call her? TGV 2.01. 9 P
love bade me swear, and love bids me forswear. 2.06. 6
i carried mistress silvia the dog you bade me. 4.04. 46 P
and she bade me tell your worship that her WIV 2.02.100 P
i bade the rascal knock upon your gate, | and SHR 1.02. 37
he bade me store up, as a triple eye, | safer AWW 2.01.108
helen, | i bade her, if her fortunes ever stood 5.03. 84
the lady bade take away the fool, therefore i TN 1.05. 52 P
sir, i bade them take away you. 1.05. 54 P
my lady bade me tell you that, though she 2.03. 96 P
i bade you never speak again of him; 3.01.107
bade me come smiling and cross-garter'd to you, 5.01.337
whom he loves | (he bade me say so) more than WT 5.01.146
your highness bade me ask for it to-day. H5 2.02. 63
but he that temper'd thee, bade thee stand up, 2.02.118
so 'a bade me lay more clothes on his feet. 2.03. 22 P
you bade me ban, and will you bid me leave? 2H6 3.02.333
bade me rely on him as on my father, | and he R3 2.02. 25
you he bade | attend him here this morning. H8 3.02. 81
bade me enjoy it, with the place and honors, 3.02.248
he bade me take a trumpet, | and to this purpose TRO 1.03.263
i bade the vile owl go learn me the tenor of the 2.01. 90 P
hector bade ask. 4.05. 71
she's well, but bade me not commend her to you. 4.05.180
in very spite of cunning, | bade him win all. 5.05. 42
at twelve year old, | i bade her come. ROM 1.03. 3
thine ears (like tapsters that bade welcome) TIM 4.03.215
as i was, i plunged in | and bade him follow; JC 1.02.106
ay, and that tongue of his that bade the romans 1.02.125
and so bestow these papers as you bade me. 1.03.151
and, being prostrate, thus he bade me say: 3.01.125
nev'r shook hands, nor bade farewell to him, MAC 1.02. 21
he bade me, from him, call thee thane of cawdor; 1.03.105
of king upon me, | and bade them speak to him; 3.01. 58
his majesty bade me signify to you that 'a has HAM 5.02.101 P
to th' very moment that he bade me tell it; OTH 1.03.133
and bade me, if i had a friend that lov'd her, 1.03.164
bade her wrong stay, and her displeasure fly; 2.01.153
bade him anon return and here speak with me, 4.01. 80
i have laid those sheets you bade me on the bed. 4.03. 22
thou not then | to do this when i bade thee? ANT 4.14. 82
antony | did tell me of you, bade me trust you, 5.02. 13
till he had done his sacrifice, | as dian bade; PER 5.02. 13
she bade love last, and yet she fell a-turning. PP 7.16
she bade good night that kept my rest away, 14. 2
for why, she sight, and bade me come to-morrow. 14.24
BADG'D 1 FR 0.0001 REL FR 1 V 0 P
hands and faces were all badg'd with blood; MAC 2.03.102
BADGE 14 FR 0.0015 REL FR 11 V 3 P
modest enough without a badge of bitterness. ADO 1.01. 23 P
black is the badge of hell, | the hue of LLL 4.03.250
bearing the badge of faith to prove them true? MND 3.02.127
for suff'rance is the badge of all our tribe. MV 1.03.110
pale, which is the badge of pusillanimity and 2H4 4.03.105 P
this hour is an honorable badge of the service; H5 4.07.101 P
and he first took exceptions at this badge, 1H6 4.01.105
not, | in that he wears the badge of somerset. 4.01.177
that slanders me with murther's crimson badge. 2H6 3.02.200
might i but know thee by thy /household badge. 5.01.201
now, by my father's badge, old nevil's crest, 5.01.202
sweet mercy is nobility's true badge. TIT 1.01.119
better than he have worn vulcan's badge. 2.01. 89
i give | a badge of fame to slander's livery, LUC 1054
BADGES 4 FR 0.0004 REL FR 4 V 0 P
mark but the badges of these men, my lords, TMP 5.01.267
and by these badges understand the king. LLL 5.02.754
smiles, | the badges of his grief and patience, R2 5.02. 33
slow | but heavy tears, badges of either's woe. SON 44.14
BADLY 1 FR 0.0001 REL FR 1 V 0 P
badly, i fear. how fares your majesty? JN 5.03. 2
BADNESS 4 FR 0.0004 REL FR 3 V 1 P
but he's more, | had i more name for badness. MM 5.01. 59
set a-work by a reprovable badness in himself. LR 3.05. 7 P
vices of thy mistress | as badness would desire. 4.06.254
all men are bad and in their badness reign. SON 121.14
BADST 2 FR 0.0002 REL FR 2 V 0 P
and, as thou badst me, | in troops i have TMP 1.02.219
and badst me bury love. ROM 2.03. 83
BAES 2 FR 0.0002 REL FR 0 V 2 P
hear her lamb when it baes will never answer a ADO 3.03. 71 P
he's a lamb indeed, that baes like a bear. COR 2.01. 11 P
BAFFLE 2 FR 0.0002 REL FR 0 V 2 P
read politic authors, i will baffle sir toby, i TN 2.05.162 P
an' i do not, call me villain and baffle me. 1H4 1.02.101 P
BAFFLED 3 FR 0.0003 REL FR 3 V 0 P
alas, poor fool, how have they baffled thee! TN 5.01.369
i am disgrac'd, impeach'd, and baffled here, R2 1.01.170
and shall good news be baffled? 2H4 5.03.105
BAG 8 FR 0.0009 REL FR 4 V 4 P
and i have a bag of money here troubles me. WIV 2.02.171 P
what, a hodge-pudding? a bag of flax? 5.05.151 P
and why dost thou deny the bag of gold? ERR 4.04. 96
a sealed bag, two sealed bags of ducats, | of MV 2.08. 18
retreat, though not with bag and baggage, yet AYL 3.02.161 P
in and out the enemy, | with bag and baggage. WT 1.02.206
my gracious lord, here is the bag of gold. TIT 2.03.280
then put up your pipes in your bag, for i'll OTH 3.01. 19 P
BAGGAGE 9 FR 0.0010 REL FR 4 V 5 P
you witch, you rag, you baggage, you poulcat, WIV 4.02.185 P
thou baggage, let me in. ERR 3.01. 57
though not with bag and baggage, yet with scrip AYL 3.02.161 P
y' are a baggage, the slys are no rogues. SHR in.1. 3 P
in and out the enemy, | with bag and baggage. WT 1.02.206
out, you baggage! ROM 3.05.156
hang thee, young baggage! 3.05.160
is dead that lay with the little baggage. PER 4.02. 23 P
if the peevish baggage would but give way to 4.06. 19 P
/BAGOT 1 FR 0.0001 REL FR 1 V 0 P
ourself and bushy, /bagot /here /and /green, R2 1.04. 23
BAGOT 5 FR 0.0005 REL FR 5 V 0 P
which they say is held | by bushy, bagot, and R2 2.03.165
where is bagot? 3.02.122
call forth bagot. 4.01. 1
now, bagot, freely speak thy mind, | what thou 4.01. 2
bagot, forbear, thou shalt not take it up. 4.01. 30
BAGPIPE 4 FR 0.0004 REL FR 2 V 2 P
and others, when the bagpipe sings i' th' nose, MV 4.01. 49
why he, a woollen bagpipe, but of force | must 4.01. 56
no, the bagpipe could not move you. WT 4.04.183 P
yea, or the drone of a lincolnshire bagpipe. 1H4 1.02. 76 P
BAGPIPER 1 FR 0.0001 REL FR 1 V 0 P
eyes, | and laugh like parrots at a bagpiper; MV 1.01. 53
BAGS 9 FR 0.0010 REL FR 9 V 0 P
than stamps in gold, or sums in sealed bags; WIV 3.04. 16
a sealed bag, two sealed bags of ducats, | of MV 2.08. 18
and that his bags shall prove. SHR 1.02.177
and ere our coming see thou shake the bags | of JN 3.03. 7
the clergy's bags | are lank and lean with thy 2H6 1.03.128
but fathers that bear bags | shall see their LR 2.04. 50
to your house, your daughter, and your bags! OTH 1.01. 80
honor, | or tie my pleasure up in silken bags, PER 3.02. 41
and entreasur'd | with full bags of spices! 3.02. 66
BAIL 17 FR 0.0019 REL FR 14 V 3 P
i spy comfort, i cry bail. MM 3.02. 41 P
i hope, sir, your good worship will be my bail. 3.02. 73 P
you will not bail me then, sir? 3.02. 81 P
first, provost, let me bail these gentle three. 5.01.357
i do obey thee, till i give thee bail. ERR 4.01. 80
in the street, | and that shall bail me. 4.01.107
i sent you money, sir, to be your bail, | by 5.01.382
i'll put in bail, my liege. AWW 5.03.285
good mother, fetch my bail. 5.03.295
sirrah, call in my /sons to be my bail. 2H6 5.01.111
shall be their father's bail, and bane to those 5.01.120
and here comes clifford to deny their bail. 5.01.123
i did, my lord, yet let me be their bail, | for TIT 2.03.295
thou shalt not bail them, see thou follow me. 2.03.299
that blow did bail it from the deep unrest | of LUC 1725
arrest | without all bail shall carry me away, SON 74. 2
then my friend's heart let my poor heart bail; 133.10
BAILIFF 1 FR 0.0001 REL FR 0 V 1 P
then a process-server, a bailiff, then he WT 4.03. 96 P
/BAILLEZ 1 FR 0.0001 REL FR 0 V 1 P
rugby, /baillez me some paper. WIV 1.04. 87 P
BAIRN *(see barne, etc.)*
BAISANT 1 FR 0.0001 REL FR 0 V 1 P
votre /grandeur en baisant la main d'une (notre H5 5.02.255 P
BAISEES 1 FR 0.0001 REL FR 0 V 1 P
demoiselles pour etre baisees devant leur noces, H5 5.02.258 P
/BAISER 1 FR 0.0001 REL FR 0 V 1 P
i cannot tell wat is /baiser en anglish. H5 5.02.262 P
/BAIT 1 FR 0.0001 REL FR 1 V 0 P
/that /my /wretchedness /doth /bait /myself, R2 4.01.238
BAIT 18 FR 0.0020 REL FR 15 V 3 P
catch a saint, | with saints dost bait thy hook! MM 2.02.180
do their gay vestments his affections bait? ERR 2.01. 94
bait the hook well, this fish will bite. ADO 2.03.108 P
and greedily devour the treacherous bait; 3.01. 28
of the false sweet bait that we lay for it. 3.01. 33
contriv'd | to bait me with this foul derision? MND 3.02.197
but fish not with this melancholy bait | for MV 1.01.101
to bait fish withal — if it will feed nothing 3.01. 53 P
if the young dace be a bait for the old pike, i 2H4 3.02.330 P
we'll bait thy bears to death, | and manacle the 2H6 5.01.148
pleas'd with this dainty bait, thus goes to bed. TRO 5.08. 20
when as the one is wounded with the bait, | the TIT 4.04. 92
she steal love's sweet bait from fearful hooks. ROM 2.pr. 8
brutus, bait not me, | i'll not endure it. JC 4.03. 28
your bait of falsehood take this carp of truth, HAM 2.01. 60
where't grows, | but worn a bait for ladies. CYM 3.04. 57
the tender nibbler would not touch the bait, PP 4.11
past reason hated as a swallowed bait | on SON 129. 7
BAITED 5 FR 0.0005 REL FR 4 V 1 P
alas, poor machabeus, how hath he been baited! LLL 5.02.631 P
and baited it with all th' unmuzzled thoughts TN 3.01.119
to be so baited, scorn'd, and stormed at. R3 1.03.108
why stay we to be baited | with one that wants COR 4.02. 43
and to be baited with the rabble's curse. MAC 5.08. 29
BAITING 1 FR 0.0001 REL FR 1 V 0 P
and here ye lie baiting of bombards, when | ye H8 5.03. 81
BAITING-PLACE 1 FR 0.0001 REL FR 1 V 0 P
if thou dar'st bring them to the baiting-place. 2H6 5.01.150
BAITS 4 FR 0.0004 REL FR 4 V 0 P
late hath beat her husband, | and now baits me! WT 2.03. 93
be caught | with cautelous baits and practice. COR 4.01. 33
than baits to fish, or honey-stalks to sheep, TIT 4.04. 91
she touch'd no unknown baits, nor fear'd no LUC 103
BAJAZETH'S 1 FR 0.0001 REL FR 0 V 1 P
mouth and buy myself another of bajazeth's mule, AWW 4.01. 42 P
BAK'D 6 FR 0.0006 REL FR 5 V 1 P
o' th' earth | when it is bak'd with frost. TMP 1.02.256
had bak'd thy blood and made it heavy, thick, JN 3.03. 43
and then to be bak'd with no date in the pie, TRO 1.02.256 P
and in that paste let their vile heads be bak'd. TIT 5.02.200
look to the bak'd meats, good angelica, | spare ROM 4.04. 5
bak'd and impasted with the parching streets, HAM 2.02.459
BAK'D-MEATS 1 FR 0.0001 REL FR 1 V 0 P
the funeral bak'd-meats | did coldly furnish HAM 1.02.180
BAKE 2 FR 0.0002 REL FR 1 V 1 P
wring, brew, bake, scour, dress meat and drink, WIV 1.04. 96 P
a fenny snake, | in the cauldron boil and bake; MAC 4.01. 13
BAKED 1 FR 0.0001 REL FR 1 V 0 P
why, there they are, both baked in this pie; TIT 5.03. 60
BAKER'S 1 FR 0.0001 REL FR 0 V 1 P
they say the owl was a baker's daughter. HAM 4.05. 43 P
BAKERS' 1 FR 0.0001 REL FR 0 V 1 P
i have given them away to bakers' wives, they 1H4 3.03. 70 P
BAKES 1 FR 0.0001 REL FR 1 V 0 P
and bakes the /elf-locks in foul sluttish hairs, ROM 1.04. 90
BAKING 1 FR 0.0001 REL FR 0 V 1 P
the cake, the heating the oven, and the baking; TRO 1.01. 25 P
/BALANCE 1 FR 0.0001 REL FR 1 V 0 P
/i /have /in /equal /balance /justly /weigh'd 2H4 4.01. 67
BALANCE 9 FR 0.0010 REL FR 6 V 3 P
shall ne'er weigh more reasons in her balance. ADO 5.01.207 P
a mote will turn the balance, which pyramus, MND 5.01.318 P
are there balance here to weigh | the flesh? MV 4.01.255
so tott'ring in the balance that i could neither AWW 1.03.124 P
if not to thy estate, | a balance more replete. 2.03.176
but in the balance of great bullingbrook, R2 3.04. 87
therefore still bear the balance and the sword, 2H4 5.02.103
words, | except a sword or sceptre balance it. 2H6 5.01. 9
commit my cause in balance to be weigh'd. TIT 1.01. 55
BALD 17 FR 0.0019 REL FR 5 V 12 P
like to lose your hair, and prove a bald jerkin. TMP 4.01.237 P
as plain as the plain bald pate of father time ERR 2.02. 70 P
to recover his hair that grows bald by nature. 2.02. 73 P
time himself is bald, and therefore, to the 2.02.106 P
to the world's end, will have bald followers. 2.02.107 P
i knew 'twould be a bald conclusion. 2.02.108 P
with age | and high top bald with dry antiquity: AYL 4.03.105
time the clock-setter, that bald sexton time! JN 3.01.324
this bald unjointed chat of his, my lord, | i 1H4 1.03. 65
precious rich crown for a pitiful bald crown! 2.04.382 P
always a little, lean, old, chopp'd, bald shot. 2H4 3.02.275 P
a curl'd pate will grow bald, a fair face will H5 5.02.161 P
some abram, some bald, but that our wits are so COR 2.03. 20 P
should the people do with these bald tribunes? 3.01.164
of the senators but they stand bald before him. 4.05.194 P
make curl'd-pate ruffians bald, | and let the TIM 4.03.160
little wit in thy bald crown when thou gav'st LR 1.04.162 P
BALD-PATE 1 FR 0.0001 REL FR 1 V 0 P
come hither, goodman bald-pate, do you know me? MM 5.01.326
BALD-PATED 1 FR 0.0001 REL FR 0 V 1 P
sir, why, you bald-pated, lying rascal, you must MM 5.01.352 P
BALDRICK 2 FR 0.0002 REL FR 1 V 1 P
or hang my bugle in an invisible baldrick, all ADO 1.01.242 P
his thigh a sword | hung by a curious baldrick, TNK 4.02. 86
BALE 1 FR 0.0001 REL FR 1 V 0 P
point of battle, | the one side must have bale. COR 1.01.163
BALEFUL 7 FR 0.0008 REL FR 7 V 0 P
deceit | contriv'd by art and baleful sorcery. 1H6 2.01. 15
voice, | by sight of these our baleful enemies. 5.04.122
thou baleful messenger, out of my sight! 2H6 3.02. 48
if we should recompt | our baleful news, and at 3H6 2.01. 97
overcome with moss and baleful mistletoe; TIT 2.03. 95
ear | the story of that baleful burning night, 5.03. 83
with baleful weeds and precious-juiced flowers. ROM 2.03. 8
BALK 2 FR 0.0002 REL FR 2 V 0 P
balk logic with acquaintance that you have, SHR 1.01. 34
or altogether balk | the prey wherein by nature LUC 696
BALK'D 2 FR 0.0002 REL FR 1 V 1 P
look'd for at your hand, and this was balk'd. TN 3.02. 24 P
balk'd in their own blood, did sir walter see 1H4 1.01. 69
BALL 6 FR 0.0006 REL FR 5 V 1 P
but when from under this terrestrial ball | he R2 3.02. 41
been an ignis fatuus or a ball of wildfire, 1H4 3.03. 40 P
the acts commenced on this ball of earth. 2H4 in 5
'tis not the balm, the sceptre, and the ball, H5 4.01.260
she would be as swift in motion as a ball; ROM 2.05. 13
hath made the ball | for them to play upon, PER 2.01. 60
BALLAD *(also ballet, etc.)*
BALLAD 11 FR 0.0012 REL FR 3 V 8 P
with a woeful ballad | made to his mistress' AYL 2.07.148
for i the ballad will repeat, | which men full AWW 1.03. 60
i love a ballad but even too well, if it be WT 4.04.188 P
here's another ballad, of a fish that appear'd 4.04.275 P
and sung this ballad against the hard hearts of 4.04.277 P
the ballad is very pitiful, and as true. 4.04.281 P
this is a merry ballad, but a very pretty one. 4.04.286 P
brooch, table-book, ballad, knife, tape, glove, 4.04.598 P
i will have it in a particular ballad else, with 2H4 4.03. 48 P
is but a prater, a rhyme is but a ballad; H5 5.02.159 P
and scald rhymers | ballad 's out a' tune. ANT 5.02.216
BALLAD-MAKER'S 1 FR 0.0001 REL FR 0 V 1 P
mine eyes with a ballad-maker's pen and hang me ADO 1.01.252 P
BALLAD-MAKERS 2 FR 0.0002 REL FR 0 V 2 P
this hour that ballad-makers cannot be able to WT 5.02. 24 P
iron, increase tailors, and breed ballad-makers. COR 4.05.220 P
BALLADS 5 FR 0.0005 REL FR 1 V 4 P
a divulged shame, | traduc'd by odious ballads; AWW 2.01.172
them as he had eaten ballads and all men's ears WT 4.04.185 P
what hast here? ballads? 4.04.259 P
and let's first see moe ballads. 4.04.274 P
and i have not ballads made on you all and sung 1H4 2.02. 45 P
BALLAST 1 FR 0.0001 REL FR 0 V 1 P
armadoes of carrects to be ballast at her nose. ERR 3.02.137 P
BALLASTING 1 FR 0.0001 REL FR 1 V 0 P
less, and so more equal ballasting | to thee, CYM 3.06. 77
BALLET *(also ballad, etc.)*
BALLET 4 FR 0.0004 REL FR 0 V 4 P
is there not a ballet, boy, of the king and the LLL 1.02.109 P
guilty of such a ballet some three ages since, 1.02.111 P
peter quince to write a ballet of this dream. MND 4.01.215 P
i love a ballet in print, a-life, for then we WT 4.04.260 P
BALLET-MONGERS 1 FR 0.0001 REL FR 1 V 0 P
than one of these same metre ballet-mongers. 1H4 3.01.128
BALLOW 1 FR 0.0001 REL FR 0 V 1 P
whither your costard or my ballow be the harder. LR 4.06.241 P
BALLS 10 FR 0.0011 REL FR 10 V 0 P
or whether, riding on the balls of mine, | seem MV 3.02.117
why, these balls bound, there's noise in it. AWW 2.03.297
when we have match'd our rackets to these balls, H5 1.02.261
of his | hath turn'd his balls to gun-stones, 1.02.282
i did present him with the paris balls. 2.04.131
bent | the fatal balls of murthering basilisks. 5.02. 17

that twofold balls and treble sceptres carry. MAC 4.01.121
or i'll spurn thine eyes | like balls before me; ANT 2.05. 64
are balls of quenchless fire to burn thy city. LUC 1554
sometime diverted their poor balls are tied | to LC 24
/BALM 1 FR 0.0001 REL FR 1 V 0 P
/mine /own /tears /i /wash /away /my /balm, R2 4.01.207
BALM 16 FR 0.0018 REL FR 16 V 0 P
with juice of balm and every precious flow'r; WIV 5.05. 62
balm his foul head in warm distilled waters, SHR in.1. 48
the which no balm can cure but his heart–blood R2 1.01.172
can wash the balm off from an anointed king; 3.02. 55
hearse | be drops of balm to sanctify thy head; 2H4 4.05.114
and i know | 'tis not the balm, the sceptre, and H5 4.01.260
thy balm wash'd off wherewith thou was anointed. 3H6 3.01. 17
my pity hath been balm to heal their wounds, 4.08. 41
life | i pour the helpless balm of my poor eyes. R3 1.02. 13
but, saying thus, in stead of oil and balm, TRO 1.01. 61
fear, | we sent to thee to give thy rages balm, TIM 5.04. 16
balm of hurt minds, great nature's second course MAC 2.02. 36
the argument of your praise, balm of your age, LR 1.01.215
as sweet as balm, as soft as air, as gentle — ANT 5.02.311
and, trembling in her passion, calls it balm, VEN 27
and drop sweet balm in priam's painted wound, LUC 1466
/BALM'D 1 FR 0.0001 REL FR 1 V 0 P
/might /yet /have /balm'd /thy /broken /sinews, LR 3.06. 98
BALM'D 1 FR 0.0001 REL FR 1 V 0 P
balm'd and entreasur'd | with full bags of PER 3.02. 65
BALMS 3 FR 0.0003 REL FR 3 V 0 P
to a gentle bath | and balms applied to you, yet COR 1.06. 64
convent in their behoof, our richest balms, TNK 1.04. 31
balms, and gums, and heavy cheers, | sacred 1.05. 4
BALMY 3 FR 0.0003 REL FR 3 V 0 P
to have their balmy slumbers wak'd with strife. OTH 2.03.258
o balmy breath, that dost almost persuade 5.02. 16
now with the drops of this most balmy time | my SON 107. 9
BALSAMUM 1 FR 0.0001 REL FR 1 V 0 P
and i have bought | the oil, the balsamum, and ERR 4.01. 89
BALSOM 1 FR 0.0001 REL FR 1 V 0 P
is this the balsom that the usuring senate TIM 3.05.109
BALTHASAR 3 FR 0.0003 REL FR 2 V 1 P
come, balthasar, we'll hear that song again. ADO 2.03. 43
yea, marry, dost thou hear, balthasar? 2.03. 84 P
how now, balthasar? ROM 5.01. 12
BALTHAZAR 5 FR 0.0005 REL FR 4 V 1 P
y' are sad, signior balthazar, pray god our ERR 3.01. 19
o, signior balthazar, either at flesh or fish, 3.01. 22
where balthazar and i did dine together. 5.01.223
now, balthazar, | as i have ever found thee MV 3.04. 45
his name is balthazar. 4.01.154 P
'BAN *(also ca–caliban, caliban)*
'BAN 2 FR 0.0002 REL FR 2 V 0 P
'ban, 'ban, ca–caliban | has a new master, get a TMP 2.02.184
'ban, 'ban, ca–caliban | has a new master, get a 2.02.184
BAN 6 FR 0.0006 REL FR 6 V 0 P
and ban thine enemies, both mine and thine! 2H6 2.04. 25
ay, every joint should seem to curse and ban; 3.02.319
you bade me ban, and will you bid me leave? 3.02.333
with hecat's ban thrice blasted, thrice HAM 3.02.258
cries, | and bitter words to ban her cruel foes; LUC 1460
strength, | and ban and brawl, and say thee nay; PP 18.32
BANBURY 1 FR 0.0001 REL FR 0 V 1 P
you banbury cheese! WIV 1.01.128 P
BAN'D 1 FR 0.0001 REL FR 1 V 0 P
to give ten thousand ducats | to have it ban'd? MV 4.01. 46
BAND* *(also bond, etc.)*
BAND* 29 FR 0.0032 REL FR 22 V 7 P
tell me, was he arrested on a band? ERR 4.02. 49
not on a band but on a stronger thing: 4.02. 50
ay, sir, the sergeant of the band: 4.03. 30 P
any man to answer it that breaks his band; 4.03. 31 P
thee | to bind our loves up in a holy band; ADO 3.01.114
captain of our fairy band, | helena is here at MND 3.02.110
chosen out of the gross band of the unfaithful; AYL 4.01.195 P
he must think us some band of strangers i' th' AWW 4.01. 14 P
now will i charge you in the band of truth, 4.02. 56
me this other day to turn him out a' th' band. 4.03.200 P
hast thou, according to thy oath and band, R2 1.01. 2
'tis nothing but some band that he is ent'red 5.02. 65
he would not take his band and yours, he lik'd 2H4 1.02. 32 P
the royal captain of this ruin'd band | walking H5 4.pr. 29
do but behold yond poor and starved band, | and 4.02. 16
we few, we happy few, we band of brothers; 4.03. 60
to ireland will you lead a band of men, 2H6 3.01.312
whiles i in ireland nourish a mighty band, | i 3.01.348
for with a band of thirty thousand men | comes 3H6 2.02. 68
with all his threat'ning band of typhon's brood, TIT 4.02. 94
who leads towards rome a band of warlike goths, 5.02.113
doth daily make revolt | in my penurious band. TIM 4.03. 93
you shall find the band that seems to tie their ANT 2.06.120 P
and as my farthest band | shall pass on thy 3.02. 26
more of thee merited than a band of clotens CYM 5.05.304
and quality i hold i may | continue in thy band. TNK 5.01.162
sometime her arms infold him like a band: VEN 225
jail of snow, | or ivory in an alablaster band, 363
fearing some hard news from the warlike band LUC 255
BANDETTO 1 FR 0.0001 REL FR 1 V 0 P
a roman sworder and bandetto slave | murder'd 2H6 4.01.135
BANDIED 1 FR 0.0001 REL FR 1 V 0 P
well bandied both, a set of wit well played. LLL 5.02. 29
BANDING 1 FR 0.0001 REL FR 1 V 0 P
and, banding themselves in contrary parts, | do 1H6 3.01. 81
BANDIT *(see bandetto)*
BAN–DOGS 1 FR 0.0001 REL FR 1 V 0 P
time when screech–owls cry and ban–dogs howl, 2H6 1.04. 18
BANDS* 15 FR 0.0017 REL FR 15 V 0 P
but release me from my bands | with the help of TMP ep 9
that must take hands | to join in hymen's bands, AYL 5.04.129
who gently would dissolve the bands of life, R2 2.02. 71
if not, the end of life cancels all bands, | and 1H4 3.02.157
in infant bands crown'd king | of france and H5 ep 9
your troops of horsemen with his bands of foot, 1H6 4.01.165
york, | and die in bands for this unmanly deed! 3H6 1.01.186
us | with some few bands of chosen soldiers, 3.03.204
joy, | to him forthwith in holy wedlock bands. 3.03.243
take your commission, hie you to your bands, COR 1.02. 26
their bands i' th' vaward are the /antiates, 1.06. 53
lost by his father, with all bands of law, | to HAM 1.02. 24
our hands | unite comutual in most sacred bands. 3.02.160
bring him through the bands. ANT 3.12. 25
not muster'd | among the bands) may drive us to CYM 4.04. 11
BANDY 7 FR 0.0008 REL FR 5 V 2 P
i will bandy with thee in faction; AYL 5.01. 55 P
to bandy word for word and frown for frown; SHR 5.02.172
i will not bandy with thee word for word, | but 3H6 1.04. 49
enjoy, | one fit to bandy with thy lawless sons, TIT 1.01.312
my words would bandy her to my sweet love, | and ROM 2.05. 14
do you bandy looks with me, you rascal? LR 1.04. 84 P
to bandy hasty words, to scant my sizes, | and 2.04.175
BANDYING 2 FR 0.0002 REL FR 2 V 0 P
this factious bandying of their favorites, | but 1H6 4.01.190
hath | forbid this bandying in verona streets. ROM 3.01. 89
BANE 7 FR 0.0008 REL FR 6 V 1 P
like rats that ravin down their proper bane, | a MM 1.02.129
and bane to those | that for my surety will 2H6 5.01.120
'twill be his death, 'twill be his bane, he TRO 4.02. 93 P
let rome herself be bane unto herself, | and she TIT 5.03. 73
i will not be afraid of death and bane, | till MAC 5.03. 59
preserv'd the britains, was the romans' bane." CYM 5.03. 58
nothing but my body's bane would cure thee." VEN 372
BANES 4 FR 0.0004 REL FR 3 V 1 P
i'll crave the day | when i shall ask the banes, SHR 2.01.180
make friends, invite, and proclaim the banes, 3.02. 16
such as had been ask'd twice on the banes, such 1H4 4.02. 17 P
and i, her husband, contradict your banes. LR 5.03. 87
BANG 1 FR 0.0001 REL FR 0 V 1 P
you'll bear me a bang for that, i fear. JC 3.03. 18 P
BANG'D 2 FR 0.0002 REL FR 1 V 1 P
you should have bang'd the youth into dumbness. TN 3.02. 23 P
the desperate tempest hath so bang'd the turks, OTH 2.01. 21
/BANISH 1 FR 0.0001 REL FR 1 V 0 P
/force /perforce /compell'd /to /banish /him; 2H4 4.01.114
BANISH 38 FR 0.0043 REL FR 30 V 8 P
who, all enrag'd, will banish valentine; TGV 2.06. 38
blushes | that banish what they sue for. MM 2.04.163
nor do not banish reason | for inequality, but 5.01. 64
and banish hence these abject lowly dreams. SHR in.2. 32
therefore we banish you our territories. R2 1.03.139
(our part therein we banish with yourselves) 1.03.181
six years we banish him, and he shall go. 1.03.248
think not the king did banish thee, | but thou 1.03.279
as 'twere to banish their affects with him. 1.04. 30
banish us both, and send the king with me. 5.01. 83
him keep with, the rest banish. 1H4 2.04.431 P
no, my good lord, banish peto, banish bardolph, 2.04.474 P
banish peto, banish bardolph, banish poins, but 2.04.474 P
banish bardolph, banish poins, but for sweet 2.04.475 P
falstaff, banish not him thy harry's company, 2.04.478 P
company, banish not him thy harry's company — 2.04.478 P
him thy harry's company — banish plump jack, 2.04.479 P
banish plump jack, and banish all the world. 2.04.480 P
till then i banish thee, on pain of death, | as 2H4 5.05. 63
henceforth we banish thee, on pain of death. 1H6 4.01. 47
and you, good uncle, banish all offense. 5.05. 96
lord, | banish the canker of ambitious thoughts! 2H6 1.02. 18
nobility, | i banish her my bed and company, 2.01.193
even from this instant, banish him our city, COR 3.03.101
men | that do corrupt my air — i banish you! 3.03.123
have the power still | to banish your defenders, 3.03.128
to banish him that strook more blows for rome 4.02. 19
when i said banish him, i said 'twas pity. 4.06.140
we banish thee for ever. TIM 3.05. 97
banish me? 3.05. 97
banish your dotage, banish usury, | that makes 3.05. 98
banish your dotage, banish usury, | that makes 3.05. 98
o, banish me, my lord, but kill me not! OTH 5.02. 78
knows | thou didst unjustly banish me; CYM 3.03.100
'twas leonatus' jewel, | whom thou didst banish; 5.05.144
heaven's sake save their lives, and banish 'em. TNK 3.06.251
of your great trespass | as but to banish you, STM II.C 125
every thing did banish moan, | save the PP 20. 7
/BANISH'D 2 FR 0.0002 REL FR 1 V 1 P
/they /say /edgar, /his /banish'd /son, /is LR 4.07. 89 P
/sir, /the /banish'd /kent, /who /in /disguise 5.03.220
BANISH'D 97 FR 0.0109 REL FR 82 V 15 P
from argier, | thou know'st, was banish'd; TMP 1.02.266
where she, at least, is banish'd from your eye, 2.01.127
to die is to be banish'd from myself, | and TGV 3.01.171
banish'd from her | is self from self, a deadly 3.01.172
that thou art banish'd — o, that's the news! 3.01.219
you | now valentine is banish'd from her sight. 3.02. 2
what, were you banish'd thence? 4.01. 23
but were you banish'd for so small a fault? 4.01. 31
indeed because you are a banish'd man, 4.01. 57
good will | i bear unto the banish'd valentine, 4.03. 15
these banish'd men, that i have kept withal, 5.04.152
the old duke is banish'd by his younger brother AYL 1.01. 99 P
duke's daughter, be banish'd with her father? 1.01.106 P
you could teach me to forget a banish'd father, 1.02. 5 P
if my uncle, thy banish'd father, had banish'd 1.02. 9 P
thy banish'd father, had banish'd thy uncle, the 1.02. 10 P
the other is daughter to the banish'd duke, 1.02.273
so was i when your highness banish'd him. 1.03. 60
she is banish'd. 1.03. 84
know'st thou not the duke | hath banish'd me, 1.03. 95
than doth your brother that hath banish'd you. 2.01. 28
here come two of the banish'd duke's pages. 5.03. 5 P
his crown bequeathing to his banish'd brother, 5.04.163
hand, whose banish'd sense | thou hast repeal'd, AWW 2.03. 48
own | from my remembrance clearly banish'd his. TN 5.01.282
o fair return of banish'd majesty! JN 3.01.321
lay on our royal sword your banish'd hands; R2 1.03.179
banish'd this frail sepulchre of our flesh | as 1.03.196
as now our flesh is banish'd from this land; 1.03.197
and i from heaven banish'd as from hence! 1.03.203
hath from the number of his banish'd years 1.03.210
thy son is banish'd upon good advice, | whereto 1.03.233
though banish'd, yet a true–born englishman. 1.03.309
the royalties and rights of banish'd herford? 2.01.190
but by the robbing of the banish'd duke. 2.01.261
the banish'd bullingbrook repeals himself, | and 2.02. 49
i wot your love pursues | a banish'd traitor. 2.03. 60
why have those banish'd and forbidden legs 2.03. 90
thou art a banish'd man, and here art come 2.03.110
as i was banish'd, i was banish'd herford, | but 2.03.113
as i was banish'd, i was banish'd herford, | but 2.03.113
many a time hath banish'd norfolk fought | for 4.01. 92
your banish'd honors and restore yourselves 1H4 1.03.181
been | a banish'd woman from my harry's bed? 2.03. 39
but all are banish'd till their conversations 2H4 5.05.100
duke | hath banish'd moody discontented fury, 1H6 3.01.123
his lady banish'd, and a limb lopp'd off. 2H6 2.03. 42
now, by the ground that i am banish'd from, 3.02.334
if it be banish'd from the frosty head, | where 5.01.167
my love, | is, of a king, become a banish'd man, 3H6 3.03. 25
alas, h'as banish'd me his bed already, | his H8 3.01.119
worms, and my poor name | banish'd the kingdom! 4.02.127
he's banish'd, and it shall be so. COR 3.03.107
but he is banish'd | as enemy to the people and 3.03.117
our enemy is banish'd, he is gone! hoo! hoo! 3.03.137
whom you have banish'd — does exceed you all. 4.02. 42
coriolanus banish'd? 4.03. 27 P
banish'd, sir. 4.03. 28 P
to rome but that | thou art thence banish'd, we 4.05.128
said we were i' th' wrong when we banish'd him. 4.06.155 P
made him fear'd, | so hated, and so banish'd; 4.07. 48
go you that banish'd him | a mile before his 5.01. 4
when we banish'd him, we respected not them; 5.04. 32 P
/unshout the noise that banish'd martius! 5.05. 4
being banish'd for't, he came unto my hearth, 5.06. 29
here stands my other son, a banish'd man, | and TIT 3.01. 99
thy other banish'd son with this dear sight 3.01.256
hence "banished" is banish'd from the world, ROM 3.03. 19
where that same banish'd runagate doth live, 3.05. 89
this is that banish'd haughty montague, | that 5.03. 49
banish'd the new–made bridegroom from this city, 5.03.235
i hate not to be banish'd, | it is a cause TIM 3.05.111
alcibiades is banish'd: hear you of it? 3.06. 53 P
alcibiades banish'd? 3.06. 54 P
ear | for the repealing of my banish'd brother? JC 3.01. 51
that i was constant cimber should be banish'd, 3.01. 72
upon thyself | hath banish'd me from scotland. MAC 4.03.113
thy banish'd trunk be found in our dominions, LR 1.01.177
kent banish'd thus? 1.02. 23
and the noble and true–hearted kent banish'd! 1.02.116 P
now, banish'd kent, | if thou canst serve where 1.04. 4
this fellow has banish'd two on 's daughters, 1.04.102 P
he said it would be thus, poor banish'd man. 3.04.164
wedded, | her husband banish'd, she imprison'd: CYM 1.01. 8
and therefore banish'd) is a creature such | as, 1.01. 19
to his mistress | (for whom he now is banish'd), 1.01. 51
a wedded lady | that hath her husband banish'd. 1.06. 3
a banish'd rascal; 2.01. 39 P
t' enjoy thy banish'd lord and this great land! 2.01. 65
what of him? he is | a banish'd traitor. 5.05.318
indeed a banish'd man, | i know not how a 5.05.319
am that belarius whom you sometime banish'd. 5.05.333
banish'd. TNK 2.02.244
banish'd the kingdom? 2.03. 1
but banish'd | the free enjoying of that face i 2.03. 2
this is the man | was begg'd and banish'd, this 3.06.143
may say, the plague is banish'd by thy breath. VEN 510
BANISHED 32 FR 0.0036 REL FR 32 V 0 P
doth silvia know that i am banished? TGV 3.01.223
myself was from verona banished | for practicing 4.01. 45
to a man disgrac'd, | banished valentine. 5.04.124
i heard the banished norfolk say | that thou, R2 4.01. 80
death, | or banished fair england's territories, 2H6 3.02.245
well assur'd, | adventure to be banished myself; 3.02.350
and banished i am, if but from thee. 3.02.351
thus is poor suffolk ten times banished, | once 3.02.357
wert thou not banished on pain of death? R3 1.03.166
then, | from these devourers to be banished! TIT 3.01. 57
lastly, myself unkindly banished, | the gates 5.03.104
tybalt is gone, and romeo banished, | romeo that ROM 3.02. 69
romeo that kill'd him, he is banished. 3.02. 70
"tybalt is dead, and romeo banished." 3.02.112
that "banished," that one word "banished," 3.02.113
that "banished," that one word "banished," 3.02.113
"romeo is banished," to speak that word, | is 3.02.122
"romeo is banished"! 3.02.124
here from verona art thou banished. 3.03. 15
hence "banished" is banish'd from the world, 3.03. 19
then "banished" | is death misterm'd. 3.03. 20
calling death "banished," | thou cut'st my head 3.03. 21
but romeo may not, he is banished. 3.03. 40
they are free men, but i am banished: 3.03. 42
ne'er so mean, | but "banished" to kill me? 3.03. 46
"banished"? 3.03. 46
to mangle me with that word "banished"? 3.03. 51
to comfort thee though thou art banished. 3.03. 56
yet "banished"? 3.03. 57
doting like me, and like me banished, | then 3.03. 67
romeo is banished, and all the world to nothing 3.05.213
thy brother by decree is banished; JC 3.01. 44
BANISHERS 1 FR 0.0001 REL FR 1 V 0 P
spite, | to be full quit of those my banishers, COR 4.05. 83
/BANISHMENT 1 FR 0.0001 REL FR 0 V 1 P
/diffidences, /banishment /of /friends, LR 1.02.147 P
BANISHMENT 40 FR 0.0045 REL FR 36 V 4 P
her | is self from self, a deadly banishment. TGV 3.01.173
/in content | to liberty, and not to banishment. AYL 1.03.138
call home thy ancient thoughts from banishment, SHR in.2. 31
but tread the stranger paths of banishment. R2 1.03.143
lent | shall point on me and gild my banishment. 1.03.147
god, | embrace each other's love in banishment, 1.03.184
return with welcome home from banishment. 1.03.212
hours | and added years to his short banishment, 1.04. 17
when time shall call him home from banishment, 1.04. 21
gloucester's death, nor herford's banishment, 2.01.165
clouds, | eating the bitter bread of banishment, 3.01. 21
provided that my banishment repeal'd | and lands 3.03. 40
that laid the sentence of dread banishment | on 3.03.134
and left me in reputeless banishment, | a fellow 1H4 3.02. 44
done, | live in your country here in banishment, 2H6 2.03. 12
welcome is banishment, welcome were my death. 2.03. 14
makes them thus forward in his banishment. 3.02.253
but i do find more pain in banishment | than R3 1.03.167
their kingdom's loss, my woeful banishment, 1.03.192
death, for fine, or banishment, then let them, COR 3.03. 15
so to heart the banishment of that worthy 4.03. 22 P
who, hearing of our martius' banishment, 4.06. 43
though we willingly consented to his banishment, 4.06.144 P

pronounc'd | my everlasting doom of banishment. TIT 3.01. 51
man, | that lucius' banishment was wrongfully, 4.04. 76
when theirs are dry, for romeo's banishment. ROM 3.02.131
not body's death, but body's banishment. 3.03. 11
ha, banishment? 3.03. 12
do not say "banishment"! 3.03. 14
turn'd that black word "death" to "banishment." 3.03 27
o, thou wilt speak again of banishment. 3.03. 53
banishment! TIM 3.05.110
freedom lives hence, and banishment is here. LR 1.01.181
to have from him as this of kent's banishment. 1.01.301 P
and then his banishment. CYM 1.04. 18 P
so | followed my banishment, and this twenty 3.03. 69
stole these children | upon my banishment; 5.05.342
lives, invent a way | safer than banishment. TNK 3.06.218
thy banishment | i not mislike, so we may fairly 3.06.258
consent | to tarquin's everlasting banishment. LUC 1855

BANISHMENTS 2 FR 0.0002 REL FR 2 V 0 P
the fair–ey'd maids shall weep our banishments, TNK 2.02. 37
upon their lives; but with their banishments. 3.06.214

BANISTER 1 FR 0.0001 REL FR 1 V 0 P
flying for succor to his servant banister, H8 2.01.109

BANK 16 FR 0.0018 REL FR 16 V 0 P
sitting on a bank, | weeping again the king my TMP 1.02.390
i know a bank where the wild thyme blows, MND 2.01.249
for i upon this bank will rest my head. 2.02. 40
how sweet the moonlight sleeps upon this bank! MV 5.01. 54
sound | that breathes upon a bank of violets, TN 1.01. 6
no, like a bank, for love to lie and play on; WT 4.04.130
here in this place | i'll set a bank of rue, R2 3.04.105
took, | when on the gentle severn's sedgy bank, 1H4 1.03. 98
and hid his crisp head in the hollow bank 1.03.106
or as the snake roll'd in a flow'ring bank, 2H6 3.01.228
and twice by awkward wind from england's bank 3.02. 83
but here, upon this bank and /shoal of time, MAC 1.07. 6
yea | (we challenge too), the bank of any nymph, TNK 3.01. 8
they are o'er the bank of their obedience, STM II.C 39
rank | perforce will force it overflow the bank. VEN 72
"witness this primrose bank whereon i lie, 151

BANK'D 1 FR 0.0001 REL FR 1 V 0 P
as i have bank'd their towns? JN 5.02.104

BANKET *(also banquet)*

BANKET 12 FR 0.0013 REL FR 11 V 1 P
i'll go seek the duke, his banket is prepar'd. AYL 2.05. 62 P
my banket is to close our stomachs up | after SHR 5.02. 9
some of these | should find a running banket, H8 1.04. 12
you have now a broken banket, but we'll mend it. 1.04. 61
is the banket ready | i' th' privy chamber? 1.04. 98
and whilst i at a banket hold him sure, | i'll TIT 5.02. 76
to, | and this the banket she shall surfeit on, 5.02.193
be every one officious | to make this banket, 5.02.202
bring in the banket quickly; ANT 1.02. 12
more than what | that banket bids thee to! TNK 1.01.186
sir, they call | the scatter'd to the banket. 3.01.109
ev'n he that led you to this banket shall 5.04. 22

/BANKROUT 1 FR 0.0001 REL FR 1 V 0 P
/since /it /is /bankrout /of /his /majesty. R2 4.01.267

BANKROUT 13 FR 0.0014 REL FR 12 V 1 P
time is a very bankrout and owes more than he's ERR 4.02. 58
make rich the ribs, but bankrout quite the wits. LLL 1.01. 27
for debt that bankrout /sleep doth sorrow owe; MND 3.02. 85
a bankrout, a prodigal, who dare scarce show his MV 3.01. 44 P
to cut the forfeiture from that bankrout there. 4.01.122
be york the next that must be bankrout so! R2 2.01.151
the /king's grown bankrout, like a broken man. 2.01.257
big mars seems bankrout in their beggar'd host, H5 4.02. 43
break, my heart, poor bankrout, break at once! ROM 3.02. 57
but blessed bankrout that by love so thriveth! VEN 466
that they prove bankrout in this poor rich gain. LUC 140
like to a bankrout beggar wails his case: 711
why should he live, now nature bankrout is, SON 67. 9

BANKRUPT 2 FR 0.0002 REL FR 1 V 1 P
word with me, i shall make your wit bankrupt. TGV 2.04. 42 P
upon that poor and broken bankrupt there?" AYL 2.01. 57

BANKRUPTS 1 FR 0.0001 REL FR 1 V 0 P
bankrupts, hold fast; TIM 4.01. 8

BANKS 19 FR 0.0021 REL FR 19 V 0 P
thy banks with pioned and twilled brims, | which TMP 4.01. 64
join | do glorify the banks that bound them in; JN 2.01.442
with the sea | that chides the banks of england, 1H4 3.01. 44
thrice from the banks of wye | and 3.01. 64
we come within our aweful banks again, | and 2H4 4.01.174
to ask those on the banks | if they were his R3 4.04.523
were his brain as barren | as banks of libya TRO 1.03.328
like to a strange soul upon the stygian banks 3.02. 9
that tiber trembled underneath her banks | to JC 1.01. 45
draw them to tiber banks, and weep your tears 1.01. 58
and cydnus swell'd above the banks, or for | the CYM 2.04. 71
upon your never–withering banks of flow'rs. 5.04. 98
and now at length they overflow their banks. PER 2.04. 24
and at the banks of /aulis meet us with | the TNK 1.01.212
than humble banks can go to law with waters 5.03. 99
being stopp'd, the bounding banks o'erflows; LUC 1119
to simois' reedy banks the red blood ran, 1437
join, and shoot their foam at simois' banks. 1442
two contracted new | come daily to the banks, SON 56.11

/BANNER 1 FR 0.0001 REL FR 1 V 0 P
/at /point | /to /show /their /open /banner. LR 3.01. 34

BANNER 4 FR 0.0004 REL FR 4 V 0 P
i will the banner from a trumpet take, | and use H5 4.02. 61
the royal banner, and all quality, | pride, pomp OTH 3.03.353
from euphrates | his conquering banner shook, ANT 1.02.102
and when his gaudy banner is display'd, | the LUC 272

BANNERETS 1 FR 0.0001 REL FR 0 V 1 P
yet the scarfs and the bannerets about thee did AWW 2.03.204 P

/BANNERS 1 FR 0.0001 REL FR 1 V 0 P
/spreads /his /banners /in /our /noiseless /land LR 4.02. 56

BANNERS 8 FR 0.0009 REL FR 8 V 0 P
play | upon the dancing banners of the french, JN 2.01.308
and nobles bearing banners, there lie dead | one H5 4.08. 82
in our ages see | their banners wave again. COR 3.01. 8
lord, | into our city with thy banners spread; TIM 5.04. 30
where the norweyan banners flout the sky | and MAC 1.02. 49
hang out our banners on the outward walls, | the 5.05. 1
how, with his banners and his well–paid ranks, ANT 3.01. 32
his banners sable, trimm'd with rich expense, PER 5.ch. 19

BANNING 2 FR 0.0002 REL FR 2 V 0 P
fell banning hag, enchantress, hold thy tongue! 1H6 5.03. 42
sits, | banning his boist'rous and unruly beast; VEN 326

BANNS *(see banes)*

BANQUET *(also banket)*

BANQUET 15 FR 0.0017 REL FR 12 V 3 P
come let us to the banquet. ADO 2.01.171 P
his words are a very fantastical banquet, just 2.03. 21 P
the mind shall banquet, though the body pine; LLL 1.01. 25
fingers, | a most delicious banquet by his bed, SHR in.1. 39
visit his countrymen, and banquet them? 1.01.197
and feast and banquet in the open streets, | to 1H6 1.06. 13
come in, and let us banquet royally, | after 1.06. 30
now a blessed troop | invite me to a banquet, H8 4.02. 88
besides the running banquet of two beadles that 5.03. 65 P
and bid him come and banquet at thy house, TIT 5.02.114
we have a trifling foolish banquet towards. ROM 1.05.122
ladies, there is an idle banquet attends you, TIM 1.02.155
it is a banquet to me. MAC 1.04. 56
"but o, what banquet wert thou to the taste, VEN 445
and to the painted banquet bids my heart; SON 47. 6

BANQUETED 1 FR 0.0001 REL FR 1 V 0 P
secure, | having all day carous'd and banqueted: 1H6 2.01. 12

BANQUETING 2 FR 0.0002 REL FR 2 V 0 P
this night in banqueting must all be spent. TRO 5.01. 46
that i profess myself in banqueting | to all the JC 1.02. 77

BANQUETS 2 FR 0.0002 REL FR 2 V 0 P
his hours fill'd up with riots, banquets, sports H5 1.01. 56
free from our feasts and banquets bloody knives; MAC 3.06. 35

BANQUO 22 FR 0.0024 REL FR 22 V 0 P
not this | our captains, macbeth and banquo? MAC 1.02. 34
so all hail, macbeth and banquo! 1.03. 68
banquo and macbeth, all hail! 1.03. 69
noble banquo, | that hast no less deserv'd, nor 1.04. 29
true, worthy banquo! 1.04. 54
banquo and donalbain! 2.03. 75
banquo! 2.03. 78
o banquo, banquo, | our royal master's murther'd 2.03. 86
o banquo, banquo, | our royal master's murther'd 2.03. 86
our fears in banquo | stick deep, and in his 3.01. 48
to make them kings — the seeds of banquo kings! 3.01. 69
and to a notion craz'd | say, "thus did banquo." 3.01. 83
both of you | know banquo was your enemy. 3.01.114
banquo, thy soul's flight, | if it find heaven, 3.01.140
is banquo gone from court? 3.02. 1
let your remembrance apply to banquo, | present 3.02. 30
thou know'st that banquo and his fleance lives. 3.02. 37
were the grac'd person of our banquo present, 3.04. 40
and to our dear friend banquo, whom we miss; 3.04. 89
and the right valiant banquo walk'd too late, 3.06. 5
thou art too like the spirit of banquo; 4.01.112
for the blood–bolter'd banquo smiles upon me, 4.01.123

BANQUO'S 5 FR 0.0005 REL FR 4 V 1 P
so, | for banquo's issue have i fil'd my mind, MAC 3.01. 64
'tis banquo's then. 3.04. 13
but banquo's safe? 3.04. 24
much, shall banquo's issue ever | reign in this 4.01.102
i tell you yet again, banquo's buried; 5.01. 63 P

BANS 2 FR 0.0002 REL FR 2 V 0 P
take thou that too, with multiplying bans! TIM 4.01. 34
sometimes with lunatic bans, sometime with LR 2.03. 19

BAPTISM 3 FR 0.0003 REL FR 3 V 0 P
conscience wash'd | as pure as sin with baptism. H5 1.02. 32
is, a fair young maid that yet wants baptism, H8 5.02.196
win the moor, were/'t to renounce his baptism, OTH 2.03.343

BAPTISTA 25 FR 0.0028 REL FR 18 V 7 P
signior baptista, will you be so strange? SHR 1.01. 85
signior baptista, for this fiend of hell, | and 1.01. 88
her father is baptista minola, | an affable and 1.02. 97
therefore this order hath baptista ta'en, | that 1.02.126
sober robes | to old baptista as a schoolmaster 1.02.133
to baptista minola. 1.02.164
way | to the house of signior baptista minola? 1.02.220
baptista is a noble gentleman, | to whom my 1.02.238
good morrow, neighbor baptista. 2.01. 39 P
signior baptista, my business asketh haste, 2.01.114
but now, baptista, to your younger daughter — 2.01.332
patience, good katherine, and baptista too. 3.02. 21
and give assurance to baptista minola, | as if 4.02. 69
signior baptista may remember me | near twenty 4.04. 3
but hast thou done thy errand to baptista? 4.04. 14
here comes baptista; 4.04. 18
signior baptista, you are happily met. 4.04. 19
you, | signior baptista, of whom i hear so well. 4.04. 37
signior baptista, shall i lead the way? 4.04. 69
baptista is safe, talking with the deceiving 4.04. 82 P
help, son! help, signior baptista! 5.01. 60 P
father baptista, i charge you see that he be 5.01. 92 P
take heed, signior baptista, lest you be 5.01. 98 P
fear not, baptista, we will content you, go to; 5.01.135 P
gonzago is the duke's name, his wife, baptista. HAM 3.02.240 P

BAPTISTA'S 6 FR 0.0006 REL FR 5 V 1 P
till by helping baptista's eldest daughter to a SHR 1.01.137 P
indeed had baptista's youngest daughter. 1.01.240
thee, | for in baptista's keep my treasure is. 1.02.118
over and beside | signior baptista's liberality, 1.02.149
you, | did you yet ever see baptista's daughter? 1.02.250
'twixt me and one baptista's daughter here. 4.02.119

BAPTIZ'D 1 FR 0.0001 REL FR 1 V 0 P
call me but love, and i'll be new baptiz'd; ROM 2.02. 50

BAR* 33 FR 0.0037 REL FR 27 V 6 P
any bar, any cross, any impediment will be ADO 2.02. 4 P
nay, but i bar to–night, you shall not gauge me MV 2.02.199
heaven, is no bar | to stop the foreign spirits, 2.07. 45
so sweet a bar | should sunder such sweet 3.02.119
i bar confusion, | 'tis i must make conclusion AYL 5.04.125
come, since this bar in law makes us friends, it SHR 1.01.135 P
bring the device to the bar and crown thee for a TN 3.04.140 P
thou shalt), we'll bar thee from succession, WT 4.04.429
right, | let it be lawful that law bar no wrong; JN 3.01.186
i will bar no honest man my house, nor no 2H4 2.04.102 P
or should, or should not, bar us in our claim; H5 1.02. 12
there is no bar | to make against your highness' 1.02. 35
the founder of this law and female bar. 1.02. 42
to bar your highness claiming from the female, 1.02. 92
of berri, | alanson, brabant, bar, and burgundy, 3.05. 42
bar harry england, that sweeps through our land 3.05. 48
the duke of burgundy, | and edward duke of bar; 4.08. 98
majesties | unto this bar and royal interview, 5.02. 27
to bar my master's heirs in true descent — R3 3.02. 54
i am their mother, who shall bar me from them? 4.01. 21
heaven and fortune bar me happy hours! 4.04.400
throng to the bar, crying all, "guilty! 5.03.199
the great duke | came to the bar; H8 2.01. 12
when he was brought again to th' bar, to hear 2.01. 31
if you cannot | bar his access to th' king, 3.02. 17
you do surely bar the door upon your own liberty HAM 3.02.338 P
all ports i'll bar, the villain shall not scape; LR 2.01. 80
though their injunction be to bar my doors, 3.04.150
/sister, | i bar it in the interest of my wife; 5.03. 85
and, to bar your offense herein too, i durst CYM 1.04.111 P
thinking to bar thee of succession, as | thou 3.03.102
greatness was no guard | to bar heaven's shaft, PER 2.04. 15
eye my heart /thy picture's sight would bar, SON 46. 3

BARBARA *(see barbary*)*

BARBARIAN 2 FR 0.0002 REL FR 0 V 2 P
among those of any wit, like a barbarian slave. TRO 2.01. 47 P
betwixt an erring barbarian and /a super–subtle OTH 1.03.356 P

BARBARIANS 1 FR 0.0001 REL FR 1 V 0 P
i would they were barbarians, as they are, COR 3.01.237

BARBARISM 4 FR 0.0004 REL FR 3 V 1 P
and though i have for barbarism spoke more LLL 1.01.112
lest barbarism (making me the precedent) WT 2.01. 84
melted, | and barbarism itself have pitied him. R2 5.02. 36
the grecians began to proclaim barbarism, and TRO 5.04. 16 P

/BARBAROUS 1 FR 0.0001 REL FR 1 V 0 P
/most /barbarous, /most /degenerate, /have /you LR 4.02. 43

BARBAROUS 21 FR 0.0023 REL FR 19 V 2 P
most barbarous intimation! LLL 4.02. 13 P
we will be singuled from the barbarous. 5.01. 82 P
and rank me with the barbarous multitudes. MV 2.09. 33
fit for the mountains and the barbarous caves, TN 4.01. 48
to choke his days | with barbarous ignorance, JN 4.02. 59
hence, did give ourself | to barbarous license; H5 1.02.271
and give our vineyards to a barbarous people. 3.05. 4
o barbarous and bloody spectacle! 2H6 4.01.144
ah, barbarous villains! 4.04. 15
from weary wars against the barbarous goths, TIT 1.01. 28
was never scythia half so barbarous. 1.01.131
thou art a roman, be not barbarous: 1.01.378
plot, | accompanied but with a barbarous moor, 2.03. 78
ay, come, semiramis, nay, barbarous tamora, 2.03.118
o barbarous, beastly villains like thyself! 5.01. 97
good uncle, take you in this barbarous moor, 5.03. 4
the barbarous scythian, | or he that makes his LR 1.01.116
christian shame, put by this barbarous brawl. OTH 2.03.172
receive us | for barbarous and unnatural revolts CYM 4.04. 6
not enough barbarous, had not o'erboard thrown PER 4.02. 66
to find a nation of such barbarous temper | that STM II.C 131

BARBARY* 11 FR 0.0012 REL FR 6 V 5 P
from lisbon, barbary, and india, | and not one MV 3.02.269
of thee than a barbary cock–pigeon over his hen, AYL 4.01.150 P
when bullingbrook rode on roan barbary, | that R2 5.05. 78
rode he on barbary? 5.05. 81
in barbary, sir, it cannot come to so much. 1H4 2.04. 75 P
he'll not swagger with a barbary hen, if her 2H4 2.04. 99 P
sir, hath wager'd with him six barbary horses, HAM 5.02.147 P
have your daughter cover'd with a barbary horse, OTH 1.01.111 P
my mother had a maid call'd barbary; 4.03. 26
all at one side | and sing it like poor barbary. 4.03. 33
luce with the white legs, and bouncing barbary. TNK 3.05. 26

BARBARY–A 1 FR 0.0001 REL FR 1 V 0 P
from the south, | from the coast of barbary–a; TNK 3.05. 60

BARBASON 2 FR 0.0002 REL FR 0 V 2 P
barbason, well; WIV 2.02.297 P
i am not barbason, you cannot conjure me. H5 2.01. 54 P

BARBED 2 FR 0.0002 REL FR 2 V 0 P
his barbed steeds to stables, and his heart | to R2 3.03.117
in stead of mounting barbed steeds | to fright R3 1.01. 10

BARBER 2 FR 0.0002 REL FR 1 V 1 P
for a barber shall never earn sixpence out of it 2H4 1.02. 25 P
or let me know | why mine own barber is unblest, TNK 1.02. 53

BARBER'D 1 FR 0.0001 REL FR 1 V 0 P
being barber'd ten times o'er, goes to the feast ANT 2.02.224

BARBER–MONGER 1 FR 0.0001 REL FR 0 V 1 P
you, you whoreson cullionly barber–monger, draw! LR 2.02. 33 P

BARBER'S 7 FR 0.0008 REL FR 2 V 5 P
stand like the forfeits in a barber's shop, | as MM 5.01.321
hath any man seen him at the barber's? ADO 3.02. 43 P
but the barber's man hath been seen with him, 3.02. 45 P
i must to the barber's, mounsieur; MND 4.01. 23 P
slash, | like to a censer in a barber's shop. SHR 4.03. 91
it is like a barber's chair that fits all AWW 2.02. 17 P
it shall to the barber's with your beard. HAM 2.02.499 P

BARB'RY 1 FR 0.0001 REL FR 0 V 1 P
six barb'ry horses against six french swords, HAM 5.02.161 P

BAR'D 2 FR 0.0002 REL FR 1 V 1 P
of the penitent to be so bar'd before his death. MM 4.02.176 P
see, | have bar'd my bosom to the thunder–stone; JC 1.03. 49

/BARD 1 FR 0.0001 REL FR 1 V 0 P
/because /a /bard /of /ireland /told /me /once R3 4.02.106

/BARDOLPH 1 FR 0.0001 REL FR 0 V 1 P
falstaff, /bardolph, /peto, and gadshill shall 1H4 1.02.162 P

BARDOLPH 57 FR 0.0064 REL FR 7 V 50 P
against your cony–catching rascals, bardolph, WIV 1.01.125 P
i will entertain bardolph; 1.03. 10 P
bardolph, follow him. 1.03. 16 P
bardolph, i say! 3.05. 1 P
bardolph! 1H4 2.02. 21 P
fair, so did you, peto, so did you, bardolph. 2.04.299 P
banish peto, banish bardolph, banish poins, but 2.04.474 P
bardolph, am i not fall'n away vilely since this 3.03. 1 P
bardolph was shav'd and lost many a hair, and 3.03. 59 P
did i, bardolph? 3.03.140 P
bardolph! 3.03.193 P
bardolph, get thee before to coventry; 4.02. 1 P
that the lord bardolph doth attend him here. 2H4 1.01. 3
what news, lord bardolph? 1.01. 7
procure him better assurance than bardolph. 1.02. 32 P
where's bardolph? 1.02. 49 P
the prince for striking him about bardolph. 1.02. 56 P
'tis very true, lord bardolph, for indeed | it 1.03. 25
to us no more, nay, not so much, lord bardolph, 1.03. 69
and that arrant malmsey–nose knave, bardolph, 2.01. 40 P
draw, bardolph, cut me off the villain's head, 2.01. 46 P
keep them off, bardolph. 2.01. 54 P
by the mass, here comes bardolph. 2.02. 69 P

and yours, most noble bardolph! 2.02. 74 P
and how doth thy master, bardolph? 2.02. 98 P
you boy, and bardolph, no word to your master 2.02.160 P
bardolph hath brought word. 2.04. 17 P
i tell thee what, corporal bardolph, i could 2.04.153 P
quoit him down, bardolph, like a shove–groat 2.04.192 P
or honest bardolph, whose zeal burns in his nose 2.04.329 P
fiend hath prick'd down bardolph irrecoverable, 2.04.332 P
good master corporate bardolph, stand my friend, 3.02.220 P
put me a caliver into wart's hand, bardolph. 3.02.271 P
bardolph, give the soldiers coats. 3.02.290 P
on, bardolph, lead the men away. 3.02.300 P
how now, bardolph? 4.03.126 P
the earl northumberland and the lord bardolph, 4.04. 97
give me your hand, master bardolph. 5.01. 55 P
thank thee with my heart, kind master bardolph, 5.01. 58 P
bardolph, look to our horses. 5.01. 61 P
give master bardolph some wine, davy. 5.03. 25 P
be merry, master bardolph, and, my little 5.03. 30 P
honest bardolph, welcome. 5.03. 55 P
i'll drink to master bardolph, and to all the 5.03. 58 P
together, ha, will you not, master bardolph? 5.03. 63 P
away, bardolph! 5.03.122 P
away, bardolph! 5.03.132 P
come, lieutenant pistol, come, bardolph. 5.05. 89 P
good morrow, lieutenant bardolph. H5 2.01. 2 P
good bardolph, put thy face between his sheets, 2.01. 83 P
bardolph, be blithe; 2.03. 4
for bardolph, he is white–liver'd and red–fac'd; 3.02. 32 P
bardolph stole a lute–case, bore it twelve 3.02. 42 P
nym and bardolph are sworn brothers in filching, 3.02. 44 P
bardolph, a soldier firm and sound of heart, 3.06. 25
be executed for robbing a church, one bardolph, 3.06.101 P
bardolph and nym had ten times more valor than 4.04. 70 P
BARDOLPH'S 3 FR 0.0003 REL FR 2 V 1 P
'a saw a flea stick upon bardolph's nose, and 'a H5 2.03. 41 P
fortune is bardolph's foe, and frowns on him; 3.06. 39
and let not bardolph's vital thread be cut 3.06. 47
BARDS 1 FR 0.0001 REL FR 1 V 0 P
/figures, scribes, bards, poets, cannot | think, ANT 3.02. 16
BARE* *(also bore*)*
BARE* 59 FR 0.0066 REL FR 47 V 12 P
dwell | in this bare island by your spell, | but TMP ep 8
it appears by their bare liveries that they live TGV 2.04. 45 P
bare liveries that they live by your bare words. 2.04. 46 P
which is much in a bare christian. 3.01.273 P
by the bare scalp of robin hood's fat friar, 4.01. 36
that from the seedness the bare fallow brings MM 1.04. 42
i thank him, i bare home upon my shoulders: ERR 2.01. 73
the hate i bare thee made me leave thee so? MND 3.02.190
how many then should cover that stand bare? MV 2.09. 44
therefore lay bare your bosom. 4.01.252
of bare distress hath ta'en from me the show AYL 2.07. 95
more honorable than the bare brow of a bachelor; 3.03. 61 P
and a half, but his right cheek is worn bare. AWW 4.05. 98 P
me, that bare eyes | to see alike mine honor as WT 1.02.309
of appetite | by bare imagination of a feast? R2 1.03.297
stand bare and naked, trembling at themselves? 3.02. 46
never did bare and rotten policy | color her 1H4 1.03.108
such poor, such bare, such lewd, such mean 3.02. 13
methinks they are exceeding poor and bare, too 4.02. 69 P
unless you call three fingers in the ribs bare. 4.02. 74 P
to melt | and drop upon our bare unarmed heads. 2H4 2.04.365
like lean, sterile, and bare land, manur'd, 4.03.119 P
wings is flown | from this bare wither'd trunk. 4.05.229
which caesar and his fortune bare at once. 1H6 1.02.139
whom with my bare fists i would execute, | if i 1.04. 36
damned wretch, the curse of her that bare thee; 2H6 4.10. 77
but then aeneas bare a living load — | nothing 5.02. 64
some tardy cripple bare the countermand, | that R3 2.01. 90
our head shall go bare till merit /crown /it. TRO 3.02. 92 P
with truth and plainness i do wear mine bare. 4.04.106
groats, to show bare heads | in congregations, COR 3.02. 10
it was a bare petition of a state | to one whom 5.01. 20
and made thy body bare | of her two branches, TIT 2.04. 17
and that bare vowel i shall poison more | than ROM 3.02. 46
art thou so bare and full of wretchedness, | and 5.01. 68
who bare my letter then to romeo? 5.02. 13
especially upon bare friendship without security TIM 3.01. 42 P
of wreakful heaven, whose bare unhoused trunks, 4.03.229
fell from their boughs, and left me open, bare, 4.03.265
is ceremony, | meeting were bare without it. MAC 3.04. 36
might his quietus make | with a bare bodkin; HAM 3.01. 75
man is no more but such a poor, bare, fork'd LR 3.04.107 P
the sea, with such a storm as his bare head | in 3.07. 59
weapons rather use | than their bare hands. OTH 1.03.175
all kind of sores and shames on my bare head, 4.02. 49
wear thy good rapier bare, and put it home. 5.01. 2
night, that dawning | may bare the raven's eye! CYM 2.02. 49
nay, my leaves, | and left me bare to weather. 3.03. 64
hast stuck to the bare fortune of that beggar 3.05.118 P
scars and bare weeds | the gain o' th' TNK 1.02. 15
what bare excuses mak'st thou to be gone! VEN 188
on, to make his stand | on her bare breast, the LUC 439
bare and unpeopled in this fearful flood. 1741
youth like summer brave, age like winter bare. PP 12. 4
which wit so poor as mine | may make seem bare, SON 26. 6
utt'ring bare truth, even so as foes commend. 69. 4
bare /ruin'd choirs, where late the sweet birds 73. 4
the argument all bare is of more worth | than 103. 3
whose bare outbragg'd the web it seem'd to wear; LC 95
BARE–ARM'D 1 FR 0.0001 REL FR 1 V 0 P
will you fight bare–arm'd? TNK 3.06. 63
BARE–BON'D 1 FR 0.0001 REL FR 1 V 0 P
shows me a bare–bon'd death by time outworn. LUC 1761
BARE–BONE 1 FR 0.0001 REL FR 0 V 1 P
here comes lean jack, here comes bare–bone. 1H4 2.04.326 P
BAREFAC'D 3 FR 0.0003 REL FR 2 V 1 P
and then you will play barefac'd. MND 1.02. 98 P
with barefac'd power sweep him from my sight, MAC 3.01.118
"they bore him barefac'd on the bier, | /hey HAM 4.05.165
BAREFOOT 7 FR 0.0008 REL FR 5 V 2 P
which | lie tumbling in my barefoot way, and TMP 2.02. 11
i must dance barefoot on her wedding–day, | and SHR 2.01. 33
that barefoot plod i the cold ground upon, AWW 3.04. 6
condition i had gone barefoot to india. TRO 1.02. 74 P
going to find a barefoot brother out, | one of ROM 5.02. 5
"run barefoot up and down, threat'ning the HAM 2.02.505
would have walk'd barefoot to palestine for a OTH 4.03. 39 P
BARE–GNAWN 1 FR 0.0001 REL FR 1 V 0 P
by treason's tooth bare–gnawn and canker–bit, LR 5.03.122
BARE–HEADED 4 FR 0.0004 REL FR 4 V 0 P
bare–headed, lower than his proud steed's neck, R2 5.02. 19
bare–headed, sweating, knocking at the taverns, 2H4 2.04.359
bare–headed plodded by my foot–cloth mule | and 2H6 4.01. 54
alack, bare–headed? LR 3.02. 60
BARELY 4 FR 0.0004 REL FR 4 V 0 P
shall i not have barely my principal? MV 4.01.342
you barely leave our thorns to prick ourselves, AWW 4.02. 19
barely in title, not in revenues. R2 2.01.226
fear'd /hopes | i barely gratify your love; CYM 2.04. 7
BARENESS 4 FR 0.0004 REL FR 3 V 1 P
ourselves, | and mock us with our bareness. AWW 4.02. 20
not where they had that, and for their bareness, 1H4 4.02. 71 P
beauty o'ersnow'd and bareness every where: SON 5. 8
what old december's bareness every where! 97. 4
BARE–PICK'D 1 FR 0.0001 REL FR 1 V 0 P
now for the bare–pick'd bone of majesty | doth JN 4.03.148
BARE–RIBB'D 1 FR 0.0001 REL FR 1 V 0 P
and in his forehead sits | a bare–ribb'd death, JN 5.02.177
BARFUL 1 FR 0.0001 REL FR 1 V 0 P
yet a barful strife! TN 1.04. 41
BARGAIN 20 FR 0.0022 REL FR 16 V 4 P
and seal the bargain with a holy kiss. TGV 2.02. 7
earnest, | upon what bargain do you give it me? ERR 2.02. 25
the boy hath sold him a bargain, a goose, that's LLL 3.01.101
to sell a bargain well is as cunning as fast and 3.01.103
short | to make a world–without–end bargain in. 5.02.789
mean to solemnize | the bargain of your faith, i MV 3.02.193
so is the bargain. AYL 5.04. 15
take hands, a bargain! WT 4.04.383
hands | to clap this royal bargain up of peace, JN 3.01.235
the devil shall have his bargain, for he was 1H4 1.02.118 P
but in the way of bargain, mark ye me, | i'll 3.01.137
i by bargain should | wear it myself. H5 4.07.174
i' faith, do, and so clap hands and a bargain. 5.02.130 P
so worthless peasants bargain for their wives, 1H6 5.05. 53
go to, a bargain made, seal it, seal it, i'll be TRO 3.02.197 P
kiss | a dateless bargain to engrossing death! ROM 5.03.115
there's a bargain made. JC 1.03.120
she was too fond of her most filthy bargain. OTH 5.02.157
lest the bargain should catch cold and starve. CYM 1.04.166 P
that's as we bargain, madam. TNK 2.02.152
BARGAIN'D 3 FR 0.0003 REL FR 2 V 1 P
'tis bargain'd 'twixt us twain, being alone, SHR 2.01.304
while his own lands are bargain'd for and sold. 2H6 1.01.231
mistress, if i have bargain'd for the joint — PER 4.02.130 P
BARGAINS 4 FR 0.0004 REL FR 3 V 1 P
on me, my bargains, and my well–won thrift, MV 1.03. 50
scorn'd my nation, thwarted my bargains, cool'd 3.01. 57 P
no bargains break that are not this day made: JN 3.01. 93
what bargains may i make, still to be sealing? VEN 512
BARGE 7 FR 0.0008 REL FR 7 V 0 P
my barge stays; H8 1.03. 63
th' have left their barge and landed, | and 1.04. 54
see the barge be ready; 2.01. 98
the barge she sat in, like a burnish'd throne, ANT 2.02.191
from the barge | a strange invisible perfume 2.02.211
and to him in his barge with fervor hies. PER 5.ch. 20
sir, there is a barge put off from meteline, 5.01. 3
BARGULUS 1 FR 0.0001 REL FR 1 V 0 P
more | than bargulus the strong illyrian pirate. 2H6 4.01.108
BARING 1 FR 0.0001 REL FR 0 V 1 P
or the baring of my beard, and to say it was in AWW 4.01. 49 P
/BARK* 1 FR 0.0001 REL FR 1 V 0 P
had not their /bark been very slow of sail; ERR 1.01.116
BARK* 50 FR 0.0056 REL FR 44 V 6 P
in few, they hurried us aboard a bark, | bore us TMP 1.02.144
the watch–dogs bark! 1.02.383
which i made of the bark of a tree with mine own 2.02.123 P
why do your dogs bark so? WIV 1.01.287 P
would bark your honor from that trunk you bear, MM 3.01. 71
if any bark put forth, come to the mart, | where ERR 3.02.150
there's a bark of epidamium | that stays but 4.01. 85
you sent me to the bay, sir, for a bark. 4.01. 99
an hour since that the bark expedition put forth 4.03. 38 P
had rather hear my dog bark at a crow than a man ADO 1.01.131 P
dumaine is mine, as sure as bark on tree. LLL 5.02.285
and neigh, and bark, and grunt, and roar, and MND 3.01.110
and when i ope my lips let no dog bark!" MV 1.01. 94
the scarfed bark puts from her native bay, 2.06. 15
look to thy bark, i'll not be long before | i WT 3.03. 8
and make conceive a bark of baser kind | by bud 4.04. 94
what became of his bark and his followers? 5.02. 67 P
/we at time of year | do wound the bark, the R2 3.04. 58
even as a splitted bark, so sunder we; 2H6 3.02.411
cry, | the rest stand all aloof and bark at him. 3H6 2.01. 17
all these the enemies to our poor bark. 5.04. 28
that dogs bark at me as i halt by them — | why, R3 1.01. 23
being a bark to brook no mighty sea — | than in 3.07.162
like a poor bark of sails and tackling reft, 4.04.234
every tree, lop, bark, and part o' th' timber; H8 1.02. 96
to village curs, | bark when their fellows do: 2.04.161
our doubtful hope, our convoy, and our bark. TRO 1.01.104
the strong–ribb'd bark through liquid mountains 1.03. 40
lo, as the bark that hath discharg'd his fraught TIT 1.01. 71
and on their skins, as on the bark of trees, 5.01.138
in one little body | thou counterfeits a bark, a ROM 3.05.131
the bark thy body is, | sailing in this salt 3.05.133
on | the dashing rocks thy sea–sick weary bark! 5.03.118
leak'd is our bark, | and we, poor mates, stand TIM 4.02. 19
thou that rig'st the bark and plough'st the foam 5.01. 50
why now blow wind, swell billow, and swim bark! JC 5.01. 67
though his bark cannot be lost, | yet it shall MAC 1.03. 24
the bark is ready, and the wind at help, | th' HAM 4.03. 44
blanch, and sweetheart, see, they bark at me. LR 3.06. 63
and yond tall anchoring bark, | diminish'd to 4.06. 18
thou hast seen a farmer's dog bark at a beggar? 4.06.155 P
his bark is stoutly timber'd, and his pilot | of OTH 2.01. 48
and let the laboring bark climb hills of seas 2.01.187
of heavy pericles think this his bark; PER 5.ch. 22
and when you bark, do it with judgment. TNK 3.05. 37
dog shall rouse thee, though a thousand bark." VEN 240
ay me, the bark pill'd from the lofty pine, LUC 1167
so must my soul, her bark being pill'd away. 1169
my saucy bark (inferior far to his) | on your SON 80. 7
it is the star to every wand'ring bark, | whose 116. 7
BARK'D 2 FR 0.0002 REL FR 2 V 0 P
mine, | and a most instant tetter bark'd about, HAM 1.05. 71
and this pine is bark'd, | that overtopp'd them ANT 4.12. 23
BARKETH 1 FR 0.0001 REL FR 1 V 0 P
or as the wolf doth grin before he barketh, | or VEN 459
BARKING 2 FR 0.0002 REL FR 2 V 0 P
the envious barking of your saucy tongue 1H6 3.04. 33
dogs, that are as often beat for barking | as COR 2.03.216
BARKLOUGHLY 1 FR 0.0001 REL FR 1 V 0 P
barkloughly castle call they this at hand? R2 3.02. 1
/BARKS* 1 FR 0.0001 REL FR 1 V 0 P
/the //deep–drawing /barks /do /there /disgorge TRO pr 12
BARKS* 5 FR 0.0005 REL FR 3 V 2 P
and in their barks my thoughts i'll character, AYL 3.02. 6
trees with writing love–songs in their barks. 3.02.260 P
plants with carving "rosalind" on their barks; 3.02.361 P
the fox barks not when he would steal the lamb. 2H6 3.01. 55
sheets, | the barks of trees thou brows'd. ANT 1.04. 66
BARK'ST 1 FR 0.0001 REL FR 0 V 1 P
beauty, ay, that thou bark'st at him. TRO 2.01. 35 P
BARKY 1 FR 0.0001 REL FR 1 V 0 P
ivy so | enrings the barky fingers of the elm. MND 4.01. 44
BARLEY 1 FR 0.0001 REL FR 1 V 0 P
thy rich leas | of wheat, rye, barley, fetches, TMP 4.01. 61
BARLEY–BREAK 1 FR 0.0001 REL FR 0 V 1 P
sometime we go to barley–break, we of the TNK 4.03. 31 P
BARLEY–BROTH 1 FR 0.0001 REL FR 1 V 0 P
drench for sur–rein'd jades, their barley–broth, H5 3.05. 19
BARM 1 FR 0.0001 REL FR 1 V 0 P
and sometime make the drink to bear no barm, MND 2.01. 38
BARN 2 FR 0.0002 REL FR 1 V 1 P
house, | my household stuff, my field, my barn, SHR 3.02.231
he loves his own barn better than he loves our 1H4 2.03. 5 P
BARNACLES 1 FR 0.0001 REL FR 1 V 0 P
and all be turn'd to barnacles, or to apes TMP 4.01.248
BARNARDINE 15 FR 0.0017 REL FR 5 V 10 P
morning are to die claudio and barnardine. MM 4.02. 8 P
call hither barnardine and claudio. 4.02. 60 P
where's barnardine? 4.02. 65
of the clock, and in the afternoon barnardine. 4.02.122 P
what is that barnardine who is to be executed in 4.02.128 P
let this barnardine be this morning executed, 4.02.170 P
sirrah, bring barnardine hither. 4.03. 20 P
master barnardine! 4.03. 21 P
you must rise and be hang'd, master barnardine! 4.03. 22 P
what ho, barnardine! 4.03. 23 P
pray, master barnardine, awake till you are 4.03. 32 P
but barnardine must die this afternoon; 4.03. 83
in secret holds, both barnardine and claudio. 4.03. 87
his name is barnardine. 5.01.467
which is that barnardine? 5.01.478
BARNARDINE'S 1 FR 0.0001 REL FR 0 V 1 P
executioner, and off with barnardine's head. MM 4.02.206 P
BARNARDO 5 FR 0.0005 REL FR 5 V 0 P
barnardo. HAM 1.01. 4
barnardo hath my place. | give you good night. 1.01. 17
holla, barnardo! 1.01. 18
down, | and let us hear barnardo speak of this. 1.01. 34
marcellus and barnardo, on their watch, | in the 1.02.197
BARNE 2 FR 0.0002 REL FR 0 V 2 P
mercy on 's, a barne? WT 3.03. 70 P
a very pretty barne! 3.03. 70 P
BARNES* 2 FR 0.0002 REL FR 0 V 2 P
for they say barnes are blessings. AWW 1.03. 25 P
doit of staffordshire, and black george barnes, 2H4 3.02. 20 P
BARNET 2 FR 0.0002 REL FR 2 V 0 P
i will away towards barnet presently, | and bid 3H6 5.01.110
we, having now the best at barnet field, | will 5.03. 20
BARNS 4 FR 0.0004 REL FR 3 V 1 P
foison plenty, | barns and garners never empty; TMP 4.01.111
enough, you'll see he shall lack no barns. ADO 3.04. 49 P
set fire on barns and haystalks in the night, TIT 5.01.133
and useless barns the harvest of his wits; LUC 859
BARON 1 FR 0.0001 REL FR 0 V 1 P
to falconbridge, the young baron of england? MV 1.02. 67 P
BARONS 6 FR 0.0006 REL FR 6 V 0 P
now when the lords and barons of the realm 1H4 4.03. 66
high dukes, great princes, barons, lords, and H5 3.05. 46
of other lords and barons, knights and squires, 4.08. 78
the rest are princes, barons, lords, knights, 4.08. 89
seven earls, twelve barons, and twenty reverend 2H6 1.01. 8
over her, are four barons | of the cinque–ports. H8 4.01. 48
BARONY 1 FR 0.0001 REL FR 1 V 0 P
honor, for a silken point | i'll give my barony. 2H4 1.01. 54
BARRABAS 1 FR 0.0001 REL FR 1 V 0 P
would any of the stock of barrabas | had been MV 4.01.296
BARR'D 12 FR 0.0013 REL FR 12 V 0 P
sweet recreation barr'd, what doth ensue | but ERR 5.01. 78
which was before barr'd up with ribs of iron! ADO 4.01.151
things hid and barr'd, you mean, from common LLL 1.01. 57
inspired merit so by breath is barr'd. AWW 2.01.148
body, from his presence | i am barr'd, like one WT 3.02. 98
purpose so barr'd, it follows | nothing is done COR 3.01.148
that was thy joy, | be barr'd his entrance here. TIT 1.01.383
nor have we herein barr'd | your better wisdoms, HAM 1.02. 14
pitying | the pangs of barr'd affections, though CYM 1.01. 82
when it is barr'd the aidance of the tongue. VEN 330
in his bedchamber to be barr'd of rest. 784
hath barr'd him from the blessed thing he sought LUC 340
BARRELS 1 FR 0.0001 REL FR 1 V 0 P
place barrels of pitch upon the fatal stake, 1H6 5.04. 57
BARREN 43 FR 0.0048 REL FR 34 V 9 P
furlongs of sea for an acre of barren ground, TMP 1.01. 66 P
springs, brine–pits, barren place and fertile. 1.02.338
but barren hate, | sour–ey'd disdain, and 4.01. 19
barren my wit? ERR 2.01. 91
o, these are barren tasks, too hard to keep, LLL 1.01. 47
and such barren plants are set before us, that 4.02. 28
and therefore, finding barren practicers, 4.03.322
mew'd, | to live a barren sister all your life, MND 1.01. 72
the shallowest thick–skin of that barren sort, 3.02. 13
take | a breed for barren metal of his friend? MV 1.03.134
marry, now i let go your hand, i am barren. TN 1.03. 79 P
ladyship takes delight in such a barren rascal. 1.05. 84 P

"madam, why laugh you at such a barren rascal? 5.01.375 P
upon a barren mountain, and still winter | in WT 3.02.212
of that kind | our rustic garden's barren, and i 4.04. 84
and dull unfeeling barren ignorance | is made my R2 1.03.168
and that small model of the barren earth | which 3.02.153
us, | and we are barren and bereft of friends, 3.03. 84
no, on the barren mountains let him starve; 1H4 1.03. 89
that wish'd him on the barren mountains starve. 1.03.159
such barren pleasures, rude society, | as thou 3.02. 14
barren, barren, barren, beggars all, beggars all 2H4 5.03. 7 P
barren, barren, barren, beggars all, beggars all 5.03. 7 P
barren, barren, barren, beggars all, beggars all 5.03. 7 P
after summer evermore succeeds | barren winter, 2H6 2.04. 3
i am not barren to bring forth complaints. R3 2.02. 67
old barren plants, to wail it with their age. 4.04.394
were his brain as barren | as banks of libya TRO 1.03.327
i must not, i need not be barren of accusations; COR 1.01. 44 P
a barren detested vale you see it is; TIT 2.03. 93
the barren, touched in this holy chase, | shake JC 1.02. 8
crown, | and put a barren sceptre in my gripe, MAC 3.01. 61
on some quantity of barren spectators to laugh HAM 3.02. 41 P
in mine ears, | that long time have been barren. ANT 2.05. 25
for beauty that made barren the swell'd boast CYM 5.05.162
thick–sighted, barren, lean, and lacking juice, VEN 136
and barren dearth of daughters and of sons, | be 754
which far exceeds his barren skill to show. LUC 81
when lofty trees i see barren of leaves, | which SON 12. 5
day | and barren rage of death's eternal cold? 13.12
with means more blessed than my barren rhyme? 16. 4
why is my verse so barren of new pride? 76. 1
did exceed | the barren tender of a poet's debt; 83. 4
BARRENLY 1 FR 0.0001 REL FR 1 V 0 P
harsh, featureless, and rude, barrenly perish: SON 11.10
BARRENNESS 1 FR 0.0001 REL FR 0 V 1 P
i found it by the barrenness, hard in the palm ERR 3.02.120 P
BARREN–SPIRITED 1 FR 0.0001 REL FR 1 V 0 P
a barren–spirited fellow; JC 4.01. 36
BARRICADO 2 FR 0.0002 REL FR 1 V 1 P
how may we barricado it against him? AWW 1.01.113 P
be it concluded, | no barricado for a belly. WT 1.02.204
BARRICADOES 1 FR 0.0001 REL FR 0 V 1 P
it hath bay windows transparent as barricadoes, TN 4.02. 37 P
BARROW 1 FR 0.0001 REL FR 0 V 1 P
in a basket like a barrow of butcher's offal? WIV 3.05. 5 P
BARR'ST 2 FR 0.0002 REL FR 2 V 0 P
thou barr'st us | our prayers to the gods, which COR 5.03.104
what, villain boy, | barr'st me my way in rome? TIT 1.01.291
BARS 14 FR 0.0015 REL FR 13 V 1 P
besides these, other bars he lays before me, WIV 3.04. 7
bars me the right of voluntary choosing. MV 2.01. 16
puts bars between the owners and their rights! 3.02. 19
with his hinds, bars me the place of a brother, AYL 1.01. 19 P
which bars a thousand harms and lengthens life. SHR in.2. 136
produce | a will that bars the title of thy son. JN 2.01.192
/wont through a secret grate of iron bars | in 1H6 1.04. 10
that they suppos'd i could rend bars of steel, 1.04. 51
which obloquy set bars before my tongue, | else 2.05. 49
god, her conscience, and these bars against me, R3 1.02.234
but life, being weary of these worldly bars, JC 1.03. 96
or as those bars which stop the hourly dial, LUC 327
whilst i, whom fortune of such triumph bars, SON 25. 3
way, | each trifle under truest bars to thrust, 48. 2
BARSON 1 FR 0.0001 REL FR 0 V 1 P
lady, i think 'a be, but goodman puff of barson. 2H4 5.03. 90 P
BARTER'D 1 FR 0.0001 REL FR 1 V 0 P
once in contempt they would have barter'd me; 1H6 1.04. 31
BARTHOL'MEW 1 FR 0.0001 REL FR 1 V 0 P
sirrah. go you to barthol'mew my page, | and see SHR in.1. 105
BARTHOLOMEW 1 FR 0.0001 REL FR 0 V 1 P
thou whoreson little tidy bartholomew boar–pig, 2H4 2.04.231 P
BARTHOLOMEW–TIDE
1 FR 0.0001 REL FR 0 V 1 P
kept, are like flies at bartholomew–tide, blind, H5 5.02.308 P
BASAN 1 FR 0.0001 REL FR 1 V 0 P
that i were | upon the hill of basan, to outroar ANT 3.13.127
BASE* *(also bass)*
/BASE* 1 FR 0.0001 REL FR 1 V 0 P
/made /glory /base, /and /sovereignty /a /slave; R2 4.01.251
BASE* 173 FR 0.0195 REL FR 151 V 22 P
it did base my trespass. TMP 3.03. 99
indeed i bid the base for proteus. TGV 1.02. 94
lest the base earth | should from her vesture 2.04.159
base men, that use them to so base effect! 2.07. 73
base men, that use them to so base effect! 2.07. 73
go, base intruder! 3.01.157
without false vantage, or base treachery. 4.01. 29
no, we detest such vile base practices. 4.01. 71
the more degenerate and base art thou | to make 5.04.136
o base hungarian wight! WIV 1.03. 20 P
i will run no base humor. 1.03. 77 P
when thou shalt lack, | base phrygian turk! 1.03. 88
noble to conserve a life | in base appliances. MM 3.01. 88
it is the base (though bitter) disposition of ADO 2.01.207 P
won, | save base authority from others' books. LLL 1.01. 87
swain, that base minnow of thy mirth" — 1.01.247 P
which the base vulgar do call three. 1.02. 48 P
and as it is base for a soldier to love, so am i 1.02. 58 P
to love, so am i in love with a base wench. 1.02. 59 P
i do affect the very ground (which is base) 1.02.167 P
not utt'red by base sale of chapmen's tongues. 2.01. 16
welcome to the wide fields too base to be mine. 2.01. 93 P
in the vulgar — o base and obscure vulgar! 4.01. 68 P
kisses the base ground with obedient breast? 4.03.221
things base and vile, holding no quantity, MND 1.01.232
'twere damnation | to think so base a thought; MV 2.07. 50
gold, silver, and base lead. 2.09. 20
or with a base and boist'rous sword enforce | a AYL 2.03. 32
all but the base. SHR 3.01. 46
the base is right, 'tis the base knave that jars 3.01. 47
base is right, 'tis the base knave that jars. 3.01. 47
late | was in my nobler thoughts most base, is AWW 2.03.171
life and in the highest compulsion of base fear, 3.06. 30 P
though i confess, on base and ground enough, TN 5.01. 75
thou art too base | to be /acknowledg'd. WT 4.04.418
war | to a most base and vile–concluded peace. JN 2.01.586
parley, and base truce | to arms invasive? 5.01. 68
or sound so base a parley, my teeth shall tear R2 1.01.192
apish nation | limps after in base imitation. 2.01. 23
base men by his endowments are made great. 2.03.139
fall to the base earth from the firmament. 2.04. 20
in the base court he doth attend | to speak with 3.03.176
in the base court? 3.03.180
base court, where kings grow base, | to come at 3.03.180
base court, where kings grow base, | to come at 3.03.180
in the base court, come down? 3.03.182
to make the base earth proud with kissing it. 3.03.191
what answer shall i make to this base man? 4.01. 20
though being all too base | to stain the temper 4.01. 28
the rod, | and fawn on rage with base humility, 5.01. 33
who doth permit the base contagious clouds | to 1H4 1.02.198
being the agents or base second means, | the 1.03.165
thou hast tir'd thyself in base comparisons, 2.04.250 P
by smiling pick–thanks and base newsmongers, | i 3.02. 25
base inclination, and the start of spleen, | to 3.02.125
what, you poor, base, rascally, cheating, 2H4 2.04.124 P
i'll ne'er bear a base mind. 3.02.235 P
faith, i'll bear no base mind. 3.02.240 P
came like itself, in base and abject routs, 4.01. 33
the ugly form | of base and bloody insurrection 4.01. 40
puff i' thy teeth, most recreant coward base! 5.03. 92
a foutre for the world and worldlings base! 5.03. 99
o base assyrian knight, what is thy news? 5.03.101
is in base durance and contagious prison, 5.05. 34
base tike, call'st thou me host? H5 2.01. 29
base is the slave that pays. 2.01. 96
rock | o'erhang and jutty his confounded base, 3.01. 13
for there is none of you so mean and base | that 3.01. 29
or art thou base, common, and popular? 4.01. 38
hand | like a base pander hold the chamber–door 4.05. 14
dost thou thirst, base troyan, | to have me fold 5.01. 19
base troyan, thou shalt die. 5.01. 31
a base wallon, to win the dolphin's grace, 1H6 1.01.137
will'd me to leave my base vocation | and free 1.02. 80
all color | of base insinuating flattery, | i 2.04. 35
perish, base prince, ignoble duke of york! 3.01.177
so will this base and envious discord breed. 3.01.193
base muleters of france! 3.02. 68
i vow'd, base knight, when i did meet thee next, 4.01. 14
"contaminated, base, | and misbegotten blood i 4.06. 21
of all base passions, fear is most accurs'd. 5.02. 18
more vile | than is a slave in base servility; 5.03.113
base ignoble wretch! 5.04. 7
that he should be so abject, base, and poor, 5.05. 49
gloucester bears this base and humble mind. 2H6 1.02. 62
away, base cullions! 1.03. 40
base dunghill villain and mechanical, | i'll 1.03.193
'tis but a base ignoble mind | that mounts no 2.01. 13
never yet did base dishonor blur our name | but 4.01. 39
base slave, thy words are blunt and so art thou. 4.01. 67
small things make base men proud. 4.01.106
and will you credit this base drudge's words, 4.02.151
and you, base peasants, do ye believe him? 4.08. 21 P
only my followers' base and ignominious treasons 4.08. 63 P
base, fearful, and despairing henry! 3H6 1.01.178
degree | to base declension and loath'd bigamy. R3 3.07.189
a base foul stone, made precious by the foil 5.03.250
a scum of britains and base lackey peasants, 5.03.317
yet i am richer than my base accusers, | that H8 2.01.104
'em, | envy and base opinion set against 'em, 3.01. 36
they are too thin and base to hide offenses. 5.02.160
o theft most base, | that we have stol'n what we TRO 2.02. 92
her possession up | on terms of base compulsion! 2.02.153
but the strong base and building of my love | is 4.02.103
when we have here her base and pillar by us. 4.05.212
with those that wore them, these base slaves, COR 1.05. 7
by jove himself, | it makes the consuls base; 3.01.108
i | with my base tongue give to my noble heart 3.02.100
their base throats tear | with giving him glory. 5.06. 52
for these base bondmen to the yoke of rome. TIT 4.01.109
'zounds, ye whore, is black so base a hue? 4.02. 71
and here's the base fruit of her burning lust. 5.01. 43
i, that with base prayers | i should repent the 5.03.185
the base o' th' mount | is rank'd with all TIM 1.01. 64
they have all been touch'd and found base metal, 3.03. 6
if 'twill not serve, 'tis not so base as you, 3.04. 58
it could not else be i should prove so base | to 3.05. 93
right, | base noble, old young, coward valiant. 4.03. 30
it serves | for the base matter to illuminate JC 1.03.110
scorning the base degrees | by which he did 2.01. 26
low–crooked curtsies, and base spaniel fawning. 3.01. 43
who is here so base that would be a bondman? 3.02. 29 P
even at the base of pompey's statue | (which all 3.02.188
now | contaminate our fingers with base bribes? 4.03. 24
cliff | that beetles o'er his base into the sea, HAM 1.04. 71
with flaming top | stoops to his base, and with 2.02.476
marriage move | are base respects of thrift, but 3.02.183
like some ore | among a mineral of metals base, 4.01. 26
to what base uses we may return, horatio! 5.01.202 P
wherefore base? LR 1.02. 6
why brand they us | with base? 1.02. 10
base, base? 1.02. 10
base, base? 1.02. 10
edmund the base | shall /top th' legitimate. 1.02. 20
nor tripp'd neither, you base football player. 1.04. 86 P
a base, proud, shallow, beggarly, three–suited, 2.02. 16 P
pension beg | to keep base life afoot. 2.04.215
and all indign and base adversities | make head OTH 1.03.273
(as they say base men being in love have then a 2.01.215 P
prerogativ'd are they less than the base; 3.03.274
some base notorious knave, some scurvy fellow. 4.02.140
like the base /indian, threw a pearl away 5.02.347
o rarely base! ANT 5.02.158
this proves me base. 5.02.300
an eye | base and illustrious as the smoky light CYM 1.06.109
such an end thou seek'st — as base as strange. 1.06.144
the contract you pretend with that base wretch, 2.03.113
the precious note of it with a base slave, | a 2.03.122
besides, thou wert too base | to be his groom. 2.03.126
father cowards and base things sire base: 4.02. 26
father cowards and base things sire base: 4.02. 26
thou villain base, | know'st me not by my 4.02. 80
the country base than to commit such slaughter, 5.03. 20
that never relish'd of a base descent. PER 2.05. 60
her bud again, | and leaves him to base briers. TNK 2.02.143
i am base, | my father the mean keeper of his 2.04. 2
base cousin, | dar'st thou break first? 3.03. 44
a noble difference, | but base disposers of it. 3.06.117
to bid the wind a base he now prepares, | and VEN 303
throwing the base thong from his bending crest, 395
estate, | hiding base sin in pleats of majesty; LUC 93
then my digression is so vile, so base, | that 202
thou nobly base, they basely dignified; 660
the cedar stoops not to the base shrub's foot, 664
thee | unto the base bed of some rascal groom, 671
base watch of woes, sin's pack–horse, virtue's 928
for who so base would such an office have | as 1000
as sland'rous deathsman to so base a slave? 1001
to let base clouds o'ertake me in my way, SON 34. 3
knife, | too base of thee to be remembered. 74.12
but if that flow'r with base infection meet, 94.11
dark'ning thy pow'r to lend base subjects light? 100. 4
nor tender feeling to base touches prone, | nor 141. 6
BASE–BORN 3 FR 0.0003 REL FR 3 V 0 P
contemptuous base–born callot as she is, | she 2H6 1.03. 83
better ten thousand base–born cades miscarry 4.08. 47
to let thy tongue detect thy base–born heart? 3H6 2.02.143
BASELESS 1 FR 0.0001 REL FR 1 V 0 P
and, like the baseless fabric of this vision, TMP 4.01.151
BASELY 13 FR 0.0014 REL FR 13 V 0 P
is not himself, but basely led | by flatterers, R2 2.01.241
but basely yielded upon compromise | that which 2.01.253
to spend that shortness basely were too long 1H4 5.02. 82
that basely fled when noble talbot stood. 1H6 4.05. 17
none basely slain in brawls. TIT 1.01.353
openly, | and basely put it up without revenge? 1.01.433
a lord | basely insinuate and send us gifts. 4.02. 38
and basely cozen'd | of that true hand that 5.03.101
and do now not basely die, | not cowardly put ANT 4.15. 55
to me than begging | to take my life so basely. TNK 3.06.267
they basely fly, and dare not stay the field. VEN 894
thou nobly base, they basely dignified; LUC 660
thy int'rest was not bought | basely with gold, 1068
BASENESS 18 FR 0.0020 REL FR 15 V 3 P
some kinds of baseness | are nobly undergone; TMP 3.01. 2
and says such baseness | had never like executor 3.01. 12
why, thou unconfinable baseness, it is as much WIV 2.02. 21 P
that thou bear'st | are nurs'd by baseness. MM 3.01. 15
it is the baseness of thy fear | that makes thee TN 5.01.146
tak'st up the princess by that forced baseness WT 2.03. 79
reflect i not on thy baseness court–contempt? 4.04.734 P
for | there is no primer baseness. H8 1.02. 67
action teach my mind | a most inherent baseness. COR 3.02.123
fly, damned baseness, | to him that worships TIM 3.01. 47
a baseness to write fair, and labor'd much | how HAM 5.02. 34
with baseness? LR 1.02. 10
the blood and baseness of our natures would OTH 1.03.328 P
mind, and made of no such baseness | as jealious 3.04. 27
dishonor that the gods | detest my baseness. ANT 4.14. 57
before him, branded | his baseness that ensued? 4.14. 77
have made my throne | a seat for baseness. CYM 1.01.142
from whose so many weights of baseness cannot 3.05. 88
BASER 14 FR 0.0015 REL FR 12 V 2 P
he throws upon the gross world's baser slaves; LLL 1.01. 30
where her shoe (which is baser) guided by her 1.02.168 P
civet is of a baser birth than tar, the very AYL 3.02. 67 P
whose baser stars do shut us up in wishes, AWW 1.01.183
and make conceive a bark of baser kind | by bud WT 4.04. 94
best | neighbor'd by fruit of baser quality; H5 1.01. 62
but with a baser man of arms by far | once in 1H6 1.04. 30
that he is worshipp'd in a baser temple | than TIM 5.01. 48
volume of my brain, | unmix'd with baser matter. HAM 1.05.104
'tis dangerous when the baser nature comes 5.02. 60
my other elements | i give to baser life. ANT 5.02.290
thou art baser in it than a cutpurse. TNK 2.02.211
hidden sun, | breaks through his baser garments. 2.05. 24
"the baser is he, coming from a king, | to shame LUC 1002
BASES* 4 FR 0.0004 REL FR 3 V 1 P
but they are most of them means and bases; WT 4.03. 43 P
troy, yet upon his bases, had been down, | and TRO 1.03. 75
i yet am unprovided | of a pair of bases. PER 2.01.161
honoring, | or laid great bases for eternity, SON 125. 3
/BASEST 1 FR 0.0001 REL FR 1 V 0 P
/is /such /as /basest /and /contemned'st LR 2.02.143
BASEST 13 FR 0.0014 REL FR 11 V 2 P
guided by her foot (which is basest) doth tread. LLL 1.02.169 P
or what is he of basest function, | that says AYL 2.07. 79
the basest horn of his hoof is more musical than H5 3.07. 17 P
that, being one o' th' lowest, basest, poorest, COR 1.01.157
who can bring noblest minds to basest ends! TIM 4.03.464
see whe'er their basest metal be not mov'd; JC 1.01. 61
to take the basest and most poorest shape | that LR 2.03. 7
our basest beggars | are in the poorest thing 2.04.264
thou basest thing, avoid hence, from my sight! CYM 1.01.125
and prostitute me to the basest groom | that PER 4.06.190
anon permit the basest clouds to ride | with SON 33. 5
meet, | the basest weed outbraves his dignity: 94.12
queen | the basest jewel will be well esteem'd, 96. 6
BASE–STRING 1 FR 0.0001 REL FR 0 V 1 P
i have sounded the very base–string of humility. 1H4 2.04. 6 P
BASE–VIOL 1 FR 0.0001 REL FR 0 V 1 P
he that went, like a base–viol, in a case of ERR 4.03. 24 P
BASHFUL *(also pashful)*
BASHFUL 8 FR 0.0009 REL FR 7 V 1 P
hence, bashful cunning, | and prompt me, plain TMP 3.01. 81
show'd | bashful sincerity and comely love. ADO 4.01. 54
her wit, | her affability and bashful modesty, SHR 2.01. 49
you virtuous ass, you bashful fool, must you be 2H4 2.02. 75 P
and bashful henry depos'd, whose cowardice 3H6 1.01. 41
make bold her bashful years with your experience
R3 4.04.326
he burns with bashful shame, she with her tears VEN 49
no, | and forth with bashful innocence doth hie. LUC 1341
BASHFULNESS 1 FR 0.0001 REL FR 1 V 0 P
no maiden shame, | no touch of bashfulness? MND 3.02.286
BASILISCO–LIKE 1 FR 0.0001 REL FR 1 V 0 P
"knight, knight," good mother, basilisco–like. JN 1.01.244
BASILISK 4 FR 0.0004 REL FR 4 V 0 P
make me not sighted like the basilisk. WT 1.02.388
come, basilisk, | and kill the innocent gazer 2H6 3.02. 52
i'll slay more gazers than the basilisk, | i'll 3H6 3.02.187
take this too, | it is a basilisk unto mine eye, CYM 2.04.107
BASILISKS 4 FR 0.0004 REL FR 4 V 0 P
of basilisks, of cannon, culverin, | of 1H4 2.03. 53
bent | the fatal balls of murthering basilisks. H5 5.02. 17

their chiefest prospect murd'ring basilisks! 2H6 3.02.324
would they were basilisks, to strike thee dead! R3 1.02.150
BASIMECU 1 FR 0.0001 REL FR 0 V 1 P
giving up of normandy unto mounsieur basimecu, 2H6 4.07. 28 P
BASIN 3 FR 0.0003 REL FR 2 V 1 P
let one attend him with a silver basin | full of SHR in.1. 55
the basin that receives your guilty blood. TIT 5.02.183
i dreamt of a silver basin and ew'r to-night. TIM 3.01. 7 P
/BASINGSTOKE 1 FR 0.0001 REL FR 1 V 0 P
at /basingstoke, my lord. 2H4 2.01.169
BASINS 1 FR 0.0001 REL FR 1 V 0 P
basins and ewers to lave her dainty hands; SHR 2.01.348
BASIS 5 FR 0.0005 REL FR 4 V 1 P
th' shore, that o'er his wave-worn basis bowed, TMP 2.01.121
build me thy fortunes upon the basis of valor. TN 3.02. 34 P
though we upon this mountain's basis by | took H5 4.02. 30
that now on pompey's basis /lies along | no JC 3.01.115
great tyranny, lay thou thy basis sure, | for MAC 4.03. 32
BASK'D 1 FR 0.0001 REL FR 1 V 0 P
who laid him down and bask'd him in the sun, AYL 2.07. 15
BASKET 20 FR 0.0022 REL FR 3 V 17 P
staggering) take this basket on your shoulders. WIV 3.03. 13 P
look, here is a basket; 3.03.129 P
when your husband ask'd who was in the basket! 3.03.181 P
liv'd to be carried in a basket like a barrow of 3.05. 5 P
being thus cramm'd in the basket, a couple of 3.05. 97 P
once or twice what they had in their basket. 3.05.103 P
the last time he search'd for him, in a basket; 4.02. 33 P
shall i put him into the basket again? 4.02. 47 P
no, i'll come no more i' th' basket. 4.02. 49 P
is he, and talks of the basket too, howsoever he 4.02. 92 P
i'll appoint my men to carry the basket again, 4.02. 95 P
my men what they shall do with the basket. 4.02.100 P
sirs, take the basket again on your shoulders. 4.02.108 P
set down the basket, villain! 4.02.116 P
youth in a basket! 4.02.117 P
empty the basket, i say! 4.02.143 P
out of my house yesterday in this basket. 4.02.147 P
secrecy, | unpeg the basket on the house's top, HAM 3.04.193
ape, | to try conclusions in the basket creep, 3.04.195
this was his basket. ANT 5.02.340
BASKET-HILT 1 FR 0.0001 REL FR 0 V 1 P
you basket-hilt stale juggler, you! 2H4 2.04.131 P
BASS *(also base*, etc.)*
BASS 1 FR 0.0001 REL FR 1 V 0 P
the mean is drown'd with /your unruly bass. TGV 1.02. 93
BASSANIO 33 FR 0.0037 REL FR 30 V 3 P
here comes bassanio, your most noble kinsman, MV 1.01. 57
my lord bassanio, since you have found antonio, 1.01. 69
i pray you, good bassanio, let me know it, | and 1.01.135
yes, yes, it was bassanio — as i think, so was 1.02.115 P
mark you this, bassanio, | the devil can cite 1.03. 97
give me your present to one master bassanio, who 2.02.109 P
signior bassanio! 2.02.175
signior bassanio, hear me: 2.02.189
the difference of old shylock and bassanio. 2.05. 2
come about, | bassanio presently will go aboard. 2.06. 65
why, man, i saw bassanio under sail, | with him 2.08. 1
duke | they were not with bassanio in his ship. 2.08. 11
i saw bassanio and antonio part: 2.08. 36
bassanio told him he would make some speed | of 2.08. 37
/slubber not business for my sake, bassanio, 2.08. 39
bassanio, lord love, if thy will it be! 2.09.101
upon the rack, bassanio! 3.02. 26
you see me, lord bassanio, where i stand, | such 3.02.149
my lord bassanio and my gentle lady, | i wish 3.02.189
with leave, bassanio, i am half yourself, | and 3.02.248
"sweet bassanio, my ships have all miscarried, 3.02.315 P
pray god bassanio come | to see me pay his debt, 3.03. 35
jessica | in place of lord bassanio and myself. 3.04. 39
meet | the lord bassanio live an upright life, 3.05. 74
you cannot better be employ'd, bassanio, | than 4.01.117
give me your hand, bassanio, fare you well! 4.01.265
be judge | whether bassanio had not once a love. 4.01.277
my lord bassanio, let him have the ring. 4.01.449
my lord bassanio upon more advice | hath sent 4.02. 6
husband, | and never be bassanio so for me — 5.01.131
my lord bassanio gave his ring away | unto the 5.01.179
here, lord bassanio, swear to keep this ring. 5.01.256
pardon me, bassanio, | for, by this ring, the 5.01.258
BASSANIO'S 7 FR 0.0008 REL FR 7 V 0 P
and we are stay'd for at bassanio's feast. MV 2.06. 48
who went with him to search bassanio's ship. 2.08. 5
wondrous sensible | he wrung bassanio's hand, 2.08. 49
o, then be bold to say bassanio's dead! 3.02.185
that steals the color from bassanio's cheek — 3.02.244
shall lose a hair through bassanio's fault. 3.02.302
how dost thou like the lord bassanio's wife? 3.05. 72
BASSIANUS' 3 FR 0.0003 REL FR 3 V 0 P
chaste | than this lavinia, bassianus' love. TIT 2.01.109
and wash their hands in bassianus' blood. 2.03. 45
womb | of this deep pit, poor bassianus' grave. 2.03.240
BASSIANUS 18 FR 0.0020 REL FR 18 V 0 P
if ever bassianus, caesar's son, | were gracious TIT 1.01. 10
so, bassianus, you have play'd your prize. 1.01.399
prince bassianus, leave to plead my deeds, 1.01.424
for you, prince bassianus, i have pass'd | my 1.01.468
become so loose, | or bassianus so degenerate, 2.01. 66
though bassianus be the emperor's brother, 2.01. 88
thee, | this is the day of doom for bassianus: 2.03. 42
no more, great empress, bassianus comes. 2.03. 52
so long, | poor i was slain when bassianus died. 2.03.171
lord bassianus lies /beray'd in blood, | all on 2.03.222
hour, | to find thy brother bassianus dead. 2.03.252
where is thy brother bassianus? 2.03.261
poor bassianus here lies murthered. 2.03.263
sweet huntsman — bassianus 'tis we mean — | do 2.03.269
same pit | where we decreed to bury bassianus. 2.03.274
that should have murthered bassianus here. 2.03.279
'twas her two sons that murdered bassianus; 5.01. 91
hole, | where the dead corpse of bassianus lay; 5.01.105
BASTA 1 FR 0.0001 REL FR 1 V 0 P
basta, content thee; SHR 1.01.198
BASTARD *(also basterd)*
/BASTARD 1 FR 0.0001 REL FR 0 V 1 P
/'tis /said, /the /bastard /son /of /gloucester. LR 4.07. 88 P
BASTARD 65 FR 0.0073 REL FR 44 V 21 P
and this demi-devil | (for he's a bastard one) TMP 5.01.273
that's as much as to say "bastard virtues," that TGV 3.01.318 P
all the world drink brown and white bastard. MM 3.02. 3 P
shame hath a bastard fame, well managed; ERR 3.02. 19
the practice of it lives in john the bastard, ADO 4.01.188
your brother the bastard is fled from messina. 5.01.190 P
were so pleas'd that thou wert but my bastard, LLL 5.01. 76 P
and that is but a kind of bastard hope neither. MV 3.05. 7 P
that were a kind of bastard hope indeed; 3.05. 13 P
that same wicked bastard of venus that was begot AYL 4.01.211 P
give her the bastard, | thou dotard, thou art WT 2.03. 74
take up the bastard, | take't up, i say; 2.03. 76
the bastard brains with these my proper hands 2.03.140
shall i live on to see this bastard kneel | and 2.03.155
save this bastard's life — for 'tis a bastard, 2.03.161
that thou carry | this female bastard hence, and 2.03.175
you had a bastard by polixenes, | and i but 3.02. 83
for he is but a bastard to the time | that doth JN 1.01.207
with them a bastard of the king's deceas'd, 2.01. 65
thy bastard shall be king | that thou mayst be a 2.01.122
my boy a bastard? 2.01.129
the bastard faulconbridge | is now in england 3.04.171
bed, | and that he is a bastard, not thy son. R2 5.02.106
score a pint of bastard in the half-moon," or so 1H4 2.04. 27 P
why then your brown bastard is your only drink! 2.04. 73 P
a bastard son of the king's? 2H4 2.04.283 P
normans, but bastard normans, norman bastards! H5 3.05. 10
to new-store france with bastard warriors. 3.05. 31
the bastard of orleance with him is join'd; 1H6 1.01. 93
bastard of orleance, thrice welcome to us. 1.02. 47
as good? | thou bastard of my grandfather! 3.01. 42
orleance the bastard, charles, burgundy, 4.04. 26
name | to make a bastard and a slave of me! 4.05. 15
the ireful bastard orleance, that drew blood 4.06. 16
i quickly shed | some of his bastard blood, and 4.06. 20
here, purposing the bastard to destroy, | came 4.06. 25
brutus' bastard hand | stabb'd julius caesar; 2H6 4.01.136
to say if that the bastard boys of york | shall 5.01.115
and not these bastard britains, whom our fathers R3 5.03.333
bastard margarelon | hath doreus prisoner, | and TRO 5.05. 7
a bastard son of priam's. 5.07. 15 P
i am a bastard too, i love bastards. 5.07. 16 P
i am bastard begot, bastard instructed, bastard 5.07. 17 P
i am bastard begot, bastard instructed, bastard 5.07. 17 P
bastard instructed, bastard in mind, bastard in 5.07. 17 P
bastard in mind, bastard in valor, in every 5.07. 18 P
bite another, and wherefore should one bastard? 5.07. 20 P
farewell, bastard. 5.07. 22 P
a getter of more bastard children than war's a COR 4.05.225 P
wouldst thou have me prove myself a bastard? TIT 2.03.148
ho, ho! i laugh to think that babe a bastard. TIM 1.02.112 P
go, thou wast born a bastard, and thou't die a 2.02. 84 P
think it a bastard, whom the oracle | hath 4.03.121
what bastard doth not? JC 5.04. 2
drop of blood that's calm proclaims me bastard, HAM 4.05.118
why bastard? LR 1.02. 6
our father's love is to the bastard edmund | as 1.02. 17
degenerate bastard, i'll not trouble thee; 1.04.254
"thou unpossessing bastard, dost thou think, 2.01. 67
for gloucester's bastard son | was kinder to his 4.06.114
comes in | like old importment's bastard) has TNK 1.03. 80
this bastard graff shall never come to growth. LUC 1062
before these bastard signs of fair were born, SON 68. 3
it might for fortune's bastard be unfather'd, 124. 2
and beauty slander'd with a bastard shame, | for 127. 4
BASTARDIZING 1 FR 0.0001 REL FR 0 V 1 P
in the firmament twinkled on my bastardizing. LR 1.02.133 P
BASTARDLY 1 FR 0.0001 REL FR 0 V 1 P
thou bastardly rogue! 2H4 2.01. 49 P
BASTARD'S 2 FR 0.0002 REL FR 2 V 0 P
to save this bastard's life — for 'tis a WT 2.03.161
now where's the bastard's braves, and charles 1H6 3.02.123
BASTARDS 18 FR 0.0020 REL FR 13 V 5 P
hang'd a man for the getting a hundred bastards, MM 3.02.118 P
sure they are bastards to the english, the AWW 2.03. 94 P
gillyvors, | which some call nature's bastards. WT 4.04. 83
in gillyvors, | and do not call them bastards. 4.04. 99
bastards, and else. JN 2.01.276
some bastards too. 2.01.279
normans, but bastard normans, norman bastards! H5 3.05. 10
well, go to, we'll have no bastards live, 1H6 5.04. 70
i wish the bastards dead, | and i would have it R3 4.02. 18
tyrrel, i mean those bastards in the tower. 4.02. 75
i am a bastard too, i love bastards. TRO 5.07. 16 P
though but bastards and syllables | of no COR 3.02. 56
bastards and all! 4.02. 27
now, gods, stand up for bastards! LR 1.02. 22
we are all bastards, | and that most venerable CYM 2.05. 2
'tis not our bringing up of poor bastards — as PER 4.02. 14 P
it with the palsy, for these bastards of dung — STM II.C 12 P
and bastards of his foul adulterate heart. LC 175
BASTARDY 9 FR 0.0010 REL FR 9 V 0 P
but once he slander'd me with bastardy. JN 1.01. 74
that thou thyself wast born in bastardy; 2H6 3.02.223
time, | infer the bastardy of edward's children. R3 3.05. 75
touch'd you the bastardy of edward's children? 3.07. 4
his tyranny for trifles, his own bastardy, | as 3.07. 9
tree, | and by his side his fruit of bastardy. TIT 5.01. 48
nobly bears, | is guilty of a several bastardy, JC 2.01.138
bastardy? LR 1.02. 10
thy issue blurr'd with nameless bastardy; LUC 522
BASTED 1 FR 0.0001 REL FR 0 V 1 P
the guards are but slightly basted on neither. ADO 1.01.287 P
BASTERD *(also bastard)*
BASTERD 1 FR 0.0001 REL FR 0 V 1 P
ish a villain, and a basterd, and a knave, and a H5 3.02.123 P
BASTES 1 FR 0.0001 REL FR 1 V 0 P
that bastes his arrogance with his own seam, TRO 2.03.185
BASTINADO 3 FR 0.0003 REL FR 1 V 2 P
will deal in poison with thee, or in bastinado, AYL 5.01. 54 P
he gives the bastinado with his tongue; JN 2.01.463
that gave amamon the bastinado and made lucifer
1H4 2.04.337 P
BASTING* 2 FR 0.0002 REL FR 0 V 2 P
basting. ERR 2.02. 58 P
choleric, and purchase me another dry basting. 2.02. 63 P
BAT* 4 FR 0.0004 REL FR 4 V 0 P
ere the bat hath flown | his cloister'd flight, MAC 3.02. 40
toe of frog, | wool of bat and tongue of dog, 4.01. 15
would from a paddock, from a bat, a gib, | such HAM 3.04.190
so slides he down upon his grained bat, | and LC 64
BATAILLES 1 FR 0.0001 REL FR 1 V 0 P
dieu de batailles! H5 3.05. 15
BATCH 1 FR 0.0001 REL FR 1 V 0 P
thou crusty batch of nature, what's the news? TRO 5.01. 5
BATE* *(also abate, etc.)*
BATE* 16 FR 0.0018 REL FR 9 V 7 P
thou did promise | to bate me a full year. TMP 1.02.250
bate, i beseech you, widow dido. 2.01.101 P
her, rather than she will bate one breath of her ADO 2.03.176 P
honor which shall bate his scythe's keen edge, LLL 1.01. 6
and bid the main flood bate his usual height; MV 4.01. 72
that bate and beat and will not be obedient. SHR 4.01.196
dram of it, and i will not bate thee a scruple. AWW 2.03.222 P
do i not bate? 1H4 3.03. 2 P
leg, and breeds no bate with telling of discreet 2H4 2.04.250 P
bate me some, and i will pay you some, and (as ep 14 P
good bawcock, bate thy rage; H5 3.02. 25
hooded valor, and when it appears, it will bate. 3.07.112 P
neither will they bate | one jot of ceremony. COR 2.02.140
wrong, you bate too much of your own merits. TIM 1.02.206
who long'st | (o, let me bate!) CYM 3.02. 54
keep the feast full, bate not an hour on't. TNK 1.01.220
BATE-BREEDING 1 FR 0.0001 REL FR 1 V 0 P
"this sour informer, this bate-breeding spy, VEN 655
BATED* 9 FR 0.0010 REL FR 8 V 1 P
of my instruction hast thou nothing bated | in TMP 3.03. 85
were the world mine, demetrius being bated, MND 1.01.190
with bated breath and whisp'ring humbleness, MV 1.03.124
these griefs and losses have so bated me | that 3.03. 32
(those bated that inherit but the fall | of the AWW 2.01. 13
flight, | and like a bated and retired flood, JN 5.04. 53
wind | bated like eagles having lately bath'd, 1H4 4.01. 99
that, on the supervise, no leisure bated, | no, HAM 5.02. 23
i cannot be bated one doit of a thousand pieces. PER 4.02. 51 P
BATELESS 1 FR 0.0001 REL FR 1 V 0 P
set | this bateless edge on his keen appetite; LUC 9
BATES* 2 FR 0.0002 REL FR 1 V 1 P
brother john bates, is not that the morning H5 4.01. 85 P
who bates mine honor shall not know my coin. TIM 3.03. 26
BATH* *(also both)*
BATH* 8 FR 0.0009 REL FR 6 V 2 P
and in the height of this bath (when i was more WIV 3.05.118 P
gud feith, gud captens bath, and i sall quit you H5 3.02.103 P
you were conducted to a gentle bath | and balms COR 1.06. 63
the death of each day's life, sore labor's bath, MAC 2.02. 35
and grew a seething bath, which yet men prove SON 153. 7
i, sick withal, the help of bath desired, | and 153.11
the bath for my help lies | where cupid got new 153.13
growing a bath and healthful remedy | for men 154.11
BATH'D 6 FR 0.0006 REL FR 6 V 0 P
tears our recountments had most kindly bath'd, AYL 4.03.140
wind | bated like eagles having lately bath'd, 1H4 4.01. 99
or bath'd thy growing with our heated bloods. 3H6 2.02.169
when he by night lay bath'd in maiden blood. TIT 2.03.232
pipes, | in which so many smiling romans bath'd, JC 2.02. 86
these often bath'd she in her fluxive eyes, LC 50
BATHE 7 FR 0.0008 REL FR 7 V 0 P
the delighted spirit | to bathe in fiery floods, MM 3.01.121
came smiling and did bathe their hands in it. JC 2.02. 79
and let us bathe our hands in caesar's blood 3.01.106
except they meant to bathe in reeking wounds, MAC 1.02. 39
or bathe my dying honor in the blood | shall ANT 4.02. 6
had i this cheek | to bathe my lips upon; CYM 1.06.100
"the crow may bathe his coal-black wings in mire
LUC 1009
BATHES 2 FR 0.0002 REL FR 2 V 0 P
she bathes in water, yet her fire must burn. VEN 94
he falls, and bathes the pale fear in his face, LUC 1775
BATHING 1 FR 0.0001 REL FR 1 V 0 P
and the chimney-piece | chaste dian bathing. CYM 2.04. 82
BATHS 1 FR 0.0001 REL FR 1 V 0 P
season the slaves | for tubs and baths, bring TIM 4.03. 87
BATING 1 FR 0.0001 REL FR 1 V 0 P
hood my unmann'd blood, bating in my cheeks, ROM 3.02. 14
BATLER 1 FR 0.0001 REL FR 0 V 1 P
the kissing of her batler and the cow's dugs AYL 2.04. 49 P
BAT'S 1 FR 0.0001 REL FR 1 V 0 P
on the bat's back i do fly | after summer TMP 5.01. 91
BATS* 3 FR 0.0003 REL FR 3 V 0 P
of sycorax, toads, beetles, bats, light on you! TMP 1.02.340
where go you | with bats and clubs? COR 1.01. 56
but make you ready your stiff bats and clubs, 1.01.161
BATTALIA 1 FR 0.0001 REL FR 1 V 0 P
why, our battalia trebles that account; R3 5.03. 11
BATTALIONS 1 FR 0.0001 REL FR 1 V 0 P
they come not single spies, | but in battalions: HAM 4.05. 79
BATTEN 2 FR 0.0002 REL FR 1 V 1 P
your function, go, and batten on cold bits. COR 4.05. 32 P
leave to feed, | and batten on this moor? HAM 3.04. 67
BATTER 3 FR 0.0003 REL FR 3 V 0 P
or with a log | batter his skull, or paunch him TMP 3.02. 90
be the ram to batter | the fortress of it; ANT 3.02. 30
(rude ram, to batter such an ivory wall!), LUC 464
BATTER'D 3 FR 0.0003 REL FR 3 V 0 P
the tyrant has not batter'd at their peace? MAC 4.03.178
have batter'd down her consecrated wall, | and LUC 723
her mansion batter'd by the enemy, | her sacred 1171
BATTERING 2 FR 0.0002 REL FR 1 V 1 P
so you would leave battering, i had rather have ERR 2.02. 36 P
their battering cannon charged to the mouths, JN 2.01.382
BATTERS 3 FR 0.0003 REL FR 3 V 0 P
so that the ram that batters down the wall, TRO 1.03.206
in commotion rages, | and batters down himself. 2.03.176
sky-planted, batters all rebelling coasts? CYM 5.04. 96
BATTERY 8 FR 0.0009 REL FR 4 V 4 P
i'll have an action of battery against him, if TN 4.01. 34 P
this union shall do more than battery can | to JN 2.01.446
talks like a knell, and his hum is a battery. COR 5.04. 21 P
and will not tell him of his action of battery? HAM 5.01.103 P
make battery to our ears with the loud music; ANT 2.07.109
of ajax cannot keep | the battery from my heart. 4.14. 39
which else an easy battery might lay flat, for CYM 1.04. 22 P
make raging battery upon shores of flint." PER 4.04. 43
BATTLE *(also pattle)*
/BATTLE 1 FR 0.0001 REL FR 1 V 0 P
/rather /lose /the /battle /than /that /sister LR 5.01. 18

BATTLE 103 FR 0.0116 REL FR 95 V 8 P
"the battle with the centaurs, to be sung | by MND 5.01. 44
occasion, | made him give battle to the lioness, AYL 4.03.130
have i not in a pitched battle heard | loud SHR 1.02.205
perchance he's hurt i' th' battle. AWW 3.05. 87 P
besides i say, and will in battle prove, | or R2 1.01. 92
this feast of battle with mine adversary. 1.03. 92
what may the king's whole battle reach unto? 1H4 4.01.129
let it be seen to–morrow in the battle | which 4.03. 13
thou see me down in the battle and bestride me, 5.01.121 P
the king will bid you battle presently. 5.02. 30
name, that in battle thus | thou crossest me? 5.03. 1
and i do haunt thee in the battle thus | because 5.03. 4
holes in an enemy's battle as thou hast done in 2H4 3.02.154 P
our battle is more full of names than yours, 4.01.152
hear | a fearful battle rend'red you in music; H5 1.01. 44
shame | when cressy battle fatally was struck, 2.04. 54
we would not seek a battle as we are, | nor, as 3.06.164
each battle sees the other's umber'd face. 4.pr. 9
and so our scene must to the battle fly; 4.pr. 48
and heads, chopp'd off in a battle, shall join 4.01.136 P
there are few die well that die in a battle; 4.01.142 P
action swarm | about our squares of battle, were 4.02. 28
to demonstrate the life of such a battle, | in 4.02. 54
the king himself is rode to view their battle. 4.03. 2
more help, could fight this royal battle! 4.03. 75
that ran from the battle ha' done this slaughter 4.07. 6 P
but in plain shock and even play of battle, 4.08.109
and rush'd into the bowels of the battle. 1H6 1.01.129
this dastard, at the battle of poictiers, | when 4.01. 19
wilt thou yet leave the battle, boy, and fly, 4.06. 28
into the clust'ring battle of the french; 4.07. 13
one, | and means to give you battle presently. 5.02. 13
that those which fly before the battle ends 2H6 4.02.178
thy chair–days, thus | to die in ruffian battle? 5.02. 49
saint albons battle won by famous york | shall 5.03. 30
and issue forth and bid them battle straight. 3H6 1.02. 70
many a battle have i won in france | when as the 1.02. 73
i saw him in the battle range about, | and 2.01. 11
darraign your battle, for they are at hand. 2.02. 72
this battle fares like to the morning's war, 2.05. 1
clifford too, | have chid me from the battle; 2.05. 17
whiles lions war and battle for their dens, 2.05. 74
cross the seas and bid false edward battle; 3.03.235
loss of some pitch'd battle against warwick? 4.04. 4
doubt | will issue out again and bid us battle. 5.01. 63
of force enough to bid his brother battle; 5.01. 77
and bid thee battle, edward, if thou dar'st. 5.01.111
here pitch our battle, hence we will not budge. 5.04. 66
in margaret's battle at saint albons slain? R3 1.03.129
which in the day of battle tire thee more | than 4.04.189
here, | a royal battle might be won and lost. 4.04.536
i'll draw the form and model of our battle, 5.03. 24
be — | prepare thy battle early in the morning, 5.03. 88
to–morrow in the battle think on me, | and fall 5.03.134
good angels guard thy battle! 5.03.138
awake, | and in a bloody battle end thy days! 5.03.155
to–morrow in the battle think on me, | and fall 5.03.162
o, in the battle think on buckingham, | and die 5.03.169
plain, | and thus my battle shall be ordered: 5.03.292
we will follow | in the main battle, whose 5.03.299
after the battle let george stanley die. 5.03.346
troy, | that find such cruel battle here within? TRO 1.01. 3
as subject all the vale, | to see the battle. 1.02. 4
cop'd hector in the battle and strook him down, 1.02. 34 P
as doth a battle, when they charge on heaps 3.02. 28
a maiden battle then? o, i perceive you. 4.05. 87
from my great purpose in to–morrow's battle. 5.01. 38
rome and her rats are at the point of battle, COR 1.01.162
and given to lartius and to martius battle. 1.06. 11
how lies their battle? 1.06. 51
and to the battle came he, where he did | run 2.02.118
and boys with stones | in puny battle slay me. 4.04. 6
why do fond men expose themselves to battle, TIM 3.05. 42
the noise of battle hurtled in the air; JC 2.02. 22
their bloody sign of battle is hung out, | and 5.01. 14
lead your battle softly on | upon the left hand 5.01. 16
mark antony, shall we give sign of battle? 5.01. 23
to set | upon one battle all our liberties. 5.01. 75
if we do lose this battle, then is this | the 5.01. 97
then, if we lose this battle, | you are 5.01.107
your right noble son, | lead our first battle. MAC 5.06. 4
do you hear aught, sir, of a battle toward? LR 4.06.209
before you fight the battle, ope this letter. 5.01. 40
we'll use | his countenance for the battle, 5.01. 63
the battle done, and they within our power, 5.01. 67
nor the division of a battle knows | more than a OTH 1.01. 23
than pertains to feats of broils and battle, 1.03. 87
his cocks do win the battle still of mine, ANT 2.03. 37
ay, and to wage this battle at pharsalia, 3.07. 31
provoke not battle | till we have done at sea. 3.08. 3
in eye of caesar's battle, from which place | we 3.09. 2
close by the battle, ditch'd, and wall'd with CYM 5.03. 14
arise my knights o' th' battle. 5.05. 20
and your three motives to the battle, with | i 5.05.388
ere the stroke | of yet this scarce–cold battle, 5.05.469
them reported in the battle to be the only doers TNK 2.01. 29 P
yet in the field to strike a battle for her; 2.02.252
are making battle, thus like knights appointed, 3.06.134
this battle shall confound | both these brave 5.01.166
whose sinowy neck in battle ne'er did bow, | who VEN 99
"on his bow–back he hath a battle set | of 619
whose waves to imitate the battle sought | with LUC 1438
the scars of battle scapeth by the flight, | and LC 244
BATTLE–AXE 1 FR 0.0001 REL FR 1 V 0 P
rome, | and rear'd aloft the bloody battle–axe, TIT 3.01.168
BATTLEMENTS 8 FR 0.0009 REL FR 8 V 0 P
and stand securely on their battlements | as in JN 2.01.374
that from this castle's tottered battlements R2 3.03. 52
paris, | from off the battlements of any tower, ROM 4.01. 78
have you climb'd up to walls and battlements, JC 1.01. 38
and fix'd his head upon our battlements. MAC 1.02. 23
fatal entrance of duncan | under my battlements. 1.05. 40
let all the battlements their ord'nance fire. HAM 5.02.270
a fuller blast ne'er shook our battlements. OTH 2.01. 6
/BATTLE'S 1 FR 0.0001 REL FR 1 V 0 P
/or /ill, /as /this /day's /battle's /fought. LR 4.07. 96
BATTLE'S 4 FR 0.0004 REL FR 4 V 0 P
charg'd our main battle's front and, breaking in 3H6 1.01. 8
and, now the battle's ended, | if friend or foe, 2.06. 44
done, | when the battle's lost and won. MAC 1.01. 4
as life for honor in fell battle's rage, | honor LUC 145
/BATTLES 1 FR 0.0001 REL FR 1 V 0 P
of my life | from year to year — the /battles, OTH 1.03.130
BATTLES 17 FR 0.0019 REL FR 17 V 0 P
like heralds 'twixt two dreadful battles set: JN 4.02. 78
on | to bloody battles and to bruising arms. 1H4 3.02.105
in sight of both our battles we may meet, | /and 2H4 4.01.177
o god of battles, steel my soldiers' hearts, H5 4.01.289
the french are bravely in their battles set, 4.03. 69
the battles of the lord of hosts he fought; 1H6 1.01. 31
in thirteen battles salisbury o'ercame; 1.04. 78
whom i encount'red as the battles join'd. 3H6 1.01. 15
our battles join'd, and both sides fiercely 2.01.121
by all the battles wherein we have fought, | by COR 1.06. 56
and in the brunt of seventeen battles since | he 2.02.100
battles thrice six | i have seen, and heard of; 2.03.128
successful in the battles that he fights, | with TIT 1.01. 66
their battles are at hand; JC 5.01. 4
labio and flavio, set our battles on. 5.03.108
your high–engender'd battles 'gainst a head | so LR 3.02. 23
know that to–morrow the last of many battles ANT 4.01. 11
BATT'RED 3 FR 0.0003 REL FR 3 V 0 P
have batt'red me like roaring cannon–shot, | and 1H6 3.03. 79
than foemen's marks upon his batt'red shield, TIT 4.01.127
his batt'red shield, his uncontrolled crest, VEN 104
BATT'RING 1 FR 0.0001 REL FR 1 V 0 P
against the wrackful siege of batt'ring days, SON 65. 6
BATT'RY 8 FR 0.0009 REL FR 7 V 1 P
or i'll have mine action of batt'ry on thee. MM 2.01.179 P
me best, | if i begin the batt'ry once again, H5 3.03. 7
where is best place to make our batt'ry next? 1H6 1.04. 65
her sighs will make a batt'ry in his breast, 3H6 3.01. 37
and make a batt'ry through his /deafen'd parts, PER 5.01. 47
for where a heart is hard they make no batt'ry." VEN 426
as they did batt'ry to the spheres intend; LC 23
to leave the batt'ry that you make 'gainst mine, 277
BATTY 1 FR 0.0001 REL FR 1 V 0 P
with leaden legs and batty wings doth creep. MND 3.02.365
BAUBLE *(also bable)*
BAUBLE 6 FR 0.0006 REL FR 4 V 2 P
cap, | a custard–coffin, a bauble, a silken pie. SHR 4.03. 82
and i would give his wife my bauble, sir, to do AWW 4.05. 30 P
how many shallow bauble boats dare sail | upon TRO 1.03. 35
i know | an idiot holds his bauble for a god, TIT 5.01. 79
venetians, and thither comes the bauble, and, OTH 4.01.135 P
senseless bauble, | art thou a feodary for this CYM 3.02. 20
BAUBLES 1 FR 0.0001 REL FR 1 V 0 P
and his shipping | (poor ignorant baubles!) CYM 3.01. 27
BAUBLING 1 FR 0.0001 REL FR 1 V 0 P
a baubling vessel was he captain of, | for TN 5.01. 54
BAVIAN 2 FR 0.0002 REL FR 2 V 0 P
where's the bavian? TNK 3.05. 33
the bavian, with long tail and eke long tool, 3.05.132
BAVIN 1 FR 0.0001 REL FR 1 V 0 P
with shallow jesters, and rash bavin wits, 1H4 3.02. 61
BAWCOCK 4 FR 0.0004 REL FR 3 V 1 P
why, how now, my bawcock? how dost thou, chuck? TN 3.04.112 P
why, that's my bawcock. WT 1.02.121
good bawcock, bate thy rage; H5 3.02. 25
the king's a bawcock, and a heart of gold, | a 4.01. 44
BAWD* 41 FR 0.0046 REL FR 17 V 24 P
pompey, you are partly a bawd, pompey, howsoever MM 2.01.219 P
by being a bawd? 2.01.225 P
mercy to thee would prove itself a bawd, | 'tis 3.01.149
fie, sirrah, a bawd, a wicked bawd! 3.02. 19
fie, sirrah, a bawd, a wicked bawd! 3.02. 19
ever your fresh whore and your powder'd bawd, an 3.02. 60 P
for being a bawd, for being a bawd. 3.02. 65 P
for being a bawd, for being a bawd. 3.02. 65 P
if imprisonment be the due of a bawd, why, 'tis 3.02. 67 P
bawd is he doubtless, and of antiquity too; 3.02. 67 P
a bawd of eleven years' continuance, may it 3.02.196 P
whipping, for you have been a notorious bawd. 4.02. 14 P
i have been an unlawful bawd time out of mind, 4.02. 15 P
he hath been a bawd. 4.02. 27 P
a bawd, sir? 4.02. 28 P
is a more penitent trade than your bawd — he 4.02. 50 P
come on, bawd, i will instruct thee in my trade; 4.02. 54 P
to be bawd to a bell–wether, and to betray a AYL 3.02. 80 P
a most intelligencing bawd! WT 2.03. 69
this bawd, this broker, this all–changing word, JN 2.01.582
and made his majesty the bawd to theirs. 3.01. 59
france is a bawd to fortune and king john, 3.01. 60
so shall my virtue be his vice's bawd, | an' he R2 5.03. 67
a bawd, a cutpurse. H5 3.06. 62 P
well, bawd i'll turn, | and something lean to 5.01. 85
by the same token, you are a bawd. TRO 1.02.281 P
a bawd, a bawd, a bawd! so ho! ROM 2.04.130 P
a bawd, a bawd, a bawd! so ho! 2.04.130 P
a bawd, a bawd, a bawd! so ho! 2.04.130 P
thou wast born a bastard, and thou't die a bawd. TIM 2.02. 85 P
habit only that is honest, | herself's a bawd. 4.03.115
her trade, | and to make whores, a bawd. 4.03.135
from what it is to a bawd than the force of HAM 3.01.111 P
one that wouldst be a bawd in way of good LR 2.02. 20 P
yet she's a simple bawd | that cannot say as OTH 4.02. 20
that /dignifies the renown of a bawd, no less PER 4.06. 39 P
and her gain | she gives the cursed bawd. 5.ch. 11
when reason is the bawd to lust's abuse. VEN 792
laud, | and mak'st fair reputation but a bawd. LUC 623
blind muffled bawd! 768
troth, | thou foul abettor, thou notorious bawd! 886
BAWD–BORN 1 FR 0.0001 REL FR 0 V 1 P
bawd–born. MM 3.02. 68 P
BAWDRY 3 FR 0.0003 REL FR 1 V 2 P
we must be married, or we must live in bawdry. AYL 3.03. 97
love–songs for maids, so without bawdry, which WT 4.04.194 P
he's for a jig or a tale of bawdry, or he sleeps HAM 2.02.500 P
BAWD'S 1 FR 0.0001 REL FR 0 V 1 P
that this house, if it be not a bawd's house, it MM 2.01. 76 P
BAWDS 5 FR 0.0005 REL FR 1 V 4 P
and the knaves, you need not to fear the bawds. MM 2.01.235 P
and clocks the tongues of bawds, and dials the 1H4 1.02. 8 P
o /traders and bawds, how earnestly are you set TRO 5.10. 37 P
and usurers' men, bawds between gold and want! TIM 2.02. 60 P
field, | and bawds and whores do churches build; LR 3.02. 92
BAWDY 8 FR 0.0009 REL FR 5 V 3 P
if bawdy talk offend you, we'll have very little MM 4.03.178 P
it is a bawdy planet, that will strike | where WT 1.02.201
come sing me a bawdy song, make me merry. 1H4 3.03. 13 P
they | that come to hear a merry, bawdy play, H8 pr 14
for every false drop in her bawdy veins, | a TRO 4.01. 70
for the bawdy hand of the dial is now upon the ROM 2.04.112 P
bloody, bawdy villain! HAM 2.02.580
the bawdy wind, that kisses all it meets, | is OTH 4.02. 78
BAWDY–HOUSE 4 FR 0.0004 REL FR 0 V 4 P
week, went to a bawdy–house not above once in a 1H4 3.03. 17 P
this house is turn'd bawdy–house, they pick 3.03. 99 P
tearing a poor whore's ruff in a bawdy–house? 2H4 2.04.145 P
will be thought we keep a bawdy–house straight. H5 2.01. 35 P
BAWDY–HOUSES 2 FR 0.0002 REL FR 0 V 2 P
tavern–reckonings, memorandums of bawdy–houses, 1H4 3.03.159 P
come, i am for no more bawdy–houses. PER 4.05. 6 P
/BAWL 1 FR 0.0001 REL FR 0 V 1 P
whether those that /bawl out the ruins of thy 2H4 2.02. 23 P
BAWLING 1 FR 0.0001 REL FR 0 V 1 P
a pox o' your throat, you bawling, blasphemous, TMP 1.01. 40 P
/BAY* 1 FR 0.0001 REL FR 1 V 0 P
/from /th' /athenian /bay | /put /forth /toward TRO pr 6
BAY* 27 FR 0.0030 REL FR 22 V 5 P
the fairest house in it after threepence a bay. MM 2.01.242 P
syracusian born | come to the bay of ephesus, he ERR 1.01. 19
you sent me to the bay, sir, for a bark. 4.01. 99
who put unluckily into this bay | against the 5.01.125
the scarfed bark puts from her native bay, MV 2.06. 15
an unknown bottom, like the bay of portugal. AYL 4.01.208 P
'tis thought your deer does hold you at a bay. SHR 5.02. 56
i'd give bay curtal and his furniture, | my AWW 2.03. 59
it hath bay windows transparent as barricadoes, TN 4.02. 36 P
a bay in britain, receiv'd intelligence | that R2 2.01.278
to rouse his wrongs and chase them to the bay. 2.03.128
and make the cowards stand aloof at bay. 1H6 4.02. 52
and i, in such a desp'rate bay of death, | like R3 4.04.233
what moves ajax thus to bay at him? TRO 2.03. 90 P
returns with precious lading to the bay | from TIT 1.01. 72
uncouple here and let us make a bay, | and wake 2.02. 3
we had a thousand roman dames | at such a bay, 4.02. 42
good words the other day of a bay courser | i TIM 1.02.211
i had rather be a dog, and bay the moon, | than JC 4.03. 27
to ride on a bay trotting–horse over four–inch'd LR 3.04. 56 P
that he may bless this bay with his tall ship, OTH 2.01. 79
iago, | go to the bay and disembark my coffers. 2.01.208
upon me, set | the dogs o' th' street to bay me; CYM 5.05.223
you had indeed, | a bright bay, i remember. TNK 3.06. 78
by this she hears the hounds are at a bay, VEN 877
ah, that i had my lady at this bay: PP 11.13
be anchor'd in the bay where all men ride, | why SON 137. 6
BAY'D 3 FR 0.0003 REL FR 3 V 0 P
when in a wood of crete they bay'd the bear MND 4.01.113
here wast thou bay'd, brave hart, | here didst JC 3.01.204
the stake, | and bay'd about with many enemies, 4.01. 49
BAYING 1 FR 0.0001 REL FR 1 V 0 P
back unarm'd, | they baying him at the heels. 2H4 1.03. 80
BAYNARD'S 2 FR 0.0002 REL FR 2 V 0 P
you thrive well, bring them to baynard's castle, R3 3.05. 98
meet me within this hour at baynard's castle. 3.05.105
BAYONNE 1 FR 0.0001 REL FR 1 V 0 P
speeches utter'd | by th' bishop of bayonne, H8 2.04.173
BAYS 2 FR 0.0002 REL FR 1 V 1 P
up, my dish of chastity with rosemary and bays! PER 4.06.151 P
that blasts my bays and my fam'd works makes TNK pr 20
BAY–TREES 1 FR 0.0001 REL FR 1 V 0 P
the bay–trees in our country are all wither'd, R2 2.04. 8
BE* *(also by)*
/BE* 44 FR 0.0049 REL FR 39 V 5 P
BE* 7335 FR 0.8291 REL FR 5393 V 1942 P
BEACH 5 FR 0.0005 REL FR 5 V 0 P
you may as well go stand upon the beach | and MV 4.01. 71
the english beach | pales in the flood with men, H5 5.pr. 9
then let the pibbles on the hungry beach COR 5.03. 58
the fishermen, that /walk upon the beach, LR 4.06. 17
the twinn'd stones | upon the number'd beach, CYM 1.06. 36
BEACHED 2 FR 0.0002 REL FR 2 V 0 P
brook, | or in the beached margent of the sea, MND 2.01. 85
upon the beached verge of the salt flood, | who TIM 5.01.216
BEACHY 1 FR 0.0001 REL FR 1 V 0 P
times to see | the beachy girdle of the ocean 2H4 3.01. 50
BEACON 5 FR 0.0005 REL FR 4 V 1 P
which as a beacon gives warning to all the rest 2H4 4.03.108 P
see, noble charles, the beacon of our friend, 1H6 3.02. 29
modest doubt is call'd | the beacon of the wise, TRO 2.02. 16
approach, thou beacon to this under globe, LR 2.02.163
men | be like a beacon fir'd t' amaze your eyes. PER 1.04. 87
BEAD 1 FR 0.0001 REL FR 1 V 0 P
you bead, you acorn. MND 3.02.330
BEADED 1 FR 0.0001 REL FR 1 V 0 P
drew, | of amber, crystal, and of beaded jet, LC 37
BEADLE 7 FR 0.0008 REL FR 4 V 3 P
love's whip, | a very beadle to a humorous sigh, LLL 3.01.175
injury | her injury, the beadle to her sin — JN 2.01.188
war is his beadle, war is his vengeance; H5 4.01.169 P
sirrah, go fetch the beadle hither straight. 2H6 2.01.137
sirrah beadle, whip him till he leap over that 2.01.145 P
thou rascal beadle, hold thy bloody hand! LR 4.06.160
i would wish no better office than to be beadle. PER 2.01. 93 P
BEADLES 2 FR 0.0002 REL FR 1 V 1 P
have you not | beadles in your town, and things 2H6 2.01.134
running banquet of two beadles that is to come. H8 5.03. 66 P
BEADS 10 FR 0.0011 REL FR 10 V 0 P
o, for my beads! ERR 2.02.188
with amber bracelets, beads, and all this SHR 4.03. 58
with these crystal beads heaven shall be brib'd JN 2.01.171
i'll give my jewels for a set of beads, | my R2 3.03.147
that beads of sweat have stood upon thy brow, 1H4 2.03. 58
my dreams, | in courtly company, or at my beads, 2H6 1.01. 27
holiness, | to number ave–maries on his beads; 1.03. 56
numb'ring our ave–maries with our beads? 3H6 2.01.162
and devout religious men | are at their beads, R3 3.07. 93
seeing those beads of sorrow stand in thine, JC 3.01.284

BEADSMAN 1 FR 0.0001 REL FR 1 V 0 P
for i will be thy beadsman, valentine. TGV 1.01. 18
BEADSMEN 1 FR 0.0001 REL FR 1 V 0 P
thy very beadsmen learn to bend their bows | of R2 3.02.116
BEAGLE 1 FR 0.0001 REL FR 0 V 1 P
she's a beagle, true-bred, and one that adores TN 2.03.179 P
BEAGLES 1 FR 0.0001 REL FR 1 V 0 P
get thee away, and take | thy beagles with thee. TIM 4.03.175
BEAK 5 FR 0.0005 REL FR 5 V 0 P
now on the beak, | now in the waist, the deck, TMP 1.02.196
although the kite soar with unbloodied beak? 2H6 3.02.193
prunes the immortal wing and cloys his beak, CYM 5.04.118
tires with her beak on feathers, flesh, and bone VEN 56
whose crooked beak threats, if he mount, he dies LUC 508
BEAKS 2 FR 0.0002 REL FR 2 V 0 P
and turn their halcyon beaks | with every gale LR 2.02. 78
who endured | the beaks of ravens, talents of TNK 1.01. 41
BE-ALL 1 FR 0.0001 REL FR 1 V 0 P
blow | might be the be-all and the end-all — MAC 1.07. 5
/BEAM 1 FR 0.0001 REL FR 0 V 1 P
if the /beam of our lives had not one scale of OTH 1.03.326 P
BEAM 11 FR 0.0012 REL FR 9 V 2 P
at | which end o' th' beam should bow. TMP 2.01.132
sometimes the beam of her view gilded my foot, WIV 1.03. 61 P
i fear not goliah with a weaver's beam, because 5.01. 22 P
but i a beam do find in each of three. LLL 4.03.160
defective scale, | shall weigh thee to the beam; AWW 2.03.155
a rush will be a beam | to hang thee on; JN 4.03.129
streams, | twinkling another counterfeited beam, 1H6 5.03. 63
whose beam stands sure, whose rightful cause 2H6 2.01.201
and stands colossus-wise, waving his beam, TRO 5.05. 9
might down stretch | below the beam of sight, COR 3.02. 5
with weight | /till our scale turn the beam. HAM 4.05.158
BEAMS 26 FR 0.0029 REL FR 26 V 0 P
but creep in crannies, when he hides his beams: ERR 2.02. 31
for gazing on your beams, fair sun, being by. 3.02. 56
quench'd in the chaste beams of the wat'ry moon,
MND 2.01.162
opening on neptune with fair blessed beams, 3.02.392
sweet moon, i thank thee for thy sunny beams; 5.01.272
how far that little candle throws his beams! MV 5.01. 90
but to the brightest beams | distracted clouds AWW 5.03. 34
and those his golden beams to you here lent R2 1.03.146
brandish'd sword did blind men with his beams; 1H6 1.01. 10
may never glorious sun reflex his beams | upon 5.04. 87
lords, cold snow melts with the sun's hot beams: 2H6 3.01.223
like to the glorious sun's transparent beams, 3.01.353
dark cloudy death o'ershades his beams of life, 3H6 2.06. 62
thy very beams will dry those vapors up, | for 5.03. 12
whose bright out-shining beams thy cloudy wrath R3 1.03.267
bright faces | cast thousand beams upon me, like H8 4.02. 89
and, having gilt the ocean with his beams, TIT 2.01. 6
her collars of the moonshine's wat'ry beams, ROM 1.04. 65
ten times faster glides than the sun's beams, 2.05. 5
sun, hide thy beams, timon hath done his reign. TIM 5.01.223
that by thy comfortable beams i may | peruse LR 2.02.164
sun, to have | the benefit of his blest beams, CYM 4.04. 42
and in the beams o' th' sun | so vanish'd; 5.05.472
whose beams upon his hairless face are fix'd, VEN 487
with thy tickling beams eyes that are sleeping; LUC 1090
best | as fast as objects to his beams assemble? SON 114. 8
BEAN-FED 1 FR 0.0001 REL FR 1 V 0 P
smile | when i a fat and bean-fed horse beguile, MND 2.01. 45
BEANS 1 FR 0.0001 REL FR 0 V 1 P
peas and beans are as dank here as a dog, and 1H4 2.01. 8 P
BEAR* *(also pear*)*
/BEAR* 5 FR 0.0005 REL FR 5 V 0 P
and, sweet sprites, /the /burthen /bear. TMP 1.02.380
/wherein /the //cub-drawn /bear /would /couch, LR 3.01. 12
/come /help /to /bear /thy /master; 3.06.100
/even /the //head-lugg'd /bear /would /lick, 4.02. 42
the holding every man shall /bear as loud | as ANT 2.07.111
BEAR* 560 FR 0.0633 REL FR 465 V 95 P
stomach, to bear up | against what should ensue. TMP 1.02.157
good instruction give | how i may bear me here. 1.02.426
bush nor shrub to bear off any weather at all. 2.02. 18 P
i'll bear him no more sticks, but follow thee, 2.02.163
bear my bottle. 2.02.175 P
sit down, | i'll bear your logs the while. 3.01. 24
o heaven, o earth, bear witness to this sound, 3.01. 68
therefore bear up and board 'em. 3.02. 2 P
bear with my weakness, my old brain is troubled. 4.01.159
help to bear this away where my hogshead of wine 4.01.250 P
i perceive i must be fain to bear with you. TGV 1.01.120 P
why, sir, how do you bear with me? 1.01.122 P
that, some whirlwind bear | unto a ragged, 1.02.117
to bear my lady's train, lest the base earth 2.04.159
wrong, | to bear a hard opinion of his truth: 2.07. 81
that stays to bear my letters to my friends, 3.01. 53
that you may bear it | under a cloak that is of 3.01.129
good will | i bear unto the banish'd valentine, 4.03. 15
of sands, | to bear me company, and go with me; 4.03. 34
bear witness, heaven, i have my wish for ever. 5.04.119
you are afraid if you see the bear loose, are WIV 1.01.292 P
go, bear thou this letter to mistress page; 1.03. 72 P
hold, sirrah, bear you these letters tightly; 1.03. 79
you'll not bear a letter for me, you rogue? 2.02. 19 P
if you will help to bear it, sir john, take all, 2.02.172 P
i pray you bear witness that me have stay six or 2.03. 35 P
whither bear you this? 3.03.152 P
why, what have you to do whither they bear it? 3.03.155 P
ay, ay; i must bear it. 3.03.209 P
i hope not, i had lief as bear so much lead. 4.02.113 P
of man's disposition is able to bear. 4.05.109 P
with the dear love i bear to fair anne page, 4.06. 9
what figure of us think you he will bear? MM 1.01. 16
bear me to prison, where i am committed. 1.02.117
how i may formally in person bear | like a true 1.03. 47
i do; and bear the shame most patiently. 2.03. 20
his life, if it be sin, | heaven let me bear it! 2.04. 70
that bear in them one and the self-same tongue, 2.04.173
would bark your honor from that trunk you bear, 3.01. 71
he who the sword of heaven will bear | should be 3.02.261
to angelo | (the provost, he shall bear them), 4.03. 94
under | the pleasing punishment that women bear)
ERR 1.01. 46
might bear him company in the quest of him: 1.01.129
mark'd | to bear the extremity of dire mishap! 1.01.141
go bear it to the centaur, where we host, | and 1.02. 9
perchance you will not bear them patiently. 1.02. 86
but, were you wedded, you would bear some sway. 2.01. 28
by the wrongs i suffer, and the blows i bear. 3.01. 16
bear a fair presence, though your heart be 3.02. 13
as from a bear a man would run for life, | so 3.02.154
no, bear it with you, lest i come not time 4.01. 41
go, dromio, there's the money, bear it straight, 4.02. 63
nay, i bear it on my shoulders, as a beggar wont 4.04. 37 P
god and the rope-maker bear me witness | that i 4.04. 90
bear me forthwith unto his creditor, | and, 4.04.120
go bear him hence. 4.04.130
his word might bear my wealth at any time. 5.01. 8
bind dromio too, and bear them to my house. 5.01. 35
him fast, | and bear him home for his recovery. 5.01. 41
why bear you these rebukes, and answer not? 5.01. 89
nor send him forth, that we may bear him hence. 5.01.158
let him bear it for a difference between himself ADO 1.01. 69 P
"in time the savage bull doth bear the yoke." 1.01.261
but if ever the sensible benedick bear it, pluck 1.01.263 P
which shall bear no less likelihood than to see 2.02. 42 P
they say i will bear myself proudly, if i 2.03.225 P
'tis a truth, i can bear them witness; 2.03.231 P
bear thee well in it, and leave us alone. 3.01. 13
bear it coldly but till midnight, and let the 3.02.129 P
therefore bear you the lanthorn. 3.03. 24 P
bear her in hand until they come to take hands, 4.01.303 P
who, i myself will bear witness, is praiseworthy 5.02. 87 P
bear this significant to the country maid LLL 3.01.130 P
see him walk before a lady and to bear her fan! 4.01.145
must thou speak," and "thus thy body bear"; 5.02.100
bear with me, i am sick; 5.02.417
of your love | but that it bear this trial, and 5.02.803
and sometime make the drink to bear no barm, MND 2.01. 38
looks upon | (be it on lion, bear, or wolf, or 2.01.180
be it ounce, or cat, or bear, | pard, or boar 2.02. 30
i am as ugly as a bear; 2.02. 94
a hog, a headless bear, sometime a fire, | and 3.01.109
horse, hound, hog, bear, fire, at every turn. 3.01.111
quiet go, | to athens will i bear my folly back, 3.02.315
sent | to bear him to my bower in fairy land. 4.01. 61
when in a wood of crete they bay'd the bear 4.01.113
some fear, | how easy is a bush suppos'd a bear! 5.01. 22
i will feed fat the ancient grudge i bear him. MV 1.03. 47
tell me once more what title thou dost bear: 2.09. 35
i'll keep my oath, | patiently to bear my wroth. 2.09. 78
know | a creature that did bear the shape of man 3.02.275
whose souls do bear an egall yoke of love, 3.04. 13
hate and a certain loathing | i bear antonio, 4.01. 61
axe, bear half the keenness | of thy sharp envy. 4.01.125
bear him away. what is thy name, young man? AYL 1.02.221
let me the knowledge of my fault bear with me: 1.03. 46
fly, | whither to go, and what to bear with us, 1.03.101
to bear your griefs yourself, and leave me out; 1.03.103
i pray you bear with me, i cannot go no further. 2.04. 9 P
part, i had rather bear with you than bear you. 2.04. 11 P
part, i had rather bear with you than bear you. 2.04. 12 P
yet i should bear no cross if i did bear you, 2.04. 12 P
yet i should bear no cross if i did bear you, 2.04. 13 P
come, i will bear thee to some shelter, and thou 2.06. 16 P
in them more feet than the verses would bear. 3.02.166 P
the feet might bear the verses. 3.02.167 P
lame and could not bear themselves without the 3.02.170 P
for no ill will i bear you. 3.05. 71
and yet it is not that i bear thee love, | but 3.05. 93
very taunting letter, | and thou shalt bear it; 3.05.135
bear this, bear all! 4.03. 14
bear this, bear all! 4.03. 14
for i must bear answer back | how you excuse my 4.03.179
this that you should bear a good opinion of my 5.02. 54 P
times remov'd (bear your body more seeming, 5.04. 68 P
o women, for the love you bear to men, to like ep 13 P
you, o men, for the love you bear to women (as i ep 15 P
another bear the ewer, the third a diaper, | and SHR in.1. 57
love, | he bear himself with honorable action, in.1. 110
and make her bear the penance of her tongue? 1.01. 89
yet, for the love i bear my sweet bianca, if i 1.01.110 P
for who shall bear your part, | and be in padua 1.01.194
be contributors | and bear his charge of wooing, 1.02.215
asses are made to bear, and so are you. 2.01.199
women are made to bear, and so are you. 2.01.200
sirrah, i will not bear these braves of thine. 3.01. 15
come, mistress kate, i'll bear you company. 4.03. 49
while he did bear my countenance in the town, 5.01.126
i'll bear it all myself. 5.02. 79
to grow there and to bear — "let me not live" AWW 1.02. 55
thoughts | a modest one, to bear me back again. 2.01.128
more i'll entreat you | written to bear along. 3.02. 95
we'll strive to bear it for your worthy sake 3.03. 5
as we'll direct her how 'tis best to bear it. 3.07. 20
and for turning away, let summer bear it out. TN 1.05. 20 P
you your leave, that i may bear my evils alone. 2.01. 6 P
between that love a woman can bear me | and that 2.04.102
to anger him we'll have the bear again, and we 2.05. 9 P
will either of you bear me a challenge to him? 3.02. 40 P
a fiend like thee might bear my soul to hell. 3.04.217
and looks pale, as if a bear were at his heels. 3.04.295 P
he will bear you easily, and reins well. 3.04.323 P
if not, how best to bear it. WT 1.02.406
trunk which you | shall bear along impawn'd, 1.02.436
though he does bear some signs of me, yet you 2.01. 57
bear the boy hence, he shall not come about her. 2.01. 59
upon, | the centre is not big enough to bear | a 2.01.102
it is but weakness | to bear the matter thus — 2.03. 2
and that thou bear it | to some remote and 2.03.175
as nature | will bear up with this exercise, so 3.02.241
to see how the bear tore out his shoulder-bone, 3.03. 95 P
poor gentleman roar'd, and the bear mock'd him, 3.03.101 P
water, nor the bear half din'd on the gentleman. 3.03.106 P
i'll go see if the bear be gone from the 3.03.129 P
leave to live, | and bear the sow-skin bouget, 4.03. 20
plackets where they should bear their faces? 4.04.243 P
if thou'lt bear a part, thou shalt hear; 4.04.292 P
i can bear my part, you must know 'tis my 4.04.295 P
friends unknown, you shall bear witness to't: 4.04.384
see the play so lies | that i must bear a part. 4.04.656
and though authority be a stubborn bear, yet he 4.04.802 P
then, good my lords, bear witness to his oath. 5.01. 72
sceptres, | and those that bear them, living. 5.01.147
that which i shall report will bear no credit, 5.01.179
he was torn to pieces with a bear. 5.02. 63 P
and that those veins | did verily bear blood? 5.03. 65
bear mine to him, and so depart in peace. JN 1.01. 23
your father's wife did after wedlock bear him; 1.01.117
from henceforth bear his name whose form thou 1.01.160
some sins do bear their privilege on earth, 1.01.261
and then our arms, like to a muzzled bear, 2.01.249
we will bear home that lusty blood again | which 2.01.255
put thee down, 'gainst whom these arms we bear, 2.01.346
and bear possession of our person here, | lord 2.01.366
well could i bear that england had this praise, 3.04. 15
i hope your warrant will bear out the deed. 4.01. 6
think you i bear the shears of destiny? 4.02. 91
bear with me, cousin, for i was amaz'd | under 4.02.137
go, bear him in thine arms. 4.03.139
bear away that child, | and follow me with speed 4.03.156
would bear thee from the knowledge of thyself, 5.02. 35
i pray you bear me hence | from forth the noise 5.04. 44
my arm shall give thee help to bear thee hence, 5.04. 58
and tempt us not to bear above our power! 5.06. 38
go bear this lance to thomas duke of norfolk. R2 1.03.103
go, bear not along | the clogging burthen of a 1.03.199
is so arm'd | to bear the tidings of calamity. 3.02.105
they might have liv'd to bear and he to taste 3.04. 62
well, bear you well in this new spring of time, 5.02. 50
created to be aw'd by man, | wast born to bear? 5.05. 92
a horse, | and yet i bear a burthen like an ass, 5.05. 93
this dead king to the living king i'll bear; 5.05.117
am as melancholy as a gib cat or a lugg'd bear. 1H4 1.02. 74 P
a head, | for, bear ourselves as even as we can, 1.03.285
to bear our fortunes in our own strong arms, 1.03.298
i'll not bear my own flesh so far afoot again 2.02. 35 P
in respect of the love i bear your house." 2.03. 2 P
of many men | i do not bear these crossings. 3.01. 35
go bear this letter to lord john of lancaster, 3.03.195
who is to bear me like a thunderbolt | against 4.01.120
bear this sealed brief | with winged haste to 4.04. 1
and westmerland, that was engag'd, did bear it, 5.02. 43
should reward valor bear the sin upon their own 5.04.150 P
bear worcester to the death and vernon too. 5.05. 14
yea-forsooth knave, to bear a gentleman in hand,
2H4 1.02. 36 P
a penny, you are too impatient to bear crosses. 1.02.226 P
go bear this letter to my lord of lancaster, 1.02.238 P
is a long one for a poor lone woman to bear, and 2.01. 33 P
an ass and a beast, to bear every knave's wrong. 2.01. 38 P
once, or to bear the inventory of thy shirts, as 2.02. 17 P
you cannot one bear with another's confirmities. 2.04. 58 P
one must bear, and that must be you, you are the 2.04. 59 P
can a weak empty vessel bear such a huge full 2.04. 62 P
you like well and bear your years very well. 3.02. 83 P
i'll ne'er bear a base mind. 3.02.235 P
faith, i'll bear no base mind. 3.02.240 P
that all their eyes may bear those tokens home 4.02. 64
which, cousin, you shall bear to comfort him, 4.03. 79
up, and bear me hence | into some other chamber. 4.04.131
but bear me to that chamber, there i'll lie, 4.05.239
or twice in a quarter bear out a knave against 5.01. 48 P
him, do bear themselves like foolish justices; 5.01. 66 P
let me but bear your love, i'll bear your cares. 5.02. 58
let me but bear your love, i'll bear your cares. 5.02. 58
therefore still bear the balance and the sword, 5.02.103
th' unstained sword that you have us'd to bear, 5.02.114
we'll have in drink, but you must bear, the 5.03. 29 P
we bear our civil swords and native fire | as 5.05.106
how smooth and even they do bear themselves! H5 2.02. 3
think you not that the pow'rs we bear with us 2.02. 15
thou that didst bear the key of all my counsels, 2.02. 96
bear them hence. 2.02.181
to-morrow shall you bear our full intent | back 2.04.114
that may be, for you bear a many superfluously, 3.07. 74 P
the mouth of a russian bear and have their heads 3.07.144 P
beat us, for they bear them on their shoulders; 4.01.226 P
we must bear all. 4.01.233
i pray thee bear my former answer back: 4.03. 90
now we bear the king | toward callice; 5.pr. 6
and bear me witness all, | that here i kiss her 5.02.357
god, these nobles should such stomachs bear! 1H6 1.03. 90
bear hence his body, i will help to bury it. 1.04. 87
will not your honors bear me company? 2.02. 53
between two horses, which doth bear him best, 2.04. 14
well | to bear with their perverse objections; 4.01.129
talbot dead, great york might bear the name. 4.04. 9
never to england shall he bear his life, | but 4.04. 38
my spirit can no longer bear these harms. 4.07. 30
that i may bear them hence | and give them 4.07. 85
i'll bear them hence; 4.07. 92
bear her this jewel, pledge of my affection. 5.01. 47
did bear him like a noble gentleman. 2H6 1.01.184
bear that proportion to my flesh and blood | as 1.01.233
and in my standard bear the arms of york, | to 1.01.256
ah, humphrey, can i bear this shameful yoke? 2.04. 37
the reverent care i bear unto my lord | made me 3.01. 34
before his legs be firm to bear his body. 3.01.190
and bear the name and port of gentlemen? 4.01. 19
more can i bear than you dare execute. 4.01.130
his body will i bear unto the king. 4.01.145
this monument of the victory will i bear, and 4.03. 11 P
hear me but speak, and bear me where you will. 4.07. 59
which i will bear in triumph to the king, 4.10. 83
i am resolv'd to bear a greater storm | than any 5.01.198
the rampant bear chain'd to the ragged staff, 5.01.203
and from thy burgonet i'll rend thy bear, | and 5.01.208
and despite the bearard that protects the bear. 5.01.210
and if thou dost not hide thee from the bear, 5.02. 2
as did aeneas old anchises bear, | so bear i 5.02. 62
bear, | so bear i thee upon my manly shoulders; 5.02. 63
and i, my lord, will bear him company. 3H6 1.03. 6
or as a bear, encompass'd round with dogs, | who 2.01. 15
henceforward will i bear | upon my target three 2.01. 39
nay, bear three daughters; 2.01. 41
richard, i bear thy name, i'll venge thy death, 2.01. 87
'tis love i bear thy glories make me speak. 2.01.158
whose hand is that the forest bear doth lick? 2.02. 13
i'll bear thee hence, where i may weep my fill. 2.05.113
i'll bear thee hence, and let them fight that 2.05.121

edward will always bear himself as king. 4.03. 45
yet, gracious madam, bear it as you may: 4.04. 14
and bear with mildness my misfortune's cross; 4.04. 20
seize on the shame–fac'd henry, bear him hence, 4.08. 52
than bear so low a sail to strike to thee. 5.01. 52
even with the dearest blood your bodies bear. 5.01. 69
live | to bear his image and renew his glories! 5.04. 54
go bear them hence, i will not hear them speak. 5.05. 4
away with her, go bear her hence perforce. 5.05. 68
nay, never bear me hence, dispatch me here; 5.05. 69
away, i say, i charge ye bear her hence. 5.05. 81
stay, you that bear the corse, and set it down. R3 1.02. 33
bear with her weakness, which i think proceeds 1.03. 28
died, | and that a winged mercury did bear; 2.01. 89
that bear this heavy mutual load of moan, | now 2.02.113
and so was i. i'll bear you company. 2.03. 47
and thither bear your treasure and your goods. 2.04. 69
uncle, your grace knows how to bear with him. 3.01.127
you mean, to bear me, not to bear with me. 3.01.128
you mean, to bear me, not to bear with me. 3.01.128
that you should bear me on your shoulders. 3.01.131
the tender love i bear your grace, my lord, 3.04. 63
as loath to bear me to the slaughter–house. 3.04. 86
bear him my head. 3.04.106
to bear the golden yoke of sovereignty, | which 3.07.146
back, | to bear her burthen whe'er i will or no, 3.07.229
i'll bear thy blame, | and take thy office from 4.01. 24
both, | to bear this tidings to the bloody king. 4.03. 22
bear with me; 4.04. 61
bear her my true love's kiss; 4.04.430
sir william brandon, you shall bear my standard. 5.03. 22
good captain blunt, bear my good–night to him, 5.03. 30
now | that bear a weighty and a serious brow, H8 pr 2
did almost sweat to bear | the pride upon them, 1.01. 24
nay, he must bear you company. 1.01.212
most pestilent to th' hearing, and, to bear 'em, 1.02. 49
(out of the great respect they bear to beauty) 1.04. 69
after all this, how did he bear himself? 2.01. 30
yet, heaven bear witness, | and if i have a 2.01. 59
the law i bear no malice for my death; 2.01. 62
my lord, you'll bear us company? 2.02. 58
have you limbs | to bear that load of title? 2.03. 39
you bear a gentle mind, and heav'nly blessings 2.03. 57
time | i know your back will bear a duchess. 2.03. 99
moe new disgraces | with these you bear already. 3.02. 6
and bear the inventory | of your best graces in 3.02.137
part of business which | i bear i' th' state; 3.02.146
so farewell — to the little good you bear me. 3.02.350
bear witness, all that have not hearts of iron, 3.02.424
they that bear | the cloth of honor over her, 4.01. 47
their practices | must bear the same proportion, 5.01.129
is as valiant as the lion, churlish as the bear, TRO 1.02. 21 P
though my heart's content firm love doth bear, 1.02.294
bear the great sway of his affairs with reason, 2.02. 35
'a should not bear it so, 'a should eat swords 2.03.217 P
through the sight i bear in things to /come, | i 3.03. 4
let diomedes bear him, | and bring us cressid 3.03. 30
and 'tis a burthen | which i am proud to bear. 3.03. 37
come, thou shalt bear a letter to him straight. 3.03.305
let me bear another to his horse, for that's the 3.03.306 P
death, 'twill be his bane, he cannot bear it. 4.02. 93 P
thou shouldst not bear from me a greekish member 4.05.130
and bear hence | a great addition earned in thy 4.05.140
that sleeve is mine that he'll bear on his helm. 5.02.169
you, | upon the love you bear me, get you in. 5.03. 78
go bear patroclus' body to achilles, | and bid 5.05. 17
one bear will not bite another, and wherefore 5.07. 18 P
and there's all the love they bear us. COR 1.01. 86 P
as children from a bear, the volsces shunning 1.03. 31
that bear the shapes of men, how have you run 1.04. 35
but is | able to bear against the great aufidius 1.06. 79
shall bear the business in some other fight, 1.06. 82
bear | th' addition nobly ever! 1.09. 65
he's a lamb indeed, that baes like a bear. 2.01. 11 P
he's a bear indeed, that lives like a lamb. 2.01. 12 P
i must be content to bear with those that say 2.01. 60 P
for your voices bear | of wounds two dozen odd; 2.03.127
your liberties and the charters that you bear 2.03.180
bear him to th' rock tarpeian, and from thence 3.01.212
lay hands upon him, | and bear him to the rock. 3.01.222
and o'erbear | what they are us'd to bear? 3.01.249
put mine armor on, | which i can scarcely bear. 3.02. 35
to my noble heart | a lie that it must bear? 3.02.101
piece | will bear the knave by th' volume. 3.03. 33
that common chances common men could bear, 4.01. 5
good man, the wounds that he does bear for rome! 4.02. 28
and displeasure | which thou shouldst bear me. 4.05. 73
and bear the palm for having bravely shed | thy 5.03.117
and you shall bear | a better witness back than 5.03.203
him, that | must bear my beating to his grave — 5.06.108
bear from hence his body, | and mourn you for 5.06.141
bear his betroth'd from all the world away. TIT 1.01.286
and so in this, to bear me down with braves. 2.01. 30
that ever death should let life bear his name, 3.01.248
head, | and in this hand the other will i bear; 3.01.280
bear thou my hand, sweet wench, between thy 3.01.282
hue, | in that it scorns to bear another hue; 4.02.100
on, you thick–lipp'd slave, i'll bear you hence, 4.02.175
wrung with wrongs more than our backs can bear. 4.03. 49
calm thee, and bear the faults of titus' age, 4.04. 29
signifies what hate they bear their emperor, 5.01. 3
"for i must bear thee to a trusty goth, | who, 5.01. 34
the child | and bear it from me to the emperess. 5.01. 54
or more than any living man could bear. 5.03.127
and bid thee bear his pretty tales in mind, 5.03.165
them, which is disgrace to them if they bear it. ROM 1.01. 43 P
nay, i do bear a brain — but, as i said, | when 1.03. 29
being but heavy, i will bear the light. 1.04. 12
that presses them and learns them first to bear, 1.04. 93
i bear no hatred, blessed man, for lo | my 2.03. 53
but you shall bear the burthen soon at night. 2.05. 76
the love i bear thee can afford | no better term 3.01. 60
bear hence this body and attend our will; 3.01.196
you could find out but a man | to bear a poison, 3.05. 97
night | shall romeo bear thee hence to mantua. 4.01.117
is, | and in her best array, bear her to church; 4.05. 81
and bear this work of heaven with patience. 5.03.261
him in itself, | it must not bear my daughter. TIM 1.01.131

we'll bear, with your lordship. 1.01.177
to revenge is no valor, but to bear. 3.05. 39
how full of valor did he bear himself | in the 3.05. 64
nothing i'll bear from thee | but nakedness, 4.01. 32
can bear great fortune | but by contempt of 4.03. 7
the /senator shall bear contempt hereditary, 4.03. 10
for every storm that blows — i to bear this, 4.03.266
wert thou a bear, thou wouldst be kill'd by the 4.03.338 P
the oaks bear mast, the briers scarlet heps; 4.03.419
you bear too stubborn and too strange a hand JC 1.02. 35
troy upon his shoulder | the old anchises bear, 1.02.114
of the majestic world | and bear the palm alone. 1.02.131
caesar doth bear me hard, but he loves brutus. 1.02.313
that part of tyranny that i do bear | i can 1.03. 99
will bear no color for the thing he is, 2.01. 29
they do) bear fire enough | to kindle cowards, 2.01.120
caius ligarius doth bear caesar hard, | who 2.01.215
purposes, | but bear it as our roman actors do, 2.01.226
can i bear that with patience, | and not my 2.01.301
time | to bear my greeting to the senators, 2.02. 61
i do beseech ye, if you bear me hard, | now, 3.01.157
bear with me, | my heart is in the coffin there 3.02.105
stand back; room, bear back! 3.02.168 P
you'll bear me a bang for that, i fear. 3.03. 18 P
he shall but bear them as the ass bears gold, 4.01. 21
that every nice offense should bear his comment. 4.03. 8
a friend should bear his friend's infirmities; 4.03. 86
have not you love enough to bear with me, | when 4.03.119
bear with him, brutus, 'tis his fashion. 4.03.135
then like a roman bear the truth i tell: 4.03.188
you, | but yet my nature could not bear it so. 4.03.195
bear with me, good boy, i am much forgetful. 4.03.255
and every one did bear | thy praises in his MAC 1.03. 98
bear welcome in your eye, | your hand, your 1.05. 64
shut the door, | not bear the knife myself. 1.07. 16
who shall bear the guilt | of our great quell? 1.07. 71
approach thou like the rugged russian bear, 3.04. 99
all harms, | was never call'd to bear my part, 3.05. 8
scorn death, and bear | his hopes 'bove wisdom, 3.05. 30
the mind i sway by, and the heart i bear, 5.03. 9
whose arms | are hir'd to bear their staves; 5.07. 18
i bear a charmed life, which must not yield | to 5.08. 12
it us befitted | to bear our hearts in grief, HAM 1.02. 3
if thou hast nature in thee, bear it not, | let 1.05. 81
grow not instant old, | but bear me /stiffly up. 1.05. 95
how strange or odd some'er i bear myself — | as 1.05.170
for who would bear the whips and scorns of time, 3.01. 69
who would fardels bear, | to grunt and sweat 3.01. 75
and makes us rather bear those ills we have, 3.01. 80
him his pranks have been too broad to bear with, 3.04. 2
they bear the mandate — they must sweep my way, 3.04.204
may take it thence, | and bear it to the chapel. 4.02. 8
to bear all smooth and even, | this sudden 4.03. 7
is the great love the general gender bear him, 4.07. 18
and you, the judges, bear a wary eye. 5.02.279
let four captains | bear hamlet, like a soldier, 5.02.396
which nor our nature nor our place can bear, LR 1.01.171
goneril, | to the great love i bear you — 1.04.312
but fathers that bear bags | shall see their 2.04. 50
father, fool me not so much | to bear it tamely; 2.04.276
thou'dst shun a bear, | but if /thy flight lay 3.04. 9
sea, | thou'dst meet the bear i' th' mouth. 3.04. 11
and i'll repair the misery thou dost bear | with 4.01. 76
if i could bear it longer, and not fall | to 4.06. 37
henceforth i'll bear | affliction till it do cry 4.06. 75
bear free and patient thoughts. 4.06. 80
you must bear with me. 4.07. 82
thy great employment | will not bear question; 5.03. 33
the gods defend her! bear him hence awhile. 5.03.257
bear them from hence. 5.03.319
so may he with more facile question bear it, OTH 1.03. 23
mane, | seems to cast water on the burning bear, 2.01. 14
it is impossible to bear it out. 2.01. 19
to show the love and duty that i bear you | with 3.03.194
it | that the probation bear no hinge nor loop 3.03.365
would you would bear your fortune like a man! 4.01. 61
prithee bear some charity to my wit, do not 4.01.120 P
o, she will sing the savageness out of a bear. 4.01.189 P
t' atone them, for the love i bear to cassio. 4.01.233
yet could i bear that too, well, very well; 4.02. 56
where either i must live or bear no life; 4.02. 58
upon her, | that true hearts cannot bear it. 4.02.117
o, for a chair, | to bear him easily hence! 5.01. 83
some good man bear him carefully from hence, 5.01. 99
o, bear him /out o' th' air. 5.01.104
they are loves i bear to you. 5.02. 40
but be prepar'd to know | the purposes i bear; ANT 1.03. 67
labor | to bear such idleness so near the heart 1.03. 94
foils, when we do bear | so great weight in his 1.04. 24
o happy horse, to bear the weight of antony! 1.05. 21
to part with unhack'd edges and bear back | our 2.06. 38
bear him ashore. i'll pledge it for him, pompey. 2.07. 85
bear the king's son's body | before our army. 3.01. 3
the mares would bear | a soldier and his horse. 3.07. 8
a charge we bear i' th' war, | and, as the 3.07. 16
no more upon't, | it is asham'd to bear me. 3.11. 2
of caesar's shall | bear us an arrant to him. 3.13.104
world | shall bear the olive freely. 4.06. 6
bear our hack'd targets like the men that owe 4.08. 31
o, bear me witness, night — 4.09. 5
shall upon record | bear hateful memory: 4.09. 9
let us bear him | to th' court of guard; 4.09. 30
a vapor sometime like a bear or lion, | a 4.14. 3
bear me, good friends, where cleopatra bides, 4.14.131
and we punish it | seeming to bear it lightly. 4.14.138
and you bear it | as answering to the weight. 5.02.101
her bed, | and bear her women from the monument. 5.02.357
you bear a graver purpose, i hope. CYM 1.04.138 P
and the primeroses, | bear to my closet. 1.05. 84
the love i bear him | made me to fan you thus, 1.06.176
sands that will not bear your enemies' boats, 3.01. 21
which neither here i'll keep nor bear again, 5.03. 82
to bear with patience | such griefs as you PER 1.02. 65
thee i lay, whose wisdom's strength can bear it. 1.02.119
i shall with aged patience bear your yoke. 2.04. 48
to the next chamber bear her. 3.02.107
behind | is left to govern it, you bear in mind, 4.04. 14
and bear his courses to be ordered | by lady 4.04. 47

bear 'em speedily | from our kind air, to them TNK 1.04. 37
at misery | and bear the chance of war yet. 2.02. 3
how bravely may he bear himself to win her, | if 2.02.254
dares any | so noble bear a guilty business? 3.01. 90
yours | will bear the curses else of after–ages 3.06.187
bear for it, master. 4.01.151
who do bear thy yoke | as 'twere a wreath of 5.01. 95
they are. | you bear a charge there too. 5.02.101
bear this hence. 5.04.109
let's go off, | and bear us like the time. 5.04.137
thus will they bear down all things. STM II.C 40
herbs for their smell, and sappy plants to bear: VEN 165
but the blunt boar, rough bear, or lion proud, 884
a thousand spleens bear her a thousand ways, 907
whose crime will bear an ever–during blame. LUC 224
with foul offenders thou perforce must bear, 612
despitefully i mean to bear thee | unto the base 670
alas, how many bear such shameful blows, | which 832
old woes, not infant sorrows, bear them mild; 1096
tear, | and with deep groans the diapason bear; 1132
men prove beasts, let beasts bear gentle minds." 1148
that lose half with greater patience bear it 1158
by and by, to bear | a letter to my lord, my 1292
that suspicion which the world might bear her. 1321
when every part a part of woe doth bear. 1327
and in their rage such signs of rage they bear, 1419
this load of wrath that burning troy doth bear; 1474
but such a face should bear a wicked mind. 1540
but kneel with me and help to bear thy part, 1830
they did conclude to bear dead lucrece thence, 1850
by a gift of learning did bear the maid away: PP 15.14
grief in heart | he with thee doth bear a part. 20.54
his tender heir might bear his memory: SON 1. 4
in singleness the parts that thou shouldst bear. 8. 8
your sweet issue your sweet form should bear. 13. 8
virtuous wish would bear your living flowers, 16. 7
to bear love's wrong than hate's known injury. 40.12
plods /dully on, to bear that weight in me, | as 50. 6
which laboring for invention bear amiss | the 59. 3
the vacant leaves thy mind's imprint will bear, 77. 3
is) | the humble as the proudest sail doth bear, 80. 6
that for thy right myself will bear all wrong. 88.14
do witness bear | thy black is fairest in my 131.11
bear thine eyes straight, though thy proud heart 140.14
lies, | what unapproved witness dost thou bear! LC 53

BEARARD *(also bear–herd, berrord)*

BEARARD 2 FR 0.0002 REL FR 2 V 0 P
and manacle the bearard in their chains, | if 2H6 5.01.149
despite the bearard that protects the bear. 5.01.210

BEAR–BAITING 2 FR 0.0002 REL FR 0 V 2 P
i have in fencing, dancing, and bear–baiting. TN 1.03. 93 P
o' favor with my lady about a bear–baiting here. 2.05. 8 P

BEAR–BAITINGS 1 FR 0.0001 REL FR 0 V 1 P
he haunts wakes, fairs, and bear–baitings. WT 4.03.102 P

BEARD *(also peard)*

BEARD 91 FR 0.0102 REL FR 42 V 49 P
tears runs down his beard like winter's drops TMP 5.01. 16
ay, by my beard, will we, for he is a proper man TGV 4.01. 10
does he not wear a great round beard, like a WIV 1.04. 20 P
with a little yellow beard, a cain–color'd beard 1.04. 23 P
a little yellow beard, a cain–color'd beard. 1.04. 23 P
shave the head, and tie the beard, and say it MM 4.02.175 P
his beard and head | just of his color. 4.03. 72
whose beard they have sing'd off with brands of ERR 5.01.171
not endure a husband with a beard on his face, i ADO 2.01. 30 P
you may light on a husband that hath no beard. 2.01. 33 P
he that hath a beard is more than a youth, and 2.01. 36 P
and he that hath no beard is less than a man; 2.01. 37 P
fetch you a hair off the great cham's beard, do 2.01.269 P
younger than he did, by the loss of a beard. 3.02. 49 P
if such a one will smile and stroke his beard, 5.01. 15
god's blessing on your beard! LLL 2.01.203
a beard, fair health, and honesty; 5.02.824
i have a beard coming. MND 1.02. 48 P
what beard were i best to play it in? 1.02. 90 P
discharge it in either your straw–color beard, 1.02. 94 P
your straw–color beard, your orange–tawny beard, 1.02. 94 P
beard, your purple–in–grain beard, or your 1.02. 95 P
or your french–crown–color beard, your perfit 1.02. 96 P
hath rotted ere his youth attain'd a beard. 2.01. 95
that did void your rheum upon my beard | and MV 1.03.117
what a beard hast thou got! 2.02. 93 P
with eyes severe and beard of formal cut, | full AYL 2.07.155
or his chin worth a beard? 3.02.207 P
nay, he hath but a little beard. 3.02.208 P
let me stay the growth of his beard, if thou 3.02.210 P
a beard neglected, which you have not — but i 3.02.375 P
for simply your having in beard is a younger 3.02.377 P
dislike the cut of a certain courtier's beard. 5.04. 70 P
me word, if i said his beard was not cut well, 5.04. 71 P
how oft did you say his beard was not well cut? 5.04. 83 P
but that his beard grew thin and hungerly, | and SHR 3.02.175
than these boys', | and writ as little beard. AWW 2.03. 61
or the baring of my beard, and to say it was in 4.01. 49 P
by my old beard, | and ev'ry hair that's on't, 5.03. 76
wherein, by the color of his beard, the shape of TN 2.03.156 P
his next commodity of hair, send thee a beard! 3.01. 45 P
will hang like an icicle on a dutchman's beard, 3.02. 28 P
i prithee put on this gown and this beard, make 4.02. 2 P
have done this without thy beard and gown, he 4.02. 65 P
by my white beard, | you offer him, if this be WT 4.04.404
in this farthel will make him scratch his beard. 4.04.708 P
whose valor plucks dead lions by the beard; JN 2.01.138
thy father's beard is turn'd white with the news 1H4 2.04.358 P
breathes upon the ground | but i will beard him. 4.01. 12
i will sooner have a beard grow in the palm of 2H4 1.02. 21 P
a yellow cheek, a white beard, a decreasing leg, 1.02.181 P
whose beard the silver hand of peace hath 4.01. 43
i will verify as much in his beard. H5 3.02. 71 P
and what a beard of the general's cut and a 3.06. 77 P
and takes him by the beard, kisses the gashes 4.06. 13
back will stoop, a black beard will turn white, 5.02.160 P
constantinople and take the turk by the beard? 5.02.209 P
do what thou dar'st, i beard thee to thy face. 1H6 1.03. 44
priest, beware your beard, | i mean to tug it 1.03. 47
his well–proportion'd beard made rough and 2H6 3.02.175
that ever was broach'd, and beard thee too. 4.10. 38 P
now play me nestor, hem, and stroke thy beard, TRO 1.03.165

me | i'll hide my silver beard in a gold beaver, 1.03.296
by this white beard, i'd fight with thee 4.05.209
if e'er again i meet him beard to beard, | he's COR 1.10. 11
if e'er again i meet him beard to beard, | he's 1.10. 11
you had more beard when i last saw you, but your 4.03. 8 P
more or a hair less in his beard than thou hast. ROM 3.01. 18 P
pity not honor'd age for his white beard, | he TIM 4.03.112
we might have met them dareful, beard to beard, MAC 5.05. 6
we might have met them dareful, beard to beard, 5.05. 6
his beard was grisl'd, no? HAM 1.02.239
com'st thou to beard me in denmark? 2.02.424 P
it shall to the barber's with your beard. 2.02.499 P
plucks off my beard and blows it in my face, 2.02.573
"his beard was as white as snow, | /all flaxen 4.05.195
that we can let our beard be shook with danger 4.07. 32
life i have spar'd at suit of his grey beard — LR 2.02. 63 P
spare my grey beard, you wagtail? 2.02. 67 P
art not asham'd to look upon this beard? 2.04.193
most ignobly done | to pluck me by the beard. 3.07. 36
if you did wear a beard upon your chin, | i'ld 3.07. 76
goneril with a white beard? 4.06. 96 P
the white hairs in my beard ere the black ones 4.06. 98 P
defeat thy favor with an usurp'd beard. OTH 1.03.341 P
did i to-day | see cassio wipe his beard with. 3.03.439
jupiter, | were i the wearer of antonio's beard, ANT 2.02. 7
so long a breeding as his white beard came to, CYM 5.03. 17
red and white, for yet no beard has blest him; TNK 4.02.107
in speech it seem'd his beard, all silver white, LUC 1405
borne on the bier with white and bristly beard: SON 12. 8
BEARDED 4 FR 0.0004 REL FR 3 V 1 P
of strange oaths, and bearded like the pard, AYL 2.07.150
four dozen of such bearded hermits' staves as 2H4 5.01. 63 P
am i dar'd and bearded to my face? 1H6 1.03. 45
think every bearded fellow that's but yok'd OTH 4.01. 66
BEARDLESS 2 FR 0.0002 REL FR 2 V 0 P
shall a beardless boy, | a cock'red silken JN 5.01. 69
the push | of every beardless vain comparative, 1H4 3.02. 67
BEARD'S 1 FR 0.0001 REL FR 1 V 0 P
so sure as this beard's grey — what will you WT 2.03.162
BEARDS 13 FR 0.0014 REL FR 5 V 8 P
good strings to your beards, new ribands to your MND 4.02. 36 P
the beards of hercules and frowning mars, | who, MV 3.02. 85
and swear by your beards that i am a knave. AYL 1.02. 72 P
by our beards (if we had them) thou art. 1.02. 74 P
as many of you as had beards that pleas'd me, ep 19 P
as many as have good beards, or good faces, or ep 21 P
'tis merry in hall when beards wags all, | and 2H4 5.03. 34
your fathers taken by the silver beards, | and H5 3.03. 36
it is not worth the wagging of your beards, and COR 2.01. 87 P
and your beards deserve not so honorable a grave 2.01. 87 P
and take our goodly aged men by th' beards, TIM 5.01.172
and yet your beards forbid me to interpret MAC 1.03. 46
rogue says here that old men have grey beards, HAM 2.02.197 P
BEARER 7 FR 0.0008 REL FR 7 V 0 P
stand aside, good bearer. LLL 4.01. 55
when thou dost pinch thy bearer, thou dost sit 2H4 4.05. 29
most renown'd, | hast eat thy bearer up." 4.05.164
fortune, do divorce | it from the bearer, 'tis a H8 2.03. 15
borne here in the face | the bearer knows not, TRO 3.03.104
when crouching marrow in the bearer strong TIM 5.04. 9
excuse the slow offense | of my dull bearer, SON 51. 2
BEARERS 2 FR 0.0002 REL FR 2 V 0 P
for bearers of this greeting to old norway, HAM 1.02. 35
he should those bearers put to sudden death, 5.02. 46
BEAREST 5 FR 0.0005 REL FR 4 V 1 P
bear his name whose form thou bearest: JN 1.01.160
admiral, thou bearest the lantern in the poop, 1H4 3.03. 25 P
yet, in faith, thou bearest thee like a king. 5.04. 36
o god, seest thou this, and bearest so long? 2H6 2.01.151
o tamora, thou bearest a woman's face — TIT 2.03.136
BEARETH 1 FR 0.0001 REL FR 1 V 0 P
and for the love he beareth to your daughter SHR 4.04. 29
BEAR-HERD *(also bearard, berrord)*
BEAR-HERD 1 FR 0.0001 REL FR 0 V 1 P
by transmutation a bear-herd, and now by present SHR in.2. 20 P
/BEARING 2 FR 0.0002 REL FR 2 V 0 P
/we /our /betters /see /bearing /our /woes, LR 3.06.102
/grief /hath /mates, /and /bearing /fellowship. 3.06.107
BEARING 44 FR 0.0049 REL FR 38 V 6 P
no, you shall have it for bearing the letter. TGV 1.01.118 P
rushing in their houses, bearing thence | rings, ERR 5.01.143
and that is claudio. i know him by his bearing. ADO 2.01.160 P
for shape, for bearing, argument, and valor, 3.01. 96
good repute, carriage, bearing, and estimation." LLL 1.01.268 P
bearing the badge of faith to prove them true? MND 3.02.127
well, we shall see your bearing. MV 2.02.198
in bearing thus the absence of your lord. 3.04. 4
tranio, "regia," bearing my port, "celsa senis," SHR 3.01. 35 P
thee more than ever the bearing of letter did. TN 4.02.112 P
and stable bearing | as i perceive she does. 4.03. 19
the manner of your bearing towards him, with WT 4.04.558
whom | (though bearing misery) i desire my life 5.01.137
bearing their birthrights proudly on their backs JN 2.01. 70
we lop away, that bearing boughs may live; R2 3.04. 64
bearing their own misfortunes on the back | of 5.05. 29
fair | when the intent of bearing them is just. 1H4 5.02. 88
that either wise bearing or ignorant carriage is 2H4 5.01. 75 P
by his blunt bearing he will keep his word, H5 4.07.177
and nobles bearing banners, there lie dead | one 4.08. 82
bearing it to the bloody slaughter-house, | even 2H6 3.01.212
with thy brave bearing should i be in love, 5.02. 20
queen, | bearing the king in my behalf along; 3H6 2.01.115
i mean, in bearing weight of government, | while 4.06. 51
satisfaction canst thou make | for bearing arms, 5.05. 15
bearing a state of mighty moment in't | and H8 2.04.214
bearing the king's will from his mouth expressly 3.02.235
viand, never bearing | like labor with the rest, COR 1.01.100
have their provand | only for bearing burthens, 2.01.252
scaling his present bearing with his past, 2.03.249
bearing his valiant sons | in coffins from the TIT 1.01. 34
scarf, | bearing a tartar's painted bow of lath, ROM 1.04. 5
if there be | such valor in the bearing, what TIM 3.05. 46
that stay at home, if bearing carry it; 3.05. 48
a turkish fleet, and bearing up to cyprus. OTH 1.03. 8
bearing with frank appearance | their purposes 1.03. 38
the bearing earth with his hard hoof he wounds, VEN 267
i had my load before, now press'd with bearing: 430
save of their lord no bearing yoke they knew, LUC 409
bearing away the wound that nothing healeth, 731
in youth, quick bearing and dexterity; 1389
bearing thy heart, which i will keep so chary SON 22.11
bearing the wanton burthen of the prime, | like 97. 7
in vowing new hate after new love bearing. 152. 4
BEARING-CLOTH 2 FR 0.0002 REL FR 1 V 1 P
look thee, a bearing-cloth for a squire's child! WT 3.03.115 P
thy scarlet robes as a child's bearing-cloth 1H6 1.03. 42
BEAR-LIKE 1 FR 0.0001 REL FR 1 V 0 P
fly, | but bear-like i must fight the course. MAC 5.07. 2
BEAR'S 2 FR 0.0002 REL FR 2 V 0 P
with the bear's fell paw | hath clapp'd his tail 2H6 5.01.153
save this, which is the lion's and the bear's, TNK 1.01. 53
BEARS* 120 FR 0.0135 REL FR 106 V 14 P
and penetrate the breasts | of ever-angry bears. TMP 1.02.289
that's a brave god, and bears celestial liquor. 2.02.117
fire, | bears no impression of the thing it was. TGV 2.04.202
he bears an honorable mind, | and will not use a 5.03. 13
be there bears i' th' town? WIV 1.01.287 P
she bears the purse too; 1.03. 68 P
th' expressure that it bears, green let it be, 5.05. 67
yet in this | that bears the name of life? MM 3.01. 39
no, | for my authority bears of a credent bulk, 4.04. 26
then she bears some breadth? ERR 3.02.112 P
comes aboard, | and then, sir, she bears away. 4.01. 87
in verity you did, my bones bears witness, 4.04. 77
and then the two bears will not bite one another ADO 3.02. 78 P
why, she that bears the bow. | finely put off! LLL 4.01.109
thy eye jove's lightning bears, thy voice his 4.02.115
folly in fools bears not so strong a note | as 5.02. 75
a heavy heart bears not a humble tongue. 5.02.737
his nail | and tom bears logs into the hall 5.02.914
this first, of gold, who this inscription bears, MV 2.07. 4
a coin that bears the figure of an angel 2.07. 56
it must appear | that malice bears down truth. 4.01.214
what is comely | envenoms him that bears it! AYL 2.03. 15
when that i say the city-woman bears | the cost 2.07. 75
wind, | through all the world bears rosalind. 3.02. 91
was writing of it, | it bears an angry tenure. 4.03. 11
i tell you, sir, she bears me fair in hand. SHR 4.02. 3
my father's bears more toward the market-place; 5.01. 9
bears in his visage no great presage of cruelty. TN 3.02. 64 P
with the same havior that your passion bears 3.04.206
nor brass nor stone nor parchment bears not one, WT 1.02.360
wolves and bears, they say, | casting their 2.03.187
much surpassing | the common praise it bears. 3.01. 3
my mother, and my nurse, that bears me yet! R2 1.03.307
who bears hard | his brother's death at bristow, 1H4 1.03.270
in the respect of the love he bears our house: 2.03. 4 P
but | mark how he bears his course, and runs me 3.01.107
his letters bears his mind, not i, my /lord. 4.01. 20
ay, by my faith, that bears a frosty sound. 4.01.128
this earth that bears /thee dead | bears not 5.04. 92
dead | bears not alive so stout a gentleman. 5.04. 93
broke loose, | and bears down all before him. 2H4 1.01. 11
of the speech of peace that bears such grace, 4.01. 48
your mistress bears well. H5 3.07. 45 P
ev'n as your horse bears your praises, who would 3.07. 76 P
two blades, which bears the better temper, 1H6 2.04. 13
he bears him on the place's privilege, | or 2.04. 86
the coward horse that bears me fall and die! 4.06. 47
while gloucester bears this base and humble mind 2H6 1.02. 62
she bears a duke's revenues on her back, | and 1.03. 80
and bears his thoughts above his falcon's pitch. 2.01. 12
scarce himself, | that bears so shrewd a maim: 2.03. 41
with what a majesty he bears himself, | how 3.01. 6
respecting what a rancorous mind he bears | and 3.01. 24
call hither to the stake my two brave bears, 5.01.144
are these thy bears? 5.01.148
we'll bait thy bears to death, | and manacle the 5.01.148
thy father bears the type of king of naples, 3H6 1.04.121
whose father bears the title of a king | (as if 2.02.140
until my misshap'd trunk that bears this head 3.02.170
with them, the two brave bears, warwick and 5.07. 10
where every horse bears his commanding rein R3 2.02.128
now thy proud neck bears half my burthen'd yoke, 4.04.111
that churchman bears a bounteous mind indeed, H8 1.03. 55
and bears his blushing honors thick upon him; 3.02.354
who's that that bears the sceptre? 4.01. 38
and bears his head | in such a rein, in full as TRO 1.03.188
after the inveterate hate he bears you. COR 2.03.226
think | upon the wounds his body bears, which 3.03. 50
appearance, and thy face | bears a command in't; 4.05. 61
he bears himself more proudlier, | even to my 4.07. 8
th' vulgar eye, that he bears all things fairly, 4.07. 21
why, there's the privilege your beauty bears. TIT 4.02.116
alone, | 'a bears him like a portly gentleman; ROM 1.05. 66
chain me with roaring bears, | or hide me 4.01. 80
lord, which bears that office to signify their TIM 1.02.120 P
who dies that bears not one spurn to their 1.02.141
destroyers, affable wolves, meek bears, | you 3.06. 95
great with tigers, dragons, wolves, and bears, 4.03.189
true; for he bears it not about him, 'tis hid. 4.03.406 P
so every bondman in his own hand bears | the JC 1.03.101
yourself | which every noble roman bears of you. 2.01. 93
every drop of blood | that every roman bears, 2.01.137
blood | that every roman bears, and nobly bears, 2.01.137
for in the ingrafted love he bears to caesar — 2.01.184
and bears with glasses, elephants with holes, 2.01.205
to think that caesar bears such rebel blood 3.01. 40
he shall but bear them as the ass bears gold, 4.01. 21
that carries anger as the flint bears fire, 4.03.111
no man bears sorrow better. portia is dead. 4.03.147
he bears too great a mind. 5.01.112
but under heavy judgment bears that life | which MAC 1.03.110
who bears a glass | which shows me many more; 4.01.119
than that which dearest father bears his son HAM 1.02.111
what is he whose grief | bears such an emphasis, 5.01.255
authority with such disposition as he bears, LR 1.01.305 P
tied by the heads, dogs and bears by th' neck, 2.04. 8 P
injuries the king now bears will be reveng'd 3.03. 12 P
he bears the sentence well that nothing bears OTH 1.03.212
he bears the sentence well that nothing bears 1.03.212
but he bears both the sentence and the sorrow 1.03.214
serious | importeth thee to know, this bears. ANT 1.02.121
'a bears the third part of the world, man; 2.07. 90 P
a woman that | bears all down with her brain, CYM 2.01. 54
and the device he bears upon his shield | is a PER 2.02. 19
and the device he bears upon his shield | is an 2.02. 25
he bears | a tempest, which his mortal vessel 4.04. 29
nothing we'll omit | that bears recovery's name. 5.01. 54
and then they fight like compell'd bears, would TNK 3.01. 68
he bears a charging-staff emboss'd with silver. 4.02.140
how horrible a shape | your innovation bears: STM II.C 93
and to collatium bears the lightless fire, LUC 4
she bears the load of lust he left behind, | and 734
here one being throng'd bears back, all boll'n 1417
that map which deep impression bears | of hard 1712
thee, | ruthless bears they will not cheer thee. PP 20.22
to him that bears the strong offense's /cross. SON 34.12
the beast that bears me, tired with my woe, 50. 5
but bears it out even to the edge of doom. 116.12
and often reading what contents it bears; LC 19
and sweetens, in the suff'ring pangs it bears, 272
BEAR'ST 8 FR 0.0009 REL FR 8 V 0 P
for all th' accommodations that thou bear'st MM 3.01. 14
thou bear'st thy heavy riches but a journey, 3.01. 27
youth, thou bear'st thy father's face; AWW 1.02. 19
thee as a father, if | thou bear'st my life off. WT 1.02.462
that bear'st a cheek for blows, a head for LR 4.02. 51
bear'st thou her face in mind? ANT 3.03. 29
whiles against a thorn thou bear'st thy part LUC 1135
for shame deny that thou bear'st love to any, SON 10. 1
BEAR'T 2 FR 0.0002 REL FR 2 V 0 P
and bear't before him, thereby shall we shadow MAC 5.04. 5
bear't that th' opposed may beware of thee. HAM 1.03. 67
BEAR-WHELP 1 FR 0.0001 REL FR 1 V 0 P
or an unlick'd bear-whelp | that carries no 3H6 3.02.161
BEAR-WHELPS 1 FR 0.0001 REL FR 1 V 0 P
but if you hunt these bear-whelps, then beware, TIT 4.01. 96
BEAST 79 FR 0.0089 REL FR 48 V 31 P
any strange beast there makes a man. TMP 2.02. 31 P
of the beast caliban and his confederates 4.01.140
i would have been a breakfast to the beast TGV 5.04. 34
it is a familiar beast to man, and signifies WIV 1.01. 21 P
what a beast am i to slack it! 3.04.111 P
love, that in some respects makes a beast a man; 5.05. 5 P
in some other, a man a beast. 5.05. 6 P
a fault done first in the form of a beast (o 5.05. 9 P
o you beast! MM 3.01.135
both work | ere this rude beast will profit. 3.02. 33
to your horse, and she would have me as a beast; ERR 3.02. 86 P
not that, i being a beast, she would have me, 3.02. 87 P
to be disturb'd, would mad or man or beast: 5.01. 84
of my tongue is better than a beast of yours. ADO 1.01.139 P
when he would play the noble beast in love. 5.04. 47
not so, gentle beast. LLL 2.01.222
this grisly beast, which lion hight by name, MND 5.01.139
a very gentle beast, and of a good conscience. 5.01.227 P
the very best at a beast, my lord, that e'er i 5.01.229 P
he is worst, he is little better than a beast. MV 1.02. 89 P
i think he be transform'd into a beast, | for i AYL 2.07. 1
meaning me a beast. 4.03. 49 P
the royal disposition of that beast | to prey on 4.03.117
o monstrous beast, how like a swine he lies! SHR in.1. 34
thou know'st winter tames man, woman, and beast; 4.01. 24 P
away, you three-inch fool! i am no beast. 4.01. 26 P
waits, | as doth a raven on a sick-fall'n beast, JN 4.03.153
aside, thou art a beast to say otherwise. 1H4 3.03.122 P
say, what beast, thou knave, thou? 3.03.124 P
what beast? why, an otter. 3.03.125 P
a woman should be made an ass and a beast, to 2H4 2.01. 38 P
it is a beast for perseus. H5 3.07. 20 P
sell the lion's skin | while the beast liv'd, 4.03. 94
even of the bonny beast he lov'd so well. 2H6 5.02. 12
not to the beast that would usurp their den. 3H6 2.02. 12
no beast so fierce but knows some touch of pity. R3 1.02. 71
but i know none, and therefore am no beast. 1.02. 72
wilt thou not, beast, abide? TRO 5.06. 30
the beast | with many heads butts me away. COR 4.01. 1
o, that i knew thy heart, and knew the beast, TIT 2.04. 34
o, what a beast was i to chide at him! ROM 3.02. 95
acts /denote | the unreasonable fury of a beast. 3.03.111
man, | and ill-beseeming beast in seeming both, 3.03.113
what a wicked beast was i to disfurnish myself TIM 3.02. 44 P
i am not able to do (the more beast, i say!) 3.02. 49 P
of man and beast the infinite malady | crust you 3.06. 98
th' unkindest beast more kinder than mankind. 4.01. 36
a beast, as thou art. 4.03. 50
of men, and remain a beast with the beasts? 4.03.325 P
what beast couldst thou be, that were not 4.03.343 P
thou be, that were not subject to a beast? 4.03.344 P
and what a beast art thou already, that seest 4.03.344 P
beast! 4.03.371
some beast read this; 5.03. 4
they could not find a heart within the beast. JC 2.02. 40
caesar should be a beast without a heart | if he 2.02. 42
what beast was't then | that made you break this MAC 1.07. 47
o god, a beast, that wants discourse of reason, HAM 1.02.150
ay, that incestuous, that adulterate beast, 1.05. 42
"the rugged pyrrhus, like th' hyrcanian beast — 2.02.450
a beast, no more. 4.04. 35
and demi-natur'd | with the brave beast. 4.07. 88
let a beast be lord of beasts, and his crib 5.02. 86 P
in contempt of man, | brought near to beast. LR 2.03. 9
thou ow'st the worm no silk, the beast no hide, 3.04.104 P
moor are /now making the beast with two backs. OTH 1.01.116 P
man, by and by a fool, and presently a beast! 2.03.306 P
a horned man's a monster and a beast. 4.01. 62
there's many a beast then in a populous city, 4.01. 63
our dungy earth alike | feeds beast as man; ANT 1.01. 36
'tis like a beast, methinks. TNK 2.02. 99
then i'll leave you; | you are a beast now. 3.03. 47
i were a beast and i'ld call it good sport. 4.03. 52 P
she is horribly in love with him, poor beast, 5.02. 62
sits, | banning his boist'rous and unruly beast; VEN 326
when as i met the boar, that bloody beast, 999
to the rough beast that knows no gentle right, LUC 545
the beast that bears me, tired with my woe, SON 50. 5
o, what excuse will my poor beast then find, 51. 5
BEAST-EATING 1 FR 0.0001 REL FR 1 V 0 P
then the beast-eating clown, and next the fool, TNK 3.05.131
BEASTLIEST 1 FR 0.0001 REL FR 0 V 1 P
so that in the beastliest sense you are pompey MM 2.01.218 P
BEASTLINESS 1 FR 0.0001 REL FR 0 V 1 P

that bolting–hutch of beastliness, that swoll'n 1H4 2.04.450 P
/BEASTLY 1 FR 0.0001 REL FR 1 V 0 P
/thou, /beastly /feeder, /art /so /full /of /him 2H4 1.03. 95
BEASTLY 21 FR 0.0023 REL FR 16 V 5 P
the form of a beast (o jove, a beastly fault!) WIV 5.05. 9 P
from their abominable and beastly touches | i MM 3.02. 24
me, but that she, being a very beastly creature, ERR 3.02. 88 P
see how beastly she doth court him! SHR 4.02. 34
misuse, | such beastly shameless transformation, 1H4 1.01. 44
he stabb'd me in mine own house, most beastly, 2H4 2.01. 14 P
not to relent is beastly, savage, devilish. R3 1.04.262
in beastly sort, dragg'd through the shameful TRO 5.10. 5
being the herdsmen of the beastly plebeians. COR 2.01. 95 P
ah, beastly creature, | the blot and enemy to TIT 2.03.182
o barbarous, beastly villains like thyself! 5.01. 97
her life was beastly and devoid of pity, | and, 5.03.199
in that beastly fury | he has been known to TIM 3.05. 70
a beastly ambition, which the gods grant thee t' 4.03.327 P
virgins to the stain | of contumelious, beastly, 5.01.174
you beastly knave, know you no reverence? LR 2.02. 69
i would have spoke | was beastly /dumb'd by him. ANT 1.05. 50
and to expound | his beastly mind to us, he hath CYM 1.06.153
we are beastly: 3.03. 40
you that | like beasts which you shun beastly, 5.03. 27
take courage, | you shall not die thus beastly. TNK 3.03. 6
BEAST'S 1 FR 0.0001 REL FR 1 V 0 P
nature needs, | man's life is cheap as beast's. LR 2.04.267
BEASTS 36 FR 0.0040 REL FR 23 V 13 P
roar | that beasts shall tremble at thy din. TMP 1.02.371
heavens keep him from these beasts! 2.01.324
needs buy and sell men and women like beasts, we MM 3.02. 2 P
the beasts, the fishes, and the winged fowls ERR 2.01. 18
it is a blessing that he bestows on beasts, and 2.02. 80 P
when beasts most graze, birds best peck, and men LLL 1.01.236 P
and leave thee to the mercy of wild beasts. MND 2.01.228
for beasts that meet me run away for fear. 2.02. 95
here come two noble beasts in, a man and a lion. 5.01.217 P
here comes a pair of very strange beasts, which AYL 5.04. 37 P
have taken | the shapes of beasts upon them. WT 4.04. 27
which art a lion and the king of beasts? R2 5.01. 34
a king of beasts indeed — if aught but beasts, 5.01. 35
a king of beasts indeed — if aught but beasts, 5.01. 35
horse, and all other jades you may call beasts. H5 3.07. 24 P
hath robb'd many beasts of their particular TRO 1.02. 19 P
nature teaches beasts to know their friends. COR 2.01. 6 P
but like beasts | and cowardly nobles gave way 4.06.121
but throw her forth to beasts and birds to prey: TIT 5.03.198
what ho, you men, you beasts! ROM 1.01. 83
give it the beasts, to be rid of the men. TIM 4.03.323 P
of men, and remain a beast with the beasts? 4.03.325 P
of athens is become a forest of beasts. 4.03.348 P
that beasts | may have the world in empire! 4.03.391
water, | as beasts and birds and fishes. 4.03.423
nor on the beasts themselves, the birds and 4.03.424
why birds and beasts from quality and kind, JC 1.03. 64
thou /art fled to brutish beasts, | and men have 3.02.104
the which we are pictures, or mere beasts; HAM 4.05. 86
let a beast be lord of beasts, and his crib 5.02. 86 P
and applause, transform ourselves into beasts! OTH 2.03.293 P
the gilded puddle | which beasts would cough at; ANT 1.04. 63
you that | like beasts which you shun beastly, CYM 5.03. 27
since men prove beasts, let beasts bear gentle LUC 1148
men prove beasts, let beasts bear gentle minds." 1148
made, | beasts did leap and birds did sing, PP 20. 5
BEAT *(also peat*, etc.)*
/BEAT 2 FR 0.0002 REL FR 2 V 0 P
/didst /thou /beat /heaven /with /blessing 2H4 1.03. 92
/beat /loud /the /taborins, let the trumpets TRO 4.05.275
BEAT-- 1 FR 0.0001 REL FR 0 V 1 P
beat— ADO 4.01.314 P
BEAT 125 FR 0.0141 REL FR 83 V 42 P
i saw him beat the surges under him, | and ride TMP 2.01.115
i could find in my heart to beat him — 2.02.156 P
beat him enough. 3.02. 85
after a little time | i'll beat him too. 3.02. 86
i am sorry i beat thee; 3.02.111 P
beat the ground | for kissing of their feet; 4.01.173
then i beat my tabor, | at which, like unback'd 4.01.175
me, and return | or ere your pulse twice beat. 5.01.103
her my house, and hath threat'ned to beat her. WIV 4.02. 87 P
trust me, he beat him most pitifully. 4.02.201 P
he beat him most unpitifully, methought. 4.02.203 P
i will tell you — he beat me grievously, in the 5.01. 20 P
pompey, i shall beat you to your tent, and prove MM 2.01.248 P
or they shall beat out my brains with billets. 4.03. 55 P
for, in conclusion, he did beat me there. ERR 2.01. 74
self–harming jealousy — fie, beat it hence! 2.01.102
or i will beat this method in your sconce. 2.02. 34
he met me on the mart, and that i beat him, 3.01. 7
that you beat me at the mart, i have your hand 3.01. 12
cry for this, minion, if i beat the door down. 3.01. 59
them, and then they laugh at him and beat him. ADO 2.01.142 P
that stole your meat, and you'll beat the post. 2.01.199 P
in angel whiteness beat away those blushes, 4.01.161
sweet chucks, beat not the bones of the buried. LLL 5.02.661 P
the more you beat me, i will fawn on you. MND 2.01.204
her, how he beat me because her horse stumbled, SHR 4.01. 77 P
that bate and beat and will not be obedient. 4.01.196
it, and beat me to death with a bottom of brown 4.03.136 P
he that knocks as he would beat down the gate? 5.01. 16 P
sir, what are you that offer to beat my servant? 5.01. 63 P
i'll beat him, by my life, if i can meet him AWW 2.03.237 P
his age than i would have of — i'll beat him, 2.03.241 P
if i were but two hours younger, i'd beat thee. 2.03.253 P
general offense, and every man should beat thee. 2.03.255 P
o, if i thought that, i'd beat him like a dog! TN 2.03.141 P
'slight, i could so beat the rogue! 2.05. 33 P
'slid, i'll after him again and beat him. 3.04.391 P
say this to him, | he's beat from his best ward. WT 1.02. 33
tongue, who late hath beat her husband, | and 2.03. 92
when living blood doth in these temples beat, JN 2.01.108
excuse it is to beat usurping down. 2.01.119
as york thrives to beat back bullingbrook. R2 2.02.144
i'll give thee scope to beat, | since foes have 3.03.140
since foes have scope to beat both thee and me. 3.03.141
and beat our watch and rob our passengers, 5.03. 9
tom, beat cut's saddle, put a few flocks in the 1H4 2.01. 5 P
if i do not beat thee out of thy kingdom with a 2.04.136 P
whose swift wrath beat down | the never–daunted 2H4 1.01.109
let's beat him before his whore. 2.04.257 P
and told john a' gaunt he beat his own name, for 3.02.324 P
is dead that you and pistol beat amongst you. 5.04. 17 P
twenty french crowns to one they will beat us, H5 4.01.226 P
now beat them hence, why do you let them stay? 1H6 1.03. 54
to beat assailing death from his weak /legions; 4.04. 16
beat down alanson, orleance, burgundy, | and 4.06. 14
thine eyes and thoughts | beat on a crown, the 2H6 2.01. 20
"a staff is quickly found to beat a dog." 3.01.171
when from thy shore the tempest beat us back, 3.02.102
o, beat away the busy meddling fiend | that lays 3.03. 21
at unawares may beat down edward's guard, | and 3H6 4.02. 23
let's levy men, and beat him back again. 4.08. 6
or shall we beat the stones about thine ears? 5.01.108
but that thy brothers beat aside the point. R3 1.02. 96
why do /you weep so oft, and beat your breast, 2.02. 3
that my pent heart may have some scope to beat, 4.01. 34
unarm'd, and unresolv'd to beat them back. 4.04.436
where is thy power then, to beat him back? 4.04.479
yet to beat down these rebels here at home. 4.04.530
no new device to beat this from his brains? H8 3.02.217
i will beat thee into handsomeness. TRO 2.01. 15 P
if thou use to beat me, i will begin at thy heel 2.01. 47 P
therefore i beat thee. 2.01. 67 P
bobb'd his brain more than he has beat my bones. 2.01. 70 P
whose present courage may beat down our foes, 2.02.201
that i could beat him, whilst he rail'd at me. 2.03. 5 P
but our great ajax bravely beat down him." 3.03.213
will you beat down the door? 4.02. 43 P
the fierce polydamas | hath beat down menon; 5.05. 7
he'll beat aufidius' head below his knee, | and COR 1.03. 46
have you run | from slaves that apes would beat! 1.04. 36
stand fast, we'll beat them to their wives, | as 1.04. 41
told me they had beat you to your trenches? 1.06. 40
so often hast thou beat me; 1.10. 8
dogs, that are as often beat for barking | as 2.03.216
on fair ground | i could beat forty of them. 3.01.242
thou hast beat me out | twelve several times, 4.05.121
and beat the messenger who bids beware | of what 4.06. 55
beat thou the drum, that it speak mournfully; 5.06.149
with frost, or grass beat down with storms. TIT 4.04. 71
and on the ragged stones beat forth our souls, 5.03.133
beat them down! ROM 1.01. 73
prick love for pricking, and you beat love down. 1.04. 28
draw, benvolio, beat down their weapons. 3.01. 86
nor that is not the lark whose notes do beat 3.05. 21
other day, and now he has beat it out of my hat. TIM 3.06.113 P
old limping sire, | with it beat out his brains! 4.01. 15
i prithee beat thy drum and get thee gone. 4.03. 97
i'll beat thee, but i should infect my hands. 4.03.364
lie where the light foam of the sea may beat 4.03.378
our enemies have beat us to the pit. JC 5.05. 23
and swearers enow to beat the honest men and MAC 4.02. 57 P
beard to beard, | and beat them backward home. 5.05. 7
beat at this gate, that let thy folly in | and LR 1.04.271
one whom i will beat into /clamorous whining, if 2.02. 23 P
up thy heels, and beat thee before the king? 2.02. 30 P
or at their chamber–door i'll beat the drum 2.04.118
i'll beat the knave into a twiggen bottle. OTH 2.03.147 P
beat me? 2.03.149 P
even so as one would beat his offenseless dog to 2.03.274 P
turk | beat a venetian and traduc'd the state, 5.02.354
the water which they beat to follow faster, | as ANT 2.02.196
and his quails ever | beat mine, inhoop'd, at 2.03. 39
head of /actium | beat th' approaching caesar. 3.07. 52
as he had power | to beat me out of egypt. 4.01. 2
we'll beat 'em into bench–holes. 4.07. 9
we have beat him to his camp. 4.08. 1
nightingale, | we have beat them to their beds. 4.08. 19
if you beat us out of it, it is yours; CYM 3.01. 80 P
hear | the rain and wind beat dark december, how 3.03. 37
thou art some fool, | i am loath to beat thee. 4.02. 86
vessels with their power | to beat us down, the PER 1.04. 68
lied so lewdly | that women ought to beat me. TNK 4.02. 36
two emulous philomels beat the ear o' th' night 5.03.124
but as reproof and reason beat it dead, | by thy LUC 489
beat at thy rocky and wrack–threat'ning heart, 590
BEATED 1 FR 0.0001 REL FR 1 V 0 P
beated and chopp'd with tann'd antiquity, | mine SON 62.10
BEATEN 47 FR 0.0053 REL FR 27 V 20 P
knight, you have beaten my men, kill'd my deer, WIV 1.01.111 P
cozen'd, for i have been cozen'd and beaten too. 4.05. 94 P
good heart, is beaten black and blue, that you 4.05.112 P
i was beaten myself into all the colors of the 4.05.115 P
i knew not what 'twas to be beaten till lately. 5.01. 26 P
go back again, and be new beaten home? ERR 2.01. 76
but i pray, sir, why am i beaten? 2.02. 39 P
nothing, sir, but that i am beaten. 2.02. 41 P
there ever any man thus beaten out of season, 2.02. 47
beaten the maids a–row, and bound the doctor, 5.01.170
melancholy and would fain have it beaten away. ADO 5.01.124 P
no, if a man will be beaten with brains, 'a 5.04.103 P
i did think to have beaten thee, but in that 5.04.110 P
so is alcides beaten by his /page, | and so may MV 2.01. 35
house, | as beaten hence by your strange lunacy. SHR in.2. 29
yet would you say ye were beaten out of door, in.2. 85
was ever man so beaten? 4.01. 2 P
ever thou be'st bound in thy scarf and beaten, AWW 2.03.226 P
you were beaten in italy for picking a kernel 2.03.258 P
with, should be once heard and thrice beaten. 2.05. 31 P
i am robb'd, sir, and beaten; WT 4.03. 61 P
are we not beaten? JN 3.04. 6
indeed your drums, being beaten, will cry out; 5.02.166
and so shall you, being beaten. 5.02.167
earl of fife and eldest son | to beaten douglas, 1H4 1.01. 72
hath beaten down young hotspur and his troops, 2H4 in 25
thus is the shepherd beaten from thy side, | and 2H6 3.01.191
mine eyes should sparkle like the beaten flint, 3.02.317
our fathers | have in their own land beaten, R3 5.03.334
as i am, beaten | a long time out of play, may H8 1.03. 44
her foes shake like a field of beaten corn, 5.04. 31
no man is beaten voluntary. TRO 2.01. 96 P
i'd have beaten him like a dog, but for COR 4.05. 51 P
thy head hath been beaten as addle as an egg for ROM 3.01. 23 P
nor stony tower, nor walls of beaten brass, JC 1.03. 93
let us be beaten, if we cannot fight. MAC 5.06. 8
but in the beaten way of friendship, what make HAM 2.02.269 P
i'ld have thee beaten for being old before thy LR 1.05. 42 P
far off methinks i hear the beaten drum. 4.06.285
cassio hath beaten thee, | and thou by that OTH 2.03.374
when thou once | was beaten from modena, where ANT 1.04. 57
the poop was beaten gold, | purple the sails, 2.02.192
they are beaten, sir, and our advantage serves 4.07. 11
was carried | from off our coast, twice beaten; CYM 3.01. 26
beaten for loyalty | excited me to treason. 5.05.344
retire, | beaten away by brain–sick rude desire. LUC 175
that patience is quite beaten from her breast; 1563
/BEATING 1 FR 0.0001 REL FR 1 V 0 P
/poor /heart /beats /with /outrageous /beating, TIT 3.02. 13
BEATING 19 FR 0.0021 REL FR 14 V 5 P
for still 'tis beating in my mind, your reason TMP 1.02.176
or two i'll walk | to still my beating mind. 4.01.163
do not infest your mind with beating on | the 5.01.246
and he will bless that cross with other beating: ERR 2.01. 79
when i am cold, he heats me with beating; 4.04. 33 P
when i am warm, he cools me with beating. 4.04. 34 P
can bide the beating of so strong a passion | as TN 2.04. 94
beating and hanging are terrors to me. WT 4.03. 29 P
a million of beating may come to a great matter. 4.03. 59 P
beating your officers, cursing yourselves, COR 3.03. 78
him, that | must bear my beating to his grave — 5.06.108
and myself, | the bell then beating one — HAM 1.01. 39
whereon his brains still beating puts him thus 3.01.174
dull ass will not mend his pace with beating, 5.01. 57 P
beating his kind embracements with her heels. VEN 312
planting oblivion, beating reason back, 557
anon his beating heart, alarum striking, | gives LUC 433
beating her bulk, that his hand shakes withal. 467
she wakes her heart by beating on her breast, 759
BEATRICE 43 FR 0.0048 REL FR 12 V 31 P
"get you to heaven, beatrice, get you to heaven, ADO 2.01. 45 P
but that my lady beatrice should know me, and 2.01.203 P
disposition of beatrice that puts the world into 2.01.208 P
the lady beatrice hath a quarrel to you. 2.01.236 P
lady beatrice, i will get you one. 2.01.321 P
and the lady beatrice into a mountain of 2.01.366 P
stomach, he shall fall in love with beatrice. 2.01.384 P
that your niece beatrice was in love with 2.03. 91 P
"benedick" and "beatrice" between the sheet? 2.03.137 P
here comes beatrice. 2.03.244 P
fair beatrice, i thank you for your pains. 2.03.249 P
there shalt thou find my cousin beatrice 3.01. 2
now, ursula, when beatrice doth come, | as we do 3.01. 15
be how benedick | is sick in love with beatrice. 3.01. 21
for look where beatrice, like a lapwing, runs 3.01. 24
so angle we for beatrice, who even now | is 3.01. 29
sure | that benedick loves beatrice so entirely? 3.01. 37
and never to let beatrice know of it. 3.01. 43
a bed | as ever beatrice shall couch upon? 3.01. 46
heart | of prouder stuff than that of beatrice. 3.01. 50
so odd and from all fashions | as beatrice is, 3.01. 73
for my life, to break with him about beatrice. 3.02. 75 P
have by this play'd their parts with beatrice, 3.02. 77 P
good ursula, wake my cousin beatrice, and desire 3.04. 1 P
ask my lady beatrice else, here she comes. 3.04. 37 P
lady beatrice, have you wept all this while? 4.01.255 P
by my sword, beatrice, thou lovest me. 4.01.274 P
what offense, sweet beatrice? 4.01.282 P
tarry, sweet beatrice. 4.01.292 P
beatrice — 4.01.295 P
hear me, beatrice — 4.01.308 P
nay, but, beatrice — 4.01.311 P
tarry, good beatrice. by this hand, i love thee. 4.01.324 P
i'll tell thee how beatrice prais'd thy wit the 5.01.159 P
and, i'll warrant you, for the love of beatrice. 5.01.196 P
hands by helping me to the speech of beatrice. 5.02. 3 P
and so i pray thee call beatrice; 5.02. 16 P
well, i will call beatrice to you, who i think 5.02. 23 P
sweet beatrice, wouldst thou come when i call'd 5.02. 42 P
an old instance, beatrice, that liv'd in the 5.02. 76 P
soft and fair, friar. which is beatrice? 5.04. 72
of his own pure brain, | fashion'd to beatrice. 5.04. 88
well hop'd thou wouldst have denied beatrice, 5.04.113 P
/BEATS 2 FR 0.0002 REL FR 2 V 0 P
/beats /in /this /hollow /prison /of /my /flesh, TIT 3.02. 10
/when /thy /poor /heart /beats /with /outrageous 3.02. 13
BEATS 24 FR 0.0027 REL FR 20 V 4 P
thy pulse | beats as of flesh and blood; TMP 5.01.114
the baby beats the nurse, and quite athwart MM 1.03. 30
an idle plume, | which the air beats for vain. 2.04. 12
weeps, sobs, beats her heart, tears her hair, ADO 2.03.147 P
proud contempt that beats his peace to heaven. JN 2.01. 88
whose rocky shore beats back the envious siege R2 2.01. 62
your pulsidge beats as extraordinarily as heart 2H4 2.04. 23 P
that beats upon the high shore of this world — H5 4.01.265
binds the wretch and beats it when it strays, 2H6 3.01.211
he beats me, and i rail at him. TRO 2.03. 3 P
my heart beats thicker than a feverous pulse, 3.02. 36
it beats as it would fall in twenty pieces. ROM 2.05. 49
scorn, with one hand beats | cold death aside, 3.01.161
his /agile arm beats down their fatal points, 3.01.166
i' th' world, and hems, and beats her heart, HAM 4.05. 5
save what beats there — filial ingratitude! LR 3.04. 14
natural luck, | he beats thee 'gainst the odds. ANT 2.03. 28
your sorrow beats so ardently upon me | that it TNK 1.01.126
now, now, it beats upon it — now, now, now! 3.04. 7
her attention, for this her mind beats upon; 4.03. 78 P
my boding heart pants, beats, and takes no rest, VEN 647
and now she beats her heart, whereat it groans, 829
part is youth, and beats these from the stage. LUC 278
and town, | the golden bullet beats it down. PP 18.18
BEAU 3 FR 0.0003 REL FR 0 V 3 P
here comes monsieur /le beau. AYL 1.02. 91 P
bon jour, monsieur le beau. 1.02. 97 P
call him hither, good monsieur le beau. 1.02.163 P
BEAUFORD 10 FR 0.0011 REL FR 10 V 0 P
here's beauford, that regards nor god nor king, 1H6 1.03. 60
fie, uncle beauford, i have heard you preach 3.01.127
or hath mine uncle beauford and myself, | with 2H6 1.01. 88
have we beauford | the imperious churchman, 1.03. 68
and york and impious beauford, that false priest 2.04. 53

myself and beauford had him in protection, | and 3.02.180
is beauford term'd a kite? 3.02.196
that cardinal beauford is at point of death; 3.02.369
speak, beauford, to thy sovereign. 3.03. 1
beauford, it is thy sovereign speaks to thee. 3.03. 7
BEAUFORD'S 3 FR 0.0003 REL FR 3 V 0 P
at beauford's pride, at somerset's ambition, 2H6 2.02. 71
beauford's red sparkling eyes blab his heart's 3.01.154
by suffolk and the cardinal beauford's means. 3.02.124
BEAUMOND 1 FR 0.0001 REL FR 1 V 0 P
the lords of ross, beaumond, and willoughby, R2 2.02. 54
BEAUMONT 2 FR 0.0002 REL FR 2 V 0 P
beaumont, grandpre, roussi, and faulconbridge, H5 3.05. 44
beaumont and marle, vaudemont and lestrake. 4.08.100
BEAUTEOUS 45 FR 0.0050 REL FR 41 V 4 P
how beauteous mankind is! TMP 5.01.183
black men are pearls in beauteous ladies' eyes. TGV 5.02. 12
between lord perigort and the beauteous heir LLL 2.01. 41
true, that thou art beauteous; 4.01. 61 P
more fairer than fair, beautiful than beauteous, 4.01. 63 P
hand of the most beauteous lady rosaline." 4.02.132 P
beauteous as ink — a good conclusion. 5.02. 41
can be) | i am belov'd of beauteous hermia. MND 1.01.104
this beauteous lady thisby is certain. 5.01.130
the beauteous scarf | veiling an indian beauty; MV 3.02. 98
with wealth enough, and young and beauteous, SHR 1.02. 86
tongue, | as is the other for beauteous modesty. 1.02.253
kindness in women, not their beauteous looks, 4.02. 41
and though that nature with a beauteous wall TN 1.02. 48
but the beauteous evil | are empty trunks 3.04.369
to seek the beauteous eye of heaven to garnish, JN 4.02. 15
which was embounded in this beauteous clay, 4.03.137
thou most beauteous inn, | why should R2 5.01. 13
of beauteous margaret hath astonish'd me. 1H6 5.05. 2
for thou hast given me in this beauteous face 2H6 1.01. 21
king, that calls your beauteous daughter wife, R3 4.04.315
i tender not thy beauteous princely daughter! 4.04.405
having lands, and blest with beauteous wives, 5.03.321
sweet blowse, you are a beauteous blossom sure. TIT 4.02. 72
county anselme and his beauteous sisters; ROM 1.02. 65 P
may prove a beauteous flow'r when next we meet. 2.02.122
beauteous and swift, the minions of their race, MAC 2.04. 15
where is the beauteous majesty of denmark? HAM 4.05. 21
the arm'd rest, courtiers of beauteous freedom, ANT 2.06. 17
farewell, my beauteous sister. TNK 1.01.219
and this beauteous morn | (the prim'st of all 3.01. 18
this beauteous combat, willful and unwilling, VEN 365
the beauteous influence that makes him bright, 862
ne'er saw the beauteous livery that he wore — 1107
lent | in the possession of his beauteous mate; LUC 18
then, beauteous niggard, why dost thou abuse SON 4. 5
seeking that beauteous roof to ruinate, | which 10. 7
makes black night beauteous and her old face new 27.12
why didst thou promise such a beauteous day, 34. 1
beauteous thou art, therefore to be assailed; 41. 6
o, how much more doth beauty beauteous seem | by 54. 1
and so of you, beauteous and lovely youth, 54.13
you to your beauteous blessings add a curse, 84.13
three beauteous springs to yellow autumn turn'd 104. 5
"his qualities were beauteous as his form, | for LC 99
BEAUTIED 1 FR 0.0001 REL FR 1 V 0 P
harlot's cheek, beautied with plast'ring art, HAM 3.01. 50
BEAUTIES 20 FR 0.0022 REL FR 18 V 2 P
"all hail, the richest beauties on the earth!" LLL 5.02.158
beauties no richer than rich taffata. 5.02.159
one that compos'd your beauties; MND 1.01. 48
i might in virtues, beauties, livings, friends, MV 3.02.156
good beauties, let me sustain no scorn; TN 1.05.175 P
outliving beauties outward, with a mind | that TRO 3.02.162
examine other beauties. ROM 1.01.228
with all the admired beauties of verona. 1.02. 84
do their amorous rites | by their own beauties, 3.02. 9
that your good beauties be the happy cause | of HAM 3.01. 38
manners, and beauties — all which the moor is OTH 2.01.230 P
she locks her beauties in her bud again, | and TNK 2.02.142
first with mine eye of all those beauties in her 2.02.168
all those beauties | she sows into the births of 4.02. 8
would root these beauties as he roots the mead. VEN 636
mortal stars as bright as heaven's beauties, LUC 13
since sweets and beauties do themselves forsake, SON 12.11
and all those beauties whereof now he's king 63. 6
thy glass will show thee how thy beauties /wear, 77. 1
as those whose beauties proudly make them cruel; 131. 2
BEAUTIFIED 3 FR 0.0003 REL FR 1 V 2 P
seeing you are beautified | with goodly shape, TGV 4.01. 53
my soul's idol, the most beautified ophelia" — HAM 2.02.109 P
a vile phrase, "beautified" is a vile phrase. 2.02.111 P
BEAUTIFUL 17 FR 0.0019 REL FR 13 V 4 P
since i saw her, and still i see her beautiful. TGV 2.01. 67 P
a virtuous gentlewoman, mild and beautiful! 4.04.180
more fairer than fair, beautiful than beauteous, LLL 4.01. 63 P
thou art as wise as thou art beautiful. MND 3.01.148
most beautiful pagan, most sweet jew! MV 2.03. 11 P
thou hast a lady far more beautiful | than any SHR in.2. 62
hold, | his youngest daughter, beautiful bianca, 1.02.120
lark, | because his feathers are more beautiful? 4.03.176
me, was yet of many accounted beautiful; TN 2.01. 26 P
o, what a deal of scorn looks beautiful | in the 3.01.145
she's beautiful; 1H6 5.03. 78
beautiful tyrant! ROM 3.02. 75
which was not half so beautiful and kind; TIM 1.02.148
eyes | were not in fault, for she was beautiful; CYM 5.05. 63
thou art alone | and only beautiful, and these TNK 4.02. 38
and beauty making beautiful old rhyme | in SON 106. 3
why, 'twas beautiful and hard, | whereto his LC 211
BEAUTIFY 5 FR 0.0005 REL FR 5 V 0 P
to blush and beautify the cheek again. 2H6 3.02.167
are brought to rome | to beautify thy triumphs, TIT 1.01.110
lover, | to beautify him, only lacks a cover. ROM 1.03. 88
to grace thy marriage–day, i'll beautify. PER 5.03. 76
each in her sleep themselves so beautify, | as LUC 404
BEAUTY 263 FR 0.0297 REL FR 235 V 28 P
to consider is | the beauty of his daughter. TMP 3.02. 99
which now shows all the beauty of the sun, | and TGV 1.03. 86
i mean that her beauty is exquisite, but her 2.01. 54 P
make her fair, that no man counts of her beauty. 2.01. 60 P
how esteem'st thou me? i account of her beauty. 2.01. 62 P
then let her beauty be her wedding–dow'r, | for 3.01. 78
say that upon the altar of her beauty | you 3.02. 72
when to her beauty i commend my vows, | she bids 4.02. 9
for beauty lives with kindness. 4.02. 45
love–letters in the holiday–time of my beauty, WIV 2.01. 2 P
the right arch'd beauty of the brow that becomes 3.03. 56 P
proclaim an enshield beauty ten times louder MM 2.04. 80
beauty ten times louder | than beauty could, 2.04. 81
hast neither heat, affection, limb, nor beauty, 3.01. 37
that is cheap in beauty makes beauty brief in 3.01.182 P
cheap in beauty makes beauty brief in goodness; 3.01.182 P
hath homely age th' alluring beauty took | from ERR 2.01. 89
the jewel best enamelled | will lose his beauty; 2.01.110
since that my beauty cannot please his eye, 2.01.114
first he did praise my beauty, then my speech. 4.02. 15
her as much in beauty as the first of may doth ADO 1.01.192 P
an obstinate heretic in the despite of beauty. 1.01.235 P
for beauty is a witch | against whose charms 2.01.179
to turn all beauty into thoughts of harm, | and 4.01.107
then write me a sonnet in praise of my beauty? 5.02. 5 P
good lord boyet, my beauty, though but mean, LLL 2.01. 13
beauty is bought by judgment of the eye, | not 2.01. 15
i thank my beauty, i am fair that shoot, | and 4.01. 11
see, see, my beauty will be sav'd by merit. 4.01. 21
ay, my continent of beauty. 4.01.109
never faith could hold, if not to beauty vowed! 4.02.106
beauty doth varnish age, as if new born, | and 4.03.240
that i may swear beauty doth beauty lack, | if 4.03.247
that i may swear beauty doth beauty lack, | if 4.03.247
without the beauty of a woman's face? 4.03.297
world | teaches such beauty as a woman's eye? 4.03.309
a light condition in a beauty dark. 5.02. 20
your beauty, ladies, | hath much deformed us, 5.02.756
none, but your beauty; MND 1.01.201
sees helen's beauty in a brow of egypt. 5.01. 11
look on beauty, | and you shall see 'tis MV 3.02. 88
the beauteous scarf | veiling an indian beauty; 3.02. 99
beauty provoketh thieves sooner than gold. AYL 1.03.110
for honesty coupled to beauty is to have honey a 3.03. 30 P
what though you have no beauty — | as, by my 3.05. 37
o yes, i saw sweet beauty in her face, | such as SHR 1.01.167
sir, | that, hearing of her beauty and her wit, 2.01. 48
thy virtues spoke of, and thy beauty sounded, 2.01.192
for by this light whereby i see thy beauty, 2.01.273
thy beauty that doth make me like thee well, 2.01.274
what stars do spangle heaven with such beauty, 4.05. 31
it blots thy beauty, as frosts do bite the meads 5.02.139
muddy, ill–seeming, thick, bereft of beauty, 5.02.143
youth, beauty, wisdom, courage — all | that AWW 2.01.181
lays down his wanton siege before her beauty, 3.07. 18
a wife | whose beauty did astonish the survey 5.03. 16
exquisite, and unmatchable beauty — i pray you TN 1.05.171 P
'tis beauty truly blent, whose red and white 1.05.239
i will give out divers schedules of my beauty. 1.05.245 P
you were crown'd | the nonpareil of beauty! 1.05.254
virtue is beauty, but the beauteous evil | are 3.04.369
were never for a piece of beauty rarer, | nor in WT 4.04. 32
and take | the winds of march with beauty; 4.04.120
i'll have thy beauty scratch'd with briers and 4.04.425
thus your verse | flow'd with her beauty once. 5.01.102
your choice is not so rich in worth as beauty, 5.01.214
if lusty love should go in quest of beauty, JN 2.01.426
such as she is, in beauty, virtue, birth, | is 2.01.432
can in this book of beauty read, "i love," | her 2.01.485
as she in beauty, education, blood, | holds hand 2.01.493
and chase the native beauty from his cheek, 3.04. 83
death, made proud with pure and princely beauty! 4.03. 35
or, when he doom'd this beauty to a grave, 4.03. 39
and stain'd the beauty of a fair queen's cheeks R2 3.01. 14
body be call'd thieves of the day's beauty. 1H4 1.02. 25 P
to smother up his beauty from the world, | that, 1.02.199
a stain | upon the beauty of all parts besides, 3.01.186
burs, | losing both beauty and utility; H5 5.02. 53
age, that ill layer–up of beauty, can do no more 5.02.230 P
that beauty am i blest with which you may see. 1H6 1.02. 86
her beauty, and the value of her dower, | he 5.01. 44
o fairest beauty, do not fear nor fly, | for i 5.03. 46
so seems this gorgeous beauty to mine eyes. 5.03. 64
could i come near your beauty with my nails, | i 2H6 1.03.141
child | that for the beauty thinks it excellent. 3.01.230
and beauty, that the tyrant oft reclaims, 5.02. 54
'tis beauty that doth oft make women proud, 3H6 1.04.128
your beauty was the cause of that effect — R3 1.02.121
your beauty, that did haunt me in my sleep | to 1.02.122
nails should rent that beauty from my cheeks. 1.02.126
thy beauty hath, and made them blind with 1.02.166
but, now thy beauty is propos'd my fee, | my 1.02.169
but 'twas thy beauty that provoked me. 1.02.180
/which in their summer beauty kiss'd each other. 4.03. 13
and i'll corrupt her manners, stain her beauty, 4.04.207
there will be | the beauty of this kingdom, i'll H8 1.03. 54
where this heaven of beauty | shall shine at 1.04. 59
(out of the great respect they bear to beauty) 1.04. 69
o beauty, | till now i never knew thee! 1.04. 75
beauty and honor in her are so mingled | that 2.03. 76
freely | the beauty of her person to the people. 4.01. 68
for virtue and true beauty of the soul, | for 4.02.144
nor his beauty. TRO 1.02. 90 P
is not birth, beauty, good shape, discourse, 1.02.253 P
honesty, my mask, to defend my beauty, and you, 1.02.262 P
and dare avow her beauty and her worth | in 1.03.271
greatness as cerberus is at proserpina's beauty, 2.01. 34 P
the pleasures such a beauty brings with it, 2.02.147
the mortal venus, the heart–blood of beauty, 3.01. 32 P
gives us more palm in beauty than we have, | yea 3.01.157
the beauty that is borne here in the face | the 3.03.103
for beauty, wit, | high birth, vigor of bone, 3.03.171
o beauty, where is thy faith? 5.02. 67
if beauty have a soul, this is not she; 5.02.138
fellow, commend my service to her beauty; 5.05. 3
why, there's the privilege your beauty bears. TIT 4.02.116
to the air | or dedicate his beauty to the /sun. ROM 1.01.153
o, she is rich in beauty, only poor | that, when 1.01.215
that, when she dies, with beauty dies her store. 1.01.216
for beauty starv'd with her severity | cuts 1.01.219
severity | cuts beauty off from all posterity. 1.01.220
what doth her beauty serve but as a note | where 1.01.235
beauty too rich for use, for earth too dear! 1.05. 47
for i ne'er saw true beauty till this night. 1.05. 53
juliet, | thy beauty hath made me effeminate, 3.01.114
and her beauty makes | this vault a feasting 5.03. 85
breath, | hath had no power yet upon thy beauty: 5.03. 93
i charm you, by my once commended beauty, | by JC 2.01.271
enough | if she unmask her beauty to the moon. HAM 1.03. 37
the beauty of the world! 2.02.307 P
should admit no discourse to your beauty. 3.01.107 P
could beauty, my lord, have better commerce than 3.01.108 P
for the power of beauty will sooner transform 3.01.110 P
honesty can translate beauty into his likeness. 3.01.112 P
than life, with grace, health, beauty, honor; LR 1.01. 58
infect her beauty, | you fen–suck'd fogs, drawn 2.04.166
tying her duty, beauty, wit, and fortunes | in OTH 1.01.135
signior, | if virtue no delighted beauty lack, 1.03.289
as having sense of beauty, do omit | their 2.01. 71
lest her body and beauty unprovide my mind again 4.01.205 P
he hath a daily beauty in his life | that makes 5.01. 19
let witchcraft join with beauty, lust with both, ANT 2.01. 22
whose beauty claims | no worse a husband than 2.02.127
if beauty, wisdom, modesty, can settle | the 2.02.240
her beauty and her brain go not together. CYM 1.02. 29 P
or let her beauty | look thorough a casement to 2.04. 33
let there be no honor | where there is beauty; 2.04.109
for beauty that made barren the swell'd boast 5.05.162
the beauty of this sinful dame | made many PER 1.ch. 31
i sought the purchase of a glorious beauty, 1.02. 72
which shows that beauty hath his power and will, 2.02. 34
as my giving out her beauty stirs up the lewdly 4.02.143 P
fair /one, all goodness that consists in beauty, 5.01. 70
she is all the beauty extant! TNK 2.02.147
what think you of this beauty? 2.02.153
yes, a matchless beauty. 2.02.154
lover, | and have as just a title to her beauty, 2.02.180
feed | upon the sweetness of a noble beauty, 2.03. 11
dearest beauty, | thus let me seal my vow'd 2.05. 38
and then to whom the birthright of this beauty 3.06. 31
treason | in service of so excellent a beauty, 3.06.162
if your vow stand, shall curse me and my beauty, 3.06.247
these the bright lamps of beauty, that command 4.02. 39
must be the sacrifice | to my unhappy beauty? 4.02. 64
you have steel'd 'em with your beauty. 4.02.149
at great feasts | sought to betray a beauty, but 5.01.103
which bred more beauty in his angry eyes: VEN 70
look in mine eyeballs, there thy beauty lies; 119
beauty within itself should not be wasted. 130
my beauty as the spring doth yearly grow, | my 141
dainties to taste, fresh beauty for the use, 164
spring from seeds and beauty breedeth beauty; 167
spring from seeds and beauty breedeth beauty; 167
would love | that inward beauty and invisible, 434
were beauty under twenty locks kept fast, | yet 575
beauty hath nought to do with such foul fiends. 638
of nature, | to mingle beauty with infirmities, 735
but in one minute's fight brings beauty under; 746
semblance he hath fed | upon fresh beauty, 796
mean | to stifle beauty and to steal his breath? 934
his breath and beauty set | gloss on the rose, 935
seeing his beauty, thou shouldst strike at it: 938
and that his beauty may the better thrive, 1011
for he being dead, with him is beauty slain, 1019
and, beauty dead, black chaos comes again. 1020
but true sweet beauty liv'd and died with him. 1080
and every beauty robb'd of his effect. 1132
honor and beauty, in the owner's arms, | are LUC 27
beauty itself doth of itself persuade | the eyes 29
within whose face beauty and virtue strived 52
virtue bragg'd, beauty would blush for shame; 54
when beauty boasted blushes, in despite | virtue 55
but beauty, in that white intituled | from 57
then virtue claims from beauty beauty's red, 59
in that high task hath done her beauty wrong, 80
all orators are dumb when beauty pleadeth, 268
desire my pilot is, beauty my prize, | then who 279
thy beauty hath ensnar'd thee to this night, 485
dead, | by thy bright beauty was it newly bred. 490
only he hath an eye to gaze on beauty, | and 496
that with my nails her beauty i may tear. 1472
that my poor beauty had purloin'd his eyes, 1651
torn, | and shiver'd all the beauty of my glass, 1763
never faith could hold, if not to beauty vowed: PP 5. 2
beauty is but a vain and doubtful good, | a 13. 1
so beauty blemish'd once, for ever lost, | in 13.11
beauty, truth, and rarity, | grace in all PHT 53
be, | beauty brag, but 'tis not she, | truth and 63
but 'tis not she, | truth and beauty buried be. 64
then being ask'd where all thy beauty lies, SON 2. 5
proving his beauty by succession thine! 2.12
thy unus'd beauty must be tomb'd with thee, 4.13
beauty o'ersnow'd and bareness every where: 5. 8
beauty's effect with beauty were bereft, | nor 5.11
age, | yet mortal looks adore his beauty still, 7. 7
that beauty still may live in thine or thee. 10.14
herein lives wisdom, beauty, and increase, 11. 5
then of thy beauty do i question make | that 12. 9
so should that beauty which you hold in lease 13. 5
art | as truth and beauty shall together thrive 14.11
if i could write the beauty of your eyes, | and 17. 5
muse | stirr'd by a painted beauty to his verse, 21. 2
for all that beauty that doth cover thee | is 22. 5
for whether beauty, birth, or wealth, or wit, 37. 5
thy beauty and thy years full well befits, | for 41. 3
and chide thy beauty and thy straying youth, 41.10
hers, by thy beauty tempting her to thee, 41.13
thee, | thine, by thy beauty being false to me. 41.14
on helen's cheek all art of beauty set, | and 53. 7
year, | the one doth shadow of your beauty show, 53.10
o, how much more doth beauty beauteous seem | by 54. 1
painting my age with beauty of thy days. 62.14
never cut from memory | my sweet love's beauty, 63.12
his beauty shall in these black lines be seen, 63.13
how with this rage shall beauty hold a plea, 65. 3
or who his spoil /of beauty can forbid? 65.12
why should poor beauty indirectly seek | roses 67. 7
when beauty liv'd and died as flowers do now, 68. 2
green, | robbing no old to dress his beauty new, 68.12
to show false art what beauty was of yore. 68.14
they look into the beauty of thy mind, | and 69. 9
the ornament of beauty is suspect, | a crow that 70. 3

beauty doth he give, | and found it in thy cheek 79.10
dumb, | for i impair not beauty being mute, 83.11
how like eve's apple doth thy beauty grow, | if 93.13
doth spot the beauty of thy budding name! 95. 3
for thy neglect of truth in beauty dy'd? 101. 2
both truth and beauty on my love depends; 101. 3
beauty no pencil, beauty's truth to lay; 101. 7
your eye i ey'd, | such seems your beauty still. 104. 3
ah, yet doth beauty, like a dial hand, | steal 104. 9
and beauty making beautiful old rhyme | in 106. 3
even such a beauty as you master now. 106. 8
tan sacred beauty, blunt the sharp'st intents, 115. 7
and beauty slander'd with a bastard shame, | for 127. 4
sweet beauty hath no name, no holy bow'r, | but 127. 7
at such who, not born fair, no beauty lack, 127.11
that every tongue says beauty should look so. 127.14
then will i swear beauty herself is black, | and 132.13
the statute of thy beauty thou wilt take, | thou 134. 9
they know what beauty is, see where it lies, 137. 3
it saw | the carcass of a beauty spent and done. LC 11
some beauty peep'd through lettice of sear'd age 14

BEAUTY'S 34 FR 0.0038 REL FR 33 V 1 P
stain'd | with grief (that's beauty's canker), TMP 1.02.416
and beauty's crest becomes the heavens well. LLL 4.03.252
of beauty's tutors have enrich'd you with? 4.03.320
sweet kate, embrace her for her beauty's sake. SHR 4.05. 34
true cuckold but calamity, so beauty's a flower. TN 1.05. 52 P
beauty's princely majesty is such, | 'confounds 1H6 5.03. 70
hath plac'd thy beauty's image and thy virtue. 3H6 3.03. 64
leaves and fruit maintain'd with beauty's sun, 3.03.126
these eyes could not endure that beauty's wrack; R3 1.02.127
and find delight writ there with beauty's pen; ROM 1.03. 82
beauty's ensign yet | is crimson in thy lips and 5.03. 94
sits here like beauty's child, whom nature gat PER 2.02. 6
then virtue claims from beauty beauty's red, LUC 59
argued by beauty's red and virtue's white; 65
had anatomiz'd | time's ruin, beauty's wrack, 1451
looks as none could look but beauty's queen. PP 4. 4
that thereby beauty's rose might never die, SON 1. 2
and dig deep trenches in thy beauty's field, 2. 2
how much more praise deserv'd thy beauty's use, 2. 9
thou spend | upon thyself thy beauty's legacy? 4. 2
beauty's effect with beauty were bereft, | nor 5.11
with beauty's treasure ere it be self–kill'd. 6. 4
but beauty's waste hath in the world an end, 9.11
thy end is truth's and beauty's doom and date. 14.14
allow | for beauty's pattern to succeeding men. 19.12
thy beauty's form in table of my heart; 24. 2
and delves the parallels in beauty's brow, 60.10
ere beauty's dead fleece made another gay: 68. 8
where beauty's veil doth cover every blot, | and 95.11
beauty no pencil, beauty's truth to lay; 101. 7
ere you were born was beauty's summer dead. 104.14
then, in the blazon of sweet beauty's best, | of 106. 5
or if it were, it bore not beauty's name; 127. 2
but now is black beauty's successive heir, | and 127. 3

BEAUTY–WANING 1 FR 0.0001 REL FR 1 V 0 P
sons, | a beauty–waning and distressed widow, R3 3.07.185

BEAVER 6 FR 0.0006 REL FR 6 V 0 P
i saw young harry with his beaver on, | his 1H4 4.01.104
and faintly through a rusty beaver peeps. H5 4.02. 44
i cleft his beaver with a downright blow. 3H6 1.01. 12
is my beaver easier than it was? R3 5.03. 50
me | i'll hide my silver beard in a gold beaver, TRO 1.03.296
o yes, my lord, he wore his beaver up. HAM 1.02.230

/BEAVERS 1 FR 0.0001 REL FR 1 V 0 P
/staves /in /charge, /their /beavers /down, 2H4 4.01.118

/BECAME 1 FR 0.0001 REL FR 1 V 0 P
/became /the /accents /of /the /valiant; 2H4 2.03. 25

BECAME 23 FR 0.0026 REL FR 18 V 5 P
whose whiteness so became them | as if but now TGV 3.01.229
there had she not been long but she became | a ERR 1.01. 49
at eighteen years became inquisitive | after his 1.01.125
what then became of them i cannot tell; 5.01.355
think the frenchman became his surety and seal'd MV 1.02. 82 P
of her nature became as a prey to her grief; AWW 4.03. 51 P
begin some speech, her eyes | became two spouts; WT 3.03. 26
jupiter | became a bull and bellow'd; 4.04. 28
pray you, became of antigonus, that carried 5.02. 59 P
what became of his bark and his followers? 5.02. 67 P
and, which became him like a prince indeed, | he 1H4 5.02. 60
became a bricklayer when he came to age. 2H6 4.02.145
since every jack became a gentleman, | there's R3 1.03. 71
following day | became the next day's master, H8 1.01. 17
in his life | became him like the leaving it. MAC 1.04. 8
our will became the servant to defect, | which 2.01. 18
of our ship, so i alone became their prisoner. HAM 4.06. 20 P
became his guide, | led him, begg'd for him, LR 5.03.191
it should be better he became her guest; ANT 2.02.221
minist'red, | and in 's spring became a harvest; CYM 1.01. 46
in hard voyages, became | the life o' th' need. 5.03. 44
what became of him | i further know not. 5.05.285
whether the horse by him became his deed, | or LC 111

BECAUSE *(also 'cause)*

/BECAUSE 2 FR 0.0002 REL FR 2 V 0 P
/because /a /bard /of /ireland /told /me /once R3 4.02.106
/because /that /like /a /jack /thou /keep'st 4.02.114

BECAUSE 197 FR 0.0222 REL FR 135 V 62 P
i think him so, because i think him so. TGV 1.02. 24
that's because the one is painted, and the other 2.01. 56 P
because love is blind. 2.01. 70 P
thee, | because thou seest me dote upon my love. 2.04.173
because thou hast not so much charity in thee as 2.05. 57 P
because myself do want my servants' fortune. 3.01.147
thou reach stars, because they shine on thee? 3.01.156
not for that neither, because i love crusts. 3.01.341 P
because we know, on valentine's report, | you 3.02. 57
indeed because you are a banish'd man, 4.01. 57
marry, mine host, because i cannot be merry. 4.02. 28 P
because methinks that she lov'd you as well | as 4.04. 79
because he loves her, he despiseth me; 4.04. 95
because i love him, i must pity him. 4.04. 96
sweet mistress' sake, because thou lov'st her. 4.04.177
had been one number more, because they say, WIV 4.01. 24 P
beam, because i know also life is a shuttle. 5.01. 22 P
find, we stoop and take't, | because we see it; MM 2.01. 25
because it is an open room and good for winter. 2.01.131 P
because he hath some offenses in him that thou 2.01.185 P
because authority, though it err like others, 2.02.134
in his house–eaves, because they are lecherous. 3.02.176 P
she is so hot, because the meat is cold: ERR 1.02. 47
the meat is cold, because you come not home: 1.02. 48
you come not home, because you have no stomach: 1.02. 49
because their business still lies out a' door. 2.01. 11
because that i familiarly sometimes | do use you 2.02. 26
because it is a blessing that he bestows on 2.02. 79 P
because i will not do them the wrong to mistrust ADO 1.01.242 P
may be i go under that title because i am merry. 2.01.205 P
sin upon purpose, because they would go thither; 2.01.259 P
because you talk of wooing, i will sing, | since 2.03. 49
because i have rail'd so long against marriage; 2.03.237 P
thou pretty, because little. LLL 1.02. 21 P
little pretty, because little. wherefore apt? 1.02. 22 P
and therefore apt, because quick. 1.02. 23 P
love her, because your heart cannot come by her; 3.01. 41 P
her, because your heart is in love with her; 3.01. 43 P
this swain, because of his great limb or joint, 5.01.127 P
because thou hast no face. 5.02.608 P
patience, | because it is a customary cross, MND 1.01.153
because in choice he is so oft beguil'd. 1.01.239
because that she as her attendant hath | a 2.01. 21
this wood, | because i cannot meet my hermia. 2.01.193
esteem, | because i am so dwarfish and so low? 3.02.295
because she is something lower than myself, 3.02.304
"bottom's dream," because it hath no bottom; 4.01.216 P
us say you are sad | because you are not merry; MV 1.01. 48
and say you are merry | because you are not sad. 1.01. 50
proof, | because what follows is pure innocence. 1.01.145
because i will not jump with common spirits, 2.09. 32
for me in heaven because i am a jew's daughter; 3.05. 33 P
and in slavish parts, | because you bought them. 4.01. 93
him for that, and do you love him because i do. AYL 1.03. 39 P
because that i am more than common tall, | that 1.03.115
is not so keen, | because thou art not seen, 2.07.178
the one sleeps easily because he cannot study, 3.02.321 P
other lives merrily because he feels no pain; 3.02.322 P
say you are, because i would be talking of her. 4.01. 89 P
abuses every one's eyes because his own are out, 4.01.214 P
because she brought stone jugs and no seal'd SHR in.2. 88
because i know you well and love you well, 1.01. 53
because she will not be annoy'd with suitors. 1.01.184
be lucentio, | because so well i love lucentio. 1.01.217
tranio, be so, because lucentio loves, | and let 1.01.218
her, how he beat me because her horse stumbled, 4.01. 77 P
lark, | because his feathers are more beautiful? 4.03.176
because his painted skin contents the eye? 4.03.178
before, because i would not fall out with thee. AWW 4.05. 57 P
because he's guilty, and he is not guilty. 5.03.289
because she will admit no kind of suit, | no, TN 1.02. 45
dost thou think, because thou art virtuous, 2.03.115 P
sir toby, because we'll be dress'd together. 5.01.204 P
not for because | your brows are blacker; WT 2.01. 7
of gambols, because they are not in't; 4.04.328 P
this other day, because i was no gentleman born. 5.02.129 P
because he hath a half–face like my father! JN 1.01. 92
but for because he hath not woo'd me yet: 2.01.588
i must pocket up these wrongs, | because — 3.01.201
bonds, | because my poor child is a prisoner. 3.04. 75
because that john hath made his peace with rome? 5.02. 96
we, | because we ever have been near the king. R2 2.02.134
because your lordship was proclaimed traitor. 2.03. 30
com'st thou because the anointed king is hence? 2.03. 96
because my power is weak and all ill left; 2.03.154
because we thought ourself thy lawful king; 3.03. 74
and for because the world is populous, | and 5.05. 3
because the king is certainly possess'd | of all 1H4 4.01. 40
good name, | because you are not of our quality, 4.03. 36
because some tell me that thou art a king. 5.03. 5
because the rest of the low countries have /made 2H4 2.02. 21 P
why, because you have been so lewd and so much 2.02. 62 P
because their legs are both of a bigness, and 'a 2.04.244 P
care, but rather, because i am unwilling, and, 3.02.224 P
because, look you, you do not love it, nor your H5 5.01. 24 P
because he could not speak english in the native 5.01. 75 P
because he hath not the gift to woo in other 5.02.154 P
gentle princess, because i love thee cruelly. 5.02.202 P
religion | because he is protector of the realm, 1H6 1.03. 66
it is because no one should sway but he, | no 3.01. 37
hearts, | because i ever found them as myself. 3.02. 98
because till now we never saw your face. 3.04. 24
which i have done, because, unworthily, | thou 4.01. 16
because, forsooth, the king of scots is crown'd. 4.01.157
thanks, | because this is in traffic of a king. 5.03.164
because you want the grace that others have, 5.04. 46
because she is a maid, | spare for no faggots, 5.04. 55
do, | because he is near kinsman unto charles. 5.05. 45
because the king, forsooth, will have it so. 2H6 1.03.115
because here is a man accused of treason. 1.03.177
french, | because in york this breeds suspicion; 1.03.206
because i wish'd this world's eternity. 2.04. 90
because i would not tax the needy commons, 3.01.116
over, | because his purpose is not executed. 3.01.256
because thy flinty heart, more hard than they, 3.02. 99
them in prison, and because they could not read, 4.07. 44 P
sweet is the country, because full of riches, 4.07. 62
because my book preferr'd me to the king; 4.07. 72
because the unconquer'd soul of cade is fled. 4.10. 64 P
run back and bite, because he was withheld, 5.01.152
i'll kill my horse, because i will not fly. 3H6 2.03. 24
because he would avoid such bitter taunts 2.06. 66
because in quarrel of the house of york | the 3.02. 6
that's soon perform'd, because i am a subject. 3.02. 54
because thy father henry did usurp, | and thou 3.03. 79
and shall have your will, because our king. 4.01. 17
'tis the more honor, because more dangerous. 4.03. 15
because my name is george. R3 1.01. 46
because i cannot flatter and look fair, | smile 1.03. 47
because i will be guiltless from the meaning. 1.04. 94
because sweet flow'rs are slow and weeds make 2.04. 15
because that i am little, like an ape, | he 3.01.130
because they have been still my adversaries; 3.02. 52
because, my lord, i would have had you heard 3.05. 56
because, my lord, you know my mother lives. 3.05. 94
boot, because both they | match'd not the high 4.04. 65
because they speak no english, thus they pray'd H8 1.04. 65
because all those things you have done of late 3.02.338
lord, because we have business of more moment, 5.02. 86
because she's kin to me, therefore she's not so TRO 1.01. 74 P
because not there. 1.01.106
because your speech hath none that tell him so? 2.02. 36
unrespective sieve, | because we now are full. 2.02. 72
courage of our minds, | because cassandra's mad. 2.02.122
bed, because it shall not speak of your pretty 3.02.208 P
"because thou canst not ease thy smart | by 4.04. 19
because i am the store–house and the shop | of COR 1.01.133
because you talk of pride now — will you not be 2.01. 25 P
because that now it lies you on to speak | to 3.02. 52
because they then less need one another. 4.05.231 P
wept, | because they died in honor's lofty bed. TIT 3.01. 11
perchance she weeps because they kill'd her 3.01.114
perchance because she knows them innocent. 3.01.115
because the law hath ta'en revenge on them. 3.01.117
and yet dear too, because i bought mine own. 3.01.199
because i would be sure to have all well, | to 5.03. 31
hand, | because she was enforc'd, stain'd, and 5.03. 38
because the girl should not survive her shame, 5.03. 41
because their breath with sweetmeats tainted are ROM 1.04. 76
to myself, | because it is an enemy to thee; 2.02. 56
no other reason but because thou hast hazel eyes 3.01. 20 P
because he hath waken'd thy dog that hath lain 3.01. 25 P
that is because the traitor murderer lives. 3.05. 84
because he married me before to romeo? 4.03. 27
because my heart itself plays "my heart is full. 4.05.106 P
marry, sir, because silver hath a sweet sound. 4.05.131 P
sound," because musicians sound for silver. 4.05.134 P
because musicians have no gold for sounding: 4.05.141 P
'tis yours, because you lik'd it. TIM 1.02.212
of me, because i have no power to be kind. 3.02. 54 P
'tis, then, because thou dost not keep a dog, 4.03.200
because thou art a woman, and disclaim'st 4.03.483
of stinking breath because caesar refus'd the JC 1.02.247 P
because i love you, i will let you know. 2.02. 74
because i knew the man, was slighted off. 4.03. 5
why, because 'a was mad. HAM 5.01.150 P
because they are not eight. LR 1.05. 37 P
because i would not see thy cruel nails | pluck 3.07. 56
that will not see | because he does not feel, 4.01. 69
because we come to do you service and you think OTH 1.01.109 P
not ours to–day, it is | because we brave her. ANT 4.04. 5
not fight with me because of the queen my mother CYM 2.01. 19 P
desert, because thine eye | presumes to reach, PER 1.01. 32
not | to ask the reason why, because we bid it. 1.01.157
it, | for who digs hills because they do aspire 1.04. 5
because he should have swallow'd me too, and 2.01. 39 P
because another | first sees the enemy, shall i TNK 2.02.193
and because you say | you are a horseman, i must 2.05. 44
thousand blossoms, | because they may be rotten? 3.06.244
because adonis' heart hath made mine hard." VEN 378
proud, | because the cry remaineth in one place, 885
some hedge, because he would not fear him; 1094
from thievish ears, because it is his own? LUC 35
because thou lov'st the one, and i the other. PP 8. 4
thou dost love her because thou know'st i love SON 42. 6
because he needs no praise, wilt thou be dumb? 101. 9
because i would not dull you with my song. 102.14

BECHANC'D 1 FR 0.0001 REL FR 1 V 0 P
that such a thing bechanc'd would make me sad? MV 1.01. 38

BECHANCE 2 FR 0.0002 REL FR 2 V 0 P
all happiness bechance to thee in milan. TGV 1.01. 61
let there bechance him pitiful mischances | to LUC 976

BECHANCED 1 FR 0.0001 REL FR 1 V 0 P
my sons, god knows what hath bechanced them; 3H6 1.04. 6

BECK 5 FR 0.0005 REL FR 4 V 1 P
on thee, | each in his office ready at thy beck. SHR in.2. 34
and they have troops of soldiers at their beck? 3H6 1.01. 68
more offenses at my beck than i have thoughts to HAM 3.01.124 P
thy beck might from the bidding of the gods ANT 3.11. 60
o, let me suffer (being at your beck) | th' SON 58. 5

BECK'D 1 FR 0.0001 REL FR 1 V 0 P
whose eye beck'd forth my wars and call'd them ANT 4.12. 26

BECKING 1 FR 0.0001 REL FR 1 V 0 P
and let us follow | the becking of our chance. TNK 1.02.116

BECK'NING 2 FR 0.0002 REL FR 2 V 0 P
mars | beck'ning with fiery truncheon my retire, TRO 5.03. 53
and with a beck'ning | informs the tapster to TNK 3.05.129

BECKON'D 1 FR 0.0001 REL FR 1 V 0 P
with one man beckon'd from the rest below, TIM 1.01. 74

/BECKONS 1 FR 0.0001 REL FR 0 V 1 P
iago /beckons me; now he begins the story. OTH 4.01.130 P

BECKONS 2 FR 0.0002 REL FR 2 V 0 P
he beckons with his hand and smiles on me, | as 1H6 1.04. 92
it beckons you to go away with it, | as if it HAM 1.04. 58

BECKS 2 FR 0.0002 REL FR 2 V 0 P
when gold and silver becks me to come on. JN 3.03. 13
serving of becks and jutting–out of bums! TIM 1.02.231

BECOM'D 2 FR 0.0002 REL FR 2 V 0 P
which might have well becom'd the best of men, ANT 3.07. 26
he would have well becom'd this place, and CYM 5.05.406

/BECOME 2 FR 0.0002 REL FR 2 V 0 P
/are /now /become /enamor'd /on /his /grave. 2H4 1.03.102
/beloved, | /if /all /could /so /become /it. LR 4.03. 24

BECOME 152 FR 0.0171 REL FR 114 V 38 P
it would become me | as well as it does you; TMP 3.01. 28
ay, lord, she will become thy bed, i warrant, 3.02.104
them, your affections | would become tender. 5.01. 19
that his issue | should become kings of naples? 5.01.206
he being her pupil, to become her tutor. TGV 2.01.138
thou that my master is become a notable lover? 2.05. 42 P
i tell thee, my master is become a hot lover. 2.05. 51 P
to be fantastic may become a youth | of greater 2.07. 47
will well become such sweet–complaining 3.02. 85
but since your falsehood shall become you well 4.02.129
face, | that now she is become as black as i. 4.04.156
dozen white louses do become an old coat well; WIV 1.01. 19 P
i will do as it shall become one that would do 1.01.233 P
shall i sir pandarus of troy become, | and by my 1.03. 75
my brows become nothing else, nor that well 3.03. 60 P
is dark, light and spirits will become it well. 5.02. 12 P
yokes | become the forest better than the town? 5.05.108
and what shall become of those in the city? MM 1.02. 97 P
what shall become of me? 1.02.105 P
become them with one half so good a grace | as 2.02. 62
this sensible warm motion to become | a kneaded 3.01.119

of his proceeding, it shall become him well; 3.02.256 P
become much more the better | for being a little 5.01.440
look sweet, speak fair, become disloyalty; ERR 3.02. 11
become the argument of his own scorn by falling ADO 2.03. 10 P
doth not my wit become me rarely? 3.04. 70 P
was such another, and now is he become a man. 3.04. 87 P
what shall become of this? what will this do? 4.01.209
for as it would ill become me to be vain, LLL 4.02. 30
antonio shall become bound — well. MV 1.03. 6 P
to become | the follower of so poor a gentleman. 2.02.147
parts that become thee happily enough | and in 2.02.182
become a christian and thy loving wife. 2.03. 21
love | as shall conveniently become you there." 2.08. 45
this favor | he presently become a christian; 4.01.387
the night | become the touches of sweet harmony. 5.01. 57
keep for me, | i will become as liberal as you, 5.01.226
me such exercises as may become a gentleman, or AYL 1.01. 72 P
to consider that tears do not become a man. 3.04. 3 P
a beggar, therefore to beg will not become me. ep 11 P
it shall become to serve all hopes conceiv'd, SHR 1.01. 15
did ever dian so become a grove | as kate this 2.01.258
as those two eyes become that heavenly face? 4.05. 32
'tis a hard bondage to become the wife | of a AWW 3.05. 64
for such disguise as haply shall become | the TN 1.02. 54
it shall become thee well to act my woes. 1.04. 26
what will become of this? 2.02. 36
thy smiles become thee well. 2.05.176 P
freedom at tray–trip, and become thy bond–slave? 2.05.191 P
am not tall enough to become the function well, 4.02. 6 P
what it please my lord, that shall become him. 5.01.116
fertile bosom, | and well become the agent; WT 1.02.114
you never spoke what did become you less | than 1.02.282
become some women best, so that there be not 2.01. 9
with such a kind of love as might become | a 3.02. 64
spring that might | become your time of day — 4.04.114
such receiving | as shall become your highness, 4.04.527
as if that joy were now become a loss, cries, "o 5.02. 51 P
now, in age, | is she become the suitor? 5.03.109
o, well did he become that lion's robe, | that JN 2.01.141
become thy great birth nor deserve a crown. 3.01. 50
of war | when he intendeth to become the field. 5.01. 55
to be a make–peace shall become my age. R2 1.01.160
for both hast thou, and both become the grave. 2.01.140
but what, a' god's name, doth become of this? 2.01.251
what is become of bushy? 3.02.123
shall ill become the flower of england's face, 3.03. 97
when triumph is become an alehouse guest? 5.01. 15
of the thieves, and so become a rare hangman. 1H4 1.02. 67 P
if i become not a cart as well as another man, a 2.04.496 P
and i care not if i do become your physician. 2H4 1.02.125 P
doth this become your place, your time, and 2.01. 66
master gower, if they become me not, he was a 2.01.191 P
what a maidenly man–at–arms are you become! 2.02. 77 P
such things become the hatch and brood of time, 3.01. 86
say my cousin william is become a good scholar. 3.02. 10 P
and now is this vice's dagger become a squire, 3.02.319 P
sherris, that he is become very hot and valiant. 4.03.122 P
sacred throne, | and make you long become it! H5 1.02. 8
bones, | ill–favoredly become the morning field. 4.02. 40
the sciences that should become our country, 5.02. 58
he doth, my lord, and is become your foe. 1H6 4.01. 65
o thou whose wounds become hard–favored death, 4.07. 23
you shall become true liegemen to his crown. 5.04.128
"first of the king: what shall of him become?" 2H6 1.04. 29
himself, | how insolent of late he is become, 3.01. 7
that head of thine doth not become a crown: 5.01. 96
where our right valiant father is become. 3H6 2.01. 10
now my soul's palace is become a prison; 2.01. 74
my love, | is, of a king, become a banish'd man, 3.03. 25
should not become my wife and england's queen. 4.01. 26
but, madam, where is warwick then become? 4.04. 25
is to become her husband and her father: R3 1.01.156
me too, | to see you are become so penitent. 1.02.220
my soul, | and to myself become an enemy. 2.02. 37
of time, | will well become the seat of majesty, 3.07.169
inter their bodies as become their births. 5.05. 15
and is become as black | as if besmear'd in hell H8 1.02.123
to hear what shall become | of the great duke of 2.01. 2
what will become of me now, wretched lady? 3.01.146
but i beseech you, what's become of katherine, 4.01. 22
lord, | become a churchman better than ambition; 5.02. 98
'twould not become him, his own's better. TRO 1.02. 91 P
you service, am become | as new into the world, 3.03. 11
what's become of the wenching rogues? 5.04. 33 P
this with our pikes, ere we become rakes; COR 1.01. 23 P
how honor would become such a person, that it 1.03. 10 P
what is become of martius? 1.04. 48
very priests must become mockers if they shall 2.01. 84 P
the wounds become him. 2.01.123 P
such as become a soldier | rather than envy you. 3.03. 56
what, is lavinia then become so loose, | or TIT 2.01. 65
with her continual tears | become a deluge, 3.01.229
thus it shall become | high–witted tamora to 4.04. 34
have got a humor there | does not become a man, TIM 1.02. 27
that answer might have become apemantus. 2.02.118 P
of athens is become a forest of beasts. 4.03.348 P
these words become your lips as they pass 5.01.195
and this man | is now become a god, and cassius JC 1.02.116
sound them, it doth become the mouth as well; 1.02.145
it would become me better than to close | in 3.01.202
so well thy words become thee as thy wounds, MAC 1.02. 43
i dare do all that may become a man; 1.07. 46
i must become a borrower of the night | for a 3.01. 26
fear) would well become | a woman's story at a 3.04. 63
to be tender–minded | does not become a sword. LR 5.03. 32
what ever shall become of michael cassio, | he's OTH 3.03. 8
and is become the bellows and the fan | to cool ANT 1.01. 9
low'ring, does become | the opposite of itself. 1.02.125
how this herculean roman does become | the 1.03. 84
and shall become you well, to entreat your 2.02. 2
for vildest things | become themselves in her, 2.02.238
dress, | which will become you both, farewell. 2.04. 5
and impatience does | become a dog that's mad. 4.15. 80
of more tenderness | than doth become a man. CYM 1.01. 95
satisfy me home, | what is become of her? 3.05. 93
and to become the geck and scorn | o' th' 5.04. 67
than a physician | would this report become? 5.05. 28
address'd, | will well become a soldier's dance. PER 2.03. 95
no visor does become black villainy | so well as 4.04. 44
could i persuade him to become a freeman, | he TNK 2.06. 24
nothing, | our business is become a nullity, 3.05. 54
what will become of 'em? 3.06.288
yet these that we count errors may become him: 4.02. 31
her mind and eye become the pranks and friskins 4.03. 80 P
all this shall become palamon, for palamon can 4.03. 86 P
and they themselves become | the executioners. 5.04.121
as striving who should best become her grief; VEN 968
make the young old, the old become a child. 1152
words, till action might become them better. LUC 1323
some one | become the public plague of many moe? 1479
as those two /mourning eyes become thy face. SON 132. 9

BECOMED 1 FR 0.0001 REL FR 1 V 0 P
cell, | and gave him what becomed love i might, ROM 4.02. 26

/BECOMES 2 FR 0.0002 REL FR 2 V 0 P
time the rod | /becomes more mock'd than fear'd; MM 1.03. 27
/the /innocent | /becomes /not /titus' /brother. TIT 3.02. 57

BECOMES 68 FR 0.0076 REL FR 58 V 10 P
beauty of the brow that becomes the ship–tire, WIV 3.03. 57 P
for all thy blessed youth | becomes as aged, and MM 3.01. 35
the deed so far, | that it becomes a virtue. 3.01.135
me, and to be merry best becomes you, for, out ADO 2.01.332 P
nothing becomes him ill that he would well. LLL 2.01. 46
and beauty's crest becomes the heavens well. 4.03.252
said | becomes a virtuous bachelor and a maid, MND 2.02. 59
skill, | reason becomes the marshal to my will, 2.02.120
it becomes | the throned monarch better than his MV 4.01.188
further offend you than becomes me for my good. AYL 1.01. 79 P
to see such a sight, it well becomes the ground. 3.02.243 P
he's proud — and yet his pride becomes him. 3.05.114
wait you on him, i charge you, as becomes, SHR 1.01.233
brought up as best becomes a gentlewoman. 1.02. 87
go with me to clothe you as becomes you. 4.02.121
katherine, that cap of yours becomes you not; 5.02.121
to you what further becomes his greatness, even AWW 3.06. 70 P
but it becomes /me well enough, does't not? TN 1.03.100 P
the office | becomes a woman best. WT 2.02. 30
to chide at your extremes it not becomes me. 4.04. 6
it becomes thy oath full well, | thou to me thy 4.04.300
his son a guest | that best becomes the table. 4.04.396
she shall be habited as it becomes | the partner 4.04.546
it becomes none but tradesmen, and they often 4.04.723 P
and it becomes | my marvel and my message. 5.01.187
becomes a sun and makes your son a shadow. JN 2.01.500
france friend with england, what becomes of me? 3.01. 35
snow, tumbled about, | anon becomes a mountain. 3.04.177
which is the birth, becomes excellent wit. 2H4 4.03.102 P
into revolt | when gold becomes her object! 4.05. 66
for, by my faith, it very well becomes you. 5.02. 50
how ill white hairs becomes a fool and jester! 5.05. 48
in peace there's nothing so becomes a man | as H5 3.01. 3
a name that in my thoughts becomes me best, | if 3.03. 6
this becomes the great. 3.05. 55
becomes it thee to taunt his valiant age, | and 1H6 3.02. 54
diamond safe | in golden palaces, as it becomes. 5.03.170
such commendations as becomes a maid, | a virgin 5.03.177
no more than well becomes | so good a quarrel 2H6 2.01. 27
becomes it thee to be thus bold in terms 3H6 2.02. 85
that king lewis | becomes your enemy, for 4.01. 30
than but once think his place becomes thee not. H8 5.02.168
i think his smiling becomes him better than any TRO 1.02.122 P
it more becomes a man | than gilt his trophy. COR 1.03. 39
this palt'ring | becomes not rome; 3.01. 59
but let us give him burial as becomes, | give TIT 1.01.347
law that threat'ned death becomes thy friend, ROM 3.03.139
and in the pulpit, as becomes a friend, | speak JC 3.01.229
o, how the wheel becomes it! HAM 4.05.172 P
too, for youth no less becomes | the light and 4.07. 78
such a sight as this | becomes the field, but 5.02.402
do you but mark how this becomes the house! LR 2.04.153
whom every thing becomes — to chide, to laugh, ANT 1.01. 49
say this becomes him | (as his composure must be 1.04. 21
or merry, | the violence of either thee becomes, 1.05. 60
thy angel | becomes a fear, as being o'erpow'r'd 2.03. 23
thy plainness, | it nothing ill becomes thee. 2.06. 79
his captain can | becomes his captain's captain; 3.01. 22
observe how antony becomes his flaw, | and what 3.12. 34
fare thee well, dame, what e'er becomes of me. 4.04. 29
which to shake off | becomes a warlike people, CYM 3.01. 52
though valor | becomes thee well enough. 4.02.156
how well this honest mirth becomes their labor! PER 2.01. 95
prepare for mirth, for mirth becomes a feast. 2.03. 7
melancholy | becomes him nobly. TNK 5.03. 50
and his full poise | becomes the rider's load. 5.04. 82
but that your trespass now becomes a fee, | mine SON 120.13
better becomes the grey cheeks of th' east, 132. 6

BECOME'T 1 FR 0.0001 REL FR 1 V 0 P
state | of that integrity which should become't; COR 3.01.159

BECOMING 8 FR 0.0009 REL FR 8 V 0 P
man, | within the limit of becoming mirth, | i LLL 2.01. 67
of like sorrow, | so fill'd, and so becoming; WT 3.03. 22
and becoming | the action of good women. H8 2.03. 54
a doubt | in such a time nothing becoming you, CYM 4.04. 15
fit you | with dignities becoming your estates. 5.05. 22
'ad been a kindness | becoming well thy /fact. PER 4.03. 12
yet so they mourn, becoming of their woe, | that SON 127.13
whence hast thou this becoming of things ill, 150. 5

BECOMINGS 1 FR 0.0001 REL FR 1 V 0 P
since my becomings kill me when they do not ANT 1.03. 96

BECOM'ST 2 FR 0.0002 REL FR 2 V 0 P
and joy that thou becom'st king henry's friend. 3H6 3.03.201
cytherea, | how bravely thou becom'st thy bed! CYM 2.02. 15

/BED 2 FR 0.0002 REL FR 2 V 0 P
and as a /bed i'll take /them, and there lie, ERR 3.02. 49
services are due, | /a fool usurps my /bed. LR 4.02. 28

BED 283 FR 0.0320 REL FR 226 V 57 P
three inches of it, | can lay to bed for ever; TMP 2.01.284
ay, lord, she will become thy bed, i warrant, 3.02.104
the union of your bed with weeds so loathly 4.01. 21
myself were mudded in that oozy bed | where my 5.01.151
my bosom as a bed | shall lodge thee till thy TGV 1.02.111
i was in love with my bed. 2.01. 81 P
this, | that presently you hie you home to bed. 4.02. 94
pay all, go to bed when she list, rise when she WIV 2.02.119 P
my bed shall be abus'd, my coffers ransack'd, my 2.02.292 P
contract | i got possession of julietta's bed. MM 1.02.146
and strip myself to death, as to a bed | that, 2.04.102
if for this night he entreat you to his bed, 3.01.263 P
her brother's ghost his paved bed would break, 5.01.435
so he would keep fair quarter with his bed! ERR 2.01.108
then fair league and truce with thy true bed, 2.02.145
'tis double wrong, to truant with your bed, 3.02. 17
of mine, | nor to her bed no homage do i owe: 3.02. 43
that thinks a man always going to bed and says, 4.03. 32 P
in bed he slept not for my urging it; 5.01. 63
when thou didst make him master of thy bed, | to 5.01.163
deserve as full as fortunate a bed | as ever ADO 3.01. 45
and bid those that are drunk get them to bed. 3.03. 43 P
the church–bench till two, and then all to bed. 3.03. 90 P
she knows the heat of a luxurious bed; 4.01. 41
hence — | i have forsworn his bed and company. MND 2.01. 62
you come | to give their bed joy and prosperity. 2.01. 73
find you out a bed; 2.02. 39
one heart, one bed, two bosoms, and one troth. 2.02. 42
here is my bed; 2.02. 64
what angel wakes me from my flow'ry bed? 3.01.129
eyes, | to have my love to bed and to arise; 3.01.171
me | to measure out my length on this cold bed. 3.02.429
come sit thee down upon this flow'ry bed, 4.01. 1
wait in your royal walks, your board, your bed! 5.01. 31
lovers, to bed, 'tis almost fairy time. 5.01.364
sweet friends, to bed. 5.01.368
but here an angel in a golden bed | lies all MV 2.07. 58
take what wife you will to bed, | i will ever be 2.09. 70
again, | no bed shall e'er be guilty of my stay, 3.02.326
i will ne'er come in your bed | until i see the 5.01.190
i have, | no, not my body nor my husband's bed. 5.01.228
or go to bed now, being two hours to day. 5.01.303
they found the bed untreasur'd of their mistress AYL 2.02. 7
you | than without candle may go dark to bed — 3.05. 39
your wive's wit going to your neighbor's bed. 4.01.169 P
juno's crown, | o blessed bond of board and bed! 5.04.142
you to a long and well–deserved bed; 5.04.190
go to thy cold bed, and warm thee. SHR in.1. 10 P
this were a bed but cold to sleep so soundly. in.1. 33
what think you, if he were convey'd to bed, in.1. 37
fingers, | a most delicious banquet by his bed, in.1. 39
take him up gently and to bed with him, | and in.1. 72
softer and sweeter than the lustful bed | on in.2. 38
being all this time abandon'd from your bed. in.2. 115
madam, undress you and come now to bed. in.2. 117
that i should yet absent me from your bed. in.2. 123
wed her, and bed her, and rid the house of her! 1.01.144 P
marry, so i mean, sweet katherine, in thy bed; 2.01.267
fault | i'll find about the making of the bed, 4.01.200
come, kate, we'll to bed. 5.02.184
on 's bed of death | many receipts he gave me; AWW 2.01.104
vows, and in your bed | find fairer fortune, if 2.03. 91
know'st she has rais'd me from my sickly bed. 2.03.111
priest i have sworn, | i will not bed her. 2.03.270
i'll to the tuscan wars, and never bed her. 2.03.273
when you have conquer'd my yet maiden bed, 4.02. 57
finger, | unless she gave it to yourself in bed, 5.03.110
prove that i husbanded her bed in florence, 5.03.126
at that time that i knew of their going to bed, 5.03.263 P
he knows himself my bed he hath defil'd, | and 5.03.300
to be up after midnight and to go to bed then, TN 2.03. 7 P
so that to go to bed after midnight is to go to 2.03. 8 P
bed after midnight is to go to bed betimes. 2.03. 9 P
i have wit enough to lie straight in my bed. 2.03.137 P
for this night, to bed, and dream on the event. 2.03.175 P
let's to bed, knight. 2.03.182 P
burn some sack, 'tis too late to go to bed now. 2.03.191 P
were big enough for the bed of ware in england, 3.02. 47 P
wilt thou go to bed, malvolio? 3.04. 29 P
to bed? ay, sweet heart, and i'll come to thee. 3.04. 30 P
get him to bed, and let his hurt be look'd to. 5.01.208 P
a fellow of the royal bed, which owe | a moi'ty WT 3.02. 38
that goes to bed wi' th' sun | and with him 4.04.105
when you are going to bed? 4.04.245 P
wife was brought to bed of twenty money–bags at 4.04.263 P
yea, | to die upon the bed my father died, | to 4.04.455
habited as it becomes | the partner of your bed. 4.04.547
to bless the bed of majesty again | with a sweet 5.01. 33
to make room for him in my husband's bed. JN 1.01.255
my bed was ever to thy son as true | as thine 2.01.124
shall gild her bridal bed and make her rich | in 2.01.491
lies in his bed, walks up and down with me, 3.04. 94
that bed, that womb, | that mettle, that self R2 1.02. 22
convey me to my bed, then to my grave; 2.01.137
and him, | broke the possession of a royal bed, 3.01. 13
suspect | that i have been disloyal to thy bed, 5.02.105
time enough to go to bed with a candle, i 1H4 2.01. 43 P
been | a banish'd woman from my harry's bed? 2.03. 39
what doth gravity out of his bed at midnight? 2.04.294 P
to the welsh lady's bed. 3.01.242 P
i prithee tell me, doth he keep his bed? 4.01. 21
come, it grows late, we'll to bed. 2H4 2.04.276 P
please it your grace | to go to bed. 3.01. 99
treason's true bed and yielder–up of breath. 4.02.123
come hither, harry, sit thou by my bed, | and 4.05.181
come, cousin silence — and then to bed. 5.03. 4 P
carry master silence to bed. 5.03.129 P
he is very sick, and would to bed. H5 2.01. 83 P
i put my hand into the bed and felt them, and 2.03. 23 P
in the wars do as every sick man in his bed, 4.01.179 P
not all these, laid in bed majestical, | can 4.01.267
which troubles oft the bed of blessed marriage, 5.02.364
and if i did but stir out of my bed, | ready 1H6 1.04. 55
affects, | must be companion of his nuptial bed. 5.05. 58
nobility, | i banish her my bed and company, 2H6 2.01.193
have you laid fair the bed? 3.02. 11
dead in his bed, my lord; gloucester is dead. 3.02. 29
thy mother took into her blameful bed | some 3.02.212
died he not in his bed? 3.03. 9
you were best to go to bed and dream again, | to 5.01.196
both from thy table, henry, and thy bed, | until 3H6 1.01.248
but when he took a beggar to his bed, | and 2.02.154
golden cup, | his body couched in a curious bed, 2.05. 53
what, will he not to bed? 4.03. 3
sun, | ere he attain his easeful western bed: 5.03. 6
will not fight for such a hope | go home to bed, 5.04. 56

in his bed? R3 1.01.142
prince | and made her widow to a woeful bed? 1.02.248
by her, in his unlawful bed, he got | this 3.07.190
o my accursed womb, the bed of death! 4.01. 53
and, when thou wed'st, let sorrow haunt thy bed; 4.01. 73
for never yet one hour in his bed | did i enjoy 4.01. 82
slander myself as false to edward's bed, | throw 4.04.208
and lead thy daughter to a conqueror's bed; 4.04.334
alas, h'as banish'd me his bed already, | his H8 3.01.119
so went to bed; 4.02. 24
i must to bed, | call in more women. 4.02.166
i must to him too, | before he go to bed. 5.01. 9
prithee to bed, and in thy pray'rs remember 5.01. 73
her bed is india, there she lies, a pearl; TRO 1.01.100
him patroclus | upon a lazy bed the livelong day 1.03.147
the large achilles, on his press'd bed lolling, 1.03.162
whereupon i will show you a chamber, which bed, 3.02.208 P
cupid grant all tongue-tied maidens here | bed, 3.02.211
to bed, to bed. 4.02. 4
to bed, to bed. 4.02. 4
i prithee now, to bed. 4.02. 7
thy master now lies thinking on his bed | of 5.02. 78
pleas'd with this dainty bait, thus goes to bed. 5.08. 20
embracements of his bed where he would show most
COR 1.03. 5 P
whose hours, whose bed, whose meal and exercise 4.04. 14
and triumphs over chance in honor's bed. TIT 1.01.178
wept, | because they died in honor's lofty bed. 3.01. 11
that left the camp to sin in lucrece' bed? 4.01. 64
his wife but yesternight was brought to bed; 4.02.153
to draw | the shady curtains from aurora's bed, ROM 1.01.136
in bed asleep, while they do dream things true. 1.04. 52
come on, then let's to bed. 1.05.125
and, on my life, hath stol'n him home to bed. 2.01. 4
head | so soon to bid good morrow to thy bed. 2.03. 34
our romeo hath not been in bed to-night. 2.03. 42
he made you for a highway to my bed, | but i, a 3.02.134
and now falls on her bed, and then starts up, 3.03.100
lady, | and bid her hasten all the house to bed, 3.03.156
wife, go you to her ere you go to bed, 3.04. 15
go you to juliet ere you go to bed; 3.04. 31
make the bridal bed | in that dim monument where 3.05.200
take thou this vial, being then in bed, | and 4.01. 93
the morning comes | to rouse thee from thy bed, 4.01.108
i'll not to bed to-night; 4.02. 42
get thee to bed and rest, for thou hast need. 4.03. 13
go, you cot-quean, go, | get you to bed. 4.04. 7
ay, let the county take you in your bed, | he'll 4.05. 10
flower, with flowers thy bridal bed i strew — 5.03. 12
why i descend into this bed of death | is partly 5.03. 28
maid, to thy master's bed, | thy mistress is o' TIM 4.01. 12
thou bright defiler | of hymen's purest bed! 4.03.383
sure | it did not lie there when i went to bed. JC 2.01. 38
get you to bed again, it is not day. 2.01. 39
betimes, | and every man hence to his idle bed; 2.01.117
y' have ungently, brutus, | stole from my bed; 2.01.238
why, so i do. good portia, go to bed. 2.01.260
and will he steal out of his wholesome bed | to 2.01.264
to keep with you at meals, comfort your bed, 2.01.284
hath made his pendant bed and procreant cradle. MAC 1.06. 8
get thee to bed. 2.01. 32
was it so late, friend, ere you went to bed, 2.03. 22
i have seen her rise from her bed, throw her 5.01. 5 P
it, afterwards seal it, and again return to bed; 5.01. 8 P
to bed, to bed; 5.01. 66 P
to bed, to bed; 5.01. 66 P
to bed, to bed, to bed. 5.01. 68 P
to bed, to bed, to bed. 5.01. 68 P
to bed, to bed, to bed. 5.01. 68 P
will she go now to bed? 5.01. 69 P
get thee to bed, francisco. HAM 1.01. 7
will /sate itself in a celestial bed | and prey 1.05. 56
let not the royal bed of denmark be | a couch 1.05. 82
dead, | when second husband kisses me in bed. 3.02.185
speak with you in her closet ere you go to bed. 3.02.332 P
liege, | i'll call upon you ere you go to bed, 3.03. 34
or in th' incestious pleasure of his bed, | at 3.03. 90
to live | in the rank sweat of an enseamed bed, 3.04. 92
good night, but go not to my uncle's bed — 3.04.159
let the bloat king tempt you again to bed, 3.04.182
sun, | and thou hadst not come to my bed.'" 4.05. 66
her cradle ere she had a husband for her bed. LR 1.01. 16 P
than doth, within a dull, stale, tired bed, | go 1.02. 13
i beg | that you'll vouchsafe me raiment, bed, 2.04.156
if he ask for me, i am ill and gone to bed. 3.03. 17 P
go to thy bed, and warm thee. 3.04. 48 P
and i'll go to bed at noon. 3.06. 85 P
then am i the prisoner, and his bed my jail; 4.06.266 P
hath rais'd me from my bed, nor doth the general OTH 1.03. 54
/couch of war | my thrice-driven bed of down. 1.03.231
why, go to bed and sleep. 1.03.304 P
you rise to play, and go to bed to work. 2.01.115
like bride and groom | devesting them for bed; 2.03.181
come away to bed. 2.03.253
his bed shall seem a school, his board a shrift, 3.03. 24
or to be naked with her friend in bed | an hour, 4.01. 3
naked in bed, iago, and not mean harm? 4.01. 5
strangle her in her bed, even the bed she hath 4.01.207 P
in her bed, even the bed she hath contaminated. 4.01.208 P
to-night | lay on my bed my wedding-sheets — 4.02.105
get you to bed on th' instant, i will be 4.03. 7 P
and hath commanded me to go to bed, | and bid me 4.03. 13
i have laid those sheets you bade me on the bed. 4.03. 22
thy bed, lust-stain'd, shall with lust's blood 5.01. 36
will you come to bed, my lord? 5.02. 24
my mistress here lies murthered in her bed — 5.02.185
look on the tragic loading of this bed; 5.02.363
our fortunes to-night, shall be — drunk to bed. ANT 1.02. 46 P
is not | amiss to tumble on the bed of ptolomy, 1.04. 17
she made great caesar lay his sword to bed; 2.02.227
ere the ninth hour, i drunk him to his bed; 2.05. 21
for the best turn i' th' bed. 2.05. 59
my death, and run into't | as to a lover's bed. 4.14.101
take up her bed, | and bear her women from the 5.02.356
more noble than that runagate to your bed, | and CYM 1.06.137
to bed. 2.02. 4
cytherea, | how bravely thou becom'st thy bed! 2.02. 15
such | th' adornment of her bed; 2.02. 26
apparent | that you have tasted her in bed, my 2.04. 57
pisanio, hath play'd the strumpet in my bed; 3.04. 22 P
false to his bed? 3.04. 40
that's false to 's bed? 3.04. 44
do't, and to bed then. 3.04.100
nights together | have made the ground my bed. 3.06. 3
if he be gone, he'll make his grave a bed. 4.02.216
for nature doth abhor to make his bed | with the 4.02.357
my queen | upon a desperate bed, and in a time 4.03. 6
that is my bed too, lads, and there i'll lie. 4.04. 52
and a hangman to help him to bed, i think he 5.04.174 P
in suit the place of 's bed and win this ring 5.05.185
flesh | by the defiling of her parent's bed; PER 1.01.131
shed | to keep his bed of blackness unlaid ope, 1.02. 89
then with what haste you can, get you to bed. 2.05. 93
hymen hath brought the bride to bed, | where, by 3.ch. 9
and he went to bed to her very description. 4.02.100 P
whom jove hath mark'd | the honor of your bed, TNK 1.01. 30
who made too proud the bed, took leave o' th' 1.03. 52
we'll to bed then. 5.02. 86
making my arms his field, his tent my bed. VEN 108
"who sees his true-love in her naked bed, 397
"here was thy father's bed, here in my breast; 1183
for then is tarquin brought unto his bed, LUC 120
and now this lustful lord leapt from his bed, 169
led, | the roman lord marcheth to lucrece' bed. 301
stalks, | and gazeth on her yet unstained bed. 366
in his clear bed might have reposed still! 382
without the bed her other fair hand was, | on 393
way, | for in thy bed i purpose to destroy thee. 514
both, | that to his borrowed bed he make retire, 573
thee | unto the base bed of some rascal groom, 671
o that prone lust should stain so pure a bed! 684
climb | his wonted height, yet ere he go to bed, 776
bred, | not spend the dowry of a lawful bed. 938
afflict him in his bed with bedred groans; 975
in the interest of thy bed | a stranger came, 1619
were kisses all the joys in bed, | one woman PP 18.47
there will i make thee a bed of roses, | with a 19. 9
weary with toil, i haste me to my bed, | the SON 27. 1

BEDABBLED 1 FR 0.0001 REL FR 1 V 0 P
bedabbled with the dew and torn with briers, | i MND 3.02.443

BEDASH'D 1 FR 0.0001 REL FR 1 V 0 P
their cheeks | like trees bedash'd with rain — R3 1.02.163

BEDAUB'D 1 FR 0.0001 REL FR 1 V 0 P
pale, pale as ashes, all bedaub'd in blood, ROM 3.02. 55

BEDAZZLED 1 FR 0.0001 REL FR 1 V 0 P
that have been so bedazzled with the sun, | that SHR 4.05. 46

BEDCHAMBER 7 FR 0.0008 REL FR 7 V 0 P
your bedchamber. R3 1.02.111
to his own hand, in 's bedchamber. H8 3.02. 77
their mother's bedchamber should not be safe TIT 4.01.108
breeds him and makes him of his bedchamber, CYM 1.01. 42
in them, i will keep them | in my bedchamber. 1.06.196
first, her bedchamber | (where i confess i slept 2.04. 66
in his bedchamber to be barr'd of rest. VEN 784

BED-CLOTHES 1 FR 0.0001 REL FR 0 V 1 P
little harm, save to his bed-clothes about him; AWW 4.03.257 P

BEDDED 3 FR 0.0003 REL FR 2 V 1 P
therefore my son i' th' ooze is bedded; TMP 3.03.100
i have wedded her, not bedded her, and sworn to AWW 3.02. 21 P
your bedded hair, like life in excrements, HAM 3.04.121

BEDE 1 FR 0.0001 REL FR 1 V 0 P
where's bede? WIV 5.05. 49

BEDECK 1 FR 0.0001 REL FR 1 V 0 P
true use indeed | which should bedeck thy shape, ROM 3.03.125

BEDECKING 1 FR 0.0001 REL FR 1 V 0 P
with such bedecking ornaments of praise? LLL 2.01. 79

BEDEW 3 FR 0.0003 REL FR 3 V 0 P
and bedew | her pasters' grass with faithful R2 3.03. 99
let all the tears that should bedew my hearse 2H4 4.05.113
wherewith you now bedew king henry's hearse, | i 1H6 1.01.104

BEDFELLOW 13 FR 0.0014 REL FR 11 V 2 P
lady, were you her bedfellow last night? ADO 4.01.147
i have this twelvemonth been her bedfellow. 4.01.149
own, | i'll have that doctor for /my bedfellow. MV 5.01.233
sweet doctor, you shall be my bedfellow — 5.01.284
stars | allots thee for his lovely bedfellow! SHR 4.05. 41
and how doth my cousin, your bedfellow? 2H4 3.02. 5 P
his pillow, | being so troublesome a bedfellow? 4.05. 22
nay, but the man that was his bedfellow, | whom H5 2.02. 8
an able man to leave | so sweet a bedfellow? H8 2.02.142
people, | but tie him not to be their bedfellow. COR 2.02. 65
go, you wild bedfellow, you cannot soothsay. ANT 1.02. 51 P
no bedfellow! CYM 4.02.295
thither frame | to seek her as a bedfellow, | in PER 1.ch. 33

BEDFELLOWS 3 FR 0.0003 REL FR 2 V 1 P
misery acquaints a man with strange bedfellows; TMP 2.02. 40 P
which now, two tender bedfellows for dust, | thy R3 4.04.385
manly courage | are bedfellows in his visage. TNK 5.03. 44

BEDFORD 10 FR 0.0011 REL FR 10 V 0 P
good morrow, brother bedford. H5 4.01. 3
then, joyfully, my noble lord of bedford, | my 4.03. 8
words, | harry the king, bedford and exeter, 4.03. 53
bedford, if thou be slack, i'll fight it out. 1H6 1.01. 99
the earl of bedford had a prisoner | call'd the 1.04. 27
dying prince, | the valiant duke of bedford. 3.02. 87
courageous bedford, let us now persuade you. 3.02. 93
heavens keep old bedford safe! 3.02.100
the noble duke of bedford late deceas'd, | but 3.02.132
and did my brother bedford toil his wits, | to 2H6 1.01. 83

BEDFORD'S 1 FR 0.0001 REL FR 1 V 0 P
shall henry's conquest, bedford's vigilance, 2H6 1.01. 96

BED-HANGERS 1 FR 0.0001 REL FR 0 V 1 P
worth a thousand of these bed-hangers and these 2H4 2.01.146 P

BEDIMM'D 1 FR 0.0001 REL FR 1 V 0 P
ye be) i have bedimm'd | the noontide sun, TMP 5.01. 41

/BEDLAM 1 FR 0.0001 REL FR 1 V 0 P
/and /get /the /bedlam | /to /lead /him /where LR 3.07.103

BEDLAM 7 FR 0.0008 REL FR 6 V 1 P
bedlam, have done. JN 2.01.183
ha, art thou bedlam? H5 5.01. 19
did instigate the bedlam brain-sick duchess | by 2H6 3.01. 51
to bedlam with him! 5.01.131
a bedlam and ambitious humor | makes him oppose 5.01.132
melancholy, with a sigh like tom o' bedlam. LR 1.02.136 P
me proof and president | of bedlam beggars, who, 2.03. 14

BED-MATE 1 FR 0.0001 REL FR 1 V 0 P
business | should rob my bed-mate of my company.
TRO 4.01. 6

BED-PRESSER 1 FR 0.0001 REL FR 0 V 1 P
this sanguine coward, this bed-presser, this 1H4 2.04.242 P

BEDRED *(also bed-rid)*

BEDRED 3 FR 0.0003 REL FR 3 V 0 P
to her decrepit, sick, and bedred father; LLL 1.01.138
who, impotent and bedred, scarcely hears | of HAM 1.02. 29
afflict him in his bed with bedred groans; LUC 975

BEDRENCH 1 FR 0.0001 REL FR 1 V 0 P
such crimson tempest should bedrench | the fresh R2 3.03. 46

BED-RID *(also bedred)*

BED-RID 1 FR 0.0001 REL FR 1 V 0 P
lies he not bed-rid? WT 4.04.401

BED-RIGHT 1 FR 0.0001 REL FR 1 V 0 P
that no bed-right shall be paid | till hymen's TMP 4.01. 96

BED-ROOM 1 FR 0.0001 REL FR 1 V 0 P
then by your side no bed-room me deny; MND 2.02. 51

BEDS' 1 FR 0.0001 REL FR 1 V 0 P
robb'd others' beds' revenues of their rents. SON 142. 8

BEDS *(also peds)*

BEDS 28 FR 0.0031 REL FR 25 V 3 P
dress meat and drink, make the beds, and do all WIV 1.04. 97 P
rest, | but seek the weary beds of people sick. LLL 5.02.822
i | upon faint primrose beds were wont to lie, MND 1.01.215
burial, | already to their wormy beds are gone. 3.02.384
let their beds | be made as soft as yours, and MV 4.01. 95
away before me to sweet beds of flow'rs, TN 1.01. 39
but when i came unto my beds, | with hey ho, etc 5.01.401
by this time from their fixed beds of lime | had JN 2.01.219
rescue those breathing lives to die in beds, 2.01.419
and send the hearers weeping to their beds. R2 5.01. 45
li'st thou with the vile | in loathsome beds, 2H4 3.01. 16
when others sleep upon their quiet beds, 1H6 2.01. 6
'twas time, i trow, to wake and leave our beds, 2.01. 41
rous'd on the sudden from their drowsy beds, 2.02. 23
by bloody hands, in sleeping on your beds! 5.03. 41
down thy youth | in different beds of lust, and TIM 4.03.257
their sleep who have died holily in their beds. MAC 5.01. 61 P
trick of fame | go to their graves like beds, HAM 4.04. 62
in your huswifery, and huswives in your beds. OTH 2.01.112
that nightly lie in those unproper beds | which 4.01. 68
the beds i' th' east are soft, and thanks to you ANT 2.06. 50
nightingale, | we have beat them to their beds. 4.08. 19
strange he hides him in fresh cups, soft beds, CYM 5.03. 71
since they love men in arms as well as beds. PER 2.03. 98
not so awake the beds of eels as my giving out 4.02.143 P
duke, think | what beds our slain kings have! TNK 1.01.140
what griefs our beds, | that our dear lords have 1.01.140
that from their dark beds once more leap her VEN 1050

BED-SWERVER 1 FR 0.0001 REL FR 1 V 0 P
that she's | a bed-swerver, even as bad as those WT 2.01. 93

BED-TIME 3 FR 0.0003 REL FR 2 V 1 P
mart, | and afterward consort you till bed-time: ERR 1.02. 28
hours | between /our after-supper and bed-time? MND 5.01. 34
i would 'twere bed-time, hal, and all well. 1H4 5.01.125 P

BED-VOW 1 FR 0.0001 REL FR 1 V 0 P
in act thy bed-vow broke, and new faith torn SON 152. 3

BEDWARD 1 FR 0.0001 REL FR 1 V 0 P
day was done | and tapers burnt to bedward! COR 1.06. 32

BED-WORK 1 FR 0.0001 REL FR 1 V 0 P
they call this bed-work, mapp'ry, closet-war, TRO 1.03.205

BEE 7 FR 0.0008 REL FR 5 V 2 P
where the bee sucks, there suck i, | in a TMP 5.01. 88
'tis seldom when the bee doth leave her comb 2H4 4.04. 79
when, like the bee, tolling from every flower 4.05. 74
some say the bee stings, but i say, 'tis the 2H6 4.02. 81 P
of these drones, that rob the bee of her honey. PER 2.01. 47 P
my honey lost, and i, a drone-like bee, | have LUC 836
and suck'd the honey which thy chaste bee kept. 840

BEECH 1 FR 0.0001 REL FR 1 V 0 P
went a-hunting, and a wood, | and a broad beech;
TNK 3.03. 41

BEEF 12 FR 0.0013 REL FR 4 V 8 P
sir, she hath eaten up all her beef, and she is MM 3.02. 56 P
me any conserves, give me conserves of beef. SHR in.2. 8 P
what say you to a piece of beef and mustard? 4.03. 23
why then the beef, and let the mustard rest. 4.03. 26
mustard, | or else you get no beef of grumio. 4.03. 28
why then the mustard without the beef. 4.03. 30
i am a great eater of beef and i believe that TN 1.03. 85 P
o, my sweet beef, i must still be good angel to 1H4 3.03.177 P
them great meals of beef and iron and steel, H5 3.07.150 P
ay, but these english are shrowdly out of beef. 3.07.152 P
clown in chines of beef ere thou sleep in thy 2H6 4.10. 57 P
a bushel, and beef at four nobles a stone, list STM II.C 3 P

BEEFS 2 FR 0.0002 REL FR 1 V 1 P
neither, | as flesh of muttons, beefs, or goats. MV 1.03.167
for him, a court, and now has he land and beefs! 2H4 3.02.328 P

BEEF-WITTED 1 FR 0.0001 REL FR 0 V 1 P
greece upon thee, thou mongrel beef-witted lord!
TRO 2.01. 13 P

BEEHIVES 1 FR 0.0001 REL FR 1 V 0 P
drones suck not eagles' blood, but rob beehives. 2H6 4.01.109

BEELZEBUB *(see belzebub)*

BEEN *(also bin)*

/BEEN 7 FR 0.0008 REL FR 3 V 4 P
/i /thought /you /had /been /willing /to /resign R2 4.01.190
/if /your /father /had /been /victor /there, 2H4 4.01.132
/there /has /been /much /to /do /on /both /sides HAM 2.02.352 P
/o, /there /has /been /much /throwing /about /of 2.02.358 P
/how /long /have /you /been /a /sectary LR 1.02.150 P
/five /fiends /have /been /in /poor /tom /at 4.01. 59 P
/am /doubtful /that /you /have /been /conjunct 5.01. 12

BEEN 745 FR 0.0842 REL FR 524 V 221 P
had i been any god of power, i would | have sunk TMP 1.02. 10
once in a month recount what thou hast been, 1.02.262
would't had been done! 1.02.349
for it hath been said, "as proper a man as ever 2.02. 60 P
trifle to abuse me | (as late i have been), i 5.01.113
you have | been justled from your senses, know 5.01.158
i have been in such a pickle since i saw you 5.01.282 P
i should have been a sore one then. 5.01.289 P
that | whereon this month i have been hammering.
TGV 1.03. 18
how long hath she been deform'd? 2.01. 64 P
and though myself have been an idle truant, 2.04. 64
should i have wish'd a thing, it had been he. 2.04. 82

should have been cherish'd by her child–like 3.01. 75
this discipline shows thou hast been in love. 3.02. 87
me happy, | or else i often had been miserable. 4.01. 35
already have i been false to valentine, | and 4.02. 1
she bids me think how i have been forsworn | in 4.02. 10
but it hath been the longest night | that e'er i 4.02.139
he did, i think verily he had been hang'd for't; 4.04. 15 P
he had not been there (bless the mark!) 4.04. 18 P
i, having been acquainted with the smell before, 4.04. 23 P
he hath stol'n, otherwise he had been executed; 4.04. 31 P
where have you been these two days loitering? 4.04. 44
she hath been fairer, madam, than she is: 4.04.149
as if the garment had been made for me; 4.04.163
had i been seized by a hungry lion, | i would 5.04. 33
i would have been a breakfast to the beast 5.04. 34
how now, simple, where have you been? WIV 1.01.200 P
the young man, he would have been horn–mad. 1.04. 50 P
if he had been throughly mov'd, you should have 1.04. 90 P
why, he hath not been thrice in my company! 2.01. 26 P
i have been content, sir, you should lay my 2.02. 5 P
yet there has been knights, and lords, and 2.02. 63 P
of them all, and yet there has been earls, nay 2.02. 76 P
and you have been a man long known to me, though 2.02.181 P
which hath been on the wing of all occasions. 2.02.201 P
shallow, you have yourself been a great fighter, 2.03. 42 P
little jack–a–lent, have you been true to us? 3.03. 27 P
i had been drown'd, but that the shore was 3.05. 14 P
what a thing should i have been when i had been 3.05. 17 P
should i have been when i had been swell'd! 3.05. 17 P
i should have been a mountain of mummy. 3.05. 18 P
be thrown into etna, as i have been into thames, 3.05.127 P
truly, i thought there had been one number more, 4.01. 23 P
you say he has been thrown in the rivers, and 4.04. 20 P
and has been grievously peaten as an old oman. 4.04. 21 P
cozen'd, for i have been cozen'd and beaten too. 4.05. 94 P
ear of the court, how i have been transform'd, 4.05. 95 P
transformation hath been wash'd and cudgell'd, 4.05. 96 P
of money, to whom you should have been a pander. 5.05.167 P
if it had not been i' th' church, i would have 5.05.185 P
if i did not think it had been anne page, would 5.05.187 P
if i had been married to him (for all he was in 5.05.191 P
have gone round | and none of them been worn; MM 1.02.169
who, if she had been a woman cardinally given, 2.01. 79 P
given, might have been accus'd in fornication, 2.01. 80 P
how long have you been in this place of 2.01.258 P
alas, it hath been great pains to you. 2.01.265 P
if he had been as you, and you as he, | you 2.02. 64
he, like you, | would not have been so stern. 2.02. 66
the law hath not been dead, though it hath slept 2.02. 90
longing, have been sick for, ere i'ld yield | my 2.04.103
so please you, this friar hath been with him, 3.02.212 P
you have not been inquir'd after. 4.01. 19 P
whipping, for you have been a notorious bawd. 4.02. 13 P
i have been an unlawful bawd time out of mind, 4.02. 15 P
he hath been a bawd. 4.02. 27 P
you rogue, i have been drinking all night, i am 4.03. 43 P
i have been drinking hard all night, and i will 4.03. 53 P
duke of dark corners had been at home, he had 4.03.157 P
she hath been a suitor to me for her brother, 5.01. 34
had he been lay, my lord, | for certain words he 5.01.128
and us, | it hath in solemn synods been decreed, ERR 1.01. 13
a heavier task could not have been impos'd 1.01. 31
for me, | and by me, had not our hap been bad: 1.01. 38
there had she not been long but she became | a 1.01. 49
whilst i had been like heedful of the other. 1.01. 82
had not their /bark been very slow of sail; 1.01.116
if thou hadst been dromio to–day in my place, 3.01. 46
if my breast had not been made of faith, and my 3.02.145
this week he hath been heavy, sour, sad, | and 5.01. 45
if here you hous'd him, here he would have been; 5.01.272
twenty years | have i been patron to antipholus, 5.01.328
women, they would else have been troubled with a ADO 1.01.129 P
yet it had not been amiss the rod had been made, 2.01.227 P
yet it had not been amiss the rod had been made, 2.01.228 P
she told me, not thinking i had been myself, 2.01.243 P
and he had been a dog that should have howl'd 2.03. 79 P
her spirit had been invincible against all 2.03.114 P
if it had been painful, i would not have come. 2.03.251 P
gallants, i am not as i have been. 3.02. 15 P
but the barber's man hath been seen with him, 3.02. 45 P
(for she has been too long a–talking of), the 3.02.103 P
you have been always call'd a merciful man, 3.03. 61 P
'a has been a vile thief this seven year; 3.03.126 P
what a hero hadst thou been, | if half thy 4.01.100
if half thy outward graces had been placed 4.01.101
i have this twelvemonth been her bedfellow. 4.01.149
a little, | for i have only been silent so long, 4.01.156
o that i had been writ down an ass! 4.02. 86 P
i doubt we should have been too young for them. 5.01.118 P
we have been up and down to seek thee, for we 5.01.122 P
so, though very many have been beside their wit. 5.01.128 P
but always hath been just and virtuous | in any 5.01.302
prov'd my lady hero hath been falsely accus'd, 5.02. 97 P
and the prince and claudio | have been deceived. 5.04. 76
mile of my court" — hath this been proclaim'd? LLL 1.01.120 P
what great men have been in love? 1.02. 65 P
of that which hath so faithfully been paid. 2.01.156
obscure precedence that hath tofore been sain. 3.01. 82
i, that have been love's whip, | a very beadle 3.01.174
am i the first that have been perjur'd so? 4.03. 49
i have been closely shrouded in this bush | and 4.03.135
at dinner have been sharp and sententious: 5.01. 3 P
they have been at a great feast of languages, 5.01. 36 P
for he hath been five thousand year a boy. 5.02. 11
had she been light, like you, | of such a merry, 5.02. 15
she might 'a' been /a grandam ere she died. 5.02. 17
i should have fear'd her had she been a devil." 5.02.106
had he been adam, he had tempted eve. 5.02.322
hath this brave /manage, this career, been run. 5.02.482
alas, poor machabeus, how hath he been baited! 5.02.631 P
than this /in our respects | have we not been, 5.02.783
if then true lovers have been ever cross'd, | it MND 1.01.150
sides, voices, and minds | had been incorporate. 3.02.208
had gone forward, we had all been made men. 4.02. 17 P
garter, it would have been a fine tragedy; 5.01.359 P
what were good to do, chapels had been churches, MV 1.02. 13 P
had you been as wise as bold, | young in limbs, 2.07. 70
old, | your answer had not been inscroll'd. 2.07. 72
we have been up and down to seek him. 3.01. 76 P
make me wish a sin, | that i had been forsworn. 3.02. 14
love | had been the very sum of my confession. 3.02. 36
the law, your exposition | hath been most sound. 4.01.238
had been her husband rather than a christian! 4.01.297
had i been judge, thou shouldst have had ten 4.01.399
have by your wisdom been this day acquitted | of 4.01.409
we have been praying for our husbands' welfare, 5.01.114
you should have been respective and have kept it 5.01.156
had you been there, i think you would have 5.01.221
my father, so thou hadst been still with me, i AYL 1.02. 11 P
i would thou hadst been son to some man else: 1.02.224
hast thou been drawn to by thy fantasy? 2.04. 31
he hath been all this day to look you. 2.05. 33 P
and i have been all this day to avoid him. 2.05. 34 P
one that hath been a courtier, | and says, if 2.07. 36
for thou thyself hast been a libertine, | as 2.07. 65
i thought that all things had been savage here, 2.07.107
if ever been where bells have knoll'd to church, 2.07.114
and have with holy bell been knoll'd to church, 2.07.121
faith, i had as lief have been myself alone. 3.02.254 P
have you not been acquainted with goldsmiths' 3.02.271 P
had not that been as proper? 3.02.307 P
i have been told so of many; 3.02.343 P
to that end i have been with sir oliver martext, 3.03. 43 P
orlando, where have you been all this while? 4.01. 39 P
if it had not been for a hot midsummer night; 4.01.102 P
i' faith, i should have been a woman by right. 4.03.175 P
i thought thy heart had been wounded with the 5.02. 22 P
and hath been tutor'd in the rudiments | of many 5.04. 31
he hath been a courtier, he swears. 5.04. 42 P
a lady, i have been politic with my friend, 5.04. 45 P
persuade him that he hath been lunatic, | and SHR in.1. 63
these fifteen years you have been in a dream, in.2. 79
we have not yet been seen in any house, | nor 1.01.199
sirrah, where have you been? 1.01.221
where have i been? 1.01.222 P
that have been more kindly beholding to you than 2.01. 78 P
scholar, that hath been long studying at rheims, 2.01. 80 P
that i have been thus pleasant with you both. 3.01. 58
than hath been taught by any of my trade; 3.01. 69
a pair of boots that have been candle–cases, one 3.02. 45 P
hath been often burst and now repair'd with 3.02. 59 P
he, as if | he had been aboard, carousing to his 3.02.171
first, tell me, have you ever been at pisa? 4.02. 93
ay, sir, in pisa have i often been, | pisa 4.02. 94
that have been so bedazzled with the sun, | that 4.05. 46
for she is chang'd, as she had never been. 5.02.115
my mind hath been as big as one of yours, | my 5.02.170
and do suppose | what hath been cannot be. AWW 1.01.226
i have been, madam, a wicked creature, as you 1.03. 35 P
of my thoughts | happily been absent then. 1.03.235
judgment shown, | when judges have been babes; 2.01.139
when miracles have by the great'st been denied. 2.01.141
this had been truth, sir. 2.04. 31 P
at overnight, | she might have been o'erta'en; 3.04. 24
my neighbor how you have been solicited by a 3.05. 14 P
many a maid hath been seduc'd by them, and the 3.05. 21 P
have prevented, if he had been there to command. 3.06. 54 P
it might have been recover'd. 3.06. 58 P
daughter–in–law had been alive at this hour, and 4.05. 4 P
i have been sometimes there. 5.01. 11
sir, been better known to you, when i have held 5.02. 2 P
whether i have been to blame or no, i know not. 5.03.129
th' sequent issue, | hath it been owed and worn. 5.03.198
my master hath been an honorable gentleman. 5.03.238 P
either tell me where thou hast been, or i will TN 1.05. 1 P
h'as been told so; 1.05.147 P
if the heavens had been pleas'd, would we had so 2.01. 20 P
he has been yonder i' the sun practicing 2.05. 16 P
having been three months married to her, sitting 2.05. 44 P
and they have been grand–jurymen since before 3.02. 16 P
i have been dear to him, lad, some two thousand 3.02. 54 P
it might have since been answer'd in repaying 3.03. 33
they say he has been fencer to the sophy. 3.04.278 P
on't, and i thought he had been valiant, and so 3.04.283 P
but if he had not been in drink, he would have 5.01.193 P
but, had it been the brother of my blood, | i 5.01.210
hath been between this lady and this lord. 5.01.258
so comes it, lady, you have been mistook; 5.01.259
you would have been contracted to a maid, | nor 5.01.261
he hath been most notoriously abus'd. 5.01.379
hath been royally attorney'd with interchange of WT 1.01. 27 P
nine changes of the wat'ry star hath been | the 1.02. 1
and our weak spirits ne'er been higher rear'd 1.02. 72
temptations have since then been born to 's: 1.02. 77
there have been | (or i am much deceiv'd) 1.02.190
little thinks she has been sluic'd in 's absence 1.02.194
but we have been | deceiv'd in thy integrity, 1.02.239
as he had seen't or been an instrument | to vice 1.02.415
i have seen a lady's nose | that has been blue, 2.01. 15
you that have been so tenderly officious | with 2.03.159
though a present death | had been more merciful. 2.03.185
sir, their speed | hath been beyond accompt. 2.03.198
twenty–three days | they have been absent. 2.03.199
as she hath | been publicly accus'd, so shall 2.03.204
as it hath been to us rare, pleasant, speedy, 3.01. 13
my past life | hath been as continent, as chaste 3.02. 34
which not to have done i think had been in me 3.02. 67
for as | thy brat hath been cast out, like to 3.02. 87
have | been both at delphos, and from thence 3.02.126
which had been done, | but that the good mind of 3.02.161
this has been some stair–work, some trunk–work, 3.03. 73 P
would i had been by, to have help'd the old man! 3.03.107 P
i would you had been by the ship side, to have 3.03.109 P
i have for the most part been air'd abroad, i 4.02. 5 P
he hath been since an ape–bearer, then a 4.03. 95 P
your greatness | hath not been us'd to fear. 4.04. 18
here has been too much homely foolery already. 4.04.332 P
as you have ever been my father's honor'd friend 4.04.493
as if my trinkets had been hallow'd and brought 4.04.601 P
what an exchange had this been, without boot! 4.04.675 P
was the farthest off you could have been to him, 4.04.704 P
then your blood had been the dearer by i know 4.04.705 P
is colder than that theme, "she had not been, 5.01.100
what might i have been, | might i a son and 5.01.176
could have seen't, the woe had been universal. 5.02. 92 P
for had i been the finder–out of this secret, it 5.02.121 P
ay, and have been so any time these four hours. 5.02.136 P
me, mine own, | where hast thou been preserv'd? 5.03.124
this might have been prevented and made whole JN 1.01. 35
if thou hadst said him nay, it had been sin. 1.01.275
their fixed beds of lime | had been dishabited, 2.01.220
that hath been forward first | to speak unto 2.01.482
been sworn my soldier, bidding me depend | upon 3.01.125
indeed i have been merrier. 4.01. 12
o, where hath our intelligence been drunk? 4.02.116
hadst not thou been by, | a fellow by the hand 4.02.220
be great in act, as you have been in thought. 5.01. 45
the legate of the pope hath been with me, | and 5.01. 62
as it on earth hath been thy servant still. 5.07. 73
since it hath been beforehand with our griefs. 5.07.111
o, had't been a stranger, not my child, | to R2 1.03.239
smooth his fault i should have been more mild. 1.03.240
we, | because we ever have been near the king. 2.02.134
and yet your fair discourse hath been as sugar, 2.03. 6
had you first died, and he been thus trod down, 2.03.126
the noble duke hath been too much abused. 2.03.137
how some have been depos'd, some slain in war, 3.02.157
the time hath been, | would you have been so 3.03. 11
would you have been so brief with him, he would 3.03. 12
have been so brief /with /you to shorten you, 3.03. 13
or that i could forget what i have been! 3.03.138
hath he been in thy heart? 5.01. 28
beasts, | i had been still a happy king of men. 5.01. 36
suspect | that i have been disloyal to thy bed, 5.02.105
i have been studying how i may compare | this 5.05. 1
for though mine enemy thou hast ever been, 5.06. 28
else he had been damn'd for cozening the devil. 1H4 1.02.122 P
my blood hath been too cold and temperate, 1.03. 1
which hath been smooth as oil, soft as young 1.03. 7
guns | he would himself have been a soldier. 1.03. 64
bit than i have been since the first cock. 2.01. 17 P
for what offense have i this fortnight been | a 2.03. 38
thy spirit within thee hath been so at war, 2.03. 56
where hast been, hal? 2.04. 3 P
o lord, i would it had been two! 2.04. 60 P
welcome, jack, where hast thou been? 2.04.113 P
tell me, where hast thou been this month? 2.04.432 P
kitten'd, though yourself had never been born. 3.01. 19
had i so lavish of my presence been, | so 3.02. 39
villainous company, hath been the spoil of me. 3.03. 10 P
not think thou hadst been an ignis fatuus or a 3.03. 39 P
i would it had been of horse. 3.03.187 P
i would the state of time had first been whole 4.01. 25
whole | ere he by sickness had been visited, 4.01. 26
but yet i would your father had been here. 4.01. 60
such as had been ask'd twice on the banes, such 4.02. 16 P
your honor had already been at shrewsbury. 4.02. 53 P
to my shame, | i have a truant been to chivalry, 5.01. 94
which would have been as speedy in your end | as 5.04. 55
many a creature else | had been alive this hour, 5.05. 8
having been well, that would have made me sick, 2H4 1.01.138
and borne, and have been fubb'd off, and fubb'd 2.01. 34 P
you should have been well on your way to york. 2.01. 67
she hath been in good case, and the truth is, 2.01.106 P
why, because you have been so lewd and so much 2.02. 62 P
your majesty hath been this fortnight ill, | and 3.01.104
and you may, but if he had been a man's tailor, he'd 3.02.152 P
a' gaunt as if he had been sworn brother to him, 3.02.321 P
lords | had not been here to dress the ugly form 4.01. 39
wherein have you been galled by the king? 4.01. 89
what peer hath been suborn'd to grate on you? 4.01. 90
the which hath been with scorn shov'd from the 4.02. 37
blood, | my father's purposes have been mistook, 4.02. 56
this had been cheerful after victory. 4.02. 88
falstaff, where have you been all this while? 4.03. 26
had they been rul'd by me, | you should have won 4.03. 66
the manner how this action hath been borne 4.04. 88
for this they have been thoughtful to invest 4.05. 72
for all my reign hath been but as a scene 4.05.197
it hath been prophesied to me many years, | i 4.05.236
master silence had been a man of this mettle. 5.03. 37 P
i have been merry twice and once ere now. 5.03. 39 P
blessed are they that have been my friends, and 5.03.137 P
there hath been a man or two kill'd about her. 5.04. 6 P
when thou dost hear i am as i have been, 5.05. 60
you would say it hath been all in all his study; H5 1.01. 42
who hath been still a giddy neighbor to us; 1.02.145
she hath been then more fear'd than harm'd, my 1.02.155
when all her chevalry hath been in france, | and 1.02.157
went away and it had been any christom child. 2.03. 11 P
the kindred of him hath been flesh'd upon us; 2.04. 50
by french fathers | had twenty years been made. 2.04. 62
of th' athversary hath been very great, 3.06. 98 P
in his cap, and i have been as good as my word. 4.08. 32 P
for had you been as i took you for, i made no 4.08. 54 P
alas, she hath from france too long been chas'd, 5.02. 38
here had the conquest fully been seal'd up, | if 1H6 1.01.130
improvident soldiers, had your watch been good, 2.01. 58
had all your quarters been as safely kept | as 2.01. 63
we had not been thus shamefully surpris'd. 2.01. 65
and what a terror he had been to france. 2.02. 17
madam, i have been bold to trouble you; 2.03. 25
long time thy shadow hath been thrall to me, 2.03. 36
faith, i have been a truant in the law, | and 2.04. 7
and even since then hath richard been obscur'd, 2.05. 26
too, | hath been enacted through your enmity. 3.01.116
we have been guided by thee hitherto, | and of 3.03. 9
that hath so long been resident in france? 3.04. 14
or been reguerdon'd with so much as thanks, 3.04. 23
i should have begg'd i might have been employ'd. 4.01. 72
had death been french, then death had died 4.07. 28
suits | have been consider'd and debated on. 5.01. 35
tush, women have been captivate ere now. 5.03.107
this argues what her kind of life hath been, 5.04. 15
had been a little ratsbane for thy sake! 5.04. 29
joan of aire hath been | a virgin from her 5.04. 49
she and the dolphin have been juggling. 5.04. 68
it's sign she hath been liberal and free. 5.04. 82
that in this quarrel have been overthrown | and 5.04.105
france, | undoing all, as all had never been! 2H6 1.01.103
realm | have been as bondmen to thy sovereignty. 1.03.127
hast thou been long blind and now restor'd? 2.01. 74

hadst thou been his mother, thou couldst have 2.01. 79
soul, god's goodness hath been great to thee. 2.01. 82
how long hast thou been blind? 2.01. 95
if thou hadst been born blind, | thou mightst as 2.01.124
and, but for owen glendower, had been king, 2.02. 41
death, at whose name i oft have been afeard, 2.04. 89
although thou hast been conduct of my shame. 2.04.101
and, had i first been put to speak my mind, | i 3.01. 43
had been the regent there in stead of me, | he 3.01.294
thy fortune, york, hadst thou been regent there, 3.01.305
and had i not been cited so by them, | yet did i 3.02.281
they have been up these two days. 4.02. 2 P
i have been so well brought up that i can write 4.02.105 P
thyself as if thou hadst been in thine own 4.03. 4 P
i fear me, love, if that i had been dead, | thou 4.04. 23
that cause they have been most worthy to live. 4.07. 45 P
my brain–pan had been cleft with a brown bill; 4.10. 12 P
time, when i have been dry and bravely marching, 4.10. 13 P
had i been there, which am a silly woman, | the 3H6 1.01.243
france | when as the enemy hath been ten to one; 1.02. 74
had he been slaughter–man to all my kin, | i 1.04.169
had he been ta'en, we should have heard the news 2.01. 4
had he been slain, we should have heard the news 2.01. 5
hadst thou been meek, our title still had slept, 2.02.160
so many days my ewes have been with young, | so 2.05. 35
your grace hath still been fam'd for virtuous, 4.06. 26
my pity hath been balm to heal their wounds, 4.08. 41
i have not been desirous of their wealth, | nor 4.08. 44
have been as piercing as the midday sun | to 5.02. 17
ah, that thy father had been so resolv'd! 5.05. 22
the bird that hath been limed in a bush, | with 5.06. 13
hadst thou been kill'd when first thou didst 5.06. 35
god make your majesty joyful, as you have been! R3 1.03. 19
but have been | an earnest advocate to plead for 1.03. 85
what you have been ere this, and what you are; 1.03.131
withal, what i have been, and what i am. 1.03.132
i thought thou hadst been resolute. 1.04.113 P
the duke shall know how slack you have been! 1.04.275
you have been factious one against the other. 2.01. 20
all | have been beholding to him in his life; 2.01.130
now, by my troth, if i had been rememb'red, | i 2.04. 23
grandam, this would have been a biting jest. 2.04. 30
because they have been still my adversaries; 3.02. 52
i have been long a sleeper; 3.04. 23
which by my presence might have been concluded. 3.04. 25
and both the princes had been breathing here, 4.04.384
plead what i will be, not what i have been; 4.04.414
they have not been commanded, mighty king. 4.04.486
such proclamation hath been made, my lord. 4.04.517
one that hath ever been god's enemy. 5.03.252
england hath long been mad and scarr'd herself: 5.05. 23
the son, compell'd, been butcher to the sire. 5.05. 26
there have been commissions | sent down among H8 1.02. 20
quoth he, "i for this had been committed — | as 1.02.193
their very noses had been councillors | to pepin 1.03. 9
i have been begging sixteen years in court | (am 2.03. 82
it hath already publicly been read, | and on all 2.04. 3
i have been to you a true and humble wife, | at 2.04. 23
that i have been your wife in this obedience 2.04. 35
and have been blest | with many children by you. 2.04. 36
who had been hither sent on the debating | /a 2.04.174
for her sake that i have been — for i feel 3.01. 77
been, out of fondness, superstitious to him? 3.01.131
show'r'd on me daily have been more than could 3.02.167
mine own ends | have been mine so, that evermore 3.02.172
i should have been beholding to your paper. 4.01. 21
god save you, sir! where have you been broiling? 4.01. 56
and had their faces | been loose, this day they 4.01. 75
faces | been loose, this day they had been lost. 4.01. 75
such things have been done. 5.01.133
should find respect | for what they have been. 5.02.111
my noble gossips, y' have been too prodigal. 5.04. 12
and't had been a green hair, i should have TRO 1.02.152 P
it now, for it has been a great while going by. 1.02.168 P
troy, yet upon his bases, had been down, | and 1.03. 75
the specialty of rule hath been neglected, | and 1.03. 78
thousand dismes, | hath been as dear as helen; 2.02. 20
carrion weight, | a troyan hath been slain. 4.01. 73
night hath been too brief. 4.02. 11
would thou hadst ne'er been born! 4.02. 86 P
i have been seeking you this hour, my lord. 5.02.182
hath nothing been but shapes and forms of 5.03. 12
i would have been much more a fresher man, | had 5.06. 20
what ever have been thought /on in this state COR 1.02. 4
then his good report should have been my son; 1.03. 20 P
thy exercise hath been too violent for | a 1.05. 15
induc'd | as you have been — that's for my 1.09. 17
i would not have been so fidius'd for all the 2.01.130 P
faith, there hath been many great men that have 2.02. 7 P
having been supple and courteous to the people, 2.02. 26 P
i would you rather had been silent. 2.02. 61
we have been call'd so of many, not that our 2.03. 18 P
you have been a scourge to her enemies, you have 2.03. 91 P
her enemies, you have been a rod to her friends; 2.03. 92 P
virtuous that i have not been common in my love. 2.03. 95 P
he has been bred i' th' wars | since 'a could 3.01.318
you might have been enough the man you are, 3.02. 19
lesser had been | the /thwartings of your 3.02. 20
come, you have been too rough, something too 3.02. 25
i have been i' th' market–place; 3.02. 93
straight, he hath been us'd | ever to conquer, 3.03. 25
i have been consul, and can show /for rome | her 3.03.110
to say, | if you had been the wife of hercules, 4.01. 17
well | my hazards still have been your solace, 4.01. 28
there hath been in rome strange insurrections; 4.03. 13 P
hath been! 4.03. 16 P
we have been down together in my sleep, 4.05.124
and he had been cannibally given, he might have 4.05.188 P
and might have been much better, if | he could 4.06. 16
can, | and three examples of the like hath been 4.06. 51
i have been | the book of his good acts, whence 5.02. 14
howsoever you have been his liar, as you say you 5.02. 31 P
i have been blown out of your gates with sighs, 5.02. 74 P
that we have been familiar, | ingrate 5.02. 85
his countenance as if | i had been mercenary. 5.06. 40
that have been thus forward in my right, | i TIT 1.01. 56
whose friend in justice thou hast ever been, 1.01.180
rome, i have been thy soldier forty years, | and 1.01.193

i have been troubled in my sleep this night, 2.02. 9
i have been broad awake two hours and more. 2.02. 17
in bootless prayer have they been held up, | and 3.01. 75
my hand hath been but idle, let it serve | to 3.01.171
o, would thou wert as thou tofore hast been! 3.01.293
have by my means been butchered wrongfully? 4.04. 55
villain, thou mightst have been an emperor. 5.01. 30
long have i been forlorn, and all for thee. 5.02. 81
death, | they have been violent to me and mine. 5.02.109
that hath been breeder of these dire events. 5.03.178
if thou hadst, thou hadst been poor–john. ROM 1.01. 31 P
many a morning hath he there been seen, | with 1.01.131
o then i see queen mab hath been with you. 1.04. 53
i should have been more strange, i must confess, 2.02.102
our romeo hath not been in bed to–night. 2.03. 42
my good son, but where hast thou been then? 2.03. 47
i have been feasting with mine enemy, | where on 2.03. 49
i had, my weapon should quickly have been out. 2.04.158 P
and yet thy head hath been beaten as addle as an 3.01. 23 P
tybalt, that an hour | hath been my cousin! 3.01.113
company, | i would have been a–bed an hour ago. 3.04. 7
still my care hath been | to have her match'd; 3.05.177
now, my headstrong, where have you been gadding? 4.02. 16
not, | for he hath still been tried a holy man. 4.03. 29
all night for lesser cause, and ne'er been sick. 4.04. 10
ay, you have been a mouse–hunt in your time, 4.04. 11
life and these lips have long been separated. 4.05. 27
at the point of death | have they been merry, 5.03. 89
how long hath he been there? 5.03.130
poison, i see, hath been his timeless end. 5.03.162
that from my first have been inclin'd to thrift, TIM 1.01.118
't 'as been prov'd. 1.02. 49 P
how had you been my friends else? 1.02. 90 P
't 'as been done; 1.02.144
when all our offices have been oppress'd | with 2.02.158
i have been bold | (for that i knew it the most 2.02.199
something hath been amiss — a noble nature 2.02.208
my knowing, timon has been this lord's father, 3.02. 67
they have all been touch'd and found base metal, 3.03. 6
have i been ever free, and must my house | be my 3.04. 80
fury | he has been known to commit outrages 3.05. 71
if thou hadst not been born the worst of men, 4.03.275
of men, | thou hadst been a knave and flatterer. 4.03.276
of his | has been but a try for his friends? 5.01. 9
and i had been a man of any occupation, if i JC 1.02.266 P
such instigations have been often dropp'd 2.01. 49
i have been up this hour, awake all night. 2.01. 88
for here have been | some six or seven, who did 2.01.276
heaven nor earth have been at peace to–night. 2.02. 1
your best friends shall wish i had been further. 2.02.125
come hither, fellow; which way hast thou been? 2.04. 21
i did not think you could have been so angry. 4.03.143
yet would not so have been, | durst i have done 5.03. 47
strato, thou hast been all this while asleep; 5.05. 32
where hast thou been, sister? MAC 1.03. 1
as one that had been studied in his death, | to 1.04. 9
of thanks and payment | might have been mine! 1.04. 20
meek, hath been | so clear in his great office, 1.07. 17
he hath been in unusual pleasure, and | sent 2.01. 13
the night has been unruly. 2.03. 54
if he had been forgotten, | it had been as a gap 3.01. 11
it had been as a gap in our great feast, | and 3.01. 12
(which still hath been both grave and prosperous 3.01. 21
which you thought had been | our innocent self? 3.01. 77
i had else been perfect, | whole as the marble, 3.04. 20
is often thus, | and hath been from his youth. 3.04. 53
blood hath been shed ere now, i' th' olden time, 3.04. 74
murthers have been perform'd | too terrible for 3.04. 76
the /time has been, | that when the brains were 3.04. 77
stones have been known to move and trees to 3.04.122
you have done | hath been but for a wayward son, 3.05. 11
only i say | things have been strangely borne. 3.06. 3
it hath been | th' untimely emptying of the 4.03. 67
and it hath been | the sword of our slain kings. 4.03. 86
the time has been, my senses would have cool'd 5.05. 10
there would have been a time for such a word. 5.05. 18
of fortinbras, | had he been vanquisher; HAM 1.01. 93
middle of the night, | been thus encount'red. 1.02.199
i would i had been there. 1.02.234
have of your audience been most free and 1.03. 93
o, my lord, my lord, i have been so affrighted! 2.01. 72
purport | as if he had been loosed out of hell 2.01. 80
thou still hast been the father of good news. 2.02. 42
hath there been such a time — i would fain know 2.02.153
of the scene | been strook so to the soul, that 2.02.591
for thou hast been | as one in suff'ring all 3.02. 65
about the world have times twelve thirties been, 3.02.158
him his pranks have been too broad to bear with, 3.04. 2
it had been so with us had we been there. 4.01. 13
it had been so with us had we been there. 4.01. 13
how long hath she been thus? 4.05. 67
you have been talk'd of since your travel much, 4.07. 71
as had he been incorps'd and demi–natur'd | with 4.07. 87
if this had not been a gentlewoman, she should 5.01. 24 P
she should have been buried out a' christian 5.01. 24 P
into the land, | as if i had never been such." 5.01. 74
how long hast thou been grave–maker? 5.01.142 P
i have been sexton here, man and boy, thirty 5.01.161 P
her obsequies have been as far enlarg'd | as we 5.01.226
she should in ground unsanctified been lodg'd 5.01.229
hop'd thou shouldst have been my hamlet's wife. 5.01.244
into france i have been in continual practice. 5.02.211 P
stage, | for he was likely, had he been put on, 5.02.397
his breeding, sir, hath been at my charge. LR 1.01. 9 P
he hath been out nine years, and away he shall 1.01. 32 P
hadst not been born than not t' have pleas'd me 1.01.234
we have made of it hath /not been little. 1.01.289 P
and soundest of his time hath been but rash; 1.01.295 P
/fut, i should have been that i am, had the 1.02.131 P
shouldst not have been old till thou hadst been 1.05. 44 P
not have been old till thou hadst been wise. 1.05. 45 P
i have been with your father, and given him 2.01. 2 P
from my sister | been well inform'd of them, and 2.01.102
though they had been but two years o' th' trade. 2.02. 59 P
fellow | who, having been prais'd for bluntness, 2.02. 96
who hath most fortunately been inform'd | of my 2.02.167
and thou hadst been set i' th' stocks for that 2.04. 64 P
what hath been seen, | either in snuffs and 3.01. 25

reserv'd a blanket, else we had been all sham'd. 3.04. 65 P
what hast thou been? 3.04. 84 P
have been tom's food for seven long year. 3.04.139
i have been your tenant, and your father's 4.01. 13
poor tom hath been scar'd out of his good wits. 4.01. 57 P
i have been worth the /whistling. 4.02. 29
had he been where he thought, | by this had 4.06. 44
he thought, | by this had thought been past. 4.06. 45
hadst thou been aught but goss'mer, feathers, 4.06. 49
had you not been their father, these white 4.07. 29
where have i been? 4.07. 51
methinks our pleasure might have been demanded 5.03. 62
by heaven, i rather would have been his hangman. OTH 1.01. 34
you have been hotly call'd for; 1.02. 44
it had been better you had not kiss'd your three 2.01.172 P
if she had been bless'd, she would never have 2.01.252 P
i have been to–night exceedingly well cudgell'd; 2.03.365 P
have your instruments been in naples, that they 3.01. 3 P
you have not been a–bed then? 3.01. 31
i have been talking with a suitor here, | a man 3.03. 42
i did not think he had been acquainted with her. 3.03. 99
mine, 'tis his, and has been slave to thousands; 3.03.158
that you have been so earnest | to have me filch 3.03.314
i had been happy, if the general camp, | pioners 3.03.345
thou hadst been better have been born a dog 3.03.362
thou hadst been better have been born a dog 3.03.362
this while with leaden thoughts been press'd, 3.04.177
aches at thee, would thou hadst never been born! 4.02. 69
how have i been behav'd, that he might stick 4.02.108
that thrust had been mine enemy indeed, | but 5.01. 24
i have been to seek you. 5.01. 81
cassio hath here been set on in the dark | by 5.01.112
had all his hairs been lives, my great revenge 5.02. 74
/nay, had she been true, | if heaven would make 5.02.143
which not to have been blest withal would have ANT 1.02.154 P
throned gods), | who have been false to fulvia? 1.03. 29
thy biddings have been done, and every hour, 1.04. 34
it hath been taught us from the primal state 1.04. 41
in mine ears, | that long time have been barren. 2.05. 25
you have been a great thief by sea. 2.06. 92 P
villainy, | in thee't had been good service. 2.07. 75
had our general | been what he knew himself, it 3.10. 26
you have been a boggler ever, | but when we in 3.13.110
since | thou hast been whipt for following him. 3.13.137
where hast thou been, my heart? 3.13.172
thou hast been rightly honest — so hast thou — 4.02. 11
me well, | and kings have been your fellows. 4.02. 13
cause, but as't had been | each man's like mine; 4.08. 6
bruised pieces, go, | you have been nobly borne. 4.14. 43
been laden with like frailties which before 5.02.123
there might have been, | but that my master CYM 1.01.161
this hath been | your faithful servant. 1.01.173
would there had been some hurt done! 1.02. 35 P
not so, unless it had been the fall of an ass, 1.02. 36 P
as since he hath been allow'd the name of. 1.04. 3 P
of his endowments had been tabled by his side, 1.04. 6 P
to whom i have been often bound for no less than 1.04. 27 P
since when i have been debtor to you for 1.04. 36 P
it had been pity you should have been put 1.04. 39 P
had been pity you should have been put together, 1.04. 40 P
had been something too fair and too good for any 1.04. 71 P
have i not been | thy pupil long? 1.05. 11
had i been thief–stol'n, | as my two brothers, 1.06. 5
if his wit had been like him that broke it, it 2.01. 8 P
would he had been one of my rank! 2.01. 15 P
she hath been reading late | the tale of tereus; 2.02. 44
never talk on't: | she hath been colted by him. 2.04.133
where horses have been nimbler than the sands 3.02. 72
this rock and these demesnes have been my world, 3.03. 70
whose love–suit hath been to me | as fearful as 3.04.133
us, for | we have been too slight in sufferance. 3.05. 35
of posthumus, most retir'd | hath her life been; 3.05. 37
would it had been so, that they | had been my 3.06. 75
that they | had been my father's sons, then had 3.06. 76
then had my prize | been less, and so more equal 3.06. 77
as juno had been sick | and he her dieter. 4.02. 50
but yields a crop | as if it had been sow'd. 4.02.181
who had not now been drooping here, if seconds 5.03. 90
thou shouldst have been, and shielded him | from 5.04. 41
thou hast been a grandsire and begot | a father 5.04.123
he hath been search'd among the dead and living; 5.05. 11
it had been vicious | to have mistrusted her; 5.05. 65
o, would | our viands had been poison'd, or at 5.05.156
so, had it been a carbuncle | of phoebus' wheel; 5.05.189
safely, had it | been all the worth of 's car. 5.05.191
that headless man | i thought had been my lord. 5.05.300
it hath been sung at festivals, | on ember–eves PER 1.ch. 5
where when men been, there's seldom ease, | for 2.ch. 28
master, if i had been the sexton, i would have 2.01. 36 P
i would have been that day in the belfry. 2.01. 37 P
me too, and when i had been in his belly, i 2.01. 40 P
what i have been i have forgot to know, | but 2.01. 71
it hath been a shield | 'twixt me and death" — 2.01.126
pericles, | my education been in arts and arms; 2.03. 82
with us at sea it hath been still observ'd, and 3.01. 51 P
't 'as been a turbulent and stormy night. 3.02. 4
i have been in many; 3.02. 5
your creatures, who by you have been restored; 3.02. 45
she hath not been | entranc'd above five hours. 3.02. 93
no cheap thing, if men were as they have been. 4.02. 61 P
't 'ad been a kindness | becoming well thy /fact 4.03. 11
one, how long have you been at this trade? 4.06. 66 P
how long have you been of this profession? 4.06. 72 P
diseases have been sold dearer than physic — 4.06. 98
i doubt not but thy training hath been noble. 4.06.112
as hath been belch'd on by infected lungs. 4.06.169
eyes, | but have been gaz'd on like a comet. 5.01. 86
and such a one | my daughter might have been. 5.01.108
thou hadst been toss'd from wrong to injury, 5.01.130
rest you said | thou hast been godlike perfit, 5.01.206
is not dead at tharsus, as she should have been, 5.01.215
for it seems | you have been noble towards her. 5.01.263
to themselves | been death's most horrid agents, TNK 1.01.144
we have been soldiers, and we cannot weep | when 1.03. 18
had they been taken | when their last hurts were 1.04. 25
'twas possible | they might have been recovered. 1.04. 27
they would have look'd had they been victors, 2.01. 33 P

what had we been, old in the court of creon, 2.02.105
you have been well advertis'd | how much i dare; 3.01. 58
my rudiments | been labor'd so long with ye, 3.05. 4
tile, | we have been fatuus, and labored vainly. 3.05. 41
ladies, if we have been merry, | and have 3.05.138
learn what maids have been her companions and 4.03. 90 P
have never been foul-mouth'd against thy law, 5.01. 98
i have been harsh | to large confessors, and 5.01.104
twenty times had been far better, | for there 5.02. 7
in the passage | the gods have been most equal. 5.04.115
till now grown up | had been ta'en from you, and STM II.C 66
"i have been wooed, as i entreat thee now, VEN 97
yet hath he been my captive, and my slave, | and 101
"thou hadst been gone," quoth she, "sweet boy, 613
"had i been tooth'd like him, i must confess, 1117
sin | to wish that i their father had not been. LUC 210
back, | for it had been dishonor to disdain him. 844
troy had been bright with fame, and not with 1491
for his approach that often there had been. PP 6. 8
"had women been so strong as men, | in faith, 18.35
but that which is | hath been before, how are SON 59. 2
how like a winter hath my absence been | from 97. 1
from you have i been absent in the spring, 98. 1
that i have frequent been with unknown minds, 117. 5
have mine eyes out of their spheres been fitted 119. 7
knows | her pretty looks have been mine enemies, 139.10
i might as yet have been a spreading flower, LC 75
for feasts of love i have been call'd unto, 181
BEER 5 FR 0.0005 REL FR 1 V 4 P
it not show vildly in me to desire small beer? 2H4 2.02. 6 P
i do now remember the poor creature, small beer. 2.02. 11 P
and here's a pot of good double beer, neighbor. 2H6 2.03. 64 P
and i will make it felony to drink small beer. 4.02. 68 P
to suckle fools and chronicle small beer. OTH 2.01.160
BEER-BARREL 1 FR 0.0001 REL FR 0 V 1 P
was converted might they not stop a beer-barrel? HAM 5.01.212 P
BEE'S 1 FR 0.0001 REL FR 0 V 1 P
the bee stings, but i say, 'tis the bee's wax; 2H6 4.02. 82 P
BEES 9 FR 0.0010 REL FR 9 V 0 P
pinch more stinging | than bees that made 'em. TMP 1.02.330
and kill the bees that yield it with your stings TGV 1.02.104
we bring it to the hive, and, like the bees, 2H4 4.05. 77
so bees with smoke and doves with noisome stench 1H6 1.05. 23
like an angry hive of bees | that want their 2H6 3.02.125
like stinging bees in hottest summer's day, TIT 5.01. 14
but for your words, they rob the hybla bees, JC 5.01. 34
be | you bees that make these locks of counsel! CYM 3.02. 36
the old bees die, the young possess their hive: LUC 1769
BEESOM *(also bisson)*
BEESOM 1 FR 0.0001 REL FR 0 V 1 P
what harm can your beesom conspectuities glean COR 2.01. 64 P
BEEST 15 FR 0.0017 REL FR 7 V 8 P
if thou beest stephano, touch me, and speak to TMP 2.02.100 P
if thou beest trinculo, come forth. 2.02.103 P
in thy life, if thou beest a good moon-calf. 3.02. 21 P
if thou beest a man, show thyself in thy 3.02.128 P
if thou beest a devil, take't as thou list. 3.02.129 P
whe'er thou beest he or no, | or some enchanted 5.01.111
if thou beest prospero, | give us particulars of 5.01.134
if thou beest rated by thy estimation, | thou MV 2.07. 26
within these ten days if that thou beest found AYL 1.03. 43
if thou beest not damn'd for this, the devil 3.02. 83 P
if thou beest yet a fresh uncropped flower, AWW 5.03.327
if ever thou beest mine, kate, as i have a H5 5.02.203 P
if thou beest death, i'll give thee england's 2H6 3.03. 2
if thou beest not immortal, look about you; JC 2.03. 6 P
if thou beest slain and with no stroke of mine, MAC 5.07. 15
BEETLE* 6 FR 0.0006 REL FR 5 V 1 P
and the poor beetle, that we tread upon, | in MM 3.01. 78
if i do, fillip me with a three-man beetle. 2H4 1.02.228 P
here are the beetle brows shall blush for me. ROM 1.04. 32
the shard-borne beetle with his drowsy hums MAC 3.02. 42
they are his shards, and he their beetle, so. ANT 3.02. 20
we find | the sharded beetle in a safer hold CYM 3.03. 20
BEETLE-HEADED 1 FR 0.0001 REL FR 1 V 0 P
a whoreson, beetle-headed, flap-ear'd knave! SHR 4.01.157
BEETLES* 4 FR 0.0004 REL FR 4 V 0 P
the charms | of sycorax, toads, beetles, bats, TMP 1.02.340
beetles black, approach not near; MND 2.02. 22
cliff | that beetles o'er his base into the sea, HAM 1.04. 71
midway air | show scarce so gross as beetles. LR 4.06. 14
BEFALL 27 FR 0.0030 REL FR 27 V 0 P
and do look to know | what doth befall you here. MM 1.01. 58
so befall my soul | as this is false he burthens ERR 5.01.208
now fair befall your mask! LLL 2.01.123
well, befall what will befall, | i'll jest a 5.02.870
well, befall what will befall, | i'll jest a 5.02.870
the worst that may befall me in this case, | if MND 1.01. 63
do best please me | that befall prepost'rously. 3.02.121
in this same enterlude it doth befall | that i, 5.01.155
now fair befall thee, good petruchio! SHR 5.02.111
but jealousy what might befall your travel, TN 3.03. 8
many years of happy days befall | my gracious R2 1.01. 20
whom fair befall in heaven 'mongst happy souls, 2.01.129
more blessed hap did ne'er befall our state. 1H6 1.06. 10
and peace, no war, befall thy parting soul! 2.05.115
o, let me stay, befall what may befall! 2H6 3.02.402
o, let me stay, befall what may befall! 3.02.402
all, | and more such days as these to us befall! 5.03. 33
what danger or what sorrow can befall thee | so 3H6 4.01. 76
in these conflicts | what may befall him, to his 4.06. 95
now fair befall thee and thy noble house! R3 1.03.281
now fair befall you! 3.05. 47
if thou wilt not, befall what may befall, | i'll TIT 5.01. 57
if thou wilt not, befall what may befall, | i'll 5.01. 57
and ours with thine, befall what fortune will. 5.03. 3
let's reason with the worst that may befall. JC 5.01. 96
at mine intent | by what did here befall me. ANT 2.02. 42
madam, all joy befall your grace, and you! CYM 3.05. 9
/BEFALL'N 1 FR 0.0001 REL FR 1 V 0 P
/what /hath /then /befall'n? 2H4 1.01.177
BEFALL'N 8 FR 0.0009 REL FR 7 V 1 P
what have befall'n of them and /thee till now. ERR 1.01.123
i come to tell you things sith then befall'n. 3H6 2.01.106
what late misfortune is befall'n king edward? 4.04. 3
of york and lancaster, | that had befall'n us. R3 1.04. 16
how now, what hath befall'n? HAM 4.03. 11
i could heartily wish this had not befall'n; OTH 2.03.301 P
sir, you shall understand what hath befall'n, 5.02.307
"what uncouth ill event | hath thee befall'n, LUC 1599
BEFALLS 1 FR 0.0001 REL FR 1 V 0 P
i cannot do for you | than what befalls myself. TN 3.04.337
BEFELL 3 FR 0.0003 REL FR 2 V 1 P
how heavily this befell to the poor gentlewoman. MM 3.01.218 P
of sweet and bitter fancy, | lo what befell! AYL 4.03.102
i'll tell thee what befell me on a day | in this 3H6 3.01. 10
BEFIT 1 FR 0.0001 REL FR 1 V 0 P
be | as doth befit our honor and your worth. PER 1.01.120
BEFITS 10 FR 0.0011 REL FR 9 V 1 P
to any business that | we say befits the hour. TMP 2.01.290
her, | as best befits her wounded reputation, ADO 4.01.241
o, how that name befits my composition! R2 2.01. 73
it well befits you should be of the peace. 2H4 3.02. 89 P
it ill befits thy state | and birth that thou 3H6 3.03. 2
such as befits the pleasure of the court? 5.07. 44
blind is his love and best befits the dark. ROM 2.01. 32
do | so far ask pardon as befits mine honor | to ANT 2.02. 97
it befits not me | unto a stranger knight to be PER 2.03. 66
thy beauty and thy years full well befits, | for SON 41. 3
BEFITTED 1 FR 0.0001 REL FR 1 V 0 P
and that it us befitted | to bear our hearts in HAM 1.02. 2
BEFITTING 1 FR 0.0001 REL FR 1 V 0 P
a breakfast, nor | befitting this first meeting. TMP 5.01.165
BEFORE *(also afore, 'fore, tofore)*
/BEFORE 6 FR 0.0006 REL FR 5 V 1 P
/king | /before /i /have /shook /off /the /regal R2 4.01.163
/standing /before /the /sun /of /bullingbrook, 4.01.261
/the /accompt /of /chance /before /you /said, 2H4 1.01.167
/before /he /was /what /thou /wouldst /have /him 1.03. 93
/here /take /my /oath /before /this /honorable LR 3.06. 47 P
/was /this /before /the /king /return'd? 4.03. 37
BEFORE 760 FR 0.0859 REL FR 579 V 181 P
remember | a time before we came unto this cell? TMP 1.02. 39
not a blemish, | but fresher than before; 1.02.219
before the time be out? no more! 1.02.246
was never grac'd before with such a paragon to 2.01. 75 P
garments sit upon me, | much feater than before. 2.01.273
if it should thunder as it did before, i know 2.02. 22 P
the sun will set before i shall discharge | what 3.01. 22
out, we will drink water — not a drop before; 3.02. 2 P
as i told thee before, i am subject to a tyrant, 3.02. 42
if thou dost break her virgin-knot before | all 4.01. 15
before you can say "come" and "go," | and 4.01. 44
i drink the air before me, and return | or ere 5.01.102
i have heard renown, | but never saw before; 5.01.194
go on before; TGV 2.04.186
how now, sir proteus, are you crept before us? 4.02. 18
are you sadder than you were before? 4.02. 55 P
i, having been acquainted with the smell before, 4.04. 23 P
hours, | unless it be to come before their time, 5.01. 5
all his successors (gone before him) hath done't WIV 1.01. 14 P
if thou seest her before me, commend me. 1.04.157 P
for they say, if money go before, all ways do 2.02.168 P
go before you like a man than follow him like a 3.02. 5 P
marry, as i told you before, john and robert, be 3.03. 9 P
i'll speak it before the best lord, i would make 3.03. 50 P
i come before to tell you. 3.03.115 P
besides these, other bars he lays before me, 3.04. 7
more wit than ever i learn'd before in my life; 4.05. 60 P
go before into the park; 5.03. 4 P
call hither, | i say, bid come before us angelo. MM 1.01. 15
mettle | before so noble and so great a figure 1.01. 49
in the thanksgiving before meat, do relish the 1.02. 15 P
and do bring in here before your good honor two 2.01. 49 P
whom i detest before heaven and your honor — 2.01. 69 P
prove it before these varlets here, thou 2.01. 86 P
respected with him before he married with her. 2.01.170 P
i respected with her before i was married to her 2.01.175 P
you let me not find you before me again upon any 2.01.246 P
kneel down before him, hang upon his gown; 2.02. 44
plays such fantastic tricks before high heaven 2.02.121
before his sister should her body stoop | to 2.04.182
he must before the deputy, sir, he has given him 3.02. 34 P
if he be a whoremonger, and comes before him, he 3.02. 36 P
me desire you to make your answer before him. 3.02.156 P
let him be call'd before us. 3.02.205 P
strangely, for he hath not us'd it before. 4.02.118 P
of the penitent to be so bar'd before his death. 4.02.176 P
and he shall bring you | before the duke; 4.03.142
i was once before him for getting a wench with 4.03.169 P
we proclaim it in an hour before his ent'ring, 4.04. 9 P
speak loud and kneel before him. 5.01. 19
are i' the wrong | to speak before your time. 5.01. 87
absence was not six months old | before herself ERR 1.01. 45
we sail'd | before the always-wind-obeying deep 1.01. 63
weeping before for what she saw must come, | and 1.01. 71
gather the sequel by that went before. 1.01. 95
was carried with more speed before the wind, 1.01.109
have denied that before you were so choleric. 2.02. 66 P
are you there, wife? you might have come before. 3.01. 63
one that before the judgment carries poor souls 4.02. 40
kneel to the duke before he pass the abbey. 5.01.129
i will determine this before i stir. 5.01.167
let's go hand in hand, not one before another. 5.01.426
that adam had left him before he transgress'd. ADO 2.01.252 P
once before he won it of me with false dice, 2.01.280 P
this the very night before the intended wedding 2.02. 45 P
note this before my notes: 2.03. 54
before god! and, in my mind, very wise. 2.03.185 P
ent'red, even the night before her wedding-day. 3.02.114 P
and there, before the whole congregation, shame 3.03.161 P
them this morning examin'd before your worship. 3.05. 47 P
which was before barr'd up with ribs of iron! 4.01.151
let them come before master constable. 4.02. 8 P
yea, marry, let them come before me. 4.02. 9 P
defend but god should go before such villains! 4.02. 20 P
to disgrace hero before the whole assembly, and 4.02. 54 P
i will go before and show him their examination. 4.02. 65 P
which before | would give preceptial med'cine to 5.01. 23
day, | before the wheels of phoebus, round about 5.03. 26
before this friar, and swear to marry her. 5.04. 57
give me your hand before this holy friar — | i 5.04. 58
boast | before the birds have any cause to sing? LLL 1.01.103
course, | before we enter his forbidden gates, 2.01. 26
to meet you, gentle lady, | before i came. 2.01. 84
submissive fall his princely feet before, | and 4.01. 90
to see him walk before a lady and to bear her 4.01.145
and such barren plants are set before us, that 4.02. 28
where, if (before repast) it shall please you to 4.02.154 P
you shall present before her the nine worthies. 5.01.117 P
and learned gentleman, before the princess, i 5.01.122 P
swore | a better speech was never spoke before. 5.02.110
then die a calf, before your horns do grow. 5.02.253
when she's dispos'd, | told our intents before; 5.02.467
and lay my arms before the legs of this sweet 5.02.555
of you, my lord berowne, | before i saw you; 5.02.842
be it so she will not here before your grace MND 1.01. 39
before the time i did lysander see, | seem'd 1.01.204
in our enterlude before the duke and the duchess 1.02. 6 P
before milk-white, now purple with love's wound, 2.01.167
it in action as we will do it before the duke. 3.01. 5 P
he goes before me and still dares me on. 3.02.413
for well i wot | thou run'st before me, shifting 3.02.423
it in the latter end of a play, before the duke. 4.01.217 P
moonshine is gone before thisby comes back and 5.01.312 P
i am sent with broom before, | to sweep the dust 5.01.389
sirrah, go before. MV 1.02.132
he stuck them up before the fulsome ewes, | who 1.03. 86
that's a month before | this bond expires, i do 1.03.157
my ships come home a month before the day. 1.03.181
or swear before you choose, if you choose wrong 2.01. 40
go you before me, sirrah, | say i will come. 2.05. 38
i will go before, sir. 2.05. 40 P
hour, | for lovers ever run before the clock. 2.06. 4
venetian, one that comes before | to signify th' 2.09. 87
as this fore-spurrer comes before his lord. 2.09. 95
bespeak him a fortnight before. 3.01.126 P
pause a day or two | before you hazard, for in 3.02. 2
some month or two | before you venture for me. 3.02. 10
before a friend of this description | shall lose 3.02.301
thou call'dst me dog before thou hadst a cause, 3.03. 6
i shall be there before thee. 3.04. 55
see our husbands | before they think of us. 3.04. 59
we were christians enow before, e'en as many as 3.05. 22 P
make room, and let him stand before our face. 4.01. 16
i pardon thee thy life before thou ask it. 4.01.369
and be a day before our husbands home. 4.02. 3
word | my mistress will before the break of day 5.01. 29
but there is come a messenger before, | to 5.01.117
know you before whom, sir? AYL 1.01. 42 P
ay, better than him i am before knows me. 1.01. 43 P
i confess your coming before me is nearer to his 1.01. 50 P
what, you wrastle to-morrow before the new duke? 1.01.120 P
he had sworn it away before ever he saw those 1.02. 79 P
you should not have mock'd me before. 1.02.209 P
had i before known this young man his son, | i 1.02.237
your praise is come too swiftly home before you. 2.03. 9
but if thou diest before i come, thou art a 2.06. 13 P
the nine days out of the wonder before you came; 3.02.175 P
i would kiss before i spoke. 4.01. 72 P
could be out, being before his belov'd mistress? 4.01. 81 P
yet he did what he could to die before, and he 4.01. 99 P
there's a girl goes before the priest, and 4.01.140 P
a woman's thought runs before her actions. 4.01.141 P
who quickly fell before him, in which hurtling 4.03.131
or else be incontinent before marriage. 5.02. 39 P
to you, to set her before your eyes to-morrow, 5.02. 66 P
before i have a husband for the elder. SHR 1.01. 51
for those defects i have before rehears'd, 1.02.124
the younger then is free, and not before. 1.02.262
if you should die before him, where's her dower? 2.01.389
"hic ibat," as i told you before, "simois," i am 3.01. 31 P
madam, before you touch the instrument, | to 3.01. 64
back and shoulder-shotten, near-legg'd before, 3.02. 56 P
to pass, | as before imparted to your worship, 3.02.130
such a mad marriage never was before. 3.02.182
i must away to-day, before night come. 3.02.190
i am sent before to make a fire, and they are 4.01. 4 P
she was, good curtis, before this frost; 4.01. 22 P
swore, how she pray'd that never pray'd before; 4.01. 80 P
where is the foolish knave i sent before? 4.01.127
here, sir — as foolish as i was before. 4.01.128
my leave, | in resolution as i swore before. 4.02. 43
and so shall mine before you touch the meat. 4.03. 46
you shall not choose but drink before you go. 5.01. 11
you, for i never saw you before in all my life. 5.01. 51 P
i heard not of it before. AWW 1.01. 35 P
man, setting down before you, will undermine you 1.01.118 P
and florence is denied before he comes. 1.02. 12
constancies | expire before their fashions." 1.02. 63
many likelihoods inform'd me of this before, 1.03.124 P
here on my knee, before high heaven and you, 1.03.192
that before you, and next unto high heaven, | i 1.03.193
beware of being captives | before you serve. 2.01. 22
most fruitfully, i am there before my legs. 2.02. 70 P
go call before me all the lords in court. 2.03. 46
before i speak, too threat'ningly replies. 2.03. 81
although before the solemn priest i have sworn, 2.03.269
sir, "before a knave th' art a knave," that's 2.04. 29 P
a knave," that's "before me th' art a knave." 2.04. 30 P
know it before the report come. 3.02. 23 P
lays down his wanton siege before her beauty, 3.07. 18
but my heart hath the fear of mars before it, 4.01. 30 P
he ne'er pays after-debts, take it before, | and 4.03.226
who pays before, but not when he does owe it. 4.03.230
i could endure any thing before but a cat, and 4.03.237 P
h'as led the drum before the english tragedians. 4.03.266 P
lord the king, | we'll be before our welcome. 4.04. 14
be a-weary of thee, and i tell thee so before, 4.05. 57 P
since you are like to see the king before me, 5.01. 30
'tis not so sweet now as it was before. TN 1.01. 8
away before me to sweet beds of flow'rs, 1.01. 39
why, let her except before excepted. 1.03. 7 P
wherefore have these gifts a curtain before 'em? 1.03.126 P
as a squash is before 'tis a peascod, or a 1.05.157 P
for some hour before you took me from the breach 2.01. 21 P
before me, she's a good wench. 2.03.178 P
at your heels than fortunes before you. 2.05.138 P
sport, mark his first approach before my lady. 2.05.198 P
at every feather | that comes before his eye. 3.01. 65
better | to fall before the lion than the wolf! 3.01.129
grand-jurymen since before noah was a sailor. 3.02. 17 P
with this ridiculous boldness before my lady? 3.04. 38 P

there, before him, | and underneath that 4.03. 24
to his use | not half an hour before. 5.01. 92
and for three months before, | no int'rim, not a 5.01. 94
what occasion now | reveals before 'tis ripe, 5.01.154
you" many thousands moe | that go before it. WT 1.02. 9
when was't before? 1.02. 90
but once before i spoke to th' purpose? 1.02.100
that puts to | before her troth-plight: 1.02.278
she is, something before her time, deliver'd. 2.02. 23
sir, before polixenes | came to your court, how 3.02. 46
open air, before | i have got strength of limit. 3.02.105
i'll not be long before | i call upon thee. 3.03. 8
thrice bow'd before me, | and, gasping to begin 3.03. 24
since my desires | run not before mine honor, 4.04. 34
that come before the swallow dares, and take 4.04.119
must be tittle-tattling before all our guests? 4.04.246 P
own report, sir, hath danc'd before the king; 4.04.338 P
me breathe my life | before this ancient sir, 4.04.361
swain seems to wash | the hand was fair before! 4.04.367
of his highness settle, | come not before him. 4.04.472
for my visitation shall i | hold up before him? 4.04.556
walk before toward the sea-side, go on the right 4.04.824 P
let's before, as he bids us. 4.04.829 P
of something wildly | by us perform'd before. 5.01.130
but i was a gentleman born before my father; 5.02.140 P
full fourteen weeks before the course of time. JN 1.01.113
nay, i would have you go before me thither. 1.01.155
that will take pains to blow a horn before her? 1.01.219
before angiers well met, brave austria. 2.01. 1
welcome before the gates of angiers, duke. 2.01. 17
we'll lay before this town our royal bones, 2.01. 41
here | before the eye and prospect of your town, 2.01.208
have brought a countercheck before your gates, 2.01.224
in warlike march these greens before your town, 2.01.242
before the dew of evening fall, shall fleet | in 2.01.285
before we will lay down our just-borne arms 2.01.345
and even before this truce, but new before, | no 3.01.233
and even before this truce, but new before, | no 3.01.233
assured loss before the match be play'd. 3.01.336
haste before, | and ere our coming see thou 3.03. 6
foot of mine doth tread, | he lies before me. 3.03. 63
before the curing of a strong disease, | even in 3.04.112
you were crown'd before, | and that high royalty 4.02. 4
pomp, | to guard a title that was rich before, 4.02. 10
than did the fault before it was so patch'd. 4.02. 34
to this effect, before you were new crown'd, 4.02. 35
was | before the child himself felt he was sick. 4.02. 88
constance in a frenzy died | three days before; 4.02.123
bring them before me. 4.02.169
the better foot before. 4.02.170
soul, | kneeling before this ruin of sweet life, 4.03. 65
prophet | say that before ascension-day at noon 5.01. 26
before i drew this gallant head of war, | and 5.02.113
seek out king john and fall before his feet; 5.04. 13
king john did fly an hour or two before | the 5.05. 17
away before; 5.06. 43
my height | before this outdar'd dastard? R2 1.01.190
i take my leave before i have begun, | for 1.02. 60
hither | before king richard in his royal lists? 1.03. 32
hand | and bow my knee before his majesty, | for 1.03. 47
are men's ends mark'd than their lives before. 2.01. 11
deposing thee before thou wert possess'd, 2.01.107
my lord, your son was gone before i came. 2.02. 86
an hour before i came, the duchess died. 2.02. 97
tongue, | before i make reply to aught you say. 2.03. 73
art come | before the expiration of thy time, 2.03.111
then set before my face the lord aumerle. 4.01. 6
my lord, | before i freely speak my mind herein, 4.01.327
lest you be cropp'd before you come to prime. 5.02. 51
spur post, and get before him to the king, | and 5.02.112
a beggar begs that never begg'd before. 5.03. 78
back | of such as have before endur'd the like. 5.05. 30
before i knew thee, hal, i knew nothing, and now 1H4 1.02. 92 P
why, we will set forth before or after them and 1.02.169 P
before the game is afoot thou still let'st slip. 1.03.278
let us share, and then to horse before day. 2.02. 99 P
i did that i did not this seven year before, i 2.04.312 P
the hour before the heavenly-harness'd team 3.01.218
of a hair was never lost in my house before. 3.03. 58 P
i was never call'd so in mine own house before. 3.03. 63 P
ignorant a kind of fear | before not dreamt of. 4.01. 75
bardolph, get thee before to coventry; 4.02. 1 P
laid gifts before him, proffer'd him their oaths 4.03. 71
yet this before my father's majesty: 5.01. 96
yet, i would be loath to pay him before his day. 5.01.128 P
prince of wales stepp'd forth before the king, 5.02. 45
nay, before god, hal, if percy be alive, thou 5.03. 50 P
before, i lov'd thee as a brother, john, | but 5.04. 19
i run before king harry's victory, | who in a 2H4 in 23
and that the king before the douglas' rage in 31
broke loose, | and bears down all before him. 1.01. 11
i knew of this before, but, to speak truth, 1.01.210
i do here walk before thee like a sow that hath 1.02. 11 P
john, i sent for you before your expedition to 1.02.101 P
faith, you said so before. 2.01.137 P
before god, i am exceeding weary. 2.02. 1 P
once set a dish of apple-johns before him, and 2.04. 5 P
i was before master tisick, the debuty, t' other 2.04. 85 P
their names upon you before you have earn'd them 2.04.143 P
an excellent good word before it was ill sorted; 2.04.149 P
let's beat him before his whore. 2.04.257 P
you speak of me /even now before this honest, 2.04.301 P
i disprais'd him before the wicked, that the 2.04.319 P
i was prick'd well enough before, and you could 3.02.111 P
what, dost thou roar before thou art prick'd? 3.02.178 P
by old nightwork before i came to clement's inn. 3.02.209 P
all | that feel the bruises of the days before, 4.01. 98
before, and greet his grace. 4.01.226
our news shall go before us to his majesty, 4.03. 78
is the warming of the blood, which before (cold 4.03.104 P
say it did so a little time before | that our 4.04.127
thee with my honors | before thy hour be ripe? 4.05. 96
that had before my face murdered my father, 4.05.167
we will accite | (as i before rememb'red) all 5.02.142
and so i kneel down before you — but, indeed, ep 16 P
before the frenchman speak a word of it. H5 1.01. 97
before we hear him, of some things of weight 1.02. 5
save those to god, that run before our business. 1.02.303
for, god before, | we'll chide this dolphin at 1.02.307
swallow'd, and digested, | appear before us? 2.02. 57
they seem to threaten | runs far before them. 2.04. 71
cannon touches, | and down goes all before them. 3.pr. 34
yet, god before, tell him we will come on, 3.06.156
that every wretch, pining and pale before, 4.pr. 41
the organs, though defunct and dead before, 4.01. 21
that have before gor'd the gentle bosom of peace 4.01.165 P
than he was before guilty of those impieties for 4.01.175 P
i'll be before thee. 4.01.288
compound, | before thy most assured overthrow; 4.03. 81
his bended sword | before him through the city. 5.pr. 19
me, | if i demand, before this royal view, 5.02. 32
which you before so urg'd, lies in his answer. 5.02. 76
but, before god, kate, i cannot look greenly, 5.02.142 P
who, though i speak it before his face, if he be 5.02.241 P
maids in france to kiss before they are married, 5.02.266 P
which before would not abide looking on. 5.02.310 P
as love is, my lord, before it loves. 5.02.315 P
say'st thou, man, before dead henry's corse? 1H6 1.01. 62
he wanted pikes to set before his archers; 1.01.116
i know thee well, though never seen before. 1.02. 67
and, whereas i was black and swart before, 1.02. 84
thou wilt answer this before the pope. 1.03. 52
before the kings and queens of france. 1.06. 27
reign, | before whose glory i was great in arms, 2.05. 24
which obloquy set bars before my tongue, | else 2.05. 49
fast | before he'll buy again at such a rate. 3.02. 43
grace may starve, perhaps, before that time. 3.02. 48
here will i sit before the walls of roan | and 3.02. 91
but yet before we go, let's not forget | the 3.02.131
lets fall his sword before your highness' feet, 3.04. 9
before we met, or that a stroke was given, 4.01. 22
before young talbot from old talbot fly | the 4.06. 46
before that england give the french the foil. 5.03. 23
be so — | what ransom must i pay before i pass? 5.03. 73
suit, | before thou make a trial of her love? 5.03. 76
before i would have yielded to this league. 2H6 1.01.127
a proper jest, and never heard before, | that 1.01.132
in france, and starv'd in france, | before — 1.01.136
pride went before, ambition follows him. 1.01.180
i cannot go before | while gloucester bears this 1.02. 61
we'll hear more of your matter before the king. 1.03. 35 P
before we make election, give me leave | to show 1.03.162
a man that ne'er saw in his life before. 2.01. 63
but cloaks and gowns, before this day, a many. 2.01.113
never, before this day, in all his life. 2.01.114
edward the black prince died before his father, 2.02. 18
of the elder son | succeed before the younger, i 2.02. 52
i must offend before i be attainted; 2.04. 59
and my consent ne'er ask'd herein before? 2.04. 72
before his legs be firm to bear his body. 3.01.190
before his chaps be stain'd with crimson blood, 3.01.259
betime, | before the wound do grow uncurable; 3.01.286
shalt have cause to fear before i leave thee. 4.01.118
for our enemies shall /fall before us, inspir'd 4.02. 35 P
that those which fly before the battle ends 4.02.178
they fell before thee like sheep and oxen, and 4.03. 3 P
we will have the mayor's sword borne before us. 4.03. 14 P
and whereas, before, our forefathers had no 4.07. 34 P
to call poor men before them about matters they 4.07. 42 P
for with these borne before us, in stead of 4.07.135 P
your wives and daughters before your faces. 4.08. 31 P
nay, before them, if we can. 5.03. 28
before i see thee seated in that throne | which 3H6 1.01. 22
as shall revenge his death before i stir. 1.01.100
and creep into it far before thy time? 1.01.237
before i would have granted to that act. 1.01.245
but thou prefer'st thy life before thine honor; 1.01.246
not took | before a true and lawful magistrate 1.02. 23
sweet clifford, hear me speak before i die: 1.03. 18
o, let me pray before i take my death! 1.03. 35
turn back and fly, like ships before the wind, 1.04. 4
not his that spoils her young before her face. 2.02. 14
before thy sovereign and thy lawful king? 2.02. 86
you said so much before, and yet you fled. 2.02.106
i'll away before. 2.05.136
for (though before his face i speak the words) 2.06. 39
before the king will grant her humble suit. 3.02. 13
bona, hear me speak | before you answer warwick. 3.03. 66
before thy coming, lewis was henry's friend. 3.03.143
i told your majesty as much before: 3.03.179
before it pleas'd his majesty | to raise my 4.01. 67
from ravenspurgh haven before the gates of york, 4.07. 8
away betimes, before his forces join, | and take 4.08. 62
let him depart before we need his help. 5.04. 49
'twas sin before, but now 'tis charity. 5.05. 76
to strut before a wanton ambling nymph; R3 1.01. 17
sent before my time | into this breathing world, 1.01. 20
go you before, and i will follow you. 1.01.144
but yet i run before my horse to market: 1.01.160
marr'd, | that will i make before i let thee go. 1.03.165
were you snarling all before i came, | ready to 1.03.187
long die thy happy days before thy death, | and, 1.03.206
before i be convict by course of law, | to 1.04.187
take heed you dally not before your king, | lest 2.01. 12
rule, | this sickly land might solace as before. 2.03. 30
before the days of change, still is it so. 2.03. 41
see | the water swell before a boist'rous storm. 2.03. 44
to fly the boar before the boar pursues | were 3.02. 28
before i'll see the crown so foul misplac'd. 3.02. 44
go on before, i'll talk with this good fellow. 3.02. 95
i shall return before your lordship thence. 3.02.120
his grace not being warn'd thereof before: 3.07. 86
dear lord, | before i positively speak in this. 4.02. 25
that had his teeth before his eyes | to worry 4.04. 49
why, what wouldst thou do there before i go? 4.04.454
your highness told me i should post before. 4.04.455
bid him bring his power | before sunrising, lest 5.03. 61
high-rear'd bulwarks, stand before our faces. 5.03.242
or has given all before, and he begins | a new H8 1.01. 71
let be call'd before us | that gentleman of 1.02. 4
not long before your highness sped to france, 1.02.151
it, | that never see 'em pace before, the spavin 1.03. 12
his master would be serv'd before a subject, if 2.02. 7 P
serv'd before a subject, if not before the king, 2.02. 8 P
all men's honors | lie like one lump before him, 2.02. 48
doctor pace | in this man's place before him? 2.02.122
have your mouth fill'd up | before you open it. 2.03. 88
that there had reign'd by many | a year before. 2.04. 50
nay, before, | or god will punish me. 2.04. 74
the which before | his highness shall speak in, 2.04.102
before you all, appeal unto the pope, | to bring 2.04.119
before the primest creature | that's paragon'd 2.04.230
such joy | i never saw before. 4.01. 76
shake the press | and make 'em reel before 'em. 4.01. 79
he stepp'd before me happily | for my example. 4.02. 10
i must to him too, | before he go to bed. 5.01. 9
fell mischiefs | our reasons laid before him, 5.01. 50
sir, i did never win of you before. 5.01. 58
that you shall | this morning come before us, 5.01.101
this morning see | you do appear before them. 5.01.145
and your appeal to us | there make before them. 5.01.152
guy, nor colbrand, | to mow 'em down before me; 5.03. 23
never, before | this happy child, did i get any 5.04. 64
before the sun rose he was harness'd light, TRO 1.02. 8
ay, if i ever saw him before and knew him. 1.02. 65 P
sith /every action that hath gone before, 1.03. 13
they place before his hand that made the engine, 1.03.208
yourself shall feast with us before you go, 1.03.308
we do allowance give | before a sleeping giant. 2.03.138
here is a man — but 'tis before his face, | i 2.03.229
ay, sir, when he goes before me. 3.01. 3 P
we will not name desert before his birth, and, 3.02. 94 P
to send their smiles before them to achilles, 3.03. 72
or, if you please, | haste there before us. 4.01. 41
that swore to ride before him to the field. 4.04.142
stints their strife before their strokes begin. 4.05. 93
i had your heart before, this follows it. 5.02. 83
like scaling sculls | before the belching whale; 5.05. 23
fall down before him like a mower's swath. 5.05. 25
before we proceed any further, hear me speak. COR 1.01. 1 P
if they set down before 's, for the remove 1.02. 28
lartius are set down before their city corioles; 1.03. 99 P
now put your shields before your hearts, and 1.04. 24
of this feast, | having fully din'd before. 1.09. 11
what you have done, before our army hear me. 1.09. 27
before the common distribution, at | your only 1.09. 35
for what he did before corioles, call him, 1.09. 63
he had, before this last expedition, twenty-five 2.01.153 P
before him he carries noise, and behind him he 2.01.158 P
/chin he drove | the bristled lips before him. 2.02. 92
before and in corioles, let me say, | i cannot 2.02.102
as weeds before | a vessel under sail, so men 2.02.105
we will be there before the stream o' th' people 2.03.261
why this was known before. 3.01. 46
that prefer | a noble life before a long, and 3.01.153
will you hence | before the tag return, whose 3.01.247
is not then respected | for what before it was. 3.01.306
your power well on | before you had worn it out. 3.02. 18
before he should thus stoop to th' /herd, but 3.02. 32
perform a part | thou hast not done before. 3.02.110
chance | that starts i' th' way before thee. 4.01. 37
son | were in arabia, and thy tribe before him, 4.02. 24
this here before you. 4.04. 11
those my banishers, | stand i before thee here. 4.05. 84
directly to say the troth on't, before corioles; 4.05.186 P
of the senators but they stand bald before him. 4.05.194 P
he will mow all down before him, and leave his 4.05.202 P
the people, which before | were in wild hurry. 4.06. 3
of the war | destroy what lies before 'em. 4.06. 42
before you punish him, where he heard this, 4.06. 53
with fire, and took | what lay before them. 4.06. 79
and you'll look pale | before you find it other. 4.06.102
you that banish'd him | a mile before his tent, 5.01. 5
i kneel'd before him; 5.01. 65
you'll see your rome embrac'd with fire before 5.02. 7
we will before the walls of rome to-morrow | set 5.03. 1
cushion than the flint | i kneel before thee, 5.03. 54
or, if you'ld ask, remember this before: 5.03. 79
and the ground shrinks before his treading. 5.04. 19 P
strew flowers before them! 5.05. 3
and | intends t' appear before the people, 5.06. 7
nature, never known before | but to be rough, 5.06. 24
what faults he made before the last, i think 5.06. 63
before this earthy prison of their bones, | that TIT 1.01. 99
come on, my lords, the better foot before. 2.03.192
death, | and let me say (that never wept before) 3.01. 25
my grief was at the height before thou cam'st, 3.01. 70
for fear they die before their pardon come. 3.01.175
before the palace gate | to brave the tribune in 4.02. 35
this before all the world do i prefer, | this 4.02.109
go thou before, to be our ambassador. 4.04.100
an hour before the worshipp'd sun | peer'd forth ROM 1.01.118
but saying o'er what i have said before: 1.02. 7
indeed i should have ask'd /thee that before. 1.02. 77
for even the day before, she broke her brow, 1.03. 38
i gave thee mine before thou didst request it; 2.02.128
before, and apace. 2.04.217 P
but all this did i know before. 2.05. 46
for wearing his new doublet before easter? 3.01. 28 P
marry, go before to field, he'll be your 3.01. 58
this day | as is the night before some festival 3.02. 29
go before, nurse; 3.03.155
either be gone before the watch be set, | or by 3.03.167
for it was bad enough before their spite. 4.01. 31
because he married me before to romeo? 4.03. 27
i wake before the time that romeo | come to 4.03. 31
the night before thy wedding-day | hath death 4.05. 35
their keepers call | a lightning before death! 5.03. 90
and romeo dead, and juliet, dead before, | warm 5.03.196
this, | to press before thy father to a grave? 5.03.215
life | be sacrific'd some hour before his time, 5.03.268
even he drops down | the knee before him, and TIM 1.01. 61
most noble timon, call the man before thee. 1.01.113
i should fear those that dance before me now 1.02.143
put out of office | before i were forc'd out! 1.02.202
had you not fully laid my state before me, 2.02.125
brought in my accompts, | laid them before you; 2.02.134
call me before th' exactest auditors, | and set 2.02.156
now, before the gods, i am asham'd on't. 3.02. 17 P
purchase the day before for a little part, and 3.02. 47 P
servilius, now before the gods, i am not able to 3.02. 48 P
if you had sent but two hours before — 3.06. 45 P
outlives incertain pomp, is crown'd before: 4.03.243
but followed | the sug'red game before thee. 4.03.259

on each bush | lays her full mess before you. 4.03.421
the day serves, before black–corner'd night, 5.01. 44
camp | but i do prize it at my love before | the 5.01.181
before proud athens he's set down by this, 5.03. 9
so thou wilt send thy gentle heart before, | to 5.04. 48
set him before me, let me see his face. JC 1.02. 20
marry, before he fell down, when he perceiv'd 1.02.263 P
perhaps, speak this | before a willing bondman; 1.03.113
by all the gods that romans bow before, | i here 2.01.320
cowards die many times before their deaths, 2.02. 32
metellus cimber throws before thy seat | an 3.01. 34
before the eyes of both our armies here | (which 4.02. 43
bid him set on his pow'rs betimes before, | and 4.03.307
here, | answering before we do demand of them. 5.01. 6
words before blows: is it so, countrymen? 5.01. 27
and very wisely threat before you sting. 5.01. 38
to see my best friend ta'en before my face! 5.03. 35
defense, | and pour'd them down before him. MAC 1.03.100
thou art so far before, | that swiftest wing of 1.04. 16
whose care is gone before to bid us welcome: 1.04. 57
by which title, before, these weird sisters 1.05. 8 P
his spur, hath holp him | to his home before us. 1.06. 24
is this a dagger which i see before me, | the 2.01. 33
gouts of blood, | which was not so before. 2.01. 47
had i but died an hour before this chance, | i 2.03. 91
bring them before us. 3.01. 47
this deed i'll do before this purpose cool. 4.01.154
or else climb upward | to what they were before. 4.02. 25
shall have more vices than it had before, | more 4.03. 47
whither indeed, before /thy here–approach, | old 4.03.133
lives | expire before the flowers in their caps, 4.03.172
what wood is this before us? 5.04. 3
and bear't before him, thereby shall we shadow 5.04. 5
to kiss the ground before young malcolm's feet, 5.08. 28
before my body | i throw my warlike shield. 5.08. 32
had he his hurts before? 5.09. 12
time | before we reckon with your several loves, 5.09. 27
before my god, i might not this believe HAM 1.01. 56
thus twice before, and jump at this dead hour, 1.01. 65
appears before them, and with solemn march 1.02.201
too oft before their buttons be disclos'd, | and 1.03. 40
here, as before, never, so help you mercy, | how 1.05.169
before you visit him, to make inquire | of his 2.01. 4
to speak of horrors — he comes before me. 2.01. 81
makes vow before his uncle never more | to give 2.02. 70
so levied, as before, against the polack, | with 2.02. 75
before my daughter told me — what might you, 2.02.134
the murther of my father | before mine uncle. 2.02.596
already order | this night to play before him. 3.01. 21
there is a play to–night before the king, | one 3.02. 75
bring him before us. 4.03. 15
i'll be with you straight — go a little before. 4.04. 31
looking before and after, gave us not | that 4.04. 37
"quoth she, 'before you tumbled me, | you 4.05. 62
if 'a be not rotten before 'a die — as we have 5.01.165 P
/comply, sir, with his dug before 'a suck'd it. 5.02.187 P
to laertes before you fall to play. 5.02.207 P
saucily to the world before he was sent for, yet LR 1.01. 22 P
i'll do't before i speak — that you make known 1.01.226
has he never before sounded you in this business 1.02. 69 P
go you before to gloucester with these letters. 1.05. 1 P
have thee beaten for being old before thy time. 1.05. 42 P
come before my father. 2.01. 31
up thy heels, and beat thee before the king? 2.02. 30 P
shoulder that i see | before me at this instant. 2.02. 95
the night before there was no purpose in them 2.04. 3
that will house | before the head has any, | the 3.02. 28
merlin shall make, for i live before his time. 3.02. 95 P
yeoman that sees his son a gentleman before him. 3.06. 14 P
pinion him like a thief, bring him before us. 3.07. 23
'tis known before; 4.04. 22
tempt me again | to die before you please! 4.06.219
before you fight the battle, ope this letter. 5.01. 40
and let her speak of me before her father. OTH 1.03.116
to you, preferring you before her father, | so 1.03.187
before, behind thee, and on every hand, 2.01. 86
marry, before your ladyship, i grant, | she puts 2.01.105
great as my content | to see you here before me. 2.01.184
but, by your leave, not before me; 2.03.109 P
lieutenant is to be sav'd before the ancient. 2.03.110 P
you see this fellow that is gone before: 2.03.121
which till to–night | i ne'er might say before. 2.03.236
love shall grow stronger than it was before. 2.03.325 P
the day had broke | before we parted. 3.01. 33
before emilia here, | i give thee warrant of thy 3.03. 19
and weigh'st thy words before thou giv'st them 3.03.119
no, iago, | i'll see before i doubt; 3.03.190
i nev'r saw this before. 3.04.100
before me! look where she comes. 4.01.145 P
build on thee a better opinion than ever before. 4.02.206 P
if i do die before /thee, prithee shroud me | in 4.03. 24
a word or two before you go. 5.02.338
smooth success | be strew'd before your feet! ANT 1.03.101
were we before our armies, and to fight, | i 2.02. 26
of this my letters | before did satisfy you. 2.02. 52
before the gods my knee shall bow my prayers 2.03. 3
journey, be at /the mount | before you, lepidus. 2.04. 7
or i'll spurn thine eyes | like balls before me; 2.05. 64
and we shall talk before we fight. 2.06. 2
have we | our written purposes before us sent, 2.06. 4
then | i came before you here a man prepar'd 2.06. 40
caesar, and (as i said before) that which is the 2.06.128 P
bear the king's son's body | before our army. 3.01. 4
's will permit, | we shall appear before him. 3.01. 37
and spurns | the rush that lies before him; 3.05. 17
that day appear'd, and oft before gave audience, 3.06. 18
honor, ne'er before | did violate so itself. 3.10. 22
run one before, | and let the queen know of our 4.08. 1
before the sun shall see 's, we'll spill the 4.08. 3
poor enobarbus did | before thy face repent! 4.09. 10
seat | of fortunate caesar, drawn before him, 4.14. 76
before i strike this bloody stroke, farewell. 4.14. 91
when such a spacious mirror's set before him, 5.01. 34
been laden with like frailties which before 5.02.123
you with your children will he send before. 5.02.202
if she went before others i have seen, as that CYM 1.04. 72 P
and do't, i' th' court, before | her father. 2.04.148
i see before me, man; 3.02. 78
false oaths prevail'd | before my perfect honor, 3.03. 67
if't be summer news, | smile to't before; 3.04. 13
ta'en thy stand, | th' elected deer before thee? 3.04.109
she hath not appear'd | before the roman, nor to 3.05. 31
call her before us, for | we have been too 3.05. 34
but even before, i was | at point to sink for 3.06. 16
before i enter'd here i call'd, and thought | to 3.06. 46
thy garments cut to pieces before /her face: 4.01. 18 P
be | doth miracle itself, lov'd before me. 4.02. 29
of my dear'st mother | it did not speak before. 4.02.191
go before | this lout as he exceeds our lords, 5.02. 8
how they wound | some slain before, some dying, 5.03. 47
naked breast | stepp'd before targes of proof, 5.05. 5
having receiv'd the punishment before | for that 5.05.343
before thee stands this fair hesperides, | with PER 1.01. 27
as these before thee, thou thyself shalt bleed. 1.01. 58
but being play'd upon before your time, | hell 1.01. 84
and punish that before that he would punish. 1.02. 33
poor men that were cast away before us even now. 2.01. 19 P
driving the poor fry before him, and at last 2.01. 31 P
where, driven before the winds, he is arriv'd 5.ch. 14
seeing this goodly vessel ride before us, | i 5.01. 18
i am the governor of this place you lie before. 5.01. 21
maid, | my lord, that ne'er before invited eyes, 5.01. 85
are met together | before the people all, 5.01.243
whose sovereigns fell before | the wrath of TNK 1.01. 39
asprays do the fish, | subdue before they touch. 1.01.139
not dreams we stand before your puissance, 1.01.155
as before, hence you, | and at the banks of 1.01.211
thebes and the temptings in't before we further 1.02. 4
or to go tiptoe | before the street be foul? 1.02. 58
our hands advanc'd before our hearts, what will 1.02.112
before one salmon, you shall take a number of 2.01. 4 P
before my liberty. 2.02.159
by any means | before the ladies see us, and do 2.03. 57
of one meal lend me — come before me then, | a 3.01. 74
/open her before the wind! 3.04. 9
and the boar, | break comely out before him; 3.05. 19
to speak, before thy noble grace, this tenner; 3.05.123
but still before that flew | the lightning of 3.06. 84
only a little let him fall before me, | that i 3.06.178
i'll be cut a–pieces | before i take this oath. 3.06.257
before us that are here, can force his cousin 3.06.294
for i came home before the business | was fully 4.01. 4
and before the gods | tender their holy prayers. 5.01. 1
before the holy altars of your helpers, | the 5.01. 12
before i turn, let me embrace thee, cousin; 5.01. 31
go with me | before the god of our profession. 5.01. 38
with his crutch, and cure him | before apollo; 5.01. 83
let us rise | and bow before the goddess. 5.01.136
will be honest, | she has the path before her. 5.02. 23
before god, that's as true as the gospel. STM II.C 88 P
let me set up before your thoughts, good friends II.C 90
being mad before, how doth she now for wits? VEN 249
now was she just before him as he sat, | and 349
who plucks the bud before one leaf put forth? 416
i had my load before, now press'd with bearing: 430
even as the wind is hush'd before it raineth, 458
or as the wolf doth grin before he barketh, | or 459
or as the berry breaks before it staineth, | or 460
before i know myself, seek not to know me, | no 525
for he the night before, in tarquin's tent, LUC 15
before you blot | with your uncleanness that 192
end thy ill aim before thy shoot be ended; 579
when thus thy vices bud before thy spring? 604
and lust, the thief, far poorer than before. 693
throng her inventions, which shall go before. 1302
as lagging fowls before the northern blast. 1335
before the which is drawn the power of greece, 1368
and that deep vow which brutus made before, | he 1847
falls, through wind, before the fall should be. PP 10. 6
they that fawn'd on him before | use his company 20.47
sets you most rich in youth before my sight, SON 15.10
moan, | which i new pay as if not paid before: 30.12
what hast thou then more than thou hadst before? 40. 2
all mine was thine, before thou hadst this more. 40. 4
but that which is | hath been before, how are 59. 2
each changing place with that which goes before, 60. 3
in days long since, before these last so bad. 67.14
before these bastard signs of fair were born, 68. 3
before the golden tresses of the dead, | the 68. 5
words come hindmost) holds his rank before. 85.12
mend, | to mar the subject that before was well? 103.10
those lines that i before have writ do lie, 115. 1
than think that we before have heard them told. 123. 8
woe, | before, a joy propos'd, behind, a dream. 129.12
to follow that which flies before her face, 143. 7

BEFORE–BREACH 1 FR 0.0001 REL FR 0 V 1 P
men are punish'd for before–breach of the king's H5 4.01.170 P

BEFOREHAND *(also aforehand, 'forehand)*

BEFOREHAND 2 FR 0.0002 REL FR 2 V 0 P
since it hath been beforehand with our griefs. JN 5.07.111
all this beforehand counsel comprehends. LUC 494

BEFORE'T 2 FR 0.0002 REL FR 2 V 0 P
and we shall have more wars before't be long. 3H6 4.06. 91
and will endure | our setting down before't. MAC 5.04. 10

BEFORE–TIME 1 FR 0.0001 REL FR 1 V 0 P
martius, and i have | before–time seen him thus. COR 1.06. 24

BEFORTUNE 1 FR 0.0001 REL FR 1 V 0 P
me, | as much i wish all good befortune you. TGV 4.03. 41

BEFRIEND 5 FR 0.0005 REL FR 4 V 1 P
thou mayst befriend me so much as to think | i JN 5.06. 10
and god befriend us, as our cause is just! 1H4 5.01.120
o earth, i will befriend thee more with rain, TIT 3.01. 16
will you befriend me so far as to use mine own TIM 3.02. 57 P
i shall beseech him to befriend himself. JC 2.04. 30

BEFRIENDED 2 FR 0.0002 REL FR 2 V 0 P
if in his death the gods have us befriended, TRO 5.09. 9
o happy man, they have befriended thee! TIT 3.01. 52

BEFRIENDS 2 FR 0.0002 REL FR 2 V 0 P
my rest and negligence befriends thee now, | but TRO 5.06. 17
that you were once unkind befriends me now, SON 120. 1

/BEG 2 FR 0.0002 REL FR 2 V 0 P
/i'll /beg /one /boon, | /and /then /be /gone R2 4.01.302
/being /so /great, /i /have /no /need /to /beg. 4.01.309

BEG 103 FR 0.0116 REL FR 88 V 15 P
a smaller boon than this i cannot beg, | and TGV 5.04. 24
that i do beg his life, if it be sin, | heaven MM 2.04. 69
as aged, and doth beg the alms | of palsied eld; 3.01. 35
and sequent death, | is all the grace i beg. 5.01.374
beg thou, or borrow, to make up the sum, | and ERR 1.01.153
lam'd me, i shall beg with it from door to door. 4.04. 39 P
how i would make him fawn, and beg, and seek, LLL 5.02. 62
beg a greater matter, | thou now requests but 5.02.207
thou bid'st me beg; 5.02.210
you cannot beg us, sir, i can assure you, sir, 5.02.490
i beg the ancient privilege of athens: MND 1.01. 41
i do but beg a little changeling boy | to be my 2.01.120
what worser place can i beg in your love | (and 2.01.208
wak'st, if she be by, | beg of her for remedy. 3.02.109
i'll to my queen and beg her indian boy; 3.02.375
i beg the law, the law, upon his head. 4.01.155
down therefore, and beg mercy of the duke. MV 4.01.363
beg that thou mayst have leave to hang thyself, 4.01.364
you taught me first to beg, and now methinks 4.01.439
beg, when that is spent? AYL 1.01. 75 P
what, wouldst thou have me go and beg my food? 2.03. 31
a beggar, therefore to beg will not become me. ep 10 P
i do beg your good will in this case. AWW 1.03. 21 P
you beg a single penny more. 5.02. 37 P
you beg more than "word" then. 5.02. 40 P
but first i beg my pardon — the young lord 5.03. 12
and on our knees we beg | (as recompense of our WT 2.03.149
a race or two of ginger, but that i may beg; 4.03. 48 P
would he do so, i'ld beg your precious mistress, 5.01.223
upon my knee i beg, go not to arms | against JN 3.01.308
i do not ask you much, | i beg cold comfort; 5.07. 42
and to beg | enfranchisement immediate on his R2 3.03.113
and beg thy pardon ere he do accuse thee. 5.02.113
yet such extenuation let me beg | as, in reproof 1H4 3.02. 22
to sue his livery and beg his peace, | with 4.03. 62
did you beg any? god forbid! 5.02. 35
they are for the town's end, to beg during life. 5.03. 38 P
it is worse shame to beg than to be on the worst 2H4 1.02. 76 P
and never shall you see that i will beg | a 5.02. 37
my duty, and my speech, to beg your pardons. ep 3 P
most humbly on my knee i beg | the leading of H5 4.03.130
here on my knee i beg mortality, | rather than 1H6 4.05. 32
hence, | i care not whither, for i beg no favor; 2H6 2.04. 92
make thee beg pardon for thy passed speech, 3.02.221
ay, but she's come to beg; 3H6 3.01. 42
i think he means to beg a child of her. 3.02. 27
call edward king and at his hands beg mercy? 5.01. 23
stroke, | and humbly beg the death upon my knee. R3 1.02.178
may | but beg one favor at thy gracious hand, 1.02.207
me, | as you would beg, were you in my distress. 1.04.266
this do i beg of /god, | when i am cold in love 2.01. 39
yet none of you would once beg for his life. 2.01.131
me, | 'twas not my purpose thus to beg a kiss. TRO 3.02.137
may i, sweet lady, beg a kiss of you? 4.05. 47
why, beg then. 4.05. 48
gifts, am bound to beg | of my lord general. COR 1.09. 80
to th' people, beg their stinking breaths. 2.01.236
should i stand here | to beg of hob and dick, 2.03.116
to beg of thee, it is my more dishonor | than 3.02.124
kneel in the streets and beg for grace in vain. TIT 1.01.455
'tis present death i beg, and one thing more 2.03.173
upon my feeble knee | i beg this boon, with 2.03.289
saturnine and his emperess | beg at the gates, 3.01.298
villains, for shame you could not beg for grace. 5.02:179
out | to beg relief among rome's enemies, | who 5.03.106
i beg for justice, which thou, prince, must give ROM 3.01.180
beg pardon of the prince, and call thee back 3.03.152
and you be not, hang, beg, starve, die in the 3.05.192
to fall prostrate here | and beg your pardon. 4.02. 21
i beg of you to know me, good my lord, | t' TIM 4.03.487
to beg enfranchisement for publius cimber. JC 3.01. 57
beg not your death of us. 3.01.164
to beg the voice and utterance of my tongue) | a 3.01.261
yea, beg a hair of him for memory, | and, dying, 3.02.134
who neither beg nor fear | your favors nor your MAC 1.03. 60
and more i beg not. 5.07. 23
what wouldst thou beg, laertes, | that shall not HAM 1.02. 45
your clemency, | we beg your hearing patiently. 3.02.151
times | virtue itself of vice must pardon beg, 3.04.154
to be blest, | i'll blessing beg of you. 3.04.172
to–morrow shall i beg leave to see your kingly 4.07. 44 P
that he could nothing do but wish and beg | your 4.07.104
such–a–one's horse, when 'a /meant to beg it, 5.01. 85 P
there's mine, beg another of thy daughters. LR 1.04.108 P
on my knees i beg | that you'll vouchsafe me 2.04.155
pension beg | to keep base life afoot. 2.04.214
he has some reason, else he could not beg. 4.01. 31
i therefore beg it not | to please the palate of OTH 1.03.261
beg often our own harms, which the wise pow'rs ANT 2.01. 6
with what gift beside | thy modesty can beg. 2.05. 72
keep decorum, must | no less beg than a kingdom. 5.02. 18
be pale, i beg but leave to air this jewel. CYM 2.04. 96
i do not bid thee beg my life, good lad, | and 5.05.101
would now be glad of bread and beg for it; PER 1.04. 41
he asks of you that never us'd to beg. 2.01. 62
no, friend, cannot you beg? 2.01. 63 P
hark you, my friend, you said you could not beg? 2.01. 86 P
to beg of you, kind friends, this coat of worth, 2.01.136
myself to beg, if i priz'd life so much | as to TNK 3.02. 23
which cannot want due mercy, i beg first. 3.06.209
an antic 'fore the duke, | and beg his pardon." 4.01. 76
boy, | 'tis but a kiss i beg, why art thou coy? VEN 96
i'll beg her love: LUC 241

BEGAN *(also can*, gan)*

/BEGAN 1 FR 0.0001 REL FR 1 V 0 P
/the /strings /of /life | /began /to /crack. LR 5.03.218

BEGAN 45 FR 0.0050 REL FR 39 V 6 P
my very visor began to assume life and scold ADO 2.01.241 P
time, | my lungs began to crow like chanticleer, AYL 2.07. 30
this carol they began that hour, | with a hey, 5.03. 26
began to scold and raise up such a storm | that SHR 1.01.172
live" — | this his good melancholy oft began, AWW 1.02. 56
yet you began rudely. TN 1.05.212 P
be), who began to be much sea–sick, and himself WT 5.02.118 P
lady, | dear queen, that ended when i but began, 5.03. 45
began to give me ground; 1H4 2.04.216 P
they surfeited with honey and began | to loathe 3.02. 71
once writ a sonnet in his praise and began thus: H5 3.07. 40 P
'tis thought, lord talbot, when the fight began, 1H6 2.02. 22

since henry monmouth first began to reign, 2.05. 23
nay, let it rest where it began at first. 4.01.121
upon my life, began her devilish practices; 2H6 3.01. 46
and when the dusky sky began to rob | my 3.02.104
how began it first? 3H6 1.02. 5
o, then began the tempest to my soul! R3 1.04. 44
first i began in private | with you, my lord of H8 2.04.207
the grecians began to proclaim barbarism, and TRO 5.04. 16 P
how youngly he began to serve his country, | how COR 2.03.236
he had continued to his country | as he began, 4.02. 31
speak, nephew, were you by when it began? ROM 1.01.105
benvolio, who began this bloody fray? 3.01.151
of sorrow stand in thine, | began to water. JC 3.01.285
new supplies of men, | began a fresh assault. MAC 1.02. 33
the thane of cawdor, began a dismal conflict, 1.02. 53
and anon methought | the wood began to move. 5.05. 34
who began this? OTH 2.03.178
give me to know | how this foul rout began; 2.03.210
then began | a stop i' th' chaser; CYM 5.03. 39
as virtue) he began | his mistress' picture, 5.05.174
was my mother, who did end | the minute i began.
PER 5.01.212
some say, began to throw | her bow away, and TNK 5.01. 93
"thrice fairer than myself," thus she began, VEN 7
by this the love–sick queen began to sweat, 175
once more the engine of her thoughts began: 367
whereat her tears began to turn their tide, 979
and their ranks began | to break upon the galled LUC 1439
"show me the strumpet that began this stir, 1471
each present lord began to promise aid, | as 1696
with this they all at once began to say, | her 1709
began to clothe his wit in state and pride, 1809
by her, | under a myrtle shade began to woo him. PP 11. 2
his phoenix down began but to appear | like LC 93

BEGAN'ST 1 FR 0.0001 REL FR 1 V 0 P
that thou began'st to twist so fine a story? ADO 1.01.311

BEGAN'T 1 FR 0.0001 REL FR 1 V 0 P
iago, who began't? OTH 2.03.217

BE–GAR 4 FR 0.0004 REL FR 0 V 4 P
ay, be–gar, and de maid is love–a me. WIV 3.02. 64 P
be–gar nor i too; there is no–bodies. 3.03.213 P
ay, be–gar, and 'tis a boy. 5.05.209 P
be–gar, i'll raise all windsor. 5.05.209 P

/BEGET 1 FR 0.0001 REL FR 1 V 0 P
/one /self /mate /and /make /could /not /beget LR 4.03. 34

BEGET 22 FR 0.0024 REL FR 18 V 4 P
did beget of him | a falsehood in its contrary, TMP 1.02. 94
of you, | but rather to beget more love in you. TGV 3.01. 97
such friends as time in padua shall beget. SHR 1.01. 45
if old sir robert did beget us both, | and were JN 1.01. 80
father, and these two beget | a generation of R2 5.05. 7
those whom you call'd fathers did beget you. H5 3.01. 23
and doth beget new courage in our breasts. 1H6 3.03. 87
not so, | i did beget her, all the parish knows. 5.04. 11
conqueror, | is likely to beget more conquerors, 5.05. 74
this deadly quarrel daily doth beget! 3H6 2.05. 91
thing you gave in charge | beget your happiness, R3 4.03. 26
i will beget | mine issue of your blood upon 4.04.297
live and beget a happy race of kings! 5.03.152
this one christening will beget a thousand, here H8 5.03. 37 P
hot thoughts, and hot thoughts beget hot deeds, TRO 3.01.130 P
will beget | a very excellent piece of villainy. TIT 2.03. 6
we may, | till time beget some careful remedy. 4.03. 30
they never do beget a coal–black calf. 5.01. 32
you must acquire and beget a temperance that may
HAM 3.02. 7 P
some blood drawn on me would beget opinion | of
LR 2.01. 33
would marry a gallows and beget young gibbets, i CYM 5.04.199 P
thou that beget'st him that did thee beget; PER 5.01.195

BEGETS 7 FR 0.0008 REL FR 4 V 3 P
his eye begets occasion for his wit, | for every LLL 2.01. 69
fear, and not love, begets his penitence. R2 5.03. 56
lies are like their father that begets them, 1H4 2.04.225 P
hot blood, and hot blood begets hot thoughts, TRO 3.01.129 P
seldom but that pity begets you a good opinion, PER 4.02.120 P
but gold that's put to use more gold begets." VEN 768
that makes him honor'd, or begets him hate; LUC 1005

BEGET'ST 1 FR 0.0001 REL FR 1 V 0 P
thou that beget'st him that did thee beget; PER 5.01.195

BEGETTING 4 FR 0.0004 REL FR 4 V 0 P
earth | might thus have stood, begetting wonder, WT 5.01.133
o heavy times, begetting such events! 3H6 2.05. 63
loins, my liege, | and blood of your begetting. CYM 5.05.331
wife, ever begetting | new births of love; TNK 2.02. 80

BEGGAR 61 FR 0.0069 REL FR 32 V 29 P
will not give a doit to relieve a lame beggar, TMP 2.02. 32 P
to speak puling, like a beggar at hallowmas. TGV 2.01. 26 P
yes, your beggar of fifty; MM 3.02.125 P
he would mouth with a beggar, though she smelt 3.02.183 P
satin, which now peaches him a beggar. 4.03. 12 P
it on my shoulders, as a beggar wont her brat; ERR 4.04. 37 P
is not marriage honorable in a beggar? ADO 3.04. 30 P
not a ballet, boy, of the king and the beggar? LLL 1.02.110 P
the pernicious and indubitate beggar zenelophon; 4.01. 66 P
to the beggar. 4.01. 73 P
the beggar. 4.01. 73 P
the beggar. 4.01. 74 P
thou the beggar, for so witnesseth thy lowliness 4.01. 79 P
a beggar, that was us'd to come so smug upon the MV 3.01. 46 P
you teach me how a beggar should be answer'd. 4.01.440
breeding, be married under a bush like a beggar? AYL 3.03. 84 P
i am not furnish'd like a beggar, therefore to ep 10 P
would not the beggar then forget himself? SHR in.1. 41
no better than a poor and loathsome beggar. in.1. 123
wilt thou needs be a beggar? AWW 1.03. 20 P
the king's a beggar, now the play is done; ep 1
the /king lies by a beggar, if a beggar dwells TN 3.01. 8 P
lies by a beggar, if a beggar dwells near him; 3.01. 9 P
hope, is not great, sir — begging but a beggar: 3.01. 55 P
cressida was a beggar. 3.01. 55 P
leave out | betwixt the prince and beggar. WT 2.01. 87
yet, | like a poor beggar, raileth on the rich. JN 2.01.592
well, whiles i am a beggar, i will rail, | and 2.01.593
a beggar begs that never begg'd before. R2 5.03. 78
and now chang'd to "the beggar and the king." 5.03. 80
then treasons make me wish myself a beggar, 5.05. 33
but when he took a beggar to his bed, | and 3H6 2.02.154
and spurn upon thee, beggar, for thy boldness. R3 1.02. 42
a begging prince what beggar pities not? 1.04.267
a beggar, brother? 3.01.112
in weightier things you'll say a beggar nay. 3.01.119
th' ensuing night | made it a fool and beggar. H8 1.01. 28
beggar the estimation which you priz'd | richer TRO 2.02. 91
this, | to show him what a beggar his heart is, TIM 1.02.195
day sent to me, i was so unfortunate a beggar. 3.06. 43 P
his poor self, | a dedicated beggar to the air, 4.02. 13
raise me this beggar, and deny't that lord, 4.03. 9
contempt hereditary, | the beggar native honor. 4.03. 11
courtier be again, | wert thou not beggar. 4.03.242
from the bone | ere thou relieve the beggar. 4.03.529
beggar that i am, i am /even poor in thanks — HAM 2.02.272 P
fat king and your lean beggar is but variable 4.03. 23 P
may go a progress through the guts of a beggar. 4.03. 31 P
nothing but the composition of a knave, beggar, LR 2.02. 21 P
madman and beggar too. 4.01. 30
a poor unfortunate beggar. 4.06. 68
thou hast seen a farmer's dog bark at a beggar? 4.06.155 P
a beggar in his drink | could not have laid such OTH 4.02.120
forget to send to antony, | shall die a beggar. ANT 1.05. 65
if your master | would have a queen his beggar, 5.02. 16
thou took'st a beggar, wouldst have made my CYM 1.01.141
flat, for taking a beggar without less quality. 1.04. 23 P
to the bare fortune of that beggar posthumus, 3.05.119 P
or what fond beggar, but to touch the crown, LUC 216
like to a bankrout beggar wails his case: 711
as, to behold desert a beggar born, | and needy SON 66. 2

BEGGAR'D 6 FR 0.0006 REL FR 6 V 0 P
lean, rent, and beggar'd by the strumpet wind! MV 2.06. 19
big mars seems bankrout in their beggar'd host, H5 4.02. 43
you to the grave, | and beggar'd yours for ever? MAC 3.01. 90
death, | wherein necessity, of matter beggar'd, HAM 4.05. 92
her own person, | it beggar'd all description: ANT 2.02.198
beggar'd of blood to blush through lively veins, SON 67.10

BEGGAR–FEAR 1 FR 0.0001 REL FR 1 V 0 P
or with pale beggar–fear impeach my height R2 1.01.189

BEGGARLY 10 FR 0.0011 REL FR 5 V 5 P
a penny and he renders me the beggarly thanks. AYL 2.05. 29 P
the rest were ragged, old, and beggarly, | yet, SHR 4.01.137
they are exceeding poor and bare, too beggarly. 1H4 4.02. 69 P
arrant, rascally, beggarly, lousy knave it is. H5 4.08. 34 P
the rascally, scald, beggarly, lousy, pragging 5.01. 5 P
my dukedom to a beggarly denier, | i do mistake R3 1.02.251
years in court | (am yet a courtier beggarly) H8 2.03. 83
his shelves | a beggarly account of empty boxes, ROM 5.01. 45
a base, proud, shallow, beggarly, three–suited, LR 2.02. 16 P
he do shake me off | to beggarly divorcement) OTH 4.02.158

BEGGAR–MAID 1 FR 0.0001 REL FR 1 V 0 P
when king cophetua lov'd the beggar–maid! ROM 2.01. 14

BEGGAR–MAN 1 FR 0.0001 REL FR 1 V 0 P
is it a beggar–man? LR 4.01. 29

BEGGAR'S 10 FR 0.0011 REL FR 8 V 2 P
hand | took up a beggar's issue at my gates, ADO 4.01.132
the beggar's. LLL 4.01. 76 P
thou, when thou command'st the beggar's knee, H5 4.01.256
a beggar's book | outworths a noble's blood. H8 1.01.122
a beggar's tongue | make motion through my lips, COR 3.02.117
being holiday, the beggar's shop is shut. ROM 5.01. 56
steal but a beggar's dog | and give it timon, TIM 2.01. 5
i had rather be a beggar's dog than apemantus. 4.03.356 P
the dung, | the beggar's nurse and caesar's. ANT 5.02. 8
let him have time a beggar's orts to crave, LUC 985

/BEGGARS' 1 FR 0.0001 REL FR 0 V 1 P
/outstretch'd /heroes /the /beggars' /shadows. HAM 2.02.264 P

/BEGGARS 1 FR 0.0001 REL FR 0 V 1 P
/then /are /our /beggars /bodies, /and /our HAM 2.02.263 P

BEGGARS 24 FR 0.0027 REL FR 19 V 5 P
beggars that come unto my father's door | upon SHR 4.03. 4
of kings, of beggars, old men, young men, maids, JN 2.01.570
not be the last — like seely beggars | who, R2 5.05. 25
nor moody beggars, starving for a time | of 1H4 5.01. 81
barren, barren, beggars all, beggars all, sir 2H4 5.03. 7 P
barren, beggars all, beggars all, sir john! 5.03. 7 P
that beggars mounted runt their horse to death. 3H6 1.04.127
it beggars any man that keeps it. R3 1.04.141 P
these famish'd beggars weary of their lives, 5.03.329
for they pass'd by me | as misers do by beggars, TRO 3.03.143
speaking is for beggars; 3.03.269 P
but that | which they have given to beggars. COR 3.01. 74
they are but beggars that can count their worth, ROM 2.06. 32
mine heir from forth the beggars of the world, TIM 1.01.138
of his) | what charitable men afford to beggars. 3.02. 75
when beggars die there are no comets seen; JC 2.02. 30
me proof and president | of bedlam beggars, who, LR 2.03. 14
our basest beggars | are in the poorest thing 2.04.264
so beggars marry many. 3.02. 30
and take a queen | worth many babes and beggars!
ANT 5.02. 48
two beggars told me | i could not miss my way. CYM 3.06. 8
and falsehood | is worse in kings than beggars. 3.06. 14
why, are /your beggars whipt then? PER 2.01. 90
for if all your beggars were whipt, i would wish 2.01. 92 P

BEGGAR–WOMAN 1 FR 0.0001 REL FR 1 V 0 P
to nurse, | was by a beggar–woman stol'n away, 2H6 4.02.143

BEGGARY 12 FR 0.0013 REL FR 10 V 2 P
and usurp the beggary he was never born to. MM 3.02. 93 P
death | of learning, late deceas'd in beggary." MND 5.01. 53
shall be | to say there is no vice but beggary. JN 2.01.596
rage, | and countenanc'd by boys and beggary — 2H4 4.01. 35
reproach and beggary | is crept into the palace 2H6 4.01.101
'a must needs, for beggary is valiant. 4.02. 54 P
delay /leads impotent and snail–pac'd beggary. R3 4.03. 53
contempt and beggary hangs upon thy back; ROM 5.01. 71
there's beggary in the love that can be reckon'd ANT 1.01. 15
pronounce | the beggary of his change; CYM 1.06.115
is no more dependancy | but brats and beggary) 2.03.119
promis'd nought | but beggary and poor looks. 5.05. 10

BEGG'D 29 FR 0.0032 REL FR 27 V 2 P
that love i begg'd for you, he begg'd of me. ERR 4.02. 12
that love i begg'd for you, he begg'd of me. 4.02. 12
her, | and she in mild terms begg'd my patience, MND 4.01. 58
clerk, | a prating boy, that begg'd it as a fee. MV 5.01.164
his ring away | unto the judge that begg'd it, 5.01.180
that took some pains in writing, he begg'd mine, 5.01.182
and begg'd the ring, the which i did deny him, 5.01.212
i think you would have begg'd | the ring of me 5.01.221
i understand you, sir. 'tis well begg'd. TN 3.01. 53 P
is bought more oft than begg'd or borrow'd. 3.04. 3
it, and exactly begg'd | your grace's pardon, R2 1.01.140
a beggar begs that never begg'd before. 5.03. 78
i should have begg'd i might have been employ'd. 1H6 4.01. 72
and given in earnest what i begg'd in jest. R3 5.01. 22
o, well begg'd! COR 1.09. 87
there's in all two worthy voices begg'd. 2.03. 81 P
he mock'd us when he begg'd our voices. 2.03.159
that saidst i begg'd the empire at thy hands. TIT 1.01.307
for 'tis not life that i have begg'd so long, 2.03.170
hath begg'd that i will stay at home to–day. JC 2.02. 82
led him, begg'd for him, sav'd him from despair; LR 5.03.192
to such a trifle), | he begg'd of me to steal't. OTH 5.02.229
whereon, i begg'd | his pardon for return. ANT 3.06. 59
cried he? and begg'd 'a pardon? 3.13.132
to have begg'd or bought what i have took. CYM 3.06. 47
this is the man | was begg'd and banish'd, this TNK 3.06.143
their knees | begg'd with such handsome pity, 4.01. 9
they that nev'r begg'd | but they prevail'd, had 4.01. 26
and begg'd for that which thou unask'd shalt VEN 102

/BEGGING 2 FR 0.0002 REL FR 2 V 0 P
/betwixt /thy /begging /and /my /meditation. R3 4.02.115
/as /begging /hermits /in /their /holy /prayers. TIT 3.02. 41

BEGGING 9 FR 0.0010 REL FR 5 V 4 P
this begging is not strange. LLL 5.02.210
hope, is not great, sir — begging but a beggar: TN 3.01. 54 P
a young knave, and begging? 2H4 1.02. 72 P
a begging prince what beggar pities not? R3 1.04.267
i have been begging sixteen years in court | (am H8 2.03. 82
my desire yet to trouble the poor with begging. COR 2.03. 70 P
gets more with begging than we can do with PER 2.01. 64 P
wrinching our holy begging in our eyes | to make TNK 1.01.156
'tis worse to me than begging | to take my life 3.06.266

BEGIN *(also gin*, etc.)*

/BEGIN 2 FR 0.0002 REL FR 2 V 0 P
/th' /obstructions /which /begin /to /stop 2H4 4.01. 65
/shalt /read /when /mine /begin /to /dazzle. TIT 3.02. 85

BEGIN 119 FR 0.0134 REL FR 84 V 35 P
i do begin to have bloody thoughts. TMP 4.01.220 P
begin to chase the ignorant fumes that mantle 5.01. 67
even as i would, when i to love begin. TGV 1.01. 10
you always end ere you begin. 2.04. 32 P
that thus without advice begin to love her? 2.04.208
i do begin to perceive that i am made an ass. WIV 5.05.119 P
thine own confession, learn to begin thy health; MM 1.02. 38 P
i now begin with grief and shame to utter. 5.01. 96
but, like a shrew, you first begin to brawl. ERR 4.01. 51
now begin, | for look where beatrice, like a ADO 3.01. 23
some riddle — come, thy l'envoy — begin. LLL 3.01. 71
now will i begin your moral, and do you follow 3.01. 93 P
how did this argument begin? 3.01.105
and, to begin, wench — so god help me, law! 5.02.414
begin, sir, you are my elder. 5.02.605 P
ver, begin. 5.02.893 P
pyramus, you begin. MND 3.01. 74 P
made senseless things begin to do them wrong, 3.02. 28
her dotage now i do begin to pity. 4.01. 47
begin these wood–birds but to couple now? 4.01.140
i'll begin it — ding, dong, bell. MV 3.02. 71
begin you to grow upon me? AYL 1.01. 85 P
you must begin, "will you, orlando" — 4.01.129 P
we'll begin these rites, | as we do trust 5.04.197
to conjure you, and i'll begin with the women. ep 12 P
horse in padua to begin his wooing that would SHR 1.01.143 P
and he begin once, he'll rail in his rope–tricks 1.02.111 P
fingering, | i must begin with rudiments of art, 3.01. 66
now i begin: 4.01. 66 P
who shall begin? 5.02. 75
come on, i say, and first begin with her. 5.02.133
i say she shall, and first begin with her. 5.02.135
possession of the bride, | /end ere i do begin. AWW 2.05. 27
of my cupid's knock'd out, and i begin to love, 3.02. 15 P
they begin to smoke me, and disgraces have of 4.01. 27 P
i begin to love him for this. 4.03.262 P
much shame, you might begin an impudent nation. 4.03.328 P
go thy ways, i begin to be a–weary of thee, and 4.05. 56 P
begin, fool. TN 2.03. 68 P
i shall never begin if i hold my peace. 2.03. 70 P
good, i' faith. come, begin. 2.03. 71 P
and, gasping to begin some speech, her eyes WT 3.03. 25
can be thought to begin from such a cottage. 4.02. 43 P
when daffadils begin to peer, | with heigh, the 4.03. 1
appear soul–vex'd, | and begin, "why to me — ?" 5.01. 60
would she begin a sect, might quench the zeal 5.01.107
sir," | thus, leaning on mine elbow, i begin, JN 1.01.194
cousin, throw up your gage, do you begin. R2 1.01.186
order the trial, marshal, and begin. 1.03. 99
desire, | attending but the signal to begin. 1.03.116
and see already how he doth begin | to make us 1H4 1.03.289
and begin to patch up thine old body for heaven? 2H4 2.04.233 P
doth begin to melt | and drop upon our bare 2.04.364
france win, | then with scotland first begin." H5 1.02.168
me best, | if i begin the batt'ry once again, 3.03. 7
i have heard a sonnet begin so to one's mistress 3.07. 41 P
stay, | we shall begin our ancient bickerings. 2H6 1.01.144
grace, | begin your suits anew, and sue to him. 1.03. 39
sweet york, begin; 2.02. 7
can so young a thorn begin to prick? 3H6 5.05. 13
i do the wrong, and first begin to brawl. R3 1.03.323
he did, my gracious lord, begin that place, 3.01. 70
and then again begin, and stop again, | as if 3.05. 3
now, ulysses, i begin to relish thy advice, TRO 1.03.386
thou use to beat me, i will begin at thy heel, 2.01. 48 P
do in our eyes begin to lose their gloss, | yea, 2.03.119
that all the greeks begin to worship ajax; 3.03.182
i'll begin. 4.05. 22
stints their strife before their strokes begin. 4.05. 93
the gods begin to mock me. COR 1.09. 79
a curse begin at very root on 's heart, | that 2.01.185
his honors | from where he should begin and end, 2.01.225
but there to end | where he was to begin, and 5.06. 65
swear that he shall, and then i will begin. TIT 5.01. 70
and stop their mouths if they begin to cry. 5.02.161
us take the law of our sides, let them begin. ROM 1.01. 39 P
should in the farthest east begin to draw | the 1.01.135
stars | shall bitterly begin his fearful date 1.04.108
not rosemary and romeo begin both with a letter? 2.04.207 P

nay, and you begin to rail on society once, i am TIM 1.02.244 P
make a mighty fire | begin it with weak straws. JC 1.03.108
never follow any thing | that other men begin. 2.01.152
and stal'd by other men, | begin his fashion. 4.01. 39
and where i did begin, there shall i end; 5.03. 24
good things of day begin to droop and drowse, MAC 3.02. 52
and begin | to doubt th' equivocation of the 5.05. 41
if it live in your memory, begin at this line — HAM 2.02.448 P
begin, murtherer, leave thy damnable faces and 3.02.252 P
murtherer, leave thy damnable faces and begin. 3.02.253 P
i stand in pause where i shall first begin, 3.03. 42
lord, | and, as the world were now but to begin, 4.05.104
come begin; 5.02.278
i begin to find an idle and fond bondage in the LR 1.02. 49 P
my wits begin to turn. 3.02. 67
to go, my lord, | his wits begin t' unsettle. 3.04.162
my tears begin to take his part so much, | they 3.06. 60
find itself abus'd, begin to heave the gorge, OTH 2.01.233 P
scurvy, and begin to find myself fopp'd in it. 4.02.194 P
begin to throw | pompey the great and all his ANT 1.02.187
we part, and let's | draw lots who shall begin. 2.06. 61
mine honesty and i begin to square. 3.13. 41
go forth, agrippa, and begin the fight. 4.06. 1
my desolation does begin to make | a better life 5.02. 1
and winking mary–buds begin to ope their golden CYM 2.03. 24
brother, begin. 4.02.254
so. begin. 4.02.257
guise o' th' world, i will begin | the fashion: 5.01. 32
well, | my peace we will begin. 5.05.459
but custom what they did begin | was with long PER 1.ch. 29
are the knights ready to begin the triumph? 2.02. 1
begin to part | their fringes of bright gold. 3.02. 99
you did begin | as if you met decays of many TNK 1.02. 28
'tis not this | i did begin to speak of. 1.02. 35
chin, | and where she ends, she doth anew begin. VEN 60
that for his prey to pray he doth begin, | as if LUC 342
first like a trumpet doth his tongue begin | to 470
that twice she doth begin ere once she speaks. 567
"with this i did begin to start and cry, | and 1639
that mine eye loves it and doth first begin. SON 114.14

BEGINNERS 2 FR 0.0002 REL FR 2 V 0 P
where are the vile beginners of this fray? ROM 3.01.141
a sin in war, | damn'd in the first beginners!), CYM 5.03. 37

/BEGINNING 1 FR 0.0001 REL FR 1 V 0 P
/those /broils, | /beginning /in /the /middle; TRO pr 28

BEGINNING 19 FR 0.0021 REL FR 11 V 8 P
end of his commonwealth forgets the beginning. TMP 2.01.159 P
but if there be no great love in the beginning, WIV 1.01.246 P
there is pretty orders beginning, i can tell you MM 2.01.236 P
she now when she is beginning to write to him; ADO 2.03.130 P
skill, | that is the true beginning of our end. MND 5.01.111
i will tell you the beginning; AYL 1.02.113 P
well, the beginning, that is dead and buried. 1.02.117 P
i could match this beginning with an old tale. 1.02.120 P
a strange beginning: "borrowed majesty"! JN 1.01. 5
end of a fray and the beginning of a feast 1H4 4.02. 79
seeds | and weak beginning lie intreasured. 2H4 3.01. 85
we see yonder the beginning of the day, but i H5 4.01. 89 P
and the end of it | unknown to the beginning. COR 3.01.327
this was an ill beginning of the night. JC 4.03.234
speak | any beginning to this peevish odds; OTH 2.03.185
i will never fail | beginning nor supplyment. CYM 3.04.179
then but beginning | to swell about the blossom) TNK 1.03. 67
this is a cold beginning. 3.05.101
find sweet beginning, but unsavory end; VEN 1138

BEGINNINGS 1 FR 0.0001 REL FR 1 V 0 P
lurking in our way | to hinder our beginnings. H5 2.02.187

/BEGINS 2 FR 0.0002 REL FR 1 V 1 P
/in /good /troth, /it /begins /so. TRO 3.01.114 P
/plumed /helm /thy /state /begins /to /threat, LR 4.02. 57

BEGINS 63 FR 0.0071 REL FR 50 V 13 P
no, it begins again. TMP 1.02.396
adrian, for a good wager, first begins to crow? 2.01. 29 P
their understanding | begins to swell, and the 5.01. 80
the sun begins to gild the western sky, | and TGV 5.01. 1
inconstancy falls off ere it begins. 5.04.113
why, here begins his morning story right: ERR 5.01.357
for the letter that begins them all, h. ADO 3.04. 56 P
peace, the peal begins. LLL 5.01. 43 P
worthies, away! the scene begins to cloud. 5.02.721
and there begins my sadness. AYL 1.01. 4 P
me, begins to mutiny against this servitude. 1.01. 23 P
you to entreaty, and there begins new matter. 4.01. 80 P
ay, marry, sir, now it begins to work. SHR 3.02.218
mine, and ever | my love, as it begins, shall so AWW 4.02. 37
it begins, "hold thy peace." TN 2.03. 68 P
m — malvolio; m — why, that begins my name. 2.05.125 P
methinks | my favor here begins to warp. WT 1.02.365
the storm begins. 3.03. 49
thine eye begins to speak, set thy tongue there; R2 5.03.125
team | begins his golden progress in the east. 1H4 3.01.219
how bloodily the sun begins to peer | above yon 5.01. 1
yet my blood begins to flatter me that thou dost H5 5.02.223 P
the day begins to break, and night is fled, 1H6 2.02. 1
there comes the ruin, there begins confusion. 4.01.194
for ere the glass, that now begins to run, 4.02. 35
this knave's tongue begins to double. 2H6 2.03. 91
whose flood begins to flow within mine eyes; 3.01.199
and when the rage allays, the rain begins. 3H6 1.04.146
ay, now begins a second storm to rise, | for 3.03. 47
for here i hope begins our lasting joy. 5.07. 46
and, for my name of george begins with g, | it R3 1.01. 58
insulting tyranny begins to jut | upon the 2.04. 51
so now prosperity begins to mellow | and drop 4.04. 1
before, and he begins | a new hell in himself. H8 1.01. 71
look, hector, how the sun begins to set, | how TRO 5.08. 5
ay, now begins our sorrows to approach. TIT 4.04. 72
no, i know it begins with some other letter — ROM 2.04.210 P
this but begins the woe others must end. 3.01.120
of health and living now begins to mend, | and TIM 5.01.187
now mark him, he begins again to speak. JC 3.02.117
when love begins to sicken and decay | it useth 4.02. 20
beast —" | 'tis not so, it begins with pyrrhus: HAM 2.02.451 P
this bad begins and worse remains behind. 3.04.179
for form, | i will pack when it begins to rain, LR 2.04. 80
he begins at curfew, and walks /till /the first 3.04.116 P
my blood begins my safer guides to rule, | and OTH 2.03.205
iago /beckons me; now he begins the story. 4.01.130 P
when it appears to you where this begins, | turn ANT 3.04. 33
when one so great begins to rage, he's hunted 4.01. 7
that means to be of note, begins betimes. 4.04. 27
your daughter's chastity — there it begins. CYM 5.05.179
seldom ease, | for now the wind begins to blow; PER 2.ch. 29
come! who begins? TNK 5.04. 21
even now | to tie the rider she begins to prove. VEN 40
he sees her coming, and begins to glow, | even 337
with blindfold fury she begins to forage; 554
she, marking them, begins a wailing note, | and 835
at last she thus begins: LUC 1303
her by the bloodless hand, | and thus begins: 1598
begins the sad dirge of her certain ending: 1612
from lips new waxen pale begins to blow | the 1663
begins to talk, but through his lips do throng 1783
but then begins a journey in my head | to work SON 27. 3

BEGNAW 1 FR 0.0001 REL FR 1 V 0 P
the worm of conscience still begnaw thy soul! R3 1.03.221

BEGNAWN 1 FR 0.0001 REL FR 0 V 1 P
with the staggers, begnawn with the bots, SHR 3.02. 54 P

BEGOT 27 FR 0.0030 REL FR 21 V 6 P
i will try thee. tell me this: who begot thee? TGV 3.01.293 P
that he was begot between two stock–fishes. MM 3.02.109 P
himself there's one | whom he begot with child), 5.01.511
these are begot in the ventricle of memory, LLL 4.02. 68 P
whose influence is begot of that loose grace 5.02.859
how begot, how nourished? MV 3.02. 65
villain that says such a father begot villains. AYL 1.01. 58 P
bastard of venus that was begot of thought, 4.01.212 P
ends | that here were well begun and well begot; 5.04.171
but whe'er i be as true begot or no, | that JN 1.01. 75
but that i am as well begot, my liege | (fair 1.01. 77
well shot, | and i am i, howe'er i was begot. 1.01.175
and they shall say, when richard me begot, | if 1.01.274
i think | his father never was so true begot — 2.01.130
what cannoneer begot this lusty blood? 2.01.461
so, | for nothing hath begot my something grief, R2 2.02. 36
let not sloth dim your honors new begot. 1H6 1.01. 79
then, | i found that the issue was not his begot; R3 3.05. 90
i am bastard begot, bastard instructed, bastard TRO 5.07. 17 P
first know thou, i begot him on the empress. TIT 5.01. 87
idle brain, | begot of nothing but vain fantasy, ROM 1.04. 98
my lord, | you have begot me, bred me, lov'd me: LR 1.01. 96
'twas this flesh begot | those pelican daughters 3.04. 74
it is a monster | begot upon itself, born on OTH 3.04.162
why should excuse be born or e'er begot? CYM 3.02. 65
thou hast been a grandsire and begot | a father 5.04.123
thou wast begot, to get it is thy duty. VEN 168

BEGOTTEN 4 FR 0.0004 REL FR 2 V 2 P
and show me a child begotten of thy body that i AWW 3.02. 59 P
his innocent babe truly begotten, and the king WT 3.02.134 P
remov'd, | leaving no heir begotten of his body) 1H6 2.05. 72
not me begotten of a shepherd swain, | but 5.04. 37

BEGRIM'D 2 FR 0.0002 REL FR 2 V 0 P
is now begrim'd and black | as mine own face. OTH 3.03.387
see the laboring pioner | begrim'd with sweat, LUC 1381

BEGS 7 FR 0.0008 REL FR 7 V 0 P
upon the humbled neck | but first begs pardon. AYL 3.05. 6
a beggar begs that never begg'd before. R2 5.03. 78
that love which virtue begs and virtue grants. 3H6 3.02. 63
she now begs | that little thought, when she set H8 3.01.182
by her, that else will take the thing she begs, LR 1.04.248
for he partly begs | to be desir'd to give. ANT 3.13. 66
want cries some, but where excess begs all. LC 42

BEG'ST 1 FR 0.0001 REL FR 1 V 0 P
what beg'st thou then? fond woman, let me go. TIT 2.03.172

BEGUIL'D 22 FR 0.0024 REL FR 19 V 3 P
treacherous man, | thou hast beguil'd my hopes! TGV 5.04. 64
sir, that beguil'd him of a chain, had the chain WIV 4.05. 32 P
very same man that beguil'd master slender of 4.05. 37 P
because in choice he is so oft beguil'd. MND 1.01.239
this palpable–gross play hath well beguil'd 5.01.367
ay me, detested! how am i beguil'd! TN 5.01.139
you have beguil'd me with a counterfeit JN 3.01. 99
hath very much beguil'd | the tediousness and R2 2.03. 11
poor ropes, you are beguil'd, | both you and i, ROM 3.02.132
beguil'd, divorced, wronged, spited, slain! 4.05. 55
most detestable death, by thee beguil'd, | by 4.05. 56
he that beguil'd you in a plain accent was a LR 2.02.111 P
art not vanquish'd, | but cozen'd and beguil'd. 5.03.155
hath thus beguil'd your daughter of herself, OTH 1.03. 66
plague | to beguile many and be beguil'd by one) 4.01. 97
in such distractions as | beguil'd all spies. ANT 3.07. 77
loose | beguil'd me to the very heart of loss. 4.12. 29
approach ho, all's not well; caesar's beguil'd. 5.02.323
to mock the subtle in themselves beguil'd, | to LUC 957
that it beguil'd attention, charm'd the sight. 1404
fortune smil'd, | thou and i were both beguil'd. PP 20.28
hath been before, how are our brains beguil'd, SON 59. 2

BEGUILD 1 FR 0.0001 REL FR 1 V 0 P
to me came tarquin armed to beguild | with LUC 1544

/BEGUILE 2 FR 0.0002 REL FR 2 V 0 P
/in /prosperity, | /thou /dost /beguile /me! R2 4.01.281
and pious bonds, | the better to /beguile. HAM 1.03.131

BEGUILE 24 FR 0.0027 REL FR 17 V 7 P
seeking light, doth light of light beguile; LLL 1.01. 77
smile | when i a fat and bean–fed horse beguile, MND 2.01. 45
how shall we beguile | the lazy time, if not 5.01. 40
see, to beguile the old folks, how the young SHR 1.02.138 P
senis," that we might beguile the old pantaloon. 3.01. 36 P
here he comes, to beguile two hours in a sleep, AWW 4.01. 22 P
well, and to beguile the supposition of that 4.03.299 P
whiles you beguile the time and feed your TN 3.03. 41
who does beguile you? who does do you wrong? 5.01.140
his work, would beguile nature of her custom, so WT 5.02. 99 P
and now you pick a quarrel to beguile me of it. 1H4 3.03. 67 P
reignier, is't thou that thinkest to beguile me? 1H6 1.02. 65
and so beguile thy sorrow, till the heavens TIT 4.01. 35
thou wert the lion, the fox would beguile thee; TIM 4.03.329 P
to beguile the time, | look like the time; MAC 1.05. 63
and fain i would beguile | the tedious day with HAM 3.02.226
when misery could beguile the tyrant's rage, LR 4.06. 63
and often did beguile her of her tears, | when i OTH 1.03.156
so let the turk of cyprus us beguile, | we lose 1.03.210
but i do beguile | the thing i am by seeming 2.01.122
plague | to beguile many and be beguil'd by one) 4.01. 97
misery of age, beguile | the gout and rheum, TNK 5.04. 7
with sweets that shall the truest sight beguile; VEN 1144
thou dost beguile the world, unless some mother SON 3. 4

BEGUILED 1 FR 0.0001 REL FR 1 V 0 P
maid, | and how she was beguiled and surpris'd, SHR in.2. 55

BEGUILES 5 FR 0.0005 REL FR 4 V 1 P
and high and low beguiles the rich and poor. WIV 1.03. 86
read it not truly, my ancient skill beguiles me; MM 4.02.155 P
beguiles the truer office of mine eyes? AWW 5.03.305
show | beguiles him as the mournful crocodile 2H6 3.01.226
rudely beguiles our lips | of all rejoindure, TRO 4.04. 35

BEGUILING 3 FR 0.0003 REL FR 2 V 1 P
parts besides, | beguiling them of commendation. 1H4 3.01.187
of beguiling virgins with the broken seals of H5 4.01.163 P
and knew the patterns of his foul beguiling, LC 170

/BEGUN 2 FR 0.0002 REL FR 1 V 1 P
tradition, /begun upon an honorable respect, and H5 5.01. 71 P
how e'er my haps, my joys /were ne'er /begun. HAM 4.03. 68

BEGUN 31 FR 0.0035 REL FR 31 V 0 P
you have often | begun to tell me what i am, but TMP 1.02. 34
i have begun, | and now i give my sensual race MM 2.04.159
ends | that here were well begun and well begot; AYL 5.04.171
my lord, 'tis but begun. SHR 1.01.252
well begun, tranio. 1.02.227
thus have i politicly begun my reign, | and 'tis 4.01.188
nay, that you shall not, since you have begun; 5.02. 44
a great while ago the world begun, | /with hey TN 5.01.405
philip, my liege, so is my name begun, | philip, JN 1.01.158
this day all things begun come to ill end, | yea 3.01. 94
good uncle, let this end where it begun; R2 1.01.158
i take my leave before i have begun, | for 1.02. 60
the french | she carry armor as she hath begun. 1H6 2.01. 24
begun through malice of the bishop's men. 3.01. 75
yet know thou, since we have begun to strike, 3H6 2.02.167
hope makes | in all designs begun on earth below TRO 1.03. 4
and when such time they have begun to cry, | let COR 3.03. 19
ne'er saw her match since first the world begun. ROM 1.02. 93
must end that work the ides of march begun. JC 5.01.113
i have begun to plant thee, and will labor | to MAC 1.04. 28
things bad begun make strong themselves by ill. 3.02. 55
but, orderly to end where i begun, | our wills HAM 3.02.210
father, | but that i know love is begun by time, 4.07.111
to my brains, | they had begun the play. 5.02. 31
o, make an end | of what i have begun. ANT 4.14.106
his meaning struck her ere his words begun. VEN 462
their copious stories, oftentimes begun, | end 845
an expir'd date, cancell'd ere well begun: LUC 26
so, the curtain drawn, his eyes begun | to wink, 374
time had not scythed all that youth begun, | nor LC 12
believ'd her eyes when they t' assail begun, 262

/BEHALF 1 FR 0.0001 REL FR 1 V 0 P
/and /rob /in /the /behalf /of /charity. TRO 5.03. 22

BEHALF 44 FR 0.0049 REL FR 33 V 11 P
let me have thy voice in my behalf. WIV 1.04.156 P
this well carried shall on her behalf | change ADO 4.01.210
and in that behalf, | bold of your worthiness, LLL 2.01. 27
in her behalf that scorns your services. MND 3.02.331
was | (as his wise mother wrought in his behalf) MV 1.03. 73
insinuate with you in the behalf of a good play! AYL ep 9 P
was very honest in the behalf of the maid; AWW 4.03.219 P
sonnet you writ to diana in behalf of the count 4.03.320 P
yet must suffer | something in my behalf. 4.04. 28
my master to speak in the behalf of my daughter, 4.05. 72 P
to whet your gentle thoughts | on his behalf. TN 3.01.106
may swear it in the behalf of his friend; WT 5.02.163 P
in right and true behalf | of thy deceased JN 1.01. 7
come | to spread his colors, boy, in thy behalf, 2.01. 8
in that behalf which we have challeng'd it? 2.01.264
is mustering in his clouds on our behalf R2 3.03. 86
my prisoners in your majesty's behalf. 1H4 1.03. 48
power | did gage them both in an unjust behalf 1.03.173
have much to say in the behalf of that falstaff. 2.04.485 P
to engross up glorious deeds on my behalf; 3.02.148
and even in thy behalf i'll thank myself | for 5.04. 97
the emperor's coming in behalf of france, | to H5 5.pr. 38
that you on my behalf would pluck a flower. 1H6 2.04.129
in your behalf still will i wear the same. 2.04.130
for every word you speak in his behalf | is 2H6 3.02.208
this hand of mine hath writ in thy behalf, | and 4.01. 63
queen, | bearing the king in my behalf along; 3H6 2.01.115
madam, in our king's behalf | i am commanded, 3.03. 59
leave | to play the broker in mine own behalf; 4.01. 63
and stafford, you in our behalf | go levy men, 4.01.130
and in the duke's behalf i'll give my voice, R3 3.04. 19
have letters from me to my son | in your behalf, 4.01. 50
be eloquent in my behalf to her. 4.04.357
of butchered princes fight in thy behalf. 5.03.122
which you say live to come in my behalf. TRO 3.03. 16
vexed, whom we see have sided | in his behalf. COR 4.02. 3
as many lies in his behalf as you have utter'd 5.02. 25 P
hath got this mortal hurt | in my behalf; ROM 3.01.111
you can with modesty speak in your own behalf; TIM 1.02. 94 P
which, in my lord's behalf, i come to entreat 3.01. 17 P
hear | (if you dare venture in your own behalf) LR 4.02. 20
i will do | all my abilities in thy behalf. OTH 3.03. 2
tell him i have mov'd my lord on his behalf, and 3.04. 19 P
than the sands | that run i' th' clock's behalf. CYM 3.02. 73

BEHALFS 2 FR 0.0002 REL FR 1 V 1 P
to his presence, whisper him in your behalfs; WT 4.04.797 P
edify the duke | most parlously in our behalfs. TNK 2.03. 53

BEHAV'D 2 FR 0.0002 REL FR 2 V 0 P
judge, | and gather by him, as he is behav'd, HAM 3.01. 34
how have i been behav'd, that he might stick OTH 4.02.108

BEHAVEDST 1 FR 0.0001 REL FR 0 V 1 P
and thou behavedst thyself as if thou hadst been 2H6 4.03. 4 P

BEHAVIOR 31 FR 0.0035 REL FR 19 V 12 P
but chiefly for thy face and thy behavior, TGV 4.04. 67
and the hardest voice of her behavior (to be WIV 1.03. 47 P
what an unweigh'd behavior hath this flemish 2.01. 23 P
gait majestical, and his general behavior vain, LLL 5.01. 12 P
behavior, what wert thou | till this madman 5.02.337
bonnet in germany, and his behavior every where. MV 1.02. 76 P
spirit, lest through thy wild behavior | i be 2.02.187
in the country as the behavior of the country is AYL 3.02. 47 P
lest, over–eyeing of his odd behavior | (for yet SHR in.1. 95
do i see | maid's mild behavior and sobriety. 1.01. 71
for learning and behavior | fit for her turn, 1.02.168

her wondrous qualities and mild behavior, | am 2.01. 50
hiding his bitter jests in blunt behavior; 3.02. 13
there is a fair behavior in thee, captain, | and TN 1.02. 47
i' the sun practicing behavior to his own shadow 2.05. 17 P
for the behavior of the young gentleman gives 3.04.185 P
king of france | in my behavior to the majesty, JN 1.01. 3
when this loose behavior i throw off | and pay 1H4 1.02.208
hath my behavior given to your displeasure, H8 2.04. 20
her wonted greatness, | to use so rude behavior. 4.02.103
and in the gown of humility, mark his behavior. COR 2.03. 41 P
therefore thou mayest think my behavior light, ROM 2.02. 99
it were a very gross kind of behavior, as they 2.04.167 P
visit him, to make inquire | of his behavior. HAM 2.01. 5
your behavior hath strook her into amazement and 3.02.326 P
often the surfeits of our own behavior — we LR 1.02.120 P
thee fight, | when i have envied thy behavior. ANT 2.06. 75
she comes, you shall perceive her behavior. TNK 4.03. 9 P
his behavior | so charm'd me that methought 5.03.118
her sad behavior feeds his vulture folly, | a LUC 556
and he stole that word | from thy behavior; SON 79.10
BEHAVIORS 8 FR 0.0009 REL FR 5 V 3 P
i will teach the children their behaviors; WIV 4.04. 67 P
a fool when he dedicates his behaviors to love, ADO 2.03. 9 P
she hath in all outward behaviors seem'd ever to 2.03. 97 P
all his behaviors did make their retire | to the LLL 2.01.234
see it so grossly shown in thy behaviors | that AWW 1.03.178
that borrow their behaviors from the great, JN 5.01. 51
which give some soil, perhaps, to my behaviors; JC 1.02. 42
and light behaviors | quite in the wrong. OTH 4.01.102
BEHEAD 1 FR 0.0001 REL FR 0 V 1 P
take him away, and behead him. 2H6 4.07. 96 P
BEHEADED 6 FR 0.0006 REL FR 5 V 1 P
how came it claudio was beheaded | at an unusual MM 5.01.457
this town, | beheaded publicly for his offense. ERR 5.01.127
so fell that noble earl | and was beheaded. 1H6 2.05. 91
well, he shall be beheaded for it ten times. 2H6 4.07. 24 P
to–day the lords you /talk'd of are beheaded. R3 3.02. 91
their fell faults our brothers were beheaded, TIT 5.03.100
BEHELD 37 FR 0.0041 REL FR 33 V 4 P
at ebb) beheld | the king my father wrack'd. TMP 1.02.436
works 'em | that if you now beheld them, your 5.01. 18
we, in all our trim, freshly beheld | our royal, 5.01.236
'tis but her picture i have yet beheld, | and TGV 2.04.209
madness i ever yet beheld seem'd but tameness, WIV 4.02. 27 P
you saw the mistress, i beheld the maid; MV 3.02.198
men alive | i never yet beheld that special face SHR 2.01. 11
you all | that have beheld me give away myself 3.02.194
too, | hast thou beheld a fresher gentlewoman? 4.05. 29
princess (she | the fairest i have yet beheld), WT 5.01. 87
there might you have beheld one joy crown 5.02. 44 P
lov'd myself | till now infixed i beheld myself JN 2.01.502
/have /you beheld, | or have you read, or heard, 4.03. 41
a woeful pageant have we here beheld. R2 4.01.321
how it ern'd my heart when i beheld | in london 5.05. 76
that she may boast she hath beheld the man 1H6 2.02. 42
days, | how many of you have mine eyes beheld! R3 2.04. 56
beheld them when they lighted, how they clung H8 1.01. 9
not virtuously on his own part beheld, | do in TRO 2.03.118
hadst thou beheld — COR 1.09. 13
part with those | that have beheld the doing. 1.09. 40
there's some among you have beheld me fighting; 3.01.223
and thou hast oft beheld | heart–hard'ning 4.01. 24
whom your goths beheld | alive and dead, and for TIT 1.01.122
beheld his tears, and laugh'd so heartily | that 5.01.116
that i beheld. ANT 3.10. 15
and golden phoebus never be beheld | of eyes 5.02.317
diamond of yours outlustres many i have beheld, CYM 1.04. 74 P
and strangers ne'er beheld but wond'red at; PER 1.04. 25
none that beheld him but, like lesser lights, 2.03. 41
ever affected any man ere she beheld palamon? TNK 4.03. 63 P
which never yet | beheld thing maculate — look 5.01.145
"when he beheld his shadow in the brook, | the VEN 1099
where herself herself beheld | a thousand times, 1129
what he beheld, on that he firmly doted, | and LUC 416
that thinks she hath beheld some ghastly sprite, 451
dwell'd, | till she despairing hecuba beheld, 1447
BEHEST 1 FR 0.0001 REL FR 1 V 0 P
let us with care perform his great behest. CYM 5.04.122
BEHESTS 3 FR 0.0003 REL FR 3 V 0 P
opposition | to you and your behests, and am ROM 4.02. 19
i have known frights, fury, friends' behests, TNK 1.04. 40
or kings be breakers of their own behests? LUC 852
/BEHIND 3 FR 0.0003 REL FR 2 V 1 P
/thou /must /not /stay /behind. LR 3.06.101
/free /things /and /happy /shows /behind, | /but 3.06.105
/who /hath /he /left /behind /him /general? 4.03. 7 P
BEHIND 110 FR 0.0124 REL FR 84 V 26 P
since | they have left their viands behind; TMP 3.03. 41
all praise | and make it halt behind her. 4.01. 11
pageant faded, | leave not a rack behind. 4.01.156
a word (for far behind his worth | comes all the TGV 2.04. 71
i vill not for the varld i shall leave behind. WIV 1.04. 64 P
not see me, i will ensconce me behind the arras. 3.03. 90 P
they threw me off from behind one of them, in a 4.05. 68 P
there's more behind that is more gratulate. MM 5.01.529
where we'll show | what's yet behind, that/'s 5.01.539
it in your face, so he break it not behind. ERR 3.01. 76
he that came behind you, sir, like an evil angel 4.03. 20 P
behind the ditches of the abbey here. 5.01.122
i whipt me behind the arras, and there heard it ADO 1.03. 61 P
no glory lives behind the back of such. 3.01.110
two men ride of a horse, one must ride behind. 3.05. 37 P
a foolish heart, that i leave here behind. MND 3.02.319
for, meeting her of late behind the wood, 4.01. 48
before, | to sweep the dust behind the door. 5.01.390
turning his face, he put his hand behind him, MV 2.08. 47
this shadow | doth limp behind the substance. 3.02.129
'tis well you offer it behind her back, | the 4.01.293
her exile, or have died to stay behind her. AYL 1.01.110 P
myself | did steal behind him as he lay along 2.01. 30
o brave oliver, | leave me not behind thee; 3.03.101
promise, or come one minute behind your hour, i 4.01.191 P
so shall i no whit be behind in duty | to fair SHR 1.02.174
hill, my master riding behind my mistress — 4.01. 67 P
h'as left me here behind to expound the meaning 4.04. 78 P
o my sweet lord, that you will stay behind us! AWW 2.01. 24
he left this ring behind him, | would i or not. TN 1.05.301
he left behind him myself and a sister, both 2.01. 19 P
and then i comes behind. 2.05.135 P
and you had any eye behind you, you might see 2.05.136 P
i could not stay behind you. 3.03. 4
to let him there a month behind the gest WT 1.02. 41
i love thee not a jar o' th' clock behind | what 1.02. 43
two lads that thought there was no more behind 1.02. 63
which hoxes honesty behind, restraining | from 1.02.244
behind the tuft of pines i met them; 2.01. 34
your grace shall stay behind | so strongly JN 3.03. 1
i do but stay behind | to do the office for thee 5.07. 70
why, foolish boy, the king is left behind, | and R2 2.03. 97
eye of heaven is hid | behind the globe, that 3.02. 38
i'll not be long behind; 5.02.114
sirrah jack, thy horse stands behind the hedge; 1H4 2.02. 70 P
go hide thee behind the arras, the rest walk up 2.04.500 P
fast asleep behind the arras, and snorting like 2.04.528 P
loseth men's hearts and leaves behind a stain 3.01.185
i fell asleep here behind the arras and had my 3.03. 97 P
king | in deputation left behind him here, 4.03. 87
stockfish, a fruiterer, behind gray's inn. 2H4 3.02. 32 P
come here, pistol, stand behind me. 5.05. 10 P
there left behind and settled certain french; H5 1.02. 47
nor leave not one behind that doth not wish 2.02. 23
some upon their wives left poor behind them, 4.01.139 P
plac'd behind | with purpose to relieve and 1H6 1.01.132
come, come from behind, | i know thee well, 1.02. 66
fortune in favor makes him lag behind. 3.03. 34
and left behind him richard, his only son, | who 2H6 2.02. 19
o monstrous coward! what, to come behind folks? 4.07. 83 P
i'll leave my son my virtuous deeds behind, 3H6 2.02. 49
look behind you, my lord. R3 1.04.268
toward /ludlow then, for we'll not stay behind. 2.02.154
but leave behind | your son, george stanley. 4.04.494
and leave me here in wretchedness behind ye? H8 4.02. 84
when suddenly a file of boys behind 'em, loose 5.03. 56 P
she's a fool to stay behind her father, let her TRO 1.01. 81 P
there's troilus will not come far behind him. 1.02. 57 P
with t' other, | ere stay behind this business. COR 1.01.243
all hurt behind! 1.04. 37
carries noise, and behind him he leaves tears: 2.01.159 P
behind the abbey wall | within this hour my man ROM 2.04.187
being spoke behind your back, than to your face. 4.01. 28
bold, and forth on, | leaving no tract behind. TIM 1.01. 50
'tis pity bounty had not eyes behind, | that man 1.02.163
like a cur, behind | strook caesar on the neck. JC 5.01. 43
the greatest is behind. MAC 1.03.117
be you and i behind an arras then, | mark the HAM 2.02.163
and thou shalt live in this fair world behind, 3.02.175
behind the arras i'll convey myself | to hear 3.03. 28
this bad begins and worse remains behind. 3.04.179
fit, | behind the arras hearing something stir, 4.01. 9
standing thus unknown, shall i leave behind me! 5.02.345
flattering his displeasure, | tripp'd me behind; LR 2.02.119
so that, dear lords, if i be left behind, | a OTH 1.03.255
othello, leave some officer behind, | and he 1.03.280
before, behind thee, and on every hand, 2.01. 86
see suitors following, and not look behind: 2.01.157
here, stand behind this /bulk, straight will he 5.01. 1
speak not against it, | i will not stay behind. ANT 3.07. 19
eyes | by looking back what i have left behind 3.11. 53
and snatch 'em up, as we take hares, behind: 4.07. 13
when i should see behind me | th' inevitable 4.14. 64
i'll throw't into the creek | behind our rock, CYM 4.02.152
pass was damm'd | with dead men hurt behind, and 5.03. 12
behind | is left to govern it, you bear in mind, PER 4.04. 13
tyre, | i left behind an ancient substitute. 5.03. 51
leave 'em all behind us | like lazy clouds, TNK 2.02. 13
in the great lake that lies behind the palace, 4.01. 53
that, believe me, | she left me far behind her. 4.01. 99
his hair hangs long behind him, black and 4.02. 83
cries, "o, that ever i did it behind the arras!" 4.03. 55 P
face the lion walk'd along | behind some hedge, VEN 1094
she bears the load of lust he left behind, | and LUC 734
the scalps of many, almost hid behind, | to jump 1413
himself behind | was left unseen, save to the 1425
that thou no form of thee hast left behind, SON 9. 6
my grief lies onward and my joy behind. 50.14
woe, | before, a joy propos'd, behind, a dream. 129.12
whilst i, thy babe, chase thee afar behind, 143.10
BEHIND–DOOR–WORK
1 FR 0.0001 REL FR 0 V 1 P
some trunk–work, some behind–door–work. WT 3.03. 74 P
BEHIND–HAND 1 FR 0.0001 REL FR 1 V 0 P
as interpreters | of my behind–hand slackness. WT 5.01.151
BEHOLD 181 FR 0.0204 REL FR 166 V 15 P
through my prison once a day | behold this maid. TMP 1.02.492
behold, sir king, | the wronged duke of milan, 5.01.106
behold her that gave aim to all thy oaths, | and TGV 5.04.101
will you go with us to behold it? WIV 2.01.206 P
behold what honest clothes you send forth to 4.02.120 P
behold, behold, where madam mitigation comes! MM 1.02. 44 P
behold, behold, where madam mitigation comes! 1.02. 44 P
and to behold his sway, | i will, as 'twere a 1.03. 43
that would behold in me this shameful sport. ERR 4.04.105
see where they come, we will behold his death. 5.01.128
most mighty duke, behold a man much wrong'd. 5.01.331
behold how like a maid she blushes here! ADO 4.01. 34
do but behold the tears that swell in me, | and LLL 4.03. 35
toward that shade i might behold address'd | the 5.02. 92
heavenly spirits, vouchsafe | not to behold" — 5.02.167
"once to behold," rogue. 5.02.168 P
"once to behold with your sun–beamed eyes, | — 5.02.169
behold the window of my heart, mine eye, | what 5.02.838
shall behold the night | of our solemnities. MND 1.01. 10
and ere a man hath power to say "behold!" 1.01.147
when phoebe doth behold | her silver visage in 1.01.209
his life hath sold | but my outside to behold. MV 2.07. 68
behold, there stand the caskets, noble prince. 2.09. 4
some that are mad if they behold a cat; 4.01. 48
o, behold this ring, | whose high respect and AWW 5.03.191
dead is quick — | and now behold the meaning. 5.03.304
heat, | shall not behold her face at ample view; TN 1.01. 26
behold, my lords, | although the print be little WT 2.03. 98
if pow'rs divine | behold our human actions (as 3.02. 29
for behold me, | a fellow of the royal bed, 3.02. 37
flaunts, behold | the sternness of his presence? 4.04. 23
with any thing | that you behold the while. 4.04. 48
ere they can behold | bright phoebus in his 4.04.123
where he is to behold him with flies blown to 4.04.790 P
behold, and say 'tis well. 5.03. 20
if you can behold it, | i'll make the statue 5.03. 87
behold, the french amaz'd vouchsafe a parle, JN 2.01.226
heralds, from off our tow'rs we might behold, 2.01.325
never | must i behold my pretty arthur more. 3.04. 89
of yours | behold another day break in the east; 5.04. 32
there to behold | our cousin herford and fell R2 1.02. 45
behold, his eye, | as bright as is the eagle's, 3.03. 68
yet look up, behold, | that you in pity may 5.01. 8
and only stays but to behold the face | of that 1H4 1.03.275
if thou didst, then behold that compound. 2.04.122 P
do you behold these exhalations? 2.04.320 P
behold yourself so by a son disdained; 2H4 5.02. 95
and monarchs to behold the swelling scene! H5 pr 4
hill | stood smiling to behold his lion's whelp 1.02.109
tertian, that it is most lamentable to behold. 2.01.120 P
and in them behold | upon the hempen tackle 3.pr. 7
behold the threaden sails, | borne with th' 3.pr. 10
you stand upon the rivage and behold | a city on 3.pr. 14
behold the ordinance on their carriages, | with 3.pr. 26
now, who will behold | the royal captain of this 4.pr. 28
fear, that mean and gentle all | behold, as may 4.pr. 46
how shall we then behold their natural tears? 4.02. 13
do but behold yond poor and starved band, | and 4.02. 16
and behold, the english beach | pales in the flood 5.pr. 9
but now behold, | in the quick forge and 5.pr. 22
right joyous are we to behold your face, | most 5.02. 9
as we are now glad to behold your eyes — | your 5.02. 14
and that hereafter ages may behold | what ruin 1H6 2.02. 10
lord of winchester, behold | my sighs and tears, 3.01.107
behold, my lord of winchester, the duke | hath 3.01.122
behold, this is the happy wedding torch | that 3.02. 26
behold the wounds, the most unnatural wounds, 3.03. 50
still | you may behold confusion of your foes. 4.01. 77
out, | must i behold thy timeless cruel death? 5.04. 5
will her ladyship behold and hear our exorcisms? 2H6 1.04. 4 P
so please your highness to behold the fight. 2.03. 51
relent, | that were unworthy to behold the same? 4.04. 18
is my apparel sumptuous to behold? 4.07.100
that this is true, father, behold his blood. 3H6 1.01. 13
i make king lewis behold | thy sly conveyance 3.03.159
deeds, | behold this pattern of thy butcheries. R3 1.02. 54
to–day shalt thou behold a subject die | for 3.03. 3
behold, mine arm | is like a blasted sapling, 3.04. 68
perish | and never more behold thy face again. 4.04.187
do through the clouds behold this present hour, 5.01. 8
let's stand close and behold him. H8 2.01. 55
here, and behold | the lady anne pass from her 4.01. 2
present, and behold | that chair stand empty; 5.02. 44
(but few now living can behold that goodness) 5.04. 21
do you with cheeks abash'd behold our works, TRO 1.03. 18
and anon behold | the strong–ribb'd bark through 1.03. 39
that most pure spirit of sense, behold itself, 3.03.106
till he behold them formed in th' applause 3.03.119
to talk with him, and to behold his visage, 3.03.240
behold thy fill. 4.05.236
behold, i pray you! 5.02. 40
you look upon that sleeve, behold it well. 5.02. 69
behold, /distraction, frenzy, and amazement, 5.03. 85
behold, these are the tribunes of the people, COR 3.01. 21
do not flatter, and | therein behold themselves. 3.01. 68
behold | dissentious numbers pest'ring streets, 4.06. 6
behold now presently, and swound for what's to 5.02. 66 P
nay, behold 's! 5.03.173
behold, the heavens do ope, | the gods look down 5.03.183
behold our patroness, the life of rome! 5.05. 1
had, | behold the poor remains, alive and dead! TIT 1.01. 81
behold, i choose thee, tamora, for my bride, 1.01.319
pit, | where never man's eye may behold my body: 2.03.177
will not permit mine eyes once to behold | the 2.03.218
shall i do | now i behold thy lively body so? 3.01.105
looking all downwards to behold our cheeks, 3.01.124
can the son's eye behold his father bleed? 5.03. 65
behold the child: 5.03.119
from the place where you behold us pleading, 5.03.130
at my poor house look to behold this night ROM 1.02. 24
this night you shall behold him at our feast; 1.03. 80
be much in years | ere i again behold my romeo! 3.05. 47
be satisfied | with romeo, till i behold him — 3.05. 94
give me some present counsel, or, behold, 4.01. 61
woeful day | that ever, ever, i did yet behold! 4.05. 51
of death | is partly to behold my lady's face, 5.03. 29
may you a better feast never behold, | you knot TIM 3.06. 88
behold, the earth hath roots; 4.03.417
let me behold thy face. 4.03.493
whiles they behold a greater than themselves, JC 1.02.209
that mothers shall but smile when they behold 3.01.267
what weep you when you but behold | our caesar's 3.02.195
come down, behold no more. 5.03. 33
behold! MAC 3.04. 68
when now i think you can behold such sights, 3.04.113
i am sick at heart | when i behold — seyton, i 5.03. 20
behold where stands | th' usurper's cursed head: 5.09. 20
but soft, behold! HAM 1.01.126
all from her father's death — and now behold! 4.05. 76
eyes, not to behold | this shameful lodging. LR 2.02.171
behold yond simp'ring dame, | whose face between 4.06.118
there thou mightst behold the great image of 4.06.158 P
behold, it is my privilege, | the privilege of 5.03.129
she lov'd and hated, | one of them we behold. 5.03.282
o, behold, | the riches of the ship is come on OTH 2.01. 82
too — and behold what innovation it makes here. 2.03. 40 P
behold her topp'd? 3.03.396
behold her well; 5.01.108
behold, i have a weapon; 5.02.259
behold and see. ANT 1.01. 13
so it is a deadly sorrow to behold a foul knave 1.02. 72 P
didst thou behold octavia? 3.03. 7
place | we may the number of the ships behold, 3.09. 3
i can behold no longer. 3.10. 1
behold this man, | commend unto his lips thy 4.08. 22
behold it stain'd | with his most noble blood. 5.01. 25
o, behold, | how pomp is followed! 5.02.150
behold, sir. 5.02.197
many there could behold the sun with as firm CYM 1.04. 12 P
jove — | once more let me behold it. 2.04. 99
behold divineness | no elder than a boy! 3.06. 43

behold their quarter'd fires, have both their 4.04. 18
behold, | here's poison and here's gold; PER 1.01.154
behold, | her eyelids, cases to those heavenly 3.02. 97
behold him. 5.01. 36
in a /glassy stream, | you may behold 'em. TNK 1.01.113
view us their mortal herd, behold who err, | and 1.04. 5
never more | must we behold those comforts, 2.02. 9
behold, and wonder! 2.02.133
who doth the world so gloriously behold | that VEN 857
and yet," quoth she, "behold two adons dead! 1070
who, peeping forth this tumult to behold, | are LUC 447
light, | she prays she never may behold the day: 746
the same disgrace which they themselves behold; 751
let not the jealous day behold that face, 800
and scarce hath eyes his treasure to behold, 857
day, | as shaming any eye should thee behold, 1143
the ear | the heavy motion that it doth behold, 1326
you might behold triumphing in their faces; 1388
o, what art | of physiognomy might one behold! 1395
outruns the eye that doth behold his haste, 1668
i often did behold | in thy sweet semblance my 1758
when i behold the violet past prime, | and sable SON 12. 3
but when in thee time's furrows i behold, | then 22. 3
as, to behold desert a beggar born, | and needy 66. 2
that time of year thou mayst in me behold | when 73. 1
for we, which now behold these present days, 106.13
yet in good faith some say that thee behold, 131. 5
that they behold and see not what they see? 137. 2
"though in me you behold | the injury of many a LC 71
"'and lo behold these talents of their hair, 204

BEHOLDEN *(see beholding*)*

BEHOLDER 1 FR 0.0001 REL FR 0 V 1 P
but the wisest beholder, that knew no more but WT 5.02. 17 P

/BEHOLDERS 2 FR 0.0002 REL FR 2 V 0 P
/like /the /sun, /did /make /beholders /wink? R2 4.01.284
/to /tell /you, /fair /beholders, /that /our TRO pr 26

BEHOLDERS 3 FR 0.0003 REL FR 2 V 1 P
them that all the beholders take his part with AYL 1.02.131 P
ground | to hurl at the beholders of my shame. 1H6 1.04. 46
and the beholders of this frantic play, | th' R3 4.04. 68

BEHOLDEST 1 FR 0.0001 REL FR 0 V 1 P
ink which here thou viewest, beholdest, LLL 1.01.244 P

/BEHOLDING* 1 FR 0.0001 REL FR 1 V 0 P
/little /are /we /beholding /to /your /love, R2 4.01.160

BEHOLDING* 30 FR 0.0034 REL FR 23 V 7 P
she is beholding to thee, gentle youth. TGV 4.04.173
sometime may be beholding to his friend for a WIV 1.01.273 P
is marvellous little beholding to your reports, MM 4.03.159 P
well, shylock, shall we be beholding to you? MV 1.03.105
you are fain to be beholding to your wives for. AYL 4.01. 60 P
to whom we all rest generally beholding. SHR 1.02.272
have been more kindly beholding to you than any, 2.01. 78 P
and here beholding | his daughter's trial! WT 3.02.120
to whom am i beholding for these limbs? JN 1.01.239
i think you are more beholding to the night than 1H4 2.01. 89 P
would, by beholding him, have wash'd his knife 2H4 4.05. 86
beholding him, plucks comfort from his looks. H5 4.pr. 42
play on the lute, beholding the towns burn: 1H6 1.04. 96
all | have been beholding to him in his life; R3 2.01.130
then he is more beholding to you than i. 3.01.107
revenge, | and now i cloy me with beholding it. 4.04. 62
my lord sands, | i am beholding to you; H8 1.04. 41
i should have been beholding to your paper. 4.01. 21
if a prince | may be beholding to a subject, i 5.02.191
and you, good brethren, i am much beholding; 5.04. 70
some thing not worth in me such rich beholding TRO 3.03. 91
should not sell him an hour from her beholding; COR 1.03. 9 P
is she not then beholding to the man | that TIT 1.01.396
we are beholding to you, good andronicus. 5.03. 33
for brutus' sake, i am beholding to you. JC 3.02. 65
sake | he finds himself beholding to us all. 3.02. 67
father are not fit for your beholding. LR 3.07. 9 P
i am beholding to you | for your sweet music PER 2.05. 25
i am wild in my beholding. 5.01.222
he ten times pines that pines beholding food, LUC 1115

BEHOLDS 4 FR 0.0004 REL FR 4 V 0 P
when helenus beholds | a grecian and his sword, TRO 2.02. 42
that eye which him beholds, as more divine, LUC 291
lie | imagine every eye beholds their blame, 1343
till lucrece' father, that beholds her bleed, 1732

BEHOLD'ST 3 FR 0.0003 REL FR 3 V 0 P
not the smallest orb which thou behold'st | but MV 5.01. 60
yet thou behold'st! COR 5.02. 93
eros, thou yet behold'st me? ANT 4.14. 1

BEHOOF 3 FR 0.0003 REL FR 3 V 0 P
parley'd unto foreign kings | for your behoof — 2H6 4.07. 78
all our surgeons | convent in their behoof, our TNK 1.04. 31
for fear of harms that preach in our behoof. LC 165

BEHOOFEFUL 1 FR 0.0001 REL FR 1 V 0 P
as are behoofeful for our state to–morrow. ROM 4.03. 8

BEHOOVE 1 FR 0.0001 REL FR 1 V 0 P
and unnoted passion | he did behoove his anger, TIM 3.05. 22

BEHOOVES 4 FR 0.0004 REL FR 3 V 1 P
abroad, therefore it behooves men to be wary. WT 4.04.254 P
behooves it us to labor for the realm. 2H6 1.01.182
as it behooves my daughter and your honor. HAM 1.03. 97
perforce, | behooves me keep at utterance. CYM 3.01. 72

BEHOVE 2 FR 0.0002 REL FR 2 V 0 P
if you know aught which does behove my knowledge WT 1.02.395
contract — o — the time for — a — my behove, HAM 5.01. 63

/BEHOWLS 1 FR 0.0001 REL FR 1 V 0 P
/lion roars, | and the wolf /behowls the moon; MND 5.01.372

/BEING 9 FR 0.0010 REL FR 8 V 1 P
/being /now /a /subject, | /i /have /a /king R2 4.01.307
/being /so /great, /i /have /no /need /to /beg. 4.01.309
/more /than /that /being /which /was /like /to 2H4 1.01.179
/and /being /now /trimm'd /in /thine /own 1.03. 94
/our /late /king /richard (/being /infected) 4.01. 58
/being /mounted /and /both /roused /in /their 4.01.116
/that /time | /have /told /me, /i /being /by, R3 4.02.101
not count it holy | /to /hurt /by /being /just; TRO 5.03. 20
/dungeons, /denmark /being /one /o' /th' /worst. HAM 2.02.246 P

BEING 738 FR 0.0834 REL FR 602 V 136 P
the prime duke, being so reputed | in dignity, TMP 1.02. 72
those being all my study, | the government i 1.02. 74
being transported | and rapt in secret studies. 1.02. 76
being once perfected how to grant suits, | how 1.02. 79
mind | with that which, but by being so retir'd, 1.02. 91
he being thus lorded, | not only with what my 1.02. 97
of naples, being an enemy | to me inveterate, 1.02.121
who being then appointed | master of this design 1.02.162
wilt not take, | being capable of all ill! 1.02.353
duke of milan | and his brave son being twain. 1.02.439
that our garments, being, as they were, drench'd 2.01. 62 P
being rather new dy'd than stain'd with salt 2.01. 64 P
scape being drunk, for want of wine. 2.01.147
the king and all our company else being drown'd, 2.02.175 P
lie, being but half a fish and half a monster? 3.02. 29 P
you 'mongst men | being most unfit to live. 3.03. 58
the dismissed bachelor loves, | being lass–lorn; 4.01. 68
they being penitent, | the sole drift of my 5.01. 28
the master and the boatswain | being awake, 5.01.100
and being so hard to me that brought your mind, TGV 1.01.138 P
being destin'd to a drier death on shore. 1.01.150
have given it you, but i, being in the way, 1.02. 39
man, | not being tried and tutor'd in the world: 1.03. 21
and yet i was last chidden for being too slow. 2.01. 12 P
for he, being in love, could not see to garter 2.01. 76 P
and you, being in love, cannot see to put on 2.01. 77 P
for being ignorant to whom it goes, | i writ at 2.01.110
he being her pupil, to become her tutor. 2.01.138
that my master, being scribe, to himself should 2.01.140
nay then he should be blind, and, being blind, 2.04. 93
but, valentine being gone, i'll quickly cross 2.06. 40
thou know'st, being stopp'd, impatiently doth 2.07. 26
being unprevented, to your timeless grave. 3.01. 21
my health and happy being at your court. 3.01. 57
which, being writ to me, shall be deliver'd 3.01.251
being entreated to it by your friend. 3.02. 45
and, being help'd, inhabits there. 4.02. 48
she, | but, being mask'd, he was not sure of it; 5.02. 40
being nimble–footed, he hath outrun us, | but 5.03. 7
and being fap, sir, was, as they say, cashier'd; WIV 1.01.178 P
my master knows not of your being here, and has 3.03. 30 P
some special suspicion of falstaff's being here, 3.03.188 P
and that, my state being gall'd with my expense, 3.04. 5
being thus cramm'd in the basket, a couple of 3.05. 97 P
the truth being known, | we'll all present 4.04. 63
bore many gentlemen (myself being one) | in hand MM 1.04. 51
as i say, this mistress elbow, being (as i say) 2.01. 98 P
with child, and being great–bellied, and longing 2.01. 98 P
you being then (if you be rememb'red) cracking 2.01.106 P
howsoever you color it in being a tapster, are 2.01.220 P
by being a bawd? 2.01.224 P
is like a good thing, being often read, | grown 2.04. 8
his filth within being cast, he would appear | a 3.01. 92
if it were damnable, he being so wise, | why 3.01.112
but grace, being the soul of your complexion, 3.01.183 P
this being granted in course — and now follows 3.01.248 P
signify that craft, being richer than innocency, 3.02. 9 P
for being a bawd, for being a bawd. 3.02. 65 P
for being a bawd, for being a bawd. 3.02. 65 P
sir, being members of my occupation, using 4.02. 37 P
being a murtherer, though he were my brother. 4.02. 62
he tyrannous, | but this being so, he's just. 4.02. 85
the matter being afoot, keep your instruction, 4.05. 3
must either punish me, not being believ'd, | or 5.01. 31
being come to knowledge that there was complaint 5.01.153
being criminal, in double violation | of sacred 5.01.404
much more the better | for being a little bad; 5.01.441
rock, | which being violently borne /upon, | our ERR 1.01.102
not being able to buy out his life | according 1.02. 5
we being strangers here, how dar'st thou trust 1.02. 60
thou flout me thus unto my face, | being forbid? 1.02. 92
why is time such a niggard of hair, being, as it 2.02. 77 P
thyself i call it, being strange to me, | that, 2.02.121
thy flesh, | being strumpeted by thy contagion. 2.02.144
who, every word by all my wit being scann'd, 2.02.150
i should kick, being kick'd, and, being at that 3.01. 17
kick, being kick'd, and, being at that pass, 3.01. 17
make us /but believe | (being compact of credit) 3.02. 22
let love, being light, be drowned if she sink! 3.02. 52
for gazing on your beams, fair sun, being by. 3.02. 56
not that, i being a beast, she would have me, 3.02. 87 P
me, but that she, being a very beastly creature, 3.02. 87 P
of his own doors being shut against his entrance 4.03. 89
house, | and tell his wife that, being lunatic, 4.03. 93
likeness of your grace, for trouble being gone, ADO 1.01.100 P
we may guess by this what you are, being a man. 1.01.110 P
being reconcil'd to the prince your brother: 1.01.155 P
as being a profess'd tyrant to their sex? 1.01.168 P
unhandsome, and being no other but as she is, i 1.01.175 P
i wonder that thou (being, as thou say'st thou 1.03. 10 P
being entertain'd for a perfumer, as i was 1.03. 58 P
so, by being too curst, god will send you no 2.01. 25 P
either to make him a garland, as being forsaken, 2.01.218 P
bind him up a rod, as being worthy to be whipt. 2.01.219 P
who, being overjoy'd with finding a bird's nest, 2.01.223 P
just cause, being her uncle and her guardian. 2.03.166 P
in them, being chosen for the prince's watch. 3.03. 6 P
door, for the wedding being there to–morrow, 3.03. 93 P
commodity, being taken up of these men's bills. 3.03.178 P
whiles we enjoy it, but being lack'd and lost, 4.01.219
being that i flow in grief, | the smallest twine 4.01.249
of age to brag | what i have done being young, 5.01. 61
i, being else by faith enforc'd | to call young 5.04. 8
i will fast, being loose. LLL 1.02.156 P
being but the one half of an entire sum 2.01.130
being out of heart that you cannot enjoy her. 3.01. 44 P
were still at odds, being but three. 3.01. 85
were still at odds, being but three. 3.01. 90
were still at odds, being but three. 3.01. 96
frame, | and never going aright, being a watch, 3.01.192
but being watch'd that it may still go right! 3.01.193
omne bene, say i, being of an old father's mind: 4.02. 32
thou being a goddess, i forswore not thee. 4.03. 63
thy grace being gain'd cures all disgrace in me. 4.03. 65
that you stand forfeit, being those that sue? 5.02.427
our love being yours, the error that love makes 5.02.771
by being once false for ever to be true | to 5.02.773
but, being over–full of self–affairs, | my mind MND 1.01.113
were the world mine, demetrius being bated, 1.01.190
but she, being mortal, of that boy did die, 2.01.135
so i, being young, till now ripe not to reason; 2.02.118
being o'er shoes in blood, plunge in the deep, 3.02. 48
durst thou have look'd upon him being awake? 3.02. 69
i wonder of their being here together. 4.01.131
methinks, being sensible, should curse again. 5.01.182 P
and, being done, thus wall away doth go. 5.01.205
and creep into the jaundies | by being peevish? MV 1.01. 86
being so full of unmannerly sadness in his youth 1.02. 49 P
fall as jacob's hire, the ewes, being rank, | in 1.03. 80
friend launcelot, being an honest man's son" — 2.02. 15 P
father, who, being more than sand–blind, high 2.02. 36 P
doth cause me, as my father, being, i hope, an 2.02.134 P
these things being bought and orderly bestowed, 2.02.170
being ten times undervalued to tried gold? 2.07. 53
and even there, his eye being big with tears, 2.08. 46
but, being season'd with a gracious voice, 3.02. 76
where every something, being blent together, 3.02.181
antonio, | being the bosom lover of my lord, 3.04. 17
shame | as to offend, himself being offended; 4.01. 58
and yet, thy wealth being forfeit to the state, 4.01.365
no note at all of our being absent hence — 5.01.120
or go to bed now, being two hours to day. 5.01.303
being ever from their cradles bred together, AYL 1.01.108 P
being native burghers of this desert city, 2.01. 23
then, being there alone, | left and abandoned of 2.01. 49
no, corin, being old, thou canst not guess, 2.04. 25
plays many parts, | his acts being seven ages. 2.07.143
for not being at court? your reason. 3.02. 39 P
her worth, being mounted on the wind, | through 3.02. 90
which time would i, being but a moonish youth, 3.02.409 P
and will you, being a man of your breeding, be 3.03. 83 P
and not being well married, it will be a good 3.03. 92 P
foul is most foul, being foul to be a scoffer. 3.05. 62
could be out, being before his belov'd mistress? 4.01. 81 P
in the hellespont and being taken with the cramp 4.01.104 P
it is no boast, being ask'd, to say we are. 4.03. 90
so sweetly tastes, being the thing i am. 4.03.137
after some small space, being strong at heart, 4.03.151
drink, being pour'd out of a cup into a glass, 5.01. 41 P
as being overjoyed | to see her noble lord SHR in.1. 120
which in a napkin (being close convey'd) | shall in.1. 127
being all this time abandon'd from your bed. in.2. 115
gave me my being and my father first, | a 1.01. 11
a servant to use his master so, being perhaps 1.02. 32 P
own, | that, being a stranger in this city here, 2.01. 89
'tis bargain'd 'twixt us twain, being alone, 2.01.304
being restrain'd to keep him from stumbling, 3.02. 58 P
that, being mad herself, she's madly mated. 3.02.244
whose hand (she being now at hand) thou shalt 4.01. 30 P
cold comfort, for being slow in thy hot office? 4.01. 31 P
your husband, being troubled with a shrew, 5.02. 28
and, being a winner, god give you good night! 5.02.187
virginity being blown down, man will quicklier AWW 1.01.123 P
virginity, by being once lost, may be ten times 1.01.130 P
by being ever kept, it is ever lost. 1.01.131 P
beware of being captives | before you serve. 2.01. 21
my being here it is that holds thee hence. 3.02.123
drum, being not ignorant of the impossibility, 4.01. 35 P
but that, my offenses being many, i would repent 4.03.242 P
his qualities being at this poor price, i need 4.03.276 P
being fool'd, by fool'ry thrive! 4.03.338
and this was it i gave him, being a–bed. 5.03.228
yet you will be hang'd for being so long absent, TN 1.05. 16 P
mourn for your brother's soul being in heaven. 1.05. 71 P
what, for being a puritan? 2.03.143 P
whose fair flow'r | being once display'd, doth 2.04. 39
she did praise my leg being cross–garter'd, and 2.05.167 P
being addicted to a melancholy as she is, that 2.05.202 P
yes, being kept together and put to use. 3.01. 50 P
your travel, | being skilless in these parts; 3.03. 9
this letter, being so excellently ignorant, will 3.04.188 P
and part being prompted by your present trouble, 3.04.343
so i, being master parson, am master parson; 4.02. 15 P
where being apprehended, his false cunning 5.01. 86
mistress | (so sovereignly being honorable). WT 1.02.323
is sleep, which being spotted | is goads, thorns 1.02.328
how accurs'd | in being so blest! 2.01. 39
if | the cause were not in being — part o' th' 2.03. 3
which being so horrible, so bloody, must | lead 2.03.152
being well arriv'd from delphos, are both landed 2.03.196
let us be clear'd | of being tyrannous, since we 3.02. 5
the pretense whereof being by circumstances 3.02. 17 P
being counted falsehood, shall (as i express it) 3.02. 27
being transported by my jealousies | to bloody 3.02.158
encourage him, | not doing it and being done. 3.02.165
(this being indeed the issue | of king polixenes 3.03. 43
no less unhappy, their issue not being gracious, 4.02. 27 P
my father nam'd me autolycus, who being, as i am 4.03. 25 P
of all kinds, | the flow'r–de–luce being one! 4.04.127
no money of me, but being enthrall'd as i am, it 4.04.232 P
one being dead, | i shall have more than you can 4.04.387
does nothing | but what he did being childish? 4.04.402
being now awake, i'll queen it no inch farther, 4.04.449
by this means being there | so soon as you 4.04.619
she being none of your flesh and blood, your 4.04.693 P
this being done, let the law go whistle; 4.04.697 P
seems to be the more noble in being fantastical. 4.04.751 P
be smil'd at, their offenses being so capital? 4.04.793 P
being something gently consider'd, i'll bring 4.04.794 P
him call me rogue for being so far officious, 4.04.839 P
being ready to leap out of himself for joy of 5.02. 49 P
luck, being in so preposterous estate as we are. 5.02.147 P
venture to be drunk, not being a tall fellow, 5.02.172 P
stone rebuke me | for being more stone than it? 5.03. 38
that the oracle | gave hope thou wast in being, 5.03.127
why, being younger born, | doth he lay claim to JN 1.01. 71
your father, | being none of his, refuse him. 1.01.127
in manners, being as like | as rain to water, or 2.01.127
being but the second generation | removed from 2.01.181
town, | being no further enemy to you | than the 2.01.243
being wrong'd as we are by this peevish town, 2.01.402
eye, | which, being but the shadow of your son, 2.01.499
and being rich, my virtue then shall be | to say 2.01.595
majesty, which, being touch'd and tried, 3.01.100
and being not done, where doing tends to ill, 3.01.272
for, being not mad, but sensible of grief, | my 3.04. 53
being create for comfort, to be us'd | in 4.01.106
being urged at a time unseasonable. 4.02. 20
a lady's tears, | being an ordinary inundation; 5.02. 48

war | plead for our interest and our being here. 5.02.165
indeed your drums, being beaten, will cry out; 5.02.166
and so shall you, being beaten. 5.02.167
belief | that, being brought into the open air, 5.07. 7
or, being open, put into his hands | that knows R2 1.03.164
for young hot colts being rag'd do rage the more 2.01. 70
old gaunt indeed, and gaunt in being old. 2.01. 74
such as it is, being tender, raw, and young, 2.03. 42
the cloak of night being pluck'd from off their 3.02. 45
for if of joy, being altogether wanting, | it 3.04. 13
or if of grief, being altogether had, | it adds 3.04. 15
lest, being over–proud in sap and blood, | with 3.04. 59
though being all too base | to stain the temper 4.01. 28
being ne'er so little urg'd, another way | to 5.01. 64
for one step i'll groan, the way being short, 5.01. 91
but that is lost for being richard's friend; 5.02. 42
pleas'd, till he be eas'd | with being nothing. 5.05. 41
we be men of good government, being govern'd, as 1H4 1.02. 27 P
doth ebb and flow like the sea, being govern'd, 1.02. 32 P
being wanted, he may be more wond'red at | by 1.02.201
i then, all smarting with my wounds being cold, 1.03. 49
being the agents or base second means, | the 1.03.165
your son in scotland being thus employed, 1.03.265
you any levers to lift me up again, being down? 2.02. 35 P
their points being broken — 2.04.214 P
thou being heir–apparent, could the world pick 2.04.366 P
why, being son to me, art thou so pointed at? 2.04.406 P
and therefore more valiant, being, as he is, old 2.04.477 P
which being sealed interchangeably | (a business 3.01. 80
where, being but young, i framed to the harp 3.01.121
by being seldom seen, i could not stir | but 3.02. 46
that, being daily swallowed by men's eyes, 3.02. 70
being with his presence glutted, gorg'd, and 3.02. 84
and, being no more in debt to years than thou, 3.02.103
my father and glendower being both away, | the 4.01.131
being men of such great leading as you are, 4.03. 17
and being fed by us you us'd us so | as that 5.01. 59
on, | and, his corruption being ta'en from us, 5.02. 22
with joyful tidings, and, being better hors'd, 2H4 1.01. 35
being bruited once, took fire and heat away 1.01.114
being sick, have (in some measure) made me well. 1.01.139
with grief, being now enrag'd with grief, | are 1.01.144
that, each heart being set | on bloody courses, 1.01.158
being upon hasty employment in the king's 2.01.127 P
being you are to take soldiers up in counties as 2.01.186 P
so, their fathers being so sick as yours at this 2.02. 30 P
or when a man is being whereby 'a may be thought 3.02. 78 P
yet notwithstanding, being incens'd, he is flint 4.04. 33
but, being moody, give him time and scope, 4.04. 39
his pillow, | being so troublesome a bedfellow? 4.05. 22
with the imputation of being near their master; 5.01. 72 P
but, being awak'd, i do despise my dream. 5.05. 51
being valu'd thus: H5 1.01. 11
as heir general, being descended | of blithild, 1.02. 66
that england, being empty of defense, | hath 1.02.153
for once the eagle (england) being in prey, | to 1.02.169
france being ours, we'll bend it to our awe, 1.02.224
and with forms being fetch'd | from glist'ring 2.02.116
look you, being as good a man as yourself, both 3.02.128 P
his cause being just and his quarrel honorable. 4.01.128 P
wherein thou art less happy, being fear'd, 4.01.248
that being dead, like to the bullet's crasing, 4.03.105
and also being a little intoxicates in his 4.07. 37 P
friend clytus, being in his ales and his cups; 4.07. 45 P
being in his right wits and his good judgments, 4.07. 46 P
being free from vainness and self–glorious pride 5.pr. 20
being a maid yet ros'd over with the virgin 5.02.295 P
as man and wife, being two, are one in love, 5.02.361
he, being in the vaward, plac'd behind | with 1H6 1.01.132
king is, | being ordain'd his special governor, 1.01.171
fie, lords, that you, being supreme magistrates, 1.03. 57
how wert thou handled, being prisoner? 1.04. 24
that, being captain of the watch to–night, | did 2.01. 61
being but fourth of that heroic line. 2.05. 78
you cannot witness for me, being slain. 4.05. 43
whom should we match with henry, being a king, 5.05. 66
we here discharge your grace from being regent 2H6 1.01. 66
he being of age to govern of himself? 1.01.166
and, being a woman, i will not be slack | to 1.02. 66
my choler being overblown | with walking once 1.03.152
being call'd | a hundred times and oft'ner, in 2.01. 87
for richard, the first son's heir, being dead, 2.02. 31
anne, | my mother, being heir unto the crown, 2.02. 44
and, being protector, stay'd the soldiers' pay, 3.01.105
who being accus'd a crafty murtherer, | his 3.01.254
for, being green, there is great hope of help. 3.01.287
and, in the end being rescued, i have seen | him 3.01.364
for humphrey being dead, as he shall be, | and 3.01.382
being all descended to the laboring heart, | who 3.02.163
as being thought to contradict your liking, 3.02.252
lest, being suffer'd in that harmful slumber, 3.02.262
thy name is gualtier, being rightly sounded. 4.01. 37
being captain of a pinnace, threatens more 4.01.107
being burnt i' th' hand for stealing of sheep. 4.02. 63 P
that parchment, being scribbled o'er, should 4.02. 80 P
the elder of them, being put to nurse, | was by 4.02.142
or why thou, being a subject as i am, | against 5.01. 19
o, let me view his visage, being dead, | that 5.01. 69
who, being suffer'd, with the bear's fell paw 5.01.153
being opposites of such repairing nature. 5.03. 22
he rose against him, being his sovereign, | and 3H6 1.01.141
being not took | before a true and lawful 1.02. 22
the smallest worm will turn, being trodden on, 2.02. 17
thou, being a king, blest with a goodly son, 2.02. 23
my father, being the earl of warwick's man, 2.05. 65
and, by god's mother, i, being but a bachelor, 3.02.103
so do i wish the crown, being so far off, | and 3.02.140
which being shallow, you shall give me leave 4.01. 62
well, i will arm me, being thus forewarn'd. 4.01.113
thy brother being carelessly encamp'd, | his 4.02. 14
embassade | then i degraded you from being king, 4.03. 33
we being thus arriv'd | from ravenspurgh haven 4.07. 7
as being well content with that alone. 4.07. 24
but being ent'red, | i doubt not, i, but we 4.07. 32
which, being suffer'd, rivers cannot quench. 4.08. 8
if not, the city being but of small defense, 5.01. 64
small joy have i in being england's queen. R3 1.03.109
in me | that i enjoy, being the queen thereof. 1.03.153
so do i ever — being well advis'd; 1.03.317
being pent from liberty, as i am now, | if two 1.04.258
have i | (thine being but a moi'ty of my moan) 2.02. 60
that i, being govern'd by the watery moon, | may 2.02. 69
and being seated, and domestic broils | clean 2.04. 60
and being but a toy, which is no grief to give. 3.01.114
being nothing like the noble duke my father. 3.05. 92
as being got, your father then in france, | and 3.07. 10
and his resemblance, being not like the duke. 3.07. 11
being the right idea of your father, | both in 3.07. 13
his grace not being warn'd thereof before: 3.07. 86
being a bark to brook no mighty sea — | than in 3.07.162
for one being sued to, one that humbly sues; 4.04.100
for she being feared of all, now fearing one; 4.04.103
to torture thee the more, being what thou art. 4.04.108
as one being best acquainted with her humor. 4.04.269
the loss you have is but a son being king, | and 4.04.307
an honest tale speeds best being plainly told. 4.04.358
lest, being seen, thy brother, tender george, 5.03. 95
you sleep in peace, the tyrant being slain; 5.03.256
still him in praise, and being present both, H8 1.01. 31
being now seen possible enough, got credit, 1.01. 37
for, being not propp'd by ancestry, whose grace 1.01. 59
a full hot horse, who being allow'd his way, 1.01.133
the duke being at the rose, within the parish 1.02.152
forg'd him some design, which, being believ'd, 1.02.181
being at greenwich, | after your highness had 1.02.188
of such a time, being my sworn servant, | the 1.02.191
th' usurper richard, who, being at salisbury, 1.02.196
being distress'd, was by that wretch betray'd, 2.01.110
would i had no being | if this salute my blood a 2.03.102
the queen being absent, 'tis a needful fitness 2.04.232
and found the blessedness of being little; 4.02. 66
which, being consider'd, | have mov'd us and our 5.01. 99
i weigh not, | being of those virtues vacant. 5.01.125
tower, | where, being but a private man again, 5.02. 90
may do, | not being torn a–pieces, we have done. 5.03. 76
the sea being smooth, | how many shallow bauble TRO 1.03. 34
degree being vizarded, | th' unworthiest shows 1.03. 83
beard, | as he being dress'd to some oration." 1.03.166
and choice (being mutual act of all our souls) 1.03.348
and, being born, his addition shall be humble. 3.02. 94 P
ere they be woo'd, they are constant being won. 3.02.111 P
summer, | and not a man, for being simply man, 3.03. 80
when they fall, as being slippery standers, 3.03. 84
the combatants being kin | half stints their 4.05. 92
soon provok'd, nor being provok'd soon calm'd; 4.05. 99
and being once subdu'd in armed tail, | sweet 5.10. 43
but that he pays himself with being proud. COR 1.01. 33 P
for that, being one o' th' lowest, basest, 1.01.157
vented their complainings, which being answer'd, 1.01.209
being mov'd, he will not spare to gird the gods. 1.01.256
for i cannot, | being a volsce, be that i am. 1.10. 5
being naked, sick, nor fane nor capitol, | the 1.10. 20
if you take it as a pleasure to you in being so. 2.01. 32 P
you blame martius for being proud? 2.01. 33 P
being the herdsmen of the beastly plebeians. 2.01. 95 P
which, being advanc'd, declines, and then men 2.01.161
of the which we being members, should bring 2.03. 12 P
where being three parts melted away with rotten 2.03. 31 P
and nobly named so, twice being censor, | was 2.03.244
you being their mouths, why rule you not their 3.01. 36
being but | the horn and noise o' th' monster's, 3.01. 94
being press'd to th' war, | even when the navel 3.01.122
being i' th' war, | their mutinies and revolts, 3.01.125
and, being angry, does forget that ever | he 3.01.258
the service of the foot | being once gangren'd, 3.01.305
lest his infection, being of catching nature, 3.01.308
art their soldier, and, being bred in broils, 3.02. 81
for they have pardons, being ask'd, as free | as 3.02. 88
being once chaf'd, he cannot | be rein'd again 3.03. 27
that being pass'd for consul with full voice, 3.03. 59
when most strook home, being gentle wounded, 4.01. 8
being now in no request of his country. 4.03. 35 P
no better entertainment | in being coriolanus. 4.05. 10
but being assur'd none but myself could move 5.02. 73 P
who being so heighten'd, | he watered his new 5.06. 21
being banish'd for't, he came unto my hearth, 5.06. 29
draw near them then in being merciful: TIT 1.01.118
and, being intercepted in your sport, | great 2.03. 80
the bull, being gall'd, gave aries such a knock 4.03. 72
too like the sire for ever being good. 5.01. 50
and, being credulous in this mad thought, | i'll 5.02. 74
and, being dead, let birds on her take pity. 5.03.200
i strike quickly, being mov'd. ROM 1.01. 6 P
and therefore women, being the weaker vessels, 1.01. 15 P
be found, | being one too many by my weary self, 1.01.128
being purg'd, a fire sparkling in lovers' eyes, 1.01.191
being vex'd, a sea nourish'd with loving tears. 1.01.192
being black, puts us in mind they hide the fair. 1.01.231
which /on more view of many, mine, being one, 1.02. 32
tut, you saw her fair, none else being by, 1.02. 94
being but heavy, i will bear the light. 1.04. 12
and, being thus frighted, swears a prayer or two 1.04. 87
and, being anger'd, puffs away from thence, 1.04.102
being held a foe, he may not have access | to 2.pr. 9
as glorious to this night, being o'er my head, 2.02. 27
being in night, all this is but a dream, | too 2.02.140
virtue itself turns vice, being misapplied, 2.03. 21
for this, being smelt, with that part cheers 2.03. 25
being tasted, stays all senses with the heart. 2.03. 26
the letter's master, how he dares, being dar'd. 2.04. 12 P
being a divine, a ghostly confessor, | a 3.03. 49
two, | for hark you, tybalt being slain so late, 3.04. 24
being our kinsman, if we revel much: 3.04. 26
being spoke behind your back, than to your face. 4.01. 28
take thou this vial, being then in bed, | and 4.01. 93
being holiday, the beggar's shop is shut. 5.01. 56
being loose, unfirm, with digging up of graves, 5.03. 6
being the time the potion's force should cease. 5.03.249
and being enfranchis'd, bid him come to me; TIM 1.01.106
is, | being of no power to make his wishes good. 1.02.196
being free itself, it thinks all others so. 2.02.233
that nature being sick of man's unkindness 4.03.176
thou hast cast away thyself, being like thyself, 4.03.220
hath a distracted and most wretched being, 4.03.246
thou shouldst desire to die, being miserable. 4.03.248
gave life and influence | to their whole being! 5.01. 64
by being what you are | make them best seen and 5.01. 68
being mechanical, you ought not walk | upon a JC 1.01. 3
being cross'd in conference by some senators. 1.02.188
and being offer'd him, he put it by with the 1.02.222 P
but life, being weary of these worldly bars, 1.03. 96
he says he does, being then most flattered. 2.01.208
my sex, | being so father'd and so husbanded? 2.01.297
and, being prostrate, thus he bade me say: 3.01.125
and, being men, hearing the will of caesar, | it 3.02.143
died | by their proscriptions, cicero being one. 4.03.178
and mayst be honor'd, being cato's son. 5.04. 11
the dues of rejoicing by being ignorant of what MAC 1.05. 12 P
which, being taught, return | to plague th' 1.07. 9
being unprepar'd, | our will became the servant 2.01. 17
i think, being too strong for him, though he 2.03. 39 P
there is none but he | whose being i do fear; 3.01. 54
that every minute of his being thrusts | against 3.01.116
being gone, | i am a man again. 3.04.106
being compar'd | with my confineless harms. 4.03. 54
him does condemn | itself for being there? 5.02. 25
and thou oppos'd, being of no woman born, | yet 5.08. 31
we do it wrong, being so majestical, | to offer HAM 1.01.143
beware | of entrance to a quarrel, but being in, 1.03. 66
being nature's livery, or fortune's star, | his 1.04. 32
do to that, | being a thing immortal as itself? 1.04. 67
to shatter all his bulk | and end his being. 2.01. 93
which, being kept close, might move | more grief 2.01.115
being of so young days brought up with him, 2.02. 11
in a dead dog, being a good kissing carrion — 2.02.182 P
ere we come to fall, | or /pardon'd being down? 3.03. 50
he, being remiss, | most generous, and free from 4.07.134
being thus benetted round with /villainies — 5.02. 29
fault undone, the issue of it being so proper. LR 1.01. 18 P
/fear'd to lose it, | thy safety being motive. 1.01.157
fairest cordelia, that art most rich being poor, 1.01.250
have thee beaten for being old before thy time. 1.05. 42 P
being oil to fire, snow to the colder moods; 2.02. 77
being down, insulted, rail'd, | and put upon him 2.02.119
sir, being his knave, i will. 2.02.137
being the very fellow which of late | display'd 2.04. 40
not ourselves | when nature, being oppress'd, 2.04.108
i pray you, father, being weak, seem so. 2.04.201
not being the worst | stands in some rank of 2.04.257
him to, being apt | to have his ear abus'd, 2.04.306
but being widow, and my gloucester with her, 4.02. 84
great ignorance, gloucester's eyes being out, 4.05. 9
and at her late being here | she gave strange 4.05. 24
i carry out my side, | her husband being alive. 5.01. 62
countenance for the battle, which being done, 5.01. 63
(being full of supper and distemp'ring draughts) OTH 1.01. 99
i fetch my life and being | from men of royal 1.02. 21
when, being not at your lodging to be found, 1.02. 45
so prepost'rously to err | (being not deficient, 1.03. 63
of being taken by the insolent foe | and sold to 1.03.137
my story being done, | she gave me for my pains 1.03.158
being strong on both sides, are equivocal. 1.03.217
in impatient thoughts | by being in his eye. 1.03.243
saints in your injuries, devils being offended, 2.01.111
she that being ang'red, her revenge being nigh, 2.01.152
she that being ang'red, her revenge being nigh, 2.01.152
(as they say base men being in love have then a 2.01.215 P
montano and myself being in speech, | there 2.03.225
that, i being absent and my place supplied, | my 3.03. 17
and, to th' advantage, i, being here, took't up. 3.03.312
and, being troubled with a raging tooth, | i 3.03.414
why then 'tis hers, my lord, and, being hers, 4.01. 12
lest, being like one of heaven, the devils 4.02. 36
being done, there is no pause. 5.02. 82
of one not easily jealous, but, being wrought, 5.02.345
she's good, being gone; ANT 1.02.126
as we rate boys who, being mature in knowledge, 1.04. 31
worth love, | comes /dear'd by being lack'd. 1.04. 44
that, being unseminar'd, thy freer thoughts 1.05. 11
which are not so — | or being, concern you not. 2.02. 30
my being in egypt, caesar, | what was't to you? 2.02. 35
your being in egypt | might be my question. 2.02. 39
being barber'd ten times o'er, goes to the feast 2.02.224
angel | becomes a fear, as being o'erpow'r'd: 2.03. 23
being done unknown, | i should have found it 2.07. 78
so is he, being a man. 3.02. 53
and, being, that we detain | all his revenue. 3.06. 29
being an abstract 'tween his lust and him. 3.06. 61
thou hast forespoke my being in these wars, 3.07. 3
refusing him at sea, | being prepar'd for land. 3.07. 40
she once being loof'd, | the noble ruin of her 3.10. 17
world oppos'd, he being | the mered question. 3.13. 9
being whipt, | bring him again; 3.13.102
the hangman thank | for being yare about him. 3.13.131
he thinks, being twenty times of better fortune, 4.02. 3
which, being dried with grief, will break to 4.09. 17
but being charg'd, we will be still by land, 4.11. 1
being so frustrate, tell him he mocks | the 5.01. 2
not being fortune, he's but fortune's knave, | a 5.02. 3
she levell'd at our purposes, and, being royal, 5.02.336
took such sorrow | that he quit being, and his CYM 1.01. 38
a drop of blood a day, and, being aged, | die of 1.01.157
being so far provok'd as i was in france, i 1.04. 67 P
to shift his being | is to exchange one misery 1.05. 54
and i am something curious, being strange, | to 1.06.191
therefore your issues, being foolish, do not 2.01. 47 P
but that you shall not say i yield being silent, 2.03. 94
your great knowing | should learn, being taught, 2.03. 98
to forget a lady's manners | by being so verbal; 2.03.106
and hated | for being preferr'd so well. 2.03.131
not a whit, | your lady being so easy. 2.04. 47
being so near the truth as i will make them, 2.04. 62
likewise reap, | being, as it is, much spoke of. 2.04. 87
who knows if one her women, being corrupted, 2.04.116
this service is not service, so being done, 3.03. 16
service, so being done, | but being so allowed. 3.03. 17
my fault being nothing (as i have told you oft) 3.03. 65
true honest men being heard, like false aeneas, 3.04. 58
the perturb'd court | for my being absent? 3.04.106
lest, being miss'd, i be suspected of | your 3.04.186
she being down, | i have the placing of the 3.05. 64
to whom being going, almost spent with hunger, 3.06. 62
am ill, but your being by me | cannot amend me; 4.02. 11

was that it was for not being such a smile; 4.02. 53
being scarce made up, | i mean, to man, he had 4.02.109
what cloten's being here to us portends, | or 4.02.182
slumber, | not as death's dart being laugh'd at; 4.02.211
and though you took his life, as being our foe, 4.02.250
newness | of cloten's death (we being not known, 4.04. 10
being an ugly monster, | 'tis strange he hides 5.03. 70
for being now a favorer to the britain, | no 5.03. 74
you rather, mine being yours; 5.04. 26
his merits due, | being all to dolors turn'd? 5.04. 80
which, being dead many years, shall after revive 5.04.141 P
the brain the heavier for being too light, the 5.04.164 P
the purse too light, being drawn of heaviness. 5.04.165 P
which, being cruel to the world, concluded 5.05. 32
for you a mortal mineral, which, being took, 5.05. 50
who, being born your vassal, | am something 5.05.113
picture, which by his tongue being made, | and 5.05.175
being thus quench'd | of hope, not longing, mine 5.05.195
that's due to all the villains past, in being, 5.05.212
o' th' earth amend | by being worse than they. 5.05.217
which, being ta'en, would cease | the present 5.05.255
which, being dead many years, shall after revive 5.05.438 P
name, | being leo–natus, doth import so much. 5.05.445
but being play'd upon before your time, | hell PER 1.01. 84
what being more known grows worse, to smother it 1.01.106
all love the womb that their first being bred, 1.01.107
and what may make him blush in being known, 1.02. 22
who seem'd my good protector, and, being here, 1.02. 82
from whence we had our being and our birth. 1.02.114
being bid to ask what he would of the king, 1.03. 5 P
being at antioch — 1.03. 18
but like to groves, being topp'd, they higher 1.04. 9
and being join'd, i'll thus your hopes destroy, 2.05. 86
with pain, | being thereto not compelled. 3.02. 26
too much money this mart by being too wenchless. 4.02. 5 P
dead, | nor none can know, leonine being gone. 4.03. 30
by you being pardoned, we commit no crime | to 4.04. 5
thetis, being proud, swallowed some part a' th' 4.04. 39
do in such a place as this, she being once gone. 4.05. 3 P
being on shore, honoring of neptune's triumphs, 5.01. 17
being demanded that, | she would sit still and 5.01.188
whereto being bound, | the interim, pray you, 5.02. 13
roses, their sharp spines being gone, | not TNK 1.01. 1
who cannot feel nor see the rain, being in't, 1.01.120
but alas, | being a natural sister of our sex, 1.01.125
what thou feel'st being able | to make mars 1.01.181
for | thou, being but mortal, makest affections 1.01.229
do, being sensually subdu'd | we lose our human 1.01.232
and here being thus together, | we are an 2.02. 78
thus mistakes, the which, to you being enemy, 3.01. 49
in, which being glu'd together | makes morris, 3.05.119
sir, your offenses | being no more than his. 3.06.183
being so few and well dispos'd, they show 4.02.122
which being laid unto | mine innocent true heart 5.01.133
being therein train'd | and of kind manage; 5.04. 68
that arcite's legs, being higher than his head, 5.04. 78
and being set, i'll smother thee with kisses. VEN 18
being wasted in such time–beguiling sport." 24
being so enrag'd, desire doth lend her force 29
being red, she loves him best, and being white, 77
being red, she loves him best, and being white, 77
who, being look'd on, ducks as quickly in; 87
being judge in love, she cannot right her cause. 220
being mad before, how doth she now for wits? 249
the strong–neck'd steed, being tied unto a tree, 263
being proud, as females are, to see him woo her, 309
and being steel'd, soft sighs can never grave it 376
to touch the fire, the weather being cold? 402
colt that's back'd and burthen'd being young, 419
being nurse and feeder of the other four! 446
fast, | or being early pluck'd is sour to taste. 528
like a wild bird being tam'd with too much 560
like lawn being spread upon the blushing rose, 590
being mov'd, he strikes, what e'er is in his way 623
being ireful, on the lion he will venter. 628
whose blood upon the fresh flowers being shed 665
"for there his smell with others being mingled, 691
many, | and, being low, never reliev'd by any. 708
like milk and blood being mingled both together, 902
being prison'd in her eye like pearls in glass, 980
for he being dead, with him is beauty slain, 1019
or as the snail, whose tender horns being hit, 1033
and being open'd, threw unwilling light | upon 1051
oft the eye mistakes, the brain being troubled. 1068
the wind would blow it off, and being gone, 1089
that thou being dead, the day should yet be 1134
the sovereignty of either being so great | that LUC 69
thither, | he makes excuses for his being there. 114
the guilt being great, the fear doth still 229
"and how her hand, in my hand being lock'd, 260
and being lighted, by the light he spies 316
the curtains being close, about he walks, 367
to wink, being blinded with a greater light: 375
being so applied, | his venom in effect is 531
the flesh being proud, desire doth fight with 712
being so bad, such numbers seek for thee? 896
the moon being clouded presently is miss'd, 1007
who, being stopp'd, the bounding banks o'erflows 1119
so must my soul, her bark being pill'd away. 1169
life, | the one will live, the other being dead: 1187
but as the earth doth weep, the sun being set, 1226
and sorrow ebbs, being blown with wind of words. 1330
his nose being shadowed by his neighbor's ear; 1416
here one being throng'd bears back, all boll'n 1417
being from the feeling of her own grief brought 1578
rage sent out, recall'd in rage, being past), 1671
being constrain'd with dreadful circumstance? 1703
which being done with speedy diligence, | the 1853
for being both to me, both to each friend, | i PP 2.11
thou being a goddess, i forswore not thee: 3. 6
thy grace being gain'd cures all disgrace in me. 3. 8
then being ask'd where all thy beauty lies, SON 2. 5
and being frank she lends to those are free: 4. 4
whose speechless song, being many, seeming one, 8.13
as thou being mine, mine is thy good report. 36.14
thee, | thine, by thy beauty being false to me. 41.14
my life, being made of four, with two alone 45. 7
his rider lov'd not speed, being made from thee. 50. 8
desire (of /perfect'st love being made) | shall 51.10
being had, to triumph, being lack'd, to hope. 52.14
being had, to triumph, being lack'd, to hope. 52.14
as call it winter, which, being full of care, 56.13
being your slave, what should i do but tend 57. 1
being your vassal bound to stay your leisure. 58. 4
o, let me suffer (being at your beck) | th' 58. 5
crawls to maturity, wherewith being crown'd, 60. 6
/thy worth the greater, being woo'd of time, 70. 6
either not assail'd, or victor being charg'd, 70.10
life, | the prey of worms, my body being dead, 74.10
or (being wrack'd) i am a worthless boat, | he 80.11
and tongues to be your being shall rehearse, 81.11
that you yourself, being extant, well might show 83. 6
which shall be most my glory, being dumb, | for 83.10
dumb, | for i impair not beauty being mute, 83.11
being fond on praise, which makes your praises 84.14
with mine own weakness being best acquainted, 88. 5
as thou being mine, mine is thy good report. 96.14
or whether doth my mind, being crown'd with you, 114. 1
so, being full of your ne'er–cloying sweetness, 118. 5
when not to be receives reproach of being, | and 121. 2
and yet thou wilt, for i, being pent in thee, 133.13
so thou, being rich in will, add to thy will 135.11
but being both from me, both to each friend, | i 144.11
when he again desires her, being sat, | her LC 66
did, | demand of him, nor being desired yielded; 149
strong o'er them, and you o'er me being strong, 257

BELARIUS 4 FR 0.0004 REL FR 4 V 0 P
myself, belarius, that am morgan call'd, | they CYM 3.03.106
great king, a subject who | was call'd belarius. 5.05.317
am that belarius whom you sometime banish'd. 5.05.333
who, by belarius stol'n, | for many years 5.05.455

BELATED *(see lated)*

BELCH 6 FR 0.0006 REL FR 3 V 3 P
sea | hath caus'd to belch up you; TMP 3.03. 56
sir toby belch! how now, sir toby belch? TN 1.03. 44 P
sir toby belch! how now, sir toby belch? 1.03. 45 P
bulk, | who almost burst to belch it in the sea. R3 1.04. 41
and when they are full | they belch us. OTH 3.04.106
(the bitterness of it i now belch from my heart) CYM 3.05.134 P

BELCH'D 1 FR 0.0001 REL FR 1 V 0 P
as hath been belch'd on by infected lungs. PER 4.06.169

BELCHES 1 FR 0.0001 REL FR 1 V 0 P
a good constraint of fortune it belches upon us. PER 3.02. 55

BELCHING 2 FR 0.0002 REL FR 2 V 0 P
like scaling sculls | before the belching whale; TRO 5.05. 23
the belching whale | and humming water must PER 3.01. 62

BELDAM 1 FR 0.0001 REL FR 1 V 0 P
beldam, i think we watch'd you at an inch. 2H6 1.04. 42

BELDAME 2 FR 0.0002 REL FR 2 V 0 P
shakes the old beldame earth, and topples down 1H4 3.01. 31
"to show the beldame daughters of her daughter, LUC 953

BELDAME'S 1 FR 0.0001 REL FR 1 V 0 P
and shapes her sorrow to the beldame's woes, LUC 1458

BELDAMES 1 FR 0.0001 REL FR 1 V 0 P
old men and beldames in the streets | do JN 4.02.185

BELDAMS 1 FR 0.0001 REL FR 1 V 0 P
have i not reason, beldams as you are? MAC 3.05. 2

BELEE'D 1 FR 0.0001 REL FR 1 V 0 P
must be belee'd and calm'd | by debitor and OTH 1.01. 30

BELFRY 1 FR 0.0001 REL FR 0 V 1 P
i would have been that day in the belfry. PER 2.01. 37 P

BELGIA 2 FR 0.0002 REL FR 1 V 1 P
where stood belgia, the netherlands? ERR 3.02.138 P
edward from belgia, | with hasty germans and 3H6 4.08. 1

BELIE 10 FR 0.0011 REL FR 8 V 2 P
to belie him i will not, and more of his AWW 4.03.267 P
for they shall yet belie thy happy years, | that TN 1.04. 30
thou art /not holy to belie me so, | i am not JN 3.04. 44
should i do so, i should belie my thoughts. R2 2.02. 77
thou dost belie him, percy, thou dost belie him; 1H4 1.03.113
thou dost belie him, percy, thou dost belie him; 1.03.113
and he doth sin that doth belie the dead, | not 2H4 1.01. 98
we say lie on her, when they belie her. OTH 4.01. 36 P
thou dost belie her, and thou art a devil. 5.02.133
rides on the posting winds and doth belie | all CYM 3.04. 36

BELIED 8 FR 0.0009 REL FR 7 V 1 P
o, on my soul, my cousin is belied! ADO 4.01.146
my soul doth tell me hero is belied, | and that 5.01. 42
i say thou hast belied mine innocent child! 5.01. 67
sixt and lastly, they have belied a lady; 5.01.218 P
i have belied a lady, | the princess of this CYM 5.02. 2
that she concludes the picture was belied. LUC 1533
as rare | as any she belied with false compare. SON 130.14
that i may not be so, nor thou belied, | bear 140.13

BELIEF 15 FR 0.0017 REL FR 12 V 3 P
grossness of the foppery into a receiv'd belief, WIV 5.05.125 P
in some little measure draw a belief from you, AYL 5.02. 57 P
my niece is already in the belief that he's mad. TN 3.04.136 P
and let belief and life encounter so | as doth JN 3.01. 31
yet doth speak, and holds belief | that, being 5.07. 6
marry, for that she's in a wrong belief, | i go 1H6 2.03. 31
king | stands not within the prospect of belief, MAC 1.03. 74
which was to my belief witness'd the rather, 4.03.184
and will not let belief take hold of him HAM 1.01. 24
my dream, | belief of it oppresses me already. OTH 1.01.143
this speed of caesar's | carries beyond belief. ANT 3.07. 75
by wounding his belief in her renown | with CYM 5.05.202
see how belief may suffer by foul show! PER 4.04. 23
friends, | if this but answer to my just belief, 5.01.238
the belief | both seal'd with eye and ear. TNK 5.03. 14

BELIEST 1 FR 0.0001 REL FR 1 V 0 P
no, not so, villain, thou beliest thyself. ADO 5.01.265

/BELIEV'D 1 FR 0.0001 REL FR 1 V 0 P
/let /pity /not /be /believ'd!" LR 4.03. 29

BELIEV'D 18 FR 0.0020 REL FR 14 V 4 P
little honor to be much believ'd, | and most MM 2.04.149
must either punish me, not being believ'd, | or 5.01. 31
great oaths would scarce make that be believ'd. AWW 4.01. 60 P
i have too much believ'd mine own suspicion. WT 3.02.151
i have heard (but not believ'd) the spirits o' 3.03. 16
i would not have believ'd him — no tongue but JN 4.01. 70
may move and what he hears may be believ'd, that 1H4 1.02.154 P
if i may be believ'd, so; 5.04.149 P
if something thou wouldst swear to be believ'd, R3 4.04.372
enough, got credit, | that bevis was believ'd. H8 1.01. 38
forg'd him some design, which, being believ'd, 1.02.181
let it not be believ'd for womanhood! TRO 5.02.129
and be these juggling fiends no more believ'd, MAC 5.08. 19
you should not have believ'd me, for virtue HAM 3.01.116 P
my lord, this would not be believ'd in venice, OTH 4.01.242
this is not strong enough to be believ'd | of CYM 2.04.131
and i | believ'd it was his, for she swore it TNK 5.01.117
believ'd her eyes when they t' assail begun, LC 262

BELIEVE 248 FR 0.0280 REL FR 173 V 75 P
lie — he did believe | he was indeed the duke, TMP 1.02.102
believe me, sir, | it carries a brave form. 1.02.411
i do well believe your highness, and did it to 2.01.172 P
now i will believe | that there are unicorns; 3.03. 21
i'll believe both; 3.03. 24
i should report this now, would they believe me? 3.03. 28
who would believe that there were mountaineers, 3.03. 44
i do believe it | against an oracle. 4.01. 11
that will /not let you | believe things certain. 5.01.125
no, believe me. TGV 2.01.155 P
so i believe; 3.02. 16
believe me, robert shallow, esquire, saith he is WIV 1.01.106 P
nay, i'll ne'er believe that; 2.01. 37 P
believe it, page, he speaks sense. 2.01.125
i will not believe such a cataian, though the 2.01.144 P
for, believe me, i hear the parson is no jester. 2.01.209 P
i do believe the swearer. what with me? 2.02. 39 P
believe it, for you know it. 2.02.231 P
believe me, there's no such thing in me. 3.03. 67 P
i believe thee; MM 1.02. 18 P
believe me, this may be. 1.02. 74 P
believe not that the dribbling dart of love 1.03. 2
do not believe it. 1.04. 39
(whom i believe to be most strait in virtue) 2.01. 9
well, believe this, | no ceremony that to great 2.02. 58
sir, believe this, | i had rather give my body 2.04. 55
believe me, on mine honor, | my words express my 2.04.147
who will believe thee, isabel? 2.04.154
did i tell this, | who would believe me? 2.04.172
i do make myself believe that you may most 3.01.199 P
canst thou believe thy living is a life, | so 3.02. 26
the duke, and i believe i know the cause of his 3.02.131 P
i can hardly believe that, since you know not 3.02.153 P
let me excuse me, and believe me so, | my mirth 4.01. 12
i do constantly believe you. 4.01. 21 P
yet i believe there comes | no countermand; 4.02. 96
believe it, royal prince, | if he be less, he's 5.01. 57
if she be mad — as i believe no other — | her 5.01. 60
we did believe no less. 5.01.142
my lord, most villainously, believe it. 5.01.149
make us /but believe | (being compact of credit) ERR 3.02. 21
a man denies, you are now bound to believe him. 5.01.307 P
not i, believe me. ADO 2.01.134 P
they will scarcely believe this without trial. 2.02. 41 P
and i | believe it better than reportingly. 3.01.116
surely i do believe your fair cousin is wrong'd. 4.01.259 P
nothing so well as you, but believe me not; 4.01.271 P
"that i believe," said she, "for he swore a 5.01.167 P
who i believe was pack'd in all this wrong, 5.01.299
but i believe, although i seem so loath, | i am LLL 1.01.159
do not believe | but i shall do thee mischief in MND 2.01.236
i believe we must leave the killing out, when 3.01. 14 P
i'll believe as soon | this whole earth may be 3.02. 52
believe me, king of shadows, i mistook. 3.02.347
i never may believe | these antic fables, nor 5.01. 2
believe me, sir, had i such venture forth, | the MV 1.01. 15
believe me, no. 1.01. 41
believe me, you are marvellously chang'd. 1.01. 76
or made her neighbors believe she wept for the 3.01. 9 P
nerissa teaches me what to believe — | i'll die 5.01.207
youth, i would i could make thee believe i love. AYL 3.02.385 P
me believe it? 3.02.387 P
may as soon make her that you love believe it, 3.02.388 P
believe then, if you please, that i can do 5.02. 58 P
dost thou believe, orlando, that the boy | can 5.04. 1
i sometimes do believe, and sometimes do not, 5.04. 3
believe me, lord, i think he cannot choose. SHR in.1. 42
believe me, sister, of all the men alive | i 2.01. 10
i tell you 'tis incredible to believe | how much 2.01.306
in time i may believe, yet i mistrust. 3.01. 51
i must believe my master, else, i promise you, 3.01. 54
not i, believe me, thus i'll visit her. 3.02.114
sir, so his mother says, if i may believe her. 5.01. 33 P
i believe 'a means to cozen somebody in this 5.01. 38 P
believe me, sir, they butt together well. 5.02. 39
i have heard of you i do not all believe. AWW 1.03. 10 P
that i could neither believe nor misdoubt. 1.03.125 P
believe not thy disdain, but presently | do 2.03.159
fare you well, my lord, and believe this of me: 2.05. 42 P
o, i believe with him. 3.05. 58
believe it, my lord, in mine own direct 3.06. 7 P
i should believe you, | for you have show'd me 3.07. 12
would you believe my oaths | when i did love you 4.02. 26
if your lordship be in't, as i believe you are, 4.03.114 P
nor believe he can have every thing in him by 4.03.145 P
close | her eyes myself could win me to believe, 5.03.119
do not believe him. 5.03.191
i will believe thou hast a mind that suits TN 1.02. 50
eater of beef and i believe that does harm to my 1.03. 85 P
no, believe me. 1.04. 8 P
dear lad, believe it; 1.04. 29
with such estimable wonder overfar believe that, 2.01. 28 P
rightly can ever believe such impossible 3.02. 72 P
will you make me believe that i am not sent for 4.01. 1 P
make him believe thou art sir topas the curate, 4.02. 2 P
believe me, i am not, i tell thee true. 4.02.115 P
nay, i'll ne'er believe a madman till i see his 4.02.116 P
believe me, i speak as my understanding WT 1.01. 19 P
believe this crack to be in my dread mistress 1.02.322
i must believe you, sir. 1.02.333
i do believe thee: 1.02.446
and i'll be sworn you would believe my saying, 2.01. 63
i do believe it. 2.02. 62
i do believe | hermione hath suffer'd death, and 3.03. 41
have it | upon his own report, and i believe it. 4.04.170
believe me, thou talkest of an admirable 4.04.202 P
so her dead likeness, i do well believe, 5.03. 15
believe me, i do not believe thee, man, | i have JN 3.01. 9
believe me, i do not believe thee, man, | i have 3.01. 9

as true as i believe you think them false | that 3.01. 27
o, if thou teach me to believe this sorrow, 3.01. 29
breast, | and i do fearfully believe 'tis done, 4.02. 74
faith | to your proceedings, yet believe me, 5.02. 11
we do believe thee, and beshrew my soul | but i 5.04. 49
i will upon all hazards well believe | thou art 5.06. 7
thrust into my hands, | never believe me. R2 2.02.111
believe me, noble lord, | i am a stranger here 2.03. 2
o king, believe not this hard–hearted man! 5.03. 87
for i well believe | thou wilt not utter what 1H4 2.03.110
he would make you believe it was done in fight, 2.04.307 P
life | make me believe that thou art only mark'd 3.02. 9
wilt thou believe me, hal, three or four bonds 3.03.101 P
i am sorry i should force you to believe | that 2H4 1.01.105
who shall believe | but you misuse the reverence 4.02. 22
believe me, i am passing light in spirit. 4.02. 85
to her), believe not the word of the noble. 4.03. 54 P
and, princes all, believe me, i beseech you, 5.02.122
for we will hear, note, and believe in heart, H5 1.02. 30
but i believe, as cold a night as 'tis, he could 4.01.114 P
and i do believe your majesty takes no scorn to 4.07.102 P
believe my words, | for they are certain and 1H6 1.02. 58
believe me, lords, my tender years can tell, 3.01. 71
believe me, lords, for flying at the brook, | i 2H6 2.01. 1
believe me, cousin gloucester, | had not your 2.01. 43
believe me, lords, were none more wise than i — 3.01.231
i do believe that violent hands were laid | upon 3.02.156
and you, base peasants, do ye believe him? 4.08. 21 P
well guess'd, believe me, for that was my 3H6 4.05. 22
either not believe | the envious slanders of her R3 1.03. 25
now they believe it, and withal whet me | to be 1.03.331
could not believe but that i was in hell, | such 1.04. 62
take the devil in thy mind, and believe him not; 1.04.147 P
and i believe will never stand upright | till 3.02. 39
/mayor, | would you imagine, or almost believe, 3.05. 35
give | their money out of hope they may believe, H8 pr 8
i believe, not any. 1.02. 92
th' are breath i not believe in. 2.02. 53
believe me, there's an ill opinion spread then, 2.02.124
i do believe | (induc'd by potent circumstances) 2.04. 75
believe me, she has had much wrong. 3.01. 48
believe it, this is true. 3.02. 25
believe it. 3.02. 37
shortly, i believe, | his second marriage shall 3.02. 67
a royal train, believe me. 4.01. 37
believe me, sir, she is the goodliest woman 4.01. 69
i do believe it, for they pass'd by me | as TRO 3.03.142
i constantly believe | (or rather call my 4.01. 41
i must not believe you. 4.05.221
an oracle to tell me so, | i'd not believe thee. 4.05.253
proud diomed, believe, | i come to lose my arm, 5.03. 95
i do believe thee, live. 5.04. 30
god–a–mercy, that thou wilt believe me, but a 5.04. 31 P
believe me, sirs, | we shall be charg'd again. COR 1.06. 3
thy day's work, | thou't not believe thy deeds: 1.09. 2
true," i'd not believe them more | than thee, 4.05.105
but, for your son, believe it — o, believe it 5.03.187
for your son, believe it — o, believe it — 5.03.187
believe me, queen, your /swart cimmerian | doth TIT 2.03. 72
that granted, how canst thou believe an oath? 5.01. 72
not i, believe me. ROM 1.04. 14
the god of my idolatry, | and i'll believe thee. 2.02.115
believe me, love, it was the nightingale. 3.05. 5
shall i believe | that unsubstantial death is 5.03.102
fie, no, do not believe it; TIM 3.02. 8 P
but believe you this, my lord, that not long ago 3.02. 10 P
i'll believe him as an enemy, and give over my 4.03.454 P
and believe it, | my most honor'd lord, | for 4.03.517
i do believe that these applauses are | for some JC 1.02.133
for, i believe, they are portentous things 1.03. 31
believe me for mine honor, and have respect to 3.02. 14 P
respect to mine honor, that you may believe. 3.02. 16 P
believe not so. 5.01. 89
i but believe it partly, | for i am fresh of 5.01. 89
i believe drink gave thee the lie last night. MAC 2.03. 37 P
what i believe, i'll wail, | what know, believe; 4.03. 8
what i believe, i'll wail, | what know, believe; 4.03. 9
i might not this believe | without the sensible HAM 1.01. 56
so have i heard and do in part believe it. 1.01.165
it fits your wisdom so far to believe it | as he 1.03. 25
do you believe his tenders, as you call them? 1.03.103
believe so much in him, that he is young, | and 1.03.124
do not believe his vows, for they are brokers, 1.03.127
my drift, | and i believe it is a fetch of wit: 2.01. 38
that i love thee best, o most best, believe it. 2.02.122 P
though i most powerfully and potently believe, 2.02.201 P
indeed, my lord, you made me believe so. 3.01.115 P
we are arrant knaves, believe none of us. 3.01.128 P
but yet do i believe | the origin and 3.01.176
i do believe you think what now you speak, | but 3.02.186
believe me, i cannot. 3.02.354 P
do not believe it. 4.02. 9 P
believe what? 4.02. 10 P
no, believe me, 'tis very cold, the wind is 5.02. 95 P
here is newly come to court laertes, believe me, 5.02.106 P
never believe it; 5.02.340
which to believe of her | must be a faith that LR 1.01.221
he will not believe a fool. 1.04.135 P
thou'lt not believe | with how deprav'd a 2.04.136
do not believe | that, from the sense of all OTH 1.01.130
you thus, | and prays you to believe him. 1.03. 42
i cannot believe that in her, she's full of most 2.01.249 P
yet surely cassio, i believe, receiv'd | from 2.03.244
i do believe 'twas he. 3.03. 40
believe me, i had rather have lost my purse 3.04. 25
i have greater reason to believe now than ever 4.02.213 P
i do believe it, and i ask your pardon. 5.02.300
believe not all, or, if you must believe, ANT 3.04. 11
believe not all, or, if you must believe, 3.04. 11
pleasure, and believe | caesar's no merchant, to 5.02.182
but he that will believe all that they say, 5.02.256 P
i do well believe you. CYM 1.01. 67
believe it, sir, i have seen him in britain. 1.04. 1 P
i could not /but believe she excell'd many. 1.04. 74 P
i do believe | (statist though i am none, nor 2.04. 15
[illegible]ake them, | must first induce you to believe; 2.04. 63
[illegible]us may poor fools | believe false teachers. 3.04. 85
[illegible] | believe her lips in opening it. 5.05. 42

i believe you, | your honor and your goodness PER 3.03. 25
believe me law, | i never kill'd a mouse, nor 4.01. 76
let pericles believe his daughter's dead, | and 4.04. 46
i will believe thee, | and make /my senses 5.01.122
you said you would believe me, | but, not to be 5.01.150
believe me, 'twere best i did give o'er. 5.01.166
i will believe you by the syllable | of what you 5.01.167
i must no more believe thee in this point TNK 1.03. 87
(though in't i know thou dost believe thyself) 1.03. 88
i believe it, | and to that destiny have 2.02. 4
believe | his mother was a wondrous handsome 2.05. 19
believe you'll find it so. 4.01. 47
with such a cry and swiftness that, believe me, 4.01. 98
believe me, one would marry a leprous witch to 4.03. 46 P
swore it was, | and who would not believe her? 5.01.118
not to believe, and yet too credulous: VEN 986
i do believe her (though i know she lies) | that PP 1. 2
who will believe my verse in time to come | if SON 17. 1
and then believe me, my love is as fair | as any 21.10
never believe, though in my nature reign'd | all 109. 9
i do believe her, though i know she lies, | that 138. 2

BELIEVED 1 FR 0.0001 REL FR 1 V 0 P
bad, | mad slanderers by mad ears believed be. SON 140.12

BELIEVES 4 FR 0.0004 REL FR 4 V 0 P
and she believes, where ever they are gone, AYL 2.02. 15
such passion fly | that he believes himself; TN 3.04.374
the quality of flesh | and not believes himself. TIM 4.03.157
for he believes | it is a thing most precious. CYM 3.05. 58

BELIEVEST 1 FR 0.0001 REL FR 1 V 0 P
thou believest no god: TIT 5.01. 71

BELIEVE'T 10 FR 0.0011 REL FR 10 V 0 P
dost thou believe't? AWW 1.03.249
such is his noble purpose, and, believe't, | the 3.02. 70
and | believe't not lightly — though i go alone COR 4.01. 29
believe't, dear lord, | you mend the jewel by TIM 1.01.171
believe't, my lord and i have made an end: 3.04. 55
believe't that we'll do any thing for gold. 4.03.150
that cassio loves her, i do well believe't; OTH 2.01.286
i'll not believe't. 3.03.279
he wail'd, | believe't — till i weep too. ANT 3.02. 59
believe't, i will. PER 2.01.153

BELIEVING 6 FR 0.0006 REL FR 2 V 4 P
no believing you indeed, sir: TGV 2.01.156 P
some woman, there is no believing old signs. ADO 3.02. 41 P
dissuade me from believing thee a vessel of too AWW 2.03.205 P
means to be sav'd by believing rightly can ever TN 3.02. 71 P
that to believing souls | gives light in 2H6 2.01. 64
the silly boy, believing she is dead, | claps VEN 467

BELIEV'ST 1 FR 0.0001 REL FR 1 V 0 P
as thou believ'st | there is another comfort MM 5.01. 48

BELIKE 43 FR 0.0048 REL FR 34 V 9 P
heavy? belike it hath some burden then? TGV 1.02. 82
belike, boy, then you are in love — for last 2.01. 79 P
belike that now she hath enfranchis'd them 2.04. 90
she is dead, belike? 4.04. 75
belike she thinks that proteus hath forsook her? 4.04.146
belike having receiv'd wrong by some person, is WIV 3.01. 53 P
lord angelo, belike, thinking me remiss in mine MM 4.02.115 P
a ghostly father, belike. 5.01.126
this' a good friar, belike! 5.01.131
belike you thought our love would last too long ERR 4.01. 25
belike his wife, acquainted with his fits, | on 4.03. 90
some merry mocking lord belike, is't so? LLL 2.01. 52
if my hand be out, then belike your hand is in. 4.01.135
belike for want of rain; MND 1.01.130
belike some noble gentleman that means SHR in.1. 75
shall i be appointed hours, as though, belike, 1.01.103
o then belike you fancy riches more: 2.01. 16
belike you mean to make a puppet of me. 4.03.103
so belike is that. AWW 4.05.100 P
belike you slew great number of his people? TN 3.03. 29
belike this is a man of that quirk. 3.04.244 P
o, belike it is the bishop of carlisle. R2 3.03. 30
belike then my appetite was not princely got, 2H4 2.02. 9 P
o then belike she was old and gentle, and you H5 3.07. 52 P
belike your lordship takes us then for fools, 1H6 3.02. 62
then you belike suspect these noblemen | as 2H6 3.02.186
belike he means, | back'd by the power of 3H6 1.01. 51
'twas odds, belike, when valiant warwick fled: 2.01.148
belike he thinks me henry. 4.01. 96
belike she minds to play the amazon. 4.01.106
belike the elder; 4.01.118
to–morrow then belike shall be the day, | if 4.03. 7
who should that be? belike unlook'd–for friends. 5.01. 14
belike his majesty hath some intent | that you R3 1.01. 49
aiming, belike, at your interior hatred, | that 1.03. 65
belike for joy the emperor hath a son. TIT 4.02. 50
belike they had some notice of the people, | how JC 3.02.270
belike this show imports the argument of the HAM 3.02.139 P
why then belike he likes it not, perdy. 3.02.294
belike | some things — i know not what. LR 4.05. 20
but that, belike, iago in the /nick | came in OTH 5.02.317
then belike my children shall have no names. ANT 1.02. 35 P
belike 'tis but a rumor. good night to you. 4.03. 5

BELL 37 FR 0.0041 REL FR 33 V 4 P
hark now i hear them — ding–dong bell. TMP 1.02.405
there suck i, | in a cowslip's bell i lie; 5.01. 89
the windsor bell hath strook twelve; WIV 5.05. 1 P
the clock hath strucken twelve upon the bell: ERR 1.02. 45
no, no, the bell, 'tis time that i were gone: 4.02. 53
he hath a heart as sound as a bell, and his ADO 3.02. 12 P
in monument than the bell rings and the widow 5.02. 79 P
i'll begin it — ding, dong, bell. MV 3.02. 71
ding, dong, bell. 3.02. 72
and have with holy bell been knoll'd to church, AYL 2.07.121
bell, book, and candle shall not drive me back, JN 3.03. 12
if the midnight bell | did with his iron tongue 3.03. 37
which strike upon my heart, | which is the bell. R2 5.05. 57
his tongue | sounds ever after as a sullen bell, 2H4 1.01.102
when that your flock, assembled by the bell, 4.02. 5
enter, go in, the market bell is rung. 1H6 3.02. 16
hark, hark, the dolphin's drum, a warning bell, 4.02. 39
my sighing breast shall be thy funeral bell; 3H6 2.05.117
i'll startle you | worse than the sacring bell, H8 3.02.295
weed, | no mournful bell shall ring her burial, TIT 5.03.197
this sight of death is as a bell | that warns my ROM 5.03.206
my drink is ready, | she strike upon the bell. MAC 2.01. 32
the bell invites me. 2.01. 62

ring the bell. 2.03. 80
and myself, | the bell then beating one — HAM 1.01. 39
and the bringing home | of bell and burial. 5.01.234
awake the snorting citizens with the bell, | or OTH 1.01. 90
hour of five till the bell have told eleven. 2.02. 10 P
who's that which rings the bell? 2.03.161
silence that dreadful bell, it frights the isle 2.03.175
let's mock the midnight bell. ANT 3.13.184
be bold to ring the bell. TNK 3.02. 20
falls, and sounds more like | a bell than blade. 5.03. 6
to one sore sick that hears the passing bell. VEN 702
woes, | for sorrow, like a heavy hanging bell, LUC 1493
no deal, | my wether's bell rings doleful knell, PP 17.18
than you shall hear the surly sullen bell | give SON 71. 2

BELLARIO 8 FR 0.0009 REL FR 8 V 0 P
this | into my /cousin's hands, doctor bellario, MV 3.04. 50
unless bellario, a learned doctor, | whom i have 4.01.105
came you from padua, from bellario? 4.01.119
from both, my lord. bellario greets your grace. 4.01.120
this letter from bellario doth commend | a young 4.01.143
you hear the learn'd bellario, what he writes, 4.01.167
come you from old bellario? 4.01.169
it comes from padua, from bellario. 5.01.268

BELLARIO'S 1 FR 0.0001 REL FR 1 V 0 P
time the court shall hear bellario's letter. MV 4.01.149

BELLE 1 FR 0.0001 REL FR 0 V 1 P
answer you, la plus belle katherine du monde, H5 5.02.216 P

BELLIED 1 FR 0.0001 REL FR 1 V 0 P
your breath with full consent bellied his sails; TRO 2.02. 74

BELLIES 2 FR 0.0002 REL FR 0 V 2 P
with hearts in their bellies no bigger than 1H4 4.02. 21 P
so they come by great bellies. TIM 1.01.207 P

BELLMAN 1 FR 0.0001 REL FR 1 V 0 P
it was the owl that shriek'd, the fatal bellman, MAC 2.02. 3

BELLONA 2 FR 0.0002 REL FR 2 V 0 P
unto the helmeted bellona use them | and pray TNK 1.01. 75
whose speed | the great bellona i'll solicit; 1.03. 13

BELLONA'S 1 FR 0.0001 REL FR 1 V 0 P
till that bellona's bridegroom, lapp'd in proof, MAC 1.02. 54

BELLOW 1 FR 0.0001 REL FR 0 V 1 P
the croaking raven doth bellow for revenge. HAM 3.02.254 P

BELLOW'D 2 FR 0.0002 REL FR 1 V 1 P
jupiter | became a bull and bellow'd; WT 4.04. 28
so strutted and bellow'd that i have thought HAM 3.02. 33 P

/BELLOWED 1 FR 0.0001 REL FR 1 V 0 P
/he /fastened /on /my /neck /and /bellowed /out LR 5.03.213

BELLOWING 2 FR 0.0002 REL FR 2 V 0 P
now, we heard a hollow burst of bellowing | like TMP 2.01.311
mad bounds, bellowing and neighing loud, | which MV 5.01. 73

BELLOWS 2 FR 0.0002 REL FR 2 V 0 P
and is become the bellows and the fan | to cool ANT 1.01. 9
him, | for flattery is the bellows blows up sin, PER 1.02. 39

BELLOWS–MENDER 2 FR 0.0002 REL FR 0 V 2 P
francis flute, the bellows–mender. MND 1.02. 42 P
flute, the bellows–mender! 4.01.202 P

BELLS 20 FR 0.0022 REL FR 15 V 5 P
but match'd in mouth like bells, | each under MND 4.01.123
if ever been where bells have knoll'd to church, AYL 2.07.114
the horse his curb, and the falcon her bells, so 3.03. 80 P
tripping measure, or the bells of saint bennet, TN 5.01. 38 P
rejoice, you men of angiers, ring your bells, JN 2.01.312
and bid the merry bells ring to thine ear | that 2H4 4.05.111
why ring not out the bells aloud throughout the 1H6 1.06. 11
shaking the bloody darts as he his bells. 2H6 3.01.366
ring bells aloud, burn bonfires clear and bright 5.01. 3
dares stir a wing if warwick shake his bells. 3H6 1.01. 47
our instruments to melancholy bells, | our ROM 4.05. 86
like sweet bells jangled, out of time and harsh; HAM 3.01.158
bells in your parlors, wild–cats in your OTH 2.01.110
whole parish, church, steeple, bells, and all. PER 2.01. 34 P
i would have kept such a jangling of the bells, 2.01. 41 P
he should never have left till he cast bells, 2.01. 42 P
spring–time's harbinger, | with her bells dim; TNK 1.01. 9
it was a hawk, | and her bells were cut away." 3.05. 71
let him play | qui passa o' th' bells and bones. 3.05. 86
trembling fear, as fowl hear falcons' bells. LUC 511

BELL–WETHER 2 FR 0.0002 REL FR 0 V 2 P
be detected with a jealious rotten bell–wether; WIV 3.05.110 P
to be bawd to a bell–wether, and to betray a AYL 3.02. 81 P

/BELLY 1 FR 0.0001 REL FR 0 V 1 P
/cries /in /tom's /belly /for /two /white LR 3.06. 30 P

BELLY 37 FR 0.0041 REL FR 13 V 24 P
view gilded my foot, sometimes my portly belly. WIV 1.03. 62 P
(with so many tuns of oil in his belly) ashore 2.01. 65 P
i have my belly full of ford. 3.05. 36 P
your belly is all putter. 5.05.140 P
i dare not for my head fill my belly; MM 4.03.154 P
quick, the child brags in her belly already. LLL 5.02.677 P
man's blood in his belly than will sup a flea. 5.02.692 P
you can the getting up of the negro's belly; MV 3.05. 39 P
in fair round belly with good capon lin'd, AYL 2.07.154
so you may put a man in your belly. 3.02.204 P
to the roof of my mouth, my heart in my belly, SHR 4.01. 8 P
be it concluded, | no barricado for a belly. WT 1.02.204
manningtree ox with the pudding in his belly, 1H4 2.04.453 P
'sblood, i would my face were in your belly! 3.03. 49 P
i am the fellow with the great belly, and he my 2H4 1.02.146 P
beard, a decreasing leg, an increasing belly? 1.02.182 P
with a white head and something a round belly. 1.02.189 P
put all my substance into that fat belly of his, 2.01. 75 P
methought 'a made a shrewd thrust at your belly. 2.04.211 P
a whole school of tongues in this belly of mine, 4.03. 18 P
and i had but a belly of any indifferency, i 4.03. 20 P
the fat knight with the great belly doublet. H5 4.07. 48 P
the fellow has mettle enough in his belly. 4.08. 63 P
so, underneath the belly of their steeds, | that 3H6 2.03. 20
upon my back, to defend my belly, upon my wit, TRO 1.02.260 P
wears his wit in his belly and his guts in his 2.01. 73 P
the body's members | rebell'd against the belly; COR 1.01. 97
the belly answer'd — 1.01.105
well, sir, what answer made the belly? 1.01.106
i may make the belly smile | as well as speak — 1.01.109
should by the cormorant belly be restrain'd, 1.01.121
did complain, | what could the belly answer? 1.01.124
your most grave belly was deliberate, | not rash 1.01.128
my good friends, this says the belly, mark me. 1.01.141
the senators of rome are this good belly, | and 1.01.148

and when i had been in his belly, i would have PER 2.01. 40 P
neck, | he on her belly falls, she on her back. VEN 594
BELLYFUL 2 FR 0.0002 REL FR 1 V 1 P
rumble thy bellyful! LR 3.02. 14
every jack slave hath his bellyful of fighting, CYM 2.01. 20 P
//BELLY–PINCHED 1 FR 0.0001 REL FR 1 V 0 P
/the /lion /and /the //belly–pinched /wolf LR 3.01. 13
BELLY'S 3 FR 0.0003 REL FR 2 V 1 P
for my belly's as cold as if i had swallow'd WIV 3.05. 22 P
your belly's answer — what? COR 1.01.114
patience awhile, you'st hear the belly's answer. 1.01.126
BELMAN 1 FR 0.0001 REL FR 1 V 0 P
why, belman is as good as he, my lord; SHR in.1. 22
BELMONT 7 FR 0.0008 REL FR 6 V 1 P
in belmont is a lady richly left, | and she is MV 1.01.161
which makes her seat of belmont colchis' strond, 1.01.171
to furnish thee to belmont, to fair portia. 1.01.182
i must go with you to belmont. 2.02.179 P
morning early will we both | fly toward belmont. 4.01.457
love did run from venice, | as far as belmont. 5.01. 17
before the break of day | be here at belmont. 5.01. 30
BELOCK'D 1 FR 0.0001 REL FR 1 V 0 P
a vow'd contract, | was fast belock'd in thine; MM 5.01.210
BELONG 18 FR 0.0020 REL FR 14 V 4 P
but that you take what doth to you belong, | it LLL 5.02.381
doth to our rose of youth rightly belong; AWW 1.03.130
belong you to the lady olivia, friends? TN 5.01. 8 P
of foot, | doth not thy embassage belong to me, R2 3.04. 93
to you | this honorable bounty shall belong. 1H4 5.05. 26
doth any name particular belong | unto the 2H4 4.05.232
give | that doth belong unto the house of york, 1H6 3.01.164
god, | for judgment only doth belong to thee. 2H6 3.02.140
as i belong to worship and affect | in honor H8 1.01. 39
good master porter, i belong to th' larder. 5.03. 4 P
belong to th' gallows, and be hang'd, ye rogue! 5.03. 6 P
spring, | your tributary drops belong to woe, ROM 3.02.103
did not you chiefly belong to my heart? TIM 1.02. 92 P
to me, and say the tears | belong to egypt. ANT 1.03. 78
such danger to resistance did belong | that LUC 1265
to you it doth belong | yourself to pardon of SON 58.11
such is my love, to thee i so belong, | that for 88.13
the broken bosoms that to me belong | have LC 254
BELONG'D *(also 'long'd, etc.)*
BELONG'D 2 FR 0.0002 REL FR 1 V 1 P
and show'd what necessity belong'd to't, and yet TIM 3.02. 13 P
(more than indeed belong'd to such a trifle), OTH 5.02.228
BELONGING 4 FR 0.0004 REL FR 4 V 0 P
belonging to whom? LLL 2.01.224
with all appertinents | belonging to his honor; H5 2.02. 88
camp, i give him, | with all his trim belonging; COR 1.09. 62
/nor /any /other /part | belonging to a man. ROM 2.02. 42
BELONGINGS 1 FR 0.0001 REL FR 1 V 0 P
thyself and thy belongings | are not thine own MM 1.01. 29
BELONGS 18 FR 0.0020 REL FR 13 V 5 P
we know what belongs to a frippery. TMP 4.01.225 P
than talk, we know what belongs to a watch. ADO 3.03. 38 P
to things of sale a seller's praise belongs: LLL 4.03.236
sounded, | yet not so deeply as to thee belongs, SHR 2.01.193
brass, and all things that belongs | to house or 2.01.355
here it is, and all that belongs to't. AWW 2.02. 35 P
that title and what shame else belongs to't. WT 4.04.841 P
or if there were, it not belongs to you. 2H4 4.01. 96
and know the office that belongs to such. 1H6 3.01. 55
knee, | disdaining duty that to us belongs. 2H6 3.01. 17
and if there be | no great offense belongs to't, H8 5.01. 12
me the duty which | to a mother's part belongs. COR 5.03.168
stay, madam, here is more belongs to her: TIT 2.03.122
i speak, | no blame belongs to thee.) TIM 2.02.222
and one that knows what belongs to reason; 3.01. 36 P
all that belongs to this. CYM 5.05.147
to hear with eyes belongs to love's fine wit. SON 23.14
i see a better state to me belongs | than that 92. 7
BELOV'D 39 FR 0.0044 REL FR 30 V 9 P
when women cannot love where they're belov'd! TGV 5.04. 44
when proteus cannot love where he's belov'd! 5.04. 45
sir, | of credit infinite, highly belov'd, ERR 5.01. 6
can be) | i am belov'd of beauteous hermia. MND 1.01.104
and no less belov'd of her uncle than his own AYL 1.01.111 P
of all sorts enchantingly belov'd, and indeed so 1.01.168 P
could be out, being before his belov'd mistress? 4.01. 81 P
i told you your son was well belov'd in padua. SHR 5.01. 25 P
image of the creature | that is belov'd. TN 2.04. 20
"to the unknown belov'd, this, and my good 2.05. 90 P
our wife, and one | of us too much belov'd. WT 3.02. 4
will i break my oath | to this my fair belov'd. 4.04.492
creep | of that same noble prelate well belov'd, 1H4 1.03.267
and the protector's wife, belov'd of him? 2H6 1.02. 44
no less belov'd | than when thou wert protector 2.03. 26
and am i then a man to be belov'd? 3H6 3.02.163
and thou, brave oxford, wondrous well belov'd, 4.08. 17
now welcome more, and ten times more belov'd, 5.01.103
ever belov'd and loving may his rule be; H8 2.01. 92
that she belov'd knows nought that knows not TRO 1.02.288
she was belov'd, /she /lov'd; 4.05.292
lest parties (as he is belov'd) break out, | and COR 3.01.313
and come home belov'd | of all the trades in 3.02.133
this man, aufidius, | was my belov'd in rome; 5.02. 93
now romeo is belov'd and loves again, | alike ROM 2.pr. 5
you see, my lord, how ample y' are belov'd. TIM 1.02.130
make the meat be belov'd more than the man that 3.06. 76 P
know unthrift that was belov'd after his means? 4.03.311 P
thou talk'st of, didst thou ever know belov'd? 4.03.314 P
meet, | mark antony, so well belov'd of caesar, JC 2.01.156
honor'd, belov'd, and haply one as kind | for HAM 3.02.176
for ever, and live the belov'd of your brother. LR 1.02. 54 P
yet edmund was belov'd! 5.03.240
of this, | that the magnifico is much belov'd, OTH 1.02. 12
i'll set a bourn how far to be belov'd. ANT 1.01. 16
and it appears he is belov'd of those | that 1.04. 37
so well master'd, but be sure | no less belov'd. CYM 4.02.384
grant, if thou wilt, thou art belov'd of many, SON 10. 3
in me, | more worthy i to be belov'd of thee. 150.14
/BELOVED 1 FR 0.0001 REL FR 1 V 0 P
/sorrow /would /be /a /rarity /most /beloved, LR 4.03. 23
BELOVED 15 FR 0.0017 REL FR 15 V 0 P
some oration fairly spoke | by a beloved prince, MV 3.02.179
of all | my best beloved and approved friend, SHR 1.02. 3
in duty | to fair bianca, so beloved of me. 1.02.175
beloved of me, and that my deeds shall prove. 1.02.176
long live lord titus, my beloved brother, TIT 1.01.169
the gods | for our beloved mother in her pains. 4.02. 47
change of mood | spurns down her late beloved, TIM 1.01. 85
beloved sons, be yours, which to confirm, | this LR 1.01.138
beloved regan, | thy sister's naught. 2.04.133
you shall be more beloving than beloved. ANT 1.02. 23
the loss | of a beloved daughter and a wife. PER 5.01. 30
band | where her beloved collatinus lies. LUC 256
i, that love and am beloved | where i may not SON 25.13
thy sweet beloved name no more shall dwell, 89.10
idolatry, | nor my beloved as an idol show, 105. 2
BELOVING 1 FR 0.0001 REL FR 1 V 0 P
you shall be more beloving than beloved. ANT 1.02. 23
BELOW 44 FR 0.0049 REL FR 38 V 6 P
i pray now keep below. TMP 1.01. 11 P
are founder'd | or night kept chain'd below. 4.01. 31
one master /brook below would fain speak with WIV 2.02.144 P
buckled below fair knighthood's bending knee: 5.05. 72
consecrated fount, | a league below the city; MM 4.03. 99
why, shall i always keep below stairs? ADO 5.02. 10 P
and place your hands below your husband's foot; SHR 5.02.177
who were below him | he us'd as creatures of AWW 1.02. 41
from below your duke to beneath your constable, 2.02. 30 P
sir, ancient pistol's below, and would speak 2H4 2.04. 69 P
you be by her aloft, while we be busy below; 2H6 1.04. 8 P
one heav'd a–high, to be hurl'd down below; R3 4.04. 86
they are as children but one step below, | even 4.04.301
i am afraid | his thinkings are below the moon, H8 3.02.134
in all designs begun on earth below | fails in TRO 1.03. 4
the general's disdain'd | by him one step below, 1.03.130
not in their liking | below their cobbled shoes. COR 1.01.196
more attain'd than by | a place below the first; 1.01.266
he'll beat aufidius' head below his knee, | and 1.03. 46
sail, so men obey'd | and fell below his stem. 2.02.107
might down stretch | below the beam of sight, 3.02. 5
again, | till thou art here aloft or i below. TIT 2.03.244
i'll dive into the burning lake below, | and 4.03. 44
sent from below | to join with him and right his 5.02. 3
with one man beckon'd from the rest below, TIM 1.01. 74
below thy sister's orb | infect the air! 4.03. 2
grize of fortune | is smooth'd by that below. 4.03. 17
stout men's pillows from below their heads. 4.03. 33
with all th' abhorred births below crisp heaven 4.03.183
of some high powers | that govern us below. JC 5.01.107
and the orb below | as hush as death, anon the HAM 2.02.485
my words fly up, my thoughts remain below: 3.03. 97
but i will delve one yard below their mines, 3.04.208
thou climbing sorrow, | thy element's below. LR 2.04. 58
as i stood here below, methought his eyes | were 4.06. 69
head | to the descent and dust below thy foot, 5.03.138
help, friends below, let's draw him hither. ANT 4.15. 13
as gentle | as zephyrs blowing below the violet, CYM 4.02.172
thunder above, and deeps below, | makes such PER 2.ch. 30
we here below | recall not what we give, and 3.01. 24
you shall hear | scenes, though below his art, TNK pr 28
clip my yellow locks an inch below mine e'e. 3.04. 20
clapping their proud tails to the ground below, VEN 923
coucheth the fowl below with his wings' shade, LUC 507
BEL'S 1 FR 0.0001 REL FR 0 V 1 P
sometime like god bel's priests in the old ADO 3.03.135 P
BELT 3 FR 0.0003 REL FR 2 V 1 P
buckles himself in my belt cannot live in less. 2H4 1.02.138 P
his distemper'd cause | within the belt of rule. MAC 5.02. 16
a belt of straw and ivy buds, | with coral PP 19.13
BELZEBUB 3 FR 0.0003 REL FR 0 V 3 P
he holds belzebub at the stave's end as well as TN 5.01.284 P
the devil is, as lucifer and belzebub himself, H5 4.07.138 P
who's there, i' th' name of belzebub? MAC 2.03. 4 P
/BEMADDING 1 FR 0.0001 REL FR 1 V 0 P
/of /how /unnatural /and /bemadding /sorrow LR 3.01. 38
BEMET 1 FR 0.0001 REL FR 1 V 0 P
our very loving sister, well bemet. LR 5.01. 20
BEMETE 1 FR 0.0001 REL FR 1 V 0 P
or i shall so bemete thee with thy yard | as SHR 4.03.112
BEMOAN'D 1 FR 0.0001 REL FR 1 V 0 P
was ever father so bemoan'd his son? 3H6 2.05.110
BEMOCK 1 FR 0.0001 REL FR 1 V 0 P
bemock the modest moon. COR 1.01.257
BEMOCK'D–AT 1 FR 0.0001 REL FR 1 V 0 P
loud winds, or with bemock'd–at stabs | kill the TMP 3.03. 63
BEMOIL'D 1 FR 0.0001 REL FR 0 V 1 P
heard in how miry a place, how she was bemoil'd, SHR 4.01. 75 P
/BEMONSTER 1 FR 0.0001 REL FR 1 V 0 P
/for /shame | /bemonster /not /thy /feature. LR 4.02. 63
BEN 3 FR 0.0003 REL FR 2 V 1 P
con tutto /il core, ben trovato, may i say. SHR 1.02. 24
alla nostra casa ben venuto, molto honorato 1.02. 25 P
it so, | petruchio, i shall be your ben venuto. 1.02.280
/BENCH 1 FR 0.0001 REL FR 1 V 0 P
/of /equity, | /bench /by /his /side. LR 3.06. 38
BENCH 8 FR 0.0009 REL FR 6 V 2 P
and be the supporter to a bench, but he'll speak TN 1.05.149 P
to pluck down justice from your aweful bench? 2H4 5.02. 86
against a graver bench | than ever frown'd in COR 3.01.106
their obedience fails | to th' greater bench. 3.01.166
that they cannot sit at ease on the old bench? ROM 2.04. 35 P
pluck the grave wrinkled senate from the bench, TIM 4.01. 5
and approbation | with senators on the bench. 4.03. 38
god, | that i from such an humble bench of birth STM III 6
BENCH'D 1 FR 0.0001 REL FR 1 V 0 P
form | have bench'd and rear'd to worship, who WT 1.02.314
BENCHER 1 FR 0.0001 REL FR 0 V 1 P
table than a necessary bencher in the capitol. COR 2.01. 82 P
BENCHES 2 FR 0.0002 REL FR 0 V 2 P
supper, and sleeping upon benches after noon, 1H4 1.02. 4 P
pluck down benches. JC 3.02.258 P
BENCH–HOLES 1 FR 0.0001 REL FR 1 V 0 P
we'll beat 'em into bench–holes. ANT 4.07. 9
/BEND 2 FR 0.0002 REL FR 2 V 0 P
/flatter, /bow, /and /bend /my /knee. R2 4.01.165
/which /makes /me /bend /makes /the /king /bow: LR 3.06.109
BEND 48 FR 0.0054 REL FR 48 V 0 P
to his crown, and bend | the dukedom yet unbow'd TMP 1.02.114
but i do bend my speech | to one that can my MM 1.01. 40
therefore homeward did they bend their course. ERR 1.01.117
yet bend not all the harm upon yourself; ADO 5.01. 39
i would bend under any heavy weight | that he'll 5.01.277
we bend to that the working of the heart; LLL 4.01. 33
or | shall i bend low and in a bondman's key, MV 1.03.123
maid, | bend thoughts and wits to achieve her. SHR 1.01.179
in hand at court, | thither we bend again. AWW 3.02. 55
who for bohemia bend, to signify | not only my WT 5.01.165
and both conjointly bend | your sharpest deeds JN 2.01.379
myself and them | bend their best studies — 4.02. 51
why do you bend such solemn brows on me? 4.02. 90
or bend one wrinkle on my sovereign's face. R2 2.01.170
thy very beadsmen learn to bend their bows | of 3.02.116
unto my mother's prayers i bend my knee. 5.03. 97
why dost thou bend thine eyes upon the earth, 1H4 2.03. 42
towards york shall bend you with your dearest 5.05. 36
france being ours, we'll bend it to our awe, H5 1.02.224
and bend up every spirit | to his full height. 3.01. 16
i'll either make thee stoop and bend thy knee, 1H6 5.01. 61
see how the ugly witch doth bend her brows, | as 5.03. 34
in duty bend thy knee to me | that bows unto the 2H6 5.01.173
o warwick, i do bend my knee with thine, | and 3H6 2.03. 33
and, lords, towards coventry bend we our course, 4.08. 58
speak gentle words and humbly bend thy knee, 5.01. 22
to bend the fatal instruments of war | against 5.01. 87
which thou once didst bend against her breast, R3 1.02. 95
and towards london do they bend their power, 4.05. 17
they were us'd to bend, | to send their smiles TRO 3.03. 71
to our own selves bend we our needful talk. 4.04.139
bend like his | that hath receiv'd an alms! COR 3.02.119
and must bend his body | if caesar carelessly JC 1.02.117
and that same eye whose bend doth awe the world 1.02.123
if thou dost bend, and pray, and fawn for him, 3.01. 45
and bend up | each corporal agent to this MAC 1.07. 79
my thoughts and wishes bend again toward france, HAM 1.02. 55
and we beseech you bend you to remain | here in 1.02.115
you, | that you do bend your eye on vacancy, 3.04.117
'gainst parricides did all the thunder bend, LR 2.01. 46
war | have glow'd like plated mars, now bend, ANT 1.01. 4
except she bend her humor, shall be assur'd | to CYM 1.05. 81
i as a tree | whose boughs did bend with fruit; 3.03. 61
now to marina bend your mind, | whom our PER 4.ch. 5
will to my sense bend no licentious ear, | but 5.03. 30
makest affections bend | to godlike honors; TNK 1.01.229
me your aid | and bend your spirits towards him. 5.01. 48
he is no woodman that doth bend his bow | to LUC 580
BENDED 7 FR 0.0008 REL FR 7 V 0 P
but neither bended knees, pure hands held up, TGV 3.01.231
against them both my true joints bended be. R2 5.03. 98
his bruised helmet and his bended sword | before H5 5.pr. 18
and humbly now upon my bended knee, | in sight 2H6 1.01. 10
the nobles bended, | as to jove's statue, and COR 2.01.265
and to the last bended their light on me. HAM 2.01. 97
my bended hook shall pierce | their slimy jaws; ANT 2.05. 12
BENDING 20 FR 0.0022 REL FR 20 V 0 P
yet always bending | towards their project. TMP 4.01.174
buckled below fair knighthood's bending knee: WIV 5.05. 72
might but my bending down | reprieve thee from MM 3.01.143
to watch the fearful bending of thy knee, R2 3.03. 73
give some supportance to the bending twigs. 3.04. 32
and bending forward strook his armed heels 2H4 1.01. 44
teacheth this prostrate and exterior bending. 4.05.148
will it give place to flexure and low bending? H5 4.01.255
our bending author hath pursu'd the story, | in ep 2
no bending knee will call thee caesar now, | no 3H6 3.01. 18
where be the bending peers that flattered thee? R3 4.04. 95
free, as debonair, unarm'd, | as bending angels; TRO 1.03.236
bending their expedition toward philippi. JC 4.03.170
whose high and bending head | looks fearfully in LR 4.01. 73
act, bending his sword | to his great master, 4.02. 74
most humbly therefore bending to your state, | i OTH 1.03.235
arms, bending down | his corrigible neck, his ANT 4.14. 73
throwing the base thong from his bending crest, VEN 395
for, bending all my loving thoughts on thee, SON 88.10
within his bending sickle's compass come, | love 116.10
BENDS 4 FR 0.0004 REL FR 4 V 0 P
his crest that prouder than blue iris bends. TRO 1.03.379
i' th' eyes, | and made their bends adornings. ANT 2.02.208
he bends her fingers, holds her pulses hard, VEN 476
finds, | or bends with the remover to remove. SON 116. 4
/BENE 1 FR 0.0001 REL FR 0 V 1 P
/bone /for /bene, priscian a little scratch'd, LLL 5.01. 28 P
BENE 1 FR 0.0001 REL FR 1 V 0 P
but omne bene, say i, being of an old father's LLL 4.02. 32
BENEATH 18 FR 0.0020 REL FR 15 V 3 P
rain from heaven | upon the place beneath. MV 4.01.186
from below your duke to beneath your constable, AWW 2.02. 30 P
so far beneath your soft and tender breeding, TN 5.01.323
you'll be found, | be you beneath the sky. WT 1.02.180
he by the next, | that next by him beneath; TRO 1.03.131
words to thee will flatter | beneath abhorring. COR 1.01.168
whom this beneath world doth embrace and hug TIM 1.01. 44
i think our country sinks beneath the yoke: MAC 4.03. 39
fadoms to the sea | and hears it roar beneath. HAM 1.04. 78
for all beneath the moon | would i not leap LR 4.06. 26
the gods inherit, | beneath is all the fiends': 4.06.127
whose heads | /do /grow beneath their shoulders. OTH 1.03.145
o, i were damn'd beneath all depth in hell | but 5.02.137
left remarkable | beneath the visiting moon. ANT 4.15. 68
it smites me | beneath the fall i have. 5.02.172
more strong, not beneath him in fortunes, beyond CYM 4.01. 11 P
sir, we have a chest beneath the hatches, PER 3.01. 70 P
of all the faults beneath the heavens, the gods 4.03. 20
BENEDICITE 2 FR 0.0002 REL FR 2 V 0 P
grace go with you, benedicite! MM 2.03. 39
benedicite! ROM 2.03. 31
BENEDICK 53 FR 0.0060 REL FR 15 V 38 P
my cousin means signior benedick of padua. ADO 1.01. 35 P
niece, you tax signior benedick too much, but 1.01. 46 P
of merry war betwixt signior benedick and her; 1.01. 62 P
if he have caught the benedick, it will cost him 1.01. 89 P
signior benedick, no, for then were you a child. 1.01.107 P
you have it full, benedick. 1.01.109 P
you will still be talking, signior benedick, 1.01.117
such meet food to feed it as signior benedick? 1.01.121
signior claudio and signior benedick — my dear

benedick, didst thou note the daughter of 1.01.162 P
but if ever the sensible benedick bear it, pluck 1.01.263 P
"here you may see benedick the married man." 1.01.267 P
in the mean time, good signior benedick, repair 1.01.275 P
the sixt of july. your loving friend, benedick. 1.01.284 P
just in the midway between him and benedick: 2.01. 7 P
well, this was signior benedick that said so. 2.01.131 P
are not you signior benedick? 2.01.161 P
thus answer i in name of benedick, | but hear 2.01.172
you have lost the heart of signior benedick. 2.01.277 P
she were an excellent wife for benedick. 2.01.351 P
to bring signior benedick and the lady beatrice 2.01.366 P
and benedick is not the unhopefullest husband 2.01.377 P
that she shall fall in love with benedick, and i 2.01.381 P
will so practice on benedick that, in despite of 2.01.382 P
see you where benedick hath hid himself? 2.03. 40
beatrice was in love with signior benedick? 2.03. 91 P
that she should so dote on signior benedick, 2.03. 96 P
it had, my lord, especially against benedick. 2.03.117 P
hath she made her affection known to benedick? 2.03.124 P
she found "benedick" and "beatrice" between the 2.03.137 P
"o sweet benedick! 2.03.148 P
it were good that benedick knew of it by some 2.03.154 P
in every thing but in loving benedick. 2.03.162 P
i pray you tell benedick of it, and hear what 'a 2.03.170 P
shall we go seek benedick, and tell him of her 2.03.199 P
i love benedick well, and i could wish he would 2.03.207 P
and down, | our talk must only be of benedick. 3.01. 17
my talk to thee must be how benedick | is sick 3.01. 20
sure | that benedick loves beatrice so entirely? 3.01. 37
but i persuaded them, if they lov'd benedick, 3.01. 41
therefore let benedick, like cover'd fire, 3.01. 77
rather i will go to benedick | and counsel him 3.01. 82
so rare a gentleman as signior benedick. 3.01. 91
signior benedick, | for shape, for bearing, 3.01. 95
and, benedick, love on, i will requite thee, 3.01.111
will only be bold with benedick for his company, 3.02. 8 P
yet benedick was such another, and now is he 3.04. 86 P
prince, the count, signior benedick, don john, 3.04. 96 P
signior benedick! 4.01.114
"here dwells benedick the married man"? 5.01.184 P
good morrow, benedick. 5.04. 40
containing her affection unto benedick. 5.04. 90
how dost thou, benedick, the married man? 5.04. 99
BENEDICK'S 3 FR 0.0003 REL FR 0 V 3 P
then half signior benedick's tongue in count ADO 2.01. 11 P
john's melancholy in signior benedick's face — 2.01. 13 P
bull's horns on the sensible benedick's head? 5.01.182 P
/BENEDICTION 1 FR 0.0001 REL FR 1 V 0 P
/that /stripp'd /her /from /his /benediction, LR 4.03. 43
BENEDICTION 5 FR 0.0005 REL FR 4 V 1 P
hallow'd and brought a benediction to the buyer; WT 4.04.602 P
royalty he leaves | the healing benediction. MAC 4.03.156
thou out of heaven's benediction com'st | to the LR 2.02.161
and hold your hand in benediction o'er me. 4.07. 57
the benediction of these covering heavens | fall CYM 5.05.350
BENEDICTUS 4 FR 0.0004 REL FR 0 V 4 P
you some of this distill'd carduus benedictus, ADO 3.04. 74 P
benedictus! 3.04. 77 P
why benedictus? 3.04. 77 P
you have some moral in this benedictus. 3.04. 78 P
BENEFACTORS 4 FR 0.0004 REL FR 0 V 4 P
your good honor two notorious benefactors. MM 2.01. 50 P
benefactors? 2.01. 51 P
what benefactors are they? 2.01. 51 P
you great benefactors, sprinkle our society with TIM 3.06. 70 P
BENEFICE 1 FR 0.0001 REL FR 1 V 0 P
asleep, | then he dreams of another benefice. ROM 1.04. 81
BENEFICIAL 4 FR 0.0004 REL FR 3 V 1 P
day | to seek thy /health by beneficial help. ERR 1.01.151
bulk | take up the rays o' th' beneficial sun, H8 1.01. 56
for, besides these beneficial news, it is the OTH 2.02. 6 P
kinsman as you force me find | a beneficial foe, TNK 3.06. 22
BENEFIT 40 FR 0.0045 REL FR 30 V 10 P
omitting the sweet benefit of time | to clothe TGV 2.04. 65
him into the water will do him a benefit. WIV 3.03.184 P
i would require is likewise your own benefit. MM 3.01.156 P
do a poor wrong'd lady a merited benefit; 3.01.201 P
the doubleness of the benefit defends the deceit 3.01.257 P
for the benefit of silence, would thou wert so 5.01.190 P
and by the benefit of his wished light | the ERR 1.01. 90
of whom i hope to make much benefit; 1.02. 25
yet have i the benefit of my senses as well as TN 5.01.305 P
to hold | shall nothing benefit your knowledge, WT 4.04.503
have done the time more benefit and grac'd 5.01. 22
would be thence that has the benefit of access? 5.02.109 P
to have | the present benefit which i possess, R2 2.03. 14
i crave the benefit of law of arms. 1H6 4.01.100
give it you | in earnest of a further benefit, 5.03. 16
sold their bodies for their country's benefit, 5.04.106
usurp'st, | of benefit proceeding from our king, 5.04.152
will make but little for his benefit. 2H6 1.03. 98
the benefit thereof is always granted | to those R3 3.01. 48
royal self | this proffer'd benefit of dignity; 3.07.196
reverent, | give mine the benefit of seniory, 4.04. 36
but benefit no further | than vainly longing. H8 1.02. 80
to give me now a little benefit | out of those TRO 3.03. 14
shall find | no public benefit which you receive COR 1.01.152
the benefit | which thou shalt thereby reap is 5.03.142
and give away | the benefit of our levies, 5.06. 66
lord, | for any benefit that points to me, TIM 4.03.519
grant that, and then is death a benefit; JC 3.01.103
death, shall receive the benefit of his dying, a 3.02. 43 P
receive at once the benefit of sleep and do the MAC 5.01. 10 P
as the winds give benefit | and convey /is HAM 1.03. 2
is wretchedness depriv'd that benefit, | to end LR 4.06. 61
distinguish betwixt a benefit and an injury, i OTH 1.03.313 P
love again, | but to know so must be my benefit; 3.04.119
you shall find | a benefit in this change; ANT 5.02.128
with the next benefit o' th' wind. CYM 4.02.342
sun, to have | the benefit of his blest beams, 4.04. 42
'tis a benefit, | a mercy i must thank 'em for; TNK 2.03. 1
plight | that am debarr'd the benefit of rest? SON 28. 2
o benefit of ill! 119. 9
/BENEFITED 1 FR 0.0001 REL FR 1 V 0 P
/a /man, /a /prince, /by /him /so /benefited! LR 4.02. 45
BENEFITS 7 FR 0.0008 REL FR 4 V 3 P
for her benefits are mightily misplac'd, and the AYL 1.02. 34 P
that dost not bite so nigh | as benefits forgot; 2.07.186
disable all the benefits of your own country; 4.01. 34 P
when these so noble benefits shall prove | not H8 1.02.115
services may prove | as benefits to thee; COR 4.05. 90
we are born to do benefits; TIM 1.02.102 P
turn all her mother's pains and benefits | to LR 1.04.286
BENETTED 1 FR 0.0001 REL FR 1 V 0 P
being thus benetted round with /villainies — HAM 5.02. 29
BENEVOLENCE 1 FR 0.0001 REL FR 0 V 1 P
be glad to do my benevolence to make atonements WIV 1.01. 33 P
BENEVOLENCES 1 FR 0.0001 REL FR 1 V 0 P
as blanks, benevolences, and i wot not what. R2 2.01.250
BENIGN 1 FR 0.0001 REL FR 1 V 0 P
a better prince and benign lord, | that will PER 2.ch. 3
BENISON 4 FR 0.0004 REL FR 4 V 0 P
god's benison go with you, and with those | that MAC 2.04. 40
without our grace, our love, our benison. LR 1.01.265
the bounty and the benison of heaven | to boot, 4.06.225
in conversation, | to whom i give my benison, PER 2.ch. 10
BENNET 2 FR 0.0002 REL FR 1 V 1 P
measure, or the bells of saint bennet, sir, may TN 5.01. 39 P
the heads of brocas and sir bennet seely, | two R2 5.06. 14
BENT 47 FR 0.0053 REL FR 43 V 4 P
us again, and madly bent on us | chas'd us away; ERR 5.01.152
it seems her affections have their full bent. ADO 2.03.223 P
two of them have the very bent of honor, | and 4.01.186
which, not to anger bent, is music and sweet LLL 4.02.116
like to a silver bow | /new bent in heaven, MND 1.01. 10
i see you all are bent | to set against me for 3.02.145
though my revenges were high bent upon him | and AWW 5.03. 10
or thy affection cannot hold the bent; TN 2.04. 37
our cannon shall be bent | against the brows of JN 2.01. 37
speak on with favor, we are bent to hear. 2.01.422
when he perceives the envious clouds are bent R2 3.03. 65
stage, | are idly bent on him that enters next, 5.02. 25
gaze, | such as is bent on sunlike majesty, 1H4 3.02. 79
come off the breach with his pike bent bravely, 2H4 2.04. 50 P
against the french that met them in their bent H5 5.02. 16
than midday sun fierce bent against their faces. 1H6 1.01. 14
but all his mind is bent to holiness, | to 2H6 1.03. 55
a sort of naughty persons, lewdly bent, | under 2.01.163
and who durst smile when warwick bent his brow? 3H6 5.02. 22
reverend fathers, | divinely bent to meditation, R3 3.07. 62
ear, | to set his /sense on /the attentive bent, TRO 1.03.252
question me | why such unplausive eyes are bent, 3.03. 43
but gives all gaze and bent of amorous view | on 4.05.282
lead on this preparation | whither 'tis bent. COR 1.02. 16
power | of high-resolved men, bent to the spoil, TIT 4.04. 64
if that thy bent of love be honorable, | thy ROM 2.02.143
for i can give his humor the true bent, | and i JC 2.01.210
in all these men, and it is bent against caesar. 2.03. 6 P
for now i am bent to know, | by the worst means, MAC 3.04.133
and here give up ourselves, in the full bent, HAM 2.02. 30
they fool me to the top of my bent. 3.02.384 P
tend, and every thing is bent | for england. 4.03. 45
the bow is bent and drawn, make from the shaft. LR 1.01.143
and my best spirits are bent | to prove upon thy 5.03.140
our lips and eyes, | bliss in our brows' bent; ANT 1.03. 36
although they wear their faces to the bent | of CYM 1.01. 13
how thaliard came full bent with sin | and hid PER 2.ch. 23
daughter, | but bent all offices to honor her. 2.05. 48
and do the deed with a bent brow. TNK 3.01.101
o, who can find the bent of woman's fancy? 4.02. 33
yet his eye | is like an engine bent, or a sharp 5.03. 42
still, | like to a mortal butcher bent to kill. VEN 618
which, not to anger bent, is music and sweet PP 5.12
what though her frowning brows be bent, | her 18.25
if to women he be bent, | they have at 20.43
now while the world is bent my deeds to cross, SON 90. 2
cries to catch her whose busy care is bent | to 143. 6
BENTII 1 FR 0.0001 REL FR 0 V 1 P
vaumond, bentii, two hundred fifty each; AWW 4.03.165 P
BENTIVOLII 1 FR 0.0001 REL FR 1 V 0 P
the world, | vincentio, come of the bentivolii; SHR 1.01. 13
BENTS 1 FR 0.0001 REL FR 1 V 0 P
to your own bents dispose you; WT 1.02.179
BENUMBED 1 FR 0.0001 REL FR 1 V 0 P
of partial indulgence | to their benumbed wills, TRO 2.02.179
BENVOLIO 6 FR 0.0006 REL FR 5 V 1 P
turn thee, benvolio, look upon thy death. ROM 1.01. 67
come between us, good benvolio, my wits faints. 2.04. 67 P
draw, benvolio, beat down their weapons. 3.01. 86
help me into some house, benvolio, | or i shall 3.01.105
benvolio, who began this bloody fray? 3.01.151
this is the truth, or let benvolio die. 3.01.175
BEPAINT 1 FR 0.0001 REL FR 1 V 0 P
else would a maiden blush bepaint my cheek | for ROM 2.02. 86
BEPAINTED 1 FR 0.0001 REL FR 1 V 0 P
whose frothy mouth bepainted all with red, VEN 901
BEPRAY 1 FR 0.0001 REL FR 0 V 1 P
i bepray you let me borrow my arms again. LLL 5.02.696 P
BEQUEATH 17 FR 0.0019 REL FR 16 V 1 P
walk — and my horns i bequeath your husbands. WIV 5.05. 26 P
and yours of helena to me bequeath, | whom i do MND 3.02.166
you to your former honor i bequeath, | your AYL 5.04.186
bequeath to death your numbness; WT 5.03.102
bequeath thy land to him, and follow me? JN 1.01.149
i do bequeath my faithful services | and true 5.07.104
so, for what can we bequeath | save our deposed R2 3.02.149
and at that time bequeath you my diseases. TRO 5.10. 56
a sister i bequeath you, whom no brother | did ANT 2.02.149
so i bequeath a happy peace to you | and all PER 1.01. 50
which my dead father did bequeath to me, | with 2.01.124
that to your sword you will bequeath this plea, TNK 3.01.115
bequeath not to their lot | the shame that from LUC 534
my stained blood to tarquin i'll bequeath, 1181
"my honor i'll bequeath unto the knife | that 1184
lost, | what legacy shall i bequeath to thee? 1192
thy discontent thou didst bequeath to me. PP 10.12
BEQUEATH'D 4 FR 0.0004 REL FR 1 V 3 P
upon this fashion bequeath'd me by will but poor AYL 1.01. 2 P
my lord, and bequeath'd to my overlooking. AWW 1.01. 38 P
her father bequeath'd her to me, and she herself 1.03.101 P
upon his death-bed he by will bequeath'd | his JN 1.01.109
BEQUEATHED 3 FR 0.0003 REL FR 3 V 0 P
house, | bequeathed down from many ancestors, AWW 4.02. 43
house, | bequeathed down from many ancestors, 4.02. 47
her contrite sighs unto the clouds bequeathed LUC 1727
BEQUEATHING 3 FR 0.0003 REL FR 3 V 0 P
his crown bequeathing to his banish'd brother, AYL 5.04.163
bequeathing it as a rich legacy | unto their JC 3.02.136
seeing | and first bequeathing of the soul to) TNK 3.06.148
BEQUEST 1 FR 0.0001 REL FR 1 V 0 P
nature's bequest gives nothing, but doth lend, SON 4. 3
/BERATTLE 1 FR 0.0001 REL FR 0 V 1 P
/and /so /berattle /the /common /stages — /so HAM 2.02.342 P
BERAY'D *(also ray'd)*
/BERAY'D 1 FR 0.0001 REL FR 1 V 0 P
lord bassianus lies /beray'd in blood, | all on TIT 2.03.222
BEREAVE 5 FR 0.0005 REL FR 4 V 1 P
thou mayest bereave him of his wits with wonder. 1H6 5.03.195
but she'll bereave you a' th' deeds too, if she TRO 3.02. 56 P
you shall bereave yourself | of my good purposes ANT 5.02.130
you, | i'll not bereave you of your servant. PER 4.01. 31
i must awhile bereave you | of your fair TNK 2.02.223
BEREAVED 2 FR 0.0002 REL FR 2 V 0 P
life, | have by my hands of life bereaved him. 3H6 2.05. 68
wisdom | in the restoring his bereaved sense? LR 4.04. 9
BEREAVES 3 FR 0.0003 REL FR 3 V 0 P
and bereaves the state | of that integrity which COR 3.01.158
which the hot tyrant stains, and soon bereaves, VEN 797
rushing from forth a cloud, bereaves our sight, LUC 373
BEREFT 22 FR 0.0024 REL FR 21 V 1 P
thee of thy son, alonso, | they have bereft; TMP 3.03. 76
but, if thou live to see like right bereft, ERR 2.01. 40
madam, you have bereft me of all words, | only MV 3.02.175
muddy, ill-seeming, thick, bereft of beauty, SHR 5.02.143
pity him, | bereft and gelded of his patrimony. R2 2.01.237
us, | and we are barren and bereft of friends, 3.03. 84
in those territories | is utterly bereft you: 2H6 3.01. 85
whose dismal tune bereft my vital pow'rs; 3.02. 41
worth, | they say is shamefully bereft of life. 3.02.269
and hath bereft thee of thy life too late. 3H6 2.05. 93
i think /his understanding is bereft. 2.06. 60
he that bereft thee, lady, of thy husband, | did R3 1.02.138
you have bereft me of all words, lady. TRO 3.02. 54 P
kind, | have here bereft my brother of his life. TIT 2.03.282
lies a wretched corse, of wretched soul bereft; TIM 5.04. 70
the rites for why i love him are bereft me, OTH 1.03.257
to have bereft a prince of all his fortunes; PER 2.01. 9
of the seas | bereft of ships and men, cast on 2.03. 89
gone, | and 'tis your fault i am bereft him so. VEN 381
"say that the sense of feeling were bereft me, 439
in me, | from me by strong assault it is bereft: LUC 835
beauty's effect with beauty were bereft, | nor SON 5.11
BERGAMO 1 FR 0.0001 REL FR 0 V 1 P
o villain, he is a sailmaker in bergamo. SHR 5.01. 78 P
BERGOMASK 2 FR 0.0002 REL FR 0 V 2 P
or to hear a bergomask dance between two of our MND 5.01.353 P
but come, your bergomask; 5.01.361 P
BERHYM'D 1 FR 0.0001 REL FR 0 V 1 P
i was never so berhym'd since pythagoras' time, AYL 3.02.176 P
BERHYME 1 FR 0.0001 REL FR 0 V 1 P
(marry, she had a better love to berhyme her), ROM 2.04. 41 P
BERKELEY 8 FR 0.0009 REL FR 8 V 0 P
your men, | and meet me presently at berkeley. R2 2.02.119
how far is it, my lord, to berkeley now? 2.03. 1
and sent me over by berkeley, to discover | what 2.03. 33
how far is it to berkeley? 2.03. 51
and in it are the lords of york, berkeley, and 2.03. 55
it is my lord of berkeley, as i guess. 2.03. 68
at berkeley castle. 1H4 1.03.249
tressel and berkeley, go along with me. R3 1.02.221
BERMOOTHES 1 FR 0.0001 REL FR 1 V 0 P
to fetch dew | from the still-vex'd bermoothes, TMP 1.02.229
BERNARDO *(see barnardo)*
BEROWNE 26 FR 0.0029 REL FR 23 V 3 P
you three, berowne, dumaine, and longaville, LLL 1.01. 15
you swore to that, berowne, and to the rest. 1.01. 53
berowne is like an envious sneaping frost | that 1.01.100
well, sit you out; go home, berowne; adieu. 1.01.110
my lord berowne, see him delivered o'er, | and 1.01.305
berowne they call him, but a merrier man, 2.01. 66
that last is berowne, the merry madcap lord. 2.01.215
have a letter from monsieur berowne to one lady 4.01. 53
from my lord berowne, a good master of mine, 4.01.104
ay, sir, from one monsieur berowne, one of the 4.02.129 P
ladyship's in all desired employment, berowne." 4.02.136 P
this berowne is one of the votaries with the 4.02.137 P
o, would the king, berowne, and longaville, 4.03.121
what will berowne say when that he shall hear 4.03.143
berowne, read it over. where hadst thou it? 4.03.193
my eyes are then no eyes, nor i berowne. 4.03.228
and, good berowne, now prove | our loving lawful 4.03.280
nay, i have verses too, i thank berowne; 5.02. 34
that same berowne i'll torture ere i go. 5.02. 60
thine, | so shall berowne take me for rosaline. 5.02.133
this pert berowne was out of count'nance quite. 5.02.272
berowne did swear himself out of all suit. 5.02.275
and quick berowne hath plighted faith to me. 5.02.283
and lord berowne (i thank him) is my dear. 5.02.457
berowne, they will shame us; 5.02.511
oft have i heard of you, my lord berowne, 5.02.841
BEROWNE'S 1 FR 0.0001 REL FR 1 V 0 P
it is berowne's writing, and here is his name. LLL 4.03.199
BERRI 2 FR 0.0002 REL FR 2 V 0 P
therefore the dukes of berri and of britain, H5 2.04. 4
you dukes of orleance, bourbon, and of berri, 3.05. 41
BERRIES 8 FR 0.0009 REL FR 8 V 0 P
wouldst give me | water with berries in't, and TMP 1.02.334
i'll pluck thee berries; 2.02.160
two lovely berries moulded on one stem; MND 3.02.211
and wholesome berries thrive and ripen best H5 1.01. 61
i'll make you feed on berries and on roots, TIT 4.02.177
we cannot live on grass, on berries, water, | as TIM 4.03.422
as those poor birds that helpless berries saw. VEN 604
fed them with his sight, they him with berries. 1104
BERRORD *(also bearard, bear-herd)*
BERRORD 2 FR 0.0002 REL FR 0 V 2 P
even take sixpence in earnest of the berrord, ADO 2.01. 40 P
times that true valor is turn'd berrord; 2H4 1.02.169 P
BERRY 3 FR 0.0003 REL FR 3 V 0 P

deign | the roughest berry on the rudest hedge; ANT 1.04. 64
own shape of bud, bird, branch, or berry, | that PER 5.ch. 6
or as the berry breaks before it staineth, | or VEN 460
BERTRAM 7 FR 0.0008 REL FR 6 V 1 P
be thou blest, bertram, and succeed thy father AWW 1.01. 61
heaven bless him! | farewell, bertram. 1.01. 74
there is no living, none, | if bertram be away. 1.01. 85
/rossillion, my good lord, | young bertram. 1.02. 19
why then, young bertram, take her, she's thy 2.03.105
know'st thou not, bertram, | what she has done 2.03.108
your unfortunate son, bertram." 3.02. 27 P
BERTRAM'S 1 FR 0.0001 REL FR 1 V 0 P
carries no favor in't but bertram's. AWW 1.01. 83
BERWICK 3 FR 0.0003 REL FR 3 V 0 P
at berwick in the north, and't like your grace. 2H6 2.01. 81
till they come to berwick, from whence they came 2.01.156
mount you, my lord, towards berwick post amain. 3H6 2.05.128
BESCREEN'D 1 FR 0.0001 REL FR 1 V 0 P
what man art thou that thus bescreen'd in night ROM 2.02. 52
BESEECH' 1 FR 0.0001 REL FR 1 V 0 P
serv'd you, and beseech' | so to esteem of us; WT 2.03.148
BESEECH *(also peseech)*
/BESEECH 1 FR 0.0001 REL FR 0 V 1 P
i beseech you, on my knees /i /beseech /you, TRO 4.02. 89 P
BESEECH 230 FR 0.0260 REL FR 154 V 76 P
beseech you, father. TMP 1.02.474
beseech you, sir, be merry; 2.01. 1
bate, i beseech you, widow dido. 2.01.101 P
i do beseech you — | chiefly that i might set 3.01. 34
i do beseech thy greatness, give him blows, 3.02. 64
i do beseech you | (that are of suppler joints) 3.03.106
i beseech you | confirm his welcome with some TGV 2.04.100
i now beseech you (for your daughter's sake) 5.04.149
and i beseech you be rul'd by your well–willers. WIV 1.01. 71 P
i beseech you be not so phlegmatic. 1.04. 75 P
i beseech you heartily, some of you go home with 3.02. 79 P
i beseech you follow; 4.02.195 P
and i beseech you, look into master froth here, MM 2.01.122 P
i beseech you, sir, ask him what this man did to 2.01.143 P
i beseech your honor, ask me. 2.01.145 P
i beseech you, sir, look in this gentleman's 2.01.147 P
nay, i beseech you mark it well. 2.01.151 P
i do beseech you let it be his fault, | and not 2.02. 35
when, i beseech you? 2.04. 39
and therefore i beseech you | look forward on 4.03. 57
i beseech you let it be proclaim'd betimes i' 4.04. 15 P
i beseech your highness do not marry me to a 5.01.514 P
have patience, i beseech. ERR 4.02. 16
whom i beseech | to give me ample satisfaction 5.01.252
but i beseech your grace pardon me, i was born ADO 2.01.329 P
be vigitant, i beseech you. 3.03. 94 P
i beseech you let it be rememb'red in his 5.01.306 P
which i beseech your worship to correct yourself 5.01.322 P
— of other men's secrets, i beseech you. LLL 1.01.230 P
i beseech you a word. what is she in the white? 2.01.197
i beseech you read it. 4.02. 92 P
i beseech your society. 4.02.159 P
i beseech your grace let this letter be read: 4.03.191
i do beseech thee remember thy courtesy; 5.01. 97 P
i beseech thee apparel thy head; 5.01. 98 P
i beseech you follow. 5.01.148 P
madam, not so, i do beseech you stay. 5.02.728
but i beseech your grace that i may know | the MND 1.01. 62
i beseech your worship's name. 3.01.179 P
your name, i beseech you, sir? 3.01.189 P
ergo, i beseech you, talk you of young master MV 2.02. 57 P
i beseech you, sir, go. 2.05. 19 P
i do beseech you | even at that time i may be 3.02.193
therefore i do beseech you | make no moe offers, 4.01. 80
i beseech you let his lack of years be no 4.01.161 P
and i beseech you | wrest once the law to your 4.01.214
most heartily i do beseech the court | to give 4.01.243
i beseech you, punish me not with your hard AYL 1.02.183 P
yes, i beseech your grace, i am not yet well 1.02.217 P
i do beseech your grace | let me the knowledge 1.03. 45
tell me, i beseech you, which is the readiest SHR 1.02.219
for what reason, i beseech you? 1.02.233
but to knock at your ear, and beseech list'ning. 4.01. 66 P
i shall beseech your highness, | in such a AWW 2.03.106
i most unfeignedly beseech your lordship to make 2.03.244 P
where do the palmers lodge, i do beseech you? 3.05. 35
i beseech you let me answer to the particular of 4.03.182 P
i shall beseech your lordship to remain with me 4.05. 86 P
i do beseech you, whither is he gone? 5.01. 27
i do beseech you, sir, | since you are like to 5.01. 29
i beseech your honor to hear me one single word. 5.02. 35 P
and i beseech your majesty to make it | natural 5.03. 5
give me leave, beseech you. TN 3.01.111
and i beseech you come again to–morrow. 3.04.210
i beseech you do me this courteous office, as to 3.04.253 P
i beseech you, what manner of man is he? 3.04.263 P
beseech you — WT 1.01. 10 P
press me not, beseech you, so. 1.02. 19
but beseech your grace | be plainer with me, let 1.02.264
in whose success we are gentle — i beseech you, 1.02.394
beseech you all, my lords, | with thoughts so 2.01.112
beseech your highness | my women may be with me, 2.01.116
beseech your highness call the queen again. 2.01.126
and i beseech you hear me, who professes 2.03. 53
beseech your highness, give us better credit. 2.03.147
beseech you tenderly apply to her | some 3.02.152
i beseech you, rather | let me be punish'd, that 3.02.224
no, i beseech you, sir. 4.03. 79 P
soft, swain, awhile, beseech you. 4.04.391
beseech you | of your own state take care. 4.04.447
beseech you, sir, | remember since you ow'd no 5.01.218
beseech you, sir, were you present at this 5.02. 1 P
i humbly beseech you, sir, to pardon me all the 5.02.149 P
"i shall beseech you" — that is question now; JN 1.01.195
i do beseech you, madam, be content. 3.01. 42
i do beseech your majesty, impute his words | to R2 2.01.141
i beseech your grace | look on my wrongs with an 2.03.115
i do beseech your grace to pardon me. 5.02. 60
i do beseech you pardon me, i may not show it. 5.02. 70
i do beseech your majesty, | to have some 5.03. 26
not yet, i thee beseech. 5.03. 92
and i beseech you, let not his report | come 1H4 1.03. 67
i do beseech your majesty may salve | the 3.02.155
i beseech your majesty make up, | lest your 5.04. 5
and i beseech your grace | i may dispose of him. 5.05. 23
and i most humbly beseech your lordship to have 2H4 1.02. 99 P
i beseech you stand to me. 2.01. 63 P
i beseech you i may have redress against them. 2.01.108 P
i beseech you, which is justice shallow? 3.02. 56 P
let me see them, i beseech you. 3.02. 95 P
and i beseech your grace let it be book'd with 4.03. 46 P
lord, i beseech you give me leave to go through 4.03. 81 P
i beseech you, sir, to countenance william visor 5.01. 38 P
therefore i beseech you let him be countenanc'd. 5.01. 51 P
and, princes all, believe me, i beseech you, 5.02.122
which i beseech you to let me have home with me. 5.05. 74 P
i beseech you, good sir john, let me have five 5.05. 82 P
one word more, i beseech you. ep 26 P
which i beseech your highness to forgive, H5 2.02.153
captain macmorris, i beseech you now, will you 3.02. 94 P
not so, i do beseech your majesty. 3.05. 65
captain, i thee beseech to do me favors. 3.06. 21
i pray you, and beseech you, that you will. 4.01. 82 P
captain, i beseech you now, come apace to the 4.08. 2 P
i beseech you take it for your own fault and not 4.08. 53 P
therefore i beseech your highness pardon me. 4.08. 55 P
i do beseech your royal majesty, | let him have 2H6 1.03.195
therefore i beseech your majesty, do not cast 1.03.201 P
i beseech your majesty give me leave to go; 2.03. 20
i beseech /god on my knees thou mayst be turn'd 4.10. 58 P
i beseech your graces both to pardon me: R3 1.01. 84
i do beseech your grace to pardon me, and withal 1.01.103
for divers unknown reasons, i beseech you, 1.02.217
i do beseech you, either not believe | the 1.03. 25
and less'ned be that small, god i beseech him! 1.03.110
i do beseech your highness | to take our brother 2.01. 76
i do beseech you send for some of them. 3.04. 33
i do beseech your grace to pardon me, | who, 3.07.105
i do beseech you take it not amiss, | i cannot 3.07.206
yes, heartily beseech you. H8 1.02.176
i do beseech your grace, for charity, | if ever 2.01. 79
beseech your lordship, | vouchsafe to speak my 2.03. 70
wherefore i humbly | beseech you, sir, to spare 2.04. 54
his highness shall speak in, i do beseech | you, 2.04.103
but i beseech you, what's become of katherine, 4.01. 22
i do beseech your lordships, | that, in this 5.02. 80
ungain'd, beseech; TRO 1.02.293
my lord, i do beseech you pardon me, | 'twas not 3.02.136
i do beseech you, as in way of taste, | to give 3.03. 13
good uncle, i beseech you, on my knees /i 4.02. 88 P
(which i beseech you call a virtuous sin) 4.04. 81
i beseech you next | to feast with me and see me 4.05.228
my lord ulysses, tell me, i beseech you, | in 4.05.277
i beseech you go. 5.02. 39
but i beseech you, | what says the other troop? COR 1.01.203
beseech you give me leave to retire myself. 1.03. 27
i do beseech you, | by all the battles wherein 1.06. 55
therefore i beseech you, | in sign of what you 1.09. 25
i do beseech you, | let me o'erleap that custom; 2.02.135
therefore, beseech you, i may be consul. 2.03.103 P
no more words, we beseech you. 3.01. 75
therefore beseech you — | you that will be less 3.01.149
beseech you, tribunes, hear me but a word. 3.01.215
be gone, beseech you. 3.01.235
calmly, i do beseech you. 3.03. 31
which is his house, beseech you? 4.04. 10
have not the face | to say, "beseech you cease." 4.06.117
sir, i beseech you, think you he'll carry rome? 4.07. 27
i beseech you peace; 5.03. 78
i beseech you follow straight. ROM 1.03.103 P
if thou meanest not well, | i do beseech thee — 2.02.151
what are they, beseech your ladyship? 3.05.106
good father, i beseech you on my knees, | hear 3.05.158
pardon, i beseech you! 4.02. 21
i do beseech you, sir, have patience. 5.01. 27
i beseech thee, youth, | put not another sin 5.03. 61
which i do beseech | your lordship to accept. TIM 1.01.155
i beseech your honor, | vouchsafe me a word, it 1.02.176
o, i beseech you pardon me, my lord, in that. 1.02.213
i do beseech you, good my lords, keep on, | i'll 2.02. 34
if i might beseech you, gentlemen, to repair 3.04. 68 P
my lords, | i do beseech you know me. 3.05. 89
beseech your honor | to make it known to us. 5.01. 89
nay, i beseech you, sir, be not out with me; JC 1.01. 16 P
i shall beseech him to befriend himself. 2.04. 30
i do beseech ye, if you bear me hard, | now, 3.01.157
i do beseech you give him leave to go. HAM 1.02. 61
and we beseech you bend you to remain | here in 1.02.115
and i beseech you instantly to visit | my too 2.02. 35
away, i do beseech you, both away. 2.02.169
i do beseech you. 3.02.355 P
i beseech you. 5.02. 28
i beseech you remember. 5.02.104 P
therefore beseech you | t' avert your liking a LR 1.01.210
i yet beseech your majesty — | if for i want 1.01.223
i beseech you, sir, pardon me. 1.02. 36 P
i beseech you pardon me, my lord, if i be 1.04. 64 P
none of these, my lord, i beseech your pardon. 1.04. 82 P
i do beseech you | to understand my purposes 1.04.238
let me beseech your grace not to do so. 2.02.140
i do beseech your grace — 3.04.171
but i beseech you, | if't be your pleasure and OTH 1.01.120
i do beseech you, | send for the lady to the 1.03.114
i humbly beseech you proceed to th' affairs of 1.03.220
in the morning i will beseech the virtuous 2.03.330 P
yet i beseech you, | if you think fit, or that 3.01. 50
whereon, i do beseech thee, grant me this, | to 3.03. 84
i do beseech you, | though i perchance am 3.03.144
i humbly do beseech you of your pardon | for too 3.03.212
and hold her free, i do beseech your honor. 3.03.255
i do beseech you | that by your virtuous means i 3.04.110
i do beseech your lordship call her back. 4.01.249
i do beseech you, sir, trouble yourself no 4.03. 1
i do beseech you | that i may speak with you. 5.02.101
that cannot go, sweet isis, i beseech thee! ANT 1.02. 64 P
good isis, i beseech thee! 1.02. 69 P
time | of stirs abroad, i shall beseech you, sir 1.04. 82
partners, | the rather for i earnestly beseech, 2.02. 23
forsake thy seat, i do beseech thee, captain, 2.07. 38
i beseech you, sir, | harm not yourself with CYM 1.01.133
beseech your patience. 1.01.153
i beseech you all be better known to this 1.04. 30 P
but i beseech your grace, without offense | (my 1.05. 6
beseech you, sir, | desire my man's abode where 1.06. 52
continues well my lord? his health, beseech you? 1.06. 56
yes, i beseech; 1.06.200
therefore i shall beseech you, if you please 1.06.205
tempters of the night | guard me, beseech ye. 2.02. 10
beseech your majesty, | forbear sharp speeches 3.05. 38
beseech your highness, | hold me your loyal 4.03. 15
take that life, beseech you, | which i so often 5.05.414
that we have, | cause it to sound, beseech you. PER 3.02. 89
i do beseech you | to learn of me, who stand /i' 4.04. 7
i beseech your honor give me leave a word, and 4.06. 46 P
i beseech you do. 4.06. 48 P
i beseech your honor one piece for me. 4.06.117 P
let us beseech you | that for our gold we may 5.01. 55
recount, i do beseech thee. 5.01.141
beseech you first, go with me to my house, 5.03. 65
and learn of him, i heartily beseech thee, | to VEN 404
BESEECH'D* *(also besieg'd)*
BESEECH'D* 3 FR 0.0003 REL FR 2 V 1 P
the town is beseech'd, and the trumpet call us H5 3.02.108 P
and he beseech'd me to entreat your majesties HAM 3.01. 22
their kind acceptance weepingly beseech'd, LC 207
BESEECHERS 1 FR 0.0001 REL FR 1 V 0 P
let no unkind, no fair beseechers kill; SON 135.13
BESEECHING 4 FR 0.0004 REL FR 4 V 0 P
beseeching god, and you, to pardon me. H5 2.02.160
beseeching thee (if with thy will it stands) 3H6 2.03. 38
beseeching him to give her virtuous breeding — H8 4.02.134
beseeching you | to give her princely training, PER 3.03. 15
BESEEK 1 FR 0.0001 REL FR 0 V 1 P
i beseek you now, aggravate your choler. 2H4 2.04.162 P
BESEEM 6 FR 0.0006 REL FR 6 V 0 P
weeds | as may beseem some well–reputed page. TGV 2.07. 43
and ill it doth beseem your holiness | to ERR 5.01.110
so qualified as may beseem | the spouse of any SHR 4.05. 66
it would beseem the lord northumberland | to say R2 3.03. 7
it seems | as may beseem a monarch like himself. 3H6 3.03.122
let it then as well beseem thy heart | to mourn SON 132.10
BESEEMETH 1 FR 0.0001 REL FR 1 V 0 P
to teach a teacher ill beseemeth me. LLL 2.01.108
BESEEMING 5 FR 0.0005 REL FR 5 V 0 P
beseeming such a wife as your fair daughter. TGV 3.01. 66
yet best beseeming me to speak the truth. R2 4.01.116
was infamous | and ill beseeming any common man, 1H6 4.01. 31
cast by their grave beseeming ornaments | to ROM 1.01. 93
did company these three | in poor beseeming; CYM 5.05.409
BESEEMS 5 FR 0.0005 REL FR 5 V 0 P
it ill beseems this presence to cry aim | to JN 2.01.196
more than well beseems | a man of thy profession 1H6 3.01. 19
and give them burial as beseems their worth. 4.07. 86
how evil it beseems thee | to flatter henry and 3H6 4.07. 84
sad pause and deep regard beseems the sage; LUC 277
BESET 7 FR 0.0008 REL FR 7 V 0 P
now, daughter silvia, you are hard beset. TGV 2.04. 49
fled — | the thicket is beset, he cannot scape. 5.03. 11
o, god defend me, how am i beset! ADO 4.01. 77
him, | i was beset with shame and courtesy, | my MV 5.01.217
forth thy weapon, we are beset with thieves; SHR 3.02.236
town, | drew to defend him when he was beset; TN 5.01. 85
lies, | do tell her she is dreadfully beset, LUC 444
BESHREW *(also beshrow, 'shrew)*
BESHREW 29 FR 0.0032 REL FR 24 V 5 P
beshrew me, but you have a quick wit. TGV 1.01.125 P
beshrew me, sir, but if he make this good, | he 2.04. 75
beshrew his hand, i scarce could understand it. ERR 2.01. 49
marry, beshrew my hand, | if it should give your ADO 5.01. 55
now much beshrew my manners and my pride, | if MND 2.02. 54
beshrew my heart, but i pity the man. 5.01.290 P
beshrew me, the knight's in admirable fooling. TN 2.03. 80 P
beshrew his soul for me, | he started one poor 4.01. 58
unsafe lunes i' th' king, beshrew them! WT 2.02. 28
and beshrew my soul | but i do love the favor JN 5.04. 49
beshrew thy very heart! 5.05. 14
beshrew thee, cousin, which didst lead me forth R2 3.02.204
beshrew your heart, | fair daughter, you do draw 2H4 2.03. 45
any thing, and wilt not call, beshrew thy heart. 5.03. 56 P
now beshrew my father's ambition! H5 5.02.225 P
beshrew the winners, for they play'd me false! 2H6 3.01.184
beshrew me, but his passions moves me so | that 3H6 1.04.150
beshrew me, i would, | and venture maidenhead H8 2.03. 24
beshrew the witch! TRO 4.02. 12
come, beshrew your heart, you'll ne'er be good, 4.02. 29
beshrew your heart for sending me about | to ROM 2.05. 51
and from my soul too, else beshrew them both. 3.05.227
she will beshrew me much that romeo | hath had 5.02. 26
beshrew me much, emilia, | i was (unhandsome OTH 3.04.150
beshrew him for't! 4.02.128
beshrew me, if i would do such a wrong | for the 4.03. 78
i have, | beshrew mine eyes for't! TNK 2.02.157
sister, beshrew my heart, you have a servant 2.05. 62
beshrew that heart that makes my heart to groan SON 133. 1
BESHROW 5 FR 0.0005 REL FR 5 V 0 P
and i beshrow all shrows, | but, katherine, what LLL 5.02. 46
beshrow me but i love her heartily, | for she is MV 2.06. 52
beshrow your eyes, | they have o'erlook'd me and 3.02. 14
beshrow my very heart, | i think you are happy ROM 3.05.221
meant to wrack thee, but beshrow my jealousy! HAM 2.01.110
BESIDE 36 FR 0.0040 REL FR 34 V 2 P
beside, she hath prosperous art | when she will MM 1.02.184
beside the charge, the shame, imprisonment, ERR 5.01. 18
so, though very many have been beside their wit. ADO 5.01.128 P
no food, | and but one meal on every day beside, LLL 1.01. 40
when she did starve the general world beside 2.01. 11
and i say beside that, 'twas a pricket that the 4.02. 48 P
over and beside | signior baptista's liberality, SHR 1.02.148
beside, so qualified as may beseem | the spouse 4.05. 66
at the saint francis here beside the port. AWW 3.05. 36
lord of thy presence and no land beside? JN 1.01.137
we pray with heart and soul, and all beside; R2 5.03.104
and to the coffers of the king beside, | a H5 1.01. 18
beside, i fear me, if thy thoughts were sifted, 1H6 3.01. 24
beside five hundred prisoners of esteem, | lets 3.04. 8
myself and divers gentlemen beside | were there 4.01. 25
beside, what infamy will there arise, | when 4.01.143

beside, my lord, the sooner to effect | and 5.01. 15
beside, his wealth doth warrant a liberal dower, 5.05. 46
than all the princes in the land beside. 2H6 1.01.176
beside the haughty protector, have we beauford 1.03. 68
to frustrate both his oath and what beside | may 3H6 2.01.175
is, beside forfeiting | our own brains and the H8 pr 19
beside that of the jewel house, is made master 5.01. 34
that hath beside well in his person wrought | to COR 2.03.246
the multitude, beside themselves with fear, JC 3.01.180
you must note beside | that we have tried the 4.03.213
provide, | your charms and every thing beside. MAC 3.05. 19
we have met with foes | that strike beside us. 5.07. 29
and i will boot thee with what gift beside | thy ANT 2.05. 71
save him, sir, | and spare no blood beside. CYM 5.05. 92
each errant step beside is torment. TNK 3.02. 34
beside, i have another oath 'gainst yours, | of 3.06.230
yet sometimes falls an orient drop beside, VEN 981
than when it hath my added praise beside. SON 103. 4
hat, | hanging her pale and pined cheek beside; LC 32
love to myself, and to no love beside. 77
BESIDES 117 FR 0.0132 REL FR 85 V 32 P
form a shape, | besides yourself, to like of. TMP 3.01. 57
besides, the gentleman | is full of virtue, TGV 3.01. 64
besides, the fashion of the time is chang'd) 3.01. 86
besides, her intercession chaf'd him so, | when 3.01.235
besides, thy staying will abridge thy life. 3.01.247
besides, she did intend confession | at 5.02. 41
and galen — and he is a knave besides, a WIV 3.01. 66 P
besides your cheer, you shall have sport; 3.02. 80 P
besides these, other bars he lays before me, 3.04. 7
who's at home besides yourself? 4.02. 13 P
besides, i'll make a present recompense. 4.06. 55
besides, you know, it draws something near to MM 1.02. 77 P
besides, upon the very siege of justice | lord 4.02. 98
besides, he tells me that, if peradventure | he 4.06. 5
married, | and i confess besides i am no maid. 5.01.185
an ass, i am a woman's man, and besides myself. ERR 3.02. 78 P
what woman's man, and how besides thyself? 3.02. 79 P
marry, sir, besides myself, i am due to a woman: 3.02. 81 P
besides, i have some business in the town. 4.01. 35
besides this present instance of his rage, | is 4.03. 87
besides, i will be sworn these ears of mine 5.01.260
besides her urging of her wrack at sea — 5.01.360
for, besides the groves, | the skies, the MND 4.01.115
besides, the lott'ry of my destiny | bars me the MV 2.01. 15
besides, antonio certified the duke | they were 2.08. 10
to wit (besides commends and courteous breath), 2.09. 90
besides, it should appear, that if he had | the 3.02.272
besides that they are fair with their feeding, AYL 1.01. 11 P
besides this nothing that he so plentifully 1.01. 16 P
besides, his cote, his flocks, and bounds of 2.04. 83
besides, our hands are hard. 3.02. 59 P
besides, the oath of /a lover is no stronger 3.04. 30 P
besides, i like you not. 3.05. 74
besides, he brings his destiny with him. 4.01. 56 P
besides two thousand ducats by the year | of SHR 2.01.369
have, besides an argosy | that now is lying in 2.01.374
besides two galliasses | and twelve tight 2.01.378
besides, possess'd with the glanders and like to 3.02. 50 P
besides, old gremio is heark'ning still, | and 4.04. 53
besides, virginity is peevish, proud, idle, made AWW 1.01.143 P
for besides that he's a fool, he's a great TN 1.03. 29 P
besides, you grow dishonest. 1.05. 42 P
for besides that it is excellently well penn'd, 1.05.173 P
besides, she uses me with a more exalted respect 2.05. 26 P
"besides, you waste the treasure of your time 2.05. 77 P
alas, sir, how fell you besides your five wits? 4.02. 86 P
besides, i have stay'd | to tire your royalty. WT 1.02. 14
besides, this place is famous for the creatures 3.03. 12
besides, the penitent king, my master, hath sent 4.02. 6 P
besides, you know, | prosperity's the very bond 4.04.572
and if it be in man besides the king to effect 4.04.798 P
besides, the gods | will have fulfill'd their 5.01. 35
besides, i met lord bigot and lord salisbury, JN 4.02.162
the love of him, and this respect besides, | for 5.04. 41
for besides i say, and will in battle prove, | or R2 1.01. 92
besides, our nearness to the king in love | is 2.02.127
scroop, besides a clergyman | of holy reverence, 3.03. 28
besides himself, are all the english peers, 3.04. 88
besides, i heard the banished norfolk say | that 4.01. 80
is there not besides the douglas? 1H4 2.03. 26 P
enough | to put him quite besides his patience. 3.01.177
a stain | upon the beauty of all parts besides, 3.01.186
you owe money here besides, sir john, for your 3.03. 72 P
besides, the king hath wasted all his rods | on 2H4 4.01.213
besides, their writers say, | king pepin, which H5 1.02. 64
besides, they are our outward consciences | and 4.01. 8
besides, there is no king, be his cause never so 4.01.158 P
besides, they all are fresh. 4.03. 4
besides, in mercy, | the constable desires thee 4.03. 83
besides, they have burn'd and carried away all 4.07. 7 P
besides, we'll cut the throats of those we have, 4.07. 63
full fifteen hundred, besides common men. 4.08. 79
besides, all french and france exclaims on thee, 1H6 3.03. 60
besides, he says there are two councils kept; R3 3.02. 12
besides, he hates me for my father warwick, 4.01. 85
besides, the king's name is a tower of strength, 5.03. 12
besides, | you'll find a most unfit time to H8 2.02. 59
besides the running banquet of two beadles that 5.03. 65 P
besides th' applause and approbation | the which TRO 1.03. 59
much, and i do fear besides | that i shall lose 3.02. 26
besides, if things go well, | opinion that so COR 1.01.270
besides, forget not | with what contempt he wore 2.03.220
besides, this sorrow is an enemy, | and would TIT 3.01.267
he owes nine thousand, besides my former sum, TIM 2.01. 2
besides, his expedition promises | present 5.02. 3
besides — i ha' not since put up my sword — JC 1.03. 19
if i know this, know all the world besides, 1.03. 98
besides the things that we have heard and seen, 2.02. 15
besides, it were a mock | apt to be render'd, 2.02. 96
unto the crown, | besides the thane of cawdor. MAC 1.03.122
besides, this duncan | hath borne his faculties 1.07. 16
agitation, besides her walking and other actual 5.01. 11 P
besides, to be demanded of a spunge, what HAM 4.02. 12 P
besides, his picture | i will send far and near, LR 2.01. 81
who's there, besides foul weather? 3.01. 1
besides, the knave is handsome, young, and hath OTH 2.01.245 P
for, besides these beneficial news, it is the 2.02. 6 P
and, besides, the moor | may unfold me to him; 5.01. 20
there is besides, in roderigo's letter, | how he 5.02.324
and say besides, that in aleppo once, | where a 5.02.352
of cneius pompey's — besides what hotter hours, ANT 3.13.118
and had (besides this gentleman in question) CYM 1.01. 34
besides, the seeing these effects will be | both 1.05. 25
and no more | but what thou art besides, thou 2.03.126
quite besides | the government of patience! 2.04.149
thee all this, | yea, and furr'd moss besides. 4.02.228
and besides, the king | hath not deserv'd my 4.04. 24
loves woman for, besides that hook of wiving, 5.05.167
besides this treasure for a fee, | the gods PER 3.02. 74
besides, the sore terms we stand upon with the 4.02. 34 P
and who to thank | (besides the gods) for this 5.03. 58
besides, my father must be hang'd to–morrow, TNK 5.02. 80
besides, his soul's fair temple is defaced, | to LUC 719
besides, of weariness he did complain him, | and 845
besides, the life and feeling of her passion 1317
who with his fear is put besides his part, | or SON 23. 2
that all the world besides methinks are dead. 112.14
BESIEG'D *(also beseech'd*)*
BESIEG'D 4 FR 0.0004 REL FR 4 V 0 P
the sea | (except this city now by us besieg'd) JN 2.01.489
so you had need, for orleance is besieg'd; 1H6 1.01.157
sirrah, thou know'st how orleance is besieg'd, 1.04. 1
on his will | till paris was besieg'd, famish'd, 2H6 1.03.172
BESIEGE 10 FR 0.0011 REL FR 9 V 1 P
the most mighty neptune | seem to besiege, and TMP 1.02.205
like one that comes here to besiege his court, LLL 2.01. 86
he owes the malady | that doth my life besiege. AWW 2.01. 10
faintly besiege us one hour in a month. 1H6 1.02. 8
intend here to besiege you in your castle. 3H6 1.02. 50
the army of the queen mean to besiege us. 1.02. 64
tool come to court, the women so besiege us? H8 5.03. 35 P
when forty winters shall besiege thy brow, | and SON 2. 1
all frailties that besiege all kinds of blood, 109.10
i held my city, | till thus he gan besiege me: LC 177
BESIEGED 2 FR 0.0002 REL FR 1 V 1 P
it is, besieged with sable–colored melancholy, i LLL 1.01.231 P
from the besieged ardea all in post, | borne by LUC 1
BESLUBBER 1 FR 0.0001 REL FR 0 V 1 P
and then to beslubber our garments with it and 1H4 2.04.310 P
BESMEAR 2 FR 0.0002 REL FR 2 V 0 P
would not let ingratitude | so much besmear it. MV 5.01.219
up to the elbows, and besmear our swords; JC 3.01.107
BESMEAR'D 4 FR 0.0004 REL FR 4 V 0 P
it was besmear'd | as black as vulcan in the TN 5.01. 52
knows they were besmear'd and over–stain'd JN 3.01.236
is become as black | as if besmear'd in hell. H8 1.02.124
unswept stone, besmear'd with sluttish time. SON 55. 4
BESMIRCH 1 FR 0.0001 REL FR 1 V 0 P
and now no soil nor cautel doth besmirch | the HAM 1.03. 15
BESMIRCH'D 1 FR 0.0001 REL FR 1 V 0 P
our gayness and our gilt are all besmirch'd H5 4.03.110
BESOM 1 FR 0.0001 REL FR 0 V 1 P
that i am the besom that must sweep the court 2H6 4.07. 31 P
BESONIAN 1 FR 0.0001 REL FR 1 V 0 P
under which king, besonian? speak, or die. 2H4 5.03.113
BESONIANS 1 FR 0.0001 REL FR 1 V 0 P
great men oft die by vild besonians: 2H6 4.01.134
BESORT 2 FR 0.0002 REL FR 2 V 0 P
depend, | to be such men as may besort your age, LR 1.04.251
with such accommodation and besort | as levels OTH 1.03.238
BESOTTED 1 FR 0.0001 REL FR 1 V 0 P
like one besotted on your sweet delights. TRO 2.02.143
BESPAKE *(also bespoke)*
BESPAKE 2 FR 0.0002 REL FR 2 V 0 P
but i bespake you fair, and hurt you not. TN 5.01.189
his proud steed's neck, | bespake them thus: R2 5.02. 20
BESPEAK 6 FR 0.0006 REL FR 4 V 2 P
do, expect spoon–meat, or bespeak a long spoon. ERR 4.03. 61 P
he did bespeak a chain for me, but had it not. 4.04.136
bespeak him a fortnight before. MV 3.01.126 P
here is the cap your worship did bespeak. SHR 4.03. 63
i will bespeak our diet, | whiles you beguile TN 3.03. 40
and my young mistress thus i did bespeak: HAM 2.02.140
BESPICE 1 FR 0.0001 REL FR 1 V 0 P
how i am gall'd — mightst bespice a cup, | to WT 1.02.316
BESPOKE *(also bespake)*
BESPOKE 5 FR 0.0005 REL FR 4 V 1 P
made it for me, sir! i bespoke it not. ERR 3.02.171
then fairly i bespoke the officer | to go in 5.01.233
i have bespoke supper to–morrow night in 1H4 1.02.129 P
blood, and in disgrace | bespoke him thus: 1H6 4.06. 21
make your loves to me, | my lady is bespoke. LR 5.03. 89
BESS 1 FR 0.0001 REL FR 1 V 0 P
come hither, bess, and let me kiss my boy. 3H6 5.07. 15
/BESSY 1 FR 0.0001 REL FR 1 V 0 P
"/come /o'er /the /bourn, /bessy, /to /me" — LR 3.06. 25
BE'ST 13 FR 0.0014 REL FR 8 V 5 P
if thou be'st the man | that hadst a wife once ERR 5.01.342
o, if thou be'st the same egeon, speak, | and 5.01.345
drunk wine — but if thou be'st not an ass, i am AWW 2.03.100 P
if ever thou be'st bound in thy scarf and beaten 2.03.225 P
for, if thou be'st capable of things serious, WT 4.04.764 P
if after three days' space thou here be'st found 2H6 3.02.295
if that thou be'st a roman, take it forth. JC 4.03.103
if thou be'st as poor for a subject as he's for LR 1.04. 21 P
if thou be'st valiant (as they say base men OTH 2.01.215 P
disprove this villain, if thou be'st a man. 5.02.172
if that thou be'st a devil, i cannot kill thee. 5.02.287
be'st thou sad or merry, | the violence of ANT 1.05. 59
if thou be'st, | as thou art spoken, great and TNK 3.06.151
/BEST 4 FR 0.0004 REL FR 4 V 0 P
/past /and /to /come /seems /best; 2H4 1.03.108
she, whom even but now was your /best object, LR 1.01.214
/secret /feet | /in /some /of /our /best /ports, 3.01. 33
/and /the /best /quarrels, /in /the /heat, /are 5.03. 56
BEST 483 FR 0.0546 REL FR 394 V 89 P
i come | to answer thy best pleasure; TMP 1.02.190
thou best know'st | what torment i did find thee 1.02.286
fetch us in fuel, and be quick, thou'rt best, 1.02.366
i am the best of them that speak this speech, 1.02.430
the best? 1.02.431
'tis best we stand upon our guard, | or that we 2.01.321
my best way is to creep under his gaberdine; 2.02. 38 P
i'll show thee the best springs; 2.02.160
full many a lady | i have ey'd with best regard, 3.01. 40
are created | of every creature's best! 3.01. 48
invert | what best is boded me to mischief! 3.01. 71
no matter, since i feel | the best is past. 3.03. 51
and the best comforter | to an unsettled fancy, 5.01. 58
the best news is, that we have safely found 5.01.221
ground be overcharg'd, you were best stick her. TGV 1.01.101 P
'twere best pound you. 1.01.103 P
then thus: of many good i think him best. 1.02. 21
yet he, of all the rest, i think best loves ye. 1.02. 28
best sing it to the tune of "light o' love." 1.02. 80
but she would be best pleas'd | to be so ang'red 1.02. 99
if you respect them, best to take them up. 1.02.131
then tell me, whither were i best to send him? 1.03. 24
why, ev'n what fashion thou best likes, lucetta. 2.07. 52
a woman sometime scorns what best contents her. 3.01. 93
how shall i best convey the ladder thither? 3.01.128
well, the best is, she hath no teeth to bite. 3.01.344 P
the best way is to slander valentine | with 3.02. 31
read over julia's heart (thy first best love), 5.04. 46
i think the best way were to entertain him with WIV 2.01. 66 P
the best courtier of them all (when the court 2.02. 61 P
and in such wine and sugar of the best, and the 2.02. 69 P
i'll speak it before the best lord, i would make 3.03. 50 P
you were best meddle with buck–washing. 3.03.155 P
there's a hole made in your best coat, master 3.05.141 P
'tis one of the best discretions of a oman as 4.04. 1 P
and he my husband best of all affects. 4.04. 87
i'll make the best in gloucestershire know on't. 5.05.180 P
and he that might the vantage best have took MM 2.02. 74
thy best of rest is sleep, | and that thou oft 3.01. 17
therefore your best appointment make with speed, 3.01. 59
a bawd, | 'tis best that thou diest quickly. 3.01.150
the best and wholesom'st spirits of the night 4.02. 73
beholding to your reports, but the best is, he 4.03.160 P
do with your injuries as seems you best, | in 5.01.256
they say best men are moulded out of faults, 5.01.439
i see the jewel best enamelled | will lose his ERR 2.01.109
in debating which was best, we shall part with 3.01. 67
offends me, and to be merry best becomes you, ADO 2.01.332 P
the best i can, my lord. 2.03. 88 P
which is the best to furnish me to–morrow. 3.01.103
her, | as best befits her wounded reputation, 4.01.241
when beasts most graze, birds best peck, and men
LLL 1.01.236 P
as i look'd for, but the best that ever i heard. 1.01.280 P
ay, the best for the worst. 1.01.281 P
as i have read, sir, and the best of them too. 1.02. 84 P
for the best ward of mine honor is rewarding my 3.01.132 P
you were best call it "daughter–beamed eyes." 5.02.172
i am best pleas'd with that. 5.02.229
with eyes best seeing, heaven's fiery eye, | by 5.02.375
that sport best pleases that doth /least know 5.02.516
to a halfpenny, pompey proves the best worthy. 5.02.561 P
no, he is best indu'd in the small. 5.02.641 P
honest plain words best pierce the ear of grief, 5.02.753
bow, | by his best arrow with the golden head, MND 1.01.170
you were best to call them generally, man by man 1.02. 2 P
what beard were i best to play it in? 1.02. 91 P
do thy best | to pluck this crawling serpent 2.02.145
and those things do best please me | that befall 3.02.120
he hath simply the best wit of any handicraft 4.02. 9 P
yea, and the best person too; 4.02. 11 P
the best in this kind are but shadows; 5.01.211 P
the very best at a beast, my lord, that e'er i 5.01.229 P
to the best bride–bed will we, | which by us 5.01.403
when he is best, he is a little worse than a man MV 1.02. 88 P
look'd upon, was the best deserving a fair lady. 1.02.118 P
feast to–night | my best esteem'd acquaintance. 2.02.172
my best endeavors shall be done herein. 2.02.173
you were best to tell antonio what you hear, 2.08. 33
i think the best grace of wit will shortly turn 3.05. 44 P
why, i were best to cut my left hand off, | and 5.01.177
and thou wert best look to't; AYL 1.01.147 P
especially of my own people, who best know him, 1.01.170 P
you may see the end, for the best is yet to do, 1.02.115 P
a fault i will not change for your best virtue. 3.02.283 P
the best thing in him | is his complexion; 3.05.115
therefore put you in your best array, bid your 5.02. 72 P
it is best | put finger in the eye, and she knew SHR 1.01. 78
i had given him the best horse in padua to begin 1.01.143 P
of all | my best beloved and approved friend, 1.02. 3
happily to wive and thrive as best i may. 1.02. 56
brought up as best becomes a gentlewoman. 1.02. 87
i charge /thee tell | whom thou lov'st best; 2.01. 9
if i be waspish, best beware my sting. 2.01.210
i must confess your offer is the best, | and let 2.01.386
old fashions please me best; 3.01. 80
house, | and revel it as bravely as the best, 4.03. 54
and if you cannot, best you stop your ears. 4.03. 76
hence, make your best of it. 4.03.100
where then do you know best | we be affied and 4.04. 48
they're busy within, you were best knock louder. 5.01. 14 P
then thou wert best say that i am not lucentio. 5.01.103 P
feast with the best, and welcome to my house. 5.02. 8
'tis the best brine a maiden can season her AWW 1.01. 48 P
he cannot want the best | that shall attend his 1.01. 72
the best wishes that can | be forg'd in your 1.01. 74
thou wert best set thy lower part where thy nose 2.03.251 P
hope, lay our best love and credence | upon thy 3.03. 2
as we'll direct her how 'tis best to bear it. 3.07. 20
drunkenness is his best virtue, for he will be 4.03.255 P
his brother is reputed one of the best that is. 4.03.289 P
grant it me, o king, in you it best lies; 5.03.145 P
for i myself am best | when least in company. TN 1.04. 37
i'll do my best | to woo your lady. 1.04. 40
make your excuse wisely, you were best. 1.05. 31 P
why, this is the best fooling, when all is done. 2.03. 29 P
the best persuaded of himself, so cramm'd (as he 2.03.150 P
to–morrow, sir. best first go see your lodging. 3.03. 20
suburbs at the elephant | is best to lodge. 3.03. 40
your ladyship were best to have some guard about 3.04. 12 P
say this to him, | he's beat from his best ward. WT 1.02. 33
what cheer? how is't with you, best brother? 1.02.148
if not, how best to bear it. 1.02.406
then, my best blood turn | to an infected jelly, 1.02.417
be yok'd with his that did betray the best! 1.02.419
become some women best, so that there be not 2.01. 9
a sad tale's best for winter. 2.01. 25

on, and do your best | to fright me with your 2.01. 27
as your charities | shall best instruct you, 2.01.114
the office | becomes a woman best. 2.02. 30
commend my best obedience to the queen. 2.02. 34
great apollo | turn all to th' best! 3.01. 15
my lord, best know | (/who least will seem to do 3.02. 32
make your best haste, and go not | too far i' 3.03. 10
they have scar'd away two of my best sheep, 3.03. 66 P
my best camillo! we must disguise ourselves. 4.02. 54 P
half a kiss to choose | who loves another best. 4.04.176
his son a guest | that best becomes the table. 4.04.396
and with my best endeavors, in your absence, 4.04.531
who | do their best office, if they can but stay 4.04.571
means i saw whose purse was best in picture, and 4.04.603 P
so his successor | was like to be the best. 5.01. 49
my best train | i have from your sicilian shores 5.01.163
you were best say these robes are not gentlemen 5.02.132 P
"o sir," says answer, "at your best command, JN 1.01.197
to cull the plots of best advantages. 2.01. 40
forth | in best appointment all our regiments. 2.01.296
equality | by our best eyes cannot be censured. 2.01.328
your breeches best may carry them. 3.01.201
handkercher about your brows | (the best i had, 4.01. 43
i am best pleas'd to be from such a deed. 4.01. 85
myself and them | bend their best studies — 4.02. 51
e'er you think, good words, i think, were best. 4.03. 28
have i not here the best cards for the game, 5.02.105
for in a night the best part of my pow'r, | as i 5.07. 61
with other princes that may best be spar'd, 5.07. 97
even in the best blood chamber'd in his bosom, R2 1.01.149
the best way is to venge my gloucester's death. 1.02. 36
i would he were the best | in all this presence 4.01. 31
yet best beseeming me to speak the truth. 4.01.116
he did confound the best part of an hour | in 1H4 1.03.100
and cuts me from the best of all my land | a 3.01. 98
'twere best he did. 5.02. 3
let each man do his best, and here draw i | a 5.02. 92
with the best blood that i can meet withal | in 5.02. 94
i am in good name and fame with the very best. 2H4 2.04. 76 P
bona /robas were and had the best of them all at 3.02. 24 P
men, and i would have you serv'd with the best. 3.02.256 P
our armor all as strong, our cause the best; 4.01.154
therefore thou best of gold art /worst /of gold. 4.05.160
in equal rank with the best govern'd nation, 5.02.137
it is best, certain. 5.05. 23 P
and wholesome berries thrive and ripen best H5 1.01. 61
no doubt, my liege, if each man do his best. 2.02. 19
to /mark /the full–fraught man and best indued 2.02.139
in cases of defense 'tis best to weigh | the 2.04. 43
heard that men of few words are the best men, 3.02. 37 P
therefore to our best mercy give yourselves, 3.03. 3
a name that in my thoughts becomes me best, | if 3.03. 6
tut, i have the best armor of the world. 3.07. 1 P
it is the best horse of europe. 3.07. 5 P
whose hours the peasant best advantages. 4.01.284
would share from me, | for the best hope i have. 4.03. 33
angers, look you, kill his best friend, clytus. 4.07. 38 P
the mayor and all his brethren in best sort, 5.pr. 25
your mightiness on both parts best can witness. 5.02. 28
should not in this best garden of the world, 5.02. 36
as your wisdoms best | shall see advantageable 5.02. 87
if he be not fellow with the best king, thou 5.02.242 P
thou shalt find the best king of good fellows. 5.02.242 P
god, the best maker of all marriages, | combine 5.02.359
by which the world's best garden he achieved, ep 7
and for his safety there i'll best devise. 1H6 1.01.172
where is best place to make our batt'ry next? 1.04. 65
as fitting best to quittance their deceit 2.01. 14
between two horses, which doth bear him best, 2.04. 14
now will it best avail your majesty | to cross 3.01.178
here is the best and safest passage in? 3.02. 22
i were best to leave him, for he will not hear. 5.03. 83
warwick may live to be the best of all. 2H6 1.03.112
that time best fits the work we have in hand. 1.04. 20
and look thyself be faultless, thou wert best. 2.01.185
where it best fits to be, in henry's hand. 2.03. 44
and with your best endeavor have stirr'd up | my 3.01.163
my lords, what to your wisdoms seemeth best, 3.01.195
ay, by the best blood that ever was broach'd, 4.10. 37 P
tell kent from me, she hath lost her best man, 4.10. 73 P
you were best to go to bed and dream again, | to 5.01.196
richard hath best deserv'd of all my sons. 3H6 1.01. 17
neither the king, nor he that loves him best, 1.01. 45
would thy best friends did know | how it doth 2.02. 54
the queen hath best success when you are absent. 2.02. 74
now one the better, then another best; 2.05. 10
they prosper best of all when i am thence. 2.05. 18
shall do and undo as him pleaseth best. 2.06.105
here stand we both and aim we at the best; 3.01. 8
i hope all's for the best. 3.03.170
we, having now the best at barnet field, | will 5.03. 20
rest, | counting myself but bad till i be best. 5.06. 91
one) | were best to do it secretly alone. R3 1.01.100
where it seems best unto your royal self. 3.01. 63
most fit | for your best health and recreation. 3.01. 67
best fitteth my degree or your condition. 3.07.143
widow, | even in the afternoon of her best days, 3.07.186
as one being best acquainted with her humor. 4.04.269
what were i best to say? 4.04.337
an honest tale speeds best being plainly told. 4.04.358
buckingham is taken — | that is the best news. 4.04.532
with best advantage will deceive the time, | and 5.03. 92
equal in lustre, were now best, now worst, | as H8 1.01. 29
therefore best | not wake him in his slumber. 1.01.121
my life itself, and the best heart of it, 1.02. 1
what we oft do best, | by sick interpreters 1.02. 81
grosser quality, is cried up | for our best act. 1.02. 85
and then let's dream | who's best in favor. 1.04.108
handsome, and of the best breed in the north. 2.02. 4 P
ay, and the best she shall have; 2.02.113
and my favor | to him that does best, god forbid 2.02.114
our content | is our best having. 2.03. 23
(well worthy the best heir o' th' world) should 2.04.196
inventory | of your best graces in your mind; 3.02.138
thee and all thy best parts bound together) 3.02.258
the best persuasions to the contrary | fail not 5.01.147
want of wisdom, you, that best should teach us, 5.02. 48
crooked malice nourishment | dare bite the best. 5.02. 80
know within a while | all the best men are ours; ep 13
shall make it good, or do his best to do it: TRO 1.03.274
main opinion crush | in taint of our best man. 1.03.373
/cull their flower, ajax shall cope the best. 2.03.264
who, in your thoughts, deserves fair helen best, 4.01. 54
but that that likes not you pleases me best. 5.02.103 P
see, our best elders. COR 1.01.226
vaward are the /antiates, | of their best trust; 1.06. 54
choice of those | that best can aid your action. 1.06. 66
out my command, | which men are best inclin'd. 1.06. 85
send us to rome | the best, with whom we may 1.09. 77
when you speak best unto the purpose, it is not 2.01. 86 P
some of the best of 'em were hereditary hangmen. 2.01. 92 P
he prov'd best man i' th' field, and for his 2.02. 97
that our best water brought by conduits hither, 2.03.242
myself | take up a brace o' th' best of them, 3.01.243
the same you are not, which, for your best ends, 3.02. 47
as best thou art experienc'd, since thou know'st 4.05.139
for his best friends, if they | should say, "be 4.06.111
that we did, we did for the best, and though we 4.06.143 P
best of my flesh, | forgive my tyranny; 5.03. 42
to accomplish, | my best and freshest men; 5.06. 34
let's make the best of it. 5.06.146
patron of virtue, rome's best champion, TIT 1.01. 65
whose fortunes rome's best citizens applaud! 1.01.164
my lord, what i have done, as best i may, 1.01.411
than prosecute the meanest or the best | for 4.04. 33
bid him demand what pledge will please him best. 4.04.106
she shall scant show well that now seems best. ROM 1.02. 99
away, be gone, the sport is at the best. 1.05.119
blind is his love and best befits the dark. 2.01. 32
i thought all for the best. 3.01.104
if love be blind, | it best agrees with night. 3.02. 10
o tybalt, tybalt, the best friend i had! 3.02. 61
back, | happiness courts thee in her best array, 3.03.142
i think it best you married with the county. 3.05.217
is, | /in thy best robes, uncovered on the bier, 4.01.110
ay, those attires are best, but, gentle nurse, 4.03. 1
but she's best married that dies married young. 4.05. 78
is, | and in her best array, bear her to church; 4.05. 81
at my dearest cost | in qualities of the best. TIM 1.01.125
the best, for the innocence. 1.01.196 P
i could wish my best friend at such a feast. 1.02. 79 P
the five best senses | acknowledge thee their 1.02.123
my lord, you take us even at the best. 1.02.152
the best of happiness, | honor, and fortunes, 1.02.228
of whom, even to the state's best health, i have 2.02.197
and the best half should have return'd to him, 3.02. 84
this was my lord's best hope, now all are fled, 3.03. 35
ever at the best, hearing well of your lordship. 3.06. 27 P
i'll ever serve his mind with my best will; 4.02. 49
best state, contentless, | hath a distracted and 4.03.245
the best, and truest; 4.03.290
good as the best. 5.01. 21
what you are | make them best seen and known. 5.01. 69
thou draw'st a counterfeit | best in all athens; 5.01. 81
th' art indeed the best, | thou counterfeit'st 5.01. 81
vacant lie, | for thy best use and wearing. 5.01.143
what dost thou with thy best apparel on? JC 1.01. 8
and do you now put on your best attire? 1.01. 48
heard | where many of the best respect in rome 1.02. 59
that your best friends shall wish i had been 2.02.125
desire you to o'er–read | (at your best leisure) 3.01. 5
with the most boldest and best hearts of rome. 3.01.121
as i slew my best lover for the good of rome, i 3.02. 45 P
'twere best he speak no harm of brutus here! 3.02. 68
ay, and truly, you were best. 3.03. 12 P
our best friends made, our means stretch'd, 4.01. 44
how covert matters may be best disclos'd, | and 4.01. 46
to see my best friend ta'en before my face! 5.03. 35
to know my deed, 'twere best not know myself. MAC 2.02. 70
we have lost | best half of our affair. 3.03. 21
but in best time | we will require her welcome. 3.04. 5
thou art the best o' th' cut–throats, | yet he's 3.04. 16
to feed were best at home; 3.04. 34
sprites, | and show the best of our delights. 4.01.128
and best knows | the fits o' th' season. 4.02. 16
how he solicits heaven, | himself best knows; 4.03.150
and thy best graces spend it at thy will! HAM 1.02. 63
i shall in all my best obey you, madam. 1.02.120
be wary then, best safety lies in fear: 1.03. 43
and they in france of the best rank and station 1.03. 73
murther most foul, as in the best it is, | but 1.05. 27
groans, but that i love thee best, o most best, 2.02.121 P
but that i love thee best, o most best, believe 2.02.122 P
the best actors in the world, either for tragedy 2.02.396 P
him where | your wisdom best shall think. 3.01.187
officers do the king best service in the end: 4.02. 17 P
i pray you pass with your best violence; 5.02.298
and in thy best consideration check | this LR 1.01.150
the best, the dearest, should in this trice of 1.01.216
the best and soundest of his time hath been but 1.01.295 P
makes the world bitter to the best of our times; 1.02. 47 P
we have seen the best of our time. 1.02.112 P
brother, i advise you to the best; 1.02.172 P
qualified in, and the best of me is diligence. 1.04. 35 P
sirrah, you were best take my coxcomb. 1.04. 97 P
best! 2.01. 14
and when he saw my best alarum'd spirits, | bold 2.01. 53
which i best /thought it fit | to answer from 2.01.123
'tis best to give him way, he leads himself. 2.04.298
the lamentable change is from the best, | the 4.01. 5
i'll bring him the best 'parel that i have, 4.01. 49
who with best meaning have incurr'd the worst. 5.03. 4
rights, | by me invested, he compeers the best. 5.03. 69
and my best spirits are bent | to prove upon thy 5.03.140
mine eyes are not o' th' best; 5.03.280
you were best go in. OTH 1.02. 30
you best know the place. 1.03.121
take up this mangled matter at the best; 1.03.173
the fortitude of the place is best known to you; 1.03.223 P
and bring them after in the best advantage. 1.03.297
thou praisest the worst best. 2.01.144 P
and passion, having my best judgment collied, 2.03.206
arm, the best of you | shall sink in my rebuke. 2.03.208
the best sometimes forget. 2.03.241
as men in rage strike those that wish them best, 2.03.243
the wars must make example | out of her best), 3.03. 66
their best conscience | is not to leave't undone 3.03.203
as i have spoken for you all my best, | and 3.04.127
what's best to do? 5.02. 95
peace, you were best. 5.02.161
well, thou dost best. 5.02.306
the gods best know — ANT 1.03. 24
at the last, best, | see when and where she died 1.03. 61
but this is not the best. 1.03. 83
no worse a husband than the best of men; 2.02.128
my arm is sore, best play with mardian. 2.05. 4
for the best turn i' th' bed. 2.05. 59
but he loves caesar best, yet he loves antony. 3.02. 15
when the best hint was given him, he not /took't 3.04. 9
let your best love draw to that point which 3.04. 21
to that point which seeks | best to preserve it. 3.04. 22
best of comfort, | and ever welcome to us. 3.06. 89
which might have well becom'd the best of men, 3.07. 26
women are not | in their best fortunes strong, 3.12. 30
let our best heads | know that to–morrow the 4.01. 10
the best you saf'd the bringer | out of the host; 4.06. 25
the foul'st best fits | my latter part of life. 4.06. 37
where their appointment we may best discover, 4.10. 8
for his best force | is forth to man his galleys 4.11. 2
to the vales, | and hold our best advantage. 4.11. 4
serv'd, who best was worthy | best to be serv'd. 5.01. 6
serv'd, who best was worthy | best to be serv'd. 5.01. 7
so, dolabella, | it shall content me best. 5.02. 68
make your best use of this. 5.02.203
go fetch | my best attires. 5.02.228
yourself some comfort | out of your best advice. CYM 1.01.156
could best express how slow his soul sail'd on, 1.03. 13
and your lord | (the best feather of our wing) 1.06.186
equal discourtesy | to your best kindness; 2.03. 97
and therewithal the best, or let her beauty 2.04. 33
madam, you're best consider. 3.02. 77
happ'ly this life is best, | if quiet life be 3.03. 29
this life is best, | if quiet life be best; 3.03. 30
report was once | first with the best of note. 3.03. 58
may the gods | direct you to the best! 3.04.193
from every one | the best she hath, and she, of 3.05. 73
i were best not call; 3.06. 19
best draw my sword; 3.06. 25
have prov'd best woodman and | are master of the 3.06. 28
but imogen is your own, do your best wills, 5.01. 16
of imogen, that best | could deem his dignity? 5.04. 56
whom best i love, i cross; 5.04.101
a man should have the best use of eyes to see 5.04.189 P
think more and more | what's best to ask. 5.05.110
with all my heart, | and lend my best attention. 5.05.117
and was the best of all | amongst the rar'st of 5.05.159
swell'd boast | of him that best could speak; 5.05.163
eye | i give my cause, who best can justify. PER 1.ch. 42
sit, | to knit in her their best perfections. 1.01. 11
i'll do my best, sir. 1.04. 20
and that in tharsus was not best | longer for 2.ch. 25
thou shalt have my best gown to make thee a pair 2.01.163 P
but you the best. 2.03.108
to–morrow all for speeding do their best. 2.03.115
that best know how to rule and how to reign, 2.04. 38
the good gods | throw their best eyes upon't! 3.01. 37
we have taken | no care to your best courses. 4.01. 38
have him here to–morrow with his best ruff on. 4.02.103 P
"the fairest, sweetest, and best lies here, 4.04. 34
believe me, 'twere best i did give o'er. 5.01.166
artesius, that best knowest | how to draw out, TNK 1.01.159
can, fitt'st time | for best solicitation? 1.01.170
those best affections that the heavens infuse 1.03. 9
each side like justice, which he loves best. 1.03. 47
doubtless | there is a best, and reason has no 1.03. 48
mercy, all our best | their best skill tender! 1.04. 46
mercy, all our best | their best skill tender! 1.04. 47
of all flow'rs | methinks a rose is best. 2.02.136
wrestled, | the best men call'd it excellent; 2.03. 76
what e'er you are, you run the best, and wrastle 2.05. 3
that knew me | would say it was my best piece; 2.05. 14
in me, | since thy best props are warp'd! 3.02. 32
the best way is, the next way to a grave; 3.02. 33
y' had best look to her, | for, if she see him 4.01.123
with all her best endowments, all those beauties 4.02. 8
he of the two pretenders that best loves me 5.01.158
and that will founder the best hobby–horse | (if 5.02. 52
he whom the gods | do of the two know best, i 5.03. 39
being red, she loves him best, and being white, VEN 77
her best is better'd with a more delight. 78
but then woos best when most his choice is 570
"in night," quoth she, "desire sees best of all. 720
since her best work is ruin'd with thy rigor." 954
as striving who should best become her grief; 968
sorrow seemeth chief, | but none is best; 971
they that love best their loves shall not enjoy. 1164
grief best is pleas'd with grief's society; LUC 1111
words," quoth she, "shall fit the trespass best, 1613
although i know my years be past the best, | i PP 1. 6
o, love's best habit's in a soothing tongue, 1.11
bad in the best, though excellent in neither. 7.18
look whom she best endow'd she gave the more; SON 11.11
and perspective it is best painter's art. 24. 4
look what is best, that best i wish in thee: 37.13
look what is best, that best i wish in thee: 37.13
when most i wink, then do mine eyes best see, 43. 1
thou, best of dearest and mine only care, | art 48. 7
shall time's best jewel from time's chest lie 65.10
now counting best to be with you alone, | then 75. 7
so all my best is dressing old words new, 76.11
with mine own weakness being best acquainted, 88. 5
all these i better in one general best. 91. 8
but best is best, if never intermix'd"? 101. 8
but best is best, if never intermix'd"? 101. 8
then, in the blazon of sweet beauty's best, | of 106. 5
and worse essays prov'd thee my best of love. 110. 8
then give me welcome, next my heaven the best, 110.13
creating every bad a perfect best | as fast as 114. 7
might i not then say, "now i love you best," 115.10
yet what the best is take the worst to be. 137. 4
although she knows my days are past the best, 138. 6
o, love's best habit is in seeming trust, | and 138.11
when all my best doth worship thy defect, 149.11
that in my mind thy worst all best exceeds? 150. 8

stood in doubt | if best were as it was, or best LC 98
doubt | if best were as it was, or best without. 98
in either's aptness, as it best deceives, | to 306
BESTAINED 1 FR 0.0001 REL FR 1 V 0 P
we will not line his thin bestained cloak | with JN 4.03. 24
BEST–BODING 1 FR 0.0001 REL FR 1 V 0 P
palamon | had the best–boding chance. TNK 5.03. 77
BEST–CONDITION'D 1 FR 0.0001 REL FR 1 V 0 P
the best–condition'd and unwearied spirit | in MV 3.02.293
BESTEAD 1 FR 0.0001 REL FR 1 V 0 P
i never saw a fellow worse bestead, | or more 2H6 2.03. 56
BESTIAL 3 FR 0.0003 REL FR 2 V 1 P
luxury | and bestial appetite in change of lust, R3 3.05. 81
now whether it be | bestial oblivion, or some HAM 4.04. 40
part of myself, and what remains is bestial. OTH 2.03.264 P
BESTIR 2 FR 0.0002 REL FR 0 V 2 P
bestir, bestir. TMP 1.01. 4 P
bestir, bestir. 1.01. 4 P
BESTIRR'D 2 FR 0.0002 REL FR 1 V 1 P
and thus hath so bestirr'd thee in thy sleep, 1H4 2.03. 57
no marvel, you have so bestirr'd your valor. LR 2.02. 53 P
BEST–MOVING 1 FR 0.0001 REL FR 1 V 0 P
single you | as our best–moving fair solicitor. LLL 2.01. 29
BESTOW 52 FR 0.0058 REL FR 44 V 8 P
must | bestow upon the eyes of this young couple TMP 4.01. 40
and bestow your luggage where you found it. 5.01.299
worth | comes all the praises that i now bestow) TGV 2.04. 72
i know you have determin'd to bestow her | on 3.01. 13
how and which way i may bestow myself | to be 3.01. 87
bestow thy fawning smiles on equal mates, | and 3.01.158
how should i bestow him? WIV 4.02. 47 P
that chain will i bestow | (be it for nothing ERR 3.01.117
that will i bestow | among my wife and /her 4.01. 16
could find in my heart to bestow it all of your ADO 3.05. 22 P
know | by favors several which they did bestow. LLL 5.02.125
royalty, bestow on me the sense of hearing. 5.02.664 P
of doves that i would bestow upon your worship, MV 2.02.136 P
rosalind, | you will bestow her on orlando here? AYL 5.04. 7
not to bestow my youngest daughter | before i SHR 1.01. 50
daughters, | i here bestow a simple instrument, 2.01. 99
me | in heedfull'st reservation to bestow them, AWW 1.03.225
i know | is free for me to ask, thee to bestow. 2.01.200
i will bestow some precepts of this virgin 3.05.100
for what is yours to bestow is not yours to TN 1.05.188 P
what bestow of him? 3.04. 2
and tell me how you would bestow yourself. JN 3.01.225
we see falstaff bestow himself to–night in his 2H4 2.02.169 P
i will bestow a breakfast to make you friends, H5 2.01. 11 P
my sovereign lord, bestow yourself with speed. 4.03. 68
lord, | we will bestow you in some better place, 1H6 3.02. 88
and justice, | and to bestow your pity on me; H8 2.04. 14
reverend fathers, | bestow your counsels on me. 3.01.182
havings, to bestow | my bounties upon you. 3.02.159
what did you swear you would bestow on me? TRO 5.02. 25
if you'll bestow a small (of what you have COR 1.01.125
ask but mock, bestow | your su'd–for tongues? 2.03.207
will ye bestow them friendly on andronicus? TIT 1.01.219
physic, | and you must needs bestow her funeral; 4.02.163
what you bestow, in him i'll counterpoise, | and TIM 1.01.145
and so bestow these papers as you bade me. JC 1.03.151
fellow, wilt thou bestow thy time with me? 5.05. 61
we'll so bestow ourselves that, seeing unseen, HAM 3.01. 32
so please you, | we will bestow ourselves. 3.01. 43
i will bestow him, and will answer well | the 3.04.176
bestow this place on us a little while. 4.01. 4
and /the fee bestow | upon the foul disease. LR 1.01.163
bosom, and bestow | your needful counsel to our 2.01.126
come, father, i'll bestow you with a friend. 4.06.286
praise couldst thou bestow on a deserving woman OTH 2.01.144 P
i will bestow you where you shall have time | to 3.01. 54
yours, | bestow it at your pleasure, and believe ANT 5.02.182
bestow your love and your affections | upon a PER 2.05. 77
a woman in him | (if he please to bestow it so) TNK 2.04. 10
a steed that emily | did first bestow on him — 5.04. 50
thy soul's thought (all naked) will bestow it; SON 26. 8
and laboring in moe pleasures to bestow them LC 139
BESTOW'D 24 FR 0.0027 REL FR 11 V 13 P
if she be otherwise, 'tis labor well bestow'd. WIV 2.01.240 P
and, i protest to you, bestow'd much on her; 2.02.195 P
and so they shall be both bestow'd. 4.05.107 P
in few, bestow'd her on her own lamentation, MM 3.01.227 P
in what safe place you have bestow'd my money; ERR 1.02. 78
don /pedro hath bestow'd much honor on a young ADO 1.01. 10 P
and the rod he might have bestow'd on you, who, 2.01.230 P
i would she had bestow'd this dotage on me, i 2.03.168 P
surely suit ill spent and labor ill bestow'd. 3.02.100 P
her gifts may henceforth be bestow'd equally. AYL 1.02. 33 P
i would i had bestow'd that time in the tongues TN 1.03. 92 P
the parts that fortune hath bestow'd upon her, 2.04. 83
servingman than ever she bestow'd upon me. 3.02. 7 P
i would have bestow'd the thousand pound i 2H4 5.05. 12 P
large gifts have i bestow'd on learned clerks, 2H6 4.07. 71
or else you would not have bestow'd the heir 3H6 4.01. 56
none so noble | whose life were ill bestow'd, or TRO 2.02.159
and wonder of good deeds evilly bestow'd! TIM 4.03.461
we hear our bloody cousins are bestow'd | in MAC 3.01. 29
my lord, will you see the players well bestow'd? HAM 2.02.523 P
where the dead body is bestow'd, my lord, | we 4.03. 12
old man and 's people | cannot be well bestow'd. LR 2.04.289
in) | bestow'd his lips on that unworthy place, ANT 3.13. 84
the kiss i gave you is bestow'd in vain, | and VEN 771
BESTOWED 8 FR 0.0009 REL FR 8 V 0 P
which (all too much) i have bestowed on thee. TGV 3.01.162
these things being bought and orderly bestowed, MV 2.02.170
how little is the cost i have bestowed | in 3.04. 19
with one consent to have her so bestowed; SHR 4.04. 35
i have bestowed to breed this present peace, 2H4 4.02. 74
and on it have bestowed more contrite tears, H5 4.01.296
thetis' birth–child on the heavens bestowed; PER 4.04. 41
o, that sad breath his spungy lungs bestowed, LC 326
BESTOWING 5 FR 0.0005 REL FR 5 V 0 P
of noble bachelors stand at my bestowing, | o'er AWW 2.03. 53
i of you shall borrow, | err in bestowing it. 3.07. 12
emperor | for not bestowing on him at his asking H8 2.01.163
(which was a sin), yet in bestowing, madam, | he 4.02. 56
and all my powers do their bestowing lose, TRO 3.02. 37
BESTOWS 5 FR 0.0005 REL FR 4 V 1 P
it is a blessing that he bestows on beasts, and ERR 2.02. 79 P
silence bestows that virtue on it, madam. MV 5.01.101
favor, and bestows himself | like a ripe sister; AYL 4.03. 86
sir, can you tell | where he bestows himself? MAC 3.06. 24
lips | as of her tongue she oft bestows on me, OTH 2.01.101
BESTOW'ST 1 FR 0.0001 REL FR 1 V 0 P
that fresh blood which youngly thou bestow'st SON 11. 3
BESTOW'T 1 FR 0.0001 REL FR 1 V 0 P
hers, | she may, i think, bestow't on any man. OTH 4.01. 13
BESTRAUGHT 1 FR 0.0001 REL FR 0 V 1 P
i am not bestraught. SHR in.2. 25 P
BEST–REGARDED 1 FR 0.0001 REL FR 1 V 0 P
i swear | the best–regarded virgins of our clime MV 2.01. 10
BESTREW *(also bestrow)*
BESTREW 1 FR 0.0001 REL FR 1 V 0 P
and discord shall bestrew | the union of your TMP 4.01. 20
BESTREW'D 1 FR 0.0001 REL FR 1 V 0 P
full of rose–water and bestrew'd with flowers, SHR in.1. 56
BESTRID 6 FR 0.0006 REL FR 6 V 0 P
when i bestrid thee in the wars, and took | deep ERR 5.01.192
that horse that thou so often hast bestrid, R2 5.05. 79
him to his horse, | three times bestrid him; 2H6 5.03. 9
he bestrid | an o'erpress'd roman, and i' th' COR 2.02. 92
his legs bestrid the ocean, his rear'd arm ANT 5.02. 82
never bestrid a horse, save one that had | a CYM 4.04. 38
/BESTRIDE 1 FR 0.0001 REL FR 1 V 0 P
/them /he /doth /bestride /a /bleeding /land, 2H4 1.01.207
BESTRIDE 8 FR 0.0009 REL FR 6 V 2 P
thou see me down in the battle and bestride me, 1H4 5.01.121 P
when i bestride him, i soar, i am a hawk; H5 3.07. 15 P
and once again bestride our foaming steeds, 3H6 2.01.183
bestride the rock, the tide will wash you off, 5.04. 31
my wedded mistress saw | bestride my threshold. COR 4.05.118
a lover may bestride the gossamers | that idles ROM 2.06. 18
man, he doth bestride the narrow world | like a JC 1.02.135
like good men | bestride our downfall birthdom. MAC 4.03. 4
BESTRIDES 1 FR 0.0001 REL FR 1 V 0 P
when he bestrides the lazy puffing clouds, | and ROM 2.02. 31
BESTROW *(also bestrew)*
BESTROW 1 FR 0.0001 REL FR 1 V 0 P
we will bestrow the ground. SHR in.2. 40
BEST'S 1 FR 0.0001 REL FR 0 V 1 P
there's best's son, the tanner of wingham — 2H6 4.02. 21 P
BEST–TEMPER'D 2 FR 0.0002 REL FR 2 V 0 P
from the best–temper'd courage in his troops, 2H4 1.01.115
heavens infuse | in their best–temper'd pieces, TNK 1.03. 10
/BE'T 3 FR 0.0003 REL FR 3 V 0 P
/and /be't /of /less /expect | /that /matter TRO 1.03. 70
/if /you /please, | /be't at her father's. OTH 1.03.240
/be't so. 5.01. 22
BE'T 15 FR 0.0017 REL FR 15 V 0 P
be't to fly, | to swim, to dive into the fire, TMP 1.02.190
be't so, lysander. MND 2.02. 39
at the queen's be't; WT 1.02.221
but be't known | (from him that has most cause 2.01. 76
be't so; 2.02. 16
prove as successful to the queen (o be't so!) 3.01. 12
be't so; proceed. H8 2.04. 5
but that you say "be't so," | i speak it in my TRO 4.04.134
be't their comfort | we are coming thither. MAC 4.03.188
then be't so, my good lord. how does the king? LR 4.07. 12
be't as our gods will have't! ANT 2.01. 50
be't so, declare thine office. 3.12. 10
still be't yours, | bestow it at your pleasure, 5.02.181
be't so; CYM 4.02.234
be't when they weav'd the sleided silk | with PER 4.ch. 21
BET 1 FR 0.0001 REL FR 0 V 1 P
that's the french bet against the danish. HAM 5.02.163 P
BETAKE 9 FR 0.0010 REL FR 5 V 4 P
sir, betake thee to thy faith, for seventeen AWW 4.01. 75 P
that defense thou hast, betake thee to't. TN 3.04.220 P
life at any price, betake you to your guard; 3.04.230 P
therefore betake thee | to nothing but despair. WT 3.02.209
treasons, makes me betake me to my heels. 2H6 4.08. 64 P
in, | but every man betake him to his legs. ROM 1.04. 34
therefore each one betake him to his rest; PER 2.03.114
again betake you to your hawthorn house. TNK 3.01. 82
charm, | doth too too oft betake him to retire, LUC 174
BETAKES 2 FR 0.0002 REL FR 2 V 0 P
fight, | and every one to rest himself betakes, LUC 125
drown'd | when as himself to singing he betakes. PP 8.12
BETEEM 2 FR 0.0002 REL FR 2 V 0 P
well | beteem them from the tempest of my eyes. MND 1.01.131
that he might not beteem the winds of heaven HAM 1.02.141
BETHINK 21 FR 0.0023 REL FR 18 V 3 P
here at hand, bethink you of some conveyance. WIV 3.03.127 P
good, good my lord, bethink you: MM 2.02. 87
i will bethink me. come again to–morrow. 2.02.144
'twas bravely done, if you bethink you of it. ADO 5.01.270
and now i do bethink me, so it is — | i came MND 4.01.150
and not bethink me straight of dangerous rocks, MV 1.01. 31
and, that i may be assur'd, i will bethink me. 1.03. 30 P
o noble lord, bethink thee of thy birth, | call SHR in.2. 30
and now i do bethink me, it was she | first told TN 5.01.348
bethink you, father, for the difference | is JN 3.01.204
but i bethink me what a weary way | from R2 2.03. 8
bethink thee on her virtues that surmount, 1H6 5.03.191
o clifford, but bethink thee once again, | and 3H6 1.04. 44
as i bethink me, you should not be king | till 1.04.101
while we bethink a means to break it off. 3.03. 39
bethink you like a careful mother | of the young R3 2.02. 96
bid him bethink | how nice the quarrel was, and ROM 3.01.153
trust to't, bethink you, i'll not be forsworn. 3.05.195
sirs, | it may be i shall otherwise bethink me. JC 4.03.251
bethink yourself wherein you may have offended LR 1.02.159 P
if you bethink yourself of any crime OTH 5.02. 26
BETHINKING 1 FR 0.0001 REL FR 1 V 0 P
thy coward heart with false bethinking grieves." VEN 1024
BETHOUGHT 6 FR 0.0006 REL FR 5 V 1 P
i have bethought me of another fault. MM 5.01.456
he hath better bethought him of his quarrel, and TN 3.04.298 P
marry, well bethought. HAM 1.03. 90
and am bethought | to take the basest and most LR 2.03. 6
bethought what was past, what might succeed. PER 1.02. 83
'tis well bethought. 5.01. 44
BETHUMP'D 1 FR 0.0001 REL FR 1 V 0 P
i was never so bethump'd with words | since i JN 2.01.466
BETID 2 FR 0.0002 REL FR 2 V 0 P
as an hair | betid to any creature in the vessel TMP 1.02. 31
/thee tales | of woeful ages long ago betid; R2 5.01. 42
BETIDE *(also 'tide)*
/BETIDE 1 FR 0.0001 REL FR 1 V 0 P
"what shall /betide the duke of somerset?" 2H6 1.04. 34
BETIDE 9 FR 0.0010 REL FR 9 V 0 P
more health and happiness betide my liege | than R2 3.02. 91
"what shall betide the duke of somerset?" 2H6 1.04. 66
provide | a salve for any sore that may betide. 3H6 4.06. 88
more direful hap betide that hated wretch | that R3 1.02. 17
ill rest betide the chamber where thou liest! 1.02.112
if he were dead, what would betide on me? 1.03. 6
and so betide to me | as well i tender you and 2.04. 71
now help, or woe betide thee evermore! TIT 4.02. 56
neither know i | what is betide to cloten, but CYM 4.03. 40
BETIDETH 2 FR 0.0002 REL FR 2 V 0 P
else | betideth here in absence of thy friend; TGV 1.01. 59
with you, | reaking as little what betideth me, 4.03. 40
BETIME 5 FR 0.0005 REL FR 5 V 0 P
put up thy sword betime, | or i'll so maul you JN 4.03. 98
send succors, lords, and stop the rage betime, 2H6 3.01.285
valentine's day, | all in the morning betime, HAM 4.05. 49
to business that we love we rise betime, | and ANT 4.04. 20
that hostler | must rise betime that cozens him. TNK 5.02. 60
BETIMES 24 FR 0.0027 REL FR 15 V 9 P
all night, and is hang'd betimes in the morning, MM 4.03. 46 P
you let it be proclaim'd betimes i' th' morn. 4.04. 16 P
but the next morn betimes, | his purpose 5.01.101
let me say amen betimes, lest the devil cross my MV 3.01. 19 P
to be a–bed after midnight is to be up betimes, TN 2.03. 2 P
to bed after midnight is to go to bed betimes. 2.03. 9 P
cur'd | of this diseas'd opinion, and betimes, WT 1.02.297
he tires betimes that spurs too fast betimes; R2 2.01. 36
he tires betimes that spurs too fast betimes; 2.01. 36
be with me betimes in the morning, and so good 1H4 2.04.548 P
i rather would have lost my life betimes | than 2H6 3.01.297
away betimes, before his forces join, | and take 3H6 4.08. 62
man, | he should have leave to go away betimes, 5.04. 45
come, let us sup betimes, that afterwards | we R3 3.01.199
let us pay betimes | a moi'ty of that mass of TRO 2.02.106
if these be motives weak, break off betimes, JC 2.01.116
bid him set on his pow'rs betimes before, | and 4.03.307
i will to–morrow | (and betimes i will) to the MAC 3.04.132
good god betimes remove | the means that makes 4.03.162
knows what is't to leave betimes, let be. HAM 5.02.224 P
i'll be with thee betimes. OTH 1.03.375 P
and betimes in the morning i will beseech the 2.03.329 P
that means to be of note, begins betimes. ANT 4.04. 27
or betimes | let's reinforce, or fly. CYM 5.02. 17
BETOKEN 1 FR 0.0001 REL FR 1 V 0 P
this doth betoken | the corse they follow did HAM 5.01.219
BETOKEN'D 1 FR 0.0001 REL FR 1 V 0 P
that ever yet betoken'd | wrack to the seaman, VEN 453
/BETOOK 1 FR 0.0001 REL FR 1 V 0 P
your lord has /betook himself to unknown travels PER 1.03. 34
BETOOK 1 FR 0.0001 REL FR 0 V 1 P
and, as i am a gentleman, betook myself to walk: LLL 1.01.234 P
BETOSSED 1 FR 0.0001 REL FR 1 V 0 P
when my betossed soul | did not attend him as we ROM 5.03. 76
BETRAY 42 FR 0.0047 REL FR 30 V 12 P
do not betray me, sir. WIV 3.03. 75 P
hope, to betray him to another punishment? 3.03.195 P
we'll betray him finely. 5.03. 20 P
those that betray them do no treachery. 5.03. 22
that modesty may more betray our sense | than MM 2.02.168
she did betray me to my own reproof. ERR 5.01. 90
i do betray myself with blushing. maid. LLL 1.02.133 P
these betray nice wenches that would be betray'd 3.01. 23 P
and to betray a she–lamb of a twelvemonth to a AYL 3.02. 81 P
and betray themselves to every modern censure 4.01. 6 P
fear, offer to betray you and deliver all the AWW 3.06. 30 P
'a will betray us all unto ourselves: 4.01. 92
will you undertake to betray the florentine? 4.03.293 P
of the letter that i dropp'd to betray him. TN 3.02. 78 P
how sometimes nature will betray its folly! WT 1.02.151
be yok'd with his that did betray the best! 1.02.419
sleeping neglection doth betray to loss | the 1H6 4.03. 49
have all lim'd bushes to betray thy wings, | and 2H6 2.04. 54
villain, thou wilt betray me, and get a thousand 4.10. 26 P
i know thee not, why then should i betray thee? 4.10. 32
her husband, knave. wouldst thou betray me? R3 1.01.102
nor to betray you any way to sorrow — | you H8 3.01. 56
to betray me. 3.01. 67
wilt thou betray thy noble mistress thus? TIT 4.02.106
hue, that will betray with blushing | the close 4.02.117
shall she live to betray this guilt of ours, | a 4.02.149
now goes | to lay a complot to betray thy foes. 5.02.147
wear them, betray with them. TIM 4.03.147
trifles, to betray 's | in deepest consequence. MAC 1.03.125
would not betray | the devil to his fellow, and 4.03.128
rustling of silks betray thy poor heart to woman LR 3.04. 95 P
yet she must die, else she'll betray more men. OTH 5.02. 6
far off, i will betray | tawny/–finn'd fishes; ANT 2.05. 11
the shes of italy should not betray | mine CYM 1.03. 29
which, to betray, dost, with thine angel's face, PER 4.03. 47
"his shackles will betray him, he'll be taken, TNK 4.01. 70
at great feasts | sought to betray a beauty, but 5.01.103
or sire, | or lain in ambush to betray my life, LUC 233
for those thine eyes betray thee unto mine. 483
how many lambs might the stern wolf betray, | if SON 96. 9
i do betray | my nobler part to my gross body's 151. 5
would yet again betray the fore–betray'd, | and LC 328
BETRAY'D 20 FR 0.0022 REL FR 18 V 2 P
wenches that would be betray'd without these; LLL 3.01. 24 P
camillo has betray'd me; WT 5.01.193
hath willfully betray'd | the lives of those 1H4 1.03. 81
for conclusion, he hath betray'd his followers, H5 3.06.134 P
aid, | unto his dastard foemen is betray'd. 1H6 1.01.144
but dies, betray'd to fortune by your strife. 4.04. 39
trust nobody, for fear you /be betray'd. 2H6 4.04. 58
either betray'd by falsehood of his guard | or 3H6 4.04. 8
poor clarence, by thy guile betray'd to death! R3 5.03.133
being distress'd, was by that wretch betray'd, H8 2.01.110
perfidiously | he has betray'd your business, COR 5.06. 91
hear | that unicorns may be betray'd with trees, JC 2.01.204
alas, he is betray'd and i undone! OTH 5.02. 76
e'er thy tongue | hath so betray'd thine act. ANT 2.07. 78
betray'd i am. 4.12. 24

she hath betray'd me, and shall die the death. 4.14. 26
who are in this | reliev'd, but not betray'd. 5.02. 41
mother was her painting) hath betray'd him. CYM 3.04. 50
though those that are betray'd | do feel the 3.04. 85
betray'd the hours thou gav'st me to repose? LUC 933
BETRAYED 5 FR 0.0005 REL FR 5 V 0 P
are we betrayed thus to thy over–view? LLL 4.03.173
not you by me, but i betrayed to you: 4.03.174
i am betrayed by keeping company | with men like 4.03.177
o, never was there queen | so mightily betrayed! ANT 1.03. 25
this foul egyptian hath betrayed me. 4.12. 10
BETRAYEDST 1 FR 0.0001 REL FR 1 V 0 P
that thou betrayedst polixenes, 'twas nothing — WT 3.02.185
BETRAYING 2 FR 0.0002 REL FR 2 V 0 P
for, by oppressing and betraying me, | thou TIM 4.03.503
for, thou betraying me, i do betray | my nobler SON 151. 5
BETRAYS 2 FR 0.0002 REL FR 2 V 0 P
hopeful son's, his babe's, betrays to slander, WT 2.03. 86
betrays | to sland'rous tongues and wretched LUC 160
BETRIMS 1 FR 0.0001 REL FR 1 V 0 P
brims, | which spungy april at thy hest betrims, TMP 4.01. 65
BETROTH'D 7 FR 0.0008 REL FR 7 V 0 P
ay, and we are betroth'd: TGV 2.04.179
to whom, thyself art witness, | i am betroth'd; 4.02.110
you are betroth'd both to a maid and man. TN 5.01.263
your highness is betroth'd | unto another lady 1H6 5.05. 26
and afterward by substitute betroth'd | to bona, R3 3.07.181
bear his betroth'd from all the world away. TIT 1.01.286
betroth'd and would have married her perforce ROM 5.03.238
BETROTHED 4 FR 0.0004 REL FR 4 V 0 P
angelo to–night shall lie | his old betrothed MM 3.02.279
my lord, | was i betrothed ere i /saw hermia; MND 4.01.172
for husbands, fathers, and betrothed lovers, H5 2.04.108
own, | my true betrothed love, and now my wife? TIT 1.01.406
BETROTHS 1 FR 0.0001 REL FR 0 V 1 P
what is he for a fool that betroths himself to ADO 1.03. 47 P
BETTED 1 FR 0.0001 REL FR 0 V 1 P
him well, and betted much money on his head. 2H4 3.02. 45 P
BETTER *(also bettre, petter)*
/BETTER 4 FR 0.0004 REL FR 3 V 1 P
/like, /if /their /means /are /no /better), HAM 2.02.350 P
/and /tears | /were /like /a /better /way: LR 4.03. 19
/town, | /who /sometime, /in /his /better /tune, 4.03. 39
thy love is /better than high birth to me, SON 91. 9
BETTER 630 FR 0.0712 REL FR 425 V 205 P
i am, nor that i am more better | than prospero, TMP 1.02. 19
my father's of a better nature, sir, | than he 1.02.497
no better than the earth he lies upon, | if he 2.01.281
has done little better than play'd the jack with 4.01.197 P
i must go send some better messenger: TGV 1.01.151
excellent device, was there ever heard a better, 2.01.139
for truth hath better deeds than words to grace 2.02. 18
to learn his wit t' exchange the bad for better. 2.06. 13
better forbear till proteus make return. 2.07. 14
only carry, therefore is she better than a jade. 3.01.277 P
he hath stay'd for a better man than thee. 3.01.376 P
makes me the better to confer with thee. 3.02. 19
would better fit his chamber than this shadow. 4.04.120
but better indeed, when you hold /your peace. 5.02. 18
i better brook than flourishing peopled towns: 5.04. 3
better have none | than plural faith, which is 5.04. 51
i wish'd your venison better, it was ill kill'd. WIV 1.01. 83 P
'twere better for you if it were known in 1.01.118 P
heaven may decrease it upon better acquaintance, 1.01.247 P
ay, for fault of a better. 1.04. 17 P
the better that it pleases your good worship to 1.04.135 P
would you desire better sympathy? 2.01. 9 P
i like it never the better for that. 2.01.179 P
in windsor leads a better life than she does: 2.02.117 P
i think myself in better plight for a lender 2.02.166 P
better three hours too soon than a minute too 2.02.312 P
i know not which pleases me better, that my 3.03.178 P
heaven make you better than your thoughts! 3.03.204 P
can tell you how things go better than i can. 3.04. 65 P
i mean it not, i seek you a better husband. 3.04. 84
he is a better scholar than i thought he was. 4.01. 80 P
better shame than murther. 4.02. 44 P
there is no better way than that they spoke of. 4.04. 16
(the better to /denote her to the doctor, | for 4.06. 39
better a little chiding than a great deal of 5.03. 9 P
yokes | become the forest better than the town? 5.05.108
none better knows than you | how i have ever MM 1.03. 7
tell me true, it shall be the better for you. 2.01.221 P
as the flesh and fortune shall better determine. 2.01.254 P
it, would much better please me | than to demand 2.04. 32
good, | but graciously to know i am no better. 2.04. 77
better it were a brother died at once, | than 2.04.106
warranted need, give him a better proclamation. 3.02.144 P
love talks with better knowledge, and knowledge 3.02.150 P
he shall know you better, sir, if i may live to 3.02.161 P
for my better satisfaction, let me have 4.02.122 P
shrift and advise him for a better place. 4.02.208 P
o, the better, sir; 4.03. 45 P
the better, given me by so holy a man. 4.03.113
he's a better woodman than thou tak'st him for. 4.03.162 P
he was drunk then, my lord, it can be no better. 5.01.189 P
not better than he, by her own report. 5.01.273 P
that life is better life, past fearing death, 5.01.397
you with all, | to buy you a better husband. 5.01.425
lord, | i crave no other, nor no better man. 5.01.426
become much more the better | for being a little 5.01.440
mercy to provide | for better times to come. 5.01.485
am better than thy dear self's better part. ERR 2.02.123
am better than thy dear self's better part. 2.02.123
better cheer may you have, but not with better 3.01. 29
cheer may you have, but not with better heart. 3.01. 29
it is thyself, mine own self's better part: 3.02. 61
ah, but i think him better than i say, | and yet 4.02. 25
he hath indeed better bett'red expectation than ADO 1.01. 15 P
how much better is it to weep at joy than to joy 1.01. 28 P
a bird of my tongue is better than a beast of 1.01.139 P
that she may be the better prepar'd for an 1.02. 22 P
and it better fits my blood to be disdain'd of 1.03. 28 P
i love you the better; the hearers may cry amen. 2.01.105 P
it were a better death than die with mocks, 3.01. 79
and i | believe it better than reportingly. 3.01.116
and aim better at me by that i now will manifest 3.02. 96 P
but it would better fit your honor to change 3.02.115 P
if they make you not then the better answer, you 3.03. 46 P
troth, i think your other rebato were better. 3.04. 7 P
will fashion the event in better shape | than i 4.01.235
that you are little better than false knaves, 4.02. 21 P
and yet a better love than my master. LLL 1.02.120 P
this civil war of wits were much better used 2.01.226
better than remuneration, aleven–pence–farthing 3.01.170 P
than remuneration, aleven–pence–farthing better; 3.01.171 P
did you ever hear better? 4.01. 95
if so, our copper buys no better treasure. 4.03.383
swore | a better speech was never spoke before. 5.02.110
well, better wits have worn plain statute–caps. 5.02.281
conster my speeches better, if you may. 5.02.341
then wish me better, i will give you leave. 5.02.342
that hid the worse and show'd the better face. 5.02.388
and, for the more better assurance, tell them MND 3.01. 19 P
this falls out better than i could devise. 3.02. 35
would you desire lime and hair to speak better? 5.01.166 P
which pyramus, which thisby, is the better: 5.01.319 P
the better part of my affections would | be with MV 1.01. 16
ye well, | we leave you now with better company. 1.01. 59
they would be better if well follow'd. 1.02. 11 P
he hath a horse better than the neapolitan's, a 1.02. 58 P
a better bad habit of frowning than the count 1.02. 59 P
he is worst, he is little better than a beast. 1.02. 89 P
thou mayst with better face | exact the penalty. 1.03.136
lichas play at dice | which is the better man, 2.01. 33
ordered, | and better in my mind not undertook. 2.04. 7
are my deserts no better? 2.09. 60
shall go hard but i will better the instruction. 3.01. 73 P
in my wish | to wish myself much better, yet, 3.02.152
i shall answer that better to the commonwealth 3.05. 37 P
know | a many fools, that stand in better place, 3.05. 68
you cannot better be employ'd, bassanio, | than 4.01.117
acceptance, whose trial shall better publish his 4.01.165 P
the throned monarch better than his crown. 4.01.189
be thought | no better a musician than the wren. 5.01.106
which speed, we hope, the better for our words. 5.01.115
and bid him keep it better than the other. 5.01.255
and i have better news in store for you | than 5.01.274
his horses are bred better, for, besides that AYL 1.01. 11 P
sir, be better employ'd and be naught a while. 1.01. 35 P
ay, better than him i am before knows me. 1.01. 43 P
the courtesy of nations allows you my better, in 1.01. 46 P
all the better; 1.02. 96 P
which may be better supplied when i have made it 1.02.192 P
thou shouldst have better pleas'd me with this 1.02.227
my better parts | are all thrown down, and that 1.02.249
hereafter, in a better world than this, | i 1.02.284
take the part of a better wrastler than myself! 1.03. 22 P
were it not better, | because that i am more 1.03.114
yet fortune cannot recompense me better | than 2.03. 75
when i was at home, i was in a better place, but 2.04. 17 P
provided that you weed your better judgments 2.07. 45
if ever you have look'd on better days, | if 2.07.113
true is it that we have seen better days, | and 2.07.120
but were i not the better part made mercy, | i 3.01. 2
a better instance, i say; 3.02. 57 P
cleopatra's majesty, | atalanta's better part, 3.02.147
i do desire we may be better strangers. 3.02.258 P
and by how much defense is better than no skill, 3.03. 62 P
but i were better to be married of him than of 3.03. 91 P
shepherdess, look on him better, | and be not 3.05. 77
youth, let me /be better acquainted with thee. 4.01. 1 P
i am so; i do love it better than laughing. 4.01. 4 P
a better jointure, i think, than you make a 4.01. 55 P
he hath a rosalind of a better leer than you. 4.01. 67 P
nay, you were better speak first, and when you 4.01. 73 P
or, to thy better understanding, diest; 5.01. 51 P
good plays prove the better by the help of good ep 6 P
trust me, i take him for the better dog. SHR in.1. 25
no better than a poor and loathsome beggar. in.1. 123
the better for him, would i were so too! 1.01.238
pedascule, i'll watch you better yet. 3.01. 50
were it better i should rush in thus: 3.02. 91
'twere well for kate and better for myself. 3.02.120
to put on better ere he go to church. 3.02.126
and better 'twere that both of us did fast, 4.01.173
he that knows better how to tame a shrew, | now 4.01.210
i never saw a better fashion'd gown, | more 4.03.101
or is the adder better than the eel, | because 4.03.177
come, sir, we will better it in pisa. 4.04. 71
better once than never, for never too late. 5.01.150
i hope better. 5.02. 85
nay, i will win my wager better yet, | and show 5.02.116
in her they are the better for their simpleness; AWW 1.01. 44 P
your date is better in your pie and your 1.01.159 P
it was formerly better, marry, yet 'tis a 1.01.163 P
i'll like a maid the better whilst i have a 2.03. 42 P
no better, if you please. 2.03. 84
i have spoken better of you than you have or 2.05. 47 P
for my respects are better than they seem, | and 2.05. 66
when better fall, for your avails they fell. 3.01. 22
i prithee, lady, have a better cheer; 3.02. 64
better 'twere | i met the ravin lion when he 3.02.116
better 'twere | that all the miseries which 3.02.118
none better than to let him fetch off his drum, 3.06. 19 P
to do, and dares better be damn'd than to do't? 3.06. 88 P
sir, been better known to you, when i have held 5.02. 2 P
which better than the first, o dear heaven, 5.03. 71
mistress accost, i desire better acquaintance. TN 1.03. 52 P
she will attend it better in thy youth | than in 1.04. 27
"better a witty fool than a foolish wit." 1.05. 36 P
decays the wise, doth ever make the better fool. 1.05. 77 P
infirmity, for the better increasing your folly! 1.05. 79 P
set kind of fools no better than the fools' 1.05. 89 P
'tis, | poor lady, she were better love a dream. 2.02. 26
he does it with a better grace, but i do it more 2.03. 82 P
my legs do better understand me, sir, than i 3.01. 79 P
how much the better | to fall before the lion 3.01.128
would it be better, madam, than i am? 3.01.143
sought is good, but given unsought is better. 3.01.156
firm, | you should find better dealing. 3.03. 18
may have mercy upon mine, but my hope is better, 3.04.168 P
he hath better bethought him of his quarrel, and 3.04.297 P
if you be no better in your wits than a fool. 4.02. 90 P
sir, the better for my foes and the worse for my 5.01. 12 P
just the contrary: the better for thy friends. 5.01. 14 P
worse for my friends and the better for my foes. 5.01. 23 P
dearest, thou never spok'st | to better purpose. WT 1.02. 89
who have sped the better | by my regard, but 1.02.389
i love you better. 2.01. 6
action i now go on | is for my better grace. 2.01.122
jove send her | a better guiding spirit! 2.03.127
beseech your highness, give us better credit. 2.03.147
better burn it now | than curse it then. 2.03.156
counsel and aid them, for their better safety, 3.02. 20 P
which i receive much better | than to be pitied 3.02.233
since fate (against thy better disposition) 3.03. 28
better not to have had thee than thus to want 4.02. 12 P
sweet sir, much better than i was: 4.03.111 P
for it is | a way to make us better friends, 4.04. 66
yet nature is made better by no mean | but 4.04. 89
he could never come better; 4.04.187 P
no, nor mean better. 4.04.381
if not, my senses, better pleas'd with madness, 4.04.484
the swifter speed the better. 4.04.669
more benefit and grac'd | your kindness better. 5.01. 23
and better us'd, would make her sainted spirit 5.01. 57
time doth boast itself | above a better gone, so 5.01. 97
shrewdly ebb'd, | to say you have seen a better. 5.01.103
to be much sea–sick, and himself little better, 5.02.119 P
a foot of honor better than i was, | but many a JN 1.01.182
madam, i would not wish a better father. 1.01.260
his | but buffets better than a fist of france. 2.01.465
the better act of purposes mistook | is to 3.01.274
and better conquest never canst thou make | than 3.01.290
upon which better part our pray'rs come in, | if 3.01.293
say, | but i will fit it with some better /time. 3.03. 26
as i, | i could give better comfort than you do. 3.04.100
what better matter breeds for you | than i have 3.04.170
with any long'd–for change or better state. 4.02. 8
when workmen strive to do better than well, 4.02. 28
the better foot before. 4.02.170
thou wert better gall the devil, salisbury. 4.03. 95
might | the better arm you to the sudden time 5.06. 26
each day still better other's happiness | until R2 1.01. 22
'tis better hope he is, | for his designs crave 2.02. 43
shouldst please me better wouldst thou weep. 3.04. 20
thou, thou little better thing than earth, 3.04. 78
better far off than, near, be ne'er the near. 5.01. 88
through both | i see some sparks of better hope, 5.03. 21
the better sort, | as thoughts of things divine, 5.05. 11
penury | persuades me i was better when a king; 5.05. 35
truly, little better than one of the wicked. 1H4 1.02. 94 P
by how much better than my word i am, | by so 1.02.210
to you | when you are better temper'd to attend. 1.03.235
christen could be better bit than i have been 2.01. 17 P
he loves his own barn better than he loves our 2.03. 5 P
i never dealt better since i was a man; 2.04.169 P
i shall think the better of myself, and thee, 2.04.273 P
i think there's no man speaks better welsh. 3.01. 49
his health was never better worth than now. 4.01. 27
they'll fill a pit as well as better. 4.02. 67 P
the better part of ours are full of rest. 4.03. 27
the better cherish'd, still the nearer death. 5.02. 15
making you ever better than his praise | by 5.02. 58
better consider what you have to do | than i, 5.02. 76
i better brook the loss of brittle life | than 5.04. 78
i could have better spar'd a better man. 5.04.104
i could have better spar'd a better man. 5.04.104
the better part of valor is discretion, in the 5.04.119 P
in the which better part i have sav'd my life. 5.04.120 P
am afraid he would prove the better counterfeit. 5.04.124 P
with joyful tidings, and, being better hors'd, 2H4 1.01. 35
you should procure him better assurance than 1.02. 31 P
thou tak'st leave, thou wert better be hang'd. 1.02. 89 P
you are as a candle, the better part burnt out. 1.02.156 P
well, god send the prince a better companion! 1.02.199 P
god send the companion a better prince! 1.02.201 P
i were better to be eaten to death with a rust 1.02.219 P
but gladly would be better satisfied | how in 1.03. 6
humors, there's not a better wench in england. 2.01.149 P
i have heard better news. 2.01.166
the tennis–court–keeper knows better than i, for 2.02. 19 P
as to one it pleases me, for fault of a better, 2.02. 42 P
the world keeps the road–way better than thine: 2.02. 59 P
better than i was. hem! 2.04. 30 P
have not seen a hulk better stuff'd in the hold. 2.04. 65 P
and ten times better than the nine worthies. 2.04.220 P
i love thee better than i love e'er a scurvy 2.04.272 P
a better than thou: 2.04.287 P
a soldier is better /accommodated than with a 3.02. 66 P
better accommodated! 3.02. 69 P
it better show'd with you | when that your flock 4.02. 4
shall better speak of you than you deserve. 4.03. 85
had the wit, 'twere better than your dukedom. 4.03. 86 P
thou hast a better place in his affection | than 4.04. 22
to thee it shall descend with better quiet, 4.05.187
better opinion, better confirmation, | for all 4.05.188
quiet, | better opinion, better confirmation, 4.05.188
i' th' court is better than a penny in purse. 5.01. 31 P
that no man could better command his servants. 5.01. 74 P
thou wert better thou hadst strook thy mother, 5.04. 9 P
this poor show doth better, this doth infer the 5.05. 13 P
patience for it and to promise you a better. ep 10 P
us, | we lose the better half of our possession; H5 1.01. 8
never was monarch better fear'd and lov'd | than 2.02. 25
i must leave them, and seek some better service. 3.02. 52 P
plow up all, if there is not better directions. 3.02. 64 P
when there is more better opportunity to be 3.02.138 P
advantage is a better soldier than rashness. 3.06.120 P
i have | almost no better than so many french; 3.06.147
told that by one that knows him better than you. 3.07.104 P
you are the better at proverbs, by how much "a 3.07.121 P
were better than a churlish turf of france. 4.01. 15
not so, my liege, this lodging likes me better, 4.01. 16
then you are a better than the king. 4.01. 43 P
which likes me better than to wish us one. 4.03. 77
and, i warrant you, it is the better for you. 4.08. 66 P
once more, with better heed | to re–survey them, 5.02. 80
the princess is the better englishwoman. 5.02.121 P
i am glad thou canst speak no better english, 5.02.123 P
the elder i wax, the better i shall appear. 5.02.229 P
wear me, if thou wear me, better and better; 5.02.233 P
wear me, if thou wear me, better and better; 5.02.233 P

better far, i guess, | that we do make our 1H6 2.01. 29
did look no better to that weighty charge. 2.01. 62
two blades, which bears the better temper, 2.04. 13
and that i'll prove on better men than somerset, 2.04. 98
will see his burial better than his life. 2.05.121
lord, | we will bestow you in some better place, 3.02. 88
let me persuade you take a better course. 4.01.132
but your discretions better can persuade | than 4.01.158
her father is no better than an earl, | although 5.05. 37
love, | but prosper better than the troyan did. 5.05.106
was better worth than all my father's lands, 2H6 1.03. 86
the cardinal's not my better in the field. 1.03.110
to this gear, the sooner the better. 1.04. 14 P
i saw not better sport these seven years' day; 2.01. 2
been his mother, thou couldst have better told. 2.01. 79
sheriff, farewell, and better than i fare, 2.04.100
which fear, if better reasons can supplant, | i 3.01. 37
for there's no better sign of a brave mind than 4.02. 19 P
better ten thousand base-born cades miscarry 4.08. 47
wife, let's in, and learn to govern better, 4.09. 48
i am far better born than is the king; 5.01. 28
my title's good, and better far than his. 3H6 1.01.130
no, i can better play the orator. 1.02. 2
it, | you love the breeder better than the male. 2.01. 42
your legs did better service than your hands. 2.02.104
now one the better, then another best; 2.05. 10
life | to be no better than a homely swain, | to 2.05. 22
'tis better said than done, my gracious lord. 3.02. 90
such | as are of better person than myself, 3.02.167
and better 'twere you troubled him than france. 3.03.155
'tis better using france than trusting france. 4.01. 42
she better would have fitted me or clarence; 4.01. 54
i like it better than a dangerous honor. 4.03. 17
better do so than tarry and be hang'd. 4.05. 26
i tell ye all | i am your better, traitors as ye 5.05. 36
'tis sin to flatter, "good" was little better: 5.06. 3
my breast can better brook thy dagger's point 5.06. 27
the better for the king of heaven that hath him. R3 1.02.105
did it to help thee to a better husband. 1.02.139
his better doth not breathe upon the earth. 1.02.140
he lives, that loves thee better than he could. 1.02.141
the self-same name, but one of better nature. 1.02.143
(whom god preserve better than you would wish!) 1.03. 59
ay, and much better blood than his or thine. 1.03.125
'tis better, sir, than to be tedious. 1.04. 89 P
who shall reward you better for my life | than 1.04.230
ill news, by'r lady — seldom comes the better. 2.03. 4
better it were they all came by his father, | or 2.03. 23
might better wear their heads | than some that 3.02. 92
the better that your lordship please to ask. 3.02. 97
'tis better with me now | than when thou met'st 3.02. 98
death, | and i in better state than e'er i was. 3.02.104
i never look'd for better at his hands | after 3.05. 50
take thou that, till thou bring better news. 4.04.508
smil'd and said, "the better for our purpose." 5.03.274
abusing better men than they can be | out of a H8 1.03. 28
they rested, | i think would better please 'em. 1.04. 13
will, much better | she ne'er had known pomp! 2.03. 12
verily, | i swear, 'tis better to be lowly born, 2.03. 19
world who shall report he has | a better wife, 2.04.136
both for your honor better and your cause; 3.01. 95
within these forty hours surrey durst better 3.02.253
you to your meditations | how to live better. 3.02.346
nor, i'll assure you, better taken, sir. 4.01. 12
sweet lady, does | deserve our better wishes. 5.01. 26
ween you of better luck, | i mean in perjur'd 5.01.135
and a soul | none better in my kingdom. 5.01.155
and our consent, for better trial of you, | from 5.02. 88
lord, | become a churchman better than ambition; 5.02. 98
he had better starve | than but once think his 5.02.167
if she be fair, 'tis better for her; TRO 1.01. 67 P
better at home, if "would i might" were "may." 1.01.114
troilus is the better man of the two. 1.02. 60 P
no, hector is not a better man than troilus. 1.02. 79 P
'twould not become him, his own's better. 1.02. 91 P
you, i think helen loves him better than paris. 1.02.107 P
smiling becomes him better than any man in all 1.02.122 P
the greeks achilles, a better man than troilus. 1.02.248 P
the lustre of the better shall exceed | by 1.03.360
and it were better parch in afric sun | than in 1.03.369
give him allowance for the better man, | for 1.03.376
our opinion still | that we have better men. 1.03.383
all the better, their fraction is more our wish 2.03. 98 P
think he thinks himself a better man than i am? 2.03.145 P
friend, know me better, i am the lord pandarus. 3.01. 11 P
i hope i shall know your honor better! 3.01. 13 P
the better. 3.03. 61
and better would it fit achilles much | to throw 3.03.207
'twere better she were kiss'd in general. 4.05. 21
the kiss you take is better than you give; 4.05. 38
thy better must. 5.02. 33
'twas one's that lov'd me better than you will. 5.02. 89
in you, | which better fits a lion than a man. 5.03. 38
better be held nor more attain'd than by | a COR 1.01.265
that it was no better than picture-like to hang 1.03. 11 P
is now, she will but disease our better mirth. 1.03.105 P
of no better report than a horse-drench. 2.01.118 P
i wish no better | than have him hold that 2.01.239
know not why, they hate upon no better a ground. 2.02. 11 P
and to make us no better thought of, a little 2.03. 14 P
better it is to die, better to starve, | than 2.03.113
better it is to die, better to starve, | than 2.03.113
this mutiny were better put in hazard | than 2.03.256
not unlike, | each way, to better yours. 3.01. 49
in a better hour, | let what is meet be said it 3.01.168
that leads my use of anger | to better vantage. 3.02. 31
i have deserv'd no better entertainment | in 4.05. 9
and might have been much better, if | he could 4.06. 16
deity than nature, | that shapes man better; 4.06. 92
shall bear | a better witness back than words, 5.03.204
a better head her glorious body fits | than his TIT 1.01.187
sheath, | till you know better how to handle it. 2.01. 42
better than he have worn vulcan's badge. 2.01. 89
the worse to her, the better lov'd of me. 2.03.167
come on, my lords, the better foot before. 2.03.192
that could have better sew'd than philomel. 2.04. 43
in some sort they are better than the tribunes, 3.01. 39
my youth can better spare my blood than you, 3.01.165
but thou art deeper read, and better skill'd; 4.01. 33
coal-black is better than another hue, | in that 4.02. 99
no better? ROM 1.01. 56 P
say "better," here comes one of my master's 1.01. 58 P
yes, better, sir. 1.01. 60 P
my life were better ended by their hate, | than 2.02. 77
(marry, she had a better love to berhyme her), 2.04. 40 P
is not this better now than groaning for love? 2.04. 88 P
though his face be better than any man's, yet 2.05. 40 P
bear thee can afford | no better term than this: 3.01. 61
but love thee better than thou canst devise, 3.01. 69
i thought thy disposition better temper'd. 3.03.115
all, | and all the better is it for the maid. 4.05. 68
by heaven, i love thee better than myself, | for 5.03. 64
that few things loves better | than to abhor TIM 1.01. 59
some better than his value — on the moment 1.01. 79
he wrought better that made the painter, and yet 1.01.198 P
and what better or properer can we call our own 1.02.102 P
farewell, and come with better music. 1.02.246 P
my horse and buy twenty moe | better than he, 2.01. 8
let it not cumber your better remembrance. 3.06. 46 P
may you a better feast never behold, | you knot 3.06. 88
master's fortunes, | "we have seen better days." 4.02. 27
who seeks for better of thee, sauce his palate 4.03. 24
i love thee better now than e'er i did. 4.03.233
that never knew but better, is some burthen: 4.03.267
thou shouldst have lov'd thyself better now. 4.03.310 P
let it go naked, men may see't the better. 5.01. 67
to digest his words | with better appetite. JC 1.02.302
impossible, | yea, get the better of them. 2.01.326
caesar's wife shall meet with better dreams." 2.02. 99
it would become me better than to close | in 3.01.202
your senses, that you may the better judge. 3.02. 17 P
caesar's better parts | shall be crown'd in 3.02. 51
you say you are a better soldier: 4.03. 51
i said an elder soldier, not a better. 4.03. 56
did i say "better"? 4.03. 57
thou lovedst him better | than ever thou lovedst 4.03.106
no man bears sorrow better. portia is dead. 4.03.147
'tis better that the enemy seek us; 4.03.199
good reasons must of force give place to better: 4.03.203
not that we love words better, as you do. 5.01. 28
good words are better than bad strokes, octavius 5.01. 29
go not my horse the better, | i must become a MAC 3.01. 25
better be with the dead, | whom we, to gain our 3.02. 19
'tis better thee without than he within. 3.04. 14
night, and better health | attend his majesty! 3.04.119
better macbeth | than such an one to reign. 4.03. 65
an older and a better soldier none | that 4.03.191
i see lives, the gashes | do better upon them. 5.08. 3
so, | for it hath cow'd my better part of man! 5.08. 18
nor have we herein barr'd | your better wisdoms, HAM 1.02. 15
and pious bonds, | the better to /beguile. 1.03.131
i am sorry that with better heed and judgment 2.01.108
but, better look'd into, he truly found | it was 2.02. 64
by what more dear a better proposer can charge 2.02.286 P
in reputation and profit, was better both ways. 2.02.330 P
your death you were better have a bad epitaph 2.02.525 P
god's bodkin, man, much better: 2.02.529 P
my lord, have better commerce than with honesty? 3.01.108 P
things that it were better my mother had not 3.01.123 P
still better, and worse. 3.02.251 P
i took thee for thy better. 3.04. 32
bad performance, | 'twere better not assay'd; 4.07.152
the king shall drink to hamlet's better breath, 5.02.271
i must love you, and sue to know you better. LR 1.01. 30 P
see better, lear, and let me still remain | the 1.01.158
better thou | hadst not been born than not t' 1.01.233
been born than not t' have pleas'd me better. 1.01.234
thou losest here, a better where to find. 1.01.261
grace, | i would prefer him to a better place. 1.01.274
you can derive from him better testimony of his 1.02. 81 P
i am better than thou art now, i am a fool, thou 1.04.193 P
striving to better, oft we mar what's well. 1.04.346
the better! 2.01. 14
i have seen better faces in my time | than 2.02. 93
when a wise man gives thee better counsel, give 2.04. 75 P
fetch me a better answer. 2.04. 91
disdains your state | better than you yourself. 2.04.150
thou better know'st | the offices of nature, 2.04.177
mend when thou canst, be better at thy leisure, 2.04.229
in a dry house is better than this rain-water 3.02. 11 P
thou wert better in a grave than to answer with 3.04.101 P
what, hath your grace no better company? 3.04.142
here is better than the open air, take it 3.06. 1 P
but better service have i never done you | than 3.07. 74
yet better thus, and known to be contemn'd, 4.01. 1
your sister is the better soldier. 4.05. 3
in better phrase and matter than thou didst. 4.06. 8
methinks y' are better spoken. 4.06. 10
better i were distract, | so should my thoughts 4.06.281
be better suited, | these weeds are memories of 4.07. 6
transported with no worse nor better guard | but OTH 1.01.124
'tis better as it is. 1.02. 6
i could never better stead thee than now. 1.03.339 P
well, | the better shall my purpose work on him. 1.03.391
it had been better you had not kiss'd your three 2.01.172 P
for the better compass of his salt and most 2.01.240 P
her will, recoiling to her better judgment, 3.03.236
i swear 'tis better to be much abus'd | than but 3.03.336
thou hadst been better have been born a dog 3.03.362
your case is better. 4.01. 69
do build on thee a better opinion than ever 4.02.205 P
but that my coat is better than thou know'st. 5.01. 25
yea, curse his better angel from his side, | and 5.02.208
a better never did itself sustain | upon a 5.02.260
but i will hope | of better deeds to-morrow. ANT 1.01. 62
o, excellent, i love long life better than figs. 1.02. 32 P
am i not an inch of fortune better than she? 1.02. 58 P
you were but an inch of fortune better than i, 1.02. 60 P
whose better issue in the war from italy, | upon 1.02. 93
you can do better yet; but this is meetly. 1.03. 81
i could have given less matter | a better ear. 2.01. 32
it should be better he became her guest; 2.02.221
and in our sports my better cunning faints 2.03. 35
better to leave undone, than by our deed 3.01. 14
for better might we | have lov'd without this 3.02. 31
three in egypt | cannot make better note. 3.03. 23
better i were not yours | than /yours so 3.04. 23
i have sixty sails, caesar none better. 3.07. 49
'tis better playing with a lion's whelp | than 3.13. 94
he thinks, being twenty times of better fortune, 4.02. 3
how wouldst thou have paid | my better service, 4.06. 32
but better 'twere | thou fell'st into my fury, 4.12. 40
which in thy absence is | no better than a sty? 4.15. 62
desolation does begin to make | a better life. 5.02. 2
i beseech you all be better known to this CYM 1.04. 31 P
was born, and i pray you be better acquainted. 1.04.122 P
i will consider your music the better; 2.03. 28 P
the very devils cannot plague them better. 2.05. 35
our crows shall fare the better for you; 3.01. 82 P
thou mayst be valiant in a better cause, | but 3.04. 72
'tis all the better, | your valiant britains 3.05. 19
all the better. 3.05. 68
as 'tis no better reckon'd, but of those | who 3.06. 54
you shall have better cheer | ere you depart, 3.06. 66
or if not, | nothing to be were better. 4.02.368
than be so, | better to cease to be. 4.04. 31
and give me leave, | i'll take the better care; 4.04. 45
must murther wives much better than themselves 5.01. 4
yet am i better | than one that's sick o' th' 5.04. 4
i repent, | i cannot do it better than in gyves, 5.04. 14
this man is better than the man he slew, | as 5.05.302
you, live, | and deal with others better. 5.05.420
a better prince and benign lord, | that will PER 2.ch. 3
i would wish no better office than to be beadle. 2.01. 92 P
and if that ever my low fortunes better, | i'll 2.01.142
he had need mean better than his outward show 2.02. 48
now, by the gods, he could not please me better. 2.03. 72
protest my ears were never better fed | with 2.05. 27
ay, and better too; 4.02. 37 P
so, 'tis the better for you that your resorters 4.06. 23 P
since they do better thee in their command. 4.06.162
any of these ways are yet better than this; 4.06.177
i/'d wish no better choice, and think me rarely 5.01. 69
but her better stars | brought her to meteline, 5.03. 9
now i know you better. 5.03. 37
i am given out to be better lin'd than it can TNK 2.01. 5 P
(better the red-ey'd god of war nev'r /ware), 2.02. 21
of any two that lov'd | better than we do, 2.02.113
and three better lads nev'r danc'd | under green 2.03. 38
i lov'd my lips the better ten days after. 2.04. 26
and somewhat better than your rank i'll use you. 2.05. 43
i like him better, prince, i shall not then 2.05. 47
durst better have endur'd cold iron than done it 2.06. 10
and for a preface, | i never heard a better. 3.05.151
take my sword, i hold it better. 3.06. 89
better they fall by th' law than one another. 3.06.225
which you'll hear of | at better time. 4.01. 30
two greater and two better never yet | made 4.02. 62
better, o' my conscience, | was never soldier's 4.02. 87
dreaming of another world and a better; 4.03. 5 P
twenty times had been far better, | for there 5.02. 7
it is much better | i am not there. 5.03. 64
better never born | than minister to such harm! 5.03. 65
that was thus good | encount'red yet his better. 5.03.123
i dare say, many a better, to prolong | your old ep 16
are better proof than thy spear's point can VEN 626
and that his beauty may the better thrive, 1011
while thou on tereus descants better skill. LUC 1134
to live or die which of the twain were better, 1154
the better so to clear her | from that suspicion 1320
words, till action might become them better. 1323
my better angel is a man (right fair), | my PP 2. 3
evil | tempteth my better angel from my side, 2. 6
brought | to march in ranks of better equipage; SON 32.12
but since he died and poets better prove, 32.13
sing, | when thou art all the better part of me? 39. 2
whether we are mended, or whe'er better they, 59.11
my spirit is thine, the better part of me. 74. 8
knowing a better spirit doth use your name, 80. 2
and their gross painting might be better us'd 82.13
comes home again, on better judgment making. 87.12
all these i better in one general best. 91. 8
i see a better state to me belongs | than that 92. 7
that did not better for my life provide | than 111. 3
true | that better is by evil still made better, 119.10
true | that better is by evil still made better, 119.10
'tis better to be vile than vile esteemed, 121. 1
better becomes the grey cheeks of th' east, 132. 6
if i might teach thee wit, better it were, 140. 5
the better angel is a man right fair, | the 144. 3
evil | tempteth my better angel from my /side, 144. 6

/BETTER'D 1 FR 0.0001 REL FR 1 V 0 P
but since he is /better'd, we have therefore HAM 5.02.263

BETTER'D 3 FR 0.0003 REL FR 2 V 1 P
which, better'd with his own learning, the MV 4.01.158 P
her best is better'd with a more delight. VEN 78
then better'd that the world may see my pleasure SON 75. 8

BETTERED 1 FR 0.0001 REL FR 1 V 0 P
which i have bettered rather than decreas'd. SHR 2.01.118

BETTERING 1 FR 0.0001 REL FR 1 V 0 P
to closeness and the bettering of my mind | with TMP 1.02. 90

/BETTERS 1 FR 0.0001 REL FR 1 V 0 P
/when /we /our /betters /see /bearing /our /woes LR 3.06.102

BETTERS 11 FR 0.0012 REL FR 10 V 1 P
your betters, sir. AYL 2.04. 68
your betters have endur'd me say my mind, | and SHR 4.03. 75
under the degree of my betters, and yet i will TN 1.03.118 P
what you do | still betters what is done. WT 4.04.136
our country manners give our betters way. JN 1.01.156
but as my betters are | that led me hither. 2H4 4.03. 65
ambitious warwick, let thy betters speak. 2H6 1.03.109
all in this presence are thy betters, warwick. 1.03.111
the sons of york, thy betters in their birth, 5.01.119
if our betters play at that game, we must not TIM 1.02. 12
rabble make servants of their betters. LR 1.04.256

/BETTING 1 FR 0.0001 REL FR 0 V 1 P
/shillings /i /won /from /you /at /betting? H5 2.01.106 P

BETTING 1 FR 0.0001 REL FR 0 V 1 P
me the eight shillings i won of you at betting? H5 2.01. 95 P

BETTRE *(also better, petter)*

BETTRE 1 FR 0.0001 REL FR 0 V 1 P
your majesty entendre bettre que moi. H5 5.02.264 P

BETT'RED 1 FR 0.0001 REL FR 0 V 1 P
hath indeed better bett'red expectation than you ADO 1.01. 16 P

BETT'RING 2 FR 0.0002 REL FR 2 V 0 P
bett'ring thy loss makes the bad causer worse; R3 4.04.122
compare them with the bett'ring of the time, SON 32. 5
BETUMBLED 1 FR 0.0001 REL FR 1 V 0 P
said, from her betumbled couch she starteth, LUC 1037
BETWEEN *(also 'tween)*
/BETWEEN 5 FR 0.0005 REL FR 2 V 3 P
/it /is /further /agreed /between /them, that 2H6 1.01. 50 P
/get /some /little /knife /between /thy /teeth, TIT 3.02. 16
/but /that /between /us /we /can /kill /a /fly 3.02. 77
/the /means /of /meeting /between /him and my HAM 2.02.212 P
/as /of /unnaturalness /between /the /child /and LR 1.02.144 P
BETWEEN 241 FR 0.0272 REL FR 150 V 91 P
to have no screen between this part he play'd TMP 1.02.107
weigh'd between loathness and obedience, at 2.01.131
rain grace | on that which breeds between 'em! 3.01. 76
the match between sir thurio and my daughter? TGV 3.02. 23
to make atonements and compremises between you.
WIV 1.01. 34 P
and desire a marriage between master abraham and 1.01. 56 P
i would i could do a good office between you. 1.01.100 P
we three to hear it and end it between them. 1.01.142 P
his hands as any is between this and his head. 1.04. 26 P
a fray to be fought between sir hugh the welsh 2.01.200 P
absence from his house between ten and eleven. 2.02. 84 P
look you, he may come and go between you both; 2.02.125 P
say i shall be with her between ten and eleven; 2.02.264 P
is such a league between my goodman and he! 3.02. 25 P
about a match between anne page and my cousin 3.02. 57 P
more to come to her, between eight and nine. 3.05. 46 P
do so. between nine and ten, say'st thou? 3.05. 53 P
what hath pass'd between me and ford's wife? 3.05. 62 P
there went but a pair of shears between us. MM 1.02. 28 P
as there may between the lists and the velvet. 1.02. 29 P
what hath pass'd between you and your sister. 3.01.161 P
between which time of the contract and limit of 3.01.215 P
that he was begot between two stock–fishes. 3.02.109 P
between you 'greed concerning her observance? 4.01. 41
but not a thousand marks between you both. ERR 1.02. 84
between you, i shall have a holy head. 2.01. 80
the salt rheum that ran between france and it. 3.02.128 P
between them they will kill the conjurer. 5.01.177
meet but there's a skirmish of wit between them. ADO 1.01. 64 P
bear it for a difference between himself and his 1.01. 69 P
just in the midway between him and benedick: 2.01. 7 P
"benedick" and "beatrice" between the sheet? 2.03.137 P
about all the hot–bloods between fourteen and 3.03.132 P
in faith, honest as the skin between his brows. 3.05. 12 P
what hath pass'd between you and claudio. 5.02. 48 P
between lord perigort and the beauteous heir LLL 2.01. 41
for what is inward between us, let it pass. 5.01. 97 P
and stand between her back, sir, and the fire, 5.02.476
flying between the cold moon and the earth, MND 2.01.156
she hath made compare | between our statures: 3.02.291
hours | between /our after–supper and bed–time? 5.01. 34
that stand'st between her father's ground and 5.01.175
now is the moon used between the two neighbors. 5.01.206 P
a bergomask dance between two of our company? 5.01.353 P
was | between these woolly breeders in the act, MV 1.03. 83
is very well parted between my master shylock 2.02.149 P
is more difference between thy flesh and hers 3.01. 39 P
thy flesh and hers than between jet and ivory, 3.01. 40 P
more between your bloods than there is between 3.01. 40 P
your bloods than there is between red wine and 3.01. 41 P
puts bars between the owners and their rights! 3.02. 19
all debts are clear'd between you and i, if i 3.02.319 P
and speak between the change of man and boy 3.04. 66
cause in controversy between the jew and antonio 4.01.155 P
with a young maid between the contract of her AYL 3.02.314 P
for they sleep between term and term, and then 3.02.332 P
between the pale complexion of true love | and 3.04. 53
between the acres of the rye, | with a hey, and 5.03. 22
that between you and the women the play may ep 17 P
let specialties be therefore drawn between us, SHR 2.01.126
of love between your daughter and himself; 4.04. 27
is there any unkindness between my lord and you,
AWW 2.05. 32 P
is heavy news within between two soldiers and my 3.02. 33 P
and between these main parcels of dispatch 4.03. 90 P
we have this dialogue between the fool and the 4.03. 98 P
i did go between them, as i said, but more than 5.03.258 P
deadly divorce step between me and you! 5.03.318
to see a huswife take thee between her legs, and TN 1.03.103 P
with him in standing water, between boy and man. 1.05.159 P
rest | between the elements of air and earth, 1.05.275
compare | between that love a woman can bear me 2.04.102
that can be can come between me and the full 3.04. 81 P
his employment between his lord and my niece 3.04.187 P
hath newly pass'd between this youth and me. 5.01.155
hath been between this lady and this lord. 5.01.258
we'll part the time between 's then; WT 1.02. 18
come between | ere you can say she's honest: 2.01. 75
i would there were no age between ten and 3.03. 59 P
is nothing in the between but getting wenches 3.03. 61 P
scene such growing | as you had slept between. 4.01. 17
was not full a month | between their births. 5.01.118
this is a match, | and made between 's by vows. 5.03.138
that e'er i put between your holy looks | my ill 5.03.148
shores | between my father and my mother lay, JN 1.01.106
between our kingdoms and our royal selves, | and 3.01.232
and go | between his purpose and his conscience, 4.02. 77
between my conscience and my cousin's death. 4.02.248
i'll make a peace between your soul and you. 4.02.250
fought | between compulsion and a brave respect! 5.02. 44
between this chastis'd kingdom and myself, | and 5.02. 84
grief, | or else he never would compare between. R2 2.01.185
towns | between that royal field of shrewsbury 2H4 in 34
as common as the way between saint albons and 2.02.167 P
i'll canvass thee between a pair of sheets. 2.04.225 P
hair will turn scales between their haberdepois. 2.04.254 P
opener and intelligencer | between the grace, 4.02. 21
ours, and here between the armies | let's drink 4.02. 62
already temp'ring between my finger and my thumb 4.03.130 P
between his greatness and thy other brethren. 4.04. 26
the river hath thrice flowed, no ebb between, 4.04.125
between the floods of sala and of /elbe; H5 1.02. 45
good bardolph, put thy face between his sheets, 2.01. 83 P
'a parted ev'n just between twelve and one, ev'n 2.03. 12 P
between the promise of his greener days | and 2.04.136
let it be a quarrel between us, if you live. 4.01.205 P
in the comparisons between macedon and monmouth, 4.07. 24 P
follow, and see there be no harm between them. 4.07.182
to order peace between them — and omit | all 5.pr. 39
and i, between saint denis and saint george, 5.02.207 P
thrust in between the /paction of these kingdoms 5.02.365
judge you, my lord of warwick, then between us. 1H6 2.04. 10
between two hawks, which flies the higher pitch, 2.04. 11
between two dogs, which hath the deeper mouth, 2.04. 12
between two blades, which bears the better 2.04. 13
between two horses, which doth bear him best, 2.04. 14
between two girls, which hath the merriest eye 2.04. 15
shall send between the red rose and the white 2.04.126
between the realms of england and of france. 5.01. 6
and peace established between these realms. 5.03. 92
between our sovereign and the french king 2H6 1.01. 41
it is agreed between the french king charles, 1.01. 43 P
it is further agreed between them, that the 1.01. 57 P
dying with mother's dug between its lips; 3.02.393
clapp'd his tail between his legs and cried; 5.01.154
for one to thrust his hand between his teeth, 3H6 1.04. 57
and yet, between my soul's desire and me — 3.02.128
for many lives stand between me and home; 3.02.173
between the duke of gloucester and your brothers
R3 1.03. 37
and between them and my lord chamberlain, | and 1.03. 38
so that between their titles and low name 1.04. 82
between these swelling wrong–incensed peers. 2.01. 52
if ever any grudge were lodg'd between us; 2.01. 66
and stand between two churchmen, good my lord — 3.07. 48
hath he set bounds between their love and me? 4.01. 20
the peace between the french and us not values H8 1.01. 88
pray sit between these ladies. 1.04. 24
a separation | between the king and katherine? 2.01.149
crack'd the league | between us and the emperor 2.02. 25
weighty difference | between the king and you, 3.01. 59
a league between his highness and ferrara. 3.02.323
there were no more comparison between the women!
TRO 1.01. 43 P
gone between and between, but small thanks for 1.01. 71 P
gone between and between, but small thanks for 1.01. 72 P
between our ilium and where she /resides, | let 1.01.101
what, not between troilus and hector? 1.02. 63 P
cut, | bounding between the two moist elements, 1.03. 41
(between whose endless jar justice resides) 1.03.117
midway between your tents and walls of troy, 1.03.278
to use between your strangeness and his pride, 3.03. 45
there is between my will and all offenses | a 5.02. 53
'tis sworn between us we shall ever strike COR 1.02. 35
in hearing a cause between an orange–wife and a 2.01. 70 P
are hearing a matter between party and party, if 2.01. 73 P
that we labor'd | (no impediment between) but 2.03.228
i shall, between this and supper, tell you most 4.03. 40 P
and vows revenge as spacious as between | the 4.06. 68
all this while | between the child and parent. 5.03. 56
there is differency between a grub and a 5.04. 11 P
doth rise and fall between thy rosed lips, TIT 2.04. 24
agree between you, i will spare my hand. 3.01.183
thou my hand, sweet wench, between thy teeth. 3.01.282
myself, | set deadly enmity between two friends, 5.01.131
the quarrel is between our masters and us their ROM 1.01. 19 P
come between us, good benvolio, my wits faints. 2.04. 67 P
why the dev'l came you between us? 3.01.103 P
and usurers' men, bawds between gold and want! TIM 2.02. 60 P
between the acting of a dreadful thing | and the JC 2.01. 63
there is some grudge between 'em; 4.03.125
nor keep peace between | th' effect and /it! MAC 1.05. 46
but god above | deal between thee and me! 4.03.121
what is between you? HAM 1.03. 98
for your desire to know what is between us, 1.05.139
between who? 2.02.194 P
as i do crawling between earth and heaven? 3.01.127 P
a fair thought to lie between maids' legs. 3.02.118 P
and never come mischance between us twain! 3.02.228
i could interpret between you and your love, if 3.02.246 P
that your grace hath screen'd and stood between 3.04. 3
o, step between her and her fighting soul. 3.04.113
between the chaste unsmirched brow | of my true 4.05.120
as love between them like the palm might 5.02. 40
between the pass and fell incensed points | of 5.02. 61
popp'd in between th' election and my hopes, 5.02. 65
that in a dozen passes between yourself and him, 5.02.166 P
come not between the dragon and his wrath; LR 1.01.122
to confirm, | this coronet part between you. 1.01.139
of leave–taking between france and him. 1.01.303 P
my boy, between a bitter fool and a sweet one? 1.04.137 P
there is division between the dukes, and a worse 3.03. 9 P
the conflict be sore between that and my blood. 3.05. 23 P
this trusty servant | shall pass between us. 4.02. 19
whose face between her forks presages snow; 4.06.119
this broken joint between you and her husband OTH 2.03.322 P
o yes, and went between us very oft. 3.03.100
there's fall'n between him and my lord | an 4.01.224
each syllable that breath made up between them. 4.02. 5
will fashion to fall out between twelve and one) 4.02.236 P
your attempt, and he shall fall between us. 4.02.238 P
what malice was between you? 5.01.102
though, between them and a great cause, they ANT 1.02.139 P
to the time o' th' year between the extremes 1.05. 51
but between both. 1.05. 58
pregnant they should square between themselves, 2.01. 45
to enforce no further | the griefs between ye: 2.02.100
therefore | make space enough between you. 2.03. 24
may be written | and seal'd between us. 2.06. 59
the greater war between him and his discretion. 2.07. 9 P
her led | between her brother and mark antony. 3.03. 10
if this division chance, ne'er stood between, 3.04. 13
you requested, | yourself shall go between 's. 3.04. 25
and throw between them all the food thou hast, 3.05. 14
their lust | since then hath made between them. 3.06. 8
to let him breathe between the heavens and earth 3.12. 14
it was divided | between her heart and lips. 4.14. 33
i would they had not come between us. CYM 1.02. 22 P
let there be covenants drawn between 's. 1.04.143 P
fiends of hell | divide themselves between you! 2.04.130
your lady seeks my life, come you between, | and PER 4.01. 89
child, and stood between | her and her fortunes. 4.03. 31
that i would pluck | and put between my breasts TNK 1.03. 67
and all the ties between us, i disclaim | if 2.02.173
and pitch between her arms to anger thee. 2.02.217
the matter's too far driven between him | and 2.03. 43
that i, poor man, might eftsoons come between, 3.01. 12
lest this match between 's | be cross'd ere met. 3.01. 97
i am persuaded this question, sick between 's, 3.01.113
willow," and between | ever was "palamon, fair 4.01. 80
i will, between the passages of this project, 4.03. 98 P
blow that nearness out that flames between ye, 5.01. 10
that the sense | could not be judge between 'em. 5.03.128
so it far'd | good space between these kinsmen; 5.03.129
warm, | and lo i lie between that sun and thee; VEN 194
done, | between this heavenly and earthly sun. 198
o, what a war of looks was then between them! 355
lest between them both it should be kill'd, LUC 74
arm, | is madly toss'd between desire and dread; 171
the locks between her chamber and his will, 302
between whose hills her head entombed is; 390
as if between them twain there were no strife, 405
between each kiss her oaths of true love PP 7. 8
so between them love did shine, | that the PHT 33
BETWIXT *(also 'twixt)*
/BETWIXT 1 FR 0.0001 REL FR 1 V 0 P
/betwixt /thy /begging /and /my /meditation. R3 4.02.115
BETWIXT 55 FR 0.0062 REL FR 42 V 13 P
speech of marriage | betwixt myself and her; MM 5.01.218
a kind of merry war betwixt signior benedick and ADO 1.01. 62 P
out at your window betwixt twelve and one? 4.01. 84
the sealing–day betwixt my love and me | for MND 1.01. 84
my blood, were there twenty brothers betwixt us. AYL 1.01. 49 P
betwixt the constant red and mingled damask. 3.05.123
when from the first to last betwixt us two 4.03.139
put such difference betwixt their two estates; AWW 1.03.112 P
share the advice betwixt you. 2.01. 3
great difference betwixt our bohemia and your WT 1.01. 4 P
and there rooted betwixt them then such an 1.01. 23 P
leave out | betwixt the prince and beggar. 2.01. 87
honor, i | will stand betwixt you and danger. 2.02. 64
betwixt the firmament and it you cannot thrust a 3.03. 85 P
things known betwixt us three, i'll write you 4.04.560
need | some messenger betwixt me and the peers, JN 4.02.179
can arbitrate this cause betwixt us twain; R2 1.01. 50
made a divorce betwixt his queen and him, 3.01. 12
me, | and then betwixt me and my married wife. 5.01. 73
betwixt that holmedon and this seat of ours; 1H4 1.01. 65
corse | betwixt the wind and his nobility. 1.03. 45
betwixt my love and your high majesty. 1.03. 69
as is the difference betwixt day and night | the 3.01.217
thee in the night betwixt tavern and tavern; 3.03. 43 P
and the villains march wide betwixt the legs, as 4.02. 40 P
borne | betwixt our armies true intelligence. 5.05. 10
betwixt the stout lord talbot and the french. 1H6 1.01.106
truce | betwixt ourselves and all our followers. 3.01.139
this late dissension grown betwixt the peers 3.01.188
law | argu'd betwixt the duke of york and him; 4.01. 96
betwixt ourselves let us decide it then. 4.01.119
mouths | to raise a mutiny betwixt yourselves. 4.01.131
betwixt our nation and the aspiring french; 5.04. 99
that trudge betwixt the king and mistress shore. R3 1.01. 73
difference | betwixt you and the cardinal. H8 1.01.102
his fears were that the interview betwixt 1.01.180
could | come pat betwixt too early and too late 2.03. 84
have blown this coal betwixt my lord and me — 2.04. 79
there is, betwixt that smile we would aspire to, 3.02.368
the cause betwixt her and this great offender. 5.02.156
up a matter of brawl betwixt my uncle and one of TIT 4.03. 93 P
themselves | betwixt your eyes and night? JC 2.01. 99
to come betwixt our sentence and our power, LR 1.01.170
i would have all well betwixt you. 2.04.120
posts shall be swift and intelligent betwixt us. 3.07. 11 P
i could distinguish betwixt a benefit and an OTH 1.03.313 P
and a frail vow betwixt an erring barbarian and 1.03.355 P
is set | betwixt us as the cement of our love, ANT 3.02. 29
that have my heart parted betwixt two friends 3.06. 77
which i had set | betwixt two charming words, CYM 1.03. 35
conditions, let us have articles betwixt us. 1.04.157 P
live, like diana's priest, betwixt cold sheets, 1.06.133
betwixt a father by thy step–dame govern'd, | a 2.01. 58
your prayers, and betwixt ye | i part my wishes. TNK 5.01. 16
betwixt mine eye and heart a league is took, SON 47. 1
BEVEL 1 FR 0.0001 REL FR 1 V 0 P
may be straight though they themselves be bevel; SON 121.11
BEVERAGE 1 FR 0.0001 REL FR 1 V 0 P
if from me he have wholesome beverage, | account
WT 1.02.346
BEVIS 1 FR 0.0001 REL FR 1 V 0 P
enough, got credit, | that bevis was believ'd. H8 1.01. 38
BEVY 2 FR 0.0002 REL FR 2 V 0 P
in all this noble bevy, has brought with her H8 1.04. 4
i'll bring a bevy, | a hundred black–ey'd maids TNK 4.01. 71
BEWAIL 2 FR 0.0002 REL FR 2 V 0 P
like tears that did their own disgrace bewail. MND 4.01. 56
a one, | which to this hour bewail the injury, COR 5.06.152
BEWAILED 1 FR 0.0001 REL FR 1 V 0 P
lest my bewailed guilt should do thee shame, SON 36.10
BEWAILING 1 FR 0.0001 REL FR 1 V 0 P
robb'd this bewailing land | of noble buckingham H8 3.02.255
BEWAILS 1 FR 0.0001 REL FR 1 V 0 P
even so myself bewails good gloucester's case 2H6 3.01.217
BEWARE 30 FR 0.0034 REL FR 23 V 7 P
keep a care, | shake off slumber, and beware. TMP 2.01.304
would keep from my heels, and beware of an ass. ERR 3.01. 18
like the parrot, "beware the rope's end." 4.04. 42 P
cause, | but, since i am a dog, beware my fangs. MV 3.03. 7
therefore beware my censure, and keep your AYL 4.01.195 P
if i be waspish, best beware my sting. SHR 2.01.210
beware of being captives | before you serve. AWW 2.01. 21
beware of them, diana; 3.05. 18 P
my liege, beware! R2 5.03. 39
but beware instinct — the lion will not touch 1H4 2.04.271 P
priest, beware your beard, | i mean to tug it 1H6 1.03. 47
clarence, beware! 3H6 5.06. 84
have not to do with him, beware of him; R3 1.03.291
the king loves you, | beware you lose it not. H8 3.01.172
o, then beware! TRO 3.03.228
and beat the messenger who bids beware | of what
COR 4.06. 55

young lords, beware! TIT 2.01. 69
but if you hunt these bear–whelps, then beware, 4.01. 96
beware the ides of march. JC 1.02. 18
a soothsayer bids you beware the ides of march. 1.02. 19
beware the ides of march. 1.02. 23
"caesar, beware of brutus; 2.03. 1 P
beware macduff, | beware the thane of fife. MAC 4.01. 71
beware macduff, | beware the thane of fife. 4.01. 72
beware | of entrance to a quarrel, but being in, HAM 1.03. 65
bear't that th' opposed may beware of thee. 1.03. 67
beware my follower. LR 3.04.140 P
pray, innocent, and beware the foul fiend. 3.06. 8 P
o, beware, my lord, of jealousy! OTH 3.03.165
"hadst thou but bid beware, then he had spoke, VEN 943

BEWEEP 4 FR 0.0004 REL FR 4 V 0 P
darkness, | i do beweep to many simple gulls — R3 1.03.327
and i'll beweep these comforts, worthy senators. TIM 5.01.158
beweep this cause again, i'll pluck ye out, LR 1.04.302
eyes, | i all alone beweep my outcast state, SON 29. 2

BEWEPT 3 FR 0.0003 REL FR 3 V 0 P
it cannot be, for he bewept my fortune, | and R3 1.04.244
i have bewept a worthy husband's death, | and 2.02. 49
which bewept to the ground did not go | with HAM 4.05. 39

BEWET 1 FR 0.0001 REL FR 1 V 0 P
his napkin, with /his true tears all bewet, TIT 3.01.146

BEWHOR'D 1 FR 0.0001 REL FR 1 V 0 P
alas, iago, my lord hath so bewhor'd her, OTH 4.02.115

BEWITCH 2 FR 0.0002 REL FR 2 V 0 P
not his smoothing words | bewitch your hearts. 2H6 1.01.157
grant that warwick's words bewitch him not! 3H6 3.03.112

BEWITCH'D 9 FR 0.0010 REL FR 7 V 2 P
this man hath bewitch'd the bosom of my child. MND 1.01. 27
pray god he be not bewitch'd! TN 3.04.101 P
and yet i am bewitch'd with the rogue's company. 1H4 2.02. 17 P
either she hath bewitch'd me with her words, 1H6 3.03. 58
look how i am bewitch'd; R3 3.04. 68
tell us what sinon hath bewitch'd our ears, | or TIT 5.03. 85
thou hast bewitch'd my daughter, and thou art PER 2.05. 49
honest fear, bewitch'd with lust's foul charm, LUC 173
consents bewitch'd, ere he desire, have granted, LC 131

BEWITCHED 1 FR 0.0001 REL FR 1 V 0 P
again, | alike bewitched by the charm of looks; ROM 2.pr. 6

BEWITCHING 1 FR 0.0001 REL FR 1 V 0 P
bewitching like the wanton mermaids' songs, VEN 777

BEWITCHMENT 1 FR 0.0001 REL FR 0 V 1 P
counterfeit the bewitchment of some popular man,
COR 2.03.101 P

/BEWRAY 1 FR 0.0001 REL FR 1 V 0 P
/and /thyself /bewray | /when /false /opinion, LR 3.06.111

BEWRAY 6 FR 0.0006 REL FR 6 V 0 P
comes the queen, whose looks bewray her anger. 3H6 1.01.211
and not bewray thy treason with a blush? 3.03. 97
and state of bodies would bewray what life | we COR 5.03. 95
write down thy mind, bewray thy meaning so, TIT 2.04. 3
did not thy hue bewray whose brat thou art, 5.01. 28
he did bewray his practice, and receiv'd | this LR 2.01.107

BEWRAY'D 3 FR 0.0003 REL FR 3 V 0 P
bewray'd the faintness of my master's heart. 1H6 4.01.107
longing to hear the hateful foe bewray'd. LUC 1698
be it said, | to hear her secrets so bewray'd. PP 18.54

/BEYOND 1 FR 0.0001 REL FR 1 V 0 P
thrice fam'd beyond, /beyond all erudition; TRO 2.03.243

BEYOND 67 FR 0.0075 REL FR 59 V 8 P
for our escape | is much beyond our loss. TMP 2.01. 3
it is — which is indeed almost beyond credit — 2.01. 60 P
even | ambition cannot pierce a wink beyond, 2.01.242
she that dwells | ten leagues beyond man's life; 2.01.247
i, | beyond all limit of what else i' th' world, 3.01. 72
i' th' filthy–mantled pool beyond your cell, 4.01.182
rejoice | beyond a common joy, and set it down 5.01.207
and such daub'ry as this is, beyond our element; WIV 4.02.178 P
for so soon as i came beyond eton, they threw me 4.05. 67 P
beyond imagination is the wrong | that she this ERR 5.01.201
hath borne himself beyond the promise of his age ADO 1.01. 14 P
and shrowd and froward, so beyond all measure, SHR 1.02. 90
and thou dost | (and that beyond commission), WT 1.02.144
for the harlot king | is quite beyond mine arm, 2.03. 5
sir, their speed | hath been beyond accompt. 2.03.198
if one jot beyond | the bound of honor, or in 3.02. 50
and beyond the imagination of his neighbors, is 4.02. 39 P
beyond the infinite and boundless reach | of JN 4.03.117
drives him beyond the bounds of patience. 1H4 1.03.200
all westward, wales beyond the severn shore, 3.01. 75
of an house | beyond his power to build it, who, 2H4 1.03. 59
stretches itself beyond the hour of death. 4.04. 57
my gracious lord, you look beyond him quite: 4.04. 67
and did seat the french | beyond the river sala, H5 1.02. 63
beyond the river we'll encamp ourselves, | and 3.06.171
the dolphin hath prevail'd beyond the seas, 2H6 1.03.125
enjoys, | is far beyond a prince's delicates — 3H6 2.05. 51
they did perform | beyond thought's compass, H8 1.01. 36
and it stretches | beyond you to your friends. 1.02.142
that ne'er dream'd a joy beyond his pleasure; 3.01.135
which went | beyond all man's endeavors. 3.02.169
in a sea of glory, | but far beyond my depth. 3.02.361
o, cromwell, | the king has gone beyond me! 3.02.408
and thy parts of nature | thrice fam'd beyond, TRO 2.03.243
they do disdain us much beyond our thoughts, COR 1.04. 26
for rome, he fought | beyond the mark of others. 2.02. 89
but now 'tis odds beyond arithmetic, | and 3.01.244
that wound beyond their feeling to the quick. TIT 4.02. 28
my lord, i /aim'd a mile beyond the moon, | your 4.03. 66
his promises fly so beyond his state | that what TIM 1.02.197
and, if it be so far beyond his health, 3.04. 74
but he hath conjur'd me beyond them, and i must 3.06. 11 P
o caesar, these things are beyond all use, | and JC 2.02. 25
thy letters have transported me beyond | this MAC 1.05. 56
this disease is beyond my practice; 5.01. 59 P
with thoughts beyond the reaches of our souls? HAM 1.04. 56
age | to cast beyond ourselves in our opinions, 2.01.112
beyond what can be valued, rich or rare, | no LR 1.01. 57
beyond all manner of so much i love you. 1.01. 61
you are abus'd | beyond the mark of thought; ANT 3.06. 87
this speed of caesar's | carries beyond belief. 3.07. 75
in you, which i account his, beyond all talents. CYM 1.06. 80
for mine's beyond beyond — say, and speak thick 3.02. 56
for mine's beyond beyond — say, and speak thick 3.02. 56
to prince it much | beyond the trick of others. 3.03. 86
a thing perplex'd | beyond self–explication. 3.04. 8
beyond him in the advantage of the time, above 4.01. 11 P
minerva, | postures beyond brief nature; 5.05.165
her face was to mine eye beyond all wonder; PER 1.02. 75
assured | beyond its power there's nothing; TNK 1.02. 65
which shall be then | beyond further requiring. 1.03. 26
punishment, a death | beyond imagination! 2.03. 5
i love him beyond love and beyond reason, | or 2.06. 11
i love him beyond love and beyond reason, | or 2.06. 11
in which you swore i went beyond all women, 3.06.206
devise extremes beyond extremity, | to make him LUC 969
above that idle rank remain | beyond all date, SON 122. 4

BEZONIAN *(see besonian, etc.)*

BIANCA 40 FR 0.0045 REL FR 36 V 4 P
i may soon make good | what i have said, bianca, SHR 1.01. 75
and let it not displease thee, good bianca, 1.01. 76
go in, bianca. 1.01. 91
stay, | for i have more to commune with bianca. 1.01.101
for the love i bear my sweet bianca, if i can by 1.01.110 P
sweet bianca! 1.01.139 P
hold, | his youngest daughter, beautiful bianca, 1.02.120
that none shall have access unto bianca | till 1.02.127
well seen in music, to instruct bianca, | that 1.02.134
about a schoolmaster for the fair bianca, | and 1.02.166
i no whit be behind in duty | to fair bianca, so 1.02.175
then well one more may fair bianca have; 1.02.243
bianca, stand aside. 2.01. 24
what, in my sight? bianca, get thee in. 2.01. 30
your daughter, | unto bianca, fair and virtuous. 2.01. 91
and i am one that love bianca more | than words 2.01.335
now on the sunday following shall bianca | be 2.01.395
b mi, bianca, take him for thy lord, | c fa ut, 3.01. 75
yet if thy thoughts, bianca, be so humble | to 3.01. 89
hope, | and marry sweet bianca with consent. 3.02.137
place, | and let bianca take her sister's room. 3.02.250
shall sweet bianca practice how to bride it? 3.02.251
that mistress bianca | doth fancy any other but 4.02. 1
you that durst swear that your mistress bianca 4.02. 12
heard | of your entire affection to bianca, 4.02. 23
forswear bianca and her love for ever. 4.02. 26
mistress bianca, bless you with such grace | as 4.02. 44
to me now, | give me bianca for my patrimony. 4.04. 22
home, | and bid bianca make her ready straight; 4.04. 63
but bid bianca farewell for ever and a day. 4.04. 97
look not pale, bianca, thy father will not frown 5.01.138 P
my fair bianca, bid my father welcome, | while i 5.02. 4
son, i'll be your half, bianca comes. 5.02. 78
the wisdom of your duty, fair bianca, | hath 5.02.127
how is't with you, my most fair bianca? OTH 3.04.170
pardon me, bianca. 3.04.176
sweet bianca, | take me this work out. 3.04.179
no, /by /my /faith, bianca. 3.04.187
now will i question cassio of bianca, | a 4.01. 93
how now, my sweet bianca? how now? how now? 4.01.156 P

BIANCA'S 6 FR 0.0006 REL FR 5 V 1 P
i that our good will effects | bianca's grief. SHR 1.01. 87
mistress and be happy rivals in bianca's love, 1.01.117 P
greatest dower | shall have my bianca's love. 2.01.344
doth watch bianca's steps so narrowly, | 'twere 3.02.139
bianca's love | made me exchange my state with 5.01.124
now, if this suit lay in bianca's /pow'r, | how OTH 4.01.107

BIAS 12 FR 0.0013 REL FR 11 V 1 P
study his bias leaves, and makes his book thine LLL 4.02.109
run, | and not unluckily against the bias. SHR 4.05. 25
but nature to her bias drew in that. TN 5.01.260
commodity, | commodity, the bias of the world —
JN 2.01.574
till this advantage, this vile–drawing bias, 2.01.577
and this same bias, this commodity, | this bawd, 2.01.581
and that my fortune runs against the bias. R2 3.04. 5
trial did draw | bias and thwart, not answering TRO 1.03. 15
till thy sphered bias cheek | outswell the colic 4.05. 8
with windlasses and with assays of bias, | by HAM 2.01. 62
the king falls from bias of nature; LR 1.02.111 P
study his bias leaves, and makes his book thine PP 5. 5

//BIAS–DRAWING 1 FR 0.0001 REL FR 1 V 0 P
/purely /from /all /hollow //bias–drawing, TRO 4.05.169

BIBBLE *(also pibble*)*

BIBBLE 1 FR 0.0001 REL FR 0 V 1 P
to sleep, and leave thy vain bibble babble. TN 4.02. 96 P

BIBLE *(see pible)*

BICKERINGS 1 FR 0.0001 REL FR 1 V 0 P
stay, | we shall begin our ancient bickerings. 2H6 1.01.144

BID* *(also pid)*

/BID* 3 FR 0.0003 REL FR 2 V 1 P
/to /bid /aeneas /tell /the /tale /twice /o'er TIT 3.02. 27
/bid a sick man in sadness /make his will — | a ROM 1.01.202
/for /a /while /no /money /bid /for /argument, HAM 2.02.354 P

BID* 353 FR 0.0399 REL FR 292 V 61 P
in the dark | out of my way, unless he bid 'em; TMP 2.02. 7
drink, servant–monster, when i bid thee. 3.02. 8 P
and to thee and thy company i bid | a hearty 5.01.110
indeed i bid the base for proteus. TGV 1.02. 94
bid him make haste and meet me at the north–gate 3.01.260
did not i bid thee still mark me and do as i do? 4.04. 36 P
wife, bid these gentlemen welcome. WIV 1.01.194 P
or bid farewell to your good life for ever. 3.03.119 P
and bid her think what a man is: 3.05. 49 P
if he bid you set it down, obey him. 4.02.110 P
time | to take her by the hand and bid her go, 4.06. 37
call hither, | i say, bid come before us angelo. MM 1.01. 15
bid herself assay him. 1.02.181
strike and gall them | for what i bid them do; 1.03. 37
for we bid this be done, | when evil deeds have 1.03. 37
and bid them bring the trumpets to the gate. 4.05. 9
duke, | you bid me seek redemption of the devil. 5.01. 29
you were not bid to speak. 5.01. 78
will not show my face | until my husband bid me. 5.01.170
we bid be quiet when we hear it cry; ERR 2.01. 35
dromio, go bid the servants spread for dinner. 2.02.187
go bid them let us in. 3.01. 30
at the door, master, bid them welcome hither. 3.01. 68
chain, and bid my wife | disburse the sum on the 4.01. 37
an evil angel, and bid you forsake your liberty. 4.03. 20 P
to what end did i bid thee hie thee home? 4.04. 15
and bid the lady abbess come to me: 5.01.166
let me bid you welcome, my lord, being ADO 1.01.154 P
my will i am sent to bid you come in to dinner. 2.03.247 P
my will i am sent to bid you come in to dinner" 2.03.257 P
us, | and bid her steal into the pleached bower, 3.01. 7
and did they bid you tell her of it, madam? 3.01. 39
you are to bid any man stand, in the prince's 3.03. 26 P
and bid those that are drunk get them to bed. 3.03. 43 P
you must call to the nurse and bid her still it. 3.03. 66 P
and bid her come hither. 3.04. 4 P
bid him bring his pen and inkhorn to the jail. 3.05. 58 P
that you have in her, bid her answer truly. 4.01. 75
come, bid me do any thing for thee. 4.01.288 P
like mine, | and bid him speak of patience; 5.01. 10
i will bid thee draw, as we do the minstrels, 5.01.128 P
he hath bid me to a calve's–head and a capon, 5.01.154 P
i cannot bid you bid my daughter live — | that 5.01.279
i cannot bid you bid my daughter live — | that 5.01.279
yea, signior, and depart when you bid me. 5.02. 44 P
why, that they have, and bid them so be gone. LLL 5.02.182
you, | as much in private, and i'll bid adieu. 5.02.241
go bid them prepare. 5.02.509 P
with the love–juice, as i did bid thee do? MND 3.02. 37
go, bid the huntsmen wake them with their horns. 4.01.138
the duke was here, and bid us follow him? 4.01.195
and he did bid us follow to the temple. 4.01.197
if i could bid the fift welcome with so good MV 1.02.127 P
with so good heart as i can bid the other four 1.02.128 P
to bid my old master the jew to sup to–night 2.04. 17 P
who bids thee call? i do not bid thee call. 2.05. 7
i am bid forth to supper, jessica. 2.05. 11
i am not bid for love, they flatter me, | but 2.05. 13
do as i bid you, shut doors after you; 2.05. 53
int'rest here | have power to bid you welcome. 3.02.222
leave, | i bid my very friends and countrymen, 3.02.223
nerissa, cheer yond stranger, bid her welcome. 3.02.237
bid your friends welcome, show a merry cheer — 3.02.312
go in, sirrah, bid them prepare for dinner. 3.05. 46 P
then bid them prepare dinner! 3.05. 50 P
go to thy fellows, bid them cover the table, 3.05. 58 P
and bid the main flood bate his usual height; 4.01. 72
take thrice thy money, bid me tear the bond. 4.01.234
bid her be judge | whether bassanio had not once 4.01.276
and bid him keep it better than the other. 5.01.255
by mine honor, but i was bid to come for you. AYL 1.02. 60 P
and bid him take that for coming a–night to jane 2.04. 47 P
my gentle phebe did bid me give you this. 4.03. 7
and i will bid the duke to the nuptial. 5.02. 43 P
put you in your best array, bid your friends; 5.02. 72 P
good my lord, bid him welcome. 5.04. 40 P
kind offer, when i make curtsy, bid me farewell. ep 23 P
bid them come near. SHR in.1. 79
bid him shed tears, as being overjoyed | to see in.1. 120
now, knock when i bid you, sirrah villain! 1.02. 19
he bid me knock him and rap him soundly, sir. 1.02. 30 P
bid them use them well. 2.01.110
if she do bid me pack, i'll give her thanks, 2.01.177
as though she bid me stay by her a week; 2.01.178
provide the feast, father, and bid the guests, 2.01.316
when i should bid good morrow to my bride | and 3.02.122
did i not bid thee meet me in the park, | and 4.01.130
and bid my cousin ferdinand come hither; 4.01.151
you bid me make it orderly and well, | according 4.03. 94
i did not bid you mar it to the time. 4.03. 97
unto thee, i bid thy master cut out the gown, 4.03.126 P
gown, but i did not bid him cut it to pieces. 4.03.127 P
home, | and bid bianca make her ready straight; 4.04. 63
but bid bianca farewell for ever and a day. 4.04. 97
go to saint luke's to bid the priest be ready to 4.04.103 P
my fair bianca, bid my father welcome, | while i 5.02. 4
go, biondello, bid your mistress come to me. 5.02. 76
the true minute when | exception bid him speak, AWW 1.02. 40
you, madam, that he bid helen come to you. 1.03. 66 P
and what dole of honor | flies where you bid it, 2.03.170
his taken labors bid him me forgive; 3.04. 12
my life, be thine, | and i'll be bid by thee. 4.02. 53
"when he swears oaths, bid him drop gold, and 4.03.223
bid the dishonest man mend himself: TN 1.05. 45 P
her steward malvolio and bid him turn you out of 2.03. 74 P
of her, she is very willing to bid you farewell. 2.03.101 P
"shall i bid him go?" 2.03.109
"shall i bid him go, and spare not?" 2.03.111
you by my lady, to bid you come speak with her, 4.01. 6 P
pray you bid | these unknown friends to 's WT 4.04. 64
on, | and bid us welcome to your sheep–shearing, 4.04. 69
pleas'd with madness, | do bid it welcome. 4.04.485
ghost that walk'd, i'ld bid you mark | her eye, 5.01. 63
make proselytes | of who she but bid follow. 5.01.109
some speedy messenger bid her repair | to our JN 2.01.554
here is my throne, bid kings come bow to it. 3.01. 74
so well, that what you bid me undertake, 3.03. 56
come forth. do as i bid you do. 4.01. 71
our suit | that you have bid us ask his liberty, 4.02. 63
face, | as bid me tell my tale in express words, 4.02.234
after such bloody toil, we bid good night, | and 5.05. 6
and none of you will bid the winter come | to 5.07. 36
face, | and bid his ears a little while be deaf, R2 1.01.112
obedience bids i should not bid again. 1.01.163
norfolk, throw down, we bid, there is no boot. 1.01.164
bid him — ah, what? 1.02. 65
you would have bid me argue like a father. 1.03.238
and, uncle, bid him so. 1.03.247
a brace of draymen bid god speed him well, | and 1.04. 32
bid him repair to us to ely house | to see this 2.01.216
bid her send me presently a thousand pound. 2.02. 91
o, call back yesterday, bid time return, | and 3.02. 69
and ere thou bid good night, to quite their 5.01. 43
until thou bid me joy | by pardoning rutland, my 5.03. 95
bid the ostler bring my gelding out of the 1H4 2.01. 96 P
bid butler lead him forth into the park. 2.03. 72
and bid you play it off. 2.04. 17 P
that daff'd the world aside | and bid it pass? 4.01. 97
bid my lieutenant peto meet me at town's end. 4.02. 9 P
my life, | if well–respected honor bid me on, 4.03. 10
the king will bid you battle presently. 5.02. 30
kiss me, and bid me fetch thee thirty shillings? 2H4 2.01.102 P
a death's–head, do not bid me remember mine end. 2.04.235 P
bid mistress tearsheet come to my master. 2.04.387 P
bid them o'er–read these letters | and well 3.01. 2
and bid the merry bells ring to thine ear | that 4.05.111
yea, marry, william cook, bid him come hither. 5.01. 11 P

for me, by heaven (i bid you be assur'd), | i'll 5.02. 56
when my legs are too, i will bid you good night. ep 33 P
comfort him, bid him 'a should not think of god; H5 2.03. 20 P
they bid us to the english dancing–schools, 3.05. 32
bid him therefore consider of his ransom, which 3.06.125 P
go bid thy master well advise himself. 3.06.159
and on to–morrow bid them march away. 3.06.172
and bid thy ceremony give thee cure! 4.01.252
bid them achieve me, and then sell my bones. 4.03. 91
bid him prepare, for i will cut his throat. 4.04. 32
if they will fight with us, bid them come down, 4.07. 58
yesterday, look you, and bid me eat my leek. 5.01. 9 P
to bid his young son welcome to his grave? 1H6 4.03. 40
laugh, | and bid me be advised how i tread. 2H6 2.04. 36
what, gone, my lord, and bid me not farewell? 2.04. 85
and bid them blow towards england's blessed 3.02. 90
and bid mine eyes be packing with my heart, 3.02.111
you bade me ban, and will you bid me leave? 3.02.333
and bid the apothecary | bring the strong poison 3.03. 17
go bid her hide him quickly from the duke. 5.01. 84
call hither clifford, bid him come amain, | to 5.01.114
bid salisbury and warwick come to me. 5.01.147
call buckingham, and bid him arm himself. 5.01.192
set, | i would speak blasphemy ere bid you fly. 5.02. 85
and issue forth and bid them battle straight. 3H6 1.02. 70
child, | to bid the father wipe his eyes withal, 1.04.139
if warwick bid him stay. 2.01.188
cross the seas and bid false edward battle; 3.03.235
and thus i seal my truth, and bid adieu. 4.08. 29
doubt | will issue out again and bid us battle. 5.01. 63
of force enough to bid his brother battle; 5.01. 77
and bid thee battle, edward, if thou dar'st. 5.01.111
then bid me kill myself, and i will do it. R3 1.02.186
bid me farewell. 1.02.222
bid gloucester think /of this, and he will weep. 1.04.239
kneel'd /at my feet and bid me be advis'd? 2.01.108
and bid my lord, for joy of this good news, 3.01.184
lord, | bid him not fear the separated council: 3.02. 20
go, bid thy master rise and come to me, | and we 3.02. 31
and so, my good lord mayor, we bid farewell. 3.05. 71
bid them both | meet me within this hour at 3.05.104
i bid them that did love their country's good 3.07. 21
and anne my wife hath bid this world good night. 4.03. 39
and bid her wipe her weeping eyes withal. 4.04.278
endur'd of her, for whom you bid like sorrow. 4.04.304
bid him levy straight | the greatest strength 4.04.449
bid him bring his power | before sunrising, lest 5.03. 60
bid my guard watch; 5.03. 76
thy nephews' souls bid thee despair and die! 5.03.149
edward's unhappy sons do bid thee flourish. 5.03.153
call up lord stanley, bid him bring his power. 5.03.290
bid him recount | the fore–recited practices, H8 1.02.126
bid him strive | to the love o' th' commonalty; 1.02.169
and once more in mine arms i bid him welcome, 2.02. 98
bid the music leave, | they are harsh and heavy 4.02. 94
get you gone, | and do as i have bid you. 5.01.156
my commission | bid ye so far forget yourselves? 5.02.177
if they hold when their ladies bid 'em clap. ep 14
and bid the cheek be ready with a blush | modest TRO 1.03.228
sweet, bid me hold my tongue, | for in this 3.02.129
bid them have patience, she shall come anon. 4.04. 52
so now, fair prince of troy, i bid good night. 5.01. 71
bid me do any thing but that, sweet greek. 5.02. 27
ho! bid my trumpet sound! 5.03. 13
your fair sword, | you bid them rise and live. 5.03. 42
and bid the snail–pac'd ajax arm for shame. 5.05. 18
tell valeria | we are fit to bid her welcome. COR 1.03. 44
bid them wash their faces, | and keep their 2.03. 60
when i am forth, | bid me farewell, and smile. 4.01. 50
bid them all home, he's gone; 4.02. 1
bid them home. 4.02. 5
do not bid me | dismiss my soldiers, or 5.03. 81
bid them repair to th' market–place, where i, 5.06. 3
i am not bid to wait upon this bride. TIT 1.01.338
this is the hole where aaron bid us hide him. 2.03.186
him | from thousand dangers, bid him bury it: 3.01.195
youth, | the hope of rome, for so he bid me say; 4.02. 13
marcus, loose when i bid. 4.03. 59
bid him demand what pledge will please him best. 4.04.106
and bid the owners quench them with their tears. 5.01.134
and bid him come and banquet at thy house, 5.02.114
bid him repair to me, and bring with him | some 5.02.124
bid him encamp his soldiers where they are. 5.02.126
and bid that strumpet, your unhallowed dam, 5.02.190
this is the feast that i have bid her to, | and 5.02.192
and bid thee bear his pretty tales in mind, 5.03.165
bid him farewell, commit him to the grave, | do 5.03.170
'twas no need, i trow, | to bid me trudge. ROM 1.03. 34
head | so soon to bid good morrow to thy bed. 2.03. 34
told you, my young lady bid me inquire you out; 2.04.163 P
what she bid me say, i will keep to myself. 2.04.164 P
bid her devise | some means to come to shrift 2.04.179
bid him bethink | how nice the quarrel was, and 3.01.153
the cords | that romeo bid thee fetch? 3.02. 35
and bid him come to take his last farewell. 3.02.143
lady, | and bid her hasten all the house to bed, 3.03.156
do so, and bid my sweet prepare to chide. 3.03.162
here, sir, a ring she bid me give you, sir. 3.03.163
son paris' love, | and bid her — mark you me? 3.04. 17
o, bid me leap, rather than marry paris, | from 4.01. 77
ways, or bid me lurk | where serpents are; 4.01. 79
or bid me go into a new–made grave, | and hide 4.01. 84
leave me, and do the thing i bid thee do. 5.01. 30
do as i bid thee, go. 5.03. 9
say | a madman's mercy bid thee run away. 5.03. 67
and with wild looks bid me devise some mean | to 5.03.240
this letter he early bid me give his father, 5.03.275
grave, | and bid me stand aloof, and so i did. 5.03.282
and being enfranchis'd, bid him come to me; TIM 1.01.106
thou art a fool to bid me farewell twice. 1.01.263
then thou mightst kill 'em — and bid me to 'em! 1.02. 82 P
present, you have bid me | return so much, i 2.02.136
could i frankly use | as i can bid thee speak. 2.02.180
bid 'em send o' th' instant | a thousand talents 2.02.198
bid him suppose some good necessity | touches 2.02.227
go, bid all my friends again, | lucius, lucullus 3.04.110
bid them flatter thee. 4.03.231
bid every noise be still; peace yet again! JC 1.02. 14
for he did bid antonio | send word to you he 1.03. 37
now bid me run, | and i will strive with things 2.01.324
go bid the priests do present sacrifice, | and 2.02. 5
bid them prepare within; 2.02.118
thus, brutus, did my master bid me kneel; 3.01.123
thus did mark antony bid me fall down; 3.01.124
and bid me say to you by word of mouth — | o 3.01.280
poor, dumb mouths, | and bid them speak for me. 3.02.226
must be taught, and train'd, and bid go forth; 4.01. 35
bid them move away; 4.02. 45
bid our commanders lead their charges off | a 4.02. 48
bid the commanders | prepare to lodge their 4.03.139
bid him set on his pow'rs betimes before, | and 4.03.307
thy life, | that whatsoever i did bid thee do, 5.03. 39
wreath of victory, | and bid me give it thee? 5.03. 83
thy brutus bid me give it thee, and i | will do 5.03. 86
whose care is gone before to bid us welcome: MAC 1.04. 57
how you shall bid god 'ield us for your pains, 1.06. 13
go bid thy mistress, when my drink is ready, 2.01. 31
do not bid me speak; 2.03. 72
and bid my will avouch it, yet i must not, | for 3.01.119
but who did bid thee join with us? 3.03. 1
bid the tree | unfix his earth–bound root? 4.01. 95
the rivals of my watch, bid them make haste. HAM 1.01. 13
itself should gape | and bid me hold my peace. 1.02.245
bid the players make haste. 3.02. 49 P
not this, by no means, that i bid you do: 3.04.181
go bid the soldiers shoot. 5.02.403
bid them farewell, cordelia, though unkind, LR 1.01.260
bid farewell to your sisters. 1.01.267
bid them come forth and hear me, | or at their 2.04.117
i do not bid the thunder–bearer shoot, | nor 2.04.227
bid her alight, | and her troth plight, | and 3.04.122
i never done you | than now to bid you hold. 3.07. 75
do as i bid thee, or rather do thy pleasure; 4.01. 47
bid me farewell, and let me hear thee going. 4.06. 31
come | to bid my king and master aye good night. 5.03.236
that will not serve god, if the devil bid you. OTH 1.01.109 P
so was i bid report here to the state | by 1.03. 15
and bid "good morrow, general." 3.01. 2
that which so often you did bid me steal. 3.03.309
seek him, bid him come hither. 3.04. 18 P
i have sent to bid cassio come speak with you. 3.04. 50
and bid me, when my fate would have me wiv'd, 3.04. 64
bid her come hither; 4.02. 19
me to go to bed, | and bid me to dismiss you. 4.03. 14
for your going, | but bid farewell, and go. ANT 1.03. 33
then bid adieu to me, and say the tears | belong 1.03. 77
alexas, bid him | report the feature of octavia, 2.05.111
bid you alexas | bring me word how tall she is. 2.05.117
do as i bid you. 2.07. 54
let neptune hear we bid a loud farewell | to 2.07.132
bid them all fly; 4.12. 15
bid them all fly, be gone. 4.12. 17
thy death and fortunes bid thy followers fly. 4.14.111
bid that welcome | which comes to punish us, and 4.14.136
go to him, dolabella, bid him yield; 5.01. 1
bid her have good heart. 5.01. 56
those things i bid you do, get them dispatch'd, CYM 1.03. 39
as i | have words to bid you, and shall find it 1.06. 30
go bid my woman | search for a jewel that too 2.03.140
go, bid my woman feign a sickness, say | she'll 3.02. 74
away, i prithee, | do as i bid thee. 3.02. 81
what villainy soe'er i bid thee do, to perform 3.05.112 P
boys, bid him welcome. 3.06. 68
i bid for you as i do buy. 3.06. 70
bid the captains look to't. 4.02.344
i do not bid thee beg my life, good lad, | and 5.05.101
not | to ask the reason why, because we bid it. PER 1.01.157
being bid to ask what he would of the king, 1.03. 5 P
for if a king bid a man be a villain, he's bound 1.03. 7 P
how? | do as i bid you, or you'll move me else. 2.03. 71
loath to bid farewell, we take our leaves. 2.05. 13
bid nestor bring me spices, ink and /paper, | my 3.01. 65
and bid nicander | bring me the satin coffin. 3.01. 66
bid him that we, whom flaming war doth scorch, TNK 1.01. 91
let us bid farewell; 5.04. 19
hath bid him rule, and will'd you to obey; STM II.C 100
"bid me discourse, i will enchant thine ear, VEN 145
to bid the wind a base he now prepares, | and 303
last, | and bid suspicion double–lock the door, 448
light | do summon us to part and bid good night. 534
"hadst thou but bid beware, then he had spoke, 943
they bid thee crop a weed, thou pluck'st a 946
mild patience bid fair lucrece speak | to the LUC 1268
one of my husband's men | bid thou be ready, by 1292
bid him with speed prepare to carry it, | the 1294
when you have bid your servant once adieu. SON 57. 8
BIDDEN 1 FR 0.0001 REL FR 0 V 1 P
if he will not stand when he is bidden, he is ADO 3.03. 31 P
BIDDING 27 FR 0.0030 REL FR 21 V 6 P
to thy strong bidding, task | ariel, and all his TMP 1.02.192
bidding the law make curtsy to their will, MM 2.04.175
to tell me i could do nothing without bidding. MV 2.05. 9 P
health, at your bidding, serve your majesty! AWW 2.01. 18
and that at my bidding you could so stand up. 2.01. 65
i shall not break your bidding, good my lord. 2.05. 88
what you mean by bidding me taste my legs. TN 3.01. 80 P
go, do our bidding; hence! WT 2.01.125
by this sword | thou wilt perform my bidding. 2.03.169
leave me, | and think upon my bidding. 2.03.207
my soldier, bidding me depend | upon thy stars, JN 3.01.125
save bidding farewell to so sweet a guest | as R2 2.02. 8
his neigh is like the bidding of a monarch, and H5 3.07. 28 P
he bids be done is finish'd with his bidding. COR 5.04. 23 P
your bidding shall i do effectually. TIT 4.04.107
no, i will do nothing at thy bidding; TIM 1.01.268 P
me give it thee, and i | will do his bidding. JC 5.03. 87
denies his person | at our great bidding? MAC 3.04.128
when the thunder would not peace at my bidding, LR 4.06.103 P
it was his bidding; OTH 4.03. 15
thy beck might from the bidding of the gods ANT 3.11. 60
but performs | the bidding of the fullest man, 3.13. 87
be thou honest, | do thou thy master's bidding. CYM 3.04. 65
do his bidding, strike. 3.04. 71
thou art too slow to do thy master's bidding 3.04. 97
or perform my bidding, or thou livest in woe; PER 5.01.247
bidding them find their sepulchres in mud, LC 46
BIDDINGS 1 FR 0.0001 REL FR 1 V 0 P
thy biddings have been done, and every hour, ANT 1.04. 34
BIDDY 1 FR 0.0001 REL FR 0 V 1 P
ay, biddy, come with me. TN 3.04.115 P
BIDE 16 FR 0.0018 REL FR 15 V 1 P
and bide the penance of each three years' day. LLL 1.01.115
lysander's love, that would not let him bide — MND 3.02.186
want of other idleness, i'll bide your proof. TN 1.05. 64 P
can bide the beating of so strong a passion | as 2.04. 94
say | my love can give no place, bide no denay. 2.04.124
to bide upon't: WT 1.02.242
of ten thousand men | must bide the touch; 1H4 4.04. 10
head, | or bide the mortal fortune of the field? 3H6 2.02. 83
there let them bide until we have devis'd | some TIT 2.03.284
nor bide th' encounter of assailing eyes, | nor ROM 1.01.213
that bide the pelting of this pitiless storm, LR 3.04. 29
where bide? CYM 3.04.128
at court, | then not in britain must you bide. 3.04.135
bide each check | without accusing you of injury SON 58. 7
is more than my o'erpress'd defense can bide? 139. 8
some in her threaden fillet still did bide, LC 33
BIDED *(see bid*)*
BIDES 4 FR 0.0004 REL FR 4 V 0 P
yet the gold bides still | that others touch and ERR 2.01.110
in whose cold blood no spark of honor bides. 3H6 1.01.184
safe in a ditch he bides, | with twenty trenched MAC 3.04. 25
bear me, good friends, where cleopatra bides, ANT 4.14.131
BIDING 3 FR 0.0003 REL FR 3 V 0 P
her, | with many bitter threats of biding there. TGV 3.01.238
me your hand, | i'll lead you to some biding. LR 4.06.224
blow these pitchy vapors from their biding, LUC 550
/BIDS 2 FR 0.0002 REL FR 2 V 0 P
/bids /thee, /with /most /divine /integrity, TRO 4.05.170
/he /runs, | /and /bids /what /will /take /all. LR 3.01. 15
BIDS 68 FR 0.0076 REL FR 59 V 9 P
come, | the very minute bids thee ope thine ear. TMP 1.02. 37
bids thee leave these, and with her sovereign 4.01. 72
love bade me swear, and love bids me forswear. TGV 2.06. 6
the law of friendship bids me to conceal, | but 3.01. 5
she bids me think how i have been forsworn | in 4.02. 10
me my cue, and my assurance bids me search — WIV 3.02. 46 P
my husband bids me, now i will unmask. MM 5.01.206
bids me a thousand times good night — i tell ADO 3.03.147 P
the princess bids you tell | how many inches LLL 5.02.192
well, the most courageous fiend bids me pack. MV 2.02. 10 P
who bids thee call? i do not bid thee call. 2.05. 7
she bids you come to her. SHR 5.02. 92
would have tears, and sorrow bids me speak. AWW 3.04. 42
our general bids you answer to what i shall ask 4.03.127 P
one | he chides to hell and bids the other grow WT 4.04.553
let's before, as he bids us. 4.04.829 P
obedience bids i should not bid again. R2 1.01.163
whom both my oath | and duty bids defend; 2.02.113
whom conscience and my kinred bids to right. 2.02.115
and bids me speak of nothing but despair. 3.02. 66
that bids me be of comfort any more. 3.02.208
and 'tis no little reason bids us speed, | to 1H4 1.03.283
she bids you on the wanton rushes lay you down, 3.01.211
he bids you name your griefs, and with all speed 4.03. 48
we are time's subjects, and time bids be gone. 2H4 1.03.110
much of your youth, | and bids you be advis'd: H5 1.02.251
he bids you then resign | your crown and kingdom 2.04. 93
and bids you, in the bowels of the lord, 2.04.102
bids them good morrow with a modest smile, | and 4.pr. 33
breathe we, lords, good fortune bids us pause, 3H6 2.06. 31
for warwick bids you all farewell, to meet in 5.02. 49
tell them that god bids us do good for evil: R3 1.03.334
when that he bids good morrow with such spirit. 3.04. 50
so foolish sorrows bids your stones farewell. 4.01.103
in brief — for so the season bids us be — 5.03. 87
harry the sixt bids thee despair and die. 5.03.127
let me speak, sir, | for heaven now bids me; H8 5.04. 15
hold my peace when achilles' /brach bids me, TRO 2.01.115 P
achilles bids me say, he is much sorry | if any 2.03.107
achilles bids you welcome. 4.05. 25
and beat the messenger who bids beware | of what COR 4.06. 55
what he bids be done is finish'd with his 5.04. 23 P
and bids thee christen it with thy dagger's TIT 4.02. 70
for though /fond nature bids us all lament, ROM 4.05. 82
a soothsayer bids you beware the ides of march. JC 1.02. 19
love | to your proceeding bids me tell you this; 2.02.103
the o'er–fraught heart, and bids it break. MAC 4.03.210
thus kent, o princes, bids you all adieu, LR 1.01.186
so your face bids me, though you say nothing. 1.04.195 P
apt | to have his ear abus'd, wisdom bids fear. 2.04.307
bids the wind blow the earth into the sea, | or 3.01. 5
hark, the land bids me tread no more upon't, ANT 3.11. 1
and bids thee study on what fair demands | thou 5.02. 10
without offense | (my conscience bids me ask), CYM 1.05. 7
his majesty bids you welcome. 3.01. 77 P
more than what | that banket bids thee to! TNK 1.01.186
bold young men that, when he bids 'em charge, 2.02.249
bids him farewell, and look well to her heart, VEN 580
bids them leave quaking, bids them fear no more 899
them leave quaking, bids them fear no more — 899
expel, | for now reviving joy bids her rejoice, 977
who bids them still consort with ugly night, 1041
the hot charge, and bids them do their liking. LUC 434
and bids her eyes hereafter still be blind; 758
and bids it leap from thence, where it may find 760
and bids lucretius give his sorrow place, | and 1773
till manly shame bids him possess his breath, 1777
and to the painted banquet bids my heart; SON 47. 6
BID'ST 5 FR 0.0005 REL FR 5 V 0 P
thou bid'st me beg; LLL 5.02.210
we shall not marry till thou bid'st us. WT 5.01. 82
if thou that bid'st me be content wert grim, JN 3.01. 43
bid'st thou me rage? 3H6 1.04.143
thou bid'st me to my loss; CYM 3.05.157
BIEN 4 FR 0.0004 REL FR 0 V 4 P
child or pupil, undertake your bien venuto; LLL 4.02.157 P
ete en angleterre, et tu bien parles le langage. H5 3.04. 1 P
ecoutez, dites–moi si je parle bien: 3.04. 18 P
c'est bien dit, madame, il est fort bon anglois. 3.04. 19 P
BIER 7 FR 0.0008 REL FR 7 V 0 P
here, | in weeping after this untimely bier. R2 5.06. 52

and thou and romeo press /one heavy bier! ROM 3.02. 60
is, | /in thy best robes, uncovered on the bier, 4.01.110
"they bore him barefac'd on the bier, | /hey HAM 4.05.165
the bier at door, | and a demand who is't shall CYM 4.02. 22
who loses, yet i'll weep upon his bier. TNK 3.06.308
borne on the bier with white and bristly beard: SON 12. 8
BI–FOLD 1 FR 0.0001 REL FR 1 V 0 P
bi–fold authority, where reason can revolt TRO 5.02.144
BIG *(also pig*)*
/BIG 1 FR 0.0001 REL FR 1 V 0 P
/whilst /i | /was /big /in /clamor, /came /there LR 5.03.209
BIG 42 FR 0.0047 REL FR 30 V 12 P
mine own, who is a dog as big as ten of yours, TGV 4.04. 57 P
he's too big to go in there. what shall i do? WIV 3.03.134 P
there is no woman's gown big enough for him; 4.02. 70 P
she's as big as he is. 4.02. 78 P
your thief, your true man thinks it big enough; MM 4.02. 45 P
if it be too big for your thief, your thief 4.02. 45 P
she is too big, i hope, for me to compass. ERR 4.01.111
thumb, he is not so big as the end of his club. LLL 5.01.131 P
"i pompey am, pompey surnam'd the big" — 5.02.550
his leg is too big for hector's. 5.02.639 P
and even there, his eye being big with tears, MV 2.08. 46
and the big round tears | cours'd one another AYL 2.01. 38
for his shrunk shank, and his big manly voice, 2.07.161
nay, look not big, nor stamp, nor stare, nor SHR 3.02.228
my mind hath been as big as one of yours, | my 5.02.170
of humility over the black gown of a big heart. AWW 1.03. 95 P
no woman's heart | so big, to hold so much; TN 2.04. 96
the sheet were big enough for the bed of ware in 3.02. 47 P
her sport herself | with that she's big with, WT 2.01. 61
upon, | the centre is not big enough to bear | a 2.01.102
if you had but look'd big and spit at him, he'ld 4.03.106 P
strive to speak big, and clap their female R2 3.02.114
if that the devil and mischance look big | upon 1H4 4.01. 58
whiles the big year, swoll'n with some other 2H4 in 13
to look with forehead bold and big enough | upon 1.03. 8
the stature, bulk, and big assemblance of a man? 3.02.259 P
big mars seems bankrout in their beggar'd host, H5 4.02. 43
and buckingham | shall lessen this big look. H8 1.01.119
full of protest, of oath and big compare, TRO 3.02.175
a carbuncle entire, as big as thou art, | were COR 1.04. 55
for i mock at death | with as big heart as thou. 3.02.128
a bump as big as a young cock'rel's stone — | a ROM 1.03. 53
not half so big as a round little worm | prick'd 1.04. 68
how big imagination | moves in this lip! TIM 1.01. 32
thy heart is big; JC 3.01.282
farewell the plumed troops and the big wars OTH 3.03.349
big of this gentleman, our theme, deceas'd | as CYM 1.01. 39
another stain, as big as hell can hold, | were 2.04.140
have not i | an arm as big as thine? 4.02. 77
a heart as big? 4.02. 77
the teeming autumn, big with rich increase, SON 97. 6
big discontent so breaking their contents. LC 56
BIGAMY 1 FR 0.0001 REL FR 1 V 0 P
degree | to base declension and loath'd bigamy. R3 3.07.189
BIG–BELLIED 1 FR 0.0001 REL FR 1 V 0 P
and grow big–bellied with the wanton wind; MND 2.01.129
BIG–BON'D 1 FR 0.0001 REL FR 1 V 0 P
no big–bon'd men fram'd of the cyclops' size, TIT 4.03. 47
BIGGEN 1 FR 0.0001 REL FR 1 V 0 P
as he whose brow with homely biggen bound 2H4 4.05. 27
BIGGER 16 FR 0.0018 REL FR 13 V 3 P
and teach me how | to name the bigger light, and TMP 1.02.335
to hide itself, | the bigger bulk it shows. 3.01. 81
that makes his opening with this bigger key. MM 4.01. 31
come let me have a bigger. SHR 4.03. 68
i'll have no bigger, this doth fit the time, 4.03. 69
are to herrings, the husband's the bigger. TN 3.01. 35 P
whose compass is no bigger than thy head, | and R2 2.01.101
in their bellies no bigger than pins' heads, and 1H4 4.02. 21 P
the spoons will be the bigger, sir. H8 5.03. 39 P
i'll run away till i am bigger, but then i'll COR 5.03.128
no less! nay, bigger: women grow by men. ROM 1.03. 95
comes | in shape no bigger than an agot–stone 1.04. 55
methinks he seems no bigger than his head. LR 4.06. 16
that had a court no bigger than this cave, CYM 3.06. 82
thy words, i grant, are bigger; 4.02. 78
he's somewhat bigger than the knight he spoke of TNK 4.02. 94
BIGGER–LOOK'D 1 FR 0.0001 REL FR 1 V 0 P
a number, for a business | more bigger–look'd. TNK 1.01.215
BIGGEST 1 FR 0.0001 REL FR 1 V 0 P
shot through and biggest tears o'ershow'r'd, PER 4.04. 26
BIGGIN *(see biggen)*
BIGNESS 1 FR 0.0001 REL FR 0 V 1 P
because their legs are both of a bigness, and 'a 2H4 2.04.244 P
BIGOT 2 FR 0.0002 REL FR 2 V 0 P
besides, i met lord bigot and lord salisbury, JN 4.02.162
lord bigot, i am none. 4.03.103
BIG–SWOLL'N 2 FR 0.0002 REL FR 2 V 0 P
the execution of my big–swoll'n heart | upon 3H6 2.02.111
the welkin with his big–swoll'n face? TIT 3.01.223
BILBERRY 1 FR 0.0001 REL FR 1 V 0 P
there pinch the maids as blue as bilberry; WIV 5.05. 45
BILBO 2 FR 0.0002 REL FR 1 V 1 P
mine, | i combat challenge of this latten bilbo. WIV 1.01.162
next, to be compass'd, like a good bilbo, in the 3.05.111 P
/BILBOES 1 FR 0.0001 REL FR 1 V 0 P
i lay | worse than the mutines in the /bilboes. HAM 5.02. 6
BILBOW *(also elbow, ilbow)*
BILBOW 1 FR 0.0001 REL FR 0 V 1 P
hand, de fingre, de nailes, d' arma, de bilbow. H5 3.04. 29 P
BILE 1 FR 0.0001 REL FR 1 V 0 P
thou art a bile, | a plague–sore, or embossed LR 2.04.223
BILES 3 FR 0.0003 REL FR 1 V 2 P
agamemnon, how if he had biles — full, all over TRO 2.01. 2 P
and those biles did run — say so — did not the 2.01. 5 P
herd of — biles and plagues | plaster you o'er, COR 1.04. 31
BILL* 17 FR 0.0019 REL FR 8 V 9 P
who writes himself armigero, in any bill, WIV 1.01. 10 P
i'll exhibit a bill in the parliament for the 2.01. 29 P
the mean time i will draw a bill of properties, MND 1.02.105 P
cock so black of hue, | with orange–tawny bill, 3.01.126
and as pigeons bill, so wedlock would be AYL 3.03. 81 P
error i' th' bill, sir, error i' th' bill! SHR 4.03.145 P
error i' th' bill, sir, error i' th' bill! 4.03.145 P
take thou the bill, give me thy mete–yard, and 4.03.151 P
the bill to him! WT 1.02.183
that self bill is urg'd | which in th' eleventh H5 1.01. 1
thus runs the bill. 1.01. 19
how now for mitigation of this bill | urg'd by 1.01. 70
my brain–pan had been cleft with a brown bill; 2H6 4.10. 12 P
my lord, here is my bill. TIM 3.04. 85 P
from the bill | that writes them all alike: MAC 3.01. 99
with charitable bill (o bill, sore shaming CYM 4.02.225
with charitable bill (o bill, sore shaming 4.02.225
BILLARDS 1 FR 0.0001 REL FR 1 V 0 P
let it alone, let's to billards. come, charmian. ANT 2.05. 3
BILLETED 2 FR 0.0002 REL FR 1 V 1 P
and their charges, distinctly billeted, already COR 4.03. 44 P
retire thee, go where thou art billeted. OTH 2.03.380
BILLETS 1 FR 0.0001 REL FR 0 V 1 P
or they shall beat out my brains with billets. MM 4.03. 55 P
BILLIARDS *(see billards)*
BILLING 1 FR 0.0001 REL FR 0 V 1 P
what, billing again? TRO 3.02. 57 P
BILLOW 5 FR 0.0005 REL FR 4 V 1 P
why now blow wind, swell billow, and swim bark! JC 5.01. 67
the chidden billow seems to pelt the clouds, OTH 2.01. 12
their vessel shakes | on neptune's billow; PER 3.ch. 45
and the brine and cloudy billow kiss the moon, i 3.01. 46 P
i never saw so huge a billow, sir, | as toss'd 3.02. 58
/BILLOWS 1 FR 0.0001 REL FR 1 V 0 P
who take the ruffian /billows by the top, 2H4 3.01. 22
BILLOWS 4 FR 0.0004 REL FR 4 V 0 P
methought the billows spoke, and told me of it; TMP 3.03. 96
a city on th' inconstant billows dancing; H5 3.pr. 15
into the tumbling billows of the main. R3 1.04. 20
heard him play, | even the billows of the sea, H8 3.01. 10
BILLS* 14 FR 0.0015 REL FR 7 V 7 P
he set up his bills here in messina, and ADO 1.01. 39 P
only, have a care that your bills be not stol'n. 3.03. 41 P
commodity, being taken up of these men's bills. 3.03.178 P
with bills on their necks, "be it known unto all AYL 1.02.123 P
for i have bills for money by exchange | from SHR 4.02. 89
distaff–women manage rusty bills | against thy R2 3.02.118
and take up commodities upon our bills? 2H6 4.07.127 P
clubs, bills, and partisans! ROM 1.01. 73
why then preferr'd you not your sums and bills TIM 3.04. 49
all our bills. 3.04. 89 P
that by proscription and bills of outlawry, JC 4.03.173
and give these bills | unto the legions on the 5.02. 1
bring up the brown bills. LR 4.06. 91 P
some other in their bills | would bring him VEN 1102
BIN *(also been)*
BIN 2 FR 0.0002 REL FR 0 V 2 P
and chud ha' bin zwagger'd out of my life, LR 4.06.238 P
life, 'twould not ha' bin zo long as 'tis by a 4.06.239 P
BIND 44 FR 0.0049 REL FR 41 V 3 P
from me, | to bind him to remember my good will; TGV 4.04. 98
o, bind him, bind him! let him not come near me. ERR 4.04.106
o, bind him, bind him! let him not come near me. 4.04.106
go bind this man, for he is frantic too. 4.04.113
bind dromio too, and bear them to my house. 5.01. 35
let us come in, that we may bind him fast, | and 5.01. 40
of more aid, | we came again to bind them. 5.01.154
as being forsaken, or to bind him up a rod, as ADO 2.01.219 P
thee | to bind our loves up in a holy band; 3.01.114
come, bind them. 4.02. 72 P
to bind me, or undo me — one of them. 5.04. 20
fast bind, fast find — | a proverb never stale MV 2.05. 54
they that reap must sheaf and bind, | then to AYL 3.02.107
we will bind and hoodwink him so, that he shall AWW 3.06. 24 P
most provident in peril, bind himself | (courage TN 1.02. 12
bind up those tresses. JN 3.04. 61
bind up your hairs. 3.04. 68
and bind the boy which you shall find with me 4.01. 4
give me the iron, i say, and bind him here. 4.01. 74
go bind thou up young dangling apricocks, R2 3.04. 29
now bind my brows with iron, and approach | the 2H4 1.01.150
a hoop of gold to bind thy brothers in, | that 4.04. 43
to effect | and surer bind this knot of amity, 1H6 5.01. 16
so shall you bind me to your highness' service. 3H6 3.02. 43
bind up my wounds! R3 5.03.177
straight they told me they would bind me here TIT 2.03.106
then into limits could i bind my woes: 3.01.220
name, | and therefore bind them, gentle publius. 5.02.157
and now i find it, therefore bind them sure, 5.02.160
look that you bind them fast. 5.02.165
to enverness, | and bind us further to you. MAC 1.04. 43
bind fast his corky arms. LR 3.07. 29
bind him, i say. 3.07. 32
to this chair bind him. 3.07. 34
let me but bind it hard, within this hour | it OTH 3.03.286
i'll bind it with my shirt. 5.01. 73
and such a twain can do't, in which i bind, ANT 1.01. 38
divisions, and bind up | the petty difference, 2.01. 48
bind the offender, | and take him from our CYM 5.05.300
upon the winds command, bind them in brass, PER 3.01. 3
stead that is distress'd | does bind me to her. TNK 1.01. 37
yet i may bind those wounds up, that must open 4.02. 1
and him bind by my place | to give the smooth STM III 10
me | under that bond that him as fast doth bind. SON 134. 8
BINDETH 1 FR 0.0001 REL FR 1 V 0 P
most of all these reasons bindeth us | in our 1H6 5.05. 60
/BINDS 1 FR 0.0001 REL FR 1 V 0 P
/with /a /double /surety /binds /his /followers. 2H4 1.01.191
BINDS 3 FR 0.0003 REL FR 2 V 1 P
according as marriage binds and blood breaks. AYL 5.04. 57 P
and binds the wretch and beats it when it strays 2H6 3.01.211
your lordship ever binds him. TIM 1.01.104
BIONDELLO 12 FR 0.0013 REL FR 8 V 4 P
if, biondello, thou wert come ashore, | we could SHR 1.01. 42
when biondello comes, he waits on thee, | but i 1.01.208
even he, biondello. 1.02.222
i love no chiders, sir. biondello, let's away. 1.02.226
what is he, biondello? 4.02. 62
sirrah biondello, | now do your duty throughly, 4.04. 10
what say'st thou, biondello? 4.04. 74 P
biondello, what of that? 4.04. 77 P
hear'st thou, biondello? 4.04. 98 P
i fly, biondello; 5.01. 2 P
go, biondello, bid your mistress come to me. 5.02. 76
sirrah biondello, go and entreat my wife | to 5.02. 86
BIRCH 2 FR 0.0002 REL FR 2 V 0 P
having bound up the threat'ning twigs of birch, MM 1.03. 24
the birch upon the breeches of the small ones, TNK 3.05.111
/BIRD 1 FR 0.0001 REL FR 1 V 0 P
hillo, ho, ho, boy! come, /bird, come. HAM 1.05.116
BIRD 49 FR 0.0055 REL FR 42 V 7 P
this was well done, my bird. TMP 4.01.184
a bird of my tongue is better than a beast of ADO 3.01.139 P
who would set his wit to so foolish a bird? MND 3.01.134 P
who would give a bird the lie, though he cry 3.01.135 P
fairy sprite | hop as light as bird from brier, 5.01.394
for his own part, knew the bird was fledge, and MV 3.01. 29 P
the world what the bird hath done to her own AYL 4.01.204 P
am i your bird? SHR 5.02. 46
this bird you aim'd at, though you hit her not; 5.02. 50
of our grandam might happily inhabit a bird. TN 4.02. 53 P
as is the falcon's flight | against a bird, do i R2 1.03. 62
so | as that ungentle gull, the cuckoo's bird, 1H4 5.01. 60
o westmerland, thou art a summer bird, | which 2H4 4.04. 91
i heard a bird so sing, | whose music, to my 5.05.107
but not as truly, | as bird doth sing on bough." H5 3.02. 19
that mounts no higher than a bird can soar. 2H6 2.01. 14
nest | but may imagine how the bird was dead, 3.02.192
forth | a bird that will revenge upon you all; 3H6 1.04. 36
nay, if thou be that princely eagle's bird, 2.01. 91
the bird that hath been limed in a bush, | with 5.06. 13
and i, the hapless male to one sweet bird, 5.06. 15
the rod, and bird of peace, and all such emblems H8 4.01. 89
but as when | the bird of wonder dies, the 5.04. 40
where like a sweet melodious bird it sung TIT 3.01. 85
and yet no farther than a wanton's bird, | that ROM 2.02.177
i would i were thy bird. 2.02.182
and yesterday the bird of night did sit | even JC 1.03. 26
but this bird | hath made his pendant bed and MAC 1.06. 7
the obscure bird | clamor'd the livelong night. 2.03. 59
poor bird, thou'dst never fear the net nor lime, 4.02. 34
this bird of dawning singeth all night long, HAM 1.01.160
o, well flown, bird! LR 4.06. 91 P
o antony! o thou arabian bird! ANT 3.02. 12
she is alone th' arabian bird, and i | have lost CYM 1.06. 17
we make a choir, as doth the prison'd bird, 3.03. 43
the bird is dead | that we have made so much on. 4.02.197
i saw jove's bird, the roman eagle, wing'd 4.02.348
his royal bird | prunes the immortal wing and 5.04.117
though they did change me to the meanest bird PER 4.06.101
composes | nature's own shape of bud, bird, 5.ch. 6
bird melodious, or bird fair, | is absent hence! TNK 1.01. 17
of the air, | bird melodious, or bird fair, | is 1.01. 17
look how a bird lies tangled in a net, | so VEN 67
like a wild bird being tam'd with too much 560
like to a new–kill'd bird she trembling lies; LUC 457
"and for, poor bird, thou sing'st not in the day 1142
she, poor bird, as all forlorn, | lean'd her PP 20. 9
let the bird of loudest lay, | on the sole PHT 1
for it no form delivers to the heart | of bird, SON 113. 6
BIRD–BOLT *(also burbolt)*
BIRD–BOLT 1 FR 0.0001 REL FR 0 V 1 P
him with thy bird–bolt under the left pap. LLL 4.03. 23 P
BIRD–BOLTS 1 FR 0.0001 REL FR 0 V 1 P
take those things for bird–bolts that you deem TN 1.05. 93 P
BIRDING–PIECES 1 FR 0.0001 REL FR 0 V 1 P
always use to discharge their birding–pieces. WIV 4.02. 58 P
BIRDLIME 1 FR 0.0001 REL FR 1 V 0 P
comes from my pate as birdlime does from frieze, OTH 2.01.126
BIRD'S 4 FR 0.0004 REL FR 2 V 2 P
who, being overjoy'd with finding a bird's nest, ADO 2.01.223 P
who, as i take it, have stol'n his bird's nest. 2.01.231 P
his merry note | unto the sweet bird's throat, AYL 2.05. 4
must climb a bird's nest soon when it is dark. ROM 2.05. 74
BIRDS 48 FR 0.0054 REL FR 46 V 2 P
whose falls | melodious birds sings madrigals; WIV 3.01. 18
"melodious birds sing madrigals — | when as i 3.01. 23
law, | setting it up to fear the birds of prey, MM 2.01. 2
boast | before the birds have any cause to sing? LLL 1.01.103
when beasts most graze, birds best peck, and men 1.01.236 P
saw | and birds sit brooding in the snow | and 5.02.923
when birds do sing, hey ding a ding, ding, AYL 5.03. 20
with hey, the sweet birds, o, how they sing! WT 4.03. 6
suppose the singing birds musicians, | the grass R2 1.03.288
and plac'd a choir of such enticing birds | that 2H6 1.03. 89
yea, man and birds are fain of climbing high. 2.01. 8
and of their feather many moe proud birds, 3H6 2.01.170
for both of you are birds of self–same feather. 3.03.161
ay, such a pleasure as incaged birds | conceive, 4.06. 12
the birds chaunt melody on every bush, | the TIT 2.03. 12
hounds and horns and sweet melodious birds | be 2.03. 27
the whilst their own birds famish in their nests 2.03.154
the eagle suffers little birds to sing, | and is 4.04. 83
but throw her forth to beasts and birds to prey: 5.03.198
and, being dead, let birds on her take pity. 5.03.200
that birds would sing and think it were not ROM 2.02. 22
leaves winter, such summer birds are men. TIM 3.06. 32 P
water, | as beasts and birds and fishes. 4.03.423
on the beasts themselves, the birds and fishes; 4.03.424
why birds and beasts from quality and kind, JC 1.03. 64
the most diminutive of birds, will fight, | her MAC 4.02. 10
as birds do, mother. 4.02. 32
poor birds they are not set for. 4.02. 36
let the birds fly, and like the famous ape, | to HAM 3.04.194
we two alone will sing like birds i' th' cage; LR 5.03. 9
sorrow to shepherds, woe unto the birds, | gusts VEN 455
the sheep are gone to fold, birds to their nest, 532
even so poor birds, deceiv'd with painted grapes 601
as those poor birds that helpless berries saw. 604
when he was by, the birds such pleasure took, 1101
birds never lim'd no secret bushes fear: LUC 88
and give the sneaped birds more cause to sing. 333
the adder hisses where the sweet birds sing, 871
the little birds that tune their morning's joy 1107
"you mocking birds," quoth she, "your tunes 1121
clear wells spring not, sweet birds sing not, PP 17.25
by whose falls | melodious birds sing madrigals. 19. 8
made, | beasts did leap and birds did sing, 20. 5
all thy fellow birds do sing, | careless of thy 20.25
for these dead birds sigh a prayer. PHT 67
/ruin'd choirs, where late the sweet birds sang. SON 73. 4
thee, | and, thou away, the very birds are mute; 97.12
yet nor the lays of birds, nor the sweet smell 98. 5
BIRNAN 10 FR 0.0011 REL FR 10 V 0 P

until | great birnan wood to high dunsinane hill MAC 4.01. 93
rise never till the wood | of birnan rise, and 4.01. 98
near birnan wood | shall we well meet them; 5.02. 5
make we our march towards birnan. 5.02. 31
till birnan wood remove to dunsinane | i cannot 5.03. 2
bane, | till birnan forest come to dunsinane. 5.03. 60
the wood of birnan. 5.04. 3
i look'd toward birnan, and anon methought | the 5.05. 33
not, till birnan wood | do come to dunsinane," 5.05. 43
though birnan wood be come to dunsinane, | and 5.08. 30
/BIRTH 1 FR 0.0001 REL FR 1 V 0 P
/for /he /himself /is /subject /to /his /birth: HAM 1.03. 18
BIRTH 91 FR 0.0102 REL FR 81 V 10 P
and a birth, indeed, | which throes thee much to TMP 2.01.230
worthy his youth and nobleness of birth. TGV 1.03. 33
but truer stars did govern proteus' birth: 2.07. 74
what says she to my birth? 5.02. 22
he doth object i am too great of birth, | and WIV 3.04. 4
worm, thou wast o'erlook'd even in thy birth. 5.05. 83
him from her, she is no equal for his birth. ADO 2.01.165 P
but on this travail look for greater birth: 4.01.213
why should i joy in any abortive birth? LLL 1.01.104
your wit | what was a month old at cain's birth, 4.02. 35
great things laboring perish in their birth. 5.02.520
i do in birth deserve her, and in fortunes, | in MV 2.07. 32
you that keeping for a gentleman of my birth, AYL 1.01. 10 P
civet is of a baser birth than tar, the very 3.02. 67 P
sly's son of burton-heath, by birth a pedlar, by SHR in.2. 19 P
o noble lord, bethink thee of thy birth, | call in.2. 30
her dowry wealthy, and of worthy birth; 4.05. 65
commission of your birth and virtue gives you AWW 2.03.262 P
our celebration keep | according to my birth. TN 4.03. 31
and died that day when viola from her birth 5.01.244
death, nor on the birth | of trembling winter, WT 4.04. 80
her breeding as | she is i' th' rear 'our birth. 4.04.581
if love ambitious sought a match of birth, JN 2.01.430
such as she is, in beauty, virtue, birth, | is 2.01.432
become thy great birth nor deserve a crown. 3.01. 50
but thou art fair, and at thy birth, dear boy, 3.01. 51
for since the birth of cain, the first male 3.04. 79
by their breed, and famous by their birth, R2 2.01. 52
myself, a prince by fortune of my birth, | near 3.01. 16
and at my birth | the frame and huge foundation 1H4 3.01. 15
at your birth | our grandam earth, having this 3.01. 32
to tell you once again that at my birth | the 3.01. 36
grant that our hopes (yet likely of fair birth) 2H4 1.03. 63
voice, the tongue, which is the birth, becomes 4.03.101 P
and in the derivation of my birth, and in other H5 3.02.130 P
dolphin, i am by birth a shepherd's daughter, 1H6 1.02. 72
and stands upon the honor of his birth, | if he 2.04. 28
body) | i was the next by birth and parentage; 2.05. 73
and, for your royal birth, | inferior to none 3.01. 95
thee, | doubting thy birth and lawful progeny. 3.03. 61
knights of the garter were of noble birth, 4.01. 34
shalt well perceive | that neither in birth, or 5.01. 59
this man | of purpose to obscure my noble birth. 5.04. 22
her peerless feature, joined with her birth, 5.05. 68
a cunning man did calculate my birth | and told 2H6 4.01. 34
by her he had two children at one birth. 4.02.139
and, ignorant of his birth and parentage, 4.02.144
the sons of york, thy betters in their birth, 5.01.119
and birth that thou shouldst stand while lewis 3H6 3.03. 3
the owl shriek'd at thy birth, an evil sign; 5.06. 44
your state of fortune, and your due of birth, R3 3.07.120
your right of birth, your empery, your own. 3.07.136
crown, | as the ripe revenue and due of birth, 3.07.158
a grievous burthen was thy birth to me, | tetchy 4.04.168
wrong not her birth, she is a royal princess. 4.04.212
her life is safest only in her birth. 4.04.214
lo at their birth good stars were opposite. 4.04.216
is not birth, beauty, good shape, discourse, TRO 1.02.253 P
shores, | the primogenity and due of birth, 1.03.106
we will not name desert before his birth, and, 3.02. 94 P
high birth, vigor of bone, desert in service, 3.03.172
even in the birth of our own laboring breath. 4.04. 38
prodigious birth of love it is to me | that i ROM 1.05.140
revolts from true birth, stumbling on abuse. 2.03. 20
why railest thou on thy birth? 3.03.119
since birth, and heaven, and earth, all three do 3.03.120
residence, and birth | scarce is dividant, touch TIM 4.03. 4
thou never com'st unto a happy birth, | but JC 5.03. 70
(from whom this tyrant holds the due of birth) MAC 3.06. 25
wherein our saviour's birth is celebrated, HAM 1.01.159
as in their birth, wherein they are not guilty 1.04. 25
of violent birth, but poor validity, | which now 3.02.189
let me, if not by birth, have lands by wit: LR 1.02.183
bring this monstrous birth to the world's light. OTH 1.03.404
though he had twinn'd with me, both at a birth, 2.03.212
what's his name and birth? CYM 1.01. 27
the advantage of the time, above him in birth, 4.01. 12 P
not seeming | so worthy as thy birth. 4.02. 94
our jovial star reign'd at his birth, and in 5.04.105
o, what, am i | a mother to the birth of three? 5.05.369
from whence we had our being and our birth. PER 1.02.114
in honor of whose birth these triumphs are, 2.02. 5
for a more blusterous birth had never babe. 3.01. 28
marina was she call'd, and at her birth, 4.04. 38
you not name a tempest, | a birth, and death? 5.03. 34
god, | that i from such an humble bench of birth STM III 6
a dearer birth than this his love had brought SON 32.11
for whether beauty, birth, or wealth, or wit, 37. 5
showing their birth and where they did proceed? 76. 8
some glory in their birth, some in their skill, 91. 1
thy love is /better than high birth to me, 91. 9
BIRTH-CHILD 1 FR 0.0001 REL FR 1 V 0 P
hath thetis' birth-child on the heavens bestowed PER 4.04. 41
BIRTHDAY 4 FR 0.0004 REL FR 3 V 1 P
messala, | this is my birthday; JC 5.01. 71
it is my birthday, | i had thought t' have held ANT 3.13.184
and to-morrow is her birthday, and there are PER 2.01.109 P
honor'd her fair birthday with your virtues, TNK 2.05. 36
BIRTHDOM 1 FR 0.0001 REL FR 1 V 0 P
like good men | bestride our downfall birthdom. MAC 4.03. 4
BIRTH-HOUR'S 1 FR 0.0001 REL FR 1 V 0 P
worse than a slavish wipe or birth-hour's blot; LUC 537
BIRTHPLACE 1 FR 0.0001 REL FR 1 V 0 P
my birthplace /hate i, and my love's upon | this COR 4.04. 23
BIRTHRIGHT 5 FR 0.0005 REL FR 5 V 0 P
and thy goodness | share with thy birthright! AWW 1.01. 64
with honor of his birthright to the crown. 2H6 2.02. 62
hath he deserv'd to lose his birthright thus? 3H6 1.01.219
should lose his birthright by his father's fault 2.02. 35
and then to whom the birthright of this beauty TNK 3.06. 31
BIRTHRIGHTS 1 FR 0.0001 REL FR 1 V 0 P
bearing their birthrights proudly on their backs JN 2.01. 70
BIRTHS 7 FR 0.0008 REL FR 7 V 0 P
was not full a month | between their births. WT 5.01.118
unfather'd heirs and loathly births of nature. 2H4 4.04.122
dear nurse of arts, plenties, and joyful births, H5 5.02. 35
inter their bodies as become their births. R3 5.05. 15
with all th' abhorred births below crisp heaven TIM 4.03.183
wife, ever begetting | new births of love; TNK 2.02. 81
she sows into the births of noble bodies, | were 4.02. 9
BIRTH-STRANGLED 1 FR 0.0001 REL FR 1 V 0 P
finger of birth-strangled babe | ditch-deliver'd MAC 4.01. 30
BIS 1 FR 0.0001 REL FR 0 V 1 P
twice sod simplicity, bis coctus! LLL 4.02. 22 P
BISCUIT 2 FR 0.0002 REL FR 1 V 1 P
which is as dry as the remainder biscuit | after AYL 2.07. 39
with his fist, as a sailor breaks a biscuit. TRO 2.01. 40 P
/BISHOP 1 FR 0.0001 REL FR 1 V 0 P
/but /now /the /bishop | /turns /insurrection 2H4 1.01.200
BISHOP 19 FR 0.0021 REL FR 19 V 0 P
o, belike it is the bishop of carlisle. R2 3.03. 30
why, bishop, is norfolk dead? 4.01.101
they say the bishop and northumberland | are 2H4 3.01. 95
with you, lord bishop, | it is even so. 4.02. 15
mowbray, the bishop scroop, hastings, and all, 4.04. 84
ay, /so the bishop be not overborne. 1H6 3.01. 53
the bishop and the duke of gloucester's men, 3.01. 78
the bishop hath a kindly gird. 3.01.131
lord bishop, set the crown upon his head. 4.01. 1
the bishop will be overborne by thee. 5.01. 60
i'll send some holy bishop to entreat; 2H6 4.04. 9
is new committed to the bishop of york, | fell 3H6 4.04. 11
is prisoner to the bishop here, at whose hands 4.05. 5
bishop, farewell! 4.05. 28
bishop of exeter, his elder brother, | with many R3 4.04.501
speeches utter'd | by th' bishop of bayonne, H8 2.04.173
he | (i mean the bishop) did require a respite, 2.04.178
this is about that which the bishop spake. 5.01. 84
at sudden commendations, | bishop of winchester. 5.02.158
BISHOP'S 4 FR 0.0004 REL FR 4 V 0 P
begun through malice of the bishop's men. 1H6 3.01. 75
stand you thus close to steal the bishop's deer? 3H6 4.05. 17
and from the bishop's huntsmen rescu'd him; 4.06. 84
you left poor henry at the bishop's palace, 5.01. 45
BISHOPS 5 FR 0.0005 REL FR 5 V 0 P
leads ancient lords and reverend bishops on | to 1H4 3.02.104
twelve barons, and twenty reverend bishops, | i 2H6 1.01. 8
with reverend fathers and well-learned bishops. R3 3.05.100
you maim'd the jurisdiction of all bishops. H8 3.02.312
what two reverend bishops | were those that went 4.01. 99
BISSON *(also beesom)*
BISSON 1 FR 0.0001 REL FR 1 V 0 P
threat'ning the flames | with bisson rheum, a HAM 2.02.506
BIT* 8 FR 0.0009 REL FR 6 V 2 P
evils, age and hunger, | i will not touch a bit. AYL 2.07.133
and with a half-cheek'd bit and a head-stall of SHR 3.02. 57 P
could be better bit than i have been since the 1H4 2.01. 17 P
and in their pale dull mouths the /gimmal'd bit H5 4.02. 49
as is the bud bit with an envious worm, | ere he ROM 1.01.151
that /it had it head bit off by it young." LR 1.04.216
though he had bit me, should have stood that 4.07. 36
the iron bit he crusheth 'tween his teeth, VEN 269
BITCH 1 FR 0.0001 REL FR 0 V 1 P
pandar, and the son and heir of a mungril bitch; LR 2.02. 23 P
BITCH'S 1 FR 0.0001 REL FR 0 V 1 P
they would have drown'd a blind bitch's puppies, WIV 3.05. 11 P
BITCH-WOLF'S 1 FR 0.0001 REL FR 0 V 1 P
thou bitch-wolf's son, canst thou not hear? TRO 2.01. 10 P
/BITE 1 FR 0.0001 REL FR 1 V 0 P
/as /despair | /that /frosts /will /bite /them. 2H4 1.03. 41
BITE 39 FR 0.0044 REL FR 22 V 17 P
that mow and chatter at me, | and after bite me; TMP 2.02. 10
lo, lo, again! bite him to death, i prithee. 3.02. 34 P
time after) | now gins to bite the spirits. 3.03.106
well, the best is, she hath no teeth to bite. TGV 3.01.344 P
a sword, and it shall bite upon my necessity. WIV 2.01.131 P
that thus can make him bite the law by th' nose, MM 3.01.108
if i had my mouth, i would bite; ADO 1.03. 35 P
bait the hook well, this fish will bite. 2.03.109 P
two bears will not bite one another when they 3.02. 78 P
that dost not bite so nigh | as benefits forgot; AYL 2.07.185
nor bite the lip, as angry wenches will, | nor SHR 2.01.248
blots thy beauty, as frosts do bite the meads, 5.02.139
dagger muzzled | lest it should bite its master, WT 1.02.157
for gnarling sorrow hath less power to bite R2 1.03.292
bite, i pray you, it is good for your green H5 5.01. 41 P
must i bite? 5.01. 44 P
so york must sit, and fret, and bite his tongue, 2H6 1.01.230
seen a hot o'erweening cur | run back and bite, 5.01.152
and bite thy tongue, that slanders him with 3H6 1.04. 47
to signify thou cam'st to bite the world; 5.06. 54
signified | that i should snarl, and bite, and 5.06. 77
but he would bite none. H8 1.04. 29
crooked malice nourishment | dare bite the best. 5.02. 80
no marvel though you bite so sharp /at reasons, TRO 2.02. 33
by vulcan's skill, | my sword should bite it. 5.02.171
one bear will not bite another, and wherefore 5.07. 19 P
to bite his lip | and hum at good cominius much COR 5.01. 48
or shall we bite our tongues, and in dumb shows TIT 3.01.131
i will bite my thumb at them, which is disgrace ROM 1.01. 42 P
do you bite your thumb at us, sir? 1.01. 44 P
i do bite my thumb, sir. 1.01. 45 P
do you bite your thumb at us, sir? 1.01. 46 P
no, sir, i do not bite my thumb at you, sir, but 1.01. 50 P
my thumb at you, sir, but i bite my thumb, sir. 1.01. 51 P
i will bite thee by the ear for that jest. 2.04. 77 P
nay, good goose, bite not. 2.04. 78 P
oft bite the holy cords a-twain | which are t' LR 2.02. 74
black or white, | tooth that poisons if it bite; 3.06. 67
again, | though i am mad, i will not bite him. ANT 2.05. 80
/BITES 1 FR 0.0001 REL FR 0 V 1 P
/the /foul /fiend /bites /my /back. LR 3.06. 17 P
BITES 10 FR 0.0011 REL FR 9 V 1 P
sour ringlets make, | whereof the ewe not bites; TMP 5.01. 38
that bites the first-born infants of the spring. LLL 1.01.101
which when it bites and blows upon my body AYL 2.01. 8
doth never rankle more | than when he bites, but R2 1.03.303
look when he fawns he bites; R3 1.03.289
and when he bites, | his venom tooth will rankle 1.03.289
he bites his lip, and starts, | stops on a H8 3.02.113
bites his lip with a politic regard, as who TRO 3.03.254 P
the air bites shrowdly, it is very cold. HAM 1.04. 1
he stamps, and bites the poor flies in his fume. VEN 316
BITING 10 FR 0.0011 REL FR 6 V 4 P
to repay that money will be a biting affliction. WIV 5.05.169 P
we have strict statutes and most biting laws MM 1.03. 19
not guiltless here | under some biting error. ADO 4.01.170
where biting cold would never let grass grow, 2H6 3.02.337
then we are like to have biting statutes, unless 4.07. 16 P
cold biting winter mars our hop'd-for hay. 3H6 4.08. 61
grandam, this would have been a biting jest. R3 2.04. 30
with my good biting falchion | i would have made LR 5.03.277
you to touch him, for his biting is immortal; ANT 5.02.246 P
how she died of the biting of it, what pain she 5.02.254 P
BITS* 6 FR 0.0006 REL FR 5 V 1 P
(the needful bits and curbs to headstrong weeds) MM 1.03. 20
and dainty bits | make rich the ribs, but LLL 1.01. 26
their mouths with stubborn bits and spur 'em H8 5.02. 58
the bits and greasy relics | of her o'er-eaten TRO 5.02.159
your function, go, and batten on cold bits. COR 4.05. 33 P
how many prodigal bits have slaves and peasants TIM 2.02.165
BITTEN 1 FR 0.0001 REL FR 0 V 1 P
at a playhouse and fight for bitten apples, that H8 5.03. 61 P
/BITTER 5 FR 0.0005 REL FR 5 V 0 P
have at you for a /bitter jest or two! SHR 5.02. 45
/will /revenge /these /bitter /woes /of /ours. TIT 3.02. 3
/leave /these /bitter /deep /laments, | /make 3.02. 46
and do such /bitter /business /as /the day HAM 3.02.391
/the /sweet /and /bitter /fool | /will LR 1.04.144
BITTER 71 FR 0.0080 REL FR 61 V 10 P
thoughts have punish'd me | with bitter fasts, TGV 2.04.131
when i was sick, you gave me bitter pills, | and 2.04.149
her, | with many bitter threats of biding there. 3.01.238
it is a bitter deputy. MM 4.02. 78
for 'tis a physic | that's bitter to sweet end. 4.06. 8
it is the base (though bitter) disposition of ADO 2.01.207 P
too bitter is thy jest. LLL 4.03.172
gall! bitter. 5.02.237
lay breath so bitter on your bitter foe. MND 3.02. 44
lay breath so bitter on your bitter foe. 3.02. 44
good hermia, do not be so bitter with me. 3.02.306
then stir demetrius up with bitter wrong; 3.02.361
freeze, freeze, thou bitter sky, | that dost not AYL 2.07.184
looks, i'll sauce her with bitter words. 3.05. 69 P
i will be bitter with him and passing short. 3.05.138
chewing the food of sweet and bitter fancy, | lo 4.03.101
how bitter a thing it is to look into happiness 5.02. 43 P
when did she cross thee with a bitter word? SHR 2.01. 28
hiding his bitter jests in blunt behavior; 3.02. 13
in the most bitter touch of sorrow that e'er i AWW 1.03.117 P
'tis bitter. 3.02. 76
the bitter past, more welcome is the sweet. 5.03.334
his revenges must | in that be made more bitter. WT 1.02.457
what wit can make heavy and vengeance bitter; 4.04.773 P
it is as bitter | upon thy tongue as in my 5.01. 18
and bitter shame hath spoil'd the sweet word's JN 3.04.110
war, | the bitter clamor of two eager tongues, R2 1.01. 49
clouds, | eating the bitter bread of banishment, 3.01. 21
nail'd | for our advantage on the bitter cross. 1H4 1.01. 27
my troth, captain, these are very bitter words. 2H4 2.04.170 P
this bitter taste | yields his engrossments to 4.05. 78
sweeten the bitter mock you sent his majesty, H5 2.04.122
and thou hast given me most bitter terms. 4.08. 42
and for those wrongs, those bitter injuries, 1H6 2.05.124
i would invent as bitter searching terms, | as 2H6 3.02.311
because he would avoid such bitter taunts 3H6 2.06. 66
your blunt upbraidings and your bitter scoffs. R3 1.03.103
thou hadst call'd me all these bitter names. 1.03.235
the bitter sentence of poor clarence' death? 1.04.186
and yet his punishment was bitter death. 2.01.106
o bitter consequence, | that edward still should 4.02. 15
hoping the consequence | will prove as bitter, 4.04. 7
and in the breath of bitter words let's smother 4.04.133
whom to leave | is only bitter to him, only H8 2.01. 74
to leave a thousandfold more bitter than | 'tis 2.03. 8
is it bitter? 2.03. 89
the bitter disposition of the time | will have TRO 4.01. 49
you are too bitter to your country-woman. 4.01. 68
she's bitter to her country. 4.01. 69
and for these bitter tears which now you see TIT 3.01. 6
and made a brine-pit with our bitter tears? 3.01.129
ease their stomachs with their bitter tongues. 3.01.233
but to torment you with my bitter tongue! 5.01.150
steel, | nor can i utter all our bitter grief, 5.03. 89
on the nipple | of my dug and felt it bitter, ROM 1.03. 31
thy wit is a very bitter sweeting, it is a most 2.04. 79 P
come, bitter conduct, come, unsavory guide! 5.03.116
'tis bitter cold, | and i am sick at heart. HAM 1.01. 8
and lack gall | to make oppression bitter, or 2.02.578
of age makes the world bitter to the best of our LR 1.02. 47 P
a bitter fool! 1.04.136 P
my boy, between a bitter fool and a sweet one? 1.04.138 P
in their power | to make this bitter to thee. OTH 1.01.104
you shall yourself read in the bitter letter 1.03. 68
i see a thing | bitter to me as death; CYM 5.05.104
bitter torture shall | winnow the truth from 5.05.133
ear | that are most /dearly sweet and bitter. TNK 5.04. 47
thy sug'red tongue to bitter wormwood taste; LUC 893
cries, | and bitter words to ban her cruel foes; 1460
no bitterness that i will bitter think, | nor SON 111.11
to bitter sauces did i frame my feeding, | and, 118. 6
BITTEREST 2 FR 0.0002 REL FR 2 V 0 P
of a doit, break out | to bitterest enmity; COR 4.04. 18
and all the bitterest terms | that ever ear did TIT 2.03.110
BITTERLY 9 FR 0.0010 REL FR 9 V 0 P
mistress, moved therewithal, | wept bitterly; TGV 4.04.171
and she will speak most bitterly and strange. MM 5.01. 36
which then blew bitterly against our faces, R2 1.04. 7
silence, | or bitterly to speak in your reproof, R3 3.07.142
more bitterly could i expostulate, | save that, 3.07.192
you speak too bitterly. 4.04.181

reproaches | most bitterly on you as putter–on H8 1.02. 24
a perilous knock — and it cried bitterly. ROM 1.03. 54
stars | shall bitterly begin his fearful date 1.04.108

BITTERNESS 11 FR 0.0012 REL FR 8 V 3 P
modest enough without a badge of bitterness. ADO 1.01. 23 P
you love me not, but say not so | in bitterness. AYL 3.05. 3
contempt nor bitterness | were in his pride or AWW 1.02. 36
that it yields nought but shame and bitterness. JN 3.04.111
of our livers with the bitterness of your galls; 2H4 1.02.175 P
from bitterness of soul | denounc'd against thee R3 1.03.178
his fits, his frenzy, and his bitterness? TIT 4.04. 12
of my despised time | is nought but bitterness. OTH 1.01.162
(the bitterness of it i now belch from my heart) CYM 3.05.133 P
you, | nor think the bitterness of absence sour, SON 57. 7
no bitterness that i will bitter think, | nor 111.11

BITT'REST 2 FR 0.0002 REL FR 2 V 0 P
deserv'd | all tongues to talk their bitt'rest. WT 3.02.216
now seeming sweet, convert to bitt'rest gall. ROM 1.05. 92

/BITUM'D 1 FR 0.0001 REL FR 1 V 0 P
how close 'tis caulk'd and /bitum'd! PER 3.02. 56

BITUM'D 1 FR 0.0001 REL FR 0 V 1 P
beneath the hatches, caulk'd and bitum'd ready. PER 3.01. 71 P

BLAB 3 FR 0.0003 REL FR 3 V 0 P
red sparkling eyes blab his heart's malice, 2H6 3.01.154
them, cannot choose | but they must blab — OTH 4.01. 29
violets whereon we lean | never can blab, nor VEN 126

BLABB'D 2 FR 0.0002 REL FR 2 V 0 P
why have i blabb'd? TRO 3.02.124
that blabb'd them with such pleasing eloquence, TIT 3.01. 83

BLABBING 1 FR 0.0001 REL FR 1 V 0 P
the gaudy, blabbing, and remorseful day | is 2H6 4.01. 1

BLABS 1 FR 0.0001 REL FR 1 V 0 P
when my tongue blabs, then let mine eyes not see TN 1.02. 63

BLACK *(also plack)*

/BLACK 2 FR 0.0002 REL FR 1 V 1 P
/sir, /it /was /a /black //ill–favor'd /fly, TIT 3.02. 66
/croak /not, /black /angel, /i /have /no /food LR 3.06. 31 P

BLACK 175 FR 0.0197 REL FR 151 V 24 P
yond same black cloud, yond huge one, looks like TMP 2.02. 20 P
though ne'er so black, say they have angels' TGV 3.01.103
why, man? how black? 3.01.287 P
why, as black as ink. 3.01.288 P
face, | that now she is become as black as i. 4.04.156
nay then the wanton lies; my face is black. 5.02. 10
black men are pearls in beauteous ladies' eyes. 5.02. 12
good heart, is beaten black and blue, that you WIV 4.05.112 P
what tellest thou me of black and blue? 4.05.114 P
my doe with the black scut? 5.05. 18 P
fairies, black, grey, green, and white, | you 5.05. 37
as these black masks | proclaim an enshield MM 2.04. 79
suck our breath, or pinch us black and blue. ERR 2.02.192
if black, why, nature, drawing of an antic, ADO 3.01. 63
which indeed is not under white and black, this 5.01.305 P
i did commend the black oppressing humor to the LLL 1.01.232 P
by heaven, thy love is black as ebony. 4.03.243
no face is fair that is not full so black. 4.03.249
black is the badge of hell, | the hue of 4.03.250
o, if in black my lady's brows be deck'd, | it 4.03.254
and therefore is she born to make black fair. 4.03.257
paints itself black, to imitate her brow. 4.03.261
to look like her are chimney–sweepers black. 4.03.262
i'll change my black gown for a faithful friend. 5.02.834
beetles black, approach not near; MND 2.02. 22
the woosel cock so black of hue, | with 3.01.125
anon | with drooping fog as black as acheron, 3.02.357
o night with hue so black! 5.01.170
fell a–bleeding on black monday last at six a' MV 2.05. 25 P
fairest lin'd | are but black to rosalind. AYL 3.02. 93
'tis not your inky brows, your black silk hair, 3.05. 46
he said mine eyes were black and my hair black, 3.05.130
he said mine eyes were black and my hair black, 3.05.130
of humility over the black gown of a big heart. AWW 1.03. 95 P
black and fearful | on the opposer. 3.01. 5
the black prince, sir, alias the prince of 4.05. 42 P
sweet, | on my black coffin let there be strown. TN 2.04. 60
and we will fool him black and blue, shall we 2.05. 10 P
not black in my mind, though yellow in my legs. 3.04. 26 P
as black as vulcan in the smoke of war. 5.01. 53
yet black brows, they say, | become some women WT 2.01. 8
driven snow, | cypress black as e'er was crow, 4.04.219
but in despair die under their black weight. JN 3.01.297
thou'rt damn'd as black — nay, nothing is so 4.03.121
damn'd as black — nay, nothing is so black — 4.03.121
whose black contagious breath | already smokes 5.04. 33
why, here walk i in the black brow of night, 5.06. 17
black, fearful, comfortless, and horrible. 5.06. 20
and myself | rescued the black prince, that R2 2.03.101
good duke of york's | that tell black tidings. 3.04. 71
of the christian cross | against black pagans, 4.01. 95
souls refin'd | should show so heinous, black, 4.01.131
lament, | and put on sullen black incontinent. 5.06. 48
like the south | borne with black vapor, doth 2H4 2.04.364
alas, a black woosel, cousin shallow! 3.02. 8 P
doit of staffordshire, and black george barnes, 3.02. 20 P
and your great–uncle's, edward the black prince, H5 1.02.105
of it stands off as gross | as black and white, 2.02.104
and 'a said it was a black soul burning in hell? 2.03. 41 P
captiv'd by the hand | of that black name, 2.04. 56
that black name, edward, black prince of wales; 2.04. 56
it will be a black matter for the king that led 4.01.144 P
as ever his black shoe trod upon god's ground 4.07.141 P
back will stoop, a black beard will turn white, 5.02.160 P
hung be the heavens with black, yield day to 1H6 1.01. 1
we mourn in black, why mourn we not in blood? 1.01. 17
and, whereas i was black and swart before, 1.02. 84
your kingdom's terror and black nemesis? 4.07. 78
black, forsooth, coal–black as jet. 2H6 2.01.110
the first, edward the black prince, prince of 2.02. 11
edward the black prince died before his father, 2.02. 18
i will stir up in england some black storm 3.01.349
but see, his face is black and full of blood, 3.02.168
and from his bosom purge this black despair! 3.03. 23
and wrap our bodies in black mourning gowns, 3H6 2.01.161
we, well cover'd with the night's black mantle, 4.02. 22
that now are dimm'd with death's black veil, 5.02. 16
i spy a black, suspicious, threat'ning cloud, 5.03. 4
what black magician conjures up this fiend | to R3 1.02. 34
black night o'ershade thy day, and death thy 1.02.131
i'll join with black despair against my soul, 2.02. 36
but if black scandal or foul–fac'd reproach 3.07.231
the consequence | will prove as bitter, black, 4.04. 7
richard yet lives, hell's black intelligencer, 4.04. 71
a black day will it be to somebody. 5.03.280
is on me | which makes my whit'st part black. H8 1.01.209
and is become as black | as if besmear'd in hell 1.02.123
he had a black mouth that said other of him. 1.03. 58
no black envy | shall make my grave. 2.01. 85
arm'd, as black defiance | as heart can think or TRO 4.01. 13
not that our heads are some brown, some black, COR 2.03. 19 P
aaron will have his soul black like his face. TIT 3.01.205
a joyless, dismal, black, and sorrowful issue! 4.02. 66
'zounds, ye whore, is black so base a hue? 4.02. 71
can never turn the swan's black legs to white, 4.02.102
look how the black slave smiles upon the father, 4.02.120
acts of black night, abominable deeds, 5.01. 64
ay, like a black dog, as the saying is. 5.01.122
provide thee two proper palfreys, black as jet, 5.02. 50
black and portendous must this humor prove, ROM 1.01.141
being black, puts us in mind they hide the fair. 1.01.231
stabb'd with a white wench's black eye, run 2.04. 14 P
this day's black fate on moe days doth depend, 3.01.119
some twenty of them fought in this black strife, 3.01.178
night, | thou sober–suited matron all in black, 3.02. 11
bating in my cheeks, | with thy black mantle; 3.02. 15
the law, | and turn'd that black word "death" to 3.03. 27
never was seen so black a day as this. 4.05. 53
turn from their office to black funeral: 4.05. 85
thus much of this will make | black white, foul TIM 4.03. 29
engenders the black toad and adder blue, | the 4.03.181
to die | in our black sentence and proscription. JC 4.01. 17
let not light see my black and deep desires; MAC 1.04. 51
ere to black hecat's summons | the shard–borne 3.02. 41
whiles night's black agents to their preys do 3.02. 53
how now, you secret, black, and midnight hags? 4.01. 48
black macbeth | will seem as pure as snow, and 4.03. 52
hath from my soul | wip'd the black scruples, 4.03.116
the devil damn thee black, thou cream–fac'd loon 5.03. 11
mother, | nor customary suits of solemn black, HAM 1.02. 78
black as his purpose, did the night resemble 2.02.453
hath now this dread and black complexion smear'd 2.02.455
nay then let the dev'l wear black, for i'll have 3.02.129 P
thoughts black, hands apt, drugs fit, and time 3.02.255
o bosom black as death! 3.03. 67
and that his soul may be as damn'd and black 3.03. 94
and there i see such black and /grained spots 3.04. 90
look'd black upon me, strook me with her tongue, LR 2.04.160
be thy mouth or black or white, | tooth that 3.06. 66
hairs in my beard ere the black ones were there. 4.06. 98 P
an old black ram | is tupping your white ewe. OTH 1.01. 88
your son–in–law is far more fair than black. 1.03.290
well prais'd! how if she be black and witty? 2.01.131
if she be black, and thereto have a wit, 2.01.132
have a measure to the health of black othello. 2.03. 32 P
haply, for i am black, | and have not those soft 3.03.263
is now begrim'd and black | as mine own face. 3.03.387
arise, black vengeance, from the hollow hell! 3.03.447
that am with phoebus' amorous pinches black, ANT 1.05. 28
these signs, | they are black vesper's pageants. 4.14. 8
damn'd paper, | black as the ink that's on thee! CYM 3.02. 20
the rest (hark in thine ear) as black as incest, PER 1.02. 76
shield | is a black ethiope reaching at the sun; 2.02. 20
no visor does become black villainy | so well as 4.04. 44
his complexion | nearer a brown than black; TNK 4.02. 79
him, black and shining | like ravens' wings; 4.02. 83
now, | by casting her black mantle over both, 5.03. 25
emily | did first bestow on him — a black one, 5.04. 50
another flap–mouth'd mourner, black and grim, VEN 920
and, beauty dead, black chaos comes again. 1020
when thou shalt charge me with so black a deed? LUC 226
with such black payment as thou hast pretended; 576
falls into thy boundless flood | black lust, 654
black stage for tragedies and murthers fell! 766
through night's black bosom should not peep 788
which underneath thy black all–hiding cloak 801
her blue blood chang'd to black in every vein, 1454
who finds his lucrece clad in mourning black, 1585
and some look'd black, and that false tarquin 1743
face | of that black blood a wat'ry rigol goes, 1745
in black mourn i, all fears scorn i, | love hath PP 17.13
makes black night beauteous and her old face new SON 27.12
his beauty shall in these black lines be seen, 63.13
that in black ink my love may still shine bright 65.14
which by and by black night doth take away, 73. 7
in the old age black was not counted fair, | or 127. 1
but now is black beauty's successive heir, | and 127. 3
therefore my mistress' eyes are raven black, 127. 9
if hairs be wires, black wires grow on her head. 130. 4
thy black is fairest in my judgment's place. 131.12
in nothing art thou black save in thy deeds, 131.13
have put on black, and loving mourners be, 132. 3
then will i swear beauty herself is black, | and 132.13
who art as black as hell, as dark as night. 147.14
would have seem'd more black and damned here!" LC 54

BLACKAMOOR 1 FR 0.0001 REL FR 0 V 1 P
i care not and she were a blackamoor, 'tis all TRO 1.01. 77 P

BLACKBERRIES 2 FR 0.0002 REL FR 0 V 2 P
if reasons were as plentiful as blackberries, i 1H4 2.04.239 P
of heaven prove a micher and eat blackberries? 2.04.408 P

BLACKBERRY 1 FR 0.0001 REL FR 0 V 1 P
ulysses, is not prov'd worth a blackberry. TRO 5.04. 12 P

BLACK–BROW'D 2 FR 0.0002 REL FR 2 V 0 P
must for aye consort with black–brow'd night. MND 3.02.387
gentle night, come, loving, black–brow'd night, ROM 3.02. 20

BLACK–CORNER'D 1 FR 0.0001 REL FR 1 V 0 P
the day serves, before black–corner'd night, TIM 5.01. 44

BLACKER 5 FR 0.0005 REL FR 5 V 0 P
words, blacker in their effect | than in their AYL 4.03. 35
not for because | your brows are blacker; WT 2.01. 8
how his piety | does my deeds make the blacker! 3.02.172
the more angel she, | and you the blacker devil! OTH 5.02.131
blush not in actions blacker than the night PER 1.01.135

BLACKEST 4 FR 0.0004 REL FR 3 V 1 P
the blackest news that ever thou heardst. TGV 3.01.286 P
vows, to the blackest devil! HAM 4.05.132
when devils will the blackest sins put on, OTH 2.03.351
the blackest sin is clear'd with absolution; LUC 354

BLACK–EY'D 1 FR 0.0001 REL FR 1 V 0 P
a hundred black–ey'd maids that love as i do, TNK 4.01. 72

BLACK–FAC'D 4 FR 0.0004 REL FR 4 V 0 P
when black–fac'd clifford shook his sword at him R3 1.02.158
for, by this black–fac'd night, desire's foul VEN 773
but when a black–fac'd cloud the world doth LUC 547
into so bright a day such black–fac'd storms, 1518

BLACK–FRIARS 1 FR 0.0001 REL FR 1 V 0 P
for such receipt of learning is black–friars; H8 2.02.138

BLACK–HAIR'D 1 FR 0.0001 REL FR 1 V 0 P
she lov'd a black–hair'd man. TNK 3.03. 31

BLACKHEATH 1 FR 0.0001 REL FR 1 V 0 P
even now | you may imagine him upon blackheath; H5 5.pr. 16

BLACKMERE 1 FR 0.0001 REL FR 1 V 0 P
lord strange of blackmere, lord verdon of alton, 1H6 4.07. 65

BLACKNESS 4 FR 0.0004 REL FR 3 V 1 P
the raven chides blackness. TRO 2.03.211 P
find a white that shall her blackness /hit. OTH 2.01.133
of heaven, | more fiery by night's blackness; ANT 1.04. 13
shed | to keep his bed of blackness unlaid ope, PER 1.02. 89

BLACKS 1 FR 0.0001 REL FR 1 V 0 P
but were they false | as o'er–dy'd blacks, as WT 1.02.132

BLADDER 1 FR 0.0001 REL FR 0 V 1 P
and grief, it blows a man up like a bladder. 1H4 2.04.333 P

BLADDERS 3 FR 0.0003 REL FR 2 V 1 P
like little wanton boys that swim on bladders, H8 3.02.359
whissing lungs, bladders full of imposthume, TRO 5.01. 21 P
green earthen pots, bladders, and musty seeds, ROM 5.01. 46

BLADE 12 FR 0.0013 REL FR 11 V 1 P
whereat, with blade, with bloody blameful blade, MND 5.01.146
whereat, with blade, with bloody blameful blade, 5.01.146
trusty sword, | come, blade, my breast imbrue! 5.01.344
natural rebellion, done i' th' blade of youth, AWW 5.03. 6
and this thy son's blood cleaving to my blade 3H6 1.03. 50
and with thy treacherous blade | unrip'st the R3 1.04.206
come, | and flourishes his blade in spite of me. ROM 1.01. 78
"by jesu, a very good blade! 2.04. 30 P
and on thy blade and dudgeon gouts of blood, MAC 2.01. 46
let fall thy blade on vulnerable crests, | i 5.08. 11
falls, and sounds more like | a bell than blade. TNK 5.03. 6
this said, he shakes aloft his roman blade, LUC 505

BLADED 2 FR 0.0002 REL FR 2 V 0 P
decking with liquid pearl the bladed grass | (a MND 1.01.211
though bladed corn be lodg'd, and trees blown MAC 4.01. 55

BLADES 3 FR 0.0003 REL FR 2 V 1 P
you break jests as braggards do their blades, ADO 5.01.187 P
between two blades, which bears the better 1H6 2.04. 13
of breaches, ambuscadoes, spanish blades, | of ROM 1.04. 84

BLAINS 1 FR 0.0001 REL FR 1 V 0 P
itches, blains, | sow all th' athenian bosoms, TIM 4.01. 28

BLAM'D 7 FR 0.0008 REL FR 4 V 3 P
are all dead, there need none to be blam'd. MND 5.01.357 P
that was not to be blam'd in the command of the AWW 3.06. 51 P
your suspicion, | be blam'd for't how you might. WT 2.01.161
you that are blam'd for it alike with us, | know H8 1.02. 39
which i have rather blam'd as mine own jealous LR 1.04. 69 P
but yet be blam'd, if thou this self deceivest SON 40. 7
that thou are blam'd shall not be thy defect, 70. 1

BLAME 94 FR 0.0106 REL FR 86 V 8 P
old lord, i cannot blame thee, | who am myself TMP 3.03. 4
jove, or who can blame me to piss my tallow? WIV 5.05. 14 P
one ne'er got me credit, the other mickle blame. ERR 3.01. 45
and i, to blame, have held him here too long. 4.01. 47
then if she fear, or be to blame, | by this you LLL 1.02.103
truly, the more to blame he; MV 3.05. 21 P
you were to blame, i must be plain with you, 5.01.166
if this be so, why blame you me to love you? AYL 5.02.103
if this be so, why blame you me to love you? 5.02.104
if this be so, why blame you me to love you? 5.02.105
you speak too, "why blame you me to love you?" 5.02.106 P
go, girl, i cannot blame thee now to weep, | for SHR 3.02. 27
signior petruchio, fie, you are to blame. 4.03. 48
amaz'd me more | than i dare blame my weakness. AWW 2.01. 85
he has much worthy blame laid upon him for 4.03. 6 P
which i presume shall render you no blame, | but 5.01. 32
whether i have been to blame or no, i know not. 5.03.129
blame not this haste of mine. TN 4.03. 22
i cannot blame him: 1H4 1.03.145
nay, then i cannot blame his cousin king, | that 1.03.158
i cannot blame him. 3.01. 13
i feel me much to blame | so idly to profane the 2H4 2.04.361
i blame you not, | for, hearing this, i must H5 4.06. 32
can you blame her then, being a maid yet ros'd 5.02.295 P
or will you blame and lay the fault on me? 1H6 2.01. 57
tush, that was but his fancy, blame him not. 4.01.178
and shall my youth be guilty of such blame? 4.05. 47
i cannot blame them all, what is't to them? 2H6 1.01.220
i know it well, lord warwick, blame me not. 3H6 2.01.157
i blame not her: 4.01.101
yet in this one thing let me blame your grace, 4.06. 30
did not offend, nor were not worthy blame, | if 5.05. 54
alas, i blame you not, for you are mortal, | and R3 1.02. 44
i cannot blame her; 1.03.305
the king mine uncle is to blame for it. 2.02. 13
i'll bear thy blame, | and take thy office from 4.01. 24
hath but wrong, and blame the due of blame. 5.01. 29
hath but wrong, and blame the due of blame. 5.01. 29
i cannot blame his conscience. H8 4.01. 47
you are to blame, | knowing she will not lose 4.02.101
if the king blame me for't, i'll lay ye all | by 5.03. 78
you blame martius for being proud? COR 2.01. 32 P
who is't can blame him? 4.06.105
the blame | may hang upon your hardness, 5.03. 90
takes from aufidius a great part of blame. 5.06.145
you are to blame, my lord, to rate her so. ROM 3.05.169
does not become a man, 'tis much to blame. TIM 1.02. 27
i speak, | no blame belongs to thee.) 2.02.222
i am to blame to be thus waited for. JC 2.02.119
i blame you not for praising caesar so, | but 3.01.214
you shall not in your funeral speech blame us, 3.01.245
poor knave, i blame thee not, thou art 4.03.241

by which i did blame cato for the death | which 5.01.101
his absence, sir, | lays blame upon his promise. MAC 3.04. 43
who then shall blame | his pester'd senses to 5.02. 22
we are oft to blame in this — | 'tis too much HAM 3.01. 45
if they come to't, | by cock, they are to blame. 4.05. 61
for his death no wind of blame shall breathe, 4.07. 66
i can no more — the king, the king's to blame. 5.02.320
as in part i understand them, are to blame. LR 1.02. 42 P
the duke's to blame in this, 'twill be ill taken 2.02.159
wholesome end | as clears her from all blame. 2.04.145
'tis his own blame hath put himself from rest, 2.04.290
canst thou blame him? 3.04.162
wrath, which men | may blame, but not control. 3.07. 27
leave, gentle wax, and, manners, blame us not: 4.06.259
and | to lay the blame upon her own despair, 5.03.255
destruction on my head if my bad blame | light OTH 1.03.177
who let us not therefore blame. 2.03. 16 P
'twas witchcraft — but i am much to blame. 3.03.211
i am to blame. 3.03.282
/i' /faith, you are to blame. 3.04. 97
your calling back, | lay not your blame on me. 4.02. 46
let nobody blame him, his scorn i approve" — 4.03. 52
but heavens know | some men are much to blame. CYM 1.06. 77
our great court | made me to blame in memory. 3.05. 51
occasion in his arms | of what we blame him for. 4.02.197
no blame be to you, sir, for all was lost | but 5.03. 3
though you did love this youth, i blame ye not, 5.05.267
blame both my lord and me, that we have taken PER 4.01. 37
fed | upon fresh beauty, blotting it with blame; VEN 796
adonis lives, and death is not to blame; 992
whose crime will bear an ever–during blame. LUC 224
discern | authority for sin, warrant for blame, 620
nurse of blame! 767
but that which doth devour, | is worthy blame. 1257
those proud lords to blame | make weak–made 1259
"the more to blame my sluggard negligence. 1278
lie | imagine every eye beholds their blame, 1343
strike, | let reason rule things worthy blame, PP 18. 3
i cannot blame thee for my love thou usest, SON 40. 6
not blame your pleasure, be it ill or well. 58.14
o, blame me not if i no more can write! 103. 5
is perjur'd, murd'rous, bloody, full of blame, 129. 3
BLAMEFUL 3 FR 0.0003 REL FR 3 V 0 P
whereat, with blade, with bloody blameful blade, MND 5.01.146
thy mother took into her blameful bed | some 2H6 3.02.212
and edward, | as blameful as the executioner? R3 1.02.119
BLAMELESS 2 FR 0.0002 REL FR 1 V 1 P
and so far blameless proves my enterprise, MND 3.02.350
"hermione is chaste, polixenes blameless, WT 3.02.133 P
BLAMES 3 FR 0.0003 REL FR 3 V 0 P
my high–repented blames, | dear sovereign, AWW 5.03. 36
the taints and blames i laid upon myself, | for MAC 4.03.124
he saith she is immodest, blames her miss; VEN 53
BLANC 1 FR 0.0001 REL FR 1 V 0 P
i have from le port blanc, | a bay in britain, R2 2.01.277
BLANCH 10 FR 0.0011 REL FR 10 V 0 P
with her her niece, the lady blanch of spain; JN 2.01. 64
that daughter there of spain, the lady blanch, 2.01.423
where should he find it fairer than in blanch? 2.01.427
where should he find it purer than in blanch? 2.01.429
whose veins bound richer blood than lady blanch? 2.01.431
shall lewis have blanch, and blanch those 3.01. 3
lewis have blanch, and blanch those provinces? 3.01. 3
lewis marry blanch? 3.01. 34
you, in the right of lady blanch your wife, 3.04.142
trey, blanch, and sweetheart, see, they bark at LR 3.06. 63
BLANCH'D 1 FR 0.0001 REL FR 1 V 0 P
your cheeks, | when mine is blanch'd with fear. MAC 3.04.115
/BLANK 1 FR 0.0001 REL FR 0 V 1 P
freely, or the /blank verse shall halt for't. HAM 2.02.325 P
BLANK 11 FR 0.0012 REL FR 8 V 3 P
writ with blank space for different names (sure, WIV 2.01. 75 P
run smoothly in the even road of a blank verse, ADO 5.02. 34 P
then god buy you, and you talk in blank verse. AYL 4.01. 32 P
a blank, my lord. TN 2.04.110
arm, out of the blank | and level of my brain — WT 2.03. 5
substitutes at home shall have blank charters, R2 1.04. 48
seals a commission to a blank of danger, | and TRO 3.03.231
infinite as all, | the other blank as nothing. 4.05. 81
diameter, | as level as the cannon to his blank, HAM 4.01. 42
me still remain | the true blank of thine eye. LR 1.01.159
and stood within the blank of his displeasure OTH 3.04.128
BLANKET 6 FR 0.0006 REL FR 3 V 3 P
i will toss the rogue in a blanket. 2H4 2.04.223 P
nor heaven peep through the blanket of the dark MAC 1.05. 53
a blanket, in the alarm of fear caught up — HAM 2.02.509
blanket my loins, elf all my hairs in knots, LR 2.03. 10
nay, he reserv'd a blanket, else we had been all 3.04. 65 P
caesar can hide the sun from us with a blanket, CYM 3.01. 43 P
/BLANKS 1 FR 0.0001 REL FR 1 V 0 P
cannot contain | commit to these waste /blanks, SON 77.10
BLANKS 4 FR 0.0004 REL FR 4 V 0 P
would they were blanks, rather than fill'd with TN 3.01.104
as blanks, benevolences, and i wot not what. R2 2.01.250
it is lots to blanks | my name hath touch'd your COR 5.02. 10
each opposite that blanks the face of joy | meet HAM 3.02.220
BLASPHEME 3 FR 0.0003 REL FR 3 V 0 P
you do blaspheme the good in mocking me. MM 1.04. 38
brother of england, you blaspheme in this. JN 3.01.161
stands accus'd, | and does blaspheme his breed? MAC 4.03.108
BLASPHEMING 2 FR 0.0002 REL FR 2 V 0 P
air, | blaspheming god and cursing men on earth. 2H6 3.02.372
digg'd i' th' dark, | liver of blaspheming jew, MAC 4.01. 26
BLASPHEMOUS 1 FR 0.0001 REL FR 0 V 1 P
you bawling, blasphemous, incharitable dog! TMP 1.01. 40 P
BLASPHEMY 3 FR 0.0003 REL FR 3 V 0 P
now, blasphemy, | that swear'st grace o'erboard, TMP 5.01.218
word, | which in the soldier is flat blasphemy. MM 2.02.131
set, | i would speak blasphemy ere bid you fly. 2H6 5.02. 85
/BLAST 2 FR 0.0002 REL FR 2 V 0 P
/and /for /one /blast /of /thy /minikin /mouth, LR 3.06. 43
to which that /blast gives heat and stronger PER 1.02. 41
BLAST 14 FR 0.0015 REL FR 14 V 0 P
but when the blast of war blows in our ears, H5 3.01. 5
now let the general trumpet blow his blast, 2H6 5.02. 43
lest with my sighs or tears i blast or drown 3H6 4.04. 23
i'll blast his harvest, /and your head were laid 5.07. 21
come, blow thy blast. COR 1.04. 12
striding the blast, or heaven's cherubin, hors'd MAC 1.07. 22
i'll cross it, though it blast me. HAM 1.01.127
that might hold | if this did blast in proof. 4.07.154
a fuller blast ne'er shook our battlements. OTH 2.01. 6
with brazen din blast you the city's ear, | make ANT 4.08. 36
virtue /preserv'd from fell destruction's blast, PER 5.03. 89
like lightning, | to blast whole armies, more! TNK 2.02. 25
or entertain'st a hope to blast my wishes, 2.02.170
as lagging fowls before the northern blast. LUC 1335
BLASTED 12 FR 0.0013 REL FR 11 V 1 P
and every part about you blasted with antiquity? 2H4 1.02.184 P
thus are my blossoms blasted in the bud, | and 2H6 3.01. 89
mine arm | is like a blasted sapling, wither'd R3 3.04. 69
be men like blasted woods, | and may diseases TIM 4.03.531
why | upon this blasted heath you stop our way MAC 1.03. 77
stature of blown youth | blasted with ecstasy. HAM 3.01.160
with hecat's ban thrice blasted, thrice 3.02.258
to see't mine eyes are blasted. ANT 3.10. 4
you were half blasted ere i knew you; 3.13.105
find | our paragon to all reports thus blasted, PER 4.01. 35
wreath | was then nor thresh'd nor blasted; TNK 1.01. 65
bud and be blasted in a breathing while, | the VEN 1142
BLASTING 4 FR 0.0004 REL FR 4 V 0 P
wit | is turn'd to folly, blasting in the bud, TGV 1.01. 48
a blasting and a scandalous breath to fall | on MM 5.01.122
mildewed ear, | blasting his wholesome brother. HAM 3.04. 65
you behold | the injury of many a blasting hour, LC 72
BLASTMENTS 1 FR 0.0001 REL FR 1 V 0 P
youth | contagious blastments are most imminent. HAM 1.03. 42
/BLASTS 1 FR 0.0001 REL FR 1 V 0 P
/the /impetuous /blasts /with /eyeless /rage LR 3.01. 8
BLASTS 10 FR 0.0011 REL FR 10 V 0 P
and there he blasts the tree, and takes the WIV 4.04. 32
that blasts of january | would blow you through WT 4.04.111
bolted | by th' northern blasts twice o'er. 4.04.365
that stand high have many blasts to shake them, R3 1.03.258
with thee airs from heaven, or blasts from hell, HAM 1.04. 41
blasts and fogs upon thee! LR 1.04.299
unto the worst | owes nothing to thy blasts. 4.01. 9
that blasts my bays and my fam'd works makes TNK pr 20
hasty spring still blasts and ne'er grows old! LUC 49
"unruly blasts wait on the tender spring, 869
BLAZ'D 2 FR 0.0002 REL FR 2 V 0 P
and ever, as it blaz'd, they threw on him ERR 5.01.172
room | hath blaz'd with lights and bray'd with TIM 2.02.161
BLAZE* 9 FR 0.0010 REL FR 8 V 1 P
his rash fierce blaze of riot cannot last, | for R2 2.01. 33
for well i wot ye blaze to burn them out. 3H6 5.04. 71
for hector in his blaze of wrath subscribes | to TRO 4.05.105
and their blaze | shall darken him for ever. COR 2.01.258
the main blaze of it is past, but a small thing 4.03. 20 P
we can find a time | to blaze your marriage, ROM 3.03.151
the heavens themselves blaze forth the death of JC 2.02. 31
i have a speech a' fire that fain would blaze, HAM 4.07.190
red cheeks and fiery eyes blaze forth her wrong; VEN 219
BLAZED 1 FR 0.0001 REL FR 1 V 0 P
that two red fires in both their faces blazed; LUC 1353
BLAZES 1 FR 0.0001 REL FR 1 V 0 P
these blazes, daughter, | giving more light than HAM 1.03.117
BLAZING 2 FR 0.0002 REL FR 1 V 1 P
woman born but /or every blazing star or at an AWW 1.03. 87 P
each one already blazing by our meeds, | should 3H6 2.01. 36
BLAZON 7 FR 0.0008 REL FR 6 V 1 P
crest, | with loyal blazon, evermore be blest! WIV 5.05. 64
lady, i think your blazon to be true, though, ADO 2.01.296 P
and spirit | do give thee fivefold blazon. TN 1.05.293
and that thy skill be more | to blazon it, then ROM 2.06. 26
but this eternal blazon must not be | to ears of HAM 1.05. 21
any gross stuff | to form me like your blazon, TNK 3.01. 47
then, in the blazon of sweet beauty's best, | of SON 106. 5
BLAZON'D 1 FR 0.0001 REL FR 1 V 0 P
with wit well blazon'd, smil'd or made some moan LC 217
BLAZONING 2 FR 0.0002 REL FR 2 V 0 P
and blazoning our unjustice every where? TIT 4.04. 18
one that excels the quirks of blazoning pens, OTH 2.01. 63
BLAZON'ST 1 FR 0.0001 REL FR 1 V 0 P
thou thyself thou blazon'st | in these two CYM 4.02.170
BLEACH 1 FR 0.0001 REL FR 1 V 0 P
daws, | and maidens bleach their summer smocks, LLL 5.02.906
BLEACHING 2 FR 0.0002 REL FR 1 V 1 P
what honest clothes you send forth to bleaching! WIV 4.02.121 P
the white sheet bleaching on the hedge, | with WT 4.03. 5
BLEAK* *(also bleat)*
/BLEAK* 1 FR 0.0001 REL FR 1 V 0 P
on, and the /bleak winds | do sorely ruffle; LR 2.04.300
BLEAK* 6 FR 0.0006 REL FR 5 V 1 P
why he hath made the ewe bleak for the lamb; MV 4.01. 74
yet thou liest in the bleak air. AYL 2.06. 15 P
steely bones | looks bleak i' th' cold wind. AWW 1.01.104
to make his bleak winds kiss my parched lips JN 5.07. 40
think'st | that the bleak air, thy boisterous TIM 4.03.222
our lodgings, standing bleak upon the sea, PER 3.02. 14
BLEAR'D 1 FR 0.0001 REL FR 1 V 0 P
while counterfeit supposes blear'd thine eyne. SHR 5.01.117
BLEARED 2 FR 0.0002 REL FR 2 V 0 P
with bleared visages, come forth to view | the MV 3.02. 59
and the bleared sights | are spectacled to see COR 2.01.205
BLEAT *(also bleak*)*
BLEAT 3 FR 0.0003 REL FR 3 V 0 P
much like to you, for you have just his bleat. ADO 5.04. 51
bleat softly then, the butcher hears you cry. LLL 5.02.255
i' th' sun, | and bleat the one at th' other. WT 1.02. 68
BLEATED 1 FR 0.0001 REL FR 1 V 0 P
the green neptune | a ram and bleated; WT 4.04. 29
BLEATS 1 FR 0.0001 REL FR 0 V 1 P
it baes will never answer a calf when he bleats. ADO 3.03. 72 P
BLED 3 FR 0.0003 REL FR 3 V 0 P
flesh away, | which all this while had bled; AYL 4.03.148
for that i have not wash'd | my nose that bled, COR 1.09. 48
and the drops | that we have bled together. 5.01. 11
/BLEED 2 FR 0.0002 REL FR 2 V 0 P
/fever, | /and /we /must /bleed /for /it; 2H4 4.01. 57
/at /this /time | /we /sweat /and /bleed: LR 5.03. 55
BLEED 39 FR 0.0044 REL FR 35 V 4 P
if you prick us, do we not bleed? MV 3.01. 64 P
to stop his wounds, lest he do bleed to death. 4.01.258
i would fain say, bleed tears; WT 5.02. 89 P
if not, bleed france, and peace ascend to heaven JN 2.01. 86
our doctors say this is no month to bleed. R2 1.01.157
our noses with speargrass to make them bleed, 1H4 2.04.310 P
not i, my lord, unless i did bleed too. 5.04. 4
they lost france, and made his england bleed; H5 ep 12
if i, my lord, for my opinion bleed, | opinion 1H6 2.04. 52
open their congeal'd mouths and bleed afresh! R3 1.02. 56
let paris bleed, 'tis but a scar to scorn; TRO 1.01.111
draw emulous factions and bleed to death upon. 2.03. 74 P
look how thy wounds do bleed at many vents! 5.03. 82
can the son's eye behold his father bleed? TIT 5.03. 65
i bleed inwardly for my lord. TIM 1.02.205
but, alas, | caesar must bleed for it! JC 2.01.171
how many times shall caesar bleed in sport, 3.01.114
did not great julius bleed for justice' sake? 4.03. 19
if he do bleed, | i'll gild the faces of the MAC 2.02. 52
bleed, bleed, poor country! 4.03. 31
bleed, bleed, poor country! 4.03. 31
with thy keen sword impress as make me bleed. 5.08. 10
they bleed on both sides. how is it, my lord? HAM 5.02.304
she sounds to see them bleed. 5.02.308
look, sir, i bleed. LR 2.01. 41
regan, i bleed apace, | untimely comes this hurt 3.07. 97
bless thy sweet eyes, they bleed. 4.01. 54
/'zounds, i bleed still, | i am hurt to th' OTH 2.03.164
nobody come? then shall i bleed to death. 5.01. 45
i bleed, sir, but not kill'd. 5.02.288
i do not see them bleed. ANT 5.02.338
as these before thee, thou thyself shalt bleed. PER 1.01. 58
i do bleed | when such i meet, and wish great TNK 1.02. 20
if you do, | your teeth will bleed extremely. 3.05. 81
must open | and bleed to death for my sake else. 4.02. 2
thought of it doth make my faint heart bleed, VEN 669
stole his blood and seem'd with him to bleed. 1056
eyes forgo their light, my false heart bleed? LUC 228
till lucrece' father, that beholds her bleed, 1732
BLEEDEST 1 FR 0.0001 REL FR 1 V 0 P
harry, withdraw thyself, thou bleedest too much. 1H4 5.04. 2
BLEEDETH 1 FR 0.0001 REL FR 1 V 0 P
end | to this debate that bleedeth at our doors, 2H4 4.04. 2
/BLEEDING 2 FR 0.0002 REL FR 2 V 0 P
/them /he /doth /bestride /a /bleeding /land, 2H4 1.01.207
/of /eggs | /to /apply /to /his /bleeding /face. LR 3.07.107
BLEEDING 32 FR 0.0036 REL FR 29 V 3 P
whose sons lie scattered on the bleeding ground. JN 2.01.304
and spit it bleeding in his high disgrace, R2 1.01.194
to open | the purple testament of bleeding war; 3.03. 94
war | all hot and bleeding will we offer them. 1H4 4.01.115
dead, | breathless and bleeding on the ground. 5.04.134
his bleeding sword 'twixt england and fair H5 5.02.355
lest, bleeding, you do paint the white rose red, 1H6 2.04. 50
i'll find friends to wear my bleeding roses, 2.04. 72
who finds the heifer dead and bleeding fresh, 2H6 3.02.188
with gobbets of thy /mother's bleeding heart. 4.01. 85
eyes, | the bleeding witness of my hatred by, R3 1.02.233
so she may live unscarr'd of bleeding slaughter, 4.04.210
slew her brothers | a pair of bleeding hearts; 4.04.272
dismiss the controversy bleeding, the more COR 2.01. 77 P
five times he hath return'd | bleeding to rome, TIT 1.01. 34
and juliet bleeding, warm, and newly dead, | who ROM 5.03.175
so they were bleeding new, my lord, there's no TIM 1.02. 78 P
nor sight of priests in holy vestments bleeding, 4.03.126
and this the bleeding business they have done. JC 3.01.168
o, pardon me, thou bleeding piece of earth, 3.01.254
would to the bleeding and the grim alarm MAC 5.02. 4
with less remorse than pyrrhus' bleeding sword HAM 2.02.491
habit | met i my father with his bleeding rings, LR 5.03.190
the testimonies whereof lies bleeding in me. CYM 3.04. 23 P
thy complaining than | thy master in bleeding. 4.02.376
sick between 's, | by bleeding must be cur'd. TNK 3.01.114
their scratch'd ears, bleeding as they go. VEN 924
which bleeding under pyrrhus' proud foot lies. LUC 1449
and then in key–cold lucrece' bleeding stream 1774
to show her bleeding body thorough rome, | and 1851
heart is bleeding, all help needing, | o cruel PP 17.15
it break, with bleeding groans they pine, | and LC 275
BLEEDS 9 FR 0.0010 REL FR 8 V 1 P
o, my heart bleeds | to think o' th' teen that i TMP 1.02. 63
her legs that one shall swear she bleeds, | and SHR in.2. 58
weep i cannot, | but my heart bleeds; WT 3.03. 52
life, | which bleeds away even as a form of wax JN 5.04. 24
my heart bleeds inwardly that my father is so 2H4 2.02. 48 P
o wife, look how our daughter bleeds! ROM 5.03.202
it weeps, it bleeds, and each new day a gash MAC 4.03. 40
for every tear he falls a troyan bleeds; LUC 1551
for his foul act by whom thy fair wife bleeds? 1824
BLEED'ST 3 FR 0.0003 REL FR 3 V 0 P
worthy sir, thou bleed'st, | thy exercise hath COR 1.05. 14
hast heavy substance, bleed'st not, speak'st, LR 4.06. 52
thou bleed'st apace. ANT 4.07. 6
/BLEMISH 1 FR 0.0001 REL FR 1 V 0 P
/thick (/which /nature /made /his /blemish) 2H4 2.03. 24
BLEMISH 9 FR 0.0010 REL FR 9 V 0 P
on their sustaining garments not a blemish, TMP 1.02.218
first, his integrity | stands without blemish; MM 5.01.108
in nature there's no blemish but the mind; TN 3.04.367
i'll give no blemish to her honor, none. WT 1.02.341
you should not blemish it, if i stood by: R3 1.02.128
rare indeed | whom these things cannot blemish), ANT 1.04. 23
thy deserving, | and blemish caesar's triumph. 4.12. 33
take, | the blemish that will never be forgot, LUC 536
more she thought he spied in her some blemish. 1358
BLEMISH'D 6 FR 0.0006 REL FR 6 V 0 P
and foolish sire | blemish'd his gracious dam; WT 3.02.198
redeem from broking pawn the blemish'd crown, R2 2.01.293
house, | to the corruption of a blemish'd stock; R3 3.07.122
thy garter, blemish'd, pawn'd his knightly 4.04.370
if in this blemish'd fort i make some hole LUC 1175
so beauty blemish'd once, for ever lost, | in PP 13.11
BLEMISHES 3 FR 0.0003 REL FR 3 V 0 P
i cannot forget | my blemishes in them, and so WT 5.01. 8
read not my blemishes in the world's report. ANT 2.03. 5
he | does pity, as constrained blemishes, | not 3.13. 59
BLENCH 5 FR 0.0005 REL FR 5 V 0 P
sometimes you do blench from this to that, | as MM 4.05. 5
could man so blench? WT 1.02.333
doth lesser blench at suff'rance than i do. TRO 1.01. 28

to blench from this and to stand firm by honor. 2.02. 68
if 'a do blench, | i know my course. HAM 2.02.597
BLENCHES 1 FR 0.0001 REL FR 1 V 0 P
these blenches gave my heart another youth, SON 110. 7
BLEND 2 FR 0.0002 REL FR 2 V 0 P
then blend your spirits with mine, | you whose TNK 5.01. 72
the heaven–hu'd sapphire and the opal blend LC 215
BLENDED 2 FR 0.0002 REL FR 2 V 0 P
half hector comes to seek | this blended knight, TRO 4.05. 86
when, both your voices blended, the great'st COR 3.01.103
BLENT 2 FR 0.0002 REL FR 2 V 0 P
where every something, being blent together, MV 3.02.181
'tis beauty truly blent, whose red and white TN 1.05.239
BLESS *(also pless, etc.)*
/BLESS 1 FR 0.0001 REL FR 0 V 1 P
/so, /bless /thee, /master! LR 4.01. 63 P
BLESS 110 FR 0.0124 REL FR 65 V 45 P
that would not bless our europe with your TMP 2.01.125
go with me | to bless this twain, that they may 4.01.104
he had not been there (bless the mark!) TGV 4.04. 19 P
/god bless them and make them his servants! WIV 2.02. 52 P
/god bless thee, bully–doctor! 2.03. 18 P
bless you, sir! 3.05. 60 P
bless you, good father friar. MM 3.02. 11 P
bless you, friar. 3.02. 77 P
and he will bless that cross with other beating: ERR 2.01. 79
can cross him any way, i bless myself every way. ADO 1.03. 68 P
god bless me from a challenge! 5.01.144 P
god bless my ladies! LLL 2.01. 77
god bless the king! 4.03.187
they did not bless us with one happy word. 5.02.370
bless thee, bottom, bless thee! MND 3.01.118 P
bless thee, bottom, bless thee! 3.01.118 P
and bless it to all fair prosperity. 4.01. 90
a paramour is, god bless us, a thing of naught. 4.02. 14 P
she for a woman, god bless us. 5.01.320 P
grace, | will we sing, and bless this place. 5.01.400
take his gait, | and each several chamber bless, 5.01.417
who, god bless the mark, is a kind of devil; MV 2.02. 24 P
god bless your worship! 2.02.120 P
error but some sober brow | will bless it, and 3.02. 79
bless you with such grace | as 'longeth to a SHR 4.02. 44
heaven bless him! | farewell, bertram. AWW 1.01. 73
bless our poor virginity from underminers and 1.01.120 P
bless you, my fortunate lady! 2.04. 14 P
bless him at home in peace, whilst i from far 3.04. 10
what angel shall | bless this unworthy husband? 3.04. 26
god bless you, captain parolles. 4.03.315 P
better than the first, o dear heaven, bless! 5.03. 71
bless you, fair shrew. TN 1.03. 47 P
god bless thee, lady! 1.05. 36 P
jove bless thee, master parson. 4.02. 11 P
now bless thyself: WT 3.03.113 P
i bless the time | when my good falcon made her 4.04. 14
bless me from marrying a usurer! 4.04.268 P
to bless the bed of majesty again | with a sweet 5.01. 33
jesus bless us! 1H4 2.02. 82 P
be honest, and god bless your expedition! 2H4 1.02.221 P
you would bless you to hear what he said. 2.04. 95 P
now, the lord bless that sweet face of thine! 2.04.292 P
sir john, the lord bless you! 3.02.292 P
god bless thy lungs, good knight. 5.05. 9 P
the lord in heaven bless thee, noble harry! H5 4.01. 33
and bless us with her former qualities. 5.02. 67
word thou shalt no sooner bless mine ear withal, 5.02.238 P
saint denis bless this happy stratagem! 1H6 3.02. 18
jesu bless him! 2H6 1.03. 5 P
o lord bless me, i pray god, for i am never able 2.03. 77 P
likely in time to bless a regal throne. 3H6 4.06. 74
"o, jesus bless us, he is born with teeth!" 5.06. 75
god bless thee, and put meekness in thy breast, R3 2.02.107
god bless your grace with health and happy days! 3.01. 18
god bless the prince from all the pack of you! 3.03. 5
if not to bless us and the land withal, | yet to 3.07.197
god bless your grace! we see it and will say it. 3.07.237
i, by attorney, bless thee from thy mother, 5.03. 83
stroke of fortune falls | will bless the king. H8 2.02. 36
paper in the packet, | to bless your eye withal. 3.02.130
ever god bless your highness! 3.02.136
god bless him! 3.02.392
heaven bless thee! 4.01. 42
the god of heaven | both now and ever bless her! 5.01.165
bless me, what a fry of fornication is at door! 5.03. 35 P
her own shall bless her; 5.04. 30
children | shall see this, and bless heaven. 5.04. 55
heaven bless thee from a tutor, and discipline TRO 2.03. 29 P
jove bless great ajax! 3.03.280 P
heavens bless my lord from fell aufidius! COR 1.03. 45
you bless me, gods! 4.05.135
first, the gods bless you for your tidings; 5.04. 58
o, bless me here with thy victorious hand, TIT 1.01.163
now god in heaven bless thee! hark you, sir. ROM 2.04.194
god in heaven bless her! 3.05.168
so the gods bless me, | when all our offices TIM 2.02.157
assurance bless your thoughts! 2.02.180
are to me nothing, so in nothing bless them, and 3.06. 83 P
knit and break religions, bless th' accurs'd, 4.03. 35
one cried, "god bless us!" MAC 2.02. 24
say "amen," | when they did say "god bless us!" 2.02. 27
bless you, fair dame! 4.02. 65
god bless you, sir. HAM 3.02.373 P
god bless you, sir. 4.06. 7 P
let him bless thee too. 4.06. 8 P
bless thy five wits! LR 3.04. 58 P
bless thee from whirlwinds, star–blasting, and 3.04. 59 P
bless thy five wits! 3.06. 57 P
bless thee, master! 4.01. 39
bless thy sweet eyes, they bleed. 4.01. 54
bless thee, good man's son, from the foul fiend! 4.01. 57 P
if edgar live, o bless him! 4.06. 40
lieutenant be, | and i (/god bless the mark!) OTH 1.01. 33
that he may bless this bay with his tall ship, 2.01. 79
/heaven bless the isle of cyprus and our noble 2.02. 11 P
/heaven bless us! 3.04. 81
holy priests | bless her when she is riggish. ANT 2.02.239
i shall pray, "o, bless my lord and husband!" 3.04. 16
by crying out as loud, | "o, bless my brother!" 3.04. 18
commend thy acts, | make her thanks bless thee. 4.08. 13
and bless the good remainders of the court! CYM 1.01.129
if you will bless me, sir, and give me leave, 4.04. 44
now the gods to bless your honor! PER 4.06. 21 P
o heavens bless my girl! 5.01.223
/i bless thee for thy vision, and will offer 5.03. 69
and lovers yet unborn shall bless my ashes. TNK 3.06.283
themselves, thither they go — jupiter bless us! 4.03. 36 P
and bless me with a sign | of thy great pleasure 5.01.128
and never did he bless | my youth with his, the VEN 1119
/BLESS'D 1 FR 0.0001 REL FR 1 V 0 P
/on | /and /bless'd /and /grac'd /and /did, 2H4 4.01.137
BLESS'D 12 FR 0.0013 REL FR 4 V 8 P
freely to estate | on the bless'd lovers. TMP 4.01. 86
is the single man therefore bless'd? AYL 3.03. 58 P
we are bless'd in this man, as i may say, even WT 4.04.827 P
bless'd in this man, as i may say, even bless'd. 4.04.828 P
never, paulina, so be bless'd my spirit! 5.01. 71
and your father's bless'd | (as he from heaven 5.01.174
and little bless'd with the soft phrase of peace OTH 1.03. 82
in her, she's full of most bless'd condition. 2.01.250 P
bless'd fig's–end! 2.01.251 P
if she had been bless'd, she would never have 2.01.252 P
bless'd pudding! 2.01.253 P
so apt, so bless'd a disposition, she holds it a 2.03.320 P
BLESSED 87 FR 0.0098 REL FR 79 V 8 P
or blessed was't we did? TMP 1.02. 61
gods, | and on this couple drop a blessed crown! 5.01.202
much turmoil | a blessed soul doth in elysium. TGV 2.07. 38
o this blessed hour! WIV 3.03. 46 P
for all thy blessed youth | becomes as aged, and MM 3.01. 34
then, o you blessed ministers above, | keep me 5.01.115
blessed be your royal grace! 5.01.137
some blessed power deliver us from hence! ERR 4.03. 44
blessed are clouds, to do as such clouds do! LLL 5.02.204
thrice blessed they that master so their blood MND 1.01. 74
for she hath blessed and attractive eyes. 2.02. 91
opening on neptune with fair blessed beams, 3.02.392
flower | hath such force and blessed power. 4.01. 74
will we, | which by us shall blessed be; 5.01.404
for, by these blessed candles of the night, MV 5.01.220
juno's crown, | o blessed bond of board and bed! AYL 5.04.142
grace | as 'longeth to a lover's blessed case! SHR 4.02. 45
nay then you lie; it is the blessed sun. 4.05. 17
then, god be blest, it /is the blessed sun, 4.05. 18
methinks in thee some blessed spirit doth speak AWW 2.01.175
now blessed be the great apollo! WT 3.02.137
how blessed are we that are not simple men! 4.04.745
the blessed gods | purge all infection from our 5.01.168
now blessed be the hour by night or day | when i JN 1.01.165
heaven, | and with a blessed and unvex'd retire, 2.01.253
he is the half part of a blessed man, | left to 2.01.437
and this blessed day | ever in france shall be 3.01. 75
and blessed shall he be that doth revolt | from 3.01.174
this blessed plot, this earth, this realm, this R2 2.01. 50
of the world's ransom, blessed mary's son; 2.01. 56
under whose blessed cross | we are impressed and 1H4 1.01. 20
over whose acres walk'd those blessed feet 1.01. 25
and the blessed sun himself a fair hot wench in 1.02. 9 P
shall the blessed sun of heaven prove a micher 2.04.407 P
and thou art a blessed fellow to think as every 2H4 2.02. 57 P
the dove, and very blessed spirit of peace, 4.01. 46
blessed are they that have been my friends, and 5.03.137 P
we are blessed in the change. H5 1.01. 37
he is not — god be praised and blessed! 3.06. 10 P
which troubles oft the bed of blessed marriage, 5.02.364
more blessed hap did ne'er befall our state. 1H6 1.06. 10
and have thee reverenc'd like a blessed saint. 3.03. 15
for blessed are the peacemakers on earth. 2H6 2.01. 34
let me be blessed for the peace i make | against 2.01. 35
bid them blow towards england's blessed shore, 3.02. 90
and that the people of this blessed land | may 3H6 4.06. 21
here | to make the blessed period of this peace. R3 2.01. 44
a blessed labor, my most sovereign lord. 2.01. 53
the holy privilege | of blessed sanctuary! 3.01. 42
o cromwell, | thou fall'st a blessed martyr! H8 3.02.449
his blessed part to heaven, and slept in peace. 4.02. 30
saw you not even now a blessed troop | invite me 4.02. 87
shade thy person | under their blessed wings! 5.01.161
o blessed heavens! COR 4.02. 20
and, touching hers, make blessed my rude hand. ROM 1.05. 51
lady, by yonder blessed moon i vow, | that tips 2.02.107
o blessed, blessed night! 2.02.139
o blessed, blessed night! 2.02.139
i bear no hatred, blessed man, for lo | my 2.03. 53
o blessed breeding sun, draw from the earth TIM 4.03. 1
i see them now, then was a blessed time. 4.03. 79
this chance, | i had liv'd a blessed time; MAC 2.03. 92
antony, octavia is | a blessed lottery to him. ANT 2.02.242
be witness to me, o thou blessed moon, | when 4.09. 7
o blessed, that i might not! CYM 1.01.139
blessed be those, | how mean soe'er, that have 1.06. 7
blessed live you long, | a lady to the worthiest 1.06.159
how far it is | to this same blessed milford. 3.02. 59
thou blessed thing, | jove knows what man thou 4.02.206
make me blessed in your care | in bringing up my PER 3.03. 31
her | as she is heavenly and a blessed goddess; TNK 2.02.163
blessed garden, | and fruit and flowers more 2.02.232
and fruit and flowers more blessed, that still 2.02.233
he's a blessed man! 2.02.247
your chance to come where the blessed spirits — 4.03. 22 P
we go to barley–break, we of the blessed. 4.03. 31 P
blessed souls be with thee! 5.04. 96
but blessed bankrout that by love so thriveth! VEN 466
barr'd him from the blessed thing he sought. LUC 340
but they must ope, this blessed league to kill, 383
with means more blessed than my barren rhyme? SON 16. 4
mine eyes be blessed made | by looking on thee 43. 9
so am i as the rich whose blessed key | can 52. 1
blessed are you, whose worthiness gives scope, 52.13
and you in every blessed shape we know. 53.12
whilst it hath thought itself so blessed never? 119. 6
upon that blessed wood whose motion sounds 128. 2
BLESSED–FAIR 1 FR 0.0001 REL FR 1 V 0 P
but what's so blessed–fair that fears no blot? SON 92.13
BLESSEDLY 2 FR 0.0002 REL FR 1 V 1 P
we heav'd thence, | but blessedly holp hither. TMP 1.02. 63
dying, the time was blessedly lost wherein such H5 4.01.181 P
BLESSEDNESS 3 FR 0.0003 REL FR 3 V 0 P
grows, lives, and dies in single blessedness. MND 1.01. 78
and found the blessedness of being little; H8 4.02. 66
so shall she leave her blessedness to one 5.04. 43
BLESSES 2 FR 0.0002 REL FR 2 V 0 P
to taint that honor every good tongue blesses, H8 3.01. 55
praise, | naming thy name blesses an ill report. SON 95. 8
BLESSETH 1 FR 0.0001 REL FR 1 V 0 P
it blesseth him that gives and him that takes. MV 4.01.187
/BLESSING 1 FR 0.0001 REL FR 1 V 0 P
/beat /heaven /with /blessing /bullingbrook 2H4 1.03. 92
BLESSING 49 FR 0.0055 REL FR 34 V 15 P
shall shun you, | ceres' blessing so is on you. TMP 4.01.117
"father, your blessing." TGV 2.03. 24 P
"blessing of your heart, you brew good ale." 3.01.304 P
blessing on your heart for't! WIV 2.02.107 P
blessing of his heart! 4.01. 13 P
because it is a blessing that he bestows on ERR 2.02. 79 P
when i have heard it, what blessing brings it? ADO 1.03. 6 P
for the which blessing i am at him upon my knees 2.01. 28 P
god's blessing on your beard! LLL 2.01.203
and thrift is blessing, if men steal it not. MV 1.03. 90
give me your blessing; 2.02. 78 P
fooling about it, but give me your blessing. 2.02. 84 P
i feel too much thy blessing; 3.02.113
life, | for, having such a blessing in his lady, 3.05. 75
charg'd my brother, on his blessing, to breed me AYL 1.01. 4 P
never have the blessing of god till i have issue AWW 1.03. 24 P
home | and pray god's blessing into thy attempt. 1.03.254
blessing upon your vows, and in your bed | find 2.03. 91
here 'tis — commends it to your blessing. WT 2.03. 67
and blessing | against this cruelty fight on thy 2.03.190
that | i kneel and then implore her blessing. 5.03. 44
madam, kneel, | and pray your mother's blessing. 5.03.120
my blessing go with thee! JN 3.03. 71
yet blessing on his heart that gives it me! R2 5.05. 64
god's blessing of your good heart! 2H4 2.04.303 P
upon my blessing i command thee go. 1H6 4.05. 36
kneel down and take my blessing, good my girl. 5.04. 25
humbly on my knee | i crave your blessing. R3 2.02.106
that is the butt–end of a mother's blessing. 2.02.110
from her | will fall some blessing to this land, H8 3.02. 51
with this kiss take my blessing: 5.04. 10
and steal immortal blessing from her lips, | who ROM 3.03. 37
i had most need of blessing, and "amen" | stuck MAC 2.02. 29
that a swift blessing | may soon return to this 3.06. 47
my pretty cousin, | blessing upon you! 4.02. 26
a double blessing is a double grace, | occasion HAM 1.03. 53
there — my blessing with thee! 1.03. 57
farewell, my blessing season this in thee! 1.03. 81
conception is a blessing, but as your daughter 2.02.185 P
to be blest, | i'll blessing beg of you. 3.04.172
and did the third a blessing against his will; LR 1.04.103 P
good nuncle, in, ask thy daughters blessing. 3.02. 12 P
when thou dost ask me blessing, i'll kneel down 5.03. 10
i ask'd his blessing, and from first to last 5.03.196
your blessing, sir. CYM 5.05.266
now blessing on thee! PER 5.01.213
and bridegroom's feet, | blessing their sense! TNK 1.01. 15
what worthy blessing | can be, but our 2.02. 76
of their fair subject, blessing every book. SON 82. 4
BLESSINGS 20 FR 0.0022 REL FR 19 V 1 P
juno sings her blessings on you. TMP 4.01.109
now all the blessings | of a glad father compass 5.01.179
for they say barnes are blessings. AWW 1.03. 26 P
tell me what blessings i have here alive, | that WT 3.02.107
and with thy blessings steel my lance's point, R2 1.03. 74
face | a world of earthly blessings to my soul, 2H6 1.01. 22
renders good for bad, blessings for curses. R3 1.02. 69
soul forsake, | shall cry for blessings on him. H8 2.01. 90
his curses and his blessings | touch me alike; 2.02. 52
which, to say sooth, are blessings; 2.03. 30
and heav'nly blessings | follow such creatures. 2.03. 57
he has run his course and sleeps in blessings, 3.02.398
dews of heaven fall thick in blessings on her! 4.02.133
upon this land a thousand thousand blessings, 5.04. 19
a pack of blessings light upon thy back, ROM 3.03.141
are crown'd, | that i account them blessings; TIM 2.02.182
and sundry blessings hang about his throne MAC 4.03.158
flow, flow, | you heavenly blessings, on her! CYM 3.05.161
i see two comforts rising, two mere blessings, TNK 2.02. 58
you to your beauteous blessings add a curse, SON 84.13
BLEST 65 FR 0.0073 REL FR 62 V 3 P
the grace that with such grace hath blest them, TGV 3.01.146
let me be blest to make this happy close; 5.04.117
i am blest in your acquaintance. WIV 2.02.268 P
crest, | with loyal blazon, evermore be blest! 5.05. 64
bound by my charity and my blest order, | i come MM 2.03. 3
god hath blest you with a good name. ADO 3.03. 14 P
no night is now with hymn or carol blest. MND 2.01.102
and the owner of it blest | ever shall in safety 5.01.419
this was a way to thrive, and he was blest; MV 1.03. 89
to make me blest or cursed'st among men. 2.01. 46
it is twice blest: 4.01.186
i thank ye, and be blest for your good comfort! AYL 2.07.135
then, god be blest, it /is the blessed sun, SHR 4.05. 18
be thou blest, bertram, and succeed thy father AWW 1.01. 61
rest | unquestion'd welcome and undoubted blest. 2.01.208
how blest am i | in my just censure! WT 2.01. 36
how accurs'd | in being so blest! 2.01. 39
now be you blest for it! 2.02. 52
and then we shall be blest | to do your pleasure JN 3.01.251
how blest this land would be | in this your R2 4.01. 18
should be the father to so blest a son — | a 1H4 1.01. 80
he was a king blest of the king of kings. 1H6 1.01. 28
that beauty am i blest with which you may see. 1.02. 86
thou, being a king, blest with a goodly son, 3H6 2.02. 23
crown, | as likely to be blest in peace and war; 4.06. 35
the heavens have blest you with a goodly son R3 1.03. 9
blest his three sons with his victorious arm, 1.04.236
if grace had blest thee with a fairer life. 4.04.221
having lands, and blest with beauteous wives, 5.03.321
and have been blest | with many children by you. H8 2.04. 36
tell him, in death i blest him, | for so i will. 4.02.163
god's blest mother! 5.01.153
in so strain'd a purity | that the blest gods, TRO 4.04. 25
it would discredit the blest gods, proud man, 4.05.247
which the rather | we shall be blest to do, if COR 2.02. 58
o, stand up blest! 5.03. 52

and cry, "be blest | for making up this peace!" 5.03.139
doth she not count her blest, | unworthy as she ROM 3.05.143
we scarce thought us blest | that god had lent 3.05.164
my dearest lord, blest to be most accurs'd. TIM 4.02. 42
fly, whilst thou art blest and free. 4.03.535
we are blest that rome is rid of him. JC 3.02. 70
and blest are those | whose blood and judgment HAM 3.02. 68
night, | and when you are desirous to be blest, 3.04.171
o the blest gods! LR 2.04.168
all blest secrets, | all you unpublish'd virtues 4.04. 15
which not to have been blest withal would have ANT 1.02.154 P
blest be | you bees that make these locks of CYM 3.02. 35
sun, to have | the benefit of his blest beams, 4.04. 42
do your best wills, | and make me blest to obey. 5.01. 17
ascension is | more sweet than our blest fields. 5.04.117
away, and, to be blest, | let us with care 5.04.121
blest pray you be, | that, after this strange 5.05.370
climb to their nostrils | from our blest altars. 5.05.478
to me and to my aid the blest infusions | that PER 3.02. 35
her hither | to have blest mine eyes with her! 3.03. 9
blest, and mine own! 5.03. 48
of mortal loathsomeness from the blest eye | of TNK 1.01. 45
hast likewise blest a /place | with thy sole 3.01. 10
therefore this blest morning | shall be the last 3.06. 13
red and white, for yet no beard has blest him; 4.02.107
that love–sick love by pleading may be blest; VEN 328
to make some special instant special blest, | by SON 52.11
return of love, more blest may be the view; 56.12
making dead wood more blest than living lips: 128.12

BLEW 4 FR 0.0004 REL FR 3 V 1 P
it was my breath that blew this tempest up, JN 5.01. 17
which then blew bitterly against our faces, R2 1.04. 7
what wind blew you hither, pistol? 2H4 5.03. 85 P
only envy at, | ye blew the fire that burns ye. H8 5.02.148

BLIND 86 FR 0.0097 REL FR 64 V 22 P
her and her blind boy's scandall'd company | i TMP 4.01. 90
that the blind mole may not | hear a foot fall; 4.01.194
because love is blind. TGV 2.01. 70 P
look you, wept herself blind at my parting. 2.03. 13 P
nay then he should be blind, and, being blind, 2.04. 93
nay then he should be blind, and, being blind, 2.04. 93
there is no reason but i shall be blind. 2.04.212
three or four of his blind brothers and sisters 4.04. 4 P
they would have drown'd a blind bitch's puppies, WIV 3.05. 11 P
of a brothel–house for the sign of blind cupid. ADO 1.01.254 P
now you strike like the blind man. 2.01.198 P
doth falsely blind the eyesight of his look. LLL 1.01. 76
bows not his vassal head and, strooken blind, 4.03.220
a lover's eyes will gaze an eagle blind. 4.03.331
nor woo in rhyme, like a blind harper's song! 5.02.405
and therefore is wing'd cupid painted blind. MND 1.01.235
/page, | and so may i, blind fortune leading me, MV 2.01. 36
but love is blind, and lovers cannot see | the 2.06. 36
he knows me as the blind man knows the cuckoo, 5.01.112
and the bountiful blind woman doth most mistake
AYL 1.02. 35 P
that blind rascally boy that abuses every one's 4.01.213 P
whom the blind waves and surges have devour'd. TN 5.01.229
eyes | blind with the pin and web but theirs, WT 1.02.291
i will bring these two moles, these blind ones, 4.04.836 P
made | upon thy feature, for my rage was blind, JN 4.02.264
do, | make blind itself with foolish tenderness. 1H4 3.02. 91
yea, strike the dolphin blind to look on us. H5 1.02.280
the blind and bloody soldier with foul hand 3.03. 34
furious fickle wheel, | that goddess blind, 3.06. 28
fortune is painted blind, with a muffler afore 3.06. 31 P
eyes, to signify to you that fortune is blind; 3.06. 32 P
true likeness, he must appear naked and blind. 5.02.294 P
the appearance of a naked blind boy in her naked 5.02.297 P
wink and yield, as love is blind and enforces. 5.02.301 P
kept, are like flies at bartholomew–tide, blind, 5.02.309 P
in the latter end, and she must be blind too. 5.02.314 P
brandish'd sword did blind men with his beams; 1H6 1.01. 10
forsooth, a blind man at saint albon's shrine, 2H6 2.01. 61
hast thou been long blind and now restor'd? 2.01. 74
born blind, and't please your grace. 2.01. 75
how long hast thou been blind? 2.01. 95
if thou hadst been born blind, | thou mightst as 2.01.124
i would be blind with weeping, sick with groans, 3.02. 62
and call'd them blind and dusky spectacles, 3.02.112
be blind with tears, and break o'ercharg'd with 3H6 2.05. 78
beauty hath, and made them blind with weeping. R3 1.02.166
and are you yet to your own souls so blind 1.04.252
dead life, blind sight, poor mortal–living ghost 4.04. 26
fall | into the blind cave of eternal night. 5.03. 62
that blind priest, like the eldest son of H8 2.02. 20
blind fear, that seeing reason leads, finds TRO 3.02. 71 P
finds safer footing than blind reason stumbling 3.02. 72 P
troy, | and blind oblivion swallow'd cities up, 3.02.187
to see him, and | the blind to hear him speak. COR 2.01.263
will you be put in mind of his blind fortune, 5.06.117
come let us go, and make thy father blind,'| for TIT 2.04. 52
for such a sight will blind a father's eye. 2.04. 53
and make them blind with tributary tears; 3.01.269
kill'd her for whom my tears have made me blind. 5.03. 49
he that is strooken blind cannot forget | the ROM 1.01.232
blind is his love and best befits the dark. 2.01. 32
if love be blind, love cannot hit the mark. 2.01. 33
heart cleft with the blind bow–boy's butt–shaft; 2.04. 16 P
by their own beauties, or, if love be blind, 3.02. 9
that wear rags | do make their children blind, LR 2.04. 49
their noses are led by their eyes but blind men, 2.04. 70 P
the time's plague, when madmen lead the blind. 4.01. 46
if you do chance to hear of that blind traitor, 4.05. 37
no, do thy worst, blind cupid, i'll not love. 4.06.137 P
(being not deficient, blind, or lame of sense), OTH 1.03. 63
drown cats and blind puppies! 1.03.336 P
eyes | are sometimes like our judgments, blind. CYM 4.02.302
the blind mole casts | copp'd hills towards PER 1.01.100
some blind priest for the purpose that will TNK 5.02. 78
on one | that two must needs be blind for't! 5.03.146
but blind they are, and keep themselves enclosed LUC 378
shame folded up in blind concealing night, 675
and bids her eyes hereafter still be blind; 758
blind muffled bawd! 768
the poor, lame, blind, halt, creep, cry out for 902
looking on darkness which the blind do see; SON 27. 8
doth part his function, and is partly blind, 113. 3
swear to thy blind soul that i was thy will, 136. 2
thou blind fool, love, what dost thou to mine 137. 1
cunning love, with tears thou keep'st me blind, 148.13
those that can see thou lov'st, and i am blind. 149.14

BLINDED 5 FR 0.0005 REL FR 5 V 0 P
if this fond love were not a blinded god? TGV 4.04.196
and give him light that it was blinded by. LLL 1.01. 83
her brow, | that is not blinded by her majesty? 4.03.224
he hath no eyes, the dust hath blinded them. 2H6 3.03. 14
to wink, being blinded with a greater light: LUC 375

BLINDFOLD 2 FR 0.0002 REL FR 2 V 0 P
and blindfold death not let me see my son. R2 1.03.224
with blindfold fury she begins to forage; VEN 554

BLINDING 2 FR 0.0002 REL FR 2 V 0 P
for sorrow's eyes, glazed with blinding tears, R2 2.02. 16
dart your blinding flames | into her scornful LR 2.04.165

BLINDLY 1 FR 0.0001 REL FR 1 V 0 P
the brother blindly shed the brother's blood, R3 5.05. 24

BLINDMAN'S 1 FR 0.0001 REL FR 1 V 0 P
that it will glimmer through a blindman's eye. 1H6 2.04. 24

BLINDNESS 5 FR 0.0005 REL FR 3 V 2 P
her eyes repair, | to help him of his blindness; TGV 4.02. 47
your false love with some show of blindness: ERR 3.02. 8
some of you, thank love for my blindness, who H5 5.02.317 P
best use of eyes to see the way of blindness! CYM 5.04.189 P
and, to enlighten thee, gave eyes to blindness, SON 152.11

/BLINDS 1 FR 0.0001 REL FR 1 V 0 P
/yet /salt /water /blinds /them /not /so /much R2 4.01.245

BLINDS 1 FR 0.0001 REL FR 0 V 1 P
angel about him, but the devil blinds him too. 2H4 2.04.336 P

BLIND–WORM'S 1 FR 0.0001 REL FR 1 V 0 P
of dog, | adder's fork and blind–worm's sting, MAC 4.01. 16

BLIND–WORMS 1 FR 0.0001 REL FR 1 V 0 P
newts and blind–worms, do no wrong, | come not MND 2.02. 11

BLINK 1 FR 0.0001 REL FR 1 V 0 P
me thy chink, to blink through with mine eyne! MND 5.01.177

BLINKING 2 FR 0.0002 REL FR 2 V 0 P
the portrait of a blinking idiot, | presenting MV 2.09. 54
christendoms | that blinking cupid gossips. AWW 1.01.175

BLISS 22 FR 0.0024 REL FR 21 V 1 P
bliss and goodness on you! MM 3.02.215 P
thus have you heard me sever'd from my bliss, ERR 1.01.118
this princess of pure white, this seal of bliss! MND 3.02.144
o wicked wall, through whom i see no bliss! 5.01.180
shadows kiss, | such have but a shadow's bliss. MV 2.09. 67
this, | and hold your fortune for your bliss, 3.02.136
at the last | unto the wished haven of my bliss. SHR 5.01.128
whereas the contrary bringeth bliss, | and is a 1H6 5.05. 64
card'nal, if thou think'st on heaven's bliss, 2H6 3.03. 27
and all that poets feign of bliss and joy. 3H6 1.02. 31
and by the hope i have of heavenly bliss, | that 3.03.182
this pretty lad will prove our country's bliss. 4.06. 70
this, | as far from help as limbo is from bliss! TIT 3.01.149
and threat me i shall never come to bliss | till 3.01.272
too fair, | to merit bliss by making me despair. ROM 1.01.222
bliss be upon you! 5.03.124
thou art a soul in bliss, but i am bound | upon LR 4.07. 45
that cuckold lives in bliss | who, certain of OTH 3.03.167
so come my soul to bliss, as i speak true; 5.02.250
our lips and eyes, | bliss in our brows' bent; ANT 1.03. 36
swelling on either side to want his bliss; LUC 389
a bliss in proof, and prov'd, /a very woe, SON 129.11

BLISSFUL 1 FR 0.0001 REL FR 1 V 0 P
the blissful dew of heaven does arrouse you. TNK 5.04.104

BLISTER 6 FR 0.0006 REL FR 6 V 0 P
blow on ye, | and blister you all o'er! TMP 1.02.324
a blister on his sweet tongue, with my heart, LLL 5.02.335
if i prove honey–mouth'd, let my tongue blister; WT 2.02. 31
for each true word, a blister, and each false TIM 5.01.132
of an innocent love | and sets a blister there, HAM 3.04. 44
by the pow'rful sun, | to fall and blister! LR 2.04.168

BLISTER'D 2 FR 0.0002 REL FR 2 V 0 P
of her own youth, | hath blister'd her report. MM 2.03. 12
blister'd be thy tongue | for such a wish! ROM 3.02. 90

BLISTERS 2 FR 0.0002 REL FR 2 V 0 P
which oft the angry mab with blisters plagues, ROM 1.04. 75
tyrant, whose sole name blisters our tongues, MAC 4.03. 12

BLIST'RED 1 FR 0.0001 REL FR 1 V 0 P
short blist'red breeches, and those types of H8 1.03. 31

BLIST'RING 1 FR 0.0001 REL FR 1 V 0 P
lords | lie blist'ring 'fore the visitating sun, TNK 1.01.146

BLITHE 4 FR 0.0004 REL FR 4 V 0 P
but let them go, | and be you blithe and bonny, ADO 2.03. 67
bardolph, be blithe; H5 2.03. 4
and now, sweet emperor, be blithe again, | and TIT 4.04.111
so buxom, blithe, and full of face | as heaven PER 1.ch. 23

BLITHER 1 FR 0.0001 REL FR 1 V 0 P
mouth, | are the blither for their drouth. PER 3.ch. 8

BLITHILD 1 FR 0.0001 REL FR 1 V 0 P
being descended | of blithild, which was H5 1.02. 67

BLOAT 1 FR 0.0001 REL FR 1 V 0 P
let the bloat king tempt you again to bed, HAM 3.04.182

BLOCK 16 FR 0.0018 REL FR 10 V 6 P
what a block art thou, that thou canst not! TGV 2.05. 26 P
provide your block and your axe to–morrow, four
MM 4.02. 52 P
is the axe upon the block, sirrah? 4.03. 37 P
after him, fellows, bring him to the block. 4.03. 65
we do condemn thee to the very block | where 5.01.414
it ever changes with the next block. ADO 1.01. 77 P
o, she misus'd me past the endurance of a block; 2.01.240 P
if silent, why, a block moved with none. 3.01. 67
up | is but a quintain, a mere liveless block. AYL 1.02.251
guard /these /traitors to the block of death, 2H4 4.02.122
stoop to the block than these knees bow to any 2H6 4.01.125
come, lead me to the block; R3 3.04.106
come lead me, officers, to the block of shame; 5.01. 28
who like a block hath denied my access to thee. COR 5.02. 78 P
this' a good block. LR 4.06.183
how thou stir'st, thou block! PER 3.02. 90

BLOCKHEAD 1 FR 0.0001 REL FR 0 V 1 P
'tis strongly wadg'd up in a blockhead; COR 2.03. 28 P

BLOCKISH 1 FR 0.0001 REL FR 1 V 0 P
and by device let blockish ajax draw | the sort TRO 1.03.374

BLOCKS 4 FR 0.0004 REL FR 4 V 0 P
heads to tender down | on twenty bloody blocks, MM 2.04.181
will draw in | more than the common blocks. WT 1.02.225
what tongueless blocks were they! R3 3.07. 42
you blocks, you stones, you worse than senseless JC 1.01. 35

BLOIS 1 FR 0.0001 REL FR 1 V 0 P
maine, blois, poictiers, and tours, are won away 1H6 4.03. 45

BLOMER (*see bulmer*)

BLOOD (*also plood, etc.*)

/BLOOD 7 FR 0.0008 REL FR 7 V 0 P
/doth /enlarge /his /rising /with /the /blood 2H4 1.01.204
/in /military /rules, /humors /of /blood, | /he 2.03. 30
with /blood and sword and fire, to win your H5 1.02.131
/by /christ's /dear /blood /shed /for /our R3 1.04.190
/orgillous, /their /high /blood /chaf'd, | /have TRO pr 2
/i /am /a /gentleman /of /blood /and /breeding, LR 3.01. 40
/to /let /these /hands /obey /my /blood, | /they 4.02. 64

BLOOD 686 FR 0.0775 REL FR 618 V 68 P
oaths are straw | to th' fire i' th' blood. TMP 4.01. 53
flesh and blood, | you, brother mine, that 5.01. 74
thy pulse | beats as of flesh and blood; 5.01.114
mind to feed on your blood than live in your air TGV 2.04. 27 P
now, as thou art a gentleman of blood, | advise 3.01.121
and /makes milch–kine yield blood, and shakes a WIV 4.04. 33
scarce confesses | that his blood flows; MM 1.03. 52
angelo, a man whose blood | is very snow–broth; 1.04. 57
or that the resolute acting of /your blood 2.01. 12
blood, thou art blood. 2.04. 15
blood, thou art blood. 2.04. 15
why does my blood thus muster to my heart, 2.04. 20
though he hath fall'n by prompture of the blood, 2.04.178
of wilderness | ne'er issu'd from his blood. 3.01.142
both in the heat of blood | and lack of temper'd 5.01.472
my blood is mingled with the crime of lust: ERR 2.02.141
nail, | a rush, a hair, a drop of blood, a pin, 4.03. 72
even for the blood | that then i lost for thee, 5.01.193
and all the conduits of my blood froze up, | yet 5.01.314
i thank god and my cold blood, i am of your ADO 1.01.130 P
that ever i lose more blood with love than i 1.01.251 P
and it better fits my blood to be disdain'd of 1.03. 28 P
against whose charms faith melteth into blood. 2.01.180
wisdom and blood combating in so tender a body, 2.03.163 P
ten proofs to one that blood hath the victory. 2.03.165 P
no true drop of blood in him to be truly touch'd 3.02. 19 P
comes not that blood as modest evidence | to 4.01. 37
but you are more intemperate in your blood 4.01. 59
deny | the story that is printed in her blood? 4.01.122
time hath not yet so dried this blood of mine, 4.01.193
i will be flesh and blood, | for there was never 5.01. 34
not this speech like iron through your blood? 5.01.245
i would see his own person in flesh and blood. LLL 1.01.185 P
thou heat'st my blood. 1.02. 30 P
alack, let it blood. 2.01.186
alone now seek to spill | the poor deer's blood, 4.01. 35
know, sanguis, in blood, ripe as the pomewater, 4.02. 4 P
she | reigns in my blood and will rememb'red be. 4.03. 94
a fever in your blood! 4.03. 95
as true we are as flesh and blood can be. 4.03.211
young blood doth not obey an old decree. 4.03.213
for native blood is counted painting now; 4.03.259
the blood of youth burns not with such excess 5.02. 73
if 'a have no more man's blood in his belly than 5.02.691 P
change not your offer made in heat of blood; 5.02.800
when blood is nipp'd and ways be /foul, | then 5.02.916
know of your youth, examine well your blood, MND 1.01. 68
thrice blessed they that master so their blood 1.01. 74
but either it was different in blood — 1.01.135
i see no blood, no wound. 2.02.101
being o'er shoes in blood, plunge in the deep, 3.02. 48
i am not guilty of lysander's blood; 3.02. 75
sighs of love, that costs the fresh blood dear. 3.02. 97
thy mantle good, | what, stain'd with blood? 5.01.283
why should a man, whose blood is warm within, MV 1.01. 83
the brain may devise laws for the blood, but a 1.02. 18 P
to prove whose blood is reddest, his or mine. 2.01. 7
be launcelot, thou art mine own flesh and blood. 2.02. 93 P
but though i am a daughter to his blood, | i am 2.03. 18
my own flesh and blood to rebel! 3.01. 34 P
i say, my daughter is my flesh and my blood. 3.01. 38 P
only my blood speaks to you in my veins, | and 3.02.176
the jew shall have my flesh, blood, bones, and 4.01.112
ere thou shalt lose for me one drop of blood. 4.01.113
this bond doth give thee here no jot of blood; 4.01.306
if thou dost shed | one drop of christian blood, 4.01.310
shed thou no blood, nor cut thou less nor more 4.01.325
which is the hot condition of their blood, | if 5.01. 74
gentle condition of blood you should so know me.
AYL 1.01. 45 P
but the same tradition takes not away my blood, 1.01. 48 P
malice | of a diverted blood and bloody brother. 2.03. 37
apply | hot and rebellious liquors in my blood, 2.03. 49
dy'd in /his blood, unto the shepherd youth 4.03.155
many will swoon when they do look on blood. 4.03.158
according as marriage binds and blood breaks. 5.04. 57 P
so workmanly the blood and tears are drawn. SHR in.2. 60
tarry in despite of the flesh and the blood. in.2. 128 P
too much sadness hath congeal'd your blood, in.2. 132
thy blood and virtue | contend for empire in AWW 1.01. 62
as you and all flesh and blood are, and indeed i 1.03. 36 P
my wife is the cherisher of my flesh and blood; 1.03. 47 P
my flesh and blood loves my flesh and blood; 1.03. 48 P
my flesh and blood loves my flesh and blood; 1.03. 48 P
he that loves my flesh and blood is my friend; 1.03. 49 P
our blood to us, this to our blood is born. 1.03.131
our blood to us, this to our blood is born. 1.03.131
does it curd thy blood | to say i am thy mother? 1.03.149
to choose from forth the royal blood of france, 2.01.196
good, | to make yourself a son out of my blood. 2.03. 97
whose great decision hath much blood let forth 3.01. 3
son, | but i do wash his name out of my blood, 3.02. 67
now his important blood will nought deny | that 3.07. 21
am i not of her blood? TN 2.03. 78 P
hands, let thy blood and spirit embrace them, 2.05.147 P
and you find so much blood in his liver as will 3.02. 61 P
this does make some obstruction in the blood, 3.04. 21 P
strong corruption | inhabits our frail blood. 3.04.357
an ounce or two of this malapert blood from you. 4.01. 44 P
this once, and let your flesh and blood obey it. 5.01. 33 P
but, had it been the brother of my blood, | i 5.01.210
be not amaz'd, right noble is his blood. 5.01.264
ne'er been higher rear'd | with stronger blood, WT 1.02. 73
in me | thoughts that would thick my blood. 1.02.171

give scandal to the blood o' th' prince my son 1.02.330
then, my best blood turn | to an infected jelly, 1.02.417
of me, yet you | have too much blood in him. 2.01. 58
i'll pawn the little blood which i have left 2.03.166
for the red blood reigns in the winter's pale. 4.03. 4
and the true blood which peeps fairly through't, 4.04.148
her something | that makes her blood look on't. 4.04.160
not hold thee of our blood, no, not our kin, 4.04.430
a changeling, and none of your flesh and blood. 4.04.689 P
she being none of your flesh and blood, your 4.04.693 P
your flesh and blood has not offended the king, 4.04.694 P
king, and so your flesh and blood is not to be 4.04.695 P
and then your blood had been the dearer by i 4.04.704 P
for i am sure my heart wept blood. 5.02. 89 P
and that those veins | did verily bear blood? 5.03. 65
here have we war for war and blood for blood, JN 1.01. 19
here have we war for war and blood for blood, 1.01. 19
arthur, that great forerunner of thy blood, 2.01. 2
wade to the market–place in frenchmen's blood, 2.01. 42
lest unadvis'd you stain your swords with blood. 2.01. 45
and then we shall repent each drop of blood 2.01. 48
an /ate, stirring him to blood and strife; 2.01. 63
when living blood doth in these temples beat, 2.01.108
we will bear home that lusty blood again | which 2.01.255
rage, | and stalk in blood to our possession? 2.01.266
hither return all gilt with frenchmen's blood. 2.01.316
blood hath bought blood, and blows have answer'd 2.01.329
blood hath bought blood, and blows have answer'd 2.01.329
france, hast thou yet more blood to cast away? 2.01.334
thou hast not sav'd one drop of blood | in this 2.01.341
when the rich blood of kings is set on fire! 2.01.351
till then, blows, blood, and death! 2.01.360
whose veins bound richer blood than lady blanch? 2.01.431
what cannoneer begot this lusty blood? 2.01.461
as she in beauty, education, blood, | holds hand 2.01.493
false blood to false blood join'd! 3.01. 2
false blood to false blood join'd! 3.01. 2
you came in arms to spill mine enemies' blood, 3.01.102
shall these hands, so lately purg'd of blood, 3.01.239
against the blood that thou hast married? 3.01.301
the sun's o'ercast with blood; 3.01.326
that nothing can allay, nothing but blood, | the 3.01.342
the blood and dearest–valued blood of france. 3.01.343
the blood and dearest–valued blood of france. 3.01.343
to ashes, ere our blood shall quench that fire. 3.01.345
had bak'd thy blood and made it heavy, thick, 3.03. 43
your mind is all as youthful as your blood. 3.04.125
for he that steeps his safety in true blood 3.04.147
that blood which ow'd the breadth of all this 4.02. 99
there is no sure foundation set on blood; 4.02.104
where is that blood | that i have seen inhabit 4.02.106
this kingdom, this confine of blood and breath, 4.02.246
not painted with the crimson spots of blood. 4.02.253
and foul imaginary eyes of blood | presented 4.02.265
leaves the print of blood where e'er it walks. 4.03. 26
and the love of soul | to stranger blood, to 5.01. 11
the blood of malice in a vein of league, | and 5.02. 38
full warm of blood, of mirth, of gossiping. 5.02. 59
by all the blood that ever fury breath'd, | the 5.02.127
too late, the life of all his blood | is touch'd 5.07. 1
to tyrannize | on unreprievable condemned blood. 5.07. 48
the blood is hot that must be cool'd for this. R2 1.01. 51
out his innocent soul through streams of blood, 1.01.103
which blood, like sacrificing abel's, cries, 1.01.104
till i have told this slander of his blood | how 1.01.113
such neighbor nearness to our sacred blood 1.01.119
even in the best blood chamber'd in his bosom, 1.01.149
let's purge this choler without letting blood. 1.01.153
the part i had in woodstock's blood | doth more 1.02. 1
hath love in thy old blood no living fire? 1.02. 10
one, | were as seven vials of his sacred blood, 1.02. 12
one vial full of edward's sacred blood, | one 1.02. 17
ah, gaunt, his blood was thine! 1.02. 22
farewell, my blood, which if to–day thou shed, 1.03. 57
o thou, the earthly author of my blood, | whose 1.03. 69
rouse up thy youthful blood, be valiant and live 1.03. 83
with that dear blood which it hath fostered; 1.03.126
and make us wade even in our kinred's blood: 1.03.138
chasing the royal blood | with fury from his 2.01.118
that blood already, like the pelican, | hast 2.01.126
thou respect'st not spilling edward's blood. 2.01.131
his hands were guilty of no kinred blood, | but 2.01.182
moe | of noble blood in this declining land. 2.01.240
yet, to wash your blood | from off my hands, 3.01. 5
a happy gentleman in blood and lineaments, | by 3.01. 9
near to the king in blood, and near in love 3.01. 17
sign, | save men's opinions and my living blood, 3.01. 26
but now the blood of twenty thousand men | did 3.02. 76
and, till so much blood thither come again, 3.02. 78
and mock not flesh and blood | with solemn 3.02.171
and lay the summer's dust with show'rs of blood 3.03. 43
for well we know no hand of blood and bone | can 3.03. 79
her pasters' grass with faithful english blood. 3.03.100
lest, being over–proud in sap and blood, | with 3.04. 59
the blood of english shall manure the ground, 4.01.137
hath with the king's blood stain'd the king's 5.05.110
as full of valure as of royal blood! 5.05.113
that blood should sprinkle me to make me grow. 5.06. 46
to wash this blood off from my guilty hand. 5.06. 50
daub her lips with her own children's blood, 1H4 1.01. 6
balk'd in their own blood, did sir walter see 1.01. 69
nor thou cam'st not of the blood royal, if thou 1.02.140 P
my blood hath been too cold and temperate, 1.03. 1
and shed my dear blood drop by drop in the dust, 1.03.134
by richard, that dead is, the next of blood? 1.03.146
the blood more stirs | to rouse a lion than to 1.03.197
hast thou lost the fresh blood in thy cheeks, 2.03. 44
with it and swear it was the blood of true men. 2.04.311 P
doth not thy blood thrill at it? 2.04.370 P
sometimes it show greatness, courage, blood — 3.01.179
charming your blood with pleasing heaviness, 3.01.215
out of my blood | he'll breed revengement and a 3.02. 6
to, | accompany the greatness of thy blood, 3.02. 16
of all the court and princes of my blood; 3.02. 35
son, | when i will wear a garment all of blood, 3.02.135
on his /altar sit | up to the ears in blood. 4.01.117
made to my father, while his blood was poor, 4.03. 76
and will, to save the blood on either side, 5.01. 99
it hath the excuse of youth and heat of blood, 5.02. 17
can lift your blood up with persuasion. 5.02. 78
with the best blood that i can meet withal | in 5.02. 94
and by, | till then in blood by noble percy lie. 5.04.110
of bold rebellion | even with the rebels' blood. 2H4 in 27
a kind of sleeping in the blood, a whoreson 1.02.113 P
durst not have attach'd one of so high blood. 2.02. 3 P
say, "there's some of the king's blood spilt." 2.02.113 P
wine, and it perfumes the blood ere one can say, 2.04. 28 P
by this light flesh and corrupt blood, thou art 2.04.295 P
turning your books to graves, your ink to blood, 4.01. 50
written on the earth | with yet appearing blood, 4.01. 82
and swear here, by the honor of my blood, | my 4.02. 55
for thin drink doth so over–cool their blood, 4.03. 92 P
excellent sherris is the warming of the blood, 4.03.103 P
for the cold blood he did naturally inherit of 4.03.118 P
when you perceive his blood inclin'd to mirth; 4.04. 38
in, | that the united vessel of their blood, 4.04. 44
the blood weeps from my heart when i do shape, 4.04. 58
when rage and hot blood are his counsellors, 4.04. 63
me | is tears and heavy sorrows of the blood, 4.05. 38
which, as immediate from thy place and blood, 4.05. 42
that tyranny, which never quaff'd but blood, 4.05. 85
but if it did infect my blood with joy, | or 4.05.169
the tide of blood in me | hath proudly flow'd in 5.02.129
health | shall drop their blood in approbation H5 1.02. 19
did contend | without much fall of blood, whose 1.02. 25
whelp | forage in blood of french nobility. 1.02.110
the blood and courage that renowned them | runs 1.02.118
as did the former lions of your blood. 1.02.124
that have so cowarded and chas'd your blood 2.02. 75
constant in spirit, not swerving with the blood, 2.02.133
to suck, to suck, the very blood to suck! 2.03. 56
the dead men's blood, the privy maidens' groans, 2.04.107
stiffen the sinews, /conjure up the blood, 3.01. 7
whose blood is fet from fathers of war–proof! 3.01. 18
be copy now to /men of grosser blood, | and 3.01. 24
decoct their cold blood to such valiant heat? 3.05. 20
and shall our quick blood, spirited with wine, 3.05. 21
with pennons painted in the blood of harflew. 3.05. 49
for th' effusion of our blood, the muster of his 3.06.130 P
we shall your tawny ground with your red blood 3.06.161
of any thing, when blood is their argument? 4.01.143 P
than from it issued forced drops of blood. 4.01.297
hands hold up | toward heaven, to pardon blood; 4.01.300
that their hot blood may spin in english eyes, 4.02. 10
what, will you have them weep our horses' blood? 4.02. 12
scarce blood enough in all their sickly veins 4.02. 20
for he to–day that sheds his blood with me 4.03. 61
out at thy throat | in drops of crimson blood. 4.04. 15
as i suck blood, i will some mercy show. 4.04. 64
from helmet to the spur all blood he was. 4.06. 6
to death, with blood he seal'd | a testament of 4.06. 26
lie drown'd and soak'd in mercenary blood; 4.07. 76
their peasant limbs | in blood of princes, and 4.07. 78
squires, | and gentlemen of blood and quality. 4.08. 90
will | that nothing do but meditate on blood — 5.02. 60
yet my blood begins to flatter me that thou dost 5.02.222 P
son, and from her blood raise up | issue to me, 5.02.348
we mourn in black, why mourn we not in blood? 1H6 1.01. 17
blood will i draw on thee — thou art a witch — 1.05. 6
for every drop of blood was drawn from him 2.02. 8
his trespass yet lives guilty in thy blood, 2.04. 94
say | this quarrel will drink blood another day. 2.04.133
parliament, | either to be restored to my blood, 2.05.128
then be at peace, except ye thirst for blood. 3.01.117
is | that richard be restored to his blood. 3.01.158
let richard be restored to his blood, | so shall 3.01.159
one drop of blood drawn from thy country's bosom 3.03. 54
else this blow should broach thy dearest blood. 3.04. 40
that doth presume to boast of gentle blood. 4.01. 44
that for a trifle that was bought with blood! 4.01.150
if we be english deer, be then in blood, | not 4.02. 48
the world will say, he is not talbot's blood, 4.05. 16
bastard orleance, that drew blood | from thee, 4.06. 16
i quickly shed | some of his bastard blood, and 4.06. 20
base, | and misbegotten blood i spill of thine, 4.06. 22
for that pure blood of mine | which thou didst 4.06. 23
and in that sea of blood my boy did drench | his 4.07. 14
did flesh his puny sword in frenchmen's blood! 4.07. 36
means | to stop effusion of our christian blood, 5.01. 9
where i was wont to feed you with my blood, 5.03. 14
i am descended of a gentler blood. 5.04. 8
stain'd with the guiltless blood of innocents, 5.04. 44
whose maiden blood, thus rigorously effus'd, 5.04. 52
my sword should shed hot blood, mine eyes no 2H6 1.01.118
consider, lords, he is the next of blood, | and 1.01.151
bear that proportion to my flesh and blood | as 1.01.233
were i a man, a duke, and next of blood, | i 1.02. 63
red, master, red as blood. 2.01.108
before his chaps be stain'd with crimson blood, 3.01.259
and temper clay with blood of englishmen. 3.01.311
see how the blood is settled in his face. 3.02.160
but see, his face is black and full of blood, 3.02.168
thou shalt be waking while i shed thy blood, 3.02.227
or with their blood stain this discolored shore. 4.01. 11
obscure and lousy swain, king henry's blood, 4.01. 50
blood, | the honorable blood of lancaster, 4.01. 51
drones suck not eagles' blood, but rob beehives. 4.01.109
but angry, wrathful, and inclin'd to blood, | if 4.02.126
ay, by the best blood that ever was broach'd, 4.10. 37 P
ne'er shall this blood be wiped from thy point, 4.10. 69
war, | and shame thine honorable age with blood? 5.01.170
that this is true, father, behold his blood. 3H6 1.01. 13
brother, here's the earl of wiltshire's blood, 1.01. 14
than drops of blood were in my father's veins. 1.01. 97
sits, | write up his title with usurping blood. 1.01.169
in whose cold blood no spark of honor bides. 1.01.184
once, | or nourish'd him as i did with my blood, 1.01.222
even in the lukewarm blood of henry's heart. 1.02. 34
my father's blood | hath stopp'd the passage 1.03. 21
then let my father's blood open it again, | he 1.03. 23
and this thy son's blood cleaving to my blade 1.03. 50
shall rust upon my weapon, till thy blood, 1.03. 51
in blood of those that had encount'red him. 1.04. 13
i stain'd this napkin with the blood | that 1.04. 79
have touch'd, would not have stain'd with blood; 1.04.153
cloth thou dipp'dst in blood of my sweet boy, 1.04.157
boy, | and i with tears do wash the blood away. 1.04.158
my soul to heaven, my blood upon your heads! 1.04.168
a napkin steeped in the harmless blood | of 2.01. 62
who thunders to his captives blood and death, 2.01.127
if thou deny, their blood upon thy head, | for 2.02.129
thy brother's blood the thirsty earth hath drunk 2.03. 15
stain'd their fetlocks in his smoking blood, 2.03. 21
then let the earth be drunken with our blood! 2.03. 23
the one his purple blood right well resembles, 2.05. 99
and much effuse of blood doth make me faint. 2.06. 28
and with the issuing blood | stifle the villain 2.06. 82
are near to warwick by blood and by alliance: 4.01.136
write in the dust this sentence with thy blood: 5.01. 56
even with the dearest blood your bodies bear. 5.01. 69
who gave his blood to lime the stones together, 5.01. 84
my blood, my want of strength, my sick heart 5.02. 8
the wrinkles in my brows, now fill'd with blood, 5.02. 19
lo, now my glory smear'd in dust and blood! 5.02. 23
thy tears would wash this cold congealed blood 5.02. 37
they that stabb'd caesar shed no blood at all, 5.05. 53
petitioners for blood thou ne'er put'st back. 5.05. 80
will the aspiring blood of lancaster | sink in 5.06. 61
throne, | repurchas'd with the blood of enemies. 5.07. 2
thou bloodless remnant of that royal blood, | be R3 1.02. 7
cursed the blood that let this blood from hence! 1.02. 16
cursed the blood that let this blood from hence! 1.02. 16
for 'tis thy presence that exhales this blood 1.02. 58
from cold and empty veins where no blood dwells. 1.02. 59
which this blood mad'st, revenge his death! 1.02. 62
which this blood drink'st, revenge his death! 1.02. 63
as thou dost swallow up this good king's blood, 1.02. 66
thy murd'rous falchion smoking in his blood; 1.02. 94
to royalize his blood i spent mine own. 1.03.124
ay, and much better blood than his or thine. 1.03.125
in the faultless blood of pretty rutland — 1.03.177
as it is won with blood, lost be it so! 1.03.271
thy garments are not spotted with our blood; 1.03.282
with bright hair | dabbled in blood, and he 1.04. 54
nearer in bloody thoughts, /but not in blood, 2.01. 93
welcome destruction, blood, and massacre! 2.04. 53
to brother, | blood to blood, self against self. 2.04. 63
to brother, | blood to blood, self against self. 2.04. 63
to–morrow are let blood at pomfret castle, | and 3.01.183
we give to thee our guiltless blood to drink. 3.03. 14
be satisfied, dear god, with our true blood, 3.03. 22
but as successively, from blood to blood, | your 3.07.135
but as successively, from blood to blood, | your 3.07.135
when scarce the blood was well wash'd from his 4.01. 67
in | so far in blood that sin will pluck on sin. 4.02. 64
unlawfully made drunk with innocent blood! 4.04. 30
to worry lambs and lap their gentle blood, 4.04. 50
i have no moe sons of the royal blood | for thee 4.04.200
did to thy father, steep'd in rutland's blood — 4.04.275
mine issue of your blood upon your daughter. 4.04.298
below, | even of your metal, of your very blood; 4.04.302
swills your warm blood like wash and makes his 5.02. 9
one rais'd in blood, and one in blood 5.03.247
rais'd in blood, and one in blood established; 5.03.247
spur your proud horses hard, and ride in blood; 5.03.340
the brother blindly shed the brother's blood, 5.05. 24
and make poor england weep in streams of blood! 5.05. 37
a beggar's book | outworths a noble's blood. H8 1.01.123
for then my guiltless blood must cry against 'em 2.01. 68
and with that blood will make 'em one day groan 2.01.106
the spaniard, tied by blood and favor to her, 2.02. 89
i had no being | if this salute my blood a jot; 2.03.103
by those claim their greatness, not by blood. 5.04. 38
when with your blood you daily paint her thus. TRO 1.01. 91
is among the greeks | a lord of troyan blood, 1.02. 13
prove this troth with my three drops of blood. 1.03.301
or is your blood | so madly hot that no 2.02.115
to the hot passion of distemp'red blood | than 2.02.169
i would not wish a drop of troyan blood | spent 2.02.197
let thy blood be thy direction till thy death; 2.03. 30 P
worth | holds in his blood such swoll'n and hot 2.03.173
i'll /let his /humors blood. 2.03.212 P
love, and that breeds hot blood, and hot blood 3.01.129 P
hot blood, and hot blood begets hot thoughts, 3.01.129 P
is this the generation of love — hot blood, hot 3.01.131 P
that doth renew swifter than blood decays! 3.02.163
they will almost | give us a prince of blood, a 3.03. 26
no love, no blood, no soul so near me | as the 4.02. 98
stretch thy chest, and let thy eyes spout blood; 4.05. 10
this ajax is half made of hector's blood, | in 4.05. 83
the obligation of our blood forbids | a gory 4.05.122
my mother's blood | runs on the dexter cheek, 4.05.127
stone will cost | a drop of grecian blood. 4.05.224
i'll heat his blood with greekish wine to–night, 5.01. 1
with too much blood and too little brain, these 5.01. 48 P
too much brain and too little blood they do, 5.01. 50 P
art thou of blood and honor? 5.04. 27
patroclus' wounds have rous'd his drowsy blood, 5.05. 32
sword, thou hast thy fill of blood and death. 5.08. 4
i send it through the rivers of your blood, COR 1.01.135
thou rascal, that art worst in blood to run, 1.01.159
his bloody brow? o jupiter, no blood! 1.03. 38
than hector's forehead when it spit forth blood 1.03. 42
the blood i drop is rather physical | than 1.05. 18
ay, if you come not in the blood of others, 1.06. 28
by th' blood we have shed together, by th' vows 1.06. 57
'tis not my blood | wherein thou seest me mask'd 1.08. 9
mother, | who has a charter to extol her blood, 1.09. 14
the blood upon your visage dries, 'tis time | it 1.09. 93
from face to foot | he was a thing of blood, 2.02.109
as for my country i have shed my blood, | not 3.01. 76
killing our enemies, the blood he hath lost 3.01.297
to your fortune and | the hazard of much blood. 3.02. 61
and the drops of blood | shed for my thankless 4.05. 69
drawn tuns of blood out of thy country's breast, 4.05. 99
his crest up again and the man in blood, they 4.05.211 P
the veins unfill'd, our blood is cold, and then 5.01. 51
these pipes and these conveyances of our blood 5.01. 54
lest i let forth your half–pint of blood. 5.02. 56 P
and in her hand | the grandchild to her blood. 5.03. 24
bravely shed | thy wife and children's blood. 5.03.118
lies, he sold the blood and labor | of our great 5.06. 46
andronicus, stain not thy tomb with blood! TIT 1.01.116
blood and revenge are hammering in my head. 2.03. 39

and wash their hands in bassianus' blood. 2.03. 45
upon whose leaves are drops of new–shed blood 2.03.200
and see a fearful sight of blood and death. 2.03.216
lord bassianus lies /beray'd in blood, | all on 2.03.222
when he by night lay bath'd in maiden blood. 2.03.232
alas, a crimson river of warm blood, | like to a 2.04. 22
and, notwithstanding all this loss of blood, 2.04. 29
for all my blood in rome's great quarrel shed, 3.01. 4
my sons' sweet blood will make it shame and 3.01. 15
so thou refuse to drink my dear sons' blood. 3.01. 22
my youth can better spare my blood than you, 3.01.165
and see their blood or die with this reproach. 4.01. 94
man but i | do execution on my flesh and blood. 4.02. 84
of that self blood that first gave life to you, 4.02.123
touch not the boy, he is of royal blood. 5.01. 49
the basin that receives your guilty blood. 5.02.183
and with your blood and it i'll make a paste, 5.02.187
receive the blood, and when that they are dead, 5.02.197
that have preserv'd her welfare in my blood, 5.03.110
where civil blood makes civil hands unclean. ROM pr 4
had she affections and warm youthful blood, 2.05. 12
now comes the wanton blood up in your cheeks, 2.05. 70
now, these hot days, is the mad blood stirring. 3.01. 4
o, the blood is spill'd | of my dear kinsman! 3.01.147
for blood of ours, shed blood of montague. 3.01.149
for blood of ours, shed blood of montague. 3.01.149
who now the price of his dear blood doth owe? 3.01.183
my blood for your rude brawls doth lie 3.01.189
hood my unmann'd blood, bating in my cheeks, 3.02. 14
pale, pale as ashes, all bedaub'd in blood, 3.02. 55
all bedaub'd in blood, | all in gore blood; 3.02. 56
o god, did romeo's hand shed tybalt's blood? 3.02. 71
with blood removed but little from her own? 3.03. 96
dry sorrow drinks our blood. 3.05. 59
her blood is settled, and her joints are stiff; 4.05. 26
alack, what blood is this, which stains | the 5.03.140
and steep'd in blood? 5.03.145
see so many dip their meat in one man's blood, TIM 1.02. 41 P
their blood is cak'd, 'tis cold, it seldom flows 2.02.216
tell out my blood. 3.04. 94
who in hot blood | hath stepp'd into the law, 3.05. 11
who cannot condemn rashness in cold blood? 3.05. 53
he forfeits his own blood that spills another. 3.05. 87
strange, unusual blood, | when man's worst sin 4.02. 38
with man's blood paint the ground, gules, gules. 4.03. 60
go, suck the subtle blood o' th' grape, | till 4.03.429
till the high fever seethe your blood to froth, 4.03.430
that comes in triumph over pompey's blood? JC 1.01. 51
when every drop of blood | that every roman 2.01.136
and in the spirit of men there is no blood; 2.01.168
of war, | which drizzled blood upon the capitol; 2.02. 21
with an hundred spouts, | did run pure blood; 2.02. 78
your statue spouting blood in many pipes, | in 2.02. 85
from you great rome shall suck | reviving blood, 2.02. 88
might fire the blood of ordinary men, | and turn 3.01. 37
to think that caesar bears such rebel blood 3.01. 40
and men are flesh and blood, and apprehensive; 3.01. 67
and let us bathe our hands in caesar's blood 3.01.106
who else must be let blood, who else is rank; 3.01.152
with the most noble blood of all this world. 3.01.156
weeping as fast as they stream forth thy blood, 3.01.201
woe to the hand that shed this costly blood! 3.01.258
blood and destruction shall be so in use, | and 3.01.265
and dip their napkins in his sacred blood; 3.02.133
mark how the blood of caesar followed it, | as 3.02.178
(which all the while ran blood) great caesar 3.02.189
nor the power of speech | to stir men's blood; 3.02.223
and drop my blood for drachmaes than to wring 4.03. 73
when grief and blood ill–temper'd vexeth him? 4.03.115
that mak'st my blood cold, and my hair to stare? 4.03.280
now is his red blood cassius' day is set! 5.03. 62
make thick my blood, | stop up th' access and MAC 1.05. 43
when we have mark'd with blood those sleepy two 1.07. 75
and on thy blade and dudgeon gouts of blood, 2.01. 46
them, and smear | the sleepy grooms with blood. 2.02. 47
will all great neptune's ocean wash this blood 2.02. 57
head, the fountain of your blood | is stopp'd, 2.03. 98
hands and faces were all badg'd with blood; 2.03.102
his silver skin lac'd with his golden blood, 2.03.112
the near in blood, | the nearer bloody. 2.03.140
there's blood upon thy face. 3.04. 13
blood hath been shed ere now, i' th' olden time, 3.04. 74
thy bones are marrowless, thy blood is cold; 3.04. 93
it will have blood, they say; 3.04.121
blood will have blood. 3.04.121
blood will have blood. 3.04.121
brought forth | the secret'st man of blood. 3.04.125
i am in blood | stepp'd in so far that, should i 3.04.135
cool it with a baboon's blood, | then the charm 4.01. 37
pour in sow's blood, that hath eaten | her nine 4.01. 64
the old man to have had so much blood in him? 5.01. 40 P
here's the smell of the blood still. 5.01. 50 P
those clamorous harbingers of blood and death. 5.06. 10
too much charg'd | with blood of thine already. 5.08. 6
as stars with trains of fire and dews of blood, HAM 1.01.117
favor, | hold it a fashion and a toy in blood, 1.03. 6
when the blood burns, how prodigal the soul 1.03.116
harrow up thy soul, freeze thy young blood, 1.05. 16
blazon must not be | to ears of flesh and blood. 1.05. 22
holds such an enmity with blood of man | that 1.05. 65
into milk, | the thin and wholesome blood. 1.05. 70
fiery mind, | a savageness in unreclaimed blood, 2.01. 34
gules, horridly trick'd | with blood of fathers, 2.02.458
whose blood and judgment are so well co–meddled, 3.02. 69
now could i drink hot blood, | and do such 3.02.390
were thicker than itself with brother's blood, 3.03. 44
at your age | the heyday in the blood is tame, 3.04. 69
want true color — tears perchance for blood. 3.04.130
for like the hectic in my blood he rages, | and 4.03. 66
excitements of my reason and my blood, | and let 4.04. 58
that drop of blood that's calm proclaims me 4.05.118
pelican, | repast them with my blood. 4.05.148
where it draws blood, no cataplasm so rare, 4.07.143
care, | propinquity and property of blood, | and LR 1.01.114
some blood drawn on me would beget opinion | of 2.01. 33
my breath and blood! 2.04.103
but yet thou art my flesh, my blood, my daughter 2.04.221
or embossed carbuncle, | in my corrupted blood. 2.04.225
our flesh and blood, my lord, is grown so vild 3.04.145
i had a son, | now outlaw'd from my blood; 3.04.167
and fum, | i smell the blood of a british man.'" 3.04.184
the conflict be sore between that and my blood. 3.05. 23 P
i am no less in blood than thou art, edmund; 5.03.168
o treason of the blood! OTH 1.01.169
that with some mixtures pow'rful o'er the blood, 1.03.104
to heaven | i do confess the vices of my blood, 1.03.123
the blood and baseness of our natures would 1.03.328 P
merely a lust of the blood and a permission of 1.03.334 P
when the blood is made dull with the act of 2.01.227 P
my blood begins my safer guides to rule, | and 2.03.205
but with a little act upon the blood | burn like 3.03.328
o blood, blood, blood! 3.03.451
o blood, blood, blood! 3.03.451
o blood, blood, blood! 3.03.451
or did the letters work upon his blood | and 4.01.275
shall with lust's blood be spotted. 5.01. 36
yet i'll not shed her blood, | nor scar that 5.02. 3
and that blood of thine | is caesar's homager; ANT 1.01. 30
higher than both in blood and life, stands up 1.02.190
you'll heat my blood; no more. 1.03. 80
the borders maritime | lack blood to think on't, 1.04. 52
when i was green in judgment, cold in blood, 1.05. 74
yet with parthian blood thy sword is warm, | the 3.01. 6
to kiss these lips, i will appear in blood; 3.13.174
or bathe my dying honor in the blood | shall 4.02. 6
we'll spill the blood | that has to–day escap'd. 4.08. 3
behold it stain'd | with his most noble blood. 5.01. 26
with tears as sovereign as the blood of hearts, 5.01. 41
there is a vent of blood, and something blown; 5.02.349
thou'rt poison to my blood. CYM 1.01.128
let her languish | a drop of blood a day, and, 1.01.157
her blood? 3.02. 13
then | the princely blood flows in his cheek, he 3.03. 93
color | i'ld let a parish of such clotens blood, 4.02.168
their royal blood enchaf'd, as the rud'st wind 4.02.174
give color to my pale cheek with thy blood, 4.02.330
did see man die, scarce ever look'd on blood, 4.04. 36
their blood thinks scorn | till it fly out and 4.04. 53
we should not, when the blood was cool, have 5.05. 77
save him, sir, | and spare no blood beside. 5.05. 92
for whom my heart drops blood, and my false 5.05.148
loins, my liege, | and blood of your begetting. 5.05.331
sleep out of mine eyes, blood from my cheeks, PER 1.02. 96
wishing it so much blood unto your life. 2.03. 77
the contrary) | as great in blood as i myself. 2.05. 80
even as my life my blood that fosters it. 2.05. 89
do not | consume your blood with sorrowing; 4.01. 23
pray walk softly, do not heat your blood. 4.01. 48
much less in blood than virtue, yet a princess 4.03. 7
for flesh and blood, sir, white and red, you 4.06. 34 P
but are you flesh and blood? 5.01.152
dear palamon, dearer in love than blood, | and TNK 1.02. 1
the blood of mine that's sib to him be suck'd 1.02. 72
not his kinsmen | in blood unless in quality. 1.02. 79
in, the blood we venture | should be as for our 1.02.109
friendship, blood, | and all the ties between us 2.02.172
am not i | part of /your blood, part of your 2.02.185
hath taken notice | both of his blood and body. 2.02.228
falsest cousin | that ever blood made kin! 3.01. 38
a good hearty draught, it breeds good blood, man 3.03. 17
and that blood we desire to shed is mutual — 3.06. 95
must now be soil'd | with blood of princes? 4.02. 60
weep not, till they weep blood. 4.02.148
know my prize | must be dragg'd out of blood; 5.01. 43
camp a cestron | brimm'd with the blood of men. 5.01. 47
that heal'st with blood | the earth when it is 5.01. 64
allow'st no more blood than will make a blush, 5.01.141
not physick'd by respect might turn our blood STM III 13
face doth reek and smoke, her blood doth boil, VEN 555
whose blood upon the fresh flowers being shed 665
disorder breeds by heating of the blood; 742
like milk and blood being mingled both together, 902
but stole his blood and seem'd with him to bleed 1056
and stains her face with his congealed blood. 1122
and in his blood that on the ground lay spill'd, 1167
resembling well his pale cheeks and the blood 1169
good | to wither in my breast as in his blood. 1182
thou art the next of blood, and 'tis thy right. 1184
who seek to stain the ocean of thy blood. LUC 655
wretched hands such wretched blood should spill; 999
me good | is to let forth my foul defiled blood. 1029
my stained blood to tarquin i'll bequeath, 1181
my blood shall wash the slander of mine ill; 1207
ere she with blood had stain'd her stain'd 1316
the more she saw the blood his cheeks replenish, 1357
the red blood reek'd, to show the painter's 1377
to simois' reedy banks the red blood ran, 1437
her blue blood chang'd to black in every vein, 1454
though my gross blood be stain'd with this abuse 1655
her blood, in poor revenge, held it in chase; 1736
that the crimson blood | circles her body in on 1738
some of her blood still pure and red remain'd, 1742
face | of that black blood a wat'ry rigol goes, 1745
woes, | corrupted blood some watery token shows, 1748
and blood untainted still doth red abide, 1749
and by this chaste blood so unjustly stained, 1836
and see thy blood warm when thou feel'st it cold SON 2.14
and that fresh blood which youngly thou 11. 3
and burn the long–liv'd phoenix in her blood; 19. 4
hours have drain'd his blood and fill'd his brow 63. 3
beggar'd of blood to blush through lively veins, 67.10
might be better us'd | where cheeks need blood, 82.14
all frailties that besiege all kinds of blood, 109.10
eyes | give salutation to my sportive blood? 121. 6
found yet moe letters sadly penn'd in blood, LC 47
cried, "o false blood, thou register of lies, 52
"nor gives it satisfaction to our blood | that 162
that abroad you see | are errors of the blood, 184
me, | of pallid pearls and rubies red as blood, 198
BLOOD–BESPOTTED 1 FR 0.0001 REL FR 1 V 0 P
o blood–bespotted neapolitan, | outcast of 2H6 5.01.117
BLOOD–BOLTER'D 1 FR 0.0001 REL FR 1 V 0 P
for the blood–bolter'd banquo smiles upon me, MAC 4.01.123
BLOOD–CONSUMING 1 FR 0.0001 REL FR 1 V 0 P
or blood–consuming sighs recall his life, | i 2H6 3.02. 61
BLOOD–DRINKING 3 FR 0.0003 REL FR 3 V 0 P
rose, | as cognizance of my blood–drinking hate, 1H6 2.04.108
look pale as primrose with blood–drinking sighs, 2H6 3.02. 63
in this detested, dark, blood–drinking pit. TIT 2.03.224
BLOODHOUND 1 FR 0.0001 REL FR 0 V 1 P
ay, come, you starv'd bloodhound. 2H4 5.04. 27 P
BLOODIED 2 FR 0.0002 REL FR 1 V 1 P
stopp'd by me to breathe his bloodied horse. 2H4 1.01. 38
look you how his sword is bloodied, and his helm TRO 1.02.233 P
BLOODIER 1 FR 0.0001 REL FR 1 V 0 P
thou bloodier villain | than terms can give thee MAC 5.08. 7
BLOODIEST 1 FR 0.0001 REL FR 1 V 0 P
this is the bloodiest shame, | the wildest JN 4.03. 47
BLOODILY 4 FR 0.0004 REL FR 4 V 0 P
how bloodily the sun begins to peer | above yon 1H4 5.01. 1
gashes | that bloodily did yawn upon his face. H5 4.06. 14
to–day at pomfret bloodily were butcher'd, | and R3 3.04. 90
princes at a shot | so bloodily hast strook? HAM 5.02.367
BLOODLESS 8 FR 0.0009 REL FR 8 V 0 P
with bloodless stroke my heart doth gore; TN 2.05.106
of ashy semblance, meagre, pale, and bloodless, 2H6 3.02.162
thou bloodless remnant of that royal blood, | be R3 1.02. 7
envious fever | of pale and bloodless emulation, TRO 1.03.134
this dear sight | struck pale and bloodless, and TIT 3.01.257
who, overcome by doubt and bloodless fear, VEN 891
at last he takes her by the bloodless hand, LUC 1597
in bloodless white and the encrimson'd mood, LC 201
BLOOD'S 2 FR 0.0002 REL FR 2 V 0 P
setting aside his high blood's royalty, | and R2 1.01. 58
king, | and lay aside my high blood's royalty, 1.01. 71
BLOODS 15 FR 0.0017 REL FR 13 V 2 P
seal'd his rigorous statutes with their bloods, ERR 1.01. 9
sweet bloods, i both may and will. LLL 5.02.708 P
more between your bloods than there is between MV 3.01. 41 P
strange is it that our bloods, | of color, AWW 2.03.118
to mingle friendship far is mingling bloods. WT 1.02.109
as many and as well–born bloods as those — JN 2.01.278
and by the royalties of both your bloods, R2 3.03.107
or bath'd thy growing with our heated bloods. 3H6 2.02.169
our bloods are now in calm, and, so long, health TRO 4.01. 16
and may diseases lick up their false bloods! TIM 4.03.532
rome, thou hast lost the breed of noble bloods! JC 1.02.151
i know young bloods look for a time of rest. 4.03.262
our bloods | no more obey the heavens than our CYM 1.01. 1
how many worthy princes' bloods were shed | to PER 1.02. 88
we'll mingle our bloods together in the earth, 1.02.113
BLOOD–SACRIFICE 1 FR 0.0001 REL FR 1 V 0 P
cannot my body nor blood–sacrifice | entreat you 1H6 5.03. 20
BLOODSHED 2 FR 0.0002 REL FR 2 V 0 P
and prove a deadly bloodshed but a jest, JN 4.03. 55
which daily grew to quarrel and to bloodshed, 2H4 4.05.194
BLOOD–SHEDDING 1 FR 0.0001 REL FR 1 V 0 P
hands are free from guiltless blood–shedding, 2H6 4.07.102
BLOOD–SIZ'D 1 FR 0.0001 REL FR 1 V 0 P
him, if he i' th' blood–siz'd field lay swoll'n, TNK 1.01. 99
BLOOD/–STAIN'D 1 FR 0.0001 REL FR 1 V 0 P
sorrowful drops upon thy blood/–stain'd face, TIT 5.03.154
BLOOD–STAINED 2 FR 0.0002 REL FR 2 V 0 P
blood–stained with these valiant combatants. 1H4 1.03.107
from this /unhallow'd and blood–stained hole? TIT 2.03.210
BLOOD–SUCKER 1 FR 0.0001 REL FR 1 V 0 P
hell, | pernicious blood–sucker of sleeping men! 2H6 3.02.226
BLOOD–SUCKERS 1 FR 0.0001 REL FR 1 V 0 P
a knot you are of damned blood–suckers. R3 3.03. 6
BLOOD–SUCKING 1 FR 0.0001 REL FR 1 V 0 P
and stop the rising of blood–sucking sighs, 3H6 4.04. 22
BLOOD–THIRSTY 1 FR 0.0001 REL FR 1 V 0 P
to me, blood–thirsty lord; 1H6 2.03. 34
/BLOODY 1 FR 0.0001 REL FR 0 V 1 P
/the /arbiterment /is /like /to /be /bloody. LR 4.07. 93 P
BLOODY 226 FR 0.0255 REL FR 213 V 13 P
nor set | a mark so bloody on the business; TMP 1.02.142
i do begin to have bloody thoughts. 4.01.220 P
lust is but a bloody fire, | kindled with WIV 5.05. 95
heads to tender down | on twenty bloody blocks, MM 2.04.181
which lion vile with bloody mouth did stain. MND 5.01.143
whereat, with blade, with bloody blameful blade, 5.01.146
he bravely broach'd his boiling bloody breast; 5.01.147
of flesh | to–morrow to my bloody creditor. MV 3.03. 34
for thy desires | are wolvish, bloody, starv'd, 4.01.138
malice | of a diverted blood and bloody brother. AYL 2.03. 37
than he that dies and lives by bloody drops? 3.05. 7
his rosalind | he sends this bloody napkin. 4.03. 93
but for the bloody napkin? 4.03.138
not to be understood without bloody succeeding. AWW 2.03.191 P
that from the bloody course of war | my dearest 3.04. 8
th' offense is not of such a bloody nature, TN 3.03. 30
might well have given us bloody argument. 3.03. 32
full of despite, bloody as the hunter, attends 3.04.223 P
the most skillful, bloody, and fatal opposite 3.04.267 P
whom thou, in terms so bloody and so dear, 5.01. 71
and has given sir toby a bloody coxcomb too. 5.01.176 P
if a bloody coxcomb be a hurt, you have hurt me. 5.01.190 P
i think you set nothing by a bloody coxcomb. 5.01.191 P
which being so horrible, so bloody, must | lead WT 2.03.152
jealousies | to bloody thoughts and to revenge, 3.02.159
the proud control of fierce and bloody war, | to JN 1.01. 17
must | with fearful bloody issue arbitrate. 1.01. 38
all preparation for a bloody siege | and 2.01.213
made | for bloody power to rush upon your peace. 2.01.221
turn face to face and bloody point to point; 2.01.390
thou dost shame | that bloody spoil. 3.01.115
of smiling peace to march a bloody host, | and 3.01.246
and bloody england into england gone, 3.04. 8
in true blood | shall find but bloody safety, 3.04.148
wrath | out of the bloody fingers' ends of john. 3.04.168
even with the fierce looks of these bloody men. 4.01. 73
this is the man should do the bloody deed; 4.02. 69
to break within the bloody house of life, | and 4.02.210
aspect, | finding thee fit for bloody villainy, 4.02.225
it is a damned and a bloody work, | the 4.03. 57
you bloody neroes, ripping up the womb | of your 5.02.152
hearts | to fierce and bloody inclination. 5.02.158
after such bloody toil, we bid good night, | and 5.05. 6
faded, | by envy's hand and murder's bloody axe. R2 1.02. 21
blood, | but bloody with the enemies of his kin. 2.01.183
bloody with spurring, fiery–red with haste. 2.03. 58
the pale–fac'd moon looks bloody on the earth, 2.04. 10
ten thousand bloody crowns of mothers' sons 3.03. 96

the bloody office of his timeless end. 4.01. 5
where they did spend a sad and bloody hour, | as 1H4 1.01. 56
who then, affrighted with their bloody looks, 1.03.104
even with the bloody payment of your deaths. 1.03.186
we must have bloody noses and crack'd crowns, 2.03. 93
on | to bloody battles and to bruising arms. 3.02.105
blood, | and stain my favors in a bloody mask, 3.02.136
though many dearer, in this bloody fray. 5.04.108
who in a bloody field by shrewsbury | hath 2H4 in 24
but these mine eyes saw him in bloody state, 1.01.107
the bloody douglas, whose well–laboring sword 1.01.127
each heart being set | on bloody courses, the 1.01.159
led on by bloody youth, guarded with rage, | and 4.01. 34
the ugly form | of base and bloody insurrection 4.01. 40
that you should seal this lawless bloody book 4.01. 91
i would make this a bloody day to somebody. 5.04. 12 P
stand for your own, unwind your bloody flag, H5 1.02.101
and he is bred out of that bloody strain | that 2.04. 51
bloody constraint; 2.04. 97
and sword and shield, | in bloody field, | doth 3.02. 10
in liberty of bloody hand, shall range, | with 3.03. 12
the blind and bloody soldier with foul hand 3.03. 34
and by his bloody side | (yoke–fellow to his 4.06. 8
that we may wander o'er this bloody field | to 4.07. 72
whose bloody deeds shall make all europe quake. 1H6 1.01.156
but, lords, in all our bloody massacre, | i muse 2.02. 18
shall dye your white rose in a bloody red. 2.04. 61
was nothing less than bloody tyranny. 2.05.100
and i'll withdraw me and my bloody power. 4.02. 8
our nation's terror and their bloody scourge! 4.02. 16
shall see thee withered, bloody, pale, and dead. 4.02. 38
turn on the bloody hounds with heads of steel, 4.02. 51
drops bloody sweat from his war–wearied limbs, 4.04. 18
knee, | his bloody sword he brandish'd over me, 4.07. 6
in, | we should have found a bloody day of this. 4.07. 34
arms | of the most bloody nurser of his harms! 4.07. 46
all will be ours, now bloody talbot's slain. 4.07. 96
that such immanity and bloody strife | should 5.01. 13
ye both be suddenly surpris'd | by bloody hands, 5.03. 41
i am with child, ye bloody homicides! 5.04. 62
unless it were a bloody murtherer, | or foul 2H6 3.01.128
murther indeed, that bloody sin, i tortur'd 3.01.131
bearing it to the bloody slaughter–house, | even 3.01.212
shaking the bloody darts as he his bells. 3.01.366
and sooner dance upon a bloody pole | than stand 4.01.127
o barbarous and bloody spectacle! 4.01.144
rather than bloody war shall cut them short, 4.04. 12
outcast of naples, england's bloody scourge! 5.01.118
the bloody parliament shall this be call'd, 3H6 1.01. 39
ah, tutor, look where bloody clifford comes! 1.03. 2
come, bloody clifford, rough northumberland, | i 1.04. 27
after the bloody fray at wakefield fought, 2.01.107
let our bloody colors wave! 2.02.173
my tears shall wipe away these bloody marks; 2.05. 71
o bloody times! 2.05. 73
and bloody steel grasp'd in their ireful hands, 2.05.132
myself, | or hew my way out with a bloody axe. 3.02.181
bloody cannibals! 5.05. 61
i guess, | to make a bloody supper in the tower. 5.05. 85
thou wast provoked by thy bloody mind, | that R3 1.02. 99
and god, not we, hath plagu'd thy bloody deed. 1.03.180
when my son | was stabb'd with bloody daggers: 1.03.211
who made thee then a bloody minister, | when 1.04.220
a bloody deed, and desperately dispatch'd! 1.04.271
nearer in bloody thoughts, /but not in blood, 2.01. 93
o thou bloody prison! 3.03. 9
o bloody richard! 3.04.103
the tyrannous and bloody act is done, | the most 4.03. 1
albeit they were flesh'd villains, bloody dogs, 4.03. 6
both, | to bear this tidings to the bloody king. 4.03. 22
age confirm'd, proud, subtle, sly, and bloody, 4.04.172
bloody thou art, bloody will be thy end; 4.04.195
bloody thou art, bloody will be thy end; 4.04.195
and dangerous success of bloody wars, | as i 4.04.237
having bought love with such a bloody spoil. 4.04.290
the wretched, bloody, and usurping boar, | that 5.02. 7
peace | by this one bloody trial of sharp war. 5.02. 16
of bloody strokes and mortal–staring war. 5.03. 90
bloody and guilty, guiltily awake, | and in a 5.03.154
awake, | and in a bloody battle end thy days! 5.03.155
dream on, dream on, of bloody deeds and death; 5.03.171
gentlemen, | a bloody tyrant and a homicide; 5.03.246
the day is ours, the bloody dog is dead. 5.05. 2
from the dead temples of this bloody wretch 5.05. 5
that would reduce these bloody days again, | and 5.05. 36
sure | thou hast a cruel nature and a bloody. H8 5.02.164
here, sister, arm'd, and bloody in intent. TRO 5.03. 8
for i have dreamt | of bloody turbulence, and 5.03. 11
and when i have the bloody hector found, 5.07. 4
his bloody brow | with his mail'd hand then COR 1.03. 34
his bloody brow? o jupiter, no blood! 1.03. 38
set up the bloody flag against all patience, and 2.01. 75 P
the other course | will prove too bloody; 3.01.326
and | with bloody passage led your wars even to 5.06. 75
to quit the bloody wrongs upon her foes. TIT 1.01.141
upon his bloody finger he doth wear | a precious 2.03.226
two of thy whelps, fell curs of bloody kind, 2.03.281
rome, | and rear'd aloft the bloody battle–axe, 3.01.168
performers of this heinous, bloody deed? 4.01. 80
and so i leave you both — like bloody villains. 4.02. 17
that bloody mind i think they learn'd of me, 5.01.101
do | see here in bloody lines i have set down: 5.02. 14
where bloody murther or detested rape | can 5.02. 37
more stern and bloody than the centaurs' feast. 5.02.203
from those bloody hands | throw your mistempered
ROM 1.01. 86
benvolio, who began this bloody fray? 3.01.151
a piteous corse, a bloody piteous corse, | pale, 3.02. 54
'twixt my extremes and me this bloody knife 4.01. 62
where bloody tybalt, yet but green in earth, 4.03. 42
tybalt, liest thou there in thy bloody sheet? 5.03. 97
the ground is bloody, search about the 5.03.172
the fault's | bloody; TIM 3.05. 2
hand, | most bloody, fiery, and most terrible. JC 1.03.130
our course will seem too bloody, caius cassius, 2.01.162
though now we must appear bloody and cruel, | as 3.01.165
let each man render me his bloody hand. 3.01.184
peace, | shaking the bloody fingers of thy foes, 3.01.198
take | the cruel issue of these bloody men, 3.01.294
whilst bloody treason flourish'd over us. 3.02.192
o most bloody sight! 3.02.202 P
but when they should endure the bloody spur, 4.02. 25
their bloody sign of battle is hung out, | and 5.01. 14
what bloody man is that? MAC 1.02. 1
steel, | which smok'd with bloody execution, 1.02. 18
that we but teach | bloody instructions, which, 1.07. 9
it is the bloody business which informs | thus 2.01. 48
and question this most bloody piece of work, 2.03.128
the near in blood, | the nearer bloody. 2.03.141
with man's act, | threatens his bloody stage. 2.04. 6
is't known who did this more than bloody deed? 2.04. 22
we hear our bloody cousins are bestow'd | in 3.01. 29
and in such bloody distance, | that every minute 3.01.115
and with thy bloody and invisible hand | cancel 3.02. 48
free from our feasts and banquets bloody knives; 3.06. 35
be bloody, bold, and resolute: 4.01. 79
i grant him bloody, | luxurious, avaricious, 4.03. 57
bloody, bawdy villain! HAM 2.02.580
o, what a rash and bloody deed is this! 3.04. 27
a bloody deed! 3.04. 28
alas, how shall this bloody deed be answer'd? 4.01. 16
my thoughts be bloody, or be nothing worth! 4.04. 66
but since, so jump upon this bloody question, 5.02.375
so shall you hear | of carnal, bloody, and 5.02.381
hide thee, thou bloody hand; LR 3.02. 53
false of heart, light of ear, bloody of hand; 3.04. 92 P
thou rascal beadle, hold thy bloody hand! 4.06.160
the bloody proclamation to escape, | that 5.03.184
what means this bloody knife? 5.03.224
the bloody book of law | you shall yourself read OTH 1.03. 67
one at other's /breast, | in opposition bloody. 2.03.184
even so my bloody thoughts, with violent pace, 3.03.457
be in me remorse, | what bloody business ever. 3.03.469
but (dost thou hear) most bloody. 4.01. 91
where be these bloody thieves? 5.01. 63
these bloody accidents must excuse my manners 5.01. 94
some bloody passion shakes your very frame. 5.02. 44
o bloody period! 5.02.357
by isis, i will give thee bloody teeth, | if ANT 1.05. 70
before i strike this bloody stroke, farewell. 4.14. 91
if my shirt were bloody, then to shift it. CYM 1.02. 5 P
(and upon warrant of bloody affirmation) his to 1.04. 59 P
are dead, and send him | some bloody sign of it; 3.04.125
this bloody man, the care on't. 4.02.297
who is this | thou mak'st thy bloody pillow? 4.02.363
yea, bloody cloth, i'll keep thee, for i wish'd 5.01. 1
a war did cease | (ere bloody hands were wash'd) 5.05.485
horse was stuff'd within | with bloody veins, PER 1.04. 94
and the bloody times | could not have brought STM II.C 66
when as i met the boar, that bloody beast, VEN 999
so at his bloody view her eyes are fled | into 1037
in bloody death and ravishment delighting, | nor LUC 430
here friend by friend in bloody channel lies, 1487
my bloody judge forbod my tongue to speak, | no 1648
her wrongs to us, and by this bloody knife, | we 1840
like a thousand vanquish'd men in bloody fight! PP 17.24
mightier way | make war upon this bloody tyrant, SON 16. 2
the bloody spur cannot provoke him on | that 50. 9
is perjur'd, murd'rous, bloody, full of blame, 129. 3
//BLOODY–FAC'D 1 FR 0.0001 REL FR 1 V 0 P
/in /a /theme /so //bloody–fac'd /as /this, 2H4 1.03. 22
BLOODY–HUNTING 1 FR 0.0001 REL FR 1 V 0 P
jewry | at herod's bloody–hunting slaughter–men. H5 3.03. 41
BLOODY–MINDED 2 FR 0.0002 REL FR 2 V 0 P
yet let not this make thee be bloody–minded; 2H6 4.01. 36
some troops pursue the bloody–minded queen, 3H6 2.06. 33
BLOODY–SCEPTRED 1 FR 0.0001 REL FR 1 V 0 P
with an untitled tyrant bloody–sceptred, | when MAC 4.03.104
BLOOM 2 FR 0.0002 REL FR 2 V 0 P
his may of youth and bloom of lustihood. ADO 5.01. 76
ripe | the bloom that promiseth a mighty fruit. JN 2.01.473
BLOOM'D 2 FR 0.0002 REL FR 2 V 0 P
that one day bloom'd and fruitful were the next. 1H6 1.06. 7
this is a solemn rite | they owe bloom'd may, TNK 3.01. 3
BLOOMING 1 FR 0.0001 REL FR 1 V 0 P
yon little tree, yon blooming apricock! TNK 2.02.236
BLOSSOM 13 FR 0.0014 REL FR 12 V 1 P
under the blossom that hangs on the bough. TMP 5.01. 94
spied a blossom passing fair | playing in the LLL 4.03.101
that cannot so much as a blossom yield | in lieu AYL 2.03. 64
blossom, speed thee well! WT 3.03. 46
o that this blossom could be kept from cankers! 2H4 2.02. 94 P
i pluck this pale and maiden blossom here, 1H6 2.04. 47
now, by this maiden blossom in my hand, | i 2.04. 75
and there died | my icarus, my blossom, in his 4.07. 16
sweet blowse, you are a beauteous blossom sure. TIT 4.02. 72
yet fruits that blossom first will first be ripe OTH 2.03.377
then but beginning | to swell about the blossom) TNK 1.03. 68
that still blossom | as her bright eyes shine on 2.02.233
was ever may, | spied a blossom passing fair, PP 16. 3
BLOSSOMING 2 FR 0.0002 REL FR 2 V 0 P
as blossoming time | that from the seedness the MM 1.04. 41
melt their sweets | on blossoming caesar; ANT 4.12. 23
BLOSSOMS 7 FR 0.0008 REL FR 6 V 1 P
weeds | nip not the gaudy blossoms of your love LLL 5.02.802
appearing in the blossoms of their fortune. WT 5.02.125 P
thus are my blossoms blasted in the bud, | and 2H6 3.01. 89
the tender leaves of hopes, to–morrow blossoms, H8 3.02.353
cut off even in the blossoms of my sin, HAM 1.05. 76
young boughs that blush with thousand blossoms, TNK 3.06.243
where rarest havings made the blossoms dote, LC 235
/BLOT 1 FR 0.0001 REL FR 1 V 0 P
/mark'd /with /a /blot, /damn'd /in /the /book R2 4.01.236
BLOT 29 FR 0.0032 REL FR 29 V 0 P
it is the lesser blot, modesty finds, | women to TGV 5.04.108
i am possess'd with an adulterate blot; ERR 2.02.140
nature, drawing of an antic, | made a foul blot; ADO 3.01. 64
who can blot that name | with any just reproach? 4.01. 80
hero, | hero itself can blot out hero's virtue. 4.01. 82
passes praise, then praise too short doth blot. LLL 4.03.237
a good grandame, boy, that would blot thee. JN 2.01.133
side, | for time hath set a blot upon my pride. R2 3.02. 81
plot | to rid the realm of this pernicious blot? 4.01.325
excuse | this deadly blot in thy digressing son. 5.03. 66
and for his sake wear the detested blot | of 1H4 1.03.162
and thus thy fall hath left a kind of blot | to H5 2.02.138
this blot that they object against your house 1H6 2.04.116
but with our sword we wip'd away the blot; 2H6 4.01. 40
to blot out me, and put his own son in. 3H6 2.01. 92
the blot and enemy to our general name! TIT 2.03.183
as shall to thee blot out what wrongs were TIM 5.01.153
that you make known | it is no vicious blot, LR 1.01.227
and that would be a blot i' th' business. TNK 5.02. 81
like misty vapors when they blot the sky, VEN 184
before you blot | with your uncleanness that LUC 192
worse than a slavish wipe or birth–hour's blot; 537
to blot old books and alter their contents, | to 948
to shun this blot, she would not blot the letter 1322
she would not blot the letter | with words, till 1322
or blot with hell–born sin such saint–like forms 1519
dost him grace when clouds do blot the heaven; SON 28.10
but what's so blessed–fair that fears no blot? 92.13
where beauty's veil doth cover every blot, | and 95.11
BLOTS 8 FR 0.0009 REL FR 8 V 0 P
and the blots of nature's hand | shall not in MND 5.01.409
it blots thy beauty, as frosts do bite the meads SHR 5.02.139
to look into the blots and stains of right. JN 2.01.114
a good mother, boy, that blots thy father. 2.01.132
full of unpleasing blots and sightless stains, 3.01. 45
with inky blots and rotten parchment bonds; R2 2.01. 64
from all the impure blots and stains thereof; R3 3.07.234
so shall those blots that do with me remain, SON 36. 3
BLOTTED 4 FR 0.0004 REL FR 4 V 0 P
unpleasant'st words | that ever blotted paper! MV 3.02.252
my name be blotted from the book of life, | and R2 1.03.202
my heart those charms, thine eyes, are blotted; OTH 5.01. 35
wit sets down is blotted straight with will; LUC 1299
BLOTTING 2 FR 0.0002 REL FR 2 V 0 P
blotting your names from books of memory, 2H6 1.01.100
fed | upon fresh beauty, blotting it with blame; VEN 796
BLOW* *(also plow, etc.)*
/BLOW* 1 FR 0.0001 REL FR 1 V 0 P
hark how her sighs doth /blow! TIT 3.01.225
BLOW* 106 FR 0.0119 REL FR 85 V 21 P
blow till thou burst thy wind, if room enough! TMP 1.01. 7 P
a south–west blow on ye, | and blister you all 1.02.323
what a blow was there given! 2.01.180 P
than to suffer | the flesh–fly blow my mouth. 3.01. 63
bud | is eaten by the canker ere it blow, | even TGV 1.01. 46
blow not a word away | till i have found each 1.02.115
as thoughts do blow them, higher and higher. WIV 5.05. 98
and most desire should meet the blow of justice; MM 2.02. 30
there was blow for blow. ERR 3.01. 56
there was blow for blow. 3.01. 56
road, | and if the wind blow any way from shore, 3.02.148
air, quoth he, thy cheeks may blow; LLL 4.03.107
blow like sweet roses in this summer air. 5.02.293
how blow? how blow? speak to be understood. 5.02.294
how blow? how blow? speak to be understood. 5.02.294
when all aloud the wind doth blow | and coughing 5.02.921
broth | would blow me to an ague when i thought MV 1.01. 23
for the four winds blow in from every coast 1.01.168
to blow on whom i please, for so fools have; AYL 2.07. 49
blow, blow, thou winter wind, | thou art not so 2.07.174
blow, blow, thou winter wind, | thou art not so 2.07.174
hortensio, but we may blow our nails together, SHR 1.01.107 P
that gives not half so great a blow to hear | as 1.02.208
yet extreme gusts will blow out fire and all; 2.01.135
that /shake not, though they blow perpetually. 2.01.141
before you, will undermine you and blow you up. AWW 1.01.119 P
military policy how virgins might blow up men? 1.01.122 P
does not toby take you a blow o' the lips then? TN 2.05. 67 P
note, that keeps you from the blow of the law. 3.04.153 P
that may blow | no sneaping winds at home, to WT 1.02. 12
of january | would blow you through and through. 4.04.112
yet we free thee | from the dead blow of it. 4.04.434
on, | which sixteen winters cannot blow away, 5.03. 50
that will take pains to blow a horn before her? JN 1.01.219
of what i mean to speak | shall blow each dust, 3.04.128
thou hast a sigh to blow away this praise, 2H4 1.01. 80
let us but blow on them, | the vapor of our H5 4.02. 23
or else this blow should broach thy dearest 1H6 3.04. 40
i shall never be able to fight a blow. 2H6 1.03.216 P
peter, have at thee with a downright blow! 2.03. 90 P
shall blow ten thousand souls to heaven or hell; 3.01.350
and bid them blow towards england's blessed 3.02. 90
tut, when struck'st thou one blow in the field? 4.07. 79 P
now let the general trumpet blow his blast, 5.02. 43
i cleft his beaver with a downright blow. 3H6 1.01. 12
look, as i blow this feather from my face, | and 3.01. 84
me again, | obeying with my wind when i do blow, 3.01. 86
closer or, good faith, you'll catch a blow. 3.02. 23
i had rather chop this hand off at a blow, | and 5.01. 50
and blow it to the source from whence it came; 5.03. 11
there is my purse to cure that blow of thine. R3 4.04.514
he stands there like a mortar–piece to blow us. H8 5.03. 46 P
can watch you for telling how i took the blow — TRO 1.02.269 P
trumpet, blow /loud, | send thy brass voice 1.03.256
which | cold lips blow to their deities, take 4.04. 27
blow, villain, till thy sphered bias cheek 4.05. 8
/loud /the /taborins, let the trumpets blow, 4.05.275
come, blow thy blast. COR 1.04. 12
can you think to blow out the intended fire your 5.02. 45 P
will blow these sands like sibyl's leaves abroad TIT 4.01.105
gregory, remember thy washing blow. ROM 1.01. 63 P
it with something, make it a word and a blow. 3.01. 40 P
breath whom thou'lt observe | blow off thy cap; TIM 4.03.213
why now blow wind, swell billow, and swim bark! JC 5.01. 67
all the other, | and the very ports they blow, MAC 1.03. 15
that but this blow | might be the be–all and the 1.07. 4
air, | shall blow the horrid deed in every eye, 1.07. 24
blow wind, come wrack, | at least we'll die with 5.05. 50
seeming to feel this blow, with flaming top HAM 2.02.475
below their mines, | and blow them at the moon. 3.04.209
opinions, and do but blow them to their trial, 5.02.193 P
bids the wind blow the earth into the sea, | or LR 3.01. 5
blow, winds, and crack your cheeks! 3.02. 1
rage, blow! 3.02. 1
the sharp hawthorn blow the /cold winds." 3.04. 47 P
may the winds blow till they have waken'd death! OTH 2.01.186
found them close together | at blow and thrust, 2.03.238
all my fond love thus do i blow to heaven. 3.03.445
blow me about in winds! 5.02.279
the blow thou hadst | shall make thy peace for ANT 2.05. 69

the sighs of octavia blow the fire up in caesar, 2.06.127 P
the least wind i' th' world will blow them down. 2.07. 3 P
let the water–flies | blow me into abhorring! 5.02. 60
or death, | i wait the sharpest blow, antiochus. PER 1.01. 55
the axe myself, | do but you strike the blow. 1.02. 59
must feel war's blow, who spares not innocence: 1.02. 93
that were to blow at fire in hope to quench it, 1.04. 4
seldom ease, | for now the wind begins to blow; 2.ch. 29
blow, and split thyself. 3.01. 44 P
how she gins | to blow into life's flower again! 3.02. 95
instrument of wrath | prest for this blow. 4.ch. 45
'tis but a blow, which never shall be known. 4.01. 2
we have, a strong wind will blow it to pieces, 4.02. 19 P
her modesty will blow so far she falls for't. TNK 2.02.144
boys in athens | blow wind i' th' breech on 's, 2.03. 47
to blow that nearness out that flames between ye 5.01. 10
ev'ry blow that falls | threats a brave life, 5.03. 3
to fan and blow them dry again she seeks. VEN 52
the wind would blow it off, and being gone, 1089
which blow these pitchy vapors from their biding LUC 550
from lips new waxen pale begins to blow | the 1663
that blow did bail it from the deep unrest | of 1725
this windy tempest, till it blow up rain, | held 1788
is it revenge to give thyself a blow | for his 1823
"air," quoth he, "thy cheeks may blow, | air, PP 16. 9
falls | under the blow of thralled discontent, SON 124. 7
BLOWED 1 FR 0.0001 REL FR 0 V 1 P
i would have blowed up the town, so chrish save H5 3.02. 91 P
BLOWERS–UP 1 FR 0.0001 REL FR 0 V 1 P
poor virginity from underminers and blowers–up! AWW 1.01.121 P
BLOWEST 2 FR 0.0002 REL FR 2 V 0 P
thou blowest for hector. TRO 4.05. 11
thou blowest the fire when temperance is thaw'd, LUC 884
/BLOWING* 1 FR 0.0001 REL FR 1 V 0 P
/the /loud /trumpet /blowing /them /together; 2H4 4.01.120
BLOWING* 7 FR 0.0008 REL FR 4 V 3 P
door, sweating, and blowing, and looking wildly, WIV 3.03. 86 P
but i with blowing the fire shall warm myself; SHR 4.01. 9 P
marry, in blowing him down again, with the AWW 1.01.124 P
what time the shepherd, blowing of his nails, 3H6 2.05. 3
the shambles, | that quicken even with blowing. OTH 4.02. 67
as gentle | as zephyrs blowing below the violet, CYM 4.02.172
growing, | marigolds on death–beds blowing, TNK 1.01. 11
/BLOWN* 1 FR 0.0001 REL FR 1 V 0 P
soul | to such exsufflicate and /blown surmises, OTH 3.03.182
BLOWN* 41 FR 0.0046 REL FR 34 V 7 P
and blown with restless violence round about MM 3.01.124
if speaking, why, a vane blown with all winds; ADO 3.01. 66
orb, | as chaste as is the bud ere it be blown; 4.01. 58
are angels /vailing clouds, or roses blown. LLL 5.02.297
have blown me full of maggot ostentation. 5.02.409
virginity being blown down, man will quicklier AWW 1.01.123 P
blown down, man will quicklier be blown up. 1.01.124 P
he is to behold him with flies blown to death. WT 4.04.791 P
the breath of heaven hath blown his spirit out, JN 4.01.109
this show'r, blown up by tempest of the soul, 5.02. 50
and now 'tis far too huge to be blown out | with 5.02. 86
how now, blown jack? how now, quilt? 1H4 4.02. 49 P
rumor is a pipe | blown by surmises, jealousies, 2H4 in 16
your air of france | hath blown that vice in me. H5 3.06.152
will go out | with titles blown from adulation? 4.01.254
ever feather so lightly blown to and fro as this 2H6 4.08. 55 P
blown with the windy tempest of my heart | upon 3H6 2.05. 86
what though the mast be now blown overboard, 5.04. 3
have blown this coal betwixt my lord and me — H8 2.04. 79
you charge me | that i have blown this coal. 2.04. 94
that hath to this maturity blown up | in rank TRO 1.03.317
or my heart will be blown up by /th' /root. 4.04. 54 P
i have been blown out of your gates with sighs, COR 5.02. 74 P
ne'er through an arch so hurried the blown tide, 5.04. 47
our chimneys were blown down, and, as they say, MAC 2.03. 55
bladed corn be lodg'd, and trees blown down; 4.01. 55
that unmatch'd form and stature of blown youth HAM 3.01.159
with all his crimes broad blown, as flush as may 3.03. 81
the wretch that thou hast blown unto the worst LR 4.01. 8
no blown ambition doth our arms incite, | but 4.04. 27
when it hath blown his ranks into the air, | and OTH 3.04.135
against the blown rose may they stop their nose ANT 3.13. 39
'tis well blown, lads. 4.04. 25
there is a vent of blood, and something blown; 5.02.349
toward ephesus | turn our blown sails; PER 5.01.255
is blown abroad, help me, thy poor well–willer, TNK 3.05.116
yet from mine ear the tempting tune is blown; VEN 778
their light blown out in some mistrustful wood, 826
my sighs are blown away, my salt tears gone, 1071
small lights are soon blown out, huge fires LUC 647
and sorrow ebbs, being blown with wind of words. 1330
/BLOWS* 2 FR 0.0002 REL FR 2 V 0 P
/so /many /blows /upon /this /face /of /mine, R2 4.01.278
/in /the /dole /of /blows /your /son /might 2H4 1.01.169
BLOWS* 77 FR 0.0087 REL FR 65 V 12 P
i do beseech thy greatness, give him blows, TMP 3.02. 64
so plainly, i could too well feel his blows; ERR 2.01. 53 P
and you use these blows long, i must get a 2.02. 37 P
that he did buffet thee, and, in his blows, 2.02.158
were parchment, and the blows you gave were ink, 3.01. 13
by the wrongs i suffer, and the blows i bear. 3.01. 16
her trim, the merry wind | blows fair from land: 4.01. 91
sir, that i might not feel your blows. 4.04. 26 P
thou art sensible in nothing but blows, and so 4.04. 27 P
nothing at his hands for my service but blows. 4.04. 32 P
leap for joy, though they are lame with blows: LLL 5.02.291
and dick the shepherd blows his nail | and tom 5.02.913
i know a bank where the wild thyme blows, MND 2.01.249
which when it bites and blows upon my body AYL 2.01. 8
gale | blows you to padua here from old verona? SHR 1.02. 49
look how imagination blows him. TN 2.05. 43 P
i am a feather for each wind that blows. WT 2.03.154
of chance, and flies | of every wind that blows. 4.04.541
bought blood, and blows have answer'd blows; JN 2.01.329
bought blood, and blows have answer'd blows; 2.01.329
till then, blows, blood, and death! 2.01.360
and let thy blows, doubly redoubled, | fall like R2 1.03. 80
which his noble ancestors achiev'd with blows. 2.01.254
to change blows with thee for our day of doom. 3.02.189
what wards, what blows, what extremities he 1H4 1.02.189 P
till fields, and blows, and groans applaud our 1.03.302
and grief, it blows a man up like a bladder. 2.04.332 P
o my poor kingdom, sick with civil blows! 2H4 4.05.133
not the ill wind which blows no man to good. 5.03. 86 P
but when the blast of war blows in our ears, H5 3.01. 5
flames a' fire, and his lips blows at his nose, 3.06.104 P
i will not answer thee with words, but blows. 1H6 1.03. 69
and interchanging blows i quickly shed | some of 4.06. 19
come, leave your drinking, and fall to blows. 2H6 2.03. 79 P
by words or blows here let us win our right. 3H6 1.01. 37
but buckler with thee blows, twice two for one. 1.04. 50
for raging wind blows up incessant showers, 1.04.145
blows and revenge for me. 2.01. 86
for strokes receiv'd and many blows repaid 2.03. 3
ill blows the wind that profits nobody. 2.05. 55
for i have bought it with an hundred blows. 2.05. 81
my face, | and as the air blows it to me again, 3.01. 85
blow, | and yielding to another when it blows, 3.01. 87
that breath fame blows, that praise, sole pure, TRO 1.03.244
his blows are well dispos'd. there, ajax! 4.05.116
and sore blows | for sinking under them. COR 2.01.252
when blows have made me stay, i fled from words. 2.02. 72
to some nation | that won you without blows! 3.03.133
fortune's blows, | when most strook home, being 4.01. 7
to banish him that strook more blows for rome 4.02. 19
moe noble blows than ever thou wise words, | and 4.02. 21
while we were interchanging thrusts and blows, ROM 1.01.113
this wind you talk of blows us from ourselves: 1.04.104
what storm is this that blows so contrary? 3.02. 64
shall demonstrate these quick blows of fortune's TIM 1.01. 91
for every storm that blows — i to bear this, 4.03.266
words before blows; is it so, countrymen? JC 5.01. 27
the posture of your blows are yet unknown; 5.01. 33
whom the vile blows and buffets of the world MAC 3.01.108
and our vain blows malicious mockery. HAM 1.01.146
plucks off my beard and blows it in my face, 2.02.573
still through the hawthorn blows the cold wind: LR 3.04. 98 P
dust which the rude wind | blows in your face. 4.02. 31
that bear'st a cheek for blows, a head for 4.02. 51
a most poor man, made tame to fortune's blows, 4.06.221
when caesar and your brother were at blows, ANT 2.06. 44
we scorn her most when most she offers blows. 3.11. 74
this blows my heart. 4.06. 33
blows dust in others' eyes, to spread itself; PER 1.01. 97
him, | for flattery is the bellows blows up sin, 1.02. 39
is this wind westerly that blows? 4.01. 50
how modestly she blows, and paints the sun TNK 2.02.139
my father ever hated — | disgrace and blows. 2.05. 59
that my embraces | might thank ye, not my blows. 3.06. 23
whose breath blows down | the teeming ceres' 5.01. 52
stay, | and blows the smoke of it into his face, LUC 312
alas, how many bear such shameful blows, | which 832
BLOWSE 1 FR 0.0001 REL FR 1 V 0 P
sweet blowse, you are a beauteous blossom sure. TIT 4.02. 72
BLUBBER'D 2 FR 0.0002 REL FR 1 V 1 P
she comes blubber'd. 2H4 2.04.390 P
think | of rotten kings or blubber'd queens? TNK 1.01.180
BLUBB'RING 2 FR 0.0002 REL FR 2 V 0 P
blubb'ring and weeping, weeping and blubb'ring. ROM 3.03. 87
blubb'ring and weeping, weeping and blubb'ring. 3.03. 87
BLUE *(also plue)*
BLUE 28 FR 0.0031 REL FR 22 V 6 P
and with each end of thy blue bow dost crown TMP 4.01. 80
good heart, is beaten black and blue, that you WIV 4.05.112 P
what tellest thou me of black and blue? 4.05.114 P
there pinch the maids as blue as bilberry; 5.05. 45
em'rald tuffs, flow'rs purple, blue, and white, 5.05. 70
suck our breath, or pinch us black and blue. ERR 2.02.192
when daisies pied and violets blue | and LLL 5.02.894
a blue eye and sunken, which you have not; AYL 3.02.373 P
on the other, gart'red with a red and blue list; SHR 3.02. 68 P
be slickly comb'd, their blue coats brush'd, and 4.01. 91 P
and we will fool him black and blue, shall we TN 2.05. 10 P
blue, my lord. WT 2.01. 13
i have seen a lady's nose | that has been blue, 2.01. 15
privileged place — | blue coats to tawny coats! 1H6 1.03. 47
the lights burn blue. R3 5.03.180
his crest that prouder than blue iris bends. TRO 1.03.379
engenders the black toad and adder blue, | the TIM 4.03.181
and when the cross blue lightning seem'd to open JC 1.03. 50
pelion, or the skyish head | of blue olympus. HAM 5.01.254
even till we make the main and th' aerial blue OTH 2.01. 39
or blue promontory | with trees upon't that nod ANT 4.14. 5
azure lac'd | with blue of heaven's own tinct. CYM 2.02. 23
with hand armipotent from forth blue clouds TNK 5.01. 54
her two blue windows faintly she upheaveth, VEN 482
her breasts like ivory globes circled with blue, LUC 407
whose ranks of blue veins, as his hand did scale 440
her blue blood chang'd to black in every vein, 1454
her tear–distained eye | blue circles stream'd, 1587
BLUE–BOTTLE 1 FR 0.0001 REL FR 0 V 1 P
swing'd for this — you blue–bottle rogue, you 2H4 5.04. 19 P
BLUE–CAPS 1 FR 0.0001 REL FR 0 V 1 P
and one mordake, and a thousand blue–caps more. 1H4 2.04.357 P
BLUE–EY'D 1 FR 0.0001 REL FR 1 V 0 P
this blue–ey'd hag was hither brought with child TMP 1.02.269
BLUES 1 FR 0.0001 REL FR 1 V 0 P
the yellows, blues, | the purple violets, and PER 4.01. 14
BLUEST 1 FR 0.0001 REL FR 1 V 0 P
and here | my bluest veins to kiss — a hand ANT 2.05. 29
BLUE–VEIN'D 1 FR 0.0001 REL FR 1 V 0 P
these blue–vein'd violets whereon we lean VEN 125
BLUISH 1 FR 0.0001 REL FR 0 V 1 P
skirts, round underborne with a bluish tinsel; ADO 3.04. 21 P
BLUNT* 45 FR 0.0050 REL FR 42 V 3 P
by some sly trick blunt thurio's dull proceeding TGV 2.06. 41
but doth rebate and blunt his natural edge MM 1.04. 60
vicious, ungentle, foolish, blunt, unkind, ERR 4.02. 21
sir, and his wits are not so blunt as, god help, ADO 3.05. 10 P
and yours as blunt as the fencer's foils, which 5.02. 13 P
is a sharp wit match'd with too blunt a will, LLL 2.01. 49
third, dull lead, with warning all as blunt, MV 2.07. 8
you are too blunt, go to it orderly. SHR 2.01. 45
hiding his bitter jests in blunt behavior; 3.02. 13
though he be blunt, i know him passing wise; 3.02. 24
a good blunt fellow. JN 1.01. 71
heads of salisbury, /spencer, blunt, and kent. R2 5.06. 8
sir walter blunt, new lighted from his horse, 1H4 1.01. 63
how now, good blunt? 3.02.162
welcome, sir walter blunt; 4.03. 32
the noble westmerland, and warlike blunt, | and 4.04. 30
a gallant knight he was, his name was blunt, 5.03. 20
sir walter blunt. 5.03. 32 P
valiant shirley, stafford, blunt are in my arms. 5.04. 41
that the blunt monster with uncounted heads, 2H4 in 18
blunt, lead him hence, and see you guard him 4.03. 75
therefore omit him not, blunt not his love, 4.04. 27
to trip the course of law and blunt the sword 5.02. 87
by his blunt bearing he will keep his word, H5 4.07.177
base slave, thy words are blunt and so art thou. 2H6 4.01. 67
with hasty germans and blunt hollanders, | hath 3H6 4.08. 2
that clarence is so harsh, so blunt, unnatural, 5.01. 86
your blunt upbraidings and your bitter scoffs. R3 1.03.103
no doubt the murd'rous knife was dull and blunt 4.04.227
oxford, redoubted pembroke, sir james blunt, 4.05. 14
good captain blunt, bear my good–night to him, 5.03. 30
sweet blunt, make some good means to speak with 5.03. 40
good night, good captain blunt. 5.03. 44
blunt wedges rive hard knots; TRO 1.03.316
what a blunt fellow is this grown to be! JC 1.02.295
me all) a plain blunt man | that love my friend, 3.02.218
blunt not the heart, enrage it. MAC 4.03.229
i am too blunt and saucy: CYM 5.05.325
but the blunt boar, rough bear, or lion proud, VEN 884
this is too curious–good, this blunt and ill: LUC 1300
in ajax' eyes blunt rage and rigor roll'd, | but 1398
onward to troy with the blunt swains he goes, 1504
devouring time, blunt thou the lion's paws, SON 19. 1
a face | that overgoes my blunt invention quite, 103. 7
tan sacred beauty, blunt the sharp'st intents, 115. 7
BLUNTED 2 FR 0.0002 REL FR 2 V 0 P
such eyes | as, sick and blunted with community, 1H4 3.02. 77
is but to whet thy almost blunted purpose. HAM 3.04.111
BLUNTER 1 FR 0.0001 REL FR 1 V 0 P
said | thy edge should blunter be than appetite, SON 56. 2
BLUNTEST 1 FR 0.0001 REL FR 1 V 0 P
he is the bluntest wooer in christendom. 3H6 3.02. 83
BLUNTING 2 FR 0.0002 REL FR 2 V 0 P
for blunting the fine point of seldom pleasure. SON 52. 4
by blunting us to make our wits more keen. LC 161
BLUNTLY 3 FR 0.0003 REL FR 2 V 1 P
no more but plain and bluntly "to the king"? 1H6 4.01. 51
or bad news, that thou com'st in so bluntly? R3 4.03. 45
telling it, and deliver a plain message bluntly. LR 1.04. 34 P
BLUNTNESS 1 FR 0.0001 REL FR 1 V 0 P
having been prais'd for bluntness, doth affect LR 2.02. 96
BLUNTS* 2 FR 0.0002 REL FR 2 V 0 P
unkindness blunts it more than marble hard. ERR 2.01. 93
and both the blunts | kill'd by the hand of 2H4 1.01. 16
BLUNT–WITTED 1 FR 0.0001 REL FR 1 V 0 P
blunt–witted lord, ignoble in demeanor! 2H6 3.02.210
BLUR 2 FR 0.0002 REL FR 2 V 0 P
never yet did base dishonor blur our name | but 2H6 4.01. 39
this blur to youth, this sorrow to the sage, LUC 222
BLURR'D 2 FR 0.0002 REL FR 2 V 0 P
time hath nothing blurr'd those lines of favor CYM 4.02.104
thy issue blurr'd with nameless bastardy; LUC 522
BLURS 1 FR 0.0001 REL FR 1 V 0 P
act | that blurs the grace and blush of modesty, HAM 3.04. 41
BLURTED 1 FR 0.0001 REL FR 1 V 0 P
whilest ours was blurted at and held a mawkin PER 4.03. 34
BLUSH 60 FR 0.0067 REL FR 53 V 7 P
o proteus, let this habit make thee blush! TGV 5.04.104
her blush is guiltiness, not modesty. ADO 4.01. 42
for blush in cheeks by faults are bred | and LLL 1.02.101
you may look pale, but i should blush, i know, 4.03.127
come, sir, you blush; 4.03.129
and mark'd you both, and for you both did blush. 4.03.136
cupid himself would blush | to see me thus MV 2.06. 38
him to thee as he is, i must blush and weep, and AYL 1.01.157 P
with safety of a pure blush thou mayst in honor 1.02. 28 P
in the which hope i blush, and hide my sword. 2.07.119
me, | "we blush that thou shouldst choose; AWW 2.03. 70
me when his wife was dead, i blush to say it, he 5.03.140 P
innocence shall make | false accusation blush, WT 3.02. 31
i should blush | to see you so attir'd — sworn, 4.04. 12
for this | i'll blush you thanks. 4.04.584
you will but make it blush | and glow with shame JN 4.01.112
of your dear mother england, blush for shame; 5.02.153
but stay'd and made the western welkin blush, 5.05. 2
wherefore blush you now? 2H4 2.02. 76 P
we hope to make the sender blush at it. H5 1.02.299
katherine, and i must not blush to affirm it. 5.02.114 P
blush for pure shame to counterfeit our roses, 1H6 2.04. 66
but be thou mild, and blush not at my shame, 2H6 2.04. 48
thou shalt not see me blush | nor change my 3.01. 98
to blush and beautify the cheek again. 3.02.167
i would assay, proud queen, to make thee blush. 3H6 1.04.118
and not bewray thy treason with a blush? 3.03. 97
blush, blush, thou lump of foul deformity; R3 1.02. 57
blush, blush, thou lump of foul deformity; 1.02. 57
now, if you can blush, and cry "guilty," H8 3.02.305
if i blush, | it is to see a nobleman want 3.02.307
and bid the cheek be ready with a blush | modest TRO 1.03.228
she does so blush, and fetches her wind so short 3.02. 31 P
come, come, what need you blush? 3.02. 40 P
you shall perceive | whether i blush or no; COR 1.09. 70
it is a part | that i shall blush in acting, and 2.02.145
his friends | blush that the world goes well, 4.06. 5
sons' sweet blood will make it shame and blush. TIT 3.01. 15
i blush to think upon this ignomy. 4.02.115
what, canst thou say all this and never blush? 5.01.121
here are the beetle brows shall blush for me. ROM 1.04. 32
else would a maiden blush bepaint my cheek | for 2.02. 86
still blush, as thinking their own kisses sin; 3.03. 39
whose blush doth thaw the consecrated snow TIM 4.03.385
act | that blurs the grace and blush of modesty, HAM 3.04. 41
o shame, where is thy blush? 3.04. 81
o, | i follow'd that i blush to look upon. ANT 3.11. 12
nay, blush not, cleopatra, i approve | your 5.02.149
blush not in actions blacker than the night PER 1.01.135
and what may make him blush in being known, 1.02. 22
(whose modest scenes blush on his marriage–day, TNK pr 4
young boughs that blush with thousand blossoms, 3.06.243
allow'st no more blood than will make a blush, 5.01.141
forgetting shame's pure blush and honor's wrack. VEN 558
virtue bragg'd, beauty would blush for shame; LUC 54

and the red rose blush at her own disgrace, 479
"where now i have no one to blush with me, | to 792
yet will she blush, here be it said, | to hear PP 18.53
beggar'd of blood to blush through lively veins, SON 67.10
to blush at speeches rank, to weep at woes, | or LC 307
BLUSH'D 10 FR 0.0011 REL FR 6 V 4 P
before, i blush'd to hear his monstrous devices. 1H4 2.04.312 P
and ever since thou hast blush'd extempore. 2.04.316 P
and helen so blush'd, and paris so chaf'd, and TRO 1.02.166 P
that pages blush'd at him, and men of heart COR 5.06. 98
i have so often blush'd to acknowledge him, that LR 1.01. 10 P
and quiet that her motion | blush'd at herself; OTH 1.03. 96
but have blush'd | at simp'ring sirs that did. TNK 5.01.103
boy, | who blush'd and pouted in a dull disdain, VEN 33
for lucrece thought he blush'd to see her shame, LUC 1344
she thought he blush'd, as knowing tarquin's 1354
BLUSHES 15 FR 0.0017 REL FR 13 V 2 P
i think the boy hath grace in him; he blushes. TGV 5.04.165
lay by all nicety and prolixious blushes | that MM 2.04.162
behold how like a maid she blushes here! ADO 4.01. 34
in angel whiteness beat away those blushes, 4.01.161
the blushes in my cheeks thus whisper me, | "we AWW 2.03. 69
cool, blushes! 4.03.337
he blushes, and 'tis hit. 5.03.195
come, quench your blushes, and present yourself WT 4.04. 67
o, he is bold, and blushes not at death. JN 4.03. 76
put off your maiden blushes, avouch the thoughts H5 5.02.235 P
these blushes of hers must be quench'd with some
PER 4.02.124 P
and paints the sun | with her chaste blushes! TNK 2.02.140
when beauty boasted blushes, in despite | virtue LUC 55
likewise lent me | of grief and blushes, aptly LC 200
of burning blushes, or of weeping water, | or 304
BLUSHEST 1 FR 0.0001 REL FR 1 V 0 P
thou blushest, antony, and that blood of thine ANT 1.01. 30
BLUSHING 28 FR 0.0031 REL FR 24 V 4 P
i have mark'd | a thousand blushing apparitions ADO 4.01.159
i do betray myself with blushing. maid. LLL 1.02.133 P
his treasons will sit blushing in his face, R2 3.02. 51
as doth the blushing discontented sun | from out 3.03. 63
indeed, | he made a blushing cital of himself, 1H4 5.02. 61
ass, you bashful fool, must you be blushing? 2H4 2.02. 76 P
did represent my master's blushing cheeks, 1H6 4.01. 93
and, if thou canst for blushing, view this face, 3H6 1.04. 46
and to my brother turn my blushing cheeks. 5.01. 99
'tis a blushing shame–fac'd spirit that mutinies R3 1.04.138 P
in your way | for more than blushing comes to. H8 2.03. 42
as from a blushing handmaid, to his highness; 2.03. 72
and bears his blushing honors thick upon him; 3.02.354
what, blushing still? TRO 3.02.100 P
face | blushing to be encount'red with a cloud. TIT 2.04. 32
hue, that will betray with blushing | the close 4.02.117
my lips, two blushing pilgrims, ready stand | to ROM 1.05. 95
this blushing virgin, should take manhood to her TNK 2.02.258
would have trembled to deny | a blushing maid — 3.06.205
like lawn being spread upon the blushing rose, VEN 590
when lo the blushing morrow | lends light to all LUC 1082
and, blushing on her, with a steadfast eye 1339
and, blushing with him, wistly on him gazed; 1355
so | that blushing red no guilty instance gave, 1511
abide, | blushing at that which is so putrefied. 1750
and blushing fled, and left her all alone. PP 9.14
/one blushing shame, another white despair; SON 99. 9
at the wood's boldness by thee blushing stand. 128. 8
BLUSTER 1 FR 0.0001 REL FR 1 V 0 P
which in the bluster of thy wrath must fall TIM 5.04. 41
BLUSTERER 1 FR 0.0001 REL FR 1 V 0 P
sometime a blusterer that the ruffle knew | of LC 58
BLUSTERING 1 FR 0.0001 REL FR 1 V 0 P
early in blustering morn this lady was | thrown PER 5.03. 22
BLUSTEROUS 1 FR 0.0001 REL FR 1 V 0 P
for a more blusterous birth had never babe. PER 3.01. 28
BLUSTERS 1 FR 0.0001 REL FR 1 V 0 P
look grimly | and threaten present blusters. WT 3.03. 4
BLUST'RING 3 FR 0.0003 REL FR 3 V 0 P
and make fair weather in your blust'ring land. JN 5.01. 21
foretells a tempest and a blust'ring day. 1H4 5.01. 6
no cloudy show of stormy blust'ring weather LUC 115
BOAR 35 FR 0.0039 REL FR 34 V 1 P
or bear, | pard, or boar with bristled hair, MND 2.02. 31
rage like an angry boar chafed with sweat? SHR 1.02.202
doth the old boar feed in the old frank? 2H4 2.02.146 P
he dreamt the boar had rased off his helm. R3 3.02. 11
to fly the boar before the boar pursues | were 3.02. 28
to fly the boar before the boar pursues | were 3.02. 28
pursues | were to incense the boar to follow us, 3.02. 29
where he shall see the boar will use us kindly. 3.02. 33
fear you the boar, and go so unprovided? 3.02. 73
stanley did dream the boar did /rase our helms, 3.04. 82
that in the sty of the most deadly boar | my son 4.05. 2
the wretched, bloody, and usurping boar, | that 5.02. 7
the chafed boar, the mountain lioness, | the TIT 4.02.138
who, like a boar too savage, doth root up | his TIM 5.01.165
the boar of thessaly | was never so emboss'd. ANT 4.13. 2
like a full–acorn'd boar, a german /one, | cried CYM 2.05. 16
that hast slain | the scythe–tusk'd boar; TNK 1.01. 79
do you, | as once did meleager and the boar, 3.05. 18
it, | unless it be a boar, and then i chase it; VEN 410
to hunt the boar with certain of his friends. 588
"the boar!" 589
that thou toldst me thou wouldst hunt the boar. 614
when thou didst name the boar, not to dissemble, 641
mine eye | the picture of an angry chafing boar, 662
if thou encounter with the boar to–morrow. 672
to make thee hate the hunting of the boar, 711
but the blunt boar, rough bear, or lion proud, 884
and with that word she spied the hunted boar, 900
but back retires to rate the boar for murther. 906
i felt a kind of fear | when as i met the boar, 999
"'tis not my fault, the boar provok'd my tongue, 1003
upon the wide wound that the boar had trench'd 1052
"but this foul, grim, and urchin–snouted boar, 1105
he ran upon the boar with his sharp spear, | who 1112
here in these brakes deep–wounded with a boar, PP 9.10
BOARD 15 FR 0.0017 REL FR 12 V 3 P
therefore bear up and board 'em. TMP 3.02. 3 P
and let her read it in thy looks at board: ERR 3.02. 18
at board he fed not for my urging it; 5.01. 64
i was as willing to grapple as he was to board. LLL 2.01.218
to us | wait in your royal walks, your board, MND 5.01. 31
juno's crown, | o blessed bond of board and bed! AYL 5.04.142
for i will board her, though she chide as loud SHR 1.02. 95
"accost" is front her, board her, woo her, TN 1.03. 57 P
and this is he that did the tiger board, | when 5.01. 62
we cannot lodge and board a dozen or fourteen H5 2.01. 33 P
fed from my trencher, kneel'd down at the board, 2H6 4.01. 57
letter, | the honorable board of council out, H8 1.01. 79
i'll board him presently. HAM 2.02.170
his bed shall seem a school, his board a shrift, OTH 3.03. 24
i would have left it on the board so soon | as i CYM 3.06. 50
BOARDED 7 FR 0.0008 REL FR 4 V 3 P
i boarded the king's ship; TMP 1.02.196
he would never have boarded me in this fury. WIV 2.01. 88 P
i would he had boarded me. ADO 2.01.143 P
and boarded her i' th' wanton way of youth. AWW 5.03.211
straightway /calm'd and boarded with a pirate. 2H6 4.09. 33
valor, and in the grapple i boarded them. HAM 4.06. 18 P
faith, he to–night hath boarded a land carract. OTH 1.02. 50
BOARDING 1 FR 0.0001 REL FR 0 V 1 P
"boarding," call you it? WIV 2.01. 90 P
BOARDS 1 FR 0.0001 REL FR 0 V 1 P
but ships are but boards, sailors but men; MV 1.03. 22 P
BOARISH 1 FR 0.0001 REL FR 1 V 0 P
in his anointed flesh /rash boarish fangs. LR 3.07. 58
BOAR–PIG 1 FR 0.0001 REL FR 0 V 1 P
thou whoreson little tidy bartholomew boar–pig, 2H4 2.04.231 P
BOAR'S 2 FR 0.0002 REL FR 2 V 0 P
good angels guard thee from the boar's annoy! R3 5.03.151
the foul boar's conquest on her fair delight, VEN 1030
BOAR–SPEAR 2 FR 0.0002 REL FR 2 V 0 P
a boar–spear in my hand, and — in my heart AYL 1.03.118
come on, come on, where is your boar–spear, man?
R3 3.02. 72
BOAST 40 FR 0.0045 REL FR 37 V 3 P
do not smile at me that i boast her /off, | for TMP 4.01. 9
my duty will i boast of, nothing else. TGV 2.04.111
give god thanks, and make no boast of it, and ADO 3.03. 20 P
why should proud summer boast | before the birds
LLL 1.01.102
i give heaven thanks, and make no boast of them. AYL 2.05. 37 P
it is no boast, being ask'd, to say we are. 4.03. 90
as every present time doth boast itself | above WT 5.01. 96
of nature's gifts thou mayst with lilies boast, JN 3.01. 53
yet can i not of such tame patience boast | as R2 1.01. 52
boast of nothing else | but that i was a 1.03.273
where e'er i wander, boast of this i can, 1.03.308
it is a conquest for a prince to boast of. 1H4 1.01. 77
i could make as true a boast as that, if i had a H5 3.07. 62 P
proclaimed through our host | to boast of this, 4.08.115
that she may boast she hath beheld the man 1H6 2.02. 42
nor should that nation boast it so with us, 3.03. 23
that doth presume to boast of gentle blood. 4.01. 44
upon my death the french can little boast; 4.05. 24
keep thou the napkin and go boast of this, | and 3H6 1.04.159
cannot make boast to have that which he hath, TRO 3.03. 98
when every thing doth make a gleeful boast? TIT 2.03. 11
where they boast | to have well–armed friends. LR 3.07. 19
but (o vain boast!) OTH 5.02.264
now boast thee, death, in thy possession lies ANT 5.02.315
are as dear as yours, | can justly boast of. CYM 2.03. 80
i had rather | you felt than make't my boast. 2.03.111
further to boast were neither true nor modest, 5.05. 18
for beauty that made barren the swell'd boast 5.05.162
with other virtues, which i'll keep from boast, PER 4.06.184
to those that boast and have not, a defier; TNK 5.01.120
what canst thou boast | of things long since, or VEN 1077
perchance his boast of lucrece' sov'reignty LUC 36
he shall not boast who did thy stock pollute 1063
my resolution, love, shall be thy boast, | by 1193
stars | of public honor and proud titles boast, SON 25. 2
then may i dare to boast how i do love thee, 26.13
as victors of my silence cannot boast; 86.11
and having thee, of all men's pride i boast: 91.12
time, thou shalt not boast that i do change: 123. 1
"'o, pardon me, in that my boast is true: LC 246
BOASTED 2 FR 0.0002 REL FR 2 V 0 P
now | that you so oft have boasted to retain? LR 3.06. 59
when beauty boasted blushes, in despite | virtue LUC 55
BOASTFUL 1 FR 0.0001 REL FR 1 V 0 P
in high and boastful neighs | piercing the H5 4.pr. 10
BOASTING 5 FR 0.0005 REL FR 4 V 1 P
out of hand, | and set upon our boasting enemy. 1H6 3.02.103
to such as boasting show their scars | a mock is TRO 4.05.290
and topping all others in boasting. COR 2.01. 20 P
no boasting like a fool; MAC 4.01.153
which, when i know that boasting is an honor, OTH 1.02. 20
BOASTS 2 FR 0.0002 REL FR 2 V 0 P
and (which is more than all these boasts can be) MND 1.01.103
and boasts himself | to have a worthy feeding; WT 4.04.168
/BOAT 1 FR 0.0001 REL FR 1 V 0 P
"/her /boat /hath /a /leak, | /and /she /must LR 3.06. 26
BOAT 10 FR 0.0011 REL FR 9 V 1 P
were down, i could drive the boat with my sighs. TGV 2.03. 53 P
the sailors sought for safety by our boat, | and ERR 1.01. 76
hung on our driving boat, i saw your brother, TN 1.02. 11
to hazard all our lives in one small boat! 1H6 4.06. 33
richmond in dorsetshire sent out a boat | unto R3 4.04.522
where's then the saucy boat | whose weak TRO 1.03. 42
my boat sails freely, both with wind and stream. OTH 2.03. 63
come down into the boat. ANT 2.07.129
convey thy deity | aboard our dancing boat, make PER 3.01. 13
or (being wrack'd) i am a worthless boat, | he SON 80.11
BOATS 6 FR 0.0006 REL FR 6 V 0 P
how many shallow bauble boats dare sail | upon TRO 1.03. 35
light boats sail swift, though greater hulks 2.03.266
that when the sea was calm all boats alike COR 4.01. 6
the banks, or for | the press of boats or pride. CYM 2.04. 72
sands that will not bear your enemies' boats, 3.01. 21
brings in some boats that are not steer'd. 4.03. 46
BOATSWAIN 5 FR 0.0005 REL FR 3 V 2 P
boatswain! TMP 1.01. 1 P
good boatswain, have care. 1.01. 9 P
"the master, the swabber, the boatswain, and i, 2.02. 46
the master and the boatswain | being awake, 5.01. 99
the boatswain whistles, and | the master calls, PER 4.01. 63
BOB* 3 FR 0.0003 REL FR 2 V 1 P
and when she drinks, against her lips i bob, MND 2.01. 49
he smart, | /not /to seem senseless of the bob; AYL 2.07. 55
you shall not bob us out of our melody. TRO 3.01. 68 P
BOBB'D* 3 FR 0.0003 REL FR 2 V 1 P
fathers | have in their own land beaten, bobb'd, R3 5.03.334
i have bobb'd his brain more than he has beat my TRO 2.01. 69 P
of gold and jewels that i bobb'd from him | as OTH 5.01. 16
BOBLIBINDO 1 FR 0.0001 REL FR 0 V 1 P
boblibindo chicurmurco. AWW 4.03.125 P
BOBTAIL 1 FR 0.0001 REL FR 1 V 0 P
or /lym, | or bobtail /tike or trundle–tail, LR 3.06. 70
BOCCHUS 1 FR 0.0001 REL FR 1 V 0 P
he hath assembled | bocchus, the king of libya; ANT 3.06. 69
BODE 7 FR 0.0008 REL FR 3 V 4 P
and i pray god his bad voice bode no mischief. ADO 2.03. 81 P
what should that bode? 3.02. 42 P
this was my dream, what it doth bode god knows. 2H6 1.02. 31
i would croak like a raven, i would bode, i TRO 5.02.191 P
croak like a raven, i would bode, i would bode. 5.02.191 P
doth that bode weeping? OTH 4.03. 59
what did thy song bode, lady? 5.02.246
BODED *(also aboded)*
BODED 2 FR 0.0002 REL FR 2 V 0 P
invert | what best is boded me to mischief! TMP 3.01. 71
what boded this, but well forewarning wind | did 2H6 3.02. 85
BODEMENTS 2 FR 0.0002 REL FR 2 V 0 P
superstitious girl | makes all these bodements. TRO 5.03. 80
sweet bodements! MAC 4.01. 96
BODES 6 FR 0.0006 REL FR 6 V 0 P
and so it is; i wonder what it bodes. SHR 5.02.107
marry, peace it bodes, and love, and quiet life, 5.02.108
what e'er it bodes, henceforward will i bear 3H6 2.01. 39
my sight is very dull, what e'er it bodes. TIT 2.03.195
which, once untangled, much misfortune bodes. ROM 1.04. 91
this bodes some strange eruption to our state. HAM 1.01. 69
BODG'D *(also boudge, bouge, budge)*
BODG'D 1 FR 0.0001 REL FR 1 V 0 P
we bodg'd again, as i have seen a swan | with 3H6 1.04. 19
BODIED 1 FR 0.0001 REL FR 1 V 0 P
ill–fac'd, worse bodied, shapeless every where; ERR 4.02. 20
/BODIES 2 FR 0.0002 REL FR 1 V 1 P
/action /of /their /bodies /from /their /souls, 2H4 1.01.195
/then /are /our /beggars /bodies, /and /our HAM 2.02.263 P
BODIES 44 FR 0.0049 REL FR 38 V 6 P
is a curer of souls, and you a curer of bodies. WIV 2.03. 39 P
guts should hale souls out of men's bodies? ADO 2.03. 60 P
so, with two seeming bodies but one heart, | two MND 3.02.212
and as imagination bodies forth | the forms of 5.01. 14
why are our bodies soft, and weak, and smooth, SHR 5.02.165
souls and bodies hath he divorc'd three, and his TN 3.04.237 P
me | to the dead bodies of my queen and son. WT 3.02.235
presently your souls must part your bodies — R2 3.01. 3
save our deposed bodies to the ground? 3.02.150
and as the soldiers bore dead bodies by, | he 1H4 1.03. 42
all the gibbets and press'd the dead bodies. 4.02. 37 P
hearts have left their bodies here in england, H5 1.02.128
o, let their bodies follow, my dear liege, 1.02.130
give | their bodies to the lust of english youth 3.05. 30
their poor bodies | must lie and fester. 4.03. 87
a many of our bodies shall no doubt | find 4.03. 95
in safety, and dispose | of their dead bodies! 4.07. 83
and have our bodies slaught'red by thy foes. 1H6 3.01.101
ta'en, | and to survey the bodies of the dead. 4.07. 57
give me their bodies, that i may bear them hence 4.07. 85
go take their bodies hence. 4.07. 91
and sold their bodies for their country's 5.04.106
and the bodies shall be dragg'd at my horse 2H6 4.03. 12 P
and wrap our bodies in black mourning gowns, 3H6 2.01.161
and all the unlook'd–for issue of their bodies 3.02.131
even with the dearest blood your bodies bear. 5.01. 69
their souls whose bodies richard murther'd R3 5.03.230
inter their bodies as become their births. 5.05. 15
and the bodies | of the duke's confessor, john H8 1.01.217
why, had your bodies | no heart among you? COR 2.03.203
and state of bodies would bewray what life | we 5.03. 95
do some villainous shame | to the dead bodies. ROM 5.03. 53
to keep those many many bodies safe | that live HAM 3.03. 9
conceit in weakest bodies strongest works, 3.04.114
give order that these bodies | high on a stage 5.02.377
take up the bodies. 5.02.401
produce the bodies, be they alive or dead. LR 5.03.231
our bodies are our gardens, to the which our OTH 1.03.320 P
but we do launch | diseases in our bodies. ANT 5.01. 37
heaven came and shrivell'd up | those bodies, PER 2.04. 10
two souls | put in two noble bodies, let 'em TNK 2.02. 65
swim with your bodies, | and carry it sweetly 3.05. 28
she sows into the births of noble bodies, | were 4.02. 9
all–fear'd gods, bow down your stubborn bodies. 5.01. 13
BODILESS 1 FR 0.0001 REL FR 1 V 0 P
this bodiless creation ecstasy | is very cunning HAM 3.04.138
BODILY 4 FR 0.0004 REL FR 1 V 3 P
in bodily health, sir. 2H4 2.02.103 P
that could be brought to bodily act ere rome COR 1.02. 5
had thought you had receiv'd some bodily wound;
OTH 2.03.267 P
enjoy'd the dearest bodily part of your mistress CYM 1.04.150 P
BODING *(also aboding)*
BODING 4 FR 0.0004 REL FR 4 V 0 P
and boding screech–owls make the consort full! 2H6 3.02.327
house, | boding to all) he had my handkerchief. OTH 4.01. 22
nor | the boding raven, nor /chough /hoar, | nor TNK 1.01. 20
my boding heart pants, beats, and takes no rest, VEN 647
BODKIN 3 FR 0.0003 REL FR 1 V 2 P
the head of a bodkin. LLL 5.02.611 P
god's bodkin, man, much better: HAM 2.02.529 P
might his quietus make | with a bare bodkin; 3.01. 75
BODKIN'S 1 FR 0.0001 REL FR 0 V 1 P
and it you cannot thrust a bodkin's point. WT 3.03. 86 P
BODY *(also pody)*
/BODY 2 FR 0.0002 REL FR 2 V 0 P
/t' /undeck /the /pompous /body /of /a /king; R2 4.01.250
/follow'd /both /with /body /and /with /mind; 2H4 1.01.203
BODY 253 FR 0.0286 REL FR 211 V 42 P
and as with age his body uglier grows, | so his TMP 4.01.191
does now speak to thee, i embrace thy body, 5.01.109
a passing shame | that i (unworthy body as i am) TGV 1.02. 18
his body for a girl that loves him not. 5.04.134
i' faith, and find any body in the house, here WIV 1.04. 4 P

i'll make more of thy old body than i have done. 2.02.139 P
good body, i thank thee. 2.02.142 P
or whether that the body public be | a horse MM 1.02.159
give up your body to such sweet uncleanness | as 2.04. 54
this, | i had rather give my body than my soul. 2.04. 56
you must lay down the treasures of your body 2.04. 96
sick for, ere i'ld yield | my body up to shame. 2.04.104
brother | by yielding up thy body to my will, 2.04.164
before his sister should her body stoop | to 2.04.182
the damned'st body to invest and cover | in 3.01. 95
complexion, shall keep the body of it ever fair. 3.01.184 P
me, hath any body inquir'd for me here to-day? 4.01. 16 P
and by an eminent body that enforc'd | the law 4.04. 22
not, but by gift of my chaste body | to his 5.01. 97
who thinks he knows that he ne'er knew my body, 5.01.203
this is the body | that took away the match from 5.01.210
soul-killing witches that deform the body, ERR 1.02.100
and that this body, consecrate to thee, | by 2.02.132
a very reverent body: 3.02. 90 P
in what part of her body stands ireland? 3.02.116 P
me, | and therewithal took measure of my body. 4.03. 9
the body of your discourse is sometime guarded ADO 1.01.285 P
wisdom and blood combating in so tender a body, 2.03.164 P
but they should suffer salvation, body and soul. 3.03. 3 P
and justly as your soul | should with your body. 4.01.249
i'll prove it on his body, if he dare, | despite 5.01. 74
the mind shall banquet, though the body pine; LLL 1.01. 25
must thou speak," and "thus thy body bear"; 5.02.100
my little body is a-weary of this great world. MV 1.02. 1 P
taken | in what part of your body pleaseth me. 1.03.151
lady, | the paper as the body of my friend, 3.02.264
i never knew so young a body with so old a head. 4.01.163 P
i have, | no, not my body nor my husband's bed. 5.01.228
i once did lend my body for his wealth, | which, 5.01.249
which when it bites and blows upon my body AYL 2.01. 8
he pierceth through | the body of /the country, 2.01. 59
cleanse the foul body of th' infected world, 2.07. 60
nature charg'd | that one body should be fill'd 3.02.142
a body would think this was well counterfeited! 4.03.165 P
times remov'd (bear your body more seeming, 5.04. 69 P
to deck thy body with his ruffling treasure. SHR 4.03. 60
for 'tis the mind that makes the body rich; 4.03.172
an hasty-witted body | would say your head and 5.02. 40
commits his body | to painful labor, both by sea 5.02.148
that wishing well had not a body in't, | which AWW 1.01.181
blessing of god till i have issue a' my body; 1.03. 25 P
my poor body, madam, requires it. 1.03. 28 P
grow to you, and our parting is a tortur'd body. 2.01. 37 P
child begotten of thy body that i am father to, 3.02. 59 P
of as able body as when he number'd thirty. 4.05. 81 P
and will continue | the standing of his body. WT 1.02.431
my second joy | and first-fruits of my body, 3.02. 97
or /hoop his body more with thy embraces, | i 4.04.439
preparation | was levied in the body of a land. JN 4.02.112
nay, in the body of this fleshly land, | this 4.02.245
in peace, and part this body and my soul | with 5.04. 47
sings | his soul and body to their lasting rest. 5.07. 24
at worcester must his body be interr'd, | for so 5.07. 99
speak | my body shall make good upon this earth, R2 1.01. 37
commit'st thy anointed body to the cure | of 2.01. 98
of him, | and learn to make a body of a limb. 3.02.187
his body to that pleasant country's earth, | and 4.01. 98
hath yielded up his body to the grave; 5.06. 21
of the night's body be call'd thieves of the 1H4 1.02. 24 P
god's body, the turkeys in my pannier are quite 2.01. 26 P
when that this body did contain a spirit, | a 5.04. 89
need i thus | my well-known body to anatomize 2H4 in 21
come, we will all put forth, body and goods. 1.01.186
i think we are so /a body strong enough, | even 1.03. 66
and begin to patch up thine old body for heaven? 2.04.233 P
that show a weak mind and an able body, for the 2.04.252 P
then you perceive the body of our kingdom | how 3.01. 38
it is but as a body yet distempered, | which to 3.01. 41
depending | hath fed upon the body of my father; 4.05.159
and mock your workings in a second body? 5.02. 90
that the great body of our state may go | in 5.02.136
make less thy body (hence) and more thy grace, 5.05. 52
be, and here i commit my body to your mercies. ep 14 P
the breath no sooner left his father's body, H5 1.01. 25
leaving his body as a paradise | t' envelop and 1.01. 30
like little body with a mighty heart, | what 2.pr. 17
forgive, | although my body pay the price of it. 2.02.154
my fault, but not my body, pardon, sovereign. 2.02.165
who, with a body fill'd and vacant mind, | gets 4.01.269
i richard's body have interred new, | and on it 4.01.295
bear hence his body, i will help to bury it. 1H6 1.04. 87
bring forth the body of old salisbury, | and 2.02. 4
mistake | the outward composition of his body. 2.03. 75
remov'd, | leaving no heir begotten of his body) 2.05. 72
my body shall | pay recompense, if you will 5.03. 18
cannot my body nor blood-sacrifice | entreat you 5.03. 20
then take my soul — my body, soul, and all, 5.03. 22
before his legs be firm to bear his body. 2H6 3.01.190
my body round engirt with misery — | for what's 3.01.200
rear up his body, wring him by the nose. 3.02. 34
it, | and so i wish'd thy body might my heart. 3.02.109
come hither, gracious sovereign, view this body. 3.02.149
soul, | or i should breathe it so into thy body, 3.02.398
there let his head and liveless body lie, 4.01.142
his body will i bear unto the king. 4.01.145
but where's the body that i should embrace? 4.04. 6
and as i thrust thy body in with my sword, | so 4.10. 78
my soul and body on the action both! 5.02. 26
house, | so was his will in his old feeble body. 5.03. 13
that this my body | might in the ground be 3H6 2.01. 75
that to my foes this body must be prey, | yet 2.03. 39
golden cup, | his body couched in a curious bed, 2.05. 53
lady's lap, | and deck my body in gay ornaments, 3.02.149
my back, | where sits deformity to mock my body; 3.02.158
together like a double shadow | to henry's body, 4.06. 50
he'll soon find means to make the body follow. 4.07. 26
what is the body when the head is off? 5.01. 41
my mangled body shows, | my blood, my want of 5.02. 7
shows, | that i must yield my body to the earth, 5.02. 9
then, since the heavens have shap'd my body so, 5.06. 78
i'll throw thy body in another room, | and 5.06. 92
thou hadst but power over his mortal body, | his R3 1.02. 47
of tailors | to study fashions to adorn my body: 1.02.257
i'll go hide the body in some hole | till that 1.04.280
upon my body with their hellish charms? 3.04. 62
not sleeping, to engross his idle body, | but 3.07. 76
cur | preys on the issue of his mother's body, 4.04. 57
the purple sap from her sweet brother's body, 4.04.277
my anointed body | by thee was punched full of 5.03.124
who set the body and the limbs | of this great H8 1.01. 46
of his own body he was ill, and gave | the 4.02. 43
body a' me, where is it? 5.02. 22
well, i would my heart were in her body. TRO 1.02. 79 P
death, | do to this body what extremes you can; 4.02.102
out | at every joint and motive of her body. 4.05. 57
in which part of his body | shall i destroy him 4.05.242
go bear patroclus' body to achilles, | and bid 5.05. 17
come, tie his body to my horse's tail, | along 5.08. 21
a gulf it did remain | i' th' midst a' th' body, COR 1.01. 99
and affection common | of the whole body. 1.01.105
be restrain'd, | who is the sink a' th' body — 1.01.122
store-house and the shop | of the whole body. 1.01.134
the repulse of tarquin seven hurts i' th' body. 2.01.150 P
your loving motion toward the common body | to 2.02. 53
that you bear | i' th' body of the weal; 2.03.181
wish | to jump a body with a dangerous physic 3.01.154
think | upon the wounds his body bears, which 3.03. 50
let me twine | mine arms about that body, where 4.05.107
shall bury | his reasons with his body. 5.06. 58
bear from hence his body, | and mourn you for 5.06.141
a better head her glorious body fits | than his TIT 1.01.187
as any mortal body hearing it | should straight 2.03.103
bind me here | unto the body of a dismal yew, 2.03.107
pit, | where never man's eye may behold my body: 2.03.177
some bring the murthered body, some the 2.03.300
and made thy body bare | of her two branches, 2.04. 17
shall i do | now i behold thy lively body so? 3.01.105
sheaf, | these broken limbs again into one body. 5.03. 72
sheathing the steel in my advent'rous body. 5.03.112
and for a hand and a foot and a body, though ROM 2.05. 42 P
bear hence this body and attend our will; 3.01.196
upon his body that hath slaughter'd him! 3.05.102
in one little body | thou counterfeits a bark, a 3.05.130
the bark thy body is, | sailing in this salt 3.05.133
calm, will overset | thy tempest-tossed body. 3.05.137
that did spit his body | upon a rapier's point. 4.03. 56
her body sleeps in capel's monument, | and her 5.01. 18
which now the public body, which doth seldom TIM 5.01.145
and must bend his body | if caesar carelessly JC 1.02.117
i may | produce his body to the market-place, 3.01.228
mark antony, here take you caesar's body. 3.01.244
prepare the body then, and follow us. 3.01.253
here comes his body, mourn'd by mark antony, who 3.02. 41 P
stand from the hearse, stand from the body. 3.02.165 P
we'll burn his body in the holy place, | and 3.02.254
take up the body. 3.02.256
what villain touch'd his body, that did stab 4.03. 20
where, where, messala, doth his body lie? 5.03. 91
come therefore, and to /thasos send his body; 5.03.104
where is duncan's body? MAC 2.04. 32
in my bosom for the dignity of the whole body. 5.01. 56 P
before my body | i throw my warlike shield. 5.08. 32
with which she followed my poor father's body, HAM 1.02.148
unto the voice and yielding of that body 1.03. 23
and makes each petty artere in this body | as 1.04. 82
the natural gates and alleys of the body, | and 1.05. 67
vile and loathsome crust, | all my smooth body. 1.05. 73
and the very age and body of the time his form 3.02. 24 P
a deed | as from the body of contraction plucks 3.04. 46
to draw apart the body he hath kill'd, | o'er 4.01. 24
fair, and bring the body | into the chapel. 4.01. 36
what have you done, my lord, with the dead body? 4.02. 5
you must tell us where the body is, and go with 4.02. 25 P
the body is with the king, but the king is not 4.02. 27 P
the king, but the king is not with the body. 4.02. 28 P
i have sent to seek him, and to find the body. 4.03. 1
where the dead body is bestow'd, my lord, | we 4.03. 12
is a sore decayer of your whoreson dead body. 5.01.172 P
and from her derogate body never spring | a babe LR 1.04.280
sword he charges home | my unprovided body, 2.01. 52
commands the mind | to suffer with the body. 2.04.109
with thy uncover'd body this extremity of the 3.04.102 P
a small spark, all the rest on 's body cold. 3.04.113 P
suits to his back, six shirts to his body — 3.04.136 P
if ever thou wilt thrive, bury my body, | and 4.06.247
when she is sated with his body, she will find OTH 1.03.350 P
pioners and all, had tasted her sweet body, | so 3.03.346
lest her body and beauty unprovide my mind again 4.01.205 P
why he hath thus ensnar'd my soul and body? 5.02.302
this common body, | like to a vagabond flag upon ANT 1.04. 44
bear the king's son's body | before our army. 3.01. 3
she shows a body rather than a life, | a statue, 3.03. 20
the soul and body rive not more in parting 4.13. 5
eros, now thy captain is | even such a body. 4.14. 13
the arm of mine own body, and the heart | where 5.01. 45
ah, but some natural notes about her body, CYM 2.02. 28
garment | that ever hath but clipt his body, is 2.03.134
my speech of insultment ended on his dead body, 3.05.141 P
the lines of my body are as well drawn as his; 4.01. 9 P
if we do fear this body hath a tail | more 4.02.144
thersites' body is as good as ajax', | when 4.02.252
he'll then instruct us of this body. 4.02.360
by those fearful objects to prepare | this body, PER 1.01. 44
makes both my body pine and soul to languish, 1.02. 32
good mariner, | i'll bring the body presently. 3.01. 81
should therein make me vile, the common body, 3.03. 21
i'll throw my body out, | and leap the garden, TNK 2.02.215
hath taken notice | both of his blood and body. 2.02.228
first | he bows his noble body, then salutes me 2.04. 23
but his body | and fiery mind illustrate a brave 2.05. 21
lovers, | cast yourselves in a body decently, 3.05. 20
the body of our sport, of no small study, | i 3.05.121
to him, a mere gipsy, | and this the noble body. 4.02. 45
tainted with extremes) runs through his body, 4.02.101
promises | in such a body yet i never look'd on. 4.02.119
arms in assurance | my body to this business. 5.01.135
they said that palamon had arcite's body 5.03. 79
"what is thy body but a swallowing grave, VEN 757
the strongest body shall it make most weak, 1145
it, | but with my body my poor soul's pollution? LUC 1157
"my body or my soul, which was the dearer, 1163
the knife | that wounds my body so dishonored. 1185
my soul and body to the skies and ground, | my 1199
that dying fear through all her body spread, 1266
body spread, | and who cannot abuse a body dead? 1267
fed, | show'd life imprison'd in a body dead. 1456
himself on her self-slaught'red body threw, 1733
blood | circles her body in on every side, | who 1739
to show her bleeding body thorough rome, | and 1851
my body is the frame wherein 'tis held, | and SON 24. 3
me untrue, | my name be buried where my body is, 72.11
life, | the prey of worms, my body being dead, 74.10
my soul doth tell my body that he may | triumph 151. 7

BODY-CURER 1 FR 0.0001 REL FR 0 V 1 P
french and welsh, soul-curer and body-curer! WIV 3.01. 98 P

BODYKINS 1 FR 0.0001 REL FR 0 V 1 P
bodykins, master page, though i now be old and WIV 2.03. 44 P

BODY'S 26 FR 0.0029 REL FR 23 V 3 P
a great charge to come under one body's hand. WIV 1.04. 99 P
earth's god, and body's fost'ring patron" — LLL 1.01.221 P
on thy soul's peril and thy body's torture, WT 2.03.181
to prove by god's grace, and my body's valor, R2 1.03. 37
for all my body's moisture | scarce serves to 3H6 2.01. 79
more than my body's parting with my soul. 2.06. 4
lands | is nothing left me but my body's length. 5.02. 26
why then all-souls' day is my body's doomsday. R3 5.01. 12
panging | as soul and body's severing. H8 2.03. 16
there was a time when all the body's members COR 1.01. 96
and by my body's action teach my mind | a most 3.02.122
doth make your honor of his body's hue, TIT 2.03. 73
not body's death, but body's banishment. ROM 3.03. 11
not body's death, but body's banishment. 3.03. 11
when the mind's free, | the body's delicate; LR 3.04. 12
that she repeals him for her body's lust, | and OTH 2.03.357
his body's a passable carcass, if he be not hurt CYM 1.02. 9 P
my body's mark'd | with roman swords, and my 3.03. 56
his body's hostage | for his return. 4.02.185
mark how his body's made for't. TNK 2.03. 71
nothing but my body's bane would cure thee." VEN 372
her body's stain her mind untainted clears, LUC 1710
to work my mind, when body's work's expired; SON 27. 4
in their wealth, some in their body's force, 91. 2
is this thy body's end? 146. 8
my nobler part to my gross body's treason; 151. 6

BOG 2 FR 0.0002 REL FR 1 V 1 P
through bog, through bush, through brake, MND 3.01.107
/ford and whirlpool, o'er bog and quagmire; LR 3.04. 53 P

BOGGLE 1 FR 0.0001 REL FR 1 V 0 P
you boggle shrewdly, every feather starts you. AWW 5.03.232

BOGGLER 1 FR 0.0001 REL FR 1 V 0 P
you have been a boggler ever, | but when we in ANT 3.13.110

BOGS 3 FR 0.0003 REL FR 1 V 2 P
infections that the sun sucks up | from bogs, TMP 2.02. 2
in her buttocks, i found it out by the bogs. ERR 3.02.118 P
so, and ride not warily, fall into foul bogs. H5 3.07. 57 P

BOHEMIA 24 FR 0.0027 REL FR 15 V 9 P
to visit bohemia on the like occasion whereon my WT 1.01. 1 P
difference betwixt our bohemia and your sicilia. 1.01. 4 P
of sicilia means to pay bohemia the visitation 1.01. 6 P
sicilia cannot show himself overkind to bohemia. 1.01. 22 P
when at bohemia | you take my lord, i'll give 1.02. 39
most understand | bohemia stays here longer. 1.02.230
the covering sky is nothing, bohemia nothing, 1.02.294
her medal hanging | about his neck, bohemia — 1.02.308
i do, and will fetch off bohemia for't; 1.02.334
feasts, keep with bohemia | and with your queen. 1.02.344
here comes bohemia. 1.02.364
adultery with polixenes, king of bohemia, and 3.02. 15 P
ship hath touch'd upon | the deserts of bohemia? 3.03. 2
oath, | places remote enough are in bohemia, 3.03. 31
that i now may be | in fair bohemia, and 4.01. 21
not a more cowardly rogue in all bohemia. 4.03.105 P
all the lawyers in bohemia can learnedly handle, 4.04.205 P
not for bohemia, nor the pomp that may | be 4.04.488
who for bohemia bend, to signify | not only my 5.01.165
sir, | bohemia greets you from himself by me; 5.01.181
where's bohemia? speak. 5.01.185
bohemia stops his ears, and threatens them 5.01.201
then asks bohemia forgiveness; 5.02. 52 P
as honest a true fellow as any is in bohemia. 5.02.157 P

BOHEMIAN 1 FR 0.0001 REL FR 0 V 1 P
a bohemian born; MM 4.02.130 P

BOHEMIAN-TARTAR 1 FR 0.0001 REL FR 0 V 1 P
here's a bohemian-tartar tarries the coming down WIV 4.05. 20 P

BOHEMIA'S 2 FR 0.0002 REL FR 2 V 0 P
tell him you are sure | all in bohemia's well; WT 1.02. 31
we are not furnish'd like bohemia's son, | nor 4.04.588

BOHUN 1 FR 0.0001 REL FR 1 V 0 P
now, poor edward bohun. H8 2.01.103

BOIL *(see bile, etc.)*

BOIL 7 FR 0.0008 REL FR 6 V 1 P
where i have seen corruption boil and bubble, MM 5.01.318
makes merit her election, and doth boil | (as TRO 1.03.349
got, | boil thou first i' th' charmed pot. MAC 4.01. 9
a fenny snake, | in the cauldron boil and bake; 4.01. 13
trouble, | like a hell-broth boil and bubble. 4.01. 19
and there boil like a gammon of bacon that will TNK 4.03. 38 P
face doth reek and smoke, her blood doth boil, VEN 555

/BOIL'D 1 FR 0.0001 REL FR 1 V 0 P
brains, | now useless, /boil'd within thy skull! TMP 5.01. 60

BOIL'D 3 FR 0.0003 REL FR 1 V 2 P
let me be boil'd to death with melancholy. TN 2.05. 3 P
given, he might have boil'd and eaten him too. COR 4.05.189 P
such boil'd stuff | as well might poison poison. CYM 1.06.125

BOIL'D-BRAINS 1 FR 0.0001 REL FR 0 V 1 P
any but these boil'd-brains of nineteen and WT 3.03. 64 P

BOILING 4 FR 0.0004 REL FR 3 V 1 P
he bravely broach'd his boiling bloody breast; MND 5.01.147
boiling | in leads or oils? WT 3.02.176
for boiling choler chokes | the hollow passage 1H6 5.04.120
such burning, frying, boiling, hissing, howling, TNK 4.03. 33 P

BOISTEROUS 3 FR 0.0003 REL FR 3 V 0 P
why, 'tis a boisterous and a cruel style, | a AYL 4.03. 31
feeling what small things are boisterous there, JN 4.01. 94
that the bleak air, thy boisterous chamberlain, TIM 4.03.222

BOISTEROUSLY 1 FR 0.0001 REL FR 1 V 0 P
must be as boisterously maintain'd as gain'd; JN 3.04.136

BOIST'ROUS 12 FR 0.0013 REL FR 11 V 1 P

or with a base and boist'rous sword enforce | a AYL 2.03. 32
here to make good the boist'rous late appeal, R2 1.01. 4
so rous'd up with boist'rous untun'd drums, 1.03.134
into the harsh and boist'rous tongue of war? 2H4 4.01. 49
but as an honor snatch'd with boist'rous hand, 4.05.191
o clifford, boist'rous clifford, thou hast slain 3H6 2.01. 70
see | the water swell before a boist'rous storm. R3 2.03. 44
too rude, too boist'rous, and it pricks like ROM 1.04. 26
consequence, | attends the boist'rous /ruin. HAM 3.03. 22
this more stubborn and boist'rous expedition. OTH 1.03.228 P
all foul means | of boist'rous and rough jad'ry, TNK 5.04. 72
sits, | banning his boist'rous and unruly beast; VEN 326
BOIST'ROUS–ROUGH 1 FR 0.0001 REL FR 1 V 0 P
alas, what need you be so boist'rous–rough? JN 4.01. 75
/BOITE 1 FR 0.0001 REL FR 0 V 1 P
and vetch me in my closet /une /boite /en verd, WIV 1.04. 45 P
BOLD *(also pold)*
/BOLD 2 FR 0.0002 REL FR 2 V 0 P
/or /what /doth /this /bold /enterprise /bring 2H4 1.01.178
/i /am /thus /bold /to /put /your /grace /in R3 4.02.110
BOLD 151 FR 0.0170 REL FR 129 V 22 P
to besiege, and make his bold waves tremble, TMP 1.02.205
his bold head | 'bove the contentious waves he 2.01.118
may i be bold | to think these spirits? 4.01.119
tow'r, | so bold leander would adventure it. TGV 3.01.120
i'll be so bold to break the seal for once. 3.01.139
i dare be bold | with our discourse to make your 5.04.162
i make bold, to press with so little preparation WIV 2.02.156 P
/brook, i will first make bold with your money; 2.02.252 P
i'll be so bold as stay, sir, till she come down 4.05. 12 P
may i be bold to say so, sir? 4.05. 53 P
ay, sir; like who more bold? 4.05. 54 P
faults may shake our frames), let me be bold. MM 2.04.133
virtue is bold, and goodness never fearful. 3.01.208 P
i will only be bold with benedick for his ADO 3.02. 8 P
bold of your worthiness, we single you | as our LLL 2.01. 28
but pardon me, i am too sudden bold; 2.01.107
making the bold wag by their praises bolder. 5.02.108
i know not by what power i am made bold, | nor MND 1.01. 59
if i cut my finger, i shall make bold with you. 3.01.184 P
art too wild, too rude, and bold of voice — MV 2.02.181
had you been as wise as bold, | young in limbs, 2.07. 70
o, then be bold to say bassanio's dead! 3.02.185
your spirits are too bold for your years. AYL 1.02.173 P
and therefore let me be thus bold with you | to SHR 1.02.104
if i may be bold, | tell me, i beseech you, 1.02.218
sir, let me be so bold as ask you, | did you yet 1.02.249
am bold to show myself a forward guest | within 2.01. 51
may i be so bold to know the cause of your 2.01. 87 P
may i be bold to acquaint his grace you are gone AWW 3.06. 78 P
of that i have made a bold charter, but i thank 4.05. 92 P
be bold you do so grow in my requital | as 5.01. 5
durst make too bold a herald of my tongue; 5.03. 46
and that may you be bold to say in your foolery. TN 1.05. 12 P
bold oxlips, and | the crown imperial; WT 4.04.125
o, he is bold, and blushes not at death. JN 4.03. 76
brought hither henry herford thy bold son, R2 1.01. 3
chest | is a bold spirit in a loyal breast. 1.01.181
the duke of norfolk, sprightfully and bold, 1.03. 3
no person be so bold | or daring–hardy as to 1.03. 42
words are but as thoughts, therefore be bold. 2.01.276
o heinous, strong, and bold conspiracy! 5.03. 59
ten thousand bold scots, two and twenty knights, 1H4 1.01. 68
sir, your presence is too bold and peremptory, 1.03. 17
day | be bold to tell you that i am your son, 3.02.134
yet doth he give us bold advertisement | that 4.01. 36
the breast of civil peace | such bold hostility, 4.03. 44
more daring or more bold, is now alive | to 5.01. 91
quenching the flame of bold rebellion | even 2H4 in 26
stopping my greedy ear with their bold deeds, 1.01. 78
to look with forehead bold and big enough | upon 1.03. 8
all these bold fears | thou seest with peril i 4.05.195
your father) | i gave bold way to my authority, 5.02. 82
"happy am i, that have a man so bold, | that 5.02.108
that you use the same | with the like bold, just 5.02.116
god, his grace is bold to trust these traitors. H5 2.02. 1
you, i will be so bold as to tell you i know the 3.02.139 P
but i will be so bold as to wear it in my cap 5.01. 11 P
i'll be so bold to take what they have left. 1H6 2.01. 78
madam, i have been bold to trouble you; 2.03. 25
must your bold verdict enter talk with lords?" 3.01. 63
conceit | to set a gloss upon his bold intent, 4.01.103
talbot, | who, ring'd about with bold adversity, 4.04. 14
to me, | for i am bold to counsel you in this. 2H6 1.03. 93
dare you be so bold? 3.02.238
and therefore am i bold and resolute. 4.04. 60
dare any be so bold to sound retreat or parley 4.08. 4 P
were he as famous and as bold in war | as he is 3H6 2.01.155
becomes it thee to be thus bold in terms 2.02. 85
and what makes robbers bold but too much lenity? 2.06. 22
not mutinous in peace, yet bold in war; 4.08. 10
boy, | bold, quick, ingenious, forward, capable: R3 3.01.155
yet who/'s so bold but says he sees it not? 3.06. 12
thy prime of manhood daring, bold, and venturous 4.04.171
make bold her bashful years with your experience 4.04.326
the ransom of my bold attempt | shall be this 5.03.265
"jockey of norfolk, be not so bold, | for dickon 5.03.304
fight, bold yeomen! 5.03.338
this makes bold mouths, | tongues spit their H8 1.02. 60
forth, and with bold spirit relate what you, 1.02.129
me | and dare be bold to weep for buckingham, 2.01. 72
so long have slept upon | this bold bad man. 2.02. 43
ye are too bold. 2.02. 70
i will be bold with time and your attention: 2.04.169
you made bold | to carry into flanders the great 3.02.318
may i be bold to ask what that contains, | that 4.01. 13
a bold brave gentleman. 4.01. 40
i shall remember this bold language. 5.02.119
do. | remember your bold life too. 5.02.120
for then the bold and coward, | the wise and TRO 1.03. 23
bold as an oracle, and sets thersites, | a slave 1.03.192
of generosity | and make bold power look pale — COR 1.01.212
bold gentleman! 1.05. 22
i will be bold to take my leave of you. 2.01. 96 P
ungrateful rome, | like a bold flood o'er–beat. 4.05.131
forbid i should be so bold to press to heaven in TIT 4.03. 91 P
be bold in us, we'll follow where thou lead'st, 5.01. 13
i am too bold, 'tis not to me she speaks. ROM 2.02. 14
that i mean to make bold withal, and, as you 3.01. 78 P
with piercing steel at bold mercutio's breast, 3.01.159
till strange love grow bold, | think true love 3.02. 15
but flies an eagle flight, bold, and forth on, TIM 1.01. 49
i have been bold | (for that i knew it the most 2.02.199
in execution | of any bold or noble enterprise, JC 1.02.298
i think we are too bold upon your rest. 2.01. 86
caesar was mighty, bold, royal, and loving. 3.01.127
which hath made them drunk hath made me bold; MAC 2.02. 1
i'll make so bold to call, | for 'tis my limited 2.03. 51
ay, and a bold one, that dare look on that 3.04. 58
be bloody, bold, and resolute: 4.01. 79
the bold winds speechless, and the orb below HAM 2.02.485
o my lord, if my duty be too bold, my love is 3.02.348 P
to mine own room again, making so bold, | my 5.02. 16
men so disorder'd, so debosh'd and bold, | that LR 1.04.242
bold in the quarrel's right, rous'd to th' 2.01. 54
show too bold malice | against the grace and 2.02.130
wherefore, bold peasant, | /durst thou support a 4.06.231
he is bold in his defense." 5.03.114 P
we then have done you bold and saucy wrongs; OTH 1.01.128
a maiden, never bold; 1.03. 94
(not surfeited to death) | stand in bold cure. 2.01. 51
captain, | left in the conduct of the bold iago, 2.01. 75
that gives me this bold show of courtesy. 2.01. 99
i have made bold, iago, | to send in to your 3.01. 33
as (to be bold with you) | not to affect many 3.03.228
here, at thy hand; be bold, and take thy stand. 5.01. 7
a great deal abus'd in too bold a persuasion, CYM 1.04.114 P
i will make bold | to send them to you, only for 1.06.197
to win the king as i am bold her honor | will 2.04. 2
they come | under the conduct of bold jachimo, 4.02.340
though with the loss | of many a bold one, whose 5.05. 71
which i'll make bold your highness | cannot deny 5.05. 89
like a bold champion i assume the lists, | nor PER 1.01. 61
not me | unto a stranger knight to be so bold. 2.03. 67
to his bold ends honor and golden ingots, TNK 1.02. 17
and call to arms | the bold young men that, when 2.02.249
you were call'd | a good knight and a bold. 3.01. 65
none but arcite | in this kind is so bold. 3.01. 92
be bold to ring the bell. 3.02. 20
what a bold gravity, and yet inviting, | has 4.02. 41
and | the two bold titlers at this instant are 5.03. 83
i am not bold, | we have no such cause. ep 11
be bold to play, our sport is not in sight; VEN 124
who is so faint that dares not be so bold | to 401
men can cover crimes with bold stern looks, LUC 1252
"but, lady, if your maid may be so bold, | she 1282
was defect | of spirit, life, and bold audacity. 1346
when their brave hope, bold hector, march'd to 1430
hold | only to flatter fools and make them bold: 1559
youth is hot and bold, age is weak and cold, PP 12. 7
therefore to give them from me was i bold, | to SON 122.11
to say they err i dare not be so bold, 131. 7
BOLD–BEATING 1 FR 0.0001 REL FR 0 V 1 P
phrases, and your bold–beating oaths, under the WIV 2.02. 28 P
BOLDEN'D 1 FR 0.0001 REL FR 1 V 0 P
art thou thus bolden'd, man, by thy distress? AYL 2.07. 91
BOLDER 7 FR 0.0008 REL FR 6 V 1 P
which makes me the bolder to chide you for yours TGV 2.01. 83 P
making the bold wag by their praises bolder. LLL 5.02.108
yet | that any of these bolder vices wanted WT 3.02. 55
makes me the bolder to salute my king | with 2H6 1.01. 29
than my lord hastings no man might be bolder, R3 3.04. 29
bolder, though not so subtle. COR 1.10. 17
a bolder traitor never trod thy ground, | a TNK 3.06.141
BOLDEST 3 FR 0.0003 REL FR 3 V 0 P
rather to put on | your boldest suit of mirth, MV 2.02.202
with the most boldest and best hearts of rome. JC 3.01.121
names concealments in | the boldest language. TNK 5.01.124
BOLD–FAC'D 2 FR 0.0002 REL FR 2 V 0 P
heart with proud desire | of bold–fac'd victory. 1H6 4.06. 12
and like a bold–fac'd suitor gins to woo him. VEN 6
/BOLDLY 1 FR 0.0001 REL FR 1 V 0 P
in murthers and in outrage /boldly here, | but R2 3.02. 40
BOLDLY 17 FR 0.0019 REL FR 16 V 1 P
boldly, at least. MM 5.01.297
that, yet thus far i will boldly publish her: TN 2.01. 28 P
we should have answer'd heaven | boldly, "not WT 1.02. 74
traitor, | which in myself i boldly will defend, R2 1.01.145
if it be so, out with it boldly, man, | quick is 2.01.233
stirr'd up by god, thus boldly for his king. 4.01.133
we may boldly spend upon the hope of what | /is 1H4 4.01. 54
and boldly did outdare | the dangers of the time 5.01. 40
but boldly stand and front him to his face. 2H6 5.01. 86
what's he approacheth boldly to our presence? 3H6 3.03. 44
sound drums and trumpets boldly and cheerfully. R3 5.03.269
and that way i am wife in, | out with it boldly: H8 3.01. 39
you shall know many dare accuse you boldly, 5.02. 91
let's kill him boldly, but not wrathfully; JC 2.01.172
none but friends: say boldly. ANT 3.13. 47
teach 'em | boldly to gaze against bright arms, TNK 2.02. 35
and in thy name | to my design march boldly. 5.01. 68
BOLD'NED 1 FR 0.0001 REL FR 1 V 0 P
but am bold'ned | under your promis'd pardon. H8 1.02. 55
BOLDNESS 16 FR 0.0018 REL FR 13 V 3 P
but, in the boldness of my cunning, i will lay MM 4.02.155 P
pardon me, sir, the boldness is mine own, | that SHR 2.01. 88
a strumpet's boldness, a divulged shame, AWW 2.01.171
'tis but the boldness of his hand, haply, 3.02. 77
with this ridiculous boldness before my lady? TN 3.04. 37 P
what foolish boldness brought thee to their 5.01. 70
and arms her with the boldness of a wife | to WT 1.02.184
if wit flow from't | as boldness from my bosom, 2.02. 51
made fault | i' th' boldness of your speech. 3.02.218
show boldness and aspiring confidence. JN 5.01. 56
you call honorable boldness impudent sauciness; 2H4 2.01.123 P
and spurn upon thee, beggar, for thy boldness. R3 1.02. 42
that i bring | will make my boldness manners. H8 5.01.159
boldness comes to me now, and brings me heart. TRO 3.02.113
boldness be my friend! CYM 1.06. 18
at the wood's boldness by thee blushing stand. SON 128. 8
/BOLDS 1 FR 0.0001 REL FR 1 V 0 P
/not /bolds /the /king, /with /others /whom, /i LR 5.01. 26
BOLD'ST 1 FR 0.0001 REL FR 1 V 0 P
bad as those | that vulgars give bold'st titles; WT 2.01. 94
BOLEYN *(see bullen, etc.)*
BOLINGBROKE *(see bullingbrook, etc.)*
BOLINGBROOK 1 FR 0.0001 REL FR 1 V 0 P
witch, | with roger bolingbrook, the conjurer? 2H6 1.02. 76
BOLINS *(also bowling*)*
BOLINS 1 FR 0.0001 REL FR 0 V 1 P
slack the bolins there! PER 3.01. 43 P
BOLL'N 1 FR 0.0001 REL FR 1 V 0 P
being throng'd bears back, all boll'n and red, LUC 1417
BOLSTER 2 FR 0.0002 REL FR 2 V 0 P
here i'll fling the pillow, there the bolster, SHR 4.01.201
if ever mortal eyes do see them bolster | more OTH 3.03.399
BOLT 11 FR 0.0012 REL FR 8 V 3 P
and rifted jove's stout oak | with his own bolt; TMP 5.01. 46
i'll make a shaft or a bolt on't. WIV 3.04. 24 P
thou rather with thy sharp and sulphurous bolt MM 2.02.115
yet mark'd i where the bolt of cupid fell. MND 2.01.165
according to the fool's bolt, sir, and such AYL 5.04. 64 P
by how much "a fool's bolt is soon shot." H5 3.07.122 P
and yet to /charge thy sulphur with a bolt COR 5.03.152
and in conclusion to oppose the bolt | against LR 2.04.176
'twas but a bolt of nothing, shot at nothing, CYM 4.02.300
me | the penitent instrument to pick that bolt, 5.04. 10
you ghosts | accuse the thunderer, whose bolt, 5.04. 95
BOLTED 3 FR 0.0003 REL FR 3 V 0 P
tooth, or the fann'd snow that's bolted | by th' WT 4.04.364
such and so finely bolted didst thou seem. H5 2.02.137
sword, and is ill school'd | in bolted language; COR 3.01.320
BOLTERS 1 FR 0.0001 REL FR 0 V 1 P
bakers' wives, they have made bolters of them. 1H4 3.03. 70 P
BOLTING 2 FR 0.0002 REL FR 0 V 2 P
but you must tarry the bolting. TRO 1.01. 17 P
ay, the bolting; 1.01. 20 P
BOLTING–HUTCH 1 FR 0.0001 REL FR 0 V 1 P
of humors, that bolting–hutch of beastliness, 1H4 2.04.450 P
/BOLTS 1 FR 0.0001 REL FR 1 V 0 P
/and /corresponsive /and /fulfilling /bolts TRO pr 18
BOLTS 4 FR 0.0004 REL FR 1 V 3 P
lay bolts enough upon him. MM 5.01.346 P
bolts and shackles! TN 2.05. 56 P
which shackles accidents and bolts up change, ANT 5.02. 6
no bolts for the dead. CYM 5.04.196 P
BOMBARD *(also bumbard)*
BOMBARD 1 FR 0.0001 REL FR 0 V 1 P
parcel of dropsies, that huge bombard of sack, 1H4 2.04.451 P
BOMBARDS 1 FR 0.0001 REL FR 1 V 0 P
and here ye lie baiting of bombards, when | ye H8 5.03. 81
BOMBAST *(also bumbast)*
BOMBAST 1 FR 0.0001 REL FR 1 V 0 P
as bombast and as lining to the time; LLL 5.02.781
/BON 1 FR 0.0001 REL FR 0 V 1 P
say you by the french lord, monsieur le /bon? MV 1.02. 55 P
BON 6 FR 0.0006 REL FR 1 V 5 P
bon jour, monsieur le beau. AYL 1.02. 97 P
je pense que je suis le bon ecolier; H5 3.04. 13 P
c'est bien dit, madame, il est fort bon anglois. 3.04. 19 P
o bon dieu! 5.02.115 P
horn and hound we'll give your grace bon jour. TIT 1.01.494
signior romeo, bon jour! ROM 2.04. 44 P
BONA* 16 FR 0.0018 REL FR 14 V 2 P
we knew where the bona /robas were and had the 2H4 3.02. 23 P
she was then a bona roba. 3.02.205 P
nothing but this; 'tis "bona terra, mala gens." 2H6 4.07. 56
france, | and ask the lady bona for thy queen. 3H6 2.06. 90
vouchsafe to grant | that virtuous lady bona, 3.03. 56
king lewis and lady bona, hear me speak | before 3.03. 65
the measure of his love | unto our sister bona. 3.03.121
disdain, | unless the lady bona quit his pain. 3.03.128
that bona shall be wife to the english king. 3.03.139
i will revenge his wrong to lady bona, | and 3.03.197
how shall bona be reveng'd | but by thy help to 3.03.212
and mine, fair lady bona, joins with yours. 3.03.217
him | about the marriage of the lady bona. 4.01. 31
but what said lady bona to my marriage? 4.01. 97
answer | lewis and the lady bona send to him. 4.03. 56
and afterward by substitute betroth'd | to bona, R3 3.07.182
BOND *(also band*, etc.)*
BOND 73 FR 0.0082 REL FR 67 V 6 P
i will discharge my bond, and thank you too. ERR 4.01. 13
master, i am here ent'red in bond for you. 4.04.125
and me | for everlasting bond of fellowship — MND 1.01. 85
i would i had your bond, for i perceive | a weak 3.02.267
bond, for i perceive | a weak bond holds you. 3.02.268
i think i may take his bond. MV 1.03. 27 P
well then, your bond; 1.03. 68
to a notary, seal me there | your single bond; 1.03.145
content, in faith, i'll seal to such a bond, 1.03.152
you shall not seal to such a bond for me, | i'll 1.03.154
that's a month before | this bond expires, i do 1.03.158
of thrice three times the value of this bond. 1.03.159
yes, shylock, i will seal unto this bond. 1.03.171
give him direction for this merry bond, | and i 1.03.173
and for the jew's bond which he hath of me, 2.08. 41
let him look to his bond. 3.01. 47 P
to call me usurer, let him look to his bond. 3.01. 48 P
a christian cur'sy, let him look to his bond. 3.01. 50 P
plea | of forfeiture, of justice, and his bond. 3.02.283
pay him six thousand, and deface the bond; 3.02.299
is very low, my bond to the jew is forfeit; 3.02.317 P
i'll have my bond, speak not against my bond, 3.03. 4
i'll have my bond, speak not against my bond, 3.03. 4
i have sworn an oath that i will have my bond. 3.03. 5
i'll have my bond; 3.03. 12
i'll have my bond, and therefore speak no more. 3.03. 13
i'll have no speaking, i will have my bond. 3.03. 17
sworn | to have the due and forfeit of my bond. 4.01. 37
i would not draw them, i would have my bond. 4.01. 87
till thou canst rail the seal from off my bond, 4.01.139
do you confess the bond? 4.01.181
the law, | the penalty and forfeit of my bond. 4.01.207
i pray you let me look upon the bond. 4.01.225
why, this bond is forfeit, | and lawfully by 4.01.230
take thrice thy money, bid me tear the bond. 4.01.234
i stay here on my bond. 4.01.242
which here appeareth due upon the bond. 4.01.249
so says the bond, doth it not, noble judge? 4.01.253
is it so nominated in the bond? 4.01.259

i cannot find it, 'tis not in the bond. 4.01.262
this bond doth give thee here no jot of blood; 4.01.306
take then thy bond, take thou thy pound of flesh 4.01.308
pay the bond thrice | and let the christian go. 4.01.318
he shall have merely justice and his bond. 4.01.339
are dearer than the natural bond of sisters. AYL 1.02.276
juno's crown, | o blessed bond of board and bed! 5.04.142
my love hath in't a bond | whereof the world AWW 1.03.188
a contract of eternal bond of love, | confirm'd TN 5.01.156
you know, | prosperity's the very bond of love, WT 4.04.573
there is /my bond of faith, | to tie thee to my R2 4.01. 76
what doth he with a bond | that he is bound to? 5.02. 67
cancel his bond of life, dear god, i pray, R3 4.04. 77
my bond to wedlock or my love and duty, H8 2.04. 40
should, notwithstanding that your bond of duty, 3.02.188
should with a bond of air, strong as the TRO 1.03. 66
all bond and privilege of nature, break! COR 5.03. 25
will strain a little, | for 'tis a bond in men. TIM 1.01.144
so fond, | to trust man on his oath or bond; 1.02. 65
what other bond | than secret romans, that have JC 2.01.124
within the bond of marriage, tell me, brutus, 2.01.280
hand | cancel and tear to pieces that great bond MAC 3.02. 49
double sure, | and take a bond of fate: 4.01. 84
i love your majesty | according to my bond, no LR 1.01. 93
and the bond crack'd 'twixt son and father. 1.02.108 P
with how manifold and strong a bond | the child 2.01. 47
the offices of nature, bond of childhood, 2.04.178
doubt not, sir, | i knew it for my bond. ANT 1.04. 84
no bond, but to do just ones. CYM 5.01. 7
but think her bond of chastity quite crack'd, 5.05.207
am i bound | by any generous bond to follow him TNK 1.02. 50
they scatter and unloose it from their bond, LUC 136
me | under that bond that him as fast doth bind. SON 134. 8
vow, bond, nor space, | in thee hath neither LC 264
BONDAGE 23 FR 0.0026 REL FR 17 V 6 P
th' harmony of their tongues hath into bondage TMP 3.01. 41
a heart as willing | as bondage e'er of freedom. 3.01. 89
i will pray, pompey, to increase your bondage. MM 3.02. 76 P
thy life into death, thy liberty into bondage. AYL 5.01. 54 P
find what it is to be proud of thy bondage. AWW 2.03.227 P
'tis a hard bondage to become the wife | of a 3.05. 64
it will also be the bondage of certain ribbons WT 4.04.233 P
a freer heart | cast off his chains of bondage, R2 1.03. 89
would you not suppose | your bondage happy, to 1H6 5.03.111
to be a queen in bondage is more vile | than is 5.03.112
bondage is hoarse, and may not speak aloud, ROM 2.02.160
cassius from bondage will deliver cassius. JC 1.03. 90
free from the bondage you are in, messala; 5.05. 54
an idle and fond bondage in the oppression of LR 1.02. 49 P
that, doting on his own obsequious bondage, OTH 1.01. 46
's free hours languish for | assured bondage?" CYM 1.06. 73
of no more bondage be to where they are made 2.04.111
prison'd bird, | and sing our bondage freely. 3.03. 44
most welcome, bondage! 5.04. 3
arms alone, | they were not born for bondage. 5.05.306
nobility enforce a freedom out of bondage. TNK 2.01. 34 P
fee, | he held such petty bondage in disdain, VEN 394
and, true to bondage, would not break from LC 34
BONDMAID 1 FR 0.0001 REL FR 1 V 0 P
to make a bondmaid and a slave of me — | that i SHR 2.01. 2
BONDMAN 9 FR 0.0010 REL FR 8 V 1 P
with him his bondman, all as mad as he — ERR 5.01.141
and is not that your bondman, dromio? 5.01.288
within this hour i was his bondman, sir, | but 5.01.289
so every bondman in his own hand bears | the JC 1.03.101
perhaps, speak this | before a willing bondman; 1.03.113
who is here so base that would be a bondman? 3.02. 29 P
check'd like a bondman, all his faults observ'd, 4.03. 97
with pindarus his bondman, on this hill. 5.03. 56
him he has | hipparchus, my enfranched bondman,
ANT 3.13.149
BONDMAN'S 1 FR 0.0001 REL FR 1 V 0 P
or | shall i bend low and in a bondman's key, MV 1.03.123
BONDMEN 4 FR 0.0004 REL FR 4 V 0 P
realm | have been as bondmen to thy sovereignty. 2H6 1.03.127
for these base bondmen to the yoke of rome. TIT 4.01.109
you are, | and make your bondmen tremble. JC 4.03. 44
and bow'd like bondmen, kissing caesar's feet; 5.01. 42
BONDS 24 FR 0.0027 REL FR 22 V 2 P
his words are bonds, his oaths are oracles, TGV 2.07. 75
you make my bonds still greater. MM 5.01. 8
till, gnawing with my teeth my bonds in sunder, ERR 5.01.250
whoever bound him, i will loose his bonds, | and 5.01.340
pigeons fly | to seal love's bonds new made, MV 2.06. 6
are very rascals since bonds disgrac'd them. TN 3.01. 21 P
i tore them from their bonds, and cried aloud, JN 3.04. 70
and will again commit them to their bonds, 3.04. 74
with inky blots and rotten parchment bonds; R2 2.01. 64
hal, three or four bonds of forty pound a-piece, 1H4 3.03.101 P
tyranny, | coupled in bonds of perpetuity, | two 1H6 4.07. 20
cressid is mine, tied with the bonds of heaven. TRO 5.02.154
the bonds of heaven are slipp'd, dissolv'd, and 5.02.156
take the bonds along with you, | and have the TIM 2.01. 34
with clamorous demands of debt, broken bonds, 2.02. 37
to grace in captive bonds his chariot-wheels? JC 1.01. 34
breathing like sanctified and pious bonds, | the HAM 1.03.130
embracements from a next | with bonds of death! CYM 1.01.117
and men in dangerous bonds pray not alike; 3.02. 37
take this life, | and cancel these cold bonds. 5.04. 28
all o'erjoy'd, | save these in bonds. 5.05.402
my bonds in thee are all determinate. SON 87. 4
call, | whereto all bonds do tie me day by day; 117. 4
and seal'd false bonds of love as oft as mine, 142. 7
BOND-SLAVE 2 FR 0.0002 REL FR 1 V 1 P
freedom at tray-trip, and become thy bond-slave?
TN 2.05.191 P
thy state of law is bond-slave to the law, | and R2 2.01.114
BOND-SLAVES 1 FR 0.0001 REL FR 1 V 0 P
bond-slaves and pagans shall our statesmen be. OTH 1.02. 99
/BONE* 3 FR 0.0003 REL FR 0 V 3 P
laus deo, /bone intelligo. LLL 5.01. 27 P
/bone? 5.01. 28 P
/bone /for /bene, priscian a little scratch'd. 5.01. 28 P
BONE* 15 FR 0.0017 REL FR 14 V 1 P
to show his teeth as white as whale's bone; LLL 5.02.332
a death's-head with a bone in his mouth than to MV 1.02. 51 P
now for the bare-pick'd bone of majesty | doth JN 4.03.148
for well we know no hand of blood and bone | can
R2 3.03. 79
thou great commander, nerves and bone of greece,
TRO 1.03. 55
must /tarre the mastiffs on, as 'twere a bone. 1.03.390
high birth, vigor of bone, desert in service, 3.03.172
here lies thy heart, thy sinews, and thy bone. 5.08. 12
her whip of cricket's bone, the lash of film, ROM 1.04. 66
in this rage, with some great kinsman's bone, 4.03. 53
you old enough that you may live | only in bone, TIM 3.05.104
but let the famish'd flesh slide from the bone 4.03.528
with her beak on feathers, flesh, and bone, VEN 56
in shape, in courage, color, pace, and bone. 294
crack'd many a ring of posied gold and bone, LC 45
BONE-ACHE 2 FR 0.0002 REL FR 0 V 2 P
or rather, the neapolitan bone-ache! TRO 2.03. 19 P
lime-kills i' th' palm, incurable bone-ache, and 5.01. 22 P
BONELESS 1 FR 0.0001 REL FR 1 V 0 P
have pluck'd my nipple from his boneless gums, MAC 1.07. 57
/BONES 1 FR 0.0001 REL FR 1 V 0 P
/dislocate /and /tear | /thy /flesh /and /bones. LR 4.02. 66
BONES 83 FR 0.0093 REL FR 70 V 13 P
fill all thy bones with aches, make thee roar TMP 1.02.370
thy father lies, | of his bones are coral made: 1.02.398
i can go no further, sir, | my old bones aches. 3.03. 2
last that i fear me will never out of my bones. 5.01.283 P
thy bones are hollow; MM 1.02. 56 P
when it lies starkly in the traveller's bones. 4.02. 67
in verity you did, my bones bears witness, ERR 4.04. 77
and sing it to her bones, sing it to-night. ADO 5.01.285
now, unto thy bones good night! 5.03. 22
sweet chucks, beat not the bones of the buried. LLL 5.02.661 P
let's have the tongs and the bones. MND 4.01. 29 P
jew shall have my flesh, blood, bones, and all, MV 4.01.112
that they take place when virtue's steely bones AWW 1.01.103
oblivion is the tomb | of honor'd bones indeed. 2.03.141
free maids that weave their thread with bones, TN 2.04. 45
my poor corpse, where my bones shall be thrown. 2.04. 62
air'd abroad, i desire to lay my bones there. WT 4.02. 6 P
father died, | to lie close by his honest bones; 4.04.456
(fair fall the bones that took the pains for me! JN 1.01. 78
we'll lay before this town our royal bones, 2.01. 41
and i will kiss thy detestable bones, | and put 3.04. 29
heaven take my soul, and england keep my bones! 4.03. 10
whose hollow womb inherits nought but bones. R2 2.01. 83
which serves as paste and cover to our bones. 3.02.154
that stands upon your royal grandsire's bones, 3.03.106
brains with care, | their bones with industry; 2H4 4.05. 69
goodman death, goodman bones! 5.04. 28 P
or lay these bones in an unworthy urn, H5 1.02.228
yond island carrions, desperate of their bones, 4.02. 39
bid them achieve me, and then sell my bones. 4.03. 91
those that leave their valiant bones in france, 4.03. 98
i have fin'd these bones of mine for ransom? 4.07. 69
till bones and flesh and sinews fall away, | so 1H6 3.01.192
hew them to pieces, hack their bones asunder, 4.07. 47
by these ten bones, my lords, he did speak them 2H6 1.03.190 P
would he were wasted, marrow, bones, and all, 3H6 3.02.125
that warwick's bones may keep thine company. 5.02. 4
and mock'd the dead bones that lay scatt'red by. R3 1.04. 33
then would i hide my bones, not rest them here. 4.04. 33
truth's sake and his conscience, that his bones, H8 3.02.397
is come to lay his weary bones among ye; 4.02. 22
bobb'd his brain more than he has beat my bones.
TRO 2.01. 70 P
and such an ache in my bones that, unless a man 5.03.105 P
a goodly medicine for my aching bones! 5.10. 35 P
though not for me, yet for /your aching bones. 5.10. 50
or i shall shake thy bones | out of thy garments COR 3.01.178
before this earthy prison of their bones, | that TIT 1.01. 99
not i, till mutius' bones be buried. 1.01.369
there lie thy bones, sweet mutius, with thy 1.01.387
hark, villains, i will grind your bones to dust, 5.02.186
let me go grind their bones to powder small, 5.02.198
o, their bones, their bones! ROM 2.04. 35 P
o, their bones, their bones! 2.04. 35 P
fie, how my bones ache! 2.05. 26
i would thou hadst my bones, and i thy news. 2.05. 27
is this the poultice for my aching bones? 2.05. 63
quite with dead men's rattling bones, | with 4.01. 82
where for this many hundred years the bones | of 4.03. 40
looks, | sharp misery had worn him to the bones; 5.01. 41
i feel't upon my bones. TIM 3.06.119
consumptions sow | in hollow bones of man, 4.03.152
the good is oft interred with their bones; JC 3.02. 76
night hangs upon mine eyes, my bones would rest, 5.05. 41
within my tent his bones to-night shall lie, 5.05. 78
his predecessors | and guardian of their bones. MAC 2.04. 35
thy bones are marrowless, thy blood is cold; 3.04. 93
fight, till from my bones my flesh be hack'd. 5.03. 32
but tell | why thy canoniz'd bones, hearsed in HAM 1.04. 47
if thou canst mutine in a matron's bones, | to 3.04. 83
no trophy, sword, nor hatchment o'er his bones, 4.05.215
did these bones cost no more the breeding, but 5.01. 91 P
strike her young bones, | you taking airs, with LR 2.04.163
and hell gnaw his bones! OTH 4.02.136
full surfeits and the dryness of his bones ANT 1.04. 27
/ooze, | where, for a monument upon thy bones, PER 3.01. 61
how will it shake the bones of that good man, TNK pr 17
to his bones sweet sleep! pr 29
he will not suffer us to burn their bones, | to 1.01. 43
give us the bones | of our dead kings, that we 1.01. 49
go and find out | the bones of your dead lords, 1.04. 7
let him play | qui passa o' th' bells and bones. 3.05. 86
shall curse my bones, and hold it for no sin LUC 209
that churl death my bones with dust shall cover, SON 32. 2
BONFIRE 2 FR 0.0002 REL FR 0 V 2 P
perpetual triumph, an everlasting bonfire light! 1H4 3.03. 41 P
go the primrose way to th' everlasting bonfire. MAC 2.03. 19 P
BONFIRES 6 FR 0.0006 REL FR 4 V 2 P
nothing but bonfires. WT 5.02. 22 P
bonfires in france forthwith i am to make, | to 1H6 1.01.153
dolphin, command the citizens make bonfires, 1.06. 12
burn bonfires clear and bright | to entertain 2H6 5.01. 3
some to dance, some to make bonfires, each man OTH 2.02. 5 P
whose youth, like wanton boys through bonfires, TNK 5.01. 86
BONI 1 FR 0.0001 REL FR 1 V 0 P
dii boni! | a tinker, damsel? TNK 3.05. 83
BONNE 2 FR 0.0002 REL FR 0 V 2 P
que vous etes le gentilhomme de bonne qualite. H5 4.04. 3 P
je suis le gentilhomme de bonne maison; 4.04. 41 P
BONNET 9 FR 0.0010 REL FR 5 V 4 P
his round hose in france, his bonnet in germany, MV 1.02. 75 P
hose should be ungarter'd, your bonnet unbanded,
AYL 3.02.379 P
off goes his bonnet to an oyster-wench, | a R2 1.04. 31
gage of thine, and i will wear it in my bonnet; H5 4.01.209 P
son, | go to them, with this bonnet in thy hand, COR 3.02. 73
/put your bonnet to his right use, 'tis for the HAM 5.02. 92 P
and with his bonnet hides his angry brow, VEN 339
"bonnet nor veil henceforth no creature wear! 1081
"and therefore would he put his bonnet on, 1087
BONNETED 1 FR 0.0001 REL FR 0 V 1 P
supple and courteous to the people, bonneted, COR 2.02. 27 P
BONNY 8 FR 0.0009 REL FR 8 V 0 P
but let them go, | and be you blithe and bonny, ADO 2.03. 67
the bonny priser of the humorous duke? AYL 2.03. 8
and bonny kate, and sometimes kate the curst; SHR 2.01.186
but for my bonny kate, she must with me. 3.02.227
even of the bonny beast he lov'd so well. 2H6 5.02. 12
a cherry lip, a bonny eye, a passing pleasing R3 1.01. 94
end — "for bonny sweet robin is all my joy." HAM 4.05.187
i can sing "the broom," | and "bonny robin." TNK 4.01.108
BONOS 1 FR 0.0001 REL FR 0 V 1 P
bonos dies, sir toby: TN 4.02. 12 P
BONUM 1 FR 0.0001 REL FR 1 V 0 P
glorious, | et bonum quo antiquius, eo melius. PER 1.ch. 10
BONVILLE 1 FR 0.0001 REL FR 1 V 0 P
of the lord bonville on your new wive's son, 3H6 4.01. 57
/BOOK 3 FR 0.0003 REL FR 3 V 0 P
/a /blot, /damn'd /in /the /book /of /heaven. R2 4.01.236
/when /i /do /see /the /very /book /indeed 4.01.274
/was /the /mark /and /glass, /copy /and /book, 2H4 2.03. 31
BOOK 90 FR 0.0101 REL FR 68 V 22 P
here, kiss the book. TMP 2.02.130 P
kiss the book. 2.02.142 P
i'll to my book, | for yet ere supper-time must 3.01. 94
did ever plummet sound | i'll drown my book. 5.01. 57
upon some book i love i'll pray for thee. TGV 1.01. 20
shillings i had my book of songs and sonnets WIV 1.01.199 P
you have not the book of riddles about you, have 1.01.201 P
book of riddles? 1.01.203 P
fenton, i'll be sworn on a book she loves you. 1.04.146 P
and a good studient from his book, and it is 3.01. 38 P
my son profits nothing in the world at his book. 4.01. 15 P
i'll be suppos'd upon a book, his face is the MM 2.01.155 P
and tire the hearer with a book of words. ADO 1.01.307
in my chamber-window lies a book; 2.03. 3 P
seal doth warrant | the tenure of my book; 4.01.167
as, painfully to pore upon a book | to seek the LLL 1.01. 74
fed of the dainties that are bred in a book; 4.02. 24
his bias leaves, and makes his book thine eyes, 4.02.109
where is a book? 4.03.246
in that each of you have forsworn his book, 4.03.293
love's stories written in love's richest book. MND 2.02.122
which doth offer to swear upon a book, i shall MV 2.02.159 P
we quarrel in print, by the book — as you have AYL 5.04. 90 P
keep house and ply his book, welcome his friends SHR 1.01.196
that, all amaz'd, the priest let fall the book, 3.02.161
such a cuff | that down fell priest and book, 3.02.164
down fell priest and book, and book and priest. 3.02.164
or four languages word for word without book, TN 1.03. 27 P
to thee the book even of my secret soul. 1.04. 14
cons state without book and utters it by great 2.03.149 P
unroll'd, and my name put in the book of virtue! WT 4.03.122 P
and then comes answer like an absey book: JN 1.01.196
can in this book of beauty read, "i love," | her 2.01.485
bell, book, and candle shall not drive me back, 3.03. 12
my name be blotted from the book of life, | and R2 1.03.202
and now i will unclasp a secret book, | and to 1H4 1.03.188
by that time will our book, i think, be drawn. 3.01.221
by this our book is drawn, we'll but seal, | and 3.01.265
as far in the devil's book as thou and falstaff, 2H4 2.02. 46 P
o god, that one might read the book of fate, 3.01. 45
would shut the book, and sit him down and die. 3.01. 56
that you should seal this lawless bloody book 4.01. 91
for in the book of numbers is it writ, | when H5 1.02. 98
o'er this bloody field | to book our dead, and 4.07. 73
yourself, | i'll note you in my book of memory, 1H6 2.04.101
such as by god's book are adjudg'd to death. 2H6 2.03. 4
h'as a book in his pocket with red letters in't. 4.02. 90 P
because my book preferr'd me to the king; 4.07. 72
good day, my lord. what, at your book so hard? 3H6 5.06. 1
made him my book, wherein my soul recorded | the
R3 3.05. 27
and see, a book of prayer in his hand — | true 3.07. 98
a book of prayers on their pillow lay, | which 4.03. 14
for by the book | he should have brav'd the east 5.03.278
a beggar's book | outworths a noble's blood. H8 1.01.122
con an oration without book than thou learn /a TRO 2.01. 18 P
book than thou learn /a prayer without book. 2.01. 18 P
o, like a book of sport thou'lt read me o'er; 4.05.239
children is enroll'd | in jove's own book, like COR 3.01.291
i have been | the book of his good acts, whence 5.02. 15
some book there is that she desires to see. TIT 4.01. 31
lucius, what book is that she tosseth so? 4.01. 41
perhaps you have learn'd it without book. ROM 1.02. 59 P
this precious book of love, this unbound lover, 1.03. 87
that book in many's eyes doth share the glory, 1.03. 91
you kiss by th' book. 1.05.110
villain, that fights by the book of arithmetic! 3.01.102 P
was ever book containing such vile matter | so 3.02. 83
one writ with me in sour misfortune's book! 5.03. 82
a picture, sir. when comes your book forth? TIM 1.01. 26
look, lucius, here's the book i sought for so; JC 4.03.252
my thane, is as a book, where men | may read MAC 1.05. 62
live | within the book and volume of my brain, HAM 1.05.103
read on this book, | that show of such an 3.01. 43
the bloody book of law | you shall yourself read OTH 1.03. 67
was this fair paper, this most goodly book, 4.02. 71
in nature's infinite book of secrecy | a little ANT 1.02. 10
makes him fine, | yet keeps his book uncross'd. CYM 3.03. 26
a book? 5.04.133
your neck, sir, is pen, book, and counters; 5.04.170 P
her face the book of praises, where is read PER 1.01. 15
who has a book of all that monarchs do, | he's 1.01. 94
shall raze you out o' th' book of trespasses TNK 1.01. 33

for princes are the glass, the school, the book, LUC 615
his bias leaves, and makes his book thine eyes, PP 5. 5
foil'd, | is from the book of honor rased quite, SON 25.11
sun, | show me your image in some antique book, 59. 7
and of this book this learning mayst thou taste. 77. 4
shall profit thee, and much enrich thy book. 77.14
of their fair subject, blessing every book. 82. 4
book both my willfulness and errors down, | and 117. 9
BOOK'D 1 FR 0.0001 REL FR 0 V 1 P
your grace let it be book'd with the rest of 2H4 4.03. 46 P
BOOKFUL 1 FR 0.0001 REL FR 0 V 1 P
of pandars, and a whole bookful of these quondam
ADO 5.02. 32 P
BOOKISH 3 FR 0.0003 REL FR 2 V 1 P
though i am not bookish, yet i can read WT 3.03. 72 P
whose bookish rule hath pull'd fair england down 2H6 1.01.259
than a spinster — unless the bookish theoric, OTH 1.01. 24
BOOK–MATES 1 FR 0.0001 REL FR 1 V 0 P
makes sport | to the prince and his book–mates. LLL 4.01.100
BOOK–MEN 2 FR 0.0002 REL FR 2 V 0 P
much better used | on navarre and his book–men, LLL 2.01.227
you two are book–men: 4.02. 34
BOOK–OATH 1 FR 0.0001 REL FR 0 V 1 P
i put thee now to thy book–oath. 2H4 2.01.103 P
BOOKS 38 FR 0.0043 REL FR 32 V 6 P
knowing i lov'd my books, he furnish'd me | from TMP 1.02.166
brain him, | having first seiz'd his books; 3.02. 89
remember | first to possess his books; 3.02. 92
burn but his books. 3.02. 95
i see, lady, the gentleman is not in your books. ADO 1.01. 79 P
won, | save base authority from others' books. LLL 1.01. 87
they are the ground, the books, the academes, 4.03.299
and in that vow we have forsworn our books. 4.03.316
they are the books, the arts, the academes, 4.03.349
we turn'd o'er many books together. MV 4.01.156 P
tongues in trees, books in the running brooks, AYL 2.01. 16
o rosalind, these trees shall be my books, | and 3.02. 5
the book — as you have books for good manners. 5.04. 91 P
my books and instruments shall be my company, SHR 1.01. 82
all books of love, see that at any hand — | and 1.02.146
well read in poetry | and other books, good ones 1.02.170
and this small packet of greek and latin books. 2.01.100
take you the lute, and you the set of books. 2.01.106
a herald, kate? o, put me in thy books! 2.01.224
your father prays you leave your books, | and 3.01. 82
i'll be sworn upon all the books in england, i 1H4 2.04. 49 P
turning your books to graves, your ink to blood, 2H4 4.01. 50
how deep you were within the books of god? 4.02. 17
unless my study and my books be false, | the 1H6 2.04. 56
and fitter is my study and my books | than 5.01. 22
blotting your names from books of memory, 2H6 1.01.100
had no other books but the score and the tally, 4.07. 35 P
which made me down to throw my books, and fly —
TIT 4.01. 25
goes toward love as schoolboys from their books, ROM 2.02.156
his land's put to their books. TIM 1.02.200
mark him, and write his speeches in their books, JC 1.02.126
all saws of books, all forms, all pressures past HAM 1.05.100
thy pen from lenders' books, and defy the foul LR 3.04. 97 P
writ in the glassy margents of such books. LUC 102
how | to cipher what is writ in learned books, 811
to blot old books and alter their contents, | to 948
poor women's faces are their own faults' books. 1253
o, let my books be then the eloquence | and dumb
SON 23. 9
/BOON 1 FR 0.0001 REL FR 1 V 0 P
/i'll /beg /one /boon, | /and /then /be /gone R2 4.01.302
BOON 11 FR 0.0012 REL FR 11 V 0 P
a smaller boon than this i cannot beg, | and TGV 5.04. 24
to grant one boon that i shall ask of you. 5.04.150
but you will take exceptions to my boon. 3H6 3.02. 46
reasons, i beseech you, | grant me this boon. R3 1.02.218
a boon, my sovereign, for my service done! 2.01. 96
upon my feeble knee | i beg this boon, with TIT 2.03.289
my boon i make it, that you know me not | till LR 4.07. 10
why, this is not a boon; OTH 3.03. 76
and ask of cymbeline what boon thou wilt, CYM 5.05. 97
my boon is, that this gentleman may render | of 5.05.135
this, my last boon, give me, | for such kindness PER 5.02. 3
BOOR 1 FR 0.0001 REL FR 0 V 1 P
what wouldst thou have, boor? WIV 4.05. 1 P
BOORISH 1 FR 0.0001 REL FR 0 V 1 P
society — which in the boorish is company — of AYL 5.01. 48 P
BOORS 1 FR 0.0001 REL FR 0 V 1 P
let boors and franklins say it, i'll swear it. WT 5.02.160 P
/BOOT* 1 FR 0.0001 REL FR 1 V 0 P
this, and saint george to /boot! R3 5.03.301
BOOT* 31 FR 0.0035 REL FR 23 V 8 P
i'll wear a boot, to make it somewhat rounder. TGV 5.02. 6
could i, with boot, change for an idle plume, MM 2.04. 11
then vail your stomachs, for it is no boot, SHR 5.02.176
he will look upon his boot and sing, mend the AWW 3.02. 6 P
grace to boot! WT 1.02. 80
it shall scarce boot me | to say "not guilty." 3.02. 25
be the worst, yet hold thee, there's some boot. 4.04.637 P
what an exchange had this been, without boot! 4.04.675 P
what a boot is here, with this exchange! 4.04.675 P
norfolk, throw down, we bid, there is no boot. R2 1.01.164
now, by my sceptre and my soul to boot, | he 1H4 3.02. 97
night, | with all appliances and means to boot, 2H4 3.01. 29
boot, boot, master shallow! 5.03.134 P
boot, boot, master shallow! 5.03.134 P
make boot upon the summer's velvet buds, | which
H5 1.02.194
then talk no more of flight, it is no boot; 1H6 4.06. 52
and thou that art his mate, make boot of this; 2H6 4.01. 13
young york he is but boot, because both they R3 4.04. 65
helen, to change, would give an eye to boot. TRO 1.02.239 P
i'll give you boot, i'll give you three for one. 4.05. 40
the tyrant's grasp, | and the rich east to boot. MAC 4.03. 37
the bounty and the benison of heaven | to boot, LR 4.06.226
and the benison of heaven | to boot, and boot! 4.06.226
with boot, and such addition as your honors 5.03.302
and i will boot thee with what gift beside | thy ANT 2.05. 71
breath, but now | make boot of his distraction: 4.01. 9
to boot, my son, | who shall take notice of these CYM 1.05. 69
nor the voice of unpav'd eunuch to boot, can 2.03. 30 P
greeks, | and mine to boot, be darted on thee! 4.02.314
and what they win in't, boot and glory; TNK 1.02. 70
will, | and will to boot, and will in overplus; SON 135. 2
BOOT–HOSE 1 FR 0.0001 REL FR 0 V 1 P
on one leg and a kersey boot–hose on the other, SHR 3.02. 67 P
BOOTIES 1 FR 0.0001 REL FR 0 V 1 P
she drops booties in my mouth. WT 4.04.832 P
BOOTLESS 23 FR 0.0026 REL FR 23 V 0 P
stopp'd | and left me to a bootless inquisition, TMP 1.02. 35
and spend his prodigal wits in bootless rhymes, LLL 5.02. 64
and bootless make the breathless huswife churn, MND 2.01. 37
speed to catch the tiger — bootless speed, 2.01.233
i'll follow him no more with bootless prayers. MV 3.03. 20
old, | and bootless 'tis to tell you we will go; 1H4 1.01. 29
him | bootless home and weather–beaten back. 3.01. 66
we may as bootless spend our vain command | upon
H5 3.03. 24
with bootless labor swim against the tide, | and 3H6 1.04. 20
bootless is flight, they follow us with wings, 2.03. 12
bootless are plaints, and cureless are my wounds 2.06. 23
clifford, repent in bootless penitence. 2.06. 70
come, come, dispatch, 'tis bootless to exclaim. R3 3.04.102
it shall be therefore bootless | that longer you H8 2.04. 61
yet plead i must, | and bootless unto them. TIT 3.01. 36
in bootless prayer have they been held up, | and 3.01. 75
doth not brutus bootless kneel? JC 3.01. 75
very bootless. LR 5.03.295
he robs himself that spends a bootless grief. OTH 1.03.209
you may, | but bootless is your sight; PER 5.01. 33
bootless toil must recompense itself | with its TNK 1.01.153
and leave this idle theme, this bootless chat; VEN 422
and trouble deaf heaven with my bootless cries, SON 29. 3
BOOTS* 26 FR 0.0029 REL FR 17 V 9 P
for you are over boots in love, | and yet you TGV 1.01. 25
over the boots? nay, give me not the boots. 1.01. 27
over the boots? nay, give me not the boots. 1.01. 27
no, i will not; for it boots thee not. 1.01. 28
by drop, and liquor fishermen's boots with me. WIV 4.05. 98 P
a pair of boots that have been candle–cases, one SHR 3.02. 45 P
you may be jogging whiles your boots are green. 3.02.211
off with my boots, you rogues! 4.01.144
shift to run into't, boots and spurs and all, AWW 2.05. 36 P
enough to drink in, and so be these boots too; TN 1.03. 12 P
it boots thee not to be compassionate, | after R2 1.03.174
and what i want it boots not to complain. 3.04. 18
give me my boots, i say, saddle my horse. 5.02. 77
bring me my boots, i will unto the king. 5.02. 84
give me my boots, i say. 5.02. 87
up and down on her, and make her their boots. 1H4 2.01. 82 P
what, the commonwealth their boots? 2.01. 83 P
home without boots, and in foul weather too! 3.01. 67
a good grace, and wears his boots very smooth, 2H4 2.04.248 P
come, come, come, off with your boots. 5.01. 54 P
i am fortune's steward — get on thy boots. 5.03.131 P
it needs not, nor it boots thee not, proud queen 3H6 1.04.125
it boots not to resist both wind and tide. 4.03. 59
what boots it thee to call thyself a sun? TIT 5.03. 18
pull off my boots; LR 4.06.173
nor boots it me to say i honor /him, | if he PER 1.02. 20
BOOTY 3 FR 0.0003 REL FR 2 V 1 P
and when they have the booty, if you and i do 1H4 1.02.165 P
so triumph thieves upon their conquer'd booty, 3H6 1.04. 63
here comes a parcel of our hopeful booty, TIT 2.03. 49
BO–PEEP 1 FR 0.0001 REL FR 1 V 0 P
sung, | that such a king should play bo–peep, LR 1.04.177
BORACHIO 4 FR 0.0004 REL FR 0 V 4 P
what news, borachio? ADO 1.03. 41 P
borachio. 4.02. 11 P
pray write down borachio. yours, sirrah? 4.02. 12 P
borachio one! 5.01.211 P
BOR'D 1 FR 0.0001 REL FR 1 V 0 P
believe as soon | this whole earth may be bor'd, MND 3.02. 53
BORDEAUX *(see burdeaux)*
BORDER 1 FR 0.0001 REL FR 1 V 0 P
his car | above the border of this horizon, 3H6 4.07. 81
/BORDERED 1 FR 0.0001 REL FR 1 V 0 P
/cannot /be /bordered /certain /in /itself. LR 4.02. 33
BORDERERS 1 FR 0.0001 REL FR 1 V 0 P
our inland from the pilfering borderers. H5 1.02.142
BORDERS 1 FR 0.0001 REL FR 1 V 0 P
the borders maritime | lack blood to think on't, ANT 1.04. 51
BORE* *(also bare*)*
/BORE* 1 FR 0.0001 REL FR 0 V 1 P
they much too light for the /bore of the matter. HAM 4.06. 26 P
BORE* 34 FR 0.0038 REL FR 27 V 7 P
durst not, | so dear the love my people bore me; TMP 1.02.141
bore us some leagues to sea, where they prepared 1.02.145
o, that you bore | the mind that i do! 2.01.266
far exceed the love | i ever bore my daughter, TGV 3.01.167
bore many gentlemen (myself being one) | in hand
MM 1.04. 51
they fell upon me, bound me, bore me thence, ERR 5.01.247
that bore thee at a burthen two fair sons. 5.01.344
the clown bore it, the fool sent it, and the LLL 4.03. 16 P
father wore it, | and thy father bore it. AYL 4.02. 16
she bore a mind that envy could not but call TN 2.01. 29 P
the love i bore your queen — lo, fool again! WT 3.02.228
and as the soldiers bore dead bodies by, | he 1H4 1.03. 42
here i lay, and thus i bore my point. 2.04.195 P
stole a lute–case, bore it twelve leagues, and H5 3.02. 43 P
methought he bore him in the thickest troop | as 3H6 2.01. 13
zeal and obedience he still bore your grace, H8 3.01. 63
you stood, confin'd | into an auger's bore. COR 4.06. 87
come to him | to wreak the love i bore my cousin ROM 3.05.101
but he which bore my letter, friar john, | was 5.03.250
through the window/–bars bore at men's eyes, TIM 4.03.117
the queen that bore thee, | oft'ner upon her MAC 4.03.109
"they bore him barefac'd on the bier, | /hey HAM 4.05.165
and, mermaid–like, awhile they bore her up, 4.07.176
'a was the first that ever bore arms. 5.01. 33 P
he hath bore me on his back a thousand times. 5.01.186 P
bore the commission of my place and person, LR 5.03. 64
with so mortal a purpose as then each bore, upon CYM 1.04. 41 P
or she that bore you was no queen, and you 1.06.127
whom she bore in hand to love | with such 5.05. 43
whose towers bore heads so high they kiss'd the PER 1.04. 24
/void'st of honor | that ev'r bore gentle token! TNK 3.01. 37
were't aught to me i bore the canopy, | with my SON 125. 1
or if it were, it bore not beauty's name; 127. 2
melting, though our drops this diff'rence bore: LC 300
BOREAS 1 FR 0.0001 REL FR 1 V 0 P
but let the ruffian boreas once enrage | the TRO 1.03. 38
BORES 3 FR 0.0003 REL FR 3 V 0 P
a little pin | bores thorough his castle wall, R2 3.02.170
at this instant | he bores me with some trick. H8 1.01.128
counsellor should fill the bores of hearing, CYM 3.02. 57
BORESPRIT 1 FR 0.0001 REL FR 1 V 0 P
the yards and boresprit, would i flame TMP 1.02.200
BORING 1 FR 0.0001 REL FR 0 V 1 P
now the ship boring the moon with her mainmast,
WT 3.03. 92 P
BORN *(also porn)*
/BORN 2 FR 0.0002 REL FR 0 V 2 P
some are /born great, some /achieve greatness, TN 2.05.145 P
/given /away, /that /thou /wast /born /with. LR 1.04.150 P
BORN 181 FR 0.0204 REL FR 134 V 47 P
if he be not born to be hang'd, our case is TMP 1.01. 32 P
thou hast. where was she born? speak. tell me. 1.02.260
a devil, a born devil, on whose nature | nurture 4.01.188
and a gentleman born, master parson, who writes WIV 1.01. 9 P
yet i live like a poor gentleman born. 1.01.276 P
as my mother was, the first hour i was born. 2.02. 38
where were you born, friend? MM 2.01.193 P
and so in progress to be hatch'd and born, | are 2.02. 97
the law than my son should be unlawfully born. 3.01.191 P
and usurp the beggary he was never born to. 3.02. 94 P
a bohemian born; 4.02.130 P
more, if any born at ephesus be seen | at any ERR 1.01. 16
if any syracusian born | come to the bay of 1.01. 18
in syracusa was i born, and wed | unto a woman, 1.01. 36
as thou say'st thou art, born under saturn) ADO 1.03. 11 P
me, i was born to speak all mirth and no matter. 2.01.330 P
out a' question, you were born in a merry hour. 2.01.333 P
was a star danc'd, and under that was i born. 2.01.335 P
no, i was not born under a rhyming planet, nor i 5.02. 40 P
for every man with his affects is born, | not by LLL 1.01.151
you were born to do me shame. 4.03.200
we cannot cross the cause why we were born; 4.03.214
beauty doth varnish age, as if new born, | and 4.03.240
and therefore is she born to make black fair. 4.03.257
and longaville was for my service born. 5.02.284
wherefore was i to this keen mockery born? MND 2.02.123
and vows so born, | in their nativity all truth 3.02.124
what stuff 'tis made of, whereof it is born, | i MV 1.01. 4
bring me the fairest creature northward born, 2.01. 4
in that you are the first born, but the same AYL 1.01. 47 P
conceiv'd of spleen, and born of madness, that 4.01.213 P
the horn, | it was a crest ere thou wast born; 4.02. 14
a fair name. wast born i' the forest here? 5.01. 22 P
born in verona, old /antonio's son. SHR 1.02.190
his name is litio, born in mantua. 2.01. 60
for i am he am born to tame you, kate, | and 2.01.276
which might be felt, that we, the poorer born, AWW 1.01.182
parolles, you were born under a charitable star. 1.01.190 P
under that you must needs be born under mars. 1.01.196 P
have a good woman born but /or every blazing 1.03. 86 P
our blood to us, this to our blood is born. 1.03.131
which challenges itself as honor's born, | and 2.03.134
king, who, so ennobled, | is as 'twere born so. 2.03.173
though my estate be fall'n, i was well born, 3.07. 4
well, for i was bred and born | not three hours' TN 1.02. 22
were we not born under taurus? 1.03.137 P
i can tell thee where that saying was born, of 1.05. 10 P
him myself and a sister, both born in an hour. 2.01. 19 P
"some are born great" — 3.04. 41 P
why, "some are born great, some achieve 5.01.370 P
crutches ere he was born desire yet their life WT 1.01. 40 P
temptations have since then been born to 's: 1.02. 77
avoid what's grown than question how 'tis born. 1.02.433
ignorant by age, | or thou wert born a fool. 2.01.174
o that ever i was born! 4.03. 50 P
house these seven years | be born another such. 4.04.579
wink of an eye some new grace will be born. 5.02.111 P
sons and daughters will be all gentlemen born. 5.02.127 P
this other day, because i was no gentleman born. 5.02.130 P
them not and think me still no gentleman born. 5.02.131 P
best say these robes are not gentlemen born. 5.02.132 P
and try whether i am not now a gentleman born. 5.02.134 P
i know you are now, sir, a gentleman born. 5.02.135 P
but i was a gentleman born before my father; 5.02.139 P
born in northamptonshire, and eldest son, | as i JN 1.01. 51
why, being younger born, | doth he lay claim to 1.01. 71
that geffrey was thy elder brother born, | and 2.01.104
to fears, | a woman, naturally born to fears; 3.01. 15
there was not such a gracious creature born. 3.04. 81
/were born to see so sad an hour as this, 5.02. 26
for you are born | to set a form upon that 5.07. 25
we were not born to sue, but to command, | which
R2 1.01.196
wherefore was i born? 2.03.122
what, was i born to this, that my sad look 3.04. 98
created to be aw'd by man, | wast born to bear? 5.05. 92
kitten'd, though yourself had never been born. 1H4 3.01. 19
i say the earth did shake when i was born. 3.01. 20
i was not born a yielder, thou proud scot, | and 5.03. 11
lord, i was born about three of the clock in the 2H4 1.02.187 P
court, | whereon this hydra son of war is born, 4.02. 38
and so success of mischief shall be born, | and 4.02. 47
town's name where alexander the pig was born? H5 4.07. 13 P
i think alexander the great was born in macedon. 4.07. 19 P
that henry born at monmouth should win all, 1H6 3.01.197
win all, | and henry born at windsor lose all: 3.01.198
son, | born to eclipse thy life this afternoon. 4.05. 53
"young talbot was not born | to be the pillage 4.07. 40
born blind, and't please your grace. 2H6 2.01. 75
where wert thou born? 2.01. 80
o, born so, master. 2.01. 96
if thou hadst been born blind, | thou mightst as 2.01.124
you, madam, for you are more nobly born, 2.03. 9
that thou thyself wast born in bastardy; 3.02.223
the field is honorable, and there was he born, 4.02. 51 P
think this word "sallet" was born to do me good; 4.10. 10 P
i am far better born than is the king; 5.01. 28
but 'twas ere i was born. 3H6 1.03. 39
like men born to renown by life or death. 1.04. 8
more than i seem, and less than i was born to; 3.01. 56
ay, thou wast born to be a plague to men. 5.05. 28

shall rue the hour that ever thou wast born. 5.06. 43
hadst thou in thy head when thou wast born, | to 5.06. 53
"o, jesus bless us, he is born with teeth!" 5.06. 75
but i was born so high, | our aery buildeth in R3 1.03.262
more than the infant that is born to–night. 2.01. 72
his nurse? why, she was dead ere thou wast born. 2.04. 33
verily, | i swear, 'tis better to be lowly born, H8 2.03. 19
and a stranger, | born out of your dominions; 2.04. 16
she's noble born; 2.04.142
he will weep you an' 'twere a man born in april. TRO 1.02.174 P
and, being born, his addition shall be humble. 3.02. 94 P
would thou hadst ne'er been born! 4.02. 86 P
got in fear, | though you were born in rome!" COR 1.03. 34
he was not born to shame: ROM 3.02. 91
well, we were born to die. 3.04. 4
o, weraday, that ever i was born! 4.05. 15
we are born to do benefits; TIM 1.02.101 P
o, joy's e'en made away ere't can be born! 1.02.106 P
go, thou wast born a bastard, and thou't die a 2.02. 84 P
world | when sects and factions were newly born. 3.05. 30
thou wast born to conquer my country. 4.03.107
if thou hadst not been born the worst of men, 4.03.275
surely, this man | was born of woman. 4.03.494
i was born free as caesar, so were you; JC 1.02. 97
i was not born to die on brutus' sword. 5.01. 58
as this very day | was cassius born. 5.01. 72
for none of woman born | shall harm macbeth. MAC 4.01. 80
was he not born of woman? 5.03. 4
no man that's born of woman | shall e'er have 5.03. 6
what's he | that was not born of woman? 5.07. 3
thou wast born of woman. 5.07. 11
brandish'd by man that's of a woman born. 5.07. 13
which must not yield | to one of woman born. 5.08. 13
and thou oppos'd, being of no woman born, | yet 5.08. 31
i am native here | and to the manner born, it is HAM 1.04. 15
spite, | that ever i was born to set it right! 1.05.189
was that very day that young hamlet was born — 5.01.147 P
hadst not been born than not t' have pleas'd me LR 1.01.234
that dowerless took | our youngest born, i could 2.04.213
when we are born, we cry that we are come | to 4.06.182
thou hadst been better have been born a dog OTH 3.03.362
i think the sun where he was born | drew all 3.04. 30
a monster | begot upon itself, born on itself. 3.04.162
aches at thee, would thou hadst never been born! 4.02. 69
who's born that day | when i forget to send to ANT 1.05. 63
serves for the matter that is then born in't. 2.02. 10
gentleman, our theme, deceas'd | as he was born. CYM 1.01. 40
let it die as it was born, and i pray you be 1.04.121 P
the remedy then born — discover to me | what 1.06. 98
why should excuse be born or e'er begot? 3.02. 65
not born where't grows, | but worn a bait for 3.04. 56
till it fly out and show them princes born. 4.04. 54
they went hence so soon as they were born. 5.04.126
sir, | in cambria are we born, and gentlemen. 5.05. 17
my boy, a britain born, | let him be ransom'd. 5.05. 84
who, being born your vassal, | am something 5.05.113
arms alone, | they were not born for bondage. 5.05.306
if you, born in those latter times, | when wit's PER 1.ch. 11
for she was born at sea, i have nam'd so, here 3.03. 13
that she may be | manner'd as she is born. 3.03. 17
maid, | born in a tempest when my mother died, 4.01. 18
when i was born, the wind was north. 4.01. 51
when i was born. 4.01. 58
if you were born to honor, show it now; 4.06. 92
she's born to undo us. 4.06.149 P
where were you born? 5.01.154
call'd marina | for i was born at sea. 5.01.156
of a king, | who died the minute i was born, 5.01.158
thou that wast born at sea, buried at tharsus, 5.01.196
born to uphold creation in that honor | first TNK 1.01. 82
better never born | than minister to such harm! 5.03. 65
strength of nature | which we are born /withal. STM III 5
my shame so dead, mine honor is new born. LUC 1190
in thy sweet semblance my old age new born, 1759
as, to behold desert a beggar born, | and needy SON 66. 2
before these bastard signs of fair were born, 68. 3
whose influence is thine, and born of thee: 78.10
ere you were born was beauty's summer dead. 104.14
and rather make them born to our desire | than 123. 7
they mourners seem | at such who, not born fair, 127.11
yet who knows not conscience is born of love? 151. 2

/BORNE 1 FR 0.0001 REL FR 1 V 0 P
/he /ne'er /had /borne /it /out /of /coventry; 2H4 4.01.133

BORNE 76 FR 0.0086 REL FR 63 V 13 P
good wombs have borne bad sons. TMP 1.02.120
i should have borne the humor'd letter to her; WIV 2.01.130 P
'tis well borne up. MM 4.01. 47
celerity, | when it is borne in high authority. 4.02.111
hath he borne himself penitently in prison? 4.02.140 P
morning executed, and his head borne to angelo. 4.02.171 P
rock, | which being violently borne /upon, | our ERR 1.01.102
him be brought forth, and borne hence for help. 5.01.160
witness you, | that he is borne about invisible: 5.01.187
he hath borne himself beyond the promise of his ADO 1.01. 13 P
the conference was sadly borne; 2.03.221 P
if overboldly we have borne ourselves | in the LLL 5.02.734
still have i borne it with a patient shrug, MV 1.03.109
(which never tender lady hath borne greater) WT 2.02. 22
i' th' love | that i have borne your father? 4.04.517
this act so evilly borne shall cool the hearts JN 3.04.149
this must not be thus borne. 4.02.101
what penny hath rome borne? 5.02. 97
where it perceives it is but faintly borne. R2 1.03.281
god, 'tis shame such wrongs are borne | in him, 2.01.238
had he done so, himself had borne the crown, 3.04. 65
the seeming sufferances that you had borne, 1H4 5.01. 51
if like a christian thou hadst truly borne 5.05. 9
for a poor lone woman to bear, and i have borne, 2H4 2.01. 33 P
to bear, and i have borne, and borne, and borne, 2.01. 33 P
and borne, and borne, and have been fubb'd off, 2.01. 34 P
like the south | borne with black vapor, doth 2.04.364
the manner how this action hath been borne 4.04. 88
foreign quarrels, that action, hence borne out, 4.05.214
purpose, and be all well borne | without defeat. H5 1.02.212
king'd, | her sceptre so fantastically borne, 2.04. 27
borne with th' invisible and creeping wind, 3.pr. 11
which must proportion the losses we have borne, 3.06.127 P
fear'd the death, they have borne life away; 4.01.172 P
where that his lords desire him to have borne 5.pr. 17
which hitherto have borne in them | against the 5.02. 15
o my dear lord, lo where your son is borne! 1H6 4.07. 17
while all is shar'd and all is borne away, 2H6 1.01.228
even so remorseless have they borne him hence; 3.01.213
we will have the mayor's sword borne before us. 4.03. 14 P
for with these borne before us, in stead of 4.07.134 P
ay, and their colors, often borne in france, 3H6 1.01.127
and never seen thee, never borne thee son, 1.01.217
i have too long borne | your blunt upbraidings R3 1.03.102
have aught committed that is hardly borne | /by 2.01. 58
ay, or surly borne — TRO 2.03.238
the beauty that is borne here in the face | the 3.03.103
troilus had rather troy were borne to greece 4.01. 47
borne to greece | than cressid borne from troy. 4.01. 48
of martius, "o, if he | had borne the business!" COR 1.01.270
but either | have borne the action of yourself, 4.07. 15
lords, how plainly | i have borne this business. 5.03. 4
and borne her cleanly by the keeper's nose? TIT 2.01. 94
these miseries are more than may be borne. 3.01.243
may this be borne as if his traitorous sons, 4.04. 53
thou shall be borne to that same ancient vault ROM 4.01.111
thou shalt not back till i have borne this corse JC 3.01.291
this duncan | hath borne his faculties so meek, MAC 1.07. 17
how you were borne in hand, how cross'd, the 3.01. 80
only i say | things have been strangely borne. 3.06. 3
he has borne all things well, and i do think 3.06. 17
which i have heavily borne, there ran a rumor 4.03.182
and impotence | was falsely borne in hand, sends HAM 2.02. 67
that it were better my mother had not borne me: 3.01.123 P
or the hard rein which both of them hath borne LR 3.01. 27
the oldest hath borne most; 5.03.326
was borne so like a soldier, that thy cheek | so ANT 1.04. 70
the trees by th' way | should have borne men, 3.06. 47
bruised pieces, go, | you have been nobly borne. 4.14. 43
this, the fool had borne | my head as i do his. CYM 4.02.116
knighthoods and honors, borne | as i wear mine, 5.02. 6
i'll show the virtue i have borne in arms. PER 2.01.145
o, had thy mother borne so hard a mind, | she VEN 203
borne by the trustless wings of false desire, LUC 2
borne on the bier with white and bristly beard: SON 12. 8
without thy help, by me be borne alone. 36. 4

BOROUGH 2 FR 0.0002 REL FR 1 V 1 P
or fourth, or fift borough, i'll answer him by SHR in.1. 13 P
proclaim'd | in every borough as we pass along, 3H6 2.01.195

BOROUGHS 1 FR 0.0001 REL FR 1 V 0 P
knee, | met him in boroughs, cities, villages, 1H4 4.03. 69

BORROW 31 FR 0.0035 REL FR 22 V 9 P
sit you down, | we'll borrow place of him. MM 5.01.362
beg thou, or borrow, to make up the sum, | and ERR 1.01.153
well, i'll break in: go borrow me a crow. 3.01. 80
i bepray you let me borrow my arms again. LLL 5.02.696 P
albeit i neither lend nor borrow | by taking nor MV 1.03. 61
methoughts you said you neither lend nor borrow 1.03. 69
you must borrow me gargantua's mouth first; AYL 3.02.225 P
why, she comes to borrow nothing of them. SHR 4.01.105 P
by the good aid that i of you shall borrow, AWW 3.07. 11
presence i'll adventure | the borrow of a week. WT 1.02. 39
that borrow their behaviors from the great, JN 5.01. 51
do me good, | and never borrow any tear of thee. R2 3.04. 23
coming in to borrow a mess of vinegar, telling 2H4 2.01. 95 P
and i dare swear you borrow not that face | of 5.02. 28
you are a lover, borrow cupid's wings, | and ROM 1.04. 17
when men come to borrow of your masters, they TIM 2.02.100 P
the lord lucullus to borrow so many talents, nay 3.02. 12 P
i am sorry, when he sent to borrow of me, that 3.06. 15 P
were your godheads to borrow of men, men would 3.06. 74 P
stay, i will lend thee money, borrow none. 3.06.101
there were no suns to borrow of. 4.03. 70
if but as /well i other accents borrow, | that LR 1.04. 1
to pay grief, must of poor patience borrow. OTH 1.03.215
if you borrow one another's love for the instant ANT 2.02.103 P
(and with what imitation you can borrow | from CYM 3.04.171
'tis much to borrow, and i will not owe it; VEN 411
from whom each lamp and shining star doth borrow 861
o, how her eyes and tears did lend and borrow! 961
light to all fair eyes that light will borrow; LUC 1083
them words, and she their looks doth borrow. 1498
good day, of night now borrow: PP 14.29

BORROW'D 11 FR 0.0012 REL FR 4 V 7 P
pluck the borrow'd veil of modesty from the WIV 3.02. 41 P
articles are borrow'd of the pronoun, and be 4.01. 40 P
in him, for he borrow'd a box of the ear of the MV 1.02. 80 P
is bought more oft than begg'd or borrow'd. TN 3.04. 3
of an hour, paid money that i borrow'd — three 1H4 3.03. 18 P
bestow'd the thousand pound i borrow'd of you. 2H4 5.05. 12 P
his feathers are but borrow'd, | for he's 2H6 3.01. 75
what would he have borrow'd of you? TIM 3.06. 20 P
as if i borrow'd mine oaths of him and might not CYM 2.01. 4 P
fairing the foul with art's false borrow'd face, SON 127. 6
which borrow'd from this holy fire of love | a 153. 5

BORROW'DST 1 FR 0.0001 REL FR 1 V 0 P
that any /drop thou borrow'dst from thy mother, TRO 4.05.133

BORROWED 16 FR 0.0018 REL FR 16 V 0 P
have him help to waste | his borrowed purse. MV 2.05. 51
or how | should i, in these my borrowed flaunts, WT 4.04. 23
the borrowed majesty, of england here. JN 1.01. 4
a strange beginning: "borrowed majesty"! 1.01. 5
a borrowed title hast thou bought too dear. 1H4 5.03. 23
the borrowed glories that by gift of heaven, H5 2.04. 79
and in this borrowed likeness of shrunk death ROM 4.01.104
to help to take her from her borrowed grave, 5.03.248
why do you dress me | in borrowed robes? MAC 1.03.109
and thirty dozen moons with borrowed sheen HAM 3.02.157
this borrowed passion stands for true old woe; PER 4.04. 24
"when cynthia with her borrowed light," etc. TNK 4.01.153
as if from thence they borrowed all their shine. VEN 488
both, | that to his borrowed bed he make retire, LUC 573
to see those borrowed tears that sinon sheeds! 1549
o, all that borrowed motion seeming owed, LC 327

BORROWER 2 FR 0.0002 REL FR 2 V 0 P
i must become a borrower of the night | for a MAC 3.01. 26
neither a borrower nor a lender /be, | for /loan HAM 1.03. 75

/BORROWER'S 1 FR 0.0001 REL FR 0 V 1 P
the answer is as ready as a /borrower's cap, "i 2H4 2.02.115 P

BORROWING 4 FR 0.0004 REL FR 3 V 1 P
shut his bosom | against our borrowing prayers. AWW 3.01. 9
borrowing only lingers and lingers it out, but 2H4 1.02.237 P
and try the argument of hearts by borrowing, TIM 2.02.178
and borrowing dulleth /th' edge of husbandry. HAM 1.03. 77

BORROWS 4 FR 0.0004 REL FR 0 V 4 P
sir thurio borrows his wit from your ladyship's TGV 2.04. 38 P
looks, and spends what he borrows kindly in your 2.04. 39 P
hanging by it, and borrows money in god's name, ADO 5.01.309 P
the sun borrows of the moon when diomed keeps TRO 5.01. 94 P

BOR'ST 1 FR 0.0001 REL FR 0 V 1 P
thou bor'st thine ass on thy back o'er the dirt. LR 1.04.161 P

BOSKO 1 FR 0.0001 REL FR 0 V 1 P
bosko chimurcho. AWW 4.03.124 P

BOSKOS 3 FR 0.0003 REL FR 0 V 3 P
boskos thromuldo boskos. AWW 4.01. 68 P
boskos thromuldo boskos. 4.01. 68 P
boskos vauvado. 4.01. 74 P

BOSKY 1 FR 0.0001 REL FR 1 V 0 P
crown | my bosky acres and my unshrubb'd down, TMP 4.01. 81

BOS'N 1 FR 0.0001 REL FR 0 V 1 P
where is the master, bos'n? TMP 1.01. 12 P

/BOSOM 1 FR 0.0001 REL FR 1 V 0 P
/thy /glutton /bosom /of /the /royal /richard, 2H4 1.03. 98

BOSOM 133 FR 0.0150 REL FR 119 V 14 P
but i feel not | this deity in my bosom. TMP 2.01.278
my bosom as a bed | shall lodge thee till thy TGV 1.02.111
my herald thoughts in thy pure bosom rest them, 3.01.144
even in the milk–white bosom of thy love. 3.01.252
one's right hand | is perjured to the bosom? 5.04. 68
dart of love | can pierce a complete bosom. MM 1.03. 3
go to your bosom, | knock there, and ask your 2.02.136
and you shall have your bosom on this wretch, 4.03.134
it | to lock it in the wards of covert bosom. 5.01. 10
and in her bosom i'll unclasp my heart, | and ADO 1.01.323
through the transparent bosom of the deep, | as LLL 4.03. 30
his loving bosom to keep down his heart. 4.03.134
this man hath bewitch'd the bosom of my child. MND 1.01. 27
that through thy bosom makes me see thy heart. 2.02.105
antonio, | being the bosom lover of my lord, MV 3.04. 17
you must prepare your bosom for his knife — 4.01.245
therefore lay bare your bosom. 4.01.252
hand with his | whose heart within his bosom is. AYL 5.04.115
and with declining head into his bosom, | bid SHR in.1. 119
stall this in your bosom, and i thank you for AWW 1.03.126 P
would in so just a business shut his bosom 3.01. 8
faith, for seventeen poniards are at thy bosom. 4.01. 76 P
through flinty tartar's bosom would peep forth 4.04. 7
in orsino's bosom. TN 1.05.224 P
in his bosom? in what chapter of his bosom? 1.05.225 P
in his bosom? in what chapter of his bosom? 1.05.225 P
my bosom is full of kindness, and i am yet so 2.01. 39 P
a cypress, not a bosom, | hides my heart. 3.01.121
i have one heart, one bosom, and one truth, 3.01.158
from heartiness, from bounty, fertile bosom, WT 1.02.113
that is entertainment | my bosom likes not, nor 1.02.119
priest–like, thou | hast cleans'd my bosom: 1.02.238
if wit flow from't | as boldness from my bosom, 2.02. 51
but that you have your father's bosom there, 4.04.563
will send destruction | into this city's bosom. JN 2.01.410
thy voluntary oath | lives in this bosom, dearly 3.03. 24
day, | i would into thy bosom pour my thoughts. 3.03. 53
i strike my foot | upon the bosom of the ground, 4.01. 3
his words do take possession of my bosom. 4.01. 32
within this bosom never ent'red yet | the 4.02.254
march | upon her gentle bosom, and fill up | her 5.02. 28
and great affections wrastling in thy bosom 5.02. 41
there is so hot a summer in my bosom | that all 5.07. 30
take their course | through my burn'd bosom, nor 5.07. 39
even in the best blood chamber'd in his bosom, R2 1.01.149
be mowbray's sins so heavy in his bosom | that 1.02. 50
march | so many miles upon her peaceful bosom, 2.03. 93
behind, | and in my loyal bosom lies his power. 2.03. 98
and when they from thy bosom pluck a flower, 3.02. 19
eyes | write sorrow on the bosom of the earth. 3.02.147
sweet peace conduct his sweet soul to the bosom 4.01.103
to whose flint bosom my condemned lord | is 5.01. 3
what seal is that, that hangs without thy bosom? 5.02. 56
i tore it from the traitor's bosom, king; 5.03. 55
shall secretly into the bosom creep | of that 1H4 1.03.266
truth, nor honesty in this bosom of thine; 3.03.154 P
against the bosom of the prince of wales. 4.01.121
deeds | even in the bosom of our adversaries. 5.05. 31
whose bosom burns | with an incensed fire of 2H4 1.03. 13
there is a thing within my bosom tells me | that 4.01.181
he's in arthur's bosom, if ever man went to H5 2.03. 10 P
bosom, if ever man went to arthur's bosom. 2.03. 10 P
i and my bosom must debate a while, | and then i 4.01. 31
gor'd the gentle bosom of peace with pillage and 4.01.165 P
neck, | and in his bosom spend my latter gasp. 1H6 2.05. 38
one drop of blood drawn from thy country's bosom 3.03. 54
feeds in the bosom of such great commanders, 4.03. 48
and from his bosom purge this black despair! 2H6 3.03. 23
day | is crept into the bosom of the sea; 4.01. 2
point | made issue from the bosom of the boy; 3H6 1.04. 81
house | in the deep bosom of the ocean buried. R3 1.01. 4
so i might live one hour in your sweet bosom. 1.02.124
spirit that mutinies in a man's bosom. 1.04.139 P
the sons of edward sleep in abraham's bosom, 4.03. 38
reft, | rush all to pieces on thy rocky bosom. 4.04.235
awake and think our wrongs in richard's bosom 5.03.144
let us be lead within thy bosom, richard, | and 5.03.147
a thousand hearts are great within my bosom. 5.03.347
bosom up my counsel, | you'll find it wholesome. H8 1.01.112
this respite shook | the bosom of my conscience, 2.04.183
cause, that she should lie i' th' bosom of | our 3.02.100
even such a passion doth embrace my bosom: TRO 3.02. 35
how shall this bosom multiplied digest | the COR 3.01.131
till i have sheath'd | my rapier in his bosom, TIT 2.01. 54
and from her bosom took the enemy's point, 5.03.111
woos | even now the frozen bosom of the north, ROM 1.04.101
clouds, | and sails upon the bosom of the air. 2.02. 32
kind | we sucking on her natural bosom find: 2.03. 12
rests, one, two, and the third in your bosom: 2.04. 23 P
thou and my bosom henceforth shall be twain. 3.05.240
thy husband in thy bosom there lies dead; 5.03.155
and it mis–sheathed in my daughter's bosom! 5.03.205
that labor on the bosom of this sphere | to TIM 1.01. 66
come freely | to gratulate thy plenteous bosom. 1.02.125
from forth thy plenteous bosom, one poor root! 4.03.186

love him, feed him, | keep in your bosom; 5.01. 97
see, | have bar'd my bosom to the thunder–stone; JC 1.03. 49
and by and by thy bosom shall partake | the 2.01.305
ran through caesar's bowels, search this bosom. 5.03. 42
of cawdor shall deceive | our bosom interest. MAC 1.02. 64
keep | my bosom franchis'd and allegiance clear, 2.01. 28
such a heart in my bosom for the dignity of the 5.01. 55 P
cleanse the stuff'd bosom of that perilous stuff 5.03. 44
and to those thorns that in her bosom lodge | to HAM 1.05. 87
"in her excellent white bosom, these, etc." 2.02.113 P
ever | the soul of nero enter this firm bosom, 3.02.394
o bosom black as death! 3.03. 67
shall to my bosom | be as well neighbor'd, LR 1.01.118
lay comforts to your bosom, and bestow | your 2.01.126
i know you are of her bosom. 4.05. 26
more, | to pluck the common bosom on his side, 5.03. 49
run from her guardage to the sooty bosom | of OTH 1.02. 70
shall have time | to speak your bosom freely. 3.01. 55
swell, bosom, with thy fraught, | for 'tis of 3.03.449
it doth abuse your bosom. 4.02. 14
her hand on her bosom, her head on her knee, 4.03. 42
will sometimes | divide me from your bosom. ANT 2.03. 2
my face, | but in my bosom shall she never come, 2.06. 55
whose bosom was my crownet, my chief end, | like 4.12. 27
the heaviness and guilt within my bosom | takes CYM 5.02. 1
i wak'd, i found | this label on my bosom, whose 5.05.430
flaming, thy /lone bosom | inflame too nicely, PER 4.01. 5
heart | leaps to be gone into my mother's bosom. 5.03. 45
that which rips my bosom | almost to th' heart's TNK 1.02. 61
in 's bosom. 1.03. 17
she swears | from his soft bosom never to remove VEN 81
within my bosom, whereon thou dost lie, | my 646
in the sweet channel of her bosom dropp'd; 958
and says, within her bosom it shall dwell, 1173
through night's black bosom should not peep LUC 788
no love toward others in that bosom sits | that SON 9.13
thy bosom is endeared with all hearts, | which i 31. 1
"that he did in the general bosom reign | of LC 127

/BOSOM'D 1 FR 0.0001 REL FR 1 V 0 P
/been /conjunct | /and /bosom'd /with /her — LR 5.01. 13

BOSOM'S 4 FR 0.0004 REL FR 4 V 0 P
of no allowance to your bosom's truth. COR 3.02. 57
my bosom's lord sits lightly in his throne, ROM 5.01. 3
which in my bosom's shop is hanging still, SON 24. 7
prison my heart in thy steel bosom's ward, | but 133. 9

BOSOMS 29 FR 0.0032 REL FR 29 V 0 P
emptying our bosoms of their counsel /sweet, MND 1.01.216
one heart, one bed, two bosoms, and one troth. 2.02. 42
two bosoms interchained with an oath, | so then 2.02. 49
oath, | so then two bosoms and a single troth. 2.02. 50
from brassy bosoms and rough hearts of flints, MV 4.01. 31
and make itself a pastime | to harder bosoms! WT 1.02.153
of the first–born cain | reign in all bosoms, 2H4 1.01.158
a nest of hollow bosoms, which he fills | with H5 2.pr. 21
as if allegiance in their bosoms sate | crowned 2.02. 4
for your own reasons turn into your bosoms, | as 2.02. 82
christian–like accord | in their sweet bosoms, 5.02.354
throw in the frozen bosoms of our part | hot 2H6 5.02. 35
i stabb'd your fathers' bosoms, split my breast. 3H6 2.06. 30
turn their own points in their masters' bosoms; R3 5.01. 24
makes his trough | in your embowell'd bosoms — 5.02. 10
should lift their bosoms higher than the shores, TRO 1.03.112
should once set footing in your generous bosoms? 2.02.155
whose double bosoms seems to wear one heart, COR 4.04. 13
when they do hug him in their melting bosoms. TIT 3.01.213
ay, with my dagger in their bosoms, grandsire. 4.01.118
sow all th' athenian bosoms, and their crop | be TIM 4.01. 29
tut, i am in their bosoms, and i know JC 5.01. 7
and i will put that business in your bosoms, MAC 3.01.103
shade, and there | weep our sad bosoms empty. 4.03. 2
to your professed bosoms i commit him, | but yet LR 1.01.272
eleven to ninety reign'st | in mortal bosoms, TNK 5.01.131
but they whose guilt within their bosoms lie LUC 1342
the humble salve which wounded bosoms fits! SON 120.12
the broken bosoms that to me belong | have LC 254

BOSS'D 1 FR 0.0001 REL FR 1 V 0 P
fine linen, turkey cushions boss'd with pearl, SHR 2.01.353

BOSWORTH 1 FR 0.0001 REL FR 1 V 0 P
pitch our tent, even here in bosworth field. R3 5.03. 1

BOTCH 2 FR 0.0002 REL FR 2 V 0 P
by treasons | do botch and bungle up damnation H5 2.02.115
and botch the words up fit to their own thoughts HAM 4.05. 10

BOTCH'D 2 FR 0.0002 REL FR 2 V 0 P
fruitless pranks | this ruffian hath botch'd up, TN 4.01. 56
'tis not well mended so, it is but botch'd; TIM 4.03.285

BOTCHER 1 FR 0.0001 REL FR 0 V 1 P
if he cannot, let the botcher mend him. TN 1.05. 47 P

BOTCHER'S 2 FR 0.0002 REL FR 0 V 2 P
'a was a botcher's prentice in paris, from AWW 4.03.185 P
a grave as to stuff a botcher's cushion, or to COR 2.01. 88 P

BOTCHES 1 FR 0.0001 REL FR 1 V 0 P
to leave no rubs nor botches in the work — MAC 3.01.133

BOTCHY 1 FR 0.0001 REL FR 0 V 1 P
were not that a botchy core? TRO 2.01. 6 P

BOTH *(also bath*)*

/BOTH 4 FR 0.0004 REL FR 3 V 1 P
/am /i /both /priest /and /clerk? R2 4.01.173
/he's /follow'd /both /with /body /and /with 2H4 1.01.203
/being /mounted /and /both /roused /in /their 4.01.116
/has /been /much /to /do /on /both /sides, /and HAM 2.02.352 P

BOTH 672 FR 0.0759 REL FR 566 V 106 P
both, both, my girl. TMP 1.02. 61
both, both, my girl. 1.02. 61
having both the key | of officer and office, set 1.02. 83
now | must by us both be spent most preciously. 1.02.241
feather from unwholesome fen | drop on you both! 1.02.323
allaying both their fury and my passion | with 1.02.393
they are both in either's pow'rs; 1.02.451
then let us both be sudden. 2.01.306
i'll believe both; 3.03. 24
weeds so loathly | that you shall hate it both. 4.01. 22
pay thy graces | home both in word and deed. 5.01. 71
o heavens, that they were living both in naples, 5.01.149
and the matter may be both at once deliver'd. TGV 1.01.130 P
we'll both attend upon your ladyship. 2.04.121
no, they are both as whole as a fish. 2.05. 19 P
for friar laurence met them both, | as he in 5.02. 37
i will be cheaters to them both, and they shall WIV 1.03. 70 P
and west indies, and i will trade to them both. 1.03. 72 P
with both the humors, i. 1.03. 94
he woos both high and low, both rich and poor, 2.01.113
he woos both high and low, both rich and poor, 2.01.113
both young and old, one with another, ford. 2.01.114
look you, he may come and go between you both; 2.02.125 P
fare thee well, commend me to them both. 2.02.131 P
do you study them both, master parson? 3.01. 45 P
boys of art, i have deceiv'd you both; 3.01.107 P
and did he send you both these letters at an 4.04. 3 P
and so they shall be both bestow'd. 4.05.107 P
can be manifested, | without the show of both. 4.06. 16
both, my good host, to go along with me. 4.06. 47
ay, and an ox too; both the proofs are extant. 5.05.120 P
the glory of a creditor, | both thanks and use. MM 1.01. 40
of your order, | visit both prince and people; 1.03. 45
to my heart, | making both it unable for itself, 2.04. 21
hooking both right and wrong to th' appetite, 2.04.176
dreaming on both, for all thy blessed youth 3.01. 34
with both, her combinate–husband, this 3.01.222 P
correction and instruction must both work | ere 3.02. 32
you are to do me both a present and a dangerous 4.02.161 P
angelo hath seen them both, and will discover 4.02.172 P
i know them both. 4.02.195 P
in secret holds, both barnardine and claudio. 4.03. 87
many and hearty thankings to you both. 5.01. 4
both in the heat of blood | and lack of temper'd 5.01.472
both by the syracusians and ourselves, | to ERR 1.01. 14
of such a burthen male, twins both alike. 1.01. 55
fortune had left to both of us alike | what to 1.01.105
but not a thousand marks between you both. 1.02. 84
nay, master, both in mind and in my shape. 2.02.197
thou hast stol'n both mine office and my name: 3.01. 44
both wind and tide stays for this gentleman, 4.01. 46
both one and other he denies me now. 4.03. 85
mistress, both man and master is possess'd: 4.04. 92
villain, thou speak'st false in both. 4.04.100
my master and his man are both broke loose, 5.01.169
they are both forsworn: 5.01.212
there left me and my man, both bound together, 5.01.249
i am sure you both of you remember me. 5.01.292
the duke, my husband, and my children both, 5.01.404
you are both sure, and will assist me? ADO 1.03. 69 P
for he both pleases men and angers them, and 2.01.141 P
me, intend a kind of zeal both to the prince and 2.02. 36 P
both which, master constable — 3.03. 17 P
both strength of limb, and policy of mind, 4.01.198
'fore god, they are both in a tale. 4.02. 31 P
good day to both of you. 5.01. 46
gentlemen both, we will not wake your patience. 5.01.102
i came to seek you both. 5.01.121 P
that were impossible — but i pray you both, 5.01.280
dead, | and she alone is heir to both of us. 5.01.290
or to forbear both. LLL 1.01.198 P
i confess both, they are both the varnish of a 1.02. 43 P
they are both the varnish of a complete man. 1.02. 43 P
no, on both in one, or one in both. 4.01. 78 P
no, on both in one, or one in both. 4.01. 78 P
by my troth, most pleasant. how both did fit it! 4.01.129
marvellous well shot, for they both did hit /it. 4.01.130
shrouded in this bush | and mark'd you both, and 4.03.136
and mark'd you both, and for you both did blush. 4.03.136
writ a' both sides the leaf, margent and all, 5.02. 8
well bandied both, a set of wit well played. 5.02. 29
i remit both twain. 5.02.459
sweet bloods, i both may and will. 5.02.708 P
ever to be true | to those that make us both — 5.02.774
i have some private schooling for you both. MND 1.01.116
in a spleen, unfolds both heaven and earth; 1.01.146
one turf shall serve as pillow for us both, 2.02. 41
and both as light as tales. 3.02.133
you both are rivals, and love hermia; 3.02.155
and now both rivals, to mock helena. 3.02.156
have with our needles created both one flower, 3.02.204
both on one sampler, sitting on one cushion, 3.02.205
both warbling of one song, both in one key, | as 3.02.206
both warbling of one song, both in one key, | as 3.02.206
two of both kinds makes up four. 3.02.438
may now perchance both quake and tremble here, 5.01.221
good signiors both, when shall we laugh? MV 1.01. 66
and by adventuring both | i oft found both. 1.01.143
and by adventuring both | i oft found both. 1.01.144
or to find both | or bring your latter hazard 1.01.150
one speak for both. what would you? 2.02.141 P
at his house and desires to speak with you both. 3.01. 75 P
methinks it should have power to steal both his 3.02.125
when we are both accoutered like young men, 3.04. 63
i fear you are damn'd both by father and mother; 3.05. 15 P
well, you are gone both ways. 3.05. 18 P
from both, my lord. bellario greets your grace. 4.01.120
antonio and old shylock, both stand forth. 4.01.175
and in the morning early will we both | fly 4.01.456
in both my eyes he doubly sees himself, | in 5.01.244
stand you both forth now. AYL 1.02. 71 P
heels, and your heart, both in an instant. 3.02.213 P
they are both the confirmer of false reckonings. 3.04. 32 P
your sorrow and my grief | were both extermin'd. 3.05. 89
orlando doth commend him to you both, | and to 4.03. 91
consent with both that we may enjoy each other. 5.02. 9 P
i' faith, and both in a tune, like two gipsies 5.03. 14 P
to have her and death were both one thing. 5.04. 17
both from his enterprise and from the world, 5.04.162
if either of you both love katherina, | because SHR 1.01. 52
our cake's dough on both sides. 1.01.109 P
upon advice, it toucheth us both, that we may 1.01.116 P
both our inventions meet and jump in one. 1.01.190
or both? 1.01.224 P
sufficeth my reasons are both good and weighty. 1.01.248
gentlemen | to my daughters, and tell them both, 2.01.109
and he of both | that can assure my daughter 2.01.342
and so i take my leave, and thank you both. 2.01.398
that i have been thus pleasant with you both. 3.01. 58
farewell, sweet masters both, i must be gone. 3.01. 85
both of one horse? 4.01. 69 P
and better 'twere that both of us did fast, 4.01.173
tranio, you jest, but have you both forsworn me? 4.02. 48
then both or one, or any thing thou wilt. 4.03. 29
or both dissemble deeply their affections; 4.04. 42
for both our sakes, i would that word were true. 5.02. 15
body | to painful labor, both by sea and land; 5.02.149
long, | but on us both did haggish age steal on, AWW 1.02. 29
sever'd in religion, their heads are both one: 1.03. 54 P
or were you both our mothers, | i care no more 1.03.163
that your dian | was both herself and love, o, 1.03.213
if both gain, all | the gift doth stretch itself 2.01. 3
as 'tis receiv'd, | and is enough for both. 2.01. 5
so i say, both of galen and paracelsus. 2.03. 11 P
o'er whom both sovereign power and father's 2.03. 54
which both thy duty owes and our power claims, 2.03.161
both my revenge and hate | loosing upon thee, in 2.03.164
which of them both | is dearest to me, i have no 3.04. 38
well in it, the duke shall both speak of it, and 3.06. 69 P
where both not sin, and yet a sinful fact. 3.07. 47
for which live long to thank both heaven and me! 4.02. 67
for thee, thou art both knave and fool. 4.05. 32 P
in the minority of them both, his majesty, out 4.05. 73 P
put upon me at once both the office of god and 5.02. 49 P
both suffer under this complaint we bring, | and 5.03.163
and both shall cease, without your remedy. 5.03.164
you must marry me, | either both or none. 5.03.175
both, both. o, pardon! 5.03.308
both, both. o, pardon! 5.03.308
(courage and hope both teaching him the practice TN 1.02. 13
or, if both break, your gaskins fall. 1.05. 25 P
him myself and a sister, both born in an hour. 2.01. 19 P
coming, | that can sing both high and low. 2.03. 41
will so fright them both that they will kill one 3.04.195 P
both day and night did we keep company. 5.01. 96
if spirits can assume both form and suit, | you 5.01.235
if nothing lets to make us happy both | but this 5.01.249
you are betroth'd both to a maid and man. 5.01.263
thou shalt be both the plaintiff and the judge 5.01.354
justly weigh'd | that have on both sides pass'd. 5.01.368
to save both, | farewell, our brother. WT 1.02. 26
see good and evil, | inclining to them both. 1.02.304
or both yourself and me | cry lost, and so good 1.02.410
well arriv'd from delphos, are both landed, 2.03.196
been in me | both disobedience and ingratitude 3.02. 68
have | been both at delphos, and from thence 3.02.126
one grave shall be for both; 3.02.236
may, if fortune please, both breed thee, pretty, 3.03. 48
both roaring louder than the sea or weather. 3.03.101 P
try all, both joy and terror | of good and bad, 4.01. 1
upon | this day she was both pantler, butler, 4.04. 56
pantler, butler, cook, | both dame and servant; 4.04. 57
grace and remembrance be to you both, | and 4.04. 76
we can both sing it. 4.04.292 P
wenches, i'll buy for you both. 4.04.312 P
his pettitoes till he had both tune and words, 4.04.607 P
who has | (his dignity and duty both cast off) 5.01.183
having both their country quitted | with this 5.01.192
both your pardons, | that e'er i put between 5.03.147
if old sir robert did beget us both, | and were JN 1.01. 80
when i have said, make answer to us both. 2.01.235
we for the worthiest hold the right from both. 2.01.282
the onset and retire | of both your armies, 2.01.327
both are alike, and both alike we like. 2.01.331
both are alike, and both alike we like. 2.01.331
yet for both. 2.01.333
and both conjointly bend | your sharpest deeds 2.01.379
so newly join'd in love, so strong in both, 3.01.240
i am with both, each army hath a hand, | and in 3.01.328
and in their rage, i having hold of both, | they 3.01.329
must you with hot irons burn out both mine eyes? 4.01. 39
i will both hear and grant you your requests. 4.02. 46
both for myself and them — but, chief of all, 4.02. 49
deed, which both our tongues held vild to name. 4.02.241
both they and we, perusing o'er these notes, 5.02. 5
high–stomach'd are they both and full of ire, R2 1.01. 18
we thank you both, yet one but flatters us, | as 1.01. 25
mine honor is my life, both grow in one, | take 1.01.182
both to defend my loyalty and truth | to god, my 1.03. 19
both who he is and why he cometh hither | thus 1.03. 27
both to defend himself and to approve | henry of 1.03.112
and both return back to their chairs again. 1.03.120
for both hast thou, and both become the grave. 2.01.140
for both hast thou, and both become the grave. 2.01.140
richly in both, if justice had her right. 2.01.227
both are my kinsmen: 2.02.111
whom both my oath | and duty bids defend; 2.02.112
both young and old rebel, | and all goes worse 3.02.119
on both his knees doth kiss king richard's hand, 3.03. 36
and by the royalties of both your bloods, 3.03.107
since foes have scope to beat both thee and me. 3.03.141
their fortunes both are weigh'd. 3.04. 84
what, is my richard both in shape and mind 5.01. 26
and hate turns one or both | to worthy danger 5.01. 67
banish us both, and send the king with me. 5.01. 83
yet through both | i see some sparks of better 5.03. 20
against them both my true joints bended be. 5.03. 98
both have i spill'd; 5.05.114
power | did gage them both in an unjust behalf 1H4 1.03.173
both in an unjust behalf | (as both of you — 1.03.174
a plague upon you both! 2.02. 21 P
o, we are undone, both we and ours for ever! 2.02. 86 P
so majestically, both in word and matter, hang 2.04.436 P
both which i have had, but their date is out, 2.04.503 P
my father and glendower being both away, | the 4.01.131
in both your armies there is many a soul | shall 5.01. 83
both he and they and you, yea, every man | shall 5.01.107
the douglas and the hotspur both together | are 5.01.116
but we rose both at an instant and fought a long 5.04.147 P
and both the blunts | kill'd by the hand of 2H4 1.01. 16
and so both the degrees prevent my curses. 1.02.231 P
her serve your uses both in purse and in person. 2.01.116 P
on, i must be fain to pawn both my plate and the 2.01.141 P
you are both, i' good truth, as rheumatic as two 2.04. 56 P
because their legs are both of a bigness, and 'a 2.04.244 P
fare you well, gentlemen both, i thank you. 3.02.289 P
indeed, | concurring both in name and quality. 4.01. 87
all members of our cause, both here and hence, 4.01.169
in sight of both our battles we may meet, | /and 4.01.177
and both against the peace of heaven and him 4.02. 29
for then both parties nobly are subdued, | and 4.02. 90
mowbray, | of capital treason i attach you both. 4.02.109

both which we doubt not but your majesty | shall 4.04. 11
will fortune never come with both hands full, 4.04.103
or peace, or both at once, may be | as things 5.02.138
for women are shrows, both short and tall; 5.03. 33
come, i charge you both go with me, for the man 5.04. 16 P
man as yourself, both in the disciplines of war, H5 3.02.129 P
gentlemen both, you will mistake each other. 3.02.134 P
as well provided of both as any prince in the 3.07. 9 P
which is both healthful and good husbandry. 4.01. 7
brothers both, | commend me to the princes in 4.01. 24
of valor as of kindness, | princely in both. 4.03. 16
with a wooden dagger, and they are both hang'd, 4.04. 72 P
that the situations, look you, is both alike. 4.07. 26 P
is to my fingers, and there is salmons in both. 4.07. 31 P
notice of the numbers dead | on both our parts. 4.07.118
my duty to you both, on equal love. 5.02. 23
your mightiness on both parts best can witness. 5.02. 28
burs, | losing both beauty and utility; 5.02. 53
appear | how much in duty i am bound to both. 1H6 2.01. 37
when arm in arm they both came swiftly running, 2.02. 29
proud pole, i will, and scorn both him and thee. 2.04. 78
what is that wrong whereof you both complain? 4.01. 87
good cousins both, of york and somerset, | quiet 4.01.114
both are my kinsmen, and i love them both. 4.01.155
both are my kinsmen, and i love them both. 4.01.155
now they meet where both their lives are done. 4.03. 38
if we both stay, we both are sure to die. 4.05. 20
if we both stay, we both are sure to die. 4.05. 20
if death be so apparent, then both fly. 4.05. 44
thought | it was both impious and unnatural 5.01. 12
your purpose is both good and reasonable; 5.01. 36
and may ye both be suddenly surpris'd | by 5.03. 40
such fierce alarums both of hope and fear, | as 5.05. 85
ay, grief, i fear me, both at first and last. 5.05.102
but i will rule both her, the king, and realm. 5.05.108
myself did win them both. 2H6 1.01.119
anjou and maine both given unto the french! 1.01.236
mine, | and, having both together heav'd it up, 1.02. 13
we'll both together lift our heads to heaven, 1.02. 14
to call them both a pair of crafty knaves. 1.02.103
and ban thine enemies, both mine and thine! 2.04. 25
but both of you were vowed duke humphrey's foes, 3.02.182
cut both the villains' throats; 4.01. 20
head, and bring them both upon two poles hither. 4.07.112 P
of one or both of us the time is come. 5.02. 13
my soul and body on the action both! 5.02. 26
and you both have vow'd revenge | on him, his 3H6 1.01. 55
he is both king and duke of lancaster, | and 1.01. 87
how hast thou injur'd both thyself and us! 1.01.179
i here divorce myself | both from thy table, 1.01.248
child, | lest thou be hated both of god and man. 1.03. 9
congeal'd with this, do make me wipe off both. 1.03. 52
my uncles both are slain in rescuing me; 1.04. 2
of naples, | of both the sicils and jerusalem, 1.04.122
battles join'd, and both sides fiercely fought; 2.01.121
to frustrate both his oath and what beside | may 2.01.175
and this for rutland, both bound to revenge, 2.04. 3
both tugging to be victors, breast to breast, 2.05. 11
swearing both | they prosper best of all when i 2.05. 17
yield both my life and them | to some man else, 2.05. 59
so shalt thou sinow both these lands together, 2.06. 91
i'll stay above the hill, so both may shoot. 3.01. 5
here stand we both and aim we at the best; 3.01. 8
herein your highness wrongs both them and me. 3.02. 75
i can tell you both | her suit is granted for 3.02.116
our people and our peers are both misled, | our 3.03. 35
for this is he that moves both wind and tide. 3.03. 48
with my talk and tears | (both full of truth) i 3.03.159
for both of you are birds of self-same feather. 3.03.161
what if both lewis and warwick be appeas'd | by 4.01. 34
clarence and somerset both gone to warwick? 4.01.127
if it be so, then both depart to him; 4.01.138
it boots not to resist both wind and tide. 4.03. 59
warwick and clarence, give me both your hands. 4.06. 38
i make you both protectors of this land, | while 4.06. 41
both him and all his brothers unto reason. 4.07. 34
as we may, we'll meet both thee and warwick. 4.07. 86
thou and thy brother both shall buy this treason 5.01. 68
two of thy name, both dukes of somerset, | have 5.01. 73
devil" were alike, | and both preposterous; 5.06. 5
and kiss your princely nephew, brothers both. 5.07. 27
i beseech your graces both to pardon me: R3 1.01. 84
not thyself, fair creature — thou art both. 1.02.132
to both their deaths shalt thou be accessary. 1.02.191
i fear me both are false. 1.02.194
wear both of them, for both of them are thine. 1.02.205
wear both of them, for both of them are thine. 1.02.205
told me, when we both lay in the field | frozen 2.01.115
my pretty cousins, you mistake me both: 2.02. 8
alas for both, both mine, edward and clarence! 2.02. 73
alas for both, both mine, edward and clarence! 2.02. 73
so hath this, both by his father and mother. 2.03. 22
uncle, my brother mocks both you and me: 3.01.129
my good lords both, with all the heed i can. 3.01.187
at crosby house, there shall you find us both. 3.01.190
to me, | and we will both together to the tower, 3.02. 32
the princes both make high account of you — 3.02. 69
and both are ready in their offices | at any 3.05. 10
and your good graces both have well proceeded, 3.05. 48
and do not doubt, right noble princes both, 3.05. 64
bid them both | meet me within this hour at 3.05.104
both in your form and nobleness of mind; 3.07. 14
these both put off, a poor petitioner, | a 3.07.183
god give your graces both | a happy and a joyful 4.01. 5
hence both are gone with conscience and remorse 4.03. 20
and so i left them both, | to bear this tidings 4.03. 21
boot, because both they | match'd not the high 4.04. 65
and both the princes had been breathing here, 4.04.384
we must both give and take, my loving lord. 5.03. 6
still him in praise, and being present both, H8 1.01. 31
or wolf, or both (for he is equal rav'nous | as 1.01.159
both | fell by our servants, by those men we 2.01.121
good day to both your graces. 2.02. 13
your late censure | both of his truth and him 3.01. 65
my lords, i thank you both for your good wills. 3.01. 68
both for your honor better and your cause; 3.01. 95
ye tell me what ye wish for both — my ruin. 3.01. 98
be ever double | both in his words and meaning. 4.02. 39
have follow'd both my fortunes faithfully, | of 4.02.141
the god of heaven | both now and ever bless her! 5.01.165
all the progress | both of my life and office, i 5.02. 68
both in his private conscience and his place, 5.02. 75
i shall both find your lordship judge and juror, 5.02. 95
fools on both sides, helen must needs be fair, TRO 1.01. 90
i give to both your speeches, which were such 1.03. 62
his experienc'd tongue, yet let it please both, 1.03. 68
for both our honor and our shame in this | are 1.03.363
paris and troilus, you have both said well, 2.02.163
a man may wear it on both sides, like a leather 3.03.264 P
both alike. 4.01. 55
both merits pois'd, each weighs nor less nor 4.01. 66
both take and give. 4.05. 37
his heart and hand both open and both free, 4.05.100
his heart and hand both open and both free, 4.05.100
there is expectance here from both the sides, 4.05.146
both taxing me and gaging me to keep | an oath 5.01. 41
to an ass, were nothing, he is both ass and ox; 5.01. 59 P
to an ox, were nothing, /he /is both ox and ass. 5.01. 60 P
good night and welcome, both /at /once, to those 5.01. 77
come both you cogging greeks, have at you both! 5.06. 11
come both you cogging greeks, have at you both! 5.06. 11
my ladies both, good day to you. COR 1.03. 48 P
how do you both? 1.03. 51 P
own, | that both our powers, with smiling fronts 1.06. 8
their cause is calling both the parties knaves. 2.01. 79 P
whom | we met here both to thank and to remember 2.02. 47
and till we call'd | both field and city ours, 2.02.121
both observe and answer | the vantage of his 2.03.259
when, both your voices blended, the great'st 3.01.103
confusion | may enter 'twixt the gap of both, 3.01.111
what may be sworn by, both divine and human, 3.01.141
on both sides more respect. 3.01.180
since that to both | it stands in like request? 3.02. 50
in | thy lying tongue both numbers, i would say 3.03. 72
hail to you both! 4.06. 12
the gods preserve you both! 4.06. 20
on our knees, | are bound to pray for you both. 4.06. 23
rather to show a noble grace to both parts 5.03.121
peace both, and hear me speak. 5.06.110
it offend you then | that both should speed? TIT 2.01.101
but to your wishes' height advance you both. 2.01.125
let not this wasp outlive, us both to sting. 2.03.132
he and his lady both are at the lodge, | upon 2.03.254
will send thee hither both thy sons alive, | and 3.01.155
o, none of both but are of high desert. 3.01.170
let me redeem my brothers both from death. 3.01.180
i'll deceive them both; 3.01.186
sons | presents that i intend to send them both. 4.01.116
and pray the roman gods confound you both! 4.02. 6
that you are both decipher'd, that's the news, 4.02. 8
and so i leave you both — like bloody villains. 4.02. 17
and tell them both the circumstance of all, 4.02.156
that down fell both the ram's horns in the court 4.03. 73
yet should both ear and heart obey my tongue. 4.04. 99
but where the bull and cow are both milk-white, 5.01. 31
that both mine eyes were rainy like to his; 5.01.117
both her sweet hands, her tongue, and that more 5.02.175
why, there they are, both baked in this pie; 5.03. 60
two households, both alike in dignity, | in fair ROM pr 1
both by myself and many other friends, | but he, 1.01.146
of honorable reckoning are you both, | and pity 1.02. 4
thee, | the more i have, for both are infinite. 2.02.135
both our remedies | within thy help and holy 2.03. 51
good morrow to you both. 2.04. 46 P
not rosemary and romeo begin both with a letter? 2.04.207 P
ay, nurse, what of that? both with an r. 2.04.208 P
romeo shall thank thee, daughter, for us both. 2.06. 22
tongue | unfold the imagin'd happiness that both 2.06. 28
a plague a' both houses! 3.01. 91
a plague a' both your houses! 3.01.100 P
a plague a' both your houses! 3.01.106
either thou or i, or both, must go with him. 3.01.129
dead," | thy father or thy mother, nay, or both, 3.02.119
beguil'd, | both you and i, for romeo is exil'd. 3.02.133
man, | and ill-beseeming beast in seeming both, 3.03.113
love, | misshapen in the conduct of them both, 3.03.131
and from my soul too, else beshrew them both. 3.05.227
turn to another, this shall slay them both. 4.01. 59
suspecting that we both were in a house | where 5.02. 9
and here i stand both to impeach and purge 5.03.226
i know them both; th' other's a jeweller. TIM 1.01. 8
take my deserts to his, and join 'em both; 3.05. 78
with all my heart, gentlemen both; 3.06. 25 P
th' athenians both within and out that wall! 4.01. 38
never knewest, but the extremity of both ends. 4.03.301 P
both too, and women's sons. 4.03.414 P
other, | and i will look on both indifferently; JC 1.02. 87
we both have fed as well, and we can both 1.02. 98
and we can both | endure the winter's cold as 1.02. 98
both meet to hear and answer such high things. 1.02.170
do so. farewell both. 1.02.294 P
you shall confess that you are both deceiv'd. 2.01.105
before the eyes of both our armies here | (which 4.02. 43
thee as thy wounds, | they smack of honor both. MAC 1.02. 44
or that with both | he labor'd in his country's 1.03.113
that the proportion both of thanks and payment 1.04. 19
greater than both, by the all-hail hereafter! 1.05. 55
and his subject, | strong both against the deed; 1.07. 14
did then adhere, and yet you would make both: 1.07. 52
that could swear in both the scales against 2.03. 9 P
good morrow, both. 2.03. 44
fortune | shall keep us both the safer. 2.03.139
still hath been both grave and prosperous) | in 3.01. 21
both of you | know banquo was your enemy. 3.01.113
for certain friends that are both his and mine, 3.01.120
of things disjoint, both the worlds suffer, 3.02. 16
present him eminence both with eye and tongue: 3.02. 31
both sides are even; 3.04. 10
wait on appetite, | and health on both! 3.04. 38
both more and less have given him the revolt, 5.04. 12
the tyrant's people on both sides do fight, 5.07. 25
where, as they had delivered, both in time, HAM 1.02.209
for /loan oft loses both itself and friend, 1.03. 76
heat, extinct in both | even in their promise, 1.03.118
i entreat you both | that, being of so young 2.02. 10
both your majesties | might, by the sovereign 2.02. 26
but we both obey, | and here give up ourselves, 2.02. 29
soul, | both to my god and to my gracious king. 2.02. 45
away, i do beseech you, both away. 2.02.169
good lads, how do you both? 2.02.226 P
their residence, both in reputation and profit, 2.02.330 P
in reputation and profit, was better both ways. 2.02.330 P
to his wonted way again, | to both your honors. 3.01. 41
whose end, both at the first and now, was and is 3.02. 21 P
and after we will both our judgments join | in 3.02. 86
both here and hence pursue me lasting strife, 3.02.222
where i shall first begin, | and both neglect. 3.03. 43
wind, when both contend | which is the mightier. 4.01. 7
majesty and skill | both countenance and excuse. 4.01. 32
friends both, go join you with some further aid: 4.01. 33
and let them know both what we mean to do | and 4.01. 39
that both the worlds i give to negligence, | let 4.05.135
swoopstake, you will draw both friend and foe, 4.05.143
weigh what convenience both of time and means 4.07.149
i do not fear it, i have seen you both; 5.02.262
they bleed on both sides. how is it, my lord? 5.02.304
(since now we will divest us both of rule, LR 1.01. 49
so farewell to you both. 1.01.275
say of what most nearly appertains to us both. 1.01.284 P
/crown i' th' middle and gav'st away both parts, 1.04.161 P
thou hast par'd thy wit o' both sides, and left 1.04.187 P
it is both he and she, | your son and daughter. 2.04. 13
good morrow to you both. 2.04.127
sith that both charge and danger | speak 'gainst 2.04.239
as full of grief as age, wretched in both. 2.04.273
i will have such revenges on you both | that all 2.04.279
or the hard rein which both of them hath borne 3.01. 27
and bring you where both fire and food is ready. 3.04.153
thou shalt meet | both welcome and protection. 3.06. 92
both stile and gate, horse-way and foot-path. 4.01. 56 P
both, both, my lord. 4.02. 81
both, both, my lord. 4.02. 81
to both these sisters have i sworn my love; 5.01. 55
both? 5.01. 58
neither can be enjoy'd | if both remain alive: 5.01. 59
i was contracted to them both; 5.03.229
hands, | both you of my inclining, and the rest. OTH 1.02. 82
my life and education both do learn me | how to 1.03.183
but he bears both the sentence and the sorrow 1.03.214
being strong on both sides, are equivocal. 1.03.217
my boat sails freely, both with wind and stream. 2.03. 63
though he had twinn'd with me, both at a birth, 2.03.212
and have their palates both for sweet and sour, 4.03. 95
caesar's, i would say — both? ANT 1.01. 28
with such full license as both truth and malice 1.02.108
higher than both in blood and life, stands up 1.02.190
both what by sea and land i can be able | to 1.04. 78
but between both. 1.05. 58
lepidus flatters both, | of both is flatter'd; 2.01. 14
lepidus flatters both, | of both is flatter'd; 2.01. 15
let witchcraft join with beauty, lust with both, 2.01. 22
i requir'd them, | the which you both denied. 2.02. 89
her love to both | would each to other and all 2.02.134
would each to other and all loves to both | draw 2.02.135
dress, | which will become you both, farewell. 2.04. 5
indeed he plied them both with excellent praises 3.02. 14
both he loves. 3.02. 19
mean, if on both parts | this be not cherish'd. 3.02. 32
ne'er stood between, | praying for both parts. 3.04. 14
till we perceiv'd both how you were wrong led 3.06. 80
both as the same, or rather ours the elder — 3.10. 13
so to them both. 3.12. 24
for both, my lord. 4.10. 2
i would they were in afric both together, CYM 1.01.167
that which makes him both without and within. 1.04. 9 P
confounded one the other, or have fall'n both. 1.04. 51 P
would hazard the winning both of first and last. 1.04. 93 P
effects will be | both noisome and infectious. 1.05. 26
that tub | both fill'd and running — ravening 1.06. 49
discover to me | what both you spur and stop. 1.06. 99
(as i have such a heart that both mine ears 1.06.130
nay, sometime hangs both thief and true man. 2.03. 72
that cures us both. 2.03.104
you, having proceeded but | by both your wills. 2.04. 56
or masterless leave both | to who shall find 2.04. 60
art, hath done you both | this cursed injury. 3.04.121
differs in dignity, | whose dust is both alike. 4.02. 5
that grief and patience, rooted in them both, 4.02. 57
fires, have both their eyes | and ears so cloy'd 4.04. 18
either both or nothing, | or senseless speaking, 5.04.146
purse and brain both empty; 5.04.163 P
whom heavens, in justice, both on her and hers, 5.05.464
where now /you're both a father and a son | by PER 1.01.127
and both like serpents are, who though they feed 1.01.132
makes both my body pine and soul to languish, 1.02. 32
shuns not to break one will crack /them both; 1.02.121
safe, | that time of both this truth shall ne'er 1.02.123
that will prove aweful both in deed and word. 2.ch. 4
a man whom both the waters and the wind, | in 2.01. 59
he's both their parent, and he is their grave, 2.03. 46
i thank both him and you, and pledge him freely. 2.03. 78
what, are you both pleased? 2.05. 88
what, are you both agreed? 2.05. 90
these surges, | which wash both heaven and hell; 3.01. 2
which makes /her both th' /heart and place | of 4.ch. 10
blame both my lord and me, that we have taken 4.01. 37
we should have both lord and lown, if the 4.06. 18 P
might equal yours, if both were justly weigh'd. 5.01. 88
griefs might equal mine, | if both were opened. 5.01.132
much follow'd both, for both much money gi'n, TNK pr 2
much follow'd both, for both much money gi'n, pr 2
both heaven and earth | friend thee for ever! 1.04. 1
so both may love. 2.02.165
hath taken notice | both of his blood and body. 2.02.228
shall be at your choice | both sword and armor. 3.01. 89
when we are arm'd | and both upon our guards, 3.06. 29
by castor, both shall die. 3.06.136
we are certainly both traitors, both despisers 3.06.137
both despisers | of thee and of thy goodness. 3.06.137
thou shalt have pity of us both, o theseus, | if 3.06.172
for, ere the sun set, both shall sleep for ever. 3.06.184
say i felt | compassion to 'em both, how would 3.06.213
they cannot both enjoy you. 3.06.275
i cannot, sir, they are both too excellent: 3.06.286

once again it stands, | or both shall die: 3.06.290
you shall both to your country, | and each 3.06.290
yes, i must, sir, | else both miscarry. 3.06.302
a great likelihood | of both their pardons; 4.01. 7
fear of my miscarrying on his scape, | or both. 4.01. 51
stand both together: 4.02. 50
cannot distinguish, but must cry for both! 4.02. 54
i had rather both, | so neither for my sake 4.02. 68
give half my state that both she and i at this 4.03. 67 P
that both mak'st and break'st | the stony girths 5.01. 55
shall confound | both these brave knights, and i 5.01.167
the belief | both seal'd with eye and ear. 5.03. 15
now, | by casting her black mantle over both, 5.03. 25
were they metamorphis'd | both into one — o, 5.03. 85
set both thine ears to th' business. 5.03. 92
we'll hear both. STM II.C 33 P
both, both, both, both! II.C 34 P
both, both, both, both! II.C 34 P
both, both, both, both! II.C 34 P
both, both, both, both! II.C 34 P
both favor, savor, hue, and qualities, | whereat VEN 747
like milk and blood being mingled both together, 902
both crystals, where they view'd each other's 963
thy weal and woe are both of them extremes; 987
could rule them both without ten women's wit." 1008
they both would strive who first should dry his 1092
which of them both should underprop her fame. LUC 53
lest between them both it should be kill'd, 74
both which, as servitors to the unjust, | so 285
by heaven and earth, and all the power of both, 572
"o time, thou tutor both to good and bad, 995
kill both thyself and her for yielding so." 1036
when both were kept for heaven and collatine? 1166
thou dead, both die, and both shall victors be." 1211
thou dead, both die, and both shall victors be." 1211
that two red fires in both their faces blazed; 1353
and both she thinks too long with her remaining. 1572
both stood like old acquaintance in a trance, 1595
for being both to me, both to each friend, | i PP 2.11
for being both to me, both to each friend, | i 2.11
one god is god of both (as poets feign), | one 8.13
one knight loves both, and both in thee remain. 8.14
one knight loves both, and both in thee remain. 8.14
nothing could be used to turn them both to gain, 15.10
fortune smil'd, | thou and i were both beguil'd. 20.28
clouds and eclipses stain both moon and sun, SON 35. 3
both find each other, and i lose both twain, 42.11
both find each other, and i lose both twain, 42.11
and both for my sake lay on me this cross. 42.12
for nimble thought can jump both sea and land 44. 7
fire, | are both with thee, where ever i abide; 45. 2
than both your poets can in praise devise. 83.14
both grace and faults are lov'd of more and less 96. 3
a third, nor red nor white, had stol'n of both, 99.10
and gives thy pen both skill and argument. 100. 8
both truth and beauty on my love depends; 101. 3
book both my willfulness and errors down, | and 117. 9
thy registers and thee i both defy, | not 123. 9
him have i lost, thou hast both him and me, | he 134.13
on both sides thus is simple truth suppress'd. 138. 8
but being both from me, both to each friend, | i 144.11
but being both from me, both to each friend, | i 144.11
in clamors of all size, both high and low. LC 21
of young, of old, and sexes both enchanted, | to 128
both fire from hence and chill extincture hath. 294
showing fair nature is both kind and tame; 311

BOTH-SIDES 1 FR 0.0001 REL FR 0 V 1 P
damnable both-sides rogue! AWW 4.03.222 P

BOTS 3 FR 0.0003 REL FR 0 V 3 P
with the staggers, begnawn with the bots, SHR 3.02. 55 P
is the next way to give poor jades the bots. 1H4 2.01. 10 P
ha, bots on't, 'tis come at last, and 'tis PER 2.01.118 P

BOTTLE* 20 FR 0.0022 REL FR 2 V 18 P
he shall taste of my bottle; TMP 2.02. 74 P
if all the wine in my bottle will recover him, i 2.02. 92 P
swear by this bottle how thou cam'st hither — i 2.02.120 P
the sailors heav'd o'erboard — by this bottle, 2.02.122 P
i'll swear upon that bottle to be thy true 2.02.125 P
when 's god's asleep, he'll rob his bottle. 2.02.151 P
bear my bottle. 2.02.176 P
give him blows, | and take his bottle from him. 3.02. 65
a pox o' your bottle! 3.02. 79 P
i will fetch off my bottle, though i be o'er 4.01.213 P
an irishman with my aqua-vitae bottle, or a WIV 2.02.304 P
for filling a bottle with a tun-dish. MM 3.02.172 P
if i do, hang me in a bottle like a cat, and ADO 1.01.257 P
i have a great desire to a bottle of hay. MND 4.01. 33 P
as wine comes out of a narrow-mouth'd bottle, AYL 3.02.201 P
fill me a bottle of sack. 1H4 4.02. 2 P
this bottle makes an angel. 4.02. 6 P
and i brandish any thing but a bottle, i would i 2H4 1.02.211 P
his cold thin drink out of his leather bottle, 3H6 2.05. 48
i'll beat the knave into a twiggen bottle. OTH 2.03.148 P

BOTTLE-ALE 2 FR 0.0002 REL FR 0 V 2 P
and the mermidons are no bottle-ale houses. TN 2.03. 28 P
away, you bottle-ale rascal! 2H4 2.04.131 P

BOTTLED 2 FR 0.0002 REL FR 2 V 0 P
why strew'st thou sugar on that bottled spider R3 1.03.241
for thee to help me curse | that bottled spider, 4.04. 81

BOTTLES* 3 FR 0.0003 REL FR 1 V 2 P
ay, but to lose our bottles in the pool — TMP 4.01.208 P
do among foaming bottles and ale-wash'd wits, is H5 3.06. 78 P
some two hundred bottles, | and twenty strike of TNK 5.02. 64

BOTTOM 51 FR 0.0057 REL FR 34 V 17 P
do so near the bottom run | by their own fear or TMP 2.01.227
to none, | you must provide to bottom it on me; TGV 3.02. 53
/and the bottom were as deep as hell, i should WIV 3.05. 13 P
me | to look into the bottom of my place. MM 1.01. 78
answer as i call you. nick bottom, the weaver. MND 1.02. 16 P
you, nick bottom, are set down for pyramus. 1.02. 20 P
what sayest thou, bully bottom? 3.01. 8 P
i pyramus am not pyramus, but bottom the weaver. 3.01. 21 P
what say you, bottom? 3.01. 66 P
o bottom, thou art chang'd! 3.01.114 P
bless thee, bottom, bless thee! 3.01.118 P
"bottom's dream," because it hath no bottom; 4.01.216 P
o sweet bully bottom! 4.02. 19 P
bottom! 4.02. 27 P
let us hear, sweet bottom. 4.02. 33 P
it, | my ventures are not in one bottom trusted, MV 1.01. 42
my affection hath an unknown bottom, like the AYL 4.01.208 P
west of this place, down in the neighbor bottom, 4.03. 78
beat me to death with a bottom of brown thread. SHR 4.03.137 P
lordship sees the bottom of /his success in't, AWW 3.06. 36 P
now i see | the bottom of your purpose. 3.07. 29
make | with the most noble bottom of our fleet, TN 5.01. 57
moon, | or dive into the bottom of the deep, 1H4 1.03.203
indent, | to rob me of so rich a bottom here. 3.01.104
we read | the very bottom and the soul of hope, 4.01. 50
i do see the bottom of justice shallow. 2H4 3.02.302 P
to sound the bottom of the after-times. 4.02. 51
come, | i'll pledge you a mile to th' bottom." 5.03. 54
praise | as is the ooze and bottom of the sea H5 1.02.164
that knew'st the very bottom of my soul, | that 2.02. 97
we then should see the bottom | of all our 2H6 5.02. 78
all scatt'red in the bottom of the sea: R3 1.04. 28
gems, | that woo'd the slimy bottom of the deep, 1.04. 32
tent that searches | to th' bottom of the worst. TRO 2.02. 17
finds bottom in th' uncomprehensive depth, 3.03.198
and i myself see not the bottom of it. 3.03.309
but the bottom of the news is, our general is COR 4.05.197 P
now to the bottom dost thou search my wound; TIT 2.03.262
is not my sorrow deep, having no bottom? 3.01.216
so low, | as one dead in the bottom of a tomb. ROM 3.05. 56
clouds, | that sees into the bottom of my grief? 3.05.197
but there's no bottom, none, | in my MAC 4.03. 60
the crimson drops | i' th' bottom of a cowslip. CYM 2.02. 39
no greater wound, | nor tent to bottom that. 3.04.115
who ever yet could sound thy bottom? 4.02.204
i'll hear you more, to th' bottom of your story, PER 5.01.164
even from the bottom of these miseries, | from TNK 2.02. 56
spun, | a bottom great wound up, greatly undone. STM III 21
sweet bottom grass and high delightful plain, VEN 236
the bottom poison, and the top o'erstraw'd 1143
for mirth doth search the bottom of annoy, | sad LUC 1109

BOTTOMLESS 3 FR 0.0003 REL FR 2 V 1 P
or rather, bottomless — that as fast as you AYL 4.01.209 P
then be my passions bottomless with them! TIT 3.01.217
o, deeper sin than bottomless conceit | can LUC 701

BOTTOM'S 2 FR 0.0002 REL FR 0 V 2 P
it shall be call'd "bottom's dream," because it MND 4.01.215 P
have you sent to bottom's house? 4.02. 1 P

BOTTOMS 2 FR 0.0002 REL FR 2 V 0 P
than now the english bottoms have waft o'er JN 2.01. 73
draw the huge bottoms through the furrowed sea, H5 3.pr. 12

BOUCIQUALT 2 FR 0.0002 REL FR 2 V 0 P
/foix, lestrake, bouciqualt, and charolois; H5 3.05. 45
john duke of bourbon, and lord bouciqualt: 4.08. 77

BOUDGE *(also bodg'd, bouge, budge)*

BOUDGE 3 FR 0.0003 REL FR 3 V 0 P
they cannot boudge till your release. TMP 5.01. 11
come, and sit you down, you shall not boudge; HAM 3.04. 18
cousin, i charge you | boudge not from athens. TNK 1.01.223

BOUGE *(also bodg'd, boudge, budge)*

BOUGE 4 FR 0.0004 REL FR 1 V 3 P
my conscience says, "launcelot, bouge not." MV 2.02. 19 P
"bouge," says the fiend. 2.02. 19 P
"bouge not," says my conscience. 2.02. 20 P
must i bouge? JC 4.03. 44

BOUGET *(also budget)*

BOUGET 1 FR 0.0001 REL FR 1 V 0 P
leave to live, | and bear the sow-skin bouget, WT 4.03. 20

BOUGH 6 FR 0.0006 REL FR 6 V 0 P
under the blossom that hangs on the bough. TMP 5.01. 94
will wing me to some wither'd bough and there WT 5.03.133
but not as truly, | as bird doth sing on bough." H5 3.02. 19
let every soldier hew him down a bough, | and MAC 5.04. 4
the studded bridle on a ragged bough | nimbly VEN 37
but that wild music burthens every bough, | and SON 102.11

BOUGHS 11 FR 0.0012 REL FR 11 V 0 P
under the shade of melancholy boughs, | lose and AYL 2.07.111
but upon the fairest boughs, | or at every 3.02.135
whose boughs were moss'd with age | and high top 4.03.104
we lop away, that bearing boughs may live; R2 3.04. 64
cometh andronicus, bound with laurel boughs, TIT 1.01. 74
one winter's brush | fell from their boughs, and TIM 4.03.265
there, on the pendant boughs her crownet weeds HAM 4.07.172
i as a tree | whose boughs did bend with fruit; CYM 3.03. 61
sweeter | than her gold buttons on the boughs, TNK 3.01. 6
the straight young boughs that blush with 3.06.243
upon those boughs which shake against the cold, SON 73. 3

BOUGHT 54 FR 0.0061 REL FR 43 V 11 P
be in love — where scorn is bought with groans; TGV 1.01. 29
however — but a folly bought with wit, | or 1.01. 34
not only bought many presents to give her, but WIV 2.02.198 P
i bought, and brought up to attend my sons. ERR 1.01. 57
a man mad as a buck to be so bought and sold. 3.01. 72
convey'd aboard, and i have bought | the oil, 4.01. 88
and show'd me silks that he had bought for me, 4.03. 8
beauty is bought by judgment of the eye, | not LLL 2.01. 15
boy's fat l'envoy, the goose that you bought, 3.01.109
then cannot we be bought; 5.02.226
i think he bought his doublet in italy, his MV 1.02. 74 P
these things being bought and orderly bestowed, 2.02.170
since you are dear bought, i will love you dear. 3.02.313
and in slavish parts, | because you bought them. 4.01. 93
i demand of him | is dearly bought as mine, and 4.01.100
he hath bought a pair of cast lips of diana. AYL 3.04. 15 P
and he hath bought the cottage and the bounds 3.05.107
till honor be bought up, and no sword worn | but AWW 2.01. 32
so, | he might have bought me at a common price. 5.03.190
inferior might | at market-price have bought. 5.03.219
for youth is bought more oft than begg'd or TN 3.04. 3
blood hath bought blood, and blows have answer'd JN 2.01.329
fly, noble english, you are bought and sold! 5.04. 10
a commodity of good names were to be bought. 1H4 1.02. 83 P
drunk me would have bought me lights as good 3.03. 45 P
i bought you a dozen of shirts to your back. 3.03. 68 P
heads, and they have bought out their services; 4.02. 22 P
rooms of them as have bought out their services, 4.02. 33 P
the lord of stafford dear to-day hath bought 5.03. 7
a borrowed title hast thou bought too dear. 5.03. 23
i bought him in paul's, and he'll buy me a horse 2H4 1.02. 52 P
that for a trifle that was bought with blood! 1H6 4.01.150
from bought and sold lord talbot, | who, ring'd 4.04. 13
on that advantage, bought with such a shame, 4.06. 44
too true, and bought his climbing very dear. 2H6 2.01. 98
bring the strong poison that i bought of him. 3.03. 18
for i have bought it with an hundred blows. 3H6 2.05. 81
shine out, fair sun, till i have bought a glass, R3 1.02.262
having bought love with such a bloody spoil. 4.04.290
for dickon thy master is bought and sold." 5.03.305
she should have bought her dignities so dear. H8 3.01.184
and thou art bought and sold among those of any TRO 2.01. 46 P
and yet dear too, because i bought mine own. TIT 3.01.199
o, i have bought the mansion of a love, | but ROM 3.02. 26
and i have bought | golden opinions from all MAC 1.07. 32
see, | so great a day as this is cheaply bought. 5.09. 3
i bought an unction of a mountebank, | so mortal HAM 4.07.141
by spells and medicines bought of mountebanks; OTH 1.03. 61
she hath bought the name of whore thus dearly. CYM 2.04.128
to have begg'd or bought what i have took. 3.06. 47
and yet the end of all is bought thus dear, PER 1.01. 98
since my master and mistress hath bought you, 4.06.196 P
lost what's dearest to me | save what is bought, TNK 5.03.113
but thou shalt know thy int'rest was not bought LUC 1067

BOULT 7 FR 0.0008 REL FR 0 V 7 P
boult! PER 4.02. 1 P
but here comes boult. 4.02. 39 P
boult, has she any qualities? 4.02. 46 P
what's her price, boult? 4.02. 50 P
boult, take you the marks of her, the color of 4.02. 57 P
boult, spend thou that in the town. 4.02.137 P
boult, take her away, use her at thy pleasure. 4.06.141 P

BOULT'S 1 FR 0.0001 REL FR 0 V 1 P
boult's return'd. PER 4.02. 92 P

BOUNC'D 2 FR 0.0002 REL FR 1 V 1 P
i saw the porpas how he bounc'd and tumbled? PER 2.01. 24 P
he spying her, bounc'd in, whereas he stood; PP 6.13

BOUNCE 2 FR 0.0002 REL FR 1 V 1 P
speaks plain cannon-fire, and smoke, and bounce, JN 2.01.462
tah," would 'a say, "bounce," would 'a say, and 2H4 3.02.284 P

BOUNCING 2 FR 0.0002 REL FR 2 V 0 P
but that, forsooth, the bouncing amazon, | your MND 2.01. 70
luce with the white legs, and bouncing barbary. TNK 3.05. 26

BOUND* 187 FR 0.0211 REL FR 147 V 40 P
had indeed no limit, | a confidence sans bound. TMP 1.02. 97
float | bound sadly home for naples, | supposing 1.02.235
my spirits, as in a dream, are all bound up. 1.02.487
bourn, bound of land, tilth, vineyard, none; 2.01.153
so shall i evermore be bound to thee; WIV 4.06. 54
having bound up the threat'ning twigs of birch, MM 1.03. 24
bound by my charity and my blest order, | i come 2.03. 3
i am bound to call upon you, and i pray you your 3.02.157 P
i am always bound to you. 4.01. 25 P
and that by great injunctions i am bound | to 4.03. 96
to him one of the other twins was bound, ERR 1.01. 81
heaven's eye | but hath his bound in earth, in 2.01. 17
now i had not, but that i am bound | to persia, 4.01. 3
for he is bound to sea, and stays but for it. 4.01. 33
they must be bound and laid in some dark room. 4.04. 94
will you be bound for nothing? 4.04.127
let's call more help | to have them bound again. 4.04.146
once did i get him bound, and sent him home, 5.01.145
beaten the maids a-row, and bound the doctor, 5.01.170
then all together | they fell upon me, bound me, 5.01.247
there left me and my man, both bound together, 5.01.249
for lately we were bound as you are now. 5.01.294
a man denies, you are now bound to believe him. 5.01.306 P
o, my old master! who hath bound him here? 5.01.339
whoever bound him, i will loose his bonds, | and 5.01.340
master constable, let these men be bound, and ADO 4.02. 64 P
two of my brother's men bound? 5.01.211 P
masters, that you are thus bound to your answer? 5.01.227 P
i am more bound to you than your fellows, for LLL 1.02.151 P
which | one part of aquitaine is bound to us, 2.01.135
where that and other specialties are bound: 2.01.164
wert immured, restrained, captivated, bound. 3.01.125 P
i am bound to serve. 4.01. 56
which, as i told you, antonio shall be bound. MV 1.03. 5 P
antonio shall become bound — well. 1.03. 6 P
ducats for three months, and antonio bound. 1.03. 10 P
he hath an argosy bound to tripolis, another to 1.03. 18 P
i am not bound to please thee with my answers. 4.01. 65
i will be bound to pay it ten times o'er, | on 4.01.211
for in my mind you are much bound to him. 4.01.407
is antonio, | to whom i am so infinitely bound. 5.01.135
you should in all sense be much bound to him, 5.01.136
for, as i hear, he was much bound for you. 5.01.137
i dare be bound again, | my soul upon the 5.01.251
on his dunghills are as much bound to him as i. AYL 1.01. 16 P
brief, i recover'd him, bound up his wound, 4.03.150
you, sir, i'll have them very fairly bound — SHR 1.02.145
and bound i am to padua, there to visit | a son 4.05. 56
when they are bound to serve, love, and obey. 5.02.164
and my appliance, | with all bound humbleness. AWW 2.01.114
well to a whipping, if you were but bound to't. 2.02. 56 P
if ever thou be'st bound in thy scarf and beaten 2.03.226 P
which should sustain the bound and high curvet 2.03.282
why, these balls bound, there's noise in it. 2.03.297
whither are bound? 3.05. 33 P
four or five, to great saint jaques bound, 3.05. 95
let me yet know of you whither you are bound. TN 2.01. 10 P
i am bound to the count orsino's court. 2.01. 42 P
i am bound to your niece, sir; 3.01. 76 P
come, we'll have him in a dark room and bound. 3.04.136 P
i shall be much bound to you for't. 3.04.270 P
if one jot beyond | the bound of honor, or in WT 3.02. 51
to see his work, so noble, | vildly bound up? 4.04. 22
i am bound to you. | there is some sap in this. 4.04.564
of this escape and whither they are bound; 4.04.663
how now, rustics, whither are you bound? 4.04.715 P
i am a soldier, and now bound to france. JN 1.01.150
whose veins bound richer blood than lady blanch? 2.01.431
join | do glorify the banks that bound them in; 2.01.442
that she is bound in honor still to do | what 2.01.522
alone which i alone | am bound to underbear. 3.01. 65
for heaven sake, hubert, let me not be bound! 4.01. 77
england, bound in with the triumphant sea, R2 2.01. 61
of wat'ry neptune, is now bound in with shame, 2.01. 63
to whose high will we bound our calm contents. 5.02. 38
bound to himself! 5.02. 67

what doth he with a bond | that he is bound to? 5.02. 68
the thieves have bound the true men. 1H4 2.02. 93 P
and bound them. 2.04.176 P
no, no, they were not bound. 2.04.177 P
you rogue, they were bound, every man of them. 2.04.178 P
we two saw you four set on four and bound them. 2.04.253 P
and all the fertile land within that bound, | to 3.01. 76
the very utmost bound | of all our fortunes. 4.01. 51
a kingdom for it was too small a bound, | but 5.04. 90
i am bound to thee, reverend feeble. 2H4 3.02.170 P
as he whose brow with homely biggen bound 4.05. 27
no less for bounty bound to us | than cambridge H5 2.02. 92
the king is not bound to answer the particular 4.01.155 P
for my love, or bound my horse for her favors, i 5.02.140 P
like captives bound to a triumphant car. 1H6 1.01. 22
appear | how much in duty i am bound to both. 2.01. 37
i am bound to you | that you on my behalf would 2.04.128
neck, | a heart it was, bound in with diamonds, 2H6 3.02.107
who can be bound by any solemn vow | to do a 5.01.184
wrong | but that he was bound by a solemn oath? 5.01.190
and this for rutland, both bound to revenge, 3H6 2.04. 3
now are our brows bound with victorious wreaths, R3 1.01. 5
i am bound by oath, and therefore pardon me. 4.01. 27
bound with triumphant garlands will i come | and 4.04.333
most rare speaker, | to nature none more bound; H8 1.02.112
these ears (for, where i am robb'd and bound, 2.04.147
it, say withal | if you are bound to us, or no. 3.02.165
thee and all thy best parts bound together) 3.02.258
but that i am bound in charity against it! 3.02.298
how much are we bound to heaven | in daily 5.02.149
to the sport abroad — are you bound thither? TRO 1.01.115
shall i, sweet lord, be bound to you so much, 4.05.284
whence he return'd, his brows bound with oak. COR 1.03. 14 P
gifts, am bound to beg | of my lord general. 1.09. 80
if you will pass | to where you are bound, you 3.01. 54
on our knees, | are bound to pray for you both. 4.06. 23
bound with an oath to yield to his conditions; 5.01. 69
whereto we are bound, together with thy victory, 5.03.108
with thy victory, | whereto we are bound? 5.03.109
no man in the world | more bound to 's mother, 5.03.159
cometh andronicus, bound with laurel boughs, TIT 1.01. 74
and faster bound to aaron's charming eyes | than 2.01. 16
herself and hers are highly bound to thee. 4.02.171
is he sure bound? 5.02.165
come, come, lavinia, look, thy foes are bound. 5.02.166
but montague is bound as well as i, | in penalty ROM 1.02. 1
not mad, but bound more than a madman is; 1.02. 54
and soar with them above a common bound. 1.04. 18
and so bound | i cannot bound a pitch above dull 1.04. 20
bound | i cannot bound a pitch above dull woe; 1.04. 21
containing such vile matter | so fairly bound? 3.02. 84
there is no end, no limit, measure, bound, | in 3.02.125
all our whole city is much bound to him. 4.02. 32
like the current flies | each bound it chases. TIM 1.01. 25
as in grateful virtue i am bound | to your free 1.02. 5
we are so virtuously bound — 1.02.226
bound servants, steal; 4.01. 10
life | is bound in shallows and in miseries. JC 4.03.221
roman, | that ever brutus will go bound to rome; 5.01.111
confin'd, bound in | to saucy doubts and fears. MAC 3.04. 23
and the survivor bound | in filial obligation HAM 1.02. 90
speak, i am bound to hear. 1.05. 6
the single and peculiar life is bound | with all 3.03. 11
and, like a man to double business bound, | i 3.03. 41
th' embassador that was bound for england — if 4.06. 11 P
to plainness honor's bound, | when majesty falls LR 1.01.148
my goddess, to thy law | my services are bound. 1.02. 2
a bond | the child was bound to th' father; 2.01. 48
all office | whereto our health is bound; 2.04.107
the revenges we are bound to take upon your 3.07. 7 P
we are bound to the like. 3.07. 10 P
in bliss, but i am bound | upon a wheel of fire, 4.07. 45
by th' law of war thou wast not bound to answer 5.03.153
if she in chains of magic were not bound, OTH 1.02. 65
to you i am bound for life and education; 1.03.182
i am much bound to you. 3.01. 55
though i am bound to every act of duty, | i am 3.03.134
i am not bound to that all slaves are free /to. 3.03.135
therefore, as i am bound, | receive it from me. 3.03.195
i am bound to thee for ever. 3.03.213
you shall think yourself bound to put it on him. 4.02.241 P
i am bound to speak. 5.02.184
and then when poisoned hours had bound me up ANT 2.02. 90
he's bound unto octavia. 2.05. 58
if i were bound to divine of this unity, i would 2.06.116 P
i have been often bound for no less than my life CYM 1.04. 27 P
desert, am bound | to load thy merit richly. 1.05. 73
whilst i am bound to wonder, i am bound | to 1.06. 81
i am bound to wonder, i am bound | to pity too. 1.06. 81
you are most bound to th' king, | who lets go by 2.03. 44
to you | which daily she was bound to proffer. 3.05. 49
whither bound? 3.06. 57
i have a kinsman who | is bound for italy; 3.06. 61
well or ill, | i am bound to you. 4.02. 46
i dare be bound he's true and shall perform 4.03. 18
he's bound by the indenture of his oath to be PER 1.03. 8 P
of this country, and a man whom i am bound to. 4.06. 54 P
govern the country, you are bound to him indeed, 4.06. 55 P
and awkward casualties | bound me in servitude. 5.01. 94
whereto being bound, | the interim, pray you, 5.02. 13
thee into | the bound thou wast o'erflowing, at TNK 1.01. 84
why am i bound | by any generous bond to follow 1.02. 49
where, having bound things scatter'd, we will 1.04. 48
a kind gentleman, and i am much bound to him. 5.02. 44
by law of nature thou art bound to breed, | that VEN 171
she would, he will not in her arms be bound; 226
those fair arms which bound him to her breast, 812
at last she sees a wretched image bound, | that LUC 1501
aid, | as bound in knighthood to her imposition, 1697
being your vassal bound to stay your leisure. SON 58. 4
bound for the prize of all–too–precious you, 86. 2
BOUND–A 1 FR 0.0001 REL FR 1 V 0 P
and whither now are you bound–a? TNK 3.05. 64
/BOUNDED 1 FR 0.0001 REL FR 0 V 1 P
/god, /i /could /be /bounded /in /a /nutshell, HAM 2.02.254 P
BOUNDED 3 FR 0.0003 REL FR 3 V 0 P
how are we park'd and bounded in a pale, | a 1H6 4.02. 45
the bounded waters | should lift their bosoms TRO 1.03.111
of our fate, | who hath bounded our last minute. TNK 1.02.103
BOUNDEN 2 FR 0.0002 REL FR 2 V 0 P
i rest much bounden to you; AYL 1.02.286
i am much bounden to your majesty. JN 3.03. 29
BOUNDETH 2 FR 0.0002 REL FR 2 V 0 P
grief boundeth where /it falls, | not with the R2 1.02. 58
yet in the eddy boundeth in his pride | back to LUC 1669
BOUNDING* 3 FR 0.0003 REL FR 3 V 0 P
speak terms of manage to thy bounding steed, 1H4 2.03. 49
cut, | bounding between the two moist elements, TRO 1.03. 41
being stopp'd, the bounding banks o'erflows; LUC 1119
/BOUNDLESS 1 FR 0.0001 REL FR 1 V 0 P
will, | to compass such a /boundless happiness! PER 1.01. 24
BOUNDLESS 9 FR 0.0010 REL FR 8 V 1 P
a callat | of boundless tongue, who late hath WT 2.03. 92
beyond the infinite and boundless reach | of JN 4.03.117
that the desire is boundless and the act a slave TRO 3.02. 83 P
my bounty is as boundless as the sea, | my love ROM 2.02.133
for there is boundless theft | in limited TIM 4.03.427
boundless intemperance | in nature is a tyranny; MAC 4.03. 66
and, of thy boundless goodness, take some note TNK 1.01. 51
and lo there falls into thy boundless flood LUC 653
brass, nor stone, nor earth, nor boundless sea, SON 65. 1
BOUNDS* 24 FR 0.0027 REL FR 23 V 1 P
lest it should burn above the bounds of reason. TGV 2.07. 23
roaming clean through the bounds of asia, | and, ERR 1.01.133
thou driv'st me past the bounds | of maiden's MND 3.02. 65
fetching mad bounds, bellowing and neighing loud MV 5.01. 73
flocks, and bounds of feed | are now on sale, AYL 2.04. 83
and he hath bought the cottage and the bounds 3.05.107
be clamorous and leap all civil bounds, | rather TN 1.04. 21
two such controlling bounds shall you be, kings, JN 2.01.444
like a proud river peering o'er his bounds? 3.01. 23
low within those bounds we have o'erlook'd, 5.04. 55
drives him beyond the bounds of patience. 1H4 1.03.200
he bounds from the earth, as if his entrails H5 3.07. 13 P
drive the english forth the bounds of france. 1H6 1.02. 54
hath he set bounds between their love and me? R3 4.01. 20
and this sinister | bounds in my father's"; TRO 4.05.129
and now like nilus it disdaineth bounds. TIT 3.01. 71
not stepping o'er the bounds of modesty. ROM 4.02. 27
of regular justice in your city's bounds, | but TIM 5.04. 61
sanctuarize, | revenge should have no bounds. HAM 4.07.128
of all these bounds, even from this line to this LR 1.01. 63
his power could give his will, bounds, comes on TNK 5.04. 67
imperiously he leaps, he neighs, he bounds, VEN 265
the sea hath bounds, but deep desire hath none, 389
what rounds, what bounds, what course, what stop LC 109
BOUNTEOUS 19 FR 0.0021 REL FR 19 V 0 P
ceres, most bounteous lady, thy rich leas | of TMP 4.01. 60
how does my bounteous sister? 4.01.103
most bounteous sir: MM 5.01.443
which with a bounteous hand was kindly lent; R3 2.02. 93
that churchman bears a bounteous mind indeed, H8 1.03. 55
call him bounteous buckingham, | the mirror of 2.01. 52
we'll share a bounteous time | in different TIM 1.01.254
with their wards | many a bounteous year, must 3.03. 38
more counsel with more money, bounteous timon. 4.03.167
the bounteous huswife nature on each bush | lays 4.03.420
according to the gift which bounteous nature MAC 3.01. 97
of your audience been most free and bounteous. HAM 1.03. 93
but to be free and bounteous to her mind. OTH 1.03.265
bounteous madam, | what ever shall become of 3.03. 7
with vain thanks, but with acceptance bounteous, 3.03.470
let's to–night | be bounteous at our meal. ANT 4.02. 10
ships and bounteous winds have brought | this PER 4.04. 17
the bounteous largess given thee to give? SON 4. 6
which bounteous gift thou shouldst in bounty 11.12
BOUNTEOUSLY 1 FR 0.0001 REL FR 1 V 0 P
i prithee (and i'll pay thee bounteously) TN 1.02. 52
BOUNTIES 5 FR 0.0005 REL FR 5 V 0 P
havings, to bestow | my bounties upon you. H8 3.02.160
as hector's leisure and your bounties shall TRO 4.05.273
timon, and to all | that of his bounties taste! TIM 1.02.123
nor came any of his bounties over me | to mark 3.02. 78
low fortunes better, | i'll pay your bounties; PER 2.01.143
BOUNTIFUL 8 FR 0.0009 REL FR 3 V 5 P
by accident most strange, bountiful fortune TMP 1.02.178
and the bountiful blind woman doth most mistake AYL 1.02. 35 P
marry, that's a bountiful answer that fits all AWW 2.02. 15 P
affable, and as bountiful | as mines of india. 1H4 3.01.166
man, and give it bountiful to the desirers. COR 2.03.102 P
athens, thy very bountiful good lord and master? TIM 3.01. 11 P
thy lord's a bountiful gentleman, but thou art 3.01. 39 P
one be prodigal, | bountiful they will him call; PP 20.38
BOUNTIFULLY 1 FR 0.0001 REL FR 0 V 1 P
commend me bountifully to his good lordship, and TIM 3.02. 52 P
/BOUNTY 1 FR 0.0001 REL FR 1 V 0 P
/for /thy /great /bounty, /that /not /only R2 4.01.300
BOUNTY 41 FR 0.0046 REL FR 34 V 7 P
to testify your bounty, i thank you, you have TGV 1.01.144 P
the gentleman | is full of virtue, bounty, worth 3.01. 65
she is a region in guiana, all gold and bounty. WIV 1.03. 69 P
work | than customary bounty can enforce you. MV 3.04. 9
had even tun'd his bounty to sing happiness to AWW 4.03. 10 P
along with you, it may awake my bounty further. TN 5.01. 44 P
sir, lullaby to your bounty till i come again. 5.01. 45 P
sir, let your bounty take a nap, i will awake it 5.01. 48 P
derive a liberty | from heartiness, from bounty, WT 1.02.113
and call this | your lack of love or bounty, you 4.04.354
fortune comes to years, | stands for my bounty. R2 2.03. 67
to you | this honorable bounty shall belong. 1H4 5.05. 26
no less for bounty bound to us | than cambridge H5 2.02. 92
may iden live to merit such a bounty, | and 2H6 5.01. 81
in peace, | your bounty, virtue, fair humility; R3 3.07. 17
that, as my hand has open'd bounty to you, | my H8 3.02.184
yet gives he not till judgment guide his bounty, TRO 4.05.102
my bounty is as boundless as the sea, | my love ROM 2.02.133
see, | magic of bounty! TIM 1.01. 6
shall we in | and taste lord timon's bounty? 1.01.274
'tis pity bounty had not eyes behind, | that man 1.02.163
o, he's the very soul of bounty! 1.02.209
heavens, have i said, the bounty of this lord! 2.02.164
no villainous bounty yet hath pass'd my heart; 2.02.173
for bounty, that makes gods, do still mar men. 4.02. 41
sir, | having often of your open bounty tasted, 5.01. 58
bounty, perseverance, mercy, lowliness, MAC 4.03. 93
they deserve, the more merit is in your bounty. HAM 2.02.532 P
that we our largest bounty may extend | where LR 1.01. 52
the bounty and the benison of heaven | to boot, 4.06.225
all thy treasure, with | his bounty overplus. ANT 4.06. 21
thou mine of bounty, how wouldst thou have paid 4.06. 31
do not abuse my master's bounty by | th' undoing 5.02. 43
for his bounty, | there was no winter in't; 5.02. 86
but yet heaven's bounty towards him might | be CYM 1.06. 78
fitting my bounty and thy state, i'll give it; 5.05. 98
of noble race, | who pour their bounty on her; PER 5.ch. 10
your tresses, | nor in more bounty spread her. TNK 1.01. 64
bounteous gift thou shouldst in bounty cherish. SON 11.12
show, | the other as your bounty doth appear, 53.11
or monarch's hands that lets not bounty fall LC 41
BOUNTY'S 1 FR 0.0001 REL FR 1 V 0 P
that thought is bounty's foe; TIM 2.02.232
BOURBIER 1 FR 0.0001 REL FR 0 V 1 P
vomissement, et la /truie lavee au bourbier." H5 3.07. 65 P
BOURBON 4 FR 0.0004 REL FR 4 V 0 P
you dukes of orleance, bourbon, and of berri, H5 3.05. 41
and he that will not follow bourbon now, | let 4.05. 12
john duke of bourbon, and lord bouciqualt: 4.08. 77
and thou, lord bourbon, our high admiral, 3H6 3.03.252
/BOURN* 2 FR 0.0002 REL FR 2 V 0 P
which, like a /bourn, a pale, a shore, confines TRO 2.03.249
"/come /o'er /the /bourn, /bessy, /to /me" — LR 3.06. 25
BOURN* 7 FR 0.0008 REL FR 7 V 0 P
bourn, bound of land, tilth, vineyard, none; TMP 2.01.153
one that fixes | no bourn 'twixt his and mine, WT 1.02.134
from whose bourn | no traveller returns, puzzles HAM 3.01. 78
from the dread summit of this chalky bourn. LR 4.06. 57
i'll set a bourn how far to be belov'd. ANT 1.01. 16
from bourn to bourn, region to region. PER 4.04. 4
from bourn to bourn, region to region. 4.04. 4
'BOUT *(also about)*
'BOUT 4 FR 0.0004 REL FR 4 V 0 P
in troops i have dispers'd them 'bout the isle. TMP 1.02.220
with ribands pendant, flaring 'bout her head; WIV 4.06. 42
her richest lockram 'bout her reechy neck, COR 2.01.209
here's a few flow'rs, but 'bout midnight, more: CYM 4.02.283
/BOUT 1 FR 0.0001 REL FR 1 V 0 P
with corns will walk /a /bout with you. ROM 1.05. 17
BOUT 4 FR 0.0004 REL FR 3 V 1 P
for his honor's sake, have one bout with you. TN 3.04.306 P
i'll have a bout with thee; 1H6 1.05. 4
damsel, i'll have a bout with you again, | or 3.02. 56
i'll play this bout first, set it by a while. HAM 5.02.284
BOUTS 1 FR 0.0001 REL FR 1 V 0 P
as make your bouts more violent to that end — HAM 4.07.158
'BOVE *(also above)*
'BOVE 4 FR 0.0004 REL FR 4 V 0 P
bold head | 'bove the contentious waves he kept, TMP 2.01.119
'bove all others? TIM 3.03. 1
death, and bear | his hopes 'bove wisdom, grace, MAC 3.05. 31
or swell the curled waters 'bove the main, LR 3.01. 6
/BOW* 2 FR 0.0002 REL FR 2 V 0 P
/flatter, /bow, /and /bend /my /knee. R2 4.01.165
/which /makes /me /bend /makes /the /king /bow: LR 3.06.109
BOW* 55 FR 0.0062 REL FR 47 V 8 P
at | which end o' th' beam should bow. TMP 2.01.132
and with each end of thy blue bow dost crown 4.01. 80
tell me, heavenly bow, | if venus or her son, as 4.01. 86
but come, the bow: LLL 4.01. 24
why, she that bears the bow. | finely put off! 4.01.109
like to a silver bow | /new bent in heaven, MND 1.01. 9
i swear to thee, by cupid's strongest bow, | by 1.01.169
and loos'd his love–shaft smartly from his bow, 2.01.159
go, | swifter than arrow from the tartar's bow. 3.02.101
even as the flourish when true subjects bow | to MV 3.02. 49
as the ox hath his bow, sir, the horse his curb, AYL 3.03. 79 P
he hath ta'en his bow and arrows and is gone 4.03. 4 P
bush, | and then pursue me as you draw your bow. SHR 5.02. 47
and most courteous feathers, which bow the head, AWW 4.05.105 P
to crush this a little, it would bow to me, for TN 2.05.140 P
here is my throne, bid kings come bow to it. JN 3.01. 74
hand | and bow my knee before his majesty, | for R2 1.03. 47
'a drew a good bow, and dead! 2H4 3.02. 43 P
you should fashion, wrest, or bow your reading, H5 1.02. 14
to re–answer, his pettiness would bow under. 3.06.129 P
but, if i bow, they'll say it was for fear. 1H6 4.05. 29
stoop to the block than these knees bow to any 2H6 4.01.125
/these | if they can brook i bow a knee to man. 5.01.110
why, warwick, hath thy knee forgot to bow? 5.01.161
and, lords, bow low to him; 3H6 1.04. 94
i am his king, and he should bow his knee. 2.02. 87
if not, that i am queen, you bow like subjects, R3 1.03.160
that freeze, | bow themselves when he did sing. H8 3.01. 5
my legs like loaden branches bow to th' earth, 4.02. 2
for, o, love's bow | shoots buck and doe. TRO 3.01.116
heaven, | and bow this feeble ruin to the earth; TIT 3.01.207
love's weak childish bow she lives uncharm'd. ROM 1.01.211
scarf, | bearing a tartar's painted bow of lath, 1.04. 5
as yours constrains a man to bow in the hams. 2.04. 53 P
by all the gods that romans bow before, | i here JC 2.01.320
and bow them to your gracious leave and pardon. HAM 1.02. 56
bow, stubborn knees, and heart, with strings of 3.03. 70
/a /wind, | would have reverted to my bow again, 4.07. 23
the bow is bent and drawn, make from the shaft. LR 1.01.143
that fellow handles his bow like a crow–keeper; 4.06. 87 P
before the gods my knee shall bow my prayers ANT 2.03. 3
up thus meanly | i' th' cave /wherein /they bow, CYM 3.03. 83
bow your knees. 5.05. 19
do't, and happy, by my silver bow! PER 5.01.248
bow not my honor. TNK 3.06.226
all–fear'd gods, bow down your stubborn bodies. 5.01. 13
say, began to throw | her bow away, and sigh. 5.01. 94
let us rise | and bow before the goddess. 5.01.136
whose sinowy neck in battle ne'er did bow, | who VEN 99
the which, by cupid's bow she doth protest, | he 581
her voice is stopp'd, her joints forget to bow, 1061
he is no woodman that doth bend his bow | to LUC 580

then jointly to the ground their knees they bow, 1846
join with the spite of fortune, make me bow, SON 90. 3
feel | needs must i under my transgression bow, 120. 3
BOW–BACK 1 FR 0.0001 REL FR 1 V 0 P
"on his bow–back he hath a battle set | of VEN 619
BOW–BOY'S 1 FR 0.0001 REL FR 0 V 1 P
heart cleft with the blind bow–boy's butt–shaft; ROM 2.04. 16 P
BOWCASE 1 FR 0.0001 REL FR 0 V 1 P
you sheath, you bowcase, you vile standing tuck 1H4 2.04.247 P
BOW'D 13 FR 0.0014 REL FR 12 V 1 P
and bow'd her hand to teach her fingering; SHR 2.01.150
and bow'd his eminent top to their low ranks, AWW 1.02. 43
thrice bow'd before me, | and, gasping to begin WT 3.03. 24
where i first bow'd my knee | unto this king of 1H4 1.03.245
but that necessity so bow'd the state | that i 2H4 3.01. 73
a threepence bow'd would hire me, | old as i am, H8 2.03. 36
then rose again and bow'd her to the people; 4.01. 85
who bow'd but in my stirrup, bend like his COR 3.02.119
he bow'd his nature, never known before | but to 5.06. 24
and bow'd like bondmen, kissing caesar's feet; JC 5.01. 42
whose heavy hand hath bow'd you to the grave, MAC 3.01. 89
sapling, and must be bow'd as i would have you. PER 4.02. 88 P
as heaven (it seem'd) to kiss the turrets bow'd. LUC 1372
BOWED 4 FR 0.0004 REL FR 4 V 0 P
th' shore, that o'er his wave–worn basis bowed, TMP 2.01.121
to me were oaks, to thee like osiers bowed. LLL 4.02.108
gentle breath, calm look, knees humbly bowed, ROM 3.01.156
to me like oaks, to thee like osiers bowed. PP 5. 4
BOWELS 23 FR 0.0026 REL FR 21 V 2 P
for thine own bowels, which do call thee /sire, MM 3.01. 29
the cannons have their bowels full of wrath, JN 2.01.210
villain, | whose bowels suddenly burst out. 5.06. 3
bosom | that all my bowels crumble up to dust. 5.07. 31
out of the bowels of the harmless earth, | which 1H4 1.03. 61
i need no more weight than mine own bowels. 5.03. 35 P
i do retort the "solus" in thy bowels, | for i H5 2.01. 51
and bids you, in the bowels of the lord, 2.04.102
and rush'd into the bowels of the battle. 1H6 1.01.129
that gnaws the bowels of the commonwealth. 3.01. 73
so, rushing in the bowels of the french, | he 4.07. 42
unrip'st the bowels of thy sov'reign's son. R3 1.04.207
tumble down | into the fatal bowels of the deep. 3.04.101
thus far into the bowels of the land | have we 5.02. 3
thou art by inches, thou thing of no bowels, TRO 2.01. 49 P
priam, | there is no lady of more softer bowels, 2.02. 11
war | into the bowels of ungrateful rome, | like COR 4.05.130
the father tearing | his country's bowels out. 5.03.103
surge | will in his brinish bowels swallow him. TIT 3.01. 97
for why my bowels cannot hide her woes, | but 3.01.23
sooner this sword shall plough thy bowels up. 4.02.
that ran through caesar's bowels, search this JC 5.03.
flows | out from the bowels of her holy altar TNK 5.01. 4
BOWER 6 FR 0.0006 REL FR 6 V 0 P
us, | and bid her steal into the pleached bower, ADO 3.01 7
lead him to my bower. MND 3.0 97
near to her close and consecrated bower, | while 3.0 7
sent | to bear him to my bower in fairy land. 4.0 61
in a fiery gulf | than flatter him in a bower. COR 3. 92
when thou didst bower the spirit of a fiend | in ROM 3. 81
BOW–HAND 1 FR 0.0001 REL FR 1 0 P
wide a' the bow–hand! LLL 1.133
BOWING 2 FR 0.0002 REL FR V 0 P
growing, | plants with goodly burthen bowing; TMP 4.01.113
bowing his head against the steepy mount | to TIM 1.01. 75
BOWL* 13 FR 0.0014 REL FR 12 V 1 P
for you at pricks, sir, challenge her to bowl. LLL 4.01.138
when roasted crabs hiss in the bowl, | then 5.02.925
and sometime lurk i in a gossip's bowl, | in MND 2.01. 47
thus the bowl should run, | and not unluckily SHR 4.05. 24
fill me a bowl of wine. R3 5.03. 63
give me a bowl of wine. 5.03. 72
let me have such a bowl may hold my thanks, H8 1.04. 39
like to a bowl upon a subtle ground, | i have COR 5.02. 20
utter your gravity o'er a gossip's bowl, | for ROM 3.05.174
lucius, a bowl of wine! JC 4.03.142
give me a bowl of wine. 4.03.158
and bowl the round nave down the hill of heaven HAM 2.02.496
you have broke his pate with your bowl. CYM 2.01. 7 P
BOWL'D 1 FR 0.0001 REL FR 1 V 0 P
th' earth, | and bowl'd to death with turnips! WIV 3.04. 87
BOWLER 1 FR 0.0001 REL FR 0 V 1 P
good neighbor, faith, and a very good bowler; LLL 5.02.583 P
BOWLINE *(see bolins, bowling*)*
BOWLING* *(also bolins)*
BOWLING* 2 FR 0.0002 REL FR 1 V 1 P
too rough for some that know little but bowling) WT 4.04.330 P
top the bowling! TNK 4.01.148
BOWLS* 3 FR 0.0003 REL FR 2 V 1 P
madam, we'll play at bowls. R2 3.04. 3
all my sad captains, fill our bowls once more; ANT 3.13.183
i have lost to–day at bowls i'll win to–night of CYM 2.01. 49 P
BOW'R 2 FR 0.0002 REL FR 2 V 0 P
sung by a fair queen in a summer's bow'r, | with 1H4 3.01.207
sweet beauty hath no name, no holy bow'r, | but SON 127. 7
BOW'RS 1 FR 0.0001 REL FR 1 V 0 P
lie rich when canopied with bow'rs. TN 1.01. 40
/BOWS* 1 FR 0.0001 REL FR 1 V 0 P
/no /less /working /than /are /swords /and /bows TRO 1.03.355
BOWS* 11 FR 0.0012 REL FR 11 V 0 P
for, like an ass whose back with ingots bows, MM 3.01. 26
bows not his vassal head and, strooken blind, LLL 4.03.220
thy very beadsmen learn to bend their bows | of R2 3.02.116
me | that bows unto the grave with mickle age. 2H6 5.01.174
his senseless sword | and, when it bows, COR 1.04. 54
my mother bows, | as if olympus to a molehill 5.03. 29
dread to speak | when power to flattery bows? LR 1.01.148
the flame o' th' taper | bows toward her, and CYM 2.02. 20
and bows you | to a morning's holy office. 3.03. 3
first | he bows his noble body, then salutes me TNK 2.04. 23
she bows her head, the new–sprung flow'r to VEN 1171
BOWSPRIT *(see boresprit)*
BOW–STRING 1 FR 0.0001 REL FR 0 V 1 P
he hath twice or thrice cut cupid's bow–string, ADO 3.02. 11 P
BOW–STRINGS 1 FR 0.0001 REL FR 0 V 1 P
enough; hold, or cut bow–strings. MND 1.02.111 P
BOW–WOW 2 FR 0.0002 REL FR 2 V 0 P
bow–wow. TMP 1.02.382
bow–wow. 1.02.384

BOX* 19 FR 0.0021 REL FR 4 V 15 P
me in my closet /une /boite /en verd, a box, a WIV 1.04. 46 P
/une /boite /en verd, a box, a green–a box. 1.04. 46 P
a green–a box. 1.04. 47 P
if he took you a box o' th' ear, you might have MM 2.01.180 P
in him, for he borrow'd a box of the ear of the MV 1.02. 80 P
he wears his honor in a box unseen, | that hugs AWW 2.03.279
wherefore that box? WT 4.04.755 P
there lies such secrets in this farthel and box, 4.04.757 P
for the box of the year that the prince gave you 2H4 1.02.194 P
by this hand i will take thee a box on the ear. H5 4.01.215 P
i have sworn to take him a box a' th' ear; 4.07.128 P
favor | may haply purchase him a box a' th' ear. 4.07.173
give him a box o' th' ear, and that will make 2H6 4.07. 86 P
the surgeon's box, or the patient's wound. TRO 5.01. 11 P
why, thou damnable box of envy, thou, what means 5.01. 25 P
faith, nothing but an empty box, sir, which, in TIM 3.01. 16 P
of his lands will scarcely lie in this box, and HAM 5.01.111 P
here is a box, i had it from the queen, | what's CYM 3.04.188
if | that box i gave you was not thought by me 5.05.241
BOXES 2 FR 0.0002 REL FR 2 V 0 P
his shelves | a beggarly account of empty boxes, ROM 5.01. 45
fetch hither all my boxes in my closet. PER 3.02. 81
BOX–TREE 1 FR 0.0001 REL FR 0 V 1 P
get ye all three into the box–tree; TN 2.05. 15 P
/BOY 4 FR 0.0004 REL FR 2 V 2 P
prithee be silent, /boy, i profit not by thy TRO 5.01. 14 P
/alas, /the /tender /boy, /in /passion /mov'd, TIT 3.02. 48
/come, /boy, /and /go /with /me, /thy /sight /is 3.02. 84
/dost /thou /call /me /fool, /boy? LR 1.04.148 P
BOY 362 FR 0.0409 REL FR 250 V 112 P
play with sparrows, | and be a boy right out. TMP 4.01.101
not so fair, boy, as well–favor'd. TGV 2.01. 49 P
belike, boy, then you are in love — for last 2.01. 79 P
no, boy, but as well as i can do them. 2.01. 92 P
ay, boy, it's for love. 2.04. 4 P
run, boy, run, run, and seek him out. 3.01.188 P
i pray thee, launce, and if thou seest my boy, 3.01.259
look to the boy. 5.04. 85
why boy! 5.04. 86 P
where is that ring, boy? 5.04. 91
i think the boy hath grace in him; he blushes. 5.04.165
i warrant you, my lord — more grace than boy. 5.04.166
i keep but three men and a boy yet, till my WIV 1.01.274 P
and "to her, boy," say i. 1.03. 55 P
and the boy never need to understand any thing; 2.02.127 P
boy, go along with this woman. 2.02.132 P
hector of greece, my boy! 2.03. 34 P
o, you are a flattering boy, now i see you'll be 3.02. 7 P
why, this boy will carry a letter twenty mile, 3.02. 32 P
going to my wife, and falstaff's boy with her. 3.02. 36 P
and falstaff's boy with her! 3.02. 38 P
thou'rt a good boy. 3.03. 33 P
help to cover your master, boy. 3.03.143 P
o boy, thou hadst a father! 3.04. 36 P
get you home, boy. 4.01. 85 P
anne page, and she's a great lubberly boy. 5.05.184 P
and 'tis a postmaster's boy. 5.05.188 P
i think so, when i took a boy for a girl. 5.05.191 P
and yet it was not anne, but a postmaster's boy. 5.05.199 P
i ha' married oon garsoon, a boy; 5.05.205 P
a boy! 5.05.206 P
ay, be–gar, and 'tis a boy. 5.05.209 P
my youngest boy, and yet my eldest care, | at ERR 1.01.124
but seven years since, in syracusa, boy, | thou 5.01.321
'twas the boy that stole your meat, and you'll ADO 2.01.199 P
boy! 2.03. 1 P
if thou kill'st me, boy, thou shalt kill a man. 5.01. 79
come follow me, boy; 5.01. 83
come, sir boy, come follow me. 5.01. 83
sir boy, i'll whip you from your foining fence, 5.01. 84
fare you well, boy, you know my mind. 5.01.185 P
boy, what sign is it when a man of great spirit LLL 1.02. 1 P
comfort me, boy: 1.02. 64 P
more authority, dear boy, name more; 1.02. 68 P
is there not a ballet, boy, of the king and the 1.02.109 P
boy, i do love that country girl that i took in 1.02.117 P
sing, boy, my spirit grows heavy in love. 1.02.122 P
his disgrace is to be called boy, but his glory 1.02.180 P
by heart and in heart, boy. 3.01. 36 P
the boy hath sold him a bargain, a goose, that's 3.01.101
constable, | a domineering pedant o'er the boy, 3.01.177
this wimpled, whining, purblind, wayward boy, 3.01.179
man when king pippen of france was a little boy, 4.01.121 P
for he hath been five thousand year a boy. 5.02. 11
the boy replied, "an angel is not evil; 5.02.105
the hedge–priest, the fool, and the boy: 5.02.543 P
so the boy love is perjur'd every where; MND 1.01.241
hath | a lovely boy stolen from an indian king; 2.01. 22
but she perforce withholds the loved boy, 2.01. 26
i do but beg a little changeling boy | to be my 2.01.120
but she, being mortal, of that boy did die, 2.01.135
die, | and for her sake do i rear up her boy; 2.01.136
give me that boy, and i will go with thee. 2.01.143
i'll to my queen and beg her indian boy; 3.02.375
and, now i have the boy, i will undo | this 4.01. 62
forbid, the boy was the very staff of my age, my MV 2.02. 66 P
but i pray you tell me, is my boy, god rest his 2.02. 71 P
i am sure you are not launcelot, my boy. 2.02. 82 P
i am launcelot, your boy that was, your son that 2.02. 85 P
here's my son, sir, a poor boy — 2.02.122 P
not a poor boy, sir, but the rich jew's man, 2.02.123 P
blush | to see me thus transformed to a boy. 2.06. 39
sweet, | even in the lovely garnish of a boy. 2.06. 45
with them the first boy for a thousand ducats. 3.02.213 P
and speak between the change of man and boy 3.04. 66
a kind of boy, a little scrubbed boy, | no 5.01.162
a youth, | a kind of boy, a little scrubbed boy, 5.01.162
clerk, | a prating boy, that begg'd it as a fee. 5.01.164
and then the boy, his clerk, | that took some 5.01.181
for that same scrubbed boy, the doctor's clerk, 5.01.261
what, boy! AYL 1.01. 52 P
remains but that i kindle the boy thither, which 1.01.173 P
'tis but a peevish boy — yet he talks well — 3.05.110
that blind rascally boy that abuses every one's 4.01.213 P
"the boy is fair, | of female favor, and bestows 4.03. 85
that the boy | can do all this that he hath 5.04. 1
i do remember in this shepherd boy | some lively 5.04. 26

but, my good lord, this boy is forest–born, 5.04. 30
i'll not budge an inch, boy; SHR in.1. 14 P
saw'st thou not, boy, how silver made it good in.1. 19
and if the boy have not a woman's gift | to rain in.1. 124
i know the boy will well usurp the grace, in.1. 131
i, faith, boy, to have the next wish after, 1.01.239
an old italian fox is not so kind, my boy. 2.01.403
why, "jack, boy! 4.01. 41 P
ho, boy!" 4.01. 41 P
but, sir, here comes your boy; 4.04. 8
my boy shall fetch the scrivener presently. 4.04. 59
and thy mind stand to't, boy, steal away bravely AWW 2.01. 29
proud scornful boy, unworthy this good gift, 2.03.151
to th' wars, my boy, to th' wars! 2.03.278
this is not well, rash and unbridled boy, | to 3.02. 28
of one count rossillion, a foolish idle boy, but 4.03.215 P
count to be a dangerous and lascivious boy, who 4.03.220 P
of that lascivious young boy the count, have i 4.03.300 P
enough for a man, nor young enough for a boy; TN 1.05.157 P
with him in standing water, between boy and man. 1.05.159 P
come hither, boy. 2.04. 15
hath it not, boy? 2.04. 25
for, boy, however we do praise ourselves, | our 2.04. 32
but died thy sister of her love, my boy? 2.04.119
did she see /thee the while, old boy? 3.02. 8 P
a very dishonest paltry boy, and more a coward 3.04.385 P
that most ingrateful boy there by your side 5.01. 77
come, boy, with me, my thoughts are ripe in 5.01.129
boy, thou hast said to me a thousand times 5.01.267
when that i was and a little tine boy, | with 5.01.389
to–morrow as to–day, | and to be boy eternal. WT 1.02. 65
mamillius, | art thou my boy? 1.02.120
yet were it true | to say this boy were like me. 1.02.135
go play, boy, play. 1.02.187
go play, boy, play. 1.02.190
how now, boy? 1.02.207
take the boy to you; 2.01. 1
give me the boy. 2.01. 56
bear the boy hence, he shall not come about her. 2.01. 59
a boy? 2.02. 24
how does the boy? 2.03. 10
a boy, or a child, i wonder? 3.03. 70 P
why, boy, how is it? 3.03. 87 P
name of mercy, when was this, boy? 3.03.103 P
but look thee here, boy. 3.03.113 P
look thee here, take up, take up, boy; 3.03.116 P
what's within, boy? 3.03.119 P
this is fairy gold, boy, and 'twill prove so. 3.03.123 P
we are lucky, boy, and to be so still requires 3.03.125 P
come, good boy, the next way home. 3.03.127 P
'tis a lucky day, boy, and we'll do good deeds 3.03.138 P
for thee, fond boy, | if i may ever know thou 4.04.426
come, boy, i am past moe children, but thy sons 5.02.126 P
and so have i, boy. 5.02.138 P
ay, thou unreverend boy, | sir robert's son! JN 1.01.227
hither is he come | to spread his colors, boy, 2.01. 8
a noble boy! who would not do thee right? 2.01. 18
till then, fair boy, | i will i not think of home, 2.01. 30
but we will make it subject to this boy. 2.01. 43
that judge hath made me guardian to this boy, 2.01.115
and this boy | liker in feature to his father 2.01.125
my boy a bastard? 2.01.129
there's a good mother, boy, that blots thy 2.01.132
there's a good grandame, boy, that would blot 2.01.133
submit thee, boy. 2.01.159
his mother shames him so, poor boy, he weeps. 2.01.166
royalties, and rights | of this oppressed boy. 2.01.177
that yon green boy shall have no sun to ripe 2.01.472
what say'st thou, boy? look in the lady's face. 2.01.495
o boy, then where art thou? 3.01. 34
but thou art fair, and at thy birth, dear boy, 3.01. 51
hubert, keep this boy. 3.02. 5
hubert, throw thine eye | on yon young boy. 3.03. 60
if that be true, i shall see my boy again; 3.04. 78
o lord, my boy, my arthur, my fair son! 3.04.103
and bind the boy which you shall find with me 4.01. 4
young boy, i must. 4.01. 40
come, boy, prepare yourself. 4.01. 89
i can heat it, boy. 4.01.104
but with my breath i can revive it, boy. 4.01.111
yet am i sworn, and i did purpose, boy, | with 4.01.123
shall a beardless boy, | a cock'red silken 5.01. 69
have you forgot the duke of /herford, boy? R2 2.03. 36
why, foolish boy, the king is left behind, | and 2.03. 97
dishonorable boy! 4.01. 65
boy, let me see the writing. 5.02. 69
poor boy, thou art amaz'd. 5.02. 85
which he, young wanton and effeminate boy, 5.03. 10
by pardoning rutland, my transgressing boy. 5.03. 96
the boy shall lead our horses down the hill. 1H4 2.02. 78 P
a lad of mettle, a good boy (by the lord, so 2.04. 12 P
give me a cup of sack, boy. 2.04.116 P
swearest thou, ungracious boy? 2.04.445 P
man by man, boy by boy, servant by servant. 3.03. 57 P
man by man, boy by boy, servant by servant. 3.03. 57 P
o, this boy | lends mettle to us all! 5.04. 23
boy, tell him i am deaf. 2H4 1.02. 66 P
boy! 1.02.232 P
and the boy that i gave falstaff. 2.02. 70 P
has not the boy profited? 2.02. 84 P
instruct us, boy, what dream, boy? 2.02. 88 P
instruct us, boy, what dream, boy? 2.02. 88 P
there 'tis, boy. 2.02. 93 P
sirrah, you boy, and bardolph, no word to your 2.02.160 P
give me my rapier, boy. 2.04.201 P
than i love e'er a scurvy young boy of them all. 2.04.273 P
or is thy boy of the wicked? 2.04.328 P
for the boy, there is a good angel about him, 2.04.335 P
now sir john, a boy, and page to thomas mowbray, 3.02. 25 P
same young sober–blooded boy doth not love me, 4.03. 88 P
cherish it, my boy; 4.04. 23
god save thee, my sweet boy! 5.05. 43
boy, bristle thy courage up; H5 2.03. 5
i am boy to them all three, but all they three, 3.02. 29 P
come hither, boy, ask me this slave in french 4.04. 23
expound unto me, boy. 4.04. 58
'tis certain there's not a boy left alive, and 4.07. 5 P
saint denis and saint george, compound a boy, 5.02.208 P

endeavor for your french part of such a boy; 5.02.214 P
of a naked blind boy in her naked seeing self? 5.02.297 P
i scorn thee and thy fashion, peevish boy. 1H6 2.04. 76
therefore, dear boy, mount on my swiftest horse, 4.05. 9
that drew blood | from thee, my boy, and had the 4.06. 17
thou didst force from talbot, my brave boy." 4.06. 24
wilt thou yet leave the battle, boy, and fly, 4.06. 28
and in that sea of blood my boy did drench | his 4.07. 14
poor boy, he smiles, methinks, as who should say 4.07. 27
in vain thou speak'st, poor boy; 3H6 1.03. 21
dicky, your boy, that with his grumbling voice 1.04. 76
point | made issue from the bosom of the boy; 1.04. 81
cloth thou dipp'dst in blood of my sweet boy, 1.04.157
were it not pity that this goodly boy | should 2.02. 34
look on the boy, | and let his manly face, which 2.02. 39
go rate thy minions, proud insulting boy! 2.02. 84
ah, boy, if any life be left in thee, | throw up 2.05. 84
o boy! 2.05. 92
my heart, sweet boy, shall be thy sepulchre, 2.05.115
peace, willful boy, or i will charm your tongue. 5.05. 31
o ned, sweet ned, speak to thy mother, boy! 5.05. 51
my poor boy, icarus; 5.06. 21
the sun that sear'd the wings of my sweet boy, 5.06. 23
come hither, bess, and let me kiss my boy. 5.07. 15
no, boy. R3 2.02. 2
ay, boy. 2.02. 32
a parlous boy! go to, you are too shrewd. 2.04. 35
come, come, my boy, we will to sanctuary. 2.04. 66
o, 'tis a perilous boy, | bold, quick, ingenious 3.01.154
boy! 4.02. 32
go call him hither, boy. 4.02. 41
the boy is foolish, and i fear not him. 4.02. 55
king, | when richmond was a little peevish boy. 4.02. 97
this burthen, 'tis too weak | ever to get a boy. H8 2.03. 44
it's one a' clock, boy, is't not? 5.01. 1
say ay, and of a boy. 5.01.163
ay, ay, my liege, | and of a lovely boy. 5.01.164
good boy, tell him i come. TRO 1.02.275 P
if my lord get a boy of you, you'll give him me. 3.02.104 P
unarm thee, go, and doubt thou not, brave boy. 5.03. 35
i'll swear 'tis a very pretty boy. COR 1.03. 58 P
honorable menenius, my boy martius approaches. 2.01.100 P
and my young boy | hath an aspect of 5.03. 31
that's my brave boy! 5.03. 76
that brought you forth this boy, to keep your 5.03.126
speak thou, boy; 5.03.156
this boy, that cannot tell what he would have, 5.03.174
name not the god, thou boy of tears! 5.06.100
"boy"? 5.06.103
"boy," false hound! 5.06.112
"boy"! 5.06.116
what, villain boy, | barr'st me my way in rome? TIT 1.01.290
why, boy, although our mother, unadvis'd, | gave 2.01. 38
ay, boy, grow ye so brave? 2.01. 45
faint-hearted boy, arise and look upon her. 3.01. 65
as for thee, boy, go get thee from my sight; 3.01.283
she loves thee, boy, too well to do thee harm. 4.01. 6
ah, boy, cornelia never with more care | read to 4.01. 12
open them, boy. 4.01. 32
and kneel, sweet boy, the roman hector's hope, 4.01. 88
boy, what say you? 4.01.106
ay, that's my boy! 4.01.110
and withal my boy | shall carry from me to the 4.01.114
no, boy, not so, i'll teach thee another course. 4.01.119
that shone so brightly when this boy was got, 4.02. 90
sir boy, let me see your archery. 4.03. 2
here, boy, "to pallas"; 4.03. 56
to it, boy! 4.03. 59
good boy, in virgo's lap; 4.03. 65
touch not the boy, he is of royal blood. 5.01. 49
to save my boy, to nourish and bring him up, 5.01. 84
come hither, boy, come, come, and learn of us 5.03.160
o now, sweet boy, give them their latest kiss! 5.03.169
ay, boy, ready. ROM 1.05. 11 P
fetch me my rapier, boy. 1.05. 55
what, goodman boy? 1.05. 77
go to, go to, | you are a saucy boy. 1.05. 83
boy, this shall not excuse the injuries | that 3.01. 66
thou wretched boy, that didst consort him here, 3.01.130
give me thy torch, boy. 5.03. 1
the boy gives warning, something doth approach. 5.03. 18
wilt thou provoke me? then have at thee, boy! 5.03. 70
lead, boy, which way? 5.03.168
good boy, wink at me, and say thou saw'st me not TIM 3.01. 44 P
is not to-morrow, boy, the /ides of march? JC 2.01. 40
boy! 2.01.229
boy, stand aside. 2.01.312
i prithee, boy, run to the senate-house; 2.04. 1
yes, bring me word, boy, if thy lord look well, 2.04. 13
hark, boy, what noise is that? 2.04. 16
sure the boy heard me. 2.04. 42
bear with me, good boy, i am much forgetful. 4.03.255
it does, my boy. 4.03.258
layest thou thy leaden mace upon my boy, | that 4.03.268
and, good boy, good night. 4.03.272
boy, lucius! 4.03.289
how goes the night, boy? MAC 2.01. 1
what's the boy malcolm? 5.03. 3
and over-red thy fear, | thou lily-liver'd boy. 5.03. 15
hillo, ho, ho, boy! come, /bird, come. HAM 1.05.116
ha, ha, boy, say'st thou so? 1.05.150
i have been sexton here, man and boy, thirty 5.01.162 P
why, my boy? LR 1.04.106 P
no, boy, nothing can be made out of nothing. 1.04.132 P
dost thou know the difference, my boy, between a 1.04.137 P
ay, boy. 1.05. 10 P
what canst tell, boy? 1.05. 17 P
come, boy. 1.05. 50 P
loyal and natural boy, i'll work the means | to 2.01. 84
with you, goodman boy, /and you please! 2.02. 45 P
come on, my boy. 3.02. 68
how dost, my boy? 3.02. 68
true, boy. come bring us to this hovel. 3.02. 78
in, boy, go first. 3.04. 26
dolphin my boy, boy, sessa! 3.04. 99 P
dolphin my boy, boy, sessa! 3.04. 99 P
while i'll place you, then the boy shall sing. ANT 2.07.110
to the boy caesar send this grizzled head, | and 3.13. 17
till like a boy you see him cringe his face, 3.13.100
he calls me boy, and chides as he had power | to 4.01. 1
to the young roman boy she hath sold me, and i 4.12. 48
some squeaking cleopatra boy my greatness | i' 5.02.220
behold divineness | no elder than a boy! CYM 3.06. 44
the boy fidele's sickness | did make my way long 4.02.148
thou diedst, a most rare boy, of melancholy. 4.02.208
friends, | the boy hath taught us manly duties. 4.02.397
boy, he's preferr'd | by thee to us, and he 4.02.400
away, boy, from the troops, and save thyself; 5.02. 14
"two boys, an old man (twice a boy), a lane, 5.03. 57
hath my poor boy done aught but well, | whose 5.04. 35
my boy, a britain born, | let him be ransom'd. 5.05. 84
boy, | thou hast look'd thyself into my grace, 5.05. 93
i know not why, wherefore, | to say "live, boy." 5.05. 96
the boy disdains me, | he leaves me, scorns me. 5.05.105
what wouldst thou, boy? 5.05.108
is not this boy reviv'd from death? 5.05.120
give answer to this boy, and do it freely, | or, 5.05.131
that was a fair boy certain, but a fool | to TNK 2.02.120
and, by the smallness of it, | a boy or woman. 4.01. 59
up to the top, boy! 4.01.150
snatch up the goodly boy and set him by him, | a 4.02. 17
narcissus was a sad boy, but a heavenly. 4.02. 32
this anatomy | had by his young fair fere a boy, 5.01.116
rein, | under her other was the tender boy, VEN 32
"o, pity," gan she cry, "flint-hearted boy, 95
is love so light, sweet boy, and may it be 155
view | how she came stealing to the wayward boy! 344
"let me excuse thy courser, gentle boy, | and 403
the silly boy, believing she is dead, | claps 467
"sweet boy," she says, "this night i'll waste in 583
been gone," quoth she, "sweet boy, ere this, 613
by this the boy that by her side lay kill'd 1165
forbade the boy he should not pass those grounds PP 9. 8
as if the boy should use like loving charms; 11. 8
nothing, sweet boy, but yet, like prayers divine SON 108. 5
o thou, my lovely boy, who in thy power | dost 126. 1
the boy for trial needs would touch my breast; 153. 9

BOYET 12 FR 0.0013 REL FR 12 V 1 P
good lord boyet, my beauty, though but mean, LLL 2.01. 13
good boyet, | you are not ignorant, all-telling 2.01. 20
here comes boyet. 2.01. 80
boyet, you can produce acquittances | for such a 2.01.160
come to our pavilion — boyet is dispos'd. 2.01.250
boyet, you can carve, | break up this capon. 4.01. 55
you still wrangle with her, boyet, and she 4.01.117
here comes boyet, and mirth is in his face. 5.02. 79
thy news, boyet? 5.02. 81
know their minds, boyet. 5.02.175
debt | pay him the due of honey-tongued boyet. 5.02.334
boyet, prepare, i will away to-night. 5.02.727

BOYISH 2 FR 0.0002 REL FR 2 V 0 P
this /unhair'd sauciness and boyish troops, JN 5.02.133
even from my boyish days | to th' very moment OTH 1.03.132

BOY-QUELLER 1 FR 0.0001 REL FR 1 V 0 P
come, come, thou boy-queller, show thy face. TRO 5.05. 45

/BOY'S 1 FR 0.0001 REL FR 0 V 1 P
/a /horse's /health, /a /boy's /love, /or /a LR 3.06. 19 P

BOY'S 6 FR 0.0006 REL FR 4 V 2 P
her and her blind boy's scandall'd company | i TMP 4.01. 90
i'll after, to rejoice in the boy's correction. TGV 3.01.384 P
then the boy's fat l'envoy, the goose that you LLL 3.01.109
looking on the lines | of my boy's face, WT 1.02.154
nay, you shall find no boy's play here, i can 1H4 5.04. 76 P
let's see the boy's face. CYM 4.02.359

BOYS' 2 FR 0.0002 REL FR 1 V 1 P
my mouth no more were broken than these boys', AWW 2.03. 60
we took him setting of boys' copies. 2H6 4.02. 88 P

BOYS* *(also poys)*

/BOYS* 1 FR 0.0001 REL FR 0 V 1 P
/do /the /boys /carry /it /away? HAM 2.02.360 P

BOYS* 92 FR 0.0104 REL FR 71 V 21 P
then to sea, boys, and let her go hang!" TMP 2.02. 54
when we were boys, | who would believe that 3.03. 43
me by the hangman's boys in the market-place; TGV 4.04. 56 P
here, boys, here, here! shall we wag? WIV 2.01.230 P
boys of art, i have deceiv'd you both; 3.01.107 P
master slender is let the boys leave to play. 4.01. 11 P
my wife, not meanly proud of two such boys, ERR 1.01. 58
troth, your town is troubled with unruly boys. 3.01. 62
boys, apes, braggarts, jacks, milksops! ADO 5.01. 91
scambling, outfacing, fashion-monging boys, 5.01. 94
and nestor play at push-pin with the boys, | and LLL 4.03.167
yes, yes, he teaches boys the horn-book. 5.01. 46 P
as waggish boys in game themselves forswear, MND 1.01.240
why, all the boys in venice follow him, | crying MV 2.08. 23
i am the youngest son of sir rowland de boys. AYL 1.01. 57 P
liege, the youngest son of sir rowland de boys. 1.02.223 P
as boys and women are for the most part cattle 3.02.414 P
tush, tush, fear boys with bugs. SHR 1.02.210
these boys are boys of ice, they'll none have AWW 2.03. 93 P
these boys are boys of ice, they'll none have 2.03. 93 P
that twenty such rude boys might tend upon | and 3.02. 82
men are to mell with, boys are not to kiss; 4.03.228
my lord's tricks and yours when you were boys. WT 1.02. 61
thy jealousies | (fancies too weak for boys, too 3.02.181
boys, with women's voices, | strive to speak big R2 3.02.113
gallants, lads, boys, hearts of gold, all the 1H4 2.04.277 P
to laugh at gibing boys, and stand the push | of 3.02. 66
i have two boys | seek percy and thyself about 5.04. 31
and rides the wild-mare with the boys, and jumps 2H4 2.04.247 P
no, faith, boys, none. 2.04.324 P
our watch-word was "hem, boys!" 3.02.218 P
rage, | and countenanc'd by boys and beggary — 4.01. 35
none of these demure boys come to any proof, for 4.03. 90 P
let us to france, like horse-leeches, my boys, H5 2.03. 55
of it, for there is none to guard it but boys. 4.04. 77 P
pales in the flood with men, wives, and boys, 5.pr. 10
and like me to the peasant boys of france, | to 1H6 4.06. 48
(in whose time boys went to span-counter for 2H6 4.02.157 P
to say if that the bastard boys of york | shall 5.01.115
those | that for my surety will refuse the boys! 5.01.121
mine, boys? not till king henry be dead. 3H6 1.02. 10
with iron-witted fools | and unrespective boys; R3 4.02. 29
my tongue should to thy ears not name my boys 4.04.231
like little wanton boys that swim on bladders, H8 3.02.359
'tis a girl | promises boys hereafter. 5.01.166
councillor, | 'mong boys, grooms, and lackeys. 5.02. 18
when suddenly a file of boys behind 'em, loose 5.03. 56 P
virgins and boys, mid-age and wrinkled /eld, TRO 2.02.104
that thy wives with spits and boys with stones COR 4.04. 5
than boys pursuing summer butterflies, | or 4.06. 94
and with these boys mine honor thou hast wounded TIT 1.01.365
and strike, brave boys, and take your turns; 2.01.129
you shall know, my boys, | your mother's hand 2.03.120
remember, boys, i pour'd forth tears in vain 2.03.163
what, what, ye sanguine, shallow-hearted boys! 4.02. 97
what say you, boys, will you abide with him, 5.02.137
cheerly, boys, be brisk a while, and the longer ROM 1.05. 15 P
as flies to wanton boys are we to th' gods, LR 4.01. 36
some wine, boys! OTH 2.03. 74 P
prithee, how many boys and wenches must i have? ANT 1.02. 36 P
as we rate boys who, being mature in knowledge, 1.04. 31
on each side her | stood pretty dimpled boys, 2.02.202
like boys unto a muss, kings would start forth 3.13. 91
young boys and girls | are level now with men; 4.15. 65
you laugh when boys or women tell their dreams; 5.02. 74
/stoop, boys, this gate | instructs you how t' CYM 3.03. 2
o boys, this story | the world may read in me: 3.03. 55
these boys know little they are sons to th' king 3.03. 80
boys, bid him welcome. 3.06. 68
hark, boys. 3.06. 80
boys, we'll go dress our hunt. 3.06. 89
thou blazon'st | in these two princely boys! 4.02.171
toys, | is jollity for apes, and grief for boys. 4.02.194
he was a queen's son, boys, | and though he came 4.02.244
have with you, boys! 4.04. 50
a narrow lane, an old man, and two boys! 5.03. 52
"two boys, an old man (twice a boy), a lane, 5.03. 57
that place them on the truth of girls and boys. 5.05.107
my boys, | there was our error. 5.05.259
why then have with ye, boys! TNK 2.03. 27
all the boys in athens | blow wind i' th' breech 2.03. 46
ha, boys, heigh for the weavers! 2.03. 49
away, boys, and hold! 2.03. 59
well, sir, | take your own time. come, boys. 2.03. 69
up with a course or two, and tack about, boys! 3.04. 10
and sweetly, by a figure, trace and turn, boys. 3.05. 21
ere, my mad boys, have at ye! 3.05. 24
mad woman? we are made, boys! 3.05. 76
ay, boys! 3.05. 92
too and have done as good boys should do, 3.05.143
and these must be boys, | he has the trick 4.01.131
who youth, like wanton boys through bonfires, 5.01. 86

BRABANT 5 FR 0.0005 REL FR 5 V 0 P
did not i dance with you in brabant once? LLL 2.01.114
did not i dance with you in brabant once? 2.01.115
of brabant and of orleance, shall make forth, H5 2.04. 5
alanson, brabant, bar, and burgundy, | jacques 3.05. 42
john duke of alanson, anthony duke of brabant, 4.08. 96

BRABANTIO 7 FR 0.0008 REL FR 7 V 0 P
what ho, brabantio, signior brabantio, ho! OTH 1.01. 78
what ho! brabantio, signior brabantio, ho! 1.01. 78
what ho, brabantio! 1.01. 79
most grave brabantio, | in simple and pure soul 1.01.106
it is brabantio. 1.02. 55
here comes brabantio and the valiant moor. 1.03. 47
good brabantio, | take up this mangled matter at 1.03.172

BRABBLE *(also prabbles, pribbles)*

BRABBLE 2 FR 0.0002 REL FR 2 V 0 P
in private brabble did we apprehend him. TN 5.01. 65
adore, | this petty brabble will undo us all. TIT 2.01. 62

BRABBLER 2 FR 0.0002 REL FR 1 V 1 P
too precious to be spent | with such a brabbler. JN 5.02.162
his mouth and promise, like brabbler the hound, TRO 5.01. 91 P

BRAC'D 1 FR 0.0001 REL FR 1 V 0 P
and even at hand a drum is ready brac'd | that JN 5.02.169

BRACE 18 FR 0.0020 REL FR 13 V 5 P
but you, my brace of lords, were i so minded, TMP 5.01.126
sweet breath as will utter a brace of words. LLL 5.02.523 P
the utterance of a brace of tongues | must needs JN 4.01. 97
a brace of draymen bid god speed him well, | and R2 1.04. 32
like a brace of greyhounds | having the fearful 3H6 2.05.129
not dallying with a brace of courtezans, | but R3 3.07. 74
you brace of warlike brothers, welcome hither. TRO 4.05.175
then you should discover a brace of unmeriting, COR 2.01. 43 P
so, here comes a brace. 2.03. 61
myself | take up a brace o' th' best of them, 3.01.243
discords too | have lost a brace of kinsmen. ROM 5.03.295
and has sent your honor two brace of greyhounds. TIM 1.02.189 P
as thine is now, held with a brace of harlots. 4.03. 80
for that it stands not in such warlike brace, OTH 1.03. 24
here without are a brace of cyprus gallants that 2.03. 31 P
so your brace of unprizable estimations, the one CYM 1.04. 90 P
me and death" — and pointed to this brace — PER 2.01.127
the year) presents me with | a brace of horses; TNK 3.01. 20

BRACELET 3 FR 0.0003 REL FR 2 V 1 P
glove, shoe-tie, bracelet, horn-ring, to keep my WT 4.04.599 P
pictures, this her bracelet | (o cunning, how i CYM 5.05.204
and here the bracelet of the truest princess 5.05.416

BRACELETS 3 FR 0.0003 REL FR 3 V 0 P
of her fantasy | with bracelets of thy hair, MND 1.01. 33
with her amber bracelets, beads, and all this SHR 4.03. 58
food, for yet | his iron bracelets are not off. TNK 2.06. 8

/BRACH 1 FR 0.0001 REL FR 0 V 1 P
hold my peace when achilles' /brach bids me, TRO 2.01.114 P

BRACH 5 FR 0.0005 REL FR 3 V 2 P
tender well my hounds | (brach merriman, the SHR in.1. 17
and couple clowder with the deep-mouth'd brach. in.1. 18
i had rather hear lady, my brach, howl in irish. 1H4 3.01.235 P
when the lady brach may stand by th' fire and LR 1.04.112 P
mongril grim, | hound or spaniel, brach or /lym, 3.06. 69

BRACY 1 FR 0.0001 REL FR 0 V 1 P
here was sir john bracy from your father; 1H4 2.04.334 P

BRAG 15 FR 0.0017 REL FR 14 V 1 P
shalt not live to brag what we have offer'd. TGV 4.01. 67
as under privilege of age to brag | what i have ADO 5.01. 60
and caesar's thrasonical brag of "i came, saw, AYL 5.02. 31 P
than you have heard him brag to you he will. TN 3.04.317

to brag and stamp and swear | upon my party! JN 3.01.122
yet, forgive me, god, | that i do brag thus! H5 3.06.151
you wisest grecians, pardon me this brag. TRO 4.05.257
to brag unto them, "thus i did, and thus!" COR 2.02.147
agree these deeds with that proud brag of thine, TIT 1.01.306
the mere lees | is left this vault to brag of. MAC 2.03. 96
if fortune brag of two she lov'd and hated, LR 5.03.281
here, but made not here his brag | of "came, and CYM 3.01. 23
o, be not proud, nor brag not of thy might, VEN 113
be, | beauty brag, but 'tis not she, | truth and PHT 63
nor shall death brag thou wand'rest in his shade SON 18.11
BRAGGADISM 1 FR 0.0001 REL FR 1 V 0 P
why, valentine, what braggadism is this? TGV 2.04.164
BRAGGARD 1 FR 0.0001 REL FR 1 V 0 P
o braggard vile and damned furious wight! H5 2.01. 60
BRAGGARDS 1 FR 0.0001 REL FR 0 V 1 P
you break jests as braggards do their blades, ADO 5.01.187 P
BRAGGART 8 FR 0.0009 REL FR 6 V 2 P
the pedant, the braggart, the hedge-priest, the LLL 5.02.542 P
you shall see | how much i was a braggart: MV 3.02.258
who knows himself a braggart, | let him fear AWW 4.03.334
that every braggart shall be found an ass. 4.03.336
which was your shame, by this unholy braggart, COR 5.06.118
a braggart, a rogue, a villain, that fights by ROM 3.01.101 P
with mine eyes, | and braggart with my tongue! MAC 4.03.231
stubborn ancient knave, you reverent braggart, LR 2.02.126
BRAGGARTS 2 FR 0.0002 REL FR 2 V 0 P
boys, apes, braggarts, jacks, milksops! ADO 5.01. 91
and let the unscarr'd braggarts of the war TIM 4.03.161
BRAGG'D 3 FR 0.0003 REL FR 2 V 1 P
may be the knave bragg'd of that he could not WIV 3.03.200 P
that was the whip of your bragg'd progeny | thou COR 1.08. 12
when virtue bragg'd, beauty would blush for LUC 54
BRAGGING *(also pragging)*
BRAGGING 8 FR 0.0009 REL FR 5 V 3 P
thou coward, art thou bragging to the stars, MND 3.02.407
and speak of frays | like a fine bragging youth, MV 3.04. 69
a thousand raw tricks of these bragging jacks, 3.04. 77
and outface the brow | of bragging horror; JN 5.01. 50
a rascal bragging slave! 2H4 2.04.228 P
this, and fig me like | the bragging spaniard. 5.03.119
under the correction of bragging be it spoken, i H5 5.02.138 P
but for bragging and telling her fantastical OTH 2.01.223 P
BRAGLESS 1 FR 0.0001 REL FR 1 V 0 P
if it be so, yet bragless let it be, | great TRO 5.09. 5
BRAGS 7 FR 0.0008 REL FR 5 V 2 P
what simple thief brags of his own /attaint? ERR 3.02. 16
quick, the child brags in her belly already. LLL 5.02.677 P
as well, were some of your brags dismounted. H5 3.07. 77 P
verona brags of him | to be a virtuous and ROM 1.05. 67
brags of his substance, not of ornament; 2.06. 31
he brags his service | as if he were of note. CYM 5.03. 93
either our brags | were crak'd of kitchen trulls 5.05.176
BRAID* *(also upbraid)*
BRAID* 2 FR 0.0002 REL FR 2 V 0 P
since frenchmen are so braid, | marry that will, AWW 4.02. 73
'twould braid yourself too near for me to tell PER 1.01. 93
BRAIDED 2 FR 0.0002 REL FR 2 V 0 P
his braided hanging mane | upon his compass'd VEN 271
though slackly braided in loose negligence. LC 35
BRAIN *(also prain, etc.)*
BRAIN 82 FR 0.0092 REL FR 58 V 24 P
there thou mayst brain him, | having first TMP 3.02. 88
bear with my weakness, my old brain is troubled. 4.01.159
no, nor no where else but in your brain. WIV 4.02.159 P
have i laid my brain in the sun and dried it, 5.05.135 P
paper bullets of the brain awe a man from the ADO 2.03.241 P
hand, | a halting sonnet of his own pure brain, 5.04. 87
that hath a mint of phrases in his brain; LLL 1.01.165
other slow arts entirely keep the brain; 4.03.321
eyes, | lives not alone immured in the brain, 4.03.325
to weed this wormwood from your fructful brain, 5.02.847
the brain may devise laws for the blood, but a MV 1.02. 18 P
and in his brain, | which is as dry as the AYL 2.07. 38
with pure love and troubled brain, he hath ta'en 4.03. 4 P
women's gentle brain | could not drop forth such 4.03. 33
when liver, brain, and heart, | these sovereign TN 1.01. 36
as much to say as i wear not motley in my brain. 1.05. 57 P
fool that has no more brain than a stone. 1.05. 85 P
arm, out of the blank | and level of my brain — WT 2.03. 6
aside, here is more matter for a hot brain. 4.04.684 P
and his pure brain | (which some suppose the JN 5.07. 2
my brain i'll prove the female to my soul, | my R2 5.05. 6
rascal, i could brain him with his lady's fan. 1H4 2.03. 23 P
the brain of this foolish-compounded clay, man, 2H4 1.02. 7 P
from study, and perturbation of the brain. 1.02.116 P
it ascends me into the brain, dries me there all 4.03. 97 P
and now my sight fails, and my brain is giddy. 4.04.110
but in gross brain little wots | what watch the H5 4.01.282
and buzz these conjurations in her brain. 2H6 1.02. 99
my brain, more busy than the laboring spider, 3.01.339
some strange commotion | is in his brain; H8 3.02.113
your brain, and every function of your power, 3.02.187
i have a young conception in my brain, | be you TRO 1.03.312
were his brain as barren | as banks of libya 1.03.327
thou hast no more brain than i have in mine 2.01. 43 P
i have bobb'd his brain more than he has beat my 2.01. 70 P
as green as ajax', and your brain so temper'd, 2.03.254
hath no arithmetic but her brain to set down her 3.03.253 P
with too much blood and too little brain, these 5.01. 48 P
if with too much brain and too little blood they 5.01. 49 P
quails, but he has not so much brain as ear-wax; 5.01. 52 P
the court, the heart, to th' seat o' th' brain, COR 1.01.136
more of your conversation would infect my brain, 2.01. 94 P
but yet a brain that leads my use of anger | to 3.02. 30
nay, i do bear a brain — but, as i said, | when ROM 1.03. 29
which are the children of an idle brain, | begot 1.04. 97
but where unbruised youth with unstuff'd brain 2.03. 37
my dull brain was wrought | with things MAC 1.03.149
that memory, the warder of the brain, | shall be 1.07. 65
proceeding from the heat-oppressed brain? 2.01. 39
raze out the written troubles of the brain, 5.03. 42
into every brain | that looks so many fadoms to HAM 1.04. 76
live | within the book and volume of my brain, 1.05.103
or else this brain of mine | hunts not the trail 2.02. 46
sleep rock thy brain, | and never come mischance 3.02.227
this is the very coinage of your brain, | this 3.04.137
a heart and brain to breed it in? LR 1.02. 57 P
lest my brain turn, and the deficient sight 4.06. 23
as if thou then hadst shut up in thy brain OTH 3.03.114
are his wits safe? is he not light of brain? 4.01.269
in a field of feasts, | keep his brain fuming; ANT 2.01. 24
it's monstrous labor when i wash my brain | and 2.07. 99
take from his heart, take from his brain, from 3.07. 11
a diminution in our captain's brain | restores 3.13.197
yet ha' we | a brain that nourishes our nerves, 4.08. 21
her beauty and her brain go not together. CYM 1.02. 30 P
a woman that | bears all down with her brain, 2.01. 54
at nothing, | which the brain makes of fumes. 4.02.301
to taint his nobler heart and brain | with 5.04. 65
such stuff as madmen | tongue and brain not; 5.04.146
purse and brain both empty; 5.04.163 P
the brain the heavier for being too light, the 5.04.164 P
to you, the liver, heart, and brain of britain, 5.05. 14
mine italian brain | gan in your duller britain 5.05.196
how her brain coins! TNK 4.03. 40 P
like the proceedings of a drunken brain, | full VEN 910
light | to the disposing of her troubled brain, 1040
oft the eye mistakes, the brain being troubled. 1068
those children nurs'd, deliver'd from thy brain, SON 77.11
that did my ripe thoughts in my brain inhearse, 86. 3
what's in the brain that ink may character 108. 1
are within my brain | full character'd with 122. 1
so long as brain and heart | have faculty by 122. 5
BRAIN'D 2 FR 0.0002 REL FR 1 V 1 P
if th' other two be brain'd like us, the state TMP 3.02. 6 P
slower foot came on, | that brain'd my purpose. MM 5.01.396
BRAINFORD 6 FR 0.0006 REL FR 0 V 6 P
my maid's aunt, the fat woman of brainford, has WIV 4.02. 76 P
he cannot abide the old woman of brainford. 4.02. 86 P
let's go dress him like the witch of brainford. 4.02. 98 P
why, it is my maid's aunt of brainford. 4.02.170 P
you, sir, was't not the wise woman of brainford? 4.05. 27 P
to be apprehended for the witch of brainford. 4.05.117 P
BRAINISH 1 FR 0.0001 REL FR 1 V 0 P
and in this brainish apprehension kills | the HAM 4.01. 11
BRAINLESS 1 FR 0.0001 REL FR 1 V 0 P
if the dull brainless ajax come safe off, TRO 1.03.380
BRAIN-PAN 1 FR 0.0001 REL FR 0 V 1 P
my brain-pan had been cleft with a brown bill; 2H6 4.10. 11 P
BRAIN'S 1 FR 0.0001 REL FR 1 V 0 P
such shadows are the weak brain's forgeries, LUC 460
BRAINS' 1 FR 0.0001 REL FR 1 V 0 P
scorn'dst our brains' flow, and those our TIM 5.04. 76
/BRAINS 1 FR 0.0001 REL FR 0 V 1 P
/has /been /much /throwing /about /of /brains. HAM 2.02.359 P
BRAINS 45 FR 0.0050 REL FR 26 V 19 P
to an unsettled fancy, cure thy brains, | now TMP 5.01. 59
has page any brains? WIV 3.02. 30 P
i'll have my brains ta'en out and butter'd, and 3.05. 7 P
scrape the figures out of your husband's brains. 4.02.216 P
or they shall beat out my brains with billets. MM 4.03. 55 P
if a man will be beaten with brains, 'a shall ADO 5.04.103 P
lovers and madmen have such seething brains, MND 5.01. 4
troilus had his brains dash'd out with a grecian AYL 4.01. 98 P
the brains of my cupid's knock'd out, and i AWW 3.02. 15 P
though i know his brains are forfeit to the next 4.03.190 P
to my niece till his brains turn o' th' toe like TN 1.03. 41 P
whose skull jove cram with brains! 1.05.114 P
ne'er believe a madman till i see his brains. 4.02.117 P
find it | and that to the infection of my brains WT 1.02.145
the bastard brains with these my proper hands 2.03.140
and rock his brains | in cradle of the rude 2H4 3.01. 19
sleep with thoughts, their brains with care, 4.05. 68
and make a quagmire of your mingled brains. 1H6 1.04.109
that many have their giddy brains knock'd out; 3.01. 83
were red-hot steel, to sear me to the brains! R3 4.01. 60
our own brains and the opinion that we bring H8 pr 20
no new device to beat this from his brains? 3.02.217
catch, and /'a knock /out either of your brains; TRO 2.01.101 P
in him when hector has knock'd out his brains, i 3.03.302 P
gallops night by night | through lovers' brains, ROM 1.04. 71
as with a club, dash out my desp'rate brains? 4.03. 54
to knock out an honest athenian's brains. TIM 1.01.192 P
old limping sire, | with it beat out his brains! 4.01. 15
which busy care draws in the brains of men; JC 2.01.232
and dash'd the brains out, had i so sworn as you MAC 1.07. 58
that when the brains were out, the man would die 3.04. 78
about, my brains! HAM 2.02.588
whereon his brains still beating puts him thus 3.01.174
o heat, dry up my brains! 4.05.155
cudgel thy brains no more about it, for your 5.01. 56 P
or i could make a prologue to my brains, | they 5.02. 30
if a man's brains were in 's heels, were't not LR 1.05. 8 P
let me have surgeons, | i am cut to th' brains. 4.06.193
from frieze, | it plucks out brains and all. OTH 2.01.127
have very poor and unhappy brains for drinking. 2.03. 34 P
in their mouths to steal away their brains! 2.03.291 P
knocking out his brains. 4.02.230 P
hercules | could have knock'd out his brains, CYM 4.02.115
live | to knock thy brains out with my shackles. TNK 2.02.219
hath been before, how are our brains beguil'd, SON 59. 2
BRAIN-SICK 6 FR 0.0006 REL FR 6 V 0 P
good lord, what madness rules in brain-sick men, 1H6 4.01.111
did instigate the bedlam brain-sick duchess | by 2H6 3.01. 51
thou mad misleader of thy brain-sick son! 5.01.163
her brain-sick raptures | cannot distaste the TRO 2.02.122
what e'er i forge to feed his brain-sick humors, TIT 5.02. 71
retire, | beaten away by brain-sick rude desire. LUC 175
BRAIN-SICKLY 1 FR 0.0001 REL FR 1 V 0 P
strength, to think | so brain-sickly of things. MAC 2.02. 43
BRAKE* *(also broke)*
/BRAKE* 1 FR 0.0001 REL FR 1 V 0 P
he has mistook the /brake i meant, is gone TNK 3.02. 1
BRAKE* 12 FR 0.0013 REL FR 10 V 2 P
passion | ne'er brake into extremity of rage. ERR 5.01. 48
our stage, this hawthorn brake our tiring-house, MND 3.01. 4 P
have spoken your speech, enter into that brake; 3.01. 75 P
bog, through bush, through brake, through brier: 3.01.107
forsook his scene, and ent'red in a brake; 3.02. 15
brake off our business for the holy land. 1H4 1.01. 48
this thick-grown brake we'll shroud ourselves, 3H6 3.01. 1
and even here brake off, and came away. R3 3.07. 41
place, and the rough brake | that virtue must go H8 1.02. 75
and all amaz'd, brake off his late intent, | for VEN 469
hasting to feed her fawn hid in some brake. 876
here kennell'd in a brake she finds a hound, 913
BRAKENBURY 3 FR 0.0003 REL FR 3 V 0 P
and please your worship, brakenbury, | you may R3 1.01. 88
we know thy charge, brakenbury, and will obey. 1.01.105
sir robert brakenbury, and sir william brandon. 5.05. 14
BRAKES* 4 FR 0.0004 REL FR 4 V 0 P
some run from brakes of ice and answer none, MM 2.01. 39
i'll run from thee and hide me in the brakes, MND 2.01.227
round rising hillocks, brakes obscure and rough, VEN 237
here in these brakes deep-wounded with a boar, PP 9.10
BRAMBLES 2 FR 0.0002 REL FR 1 V 1 P
odes upon hawthorns and elegies on brambles; AYL 3.02.362 P
the thorny brambles and embracing bushes, | as VEN 629
BRAN 7 FR 0.0008 REL FR 3 V 4 P
i am fain to dine and sup with water and bran; MM 4.03.153 P
you shall fast a week with bran and water. LLL 1.01.301 P
chaff and bran, chaff and bran! TRO 1.02.241 P
chaff and bran, chaff and bran! 1.02.242 P
the flour of all, | and leave me but the bran." COR 1.01.146
meal and bran together | he throws without 3.01.320
nature hath meal and bran, contempt and grace. CYM 4.02. 27
BRANCH 15 FR 0.0017 REL FR 13 V 2 P
it is a branch and parcel of mine oath, | a ERR 5.01.106
in every lineament, branch, shape, and form; ADO 5.01. 14
down | that violates the smallest branch herein. LLL 1.01. 21
horns upon his head, for a branch of victory. AYL 4.02. 5 P
with any branch or image of thy state; AWW 2.01.198
affection, which cannot choose but branch now. WT 1.01. 24 P
one flourishing branch of his most royal root, R2 1.02. 18
arms, | not to break peace, or any branch of it, 2H4 4.01. 85
line, | in every branch truly demonstrative; H5 2.04. 89
and, as a branch and member of this royalty, 5.02. 5
not contented that he lopp'd the branch | in 3H6 2.06. 47
from his loins no hopeful branch may spring, 3.02.126
adjudg'd an olive branch and laurel crown, | as 4.06. 34
but his present is | a withered branch, that's PER 2.02. 43
own shape of bud, bird, branch, or berry, | that 5.ch. 6
BRANCH'D 1 FR 0.0001 REL FR 0 V 1 P
officers about me, in my branch'd velvet gown; TN 2.05. 47 P
BRANCHES 16 FR 0.0018 REL FR 12 V 4 P
sisters three, and such branches of learning, is MV 2.02. 63 P
that wear upon your virgin branches yet | your WT 4.04.115
or seven fair branches springing from one root. R2 1.02. 13
some of those branches by the destinies cut; 1.02. 15
superfluous branches | we lop away, that bearing 3.04. 63
that droops his sapless branches to the ground. 1H6 2.05. 12
why grow the branches when the root is gone? R3 2.02. 41
my legs like loaden branches bow to th' earth, H8 4.02. 2
and like a mountain cedar reach his branches 5.04. 53
and made thy body bare | of her two branches, TIT 2.04. 18
and an act hath three branches — it is to act, HAM 5.01. 11 P
from a stately cedar shall be lopp'd branches, CYM 5.04.141 P
abridgment | hath to it circumstantial branches, 5.05.383
from a stately cedar shall be lopp'd branches, 5.05.438 P
and thy lopp'd branches point | thy two sons 5.05.454
the branches of another root are rotted, | and LUC 823
BRANCHLESS 1 FR 0.0001 REL FR 1 V 0 P
i were not yours | than /yours so branchless. ANT 3.04. 24
BRAND 11 FR 0.0012 REL FR 11 V 0 P
and blood | as did the fatal brand althaea burnt 2H6 1.01.234
and suffer it | a brand to th' end a' th' world. COR 3.01.302
if he were putting to my house the brand | that 4.06.115
why brand they us | with base? LR 1.02. 9
that parts us shall bring a brand from heaven, 5.03. 22
brand not my forehead with thy piercing light, LUC 1091
thence comes it that my name receives a brand, SON 111. 5
cupid laid by his brand and fell asleep: 153. 1
but at my mistress' eye love's brand new fired, 153. 9
laid by his side his heart-inflaming brand, 154. 2
this brand she quenched in a cool well by, 154. 9
BRANDED 4 FR 0.0004 REL FR 4 V 0 P
with a golden crown | where should be branded, R3 4.04.141
vainglory) | never yet branded with suspicion? H8 3.01.128
before him, branded | his baseness that ensued? ANT 4.14. 76
man that hates his country, | a branded villain! TNK 2.02.200
BRANDISH 3 FR 0.0003 REL FR 2 V 1 P
and never brandish more revengeful steel | over R2 4.01. 50
hot day, and i brandish any thing but a bottle, 2H4 1.02.211 P
brandish your crystal tresses in the sky, | and 1H6 1.01. 3
BRANDISH'D 4 FR 0.0004 REL FR 4 V 0 P
his brandish'd sword did blind men with his 1H6 1.01. 10
knee, | his bloody sword he brandish'd over me, 4.07. 6
disdaining fortune, with his brandish'd steel, MAC 1.02. 17
brandish'd by man that's of a woman born. 5.07. 13
BRANDON 3 FR 0.0003 REL FR 3 V 0 P
sir william brandon, you shall bear my standard. R3 5.03. 22
my lord of oxford — you, sir william brandon — 5.03. 27
sir robert brakenbury, and sir william brandon. 5.05. 14
BRANDS 8 FR 0.0009 REL FR 7 V 1 P
beard they have sing'd off with brands of fire, ERR 5.01.171
now the wasted brands do glow, | whilst the MND 5.01.375
(these petty brands | that calumny doth use — o WT 2.01. 71
the senseless brands will sympathize | the heavy R2 5.01. 46
and with the brands fire the traitors' houses. JC 3.02.255
come, brands ho, fire-brands! 3.03. 35 P
to my father, brands the harlot | even here, HAM 4.05.119
standing, nicely | depending on their brands. CYM 2.04. 91
BRAS 2 FR 0.0002 REL FR 0 V 2 P
dites-moi l'anglois pour le bras. H5 3.04. 21 P
impossible d'echapper la force de ton bras? 4.04. 17 P
BRASS 19 FR 0.0021 REL FR 19 V 0 P
when it deserves, with characters of brass, | a MM 5.01. 11
can any face of brass hold longer out? LLL 5.02.395
pewter and brass, and all things that belongs SHR 2.01.355
nor brass nor stone nor parchment bears not one, WT 1.02.360
walls about our life | were brass impregnable; R2 3.02.168
the portage of the head | like the brass cannon; H5 3.01. 11
shall witness live in brass of this day's work. 4.03. 97
brass, cur! 4.04. 18
luxurious mountain goat, | offer'st me brass? 4.04. 20
men's evil manners live in brass, their virtues H8 4.02. 45
hand of greece | should hold up high in brass, TRO 1.03. 64
send thy brass voice through all these lazy 1.03.257
and come, i will go get a leaf of brass, | and TIT 4.01.102
nor stony tower, nor walls of beaten brass, JC 1.03. 93
upon the winds command, bind them in brass, PER 3.01. 3
rased, | and brass eternal slave to mortal rage; SON 64. 4
since brass, nor stone, nor earth, nor boundless 65. 1

tyrants' crests and tombs of brass are spent. 107.14
unless my nerves were brass or hammered steel. 120. 4
BRASS'D 1 FR 0.0001 REL FR 1 V 0 P
if damned custom have not brass'd it so | that HAM 3.04. 37
BRASSY 1 FR 0.0001 REL FR 1 V 0 P
from brassy bosoms and rough hearts of flints, MV 4.01. 31
BRAT 8 FR 0.0009 REL FR 7 V 1 P
it on my shoulders, as a beggar wont her brat; ERR 4.04. 38 P
this brat is none of mine, | it is the issue of WT 2.03. 93
for as | thy brat hath been cast out, like to 3.02. 87
strumpet, thy words condemn thy brat and thee. 1H6 5.04. 84
as for the brat of this accursed duke, | whose 3H6 1.03. 4
by heaven, brat, i'll plague ye for that word. 5.05. 27
should all but answer for that peevish brat? R3 1.03.193
did not thy hue bewray whose brat thou art, TIT 5.01. 28
BRAT'S 1 FR 0.0001 REL FR 1 V 0 P
will you adventure | to save this brat's life? WT 2.03.163
BRATS 3 FR 0.0003 REL FR 3 V 0 P
to draw the brats of clarence out of sight, R3 3.05.107
him | against us brats with no less confidence COR 4.06. 93
is no more dependancy | but brats and beggary) CYM 2.03.119
BRAV'D 6 FR 0.0006 REL FR 4 V 2 P
brav'd in mine own house with a skein of thread? SHR 4.03.110
thou hast brav'd many men, brave not me; 4.03.124 P
i will neither be fac'd nor brav'd. 4.03.125 P
how i am brav'd, and must perforce endure it! 1H6 2.04.115
he should have brav'd the east an hour ago. R3 5.03.279
hated by one he loves, brav'd by his brother, JC 4.03. 96
BRAVE *(also prave)*
/BRAVE 1 FR 0.0001 REL FR 1 V 0 P
/greeks /do /pitch | /their /brave /pavilions. TRO pr 15
BRAVE 174 FR 0.0196 REL FR 136 V 38 P
a brave vessel | (who had, no doubt, some noble TMP 1.02. 6
my brave spirit! 1.02.206
believe me, sir, | it carries a brave form. 1.02.412
duke of milan | and his brave son being twain. 1.02.439
you are gentlemen of brave mettle; 2.01.182 P
that's a brave god, and bears celestial liquor. 2.02.117
o brave monster! lead the way. 2.02.188 P
he were a brave monster indeed if they were set 3.02. 11 P
he has brave utensils (for so he calls them) 3.02. 96
is it so brave a lass? 3.02.103
i warrant, | and bring thee forth brave brood. 3.02.105
this will prove a brave kingdom to me, where i 3.02.144 P
o brave new world | that has such people in't! 5.01.183
o setebos, these be brave spirits indeed! 5.01.261
and brave master shoe-tie the great traveller, MM 4.03. 16 P
i'll devise thee brave punishments for him. ADO 5.04.128 P
therefore, brave conquerors — for so you are, LLL 1.01. 8
full merrily | hath this brave /manage, this 5.02.482
speak, brave hector, we are much delighted. 5.02.665 P
o brave touch! MND 3.02. 70
"for the heavens, rouse up a brave mind," says MV 2.02. 12 P
not — o sweet oliver, | o brave oliver, | leave AYL 3.03.100
o, that's a brave man! 3.04. 40 P
he writes brave verses, speaks brave words, 3.04. 40 P
he writes brave verses, speaks brave words, 3.04. 41 P
speaks brave words, swears brave oaths, and 3.04. 41 P
but all's brave that youth mounts and folly 3.04. 45 P
and brave attendants near him when he wakes, SHR in.1. 40
thou hast brav'd many men, brave not me; 4.03.125 P
o, 'tis brave wars! AWW 2.01. 25
this is a brave fellow. WT 4.04.201 P
amity too, of your brave father, whom | (though 5.01.136
before angiers well met, brave austria. JN 2.01. 1
by this brave duke came early to his grave; 2.01. 5
out, dunghill! dar'st thou brave a nobleman? 4.03. 87
a cock'red silken wanton, brave our fields, 5.01. 70
fought | between compulsion and a brave respect! 5.02. 44
there end thy brave, and turn thy face in peace; 5.02.159
brave soldier, pardon me | that any accent 5.06. 13
lord of such hot youth | as when brave gaunt, R2 2.03.100
there, | young harry percy, and brave archibald, 1H4 1.01. 53
by the lord, i'll be a brave judge. 1.02. 64 P
brave world! 3.03.205
thrown | a brave defiance in king henry's teeth, 5.02. 42
if die, brave death, when princes die with us! 5.02. 86
for worms, brave percy. 5.04. 87
the chevalry of england move | to do brave acts. 2H4 2.03. 21
a rascal! to brave me? 2.04.215 P
and his brave fleet | with silken streamers the H5 3.pr. 5
o brave spirit! 4.02. 3
take it, brave york. 4.03.132
unless thou give me crowns, brave crowns; 4.04. 38
chevalier, je pense, le plus brave, vaillant, et 4.04. 56 P
of one (as he thinks) the most brave, valorous, 4.04. 62 P
in which array, brave soldier, doth he lie, 4.06. 7
of france, the brave sir guichard dolphin, 4.08. 95
call'd the brave lord ponton de santrailles, 1H6 1.04. 28
ascend, brave talbot, we will follow thee. 2.01. 28
and now no more ado, brave burgundy, | but 3.02.101
brave burgundy, undoubted hope of france, | stay 3.03. 41
welcome, brave duke, thy friendship makes us 3.03. 86
welcome, brave captain and victorious lord! 3.04. 16
then god take mercy on brave talbot's soul, 4.03. 34
if he be dead, brave talbot, then adieu! 4.04. 45
thou didst force from talbot, my brave boy." 4.06. 24
brave death by speaking, whether he will or no; 4.07. 25
welcome, brave earl, into our territories! 5.03.146
brave peers of england, pillars of the state, 2H6 1.01. 75
brave york, salisbury, and victorious warwick, 1.01. 86
no better sign of a brave mind than a hard hand. 4.02. 20 P
be brave then, for your captain is brave, and 4.02. 64 P
be brave then, for your captain is brave, and 4.02. 64 P
o, brave! 4.07.129 P
what, buckingham and clifford, are ye so brave? 4.08. 21 P
but thou wilt brave me with these saucy terms? 4.10. 36
brave thee? 4.10. 37 P
call hither to the stake my two brave bears, 5.01.144
with thy brave bearing should i be in love, 5.02. 20
brave warriors, clifford and northumberland, 3H6 1.04. 66
field, | that we, the sons of brave plantagenet, 2.01. 35
where your brave father breath'd his latest gasp 2.01.108
all the friends that thou, brave earl of march, 2.01.179
why then it sorts, brave warriors. let's away. 2.01.209
welcome, my lord, to this brave town of york. 2.02. 1
welcome, brave warwick! 3.03. 46
is lewis so brave? 4.01. 96
thanks, brave montgomery, and thanks unto you 4.07. 77
come on, brave soldiers; 4.07. 87
and thou, brave oxford, wondrous well belov'd, 4.08. 17
brave warriors, march amain towards coventry. 4.08. 64
o brave young prince! 5.04. 52
brave followers, yonder stands the thorny wood, 5.04. 67
with them, the two brave bears, warwick and 5.07. 10
hath she forgot already that brave prince, R3 1.02.239
when gallant-springing brave plantagenet, | that 1.04.221
we must be brief when traitors brave the field. 4.03. 57
a bold brave gentleman. H8 4.01. 40
is not that a brave man? TRO 1.02.186 P
there's a brave man, niece. 1.02.200 P
o brave hector! 1.02.201 P
is't not a brave man? 1.02.202 P
o, a brave man! 1.02.203 P
why, this is brave now. 1.02.214 P
brave troilus, the prince of chivalry! 1.02.228 P
o brave troilus! 1.02.231 P
for i presume brave hector would not lose | so 2.02.203
as if his foot were on brave hector's breast 3.03.140
this brave shall oft make thee to hide thy head. 4.04.137
welcome, brave hector, welcome, princes all. 5.01. 70
unarm thee, go, and doubt thou not, brave boy, 5.03. 35
advance, brave titus! COR 1.04. 25
if any think brave death outweighs bad life, 1.06. 71
that's a brave fellow; 2.02. 5 P
you have done a brave deed. 4.02. 38
are you so brave? 4.05. 17 P
wife, his child, | and this brave fellow too: 5.01. 30
that's my brave boy! 5.03. 76
ay, boy, grow ye so brave? TIT 2.01. 45
and strike, brave boys, and take your turns; 2.01.129
lucius and i'll go brave it at the court. 4.01.121
to brave the tribune in his brother's hearing. 4.02. 36
so, brave lords, when we join in league | i am a 4.02.136
league | i am a lamb, but if you brave the moor, 4.02.137
brave slip, sprung from the great andronicus, 5.01. 9
o romeo, romeo, brave mercutio is dead! ROM 3.01.116
romeo, | that slew thy kinsman, brave mercutio. 3.01.145
a brave fellow! TIM 1.02. 55 P
i have but little gold of late, brave timon, 4.03. 91
o, what a time have you chose out, brave caius, JC 2.01.314
brave son, deriv'd from honorable loins! 2.01.322
here wast thou bay'd, brave hart, | here didst 3.01.204
why didst thou send me forth, brave cassius? 5.03. 80
brave titinius! 5.03. 96
hail, brave friend! MAC 1.02. 5
for brave macbeth (well he deserves that name), 1.02. 16
look you, this brave o'erhanging firmament, this HAM 2.02.300 P
this is most brave, | that i, the son of a dear 2.02.582
and demi-natur'd | with the brave beast. 4.07. 88
this is a brave night to cool a courtezan. LR 3.02. 79 P
adieu, brave moor, use desdemona well. OTH 1.03.291
in | as to throw out our eyes for brave othello, 2.01. 38
o brave iago, honest and just, | that hast such 5.01. 31
that he made him | brave me upon the watch, 5.02.326
how goes it with my brave mark antony? ANT 1.05. 38
o that brave caesar! 1.05. 67
say "the brave antony." 1.05. 69
ha, my brave emperor! 2.07.103
no practice had | in the brave squares of war; 3.11. 40
my womb, | together with my brave egyptians all, 3.13.164
that's my brave lord! 3.13.176
'tis a brave army, | and full of purpose. 4.03. 11
not ours to-day, it is | because we brave her. 4.04. 5
o my brave emperor, this is fought indeed! 4.07. 4
have by their brave instruction got upon me | a 4.14. 98
and then, what's brave, what's noble, | let's 4.15. 86
o brave sir! CYM 1.01.166
gods please — to hold here a brave patience, TNK 2.02. 59
body | and fiery mind illustrate a brave father. 2.05. 22
and brave souls in shades, | that have died 3.01. 78
but this — | that thou art brave and noble. 3.01. 81
and there he met with brave gallants of war, 3.05. 61
thou art so brave an enemy | that no man but thy 3.06. 43
urge it home, brave lady. 3.06.233
his body, | and guides his arm to brave things. 4.02.102
shall confound | both these brave knights, and i 5.01.167
ev'ry blow that falls | threats a brave life, 5.03. 4
anon | th' assistants made a brave redemption, 5.03. 82
he speaks now of as brave a knight as e'er | did 5.03.115
thy brave soul seek elysium! 5.04. 95
when their brave hope, bold hector, march'd to LUC 1430
youth like summer brave, age like winter bare. PP 12. 4
and see the brave day sunk in hideous night; SON 12. 2
breed, to brave him when he takes thee hence. 12.14
and wear their brave state out of memory: 15. 8
BRAVED 2 FR 0.0002 REL FR 2 V 0 P
that fac'd and braved me in this matter so? SHR 5.01.121
my nobles leave me, and my state is braved, JN 4.02.243
BRAVELY 39 FR 0.0044 REL FR 29 V 10 P
bravely the figure of this harpy hast thou TMP 3.03. 83
and bravely rigg'd as when | we first put out to 5.01.224
bravely, my diligence. thou shalt be free. 5.01.241
'twas bravely done, if you bethink you of it. ADO 5.01.270
he bravely broach'd his boiling bloody breast; MND 5.01.147
swears brave oaths, and breaks them bravely, AYL 3.04. 42 P
house, | and revel it as bravely as the best, SHR 4.03. 54
thy mind stand to't, boy, steal away bravely. AWW 2.01. 29
therefore away, and leave her bravely; 2.03.299
bravely, coraggio! 2.05. 92
whatsome'er he is, | he's bravely taken here. 3.05. 52
how she came to't bravely confess'd and lamented WT 5.02. 85 P
o, bravely came we off, | when with a volley of JN 5.05. 4
full bravely hast thou flesh'd | thy maiden 1H4 5.04.130
for to serve bravely is to come halting off, you 2H4 2.04. 49 P
come off the breach with his pike bent bravely, 2.04. 50 P
his pike bent bravely, and to surgery bravely; 2.04. 51 P
to venture upon the charg'd chambers bravely — 2.04. 52 P
who came off bravely, who was shot, who H5 3.06. 73 P
the french are bravely in their battles set, 4.03. 69
she takes upon her bravely at first dash. 1H6 1.02. 71
pucelle hath bravely play'd her part in this, 3.03. 88
when i have been dry and bravely marching, it 2H6 4.10. 13 P
march on, join bravely, let us to it pell-mell; R3 5.03.312
excellent place, here we may see most bravely. TRO 1.02.182 P
but our great ajax bravely beat down him." 3.03.213
and bear the palm for having bravely shed | thy COR 5.03.117
i'll be at hand, sir, see you do it bravely. TIT 4.03.113 P
why, now thou diest as bravely as titinius, JC 5.04. 10
fight, | the noble thanes do bravely in the war, MAC 5.07. 26
i will die bravely, like a smug bridegroom. LR 4.06.198
and bravely, horse, for wot'st thou whom thou ANT 1.05. 22
cytherea, | how bravely thou becom'st thy bed! CYM 2.02. 15
a piece of work | so bravely done, so rich, that 2.04. 73
country's cause | fell bravely and were slain, 5.04. 72
how bravely may he bear himself to win her, | if TNK 2.02.254
fight bravely, cousin. 3.06.101
show | bravely about the titles of two kingdoms. 4.02.145
to disseat | his lord that kept it bravely. 5.04. 73
BRAVER 10 FR 0.0011 REL FR 9 V 1 P
and his more braver daughter could control thee, TMP 1.02.440
two, | and wear my dagger with the braver grace, MV 3.04. 65
a braver choice of dauntless spirits | than now JN 2.01. 72
but a braver place | in my heart's love hath no 1H4 4.01. 7
his head, | i do not think a braver gentleman, 5.01. 89
a braver soldier never couched lance, | a 1H6 3.02.134
but is not this braver? 2H6 4.07.130 P
two braver men | ne'er spurr'd their coursers at 3H6 5.07. 8
a nobler man, a braver warrior, | lives not this TIT 1.01. 25
six braver spirits | than these they have TNK 4.02. 73
/BRAVERY 2 FR 0.0002 REL FR 2 V 0 P
/but /sure /the /bravery /of /his /grief /did HAM 5.02. 79
upon malicious /bravery dost thou come | to OTH 1.01.100
BRAVERY 5 FR 0.0005 REL FR 5 V 0 P
where youth, and cost, witless bravery keeps. MM 1.03. 10
that says his bravery is not on my cost, AYL 2.07. 80
and come down | with fearful bravery, thinking JC 5.01. 10
with | the natural bravery of your isle, which CYM 3.01. 18
there shall want no bravery. TNK 4.02.154
BRAVES 4 FR 0.0004 REL FR 4 V 0 P
sirrah, i will not bear these braves of thine. SHR 3.01. 15
now where's the bastard's braves, and charles 1H6 3.02.123
and so in this, to bear me down with braves. TIT 2.01. 30
with that painted hope braves your mightiness; 2.03.126
BRAVEST 4 FR 0.0004 REL FR 4 V 0 P
of the time, and was | discipled of the bravest. AWW 1.02. 28
to wed it, when | the bravest questant shrinks. 2.01. 16
bravest at the last, | she levell'd at our ANT 5.02.335
from this most bravest vessel of the world CYM 4.02.319
BRAVING 4 FR 0.0004 REL FR 4 V 0 P
equal fortune, and continue | a braving war. AWW 1.02. 3
time, | in braving arms against thy sovereign. R2 2.03.112
but in this kind to come, in braving arms, | be 2.03.143
braving compare, disdainfully did sting | his LUC 40
BRAV'RY 2 FR 0.0002 REL FR 2 V 0 P
scarfs and fans, and double change of brav'ry, SHR 4.03. 57
way, | hiding thy brav'ry in their rotten smoke? SON 34. 4
BRAWL* 17 FR 0.0019 REL FR 13 V 4 P
but, like a shrew, you first begin to brawl. ERR 4.01. 51
will you win your love with a french brawl? LLL 3.01. 9 P
and if she chance to nod i'll rail and brawl, SHR 4.01.206
but he is a devil in private brawl. TN 3.04.237 P
and let no quarrel nor no brawl to come | taint 5.01.356
for his divisions, as the times do brawl, | /are 2H4 1.03. 70
this will grow to a brawl anon. 2.04.173 P
(right ill dispos'd, in brawl ridiculous) | the H5 4.pr. 51
this brawl to-day, | grown to this faction in 1H6 2.04.124
i do the wrong, and first begin to brawl. R3 1.03.323
take up a matter of brawl betwixt my uncle and TIT 4.03. 93 P
and if we meet we shall not scape a brawl, | for ROM 3.01. 3
all | the unlucky manage of this fatal brawl: 3.01.143
christian shame, put by this barbarous brawl. OTH 2.03.172
silence those whom this vild brawl distracted. 2.03.256
authority quite silenc'd by your brawl, | and STM II.C 78
strength, | and ban and brawl, and say thee nay; PP 18.32
BRAWL'D 1 FR 0.0001 REL FR 1 V 0 P
their soul-fearing clamors have brawl'd down JN 2.01.383
BRAWLING 7 FR 0.0008 REL FR 5 V 2 P
hath often still'd my brawling discontent. MM 4.01. 9
how meanest thou? brawling in french? LLL 3.01. 10 P
i know she is an irksome brawling scold. SHR 1.02.187
with oaths kept waking, and with brawling fed; 4.03. 10
what a brawling dost thou keep! 1H4 2.02. 6 P
what are you brawling here? 2H4 2.01. 65
why then, o brawling love! ROM 1.01.176
BRAWLS *(also prawls)*
BRAWLS 6 FR 0.0006 REL FR 6 V 0 P
say'st his sports were hind'red by thy brawls: ERR 5.01. 77
but with thy brawls thou hast disturb'd our MND 2.01. 87
upon the brook that brawls along this wood, | to AYL 2.01. 32
none basely slain in brawls. TIT 1.01.353
three civil brawls, bred of an airy word, | by ROM 1.01. 89
blood for your rude brawls doth lie a-bleeding; 3.01.189
BRAWN 3 FR 0.0003 REL FR 2 V 1 P
and that damn'd brawn shall play dame mortimer 1H4 2.04.110 P
and harry monmouth's brawn, the hulk sir john, 2H4 1.01. 19
once more to hew thy target from thy brawn, | or COR 4.05.120
BRAWN-BUTTOCK 1 FR 0.0001 REL FR 0 V 1 P
the quatch-buttock, the brawn-buttock, or any AWW 2.02. 18 P
BRAWNS 2 FR 0.0002 REL FR 2 V 0 P
and in my vambrace put my withered brawns, | and TRO 1.03.297
his martial thigh, | the brawns of hercules; CYM 4.02.311
BRAWNY 2 FR 0.0002 REL FR 2 V 0 P
his arms are brawny, | lin'd with strong sinews; TNK 4.02.126
"his brawny sides, with hairy bristles armed, VEN 625
BRAY 2 FR 0.0002 REL FR 2 V 0 P
with harsh-resounding trumpets' dreadful bray, R2 1.03.135
the kettle-drum and trumpet thus bray out | the HAM 1.04. 11
BRAY'D 1 FR 0.0001 REL FR 1 V 0 P
blaz'd with lights and bray'd with minstrelsy, TIM 2.02.161
BRAYING 1 FR 0.0001 REL FR 1 V 0 P
shall braying trumpets and loud churlish drums, JN 3.01.303
BRAZ'D 1 FR 0.0001 REL FR 0 V 1 P
to acknowledge him, that now i am braz'd to't. LR 1.01. 11 P
BRAZEN 11 FR 0.0012 REL FR 11 V 0 P
lives, | live regist'red upon our brazen tombs, LLL 1.01. 2
bell | did with his iron tongue and brazen mouth JN 3.03. 38
through brazen trumpet send the breath of parley R2 3.03. 33
i had rather hear a brazen canstick turn'd, | or 1H4 3.01.129
loves | are brazen images of canonized saints. 2H6 1.03. 60
he that loos'd them forth their brazen caves, 3.02. 89
yet that thy brazen gates of heaven may ope 3H6 2.03. 40

wert thou environ'd with a brazen wall. 2.04. 4
now crack thy lungs, and split thy brazen pipe. TRO 4.05. 7
and /why such daily /cast of brazen cannon, HAM 1.01. 73
with brazen din blast you the city's ear, | make ANT 4.08. 36
BRAZEN–FAC'D 1 FR 0.0001 REL FR 0 V 1 P
what a brazen–fac'd varlet art thou, to deny LR 2.02. 28 P
BRAZEN–FACE 1 FR 0.0001 REL FR 0 V 1 P
well said, brazen–face! WIV 4.02.135 P
BRAZIER 1 FR 0.0001 REL FR 0 V 1 P
the door, he should be a brazier by his face, H8 5.03. 41 P
BREACH 36 FR 0.0040 REL FR 27 V 9 P
your breach of promise to the porpentine: ERR 4.01. 49
at my hand | as honor (without breach of honor) LLL 2.01.169
him down again, with the breach yourselves made, AWW 1.01.125 P
you took me from the breach of the sea was my TN 2.01. 22 P
as patches set upon a little breach | discredit JN 4.02. 32
to come off the breach with his pike bent 2H4 2.04. 50 P
came pouring like the tide into a breach, | with H5 1.02.149
once more unto the breach, dear friends, once 3.01. 1
to the breach, to the breach! 3.02. 1 P
to the breach, to the breach! 3.02. 2 P
up to the breach, you dogs! 3.02. 20 P
and the trumpet call us to the breach, and we 3.02.109 P
at such and such a sconce, at such a breach, at 3.06. 73 P
but weakly guarded, where the breach was made. 1H6 2.01. 74
through which our policy must make a breach. 3.02. 2
away, | but i in danger for the breach of law. 2H6 2.04. 66
a breach that craves a quick expedient stop! 3.01.288
and where this breach now in our fortunes made 5.02. 82
be put | to no apparent likelihood of breach, R3 2.02.136
of this peace, aboded | the sudden breach on't. H8 1.01. 94
our breach of duty this way | is business of 2.02. 68
however, yet there is no great breach; 4.01.106
and make distinct the very breach whereout TRO 4.05.245
his gash'd stabs look'd like a breach in nature MAC 2.03.113
more honor'd in the breach than the observance. HAM 1.04. 16
cure this great breach in his abused nature, LR 4.07. 14
scapes i' th' imminent deadly breach, | of being OTH 1.03.136
between him and my lord | an unkind breach; 4.01.225
faith be not tainted with the breach of hers. CYM 3.04. 27 P
the breach of custom | is breach of all. 4.02. 10
the breach of custom | is breach of all. 4.02. 11
makes more gashes where no breach should be. VEN 1066
and in the breach appears | green–dropping sap, 1175
to make the breach and enter this sweet city. LUC 469
decay, | the impious breach of holy wedlock vow; 809
but why of two oaths' breach do i accuse thee, SON 152. 5
/BREACHES 1 FR 0.0001 REL FR 0 V 1 P
/dissipation /of /cohorts, /nuptial /breaches, LR 1.02.148 P
BREACHES 1 FR 0.0001 REL FR 1 V 0 P
of breaches, ambuscadoes, spanish blades, | of ROM 1.04. 84
BREAD *(also pread)*
BREAD 26 FR 0.0029 REL FR 16 V 10 P
i detest, an honest maid as ever broke bread. WIV 1.04.151 P
i love not the humor of bread and cheese /and 2.01.136 P
that his appetite | is more to bread than stone: MM 1.03. 53
beggar, though she smelt brown bread and garlic. 3.02.184 P
sir, by my troth he is, as ever broke bread; ADO 3.05. 39 P
that work for bread upon athenian stalls, | were MND 3.02. 10
as full of sanctity as the touch of holy bread. AYL 3.04. 14 P
clouds, | eating the bitter bread of banishment, R2 3.01. 21
i live with bread like you, feel want, | taste 3.02.175
that jade hath eat bread from my royal hand, 5.05. 85
item, bread ... ob., 1H4 2.04.539 P
one half–pennyworth of bread to this intolerable 2.04.541 P
a good pantler, 'a would 'a' chipp'd bread well. 2H4 2.04.238 P
him to rest, cramm'd with distressful bread, H5 4.01.270
good morrow, gallants, want ye corn for bread? 1H6 3.02. 41
the gods know i speak this in hunger for bread, COR 1.01. 24 P
god's bread, it makes me mad! ROM 3.05.176
that sits next him, now parts bread with him, TIM 1.02. 47 P
'a took my father grossly, full of bread, | with HAM 3.03. 80
ere i taste bread, thou art in nothing less LR 5.03. 94
her desires | buys herself bread and /clothes. OTH 4.01. 95
would now be glad of bread and beg for it; PER 1.04. 41
are stor'd with corn to make your needy bread, 1.04. 95
and his army full | of bread and sloth. TNK 1.01.159
she swore by wine and bread she would not break. 3.05. 47
friend, you must eat no white bread; 3.05. 80
BREAD–CHIPPER 1 FR 0.0001 REL FR 0 V 1 P
me, and call me pantler and bread–chipper, and i 2H4 2.04.315 P
BREADTH 9 FR 0.0010 REL FR 4 V 5 P
and i profess requital to a hair's breadth, not WIV 4.02. 3 P
then she bears some breadth? ERR 3.02.112 P
measure his woe the length and breadth of mine, ADO 5.01. 11
if there be breadth enough in the world, i will AWW 3.02. 23 P
blood which ow'd the breadth of all this isle, JN 4.02. 99
and yet the spacious breadth of this division TRO 5.02.150
/too, than the length and breadth of a pair of HAM 5.01.110 P
itself, and it is as broad as it hath breadth. ANT 2.07. 43 P
he will repent the breadth of his great voyage, PER 4.01. 36
/BREAK 2 FR 0.0002 REL FR 2 V 0 P
that life looks through /and /will /break /out. 2H4 4.04.120
shipwracking storms and direful thunders /break, MAC 1.02. 26
BREAK 273 FR 0.0308 REL FR 231 V 42 P
i had rather crack my sinews, break my back, TMP 3.01. 26
but | if thou dost break her virgin–knot before 4.01. 15
my charms i'll break, their senses i'll restore, 5.01. 31
this airy charm is for, i'll break my staff, 5.01. 54
now will we break with him. TGV 1.03. 44
now can i break my fast, dine, sup, and sleep, 2.04.141
i am to break with thee of some affairs | that 3.01. 59
i'll be so bold to break the seal for once. 3.01.139
which he will break | as easily as i do tear his 4.04.130
she will not fail, for lovers break not hours, 5.01. 4
they will break their hearts but they will WIV 2.02.308 P
and i would not break with her for more money 3.02. 55 P
break their talk, mistress quickly, my kinsman 3.04. 22 P
forsworn, | and those eyes, the break of day, MM 4.01. 3
break off thy song, and haste thee quick away. 4.01. 7
her brother's ghost his paved bed would break, 5.01.435
nay, forward, old man, do not break off so, ERR 1.01. 96
or i shall break that merry sconce of yours 1.02. 79
back, slave, or i will break thy pate across. 2.01. 78
and break it with a deep–divorcing vow? 2.02.138
ay, and let none enter, lest i break your pate. 2.02.218
go fetch me something: i'll break ope the gate. 3.01. 73
break any breaking here, and i'll break your 3.01. 74
breaking here, and i'll break your knave's pate. 3.01. 74
a man may break a word with /you, sir, and words 3.01. 75
ay, and break it in your face, so he break it 3.01. 76
it in your face, so he break it not behind. 3.01. 76
well, i'll break in: go borrow me a crow. 3.01. 80
if by strong hand you offer to break in | now in 3.01. 98
fear me not, man, i will not break away; 4.04. 1
did he break out into tears? ADO 1.01. 24 P
and i will break with her, and with her father, 1.01.309
then after to her father will i break, | and the 1.01.326
by the top, and instantly break with you of it. 1.02. 15 P
do, he'll but break a comparison or two on me, 2.01.146 P
withdrawn her father to break with him about it. 2.01.156 P
if he break the peace, he ought to enter into a 2.03.194 P
for my life, to break with him about beatrice. 3.02. 74 P
you break jests as braggards do their blades, 5.01.187 P
study to break it and not break my troth. LLL 1.01. 66
study to break it and not break my troth. 1.01. 66
this article, my liege, yourself must break, 1.01.133
if i break faith, this word shall speak for me: 1.01.153
why, will shall break it, will, and nothing else 2.01.100
keep that oath, my lord, | and sin to break it. 2.01.106
boyet, you can carve, | break up this capon. 4.01. 56
break the neck of the wax, and every one give 4.01. 59
you would for paradise break faith and troth, 4.03.141
hold it sin | to break the vow i am engaged in. 4.03.176
one word more, my maids, break off, break off. 5.02.262
one word more, my maids, break off, break off. 5.02.262
the virtue of your eye must break my oath. 5.02.348
despise me when i break this oath of mine. 5.02.441
and shivering shocks | shall break the locks MND 1.02. 33
and make him with fair /aegles break his faith, 2.01. 79
he'll | seem to break loose — take on as you 3.02.258
here will i rest me till the break of day. 3.02.446
have a care the honey–bag break not, i would be 4.01. 15 P
now, until the break of day, | through this 5.01.401
meet me all by break of day. 5.01.422
ripe wants of my friend, | i'll break a custom. MV 1.03. 64
who, if he break, thou mayst with better face 1.03.136
if he should break his day, what should i gain 1.03.163
and it shall please you to break up this, it 2.04. 10 P
to venice that swear he cannot choose but break. 3.01.115 P
is | as are those dulcet sounds in break of day 3.02. 51
my mistress will before the break of day | be 5.01. 29
i never more will break an oath with thee. 5.01.248
lord | will never more break faith advisedly. 5.01.253
as lief thou didst break his neck as his finger. AYL 1.01.146 P
i will, and when i break that oath, let me turn 1.02. 22 P
'gainst the lady | will suddenly break forth. 1.02.283
mine own wit till i break my shins against it. 2.04. 59 P
break an hour's promise in love! 4.01. 44 P
and break but a part of the thousand part of a 4.01. 46 P
dangerous, if you break one jot of your promise, 4.01.190 P
you break into some merry passion | and so SHR in.1. 97
and if you break the ice and do this /feat, 1.02.265
why then thou canst not break her to the lute? 2.01.147
or else my heart concealing it will break, | and 4.03. 78
to break a jest | upon the company you overtake? 4.05. 72
if i break time, or flinch in property | of what AWW 2.01.187
i shall not break your bidding, good my lord. 2.05. 88
that if one break, the other will hold; TN 1.05. 24 P
or, if both break, your gaskins fall. 1.05. 25 P
and then to break promise with him and make a 2.03.128 P
patience, or we break the sinews of our plot! 2.05. 75 P
you have not dar'd to break the holy seal | nor WT 3.02.129
break up the seals, and read. 3.02.131
lace, lest my heart, cracking it, | break too! 3.02.174
the fury spent, anon | did this break from her: 3.03. 27
mean mischief and break a foul gap into the 4.04.197 P
will i break my oath | to this my fair belov'd. 4.04.491
he shall feel, will break the back of man, the 4.04.770 P
reason | as my antigonus to break his grave 5.01. 42
women and fools, break off your conference. JN 2.01.150
since kings break faith upon commodity, | gain, 2.01.597
no bargains break that are not this day made: 3.01. 93
to break into this dangerous argument: 4.02. 54
his passion is so ripe, it needs must break. 4.02. 79
this will break out | to all our sorrows, and 4.02.101
to break within the bloody house of life, | and 4.02.210
shame had struck me dumb, made me break off, 4.02.235
if i get down, and do not break my limbs, | i'll 4.03. 6
of yours | behold another day break in the east; 5.04. 32
that they may break his foaming courser's back, R2 1.02. 51
heart is great, but it must break with silence, 2.01.228
for i am loath to break our country's laws. 2.03.169
they break their faith to god as well as us. 3.02.101
gathering head | shall break into corruption. 5.01. 59
when weeping made you break the story off, | of 5.02. 2
open the door, or i will break it open. 5.03. 45
and break the neck | of that proud man that did 5.05. 88
fool | art thou to break into this woman's mood, 1H4 1.03.237
as good deed as drink to break the pate on thee, 2.01. 29 P
the squier further afoot, i shall break my wind. 2.02. 13 P
in faith, i'll break thy little finger, harry, 2.03. 87
break with your wives of your departure hence. 3.01.142
ere break the smallest parcel of this vow. 3.02.159
nay, and i do, i pray god my girdle break. 3.03.151 P
for you my staff of office did i break | in 5.01. 34
gathering head, | shall break into corruption": 2H4 3.01. 77
i see him break scoggin's head at the court–gate 3.02. 30 P
not to break peace, or any branch of it, | but 4.01. 85
will you thus break your faith? 4.02.112
one time or other break some gallows' back. 4.03. 29
pluck down my officers, break my decrees, | for 4.05.117
an ill venture it come unluckily home, i break, ep 12 P
bend it to our awe, | or break it all to pieces. H5 1.02.225
with their howls confus'd | do break the clouds, 3.03. 40
break up their drowsy grave, and newly move 4.01. 22
break out into a second course of mischief, 4.03.106
use till urg'd, nor never break for urging. 5.02.145 P
break thy mind to me in broken english — wilt 5.02.245 P
break up the gates, i'll be your warrantize. 1H6 1.03. 13
thus contumeliously should break the peace! 1.03. 58
but we shall meet, and break our minds at large. 1.03. 81
how, or which way, should they first break in? 2.01. 71
the day begins to break, and night is fled, 2.02. 1
love, | and will at last break out into a flame: 3.01.190
break a lance, | and run a–tilt at death within 3.02. 50
i break my warlike word; 4.03. 31
drive you to break your necks or hang yourselves 5.04. 91
break thou in pieces and consume to ashes, 5.04. 92
although you break it when your pleasure serves. 5.04.164
spirits walk, and ghosts break up their graves, 2H6 1.04. 19
my lord, break we off; 2.02. 77
and so break off, the day is almost spent; 3.01.325
answer from the king, or we will all break in! 3.02.278
and even now my burthen'd heart would break, 3.02.320
break open the jails and let out the prisoners. 4.03. 15 P
and then break into his son–in–law's house, sir 4.07.110 P
let them break your backs with burthens, take 4.08. 29 P
is't not enough to break into my garden, | and 4.10. 33
hath made her break out into terms of rage! 3H6 1.01.265
i would break a thousand oaths to reign one year 1.02. 17
ah, would she break from hence, that this my 2.01. 75
break off the parley, for scarce i can refrain 2.02.110
with tears, and break o'ercharg'd with grief. 2.05. 78
but did you never swear and break an oath? 3.01. 72
but do not break your oaths, for of that sin 3.01. 90
while we bethink a means to break it off. 3.03. 39
heave it shall some weight, or break my back: 5.07. 24
to hurl upon their heads that break his law. R3 1.04.200
to the name of god | didst break that vow, and 1.04.206
the new–heal'd wound of malice should break out, 2.02.125
age, | you break not sanctuary in seizing him. 3.01. 47
you break no privilege nor charter there. 3.01. 54
be thou so too, and so break off the talk, | and 3.01.177
on it still shall i till heart–strings break. 4.04.365
if thou didst fear to break an oath with him, 4.04.378
if thou hadst fear'd to break an oath by him, 4.04.381
and like a glass | did break i' th' wrenching. H8 1.01.167
king's course, | and break the foresaid peace. 1.01.190
break up the court! 2.04.241
should the approach of this wild river break, 3.02.198
go break among the press, and find a way out 5.03. 84
fool slides o'er the ice that you should break. TRO 3.03.215
for if hector break not his neck i' th' combat, 3.03.258 P
my clear voice with sobs and break my heart 4.02.108
i will not break it. 5.01. 42
you will break out. 5.02. 51
i must not break my faith. 5.03. 71
wilt believe me, but a plague break thy neck — 5.04. 32 P
to break the heart of generosity | and make bold COR 1.01.211
we'll break our walls | rather than they shall 1.04. 16
in time | break ope the locks a' th' senate, and 3.01.138
lest parties (as he is belov'd) break out, | and 3.01.313
there which looks | with us to break his neck. 3.03. 30
of a doit, break out | to bitterest enmity; 4.04. 17
it cannot be | the volsces dare break with us. 4.06. 49
left undone | that which shall break his neck, 4.07. 25
all bond and privilege of nature, break! 5.03. 25
and, he returning to break our necks, they 5.04. 33 P
weep, | or, if not so, thy noble heart to break: TIT 3.01. 60
and do not break into these deep extremes. 3.01.215
make poor men's cattle break their necks, | set 5.01.132
rome's emperor, and nephew, break the parle, 5.03. 19
and break my utt'rance, even in the time | when 5.03. 91
from ancient grudge break to new mutiny, | where ROM pr 3
o, break, my heart, poor bankrout, break at once 3.02. 57
break, my heart, poor bankrout, break at once! 3.02. 57
or by the break of day /disguis'd from hence. 3.03.168
then be not poor, but break it, and take this. 5.01. 74
but must not break my back to heal his finger. TIM 2.01. 24
yellow slave | will knit and break religions, 4.03. 35
within this mile break forth a hundred springs; 4.03.418
to athens go, | break open shops; 4.03.447
and pursy insolence shall break his wind | with 5.04. 12
here lies the east; doth not the day break here? JC 2.01.101
if these be motives weak, break off betimes, 2.01.116
if he do break the smallest particle | of any 2.01.139
let us not break with him, | for he will never 2.01.150
say, | "break up the senate till another time, 2.02. 98
fret till your proud heart break; 4.03. 42
that made you break this enterprise to me? MAC 1.07. 48
the o'er–fraught heart, and bids it break. 4.03.210
promise to our ear, | and break it to our hope. 5.08. 22
peace, break thee off! HAM 1.01. 40
break we our watch up, and, by my advice, | let 1.01.168
but break my heart, for i must hold my tongue. 1.02.159
break all the spokes and /fellies from her wheel 2.02.495
speak, | but what we do determine, oft we break. 3.02.187
if she should break it now! 3.02.224 P
basket creep, | and break your own neck down. 3.04.196
break not your sleeps for that. 4.07. 30
thou hast sought to make us break our /vow — LR 1.01.168
these hot tears, which break from me perforce, 1.04.298
a hill, lest it break thy neck with following; 2.04. 73 P
shall break into a hundred thousand flaws | or 2.04.285
wilt break my heart? 3.04. 4
i had rather break mine own. 3.04. 5
break, heart, i prithee break! 5.03.313
break, heart, i prithee break! 5.03.313
or else break out in peevish jealousies, OTH 4.03. 89
almost persuade | justice to break her sword! 5.02. 17
these strong egyptian fetters i must break, | or ANT 1.02.116
i must from this enchanting queen break off; 1.02.128
i shall break | the cause of our expedience to 1.02.177
vows, | which break themselves in swearing! 1.03. 31
if swift thought break it not, a swifter mean 4.06. 34
being dried with grief, will break to powder, 4.09. 17
then in the midst a tearing groan did break 4.14. 31
that the false huswife fortune break her wheel, 4.15. 44
o, break! o, break! 5.02.310
o, break! o, break! 5.02.310
to break it with a fearful dream of him, | and CYM 3.04. 43
might break out and swear | he'ld fetch us in; 4.02.140
who shuns not to break one will crack /them both PER 1.02.121
and on her virgin honor will not break it. 2.05. 12
by break of day, if the wind cease. 3.01. 76 P
let them break and fall | off me with that TNK 1.02. 73
i' th' deliverance, will break from one of them; 2.01. 42 P
her bright eyes break each morning 'gainst thy 2.03. 9
but your silence | should break out, though i' 3.01. 62
base cousin, | dar'st thou break first? 3.03. 45

and the boar, | break comely out before him; 3.05. 19
she swore by wine and bread she would not break. 3.05. 47
dreadful clap of thunder | break from the troop. 3.06. 84
when neither curb would crack, girth break, nor 5.04. 74
and now her sobs do her intendments break. VEN 222
they drown their eyes or break their hearts. LUC 1239
"on what occasion break | those tears from thee, 1270
myself was stirring ere the break of day, | and 1280
ranks began | to break upon the galled shore, 1440
here with a sigh, as if her heart would break, 1716
what fool is not so wise | to break an oath, to PP 3.14
(like to the lark at break of day arising | from SON 29.11
not enough that through the cloud thou break, 34. 5
where thou art forc'd to break a twofold truth: 41.12
breach do i accuse thee, | when i break twenty? 152. 6
true to bondage, would not break from thence, LC 34
feeling it break, with bleeding groans they pine 275
BREAKER 2 FR 0.0002 REL FR 1 V 1 P
for he was never yet a breaker of proverbs. 1H4 1.02.118 P
cardinal, i'll be no breaker of the law; 1H6 1.03. 80
BREAKERS 1 FR 0.0001 REL FR 1 V 0 P
or kings be breakers of their own behests? LUC 852
BREAKETH 3 FR 0.0003 REL FR 3 V 0 P
breaketh his rein, and to her straight goes he. VEN 264
with this he breaketh from the sweet embrace 811
she wildly breaketh from their strict embrace, 874
BREAKFAST 16 FR 0.0018 REL FR 6 V 10 P
not a relation for a breakfast, nor | befitting TMP 5.01.164
well, that fault may be mended with a breakfast. TGV 3.01.326 P
i would have been a breakfast to the beast 5.04. 34
you to-morrow morning to my house to breakfast; WIV 3.03.230 P
some six or seven dozen of scots at a breakfast, 1H4 2.04.103 P
go make ready breakfast; 3.03.171 P
hostess, my breakfast, come! 3.03.205
i will bestow a breakfast to make you friends, H5 2.01. 11 P
that dare eat his breakfast on the lip of a lion 3.07.146 P
a sorry breakfast for my lord protector. 2H6 1.04. 75
that call'd your grace | to breakfast once, R3 4.04.177
and then to breakfast with | what appetite you H8 3.02.202
had rather be at a breakfast of enemies than a TIM 1.02. 76 P
thou liv'dst but as a breakfast to the wolf; 4.03.333 P
eight wild-boars roasted whole at a breakfast, ANT 2.02.179 P
is not worth a breakfast in the cheapest country PER 4.06.123 P
BREAKING 29 FR 0.0032 REL FR 24 V 5 P
in breaking faith with julia whom i lov'd; TGV 4.02. 11
fall | a drop of water in the breaking gulf, ERR 2.02.126
break any breaking here, and i'll break your 3.01. 74
it seems thou want'st breaking, out upon thee, 3.01. 77
such eruptions and sudden breaking out of mirth, LLL 5.01.115 P
so much i hate a breaking cause to be | of 5.02.355
that ever i heard breaking of ribs was sport for AYL 1.02.138 P
the turn, or the breaking of my spanish sword. AWW 4.01. 47 P
in breaking 'em he is stronger than hercules. 4.03.252 P
the army breaking, | my husband hies him home, 4.04. 11
sigh (a note infallible | of breaking honesty)? WT 1.02.288
me | that any accent breaking from thy tongue JN 5.06. 14
after your late tossing on the breaking seas? R2 3.02. 3
at | by breaking through the foul and ugly mists 1H4 1.02.202
limb united, | grow stronger for the breaking. 2H4 4.01.221
to keep the horsemen off from breaking in. 1H6 1.01.119
our main battle's front and, breaking in, | were 3H6 1.01. 8
heart, | why sigh'st thou without breaking?" TRO 4.04. 17
is almost mature for the violent breaking out. COR 4.03. 26 P
breaking his oath and resolution like | a twist 5.06. 94
then this breaking of his | has been but a try TIM 5.01. 8
oft breaking down the pales and forts of reason, HAM 1.04. 28
breaking forth | in rank and not-to-be-endur'd LR 1.04.203
your letters did withhold our breaking forth, ANT 3.06. 79
the breaking of so great a thing should make | a 5.01. 14
you perish instantly | for breaking prison, and TNK 3.06.114
temper | that breaking out in hideous violence STM II.C 132
tearing of papers, breaking rings a-twain, LC 6
big discontent so breaking their contents. 56
BREAK-NECK 1 FR 0.0001 REL FR 1 V 0 P
to do't, or no, is certain | to me a break-neck. WT 1.02.363
BREAK-PROMISE 1 FR 0.0001 REL FR 0 V 1 P
think you the most pathetical break-promise, and AYL 4.01.192 P
BREAKS 36 FR 0.0040 REL FR 29 V 7 P
but, too unruly deer, he breaks the pale, | and ERR 2.01.100
any man to answer it that breaks his band; 4.03. 31 P
and he that breaks them in the least degree LLL 1.01.156
for virtue's office never breaks men's troth. 5.02.350
swears brave oaths, and breaks them bravely, AYL 3.04. 42 P
one side, breaks his staff like a noble goose. 3.04. 44 P
according as marriage binds and blood breaks. 5.04. 57 P
and as the sun breaks through the darkest clouds SHR 4.03.173
that broker that still breaks the pate of faith, JN 2.01.568
and when it breaks, i fear will issue thence 4.02. 80
and let him never see joy that breaks that oath! R2 2.03.151
diseased nature oftentimes breaks forth | in 1H4 3.01. 26
breaks like a fire | out of his keeper's arms, 2H4 1.01.142
by the means whereof 'a breaks words, and keeps H5 3.02. 35 P
is not that the morning which breaks yonder? 4.01. 86 P
that he that breaks a stick of gloucester's 2H6 1.02. 33
sorrow breaks seasons and reposing hours, R3 1.04. 76
on, | and flaky darkness breaks within the east. 5.03. 86
yea, such which breaks | the sides of loyalty, H8 1.02. 27
bed the livelong day | breaks scurril jests, TRO 1.03.148
with his fist, as a sailor breaks a biscuit. 2.01. 40 P
soft, what light through yonder window breaks? ROM 2.02. 2
who calls me villain, breaks my pate across, HAM 2.02.572
that inward breaks, and shows no cause without 4.04. 28
it is, | and my heart breaks at it. LR 4.06.142
and the strong lance of justice hurtless breaks; 4.06.166
and by and by | breaks out to savage madness. OTH 4.01. 55
wherefore breaks that sigh | from th' inward of CYM 3.04. 5
hidden sun, | breaks through his baser garments. TNK 2.05. 24
and now his woven girths he breaks asunder; VEN 266
the client breaks, as desperate in his suit. 336
or as the berry breaks before it staineth, | or 460
yet love breaks through, and picks them all at 576
through the flood-gates breaks the silver rain, 959
she much amaz'd breaks ope her lock'd-up eyes, LUC 446
and midst the sentence so her accent breaks, 566
BREAK'ST 2 FR 0.0002 REL FR 2 V 0 P
if thou dost nod, thou break'st thy instrument, JC 4.03.271
that both mak'st and break'st | the stony girths TNK 5.01. 55
BREAK'T 1 FR 0.0001 REL FR 0 V 1 P
th' combat, he'll break't himself in vainglory. TRO 3.03.259 P
BREAK-VOW 1 FR 0.0001 REL FR 1 V 0 P
that daily break-vow, he that wins of all, | of JN 2.01.569
/BREAST 4 FR 0.0004 REL FR 4 V 0 P
thoughts | in any /breast of strong authority, JN 2.01.113
/father /from /the /breast /of /bullingbrook, 2H4 4.01.122
/is /left /to /tyrannize /upon /my /breast, TIT 3.02. 8
swords out, and tilting one at other's /breast, OTH 2.03.183
BREAST 114 FR 0.0128 REL FR 113 V 1 P
o thou that dost inhabit in my breast, | leave TGV 5.04. 7
think, if my breast had not been made of faith, ERR 3.02.145
a yielding 'gainst some reason in my breast, LLL 2.01.151
all about the breast! 4.03.171
a gait, a state, a brow, a breast, a waist, | a 4.03.183
kisses the base ground with obedient breast? 4.03.221
hence /hermit then — my heart is in thy breast. 5.02.816
to pluck this crawling serpent from my breast! MND 2.02.146
he bravely broach'd his boiling bloody breast; 5.01.147
trusty sword, | come, blade, my breast imbrue! 5.01.344
ay, his breast, | so says the bond, doth it not, MV 4.01.252
and you must cut this flesh from off his breast, 4.01.302
whoever charges on his forward breast, | i am AWW 3.02.113
by my troth, the fool has an excellent breast. TN 2.03. 20 P
(starr'd most unluckily) is from my breast WT 3.02. 99
what means that hand upon that breast of thine? JN 3.01. 21
/doth show the mood of a much troubled breast, 4.02. 73
chest | is a bold spirit in a loyal breast. R2 1.01.181
that it may enter butcher mowbray's breast! 1.02. 48
truth hath a quiet breast. 1.03. 96
i may longest keep | thy sorrow in my breast. 3.04. 96
i have a thousand spirits in one breast, | to 4.01. 58
words come from his mouth, ours from our breast; 5.03.102
you conjure from the breast of civil peace 1H4 4.03. 43
reigns solely in the breast of every man. H5 2.pr. 4
my breast i'll burst with straining of my 1H6 1.05. 10
well, i will lock his counsel in my breast, 2.05.118
and that engenders thunder in his breast, | and 3.01. 39
undaunted spirit in a dying breast! 3.02. 99
which thou thyself hast given her woeful breast. 3.03. 51
mother gave thee, when thou suck'dst her breast, 5.04. 28
i feel such sharp dissension in my breast, 5.05. 84
wren, | by crying comfort from a hollow breast, 2H6 3.02. 43
here may his head lie on my throbbing breast; 4.04. 5
this breast from harboring foul deceitful 4.07.103
is kindling coals that fires all my breast, 3H6 2.01. 83
both tugging to be victors, breast to breast, 2.05. 11
both tugging to be victors, breast to breast, 2.05. 11
my sighing breast shall be thy funeral bell; 2.05.117
i stabb'd your fathers' bosoms, split my breast. 2.06. 30
her sighs will make a batt'ry in his breast, 3.01. 37
words, | infuse his breast with magnanimity, 5.04. 41
my breast can better brook thy dagger's point 5.06. 27
advance thy halberd higher than my breast, | or, R3 1.02. 40
which thou once didst bend against her breast, 1.02. 95
if thou please to hide in this true breast, 1.02.175
even so thy breast encloseth my poor heart: 1.02.204
why do /you weep so oft, and beat your breast, 2.02. 3
god bless thee, and put meekness in thy breast, 2.02.107
another spread on 's breast, mounting his eyes, H8 1.02.205
and made to tremble | the region of my breast, 2.04.185
strikes his breast hard, and anon he casts | his 3.02.117
take notice, lords, he has a loyal breast, | for 3.02.200
boats dare sail | upon her /patient breast, TRO 1.03. 36
as if his foot were on brave hector's breast 3.03.140
never stood | to ease his breast with panting. COR 2.02.122
what his breast forges, that his tongue must 3.01.257
drawn tuns of blood out of thy country's breast, 4.05. 99
sung thee asleep, his loving breast thy pillow; TIT 5.03.163
griefs of mine own lie heavy in my breast, ROM 1.01.186
of a despised life clos'd in my breast | by some 1.04.110
come to thy heart as that within my breast! 2.02.124
dwell upon thine eyes, peace in thy breast! 2.02.186
with piercing steel at bold mercutio's breast, 3.01.159
here on his manly breast. 3.02. 53
whose womb unmeasurable and infinite breast TIM 4.03.178
master, in whose breast | doubt and suspect, 4.03.511
by means whereof this breast of mine hath buried JC 1.02. 49
lightning seem'd to open | the breast of heaven, 1.03. 51
there is my dagger, | and here my naked breast; 4.03.101
o my breast, | thy hope ends here! MAC 4.03.113
is it a fee-grief | due to some single breast? 4.03.197
such love must needs be treason in my breast. HAM 3.02.178
who has that breast so pure | /but /some OTH 3.03.138
man but a rush against othello's breast, | and 5.02.270
fights hath burst | the buckles on his breast, ANT 1.01. 8
dost thou not see my baby at my breast, | that 5.02.309
here, on her breast, | there is a vent of blood, 5.02.348
on her left breast | a mole cinque-spotted, like CYM 2.02. 37
seek | for further satisfying, under her breast 2.04.134
this tablet lay upon his breast, wherein | our 5.04.109
whose naked breast | stepp'd before targes of 5.05. 4
that have inflam'd desire in my breast | to PER 1.01. 20
joy and all comfort in your sacred breast! 1.02. 34
made louder by the o'erfed breast | of this most 3.ch. 3
in | the circuit of my breast any gross stuff TNK 3.01. 46
like a nightingale, | to put my breast against! 3.04. 26
broad breast, full eye, small head, and nostril VEN 296
enfranchising his mouth, his back, his breast. 396
he carries thence incaged in his breast. 582
like an earthquake, shakes thee on my breast. 648
run | into the quiet closure of my breast, | and 782
those fair arms which bound him to her breast, 812
from whose silver breast | the sun ariseth in 855
good | to wither in my breast as in his blood. 1182
"here was thy father's bed, here in my breast; 1183
on, to make his stand | on her bare breast, the LUC 439
his hand, that yet remains upon her breast 463
she wakes her heart by beating on her breast, 759
that patience is quite beaten from her breast; 1563
even here she sheathed in her harmless breast 1723
and bubbling from her breast, it doth divide 1737
this said, he strook his hand upon his breast, 1842
forlorn, | lean'd her breast up-till a thorn, PP 20.10
and the turtle's loyal breast | to eternity doth PHT 57
which in thy breast doth live, as thine in me: SON 22. 7
and dumb presagers of my speaking breast, | who 23.10
and thine for me | are windows to my breast, 24.11
art, | within the gentle closure of my breast, 48.11
as from my soul, which in thy breast doth lie: 109. 4
even to thy pure and most most loving breast. 110.14
the boy for trial needs would touch my breast; 153.10
as compound love to physic your cold breast. LC 259
what breast so cold that is not warmed here? 292
BREAST-DEEP 1 FR 0.0001 REL FR 1 V 0 P
set him breast-deep in earth and famish him, TIT 5.03.179
BREASTED 1 FR 0.0001 REL FR 1 V 0 P
and breasted | the surge most swoll'n that met TMP 2.01.117
BREASTING 1 FR 0.0001 REL FR 1 V 0 P
the furrowed sea, | breasting the lofty surge. H5 3.pr. 13
BREASTPLATE 1 FR 0.0001 REL FR 1 V 0 P
what stronger breastplate than a heart untainted 2H6 3.02.232
BREASTS 14 FR 0.0015 REL FR 14 V 0 P
and penetrate the breasts | of ever-angry bears. TMP 1.02.288
such men | whose heads stood in their breasts? 3.03. 47
is pale cold cowardice in noble breasts. R2 1.02. 34
and doth beget new courage in our breasts. 1H6 3.03. 87
who, cherish'd in your breasts, will sting your 2H6 3.01.344
may plant courage in their quailing breasts, 3H6 2.03. 54
the breasts of hecuba, | when she did suckle COR 1.03. 40
my remission lies | in volscian breasts. 5.02. 85
come to my woman's breasts, | and take my milk MAC 1.05. 47
that i would pluck | and put between my breasts TNK 1.03. 67
her breasts like ivory globes circled with blue, LUC 407
or tyrant folly lurk in gentle breasts? 851
within your hollow swelling feathered breasts, 1122
if snow be white, why then her breasts are dun; SON 130. 3
/BREATH 2 FR 0.0002 REL FR 2 V 0 P
/with /mine /own /breath /release /all /duteous R2 4.01.210
no warmth, no /breath shall testify thou livest; ROM 4.01. 98
BREATH 240 FR 0.0271 REL FR 209 V 31 P
side-stitches, that shall pen thy breath up; TMP 1.02.326
of truth, their words | are natural breath; 5.01.157
gentle breath of yours my sails | must fill, or ep 11
here's my mother's breath up and down. TGV 2.03. 29 P
be /kiss'd fasting, in respect of her breath." 3.01.324 P
that makes amends for her sour breath. 3.01.328 P
a breath thou art, | servile to all the skyey MM 3.01. 8
a blasting and a scandalous breath to fall | on 5.01.122
comes light from heaven, and words from breath, 5.01.225
they'll suck our breath, or pinch us black and ERR 2.02.192
when the sweet breath of flattery conquers 3.02. 28
but i felt it hot in her breath. 3.02.132 P
their rich aspect to the hot breath of spain, 3.02.136 P
fie, now you run this humor out of breath. 4.01. 57
how hast thou lost thy breath? 4.02. 30
if her breath were as terrible as her ADO 2.01.248 P
than she will bate one breath of her accustom'd 2.03.176 P
thou the slave that with thy breath hast kill'd 5.01.263
wind, and foul wind is but foul breath, and foul 5.02. 53 P
is but foul breath, and foul breath is noisome; 5.02. 53 P
th' endeavor of this present breath may buy LLL 1.01. 5
vows are but breath, and breath a vapor is; 4.03. 66
vows are but breath, and breath a vapor is; 4.03. 66
to death, | /wish'd himself the heavens' breath. 4.03.106
are they | that charge their breath against us? 5.02. 88
of thy royal sweet breath as will utter a brace 5.02.523 P
for mine own part, i breathe free breath. 5.02.722 P
borne ourselves | in the converse of breath — 5.02.735
uttering such dulcet and harmonious breath MND 2.01.151
o, i am out of breath in this fond chase! 2.02. 88
so hath thy breath, my dearest thisby dear. 3.01. 85
lay breath so bitter on your bitter foe. 3.02. 44
never did mockers waste more idle breath. 3.02.168
nor garlic, for we are to utter sweet breath; 4.02. 43 P
with bated breath and whisp'ring humbleness, MV 1.03.124
to wit (besides commends and courteous breath), 2.09. 90
are sever'd lips, | parted with sugar breath; 3.02.119
appears | than any that draws breath in italy. 3.02.296
art not seen, | although thy breath be rude. AYL 2.07.179
which seem to move and wanton with her breath, SHR in.2. 52
and with her breath she did perfume the air. 1.01.175
inspired merit so by breath is barr'd. AWW 2.01.148
made a groan of her last breath, and now she 4.03. 52 P
i had such a leg, and so sweet a breath to sing, TN 2.03. 21 P
a contagious breath. 2.03. 54 P
/fly away, /fly away, breath, | i am slain by a 2.04. 53
till our very pastime, tir'd out of breath, 3.04.138 P
heat outwardly or breath within, i'll serve you WT 3.02.206
the lids of juno's eyes | or cytherea's breath; 4.04.122
be when your first queen's again in breath; 5.01. 83
eternity and could put breath into his work, 5.02. 98 P
what fine chisel | could ever yet cut breath? 5.03. 79
with this abundance of superfluous breath? JN 2.01.148
zeal, now melted by the windy breath | of soft 2.01.477
word | is but the vain breath of a common man. 3.01. 8
can taste the free breath of a sacred king? 3.01.148
the latest breath that gave the sound of words 3.01.230
will, | in the vild prison of afflicted breath. 3.04. 19
and stop this gap of breath with fulsome dust, 3.04. 32
no, no, i will not, having breath to cry. 3.04. 37
for even the breath of what i mean to speak 3.04.127
one minute, nay, one quiet breath of rest. 3.04.134
the breath of heaven hath blown his spirit out, 4.01.109
but with my breath i can revive it, boy. 4.01.111
this kingdom, this confine of blood and breath, 4.02.246
be guilty of the stealing that sweet breath 4.03.136
it was my breath that blew this tempest up, 5.01. 17
set the name of right | with holy breath. 5.02. 68
your breath first kindled the dead coal of wars 5.02. 83
whose black contagious breath | already smokes 5.04. 33
but lusty, young, and cheerly drawing breath. R2 1.03. 66
draws the sweet infant breath of gentle sleep; 1.03.133
robs my tongue from breathing native breath? 1.03.173
such is the breath of kings. 1.03.215
but dead, thy kingdom cannot buy my breath. 1.03.232
not yourself, nor strive not with your breath, 2.01. 3
'tis breath thou lack'st, and that breath wilt 2.01. 30
thou lack'st, and that breath wilt thou lose. 2.01. 30
and sigh'd my english breath in foreign clouds, 3.01. 20
the breath of worldly men cannot depose | the 3.02. 56
allowing him a breath, a little scene, | to 3.02.164
where fearing dying pays death servile breath. 3.02.185
through brazen trumpet send the breath of parley 3.03. 33
be judg'd by subject and inferior breath, | and 4.01.128

recover breath, tell us how near is danger 5.03. 47
giving him breath, | the traitor lives, the true 5.03. 72
such as we see when men restrain their breath 1H4 2.03. 61
o for breath to utter what is like thee! 2.04.246 P
hark how hard he fetches breath. 2.04.530 P
and that no man might draw short breath to–day 5.02. 48
i grant you i was down and out of breath, and so 5.04.147 P
he sure means brevity in breath, short–winded. 2H4 2.02.124 P
treason's true bed and yielder–up of breath. 4.02.123
by his gates of breath | there lies a downy 4.05. 31
found no course of breath within your majesty, 4.05.150
the breath no sooner left his father's body, H5 1.01. 25
a night is but small breath, and little pause, 2.04.145
hold hard the breath, and bend up every spirit 3.01. 16
subject to the breath | of every fool whose 4.01.234
if that my fading breath permit | and death 1H6 2.05. 61
vexation almost stops my breath, | that sund'red 4.03. 41
pause, and take thy breath; 4.06. 4
speak to thy father ere thou yield thy breath! 4.07. 24
tide, | so am i driven by breath of her renown, 5.05. 7
and would have kept so long as breath did last! 2H6 1.01.211
for his breath stinks with eating toasted cheese 4.07. 12 P
color, | murther thy breath in middle of a word, R3 3.05. 2
give me some little breath, some pause, dear 4.02. 24
with me untir'd, | and stops he now for breath? 4.02. 45
a sign of dignity, a breath, a bubble; 4.04. 90
and in the breath of bitter words let's smother 4.04.133
despairing, yield thy breath! 5.03.172
now, | he would kiss you twenty with a breath. H8 1.04. 30
th' are breath i not believe in. 2.02. 53
that breath fame blows, that praise, sole pure, TRO 1.03.244
your breath with full consent bellied his sails; 2.02. 74
disgestion sake, | an after–dinner's breath. 2.03.112
she fetches her breath as short as a new–ta'en 3.02. 34 P
than breath or pen can give expressure to. 3.03.204
she hath not given so many good words breath 4.01. 74
even in the birth of our own laboring breath. 4.04. 38
with distinct breath and consign'd kisses to 4.04. 45
it, either to the uttermost, | or else a breath. 4.05. 92
nor dignifies an impare thought with breath; 4.05.103
and i have seen thee pause and take thy breath, 4.05.192
not a stroke, but keep yourselves in breath, 5.07. 3
is my day's work done, i'll take /good breath. 5.08. 3
i utter, and spend my malice in my breath. COR 2.01. 54 P
them for the hire | of their breath only! 2.02.150
i am out of breath, | confusion's near, i cannot 3.01.188
whose breath i hate | as reek a' th' rotten fens 3.03.120
never man | sigh'd truer breath; 4.05.115
of occupation and | the breath of garlic–eaters! 4.06. 98
to flame in, with such weak breath as this? 5.02. 47 P
lips, | coming and going with thy honey breath. TIT 2.04. 25
because their breath with sweetmeats tainted are ROM 1.04. 76
this bud of love, by summer's ripening breath, 2.02.121
do you not see that i am out of breath? 2.05. 30
how art thou out of breath, when thou hast 2.05. 31
when thou hast breath | to say to me that thou 2.05. 31
to say to me that thou art out of breath? 2.05. 32
then sweeten with thy breath | this neighbor air 2.06. 26
this, uttered | with gentle breath, calm look, 3.01.156
not i, unless the breath of heart–sick groans 3.03. 72
and that the trunk may be discharg'd of breath 5.01. 63
death, that hath suck'd the honey of thy breath, 5.03. 92
lips, o you | the doors of breath, seal with a 5.03.114
grief of my son's exile hath stopp'd her breath. 5.03.211
for my short date of breath | is not so long as 5.03.229
pledges the breath of him in a divided draught, TIM 1.02. 47 P
give me breath. 2.02. 33
were it all yours to give it in a breath, | how 2.02.153
the breath is gone whereof this praise is made. 2.02.170
they have e'en put my breath from me, the slaves 3.04.103
breath infect breath, | that their society (as 4.01. 30
breath infect breath, | that their society (as 4.01. 30
and he whose pious breath seeks to convert you, 4.03.141
and let his very breath whom thou'lt observe 4.03.212
not by his breath that is more miserable. 4.03.249
a deal of stinking breath because caesar refus'd JC 1.02.247 P
corporal melted, | as breath into the wind. MAC 1.03. 82
who, almost dead for breath, had scarcely more 1.05. 36
that the heaven's breath | smells wooingly here; 1.06. 5
to the heat of deeds too cold breath gives. 2.01. 61
pay his breath | to time and mortal custom. 4.01. 99
curses, not loud but deep, mouth–honor, breath, 5.03. 27
all our trumpets speak, give them all breath, 5.06. 9
black, | nor windy suspiration of forc'd breath, HAM 1.02. 79
words of so sweet breath compos'd | as made 3.01. 97
and /thumbs, give it breath with your mouth, and 3.02.358 P
be thou assur'd, if words be made of breath, 3.04.197
and breath of life, i have no life to breathe 3.04.198
we wrap the gentleman in our more rawer breath? 5.02.123 P
the king shall drink to hamlet's better breath, 5.02.271
he's fat, and scant of breath. 5.02.287
and in this harsh world draw thy breath in pain 5.02.348
a love that makes breath poor, and speech unable
LR 1.01. 60
then 'tis like the breath of an unfee'd lawyer, 1.04.129 P
i am scarce in breath, my lord. 2.02. 52 P
my breath and blood! 2.04.103
you ever–gentle gods, take my breath from me, 4.06.217
if that her breath will mist or stain the stone, 5.03.263
a rat, have life, | and thou no breath at all? 5.03.308
swell his sail with thine own pow'rful breath, OTH 2.01. 78
thy words before thou giv'st them breath, 3.03.119
each syllable that breath made up between them. 4.02. 5
o balmy breath, that dost almost persuade 5.02. 16
whose breath, indeed, these hands have newly 5.02.202
and having lost her breath, she spoke, and ANT 2.02.230
our fortune on the sea is out of breath, | and 3.10. 24
from his all–obeying breath i hear | the doom of 3.13. 77
give him no breath, but now | make boot of his 4.01. 8
outwent her, | motion and breath left out. CYM 2.04. 85
whose breath | rides on the posting winds and 3.04. 35
not to slander, | outsweet'ned not thy breath. 4.02.224
even for whom my life | is every breath a death; 5.01. 27
on either side i come to spend my breath; 5.03. 81
his celestial breath | was sulphurous to smell; 5.04.114
who tells us life's but breath, to trust it PER 1.01. 46
the breath is gone, and the sore eyes see clear 1.01. 99
let your breath cool yourself, telling your 1.01.159
fetch breath that may proclaim them louder, that 1.04. 15
and, wanting breath to speak, help me with tears 1.04. 19
and left /me breath | nothing to think on but 2.01. 6
or know what ground's made happy by his breath. 2.04. 28
y' are out of breath, | and this high–speeded TNK 1.03. 82
we seek not | thy breath of mercy, theseus. 3.06.158
and with the same breath smil'd, and kiss'd her 4.01. 93
the hearts of lions and | the breath of tigers, 5.01. 40
whose breath blows down | the teeming ceres' 5.01. 52
i'll sigh celestial breath, whose gentle wind VEN 189
laughs and weeps, and all but with a breath. 414
of thy face excelling | comes breath perfum'd, 444
till his breath breatheth life in her again. 474
may say, the plague is banish'd by thy breath. 510
so she at these sad signs draws up her breath, 929
mean | to stifle beauty and to steal his breath? 934
his breath and beauty set | gloss on the rose, 935
to smell, | comparing it to her adonis' breath, 1172
a dream, a breath, a froth of fleeting joy. LUC 212
like golden threads play'd with her breath — 400
to make more vent for passage of her breath, 1040
revenge on him that made me stop my breath. 1180
and from his lips did fly | thin winding breath, 1407
what he breathes out his breath drinks up again. 1666
till manly shame bids him possess his breath, 1777
my vow was breath, and breath a vapor is, | then PP 3. 9
my vow was breath, and breath a vapor is, | then 3. 9
and as she fetched breath, away he skips, | and 11.11
youth is full of sport, age's breath is short, 12. 5
to death, | wish'd himself the heavens' breath. 16. 8
mak'st | with the breath thou giv'st and tak'st, PHT 19
when summer's breath their masked buds discloses
SON 54. 8
o, how shall summer's honey breath hold out 65. 5
where breath most breathes, even in the mouths 81.14
then others for the breath of words respect, 85.13
that smells, | if not from my love's breath? 99. 3
and to his robb'ry had annex'd thy breath, | but 99.11
than in the breath that from my mistress reeks. 130. 8
o, that sad breath his spungy lungs bestowed, LC 326

/BREATH'D 1 FR 0.0001 REL FR 1 V 0 P
/need /to /be /reviv'd /and /breath'd /in /me? 2H4 4.01.112

BREATH'D 23 FR 0.0026 REL FR 22 V 1 P
i have not breath'd almost since i did see it. ERR 5.01.181
i have toward heaven breath'd a secret vow | to MV 3.04. 27
beseech your grace, i am not yet well breath'd. AYL 1.02.218 P
the faithfull'st off'rings have breath'd out TN 5.01.114
see, my lord, | would you not deem it breath'd? WT 5.03. 64
you were new crown'd, | we breath'd our counsel; JN 4.02. 36
by all the blood that ever fury breath'd, | the 5.02.127
his heart–blood | which breath'd this poison. R2 1.01.173
three times they breath'd and three times did 1H4 1.03.102
whom a thousand sighs are breath'd for thee! 2H6 3.02.345
your brave father breath'd his latest gasp, 3H6 2.01.108
montague hath breath'd his last, | and to the 5.02. 40
thus have you breath'd your curse against R3 1.03.239
that breath'd upon the earth a christian; 3.05. 26
that he hath breath'd in my dishonor here. TIT 2.01. 56
which, as he breath'd defiance to my ears, | he ROM 1.01.110
and breath'd such life with kisses in my lips 5.01. 8
a most incomparable man, breath'd, as it were, TIM 1.01. 10
arms, and breath'd | our sufferance vainly. 5.04. 7
i will be treble–sinew'd, hearted, breath'd, ANT 3.13.177
if | thou knew'st my mistress breath'd on me, TNK 3.01. 28
i say again, | that sigh was breath'd for emily. 3.03. 44
breath'd forth the sound that said "i hate" | to SON 145. 2

BREATHE 66 FR 0.0074 REL FR 60 V 6 P
and "go," | and breathe twice, and cry "so, so," TMP 4.01. 45
if so — i pray thee breathe it in mine ear, TGV 3.01.241
i dare thee but to breathe upon my love. 5.04.131
speak, breathe, discuss; WIV 4.05. 2 P
and mercy then will breathe within your lips, MM 2.02. 78
for mine own part, i breathe free breath. LLL 5.02.722 P
see, doth he breathe? SHR in.1. 31
here let us breathe and haply institute | a 1.01. 8
that's able to breathe life into a stone, AWW 2.01. 73
created for men to breathe themselves upon thee. 2.03.256 P
what thriftless sighs shall poor olivia breathe? TN 2.02. 39
o, hear me breathe my life | before this ancient WT 4.04.360
let the church, our mother, breathe her curse, JN 3.01.256
but now i breathe again | aloft the flood, and 4.02.138
you breathe these dead news in as dead an ear. 5.07. 65
of "never to return" | breathe i against thee, R2 1.03.153
to breathe the abundant dolor of the heart. 1.03.257
come, that i may breathe my last | in wholesome 2.01. 1
for they breathe truth that breathe their words 2.01. 8
breathe truth that breathe their words in pain. 2.01. 8
i am in health, i breathe, and see thee ill. 2.01. 92
little joy have i | to breathe this news, yet 3.04. 82
if i dare eat, or drink, or breathe, or live, 4.01. 73
and breathe short–winded accents of new broils 1H4 1.01. 3
scarlet, and when you breathe in your watering, 2.04. 16 P
well, breathe a while, and then to it again, and 2.04.249 P
hal, i prithee give me leave to breathe a while. 5.03. 44 P
we breathe too long. 5.04. 15
stay and breathe a while. 5.04. 47
stopp'd by me to breathe his bloodied horse. 2H4 1.01. 38
very latest counsel | that ever i shall breathe. 4.05.183
and suffer you to breathe in fruitful peace, 1H6 5.04.127
he shall not breathe infection in this air | but 2H6 3.02.287
here could i breathe my soul into the air, | as 3.02.391
soul, | or i should breathe it so into thy body, 3.02.398
breathe foul contagious darkness in the air. 4.01. 7
giving the house of lancaster leave to breathe, 3H6 1.02. 13
breathe out invectives 'gainst the officers. 1.04. 43
and, whilest we breathe, take time to do him 1.04.108
race, | i lay me down a little while to breathe; 2.03. 2
now breathe we, lords, good fortune bids us 2.06. 31
do i not breathe a man? 3.01. 82
durst the traitor breathe out so proud words? 4.01.112
if she have time to breathe, be well assur'd 5.03. 16
his better doth not breathe upon the earth. R3 1.02.140
the lips of those that breathe them in the air. 1.03.285
else wherefore breathe i in a christian land? 3.07.116
breathe you, my friends. COR 1.06. 1
or with our sighs we'll breathe the welkin dim, TIT 3.01.211
where life hath no more interest but to breathe! 3.01.249
to breathe such vows as lovers use to swear, ROM 2.pr. 10
wisely suffer | the worst that man can breathe, TIM 3.05. 32
you breathe in vain. 3.05. 59
but breathe his faults so quaintly | that they HAM 2.01. 31
crimes | the youth you breathe of guilty, be 2.01. 44
i have no life to breathe | what thou hast said 3.04.198
for his death no wind of blame shall breathe, 4.07. 66
but thou dost breathe, | hast heavy substance, LR 4.06. 51
i may not breathe my censure | what he might be. OTH 4.01.270
and, breathless, pow'r breathe forth. ANT 2.02.232
to let him breathe between the heavens and earth 3.12. 14
breathe not where princes are. CYM 5.05.238
yet they breathe | and have the name of men. TNK 1.04. 27
so long as men can breathe or eyes can see, | so SON 18.13
subject to invent | while thou dost breathe, 38. 2
when winds breathe sweet, unruly though they be.
LC 103

BREATHED 5 FR 0.0005 REL FR 4 V 1 P
a man so breathed, that certain he would fight, LLL 5.02.653
when he breathed, he was a man. 5.02.662 P
thy greyhounds are as swift | as breathed stags; SHR in.2. 48
this day i breathed first: JC 5.03. 23
of that polluted prison where it breathed. LUC 1726

BREATHER 3 FR 0.0003 REL FR 2 V 1 P
once can touch | but it confounds the breather. MM 4.04. 28
i will chide no breather in the world but myself AYL 3.02.280 P
rather than a life, | a statue, than a breather. ANT 3.03. 21

BREATHERS 1 FR 0.0001 REL FR 1 V 0 P
when all the breathers of this world are dead; SON 81.12

/BREATHES 2 FR 0.0002 REL FR 2 V 0 P
churchyards yawn and hell itself /breathes out HAM 3.02.389
nature awakes, | a warmth /breathes out of her. PER 3.02. 93

BREATHES 12 FR 0.0013 REL FR 10 V 2 P
the air breathes upon us here most sweetly. TMP 2.01. 47 P
so again while stephano breathes at' nostrils. 2.02. 63 P
he breathes, my lord. SHR in.1. 32
sound | that breathes upon a bank of violets, TN 1.01. 6
head lie there, | while philip breathes. JN 3.02. 4
no man so potent breathes upon the ground | but 1H4 4.01. 11
clarence still breathes, edward still lives and R3 1.01.161
whose foul mouth no healthsome air breathes in, ROM 4.03. 34
that thy tongue some say of breeding breathes, LR 5.03.144
with grief thus breathes she forth her spite LUC 762
what he breathes out his breath drinks up again. 1666
where breath most breathes, even in the mouths SON 81.14

BREATHEST 1 FR 0.0001 REL FR 1 V 0 P
and though thou livest and breathest, | yet art R2 1.02. 24

BREATHETH 2 FR 0.0002 REL FR 2 V 0 P
panting he lies, and breatheth in her face. VEN 62
till his breath breatheth life in her again. 474

BREATHING 27 FR 0.0030 REL FR 24 V 3 P
smote the air | for breathing in their faces; TMP 4.01.173
you shake the head at so long a breathing, but i ADO 2.01.363 P
kiss this shrine, this mortal breathing saint. MV 2.07. 40
no sighs but a' my breathing, no tears but a' my 3.01. 96 P
therefore i scant this breathing courtesy. 5.01.141
who are sick | for breathing and exploit. AWW 1.02. 17
rescue those breathing lives to die in beds, JN 2.01.419
and breathing to his breathless excellence | the 4.03. 66
even this ill night your breathing shall expire, 5.04. 36
robs my tongue from breathing native breath? R2 1.03.173
to the extremest point | of mortal breathing. 4.01. 48
there thou stand'st, a breathing valiant man, 1H6 4.02. 31
be my last breathing in this mortal world! 2H6 1.02. 21
sent before my time | into this breathing world, R3 1.01. 21
cannot be quiet scarce a breathing while | but 1.03. 60
but, like dumb statues or breathing stones, 3.07. 25
joys, | poor breathing orators of miseries, 4.04.129
and both the princes had been breathing here, 4.04.384
how ugly night comes breathing at his heels; TRO 5.08. 6
breathing like sanctified and pious bonds, | the HAM 1.03.130
it is the breathing time of day with me. 5.02.174 P
i am sorry to give breathing to my purpose — ANT 1.03. 14
and like the tyrannous breathing of the north CYM 1.03. 36
'tis her breathing that | perfumes the chamber 2.02. 18
sir, here's a lady that wants breathing too, PER 2.03.100
value's shortness, | to any lady breathing. TNK 5.03. 89
bud and be blasted in a breathing while, | the VEN 1142

BREATHINGS 1 FR 0.0001 REL FR 1 V 0 P
untimely breathings, sick and short assays, LUC 1720

BREATHLESS 13 FR 0.0014 REL FR 13 V 0 P
and bootless make the breathless huswife churn, MND 2.01. 37
and breathing to his breathless excellence | the JN 4.03. 66
herein all breathless lies | the mightiest of R2 5.06. 31
breathless and faint, leaning upon my sword, 1H4 1.03. 32
done, all's won, here breathless lies the king. 5.03. 16
dead, | breathless and bleeding on the ground. 5.04.134
enter his chamber, view his breathless corpse, 2H6 3.02.132
now breathless wrong | shall sit and pant in TIM 5.04. 10
why are you breathless, and why stare you so? JC 1.03. 2
stew'd in his haste, half breathless, /panting LR 2.04. 31
and, breathless, pow'r breathe forth. ANT 2.02.232
and almost breathless swim | in this deep water. TNK pr 24
till breathless he disjoin'd, and backward drew VEN 541

BREATHS 8 FR 0.0009 REL FR 4 V 4 P
they are, with your sweet breaths puff'd out. LLL 5.02.267
that lik'd me, and breaths that i defied not; AYL ep 20 P
beards, or good faces, or sweet breaths, will, ep 22 P
they say poor suitors have strong breaths; COR 1.01. 60 P
to th' people, beg their stinking breaths. 2.01.236
their lips that their breaths embrac'd together. OTH 2.01.259 P
in their thick breaths, | rank of gross diet, ANT 5.02.211
let their exhal'd unwholesome breaths make sick LUC 779

BRECKNOCK 1 FR 0.0001 REL FR 1 V 0 P
gone | to brecknock while my fearful head is on! R3 4.02.122

BRED 55 FR 0.0062 REL FR 48 V 7 P
but here nurs'd up and bred, one that is a MM 4.02.131 P
thereof the raging fire of fever bred, | and ERR 5.01. 75
their pride | against that power that bred it. ADO 3.01. 11
for blush in cheeks by faults are bred | and LLL 1.02.101
fed of the dainties that are bred in a book; 4.02. 24
my hounds are bred out of the spartan kind; MND 4.01.119
sun, | to whom i am a neighbor and near bred. MV 2.01. 3
tell me where is fancy bred, | or in the heart 3.02. 63
the skull that bred them in the sepulchre. 3.02. 96
she is not bred so dull but she can learn; 3.02.162
his horses are bred better, for, besides that AYL 1.01. 11 P
being ever from their cradles bred together, 1.01.108 P
yet am i inland bred | and know some nurture. 2.07. 96

well, for i was bred and born | not three hours' TN 1.02. 22
would not a pair of these have bred, sir? 3.01. 49 P
companion that e'er man | bred his hopes out of. WT 5.01. 12
might have kept | this calf, bred from his cow, JN 1.01.124
all of one nature, of one substance bred, | did 1H4 1.01. 11
a gentleman well bred and of good name, | that 2H4 1.01. 26
'tis true bred! 5.03. 67 P
and he is bred out of that bloody strain | that H5 2.04. 51
and plainly say | our mettle is bred out, and 3.05. 29
england all olivers and rolands bred | during 1H6 1.02. 30
the wound that bred this meeting here | cannot 3H6 2.02.121
and that thy summer bred us no increase, | we 2.02.164
love, | but from deceit bred by necessity; 3.03. 68
word "judgment" hath bred a kind of remorse in R3 1.04.108 P
he has been bred i' th' wars | since 'a could COR 3.01.318
art their soldier, and, being bred in broils, 3.02. 81
eating the flesh that she herself hath bred. TIT 5.03. 62
three civil brawls, bred of an airy word, | by ROM 1.01. 89
and i have bred her at my dearest cost | in TIM 1.01.124
the strain of man's bred out | into baboon and 1.01.250
arm | with favor never clasp'd, but bred a dog. 4.03.251
my lord, | you have begot me, bred me, lov'd me: LR 1.01. 96
a servant that he bred, thrill'd with remorse, 4.02. 73
serpent of egypt is bred now of your mud by the ANT 2.07. 26 P
must i be unfolded | with one that i have bred? 5.02.171
you bred him as my playfellow, and he is | a man CYM 1.01.145
one bred of alms and foster'd with cold dishes, 2.03.114
all love the womb that their first being bred, PER 1.01.107
where were you bred? 5.01.115
well, where were you bred? 5.01.163
where were you bred? 5.01.169
where were you bred you know it not? TNK 2.03. 63
what country bred you? 2.05. 5
we were not bred to talk, man. 3.06. 28
which bred more beauty in his angry eyes: VEN 70
alone, | thing like a man, but of no woman bred! 214
these worlds in tarquin new ambition bred, | who LUC 411
dead, | by thy bright beauty was it newly bred. 490
of foes, | to eat up errors by opinion bred, 937
so of shame's ashes shall my fame be bred, | for 1188
finding the first conceit of love there bred, SON 108.13
you are so strongly in my purpose bred | that 112.13
BREECH 2 FR 0.0002 REL FR 2 V 0 P
and ne'er have stol'n the breech from lancaster. 3H6 5.05. 24
boys in athens | blow wind i' th' breech on 's, TNK 2.03. 47
BREECH'D 1 FR 0.0001 REL FR 1 V 0 P
their daggers | unmannerly breech'd with gore. MAC 2.03.116
BREECHES *(also preeches)*
BREECHES 8 FR 0.0009 REL FR 6 V 2 P
what fashion, madam, shall i make your breeches?
TGV 2.07. 49
a pair of old breeches thrice turn'd; SHR 3.02. 44 P
your breeches best may carry them. JN 3.01.201
in this place most master wear no breeches, 2H6 1.03.146
short blist'red breeches, and those types of H8 1.03. 31
and put'st down thine own breeches, "then they LR 1.04.174 P
peer, | his breeches cost him but a crown; OTH 2.03. 90
the birch upon the breeches of the small ones, TNK 3.05.111
BREECHING 1 FR 0.0001 REL FR 1 V 0 P
i am no breeching scholar in the schools, | i'll SHR 3.01. 18
/BREED 1 FR 0.0001 REL FR 1 V 0 P
/i /would /breed /from /hence /occasions, /and LR 1.03. 24
BREED 58 FR 0.0065 REL FR 47 V 11 P
how use doth breed a habit in a man! TGV 5.04. 1
are these the breed of wits so wondered at? LLL 5.02.266
i cannot tell, i make it breed as fast. MV 1.03. 96
take | a breed for barren metal of his friend? 1.03.134
my brother, on his blessing, to breed me well; AYL 1.01. 4 P
herself, for she will breed it like a fool! 4.01.176 P
and these breed honor. AWW 2.03.133
ignorant, will breed no terror in the youth; TN 3.04.189 P
of what may chance | or breed upon our absence. WT 1.02. 12
may, if fortune please, both breed thee, pretty, 3.03. 48
and only therefore | desire to breed by me. 4.04.103
fifteen thousand hearts of england's breed — JN 2.01.275
this happy breed of men, this little world, R2 2.01. 45
fear'd by their breed, and famous by their birth 2.01. 52
he'll breed revengement and a scourge for me; 1H4 3.02. 7
and breed a kind of question in our cause. 4.01. 68
i have bestowed to breed this present peace, 2H4 4.02. 74
lest example | breed, by his sufferance, more of H5 2.02. 46
smell whereof shall breed a plague in france. 4.03.103
where i could not breed no contention with him; 5.01. 11 P
so will this base and envious discord breed. 1H6 3.01.193
one sudden foil shall never breed distrust. 3.03. 11
do breed love's settled passions in my heart, 5.05. 4
where in that nest of spicery they will breed R3 4.04.424
through their amity | breed him some prejudice; H8 1.01.182
handsome, and of the best breed in the north. 2.02. 4 P
i am sorry my integrity should breed | (and 3.01. 51
or, shedding, breed a nursery of like evil, | to TRO 1.03.319
are pleas'd to breed out your inheritors. 4.01. 65
iron, increase tailors, and breed ballad–makers. COR 4.05.220 P
make war breed peace, make peace stint war, make
TIM 5.04. 83
rome, thou hast lost the breed of noble bloods! JC 1.02.151
that ever rome | should breed thy fellow. 5.03.101
where they /most breed and haunt, i have MAC 1.06. 9
hath nature that in time will venom breed, | no 3.04. 29
stands accus'd, | and does blaspheme his breed? 4.03.108
unnatural deeds | do breed unnatural troubles; 5.01. 72
for if the sun breed maggots in a dead dog, HAM 2.02.181 P
lord, this courtesy is not of the right breed. 3.02.315 P
and many more of the same breed that i know the 5.02.189 P
a heart and brain to breed it in? LR 1.02. 57 P
diet, | or breed itself so out of circumstances, OTH 3.03. 16
the worms were hallowed that did breed the silk, 3.04. 73
and doth affection breed it? 4.03. 98
two domestic powers | breed scrupulous faction; ANT 1.03. 48
breed of greatness! CYM 4.02. 25
i feed | on mother's flesh which did me breed. PER 1.01. 65
on sweetest flowers, yet they poison breed. 1.01.133
where grief should sleep, can breed me quiet? 1.02. 5
you talk of feeding me to breed me strength; TNK 3.01.119
their lives | might breed the ruin of my name, 3.06.240
they breed sore eyes and 'tis enough to infect STM II.C 10 P
by law of nature thou art bound to breed, | that VEN 171
that on the earth would breed a scarcity | and 753

wrong, what shame, what sorrow i shall breed, LUC 499
my flocks feed not, my ewes breed not, | my rams PP 17. 1
that's for thyself to breed another thee, | or SON 6. 7
time's scythe can make defense | save breed, to 12.14
BREED–BATE 1 FR 0.0001 REL FR 0 V 1 P
i warrant you, no tell–tale nor no breed–bate. WIV 1.04. 12 P
BREEDER 8 FR 0.0009 REL FR 7 V 1 P
time is the nurse and breeder of all good. TGV 3.01.245
it, | you love the breeder better than the male. 3H6 2.01. 42
and see where comes the breeder of my sorrow! 3.03. 43
that hath been breeder of these dire events. TIT 5.03.178
why wouldst thou be a breeder of sinners? HAM 3.01.121 P
i am sure | it has a noble breeder and a pure, TNK pr 10
eye | of the fair breeder that is standing by." VEN 282
when lo the unback'd breeder, full of fear, 320
BREEDERS 2 FR 0.0002 REL FR 2 V 0 P
was | between these woolly breeders in the act, MV 1.03. 83
amongst the fair–fac'd breeders of our clime. TIT 4.02. 68
BREEDETH 2 FR 0.0002 REL FR 2 V 0 P
spring from seeds and beauty breedeth beauty; VEN 167
breath perfum'd, that breedeth love by smelling. 444
/BREEDING 1 FR 0.0001 REL FR 1 V 0 P
/i /am /a /gentleman /of /blood /and /breeding, LR 3.01. 40
BREEDING 27 FR 0.0030 REL FR 16 V 11 P
you are a gentleman of excellent breeding, WIV 2.02.225 P
in graces, and in qualities of breeding; MV 2.07. 33
may complain of good breeding or comes of a very
AYL 3.02. 30 P
being a man of your breeding, be married under a 3.03. 83 P
now put you to the height of your breeding. AWW 2.02. 2 P
she had her breeding at my father's charge — 2.03.114
him out to be of good capacity and breeding; TN 3.04.186 P
so far beneath your soft and tender breeding, 5.01.323
so leaves me to consider what is breeding | that WT 1.02.374
she's as forward of her breeding as | she is i' 4.04.580
breeding? 4.04.719 P
nobleness which nature shows above her breeding; 5.02. 37 P
among wits of no higher breeding than thine. 2H4 2.02. 36 P
honest gentleman, i know not your breeding. 5.03.107 P
let us swear | that you are worth your breeding, H5 3.01. 28
beseeching him to give her virtuous breeding — H8 4.02.134
o blessed breeding sun, draw from the earth TIM 4.03. 1
did these bones cost no more the breeding, but HAM 5.01. 92 P
his breeding, sir, hath been at my charge. LR 1.01. 9 P
that thy tongue some say of breeding breathes, 5.03.144
and besort | as levels with her breeding. OTH 1.03.239
'tis my breeding | that gives me this bold show 2.01. 98
much is breeding, | which, like the courser's ANT 1.02.192
who find in my exile the want of breeding, | the CYM 4.04. 26
so long a breeding as his white beard came to, 5.03. 17
my breeding was, sir, as | your highness knows. 5.05.339
a breeding jennet, lusty, young, and proud, VEN 260
BREEDS 30 FR 0.0034 REL FR 23 V 7 P
rain grace | on that which breeds between 'em! TMP 3.01. 76
'tis | such sense that my sense breeds with it. MM 2.02.142
there is no measure in the occasion that breeds, ADO 1.03. 4 P
virginity breeds mites, much like a cheese, AWW 1.01.141 P
and choice breeds | a native slip to us from 1.03.145
what better matter breeds for you | than i have JN 3.04.170
watching breeds leanness, leanness is all gaunt. R2 2.01. 78
and your chamber–lye breeds fleas like a loach. 1H4 2.01. 21 P
leg, and breeds no bate with telling of discreet 2H4 2.04.249 P
island of england breeds very valiant creatures; H5 3.07.140 P
but more, when envy breeds unkind division: 1H6 4.01.193
french, | because in york this breeds suspicion; 2H6 1.03.206
love, and that breeds hot blood, and hot blood TRO 3.01.129 P
here never shines the sun, here nothing breeds, TIT 2.03. 96
yet every mother breeds not sons alike — | do 2.03.146
to him | but breeds the giver a return exceeding TIM 1.01.279
that feeds and breeds by a composture stol'n 4.03.441
see what breeds about her heart. LR 3.06. 77 P
love no friend, sith love breeds such offense. OTH 3.03.380
breeds him and makes him of his bedchamber, CYM 1.01. 42
plenty and peace breeds cowards; 3.06. 21
th' imperious seas breeds monsters; 4.02. 35
joy, | which breeds a deeper longing, cure their TNK 1.01.190
a good hearty draught, it breeds good blood, man 3.03. 17
disorder breeds by heating of the blood; VEN 742
this momentary joy breeds months of pain, | this LUC 690
sing, | what virtue breeds iniquity devours: 872
advice is sporting while infection breeds. 907
fair sun that breeds the fat earth's store, | by 1837
than public means which public manners breeds. SON 111. 4
BREEZE* 2 FR 0.0002 REL FR 2 V 0 P
the herd hath more annoyance by the breeze TRO 1.03. 48
the breeze upon her, like a cow in /june — ANT 3.10. 14
BREFF *(also brief*, prief)*
BREFF 1 FR 0.0001 REL FR 0 V 1 P
i suerly do, that is the breff and the long. H5 3.02.118 P
BRENTFORD *(see brainford)*
BRETAGNE *(also britain*, brittany*)*
BRETAGNE 1 FR 0.0001 REL FR 1 V 0 P
of orleance, calaber, bretagne, and alanson, 2H6 1.01. 7
BRETHEREN 3 FR 0.0003 REL FR 3 V 0 P
make way to lay them by their bretheren. TIT 1.01. 89
give mutius burial with our bretheren. 1.01.348
for him, | he must be buried with his bretheren. 1.01.357
BRETHREN 16 FR 0.0018 REL FR 15 V 1 P
adam's sons are my brethren, and truly i hold it ADO 2.01. 64 P
my friends and brethren in these great affairs, 2H4 4.01. 6
between his greatness and thy other brethren. 4.04. 26
the mayor and all his brethren in best sort, H5 5.pr. 25
had i thy brethren here, their lives and thine 3H6 1.03. 25
will not the mayor then and his brethren come? R3 3.07. 44
i, her frail son, amongst my brethren mortal, H8 3.02.148
and you, good brethren, i am much beholding; 5.04. 70
my spritely brethren, i propend to you | in TRO 2.02.190
brethren and sisters of the hold–door trade, 5.10. 51
when | some certain of your brethren roar'd, and COR 2.03. 53
stay, roman brethren! TIT 1.01.104
these are their brethren, whom your goths beheld 1.01.122
and for their brethren slain | religiously they 1.01.123
remaineth nought but to inter our brethren, 1.01.146
i train'd thy brethren to that guileful hole, 5.01.104
BRETHREN'S 1 FR 0.0001 REL FR 1 V 0 P
tears | i render for my brethren's obsequies; TIT 1.01.160
BRETON *(see britain*, etc.)*
BREVIS 1 FR 0.0001 REL FR 1 V 0 P

my lords, "ira furor brevis est," | but yond man TIM 1.02. 28
BREVITY 4 FR 0.0004 REL FR 2 V 2 P
will imitate the honorable romans in brevity." 2H4 2.02.123 P
he sure means brevity in breath, short–winded. 2.02.124 P
with the rude brevity and discharge of one. TRO 4.04. 41
therefore, /since brevity is the soul of wit, HAM 2.02. 90
BREW 4 FR 0.0004 REL FR 1 V 3 P
"blessing of your heart, you brew good ale." TGV 3.01.305 P
and i wash, wring, brew, bake, scour, dress meat WIV 1.04. 96 P
go, brew me a pottle of sack finely. 3.05. 28 P
or brew it to a weak and colder palate, | the TRO 4.04. 7
BREWAGE 1 FR 0.0001 REL FR 0 V 1 P
i'll no pullet–sperm in my brewage. WIV 3.05. 32 P
/BREW'D 1 FR 0.0001 REL FR 1 V 0 P
/brew'd /with /her /sorrow, /mesh'd /upon /her TIT 3.02. 38
BREW'D 2 FR 0.0002 REL FR 2 V 0 P
even then that sunshine brew'd a show'r for him, 3H6 2.02.156
let's away, | our tears are not yet brew'd. MAC 2.03.124
BREWER'S 2 FR 0.0002 REL FR 0 V 2 P
is made of, i am a peppercorn, a brewer's horse. 1H4 3.03. 9 P
than he that gibbets on the brewer's bucket. 2H4 3.02.264 P
BREWERS 1 FR 0.0001 REL FR 1 V 0 P
when brewers mar their malt with water; LR 3.02. 82
BREW–HOUSE 1 FR 0.0001 REL FR 0 V 1 P
be ready here hard by in the brew–house, and WIV 3.03. 10 P
BREWING 1 FR 0.0001 REL FR 0 V 1 P
and another storm brewing, i hear it sing i' th' TMP 2.02. 19 P
BREWS 1 FR 0.0001 REL FR 0 V 1 P
"item, she brews good ale." TGV 3.01.303 P
BRIAREUS 1 FR 0.0001 REL FR 0 V 1 P
so out of joint that he is a gouty briareus, TRO 1.02. 29 P
BRIB'D 3 FR 0.0003 REL FR 2 V 1 P
with these crystal beads heaven shall be brib'd JN 2.01.171
for if i should be brib'd too, there would be TIM 1.02.238 P
"and therefore hath she brib'd the destinies VEN 733
BRIB'D–BUCK 1 FR 0.0001 REL FR 0 V 1 P
divide me like a brib'd–buck, each a haunch. WIV 5.05. 24 P
BRIBE 5 FR 0.0005 REL FR 5 V 0 P
hark how i'll bribe you. MM 2.02.145
how? bribe me? 2.02.146
pay, | nor ever had one penny bribe from france. 2H6 3.01.109
she did corrupt frail nature with some bribe, 3H6 3.02.155
heart consent to take | a bribe to pay my sword. COR 1.09. 38
BRIBER 1 FR 0.0001 REL FR 1 V 0 P
were a sufficient briber for his life. TIM 3.05. 61
BRIBES 3 FR 0.0003 REL FR 3 V 0 P
my lord, that you took bribes of france, | and, 2H6 3.01.104
pella | for taking bribes here of the sardians; JC 4.03. 3
now | contaminate our fingers with base bribes? 4.03. 24
BRICK 2 FR 0.0002 REL FR 1 V 1 P
he hath a garden circummur'd with brick, | whose MM 4.01. 28
on a brick wall have i climb'd into this garden, 2H6 4.10. 7 P
BRICKLAYER 2 FR 0.0002 REL FR 1 V 1 P
he was an honest man, and a good bricklayer. 2H6 4.02. 41 P
became a bricklayer when he came to age. 4.02.145
BRICKS 1 FR 0.0001 REL FR 0 V 1 P
and the bricks are alive at this day to testify 2H6 4.02.149 P
BRICK–WALL 1 FR 0.0001 REL FR 0 V 1 P
shall he be set against a brick–wall, the sun WT 4.04.789 P
BRIDAL 8 FR 0.0009 REL FR 8 V 0 P
gentlemen, forward to the bridal dinner. SHR 3.02.219
come, i will bring thee to thy bridal chamber. 4.01.178
shall gild her bridal bed and make her rich | in JN 2.01.491
and grac'd thy poor sire with his bridal day, 3H6 2.02.155
make the bridal bed | in that dim monument where
ROM 3.05.200
our bridal flowers serve for a buried corse; 4.05. 89
flower, with flowers thy bridal bed i strew — 5.03. 12
look for such observancy | as fits the bridal. OTH 3.04.150
BRIDE 40 FR 0.0045 REL FR 39 V 1 P
die, | i will encounter darkness as a bride, MM 3.01. 83
sunday following shall bianca | be bride to you, SHR 2.01.396
where is my lovely bride? 3.02. 92
see not your bride in these unreverent robes, 3.02.112
when i should bid good morrow to my bride | and 3.02.122
and is the bride and bridegroom coming home? 3.02.151
he took the bride about the neck | and kiss'd 3.02.177
obey the bride, you that attend on her. 3.02.223
though bride and bridegroom wants | for to 3.02.246
shall sweet bianca practice how to bride it? 3.02.251
ay, mistress bride, hath that awakened you? 5.02. 42
when i should take possession of the bride, AWW 2.05. 26
here | in likeness of a new untrimmed bride. JN 3.01.209
worth | to be the princely bride of such a lord, 1H6 5.03.152
with his new bride and england's dear–bought 2H6 1.01.252
'tis not his new–made bride shall succor him, 3H6 3.03.207
to revel it with him and his new bride. 3.03.225
and his well–chosen bride. 4.01. 7
scales | unto the brother of your loving bride. 4.01. 53
but in your bride you bury brotherhood. 4.01. 55
to revel it with him and his new bride." 4.01. 95
behold, i choose thee, tamora, for my bride, TIT 1.01.319
place | i lead espous'd my bride along with me. 1.01.328
your noble emperor and his lovely bride, | sent 1.01.334
i am not bid to wait upon this bride. 1.01.338
god give you joy, sir, of your gallant bride! 1.01.400
and wake the emperor and his lovely bride, | and 2.02. 4
ere we may think her ripe to be a bride. ROM 1.02. 11
shall happily make thee there a joyful bride. 3.05.115
he shall not make me there a joyful bride. 3.05.117
wrought | so worthy a gentleman to be her bride? 3.05.145
why, bride! 4.05. 3
come, is the bride ready to go to church? 4.05. 33
the maid is fair, a' th' youngest for a bride, TIM 1.01.123
and in terms like bride and groom | devesting OTH 2.03.180
clothed like a bride | for embracements even of PER 1.01. 6
hymen hath brought the bride to bed, | where, by 3.ch. 9
for your bride goes to that with shame which is 4.02.127 P
sweet, | lie 'fore bride and bridegroom's feet, TNK 1.01. 14
pirithous, | lead on the bride. 1.01.208
BRIDE–BED 2 FR 0.0002 REL FR 2 V 0 P
to the best bride–bed will we, | which by us MND 5.01.403
i thought thy bride–bed to have deck'd, sweet HAM 5.01.245
BRIDED 1 FR 0.0001 REL FR 1 V 0 P
i told them — who | a lass of fourteen brided. TNK 5.01.109
BRIDEGROOM 12 FR 0.0013 REL FR 12 V 0 P
to want the bridegroom when the priest attends SHR 3.02. 5
and is the bride and bridegroom coming home? 3.02.151

a bridegroom, say you? 3.02.152
this mad–brain'd bridegroom took him such a cuff 3.02.163
though bride and bridegroom wants | for to 3.02.246
fresh as a bridegroom, and his chin new reap'd 1H4 1.03. 34
when the bridegroom in the morning comes | to ROM 4.01.107
make haste, the bridegroom he is come already, 4.04. 27
banish'd the new–made bridegroom from this city, 5.03.235
till that bellona's bridegroom, lapp'd in proof, MAC 1.02. 54
i will die bravely, like a smug bridegroom. LR 4.06.198
but i will be | a bridegroom in my death, and ANT 4.14.100
/BRIDEGROOM'S 1 FR 0.0001 REL FR 1 V 0 P
/with /a /bridegroom's /fresh /alacrity | /let TRO 4.04.145
BRIDEGROOM'S 3 FR 0.0003 REL FR 3 V 0 P
that creep into the dreaming bridegroom's ear, MV 3.02. 52
you shall supply the bridegroom's place, | and SHR 3.02.249
sweet, | lie 'fore bride and bridegroom's feet, TNK 1.01. 14
BRIDEGROOMS 2 FR 0.0002 REL FR 2 V 0 P
and you brides and bridegrooms all, | with AYL 5.04.178
end | the visages of bridegrooms we'll put on TNK 5.04.127
BRIDE–HABITED 1 FR 0.0001 REL FR 1 V 0 P
i am bride–habited, | but maiden–hearted. TNK 5.01.150
BRIDEHOUSE 1 FR 0.0001 REL FR 1 V 0 P
pie, | may on our bridehouse perch or sing, | or TNK 1.01. 22
BRIDES 2 FR 0.0002 REL FR 2 V 0 P
and you brides and bridegrooms all, | with AYL 5.04.178
if the emperor's court can feast two brides, TIT 1.01.489
BRIDGE *(also pridge)*
BRIDGE 13 FR 0.0014 REL FR 7 V 6 P
what need the bridge much broader than the flood
ADO 1.01.316
now, captain fluellen, come you from the bridge? H5 3.06. 2 P
very excellent services committed at the bridge. 3.06. 4 P
the world, but keeps the bridge most valiantly, 3.06. 11 P
how now, fluellen, cam'st thou from the bridge? 3.06. 89 P
march to the bridge, it now draws toward night; 3.06.170
and i here, at the bulwark of the bridge. 1H6 1.04. 67
as well at london bridge as at the tower. 3.01. 23
jack cade hath gotten london bridge: 2H6 4.04. 49
for they have won the bridge, killing all those 4.05. 3 P
but first go and set london bridge on fire, and, 4.06. 14 P
for they account his head upon the bridge. R3 3.02. 70
take the bridge quite away | of him that, his TIM 4.03.158
BRIDGENORTH 2 FR 0.0002 REL FR 2 V 0 P
our meeting | is bridgenorth. 1H4 3.02.175
our general forces at bridgenorth shall meet. 3.02.178
BRIDGES 2 FR 0.0002 REL FR 1 V 1 P
attended him on bridges, stood in lanes, | laid 1H4 4.03. 70
a bay trotting–horse over four–inch'd bridges, LR 3.04. 57 P
BRIDGET 3 FR 0.0003 REL FR 1 V 2 P
and when mistress bridget lost the handle of her WIV 2.02. 12 P
does bridget paint still, pompey? ha? MM 3.02. 79 P
maud, bridget, marian, cic'ly, gillian, ginn! ERR 3.01. 31
BRIDLE 6 FR 0.0006 REL FR 4 V 2 P
o, know he is the bridle of your will. ERR 2.01. 13
the horses ran away, how her bridle was burst; SHR 4.01. 81 P
in what we can to bridle and suppress | the 2H6 1.01.200
but i'll bridle it. 4.07.106 P
this is it that makes me bridle passion, | and 3H6 4.04. 19
the studded bridle on a ragged bough | nimbly VEN 37
BRIDLED 2 FR 0.0002 REL FR 1 V 1 P
there's none but asses will be bridled so. ERR 2.01. 14
mine was not bridled. H5 3.07. 51 P
BRIEF* *(also breff, prief)*
/BRIEF* 1 FR 0.0001 REL FR 1 V 0 P
/in /brief, | /sorrow /would /be /a /rarity LR 4.03. 22
BRIEF* 94 FR 0.0106 REL FR 74 V 20 P
come, come, open the matter in brief: TGV 1.01.127 P
be brief, my good she–mercury. WIV 2.02. 79 P
you are a scholar (i will be brief with you), 2.02.181 P
give your men the charge, we must be brief. 3.03. 8 P
brief, short, quick, snap. 4.05. 2 P
man, | dress'd in a little brief authority, MM 2.02.118
cheap in beauty makes beauty brief in goodness; 3.01.182 P
possess'd him my most stay | can be but brief; 4.01. 44
be brief. 5.01. 26
in brief, to set the needless process by — 5.01. 92
say in brief the cause | why thou departedst ERR 1.01. 28
hence a just sevennight, and a time too brief, ADO 2.01.360 P
brief, i pray you, for you see it is a busy time 3.05. 4 P
friar francis, be brief — only to the plain 4.01. 1 P
in brief, since i do purpose to marry, i will 5.04.104 P
brief as the lightning in the collied night, MND 1.01.145
there is a brief how many sports are ripe. 5.01. 42
"a tedious brief scene of young pyramus | and 5.01. 56
tedious and brief? 5.01. 58
which is as brief as i have known a play; 5.01. 62
i hope she will be brief. 5.01.317 P
to be brief, the very truth is that the jew, MV 2.02.132 P
in very brief, the suit is impertinent to myself 2.02.137 P
but with all brief and plain conveniency | let 4.01. 82
how brief the life of man | runs his erring AYL 3.02.129
/in brief, he led me to the gentle duke, | who 4.03.142
brief, i recover'd him, bound up his wound, 4.03.150
in brief, sir, study what you most affect. SHR 1.01. 40
in brief, sir, sith it your pleasure is, | and i 1.01.211
well, sir, in brief, the gown is not for me. 4.03.155
that is the brief and the tedious of it, and AWW 2.03. 29 P
shall seem expedient on the now–born brief, 2.03.179
in a sweet verbal brief, it did concern | your 5.03.137
if you have reason, be brief. TN 1.05.200 P
write it in a martial hand, be curst and brief. 3.02. 43 P
very brief, and to exceeding good sense — less. 3.04.158 P
in brief, a braver choice of dauntless spirits JN 2.01. 72
shall draw this brief into as huge a volume. 2.01.103
in brief, we are the king of england's subjects: 2.01.267
i must be brief, lest resolution drop | out at 4.01. 35
a thousand businesses are brief in hand, | and 4.03.158
brief then; and what's the news? 5.06. 18
only to be brief | left i his title out. R2 3.03. 10
would you have been so brief with him, he would 3.03. 12
have been so brief /with /you to shorten you, 3.03. 13
come, come, in wooing sorrow let's be brief, 5.01. 93
bear this sealed brief | with winged haste to 1H4 4.04. 1
that makes such waste in brief mortality. H5 1.02. 28
therefore, in brief, | tell me their words as 3H6 4.01. 89
what, so brief? R3 1.04. 88
if die, be brief, | that our swift–winged souls 2.02. 43
speak suddenly, be brief. 4.02. 20
we must be brief when traitors brave the field. 4.03. 57
brief abstract and record of tedious days, 4.04. 28
and brief, good mother, for i am in haste. 4.04.162
be brief, lest that the process of thy kindness 4.04.254
in brief — for so the season bids us be — 5.03. 87
to steal from spiritual leisure a brief span H8 3.02.140
night hath been too brief. TRO 4.02. 11
thou art too brief. 4.05.237
i say, at once, let your brief plagues be mercy, 5.10. 8
doubt prevailing, and to make it brief wars. COR 1.03.100 P
a brief farewell. 4.01. 1
thus then in brief: ROM 1.03. 73
brief sounds determine my weal or woe. 3.02. 51
it were a grief, so brief to part with thee. 3.03.174
then i'll be brief. 5.03.169
i will be brief, for my short date of breath 5.03.229
the sweet degrees that this brief world affords TIM 4.03.253
out, out, brief candle! MAC 5.05. 23
i scent the morning air, | brief let me be. HAM 1.05. 59
on fortinbras, which he, in brief, obeys, 2.02. 68
limbs and outward flourishes, | i will be brief. 2.02. 92
are the abstract and brief chronicles of the 2.02.524 P
'tis brief, my lord. 3.02.153 P
list a brief tale, | and when 'tis told, o, that LR 5.03.182
quickly send | (be brief in it) to th' castle, 5.03.246
when i came back | (for this was brief), i found OTH 2.03.237
something that's brief; 3.01. 2
give me advantage of some brief discourse | with 3.01. 52
well, do it, and be brief, i will walk by. 5.02. 30
this is the brief: ANT 5.02.138
be brief, i pray you. CYM 1.01.101
nay, be brief: 3.04.165
minerva, | postures beyond brief nature; 5.05.165
and, to be brief, my practice so prevail'd, 5.05.199
brief, he must hence depart to tyre: PER 3.ch. 39
brief, i am | to those that prate and have done, TNK 5.01.118
"this brief abridgment of my will i make: LUC 1198
my woes are tedious, though my words are brief." 1309
nor can i fortune to brief minutes tell, SON 14. 5
love alters not with his brief hours and weeks, 116.11
our dates are brief, and therefore we admire 123. 5
in brief the grounds and motives of her woe. LC 63
BRIEFER 1 FR 0.0001 REL FR 1 V 0 P
art, | to teach you gamouth in a briefer sort, SHR 3.01. 67
BRIEFEST 1 FR 0.0001 REL FR 1 V 0 P
no friend | but resolution and the briefest end. ANT 4.15. 91
BRIEFLY 21 FR 0.0023 REL FR 11 V 10 P
briefly — i do mean to make love to ford's wife WIV 1.03. 43 P
briefly, i have pursu'd her as love hath pursu'd 2.02.200 P
show me briefly how. ADO 2.02. 11 P
and, briefly, i desire nothing but the reward of 5.01.243 P
instance, briefly; come, instance. AYL 3.02. 52 P
what england says, say briefly, gentle lord, JN 2.01. 52
briefly, to this end: 2H4 4.01. 54
you have enschedul'd briefly in your hands. H5 5.02. 73
briefly we heard their drums. COR 1.06. 16
speak briefly then, | for we are peremptory to 3.01.283
speak briefly, can you like of paris' love? ROM 1.03. 96
ay, and briefly. JC 3.03. 10 P
then to answer every man directly and briefly, 3.03. 15 P
for your dwelling — briefly. 3.03. 24 P
briefly, i dwell by the capitol. 3.03. 25 P
let's briefly put on manly readiness, | and meet MAC 2.03.133
old unhappy traitor, | briefly thyself remember; LR 4.06.229
briefly, sir. ANT 4.04. 10
briefly die their joys | that place them on the CYM 5.05.106
and time that is so briefly spent | with your PER 3.ch. 12
therefore briefly yield 'er, for she must 3.01. 53 P
BRIEFNESS 3 FR 0.0003 REL FR 3 V 0 P
briefness and fortune, work! LR 2.01. 18
i hope the briefness of your answer made | the CYM 2.04. 30
in feather'd briefness sails are fill'd, | and PER 5.02. 15
BRIER 7 FR 0.0008 REL FR 7 V 0 P
usurping ivy, brier, or idle moss, | who, all ERR 2.02.178
over dale, | thorough bush, thorough brier, MND 2.01. 3
of color like the red rose on triumphant brier, 3.01. 94
bog, through bush, through brake, through brier: 3.01.107
fairy sprite | hop as light as bird from brier, 5.01.394
from off this brier pluck a white rose with me. 1H6 2.04. 30
each envious brier his weary legs do scratch, VEN 705
BRIERS 10 FR 0.0011 REL FR 9 V 1 P
my lowing follow'd through | tooth'd briers, TMP 4.01.180
for briers and thorns at their apparel snatch; MND 3.02. 29
bedabbled with the dew and torn with briers, | i 3.02.443
o, how full of briers is this working–day world! AYL 1.03. 12 P
when briers shall have leaves as well as thorns, AWW 4.04. 32
have thy beauty scratch'd with briers and made WT 4.04.425
scratches with briers, | scars to move laughter COR 3.03. 51
whose mouth is covered with rude–growing briers,
TIT 2.03.199
the oaks bear mast, the briers scarlet heps; TIM 4.03.419
her bud again, | and leaves him to base briers. TNK 2.02.143
BRIGHT 92 FR 0.0104 REL FR 90 V 2 P
she is too bright to be look'd against. WIV 2.02.245 P
thus wisdom wishes to appear most bright | when MM 2.04. 78
nor shines the silver moon one half so bright LLL 4.03. 29
and since her time are colliers counted bright. 4.03.263
as sweet and musical | as bright apollo's lute, 4.03.340
vouchsafe, bright moon, and these thy stars, to 5.02.205
so quick bright things come to confusion. MND 1.01.149
how came her eyes so bright? 2.02. 92
you, the murtherer, look as bright, as clear, 3.02. 60
i thank thee, moon, for shining now so bright; 5.01.273
the moon shines bright. MV 5.01. 1
is thick inlaid with patens of bright gold. 5.01. 59
and thou wilt show more bright and seem more AYL 1.03. 81
"if the scorn of your bright eyne | have power 4.03. 50
lord, how bright and goodly shines the moon! SHR 4.05. 2
i say it is the moon that shines so bright. 4.05. 4
i know it is the sun that shines so bright. 4.05. 5
that i should love a bright particular star AWW 1.01. 86
in his bright radiance and collateral light 1.01. 88
they can behold | bright phoebus in his strength WT 4.04.124
i think, | that e'er the sun shone bright on. 5.01. 95
your sword is bright, sir, put it up again. JN 4.03. 79
your fearful land | with hard bright steel, and R2 3.02.111
track | of his bright passage to the occident. 3.03. 67
as bright as is the eagle's, lightens forth 3.03. 69
and like bright metal on a sullen ground, | my 1H4 1.02.212
to pluck bright honor from the pale–fac'd moon, 1.03.202
for it shines bright and never changes, but H5 5.02.164 P
soul will make | than julius caesar or bright — 1H6 1.01. 56
bright star of venus, fall'n down on the earth, 1.02.144
to save a paltry life and slay bright fame, 4.06. 45
burn bonfires clear and bright | to entertain 2H6 5.01. 3
whose bright out–shining beams thy cloudy wrath R3 1.03.267
an angel, with bright hair | dabbled in blood, 1.04. 53
and by the bright tract of his fiery car | gives 5.03. 20
fall | like a bright exhalation in the evening, H8 3.02.226
whose bright faces | cast thousand beams upon me 4.02. 88
where ever the bright sun of heaven shall shine, 5.04. 50
dear my lord, | keeps honor bright; TRO 3.03.151
tear my bright hair and scratch my praised 4.02.107
more bright in zeal than the devotion which 4.04. 26
on whose bright crest fame with her loud'st oyes 4.05.143
and tapers burn so bright, and every thing | in TIT 1.01.324
i will be bright, and shine in pearl and gold, 2.01. 19
the hunt is up, the /morn is bright and grey, 2.02. 1
feather of lead, bright smoke, cold fire, sick ROM 1.01.180
o, she doth teach the torches to burn bright! 1.05. 44
i conjure thee by rosaline's bright eyes, | by 2.01. 17
would through the airy region stream so bright 2.02. 21
o, speak again, bright angel, for thou art | as 2.02. 26
thou bright defiler | of hymen's purest bed! TIM 4.03.382
it is the bright day that brings forth the adder JC 2.01. 14
be bright and jovial among your guests to–night. MAC 3.02. 28
angels are bright still, though the brightest 4.03. 22
keep up your bright swords, for the dew will OTH 1.02. 59
finish, good lady, the bright day is done, | and ANT 5.02.193
made lud's–town with rejoicing fires bright, CYM 3.01. 32
begin to part | their fringes of bright gold. PER 3.02.100
madam, | by bright diana, whom we honor, all 3.03. 28
teach 'em | boldly to gaze against bright arms, TNK 2.02. 35
still blossom | as her bright eyes shine on ye, 2.02.234
her bright eyes break each morning 'gainst thy 2.03. 9
to this lady, | this bright young virgin. 2.05. 35
the next, the lord of may and lady bright, | the 3.05.125
you had indeed, | a bright bay, i remember. 3.06. 78
that fortunate bright star, the fair emilia, 3.06.146
these the bright lamps of beauty, that command 4.02. 39
let the temples | burn bright with sacred fires, 5.01. 3
mine eyes are grey, and bright, and quick in VEN 140
and as the bright sun glorifies the sky, | so is 485
look how a bright star shooteth from the sky, 815
the beauteous influence that makes him bright, 862
mortal stars as bright as heaven's beauties, LUC 13
whether it is that she reflects so bright | that 376
dead, | by thy bright beauty was it newly bred. 490
wip'd the brinish pearl from her bright eyes, 1213
to see their youthful sons bright weapons wield, 1432
seemed to appear | (like bright things stain'd) 1435
troy had been bright with fame, and not with 1491
into so bright a day such black–fac'd storms, 1518
bright orient pearl, alack, too timely shaded! PP 10. 3
but thou, contracted to thine own bright eyes, SON 1. 5
an eye more bright than theirs, less false in 20. 5
though not so bright | as those gold candles 21.11
i tell the day, to please him, thou art bright, 28. 9
and, darkly bright, are bright in dark directed. 43. 4
and, darkly bright, are bright in dark directed. 43. 4
thou, whose shadow shadows doth make bright, 43. 5
and nights bright days when dreams do show thee 43.14
you shall shine more bright in these contents 55. 3
in black ink my love may still shine bright. 65.14
i have sworn thee fair, and thought thee bright, 147.13
BRIGHT–BURNING 1 FR 0.0001 REL FR 1 V 0 P
or brought a faggot to bright–burning troy? TIT 3.01. 69
BRIGHTEN 1 FR 0.0001 REL FR 1 V 0 P
for yours, the god of heaven brighten it! 2H4 2.03. 17
BRIGHTER 1 FR 0.0001 REL FR 1 V 0 P
brighter than glass, and yet as glass is, PP 7. 3
BRIGHTEST 4 FR 0.0004 REL FR 4 V 0 P
but to the brightest beams | distracted clouds AWW 5.03. 34
ascend | the brightest heaven of invention! H5 pr 2
thus sometimes hath the brightest day a cloud, 2H6 2.04. 1
are bright still, though the brightest fell. MAC 4.03. 22
BRIGHTLY 2 FR 0.0002 REL FR 2 V 0 P
a substitute shines brightly as a king | until a MV 5.01. 94
that shone so brightly when this boy was got, TIT 4.02. 90
BRIGHTNESS 3 FR 0.0003 REL FR 3 V 0 P
for in her ray and brightness | the herd hath TRO 1.03. 47
the brightness of her cheek would shame those ROM 2.02. 19
and swear that brightness doth not grace the day SON 150. 4
BRIGHT–SHINING 1 FR 0.0001 REL FR 1 V 0 P
but, in the midst of this bright–shining day, 3H6 5.03. 3
BRIM 7 FR 0.0008 REL FR 7 V 0 P
o'erflow with joy | and pleasure drown the brim. AWW 2.04. 47
with ample and brim fullness of his force, H5 1.02.150
bring me but to the very brim of it, | and i'll LR 4.01. 75
and he will fill thy wishes to the brim | with ANT 3.13. 18
here, with a cup that's /stor'd unto the brim — PER 2.03. 50
on, | under whose brim the gaudy sun would peep;
VEN 1088
and stood stark naked on the brook's green brim. PP 6.10
BRIMFUL 4 FR 0.0004 REL FR 4 V 0 P
over them, | brimful of sorrow and dismay; TMP 5.01. 14
when richard, with his eye brimful of tears, 2H4 3.01. 67
our legions are brimful, our cause is ripe: JC 4.03.215
yet wild, the people's hearts brimful of fear, OTH 2.03.214
BRIMM'D 1 FR 0.0001 REL FR 1 V 0 P
camp a cestron | brimm'd with the blood of men. TNK 5.01. 47
BRIMS 1 FR 0.0001 REL FR 1 V 0 P
thy banks with pioned and twilled brims, | which TMP 4.01. 64
BRIMSTONE 3 FR 0.0003 REL FR 1 V 2 P
fire and brimstone! TN 2.05. 50 P
fire in your heart, and brimstone in your liver. 3.02. 20 P
fire and brimstone! OTH 4.01.234
BRINDED 1 FR 0.0001 REL FR 1 V 0 P
thrice the brinded cat hath mew'd. MAC 4.01. 1
/BRINE 1 FR 0.0001 REL FR 1 V 0 P
save when my lids scour'd off their /brine. TNK 3.02. 28
BRINE 10 FR 0.0011 REL FR 8 V 2 P
all but mariners | plung'd in the foaming brine, TMP 1.02.211
he shall drink nought but brine, for i'll not 3.02. 66
'tis the best brine a maiden can season her AWW 1.01. 48 P
her chamber round | with eye–offending brine; TN 1.01. 29

what a deal of brine | hath wash'd thy sallow ROM 2.03. 69
shalt be whipt with wire, and stew'd in brine, ANT 2.05. 65
and the brine and cloudy billow kiss the moon, i PER 3.01. 45 P
eat them) | the brine they wept at killing 'em. TNK 1.03. 22
the earth with show'rs of silver brine, LUC 796
laund'ring the silken figures in the brine LC 17
BRINE–PIT 1 FR 0.0001 REL FR 1 V 0 P
and made a brine–pit with our bitter tears? TIT 3.01.129
BRINE–PITS 1 FR 0.0001 REL FR 1 V 0 P
the fresh springs, brine–pits, barren place and TMP 1.02.338
/BRING 5 FR 0.0005 REL FR 5 V 0 P
/doth /this /bold /enterprise /bring /forth 2H4 1.01.178
/come, /bring /forth /the /prisoners. R3 3.03. 1
/trial /first, /bring /in /their /evidence. LR 3.06. 35
/sir, /i'll /bring /you /to /our /master /lear, 4.03. 50
spirits, | /and /bring /all /cyprus /comfort! OTH 2.01. 82
BRING 483 FR 0.0546 REL FR 388 V 95 P
bring her to try with main–course. TMP 1.01. 35 P
and then i'll bring thee to the present business 1.02.136
of it in the sea, bring forth more islands. 2.01. 94 P
making | than we bring men to comfort them. 2.01.135
the sore, | when you should bring the plaster. 2.01.140
but nature should bring forth, | of it own kind, 2.01.163
i'll bring my wood home faster. 2.02. 71 P
i prithee let me bring thee where crabs grow; 2.02.167
i'll bring thee | to clust'ring filberts, and 2.02.170
canst thou bring me to the party? 3.02. 59 P
i warrant, | and bring thee forth brave brood. 3.02.105
each putter–out of five for one will bring us 3.03. 48
go bring the rabble | (o'er whom i give thee 4.01. 37
bring a corollary, | rather than want a spirit. 4.01. 57
the trumpery in my house, go bring it hither, 4.01.186
for the prize i'll bring thee to | shall 4.01.205
at least bring forth a wonder, to content ye 5.01.170
and in the morn | i'll bring you to your ship, 5.01.308
and thither will i bring thee, valentine. TGV 1.01. 55
come, go with us, we'll bring thee to our crews, 4.01. 72
i'll bring you where you shall hear music and 4.02. 30 P
to her let us garlands bring. 4.02. 53
to bring me where to speak with madam silvia. 4.04.109
ursula, bring my picture there. 4.04.117
we must bring you to our captain. 5.03. 2
come, bring her away. 5.03. 5
come, i must bring you to our captain's cave. 5.03. 12
and i will bring the doctor about by the fields. WIV 2.03. 78 P
i will bring thee where mistress anne page is, 2.03. 86 P
he promise to bring me where is anne page; 3.01.123 P
i have suffer'd to bring this woman to evil for 3.05. 96 P
i'll but bring my young man here to school. 4.01. 8 P
go up, i'll bring linen for him straight. 4.02.100 P
and let us two devise to bring him thither. 4.04. 27
hearts, what ado here is to bring you together! 4.05.124 P
bring you the maid, you shall not lack a priest. 4.06. 53
sir, we'll bring you to windsor, to one master 5.05.165 P
that we may bring you something on the way. MM 1.01. 61
lead forth and bring you back in happiness! 1.01. 74
stead me | as bring me to the sight of isabella, 1.04. 18
bring him his confessor, let him be prepar'd, 2.01. 35
come, bring them away. 2.01. 41 P
bring them away. 2.01. 43 P
and do bring in here before your good honor two 2.01. 49 P
look you bring me in the names of some six or 2.01.272 P
bring /me to hear /them speak, where i may be 3.01. 52 P
answer'd, he would never bring them to light. 3.02.178 P
but my kisses bring again, bring again, | seals 4.01. 5
but my kisses bring again, bring again, | seals 4.01. 5
to bring you thus together 'tis no sin, | sith 4.01. 72
sirrah, bring barnardine hither. 4.03. 20 P
after him, fellows, bring him to the block. 4.03. 65
and he shall bring you | before the duke; 4.03.141
and bid them bring the trumpets to the gate. 4.05. 9
so bring us to our palace, where we'll show 5.01.538
and that to–morrow you will bring it home. ERR 3.01. 5
bring it, i pray you, to the porpentine, | for 3.01.116
buy thou a rope, and bring it home to me. 4.01. 20
then you will bring the chain to her yourself? 4.01. 40
and bring thy master home immediately. 4.02. 64
come, jailer, bring me where the goldsmith is, 4.04.142
then let your servants bring my husband forth. 5.01. 93
promising to bring it to the porpentine, | where 5.01.222
from you, | and dromio my man did bring them me. 5.01.386
bring you the length of prester john's foot, ADO 2.01.267 P
to bring signior benedick and the lady beatrice 2.01.366 P
and bring them to see this the very night before 2.02. 44 P
bring it hither to me in the orchard. 2.03. 3 P
i'll bring you thither, my lord, if you'll 3.02. 3 P
you'll be made bring deformed forth, i warrant 3.03.172 P
their examination yourself, and bring it me. 3.05. 49 P
bid him bring his pen and inkhorn to the jail. 3.05. 58 P
bring him away. 4.02. 86 P
bring me a father that so lov'd his child, 5.01. 8
with candle–wasters, bring him yet to me, | and 5.01. 18
come, bring away the plaintiffs. 5.01.253 P
bring you these fellows on. 5.01.331
least of thy sweet notice, bring her to trial. LLL 1.01.275 P
to the swain, bring him festinately hither. 3.01. 5 P
for the news i bring | is heavy in my tongue. 5.02.718
no, madam, we will bring you on your way. 5.02.873
four happy days bring in | another moon; MND 1.01. 2
ought to consider with /yourselves, to bring in 3.01. 30 P
that is, to bring the moonlight into a chamber; 3.01. 48 P
you can never bring in a wall. 3.01. 65 P
tie up my lover's tongue, bring him silently. 3.01.201
by some illusion see thou bring her here. 3.02. 98
and, good mounsieur, bring me the honey–bag. 4.01. 13 P
go bring them in; 5.01. 84
both | or bring your latter hazard back again, MV 1.01.151
a thing not in his power to bring to pass, | but 1.03. 92
bring me the fairest creature northward born, 2.01. 4
nor will not. come bring me unto my chance. 2.01. 43
when it is paid, bring your true friend along. 3.02.308
bring them i pray thee with imagin'd speed 3.04. 52
bring us the letters; call the messenger. 4.01.110
to bring thee to the gallows, not to the font. 4.01.400
give him the ring, and bring him, if thou canst, 4.01.453
and i bring word | my mistress will before the 5.01. 28
hand, | and bring your music forth into the air. 5.01. 53
i'll bring you to him straight. AYL 2.01. 69
if he be absent, bring his brother to me; 2.02. 18
quail | to bring again these foolish runaways. 2.02. 21
bring us where we may rest ourselves and feed. 2.04. 73
be food for it or bring it for food to thee. 2.06. 7 P
and if i bring thee not something to eat, i will 2.06. 11 P
bring him dead or living | within this 3.01. 6
in you, to bring the ewes and the rams together, 3.02. 78 P
you bring me out. soft, comes he not here? 3.02.251 P
bring us to this sight, and you shall say | i'll 3.04. 58
you say, if i bring in your rosalind, | you will 5.04. 6
and you say you will have her, when i bring her. 5.04. 9
that bring these tidings to this fair assembly. 5.04.153
well, bring our lady hither to our sight, | and SHR in.2. 74
kate, | and bring you from a wild kate to a kate 2.01.277
'twill bring you gain, or perish on the seas. 2.01.329
her father's liking, which to bring to pass, 3.02.129
i'll bring mine action on the proudest he | that 3.02.234
and bring along these rascal knaves with thee? 4.01.131
bring it from the dresser | and serve it thus to 4.01.163
come, i will bring thee to thy bridal chamber. 4.01.178
to dress thy meat myself, and bring it thee. 4.03. 40
him, | and bring our horses unto long–lane end; 4.03.185
what if a man bring him a hundred pound or two, 5.01. 21 P
away, i say, and bring them hither straight. 5.02.105
too, | since i nor wax nor honey can bring home, AWW 1.02. 65
bring in the admiration, that we with thee | may 2.01. 88
ere twice the horses of the sun shall bring 2.01.161
to bring me down | must answer for your raising? 2.03.112
to which title age cannot bring thee. 2.03.199 P
i will bring you | where you shall host. 3.05. 93
adversaries, when we bring him to our own tents. 3.06. 27 P
in stratagem can bring this instrument of honor 3.06. 65 P
come, bring forth this counterfeit module, h'as 4.03. 98 P
bring him forth, h'as sat i' th' stocks all 4.03.101 P
but with the word the time will bring on summer, 4.04. 31
my lord, to bring me in some grace, for you did 5.02. 46 P
me in some grace, for you did bring me out. 5.02. 47 P
on thee, lafew, | to bring forth this discov'ry. 5.03.151
go speedily and bring again the count. 5.03.152
both suffer under this complaint we bring, | and 5.03.163
find him, and bring him hither. 5.03.204
i pray you bring your hand to th' butt'ry–bar, TN 1.03. 70 P
i bring no overture of war, no taxation of 1.05.208 P
sir, to bring a cressida to this troilus. 3.01. 52 P
come bring us, bring us where he is. 3.02. 84 P
come bring us, bring us where he is. 3.02. 84 P
at which time we will bring the device to the 3.04.140 P
voice, and bring me word how thou find'st him. 4.02. 66 P
to speak with her, and bring her along with you, 5.01. 43 P
i'll bring you to a captain in this town, 5.01.254
the captain that did bring me first on shore 5.01.274
see him deliver'd, fabian, bring him hither. 5.01.315
they shall not see | to bring false generations. WT 2.01.148
from the oracle | they will bring all, whose 2.01.186
your attendants, i | shall bring emilia forth. 2.02. 14
so hot, good sir, | i come to bring him sleep. 2.03. 33
within this hour bring me word 'tis done | (and 2.03.136
therefore bring forth, | and in apollo's name, 3.02.117
if you can bring | tincture or lustre in her lip 3.02.204
prithee bring me | to the dead bodies of my 3.02.234
shall i bring thee on the way? 4.03.114 P
if i make not this cheat bring out another, and 4.03.121 P
she shall bring him that | which he not dreams 4.04.179
prithee bring him in, and let him approach 4.04.211 P
come bring away thy pack after me. 4.04.311 P
strive to qualify, | and bring him up to liking. 4.04.533
consider'd, i'll bring you where he is aboard, 4.04.795 P
this young man in pawn till i bring it you. 4.04.809 P
i will bring these two moles, these blind ones, 4.04.836 P
friends, | bring them to our embracement. 5.01.114
will bring me to consider that which may 5.01.122
my lord chatillion may from england bring | that JN 2.01. 46
and if not that, i bring you witnesses, | twice 2.01.274
pains | will bring this labor to an happy end. 3.02. 10
bring them before me. 4.02.169
but to my closet bring | the angry lords with 4.02.267
change their moons and bring their times about, R2 1.03.220
come, come, my son, i'll bring thee on thy way; 1.03.304
carts, | and bring away the armor that is there. 2.02.107
bring forth these men. 3.01. 1
bring me my boots, i will unto the king. 5.02. 84
which elder years | may happily bring forth. 5.03. 22
"lay by," and spent with crying "bring in"; 1H4 1.02. 36 P
to bring a slovenly unhandsome corse | betwixt 1.03. 44
face | of that occasion that shall bring it on. 1.03.276
bid the ostler bring my gelding out of the 2.01. 96 P
and bring him out that is but woman's son | can 3.01. 46
thou have power to raise him, bring him hither, 3.01. 59
early shall mine uncle | bring him our purposes. 4.03.111
cousin, and bring me word | what he will do. 5.01.109
which cannot choose but bring him quickly on. 5.02. 44
come bring your luggage nobly on your back. 5.04.156
tongues | they bring smooth comforts false, 2H4 in 40
i bring you certain news from shrewsbury. 1.01. 12
ragged'st hour that time and spite dare bring 1.01.151
good people, bring a rescue or two. 2.01. 56 P
look to see his father | bring up his powers; 2.03. 14
forth | shall bring this prize in very easily. 3.01.101
we bring it to the hive, and, like the bees, 4.05. 77
and tidings do i bring, and lucky joys, | and 5.03. 95
what? i do bring good news? 5.03.128
come, you rogue, come bring me to a justice. 5.04. 26 P
on this unworthy scaffold to bring forth | so H5 pr 10
at one time | bring in to any of your ancestors. 1.02.135
which pillage they with merry march bring home 1.02.195
and bring you back, charming the narrow seas 2.pr. 38
didst bring in | wonder to wait on treason and 2.02.109
husband, let me bring thee to staines. 2.03. 1 P
go, and bring them. 2.04. 67
here, | to whom expressly i bring greeting too. 2.04.112
chariot into roan | bring him our prisoner. 3.05. 55
and quickly bring us word of england's fall. 3.05. 68
bring me just notice of the numbers dead | on 4.07.117
pray thee go seek him, and bring him to my tent. 4.07.167 P
there must we bring him; 5.pr. 42
to bring your most imperial majesties | unto 5.02. 26
sad tidings bring i to you out of france, | of 1H6 1.01. 58
or bring him in obedience to your yoke. 1.01.164
a holy maid hither with me i bring, | which by a 1.02. 51
if thou spy'st any, run and bring me word, | and 1.04. 19
bring forth the body of old salisbury, | and 2.02. 4
and when you have done so, bring the keys to me. 2.03. 2
he | from john of gaunt doth bring his pedigree, 2.05. 77
work | to bring this matter to the wished end. 3.03. 28
should bring thy father to his drooping chair. 4.05. 5
bring forth that sorceress condemn'd to burn. 5.04. 1
dame eleanor gives gold to bring the witch; 2H6 1.02. 91
bring him near the king, | his highness' 2.01. 70
will bring thy head with sorrow to the ground! 2.03. 19
which time will bring to light in smooth duke 3.01. 65
betimes | than bring a burthen of dishonor home 3.01.298
bring me unto my trial when you will. 3.03. 8
bring the strong poison that i bought of him. 3.03. 18
therefore bring forth the soldiers of our prize, 4.01. 8
head, and bring them both upon two poles hither. 4.07.111 P
or dare to bring thy force so near the court. 5.01. 22
then what intends these forces thou dost bring? 5.01. 60
if thou dar'st bring them to the baiting–place. 5.01.150
may bring forth | a bird that will revenge upon 3H6 1.04. 35
would bring white hairs unto a quiet grave. 2.05. 40
bring forth that fatal screech–owl to our house 2.06. 56
and i'll be chief to bring him down again; 3.03.263
the bruit thereof will bring you many friends. 4.07. 64
bring forth the gallant, let us hear him speak. 5.05. 12
i am not barren to bring forth complaints. R3 2.02. 67
you thrive well, bring them to baynard's castle, 3.05. 98
myself, | no doubt we bring it to a happy issue. 3.07. 54
then bring me to their sights. 4.01. 24
take thou that, till thou bring better news. 4.04.508
but this good comfort bring i to your highness: 4.04.520
bid him bring his power | before sunrising, lest 5.03. 60
call up lord stanley, bid him bring his power. 5.03.290
you sleeping safe, they bring to you unrest; 5.03.320
will he bring his power? 5.03.342
our own brains and the opinion that we bring H8 pr 20
may bring his plain–song | and have an hour of 1.03. 45
to bring my whole cause 'fore his holiness, 2.04.120
the cordial that ye bring a wretched lady, | a 3.01.106
bring me a constant woman to her husband, | one 3.01.134
in spite of fortune | will bring me off again. 3.02.220
ye appear in every thing may bring my ruin! 3.02.242
bring him to us. 5.01. 83
i should have ta'en some pains to bring together 5.01.119
the tidings that i bring | will make my boldness 5.01.158
blessings, | which time shall bring to ripeness. 5.04. 20
arithmetic may soon bring his particulars TRO 1.02.113 P
to bring, uncle? 1.02.279 P
that the prais'd himself bring the praise forth; 1.03.242
i bring a trumpet to awake his ear, | to set his 1.03.251
be you my time to bring it to some shape. 1.03.313
that can from hector bring those honors off, 1.03.334
"bring action hither, this cannot go to war." 2.03.136
i shall, and bring his answer presently. 2.03.139
here i' th' orchard, i'll bring her straight. 3.02. 16 P
i have taken such pain to bring you together, 3.02.200 P
bear him, | and bring us cressid hither; 3.03. 31
withal bring word if hector will to–morrow | be 3.03. 34
'twas to bring this greek | to calchas' house, 4.01. 37
you bring me to do — and then you flout me too. 4.02. 26
i'll bring her to the grecian presently; 4.03. 6
and bring aeneas and the grecian with you. 4.04.100
lady, a word. i'll bring you to your father. 4.05. 53
alone | till accident or purpose bring you to't. 4.05.262
from agamemnon's tent, | to bring me thither? 4.05.286
i'll bring you to the gates. 5.02.188
i'll be ta'en too, | or bring him off. 5.06. 25
before 's, for the remove | bring up your army; COR 1.02. 29
confound an hour, | and bring thy news so late? 1.06. 18
bring me word thither | how the world goes, that 1.10. 31
should bring ourselves to be monstrous members. 2.03. 12 P
i cannot bring | my tongue to such a pace. 2.03. 50
and bring in | the crows to peck the eagles. 3.01.138
flat, | to bring the roof to the foundation, 3.01.204
him, and undertake to bring him | where he shall 3.01.322
where if you bring not martius, we'll proceed 3.01.331
i'll bring him to you. 3.01.332
bring me but out at gate. 4.01. 47
mark what mercy his mother shall bring from him. 5.04. 27 P
if | the roman ladies bring not comfort home, 5.04. 38
these that i bring unto their latest home, TIT 1.01. 83
follow, my lord, and i'll soon bring her back. 1.01.289
song | of lullaby to bring her babe asleep. 2.03. 29
bring thou her husband; 2.03.185
straight will i bring you to the loathsome pit 2.03.193
then all too late i bring this fatal writ, | the 2.03.264
some bring the murthered body, some the 2.03.300
i bring consuming sorrow to thine age. 3.01. 61
and bring you up | to be a warrior and command a 4.02.179
to save my boy, to nourish and bring him up, 5.01. 84
bring down the devil, for he must not die | so 5.01.145
i will bring in the empress and her sons, | the 5.02.116
to me, and bring with him | some of the chiefest 5.02.124
so, now bring them in, for i'll play the cook, 5.02.204
and bring our emperor gently in thy hand, 5.03.138
and bring thee cords made like a tackled stair, ROM 2.04.189
west, | and bring in cloudy night immediately. 3.02. 4
i will bring you thither. 3.02.129
i bring thee tidings of the prince's doom. 3.03. 8
and art | could to no issue of true honor bring. 4.01. 65
for shame, bring juliet forth, her lord is come. 4.05. 22
dost thou not bring me letters from the friar? 5.01. 13
again — | nor get a messenger to bring it thee, 5.02. 15
iron crow, and bring it straight | unto my cell. 5.02. 21
brother, i'll go and bring it thee. 5.02. 23
bring forth the parties of suspicion. 5.03.222
the little casket bring me hither. TIM 1.02.158
they labor'd | to bring manslaughter into form, 3.05. 27
to his heart, | to bring it into danger. 3.05. 35
come, bring in all together! 3.06. 47 P
bring down rose–cheek'd youth | to the /tub–fast 4.03. 87
womb, | let it no more bring out ingrateful man! 4.03.188
who can bring noblest minds to basest ends! 4.03.464
bring us to his cave. 5.01.119
bring us to him, | and /chance it as it may. 5.01.125
we stand much hazard if they bring not timon. 5.02. 5
bring in thy ranks, but leave without thy rage; 5.04. 39

bring me into your city, | and i will use the 5.04. 81
look in the calendar, and bring me word. JC 2.01. 42
bent, | and i will bring him to the capitol. 2.01.211
and bring me their opinions of success. 2.02. 6
yes, bring me word, boy, if thy lord look well, 2.04. 13
and bring me word what he doth say to thee. 2.04. 46
bring him with triumph home unto his house. 3.02. 49
we'll bring him to his house | with shouts and 3.02. 52
bring me to octavius. 3.02.271
and bring messala with you | immediately to us. 4.03.141
and bring us word unto octavius' tent | how 5.04. 31
bring forth men–children only! MAC 1.07. 72
why did you bring these daggers from the place? 2.02. 45
i'll bring you to him. 2.03. 47
bring them before us. 3.01. 47
that bring you word | macduff is fled to england 4.01.141
come bring me where they are. 4.01.156
bring thou this fiend of scotland and myself; 4.03.233
bring me no more reports, let them fly all. 5.03. 1
bring it after me. 5.03. 58
bring with thee airs from heaven, or blasts from HAM 1.04. 41
and bring these gentlemen where hamlet is. 2.02. 37
thyself do grace to them, and bring them in. 2.02. 53
when we would bring him on to some confession 3.01. 9
will bring him to his wonted way again, | to 3.01. 40
bring me to the test, | and /i the matter will 3.04.142
fair, and bring the body | into the chapel. 4.01. 36
of nothing, bring me to him. 4.02. 30 P
bring him before us. 4.03. 15
ho, bring in the lord. 4.03. 15
these good fellows will bring thee where i am. 4.06. 27 P
frenchman gave you, bring you in fine together, 4.07.133
that infirm and choleric years bring with them. LR 1.01.299 P
whence i will fitly bring you to hear my lord 1.02.169 P
come, bring away the stocks! 2.02.139
i entreat you | to bring but five and twenty; 2.04.248
true, boy. come bring us to this hovel. 3.02. 78
and bring you where both fire and food is ready. 3.04.153
pinion him like a thief, bring him before us. 3.07. 23
and bring some covering for this naked soul, 4.01. 44
i'll bring him the best 'parel that i have, 4.01. 49
bring me but to the very brim of it, | and i'll 4.01. 75
high–grown field, | and bring him to our eye. 4.04. 8
bring up the brown bills. 4.06. 91 P
self–reproving — bring his constant pleasure. 5.01. 4
i return to you again, | i'll bring you comfort. 5.02. 4
that parts us shall bring a brand from heaven, 5.03. 22
and more, much more, the time will bring it out. 5.03.164
business of the state, | to bring me to him? OTH 1.02. 91
bring him away; 1.02. 94
and he shall our commission bring to you; 1.03.281
and bring them after in the best advantage. 1.03.297
must bring this monstrous birth to the world's 1.03.404
bring thou the master to the citadel; 2.01.209
do this, if you can bring it to any opportunity. 2.01.281 P
and bring him jump when he may cassio find 2.03.386
/by /the /front | to bring you in again. 3.01. 50
part — to have so much to do | to bring him in! 3.03. 74
i think, | to bring them to that prospect; 3.03.398
i pray you bring me on the way a little, | and 3.04.197
'tis but a little way that i can bring you, 3.04.199
where is that viper? bring the villain forth. 5.02.285
come, bring away. 5.02.337
bring in the banket quickly; ANT 1.02. 12
seek him, and bring him hither. where's alexas? 1.02. 85
then we bring forth weeds | when our quick winds 1.02.109
i bring thee word | menecrates and menas, famous 1.04. 47
bring it to that, | the gold i give thee will i 2.05. 33
"but yet" is as a jailer to bring forth | some 2.05. 52
i that do bring the news made not the match. 2.05. 67
be honest, it is never good | to bring bad news. 2.05. 86
bring me word quickly. 2.05.114
bid you alexas | bring me word how tall she is. 2.05.118
spring, | and these the showers to bring it on. 3.02. 44
thou shalt bring him to me | where i will write. 3.03. 46
bring me to antony. 3.05. 23
bring him through the bands. 3.12. 25
being whipt, | bring him again; 3.13.103
fight, | follow me close, i'll bring you to't. 4.04. 34
i'll bring thee word | straight how 'tis like to 4.12. 2
mardian, | and bring me how he takes my death. 4.13. 10
and with your speediest bring us what she says, 5.01. 67
bring our crown and all. 5.02.232
would not suffer me | to bring him to the haven; CYM 1.01.171
and i will bring from thence that honor of hers 1.04.130 P
if i bring you no sufficient testimony that i 1.04.148 P
when thou shalt bring me word she loves my son, 1.05. 49
bring this apparel to my chamber. 3.05.151 P
so far have rav'd | to bring him here alone; 4.02.136
return, and bring him | to dinner presently. 4.02.165
us portends, | or what his death will bring us. 4.02.183
bring thee all this, | yea, and furr'd moss 4.02.227
and bring me word how 'tis with her. 4.03. 1
bring him to th' king. 5.03. 94
his manacles, bring your prisoner to the king. 5.04.191 P
man sing | may to your wishes pleasure bring, PER 1.ch. 14
bring in our daughter, clothed like a bride 1.01. 6
are arms to princes and bring joys to subjects. 1.02. 74
white flags display'd, they bring us peace, 1.04. 72
but bring they what they will and what they can, 1.04. 76
mighty king | his child, i wis, to incest bring; 2.ch. 2
ha, come and bring away the nets! 2.01. 13 P
and i'll bring thee to the court myself. 2.01.163 P
i'll bring you in subjection. 2.05. 75
bid nestor bring me spices, ink and /paper, | my 3.01. 65
and bid nicander | bring me the satin coffin. 3.01. 67
good mariner, | i'll bring the body presently. 3.01. 81
we'll bring your grace e'en to the edge a' th' 3.03. 35
i'll bring home some to–night. 4.02.144 P
come bring me to some private place. 4.06. 90 P
this is the fear we bring; TNK pr 21
perch or sing, | or with them any discord bring, 1.01. 23
'twould bring us to an eddy | where we should 1.02. 10
urns and odors bring away, | vapors, sighs, 1.05. 1
i would bring her fruit | fit for the gods to 2.02.238
bring him to th' plains, his learning makes no 2.03. 54
i come in | to bring him water in a morning, 2.04. 22
i'll bring you every needful thing. 3.01. 99
i'll come again some two hours hence and bring 3.03. 49
and with him bring | two swords and two good 3.06. 2
hourly bring your honor | in public question 3.06.221
i bring you news, | good news. 4.01. 17
ye are a good man | and ever bring good news. 4.01. 25
i'll bring a bevy, | a hundred black–ey'd maids 4.01. 71
i'll bring it to–morrow. 4.01.109
duke your brother, | madam, i bring you news. 4.02. 56
bring 'em in | quickly, by any means, i long to 4.02. 64
you must bring a piece of silver on the tip of 4.03. 20 P
this may bring her to eat, to sleep, and reduce 4.03. 94 P
which doubt not will bring forth comfort. 4.03.101 P
pray bring her in | and let's see how she is. 5.02. 24
they bring in strange roots, which is merely to STM II.C 8 P
sometime true news, sometime false doth bring, VEN 658
would bring him mulberries and ripe–red cherries 1103
"i see what crosses my attempt will bring, | i LUC 491
and bring him where his suit may be obtained? 898
to unmask falsehood and bring truth to light, 940
not, | green plants bring not forth their dye; PP 17.26
for to thy sensual fault i bring in sense — SON 35. 9
let him bring forth | eternal numbers to outlive 38.11
what can mine own praise to mine own self bring? 39. 3
can bring him to his sweet up–locked treasure, 52. 2
for i am sham'd by that which i bring forth, 72.13
when others would give life and bring a tomb. 83.12
so that myself bring water for my stain. 109. 8
bring me within the level of your frown, | but 117.11

BRINGER 3 FR 0.0003 REL FR 3 V 0 P
joy, | it comprehends some bringer of that joy; MND 5.01. 20
yet the first bringer of unwelcome news | hath 2H4 1.01.100
best you saf'd the bringer | out of the host; ANT 4.06. 25

BRINGETH 2 FR 0.0002 REL FR 2 V 0 P
lord, | from whom he bringeth sensible regreets: MV 2.09. 89
whereas the contrary bringeth bliss, | and is a 1H6 5.05. 64

BRINGING 14 FR 0.0015 REL FR 12 V 2 P
and to torment me | for bringing wood in slowly. TMP 2.02. 16
witness good bringing up, fortune, and truth: TGV 4.04. 69
i should have chid you for not bringing it, ERR 4.01. 50
well as another man, a plague on my bringing up! 1H4 2.04.497 P
bringing rebellion broached on his sword, | how H5 5.pr. 32
ireland, | in bringing them to civil discipline, 2H6 1.01.195
the ceremony | of bringing back the prisoner. H8 2.01. 5
hark, our drums | are bringing forth our youth. COR 1.04. 16
o, pardon me for bringing these ill news, ROM 5.01. 22
and the bringing home | of bell and burial. HAM 5.01.233
bringing the murderous coward to the stake; LR 2.01. 62
most like, | bringing me here to kill me. CYM 3.04.117
blessed in your care | in bringing up my child. PER 3.03. 32
'tis not our bringing up of poor bastards — as 4.02. 13 P

BRINGINGS–FORTH 1 FR 0.0001 REL FR 0 V 1 P
be but testimonied in his own bringings–forth, MM 3.02.145 P

BRINGING–UP 1 FR 0.0001 REL FR 1 V 0 P
to mine own children in good bringing–up, | and SHR 1.01. 99

BRINGS *(also prings)*

BRINGS 57 FR 0.0064 REL FR 46 V 11 P
that from the seedness the bare fallow brings MM 1.04. 42
he that brings any man to answer it that breaks ERR 4.03. 31 P
i think he brings the money. 4.04. 8
when the achiever brings home full numbers. ADO 1.01. 9 P
when i have heard it, what blessing brings it? 1.03. 7 P
they do not mark me, and that brings me out. LLL 5.02.173
the deepest loathing to the stomach brings, | or MND 2.02.138
who brings word the prince his master will be MV 1.02.125 P
and brings down | the rate of usance here with 1.03. 44
of any thing | that this same paper brings you. 3.02.250
besides, he brings his destiny with him. AYL 4.01. 57 P
he that brings this love to thee | little knows 4.03. 56
left on your right hand brings you to the place. 4.03. 80
and brings your froward wives | as prisoners to SHR 5.02.119
the mightiest space in fortune nature brings AWW 1.01.222
brings in the champion honor on my part, 4.02. 50
one brings thee in grace and the other brings 5.02. 50 P
thee in grace and the other brings thee out. 5.02. 50 P
the whirligig of time brings in his revenges. TN 5.01.376 P
what brings you here to court so hastily? JN 1.01.221
the yearly course that brings this day about 3.01. 81
and brings from him such offers of our peace 5.07. 84
that brings me food to make misfortune live? R2 5.05. 71
and not a man of them brings other news | than 2H4 in 38
to match with her that brings no vantages. 2H6 1.01.131
him, | and he that brings his head unto the king 4.08. 66
as brings a thousandfold more care to keep 3H6 2.02. 52
complete, | how many hours brings about the day, 2.05. 27
what brings thee to france? 3.03. 46
he is, and see, he brings the mayor along. R3 3.05. 13
reward to him that brings the traitor in? 4.04.516
and every tongue brings in a several tale, | and 5.03.194
and he brings his physic | after his patient's H8 3.02. 40
the pleasures such a beauty brings with it, TRO 2.02.147
boldness comes to me now, and brings me heart. 3.02.113
brings 'a victory in his pocket? COR 2.01.122 P
o, here comes my nurse, | and she brings news; ROM 3.02. 32
a glooming peace this morning with it brings, 5.03.305
o, the fierce wretchedness that glory brings us! TIM 4.02. 30
to mend, | and nothing brings me all things. 5.01.188
what conquest brings he home? JC 1.01. 32
is the bright day that brings forth the adder, 2.01. 14
fray, | and the wind brings it from the capitol. 2.04. 19
give him tending, | he brings great news. MAC 1.05. 38
who brings back to him that you attend him in HAM 5.02.196 P
your old smock brings forth a new petticoat, and ANT 1.02.168 P
he brings you figs. 5.02.235
he brings me liberty. 5.02.237
and brings the dire occasion in his arms | of CYM 4.02.196
fortune brings in some boats that are not 4.03. 46
one sorrow never comes but brings an heir | that PER 1.04. 63
in him, he brings not | a jot of terror to us. TNK 1.02. 94
this funeral path brings to your household's 1.05. 11
but in one minute's fight brings beauty under; VEN 746
back, | brings home his lord and other company, LUC 1584
thy sweet love rememb'red such wealth brings, SON 29.13
alack, what poverty my muse brings forth, | that 103. 1

BRING'ST 6 FR 0.0006 REL FR 4 V 2 P
thou bring'st me out of tune. AYL 3.02.248 P
thou bring'st me happiness and peace, son john, 2H4 4.05.227
hands, | unless thou bring'st them with thee. JC 5.01. 57
thou bring'st good news, i am call'd to be made CYM 5.04.193 P
out thy sorrows which /thou bring'st in haste, PER 1.04. 58
thou bring'st such pelting scurvy news TNK 2.02.266

BRINISH 4 FR 0.0004 REL FR 4 V 0 P
to hear and see her plaints, her brinish tears. 3H6 3.01. 41
surge | will in his brinish bowels swallow him. TIT 3.01. 97
and wip'd the brinish pearl from her bright eyes LUC 1213
with brinish current downward flow'd apace: LC 284

BRINK 2 FR 0.0002 REL FR 2 V 0 P
i have no strength to pluck thee to the brink. TIT 2.03.241
surprise me to the very brink of tears. TIM 5.01.156

BRISK 4 FR 0.0004 REL FR 3 V 1 P
of these most brisk and giddy–paced times. TN 2.04. 6
to see him shine so brisk and smell so sweet, 1H4 1.03. 54
"a cup of wine that's brisk and fine, | and 2H4 5.03. 46
boys, be brisk a while, and the longer liver ROM 1.05. 15 P

BRISKY 1 FR 0.0001 REL FR 1 V 0 P
most brisky juvenal and eke most lovely jew, MND 3.01. 95

BRISTLE 4 FR 0.0004 REL FR 3 V 1 P
not open my lips so wide as a bristle may enter, TN 1.05. 2 P
doth dogged war bristle his angry crest, | and JN 4.03.149
and bristle up | the crest of youth against your 1H4 1.01. 98
boy, bristle thy courage up; H5 2.03. 5

BRISTLED 2 FR 0.0002 REL FR 2 V 0 P
or bear, | pard, or boar with bristled hair, MND 2.02. 31
/chin he drove | the bristled lips before him. COR 2.02. 92

BRISTLES 1 FR 0.0001 REL FR 1 V 0 P
"his brawny sides, with hairy bristles armed, VEN 625

BRISTLY 2 FR 0.0002 REL FR 2 V 0 P
of bristly pikes that ever threat his foes, VEN 620
borne on the bier with white and bristly beard: SON 12. 8

BRISTOW 5 FR 0.0005 REL FR 5 V 0 P
i will for refuge straight to bristow castle: R2 2.02.135
your grace to go with us | to bristow castle, 2.03.164
ay, all of them at bristow lost their heads. 3.02.142
who bears hard | his brother's death at bristow, 1H4 1.03.271
fourteen days | at bristow i expect my soldiers, 2H6 3.01.328

BRITAIN* *(also bretagne, brittany*)*

BRITAIN* 47 FR 0.0053 REL FR 41 V 6 P
queen guinover of britain was a little wench, as LLL 4.01.123 P
arthur of britain, yield thee to my hand, | and JN 2.01.156
and let young arthur, duke of britain, in, | who 2.01.301
arthur of britain england's king and yours. 2.01.311
for we'll create young arthur duke of britain 2.01.551
a bay in britain, receiv'd intelligence | that R2 2.01.278
well furnished by the duke of britain | with 2.01.285
therefore the dukes of berri and of britain, H5 2.04. 4
for i know the britain richmond aims | at young R3 4.03. 40
the britain navy is dispers'd by tempest. 4.04.521
sail, and made his course again for britain. 4.04.527
long kept in britain at our mother's cost? 5.03.324
and, to–morrow, they | made britain india: H8 1.01. 21
believe it, sir, i have seen him in britain. CYM 1.04. 1 P
here comes the britain. 1.04. 28 P
and straight away for britain, lest the bargain 1.04.166 P
he is call'd | the britain reveller. 1.06. 61
thick sighs from him, whiles the jolly britain 1.06. 67
my lord, i fear, | has forgot britain. 1.06.113
in our not–fearing britain than have tidings 2.04. 19
was caius lucius in the britain court | when you 2.04. 37
sweet shortness which | was mine in britain, for 2.04. 45
be theme and hearing ever) was in this britain, 3.01. 4
who was the first of britain which did put | his 3.01. 59
the heir of cymbeline and britain, who | the 3.03. 87
at court, | then not in britain must you bide. 3.04.135
hath britain all the sun that shines? 3.04.136
are they not but in britain? 3.04.137
th' world's volume | our britain seems as of it, 3.04.138
prithee think | there's livers out of britain. 3.04.140
from whence he moves | his war for britain. 3.05. 26
a very valiant britain, and a good, | that here 4.02.369
'tis enough | that, britain, i have kill'd thy 5.01. 20
and suit myself | as does a britain peasant; 5.01. 24
if that thy gentry, britain, go before | this 5.02. 8
for being now a favorer to the britain, | no 5.03. 74
no more a britain, i have resum'd again | the 5.03. 75
in britain where was he | that could stand up 5.04. 53
britain be fortunate and flourish in peace and 5.04.144 P
to you, the liver, heart, and brain of britain, 5.05. 14
like romans, | and not o' th' court of britain. 5.05. 25
my boy, a britain born, | let him be ransom'd. 5.05. 84
he hath done no britain harm, | though he have 5.05. 90
away to britain | post i in this design. 5.05.191
brain | gan in your duller britain operate 5.05.197
britain be fortunate and flourish in peace and 5.05.441 P
whose issue | promises britain peace and plenty. 5.05.458

BRITAIN'S 3 FR 0.0003 REL FR 3 V 0 P
is this the government of britain's isle, | and 2H6 1.03. 44
britain's a world | by itself, and we will CYM 3.01. 12
"our britain's harts die flying, not our men. 5.03. 24

BRITAINS* 11 FR 0.0012 REL FR 11 V 0 P
a scum of britains and base lackey peasants, R3 5.03.317
and not these bastard britains, whom our fathers 5.03.333
fires bright, | and britains strut with courage. CYM 3.01. 33
which not to read would show the britains cold. 3.01. 75
your valiant britains have their wishes in it. 3.05. 20
our wars against | the fall'n–off britains, that 3.07. 6
must or for britains slay us or receive us | for 4.04. 5
and but the backs of britains seen, all flying 5.03. 6
preserv'd the britains, was the romans' bane." 5.03. 58
great the answer be | britains must take. 5.03. 80
that | the britains have ras'd out, though with 5.05. 70

BRITISH 4 FR 0.0004 REL FR 4 V 0 P
and fum, | i smell the blood of a british man.'" LR 3.04.184
the british pow'rs are marching hitherward. 4.04. 21
down, | i have the placing of the british crown. CYM 3.05. 65
let | a roman and a british ensign wave 5.05.480

BRITON *(see britain*, etc.)*

BRITTANY* *(also bretagne, britain*)*

BRITTANY* 4 FR 0.0004 REL FR 3 V 1 P
and then to brittany i'll cross the sea | to 3H6 2.06. 97
forthwith we'll send him hence to brittany, 4.06. 97
he shall to brittany. 4.06.101
too fair and too good for any lady in brittany. CYM 1.04. 72 P

/BRITTLE 2 FR 0.0002 REL FR 2 V 0 P
/a /brittle /glory /shineth /in /this /face, R2 4.01.287
/as /brittle /as /the /glory /is /the /face, 4.01.288

BRITTLE 4 FR 0.0004 REL FR 4 V 0 P
i better brook the loss of brittle life | than 1H4 5.04. 78

or else my kingdom stands on brittle glass. R3 4.02. 61
than glass, and yet as glass is, brittle, PP 7. 3
bud, | a brittle glass that's broken presently: 13. 4

BROACH 4 FR 0.0004 REL FR 4 V 0 P
else this blow should broach thy dearest blood. 1H6 3.04. 40
i | did broach this business to your highness, H8 2.04.150
i'll broach the tadpole on my rapier's point. TIT 4.02. 85
if i would broach the vessels of my love, | and TIM 2.02.177

BROACH'D 8 FR 0.0009 REL FR 6 V 2 P
he bravely broach'd his boiling bloody breast; MND 5.01.147
in, | i will continue that i broach'd in jest. SHR 1.02. 84
by the best blood that ever was broach'd, and 2H6 4.10. 38 P
for what hath broach'd this tumult but thy pride 3H6 2.02.159
broach'd with the steely point of clifford's 2.03. 16
that for her love such quarrels may be broach'd, TIT 2.01. 67
the business you have broach'd here cannot be ANT 1.02.173 P
or tell of babes broach'd on the lance, or women TNK 1.03. 20

BROACHED 3 FR 0.0003 REL FR 3 V 0 P
of broached mischief to the unborn times? 1H4 5.01. 21
bringing rebellion broached on his sword, | how H5 5.pr. 32
the business she hath broached in the state ANT 1.02.171

BROAD 21 FR 0.0023 REL FR 16 V 5 P
way that leads to the broad gate and the great AWW 4.05. 54 P
till by broad spreading it disperse to nought. 1H6 1.02.135
i'll canvass thee in thy broad cardinal's hat, 1.03. 36
distinction, with a broad and powerful fan, TRO 1.03. 27
in full as proud a place | as broad achilles; 1.03.190
i have been broad awake two hours and more. TIT 2.02. 17
stretches from an inch narrow to an ell broad! ROM 2.04. 84 P
i stretch it out for that word "broad," which, 2.04. 85 P
goose, proves thee far and wide a broad goose. 2.04. 87 P
be patient, for the world is broad and wide. 3.03. 16
against those honors deep and broad wherewith MAC 1.06. 17
rock, | as broad and general as the casing air; 3.04. 22
for from broad words, and 'cause he fail'd | his 3.06. 21
with all his crimes broad blown, as flush as may HAM 3.03. 81
him his pranks have been too broad to bear with, 3.04. 2
itself, and it is as broad as it hath breadth. ANT 2.07. 42 P
went a-hunting, and a wood, | and a broad beech; TNK 3.03. 41
his shoulders broad and strong, | arm'd long and 4.02. 84
broad breast, full eye, small head, and nostril VEN 296
mane, thick tail, broad buttock, tender hide; 298
his) | on your broad main doth willfully appear. SON 80. 8

BROADER 2 FR 0.0002 REL FR 1 V 1 P
need the bridge much broader than the flood? ADO 1.01.316
who can speak broader than he that has no house TIM 3.04. 63 P

BROAD-FRONTED 1 FR 0.0001 REL FR 1 V 0 P
broad-fronted caesar, | when thou wast here ANT 1.05. 29

BROADSIDES 1 FR 0.0001 REL FR 1 V 0 P
fear we broadsides? 2H4 2.04.182

BROAD-SPREADING 1 FR 0.0001 REL FR 1 V 0 P
the weeds which his broad-spreading leaves did R2 3.04. 50

BROCAS 1 FR 0.0001 REL FR 1 V 0 P
the heads of brocas and sir bennet seely, | two R2 5.06. 14

BROCK 1 FR 0.0001 REL FR 0 V 1 P
marry, hang thee, brock! TN 2.05.103 P

BROGUES 1 FR 0.0001 REL FR 1 V 0 P
and put | my clouted brogues from off my feet, CYM 4.02.214

BROIL 5 FR 0.0005 REL FR 5 V 0 P
it seems then that the tidings of this broil 1H4 1.01. 47
you of my household, leave this peevish broil, 1H6 3.01. 92
methinks already in this civil broil | i see 2H6 4.08. 44
stop, | or all will fall in broil. COR 3.01. 33
say to the king the knowledge of the broil | as MAC 1.02. 6

BROIL'D 1 FR 0.0001 REL FR 1 V 0 P
how say you to a fat tripe finely broil'd? SHR 4.03. 20

BROILING 1 FR 0.0001 REL FR 1 V 0 P
god save you, sir! where have you been broiling? H8 4.01. 56

/BROILS* 1 FR 0.0001 REL FR 1 V 0 P
/the /vaunt /and /firstlings /of /those /broils, TRO pr 27

BROILS* 12 FR 0.0013 REL FR 12 V 0 P
and breathe short-winded accents of new broils 1H4 1.01. 3
prosper this realm, keep it from civil broils, 1H6 1.01. 53
if holy churchmen take delight in broils? 3.01.111
rancorous spite, more furious raging broils, 4.01.185
mov'd with remorse of these outrageous broils, 5.04. 97
now here a period of tumultuous broils. 3H6 5.05. 1
seated, and domestic broils | clean overblown, R3 2.04. 60
who broils in loud applause, and make him fall TRO 1.03.378
art their soldier, and, being bred in broils, COR 3.02. 81
for these domestic and particular broils | are LR 5.01. 30
than pertains to feats of broils and battle, OTH 1.03. 87
and broils root out the work of masonry, | nor SON 55. 6

BROKE *(also brake*)*

/BROKE 1 FR 0.0001 REL FR 1 V 0 P
/pardon /all /oaths /that /are /broke /to /me! R2 4.01.214

BROKE 88 FR 0.0099 REL FR 69 V 19 P
o my father, | i have broke your hest to say so! TMP 3.01. 37
her waspish-headed son has broke his arrows, 4.01. 99
my men, kill'd my deer, and broke open my lodge. WIV 1.01.112 P
slender, i broke your head; 1.01.122 P
i detest, an honest maid as ever broke bread. 1.04.151 P
which are as easy broke as they make forms. MM 2.04.126
which was broke off, | partly for that her 5.01.218
you have no stomach, having broke your fast: ERR 1.02. 50
he broke from those that had the guard of him, 5.01.149
my master and his man are both broke loose, 5.01.169
i have broke with her father, and his good will ADO 2.01.299 P
sir, by my troth he is, as ever broke bread; 3.05. 39 P
him another staff, this last was broke cross. 5.01.139 P
fell over the threshold, and broke my shin. LLL 3.01.117
vows for thee broke deserve not punishment. 4.03. 61
if by me broke, what fool is not so wise | to 4.03. 70
your oath once broke, you force not to forswear. 5.02.440
by all the vows that ever men have broke | (in MND 1.01.175
and in conclusion dumbly have broke off, | not 5.01. 98
a moment threw him, and broke three of his ribs, AYL 1.02.127 P
or if thou hast not broke from company 2.04. 40
when i was in love i broke my sword upon a stone 2.04. 47 P
why no, for she hath broke the lute to me. SHR 2.01.148
i would i had, so i had broke thy pate, | and AWW 2.01. 66
h'as broke my head across and has given sir toby TN 5.01.175 P
you broke my head for nothing, and that that i 5.01.184 P
me | upon good friday and ne'er broke his fast. JN 1.01.235
i faintly broke with thee of arthur's death; 4.02.227
and broke out | to acquaint you with this evil, 5.06. 24
that late broke from the duke of exeter, | his R2 2.01.281
and him, | broke the possession of a royal bed, 3.01. 13
how sour sweet music is | when time is broke, 5.05. 43
to check time broke in a disordered string; 5.05. 46
had not an ear to hear my true time broke. 5.05. 48
broke oath on oath, committed wrong on wrong, 1H4 4.03.101
full of high feeding, madly hath broke loose, 2H4 1.01. 10
when the prince broke thy head for liking his 2.01. 89 P
that you broke your word | when you were more 2.03. 10
west, north, south, or, like a school broke up, 4.02.104
fathers | have broke their sleep with thoughts, 4.05. 68
what was th' impediment that broke this off? H5 1.01. 90
for 'a never broke any man's head but his own, 3.02. 40 P
why, all our ranks are broke. 4.05. 6
then broke i from the officers that led me, 1H6 1.04. 44
our windows are broke down in every street, 3.01. 84
the regent hath with talbot broke his word, 4.06. 2
and therefore may be broke without offense. 5.05. 35
was broke in twain (by whom i have forgot, | but 2H6 1.02. 26
broke be my sword, my arms torn and defac'd, 4.01. 42
my sword therefore broke through london gates, 4.08. 23 P
is crown'd so soon, and broke his solemn oath? 3H6 1.04.100
since when, his oath is broke; 2.02. 89
a thousand men have broke their fasts to-day 2.02.127
our ranks are broke, and ruin follows us. 2.03. 10
and tell me then, have you not broke your oaths? 3.01. 79
the cable broke, the holding-anchor lost, | and 5.04. 4
when thou hast broke it in such dear degree? R3 1.04.210
have broke their backs with laying manors on 'em H8 1.01. 84
not consulting, broke | into a general prophecy: 1.01. 91
my high-blown pride | at length broke under me, 3.02.362
you have broke it, cousin; TRO 3.01. 50 P
i would they had broke 's neck! 4.02. 76 P
that hunger broke stone walls, that dogs must COR 1.01.206
passions and whose plots have broke their sleep 4.04. 19
my grained ash an hundred times hath broke, 4.05.108
and almost broke my heart with extreme laughter. TIT 5.01.113
for even the day before, she broke her brow, ROM 1.03. 38
the day is broke, be wary, look about. 3.05. 40
such a house broke? TIM 4.02. 5
how has the ass broke the wall, that thou art 4.03.349 P
cunning in excess, | hath broke their hearts. 5.04. 29
most sacrilegious murther hath broke ope | the MAC 2.03. 67
turn'd wild in nature, broke their stalls, flung 2.04. 16
displac'd the mirth, broke the good meeting, 3.04.108
at no time broke my faith, would not betray 4.03.128
the doors are broke. HAM 4.05.112
clamb'ring to hang, an envious sliver broke, 4.07.173
and broke them in the sweet face of heaven: LR 3.04. 88 P
the day had broke | before we parted. OTH 3.01. 32
i would have broke mine eye-strings, crack'd CYM 1.03. 17
you have broke his pate with your bowl. 2.01. 6 P
if his wit had been like him that broke it, it 2.01. 9 P
he broke his whipstock and exclaim'd against TNK 1.02. 86
cannot love thee, he that broke thy prison — 3.06.139
vows for thee broke deserve not punishment. PP 3. 4
if by me broke, what fool is not so wise | to 3.13
one of her feathered creatures broke away, SON 143. 2
in act thy bed-vow broke, and new faith torn 152. 3

/BROKEN 1 FR 0.0001 REL FR 1 V 0 P
/might /yet /have /balm'd /thy /broken /sinews, LR 3.06. 98

BROKEN 69 FR 0.0078 REL FR 48 V 21 P
what, are they broken? TGV 2.05. 18 P
unheedful vows may heedfully be broken, | and he 2.06. 11
odd quirks and remnants of wit broken on me, ADO 2.03.236 P
here's a costard broken in a shin. LLL 3.01. 70
by saying that a costard was broken in a shin. 3.01.106
me, how was there a costard broken in a shin? 3.01.111 P
if broken then, it is no fault of mine: 4.03. 69
me without some broken limb shall acquit him AYL 1.01.127 P
longs to see this broken music in his sides? 1.02.141 P
upon that poor and broken bankrupt there?" 2.01. 57
crop | to glean the broken ears after the man 3.05.102
that you might excuse | his broken promise, and 4.03.154
out of the town armory, with a broken hilt, and SHR 3.02. 47 P
with two broken points; 3.02. 48 P
my mouth no more were broken than these boys', AWW 2.03. 60
most sorry, you have broken from his liking, WT 5.01.212
i make a broken delivery of the business; 5.02. 9 P
a deal of wonder is broken out within this hour 5.02. 24 P
upon our sides it never shall be broken. JN 5.02. 8
the /king's grown bankrout, like a broken man. R2 2.01.257
imp out our drooping country's broken wing, 2.01.292
the earl of worcester | hath broken his staff, 2.02. 59
broken his staff of office, and dispers'd | the 2.03. 27
their points being broken — 1H4 2.04.214 P
wouldst thou have thy head broken? 3.01.237 P
is not your voice broken, your wind short, your 2H4 1.02.182 P
our peace will, like a broken limb united, 4.01.220
virgins with the broken seals of perjury; H5 4.01.163 P
away, the skin is good for your broken coxcomb. 5.01. 55 P
come, your answer in broken music; 5.02.243 P
for thy voice is music and thy english broken; 5.02.244 P
break thy mind to me in broken english — wilt 5.02.246 P
and on the pieces of the broken wand | were 2H6 1.02. 28
false king, why hast thou broken faith with me, 5.01. 91
i will, | for hither we have broken in by force. 3H6 1.01. 29
but for a kingdom any oath may be broken: 1.02. 16
(for trust not him that hath once broken faith), 4.04. 30
methoughts that i had broken from the tower R3 1.04. 9
the broken rancor of your high-swoll'n hates, 2.02.117
king my husband made | thou hadst not broken, 4.04.380
thy broken faith hath made the prey for worms. 4.04.386
amaze the welkin with your broken staves! 5.03.341
you have now a broken banket, but we'll mend it. H8 1.04. 61
an old man, broken with the storms of state, 4.02. 21
which they moved | have broken with the king, 5.01. 47
fair prince, here is good broken music. TRO 3.01. 49 P
kiss, | distasted with the salt of broken tears. 4.04. 48
as subtle | as ariachne's broken woof to enter. 5.02.152
sheaf, | these broken limbs again into one body. TIT 5.03. 72
for your broken shin. ROM 1.02. 52
with clamorous demands of debt, broken bonds, TIM 2.02. 37
all broken implements of a ruin'd house. 4.02. 16
a broken voice, an' his whole function suiting HAM 2.02.556
a knave, a rascal, an eater of broken meats; LR 2.02. 15 P
men do their broken weapons rather use | than OTH 1.03.174
this broken joint between you and her husband 2.03.322 P
you have broken | the article of your oath, ANT 2.02. 81
of his wings destitute, the army broken, | and CYM 5.03. 5
men, | who of their broken debtors take a third, 5.04. 19
knights have done, | h'as broken a staff or so; PER 2.03. 35
and what broken piece of matter soe'er she's TNK 4.03. 6 P
kissing speaks, with lustful language broken, VEN 47
"poor broken glass, i often did behold | in thy LUC 1758
if broken, then it is no fault of mine. PP 3.12
bud, | a brittle glass that's broken presently: 13. 4
lost, vaded, broken, dead within an hour. 13. 6
ground, | as broken glass no cement can redress: 13.10
dost thou desire my slumbers should be broken SON 61. 3
the broken bosoms that to me belong | have LC 254

BROKENLY 1 FR 0.0001 REL FR 0 V 1 P
hear you confess it brokenly with your english H5 5.02.106 P

BROKER 7 FR 0.0008 REL FR 7 V 0 P
now, by my modesty, a goodly broker! TGV 1.02. 41
that broker that still breaks the pate of faith, JN 2.01.568
this bawd, this broker, this all-changing word, 2.01.582
"a crafty knave does need no broker," | yet am i 2H6 1.02.100
yet am i suffolk and the cardinal's broker. 1.02.101
leave | to play the broker in mine own behalf; 3H6 4.01. 63
hence, broker, lackey! TRO 5.10. 33

BROKERS 2 FR 0.0002 REL FR 2 V 0 P
do not believe his vows, for they are brokers, HAM 1.03.127
knew vows were ever brokers to defiling, LC 173

BROKERS-BETWEEN 1 FR 0.0001 REL FR 0 V 1 P
women cressids, and all brokers-between pandars! TRO 3.02.203 P

BROKES 1 FR 0.0001 REL FR 1 V 0 P
and brokes with all that can in such a suit AWW 3.05. 71

BROKING 1 FR 0.0001 REL FR 1 V 0 P
redeem from broking pawn the blemish'd crown, R2 2.01.293

BROOCH 6 FR 0.0006 REL FR 2 V 4 P
saint george's half-cheek in a brooch. LLL 5.02.616 P
ay, and in a brooch of lead. 5.02.617 P
just like the brooch and the toothpick, which AWW 1.01.158 P
glass, pomander, brooch, table-book, ballad, WT 4.04.598 P
is a strange brooch in this all-hating world. R2 5.05. 66
he is the brooch indeed | and gem of all the HAM 4.07. 93

BROOCH'D 1 FR 0.0001 REL FR 1 V 0 P
caesar ever shall | be brooch'd with me, if ANT 4.15. 25

BROOCHES 1 FR 0.0001 REL FR 0 V 1 P
"your brooches, pearls, and ouches." 2H4 2.04. 48 P

BROOD 9 FR 0.0010 REL FR 9 V 0 P
i warrant, | and bring thee forth brave brood. TMP 3.02.105
such things become the hatch and brood of time, 2H4 3.01. 86
why, what a brood of traitors have we here! 2H6 5.01.141
and doves will peck in safeguard of their brood. 3H6 2.02. 18
when she, poor hen, fond of no second brood, COR 5.03.162
with all his threat'ning band of typhon's brood, TIT 4.02. 94
soul | o'er which his melancholy sits on brood, HAM 3.01.165
for it was lent thee all that brood to kill. LUC 627
and make the earth devour her own sweet brood; SON 19. 2

BROODED 1 FR 0.0001 REL FR 1 V 0 P
then, in despite of brooded watchful day, | i JN 3.03. 52

BROODING 1 FR 0.0001 REL FR 1 V 0 P
saw | and birds sit brooding in the snow | and LLL 5.02.923

BROOK* *(also abrook)*

/BROOK* 41 FR 0.0046 REL FR 2 V 39 P
to him and tell him my name is /brook — only WIV 2.01.216 P
and thy name shall be /brook. 2.01.219 P
there's one master /brook below would fain speak 2.02.144 P
/brook is his name? 2.02.148 P
my name is /brook. 2.02.161 P
good master /brook, i desire more acquaintance 2.02.162 P
speak, good master /brook, i shall be glad to be 2.02.178 P
master /brook, i will first make bold with your 2.02.252 P
want no mistress ford, master /brook, you shall 2.02.260 P
master /brook, thou shalt know i will 2.02.281 P
thou, master /brook, shalt know him for knave, 2.02.285 P
i marvel i hear not of master /brook; 3.05. 57 P
now, master /brook, you come to know what hath 3.05. 61 P
master /brook, i will not lie to you. 3.05. 64 P
very ill-favoredly, master /brook. 3.05. 67 P
no, master /brook, but the peaking cornuto her 3.05. 70 P
the peaking cornuto her husband, master /brook, 3.05. 71 P
that, master /brook, there was the rankest 3.05. 91 P
nay, you shall hear, master /brook, what i have 3.05. 95 P
but mark the sequel, master /brook. 3.05.107 P
hissing-hot — think of that, master /brook. 3.05.122 P
master /brook, i will be thrown into etna, as i 3.05.126 P
eight and nine is the hour, master /brook. 3.05.131 P
you shall have her, master /brook. 3.05.137 P
master /brook, you shall cuckold ford. 3.05.137 P
nay, i'll to him again in name of /brook; 4.04. 76
how now, master /brook? 5.01. 9 P
master /brook, the matter will be known to-night 5.01. 9 P
i went to her, master /brook, as you see, like a 5.01. 15 P
but i came from her, master /brook, like a poor 5.01. 17 P
mad devil of jealousy in him, master /brook, 5.01. 19 P
for in the shape of man, master /brook, i fear 5.01. 21 P
along with me, i'll tell you all, master /brook. 5.01. 24 P
strange things in hand, master /brook! 5.01. 30 P
master /brook, falstaff's a knave, a cuckoldly 5.05.110 P
here are his horns, master /brook; 5.05.111 P
and, master /brook, he hath enjoy'd nothing of 5.05.112 P
of money, which must be paid to master /brook. 5.05.114 P
his horses are arrested for it, master /brook. 5.05.115 P
to one master /brook that you have cozen'd of 5.05.166 P
to master /brook you yet shall hold your word, 5.05.244

BROOK* 44 FR 0.0049 REL FR 42 V 2 P
have learn'd me how to brook this patiently. TGV 5.03. 4
i better brook than flourishing peopled towns: 5.04. 3
my business cannot brook this dalliance. ERR 4.01. 59
many can brook the weather that love not the LLL 4.02. 33
or mead, | by paved fountain or by rushy brook, MND 2.01. 84
they come | as o'er a brook to see fair portia. MV 2.07. 47
as doth an inland brook | into the main of 5.01. 96
or brook such disgrace well as he shall run into AYL 1.01.133 P
upon the brook that brawls along this wood, | to 2.01. 32
stood on th' extremest verge of the swift brook, 2.01. 42
he is drown'd in the brook; 3.02.287 P
straight | adonis painted by a running brook, SHR in.2. 50

i cannot brook thy sight, | this news hath made JN 3.01. 36
nor can one england brook a double reign | of 1H4 5.04. 66
i can no longer brook thy vanities. 5.04. 74
i better brook the loss of brittle life | than 5.04. 78
then brook abridgment, and your eyes advance H5 5.pr. 44
henry, our late sovereign, ne'er could brook? 1H6 1.03. 24
let him perceive how ill we brook his treason, 4.01. 74
this weighty business will not brook delay, 2H6 1.01.170
believe me, lords, for flying at the brook, | i 2.01. 1
smooth runs the water where the brook is deep, 3.01. 53
for he is fierce and cannot brook hard language. 4.09. 45
with me, | knowing how hardly i can brook abuse? 5.01. 92
/these |-if they can brook i bow a knee to man. 5.01.110
whose warlike ears could never brook retreat, 3H6 1.01. 5
my heart for anger burns, i cannot brook it. 1.01. 60
right gracious lord, i cannot brook delay. 3.02. 18
my breast can better brook thy dagger's point 5.06. 27
in that you brook it ill, it makes him worse; R3 1.03. 3
being a bark to brook no mighty sea — | than in 3.07.162
that cannot brook the accent of reproof. 4.04.159
wonder | his insolence can brook to be commanded COR 1.01.262
they be, | and cannot brook competitors in love? TIT 2.01. 77
soldiers should brook as little wrongs as gods. TIM 3.05.116
will the cold brook, | candied with ice, caudle 4.03.225
there is a willow grows askaunt the brook, HAM 4.07.166
and herself | fell in the weeping brook. 4.07.175
spreads like a plane | fast by a brook, and TNK 2.06. 6
and died to kiss his shadow in the brook. VEN 162
"when he beheld his shadow in the brook, | the 1099
sitting by a brook | with young adonis, lovely, PP 4. 1
adonis made | under an osier growing by a brook, 6. 5
a brook where adon us'd to cool his spleen. 6. 6
BROOK'D 3 FR 0.0003 REL FR 2 V 1 P
nature of our quarrel yet never brook'd parle, SHR 1.01.115 P
how hath your lordship brook'd imprisonment? R3 1.01.125
there was a brutus once that would have brook'd JC 1.02.159
BROOK'S 1 FR 0.0001 REL FR 1 V 0 P
and stood stark naked on the brook's green brim. PP 6.10
/BROOKS* 1 FR 0.0001 REL FR 0 V 1 P
such /brooks are welcome to me, that o'erflows WIV 2.02.150 P
BROOKS* 7 FR 0.0008 REL FR 7 V 0 P
nymphs, call'd naiades, of the windring brooks, TMP 4.01.128
ye elves of hills, brooks, standing lakes, and 5.01. 33
tongues in trees, books in the running brooks, AYL 2.01. 16
how brooks your grace the air | after your late R2 3.02. 2
and hair of our attempt | brooks no division. 1H4 4.01. 62
are the fount that makes small brooks to flow; 3H6 4.08. 54
a woeful hostess brooks not merry guests. LUC 1125
BROOM 2 FR 0.0002 REL FR 2 V 0 P
i am sent with broom before, | to sweep the dust MND 5.01.389
i can sing "the broom," | and "bonny robin." TNK 4.01.107
BROOM-GROVES 1 FR 0.0001 REL FR 1 V 0 P
and thy broom-groves, | whose shadow the TMP 4.01. 66
BROOM-STAFF 1 FR 0.0001 REL FR 0 V 1 P
at length they came to th' broom-staff to me, i H8 5.03. 54 P
BROTH 1 FR 0.0001 REL FR 1 V 0 P
my wind cooling my broth | would blow me to an MV 1.01. 22
BROTHEL 4 FR 0.0004 REL FR 4 V 0 P
master's bed, | thy mistress is o' th' brothel! TIM 4.01. 13
of sale," | videlicet, a brothel, or so forth. HAM 2.01. 59
makes it more like a tavern or a brothel | than LR 1.04.245
marina thus the brothel scapes, and chances PER 5.ch. 1
BROTHEL-HOUSE 1 FR 0.0001 REL FR 0 V 1 P
at the door of a brothel-house for the sign of ADO 1.01.253 P
BROTHELS 1 FR 0.0001 REL FR 0 V 1 P
keep thy foot out of brothels, thy hand out of LR 3.04. 96 P
/BROTHER 5 FR 0.0005 REL FR 4 V 1 P
o, spare me not, my /brother edward's son, | for R2 2.01.124
transformation of jupiter there, his /brother, TRO 5.01. 54 P
/fie, /brother, /fie, /teach /her /not /thus /to TIT 3.02. 21
/the /innocent | /becomes /not /titus' /brother. 3.02. 57
/could /my /good /brother /suffer /you /to /do LR 4.02. 44
BROTHER 536 FR 0.0605 REL FR 450 V 86 P
"farewell, brother!" TMP 1.01. 62
my brother and thy uncle, call'd antonio — | i 1.02. 66
me — that a brother should | be so perfidious! 1.02. 67
study, | the government i cast upon my brother, 1.02. 75
in my false brother | awak'd an evil nature, and 1.02. 92
then tell me | if this might be a brother. 1.02.118
fair milan | with all the honors on my brother; 1.02.127
you did supplant your brother prospero. 2.01.271
here lies your brother, | no better than the 2.01.280
brother, my lord the duke, | stand to, and do as 3.03. 51
king, | his brother, and yours, abide all three 5.01. 12
thy brother was a furtherer in the act. 5.01. 73
you, brother mine, that /entertain'd ambition, 5.01. 75
sir, whom to call brother | would even infect my 5.01.130
and ferdinand, her brother, found a wife | where 5.01.210
wherewith my brother held you in the cloister? TGV 1.03. 2
i will, as 'twere a brother of your order, MM 1.03. 44
fair sister | to her unhappy brother claudio? 1.04. 20
why "her unhappy brother"? 1.04. 21
gentle and fair, your brother kindly greets you. 1.04. 24
your brother and his lover have embrac'd. 1.04. 40
of business 'twixt you and your poor brother. 1.04. 71
commend me to my brother. 1.04. 88
i have a brother is condemn'd to die; 2.02. 34
you let it be his fault, | and not my brother. 2.02. 36
i had a brother then. 2.02. 42
your brother is a forfeit of the law, | and you 2.02. 71
it is the law, not i, condemn your brother. 2.02. 80
were he my kinsman, brother, or my son, | it 2.02. 81
your brother dies to-morrow; 2.02.105
we cannot weigh our brother with ourself. 2.02.126
o, let her brother live! 2.02.174
your brother cannot live. 2.04. 33
your brother is to die. 2.04. 83
could fetch your brother from the manacles | of 2.04. 93
as much for my poor brother as myself: 2.04. 99
then must your brother die. 2.04.104
better it were a brother died at once, | than 2.04.106
and rather prov'd the sliding of your brother 2.04.115
else let my brother die, | if not a fedary, but 2.04.121
my brother did love juliet, | and you tell me 2.04.142
sign me a present pardon for my brother, | or 2.04.152
redeem thy brother | by yielding up thy body to 2.04.163
i'll to my brother. 2.04.177
then, isabel, live chaste, and, brother, die; 2.04.184
more than our brother is our chastity. 2.04.185
yes, brother, you may live; 3.01. 63
there spake my brother; 3.01. 85
what says my brother? 3.01.115
this substitute, and to save your brother? 3.01.188 P
i had rather my brother die by the law than my 3.01.190 P
redeem your brother from the angry law; 3.01.201 P
her brother frederick was wrack'd at sea, having 3.01.216 P
there she lost a noble and renown'd brother, in 3.01.220 P
and the cure of it not only saves your brother, 3.01.236 P
and here, by this is your brother sav'd, your 3.01.253 P
and you, good brother father. 3.02. 13 P
provost, my brother angelo will not be alter'd, 3.02.207 P
if my brother wrought by my pity, it should not 3.02.210 P
i am a brother | of gracious order, late come 3.02.218
whose persuasion is | i come about my brother. 4.01. 47
but, soft and low, | "remember now my brother." 4.01. 69
being a murtherer, though he were my brother. 4.02. 62
by my troth, isabel, i lov'd thy brother. 4.03.156 P
she hath been a suitor to me for her brother, 5.01. 34
of a sisterhood) | was sent to by my brother; 5.01. 73
intemperate lust, | release my brother; 5.01. 99
he would have weigh'd thy brother by himself, 5.01.111
it your comfort, | so happy is your brother. 5.01.399
but as he adjudg'd your brother — | being 5.01.403
on this man condemn'd | as if my brother liv'd. 5.01.445
my brother had but justice, | in that he did the 5.01.448
if he be like your brother, for his sake | is he 5.01.490
say you will be mine, | he is my brother too. 5.01.493
years became inquisitive | after his brother; ERR 1.01.126
reft of his brother, but retain'd his name — 1.01.128
so i, to find a mother and a brother, | in quest 1.02. 39
fie, brother, how the world is chang'd with you: 2.02.152
then, gentle brother, get you in again; 3.02. 25
i would not spare my brother in this case, | if 4.01. 77
her sister here, | did call me brother. 5.01.375
embrace thy brother there, rejoice with him. 5.01.414
methinks you are my glass, and not my brother: 5.01.418
we came into the world like brother and brother; 5.01.425
we came into the world like brother and brother; 5.01.425
he hath every month a new sworn brother. ADO 1.01. 73 P
being reconcil'd to the prince your brother: 1.01.155 P
how now, brother, where is my cousin, your son? 1.02. 1 P
but, brother, i can tell you strange news that 1.02. 3 P
you have of late stood out against your brother, 1.03. 21 P
the prince your brother is royally entertain'd 1.03. 43 P
the revellers are ent'ring, brother, make good 2.01. 84 P
sure my brother is amorous on hero and hath 2.01.155 P
you are very near my brother in his love. 2.01.163 P
hath your grace ne'er a brother like you? 2.01.323 P
go you to the prince your brother; 2.02. 22 P
my lord and brother, god save you! 3.02. 80 P
good den, brother. 3.02. 81 P
for my brother, i think he holds you well, and 3.02. 97 P
large, | but, as a brother to his sister, show'd 4.01. 53
is this the prince's brother? 4.01. 70
myself, my brother, and this grieved count | did 4.01. 89
sir, that don john, the prince's brother, was a 4.02. 40 P
perjury, to call a prince's brother villain. 4.02. 42 P
man, for, brother, men | can counsel and speak 5.01. 20
brother — 5.01. 86
brother anthony — 5.01. 91
but, brother anthony — 5.01.100
no? come, brother, away! i will be heard. 5.01.108
leonato and his brother. 5.01.117 P
your brother the bastard is fled from messina. 5.01.190 P
did he not say my brother was fled? 5.01.204 P
how don john your brother incens'd me to slander 5.01.236 P
but did my brother set thee on to this? 5.01.247
my brother hath a daughter, | almost the copy of 5.01.288
all this wrong, | hir'd to it by your brother. 5.01.300
you know your office, brother: 5.04. 14
call her forth, brother, here's the friar ready. 5.04. 39
my lord, your brother john is ta'en in flight, 5.04.125
and, as thou say'st, charg'd my brother, on his AYL 1.01. 3 P
my brother jaques he keeps at school, and report 1.01. 5 P
but i, his brother, gain nothing under him but 1.01. 14 P
his hinds, bars me the place of a brother, and, 1.01. 20 P
yonder comes my master, your brother. 1.01. 26 P
god made, a poor unworthy brother of yours, with 1.01. 33 P
i know you are my eldest brother, and in the 1.01. 44 P
come, elder brother, you are too young in this. 1.01. 53 P
wert thou not my brother, i would not take this 1.01. 59 P
is banish'd by his younger brother the new duke, 1.01.100 P
to understand that your younger brother, orlando 1.01.124 P
your brother is but young and tender, and for 1.01.128 P
contriver against me his natural brother; 1.01.145 P
from tyrant duke unto a tyrant brother. 1.02.288
than doth your brother that hath banish'd you. 2.01. 28
send to his brother; 2.02. 17
if he be absent, bring his brother to me; 2.02. 18
your brother — no, no brother, yet the son 2.03. 19
your brother — no, no brother, yet the son 2.03. 19
malice | of a diverted blood and bloody brother. 2.03. 37
find out thy brother, wheresoe'er he is; 3.01. 5
i never lov'd my brother in my life. 3.01. 14
young master ganymed, my new mistress's brother. 3.02. 87 P
the woman low, | and browner than her brother." 4.03. 88
approach the man | and found it was his brother, 4.03.120
and found it was his brother, his elder brother. 4.03.120
o, i have heard him speak of that same brother, 4.03.121
are you his brother? 4.03.133
i pray you tell your brother how well i 4.03.167 P
bear answer back | how you excuse my brother, 4.03.180
god save you, brother. 5.02. 17 P
did your brother tell you how i counterfeited to 5.02. 25 P
for your brother and my sister no sooner met but 5.02. 32 P
i shall think my brother happy in having what he 5.02. 47 P
cries it out, when your brother marries aliena, 5.02. 63 P
methought he was a brother to your daughter. 5.04. 29
purposely to take | his brother here, and put 5.04.158
his crown bequeathing to his banish'd brother, 5.04.163
brother petruchio, sister katherina, | and thou, SHR 5.02. 6
the count rossillion cannot be my brother: AWW 1.03.155
he must not be my brother. 1.03.160
so that my lord your son were not my brother — 1.03.162
but, i your daughter, he must be my brother? 1.03.166
with his own hand he slew the duke's brother. 3.05. 7 P
your brother he shall go along with me. 3.06.108
go tell the count rossillion, and my brother, 4.01. 89
what's his brother, the other captain dumaine? 4.03.282 P
he excels his brother for a coward, yet his 4.03.288 P
yet his brother is reputed one of the best that 4.03.289 P
to pay this debt of love but to a brother, | how TN 1.01. 33
my brother he is in elysium. 1.02. 4
o my poor brother! and so perchance may he be. 1.02. 7
hung on our driving boat, i saw your brother, 1.02. 11
her | in the protection of his son, her brother, 1.02. 38
my niece to take the death of her brother thus? 1.03. 2 P
that i, dear brother, be now ta'en for you! 3.04.376
i my brother know | yet living in my glass; 3.04.379
even such and so | in favor was my brother, and 3.04.381
but, had it been the brother of my blood, | i 5.01.210
i never had a brother; 5.01.226
father — | such a sebastian was my brother too; 5.01.233
as long again | would be fill'd up, my brother, WT 1.02. 4
we are tougher, brother, | than you can put us 1.02. 15
to save both, | farewell, our brother. 1.02. 27
what cheer? how is't with you, best brother? 1.02.148
my brother, | are you so fond of your young 1.02.163
and reconcil'd king, my brother, whose loss of 4.02. 23 P
ay, good brother, or go about to think. 4.04.217 P
and trust, his sworn brother, a very simple 4.04.596 P
(his very air) that i should call you brother, 5.01.128
that a king, at friend, | can send his brother; 5.01.141
o my brother, | good gentleman! 5.01.147
father of this seeming lady and | her brother, 5.01.192
son took me by the hand, and call'd me brother; 5.02.141 P
and then the two kings call'd my father brother; 5.02.142 P
and then the prince, my brother, and the 5.02.143 P
with your crown'd brother and these your 5.03. 5
dear my brother, | let him that was the cause of 5.03. 53
look upon my brother. 5.03.147
behalf | of thy deceased brother geffrey's son, JN 1.01. 8
your brother did employ my father much — 1.01. 96
sirrah, your brother is legitimate, | your 1.01.116
tell me, how if my brother, | who, as you say, 1.01.120
my brother might not claim him, nor your father, 1.01.126
and like thy brother, to enjoy thy land; 1.01.135
and if my brother had my shape | and i had his, 1.01.138
brother, take you my land, i'll take my chance. 1.01.151
brother by th' mother's side, give me your hand; 1.01.163
brother, adieu, good fortune come to thee! 1.01.180
where is that slave, thy brother? 1.01.222
my brother robert, old sir robert's son? 1.01.224
hast thou conspired with thy brother too, | that 1.01.241
look here upon thy brother geffrey's face: 2.01. 99
that geffrey was thy elder brother born, | and 2.01.104
son to the elder brother of this man, | and king 2.01.239
brother of england, how may we content | this 2.01.547
brother of england, you blaspheme in this. 3.01.161
were he my brother, nay, my kingdom's heir, | as R2 1.01.116
in that thou seest thy wretched brother die, 1.02. 27
in suff'ring thus thy brother to be slaught'red, 1.02. 30
commend me to thy brother, edmund york. 1.02. 62
wert thou not brother to great edward's son, 2.01.121
my brother gloucester, plain well-meaning soul, 2.01.128
his brother, archbishop late of canterbury, 2.01.282
sent from my brother worcester, whencesoever. 2.03. 22
i am sworn brother, sweet, | to grim necessity, 5.01. 20
brother, the king hath made your nephew mad. 1H4 1.03.138
the ransom once again | of my wive's brother, 1.03.142
then | proclaim my brother edmund mortimer 1.03.156
farewell, good brother, we shall thrive, i trust 1.03.300
i fear my brother mortimer doth stir | about his 2.03. 81
i am sworn brother to a leash of drawers, and 2.04. 7 P
which by thy younger brother is supplied, | and 3.02. 33
to lord john of lancaster, | to my brother john; 3.03.196
it was myself, my brother, and his son, | that 5.01. 39
unless a brother should a brother dare | to 5.02. 53
unless a brother should a brother dare | to 5.02. 53
before, i lov'd thee as a brother, john, | but 5.04. 19
come, brother john, full bravely hast thou 5.04.130
this is the strangest fellow, brother john. 5.04.155
come, brother, let us to the highest of the 5.04.160
then, brother john of lancaster, to you | this 5.05. 25
how doth my son and brother? 2H4 1.01. 67
your brother thus; 1.01. 77
ending with "brother, son, and all are dead." 1.01. 81
douglas is living, and your brother yet, | but, 1.01. 82
can say of me is that i am a second brother, and 2.02. 67 P
and art not thou poins his brother? 2.04.284 P
soul, | who like a brother toil'd in my affairs, 3.01. 62
a' gaunt as if he had been sworn brother to him, 3.02.321 P
my brother general, the commonwealth, | i make 4.01. 93
gloucester, | where is the prince your brother? 4.04. 13
is not his brother thomas of clarence with him? 4.04. 16
chance thou art not with the prince thy brother? 4.04. 20
i am here, brother, full of heaviness. 4.05. 8
we left the prince my brother here, my liege, 4.05. 51
i'll be your father and your brother too. 5.02. 57
your brother kings and monarchs of the earth H5 1.02.122
from our brother of england? 2.04. 75
full intent | back to our brother of england. 2.04.115
look you, he were my brother, i would desire the 3.06. 54 P
we are in god's hand, brother, not in theirs. 3.06.169
good morrow, brother bedford. 4.01. 3
brother john bates, is not that the morning 4.01. 85 P
my brother gloucester's voice? 4.01.307
sheds his blood with me | shall be my brother; 4.03. 62
my lord of warwick, and my brother gloucester, 4.07.170
brabant, | the brother to the duke of burgundy, 4.08. 97
unto our brother france, and to our sister, 5.02. 2
face, | most worthy brother england, fairly met! 5.02. 10
so happy be the issue, brother /england, | of 5.02. 12
brother, we shall. 5.02. 83
exeter, | and brother clarence, and you, brother 5.02. 84
brother clarence, and you, brother gloucester, 5.02. 84
our gracious brother, i will go with them. 5.02. 92
brother, so denied, | but your request shall 5.02.343
cain, | to slay thy brother abel, if thou wilt. 1H6 1.03. 40
did my brother henry spend his youth, | his 2H6 1.01. 78
and did my brother bedford toil his wits, | to 1.01. 83
and, brother york, thy acts in ireland, | in 1.01.194
humphrey stafford and his brother are hard by, 4.02.114 P

and, brother, here's the earl of wiltshire's 3H6 1.01. 14
good brother, as thou lov'st and honorest arms, 1.01.116
brother, though i be youngest, give me leave. 1.02. 1
why, how now, sons and brother, at a strife? 1.02. 4
brother, thou shalt to london presently, | and 1.02. 36
me, | my brother montague shall post to london. 1.02. 55
brother, i go; 1.02. 60
how fares my brother? 2.01. 8
i think it cites us, brother, to the field, 2.01. 34
lord george your brother, norfolk, and myself, 2.01.138
and for your brother, he was lately sent | from 2.01.145
out, | and therefore comes my brother montague. 2.01.167
as thou didst kill our tender brother rutland, 2.02.115
and ne'er was agamemnon's brother wrong'd | by 2.02.148
brother, revenge my death!" 2.03. 19
brother, give me thy hand, and gentle warwick, 2.03. 44
and this the hand that slew thy brother rutland, 2.04. 7
these hands that slew thy sire and brother | to 2.04. 9
your brother richard mark'd him for the grave, 2.06. 40
brother of gloucester, at saint albons field 3.02. 1
king by whose injurious doom | my elder brother, 3.03.102
sent from your brother, marquess montague. 3.03.164
dear brother, how shall bona be reveng'd | but 3.03.212
now tell me, brother clarence, what think you 4.01. 1
hath not our brother made a worthy choice? 4.01. 3
now, brother of clarence, how like you our 4.01. 9
yea, brother richard, are you offended too? 4.01. 19
scales | unto the brother of your loving bride. 4.01. 53
now, brother king, farewell, and sit you fast, 4.01.119
now, brother richard, will you stand by us? 4.01.145
might i think that clarence, edward's brother, 4.02. 10
thy brother being carelessly encamp'd, | his 4.02. 14
yea, brother of clarence, art thou here too? 4.03. 41
duke edward be convey'd | unto my brother, 4.03. 53
why, brother rivers, are you yet to learn | what 4.04. 2
fell warwick's brother, and by that our foe. 4.04. 12
you know our king, my brother, | is prisoner to 4.05. 4
now, brother of gloucester, lord hastings, and 4.05. 16
brother, the time and case requireth haste, 4.05. 18
that edward is escaped from your brother, | and 4.06. 78
my brother was too careless of his charge. 4.06. 86
now, brother richard, lord hastings, and the 4.07. 1
brother, i like not this; 4.07. 10
brother, this is sir john montgomery, | our 4.07. 40
why, brother, wherefore stand you on nice points 4.07. 58
brother, we will proclaim you out of hand, | the 4.07. 63
thee | to flatter henry and forsake thy brother! 4.07. 85
thou, brother montague, in buckingham, 4.08. 14
how far off is our brother montague? 5.01. 4
'twas i that gave the kingdom to thy brother. 5.01. 34
thou and thy brother both shall buy this treason 5.01. 68
of force enough to bid his brother battle; 5.01. 77
war | against his brother and his lawful king? 5.01. 88
and to my brother turn my blushing cheeks. 5.01. 99
if thou be there, sweet brother, take my hand, 5.02. 34
for, brother, if thou didst, | thy tears would 5.02. 36
and said, "commend me to my valiant brother." 5.02. 42
clarence, excuse me to the king my brother; 5.05. 46
the wings of my sweet boy, | thy brother edward; 5.06. 24
i have no brother, i am like no brother; 5.06. 80
i have no brother, i am like no brother; 5.06. 80
/thanks, noble clarence, worthy brother, thanks. 5.07. 30
to set my brother clarence and the king | in R3 1.01. 34
brother, good day. 1.01. 42
worship, | anthony woodvile, her brother there, 1.01. 67
since that our brother dubb'd them gentlewomen, 1.01. 82
(of what degree soever) with your brother. 1.01. 87
brother, farewell, i will unto the king, | and 1.01.107
brother of gloucester, you mistake the matter: 1.03. 62
come, we know your meaning, brother gloucester; 1.03. 73
our brother is imprison'd by your means, 1.03. 77
that stir the king against the duke my brother. 1.03.330
and in my company my brother gloucester, | who 1.04. 11
for edward, for my brother, for his sake. 1.04.212
/o, if you love my brother, hate not me! 1.04.226
i am his brother and i love him well. 1.04.227
and i will send you to my brother gloucester, 1.04.229
are deceiv'd, your brother gloucester hates you. 1.04.232
i would he knew that i had sav'd his brother! 1.04.276
there wanteth now our brother gloucester here 2.01. 43
to take our brother clarence to your grace. 2.01. 77
my brother kill'd no man, his fault was thought, 2.01.105
and said, "dear brother, live, and be a king"? 2.01.114
but for my brother not a man would speak, | nor 2.01.127
talk'd how i did grow | more than my brother. 2.04. 12
make war upon themselves, brother to brother, 2.04. 62
make war upon themselves, brother to brother, 2.04. 62
i thought my mother and my brother york | would 3.01. 20
i, | the queen your mother and your brother york 3.01. 27
of york | unto his princely brother presently? 3.01. 34
say, uncle gloucester, if our brother come, 3.01. 61
richard of york, how fares our loving brother? 3.01. 96
ay, brother, to our grief, as it is yours. 3.01. 98
the prince my brother hath outgrown me far. 3.01.104
a beggar, brother? 3.01.112
uncle, my brother mocks both you and me: 3.01.129
whereof the king my brother was possess'd. 3.01.196
toad, thou toad, where is thy brother clarence? 4.04.145
familiarly shall call thy dorset brother; 4.04.316
her father's brother | would be her lord? 4.04.337
prelate, | bishop of exeter, his elder brother, 4.04.501
lest, being seen, thy brother, tender george, 5.03. 95
the brother blindly shed the brother's blood, 5.05. 24
learn this, brother, | we live not to be grip'd H8 2.02.134
the heads of all thy brother cardinals | (with 3.02.257
you a brother of us, | it fits we thus proceed, 5.01.106
three pound, lift as much as his brother hector. TRO 1.02.116 P
fie, fie, my brother! 2.02. 25
you are for dreams and slumbers, brother priest, 2.02. 37
brother, she is not worth what she doth cost 2.02. 51
our fire–brand brother, paris, burns us all. 2.02.110
why, brother hector, | we may not think the 2.02.118
most esteem'd friend, your brother troilus — 3.01. 64 P
how chance my brother troilus went not? 3.01.138 P
my brother troilus lodges there to–night. 4.01. 43
there is at hand | paris your brother, and 4.02. 61
good my brother troilus, | tell you the lady 4.03. 3
altar, and thy brother troilus | a priest there 4.03. 8
brother troilus! 4.04. 99
good brother, come you hither, | and bring 4.04. 99
aeneas, call my brother troilus to me, | and 4.05.154
where is my brother hector? 5.03. 7
notes of sally, for the heavens, sweet brother. 5.03. 14
brother, you have a vice of mercy in you, 5.03. 37
nor you, my brother, with your true sword drawn, 5.03. 56
o, well fought, my youngest brother! 5.06. 12
how now, my brother? 5.06. 21
will, sir, flatter my sworn brother, the people, COR 2.03. 96 P
thine, | thy noble brother titus and his sons, TIT 1.01. 50
long live lord titus, my beloved brother, 1.01.169
thanks, gentle tribune, noble brother marcus. 1.01.171
unworthy brother, and unworthy sons! 1.01.346
brother, for in that name doth nature plead — 1.01.370
suffer thy brother marcus to inter | his noble 1.01.375
though bassianus be the emperor's brother, 2.01. 88
the king my brother shall have notice of this. 2.03. 85
vain | to save your brother from the sacrifice, 2.03.164
speak, brother, hast thou hurt thee with the 2.03.203
o brother, with the dismall'st object hurt 2.03.204
how these were they that made away his brother. 2.03.208
o brother, help me with thy fainting hand — 2.03.233
hour, | to find thy brother bassianus dead. 2.03.252
my brother dead! 2.03.253
where is thy brother bassianus? 2.03.261
kind, | have here bereft my brother of his life. 2.03.282
but who comes with our brother marcus here? 3.01. 58
man, | and here my brother, weeping at my woes; 3.01.100
shall thy good uncle, and thy brother lucius, 3.01.122
brother, well i wot, | thy napkin cannot drink a 3.01.139
say | that to her brother which i said to thee: 3.01.145
o brother, speak with possibility, | and do not 3.01.214
struck pale and bloodless, and thy brother, i, 3.01.257
come, brother, take a head, | and in this hand 3.01.279
see, brother, see, note how she cotes the leaves 4.01. 50
brother, sit down by me. 4.01. 65
murtherous villains, will you kill your brother? 4.02. 88
he is your brother, lords, sensibly fed | of 4.02.122
nay, he is your brother by the surer side, 4.02.126
that died by law for murther of our brother, 4.04. 54
marcus, my brother! 5.02.121
me, | or else i'll call my brother back again, 5.02.135
were they that murd'red our emperor's brother, 5.03. 98
kiss, | thy brother marcus tenders on thy lips. 5.03.157
mercutio and his brother valentine; ROM 1.02. 67 P
holy franciscan friar! brother, ho! 5.02. 1
going to find a barefoot brother out, | one of 5.02. 5
brother, i'll go and bring it thee. 5.02. 23
o brother montague, give me thy hand. 5.03.296
i do not always follow lover, elder brother, and TIM 2.02.121 P
welcome, good brother. 3.04. 7
friend, or brother, | he forfeits his own blood 3.05. 86
sir, 'tis your brother cassius at the door, JC 2.01. 70
thy brother by decree is banished; 3.01. 44
ear | for the repealing of my banish'd brother? 3.01. 51
your brother too must die; consent you, lepidus? 4.01. 2
most noble brother, you have done me wrong. 4.02. 37
and if not so, how should i wrong a brother? 4.02. 39
hated by one he loves, brav'd by his brother, 4.03. 96
hear me, good brother. 4.03.212
o my dear brother! 4.03.233
good night, good brother. 4.03.237
by and by | on business to my brother cassius. 4.03.248
go and commend me to my brother cassius; 4.03.306
who knows if donalbain be with his brother? MAC 5.02. 7
all bands of law, | to our most valiant brother. HAM 1.02. 25
my father's brother, but no more like my father 1.02.152
but, good my brother, | do not, as some 1.03. 46
say, voltemand, what from our brother norway? 2.02. 59
as kill a king, and marry with his brother. 3.04. 29
mildewed ear, | blasting his wholesome brother. 3.04. 65
my brother shall know of it, and so i thank you 4.05. 70 P
her brother is in secret come from france, 4.05. 88
my arrow o'er the house | and hurt my brother. 5.02.244
or fourteen moonshines | lag of a brother? LR 1.02. 6
is a letter from my brother that i have not all 1.02. 37 P
for ever, and live the belov'd of your brother. 1.02. 54 P
against my brother till you can derive from him 1.02. 81 P
how now, brother edmund, what serious 1.02.138 P
i am thinking, brother, of a prediction i read 1.02.140 P
arm'd, brother? 1.02.171 P
brother, i advise you to the best; 1.02.172 P
a credulous father and a brother noble, | whose 1.02.179
my father hath set guard to take my brother, 2.01. 16
brother, a word! 2.01. 19
brother, i say! 2.01. 19
fly, brother. 2.01. 32
'twas her brother that, in pure kindness to his 2.04.125 P
back, edmund, to my brother, | hasten his 4.02. 15
husband's life, | and the exchange my brother! 4.06.273
but a subject of this war, | not as a brother. 5.03. 61
well stand up, | and call itself your brother. 5.03. 66
false to thy gods, thy brother, and thy father, 5.03.135
call up my brother. OTH 1.01.175
from his very arm | puff'd his own brother — 3.04.137
how is't, brother? 5.01. 71
against my brother lucius? ANT 1.02. 89
his brother /warr'd upon him, although i think 2.01. 41
your wife and brother | made wars upon me, and 2.02. 42
my brother never | did urge me in his act. 2.02. 45
you, whom no brother | did ever love so dearly. 2.02.149
when caesar and your brother were at blows, 2.06. 44
good brother, | let me request you /off, our 2.07.119
my noble brother! 3.02. 42
her led | between her brother and mark antony. 3.03. 10
by crying out as loud, | "o, bless my brother!" 3.04. 18
husband win, win brother, | prays, and destroys 3.04. 18
preparation of a war | shall stain your brother. 3.04. 27
brother, good night; to–morrow is the day. 4.03. 1
that thou, my brother, my competitor | in top of 5.01. 42
the younger brother, cadwal, | once arviragus, CYM 3.03. 95
he is a man, i'll love him as my brother: 3.06. 71
brother, stay here. | are we not brothers? 4.02. 2
brother, farewell. 4.02. 30
you and my brother search | what companies are 4.02. 68
i wish my brother make good time with him, | you 4.02.108
but see, thy brother. 4.02.112
howsoe'er, | my brother hath done well. 4.02.147
where's my brother? 4.02.183
my brother wears thee not the one half so well 4.02.202
brother, begin. 4.02.254
the conduct of bold jachimo, | sienna's brother. 4.02.341
i and my brother are not known; 4.04. 32
you call'd me brother, | when i was but your 5.05.376
thou art my brother, so we'll hold thee ever. 5.05.399
sir, | as you did mean indeed to be our brother; 5.05.423
remember me | to our all–royal brother, for TNK 1.03. 12
most royal brother — 3.06.195
o my noble brother, | that oath was rashly made, 3.06.226
her — one of 'em | i knew to be your brother; 4.01.101
for, if my brother but even now had ask'd me 4.02. 47
now, come ask me, brother — | alas, i know not! 4.02. 50
from the noble duke your brother, | madam, i 4.02. 55
and 'a made my brother arthur watchins sergeant STM II.C 43 P
thy good worship for my brother arthur watchins. II.C 59 P
guilt would seem death–worthy in thy brother. LUC 635
as they must needs (the sister and the brother), PP 8. 2

BROTHERHOOD 6 FR 0.0006 REL FR 6 V 0 P
finds brotherhood in thee no sharper spur? R2 1.02. 9
and friendship shall combine, and brotherhood. H5 2.01.109
but in your bride you bury brotherhood. 3H6 4.01. 55
this deep disgrace in brotherhood | touches me R3 1.01.111
who spoke of brotherhood? 2.01.109
by my brotherhood, | the letter was not nice but ROM 5.02. 17

BROTHERHOODS 1 FR 0.0001 REL FR 1 V 0 P
degrees in schools, and brotherhoods in cities, TRO 1.03.104

BROTHER–IN–LAW 4 FR 0.0004 REL FR 2 V 2 P
go about to make me the king's brother–in–law. WT 4.04.702 P
indeed brother–in–law was the farthest off you 4.04.703 P
but for our trusty brother–in–law and the abbot, R2 5.03.137
shall ransom straight | his brother–in–law, the 1H4 1.03. 80

BROTHER–JUSTICE 1 FR 0.0001 REL FR 0 V 1 P
but my brother–justice have i found so severe, MM 3.02.252 P

BROTHER–LIKE 1 FR 0.0001 REL FR 1 V 0 P
welcome, good clarence, this is brother–like. 3H6 5.01.105

BROTHER–LOVE 1 FR 0.0001 REL FR 1 V 0 P
with a true heart | and brother–love i do it. H8 5.02.206

BROTHERLY 3 FR 0.0003 REL FR 2 V 1 P
i speak but brotherly of him, but should i AYL 1.01.155 P
wife, | nor how to use your brothers brotherly, 3H6 4.03. 38
i love thee brotherly, but envy much | thou hast CYM 4.02.158

/BROTHER'S 1 FR 0.0001 REL FR 0 V 1 P
in a chain, /hanging at his /brother's leg — to TRO 5.01. 56 P

BROTHER'S 80 FR 0.0090 REL FR 69 V 11 P
to me inveterate, hearkens my brother's suit, TMP 1.02.122
true, my brother's daughter 's queen of tunis, 2.01.255
my brother's servants | were then my fellows, 2.01.273
under whose heavy sense your brother's life MM 1.04. 65
it doth know | that's like my brother's fault. 2.02.138
upon your tongue | against my brother's life. 2.02.141
most just law | now took your brother's life, 2.04. 53
pronounce a sentence on your brother's life; 2.04. 62
a charity in sin | to save this brother's life? 2.04. 64
what sin you do to save a brother's life, 3.01.133
if yet her brother's pardon be come hither. 4.03.108
hath yet the deputy sent my brother's pardon? 4.03.114
lord angelo, | for her poor brother's pardon. 5.01. 77
he sends a warrant | for my poor brother's head. 5.01.103
your brother's death i know sits at your heart; 5.01.389
thereon dependant, for your brother's life — 5.01.406
her brother's ghost his paved bed would break, 5.01.435
marry, it is your brother's right hand. ADO 1.03. 49 P
as in love of your brother's honor, who hath 2.02. 37 P
two of my brother's men bound? 5.01.210 P
you must be father to your brother's daughter, 5.04. 15
to–day to marry with my brother's daughter? 5.04. 37
her brother's noontide with th' antipodes. MND 3.02. 55
myself notice of my brother's purpose herein, AYL 1.01.139 P
till thou canst quit thee by thy brother's mouth 3.01. 11
in beard is a younger brother's revenue — then 3.02.377 P
committing me unto my brother's love, | who led 4.03.144
all this to season | a brother's dead love, TN 1.01. 30
good fool, for my brother's death. 1.05. 67 P
to mourn for your brother's soul being in heaven 1.05. 71 P
thou lov'st us, show in our brother's welcome; WT 1.02.174
that is my brother's plea and none of mine, JN 1.01. 67
what doth move you to claim your brother's land? 1.01. 91
then, if he were my brother's, | my brother 1.01.125
since i first call'd my brother's father dad. 2.01.467
heir, | as he is but my father's brother's son, R2 1.01.117
thy sometimes brother's wife | with her 1.02. 54
the king had cut off my head with my brother's. 2.02.102
who bears hard | his brother's death at bristow, 1H4 1.03.271
sir humphrey stafford and his brother's death 2H6 4.04. 34
thy brother's blood the thirsty earth hath drunk 3H6 2.03. 15
king, | and not be tied unto his brother's will. 4.01. 66
more than the nature of a brother's love! 5.01. 79
that, to deserve well at my brother's hands, | i 5.01. 93
my brother's love, the devil, and my rage. R3 1.04.223
thy brother's love, our duty, and thy faults 1.04.224
have i a tongue to doom my brother's death, 2.01.103
you say that edward is your brother's son: 3.07.177
loath to depose the child, your brother's son; 3.07.209
your brother's son shall never reign our king, 3.07.215
i must be married to my brother's daughter, | or 4.02. 60
at young elizabeth, my brother's daughter, | and 4.03. 41
the purple sap from her sweet brother's body, 4.04.277
the brother blindly shed the brother's blood, 5.05. 24
it seems the marriage with his brother's wife H8 2.02. 16
the dowager, | sometimes our brother's wife. 2.04.182
you'll remember your brother's excuse? TRO 3.01.142 P
let me confirm my princely brother's greeting: 4.05.174
were it | at home, upon my brother's guard, even COR 1.10. 25
marcus, for thy sake and thy brother's here, TIT 1.01.482
choice, | lavinia is thine elder brother's hope. 2.01. 74
now let me show a brother's love to thee. 3.01.182
to brave the tribune in his brother's hearing. 4.02. 36
o my brother's child! ROM 3.01.146
but for the sunset of my brother's son | it 3.05.127
it is the paster lards the brother's sides, TIM 4.03. 12
though yet of hamlet our dear brother's death HAM 1.02. 1
or thinking by our late dear brother's death 1.02. 19
i, sleeping, by a brother's hand | of life, of 1.05. 74
eldest curse upon't, | a brother's murther. 3.03. 38
were thicker than itself with brother's blood, 3.03. 44

are the queen, your husband's brother's wife, 3.04. 15
and will this brother's wager frankly play. 5.02.253
i hope, for my brother's justification, he wrote LR 1.02. 44 P
you know the character to be your brother's? 1.02. 62 P
not altogether your brother's evil disposition 3.05. 6 P
but are my brother's pow'rs set forth? 4.05. 1
but have you never found my brother's way | to 5.01. 10
so, sir, i yoke me | in my good brother's fault. CYM 4.02. 20
a counter–reflect 'gainst | my brother's heart, TNK 1.01.128

BROTHERS' 4 FR 0.0004 REL FR 4 V 0 P
thou offer'st fairly to thy brothers' wedding: AYL 5.04.167
having my country's peace and brothers' loves. 3H6 5.07. 36
therefore mine shall save my brothers' lives. TIT 3.01.166
and our hearts | of brothers' temper, do receive JC 3.01.175

/BROTHERS 1 FR 0.0001 REL FR 1 V 0 P
how parted with your /brothers? CYM 5.05.386

BROTHERS 68 FR 0.0076 REL FR 56 V 12 P
four of his blind brothers and sisters went to TGV 4.04. 4 P
of master ford's brothers watch the door with WIV 4.02. 51 P
hearing them, would call their brothers fools. MV 1.01. 99
my blood, were there twenty brothers betwixt us. AYL 1.01. 48 P
now, my co–mates and brothers in exile, | hath 2.01. 1
and they shook hands and swore brothers. 5.04.102 P
and all the brothers too — and yet i know not. TN 2.04.121
younger sons to younger brothers, revolted 1H4 4.02. 28 P
/familiars, john with my brothers and sisters, 2H4 2.02.133 P
place in his affection | than all thy brothers. 4.04. 23
a hoop of gold to bind thy brothers in, | that 4.04. 43
brothers, you /mix your sadness with some fear: 5.02. 46
yet be sad, good brothers, | for, by my faith, 5.02. 49
but entertain no more of it, good brothers, 5.02. 54
and we'll be all three sworn brothers to france. H5 2.01. 12 P
nym and bardolph are sworn brothers in filching, 3.02. 44 P
and calls them brothers, friends, and countrymen 4.pr. 34
brothers both, | commend me to the princes in 4.01. 24
go with my brothers to my lords of england. 4.01. 30
we few, we happy few, we band of brothers; 4.03. 60
that they may agree like brothers, and worship 2H6 4.02. 75 P
brothers, you muse what chat we two have had. 3H6 3.02.109
well, jest on, brothers. 3.02.116
and go we, brothers, to the man that took him, 3.02.121
and leave your brothers to go speed elsewhere. 4.01. 58
wife, | nor how to use your brothers brotherly, 4.03. 38
both him and all his brothers unto reason. 4.07. 34
there's no hop'd–for mercy with the brothers 5.04. 35
and kiss your princely nephew, brothers both. 5.07. 27
but that thy brothers beat aside the point. R3 1.02. 96
the duke of gloucester and your brothers, | and 1.03. 37
shows itself | against my children, brothers, 1.03. 67
the queen's sons and brothers haught and proud! 2.03. 28
murther her brothers and then marry her — 4.02. 62
where be thy brothers? 4.04. 92
and the dire death of my poor sons and brothers? 4.04.143
and only in that safety died her brothers. 4.04.215
thy soul's love didst thou love her brothers, 4.04.260
send to her by the man that slew her brothers 4.04.271
or he that slew her brothers and her uncles? 4.04.339
thou hadst not broken, nor my brothers died. 4.04.380
or the limbs of limehouse, their dear brothers, H8 5.03. 63 P
you brace of warlike brothers, welcome hither. TRO 4.05.175
brothers, help to convey her hence away, | and TIT 1.01.287
ah, lucius, for thy brothers let me plead. 3.01. 30
to rescue my two brothers from their death, 3.01. 49
and for his death | thy brothers are condemn'd, 3.01.109
when i did name her brothers, then fresh tears 3.01.111
let me redeem my brothers both from death. 3.01.180
two of her brothers were condemn'd to death, 5.02.173
their fell faults our brothers were beheaded, 5.03.100
to have so many like brothers commanding one TIM 1.02.104 P
twinn'd brothers of one womb, | whose 4.03. 3
here come our brothers. 5.02. 13
the counterfeit presentment of two brothers. HAM 3.04. 54
forty thousand brothers | could not with all 5.01.269
cools, friendship falls off, brothers divide: LR 1.02.107 P
himself, | or any of my brothers of the state, OTH 1.02. 96
to make you brothers, and to knit your hearts ANT 2.02.125
the heart of brothers govern in our loves, | and 2.02.147
what, are the brothers parted? 3.02. 1
been thief–stol'n, | as my two brothers, happy! CYM 1.06. 6
if brothers. 3.06. 75
brother, stay here. | are we not brothers? 4.02. 3
thou hast created | a mother and two brothers. 5.04.125
o my gentle brothers, | have we thus met? 5.05.374
i you brothers, | when we were so indeed. 5.05.377
throws her eye | on him, her brothers, me, her 5.05.395

BROTHS 1 FR 0.0001 REL FR 1 V 0 P
and sauc'd our broths, as juno had been sick CYM 4.02. 50

/BROUGHT 2 FR 0.0002 REL FR 2 V 0 P
/have /brought /ourselves /into /a /burning 2H4 4.01. 56
/yet /i /think /we /are /not /brought /so /low, TIT 3.02. 76

BROUGHT 209 FR 0.0236 REL FR 171 V 38 P
lady) hath mine enemies | brought to this shore; TMP 1.02.180
blue–ey'd hag was hither brought with child, 1.02.269
hath into bondage | brought my too diligent ear. 3.01. 42
hath sever'd us, | and brought us thus together? 5.01.188
chalk'd forth the way | which brought us hither. 5.01.204
from them, | and were brought moping hither. 5.01.240
and being so hard to me that brought your mind, TGV 1.01.138 P
till the last step have brought me to my love, 2.07. 36
one that i brought up of a puppy; 4.04. 2 P
here have i brought him back again. 4.04. 53 P
and julia herself hath brought it hither. 5.04. 99
you have brought her into such a canaries as WIV 2.02. 60 P
could never have brought her to such a canary. 2.02. 62 P
we do not know what's brought to pass under the 4.02.175 P
in this shape when you have brought him thither, 4.04. 45
forced marriage would have brought upon her. 5.05.230
as that the sin hath brought you to this shame, MM 2.03. 31
that brought you home | the head of ragozine for 5.01.532
i bought, and brought up to attend my sons. ERR 1.01. 57
i brought you word an hour since that the bark 4.03. 37 P
till i have brought him to his wits again, | or 5.01. 96
with thy command | let him be brought forth, and 5.01.160
along with them | they brought one pinch, a 5.01.238
brought to this town by that most famous warrior 5.01.368
by dromio, but i think he brought it not. 5.01.383
that she brought me up, i likewise give her most ADO 1.01.239 P
i have brought count claudio, whom you sent me 2.01.287 P
these men be bound, and brought to leonato's. 4.02. 64 P
these shallow fools have brought to light, who 5.01.234 P
how you were brought into the orchard and saw me 5.01.237 P
man | shall face to face be brought to margaret, 5.01.298
and brought with armed men back to messina. 5.04.126
signs | have brought about the annual reckoning. LLL 5.02.798
mine ear, i thank it, brought me to thy sound. MND 3.02.182
i have brought him a present. MV 2.02.100 P
thy daughter, | hymen from heaven brought her, AYL 5.04.112
heaven brought her, | yea, brought her hither, 5.04.113
because she brought stone jugs and no seal'd SHR in.2. 88
vincentio's son, brought up in florence, | it 1.01. 14
brought up as best becomes a gentlewoman. 1.02. 87
who brought it? 4.01.160
daughter is to be brought by you to the supper. 4.04. 85 P
now we are undone and brought to nothing. 5.01. 44 P
i have brought him up ever since he was three 5.01. 82 P
sigh, | till i be brought to such a silly pass! 5.02.124
here's a man stands that has brought his pardon. AWW 2.01. 63
brought you this letter, gentlemen? 3.02. 62
hath brought me up to be your daughter's dower, 4.04. 19
knight that you brought in one night here to be TN 1.03. 16 P
you know he brought me out o' favor with my lady 2.05. 7 P
foolish boldness brought thee to their mercies 5.01. 70
is good) hath brought you forth a daughter — WT 2.03. 66
and from thence have brought | this seal'd–up 3.02.126
i witness to | the times that brought them in; 4.01. 12
time's news | be known when 'tis brought forth. 4.01. 27
how a usurer's wife was brought to bed of twenty 4.04.263 P
been hallow'd and brought a benediction to the 4.04.602 P
as he says, your pawn till it be brought you. 4.04.823 P
i brought the old man and his son aboard the 5.02.114 P
have brought a countercheck before your gates, JN 2.01.224
whom zeal and charity brought to the field | as 2.01.565
and here's a prophet that i brought with me 4.02.147
who brought that letter from the cardinal? 4.03. 14
and brought in matter that should feed this fire 5.02. 85
this news was brought to richard but even now. 5.03. 12
and brought prince henry in their company, | at 5.06. 34
belief | that, being brought into the open air, 5.07. 7
let him be brought into the orchard here. 5.07. 10
brought hither henry herford thy bold son, R2 1.01. 3
how far brought you high herford on his way? 1.04. 2
i brought high herford, if you call him so, 1.04. 3
now hath my soul brought forth her prodigy, 2.02. 64
richard of burdeaux, by me hither brought. 5.06. 33
for he that brought them, in the very heat | and 1H4 1.01. 59
and he hath brought us smooth and welcome news. 1.01. 66
wild of kent hath brought three hundred marks 2.01. 55 P
hath butler brought those horses from the 2.03. 67
one horse, my lord, he brought even now. 2.03. 68
in general journey–bated and brought low. 4.03. 26
that brought you home, and boldly did outdare 5.01. 40
in this fair rescue thou hast brought to me. 5.04. 50
the world, let him be brought in to his answer. 2H4 2.01. 31 P
what the devil hast thou brought there? 2.04. 1 P
bardolph hath brought word. 2.04. 18 P
fondly brought here and foolishly sent hence. 4.02.119
are brought to the correction of your law. 4.04. 85
that this fair action may on foot be brought. H5 1.02.310
since god so graciously hath brought to light 2.02.185
that erst brought sweetly forth | the freckled 5.02. 48
if i now had him brought into my power. 1H6 1.04. 37
had york and somerset brought rescue in, | we 4.07. 33
see them guarded | and safely brought to dover, 5.01. 49
till we have brought duke humphrey in disgrace. 2H6 1.03. 96
my use, | be brought against me at my trial day! 3.01.114
if wind and fuel be brought to feed it with. 3.01.303
i have been so well brought up that i can write 4.02.105 P
the cause why i have brought this army hither 5.01. 35
were brought me of your loss and his depart. 3H6 2.01.110
and brought your prisoner to your palace gate. 3.02.119
when nature brought him to the door of death? 3.03.105
and brought from thence the thracian fatal 4.02. 21
seas, | and brought desired help from burgundy. 4.07. 6
queen from france hath brought a puissant power; 5.02. 31
and yet brought forth less than a mother's hope, 5.06. 50
it, | prodigious, and untimely brought to light, R3 1.02. 22
that they which brought me in my master's hate, 3.02. 58
some one take order buckingham be brought | to 4.04.537
he was brought to this | by a vain prophecy of H8 1.02.146
bevy, has brought with her | one care abroad. 1.04. 4
desir'd | to him brought viva voce to his face; 2.01. 18
when he was brought again to th' bar, to hear 2.01. 31
could but be brought to know our ends are honest 3.01.154
in which you brought the king | to be your 3.02.315
having brought the queen | to a prepar'd place 4.01. 63
arrested him at york, and brought him forward, 4.02. 13
and brought me garlands, griffith, which i feel 4.02. 91
sir, i have brought my lord the archbishop, | as 5.01. 80
he brought a grecian queen, whose youth and TRO 2.02. 78
you'll confess /he brought home worthy prize — 2.02. 86
what have i brought you to do? 4.02. 28 P
that could be brought to bodily act ere rome COR 1.02. 5
i, sir, | half an hour since brought my report. 1.06. 21
we do, sir, tell us what hath brought you to't. 2.03. 63 P
that our best water brought by conduits hither, 2.03.242
this extremity | hath brought me to thy hearth; 4.05. 79
you have brought | a trembling upon rome, such 4.06.118
say not we brought it. 4.06.120
mother's womb | that brought thee to this world. 5.03.125
that brought you forth this boy, to keep your 5.03.126
our spoils we have brought home | doth more than 5.06. 76
and brought to yoke, the enemies of rome. TIT 1.01. 69
sufficeth not that we are brought to rome | to 1.01.109
that brought her for this high good turn so far? 1.01.397
brought hither in a most unlucky hour, | to find 2.03.251
or brought a faggot to bright–burning troy? 3.01. 69
i mean she is brought a–bed. 4.02. 62
his wife but yesternight was brought to bed; 4.02.153
i have brought you a letter and a couple of 4.04. 43 P
then i have brought up a neck to a fair end. 4.04. 48 P
and brought him hither | to use as you think 5.01. 38
till he be brought unto the empress' face | for 5.03. 7
or who hath brought the fatal engine in | that 5.03. 86
i brought my master news of juliet's death, ROM 5.03.272
lord, | at many times i brought in my accompts, TIM 2.02.133
poor honest lord, brought low by his own heart, 4.02. 37
which | with wax i brought away, whose soft 5.04. 68
brought you caesar home? JC 1.03. 1
he hath brought many captives home to rome, 3.02. 88
and having brought our treasure where we will, 4.01. 24
he was but a fool that brought | my answer back. 4.03. 84
till he have brought thee up to yonder troops 5.03. 16
maggot–pies and choughs and rooks brought forth MAC 3.04.124
ay, and brought off the field. 5.09. 10
being of so young days brought up with him, HAM 2.02. 11
direct me | to him from whom you brought them. 4.06. 34
from hamlet? who brought them? 4.07. 38
he receiv'd them | of him that brought them. 4.07. 41
and to such wondrous doing brought his horse, 4.07. 86
let the foils be brought, the gentleman willing, 5.02.175 P
who brought it? LR 1.02. 58 P
it was not brought me, my lord; 1.02. 59 P
in contempt of man, | brought near to beast. 2.03. 9
i could as well be brought | to knee his throne, 2.04.213
has his daughters brought him to this pass? 3.04. 63
general curse | which twain have brought her to. 4.06.207
let the trumpet sound | for him that brought it. 5.01. 42
for the state affairs | hath hither brought. OTH 1.03. 73
i have brought you from venice. 2.01.264 P
those legs that brought me to a part of it. 2.03.187
fought'st against | (though daintily brought up) ANT 1.04. 60
merchandise which thou hast brought from rome 2.05.104
monument, | his guard have brought him thither. 4.15. 9
antony | shall be brought drunken forth, and i 5.02.219
a simple countryman, that brought her figs. 5.02.339
his glory which | brought them to be lamented. 5.02.363
master doctor, have you brought those drugs? CYM 1.05. 4
had i not brought | the knowledge of your 2.04. 50
i am brought hither | among th' italian gentry, 5.01. 17
tidings to the contrary | are brought your eyes; PER 2.ch. 16
hymen hath brought the bride to bed, | where, by 3.ch. 9
court of king simonides | are letters brought, 3.ch. 24
the sum of this, | brought hither to pentapolis, 3.ch. 34
fates had pleas'd you had brought her hither 3.03. 8
as i think, i have brought up some eleven — 4.02. 14 P
ay, to eleven, and brought them down again. 4.02. 16 P
well, as for him, he brought his disease hither; 4.02.110 P
ships and bounteous winds have brought | this 4.04. 17
had i brought hither a corrupted mind, | thy 4.06.104
yet i was mortally brought forth, and am | no 5.01.104
brought me to meteline. 5.01.175
but brought forth | a maid–child call'd marina, 5.03. 5
but her better stars | brought her to meteline, 5.03. 10
riding, her fortunes brought the maid aboard us, 5.03. 11
sir, they shall be brought you to my house, 5.03. 26
yet fate hath brought them off. TNK 1.03. 41
and out i have brought him to a little wood | a 2.06. 3
i have brought you food and files. 3.03. 2
as i have brought my life here to confirm it, 3.06.164
braver spirits | than these they have brought 4.02. 74
i think he might be brought to play at tennis. 5.02. 56
could not have brought you to the state of men. STM II.C 67
she had not brought forth thee, but died unkind. VEN 204
for then is tarquin brought unto his bed, LUC 120
and by their mortal fault brought in subjection 724
being from the feeling of her own grief brought 1578
a dearer birth than this his love had brought SON 32.11
for then, despite of space, i would be brought, 44. 3
and brought to medicine a healthful state 118.11
the accident which brought me to her eye | upon LC 247

BROW 81 FR 0.0091 REL FR 74 V 7 P
how angerly i taught my brow to frown, | when TGV 1.02. 62
right arch'd beauty of the brow that becomes the WIV 3.03. 56 P
there is written in your brow, provost, honesty MM 4.02.154 P
and tear the stain'd skin off my harlot brow, ERR 2.02.136
but speak you this with a sad brow? ADO 1.01.183 P
of all, | a whitely wanton with a velvet brow, LLL 3.01.196
where fair is not, praise cannot mend the brow. 4.01. 17
with her, boyet, and she strikes at the brow. 4.01.117
a gait, a state, a brow, a breast, a waist, | a 4.03.183
eye | dares look upon the heaven of her brow, 4.03.223
paints itself black, to imitate her brow. 4.03.261
and though the mourning brow of progeny | forbid 5.02.744
sees helen's beauty in a brow of egypt. MND 5.01. 11
what damned error but some sober brow | will MV 3.02. 78
to view with hollow eye and wrinkled brow | an 4.01.270.
speak sad brow and true maid. AYL 3.02.215 P
more honorable than the bare brow of a bachelor; 3.03. 61 P
i guess | by the stern brow and waspish action 4.03. 9
fie, fie, unknit that threat'ning unkind brow, SHR 5.02.136
my father had a mole upon his brow. TN 5.01.242
as if you held a brow of much distraction. WT 1.02.149
hang'd in the frowning wrinkle of her brow! JN 2.01.505
and make a riot on the gentle brow | of true 3.01.247
and outface the brow | of bragging horror; 5.01. 49
lift up thy brow, renowned salisbury, | and with 5.02. 54
why, here walk i in the black brow of night, 5.06. 17
and frowning brow to brow, ourselves will hear R2 1.01. 16
and frowning brow to brow, ourselves will hear 1.01. 16
see riot and dishonor stain the brow | of my 1H4 1.01. 85
endure | the moody frontier of a servant brow. 1.03. 19
that beads of sweat have stood upon thy brow, 2.03. 58
this seeming brow of justice, did he win | the 4.03. 83
yea, this man's brow, like to a title–leaf, 2H4 1.01. 60
it is not a confident brow, nor the throng of 2.01.111 P
as he whose brow with homely biggen bound 4.05. 27
and a jest with a sad brow will do with a fellow 5.01. 82 P
let the brow o'erwhelm it | as fearfully as doth H5 3.01. 11
day, | he knits his brow and shows an angry eye, 2H6 3.01. 15
and suffolk's cloudy brow his stormy hate; 3.01.155
and, like a gallant in the brow of youth, 5.03. 4
and who durst smile when warwick bent his brow? 3H6 5.02. 22
of golden metal that must round my brow | were R3 4.01. 59
now | that bear a weighty and a serious brow, H8 pr 2
his bloody brow | with his mail'd hand then COR 1.03. 34
his bloody brow? o jupiter, no blood! 1.03. 38
prepare thy brow to frown. know'st thou me yet? 4.05. 63
for even the day before, she broke her brow, ROM 1.03. 38
and yet i warrant it had upon it brow | a bump 1.03. 52
upon his brow shame is asham'd to sit; 3.02. 92
'tis but the pale reflex of cynthia's brow; 3.05. 20
the angry spot doth glow on caesar's brow, | and JC 1.02.183

thou to show thy dang'rous brow by night, | when 2.01. 78
but hold thee, take this garland on thy brow; 5.03. 85
thou other gold–bound brow, is like the first. MAC 4.01.114
kingdom | to be contracted in one brow of woe, HAM 1.02. 4
and, with his other hand thus o'er his brow, 2.01. 86
see what a grace was seated on this brow: 3.04. 55
between the chaste unsmirched brow | of my true 4.05.120
let it stamp wrinkles in her brow of youth, LR 1.04.284
on the brow o' th' sea | stand ranks of people, OTH 2.01. 53
and didst contract and purse thy brow together, 3.03.113
would stand and make his eyes grow in my brow; ANT 1.05. 32
an angry brow, dread lord. PER 1.02. 52
and do the deed with a bent brow. TNK 3.01.101
what a brow, | of what a spacious majesty, he 4.02. 18
a most menacing aspect, his brow | is grav'd, 5.03. 45
even so she kiss'd his brow, his cheek, his chin VEN 59
"thou canst not see one wrinkle in my brow, 139
and with his bonnet hides his angry brow, 339
with heavy eye, knit brow, and strengthless pace LUC 709
how | to cloak offenses with a cunning brow. 749
the light will show, character'd in my brow, 807
a brow unbent, that seem'd to welcome woe, 1509
when forty winters shall besiege thy brow, | and SON 2. 1
o, carve not with thy hours my love's fair brow, 19. 9
shine | with all–triumphant splendor on my brow, 33.10
and delves the parallels in beauty's brow, 60.10
hours have drain'd his blood and fill'd his brow 63. 3
were born, | or durst inhabit on a living brow; 68. 4
of hand, of foot, of lip, of eye, of brow, | i 106. 6
which vulgar scandal stamp'd upon my brow, | for 112. 2
BROW–BOUND 1 FR 0.0001 REL FR 1 V 0 P
and for his meed | was brow–bound with the oak. COR 2.02. 98
BROWN 24 FR 0.0027 REL FR 8 V 16 P
ground, long heath, brown /furze, any thing. TMP 1.01. 66 P
she has brown hair, and speaks small like a WIV 1.01. 47 P
all the world drink brown and white bastard. MM 3.02. 3 P
beggar, though she smelt brown bread and garlic. 3.02.183 P
in for a commodity of brown paper and old ginger 4.03. 5 P
for a high praise, too brown for a fair praise, ADO 1.01.172 P
slender, and as brown in hue | as hazel–nuts, SHR 2.01.254
beat me to death with a bottom of brown thread. 4.03.137 P
why then your brown bastard is your only drink! 1H4 2.04. 73 P
my brain–pan had been cleft with a brown bill; 2H6 4.10. 12 P
when the brown wench | lay kissing in your arms, H8 3.02.295
th' other day that troilus, for a brown favor TRO 1.02. 93 P
so 'tis, i must confess) — not brown neither — 1.02. 94 P
no, but brown. 1.02. 95 P
faith, to say truth, brown and not brown. 1.02. 96 P
faith, to say truth, brown and not brown. 1.02. 96 P
not that our heads are some brown, some black, COR 2.03. 19 P
bring up the brown bills. LR 4.06. 91 P
brown, madam; ANT 3.03. 33
for the white | reprove the brown for rashness, 3.11. 14
do something mingle with our younger brown, yet 4.08. 20
a pretty brown wench 'tis. TNK 3.03. 39
and yet inviting, | has this brown manly face! 4.02. 42
his complexion | nearer a brown than black; 4.02. 79
BROWNER 3 FR 0.0003 REL FR 1 V 2 P
excellently, if the hair were a thought browner; ADO 3.04. 14 P
something browner than judas's. AYL 3.04. 8 P
the woman low, | and browner than her brother." 4.03. 88
BROWNIST 1 FR 0.0001 REL FR 0 V 1 P
i had as lief be a brownist as a politician. TN 3.02. 31 P
BROWNY 1 FR 0.0001 REL FR 1 V 0 P
"his browny locks did hang in crooked curls, LC 85
BROW'S 1 FR 0.0001 REL FR 1 V 0 P
had not his clouded with his brow's repine; VEN 490
BROWS' 1 FR 0.0001 REL FR 1 V 0 P
our lips and eyes, | bliss in our brows' bent; ANT 1.03. 36
BROWS 48 FR 0.0054 REL FR 44 V 4 P
my brows become nothing else, nor that well WIV 3.03. 59 P
in faith, honest as the skin between his brows. ADO 3.05. 12 P
o, if in black my lady's brows be deck'd, | it LLL 4.03.254
help, hold his brows! 5.02.392
till o'er their brows death–counterfeiting sleep MND 3.02.364
'tis not your inky brows, your black silk hair, AYL 3.05. 46
to sit and draw | his arched brows, his hawking AWW 1.01. 94
my bosom likes not, nor my brows! WT 1.02.119
of my brains | (and hard'ning of my brows). 1.02.146
not for because | your brows are blacker; 2.01. 8
yet black brows, they say, | become some women 2.01. 8
sweetheart's hat | and pluck it o'er your brows, 4.04.651
bent | against the brows of this resisting town. JN 2.01. 38
these eyes, these brows, were moulded out of his 2.01.100
and put my eyeballs in thy vaulty brows, | and 3.04. 30
i knit my handkercher about your brows | (the 4.01. 42
why do you bend such solemn brows on me? 4.02. 90
makes fearful action | with wrinkled brows, with 4.02.192
i see your brows are full of discontent, | your R2 4.01.331
now bind my brows with iron, and approach | the 2H4 1.01.150
fury, | as by his smoothed brows it doth appear. 1H6 3.01.124
see how the ugly witch doth bend her brows, | as 5.03. 34
why doth the great duke humphrey knit his brows, 2H6 1.02. 3
that gold must round engirt these brows of mine, 5.01. 99
thou smiling while he knit his angry brows: 3H6 2.02. 20
the widow likes him not, she knits her brows. 3.02. 82
the wrinkles in my brows, now fill'd with blood, 5.02. 19
now are our brows bound with victorious wreaths, R3 1.01. 5
thou didst crown his warlike brows with paper, 1.03.174
have i pluck'd off to grace thy brows withal. 5.05. 6
whence he return'd, his brows bound with oak. COR 1.03. 14 P
on 's brows. 2.01.124 P
these happy masks that kiss fair ladies' brows, ROM 1.01.230
here are the beetle brows shall blush for me. 1.04. 32
in tatt'red weeds, with overwhelming brows, 5.01. 39
to thee, | all the charactery of my sad brows. JC 2.01.308
they | put on my brows this wreath of victory, 5.03. 82
all things foul would wear the brows of grace, MAC 4.03. 23
what, man, ne'er pull your hat upon your brows; 4.03.208
near 's as doth hourly grow | out of his brows. HAM 3.03. 7
here, hamlet, take my napkin, rub thy brows. 5.02.288
who hast not in thy brows an eye discerning LR 4.02. 52
put | his brows within a golden crown and call'd CYM 3.01. 60
my queen's square brows, | her stature to an PER 5.01.108
whether my brows may not be girt with garlands, TNK 2.03. 80
his low'ring brows o'erwhelming his fair sight, VEN 183
to mask their brows and hide their infamy, | but LUC 794
what though her frowning brows be bent, | her PP 18.25
BROWS'D 1 FR 0.0001 REL FR 1 V 0 P
sheets, | the barks of trees thou brows'd. ANT 1.04. 66
BROWSE 1 FR 0.0001 REL FR 1 V 0 P
cave, we'll browse on that | whilst what we have CYM 3.06. 38
BROWSING 1 FR 0.0001 REL FR 0 V 1 P
them, 'tis by the sea–side, browsing of ivy. WT 3.03. 68 P
BRUIS'D 5 FR 0.0005 REL FR 4 V 1 P
i bruis'd my shin th' other day with playing at WIV 1.01.283 P
a wretched soul, bruis'd with adversity, | we ERR 2.01. 34
he was so bruis'd | that the pursuers took him. 1H4 5.05. 21
bruis'd underneath the yoke of tyranny, | thus R3 5.02. 2
that the bruis'd heart was pierced through the OTH 1.03.219
BRUISE 9 FR 0.0010 REL FR 8 V 1 P
cut a little, | than fall, and bruise to death. MM 2.01. 6
and, with grey hairs and bruise of many days, ADO 5.01. 65
bruise me with scorn, confound me with a flout, LLL 5.02.397
nor bruise her flow'rets with the armed hoofs 1H4 1.01. 8
on earth | was parmaciti for an inward bruise, 1.03. 58
we thought not good to bruise an injury till it H5 3.06.122 P
most true; the law shall bruise 'em. TIM 3.05. 4
for they yet glance by and scarcely bruise, LR 5.03.149
thee but my sword, | a bruise would be dishonor. TNK 3.06. 88
BRUISED 5 FR 0.0005 REL FR 5 V 0 P
borne | his bruised helmet and his bended sword H5 5.pr. 18
our bruised arms hung up for monuments, | our R3 1.01. 6
or slain, and palamedes | sore hurt and bruised. TRO 5.05. 14
bruised pieces, go, | you have been nobly borne. ANT 4.14. 42
with bruised arms and wreaths of victory. LUC 110
BRUISES 1 FR 0.0001 REL FR 1 V 0 P
all | that feel the bruises of the days before, 2H4 4.01. 98
BRUISING 4 FR 0.0004 REL FR 4 V 0 P
i throw thy name against the bruising stones, TGV 1.02.108
on | to bloody battles and to bruising arms. 1H4 3.02.105
put in their hands thy bruising irons of wrath, R3 5.03.110
that his contempt shall not be bruising to you COR 2.03.202
BRUIT 4 FR 0.0004 REL FR 4 V 0 P
the bruit thereof will bring you many friends. 3H6 4.07. 64
the bruit is, hector's slain, and by achilles. TRO 5.09. 4
the common wrack, | as common bruit doth put it. TIM 5.01.193
the king's rouse the heaven shall bruit again, HAM 1.02.127
BRUITED 3 FR 0.0003 REL FR 3 V 0 P
being bruited once, took fire and heat away 2H4 1.01.114
i find thou art no less than fame hath bruited, 1H6 2.03. 68
clatter, one of greatest note | seems bruited. MAC 5.07. 22
BRUNDUSIUM 1 FR 0.0001 REL FR 1 V 0 P
that from tarentum and brundusium | he could so ANT 3.07. 21
BRUNT 1 FR 0.0001 REL FR 1 V 0 P
and in the brunt of seventeen battles since | he COR 2.02.100
BRUSH 2 FR 0.0002 REL FR 2 V 0 P
forgets | aged contusions and all brush of time, 2H6 5.03. 3
have with one winter's brush | fell from their TIM 4.03.264
BRUSH'D 2 FR 0.0002 REL FR 1 V 1 P
as wicked dew as e'er my mother brush'd | with TMP 1.02.321
be slickly comb'd, their blue coats brush'd, and SHR 4.01. 91 P
BRUSHES* 2 FR 0.0002 REL FR 1 V 1 P
'a brushes his hat a' mornings; ADO 3.02. 41 P
and tempt not yet the brushes of the war. TRO 5.03. 34
BRUTE* 2 FR 0.0002 REL FR 1 V 1 P
et tu, brute? — then fall, caesar! JC 3.01. 77
it was a brute part of him to kill so capital a HAM 3.02.105 P
BRUTISH 6 FR 0.0006 REL FR 4 V 2 P
but wouldst gabble like | a thing most brutish, TMP 1.02.357
as sensual as the brutish sting itself, | and AYL 2.07. 66
all this from my remembrance brutish wrath R3 2.01.119
thou /art fled to brutish beasts, | and men have JC 3.02.104
unnatural, detested, brutish villain! LR 1.02. 76 P
worse than brutish! 1.02. 77 P
BRUTUS' 12 FR 0.0013 REL FR 10 V 2 P
to cato's daughter, brutus' portia. MV 1.01.166
brutus' bastard hand | stabb'd julius caesar; 2H6 4.01.136
set this up with wax | upon old brutus' statue. JC 1.03.146
more, | portia is brutus' harlot, not his wife. 2.01.287
that brutus' love to caesar was no less than his 3.02. 19 P
for brutus' sake, i am beholding to you. 3.02. 65
for brutus' sake | he finds himself beholding to 3.02. 66
to brutus', to cassius'; 3.03. 36 P
i cannot drink too much of brutus' love. 4.03.162
i was not born to die on brutus' sword. 5.01. 58
octavius | is overthrown by noble brutus' power, 5.03. 52
once, for brutus' tongue | hath almost ended his 5.05. 39
BRUTUS 146 FR 0.0165 REL FR 141 V 5 P
were but the outside of the roman brutus, H5 2.04. 37
one's junius brutus, | sicinius velutus, and i COR 1.01.216
brutus! 3.01.186
lord junius brutus sware for lucrece' rape, TIT 4.01. 91
brutus, i do observe you now of late; JC 1.02. 32
than that poor brutus, with himself at war, 1.02. 46
then, brutus, i have much mistook your passion, 1.02. 48
tell me, good brutus, can you see your face? 1.02. 51
just, | and it is very much lamented, brutus, 1.02. 55
speaking of brutus | and groaning underneath 1.02. 60
have wish'd that noble brutus had his eyes. 1.02. 62
therefore, good brutus, be prepar'd to hear; 1.02. 66
and be not jealous on me, gentle brutus: 1.02. 71
i know that virtue to be in you, brutus, | as 1.02. 90
the fault, dear brutus, is not in our stars, 1.02.140
brutus and caesar: 1.02.142
"brutus" will start a spirit as soon as "caesar. 1.02.147
there was a brutus once that would have brook'd 1.02.159
brutus had rather be a villager | than to repute 1.02.172
struck but thus much show of fire from brutus. 1.02.177
well, brutus, thou art noble; 1.02.308
caesar doth bear me hard, but he loves brutus. 1.02.313
if i were brutus now and he were cassius, | he 1.02.314
could | but win the noble brutus to our party — 1.03.141
praetor's chair, | where brutus may but find it; 1.03.144
is decius brutus and trebonius there? 1.03.148
i will yet, ere day, | see brutus at his house. 1.03.154
"brutus, thou sleep'st; 2.01. 46
"brutus, thou sleep'st; 2.01. 48
thy full petition at the hand of brutus! 2.01. 58
good morrow, brutus, do we trouble you? 2.01. 87
this, decius brutus. 2.01. 95
we'll leave you, brutus, | and, friends, 2.01.221
brutus, my lord! 2.01.233
y' have ungently, brutus, | stole from my bed; 2.01.237
your condition, | i should not know you brutus. 2.01.255
brutus is wise, and, were he not in health, | he 2.01.258
is brutus sick? 2.01.261
what, is brutus sick? 2.01.263
no, my brutus, | you have some sick offense 2.01.267
i should not need, if you were gentle brutus. 2.01.279
within the bond of marriage, tell me, brutus, 2.01.280
withal | a woman that lord brutus took to wife. 2.01.293
if brutus have in hand | any exploit worthy the 2.01.316
but it sufficeth | that brutus leads me on. 2.01.334
here's decius brutus, he shall tell them so. 2.02. 57
what, brutus, are you stirr'd so early too? 2.02.110
the heart of brutus earns to think upon! 2.02.129
"caesar, beware of brutus; 2.03. 1 P
decius brutus loves thee not; 2.03. 4 P
o brutus, | the heavens speed thee in thine 2.04. 40
brutus hath a suit | that caesar will not grant. 2.04. 42
brutus, what shall be done? 3.01. 20
for look you, brutus, | he draws mark antony out 3.01. 25
what, brutus? 3.01. 55
doth not brutus bootless kneel? 3.01. 75
go to the pulpit, brutus. 3.01. 84
brutus shall lead, and we will grace his heels 3.01.120
thus, brutus, did my master bid me kneel; 3.01.123
brutus is noble, wise, valiant, and honest; 3.01.126
say, i love brutus, and i honor him; 3.01.128
if brutus will vouchsafe that antony | may 3.01.130
not love caesar dead | so well as brutus living; 3.01.134
the fortunes and affairs of noble brutus 3.01.135
first, marcus brutus, will i shake with you; 3.01.185
now, decius brutus, yours; 3.01.187
brutus, a word with you. 3.01.231
i will hear brutus speak. 3.02. 8
the noble brutus is ascended; silence! 3.02. 11
friend demand why brutus rose against caesar, 3.02. 20 P
none, brutus, none. 3.02. 35
no more to caesar than you shall do to brutus. 3.02. 37 P
live, brutus, live, live! 3.02. 48
better parts | shall be crown'd in brutus. 3.02. 52
peace, silence! brutus speaks. 3.02. 54
what does he say of brutus? 3.02. 66
'twere best he speak no harm of brutus here! 3.02. 68
the noble brutus | hath told you caesar was 3.02. 77
here, under leave of brutus and the rest | (for 3.02. 81
and the rest | (for brutus is an honorable man, 3.02. 82
but brutus says he was ambitious, | and brutus 3.02. 86
was ambitious, | and brutus is an honorable man. 3.02. 87
yet brutus says he was ambitious, | and brutus 3.02. 93
was ambitious, | and brutus is an honorable man. 3.02. 94
yet brutus says he was ambitious, | and sure he 3.02. 98
i speak not to disprove what brutus spoke, | but 3.02.100
i should do brutus wrong, and cassius wrong, 3.02.123
through this the well–beloved brutus stabb'd, 3.02.176
resolv'd | if brutus so unkindly knock'd or no; 3.02.180
for brutus, as you know, was caesar's angel. 3.02.181
i am no orator, as brutus is; 3.02.217
but were i brutus, | and brutus antony, there 3.02.226
and brutus antony, there were an antony | would 3.02.227
we'll burn the house of brutus. 3.02.231
brutus and cassius | are rid like madmen through 3.02.268
brutus and cassius | are levying powers; 4.01. 41
brutus, this sober form of yours hides wrongs, 4.02. 40
you know that you are brutus that speaks this, 4.03. 13
brutus, bait not me, | i'll not endure it. 4.03. 28
you wrong me, brutus: 4.03. 55
when marcus brutus grows so covetous | to lock 4.03. 79
brutus hath riv'd my heart. 4.03. 85
but brutus makes mine greater than they are. 4.03. 87
to be but mirth and laughter to his brutus, 4.03.114
o brutus! 4.03.118
when you are over–earnest with your brutus, 4.03.122
bear with him, brutus, 'tis his fashion. 4.03.135
let it not, brutus. 4.03.236
good night, lord brutus. 4.03.238
thy evil spirit, brutus. 4.03.282
in your bad strokes, brutus, you give good words 5.01. 30
now, brutus, thank yourself; 5.01. 45
now, most noble brutus, | the gods to–day stand 5.01. 92
roman, | that ever brutus will go bound to rome; 5.01.111
for ever, and for ever, farewell, brutus! 5.01.119
o cassius, brutus gave the word too early, | who 5.03. 5
whilst i go to meet | the noble brutus, 5.03. 74
shall be as welcome to the ears of brutus | as 5.03. 77
thy brutus bid me give it thee, and i | will do 5.03. 86
brutus, come apace, | and see how i regarded 5.03. 87
and i am brutus, marcus brutus, i, | brutus, my 5.04. 7
and i am brutus, marcus brutus, i, | brutus, my 5.04. 7
marcus brutus, i, | brutus, my country's friend; 5.04. 8
know me for brutus! 5.04. 8
kill brutus, and be honor'd in his death. 5.04. 14
room ho! tell antony, brutus is ta'en. 5.04. 16
brutus is ta'en, brutus is ta'en, my lord! 5.04. 18
brutus is ta'en, brutus is ta'en, my lord! 5.04. 18
safe, antony, brutus is safe enough. 5.04. 20
enemy | shall ever take alive the noble brutus; 5.04. 22
he will be found like brutus, like himself. 5.04. 25
this is not brutus, friend, but, i assure you, 5.04. 26
go on, | and see whe'er brutus be alive or dead, 5.04. 30
what ill request did brutus make to thee? 5.05. 11
for brutus only overcame himself, | and no man 5.05. 56
so brutus should be found. 5.05. 58
i thank thee, brutus, | that thou hast prov'd 5.05. 58
all that serv'd brutus, i will entertain them. 5.05. 60
brutus kill'd me. HAM 3.02.104 P
who at philippi the good brutus ghosted, | there ANT 2.06. 13
what | made all–honor'd, honest, roman brutus, 2.06. 16
wept | when at philippi he found brutus slain. 3.02. 56
and 'twas i | that the mad brutus ended. 3.11. 38
and from the purple fountain brutus drew | the LUC 1734
brutus, who pluck'd the knife from lucrece' side 1807
and that deep vow which brutus made before, | he 1847
BUBBLE 8 FR 0.0009 REL FR 7 V 1 P
where i have seen corruption boil and bubble, MM 5.01.318
seeking the bubble reputation | even in the AYL 2.07.152
on my life, my lord, a bubble. AWW 3.06. 5 P
a sign of dignity, a breath, a bubble; R3 4.04. 90
fire burn, and cauldron bubble. MAC 4.01. 11

trouble, | like a hell–broth boil and bubble. 4.01. 19
fire burn, and cauldron bubble. 4.01. 21
fire burn, and cauldron bubble. 4.01. 36
BUBBLES 3 FR 0.0003 REL FR 2 V 1 P
brow, | like bubbles in a late–disturbed stream, 1H4 2.03. 59
the earth hath bubbles, as the water has, | and MAC 1.03. 79
blow them to their trial, the bubbles are out. HAM 5.02.193 P
BUBBLING 2 FR 0.0002 REL FR 2 V 0 P
like to a bubbling fountain stirr'd with wind, TIT 2.04. 23
and bubbling from her breast, it doth divide LUC 1737
BUBUKLES 1 FR 0.0001 REL FR 0 V 1 P
his face is all bubukles, and whelks, and knobs, H5 3.06.102 P
BUCK* 10 FR 0.0011 REL FR 2 V 8 P
buck! WIV 3.03.157 P
i would i could wash myself of the buck! 3.03.158 P
buck, buck, buck! 3.03.158 P
buck, buck, buck! 3.03.158 P
buck, buck, buck! 3.03.158 P
ay, buck! 3.03.158 P
i warrant you, buck, and of the season too, it 3.03.159 P
make a man mad as a buck to be so bought and ERR 3.01. 72
i assure ye it was a buck of the first head. LLL 4.02. 10 P
for, o, love's bow | shoots buck and doe. TRO 3.01.117
BUCK–BASKET 5 FR 0.0005 REL FR 0 V 5 P
quickly, quickly! is the buck–basket — WIV 3.03. 2 P
they convey'd me into a buck–basket. 3.05. 86 P
a buck–basket? 3.05. 88 P
/by /the /lord, a buck–basket! 3.05. 89 P
enjoy'd nothing of ford's but his buck–basket, 5.05.113 P
BUCK–BASKETS 1 FR 0.0001 REL FR 0 V 1 P
this 'tis to have linen and buck–baskets! WIV 3.05.143 P
/BUCKET 1 FR 0.0001 REL FR 1 V 0 P
/that /bucket /down /and /full /of /tears /am /i R2 4.01.188
BUCKET 2 FR 0.0002 REL FR 0 V 2 P
than he that gibbets on the brewer's bucket. 2H4 3.02.264 P
sir, a new link to the bucket must needs be had; 5.01. 22 P
/BUCKETS 1 FR 0.0001 REL FR 1 V 0 P
/a /deep /well | /that /owes /two /buckets, R2 4.01.185
BUCKETS 1 FR 0.0001 REL FR 1 V 0 P
to dive like buckets in concealed wells, | to JN 5.02.139
BUCKING 1 FR 0.0001 REL FR 0 V 1 P
linen upon him, as if it were going to bucking; WIV 3.03.131 P
/BUCKINGHAM 1 FR 0.0001 REL FR 1 V 0 P
/o, /do /not /swear, /my /lord /of /buckingham. R3 3.07.220
BUCKINGHAM 73 FR 0.0082 REL FR 72 V 1 P
gloucester, york, buckingham, somerset, 2H6 1.01. 69
have you yourselves, somerset, buckingham, 1.01. 85
cousin of buckingham, though humphrey's pride 1.01.172
the imperious churchman, somerset, buckingham, 1.03. 69
peace, son, and show some reason, buckingham, 1.03.113
lord buckingham, methinks you watch'd her well. 1.04. 55
what tidings with our cousin buckingham? 2.01.161
at buckingham, and all the crew of them, | till 2.02. 72
my lord of suffolk, buckingham, and york, 3.01. 39
sharp buckingham unburthens with his tongue 3.01.156
what, buckingham and clifford, are ye so brave? 4.08. 20 P
why, buckingham, is the traitor cade surpris'd? 4.09. 8
i pray thee, buckingham, go and meet him, | and 4.09. 36
buckingham, to disturb me? 5.01. 12
humphrey of buckingham, i accept thy greeting. 5.01. 15
buckingham, i prithee pardon me, | that i have 5.01. 32
then, buckingham, i do dismiss my pow'rs. 5.01. 44
buckingham, doth york intend no harm to us 5.01. 56
see, buckingham, somerset comes with th' queen. 5.01. 83
call buckingham, and bid him arm himself. 5.01.192
call buckingham, and all the friends thou hast, 5.01.193
lord stafford's father, duke of buckingham, | is 3H6 1.01. 10
thou, brother montague, in buckingham, 4.08. 14
here /come the /lords of buckingham and derby. R3 1.03. 17
but now the duke of buckingham and i | are come 1.03. 31
o princely buckingham, i'll kiss thy hand | in 1.03.279
o buckingham, take heed of yonder dog! 1.03.288
what doth she say, my lord of buckingham? 1.03.294
namely, to derby, hastings, buckingham — | and 1.03.328
buckingham, nor you; 2.01. 19
now, princely buckingham, seal thou this league 2.01. 29
when ever buckingham doth turn his hate | upon 2.01. 32
a pleasing cordial, princely buckingham, | is 2.01. 41
of you, my noble cousin buckingham, | if ever 2.01. 65
with some little train, my lord of buckingham? 2.02.123
therefore i say with noble buckingham, | that it 2.02.138
the mighty dukes, | gloucester and buckingham. 2.04. 45
my lord of buckingham, if my weak oratory | can 3.01. 37
i'll tell you what, my cousin buckingham — 3.01. 89
myself and my good cousin buckingham | will to 3.01.137
dear | to princely richard and to buckingham. 3.02. 68
curs'd she richard, then curs'd she buckingham, 3.03. 18
cousin of buckingham, a word with you. 3.04. 35
go after, after, cousin buckingham. 3.05. 72
cousin of buckingham, and sage grave men, 3.07.227
stand all apart. cousin of buckingham — 4.02. 1
ah, buckingham, now do i play the touch, | to 4.02. 8
why, buckingham, i say i would be king. 4.02. 12
high–reaching buckingham grows circumspect. 4.02. 31
the deep–revolving witty buckingham | no more 4.02. 42
and buckingham, back'd with the hardy welshmen, 4.03. 47
than buckingham and his rash–levied strength. 4.03. 50
the petty rebel, dull–brain'd buckingham, 4.04.332
the aid | of buckingham to welcome them ashore. 4.04.439
stirr'd up by dorset, buckingham, and morton, 4.04.467
my lord, the army of great buckingham — 4.04.506
him, they came from buckingham | upon his party. 4.04.525
my liege, the duke of buckingham is taken — 4.04.531
some one take order buckingham be brought | to 4.04.537
o, in the battle think on buckingham, | and die 5.03.169
and buckingham | shall lessen this big look. H8 1.01.118
my lord the duke of buckingham and earl | of 1.01.199
i am the shadow of poor buckingham, | whose 1.01.224
i am sorry that the duke of buckingham | is run 1.02.109
have collected | out of the duke of buckingham. 1.02.131
shall become | of the great duke of buckingham. 2.01. 3
call him bounteous buckingham, | the mirror of 2.01. 52
me | and dare be bold to weep for buckingham, 2.01. 72
and, if he speak of buckingham, pray tell him 2.01. 87
lord high constable | and duke of buckingham; 2.01.103
my noble father, henry of buckingham, | who 2.01.107
this bewailing land | of noble buckingham, my 3.02.256
the duke of buckingham came from his trial. 4.01. 5
BUCKINGHAM'S 4 FR 0.0004 REL FR 4 V 0 P
with somerset's and buckingham's ambition; 2H6 1.01.202
buckingham's army is dispers'd and scatter'd, R3 4.04.511
the duke of buckingham's surveyor? H8 1.01.115
before us | that gentleman of buckingham's; 1.02. 5
BUCKLE 8 FR 0.0009 REL FR 8 V 0 P
like strengthless hinges, buckle under life, 2H4 1.01.141
in single combat thou shalt buckle with me; 1H6 1.02. 95
and hell too strong for me to buckle with: 5.03. 28
men, | since you will buckle fortune on my back, R3 3.07.228
your friends are up and buckle on their armor. 5.03.211
and buckle in a waist most fathomless | with TRO 2.02. 30
certain | he cannot buckle his distemper'd cause MAC 5.02. 15
cousin, thrust the buckle | through far enough. TNK 3.06. 61
BUCKLED 7 FR 0.0008 REL FR 6 V 1 P
buckled below fair knighthood's bending knee: WIV 5.05. 72
boots that have been candle–cases, one buckled, SHR 3.02. 46 P
and france, whose armor conscience buckled on, JN 2.01.564
with a sally of the very town | be buckled with. 1H6 4.04. 5
and when we have our armors buckled on, | the TRO 5.03. 46
is not this buckled well? ANT 4.04. 11
more buckled with strong judgment, and their TNK 1.03. 57
BUCKLER 4 FR 0.0004 REL FR 3 V 1 P
i'll buckler thee against a million. SHR 3.02.239
the hose, my buckler cut through and through, my 1H4 2.04.167 P
but buckler with thee blows, twice two for one. 3H6 1.04. 50
right, | now buckler falsehood with a pedigree? 3.03. 99
BUCKLERS 3 FR 0.0003 REL FR 1 V 2 P
i give thee the bucklers. ADO 5.02. 17 P
give us the swords, we have bucklers of our own. 5.02. 18 P
but that the guilt of murther bucklers thee, 2H6 3.02.216
BUCKLERSBURY 1 FR 0.0001 REL FR 0 V 1 P
and smell like bucklersbury in simple time — i WIV 3.03. 72 P
BUCKLES 4 FR 0.0004 REL FR 3 V 1 P
of a span | buckles in his sum of age; AYL 3.02.132
he that buckles himself in my belt cannot live 2H4 1.02.138 P
his stubborn buckles, | with /these your white TRO 3.01.150
fights hath burst | the buckles on his breast, ANT 1.01. 8
BUCKLE'T 1 FR 0.0001 REL FR 1 V 0 P
i'll buckle't close. TNK 3.06. 57
BUCKRAM 1 FR 0.0001 REL FR 0 V 1 P
thou say, thou serge, nay, thou buckram lord! 2H6 4.07. 25 P
BUCKROM 7 FR 0.0008 REL FR 0 V 7 P
sirrah, i have cases of buckrom for the nonce, 1H4 1.02.179 P
sure i have paid, two rogues in buckrom suits. 2.04.193 P
four rogues in buckrom let drive at me — 2.04.196 P
in buckrom? 2.04.204 P
ay, four, in buckrom suits. 2.04.205 P
these nine in buckrom that i told thee of — 2.04.212 P
eleven buckrom men grown out of two. 2.04.219 P
BUCKS 1 FR 0.0001 REL FR 0 V 1 P
her furr'd pack, she washes bucks here at home. 2H6 4.02. 48 P
BUCK–WASHING 1 FR 0.0001 REL FR 0 V 1 P
you were best meddle with buck–washing. WIV 3.03.155 P
BUD 22 FR 0.0024 REL FR 22 V 0 P
as in the sweetest bud | the eating canker TGV 1.01. 42
as the most forward bud | is eaten by the canker 1.01. 45
wit | is turn'd to folly, blasting in the bud, 1.01. 48
orb, | as chaste as is the bud ere it be blown; ADO 4.01. 58
fair ladies mask'd are roses in their bud; LLL 5.02.295
dian's bud o'er cupid's flower | hath such force MND 4.01. 73
but let concealment, like a worm i' th' bud, TN 2.04.111
a bark of baser kind | by bud of nobler race. WT 4.04. 95
but now will canker–sorrow eat my bud, | and JN 3.04. 82
thus are my blossoms blasted in the bud, | and 2H6 3.01. 89
as is the bud bit with an envious worm, | ere he ROM 1.01.151
this bud of love, by summer's ripening breath, 2.02.121
her neele composes | nature's own shape of bud, PER 5.ch. 6
she locks her beauties in her bud again, | and TNK 2.02.142
who plucks the bud before one leaf put forth? VEN 416
bud and be blasted in a breathing while, | the 1142
when thus thy vices bud before thy spring? LUC 604
"why should the worm intrude the maiden bud? 848
pluck'd in the bud, and vaded in the spring! PP 10. 2
a flower that dies when first it gins to bud, 13. 3
within thine own bud buriest thy content, | and, SON 1.11
and loathsome canker lives in sweetest bud. 35. 4
BUDDED 1 FR 0.0001 REL FR 1 V 0 P
which is budded out, | for france hath flaw'd H8 1.01. 94
BUDDING 3 FR 0.0003 REL FR 3 V 0 P
young budding virgin, fair, and fresh, and sweet SHR 4.05. 37
and all the budding honors on thy crest | i'll 1H4 5.04. 72
doth spot the beauty of thy budding name! SON 95. 3
BUDGE *(also bodg'd, boudge, bouge)*
BUDGE 6 FR 0.0006 REL FR 4 V 2 P
i'll not budge an inch, boy; SHR in.1. 14 P
ye cuckoo, but afoot he will not budge a foot. 1H4 2.04.354 P
nay, stand thou back, i will not budge a foot: 1H6 1.03. 38
here pitch our battle, hence we will not budge. 3H6 5.04. 66
mouse ne'er shunn'd the cat as they did budge COR 1.06. 44
i will not budge for no man's pleasure, i. ROM 3.01. 55
BUDGER 1 FR 0.0001 REL FR 1 V 0 P
let the first budger die the other's slave, COR 1.08. 5
BUDGET *(also bouget)*
BUDGET 3 FR 0.0003 REL FR 0 V 3 P
she cries "budget"; WIV 5.02. 6 P
what needs either your "mum" or her "budget"? 5.02. 9 P
/white and cried "mum," and she cried "budget," 5.05.198 P
/BUDS 1 FR 0.0001 REL FR 1 V 0 P
/early /spring | /we /see /th' /appearing /buds, 2H4 1.03. 39
BUDS 15 FR 0.0017 REL FR 14 V 1 P
like a many of these lisping hawthorn buds, that WIV 3.03. 71 P
when wheat is green, when hawthorn buds appear. MND 1.01.185
an odorous chaplet of sweet summer buds | is, as 2.01.110
some to kill cankers in the musk–rose buds, 2.02. 3
which sometime on the buds | was wont to swell 4.01. 53
thy fame, as whirlwinds shake fair buds, | and SHR 5.02.140
make boot upon the summer's velvet buds, | which H5 1.02.194
among fresh fennel buds shall you this night ROM 1.02. 29
stop their nose | that kneel'd unto the buds. ANT 3.13. 40
of the north | shakes all our buds from growing. CYM 1.03. 37
a belt of straw and ivy buds, | with coral PP 19.13
rough winds do shake the darling buds of may, SON 18. 3
summer's breath their masked buds discloses; 54. 8
for canker vice the sweetest buds doth love, 70. 7
and buds of marjerom had stol'n thy hair; 99. 7
BUFF 4 FR 0.0004 REL FR 2 V 2 P
a wolf, nay worse, a fellow all in buff; ERR 4.02. 36
but /'a's in a suit of buff which 'rested him, 4.02. 45
and is not a buff jerkin a most sweet robe of 1H4 1.02. 42 P
what a plague have i to do with a buff jerkin? 1.02. 46 P
BUFFET 4 FR 0.0004 REL FR 3 V 1 P
that he did buffet thee, and, in his blows, ERR 2.02.158
or if i might buffet for my love, or bound my H5 5.02.140 P
and we did buffet it | with lusty sinews, JC 1.02.107
and stand the buffet | with knaves that smells ANT 1.04. 20
BUFFETING 1 FR 0.0001 REL FR 0 V 1 P
come a hot june and this civil buffeting hold, 1H4 2.04.362 P
BUFFETS 5 FR 0.0005 REL FR 3 V 2 P
and so buffets himself on the forehead, crying, WIV 4.02. 25 P
his | but buffets better than a fist of france. JN 2.01.465
o, i could divide myself and go to buffets, for 1H4 2.03. 32 P
whom the vile blows and buffets of the world MAC 3.01.108
a man that fortune's buffets and rewards | hast HAM 3.02. 67
BUG 2 FR 0.0002 REL FR 2 V 0 P
the bug which you would fright me with, i seek. WT 3.02. 92
for warwick was a bug that fear'd us all. 3H6 5.02. 2
BUGBEAR 1 FR 0.0001 REL FR 0 V 1 P
a bugbear take him! TRO 4.02. 33 P
BUGLE* 2 FR 0.0002 REL FR 1 V 1 P
or hang my bugle in an invisible baldrick, all ADO 1.01.241 P
your bugle eyeballs, nor your cheek of cream AYL 3.05. 47
BUGLE–BRACELET 1 FR 0.0001 REL FR 1 V 0 P
bugle–bracelet, necklace amber, | perfume for a WT 4.04.222
BUGS 3 FR 0.0003 REL FR 3 V 0 P
tush, tush, fear boys with bugs. SHR 1.02.210
with, ho, such bugs and goblins in my life, HAM 5.02. 22
resist are grown | the mortal bugs o' th' field. CYM 5.03. 51
/BUILD 4 FR 0.0004 REL FR 4 V 0 P
/when /we /mean /to /build, | /we /first /survey 2H4 1.03. 41
/or /at /least /desist | /to /build /at /all? 1.03. 48
/of /any /ground | /to /build /a /grief /on. 4.01.108
/if /on /my /credit /you /dare /build /so /far LR 3.01. 35
BUILD 20 FR 0.0022 REL FR 13 V 7 P
i mine, to build upon a foolish woman's promise. WIV 3.05. 41 P
sparrows must not build in his house–eaves, MM 3.02.175 P
it serve for any model to build mischief on? ADO 1.03. 46 P
disdain'st in her, the which | i can build up. AWW 2.03.118
why then build me thy fortunes upon the basis of TN 3.02. 33 P
in those foundations which i build upon, | the WT 2.01.101
of an house | beyond his power to build it, who, 2H4 1.03. 59
a pretty plot, well chosen to build upon! 2H6 1.04. 56
for in thy shoulder do i build my seat, | and 3H6 2.06.100
did julius caesar build that place, my lord? R3 3.01. 69
nor build their evils on the graves of great men H8 2.01. 67
build there, carpenter, the air is sweet. TRO 3.02. 50 P
o, why should nature build so foul a den, TIT 4.01. 59
to build his fortune i will strain a little, TIM 1.01.143
thou shalt build from men; 4.03.526
by'r lady, 'a must build churches then, or else HAM 3.02.133 P
field, | and bawds and whores do churches build; LR 3.02. 92
nor build yourself a trouble | out of his OTH 3.03.150
even from this instant do build on thee a better 4.02.205 P
does, | build his statue to make him glorious. PER 2.ch. 14
BUILDED 3 FR 0.0003 REL FR 3 V 0 P
to keep it builded, be the ram to batter | the ANT 3.02. 30
no, it was builded far from accident; SON 124. 5
experience for me many bulwarks builded | of LC 152
/BUILDETH 1 FR 0.0001 REL FR 1 V 0 P
/hath /he /that /buildeth /on /the /vulgar 2H4 1.03. 90
BUILDETH 2 FR 0.0002 REL FR 2 V 0 P
our aery buildeth in the cedar's top | and R3 1.03.263
your aery buildeth in our aery's nest: 1.03.269
/BUILDING 1 FR 0.0001 REL FR 1 V 0 P
shall love, in /building, grow so /ruinous? ERR 3.02. 4
BUILDING 9 FR 0.0010 REL FR 9 V 0 P
the building fall | and leave no memory of what TGV 5.04. 9
the singing masons building roofs of gold, | the H5 1.02.198
but the strong base and building of my love | is TRO 4.02.103
did fix mine eye | upon the wasted building, TIT 5.01. 23
and stole thence | the life o' th' building! MAC 2.03. 69
may all the building in my fancy pluck | upon my LR 4.02. 85
speaks that sometime | it was a worthy building. CYM 4.02.355
sea, | this jewel holds his building on my arm. PER 2.01.156
boat, | he of tall building and of goodly pride. SON 80.12
BUILDINGS 6 FR 0.0006 REL FR 5 V 1 P
peruse the traders, gaze upon the buildings, ERR 1.02. 13
thy sumptuous buildings and thy wive's attire 2H6 1.03.130
my very wishes | and the buildings of my fancy; COR 2.01.200
such may rail against great buildings. TIM 3.04. 65 P
like goodly buildings left without a roof | soon PER 2.04. 36
to ruinate proud buildings with thy hours, | and LUC 944
BUILDS 6 FR 0.0006 REL FR 3 V 3 P
builds in the weather on the outward wall, MV 2.09. 29
when the kite builds, look to lesser linen. WT 4.03. 23 P
who builds his hope in air of your good looks R3 3.04. 98
what is he that builds stronger than either the HAM 5.01. 41 P
who builds stronger than a mason, a shipwright, 5.01. 50 P
but since the cuckoo builds not for himself, ANT 2.06. 28
BUILT 17 FR 0.0019 REL FR 13 V 4 P
and built so shelving that one cannot climb it TGV 3.01.115
like a fair house built on another man's ground, WIV 2.02.215 P
this fortress built by nature for herself R2 2.01. 43
for /'s apparel is built upon his back, and the 2H4 3.02.143 P
and i have built | two chauntries, where the sad H5 4.01.300
and dignity, thou hast built a paper–mill. 2H6 4.07. 37 P
successively from age to age, he built it? R3 3.01. 73
a second hope, as fairly built as hector. TRO 4.05.109
you deserve | to have a temple built you. COR 5.03.207
he was a gentleman on whom i built | an absolute MAC 1.04. 13
to say the gallows is built stronger than the HAM 5.01. 48 P
swallows have built | in cleopatra's sails their ANT 4.12. 3
who cannot be new built, nor has no friends | so CYM 1.05. 59
built up this city for his chiefest seat, | the PER 1.ch. 18
hath built lord cerimon | such strong renown as 3.02. 47
and ruin'd love, when it is built anew, | grows SON 119.11
thy pyramids built up with newer might | to me 123. 2
/BULK* 2 FR 0.0002 REL FR 2 V 0 P
does not grow alone | in thews and /bulk, but, HAM 1.03. 12
here, stand behind this /bulk, straight will he OTH 5.01. 1
BULK* 14 FR 0.0015 REL FR 13 V 1 P
to hide itself, | the bigger bulk it shows. TMP 3.01. 81
no, | for my authority bears of a credent bulk, MM 4.04. 26

of, | for shallow draught and bulk unprizable, TN 5.01. 55
she is spread of late | into a goodly bulk. WT 2.01. 20
grew by our feeding to so great a bulk | that 1H4 5.01. 62
the stature, bulk, and big assemblance of a man? 2H4 3.02.259 P
air, | but smother'd it within my panting bulk, R3 1.04. 40
that such a keech can with his very bulk | take H8 1.01. 55
making their way | with those of nobler bulk! TRO 1.03. 37
though the great bulk achilles be thy guard, 4.04.128
cover | the monstrous bulk of this ingratitude TIM 5.01. 65
as it did seem to shatter all his bulk | and end HAM 2.01. 92
with half the bulk o' th' world play'd as i ANT 3.11. 64
beating her bulk, that his hand shakes withal. LUC 467

BULKS 1 FR 0.0001 REL FR 1 V 0 P
stalls, bulks, windows, | are smother'd up, COR 2.01.210

BULKY 1 FR 0.0001 REL FR 1 V 0 P
the sun begins to peer | above yon bulky hill! 1H4 5.01. 2

BULL 16 FR 0.0018 REL FR 9 V 7 P
jove, thou wast a bull for thy europa, love set WIV 5.05. 3 P
"in time the savage bull doth bear the yoke." ADO 1.01.261
the savage bull may, but if ever the sensible 1.01.262 P
i think he thinks upon the savage bull. 5.04. 43
bull jove, sir, had an amiable low, | and some 5.04. 48
and some such strange bull leapt your father's 5.04. 49
upon | (be it on lion, bear, or wolf, or bull, MND 2.01.180
jupiter | became a bull and bellow'd; WT 4.04. 28
kin as the parish heckfers are to the town bull. 2H4 2.02.158 P
from a god to a bull? 2.02.173 P
fled, | and warwick rages like a chafed bull. 3H6 2.05.126
his /brother, the bull, the primitive statue and TRO 5.01. 54 P
now, bull! 5.07. 10 P
the bull has the game, ware horns ho! 5.07. 11 P
the bull, being gall'd, gave aries such a knock TIT 4.03. 72
but where the bull and cow are both milk–white, 5.01. 31

BULL–BEARING 1 FR 0.0001 REL FR 1 V 0 P
bull–bearing milo his addition yield | to sinowy TRO 2.03.247

BULL–BEEVES 1 FR 0.0001 REL FR 1 V 0 P
want their porridge and their fat bull–beeves: 1H6 1.02. 9

BULL–CALF 1 FR 0.0001 REL FR 0 V 1 P
still run and roar'd, as ever i heard bull–calf. 1H4 2.04.260 P

BULLCALF 7 FR 0.0008 REL FR 0 V 7 P
peter bullcalf o' th' green! 2H4 3.02.172 P
yea, marry, let's see bullcalf. 3.02.173 P
come prick bullcalf till he roar again. 3.02.176 P
i have three pound to free mouldy and bullcalf. 3.02.244 P
then, mouldy, bullcalf, feeble, and shadow. 3.02.248 P
mouldy and bullcalf! 3.02.250 P
and for your part, bullcalf, grow till you come 3.02.252 P

BULLEN 3 FR 0.0003 REL FR 3 V 0 P
a creature of the queen's, lady anne bullen." H8 3.02. 36
anne bullen? 3.02. 87
bullen? 3.02. 88

BULLEN'S 1 FR 0.0001 REL FR 1 V 0 P
your grace, sir thomas bullen's daughter — H8 1.04. 92

BULLENS 2 FR 0.0002 REL FR 2 V 0 P
i'll no anne bullens for him, | there's more H8 3.02. 87
no, we'll no bullens. 3.02. 89

BULLET 4 FR 0.0004 REL FR 3 V 1 P
he reputes me a cannon, and the bullet, that's LLL 3.01. 64
you think me a swallow, an arrow, or a bullet? 2H4 4.03. 33 P
staineth, | or like the deadly bullet of a gun, VEN 461
and town, | the golden bullet beats it down. PP 18.18

BULLET'S 1 FR 0.0001 REL FR 1 V 0 P
that being dead, like to the bullet's crasing, H5 4.03.105

BULLETS 7 FR 0.0008 REL FR 4 V 3 P
and these paper bullets of the brain awe a man ADO 2.03.241 P
have wings | fleeter than arrows, bullets, wind, LLL 5.02.261
and now, instead of bullets wrapp'd in fire, JN 2.01.227
shall rain their drift of bullets on this town. 2.01.412
discharge upon her, sir john, with two bullets. 2H4 2.04.115 P
come, i'll drink no proofs nor no bullets. 2.04.118 P
o, were mine eyeballs into bullets turn'd, 1H6 4.07. 79

/BULLINGBROOK 9 FR 0.0010 REL FR 9 V 0 P
/state /and /crown | /to /henry /bullingbrook. R2 4.01.180
/standing /before /the /sun /of /bullingbrook, 4.01.261
/was /at /last //out–fac'd /by /bullingbrook? 4.01.286
/gasping /for /life /under /great /bullingbrook, 2H4 1.01.208
/beat /heaven /with /blessing /bullingbrook 1.03. 92
/after /th' /admired /heels /of /bullingbrook, 1.03.105
/and /then /that /henry /bullingbrook /and /he, 4.01.115
/father /from /the /breast /of /bullingbrook, 4.01.122
/have /since /miscarried /under /bullingbrook. 4.01.127

BULLINGBROOK 53 FR 0.0060 REL FR 53 V 0 P
then, bullingbrook, as low as to thy heart R2 1.01.124
no, bullingbrook, if ever i were traitor, | my 1.03.201
nor the prevention of poor bullingbrook | about 2.01.167
the banish'd bullingbrook repeals himself, | and 2.02. 49
servants fled with him | to bullingbrook. 2.02. 61
woe, | and bullingbrook my sorrow's dismal heir. 2.02. 63
as york thrives to beat back bullingbrook. 2.02.144
of death to me | than bullingbrook to england. 3.01. 32
whilst bullingbrook, through our security, 3.02. 34
so when this thief, this traitor bullingbrook, 3.02. 47
for every man that bullingbrook hath press'd 3.02. 58
are gone to bullingbrook, dispers'd and fled. 3.02. 74
strives bullingbrook to be as great as we? 3.02. 97
his limits swells the rage | of bullingbrook, 3.02.110
warrant they have made peace with bullingbrook. 3.02.127
proud bullingbrook, i come | to change blows 3.02.188
your uncle york is join'd with bullingbrook, 3.02.200
henry bullingbrook | on both his knees doth kiss 3.03. 35
how far off from the mind of bullingbrook | it 3.03. 45
tell bullingbrook — for yon methinks he stands 3.03. 91
harry bullingbrook, doth humbly kiss thy hand, 3.03.104
northumberland comes back from bullingbrook. 3.03.142
northumberland, | what says king bullingbrook? 3.03.173
you make a leg, and bullingbrook says ay. 3.03.175
are pluck'd up root and all by bullingbrook, | i 3.04. 52
and bullingbrook | hath seiz'd the wasteful king 3.04. 54
he is in the mighty hold | of bullingbrook; 3.04. 84
but in the balance of great bullingbrook, 3.04. 87
should grace the triumph of great bullingbrook? 3.04. 99
is doom'd a prisoner by proud bullingbrook. 5.01. 4
hath bullingbrook depos'd | thine intellect? 5.01. 27
my lord, the mind of bullingbrook is chang'd, 5.01. 51
the mounting bullingbrook ascends my throne, 5.01. 56
then, as i said, the duke, great bullingbrook, 5.02. 7
tongues cried, "god save /thee, bullingbrook!" 5.02. 11
welcome, bullingbrook!" 5.02. 17
to bullingbrook are we sworn subjects now, 5.02. 39
ground | till bullingbrook have pardoned thee. 5.02.117
by | think that i am unking'd by bullingbrook, 5.05. 37
when bullingbrook rode on roan barbary, | that 5.05. 78
so proud that bullingbrook was on his back! 5.05. 84
gall'd, and tir'd by jauncing bullingbrook. 5.05. 94
as this ingrate and cank'red bullingbrook. 1H4 1.03.137
and plant this thorn, this canker, bullingbrook? 1.03.176
save how to gall and pinch this bullingbrook, 1.03.229
i hear | of this vile politician, bullingbrook. 1.03.241
unto this king of smiles, this bullingbrook — 1.03.246
three times hath henry bullingbrook made head 3.01. 63
would say, "where, which is bullingbrook?" 3.02. 49
my cousin bullingbrook ascends my throne" 2H4 3.01. 71
(succeeding his father bullingbrook) did reign, 1H6 2.05. 83
death reign'd as king | till henry bullingbrook, 2H6 2.02. 21
this edmund, in the reign of bullingbrook, | as 2.02. 39

BULLINGBROOK'S 4 FR 0.0004 REL FR 4 V 0 P
lands, our lives, and all are bullingbrook's, R2 3.02.151
from richard's night to bullingbrook's fair day. 3.02.218
crowns | than bullingbrook's return to england, 4.01. 17
runs posting on in bullingbrook's proud joy, 5.05. 59

BULLOCKS 2 FR 0.0002 REL FR 0 V 2 P
so they sell bullocks. ADO 2.01.195 P
how a good yoke of bullocks at /stamford fair? 2H4 3.02. 38 P

BULL'S 3 FR 0.0003 REL FR 0 V 3 P
pluck off the bull's horns and set them in my ADO 1.01.263 P
we set the savage bull's horns on the sensible 5.01.181 P
you dried neat's tongue, you bull's pizzle, you 1H4 2.04.245 P

BULLS 4 FR 0.0004 REL FR 4 V 0 P
heard a hollow burst of bellowing | like bulls, TMP 2.01.312
dew–lapp'd, like bulls, whose throats had 3.03. 45
and dewlapp'd like thessalian bulls; MND 4.01.122
wanton as youthful goats, wild as young bulls. 1H4 4.01.103

BULLY 12 FR 0.0013 REL FR 1 V 11 P
discard, bully hercules, cashier; WIV 1.03. 6 P
said i well, bully hector? 1.03. 11 P
my hand, bully; 2.01.217 P
ha, bully? 2.03. 28 P
in our english tongue, is valor, bully. 2.03. 61 P
he will clapper–claw thee tightly, bully. 2.03. 65 P
and moreover, bully — but first, master guest, 2.03. 73 P
bully sir john! 4.05. 16 P
let her descend, bully, let her descend; 4.05. 21 P
what sayest thou, bully bottom? MND 3.01. 8 P
o sweet bully bottom! 4.02. 19 P
and from heart–string | i love the lovely bully. H5 4.01. 48

BULLY–DOCTOR 1 FR 0.0001 REL FR 0 V 1 P
/god bless thee, bully–doctor! WIV 2.03. 18 P

BULLY–KNIGHT 1 FR 0.0001 REL FR 0 V 1 P
bully–knight. WIV 4.05. 16 P

BULLY–MONSTER 1 FR 0.0001 REL FR 0 V 1 P
coraggio, bully–monster, coraggio! TMP 5.01.258 P

BULLY–ROOK 4 FR 0.0004 REL FR 0 V 4 P
what says my bully–rook? WIV 1.03. 2 P
how now, bully–rook! 2.01.193 P
tell him, bully–rook. 2.01.198 P
what say'st thou, my bully–rook? 2.01.205 P

BULLY–STALE 1 FR 0.0001 REL FR 0 V 1 P
is he dead, bully–stale? WIV 2.03. 30 P

/BULMER 1 FR 0.0001 REL FR 1 V 0 P
reprov'd the duke | about sir william /bulmer — H8 1.02.190

BULRUSH 1 FR 0.0001 REL FR 1 V 0 P
careless tresses | a /wreath of bulrush rounded; TNK 4.01. 84

BULWARK 4 FR 0.0004 REL FR 3 V 1 P
that water–walled bulwark, still secure | and JN 2.01. 27
making the wars their bulwark, that have before H5 4.01.164 P
and i here, at the bulwark of the bridge. 1H6 1.04. 67
so | that it be proof and bulwark against sense. HAM 3.04. 38

BULWARKS 4 FR 0.0004 REL FR 4 V 0 P
let us resolve to scale their flinty bulwarks. 1H6 2.01. 27
roan, i'll shake thy bulwarks to the ground. 3.02. 17
like high–rear'd bulwarks, stand before our R3 5.03.242
experience for me many bulwarks builded | of LC 152

BUM 3 FR 0.0003 REL FR 1 V 2 P
bum, sir. MM 2.01.216 P
and your bum is the greatest thing about you, so 2.01.217 P
then slip i from her bum, down topples she, MND 2.01. 53

BUM–BAILY 1 FR 0.0001 REL FR 0 V 1 P
at the corner of the orchard like a bum–baily. TN 3.04.177 P

BUMBARD *(also bombard)*

BUMBARD 1 FR 0.0001 REL FR 0 V 1 P
looks like a foul bumbard that would shed his TMP 2.02. 21 P

BUMBAST *(also bombast)*

BUMBAST 2 FR 0.0002 REL FR 1 V 1 P
my sweet creature of bumbast, how long is't ago, 1H4 2.04.327 P
evades them with a bumbast circumstance OTH 1.01. 13

BUMP 1 FR 0.0001 REL FR 1 V 0 P
a bump as big as a young cock'rel's stone — | a ROM 1.03. 53

BUMS 1 FR 0.0001 REL FR 1 V 0 P
serving of becks and jutting–out of bums! TIM 1.02.231

BUNCH 2 FR 0.0002 REL FR 0 V 2 P
sir — 'twas in the bunch of grapes, where MM 2.01.129 P
not with fifty of them, i am a bunch of radish. 1H4 2.04.186 P

BUNCH–BACK'D 2 FR 0.0002 REL FR 2 V 0 P
thee curse this poisonous bunch–back'd toad. R3 1.03.245
bottled spider, that foul bunch–back'd toad! 4.04. 81

BUNCHES 2 FR 0.0002 REL FR 1 V 1 P
vines with clust'ring bunches growing, | plants TMP 4.01.112
shoes, and bunches of keys at their girdles, and 2H4 1.02. 39 P

BUNG 1 FR 0.0001 REL FR 0 V 1 P
you filthy bung, away! 2H4 2.04.128 P

BUNGHOLE 1 FR 0.0001 REL FR 0 V 1 P
alexander, till 'a find it stopping a bunghole? HAM 5.01.204 P

BUNGLE 1 FR 0.0001 REL FR 1 V 0 P
by treasons | do botch and bungle up damnation H5 2.02.115

BUNTING 1 FR 0.0001 REL FR 0 V 1 P
i took this lark for a bunting. AWW 2.05. 7 P

BUOY 1 FR 0.0001 REL FR 1 V 0 P
her cock, a buoy | almost too small for sight. LR 4.06. 19

BUOY'D 1 FR 0.0001 REL FR 1 V 0 P
would have buoy'd up | and quench'd the stelled LR 3.07. 60

BUR 2 FR 0.0002 REL FR 1 V 1 P
nay, friar, i am a kind of bur, i shall stick. MM 4.03.179 P
hang off, thou cat, thou bur! MND 3.02.260

BURBOLT *(also bird–bolt)*

BURBOLT 1 FR 0.0001 REL FR 0 V 1 P
for cupid, and challeng'd him at the burbolt. ADO 1.01. 42 P

BURDEAUX 8 FR 0.0009 REL FR 7 V 1 P
richard of burdeaux, by me hither brought. R2 5.06. 33
merchant's venture of burdeaux stuff in him, you 2H4 2.04. 64 P
go to the gates of burdeaux, trumpeter, | summon 1H6 4.02. 1
that he is march'd to burdeaux with his power 4.03. 4
with him and made their march for burdeaux. 4.03. 8
to burdeaux, warlike duke! 4.03. 22
to burdeaux, york! 4.03. 22
attach'd | our merchants' goods at burdeaux. H8 1.01. 96

BURDEN *(also burthen, etc.)*

BURDEN 8 FR 0.0009 REL FR 6 V 2 P
heavy? belike it hath some burden then? TGV 1.02. 82
that goes without a burden. ADO 3.04. 45 P
sake | with burden of our armor here we sweat. JN 2.01. 92
than a joint burden laid upon us all. 2H4 5.02. 55
o, 'tis a burden, cromwell, 'tis a burden | too H8 3.02.384
'tis a burden | too heavy for a man that hopes 3.02.384
thy burden at the sea, and call'd marina | for PER 5.03. 47
the burden on't was "down–a, down–a," and penn'd TNK 4.03. 11 P

BURDENED 1 FR 0.0001 REL FR 1 V 0 P
seeming as burdened | with lesser weight, but ERR 1.01.107

BURD'NED 1 FR 0.0001 REL FR 1 V 0 P
but were we burd'ned with like weight of pain, ERR 2.01. 36

BURGHER 1 FR 0.0001 REL FR 0 V 1 P
too, but that a wise burgher put in for them. MM 1.02.100 P

BURGHERS 2 FR 0.0002 REL FR 2 V 0 P
like signiors and rich burghers on the flood, MV 1.01. 10
being native burghers of this desert city, AYL 2.01. 23

BURGLARY 1 FR 0.0001 REL FR 0 V 1 P
flat burglary as ever was committed. ADO 4.02. 50 P

BURGOMASTERS 1 FR 0.0001 REL FR 0 V 1 P
and tranquility, burgomasters and great oney'rs, 1H4 2.01. 76 P

BURGONET 4 FR 0.0004 REL FR 4 V 0 P
and that i'll write upon thy burgonet, | might i 2H6 5.01.200
staff, | this day i'll wear aloft my burgonet, 5.01.204
and from thy burgonet i'll rend thy bear, | and 5.01.208
of this earth, the arm | and burgonet of men. ANT 1.05. 24

BURGUNDY 41 FR 0.0046 REL FR 41 V 0 P
of berri, | alanson, brabant, bar, and burgundy, H5 3.05. 42
brabant, | the brother to the duke of burgundy, 4.08. 97
contriv'd, | we do salute you, duke of burgundy, 5.02. 7
if, duke of burgundy, you would the peace, 5.02. 68
my lord of burgundy, we'll take your oath, | and 5.02.371
lord regent, and redoubted burgundy, | by whose 1H6 2.01. 8
i think the duke of burgundy will fast | before 3.02. 42
vow, burgundy, by honor of thy house, | prick'd 3.02. 77
and now no more ado, brave burgundy, | but 3.02.101
this is a double honor, burgundy; 3.02.116
talbot, burgundy | enshrines thee in his heart, 3.02.118
what wills lord talbot pleaseth burgundy. 3.02.130
we will entice the duke of burgundy | to leave 3.03. 19
a parley with the duke of burgundy! 3.03. 36
who craves a parley with the burgundy? 3.03. 37
brave burgundy, undoubted hope of france, | stay 3.03. 41
in spite of burgundy and all his friends. 3.03. 73
writ to your grace from th' duke of burgundy. 4.01. 12
shame to the duke of burgundy and thee! 4.01. 13
letter | sent from our uncle duke of burgundy. 4.01. 49
what? doth my uncle burgundy revolt? 4.01. 64
orleance the bastard, charles, burgundy, 4.04. 26
rage, | beat down alanson, orleance, burgundy, 4.06. 14
and when came george from burgundy to england? 3H6 2.01.143
sent | from your kind aunt, duchess of burgundy, 2.01.146
and fled (as he hears since) to burgundy. 4.06. 79
for doubtless burgundy will yield him help, 4.06. 90
seas, | and brought desired help from burgundy. 4.07. 6
tower | and was embark'd to cross to burgundy, R3 1.04. 10
attend the lords of france and burgundy, LR 1.01. 34
the princes, france and burgundy, | great rivals 1.01. 45
love | the vines of france and milk of burgundy 1.01. 84
call burgundy. 1.01.127
here's france and burgundy, my noble lord. 1.01.188
my lord of burgundy, | we first address toward 1.01.189
right noble burgundy, | when she was dear to us, 1.01.195
my lord of burgundy, | what say you to the lady? 1.01.237
cordelia by the hand, | duchess of burgundy. 1.01.244
peace be with burgundy! 1.01.247
not all the dukes of wat'rish burgundy | can buy 1.01.258
come, noble burgundy. 1.01.266

BURIAL 22 FR 0.0024 REL FR 19 V 3 P
and do all rites | that appertain unto a burial. ADO 4.01.208
all, | that in crossways and floods have burial, MND 3.02.383
top lower than her ribs | to kiss her burial. MV 1.01. 29
take hence the rest, and give them burial here. R2 5.05.118
will see his burial better than his life. 1H6 2.05.121
and give them burial as beseems their worth. 4.07. 86
till that the duke give order for his burial; R3 1.04.281
home, | with burial amongst their ancestors. TIT 1.01. 84
but let us give him burial as becomes, | give 1.01.347
give mutius burial with our bretheren. 1.01.348
and give him burial in his fathers' grave. 5.03.192
weed, | no mournful bell shall ring her burial, 5.03.197
our wedding cheer to a sad burial feast; ROM 4.05. 87
earth | with carrion men, groaning for burial. JC 3.01.275
use him, | with all respect and rites of burial. 5.05. 77
nor would we deign him burial of his men | till MAC 1.02. 60
be buried in christian burial when she willfully HAM 5.01. 1 P
hath sate on her, and finds it christian burial. 5.01. 5 P
should have been buried out a' christian burial. 5.01. 25 P
and the bringing home | of bell and burial. 5.01.234
have scarce strength left to give them burial. PER 1.04. 49
scorn now their hand should give them burial. 2.04. 12

BURIED 63 FR 0.0071 REL FR 50 V 13 P
like a young wench that had buried her grandam; TGV 2.01. 23 P
for i am sure she is not buried. 4.02.107
/his grave | assure thyself my love is buried. 4.02.114
and must be buried but as an intent | that MM 5.01.452
buried some dear friend? ERR 5.01. 50
she shall be buried with her face upwards. ADO 3.02. 68 P
and she lies buried with her ancestors — | o, 5.01. 69
die in thy lap, and be buried in thy eyes; 5.02.103 P
sweet chucks, beat not the bones of the buried. LLL 5.02.661 P
the carcasses of many a tall ship lie buried, as MV 3.01. 6 P
well, the beginning, that is dead and buried. AYL 1.02.117 P
and should be buried in highways out of all AWW 1.01.139 P
therefore i'll lie with him | when i am buried. 4.02. 73

buried a wife, mourn'd for her, writ to my lady 4.03. 88 P
or if — not to be buried, | but quick and in WT 4.04.131
that words seem'd buried in my sorrow's grave. R2 1.04. 15
head, | and by the buried hand of warlike gaunt, 3.03.109
or i'll be buried in the king's high way, | some 3.03.155
i live, | and buried once, why not upon my head? 3.03.159
within this coffin i present | thy buried fear. 5.06. 31
harflew | till in her ashes she lies buried. H5 3.03. 9
dying like men, though buried in your dunghills, 4.03. 99
town | great cordelion's heart was buried, | so 1H6 3.02. 83
and me — | the lustful edward's title buried — 3H6 3.02.129
house | in the deep bosom of the ocean buried. R3 1.01. 4
that came too lag to see him buried. 2.01. 91
and buried, gentle tyrrel? 4.03. 28
the chaplain of the tower hath buried them, 4.03. 29
buried this sigh in wrinkle of a smile, | but TRO 1.01. 38
and buried one and twenty valiant sons, TIT 1.01.195
for him, | he must be buried with his bretheren. 1.01.357
not i, till mutius' bones be buried. 1.01.369
and this shall all be buried in my death, 5.01. 67
bones | of all my buried ancestors are pack'd, ROM 4.03. 41
is dead, | and with my child my joys are buried. 4.05. 64
our bridal flowers serve for a buried corse; 4.05. 89
dead, | who here hath lain this two days buried. 5.03.176
ventidius lately | buried his father, by whose TIM 2.02.223
so his familiars to his buried fortunes | slink 4.02. 10
by means whereof this breast of mine hath buried JC 1.02. 49
and half their faces buried in their cloaks, 2.01. 74
whit appear, | but all be buried in his gravity. 2.01.149
i tell you yet again, banquo's buried; MAC 5.01. 64 P
in which the majesty of buried denmark | did HAM 1.01. 48
is she to be buried in christian burial when she 5.01. 1 P
she should have been buried out a' christian 5.01. 24 P
who is to be buried in't? 5.01.134 P
alexander died, alexander was buried, alexander 5.01.209 P
be buried quick with her, and so will i. 5.01.279
and gnats of nile | have buried them for prey! ANT 3.13.167
she rend'red life, | thy name so buried in her. 4.14. 34
she shall be buried by her antony; 5.02.358
for that i am a man, pray you see me buried. PER 2.01. 77
this cannot be | my daughter — buried! 5.01.163
thou that wast born at sea, buried at tharsus, 5.01.196
be buried | a second time within these arms. 5.03. 43
slain, | he might be buried in a tomb so simple, VEN 244
but 'tis not she, | truth and beauty buried be. PHT 64
and in themselves their pride lies buried, | for SON 25. 7
and all those friends which i thought buried. 31. 4
thou art the grave where buried love doth live, 31. 9
the rich proud cost of outworn buried age; 64. 2
me untrue, | my name be buried where my body is, 72.11

BURIER 1 FR 0.0001 REL FR 1 V 0 P
end, | and darkness be the burier of the dead! 2H4 1.01.160

BURIEST 1 FR 0.0001 REL FR 1 V 0 P
within thine own bud buriest thy content, | and, SON 1.11

BURLY–BON'D 1 FR 0.0001 REL FR 0 V 1 P
or cut not out the burly–bon'd clown in chines 2H6 4.10. 57 P

BURN 89 FR 0.0100 REL FR 74 V 15 P
sometime i'ld divide, | and burn in many places; TMP 1.02.199
and how the less, | that burn by day and night; 1.02.336
burn but his books. 3.02. 95
i care not, though he burn himself in love. TGV 2.05. 53 P
lest it should burn above the bounds of reason. 2.07. 23
car, | and with thy daring folly burn the world? 3.01.155
we burn daylight. WIV 2.01. 54 P
him sound, | and burn him with their tapers. 4.04. 63
also, to burn the knight with my taber. 4.04. 68 P
pinch him, and burn him, and turn him about, 5.05.101
"your meat doth burn," quoth i: ERR 2.01. 63
the tallow in them will burn a poland winter: 3.02. 99 P
she'll burn a week longer than the whole world. 3.02.100 P
light is an effect of fire, and fire will burn: 4.03. 56 P
ergo, light wenches will burn. 4.03. 57 P
no, and he were, i would burn my study. ADO 1.01. 80 P
to burn the errors that these princes hold 4.01.163
neigh, and bark, and grunt, and roar, and burn, MND 3.01.110
to burn the lodging where you use to lie, | and AYL 2.03. 23
the property of rain is to wet and fire to burn; 3.02. 27 P
and burn sweet wood to make the lodging sweet. SHR in.1. 49
tranio, i burn, i pine, i perish, tranio, | if i 1.01.155
come, i'll go burn some sack, 'tis too late to TN 2.03.190 P
better burn it now | than curse it then. WT 2.03.156
honor, nor my lusts | burn hotter than my faith. 4.04. 35
thy rage shall burn thee up, and thou shalt turn JN 3.01.344
must you with hot irons burn out both mine eyes? 4.01. 39
and with hot irons must i burn them out. 4.01. 59
with this same very iron to burn them out. 4.01.124
they burn in indignation. 4.02.103
for violent fires soon burn out themselves; R2 2.01. 34
that hand shall burn in never–quenching fire 5.05.108
impatiently i burn with thy desire; 1H6 1.02.108
play on the lute, beholding the towns burn: 1.04. 96
bring forth that sorceress condemn'd to burn. 5.04. 1
o, burn her, burn her! 5.04. 33
o, burn her, burn her! 5.04. 33
fire, and, if you can, burn down the tower too. 2H6 4.06. 15 P
away, burn all the records of the realm, my 4.07. 14 P
burn bonfires clear and bright | to entertain 5.01. 3
heed, lest by your heat you burn yourselves. 5.01.160
for well i wot ye blaze to burn them out. 3H6 5.04. 71
the lights burn blue. R3 5.03.180
cooling too, or ye may chance burn your lips. TRO 1.01. 26 P
ay, and burn too. COR 3.02. 24
if he could burn us all into one coal, | we have 4.06.137
sit in gold, his eye | red as 'twould burn rome; 5.01. 64
and tapers burn so bright, and every thing | in TIT 1.01.324
thrash the corn, then after burn the straw. 2.03.123
doth burn the heart to cinders where it is. 2.04. 37
a devil, | to live and burn in everlasting fire, 5.01.148
come, we burn daylight, ho! ROM 1.04. 43
o, she doth teach the torches to burn bright! 1.05. 44
is the place, there where the torch doth burn. 5.03.171
burn, house! TIM 3.06.104
be strong in whore, allure him, burn him up, 4.03.142
thou sun that comforts, burn! 5.01.131
which did flame and burn | like twenty torches JC 1.03. 16
burn! 3.02.204 P
we'll burn the house of brutus. 3.02.231
we'll burn his body in the holy place, | and 3.02.254
burn all! 3.03. 36 P
fire burn, and cauldron bubble. MAC 4.01. 11
fire burn, and cauldron bubble. 4.01. 21
fire burn, and cauldron bubble. 4.01. 36
revenges burn in them; 5.02. 3
since frost itself as actively doth burn, | and HAM 3.04. 87
burn out the sense and virtue of mine eye! 4.05.156
fierce, but thine | do comfort, and not burn. LR 2.04.173
loathed part of nature should | burn itself out. 4.06. 40
upon the blood | burn like the mines of sulphur. OTH 3.03.329
cheeks, | that would to cinders burn up modesty, 4.02. 75
our overplus of shipping will we burn, | and, ANT 3.07. 50
desire you | to burn this night with torches. 4.02. 41
o sun, | burn the great sphere thou mov'st in! 4.15. 10
that him and his they in his palace burn; PER 5.03. 98
he will not suffer us to burn their bones, | to TNK 1.01. 43
let the temples | burn bright with sacred fires, 5.01. 3
she bathes in water, yet her fire must burn. VEN 94
the sun doth burn my face, i must remove." 186
if they burn too, i'll quench them with my tears 192
do burn themselves for having so offended." 810
"fair torch, burn out thy light, and lend it not LUC 190
to burn the guiltless casket where it lay! 1057
are balls of quenchless fire to burn thy city. 1554
he finds means to burn his troy with water." 1561
and burn the long–liv'd phoenix in her blood; SON 19. 4
mars his sword nor war's quick fire shall burn 55. 7
most full flame should afterwards burn clearer. 115. 4

BURN'D 10 FR 0.0011 REL FR 9 V 1 P
"the pig," quoth i, "is burn'd": ERR 2.01. 66
and by that fire which burn'd the carthage queen MND 1.01.173
turn'd, | that a maiden's heart hath burn'd?" AYL 4.03. 41
within the scorched veins of one new burn'd. JN 3.01.278
france, i am burn'd up with inflaming wrath, | a 3.01.340
take their course | through my burn'd bosom, nor 5.07. 39
the tackle of my heart is crack'd and burn'd, 5.07. 52
they have burn'd and carried away all that was H5 4.07. 7 P
no heretics burn'd, but wenches' suitors; LR 3.02. 84
three april perfumes in three hot junes burn'd, SON 104. 7

BURNED 1 FR 0.0001 REL FR 1 V 0 P
your temples burned in their cement, and | your COR 4.06. 85

BURNET 1 FR 0.0001 REL FR 1 V 0 P
sweetly forth | the freckled cowslip, burnet, H5 5.02. 49

BURNETH 5 FR 0.0005 REL FR 5 V 0 P
i discern, | it burneth in the capels' monument. ROM 5.03.127
the taper burneth in your closet, sir. JC 2.01. 35
thine eye darts forth the fire that burneth me, VEN 196
burneth more hotly, swelleth with more rage; 332
thy eye kindled the fire that burneth here, LUC 1475

/BURNING 2 FR 0.0002 REL FR 2 V 0 P
/brought /ourselves /into /a /burning /fever, 2H4 4.01. 56
/that /burning /shame | /detains /him /from LR 4.03. 46

BURNING 51 FR 0.0057 REL FR 44 V 7 P
have i shunn'd the fire for fear of burning, TGV 1.03. 78
with liver burning hot. WIV 2.01.117
than the aims and ends | of burning youth. MM 1.03. 6
be sometime honor'd for his burning throne! 5.01.293
that light we see is burning in my hall. MV 5.01. 89
there is no malice in this burning coal; JN 4.01.108
figur'd quite o'er with burning meteors. 5.02. 53
already smokes about the burning crest | of the 5.04. 34
it would allay the burning quality | of that 5.07. 8
was full of fiery shapes | of burning cressets, 1H4 3.01. 15
thou art the knight of the burning lamp. 3.03. 27 P
for there he is in his robes, burning, burning. 3.03. 33 P
for there he is in his robes, burning, burning. 3.03. 33 P
the land is burning, percy stands on high, | and 3.03.203
he is so shak'd of a burning quotidian tertian, H5 2.01.119 P
and 'a said it was a black soul burning in hell? 2.03. 42 P
but burning fatal to the talbonites! 1H6 3.02. 28
the burning torch in yonder turret stands. 3.02. 30
descend to darkness and the burning lake! 2H6 1.04. 39
his father's acts commenc'd in burning troy! 3.02.118
thy burning car never had scorch'd the earth. 3H6 2.06. 13
a burning devil take them! TRO 5.02.195 P
th' wanton spoil | of phoebus' burning kisses — COR 2.01.218
himself a name a' th' fire | of burning rome. 5.01. 15
now, by the burning tapers of the sky, | that TIT 4.02. 89
i'll dive into the burning lake below, | and 4.03. 44
and here's the base fruit of her burning lust. 5.01. 43
ear | the story of that baleful burning night, 5.03. 83
tut, man, one fire burns out another's burning, ROM 1.02. 45
now, ere the sun advance his burning eye, | the 2.03. 5
have made milch the burning eyes of heaven, HAM 2.02.517
singeing his pate against the burning zone, 5.01.282
to have a thousand with red burning spits | come LR 3.06. 15
there is the sulphurous pit, burning, scalding, 4.06.128
mane, | seems to cast water on the burning bear, OTH 2.01. 14
she's like a liar gone to burning hell: 5.02.129
take not away the taper, leave it burning; CYM 2.02. 5
a burning torch that's turned upside down; PER 2.02. 32
the cat, with eyne of burning coal, | now 3.ch. 5
they have i' th' tother place, such burning, TNK 4.03. 32 P
doth quench the maiden burning of his cheeks; VEN 50
my flesh is soft and plump, my marrow burning, 142
with burning eye did hotly overlook them, 178
"as burning fevers, agues pale and faint, 739
'tween frozen conscience and hot burning will, LUC 247
his drumming heart cheers up his burning eye, 435
this load of wrath that burning troy doth bear; 1474
and in that cold, hot burning fire doth dwell; 1557
the gracious light | lifts up his burning head, SON 7. 2
with sighs that burning lungs did raise; LC 228
of burning blushes, or of weeping water, | or 304

BURNING–GLASS 1 FR 0.0001 REL FR 0 V 1 P
did seem to scorch me up like a burning–glass! WIV 1.03. 67 P

BURNISH'D 3 FR 0.0003 REL FR 3 V 0 P
the shadowed livery of the burnish'd sun, | to MV 2.01. 2
the barge she sat in, like a burnish'd throne, ANT 2.02.191
that cedar tops and hills seem burnish'd gold. VEN 858

BURNS 31 FR 0.0035 REL FR 28 V 3 P
when this burns, | 'twill weep for having TMP 3.01. 18
fire that's closest kept burns most of all. TGV 1.02. 30
the more thou dam'st it up, the more it burns: 2.07. 24
the capon burns, the pig falls from the spit; ERR 1.02. 44
the blood of youth burns not with such excess LLL 5.02. 73
for reason's force, | o'erbears it and burns on. AWW 5.03. 8
that honorable grief lodg'd here which burns WT 2.01.111
that makes the fire, | not she which burns in't. 2.03.116
ay me, this tyrant fever burns me up, | and will JN 5.03. 14
whose bosom burns | with an incensed fire of 2H4 1.03. 13
honest bardolph, whose zeal burns in his nose, 2.04.329 P
she's in hell already, and burns poor souls; 2.04.339 P
burns under feigned ashes of forg'd love, | and 1H6 3.01.189
burns with revenging fire, whose hopeful colors 2H6 4.01. 97
my heart for anger burns, i cannot brook it. 3H6 1.01. 60
and burns me up with flames that tears would 2.01. 84
here burns my candle out; 2.06. 1
earth gapes, hell burns, fiends roar, saints R3 4.04. 75
this candle burns not clear, 'tis i must snuff H8 3.02. 96
only envy at, | ye blew the fire that burns ye. 5.02.148
our fire–brand brother, paris, burns us all. TRO 2.02.110
troy burns, or else let helen go. 2.02.112
and add more coals to cancer when he burns 2.03.196
tut, man, one fire burns out another's burning, ROM 1.02. 45
how ill this taper burns! JC 4.03.275
illume that part of heaven | where now it burns, HAM 1.01. 38
when the blood burns, how prodigal the soul 1.03.116
and there th' offending part burns, and the TNK 4.03. 44 P
he burns with bashful shame, she with her tears VEN 49
the lamp that burns by night | dries up his oil 755
with my tears quench troy that burns so long, LUC 1468

/BURNT 1 FR 0.0001 REL FR 1 V 0 P
/how /troy /was /burnt /and /he /made /miserable TIT 3.02. 28

BURNT 28 FR 0.0031 REL FR 23 V 5 P
burnt up those logs that you are enjoin'd to TMP 3.01. 17
i'll give you a pottle of burnt sack to give me WIV 2.01.215 P
are whole, and let burnt sack be the issue. 3.01.109 P
'tis burnt, and so is all the meat. SHR 4.01.161
i tell thee, kate, 'twas burnt and dried away, 4.01.170
i'll ha' thee burnt. WT 2.03.114
my inch of taper will be burnt and done, | and R2 1.03.223
soon kindled and soon burnt, carded his state, 1H4 3.02. 62
and would have told him half his troy was burnt; 2H4 1.01. 73
you are as a candle, the better part burnt out. 1.02.157 P
as did the fatal brand althaea burnt | unto the 2H6 1.01.234
the witch in smithfield shall be burnt to ashes, 2.03. 7
being burnt i' th' hand for stealing of sheep. 4.02. 63 P
better | have burnt that tongue than said so. H8 3.02.254
day was done | and tapers burnt to bedward! COR 1.06. 32
we must be burnt for you. 5.01. 32
die, | transparent heretics, be burnt for liars! ROM 1.02. 91
night's candles are burnt out, and jocund day 3.05. 9
when i burnt in desire to question them further, MAC 1.05. 4 P
my days of nature | are burnt and purg'd away. HAM 1.05. 13
like a burnish'd throne, | burnt on the water. ANT 2.02.192
let's part, | you see we have burnt our cheeks. 2.07.122
where lo, two lamps burnt out in darkness lies; VEN 1128
like dying coals burnt out in tedious nights. LUC 1379
words like wildfire burnt the shining glory | of 1523
she burnt with love, as straw with fire flameth, PP 7.13
she burnt out love, as soon as straw out–burneth 7.14
when he most burnt in heart–wish'd luxury, | he LC 314

BURROWS 1 FR 0.0001 REL FR 0 V 1 P
they will out of their burrows, like conies COR 4.05.211 P

BURS 4 FR 0.0004 REL FR 1 V 3 P
they are but burs, cousin, thrown upon thee in AYL 1.03. 13 P
these burs are in my heart. 1.03. 17 P
hateful docks, rough thistles, kecksies, burs, H5 5.02. 52
they are burs, i can tell you, they'll stick TRO 3.02.111 P

/BURST 1 FR 0.0001 REL FR 1 V 0 P
/and /bellowed /out | /as /he'd /burst /heaven, LR 5.03.214

BURST 29 FR 0.0032 REL FR 23 V 6 P
blow till thou burst thy wind, if room enough! TMP 1.01. 7 P
now, we heard a hollow burst of bellowing | like 2.01.311
you will not pay for the glasses you have burst? SHR in.1. 8 P
hath been often burst and now repair'd with 3.02. 59 P
the horses ran away, how her bridle was burst; 4.01. 81 P
if my heart were great, | 'twould burst at this. AWW 4.03.331
the burst | and the ear–deaf'ning voice o' th' WT 3.01. 8
villain, | whose bowels suddenly burst out. JN 5.06. 30
if my heart be not ready to burst — well, sweet 2H4 2.04.380 P
and then he burst his head for crowding among 3.02.323 P
will make him burst his lead and rise from death 1H6 1.01. 64
or we'll burst them open, if that you come not 1.03. 28
my breast i'll burst with straining of my 1.05. 10
for, had the passions of thy heart burst out, 4.01.183
no, no, my heart will burst and if i speak, 3H6 5.05. 59
and i will speak, that so my heart may burst. 5.05. 60
bulk, | who almost burst to belch it in the sea. R3 1.04. 41
would thou wouldst burst! TIM 4.03.369
then burst his mighty heart, | and, in his JC 3.02.186
let me not burst in ignorance, but tell | why HAM 1.04. 46
hearsed in death, | have burst their cerements; 1.04. 48
the instant burst of clamor that she made, 2.02.515
when 'tis told, o, that my heart would burst! LR 5.03.183
of passion, joy and grief, | burst smilingly. 5.03.200
your heart is burst, you have lost half your OTH 1.01. 87
which in the scuffles of great fights hath burst ANT 1.01. 7
his voice, | and burst of speaking, were as his. CYM 4.02.106
endur'd a sea | that almost burst the deck. PER 4.01. 56
this burst of clamor | is sure th' end o' th' TNK 5.03. 77

BURSTING 1 FR 0.0001 REL FR 1 V 0 P
stretch his leathern coat | almost to bursting, AYL 2.01. 38

BURSTS 1 FR 0.0001 REL FR 1 V 0 P
sheets of fire, such bursts of horrid thunder, LR 3.02. 46

BURTHEN *(also burden, etc.)*

/BURTHEN 2 FR 0.0002 REL FR 2 V 0 P
and, sweet sprites, /the /burthen /bear. TMP 1.02.380
/matter /needless, /of /importless /burthen, TRO 1.03. 71

BURTHEN 40 FR 0.0045 REL FR 35 V 5 P
under my burthen groan'd, which rais'd in me TMP 1.02.156
growing, | plants with goodly burthen bowing; 4.01.113
let us not burthen our remembrances with | a 5.01.199
woman was delivered | of such a burthen male, ERR 1.01. 55
and this is false you burthen me withal. 5.01.269
that bore thee at a burthen two fair sons. 5.01.344
hour | my heavy burthen /ne'er delivered. 5.01.403
set down your venerable burthen, | and let him AYL 2.07.167
i would sing my song without a burthen; 3.02.247 P
the one lacking the burthen of lean and wasteful 3.02.323 P
the other knowing no burthen of heavy tedious 3.02.324 P
wife | (as wealth is burthen of my wooing dance) SHR 1.02. 68
alas, good kate, i will not burthen thee, | for 2.01.202
believing thee a vessel of too great a burthen. AWW 2.03.205 P

we have left our throne | without a burthen. WT 1.02. 3
she lives | my heart will be a burthen to me. 2.03.206
to bed of twenty money–bags at a burthen, and 4.04.264 P
but, ass, i'll take that burthen from your back, JN 2.01.145
along | the clogging burthen of a guilty soul. R2 1.03.200
a horse, | and yet i bear a burthen like an ass, 5.05. 93
betimes | than bring a burthen of dishonor home 2H6 3.01.298
can my tongue unload my heart's great burthen, 3H6 2.01. 81
back, | to bear her burthen whe'er i will or no, R3 3.07.229
head, | and leave the burthen of it all on thee. 4.04.113
a grievous burthen was thy birth to me, | tetchy 4.04.168
if your back | cannot vouchsafe this burthen, H8 2.03. 43
once | the burthen of my sorrows fall upon ye. 3.01.111
to th' earth, | willing to leave their burthen. 4.02. 3
god safely quit her of her burthen, and | with 5.01. 70
and 'tis a burthen | which i am proud to bear. TRO 3.03. 36
under love's heavy burthen do i sink. ROM 1.04. 22
and, to sink in it, should you burthen love — 1.04. 23
but you shall bear the burthen soon at night. 2.05. 76
that never knew but better, is some burthen: TIM 4.03.267
o heavy burthen! HAM 3.01. 53
at whose burthen | the anger'd ocean foams, with ANT 2.06. 20
behind, | and he the burthen of a guilty mind. LUC 735
o'ercharg'd with burthen of mine own love's SON 23. 8
amiss | the second burthen of a former child! 59. 4
bearing the wanton burthen of the prime, | like 97. 7
BURTHEN'D 3 FR 0.0003 REL FR 3 V 0 P
and even now my burthen'd heart would break, 2H6 3.02.320
now thy proud neck bears half my burthen'd yoke, R3 4.04.111
colt that's back'd and burthen'd being young, VEN 419
BURTHENING 1 FR 0.0001 REL FR 1 V 0 P
weak shoulders, overborne with burthening grief, 1H6 2.05. 10
BURTHENOUS 1 FR 0.0001 REL FR 1 V 0 P
his burthenous taxations notwithstanding, | but R2 2.01.260
BURTHENS 9 FR 0.0010 REL FR 7 V 2 P
soul | as this is false he burthens me withal! ERR 5.01.209
why sweat they under burthens? MV 4.01. 95
with such delicate burthens of dildos and WT 4.04.194 P
pray that their burthens may not fall this day, JN 3.01. 90
in | their heavy burthens at his narrow gate, H5 1.02.201
let them break your backs with burthens, take 2H6 4.08. 29 P
have their provand | only for bearing burthens, COR 2.01.252
poor thin roofs | with burthens of the dead — TIM 4.03.146
but that wild music burthens every bough, | and SON 102.11
BURTHEN–WISE 1 FR 0.0001 REL FR 1 V 0 P
for burthen–wise i'll hum on tarquin still, LUC 1133
BURTON 1 FR 0.0001 REL FR 1 V 0 P
methinks my moi'ty, north from burton here, | in 1H4 3.01. 95
BURTON–HEATH 1 FR 0.0001 REL FR 0 V 1 P
old sly's son of burton–heath, by birth a pedlar SHR in.2. 18 P
BURY* 45 FR 0.0050 REL FR 42 V 3 P
my staff, | bury it certain fadoms in the earth, TMP 5.01. 55
then in dumb silence will i bury mine, | for TGV 3.01.208
moonshine and lion are left to bury the dead. MND 5.01.348 P
my son from me, i bury a second husband. AWW 1.01. 1 P
and deeper than oblivion we do bury | th' 5.03. 24
if it be so, | we need no grave to bury honesty, WT 2.01.155
if there be any of him left, i'll bury it. 3.03.132 P
away toward bury, to the dolphin there! JN 4.03.114
only take the sacrament | to bury mine intents, R2 4.01.329
field | to book our dead, and then to bury them; H5 4.07. 73
bear hence his body, i will help to bury it. 1H6 1.04. 87
holden at bury the first of this next month. 2H6 2.04. 71
the trait'rous warwick, with the men of bury, 3.02.240
lie, | until the queen his mistress bury it. 4.01.143
but in your bride you bury brotherhood. 3H6 4.01. 55
but in your daughter's womb i bury them; R3 4.04.423
hangmen would | bury with those that wore them, COR 1.05. 7
and bury all, which yet distinctly ranges, | in 3.01.205
after your way his tale pronounc'd shall bury 5.06. 57
bury him where you can, he comes not here. TIT 1.01.354
what, would you bury him in my despite? 1.01.361
of thee | to pardon mutius and to bury him. 1.01.363
the greeks upon advice did bury ajax | that slew 1.01.379
well, bury him, and bury me the next. 1.01.386
well, bury him, and bury me the next. 1.01.386
i had none, | to bury so much gold under a tree, 2.03. 2
same pit | where we decreed to bury bassianus. 2.03.274
him | from thousand dangers, bid him bury it: 3.01.195
again, | and bury all thy fear in my devices. 4.04.112
doth with their death bury their parents' strife ROM pr 8
and badst me bury love. 2.03. 83
i'll bury thee in a triumphant grave. 5.03. 83
th' art quick, | but yet i'll bury thee; TIM 4.03. 46
i come to bury caesar, not to praise him. JC 3.02. 74
in this i bury all unkindness, cassius. 4.03.159
our graves must send | those that we bury back, MAC 3.04. 71
if ever thou wilt thrive, bury my body, | and LR 4.06.247
good sirs, take heart, | we'll bury him; ANT 4.15. 86
let us bury him, | and not protract with CYM 4.02.231
as being our foe, | yet bury him as a prince. 4.02.251
now bury me. TNK 2.02.277
and in that i'll bury | thee and all crosses 3.06.126
and she must gather flowers to bury you, | and 4.01. 78
is grav'd, and seems to bury what it frowns on, 5.03. 46
grave, | seeming to bury that posterity, | which VEN 758
BURYING 3 FR 0.0003 REL FR 3 V 0 P
what is her burying grave, that is her womb; ROM 2.03. 10
who finds her, give her burying, | she was the PER 3.02. 72
burying in lucrece' wound his folly's show. LUC 1810
BURYING–PLACE 1 FR 0.0001 REL FR 0 V 1 P
and be henceforth a burying–place to all that do 2H6 4.10. 63 P
BUSH 26 FR 0.0029 REL FR 21 V 5 P
here's neither bush nor shrub to bear off any TMP 2.02. 18 P
show'd me thee, and thy dog, and thy bush. 2.02.141
i have a fine hawk for the bush. WIV 3.03.231 P
where is the bush | that we must stand and play LLL 4.01. 7
i have been closely shrouded in this bush | and 4.03.135
thorough bush, thorough brier, | over park, over MND 2.01. 3
must come in with a bush of thorns and a lantern 3.01. 59 P
through bog, through bush, through brake, 3.01.107
in some bush? 3.02.406
some fear, | how easy is a bush suppos'd a bear! 5.01. 22
this man, with lantern, dog, and bush of thorn, 5.01.135
breeding, be married under a bush like a beggar? AYL 3.03. 84 P
indented glides did slip away | into a bush, 4.03.113
if it be true that good wine needs no bush, 'tis ep 4 P
i mean to shift my bush, | and then pursue me as SHR 5.02. 46
madam, myself have lim'd a bush for her, | and 2H6 1.03. 88
gives not the hawthorn bush a sweeter shade | to 3H6 2.05. 42
the thief doth fear each bush an officer. 5.06. 12
the bird that hath been limed in a bush, | with 5.06. 13
with trembling wings misdoubteth every bush; 5.06. 14
the birds chaunt melody on every bush, | the TIT 2.03. 12
the bounteous huswife nature on each bush | lays TIM 4.03.420
for many miles about | there's scarce a bush. LR 2.04.302
by yond bush? CYM 4.02.292
and safely presently | into your bush again, sir TNK 3.06.111
shape every bush a hideous shapeless devil. LUC 973
BUSHEL 1 FR 0.0001 REL FR 0 V 1 P
meal at nine shillings a bushel, and beef at STM II.C 3 P
BUSHELS 1 FR 0.0001 REL FR 0 V 1 P
two grains of wheat hid in two bushels of chaff; MV 1.01.116 P
BUSHES 6 FR 0.0006 REL FR 5 V 1 P
telling the bushes that thou look'st for wars, MND 3.02.408
yet to good wine they do use good bushes; AYL ep 6 P
have all lim'd bushes to betray thy wings, | and 2H6 2.04. 54
the thorny brambles and embracing bushes, | as VEN 629
and as she runs, the bushes in the way, | some 871
birds never lim'd no secret bushes fear: LUC 88
BUSH'S 1 FR 0.0001 REL FR 1 V 0 P
a bush, under which bush's shade | a lioness, AYL 4.03.113
/BUSHY 1 FR 0.0001 REL FR 1 V 0 P
/bushy, /what /news? R2 1.04. 53
BUSHY 7 FR 0.0008 REL FR 7 V 0 P
ourself and bushy, /bagot /here /and /green, R2 1.04. 23
go, bushy, to the earl of wiltshire straight, 2.01.215
which they say is held | by bushy, bagot, and 2.03.165
bushy and green, i will not vex your souls — 3.01. 2
what is become of bushy? 3.02.123
is bushy, green, and the earl of wiltshire dead? 3.02.141
i mean the earl of wiltshire, bushy, green. 3.04. 53
BUSIED 4 FR 0.0004 REL FR 3 V 1 P
/except they are busied about a counterfeit SHR 4.04. 91 P
who, busied in his /majesty, surveys | the H5 1.02.197
were busied with a whitsun morris–dance; 2.04. 25
as with a man busied about decrees: COR 1.06. 34
/BUSIL'EST 1 FR 0.0001 REL FR 1 V 0 P
my labors, | most /busil'est when i do it. TMP 3.01. 15
BUSILY 2 FR 0.0002 REL FR 2 V 0 P
scroop, | who, as we hear, are busily in arms. 1H4 5.05. 38
soft, so busily she turns the leaves! TIT 4.01. 45
BUSINESS' 1 FR 0.0001 REL FR 1 V 0 P
moe widows in them of this business' making TMP 2.01.134
/BUSINESS 3 FR 0.0003 REL FR 3 V 0 P
and do such /bitter /business /as /the day HAM 3.02.391
/what /is /the /issue /of /the /business /there. 5.02. 72
/for /this /business, | /it /touches /us, /as LR 5.01. 24
BUSINESS 243 FR 0.0274 REL FR 198 V 45 P
and then i'll bring thee to the present business TMP 1.02.136
nor set | a mark so bloody on the business; 1.02.142
to do me business in the veins o' th' earth 1.02.255
forth, i say, there's other business for thee. 1.02.315
quick, thou'rt best, | to answer other business. 1.02.367
this is no mortal business, nor no sound | that 1.02.407
but this swift business | i must uneasy make, 1.02.451
they'll tell the clock to any business that | we 2.01.289
must i perform | much business appertaining. 3.01. 96
but remember | (for that's my business to you) 3.03. 69
and there is in this business more than nature 5.01.243
beating on | the strangeness of this business. 5.01.247
that can with some discretion do my business — TGV 4.04. 65
that indeed, sir john, is my business. WIV 3.05. 63 P
turn you the key, and know his business of him; MM 1.04. 8
of business 'twixt you and your poor brother. 1.04. 71
my business is a word or two with claudio. 3.01. 48
ever return to have hearing of this business. 3.01.204 P
of his life, and the business he hath helm'd, 3.02.142 P
/see, | in special business from his holiness. 3.02.220
and when you have | a business for yourself, 5.01. 81
my business in this state | made me a looker–on 5.01.316
then | advertising and holy to your business, 5.01.383
my present business calls me from you now. ERR 1.02. 29
because their business still lies out a' door. 2.01. 11
besides, i have some business in the town. 4.01. 35
my business cannot brook this dalliance. 4.01. 59
when i am drowsy, and tend on no man's business; ADO 1.03. 16 P
to the next willow, about your own business, 2.01.188 P
on serious business craving quick dispatch, LLL 2.01. 31
i must employ you in some business | against our MND 1.01.124
we may effect this business yet ere day. 3.02.395
i take it your own business calls on you, | and MV 1.01. 63
but fare you well, | i have some business. 2.02.204
/slubber not business for my sake, bassanio, 2.08. 39
o love! dispatch all business, and be gone! 3.02.323
man | in all your business and necessities. AYL 2.03. 55
signior baptista, my business asketh haste, SHR 2.01.114
into, | and watch our vantage in this business. 3.02.144
if you knew my business, | you would entreat me 3.02.191
till you have done your business in the city. 4.02.111
we'll pass the business privately and well. 4.04. 57
lest you be cony–catch'd in this business. 5.01. 99 P
our dearest friend | prejudicates the business, AWW 1.02. 8
the business is for helen to come hither. 1.03. 96 P
for that is her demand — and know her business? 2.01. 86
now, fair one, does your business follow us? 2.01. 99
i know my business is but to the court. 2.02. 4 P
/an end, sir, to your business! 2.02. 63
in such a business, give me leave to use | the 2.03.107
a very serious business calls on him. 2.04. 40
prepar'd i was not | for such a business; 2.05. 62
would in so just a business shut his bosom 3.01. 8
great and trusty business in a main danger fail 3.06. 15 P
so confidently seems to undertake this business, 3.06. 87 P
if the business be of any difficulty, and this 4.03. 93 P
i mean the business is not ended, as fearing to 4.03. 96 P
to whose trust | your business was more welcome. 4.04. 16
i am for other business. 5.02. 34 P
her business looks in her | with an importing 5.03.135
that their business might be every thing and TN 2.04. 76 P
petitions, made | his business more material. WT 1.02.216
perchance are to this business purblind? 1.02.228
business, my lord? 1.02.229
your followers i will whisper to the business, 1.02.437
you smell this business with a sense as cold 2.01.151
for this business | will raise us all. 2.01.197
carriage of it | will clear or end the business. 3.01. 18
what is the business? 3.02.142
howe'er the business goes, you have made fault 3.02.217
am glad at heart | to be so rid o' th' business. 3.03. 15
for this ungentle business, | put on thee by my 3.03. 34
prithee be my present partner in this business, 4.02. 51 P
should hold some counsel | in such a business. 4.04.410
i not acquaint | my father of this business. 4.04.413
i am so fraught with curious business that | i 4.04.514
i understand the business, i hear it. 4.04.670 P
/that toze from thee thy business, i am 4.04.735 P
either push on or pluck back thy business there; 4.04.737 P
my business, sir, is to the king. 4.04.739 P
sir, to undertake the business for us, here is 4.04.806 P
are you a party in this business? 4.04.813 P
old man does when the business is perform'd, and 4.04.822 P
i make a broken delivery of the business; 5.02. 9 P
those that think it is unlawful business | i am 5.03. 96
sweat in this business and maintain this war? JN 5.02.102
will post | to consummate this business happily. 5.07. 95
to us to ely house | to see this business. R2 2.01.217
o, full of careful business are his looks! 2.02. 75
brake off our business for the holy land. 1H4 1.01. 48
be his dole, say i, every man to his business. 2.02. 77 P
some heavy business hath my lord in hand, | and 2.03. 63
i'll know your business, harry, that i will. 2.03. 80
(a business that this night may execute), 3.01. 81
so hath the business that i come to speak of. 3.02.163
our business valued, some twelve days hence 3.02.177
our hands are full of business, let's away, 3.02.179
day, | and since this business so fair is done, 5.05. 43
this become your place, your time, and business? 2H4 2.01. 66
thy sight | my worldly business makes a period. 4.05.230
well conceited, davy. about thy business, davy. 5.01. 36 P
save those to god, that run before our business. H5 1.02.303
you may call the business of the master the 4.01.153 P
this weighty business will not brook delay, 2H6 1.01.170
the business asketh silent secrecy. 1.02. 90
again, | to look into this business thoroughly, 2.01.198
i like you, lads, about your business straight. R3 1.03.353
you go | to give your censures in this business? 2.02.144
good catesby, go effect this business soundly. 3.01.186
catesby hath sounded hastings in our business, 3.04. 36
let us consult upon to–morrow's business. 5.03. 45
that promises no element | in such a business. H8 1.01. 49
why, all this business | our reverend cardinal 1.01. 99
from liberty, to look on | the business present. 1.01.206
and lately, | as all think, for this business. 2.01.161
how holily he works in all his business! 2.02. 23
and with some other business put the king | from 2.02. 56
breach of duty this way | is business of estate; 2.02. 69
i'll make ye know your times of business. 2.02. 71
in the unpartial judging of this business. 2.02.106
there ye shall meet about this weighty business. 2.02.139
it was a gentle business, and becoming | the 2.03. 54
of every realm, that did debate this business, 2.04. 52
more | upon this business my appearance make 2.04.133
i | did broach this business to your highness, 2.04.150
have wish'd the sleeping of this business, never 2.04.164
i' th' progress of this business, | ere a 2.04.176
what can be their business | with me, a poor 3.01. 19
if your business | seek me out, and that way i 3.01. 37
looking | either for such men or such business. 3.01. 76
(if you please | to trust us in your business), 3.01.173
hath ta'en much pain | in the king's business. 3.02. 73
to think upon the part of business which | i 3.02.145
the lord increase this business! 3.02.161
with all the business | i writ to 's holiness. 3.02.221
'tis all my business. 4.01. 4
how goes her business? 4.01. 23
your friend | some touch of your late business. 5.01. 13
in them a wilder nature than the business | that 5.01. 15
speak to the business, master secretary. 5.02. 36
lord, because we have business of more moment, 5.02. 86
day, no man think | h'as business at his house; 5.04. 75
assault upon him, for my business seethes. TRO 3.01. 40 P
sodden business! there's a stew'd phrase indeed! 3.01. 41 P
i have business to my lord, dear queen. 3.01. 58 P
nothing but heavenly business | should rob my 4.01. 5
what business, lord, so early? 4.01. 35
i cannot, lord, i have important business, | the 5.01. 82
our business is not unknown to th' senate; COR 1.01. 57 P
with t' other, | ere stay behind this business. 1.01.243
of martius, "o, if he | had borne the business!" 1.01.270
but had he died in the business, madam, how then 1.03. 18 P
shall bear the business in some other fight, 1.06. 82
you are like to do such business. 3.01. 48
(for in such business | action is eloquence, and 3.02. 75
you have ended my business, and i will merrily 4.03. 39 P
lords, how plainly | i have borne this business. 5.03. 4
perfidiously | he has betray'd your business, 5.06. 91
life, | and set abroad new business for you all? TIT 1.01.192
now will i hence about thy business, | and take 5.02.132
having some business, /do entreat her eyes | to ROM 2.02. 16
good mercutio, my business was great, and in 2.04. 49 P
hands full all, | in this so sudden business. 4.03. 12
is't not your business too? TIM 2.02. 10
the time is unagreeable to this business. 2.02. 40
and i think | one business does command us all; 3.04. 4
manner was i in debt to my importunate business, 3.06. 14 P
and this the bleeding business they have done. JC 3.01.168
gold, | to groan and sweat under the business, 4.01. 22
by and by | on business to my brother cassius. 4.03.248
the end of this day's business ere it come! 5.01.123
this night's great business into my dispatch, MAC 1.05. 68
were poor and single business to contend 1.06. 16
we will proceed no further in this business: 1.07. 31
would spend it in some words upon that business, 2.01. 23
it is the bloody business which informs | thus 2.01. 48
what's the business, | that such a hideous 2.03. 81
and i will put that business in your bosoms, 3.01.103
masking the business from the common eye | for 3.01.124
great business must be wrought ere noon: 3.05. 22
time of meeting, | thus much the business is: HAM 1.02. 27
personal power | to business with the king, more 1.02. 37
as your business and desire shall point you, 1.05.129

you, | for every man hath business and desire, 1.05.130
read, | answer, and think upon this business. 2.02. 82
this business is well ended. 2.02. 85
and my return shall be the end of /my business. 3.02.318 P
and, like a man to double business bound, | i 3.03. 41
has this fellow no feeling of his business? 5.01. 65 P
to shake all cares and business from our age, LR 1.01. 39
he never before sounded you in this business? 1.02. 70 P
frame the business after your own wisdom. 1.02. 98 P
convey the business as i shall find means, and 1.02.102 P
i do serve you in this business. 1.02.178 P
i see the business. 1.02.182
this weaves itself perforce into my business. 2.01. 15
be certain, you have mighty business in hand. 3.05. 16 P
father, | it is thy business that i go about; 4.04. 24
my lady charg'd my duty in this business. 4.05. 18
that of thy death and business i can tell. 4.06.278
your business of the world hath so an end, | and 5.01. 45
our present business | is general woe. 5.03.319
fadom they have none | to lead their business; OTH 1.01.153
it is a business of some heat. 1.02. 40
side, | upon some present business of the state, 1.02. 90
now? what's the business? 1.03. 13
neither my place, nor aught i heard of business, 1.03. 53
i will your serious and great business scant 1.03.267
that my disports corrupt and taint my business, 1.03.271
gentlemen, let's look to our business. 2.03.112 P
that your converse and business | may be more 3.01. 38
when i shall turn the business of my soul | to 3.03.181
be in me remorse, | what bloody business ever. 3.03.469
the business of the state does him offense, 4.02.166
the business she hath broached in the state ANT 1.02.171
and the business you have broach'd here cannot 1.02.173 P
till which encounter, | it is my business too. 1.04. 80
you do mistake your business, my brother never 2.02. 45
dispatch we | the business we have talk'd of. 2.02.166
our graver business | frowns at this levity. 2.07.120
i find thee | most fit for business. 3.03. 37
thy business? 3.07. 53
to business that we love we rise betime, | and 4.04. 20
the business of this man looks out of him; 5.01. 50
noble friends | are partners in the business. CYM 1.06.184
since i receiv'd command to do this business | i 3.04. 99
'tis not sleepy business, | but must be look'd 3.05. 26
that we do incite | the gentry to this business. 3.07. 7
there's business in these faces. 5.05. 23
and the number | to carry such a business, forth TNK 1.01.162
prorogue this business we are going about, and 1.01.196
a number, for a business | more bigger–look'd. 1.01.214
but | playing o'er business in his hand, another 1.03. 31
chanc'd to name you here, upon the old business. 2.01. 17 P
a wife might part us lawfully, or business, 2.02. 89
dares any | so noble bear a guilty business? 3.01. 90
nothing, | our business is become a nullity, 3.05. 54
for i came home before the business | was fully 4.01. 4
that she farces ev'ry business withal, fits it 4.03. 8 P
strove to show | mine enemy in this business, 5.01. 21
arms in assurance | my body to this business. 5.01.135
and that would be a blot i' th' business. 5.02. 81
set both thine ears to th' business. 5.03. 92
BUSINESSES 6 FR 0.0006 REL FR 3 V 3 P
i am so full of businesses, i cannot answer thee AWW 1.01.206 P
nothing acquainted with these businesses, | and 3.07. 5
i have to–night dispatch'd sixteen businesses, a 4.03. 85 P
having made me businesses which none without WT 4.02. 14 P
a thousand businesses are brief in hand, | and JN 4.03.158
bestow | your needful counsel to our businesses, LR 2.01.127
BUSKIN'D 1 FR 0.0001 REL FR 1 V 0 P
your buskin'd mistress and your warrior love, MND 2.01. 71
BUSS 2 FR 0.0002 REL FR 2 V 0 P
think thou smil'st, | and buss thee as thy wife. JN 3.04. 35
towers, whose wanton tops do buss the clouds, TRO 4.05.220
BUSSES 1 FR 0.0001 REL FR 0 V 1 P
thou dost give me flattering busses. 2H4 2.04.268 P
BUSSING 1 FR 0.0001 REL FR 1 V 0 P
thy knee bussing the stones (for in such COR 3.02. 75
BUSTLE 3 FR 0.0003 REL FR 3 V 0 P
and leave the world for me to bustle in! R3 1.01.152
come, bustle, bustle! 5.03.289
come, bustle, bustle! 5.03.289
BUSTLING 1 FR 0.0001 REL FR 1 V 0 P
i heard a bustling rumor, like a fray, | and the JC 2.04. 18
BUSY 29 FR 0.0032 REL FR 23 V 6 P
he is very busy about it. ADO 1.02. 3 P
good cousin, have a care this busy time. 1.02. 27 P
pray you, for you see it is a busy time with me. 3.05. 4 P
on meddling monkey, or on busy ape), | she shall MND 2.01.181
say | i'll prove a busy actor in their play. AYL 3.04. 59
they're busy within, you were best knock louder. SHR 5.01. 14 P
my mistress sends you word | that she is busy, 5.02. 81
she is busy, and she cannot come! 5.02. 82
be it thy course to busy giddy minds | with 2H4 4.05.213
law, | whiles i was busy for the commonwealth, 5.02. 76
knights, | with busy hammers closing rivets up, H5 4.pr. 13
you be by her aloft, while we be busy below; 2H6 1.04. 8 P
my brain, more busy than the laboring spider, 3.01.339
o, beat away the busy meddling fiend | that lays 3.03. 21
my lord of gloucester, in those busy days, R3 1.03.144
no delay, | for, lords, to–morrow is a busy day. 5.03. 18
we are busy; go. H8 2.02. 80
but that the busy day, | wak'd by the lark, hath TRO 4.02. 8
what, are you busy, ho? need you my help? ROM 4.03. 6
which busy care draws in the brains of men; JC 2.01.232
thou find'st to be too busy is some danger. HAM 3.04. 33
do you busy yourself with that? LR 1.02.142 P
let me be thought too busy in my fears | (as OTH 3.03.253
he's busy in the paper. 4.01.230
villain, | some busy and insinuating rogue, 4.02.131
for all my mind, my thought, my busy care, | is VEN 383
busy yourselves in skill–contending schools, LUC 1018
at last it rains, and busy winds give o'er: 1790
cries to catch her whose busy care is bent | to SON 143. 6
/BUT 57 FR 0.0064 REL FR 51 V 6 P
BUT 6655 FR 0.7522 REL FR 5067 V 1588 P
BUTCHER 20 FR 0.0022 REL FR 15 V 5 P
bleat softly then, the butcher hears you cry. LLL 5.02.255
mind | than to be butcher of an innocent child. JN 4.02.259
teaching stern murder how to butcher thee. R2 1.02. 32
that it may enter butcher mowbray's breast! 1.02. 48
i could lay on like a butcher and sit like a H5 5.02.141 P
and as the butcher takes away the calf | and 2H6 3.01.210
fresh, | and sees fast by a butcher with an axe, 3.02.189
are you the butcher, suffolk? 3.02.195
and dick the butcher — 4.02. 25 P
where's dick, the butcher of ashford? 4.03. 1 P
too, as myself, for example, that am a butcher. 4.07. 53 P
are you there, butcher? o, i cannot speak! 3H6 2.02. 95
where is that devil's butcher, | hard–favor'd 5.05. 77
the son, compell'd, been butcher to the sire. R3 5.05. 26
were he the butcher of my son, he should | be COR 1.09. 88
the very butcher of a silk button, a duellist, a ROM 2.04. 23 P
of this dead butcher and his fiend–like queen, MAC 5.09. 35
dispatch, | the lamb entreats the butcher. CYM 3.04. 96
still, | like to a mortal butcher bent to kill. VEN 618
or butcher sire that reaves his son of life: 766
BUTCHER'D 3 FR 0.0003 REL FR 3 V 0 P
and shamefully my hopes, by you, are butcher'd. R3 1.03.275
to–day at pomfret bloodily were butcher'd, 3.04. 90
parents live whose children thou hast butcher'd, 4.04.393
BUTCHERED 4 FR 0.0004 REL FR 4 V 0 P
taken, | a thousand of his people butchered, 1H4 1.01. 42
which his hell–govern'd arm hath butchered! R3 1.02. 67
of butchered princes fight in thy behalf. 5.03.122
have by my means been butchered wrongfully? TIT 4.04. 55
BUTCHERIES 2 FR 0.0002 REL FR 2 V 0 P
deeds, | behold this pattern of thy butcheries. R3 1.02. 54
that never dream'st on aught but butcheries. 1.02.100
BUTCHERLY 1 FR 0.0001 REL FR 1 V 0 P
how butcherly? 3H6 2.05. 89
BUTCHER'S 4 FR 0.0004 REL FR 2 V 2 P
in a basket like a barrow of butcher's offal? WIV 3.05. 5 P
did not goodwife keech, the butcher's wife, come 2H4 2.01. 94 P
and next his throat unto the butcher's knife. 3H6 5.06. 9
this butcher's cur is venom'd–mouth'd, and i H8 1.01.120
BUTCHERS 7 FR 0.0008 REL FR 7 V 0 P
should be called tyrants, butchers, murtherers! AYL 3.05. 14
to stir against the butchers of his life! R2 1.02. 3
butchers and villains! 3H6 5.05. 61
you have no children, butchers; 5.05. 63
summer butterflies, | or butchers killing flies. COR 4.06. 95
let's be sacrificers, but not butchers, caius. JC 2.01.166
that i am meek and gentle with these butchers! 3.01.255
BUTCHERY 3 FR 0.0003 REL FR 3 V 0 P
this is no place, this house is but a butchery; AYL 2.03. 27
shock | and furious close of civil butchery, 1H4 1.01. 13
suborn | to do this piece of /ruthless butchery, R3 4.03. 5
BUTLER 4 FR 0.0004 REL FR 4 V 0 P
is not this stephano, my drunken butler? TMP 5.01.277
upon | this day she was both pantler, butler, WT 4.04. 56
hath butler brought those horses from the 1H4 2.03. 67
bid butler lead him forth into the park. 2.03. 72
BUTT* 12 FR 0.0013 REL FR 8 V 4 P
they prepared | a rotten carcass of a butt, not TMP 1.02.146
i escap'd upon a butt of sack which the sailors 2.02.121 P
the whole butt, man. 2.02.134 P
when the butt is out, we will drink water — not 3.02. 1 P
look how you butt yourself in these sharp mocks! LLL 5.02.251
believe me, sir, they butt together well. SHR 5.02. 39
head, and butt! 5.02. 40
would say your head and butt were head and horn. 5.02. 41
to which is fixed, as an aim or butt, H5 1.02.186
i am your butt, and i abide your shot. 3H6 1.04. 29
why, no, you ruinous butt, you whoreson TRO 5.01. 28 P
here is my butt | and very sea–mark of my utmost OTH 5.02.267
BUTT–END 1 FR 0.0001 REL FR 1 V 0 P
that is the butt–end of a mother's blessing. R3 2.02.110
BUTTER *(also putter)*
BUTTER 8 FR 0.0009 REL FR 1 V 7 P
i will rather trust a fleming with my butter, WIV 2.02.302 P
of that — that am as subject to heat as butter; 3.05.116 P
will serve to be prologue to an egg and butter. 1H4 1.02. 21 P
are up already, and call for eggs and butter. 2.01. 60 P
thou never see titan kiss a dish of butter, 2.04.121 P
as fat as butter. 2.04.511
for thy theft hath already made thee butter. 4.02. 61 P
at a harry groat, butter at alevenpence a pound, STM II.C 2 P
BUTTER'D 2 FR 0.0002 REL FR 0 V 2 P
i'll have my brains ta'en out and butter'd, and WIV 3.05. 8 P
in pure kindness to his horse, butter'd his hay. LR 2.04.126 P
BUTTERFLIES 4 FR 0.0004 REL FR 4 V 0 P
and pluck the wings from painted butterflies, MND 3.01.172
for men, like butterflies, | show not their TRO 3.03. 78
than boys pursuing summer butterflies, | or COR 4.06. 94
and laugh | at gilded butterflies, and hear poor LR 5.03. 13
BUTTERFLY 3 FR 0.0003 REL FR 0 V 3 P
i saw him run after a gilded butterfly, and when COR 1.03. 60 P
is difference between a grub and a butterfly, 5.04. 12 P
and a butterfly, yet your butterfly was a grub. 5.04. 12 P
BUTTER–WOMAN'S 1 FR 0.0001 REL FR 0 V 1 P
must put you into a butter–woman's mouth and buy AWW 4.01. 41 P
BUTTER–WOMEN'S 1 FR 0.0001 REL FR 0 V 1 P
it is the right butter–women's rank to market. AYL 3.02. 98 P
BUTTERY 1 FR 0.0001 REL FR 1 V 0 P
go, sirrah, take them to the buttery, | and give SHR in.1. 102
BUTTOCK 4 FR 0.0004 REL FR 2 V 2 P
the brawn–buttock, or any buttock. AWW 2.02. 19 P
more with the buttock of the night than with the COR 2.01. 52 P
mane, thick tail, broad buttock, tender hide; VEN 298
cool shadow to his melting buttock lent; 315
BUTTOCKS 2 FR 0.0002 REL FR 0 V 2 P
sir, in her buttocks, i found it out by the bogs ERR 3.02.117 P
is like a barber's chair that fits all buttocks: AWW 2.02. 17 P
BUTTON 3 FR 0.0003 REL FR 1 V 2 P
the very butcher of a silk button, a duellist, a ROM 2.04. 23 P
on fortune's /cap we are not the very button. HAM 2.02.229 P
pray you undo this button. LR 5.03.310
BUTTON'D 1 FR 0.0001 REL FR 1 V 0 P
/one whose hard heart is button'd up with steel; ERR 4.02. 34
BUTTON–HOLE 1 FR 0.0001 REL FR 0 V 1 P
master, let me take you a button–hole lower. LLL 5.02.700 P
BUTTONS 3 FR 0.0003 REL FR 2 V 1 P
he will carry't — 'tis in his buttons — he WIV 3.02. 70 P
too oft before their buttons be disclos'd, | and HAM 1.03. 40
sweeter | than her gold buttons on the boughs, TNK 3.01. 6
BUTTRESS 1 FR 0.0001 REL FR 1 V 0 P
buttress, nor coign of vantage, but this bird MAC 1.06. 7
BUTT'RING 1 FR 0.0001 REL FR 0 V 1 P
henceforth eat no fish of fortune's butt'ring. AWW 5.02. 8 P
BUTT'RY–BAR 1 FR 0.0001 REL FR 0 V 1 P
i pray you bring your hand to th' butt'ry–bar, TN 1.03. 70 P
BUTTS* 4 FR 0.0004 REL FR 4 V 0 P
'tis butts, | the king's physician. H8 5.02. 10
what's that, butts? 5.02. 20
by holy mary, butts, there's knavery. 5.02. 33
the beast | with many heads butts me away. COR 4.01. 2
BUTT–SHAFT 2 FR 0.0002 REL FR 0 V 2 P
cupid's butt–shaft is too hard for hercules' LLL 1.02.176 P
heart cleft with the blind bow–boy's butt–shaft; ROM 2.04. 16 P
BUXOM 2 FR 0.0002 REL FR 2 V 0 P
and of buxom valor, hath, by cruel fate, | and H5 3.06. 26
so buxom, blithe, and full of face | as heaven PER 1.ch. 23
BUY* 117 FR 0.0132 REL FR 81 V 36 P
will money buy 'em? TMP 5.01.265
i'll go buy them vizards. WIV 4.04. 70
that silk will i go buy. 4.04. 73
that you will needs buy and sell men and women MM 3.02. 2 P
you with all, | to buy you a better husband. 5.01.425
not being able to buy out his life | according ERR 1.02. 5
house, go thou | and buy a rope's end; 4.01. 16
buy thou a rope, and bring it home to me. 4.01. 20
i buy a thousand pound a year! i buy a rope! 4.01. 21
i buy a thousand pound a year! i buy a rope! 4.01. 21
you shall buy this sport as dear | as all the 4.01. 81
some offer me commodities to buy. 4.03. 6
would you buy her, that you inquire after her? ADO 1.01.179 P
can the world buy such a jewel? 1.01.181 P
th' endeavor of this present breath may buy LLL 1.01. 5
as jewels in crystal for some prince to buy, 2.01.243
did point you to buy them, along as you pass'd; 2.01.245
i will never buy and sell out of this word. 3.01.142 P
ribbon may a man buy for a remuneration? 3.01.146 P
world, thou shouldst have it to buy gingerbread. 5.01. 72 P
thou shalt buy this dear, | if ever i thy face MND 3.02.426
they lose it that do buy it with much care. MV 1.01. 75
i will buy with you, sell with you, talk with 1.03. 35 P
to buy his favor, i extend this friendship. 1.03.168
testament, with that i will go buy my fortunes. AYL 1.01. 74 P
can in this desert place buy entertainment, 2.04. 72
what is he that shall buy his flock and pasture? 2.04. 88
buy thou the cottage, pasture, and the flock, 2.04. 92
be, | and buy it with your gold right suddenly. 2.04.100
god buy you, let's meet as little as we can. 3.02.257 P
nay then god buy you, and you talk in blank 4.01. 31 P
god buy you, and god mend your voices! 5.03. 40 P
venice | to buy apparel 'gainst the wedding–day. SHR 2.01.315
and let me buy your friendly help thus far, AWW 3.07. 15
to buy his will, it would not seem too dear, 3.07. 27
mouth and buy myself another of bajazeth's mule, 4.01. 42 P
i will buy me a son–in–law in a fair, and toll 5.03.148 P
where did you buy it? or who gave it you? 5.03.271
it was not given me, nor i did not buy it. 5.03.272
god buy you, good sir topas. TN 4.02.100 P
what am i to buy for our sheep–shearing feast? WT 4.03. 37 P
i must go buy spices for our sheep–shearing. 4.03.116 P
when you sing, | i'ld have you buy and sell so; 4.04.138
come buy of me, come; 4.04.228
come buy, come buy, | buy, lads, or else your 4.04.228
come buy, come buy, | buy, lads, or else your 4.04.228
come buy, | buy, lads, or else your lasses cry: 4.04.229
come buy. 4.04.230
pray now buy some. 4.04.260 P
pray you now buy it. 4.04.272 P
we'll buy the other things anon. 4.04.274 P
wenches, i'll buy for you both. 4.04.312 P
will you buy any tape, | or lace for your cape, 4.04.315
they throng who should buy first, as if my 4.04.601 P
dreading the curse that money may buy out, | and JN 3.01.164
but dead, thy kingdom cannot buy my breath. R2 1.03.232
shall we buy treason? 1H4 1.03. 87
you may buy land now as cheap as stinking 2.04.359 P
we shall buy maidenheads as they buy hobnails, 2.04.362 P
we shall buy maidenheads as they buy hobnails, 2.04.363 P
/into smithfield to buy your worship a horse. 2H4 1.02. 50 P
paul's, and he'll buy me a horse in smithfield; 1.02. 52 P
(saving your manhoods) to buy a saddle, and he 2.01. 27 P
they sell the pasture now to buy the horse, H5 2.pr. 5
to buy a slobb'ry and a dirty farm | in that 3.05. 13
god buy you, princes all; 4.03. 6
a woodmonger, and buy nothing of me but cudgels. 5.01. 65 P
god buy you, and keep you, and heal your pate. 5.01. 66 P
you must buy that peace | with full accord to 5.02. 70
think i had sold my farm to buy my crown. 5.02.125 P
fast | before he'll buy again at such a rate. 1H6 3.02. 43
god buy, my lord, we came but to tell you | that 3.02. 73
who would not buy thee dear? 2H6 5.01. 5
if this right hand would buy two hours' life 3H6 2.06. 80
thou and thy brother both shall buy this treason 5.01. 68
though 'twere to buy a world of happy days — R3 1.04. 6
only reserv'd their factor to buy souls | and 4.04. 72
does buy and sell his honor as he pleases, | and H8 1.01.192
/i will buy nine sparrows for a penny, and his TRO 2.01. 71 P
great princes, | and he shall buy my daughter; 3.03. 28
god buy you, with all my heart. 3.03.293 P
dispraise the thing that they desire to buy, 4.01. 77
so many thousand sighs | did buy each other, 4.04. 40
as i would buy thee, view thee limb by limb. 4.05.238
i'll buy him of you. COR 1.04. 5
things created | to buy and sell with groats, to 3.02. 10
i would not buy | their mercy at the price of 3.03. 90
would half my wealth | would buy this for a lie! 4.06.160
any man should buy the fee–simple of my life for ROM 3.01. 32 P
buy food, and get thyself in flesh. 5.01. 84
and here he writes that he did buy a poison | of 5.03.288
if i would sell my horse and buy twenty moe TIM 2.01. 7
when the means are gone that buy this praise, 2.02.169
and buy men's voices to commend our deeds. JC 2.01.146
why, i can buy me twenty at any market. MAC 4.02. 40
then you'll buy 'em to sell again. 4.02. 41
costly thy habit as thy purse can buy, | but not HAM 1.03. 70
god buy ye, fare ye well. 2.01. 66
ay, so god buy to you! 2.02.549
god buy you, sir. 4.04. 30
god buy you. 4.05.200 P

can buy this unpriz'd precious maid of me. LR 1.01.259
the slaughter, | if my cap would buy a halter, 1.04.320
god buy you; OTH 3.03.375
do him wrong | but he does buy my injuries, to CYM 1.01.105
if you buy ladies' flesh at a million a dram, 1.04.135 P
mingled sums | to buy a present for the emperor; 1.06.187
i bid for you as i do buy. 3.06. 70
money enough in the end to buy him a wooden one? PER 4.06.173 P
i would buy you | t' instruct me 'gainst a TNK 1.01.122
"he s' buy me a white cut, forth for to ride, 3.04. 22
to buy you i have lost what's dearest to me 5.03.112
and many will not buy | his goodness with this 5.04. 52
that nought could buy | dear love but loss of 5.04.111
so thou wilt buy, and pay, and use good dealing, VEN 514
they buy thy help, but sin ne'er gives a fee, LUC 913
buy terms divine in selling hours of dross; SON 146.11

BUYER 2 FR 0.0002 REL FR 0 V 2 P
hallow'd and brought a benediction to the buyer; WT 4.04.602 P
might be in 's time a great buyer of land, with HAM 5.01.104 P

BUYING 1 FR 0.0001 REL FR 1 V 0 P
that little cares for buying any thing. AYL 2.04. 90

BUYS 11 FR 0.0012 REL FR 11 V 0 P
money buys lands, and wives are sold by fate. WIV 5.05.233
if so, our copper buys no better treasure. LLL 4.03.383
price you yourselves; what buys your company? 5.02.224
the fairy land buys not the child of me. MND 2.01.122
for him, which buys | a place next to the king. H8 1.01. 65
(/an honor in him which buys out his fault), TIM 3.05. 17
seen the wicked prize itself | buys out the law. HAM 3.03. 60
her desires | buys herself bread and /clothes. OTH 4.01. 95
'tis gold | which buys admittance (oft it doth), CYM 2.03. 68
"a thousand kisses buys my heart from me, | and VEN 517
who buys a minute's mirth to wail a week? LUC 213

/BUZZ* 1 FR 0.0001 REL FR 1 V 0 P
/and /buzz /lamenting /doings /in /the /air! TIT 3.02. 62

BUZZ* 10 FR 0.0011 REL FR 8 V 2 P
should be! should — buzz! SHR 2.01.206
and buzz these conjurations in her brain. 2H6 1.02. 99
yet look to have them buzz to offend thine ears. 3H6 2.06. 95
for i will buzz abroad such prophecies | that 5.06. 86
there be moe wasps that buzz about his nose H8 3.02. 55
of our peace | buzz in the people's ears, there TIT 4.04. 7
buzz, buzz! HAM 2.02.393 P
buzz, buzz! 2.02.393 P
each buzz, each fancy, each complaint, dislike, LR 1.04.325
buzz! TNK 3.05. 79

BUZZARD* 3 FR 0.0003 REL FR 3 V 0 P
well ta'en, and like a buzzard. SHR 2.01.206
o slow–wing'd turtle, shall a buzzard take thee? 2.01.207
ay, for a turtle, as he takes a buzzard. 2.01.208

BUZZARDS 1 FR 0.0001 REL FR 1 V 0 P
whiles kites and buzzards /prey at liberty. R3 1.01.133

BUZZ'D 1 FR 0.0001 REL FR 1 V 0 P
that is not quickly buzz'd into his ears? R2 2.01. 26

BUZZERS 1 FR 0.0001 REL FR 1 V 0 P
and wants not buzzers to infect his ear | with HAM 4.05. 90

/BUZZING 1 FR 0.0001 REL FR 1 V 0 P
/that, /with /his /pretty /buzzing /melody, TIT 3.02. 64

BUZZING 4 FR 0.0004 REL FR 4 V 0 P
appear | among the buzzing pleased multitude, MV 3.02.180
and hush'd with buzzing night–flies to thy 2H4 3.01. 11
of late days hear | a buzzing of a separation H8 2.01.148
for you have stol'n their buzzing, antony, | and JC 5.01. 37

BY' *(also by'r)*

BY' 2 FR 0.0002 REL FR 0 V 2 P
by' lady, then i have brought up a neck to a TIT 4.04. 48 P
by' lady, your ladyship is nearer to heaven than HAM 2.02.425 P

BY *(also be*)*

/BY 47 FR 0.0053 REL FR 37 V 10 P

BY 3981 FR 0.4500 REL FR 3123 V 858 P

BY–DEPENDANCES 1 FR 0.0001 REL FR 1 V 0 P
be demanded, | and all the other by–dependances, CYM 5.05.390

BY–DRINKINGS 1 FR 0.0001 REL FR 0 V 1 P
for your diet and by–drinkings, and money lent 1H4 3.03. 73 P

BY–GONE 2 FR 0.0002 REL FR 2 V 0 P
this satisfaction | the by–gone day proclaim'd. WT 1.02. 32
thy by–gone fooleries were but spices of it. 3.02.184

BY–PAST 1 FR 0.0001 REL FR 1 V 0 P
content, | to put the by–past perils in her way? LC 158

BY–PATHS 1 FR 0.0001 REL FR 1 V 0 P
by what by–paths and indirect crook'd ways | i 2H4 4.05.184

BY–PEEPING 1 FR 0.0001 REL FR 1 V 0 P
then by–peeping in an eye | base and illustrious CYM 1.06.108

BY'R *(also by', py'r)*

/BY'R 1 FR 0.0001 REL FR 1 V 0 P
/by'r /lady, i could do much — OTH 3.03. 74

BY'R 15 FR 0.0017 REL FR 5 V 10 P
by'r lakin, i can go no further, sir, | my old TMP 3.03. 1
nay, by'r lady, that i think 'a cannot. ADO 3.03. 77 P
by'r lady, i think it be so. 3.03. 83 P
nay, by'r lady, i am not such a fool to think 3.04. 82 P
by'r lakin, a parlous fear. MND 3.01. 13 P
by'r lady, sir, and some dogs will catch well. TN 2.03. 62 P
by'r lady, a long lease for the clinking of 1H4 2.04. 45 P
now, sirs, by'r lady, you fought fair, so did 2.04.298 P
fifty, or, by'r lady, inclining to threescore; 2.04.424 P
by'r lady, he is a good musician. 3.01.231
by'r lady, i think 'a be, but goodman puff of 2H4 5.03. 89 P
ill news, by'r lady — seldom comes the better. R3 2.03. 4
and have an hour of hearing, and, by'r lady, H8 1.03. 46
by'r lady, thirty years. ROM 1.05. 33
but, by'r lady, 'a must build churches then, or HAM 3.02.133 P

BY–ROOM 1 FR 0.0001 REL FR 0 V 1 P
i prithee do thou stand in some by–room, while i 1H4 2.04. 29 P

BY'T 9 FR 0.0010 REL FR 6 V 3 P
keep it not, you cannot choose but lose by't. AWW 1.01.146 P
to accuse it, and | disdainful to be tried by't: H8 2.04.123
though they themselves did suffer by't, behold COR 4.06. 6
he cross'd himself by't; TIM 3.03. 29 P
you stay'd well by't in egypt. ANT 2.02.176 P
for i have gain'd by't. 2.06. 52
very true, | and so i hope he came by't. CYM 2.04.118
i have got two worlds by't. 5.05.374
i have spoke, your arcite | did not lose by't; TNK 5.03.122

BY–WORDS 1 FR 0.0001 REL FR 1 V 0 P
hath made us by–words to our enemies. 3H6 1.01. 42

BYZANTIUM 1 FR 0.0001 REL FR 1 V 0 P
his service done | at lacedaemon and byzantium TIM 3.05. 60

C 1 FR 0.0001 REL FR 1 V 0 P
lord, | c fa ut, that loves with all affection. SHR 3.01. 76

CA 1 FR 0.0001 REL FR 0 V 1 P
ca, ha! H5 3.07. 13 P

CABBAGE 1 FR 0.0001 REL FR 0 V 1 P
good cabbage. WIV 1.01.121 P

CABILEROS *(also cavaleiro, cavalery, cavaliers, cavalleria)*

CABILEROS 1 FR 0.0001 REL FR 0 V 1 P
bardolph, and to all the cabileros about london. 2H4 5.03. 59 P

CABIN 11 FR 0.0012 REL FR 9 V 2 P
to cabin! TMP 1.01. 17 P
ready in your cabin for the mischance of the 1.01. 25 P
now in the waist, the deck, in every cabin, | i 1.02.197
make me a willow cabin at your gate, | and call TN 1.05.268
she did approach | my cabin where i lay; WT 3.03. 24
who from my cabin tempted me to walk | upon the R3 1.04. 12
and cabin in a cave, and bring you up | to be a TIT 4.02.179
up from my cabin, | my sea–gown scarf'd about me HAM 5.02. 12
no, to my cabin. ANT 2.07.130
"o, let him keep his loathsome cabin still! VEN 637
and daff'd me to a cabin hang'd with care, | to PP 14. 3

CABIN'D 2 FR 0.0002 REL FR 2 V 0 P
but now i am cabin'd, cribb'd, confin'd, bound MAC 3.04. 23
they two have cabin'd | in many as dangerous as TNK 1.03. 35

CABINET 2 FR 0.0002 REL FR 2 V 0 P
from his moist cabinet mounts up on high, | and VEN 854
must'ring to the quiet cabinet | where their LUC 442

CABINS 2 FR 0.0002 REL FR 1 V 1 P
keep your cabins; TMP 1.01. 14 P
fled | into the deep–dark cabins of her head, VEN 1038

CABLE 4 FR 0.0004 REL FR 3 V 1 P
make the rope of his destiny our cable, for our TMP 1.01. 31 P
the cable broke, the holding–anchor lost, | and 3H6 5.04. 4
might to enforce it on) | will give him cable. OTH 1.02. 17
let me cut the cable, | and, when we are put off ANT 2.07. 71

CABLES 1 FR 0.0001 REL FR 0 V 1 P
knit to thy deserving with cables of perdurable OTH 1.03.338 P

CA–CALIBAN *(also 'ban, caliban)*

CA–CALIBAN 1 FR 0.0001 REL FR 1 V 0 P
'ban, ca–caliban | has a new master, get a new TMP 2.02.184

CACKLING 2 FR 0.0002 REL FR 2 V 0 P
when every goose is cackling, would be thought MV 5.01.105
plain, | i'ld drive ye cackling home to camelot. LR 2.02. 84

CACODEMON 1 FR 0.0001 REL FR 1 V 0 P
world, | thou cacodemon, there thy kingdom is. R3 1.03.143

CADDISES 1 FR 0.0001 REL FR 0 V 1 P
inkles, caddises, cambrics, lawns. WT 4.04.207 P

CADDIS–GARTER 1 FR 0.0001 REL FR 0 V 1 P
puke–stocking, caddis–garter, smooth–tongue, 1H4 2.04. 70 P

CADE* 27 FR 0.0030 REL FR 18 V 9 P
a headstrong kentishman, | john cade of ashford, 2H6 3.01.357
in ireland have i seen this stubborn cade 3.01.360
thee, jack cade the clothier means to dress the 4.02. 4 P
we john cade, so term'd of our suppos'd father 4.02. 31 P
or rather, of stealing a cade of herrings. 4.02. 33 P
jack cade, the duke of york hath taught you this 4.02.154
proclaim them traitors that are up with cade, 4.02.177
will parley with jack cade their general. 4.04. 13
lord say, jack cade hath sworn to have thy head. 4.04. 19
jack cade proclaims himself lord mortimer, 4.04. 28
jack cade hath gotten london bridge: 4.04. 49
how now? is jack cade slain? 4.05. 1
jack cade! jack cade! 4.06. 7 P
jack cade! jack cade! 4.06. 7 P
be wise, he'll never call ye jack cade more. 4.06. 10 P
know, cade, we come ambassadors from the king 4.08. 7
we'll follow cade, we'll follow cade! 4.08. 33 P
we'll follow cade, we'll follow cade! 4.08. 33 P
is cade the son of henry the fift, | that thus 4.08. 34
why, buckingham, is the traitor cade surpris'd? 4.09. 8
my state, 'twixt cade and york distress'd, 4.09. 31
but now is cade driven back, his men dispers'd, 4.09. 34
because the unconquer'd soul of cade is fled. 4.10. 65 P
is't cade that i have slain, that monstrous 4.10. 66
and fight against that monstrous rebel cade, 5.01. 62
head, | the head of cade, whom i in combat slew. 5.01. 67
the head of cade! 5.01. 68

CADENCE 1 FR 0.0001 REL FR 0 V 1 P
facility, and golden cadence of poesy, caret. LLL 4.02.122 P

CADENT 1 FR 0.0001 REL FR 1 V 0 P
with cadent tears fret channels in her cheeks, LR 1.04.285

CADES 1 FR 0.0001 REL FR 1 V 0 P
better ten thousand base–born cades miscarry 2H6 4.08. 47

CADMUS 1 FR 0.0001 REL FR 1 V 0 P
i was with hercules and cadmus once, | when in a MND 4.01.112

CADUCEUS 1 FR 0.0001 REL FR 0 V 1 P
lose all the serpentine craft of thy caduceus, TRO 2.03. 12 P

CADWAL 7 FR 0.0008 REL FR 7 V 0 P
the younger brother, cadwal, | once arviragus, CYM 3.03. 95
cadwal and i | will play the cook and servant, 3.06. 29
occasion | hath cadwal now to give it motion? 4.02.188
is cadwal mad? 4.02.195
cadwal, | i cannot sing. 4.02.239
nay, cadwal, we must lay his head to th' east, 4.02.255
this gentleman, my cadwal, arviragus, | your 5.05.359

CADWALLADER 1 FR 0.0001 REL FR 1 V 0 P
not for cadwallader and all his goats. H5 5.01. 28

CAELESTIBUS 1 FR 0.0001 REL FR 1 V 0 P
tantaene animis caelestibus irae? 2H6 2.01. 24

CAELIUS 1 FR 0.0001 REL FR 1 V 0 P
justeius, | publicola, and caelius, are for sea; ANT 3.07. 73

CAELO 1 FR 0.0001 REL FR 0 V 1 P
now hangeth like a jewel in the ear of caelo, LLL 4.02. 5 P

/CAESAR 1 FR 0.0001 REL FR 1 V 0 P
case thou stand'st | further than he is /caesar. ANT 3.13. 55

CAESAR 346 FR 0.0391 REL FR 318 V 28 P
thou'rt an emperor — caesar, keiser, and WIV 1.03. 9 P
to your tent, and prove a shrewd caesar to you; MM 2.01.249 P
what, at the wheels of caesar? 3.02. 44 P
a disaster of war that caesar himself could not AWW 3.06. 53 P
go forth and fetch their conqu'ring caesar in; H5 5.pr. 28
soul will make | than julius caesar or bright — 1H6 1.01. 56
which caesar and his fortune bare at once. 1.02.139
brutus' bastard hand | stabb'd julius caesar; 2H6 4.01.137
kent, in the commentaries caesar writ, | is 4.07. 60
no bending knee will call thee caesar now, | no 3H6 3.01. 18
they that stabb'd caesar shed no blood at all, 5.05. 53
did julius caesar build that place, my lord? R3 3.01. 69
that julius caesar was a famous man; 3.01. 84
she shall be sole victoress, caesar's caesar. 4.04.336
we make holiday to see caesar, and to rejoice in JC 1.01. 31 P
peace ho, caesar speaks. 1.02. 1
caesar, my lord? 1.02. 5
when caesar says, "do this," it is perform'd. 1.02. 10
caesar! 1.02. 12
shriller than all the music | cry "caesar!" 1.02. 17
speak, caesar is turn'd to hear. 1.02. 17
fellow, come from the throng, look upon caesar. 1.02. 21
best respect in rome | (except immortal caesar), 1.02. 60
fear the people | choose caesar for their king. 1.02. 80
i was born free as caesar, so were you; 1.02. 97
caesar said to me, "dar'st thou, cassius, now 1.02.102
caesar cried, "help me, cassius, or i sink!" 1.02.111
the waves of tiber | did i the tired caesar. 1.02.115
his body | if caesar carelessly but nod on him. 1.02.118
for some new honors that are heap'd on caesar. 1.02.134
brutus and caesar: 1.02.142
what should be in that "caesar"? 1.02.142
will start a spirit as soon as "caesar." 1.02.147
upon what meat doth this our caesar feed | that 1.02.149
the games are done, and caesar is returning. 1.02.178
caesar? 1.02.191
fear him not, caesar, he's not dangerous, | he 1.02.196
for always i am caesar. 1.02.212
hath chanc'd to–day | that caesar looks so sad. 1.02.218
breath because caesar refus'd the crown, that it 1.02.247 P
it had, almost, chok'd caesar, for he swounded, 1.02.248 P
but soft, i pray you; what, did caesar swound? 1.02.251
no, caesar hath it not; 1.02.255
mean by that, but i am sure caesar fell down. 1.02.258 P
if caesar had stabb'd their mothers, they would 1.02.274 P
caesar doth bear me hard, but he loves brutus. 1.02.313
and after this let caesar seat him sure, | for 1.02.321
brought you caesar home? 1.03. 1
comes caesar to the capitol to–morrow? 1.03. 36
'tis caesar that you mean; is it not, cassius? 1.03. 79
to–morrow | mean to establish caesar as a king; 1.03. 86
and why should caesar be a tyrant then? 1.03.103
to illuminate | so vile a thing as caesar! 1.03.111
and to speak truth of caesar, | i have not known 2.01. 19
so caesar may; 2.01. 27
since cassius first did whet me against caesar, 2.01. 61
shall no man else be touch'd but only caesar? 2.01.154
meet, | mark antony, so well belov'd of caesar, 2.01.156
well belov'd of caesar, | should outlive caesar. 2.01.157
prevent, | let antony and caesar fall together. 2.01.161
for antony is but a limb of caesar. 2.01.165
we all stand up against the spirit of caesar, 2.01.167
by caesar's spirit, | and not dismember caesar! 2.01.170
but, alas, | caesar must bleed for it! 2.01.171
for in the ingrafted love he bears to caesar — 2.01.184
if he love caesar, all that he can do | is to 2.01.186
to himself — take thought and die for caesar; 2.01.187
whether caesar will come forth to–day or no; 2.01.194
caius ligarius doth bear caesar hard, | who 2.01.215
they murther caesar!" 2.02. 3
what mean you, caesar? 2.02. 8
caesar shall forth; 2.02. 10
when they shall see | the face of caesar, they 2.02. 12
caesar, i never stood on ceremonies, | yet now 2.02. 13
o caesar, these things are beyond all use, | and 2.02. 25
yet caesar shall go forth; 2.02. 28
are to the world in general as to caesar. 2.02. 29
caesar should be a beast without a heart | if he 2.02. 42
no, caesar shall not; 2.02. 44
well | that caesar is more dangerous than he. 2.02. 45
and caesar shall go forth. 2.02. 48
caesar, all hail! 2.02. 58
good morrow, worthy caesar, | i come to fetch 2.02. 58
shall caesar send a lie? 2.02. 65
decius, go tell them caesar will not come. 2.02. 68
most mighty caesar, let me know some cause, 2.02. 69
to give this day a crown to mighty caesar. 2.02. 94
if caesar hide himself, shall they not whisper, 2.02.100
shall they not whisper, | "lo caesar is afraid"? 2.02.101
pardon me, caesar, for my dear dear love | to 2.02.102
good morrow, caesar. 2.02.109
caesar was ne'er so much your enemy | as that 2.02.112
caesar, 'tis strucken eight. 2.02.114
so to most noble caesar. 2.02.118
caesar, i will; 2.02.124
that every like is not the same, o caesar, | the 2.02.128
"caesar, beware of brutus; 2.03. 1 P
in all these men, and it is bent against caesar. 2.03. 6 P
here will i stand till caesar pass along, | and 2.03. 11
if thou read this, o caesar, thou mayest live; 2.03. 15
and take good note | what caesar doth, what 2.04. 15
is caesar yet gone to the capitol? 2.04. 24
thou hast some suit to caesar, hast thou not? 2.04. 27
if it will please caesar | to be so good to 2.04. 28
caesar | to be so good to caesar as to hear me: 2.04. 29
the throng that follows caesar at the heels, 2.04. 34
there | speak to great caesar as he comes along. 2.04. 38
brutus hath a suit | that caesar will not grant. 2.04. 43
ay, caesar, but not gone. 3.01. 2
hail, caesar! read this schedule. 3.01. 3
o caesar, read mine first; 3.01. 6
for mine's a suit | that touches caesar nearer. 3.01. 7
read it, great caesar. 3.01. 7
delay not, caesar, read it instantly. 3.01. 9
look how he makes to caesar; mark him. 3.01. 18
cassius or caesar never shall turn back, | for i 3.01. 21
for look he smiles, and caesar doth not change. 3.01. 24
go | and presently prefer his suit to caesar. 3.01. 28
amiss | that caesar and his senate must redress? 3.01. 32
high, most mighty, and most puissant caesar, 3.01. 33
to think that caesar bears such rebel blood 3.01. 40
know, caesar doth not wrong, nor without cause 3.01. 47
i kiss thy hand, but not in flattery, caesar; 3.01. 52
pardon, caesar! 3.01. 55
caesar, pardon! 3.01. 55
o caesar — 3.01. 74

great caesar — 3.01. 75
et tu, brute? — then fall, caesar! 3.01. 77
how many times shall caesar bleed in sport, 3.01.114
caesar was mighty, bold, royal, and loving. 3.01.127
say, i fear'd caesar, honor'd him, and lov'd him 3.01.129
how caesar hath deserv'd to lie in death, | mark 3.01.132
mark antony shall not love caesar dead | so well 3.01.133
o mighty caesar! 3.01.148
as here by caesar, and by you cut off, | the 3.01.162
so pity pity — | hath done this deed on caesar. 3.01.172
why i, that did love caesar when i strook him, 3.01.182
that i did love thee, caesar, o, 'tis true; 3.01.194
the enemies of caesar shall say this: 3.01.212
i blame you not for praising caesar so, | but 3.01.214
from the point, by looking down on caesar. 3.01.219
why, and wherein, caesar was dangerous. 3.01.222
that were you, antony, the son of caesar, | you 3.01.225
and that we are contented caesar shall | have 3.01.240
but speak all good you can devise of caesar, 3.01.246
you serve octavius caesar, do you not? 3.01.276
caesar did write for him to come to rome. 3.01.278
me say to you by word of mouth — | o caesar! 3.01.281
that brutus' love to caesar was no less than his 3.02. 19 P
friend demand why brutus rose against caesar, 3.02. 21 P
not that i lov'd caesar less, but that i lov'd 3.02. 22 P
had you rather caesar were living, and die all 3.02. 23 P
and die all slaves, than that caesar were dead, 3.02. 24 P
as caesar lov'd me, i weep for him; 3.02. 24 P
have done no more to caesar than you shall do to 3.02. 37 P
let him be caesar. 3.02. 51
this caesar was a tyrant. 3.02. 69
i come to bury caesar, not to praise him. 3.02. 74
so let it be with caesar. 3.02. 77
brutus | hath told you caesar was ambitious; 3.02. 78
fault, | and grievously hath caesar answer'd it. 3.02. 80
did this in caesar seem ambitious? 3.02. 90
when that the poor have cried, caesar hath wept; 3.02. 91
my heart is in the coffin there with caesar, 3.02.106
of the matter, | caesar has had great wrong. 3.02.110
but yesterday the word of caesar might | have 3.02.118
but here's a parchment with the seal of caesar, 3.02.128
it is not meet you know how caesar lov'd you: 3.02.141
and, being men, hearing the will of caesar, | it 3.02.143
men | whose daggers have stabb'd caesar; 3.02.152
then make a ring about the corpse of caesar, 3.02.158
remember | the first time ever caesar put it on; 3.02.171
mark how the blood of caesar followed it, | as 3.02.178
judge, o you gods, how dearly caesar lov'd him! 3.02.182
for when the noble caesar saw him stab, 3.02.184
all the while ran blood) great caesar fell. 3.02.189
o noble caesar! 3.02.199 P
and put a tongue | in every wound of caesar, 3.02.229
wherein hath caesar thus deserv'd your loves? 3.02.236
most noble caesar! we'll revenge his death. 3.02.243
o royal caesar! 3.02.244 P
here was a caesar! 3.02.252
i dreamt to–night that i did feast with caesar, 3.03. 1
when caesar liv'd, he durst not thus have mov'd 4.03. 58
strike as thou didst at caesar; 4.03.105
no, caesar, we will answer on their charge. 5.01. 24
hail, caesar!" 5.01. 32
hack'd one another in the sides of caesar. 5.01. 40
like a cur, behind | strook caesar on the neck. 5.01. 44
or till another caesar | have added slaughter to 5.01. 54
caesar, thou canst not die by traitors' hands, 5.01. 56
caesar, thou art reveng'd, | even with the sword 5.03. 45
o julius caesar, thou art mighty yet! 5.03. 94
the ghost of caesar hath appear'd to me | two 5.05. 17
caesar, now be still, | i kill'd not thee with 5.05. 50
he, | did that they did in envy of great caesar; 5.05. 70
as it is said | mark antony's was by caesar. MAC 3.01. 56
i did enact julius caesar. HAM 3.02.103 P
imperious caesar, dead and turn'd to clay, 5.01.213
he's a soldier fit to stand by caesar | and give OTH 2.03.122
if the scarce–bearded caesar have not sent | his ANT 1.01. 21
your dismission | is come from caesar, therefore 1.01. 27
is caesar with antonius priz'd so slight? 1.01. 56
find me to marry me with octavius caesar, and 1.02. 30 P
of them, jointing their force 'gainst caesar, 1.02. 92
pompeius | /hath given the dare to caesar, and 1.02.184
most noble caesar, shalt thou have report | how 1.04. 35
belov'd of those | that only have fear'd caesar; 1.04. 38
caesar, i bring thee word | menecrates and menas 1.04. 47
to–morrow, caesar, | i shall be furnish'd to 1.04. 76
broad–fronted caesar, | when thou wast here 1.05. 29
did i, charmian, | ever love caesar so? 1.05. 67
o that brave caesar! 1.05. 67
the valiant caesar! 1.05. 69
if thou with caesar paragon again | my man of 1.05. 71
caesar gets money where | he loses hearts. 2.01. 13
caesar and lepidus | are in the field, a mighty 2.01. 16
caesar and antony shall well greet together: 2.01. 39
his wife that's dead did trespasses to caesar; 2.01. 40
if caesar move him, | let antony look over 2.02. 4
and yonder, caesar. 2.02. 14
my being in egypt, caesar, | what was't to you? 2.02. 35
so much uncurbable her garboils, caesar, | made 2.02. 67
soft, caesar! 2.02. 83
but on, caesar, | the article of my oath. 2.02. 86
give me leave, caesar — 2.02.116
i am not married, caesar; 2.02.122
will caesar speak? 2.02.138
the power of caesar, and | his power unto 2.02.142
half the heart of caesar, worthy maecenas! 2.02.172 P
she made great caesar lay his sword to bed; 2.02.227
or friends with caesar, or not captive to him, 2.05. 44
and friends with caesar. 2.05. 47
caesar and he are greater friends than ever. 2.05. 48
he's friends with caesar, | in state of health 2.05. 55
in praising antony i have disprais'd caesar. 2.05.107
having a son and friends, since julius caesar, 2.06. 12
when caesar and your brother were at blows, 2.06. 44
i have heard that julius caesar | grew fat with 2.06. 64
a certain queen to caesar in a mattress. 2.06. 70
then is caesar and he for ever knit together. 2.06.115 P
the sighs of octavia blow the fire up in caesar, 2.06.127 P
here's to caesar! 2.07. 98
caesar and antony have ever won | more in their 3.01. 16
caesar is sad, and lepidus, | since pompey's 3.02. 4
a very fine one. o, how he loves caesar! 3.02. 7
caesar? why, he's the jupiter of men. 3.02. 9
spake you of caesar? how, the nonpareil! 3.02. 11
would you praise caesar, say "caesar," go no 3.02. 13
would you praise caesar, say "caesar," go no 3.02. 13
but he loves caesar best, yet he loves antony. 3.02. 15
but as for caesar, | kneel down, kneel down, and 3.02. 18
will caesar weep? 3.02. 50
when antony found julius caesar dead, | he cried 3.02. 54
caesar and lepidus have made wars upon pompey. 3.05. 4 P
caesar, having made use of him in the wars 3.05. 7 P
for italy and caesar. 3.05. 20
caesar, and that, having in sicily | sextus 3.06. 24
hail, caesar, and my lord! 3.06. 39
hail, most dear caesar! 3.06. 39
at pharsalia, | where caesar fought with pompey. 3.07. 32
i have sixty sails, caesar none better. 3.07. 49
head of /actium | beat th' approaching caesar. 3.07. 52
caesar has taken toryne. 3.07. 55
to caesar will i render | my legions and my 3.10. 32
fly, | and make your peace with caesar. 3.11. 6
caesar, 'tis his schoolmaster, | an argument 3.12. 2
caesar, i go. 3.12. 33
caesar, i shall. 3.12. 36
to the boy caesar send this grizzled head, | and 3.13. 17
a child as soon | as i' th' command of caesar. 3.13. 25
high–battled caesar will | unstate his happiness 3.13. 29
the full caesar will | answer his emptiness! 3.13. 35
caesar, thou hast subdu'd | his judgment too. 3.13. 36
a messenger from caesar. 3.13. 37
he needs as many, sir, as caesar has, | or needs 3.13. 49
if caesar please, our master | will leap to be 3.13. 50
caesar entreats | not to consider in what case 3.13. 53
shall i say to caesar | what you require of him? 3.13. 65
say to great caesar this in /deputation: 3.13. 74
tributaries | that do acknowledge caesar, should 3.13. 97
be thou sorry | to follow caesar in his triumph, 3.13.136
get thee back to caesar, | tell him thy 3.13.139
to flatter caesar, would you mingle eyes | with 3.13.156
caesar sets down in alexandria, where | i will 3.13.168
dares me to personal combat, | caesar to antony. 4.01. 4
caesar must think, | when one so great begins to 4.01. 6
that he and caesar might | determine this great 4.04. 36
sir, | he is with caesar. 4.05. 10
caesar, i shall. 4.06. 3
great herod to incline himself to caesar | and 4.06. 13
for this pains | caesar hath hang'd him. 4.06. 15
caesar himself has work, and our oppression 4.07. 2
for the things he speaks | may concern caesar. 4.09. 25
melt their sweets | on blossoming caesar; 4.12. 23
than she which by her death our caesar tells, 4.14. 61
strik'st not me, 'tis caesar thou defeat'st. 4.14. 68
whilst the wheel'd seat | of fortunate caesar, 4.14. 76
this sword but shown to caesar, with this 4.14.112
you did suspect | she had dispos'd with caesar, 4.14.123
of the full–fortun'd caesar ever shall | be 4.15. 24
of caesar seek your honor, with your safety. 4.15. 46
none about caesar trust but proculeius. 4.15. 48
and my hands i'll trust, | none about caesar. 4.15. 50
caesar, i shall. 5.01. 3
me to thee, as i was to him | i'll be to caesar; 5.01. 11
i say, o caesar, antony is dead. 5.01. 13
he is dead, caesar, | not by a public minister 5.01. 19
caesar is touch'd. 5.01. 33
for caesar cannot /live | to be ungentle. 5.01. 59
caesar, i shall. 5.01. 68
'tis paltry to be caesar; 5.02. 2
caesar sends greeting to the queen of egypt, 5.02. 9
guard her till caesar come. 5.02. 36
mortal house i'll ruin, | do caesar what he can. 5.02. 52
further than you shall | find cause in caesar. 5.02. 64
what thou hast done thy master caesar knows, 5.02. 65
to caesar i will speak what you shall please, 5.02. 69
know you what caesar means to do with me? 5.02.106
make way there! caesar! 5.02.111
see, caesar! 5.02.150
o caesar, what a wounding shame is this, | that 5.02.159
say, good caesar, | that i some lady trifles 5.02.164
caesar through syria | intends his journey, and 5.02.200
adieu, good queen, i must attend on caesar. 5.02.206
i hear him mock | the luck of caesar, which the 5.02.286
that i might hear thee call great caesar ass 5.02.307
caesar hath sent — 5.02.321
there's dolabella sent from caesar; call him. 5.02.324
caesar, thy thoughts | touch their effects in 5.02.329
a way there, a way for caesar! 5.02.333
o caesar, | this charmian liv'd but now, she 5.02.340
are men more order'd than when julius caesar CYM 2.04. 21
now say, what would augustus caesar with us? 3.01. 1
when julius caesar (whose remembrance yet 3.01. 2
a kind of conquest | caesar made here, but made 3.01. 23
if caesar can hide the sun from us with a 3.01. 42 P
we do say then to caesar, | our ancestor was 3.01. 53
whose use the sword of caesar | hath too much 3.01. 55
that i am to pronounce augustus caesar | (caesar 3.01. 62
i am to pronounce augustus caesar | (caesar, 3.01. 63
thy caesar knighted me; 3.01. 69
so caesar shall not find them. 3.01. 76
long live caesar! 3.07. 10
although the victor, we submit to caesar, | and 5.05.460
th' imperial caesar, should again unite | his 5.05.474

CAESARION 2 FR 0.0002 REL FR 2 V 0 P
at the feet sat | caesarion, whom they call my ANT 3.06. 6
the next caesarion /smite, | till by degrees the 3.13.162

CAESAR'S 71 FR 0.0080 REL FR 65 V 6 P
the pommel of caesar's falchion. LLL 5.02.614 P
rams, and caesar's thrasonical brag of "i came, AYL 5.02. 31 P
the way | to julius caesar's ill–erected tower, R2 5.01. 2
to dignify the times, | since caesar's fortunes. 2H4 1.01. 23
she shall be sole victoress, caesar's caesar. R3 4.04.336
of my right, | if ever bassianus, caesar's son, TIT 1.01. 10
let no images | be hung with caesar's trophies. JC 1.01. 69
growing feathers pluck'd from caesar's wing 1.01. 72
the ninety spot doth glow on caesar's brow, | and 1.02.183
for pulling scarfs off caesar's images, are put 1.02.286 P
caesar's ambition shall be glanced at. 1.02.320
o, that we then could come by caesar's spirit, 2.01.169
for he can do no more than caesar's arm | when 2.01.182
than caesar's arm | when caesar's head is off. 2.01.183
when caesar's wife shall meet with better dreams 2.02. 99
to sound more sweetly in great caesar's ear 3.01. 50
lest some friend of caesar's | should chance — 3.01. 87
so are we caesar's friends, that have abridg'd 3.01.104
and let us bathe our hands in caesar's blood 3.01.106
is no hour so fit | as caesar's death's hour, 3.01.154
and show the reason of our caesar's death. 3.01.237
mark antony, here take you caesar's body. 3.01.244
and caesar's spirit, ranging for revenge, | with 3.01.270
reasons shall be rendered | of caesar's death. 3.02. 8
any dear friend of caesar's, to him i say, that 3.02. 18 P
caesar's better parts | shall be crown'd in 3.02. 51
do grace to caesar's corpse, and grace his 3.02. 57
grace his speech | tending to caesar's glories, 3.02. 58
men), | come i to speak in caesar's funeral. 3.02. 84
and they would go and kiss dead caesar's wounds, 3.02.132
the will, the will! we will hear caesar's will. 3.02.139
you shall read us the will, caesar's will. 3.02.148
for brutus, as you know, was caesar's angel. 3.02.181
you but behold | our caesar's vesture wounded? 3.02.196
show you sweet caesar's wounds, poor, poor, dumb 3.02.225
here is the will, and under caesar's seal: 3.02.240
he and lepidus are at caesar's house. 3.02.264
directly, i am going to caesar's funeral. 3.03. 20 P
but, lepidus, go you to caesar's house; 4.01. 7
witness the hole you made in caesar's heart, 5.01. 31
and bow'd like bondmen, kissing caesar's feet; 5.01. 42
till caesar's three and thirty wounds | be well 5.01. 53
that ran through caesar's bowels, search this 5.03. 42
caesar's, i would say — both? ANT 1.01. 28
and that blood of thine | is caesar's homager; 1.01. 31
it is not caesar's natural vice to hate | /our 1.04. 2
let antony look over caesar's head | and speak 2.02. 5
fortunes shall rise higher, | caesar's or mine? 2.03. 17
caesar's. 2.03. 18
high unmatchable, | where caesar's is not; 2.03. 22
caesar's sister is call'd octavia. 2.06.109 P
you come not | like caesar's sister. 3.06. 43
in caesar's fleet | are those that often have 3.07. 36
this speed of caesar's | carries beyond belief. 3.07. 74
in eye of caesar's battle, from which place | we 3.09. 2
caesar's will? 3.13. 46
whose he is, we are, and that is caesar's. 3.13. 52
your caesar's father oft | (when he hath mus'd 3.13. 82
the jack of caesar's shall | bear us an arrant 3.13.103
as a morsel, cold upon | dead caesar's trencher; 3.13.117
or from caesar's camp | say "i am none of thine. 4.05. 8
thy deserving, | and blemish caesar's triumph. 4.12. 33
she, eros, has | pack'd cards with caesar's, and 4.14. 19
not caesar's valor hath o'erthrown antony, | but 4.15. 14
the dung, | the beggar's nurse and caesar's. 5.02. 8
and believe | caesar's no merchant, to make 5.02.183
approach ho, all's not well; caesar's beguil'd. 5.02.323
thine uncle | (famous in caesar's praises, no CYM 3.01. 6
to master caesar's sword, | made lud's–town with 3.01. 31
caesar's ambition, | which swell'd so much that 3.01. 48
in caesar's name pronounce i 'gainst thee; 3.01. 66

CAESARS 3 FR 0.0003 REL FR 2 V 1 P
compare with caesars and with cannibals | and 2H4 2.04.166
there be many caesars, | ere such another julius CYM 3.01. 11
and, as i said, there is no moe such caesars. 3.01. 36 P

CAGE 7 FR 0.0008 REL FR 4 V 3 P
therefore i have decreed not to sing in my cage. ADO 1.03. 34 P
in which cage of rushes i am sure you /are not AYL 3.02.371 P
for his father had never a house but the cage. 2H6 4.02. 52 P
is torn from forth that pretty hollow cage, TIT 3.01. 84
i must up–fill this osier cage of ours | with ROM 2.03. 7
we two alone will sing like birds i' th' cage; LR 5.03. 9
our cage | we make a choir, as doth the prison'd CYM 3.03. 42

CAGED 2 FR 0.0002 REL FR 2 V 0 P
plays, | and twenty caged nightingales do sing. SHR in.2. 36
and now she would the caged cloister fly: LC 249

CAGION *(also occasion)*
/CAGION 1 FR 0.0001 REL FR 0 V 1 P
chill not let go, zir, without vurther /cagion. LR 4.06.235 P

CAIN 4 FR 0.0004 REL FR 4 V 0 P
for since the birth of cain, the first male JN 3.04. 79
with cain go wander thorough shades of night, R2 5.06. 43
but let one spirit of the first–born cain 2H4 1.01.157
this be damascus, be thou cursed cain, | to slay 1H6 1.03. 39

CAIN–COLOR'D 1 FR 0.0001 REL FR 0 V 1 P
a little yellow beard, a cain–color'd beard. WIV 1.04. 23 P

CAIN'S 2 FR 0.0002 REL FR 1 V 1 P
your wit | what was a month old at cain's birth, LLL 4.02. 35
it to the ground, as if 'twere cain's jaw–bone, HAM 5.01. 77 P

CAITIFF 12 FR 0.0013 REL FR 10 V 2 P
o thou caitiff! MM 2.01.174 P
pleasure i shall do with this wicked caitiff? 2.01.184 P
but one, the wicked'st caitiff on the ground, 5.01. 53
i went | to this pernicious caitiff deputy — 5.01. 88
i am the caitiff that do hold him to't; AWW 3.02.114
for queen, a very caitiff crown'd with care; R3 4.04.101
here lives a caitiff wretch would sell it him." ROM 5.01. 52
i flatter not, but say thou art a caitiff. TIM 4.03.235
caitiff, to pieces shake, | that under covert LR 3.02. 55
alas, poor caitiff! OTH 4.01.108
o thou pernicious caitiff! 5.02.318
and asks the weary caitiff for his master, | and VEN 914

CAITIFFS 1 FR 0.0001 REL FR 1 V 0 P
a plague consume you, wicked caitiffs left! TIM 5.04. 71

CAITIVE 1 FR 0.0001 REL FR 1 V 0 P
a caitive recreant to my cousin herford! R2 1.02. 53

CAIUS' 2 FR 0.0002 REL FR 0 V 2 P
and ask of doctor caius' house which is the way; WIV 1.02. 1 P
daughter, she is, by this, doctor caius' wife. 5.05.175 P

CAIUS* 50 FR 0.0056 REL FR 37 V 13 P
if you can see my master, master doctor caius, WIV 1.04. 3 P
the welsh priest and caius the french doctor. 2.01.201 P
i myself dwell with master doctor caius — 2.02. 46 P
/god save you, master doctor caius! 2.03. 19 P
master doctor caius, i am come to fetch you home 2.03. 52 P
which way have you look'd for master caius, that 3.01. 3 P
master doctor caius, the renown'd french 3.01. 61 P
here comes doctor caius. 3.01. 72 P
against that match | and firm for doctor caius) 4.06. 28
you know caius martius is chief enemy to the COR 1.01. 7 P

you proceed especially against caius martius? 1.01. 26 P
where's caius martius? 1.01.223
no, caius martius, | i'll lean upon one crutch, 1.01.241
if we and caius martius chance to meet, | 'tis 1.02. 34
that caius martius | wears this war's garland; 1.09. 59
clamor of the host, | martius caius coriolanus! 1.09. 65
martius caius coriolanus! 1.09. 67
hath won, | with fame, a name to martius caius; 2.01.164
my gentle martius, worthy caius, and | by 2.01.172
work perform'd | by martius caius coriolanus, 2.02. 46
my name is caius martius, who hath done | to 4.05. 65
was wont to thwack our general, caius martius. 4.05.179 P
caius martius was | a worthy officer i' th' war, 4.06. 29
led by caius martius | associated with aufidius, 4.06. 75
when, caius, rome is thine, | thou art poor'st 4.07. 56
ay, martius, caius martius! 5.06. 87
"to /saturn," caius, not to saturnine: TIT 4.03. 57
caius and valentine! 5.02.151
caius and valentine, lay hands on them. 5.02.158
our course will seem too bloody, caius cassius, JC 2.01.162
let's be sacrificers, but not butchers, caius. 2.01.166
caius ligarius doth bear caesar hard, | who 2.01.215
caius ligarius, that metellus spake of. 2.01.311
caius ligarius, how? 2.01.312
o, what a time have you chose out, brave caius, 2.01.314
what it is, my caius, | i shall unfold to thee, 2.01.329
caius ligarius, | caesar was ne'er so much your 2.02.111
thou hast wrong'd caius ligarius. 2.03. 4 P
next, caius cassius, do i take your hand; 3.01.186
pardon me, caius cassius! 3.01.211
should i have answer'd caius cassius so? 4.03. 78
apace, | and see how i regarded caius cassius. 5.03. 88
where is your servant caius? LR 5.03.284
true, sir, she was the wife of caius marcellus. ANT 2.06.110 P
the one is caius lucius. CYM 2.03. 55
caius lucius | will do 's commission throughly. 2.04. 11
was caius lucius in the britain court | when you 2.04. 37
thou art welcome, caius. 3.01. 68
thou com'st not, caius, now for tribute; 5.05. 69
and, caius lucius, | although the victor, we 5.05.459

CAK'D 1 FR 0.0001 REL FR 1 V 0 P
their blood is cak'd, 'tis cold, it seldom flows TIM 2.02.216

CAKE 4 FR 0.0004 REL FR 2 V 2 P
your cake here is warm within: ERR 3.01. 71
my cake is dough, but i'll in among the rest, SHR 5.01.140
he that will have a cake out of the wheat must TRO 1.01. 15 P
the kneading, the making of the cake, the 1.01. 24 P

CAKE'S 1 FR 0.0001 REL FR 0 V 1 P
our cake's dough on both sides. SHR 1.01.108 P

CAKES 4 FR 0.0004 REL FR 1 V 3 P
virtuous, there shall be no more cakes and ale? TN 2.03.116 P
lives upon mouldy stew'd pruins and dried cakes. 2H4 2.04.147 P
do you look for ale and cakes here, you rude H8 5.03. 10 P
and old cakes of roses | were thinly scattered, ROM 5.01. 47

CALABER 1 FR 0.0001 REL FR 1 V 0 P
the dukes of orleance, calaber, bretagne, and 2H6 1.01. 7

CALAIS *(see callice)*

CALAMITIES 1 FR 0.0001 REL FR 1 V 0 P
wits | are drown'd and lost in his calamities. TIM 4.03. 90

CALAMITY 10 FR 0.0011 REL FR 9 V 1 P
as there is no true cuckold but calamity, so TN 1.05. 51 P
i feel | the different plague of each calamity. JN 3.04. 60
faithful loves, | sticking together in calamity. 3.04. 67
is so arm'd | to bear the tidings of calamity. R2 3.02.105
vocation | and free my country from calamity. 1H6 1.02. 81
why should calamity be full of words? R3 4.04.126
you are transported by calamity | thither where COR 1.01. 75
we must find | an evident calamity, though we 5.03.112
of thy parts, | and thou art wedded to calamity. ROM 3.03. 3
respect | that makes calamity of so long life: HAM 3.01. 68

CALCHAS' 4 FR 0.0004 REL FR 3 V 1 P
'twas to bring this greek | to calchas' house, TRO 4.01. 38
is not yond diomed, with calchas' daughter? 4.05. 13
follow his torch, he goes to calchas' tent. 5.01. 85
troyan drab, and uses the traitor calchas' tent. 5.01. 97 P

CALCHAS 3 FR 0.0003 REL FR 3 V 0 P
calchas shall have | what he requests of us. TRO 3.03. 31
in what place of the field doth calchas keep? 4.05.278
diomed. calchas, i think. where's your daughter? 5.02. 3

CALCULATE 2 FR 0.0002 REL FR 2 V 0 P
a cunning man did calculate my birth | and told 2H6 4.01. 34
why old men, fools, and children calculate, JC 1.03. 65

/CALEN 1 FR 0.0001 REL FR 0 V 1 P
/calen /o custure me! H5 4.04. 4 P

CALENDAR 9 FR 0.0010 REL FR 4 V 5 P
a calendar, a calendar! MND 3.01. 53 P
a calendar, a calendar! 3.01. 53 P
be found in the calendar of my past endeavors, AWW 1.03. 4 P
be set | among the high tides in the calendar? JN 3.01. 86
give me a calendar. R3 5.03.276
look in the calendar, and bring me word. JC 2.01. 42
hour | stand aye accursed in the calendar! MAC 4.01.134
of him, he is the card or calendar of gentry; HAM 5.02.109 P
be a day fits you, search out of the calendar, PER 2.01. 54 P

CALENDARS 1 FR 0.0001 REL FR 1 V 0 P
both, | and you the calendars of their nativity, ERR 5.01.405

CALF* *(also cauf)*

CALF* 17 FR 0.0019 REL FR 12 V 5 P
it baes will never answer a calf when he bleats. ADO 3.03. 71 P
and got a calf in that same noble feat | much 5.04. 50
he clepeth a calf, "cauf"; LLL 5.01. 22 P
"veal," quoth the dutchman. is not veal a calf? 5.02.247
a calf, fair lady! 5.02.248
no, a fair lord calf. 5.02.248
then die a calf, before your horns do grow. 5.02.253
more calf, certain. 5.02.640 P
the heckfer, and the calf | are all call'd neat. WT 1.02.124
how now, you wanton calf, | art thou my calf? 1.02.126
how now, you wanton calf, | art thou my calf? 1.02.127
your father might have kept | this calf, bred JN 1.01.124
and as the butcher takes away the calf | and 2H6 3.01.210
an ox, and iniquity's throat cut like a calf. 4.02. 27 P
as fox to lamb, or wolf to heifer's calf, | pard TRO 3.02.193
they never do beget a coal–black calf. TIT 5.01. 32
part of him to kill so capital a calf there. HAM 3.02.106 P

CALF–LIKE 1 FR 0.0001 REL FR 1 V 0 P
that calf–like they my lowing follow'd through TMP 4.01.179

CALF'S–HEAD *(see calve's–head)*

CALF'S–SKIN *(see calve's–skin)*

CALIBAN *(also 'ban, ca–caliban)*

CALIBAN 10 FR 0.0011 REL FR 10 V 0 P
yes — caliban her son. TMP 1.02.284
he, that caliban | whom now i keep in service. 1.02.285
we'll visit caliban my slave, who never | yields 1.02.308
caliban! 1.02.313
shapes as he, | having seen but him and caliban. 1.02.480
wench, | to th' most of men this is a caliban, 1.02.481
of the beast caliban and his confederates 4.01.140
spirit, | we must prepare to meet with caliban. 4.01.166
island | thine own for ever, and i, thy caliban, 4.01.218
set caliban and his companions free; 5.01.252

CALIBANS 1 FR 0.0001 REL FR 1 V 0 P
i had peopled else | this isle with calibans. TMP 1.02.351

CALIPOLIS 1 FR 0.0001 REL FR 1 V 0 P
then feed and be fat, my fair calipolis. 2H4 2.04.179

CALIVER 3 FR 0.0003 REL FR 0 V 3 P
fear the report of a caliver worse than a struck 1H4 4.02. 19 P
put me a caliver into wart's hand, bardolph. 2H4 3.02.270 P
come manage me your caliver. 3.02.273 P

CALKINS 1 FR 0.0001 REL FR 1 V 0 P
which the calkins | did rather tell than trample TNK 5.04. 55

/CALL 5 FR 0.0005 REL FR 2 V 3 P
/call /i the deer the princess kill'd a pricket. LLL 4.02. 52 P
/know /not /now /what /name /to /call /myself! R2 4.01.259
/the /common /stages — /so /they /call /them — HAM 2.02.343 P
/dost /thou /call /me /fool, /boy? LR 1.04.148 P
/with /her — /as /far /as /we /call /hers. 5.01. 13

CALL 592 FR 0.0669 REL FR 430 V 162 P
thou mightst call him | a goodly person. TMP 1.02.416
i might call him | a thing divine, for nothing 1.02.418
doth thy other mouth call me? 2.02. 97 P
have i seen | more that i may call men than you, 3.01. 51
do not approach | till thou dost hear me call. 4.01. 50
sir, whom to call brother | would even infect my 5.01.130
much weaker | than you may call to comfort you; 5.01.147
should wrangle, | and i would call it fair play. 5.01.175
so, by your circumstance, you call me fool. TGV 1.01. 36
it were a shame to call her back again, | and 1.02. 51
to call lucetta back | and ask remission for my 1.02. 64
why, sir, who bade you call her? 2.01. 9 P
come; come away, man — i was sent to call thee. 2.03. 55 P
sir — call me what thou dar'st. 2.03. 57 P
call her divine. 2.04.147
fie, fie, unreverend tongue, to call her bad, 2.06. 14
but when i call to mind your gracious favors 3.01. 6
a sea of melting pearl, which some call tears; 3.01.226
go to thy lady's grave and call hers thence, 4.02.116
silvia | entreated me to call and know her mind. 4.03. 2
"convey," the wise it call. WIV 1.03. 29 P
my master (i may call him my master, look you, 1.04. 94 P
"boarding," call you it? 2.01. 90 P
call him in. 2.02.150 P
yet i wrong him to call him poor. 2.02.271 P
what do you call your knight's name, sirrah? 3.02. 20 P
in the brew–house, and when i suddenly call you, 3.03. 11 P
be not amaz'd, call all your senses to you, 3.03.118 P
call your men, mistress ford. 3.03.143 P
call her in. 3.05. 24 P
fast enough of themselves, and to call "horum," 4.01. 67 P
somebody call my wife. 4.02.116 P
ay, sir; i'll call /them to you. 4.05. 7 P
go, knock and call; 4.05. 9 P
i'll call. 4.05. 16 P
call hither, | i say, bid come before us angelo. MM 1.01. 14
call it so. 1.02.140
i, that do speak a word, | may call it again. 2.02. 58
nay, call us ten times frail, | for we are soft 2.04.128
for thine own bowels, which do call thee /sire, 3.01. 29
at that place call upon me, and dispatch with 3.01.266 P
i am bound to call upon you, and i pray you your 3.02.158 P
may be i will call upon you anon for some 4.01. 23 P
heavy | middle of the night to call upon him. 4.01. 35
do you call, sir? 4.02. 21 P
but that you have a hanging look — do you call, 4.02. 34 P
call hither barnardine and claudio. 4.02. 60 P
call your executioner, and off with barnardine's 4.02.206 P
i'll call you at your house. 4.04. 16 P
go call at flavio's house, | and tell him where 4.05. 6
call that same isabel here once again, i would 5.01.269 P
speak not you to him till we call upon you. 5.01.286 P
to call him villain, and then to glance from him 5.01.309
sconce call you it? ERR 2.02. 35 P
thyself i call it, being strange to me, | that, 2.02.121
how can she thus then call us by our names, 2.02.166
comfort my sister, cheer her, call her /wife: 3.02. 26
why call you me love? call my sister so. 3.02. 59
why call you me love? call my sister so. 3.02. 59
call thyself sister, sweet, for i am thee: 3.02. 66
she that doth call me husband, even my soul 3.02.158
friend, | and every one doth call me by my name: 4.03. 3
let's call more help | to have them bound again. 4.04.145
go call the abbess hither. 5.01.281
and so do i, yet did she call me so; 5.01.373
her sister here, | did call me brother. 5.01.375
her chamber–window, hear me call margaret hero, ADO 2.02. 43 P
let us send her to call him in to dinner. 2.03.218 P
him go, and presently call the rest of the watch 3.03. 29 P
well, you are to call at all the alehouses, and 3.03. 42 P
you must call to the nurse and bid her still it. 3.03. 66 P
be any matter of weight chances, call up me. 3.03. 85 P
call up the right master constable. 3.03.166 P
what kind of catechising call you this? 4.01. 78
call me a fool, | trust not my reading, nor my 4.01.164
you must call forth the watch that are their 4.02. 34 P
perjury, to call a prince's brother villain. 4.02. 42 P
plaintiff here, the offender, did call me ass. 5.01.306 P
and so i pray thee call beatrice; 5.02. 16 P
well, i will call beatrice to you, who i think 5.02. 23 P
to call young claudio to a reckoning for it. 5.04. 9
call her forth, brother, here's the friar ready. 5.04. 39
which the base vulgar do call three. LLL 1.02. 48 P
berowne they call him, but a merrier man, 2.01. 66
name her name, | and rosaline they call her. 3.01.167
do not call it sin in me, | that i am forsworn 4.03.113
as it were, too peregrinate, as i may call it. 5.01. 14 P
which he would call "abbominable"; 5.01. 24 P
which the rude multitude call the afternoon. 5.01. 90 P
you were best call it "daughter–beamed eyes." 5.02.172
the ladies call him sweet; 5.02.329
i dare not call them fools; 5.02.371
call them forth quickly, we will do so. 5.02.889 P
call you me fair? MND 1.01.181
you were best to call them generally, man by man 1.02. 2 P
quince, call forth your actors by the scroll. 1.02. 14 P
answer as i call you. nick bottom, the weaver. 1.02. 16 P
those, that hobgoblin call you, and sweet puck, 2.01. 40
wound, | and maidens call it love–in–idleness. 2.01.168
to call me goddess, nymph, divine and rare, 3.02.226
titania, music call, and strike more dead | than 4.01. 81
when my cue comes, call me, and i will answer. 4.01.200 P
call philostrate. 5.01. 38
else the puck a liar call. 5.01.435
hearing them, would call their brothers fools. MV 1.01. 99
you call me misbeliever, cut–throat dog, | and 1.03.111
i am as like to call thee so again, | to spet on 1.03.130
who bids thee call? i do not bid thee call. 2.05. 7
who bids thee call? i do not bid thee call. 2.05. 7
call you? what is your will? 2.05. 10
the goodwins, i think they call the place, a 3.01. 4 P
he was wont to call me usurer, let him look to 3.01. 48 P
first go with me to church and call me wife, 3.02.303
go one, and call the jew into the court. 4.01. 14
bring us the letters; call the messenger. 4.01.110
for call you that keeping for a gentleman of my AYL 1.01. 9 P
call him in. 1.01. 93 P
call him hither, good monsieur le beau. 1.02.163 P
did you call, sir? 1.02.253
what shall i call thee when thou art a man? 1.03.123
page, | and therefore look you call me ganymed. 1.03.125
son | (yet not the son, i will not call him son) 2.03. 20
son) | of him i was about to call his father — 2.03. 21
call you 'em stanzos? 2.05. 18 P
but that they call compliment is like th' 2.05. 26 P
a greek invocation, to call fools into a circle. 2.05. 59 P
he, | "call me not fool till heaven hath sent me 2.07. 19
lands and all things that thou dost call thine 3.01. 9
if you would but call me rosalind and come every 3.02.426 P
nay, you must call me rosalind. 3.02.434 P
it pleases him to call you so; 4.01. 66 P
and the most unworthy of her you call rosalind, 4.01.194 P
call you this railing? 4.03. 43
call you this chiding? 4.03. 64
youth | that he in sport doth call his rosalind. 4.03.156
neither call the giddiness of it in question, 5.02. 5 P
chamber, | and call him madam, do him obeisance. SHR in.1. 108
i long to hear him call the drunkard husband, in.1. 133
sly, call not me honor nor lordship. in.2. 5 P
call home thy ancient thoughts from banishment, in.2. 31
sometimes you would call out for cicely hacket. in.2. 89
are you my wife and will not call me husband? in.2. 104
my men should call me "lord"; in.2. 105
i know it well. what must i call her? in.2. 108
madam, and nothing else — so lords call ladies. in.2. 111
she may perhaps call him half a score knaves or 1.02.110 P
what may i call your name? 2.01. 67
devilish spirit, | "frets, call you these?" 2.01.152
while she did call me rascal fiddler | and 2.01.157
they call me katherine that do talk of me. 2.01.184
call you me daughter? 2.01.285
call you this gamouth? 3.01. 79
but so it is, my haste doth call me hence, | and 3.02.187
call forth nathaniel, joseph, nicholas, philip, 4.01. 89 P
call them forth. 4.01. 97 P
i call them forth to credit her. 4.01.104 P
to make her come and know her keeper's call, 4.01.194
go call my men, and let us straight to him, 4.03.184
this is the house, please it you that i call? 4.04. 1
and if you please to call it a rush–candle, 4.05. 14
call forth an officer. 5.01. 91 P
fie, what a foolish duty call you this? 5.02.125
all | that happiness and prime can happy call. AWW 2.01.182
go call before me all the lords in court. 2.03. 46
not worth another word, else i'd call you knave. 2.03.263 P
body that i am father to, then call me husband; 3.02. 59 P
might tend upon | and call her hourly mistress. 3.02. 83
well, call him hither, | we are reconcil'd, and 5.03. 20
that you call in question the continuance of his TN 1.04. 6 P
as thy lord, | to call his fortunes thine. 1.04. 40
let him approach. call in my gentlewoman. 1.05.163 P
gate, | and call upon my soul within the house; 1.05.269
bore a mind that envy could not but call fair. 2.01. 29 P
i shall be constrain'd in't to call thee knave, 2.03. 66 P
time i have constrain'd one to call me knave. 2.03. 68 P
if thou hast her not i' th' end, call me cut. 2.03.187 P
i knew 'twas i, for many do call me fool. 2.05. 81 P
we'll call thee at the cubiculo. go. 3.02. 52 P
go call him hither. 3.04. 14
admire not in thy mind, why i do call thee so, 3.04.151 P
i'll call sir toby the whilst. 4.02. 3 P
i call thee by the most modest terms, for i am 4.02. 31 P
call forth the holy father. 5.01.142
which i'll not call a creature of thy place, WT 2.01. 83
beseech your highness call the queen again. 2.01.126
the keeper of the prison, call to him; 2.02. 1
i pray now call her. | withdraw yourselves. 2.02. 14
all doubt | you'ld call your children yours. 2.03. 82
i'll not call you tyrant; 2.03.116
she durst not call me so, | if she did know me 2.03.123
to see this bastard kneel | and call me father? 2.03.156
i'll not be long before | i call upon thee. 3.03. 9
some call him autolycus. 4.03.100 P
gillyvors, | which some call nature's bastards. 4.04. 83
in gillyvors, | and do not call them bastards. 4.04. 99
they call him doricles, and boasts himself | to 4.04.168
they call themselves saltiers, and they have a 4.04.326 P
and call this | your lack of love or bounty, you 4.04.353
divorce, young sir, | whom son i dare not call. 4.04.418
so call it; 4.04.486
that i may call thee something more than man 4.04.535
now meet my father, | he would not call me son. 4.04.658
let him call me rogue for being so far officious 4.04.839 P
(his very air) that i should call you brother, 5.01.128

i am thy grandame, richard, call me so. JN 1.01.168
and if his name be george, i'll call him peter; 1.01.186
call for our chiefest men of discipline | to 2.01. 39
who is it thou dost call usurper, france? 2.01.120
of heaven and earth, | call not me slanderer! 2.01.175
then tell us, shall your city call us lord, | in 2.01.263
call the lady constance; 2.01.553
away his natural cause | and call them meteors, 3.04.157
they would be as a call | to train ten thousand 3.04.174
my love was crafty love, | and call it cunning. 4.01. 54
then call them to our presence; R2 1.01. 15
call him a slanderous coward, and a villain, 1.01. 61
call it not patience, gaunt, it is despair. 1.02. 29
call it a travel that thou tak'st for pleasure. 1.03.262
i brought high herford, if you call him so, 1.04. 3
when time shall call him home from banishment, 1.04. 21
call in the letters–patents that he hath | by 2.01.202
for him, | unless you call it good to pity him, 2.01.236
barkloughly castle call they this at hand? 3.02. 1
o, call back yesterday, bid time return, | and 3.02. 69
and nothing can we call our own but death, | and 3.02.152
shall we call back northumberland, and send 3.03.129
call forth bagot. 4.01. 1
my lord of herford here, whom you call king, 4.01.134
and, madam, you must call him rutland now. 5.02. 43
did i ever call for thee to pay thy part? 1H4 1.02. 51 P
an' i do not, call me villain and baffle me. 1.02.101 P
in richard's time — what do you call the place? 1.03.242
neighbor mugs, we'll call up the gentlemen. 2.01. 44 P
are up already, and call for eggs and butter. 2.01. 59 P
and can call them all by their christen names, 2.04. 7 P
a good boy (by the lord, so they call me!), 2.04. 13 P
they call drinking deep, dyeing scarlet, and 2.04. 15 P
away, you rogue, dost thou not hear them call? 2.04. 79 P
i prithee call in falstaff. 2.04.109 P
call in ribs, call in tallow. 2.04.111 P
call in ribs, call in tallow. 2.04.111 P
ye fat paunch, and ye call me coward, by the 2.04.144 P
i call thee coward! 2.04.146 P
i'll see thee damn'd ere i call thee coward, but 2.04.147 P
call you that backing of your friends? 2.04.150 P
i know not what you call all, but if i fought 2.04.185 P
tell thee a lie, spit in my face, call me horse. 2.04.194 P
of a welsh hook — what a plague call you him? 2.04.339 P
never call a true piece of gold a counterfeit. 2.04.491 P
call in the sheriff. 2.04.505 P
go call him forth. 2.04.527 P
i can call spirits from the vasty deep. 3.01. 52
but will they come when you do call for them? 3.01. 54
and i will call him to so strict account | that 3.02.149
what call you rich? 3.03. 77 P
aside, thou art a knave to call me so. 3.03.121 P
unless you call three fingers in the ribs bare. 4.02. 73 P
what, to york? call him back again. 2H4 1.02. 64 P
and will you yet call yourself young? 1.02.185 P
wife, come in then and call me gossip quickly? 2.01. 94 P
saying that ere long they should call me madam? 2.01.101 P
you call honorable boldness impudent sauciness; 2.01.123 P
for fault of a better, to call my friend — i 2.02. 42 P
fire–brand, and therefore i call him her dream. 2.02. 90 P
call him up, drawer. 2.04.100 P
cheater, call you him? 2.04.102 P
me, and call me pantler and bread–chipper, and i 2.04.314 P
go call the earls of surrey and of warwick; 3.01. 1
phrase call you it? 3.02. 74 P
let them appear as i call; 3.02. 99 P
or to the place of diff'rence call the swords 4.01.179
call in the powers, good cousin westmerland. 4.03. 25
that may do me good, and call it what you will. 4.03. 60 P
call for the music in the other room. 4.05. 4
doth the king call? 4.05. 48
now call we our high court of parliament, | and 5.02.134
if thou want'st any thing, and wilt not call, 5.03. 56 P
shall we call in th' ambassador, my liege? H5 1.02. 3
call in the messengers sent from the dolphin. 1.02.221
he'll call you to so hot an answer of it | that 2.04.123
they will steal any thing, and call it purchase. 3.02. 42 P
and the trumpet call us to the breach, and we 3.02.108 P
poor we call them in their native lords! 3.05. 26
what do you call him? 3.06. 17 P
horse, and all other jades you may call beasts. 3.07. 24 P
you may call the business of the master the 4.01.153 P
what call you the town's name where alexander 4.07. 12 P
they call it agincourt. 4.07. 89
then call we this the field of agincourt, 4.07. 90
call yonder fellow hither. 4.07.118
call him hither to me, soldier. 4.07.151 P
that i kiss your hand, and i call you my queen. 5.02.251 P
these tidings would call forth her flowing tides 1H6 1.01. 83
speak, shall i call her in? 1.02. 58
go call her in. 1.02. 60
i'll call for clubs, if you will not away. 1.03. 84
princely train | call ye the warlike talbot, for 2.02. 35
call we to mind, and mark but this for proof: 3.03. 68
be humble to us, call my sovereign yours, | and 4.02. 6
o, that i could but call these dead to life, 4.07. 81
yet call th' embassadors, and as you please, 5.01. 24
i'll call for pen and ink, and write my mind. 5.03. 66
then call our captains and our colors forth, 5.03.128
to call them both a pair of crafty knaves. 2H6 1.02.103
what call you this? 1.04. 49
oft | myself have heard a voice to call him so. 2.01. 92
and call these foul offenders to their answers, 2.01.199
if it be fond, call it a woman's fear; 3.01. 36
go call our uncle to our presence straight. 3.02. 15
i'll call him presently, my noble lord. 3.02. 18
ungentle queen, to call him gentle suffolk! 3.02.290
normans thorough thee | disdain to call us lord, 4.01. 88
they call false caterpillars, and intend their 4.04. 37
be wise, he'll never call ye jack cade more. 4.06. 9 P
to call poor men before them about matters they 4.07. 41 P
king did i call thee? 5.01. 93
sirrah, call in my /sons to be my bail. 5.01.111
call hither clifford, bid him come amain, | to 5.01.114
look in a glass, and call thy image so. 5.01.142
call hither to the stake my two brave bears, 5.01.144
call buckingham, and bid him arm himself. 5.01.192
call buckingham, and all the friends thou hast, 5.01.193
london, | to call a present court of parliament. 5.03. 25
and call them pillars that will stand to us; 3H6 2.03. 51
can neither call it perfect day nor night. 2.05. 4
no bending knee will call thee caesar now, | no 3.01. 18
your grace my sons should call you father. 3.02.100
no more than when my daughters call thee mother. 3.02.101
for shame, leave henry, and call edward king. 3.03.100
call him my king by whose injurious doom | my 3.03.101
call edward king and at his hands beg mercy? 5.01. 23
down, | call warwick patron, and be penitent? 5.01. 27
thou wilt, if warwick call. 5.01. 80
this word "love," which greybeards call divine, 5.06. 81
were it to call king edward's widow sister, | i R3 1.01.109
i call thee not. 1.03.233
madam, his majesty doth call for you, | and for 1.03.319
and call us orphans, wretches, castaways, | if 2.02. 6
well, my dread lord — so must i call you now. 3.01. 97
i would, that i might thank you as you call me. 3.01.123
this edward, whom our manners call the prince. 3.07.191
call him again, sweet prince, accept their suit. 3.07.221
call them again. 3.07.224
go call him hither, boy. 4.02. 41
this fair alliance quickly shall call home | to 4.04.313
familiarly shall call thy dorset brother; 4.04.316
therefore, dear mother — i must call you so — 4.04.412
call for some men of sound direction: 5.03. 16
call up lord stanley, bid him bring his power. 5.03.290
he is attach'd, | call him to present trial. H8 1.02.211
call him bounteous buckingham, | the mirror of 2.01. 52
prithee call gardiner to me, my new secretary. 2.02.115
call to mind | that i have been your wife in 2.04. 34
call her again. 2.04.125
made to the queen to call back her appeal | she 2.04.235
to heaven, is all | i dare now call mine own. 3.02.454
you must no more call it york–place, that's past 4.01. 95
it is not you i call for; 4.02. 85
i must to bed, | call in more women. 4.02.167
(when heaven shall call her from this cloud of 5.04. 44
call here my varlet, i'll unarm again. TRO 1.01. 1
blood, nephew to hector, | they call him ajax. 1.02. 14
and call them shames which are indeed nought 1.03. 19
they tax our policy, and call it cowardice, 1.03.197
they call this bed–work, mapp'ry, closet–war, 1.03.205
one voice | call agamemnon head and general. 1.03.222
sir, you of troy, call you yourself aeneas? 1.03.245
and will to–morrow with his trumpet call, 1.03.277
to–morrow morning call some knight to arms 2.01.124
you may call it melancholy, if you will favor 2.03. 87 P
and this noble state | to call upon him. 2.03.110
shall i call you father? 2.03.256
general | to call together all his state of war. 2.03.260
you, that if the king call for him at supper, 3.01. 77 P
too, if she call your activity in question. 3.02. 56 P
call them all pandars. 3.02.202 P
time prompts me aloud | to call for recompense. 3.03. 3
go call thersites hither, sweet patroclus. 3.03.234
(or rather call my thought a certain knowledge) 4.01. 42
then, sweet my lord, i'll call mine uncle down, 4.02. 2
(which i beseech you call a virtuous sin) 4.04. 81
in this i do not call your faith in question 4.04. 84
they call him troilus, and on him erect | a 4.05.108
aeneas, call my brother troilus to me, | and 4.05.154
spout | which shipmen do the hurricano call, 5.02.172
cassandra, call my father to persuade. 5.03. 30
and call him noble, that was now your hate; COR 1.01.183
methinks i see him stamp thus, and call thus: 1.03. 32
call thither all the officers a' th' town, 1.05. 27
call him hither. 1.06. 41
for what he did before corioles, call him, 1.09. 63
as you are (i cannot call you lycurguses), if 2.01. 55 P
coriolanus must i call thee? 2.01.174
we call a nettle but a nettle, and | the faults 2.01.190
call coriolanus. 2.02.130
he himself stuck not to call us the many–headed 2.03. 16 P
and make the rabble | call our cares fears; 3.01.137
go call the people, in whose name myself 3.01.173
who was wont | to call them woollen vassals, 3.02. 9
call me their traitor, thou injurious tribune! 3.03. 69
prithee call my master to him. 4.05. 21 P
yet one time he did call me by my name. 5.01. 9
call all your tribes together, praise the gods, 5.05. 2
it your honors | to call me to your senate, i'll 5.06.139
rape call you it, my lord, to seize my own, | my TIT 1.01.405
go home, call for sweet water, wash thy hands. 2.04. 6
she hath no tongue to call, nor hands to wash, 2.04. 7
let fools do good, and fair men call for grace, 3.01.204
power pities wretched tears, | to that i call! 3.01.209
me, | or else i'll call my brother back again, 5.02.135
what boots it thee to call thyself a sun? 5.03. 18
a crutch, a crutch! why call you for a sword? ROM 1.01. 76
'tis the way | to call hers, exquisite, in 1.01.229
call her forth to me. 1.03. 1
call, good mercutio. 2.01. 6
were that kind of fruit | as maids call medlars, 2.01. 36
that which we call a rose | by any other word 2.02. 43
call me but love, and i'll be new baptiz'd; 2.02. 50
i have forgot why i did call thee back. 2.02.170
he dare, | it is enough i may but call her mine. 2.06. 8
your worship in that sense may call him man. 3.01. 59
prince, and call thee back | with twenty hundred 3.03.152
very late that we | may call it early by and by. 3.04. 35
o fortune, fortune, all men call thee fickle; 3.05. 60
for still thy eyes, which i may call the sea, 3.05.132
no help, | do thou but call my resolution wise, 4.01. 53
i'll call them back again to comfort me. 4.03. 17
they call for dates and quinces in the pastry. 4.04. 2
call peter, he will show thee where they are. 4.04. 17
call help. 4.05. 21
o lord, they fight! i will go call the watch. 5.03. 71
which their keepers call | a lightning before 5.03. 89
o, how may i | call this a lightning? 5.03. 91
on him, | and then i ran away to call the watch. 5.03.285
most noble timon, call the man before thee. TIM 1.01.113
i call the gods to witness, i will choose | mine 1.01.137
why dost thou call them knaves? 1.01.181
my father's age, | and call him to long peace. 1.02. 3
or properer can we call our own than the riches 1.02.102 P
i'll tell you true, i'll call to you. 1.02.217
awak'd by great occasion | to call upon his own, 2.02. 22
call me before th' exactest auditors, | and set 2.02.156
who can call him | his friend that dips in the 3.02. 65
call him, call him. 3.04. 42
call him, call him. 3.04. 42
call me to your remembrances. 3.05. 91
most vicious strain, | and call it excellent. 4.03.214
call the creatures | whose naked natures live in 4.03.227
when it is lighted, come and call me here. JC 2.01. 8
call it my fear | that keeps you in the house, 2.02. 50
remember that you call on me to–day; 2.02.122
here, | and call in question our necessities. 4.03.165
call claudio and some other of my men, | i'll 4.03.242
so call the field to rest, and let's away, | to 5.05. 80
he bade me, from him, call thee thane of cawdor; MAC 1.03.105
lest occasion call us | and show us to be 2.02. 67
he did command me to call timely on him, | i 2.03. 46
i'll make so bold to call, | for 'tis my limited 2.03. 51
ay, my good lord. our time does call upon 's. 3.01. 36
now go to the door, and stay there till we call. 3.01. 72
i'll call upon you straight; 3.01.139
call 'em; let me see 'em. 4.01. 63
it, when none can call our pow'r to accompt? 5.01. 38 P
that lesser hate him | do call it valiant fury; 5.02. 14
do you believe his tenders, as you call them? HAM 1.03.103
ay, fashion you may call it. go to, go to. 1.03.112
i'll call thee hamlet, | king, father, royal 1.04. 44
so call it, | sith nor th' exterior nor the 2.02. 5
mad call i it, for, to define true madness, 2.02. 93
if you call me jephthah, my lord, i have a 2.02.411 P
what do you call the play? 3.02.236 P
call me what instrument you will, though you 3.02.370 P
liege, | i'll call upon you ere you go to bed, 3.03. 34
you cannot call it love, for at your age | the 3.04. 68
pinch wanton on your cheek, call you his mouse, 3.04.183
we'll call up our wisest friends | and let them 4.01. 38
the rabble call him lord, | and, as the world 4.05.103
"a–down, a–down," and you call him a–down–a. 4.05.172 P
we may call it herb of grace a' sundays. 4.05.182 P
our crown, our life, and all that we call ours, 4.05.209
uncharge the practice, | and call it accident. 4.07. 68
cull–cold maids do dead men's fingers call them. 4.07.171
what call you the carriages? 5.02.154 P
why is this all /impawn'd, /as you call it? 5.02.164 P
hear it, | and call the noblest to the audience. 5.02.387
call france. LR 1.01.126
call burgundy. 1.01.127
and like a sister am most loath to call | your 1.01.270
your countenance which i would fain call master. 1.04. 28 P
go you and call my fool hither. 1.04. 43 P
call the clotpole back. 1.04. 46 P
go you call hither my fool. 1.04. 77 P
then necessity | will call discreet proceeding. 1.04.214
call my train together! 1.04.253
since i came hither | (which i can call but now) 2.01. 87
why dost thou call him knave? what is his fault? 2.02. 89
call not your stocks for me, i serve the king, 2.02.128
in my flesh, | which i must needs call mine. 2.04.223
let shame come when it will, i do not call it. 2.04.226
but yet i call you servile ministers, | that 3.02. 21
you, | i pray desire her call her wisdom to her. 4.05. 35
well stand up, | and call itself your brother. 5.03. 66
call by the trumpet; 5.03. 99
why he appears | upon this call o' th' trumpet. 5.03.119
call up her father. OTH 1.01. 67
here is her father's house, i'll call aloud. 1.01. 74
call up all my people! 1.01.141
call up my brother. 1.01.175
at every house i'll call | (i may command at 1.01.180
course of direct session | call thee to answer. 1.02. 87
i take this that you call love to be a sect or 1.03.332 P
here, at the door; i pray you call them in. 2.03. 46 P
no name to be known by, let us call thee devil! 2.03.282 P
i prithee call him back. 3.03. 51
good love, call him back. 3.03. 54
that we can call these delicate creatures ours, 3.03.269
he did not call; 4.01.230
i do beseech your lordship call her back. 4.01.249
our full senate | call all in all sufficient? 4.01.265
and call thy husband hither. 4.02.106
why should he call her whore? 4.02.137
and /mak'st me call what i intend to do | a 5.02. 64
call in the messengers. ANT 1.01. 29
we cannot call her winds and waters sighs and 1.02.147 P
the dryness of his bones | call on him for't. 1.04. 28
the east, | say thou, shall call her mistress." 1.05. 47
call the slave again, | though i am mad, i will 2.05. 79
call! 2.05. 80
sat | caesarion, whom they call my father's son, 3.06. 6
already, will their good thoughts call from him. 3.06. 21
that ever i should call thee castaway! 3.06. 40
call to me | all my sad captains, fill our bowls 3.13.182
call all his noble captains to my lord. 3.13.188
call forth my household servants, let's to–night 4.02. 9
call for enobarbus, | he shall not hear thee, or 4.05. 7
too late, good diomed. call my guard, i prithee. 4.14.128
methinks i hear | antony call; 5.02.284
that i might hear thee call great caesar ass 5.02.307
there's dolabella sent from caesar; call him. 5.02.324
though your attempt (as you call it) deserve CYM 1.04.118 P
call my women. 1.05. 74
awake by four o' th' clock, | i prithee call me. 2.02. 7
do you call me fool? 2.03.101
if you will make't an action, call witness to't. 2.03.151
most venerable man which i | did call my father, 2.05. 4
a storm or robbery (call it what you will) 3.03. 62
call her before us, for | we have been too 3.05. 34
i were best not call; 3.06. 19
i dare not call; 3.06. 19
that call me father | and think they are my sons 5.05.328
this gentleman, whom i call polydore, | most 5.05.357
my lord of rome, | call forth your soothsayer. 5.05.426
which we call mollis aer, and mollis aer | we 5.05.447
doth your highness call? PER 1.01.150
when all, for mine, if i may call offense, 1.02. 92
the good simonides, do you call him? 2.01.101
call it by what you will, the day is /yours, 2.03. 13
doth my lord call? 3.02. 2

and hundreds call themselves | your creatures, 3.02. 44
and though you call my course unnatural, | you 4.03. 36
well, call forth, call forth. 4.06. 33 P
well, call forth, call forth. 4.06. 33 P
that he have his. call up some gentlemen. 5.01. 6
doth your lordship call? 5.01. 8
thou dost startle me | to call thyself marina. 5.01.147
call | and give them repetition to the /life. 5.01.245
he shall see thebes again and call to arms | the TNK 2.02.248
sir, they call | the scatter'd to the banket. 3.01.108
if he not answer'd, i should call a wolf, | and 3.02. 10
of his gyves | might call fell things to listen, 3.02. 15
and i have heard some call him arcite, and — 3.03. 32
else, | to call the maids and pay the minstrels, 4.01.111
i were a beast and i'ld call it good sport. 4.03. 52 P
to call the fiercest tyrant from his rage, | and 5.01. 78
and call your lovers from the stage of death, 5.04.123
doth call himself affection's sentinel, | gives VEN 650
"call it not love, for love to heaven is fled, 793
shrill–tongu'd tapsters answering every call, 849
even in the moment that we call them ours. LUC 868
then call them not the authors of their ill, 1244
the one doth call her his, the other his, | yet 1793
one be prodigal, | bountiful they will him call; PP 20.38
youngly thou bestow'st | thou mayst call thine, SON 11. 4
love, my love, that thou mayst true love call, 40. 3
as call it winter, which, being full of care, 56.13
whilst i alone did call upon thy aid, | my verse 79. 1
for nothing this wide universe i call, | save 109.13
repay, | forgot upon your dearest love to call, 117. 3
to this i witness call the fools of time, 124.13
o, call not me to justify the wrong | that thy 139. 1
who hateth thee that i do call my friend? 149. 5
no want of conscience hold it that i call | her 151.13

CALLAT *(also callet, callot)*

CALLAT 1 FR 0.0001 REL FR 1 V 0 P
a callat | of boundless tongue, who late hath WT 2.03. 91

/CALL'D 1 FR 0.0001 REL FR 1 V 0 P
/and /call'd /it //rouge–mount, /at /which /name R3 4.02.105

CALL'D 207 FR 0.0234 REL FR 151 V 56 P
my brother and thy uncle, call'd antonio — | i TMP 1.02. 66
i have from their confines call'd to enact | my 4.01.121
you nymphs, call'd naiades, of the windring 4.01.128
noontide sun, call'd forth the mutinous winds, 5.01. 42
be gone, and come when you are call'd. WIV 3.03. 20 P
were call'd forth by their mistress to carry me 3.05. 98 P
let him be call'd before us. MM 3.02.205 P
who call'd here of late? 4.02. 74
he is call'd up. 4.02. 91
or diviner laid claim to me, call'd me dromio, ERR 3.02.141 P
even now a tailor call'd me in his shop, | and 4.03. 7
is not your name, sir, call'd antipholus? 5.01.287
the man | that hadst a wife once call'd aemilia, 5.01.343
much honor on a young florentine call'd claudio. ADO 1.01. 11 P
him be clapp'd on the shoulder, and call'd adam. 1.01.259 P
that jealousy shall be call'd assurance, and all 2.02. 49 P
you have been always call'd a merciful man, 3.03. 61 P
beatrice, wouldst thou come when i call'd thee? 5.02. 42 P
then call'd you for the l'envoy. LLL 3.01.107 P
to a lady of france that he call'd rosaline. 4.01.105
his heart, | and trow you what he call'd me? 5.02.279
and knavish sprite | call'd robin goodfellow. MND 2.01. 34
it shall be call'd "bottom's dream," because it 4.01.215 P
it was bassanio — as i think, so was he call'd. MV 1.02.116 P
me such a day, another time | you call'd me dog; 1.03.128
but what will you /be call'd? AYL 1.03.126
it may well be call'd jove's tree, when it drops 3.02.236 P
beasts, which in all tongues are call'd fools. 5.04. 38 P
this is call'd the retort courteous. 5.04. 72 P
this is call'd the quip modest. 5.04. 75 P
this is call'd the reply churlish. 5.04. 76 P
this is call'd the reproof valiant. 5.04. 78 P
this is call'd the countercheck quarrelsome; 5.04. 80 P
pray have you not a daughter | call'd katherina, SHR 2.01. 43
i have a daughter, sir, call'd katherina. 2.01. 44
lie, in faith, for you are call'd plain kate, 2.01.185
suppos'd lucentio | must get a father, call'd — 2.01.408
was ajax, call'd so from his grandfather. 3.01. 53
and therefore 'tis call'd a sensible tale; 4.01. 64 P
know, sir, that i am call'd hortensio. 4.02. 21
my name is call'd vincentio, my dwelling pisa, 4.05. 55
how call'd you the man you speak of, madam? AWW 1.01. 24 P
i cannot give thee less, to be call'd grateful. 2.01.129
be the officer at a place there call'd mile–end, 4.03.270 P
that scorn'd to serve | humbly call'd mistress. 5.03. 19
she call'd the saints to surety | that she would 5.03.108
my name is sebastian, which i call'd rodorigo; TN 2.01. 17 P
if my lady have not call'd up her steward 2.03. 73 P
alas, their love may be call'd appetite, | no 2.04. 97
since lowly feigning was call'd compliment. 3.01. 99
none can be call'd deform'd but the unkind. 3.04.368
and since you call'd me master for so long, 5.01.324
the heckfer, and the calf | are all call'd neat. WT 1.02.125
this news, which is call'd true, is so like an 5.02. 28 P
son took me by the hand, and call'd me brother; 5.02.141 P
and then the two kings call'd my father brother; 5.02.142 P
princess, my sister, call'd my father father; 5.02.143 P
how comes it then that thou art call'd a king, JN 2.01.107
our trumpet call'd you to this gentle parle — 2.01.205
since i first call'd my brother's father dad. 2.01.467
and meritorious shall that hand be call'd, 3.01.176
and this land be call'd | the field of golgotha R2 4.01.143
lay, | and call'd mine percy, his plantagenet! 1H4 1.01. 89
the night's body be call'd thieves of the day'i 1.02. 24 P
thou hast call'd her to a reckoning many a time 1.02. 49 P
he call'd them untaught knaves, unmannerly, | to 1.03. 43
i was never call'd so in mine own house before. 3.03. 63 P
my lord, he call'd you jack, and said he would 3.03.138 P
art thou not asham'd to be call'd captain? 2H4 2.04.141 P
may sleep when the man of action is call'd on. 2.04.377 P
you were call'd lusty shallow then, cousin. 3.02. 16 P
by the mass, i was call'd any thing, and i would 3.02. 17 P
here is two more call'd than your number, you 3.02.188 P
as a monkey, and the whores call'd him mandrake. 3.02.315 P
what is this forest call'd? 4.01. 1
'tis call'd jerusalem, my noble lord. 4.05.234
i would his majesty had call'd me with him; 5.02. 6
the king hath call'd his parliament, my lord. 5.05.103
sala, | is at this day in germany call'd meisen. H5 1.02. 53
that those whom you call'd fathers did beget you 3.01. 23
he is call'd aunchient pistol. 3.06. 18 P
my name is pistol call'd. 4.01. 62
this day is call'd the feast of crispian: 4.03. 40
it is call'd wye at monmouth; 4.07. 28 P
what is this castle call'd that stands hard by? 4.07. 88
you call'd me yesterday mountain–squire, but i 5.01. 35 P
call'd the brave lord ponton de santrailles, 1H6 1.04. 28
they call'd us for our fierceness english dogs, 1.05. 25
call'd for the truce of winchester and 2.04.118
and call'd unto a cardinal's degree? 5.01. 29
an earl i am, and suffolk am i call'd. 5.03. 53
as to be call'd but viceroy of the whole? 5.04.143
being call'd | a hundred times and oft'ner, in 2H6 2.01. 87
beadles in your town, and things call'd whips? 2.01.134
and call'd them blind and dusky spectacles, 3.02.112
how art thou call'd? and what is thy degree? 5.01. 73
the bloody parliament shall this be call'd, 3H6 1.01. 39
(as if a channel should be call'd the sea), 2.02.141
my crown is call'd content, | a crown it is that 3.01. 64
that thou hadst call'd me all these bitter names R3 1.03.235
in common worldly things 'tis call'd ungrateful 2.02. 91
i call'd thee then vain flourish of my fortune; 4.04. 82
i call'd thee then poor shadow, painted queen, 4.04. 83
that call'd your grace | to breakfast once, 4.04.176
you have a daughter call'd elizabeth, | virtuous 4.04.204
nor call'd upon | for high feats done to th' H8 1.01. 60
let be call'd before us | that gentleman of 1.02. 4
madam, you are call'd back. 2.04.128
when you are call'd, return. 2.04.130
katherine no more | shall be call'd queen, but 3.02. 70
'tis now the king's, and call'd whitehall. 4.01. 97
your grace must wait till you be call'd for. 5.02. 7
let it be call'd the wild and wand'ring flood, TRO 1.01.102
here in troy | a prince call'd hector — priam 1.03.261
but modest doubt is call'd | the beacon of the 2.02. 15
goers–between be call'd to the world's end after 3.02.201 P
you have a troyan prisoner call'd antenor, 3.03. 18
hark, you are call'd. 4.04. 50
as thou unworthy to be call'd her servant. 4.04.125
so much | that proof is call'd impossibility. 5.05. 29
let him that will a scritch–owl aye be call'd 5.10. 16
and till we call'd | both field and city ours, COR 2.02.120
he's right noble. | let him be call'd for. 2.02.130
we have been call'd so of many, not that our 2.03. 18 P
as cause had call'd you up, have held him to; 2.03.194
so he might | be call'd your vanquisher. 3.01. 17
for the people, call'd them | time–pleasers, 3.01. 44
and manhood is call'd foolery when it stands 3.01.245
he call'd me father; 5.01. 3
and then they call'd me foul adulteress, TIT 2.03.109
or be ye not henceforth call'd my children. 2.03.115
o tamora, be call'd a gentle queen, | and with 2.03.168
if that be call'd deceit, i will be honest, 3.01.188
are /they thy ministers? what are they call'd? 5.02. 61
supper serv'd up, you call'd, my young lady ROM 1.03.101 P
you are look'd for and call'd for, ask'd for and 1.05. 12 P
so romeo would, were he not romeo call'd, 2.02. 45
thou know'st i do, i call'd thee by thy name. TIM 1.01.186 P
these debts may well be call'd desperate ones, 3.04.102 P
call'd you, my lord? JC 2.01. 6
the tarquin drive when he was call'd a king. 2.01. 54
we shall be call'd purgers, not murderers. 2.01.180
so often shall the knot of us be call'd | the 3.01.117
how far is't call'd to /forres? MAC 1.03. 39
all harms, | was never call'd to bear my part, 3.05. 8
hark, i am call'd; 3.05. 34
'tis call'd the evil: 4.03.146
it cannot | be call'd our mother, but our grave; 4.03.166
still am i call'd. HAM 1.04. 84
of affection, but call'd it an honest method, as 2.02.444 P
came not the slave back to me when i call'd him? LR 1.04. 53 P
i never gave you kingdom, call'd you children; 3.02. 17
modo he's call'd, and mahu. 3.04.144 P
when i inform'd him, then he call'd me sot, 4.02. 8
you have been hotly call'd for; OTH 1.02. 44
too dear, | with that he call'd the tailor lown; 2.03. 92
leave him now till cassio | be call'd to him. 3.04. 33
he call'd her whore. 4.02.120
to be call'd whore? 4.02.127
my mother had a maid call'd barbary; 4.03. 26
"i call'd my love false love; 4.03. 55
hath kill'd a young venetian | call'd roderigo. 5.02.113
name cleopatra as she is call'd in rome. ANT 1.02.106
that call'd me timelier than my purpose hither; 2.06. 51
caesar's sister is call'd octavia. 2.06.109 P
to be call'd into a huge sphere, and not to be 2.07. 14 P
where's this cup i call'd for? 2.07. 54
you have not call'd me so, nor have you cause. 3.06. 41
eye beck'd forth my wars and call'd them home, 4.12. 26
i am call'd decretas; 5.01. 5
his father | was call'd sicilius, who did join CYM 1.01. 29
he is call'd | the britain reveller. 1.06. 60
worthiest sir that ever | country call'd his; 1.06.161
put | his brows within a golden crown and call'd 3.01. 60
who | the king his father call'd guiderius — 3.03. 88
myself, belarius, that am morgan call'd, | they 3.03.106
before i enter'd here i call'd, and thought | to 3.06. 46
who call'd me traitor, mountaineer, and swore 4.02.120
is, you shall be call'd to no more payments, 5.04.158 P
bring'st good news, i am call'd to be made free. 5.04.193 P
nothing but our lives | may be call'd ransom, 5.05. 80
every villain | be call'd posthumus leonatus, 5.05.224
great king, a subject who | was call'd belarius. 5.05.317
you call'd me brother, | when i was but your 5.05.376
this /is call'd pentapolis, and our king the PER 2.01. 99 P
he deserves so to be call'd for his peaceable 2.01.102 P
in brass, | having call'd them from the deep! 3.01. 4
marina was she call'd, and at her birth, 4.04. 38
how, a king's daughter? | and call'd marina? 5.01.150
and wherefore call'd marina? 5.01.155
call'd marina | for i was born at sea. 5.01.155
but brought forth | a maid–child call'd marina, 5.03. 6
and call'd marina | for she was yielded there. 5.03. 47
can you remember what i call'd the man? 5.03. 52
the maid flavina) | love any that's call'd man. TNK 1.03. 85
'tis call'd narcissus, madam. 2.02.119
have i call'd thee friend? 2.02.182
wrestled, | the best men call'd it excellent; 2.03. 76
you were call'd | a good knight and a bold. 3.01. 64
most trusty lover, | i call'd him now to answer. 3.06.151
it was not she that call'd him all to naught: VEN 993
silver cheeks, and call'd it then their shield, LUC 61
then let it not be call'd impiety, | if in this 1174
and that deep torture may be call'd a hell, 1287
sum, | call'd to that audit by advis'd respects; SON 49. 4
let not my love be call'd idolatry, | nor my 105. 1
for feasts of love i have been call'd unto, LC 181

CALL'DST 3 FR 0.0003 REL FR 3 V 0 P
thou call'dst me up at midnight to fetch dew TMP 1.02.228
thou call'dst me dog before thou hadst a cause, MV 3.03. 6
when we parted, | thou call'dst me king. 3H6 4.03. 31

CALLED 12 FR 0.0013 REL FR 7 V 5 P
if thy name be called luce — luce, thou hast ERR 3.01. 53
down to that nourishment which is called supper: LLL 1.01.237 P
jaquenetta (so is the weaker vessel called), 1.01.273 P
his disgrace is to be called boy, but his glory 1.02.180 P
nominated, or called, don adriano de armado. 5.01. 8 P
should be called tyrants, butchers, murtherers! AYL 3.05. 14
to–day, as i came by, i called there — | but i R2 2.02. 94
his father was called philip of macedon, as i H5 4.07. 20 P
and hast a thing within thee called conscience, TIT 5.01. 75
therefore called so | 'cause they take vengeance 5.02. 62
/wi' leave, they're called | arcite and palamon. TNK 1.04. 22
double name | neither two nor one was called. PHT 40

CALLET *(also callat, callot)*

CALLET 2 FR 0.0002 REL FR 2 V 0 P
to make this shameless callet know herself. 3H6 2.02.145
could not have laid such terms upon his callet. OTH 4.02.121

CALLICE 12 FR 0.0013 REL FR 11 V 1 P
on toward callice, ho! JN 3.03. 73
three parts of that receipt i had for callice R2 1.01.126
the restful english court | as far as callice, 4.01. 13
thy men | to execute the noble duke at callice. 4.01. 82
and in callice they stole a fire–shovel. H5 3.02. 45 P
upon our soldiers, we will retire to callice. 3.03. 56
but could be willing to march on to callice 3.06.141
and then to callice, and to england then, 4.08.125
now we bear the king | toward callice; 5.pr. 7
my gracious sovereign, as i rode from callice, 1H6 4.01. 9
after some respite, will return to callice; 4.01.170
warwick is chancellor and the lord of callice, 3H6 1.01.238

CALLING 18 FR 0.0020 REL FR 11 V 7 P
and the prisoner the very debt of your calling. MM 3.02.250 P
my reverence, calling, nor divinity, | if this ADO 4.01.168
son — and would not change that calling | to be AYL 1.02.233
of them all shall flout me out of my calling. 3.03.107 P
calling my officers about me, in my branch'd TN 2.05. 47 P
and do thou never leave calling "francis," that 1H4 2.04. 31 P
stand'st thou still, and hear'st such a calling? 2.04. 81 P
or raise myself, but keep my wonted calling? 1H6 3.01. 32
him, | calling him "humphrey, the good duke of 2H6 1.01.159
warwick is hoarse with calling thee to arms. 5.02. 7
you sign your place and calling, in full seeming H8 2.04.108
but reverence to your calling makes me modest. 5.02.104
make in their cause is calling both the parties COR 2.01. 78 P
calling death "banished," | thou cut'st my head ROM 3.03. 21
as calling home our exil'd friends abroad | that MAC 5.09. 32
an instrument of this your calling back, | lay OTH 4.02. 45
is our profession any trade, it's no calling. PER 4.02. 39 P
either of honor, office, wealth, and calling, STM III 15

CALLOT *(also callat, callet)*

CALLOT 1 FR 0.0001 REL FR 1 V 0 P
contemptuous base–born callot as she is, | she 2H6 1.03. 83

/CALLS 1 FR 0.0001 REL FR 1 V 0 P
english john talbot, captains, /calls you forth, 1H6 4.02. 3

CALLS 101 FR 0.0114 REL FR 81 V 20 P
he has brave utensils (for so he calls them) TMP 3.02. 96
he himself | calls her a nonpareil. 3.02.100
sir proteus, your /father calls for you: TGV 1.03. 88
who calls? 4.03. 4
caius, that calls himself doctor of physic? WIV 3.01. 4 P
she calls you, coz. 3.04. 53 P
it is thine host, thine ephesian, calls. 4.05. 18 P
who's that which calls? MM 1.04. 6
he calls again; 1.04. 14
peace and prosperity! who is't that calls? 1.04. 15
look, th' unfolding star calls up the shepherd. 4.02.203 P
my present business calls me from you now. ERR 1.02. 29
he murther cries, and help from athens calls. MND 3.02. 26
when i come where he calls, then he is gone. 3.02.414
i take it your own business calls on you, | and MV 1.01. 63
my well–won thrift, | which he calls interest. 1.03. 51
who calls? 5.01. 40 P
calls your worship? AYL 1.01. 88 P
the challenger, the princess calls for you. 1.02.166 P
he calls us back. 1.02.252
who calls? 2.04. 67
she calls me proud, and that she could not love 4.03. 16
and to that youth he calls his rosalind | he 4.03. 92
after many ceremonies done, | he calls for wine. SHR 3.02.170
who is that calls so coldly? 4.01. 13 P
that calls for company to countenance her. 4.01.102 P
monsieur parolles, my lord calls for you. AWW 1.01.187 P
a very serious business calls on him. 2.04. 40
he calls for the tortures. 4.03.120 P
gentlewoman, my lady calls. TN 1.05.164 P
who calls there? 4.02. 20 P
"she loves another" — who calls, ha? 4.02. 79 P
our prerogative | calls not your counsels, but WT 2.01.164
to come at traitors' calls and do them grace. R2 3.03.181
which calls me pupil or hath read to me? 1H4 3.01. 45
i be so forward with him that calls not on me? 5.01.129 P
he calls us rebels, traitors, and will scourge 5.02. 39
'a calls me /e'en /now, my lord, through a red 2H4 2.02. 79 P
and calls them brothers, friends, and countrymen H5 4.pr. 34
open the gates, 'tis gloucester that calls. 1H6 1.03. 4
sometime he calls the king, | and whispers to 2H6 3.02.374
and calls your grace usurper, openly, | and vows 4.04. 30
be treason for any that calls me other than lord 4.06. 6 P
clifford of cumberland, 'tis warwick calls! 5.02. 1
king, that calls your beauteous daughter wife, R3 4.04.315
sir, it calls, | i fear, too many curses on H8 2.01.137
action, | which, slanderer, he imitation calls, TRO 1.03.150
hands shall strike | when fitness calls them on, 1.03.202

who calls? 5.02. 2
custom calls me to't. COR 2.03.117
where's cotus? my master calls for him. cotus! 4.05. 3 P
'tis sad titus calls. TIT 5.02.121
and calls herself revenge, and thinks me mad. 5.02.185
how now, who calls? ROM 1.03. 5
it is my soul that calls upon my name. 2.02.164
thy fault our law calls death, but the kind 3.03. 25
and tybalt calls, and then on romeo cries, | and 3.03.101
but that a joy past joy calls out on me, | it 3.03.173
who is't that calls? 3.05. 65
who calls so loud? 5.01. 57
that calls our person from our morning rest? 5.03.189
ha? who calls? JC 1.02. 13
who is it in the press that calls on me? 1.02. 15
calls my lord? 4.03.245
paddock calls. MAC 1.01. 9
that such a hideous trumpet calls to parley 2.03. 82
and what needful else | that calls upon us, by 5.09. 38
who calls me villain, breaks my pate across, HAM 2.02.572
calls virtue hypocrite, takes off the rose 3.04. 42
who calls on hamlet? 4.02. 3 P
and that he calls for drink, i'll have preferr'd 4.07.159
let pride, which she calls plainness, marry her. LR 1.01.129
from those that she calls servants or from mine? 2.04.244
he calls to horse, but will i know not whither. 2.04.297
frateretto calls me, and tells me nero is an 3.06. 6 P
my master calls me, i must not say no. 5.03.323
he calls me to a restitution large | of gold and OTH 5.01. 15
your honor calls you hence, | therefore be deaf ANT 1.03. 97
(for so he calls me). 1.05. 26
time calls upon 's. 2.02.157
the emperor calls canidius. 3.07. 79
he calls me boy, and chides as he had power | to 4.01. 1
come, your lord calls! 4.14.130
to his protection, calls him posthumus leonatus, CYM 1.01. 41
that calls me traitor, i return the lie. PER 2.05. 57
and | the master calls, and trebles their 4.01. 64
ho, gentlemen! my lord calls. 5.01. 7
calls my lord? 5.01.181
the king calls for you; TNK 1.02. 84
chirp, the screech–owl | calls in the dawn! 3.02. 36
where this man calls me traitor, | let me say 3.06.160
him his own name, | calls him a god on earth. STM II.C 104
and, trembling in her passion, calls it balm, VEN 27
and calls it heavenly moisture, air of grace, 64
with untun'd tongue she hoarsely calls her maid, LUC 1214
at last she calls to mind where hangs a piece 1366
thee | calls back the lovely april of her prime, SON 3.10
then how when nature calls thee to be gone, 4.11
and he that calls on thee, let him bring forth 38.11
for what care i who calls me well or ill, | so 112. 3
whereto th' inviting time our fashion calls; 124. 8
CALL'ST 12 FR 0.0013 REL FR 10 V 2 P
for wenches, that thou call'st for such store, ERR 3.01. 34
call'st thou my love "hobby–horse"? LLL 3.01. 30 P
what a' devil's name, tailor, call'st thou this? SHR 4.03. 92
thy life, | with what thou else call'st thine. WT 2.03.138
of that penitent (as thou call'st him) and 4.02. 22 P
base tike, call'st thou me host? H5 2.01. 29
i slew thy father, call'st thou him a child? 3H6 2.02.113
detestable villain, call'st thou that trimming? TIT 5.01. 94
call'st thou that harm? TIM 4.03.173
though thou call'st thyself a hotter name | than MAC 5.07. 6
thou call'st on him that hates thee. LR 3.07. 88
call'st thou her thine? TNK 3.01. 38
CALL'T 3 FR 0.0003 REL FR 3 V 0 P
lost for ever, perdita | i prithee call't. WT 3.03. 34
call't not a plot. COR 3.01. 41
to earth, | that i must call't in question. HAM 4.05.218
CALM* *(also qualm)*
CALM* 36 FR 0.0040 REL FR 33 V 3 P
and promise you calm seas, auspicious gales, TMP 5.01.315
be calm, good wind, blow not a word away | till TGV 1.02.115
death, | would i not undergo for one calm look? 5.04. 42
of his wished light | the seas wax'd calm, and ERR 1.01. 91
they shoot but calm words folded up in smoke, JN 2.01.229
we'll calm the duke of norfolk, you your son. R2 1.01.159
to whose high will we bound our calm contents. 5.02. 38
the cankers of a calm world and a long peace, 1H4 4.02. 30 P
sick of a calm, yea, good faith. 2H4 2.04. 36 P
and they be once in a calm, they are sick. 2.04. 37 P
beams, | do calm the fury of this mad–bred flaw. 2H6 3.01.354
he dares not calm his contumelious spirit, | nor 3.02.204
that led calm henry, though he were a king, | as 3H6 2.06. 34
renowned queen, with patience calm the storm, 3.03. 38
noble temper, | a soul as even as a calm; H8 3.01.166
the unity and married calm of states | quite TRO 1.03.100
our bloods are now in calm, and, so long, health 4.01. 16
be calm, be calm. COR 3.01. 37
be calm, be calm. 3.01. 37
let's be calm. 3.01. 57
that when the sea was calm all boats alike 4.01. 6
how fair the tribune speaks to calm my thoughts! TIT 1.01. 46
to cool this heat, a charm to calm these fits, 2.01.134
o, calm thee, gentle lord, although i know 4.01. 83
to calm this tempest whirling in the court; 4.02.160
calm thee, and bear the faults of titus' age, 4.04. 29
o calm, dishonorable, vile submission! ROM 3.01. 73
uttered | with gentle breath, calm look, knees 3.01.156
without a sudden calm, will overset | thy 3.05.136
drop of blood that's calm proclaims me bastard, HAM 4.05.118
how much i had to do to calm his rage! 4.07.192
how calm and gentle i proceeded still | in all ANT 5.01. 75
therein | he was as calm as virtue) he began CYM 5.05.174
"time's glory is to calm contending kings, | to LUC 939
the harmless show | an humble gait, calm looks, 1508
be bent, | her cloudy looks will calm yer night, PP 18.26
/CALM'D 1 FR 0.0001 REL FR 1 V 0 P
is straightway /calm'd and boarded with a pirate 2H6 4.09. 33
CALM'D 4 FR 0.0004 REL FR 4 V 0 P
myself have calm'd their spleenful mutiny, 2H6 3.02.128
soon provok'd, nor being provok'd soon calm'd; TRO 4.05. 99
must be belee'd and calm'd | by debitor and OTH 1.01. 30
it in rage, though calm'd have given't again. PER 2.01.132
CALMEST 1 FR 0.0001 REL FR 1 V 0 P
and in the calmest and most stillest night, 2H4 3.01. 28
CALMLY 3 FR 0.0003 REL FR 3 V 0 P
and calmly run on in obedience | even to our JN 5.04. 56
calmly, i do beseech you. COR 3.03. 31
calmly, good laertes. HAM 4.05.117
CALMNESS 1 FR 0.0001 REL FR 1 V 0 P
or defend yourself | by calmness or by absence. COR 3.02. 95
CALMS 1 FR 0.0001 REL FR 1 V 0 P
if after every tempest come such calms, | may OTH 2.01.185
CALPHURNIA 6 FR 0.0006 REL FR 6 V 0 P
calphurnia! JC 1.02. 1
calphurnia! 1.02. 1
in your speed, antonio, | to touch calphurnia; 1.02. 7
thrice hath calphurnia in her sleep cried out, 2.02. 2
calphurnia here, my wife, stays me at home: 2.02. 75
how foolish do your fears seem now, calphurnia! 2.02.105
CALPHURNIA'S 2 FR 0.0002 REL FR 2 V 0 P
calphurnia's cheek is pale, and cicero | looks JC 1.02.185
this by calphurnia's dream is signified. 2.02. 90
CALUMNIATE 1 FR 0.0001 REL FR 1 V 0 P
functions, | created only to calumniate. TRO 5.02.124
CALUMNIATING 1 FR 0.0001 REL FR 1 V 0 P
subjects all | to envious and calumniating time. TRO 3.03.174
CALUMNIOUS 3 FR 0.0003 REL FR 2 V 1 P
ever be a foul–mouth'd and calumnious knave? AWW 1.03. 57 P
none stands under more calumnious tongues | than H8 5.01.112
virtue itself scapes not calumnious strokes. HAM 1.03. 38
CALUMNY 5 FR 0.0005 REL FR 4 V 1 P
in your own report, | and smell of calumny. MM 2.04.159
back–wounding calumny | the whitest virtue 3.02.186
(these petty brands | that calumny doth use — o WT 2.01. 72
does, for calumny will sear | virtue itself), 2.01. 73
as pure as snow, thou shalt not escape calumny. HAM 3.01.136 P
CALVED 1 FR 0.0001 REL FR 1 V 0 P
though calved i' th' porch o' th' capitol! COR 3.01.239
CALVES 1 FR 0.0001 REL FR 0 V 1 P
they are sheep and calves which seek out HAM 5.01.116 P
CALVES'–GUTS 1 FR 0.0001 REL FR 0 V 1 P
which horsehairs and calves'–guts, nor the voice CYM 2.03. 29 P
CALVE'S–HEAD 1 FR 0.0001 REL FR 0 V 1 P
he hath bid me to a calve's–head and a capon, ADO 5.01.155 P
CALVE'S–SKIN 7 FR 0.0008 REL FR 6 V 1 P
he that goes in the calve's–skin that was kill'd ERR 4.03. 19 P
and hang a calve's–skin on those recreant limbs. JN 3.01.129
and hang a calve's–skin on those recreant limbs. 3.01.131
and hang a calve's–skin on those recreant limbs. 3.01.133
and hang a calve's–skin on his recreant limbs. 3.01.199
hang nothing but a calve's–skin, most sweet lout 3.01.220
will not a calve's–skin stop that mouth of thine 3.01.299
CALVES'–SKINS 1 FR 0.0001 REL FR 0 V 1 P
ay, my lord, and of calves'–skins too. HAM 5.01.115 P
CALYDON 1 FR 0.0001 REL FR 1 V 0 P
burnt | unto the prince's heart of calydon. 2H6 1.01.235
CAM *(see kam)*
CAMBIO 8 FR 0.0009 REL FR 5 V 3 P
his name is cambio; SHR 2.01. 83 P
welcome, good cambio. 2.01. 85 P
cambio, hie you home, | and bid bianca make her 4.04. 62
cambio! 4.04. 73 P
it shall go hard if cambio go without her. 4.04.108
i marvel cambio comes not all this while. 5.01. 7
why, tell me, is not this my cambio? 5.01.122
cambio is chang'd into lucentio. 5.01.123
CAMBRIA 2 FR 0.0002 REL FR 1 V 1 P
take notice that i am in cambria, at CYM 3.02. 43 P
sir, | in cambria are we born, and gentlemen. 5.05. 17
CAMBRIC 2 FR 0.0002 REL FR 1 V 1 P
come, i would your cambric were sensible as your COR 1.03. 84 P
she would with sharp needle wound | the cambric, PER 4.ch. 24
CAMBRICS 1 FR 0.0001 REL FR 0 V 1 P
inkles, caddises, cambrics, lawns. WT 4.04.207 P
CAMBRIDGE 11 FR 0.0012 REL FR 10 V 1 P
one, richard earl of cambridge, and the second, H5 2.pr. 23
my lord of cambridge, and my kind lord of masham 2.02. 13
though cambridge, scroop, and grey, in their 2.02. 58
then, richard earl of cambridge, there is yours; 2.02. 66
my lord of cambridge here, | you know how apt 2.02. 85
less for bounty bound to us | than cambridge is, 2.02. 93
by the name of richard earl of cambridge. 2.02.146 P
was not thy father, richard earl of cambridge, 1H6 2.04. 90
the cause | my father, earl of cambridge, lost 2.05. 54
thy father, earl of cambridge then, deriv'd 2.05. 84
married richard earl of cambridge, who was | to 2H6 2.02. 45
CAMBYSES' 1 FR 0.0001 REL FR 0 V 1 P
and i will do it in king cambyses' vein. 1H4 2.04.387 P
/CAME 5 FR 0.0005 REL FR 5 V 0 P
/through /proud /london /he /came /sighing /on 2H4 1.03.104
/melody, | /came /here /to /make /us /merry! TIT 3.02. 65
as thick as tale | /came post with post, and MAC 1.03. 98
/was /big /in /clamor, /came /there /in /a /man, LR 5.03.209
/came for additions, yet their purpos'd trim LC 118
CAME 362 FR 0.0409 REL FR 279 V 83 P
remember | a time before we came unto this cell? TMP 1.02. 39
what foul play had we, that we came from thence? 1.02. 60
how came we ashore? 1.02.158
this is unwonted | which now came from him. 1.02.499
how came that widow in? 2.01. 78 P
and the rarest that e'er came there. 2.01.100 P
i not doubt | he came alive to land. 2.01.123
say, how came you hither? 5.01.228
accidents gone by | since i came to this isle. 5.01.307
deliver'd by a friend that came from him. TGV 1.03. 54
now trust me, madam, it came hardly off; 2.01.109
now tell me: how do all from whence you came? 2.04.122
whence came you? 4.01. 18
and i came no sooner into the dining–chamber but 4.04. 8 P
unhappy were you, madam, ere i came; 5.04. 29
he came of an errand to me from parson hugh. WIV 1.04. 76 P
even as you came in to me, her assistant or 2.02.262 P
he knew your worship would kill him if he came. 2.03. 11 P
otherwise you might slip away ere he came. 4.02. 53 P
for so soon as i came beyond eton, they threw me 4.05. 67 P
like a poor old man, but i came from her, master 5.01. 16 P
i came yonder at eton to marry mistress anne 5.05.183 P
this we came not to, | only for propagation of a MM 1.02.149
sir, she came in great with child; 2.01. 89 P
how came it that the absent duke had not either 4.02.132 P
of lord angelo, came not to an undoubtful proof. 4.02.137 P
i came to her from claudio, and desir'd her | to 5.01. 75
intended 'gainst lord angelo, came i hither, 5.01.154
proportions | came short of composition, but in 5.01.220
which i did think with slower foot came on, 5.01.395
how came it claudio was beheaded | at an unusual 5.01.457
too soon | we came aboard. ERR 1.01. 61
but ere they came — o, let me say no more! 1.01. 94
asia, | and, coasting homeward, came to ephesus; 1.01.134
let him walk from whence he came, lest he catch 3.01. 37
but neither chain nor goldsmith came to me: 4.01. 24
were chain'd together, and therefore came not. 4.01. 26
he that came behind you, sir, like an evil angel 4.03. 20 P
you, | by dromio here, who came in haste for it. 4.04. 84
he came to me, and i deliver'd it. 4.04. 88
husband all in rage to–day | came to my house, 4.04.138
and thereof came it that the man was mad. 5.01. 68
of more aid, | we came again to bind them. 5.01.154
i never came within these abbey walls, | nor 5.01.266
no, sir, not i, i came from syracuse. 5.01.364
i came from corinth, my most gracious lord — 5.01.366
we came into the world like brother and brother; 5.01.425
never came trouble to my house in the likeness ADO 1.01. 99 P
i came yonder from a great supper. 1.03. 42 P
how came you to this? 1.03. 57 P
of passion came so near the life of passion as 2.03.105 P
i came hither to tell you, and, circumstances 3.02.102 P
i came to seek you both. 5.01.121 P
ere i go, let me go with that i came, which is, 5.02. 47 P
to meet you, gentle lady, | before i came. LLL 2.01. 84
until the goose came out of door, | and stayed 3.01. 91
until the goose came out of door, | staying the 3.01. 97
thus came your argument in; 3.01.108
videlicet, he came, /saw, and overcame: 4.01. 69 P
he came, one; 4.01. 70 P
who came? 4.01. 71 P
to whom came he? 4.01. 73 P
not to five weeks when he came to fivescore. 4.02. 40
madam, came nothing else along with that? 5.02. 5
lord longaville said i came o'er his heart, 5.02.278
we came to visit you, and purpose now | to lead 5.02.343
how came her eyes so bright? MND 2.02. 92
then, what it was that next came in her eye, 3.02. 2
when in that moment (so it came to pass) 3.02. 33
how came these things to pass? 4.01. 78
in our flight | tell me how it came this night 4.01.100
intent, | came here in grace of our solemnity. 4.01.134
i swear, | i cannot truly say how i came here. 4.01.148
me, so it is — | i came with hermia hither. 4.01.151
when i from thebes came last a conqueror. 5.01. 51
and then came pyramus. 5.01.270 P
but how i caught it, found it, or came by it, MV 1.01. 3
that came hither in company of the marquis of 1.02.113 P
he came too late, the ship was under sail, | but 2.08. 6
with one fool's head i came to woo, | but i go 2.09. 75
a day in april never came so sweet, | to show 2.09. 93
i often came where i did hear of her, but cannot 3.01. 81 P
there came divers of antonio's creditors in my 3.01.113 P
came you from padua, from bellario? 4.01.119
but in the instant that your messenger came, in 4.01.152 P
and i came to acquaint you with a matter. AYL 1.01.122 P
to you, i came hither to acquaint you withal, 1.01.132 P
i am heartily glad i came hither to you. 1.01.159 P
the nine days out of the wonder before you came; 3.02.175 P
till his fellow–fault came to match it. 3.02.355 P
marry, to say she came to seek you there. 4.01.171 P
as how i came into that desert place — | /in 4.03.141
and caesar's thrasonical brag of "i came, saw, 5.02. 31 P
and to the skirts of this wild wood he came; 5.04.159
we came in with richard conqueror. SHR in.1. 4 P
for in a quarrel since i came ashore | i kill'd 1.01.231
why came i hither but to that intent? 1.02.198
one, | though paris came in hope to speed alone. 1.02.245
that "only" came well in. 2.01.363
who? that petruchio came? 3.02. 77 P
ay, that petruchio came. 3.02. 78 P
signior gremio, came you from the church? 3.02.149
as willingly as e'er i came from school. 3.02.150
and i, seeing this, came thence for very shame, 3.02.180
inprimis, we came down a foul hill, my master 4.01. 66 P
we met him thitherward, for thence we came; AWW 3.02. 53
you came, i think, from france? 3.05. 46
they will say, "came you off with so little?" 4.01. 39 P
thence it came | that she whom all men prais'd 5.03. 52
it came o'er my ear like the sweet sound | that TN 1.01. 5
whence came you, sir? 1.05.177 P
when came he to this town? 5.01. 93
but when i came to man's estate, | with hey ho, 5.01.393
but when i came, alas, to wive, | with hey ho, 5.01.397
but when i came unto my beds, | with hey ho, etc 5.01.401
greatest promise that ever came into my note. WT 1.01. 36 P
hold, | when you cast out, it still came home. 1.02.214
how came the posterns | so easily open? 2.01. 52
as by strange fortune | it came to us, i do in 2.03.180
before polixenes | came to your court, how i was 3.02. 47
since he came, | with what encounter so 3.02. 48
good my lord, | she came from libya. 5.01.157
i now came from him. 5.01.186
the manner how she came to't bravely confess'd 5.02. 85 P
but we came | to see the statue of our queen. 5.03. 9
not | that which my daughter came to look upon, 5.03. 13
you came not of one mother then, it seems. JN 1.01. 58
he came into the world | full fourteen weeks 1.01.112
by this brave duke came early to his grave; 2.01. 5
which here we came to spout against your town, 2.01.256
in her right we came, | which we, god knows, 2.01.548
you came in arms to spill mine enemies' blood, 3.01.102
under whose conduct came those pow'rs of france 4.02.129
o, bravely came we off, | when with a volley of 5.05. 4
who half an hour since came from the dolphin, 5.07. 83
my lord, your son was gone before i came. R2 2.02. 86
to–day, as i came by, i called there — | but i 2.02. 94
an hour before i came, the duchess died. 2.02. 97
letters came last night | to a dear friend of 3.04. 69
pomp | she came adorned hither like sweet may, 5.01. 79
who | lately came from the king, commands the 5.05.101
when all athwart there came | a post from wales 1H4 1.01. 36
uneven and unwelcome news | came from the north, 1.01. 51
came there a certain lord, neat, and trimly 1.03. 33

who therewith angry, when it next came there, 1.03. 40
when you and he came back from ravenspurgh — 1.03.248
"look when his infant fortune came to age" | and 1.03.253
these four came all afront, and mainly thrust at 2.04.200 P
but i follow'd me close, came in, foot and hand, 2.04.217 P
in kendal green came at my back and let drive at 2.04.222 P
in earnest, how came falstaff's sword so hack'd? 2.04.303 P
your uncle worcester's horses came but to-day, 4.03. 21
to god | he came but to be duke of lancaster, 4.03. 61
the more and less came in with cap and knee, 4.03. 68
tut, i came not to hear this. 4.03. 89
won, | came not till now to dignify the times, 2H4 1.01. 22
came you from shrewsbury? 1.01. 24
spake with one, my lord, that came from thence, 1.01. 25
after him came spurring hard | a gentleman, 1.01. 36
so came i a widow, | and never shall have length 2.03. 57
and as i came along | i met and overtook a dozen 2.04.357
by old nightwork before i came to clement's inn. 3.02.209 P
'a came /ever in the rearward of the fashion, 3.02.315 P
if that rebellion | came like itself, in base 4.01. 33
"there, cousin, i came, saw, and overcame." 4.03. 42 P
he came not through the chamber where we stay'd. 4.05. 56
god witness with me, when i here came in, | and 4.05.149
how i came by the crown, o god forgive, | and 4.05.218
consideration like an angel came | and whipt th' H5 1.01. 28
never came reformation in a flood | with such a 1.01. 33
came pouring like the tide into a breach, | with 1.02.149
who came off bravely, who was shot, who 3.06. 73 P
upon these words i came and cheer'd him up. 4.06. 20
and all my mother came into mine eyes | and gave 4.06. 31
i was not angry since i came to france | until 4.07. 55
never came any from mine that might offend your 4.08. 47 P
your majesty came not like yourself. 4.08. 50 P
when arm in arm they both came swiftly running, 1H6 2.02. 29
we came but to tell you | that we are here. 3.02. 73
came to the field and vanquished his foes. 3.02. 96
and therefore, as we hither came in peace, | so 4.01.160
the bastard to destroy, | came in strong rescue. 4.06. 26
as i was cause | your highness came to england, 2H6 1.03. 66
they come to berwick, from whence they came. 2.01.156
his poor queen to france, from whence she came, 2.02. 25
came he right now to sing a raven's note, 3.02. 40
merry world in england since gentlemen came up. 4.02. 9 P
became a bricklayer when he came to age. 4.02.145
and i unto the sea, from whence i came. 3H6 1.01.209
and full as oft came edward to my side | with 1.04. 11
their weapons like to lightning came and went; 2.01.129
and when came george from burgundy to england? 2.01.143
why, therefore warwick came to seek you out, 2.01.166
came on the part of york, press'd by his master; 2.05. 66
therefore i came unto your majesty. 3.02. 41
of york | my father came untimely to his death? 3.03.187
i came from edward as ambassador, | but i return 3.03.256
again, | i came to serve a king and not a duke. 4.07. 49
where is the post that came from valiant oxford? 5.01. 1
where is the post that came from montague? 5.01. 5
and blow it to the source from whence it came; 5.03. 11
i came into the world with my legs forward. 5.06. 71
never came poison from so sweet a place. R3 1.02.146
were you snarling all before i came, | ready to 1.03.187
then came wand'ring by | a shadow like an angel, 1.04. 52
with clarence, and i came hither on my legs. 1.04. 87 P
two such murtherers as yourselves came to you, 1.04.259
that came too lag to see him buried. 2.01. 91
better it were they all came by his father, | or 2.03. 23
man | the men you talk of came into my mind. 3.02.117
die | until your lordship came to see his end, 3.05. 53
and even here brake off, and came away. 3.07. 41
now | came to me as i follow'd henry's corse, 4.01. 66
and came i not at last to comfort you? 4.04.165
him, they came from buckingham | upon his party. 4.04.525
of all that i had murther'd | came to my tent, 5.03.205
came to my tent and cried on victory. 5.03.231
his color, but he came | to whisper wolsey), H8 1.01.178
the great duke | came to the bar; 2.01. 12
when i came hither, i was lord high constable 2.01.102
thus it came; 2.04.170
how came | his practices to light? 3.02. 28
and came to th' eye o' th' king, wherein was 3.02. 31
the duke of buckingham came from his trial. 4.01. 5
and with modest paces | came to the altar, where 4.01. 83
at last, with easy roads, he came to leicester, 4.02. 17
came you from the king, my lord? 5.01. 6
i am glad | i came this way so happily; 5.02. 9
at length they came to th' broom-staff to me, i 5.03. 54 P
what were you talking of when i came? TRO 1.02. 47 P
was hector arm'd and gone ere ye came to ilium? 1.02. 48 P
she came to him th' other day into the compass'd 1.02.110 P
she came and puts me her white hand to his 1.02.119 P
juno have mercy! how came it cloven? 1.02.120 P
who said he came hurt home to-day? 1.02.214 P
for my own part, i came in late. 4.02. 52 P
i came to kill thee, cousin, and bear hence | a 4.05.140
which ne'er came from the lungs, but even thus COR 1.01.108
there came news from him last night. 1.03. 92 P
their trenches driven, | and then i came away. 1.06. 13
aidless came off, | and with a sudden 2.02.112
and to the battle came he, where he did | run 2.02.118
from whence came | that ancus martius, numa's 2.03.238
on safeguard he came to me, and did curse 3.01. 9
being banish'd for't, he came unto my hearth, 5.06. 29
alas, sir, i never came there. TIT 4.03. 90 P
in the instant came | the fiery tybalt, with his ROM 1.01.108
came more and more, and fought on part and part, 1.01.114
till the prince came, who parted either part. 1.01.115
"marry" is the very theme | i came to talk of. 1.03. 64
came he not home to-night? 2.04. 2
why the dev'l came you between us? 3.01.103 P
i dreamt my lady came and found me dead — 5.01. 6
i must indeed, and therefore came i hither. 5.03. 58
came i to take her from her kindred's vault, 5.03.254
but when i came, some minute ere the time | of 5.03.257
and then in post he came from mantua | to this 5.03.273
he came with flowers to strew his lady's grave, 5.03.281
and therewithal | came to this vault to die, and 5.03.290
nor came any of his bounties over me | to mark TIM 3.02. 78
and came into the world | when sects and 3.05. 29
how came the noble timon to this change? 4.03. 67
lord, but therefore | came not my friend nor i. 5.01. 79
you came for gold, ye slaves. 5.01.112
what said he when he came unto himself? JC 1.02.262
when he came to himself again, he said, if he 1.02.269 P
and after that, he came thus sad away? 1.02.276
throw, | as if they came from several citizens, 1.02.317
came smiling and did bathe their hands in it. 2.02. 79
for with her death | that tidings came. 4.03.155
torchlight, but, my lord, | he came not back. 5.05. 3
the wonder of it, came missives from the king, MAC 1.05. 6 P
came they not by you? 4.01.137
who was't came by? 4.01.140
when i came hither to transport the tidings, 4.03.181
how came she by that light? 5.01. 21 P
from whence though willingly i came to denmark HAM 1.02. 52
my lord, i came to see your father's funeral. 1.02.176
came this from hamlet to her? 2.02.114
"then came each actor on his ass" — 2.02.395
you know, "it came to pass, as most like it was" 2.02.418
how came he dead? 4.05.131
it came from th' embassador that was bound for 4.06. 10 P
i came to't that day that our last king hamlet 5.01.143 P
how came he mad? 5.01.156 P
unknowing world | how these things came about. 5.02.380
though this knave came something saucily to the LR 1.01. 21 P
when came you to this? 1.02. 58 P
why came not the slave back to me when i call'd 1.04. 52 P
since i came hither | (which i can call but now) 2.01. 86
you know not why we came to visit you? 2.01.118
my duty kneeling, came there a reeking post, 2.04. 30
how came my man i' th' stocks? 2.04.198
"child rowland to the dark tower came, | his 3.04.182
which came from one that's of a neutral heart, 3.07. 48
my son | came then into my mind, and yet my mind 4.01. 34
when the rain came to wet me once, and the wind 4.06.101 P
we came crying hither. 4.06.178
it came even from the heart of — o, she's dead! 5.03.225
or came it by request, and such fair question OTH 1.03.113
when i came back | (for this was brief), i found 2.03.236
how came you thus recover'd? 2.03.295 P
that came a-wooing with you, and so many a time, 3.03. 71
o cassio, whence came this? 3.04.180
/unsuiting such a man), | cassio came hither. 4.01. 78
iago in the /nick | came in and satisfied him. 5.02.318
how came you, cassio, by that handkerchief 5.02.319
the watch, whereon it came | that i was cast; 5.02.326
fulvia thy wife first came into the field. ANT 1.02. 88
then | i came before you here a man prepar'd 2.06. 40
your mother came to sicily and did find | her 2.06. 45
we came hither to fight with you. 2.06.102 P
the messenger | came on my guard, and at thy 4.06. 22
why came you from your master? CYM 1.01.169
it came in too suddenly, let it die as it was 1.04.120 P
very true, | and so i hope he came by't. 2.04.118
but made not here his brag | of "came, and saw, 3.01. 24
thou toldst me, when we came from horse, the 3.04. 1
and though he came our enemy, remember | he was 4.02.245
so long a breeding as his white beard came to, 5.03. 17
i have resum'd again | the part i came in. 5.03. 76
ripp'd, | came crying 'mongst his foes, | a 5.04. 46
for this from stiller seats we came, | our 5.04. 69
he came in thunder, his celestial breath | was 5.04.114
upon your finger, say | how came it yours? 5.05.138
missing, came to me | with his sword drawn, 5.05.275
and when came you to serve our roman captive? 5.05.385
my riches to the earth from whence they came; PER 1.01. 52
how i might stop this tempest ere it came, | and 1.02. 98
now message must return from whence it came. 1.03. 35
how thaliard came full bent with sin | and hid 2.ch. 23
him, | a fire from heaven came and shrivell'd up 2.04. 9
i came unto your court for honor's cause, | and 2.05. 61
yet none does know but you how she came dead, 4.03. 29
but there never came her like in meteline. 4.06. 28 P
have plac'd me in this sty, where, since i came, 4.06. 97
you thoughten | that i came with no ill intent, 4.06.109
assur'd | came of a gentle kind and noble stock, 5.01. 68
how came you in these parts? 5.01.169
do't, | a crew of pirates came and rescued me; 5.01.174
how she came plac'd here in the temple; 5.03. 67
the intelligence of state came in the instant TNK 1.02.106
the duke himself came privately in the night, 2.01. 46 P
"the george alow came from the south, | from the 3.05. 59
makes morris, and the cause that we came hither. 3.05.120
for i came home before the business | was fully 4.01. 4
left my angle | to his own skill, came near, but 4.01. 60
them with her | and hither came to tell you. 4.01.103
within this half hour she came smiling to me 5.02. 4
as they say, from iron | came music's origin), 5.04. 61
foreknowing well, if there he came to lie, | why VEN 245
view | how she came stealing to the wayward boy! 344
but tarquin's shape came in her mind the while, LUC 1536
to me came tarquin armed to beguild | with 1544
in the interest of thy bed | a stranger came, 1620
with shining falchion in my chamber came | a 1626
his scarlet lust came evidence to swear | that 1650
(speaking to those that came with collatine), 1689
use, | and sue a friend came debtor for my sake, SON 134.11
vow'd chaste life to keep | came tripping by, 154. 4
came there for cure, and this by that i prove: 154.13
"that not a heart which in his level came LC 309

CAMEL 5 FR 0.0005 REL FR 1 V 4 P
"it is as hard to come as for a camel | to R2 5.05. 16
achilles! a drayman, a porter, a very camel. TRO 1.02.249 P
mars his idiot! do, rudeness, do, camel, do, do. 2.01. 53 P
yonder cloud that's almost in shape of a camel? HAM 3.02.377 P
by th' mass and 'tis, like a camel indeed. 3.02.378 P

CAMELOT 1 FR 0.0001 REL FR 1 V 0 P
plain, | i'ld drive ye cackling home to camelot. LR 2.02. 84

CAMELS 1 FR 0.0001 REL FR 1 V 0 P
for the world | than camels in their war, who COR 2.01.251

CAMEST 1 FR 0.0001 REL FR 1 V 0 P
how camest thou hither, tell me, and wherefore? ROM 2.02. 62

CAME'T 2 FR 0.0002 REL FR 2 V 0 P
how came't, camillo, | that he did stay? WT 1.02.219
how came't? CYM 4.02.366

CAMILLO 41 FR 0.0046 REL FR 33 V 8 P
if you shall chance, camillo, to visit bohemia WT 1.01. 1 P
why, that's some comfort. | what? camillo there? 1.02.209
camillo, this great sir will yet stay longer. 1.02.212
how came't, camillo, | that he did stay? 1.02.219
i have trusted thee, camillo, | with all the 1.02.235
ha' not you seen, camillo | (but that's past 1.02.267
i say thou liest, camillo, and i hate thee, 1.02.300
good day, camillo. 1.02.366
good camillo, | your chang'd complexions are to 1.02.380
camillo — | as you are certainly a gentleman, 1.02.390
dost thou hear, camillo, | i conjure thee, by 1.02.399
on, good camillo. 1.02.411
by whom, camillo? 1.02.413
come, camillo, | i will respect thee as a father 1.02.460
was he met there? his train? camillo with him? 2.01. 33
camillo was his help in this, his pandar. 2.01. 46
a traitor, and camillo is | a federary with her, 2.01. 89
camillo and polixenes | laugh at me; 2.03. 23
and conspiring with camillo to take away the 3.02. 16 P
know of it | is that camillo was an honest man; 3.02. 74
polixenes blameless, camillo a true subject, 3.02.133 P
new woo my queen, recall the good camillo, 3.02.156
i chose | camillo for the minister to poison 3.02.160
but that the good mind of camillo tardied | my 3.02.162
i pray thee, good camillo, be no more 4.02. 1 P
as thou lov'st me, camillo, wipe not out the 4.02. 10 P
i have consider'd so much, camillo, and with 4.02. 34 P
my best camillo! we must disguise ourselves. 4.02. 54 P
i not purpose it. | i think, camillo? 4.04.473
camillo, | not for bohemia, nor the pomp that 4.04.487
now, good camillo, | i am so fraught with 4.04.513
how, camillo, | may this (almost a miracle) be 4.04.533
worthy camillo, | what color for my visitation 4.04.554
my good camillo, | she's as forward of her 4.04.579
camillo, | preserver of my father, now of me, 4.04.585
thus we set on, camillo, to th' sea-side. 4.04.668
camillo has betray'd me; 5.01.193
who? camillo? 5.01.196
camillo, sir; 5.01.197
in the king and camillo were very notes of 5.02. 10 P
come, camillo, | and take her by the hand, whose 5.03.143

CAMILLO'S 2 FR 0.0002 REL FR 2 V 0 P
camillo's flight, | added to their familiarity WT 2.01.174
thou wouldst have poison'd good camillo's honor, 3.02.188

CAMLET *(see chamblet)*

CAMOMILE 1 FR 0.0001 REL FR 0 V 1 P
for though the camomile, the more it is trodden 1H4 2.04.400 P

CAMP 27 FR 0.0030 REL FR 21 V 6 P
and all the secrets of our camp i'll show, AWW 4.01. 84
whether one captain dumaine be i' th' camp, a 4.03.176 P
is this captain in the duke of florence's camp? 4.03.193 P
lord, | and was a common gamester to the camp. 5.03.188
all that | he gave it to a commoner a' th' camp, 5.03.194
'tis catching hither, even to our camp. 1H4 4.01. 30
fire | even to the dullest peasant in his camp, 2H4 1.01.113
for i shall sutler be | unto the camp, and H5 2.01.112
a horrid suit of the camp will do among foaming 3.06. 77 P
from camp to camp, through the foul womb of 4.pr. 4
from camp to camp, through the foul womb of 4.pr. 4
both, | commend me to the princes in our camp; 4.01. 25
taddle nor pibble babble in pompey's camp. 4.01. 71 P
absence, | seek through your camp to find you. 4.01.286
with the lackeys with the luggage of our camp. 4.04. 75 P
after this, the vengeance on the whole camp! TRO 2.03. 18 P
our guider, come, to th' roman camp conduct us. COR 1.07. 7
my noble steed, known to the camp, i give him, 1.09. 61
that left the camp to sin in lucrece' bed? TIT 4.01. 64
you up | to be a warrior and command a camp. 4.02.180
there's not a whittle in th' unruly camp | but i TIM 5.01.180
his funerals shall not be in our camp, | lest it JC 5.03.105
i had been happy, if the general camp, | pioners OTH 3.03.345
or from caesar's camp | say "i am none of thine. ANT 4.05. 8
we have beat him to his camp. 4.08. 1
great palace the capacity | to camp this host, 4.08. 33
must be to him that makes the camp a cestron TNK 5.01. 46

CAMPEIUS 3 FR 0.0003 REL FR 3 V 0 P
cardinal campeius is arriv'd, and lately, | as H8 2.01.160
this just and learned priest, card'nal campeius, 2.02. 96
cardinal campeius | is stol'n away to rome, hath 3.02. 56

CAMPING 1 FR 0.0001 REL FR 1 V 0 P
from courtly friends, with camping foes to live, AWW 3.04. 14

/CAM'ST 1 FR 0.0001 REL FR 1 V 0 P
and how, | /cam'st thou by this ill tidings? R2 3.04. 80

CAM'ST 29 FR 0.0032 REL FR 24 V 5 P
if thou rememb'rest aught ere thou cam'st here, TMP 1.02. 51
cam'st here, | how thou cam'st here thou mayst. 1.02. 52
when thou cam'st first, | thou strok'st me and 1.02.332
how cam'st thou to be the siege of this 2.02.106 P
how cam'st thou hither? 2.02.119 P
swear by this bottle how thou cam'st hither — i 2.02.120 P
arise, and say how thou cam'st here. 5.01.181
how cam'st thou in this pickle? 5.01.281
but how cam'st thou by this ring? TGV 5.04. 96
by whose advice | thou cam'st here to complain. MM 5.01.114
and for what cause thou cam'st to ephesus. ERR 1.01. 30
antipholus, thou cam'st from corinth first? 5.01.363
from whence thou cam'st, how tended on, but rest AWW 2.01.207
then cam'st in smiling, | and in such forms TN 5.01.349
in thee, nor thou cam'st not of the blood royal, 1H4 1.02.140 P
how now, fluellen, cam'st thou from the bridge? H5 3.06. 88 P
cam'st thou here by chance | or of devotion, to 2H6 2.01. 85
how cam'st thou so? 2.01. 94
to tell thee whence thou cam'st, of whom deriv'd 3H6 1.04.119
to signify thou cam'st to bite the world; 5.06. 54
be true which i have heard, | thou cam'st — 5.06. 56
and how cam'st thou hither? R3 1.04. 85
thou cam'st on earth to make the earth my hell. 4.04.167
yet cam'st thou to a morsel of this feast, COR 1.09. 10
my grief was at the height before thou cam'st, TIT 3.01. 70
time, why cam'st thou now | to murther, murther ROM 4.05. 60
whence cam'st thou, worthy thane? MAC 1.02. 48
cam'st thou from where they made the stand? CYM 5.03. 1
thee — that thou cam'st | from good descending? PER 5.01.127

CAN* *(also began, gan)*

/CAN* 6 FR 0.0006 REL FR 4 V 2 P
every one /can master a grief but he that has it ADO 3.02. 28 P
/but /they /can /see /a /sort /of /traitors R2 4.01.246
/what /violent /hands /can /she /lay /on /her TIT 3.02. 25
/i /can /interpret /all /her /martyr'd /signs: 3.02. 36

/but /that /between /us /we /can /kill /a /fly 3.02. 77
/quality /no /longer /than /they /can /sing? HAM 2.02.347 P
CAN* 1309 FR 0.1479 REL FR 962 V 347 P
if you can command these elements to silence, TMP 1.01. 21 P
certainly, sir, i can. 1.02. 41
thee more profit | than other princess' can, 1.02.173
there's nothing ill can dwell in such a temple. 1.02.458
for i can here disarm thee with this stick, 1.02.473
few in millions | can speak like us. 2.01. 8
she that from naples | can have no note, unless 2.01.248
there be that can rule naples | as well as he 2.01.262
lords that can prate | as amply and 2.01.263
three inches of it, | can lay to bed for ever; 2.01.284
if i can recover him, and keep him tame, and get 2.02. 68 P
if i can recover him, and keep him tame, i will 2.02. 76 P
this will shake your shaking, i can tell you, 2.02. 84 P
can he vent trinculos? 2.02.106 P
i can swim like a duck, i'll be sworn. 2.02.128 P
nor can imagination form a shape, | besides 3.01. 56
but my rejoicing | at nothing can be more. 3.01. 94
this can sack and drinking do. 3.02. 79 P
by'r lakin, i can go no further, sir, | my old 3.03. 1
(worse than any death | can be at once) shall 3.03. 78
strong'st suggestion | our worser genius can, 4.01. 27
before you can say "come" and "go," | and 4.01. 44
on whose nature | nurture can never stick; 4.01.189
nay, that i can deny by a circumstance. TGV 1.01. 84 P
give me a note, your ladyship can set. 1.02. 78
i look on you, i can hardly think you my master. 2.01. 31 P
no, boy, but as well as i can do them. 2.01. 92 P
though the chameleon love can feed on the air, i 2.01.173 P
when possibly i can, i will return. 2.02. 3
upon a homely object love can wink. 2.04. 98
now can i break my fast, dine, sup, and sleep, 2.04.141
proteus, all i can is nothing | to her, whose 2.04.165
if i can check my erring love, i will; 2.04.213
that longs for every thing that he can come by. 3.01.125
can nothing speak? master, shall i strike? 3.01.199 P
"inprimis, she can fetch and carry." 3.01.275 P
why, a horse can do no more; 3.01.276 P
"item, she can milk." 3.01.278 P
thou liest; i can. 3.01.292 P
"inprimis, she can milk." 3.01.301 P
ay, that she can. 3.01.302 P
"item, she can sew." 3.01.306 P
that's as much as to say, "can she so?" 3.01.307 P
"item, she can knit." 3.01.308 P
with a wench, when she can knit him a stock? 3.01.310 P
"item, she can wash and scour." 3.01.311 P
"item, she can spin." 3.01.314 P
on wheels, when she can spin for her living. 3.01.316 P
him, | your slander never can endamage him; 3.02. 43
if i can do it | by aught that i can speak in 3.02. 46
it | by aught that i can speak in his dispraise, 3.02. 47
as much as i can do, i will effect. 3.02. 66
in what you please; i'll do what i can. 4.04. 42
that can with some discretion do my business — 4.04. 65
alas, how love can trifle with itself! 4.04.183
in her, | but i can make respective in myself, 4.04.195
here can i sit alone, unseen of any, | and to 5.04. 4
words | can no way change you to a milder form, 5.04. 56
dog, and a fair dog — can there be more said? WIV 1.01. 96 P
where's simple, my man? can you tell, cousin? 1.01.134 P
the cause with as great discreetly as we can. 1.01.146 P
but can you affection the oman? 1.01.227 P
can you carry your good will to the maid? 1.01.230 P
cousin abraham slender, can you love her? 1.01.232 P
if you can carry her your desires towards her. 1.01.236 P
can you love the maid? 1.01.243 P
i can construe the action of her familiar style, 1.03. 46 P
the casement, and see if you can see my master, 1.04. 2 P
evans i will do what i can for your master. 1.04. 34 P
man, i'll do /you your master what good i can; 1.04. 93 P
than i do, nor can do more than i do with her, i 1.04.129 P
i can tell you that by the way, i praise heaven 1.04.140 P
if the love of a soldier can suffice — that i 2.01. 11 P
it is as much as i can do to keep the terms of 2.02. 21 P
he, he — i can never hit on 's name. 3.02. 24 P
my uncle can tell you good jests of him. 3.04. 39 P
they can tell you how things go better than i 3.04. 65 P
can tell you how things go better than i can. 3.04. 66 P
i will do what i can for them all three, for so 3.04.107 P
if they can find in their hearts the poor 4.02.217 P
that neither, singly, can be manifested, 4.06. 15
and i'll do what i can to get you a pair of 5.01. 6 P
jove, or who can blame me to piss my tallow? 5.05. 14 P
are now so sure that nothing can dissolve us. 5.05.224
lists of all advice | my strength can give you. MM 1.01. 7
to one that can my part in him advertise. 1.01. 41
thus can the demigod, authority, | make us pay 1.02.120
seat, that it may know | he can command, lets it 1.02.162
and discourse, | and well she can persuade. 1.02.186
dart of love | can pierce a complete bosom. 1.03. 3
can you so stead me | as bring me to the sight 1.04. 17
i'll see what i can do. 1.04. 84
is pretty orders beginning, i can tell you: 2.01.236 P
but can you if you would? 2.02. 51
can it be | that modesty may more betray our 2.02.167
for i can speak | against the thing i say. 2.04. 59
as for you, | say what you can: 2.04.170
think you i can a resolution fetch | from 3.01. 81
that thus can make him bite the law by th' nose, 3.01.108
imprisonment | can lay on nature is a paradise 3.01.130
if ever he return, and i can speak to him, i 3.01.192 P
can this be so? did angelo so leave her? 3.01.224 P
but how out of this can she avail? 3.01.234 P
i know none. can you tell me of any? 3.02. 87 P
but this i can let you understand, the greater 3.02.135 P
i can hardly believe that, since you know not 3.02.153 P
but indeed i can do you little harm; 3.02.166 P
nor greatness in mortality | can censure scape; 3.02.186
can tie the gall up in the slanderous tongue? 3.02.188
possess'd him my most stay | can be but brief; 4.01. 44
can you cut off a man's head? 4.02. 1 P
if the man be a bachelor, sir, i can; 4.02. 3 P
head, and i can never cut off a woman's head. 4.02. 4 P
who can do good on him? 4.02. 68
nor persuasion can with ease attempt you, i will 4.02.190 P
if you can, pace your wisdom | in that good path 4.03.132
i can tell thee pretty tales of the duke. 4.03.165 P
that no particular scandal once can touch | but 4.04. 27
he was drunk then, my lord, it can be no better. 5.01.188 P
what can you vouch | against him, signior lucio? 5.01.323
or impudence, | that yet can do thee office? 5.01.364
guiltiness, | to think i can be undiscernible, 5.01.368
yet will i favor thee in what i can; ERR 1.01.149
they can be meek that have no other cause: 2.01. 33
hands with me, and that my two ears can witness. 2.01. 46 P
what ruins are in me that can be found, | by him 2.01. 96
unfeeling fools can with such wrongs dispense: 2.01.103
how can she thus then call us by our names, 2.02.166
can you tell? 3.01. 52
can you tell for whose sake? 3.01. 57
suit of buff which 'rested him, that can i tell. 4.02. 45
this chain you had of me, can you deny it? 5.01. 22
he cries for you, and vows, if he can take you, 5.01.182
city, | can witness with me that it is not so. 5.01.325
only this commendation i can afford her, that ADO 1.01.173 P
can the world buy such a jewel? 1.01.181 P
i can see yet without spectacles, and i see no 1.01.189 P
count claudio, i can be secret as a dumb man; 1.01.209 P
i can tell you strange news that you yet dreamt 1.02. 4 P
can you make no use of your discontent? 1.03. 38 P
and i can give you intelligence of an intended 1.03. 44 P
if i can cross him any way, i bless myself every 1.03. 67 P
i never can see him but i am heart–burn'd an 2.01. 4 P
good eye, uncle, i can see a church by daylight. 2.01. 82 P
can virtue hide itself? 2.01.122 P
the antipodes that you can devise to send me on; 2.01.265 P
thus far can i praise him: 2.01.378 P
if we can do this, cupid is no longer an archer; 2.01.384 P
yea, my lord, but i can cross it. 2.02. 3 P
i can, at any unseasonable instant of the night, 2.02. 16 P
grow this to what adverse issue it can, i will 2.02. 51 P
the best i can, my lord. 2.03. 88 P
this can be no trick: 2.03.220 P
their detractions and can put them to mending. 2.03.230 P
'tis a truth, i can bear them witness; 2.03.231 P
can this be true? 3.01.107
can you smell him out by that? 3.02. 50 P
or george seacole, for they can write and read. 3.03. 12 P
nor i list not to think what i can, nor indeed i 3.04. 83 P
you will be in love, or that you can be in love. 3.04. 86 P
of truth | can cunning sin cover itself withal! 4.01. 36
who can blot that name | with any just reproach? 4.01. 80
marry, that can hero, | hero itself can blot out 4.01. 81
hero, | hero itself can blot out hero's virtue. 4.01. 82
shape | than i can lay it down in likelihood. 4.01.236
with no sauce that can be devis'd to it. 4.01.279 P
and this is more, masters, than you can deny. 4.02. 60 P
can counsel and speak comfort to that grief 5.01. 21
penance your invention | can lay upon my sin; 5.01.274
if your love | can labor aught in sad invention, 5.01.283
i can find out no rhyme to "lady" but "baby," an 5.02. 37 P
all this amazement can i qualify, | when after 5.04. 67
any purpose that the world can say against it, 5.04.106 P
i can but say their protestation over: LLL 1.01. 33
and every godfather can give a name. 1.01. 93
than for that angel knowledge you can say, | yet 1.01.113
as the rest of the court can possible devise." 1.01.131 P
as another man, and therefore i can be quiet. 1.02.166 P
and how can that be true love, which is falsely 1.02.171 P
you can produce acquittances | for such a sum 2.01.160
boyet, you can carve, | break up this capon. 4.01. 55
cannot, cannot, | and i cannot, another can. 4.01.128
many can brook the weather that love not the 4.02. 33
can you tell me by your wit | what was a month 4.02. 34
is that tongue that well can thee commend, | all 4.02.112
how far dost thou excel | no thought can think, 4.03. 40
once more i'll mark how love can vary wit. 4.03. 98
leaves the wind, | all unseen, can passage find; 4.03.104
as true we are as flesh and blood can be. 4.03.211
o, who can give an oath? 4.03.246
say, can you fast? 4.03.290
can you still dream and pore and thereon look? 4.03.294
the law, | and who can sever love from charity? 4.03.362
such as the shortness of the time can shape, 4.03.375
we can afford no more at such a price. 5.02.223
that can never be. 5.02.225
since you can cog, i'll play no more with you. 5.02.235
for it can never be | they will digest this 5.02.288
'a can carve too, and lisp; 5.02.323
nay, he can sing | a mean most meanly and in 5.02.327
most meanly and in hushering | mend him who can. 5.02.329
can any face of brass hold longer out? 5.02.395
it is not so, for how can this be true, | that 5.02.426
you cannot beg us, sir, i can assure you, sir, 5.02.490
choice, | you can endure the livery of a nun, MND 1.01. 70
and (which is more than all these boasts can be) 1.01.103
how happy some o'er other some can be! 1.01.226
love can transpose to form and dignity. 1.01.233
you can play no part but pyramus; 1.02. 85 P
again | ere the leviathan can swim a league. 2.01.174
her sight | (as i can take it with another herb) 2.01.184
what worser place can i beg in your love | (and 2.01.208
then how can it be said i am alone, | when all 2.01.225
knit, | so that but one heart we can make of it; 2.02. 48
man, | that i did never, no, never can, 2.02.126
you can never bring in a wall. 3.01. 65 P
will not stir from this place, do what they can. 3.01.122 P
nay, i can gleek upon occasion. 3.01.146 P
nor is he dead, for aught that i can tell. 3.02. 76
how can these things in me seem scorn to you, 3.02.126
can you not hate me, as i know you do, | but you 3.02.149
if she cannot entreat, i can compel. 3.02.248
i say i love thee more than he can do. 3.02.254
can you do me greater harm than hate? 3.02.271
but that my nails can reach unto thine eyes. 3.02.298
lower than myself, | that i can match her. 3.02.305
briers, | i can no further crawl, no further go; 3.02.444
my legs can keep no pace with my desires. 3.02.445
we the globe can compass soon, | swifter than 4.01. 97
i was — there is no man can tell what. 4.01.208 P
one sees more devils than vast hell can hold; 5.01. 9
unless you can find sport in their intents, 5.01. 79
for never any thing can be amiss, | when 5.01. 82
he says they can do nothing in this kind. 5.01. 88
chink, | to spy and i can hear my thisby's face. 5.01.193
how can it be? 5.01.280
go forth, | try what my credit can in venice do. MV 1.01.180
i can easier teach twenty what were good to be 1.02. 15 P
his own good parts that he can shoe him himself. 1.02. 42 P
but, alas, who can converse with a dumb show? 1.02. 73 P
with so good heart as i can bid the other four 1.02.128 P
if i can catch him once upon the hip, | i will 1.03. 46
the devil can cite scripture for his purpose. 1.03. 98
a cur can lend three thousand ducats?" 1.03.122
come on, in this there can be no dismay, | my 1.03.180
can you tell me whether one launcelot, that 2.02. 46 P
for she is wise, if i can judge of her, | and 2.06. 53
of venice, i can make what merchandise i will. 3.01.128 P
she is not bred so dull but she can learn; 3.02.162
i wish you all the joy that you can wish; 3.02.190
for i am sure you can wish none from me; 3.02.191
my eyes, my lord, can look as swift as yours: 3.02.197
but none can drive him from the envious plea 3.02.282
work | than customary bounty can enforce you. 3.04. 9
is but one hope in it that can do you any good, 3.05. 6 P
commonwealth than you can the getting up of the 3.05. 38 P
how every fool can play upon the word! 3.05. 43 P
and that no lawful means can carry me | out of 4.01. 9
so can i give no reason, nor i will not, | more 4.01. 59
but no metal can, | no, not the hangman's axe, 4.01.124
can no prayers pierce thee? 4.01.126
in venice | can alter a decree established. 4.01.219
what mercy can you render him, antonio? 4.01.378
i'll see if i can get my husband's ring, | which 4.02. 13
can you tell if rosalind, the duke's daughter, AYL 1.01.105 P
will take little delight in it, i can tell you, 1.02.158 P
speak to him, ladies, see if you can move him. 1.02.162 P
in mine eye, i can tell who should down. 1.02.214 P
can i not say, i thank you? 1.02.249
but i can tell you that of late this duke | hath 1.02.277
that can translate the stubbornness of fortune 2.01. 19
can it be possible that no man saw them? 2.02. 1
yet this i will not do, do how i can. 2.03. 35
can in this desert place buy entertainment, 2.04. 72
i can suck melancholy out of a song, as a weasel 2.05. 12 P
i'll go sleep, if i can; 2.05. 60 P
dear master, i can go no further. 2.06. 1 P
beast, | for i can no where find him like a man. 2.07. 2
fie on thee! i can tell what thou wouldst do. 2.07. 62
pride | that can therein tax any private party? 2.07. 71
who can come in and say that i mean her, | when 2.07. 77
i scarce can speak to thank you for myself. 2.07.170
i was an irish rat, which i can hardly remember. 3.02.177 P
god buy you, let's meet as little as we can. 3.02.257 P
for though he go as softly as foot can fall, he 3.02.328 P
can you remember any of the principal evils that 3.02.351 P
neither rhyme nor reason can express how much. 3.02.398 P
a good priest that can tell you what marriage is 3.03. 85 P
and if mine eyes can wound, now let them kill 3.05. 16
there is no force in eyes | that can do hurt. 3.05. 27
that can entame my spirits to your worship. 3.05. 48
than any of her lineaments can show her. 3.05. 56
sell when you can, you are not for all markets. 3.05. 60
then, can one desire too much of a good thing? 4.01.123 P
why now, as fast as she can marry us. 4.01.134 P
can a woman rail thus? 4.03. 42 P
offer take | of me and all that i can make, | or 4.03. 61
i can live no longer by thinking. 5.02. 50 P
if you please, that i can do strange things. 5.02. 59 P
i will help you if i can. 5.02.111 P
the boy | can do all this that he hath promised? 5.04. 2
can you nominate in order now the degrees of the 5.04. 88 P
hand, | wherein your cunning can assist me much. SHR in.1. 92
fear not, my lord, we can contain ourselves, in.1. 100
if i can by any means light on a fit man to 1.01.110 P
nor can we be distinguish'd by our faces | for 1.01.200
i'll try how you can sol, fa, and sing it. 1.02. 17
i can, petruchio, help thee to a wife | with 1.02. 85
think you a little din can daunt mine ears? 1.02.199
and weep, | till i can find occasion of revenge. 2.01. 36
a meacock wretch can make the curstest shrew. 2.01.313
that love bianca more | than words can witness, 2.01.336
words can witness, or your thoughts can guess. 2.01.336
that can assure my daughter greatest dower 2.01.343
say, signior gremio, what can you assure her? 2.01.345
and she can have no more than all i have; 2.01.382
now let me see if i can conster it: 3.01. 41
me, | as i can change these poor accoutrements, 3.02.119
but yet not stay, entreat me how you can. 3.02.203
faith, as cold as can be. 4.03. 37
then come back to my /master's as soon as i can. 5.01. 6 P
do what you can, yours will not be entreated. 5.02. 89
best bring a maiden can season her praise in. AWW 1.01. 48 P
the best wishes that can | be forg'd in your 1.01. 74
there's little can be said in't, 'tis against 1.01.135 P
if i can remember thee, i will think of thee at 1.01.188 P
he had the wit which i can well observe | to–day 1.02. 32
ere they can hide their levity in honor. 1.02. 35
too, | since i nor wax nor honey can bring home, 1.02. 65
can 't no other, | but, i your daughter, he must 1.03.165
what i can help thee to thou shalt not miss. 1.03.256
that laboring art can never ransom nature | from 2.01.118
what i can do can do no hurt to try, | since you 2.01.134
what i can do can do no hurt to try, | since you 2.01.134
for all that life can rate | worth name of life 2.01.179
all | that happiness and prime can happy call. 2.01.182
sir, you can eat none of this homely meat. 2.02. 46 P
disdain'st in her, the which | i can build up. 2.03.118
creature as a maid, | i can create the rest. 2.03.143
my life, if i can meet him with any convenience, 2.03.238 P
there can be no kernel in this light nut; 2.05. 43 P
sir, i can nothing say, | but that i am your 2.05. 71
whilst i can shake my sword or hear the drum. 2.05. 91
and all the honors that can fly from us | shall 3.01. 20
of neither on the start | can woman me unto't. 3.02. 51
to tell him that his sword can never win | the 3.02. 93
and brokes with all that can in such a suit 3.05. 71
mystery in stratagem can bring this instrument 3.06. 65 P
he can come no other way but by this 4.01. 1 P
i understand thee, and can speak thy tongue. 4.01. 74 P
there, if they were more than they can commend. 4.03. 81 P

he can say nothing of me. 4.03.116 P
if ye pinch me like a pasty, i can say no more. 4.03.123 P
nor believe he can have every thing in him by 4.03.145 P
i would do the man what honor i can, but of this 4.03.271 P
held, can serve the world for no honest use; 4.03.306 P
ere i can perfect mine intents, to kneel. 4.04. 4
that can such sweet use make of what they hate, 4.04. 22
you, i can serve as great a prince as you are. 4.05. 36 P
grow in my requital | as nothing can unroot you. 5.01. 6
foot of time | steals ere we can effect them. 5.03. 42
i neither can nor will deny | but that i know 5.03.166
"when from my finger you can get this ring | and 5.03.312
if she, my liege, can make me know this clearly, 5.03.315
for i can guess that by thy honest aid | thou 5.03.329
for i can sing | and speak to him in many sorts TN 1.02. 57
i am not such an ass but i can keep my hand dry. 1.03. 75 P
faith, i can cut a caper. 1.03.121 P
and i can cut the mutton to't. 1.03.122 P
i can tell thee where that saying was born, of 1.05. 9 P
can you do it? 1.05. 59 P
i can say little more than i have studied, and 1.05.178 P
i hate it as an unfill'd can. 2.03. 7 P
coming, | that can sing both high and low. 2.03. 41
if you can separate yourself and your 2.03. 98 P
i know i can do it. 2.03.137 P
i can write very like my lady your niece; 2.03.159 P
on a forgotten matter we can hardly make 2.03.160 P
can bide the beating of so strong a passion | as 2.04. 94
as hungry as the sea, | and can digest as much. 2.04.101
between that love a woman can bear me | and that 2.04.102
say | my love can give no place, bide no denay. 2.04.124
sir, i can yield you none without words, and 3.01. 23 P
thoughts | that tyrannous heart can think? 3.01.120
pride, | nor wit nor reason can my passion hide. 3.01.152
in the world can more prevail in man'i 3.02. 37 P
sav'd by believing rightly can ever believe such 3.02. 72 P
i can hardly forbear hurling things at him. 3.02. 81 P
i can no other answer make but thanks, | and 3.03. 14
or unsafe circumstance — what can be said? 3.04. 81 P
nothing that can be can come between me and the 3.04. 81 P
nothing that can be can come between me and the 3.04. 81 P
skill, and wrath can furnish man withal. 3.04.232 P
that satisfaction can be none but by pangs of 3.04.239 P
i will make your peace with him if i can. 3.04.269 P
fabian can scarce hold him yonder. 3.04.282 P
that my deserts to you | can lack persuasion? 3.04.349
none can be call'd deform'd but the unkind. 3.04.368
and do all they can to face me out of my wits. 4.02. 93 P
how can that be? 5.01. 16 P
you can fool no more money out of me at this 5.01. 41 P
how can this be? 5.01. 92
ay, husband. can he that deny? 5.01.144
nor can there be that deity in my nature | of 5.01.227
if spirits can assume both form and suit, | you 5.01.235
write from it, if you can, in hand or phrase, 5.01.332
you can say none of this. 5.01.334
tougher, brother, | than you can put us to't. WT 1.02. 16
can thy dam? 1.02.137
communicat'st with dreams (how can this be?), 1.02.140
come between | ere you can say she's honest: 2.01. 76
you scarce can right me throughly, then, to say 2.01. 99
but she | i can hook to me — say that she were 2.03. 7
from all dishonesty he can. 2.03. 47
unworthy and unnatural lord | can do no more. 2.03.114
fellows, if they please, | can clear me in't. 2.03.144
we can. 2.03.144
which is more | than history can pattern, though 3.02. 36
to me can life be no commodity; 3.02. 93
if you can bring | tincture or lustre in her lip 3.02.204
they are heavier | than all thy woes can stir; 3.02.209
yet i can read waiting–gentlewoman in the scape. 3.03. 72 P
which none without thee can sufficiently manage, 4.02. 14 P
is extended more than can be thought to begin 4.02. 43 P
i can stand and walk. 4.03.111 P
ere they can behold | bright phoebus in his 4.04.123
no milliner can so fit his customers with gloves 4.04.192 P
all the lawyers in bohemia can learnedly handle, 4.04.206 P
'tis in request, i can tell you. 4.04.291 P
we can both sing it. 4.04.292 P
i can bear my part, you must know 'tis my 4.04.295 P
i shall have more than you can dream of yet, 4.04.388
can he speak? 4.04.399
i am sorry that by hanging thee i can | but 4.04.421
if they can but stay you | where you'll be loath 4.04.571
and, as you can, disliken | the truth of your 4.04.652
alone shall suffer what wit can make heavy and 4.04.772 P
that a king, at friend, | can send his brother; 5.01.141
lady paulina's steward, he can deliver you more. 5.02. 26 P
no settled senses of the world can match | the 5.03. 72
if you can behold it, | i'll make the statue 5.03. 87
what you can make her do, | i am content to look 5.03. 91
the which if he can prove, 'a pops me out | at JN 1.01. 68
well, now can i make any joan a lady. 1.01.184
than e'er the coward hand of france can win. 2.01.158
i can produce | a will that bars the title of 2.01.191
walls | can hide you from our messengers of war, 2.01.260
that can we not; 2.01.270
this union shall do more than battery can | to 2.01.446
with swifter spleen than powder can enforce, 2.01.448
can in this book of beauty read, "i love," | her 2.01.485
i can with ease translate it to my will; 2.01.513
judge, | that i can find should merit any hate. 2.01.520
then, prince dolphin, can you love this lady? 2.01.524
nay, ask me if i can refrain from love, | for i 2.01.525
but the huge firm earth | can hold it up. 3.01. 73
can taste the free breath of a sacred king? 3.01.148
when law can do no right, | let it be lawful 3.01.185
how can the law forbid my tongue to curse? 3.01.190
that nothing can allay, nothing but blood, | the 3.01.342
what can go well, when we have run so ill? 3.04. 5
there's nothing in this world can make me joy: 3.04.107
can you not read it? 4.01. 37
i can heat it, boy. 4.01.104
but with my breath i can revive it, boy. 4.01.111
flood, and can give audience | to any tongue, 4.02.139
now happy he whose cloak and center can | hold 4.03.155
can arbitrate this cause betwixt us twain; R2 1.01. 50
yet can i not of such tame patience boast | as 1.01. 52
it must be great that can inherit us | so much 1.01. 85
the which no balm can cure but his heart–blood 1.01.172
farewell, my liege, now no way can i stray; 1.03.206
can change their moons and bring their times 1.03.220
who can hold a fire in his hand | by thinking on 1.03.294
where e'er i wander, boast of this i can, 1.03.308
can sick men play so nicely with their names? 2.01. 84
what will ensue hereof, there's none can tell; 2.01.212
that their events can never fall out good. 2.01.214
no good at all that i can do for him, | unless 2.01.235
can wash the balm off from an anointed king; 3.02. 55
than can my care–tun'd tongue deliver him! 3.02. 92
so, for what can we bequeath | save our deposed 3.02.149
and nothing can we call our own but death, | and 3.02.152
thus, | how can you say to me i am a king? 3.02.177
and be slain — no worse can come to fight, 3.02.183
can gripe the sacred handle of our sceptre, 3.03. 80
my legs can keep no measure in delight, | when 3.04. 7
and you can witness with me this is true. 4.01. 63
what subject can give sentence on his king? 4.01.121
can no man tell me of my unthrifty son? 5.03. 1
love loving not itself, none other can. 5.03. 88
to be done | than out of anger can be uttered. 1H4 1.01.107
as well as waiting in the court, i can tell you. 1.02. 70 P
a head, | for, bear ourselves as even as we can, 1.03.285
and great oney'rs, such as can hold in, such as 2.01. 77 P
and can call them all by their christen names, 2.04. 7 P
that i can drink with any tinker in his own 2.04. 18 P
it, yea, and can show it you here in the house; 2.04.257 P
son | can trace me in the tedious ways of art, 3.01. 47
i can call spirits from the vasty deep. 3.01. 52
why, so can i, or so can any man, | but will 3.01. 53
why, so can i, or so can any man, | but will 3.01. 53
why, i can teach you, cousin, to command | the 3.01. 55
and i can teach thee, coz, to shame the devil 3.01. 57
i can speak english, lord, as well as you, | for 3.01.119
my wife can speak no english, i no welsh. 3.01.191
one that no persuasion can do good upon. 3.01.197
as well as i am doubtless i can purge | myself 3.02. 20
where shall i find one that can steal well? 3.03.188 P
i can but thank you. 4.01. 13
if we without his help can make a head | to push 4.01. 80
as heart can think. 4.01. 84
the king, i can tell you, looks for us all, we 4.02. 56 P
for nothing can seem foul to those that win. 5.01. 8
nothing but a colossus can do thee that 5.01.123 P
can honor set to a leg? 5.01.131 P
look how we can, or sad or merrily, 5.02. 12
can lift your blood up with persuasion. 5.02. 78
with the best blood that i can meet withal | in 5.02. 94
give me life, which if i can save, so; 5.03. 60 P
nor can one england brook a double reign | of 5.04. 66
i can no longer brook thy vanities. 5.04. 74
shall find no boy's play here, i can tell you. 5.04. 76 P
to be either earl or duke, i can assure you. 5.04.142 P
wav'ring multitude, | can play upon it. 2H4 in 20
as good as heart can wish: 1.01. 13
but he's almost out of mine, i can assure him. 1.02. 28 P
the name of rebellion can tell how to make it. 1.02. 77 P
not a dangerous action can peep out his head but 1.02.213 P
a man can no more separate age and covetousness 1.02.229 P
covetousness than 'a can part young limbs and 1.02.230 P
i can get no remedy against this consumption of 1.02.236 P
if i can close with him, i care not for his 2.01. 18 P
you, can thrust me from a level consideration. 2.01.113 P
well spoke on, i can hear it with mine own ears. 2.02. 65 P
the worst that they can say of me is that i am a 2.02. 66 P
and, but my going, nothing can redeem it. 2.03. 8
i'll see if i can find out sneak. 2.04. 21 P
wine, and it perfumes the blood ere one can say, 2.04. 28 P
can a weak empty vessel bear such a huge full 2.04. 62 P
now 'a said so, i can tell whereupon. 2.04. 91 P
you can do it, sir, you can do it, i commend you 3.02.146 P
do it, sir, you can do it, i commend you well. 3.02.146 P
will do my good will, sir, you can have no more. 3.02.156 P
a man can die but once, we owe god a death. 3.02.234 P
me | that no conditions of our peace can stand. 4.01.182
if we can make our peace | upon such large terms 4.01.183
by thee, i can assure thee that 'a will not out, 5.03. 66 P
why then say an old man can do somewhat. 5.03. 78 P
that can hardly be, master shallow. 5.05. 76 P
can this cockpit hold | the vasty fields of H5 pr 11
cat, | to 'tame and havoc more than she can eat. 1.02.173
france | that can be with a nimble galliard won; 1.02.252
for i can take, and pistol's cock is up, | and 2.01. 52
"i can never win | a soul so easy as that 2.02.124
what rein can hold licentious wickedness | when 3.03. 22
can sodden water, | a drench for sur–rein'd 3.05. 18
i can tell your majesty, the duke is a prave man 3.06. 96 P
for how can they charitably dispose of any thing 4.01.142 P
can try it out with all unspotted soldiers. 4.01.160 P
native punishment, though they can outstrip men, 4.01.168 P
a private displeasure can do against a monarch! 4.01.199 P
of every fool whose sense no more can feel | but 4.01.235
can sleep so soundly as the wretched slave; 4.01.268
though all that i can do is nothing worth, 4.01.303
of knavery, mark you now, as can be offert; 4.07. 3 P
plood out of your pody, i can tell you that. 4.07.107 P
or if i can see my glove in his cap, which he 4.07.128 P
me as great honors as can be desir'd in the 4.07.160 P
i can tell you it will serve you to mend your 4.08. 68 P
if you can mock a leek, you can eat a leek. 5.01. 37 P
if you can mock a leek, you can eat a leek. 5.01. 37 P
your mightiness on both parts best can witness. 5.02. 28
that can rhyme themselves into ladies' favors, 5.02.156 P
can any of your neighbors tell, kate? 5.02.196 P
of beauty, can do no more spoil upon my face. 5.02.231 P
can you blame her then, being a maid yet ros'd 5.02.294 P
i'll to the tower with all the haste i can, | to 1H6 1.01.167
what's past and what's to come she can descry. 1.02. 57
now do thou watch, for i can stay no longer. 1.04. 18
heavens, can you suffer hell so to prevail? 1.05. 9
how can these contrarieties agree? 2.03. 59
believe me, lords, my tender years can tell, 3.01. 71
can you, my lord of winchester, behold | my 3.01.107
can this be so? 4.01. 61
but your discretions better can persuade | than 4.01.158
broils, | than yet can be imagin'd or suppos'd. 4.01.186
lucy, farewell, no more my fortune can, | but 4.03. 43
upon my death the french can little boast; 4.05. 24
no more can i be severed from your side | than 4.05. 48
than can yourself yourself in twain divide. 4.05. 49
my spirit can no longer bear these harms. 4.07. 30
charms, | and try if they can gain your liberty. 5.03. 32
no shape but his can please your dainty eye. 5.03. 38
a wife, | then how can margaret be thy paramour? 5.03. 82
yet, can testify | she was the first fruit of my 5.04. 12
i can express no kinder sign of love | than this 2H6 1.01. 18
dimm'd mine eyes, that i can read no further. 1.01. 55
ay, uncle, we will keep it, if we can; 1.01.107
in what we can to bridle and suppress | the 1.01.200
but can do more in england than the king. 1.03. 71
and he of these that can do most of all | cannot 1.03. 72
what, minion, can ye not? 1.03.138
that can i witness, and a fouler fact | did 1.03.173
have done, for more i hardly can endure. 1.04. 38
these news, as fast as horse can carry them — 1.04. 74
that mounts no higher than a bird can soar. 2.01. 14
with such holiness can you do it? 2.01. 26
shall find their deaths, if york can prophesy. 2.02. 76
nell, ill can thy noble mind abrook | the abject 2.04. 10
ah, humphrey, can i bear this shameful yoke? 2.04. 37
he that can do all in all | with her that hateth 2.04. 51
robes, | and show itself, attire me how i can. 2.04.109
can you not see? 3.01. 4
which fear, if better reasons can supplant, | i 3.01. 37
and york, | reprove my allegation if you can, 3.01. 40
who can accuse me? 3.01.103
but i can give the loser leave to chide. 3.01.182
and can do nought but wail her darling's loss, 3.01.216
ere you can take due orders for a priest. 3.01.274
to make commotion, as full well he can, | under 3.01.358
i know no pain they can inflict upon him | will 3.01.377
can chase away the first–conceived sound? 3.02. 44
ay me, i can no more! 3.02.120
i can no more: 3.02.365
can i make men live, whe'er they will or no? 3.03. 10
more can i bear than you dare execute. 4.01.130
come, soldiers, show what cruelty ye can, | that 4.01.132
he can write and read and cast accompt. 4.02. 85 P
nay, he can make obligations, and write 4.02. 93 P
so well brought up that i can write my name. 4.02.106 P
his son am i, deny it if you can. 4.02.146
and more than that, he can speak french, and 4.02.166 P
nay, answer if you can. 4.02.169 P
can he that speaks with the tongue of an enemy 4.02.170 P
but who can cease to weep and look on this? 4.04. 4
such aid as i can spare you shall command, | but 4.05. 6
fire, and, if you can, burn down the tower too. 4.06. 14 P
words as no christian ear can endure to hear. 4.07. 40 P
be as free as heart can wish or tongue can tell. 4.07.125 P
be as free as heart can wish or tongue can tell. 4.07.125 P
into this garden, to see if i can eat grass, or 4.10. 8 P
scarce can i speak, my choler is so great. 5.01. 23
with me, | knowing how hardly i can brook abuse? 5.01. 92
/these | if they can brook i bow a knee to man. 5.01.110
who can be bound by any solemn vow | to do a 5.01.184
can we outrun the heavens? good margaret, stay. 5.02. 73
and to secure us | by what we can, which can no 5.02. 77
us | by what we can, which can no more but fly. 5.02. 77
of salisbury, who can report of him, | that 5.03. 1
nay, before them, if we can. 5.03. 28
proud, | can set the duke up in despite of me. 3H6 1.01.158
who can be patient in such extremes? 1.01.215
no, i can better play the orator. 1.02. 2
scorning what e'er you can afflict me with. 1.04. 38
so cowards fight when they can fly no further, 1.04. 40
and if thine eyes can water for his death, | i 1.04. 82
that not a tear can fall for rutland's death? 1.04. 88
so | that hardly can i check my eyes from tears. 1.04.151
nor can my tongue unload my heart's great 2.01. 81
can pluck the diadem from faint henry's head, 2.01.153
for scarce i can refrain | the execution of my 2.02.110
can neither call it perfect day nor night. 2.05. 4
for how can i help them and not myself? 3.01. 21
she, poor wretch, for grief can speak no more; 3.01. 47
i can tell you both | her suit is granted for 3.02.116
to take their rooms, ere i can place myself: 3.02.132
what other pleasure can the world afford? 3.02.147
why, i can smile, and murther whiles i smile, 3.02.182
i can add colors to the chameleon, | change 3.02.191
can i do this, and cannot get a crown? 3.02.194
it shall be eas'd if france can yield relief. 3.03. 20
for how can tyrants safely govern home, | unless 3.03. 69
can oxford, that did ever fence the right, | now 3.03. 98
that your estate requires and mine can yield. 3.03.150
where having nothing, nothing can he lose. 3.03.152
be appeas'd | by such invention as i can devise? 4.01. 35
what danger or what sorrow can befall thee | so 4.01. 76
yet am i arm'd against the worst can happen; 4.01.128
"wind–changing warwick now can change no more." 5.01. 57
and, live we how we can, yet die we must. 5.02. 28
say you can swim, alas, 'tis but a while; 5.04. 29
can so young a thorn begin to prick? 5.05. 13
my breast can better brook thy dagger's point 5.06. 27
point | than can my ears that tragic history. 5.06. 28
but, as i can learn, | he hearkens after R3 1.01. 53
can you deny all this? 1.01. 96
touches me deeper than you can imagine. 1.01.112
the death of thee | than i can wish to wolves — 1.02. 19
fairer than tongue can name thee, let me have 1.02. 81
fouler than heart can think thee, thou canst 1.02. 83
i can no longer hold me patient. 1.03.156
than death can yield me here by my abode. 1.03.168
can curses pierce the clouds and enter heaven? 1.03.194
exceeding those that i can wish upon thee, | o, 1.03.217
can this dark monarchy afford false clarence?" 1.04. 51
him, from the which no warrant can defend me. 1.04.112 P
grandam, we can; 2.02. 20
how can we aid you with our kindred tears? 2.02. 63
but none can help our harms by wailing them. 2.02.103
the sum of all i can i have disclos'd. 2.04. 46
nor more can you distinguish of a man | than of 3.01. 9
can from his mother win the duke of york, | anon 3.01. 38
my good lords both, with all the heed i can. 3.01.187
where nothing can proceed that toucheth us 3.02. 23

can lesser hide his love or hate than he, | for		3.04. 52
tut, i can counterfeit the deep tragedian,		3.05. 5
for them | as i can say nay to thee for myself,		3.07. 53
and die ere men can say, "god save the queen!"		4.01. 62
lo, ere i can repeat this curse again, | within		4.01. 77
if sorrow can admit society, | /tell /over /your		4.04. 38
heaven, | to be discover'd, that can do me good?		4.04.241
therefore accept such kindness as i can.		4.04.310
can make seem pleasing to her tender years?		4.04.342
greatest strength and power that he can make,		4.04.450
all comfort that the dark night can afford | be		5.03. 80
than can the substance of ten thousand soldiers		5.03.218
those that can pity, here | may (if they think	H8	pr 5
and, if you can be merry then, i'll say | a man		pr 31
that such a keech can with his very bulk | take		1.01. 55
but i can see his pride | peep through each part		1.01. 68
not a man in england | can advise me like you;		1.01.135
he answer'd, "tush, | it can do me no damage";		1.02.183
i can, my liege.		1.02.188
abusing better men than they can be | out of a		1.03. 28
good wine, good welcome, | can make good people.		1.04. 7
you can speak the french tongue;		1.04. 57
yet i can give you inkling | of an ensuing evil,		2.01.140
who can be angry now?		2.02. 88
the most convenient place that i can think of		2.02.137
yet prayers and wishes | are all i can return.		2.03. 70
and process of this time, you can report, | and		2.04. 38
what can be their business | with me, a poor		3.01. 19
can you think, lords, | that any englishman dare		3.01. 83
there sits a judge | that no king can corrupt.		3.01.101
what can happen | to me above this wretchedness?		3.01.122
what we can do to him (though now the time		3.02. 15
i | can nothing render but allegiant thanks,		3.02.176
else | this talking lord can lay upon my credit,		3.02.265
his noble jury and foul cause can witness.		3.02.269
dare mate a sounder man than surrey can be,		3.02.274
lords, | can ye endure to hear this arrogance?		3.02.278
now, if you can blush, and cry "guilty,"		3.02.305
can thy spirit wonder | a great man should		3.02.374
how can man then | (the image of his maker) hope		3.02.441
that i can tell you too.		4.01. 24
something i can command.		4.01.116
i can no more.		4.02.173
i fear nothing | what can be said against me.		5.01.126
the upper germany, can dearly witness, | yet		5.02. 65
lay all the weight ye can upon my patience, | i		5.02.101
(but few now living can behold that goodness)		5.04. 21
'tis ten to one this play can never please | all		ep 1
lay about him to-day, i can tell them that, and	TRO	1.02. 56 P
i can tell them that too.		1.02. 58 P
he's one of the flowers of troy, i can tell you.		1.02.187 P
he has a shrowd wit, i can tell you, and he's		1.02.191 P
can helenus fight, uncle?		1.02.222 P
i can watch you for telling how i took the blow		1.02.268 P
that can from hector bring those honors off,		1.03.334
there can be no evasion | to blench from this		2.02. 67
success in a bad cause, | can qualify the same?		2.02.118
for what, alas, can these my single arms?		2.02.135
can it be | that so degenerate a strain as this		2.02.153
can he not be sociable?		2.03.210 P
to cressid as what envy can say worst shall be a		3.02. 96 P
and what truth can speak truest not truer than		3.02. 97 P
they are burs, i can tell you, they'll stick		3.02.111 P
as, if it can, i will presume in you — | to		3.02.159
than breath or pen can give expressure to.		3.03.204
how can that be?		3.03.250 P
as heart can think or courage execute.		4.01. 14
no man alive can love in such a sort | the thing		4.01. 24
death, | do to this body what extremes you can;		4.02.102
how can i moderate it?		4.04. 5
but i can tell that in each grace of these		4.04. 89
can scarce entreat you to be odd with him.		4.05.265
any man may sing her, if he can take her cliff;		5.02. 10 P
she done, prince, that can /soil our mothers?		5.02.134
where reason can revolt | without perdition, and		5.02.144
soft-conscienc'd men can be content to say it	COR	1.01. 37 P
of more strong link asunder than can ever		1.01. 71
yet i can make my audit up, that all | from me		1.01.144
wonder | his insolence can brook to be commanded		1.01.262
we shall ever strike | till one can do no more.		1.02. 36
o, good madam, there can be none yet.		1.03. 91 P
choice of those | that best can aid your action.		1.06. 66
done | as you have done — that's what i can;		1.09. 16
what good condition can a treaty find | i' th'		1.10. 6
i know you can do very little alone, for your		2.01. 35 P
what harm can your beesom conspectuities glean		2.01. 64 P
greater devotion than they can render it him,		2.02. 19 P
your multiplying spawn how can he flatter —		2.02. 78
must these have voices, that can yield them now,		3.01. 34
consul's worthiness, | so can i name his faults.		3.01.277
put mine armor on, | which i can scarcely bear.		3.02. 35
though therein you can never be too noble, | but		3.02. 40
show our general louts | how you can frown, than		3.02. 67
serve, if he | can thereto frame his spirit.		3.02. 97
or never trust to what my tongue can do | i' th'		3.02.136
nor check my courage for what they can give,		3.03. 92
and can show /for rome | her enemies' marks upon		3.03.110
that's worthily | as any ear can hear.		4.01. 54
that can judge as fitly of his worth | as i can		4.02. 34
worth | as i can of those mysteries which heaven		4.02. 35
this lies glowing, i can tell you, and is almost		4.03. 25 P
o slaves, i can tell you news — news, you		4.05.172 P
he's as like to do't as any man i can imagine.		4.05.203 P
we have record that very well it can, | and		4.06. 50
he and aufidius can | no more atone than		4.06. 72
who is't can blame him?		4.06.105
and defense | that rome can make against them.		4.06.128
he knows not | what i can urge against him.		4.07. 19
more than the instant army we can make, | might		5.01. 37
only make trial what your love can do | for rome		5.01. 40
can you, when you have push'd out your gates the		5.02. 39 P
can you think to blow out the intended fire your		5.02. 45 P
things as you, i can scarce think there's any,		5.02.103 P
doves' eyes, | which can make gods forsworn?		5.03. 28
for how can we, | alas!		5.03.106
how can we, for our country pray, | whereto we		5.03.107
will move him more | than can our reasons.		5.03.158
that so short a time can alter the condition of		5.04. 9 P
can make you greater than the queen of goths.	TIT	1.01.269
bury him where you can, he comes not here.		1.01.354
(whether by device or no, the heavens can tell).		1.01.395
if the emperor's court can feast two brides,		1.01.489
my heart suspects more than mine eye can see.		2.03.213
and wonder greatly that man's face can fold | in		2.03.266
look, sirs, if you can find the huntsman out,		2.03.278
so now go tell, and if thy tongue can speak,		2.04. 1
see how with signs and tokens she can scrowl.		2.04. 5
can do no service on her sorrowful cheeks.		3.01.147
my youth can better spare my blood than you,		3.01.165
my lord, i know not, i, nor can i guess,		4.01. 16
can you hear a good man groan | and not relent,		4.01.123
can never turn the swan's black legs to white,		4.02.102
age | to keep mine own, excuse it how she can.		4.02.105
wrung with wrongs more than our backs can bear.		4.03. 49
sir, that is as fit as can be to serve for your		4.03. 95 P
can you deliver an oration to the emperor with a		4.03. 98 P
can you with a grace deliver up a supplication?		4.03.106 P
wings | he can at pleasure stint their melody;		4.04. 86
for i can smooth and fill his aged ears | with		4.04. 96
no, not a word, how can i grace my talk,		5.02. 17
murther or detested rape | can couch for fear,		5.02. 38
can the son's eye behold his father bleed?		5.03. 65
steel, | nor can i utter all our bitter grief,		5.03. 89
my scars can witness, dumb although they are,		5.03.114
i neither know it, nor can learn of him.	ROM	1.01.144
ere he can spread his sweet leaves to the air		1.01.152
and can never find what names the writing person		1.02. 43 P
god gi' god-den. i pray, sir, can you read?		1.02. 57 P
but, i pray, can you read any thing you see?		1.02. 60 P
stay, fellow, i can read.		1.02. 63 P
faith, i can tell her age unto an hour.		1.03. 11
can you love the gentleman?		1.03. 79
speak briefly, can you like of paris' love?		1.03. 96
he that can lay hold of her | shall have the		1.05.116
can i go forward when my heart is here?		2.01. 1
and what love can do, that dares love attempt;		2.02. 68
doth cease to be | ere one can say it lightens.		2.02.120
any man that can write may answer a letter.		2.04. 10 P
the slip, sir, the slip, can you not conceive?		2.04. 48 P
can any of you tell me where i may find the		2.04.118 P
i can tell you, but young romeo will be older		2.04.120 P
can you not stay a while?		2.05. 29
but come what sorrow can, | it cannot		2.06. 3
they are but beggars that can count their worth,		2.06. 32
the love i bear thee can afford | no better term		3.01. 60
i can discover all | the unlucky manage of this		3.01.142
lovers can see to do their amorous rites | by		3.02. 8
can heaven be so envious?		3.02. 40
romeo can, | though heaven cannot.		3.02. 40
that word's death, no words can that woe sound.		3.02.126
unless philosophy can make a juliet, | displant		3.03. 58
where thou shalt live till we can find a time		3.03.150
proud can i never be of what i hate, | but		3.05.147
for i'll try if they can lick their fingers.		4.02. 4 P
again, | for nothing can be ill if she be well.		5.01. 16
then she is well and nothing can be ill:		5.01. 17
can vengeance be pursued further than death?		5.03. 55
o, what more favor can i do to thee, | than with		5.03. 98
a greater power than we can contradict | hath		5.03.153
a while, | till we can clear these ambiguities,		5.03.217
what can he say to this?		5.03.271
daughter's jointure, for no more | can i demand.		5.03.298
but i can give thee more, | for i will /raise		5.03.298
a thousand moral paintings i can show | that	TIM	1.01. 90
none | can truly say he gives if he receives.		1.02. 11
you to myself than you can with modesty speak in		1.02. 93 P
better or properer can we call our own than the		1.02.102 P
o, joy's e'en made away ere't can be born!		1.02.106 P
man | can justly praise but what he does affect.		1.02.215
hold, no reason | can sound his state in safety.		2.01. 13
could i frankly use | as i can bid thee speak.		2.02.180
is't true? can 't be?		2.02.203
timon's fortunes 'mong his friends can sink.		2.02.231
but i can tell you one thing, my lord, and which		3.02. 4 P
lord timon myself, these gentlemen can witness;		3.02. 51 P
who can call him | his friend that dips in the		3.02. 65
i'm weary of this charge, the gods can witness.		3.04. 25
who can speak broader than he that has no house		3.04. 63 P
he's truly valiant that can wisely suffer | the		3.05. 31
wisely suffer | the worst that man can breathe,		3.05. 32
not that, if money and the season can yield it.		3.06. 51 P
the meat cool ere we can agree upon the first		3.06. 68 P
supply his life, or that which can command it.		4.02. 47
can bear great fortune | but by contempt of		4.03. 7
nothing can you steal | but thieves do lose it.		4.03.447
who can bring noblest minds to basest ends!		4.03.464
can you eat roots and drink cold water?		5.01. 74
what we can do, we'll do, to do you service.		5.01. 75
than their offense can weigh down by the dram;		5.01.151
yet if you be out, sir, i can mend you.	JC	1.01. 17 P
tell me, good brutus, can you see your face?		1.02. 51
and we can both | endure the winter's cold as		1.02. 98
i can as well be hang'd as tell the manner of it		1.02.235 P
can be retentive to the strength of spirit;		1.03. 95
that i do bear | i can shake off at pleasure.		1.03.100
so can i;		1.03.100
for he can do no more than caesar's arm | when		2.01.182
caesar, all that he can do | is to himself —		2.01.186
if he be so resolv'd, | i can o'ersway him;		2.01.203
for i can give his humor the true bent, | and i		2.01.210
can i bear that with patience, | and not my		2.01.301
what can be avoided | whose end is purpos'd by		2.02. 26
i have, when you have heard what i can say;		2.02. 92
ere i can tell thee what thou shouldst do there.		2.04. 5
but speak all good you can devise of caesar,		3.01.246
peace, let us hear what antony can say.		3.02. 71
for i can raise no money by vile means.		4.03. 71
the conquerors can but make a fire of him;		5.05. 55
he can report, | as seemeth by his plight, of	MAC	1.02. 1
speak, if you can: what are you?		1.03. 47
if you can look into the seeds of time, | and		1.03. 58
what, can the devil speak true?		1.03.107
more is thy due than more than all can pay.		1.04. 21
yet when we can entreat an hour to serve, | we		2.01. 22
'tis not for you to hear what i can speak:		2.03. 84
who can be wise, amaz'd, temp'rate, and furious,		2.03.108
threescore and ten i can remember well, | within		2.04. 1
in your nature | that you can let this go?		3.01. 87
foreign levy, nothing, | can touch him further.		3.02. 26
can such things be, | and overcome us like a		3.04.109
when now i think you can behold such sights,		3.04.113
your thoughts, | which can interpret farther;		3.06. 2
sir, can you tell | where he bestows himself?		3.06. 23
t' hold what distance | his wisdom can provide.		3.06. 45
who can impress the forest, bid the tree | unfix		4.01. 95
if your art | can tell so much, shall banquo's		4.01.102
why, i can buy me twenty at any market.		4.02. 40
and what i can redress, | as i shall find the		4.03. 9
of horrid hell can come a devil more damn'd | in		4.03. 56
you, but can perceive no truth in your report.		5.01. 1 P
it, when none can call our pow'r to accompt?		5.01. 38 P
bloodier villain | than terms can give thee out!		5.08. 8
who is't that can inform me?	HAM	1.01. 79
that can i.		1.01. 79
/shapes of grief, | that can /denote me truly.		1.02. 83
costly thy habit as thy purse can buy, | but not		1.03. 70
fee, | and for my soul, what can it do to that,		1.04. 66
dear a better proposer can charge you withal, be		2.02.287 P
can you play "the murther of gonzago"*		2.02.537 P
unpregnant of my cause, | and can say nothing;		2.02.569
an' can you by no drift of conference | get from		3.01. 1
the force of honesty can translate beauty into		3.01.112 P
but, sir, such answer as i can make, you shall		3.02.322 P
o wonderful son, that can so stonish a mother!		3.02.328 P
how can that be, when you have the voice of the		3.02.341 P
pray can i not, | though inclination be as sharp		3.03. 38
but, o, what form of prayer | can serve my turn?		3.03. 52
try what repentance can.		3.03. 65
what can it not?		3.03. 65
yet what can it, when one can not repent?		3.03. 66
yet what can it, when one can not repent?		3.03. 66
nay, then i'll set those to you that can speak.		3.04. 17
for use almost can change the stamp of nature,		3.04.168
that i can keep your counsel and not mine own.		4.02. 11 P
that treason can but peep to what it would,		4.05.125
that we can let our beard be shook with danger		4.07. 32
can you devise me?		4.07. 53
and they can well on horseback, but this gallant		4.07. 84
can save the thing from death | that is but		4.07.145
how can that be, unless she drown'd herself in		5.01. 6 P
marry, now i can tell.		5.01. 53 P
every fool can tell that.		5.01.146 P
hold his purpose, i will win for him and i can;		5.02.177 P
no med'cine in the world can do thee good;		5.02.314
i can no more — the king, the king's to blame.		5.02.320
all this can i | truly deliver.		5.02.385
curiosity in neither can make choice of either's	LR	1.01. 6 P
love you more than /words can wield the matter,		1.01. 55
beyond what can be valued, rich or rare, | no		1.01. 57
what can you say to draw | a third more opulent		1.01. 85
or, whilst i can vent clamor from my throat,		1.01.165
which nor our nature nor our place can bear,		1.01.171
can buy this unpriz'd precious maid of me.		1.01.259
my brother till you can derive from him better		1.02. 81 P
the wisdom of nature can reason it thus and thus		1.02.105 P
all with me's meet that i can fashion fit.		1.02.184
that can my speech defuse, my good intent | may		1.04. 2
i can keep honest counsel, ride, run, mar a		1.04. 32 P
can you make no use of nothing, nuncle?		1.04.130 P
no, boy, nothing can be made out of nothing.		1.04.132 P
a schoolmaster that can teach thy fool to lie —		1.04.179 P
who is it that can tell me who i am?		1.04.230
like an apple, yet i can tell what i can tell.		1.05. 16 P
like an apple, yet i can tell what i can tell.		1.05. 16 P
but i can tell why a snail has a house.		1.05. 27 P
since i came hither | (which i can call but now)		2.01. 87
comes too short | which can pursue th' offender.		2.01. 89
not a nose among twenty but can smell him that's		2.04. 71 P
i can scarce speak to thee;		2.04.136
i can be patient, i can stay with regan, | i and		2.04.230
i can be patient, i can stay with regan, | i and		2.04.230
is strange | and can make vild things precious.		3.02. 71
piece out the comfort with what addition i can.		3.06. 3 P
gone, | thy comforts can do me no good at all;		4.01. 16
who is't can say, "i am at the worst"?		4.01. 25
the worst is not | so long as we can say, "this		4.01. 28
these our nether crimes | so speedily can venge!		4.02. 80
what can man's wisdom | in the restoring his		4.04. 8
one hears that, | which can distinguish sound.		4.06.211
that of thy death and business i can tell.		4.06.278
i can produce a champion that will prove | what		5.01. 43
neither can be enjoy'd | if both remain alive:		5.01. 58
who can arraign me for't?		5.03.160
he's a good fellow, i can tell you that;		5.03.285
wherein the /toged consuls can propose | as	OTH	1.01. 25
the thick-lips owe | if he can carry't thus!		1.01. 67
i think i can discover him, if you please | to		1.01.178
what, in your own part, can you say to this?		1.03. 74
and little of this great world can i speak		1.03. 86
we lose it not, so long as we can smile.		1.03.211
what from the cape can you discern at sea?		2.01. 1
mountains melt on them, | can hold the mortise?		2.01. 9
what tidings can you tell /me of my lord?		2.01. 88
that /has an eye can stamp and counterfeit		2.01.243 P
do this, if you can bring it to any opportunity.		2.01.281 P
and nothing can or shall content my soul | till		2.01.298
if i can fasten but one cup upon him, | with		2.03. 48
a vomit ere the next pottle can be fill'd.		2.03. 85 P
i can stand well enough, and i speak well enough		2.03.115 P
your officer, iago, can inform you — | while i		2.03.198
that we can call these delicate creatures ours,		3.03.269
can any thing be made of this?		3.04. 10 P
can you inquire him out, and be edified by		3.04. 14 P
why, so i can, /sir, but i will not now.		3.04. 86
futurity, | can ransom me into his love again,		3.04.118
what i can do, i will;		3.04.130
can he be angry?		3.04.134
'tis but a little way that i can bring you,		3.04.199
sir, she can turn, and turn,		4.01.253
and she can weep, sir, weep;		4.01.254
wherein none can be so determinate as the		4.02.227 P
i can again thy former light restore, | should i		5.02. 9
promethean heat | that can thy light relume.		5.02. 13
who can control his fate?		5.02.265

any cunning cruelty | that can torment him much, 5.02.334
beggary in the love that can be reckon'd. ANT 1.01. 15
such a mutual pair | and such a twain can do't, 1.01. 38
infinite book of secrecy | a little i can read. 1.02. 11
storms and tempests than almanacs can report. 1.02.149 P
why should i think you can be mine, and true 1.03. 27
can fulvia die? 1.03. 58
you can do better yet; but this is meetly. 1.03. 81
no vessel can peep forth, but 'tis as soon 1.04. 53
both what by sea and land i can be able | to 1.04. 78
for i can do nothing | but what indeed is honest 1.05. 15
can from the lap of egypt's widow pluck | the 2.01. 37
graces speak | that which none else can utter. 2.02.130
modesty, can settle | the heart of antony, 2.02.240
if you can, your reason? 2.03. 13
as well as i can, madam. 2.05. 7
with what gift beside | thy modesty can beg. 2.05. 72
yes, something you can deny for your own safety: 2.06. 91 P
/bear as loud | as his strong sides can volley. 2.07.112
who does i' th' wars more than his captain can 3.01. 21
heart, nor can | her heart inform her tongue — 3.02. 47
faults | can never be so equal that your love 3.04. 35
that your love | can equally move with them. 3.04. 36
but if we fail, | we then can do't at land. 3.07. 53
can he be there in person? 3.07. 56
i can behold no longer. 3.10. 1
yet he that can endure | to follow with 3.13. 43
if that the former dare but what it can, | no 3.13. 80
though you can guess what temperance should be, 3.13.121
nerves, and can | get goal for goal of youth. 4.08. 21
death of one person can be paid but once, | and 4.14. 27
now my spirit is going, | i can no more. 4.15. 59
go with me, and see | what i can show in this. 5.01. 77
mortal house i'll ruin, | do caesar what he can. 5.02. 52
if thou and nature can so gently part, | the 5.02.294
so soon as i can win th' offended king, | i will CYM 1.01. 75
fine this tyrant | can tickle where she wounds! 1.01. 85
my holy duty) what | his rage can do on me. 1.01. 88
remain thou here, | while sense can keep it on. 1.01.118
can we, with manners, ask what was the 1.04. 52 P
and shall find it so | in all that i can do. 1.06. 31
which can distinguish 'twixt | the fiery orbs 1.06. 34
and can we not | partition make with spectacles 1.06. 36
can my sides hold, to think that man, who knows 1.06. 69
for gold | which rottenness can lend nature; 1.06.125
up and down like a cock that nobody can match. 2.01. 21 P
if you can penetrate her with your fingering, so 2.03. 14 P
of unpav'd eunuch to boot, can never amend. 2.03. 30 P
what | can it not do, and undo? 2.03. 73
are as dear as yours, | can justly boast of. 2.03. 80
am poor of thanks, | and scarce can spare them. 2.03. 90
he never can meet more mischance than come | to 2.03.132
and your company | o'erpays all i can do. 2.04. 10
if you can make't apparent | that you have 2.04. 56
then, if you can | be pale, i beg but leave to 2.04. 95
another stain, as big as hell can hold, | were 2.04.140
we have yet many among us can gripe as hard as 3.01. 40 P
if caesar can hide the sun from us with a 3.01. 43 P
therein false strook, can take no greater wound, 3.04.114
(and with what imitation you can borrow | from 3.04.171
how | can her contempt be answer'd? 3.05. 42
and my end | can make good use of either. 3.05. 64
alas, my lord, | how can she be with him? 3.05. 90
she can scarce be there yet. 3.05.150 P
weariness | can snore upon the flint, when resty 3.06. 34
i am not very sick, | since i can reason of it. 4.02. 14
no single soul | can we set eye on; 4.02.131
can it be six mile yet? 4.02.293
flies, as deep | as these poor pickaxes can dig; 4.02.389
it said a century of prayers | (such as i can) 4.02.392
us | find out the prettiest daisied plot we can, 4.02.398
us, and he shall be interr'd | as soldiers can. 4.02.402
your preparation can affront no less | than what 4.03. 29
we fear not | what can from italy annoy us, but 4.03. 34
but none of 'em can be found. 5.03. 88
he shall be happy that can find him, if | our 5.05. 6
can find him, if | our grace can make him so. 5.05. 7
these her women | can trip me, if i err, who 5.05. 35
who is't can read a woman? 5.05. 48
a roman with a roman's heart can suffer. 5.05. 81
for more probation | i can with ease produce. 5.05.363
hardness, that i can | make no collection of it. 5.05.431
eye | i give my cause, who best can justify. PER 1.ch. 42
if i can get him within my pistol's length, 1.01.166
dead, | my heart can lend no succor to my head. 1.01.169
where grief should sleep, can breed me quiet? 1.02. 5
yet neither pleasure's art can joy my spirits, 1.02. 9
since he's so great can make his will his act, 1.02. 18
thee i lay, whose wisdom's strength can bear it. 1.02.119
it, | or can conceal his hunger till he famish? 1.04. 12
but see what heaven can do by this our change: 1.04. 33
but bring they what they will and what they can, 1.04. 76
each man | thinks all is writ he /speken can; 2.ch. 12
i can compare our rich misers to nothing so 2.01. 29 P
more with begging than we can do with working. 2.01. 65 P
which can as well inflame as it can kill. 2.02. 35
which can as well inflame as it can kill. 2.02. 35
show | can any way speak in his just commend; 2.02. 49
who can be other in this royal presence? 2.03. 49
known, | which from her by no means can i get. 2.05. 6
here comes my daughter, she can witness it. 2.05. 66
i know, | may be (nor can i think the contrary) 2.05. 79
and then with what haste you can, get you to bed 2.05. 93
and sail and high expense | can stead the quest. 3.ch. 21
round, | and every one with claps can sound, 3.ch. 36
and heaven can make | to herald thee from the 3.01. 33
thy loss is more than can thy portage quit 3.01. 35
there's nothing can be minist'red to nature 3.02. 8
be minist'red to nature | that can recover him. 3.02. 9
and can speak of the disturbances | that nature 3.02. 37
care not for me, | i can go home alone. 4.01. 42
as i can remember, by my troth, | i never did 4.01. 73
three, and they can do no more than they can do; 4.02. 7 P
three, and they can do no more than they can do; 4.02. 8 P
necessity of qualities can make her be refus'd. 4.02. 49 P
why /are you foolish? can it be undone? 4.03. 1
who can cross it? 4.03. 16
dead, | nor none can know, leonine being gone. 4.03. 30
o, sir, i can be modest. 4.06. 38 P
the stalk, never pluck'd yet, i can assure you. 4.06. 42 P
e'er since i can remember. 4.06. 73 P
proclaim that i can sing, weave, sew, and dance, 4.06.183
but can you teach all this you speak of? 4.06.188 P
well, i will see what i can do for thee. 4.06.192 P
if i can place thee, i will. 4.06.193 P
come, i'll do for thee what i can; 4.06.200 P
he can resolve you. 5.01. 1
this is the man that can, in aught you would, 5.01. 12
can draw him but to answer thee in aught, | thy 5.01. 73
receive such pay | as thy desires can wish. 5.01. 75
that, | for truth can never be confirm'd enough, 5.01.201
that he can hither come so soon | is by your 5.02. 19
can you remember what i call'd the man? 5.03. 52
that can | from first to last resolve you. 5.03. 60
the gods can have no mortal officer | more like 5.03. 62
grief | cull forth, as unpang'd judgment can, TNK 1.01.169
that i have foregone | or futurely can cope. 1.01.174
/aulis meet us with | the forces you can raise, 1.01.213
shall be returning | ere you can end this feast, 1.01.224
(unless we fear that apes can tutor 's) to | be 1.02. 43
better lin'd than it can appear to me report is 2.01. 6 P
i can tell you they are princes. 2.01. 20 P
from all that fortune can inflict upon us, | i 2.02. 57
what worthy blessing | can be, but our 2.02. 77
we'll see how near art can come near their 2.02.149
come what can come, | the worst is death: 2.03. 17
best, and wrastle, | that these times can allow. 2.05. 4
unarm'd, and can | smell where resistance is. 3.02. 16
and she fail me once — you can tell, arcas, 3.05. 46
if we can get her dance, we are made again. 3.05. 74
i can tell your fortune. 3.05. 78
then come what can come, | thou shalt know, 3.06.127
can these two live, | and have the agony of love 3.06.218
and, if you can love, end this difference. 3.06.278
can force his cousin | by fair and knightly 3.06.294
i can sing twenty more. 4.01.106
i think you can. 4.01.106
yes, truly, can i. 4.01.107
i can sing "the broom," | and "bonny robin." 4.01.107
o, who can find the bent of woman's fancy? 4.02. 33
this shall become palamon, for palamon can sing, 4.03. 86 P
can he write and read too? 5.02. 57
than humble banks can go to law with waters 5.03. 99
to me deserving | than i can quite or speak of. 5.04. 35
can that be, when | venus i have said is false? 5.04. 44
have at the worst can come, then! ep 10
forgiven | is safer wars than ever you can make, STM II.C 112
are incident, by his name | can still the rout? II.C 116
or how can well that proclamation sound | when II.C 117
look how he can, she cannot choose but love, VEN 79
violets whereon we lean | never can blab, nor 126
can thy right hand seize love upon thy left? 158
being steel'd, soft sighs can never grave it. 376
fair fall the wit that can so well defend her! 472
to sell myself i can be well contented, | so 513
while she takes all she can, not all she listeth 564
for pity now she can no more detain him; 577
better proof than thy spear's point can enter; 626
so to so, | for love can comment upon every woe. 714
what excuse can my invention make | when thou LUC 225
and extreme fear can neither fight nor fly, 230
fact, | how can they then assist me in the act? 350
but nothing can affection's course control, | or 500
the shame that from them no device can take, 535
thing | from vassal actors can be wip'd away; 608
conceit | can comprehend in still imagination! 702
receipt | ere he can see his own abomination. 704
no exclamation | can curb his heat, or rein his 706
"they think not but that every eye can see | the 750
we have no good that we can say is ours, | but 873
thy violent vanities can never last. 894
though men can cover crimes with bold stern 1252
yet with the fault i thus far can dispense: 1279
for more it is than i can well express, | and 1286
she would have said, "can lurk in such a look"; 1535
and from her tongue "can lurk" from "cannot" 1537
ere once she can discharge one word of woe; 1605
where no excuse can give the fault amending. 1614
glass, | that i no more can see what once i was! 1764
those pleasures live that art can comprehend. PP 5. 6
is that tongue that well can thee commend, | all 5. 8
ground, | as broken glass no cement can redress: 13.10
my shepherd's pipe can sound no deal, | my 17.17
smell — | a cripple soon can find a halt — 18.10
in surplice white, | that defunctive music can, PHT 14
reason none, | if what parts, can so remain." 48
nothing 'gainst time's scythe can make defense SON 12.13
nor can i fortune to brief minutes tell, 14. 5
can make you live yourself in eyes of men: 16.12
so long as men can breathe or eyes can see, | so 18.13
so long as men can breathe or eyes can see, | so 18.13
how can i then be elder than thou art? 22. 8
how can i then return in happy plight | that am 28. 1
then can i drown an eye (unus'd to flow) | for 30. 5
then can i grieve at grievances foregone, | and 30. 9
for no man well of such a salve can speak | that 34. 7
nor can thy shame give physic to my grief, 34. 9
how can my muse want subject to invent | while 38. 1
what can mine own praise to mine own self bring? 39. 3
for nimble thought can jump both sea and land 44. 7
laws, | since why to love i can allege no cause. 49.14
thus can my love excuse the slow offense | of my 51. 1
find, | when swift extremity can seem but slow? 51. 6
then can no horse with my desire keep pace; 51. 9
can bring him to his sweet up-locked treasure, 52. 2
and you, but one, can every shadow lend: 53. 4
or what strong hand can hold his swift foot back 65.11
or who his spoil /of beauty can forbid? 65.12
nothing that the thought of hearts can mend; 69. 2
quite, | for you in me can nothing worthy prove; 72. 4
the earth can have but earth, which is his due, 74. 7
he can afford | no praise to thee but what in 79.11
the earth can yield me but a common grave, 81. 7
what strained touches rhetoric can lend, | thou, 82.10
than both your poets can in praise devise. 83.14
which can say more | than this rich praise, that 84. 1
of you, if he can tell | that you are you, so 84. 7
upon thy part i can set down a story | of faults 88. 6
for there can live no hatred in thine eye, 93. 5
and all things turns to fair that eyes can see! 95.12
o, blame me not if i no more can write! 103. 5
and more, much more than in my verse can sit, 103.13
to me, fair friend, you never can be old, | for 104. 1
can yet the lease of my true love control, 107. 3
part | of thee, thy record never can be miss'd. 122. 8
is more than my o'erpress'd defense can bide? 139. 8
but my five wits nor my five senses can 141. 9
no, | how can it? 148. 9
o, how can love's eye be true, | that is so 148. 9
those that can see thou lov'st, and i am blind. 149.14

CANAKIN 2 FR 0.0002 REL FR 2 V 0 P
"and let me the canakin clink, clink; OTH 2.03. 69
and let me the canakin clink. 2.03. 70

CANARIES 2 FR 0.0002 REL FR 0 V 2 P
her into such a canaries as 'tis wonderful. WIV 2.02. 60 P
you have drunk too much canaries, and that's a 2H4 2.04. 26 P

CANARY 6 FR 0.0006 REL FR 1 V 5 P
could never have brought her to such a canary. WIV 2.02. 63 P
knight falstaff, and drink canary with him. 3.02. 88 P
the tongue's end, canary to it with your feet, LLL 3.01. 12 P
and make you dance canary | with spritely fire AWW 2.01. 74
o knight, thou lack'st a cup of canary. TN 1.03. 80 P
i think, unless you see canary put me down. 1.03. 83 P

/CANCEL 1 FR 0.0001 REL FR 1 V 0 P
we might proceed to /cancel of your days; PER 1.01.113

CANCEL 5 FR 0.0005 REL FR 5 V 0 P
cancel all grudge, repeal thee home again, TGV 5.04.143
cancel his bond of life, dear god, i pray, R3 4.04. 77
hand bears | the power to cancel his captivity. JC 1.03.102
hand | cancel and tear to pieces that great bond MAC 3.02. 49
take this life, | and cancel these cold bonds. CYM 5.04. 28

CANCELL'D 6 FR 0.0006 REL FR 6 V 0 P
his statutes cancell'd, and his treasure spent; 3H6 5.04. 79
says | my conceal'd lady to our cancell'd love? ROM 3.03. 98
an expir'd date, cancell'd ere well begun: LUC 26
cancell'd my fortunes, and enchained me | to 934
live's lasting date from cancell'd destiny. 1729
and weep afresh love's long since cancell'd woe, SON 30. 7

CANCELLING 1 FR 0.0001 REL FR 1 V 0 P
fatal this marriage, cancelling your fame, 2H6 1.01. 99

CANCELS 1 FR 0.0001 REL FR 1 V 0 P
if not, the end of life cancels all bands, | and 1H4 3.02.157

CANCER 1 FR 0.0001 REL FR 1 V 0 P
and add more coals to cancer when he burns TRO 2.03.196

CANDIDATUS 1 FR 0.0001 REL FR 1 V 0 P
be candidatus then and put it on, | and help to TIT 1.01.185

CANDIED 3 FR 0.0003 REL FR 3 V 0 P
that stand 'twixt me and milan, candied be they, TMP 2.01.279
candied with ice, caudle thy morning taste | to TIM 4.03.226
no, let the candied tongue lick absurd pomp, HAM 3.02. 60

CANDLE 16 FR 0.0018 REL FR 10 V 6 P
he dares not come there for the candle; MND 5.01.249 P
what, must i hold a candle to my shames? MV 2.06. 41
thus hath the candle sing'd the moth. 2.09. 79
how far that little candle throws his beams! 5.01. 90
when the moon shone, we did not see the candle. 5.01. 92
seek him with candle; AYL 3.01. 6
you | than without candle may go dark to bed — 3.05. 39
deserve well at my hand, help me to a candle, TN 4.02. 81 P
bell, book, and candle shall not drive me back, JN 3.03. 12
time enough to go to bed with a candle, i 1H4 2.01. 43 P
what, you are as a candle, the better part burnt 2H4 1.02.156 P
a wassail candle, my lord, all tallow; 1.02.158 P
here burns my candle out; 3H6 2.06. 1
this candle burns not clear, 'tis i must snuff H8 3.02. 96
out, out, brief candle! MAC 5.05. 23
so out went the candle, and we were left LR 1.04.217 P

CANDLE-CASES 1 FR 0.0001 REL FR 0 V 1 P
a pair of boots that have been candle-cases, one SHR 3.02. 45 P

CANDLE-HOLDER 1 FR 0.0001 REL FR 1 V 0 P
phrase, | i'll be a candle-holder and look on: ROM 1.04. 38

CANDLE-MINE 1 FR 0.0001 REL FR 0 V 1 P
you whoreson candle-mine, you, how vildly did 2H4 2.04.300 P

CANDLES' 1 FR 0.0001 REL FR 0 V 1 P
and drinks off candles' ends for flap-dragons, 2H4 2.04.246 P

CANDLES 6 FR 0.0006 REL FR 6 V 0 P
till candles, and starlight, and moonshine be WIV 5.05.102
dark needs no candles now, for dark is light. LLL 4.03.265
for, by these blessed candles of the night, MV 5.01.220
night's candles are burnt out, and jocund day ROM 3.05. 9
in heaven, | their candles are all out. MAC 2.01. 5
as those gold candles fix'd in heaven's air: SON 21.12

CANDLESTICKS *(also canstick)*

CANDLESTICKS 1 FR 0.0001 REL FR 1 V 0 P
the horsemen sit like fixed candlesticks, | with H5 4.02. 45

CANDLE-WASTERS 1 FR 0.0001 REL FR 1 V 0 P
make misfortune drunk | with candle-wasters, ADO 5.01. 18

CANDY* 2 FR 0.0002 REL FR 2 V 0 P
took the phoenix and her fraught from candy, TN 5.01. 61
what a candy deal of courtesy | this fawning 1H4 1.03.251

CANIDIUS 5 FR 0.0005 REL FR 5 V 0 P
is it not strange, canidius, | that from ANT 3.07. 20
canidius, we | will fight with him by sea. 3.07. 27
canidius, | our nineteen legions thou shalt hold 3.07. 57
the emperor calls canidius. 3.07. 79
canidius and the rest | that fell away have 4.06. 15

/CANKER 1 FR 0.0001 REL FR 1 V 0 P
/to /let /this /canker /of /our /nature /come HAM 5.02. 69

CANKER 17 FR 0.0019 REL FR 16 V 1 P
stain'd | with grief (that's beauty's canker), TMP 1.02.416
in the sweetest bud | the eating canker dwells, TGV 1.01. 43
bud | is eaten by the canker ere it blow, | even 1.01. 46
i had rather be a canker in a hedge than a rose ADO 1.03. 27 P
and heal the inveterate canker of one wound | by JN 5.02. 14
and plant this thorn, this canker, bullingbrook? 1H4 1.03.176
hath not thy rose a canker, somerset? 1H6 2.04. 68
whiles thy consuming canker eats his falsehood. 2.04. 71
lord, | banish the canker of ambitious thoughts! 2H6 1.02. 18
full soon the canker death eats up that plant. ROM 2.03. 30
the canker gnaw thy heart, | for showing me TIM 4.03. 50
the canker galls the infants of the spring | too HAM 1.03. 39
this canker that eats up love's tender spring, VEN 656
and loathsome canker lives in sweetest bud. SON 35. 4
for canker vice the sweetest buds doth love, 70. 7

which, like a canker in the fragrant rose, 95. 2
growth | a vengeful canker eat him up to death. 99.13
CANKER–BIT 1 FR 0.0001 REL FR 1 V 0 P
by treason's tooth bare–gnawn and canker–bit, LR 5.03.122
CANKER–BLOOMS 1 FR 0.0001 REL FR 1 V 0 P
the canker–blooms have full as deep a dye | as SON 54. 5
CANKER–BLOSSOM 1 FR 0.0001 REL FR 1 V 0 P
you canker–blossom! MND 3.02.282
CANKERS 4 FR 0.0004 REL FR 2 V 2 P
his body uglier grows, | so his mind cankers. TMP 4.01.192
some to kill cankers in the musk–rose buds, MND 2.02. 3
the cankers of a calm world and a long peace, 1H4 4.02. 29 P
o that this blossom could be kept from cankers! 2H4 2.02. 95 P
CANKER–SORROW 1 FR 0.0001 REL FR 1 V 0 P
but now will canker–sorrow eat my bud, | and JN 3.04. 82
CANK'RED 6 FR 0.0006 REL FR 6 V 0 P
a woman's will, a cank'red grandam's will! JN 2.01.194
as this ingrate and cank'red bullingbrook. 1H4 1.03.137
the cank'red heaps of strange–achieved gold; 2H4 4.05. 71
against my cank'red country with the spleen | of COR 4.05. 91
cank'red with peace, to part your cank'red hate; ROM 1.01. 95
cank'red with peace, to part your cank'red hate; 1.01. 95
CANK'RING 1 FR 0.0001 REL FR 1 V 0 P
foul cank'ring rust the hidden treasure frets, VEN 767
CANNIBALLY 1 FR 0.0001 REL FR 0 V 1 P
and he had been cannibally given, he might have COR 4.05.188 P
CANNIBALS 4 FR 0.0004 REL FR 4 V 0 P
compare with caesars and with cannibals | and 2H4 2.04.166
that face of his the hungry cannibals | would 3H6 1.04.152
bloody cannibals! 5.05. 61
and of the cannibals that each /other eat, | the OTH 1.03.143
CANNIKIN *(see canakin)*
CANNON 15 FR 0.0017 REL FR 13 V 2 P
mile, as easy as a cannon will shoot point–blank WIV 3.02. 33 P
he reputes me a cannon, and the bullet, that's LLL 3.01. 64
the thunder of my cannon shall be heard. JN 1.01. 26
our cannon shall be bent | against the brows of 2.01. 37
their battering cannon charged to the mouths, 2.01.382
of basilisks, of cannon, culverin, | of 1H4 2.03. 53
with linstock now the devilish cannon touches, H5 3.pr. 33
the portage of the head | like the brass cannon; 3.01. 11
spoke, | which sounded like a cannon in a vault, 3H6 5.02. 44
and /why such daily /cast of brazen cannon, HAM 1.01. 73
but the great cannon to the clouds shall tell, 1.02.126
diameter, | as level as the cannon to his blank, 4.01. 42
matter, if we could carry a cannon by our sides; 5.02.159 P
i have seen the cannon | when it hath blown his OTH 3.04.134
or that which from discharged cannon fumes. LUC 1043
CANNON–BULLETS 1 FR 0.0001 REL FR 0 V 1 P
for bird–bolts that you deem cannon–bullets. TN 1.05. 93 P
CANNONEER 2 FR 0.0002 REL FR 2 V 0 P
what cannoneer begot this lusty blood? JN 2.01.461
speak, | the trumpet to the cannoneer without, HAM 5.02.276
CANNON–FIRE 1 FR 0.0001 REL FR 1 V 0 P
he speaks plain cannon–fire, and smoke, and JN 2.01.462
CANNON'S 2 FR 0.0002 REL FR 2 V 0 P
bubble reputation | even in the cannon's mouth. AYL 2.07.153
fir'd | doth hurry from the fatal cannon's womb. ROM 5.01. 65
CANNONS' 1 FR 0.0001 REL FR 1 V 0 P
our cannons' malice vainly shall be spent JN 2.01.251
CANNONS 4 FR 0.0004 REL FR 4 V 0 P
the cannons have their bowels full of wrath, JN 2.01.210
we sweep 'em from the door with cannons — | to H8 5.03. 13
as cannons overcharg'd with double cracks, so MAC 1.02. 37
the cannons to the heavens, the heaven to earth, HAM 5.02.277
CANNON–SHOT 1 FR 0.0001 REL FR 1 V 0 P
have batt'red me like roaring cannon–shot, | and 1H6 3.03. 79
/CANNOT 9 FR 0.0010 REL FR 7 V 2 P
/and /water /cannot /wash /away /your /sin. R2 4.01.242
/eyes /are /full /of /tears, /i /cannot /see; 4.01.244
he /cannot draw his power this fourteen days. 1H4 4.01.126
i /cannot say your worships have deliver'd the COR 2.01. 57 P
/and /cannot /passionate /our /tenfold /grief TIT 3.02. 6
/for, /by /my /fay, /i /cannot /reason. HAM 2.02.265 P
/she /cannot /deny /it. LR 3.06. 51
/cannot /be /bordered /certain /in /itself. 4.02. 33
/i /cannot /draw /a /cart, /nor /eat /dried 5.03. 38
CANNOT 819 FR 0.0925 REL FR 571 V 248 P
if you cannot, give thanks you have liv'd so TMP 1.01. 23 P
but, as 'tis, | we cannot miss him. 1.02.311
even | ambition cannot pierce a wink beyond, 2.01.242
yond same cloud cannot choose but fall by 2.02. 23 P
went on four legs cannot make him give ground"; 2.02. 61 P
you cannot tell who's your friend. 2.02. 85 P
so glad of this as they i cannot be, | who are 3.01. 92
for my part, the sea cannot drown me; 3.02. 13 P
old lord, i cannot blame thee, | who am myself 3.03. 4
they | will not, nor cannot, use such vigilance 3.03. 16
i cannot too much muse | such shapes, such 3.03. 36
they cannot boudge till your release. 5.01. 11
whose honor cannot | be measur'd or confin'd. 5.01.121
your eld'st acquaintance cannot be three hours. 5.01.186
and yet it cannot overtake your slow purse. TGV 1.01.126 P
wrack, | which cannot perish having thee aboard, 1.01.149
i cannot reach so high. 1.02. 84
of time, | and how he cannot be a perfect man, 1.03. 20
my lord, i cannot be so soon provided: 1.03. 72
without me? they cannot. 2.01. 35 P
if you love her, you cannot see her. 2.01. 68 P
being in love, cannot see to put on your hose. 2.01. 77 P
it cannot speak, | for truth hath better deeds 2.02. 17
nay, that cannot be so neither; 2.03. 16 P
i cannot leave to love, and yet i do; 2.06. 17
i cannot now prove constant to myself, | without 2.06. 31
and thence she cannot be convey'd away. 3.01. 37
cannot your grace win her to fancy him? 3.01. 67
man, | if with his tongue he cannot win a woman. 3.01.105
and built so shelving that one cannot climb it 3.01.115
my ears are stopp'd and cannot hear good news, 3.01.206
nay, a horse cannot fetch, but only carry, 3.01.276 P
was eve's legacy, and cannot be ta'en from her. 3.01.339 P
of her tongue she cannot, for that's writ down 3.01.349 P
another thing she may, and that cannot i help. 3.01.352 P
where your good word cannot advantage him, 3.02. 42
and cannot soon revolt and change your mind. 3.02. 59
love | will creep in service where it cannot go. 4.02. 20
marry, mine host, because i cannot be merry. 4.02. 28 P
foul thing when a cur cannot keep himself in all 4.04. 10 P
i cannot choose | but pity her. 4.04. 77
but cannot be true servant to my master, 4.04.104
fled — | the thicket is beset, he cannot scape. 5.03. 11
a smaller boon than this i cannot beg, | and 5.04. 24
and less than this, i am sure you cannot give. 5.04. 25
and full as much (for more there cannot be) | i 5.04. 38
when women cannot love where they're belov'd! 5.04. 44
when proteus cannot love where he's belov'd! 5.04. 45
for though i cannot remember what i did when you WIV 1.01.171 P
i cannot abide the smell of hot meat since. 1.01.285 P
women, indeed, cannot abide 'em, they are very 1.01.298 P
i cannot be thus satisfied. 2.01.188 P
yet i cannot put off my opinion so easily. 2.01.234 P
alas, sir, i cannot fence. 2.03. 15 P
i cannot tell what the dickens his name is my 3.02. 19 P
mistress ford, i cannot cog, i cannot prate, 3.03. 48 P
i cannot cog, i cannot prate, mistress ford. 3.03. 48 P
i cannot cog and say thou art this and that, 3.03. 70 P
like bucklersbury in simple time — i cannot; 3.03. 73 P
in the house you cannot hide him. 3.03.128 P
i cannot find him. 3.03.199 P
i see i cannot get thy father's love, 3.04. 1
and humblest suit | cannot attain it, why then 3.04. 21
he cannot scape me; 3.05.145 P
he cannot creep into a halfpenny purse, nor into 3.05.146 P
though what i am i cannot avoid, yet to be what 3.05.149 P
he cannot abide the old woman of brainford. 4.02. 85 P
we cannot misuse /him enough. 4.02.102 P
i cannot tell vat is dat; 4.05. 86 P
that you cannot see a white spot about her. 4.05.112 P
that cannot choose but amaze him. 5.03. 17 P
what cannot be eschew'd must be embrac'd. 5.05.237
he cannot, sir; he's out at elbow. MM 2.01. 61 P
sir, your honor cannot come to that yet. 2.01.119 P
look, what i will not, that i cannot do. 2.02. 52
we cannot weigh our brother with ourself. 2.02.126
your brother cannot live. 2.04. 33
o heavens, it cannot be. 3.01. 98
the deputy cannot abide a whoremaster. 3.02. 35 P
he cannot plead his estimation with you; 4.02. 26 P
if i should be hang'd, i cannot imagine. 4.02. 40 P
cannot but yield you forth to public thanks, 5.01. 7
and yet here's one in place i cannot pardon. 5.01.499
rate, | cannot amount unto a hundred marks, ERR 1.01. 24
commends me to the thing i cannot get: 1.02. 34
since that my beauty cannot please his eye, 2.01.114
is something in the wind, that we cannot get in. 3.01. 69
what i should think of this, i cannot tell: 3.02.179
my business cannot brook this dalliance. 4.01. 59
i cannot, nor i will not, hold me still, | my 4.02. 17
it cannot be that she hath done thee wrong. 5.01.135
all these old witnesses — i cannot err — 5.01.318
what then became of them i cannot tell; 5.01.355
is the opinion that fire cannot melt out of me; ADO 1.01.232 P
i cannot hide what i am. 1.03. 13 P
this (though i cannot be said to be a flattering 1.03. 30 P
dish i love not, i cannot endure my lady tongue. 2.01.274 P
or, if you cannot, stop his mouth with a kiss, 2.01.310 P
she cannot endure to hear tell of a husband. 2.01.347 P
i cannot tell; 2.03. 23 P
i cannot tell what to think of it but that she 2.03. 99 P
knavery cannot sure hide himself in such 2.03.119 P
'tis so, i cannot reprove it; 2.03.232 P
in his youth that he cannot endure in his age. 2.03.239 P
she cannot love, | nor take no shape nor project 3.01. 54
as beatrice is, cannot be commendable. 3.01. 73
she cannot be so much without true judgment — 3.01. 88
for i cannot see how sleeping should offend; 3.03. 40 P
nay, by'r lady, that i think 'a cannot. 3.03. 77 P
i am stuff'd, cousin, i cannot smell. 3.04. 64 P
to think what i can, nor indeed i cannot think, 3.04. 84 P
friar, it cannot be. 4.01.170
i cannot be a man with wishing, therefore i will 4.01.322 P
if justice cannot tame you, she shall ne'er 5.01.206 P
i cannot bid you bid my daughter live — | that 5.01.279
marry, i cannot show it in rhyme; 5.02. 36 P
planet, nor i cannot woo in festival terms. 5.02. 41 P
of wit–crackers cannot flout me out of my humor. 5.04.101 P
i cannot stay thanksgiving. LLL 2.01.193
love her, because your heart cannot come by her; 3.01. 42 P
being out of heart that you cannot enjoy her. 3.01. 44 P
where fair is not, praise cannot mend the brow. 4.01. 17
and i cannot, cannot, cannot, | and i cannot, 4.01.127
and i cannot, cannot, cannot, | and i cannot, 4.01.127
and i cannot, cannot, cannot, | and i cannot, 4.01.127
cannot, cannot, | and i cannot, another can. 4.01.128
'gainst whom the world cannot hold argument, 4.03. 59
we cannot cross the cause why we were born; 4.03.214
then cannot we be bought; 5.02.226
i cannot give you less. 5.02.384
you cannot beg us, sir, i can assure you, sir, 5.02.490
whole world again | cannot pick out five such, 5.02.545
this cannot be hector. 5.02.642 P
it cannot be, it is impossible: 5.02.856
mirth cannot move a soul in agony. 5.02.857
place the sharp athenian law | cannot pursue us. MND 1.01.163
this wood, | because i cannot meet my hermia. 2.01.193
tell you i do not /nor i cannot love you? 2.01.201
we cannot fight for love, as men may do. 2.01.241
which the ladies cannot abide. 3.01. 12 P
it cannot be but thou hast murd'red him; 3.02. 56
you speak not as you think. it cannot be. 3.02.191
if she cannot entreat, i can compel. 3.02.248
i swear, | i cannot truly say how i came here. 4.01.148
he cannot be heard of. 4.02. 3 P
and what poor duty cannot do, noble respect 5.01. 91
for his valor cannot carry his discretion, and 5.01.233 P
discretion, i am sure, cannot carry his valor; 5.01.235 P
nerissa, that i cannot choose one, nor refuse MV 1.02. 26 P
i cannot instantly raise up the gross | of full 1.03. 55
i cannot tell, i make it breed as fast. 1.03. 96
murder cannot be hid long; 2.02. 79 P
i cannot think you are my son. 2.02. 87 P
i cannot get a service, no; 2.02.156 P
and lovers cannot see | the pretty follies that 2.06. 36
a third cannot be match'd, unless the devil 3.01. 78 P
where i did hear of her, but cannot find her. 3.01. 82 P
to venice that swear he cannot choose but break. 3.01.114 P
the duke cannot deny the course of law; 3.03. 26
sings i' th' nose, | cannot contain their urine: 4.01. 50
be rend'red | why he cannot abide a gaping pig; 4.01. 54
you cannot better be employ'd, bassanio, | than 4.01.117
the greatness whereof i cannot enough commend, 4.01.159 P
law | cannot impugn you as you do proceed. 4.01.179
it cannot be. 4.01.222
i cannot find it, 'tis not in the bond. 4.01.262
that cannot be. 4.02. 8
doth grossly close it in, we cannot hear it. 5.01. 65
he cannot speak, my lord. AYL 1.02.220
i cannot speak to her, yet she urg'd conference. 1.02.258
yet your mistrust cannot make me a traitor. 1.03. 56
my liege, | i cannot live out of her company. 1.03. 86
it cannot be. 2.02. 2
i cannot hear of any that did see her. 2.02. 4
that cannot so much as a blossom yield | in lieu 2.03. 64
yet fortune cannot recompense me better | than 2.03. 75
i pray you bear with me, i cannot go no further. 2.04. 9 P
my voice is ragged, i know i cannot please you. 2.05. 15 P
if i cannot, i'll rail against all the 2.05. 60 P
sir, sir, that cannot be. 3.01. 1
i cannot see else how thou shouldst scape. 3.02. 85 P
the one sleeps easily because he cannot study, 3.02.321 P
when a man's verses cannot be understood, nor a 3.03. 12 P
i cannot say the words. 4.01.128 P
o, that woman that cannot make her fault her 4.01.174 P
alas, dear love, i cannot lack thee two hours! 4.01.179 P
but it cannot be sounded; 4.01.207 P
aliena, i cannot be out of the sight of orlando. 4.01.216 P
we cannot hold. 5.01. 12 P
clubs cannot part them. 5.02. 41 P
why then to–morrow i cannot serve your turn for 5.02. 48 P
nor cannot insinuate with you in the behalf of a ep 8 P
believe me, lord, i think he cannot choose. SHR in.1. 42
i cannot tell; 1.01.131 P
haste, | and every day i cannot come to woo. 2.01.115
go, girl, i cannot blame thee now to weep, | for 3.02. 27
it cannot be. 3.02.200
i cannot tell, i fear 'tis choleric. 4.03. 22
and if you cannot, best you stop your ears. 4.03. 76
for curious i cannot be with you, | signior 4.04. 36
i cannot tell — /except they are busied about a 4.04. 91 P
i cannot tarry. 4.04. 99 P
word | that she is busy, and she cannot come. 5.02. 81
she is busy, and she cannot come! 5.02. 82
he cannot want the best | that shall attend his AWW 1.01. 72
keep it not, you cannot choose but lose by't. 1.01.146 P
of businesses, i cannot answer thee acutely. 1.01.206 P
that makes me see, and cannot feed mine eye? 1.01.221
and do suppose | what hath been cannot be. 1.01.226
the count rossillion cannot be my brother: 1.03.155
to her whose state is such that cannot choose 1.03.214
he, that they cannot help him, | they, that they 1.03.238
cannot help him, | they, that they cannot help. 1.03.239
no, no, it cannot be; 2.01. 8
i cannot give thee less, to be call'd grateful. 2.01.129
he that cannot make a leg, put off 's cap, kiss 2.02. 10 P
i cannot love her, nor will strive to do't. 2.03.145
to which title age cannot bring thee. 2.03.199 P
since i cannot yet find in my heart to repent. 2.05. 12 P
lord, | the reasons of our state i cannot yield, 3.01. 10
he cannot thrive, | unless her prayers, whom 3.04. 26
cannot for all that dissuade succession, but 3.05. 22 P
entertainment, your inclining cannot be remov'd. 3.06. 39 P
well, we cannot greatly condemn our success. 3.06. 55 P
and then you cannot, | by the good aid that i of 3.07. 10
we cannot afford you so. 4.01. 48 P
they cannot be too sweet for the king's tartness 4.03. 82 P
who cannot be crush'd with a plot? 4.03.325 P
sir, if i cannot serve you, i can serve as great 4.05. 36 P
we cannot help it. 5.01. 2
if he cannot, let the botcher mend him. TN 1.05. 46 P
your lord does know my mind, i cannot love him, 1.05.257
but yet i cannot love him. 1.05.262
i cannot love him; 1.05.280
if i cannot recover your niece, i am a foul way 2.03.184 P
or thy affection cannot hold the bent; 2.04. 37
but if she cannot love you, sir? 2.04. 87
/i cannot be so answer'd. 2.04. 88
you cannot love her; 2.04. 91
is, that it cannot but turn him into a notable 2.05.203 P
oxen and wain–ropes cannot hale them together. 3.02. 60 P
if this letter move him not, his legs cannot. 3.04.171 P
he cannot by the duello avoid it; 3.04.307 P
much more for what i cannot do for you | than 3.04.336
with my niece that i cannot pursue with any 4.02. 70 P
we cannot with such magnificence — in so rare WT 1.01. 12 P
may, though they cannot praise us, as little 1.01. 15 P
sicilia cannot show himself overkind to bohemia. 1.01. 21 P
affection, which cannot choose but branch now. 1.01. 24 P
to a vision so apparent rumor | cannot be mute), 1.02.271
but i cannot | believe this crack to be in my 1.02.321
know, you must, | and cannot say you dare not. 1.02.380
but | i cannot name the disease, and it is 1.02.386
or stupefied | or seeming so in skill — cannot, 2.01.166
that your free undertaking cannot miss | a 2.02. 42
it is a curse | he cannot be compell'd to't) 2.03. 89
all the husbands | that cannot do that feat, 2.03.111
weep i cannot, | but my heart bleeds; 3.03. 51
firmament and it you cannot thrust a bodkin's 3.03. 85 P
not enough consider'd (as too much i cannot), to 4.02. 18 P
i cannot do't without compters. 4.03. 36 P
i cannot tell, good sir, for which of his 4.03. 88 P
your resolution cannot hold when 'tis | oppos'd 4.04. 36
for i cannot be | mine own, nor any thing to any 4.04. 43
i cannot speak | so well, nothing so well; 4.04.380
i cannot speak, nor think, | nor dare to know 4.04.451
it cannot fail, but by | the violation of my 4.04.476
sea | with her who here i cannot hold on shore; 4.04.499
i cannot say 'tis pity | she lacks instructions, 4.04.581
earnest, but i cannot with conscience take it. 4.04.645 P
this cannot be but a great courtier. 4.04.748 P
virtues, i cannot forget | my blemishes in them, 5.01. 7
that ballad–makers cannot be able to express it. 5.02. 25 P
sight which was to be seen, cannot be spoken of. 5.02. 43 P
on, | which sixteen winters cannot blow away, 5.03. 50

well, sir, by this you cannot get my land; JN 1.01. 97
it cannot be, and if thou wert his mother. 2.01.131
equality | by our best eyes cannot be censured. 2.01.328
it cannot be, thou dost but say 'tis so. 3.01. 6
with my vex'd spirits i cannot take a truce, 3.01. 17
i cannot brook thy sight, | this news hath made 3.01. 36
law cannot give my child his kingdom here, | for 3.01.187
husband, i cannot pray that thou mayst win; 3.01.331
which cannot hear a lady's feeble voice, | which 3.04. 41
hath seiz'd arthur, and it cannot be | that, 3.04.131
so be it, for it cannot be but so. 3.04.140
we cannot hold mortality's strong hand. 4.02. 82
perchance the cardinal cannot make your peace; 5.01. 74
we cannot deal but with the very hand | of stern 5.02. 22
which since we cannot do to make you friends, R2 1.01.197
since we cannot atone you, we shall see 1.01.202
which made the fault that we cannot correct, 1.02. 5
but dead, thy kingdom cannot buy my breath. 1.03.232
his rash fierce blaze of riot cannot last, | for 2.01. 33
which honor and allegiance cannot think. 2.01.208
king i did, to please myself | i cannot do it; 2.02. 6
howe'er it be, | i cannot but be sad; 2.02. 30
is that is not yet known what, | i cannot name; 2.02. 40
who, weak with age, cannot support myself. 2.02. 83
i cannot mend it, i must needs confess, 2.03.153
but since i cannot, be it known unto you | i do 2.03.158
the breath of worldly men cannot depose | the 3.02. 56
that we cannot mend, | they break their faith to 3.02.100
of holy reverence, who, i cannot learn. 3.03. 29
is not a creature but myself, | i cannot do it; 5.05. 5
and, for they cannot, die in their own pride. 5.05. 22
a jest to execute that i cannot manage alone. 1H4 1.02.162 P
i cannot blame him: 1.03.145
nay, then i cannot blame his cousin king, | that 1.03.158
why, it cannot choose but be a noble plot. 1.03.279
upon it when thieves cannot be true one to 2.02. 27 P
now cannot i strike him, if i should be hang'd. 2.02. 73 P
in barbary, sir, it cannot come to so much. 2.04. 75 P
i cannot blame him. 3.01. 13
i cannot choose. 3.01.146
john, you are so fretful you cannot live long. 3.03. 11 P
by god, i cannot flatter, i do defy | the 4.01. 6
he cannot come, my lord, he is grievous sick. 4.01. 16
it is not possible, it cannot be, | the king 5.02. 4
which cannot choose but bring him quickly on. 5.02. 44
i cannot read them now. 5.02. 80
i cannot think, my lord, your son is dead. 2H4 1.01.104
and yet cannot he see, though he have his own 1.02. 47 P
buckles himself in my belt cannot live in less. 1.02.138 P
and yet in some respects i grant i cannot go. 1.02.167 P
i cannot tell. 1.02.168 P
i cannot rid my hands of him. 1.02.202 P
well, i cannot last ever, but it was alway yet 1.02.214 P
and those two things i confess i cannot help. 2.02. 69 P
knowest sir john cannot endure an apple–john. 2.04. 2 P
you cannot one bear with another's confirmities. 2.04. 57 P
i cannot abide swagg'rers. 2.04.109 P
asia, | which cannot go but thirty mile a day, 2.04.165
i cannot endure such a fustian rascal. 2.04.189 P
i cannot speak. 2.04.379 P
it cannot be, my lord. 3.01. 96
i cannot put him to a private soldier that is 3.02.165 P
go drink with you, but i cannot tarry dinner. 3.02.191 P
she must be old, she cannot choose but be old, 3.02.207 P
gone, and she is old, and cannot help herself. 3.02.232 P
he knows | he cannot so precisely weed this land 4.01.203
not love me, nor a man cannot make him laugh, 4.03. 88 P
no, no, he cannot long hold out these pangs. 4.04.117
those precepts cannot be serv'd; 5.01. 13 P
and i cannot once or twice in a quarter bear out 5.01. 48 P
which cannot look more hideously upon me | than 5.02. 12
i cannot perceive how, unless you give me your 5.05. 81 P
i cannot now speak, i will hear you soon. 5.05. 94
if my tongue cannot entreat you to acquit me, ep 18 P
cannot defend our own doors from the dog, | let H5 1.02.218
you cannot revel into dukedoms there. 1.02.253
and when i cannot live any longer, i will do as 2.01. 15 P
i cannot tell — things must be as they may. 2.01. 20 P
must be conclusions — well, i cannot tell. 2.01. 25 P
for we cannot lodge and board a dozen or 2.01. 32 P
i am not barbason, you cannot conjure me. 2.01. 54 P
i cannot kiss, that is the humor of it; 2.03. 60 P
the man hath no wit that cannot, from the rising 3.07. 31 P
description cannot suit itself in words | to 4.02. 53
all the water in wye cannot wash your majesty's 4.07.106 P
which cannot in their huge and proper life | be 5.pr. 5
shall mock at me, i cannot speak your england. 5.02.102 P
pardonnez–moi, i cannot tell wat is "like me." 5.02.108 P
kate, i cannot look greenly, nor gasp out my 5.02.143 P
i cannot tell wat is dat. 5.02.177 P
i cannot tell. 5.02.195 P
i cannot tell wat is /baiser en anglish. 5.02.262 P
you and i cannot be confin'd within the weak 5.02.269 P
i cannot so conjure up the spirit of love in her 5.02.288 P
who cannot see many a fair french city for one 5.02.317 P
it irks his heart he cannot be reveng'd. 1H6 1.04.105
our english troops retire, i cannot stay them; 1.05. 2
it cannot be this weak and writhled shrimp 2.03. 23
that was, | for i am ignorant and cannot guess. 2.05. 60
villain | and cannot help the noble chevalier. 4.03. 14
can, | but curse the cause i cannot aid the man. 4.03. 44
it is too late, i cannot send them now. 4.04. 1
flight cannot stain the honor you have won, 4.05. 26
you cannot witness for me, being slain. 4.05. 43
cannot my body nor blood–sacrifice | entreat you 5.03. 20
any passion of inflaming /love, | i cannot tell; 5.05. 83
i cannot blame them all, what is't to them? 2H6 1.01.220
i cannot go before | while gloucester bears this 1.02. 61
gold cannot come amiss, were she a devil. 1.02. 92
all | cannot do more in england than the nevils: 1.03. 73
first, for i cannot flatter thee in pride; 1.03.166
alas, my lord, i cannot fight; 1.03.213 P
i cannot justify whom the law condemns. 2.03. 16
witness my tears, i cannot stay to speak. 2.04. 86
who cannot steal a shape that means deceit? 3.01. 79
whereof you cannot easily purge yourself. 3.01.135
eyes | look after him, and cannot do him good, 3.01.219
it cannot be but he was murd'red here, | the 3.02.177
if i depart from thee, i cannot live, | and in 3.02.388
spirits | you cannot but forbear to murther me. 4.07. 76
for he is fierce and cannot brook hard language. 4.09. 45
i cannot give due action to my words, | except a 5.01. 8
my heart for anger burns, i cannot brook it. 3H6 1.01. 60
i cannot stay to hear these articles. 1.01.180
father, you cannot disinherit me. 1.01.226
i cannot rest | until the white rose that i wear 1.02. 32
and i am faint, and cannot fly their fury; 1.04. 23
york cannot speak unless he wear a crown. 1.04. 93
i cannot joy, until i be resolv'd | where our 2.01. 9
i cannot weep; 2.01. 79
his captives blood and death, | i cannot judge: 2.01.128
are you there, butcher? o, i cannot speak! 2.02. 95
this meeting here | cannot be cur'd by words; 2.02.122
and weak we are and cannot shun pursuit. 2.03. 13
when clifford cannot spare his friends an oath. 2.06. 78
for though they cannot greatly sting to hurt, 2.06. 94
that cannot be, the noise of thy cross–bow 3.01. 6
lands, | which we in justice cannot well deny, 3.02. 5
right gracious lord, i cannot brook delay. 3.02. 18
no, gracious lord, except i cannot do it. 3.02. 47
can i do this, and cannot get a crown? 3.02.194
scotland hath will to help, but cannot help; 3.03. 34
by living low, where fortune cannot hurt me, 4.06. 20
which, being suffer'd, rivers cannot quench. 4.08. 8
what cannot be avoided | 'twere childish 5.04. 37
since i cannot prove a lover | to entertain R3 1.01. 28
he cannot live, i hope, and must not die | till 1.01.145
and mortal eyes cannot endure the devil. 1.02. 45
if thy revengeful heart cannot forgive, | lo 1.02.173
the spacious world cannot again afford. 1.02.245
upon my life, she finds (although i cannot) 1.02.253
because i cannot flatter and look fair, | smile 1.03. 47
cannot a plain man live and think no harm, | but 1.03. 51
cannot be quiet scarce a breathing while | but 1.03. 60
i cannot tell, the world is grown so bad | that 1.03. 69
i cannot blame her; 1.03.305
if my deep pray'rs cannot appease thee, | but 1.04. 69
a man cannot steal, but it accuseth him; 1.04.135 P
a man cannot swear, but it checks him; 1.04.136 P
a man cannot lie with his neighbor's wife, but 1.04.136 P
i am strong–fram'd, he cannot prevail with me. 1.04.150 P
and therefore cannot have the hearts to do it. 1.04.176
it cannot be, for he bewept my fortune, | and 1.04.244
you cannot guess who caus'd your father's death. 2.02. 19
i cannot think it. hark, what noise is this? 2.02. 33
you cannot reason (almost) with a man | that 2.03. 39
if 'twere not she, i cannot tell who told me. 2.04. 34
and therefore, in mine opinion, cannot have it. 3.01. 52
cannot my lord stanley sleep these tedious 3.02. 6
i do, my lord, but long i cannot stay there. 3.02.119
so gross | that cannot see this palpable device? 3.06. 11
i cannot tell if to depart in silence, | or 3.07.141
amiss, | i cannot nor i will not yield to you. 3.07.207
that cannot brook the accent of reproof. 4.04.159
nay then indeed she cannot choose but hate thee, 4.04.289
look what is done cannot be now amended: 4.04.291
i cannot make you what amends i would, 4.04.309
it cannot be avoided but by this; 4.04.410
unless for that, my liege, i cannot guess. 4.04.474
you cannot guess wherefore the welshman comes. 4.04.476
i, as i may — that which i would i cannot — 5.03. 91
i cannot tell | what heaven hath given him — H8 1.01. 66
for worthy wolsey | (who cannot err), he did it. 1.01.174
whereof | we cannot feel too little, hear too 1.02.128
you cannot show me. 1.04. 48
there cannot be those numberless offenses 2.01. 84
'gainst me, that i cannot take peace with; 2.01. 85
sir, you cannot. 2.02. 78
but this cannot continue. 2.02. 83
if your back | cannot vouchsafe this burthen, 2.03. 43
the cardinal | cannot stand under them. 3.02. 3
i cannot promise | but that you shall sustain 3.02. 4
if you cannot | bar his access to th' king, 3.02. 16
words cannot carry | authority so weighty. 3.02.233
this cannot save you. 3.02.302
i cannot blame his conscience. 4.01. 47
you cannot with such freedom purge yourself 5.01.102
yes, my lord; but yet i cannot help you. 5.02. 5
nay, my lord, | that cannot be; 5.02. 84
to me you cannot reach you play the spaniel, 5.02.161
an army cannot rule 'em. 5.03. 77
i cannot fight upon this argument; TRO 1.01. 92
i cannot come to cressid but by pandar, | and 1.01. 95
i cannot choose but laugh to think how she 1.02.135 P
if i cannot ward what i would not have hit, i 1.02.267 P
cannot distaste the goodness of a quarrel 2.02.123
the world's large spaces cannot parallel. 2.02.162
with scorn, | cannot outfly our apprehensions. 2.03.115
"bring action hither, this cannot go to war." 2.03.136
he must, he is, he cannot but be wise. 2.03.252
you cannot shun yourself. 3.02.146
cannot make boast to have that which he hath, 3.03. 98
death, 'twill be his bane, he cannot bear it. 4.02. 93 P
i cannot sing, | nor heel the high lavolt, nor 4.04. 85
i cannot, lord, i have important business, | the 5.01. 82
in faith, i cannot. what would you have me do? 5.02. 23
one cannot speak a word | but it straight starts 5.02.100
i cannot conjure, troyan. 5.02.125
were curs'd, i cannot tell what to think on't. 5.03.106 P
or if you cannot weep, yet give some groans, 5.10. 49
what he cannot help in his nature, you account a COR 1.01. 41 P
we cannot, sir, we are undone already. 1.01. 64
"though all at once cannot | see what i do 1.01.142
cannot | better be held nor more attain'd than 1.01.264
but i cannot go thither. 1.03. 79 P
if we lose the field, | we cannot keep the town. 1.07. 5
but cannot make my heart consent to take | a 1.09. 37
i would i were a roman, for i cannot, | being a 1.10. 4
as you are (i cannot call you lycurguses), if 2.01. 55 P
he cannot temp'rately transport his honors 2.01.224
the man i speak of cannot in the world | be 2.02. 86
corioles, let me say, | i cannot speak him home. 2.02.103
he cannot but with measure fit the honors 2.02.123
for i cannot | put on the gown, stand naked, and 2.02.136
i cannot bring | my tongue to such a pace. 2.03. 50
and cannot go without any honest man's voice. 2.03.132 P
suffer't, and live with such as cannot rule, 3.01. 40
cannot conclude but by the yea and no | of 3.01.145
of breath, | confusion's near, i cannot speak. 3.01.189
'tis a sore upon us | you cannot tent yourself. 3.01.235
i cannot do it to the gods, | must i then do't 3.02. 38
he cannot | be rein'd again to temperance; 3.03. 27
he cannot choose. 4.03. 37 P
i cannot get him out o' th' house. 4.05. 20 P
and cannot live but to thy shame, unless | it be 4.05.100
face, methought — i cannot tell how to term it. 4.05.156 P
look you, one cannot tell how to say that. 4.05.169 P
so it cannot be denied but peace is a great 4.05.228 P
it cannot be | the volsces dare break with us. 4.06. 48
cannot be? 4.06. 49
tell not me! | i know this cannot be. 4.06. 57
the tribunes cannot do't for shame; 4.06.109
i cannot help it now, | unless by using means i 4.07. 6
and i must excuse | what cannot be amended. 4.07. 12
into his kindness, | and cannot lose your way. 5.01. 60
true under him, must say you cannot pass. 5.02. 33 P
that a jack guardant cannot office me from my 5.02. 62 P
which they did refuse | and cannot now accept, 5.03. 15
to make | what cannot be, slight work. 5.03. 62
if i cannot persuade thee | rather to show a 5.03.120
this boy, that cannot tell what he would have, 5.03.174
aufidius, though i cannot make true wars, | i'll 5.03.190
sir, i cannot tell, | we must proceed as we do 5.06. 14
provok'd by him, you cannot) the great danger 5.06.136
they be, | and cannot brook competitors in love? TIT 2.01. 77
that what you cannot as you would achieve, | you 2.01.106
who, though they cannot answer my distress, 3.01. 38
i wot, | thy napkin cannot drink a tear of mine, 3.01.140
for why my bowels cannot hide her woes, | but 3.01.230
but that i cannot do ten thousand more. 5.01.144
cannot induce you to attend my words. 5.03. 79
o lord, i cannot speak to him for weeping, | my 5.03.174
he that is strooken blind cannot forget | the ROM 1.01.232
yet i cannot choose but laugh | to think it 1.03. 50
lead | so stakes me to the ground i cannot move. 1.04. 16
bound | i cannot bound a pitch above dull woe; 1.04. 21
we cannot be here and there too. 1.05. 14 P
this cannot anger him; 2.01. 23
if love be blind, love cannot hit the mark. 2.01. 33
walls, | for stony limits cannot hold love out, 2.02. 67
that they cannot sit at ease on the old bench? 2.04. 34 P
and if i cannot, i'll find those that shall. 2.04.152 P
perchance she cannot meet him — that's not so. 2.05. 3
it cannot countervail the exchange of joy | that 2.06. 4
excess | i cannot sum up sum of half my wealth. 2.06. 34
courage, man, the hurt cannot be much. 3.01. 95
romeo can, | though heaven cannot. 3.02. 41
i cannot choose but ever weep the friend. 3.05. 77
and cannot come to him | to wreak the love i 3.05.100
to answer, "i'll not wed, i cannot love; 3.05.185
an ill cook that cannot lick his own fingers; 4.02. 6 P
therefore he that cannot lick his fingers goes 4.02. 7 P
woes | we cannot without circumstance descry. 5.03.181
mine eyes cannot hold out water, methinks. TIM 1.02.106 P
it cannot hold, it will not. 2.01. 4
it cannot hold, no reason | can sound his state 2.01. 12
want treasure, cannot | do what they would, are 2.02.205
he cannot want for money. 3.02. 8 P
he cannot want fifty — five hundred talents. 3.02. 38
say, that i cannot pleasure such an honorable 3.02. 56 P
and i cannot think but, in the end, the 3.03. 29 P
who cannot keep his wealth must keep his house. 3.03. 41
we cannot take this for answer, sir. 3.04. 77
you cannot make gross sins look clear; 3.05. 38
who cannot condemn rashness in cold blood? 3.05. 53
i cannot think but your age has forgot me, | it 3.05. 92
when gouty keepers of thee cannot stand. 4.03. 47
keep it, i cannot eat it. 4.03.101
we cannot live on grass, on berries, water, | as 4.03.422
the place, it cannot be far | where he abides. 5.01. 1
i am rapt and cannot cover | the monstrous bulk 5.01. 64
i cannot choose but tell him that i care not, 5.01.177
what's on this tomb | i cannot read; 5.03. 6
and since you know you cannot see yourself | so JC 1.02. 67
i cannot tell what you and other men | think of 1.02. 93
for who so firm that cannot be seduc'd? 1.02.312
i cannot by the progress of the stars | give 2.01. 2
cannot, is false; 2.02. 63
my heart laments that virtue cannot live | out 2.03. 13
i cannot drink too much of brutus' love. 4.03.162
or memorize another golgotha, | i cannot tell — MAC 1.02. 41
though his bark cannot be lost, | yet it shall 1.03. 24
this supernatural soliciting | cannot be ill; 1.03.131
cannot be good. 1.03.131
what cannot you and i perform upon | th' 1.07. 69
my young remembrance cannot parallel | a fellow 2.03. 62
nor heart | cannot conceive nor name thee! 2.03. 65
who cannot want the thought, how monstrous | it 3.06. 8
which you are, my thoughts cannot transpose: 4.03. 21
there cannot be | that vulture in you to devour 4.03. 73
it cannot | be call'd our mother, but our grave; 4.03.165
i cannot but remember such things were, | that 4.03.222
he cannot come out on 's grave. 5.01. 64 P
what's done cannot be undone. 5.01. 68 P
certain | he cannot buckle his distemper'd cause 5.02. 15
remove to dunsinane | i cannot taint with fear. 5.03. 3
slaughterous thoughts, | cannot once start me. 5.05. 15
let us be beaten, if we cannot fight. 5.06. 8
i cannot fly, | but bear–like i must fight the 5.07. 1
i cannot strike at wretched kerns, whose arms 5.07. 17
you cannot speak of reason to the dane | and HAM 1.02. 44
it is not, nor it cannot come to good, | but 1.02.158
guilty | (since nature cannot choose his origin) 1.04. 26
understanding of himself, | i cannot dream of. 2.02. 10
you cannot take from me any thing that i will 2.02.215 P
seneca cannot be too heavy, nor plautus too 2.02.400 P
for it cannot be | but i am pigeon–liver'd, and 2.02.576
for virtue cannot so /inoculate our old stock 3.01.117 P
laugh, cannot but make the judicious grieve; 3.02. 26 P
promise–cramm'd — you cannot feed capons so. 3.02. 94 P
the players cannot keep /counsel, they'll tell 3.02.142 P
sir, i cannot. 3.02.319 P
my lord, i cannot. 3.02.352 P
believe me, i cannot. 3.02.354 P

but these cannot i command to any utt'rance of 3.02.361 P
this little organ, yet cannot you make it speak. 3.02.369 P
you fret me, /yet you cannot play upon me. 3.02.372 P
that cannot be, since i am still possess'd | of 3.03. 53
you cannot call it love, for at your age | the 3.04. 68
is bestow'd, my lord, | we cannot get from him. 4.03. 13
plot | whereon the numbers cannot try the cause, 4.04. 63
but i cannot choose but weep to think they would 4.05. 69 P
it must be /se /offendendo, it cannot be else. 5.01. 9 P
mass, i cannot tell. 5.01. 55 P
cannot you tell that? 5.01.146 P
very sultry — as 'twere — i cannot tell how. 5.02.101 P
i cannot live to hear the news from england, 5.02.354
i cannot conceive you. LR 1.01. 12 P
i cannot wish the fault undone, the issue of it 1.01. 17 P
i am, i cannot heave | my heart into my mouth. 1.01. 91
from us till our oldness cannot relish them. 1.02. 48 P
he cannot be such a monster — 1.02. 94 P
to fear judgment, to fight when i cannot choose, 1.04. 16 P
for my duty cannot be silent when i think your 1.04. 65 P
i cannot be so partial, goneril, | to the great 1.04.311
how far your eyes may pierce i cannot tell: 1.04.345
side 's nose, that what a man cannot smell out, 1.05. 23 P
he cannot flatter, he, | an honest mind and 2.02. 98
i cannot think my sister in the least | would 2.04.141
old man and 's people | cannot be well bestow'd. 2.04.289
man's nature cannot carry | th' affliction nor 3.02. 48
my duty cannot suffer | t' obey in all your 3.04.148
you cannot see your way. 4.01. 17
poor tom's a–cold. i cannot daub it further. 4.01. 52
idle pebble chafes, | cannot be heard so high. 4.06. 22
lark so far | cannot be seen or heard. 4.06. 59
no, they cannot touch me for /coining; 4.06. 83 P
we cannot all be masters, nor all masters OTH 1.01. 43
nor all masters | cannot be truly follow'd. 1.01. 44
cannot with safety cast him, for he's embark'd 1.01.149
cannot but feel this wrong as 'twere their own; 1.02. 97
this cannot be | by no assay of reason; 1.03. 17
what cannot be preserv'd when fortune takes, 1.03.206
it cannot be. 1.03.333 P
it cannot be long that desdemona should continue 1.03.342 P
i cannot, 'twixt the heaven and the main, 2.01. 3
i cannot speak enough of this content, | it 2.01.196
i cannot believe that in her, she's full of most 2.01.249 P
jealousy so strong | that judgment cannot cure. 2.01.302
i cannot speak | any beginning to this peevish 2.03.184
i pray you pardon me, i cannot speak. 2.03.189
more of this matter cannot i report. 2.03.240
no, sure, i cannot think it, | that he would 3.03. 38
from the heart, | that passion cannot rule. 3.03.124
you cannot, if my heart were in your hand, | nor 3.03.163
i cannot speak of this. come now, your promise. 3.04. 48
them, cannot choose | but they must blab — 4.01. 28
cannot restrain | from the excess of laughter. 4.01. 98
she's a simple bawd | that cannot say as much. 4.02. 21
i cannot weep, nor answers have i none | but 4.02.103
i cannot tell. 4.02.111
upon her, | that true hearts cannot bear it. 4.02.117
i cannot say "whore." 4.02.161
i cannot go to, man, nor 'tis not very well. 4.02.192 P
of them is hereabout, | and cannot make away. 5.01. 58
thy rose, | i cannot give it vital growth again, 5.02. 14
cannot remove nor choke the strong conception 5.02. 55
if that thou be'st a devil, i cannot kill thee. 5.02.287
go, you wild bedfellow, you cannot soothsay. ANT 1.02. 51 P
prognostication, i cannot scratch mine ear. 1.02. 53 P
let him marry a woman that cannot go, sweet isis 1.02. 64 P
we cannot call her winds and waters sighs and 1.02.147 P
this cannot be cunning in her; 1.02.150 P
in the state | cannot endure my absence. 1.02.172
you have broach'd here cannot be without you, 1.02.174 P
it cannot be thus long, the sides of nature 1.03. 16
what he cannot change, | than what he chooses. 1.04. 14
rare indeed | whom these things cannot blemish), 1.04. 23
i cannot hope | caesar and antony shall well 2.01. 38
for't cannot be | we shall remain in friendship, 2.02.112
age cannot wither her, nor custom stale | her 2.02.234
i cannot hate thee worser than i do, | if thou 2.05. 90
though it cannot be denied what i have done by 2.06. 89 P
if he do, sure he cannot weep't back again. 2.06.106 P
bards, poets, cannot | think, speak, cast, write 3.02. 16
that's not so good. he cannot like her long. 3.03. 14
three in egypt | cannot make better note. 3.03. 23
auguries | say they know not, they cannot tell, 4.12. 5
yet cannot hold this visible shape, my knave. 4.14. 14
the sevenfold shield of ajax cannot keep | the 4.14. 38
for caesar cannot /live | to be ungentle. 5.01. 59
i cannot tell. 5.02. 72
i cannot project mine own cause so well | to 5.02.121
i cannot delve him to the root: CYM 1.01. 28
there cannot be a pinch in death | more sharp 1.01.130
a dram, you cannot preserve it from tainting. 1.04.135 P
return he cannot, nor | continue where he is. 1.05. 53
who cannot be new built, nor has no friends | so 1.05. 59
it cannot be i' th' eye: 1.06. 39
yea, what she cannot choose | but must be, will 1.06. 71
of a sir so rare, | which you know cannot err. 1.06.176
you cannot derogate, my lord. 2.01. 44 P
and this her son | cannot take two from twenty, 2.01. 55
he cannot choose but take this service i have 2.03. 34 P
the very devils cannot plague them better. 2.05. 35
have a fog in them | that i cannot look through. 3.02. 80
it cannot be | but that my master is abus'd. 3.04.119
from whose so many weights of baseness cannot 3.05. 88
am ill, but your being by me | cannot amend me; 4.02. 12
i cannot find those runagates, that villain 4.02. 62
villain, be thy name, | i cannot tremble at it. 4.02. 90
i cannot tell; 4.02.103
cadwal, | i cannot sing. 4.02.240
thereto so o'ergrown, | cannot be question'd. 4.04. 34
i repent, | i cannot do it better than in gyves, 5.04. 14
or a speaking such | as sense cannot untie. 5.04.148
stepp'd before targes of proof, cannot be found. 5.05. 5
i'll make bold your highness | cannot deny. 5.05. 90
please, | i cannot be much lower than my knees. PER 1.02. 47
no, friend, cannot you beg? 2.01. 63 P
and what a man cannot get, he may lawfully deal 2.01.114 P
but if i cannot win you to this love, | go 2.04. 49

cleon, for the babe | cannot hold out to tyrus. 3.01. 79
we cannot but obey | the powers above us. 3.03. 9
by the holy gods | i cannot rightly say. 3.04. 8
i cannot be bated one doit of a thousand pieces. 4.02. 51 P
why, i cannot name/'t but i shall offend. 4.06. 69 P
i cannot be offended with my trade. 4.06. 70 P
prove that i cannot, take me home again | and 4.06.189
falseness cannot come from thee, for thou 5.01.120
this cannot be | my daughter — buried! 5.01.162
you cannot read it there. TNK 1.01.111
who cannot feel nor see the rain, being in't, 1.01.120
and we cannot weep | when our friends don their 1.03. 18
i think | theseus cannot be umpire to himself, 1.03. 45
sure there cannot. 2.02.113
till our deaths it cannot, | and after death our 2.02.115
i cannot tell what you have done; 2.02.156
sure he cannot | be so unmanly as to leave me 2.06. 18
to you being enemy, | cannot to me be kind. 3.01. 50
your attendance | cannot please heaven, and i 3.01.111
i cannot hallow. 3.02. 9
he cannot run, the jingling of his gyves | might 3.02. 14
that cannot love thee, he that broke thy prison 3.06.139
which cannot want due mercy, i beg first. 3.06.209
they cannot both enjoy you. 3.06.275
i cannot, sir, they are both too excellent: 3.06.286
it cannot be. 4.01. 46
cannot distinguish, but must cry for both! 4.02. 54
fear he cannot, | he shows no such soft temper. 4.02.102
i cannot stay — | their fame has fir'd me so — 4.02.152
a perturb'd mind, which i cannot minister to. 4.03. 60 P
the glass is running now that cannot finish 5.01. 18
to those that would and cannot, a rejoicer. 5.01.121
but, as it is with schoolboys, cannot say; ep 2
the dev'l cannot rule them. STM II.C 54 P
you | to lead those that the dev'l cannot rule. II.C 56
which cannot choose but much advantage the poor II.C 70 P
your hurly | cannot proceed but by obedience. II.C 114
look how he can, she cannot choose but love, VEN 79
her help she sees, but help she cannot get, 93
being judge in love, she cannot right her cause. 220
his short thick neck cannot be easily harmed; 627
"what have you urg'd that i cannot reprove? 787
"if he be dead — o no, it cannot be, | seeing 937
"my tongue cannot express my grief for one, 1069
mar not the thing that cannot be amended. LUC 578
then kings' misdeeds cannot be hid in clay. 609
gain | but torment that it cannot cure his pain. 861
"so then he hath it when he cannot use it, | and 862
so am i now — o no, that cannot be! 1049
maze, | that cannot tread the way out readily, 1152
body spread, | and who cannot abuse a body dead? 1267
be told, | the repetition cannot make it less; 1285
the weary time she cannot entertain, | for now 1361
"it cannot be," quoth she, "that so much guile" 1534
from her tongue "can lurk" from "cannot" took: 1537
"it cannot be" she in that sense forsook, | and 1538
and turn'd it thus, "it cannot be, i find, | but 1539
crabbed age and youth cannot live together: PP 12. 1
as take the pain but cannot pluck the pelf. 14.12
senseless trees they cannot hear thee, 20.21
if thou wake, he cannot sleep; 20.52
truth may seem, but cannot be, | beauty brag, PHT 62
for who's so dumb that cannot write to thee, SON 38. 7
i cannot blame thee for my love thou usest, 40. 6
the bloody spur cannot provoke him on | that 50. 9
which cannot choose | but weep to have that 64.13
yet this thy praise cannot be so thy praise | to 70.11
look what thy memory cannot contain | commit to 77. 9
from hence your memory death cannot take, 81. 3
as victors of my silence cannot boast; 86.11
therefore in that i cannot know thy change. 93. 6
cannot dispraise but in a kind of praise, 95. 7

CANON 7 FR 0.0008 REL FR 5 V 2 P
proclaimed edict and continent canon; LLL 1.01.260 P
which is the most inhibited sin in the canon. AWW 1.01.145 P
child, | the canon of the law is laid on him, JN 2.01.180
against the hospitable canon, would i | wash my COR 1.10. 26
'twas from the canon. 3.01. 90
not fix'd | his canon 'gainst /self–slaughter! HAM 1.02.132
what canon is there | that does command my TNK 1.02. 55

CANONIZ'D 2 FR 0.0002 REL FR 2 V 0 P
me mad, | and thou shalt be canoniz'd, cardinal; JN 3.04. 52
but tell | why thy canoniz'd bones, hearsed in HAM 1.04. 47

CANONIZE 1 FR 0.0001 REL FR 1 V 0 P
foes, | and fame in time to come canonize us, TRO 2.02.202

CANONIZED 2 FR 0.0002 REL FR 2 V 0 P
call'd, | canonized and worshipp'd as a saint, JN 3.01.177
loves | are brazen images of canonized saints. 2H6 1.03. 60

CANONS 1 FR 0.0001 REL FR 1 V 0 P
religious canons, civil laws are cruel; TIM 4.03. 61

CANOPIED 3 FR 0.0003 REL FR 3 V 0 P
lie rich when canopied with bow'rs. TN 1.01. 40
lights, now canopied | under these windows, CYM 2.02. 21
light, | and canopied in darkness sweetly lay, LUC 398

CANOPIES 2 FR 0.0002 REL FR 2 V 0 P
costly apparel, tents, and canopies, | fine SHR 2.01.352
the great, | under the canopies of costly state, 2H4 3.01. 13

CANOPY 8 FR 0.0009 REL FR 5 V 3 P
than doth a rich embroider'd canopy | to kings 3H6 2.05. 44
under the canopy. COR 4.05. 38 P
under the canopy? 4.05. 39 P
strew — | o woe, thy canopy is dust and stones! ROM 5.03. 13
their shadows seem | a canopy most fatal, under JC 5.01. 87
this most excellent canopy, the air, look you, HAM 2.02.300 P
which erst from heat did canopy the herd, | and SON 12. 6
were't aught to me i bore the canopy, | with my 125. 1

/CANST 2 FR 0.0002 REL FR 2 V 0 P
and how accompanied? /canst /thou /tell /that? 2H4 4.04. 52
/thou /canst /not /strike /it /thus /to /make TIT 3.02. 14

CANST 190 FR 0.0214 REL FR 144 V 46 P
canst thou remember | a time before we came unto TMP 1.02. 38
i do not think thou canst, for then thou wast 1.02. 40
i know thou canst not choose. 1.02.186
how now? moody? | what is't thou canst demand? 1.02.245
though thou canst swim like a duck, thou art 2.02.131 P
canst thou bring me to the party? 3.02. 58 P
thou liest, thou canst not. 3.02. 62

what a block art thou, that thou canst not! TGV 2.05. 26 P
cease to lament for that thou canst not help, 3.01.243
here if thou stay, thou canst not see thy love; 3.01.246
fie on thee, jolthead, thou canst not read. 3.01.290 P
this proves that thou canst not read. 3.01.297 P
come, thou canst not hide it. WIV 3.03. 66 P
canst thou believe thy living is a life, | so MM 3.02. 26
canst thou tell if claudio die to–morrow, or no? 3.02.169 P
i know thou canst, and therefore see thou do it. ERR 2.02.139
how canst thou cross this marriage? ADO 2.02. 7 P
canst thou so daff me? 5.01. 78
how canst thou part sadness and melancholy, my LLL 1.02. 7 P
thou canst not hit it, hit it, hit it, | thou 4.01.125
hit it, | thou canst not hit it, my good man. 4.01.126
how canst thou thus for shame, titania, | glance MND 2.01. 74
thou canst compel no more than she entreat. 3.02.249
with all my heart, so thou canst get a wife. MV 3.02.195
till thou canst rail the seal from off my bond, 4.01.139
give him the ring, and bring him, if thou canst, 4.01.453
say what thou canst, i'll go along with thee. AYL 1.03.105
no, corin, being old, thou canst not guess, 2.04. 25
till thou canst quit thee by thy brother's mouth 3.01. 11
or if thou canst not, o, for shame, for shame, 3.05. 18
but since that thou canst talk of love so well, 3.05. 94
this dispatch'd with all the haste thou canst; SHR in.1. 129
counsel me, tranio, for i know thou canst; 1.01.157
why then thou canst not break her to the lute? 2.01.147
thou canst not frown, thou canst not look 2.01.247
canst not frown, thou canst not look askaunce, 2.01.247
youngling, thou canst not love so dear as i. 2.01.337
do what thou canst, i will not go to–day, | no, 3.02.208
if thou canst like this creature as a maid, | i AWW 2.03.142
that canst not dream | we, poising us in her 2.03.153
ev'n as soon as thou canst, for thou hast to 2.03.224 P
"when thou canst get the ring upon my finger, 3.02. 57 P
already, unless thou canst say they are married. 5.03.268 P
"thou canst not choose but know who i am. TN 2.05.174 P
canst with thine eyes at once see good and evil, WT 1.02.303
what? canst not rule her? 2.03. 46
thou canst not speak too much, i have deserv'd 3.02.215
how now? canst stand? 4.03. 74 P
for ere thou canst report, i will be there; JN 1.01. 25
thou canst not, cardinal, devise a name | so 3.01.149
what canst thou say but will perplex thee more, 3.01.222
and better conquest never canst thou make | than 3.01.290
we grant thou canst outscold us. 5.02.160
what i have spoke, or thou canst worse devise. R2 1.01. 77
but not a minute, king, that thou canst give. 1.03.226
shorten my days thou canst with sullen sorrow, 1.03.227
thou canst help time to furrow me with age, 1.03.229
the worst is worldly loss thou canst unfold. 3.02. 94
canst not hear? 1H4 2.01. 28 P
ay, when, canst tell? 2.01. 39 P
ground, and list if thou canst hear the tread of 2.02. 33 P
pound i could run as fast as thou canst. 2.04.148 P
canst thou now find out to hide thee from this 2.04.263 P
canst thou deny it? 2H4 2.01. 93 P
deny it if thou canst. 2.01.103 P
let it be ten pound, if thou canst. 2.01.147 P
and see if thou canst find out sneak's noise. 2.04. 11 P
canst thou, o partial sleep, give /then repose 3.01. 26
what, canst thou not forbear me half an hour? 4.05.109
canst thou, when thou command'st the beggar's H5 4.01.256
how canst thou make me satisfaction? 4.08. 45
i am glad thou canst speak no better english, 5.02.123 P
if thou canst love a fellow of this temper, kate 5.02.146 P
if thou canst love me for this, take me! 5.02.150 P
canst thou love me? 5.02.193 P
ask me what question thou canst possible, | and 1H6 1.02. 87
woman, do what thou canst to save our honors; 1.02.147
come, officer, as loud as e'er thou canst, | cry 1.03. 72
at least, if thou canst, speak. 1.04. 73
o'ertake me if thou canst, i scorn thy strength. 1.05. 15
humphrey of gloucester, if thou canst accuse, 3.01. 3
purpose to answer what thou canst object. 3.01. 7
on us thou canst not enter but by death; 4.02. 18
and no way canst thou turn thee for redress, 4.02. 25
thou never hadst renown, nor canst not lose it. 4.05. 40
chang'd to a worser shape thou canst not be. 5.03. 36
how canst thou tell she will deny thy suit, 5.03. 75
and, fly thou how thou canst, they'll tangle 2H6 2.04. 55
what canst thou answer to my majesty for giving 4.07. 27 P
see if thou canst outface me with thy looks. 4.10. 46
dar'st not, no, nor canst not rule a traitor. 5.01. 95
canst thou dispense with heaven for such an oath 5.01.181
storm | than any thou canst conjure up to–day; 5.01.199
stigmatic, that's more than thou canst tell. 5.01.215
thou canst not, son; it is impossible. 3H6 1.02. 21
and, if thou canst for blushing, view this face, 1.04. 46
amongst the loving welshmen canst procure, 2.01.180
ay, but thou canst do what i mean to ask. 3.02. 48
warwick, canst thou speak against thy liege, 3.03. 95
me their words as near as thou canst guess them. 4.01. 90
sail how thou canst, have wind and tide thy 5.01. 53
what satisfaction canst thou make | for bearing 5.05. 14
canst thou not speak? 5.05. 52
his mortal body, | his soul thou canst not have. R3 1.02. 48
thou canst make | no excuse current but to hang 1.02. 83
how canst thou urge god's dreadful law to us, 1.04.209
but canst thou guess that he doth aim at it? 3.02. 45
cousin, canst thou quake and change thy color, 3.05. 1
a grave | as thou canst yield a melancholy seat! 4.04. 32
what comfortable hour canst thou name | that 4.04.174
honor, | canst thou demise to any child of mine? 4.04.248
how canst thou woo her? 4.04.268
what canst thou swear by now? 4.04.387
canst thou say further? H8 1.02.187
sing, and disperse 'em if thou canst. 3.01. 2
thou bitch–wolf's son, canst thou not hear? TRO 2.01. 10 P
thou canst strike, canst thou? 2.01. 19 P
thou canst strike, canst thou? 2.01. 19 P
soft infancy, that nothing canst but cry, | add 2.02.105
"because thou canst not ease thy smart | by 4.04. 19
has he din'd, canst thou tell? COR 5.02. 34 P
proud and ambitious tribune, canst thou tell? TIT 1.01.202
thou canst not come to me — i come to thee. 2.03.245
canst thou not guess wherefore she plies thee 4.01. 15
guide, if thou canst, | this after me. 4.01. 69

that which thou canst not undo. 4.02. 74
that granted, how canst thou believe an oath? 5.01. 72
what, canst thou say all this and never blush? 5.01.121
farewell, thou canst not teach me to forget. ROM 1.01.237
what satisfaction canst thou have to-night? 2.02.126
but love thee better than thou canst devise, 3.01. 69
thou canst not speak of that thou dost not feel. 3.03. 64
set, | for then thou canst not pass to mantua, 3.03.149
if in thy wisdom thou canst give no help, | do 4.01. 52
how canst thou try them so? 4.02. 5
canst not read? TIM 2.02. 80 P
canst thou the conscience lack | to think i 2.02.175
and canst use the time well, if the time use 3.01. 36 P
things in the world canst thou nearest compare 4.03.318 P
thou canst not paint a man | so bad as is 5.01. 31
canst thou hold up thy heavy eyes awhile, | and JC 4.03.256
caesar, thou canst not die by traitors' hands, 5.01. 56
thou canst not say i did it; MAC 3.04. 49
if thou canst nod, speak too. 3.04. 69
canst thou not minister to a mind diseas'd, 5.03. 40
day, | thou canst not then be false to any man. HAM 1.03. 80
said, old mole, canst work i' th' earth so fast? 1.05.162
if thou canst mutine in a matron's bones, | to 3.04. 83
if thou canst serve where thou dost stand LR 1.04. 5
what services canst do? 1.04. 31 P
nay, and thou canst not smile as the wind sits, 1.04.100 P
what canst tell, boy? 1.05. 17 P
thou canst tell why one's nose stands i' th' 1.05. 19 P
canst tell how an oyster makes his shell? 1.05. 25 P
for thy daughters as thou canst tell in a year. 2.04. 55 P
mend when thou canst, be better at thy leisure, 2.04.229
canst thou blame him? 3.04.162
make all the money thou canst. OTH 1.03.354 P
if thou canst cuckold him, thou dost thyself a 1.03.368 P
for nothing canst thou to damnation add 3.03.372
hark, canst thou hear me? 5.02.247
thou canst not fear us, pompey, with thy sails; ANT 2.06. 24
and if thou canst awake by four o' th' clock, CYM 2.02. 6
of that beggar posthumus, thou canst not, in the 3.05.119 P
canst thou catch any fishes then? PER 2.01. 66 P
be got now-a-days unless thou canst fish for't. 2.01. 69 P
portage quit | with all thou canst find here. 3.01. 36
when canst thou reach it? 3.01. 75
thou canst not do a thing in the world so soon 4.01. 3
what canst thou say | when noble pericles shall 4.03. 12
what canst thou wish thine enemy to be? 4.06.158
most wise in general, tell me, if thou canst, 5.01.183
that equally canst poise sternness with pity, TNK 1.01. 86
canst not thou work such flowers in silk, wench? 2.02.127
not, fool, thou canst not, thou art feeble. 2.02.214
any death thou canst invent, duke. 3.06.281
that canst make | a cripple flourish with his 5.01. 81
thy flame — at seventy thou canst catch, | and 5.01. 87
"thou canst not see one wrinkle in my brow, VEN 139
art thou a woman's son and canst not feel | what 201
"what, canst thou talk?" 427
what canst thou boast | of things long since, or 1077
thy princely office how canst thou fulfill, LUC 628
so great a sum of sums, yet canst not live? SON 4. 8
gone, | what acceptable audit canst thou leave? 4.12
thou /not farther than my thoughts canst move, 47.11
thou canst not, love, disgrace me half so ill, 89. 5
thou canst not vex me with inconstant mind, 92. 9
thou canst not then use rigor in my jail: 133.12
canst thou, o cruel, say i love thee not, | when 149. 1
CANSTICK *(also candlesticks)*
CANSTICK 1 FR 0.0001 REL FR 1 V 0 P
i had rather hear a brazen canstick turn'd, | or 1H4 3.01.129
CANTERBURY 15 FR 0.0017 REL FR 14 V 1 P
chosen archbishop | of canterbury, from that JN 3.01.144
his brother, archbishop late of canterbury, R2 2.01.282
pilgrims going to canterbury with rich offerings 1H4 1.02.126 P
where is my gracious lord of canterbury? H5 1.02. 1
my lord of canterbury, and got your leave | to H8 2.04.219
install'd lord archbishop of canterbury. 3.02.401
the archbishop | of canterbury, accompanied with 4.01. 25
when by the archbishop of canterbury | she had 4.01. 86
ha? canterbury? 5.01. 81
my good and gracious lord of canterbury. 5.01. 92
stand up, good canterbury! 5.01.113
the high promotion of his grace of canterbury, 5.02. 23
chief cause concerns his grace of canterbury. 5.02. 38
my lord of canterbury, | i have a suit which you 5.02.194
thus, "do my lord of canterbury | a shrewd turn, 5.02.210
CANTHERIZING 1 FR 0.0001 REL FR 1 V 0 P
be as a cantherizing to the root o' th' tongue, TIM 5.01.133
/CANTLE 1 FR 0.0001 REL FR 1 V 0 P
a huge half-moon, a monstrous /cantle out. 1H4 3.01. 99
CANTLE 1 FR 0.0001 REL FR 1 V 0 P
the greater cantle of the world is lost | with ANT 3.10. 6
CANTONS 1 FR 0.0001 REL FR 1 V 0 P
write loyal cantons of contemned love, | and TN 1.05.270
CANUS 1 FR 0.0001 REL FR 1 V 0 P
club kill'd cerberus, that three-headed canus; LLL 5.02.589
CANVAS 1 FR 0.0001 REL FR 0 V 1 P
francis, your white canvas doublet will sully. 1H4 2.04. 74 P
CANVAS-CLIMBER 1 FR 0.0001 REL FR 1 V 0 P
the ladder-tackle washes off | a canvas-climber. PER 4.01. 61
CANVASS 2 FR 0.0002 REL FR 1 V 1 P
i'll canvass thee between a pair of sheets. 2H4 2.04.225 P
i'll canvass thee in thy broad cardinal's hat, 1H6 1.03. 36
/CANZONET 1 FR 0.0001 REL FR 0 V 1 P
let me supervise the /canzonet. LLL 4.02.120 P
/CAP 1 FR 0.0001 REL FR 0 V 1 P
on fortune's /cap we are not the very button. HAM 2.02.229 P
CAP 47 FR 0.0053 REL FR 24 V 23 P
one man but he will wear his cap with suspicion? ADO 1.01.198 P
not seen enough, you should wear it in your cap. 3.04. 72 P
what's her name in the cap? LLL 2.01.209
ay, and worn in the cap of a tooth-drawer. 5.02.618 P
here is the cap your worship did bespeak. SHR 4.03. 63
a knack, a toy, a trick, a baby's cap. 4.03. 67
why, thou say'st true, it is /a paltry cap, | a 4.03. 81
love me, or love me not, i like the cap, | and 4.03. 84
i see she's like to have neither cap nor gown. 4.03. 93
katherine, that cap of yours becomes you not; 5.02.121
an old courtier, wears her cap out of fashion, AWW 1.01.156 P
for they wear themselves in the cap of the time; 2.01. 53 P
he that cannot make a leg, put off 's cap, kiss 2.02. 10 P
nothing, has neither leg, hands, lip, nor cap; 2.02. 11 P
the more and less came in with cap and knee, 1H4 4.03. 68
to be worn in my cap than to wait at my heels. 2H4 1.02. 15 P
the answer is as ready as a /borrower's cap, "i 2.02.116 P
money a' thursday, shalt have a cap to-morrow. 2.04.275 P
i will cap that proverb with "there is flattery H5 3.07.114 P
not you wear your dagger in your cap that day, 4.01. 56 P
this will i also wear in my cap. 4.01.213 P
and with his cap in hand | like a base pander 4.05. 13
soldier, why wear'st thou that glove in thy cap? 4.07.121 P
or if i can see my glove in his cap, which he 4.07.128 P
thou this favor for me and stick it in thy cap. 4.07.154 P
it to in change promis'd to wear it in his cap. 4.08. 30 P
i met this man with my glove in his cap, and i 4.08. 31 P
and wear it for an honor in thy cap | till i do 4.08. 59
bold as to wear it in my cap till i see him once 5.01. 12 P
he'll make his cap co-equal with the crown." 1H6 5.01. 33
fling up his cap, and say, "god save his majesty 2H6 4.08. 15
and he that throws not up his cap for joy 3H6 2.01.196
forward, | and dare us with his cap, like larks. H8 3.02.282
take my cap, jupiter, and i thank thee. COR 2.01.105 P
"commend me to your master" and the cap | plays TIM 2.01. 18
push, did you see my cap? 3.06.109 P
did you see my cap? 3.06.115 P
breath whom thou'lt observe | blow off thy cap; 4.03.213
thou art the cap of all the fools alive. 4.03.358
a very riband in the cap of youth, | yet needful HAM 4.07. 77
the slaughter, | if my cap would buy a halter, LR 1.04.320
wore gloves in my cap; 3.04. 86 P
i have ever held my cap off to thy fortunes. ANT 2.07. 57
hoo, says 'a. there's my cap. 2.07.134
such gain the cap of him that makes him fine, CYM 3.03. 25
at length | i fling my cap up; TNK 3.05. 17
a cap of flowers, and a kirtle | embroidered all PP 19.11
CAPABILITY 1 FR 0.0001 REL FR 1 V 0 P
gave us not | that capability and godlike reason HAM 4.04. 38
/CAPABLE 1 FR 0.0001 REL FR 1 V 0 P
/you /were /advis'd /his /flesh /was /capable 2H4 1.01.172
CAPABLE 15 FR 0.0017 REL FR 10 V 5 P
wilt not take, | being capable of all ill! TMP 1.02.353
if their daughters be capable, i will put it to LLL 4.02. 79 P
the cicatrice and capable impressure | thy palm AYL 3.05. 23
heart too capable | of every line and trick of AWW 1.01. 95
so thou wilt be capable of a courtier's counsel 1.01.209 P
for, if thou be'st capable of things serious, WT 4.04.764 P
their souls | are capable of this ambition, JN 2.01.476
me, | for i am sick and capable of fears, 3.01. 12
boy, | bold, quick, ingenious, forward, capable: R3 3.01.155
own natures frail, and capable | of our flesh; H8 5.02. 46
his horse, for that's the more capable creature. TRO 3.03.307 P
who for the most part are capable of nothing but HAM 3.02. 11 P
preaching to stones, | would make them capable. 3.04.127
boy, i'll work the means | to make thee capable. LR 2.01. 85
till that a capable and wide revenge | swallow OTH 3.03.459
CAPACITIES 2 FR 0.0002 REL FR 1 V 1 P
consider not the capacities of us that are young 2H4 1.02.174 P
you most coarse frieze capacities, ye /jane TNK 3.05. 8
CAPACITY 11 FR 0.0012 REL FR 7 V 4 P
the matter to you, if you be capacity of it. WIV 1.01.215 P
god comfort thy capacity! LLL 4.02. 44 P
your capacity | is of that nature that to your 5.02.376
in least speak most, to my capacity. MND 5.01.105
notwithstanding thy capacity | receiveth as the TN 1.01. 10
this is evident to any formal capacity, there is 2.05.117 P
him out to be of good capacity and breeding; 3.04.186 P
the capacity | of your soft cheveril conscience H8 2.03. 31
sweetness | for the capacity of my ruder powers. TRO 3.02. 25
holding them, | in human action and capacity, COR 2.01.249
had our great palace the capacity | to camp this ANT 4.08. 32
CAP-AND-KNEE 1 FR 0.0001 REL FR 1 V 0 P
cap-and-knee slaves, vapors, and minute-jacks! TIM 3.06. 97
CAPANEUS 1 FR 0.0001 REL FR 1 V 0 P
king capaneus was your lord. TNK 1.01. 59
CAP-A-PE 2 FR 0.0002 REL FR 1 V 1 P
i am courtier cap-a-pe, and one that will either WT 4.04.736 P
your father, | armed at point exactly, cap-a-pe, HAM 1.02.200
CAPARISON 3 FR 0.0003 REL FR 2 V 1 P
with die and drab i purchas'd this caparison, WT 4.03. 27 P
caparison my horse! R3 5.03.289
here is the steed, we the caparison. COR 1.09. 12
CAPARISON'D 2 FR 0.0002 REL FR 0 V 2 P
thou think, though i am caparison'd like a man, AYL 3.02.195 P
for all the world caparison'd like the horse; SHR 3.02. 65 P
CAPARISONS 1 FR 0.0001 REL FR 1 V 0 P
spur, | for rich caparisons or trappings gay? VEN 286
CAPE* 5 FR 0.0005 REL FR 3 V 2 P
"with a small compass'd cape" — SHR 4.03.139 P
i confess the cape. 4.03.140 P
will you buy any tape, | or lace for your cape, WT 4.04.316
and on this north side win this cape of land, 1H4 3.01.112
what from the cape can you discern at sea? OTH 2.01. 1
CAPEL'S *(also capulet's, etc.)*
CAPEL'S 1 FR 0.0001 REL FR 1 V 0 P
her body sleeps in capel's monument, | and her ROM 5.01. 18
CAPELS' 1 FR 0.0001 REL FR 1 V 0 P
i discern, | it burneth in the capels' monument. ROM 5.03.127
CAPELS 1 FR 0.0001 REL FR 1 V 0 P
the day is hot, the capels /are abroad, | and if ROM 3.01. 2
CAPER* 6 FR 0.0006 REL FR 1 V 5 P
then is there here one master caper, at the suit MM 4.03. 9 P
faith, i can cut a caper. TN 1.03.121 P
let me see thee caper. 1.03.141 P
and he that will caper with me for a thousand 2H4 1.02.193 P
seen | him caper upright like a wild morisco, 2H6 3.01.365
he offer'd to cut a caper at the proclamation, PER 4.02.107 P
CAPER'D 1 FR 0.0001 REL FR 1 V 0 P
the third he caper'd, and cried, "all goes well. LLL 5.02.113
CAPERS 3 FR 0.0003 REL FR 1 V 2 P
he capers, he dances, he has eyes of youth; WIV 3.02. 67 P
we that are true lovers run into strange capers; AYL 2.04. 55 P
he capers nimbly in a lady's chamber | to the R3 1.01. 12
CAPET 2 FR 0.0002 REL FR 2 V 0 P
hugh capet also, who usurp'd the crown | of H5 1.02. 69
tenth, | who was sole heir to the usurper capet, 1.02. 78
CAPET'S 1 FR 0.0001 REL FR 1 V 0 P
king pepin's title and hugh capet's claim, H5 1.02. 87
CAPHIS 2 FR 0.0002 REL FR 2 V 0 P
caphis ho! TIM 2.01. 13
caphis, i say! 2.01. 14
CAPILET* 3 FR 0.0003 REL FR 1 V 2 P
diana capilet." AWW 5.03.147 P
florentine, | derived from the ancient capilet. 5.03.159
slip, and i'll give him my horse, grey capilet. TN 3.04.287 P
CAPITAINE 1 FR 0.0001 REL FR 0 V 1 P
suivez-vous le grand capitaine. H5 4.04. 66 P
CAPITAL 15 FR 0.0017 REL FR 13 V 2 P
be smil'd at, their offenses being so capital? WT 4.04.793 P
pains, | of capital treason we arrest you here. R2 4.01.151
chief majority | and military title capital 1H4 3.02.110
mowbray, | of capital treason i attach you both. 2H4 4.02.109
shall we stretch our eye | when capital crimes, H5 2.02. 56
she is our capital demand, compris'd | within 5.02. 96
of capital treason 'gainst the king and crown. 2H6 5.01.107
this | so criminal, and in such capital kind, COR 3.03. 81
and to poor we | thine enmity's most capital; 5.03.104
but treasons capital, confess'd and prov'd, MAC 1.03.115
part of him to kill so capital a calf there. HAM 3.02.105 P
feats, | so criminal and so capital in nature, 4.07. 7
edmund, i arrest thee | on capital treason, and, LR 5.03. 83
in store, | due to this heinous capital offense, PER 2.04. 5
t' instruct me 'gainst a capital grief indeed — TNK 1.01.123
CAPITE 1 FR 0.0001 REL FR 0 V 1 P
men shall hold of me in capite; 2H6 4.07.123 P
CAPITOL 39 FR 0.0044 REL FR 33 V 6 P
to th' capitol! COR 1.01. 48 P
presume to know | what's done i' th' capitol; 1.01.192
your company to th' capitol, where i know | our 1.01.244
being naked, sick, nor fane nor capitol, | the 1.10. 20
table than a necessary bencher in the capitol. 2.01. 83 P
on, to the capitol! 2.01.204
you are sent for to the capitol. 2.01.260
let's to the capitol, | and carry with us ears 2.01.268
have drawn your number, | repair to th' capitol. 2.03.254
to th' capitol, come. 2.03.260
though calved i' th' porch o' th' capitol! 3.01.239
as far as doth the capitol exceed | the meanest 4.02. 39
shall 's to the capitol? 4.06.147
let's to the capitol. 4.06.159
see you yond coign a' th' capitol, yond 5.04. 1 P
rome, | keep then this passage to the capitol, TIT 1.01. 12
and in the capitol and senate's right, | whom 1.01. 41
thou great defender of this capitol, | stand 1.01. 77
go you down that way towards the capitol, | this JC 1.01. 63
fiery eyes | as we have seen him in the capitol, 1.02.187
my sword — | against the capitol i met a lion, 1.03. 20
comes caesar to the capitol to-morrow? 1.03. 36
and roars | as doth the lion in the capitol — 1.03. 75
and the high east | stands, as the capitol, 2.01.111
augurers | may hold him from the capitol to-day. 2.01.201
bent, | and i will bring him to the capitol. 2.01.211
of war, | which drizzled blood upon the capitol; 2.02. 21
run to the capitol, and nothing else? 2.04. 11
fray, | and the wind brings it from the capitol. 2.04. 19
is caesar yet gone to the capitol? 2.04. 24
my stand, | to see him pass on to the capitol. 2.04. 26
come to the capitol. 3.01. 12
of his death is enroll'd in the capitol: 3.02. 38 P
briefly, i dwell by the capitol. 3.03. 25 P
or here or at the capitol. 4.01. 11
i was kill'd i' th' capitol; HAM 3.02.104 P
to drench the capitol, but that they would ANT 2.06. 18
common as the stairs | that mount the capitol; CYM 1.06.106
"now by the capitol that we adore, | and by this LUC 1835
CAPITULATE 2 FR 0.0002 REL FR 2 V 0 P
mortimer, | capitulate against us, and are up. 1H4 3.02.120
or capitulate | again with rome's mechanics. COR 5.03. 82
/CAPOCCHIA 1 FR 0.0001 REL FR 0 V 1 P
a poor /capocchia! TRO 4.02. 31 P
CAPON 8 FR 0.0009 REL FR 4 V 4 P
the capon burns, the pig falls from the spit; ERR 1.02. 44
mome, malt-horse, capon, coxcomb, idiot, patch! 3.01. 32
he hath bid me to a calve's-head and a capon, ADO 5.01.155 P
boyet, you can carve, | break up this capon. LLL 4.01. 56
in fair round belly with good capon lin'd, AYL 2.07.154
and cleanly, but to carve a capon and eat it? 1H4 2.04.456 P
item, a capon ... 2s.2d.. 2.04.535 P
you are cock and capon too, and you crow, cock, CYM 2.01. 23 P
CAPON'S 2 FR 0.0002 REL FR 0 V 2 P
me to her trencher and steals her capon's leg. TGV 4.04. 9 P
for a cup of madeira and a cold capon's leg? 1H4 1.02.116 P
CAPONS 2 FR 0.0002 REL FR 0 V 2 P
hours were cups of sack, and minutes capons, and 1H4 1.02. 7 P
promise-cramm'd — you cannot feed capons so. HAM 3.02. 94 P
CAPPADOCIA 1 FR 0.0001 REL FR 1 V 0 P
archelaus | of cappadocia; ANT 3.06. 70
CAPRICCIO 1 FR 0.0001 REL FR 1 V 0 P
will this capriccio hold in thee, art sure? AWW 2.03.293
CAPRICIOUS 1 FR 0.0001 REL FR 0 V 1 P
thee and thy goats, as the most capricious poet, AYL 3.03. 8 P
CAP'RING 2 FR 0.0002 REL FR 2 V 0 P
our master | cap'ring to eye her. TMP 5.01.238
mingled his royalty with cap'ring fools, | had 1H4 3.02. 63
CAPS 14 FR 0.0015 REL FR 10 V 4 P
with silken coats and caps, and golden rings, SHR 4.03. 55
time, | and gentlewomen wear such caps as these. 4.03. 70
wearing leeks in their monmouth caps, which, H5 4.07.100 P
at lower end of the hall, hurl'd up their caps, R3 3.07. 35
they threw their caps | as they would hang them COR 1.01.212
are ambitious for poor knaves' caps and legs. 2.01. 68 P
a shower and thunder with their caps and shouts. 2.01.267
cast | your stinking greasy caps in hooting at 4.06.131
as you threw caps up will he tumble down, | and 4.06.135
our masters may throw their caps at their money. TIM 3.04.101 P
lives | expire before the flowers in their caps, MAC 4.03.172
caps, hands, and tongues applaud it to the HAM 4.05.108
petticoats, nor caps, nor any petty exhibition; OTH 4.03. 74 P
they cast their caps up and carouse together ANT 4.12. 12
/CAPTAIN 1 FR 0.0001 REL FR 1 V 0 P
/the /captain — | give it the captain. LR 5.03.251
CAPTAIN 130 FR 0.0147 REL FR 63 V 67 P
say "ay" and be the captain of us all: TGV 4.01. 63
we must bring you to our captain. 5.03. 2
there is our captain. 5.03. 10

to command the captain and all the rest from MM 1.02. 13 P
captain of our fairy band, | helena is here at MND 3.02.110
a phoenix, captain, and an enemy, | a guide, a AWW 1.01.168
farewell, captain. 2.01. 38 P
the regiment of the spinii one captain spurio, 2.01. 42 P
we shall, noble captain. 2.01. 46 P
god save you, captain. 2.05. 31 P
good captain, let me be th' interpreter. 4.01. 7 P
captain, i will. 4.01. 91
him, whether one captain dumaine be i' th' camp, 4.03.176 P
do you know this captain dumaine? 4.03.184 P
is this captain in the duke of florence's camp? 4.03.192 P
therefore once more to this captain dumaine. 4.03.247 P
what's his brother, the other captain dumaine? 4.03.282 P
ay, and the captain of his horse, count 4.03.294 P
good morrow, noble captain. 4.03.314 P
god bless you, captain parolles. 4.03.315 P
god save you, noble captain. 4.03.316 P
captain, what greeting will you to my lord lafew 4.03.317 P
good captain, will you give me a copy of the 4.03.319 P
you are undone, captain, all but your scarf; 4.03.323 P
captain i'll be no more, | but i will eat and 4.03.331
and drink, and sleep as soft | as captain shall. 4.03.333
there is a fair behavior in thee, captain, | and TN 1.02. 47
a baubling vessel was he captain of, | for 5.01. 54
i'll bring you to a captain in this town, 5.01.254
the captain that did bring me first on shore 5.01.274
he hath not told us of the captain yet. 5.01.381
come, captain, | we must be neat; WT 1.02.122
not neat, but cleanly, captain: 1.02.123
and his pure soul unto his captain christ, R2 4.01. 99
his captain, steward, deputy, elect, | anointed, 4.01.126
will you give me money, captain? 1H4 4.02. 4 P
i will, captain, farewell. 4.02. 10 P
no, good captain pistol, not here, sweet captain 2H4 2.04.138 P
good captain pistol, not here, sweet captain. 2.04.139 P
captain? 2.04.140 P
art thou not asham'd to be call'd captain? 2.04.141 P
you a captain! 2.04.144 P
he a captain! 2.04.146 P
a captain! 2.04.147 P
good captain peesel, be quiet, 'tis very late, 2.04.161 P
by my troth, captain, these are very bitter 2.04.170 P
a' my word, captain, there's none such here. 2.04.176 P
my captain, sir, commends him to you, my captain 3.02. 60 P
sir, commends him to you, my captain, sir john 3.02. 61 P
o lord, good my lord captain — 3.02.177 P
good master corporal captain, for my old dame's 3.02.229 P
go, captain, and deliver to the army | this news 4.02. 69
hie thee, captain. 4.02. 71
petty spirits muster me all to their captain, 4.03.111 P
captain fluellen, you must come presently to the H5 3.02. 54 P
it is captain macmorris, is it not? 3.02. 68 P
here 'a comes, and the scots captain, captain 3.02. 74 P
and the scots captain, captain jamy, with him. 3.02. 74 P
captain jamy is a marvellous falorous gentleman, 3.02. 76 P
i say gud day, captain fluellen. 3.02. 83 P
god–den to your worship, good captain james. 3.02. 84 P
how now, captain macmorris, have you quit the 3.02. 86 P
captain macmorris, i beseech you now, will you 3.02. 94 P
captain macmorris, i think, look you, under your 3.02.120 P
otherwise than is meant, captain macmorris, 3.02.126 P
captain macmorris, when there is more better 3.02.138 P
how now, captain fluellen, come you from the 3.06. 1 P
captain, i thee beseech to do me favors. 3.06. 21
speak, captain, for his life, and i will thee 3.06. 49
i tell you what, captain gower: 3.06. 82 P
behold | the royal captain of this ruin'd band 4.pr. 29
captain fluellen! 4.01. 64 P
under what captain serve you? 4.01. 93 P
ay, he was porn at monmouth, captain gower. 4.07. 11 P
i tell you, captain, if you look in the maps of 4.07. 23 P
what think you, captain fluellen? 4.07.131 P
under captain gower, my liege. 4.07.148 P
gower is a good captain, and is good knowledge 4.07.149 P
i warrant it is to knight you, captain. 4.08. 1 P
and his pleasure, captain, i beseech you now, 4.08. 2 P
stand away, captain gower, i will give treason 4.08. 13 P
and, captain, you must needs be friends with him 4.08. 61
yes, captain; 4.08.119
i will tell you asse my friend, captain gower: 5.01. 5 P
enough, captain, you have astonish'd him. 5.01. 39 P
that, being captain of the watch to–night, | did 1H6 2.01. 61
come hither, captain. 2.02. 59
welcome, brave captain and victorious lord! 3.04. 16
much more a knight, a captain, and a leader. 4.01. 32
and whiles the honorable captain there | drops 4.04. 17
hear ye, captain? are you not at leisure? 5.03. 97
speak, captain, shall i stab the forlorn swain? 2H6 4.01. 65
being captain of a pinnace, threatens more 4.01.107
be brave then, for your captain is brave, and 4.02. 64 P
where's captain margaret, to fence you now? 3H6 2.06. 75
a wise stout captain, and soon persuaded! 4.07. 30
good captain blunt, bear my good–night to him, R3 5.03. 30
yet one thing more, good captain, do for me — 5.03. 33
good night, good captain blunt. 5.03. 44
o thou whose captain i account myself, | look on 5.03.108
but, by great mars, the captain of us all, TRO 4.05.198
sirrah, if thy captain knew i were here, he COR 5.02. 51 P
come, my captain knows you not. 5.02. 53 P
here's rome's young captain, let him tell the TIT 5.03. 94
o, he's the courageous captain of compliments. ROM 2.04. 20 P
captain alcibiades, your heart's in the field TIM 1.02. 73 P
why, how now, captain, what do you in this wise 2.02. 73 P
now, captain? 3.05. 6
favor, pardon me | if i speak like a captain. 3.05. 41
and the ass more captain than the lion, the 3.05. 49
our captain hath in every figure skill, | an 5.03. 7
go, captain, from me greet the danish king. HAM 4.04. 1
come hither, captain; LR 5.03. 26
/the /captain — | give it the captain. 5.03.252
marry, to — come, captain, will you go? OTH 1.02. 53
that i spake of, our great captain's captain, 2.01. 74
to entreat your captain | to soft and gentle ANT 2.02. 2
forsake thy seat, i do beseech thee, captain, 2.07. 38
ho, noble captain, come. 2.07.135
so thy grand captain, antony, | shall set thee 3.01. 9
who does i' th' wars more than his captain can 3.01. 21
his captain can | becomes his captain's captain; 3.01. 22
eros, now thy captain is | even such a body. 4.14. 12
my dear master, | my captain, and my emperor: 4.14. 90
what rebel captain, | as mutines are incident, STM II.C 114
soldiers when their captain once doth yield, VEN 893
affection is my captain, and he leadeth; LUC 271
and as their captain, so their pride doth grow, 298
placed are, | or captain jewels in the carcanet. SON 52. 8
and captive good attending captain ill: 66.12
CAPTAIN–GENERAL 1 FR 0.0001 REL FR 0 V 1 P
captain–general of the army, agamemnon, /et TRO 3.03.277 P
CAPTAIN'S 6 FR 0.0006 REL FR 6 V 0 P
come, i must bring you to our captain's cave. TGV 5.03. 12
that in the captain's but a choleric word, MM 2.02.130
that i spake of, our great captain's captain, OTH 2.01. 74
his captain's heart, | which in the scuffles of ANT 1.01. 6
his captain can | becomes his captain's captain; 3.01. 22
a diminution in our captain's brain | restores 3.13.197
CAPTAINS' 1 FR 0.0001 REL FR 1 V 0 P
usuring senate | pours into captains' wounds? TIM 3.05.110
CAPTAINS 14 FR 0.0015 REL FR 12 V 2 P
and captains were of my mind, they would 2H4 2.04.141 P
therefore captains had need look to't. 2.04.150 P
along | i met and overtook a dozen captains, 2.04.358
a dozen captains stay at door for you. 2.04.372
away, captains, let's get us from the walls, 1H6 3.02. 71
english john talbot, captains, /calls you forth, 4.02. 3
then call our captains and our colors forth, 5.03.128
so many captains, gentlemen, and soldiers, 5.04.104
dismay'd not this | our captains, macbeth and MAC 1.02. 34
let four captains | bear hamlet, like a soldier, HAM 5.02.395
i meet the captains at the citadel. OTH 3.03. 59
call to me | all my sad captains, fill our bowls ANT 3.13.183
call all his noble captains to my lord. 3.13.188
bid the captains look to't. CYM 4.02.344
CAPTAINSHIP 2 FR 0.0002 REL FR 2 V 0 P
to take | the captainship, thou shalt be met TIM 5.01.161
should not then | have nick'd his captainship, ANT 3.13. 8
CAPTENS 1 FR 0.0001 REL FR 0 V 1 P
gud feith, gud captens bath, and i sall quit you H5 3.02.102 P
CAPTIOUS 1 FR 0.0001 REL FR 1 V 0 P
yet in this captious and intenible sieve | i AWW 1.03.202
CAPTIVATE 3 FR 0.0003 REL FR 3 V 0 P
and sent our sons and husbands captivate. 1H6 2.03. 42
tush, women have been captivate ere now. 5.03.107
and this i do to captivate the eye | of the fair VEN 281
CAPTIVATED 1 FR 0.0001 REL FR 0 V 1 P
wert immured, restrained, captivated, bound. LLL 3.01.125 P
CAPTIVATES 1 FR 0.0001 REL FR 1 V 0 P
trull | upon their woes whom fortune captivates! 3H6 1.04.115
CAPTIV'D 1 FR 0.0001 REL FR 1 V 0 P
and all our princes captiv'd by the hand | of H5 2.04. 55
CAPTIVE 18 FR 0.0020 REL FR 17 V 1 P
the captive is enrich'd; LLL 4.01. 75 P
richest eyes, whose words all ears took captive, AWW 5.03. 17
never did captive with a freer heart | cast off R2 1.03. 88
and in a captive chariot into roan | bring him H5 3.05. 54
seat, | and turn'd my captive state to liberty, 3H6 4.06. 3
for god's sake, take away this captive scold. 5.05. 29
heart | grossly grew captive to his honey words, R3 4.01. 79
for an old aunt whom the greeks held captive, TRO 2.02. 77
when many times the captive grecian falls, 5.03. 40
return | captive to thee and to thy roman yoke; TIT 1.01.111
to grace in captive bonds his chariot–wheels? JC 1.01. 34
or friends with caesar, or not captive to him, ANT 2.05. 44
and when came you to serve our roman captive? CYM 5.05.385
wast near to make the male | to thy sex captive, TNK 1.01. 81
yet hath he been my captive, and my slave, | and VEN 101
the coward captive vanquished doth yield | to LUC 75
a captive victor that hath lost in gain, 730
and captive good attending captain ill: SON 66.12
CAPTIVES 8 FR 0.0009 REL FR 8 V 0 P
beware of being captives | before you serve. AWW 2.01. 21
like captives bound to a triumphant car. 1H6 1.01. 22
who thunders to his captives blood and death, 3H6 2.01.127
you as most | abated captives to some nation COR 3.03.132
so, | captives, to be advanced to this height? TIT 4.02. 34
he hath brought many captives home to rome, JC 3.02. 88
you have the captives | who were the opposites LR 5.03. 41
appeas'd with slaughter | of you their captives, CYM 5.05. 73
CAPTIVITY 8 FR 0.0009 REL FR 7 V 1 P
triumphant death, smear'd with captivity, 1H6 4.07. 3
king, | who kept him in captivity till he died. 2H6 2.02. 42
and men | to set him free from his captivity. 3H6 4.05. 13
hand bears | the power to cancel his captivity. JC 1.03.102
and hardy soldier fought | 'gainst my captivity. MAC 1.02. 5
given to captivity me and my utmost hopes, | i OTH 4.02. 51
more sense of their captivity than i of ruling TNK 2.01. 38 P
arcite) almost wanton | with my captivity. 2.02. 97
CAPTUM 1 FR 0.0001 REL FR 1 V 0 P
but so, | "redime te captum quam queas minimo." SHR 1.01.162
CAPUCHIUS 1 FR 0.0001 REL FR 1 V 0 P
my royal nephew, and your name capuchius. H8 4.02.110
CAPULET 13 FR 0.0014 REL FR 11 V 2 P
thou villain capulet! — hold me not, let me go. ROM 1.01. 79
by thee, old capulet, and montague, | have 1.01. 90
you, capulet, shall go along with me, | and, 1.01. 99
mine uncle capulet, his wife, and daughters; 1.02. 68 P
my master is the great rich capulet, and if you 1.02. 79 P
nay, sit, nay, sit, good cousin capulet, | for 1.05. 30
is she a capulet? 1.05.117
my love, | and i'll no longer be a capulet. 2.02. 36
is set | on the fair daughter of rich capulet. 2.03. 58
tybalt, the kinsman to old capulet, | hath sent 2.04. 6
and so, good capulet — which name i tender | as 3.01. 71
my father capulet will have it so, | and i am 4.01. 2
capulet! 5.03.291
CAPULET'S *(also capel's, etc.)*
CAPULET'S 1 FR 0.0001 REL FR 1 V 0 P
at this same ancient feast of capulet's | sups ROM 1.02. 82
CAPULETS 4 FR 0.0004 REL FR 3 V 1 P
down with the capulets! ROM 1.01. 74
by my head, here comes the capulets. 3.01. 35 P
where all the kindred of the capulets lie. 4.01.112
go tell the prince, run to the capulets, | raise 5.03.177
CAR* 15 FR 0.0017 REL FR 14 V 1 P
wilt thou aspire to guide the heavenly car, TGV 3.01.154
and phibbus' car | shall shine from far, | and MND 1.02. 35
car ce soldat ici est dispose tout /a /cette H5 4.04. 35 P
like captives bound to a triumphant car. 1H6 1.01. 22
now phaeton hath tumbled from his car, | and 3H6 1.04. 33
thy burning car never had scorch'd the earth. 2.06. 13
and when the morning sun shall raise his car 4.07. 80
and by the bright tract of his fiery car | gives R3 5.03. 20
of the duke's confessor, john de la car, | one H8 1.01.218
to me, wishing me to permit | john de la car, my 1.02.162
sir gilbert /perk his chancellor, and john car, 2.01. 20
and when thy car is loaden with their heads, | i TIT 5.02. 53
it, were it carbuncled | like holy phoebus' car. ANT 4.08. 29
safely, had it | been all the worth of 's car. CYM 5.05.191
but when from highmost pitch, with weary car, SON 7. 9
CARACTS 1 FR 0.0001 REL FR 1 V 0 P
in all his dressings, caracts, titles, forms, MM 5.01. 56
CARAT *(also charect)*
CARAT 1 FR 0.0001 REL FR 1 V 0 P
other, less fine in carat, /is more precious, 2H4 4.05.161
CARAWAYS 1 FR 0.0001 REL FR 0 V 1 P
of mine own graffing, with a dish of caraways, 2H4 5.03. 3 P
CARBINADO 1 FR 0.0001 REL FR 0 V 1 P
scotch'd him and notch'd him like a carbinado. COR 4.05.187 P
CARBINADO'D 1 FR 0.0001 REL FR 0 V 1 P
but it is your carbinado'd face. AWW 4.05.101 P
CARBONADO 2 FR 0.0002 REL FR 0 V 2 P
his willingly, let him make a carbonado of me. 1H4 5.03. 58 P
you rogue, or i'll so carbonado your shanks! LR 2.02. 38 P
CARBONADO'D 1 FR 0.0001 REL FR 0 V 1 P
to eat adders' heads, and toads carbonado'd. WT 4.04.265 P
CARBUNCLE 3 FR 0.0003 REL FR 3 V 0 P
a carbuncle entire, as big as thou art, | were COR 1.04. 55
a bile, | a plague–sore, or embossed carbuncle, LR 2.04.224
so, had it been a carbuncle | of phoebus' wheel; CYM 5.05.189
CARBUNCLED 1 FR 0.0001 REL FR 1 V 0 P
it, were it carbuncled | like holy phoebus' car. ANT 4.08. 28
CARBUNCLES 2 FR 0.0002 REL FR 1 V 1 P
all o'er embellish'd with rubies, carbuncles, ERR 3.02.135 P
with eyes like carbuncles, the hellish pyrrhus HAM 2.02.463
CARCANET 2 FR 0.0002 REL FR 2 V 0 P
your shop | to see the making of her carcanet, ERR 3.01. 4
placed are, | or captain jewels in the carcanet. SON 52. 8
CARCASS 6 FR 0.0006 REL FR 5 V 1 P
they prepared | a rotten carcass of a butt, not TMP 1.02.146
i had rather give his carcass to my hounds. MND 3.02. 64
that shakes the rotten carcass of old death JN 2.01.456
gods, | not hew him as a carcass fit for hounds; JC 2.01.174
his body's a passable carcass, if he be not hurt CYM 1.02. 9 P
it saw | the carcass of a beauty spent and done. LC 11
CARCASSES 3 FR 0.0003 REL FR 2 V 1 P
where the carcasses of many a tall ship lie MV 3.01. 5 P
i prize | as the dead carcasses of unburied men COR 3.03.122
their honors | to have sav'd their carcasses! CYM 5.03. 67
CAR'D 4 FR 0.0004 REL FR 1 V 3 P
and margery, | but none of us car'd for kate; TMP 2.02. 49
which she wept heartily and said she car'd not. ADO 5.01.175 P
himself, and he said he car'd not who knew it. H5 3.07.108 P
they ne'er car'd for us yet. COR 1.01. 80 P
CARD 6 FR 0.0006 REL FR 4 V 2 P
yet i have fac'd it with a card of ten. SHR 2.01.405
there all is marr'd; there lies a cooling card. 1H6 5.03. 84
mother, | as sure a card as ever won the set; TIT 5.01.100
quarters that they know | i' th' shipman's card. MAC 1.03. 17
we must speak by the card, or equivocation will HAM 5.01.138 P
of him, he is the card or calendar of gentry; 5.02.109 P
CARDECUE 2 FR 0.0002 REL FR 0 V 2 P
for a cardecue he will sell the fee–simple of AWW 4.03.278 P
there's a cardecue for you. 5.02. 33 P
CARDED 1 FR 0.0001 REL FR 1 V 0 P
soon kindled and soon burnt, carded his state, 1H4 3.02. 62
CARDERS 1 FR 0.0001 REL FR 1 V 0 P
have put off | the spinsters, carders, fullers, H8 1.02. 33
CARDINAL 75 FR 0.0084 REL FR 75 V 0 P
i pandulph, of fair milan cardinal, | and from JN 3.01.138
thou canst not, cardinal, devise a name | so 3.01.149
good father cardinal, cry thou amen | to my keen 3.01.181
king philip, listen to the cardinal. 3.01.198
philip, what say'st thou to the cardinal? 3.01.202
what should he say, but as the cardinal? 3.01.203
me mad, | and thou shalt be canoniz'd, cardinal; 3.04. 52
and, father cardinal, i have heard you say 3.04. 76
who brought that letter from the cardinal? 4.03. 14
perchance the cardinal cannot make your peace; 5.01. 74
the cardinal pandulph is within at rest, | who 5.07. 82
and quarrel | to the disposing of the cardinal, 5.07. 92
not open, | the cardinal of winchester forbids. 1H6 1.03. 19
cardinal, i'll be no breaker of the law; 1.03. 80
"if once he come to be a cardinal, | he'll make 5.01. 32
to us, | yet let us watch the haughty cardinal; 2H6 1.01.174
despite duke humphrey or the cardinal. 1.01.179
oft have i seen the haughty cardinal, | more 1.01.185
the pride of suffolk and the cardinal, | with 1.01.201
but, as i think, it was by th' cardinal), | and 1.02. 27
i dare not say from the rich cardinal | and from 1.02. 94
although we fancy not the cardinal, | yet must 1.03. 94
lord cardinal, i will follow eleanor, | and 1.03.148
ay, my lord cardinal, how think you by that? 2.01. 16
what, cardinal? 2.01. 23
cardinal, i am with you. 2.01. 48
and here commit you to my lord cardinal | to 3.01.137
lord cardinal, he is your prisoner. 3.01.187
but, my lord cardinal, and you, my lord of 3.01.246
by suffolk and the cardinal beauford's means. 3.02.124
that cardinal beauford is at point of death; 3.02.369
lord cardinal, will your grace | persuade the R3 3.01. 32
of the right reverend cardinal of york. H8 1.01. 51
this business | our reverend cardinal carried. 1.01.100
difference | betwixt you and the cardinal. 1.01.102
this cunning cardinal | the articles o' th' 1.01.168
him — privily | deals with our cardinal, and, 1.01.184
that thus the cardinal | does buy and sell his 1.01.191
the o'er–great cardinal | hath show'd him gold; 1.01.222
my good lord cardinal, they vent reproaches 1.02. 23
my lord cardinal, | you that are blam'd for it 1.02. 38
by oath he menac'd | revenge upon the cardinal. 1.02.138
my learn'd lord cardinal, | deliver all with 1.02.142
had the cardinal | but half my lay–thoughts in 1.04. 10
ye have found him, cardinal. 1.04. 86

are a churchman, or, i'll tell you, cardinal, 1.04. 88
let's be merry, | good my lord cardinal: 1.04.105
certainly | the cardinal is the end of this. 2.01. 40
either the cardinal, | or some about him near, 2.01.156
cardinal campeius is arriv'd, and lately, | as 2.01.160
'tis the cardinal; 2.01.161
the cardinal | will have his will, and she must 2.01.166
my good lord cardinal? 2.02. 73
my lord | cardinal of york, are join'd with me 2.02.105
cardinal, | prithee call gardiner to me, my new 2.02.114
spread then, | even of yourself, lord cardinal. 2.02.125
lord cardinal, | to you i speak. 2.04. 68
my lord cardinal, | i do excuse you; 2.04.156
lord cardinal, | the willing'st sin i ever yet 3.01. 48
upon my soul, two reverend cardinal virtues; 3.01.103
but cardinal sins and hollow hearts i fear ye. 3.01.104
the cardinal | cannot stand under them. 3.02. 2
how that the cardinal did entreat his holiness 3.02. 32
cardinal campeius | is stol'n away to rome, hath 3.02. 56
and | is posted, as the agent of our cardinal, 3.02. 59
'tis so. | the cardinal! 3.02. 75
now, my lords, | saw you the cardinal? 3.02.111
hear the king's pleasure, cardinal! 3.02.228
wench | lay kissing in your arms, lord cardinal. 3.02.296
if you can blush, and cry "guilty," cardinal, 3.02.305
lord cardinal, the king's further pleasure is — 3.02.337
so fare you well, my little good lord cardinal. 3.02.349
for since the cardinal fell that title's lost. 4.01. 96
that the great child of honor, cardinal wolsey, 4.02. 6
this cardinal, | though from an humble stock, 4.02. 48

CARDINALLY 1 FR 0.0001 REL FR 0 V 1 P
if she had been a woman cardinally given, might MM 2.01. 80 P

CARDINAL'S 14 FR 0.0015 REL FR 12 V 2 P
i'll canvass thee in thy broad cardinal's hat, 1H6 1.03. 36
under my feet i stamp thy cardinal's hat; 1.03. 49
this cardinal's more haughty than the devil. 1.03. 85
and call'd unto a cardinal's degree? 5.01. 29
yet am i suffolk and the cardinal's broker. 2H6 1.02.101
against john goodman, my lord cardinal's man, 1.03. 17 P
the cardinal's not my better in the field. 1.03.110
you read | the cardinal's malice and his potency H8 1.01.105
the cardinal's and sir thomas lovell's heads 1.02.185
to the cardinal's. 1.03. 50
set out for london, a man of my lord cardinal's, 2.02. 5 P
this is the cardinal's doing. 2.02. 19
the cardinal's letters to the pope miscarried, 3.02. 30
the king | digest this letter of the cardinal's? 3.02. 53

CARDINALS 4 FR 0.0004 REL FR 4 V 0 P
i would the college of the cardinals | would 2H6 1.03. 61
i may perceive | these cardinals trifle with me; H8 2.04.237
the two great cardinals | wait in the presence. 3.01. 16
the heads of all thy brother cardinals | (with 3.02.257

CARD-MAKER 1 FR 0.0001 REL FR 0 V 1 P
by birth a pedlar, by education a card-maker, by SHR in.2. 19 P

CARD'NAL 5 FR 0.0005 REL FR 5 V 0 P
lord card'nal, if thou think'st on heaven's 2H6 3.03. 27
the card'nal instantly will find employment, H8 2.01. 48
this just and learned priest, card'nal campeius, 2.02. 96
i speak my good lord card'nal to this point, 2.04.167
into your own hands, card'nal, by extortion; 3.02.285

CARDS 3 FR 0.0003 REL FR 3 V 0 P
have i not here the best cards for the game, JN 5.02.105
she, eros, has | pack'd cards with caesar's, and ANT 4.14. 19
go to dinner, | and then we'll play at cards. TNK 5.02.108

CARDUUS 1 FR 0.0001 REL FR 0 V 1 P
you some of this distill'd carduus benedictus, ADO 3.04. 73 P

/CARE 8 FR 0.0009 REL FR 7 V 1 P
/my /care /is /loss /of /care, /by /old /care R2 4.01.196
/my /care /is /loss /of /care, /by /old /care 4.01.196
/care /is /loss /of /care, /by /old /care /done, 4.01.196
/your /care /is /gain /of /care, /by /new /care 4.01.197
/your /care /is /gain /of /care, /by /new /care 4.01.197
/care /is /gain /of /care, /by /new /care /won; 4.01.197
but what /care i? TRO 1.01. 77 P
/i'll /never /care /what /wickedness /i /do, LR 3.07. 99

CARE 227 FR 0.0256 REL FR 169 V 58 P
good boatswain, have care. TMP 1.01. 9 P
i have done nothing, but in care of thee | (of 1.02. 16
(filth as thou art) with human care, and lodg'd 1.02.346
if of life you keep a care, | shake off slumber, 2.01.303
the rest, and let no man take care for himself; 5.01.257 P
yet i will not name it — and yet i care not — TGV 2.01.117
i tell thee, i care not, though he burn himself 2.05. 52 P
proteus, i thank thee for thine honest care, 3.01. 22
what need a man care for a stock with a wench, 3.01.309 P
i care not for that neither, because i love 3.01.341 P
sir valentine, i care not for her, i; 5.04.132
i care not for that, but that i am afeard. WIV 3.04. 27 P
have a care of your entertainments. 4.05. 75 P
thanks, provost, for thy care and secrecy, | we MM 5.01.530
and /the great care of goods at randon left, ERR 1.01. 42
i, | fixing our eyes on whom our care was fix'd, 1.01. 84
my youngest boy, and yet my eldest care, | at 1.01.124
oft, | when i am dull with care and melancholy, 1.02. 20
it seems he hath great care to please his wife. 2.01. 56
is wand'red forth, in care to seek me out. 2.02. 3
good cousin, have a care this busy time. ADO 1.02. 27 P
poor fool, it keeps on the windy side of care. 2.01.315 P
only, have a care that your bills be not stol'n. 3.03. 41 P
what though care kill'd a cat, thou hast mettle 5.01.132 P
thou hast mettle enough in thee to kill care. 5.01.134 P
i thank thee for thy care and honest pains. 5.01.314
dost thou think i care for a satire or an 5.04.102 P
by the world, i would not care a pin, if the LLL 4.03. 18 P
you weigh me not? o, that's you care not for me. 5.02. 27
great reason: for past care is still past cure. 5.02. 28
we will take some care. 5.02.510
effect it with some care, that he may prove MND 2.01.265
mounsieur, have a care the honey-bag break not, 4.01. 15 P
they lose it that do buy it with much care. MV 1.01. 75
but my chief care | is to come fairly off from 1.01.127
to see me pay his debt, and then i care not! 3.03. 36
i care not for my spirits, if my legs were not AYL 2.04. 2 P
nay, i care not for their names, they owe me 2.05. 21 P
he talks well — | but what care i for words? 3.05.111
i care not if i have. 5.02. 79
doubt not her care should be | to comb your SHR 1.01. 63
advis'd, he took some care | to get her cunning 1.01.186
i care not. 2.01.239
that all is done in reverend care of her, | and, 4.01.204
i care not what, so it be wholesome food. 4.03. 16
long, | i am content, in a good father's care, 4.04. 31
madam, the care i have had to even your content, AWW 1.03. 3 P
bosom, and i thank you for your honest care. 1.03.127 P
groan, | yet i express to you a mother's care. 1.03.148
i care no more for than i do for heaven, | so i 1.03.164
or i will throw thee from my care for ever 2.03.162
when i lose thee again, i care not; 2.03.206 P
let him be the devil, and he will, i care not; TN 1.05.128 P
ay, ay. i care not for good life. 2.03. 38 P
not so, sir, i do care for something; 3.01. 28 P
in my conscience, sir, i do not care for you. 3.01. 29 P
if that be to care for nothing, sir, i would it 3.01. 29 P
some of my people have a special care of him. 3.04. 62 P
toby, my lady prays you to have a care of him. 3.04. 93 P
i care not who knows so much of my mettle. 3.04.272 P
i care not: WT 2.03.114
camillo, and with some care, so far that i have 4.02. 35 P
barren, and i care not | to get slips of them. 4.04. 84
at least if you make a care | of happy holding 4.04.355
beseech you | of your own state take care. 4.04.448
not little of his care | to have them 4.04.519
it shall be so my care | to have you royally 4.04.591
care not for issue, | the crown will find an 5.01. 46
i would not care, i then would be content, | for JN 3.01. 48
where is my mother's care, | that such an army 4.02.117
keep good quarter and good care to-night; 5.05. 20
things past redress are now with me past care. R2 2.03.171
take special care my greetings be delivered. 3.01. 39
why, 'twas my care, | and what loss is it to be 3.02. 95
care, | and what loss is it to be rid of care? 3.02. 96
to drive away the heavy thought of care? 3.04. 2
madam, i know not, nor i greatly care not, | god 5.02. 48
so shaken as we are, so wan with care, | find we 1H4 1.01. 1
i care not. 1.02.148 P
i love thee not, | i care not for thee, kate. 2.03. 91
the shoulders, you care not who sees your back. 2.04.149 P
i do not care. 3.01.135
lordship to have a reverend care of your health. 2H4 1.02.100 P
and i care not if i do become your physician. 1.02.124 P
i can close with him, i care not for his thrust. 2.01. 18 P
well, sweet jack, have a care of thyself. 2.04.380 P
mine own part, sir, i do not care, but rather, 3.02.224 P
else, sir, i did not care, for mine own part, so 3.02.226 P
by my troth, i care not; 3.02.234 P
care i for the limb, the thews, the stature, 3.02.258 P
i will perform with a most christian care. 4.02.115
i shall observe him with all care and love. 4.04. 49
th' incessant care and labor of his mind | hath 4.04.118
golden care! 4.05. 23
sleep with thoughts, their brains with care, 4.05. 68
when that my care could not withhold thy riots, 4.05.134
what wilt thou do when riot is thy care? 4.05.135
"the care on thee depending | hath fed upon the 4.05.158
for my part, i care not; H5 2.01. 5 P
your too much love and care of me | are heavy 2.02. 52
in their dear care | and tender preservation of 2.02. 58
there is much care and valor in this welshman. 4.01. 84
gold, | nor care i who doth feed upon my cost; 4.03. 25
majesty's countryman, i care not who know it. 4.07.112 P
father, i warrant you, take you no care, | i'll 1H6 1.04. 21
of death, | nestor-like aged, in an age of care, 2.05. 6
but yet be wary in thy studious care. 2.05. 97
care is no cure, but rather corrosive, | for 3.03. 3
speak, thy father's care: 4.06. 26
for my part, noble lords, i care not which, | or 2H6 1.03.101
hence, | i care not whither, for i beg no favor; 2.04. 92
the reverent care i bear unto my lord | made me 3.01. 34
the care you have of us | to mow down thorns 3.01. 66
if those that care to keep your royal person 3.01.173
and care not who they sting in his revenge. 3.02.127
they say, in care of your most royal person, 3.02.254
me, | i thank them for their tender loving care; 3.02.280
'tis not the land i care for, wert thou thence; 3.02.359
gualtier or walter, which it is, i care not. 4.01. 38
or gather wealth, i care not with what envy. 4.10. 21
as brings a thousandfold more care to keep 3H6 2.02. 52
when care, mistrust, and treason waits on him. 2.05. 54
sad-hearted men, much overgone with care, | here 2.05.123
that | of whom you seem to have so tender care? 4.06. 66
alas, why would you heap this care on me? R3 3.07.204
full of wise care is this your counsel, madam; 4.01. 47
for queen, a very caitiff crown'd with care; 4.04.101
heart of it, | thanks you for this great care. H8 1.02. 2
and with a care exempt themselves from fear; 1.02. 89
i put it to your care. 1.02.102
bevy, has brought with her | one care abroad. 1.04. 5
your lordship sent for, with all the care i had, 2.02. 2 P
lord, have great care | i be not found a talker. 2.02. 77
that's christian care enough. 2.02.130
killing care and grief of heart | fall asleep, 3.01. 13
my lords, i care not (so much i am happy | above 3.01. 33
grace | and princely care foreseeing those fell 5.01. 49
i care not and she were a blackamoor, 'tis all TRO 1.01. 77 P
i do not care whether you do or no. 1.01. 80 P
nay, i care not for such words, no, no. 3.01. 75 P
or a herring without a roe, i would not care; 5.01. 63 P
for i care not to be the louse of a lazar, so i 5.01. 65 P
but advantageous care | withdrew me from the 5.04. 21
with such a careless force and forceless care 5.05. 40
most charitable care | have the patricians of COR 1.01. 65
o' th' state, who care for you like fathers, 1.01. 77
care for us? 1.01. 79 P
fear not our care, sir. 1.07. 5
coriolanus neither to care whether they love or 2.02. 12 P
if he did not care whether he had their love or 2.02. 16 P
i neither care for th' world nor your general; 5.02.102 P
i care not, i, knew she and all the world, | i TIT 2.01. 71
and for our father's sake, and mother's care, 3.01.181
cornelia never with more care | read to her sons 4.01. 12
for this care of tamora, | herself and hers are 4.02.170
witness these trenches made by grief and care, 5.02. 23
what care i | what curious eye doth cote ROM 1.04. 30
care keeps his watch in every old man's eye, 2.03. 35
and where care lodges, sleep will never lie; 2.03. 36
by my heel, i care not. 3.01. 36 P
i have more care to stay than will to go. 3.05. 23
still my care hath been | to have her match'd; 3.05.177
no care, no stop, so senseless of expense, TIM 2.02. 1
nor /resumes no care | of what is to continue. 2.02. 4
be it not in thy care; 3.04.115
and these looks of care? 4.03.205
if he care not for't, he will supply us easily; 4.03.403 P
unmatched mind, | care of your food and living; 4.03.517
i cannot choose but tell him that i care not, 5.01.177
take't at worst — for their knives care not, 5.01.178
which busy care draws in the brains of men; JC 2.01.232
if you did, i care not. 4.03. 57
whose care is gone before to bid us welcome: MAC 1.04. 57
sleep that knits up the ravell'd sleave of care, 2.02. 34
why, what care i? 3.04. 69
proud, and take no care | who chafes, who frets, 4.01. 90
sooth, | i care not if thou dost for me as much. 5.05. 40
half my love with him, half my care and duty. LR 1.01.102
here i disclaim all my paternal care, 1.01.113
thou hadst no need to care for her frowning, now 1.04.192 P
why then i care not for thee. 2.02. 8 P
lipsbury pinfold, i would make thee care for me. 2.02. 10 P
o, i have ta'en | too little care of this! 3.04. 33
nor doth the general care | take hold on me; OTH 1.03. 54
iago, look with care about the town, | and 2.03.255
to hear music the general does not greatly care. 3.01. 17 P
i care not for thy sword, i'll make thee known, 5.02.165
hast thou no care of me? ANT 4.15. 60
you, but | i do not greatly care to be deceiv'd, 5.02. 14
our care and pity is so much upon you, | that we 5.02.188
take thou no care, it shall be heeded. 5.02.268
by th' very truth of it, i care not for you, CYM 2.03.108
care no more to clothe and eat, | to thee the 4.02.266
this bloody man, the care on't. 4.02.297
and give me leave, | i'll take the better care; 4.04. 45
should reserve | my crack'd one to more care. 4.04. 50
no care of yours it is, you know 'tis ours. 5.04.100
let us with care perform his great behest. 5.04.122
and so much | for my peculiar care. 5.05. 83
good sooth, i care not for you. PER 1.01. 86
have after-nourishment and life by care; 1.02. 13
which care of them, not pity of myself — | who 1.02. 29
the care i had and have of subjects' good | on 1.02.118
and cloudy billow kiss the moon, i care not. 3.01. 46 P
leaving her | the infant of your care, 3.03. 15
make me blessed in your care | in bringing up my 3.03. 31
we have taken | no care to your best courses. 4.01. 38
care not for me, | i can go home alone. 4.01. 41
what, i must have care of you. 4.01. 49
and care in us | at whose expense 'tis done. 4.03. 45
what care | for what thou feel'st not? TNK 1.01.180
i care not, i am desperate. 2.06. 13
thing, | i care for nothing, and that's palamon. 3.02. 6
you care not for a grand-guard? 3.06. 58
yes, but you care not for me. 5.02. 83
for all my mind, my thought, my busy care, | is VEN 383
and with what care | he cranks and crosses with 681
swift subtle post, carrier of grisly care, LUC 926
so she, deep drenched in a sea of care, | holds 1100
youth is full of pleasance, age is full of care, PP 12. 2
and daff'd me to a cabin hang'd with care, | to 14. 3
thou, best of dearest and mine only care, | art SON 48. 7
as call it winter, which, being full of care, 56.13
for what care i who calls me well or ill, | so 112. 3
in so profound abysm i throw all care | of 112. 9
cries to catch her whose busy care is bent | to 143. 6
past cure i am, now reason is past care, | and 147. 9

CARE-CRAZ'D 1 FR 0.0001 REL FR 1 V 0 P
a care-craz'd mother to a many sons, | a R3 3.07.184

CAREER 6 FR 0.0006 REL FR 4 V 2 P
brain awe a man from the career of his humor? ADO 2.03.241 P
i shall meet your wit in the career, and you 5.01.135 P
merrily | hath this brave /manage, this career, LLL 5.02.482
stopping the career | of laughter with a sigh (a WT 1.02.286
or, if misfortune miss the first career, | be R2 1.02. 49
when down the hill he holds his fierce career? H5 3.03. 23

CAREERS 2 FR 0.0002 REL FR 0 V 2 P
and so conclusions pass'd the careers. WIV 1.01.179 P
he passes some humors and careers. H5 2.01.126 P

CAREFUL 25 FR 0.0028 REL FR 21 V 4 P
for vainer hours, and tutors not so careful. TMP 1.02.174
my wife, more careful for the latter-born, | had ERR 1.01. 78
and careful hours with time's deformed hand 5.01.299
as fairly as to say a careful man and a great TN 4.02. 9 P
session, hanging, yields a careful man work. WT 4.04.686 P
o, full of careful business are his looks! R2 2.02. 75
done the part of a careful friend and a true 2H4 2.04.322 P
our souls, | our debts, our careful wives, | our H5 4.01.231
by him that rais'd me to this careful height R3 1.03. 82
bethink you like a careful mother | of the young 2.02. 96
use careful watch, choose trusty /sentinels. 5.03. 54
most like a careful subject, have collected H8 1.02.130
go get you gone, and pray be careful all, | and TIT 4.03. 21
we may, | till time beget some careful remedy. 4.03. 30
and is not careful what they mean thereby, 4.04. 84
which i have seen thee careful to observe, 5.01. 77
the feast is ready which the careful titus 5.03. 21
well, well, thou hast a careful father, child, ROM 3.05.107
things toward, edmund, pray you be careful. LR 3.03. 20 P
soldiers, have careful watch. ANT 4.03. 7
fled, | under the covering of a careful night, PER 1.02. 81
painful perch, | of pericles the careful search, 3.ch. 16
there i'll leave it | at careful nursing. 3.01. 80
how careful was i, when i took my way, | each SON 48. 1
lo as a careful huswife runs to catch | one of 143. 1

CAREFULLY 8 FR 0.0009 REL FR 7 V 1 P
i promis'd to inquire carefully | about a SHR 1.02.165
that horse that i so carefully have dress'd! R2 5.05. 80
and more than carefully it us concerns | to H5 2.04. 2
to attend the emperor's person carefully. TIT 2.02. 8
by day and night t' attend him carefully, | and 4.03. 28
you come most carefully upon your hour. HAM 1.01. 6
it shall lose thee nothing, do it carefully. LR 1.02.115 P
some good man bear him carefully from hence, OTH 5.01. 99

CARELESS 21 FR 0.0023 REL FR 19 V 2 P
sleep she as sound as careless infancy; WIV 5.05. 52
dreadfully but as a drunken sleep, careless, MM 4.02.143 P
anon a careless herd, | full of the pasture, AYL 2.01. 52

about you demonstrating a careless desolation. 3.02.381 P
and come to padua, careless of your life? SHR 4.02. 79
into the staggers and the careless lapse | of AWW 2.03.163
and thou, too careless patient as thou art, R2 2.01. 97
grace | by seeming cold or careless of his will, 2H4 4.04. 29
got, | my careless father fondly gave away"? 3H6 2.02. 38
my brother was too careless of his charge. 4.06. 86
with such a careless force and forceless care TRO 5.05. 40
titus, unkind and careless of thine own, | why TIT 1.01. 86
thing he ow'd, | as 'twere a careless trifle. MAC 1.04. 11
the light and careless livery that it wears HAM 4.07. 79
careless heirs | may the two latter darken and PER 3.02. 28
pass'd slightly | his careless execution, where TNK 1.03. 29
though happily her careless /wear) i followed 1.03. 73
her careless tresses | a /wreath of bulrush 4.01. 83
and careless lust stirs up a desperate courage, VEN 556
birds do sing, | careless of thy sorrowing. PP 20.26
proclaim'd in her a careless hand of pride; LC 30

CARELESSLY 5 FR 0.0005 REL FR 4 V 1 P
and fleet the time carelessly, as they did in AYL 1.01.118 P
thy brother being carelessly encamp'd, | his 3H6 4.02. 14
it may be thought we held him carelessly, ROM 3.04. 25
to wear them like his raiment, carelessly, | and TIM 3.05. 33
his body | if caesar carelessly but nod on him. JC 1.02.118

CARELESSNESS 1 FR 0.0001 REL FR 0 V 1 P
out of his noble carelessness lets them plainly COR 2.02. 14 P

CARE'S 2 FR 0.0002 REL FR 1 V 1 P
i am sure care's an enemy to life. TN 1.03. 2 P
ruin, beauty's wrack, and grim care's reign; LUC 1451

/CARES 4 FR 0.0004 REL FR 4 V 0 P
/part /of /your /cares /you /give /me /with R2 4.01.194
/your /cares /set /up /do /not /pluck /my /cares 4.01.195
/set /up /do /not /pluck /my /cares /down: 4.01.195
/the /cares /i /give /i /have, /though /given 4.01.198

CARES 41 FR 0.0046 REL FR 34 V 7 P
what cares these roarers for the name of king? TMP 1.01. 16 P
you dote on her that cares not for your love. TGV 4.04. 82
for he cares not what he puts into the press, WIV 2.01. 78 P
son | knows not my feeble key of untun'd cares? ERR 5.01.311
that little cares for buying any thing. AYL 2.04. 90
'tis with cares. SHR 2.01.238
one that cares for thee, | and for thy 5.02.147
undone, and forfeited to cares for ever! AWW 2.03.267
where nothing lives but crosses, cares, and R2 2.02. 79
'a cares not what mischief he does, if his 2H4 2.01. 15 P
see thee again or no, there is nobody cares. 2.04. 68 P
exceeding well, his cares are now all ended. 5.02. 3
let me but bear your love, i'll bear your cares. 5.02. 58
the ceremonies of the wars, and the cares of it, H5 4.01. 72 P
i rest perplexed with a thousand cares. 1H6 5.05. 95
so cares and joys abound, as seasons fleet. 2H6 2.04. 4
my tongue, while heart is drown'd in cares. 3H6 3.03. 14
they often feel a world of restless cares; R3 1.04. 81
will you enforce me to a world of cares? 3.07.223
any thing, he cares not; TRO 1.02.210 P
he cares not, he'll obey conditions. 4.05. 72
for examine | their counsels and their cares; COR 1.01.150
and make the rabble | call our cares fears; 3.01.137
my general cares not for you. 5.02. 55 P
he cares not for your weeping. 5.03.156
know this of timon, | that timon cares not. TIM 5.01.171
what watchful cares do interpose themselves JC 2.01. 98
to shake all cares and business from our age, LR 1.01. 39
interest of territory, cares of state), | which 1.01. 50
he neither loves, | nor either cares for him. ANT 2.01. 16
in thy fats our cares be drown'd, | with thy 2.07.115
a court | he little cares for and a daughter who CYM 1.06.154
grows elder now, and cares it be not done. PER 1.02. 15
but let your cares o'erlook | what shipping and 1.02. 48
what cares he now for curb or pricking spur, VEN 285
now nature cares not for thy mortal vigor, 953
save thieves, and cares, and troubled minds that LUC 126
to whose weak ruins muster troops of cares, | to 720
many she sees where cares have carved some, 1445
his face, though full of cares, yet show'd 1503
her lively color kill'd with deadly cares. 1593

CARET 2 FR 0.0002 REL FR 0 V 2 P
remember, william, focative is caret. WIV 4.01. 53 P
facility, and golden cadence of poesy, caret. LLL 4.02.123 P

CARE-TUN'D 1 FR 0.0001 REL FR 1 V 0 P
than can my care-tun'd tongue deliver him! R2 3.02. 92

CARGO 7 FR 0.0008 REL FR 0 V 7 P
throca movousus, cargo, cargo, cargo. AWW 4.01. 65 P
throca movousus, cargo, cargo, cargo. 4.01. 65 P
throca movousus, cargo, cargo, cargo. 4.01. 65 P
cargo, cargo, cargo, villianda par corbo, cargo. 4.01. 66 P
cargo, cargo, cargo, villianda par corbo, cargo. 4.01. 66 P
cargo, cargo, cargo, villianda par corbo, cargo. 4.01. 66 P
cargo, cargo, cargo, villianda par corbo, cargo. 4.01. 66 P

CARL 1 FR 0.0001 REL FR 1 V 0 P
revengingly enfeebles me, or could this carl, CYM 5.02. 4

CARLISLE 3 FR 0.0003 REL FR 3 V 0 P
o, belike it is the bishop of carlisle. R2 3.03. 30
but here is carlisle living, to abide | thy 5.06. 22
carlisle, this is your doom: 5.06. 24

CARLOT 1 FR 0.0001 REL FR 1 V 0 P
bounds | that the old carlot once was master of. AYL 3.05.108

CARMAN 1 FR 0.0001 REL FR 1 V 0 P
no, no, let carman whip his jade, | the valiant MM 2.01.255

CARMEN 1 FR 0.0001 REL FR 0 V 1 P
huswives that he heard the carmen whistle, and 2H4 3.02.317 P

CARNAL 3 FR 0.0003 REL FR 2 V 1 P
how do i thank thee that this carnal cur | preys R3 4.04. 56
so shall you hear | of carnal, bloody, and HAM 5.02.381
to cool our raging motions, our carnal stings, OTH 1.03.330 P

CARNALLY 1 FR 0.0001 REL FR 1 V 0 P
carnally, she says. MM 5.01.214

CARNARVONSHIRE 1 FR 0.0001 REL FR 1 V 0 P
i myself | would for carnarvonshire, although H8 2.03. 48

CARNATION 2 FR 0.0002 REL FR 0 V 2 P
how much carnation ribbon may a man buy for a LLL 3.01.145 P
'a could never abide carnation — 'twas a color H5 2.03. 33 P

CARNATIONS 1 FR 0.0001 REL FR 1 V 0 P
are our carnations and streak'd gillyvors, WT 4.04. 82

CAROL 2 FR 0.0002 REL FR 2 V 0 P
no night is now with hymn or carol blest. MND 2.01.102
this carol they began that hour, | with a hey, AYL 5.03. 26

CAROUS'D 3 FR 0.0003 REL FR 3 V 0 P
hast thou tapp'd out and drunkenly carous'd. R2 2.01.127
secure, | having all day carous'd and banqueted: 1H6 2.01. 12
to desdemona hath to-night carous'd | potations OTH 2.03. 53

CAROUSE 2 FR 0.0002 REL FR 2 V 0 P
carouse full measure to her maidenhead, | be mad SHR 3.02.225
they cast their caps up and carouse together ANT 4.12. 12

CAROUSES *(also rouse*)*

CAROUSES 3 FR 0.0003 REL FR 3 V 0 P
and quaff carouses to our mistress' health, SHR 1.02.275
the queen carouses to thy fortune, hamlet. HAM 5.02.289
and drink carouses to the next day's fate, ANT 4.08. 34

CAROUSING 2 FR 0.0002 REL FR 1 V 1 P
aboard, carousing to his mates | after a storm, SHR 3.02.171
sir, we were carousing till the second cock; MAC 2.03. 24 P

CARP* 3 FR 0.0003 REL FR 2 V 1 P
sir, use the carp as you may, for he looks like AWW 5.02. 22 P
your bait of falsehood take this carp of truth, HAM 2.01. 60
insolent retinue | do hourly carp and quarrel, LR 1.04.203

CARP'D 1 FR 0.0001 REL FR 1 V 0 P
in fear our motion will be mock'd or carp'd at, H8 1.02. 86

CARPENTER 6 FR 0.0006 REL FR 1 V 5 P
a good hare-finder and vulcan a rare carpenter? ADO 1.01.185 P
he talks of wood; it is some carpenter. 1H6 5.03. 90
build there, carpenter, the air is sweet. TRO 3.02. 51 P
why, sir, a carpenter. JC 1.01. 6 P
the mason, the shipwright, or the carpenter? HAM 5.01. 42 P
than a mason, a shipwright, or a carpenter? 5.01. 51 P

CARPER 1 FR 0.0001 REL FR 1 V 0 P
woods | by putting on the cunning of a carper. TIM 4.03.209

CARPET 3 FR 0.0003 REL FR 2 V 1 P
unhatch'd rapier and on carpet consideration, TN 3.04.236 P
we march | upon the grassy carpet of this plain. R2 3.03. 50
shall as a carpet hang upon thy grave | while PER 4.01. 16

CARPET-MONGERS 1 FR 0.0001 REL FR 0 V 1 P
a whole bookful of these quondam carpet-mongers, ADO 5.02. 32 P

CARPETS 1 FR 0.0001 REL FR 0 V 1 P
the gills fair without, the carpets laid, and SHR 4.01. 50 P

CARPING 3 FR 0.0003 REL FR 3 V 0 P
sure, sure, such carping is not commendable. ADO 3.01. 71
this fellow here, with envious carping tongue, 1H6 4.01. 90
t' avoid the censures of the carping world. R3 3.05. 68

CARRACT 1 FR 0.0001 REL FR 1 V 0 P
faith, he to-night hath boarded a land carract. OTH 1.02. 50

CARRECK 1 FR 0.0001 REL FR 1 V 0 P
then would i make | a carreck of a cockleshell, TNK 3.04. 14

CARRECTS 1 FR 0.0001 REL FR 0 V 1 P
whole armadoes of carrects to be ballast at her ERR 3.02.137 P

/CARRIAGE 1 FR 0.0001 REL FR 1 V 0 P
passage and whole /carriage /of /this /action TRO 2.03.131

CARRIAGE 21 FR 0.0023 REL FR 12 V 9 P
and time | goes upright with his carriage. TMP 5.01. 3
all, or half, for easing me of the carriage. WIV 2.02.173 P
teach sin the carriage of a holy saint; ERR 3.02. 14
than to fashion a carriage to rob love from any. ADO 1.03. 29 P
dull, a man of good repute, carriage, bearing, LLL 1.01.268 P
let them be men of good repute and carriage. 1.02. 69 P
he was a man of good carriage, great carriage, 1.02. 71 P
he was a man of good carriage, great carriage, 1.02. 71 P
and their rough carriage so ridiculous, | should 5.02.306
a sad face, a reverend carriage, a slow tongue, TN 3.04. 73 P
the violent carriage of it | will clear or end WT 3.01. 17
a pleasing eye, and a most noble carriage, and, 1H4 2.04.424 P
wise bearing or ignorant carriage is caught, as 2H4 5.01. 76 P
from the king's acquaintance, by this carriage. H8 3.01.161
of the soul, | for honesty and decent carriage, 4.02.145
to bear, | making them women of good carriage. ROM 1.04. 94
illustrious virtue, | and honorable carriage, TIM 3.02. 81
comart | and carriage of the article /design'd, HAM 1.01. 94
roman does become | the carriage of his chafe. ANT 1.03. 85
be suspected of | your carriage from the court. CYM 3.04.187
sometimes her levell'd eyes their carriage ride, LC 22

/CARRIAGES 1 FR 0.0001 REL FR 0 V 1 P
the /carriages, sir, are the hangers. HAM 5.02.157 P

CARRIAGES 6 FR 0.0006 REL FR 2 V 4 P
for many carriages he hath dispatch'd | to the JN 5.07. 90
behold the ordinance on their carriages, | with H5 3.pr. 26
three of the carriages, in faith, are very dear HAM 5.02.151 P
to the hilts, most delicate carriages, and of 5.02.152 P
what call you the carriages? 5.02.154 P
assigns, and three liberal-conceited carriages; 5.02.162 P

/CARRIED 1 FR 0.0001 REL FR 0 V 1 P
/they /carried /me /to /the /tavern /and /made WIV 1.01.125 P

CARRIED 27 FR 0.0030 REL FR 14 V 13 P
i carried mistress silvia the dog you bade me. TGV 4.04. 45 P
have i liv'd to be carried in a basket like a WIV 3.05. 4 P
of none but him, and swears he was carried out, 4.02. 32 P
yonder arrested and carried to prison was worth MM 1.02. 61 P
saw him carried away; 1.02. 68 P
yonder man is carried to prison. 1.02. 86 P
already he hath carried | notice to escalus and 4.03.129
was carried towards corinth, as we thought. ERR 1.01. 87
was carried with more speed before the wind, 1.01.109
this well carried shall on her behalf | change ADO 4.01.210
for he carried the town gates on his back like a LLL 1.02. 71 P
this sport, well carried, shall be chronicled. MND 3.02.240
other but that he is carried into the leaguer of AWW 3.06. 26 P
late, | like a remorseful pardon slowly carried, 5.03. 58
of antigonus, that carried hence the child? WT 5.02. 60 P
falstaff, you carried your guts away as nimbly, 1H4 2.04.258 P
thou art violently carried away from grace, 2.04.446 P
and carried you a forehand shaft a fourteen and 2H4 3.02. 47 P
they have burn'd and carried away all that was H5 4.07. 7 P
this business | our reverend cardinal carried. H8 1.01.100
nobility she has | carried herself towards me. 2.04.144
heaven, that kiss | i carried from thee, dear; COR 5.03. 47
when he had carried rome and that we look'd 5.06. 42
carried to colmekill, | the sacred store-house MAC 2.04. 33
and i have heard, apollodorus carried — ANT 2.06. 68
him) he was carried | from off our coast, twice CYM 3.01. 25
only i carried winged time | post /on the lame PER 4.ch. 47

CARRIER 4 FR 0.0004 REL FR 3 V 1 P
sirrah carrier, what time do you mean to come to 1H4 2.01. 41 P
why, villain, art not thou the carrier? TIT 4.03. 87
were he | a quarter carrier of that honor which TNK 1.02.108
swift subtle post, carrier of grisly care, LUC 926

CARRIERS 2 FR 0.0002 REL FR 1 V 1 P
this punk is one of cupid's carriers. WIV 2.02.135
good morrow, carriers, what's a' clock? 1H4 2.01. 32 P

CARRIES 25 FR 0.0028 REL FR 15 V 10 P
believe me, sir, | it carries a brave form. TMP 1.02.412
before the judgment carries poor souls to hell. ERR 4.02. 40
why, it carries it. LLL 3.01.140 P
his discretion, and the fox carries the goose. MND 5.01.234 P
for the goose carries not the fox. 5.01.236 P
the second, silver, which this promise carries, MV 2.07. 6
comes slowly, he carries his house on his head; AYL 4.01. 55 P
an unclean mind carries virtuous qualities, AWW 1.01. 42 P
carries no favor in't but bertram's. 1.01. 83
be a very plausive invention that carries it. 4.01. 27 P
what is it carries you away? 1H4 2.03. 75
that carries no impression like the dam. 3H6 3.02.162
it, she that carries up the train | is that old H8 4.01. 51
justice and the truth o' th' question carries 5.01.130
man an attaint but he carries some stain of it. TRO 1.02. 25 P
none, | but carries on the stream of his dispose 2.03.164
before him he carries noise, and behind him he COR 2.01.159 P
that's no matter, the greater part carries it, i 2.03. 37 P
alla stoccato carries it away. ROM 3.01. 74
the noblest mind he carries | that ever govern'd TIM 1.01.280
that carries anger as the flint bears fire, JC 4.03.111
which carries them through and through the most HAM 5.02.191 P
this speed of caesar's | carries beyond belief. ANT 3.07. 75
brow, | of what a spacious majesty, he carries, TNK 4.02. 19
he carries thence incaged in his breast. VEN 582

CARRION 13 FR 0.0014 REL FR 10 V 3 P
shall we send that foolish carrion, mistress WIV 3.03.193 P
do as the carrion does, not as the flow'r, MM 2.02.166
a carrion death, within whose empty eye | there MV 2.07. 63
out upon it, old carrion! 3.01. 35 P
have | a weight of carrion flesh than to receive 4.01. 41
dust, | and be a carrion monster like thyself. JN 3.04. 33
bee doth leave her comb | in the dead carrion. 2H4 4.04. 80
and made a prey for carrion kites and crows 2H6 5.02. 11
scruple | of her contaminated carrion weight, TRO 4.01. 72
courtship lives | in carrion flies than romeo; ROM 3.03. 35
out, you green-sickness carrion! 3.05.156
shall smell above the earth | with carrion men, JC 3.01.275
dog, being a good kissing carrion — have you a HAM 2.02.182 P

CARRIONS 2 FR 0.0002 REL FR 2 V 0 P
yond island carrions, desperate of their bones, H5 4.02. 39
old feeble carrions, and such suffering souls JC 2.01.130

/CARRY 1 FR 0.0001 REL FR 0 V 1 P
/do /the /boys /carry /it /away? HAM 2.02.360 P

CARRY 88 FR 0.0099 REL FR 48 V 40 P
i think he will carry this island home in his TMP 2.01. 91 P
pray give me that, | i'll carry it to the pile. 3.01. 25
go to, carry this. 4.01.252 P
whereof, henceforth carry your letters yourself: TGV 1.01.145 P
"inprimis, she can fetch and carry." 3.01.275 P
a horse cannot fetch, but only carry, therefore 3.01.277 P
he must carry for a present to his lady. 4.02. 79 P
to carry that which i would have refus'd, | to 4.04.101
daughter, carry the wine in, we'll drink within. WIV 1.01.188 P
can you carry your good will to the maid? 1.01.231 P
if you can carry her your desires towards her. 1.01.236 P
why, this boy will carry a letter twenty mile, 3.02. 32 P
and carry it among the whitsters in datchet-mead 3.03. 14 P
carry them to the laundress in datchet-mead; 3.03.147 P
i must carry her word quickly. 3.05. 46 P
by their mistress to carry me in the name of 3.05. 99 P
i'll appoint my men to carry the basket again, 4.02. 95 P
repent you, fair one, of the sin you carry? MM 2.03. 19
if you think well to carry this as you may, the 3.01.256 P
oft awak'd him, as if to carry him to execution, 4.02.151 P
here is the head, i'll carry it myself. 4.03.102
must your daughter and her gentlewomen carry. ADO 2.03.215 P
hither the swain, he must carry me a letter. LLL 3.01. 49 P
weep, | no drop but as a coach doth carry thee; 4.03. 33
for his valor cannot carry his discretion, and MND 5.01.233 P
discretion, i am sure, cannot carry his valor; 5.01.235 P
and that no lawful means can carry me | out of MV 4.01. 9
carry him gently to my fairest chamber, | and SHR in.1. 46
carry this mad knave to the jail. 5.01. 92 P
carry me to the jail? 5.01. 94 P
before her beauty, | /resolv'd to carry her. AWW 3.07. 19
yet slight ones will not carry it. 4.01. 38 P
how does he carry himself? 4.03.104 P
the stocks carry him. 4.03.106 P
carry his water to th' wise woman. TN 3.04.102 P
we may carry it thus, for our pleasure and his 3.04.137 P
us, that thou carry | this female bastard hence, WT 2.03.174
why should i carry lies abroad? 4.04.271 P
your breeches best may carry them. JN 3.01.201
carry master silence to bed. 2H4 5.03.129 P
go carry sir john falstaff to the fleet. 5.05. 91
carry them here and there, jumping o'er times, H5 pr 29
we carry not a heart with us from hence | that 2.02. 21
that piece of service the men would carry coals. 3.02. 46 P
i'll use to carry thee out of this place. 1H6 1.03. 43
the french | she carry armor as she hath begun. 2.01. 24
men, | forbidden late to carry any weapon, 3.01. 79
would choose him pope and carry him to rome, 2H6 1.03. 62
these news, as fast as horse can carry them — 1.04. 74
he'll carry it so | to make the sceptre his. H8 1.02.134
words cannot carry | authority so weighty. 3.02.233
bold | to carry into flanders the great seal. 3.02.319
still in thy right hand carry gentle peace | to 3.02.445
shall the elephant ajax carry it thus? TRO 2.03. 2 P
shall pride carry it? 2.03.218 P
and 'twould, you'd carry half. 2.03.219 P
glorious heaven, | he shall not carry him; 5.06. 24
this will i carry to rome. COR 1.05. 1 P
than carry it but by the suit of the gentry to 2.01.238
and carry with us ears and eyes for th' time, 2.01.269
thought of every one coriolanus will carry it. 2.02. 4 P
sir, i beseech you, think you he'll carry rome? 4.07. 27
them, but he could not | carry his honors even. 4.07. 37
and shall she carry this unto her grave? TIT 2.03.127
boy | shall carry from me to the empress' sons 4.01.115
gregory, on my word, we'll not carry coals. ROM 1.01. 1 P
i will carry no crotchets, i'll re you, i'll fa 4.05.118 P
that stay at home, if bearing carry it; TIM 3.05. 48
go carry them, and smear | the sleepy grooms MAC 2.02. 46
that twofold balls and treble sceptres carry. 4.01.121

things in doubt | that carry but half sense. HAM 4.05. 7
matter, if we could carry a cannon by our sides; 5.02.159 P
lord whose hand must take my plight shall carry LR 1.01.101
if our father carry authority with such 1.01.304 P
may carry through itself to that full issue 1.04. 3
man's nature cannot carry | th' affliction nor 3.02. 48
goneril, | and hardly shall i carry out my side, 5.01. 61
and carry it so | as i have set it down. 5.03. 36
are in the field, a mighty strength they carry. ANT 2.01. 17
and carry back to sicily much tall youth | that 2.06. 7
i have led you oft, carry me now, good friends, 4.14.139
themselves upon her, | not carry her aboard. PER 4.01.101
and the number | to carry such a business, forth TNK 1.01.162
bodies, | and carry it sweetly and deliverly, 3.05. 29
carry your tail without offense | or scandal to 3.05. 34
so we may fairly carry | our swords and cause 3.06.259
bid him with speed prepare to carry it, | the LUC 1294
arrest | without all bail shall carry me away, SON 74. 2

CARRYING 5 FR 0.0005 REL FR 2 V 3 P
a pound shall serve me for carrying your letter. TGV 1.01.106 P
too little for carrying a letter to your lover. 1.01.109
as much as thou didst me in carrying gates. LLL 1.02. 75 P
crowns of the king by carrying my head to him, 2H6 4.10. 27 P
men, | carrying, i say, the stamp of one defect, HAM 1.04. 31

CARRY'T 5 FR 0.0005 REL FR 2 V 3 P
he smells april and may — he will carry't, he WIV 3.02. 69 P
he will carry't, he will carry't — 'tis in his 3.02. 69 P
'tis in his buttons — he will carry't. 3.02. 70 P
the thick-lips owe | if he can carry't thus! OTH 1.01. 67
done me, yea, my life, | if then thou carry't; TNK 3.01. 78

CARRY-TALE 2 FR 0.0002 REL FR 2 V 0 P
some carry-tale, some please-man, some slight LLL 5.02.463
this carry-tale, dissentious jealousy, | that VEN 657

CARS 1 FR 0.0001 REL FR 0 V 1 P
though our silence be drawn from us with cars, TN 2.05. 64 P

CAR'ST 1 FR 0.0001 REL FR 0 V 1 P
thou art a merry fellow and car'st for nothing. TN 3.01. 26 P

/CART 1 FR 0.0001 REL FR 1 V 0 P
/i /cannot /draw /a /cart, /nor /eat /dried LR 5.03. 38

CART 5 FR 0.0005 REL FR 3 V 2 P
sheaf and bind, | then to cart with rosalind. AYL 3.02.108
to cart her rather; SHR 1.01. 55
if i become not a cart as well as another man, a 1H4 2.04.496 P
full thirty times hath phoebus' cart gone round HAM 3.02.155
not an ass know when the cart draws the horse? LR 1.04.223 P

CARTERS 3 FR 0.0003 REL FR 2 V 1 P
master, there is three carters, three shepherds, WT 4.04.324 P
but when your carters or your waiting vassals R3 2.01.122
for a state, | but keep a farm and carters. HAM 2.02.167

CARTHAGE 7 FR 0.0008 REL FR 3 V 4 P
she was of carthage, not of tunis. TMP 2.01. 83 P
this tunis, sir, was carthage. 2.01. 84 P
carthage? 2.01. 85 P
i assure you, carthage. 2.01. 86 P
and by that fire which burn'd the carthage queen MND 1.01.173
and waft her love | to come again to carthage. MV 5.01. 12
as dear | as anna to the queen of carthage was: SHR 1.01.154

CARTS 1 FR 0.0001 REL FR 1 V 0 P
go, fellow, get thee home, provide some carts, R2 2.02.106

CARV'D 7 FR 0.0008 REL FR 5 V 2 P
spake, or look'd, or touch'd, or carv'd to thee. ERR 2.02.118
should be hang'd and carv'd upon these trees? AYL 3.02.173 P
what, up and down carv'd like an apple-tart? SHR 4.03. 89
a head fantastically carv'd upon it with a knife 2H4 3.02.311 P
carv'd out his passage | till he fac'd the slave MAC 1.02. 19
of hard misfortune, carv'd /in /it with tears. LUC 1713
she carv'd thee for her seal, and meant thereby SON 11.13

CARV'D-BONE 1 FR 0.0001 REL FR 0 V 1 P
the carv'd-bone face on a flask. LLL 5.02.615 P

/CARVE 1 FR 0.0001 REL FR 0 V 1 P
desire to eat with her, /carve her, drink to her TNK 4.03. 88 P

CARVE 10 FR 0.0011 REL FR 8 V 2 P
the which if i do not carve most curiously, say ADO 5.01.155 P
boyet, you can carve, | break up this capon. LLL 4.01. 55
'a can carve too, and lisp; 5.02.323
orlando, carve on every tree | the fair, the AYL 3.02. 9
and cleanly, but to carve a capon and eat it? 1H4 2.04.456 P
to carve out dials quaintly, point by point, 3H6 2.05. 24
let's carve him as a dish fit for the gods, JC 2.01.173
carve for himself, for on his choice depends HAM 1.03. 20
he that stirs next to carve for his own rage OTH 2.03.173
o, carve not with thy hours my love's fair brow, SON 19. 9

CARVED 3 FR 0.0003 REL FR 3 V 0 P
my subjects for a pair of carved saints, | and R2 3.03.152
have with my knife carved in roman letters, TIT 5.01.139
many she sees where cares have carved some, LUC 1445

CARVER 1 FR 0.0001 REL FR 1 V 0 P
arms, | be his own carver and cut out his way, R2 2.03.144

CARVER'S 1 FR 0.0001 REL FR 1 V 0 P
so much the more our carver's excellence, WT 5.03. 30

CARVES 1 FR 0.0001 REL FR 0 V 1 P
she discourses, she carves, she gives the leer WIV 1.03. 45 P

CARVING 2 FR 0.0002 REL FR 0 V 2 P
he lie ten nights awake carving the fashion of a ADO 2.03. 17 P
young plants with carving "rosalind" on their AYL 3.02.360 P

CASA 1 FR 0.0001 REL FR 0 V 1 P
alla nostra casa ben venuto, molto honorato SHR 1.02. 25 P

CASCA 25 FR 0.0028 REL FR 23 V 2 P
as they pass by, pluck casca by the sleeve, JC 1.02.179
casca will tell us what the matter is. 1.02.189
ay, casca, tell us what hath chanc'd to-day 1.02.217
i should not then ask casca what had chanc'd. 1.02.220
tell us the manner of it, gentle casca. 1.02.234
and honest casca, we have the falling sickness. 1.02.256
will you sup with me to-night, casca? 1.02.288 P
good even, casca; 1.03. 1
good night then, casca; 1.03. 39
casca, by your voice. 1.03. 41
and, thus unbraced, casca, as you see, | have 1.03. 48
you are dull, casca; 1.03. 57
now could i, casca, name to thee a man | most 1.03. 72
you speak to casca, and to such a man | that is 1.03.116
now know you, casca, i have mov'd already | some 1.03.121
no, it is casca, one incorporate | to our 1.03.135
come, casca, you and i will yet, ere day, | see 1.03.153
this, casca; 2.01. 96
good morrow, casca. 2.02.111
come not near casca; 2.03. 2 P
casca, be sudden, for we fear prevention. 3.01. 19
casca, you are the first that rears your hand. 3.01. 30
and, my valiant casca, yours; 3.01.188
see what a rent the envious casca made; 3.02.175
whilst damned casca, like a cur, behind | strook 5.01. 43

CASCA'S 1 FR 0.0001 REL FR 0 V 1 P
some to decius' house, and some to casca's; JC 3.03. 37 P

/CAS'D 1 FR 0.0001 REL FR 1 V 0 P
her eyes as jewel-like | and /cas'd as richly, PER 5.01.111

CAS'D 2 FR 0.0002 REL FR 2 V 0 P
a harp, | or like a cunning instrument cas'd up, R2 1.03.163
fairer | than those for preservation cas'd, or CYM 5.03. 22

CASE* 107 FR 0.0121 REL FR 66 V 41 P
be not born to be hang'd, our case is miserable. TMP 1.01. 33 P
let's assist them, | for our case is as theirs. 1.01. 55
thy case, dear friend, | shall be my president: 2.01.290
monster, i am in case to justle a constable. 3.02. 26 P
and in any case have a nay-word, that you may WIV 2.02.126 P
well, what is your accusative case? 4.01. 44 P
what is the focative case, william? 4.01. 51 P
what is your genitive case plural, william? 4.01. 57 P
genitive case? 4.01. 59 P
vengeance of jinny's case! 4.01. 62 P
how often dost thou with thy case, thy habit, MM 2.04. 13
i may make my case as claudio's, to cross this 4.02.168 P
me | that his attendant — so his case was like, ERR 1.01.127
in this service, you must case me in leather. 2.01. 85
i would not spare my brother in this case, | if 4.01. 77
what observation mad'st thou in this case | /of 4.02. 5
not know the matter, he is 'rested on the case. 4.02. 42
why, 'tis a plain case: 4.03. 23 P
went, like a base-viol, in a case of leather; 4.03. 24 P
yea, and a case to put it into. ADO 1.01.182 P
for god defend the lute should be like the case! 2.01. 95 P
and let my counsel sway you in this case. 4.01.201
as his your case is such; LLL 4.03.129
that superfluous case | that hid the worse and 5.02.387
to our law | immediately provided in that case. MND 1.01. 45
the worst that may befall me in this case, | if 1.01. 63
in any case, let thisby have clean linen; 4.02. 39 P
what a case am i in then, that am neither a good AYL ep 7 P
but in this case of wooing, | a child shall get SHR 2.01.410
grace | as 'longeth to a lover's blessed case! 4.02. 45
well, and hold your own in any case | with such 4.04. 6
i do beg your good will in this case. AWW 1.03. 21 P
in what case? 1.03. 22 P
in isbel's case and mine own. 1.03. 23 P
you some sport with the fox ere we case him. 3.06.103 P
my life, sir, in any case! 4.03.241 P
be | when time hath sow'd a grizzle on thy case? TN 5.01.165
stave's end as well as a man in his case may do. 5.01.285 P
but, for me, | what case stand i in? WT 1.02.352
(for, as the case now stands, it is a curse | he 2.03. 88
but though my case be a pitiful one, i hope i 4.04.814 P
o, that's the case of the shepherd's son. 4.04.816 P
it would not be sir nob in any case. JN 1.01.147
disgrace | neglected my sworn duty in that case. R2 1.01.134
case ye, case ye, on with your vizards. 1H4 2.02. 53 P
case ye, case ye, on with your vizards. 2.02. 53 P
know, | in any case, the offer of the king. 5.02. 25
give it me. what? is it in the case? 5.03. 52 P
is ent'red and my case so openly known to the 2H4 2.01. 30 P
she hath been in good case, and the truth is, 2.01.106 P
it was jove's case. 2.02.174 P
the case of a treble hoboy was a mansion for him 3.02.326 P
a rotten case abides no handling. 4.01.159
your royal thoughts, make the case yours: 5.02. 91
for mine own part, i have not a case of lives. H5 3.02. 4 P
question, my lords, no further of the case, 1H6 2.01. 72
dare no man answer in a case of truth? 2.04. 2
then for the truth and plainness of the case, 2.04. 46
this day, in argument upon a case, | some words 2.05. 45
content | to be mine own attorney in this case. 5.03.166
for god's sake pity my case. 2H6 1.03.214 P
even so myself bewails good gloucester's case 3.01.217
in any case, be not too rough in terms, | for he 4.09. 44
and haste is needful in this desp'rate case. 3H6 4.01.129
ay, but the case is alter'd. 4.03. 31
thus /stands the case: 4.05. 4
brother, the time and case requireth haste, 4.05. 18
if case some one of you would fly from us, 5.04. 34
death, | but that the extreme peril of the case, R3 3.05. 44
that, in this case of justice, my accusers, | be H8 5.02. 81
alive | and case thy reputation in thy tent, TRO 3.03.187
ay, ay, ay, ay, 'tis too plain a case. 4.04. 29 P
in such a case the gods will not be good unto us COR 5.04. 31 P
o publius, is not this a heavy case, | to see TIT 4.03. 25
to know our farther pleasure in this case, | to ROM 1.01.101
give me a case to put my visage in, | a visor 1.04. 29
and in such a case as mine a man may strain 2.04. 50 P
such a case as yours constrains a man to bow in 2.04. 52 P
o, he is even in my mistress' case, | just in 3.03. 84
even in my mistress' case, | just in her case. 3.03. 85
then, since the case so stands as now it doth, 3.05.216
up, | for well you know this is a pitiful case. 4.05. 99
ay, /by my troth, the case may be amended. 4.05.100 P
what a strange case was that! TIM 3.02. 17 P
you wrong'd yourself to write in such a case. JC 4.03. 6
whose motive, in this case, should stir me most HAM 5.02.245
daughters, and leave his horns without a case. LR 1.05. 31 P
when every case in law is right; 3.02. 87
what, with the case of eyes? 4.06.144
your eyes are in a heavy case, your purse in a 4.06.147 P
your case is better. OTH 4.01. 69
you indeed a cut, and the case to be lamented. ANT 1.02.167 P
as befits mine honor | to stoop in such a case. 2.02. 98
not to consider in what case thou stand'st 3.13. 54
than thy continent, | crack thy frail case! 4.14. 41
this case of that huge spirit now is cold. 4.15. 89
thy mistress how | the case stands with her; CYM 1.05. 67
for idiots in this case of favor would | be 1.06. 42
me, for | i yet not understand the case myself. 2.03. 75
yet the traitor | stands in worse case of woe. 3.04. 87
thirds his own worth (the case is each of ours), TNK 1.02. 96
this is the strangers' case | and this your STM II.C 139
face, | extinguishing his conduct in this case; LUC 313
like to a bankrout beggar wails his case: 711
since that my case is past the help of law. 1022
so that eternal love in love's fresh case SON 108. 9
accomplish'd in himself, not in his case; LC 116

CASED 1 FR 0.0001 REL FR 1 V 0 P
by the tongue, | a cased lion by the mortal paw, JN 3.01.259

CASEMENT 9 FR 0.0010 REL FR 3 V 6 P
i pray thee go to the casement, and see if you WIV 1.04. 2 P
may you leave a casement of the great chamber MND 3.01. 56 P
open, and the moon may shine in at the casement. 3.01. 58 P
a woman's wit, and it will out at the casement; AYL 4.01.162 P
thy casement i need not open, for i look through AWW 2.03.214 P
in florence was it from a casement thrown me, 5.03. 93
false, you threw it him | out of a casement. 5.03.230
found it thrown in at the casement of my closet. LR 1.02. 60 P
look thorough a casement to allure false hearts, CYM 2.04. 34

CASEMENTS 3 FR 0.0003 REL FR 3 V 0 P
clamber not you up to the casements then, | nor MV 2.05. 31
but stop my house's ears, i mean my casements; 2.05. 34
through casements darted their desiring eyes R2 5.02. 14

CASES* 11 FR 0.0012 REL FR 6 V 5 P
for thy cases and the numbers of the genders? WIV 4.01. 70 P
they were all in lamentable cases! LLL 5.02.273
on one another, to tear the cases of their eyes. WT 5.02. 12 P
sirrah, i have cases of buckrom for the nonce, 1H4 1.02.179 P
in cases of defense 'tis best to weigh | the H5 2.04. 43
hung up in cases that keeps their sounds to TIM 1.02. 99 P
but in these cases | we still have judgment here MAC 1.07. 7
now, his quillities, his cases, his tenures, and HAM 5.01.100 P
(as in these cases where the aim reports, | 'tis OTH 1.03. 6
and in such cases | men's natures wrangle with 3.04.143
cases to those heavenly jewels | which pericles PER 3.02. 98

CASH 1 FR 0.0001 REL FR 1 V 0 P
in cash, most justly paid. H5 2.01.115

CASHIER 1 FR 0.0001 REL FR 0 V 1 P
discard, bully hercules, cashier; WIV 1.03. 6 P

CASHIER'D 4 FR 0.0004 REL FR 2 V 2 P
and being fap, sir, was, as they say, cashier'd; WIV 1.01.179 P
how? what does his cashier'd worship mutter? TIM 3.04. 60 P
but provender, and when he's old, cashier'd. OTH 1.01. 48
thou by that small hurt /hast cashier'd cassio. 2.03.375

CASING 1 FR 0.0001 REL FR 1 V 0 P
rock, | as broad and general as the casing air; MAC 3.04. 22

CASK 1 FR 0.0001 REL FR 1 V 0 P
lock'd into the woefull'st cask | that ever did 2H6 3.02.409

CASKET 12 FR 0.0013 REL FR 10 V 2 P
and choose the right casket, you should refuse MV 1.02. 93 P
glass of rhenish wine on the contrary casket, 1.02. 97 P
here, catch this casket, it is worth the pains. 2.06. 33
what says this leaden casket? 2.07. 15
this casket threatens. 2.07. 18
unfold to any one | which casket 'twas i chose; 2.09. 11
if i fail | of the right casket, never in my 2.09. 12
an empty casket, where the jewel of life | by JN 5.01. 40
the little casket bring me hither. TIM 1.02.158
were not this glorious casket stor'd with ill. PER 1.01. 77
ink and /paper, | my casket and my jewels; 3.01. 66
to burn the guiltless casket where it lay! LUC 1057

CASKETED 1 FR 0.0001 REL FR 1 V 0 P
i have writ my letters, casketed my treasure, AWW 2.05. 24

CASKETS 6 FR 0.0006 REL FR 5 V 1 P
father's imposition depending on the caskets. MV 1.02.105 P
therefore i pray you lead me to the caskets | to 2.01. 23
the several caskets to this noble prince. 2.07. 2
behold, there stand the caskets, noble prince. 2.09. 4
but let me to my fortune and the caskets. 3.02. 39
your fortune stood upon the caskets there, | and 3.02.201

CASQUE 4 FR 0.0004 REL FR 4 V 0 P
fall like amazing thunder on the casque | of thy R2 1.03. 81
were it a casque compos'd by vulcan's skill, TRO 5.02.170
not moving | from th' casque to th' cushion, but COR 4.07. 43
my casque now. TNK 3.06. 62

CASQUES 1 FR 0.0001 REL FR 1 V 0 P
within this wooden o the very casques | that did H5 pr 13

CASSADO 1 FR 0.0001 REL FR 1 V 0 P
sent a large commission | to gregory de cassado, H8 3.02.321

CASSANDRA 4 FR 0.0004 REL FR 3 V 1 P
and cassandra laugh'd. TRO 1.02.145 P
it is cassandra. 2.02.100
cassandra, call my father to persuade. 5.03. 30
cassandra doth foresee, and i myself | am like a 5.03. 64

CASSANDRA'S 2 FR 0.0002 REL FR 1 V 1 P
will not dispraise your sister cassandra's wit, TRO 1.01. 46 P
courage of our minds, | because cassandra's mad. 2.02.122

CASSIBELAN 4 FR 0.0004 REL FR 3 V 1 P
his honor | against the romans with cassibelan, CYM 1.01. 30
and conquer'd it, cassibelan, thine uncle 3.01. 5
for joy whereof | the fam'd cassibelan, who was 3.01. 30
many among us can gripe as hard as cassibelan. 3.01. 41 P

/CASSIO 1 FR 0.0001 REL FR 1 V 0 P
/i /pray /talk /me /of /cassio. OTH 3.04. 92

CASSIO 111 FR 0.0125 REL FR 99 V 12 P
one michael cassio, a florentine | (a fellow OTH 1.01. 20
a veronesa, michael cassio, | lieutenant to the 2.01. 26
but this same cassio, though he speak of comfort 2.01. 31
i thank you, valiant cassio. 2.01. 87
how say you, cassio? 2.01.163 P
as this will i ensnare as great a fly as cassio. 2.01.169 P
in the degree of this fortune as cassio does? 2.01.237 P
cassio knows you not. 2.01.265 P
do you find some occasion to anger cassio, 2.01.267 P
taste again but by the displanting of cassio. 2.01.276 P
that cassio loves her, i do well believe't; 2.01.286
on, | i'll have our michael cassio on the hip, 2.01.305
garb | (for i fear cassio with my night-cap too) 2.01.307
am i to put our cassio in some action | that may 2.03. 60
prizes the virtue that appears in cassio, | and 2.03.134
i do love cassio well; 2.03.143
than it should do offense to michael cassio; 2.03.222
and cassio following him with determin'd sword 2.03.227
steps in to cassio and entreats his pause; 2.03.229
and fall of swords, | and cassio high in oath; 2.03.235
though cassio did some little wrong to him, | as 2.03.242
yet surely cassio, i believe, receiv'd | from 2.03.244
mince this matter, | making it light to cassio. 2.03.248
cassio, i love thee, | but never more be officer 2.03.248
to counsel cassio to this parallel course, 2.03.349
cassio hath beaten thee, | and thou by that 2.03.374
thou by that small hurt /hast cashier'd cassio. 2.03.375
my wife must move for cassio to her mistress — 2.03.383

and bring him jump when he may cassio find 2.03.386
tell her there's one cassio entreats her a 3.01. 26 P
be thou assur'd, good cassio, i will do | all my 3.03. 1
do not doubt, cassio, | but i will have my lord 3.03. 5
what ever shall become of michael cassio, | he's 3.03. 8
therefore be merry, cassio, | for thy solicitor 3.03. 26
was not that cassio parted from my wife? 3.03. 37
cassio, my lord? 3.03. 38
why, your lieutenant, cassio. 3.03. 45
michael cassio, | that came a–wooing with you, 3.03. 70
did michael cassio, when /you woo'd my lady, 3.03. 94
lik'st not that, | when cassio left my wife. 3.03.110
for michael cassio, | i dare be sworn i think 3.03.124
look to your wife, observe her well with cassio, 3.03.197
although 'tis fit that cassio have his place — 3.03.246
i lay with cassio lately, | and, being troubled 3.03.413
one of this kind is cassio. 3.03.418
did i to–day | see cassio wipe his beard with. 3.03.439
you know, sirrah, where lieutenant cassio lies? 3.04. 2 P
i will not leave him now till cassio | be call'd 3.04. 32
i have sent to bid cassio come speak with you. 3.04. 50
pray you let cassio be receiv'd again. 3.04. 88
look you, cassio and my husband! 3.04.106
how now, good cassio, what's the news with you? 3.04.109
alas, thrice–gentle cassio, | my advocation is 3.04.122
cassio, walk hereabout; 3.04.165
'save you, friend cassio! 3.04.169
and i was going to your lodging, cassio. 3.04.172
o cassio, whence came this? 3.04.180
how now, cassio? 4.01. 48
/unsuiting such a man), | cassio came hither. 4.01. 78
now will i question cassio of bianca, | a 4.01. 93
it is a creature | that dotes on cassio (as 'tis 4.01. 96
do you hear, cassio? 4.01.113
crying, "o dear cassio!" 4.01.137 P
and for cassio, let me be his undertaker. 4.01.211 P
i thank you. how does lieutenant cassio? 4.01.222
is there division 'twixt my lord and cassio? 4.01.231
t' atone them, for the love i bear to cassio. 4.01.233
him home, | deputing cassio in his government. 4.01.237
cassio shall have my place. 4.01.261
yes, you have seen cassio and she together. 4.02. 3
from venice to depute cassio in othello's place. 4.02.221 P
can be so determinate as the removing of cassio. 4.02.227 P
now, whether he kill cassio, | or cassio him, or 5.01. 12
or cassio him, or each do kill the other, 5.01. 13
if cassio do remain, | he hath a daily beauty in 5.01. 18
the voice of cassio! iago keeps his word. 5.01. 28
i cry you mercy. here's cassio hurt by villains. 5.01. 69
cassio? 5.01. 70
o my dear cassio, my sweet cassio! 5.01. 76
o my dear cassio, my sweet cassio! 5.01. 76
o cassio, cassio, cassio! 5.01. 77
o cassio, cassio, cassio! 5.01. 77
o cassio, cassio, cassio! 5.01. 77
cassio, may you suspect | who they should be 5.01. 78
alas, he faints! o cassio, cassio, cassio! 5.01. 84
alas, he faints! o cassio, cassio, cassio! 5.01. 84
alas, he faints! o cassio, cassio, cassio! 5.01. 84
patience awhile, good cassio. 5.01. 87
how do you, cassio? o, a chair, a chair! 5.01. 96
he that lies slain here, cassio, | was my dear 5.01.101
cassio hath here been set on in the dark | by 5.01.112
alas, good gentleman! alas, good cassio! 5.01.115
go know of cassio where he supp'd to–night. 5.01.117
gentlemen, let's go see poor cassio dress'd. 5.01.124
lov'd, and gave thee, | thou gav'st to cassio. 5.02. 49
never lov'd cassio | but with such general 5.02. 59
cassio, my lord, hath kill'd a young venetian 5.02.112
roderigo kill'd? | and cassio kill'd? 5.02.114
no, cassio is not kill'd. 5.02.114
not cassio kill'd? 5.02.115
cassio did top her; 5.02.136
ay, with cassio. 5.02.143
she false with cassio? 5.02.182
did you say with cassio? 5.02.182
with cassio, mistress. go to, charm your tongue. 5.02.183
that she with cassio hath the act of shame | a 5.02.211
cassio confess'd it, | and she did gratify his 5.02.212
she give it cassio? 5.02.230
imports | the death of cassio to be undertook 5.02.311
how came you, cassio, by that handkerchief 5.02.319
is taken off, | and cassio rules in cyprus. 5.02.332

CASSIO'S 10 FR 0.0011 REL FR 10 V 0 P
cassio's a proper man. OTH 1.03.392
every thing he does | with cassio's suit. 3.03. 26
why then i think cassio's an honest man. 3.03.129
cassio's my worthy friend — | my lord, i see y' 3.03.223
i will in cassio's lodging lose this napkin, 3.03.321
i found not cassio's kisses on her lips. 3.03.341
let me hear thee say | that cassio's not alive. 3.03.473
jealousy must /conster | poor cassio's smiles, 4.01.102
'tis like she comes to speak of cassio's death; 5.02. 92
did you and he consent in cassio's death? 5.02.297

CASSIUS' 5 FR 0.0005 REL FR 4 V 1 P
look, in this place ran cassius' dagger through; JC 3.02.174
to brutus', to cassius'; 3.03. 36 P
power, | as cassius' legions are by antony. 5.03. 53
so in his red blood cassius' day is set! 5.03. 62
come, cassius' sword, and find titinius' heart. 5.03. 90

CASSIUS 72 FR 0.0081 REL FR 71 V 1 P
let me not hinder, cassius, your desires; JC 1.02. 30
cassius, | be not deceiv'd. 1.02. 36
(among which number, cassius, be you one), | nor 1.02. 44
no, cassius; 1.02. 52
into what dangers would you lead me, cassius, 1.02. 63
i would not, cassius, yet i love him well. 1.02. 82
me, "dar'st thou, cassius, now | leap in with me 1.02.102
caesar cried, "help me, cassius, or i sink!" 1.02.111
a god, and cassius is | a wretched creature, and 1.02.116
but look you, cassius, | the angry spot doth 1.02.182
yond cassius has a lean and hungry look, | he 1.02.194
i should avoid | so soon as that spare cassius. 1.02.201
if i were brutus now and he were cassius, | he 1.02.314
your ear is good. cassius, what night is this! 1.03. 42
'tis caesar that you mean; is it not, cassius? 1.03. 79
cassius from bondage will deliver cassius. 1.03. 90
cassius from bondage will deliver cassius. 1.03. 90
o cassius, if you could | but win the noble 1.03.140
since cassius first did whet me against caesar, 2.01. 61
sir, 'tis your brother cassius at the door, 2.01. 70
our course will seem too bloody, caius cassius, 2.01.162
alas, good cassius, do not think of him. 2.01.185
take heed of cassius; 2.03. 2 P
cassius or caesar never shall turn back, | for i 3.01. 21
cassius, be constant; 3.01. 22
as low as to thy foot doth cassius fall, | to 3.01. 56
and cassius too. 3.01. 84
next, caius cassius, do i take your hand; 3.01.186
pardon me, caius cassius! 3.01.211
cassius, go you into the other street, | and 3.02. 3
those that will follow cassius, go with him; 3.02. 6
i will hear cassius, and compare their reasons, 3.02. 9
i should do brutus wrong, and cassius wrong, 3.02.123
brutus and cassius | are rid like madmen through 3.02.268
brutus and cassius | are levying powers; 4.01. 41
what now, lucilius, is cassius near? 4.02. 3
the horse in general, | are come with cassius. 4.02. 30
cassius, be content, | speak your griefs softly; 4.02. 41
then in my tent, cassius, enlarge your griefs, 4.02. 46
let me tell you, cassius, you yourself | are 4.03. 9
the name of cassius honors this corruption, 4.03. 15
go to; you are not, cassius. 4.03. 32
there is no terror, cassius, in your threats; 4.03. 66
was that done like cassius? 4.03. 77
should i have answer'd caius cassius so? 4.03. 78
come, | revenge yourselves alone on cassius, 4.03. 94
cassius, | for cassius is a–weary of the world; 4.03. 95
him better | than ever thou lovedst cassius. 4.03.107
o cassius, you are yoked with a lamb | that 4.03.110
hath cassius liv'd | to be but mirth and 4.03.113
yes, cassius, and, from henceforth, | when you 4.03.121
o cassius, i am sick of many griefs. 4.03.144
in this i bury all unkindness, cassius. 4.03.159
noble, noble cassius, | good night, and good 4.03.232
by and by | on business to my brother cassius. 4.03.248
go and commend me to my brother cassius; 4.03.306
so to–day, | if cassius might have rul'd. 5.01. 47
old cassius still! 5.01. 63
as this very day | was cassius born. 5.01. 72
no, cassius, no. 5.01.110
for ever, and for ever, farewell, cassius! 5.01.116
o cassius, brutus gave the word too early, | who 5.03. 5
fly therefore, noble cassius, fly far off. 5.03. 11
o cassius, | far from this country pindarus 5.03. 48
these tidings will well comfort cassius. 5.03. 54
this was he, messala, | but cassius is no more. 5.03. 60
why didst thou send me forth, brave cassius? 5.03. 80
apace, | and see how i regarded caius cassius. 5.03. 88
look whe'er he have not crown'd dead cassius! 5.03. 97
i shall find time, cassius; 5.03.103
was't | that mov'd pale cassius to conspire? ANT 2.06. 15
while i strook | the lean and wrinkled cassius, 3.11. 37

CASSOCKS 1 FR 0.0001 REL FR 0 V 1 P
dare not shake the snow from off their cassocks, AWW 4.03.169 P

/CAST 3 FR 0.0003 REL FR 3 V 0 P
/you /cast /th' /event /of /war, /my /noble 2H4 1.01.166
/thou /provok'st /thyself /to /cast /him /up. 1.03. 96
and /why such daily /cast of brazen cannon, HAM 1.01. 73

CAST 107 FR 0.0121 REL FR 78 V 29 P
study, | the government i cast upon my brother, TMP 1.02. 75
all were sea–swallow'd, though some cast again, 2.01.251
with mine own hands since i was cast ashore. 2.02.123 P
and wouldst thou have me cast my love on him? TGV 1.02. 25
ay — if you thought your love not cast away. 1.02. 26
to cast up, with a pair of anchoring hooks, 3.01.118
i, "will you cast away your child on a fool, and WIV 3.04. 96 P
his filth within being cast, he would appear | a MM 3.01. 92
the honest troyan, the poor wench is cast away. LLL 5.02.676 P
hath an argosy cast away, coming from tripolis. MV 3.01.100 P
are too precious to be cast away upon curs, AYL 1.03. 4 P
i will not cast away my physic but on those that 3.02.358 P
and to cast away honesty upon a foul slut were 3.03. 35 P
he hath bought a pair of cast lips of diana. 3.04. 15 P
'tis but one cast away, and so, come death! 4.01.185 P
to cast thy wand'ring eyes on every stale, SHR 3.01. 90
cast on no water. 4.01. 20 P
i would be loath to cast away my speech; TN 1.05.172 P
my fortunes, having cast me on your niece, give 2.05. 70 P
to be, cast thy humble slough and appear fresh. 2.05.148 P
"cast thy humble slough," says she; 3.04. 68 P
since you to non–regardance cast my faith, | and 5.01.121
hold, | when you cast out, it still came home. WT 1.02.214
for as | thy brat hath been cast out, like to 3.02. 87
cast your good counsels | upon his passion. 4.04.495
who has | (his dignity and duty both cast off) 5.01.183
france, hast thou yet more blood to cast away? JN 2.01.334
they found him dead and cast into the streets, 5.01. 39
are cast away, and sunk on goodwin sands. 5.05. 13
dead, forsook, cast off, | and none of you will 5.07. 35
however god or fortune cast my lot, | there R2 1.03. 85
a freer heart | cast off his chains of bondage, 1.03. 89
a maim | as to be cast forth in the common air, 1.03.157
wealth of all our states | all at one cast? 1H4 4.01. 47
perfectness of time | cast off his followers, 2H4 4.04. 75
let it be cast and paid. 5.01. 20 P
weak stomach, and therefore i must cast it up. H5 3.02. 53 P
for more, | be cast from possibility of all. 1H6 5.04.146
do not cast away an honest man for a villain's 2H6 1.03.202 P
he can write and read and cast accompt. 4.02. 86 P
to whom do lions cast their gentle looks? 3H6 2.02. 11
clarence, who i indeed have cast in darkness, R3 1.03.326
slave, i have set my life upon a cast, | and i 5.04. 9
lord sands, | your colt's tooth is not cast yet? H8 1.03. 48
and saint–like | cast her fair eyes to heaven, 4.01. 84
bright faces | cast thousand beams upon me, like 4.02. 89
along, | how earnestly he cast his eyes upon me! 5.02. 12
souls with modesty again, | cast none away. 5.02.100
let us cast away nothing, for we may live to TRO 4.04. 21 P
i doubt not but | our rome will cast upon thee. COR 2.01.202
but that you must | cast your election on him. 2.03.229
and from thence | into destruction cast him. 3.01.213
when you cast | your stinking greasy caps in 4.06.130
shall | go sound the ocean, and cast your nets; TIT 4.03. 7
cast by their grave beseeming ornaments | to ROM 1.01. 93
cast it off. 2.02. 9
o sweet my mother, cast me not away! 3.05.198
plain–dealing, which will not cast a man a doit. TIM 1.01.212 P
are we undone, cast off, nothing remaining? 4.02. 2
and ulcerous sores | would cast the gorge at, 4.03. 41
thou hast cast away thyself, being like thyself, 4.03.220
and put on fear, and cast yourself in wonder, JC 1.03. 60
and conn'd by rote, | to cast into my teeth. 4.03. 99
in their newest gloss, | not cast aside so soon. MAC 1.07. 35
legs sometime, yet i made a shift to cast him. 2.03. 41 P
doctor, cast | the water of my land, find her 5.03. 50
good hamlet, cast thy nighted color off, | and HAM 1.02. 68
and marble jaws | to cast thee up again. 1.04. 51
age | to cast beyond ourselves in our opinions, 2.01.112
is sicklied o'er with the pale cast of thought, 3.01. 84
he is gone, he is gone, | and we cast away moan, 4.05.198
upon, | be it lawful i take up what's cast away. LR 1.01.253
judgment he hath now cast her off appears too 1.01.291 P
and cast you, with the waters that you loose, 1.04.303
thou dost think | i have cast off for ever. 1.04.310
and dizzy 'tis, to cast one's eyes so low! 4.06. 12
for thee, oppressed king, i am cast down, 5.03. 5
cannot with safety cast him, for he's embark'd OTH 1.01.149
mane, | seems to cast water on the burning bear, 2.01. 14
our general cast us thus early for the love of 2.03. 14 P
you are but now cast in his mood, a punishment 2.03.273 P
the watch, whereon it came | that i was cast; 5.02.327
it were pity to cast them away for nothing, ANT 1.02.138 P
the city cast | her people out upon her; 2.02.213
that despiteful rome | cast on my noble father. 2.06. 23
poets, cannot | think, speak, cast, write, sing, 3.02. 17
they cast their caps up and carouse together 4.12. 12
though forfeiters you cast in prison, yet | you CYM 3.02. 38
seat, and cast | from her his dearest one, 5.04. 60
and throw stones, cast mire upon me, set | the 5.05.222
throws down one mountain to cast up a higher. PER 1.04. 6
alas, the seas hath cast me on the rocks, 2.01. 5
poor men that were cast away before us even now. 2.01. 19 P
he should never have left till he cast bells, 2.01. 42 P
may see the sea hath cast upon your coast — 2.01. 56
knave was the sea to cast thee in our way! 2.01. 57 P
bereft of ships and men, cast on this shore. 2.03. 89
but straight | must cast thee, scarcely coffin'd 3.01. 60
did the sea cast it up? 3.02. 57
which | even women have cast off, melt thee, but 4.01. 7
on her, | but cast their gazes on marina's face; 4.03. 33
something i may cast to you, not much. TNK 2.01. 2 P
lovers, | cast yourselves in a body decently, 3.05. 20
nev'r cast your child away for honesty. 5.02. 21
why hast thou cast into eternal sleeping | those VEN 951
when as thy love hath cast his utmost sum, SON 49. 3
then if he thrive and i be cast away, | the 80.13

CASTALION–KING–URINAL 1 FR 0.0001 REL FR 0 V 1 P
thou art a castalion–king–urinal! WIV 2.03. 33 P

CASTAWAY 3 FR 0.0003 REL FR 3 V 0 P
to, | like a forlorn and desperate castaway, TIT 5.03. 75
that ever i should call thee castaway! ANT 3.06. 40
she there remains a hopeless castaway; LUC 744

CASTAWAYS 1 FR 0.0001 REL FR 1 V 0 P
and call us orphans, wretches, castaways, | if R3 2.02. 6

CASTED 1 FR 0.0001 REL FR 1 V 0 P
move | with casted slough and fresh legerity. H5 4.01. 23

CASTIGATE 1 FR 0.0001 REL FR 1 V 0 P
sour cold habit on | to castigate thy pride, TIM 4.03.240

CASTIGATION 1 FR 0.0001 REL FR 1 V 0 P
much castigation, exercise devout, | for here's OTH 3.04. 41

CASTILIANO 1 FR 0.0001 REL FR 0 V 1 P
castiliano vulgo! TN 1.03. 42 P

CASTING 4 FR 0.0004 REL FR 3 V 1 P
casting their savageness aside, have done | like WT 2.03.188
the casting forth to crows thy baby–daughter 3.02.191
there was casting up of eyes, holding up of 5.02. 46 P
now, | by casting her black mantle over both, TNK 5.03. 25

/CASTLE 1 FR 0.0001 REL FR 1 V 0 P
/mayor /in /courtesy /show'd /me /the /castle, R3 4.02.104

CASTLE 37 FR 0.0041 REL FR 33 V 4 P
in this kind for the wealth of windsor castle. WIV 3.03.217 P
his house, his castle, his standing–bed and 4.05. 6 P
search windsor castle, elves, within and out. 5.05. 56
nothing there holds out | but dover castle. JN 5.01. 31
i will for refuge straight to bristow castle: R2 2.02.135
there stands the castle, by yon tuft of trees, 2.03. 53
unless you please to enter in the castle, | and 2.03.160
your grace to go with us | to bristow castle, 2.03.164
barkloughly castle call they this at hand? 3.02. 1
a little pin | bores thorough his castle wall, 3.02.170
go to flint castle, there i'll pine away — | a 3.02.209
what, will not this castle yield? 3.03. 20
the castle royally is mann'd, my lord, | against 3.03. 21
go to the rude ribs of that ancient castle; 3.03. 32
as the honey of hybla, my old lad of the castle. 1H4 1.02. 42 P
at berkeley castle. 1.03.249
we steal as in a castle, cock–sure; 2.01. 86 P
what is this castle call'd that stands hard by? H5 4.07. 88
to visit her poor castle where she lies, | that 1H6 2.02. 41
as an outlaw in a castle keeps | and useth it to 3.01. 47
at your father's castle walls | we'll crave a 5.03.129
the castle in saint albons, somerset | hath made 2H6 5.02. 68
farewell, my gracious lord, i'll to my castle. 3H6 1.01.206
intend here to besiege you in your castle. 1.02. 50
away with oxford to hames castle straight; 5.05. 2
to–morrow are let blood at pomfret castle, | and R3 3.01.183
you thrive well, bring them to baynard's castle, 3.05. 98
meet me within this hour at baynard's castle. 3.05.105
stand fast, and wear a castle on thy head! TRO 5.02.187
writing destruction on the enemy's castle? TIT 3.01.169
this castle hath a pleasant seat, the air MAC 1.06. 1
the castle of macduff i will surprise, | seize 4.01.150
your castle is surpris'd; 4.03.204
enter, sir, the castle. 5.07. 29
(be brief in it) to th' castle, for my writ | is LR 5.03.246
let us to the castle. OTH 2.01.201
the strongest castle, tower, and town, | the PP 18.17

CASTLE–DITCH 1 FR 0.0001 REL FR 0 V 1 P
couch i' th' castle–ditch till we see the light WIV 5.02. 1 P

CASTLE'S 3 FR 0.0003 REL FR 3 V 0 P
that from this castle's tottered battlements R2 3.03. 52
our castle's strength | will laugh a siege to MAC 5.05. 2

this way, my lord, the castle's gently rend'red: 5.07. 24
CASTLES 8 FR 0.0009 REL FR 8 V 0 P
and all your northern castles yielded up, | and R2 3.02.201
girding with grievous siege castles and towns; H5 1.02.152
mock mothers from their sons, mock castles down; 1.02.286
let him shun castles. 2H6 1.04. 35
sandy plains | than where castles mounted stand. 1.04. 37
"let him shun castles; 1.04. 67
plains | than where castles mounted stand." 1.04. 69
though castles topple on their warders' heads; MAC 4.01. 56
CASTOR 1 FR 0.0001 REL FR 1 V 0 P
by castor, both shall die. TNK 3.06.136
CASTS 5 FR 0.0005 REL FR 5 V 0 P
was put into you, ever casts | such doubts, as H8 3.01.170
and anon he casts | his eye against the moon. 3.02.117
what counts harsh fortune casts upon my face, ANT 2.06. 54
the blind mole casts | copp'd hills towards PER 1.01.100
and casts himself th' accounts | of all his hay TNK 5.02. 58
CASUAL 2 FR 0.0002 REL FR 1 V 1 P
of accidental judgments, casual slaughters, | of HAM 5.02.382
the one is but frail and the other casual. CYM 1.04. 91 P
CASUALLY 1 FR 0.0001 REL FR 1 V 0 P
search for a jewel that too casually | hath left CYM 2.03.141
/CASUALTIES 1 FR 0.0001 REL FR 1 V 0 P
/turn'd /her | /to /foreign /casualties, /gave LR 4.03. 44
CASUALTIES 1 FR 0.0001 REL FR 1 V 0 P
and to the world and awkward casualties | bound PER 5.01. 93
CASUALTY 1 FR 0.0001 REL FR 1 V 0 P
wall, | even in the force and road of casualty. MV 2.09. 30
/CAT 1 FR 0.0001 REL FR 0 V 1 P
/purr /the /cat /is /grey. LR 3.06. 45 P
CAT 35 FR 0.0039 REL FR 18 V 17 P
they'll take suggestion as a cat laps milk; TMP 2.01.288
is that which will give language to you, cat. 2.02. 83 P
make them | than pard or cat o' mountain. 4.01.261
our maid howling, our cat wringing her hands, TGV 2.03. 8 P
hang me in a bottle like a cat, and shoot at me, ADO 1.01.257 P
what though care kill'd a cat, thou hast mettle 5.01.133 P
play ercles rarely, or a part to tear a cat in, MND 1.02. 30 P
be it ounce, or cat, or bear, | pard, or boar 2.02. 30
hang off, thou cat, thou bur! 3.02.260
some that are mad if they behold a cat; MV 4.01. 48
why he, a harmless necessary cat; 4.01. 55
than tar, the very uncleanly flux of a cat. AYL 3.02. 68 P
if the cat will after kind, | so be sure will 3.02.103
have no more eyes to see withal than a cat. SHR 1.02.115 P
i could endure any thing before but a cat, and AWW 4.03.237 P
before but a cat, and now he's a cat to me. 4.03.238 P
a pox upon him for me, he's more and more a cat. 4.03.264 P
a pox on him, he's a cat still. 4.03.275 P
sir, or of fortune's cat — but not a musk–cat 5.02. 19 P
am as melancholy as a gib cat or a lugg'd bear. 1H4 1.02. 74 P
at the same season if your mother's cat had 3.01. 18
raven, | a couching lion and a ramping cat, 3.01.151
me, i am as vigilant as a cat to steal cream. 4.02. 58 P
eggs, | playing the mouse in absence of the cat, H5 1.02.172
it follows then the cat must stay at home, | yet 1.02.174
to be a /dog, a moile, a cat, a fitchook, a toad TRO 5.01. 61 P
mouse ne'er shunn'd the cat as they did budge COR 1.06. 44
rat, a mouse, a cat, to scratch a man to death! ROM 3.01.101 P
lives, and every cat and dog | and little mouse, 3.03. 30
"i would," | like the poor cat i' th' adage? MAC 1.07. 45
thrice the brinded cat hath mew'd. 4.01. 1
the cat will mew, and dog will have his day. HAM 5.01.292
no hide, the sheep no wool, the cat no perfume. LR 3.04.105 P
the cat, with eyne of burning coal, | now PER 3.ch. 5
yet, foul night–waking cat, he doth but dally, LUC 554
CATAIAN 2 FR 0.0002 REL FR 0 V 2 P
i will not believe such a cataian, though the WIV 2.01.144 P
my lady's a cataian, we are politicians, TN 2.03. 75 P
CATALOGUE 4 FR 0.0004 REL FR 3 V 1 P
and put you in the catalogue of those | that AWW 1.03.143
have you a catalogue | of all the voices that we COR 3.03. 8
ay, in the catalogue ye go for men, | as hounds MAC 3.01. 91
though the catalogue of his endowments had been CYM 1.04. 5 P
CAT–A–MOUNTAIN 1 FR 0.0001 REL FR 0 V 1 P
ensconce your rags, your cat–a–mountain looks, WIV 2.02. 26 P
CATAPLASM 1 FR 0.0001 REL FR 1 V 0 P
where it draws blood, no cataplasm so rare, HAM 4.07.143
CATARACTS 1 FR 0.0001 REL FR 1 V 0 P
you cataracts and hurricanoes, spout | till you LR 3.02. 2
/CATARRHS 1 FR 0.0001 REL FR 0 V 1 P
ruptures, /catarrhs, loads a' gravel in the back TRO 5.01. 19 P
CATASTROPHE 4 FR 0.0004 REL FR 1 V 3 P
the catastrophe is a nuptial; LLL 4.01. 77 P
began, | on the catastrophe and heel of pastime, AWW 1.02. 57
i'll tickle your catastrophe. 2H4 2.01. 60 P
he comes like the catastrophe of the old comedy. LR 1.02.134 P
/CATCH 1 FR 0.0001 REL FR 1 V 0 P
/with /eyeless /rage | /catch /in /their /fury, LR 3.01. 9
CATCH 73 FR 0.0082 REL FR 55 V 18 P
will you troll the catch | you taught me but TMP 3.02.117
this is the tune of our catch, play'd by the 3.02.126 P
it hither, | for stale to catch these thieves. 4.01.187
that shall catch | your royal fleet far off. 5.01.316
o cunning enemy, that, to catch a saint, | with MM 2.02.179
whence he came, lest he catch cold on 's feet. ERR 3.01. 37
for every object that the one doth catch | the LLL 2.01. 70
/yours /would i catch, fair hermia, ere i go; MND 1.01.187
my ear should catch your voice, my eye your eye, 1.01.188
my tongue should catch your tongue's sweet 1.01.189
mild hind | makes speed to catch the tiger — 2.01.233
some hats, from yielders all things catch. 3.02. 30
if i can catch him once upon the hip, | i will MV 1.03. 46
here, catch this casket, it is worth the pains. 2.06. 33
to catch the strong fellow by the leg. AYL 1.02.211 P
paths, our very petticoats will catch them. 1.03. 15 P
too light for such a swain as you to catch, SHR 2.01.204
no doubt but he hath got a quiet catch. 2.01.331
even so quickly may one catch the plague? TN 1.05.295
welcome, ass. now let's have a catch. 2.03. 18 P
the night–owl in a catch that will draw three 2.03. 58 P
i am dog at a catch. 2.03. 61 P
by'r lady, sir, and some dogs will catch well. 2.03. 62 P
most certain. let our catch be "thou knave." 2.03. 63 P
night, | and have is have, however men do catch. JN 1.01.173
you, | and 'a may catch your hide and you alone. 2.01.136
i'll smoke your skin–coat and i catch you right. 2.01.139
up gadshill in the night to catch my horse, if i 1H4 3.03. 38 P
we catch of you, doll, we catch of you. 2H4 2.04. 45 P
we catch of you, doll, we catch of you. 2.04. 46 P
and pretty traps to catch the petty thieves. H5 1.02.177
and so i shall catch the fly, your cousin, in 5.02.313 P
makes him gasp, and stare, and catch the air, 2H6 3.02.371
like lime–twigs set to catch my winged soul. 3.03. 16
closer or, good faith, you'll catch a blow. 3H6 3.02. 23
torment myself to catch the english crown; 3.02.179
came, | ready to catch each other by the throat, R3 1.03.188
our swift–winged souls may catch the king's, 2.02. 44
and am right glad to catch this good occasion H8 5.01.109
hector shall have a great catch, and /'a knock TRO 2.01.100 P
since things in motion sooner catch the eye 3.03.183
you will catch cold and curse me. 4.02. 15
i with great truth catch mere simplicity; 4.04.104
think'st thou to catch my life so pleasantly 4.05.249
us, yet sought | the very way to catch them. COR 3.01. 80
happily you may catch her in the sea; TIT 4.03. 8
to catch my death with jauncing up and down! ROM 2.05. 52
a noble nature | may catch a wrench — would all TIM 2.02.209
consumption catch thee! 4.03.201
i will fear to catch it, and give way. 4.03.352 P
the plague, | could i but catch it for them. 5.01.138
of human kindness | to catch the nearest way. MAC 1.05. 18
the consequence, and catch | with his surcease, 1.07. 3
profound, | i'll catch it ere it come to ground; 3.05. 25
ay, springes to catch woodcocks. HAM 1.03.115
wherein i'll catch the conscience of the king. 2.02.605
as the wind sits, thou'lt catch cold shortly. LR 1.04.101 P
perdition catch my soul, | but i do love thee! OTH 3.03. 90
you may be pleas'd to catch at mine intent | by ANT 2.02. 41
but i'll catch thine eyes | though they had 5.02.156
saucy lictors | will catch at us like strumpets, 5.02.215
as she would catch another antony | in her 5.02.347
lest the bargain should catch cold and starve. CYM 1.04.166 P
canst thou catch any fishes then? PER 2.01. 66 P
him lead his line | to catch one at my heart. TNK 1.01.117
this will catch her attention, for this her mind 4.03. 78 P
thy flame — at seventy thou canst catch, | and 5.01. 87
some catch her by the neck, some kiss her face, VEN 872
dove sleeps fast that this night–owl will catch; LUC 360
nor his own vision holds what it doth catch; SON 113. 8
lo as a careful huswife runs to catch | one of 143. 1
cries to catch her whose busy care is bent | to 143. 6
but if thou catch thy hope, turn back to me, 143.11
CATCH'D 4 FR 0.0004 REL FR 3 V 1 P
are so surely caught, when they are catch'd, LLL 5.02. 69
my fear hath catch'd your fondness! AWW 1.03.170
catch'd it again: COR 1.03. 63 P
and cruel death hath catch'd it from my sight! ROM 4.05. 48
CATCHES 4 FR 0.0004 REL FR 1 V 3 P
as quick as the greyhound's mouth — it catches. ADO 5.02. 12 P
which runs himself, and catches for his master. SHR 5.02. 53
out your coziers' catches without any mitigation TN 2.03. 90 P
we did keep time, sir, in our catches. sneck up! 2.03. 93 P
CATCHING 11 FR 0.0012 REL FR 9 V 2 P
yet here they shall not lie, for catching cold. TGV 1.02.133
there's goodly catching of cold. ADO 3.04. 66 P
sickness is catching; MND 1.01.186
'tis catching hither, even to our camp. 1H4 4.01. 30
physic, their diseases | are grown so catching. H8 1.03. 37
lest his infection, being of catching nature, COR 3.01.308
passion, i see, is catching, /for mine eyes, JC 3.01.283
cleopatra, catching but the least noise of this, ANT 1.02.140 P
which is not catching | where there is faith? TNK 1.02. 45
jealous of catching, swiftly doth forsake him, VEN 321
catching all passions in his craft of will, LC 126
CATECHISING 1 FR 0.0001 REL FR 1 V 0 P
what kind of catechising call you this? ADO 4.01. 78
CATECHISM 2 FR 0.0002 REL FR 0 V 2 P
is more than to answer in a catechism. AYL 3.02.228 P
and so ends my catechism. 1H4 5.01.141 P
CATECHIZE 3 FR 0.0003 REL FR 1 V 2 P
i must catechize you for it, madonna. TN 1.05. 62 P
and catechize | my picked man of countries. JN 1.01.192
i will catechize the world for him, that is, OTH 3.04. 16 P
CATE–LOG 1 FR 0.0001 REL FR 0 V 1 P
here is the cate–log of her condition. TGV 3.01.274 P
CATER–COUSINS 1 FR 0.0001 REL FR 0 V 1 P
worship's reverence) are scarce cater–cousins — MV 2.02.131 P
CATERPILLAR 1 FR 0.0001 REL FR 1 V 0 P
god | for every graff would send a caterpillar, PER 5.01. 60
CATERPILLARS 6 FR 0.0006 REL FR 5 V 1 P
the caterpillars of the commonwealth, | which i R2 2.03.166
wholesome herbs | swarming with caterpillars? 3.04. 47
ah, whoreson caterpillars! 1H4 2.02. 84 P
the bud, | and caterpillars eat my leaves away; 2H6 3.01. 90
they call false caterpillars, and intend their 4.04. 37
as caterpillars do the tender leaves. VEN 798
CATERS 1 FR 0.0001 REL FR 1 V 0 P
feed, | yea, providently caters for the sparrow, AYL 2.03. 44
CATERWAULING 2 FR 0.0002 REL FR 1 V 1 P
what a caterwauling do you keep here! TN 2.03. 72 P
why, what a caterwauling dost thou keep! TIT 4.02. 57
CATES 4 FR 0.0004 REL FR 4 V 0 P
but though my cates be mean, take them in good ERR 3.01. 28
than feed on cates and have him talk to me | in 1H4 3.01.161
taste of your wine and see what cates you have, 1H6 2.03. 79
these cates resist me, he not thought upon. PER 2.03. 29
CATESBY 23 FR 0.0026 REL FR 23 V 0 P
catesby, i come. lords, will you go with me? R3 1.03.321
come hither, catesby. 3.01.157
go, gentle catesby, | and, as it were far off, 3.01.169
tell him, catesby, | his ancient knot of 3.01.181
good catesby, go effect this business soundly. 3.01.186
shall we hear from you, catesby, ere we sleep? 3.01.188
and at the other is my good friend catesby; 3.02. 22
good morrow, catesby, you are early stirring. 3.02. 36
well, catesby, ere a fortnight make me older, 3.02. 60
my lord, good morrow, good morrow, catesby. 3.02. 74
catesby hath sounded hastings in our business, 3.04. 36
but what, is catesby gone? 3.05. 12
catesby, o'erlook the walls. 3.05. 17
for yesternight by catesby was it sent me; 3.06. 6
now, catesby, what says your lord to my request? 3.07. 58
return, good catesby, to the gracious duke, 3.07. 65
here catesby comes again. 3.07. 82
now, catesby, what says his grace? 3.07. 83
come hither, catesby. 4.02. 50
ratcliffe, thyself — or catesby — where is he? 4.04.441
catesby, fly to the duke. 4.04.442
o, true, good catesby. 4.04.449
catesby! 5.03. 58
CATHEDRAL 1 FR 0.0001 REL FR 1 V 0 P
in the cathedral church of westminster, | and in 2H6 1.02. 37
CAT–LIKE 1 FR 0.0001 REL FR 1 V 0 P
couching, head on ground, with cat–like watch, AYL 4.03.115
CATLING 1 FR 0.0001 REL FR 0 V 1 P
what say you, simon catling? ROM 4.05.130 P
CATLINGS 1 FR 0.0001 REL FR 0 V 1 P
apollo get his sinews to make catlings on. TRO 3.03.304 P
CATO 5 FR 0.0005 REL FR 5 V 0 P
by which i did blame cato for the death | which JC 5.01.101
and come, young cato, let us to the field. 5.03.107
i am the son of marcus cato, ho! 5.04. 4
i am the son of marcus cato, ho! 5.04. 6
o young and noble cato, art thou down? 5.04. 9
/CATO'S 1 FR 0.0001 REL FR 1 V 0 P
thou wast a soldier | even to /cato's wish, not COR 1.04. 57
CATO'S 3 FR 0.0003 REL FR 3 V 0 P
nothing undervalu'd | to cato's daughter, MV 1.01.166
withal | a woman well reputed, cato's daughter. JC 2.01.295
and mayst be honor'd, being cato's son. 5.04. 11
CATS 6 FR 0.0006 REL FR 3 V 3 P
cats, that can judge as fitly of his worth | as COR 4.02. 34
more than prince of cats. ROM 2.04. 19 P
good king of cats, nothing but one of your nine 3.01. 77 P
drown cats and blind puppies! OTH 1.03.336 P
first, perchance, she'll prove on cats and dogs, CYM 1.05. 38
creatures vild, as cats and dogs | of no esteem. 5.05.252
CATTLE 5 FR 0.0005 REL FR 3 V 2 P
there he blasts the tree, and takes the cattle, WIV 4.04. 32
to get your living by the copulation of cattle; AYL 3.02. 80 P
are for the most part cattle of this color; 3.02.415 P
make poor men's cattle break their necks, | set TIT 5.01.132
a reverend man that graz'd his cattle nigh, LC 57
CAUCASUS 2 FR 0.0002 REL FR 2 V 0 P
his hand | by thinking on the frosty caucasus? R2 1.03.295
eyes | than is prometheus tied to caucasus. TIT 2.01. 17
/CAUDLE 1 FR 0.0001 REL FR 0 V 1 P
ye shall have a hempen /caudle then, and the 2H6 4.07. 90 P
CAUDLE 2 FR 0.0002 REL FR 2 V 0 P
a caudle ho! LLL 4.03.172
with ice, caudle thy morning taste | to cure thy TIM 4.03.226
CAU'DRON *(also cauldron)*
CAU'DRON 1 FR 0.0001 REL FR 1 V 0 P
chawdron, | for th' ingredience of our cau'dron. MAC 4.01. 34
CAUF *(also calf*)*
CAUF 1 FR 0.0001 REL FR 0 V 1 P
he clepeth a calf, "cauf"; LLL 5.01. 22 P
CAUGHT 32 FR 0.0036 REL FR 24 V 8 P
"have i caught thee, my heavenly jewel?" WIV 3.03. 43
he is sooner caught than the pestilence, and the ADO 1.01. 87 P
if he have caught the benedick, it will cost him 1.01. 89 P
we have caught her, madam. 3.01.104
none are so surely caught, when they are catch'd LLL 5.02. 69
have the plague, and caught it of your eyes. 5.02.421
but how i caught it, found it, or came by it, MV 1.01. 3
that thou with license of free foot hast caught, AYL 2.07. 68
therefore fire, for i have caught extreme cold. SHR 4.01. 44 P
i must go look my twigs. he shall be caught. AWW 3.06.107
we have caught the woodcock, and will keep him 4.01. 90
the trout that must be caught with tickling. TN 2.05. 22 P
and it is caught | of you that yet are well. WT 1.02.386
how caught of me? 1.02.387
a sickness caught of me, and yet i well? 1.02.398
for most it caught me, the celestial habits 3.01. 4
mine eyes (caught the water though not the fish) 5.02. 83 P
sir, which i caught with ringing in the king's 2H4 3.02.182 P
wise bearing or ignorant carriage is caught, as 5.01. 76 P
eye | where my poor young was lim'd, was caught, 3H6 5.06. 17
are so mingled | that they have caught the king; H8 2.03. 77
after a gilded butterfly, and when he caught it, COR 1.03. 61 P
will or exceed the common or be caught | with 4.01. 32
h'as caught me in his eye, i will present | my TIM 4.03.469
a blanket, in the alarm of fear caught up — HAM 2.02.509
till i have caught her once more in mine arms. 5.01.250
a fox, when one has caught her, | and such a LR 1.04.317
have i caught thee? 5.03. 21
thus credulous fools are caught, | and many OTH 4.01. 45
y' are caught." ANT 2.05. 15
when you caught hurt in parting two that fought; PER 4.01. 87
now quick desire hath caught the yielding prey, VEN 547
CAULDRON *(also cau'dron)*
CAULDRON 8 FR 0.0009 REL FR 7 V 1 P
round about the cauldron go; MAC 4.01. 4
fire burn, and cauldron bubble. 4.01. 11
a fenny snake, | in the cauldron boil and bake; 4.01. 13
fire burn, and cauldron bubble. 4.01. 21
fire burn, and cauldron bubble. 4.01. 36
and now about the cauldron sing, | like elves 4.01. 41
why sinks that cauldron? 4.01.106
we be put in a cauldron of lead and usurers' TNK 4.03. 36 P
CAULK'D 2 FR 0.0002 REL FR 1 V 1 P
beneath the hatches, caulk'd and bitum'd ready. PER 3.01. 71 P
how close 'tis caulk'd and /bitum'd it. 3.02. 56
CAUS'D 11 FR 0.0012 REL FR 9 V 2 P
sea | hath caus'd to belch up you; TMP 3.03. 56
hath caus'd his death, the which if wrongfully, R2 1.02. 39
hath caus'd every soldier to cut his prisoner's H5 4.07. 9 P
the tally, thou hast caus'd printing to be us'd, 2H6 4.07. 36 P
have caus'd him, by new act of parliament, | to 3H6 2.02. 91
you cannot guess who caus'd your father's death. R3 2.02. 19
you have caus'd | your holy hat to be stamp'd on H8 3.02.324
that letter | i caus'd you write yet sent away? 4.02.128
lord, and that it was which caus'd | our swifter COR 3.01. 2
your plight is pitied | of him that caus'd it. ANT 5.02. 34
that caus'd a lesser villain than myself, | a CYM 5.05.219
'CAUSE *(also because)*
'CAUSE 2 FR 0.0002 REL FR 2 V 0 P
'cause they take vengeance of such kind of men. TIT 5.02. 63
and 'cause he fail'd | his presence at the MAC 3.06. 21
/CAUSE 9 FR 0.0010 REL FR 9 V 0 P

/that /not /only /giv'st | /me /cause /to /wail, R2 4.01.301
/me /the /way | /how /to /lament /the /cause. 4.01.302
/from /heaven /his /quarrel /and /his /cause; 2H4 1.01.206
/the /instant /action, /a /cause /on /foot — 1.03. 37
with all your just proceedings in this /cause. R3 3.05. 66
now judge what /cause had titus to revenge TIT 5.03.125
/for /by /the /image /of /my /cause /i /see HAM 5.02. 77
/sorrow | /the /king /hath /cause /to /plain. LR 3.01. 39
/some /dear /cause | /will /in /concealment 4.03. 51

CAUSE 354 FR 0.0400 REL FR 301 V 53 P

you have cause | (so have we all) of joy; TMP 2.01. 1
eye, | who hath cause to wet the grief on't. 2.01.128
merciful, | i have curs'd them without cause. 5.01.179
and that's her cause of sorrow. TGV 4.04.147
ork upon the cause with as great discreetly as WIV 1.01.146 P
far from jealousy as i am from giving him cause, 2.01.104 P
husband, to give him such cause of suspicion! 3.03.101 P
what cause of suspicion? 3.03.102 P
what cause of suspicion? 3.03.103 P
if i suspect without cause, why then make sport 3.03.150 P
i suspect without cause, mistress, do i? 4.02.132 P
elbow's wife, that he hath cause to complain of? MM 2.01.117 P
and leave you to the hearing of the cause, 2.01.136
hoping you'll find good cause to whip them all. 2.01.137
he's hearing of a cause; 2.02. 1
i believe i know the cause of his withdrawing. 3.02.131 P
what, i prithee, might be the cause? 3.02.133 P
forbear it therefore, give your cause to heaven. 4.03.124
her cause and yours | i'll perfect him withal, 4.03.140
from this to that, | as cause doth minister. 4.05. 6
be you judge | of your own cause. 5.01.167
i would he had some cause | to prattle for 5.01.181
then is your cause gone too. 5.01.300
say in brief the cause | why thou departedst ERR 1.01. 28
and for what cause thou cam'st to ephesus. 1.01. 30
they can be meek that have no other cause: 2.01. 33
plead on /her part some cause to you unknown; 3.01. 91
upon what cause? 5.01.123
i must be sad when i have cause, and smile at no ADO 1.03. 14 P
i am sorry for her, as i have just cause, being 2.03.166 P
if it should give your age such cause of fear. 5.01. 56
boast | before the birds have any cause to sing? LLL 1.01.103
as the style shall give us cause to climb in the 1.01.199 P
the first and second cause will not serve my 1.02.178 P
we cannot cross the cause why we were born; 4.03.214
so much i hate a breaking cause to be | of 5.02.355
if for my love (as there is no such cause) | you 5.02.792
auditor, | an actor too perhaps, if i see cause. MND 3.01. 80
for thou, i fear, hast given me cause to curse. 3.02. 46
noise they make | will cause demetrius to awake. 3.02.117
jew, having done me wrong, doth cause me, as my MV 2.02.133 P
thou call'dst me dog before thou hadst a cause, 3.03. 6
him with the cause in controversy between the 4.01.155 P
i am informed throughly of the cause. 4.01.173
you give your wife too unkind a cause of grief; 5.01.175
i have more cause. AYL 1.03. 93
and that a great cause of the night is lack of 3.02. 28 P
but have i not cause to weep? 3.04. 4 P
as good cause as one would desire, therefore 3.04. 5 P
have more cause to hate him than to love him, 3.05.128
found the quarrel was upon the seventh cause. 5.04. 50 P
how seventh cause? 5.04. 51 P
but for the seventh cause — how did you find 5.04. 66 P
did you find the quarrel on the seventh cause? 5.04. 67 P
this be not a lawful cause for me to leave his SHR 1.02. 29 P
i be so bold to know the cause of your coming? 2.01. 87 P
far | to know the cause why music was ordain'd! 3.01. 10
faith, mistress, then i have no cause to stay. 3.01. 86
but i have cause to pry into this pedant. 3.01. 87
know you not the cause? 4.02. 82
made me acquainted with a weighty cause | of 4.04. 26
lord, let me never have a cause to sigh, | till 5.02.123
"was this fair face the cause," quoth she, AWW 1.03. 70
with that malignant cause wherein the honor | of 2.01.111
not, i am the cause | his death was so effected. 3.02.115
alas, /our frailty is the cause, not we! TN 2.02. 31
him will my revenge find notable cause to work. 2.03.153 P
for that i woo, thou therefore hast no cause; 3.01.154
you drew your sword upon me without cause, | but 5.01.188
plaintiff and the judge | of thine own cause. 5.01.355
him that has most cause to grieve it should be) WT 2.01. 77
do not weep, good fools, | there is no cause. 2.01.119
if | the cause were not in being — part o' th' 2.03. 3
cause were not in being — part o' th' cause, 2.03. 3
such as you | nourish the cause of his awaking. 2.03. 36
not uneasy to get the cause of my son's resort 4.02. 50 P
now jove afford you cause! 4.04. 16
had she such power, | she had just cause. 5.01. 61
let him that was the cause of this have pow'r 5.03. 54
that give you cause to prove my saying true. JN 3.01. 28
you shall have no cause | to curse the fair 3.01. 96
good friend, thou hast no cause to say so yet, 3.03. 30
such temperate order in so fierce a cause, 3.04. 12
but they will pluck away his natural cause | and 3.04.156
i had a mighty cause | to wish him dead, but 4.02.205
weep | upon the spot of this enforced cause — 5.02. 30
and put his cause and quarrel | to the disposing 5.07. 91
us, | as well appeareth by the cause you come: R2 1.01. 26
can arbitrate this cause betwixt us twain; 1.01. 50
the cause of his arrival here in arms; 1.03. 8
to swear him in the justice of his cause. 1.03. 10
law, | depose him in the justice of his cause. 1.03. 30
cousin of herford, as thy cause is right, | so 1.03. 55
god in thy good cause make thee prosperous! 1.03. 78
had i thy youth and cause, i would not stay. 1.03.305
yet i know no cause | why i should welcome such 2.02. 6
'tis well that thou hast cause, | but thou 3.04. 19
that thou wert cause of noble gloucester's death 4.01. 37
thy revengeful hand, thou hast no cause to fear. 5.03. 42
and for this cause a while we must neglect | our 1H4 1.01.101
and breed a kind of question in our cause. 4.01. 68
want | such water-colors to impaint his cause, 5.01. 80
and god befriend us, as our cause is just! 5.01.120
myself, but the cause that wit is in other men. 2H4 1.02. 10 P
i have read the cause of his effects in galen, 1.02.116 P
have you heard our cause and known our means, 1.03. 1
it was young hotspur's cause at shrewsbury. 1.03. 26
of wrenching the true cause the false way. 2.01.110 P
our armor all as strong, our cause the best; 4.01.154
all members of our cause, both here and hence, 4.01.169
that every slight and false-derived cause, | yea 4.01.188
your majesty hath no just cause to hate me. 5.02. 66
no prince nor peer shall have just cause to say, 5.02.144
turn him to any cause of policy, | the gordian H5 1.01. 45
they know your grace hath cause, and means, and 1.02.125
that shall have cause to curse the dolphin's 1.02.288
my rightful hand in a well-hallow'd cause. 1.02.293
we therefore have great cause of thankfulness, 2.02. 32
working so grossly in /a natural cause | that 2.02.107
what is't to me, when you yourselves are cause, 3.03. 19
but we have no great cause to desire the 4.01. 87 P
his cause being just and his quarrel honorable. 4.01.127 P
if his cause be wrong, our obedience to the king 4.01.132 P
but if the cause be not good, the king himself 4.01.134 P
is no king, be his cause never so spotless, if 4.01.159 P
much more, and much more cause, | did they this 5.pr. 34
these news would cause him once more yield the 1H6 1.01. 67
to know the cause of your abrupt departure. 2.03. 30
and for that cause i train'd thee to my house. 2.03. 35
alliance sake, declare the cause | my father, 2.05. 53
that cause, fair nephew, that imprison'd me 2.05. 55
discover more at large what cause that was, 2.05. 59
"i have, upon especial cause, | mov'd with 4.01. 55
when for so slight and frivolous a cause | such 4.01.112
quite to forget this quarrel, and the cause. 4.01.136
can, | but curse the cause i cannot aid the man. 4.03. 44
sweet madam, give me hearing in a cause. 5.03.106
and so says york — for he hath greatest cause. 2H6 1.01.207
with thy confederates in this weighty cause. 1.02. 86
as i was cause | your highness came to england, 1.03. 65
injurious duke, that threatest where's no cause. 1.04. 48
and poise the cause in justice' equal scales, 2.01.200
beam stands sure, whose rightful cause prevails. 2.01.201
what counsel give you in this weighty cause? 3.01.289
thou shalt have cause to fear before i leave 4.01.118
only for that cause they have been most worthy 4.07. 45 P
the cause why i have brought this army hither 5.01. 35
then let me die, for now thou hast no cause. 3H6 1.03. 45
no cause? 1.03. 46
i cheer'd them up with justice of our cause, 2.01.133
from such a cause as fills mine eyes with tears 3.03. 13
this is the cause that i, poor margaret, | with 3.03. 30
suppose they take offense without a cause; 4.01. 14
and hastings as he favors edward's cause! 4.01.144
upon what cause? R3 1.01. 46
thanks | that were the cause of my imprisonment. 1.01.128
thou wast the cause, and most accurs'd effect. 1.02.120
your beauty was the cause of that effect — 1.02.121
to him that hath most cause to be a mourner, 1.02.211
god pardon them that are the cause thereof! 1.03.314
o, what cause have i | (thine being but a moi'ty 2.02. 59
all of us have cause | to wail the dimming of 2.02.101
you have no cause. 2.04. 68
and they indeed had no cause to mistrust; 3.02. 85
the cause why we are met | is to determine of 3.04. 1
in this just cause come i to move your grace. 3.07.140
ah, who hath any cause to mourn but we? 4.04. 34
though far more cause, yet much less spirit to 4.04.197
you have no cause to hold my friendship doubtful 4.04.492
god and our good cause fight upon our side; 5.03.240
the cause | he may a little grieve at. H8 2.01. 38
what's the cause? 2.02. 15
what cause | hath my behavior given to your 2.04. 19
land, who are assembled | to plead your cause. 2.04. 61
to bring my whole cause 'fore his holiness, 2.04.120
shall give you | the full cause of our coming. 3.01. 29
a strange tongue makes my cause more strange, 3.01. 45
our just opinions | and comforts to /your cause. 3.01. 61
let me have time and counsel for my cause. 3.01. 79
put your main cause into the king's protection, 3.01. 93
both for your honor better and your cause; 3.01. 95
put my sick cause into his hands that hates me? 3.01.118
we, good lady, | upon what cause, wrong you? 3.01.156
has left the cause o' th' king unhandled, and 3.02. 58
and not wholesome to | our cause, that she 3.02.100
yoke together | (as i will lend you cause) my 3.02.151
his noble jury and foul cause can witness. 3.02.269
cause the musicians play me that sad note | i 4.02. 78
the chief cause concerns his grace of canterbury 5.02. 38
i take my cause | out of the gripes of cruel men 5.02.134
the cause betwixt her and this great offender. 5.02.156
what was his cause of anger? TRO 1.02. 11
he is melancholy without cause, and merry 1.02. 26 P
i know the cause too. 1.02. 55 P
nor fear of bad success in a bad cause, | can 2.02.117
and on the cause and question now in hand | have 2.02.164
for 'tis a cause that hath no mean dependance 2.02.192
let him show us a cause. 2.03. 89 P
wars since you refus'd | the grecians' cause. 4.05.268
that cause sets up, with and against itself, 5.02.143
in some other fight, | as cause will be obey'd. COR 1.06. 83
wholesome forenoon in hearing a cause between an 2.01. 70 P
you make in their cause is calling both the 2.01. 78 P
he has more cause to be proud. 2.01.146 P
with the least cause these his new honors, which 2.01.229
you know the cause, sir, of my standing here. 2.03. 62
as cause had call'd you up, have held him to; 2.03.194
i wish i had a cause to seek him there, | to 3.01. 19
all cause unborn, could never be the native | of 3.01.129
where /one part does disdain with cause, the 3.01.143
leave us to cure this cause. 3.01.234
and power i' th' truth a' th' cause. 3.03. 18
the time thrust forth | a cause for thy repeal, 4.01. 41
them home, | and, by my troth, you have cause. 4.02. 49
sir, i have the most cause to be glad of yours. 4.03. 51 P
what cause do you think i have to swound? 5.02.100 P
you, and pray you | stand to me in this cause. 5.03.199
we have all | great cause to give great thanks. 5.04. 60
defend the justice of my cause with arms; TIT 1.01. 2
since first he undertook | this cause of rome, 1.01. 32
commit my cause in balance to be weigh'd. 1.01. 55
commit myself, my person, and the cause. 1.01. 59
for valiant doings in their country's cause? 1.01.113
nest, | that died in honor and lavinia's cause. 1.01.377
he lives in fame, that died in virtue's cause. 1.01.390
the cause were known to them it most concerns, 2.01. 50
and 'twere my cause, i should go hang myself. 2.04. 9
rome never had more cause. 4.04. 62
and what not done, that thou hast cause to rue, 5.01.109
and have a thousand times more cause than he 5.03. 51
unless good counsel may the cause remove. ROM 1.01.142
my noble uncle, do you know the cause? 1.01.143
very first house, of the first and second cause. 2.04. 25 P
what unaccustom'd cause procures her hither? 3.05. 67
watch'd ere now | all night for lesser cause, 4.04. 10
it is a cause worthy my spleen and fury, | that TIM 3.05.112
ay, timon, and have cause. 4.03.103
his fellowship i' th' cause against your city, 5.02. 12
ere thou hadst power or we had cause of fear, 5.04. 15
but if you would consider the true cause | why JC 1.03. 62
i know no personal cause to spurn at him, | but 2.01. 11
what need we any spur but our own cause | to 2.01.123
to think that or our cause or our performance 2.01.135
make me acquainted with your cause of grief. 2.01.256
most mighty caesar, let me know some cause, 2.02. 69
the cause is in my will, i will not come: 2.02. 71
wrong, nor without cause | will he be satisfied. 3.01. 47
and then we will deliver you the cause | why i, 3.01.181
and lovers, hear me for my cause, and be silent, 3.02. 13 P
you all did love him once, not without cause; 3.02.102
what cause withholds you then to mourn for him? 3.02.103
hath given me some worthy cause to wish | things 4.02. 8
our legions are brimful, our cause is ripe: 4.03.215
come, come, the cause. 5.01. 48
when therewithal we shall have cause of state MAC 3.01. 33
the general cause? 4.03.196
he cannot buckle his distemper'd cause | within 5.02. 15
your cause of sorrow | must not be measur'd by 5.09. 10
have found | the very cause of hamlet's lunacy. HAM 2.02. 49
that we find out the cause of this effect, | or 2.02.101
or rather say, the cause of this defect, | for 2.02.102
for this effect defective comes by cause: 2.02.103
like john-a-dreams, unpregnant of my cause, 2.02.568
but from what cause 'a will by no means speak. 3.01. 6
that your good beauties be the happy cause | of 3.01. 38
good my lord, what is your cause of distemper? 3.02.337 P
his form and cause conjoin'd, preaching to 3.04.126
and shows no cause without | why the man dies. 4.04. 28
thing's to do," | sith i have cause, and will, 4.04. 45
plot | whereon the numbers cannot try the cause, 4.04. 63
what is the cause, laertes, | that thy rebellion 4.05.121
report me and my cause aright | to the 5.02.339
of deaths put on by cunning and /forc'd cause, 5.02.383
of that i shall have also cause to speak, | and 5.02.391
beweep this cause again, i'll pluck ye out, LR 1.04.302
if you yourselves are old, | make it your cause; 2.04.192
i have full cause of weeping, but this heart 2.04.284
what is the cause of thunder? 3.04.155
is there any cause in nature that make these 3.06. 77 P
what was thy cause? 4.06.109
though that the queen on special cause is here, 4.06.215
you have some cause, they have not. 4.07. 74
no cause, no cause. 4.07. 74
no cause, no cause. 4.07. 74
mine's not an idle cause. OTH 1.02. 95
and therefore little shall i grace my cause | in 1.03. 88
my cause is hearted; 1.03.366 P
you have little cause to say so. 2.01.108
even out of that will i cause these of cyprus to 2.01.274 P
grieves my husband | as if the cause were his. 3.03. 4
shall rather die | than give thy cause away. 3.03. 28
my fears | (as worthy cause i have to fear i am) 3.03.254
but, sith i am ent'red in this cause so far 3.03.411
alas the day, i never gave him cause. 3.04.158
they are not ever jealious for the cause, | but 3.04.160
to the felt absence now i feel a cause. 3.04.182
it is the cause, it is the cause, my soul. 5.02. 1
it is the cause, it is the cause, my soul. 5.02. 1
it to you, you chaste stars, | it is the cause. 5.02. 3
dear general, i never gave you cause. 5.02.299
between them and a great cause, they should be ANT 1.02.139 P
the cause of our expedience to the queen, | and 1.02.178
for they have entertained cause enough | to draw 2.01. 46
against my stomach, | having alike your cause? 2.02. 51
i, | your partner in the cause 'gainst which he 2.02. 59
we have cause to be glad that matters are so 2.02.175 P
since i myself | have given myself the cause. 2.05. 84
the least cause | for what you seem to fear. 3.02. 35
you have not call'd me so, nor have you cause. 3.06. 41
by my affection, would | obey it on all cause. 3.11. 68
for i have savage cause, | and to proclaim it 3.13.128
say that i wish he never find more cause | to 4.05. 15
and have fought | not as you serv'd the cause, 4.08. 6
proportion'd to our cause, must be as great | as 4.15. 5
further than you shall | find cause in caesar. 5.02. 64
i cannot project mine own cause so well | to 5.02.121
lest i give cause | to be suspected of more CYM 1.01. 93
your cause doth strike my heart | with pity that 1.06.118
thou mayst be valiant in a better cause, | but 3.04. 72
but it honors us | that we have given him cause. 3.05. 19
wherein i should have cause to use thee with a 3.05.111 P
defect of judgment | is oft the cause of fear. 4.02.112
that striking in our country's cause | fell 5.04. 71
to the judgment of your eye | i give my cause, PER 1.ch. 42
royal antiochus, on what cause i know not, 1.03. 19
or, dead, give 's cause to mourn his funeral, 2.04. 32
try honor's cause; 2.04. 41
i came unto your court for honor's cause, | and 2.05. 61
that is the cause we trouble you so early, 3.02. 19
that we have, | cause it to sound, beseech you. 3.02. 89
let me entreat to know at large the cause | of 5.01. 62
o, help now! | our cause cries for your knee. TNK 1.01.200
the cause i know not yet. 2.02.222
makes morris, and the cause that we came hither. 3.05.120
i'll give you cause, sweet cousin. 3.06. 69
my cause and honor guard me! 3.06. 92
i know your cunning, and i know your cause. 3.06.120
may fairly carry | our swords and cause along; 3.06.260
for, and so apter | to make this cause his own. 4.02. 98
i wish it, | but not the cause, my lord. 4.02.144
you whose free nobleness do make my cause | your 5.01. 73
i am not bold, | we have no such cause. ep 12
being judge in love, she cannot right her cause. VEN 220

"it shall suspect where is no cause of fear, 1153
"it shall be cause of war and dire events, | and 1159
and give the sneaped birds more cause to sing. LUC 333
have heard the cause of my untimely death, 1178
the other takes in hand | no cause, but company, 1236
the cause craves haste, and it will soon be writ 1295
i weep for thee, and yet no cause i have, | for PP 10. 7
for a sweet content, the cause of all my /moan. 17.34
laws, | since why to love i can allege no cause. SON 49.14
the cause of this fair gift in me is wanting, 87. 7
the more i hear and see just cause of hate? 150.10
CAUSELESS 4 FR 0.0004 REL FR 3 V 1 P
and familiar things supernatural and causeless. AWW 2.03. 3 P
causeless have laid disgraces on my head, | and 2H6 3.01.162
throw my books, and fly — | causeless, perhaps. TIT 4.01. 26
she tells them 'tis a causeless fantasy | and VEN 897
CAUSER 4 FR 0.0004 REL FR 4 V 0 P
eyes, | and study too, the causer of your vow. LLL 4.03.307
is not the causer of the timeless deaths | of R3 1.02.117
bett'ring thy loss makes the bad causer worse; 4.04.122
defying, | heart's denying, causer of this. PP 17. 4
/CAUSES 1 FR 0.0001 REL FR 1 V 0 P
/most /just /and /heavy /causes /make /oppose. LR 5.01. 27
CAUSES 14 FR 0.0015 REL FR 12 V 2 P
there is reasons and causes for it. WIV 3.01. 48 P
forms | all causes to the purpose of his speed, LLL 5.02.741
them shall | the causes of their death appear WT 3.02.237
now, | for suffering so the causes of our wrack. R2 2.01.269
men | i will unfold some causes of your deaths: 3.01. 7
and in regard of causes now in hand, | which i H5 1.01. 77
and now to our french causes. 2.02. 60
is occasions and causes why and wherefore in all 5.01. 3 P
long sitting to determine poor men's causes 2H6 4.07. 88
for a thousand causes | i would prolong a while 3H6 1.04. 51
it, | and so, i say, i'll cut the causes off, 3.02.142
unto bad causes swear | such creatures as men JC 2.01.131
for mine own good | all causes shall give way. MAC 3.04.135
for their dear causes | would to the bleeding 5.02. 3
CAUSEST 1 FR 0.0001 REL FR 1 V 0 P
the evil that thou causest to be done, | that is MM 3.02. 20
CAUSETH 1 FR 0.0001 REL FR 1 V 0 P
in a sense as strong | as that which causeth it. TRO 4.04. 5
CAUTEL 1 FR 0.0001 REL FR 1 V 0 P
and now no soil nor cautel doth besmirch | the HAM 1.03. 15
CAUTELOUS 2 FR 0.0002 REL FR 2 V 0 P
be caught | with cautelous baits and practice. COR 4.01. 33
swear priests and cowards, and men cautelous, JC 2.01.129
CAUTELS 1 FR 0.0001 REL FR 1 V 0 P
applied to cautels, all strange forms receives, LC 303
CAUTERIZING *(see cantherizing)*
CAUTION 6 FR 0.0006 REL FR 6 V 0 P
with caution, that the florentine will move us AWW 1.02. 6
did throng | and press'd in with this caution. H8 2.04.187
but yet my caution was more pertinent | than the COR 2.02. 63
and that well might | advise him to a caution, MAC 3.06. 44
what e'er thou art, for thy good caution, thanks 4.01. 73
and that in way of caution — i must tell you, HAM 1.03. 95
CAUTIONS 1 FR 0.0001 REL FR 1 V 0 P
well inform'd of them, and with such cautions, LR 2.01.102
CAVALEIRO *(also cabileros, cavalery, cavaliers, cavalleria)*
CAVALEIRO 3 FR 0.0003 REL FR 0 V 3 P
cavaleiro justice, i say! WIV 2.01.194 P
tell him, cavaleiro justice; 2.01.198 P
and master page, and eke cavaleiro slender, go 2.03. 74 P
CAVALERY 1 FR 0.0001 REL FR 0 V 1 P
but to help cavalery cobweb to scratch. MND 4.01. 23 P
CAVALIERS 1 FR 0.0001 REL FR 1 V 0 P
cull'd and choice–drawn cavaliers to france? H5 3.pr. 24
CAVALLERIA 1 FR 0.0001 REL FR 0 V 1 P
or she'll disfurnish us of all our cavalleria, PER 4.06. 12 P
CAVE 24 FR 0.0027 REL FR 24 V 0 P
come, i must bring you to our captain's cave. TGV 5.03. 12
slip, | even like an o'ergrown lion in a cave, MM 1.03. 22
of your fortune, | go to my cave and tell me. AYL 2.07.197
love, | who led me instantly unto his cave, 4.03.145
have | i'll stay to know at your abandon'd cave. 5.04.196
as lean–fac'd envy in her loathsome cave. 2H6 3.02.315
fall | into the blind cave of eternal night. R3 5.03. 62
and curtain'd with a counsel–keeping cave, | we TIT 2.03. 24
then which way shall i find revenge's cave? 3.01.270
and cabin in a cave, and bring you up | to be a 4.02.179
there's not a hollow cave or lurking–place, | no 5.02. 35
else would i tear the cave where echo lies, ROM 2.02.161
did ever dragon keep so fair a cave? 3.02. 74
bring us to his cave. TIM 5.01.119
here is his cave. 5.01.126
from alcibiades to timon's cave | with letters 5.02. 10
in this our pinching cave, shall we discourse CYM 3.03. 38
up thus meanly | i' th' cave /wherein /they bow, 3.03. 83
there is cold meat i' th' cave, we'll browse on 3.06. 38
that had a court no bigger than this cave, 3.06. 82
remain here in the cave, | we'll come to you 4.02. 1
be heard at court that such as we | cave here, 4.02.138
shrinks backward in his shelly cave with pain, VEN 1034
grim cave of death! LUC 769
CAVE–KEEPER 1 FR 0.0001 REL FR 1 V 0 P
for so i thought i was a cave–keeper, | and cook CYM 4.02.298
CAVE–KEEPING 1 FR 0.0001 REL FR 1 V 0 P
cave–keeping evils that obscurely sleep. LUC 1250
CAVERN 1 FR 0.0001 REL FR 1 V 0 P
where wilt thou find a cavern dark enough | to JC 2.01. 80
CAVERNS 1 FR 0.0001 REL FR 1 V 0 P
even from the tongueless caverns of the earth, R2 1.01.105
/CAVES 1 FR 0.0001 REL FR 1 V 0 P
and find out /murderers in their guilty /caves; TIT 5.02. 52
CAVES 7 FR 0.0008 REL FR 7 V 0 P
fit for the mountains and the barbarous caves, TN 4.01. 48
of it | that caves and womby vaultages of france H5 2.04.124
he that loos'd them forth their brazen caves, 2H6 3.02. 89
of the dark, | and make them keep their caves. LR 3.02. 45
as th' aspic leaves | upon the caves of nile. ANT 5.02.353
these lovely caves, these round enchanting pits, VEN 247
that all the neighbor caves, as seeming troubled 830
CAVETO 1 FR 0.0001 REL FR 1 V 0 P
therefore caveto be thy counsellor. H5 2.03. 53
CAVIARY 1 FR 0.0001 REL FR 0 V 1 P
not the million, 'twas caviary to the general, HAM 2.02.437 P
CAVIL 6 FR 0.0006 REL FR 6 V 0 P
'tis love you cavil at; i am not love. TGV 1.01. 38
that's but a cavil; he is old, i young. SHR 2.01.390
ye me, | i'll cavil on the ninth part of a hair. 1H4 3.01.138
to cavil in the course of this contract. 1H6 5.04.156
you cavil, widow, i did mean my queen. 3H6 3.02. 99
night, | in vain i cavil with mine infamy, | in LUC 1025
CAVILLING 1 FR 0.0001 REL FR 1 V 0 P
fight it out, and not stand cavilling thus. 3H6 1.01.117
CAVILS 1 FR 0.0001 REL FR 1 V 0 P
thus cavils she with every thing she sees: LUC 1093
CAWDOR 21 FR 0.0023 REL FR 20 V 1 P
the thane of cawdor, began a dismal conflict, MAC 1.02. 53
no more that thane of cawdor shall deceive | our 1.02. 63
hail, macbeth, hail to thee, thane of cawdor! 1.03. 49
know i am thane of glamis, | but how of cawdor? 1.03. 72
the thane of cawdor lives | a prosperous 1.03. 72
prospect of belief, | no more than to be cawdor. 1.03. 75
and thane of cawdor too; went it not so? 1.03. 87
he bade me, from him, call thee thane of cawdor; 1.03.105
the thane of cawdor lives; 1.03.108
glamis, and thane of cawdor! 1.03.116
when those that gave the thane of cawdor to me 1.03.119
unto the crown, | besides the thane of cawdor. 1.03.122
i am thane of cawdor. 1.03.133
is execution done on cawdor? 1.04. 1
my worthy cawdor! 1.04. 47
who all–hail'd me 'thane of cawdor,' by which 1.05. 7 P
glamis thou art, and cawdor, and shalt be | what 1.05. 15
worthy cawdor! 1.05. 54
where's the thane of cawdor? 1.06. 20
and therefore cawdor | shall sleep no more — 2.02. 39
king, cawdor, glamis, all, | as the weird women 3.01. 1
CAWING 1 FR 0.0001 REL FR 1 V 0 P
sort, | rising and cawing at the gun's report, MND 3.02. 22
CE 2 FR 0.0002 REL FR 0 V 2 P
vous deja oublie ce que je vous ai enseigne? H5 3.04. 42 P
car ce soldat ici est dispose tout /a /cette 4.04. 35 P
CEAS'D 4 FR 0.0004 REL FR 4 V 0 P
she ceas'd | in heavy satisfaction and would AWW 5.03. 99
for miracles are ceas'd; H5 1.01. 67
my moneys, be not ceas'd | with slight denial; TIM 2.01. 16
when he hath ceas'd his ill–resounding noise, VEN 919
CEASE *(also cess*, cesse)*
CEASE 48 FR 0.0054 REL FR 46 V 2 P
here cease more questions. TMP 1.02.184
time, my lord, | you said our work should cease. 5.01. 5
cease to persuade, my loving proteus: TGV 1.01. 1
you were set, so your affection would cease. 2.01. 86 P
cease to lament for that thou canst not help, 3.01.243
i pray thee cease thy counsel, | which falls ADO 5.01. 3
heaven cease this idle humor in your honor! SHR in.2. 13
and both shall cease, without your remedy. AWW 5.03.164
cease, no more. WT 2.01.150
cease. 5.01.119
how that ambitious constance would not cease JN 1.01. 32
other's happiness, | may cease their hatred; H5 5.02.352
cease, cease these jars and rest your minds in 1H6 1.01. 44
cease these jars and rest your minds in peace. 1.01. 44
here sound retreat, and cease our hot pursuit. 2.02. 3
and this fell tempest shall not cease to rage 2H6 3.01.351
nor cease to be an arrogant controller, | though 3.02.205
cease, gentle queen, these execrations, | and 3.02.305
o, let me entreat thee cease. 3.02.339
think therefore on revenge and cease to weep. 4.04. 3
but who can cease to weep and look on this? 4.04. 4
particularities and petty sounds | to cease! 5.02. 45
thou take an oath | to cease this civil war, and 3H6 1.01.197
lamb, | the lamb will never cease to follow him. 4.08. 50
if not, why cease you till you are so? COR 1.06. 48
let them not cease, but with a din confus'd 3.03. 20
have not the face | to say, "beseech you cease." 4.06.117
sweet father, cease your tears, for at your TIT 3.01.136
which doth cease to be | ere one can say it ROM 2.02.119
to cease thy /suit, and leave me to my grief. 2.02.152
being the time the potion's force should cease. 5.03.249
to maintain it, | nor cease his flow of riot. TIM 2.02. 3
your importunacy cease till after dinner, | that 2.02. 41
things at the worst will cease, or else climb MAC 4.02. 24
if aught of woe or wonder, cease your search. HAM 5.02.363
orbs, | from whom we do exist and cease to be; LR 1.01.112
dower with her, | or cease your quest of love? 1.01.193
that things might change or cease, /tears /his 3.01. 7
fall, and cease! 5.03.265
which are, or cease, | as you shall give th' ANT 1.03. 67
than be so, | better to cease to be. CYM 4.04. 31
ta'en, would cease | the present pow'r of life, 5.05.255
never was a war did cease | (ere bloody hands 5.05.484
yet cease your ire, you angry stars of heaven! PER 2.01. 1
by break of day, if the wind cease. 3.01. 76 P
patience, good sir! | or here i'll cease. 5.01.145
time, cease thou thy course and last no longer, LUC 1765
if all were minded so, the times should cease, SON 11. 7
CEASELESS 1 FR 0.0001 REL FR 1 V 0 P
"thou ceaseless lackey to eternity, | with some LUC 967
CEASES 1 FR 0.0001 REL FR 1 V 0 P
world hath so an end, | and machination ceases. LR 5.01. 46
CEASETH 1 FR 0.0001 REL FR 1 V 0 P
water, | which never ceaseth to enlarge itself, 1H6 1.02.134
CEASING 1 FR 0.0001 REL FR 1 V 0 P
ceasing their clamorous cry till they have VEN 693
CEDAR 12 FR 0.0013 REL FR 10 V 2 P
by the spurs pluck'd up | the pine and cedar. TMP 5.01. 48
as upright as the cedar. LLL 4.03. 87
as on a mountain top the cedar shows | that 2H6 5.01.205
thus yields the cedar to the axe's edge, | whose 3H6 5.02. 11
and like a mountain cedar reach his branches H8 5.04. 53
and when from a stately cedar shall be lopp'd CYM 5.04.140 P
and when from a stately cedar shall be lopp'd 5.05.438 P
the lofty cedar, royal cymbeline, | personates 5.05.453
to the majestic cedar join'd, whose issue 5.05.457
i have sent him where a cedar, | higher than all TNK 2.06. 4
that cedar tops and hills seem burnish'd gold. VEN 858
the cedar stoops not to the base shrub's foot, LUC 664
CEDAR'S 2 FR 0.0002 REL FR 2 V 0 P
our aery buildeth in the cedar's top | and R3 1.03.263
but low shrubs wither at the cedar's root. LUC 665
CEDARS 2 FR 0.0002 REL FR 2 V 0 P
strike the proud cedars 'gainst the fiery sun, COR 5.03. 60
marcus, we are but shrubs, no cedars we, | no TIT 4.03. 46
CEDIUS 1 FR 0.0001 REL FR 1 V 0 P
corses of the kings | epistrophus and cedius; TRO 5.05. 11
CELEBRATE 6 FR 0.0006 REL FR 6 V 0 P
a contract of true love to celebrate, | and some TMP 4.01. 84
and help to celebrate | a contract of true love; 4.01.132
more than my dancing soul doth celebrate | this R2 1.03. 91
to celebrate the joy that god hath given us. 1H6 1.06. 14
egyptian bacchanals | and celebrate our drink? ANT 2.07.105
we'll celebrate their nuptials, and ourselves PER 5.03. 80
CELEBRATED 2 FR 0.0002 REL FR 2 V 0 P
us, will not have | our contract celebrated. WT 5.01.204
wherein our saviour's birth is celebrated, HAM 1.01.159
CELEBRATES 1 FR 0.0001 REL FR 1 V 0 P
witchcraft celebrates | pale hecat's off'rings; MAC 2.01. 51
CELEBRATION 7 FR 0.0008 REL FR 6 V 1 P
take away | the edge of that day's celebration, TMP 4.01. 29
note, | what time we will our celebration keep TN 4.03. 30
were the day | of celebration of that nuptial, WT 4.04. 50
forward | in celebration of this day with shows, H8 4.01. 10
news, it is the celebration of his nuptial. OTH 2.02. 7 P
o, this celebration | will long last and be more TNK 1.01.131
not any thing | in the pretended celebration. 1.01.210
CELERITY 7 FR 0.0008 REL FR 6 V 1 P
hence hath offense his quick celerity, | when it MM 4.02.110
maid, | it was the swift celerity of his death, 5.01.394
in motion of no less celerity | than that of H5 3.pr. 2
ay, with celerity, find hector's purpose TRO 1.03.330
act upon her, she hath such a celerity in dying. ANT 1.02.144 P
celerity is never more admir'd | than by the 3.07. 24
with that celerity and nature, which | she makes TNK 1.01.202
CELESTIAL 20 FR 0.0022 REL FR 18 V 2 P
that's a brave god, and bears celestial liquor. TMP 2.02.117
star, | but now i worship a celestial sun. TGV 2.06. 10
to climb celestial silvia's chamber–window, 2.06. 34
give me thy hand, celestial; WIV 3.01.106 P
celestial as thou art, o, pardon love this wrong LLL 4.02.117
there stay until the twelve celestial signs 5.02.797
nymph, divine and rare, | precious, celestial? MND 3.02.227
for most it caught me, the celestial habits WT 3.01. 4
t' envelop and contain celestial spirits. H5 1.01. 31
from above, | by inspiration of celestial grace, 1H6 5.04. 40
bliss, | and is a pattern of celestial peace. 5.05. 65
ravish'd | on that celestial harmony i go to. H8 4.02. 80
will /sate itself in a celestial bed | and prey HAM 1.05. 56
"to the celestial and my soul's idol, the most 2.02.109 P
his celestial breath | was sulphurous to smell; CYM 5.04.114
to taste the fruit of yon celestial tree | (or PER 1.01. 21
celestial dian, goddess argentine, | i will obey 5.01.250
i'll sigh celestial breath, whose gentle wind VEN 189
celestial as thou art, o, do not love that wrong PP 5.13
to ride | with ugly rack on his celestial face, SON 33. 6
CELIA 3 FR 0.0003 REL FR 2 V 1 P
dear celia — i show more mirth than i am AYL 1.02. 3 P
ay, celia, we stay'd her for your sake, | else 1.03. 67
no longer celia, but aliena. 1.03.128
CELL 30 FR 0.0034 REL FR 30 V 0 P
than prospero, master of a full poor cell, | and TMP 1.02. 20
remember | a time before we came unto this cell? 1.02. 39
and lodg'd thee | in mine own cell, till thou 1.02.347
if you be pleas'd, retire into my cell, | and 4.01.161
i' th' filthy–mantled pool beyond your cell, 4.01.182
we now are near his cell. 4.01.195
thou here, | this is the mouth o' th' cell. 4.01.216
in the line–grove which weather–fends your cell; 5.01. 10
ariel, | fetch me the hat and rapier in my cell. 5.01. 84
go, sirrah, to my cell; 5.01.292
your highness and your train | to my poor cell, 5.01.302
at friar patrick's cell, | where i intend holy TGV 4.03. 43
silvia at friar patrick's cell should meet me. 5.01. 3
intend confession | at patrick's cell this even, 5.02. 42
of my joys, | sweet cell of virtue and nobility, TIT 1.01. 93
hence will i to my ghostly /sire's close cell, ROM 2.02.188
and there she shall at friar lawrence' cell | be 2.04.181
then hie you hence to friar lawrence' cell, 2.05. 68
go, i'll to dinner, hie you to the cell. 2.05. 77
i'll to him, he is hid at lawrence' cell. 3.02.141
having displeas'd my father, to lawrence' cell, 3.05.232
look, sir, here comes the lady toward my cell. 4.01. 17
i met the youthful lord at lawrence' cell, | and 4.02. 25
iron crow, and bring it straight | unto my cell. 5.02. 22
and keep her at my cell till romeo come — 5.02. 29
or in my cell there would she kill herself. 5.03.242
vault, | meaning to keep her closely at my cell, 5.03.255
what feast is toward in thine eternal cell, HAM 5.02.365
but unto us it is | a cell of ignorance, CYM 3.03. 33
and in thy shady cell, where none may spy him, LUC 881
CELLAR 1 FR 0.0001 REL FR 0 V 1 P
my cellar is in a rock by th' sea–side, where my TMP 2.02.134 P
CELLARAGE 1 FR 0.0001 REL FR 1 V 0 P
come on, you hear this fellow in the cellarage, HAM 1.05.151
CELL'S 1 FR 0.0001 REL FR 1 V 0 P
this cell's my court. TMP 5.01.166
CELSA 3 FR 0.0003 REL FR 1 V 2 P
hic steterat priami regia celsa senis." SHR 3.01. 29
bearing my port, "celsa senis," that we might 3.01. 36 P
presume not, "celsa senis," despair not. 3.01. 44 P
CEMENT 4 FR 0.0004 REL FR 4 V 0 P
your temples burned in their cement, and | your COR 4.06. 85
how the fear of us | may cement their divisions, ANT 2.01. 48
is set | betwixt us as the cement of our love, 3.02. 29
ground, | as broken glass no cement can redress: PP 13.10
CENSER 2 FR 0.0002 REL FR 1 V 1 P
slash, | like to a censer in a barber's shop. SHR 4.03. 91
i'll tell you what, you thin man in a censer, i 2H4 5.04. 18 P
CENSOR 1 FR 0.0001 REL FR 1 V 0 P
and nobly named so, twice being censor, | was COR 2.03.244
/CENSORINUS 1 FR 0.0001 REL FR 1 V 0 P
/and /censorinus /that /was /so /surnam'd, | and COR 2.03.243
CENSUR'D 5 FR 0.0005 REL FR 1 V 4 P
h'as censur'd him | already, and, as i hear, the MM 1.04. 72
i hear how i am censur'd: ADO 2.03.225 P
two know how you are censur'd here in the city, COR 2.01. 22 P
why? how are we censur'd? 2.01. 24 P
my lord, i may be censur'd, that nature thus LR 3.05. 2 P
CENSURE 29 FR 0.0032 REL FR 25 V 4 P
i am) | should censure thus on lovely gentlemen. TGV 1.02. 19
err'd in this point which now you censure him, MM 2.01. 15

when i, that censure him, do so offend, | let 2.01. 29
nor greatness in mortality | can censure scape; 3.02.186
to every modern censure worse than drunkards. AYL 4.01. 7 P
therefore beware my censure, and keep your 4.01.196 P
how blest am i | in my just censure! WT 2.01. 37
to give their censure of these rare reports. 1H6 2.03. 10
if you do censure me by what you were, | not 5.05. 97
is old enough himself | to give his censure. 2H6 1.03.117
say you consent, and censure well the deed, 3.01.275
no discerner | durst wag his tongue in censure. H8 1.01. 33
your late censure | both of his truth and him 3.01. 64
and giddy censure | will then cry out of martius COR 1.01.268
to suffer lawful censure for such faults | as 3.03. 46
servant, or endure | your heaviest censure. 5.06.141
censure me in your wisdom, and awake your senses
JC 3.02. 16 P
take each man's censure, but reserve thy HAM 1.03. 69
shall in the general censure take corruption 1.04. 35
the censure of which one must, in your allowance 3.02. 27 P
our judgments join | in censure of his seeming. 3.02. 87
the fault | would not scape censure, nor the LR 1.04.210
first be known | that are to censure them. 5.03. 3
name is great | in mouths of wisest censure. OTH 2.03.193
i may not breathe my censure | what he might be. 4.01.270
remains the censure of this hellish villain, 5.02.368
what's worse, | must curtsy at the censure. CYM 3.03. 55
fear not slander, censure rash. 4.02.272
whose death indeed the strongest in our censure, PER 2.04. 34
CENSURED 1 FR 0.0001 REL FR 1 V 0 P
equality | by our best eyes cannot be censured. JN 2.01.328
CENSURERS 1 FR 0.0001 REL FR 1 V 0 P
in the fear | to cope malicious censurers, which H8 1.02. 78
CENSURES 4 FR 0.0004 REL FR 4 V 0 P
you go | to give your censures in this business? R3 2.02.144
t' avoid the censures of the carping world. 3.05. 68
let our just censures | attend the true event, MAC 5.04. 14
that censures falsely what they see aright? SON 148. 4
CENSURING 1 FR 0.0001 REL FR 1 V 0 P
me to the shouting varlotry | of censuring rome? ANT 5.02. 57
CENTAUR 7 FR 0.0008 REL FR 7 V 0 P
go bear it to the centaur, where we host, | and ERR 1.02. 9
i'll to the centaur to go seek this slave; 1.02.104
gave to dromio is laid up | safe at the centaur, 2.02. 2
you know no centaur? 2.02. 9
home to the centaur with the gold you gave me. 2.02. 16
come to the centaur, fetch our stuff from thence 4.04.149
goods that lay at host, sir, in the centaur. 5.01.411
CENTAURS' 1 FR 0.0001 REL FR 1 V 0 P
more stern and bloody than the centaurs' feast. TIT 5.02.203
CENTAURS 2 FR 0.0002 REL FR 2 V 0 P
"the battle with the centaurs, to be sung | by MND 5.01. 44
down from the waist they are centaurs, | though LR 4.06.124
CENTER 1 FR 0.0001 REL FR 1 V 0 P
now happy he whose cloak and center can | hold JN 4.03.155
CENTRE *(also centry, centure)*
CENTRE 12 FR 0.0013 REL FR 12 V 0 P
that the moon | may through the centre creep, MND 3.02. 54
thy intention stabs the centre. WT 1.02.138
upon, | the centre is not big enough to bear | a 2.01.102
as many lines close in the dial's centre; H5 1.02.210
the planets, and this centre | observe degree, TRO 1.03. 85
as iron to adamant, as earth to th' centre, 3.02.179
of my love | is as the very centre of the earth, 4.02.104
and pierce the inmost centre of the earth; TIT 4.03. 12
turn back, dull earth, and find thy centre out. ROM 2.01. 2
though it were hid indeed | within the centre. HAM 2.02.159
know o' th' earth | must know the centre too; TNK 1.01.115
poor soul, the centre of my sinful earth, | /... SON 146. 1
CENTRY 1 FR 0.0001 REL FR 1 V 0 P
swine | is now even in the centry of this isle, R3 5.02. 11
CENTS 1 FR 0.0001 REL FR 0 V 1 P
ma vie, et je vous donnerai deux cents ecus. H5 4.04. 42 P
CENTURE *(also centre, centry)*
CENTURE 1 FR 0.0001 REL FR 1 V 0 P
the middle centure of this cursed town. 1H6 2.02. 6
CENTURIES 1 FR 0.0001 REL FR 1 V 0 P
do send, dispatch | those centuries to our aid; COR 1.07. 3
CENTURIONS 1 FR 0.0001 REL FR 0 V 1 P
the centurions and their charges, distinctly COR 4.03. 43 P
/CENTURY* 1 FR 0.0001 REL FR 1 V 0 P
a /century send forth; LR 4.04. 6
CENTURY* 1 FR 0.0001 REL FR 1 V 0 P
and on it said a century of prayers | (such as i CYM 4.02.391
CEPHALUS *(see shafalus)*
CERBERUS 4 FR 0.0004 REL FR 3 V 1 P
whose club kill'd cerberus, that three-headed LLL 5.02.589
rather damn them with | king cerberus, and let 2H4 2.04.168
at his greatness as cerberus is at proserpina's TRO 2.01. 34 P
as cerberus at the thracian poet's feet. TIT 2.04. 51
CERE 1 FR 0.0001 REL FR 1 V 0 P
and cere up my embracements from a next | with CYM 1.01.116
CERECLOTH 1 FR 0.0001 REL FR 1 V 0 P
to rib her cerecloth in the obscure grave. MV 2.07. 51
CEREMENTS 1 FR 0.0001 REL FR 1 V 0 P
hearsed in death, | have burst their cerements; HAM 1.04. 48
CEREMONIAL 1 FR 0.0001 REL FR 1 V 0 P
to speak the ceremonial rites of marriage? SHR 3.02. 6
CEREMONIES 9 FR 0.0010 REL FR 7 V 2 P
all sanctimonious ceremonies may | with full and TMP 4.01. 16
but after many ceremonies done, | he calls for SHR 3.02.169
you shall find the ceremonies of the wars, and H5 4.01. 72 P
his ceremonies laid by, in his nakedness he 4.01.104 P
with twenty popish tricks and ceremonies, TIT 5.01. 76
if you do find them deck'd with ceremonies. JC 1.01. 65
once | of fantasy, of dreams, and ceremonies. 2.01.197
caesar, i never stood on ceremonies, | yet now 2.02. 13
have all true rites and lawful ceremonies. 3.01.241
CEREMONIOUS 7 FR 0.0008 REL FR 6 V 1 P
how ceremonious, solemn, and unearthly | it was WT 3.01. 7
then let us take a ceremonious leave | and R2 1.03. 50
tradition, form, and ceremonious duty, | for you 3.02.173
my lord, | too ceremonious and traditional. R3 3.01. 45
time | cuts off the ceremonious vows of love 5.03. 98
or the men of troy | are ceremonious courtiers. TRO 1.03.234
with that ceremonious affection as you were wont
LR 1.04. 59 P
CEREMONIOUSLY 1 FR 0.0001 REL FR 1 V 0 P
and ceremoniously let us prepare | some welcome MV 5.01. 37
CEREMONY 31 FR 0.0035 REL FR 28 V 3 P
accoustrement, complement, and ceremony of it. WIV 4.02. 6 P
marrying, | to give our hearts united ceremony. 4.06. 51
this, | no ceremony that to great ones 'longs, MM 2.02. 59
critical, | not sorting with a nuptial ceremony. MND 5.01. 55
modesty | to urge the thing held as a ceremony? MV 5.01.206
use a more spacious ceremony to the noble lords; AWW 2.01. 50 P
whose ceremony | shall seem expedient on the 2.03.178
and all the ceremony of this compact | seal'd in TN 5.01.160
curious business that | i leave out ceremony. WT 4.04.515
not too, | save ceremony, save general ceremony? H5 4.01.239
not too, | save ceremony, save general ceremony? 4.01.239
and what art thou, thou idol ceremony? 4.01.240
o ceremony, show me but thy worth! 4.01.244
and bid thy ceremony give thee cure! 4.01.252
no, not all these, thrice-gorgeous ceremony, 4.01.266
and, but for ceremony, such a wretch, | winding 4.01.278
all's now done but the ceremony | of bringing H8 2.01. 4
you saw | the ceremony? 4.01. 60
neither will they bate | one jot of ceremony. COR 2.02.141
ceremony was but devis'd at first | to set a TIM 1.02. 15
set on, and leave no ceremony out. JC 1.02. 11
and decay | it useth an enforced ceremony. 4.02. 21
from thence, the sauce to meat is ceremony, MAC 3.04. 35
appurtenance of welcome is fashion and ceremony.
HAM 2.02.372 P
what ceremony else? 5.01.223
what ceremony else? 5.01.225
what, no more ceremony? ANT 3.13. 38
leave not out a jot | o' th' sacred ceremony. TNK 1.01.131
and honor them | with treble ceremony — rather 1.04. 8
the athenians pay it | to th' heart of ceremony. 3.01. 4
to say | the perfect ceremony of love's /rite, SON 23. 6
CERES' 3 FR 0.0003 REL FR 3 V 0 P
shall shun you, | ceres' blessing so is on you. TMP 4.01.117
hanging the head at ceres' plenteous load? 2H6 1.02. 2
breath blows down | the teeming ceres' foison, TNK 5.01. 53
CERES 4 FR 0.0004 REL FR 4 V 0 P
ceres, most bounteous lady, thy rich leas | of TMP 4.01. 60
approach, rich ceres, her to entertain. 4.01. 75
juno and ceres whisper seriously; 4.01.125
when i presented ceres, | i thought to have told 4.01.167
CERIMON 5 FR 0.0005 REL FR 5 V 0 P
hath built lord cerimon | such strong renown as PER 3.02. 47
lord cerimon, my lord; 5.03. 59
lord cerimon hath letters of good credit, sir, 5.03. 77
lord cerimon, we do our longing stay | to hear 5.03. 83
in reverend cerimon there well appears | the 5.03. 93
'CERNS *(also concerns)*
'CERNS 1 FR 0.0001 REL FR 0 V 1 P
what 'cerns it you if i wear pearl and gold? SHR 5.01. 75 P
/CERTAIN 2 FR 0.0002 REL FR 1 V 1 P
/cannot /be /bordered /certain /in /itself. LR 4.02. 33
/most /certain, /sir. 4.07. 86 P
CERTAIN 172 FR 0.0194 REL FR 117 V 55 P
that's most certain. TMP 3.02. 56 P
my staff, | bury it certain fadoms in the earth, 5.01. 55
that will /not let you | believe things certain. 5.01.125
know for certain | that i am prospero and that 5.01.158
nay, that's certain; TGV 2.01. 36 P
to a place till some certain shot be paid and 2.05. 6 P
but 'tis most certain your husband's coming, WIV 3.03.113 P
i would send for certain of my creditors; MM 1.02.132 P
i'll send him certain word of my success. 1.04. 89
thou art not certain, | for thy complexion 3.01. 23
but it is certain that when he makes water his 3.02.110 P
not consent to die this day, that's certain. 4.03. 56 P
for certain words he spake against your grace 5.01.129
i am invited, sir, to certain merchants, | of ERR 1.02. 24
certain ones then. 2.02. 95 P
and sent my peasant home | for certain ducats; 5.01.232
but it is certain i am lov'd of all ladies, only ADO 1.01.125 P
'tis certain so, the prince woos for himself. 2.01.174
rich she shall be, that's certain; 2.03. 30 P
nay, that's certain, we have the exhibition to 4.02. 5 P
"certain," said she, "a wise gentleman." 5.01.165 P
and, as a certain father saith — LLL 4.02.148 P
at the father's of a certain pupil of mine, 4.02.153 P
there is no certain princess that appears; 4.03.154
some certain treason. 4.03.188
some certain special honors it pleaseth his 5.01.106 P
more calf, certain. 5.02.640 P
a man so breathed, that certain he would fight, 5.02.653
yield | thy crazed title to my certain right. MND 1.01. 92
and certain stars shot madly from their spheres, 2.01.153
a certain aim he took | at a fair vestal throned 2.01.157
be certain! 3.02.280
this beauteous lady thisby is certain. 5.01.130
the skillful shepherd pill'd me certain wands, MV 1.03. 84
lorenzo, certain, and my love indeed, | for who 2.06. 29
that's certain. 3.01. 26 P
that's certain, if the devil may be her judge. 3.01. 32 P
more than a lodg'd hate and a certain loathing 4.01. 60
for here i read for certain that my ships | are 5.01.287
of a certain knight, that swore by his honor AYL 1.02. 63 P
dislike the cut of a certain courtier's beard. 5.04. 70 P
certain it is that he will steal himself into a AWW 3.06. 91 P
what honor i can, but of this i am not certain. 4.03.272 P
certain it is i lik'd her, | and boarded her i' 5.03.210
most certain, if you are she, you do usurp TN 1.05.187 P
most certain. let our catch be "thou knave." 2.03. 63 P
nay, that's certain. 3.01. 14 P
for meddle you must, that's certain, or forswear 3.04.252 P
to do't, or no, is certain | to me a break-neck. WT 1.02.362
be certain what you do, sir, lest your justice 2.01.127
be the bondage of certain ribbons and gloves. 4.04.233 P
shores, most certain | to miseries enough; 4.04.567
nothing so certain as your anchors, who | do 4.04.570
most certain of one mother, mighty king — JN 1.01. 59
but for the certain knowledge of that truth | i 1.01. 61
be by some certain king purg'd and depos'd. 2.01.372
no certain life achiev'd by others' death. 4.02.105
came there a certain lord, neat, and trimly 1H4 1.03. 33
undertake is dangerous" — why, that's certain. 2.03. 8 P
cry | hath followed certain men unto this house. 2.04.508
his is certain, ours is doubtful. 4.03. 4
certain horse | of my cousin vernon's are not 4.03. 19
some certain edicts and some strait decrees 4.03. 79
no, that's certain, i am not a double man; 5.04.138 P
i bring you certain news from shrewsbury. 2H4 1.01. 12
your spirit is too true, your fears too certain. 1.01. 92
i hear for certain and dare speak the truth, 1.01.188
against the french, | i have no certain notice. 1.03. 85
a certain instance that glendower is dead. 3.01.103
certain, 'tis certain, very sure, very sure. 3.02. 36 P
certain, 'tis certain, very sure, very sure. 3.02. 36 P
as the psalmist saith, is certain to all, all 3.02. 37 P
death is certain. 3.02. 40 P
she cannot choose but be old, certain she's old, 3.02.208 P
this apoplexy will certain be his end. 4.04.130
it is certain that either wise bearing or 5.01. 75 P
it is best, certain. 5.05. 23 P
of his true titles to some certain dukedoms, H5 1.01. 87
there left behind and settled certain french; 1.02. 47
did claim some certain dukedoms, in the right 1.02.247
live so long as i may, that's the certain of it; 2.01. 15 P
it is certain, corporal, that he is married to 2.01. 17 P
marvellous falorous gentleman, that is certain, 3.02. 77 P
'tis certain he hath pass'd the river somme. 3.05. 1
'tis certain, every man that dies ill, the ill 4.01.186 P
'tis certain there's not a boy left alive, and 4.07. 5 P
my words, | for they are certain and unfallible. 1H6 1.02. 59
the truth | about a certain question in the law 4.01. 95
some certain dregs of conscience are yet within R3 1.04.121 P
'twould prove the verity of certain words H8 1.02.159
me, | this from a dying man receive as certain: 2.01.125
and held for certain | the king will venture at 2.01.155
certain | the daughter of a king, my drops of 2.04. 71
on certain speeches utter'd | by th' bishop of 2.04.172
for certain | this is of purpose laid by some 5.02. 13
'tis now too certain. 5.02.142
myself | from certain and possess'd conveniences TRO 3.03. 7
'tis certain, greatness, once fall'n out with 3.03. 75
(or rather call my thought a certain knowledge) 4.01. 42
a certain number | (though thanks to all) must i COR 1.06. 80
yes certain, there's a letter for you, i saw't. 2.01.113 P
when | some certain of your brethren roar'd, and 2.03. 53
and to keep him here | our certain death; 3.01.287
but this certain, | that, if thou conquer rome, 5.03.141
friend, | art thou certain this is true? 5.04. 44
is't most certain? 5.04. 44
as certain as i know the sun is fire. 5.04. 45
for certain drops of salt, your city rome, | i 5.06. 92
why then it seems some certain snatch or so TIT 2.01. 95
that's a certain text. ROM 4.01. 21
lord, there are certain ladies most desirous of TIM 1.02.116 P
there are certain nobles of the senate | newly 1.02.174
my lord, here is a note of certain dues. 2.02. 16
with certain half-caps and cold-moving nods, 2.02.212
we wait for certain money here, sir. 3.04. 46
ay, | if money were as certain as your waiting, 3.04. 47
certain. 5.01. 4
some certain of the noblest-minded romans | to JC 1.03.122
nay, that's certain: 3.02. 69
therefore 'tis certain he was not ambitious. 3.02.113
i did send to you | for certain sums of gold, 4.03. 70
for certain she is dead, and by strange manner. 4.03.189
horses (a thing most strange and certain), MAC 2.04. 14
for certain friends that are both his and mine, 3.01.120
for certain, sir, he is not; 5.02. 8
but for certain | he cannot buckle his 5.02. 14
but certain issue strokes must arbitrate, 5.04. 20
doom'd for a certain term to walk the night, HAM 1.05. 10
madam, it so fell out that certain players | we 3.01. 16
a certain convocation of politic worms are e'en 4.03. 20 P
that is most certain. 5.02. 11
that's most certain, and with you; LR 1.01.286 P
of his intent, you should run a certain course; 1.02. 82 P
if the matter of this paper be certain, you have 3.05. 15 P
'tis certain then for cyprus. OTH 1.03. 43
general, that upon certain tidings now arriv'd, 2.02. 2 P
certain, men should be what they seem. 3.03.128
lives in bliss | who, certain of his fate, loves 3.03.168
o, thou art wise; 'tis certain. 4.01. 74
talking on the sea-bank with certain venetians, 4.01.134 P
nay, that's certain. 4.01.195 P
this is most certain that i shall deliver: ANT 2.01. 28
i know you could not lack, i am certain on't, 2.02. 57
a certain queen to caesar in a mattress. 2.06. 70
o' th' nile | by certain scales i' th' pyramid; 2.07. 18
is this certain? 3.03. 21
most certain. 3.06. 97
most certain. 4.05. 11
nay, 'tis most certain, iras. 5.02.214
nay, that's certain. 5.02.222
how i would think on him at certain hours | such CYM 1.03. 27
whose top to climb | is certain falling, or so 3.03. 48
strong as my grief and as certain as i expect my 3.04. 24 P
to strike and to make me certain it is done, 3.04. 30 P
'tis certain she is fled. 3.05. 66
did compound for her | a certain stuff, which, 5.05.255
then were it certain you were not so bad | as PER 1.01.125
there are certain condolements, certain vails. 2.01.150 P
there are certain condolements, certain vails. 2.01.151 P
this letter and some certain jewels | lay with 3.04. 1
and it is said | for certain in our story, she 4.ch. 19
'tis most certain. 5.03. 20
where ev'ry seeming good's | a certain evil; TNK 1.02. 40
that was a fair boy certain, but a fool | to 2.02.120
my masters, i'll be there, that's certain. 2.03. 24
most certain | you love me not; 3.01.101
is as momentary | as to us death is certain. 5.04. 18
to hunt the boar with certain of his friends. VEN 588
her woe, | her certain sorrow writ uncertainly. LUC 1311
begins the sad dirge of her certain ending: 1612
these are certain signs to know | faithful PP 20.55
best," | when i was certain o'er incertainty, SON 115.11
CERTAINER 1 FR 0.0001 REL FR 1 V 0 P
nothing certainer: ADO 5.04. 62
CERTAINLY 29 FR 0.0032 REL FR 16 V 13 P
certainly, sir, i can. TMP 1.02. 41
no wonder, sir, | but certainly a maid. 1.02.429
no, certainly. speak louder. WIV 4.02. 16 P
some scholar would conjure her, for certainly, ADO 2.01.257 P
and therefore certainly it were not good | she 3.01. 57
certainly my conscience will serve me to run MV 2.02. 1 P

certainly the jew is the very devil incarnation, 2.02. 27 P
but antonio is certainly undone. 3.01.124 P
nay certainly there is no truth in him. AYL 3.04. 20 P
and certainly a woman's thought runs before her 4.01.140 P
as you are certainly a gentleman, thereto WT 1.02.391
but he was certainly whipt out of the court. 4.03. 89 P
if you had won it, certainly you had. JN 3.04.118
because the king is certainly possess'd | of all 1H4 4.01. 40
nell quickly, and certainly she did you wrong, H5 2.01. 18 P
certainly, aunchient, it is not a thing to 3.06. 53 P
for certainly thou art so near the gulf, | thou 4.03. 82
yes, certainly, and out of doubt and out of 5.01. 45 P
and therefore are we certainly resolv'd | to 1H6 5.01. 37
certainly | the cardinal is the end of this. H8 2.01. 39
hedge us out, we'll hear you sing, certainly. TRO 3.01. 61 P
certainly, | he flouted us downright. COR 2.03.159
our sister's man is certainly miscarried. LR 5.01. 5
and certainly in strange unquietness. OTH 3.04.133
nay certainly, i have heard the ptolomies' ANT 2.07. 34 P
nay, certainly to–night, | for look how fresh PER 3.02. 78
certainly | 'tis a main goodness, cousin, that TNK 2.02. 62
we are certainly both traitors, both despisers 3.06.137
nay, certainly you are, | for to the king god STM II.C 97
CERTAIN'ST 1 FR 0.0001 REL FR 1 V 0 P
fortune, | who, at her certain'st, reels. TNK 5.04. 21
CERTAINTIES 3 FR 0.0003 REL FR 3 V 0 P
and he is furnish'd with no certainties | more 2H4 1.01. 31
o, doubt not that, | i speak from certainties. COR 1.02. 31
for certainties | either are past remedies, or, CYM 1.06. 96
CERTAINTY 8 FR 0.0009 REL FR 5 V 3 P
not a resemblance, but a certainty; MM 4.02.188 P
tell me for more certainty, | albeit i'll swear MV 2.06. 26
we here receive it | a certainty, vouch'd from AWW 1.02. 5
upon thy certainty and confidence | what dar'st 2.01.169
encourage myself in my certainty, put myself 3.06. 76 P
evidences proclaim her, with all certainty, to WT 5.02. 38 P
if you desire to know the certainty | of your HAM 4.05.141
the certainty of this hard life, aye hopeless CYM 4.04. 27
CERTES 5 FR 0.0005 REL FR 4 V 1 P
(for, certes, these are people of the island), TMP 3.03. 30
certes she did, the kitchen vestal scorn'd you. ERR 4.04. 75
and certes the text most infallibly concludes it LLL 4.02.163 P
one, certes, that promises no element | in such H8 1.01. 48
for, "certes," says he, | "i have already chose OTH 1.01. 16
CERTIFICATE 1 FR 0.0001 REL FR 0 V 1 P
why, this is a certificate. 2H4 2.02.121 P
CERTIFIED 2 FR 0.0002 REL FR 2 V 0 P
antonio certified the duke | they were not with MV 2.08. 10
when foreign princes shall be certified | that 1H6 4.01.144
CERTIFIES 1 FR 0.0001 REL FR 1 V 0 P
then certifies your lordship that this night R3 3.02. 10
CERTIFY 1 FR 0.0001 REL FR 1 V 0 P
belief, | i go to certify her talbot's here. 1H6 2.03. 32
CES 1 FR 0.0001 REL FR 0 V 1 P
je ne voudrais prononcer ces mots devant les H5 3.04. 55 P
CESARIO 18 FR 0.0020 REL FR 14 V 4 P
duke continue these favors towards you, cesario, TN 1.04. 2 P
who saw cesario, ho? 1.04. 10
cesario, | thou know'st no less but all. 1.04. 12
now, good cesario, but that piece of song, 2.04. 2
mark it, cesario, it is old and plain. 2.04. 43
once more, cesario, | get thee to yond same 2.04. 79
cesario is your servant's name, fair princess. 3.01. 97
cesario, by the roses of the spring, | by 3.01.149
nor your name is not master cesario, nor this is 4.01. 7 P
be not offended, dear cesario. 4.01. 50
cesario, you do not keep promise with me. 5.01.103
what do you say, cesario? good my lord — 5.01.106
where goes cesario? 5.01.134
whither, my lord? cesario, husband, stay. 5.01.143
fear not, cesario, take thy fortunes up, | be 5.01.148
the count's gentleman, one cesario. 5.01.180 P
my gentleman, cesario? 5.01.183 P
cesario, come — | for so you shall be while you 5.01.385
CESS* *(also cease, cesse)*
CESS* 2 FR 0.0002 REL FR 1 V 1 P
jade is wrung in the withers, out of all cess. 1H4 2.01. 7 P
the cess of majesty | dies not alone, but, like HAM 3.03. 15
CESSE *(also cease, cess*)*
CESSE 1 FR 0.0001 REL FR 1 V 0 P
or, ere they meet, in me, o nature, cesse! AWW 5.03. 72
C'EST 2 FR 0.0002 REL FR 0 V 2 P
c'est bien dit, madame, il est fort bon anglois. H5 3.04. 19 P
c'est assez pour une fois: allons–nous a diner. 3.04. 61 P
CESTERN *(also cestron)*
CESTERN 3 FR 0.0003 REL FR 3 V 0 P
could not fill up | the cestern of my lust, and MAC 4.03. 63
or keep it as a cestern for foul toads | to knot OTH 4.02. 61
and made | a cestern for scal'd snakes! ANT 2.05. 95
CESTERNS 1 FR 0.0001 REL FR 1 V 0 P
like ivory conduits coral cesterns filling: LUC 1234
CESTRON *(also cestern, etc.)*
CESTRON 1 FR 0.0001 REL FR 1 V 0 P
must be to him that makes the camp a cestron TNK 5.01. 46
/CETERA 1 FR 0.0001 REL FR 0 V 1 P
of the army, agamemnon, /et /cetera. TRO 3.03.278 P
/CETTE 1 FR 0.0001 REL FR 0 V 1 P
ici est dispose tout /a /cette /heure de couper H5 4.04. 35 P
CHACES *(also chases)*
CHACES 1 FR 0.0001 REL FR 1 V 0 P
of france will be disturb'd | with chaces. H5 1.02.266
/CHAF'D 1 FR 0.0001 REL FR 1 V 0 P
/orgillous, /their /high /blood /chaf'd, | /have TRO pr 2
CHAF'D 4 FR 0.0004 REL FR 3 V 1 P
besides, her intercession chaf'd him so, | when TGV 3.01.235
what, are you chaf'd? H8 1.01.123
and helen so blush'd, and paris so chaf'd, and TRO 1.02.166 P
being once chaf'd, he cannot | be rein'd again COR 3.03. 27
CHAFE 5 FR 0.0005 REL FR 4 V 1 P
of falstaff as he will chafe at the doctor's WIV 5.03. 8 P
i chafe you if i tarry. let me go. SHR 2.01.241
fain would i go to chafe his paly lips | with 2H6 3.02.141
do not chafe thee, cousin, | and you, achilles, TRO 4.05.260
roman does become | the carriage of his chafe. ANT 1.03. 85
CHAFED 4 FR 0.0004 REL FR 4 V 0 P
rage like an angry boar chafed with sweat? SHR 1.02.202
fled, | and warwick rages like a chafed bull. 3H6 2.05.126
so looks the chafed lion | upon the daring H8 3.02.206
the chafed boar, the mountain lioness, | the TIT 4.02.138
CHAFES 4 FR 0.0004 REL FR 3 V 1 P
i would you did but see how it chafes, how it WT 3.03. 88 P
proud, and take no care | who chafes, who frets, MAC 4.01. 91
that on th' unnumb'red idle pebble chafes, LR 4.06. 21
he chafes her lips, a thousand ways he seeks VEN 477
CHAFF 10 FR 0.0011 REL FR 6 V 4 P
two grains of wheat hid in two bushels of chaff; MV 1.01.116 P
pick'd from the chaff and ruin of the times | to 2.09. 48
and scar'd my choughs from the chaff, i had not WT 4.04.617 P
that even our corn shall seem as light as chaff, 2H4 4.01.193
where my chaff | and corn shall fly asunder; H8 5.01.110
chaff and bran, chaff and bran! TRO 1.02.241 P
chaff and bran, chaff and bran! 1.02.241 P
to pick them in a pile | of noisome musty chaff. COR 5.01. 26
you are the musty chaff, and you are smelt 5.01. 31
fan | from me the witless chaff of such a writer TNK pr 19
CHAFFLESS 1 FR 0.0001 REL FR 1 V 0 P
gods made you | (unlike all others) chaffless. CYM 1.06.178
CHAFFY 1 FR 0.0001 REL FR 1 V 0 P
and art | a very thief in love, a chaffy lord, TNK 3.01. 41
CHAFING 3 FR 0.0003 REL FR 3 V 0 P
the troubled tiber chafing with her shores, JC 1.02.101
all swoll'n with chafing, down adonis sits, VEN 325
mine eye | the picture of an angry chafing boar, 662
CHAIN 63 FR 0.0071 REL FR 52 V 11 P
twenty times, and have taken him by the chain; WIV 1.01.296 P
and shakes a chain | in a most hideous and 4.04. 33
that beguil'd him of a chain, had the chain or 4.05. 32 P
beguil'd him of a chain, had the chain or no. 4.05. 33 P
master slender of his chain cozen'd him of it. 4.05. 37 P
i'll provide you a chain, and i'll do what i can 5.01. 5 P
sister, you know he promis'd me a chain; ERR 2.01.106
get you home | and fetch the chain; 3.01.115
that chain will i bestow | (be it for nothing 3.01.117
lo here's the chain. 3.02.166
the chain unfinish'd made me stay thus long. 3.02.168
you, | and then receive my money for the chain. 3.02.175
for fear you ne'er see chain nor money more. 3.02.177
that would refuse so fair an offer'd chain. 3.02.181
that i met with you | he had of me a chain. 4.01. 10
i promised your presence and the chain, | but 4.01. 23
but neither chain nor goldsmith came to me: 4.01. 24
how much your chain weighs to the utmost charect 4.01. 28
and with you take the chain, and bid my wife 4.01. 37
then you will bring the chain to her yourself? 4.01. 40
well, sir, i will. have you the chain about you? 4.01. 42
nay, come, i pray you, sir, give me the chain: 4.01. 45
you hear how he importunes me — the chain! 4.01. 53
either send the chain, or send me by some token. 4.01. 56
come, where's the chain? 4.01. 58
the money that you owe me for the chain. 4.01. 63
i owe you none, till i receive the chain. 4.01. 64
a chain, a chain! 4.02. 51
a chain, a chain! 4.02. 51
what, the chain? 4.02. 52
is that the chain you promis'd me to–day? 4.03. 47
or, for my diamond, the chain you promis'd, 4.03. 69
but she, more covetous, would have a chain. 4.03. 74
the devil will shake her chain, and fright us 4.03. 76
i pray you, sir, my ring, or else the chain; 4.03. 77
and for the same he promis'd me a chain: 4.03. 84
due for a chain your husband had of him. 4.04.135
he did bespeak a chain for me, but had it not. 4.04.136
straight after did i meet him with a chain. 4.04.140
you, | but i protest he had the chain of me, 5.01. 2
and that self chain about his neck, | which he 5.01. 10
deny | this chain which now you wear so openly. 5.01. 17
this chain you had of me, can you deny it? 5.01. 22
then, | who parted with me to go fetch a chain, 5.01.221
that i this day of him receiv'd the chain, 5.01.228
but had he such a chain of thee, or no? 5.01.257
these people saw the chain about his neck. 5.01.259
heard you confess you had the chain of him, 5.01.261
i never saw the chain, so help me heaven; 5.01.268
that is the chain, sir, which you had of me. 5.01.378
and you, sir, for this chain arrested me. 5.01.380
about your neck, like an usurer's chain? ADO 2.01.190 P
the chain were longer and the letter short? LLL 5.02. 56
his speech was like a tangled chain; MND 5.01.125 P
and a chain, that you once wore, about his neck. AYL 3.02.181 P
go, sir, rub your chain with crumbs. TN 2.03.119 P
and i will chain these legs and arms of thine, 1H6 2.03. 39
and in this vow do chain my soul to thine! 3H6 2.03. 34
a thrifty shoeing–horn in a chain, /hanging at TRO 5.01. 56 P
statutes daily to chain up and restrain the poor COR 1.01. 84 P
chain me with roaring bears, | or hide me ROM 4.01. 80
chain mine arm'd neck, leap thou, attire and all ANT 4.08. 14
leading him prisoner in a red rose chain; VEN 110
CHAIN'D 3 FR 0.0003 REL FR 3 V 0 P
are founder'd | or night kept chain'd below. TMP 4.01. 31
last too long | if it were chain'd together, and ERR 4.01. 26
the rampant bear chain'd to the ragged staff, 2H6 5.01.203
CHAINED 1 FR 0.0001 REL FR 1 V 0 P
free that soul which wretchedness hath chained? LUC 900
CHAINS 12 FR 0.0013 REL FR 10 V 2 P
of roaring, shrieking, howling, jingling chains, TMP 5.01.233
were't not affection chains thy tender days | to TGV 1.01. 3
i would have fil'd keys off that hung in chains. WT 4.04.612 P
a freer heart | cast off his chains of bondage, R2 1.03. 89
yea, joy, our chains and our jewels. 2H4 2.04. 47 P
that with the very shaking of their chains 2H6 5.01.145
and manacle the bearard in their chains, | if 5.01.149
and hung their rotten coffins up in chains, | it 3H6 1.03. 28
that in their chains fetter'd the kingly lion, 5.07. 11
hast prisoner held, fett'red in amorous chains, TIT 2.01. 15
if she in chains of magic were not bound, OTH 1.02. 65
pyramides my gibbet, | and hang me up in chains! ANT 5.02. 62
CHAIR 29 FR 0.0032 REL FR 26 V 3 P
sir, sitting (as i say) in a lower chair, sir — MM 2.01.128 P
it is like a barber's chair that fits all AWW 2.02. 17 P
you shall find with me | fast to the chair. JN 4.01. 5
this chair shall be my state, this dagger my 1H4 2.04.378 P
dost thou so hunger for mine empty chair | that 2H4 4.05. 94
lance, | and run a–tilt at death within a chair? 1H6 3.02. 51
should bring thy father to his drooping chair. 4.05. 5
and in that chair where kings and queens were 2H6 1.02. 38
sturdy rebel sits, | even in the chair of state. 3H6 1.01. 51
and over the chair of state, where now he sits, 1.01.168
ay, this is he that took king henry's chair, 1.04. 97
his dukedom and his chair with me is left. 2.01. 90
for chair and dukedom, throne and kingdom say, 2.01. 93
and thou this day hadst kept thy chair in peace. 2.06. 20
resign thy chair, and where i stand kneel thou, 5.05. 19
is the chair empty? R3 4.04.469
made precious by the foil | of england's chair, 5.03.251
in a rich chair of state, opposing freely | the H8 4.01. 67
reach a chair. 4.02. 3
present, and behold | that chair stand empty; 5.02. 45
hath not a tomb so evident as a chair | t' extol COR 4.07. 52
and look you lay it in the praetor's chair, JC 1.03.143
let him go up into the public chair, | we'll 3.02. 63
to this chair bind him. LR 3.07. 34
fellows, hold the chair, | upon these eyes of 3.07. 67
o, for a chair, | to bear him easily hence! OTH 5.01. 82
how do you, cassio? o, a chair, a chair! 5.01. 96
how do you, cassio? o, a chair, a chair! 5.01. 96
the chair. 5.01. 98
CHAIR–DAYS 1 FR 0.0001 REL FR 1 V 0 P
in thy reverence and thy chair–days, thus | to 2H6 5.02. 48
CHAIRS 5 FR 0.0005 REL FR 5 V 0 P
the several chairs of order look you scour WIV 5.05. 61
and both return back to their chairs again. R2 1.03.120
and the chairs of justice | supplied with worthy COR 3.03. 34
shall sit and pant in your great chairs of ease, TIM 5.04. 11
cleopatra and himself in chairs of gold | were ANT 3.06. 4
CHALIC'D 1 FR 0.0001 REL FR 1 V 0 P
those springs | on chalic'd flow'rs that lies; CYM 2.03. 23
CHALICE 2 FR 0.0002 REL FR 2 V 0 P
commends th' ingredience of our poison'd chalice MAC 1.07. 11
have preferr'd him | a chalice for the nonce, HAM 4.07.160
CHALICES 1 FR 0.0001 REL FR 0 V 1 P
take away these chalices. WIV 3.05. 28 P
CHALK'D 1 FR 0.0001 REL FR 1 V 0 P
for it is you that have chalk'd forth the way TMP 5.01.203
CHALKS 1 FR 0.0001 REL FR 1 V 0 P
whose grace | chalks successors their way, nor H8 1.01. 60
CHALKY 3 FR 0.0003 REL FR 2 V 1 P
i look'd for the chalky cliffs, but i could find ERR 3.02.126 P
as far as i could ken thy chalky cliffs, | when 2H6 3.02.101
from the dread summit of this chalky bourn. LR 4.06. 57
CHALLENG'D 9 FR 0.0010 REL FR 4 V 5 P
in messina, and challeng'd cupid at the flight, ADO 1.01. 40 P
for cupid, and challeng'd him at the burbolt. 1.01. 42 P
and hath challeng'd thee? 5.01.197 P
man, have you challeng'd charles the wrastler? AYL 1.02.168 P
seen him damn'd ere i'd have challeng'd him. TN 3.04.285 P
in that behalf which we have challeng'd it? JN 2.01.264
and, nephew, challeng'd you to single fight. 1H4 5.02. 46
by their heralds challeng'd | the noble spirits H8 1.01. 34
it on thy horn, | it should be challeng'd. TRO 5.02. 96
CHALLENGE *(also shallenge)*
CHALLENGE 51 FR 0.0057 REL FR 30 V 21 P
mine, | i combat challenge of this latten bilbo. WIV 1.01.162
and my uncle's fool, reading the challenge, ADO 1.01. 41 P
enough, i am engag'd, i will challenge him. 4.01.331 P
days, | do challenge thee to trial of a man. 5.01. 66
god bless me from a challenge! 5.01.144 P
claudio undergoes my challenge, and either i 5.02. 57 P
for you at pricks, sir, challenge her to bowl. LLL 4.01.138
when she shall challenge this, you will reject 5.02.438
hector will challenge him. 5.02.690 P
by the north pole, i do challenge thee. 5.02.693 P
pompey hath made the challenge. 5.02.707 P
come challenge me, challenge me by these deserts 5.02.805
challenge me, challenge me by these deserts, 5.02.805
a man's a–hungry, to challenge him the field, TN 2.03.127 P
i'll write thee a challenge, or i'll deliver thy 2.03.129 P
challenge me the count's youth to fight with him 3.02. 34 P
will either of you bear me a challenge to him? 3.02. 40 P
here's the challenge, read it. 3.04.143 P
that is not the matter i challenge thee for." 3.04.157 P
i will deliver his challenge by word of mouth, 3.04.191 P
while upon some horrid message for a challenge. 3.04.200 P
i am a subject, | and i challenge law. R2 2.03.134
life | did hear a challenge urg'd more modestly, 1H4 5.02. 52
if ever i live to see it, i will challenge it. H5 4.01.217 P
if alive and ever dare to challenge this glove, 4.07.127 P
if any man challenge this, he is a friend to 4.07.156 P
i know this, and thus i challenge it. 4.08. 8 P
an honor in thy cap | till i do challenge it. 4.08. 60
our king, | and not of any challenge of desert, 1H6 5.04.153
all her perfections challenge sovereignty: 3H6 3.02. 86
subjects may challenge nothing of their 4.06. 6
why, and i challenge nothing but my dukedom, 4.07. 23
by this i challenge him to single fight. 4.07. 75
no, exeter, these graces challenge grace; 4.08. 48
and make my challenge | you shall not be my H8 2.04. 77
other arms than hers — to him this challenge! TRO 1.03.272
this challenge that the gallant hector sends, 1.03.321
i have a roisting challenge sent amongst | the 2.02.208
will to–morrow | be answered in his challenge: 3.03. 35
grieve his spirit that dares not challenge it. 5.02. 94
a challenge, on my life. ROM 2.04. 8 P
that he dares ne'er come back to challenge you; 3.05.214
who may i rather challenge for unkindness | than MAC 3.04. 41
extend | where nature doth with merit challenge? LR 1.01. 53
read thou this challenge; 4.06.138 P
these white flakes | did challenge pity of them. 4.07. 30
so much i challenge that i may profess | due to OTH 1.03.188
his worthiness | does challenge much respect. 2.01.211
mean time | laugh at his challenge. ANT 4.01. 6
yea | (we challenge too), the bank of any nymph, TNK 3.01. 8
venus' doves, doth challenge that fair field; LUC 58
CHALLENGED 1 FR 0.0001 REL FR 1 V 0 P
dishonored thus and challenged of wrongs? TIT 1.01.340
CHALLENGER 5 FR 0.0005 REL FR 3 V 2 P
monsieur the challenger, the princess calls for AYL 1.02.165 P
he is the general challenger. 1.02.170 P
that | he would unhorse the lustiest challenger. R2 5.03. 19
held | from him, the native and true challenger. H5 2.04. 95
stood challenger on mount of all the age | for HAM 4.07. 28
CHALLENGER'S 1 FR 0.0001 REL FR 0 V 1 P
in pity of the challenger's youth i would fain AYL 1.02.160 P
CHALLENGERS 1 FR 0.0001 REL FR 1 V 0 P
and a cruel style, | a style for challengers. AYL 4.03. 32

CHALLENGES 1 FR 0.0001 REL FR 1 V 0 P
which challenges itself as honor's born, | and AWW 2.03.134
/CHAMBER 1 FR 0.0001 REL FR 0 V 1 P
now get you to my lady's /chamber, and tell her, HAM 5.01.193 P
CHAMBER 95 FR 0.0107 REL FR 68 V 27 P
good proteus, go with me to my chamber, | in TGV 2.04.184
him, | and presently go with me to my chamber, 2.07. 83
her chamber is aloft, far from the ground, | and 3.01.114
the picture that is hanging in your chamber; 4.02.121
a pissing–while, but all the chamber smelt him. 4.04. 19 P
me no more ado, but whips me out of the chamber. 4.04. 29 P
that's her chamber. 4.04. 86
your message done, hie home unto my chamber, 4.04. 88
would better fit his chamber than this shadow. 4.04.120
i will make a star chamber matter of it. WIV 1.01. 2 P
never come in mine own great chamber again else, 1.01.154 P
step into th' chamber, sir john. 4.02. 11 P
my husband will come into the chamber. 4.02.168 P
there's his chamber, his house, his castle, his 4.05. 6 P
woman, a fat woman, gone up into his chamber. 4.05. 12 P
sir — let me speak with you in your chamber. 4.05.121 P
come up into my chamber. 4.05.127 P
all, | withdraw into a chamber by yourselves, ADO 5.04. 11
that is, to bring the moonlight into a chamber; MND 3.01. 48 P
you leave a casement of the great chamber window 3.01. 57 P
we must have a wall in the great chamber; 3.01. 63 P
take his gait, | and each several chamber bless, 5.01.417
the ladies, her attendants of her chamber, | saw AYL 2.02. 5
carry him gently to my fairest chamber, | and SHR in.1. 46
done, conduct him to the drunkard's chamber, in.1. 107
for though you lay here in this goodly chamber, in.2. 84
as kate this chamber with her princely gait? 2.01.259
and help to dress your sister's chamber up. 3.01. 83
go to my chamber, put on clothes of mine. 3.02.113
come, i will bring thee to thy bridal chamber. 4.01.178
in her chamber, making a sermon of continency to 4.01.182 P
go with me to my chamber, and advise me. AWW 2.03.294
and water once a day her chamber round | with TN 1.01. 28
come by and by to my chamber. 4.02. 71 P
your allegiance, | out of the chamber with her! WT 2.03.122
necklace amber, | perfume for a lady's chamber; 4.04.223
we were all commanded out of the chamber; 5.02. 6 P
sitting in my dolphin chamber, at the round 2H4 2.01. 87 P
up, and bear me hence | into some other chamber. 4.04.132
he came not through the chamber where we stay'd. 4.05. 56
depart the chamber, leave us here alone. 4.05. 90
but bear me to that chamber, there i'll lie, 4.05.239
we sent unto the temple, unto his chamber, | and 1H6 2.05. 19
enter his chamber, view his breathless corpse, 2H6 3.02.132
he capers nimbly in a lady's chamber | to the R3 1.01. 12
ill rest betide the chamber where thou liest! 1.02.112
sweet prince, to london, to your chamber. 3.01. 1
stay'd me a prisoner in my chamber when | those H8 1.01. 5
is the banket ready | i' th' privy chamber? 1.04. 99
fresher air, my lord, | in the next chamber. 1.04.102
to withdraw | into your private chamber, we 3.01. 28
whereupon i will show you a chamber, which bed, TRO 3.02.207 P
all tongue–tied maidens here | bed, chamber, 3.02.211
my lord, come you again into my chamber. 4.02. 36
son, | and private in his chamber pens himself, ROM 1.01.138
ask'd for and sought for, in the great chamber. 1.05. 13 P
hie to your chamber. 3.02.138
ascend her chamber, hence and comfort her. 3.03.147
light to my chamber ho! 3.04. 33
your lady mother is coming to your chamber. 3.05. 39
let not the nurse lie with thee in thy chamber. 4.01. 92
he's much out of health, and keeps his chamber. TIM 3.04. 72 P
why have you left the chamber? MAC 1.07. 29
blood those sleepy two | of his own chamber, and 1.07. 76
hark! who lies i' th' second chamber? 2.02. 17
retire we to our chamber. 2.02. 63
approach the chamber, and destroy your sight 2.03. 71
those of his chamber, as it seem'd, had done't. 2.03.101
you do this, keep close within your chamber. HAM 4.07.129
if she be in her chamber or your house, | let OTH 1.01.138
i found it in my chamber. 3.04.188
now he tells how she pluck'd him to my chamber. 4.01.142 P
that you should find it in your chamber, and 4.01.152 P
i have another weapon in this chamber; 5.02.252
i found it in my chamber: 5.02.320
lead me to my chamber. ANT 2.05.119
please you retire to your chamber? 4.04. 35
come, i'll to my chamber. CYM 1.02. 34 P
her breathing that | perfumes the chamber thus. 2.02. 19
to note the chamber, i will write all down: 2.02. 24
ay, | to keep her chamber. 2.03. 82
the chimney | is south the chamber, and the 2.04. 81
the roof o' th' chamber | with golden cherubins 2.04. 87
of what is in her chamber nothing saves | the 2.04. 94
bring this apparel to my chamber. 3.05.151 P
and his glass to confer in his own chamber — i 4.01. 9 P
thaliard — you are of our chamber, thaliard, PER 1.01.151
she hath so strictly tied | her to her chamber, 2.05. 9
to the next chamber bear her. 3.02.107
these strewings are for their chamber. TNK 2.01. 21 P
and they have all the world in their chamber. 2.01. 25 P
the locks between her chamber and his will, LUC 302
now is he come unto the chamber door | that 337
into the chamber wickedly he stalks, | and 365
with shining falchion in my chamber came | a 1626
CHAMBER–COUNCILS 1 FR 0.0001 REL FR 1 V 0 P
heart, as well | my chamber–councils, wherein, WT 1.02.237
CHAMBER'D 1 FR 0.0001 REL FR 1 V 0 P
even in the best blood chamber'd in his bosom, R2 1.01.149
CHAMBER–DOOR 4 FR 0.0004 REL FR 4 V 0 P
hand | like a base pander hold the chamber–door H5 4.05. 14
wait like a lousy footboy | at chamber–door? H8 5.02.175
his clo'es, | and dupp'd the chamber–door, | let HAM 4.05. 53
or at their chamber–door i'll beat the drum LR 2.04.118
CHAMBER–DOORS 1 FR 0.0001 REL FR 1 V 0 P
beds, | hearing alarums at our chamber–doors. 1H6 2.01. 42
CHAMBERERS 1 FR 0.0001 REL FR 1 V 0 P
parts of conversation | that chamberers have, or OTH 3.03.265
CHAMBER–HANGING 1 FR 0.0001 REL FR 1 V 0 P
averring notes | of chamber–hanging, pictures, CYM 5.05.204
CHAMBERLAIN 12 FR 0.0013 REL FR 10 V 2 P
what ho! chamberlain! 1H4 2.01. 47 P
as fair as — at hand, quoth the chamberlain; 2.01. 50 P
her deity | got my lord chamberlain his liberty. R3 1.01. 77
as much unto my good lord chamberlain! 1.01.123
and between them and my lord chamberlain, | and 1.03. 38
what, talking with a priest, lord chamberlain? 3.02.113
good lord chamberlain, | go, give 'em welcome: H8 1.04. 56
say, lord chamberlain, | they have done my poor 1.04. 72
my lord chamberlain, | prithee come hither. 1.04. 90
well met, my lord chamberlain. 2.02. 12
thanks, my good lord chamberlain. 2.02. 61
that the bleak air, thy boisterous chamberlain, TIM 4.03.222
CHAMBERLAINS 1 FR 0.0001 REL FR 1 V 0 P
his two chamberlains | will i with wine and MAC 1.07. 63
CHAMBER–LYE 1 FR 0.0001 REL FR 0 V 1 P
and your chamber–lye breeds fleas like a loach. 1H4 2.01. 20 P
CHAMBERMAID 2 FR 0.0002 REL FR 1 V 1 P
my niece's chambermaid. TN 1.03. 51 P
the chambermaid and servingman, by night | that TNK 3.05.126
/CHAMBERMAIDS 1 FR 0.0001 REL FR 0 V 1 P
/who /since /possesses /chambermaids /and LR 4.01. 62 P
CHAMBERMAIDS 1 FR 0.0001 REL FR 1 V 0 P
i remain | with worms that are thy chambermaids; ROM 5.03.109
CHAMBER–POT 1 FR 0.0001 REL FR 0 V 1 P
and, in roaring for a chamber–pot, dismiss the COR 2.01. 76 P
CHAMBER'S 1 FR 0.0001 REL FR 1 V 0 P
the whole time | i was my chamber's prisoner. H8 1.01. 13
CHAMBERS 9 FR 0.0010 REL FR 5 V 4 P
ascend my chambers, search, seek, find out. WIV 3.03.162 P
be any pody in the house, and in the chambers, 3.03.211 P
my chambers are honorable. 4.05. 22 P
that in your chambers gave you chastisement? JN 5.02.147
to venture upon the charg'd chambers bravely — 2H4 2.04. 52 P
than in the perfum'd chambers of the great, 3.01. 12
many do keep their chambers are not sick; TIM 3.04. 73
are near at hand | that chambers will be safe. MAC 5.04. 2
her chambers are all lock'd, and there's no CYM 3.05. 43
CHAMBER–WINDOW 11 FR 0.0012 REL FR 5 V 6 P
to climb celestial silvia's chamber–window, TGV 2.06. 34
a mean | how he her chamber–window will ascend, 3.01. 39
visit by night your lady's chamber–window | with 3.02. 82
her to look out at her lady's chamber–window. ADO 2.02. 17 P
likelihood than to see me at her chamber–window, 2.02. 43 P
in my chamber–window lies a book; 2.03. 3 P
would have it at the lady hero's chamber–window. 2.03. 87 P
you shall see her chamber–window ent'red, even 3.02.113 P
leans me out at her mistress' chamber–window, 3.03.147 P
talk with a ruffian at her chamber–window, | who 4.01. 91
when midnight comes, knock at my chamber–window; AWW 4.02. 54
CHAMBLET 1 FR 0.0001 REL FR 1 V 0 P
you i' th' chamblet, get up o' th' rail, | i'll H8 5.03. 89
CHAMELEON 3 FR 0.0003 REL FR 1 V 2 P
though the chameleon love can feed on the air, i TGV 2.01.172 P
him leave, madam, he is a kind of chameleon. 2.04. 26 P
i can add colors to the chameleon, | change 3H6 3.02.191
CHAMELEON'S 1 FR 0.0001 REL FR 0 V 1 P
i' faith — of the chameleon's dish, i eat the HAM 3.02. 93 P
CHAMP 1 FR 0.0001 REL FR 1 V 0 P
richard du champ. CYM 4.02.377
CHAMPAIGN *(also champains, champian)*
CHAMPAIGN 1 FR 0.0001 REL FR 1 V 0 P
their smoothness, like a goodly champaign plain, LUC 1247
CHAMPAIGNE 1 FR 0.0001 REL FR 1 V 0 P
guienne, champaigne, rheims, orleance, | paris, 1H6 1.01. 60
CHAMPAINS *(also champaign, champian)*
CHAMPAINS 1 FR 0.0001 REL FR 1 V 0 P
with shadowy forests and with champains rich'd, LR 1.01. 64
CHAMPIAN *(also champaign, champains)*
CHAMPIAN 1 FR 0.0001 REL FR 0 V 1 P
daylight and champian discovers not more. TN 2.05.160 P
CHAMPION 15 FR 0.0017 REL FR 14 V 1 P
brings in the champion honor on my part, AWW 4.02. 50
thou fortune's champion that dost never fight JN 3.01.118
be champion of our church, | or let the church, 3.01.255
that is, to be the champion of our church! 3.01.267
to god, the widow's champion and defense. R2 1.02. 43
demand of yonder champion | the cause of his 1.03. 7
his new–come champion, virtuous joan of /aire, 1H6 2.02. 20
said | a stouter champion never handled sword. 3.04. 19
the most complete champion that ever i heard! 2H6 4.10. 55 P
himself, | and now will i be edward's champion. 3H6 4.07. 68
patron of virtue, rome's best champion, TIT 1.01. 65
the list, | and champion me to th' utterance! MAC 3.01. 71
i can produce a champion that will prove | what LR 5.01. 43
like a bold champion i assume the lists, | nor PER 1.01. 61
her champion mounted for the hot encounter: VEN 596
CHAMPIONS 4 FR 0.0004 REL FR 4 V 0 P
why then the champions are prepar'd, and stay R2 1.03. 5
his champions are the prophets and apostles, 2H6 1.03. 57
/renown'd | for hardy and undoubted champions; 3H6 5.07. 6
rome's readiest champions, repose you here in TIT 1.01.151
CHAM'S 1 FR 0.0001 REL FR 0 V 1 P
fetch you a hair off the great cham's beard, do ADO 2.01.269 P
CHANC'D 9 FR 0.0010 REL FR 8 V 1 P
omit | all the occurrences, what ever chanc'd, H5 5.pr. 40
tell us what hath chanc'd to–day | that caesar JC 1.02.217
i should not then ask casca what had chanc'd. 1.02.220
back with speed, and tell him what hath chanc'd. 3.01.287
octavius' tent | how every thing is chanc'd. 5.04. 32
think upon what hath chanc'd; MAC 1.03.153
if then they chanc'd to slack ye, | we could LR 2.04.245
this chanc'd to–night. PER 3.02. 77
your friend and i have chanc'd to name you here, TNK 2.01. 16 P
/CHANCE 5 FR 0.0005 REL FR 5 V 0 P
/the /accompt /of /chance /before /you /said, 2H4 1.01.167
/how /chance /the /prophet /could /not /at /that R3 4.02.100
/or /bad, /'tis /but /the /chance /of /war. TRO pr 31
though /chance of war hath wrought this change TIT 1.01.264
bring us to him, | and /chance it as it may. TIM 5.01.126
CHANCE 111 FR 0.0125 REL FR 94 V 17 P
should from her vesture chance to steal a kiss, TGV 2.04.160
numbers, either in nativity, chance, or death. WIV 5.01. 4 P
how chance you went not with master slender? 5.05.217 P
though my chance is now | to use it for my time. MM 3.02.217
wherein if he chance to fail, he hath sentenc'd 3.02.257 P
but, by chance, nothing of what is writ. 4.02.202 P
how chance thou art return'd so soon? ERR 1.02. 42
i may chance have some odd quirks and remnants ADO 2.03.235 P
and made a push at chance and sufferance. 5.01. 38
since you are strangers and come here by chance, LLL 5.02.218
along this coast, i here am come by chance, 5.02.554
how chance the roses there do fade so fast? MND 1.01.129
how chance moonshine is gone before thisby comes 5.01.312 P
you must take your chance, | and either not MV 2.01. 38
nor will not. come bring me unto my chance. 2.01. 43
the view, | chance as fair, and choose as true: 3.02.132
and if he chance to speak, be ready straight, SHR in.1. 52
why, this' a heavy chance 'twixt him and you, 1.02. 46
here is a gentleman whom by chance i met, | upon 1.02.181
and if she chance to nod i'll rail and brawl, 4.01.206
but they may chance to need thee at home, 5.01. 2 P
true, madam, and, to comfort you with chance, TN 1.02. 8
home, where if it be thy chance to kill me" — 3.04.160 P
if you shall chance, camillo, to visit bohemia WT 1.01. 1 P
i am question'd by my fears of what may chance 1.02. 11
some place | where chance may nurse or end it. 2.03.183
profess | ourselves to be the slaves of chance, 4.04.540
naturally honest, i am so sometimes by chance. 4.04.713 P
brother, take you my land, i'll take my chance. JN 1.01.151
madam, by chance, but not by truth; 1.01.169
where but by chance a silver drop hath fall'n, 3.04. 63
and so by chance | did grace our hollow parting R2 1.04. 8
my sovereign liege, | but by the chance of war; 1H4 1.03. 95
and your unthought–of harry chance to meet. 3.02.141
it may chance cost some of us our lives, for he 2H4 2.01. 11 P
of the main chance of things | as yet not come 3.01. 83
how chance thou art not with the prince thy 4.04. 20
what chance is this that suddenly hath cross'd 1H6 1.04. 72
that, if it chance the one of us do fail, | the 2.01. 31
and, now it is my chance to find thee out, 5.04. 4
main chance, father, you meant, but i meant 2H6 1.01.212
cam'st thou here by chance | or of devotion, to 2.01. 85
i fear her not, unless she chance to fall. 3H6 3.02. 24
but if you ever chance to have a child, | look 5.05. 65
me once restore a purse of gold that (by chance) R3 1.04.140 P
if i chance to talk a little wild, forgive me; H8 1.04. 26
if they shall chance, | in charging you with 5.01.145
cooling too, or ye may chance burn your lips. TRO 1.01. 26 P
in the reproof of chance | lies the true proof 1.03. 33
how chance my brother troilus went not? 3.01.137 P
an act that very chance doth throw upon him — 3.03.131
we met by chance, you did not find me here. 4.02. 71
where injury of chance | puts back leave–taking, 4.04. 33
as seld i have the chance — i would desire | my 4.05.150
if we and caius martius chance to meet, | 'tis COR 1.02. 34
if you chance to be pinch'd with the colic, you 2.01. 74 P
execution | of what we chance to sentence. 3.03. 22
more than a wild exposture to each chance | that 4.01. 36
to take the one the other, by some chance, 4.04. 20
lest you shall chance to whip your information, 4.06. 54
in corioles, and his child | like him by chance. 5.03.180
and triumphs over chance in honor's bed. TIT 1.01.178
woe to her chance, and damn'd her loathed choice 4.02. 78
this trick may chance to scath you. ROM 1.05. 84
well, he may chance to do some good on her. 4.02. 13
hour | is guilty of this lamentable chance! 5.03.146
i know will be, much that i fear may chance. JC 2.04. 32
lest some friend of caesar's | should chance — 3.01. 88
if chance will have me king, why, chance may MAC 1.03.143
why, chance may crown me | without my stir. 1.03.143
had i but died an hour before this chance, | i 2.03. 91
that i would set my life on any chance, | to 3.01.112
and the chance of goodness | be like our 4.03.136
if he by chance escape your venom'd stuck, | our HAM 4.07.161
you that look pale, and tremble at this chance, 5.02.334
dow'rless daughter, king, thrown to my chance, LR 1.01.256
how chance the king comes with so small a number 2.04. 63
nay then come on, and take the chance of anger. 3.07. 79
if you do chance to hear of that blind traitor, 4.05. 37
it is a chance which does redeem all sorrows 5.03.267
well, i may chance to see you; OTH 4.01.166 P
the shot of accident nor dart of chance | could 4.01.267
my better cunning faints | under his chance. ANT 2.03. 36
if this division chance, ne'er stood between, 3.04. 13
give up yourself merely to chance and hazard, 3.07. 47
i'll yet follow | the wounded chance of antony, 3.10. 35
dare but what it can, | no chance may shake it. 3.13. 81
shall remember | as things but done by chance. 5.02.120
of my spirits | through th' ashes of my chance. 5.02.174
think what a chance thou changest on, but think CYM 1.05. 68
may seem to those | which chance to find us. 4.02.332
wilt take thy chance with me? 4.02.382
if in your country wars you chance to die, 4.04. 51
this was strange chance. 5.03. 51
that have this golden chance and know not why. 5.04.132
sir, the chance of war, the day | was yours by 5.05. 75
other by–dependances, | from chance to chance; 5.05.391
other by–dependances, | from chance to chance; 5.05.391
how chance my daughter is not with you? PER 4.01. 22
in a fever, and deifies alone | voluble chance; TNK 1.02. 67
and let us follow | the becking of our chance. 1.02.116
at misery | and bear the chance of war yet. 2.02. 3
thrice–blessed chance, | to drop on such a 3.01. 13
if it be your chance to come where the blessed 4.03. 21 P
o, what pity | enough for such a chance! 5.03. 60
what is the chance? 5.03. 66
chance would have it so. 5.03. 75
palamon | had the best–boding chance. 5.03. 77
far from home, wond'ring each other's chance. LUC 1596
may any terms acquit me from this chance? 1706
by chance or nature's changing course untrimm'd: SON 18. 8
/CHANCED 1 FR 0.0001 REL FR 1 V 0 P
/sad /stories /chanced /in /the /times /of /old. TIT 3.02. 83
CHANCED 2 FR 0.0002 REL FR 2 V 0 P
strange accident | i chanced on this letter. MV 5.01.279
others' years | that what he fear'd is chanced. 2H4 1.01. 87
/CHANCELLOR 1 FR 0.0001 REL FR 1 V 0 P
la car, | one gilbert /perk, his /chancellor — H8 1.01.219
CHANCELLOR 3 FR 0.0003 REL FR 3 V 0 P
warwick is chancellor and the lord of callice, 3H6 1.01.238
sir gilbert /perk his chancellor, and john car, H8 2.01. 20
more is chosen | lord chancellor in your place. 3.02.394
CHANCE'S 1 FR 0.0001 REL FR 1 V 0 P

how chance's mocks | and changes fill the cup of 2H4 3.01. 51
CHANCES 14 FR 0.0015 REL FR 12 V 2 P
but it chances | the stealth of our most mutual MM 1.02.153
and there be any matter of weight chances, call ADO 3.03. 85 P
against ill chances men are ever merry, | but 2H4 4.02. 81
how will the country for these woeful chances 3H6 2.05.107
that common chances common men could bear, COR 4.01. 5
to fail in the disposing of those chances 4.07. 40
rest, | secure from worldly chances and mishaps! TIT 1.01.152
time | every good hap to you that chances here. ROM 3.03.171
so, oft it chances in particular men, | that for HAM 1.04. 23
how chances it they travel? 2.02.329 P
wherein i spoke of most disastrous chances: OTH 1.03.134
italy annoy us, but | we grieve at chances here. CYM 4.03. 35
scapes, and chances | into an honest house, our PER 5.ch. 1
a thousand chances, | were we from hence, would TNK 2.02. 94
CHANDLER'S 1 FR 0.0001 REL FR 0 V 1 P
good cheap at the dearest chandler's in europe. 1H4 3.03. 46 P
/CHANG'D 1 FR 0.0001 REL FR 0 V 1 P
/i /am /chang'd. OTH 1.03.379 P
CHANG'D 39 FR 0.0044 REL FR 32 V 7 P
creatures that were mine, i say, or chang'd 'em, TMP 1.02. 82
at the first sight | they have chang'd eyes. 1.02.442
besides, the fashion of the time is chang'd) TGV 3.01. 86
fie, brother, how the world is chang'd with you: ERR 2.02.152
if thou art chang'd to aught, 'tis to an ass. 2.02.199
thou wouldst have chang'd thy face for a name, 3.01. 47
grief hath chang'd me since you saw me last, 5.01.298
the story shall be chang'd: MND 2.01.230
o bottom, thou art chang'd! 3.01.114 P
believe me, you are marvellously chang'd. MV 1.01. 76
lord, how art thou chang'd! 2.02. 99 P
your mouth, | tranio is chang'd into lucentio. SHR 1.01.237
cambio is chang'd into lucentio. 5.01.123
for she is chang'd, as she had never been. 5.02.115
on the reading it he chang'd almost into another AWW 4.03. 5 P
what we chang'd | was innocence for innocence; WT 1.02. 68
your chang'd complexions are to me a mirror 1.02.381
me a mirror | which shows me mine chang'd too; 1.02.382
who was most marble there chang'd color; 5.02. 90 P
she is corrupted, chang'd, and won from thee; JN 3.01. 55
my lord, the mind of bullingbrook is chang'd, R2 5.01. 51
and now chang'd to "the beggar and the king." 5.03. 80
means his grace, that he hath chang'd his style? 1H6 4.01. 50
chang'd to a worser shape thou canst not be. 5.03. 36
our stern alarums chang'd to merry meetings, R3 1.01. 7
/once," quoth forrest, "almost chang'd my mind; 4.03. 15
my mind is chang'd. stanley, what news with you? 4.04.456
thou art chang'd for antenor. TRO 4.02. 91 P
the sorrow that delivers us thus chang'd | makes COR 5.03. 39
and art thou chang'd? ROM 2.03. 79
o, now i would they had chang'd voices too, 3.05. 32
say they are persian, but let them be chang'd. LR 3.06. 81 P
madam, within, but never man so chang'd. 4.02. 3
in nothing am i chang'd | but in my garments. 4.06. 9
he is much chang'd. OTH 4.01.268
lord, how your favor's chang'd | with this PER 4.01. 24
ay, by my faith, they shall not be chang'd yet. 4.02.135 P
her blue blood chang'd to black in every vein, LUC 1454
sorrow chang'd to solace, and solace mix'd with PP 14.23
/CHANGE 2 FR 0.0002 REL FR 1 V 1 P
to /change true rules for /odd inventions. SHR 3.01. 81
/she /must /have /change, /she /must; OTH 1.03.352 P
CHANGE 162 FR 0.0183 REL FR 136 V 26 P
what, angry, sir thurio? do you change color? TGV 2.04. 23 P
and cannot soon revolt and change your mind. 3.02. 59
hark, what fine change is in the music. 4.02. 68 P
ay; that change is the spite. 4.02. 69 P
words | can no way change you to a milder form, 5.04. 56
women to change their shapes than men their 5.04.109
how so, sir? did she change her determination? WIV 3.05. 68 P
why, here's a change indeed in the commonwealth! MM 1.02.104 P
though you change your place, you need not 1.02.107 P
your place, you need not change your trade; 1.02.108 P
if power change purpose, what our seemers be. 1.03. 54
as school–maids change their names | by vain 1.04. 47
could i, with boot, change for an idle plume, 2.04. 11
sir, change persons with me, ere you make that 5.01.336 P
dark–working sorcerers that change the mind, ERR 1.02. 99
if my passion change not shortly, god forbid it ADO 1.01.219 P
would better fit your honor to change your mind. 3.02.116 P
maintain'd the change of words with any creature 4.01.183
shall on her behalf | change slander to remorse; 4.01.211
and change you favors too, so shall your loves LLL 5.02.134
then in our measure do but vouchsafe one change. 5.02.209
thus change i like the moon. 5.02.212
will you vouchsafe with me to change a word? 5.02.238
therefore change favors, and, when they repair, 5.02.292
once disclos'd, | the ladies did change favors; 5.02.468
these four will change habits, and present the 5.02.539
change not your offer made in heat of blood; 5.02.800
i'll change my black gown for a faithful friend. 5.02.834
angry winter, change | their wonted liveries; MND 2.01.112
who will not change a raven for a dove? 2.02.114
what change is this, | sweet love? 3.02.262
would he would change! 5.01.252 P
i would not change this hue, | except to steal MV 2.01. 11
and speak between the change of man and boy 3.04. 66
entreat some power to change this currish jew. 4.01.292
but music for the time doth change his nature. 5.01. 82
son — and would not change that calling | to be AYL 1.02.233
wilt thou change fathers? 1.03. 91
and do not seek to take your change upon you, 1.03.102
i would not change it. 2.01. 18
change you color? 3.02.182 P
a fault i will not change for your best virtue. 3.02.283 P
me, | as i can change these poor accoutrements, SHR 3.02.119
scarfs and fans, and double change of brav'ry, 4.03. 57
not so, but as we change our courtesies. AWW 3.02. 97
change it, change it! 4.02. 31
change it, change it! 4.02. 31
and to come) that you do change this purpose, WT 2.03.151
will speak, that you must change this purpose, 4.04. 39
which does mend nature — change it rather; 4.04. 96
this robe of mine | does change my disposition. 4.04.135
if you will not change your purpose | but 4.04.542
in't) and change garments with this gentleman. 4.04.634 P
pow'r no jot | hath she to change our loves. 5.01.218
yea, faith itself to hollow falsehood change! JN 3.01. 95
him, | and kiss the lips of unacquainted change, 3.04.166
with any long'd–for change or better state. 4.02. 8
their thimbles into armed gauntlets change, 5.02.156
yea, but not change his spots. R2 1.01.175
can change their moons and bring their times 1.03.220
and lean–look'd prophets whisper fearful change, 2.04. 11
to change blows with thee for our day of doom. 3.02.189
change the complexion of her maid–pale peace 3.03. 98
state, for every one doth so | against a change; 3.04. 28
our vizards we will change after we leave them; 1H4 1.02.178 P
the seasons change their manners, as the year 2H4 4.04.123
world | the noble change that i have purposed! 4.05.154
we are blessed in the change. H5 1.01. 37
look ye how they change! 2.02. 73
i will not change my horse with any that treads 3.07. 11 P
that i gave it to in change promis'd to wear it 4.08. 29 P
silling, i warrant you, or i will change it. 4.08. 71 P
shall change all griefs and quarrels into love. 5.02. 20
comets, importing change of times and states, 1H6 1.01. 2
four of their lords i'll change for one of ours. 1.01.151
as if, with circe, she would change my shape! 5.03. 35
to change two dukedoms for a duke's fair 2H6 1.01.219
nor change my countenance for this arrest; 3.01. 99
thoughts, | and change misdoubt to resolution; 3.01.332
is able with the change to kill and cure. 5.01.101
change shapes with proteus for advantages, | and 3H6 3.02.192
madam, what makes you in this sudden change? 4.04. 1
"wind–changing warwick now can change no more." 5.01. 57
hope this passionate humor of mine will change. R3 1.04.118 P
before the days of change, still is it so. 2.03. 41
cousin, canst thou quake and change thy color, 3.05. 1
luxury | and bestial appetite in change of lust, 3.05. 81
and i warrant helen, to change, would give an TRO 1.02.239 P
of blood, a son of priam, | in change of him. 3.03. 27
it is prodigious, there will come some change; 5.01. 93 P
wind, to wind, there turn and change together. 5.03.110
with every minute you do change a mind, | and COR 1.01.182
greetings, | but with them change of honors. 2.01.198
may i change these garments? 2.03.146
what makes this change? 3.01. 27
of state | more than you doubt the change on't; 3.01.152
of war hath wrought this change of cheer, | thou TIT 1.01.264
she hath not seen the change of fourteen years; ROM 1.02. 9
holy saint francis, what a change is here! 2.03. 65
some say the lark and loathed toad change eyes; 3.05. 31
our solemn hymns to sullen dirges change; 4.05. 88
and all things change them to the contrary. 4.05. 90
when fortune in her shift and change of mood TIM 1.01. 84
how came the noble timon to this change? 4.03. 67
melancholy sprung | from change of future. 4.03.204
why all these things change from their ordinance JC 1.03. 66
will change to virtue and to worthiness. 1.03.160
how that might change his nature, there's the 2.01. 13
you will not come, | their minds may change. 2.02. 96
for look he smiles, and caesar doth not change. 3.01. 24
in his own change, or by ill officers, | hath 4.02. 7
now i change my mind, | and partly credit things 5.01. 77
it is but change, titinius; 5.03. 51
good friend — i'll change that name with you. HAM 1.02.163
even our loves should with our fortunes change: 3.02.201
for use almost can change the stamp of nature, 3.04.168
that things might change or cease, /tears /his LR 3.01. 7
the lamentable change is from the best, | the 4.01. 5
i must change names at home, and give the 4.02. 17
change places, and, handy–dandy, which is the 4.06.153 P
he is advis'd by aught | to change the course. 5.01. 3
how say you by this change? OTH 1.03. 17
hen, i would change my humanity with a baboon. 1.03.316 P
she must change for youth; 1.03.349 P
to change the cod's head for the salmon's tail; 2.01.155
patience, i say; your mind /perhaps may change. 3.03.452
here's a change indeed! 4.02.106
that they do | when they change us for others? 4.03. 97
you say, must change his horns with garlands! ANT 1.02. 4 P
of rest, would purge | by any desperate change. 1.03. 54
what he cannot change, | than what he chooses. 1.04. 14
i saw you last, | there's a change upon you. 2.06. 53
authority abus'd, | and did deserve his change. 3.06. 34
he never find more cause | to change a master. 4.05. 16
the miserable change now at my end | lament nor 4.15. 51
which shackles accidents and bolts up change, 5.02. 6
you shall find | a benefit in this change; 5.02.128
change you, madam? CYM 1.06. 11
pronounce | the beggary of his change; 1.06.115
but abide the change of time, | quake in the 2.04. 4
ambitions, covetings, change of prides, disdain, 2.05. 25
change | command into obedience; 3.04.154
i'ld change my sex to be companion with them, 3.06. 87
i think he would change places with his officer; 5.04.175 P
why should this change of thoughts, | the sad PER 1.02. 1
but see what heaven can do by this our change: 1.04. 33
though they did change me to the meanest bird 4.06.101
fiend | of hell would not in reputation change. 4.06.164
if all these petty ills shall change thy good, LUC 656
stern, sad tunes to change their kinds; 1147
o, change thy thought, that i may change my mind SON 10. 9
change thy thought, that i may change my mind! 10. 9
to change your day of youth to sullied night, 15.12
but not acquainted | with shifting change, as is 20. 4
that then i scorn to change my state with kings. 29.14
so far from variation or quick change? 76. 2
so ill, | to set a form upon desired change, 89. 6
therefore in that i cannot know thy change. 93. 6
and in this change is my invention spent, 105.11
in 'twixt vows, and change decrees of kings, 115. 6
time, thou shalt not boast that i do change: 123. 1
they would change their state | and situation 128. 9
/CHANGEABLE 1 FR 0.0001 REL FR 0 V 1 P
/report /is /changeable. LR 4.07. 91 P
CHANGEABLE 3 FR 0.0003 REL FR 0 V 3 P
be effeminate, changeable, longing and liking, AYL 3.02.411 P
tailor make thy doublet of changeable taffata, TN 2.04. 74 P
these moors are changeable in their wills — OTH 1.03.346 P
/CHANGED 1 FR 0.0001 REL FR 1 V 0 P
/thou /changed /and //self–cover'd /thing, /for LR 4.02. 62
CHANGED 2 FR 0.0002 REL FR 2 V 0 P
took the moon at full, but now she's changed. LLL 5.02.214
instantly to visit | my too much changed son. HAM 2.02. 36
CHANGEFUL 1 FR 0.0001 REL FR 1 V 0 P
powers, | presuming on their changeful potency. TRO 4.04. 97
CHANGELING 8 FR 0.0009 REL FR 6 V 2 P
she never had so sweet a changeling. MND 2.01. 23
i do but beg a little changeling boy | to be my 2.01.120
i then did ask of her her changeling child; 4.01. 59
this is some changeling; WT 3.03.118 P
way but to tell the king she's a changeling, and 4.04.688 P
yet his nature | in that's no changeling, and i COR 4.07. 11
plac'd it safely, | the changeling never known. HAM 5.02. 53
thou art a changeling to him, a mere gipsy, TNK 4.02. 44
CHANGELINGS 1 FR 0.0001 REL FR 1 V 0 P
of fickle changelings and poor discontents, 1H4 5.01. 76
/CHANGES 1 FR 0.0001 REL FR 1 V 0 P
joy, | yet throw such /changes of vexation on't, OTH 1.01. 72
CHANGES 18 FR 0.0020 REL FR 12 V 6 P
it ever changes with the next block. ADO 1.01. 76 P
by this light, he changes more and more. 5.01.140 P
maids, but the sky changes when they are wives. AYL 4.01.149 P
and the moon changes even as your mind. SHR 4.05. 20
nine changes of the wat'ry star hath been | the WT 1.02. 1
is breeding | that changes thus his manners. 1.02.375
but the changes i perceiv'd in the king and 5.02. 10 P
mocks | and changes fill the cup of alteration 2H4 3.01. 52
his eye is hollow, and he changes much. 4.05. 6
and now my death | changes the mood, for what in 4.05.199
for it shines bright and never changes, but H5 5.02.164 P
frights, changes, horrors, | divert and crack, TRO 1.03. 98
that monthly changes in her /circled orb, | lest ROM 2.02.110
for this "would" changes, | and hath abatements HAM 4.07.119
you see how full of changes his age is; LR 1.01.288 P
to follow still the changes of the moon | with OTH 3.03.178
the moor already changes with my poison: 3.03.325
that my steel'd sense or changes right or wrong. SON 112. 8
CHANGEST 1 FR 0.0001 REL FR 1 V 0 P
think what a chance thou changest on, but think CYM 1.05. 68
CHANGING 12 FR 0.0013 REL FR 11 V 1 P
continue in it five weeks without changing. TMP 2.01.184 P
one julia, that his changing thoughts forget, TGV 4.04.119
not changing heart with habit, i am still MM 5.01.384
but in this changing, what is your intent? LLL 5.02.137
hortensio will be quit with thee by changing. SHR 3.01. 92
sweet love, i see, changing his property, R2 3.02.135
in changing hardiment with great glendower. 1H4 1.03.101
relenting fool, and shallow, changing woman! R3 4.04.431
ways, go give that changing piece | to him that TIT 1.01.309
they are not constant, but are changing still: CYM 2.05. 30
by chance or nature's changing course untrimm'd: SON 18. 8
each changing place with that which goes before, 60. 3
CHANNEL 13 FR 0.0014 REL FR 10 V 3 P
shall leave his native channel and o'erswell JN 2.01.337
no more shall trenching war channel her fields, 1H4 1.01. 7
shall run | in a new channel fair and evenly. 3.01.102
villain's head, throw the quean in the channel. 2H4 2.01. 47 P
throw me in the channel? 2.01. 48 P
i'll throw thee in the channel. 2.01. 49 P
i charge thee waft me safely cross the channel. 2H6 4.01.115
(as if a channel should be call'd the sea), 3H6 2.02.141
current in a ditch, | and make your channel his? COR 3.01. 97
and weep your tears | into the channel, till the JC 1.01. 59
in the sweet channel of her bosom dropp'd; VEN 958
here friend by friend in bloody channel lies, LUC 1487
o, how the channel to the stream gave grace! LC 285
CHANNELS 2 FR 0.0002 REL FR 2 V 0 P
leave your crisp channels, and on this green TMP 4.01.130
with cadent tears fret channels in her cheeks, LR 1.04.285
CHANSON 1 FR 0.0001 REL FR 0 V 1 P
row of the pious chanson will show you more, for HAM 2.02.419 P
CHANT *(see chaunt, etc.)*
CHANTICLEER 2 FR 0.0002 REL FR 2 V 0 P
i hear | the strain of strutting chanticleer: TMP 1.02.386
time, | my lungs began to crow like chanticleer, AYL 2.07. 30
CHANTRY *(also chauntries)*
CHANTRY 1 FR 0.0001 REL FR 1 V 0 P
me and with this holy man | into the chantry by; TN 4.03. 24
CHAOS 6 FR 0.0006 REL FR 6 V 0 P
like to a chaos, or an unlick'd bear–whelp 3H6 3.02.161
this chaos, when degree is suffocate, | follows TRO 1.03.125
misshapen chaos of well/–seeming forms, ROM 1.01.179
and when i love thee not, | chaos is come again. OTH 3.03. 92
and, beauty dead, black chaos comes again. VEN 1020
vast sin–concealing chaos! LUC 767
CHAPE 1 FR 0.0001 REL FR 0 V 1 P
and the practice in the chape of his dagger. AWW 4.03.143 P
CHAPEL 10 FR 0.0011 REL FR 9 V 1 P
familiar, | and to the chapel let us presently. ADO 5.04. 71
tree, or shall we go with you to your chapel? AYL 3.03. 66 P
a day i'll visit | the chapel where they lie, WT 3.02.239
quit presently the chapel, or resolve you | for 5.03. 86
for at saint mary's chapel presently | the rites JN 2.01.538
view'd in open as his queen, | going to chapel; H8 3.02.405
fair, and bring the body | into the chapel. HAM 4.01. 37
may take it thence, | and bear it to the chapel. 4.02. 8
but as a monument, | thus in a chapel lying! CYM 2.02. 33
of our dead kings, that we may chapel them; TNK 1.01. 50
CHAPELESS 1 FR 0.0001 REL FR 0 V 1 P
town armory, with a broken hilt, and chapeless; SHR 3.02. 48 P
CHAPELS 1 FR 0.0001 REL FR 0 V 1 P
what were good to do, chapels had been churches, MV 1.02. 13 P
CHAPLAIN 4 FR 0.0004 REL FR 4 V 0 P
chaplain, away, thy priesthood saves thy life. 3H6 1.03. 3
the chaplain of the tower hath buried them, R3 4.03. 29
me to permit | john de la car, my chaplain, a H8 1.02.162
he spoke | my chaplain to no creature living but 1.02.166
CHAPLAINS' 1 FR 0.0001 REL FR 1 V 0 P
whole realm by your teaching and your chaplains' H8 5.02. 51
/CHAPLESS 1 FR 0.0001 REL FR 1 V 0 P
with reeky shanks and yellow /chapless skulls; ROM 4.01. 83
CHAPLET 1 FR 0.0001 REL FR 1 V 0 P
crown | an odorous chaplet of sweet summer buds MND 2.01.110
CHAPLETS 1 FR 0.0001 REL FR 1 V 0 P

with chaplets on their heads of daffadillies, TNK 4.01. 73
CHAPMEN 1 FR 0.0001 REL FR 1 V 0 P
fair diomed, you do as chapmen do, | dispraise TRO 4.01. 76
CHAPMEN'S 1 FR 0.0001 REL FR 1 V 0 P
not utt'red by base sale of chapmen's tongues. LLL 2.01. 16
CHAPS* *(also chops*)*
CHAPS* 6 FR 0.0006 REL FR 4 V 2 P
open your chaps again. TMP 2.02. 86 P
now doth death line his dead chaps with steel, JN 2.01.352
i'll thrust my knife in your mouldy chaps, and 2H4 2.04.130 P
before his chaps be stain'd with crimson blood, 2H6 3.01.259
but if my frosty signs and chaps of age, | grave TIT 5.03. 77
/world, thou /hast a pair of chaps — no more, ANT 3.05. 13
CHAPTER 1 FR 0.0001 REL FR 0 V 1 P
in his bosom? in what chapter of his bosom? TN 1.05.225 P
CHARACTER 20 FR 0.0022 REL FR 15 V 5 P
there is a kind of character in thy life, | that MM 1.01. 27
with character too gross is writ on juliet. 1.02.155
you know the character, i doubt not, and the 4.02.193 P
and in their barks my thoughts i'll character, AYL 3.02. 6
with this thy fair and outward character. TN 1.02. 51
though, i confess, much like the character; 5.01.346
there lie, and there thy character; WT 3.03. 47
with it, which they know to be his character; 5.02. 35 P
conspectuities glean out of this character, if i COR 2.01. 65 P
i paint him in the character. 5.04. 26 P
the character i'll take with wax; TIM 5.03. 6
precepts in thy memory | look thou character. HAM 1.03. 59
'tis hamlet's character. 4.07. 51
you know the character to be your brother's? LR 1.02. 62 P
though thou didst produce | my very character), 2.01. 72
know you the character? PER 3.04. 3
his nose stands high, a character of honor; TNK 4.02.110
since mind at first in character was done! SON 59. 8
reserve their character with golden quill | and 85. 3
what's in the brain that ink may character 108. 1
CHARACTER'D 4 FR 0.0004 REL FR 4 V 0 P
thoughts | are visibly character'd and engrav'd, TGV 2.07. 4
show me one scar character'd on thy skin: 2H6 3.01.300
the light will show, character'd in my brow, LUC 807
my brain | full character'd with lasting memory, SON 122. 2
CHARACTERLESS 1 FR 0.0001 REL FR 1 V 0 P
and mighty states characterless are grated | to TRO 3.02.188
CHARACTERS 12 FR 0.0013 REL FR 11 V 1 P
when it deserves, with characters of brass, | a MM 5.01. 11
written down old with all the characters of age? 2H4 1.02.180 P
memory, | rasing the characters of your renown, 2H6 1.01.101
i say, without characters fame lives long. R3 3.01. 81
whose grossness little characters sum up; TRO 1.03.325
well | in characters as red as mars his heart 5.02.164
that knew the stars as i his characters; CYM 3.02. 28
he cut our roots in characters, | and sauc'd our 4.02. 49
apollo, perfect me in the characters! PER 3.02. 67
in glitt'ring golden characters express | a 4.03. 44
eyne, | which on it had conceited characters, LC 16
thought characters and words merely but art, 174
CHARACTERY 2 FR 0.0002 REL FR 2 V 0 P
fairies use flow'rs for their charactery. WIV 5.05. 73
to thee, | all the charactery of my sad brows. JC 2.01.308
CHARBON 1 FR 0.0001 REL FR 0 V 1 P
for young charbon the puritan and old poysam the AWW 1.03. 52 P
CHAR'D 1 FR 0.0001 REL FR 1 V 0 P
all's char'd when he is gone. TNK 3.02. 21
CHARE 1 FR 0.0001 REL FR 1 V 0 P
and when thou hast done this chare, i'll give ANT 5.02.231
CHARECT *(also carat)*
CHARECT 1 FR 0.0001 REL FR 1 V 0 P
much your chain weighs to the utmost charect, ERR 4.01. 28
CHARES 1 FR 0.0001 REL FR 1 V 0 P
maid that milks | and does the meanest chares. ANT 4.15. 75
/CHARG'D 1 FR 0.0001 REL FR 1 V 0 P
/and /charg'd /us /from /his /soul /to /love R3 1.04.237
CHARG'D 33 FR 0.0037 REL FR 27 V 6 P
my master charg'd me to deliver a ring to madam TGV 5.04. 88 P
and charg'd him with a thousand marks in gold, ERR 3.01. 8
she was charg'd with nothing | but what was true ADO 5.01.104
and, as thou say'st, charg'd my brother, on his AYL 1.01. 3 P
my father charg'd you in his will to give me 1.01. 67 P
therefore heaven nature charg'd | that one body 3.02.141
for your physicians have expressly charg'd, | in SHR in.2. 121
for so your father charg'd me at our parting; 1.01.213
since i am charg'd in honor and by him | that i WT 1.02.407
i charg'd thee that she should not come about me 2.03. 43
man, | for any thing he shall be charg'd withal, 1H4 2.04.517
can purge | myself of many i am charg'd withal; 3.02. 21
to venture upon the charg'd chambers bravely — 2H4 2.04. 51 P
charg'd our main battle's front and, breaking in 3H6 1.01. 8
with this we charg'd again; 1.04. 18
the king hath strictly charg'd the contrary. R3 4.01. 17
believe me, sirs, | we shall be charg'd again. COR 1.06. 4
shall i be charg'd no further than this present? 3.03. 42
they charg'd him even | as those should do that 4.06.112
the heart is sorely charg'd. MAC 5.01. 54 P
my soul is too much charg'd | with blood of 5.08. 5
charg'd me on pain of perpetual displeasure LR 3.03. 4 P
wast thou not charg'd at peril — 3.07. 52
my lady charg'd my duty in this business. 4.05. 18
what you have charg'd me with, that have i done, 5.03.163
i have charg'd thee not to haunt about my doors. OTH 1.01. 96
(for such proceeding i am charg'd withal) | i 1.03. 93
but being charg'd, we will be still by land, ANT 4.11. 1
hath charg'd you you should not speak together. CYM 1.01. 83
or have charg'd him, | at the sixt hour of morn, 1.03. 30
when you charg'd | upon the left wing of the TNK 3.06. 74
either not assail'd, or victor being charg'd, SON 70.10
nature hath charg'd me that i hoard them not, LC 220
/CHARGE 2 FR 0.0002 REL FR 2 V 0 P
/their /armed /staves /in /charge, /their 2H4 4.01.118
and yet to /charge thy sulphur with a bolt COR 5.03.152
CHARGE 210 FR 0.0237 REL FR 164 V 46 P
ariel, thy charge | exactly is perform'd; TMP 1.02.237
i charge thee | that thou attend me. 1.02.453
charge my goblins that they grind their joints 4.01.258
in the same fashion as you gave in charge, 5.01. 8
my ariel, chick, | that is thy charge. 5.01.318
'tis a great charge to come under one body's WIV 1.04. 98 P
you shall find it a great charge; 1.04.101 P
i sue for yours — not to charge you, for i must 2.02.165 P
give your men the charge, we must be brief. 3.03. 7 P
but from lord angelo by special charge. MM 1.02.119
you this note, and by me this further charge: 4.02.103 P
so great a charge from thine own custody? ERR 1.02. 61
where is the gold i gave in charge to thee? 1.02. 70
and tell me how thou hast dispos'd thy charge. 1.02. 73
my charge was but to fetch you from the mart 1.02. 74
and charge you in the duke's name to obey me. 4.01. 70
sathan, avoid! i charge thee tempt me not. 4.03. 48
i charge thee, sathan, hous'd within this man, 4.04. 54
beside the charge, the shame, imprisonment, 5.01. 18
you embrace your charge too willingly. ADO 1.01.103 P
i charge thee on thy allegiance. 1.01.208 P
well, give them their charge, neighbor dogberry. 3.03. 7 P
this is your charge: 3.03. 24 P
this is the end of the charge: 3.03. 74 P
well, masters, we hear our charge. 3.03. 88 P
we charge you, in the prince's name, stand! 3.03.164 P
never speak, we charge you; 3.03.175 P
i charge you on your souls to utter it. 4.01. 13 P
i charge thee do so, as thou art my child. 4.01. 76
i charge you in the prince's name accuse these 4.02. 37 P
wit in the career, and you charge it against me. 5.01.136 P
and, to conclude, what you lay to their charge. 5.01.223 P
are they | that charge their breath against us? LLL 5.02. 88
i charge thee hence, and do not haunt me thus. MND 2.02. 85
i charge you by the law, | whereof you are a MV 4.01.238
have by some surgeon, shylock, on your charge, 4.01.257
thou must be hang'd at the state's charge. 4.01.367
in, | and charge us there upon inter'gatories, 5.01.298
i charge thee be not thou more griev'd than i am AYL 1.03. 92
evils that he laid to the charge of women? 3.02.352 P
that if she love me, i charge her to love thee; 4.03. 71 P
i charge you, o women, for the love you bear to ep 12 P
and i charge you, o men, for the love you bear ep 14 P
huntsman, i charge thee, tender well my hounds SHR in.1. 16
wait you on him, i charge you, as becomes, 1.01.233
be contributors | and bear his charge of wooing, 1.02.215
of all thy suitors here i charge /thee tell 2.01. 8
lay hold on him, i charge you, in the duke's 5.01. 88 P
i charge you see that he be forthcoming. 5.01. 93 P
i charge thee tell these headstrong women | what 5.02.130
howe'er, i charge thee, | as heaven shall work AWW 1.03.183
she had her breeding at my father's charge — 2.03.114
it is | a charge too heavy for my strength, but 3.03. 4
the charge and thanking | shall be for me, and, 3.05. 98
to charge in with our horse upon our own wings, 3.06. 48 P
knew the crafts | that you do charge men with. 4.02. 34
now will i charge you in the band of truth, 4.02. 56
do they charge me further? 5.03.167
me, sirrah — but tell me true, i charge you, 5.03.234
hold, toby, on thy life i charge thee hold! TN 4.01. 45
i charge thee by thy reverence | here to unfold, 5.01.151
my stay, | to you a charge and trouble. WT 1.02. 26
you, sir, | charge him too coldly. 1.02. 30
might we lay th' old proverb to your charge, 2.03. 97
it came to us, i do in justice charge thee, | on 2.03.180
sir, for i have about me many parcels of charge. 4.04.258 P
to execute the charge my father gave me | for 5.01.162
lay't so to his charge: 5.01.195
priories shall pay | this /expedition's charge. JN 1.01. 49
lay not my transgression to my charge | that art 1.01.256
to charge me to an answer, as the pope. 3.01.151
done, | what we so fear'd he had a charge to do. 4.02. 75
is't not i | that undergo this charge? 5.02.100
what doth our cousin lay to mowbray's charge? R2 1.01. 84
and, for these great affairs do ask some charge, 2.01.159
be it your charge | to keep him safely till his 4.01.152
and many limits of the charge set down | but 1H4 1.01. 35
that we at our own charge shall ransom straight 1.03. 79
along with company, for they have great charge. 2.01. 46 P
one that hath abundance of charge too — god 2.01. 58 P
i'll procure this fat rogue a charge of foot, 2.04.546 P
yea, but a little charge will trench him here, 3.01.111
i'll have it so, a little charge will do it. 3.01.114
thou shalt have charge and sovereign trust 3.02.161
charge an honest woman with picking thy pocket! 3.03.155 P
i have procur'd thee, jack, a charge of foot. 3.03.186 P
there shalt thou know thy charge, and there 3.03.201
and now my whole charge consists of ancients, 4.02. 23 P
but to my charge. 4.03. 41
hence therefore, every leader to his charge, 5.01.118
now going with some charge to the lord john of 2H4 1.02. 63 P
pistol, i charge you with a cup of sack, do you 2.04.112 P
to you, mistress dorothy, i will charge you. 2.04.121 P
charge me? 2.04.123 P
'a shall charge you and discharge you with the 3.02.261 P
the leaders, having charge from you to stand, 4.02. 99
come, i charge you both go with me, for the man 5.04. 15 P
be it your charge, my lord, | to see perform'd 5.05. 70
or nicely charge your understanding soul | with H5 1.02. 15
we charge you, in the name of god, take heed; 1.02. 23
leave | freely to render what we have in charge? 1.02.238
and upon this charge | cry, "god for harry, 3.01. 33
and we give express charge that, in our marches 3.06.108 P
i'll to my charge. 4.03. 6
and will with all expedience charge on us. 4.03. 70
i charge you in his majesty's name, apprehend 4.08. 16 P
peace and the king's, we charge and command you, 1H6 1.03. 76 P
did look no better to that weighty charge. 2.01. 62
porter, remember what i gave in charge, | and 2.03. 1
or aught intend'st to lay unto my charge, | do 3.01. 4
we charge you, on allegiance to ourself, | to 3.01. 86
henceforth i charge you, as you love our favor, 4.01.135
thy father's charge shall clear thee from that 4.05. 42
for your expenses and sufficient charge, | among 5.05. 92
i had in charge at my depart for france, | as 2H6 1.01. 2
so am i given in charge, may't please your grace 2.04. 80
but mightier crimes are laid unto your charge, 3.01.134
a charge, lord york, that i will see perform'd. 3.01.321
and charge that no man should disturb your rest 3.02.256
i charge thee waft me safely cross the channel. 4.01.115
upon london stone, i charge and command that, of 4.06. 2 P
and we charge and command that their wives be as 4.07.124 P
warriors did retire, | richard cried, "charge! 3H6 1.04. 15
foaming steeds, | and once again cry "charge!" 2.01.184
we charge you, in god's name and the king's, 3.01. 97
matter of marriage was the charge he gave me, 3.03.258
and warwick, doing what you gave in charge, | is 4.01. 32
my brother was too careless of his charge. 4.06. 86
for once allow'd the skillful pilot's charge? 5.04. 20
away, i say, i charge ye bear her hence. 5.05. 81
his majesty hath straitly given in charge | that R3 1.01. 85
we know thy charge, brakenbury, and will obey. 1.01.105
i lay unto the grievous charge of others. 1.03.325
that thus i have resign'd to you my charge. 1.04. 97
i charge you, as you hope /to /have /redemption 1.04.189
your gracious self to take on you the charge 3.07.131
if to have done the thing you gave in charge 4.03. 25
limit each leader to his several charge, | and 5.03. 25
good norfolk, hie thee to thy charge, | use 5.03. 53
go, gentlemen, every man unto his charge. 5.03.307
such | to whom as great a charge as little honor H8 1.01. 77
you charge not in your spleen a noble person 1.02.174
you that side, i'll take the charge of this. 1.04. 20
then give my charge up to sir nicholas vaux, 2.01. 96
you charge me | that i have blown this coal. 2.04. 93
this is my charge. 3.02.344
cromwell, i charge thee, fling away ambition! 3.02.440
once more, my lord of winchester, i charge you, 5.02.204
when they charge on heaps | the enemy flying. TRO 3.02. 28
with such a hell of pain and world of charge; 4.01. 58
i charge thee use her well, even for my charge; 4.04.126
i charge thee use her well, even for my charge; 4.04.126
and know you, lord, | i'll nothing do on charge. 4.04.133
how now, my charge? 5.02. 6
mend and charge home, | or, by the fires of COR 1.04. 38
obey, i charge thee, | and follow to thine 3.01.175
in this point charge him home, that he affects 3.03. 1
we charge you, that you have contriv'd to take 3.03. 63
we need not put new matter to his charge. 3.03. 76
answering us | with our own charge, making a 5.06. 67
sons, let it be your charge, as it is ours, | to TIT 2.02. 7
i charge thee in the prince's name, obey. ROM 3.01.140
the letter was not nice but full of charge, | of 5.02. 18
upon thy life i charge thee, | what e'er thou 5.03. 25
i'm weary of this charge, the gods can witness. TIM 3.04. 25
go, i charge thee, invite them all, let in the 3.04.116
and things unluckily charge my fantasy. JC 3.03. 2
how to cut off some charge in legacies. 4.01. 9
no, caesar, we will answer on their charge. 5.01. 24
speak, i charge you. MAC 1.03. 78
grooms | do mock their charge with snores. 2.02. 6
nature may recoil | in an imperial charge. 4.03. 20
by heaven i charge thee speak! HAM 1.01. 49
stay! speak, speak, i charge thee speak! 1.01. 51
look to't, i charge you. 1.03.135
faith, as you may season it in the charge: 2.01. 28
dear a better proposer can charge you withal, be 2.02.287 P
when the compulsive ardure gives the charge, 3.04. 86
witness this army of such mass and charge | led 4.04. 47
and many such-like /as's of great charge, | that 5.02. 43
his breeding, sir, hath been at my charge. LR 1.01. 9 P
his goatish disposition on the charge of a star! 1.02.128 P
sith that both charge and danger | speak 'gainst 2.04.239
will you that i go | to answer this your charge? OTH 1.02. 85
on thy love, i charge thee! 2.03.178
you charge me most unjustly. 4.02.184 P
o, did he so? i charge you go with me. 5.01.120
what, are you mad? i charge you, get you home. 5.02.194
you shall never | have tongue to charge me with. ANT 2.02. 83
a charge we bear i' th' war, | and, as the 3.07. 16
look'st like him that knows a warlike charge. 4.04. 19
do it, | detain no jot, i charge thee. 4.05. 13
go charge agrippa | plant those that have 4.06. 7
if sleep charge nature, | to break it with a CYM 3.04. 42
with this strict charge, even as he left his PER 2.01.125
patience, good sir, | even for this charge. 3.01. 27
nam'd so, here | i charge your charity withal; 3.03. 14
cousin, i charge you | boudge not from athens. TNK 1.01.222
and let mine honor down, and never charge? 2.02.195
bold young men that, when he bids 'em charge, 2.02.249
my lord, for you | i have this charge too — 2.02.269
when i saw you charge first, | methought i heard 3.06. 82
they are. | you bear a charge there too. 5.02.101
and charge me live to comfort this unfriended, 5.03.141
peace ho, peace, i charge you keep the peace! STM II.C 28
then what a rough and riotous charge have you II.C 55
when thou shalt charge me with so black a deed? LUC 226
gives the hot charge, and bids them do their 434
my heart doth charge the watch; PP 14.14
inheritors of this excess, | eat up thy charge? SON 146. 8
CHARGED 2 FR 0.0002 REL FR 2 V 0 P
their battering cannon charged to the mouths, JN 2.01.382
soul | shall stand sore charged for the wasteful H5 1.02.283
CHARGEFUL 1 FR 0.0001 REL FR 1 V 0 P
the fineness of the gold, and chargeful fashion, ERR 4.01. 29
CHARGE-HOUSE 1 FR 0.0001 REL FR 0 V 1 P
youth at the charge-house on the top of the LLL 5.01. 83 P
CHARGES 14 FR 0.0015 REL FR 11 V 3 P
and charges him, my lord, with such a time MM 5.01.197
charges she moe than me? 5.01.200
whoever charges on his forward breast, | i am AWW 3.02.113
therefore it charges me in manners the rather to TN 2.01. 14 P
king of england's own proper cost and charges, 2H6 1.01. 61 P
for costs and charges in transporting her! 1.01.134
i'll be at charges for a looking-glass, | and R3 1.02.255
till further trial in those charges | which will H8 5.01.103
we have heard | the charges of our friends. COR 1.06. 6
the centurions and their charges, distinctly 4.03. 44 P
a full third part | the charges of the action. 5.06. 78
mean while here's money for thy charges. TIT 4.03.105
bid our commanders lead their charges off | a JC 4.02. 48
with his prepared sword he charges home | my LR 2.01. 51
CHARGETH 1 FR 0.0001 REL FR 1 V 0 P
in this the madman justly chargeth them. ERR 5.01.213
CHARGING 2 FR 0.0002 REL FR 2 V 0 P
in charging you with matters, to commit you, H8 5.01.146
charging the sour-fac'd groom to hie as fast LUC 1334
CHARGING-STAFF 1 FR 0.0001 REL FR 1 V 0 P
he bears a charging-staff emboss'd with silver. TNK 4.02.140
CHARIEST 1 FR 0.0001 REL FR 1 V 0 P
the chariest maid is prodigal enough | if she HAM 1.03. 36
CHARINESS 1 FR 0.0001 REL FR 0 V 1 P

that may not sully the chariness of our honesty. WIV 2.01. 99 P
CHARING–CROSS 1 FR 0.0001 REL FR 0 V 1 P
ginger, to be deliver'd as far as charing–cross. 1H4 2.01. 25 P
CHARIOT 7 FR 0.0008 REL FR 7 V 0 P
and in a captive chariot into roan | bring him H5 3.05. 54
do i consecrate | my sword, my chariot, and my TIT 1.01.249
her chariot is an empty hazel–nut, | made by the ROM 1.04. 59
and when you saw his chariot but appear, | have JC 1.01. 43
follow his chariot, like the greatest spot | of ANT 4.12. 35
glory, | when he was seated in a chariot | of an PER 2.04. 7
in her light chariot, quickly is convey'd, VEN 1192
CHARIOTS 3 FR 0.0003 REL FR 3 V 0 P
come on then, horse and chariots let us have, TIT 2.02. 18
shall set thee on triumphant chariots, and | put ANT 3.01. 10
our chariots and our horsemen be in readiness. CYM 3.05. 23
CHARIOT–WHEELS 3 FR 0.0003 REL FR 3 V 0 P
that erst did follow thy proud chariot–wheels 2H6 2.04. 13
stab them, or tear them on thy chariot–wheels, TIT 5.02. 47
to grace in captive bonds his chariot–wheels? JC 1.01. 34
/CHARITABLE 1 FR 0.0001 REL FR 1 V 0 P
/for /thou /hast /done /a /charitable /deed. TIT 3.02. 70
CHARITABLE 18 FR 0.0020 REL FR 14 V 4 P
divines, and have all charitable preparation. MM 3.02.209 P
of mine oath, | a charitable duty of my order, ERR 5.01.107
why had i not with charitable hand | took up a ADO 4.01.131
parolles, you were born under a charitable star. AWW 1.01.191 P
you ha' done me a charitable office. WT 4.03. 76 P
swords | in such a just and charitable war. JN 2.01. 36
i come to thee for charitable license, | that we H5 4.07. 71
this fiend | to stop devoted charitable deeds? R3 1.02. 35
most charitable care | have the patricians of COR 1.01. 65
do this, and be a charitable murderer. TIT 2.03.178
a charitable wish, and full of love. 4.02. 43
why have you that charitable title from TIM 1.02. 91 P
of his) | what charitable men afford to beggars. 3.02. 75
hell, | be thy intents wicked, or charitable, HAM 1.04. 42
for charitable prayers, | /shards, flints, and 5.01.230
with charitable bill (o bill, sore shaming CYM 4.02.225
and retain anew | her charitable heart, now hard TNK 1.02. 25
thou grant'st no time for charitable deeds: LUC 908
CHARITABLY 1 FR 0.0001 REL FR 0 V 1 P
for how can they charitably dispose of any thing H5 4.01.142 P
CHARITIES 1 FR 0.0001 REL FR 1 V 0 P
with thoughts so qualified as your charities WT 2.01.113
/CHARITY 1 FR 0.0001 REL FR 1 V 0 P
/and /rob /in /the /behalf /of /charity. TRO 5.03. 22
CHARITY 59 FR 0.0066 REL FR 51 V 8 P
out of his charity, who being then appointed TMP 1.02.162
hast not so much charity in thee as to go to the TGV 2.05. 57 P
bound by my charity and my blest order, | i come MM 2.03. 3
might there not be a charity in sin | to save 2.04. 63
to my soul, | it is no sin at all, but charity. 2.04. 66
soul, | were equal poise of sin and charity. 2.04. 68
sir, induc'd by my charity, and hearing how 4.03. 50 P
dumaine, thy love is far from charity, | that in LLL 4.03.125
for charity itself fulfills the law, | and who 4.03.361
the law, | and who can sever love from charity? 4.03.362
that he hath a neighborly charity in him, for he MV 1.02. 79 P
'twere good you do so much for charity. 4.01.261
'tis charity to shew. SHR 4.01.211
if not, elsewhere they meet with charity; 4.03. 6
of charity, what kin are you to me? TN 5.01.230
there your charity would have lack'd footing. WT 3.03.110 P
whom zeal and charity brought to the field | as JN 2.01.565
ransacking the church, | offending charity. 3.04.173
your pernicious lives, | for 'twere no charity; R2 3.01. 5
and a hand | open as day for /meting charity; 2H4 4.04. 32
deum, | the dead with charity enclos'd in clay; H5 4.08.124
and charity chas'd hence by rancor's hand; 2H6 3.01.144
charity, for shame! 5.01.213
'twas sin before, but now 'tis charity. 3H6 5.05. 76
sweet saint, for charity, be not so curst. R3 1.02. 49
lady, you know no rules of charity, | which 1.02. 68
peace, peace, for shame! if not, for charity. 1.03.272
urge neither charity nor shame to me. 1.03.273
my charity is outrage, life my shame, | and in 1.03.276
gloucester, we have done deeds of charity, 2.01. 50
love, charity, obedience, and true duty! 2.02.108
lord cardinal, | deliver all with charity. H8 1.02.143
i do beseech your grace, for charity, | if ever 2.01. 79
who ever yet | have stood to charity, and 2.04. 86
wish ye half my miseries, | i have more charity. 3.01.109
but that i am bound in charity against it! 3.02.298
give him a little earth for charity!" 4.02. 23
me leave to speak him, | and yet with charity. 4.02. 33
love, friendship, charity, are subjects all | to TRO 3.03.173
alms empoison'd, | and with his charity slain. COR 5.06. 11
this was but a deed of charity | to that which TIT 5.01. 89
seldom rich, | it comes in charity to thee; TIM 1.02.223
hate all, curse all, show charity to none, | but 4.03.527
"by gis, and by saint charity, | alack, and fie HAM 4.05. 58
sometime with prayers, | enforce their charity. LR 2.03. 20
duke, that my charity be not of him perceiv'd. 3.03. 16 P
do poor tom some charity, whom the foul fiend 3.04. 60 P
let's exchange charity. 5.03.167
prithee bear some charity to my wit, do not OTH 4.01.120 P
and am so near the lack of charity | to accuse CYM 2.03.109
clotens blood, | and praise myself for charity. 4.02.169
o, the charity of a penny cord! 5.04.166 P
thought it princely charity to grieve for them. PER 1.02.100
has through ephesus pour'd forth | your charity, 3.02. 44
for a fee, | the gods requite his charity!" 3.02. 75
nam'd so, here | i charge your charity withal; 3.03. 14
the worth that learned charity aye wears. 5.03. 94
rusty, and the charity | of one meal lend me — TNK 3.01. 73
assuage, | 'tis promis'd in the charity of age. LC 70
CHARLEMAIN 2 FR 0.0002 REL FR 2 V 0 P
to give great charlemain a pen in 's hand | and AWW 2.01. 77
daughter to charlemain, who was the son | to H5 1.02. 75
CHARLES' 1 FR 0.0001 REL FR 0 V 1 P
charles' wain is over the new chimney, and yet 1H4 2.01. 2 P
CHARLES 53 FR 0.0060 REL FR 44 V 9 P
from special officers | of charles his father. LLL 2.01.162
was not charles, the duke's wrastler, here to AYL 1.01. 89 P
good monsieur charles, what's the new news at 1.01. 96 P
charles, i thank thee for thy love to me, which 1.01.137 P
i'll tell thee, charles, it is the stubbornest 1.01.142 P
farewell, good charles. 1.01.163 P
the eldest of the three wrastled with charles, 1.02.126 P
wrastler, which charles in a moment threw him, 1.02.126 P
man, have you challeng'd charles the wrastler? 1.02.168 P
how dost thou, charles? 1.02.219
or charles, or something weaker, masters thee. 1.02.260
that did but lately foil the sinowy charles, 2.02. 14
where charles the great, having subdu'd the H5 1.02. 46
and charles the great | subdu'd the saxons, and 1.02. 61
the crown | of charles the duke of lorraine, 1.02. 70
of the true line and stock of charles the great, 1.02. 71
and lewis the son | of charles the great. 1.02. 77
daughter to charles, the foresaid duke of 1.02. 83
the which marriage the line of charles the great 1.02. 84
charles delabreth, high constable of france, 3.05. 40
charles duke of orleance, nephew to the king, 4.08. 76
charles delabreth, high constable of france, 4.08. 92
the dolphin charles is crowned king in rheims; 1H6 1.01. 92
here cometh charles, i marvel how he sped. 2.01. 48
wherefore is charles impatient with his friend? 2.01. 54
that charles the dolphin may encounter them. 3.02. 9
see, noble charles, the beacon of our friend, 3.02. 29
the bastard's braves, and charles his glikes? 3.02.123
the princely charles of france, thy countryman. 3.03. 38
what say'st thou, charles? 3.03. 39
charles and the rest will take thee in their 3.03. 77
pernicious faction | and join'd with charles, 4.01. 60
with charles, alanson, and that traitorous rout. 4.01.173
orleance the bastard, charles, burgundy, 4.04. 26
the earl of arminack, near knit to charles, | a 5.01. 17
then march to paris, royal charles of france, 5.02. 4
command the conquest, charles, it shall be thine 5.02. 19
o, charles the dolphin is a proper man, | no 5.03. 37
a plaguing mischief light on charles and thee! 5.03. 39
live, | especially since charles must father it. 5.04. 71
'twas neither charles nor yet the duke i nam'd, 5.04. 77
charles, and the rest, it is enacted thus: 5.04.123
and, charles, upon condition thou wilt swear 5.04.129
insulting charles, hast thou by secret means 5.04.147
how say'st thou, charles? 5.04.165
do, | because he is near kinsman unto charles. 5.05. 45
our sovereign and the french king charles, | for 2H6 1.01. 41
it is agreed between the french king charles, 1.01. 44 P
to th' old dam, treason), charles the emperor, H8 1.01.176
charles, i will play no more to–night, | my 5.01. 56
but little, charles, | nor shall not, when my 5.01. 59
'tis midnight, charles, | prithee to bed, and in 5.01. 72
charles, good night. | well, sir, what follows? 5.01. 78
CHARM 35 FR 0.0039 REL FR 33 V 2 P
with a charm join'd to their suff'red labor, | i TMP 1.02.231
done | some wanton charm upon this man and maid, 4.01. 95
your charm so strongly works 'em | that if you 5.01. 17
upon their senses that | this airy charm is for, 5.01. 54
the charm dissolves apace, | and as the morning 5.01. 64
though music oft hath such a charm | to make bad MM 4.01. 14
yet is this no charm for the toothache. ADO 3.02. 70 P
charm ache with air, and agony with words. 5.01. 26
and ere i take this charm from off her sight MND 2.01.183
never harm, | nor spell, nor charm, | come our 2.02. 17
i throw | all the power this charm doth owe. 2.02. 79
i'll charm his eyes against she do appear. 3.02. 99
but i will charm him first to keep his tongue. SHR 1.01.209
to tame a shrew and charm her chattering tongue. 4.02. 58
and therefore shall it charm thy riotous tongue. 2H6 4.01. 64
peace, willful boy, or i will charm your tongue. 3H6 5.05. 31
have done thy charm, thou hateful with'red hag. R3 1.03.214
this siren that will charm rome's saturnine, TIT 2.01. 23
to cool this heat, a charm to calm these fits, 2.01.134
again, | alike bewitched by the charm of looks; ROM 2.pr. 6
and upon my knees | i charm you, by my once JC 2.01.271
wing, | for a charm of pow'rful trouble, | like MAC 4.01. 18
blood, | then the charm is firm and good. 4.01. 38
i'll charm the air to give a sound, | while you 4.01.129
despair thy charm, | and let the angel whom thou 5.08. 13
no fairy takes, nor witch hath power to charm, HAM 1.01.163
with cassio, mistress. go to, charm your tongue. OTH 5.02.183
i will not charm my tongue; 5.02.184
for when i am reveng'd upon my charm, | i have ANT 4.12. 16
this grave charm, | whose eye beck'd forth my 4.12. 25
nor no witchcraft charm thee! CYM 4.02.277
now for this charm that i told you of, you must TNK 4.03. 19 P
honest fear, bewitch'd with lust's foul charm, LUC 173
"and for my sake when i might charm thee so, 1681
"'my parts had pow'r to charm a sacred /nun, LC 260
CHARM'D 7 FR 0.0008 REL FR 6 V 1 P
so i charm'd their ears | that calf–like they my TMP 4.01.178
fortune forbid my outside have not charm'd her! TN 2.02. 18
whose dangerous eyes may well be charm'd asleep 2H4 4.02. 39
h'as almost charm'd me from my profession, by TIM 4.03.450 P
i, in mine own woe charm'd, | could not find CYM 5.03. 68
so charm'd me that methought alcides was | to TNK 5.03.119
that it beguil'd attention, charm'd the sight. LUC 1404
CHARMED 5 FR 0.0005 REL FR 5 V 0 P
and then i will her charmed eye release | from MND 3.02.376
got, | boil thou first i' th' charmed pot. MAC 4.01. 9
i bear a charmed life, which must not yield | to 5.08. 12
art, | threw my affections in his charmed power, LC 146
teen, | or any of my leisures ever charmed. 193
CHARMER 1 FR 0.0001 REL FR 1 V 0 P
she was a charmer, and could almost read | the OTH 3.04. 57
CHARMERS 1 FR 0.0001 REL FR 1 V 0 P
o you heavenly charmers, | what things you make TNK 5.04.131
CHARMETH 1 FR 0.0001 REL FR 1 V 0 P
music, ho, music, such as charmeth sleep! MND 4.01. 83
CHARMIAN 25 FR 0.0028 REL FR 25 V 0 P
help me away, dear charmian, i shall fall. ANT 1.03. 15
cut my lace, charmian, come! 1.03. 71
look, prithee, charmian, | how this herculean 1.03. 83
charmian! 1.05. 1
o charmian! 1.05. 18
him, | note him, good charmian, 'tis the man; 1.05. 54
ink and paper, charmian. 1.05. 65
did i, charmian, | ever love caesar so? 1.05. 66
let it alone, let's to billards. come, charmian. 2.05. 3
i am pale, charmian. 2.05. 59
i faint, o iras, charmian! 2.05.110
let him for ever go — let him not, charmian — 2.05.115
pity me, charmian, | but do not speak to me. 2.05.118
i think so, charmian: 3.03. 16
widow? charmian, hark. 3.03. 27
one thing more to ask him yet, good charmian — 3.03. 45
o charmian, i will never go from hence. 4.15. 1
help, charmian, help, iras, help; 4.15. 12
why, how now, charmian? 4.15. 83
but hark thee, charmian. 5.02.192
now, charmian! 5.02.226
now, noble charmian, we'll dispatch indeed, 5.02.230
farewell, kind charmian, iras, long farewell. 5.02.292
what work is here, charmian? is this well done? 5.02.325
this charmian liv'd but now, she stood and spake 5.02.341
CHARMING 6 FR 0.0006 REL FR 6 V 0 P
charming your blood with pleasing heaviness, 1H4 3.01.215
charming the narrow seas | to give you gentle H5 2.pr. 38
now help, ye charming spells and periapts, | and 1H6 5.03. 2
and faster bound to aaron's charming eyes | than TIT 2.01. 16
which i had set | betwixt two charming words, CYM 1.03. 35
place, more charming | with their own nobleness, 5.03. 32
CHARMINGLY 1 FR 0.0001 REL FR 1 V 0 P
majestic vision, and | harmonious charmingly. TMP 4.01.119
CHARM'S 1 FR 0.0001 REL FR 1 V 0 P
peace, the charm's wound up. MAC 1.03. 37
CHARMS 23 FR 0.0026 REL FR 20 V 3 P
all the charms | of sycorax, toads, beetles, TMP 1.02.339
my high charms work, | and these, mine enemies, 3.03. 88
my charms crack not; 5.01. 2
my charms i'll break, their senses i'll restore, 5.01. 31
now my charms are all o'erthrown, | and what ep 1
surely i think you have charms, la; WIV 2.02.104 P
of my good parts aside, i have no other charms. 2.02.106 P
she works by charms, by spells, by th' figure, 4.02.176 P
against whose charms faith melteth into blood. ADO 2.01.180
unchain your spirits now with spelling charms, 1H6 5.03. 31
upon my body with their hellish charms? R3 3.04. 62
and her great charms | misguide thy opposers' COR 1.05. 21
and i, the mistress of your charms, | the close MAC 3.05. 6
provide, | your charms and every thing beside. 3.05. 19
mumbling of wicked charms, conjuring the moon LR 2.01. 39
whose age had charms in it, whose title more, 5.03. 48
is there not charms | by which the property of OTH 1.01.171
thou hast practic'd on her with foul charms, 1.02. 73
whole course of love — what drugs, what charms, 1.03. 91
/forth of my heart those charms, thine eyes, are 5.01. 35
but all the charms of love, | salt cleopatra, ANT 2.01. 20
to my tongue | charms this report out. CYM 1.06.117
as if the boy should use like loving charms; PP 11. 8
CHARNECO 1 FR 0.0001 REL FR 0 V 1 P
and here, neighbor, here's a cup of charneco. 2H6 2.03. 63 P
CHARNEL–HOUSE 1 FR 0.0001 REL FR 1 V 0 P
bears, | or hide me nightly in a charnel–house, ROM 4.01. 81
CHARNEL–HOUSES 1 FR 0.0001 REL FR 1 V 0 P
if charnel–houses and our graves must send MAC 3.04. 70
CHAROLOIS 1 FR 0.0001 REL FR 1 V 0 P
/foix, lestrake, bouciqualt, and charolois; H5 3.05. 45
CHARON 1 FR 0.0001 REL FR 1 V 0 P
o, be thou my charon, | and give me swift TRO 3.02. 10
CHARTAM 1 FR 0.0001 REL FR 0 V 1 P
the clerk of chartam. 2H6 4.02. 85 P
CHARTER 8 FR 0.0009 REL FR 7 V 1 P
upon your charter and your city's freedom! MV 4.01. 39
withal, as large a charter as the wind, | to AYL 2.07. 48
of that i have made a bold charter, but i thank AWW 4.05. 92 P
you break no privilege nor charter there. R3 3.01. 54
mother, | who has a charter to extol her blood, COR 1.09. 14
and let me find a charter in your voice | t' OTH 1.03.245
be where you list, your charter is so strong, SON 58. 9
the charter of thy worth gives thee releasing; 87. 3
CHARTER'D 2 FR 0.0002 REL FR 2 V 0 P
the air, a charter'd libertine, is still, | and H5 1.01. 48
to your comforts, | but charter'd unto them? STM II.C 138
CHARTERS 3 FR 0.0003 REL FR 3 V 0 P
substitutes at home shall have blank charters, R2 1.04. 48
time | his charters and his customary rights; 2.01.196
your liberties and the charters that you bear COR 2.03.180
CHARTHAM *(see chartam)*
CHARTREUX 2 FR 0.0002 REL FR 2 V 0 P
a monk o' th' chartreux. H8 1.01.221
sir, a chartreux friar, | his confessor, who fed 1.02.148
CHARY 1 FR 0.0001 REL FR 1 V 0 P
which i will keep so chary | as tender nurse her SON 22.11
CHARYBDIS 1 FR 0.0001 REL FR 0 V 1 P
your father, i fall into charybdis, your mother. MV 3.05. 17 P
CHAS'D 8 FR 0.0009 REL FR 8 V 0 P
love hath chas'd sleep from my enthralled eyes, TGV 2.04.134
night–dogs run, all sorts of deer are chas'd. WIV 5.05.238
us again, and madly bent on us | chas'd us away; ERR 5.01.153
that have so cowarded and chas'd your blood H5 2.02. 75
alas, she hath from france too long been chas'd, 5.02. 38
and charity chas'd hence by rancor's hand; 2H6 3.01.144
we are those which chas'd you from the field, 3H6 1.01. 90
ten chas'd by one | are now each one the CYM 5.03. 48
CHASE 40 FR 0.0045 REL FR 36 V 4 P
printless foot | do chase the ebbing neptune, TMP 5.01. 35
begin to chase the ignorant fumes that mantle 5.01. 67
law, | have some unhappy passenger in chase. TGV 5.04. 15
apollo flies, and daphne holds the chase; MND 2.01.231
o, i am out of breath in this fond chase! 2.02. 88
by this kind of chase, i should hate him, for my AYL 1.03. 32 P
down his innocent nose | in piteous chase; 2.01. 40
is't i | that chase thee from thy country, and AWW 3.02.103
you did here, | a ring in chase of you; TN 3.01.113
this is the chase; WT 3.03. 57
court | whiles he was hast'ning (in the chase, 5.01.189
should chase us with my father, pow'r no jot 5.01.217
that holds in chase mine honor up and down? JN 1.01.223
and chase the native beauty from his cheek, 3.04. 83
to rouse his wrongs and chase them to the bay. R2 2.03.128
to chase these pagans in those holy fields, 1H4 1.01. 24
you see this chase is hotly followed, friends. H5 2.04. 68
thee i'll chase hence, thou wolf in sheep's 1H6 1.03. 55
can chase away the first–conceived sound? 2H6 3.02. 44
seek thee out some other chase, | for i myself 5.02. 14
nay, warwick, single out some other chase, | for 3H6 2.04. 12
and make pursuit where he did mean no chase. R3 3.02. 30
thy womb let loose to chase us to our graves. 4.04. 54
spies of the volsces | held me in chase, that i COR 1.06. 19

will rouse the proudest panther in the chase, TIT 2.02. 21
upon the north side of this pleasant chase; 2.03.255
if our wits run the wild–goose chase, i am done; ROM 2.04. 71 P
say, | the barren, touched in this holy chase, JC 1.02. 8
of very warlike appointment gave us chase. HAM 4.06. 17 P
i do follow here in the chase, not like a hound OTH 2.03.363 P
our valor is to chase what flies. CYM 3.03. 42
in mortal bosoms, whose chase is this world, TNK 5.01.131
rose–cheek'd adonis hied him to the chase; VEN 3
it, | unless it be a boar, and then i chase it; 410
as if another chase were in the skies. 696
for now she knows it is no gentle chase, | but 883
to chase injustice with revengeful arms: LUC 1693
her blood, in poor revenge, held it in chase; 1736
whilst her neglected child holds her in chase, SON 143. 5
whilst i, thy babe, chase thee afar behind, 143.10

CHASED 4 FR 0.0004 REL FR 4 V 0 P
are, | are with more spirit chased than enjoy'd. MV 2.06. 13
when i have chased all thy foes from hence, 1H6 1.02.115
rome, | who this accomplishment so hotly chased, LUC 716
strong arms from forth her fair streets chased. 1834

CHASER 1 FR 0.0001 REL FR 1 V 0 P
then began | a stop i' th' chaser; CYM 5.03. 40

CHASES *(also chaces)*

CHASES 1 FR 0.0001 REL FR 1 V 0 P
like the current flies | each bound it chases. TIM 1.01. 25

CHASETH 1 FR 0.0001 REL FR 1 V 0 P
a woman clad in armor chaseth them. 1H6 1.05. 3

CHASING 2 FR 0.0002 REL FR 2 V 0 P
chasing the royal blood | with fury from his R2 2.01.118
as the fleet–foot roe that's tir'd with chasing, VEN 561

CHASTE 51 FR 0.0057 REL FR 43 V 8 P
betrims, | to make cold nymphs chaste crowns; TMP 4.01. 66
twenty lascivious turtles ere one chaste man. WIV 2.01. 81 P
if he be chaste, the flame will back descend 5.05. 85
then, isabel, live chaste, and, brother, die; MM 2.04.184
not, but by gift of my chaste body | to his 5.01. 97
orb, | as chaste as is the bud ere it be blown; ADO 4.01. 58
will you give horns, chaste lady? LLL 5.02.252
quench'd in the chaste beams of the wat'ry moon, MND 2.01.162
old as sibylla, i will die as chaste as diana, MV 1.02.107 P
survey | with thy chaste eye, from thy pale AYL 3.02. 3
carve on every tree | the fair, the chaste, and 3.02. 10
and then let kate be chaste and dian sportful! SHR 2.01.261
here in florence, of a most chaste renown, and AWW 4.03. 15 P
past life | hath been as continent, as chaste, WT 3.02. 34
"hermione is chaste, polixenes blameless, 3.02.132 P
nor in a way so chaste, since my desires | run 4.04. 33
is, by our noble and chaste mistress the moon, 1H4 1.02. 28 P
chaste, and immaculate in very thought, | whose 1H6 5.04. 51
command, i mean, of virtuous chaste intents, 5.05. 20
to his goodness | the model of our chaste loves, H8 4.02.132
may know | i was a chaste wife to my grave. 4.02.170
grandam, and as chaste | as may be in the world. TRO 1.03.299
chaste as the icicle | that's curdied by the COR 5.03. 65
lucrece was not more chaste | than this lavinia, TIT 2.01.108
and father of that chaste dishonored dame, 4.01. 90
she hath sworn that she will still live chaste? ROM 1.01.217
or your chaste treasure open | to his unmast'red HAM 1.03. 31
be thou as chaste as ice, as pure as snow, thou 3.01.135 P
between the chaste unsmirched brow | of my true 4.05.120
and many worthy and chaste dames even thus, OTH 4.01. 46
in a secure couch, | and to suppose her chaste! 4.01. 72
for, if she be not honest, chaste, and true, 4.02. 17
let me not name it to you, you chaste stars, 5.02. 2
moor, she was chaste; 5.02.249
virtuous, wise, chaste, constant, qualified, and CYM 1.04. 60 P
and the chimney–piece | chaste dian bathing. 2.04. 82
that i thought her | as chaste as unsunn'd snow. 2.05. 13
of your chaste daughter the wide difference 5.05.194
it gives a good report to a number to be chaste. PER 4.06. 40 P
and paints the sun | with her chaste blushes! TNK 2.02.140
by all the chaste nights i have ever pleas'd you 3.06.200
what sins have i committed, chaste diana, | that 4.02. 58
sweet, solitary, white as chaste, and pure | as 5.01.139
of collatine's fair love, lucrece the chaste. LUC 7
happ'ly that name of "chaste" unhapp'ly set 8
thou seest our mistress' ornaments are chaste." 322
and suck'd the honey which thy chaste bee kept. 840
and by this chaste blood so unjustly stained, 1836
and by chaste lucrece' soul that late complained 1839
trumpet be, | to whose sound chaste wings obey. PHT 4
many nymphs that vow'd chaste life to keep SON 154. 3

CHASTELY 3 FR 0.0003 REL FR 2 V 1 P
flame of liking | wish chastely and love dearly, AWW 1.03.212
fill the time, | herself most chastely absent. 3.07. 34
it were as virtuous to lie as to live chastely. COR 5.02. 27 P

CHASTEST 1 FR 0.0001 REL FR 1 V 0 P
cooling his hot face in the chastest tears LUC 682

CHASTIS'D 3 FR 0.0003 REL FR 3 V 0 P
between this chastis'd kingdom and myself, | and JN 5.02. 84
tell her i have chastis'd the amorous troyan, TRO 5.05. 4
nor once be chastis'd with the sober eye | of ANT 5.02. 54

CHASTISE 6 FR 0.0006 REL FR 6 V 0 P
i am afraid | he will chastise me. TMP 5.01.263
and by whose help i mean to chastise it. JN 2.01.117
now prisoner to the palsy, chastise thee, | and R2 2.03.104
but i will chastise this high–minded strumpet. 1H6 1.05. 12
and chastise with the valor of my tongue | all MAC 1.05. 27
behold who err, | and in their time chastise. TNK 1.04. 6

CHASTISED 2 FR 0.0002 REL FR 2 V 0 P
and when this arm of mine hath chastised | the R3 4.04.331
and chastised with arms | our enemies' pride; TIT 1.01. 32

CHASTISEMENT 9 FR 0.0010 REL FR 9 V 0 P
as seems you best, | in any chastisement. MM 5.01.257
that in your chambers gave you chastisement? JN 5.02.147
to me for justice and rough chastisement; R2 1.01.106
on equal terms to give /him chastisement? 4.01. 22
lack | the very instruments of chastisement, 2H4 4.01.215
him, | and give him chastisement for this abuse. 1H6 4.01. 69
make us thy ministers of chastisement, | that we R3 5.03.113
and chastisement doth therefore hide his head. JC 4.03. 16
chastisement? 4.03. 17

CHASTITY 28 FR 0.0031 REL FR 23 V 5 P
upon whose grave thou vow'dst pure chastity. TGV 4.03. 21
more than our brother is our chastity. MM 2.04.185
of sacred chastity and of promise–breach, 5.01.405
there is not chastity enough in language ADO 4.01. 97
flower, | lamenting some enforced chastity. MND 3.01.200
the very ice of chastity is in them. AYL 3.04. 17 P
grissel, | and roman lucrece for her chastity; SHR 2.01.296
to–day, | to force a spotless virgin's chastity, 2H6 5.01.186
to–day, | thy sons make pillage of her chastity, TIT 2.03. 44
this minion stood upon her chastity, | upon her 2.03.124
than hands or tongue, her spotless chastity, 5.02.176
and, in strong proof of chastity well arm'd, ROM 1.01.210
even like thy chastity. OTH 5.02.276
there's a palm presages chastity, if nothing ANT 1.02. 47 P
and th' assault you have made to her chastity, CYM 1.04.163 P
rushes ere he waken'd | the chastity he wounded. 2.02. 14
your daughter's chastity — there it begins. 5.05.179
but think her bond of chastity quite crack'd, 5.05.207
if your peevish chastity, which is not worth a PER 4.06.122 P
up, my dish of chastity with rosemary and bays! 4.06.150 P
her, | rude and impatient, then, like chastity, TNK 2.02.141
and my chastity | be made the altar where the 4.02. 60
"therefore, despite of fruitless chastity, VEN 751
pure chastity is rifled of her store, | and lust LUC 692
touches so soft still conquer chastity. PP 4. 8
not their infirmity, | it was married chastity. PHT 61
there my white stole of chastity i daff'd, LC 297
preach'd pure maid, and prais'd cold chastity. 315

CHASTITY'S 2 FR 0.0002 REL FR 2 V 0 P
a ring, | my chastity's the jewel of our house, AWW 4.02. 46
my brow, | the story of sweet chastity's decay, LUC 808

CHAT 14 FR 0.0015 REL FR 14 V 0 P
i myself could make | a chough of as deep chat. TMP 2.01.266
do use you for my fool, and chat with you, ERR 2.02. 27
then leave this chat, and, good berowne, now LLL 4.03.280
if you deny to dance, let's hold more chat. 5.02.228
o, how i long to have some chat with her! SHR 2.01.162
and therefore, setting all this chat aside, 2.01.268
but what a fool am i to chat with you, | when i 3.02.121
down, | for now we sit to chat as well as eat. 5.02. 11
this bald unjointed chat of his, my lord, | i 1H4 1.03. 65
come, come, no more of this unprofitable chat. 3.01. 62
brothers, you muse what chat we two have had. 3H6 3.02.109
and trim her up, | i'll go and chat with paris. ROM 4.04. 26
and leave this idle theme, this bootless chat; VEN 422
as palmers' chat makes short their pilgrimage. LUC 791

CHATHAM *(see chartam)*

CHATILLION 7 FR 0.0008 REL FR 7 V 0 P
now say, chatillion, what would france with us? JN 1.01. 1
farewell, chatillion. 1.01. 30
my lord chatillion may from england bring | that 2.01. 46
thy wish | our messenger chatillion is arriv'd! 2.01. 51
chatillion, speak. 2.01. 53
jacques chatillion, rambures, vaudemont, H5 3.05. 43
jacques of chatillion, admiral of france, | the 4.08. 93

CHATS 1 FR 0.0001 REL FR 1 V 0 P
rapture lets her baby cry | while she chats him; COR 2.01.208

/CHATTELS 1 FR 0.0001 REL FR 1 V 0 P
/chattels, and whatsoever, and to be | out of H8 3.02.343

CHATTELS 2 FR 0.0002 REL FR 2 V 0 P
she is my goods, my chattels, she is my house, SHR 3.02.230
look to my chattels and my moveables. H5 2.03. 48

CHATTER 3 FR 0.0003 REL FR 2 V 1 P
sometime like apes that mow and chatter at me, TMP 2.02. 9
once, and the wind to make me chatter, when the LR 4.06.102 P
'twixt two such shes would chatter this way, and CYM 1.06. 40

CHATTERING 1 FR 0.0001 REL FR 1 V 0 P
to tame a shrew and charm her chattering tongue. SHR 4.02. 58

CHATT'RING 3 FR 0.0003 REL FR 2 V 1 P
and chatt'ring pies in dismal discords sung; 3H6 5.06. 48
raven, nor /chough /hoar, | nor chatt'ring pie, TNK 1.01. 21
boiling, hissing, howling, chatt'ring, cursing! 4.03. 33 P

CHAUCER 1 FR 0.0001 REL FR 1 V 0 P
chaucer (of all admir'd) the story gives; TNK pr 13

/CHAUD 1 FR 0.0001 REL FR 0 V 1 P
ma foi, il fait fort /chaud. WIV 1.04. 51 P

CHAUNT 3 FR 0.0003 REL FR 3 V 0 P
their thread with bones, | do use to chaunt it. TN 2.04. 46
the birds chaunt melody on every bush, | the TIT 2.03. 12
anon she hears them chaunt it lustily, | and all VEN 869

CHAUNTED 1 FR 0.0001 REL FR 1 V 0 P
which time she chaunted snatches of old lauds, HAM 4.07.177

CHAUNTING 1 FR 0.0001 REL FR 1 V 0 P
chaunting faint hymns to the cold fruitless moon MND 1.01. 73

CHAUNTRIES *(also chantry)*

CHAUNTRIES 1 FR 0.0001 REL FR 1 V 0 P
and i have built | two chauntries, where the sad H5 4.01.301

CHAUNTS 3 FR 0.0003 REL FR 2 V 1 P
the lark, that tirra–lyra chaunts, | with heigh, WT 4.03. 9
he so chaunts to the sleeve–hand and the work 4.04.209 P
who chaunts a doleful hymn to his own death, JN 5.07. 22

CHAW'D–GRASS 1 FR 0.0001 REL FR 1 V 0 P
the /gimmal'd bit | lies foul with chaw'd–grass, H5 4.02. 50

CHAWDRON 1 FR 0.0001 REL FR 1 V 0 P
add thereto a tiger's chawdron, | for th' MAC 4.01. 33

CHE* *(also i*)*

CHE* 3 FR 0.0003 REL FR 2 V 1 P
che non te /vede, che non te /prechia. LLL 4.02. 98
che non te /vede, che non te /prechia. 4.02. 98
keep out, che vor' ye, or ice try whither your LR 4.06.240 P

CHEAP 17 FR 0.0019 REL FR 11 V 6 P
the goodness that is cheap in beauty makes MM 3.01.182 P
i hold your dainties cheap, sir, and your ERR 3.01. 21
let what is dear in sicily be cheap. WT 1.02.175
may buy land now as cheap as stinking mack'rel. 1H4 2.04.360 P
of men, | so stale and cheap to vulgar company, 3.02. 41
bought me lights as good cheap at the dearest 3.03. 45 P
year, | when flesh is cheap and females dear, 2H4 5.03. 19
and hold their manhoods cheap whiles any speaks H5 4.03. 66
pirates may make cheap pennyworths of their 2H6 1.01.222
who, in a cheap estimation, is worth all your COR 2.01. 91 P
i hope to see romans as cheap as volscians. 4.05.233 P
have wrack'd for rome | to make coals cheap! 5.01. 17
which are | as cheap as lies, he sold the blood 5.06. 46
nature needs, | man's life is cheap as beast's. LR 2.04.267
such a maidenhead were no cheap thing, if men PER 4.02. 60 P
laid down, | you have sold 'em too too cheap. TNK 5.04. 15
mine own thoughts, sold cheap what is most dear, SON 110. 3

CHEAPEN 2 FR 0.0002 REL FR 0 V 2 P
virtuous, or i'll never cheapen her; ADO 2.03. 31 P
the devil, if he should cheapen a kiss of her. PER 4.06. 10 P

CHEAPER 1 FR 0.0001 REL FR 1 V 0 P
and 'twere the cheaper way. MM 2.04.105

CHEAPEST 2 FR 0.0002 REL FR 1 V 1 P
the cheapest of us is ten groats too dear. R2 5.05. 68
a breakfast in the cheapest country under the PER 4.06.123 P

CHEAPLY 2 FR 0.0002 REL FR 2 V 0 P
see, | so great a day as this is cheaply bought. MAC 5.09. 3
save what is bought, and yet i purchase cheaply, TNK 5.03.113

CHEAPSIDE 2 FR 0.0002 REL FR 0 V 2 P
and in cheapside shall my palfrey go to grass; 2H6 4.02. 69 P
lord, when shall we go to cheapside and take up 4.07.126 P

CHEAT 4 FR 0.0004 REL FR 2 V 2 P
i hope you do not mean to cheat me so? ERR 4.03. 78
tricks, some quillets, how to cheat the devil. LLL 4.03.284
caparison, and my revenue is the silly cheat. WT 4.03. 28 P
if i make not this cheat bring out another, and 4.03.120 P

CHEATED 3 FR 0.0003 REL FR 3 V 0 P
we are merely cheated of our lives by drunkards. TMP 1.01. 56
by his cunning hath | cheated me of the island. 3.02. 44
cheated of feature by dissembling nature, R3 1.01. 19

CHEATER 6 FR 0.0006 REL FR 2 V 4 P
no swagg'rer, hostess, a tame cheater, i' faith, 2H4 2.04. 97 P
cheater, call you him? 2.04.102 P
will bar no honest man my house, nor no cheater, 2.04.103 P
thou abominable damn'd cheater, art thou not 2.04.140 P
i play'd the cheater for thy father's hand, TIT 5.01.111
then, gentle cheater, urge not my amiss, | lest SON 151. 3

CHEATERS 2 FR 0.0002 REL FR 1 V 1 P
i will be cheaters to them both, and they shall WIV 1.03. 70 P
disguised cheaters, prating mountebanks, | and ERR 1.02.101

CHEATING 1 FR 0.0001 REL FR 0 V 1 P
poor, base, rascally, cheating, lack–linen mate! 2H4 2.04.124 P

CHEATS 1 FR 0.0001 REL FR 1 V 0 P
the word "maid," cheats the poor maid of that, JN 2.01.572

/CHECK 1 FR 0.0001 REL FR 1 V 0 P
/king /his /master | /will /check /him /for't. LR 2.02.142

CHECK 26 FR 0.0029 REL FR 23 V 3 P
if i can check my erring love, i will; TGV 2.04.213
to check their folly, passion's solemn tears. LLL 5.02.118
nay, you might keep that check for it, till you AYL 4.01.167 P
check thy contempt; AWW 2.03.157
check at every feather | that comes before his TN 3.01. 64
that thou mayst be a queen, and check the world! JN 2.01.123
advantage shall step forth | to check his reign, 3.04.152
with colors idlely spread, | and find no check? 5.01. 73
to check time broke in a disordered string; R2 5.05. 46
sway, | meeting the check of such another day, 1H4 5.05. 42
yet but rebuke and check was the reward of valor 2H4 4.03. 31 P
so | that hardly can i check my eyes from tears. 3H6 1.04.151
that phaeton should check thy fiery steeds, 2.06. 12
affords no joy to me | but to command, to check, 3.02.166
of a king, | sans check, to good and bad. TRO 1.03. 94
nor check my courage for what they can give, COR 3.03. 92
basis sure, | for goodness dare not check thee; MAC 4.03. 33
and in thy best consideration check | this LR 1.01.150
(how ever this may gall him with some check) OTH 1.01.148
desperate of my fortunes if they check me /here. 2.03.331 P
not almost a fault | t' incur a private check. 3.03. 67
rebukable | and worthy shameful check it were, ANT 4.04. 31
life | is nobler than attending for a check; CYM 3.03. 22
to check the tears in collatinus' eyes. LUC 1817
bide each check | without accusing you of injury SON 58. 7
if thy soul check thee that i come so near, 136. 1

CHECK'D 9 FR 0.0010 REL FR 8 V 1 P
be check'd for silence, | but never tax'd for AWW 1.01. 67
i have check'd him for it, and the young lion 2H4 1.02.196 P
then check'd and rated by northumberland, | did 3.01. 68
my dreams unto myself, | and not be check'd. 2H6 1.02. 54
then, on the other side, i check'd my friends. R3 3.07.150
check'd like a bondman, all his faults observ'd, JC 4.03. 97
had doting priam check'd his son's desire, LUC 1490
sap check'd with frost and lusty leaves quite SON 5. 7
cheered and check'd even by the self–same sky, 15. 6

CHECKER'D 2 FR 0.0002 REL FR 2 V 0 P
with shining checker'd slough, doth sting a 2H6 3.01.229
and make a checker'd shadow on the ground. TIT 2.03. 15

/CHECKING 1 FR 0.0001 REL FR 1 V 0 P
as /checking at his voyage, and that he means HAM 4.07. 62

CHECK'RED 1 FR 0.0001 REL FR 1 V 0 P
a purple flow'r sprung up, check'red with white, VEN 1168

CHECK'RING 1 FR 0.0001 REL FR 1 V 0 P
check'ring the eastern clouds with streaks of ROM 2.03. 2

/CHECKS 1 FR 0.0001 REL FR 1 V 0 P
/must /be /us'd | /with /checks /as /flatteries, LR 1.03. 20

CHECKS 7 FR 0.0008 REL FR 5 V 2 P
do, | perforce, against all checks, rebukes, and WIV 3.04. 80
or so devote to aristotle's checks | as ovid be SHR 1.01. 32
and with what wing the /staniel checks at it! TN 2.05.113 P
a man cannot swear, but it checks him; R3 1.04.136 P
checks and disasters | grow in the veins of TRO 1.03. 5
i did endure | not seldom, nor no slight checks, TIM 2.02.140
that even his stubbornness, his checks, his OTH 4.03. 20

/CHEEK 1 FR 0.0001 REL FR 1 V 0 P
/tear /trill'd /down | /her /delicate /cheek. LR 4.03. 13

CHEEK 89 FR 0.0100 REL FR 79 V 10 P
that the sea, mounting to th' welkin's cheek, TMP 1.02. 4
the setting of thine eye and cheek proclaim | a 2.01.229
my mistress made it one upon my cheek: ERR 1.02. 46
th' alluring beauty took | from my poor cheek? 2.01. 90
old ornament of his cheek hath already stuff'd ADO 3.02. 46 P
do meet, as at a fair, in her fair cheek, LLL 4.03.231
that smiles his cheek in years and knows the 5.02.465
why is your cheek so pale? MND 1.01.128
follow? nay; i'll go with thee, cheek by jowl. 3.02.338
is like a villain with a smiling cheek, | a MV 1.03.100
that steals the color from bassanio's cheek — 3.02.244
nature presently distill'd | helen's cheek, but AYL 3.02.145
a lean cheek, which you have not; 3.02.373 P
you meet in some fresh cheek the power of fancy, 3.05. 29
nor your cheek of cream | that can entame my 3.05. 47
more lusty red | than that mix'd in his cheek; 3.05.122
her sorrows takes all livelihood from her cheek. AWW 1.01. 51 P
your pie and your porridge than in your cheek; 1.01.160 P
an emblem of war, here on his sinister cheek; 2.01. 44 P
let the white death sit on thy cheek for ever, 2.03. 71

his left cheek is a cheek of two pile and a half 4.05. 97 P
his left cheek is a cheek of two pile and a half 4.05. 97 P
and a half, but his right cheek is worn bare. 4.05. 98 P
a worm i' th' bud, | feed on her damask cheek. TN 2.04.112
i should my tears let fall upon your cheek, 5.01.240
is leaning cheek to cheek? WT 1.02.285
is leaning cheek to cheek? 1.02.285
the pretty dimples of his chin and cheek, his 2.03.102
i think affliction may subdue the cheek, | but 4.04.576
upon thy cheek lay i this zealous kiss | as seal JN 2.01. 19
and chase the native beauty from his cheek, 3.04. 83
thy frozen admonition | make pale our cheek, R2 2.01.118
have ever made me sour my patient cheek, | or 2.01.169
my wive's brother, then his cheek look'd pale, 1H4 1.03.142
doth speak of you, his cheek looks pale, and 3.01. 9
and the whiteness in thy cheek | is apter than 2H4 1.01. 68
of my hand than he shall get one /of his cheek, 1.02. 22 P
eye, a dry hand, a yellow cheek, a white beard, 1.02.181 P
to blush and beautify the cheek again. 2H6 3.02.167
and pitied me, and kindly kiss'd my cheek; R3 2.02. 24
heart | her eyes, her hair, her cheek, her gait, TRO 1.01. 54
and bid the cheek be ready with a blush | modest 1.03.228
the lustre in your eye, heaven in your cheek, 4.04.118
till thy sphered bias cheek | outswell the colic 4.05. 8
there's language in her eye, her cheek, her lip, 4.05. 55
my mother's blood | runs on the dexter cheek, 4.05.128
she strokes his cheek! 5.02. 51
it seems she hangs upon the cheek of night | as ROM 1.05. 45
the brightness of her cheek would shame those 2.02. 19
see how she leans her cheek upon her hand! 2.02. 23
upon that hand, | that i might touch that cheek! 2.02. 25
else would a maiden blush bepaint my cheek | for 2.02. 86
lo here upon thy cheek the stain doth sit | of 2.03. 75
let not the virgin's cheek | make soft thy TIM 4.03.115
calphurnia's cheek is pale, and cicero | looks JC 1.02.185
the harlot's cheek, beautied with plast'ring art HAM 3.01. 50
pinch wanton on your cheek, call you his mouse, 3.04.183
that bear'st a cheek for blows, a head for LR 4.02. 51
else so thy cheek pays shame | when ANT 1.01. 31
soldier, that thy cheek | so much as lank'd not. 1.04. 70
put color in thy cheek. 4.14. 69
had i this cheek | to bathe my lips upon; CYM 1.06. 99
then | the princely blood flows in his cheek, he 3.03. 93
forget that rarest treasure of your cheek, 3.04.160
his right cheek | reposing on a cushion. 4.02.211
give color to my pale cheek with thy blood, 4.02.330
but there is something glows upon my cheek, PER 5.01. 95
fortune at you | dimpled her cheek with smiles. TNK 1.01. 66
stand up, | your grief is written in your cheek. 1.01.110
now doth she stroke his cheek, now doth he frown VEN 45
even so she kiss'd his brow, his cheek, his chin 59
that in each cheek appears a pretty dimple; 242
to love a cheek that smiles at thee in scorn! 252
but now her cheek was pale, and by and by | it 347
her other tender hand his fair cheek feels: 352
his tend'rer cheek receives her soft hand's 353
claps her pale cheek, till clapping makes it red 468
upon the blushing rose, | usurps her cheek; 591
which her cheek melts, as scorning it should 982
her lily hand her rosy cheek lies under, LUC 386
and then with lank and lean discolor'd cheek, 708
on helen's cheek all art of beauty set, | and SON 53. 7
why should false painting imitate his cheek, 67. 5
thus is his cheek the map of days outworn, 68. 1
doth he give, | and found it in thy cheek; 79.11
which on thy soft cheek for complexion dwells 99. 4
hat, | hanging her pale and pined cheek beside; LC 32
each cheek a river running from a fount | with 283
o, that false fire which in his cheek so glowed, 324
CHEEK–ROSES 1 FR 0.0001 REL FR 1 V 0 P
as those cheek–roses | proclaim you are no less! MM 1.04. 16
CHEEK'S 1 FR 0.0001 REL FR 1 V 0 P
one of thy eyes and thy cheek's side struck off! 1H6 1.04. 75
/CHEEKS 1 FR 0.0001 REL FR 1 V 0 P
/with /her /sorrow, /mesh'd /upon /her /cheeks. TIT 3.02. 38
CHEEKS 93 FR 0.0105 REL FR 91 V 2 P
the air hath starv'd the roses in her cheeks, TGV 4.04.154
for blush in cheeks by faults are bred | and LLL 1.02.101
for still her cheeks possess the same | which 1.02.105
the night of dew that on my cheeks down flows; 4.03. 28
air, quoth he, thy cheeks may blow; 4.03.107
bed, | while i thy amiable cheeks do coy, | and MND 4.01. 2
this cherry nose, | these yellow cowslip cheeks, 5.01.332
such war of white and red within her cheeks! SHR 4.05. 30
for look, thy cheeks | confess it, /t' /one to AWW 1.03.176
the blushes in my cheeks thus whisper me, | "we 2.03. 69
save unscratch'd your city's threat'ned cheeks, JN 2.01.225
and strain their cheeks to idle merriment — | a 3.03. 46
that i have seen inhabit in those cheeks? 4.02.107
that silverly doth progress on thy cheeks. 5.02. 46
and stain'd the beauty of a fair queen's cheeks R2 3.01. 14
at meeting tears the cloudy cheeks of heaven. 3.03. 57
hast thou lost the fresh blood in thy cheeks, 1H4 2.03. 44
them coin his nose, let them coin his cheeks. 3.03. 79 P
washing with kindly tears his gentle cheeks, 2H4 4.05. 83
their cheeks are paper. H5 2.02. 74
investing lank–lean cheeks and war–worn coats, 4.pr. 26
and to sun's parching heat display'd my cheeks, 1H6 1.02. 77
here by the cheeks i'll drag thee up and down. 1.03. 51
mean time your cheeks do counterfeit our roses; 2.04. 62
anger, that thy cheeks | blush for pure shame to 2.04. 65
o, tell me when my lips do touch his cheeks, 2.05. 39
did represent my master's blushing cheeks, 4.01. 93
these cheeks are pale for watching for your good 2H6 4.07. 85
i give thee this to dry thy cheeks withal. 3H6 1.04. 83
the ruthless queen gave him to dry his cheeks 2.01. 61
the other his pale cheeks, methinks, presenteth. 2.05.100
and wet my cheeks with artificial tears, | and 3.02.184
and to my brother turn my blushing cheeks. 5.01. 99
nails should rent that beauty from my cheeks. R3 1.02.126
that all the standers–by had wet their cheeks 1.02.162
but his red color hath forsook his cheeks. 2.01. 86
red wine first must rise | in their fair cheeks, H8 1.04. 44
grief hath set these jaundies o'er your cheeks? TRO 1.03. 2
do you with cheeks abash'd behold our works, 1.03. 18
my bright hair and scratch my praised cheeks, 4.02.107
their nicely gawded cheeks to th' wanton spoil COR 2.01.217
the smiles of knaves | tent in my cheeks, and 3.02.116
to tear with thunder the wide cheeks a' th' air, 5.03.151
doth shine upon the dead man's earthy cheeks, TIT 2.03.229
yet do thy cheeks look red as titan's face 2.04. 31
see | filling the aged wrinkles in my cheeks, 3.01. 7
then fresh tears | stood on her cheeks, as doth 3.01.112
looking all downwards to behold our cheeks, 3.01.124
ah, my lavinia, i will wipe thy cheeks. 3.01.142
can do no service on her sorrowful cheeks. 3.01.147
hath wash'd thy sallow cheeks for rosaline! ROM 2.03. 70
now comes the wanton blood up in your cheeks, 2.05. 70
hood my unmann'd blood, bating in my cheeks, 3.02. 14
the roses in thy lips and cheeks shall fade | to 4.01. 99
famine is in thy cheeks, | need and oppression 5.01. 69
yet | is crimson in thy lips and in thy cheeks, 5.03. 95
and keep the natural ruby of your cheeks, | when MAC 3.04.114
those linen cheeks of thine | are counsellors to 5.03. 16
with cadent tears fret channels in her cheeks, LR 1.04.285
weapons, water–drops, | stain my man's cheeks! 2.04.278
blow, winds, and crack your cheeks! 3.02. 1
i should make very forges of my cheeks, | that OTH 4.02. 74
/glow the delicate cheeks which they did cool, ANT 2.02.204
should be, which pitifully disaster the cheeks. 2.07. 16 P
let's part, | you see we have burnt our cheeks. 2.07.122
err, who with wet cheeks | were present when she CYM 5.05. 35
and with dead cheeks advise thee to desist | for PER 1.01. 39
sleep out of mine eyes, blood from my cheeks, 1.02. 96
our cheeks and hollow eyes do witness it. 1.04. 51
with cherry lips and cheeks of damask roses, TNK 4.01. 74
doth quench the maiden burning of his cheeks; VEN 50
wishing her cheeks were gardens full of flowers, 65
long have rain'd, making her cheeks all wet, 83
souring his cheeks, cries, "fie, no more of love 185
red cheeks and fiery eyes blaze forth her wrong; 219
wrings her nose, he strikes her on the cheeks, 475
the crystal tide that from her two cheeks fair 957
sighs dry her cheeks, tears make them wet again. 966
resembling well his pale cheeks and the blood 1169
the golden age to gild | their silver cheeks, LUC 61
upon my cheeks what helpless shame i feel." 756
poor lucrece' cheeks unto her maid seem so | as 1217
nor why her fair cheeks over–wash'd with woe. 1225
from thee, that down thy cheeks are raining? 1271
the more she saw the blood his cheeks replenish, 1357
her cheeks with chops and wrinkles were 1452
cheeks neither red nor pale, but mingled so 1510
o, from thy cheeks my image thou hast torn, 1762
"air," quoth he, "thy cheeks may blow, | air, PP 16. 9
might be better us'd | where cheeks need blood, SON 82.14
though rosy lips and cheeks | within his bending 116. 9
white, | but no such roses see i in her cheeks, 130. 6
better becomes the grey cheeks of th' east, 132. 6
CHEER 79 FR 0.0089 REL FR 68 V 11 P
here, master; what cheer? TMP 1.01. 2 P
i have good cheer at home, and i pray you all go WIV 3.02. 51 P
besides your cheer, you shall have sport; 3.02. 80 P
pray god our cheer | may answer my good will and ERR 3.01. 19
small cheer and great welcome makes a merry 3.01. 26
better cheer may you have, but not with better 3.01. 29
here is neither cheer, sir, nor welcome: 3.01. 66
comfort my sister, cheer her, call her /wife: 3.02. 26
take it, and much thanks for my good cheer. 5.01.393
their cheer is the greater that i am subdu'd. ADO 1.03. 71 P
well, i will meet you, so i may have good cheer. 5.01.152 P
what cheer, my love? MND 1.01.122
all fancy–sick she is and pale of cheer | with 3.02. 96
that lov'd, that lik'd, that look'd with cheer. 5.01.294
nerissa, cheer yond stranger, bid her welcome. MV 3.02.237
bid your friends welcome, show a merry cheer — 3.02.312
therefore be a' good cheer, for truly i think 3.05. 5 P
good cheer, antonio! 4.01.111
comfort a little, cheer thyself a little. AYL 2.06. 5 P
be of good cheer, youth. 4.03.163
marry, i fare well, for here is cheer enough. SHR in.2. 101
and have prepar'd great store of wedding cheer, 3.02.186
mistress, what cheer? 4.03. 37
one mess is like to be your cheer. 4.04. 70
and by all likelihood some cheer is toward. 5.01. 13
our stomachs up | after our great good cheer. 5.02. 10
i prithee, lady, have a better cheer; AWW 3.02. 64
what cheer? how is't with you, best brother? WT 1.02.148
my sovereign lord, cheer up yourself, look up. 2H4 4.04.113
shall "do nothing but eat, and make good cheer, 5.03. 17
and she shall have whipping cheer, i warrant her 5.04. 5 P
be a' good cheer." H5 2.03. 18 P
methinks your looks are sad, your cheer appal'd. 1H6 1.02. 48
salisbury, cheer thy spirit with this comfort, 1.04. 90
go, go, cheer up thy hungry–starved men; 1.05. 16
news, my lords, may cheer our drooping spirits: 5.02. 1
voice | was wont to cheer his dad in mutinies? 3H6 1.04. 77
doth not the object cheer your heart, my lord? 2.02. 4
as the rocks cheer them that fear their wrack: 2.02. 5
my lord, cheer up your spirits, our foes are 2.02. 56
my royal father, cheer these noble lords, | and 2.02. 78
and cheer his grace with quick and merry eyes. R3 1.03. 5
now cheer each other in each other's love. 2.02.114
be of good cheer. mother, how fares your grace? 4.01. 37
nor cheer of mind that i was wont to have. 5.03. 74
but cheer thy heart, and be thou not dismay'd. 5.03.174
cheer your neighbors. H8 1.04. 41
be of good cheer, | they shall no more prevail 5.01.142
go in and cheer the town. TRO 5.03. 92
of war hath wrought this change of cheer, | thou TIT 1.01.264
and cheer the heart | that dies in tempest of 1.01.457
ne'er let my heart know merry cheer indeed 2.03.188
then cheer thy spirit, for know thou, emperor, 4.04. 88
although the cheer be poor, | 'twill fill your 5.03. 28
the day to cheer and night's dank dew to dry, ROM 2.03. 6
our wedding cheer to a sad burial feast; 4.05. 87
i'll cheer up | my discontented troops, and lay TIM 3.05.113
ah, my good friend, what cheer? 3.06. 40 P
royal cheer, i warrant you. 3.06. 49 P
publius, good cheer, | there is no harm intended JC 3.01. 89
my royal lord, | you do not give the cheer. MAC 3.04. 32
come, sisters, cheer we up his sprites, | and 4.01.127
receive what cheer you may, | the night is long 4.03.239
this push | will cheer me ever, or /disseat me 5.03. 21
here in the cheer and comfort of our eye, | our HAM 1.02.116
so far from cheer and from /your former state, 3.02.164
/an anchor's cheer in prison be my scope! 3.02.219
cheer your heart, | be you not troubled with the ANT 3.06. 81
what, what, good cheer! 4.15. 83
be of good cheer; 5.02. 21
what cheer, madam? CYM 3.04. 39
go in and cheer the king, he rages, none | dare 3.05. 67
you shall have better cheer | ere you depart, 3.06. 66
good cheer, ladies! TNK 1.01.233
so guiltless she securely gives good cheer | and LUC 89
whereat she smiled with so sweet a cheer | that 264
to cheer the ploughman with increaseful crops, 958
thee, | ruthless bears they will not cheer thee. PP 20.22
'tis with so dull a cheer | that leaves look SON 97.13
CHEER'D 6 FR 0.0006 REL FR 6 V 0 P
was never hollow'd to, nor cheer'd with horn, MND 4.01.125
still and anon cheer'd up the heavy time, JN 4.01. 47
upon these words i came and cheer'd him up. H5 4.06. 20
cheer'd up the drooping army, and himself, 3H6 1.01. 6
i cheer'd them up with justice of our cause, 2.01.133
therefore be cheer'd, | make not your thoughts ANT 5.02.184
CHEERED 2 FR 0.0002 REL FR 2 V 0 P
as all the world is cheered by the sun, | so i R3 1.02.129
cheered and check'd even by the self–same sky, SON 15. 6
CHEERER 1 FR 0.0001 REL FR 1 V 0 P
her vine, the merry cheerer of the heart, H5 5.02. 41
CHEERFUL 18 FR 0.0020 REL FR 16 V 2 P
be cheerful, sir. TMP 4.01.147
be cheerful | and think of each thing well. 5.01.250
yet be cheerful, knight. WIV 5.05.170 P
thou hast not, cousin, | prithee be cheerful. AYL 1.03. 94
and look'd upon, i hope, with cheerful eyes. JN 4.02. 2
and entertain a cheerful disposition. R2 2.02. 4
and a corpulent, of a cheerful look, a pleasing 1H4 2.04.423 P
this had been cheerful after victory. 2H4 4.02. 88
with cheerful semblance and sweet majesty; H5 4.pr. 40
lords, with one cheerful voice welcome my love. 2H6 1.01. 36
o cheerful colors! see where oxford comes! 3H6 5.01. 58
i, | "this general applause and cheerful shout R3 3.07. 39
be cheerful, richmond, for the wronged souls 5.03.121
the /snake lies rolled in the cheerful sun, TIT 2.03. 13
me above the ground with cheerful thoughts. ROM 5.01. 5
be cheerful. ANT 3.02. 44
be cheerful; CYM 4.02.402
walk, and be cheerful once again, reserve | that PER 4.01. 39
CHEERFULLY 10 FR 0.0011 REL FR 8 V 2 P
pluck up thy spirits, look cheerfully upon me. SHR 4.03. 38
thou speak'st cheerfully. H5 4.01. 34
ay, he said so, to make us fight cheerfully; 4.01.192 P
go cheerfully together and digest | your angry 1H6 4.01.167
madam, good hope, his grace speaks cheerfully. R3 1.03. 34
his grace looks cheerfully and smooth this 3.04. 48
sound drums and trumpets boldly and cheerfully. 5.03.269
for look you how cheerfully my mother looks, and HAM 3.02.126 P
how cheerfully on the false trail they cry! 4.05.110
we'll follow cheerfully. TNK 5.04. 39
CHEERING 3 FR 0.0003 REL FR 3 V 0 P
cheering a rout of rebels with your drum, 2H4 4.02. 9
went through the army, cheering up the soldiers. R3 5.03. 71
till, cheering up her senses all dismay'd, | she VEN 896
CHEERLESS 1 FR 0.0001 REL FR 1 V 0 P
all's cheerless, dark, and deadly. LR 5.03.291
CHEERLY 14 FR 0.0015 REL FR 8 V 6 P
cheerly, cheerly, my hearts! TMP 1.01. 5 P
cheerly, cheerly, my hearts! 1.01. 5 P
cheerly, good hearts! 1.01. 26 P
thou look'st cheerly, and i'll be with thee AYL 2.06. 14 P
cheerly, good adam! 2.06. 18 P
but lusty, young, and cheerly drawing breath. R2 1.03. 66
cheerly, my lord, how fares your grace? 1H4 5.04. 44
cheerly to sea! H5 2.02.192
but cheerly seek how to redress their harms. 3H6 5.04. 2
in god's name cheerly on, courageous friends, R3 5.02. 14
cheerly, boys, be brisk a while, and the longer ROM 1.05. 14 P
cheerly, my hearts! 1.05. 88
prithee, man, look cheerly. TIM 2.02.214
come weigh, my hearts, cheerly! TNK 4.01.146
CHEERS 7 FR 0.0008 REL FR 6 V 1 P
and cheers these hands that slew thy sire and 3H6 2.04. 9
this cheers my heart, to see your forwardness. 5.04. 65
being smelt, with that part cheers each part, ROM 2.03. 25
and all the madness is, he cheers them up too. TIM 1.02. 42 P
balms, and gums, and heavy cheers, | sacred TNK 1.05. 4
when in his fresh array | he cheers the morn, VEN 484
his drumming heart cheers up his burning eye, LUC 435
CHEER'ST 1 FR 0.0001 REL FR 1 V 0 P
how cheer'st thou, jessica? MV 3.05. 70
CHEESE *(also seese)*
CHEESE 13 FR 0.0014 REL FR 1 V 12 P
you banbury cheese! WIV 1.01.128 P
there's pippins and cheese to come. 1.02. 12 P
the humor of bread and cheese /and /there's /the 2.01.136 P
parson hugh the welshman with my cheese, an 2.02.303 P
lest he transform me to a piece of cheese! 5.05. 82 P
i were chok'd with a piece of toasted cheese. 5.05.139 P
virginity breeds mites, much like a cheese, AWW 1.01.142 P
live | with cheese and garlic in a windmill, far 1H4 3.01.160
it will toast cheese, and it will endure cold as H5 2.01. 9 P
his breath stinks with eating toasted cheese. 2H6 4.07. 12 P
why, my cheese, my digestion, why hast thou not TRO 2.03. 41 P
that stale old mouse–eaten dry cheese, nestor, 5.04. 11 P
peace, this piece of toasted cheese will do't. LR 4.06. 89 P
CHEESE–PARING 1 FR 0.0001 REL FR 0 V 1 P
like a man made after supper of a cheese–paring. 2H4 3.02.309 P
CHEQUINS 1 FR 0.0001 REL FR 0 V 1 P
three or four thousand chequins were as pretty a PER 4.02. 26 P
CHER 2 FR 0.0002 REL FR 0 V 2 P
du monde, mon tres cher et devin deesse? H5 5.02.217 P
in french, notre tres cher fils henri, roi 5.02.339 P
CHERISH 21 FR 0.0023 REL FR 19 V 2 P
if you but knew how you the purpose cherish TMP 2.01.224
thou gentle nymph, cherish thy forlorn swain. TGV 5.04. 12
if thou dost love fair hero, cherish it, | and i ADO 1.01.308
they cherish it to make it stay there; WT 4.03. 92 P
this juggling witchcraft with revenue cherish, JN 3.01.169
to check his reign, but they will cherish it; 3.04.152

kind | cherish rebellion and are rebels all. R2 2.03.147
look to thy servants, cherish thy guesse. 1H4 3.03.172 P
have taught us how to cherish such high deeds 5.05. 30
cherish it, my boy; 2H4 4.04. 23
cherish duke humphrey's deeds | while they do 2H6 1.01.203
for what doth cherish weeds but gentle air? 3H6 2.06. 21
whom thou wast sworn to cherish and defend. R3 1.04.208
all duteous love | doth cherish you and yours, 2.01. 34
last, cherish those hearts that hate thee; H8 3.02.443
that love which thou hast vow'd to cherish; ROM 3.03.129
known to commit outrages | and cherish factions. TIM 3.05. 72
honor and honesty | i cherish and depend on, TNK 3.01. 51
to dry the old oak's sap and cherish springs, LUC 950
as priam him did cherish, | so did i tarquin, so 1546
bounteous gift thou shouldst in bounty cherish. SON 11.12
CHERISH'D 8 FR 0.0009 REL FR 7 V 1 P
should have been cherish'd by her child–like TGV 3.01. 75
foster'd, illumin'd, cherish'd, kept alive. 3.01.184
if they were not cherish'd by our virtues. AWW 4.03. 74 P
who, never so tame, so cherish'd and lock'd up, 1H4 5.02. 10
the better cherish'd, still the nearer death. 5.02. 15
who, cherish'd in your breasts, will sting your 2H6 3.01.344
must gently be preserv'd, cherish'd, and kept. R3 2.02.119
mean, if on both parts | this be not cherish'd. ANT 3.02. 33
CHERISHED 1 FR 0.0001 REL FR 1 V 0 P
oath | lives in this bosom, dearly cherished. JN 3.03. 24
CHERISHER 1 FR 0.0001 REL FR 0 V 1 P
my wife is the cherisher of my flesh and blood; AWW 1.03. 46 P
CHERISHES 1 FR 0.0001 REL FR 0 V 1 P
he that cherishes my flesh and blood loves my AWW 1.03. 47 P
CHERISHING 2 FR 0.0002 REL FR 2 V 0 P
than cherishing th' exhibiters against us; H5 1.01. 74
yet i should kill thee with much cherishing. ROM 2.02.183
CHERRIES 3 FR 0.0003 REL FR 3 V 0 P
ripe in show | thy lips, those kissing cherries, MND 3.02.140
her twinning cherries shall their sweetness fall TNK 1.01.178
bring him mulberries and ripe–red cherries: VEN 1103
CHERRY 9 FR 0.0010 REL FR 9 V 0 P
like to a double cherry, seeming parted, | but MND 3.02.209
my cherry lips have often kiss'd thy stones, 5.01.190
these lily lips, | this cherry nose, | these 5.01.331
and it grandame will | give it a plum, a cherry, JN 2.01.162
a cherry lip, a bonny eye, a passing pleasing R3 1.01. 94
'tis as like you | as cherry is to cherry. H8 5.01.169
'tis as like you | as cherry is to cherry. 5.01.169
her inkle, silk, /twin with the rubied cherry, PER 5.ch. 8
with cherry lips and cheeks of damask roses, TNK 4.01. 74
CHERRY–PIT 1 FR 0.0001 REL FR 0 V 1 P
for gravity to play at cherry–pit with sathan. TN 3.04.116 P
CHERRY–STONE 1 FR 0.0001 REL FR 1 V 0 P
a drop of blood, a pin, | a nut, a cherry–stone; ERR 4.03. 73
CHERTSEY 3 FR 0.0003 REL FR 3 V 0 P
come now towards chertsey with your holy load, R3 1.02. 29
at chertsey monast'ry this noble king, | and wet 1.02.214
towards chertsey, noble lord? 1.02.225
CHERUB 1 FR 0.0001 REL FR 0 V 1 P
i see a cherub that sees them. HAM 4.03. 48 P
CHERUBIN 5 FR 0.0005 REL FR 5 V 0 P
o, a cherubin | thou wast that did preserve me. TMP 1.02.152
than thy sword, | for all her cherubin look. TIM 4.03. 64
striding the blast, or heaven's cherubin, hors'd MAC 1.07. 22
patience, thou young and rose–lipp'd cherubin — OTH 4.02. 63
which like a cherubin above them hover'd. LC 319
CHERUBINS 5 FR 0.0005 REL FR 4 V 1 P
still quiring to the young–ey'd cherubins; MV 5.01. 62
their dwarfish pages were | as cherubins, all H8 1.01. 23
fears make devils of cherubins, they never see TRO 3.02. 69 P
th' chamber | with golden cherubins is fretted. CYM 2.04. 88
such cherubins as your sweet self resemble, SON 114. 6
CHESHU *(also jeshu, jesu)*
CHESHU 3 FR 0.0003 REL FR 0 V 3 P
by cheshu, i think 'a will plow up all, if there H5 3.02. 63 P
by cheshu, he is an ass, as in the world; 3.02. 70 P
by cheshu, he will maintain his argument as well 3.02. 79 P
CHEST 12 FR 0.0013 REL FR 10 V 2 P
neither press, coffer, chest, trunk, well, vault WIV 4.02. 61 P
what says the golden chest? MV 2.09. 23
a jewel in a ten–times–barr'd–up chest | is a R2 1.01.180
from his deep chest laughs out a loud applause, TRO 1.03.163
come, stretch thy chest, and let thy eyes spout 4.05. 10
that have their alms out of the empress' chest. TIT 2.03. 9
sir, we have a chest beneath the hatches, PER 3.01. 70 P
did the sea toss up upon our shore this chest. 3.02. 50
find | some purer chest to close so pure a mind. LUC 761
thee have i not lock'd up in any chest, | save SON 48. 9
so is the time that keeps you as my chest, | or 52. 9
time's best jewel from time's chest lie hid? 65.10
CHESTER 1 FR 0.0001 REL FR 1 V 0 P
he ask'd the way to chester, and of him | i did 2H4 1.01. 39
CHESTNUT 3 FR 0.0003 REL FR 2 V 1 P
your chestnut was ever the only color. AYL 3.04. 11 P
to hear | as will a chestnut in a farmer's fire? SHR 1.02.209
you know | the chestnut mare the duke has? TNK 5.02. 61
CHESTNUTS 1 FR 0.0001 REL FR 1 V 0 P
a sailor's wife had chestnuts in her lap, | and MAC 1.03. 4
CHESTS 6 FR 0.0006 REL FR 4 V 2 P
he hath devis'd in these three chests of gold, MV 1.02. 30 P
in cypress chests my arras counterpoints, SHR 2.01.351
lie like pawns lock'd up in chests and trunks, JN 5.02.141
are my chests fill'd up with extorted gold? 2H6 4.07. 99
been so fidius'd for all the chests in corioles, COR 2.01.131 P
his chests and treasure | he has not with him. ANT 4.05. 10
/CHETAS 1 FR 0.0001 REL FR 1 V 0 P
/and /timbria, /helias, /chetas, /troien, | /and TRO pr 16
CHEVAL 2 FR 0.0002 REL FR 1 V 1 P
le cheval volant, the pegasus, chez les narines H5 3.07. 14 P
montez /a cheval! my horse, varlot lackey! ha! 4.02. 2
CHEVALIER 2 FR 0.0002 REL FR 1 V 1 P
que je tombe entre les mains d'un chevalier, je H5 4.04. 56 P
villain | and cannot help the noble chevalier. 1H6 4.03. 14
CHEVALIERS 1 FR 0.0001 REL FR 1 V 0 P
amen, amen! mount, chevaliers! to arms! JN 2.01.287
CHEVALRY *(also chivalry)*
CHEVALRY 3 FR 0.0003 REL FR 3 V 0 P
his light | did all the chevalry of england move 2H4 2.03. 20
when all her chevalry hath been in france, | and H5 1.02.157
slain | the flow'r of europe for his chevalry, 3H6 2.01. 71
CHEVEREL 1 FR 0.0001 REL FR 0 V 1 P
o, here's a wit of cheverel, that stretches from ROM 2.04. 83 P
CHEVERIL 1 FR 0.0001 REL FR 1 V 0 P
of your soft cheveril conscience would receive H8 2.03. 32
CHEV'RIL 1 FR 0.0001 REL FR 0 V 1 P
a sentence is but a chev'ril glove to a good wit TN 3.01. 12 P
CHEW 2 FR 0.0002 REL FR 2 V 0 P
my mouth, | as if i did but only chew his name, MM 2.04. 5
till then, my noble friend, chew upon this: JC 1.02.171
CHEW'D 2 FR 0.0002 REL FR 1 V 1 P
veriest varlet that ever chew'd with a tooth. 1H4 2.02. 24 P
stretch our eye | when capital crimes, chew'd, H5 2.02. 56
CHEW'D–GRASS *(see chaw'd–grass)*
CHEWET 1 FR 0.0001 REL FR 0 V 1 P
peace, chewet, peace! 1H4 5.01. 29 P
CHEWING 1 FR 0.0001 REL FR 1 V 0 P
chewing the food of sweet and bitter fancy, | lo AYL 4.03.101
CHEZ 1 FR 0.0001 REL FR 0 V 1 P
volant, the pegasus, chez les narines de feu! H5 3.07. 14 P
CHICK 1 FR 0.0001 REL FR 1 V 0 P
my ariel, chick, | that is thy charge. TMP 5.01.317
CHICKEN 3 FR 0.0003 REL FR 3 V 0 P
set | to guard the chicken from a hungry kite, 2H6 3.01.249
so the poor chicken should be sure of death. 3.01.251
alas, poor chicken! TNK 5.02. 96
CHICKENS 4 FR 0.0004 REL FR 2 V 2 P
idle head, you would eat chickens i' th' shell. TRO 1.02.134 P
on water to scald such chickens as you are. TIM 2.02. 69 P
what, all my pretty chickens, and their dam, MAC 4.03.218
forthwith they fly | chickens, the way which CYM 5.03. 42
CHICURMURCO 1 FR 0.0001 REL FR 0 V 1 P
boblibindo chicurmurco. AWW 4.03.125 P
CHID 21 FR 0.0023 REL FR 18 V 3 P
and pray her to a fault for which i chid her. TGV 1.02. 52
how churlishly i chid lucetta hence, | when 1.02. 60
wont to have when you chid at sir proteus for 2.01. 72 P
i should have chid you for not bringing it, ERR 4.01. 50
chid i for that at frugal nature's frame? ADO 4.01.128
when we have chid the hasty–footed time | for MND 3.02.200
but he hath chid me hence and threat'ned me | to 3.02.312
whiles you chid me, i did love; AYL 4.03. 54
alas, i then have chid away my friend! JN 4.01. 86
thou wilt be horribly chid to–morrow when thou 1H4 2.04.373 P
and chid his truant youth with such a grace | as 5.02. 62
and traitors' rage | be thus upbraided, chid, 2H6 3.01.175
clifford too, | have chid me from the battle; 3H6 2.05. 17
he chid andromache and strook his armorer, | and TRO 1.02. 6
look who comes here; will you be chid? TIM 1.01.176
he chid the sisters | when first they put the MAC 3.01. 56
he might have chid me so; OTH 4.02.113
as his own state and ours, 'tis to be chid — ANT 1.04. 30
that i could wish myself a sigh to be so chid, TNK 2.01. 44 P
hath chid down all the majesty of england, STM II.C 73
and chid the painter for his wondrous skill, LUC 1528
CHIDDEN 4 FR 0.0004 REL FR 3 V 1 P
and yet i was last chidden for being too slow. TGV 2.01. 12 P
heels | and fly like chidden mercury from jove, TRO 2.02. 45
and all the rest look like a chidden train: JC 1.02.184
the chidden billow seems to pelt the clouds, OTH 2.01. 12
/CHIDE 1 FR 0.0001 REL FR 1 V 0 P
him offense, | /and /he /does /chide /with /you. OTH 4.02.167
CHIDE 53 FR 0.0060 REL FR 49 V 4 P
one word more | shall make me chide thee, if not TMP 1.02.477
makes me the bolder to chide you for yours. TGV 2.01. 83 P
if she do chide, 'tis not to have you gone, 3.01. 98
and by and by intend to chide myself | even for 4.02.103
you chide at him, offending twice as much. LLL 4.03.130
we shall chide downright, if i longer stay. MND 2.01.145
now i but chide; 3.02. 45
our sex, as well as i, may chide you for it, 3.02.218
i will chide no breather in the world but myself AYL 3.02.280 P
sweet youth, i pray you chide a year together, 3.05. 64
i had rather hear you chide than this man woo. 3.05. 65
him, | for what had he to do to chide at me? 3.05.129
and almost chide god for making you that 4.01. 36 P
master, it is no time to chide you now, SHR 1.01.159
though she chide as loud | as thunder when the 1.02. 95
nothing steads us | to chide him from our eaves, AWW 3.07. 42
of your pains, | i will no further chide you. TN 3.03. 3
to chide at your extremes it not becomes me. WT 4.04. 6
chide me, dear stone, that i may say indeed 5.03. 24
chide him for faults, and do it reverently, 2H4 4.04. 37
find him, my lord of warwick, chide him hither. 4.05. 62
we'll chide this dolphin at his father's door. H5 1.02.308
shall chide your trespass and return your mock 2.04.125
and chide the cripple tardy–gaited night, | who 4.pr. 20
nay, eleanor, then must i chide outright. 2H6 1.02. 41
but i can give the loser leave to chide. 3.01.182
and so i chide the means that keeps me from it, 3H6 3.02.141
as good to chide the waves as speak them fair. 5.04. 24
weep, | to chide my fortune, and torment myself? R3 2.02. 35
if he flinch, chide me for it. TRO 3.02.106 P
good troilus, chide me for it. 5.03. 39
chide me no more. COR 3.02.132
i pray thee chide me not. ROM 2.03. 85
that after–hours with sorrow chide us not! 2.06. 2
o, what a beast was i to chide at him! 3.02. 95
do so, and bid my sweet prepare to chide. 3.03.162
a thing like death to chide away this shame, 4.01. 74
an act of rage, | and after seem to chide 'em. JC 2.01.177
do you not come your tardy son to chide, | that, HAM 3.04.106
but i'll not chide thee, | let shame come when LR 2.04.225
do not you chide; i have a thing for you. OTH 3.03.301
whom every thing becomes — to chide, to laugh, ANT 1.01. 49
with mars fall out, with juno chide, | that thy CYM 5.04. 32
when i spur | my horse, i chide him /not; TNK 3.01.107
and gins to chide, but soon she stops his lips, VEN 46
"if thou wilt chide, thy lips shall never open." 48
"thus i forestall thee, if thou mean to chide, LUC 484
but chide rough winter that the flow'r hath 1255
they do but sweetly chide thee, who confounds SON 8. 7
and chide thy beauty and thy straying youth, 41.10
nor dare i chide the world–without–end hour, 57. 5
the forward violet thus did i chide: 99. 1
o, for my sake do you /with fortune chide, | the 111. 1
CHIDERS 1 FR 0.0001 REL FR 1 V 0 P
i love no chiders, sir. biondello, let's away. SHR 1.02.226
CHIDES 11 FR 0.0012 REL FR 10 V 1 P
at tables, chides the dice | in honorable terms; LLL 5.02.326
not her that chides, sir, at any hand, i pray. SHR 1.02.225
one | he chides to hell and bids the other grow WT 4.04.553
with the sea | that chides the banks of england, 1H4 3.01. 44
and chides the sea that sunders him from thence, 3H6 3.02.138
the raven chides blackness. TRO 2.03.211 P
he'll think your mother chides, and leave you so JC 4.03.123
little in her heart, | and chides with thinking. OTH 2.01.107
and chides as he had power | to beat me out of ANT 4.01. 1
divorce of love" — thus chides she death — VEN 932
runs, and chides his vanish'd loath'd delight. LUC 742
CHIDING 13 FR 0.0014 REL FR 12 V 1 P
better a little chiding than a great deal of WIV 5.03. 9 P
never did i hear | such gallant chiding; MND 4.01.115
and churlish chiding of the winter's wind, AYL 2.01. 7
most mischievous foul sin, in chiding sin: 2.07. 64
call you this chiding? 4.03. 64
or rather, thou art she | in thy not chiding; WT 5.03. 26
as doth a rock against the chiding flood, H8 3.02.197
in self–same key | retires to chiding fortune. TRO 1.03. 54
strike my gentleman for chiding of his fool? LR 1.03. 1
for, in good faith, | i am a child to chiding. OTH 4.02.114
thou hast as chiding a nativity | as fire, air, PER 3.01. 32
'tis but a chiding. TNK 2.03. 27
chiding that tongue that, ever sweet, | was us'd SON 145. 6
CHID'ST 1 FR 0.0001 REL FR 1 V 0 P
thou chid'st me well. R2 3.02.188
CHIDST 1 FR 0.0001 REL FR 1 V 0 P
thou chidst me oft for loving rosaline. ROM 2.03. 81
CHIEF 40 FR 0.0045 REL FR 36 V 4 P
out with't, and place it for her chief virtue. TGV 3.01.335 P
but in chief | for that her reputation was MM 5.01.220
are not you the chief woman? LLL 4.01. 51
the rest — yet my chief humor is for a tyrant. MND 1.02. 28 P
but my chief care | is to come fairly off from MV 1.01.127
of my dear father's gift stands chief in power, AWW 2.01.112
both for myself and them — but, chief of all, JN 4.02. 49
holds from all soldiers chief majority | and 1H4 3.02.109
unto your grace do i in chief address | the 2H4 4.01. 31
how now, my lord chief justice, whither away? 5.02. 1
my friends, and woe to my lord chief justice! 5.03.138 P
my lord chief justice, speak to that vain man. 5.05. 44
all france with their chief assembled strength 1H6 1.01.139
chief master gunner am i of this town, 1.04. 6
teach, | but prove a chief offender in the same? 3.01.130
regard, | king henry's peers and chief nobility 4.01.146
the chief perfections of that lovely dame | (had 5.05. 12
i was the chief that rais'd him to the crown, 3H6 3.03.262
and i'll be chief to bring him down again; 3.03.263
that his chief followers lodge in towns about 4.03. 13
but, with the first of all your chief affairs, 4.06. 58
the chief cause concerns his grace of canterbury H8 5.02. 38
makes the church | the chief aim of his honor, 5.02.153
know caius martius is chief enemy to the people. COR 1.01. 7 P
ever verified my friends | (of whom he's chief) 5.02. 18
chief architect and plotter of these woes. TIT 5.03.122
great fortunes | are made thy chief afflictions. TIM 4.02. 44
course, | chief nourisher in life's feast. MAC 2.02. 37
here's our chief guest. 3.01. 11
and the chief head | of this post–haste and HAM 1.01.106
of a most select and generous chief in that. 1.03. 74
if his chief good and market of his time | be 4.04. 34
this great world, | chief factors for the gods: ANT 2.06. 10
whose bosom was my crownet, my chief end, | like 4.12. 27
farewell, great chief. shall i strike now? 4.14. 93
were i chief lord of all this spacious world, PER 4.03. 5
"the field's chief flower, sweet above compare, VEN 8
so, | that every present sorrow seemeth chief, 970
which to repair should be thy chief desire. SON 10. 8
that she hath thee, is of my wailing chief, | a 42. 3
CHIEFEST 15 FR 0.0017 REL FR 14 V 1 P
and employ your chiefest thoughts | to courtship MV 2.08. 43
call for our chiefest men of discipline | to JN 2.01. 39
and sit at chiefest stern of public weal. 1H6 1.01.177
within their chiefest temple i'll erect | a tomb 2.02. 12
their chiefest prospect murd'ring basilisks! 2H6 3.02.324
the lord hastings, the king's chiefest friend. 3H6 4.03. 11
hither | into this chiefest thicket of the park. 4.05. 3
shall be well winged with our chiefest horse. R3 5.03.300
and that's one of the chiefest of them too. TRO 1.02.267 P
it is held | that valor is the chiefest virtue, COR 2.02. 84
help, three a' th' chiefest soldiers; 5.06.148
him | some of the chiefest princes of the goths. TIT 5.02.125
all know, security | is mortals' chiefest enemy. MAC 3.05. 33
our chiefest courtier, cousin, and our son. HAM 1.02.117
built up this city for his chiefest seat, | the PER 1.ch. 18
CHIEFLY 15 FR 0.0017 REL FR 11 V 4 P
chiefly that i might set it in my prayers — TMP 3.01. 35
but chiefly | him that you term'd, sir, "the 5.01. 14
but chiefly for thy face and thy behavior, TGV 4.04. 67
did deceive them, but chiefly by my villainy, ADO 3.03.158 P
chiefly one, | which, as the dearest issue of AWW 2.01.105
but chiefly a villainous trick of thine eye, and 1H4 2.04.403 P
and chiefly therefore i thank god and thee. 3H6 4.06. 17
but chiefly to take thence from her dead finger ROM 5.03. 30
did not you chiefly belong to my heart? TIM 1.02. 92 P
one speech in't i chiefly lov'd, 'twas aeneas' HAM 2.02.446 P
offended, and with you | chiefly i' th' world; ANT 2.02. 33
and then myself, i chiefly, | that set thee on CYM 1.05. 72
chiefly in love, whose leave exceeds commission: VEN 568
and i in deep delight am chiefly drown'd | when PP 8.11
and chiefly there | where thy desert may merit 18.14
CHIEN 1 FR 0.0001 REL FR 0 V 1 P
"le chien est retourne a son propre vomissement, H5 3.07. 64 P
/CHILD 1 FR 0.0001 REL FR 0 V 1 P
/between /the /child /and /the /parent, /death, LR 1.02.144 P
CHILD 244 FR 0.0275 REL FR 195 V 49 P
blue–ey'd hag was hither brought with child, TMP 1.02.269
didst seek to violate | the honor of my child. 1.02.348
hath requit it) | him, and his innocent child; 3.03. 72
it sound that i | must ask my child forgiveness! 5.01.198
duty, | neither regarding that she is my child, TGV 3.01. 70
for love is like a child, | that longs for every 3.01.124
good master fenton, come not to my child. WIV 3.04. 72
"will you cast away your child on a fool, and a 3.04. 96 P
i pray you have your remembrance, child. 4.01. 47 P
never name her, child, if she be a whore. 4.01. 63 P

you do ill to teach the child such words. 4.01. 65 P
why, now is cupid a child of conscience, he 5.05. 28 P
and it is for getting madam julietta with child. MM 1.02. 73 P
what? is there a maid with child by him? 1.02. 91 P
with child, perhaps? 1.02.156
he hath got his friend with child. 1.04. 29
some one with child by him? my cousin juliet? 1.04. 45
sir, she came in great with child; 2.01. 89 P
(as i say) with child, and being great–bellied, 2.01. 98 P
was ever respected with man, woman, or child. 2.01.169 P
she is with child, | and he that got it, 2.03. 12
keepdown was with child by him in the duke's 3.02.199 P
his child is a year and a quarter old come 3.02.201 P
once before him for getting a wench with child. 4.03.170 P
himself there's one | whom he begot with child), 5.01.511
signior benedick, no, for then were you a child. ADO 1.01.108 P
no child but hero, she's his only heir. 1.01.295
marriage as to show a child his new coat and 3.02. 6 P
if you hear a child cry in the night, you must 3.03. 65 P
peace, and let the child wake her with crying, 3.03. 70 P
i charge thee do so, as thou art my child. 4.01. 76
bring me a father that so lov'd his child, 5.01. 8
thou hast so wrong'd mine innocent child and me 5.01. 63
i say thou hast belied mine innocent child! 5.01. 67
thou hast kill'd my child. 5.01. 78
thy breath hast kill'd | mine innocent child? 5.01.264
almost the copy of my child that's dead, | and 5.01.289
this child of fancy, that armado hight, | for LLL 1.01.170
"with a child of our grandmother eve, a female; 1.01.263 P
and, sweet my child, let them be men of good 1.02. 68 P
sweet invocation of a child, most pretty and 1.02. 97 P
warble, child, make passionate my sense of 3.01. 1 P
with the parents of the foresaid child or pupil, 4.02.157 P
stoop, i say, | her shoulder is with child. 4.03. 88
offer'd by a child to an old man: 5.01. 62 P
and when he was a babe, a child, a shrimp, 5.02.590
quick, the child brags in her belly already. 5.02.676 P
all wanton as a child, skipping and vain, 5.02.761
with complaint | against my child, my daughter MND 1.01. 23
this man hath bewitch'd the bosom of my child. 1.01. 27
and interchang'd love–tokens with my child; 1.01. 29
of great revenue, and she hath no child. 1.01.158
and therefore is love said to be a child, 1.01.238
and jealous oberon would have the child | knight 2.01. 24
the fairy land buys not the child of me. 2.01.122
come, recreant, come, thou child, | i'll whip 3.02.409
i then did ask of her her changeling child; 4.01. 59
on this prologue like a child on a recorder — a 5.01.123 P
it is a wise father that knows his own child. MV 2.02. 77 P
was, your son that is, your child that shall be. 2.02. 85 P
in me | to be ashamed to be my father's child! 2.03. 17
the moor is with child by you, launcelot. 3.05. 39 P
you know my father hath no child but i, nor none AYL 1.02. 17 P
man's good wit seconded with the forward child, 3.03. 14 P
let her never nurse her child herself, for she 4.01.175 P
a child shall get a sire, if i fail not of my SHR 2.01.411
i am no child, no babe; 4.03. 74
happy the parents of so fair a child! 4.05. 39
his sole child, my lord, and bequeath'd to my AWW 1.01. 38 P
and show me a child begotten of thy body that i 3.02. 58 P
out of my blood, | and thou art all my child. 3.02. 68
whipt for getting the shrieve's fool with child, 4.03.187 P
and at that time he got his wife with child. 5.03.301
can get this ring | and /are by me with child, 5.03.313
it is a gallant child; WT 1.01. 38 P
how he may soften at the sight o' th' child: 2.02. 38
this child was prisoner to the womb and is | by 2.02. 57
my child? 2.03.132
in the between but getting wenches with child, 3.03. 62 P
a boy, or a child, i wonder? 3.03. 70 P
look thee, a bearing–cloth for a squire's child! 3.03.116 P
not have an heir | till his lost child be found? 5.01. 40
i heard the shepherd say, he found the child. 5.02. 7 P
of antigonus, that carried hence the child? 5.02. 60 P
aided to expose the child were even then lost 5.02. 71 P
to dispossess that child which is not his? JN 1.01.131
come to thy grandame, child. 2.01.159
do, child, go to it grandame, child, | give 2.01.160
do, child, go to it grandame, child, | give 2.01.160
thy sins are visited in this poor child, | the 2.01.179
all punish'd in the person of this child, | and 2.01.189
zeal | in the relief of this oppressed child 2.01.245
let wives with child | pray that their burthens 3.01. 89
law cannot give my child his kingdom here, | for 3.01.187
bonds, | because my poor child is a prisoner. 3.04. 75
since the birth of cain, the first male child, 3.04. 79
you are as fond of grief as of your child. 3.04. 92
grief fills the room up of my absent child, 3.04. 93
and, pretty child, sleep doubtless and secure 4.01.129
was | before the child himself felt he was sick. 4.02. 88
and find th' inheritance of this poor child, 4.02. 97
mind | than to be butcher of an innocent child. 4.02.259
as thou shalt be, if thou didst kill this child. 4.03.124
bear away that child, | and follow me with speed 4.03.156
o, had't been a stranger, not my child, | to R2 1.03.239
as a long–parted mother with her child | plays 3.02. 8
lest child, child's children, cry against you 4.01.149
that this same child of honor and renown, | this 1H4 3.02.139
is thought with child by the stern tyrant war, 2H4 in 14
he will spare neither man, woman, nor child. 2.01. 17 P
rascal, and the child i go with do miscarry, 5.04. 9 P
went away and it had been any christom child. H5 2.03. 12 P
never sees horrid night, the child of hell; 4.01.271
alas, this is a child, a silly dwarf! 1H6 2.03. 22
what, shall a child instruct you what to do? 3.01.133
thanks, reignier, happy for so sweet a child, 5.03.148
i am with child, ye bloody homicides! 5.04. 62
now heaven forfend, the holy maid with child? 5.04. 65
you are deceiv'd, my child is none of his, | it 5.04. 72
years | should be to be protected like a child. 2H6 2.03. 29
doth sting a child | that for the beauty thinks 3.01.229
ah, clifford, murther not this innocent child, 3H6 1.03. 8
couldst thou drain the life–blood of the child, 1.04.138
fault, | and long hereafter say unto his child, 2.02. 36
i slew thy father, call'st thou him a child? 2.02.113
i think he means to beg a child of her. 3.02. 27
this, in respect, a child, | and men ne'er spend 5.05. 56
and men ne'er spend their fury on a child. 5.05. 57
but if you ever chance to have a child, | look 5.05. 65
if ever he have child, abortive be it, R3 1.02. 21
nor when thy warlike father, like a child, 1.02.159
and he would love me dearly as a child. 2.02. 26
i, as a child, will go by thy direction. 2.02.153
woe to that land that's govern'd by a child! 2.03. 11
good madam, be not angry with the child. 2.04. 36
his head ere give consent | his master's child, 3.04. 39
when that my mother went with child | of that 3.05. 86
loath to depose the child, your brother's son; 3.07.209
honor, | canst thou demise to any child of mine? 4.04.248
all — | will i withal endow a child of thine; 4.04.250
had grac'd the tender temples of my child, | and 4.04.383
that the great child of honor, cardinal wolsey, H8 4.02. 6
before | this happy child, did i get any thing. 5.04. 65
i shall desire | to see what this child does, 5.04. 68
indeed la, 'tis a noble child. COR 1.03. 67 P
his mother, wife, his child, | and this brave 5.01. 29
wife, mother, child i know not. 5.02. 82
all this while | between the child and parent. 5.03. 56
wife, and child to see | the son, the husband, 5.03.101
requires nor child nor woman's face to see. 5.03.130
in corioles, and his child | like him by chance. 5.03.179
now | was i a child to fear i know not what. TIT 2.03.221
save thou the child, so we may all be safe. 4.02.131
how many women saw this child of his? 4.02.135
but say again, how many saw the child? 4.02.140
his child is like to her, fair as you are. 4.02.154
and how by this their child shall be advanc'd, 4.02.157
i heard a child cry underneath a wall. 5.01. 24
first hang the child, that he may see it sprawl 5.01. 51
save the child | and bear it from me to the 5.01. 53
thy child shall live, and i will see it 5.01. 60
unless thou swear to me my child shall live. 5.01. 68
tell on thy mind, i say thy child shall live. 5.01. 69
behold the child: 5.03.119
my child is yet a stranger in the world, | she ROM 1.02. 8
'a was a merry man — took up the child. 1.03. 40
o my brother's child! 3.01.146
to an impatient child that hath new robes | and 3.02. 30
well, well, thou hast a careful father, child, 3.05.107
marry, my child, early next thursday morn, | the 3.05.112
that god had lent us but this only child, | but 3.05.165
o me, o me, my child, my only life! 4.05. 19
but one, poor one, one poor and loving child, 4.05. 46
o child, o child! 4.05. 62
o child, o child! 4.05. 62
my soul, and not my child! 4.05. 62
alack, my child is dead, | and with my child my 4.05. 63
is dead, | and with my child my joys are buried. 4.05. 64
you love your child so ill | that you run mad, 4.05. 75
whereof thy proud child, arrogant man, is puff'd TIM 4.03.180
o hateful error, melancholy's child, | why dost JC 5.03. 67
why in that rawness left you wife and child, MAC 4.03. 26
child of integrity, hath from my soul | wip'd 4.03.115
them, for they say an old man is twice a child. HAM 2.02.385 P
speak | like a good child and a true gentleman. 4.05.149
as much as child e'er lov'd, or father found; LR 1.01. 59
there's father against child. 1.02.112 P
more hideous when thou show'st thee in a child 1.04.260
create her child of spleen, that it may live 1.04.282
tooth it is | to have a thankless child! 1.04.289
a bond | the child was bound to th' father; 2.01. 48
i will not trouble thee, my child; 2.04.219
"child rowland to the dark tower came, | his 3.04.182
i have serv'd you ever since i was a child; 3.07. 73
i think this lady | to be my child cordelia. 4.07. 69
i had rather to adopt a child than get it. OTH 1.03.191
i am glad at soul i have no other child, | for 1.03.196
for, in good faith, | i am a child to chiding. 4.02.114
let me have a child at fifty, to whom herod of ANT 1.02. 28 P
be a child o' th' time. 2.07.100
under the service of a child as soon | as i' th' 3.13. 24
and to the graver | a child that guided dotards. CYM 1.01. 50
you tell me, | is she sole child to th' king? 1.01. 56
his only child. 1.01. 56
my child? 5.05.264
bad child, worse father, to entice his own | to PER 1.ch. 27
i mother, wife — and yet his child. 1.01. 69
son | by your untimely claspings with your child 1.01.128
here have you seen a mighty king | his child, i 2.ch. 2
sits here like beauty's child, whom nature gat 2.02. 6
his queen, with child, makes her desire — 3.ch. 40
to this world | that ever was prince's child. 3.01. 31
upon you, | must in your child be thought on. 3.03. 20
blessed in your care | in bringing up my child. 3.03. 32
i think you'll turn a child again. 4.03. 4
when noble pericles shall demand his child? 4.03. 13
she did /distain my child, and stood between 4.03. 31
you not your child well loving, yet i find | it 4.03. 37
rise, th' art my child. 5.01.213
and the first sound this child hear be a hiss, TNK pr 16
primrose, first–born child of ver, | merry 1.01. 7
you play the child extremely. 2.02.204
o love, | what a stout–hearted child thou art! 2.06. 9
is at least two hundred now with child by him — 4.01.129
what a mere child is fancy, | that, having two 4.02. 52
and courtiers that have got maids with child, 4.03. 42 P
nev'r cast your child away for honesty. 5.02. 21
come, your love palamon stays for you, child, 5.02. 41
state | stands many a father with his child. 5.04. 3
make the young old, the old become a child. VEN 1152
"were tarquin night, as he is but night's child, LUC 785
"the nurse, to still her child, will tell my 813
to make the child a man, the man a child, | to 954
to make the child a man, the man a child, | to 954
true grief is fond and testy as a child, | who 1094
if in the child the father's image lies, | where 1753
"this fair child of mine | shall sum my count, SON 2.10
resembling sire, and child, and happy mother, 8.11
but were some child of yours alive that time, 17.13
me, my love is as fair | as any mother's child, 21.11
to see his active child do deeds of youth, | so 37. 2
amiss | the second burthen of a former child! 59. 4
if my dear love were but the child of state, 124. 1
whilst her neglected child holds her in chase, 143. 5

CHILD–BED 3 FR 0.0003 REL FR 3 V 0 P
hatred | the child–bed privilege denied, which WT 3.02.103
a terrible child–bed hast thou had, my dear, PER 3.01. 56
at sea in child–bed died she, but brought forth 5.03. 5

CHILD–CHANGED 1 FR 0.0001 REL FR 1 V 0 P
o, wind up | of this child–changed father! LR 4.07. 16

/CHILDED 1 FR 0.0001 REL FR 1 V 0 P
/he /childed /as /i /fathered! LR 3.06.110

CHILDERIC 1 FR 0.0001 REL FR 1 V 0 P
say, | king pepin, which deposed childeric, H5 1.02. 65

CHILDHOOD 6 FR 0.0006 REL FR 6 V 0 P
all school–days friendship, childhood innocence? MND 3.02.202
gaud | which in my childhood i did dote upon; 4.01.168
i urge this childhood proof, | because what MV 1.01.144
now i have stain'd the childhood of our joy ROM 3.03. 95
'tis the eye of childhood | that fears a painted MAC 2.02. 51
the offices of nature, bond of childhood, LR 2.04.178

CHILDHOODS 1 FR 0.0001 REL FR 0 V 1 P
they were train'd together in their childhoods; WT 1.01. 22 P

CHILDING 1 FR 0.0001 REL FR 1 V 0 P
the childing autumn, angry winter, change MND 2.01.112

CHILDISH 11 FR 0.0012 REL FR 11 V 0 P
turning again toward childish treble, pipes AYL 2.07.162
does nothing | but what he did being childish? WT 4.04.402
nor hold the sceptre in his childish fist, | nor 2H6 1.01.245
'twere childish weakness to lament or fear. 3H6 5.04. 38
their aspects with store of childish drops: R3 1.02.154
out of our easiness and childish pity | to one H8 5.02. 60
of such childish friendliness | to yield your COR 2.03.175
arm'd, | from love's weak childish bow she lives ROM 1.01.211
and childish error that they are afraid; VEN 898
"then childish fear, avaunt, debating, die! LUC 274
such childish humor from weak minds proceeds; 1825

CHILDISH–FOOLISH 1 FR 0.0001 REL FR 1 V 0 P
i am too childish–foolish for this world. R3 1.03.141

CHILDISHLY 1 FR 0.0001 REL FR 1 V 0 P
me | so far from what she was, so childishly, TNK 4.01. 39

CHILDISHNESS 3 FR 0.0003 REL FR 3 V 0 P
is second childishness and mere oblivion, | sans AYL 2.07.165
perhaps thy childishness will move him more COR 5.03.157
give me freedom, | it does from childishness. ANT 1.03. 58

CHILD–KILLER 1 FR 0.0001 REL FR 1 V 0 P
upon that clifford, that cruel child–killer. 3H6 2.02.112

CHILD–LIKE 2 FR 0.0002 REL FR 2 V 0 P
have been cherish'd by her child–like duty, | i TGV 3.01. 75
have shown your father | a child–like office. LR 2.01.106

CHILDNESS 1 FR 0.0001 REL FR 1 V 0 P
and with his varying childness cures in me WT 1.02.170

/CHILDREN 2 FR 0.0002 REL FR 0 V 2 P
/sir, /an /aery /of /children, /little /eyases, HAM 2.02.339 P
/what, /are /they /children? 2.02.345 P

CHILDREN 112 FR 0.0126 REL FR 100 V 12 P
"farewell, my wife and children!" TMP 1.01. 61
for 'tis not good that children should know any WIV 2.02.128 P
the children must | be practic'd well to this, 4.04. 65
i will teach the children their behaviors; 4.04. 67 P
the children thus dispos'd, my wife and i, ERR 1.01. 83
these are the parents to these children, | which 5.01.361
the duke, my husband, and my children both, 5.01.404
therein do men from children nothing differ. ADO 5.01. 33
in nativity, | shall upon their children be. MND 5.01.414
of the father are to be laid upon the children; MV 3.05. 2 P
marry, his kisses are judas's own children. AYL 3.04. 9 P
makes the world full of ill–favor'd children. 3.05. 53
to mine own children in good bringing–up, | and SHR 1.01. 99
fathers commonly | do get their children; 2.01.410
'tis a good hearing when children are toward. 5.02.182
of men, though it be the getting of children. AWW 3.02. 42 P
all doubt | you'ld call your children yours. WT 2.03. 82
as he does, | her children not her husband's! 2.03.108
i'll speak of her no more, nor of your children; 3.02.229
precious queen and children are even now to be 4.02. 24 P
jewel of children, seen this hour, he had pair'd 5.01.116
boy, i am past moe children, but thy sons and 5.02.126 P
of that i doubt, as all men's children may. JN 1.01. 63
and leave your children, wives, and you in peace 2.01.257
make such unconstant children of ourselves, | as 3.01.243
that we, the sons and children of this isle, 5.02. 25
us, our lives, our children, and our heirs. R2 2.01.245
strike | your children yet unborn and unbegot, 3.03. 88
which like unruly children make their sire 3.04. 30
lest child, child's children, cry against you 4.01.149
the children yet unborn | shall feel this day as 4.01.322
in cradle–clothes our children where they lay, 1H4 1.01. 88
that men would tell their children, "this is he" 3.02. 48
midwives say the children are not in the fault, 2H4 2.02. 25 P
do, | were all thy children kind and natural! H5 2.pr. 19
| they owe, some upon their children rawly left. 4.01.141 P
our children, and our sins lay on the king! 4.01.232
even so our houses, and ourselves, and children, 5.02. 56
the scarecrow that affrights our children so. 1H6 1.04. 43
we and our wives and children all will fight, 3.01.100
by her he had two children at one birth. 2H6 4.02.139
how many children hast thou, widow? tell me. 3H6 3.02. 26
now tell me, madam, do you love your children? 3.02. 36
therein thou wrong'st thy children mightily. 3.02. 74
thou art a widow, and thou hast some children, 3.02.102
women and children of so high a courage, | and 5.04. 50
you have no children, butchers; 5.05. 63
action shows itself | against my children, R3 1.03. 67
o, spare my guiltless wife and my poor children! 1.04. 72
peace, children, peace, the king doth love you 2.02. 17
and hast the comfort of thy children left; 2.02. 56
men, | but sanctuary children never till now. 3.01. 56
time, | infer the bastardy of edward's children. 3.05. 75
touch'd you the bastardy of edward's children? 3.07. 4
thy mother's name is ominous to children. 4.01. 40
wept like /two children in their deaths' sad 4.03. 8
me, thou villain–slave, where are my children? 4.04.144
and there the little souls of edward's children 4.04.192
th' advancement of your children, gentle lady. 4.04.242
they are as children but one step below, | even 4.04.301
your children were vexation to your youth, | but 4.04.305
the children live whose fathers thou hast 4.04.391
parents live whose children thou hast butcher'd, 4.04.393
yet thou didst kill my children. 4.04.422
hastings, and edward's children, grey and rivers 5.01. 3
false to his children and his wive's allies; 5.01. 15
if you do free your children from the sword, 5.03.261
your children's children quits it in your age. 5.03.262

and have been blest | with many children by you. H8 2.04. 37
our children's children | shall see this, and 5.04. 54
my thoughts were like unbridled children grown TRO 3.02.122
as children from a bear, the volsces shunning COR 1.03. 31
towards her deserved children is enroll'd | in 3.01.290
of more bastard children than war's a destroyer 4.05.225 P
our wives, and children, on our knees, | are 4.06. 22
whose children he hath slain, their base throats 5.06. 52
or be ye not henceforth call'd my children. TIT 2.03.115
some say that ravens foster forlorn children 2.03.153
which are the children of an idle brain, | begot ROM 1.04. 97
and from her womb children of divers kind | we 2.03. 11
obedience, fail in children! TIM 4.01. 4
why old men, fools, and children calculate, JC 1.03. 65
and first decree | into the /law of children. 3.01. 39
men, wives, and children stare, cry out, and run 3.01. 97
your children shall be kings. MAC 1.03. 86
do you not hope your children shall be kings, 1.03.118
to your throne and state, children and servants; 1.04. 25
and all my children? 4.03.177
my children too? 4.03.211
wife, children, servants, all | that could be 4.03.211
he has no children. 4.03.216
as the indifferent children of the earth. HAM 2.02.227 P
that wear rags | do make their children blind, LR 2.04. 49
that bear bags | shall see their children kind. 2.04. 51
i never gave you kingdom, call'd you children; 3.02. 17
the winged vengeance overtake such children. 3.07. 66
then belike my children shall have no names. ANT 1.02. 35 P
and put your children | to that destruction 5.02.131
you with your children will he send before. 5.02.202
that a king's children should be so convey'd, CYM 1.01. 63
so children temporal fathers do appease; 5.04. 12
stole these children | upon my banishment; 5.05.341
i lost my children; 5.05.354
be it our wives, our children, or ourselves, PER 1.04.103
all dear nature's children sweet, | lie 'fore TNK 1.01. 13
have told 's | they are sisters' children, 1.04. 16
honor) lastly | children of grief and ignorance. 2.02. 55
we shall have many children. 5.02. 94
are sorry, still | are children in some kind. 5.04.134
and sung by children in succeeding times. LUC 525
if children predecease progenitors, | we are 1756
and thou shalt find | those children nurs'd, SON 77.11
CHILDREN'S 15 FR 0.0017 REL FR 15 V 0 P
only to stick it in their children's sight | for MM 1.03. 25
my strict fast — i mean, my children's looks; R2 2.01. 80
daub her lips with her own children's blood, 1H4 1.01. 6
much, when sceptres are in children's hands; 1H6 4.01.192
may, even in their wives' and children's sight, 2H6 4.02.179
mayst thou live to wail thy children's death, R3 1.03.203
your children's children quits it in your age. 5.03.262
our children's children | shall see this, and H8 5.04. 54
have i had children's voices? COR 3.01. 30
bravely shed | thy wife and children's blood. 5.03.118
which, but their children's end, nought could ROM pr 11
my wife and children's ghosts will haunt me MAC 5.07. 16
nor children's tears nor mothers' groans LUC 431
"then for thy husband and thy children's sake, 533
by children's eyes, her husband's shape in mind. SON 9. 8
CHILD'S 5 FR 0.0005 REL FR 4 V 1 P
no, some of it is for my child's father. AYL 1.03. 11 P
the foul corruption of a sweet child's death. JN 4.02. 81
lest child, child's children, cry against you R2 4.01.149
thy scarlet robes as a child's bearing–cloth 1H6 1.03. 42
make a desperate tender | of my child's love. ROM 3.04. 13
CHILL* 6 FR 0.0006 REL FR 2 V 4 P
but the many will be too chill and tender, and AWW 4.05. 53 P
chill not let go, zir, without vurther /cagion. LR 4.06.235 P
chill be plain with you. 4.06.242 P
chill pick your teeth, zir. 4.06.244 P
a man throng'd up with cold, my veins are chill, PER 2.01. 73
both fire from hence and chill extincture hath. LC 294
CHILLING 1 FR 0.0001 REL FR 1 V 0 P
a chilling sweat o'erruns my trembling joints, TIT 2.03.212
CHIME 2 FR 0.0002 REL FR 2 V 0 P
'tis like a chime a–mending, with terms TRO 1.03.159
time, | hell only danceth at so harsh a chime. PER 1.01. 85
CHIMES 1 FR 0.0001 REL FR 0 V 1 P
we have heard the chimes at midnight, master 2H4 3.02.214 P
CHIMNEY 6 FR 0.0006 REL FR 1 V 5 P
what shall i do? i'll creep up into the chimney. WIV 4.02. 56 P
'twill fly with the smoke out at the chimney. AYL 4.01.164 P
charles' wain is over the new chimney, and yet 1H4 2.01. 2 P
and then we leak in your chimney, and your 2.01. 20 P
sir, he made a chimney in my father's house, and 2H6 4.02.148 P
the chimney | is south the chamber, and the CYM 2.04. 80
CHIMNEY–PIECE 1 FR 0.0001 REL FR 1 V 0 P
and the chimney–piece | chaste dian bathing. CYM 2.04. 81
CHIMNEY'S 1 FR 0.0001 REL FR 1 V 0 P
the raven rook'd her on the chimney's top, | and 3H6 5.06. 47
CHIMNEYS 2 FR 0.0002 REL FR 2 V 0 P
cricket, to windsor chimneys shalt thou leap; WIV 5.05. 43
our chimneys were blown down, and, as they say, MAC 2.03. 55
CHIMNEY–SWEEPERS 2 FR 0.0002 REL FR 2 V 0 P
to look like her are chimney–sweepers black. LLL 4.03.262
all must, | as chimney–sweepers, come to dust. CYM 4.02.263
CHIMNEY–TOPS 1 FR 0.0001 REL FR 1 V 0 P
to tow'rs and windows, yea, to chimney–tops, JC 1.01. 39
CHIMURCHO 1 FR 0.0001 REL FR 0 V 1 P
bosko chimurcho. AWW 4.03.124 P
CHIN *(also sin*)*
/CHIN 1 FR 0.0001 REL FR 1 V 0 P
when with his amazonian /chin he drove | the COR 2.02. 91
CHIN 28 FR 0.0031 REL FR 11 V 17 P
but i guess, it stood in her chin, by the salt ERR 3.02.128 P
hast got more hair on thy chin than dobbin my MV 2.02. 94 P
or his chin worth a beard? AYL 3.02.206 P
if thou delay me not the knowledge of his chin. 3.02.211 P
item, one neck, one chin, and so forth. TN 1.05.248 P
though i would not have it grow on my chin. 3.01. 48 P
the pretty dimples of his chin and cheek, his WT 2.03.102
and his chin new reap'd | show'd like a 1H4 1.03. 34
your master, whose chin is not yet fledge. 2H4 1.02. 20 P
your wind short, your chin double, your wit 1.02.183 P
i perceiv'd the first white hair of my chin. 1.02.242 P
whose chin is but enrich'd | with one appearing H5 3.pr. 22
de chin. 3.04. 35 P
has not past three or four hairs on his chin — TRO 1.02.112 P
and puts me her white hand to his cloven chin — 1.02.119 P
but laugh to think how she tickled his chin. 1.02.136 P
takes upon her to spy a white hair on his chin. 1.02.140 P
alas, poor chin! many a wart is richer. 1.02.141 P
white hair that helen spied on troilus' chin. 1.02.151 P
"here's but two and fifty hairs on your chin — 1.02.158 P
these hairs which thou dost ravish from my chin LR 3.07. 38
if you did wear a beard upon your chin, | i'ld 3.07. 76
with him | my poor chin too, for 'tis not TNK 1.02. 54
so she kiss'd his brow, his cheek, his chin, VEN 59
upon this promise did he raise his chin, | like 85
her coral lips, her snow–white dimpled chin. LUC 420
who o'er the white sheet peers her whiter chin, 472
"small show of man was yet upon his chin, | his LC 92
CHINA 1 FR 0.0001 REL FR 0 V 1 P
they are not china dishes, but very good dishes. MM 2.01. 94 P
CHINE 2 FR 0.0002 REL FR 1 V 1 P
with the glanders and like to mose in the chine, SHR 3.02. 51 P
let me ne'er hope to see a chine again, | and H8 5.03. 26
CHINES 1 FR 0.0001 REL FR 0 V 1 P
the burly–bon'd clown in chines of beef ere thou 2H6 4.10. 57 P
CHINK 5 FR 0.0005 REL FR 4 V 1 P
the story) did talk through the chink of a wall. MND 3.01. 64 P
and through wall's chink, poor souls, they are 5.01.133
that had in it a crannied hole or chink, 5.01.158
show me thy chink, to blink through with mine 5.01.177
now will i to the chink, | to spy and i can hear 5.01.192
CHINKS 1 FR 0.0001 REL FR 1 V 0 P
can lay hold of her | shall have the chinks. ROM 1.05.117
CHINS 4 FR 0.0004 REL FR 3 V 1 P
till new–born chins | be rough and razorable; TMP 2.01.249
there dancing up to th' chins, that the foul 4.01.183
sand, wear yet upon their chins | the beards of MV 3.02. 84
stroke your chins, and swear by your beards that AYL 1.02. 72 P
CHIPP'D 2 FR 0.0002 REL FR 1 V 1 P
a good pantler, 'a would 'a' chipp'd bread well. 2H4 2.04.238 P
handless, hack'd and chipp'd, come to him, TRO 5.05. 34
CHIPS 1 FR 0.0001 REL FR 1 V 0 P
state | and situation with those dancing chips, SON 128.10
CHIRON 7 FR 0.0008 REL FR 7 V 0 P
chiron, thy years wants wit, thy wits wants edge TIT 2.01. 26
chiron, we hunt not, we, with horse nor hound, 2.02. 25
"stuprum — chiron — demetrius." 4.01. 78
the empress' sons i take them, chiron, demetrius 5.02.154
o villains, chiron and demetrius! 5.02.169
not i, 'twas chiron and demetrius: 5.03. 56
to you | that chiron and the damn'd demetrius 5.03. 97
CHIRP 1 FR 0.0001 REL FR 1 V 0 P
lo | the moon is down, the crickets chirp, the TNK 3.02. 35
CHIRPING 1 FR 0.0001 REL FR 1 V 0 P
and thinks he that the chirping of a wren, | by 2H6 3.02. 42
CHIRRAH *(also sirrah)*
CHIRRAH 2 FR 0.0002 REL FR 0 V 2 P
chirrah! LLL 5.01. 32 P
/quare chirrah, not sirrah? 5.01. 33 P
CHIRURGEONLY 1 FR 0.0001 REL FR 1 V 0 P
and most chirurgeonly. TMP 2.01.141
CHISEL 1 FR 0.0001 REL FR 1 V 0 P
what fine chisel | could ever yet cut breath? WT 5.03. 78
CHITOPHER 1 FR 0.0001 REL FR 0 V 1 P
mine own company, chitopher, vaumond, bentii, AWW 4.03.165 P
CHIVALROUS 1 FR 0.0001 REL FR 1 V 0 P
degree | or chivalrous design of knightly trial; R2 1.01. 81
CHIVALRY *(also chevalry)*
/CHIVALRY 1 FR 0.0001 REL FR 1 V 0 P
/on /his /fair /worth /and /single /chivalry. TRO 4.04.148
CHIVALRY 9 FR 0.0010 REL FR 8 V 1 P
see | justice design the victor's chivalry. R2 1.01.203
home, | for christian service and true chivalry, 2.01. 54
to my shame, | i have a truant been to chivalry, 1H4 5.01. 94
field | we kept together in our chivalry!" H5 4.06. 19
fly, | now thou art seal'd the son of chivalry? 1H6 4.06. 29
brave troilus, the prince of chivalry! TRO 1.02.229 P
youth, | i am to–day i' th' vein of chivalry. 5.03. 32
and his device, a wreath of chivalry; PER 2.02. 29
name, | made glorious by his manly chivalry, LUC 109
/CHOICE 1 FR 0.0001 REL FR 1 V 0 P
/commonwealth /is /sick /of /their /own /choice, 2H4 1.03. 87
CHOICE 77 FR 0.0087 REL FR 66 V 11 P
this is my father's choice. WIV 3.04. 31
we have with a leaven'd and prepared choice MM 1.01. 51
mind, | ability in means, and choice of friends, ADO 4.01.199
a most singular and choice epithet. LLL 5.01. 15 P
if you yield not to your father's choice, | you MND 1.01. 69
or else it stood upon the choice of friends — 1.01.139
or, if there were a sympathy in choice, | war, 1.01.141
because in choice he is so oft beguil'd. 1.01.239
that hermia should give answer of her choice? 4.01.136
make choice of which your highness will see 5.01. 43
in terms of choice i am not soly led | by nice MV 2.01. 13
now make your choice. 2.07. 3
lastly, | if i do fail in fortune of my choice, 2.09. 15
well, but to my choice: 2.09. 49
let music sound while he doth make his choice; 3.02. 43
you say, there's small choice in rotten apples. SHR 1.01.134 P
that she's the choice love of signior gremio. 1.02.234
to strive for that which resteth in my choice. 3.01. 17
and choice breeds | a native slip to us from AWW 1.03.145
so make the choice of thy own time, for i, | thy 2.01.203
make choice and see, | who shuns thy love shuns 2.03. 72
rather be in this choice than throw ames–ace for 2.03. 78 P
this ring he holds | in most rich choice; 3.07. 26
at first | i stuck my choice upon her, ere my 5.03. 45
pedlar, let's have the first choice. WT 4.04.313 P
not need to grieve | at knowing of thy choice. 4.04.416
your choice is not so rich in worth as beauty, 5.01.214
a braver choice of dauntless spirits | than now JN 2.01. 72
to five and twenty thousand men of choice, | and 2H4 1.03. 11
i shall be well content with any choice | tends 1H6 5.01. 26
and ye choice spirits that admonish me | and 5.03. 3
wife | and have no portion in the choice myself. 5.03.125
so full replete with choice of all delights, 5.05. 17
hath not our brother made a worthy choice? 3H6 4.01. 3
brother of clarence, how like you our choice, 4.01. 9
a choice hour | to hear from him a matter of H8 1.02.162
here i'll make | my royal choice. 1.04. 86
you have here, lady | (and of your choice), 2.04. 58
a daughter a goddess, he should take his choice. TRO 1.02.237 P
he that meets hector issues from our choice, 1.03.347
and choice (being mutual act of all our souls) 1.03.348
their vulgar wisdoms, | of their own choice. COR 1.01.216
take your choice of those | that best can aid 1.06. 65
the common distribution, at | your only choice. 1.09. 36
the wisdom of their choice is rather to have my 2.03. 98 P
at thy choice then. 3.02.123
and, romans, fight for freedom in your choice. TIT 1.01. 17
if thou be pleas'd with this my sudden choice, 1.01.318
queen of goths, dost thou applaud my choice? 1.01.321
learn thou to make some meaner choice, | lavinia 2.01. 73
come and take choice of all my library, | and so 4.01. 34
to her chance, and damn'd her loathed choice! 4.02. 78
within her scope of choice | lies my consent and ROM 1.02. 18
you have made a simple choice, you know not how 2.05. 38 P
the choice and master spirits of this age. JC 3.01.163
for on his choice depends | the safety and HAM 1.03. 20
and therefore must his choice be circumscrib'd 1.03. 22
since my dear soul was mistress of her choice 3.02. 63
is extant, and written in very choice italian. 3.02.263 P
but it reserv'd some quantity of choice, | to 3.04. 75
make choice of whom your wisest friends you will 4.05.205
in neither can make choice of either's moi'ty. LR 1.01. 6 P
most choice forsaken, and most lov'd despis'd, 1.01.251
my train are men of choice and rarest parts, 1.04.263
at your choice, sir. 2.04.217
body, she will find the /error of her choice. OTH 1.03.351 P
her in it and compel her to some second choice. 2.01.235 P
rather makes choice of loss | than gain which ANT 3.01. 23
well, mistress, your choice agrees with mine; PER 2.05. 18
well, i do commend her choice, | and will no 2.05. 21
i/'d wish no better choice, and think me rarely 5.01. 69
take your choice, and what | you want at any TNK 2.05. 54
there shall be at your choice | both sword and 3.01. 88
make choice then. 3.06.285
i have no choice, and i have lied so lewdly 4.02. 35
my cousin palamon | has made so fair a choice. 5.02. 92
then woos best when most his choice is froward. VEN 570
CHOICE–DRAWN 1 FR 0.0001 REL FR 1 V 0 P
these cull'd and choice–drawn cavaliers to H5 3.pr. 24
CHOICELY 1 FR 0.0001 REL FR 1 V 0 P
collected choicely, from each county some, | and 2H6 3.01.313
CHOICEST 1 FR 0.0001 REL FR 1 V 0 P
with all the choicest music of the kingdom, H8 4.01. 91
CHOIR *(also quier'd, quire, etc.)*
CHOIR 5 FR 0.0005 REL FR 5 V 0 P
and plac'd a choir of such enticing birds | that 2H6 1.03. 89
the queen | to a prepar'd place in the choir, H8 4.01. 64
which perform'd, the choir, | with all the 4.01. 90
our cage | we make a choir, as doth the prison'd CYM 3.03. 43
woe, | and still the choir of echoes answer so. VEN 840
CHOIRS 1 FR 0.0001 REL FR 1 V 0 P
bare /ruin'd choirs, where late the sweet birds SON 73. 4
CHOK'D 13 FR 0.0014 REL FR 11 V 2 P
'tis time i were chok'd with a piece of toasted WIV 5.05.139 P
what, have i chok'd you with an argosy? SHR 2.01.376
is full of weeds, her fairest flowers chok'd up, R2 3.04. 44
chok'd the respect of likely peril fear'd, | and 2H4 1.01.184
go forward, and be chok'd with thy ambition! 1H6 2.04.112
chok'd with ambition of the meaner sort; 2.05.123
virtue is chok'd with foul ambition, | and 2H6 3.01.143
and give thanks | to you that chok'd it. H8 1.02. 4
it had, almost, chok'd caesar, for he swounded, JC 1.02.248 P
all pity chok'd with custom of fell deeds; 3.01.269
be chok'd with such another emphasis! ANT 1.05. 68
her judgment | that what's else rare is chok'd; CYM 3.05. 77
fear | is almost chok'd by unresisted lust. LUC 282
CHOKE 17 FR 0.0019 REL FR 15 V 2 P
your life, | and choke your good to come. MM 5.01.422
upon a knive's point and choke a daw withal. ADO 2.03.255 P
why, that's the way to choke a gibing spirit, LLL 5.02.858
and having that do choke their service up | even AYL 2.03. 61
and to choke his days | with barbarous ignorance JN 4.02. 58
with eager feeding food doth choke the feeder; R2 2.01. 37
leaving their earthly parts to choke your clime, H5 4.03.102
i trust ere long to choke thee with thine own, 1H6 3.02. 46
and choke the herbs for want of husbandry. 2H6 3.01. 33
he has a merit | to choke it in the utt'rance. COR 4.07. 49
my tears will choke me if i ope my mouth. TIT 5.03.175
i scorn thy meat, 'twould choke me; TIM 1.02. 38 P
fearful scouring | doth choke the air with dust. 5.02. 16
that do cling together | and choke their art. MAC 1.02. 9
cannot remove nor choke the strong conception OTH 5.02. 55
good lord i prove untrue, | i'll choke myself. CYM 1.05. 87
to choke mars's drum | and turn th' alarm to TNK 5.01. 80
CHOKES 2 FR 0.0002 REL FR 2 V 0 P
for boiling choler chokes | the hollow passage 1H6 5.04.120
said, impatience chokes her pleading tongue, VEN 217
CHOKING 2 FR 0.0002 REL FR 2 V 0 P
when degree is suffocate, | follows the choking, TRO 1.03.126
a choking gall, and a preserving sweet. ROM 1.01.194
CHOLER 26 FR 0.0029 REL FR 19 V 7 P
thy impatience, throw cold water on thy choler. WIV 2.03. 85 P
nay, my choler is ended. LLL 2.01.206
for it engenders choler, planteth anger, | and SHR 4.01.172
let's purge this choler without letting blood. R2 1.01.153
drunk with choler? 1H4 1.03.129
choler, my lord, if rightly taken. 2.04.324 P
i beseek you now, aggravate your choler. 2H4 2.04.162 P
fluellen valiant | and, touch'd with choler, hot H5 4.07.180
and digest | your angry choler on your enemies. 1H6 4.01.168
for boiling choler chokes | the hollow passage 5.04.120
my choler being overblown | with walking once 2H6 1.03.152
scarce can i speak, my choler is so great. 5.01. 23
and let your reason with your choler question H8 1.01.130
and something spoke in choler, ill, and hasty. 2.01. 34
should have ta'en th' advantage of his choler, COR 2.03.198
what, what? his choler? 3.01. 83
choler? 3.01. 84
put him to choler straight, he hath been us'd 3.03. 25
i mean, and we be in choler, we'll draw. ROM 1.01. 3 P
patience perforce with willful choler meeting 1.05. 89
choler does kill me that thou art alive; TIM 4.03.367
must i give way and room to your rash choler? JC 4.03. 39
no, my lord, with choler. HAM 3.02.303 P
would perhaps plunge him into more choler. 3.02.307

and france in choler parted? LR 1.02. 23
he's rash and very sudden in choler, and happily OTH 2.01.272 P
CHOLERIC 10 FR 0.0011 REL FR 7 V 3 P
that in the captain's but a choleric word, MM 2.02.130
lest it make you choleric, and purchase me ERR 2.02. 62 P
have denied that before you were so choleric. 2.02. 67 P
since, of ourselves, ourselves are choleric, SHR 4.01.174
i fear it is too choleric a meat. 4.03. 19
i cannot tell, i fear 'tis choleric. 4.03. 22
are you so choleric | with eleanor, for telling 2H6 1.02. 51
go show your slaves how choleric you are, | and JC 4.03. 43
that infirm and choleric years bring with them. LR 1.01.299 P
to the choleric fisting of every rogue | thy ear PER 4.06.167
CHOLERS 1 FR 0.0001 REL FR 0 V 1 P
and his his wraths, and his cholers, and his moods, H5 4.07. 35 P
CHOLLORS 1 FR 0.0001 REL FR 0 V 1 P
how full of chollors i am and trempling of mind! WIV 3.01. 11 P
CHOOSE 109 FR 0.0123 REL FR 78 V 31 P
i know thou canst not choose. TMP 1.02.186
same cloud cannot choose but fall by pailfuls. 2.02. 24 P
i cannot choose | but pity her. TGV 4.04. 77
by cock and pie, you shall not choose, sir! WIV 1.01.303 P
that cannot choose but amaze him. 5.03. 17 P
are chosen, they are glad to choose me for them. MM 2.01.269 P
this course | fittest choose, | for forty ducats ERR 4.03. 95
i pray you choose another subject. ADO 5.01.136 P
choose your revenge yourself, | impose me to 5.01.272
if we choose by the horns, yourself come not LLL 4.01.115
o hell! to choose love by another's eyes. MND 1.01.140
is not in the fashion to choose me a husband. MV 1.02. 22 P
o me, the word choose! 1.02. 23 P
i may neither choose who i would, nor refuse who 1.02. 23 P
nerissa, that i cannot choose one, nor refuse 1.02. 26 P
should say, "and you will not have me, choose." 1.02. 47 P
if he should offer to choose, and choose the 1.02. 92 P
offer to choose, and choose the right casket, 1.02. 92 P
temptation without, i know he will choose it. 1.02. 98 P
and either not attempt to choose at all, | or 2.01. 39
or swear before you choose, if you choose wrong 2.01. 40
if you choose wrong | never to speak to lady 2.01. 40
how shall i know if i do choose the right? 2.07. 10
if you choose that, then i am yours withal. 2.07. 12
here do i choose, and thrive i as i may! 2.07. 60
let all of his complexion choose me so. 2.07. 79
if you choose that wherein i am contain'd, 2.09. 5
by the fool multitude, that choose by show, 2.09. 26
i will not choose what many men desire, 2.09. 31
that judgment is, | that did never choose amiss. 2.09. 65
when they do choose, | they have the wisdom by 2.09. 80
to venice that swear he cannot choose but break. 3.01.114 P
i could teach you | how to choose right, but 3.02. 11
let me choose, | for as i am, i live upon the 3.02. 24
me more than eloquence, | and here choose i. 3.02.107
"you that choose not by the view, | chance as 3.02.131
the view, | chance as fair, and choose as true: 3.02.132
you'll ask me why i rather choose to have | a 4.01. 40
believe me, lord, i think he cannot choose. SHR in.1. 42
be patient, gentlemen, i choose her for myself. 2.01.302
you shall not choose but drink before you go. 5.01. 11
i hope i may choose, sir. 5.01. 47 P
keep it not, you cannot choose but lose by't. AWW 1.01.146 P
to her whose state is such that cannot choose 1.03.214
to choose from forth the royal blood of france, 2.01.196
thou hast power to choose, and they none to 2.03. 56
me, | "we blush that thou shouldst choose; 2.03. 70
thyself, if thou shouldst strive to choose. 2.03.146
choose thou thy husband, and i'll pay thy dower, 5.03.328
"thou canst not choose but know who i am. TN 2.05.174 P
thou shalt not choose but go; 4.01. 57
affection, which cannot choose but branch now. WT 1.01. 24 P
i think there is not half a kiss to choose | who 4.04.175
reason my son | should choose himself a wife, 4.04.407
give me the office | to choose you a queen. 5.01. 78
direct not him whose way himself will choose, R2 2.01. 29
let's choose executors and talk of wills; 3.02.148
choose out some secret place, some reverent room 5.06. 25
why, it cannot choose but be a noble plot. 1H4 1.03.279
i cannot choose. 3.01.146
which cannot choose but bring him quickly on. 5.02. 44
she must be old, she cannot choose but be old, 2H4 3.02.207 P
do you choose for me. 3.02.247 P
tell me, master shallow, how to choose a man? 3.02.258 P
and let us choose such limbs of noble counsel 5.02.135
choose what office thou wilt in the land, 'tis 5.03.123 P
and rather choose to hide them in a net | than H5 1.02. 93
to choose for wealth and not for perfect love. 1H6 5.05. 50
would choose him pope and carry him to rome, 2H6 1.03. 62
and i choose clarence only for protector. 3H6 4.06. 37
nay then indeed she cannot choose but hate thee, R3 4.04.289
use careful watch, choose trusty /sentinels. 5.03. 54
i cannot choose but laugh to think how she TRO 1.02.135 P
thus | given hydra here to choose an officer, COR 3.01. 93
they choose their magistrate, | and such a one 3.01.104
he cannot choose. 4.03. 37 P
nay, let him choose | out of my files, his 5.06. 32
hue | that i would choose were i to choose anew. TIT 1.01.262
hue | that i would choose were i to choose anew. 1.01.262
behold, i choose thee, tamora, for my bride, 1.01.319
and told the moor he should not choose | but 4.03. 75
yet i cannot choose but laugh | to think it ROM 1.03. 50
simple choice, you know not how to choose a man. 2.05. 39 P
i cannot choose but ever weep the friend. 3.05. 77
i will choose | mine heir from forth the beggars TIM 1.01.137
i cannot choose but tell him that i care not, 5.01.177
fear the people | choose caesar for their king. JC 1.02. 80
i rather choose | to wrong the dead, to wrong 3.02.125
guilty | (since nature cannot choose his origin) HAM 1.04. 26
but i cannot choose but weep to think they would 4.05. 69 P
/they cry, "choose we, laertes shall be king!" 4.05.107
under the which he shall not choose but fall; 4.07. 65
shuffling, you may choose | a sword unbated, and 4.07.137
to fight when i cannot choose, and to eat no LR 1.04. 17 P
and choose | to wage against the enmity o' th' 2.04.208
them, cannot choose | but they must blab — OTH 4.01. 28
better than i, where would you choose it? ANT 1.02. 60 P
choose your own company, and command what cost 3.04. 37
what lady would you choose to assail? CYM 1.04.125 P
...a, what she cannot choose | but must be, will 1.06. 71

he cannot choose but take this service i have 2.03. 34 P
i am well and lusty, choose your arms. TNK 3.06. 45
choose you, sir. 3.06. 45
i'll choose, | and end their strife. 4.02. 2
out of two i should | choose one, and pray for 5.01.153
which cannot choose but much advantage the poor STM II.C 70 P
look how he can, she cannot choose but love, VEN 79
prove unjust, | press never thou to choose anew. PP 18.22
which cannot choose | but weep to have that SON 64.13
CHOOSER 1 FR 0.0001 REL FR 1 V 0 P
(so far forth as herself might be her chooser) WIV 4.06. 11
CHOOSES 3 FR 0.0003 REL FR 1 V 2 P
whereof who chooses his meaning chooses you, MV 1.02. 31 P
whereof who chooses his meaning chooses you, 1.02. 31 P
what he cannot change, | than what he chooses. ANT 1.04. 15
CHOOSETH 11 FR 0.0012 REL FR 11 V 0 P
"who chooseth me shall gain what many men MV 2.07. 5
"who chooseth me shall get as much as he 2.07. 7
"who chooseth me must give and hazard all he 2.07. 9
"who chooseth me must give and hazard all he 2.07. 16
"who chooseth me shall get as much as he 2.07. 23
"who chooseth me shall gain what many men desire 2.07. 37
"who chooseth me must give and hazard all he 2.09. 21
"who chooseth me shall gain what many men desire 2.09. 24
"who chooseth me shall get as much as he 2.09. 36
"who chooseth me shall get as much as he 2.09. 50
"who chooseth me shall have as much as he 2.09. 58
CHOOSING 4 FR 0.0004 REL FR 4 V 0 P
bars me the right of voluntary choosing. MV 2.01. 16
for in choosing wrong | i lose your company; 3.02. 2
in choosing for yourself, you show'd your 3H6 4.01. 61
for choosing me when clarence is in place. 4.06. 31
CHOP 9 FR 0.0010 REL FR 8 V 1 P
and chop away that factious pate of his. 2H6 5.01.135
rail at him, | this hand should chop it off; 3H6 2.06. 82
i had rather chop this hand off at a blow, | and 5.01. 50
chop off his head! R3 3.01.193
give me a sword, i'll chop off my hands too, TIT 3.01. 72
chop off your hand | and send it to the king; 3.01.153
good aaron, wilt thou help to chop it off? 3.01.161
i will chop her into messes. cuckold me! OTH 4.01.200 P
come between, | and chop on some cold thought! TNK 3.01. 13
CHOP-FALL'N 1 FR 0.0001 REL FR 0 V 1 P
to mock your own grinning — quite chop-fall'n? HAM 5.01.192 P
CHOPINE 1 FR 0.0001 REL FR 0 V 1 P
i saw you last, by the altitude of a chopine. HAM 2.02.427 P
CHOPLESS 1 FR 0.0001 REL FR 0 V 1 P
and now my lady worm's, chopless, and knock'd HAM 5.01. 89 P
CHOPP'D 7 FR 0.0008 REL FR 2 V 5 P
these three days his head to be chopp'd off. MM 1.02. 69 P
dugs that her pretty chopp'd hands had milk'd; AYL 2.04. 50 P
always a little, lean, old, chopp'd, bald shot. 2H4 3.02.275 P
and heads, chopp'd off in a battle, shall join H5 4.01.136 P
how how, how how, chopp'd logic! ROM 3.05.149
howted, and clapp'd their chopp'd hands, and JC 1.02.245 P
beated and chopp'd with tann'd antiquity, | mine SON 62.10
CHOPPING 1 FR 0.0001 REL FR 1 V 0 P
the chopping french we do not understand. R2 5.03.124
CHOPPY 1 FR 0.0001 REL FR 1 V 0 P
by each at once her choppy finger laying | upon MAC 1.03. 44
CHOPS* *(also chaps*)*
CHOPS* 4 FR 0.0004 REL FR 2 V 2 P
you will, chops? 1H4 1.02.136 P
come on, you whoreson chops. 2H4 2.04.218 P
till he unseam'd him from the nave to th' chops, MAC 1.02. 22
her cheeks with chops and wrinkles were LUC 1452
CHORIS *(also chorus)*
CHORIS 1 FR 0.0001 REL FR 1 V 0 P
a rable, | or company, or by a figure, choris, TNK 3.05.107
CHORL *(also churl)*
CHORL 1 FR 0.0001 REL FR 1 V 0 P
and, tender chorl, mak'st waste in niggarding: SON 1.12
CHORUS *(also choris)*
CHORUS 3 FR 0.0003 REL FR 2 V 1 P
which supply, | admit me chorus to this history; H5 pr 32
you are as good as a chorus, my lord. HAM 3.02.245 P
of love, | as chorus to their tragic scene. PHT 52
CHORUS-LIKE 1 FR 0.0001 REL FR 1 V 0 P
with tears which chorus-like her eyes did rain. VEN 360
CHOSE 19 FR 0.0021 REL FR 18 V 1 P
i chose her when i could not ask my father | for TMP 5.01.190
sake, i rather chose | to cross my friend in his TGV 3.01. 17
wrong | have chose as umpeer of their mutiny. LLL 1.01.169
the word is well cull'd, chose, sweet, and apt, 5.01. 93 P
what if i stray'd no farther, but chose here? MV 2.07. 35
unfold to any one | which casket 'twas i chose; 2.09. 11
i chose | camillo for the minister to poison WT 3.02.159
tell me for what dull part in't | you chose her; 5.01. 65
out of a great deal of old iron i chose forth. 1H6 1.02.101
distaste what it elected) | the wife i chose? TRO 2.02. 67
how now, my masters, have you chose this man? COR 2.03.155
they have chose a consul that will from them 2.03.214
say you chose him | more after our commandment 2.03.229
o, what a time have you chose out, brave caius, JC 2.01.314
says he, | "i have already chose my officer." OTH 1.01. 17
of her revolt, | for she had eyes, and chose me. 3.03.189
i chose an eagle, | and did avoid a puttock. CYM 1.01.139
when as thine eye hath chose the dame, | and PP 18. 1
got | which for their habitation chose out thee, SON 95.10
CHOSEN 20 FR 0.0022 REL FR 15 V 5 P
as they are chosen, they are glad to choose me MM 2.01.269 P
in them, being chosen for the prince's watch. ADO 3.03. 6 P
no doubt never be chosen by any rightly but one MV 1.02. 32 P
that may be chosen out of the gross band of the AYL 4.01.194 P
that she's the chosen of signior hortensio. SHR 1.02.235
langton, chosen archbishop | of canterbury, from JN 3.01.143
wherefore a guard of chosen shot i had | that 1H6 1.04. 53
virtuous and holy, chosen from above, | by 5.04. 39
a pretty plot, well chosen to build upon! 2H6 1.04. 56
to link with him that were not lawful chosen. 3H6 3.03.115
us | with some few bands of chosen soldiers, 3.03.204
to rank our chosen truth with such a show | as H8 pr 18
for, with all the care i had, i saw well chosen, 2.02. 2 P
that sir thomas more is chosen | lord chancellor 3.02.393
that were the servants to this chosen infant, 5.04. 48
when we were chosen tribunes for the people — COR 1.01.254
what must be, was law, | then were they chosen; 3.01.168

chosen andronicus, surnamed pius | for many good TIT 1.01. 23
be chosen with proclamations to-day, | to-morrow 1.01.190
and other chosen attractions, would allure | and PER 5.01. 46
/CHOUGH 1 FR 0.0001 REL FR 1 V 0 P
nor | the boding raven, nor /chough /hoar, | nor TNK 1.01. 20
CHOUGH 2 FR 0.0002 REL FR 1 V 1 P
i myself could make | a chough of as deep chat. TMP 2.01.266
'tis a chough, but, as i say, spacious in the HAM 5.02. 87 P
CHOUGHS' 1 FR 0.0001 REL FR 0 V 1 P
choughs' language, gabble enough, and good AWW 4.01. 19 P
CHOUGHS 4 FR 0.0004 REL FR 3 V 1 P
or russet-pated choughs, many in sort, | rising MND 3.02. 21
son, and scar'd my choughs from the chaff, i had WT 4.04.617 P
by maggot-pies and choughs and rooks brought MAC 3.04.124
the crows and choughs that wing the midway air LR 4.06. 13
CHRISH *(also christ)*
CHRISH 5 FR 0.0005 REL FR 0 V 5 P
by chrish law, 'tish ill done! H5 3.02. 88 P
have blowed up the town, so chrish save me law, 3.02. 92 P
it is no time to discourse, so chrish save me. 3.02.105 P
breach, and we talk, and, be chrish, do nothing. 3.02.109 P
so chrish save me, i will cut off your head. 3.02.133 P
CHRISOM *(see christom)*
CHRIST *(also chrish)*
/CHRIST 1 FR 0.0001 REL FR 1 V 0 P
/so /judas /did /to /christ; R2 4.01.170
CHRIST 7 FR 0.0008 REL FR 5 V 2 P
for jesu christ in glorious christian field, R2 4.01. 93
and his pure soul unto his captain christ, 4.01. 99
as far as to the sepulchre of christ — | whose 1H4 1.01. 19
all the kingdoms that acknowledge christ. 3.02.111
there ish nothing done, so christ sa' me law! H5 3.02.113 P
in the name of jesu christ, speak fewer. 4.01. 65 P
for you shall sup with jesu christ to-night. 2H6 5.01.214
CHRISTEN *(also christian)*
CHRISTEN 3 FR 0.0003 REL FR 1 V 2 P
is ne'er a king christen could be better bit 1H4 2.01. 17 P
and can call them all by their christen names, 2.04. 8 P
and bids thee christen it with thy dagger's TIT 4.02. 70
CHRISTEN'D 2 FR 0.0002 REL FR 1 V 1 P
thought of pleasing you when she was christen'd. AYL 3.02.267 P
and on /other grounds | christen'd and heathen, OTH 1.01. 30
CHRISTENDOM 17 FR 0.0019 REL FR 15 V 2 P
me up for the lying'st knave in christendom. SHR in.2. 24 P
but kate, the prettiest kate in christendom, 2.01.187
tide | to do offense and scathe in christendom. JN 2.01. 75
though you and all the kings of christendom 3.01.162
by my christendom, | so i were out of prison and 4.01. 16
be damn'd for never a king's son in christendom. 1H4 1.02. 97 P
talk to me | in any summer house in christendom. 3.01.162
my words | on any plot of ground in christendom. 1H6 2.04. 89
for know, my lords, the states of christendom, 5.04. 96
sit there, the lying'st knave | in christendom. 2H6 2.01.124
he is the bluntest wooer in christendom. 3H6 3.02. 83
i think there's never a man in christendom | can R3 3.04. 51
to't, | that sure th' have worn out christendom. H8 1.03. 15
your scruple to the voice of christendom. 2.02. 87
all famous colleges | almost in christendom. 3.02. 67
that christendom shall ever speak his virtue. 4.02. 63
soldier none | that christendom gives out. MAC 4.03.192
CHRISTENDOMS 1 FR 0.0001 REL FR 1 V 0 P
adoptious christendoms | that blinking cupid AWW 1.01.174
CHRISTENING 3 FR 0.0003 REL FR 2 V 1 P
this one christening will beget a thousand, here H8 5.03. 37 P
when they pass back from the christening. 5.03. 74
th' are come already from the christening. 5.03. 83
CHRISTENINGS 1 FR 0.0001 REL FR 0 V 1 P
you must be seeing christenings? H8 5.03. 10 P
CHRISTIAN *(also christen)*
CHRISTIAN 67 FR 0.0075 REL FR 45 V 22 P
a jew, and not worth the name of a christian. TGV 2.05. 55 P
in thee as to go to the ale with a christian. 2.05. 58 P
which is much in a bare christian. 3.01.273 P
thou art as foolish christian creatures as i WIV 4.01. 71 P
now, as i am a christian, answer me, | in what ERR 1.02. 77
i hate him for he is a christian; MV 1.03. 42
the hebrew will turn christian, he grows kind. 1.03.178
if a christian do not play the knave and get 2.03. 11 P
become a christian and thy loving wife. 2.03. 21
sup to-night with my new master the christian. 2.04. 18 P
in hate, to feed upon | the prodigal christian. 2.05. 15
to gaze on christian fools with varnish'd faces; 2.05. 33
for all this — there will come a christian by, 2.05. 42
fled with a christian! 2.08. 16
o my christian ducats! 2.08. 16
was wont to lend money for a christian cur'sy, 3.01. 49 P
the same winter and summer, as a christian is? 3.01. 64 P
if a jew wrong a christian, what is his humility 3.01. 68 P
if a christian wrong a jew, what should his 3.01. 69 P
should his sufferance be by christian example? 3.01. 70 P
and sigh, and yield | to christian intercessors. 3.03. 16
by my husband, he hath made me a christian! 3.05. 20 P
these be the christian husbands. 4.01.295
had been her husband rather than a christian! 4.01.297
if thou dost shed | one drop of christian blood, 4.01.310
pay the bond thrice | and let the christian go. 4.01.319
this favor | he presently become a christian; 4.01.387
why, she defies me, | like turk to christian. AYL 4.03. 33
apparel, and not like a christian footboy or a SHR 3.02. 70 P
one of the greatest in the christian world AWW 4.04. 2
no more wit than a christian or an ordinary man TN 1.03. 84 P
for there is no christian that means to be sav'd 3.02. 71 P
where these two christian armies might combine JN 5.02. 37
home, | for christian service and true chivalry, R2 2.01. 54
some honest christian trust me with a gage — 4.01. 83
for jesu christ in glorious christian field, 4.01. 93
streaming the ensign of the christian cross 4.01. 94
god, | that in a christian climate souls refin'd 4.01.130
if like a christian thou hadst truly borne 1H4 5.05. 9
'a had him from me christian, and look if the 2H4 2.02. 71 P
i will perform with a most christian care. 4.02.115
we are no tyrant, but a christian king, | unto H5 1.02.241
following the mirror of all christian kings, 2.pr. 6
upon no christian soul but english talbot. 1H6 4.02. 30
means | to stop effusion of our christian blood, 5.01. 9
as i would embrace | the christian prince, king 5.03.172
words as no christian ear can endure to hear. 2H6 4.07. 40 P

that, as i am a christian faithful man, | i R3 1.04. 4
that breath'd upon the earth a christian; 3.05. 26
two props of virtue for a christian prince, | to 3.07. 96
of thy devotion and right christian zeal. 3.07.103
else wherefore breathe i in a christian land? 3.07.116
herself, the land, and many a christian soul, 4.04.408
(i mean the learned ones in christian kingdoms) H8 2.02. 92
that's christian care enough. 2.02.130
is this your christian counsel? 3.01. 99
you have christian warrant for 'em, and no doubt 3.02.244
as you wish christian peace to souls departed, 4.02.156
long | to have this young one made a christian. 5.02.213
on my christian conscience, this one christening 5.03. 36 P
susan and she — god rest all christian souls! ROM 1.03. 18
accent of christians nor the gait of christian, HAM 3.02. 32 P
is she to be buried in christian burial when she 5.01. 1 P
hath sate on her, and finds it christian burial. 5.01. 5 P
should have been buried out a' christian burial. 5.01. 25 P
for christian shame, put by this barbarous brawl OTH 2.03.172
no, as i am a christian. 4.02. 82
CHRISTIAN–LIKE 4 FR 0.0004 REL FR 3 V 1 P
undertakes them with a most christian–like fear. ADO 2.03.192 P
plant neighborhood and christian–like accord H5 5.02.353
yet he most christian–like laments his death; 2H6 3.02. 58
a virtuous and a christian–like conclusion — R3 1.03.315
CHRISTIANS' 1 FR 0.0001 REL FR 0 V 1 P
and of all christians' souls, /i /pray /god. HAM 4.05.200 P
CHRISTIANS 8 FR 0.0009 REL FR 2 V 6 P
it is spoke as a christians ought to speak. WIV 1.01.101 P
in the world that good christians ought to have. MM 2.01. 56 P
o father abram, what these christians are, MV 1.03.160
we were christians enow before, e'en as many as 3.05. 22 P
this making of christians will raise the price 3.05. 23 P
for in converting jews to christians, you raise 3.05. 35 P
that sought it i could wish more christians. H8 2.01. 64
having th' accent of christians nor the gait of HAM 3.02. 31 P
CHRISTIANS–SOUL 1 FR 0.0001 REL FR 0 V 1 P
as i am a christians–soul, now look you; WIV 3.01. 94 P
CHRISTMAS 3 FR 0.0003 REL FR 2 V 1 P
at christmas i no more desire a rose | than wish LLL 1.01.105
merriment, | to dash it like a christmas comedy. 5.02.462
is not a comonty a christmas gambold, or a SHR in.2. 138 P
CHRIST'NED 1 FR 0.0001 REL FR 1 V 0 P
that you should be new christ'ned in the tower. R3 1.01. 50
CHRIST'NING 1 FR 0.0001 REL FR 1 V 0 P
in christ'ning shalt thou have two godfathers: MV 4.01.398
CHRISTOM 1 FR 0.0001 REL FR 0 V 1 P
went away and it had been any christom child. H5 2.03. 12 P
CHRISTOPHER 3 FR 0.0003 REL FR 2 V 1 P
am not i christopher sly, old sly's son of SHR in.2. 18 P
indeed | and not a tinker nor christopher sly. in.2. 73
sir christopher, tell richmond this from me: R3 4.05. 1
CHRISTOPHERO 1 FR 0.0001 REL FR 0 V 1 P
i am christophero sly, call not me honor nor SHR in.2. 5 P
/CHRIST'S 1 FR 0.0001 REL FR 1 V 0 P
/by /christ's /dear /blood /shed /for /our R3 1.04.190
CHRIST'S 1 FR 0.0001 REL FR 1 V 0 P
christ's mother helps me, else i were too weak. 1H6 1.02.106
CHRONICLE 9 FR 0.0010 REL FR 8 V 1 P
of this, | for 'tis a chronicle of day by day, TMP 5.01.163
spoke your deservings like a chronicle, | making 1H4 5.02. 57
and make /her chronicle as rich with praise | as H5 1.02.163
his own trumpet, his own chronicle, and whatever TRO 2.03.156 P
let me embrace thee, good old chronicle, | that 4.05.202
whose chronicle thus writ: COR 5.03.145
to suckle fools and chronicle small beer. OTH 2.01.160
i and my sword will earn our chronicle. ANT 3.13.175
when in the chronicle of wasted time | i see SON 106. 1
CHRONICLED 3 FR 0.0003 REL FR 3 V 0 P
methinks should not be chronicled for wise. TGV 1.01. 41
this sport, well carried, shall be chronicled. MND 3.02.240
says that this deed is chronicled in hell. R2 5.05.116
CHRONICLER 1 FR 0.0001 REL FR 1 V 0 P
but such an honest chronicler as griffith. H8 4.02. 72
CHRONICLERS 1 FR 0.0001 REL FR 0 V 1 P
and the foolish chroniclers of that age found it AYL 4.01.105 P
CHRONICLES 6 FR 0.0006 REL FR 3 V 3 P
look in the chronicles; SHR in.1. 4 P
days, | or fill up chronicles in time to come, 1H4 1.03.171
and the old folk (time's doting chronicles) 2H4 4.04.126
as i have read in the chronicles, fought a most H5 4.07. 94 P
yet will be | the chronicles of my doing, let me H8 1.02. 74
the abstract and brief chronicles of the time. HAM 2.02.524 P
CHRYSOLITE 1 FR 0.0001 REL FR 1 V 0 P
world | of one entire and perfect chrysolite, OTH 5.02.145
CHUCK 7 FR 0.0008 REL FR 5 V 2 P
would have me present the princess (sweet chuck) LLL 5.01.111 P
why, how now, my bawcock? how dost thou, chuck? TN 3.04.113 P
use lenity, sweet chuck! H5 3.02. 25
be innocent of the knowledge, dearest chuck, MAC 3.02. 45
what promise, chuck? OTH 3.04. 49
pray you, chuck, come hither. 4.02. 24
no, my chuck. ANT 4.04. 2
CHUCKS 1 FR 0.0001 REL FR 0 V 1 P
sweet war–man is dead and rotten, sweet chucks, LLL 5.02.661 P
CHUD 1 FR 0.0001 REL FR 0 V 1 P
and chud ha' bin zwagger'd out of my life, LR 4.06.238 P
CHUFFS 1 FR 0.0001 REL FR 0 V 1 P
no, ye fat chuffs, i would your store were here! 1H4 2.02. 89 P
CHURCH 61 FR 0.0069 REL FR 35 V 26 P
disparagements unto you, i am of the church, and WIV 1.01. 32 P
procure the vicar | to stay for me at church, 4.06. 49
if it had not been i' th' church, i would have 5.05.185 P
good eye, uncle, i can see a church by daylight. ADO 2.01. 82 P
county claudio, when mean you to go to church? 2.01.356 P
of the town are come to fetch you to church. 3.04. 97 P
should i go to church | and see the holy edifice MV 1.01. 29
first go with me to church and call me wife, 3.02.303
the "why" is plain as way to parish church: AYL 2.07. 52
if ever been where bells have knoll'd to church, 2.07.114
and have with holy bell been knoll'd to church, 2.07.121
get you to church, and have a good priest that 3.03. 85 P
the morning wears, 'tis time we were at church. SHR 3.02.111
to put on better ere he go to church. 3.02.126
signior gremio, came you from the church? 3.02.149
that at the parting all the church did echo. 3.02.179
of saint luke's church is at your command at all 4.04. 88 P
to th' church take the priest, clerk, and some 4.04. 94 P
faith, i'll see the church a' your back, and 5.01. 4 P
i have seen them in the church together, god 5.01. 41 P
why dost thou not go to church in a galliard and TN 1.03.128 P
no, sir, i live by the church. 3.01. 3 P
i do live by the church; 3.01. 5 P
my house, and my house doth stand by the church. 3.01. 7 P
or, the church stands by thy tabor, if thy tabor 3.01. 9 P
by thy tabor, if thy tabor stand by the church. 3.01. 10 P
like a pedant that keeps a school i' th' church. 3.02. 76 P
every lane's end, every shop, church, session, WT 4.04.685 P
demand | why thou against the church, our holy JN 3.01.141
be champion of our church, | or let the church, 3.01.255
or let the church, our mother, breathe her curse 3.01.256
that is, to be the champion of our church! 3.01.267
is now in england ransacking the church, 3.04.172
in, | that so stood out against the holy church, 5.02. 71
what the inside of a church is made of, i am a 1H4 3.03. 8 P
the inside of a church! 3.03. 9 P
ephesians, my lord, of the old church. 2H4 2.02.150 P
i' faith, and thou follow'dst him like a church. 2.04.230 P
devout | by testament have given to the church, H5 1.01. 10
and a true lover of the holy church. 1.01. 23
is like to be executed for robbing a church, one 3.06.101 P
the church? 1H6 1.01. 33
ne'er throughout the year to church thou go'st 1.01. 42
in spite of pope or dignities of church, | here 1.03. 50
and am not i a prelate of the church? 3.01. 46
more like a soldier than a man o' th' church, 2H6 1.01.186
in the cathedral church of westminster, | and in 1.02. 37
makes the church | the chief aim of his honor, H8 5.02.152
hie you to church, i must another way, | to ROM 2.05. 72
alone | till holy church incorporate two in one. 2.06. 37
the county paris, at saint peter's church, 3.05.114
now, by saint peter's church and peter too, | he 3.05.116
to go with paris to saint peter's church, | or i 3.05.154
get thee to church a' thursday, | or never after 3.05.161
nurse, go with her, we'll to church to–morrow. 4.02. 37
come, is the bride ready to go to church? 4.05. 33
is, | and in her best array, bear her to church; 4.05. 81
to cut his throat i' th' church. HAM 4.07.126
the gallows is built stronger than the church; 5.01. 48 P
till they swallow'd the whole parish, church, PER 2.01. 34 P
bells, steeple, church, and parish up again. 2.01. 42 P
CHURCH–BENCH 1 FR 0.0001 REL FR 0 V 1 P
us go sit here upon the church–bench till two, ADO 3.03. 89 P
CHURCH–DOOR 1 FR 0.0001 REL FR 0 V 1 P
so deep as a well, nor so wide as a church–door, ROM 3.01. 97 P
CHURCHES 5 FR 0.0005 REL FR 3 V 2 P
what were good to do, chapels had been churches, MV 1.02. 13 P
proclaim'd at market–crosses, read in churches, 1H4 5.01. 73
and let them fight | against the churches; MAC 4.01. 53
by'r lady, 'a must build churches then, or else HAM 3.02.133 P
field, | and bawds and whores do churches build; LR 3.02. 92
CHURCH–LIKE 1 FR 0.0001 REL FR 1 V 0 P
whose church–like humors fits not for a crown. 2H6 1.01.247
CHURCHMAN 7 FR 0.0008 REL FR 5 V 2 P
hath shown himself a wise and patient churchman. WIV 2.03. 55 P
art thou a churchman? TN 3.01. 4 P
have we beauford | the imperious churchman, 2H6 1.03. 69
ambitious churchman, leave to afflict my heart. 2.01.178
that churchman bears a bounteous mind indeed, H8 1.03. 55
you are a churchman, or, i'll tell you, cardinal 1.04. 88
lord, | become a churchman better than ambition; 5.02. 98
CHURCHMEN 6 FR 0.0006 REL FR 5 V 1 P
we are justices and doctors and churchmen, WIV 2.03. 47 P
had not churchmen pray'd, | his thread of life 1H6 1.01. 33
awe, | more than god or religious churchmen may. 1.01. 40
if holy churchmen take delight in broils? 3.01.111
churchmen so hot? 2H6 2.01. 25
and stand between two churchmen, good my lord — R3 3.07. 48
CHURCHMEN'S 1 FR 0.0001 REL FR 1 V 0 P
if ye be any thing but churchmen's habits) | put H8 3.01.117
CHURCH'S 1 FR 0.0001 REL FR 1 V 0 P
the church's prayers made him so prosperous. 1H6 1.01. 32
CHURCH–WAY 1 FR 0.0001 REL FR 1 V 0 P
his sprite, | in the church–way paths to glide. MND 5.01.382
CHURCH–WINDOW 1 FR 0.0001 REL FR 0 V 1 P
like good bel's priests in the old church–window, ADO 3.03.135 P
CHURCHYARD 9 FR 0.0010 REL FR 9 V 0 P
dwelt by a churchyard. WT 2.01. 30
if this same were a churchyard where we stand, JN 3.03. 40
at touraine, in saint katherine's churchyard, 1H6 1.02.100
which show | like graves i' th' holy churchyard. COR 3.03. 51
so shall no foot upon the churchyard tread, ROM 5.03. 5
afraid to stand alone | here in the churchyard, 5.03. 11
and strew this hungry churchyard with thy limbs. 5.03. 36
ground is bloody, search about the churchyard. 5.03.172
romeo's man, we found him in the churchyard. 5.03.182
CHURCHYARD'S 1 FR 0.0001 REL FR 1 V 0 P
as he was coming from this churchyard's side. ROM 5.03.186
CHURCHYARDS 2 FR 0.0002 REL FR 2 V 0 P
here and there, | troop home to churchyards. MND 3.02.382
when churchyards yawn and hell itself /breathes HAM 3.02.389
CHURL *(also chorl)*
CHURL 8 FR 0.0009 REL FR 8 V 0 P
that every churl affords. ERR 3.01. 24
churl, upon thy eyes i throw | all the power MND 2.02. 78
thou, churl, for this time, | though full of our WT 4.04.432
her blameful bed | some stern, untutor'd churl; 2H6 3.02.213
lavinia, though you left me like a churl, | i TIT 1.01.486
o churl, drunk all, and left no friendly drop ROM 5.03.163
fie, th' art a churl. TIM 1.02. 26
when that churl death my bones with dust shall SON 32. 2
CHURLISH 18 FR 0.0020 REL FR 15 V 3 P
at her father's churlish feet she tender'd, TGV 3.01.227
and churlish chiding of the winter's wind, AYL 2.01. 7
my master is of churlish disposition, | and 2.04. 80
this is call'd the reply churlish. 5.04. 77 P
the third, the reply churlish; 5.04. 94 P
passion | invites me in this churlish messenger. TN 2.02. 23
the interruption of their churlish drums | cuts JN 2.01. 76
though churlish thoughts themselves should be 2.01.519
shall braying trumpets and loud churlish drums, 3.01.303
unknit | this churlish knot of all–abhorred war? 1H4 5.01. 16
and waste for churlish winter's tyranny. 2H4 1.03. 62
were better than a churlish turf of france. H5 4.01. 15
or doth this churlish superscription | pretend 1H6 4.01. 53
is as valiant as the lion, churlish as the bear, TRO 1.02. 21 P
i tell thee, churlish priest, | a minist'ring HAM 5.01.240
scorning his churlish drum and ensign red, VEN 107
ill–nurtur'd, crooked, churlish, harsh in voice, 134
with javeling's point a churlish swine to gore, 616
CHURLISHLY 1 FR 0.0001 REL FR 1 V 0 P
how churlishly i chid lucetta hence, | when TGV 1.02. 60
CHURLS 2 FR 0.0002 REL FR 2 V 0 P
prithee, fair youth, | think us no churls; CYM 3.06. 64
then, churls, their thoughts (although their SON 69.11
CHURN 1 FR 0.0001 REL FR 1 V 0 P
and bootless make the breathless huswife churn, MND 2.01. 37
CHUS 1 FR 0.0001 REL FR 1 V 0 P
i have heard him swear | to tubal and to chus, MV 3.02.285
CICATRICE 3 FR 0.0003 REL FR 2 V 1 P
the cicatrice and capable impressure | thy palm AYL 3.05. 23
spinii one captain spurio, /with his cicatrice, AWW 2.01. 43 P
since yet thy cicatrice looks raw and red HAM 4.03. 60
CICATRICES 1 FR 0.0001 REL FR 0 V 1 P
will be large cicatrices to show the people, COR 2.01.148 P
CICELY *(also cic'ly)*
CICELY 2 FR 0.0002 REL FR 2 V 0 P
sometimes you would call out for cicely hacket. SHR in.2. 89
would | be here, cicely the sempster's daughter. TNK 3.05. 44
CICERO 8 FR 0.0009 REL FR 8 V 0 P
and cicero | looks with such ferret and such JC 1.02.185
did cicero say any thing? 1.02.278
o cicero, | i have seen tempests when the 1.03. 4
farewell, cicero. 1.03. 40
but what of cicero? 2.01.141
died | by their proscriptions, cicero being one. 4.03.178
cicero one? 4.03.179
cicero is dead, | and by that order of 4.03.179
CICETER 1 FR 0.0001 REL FR 1 V 0 P
fire | our town of ciceter in gloucestershire, R2 5.06. 3
CIC'LY *(also cicely)*
CIC'LY 1 FR 0.0001 REL FR 1 V 0 P
maud, bridget, marian, cic'ly, gillian, ginn! ERR 3.01. 31
'CIDE *(also decide)*
/'CIDE 1 FR 0.0001 REL FR 1 V 0 P
to /'cide this title is impanelled | a quest of SON 46. 9
/CIEUX 1 FR 0.0001 REL FR 1 V 0 P
/cieux! H5 4.02. 6
CILICIA 1 FR 0.0001 REL FR 1 V 0 P
to ptolomy he assign'd | syria, cilicia, and ANT 3.06. 16
CIMBER 10 FR 0.0011 REL FR 9 V 1 P
to find out you. who's that? metellus cimber? JC 1.03.134
all but metellus cimber, and he's gone | to seek 1.03.149
and this, metellus cimber. 2.01. 96
mark well metellus cimber; 2.03. 3 P
where is metellus cimber? 3.01. 27
metellus cimber throws before thy seat | an 3.01. 34
i must prevent thee, cimber. 3.01. 35
desiring thee that publius cimber may | have an 3.01. 53
to beg enfranchisement for publius cimber. 3.01. 57
that i was constant cimber should be banish'd, 3.01. 72
CIMMERIAN 1 FR 0.0001 REL FR 1 V 0 P
your /swart cimmerian | doth make your honor of TIT 2.03. 72
CINDERS 5 FR 0.0005 REL FR 4 V 1 P
as the full moon doth the cinders of the element 2H4 4.03. 52 P
doth burn the heart to cinders where it is. TIT 2.04. 37
cheeks, | that would to cinders burn up modesty, OTH 4.02. 75
or i shall show the cinders of my spirits ANT 5.02.173
all simplicity, | here enclos'd, in cinders lie. PHT 55
CINNA 13 FR 0.0014 REL FR 7 V 6 P
'tis cinna, i do know him by his gait, | he is a JC 1.03.132
cinna, where haste you so? 1.03.133
am i not stay'd for, cinna? 1.03.136
good cinna, take this paper, | and look you lay 1.03.142
this, cinna; 2.01. 96
now, cinna; 2.02.120
have an eye to cinna; 2.03. 2 P
yours, cinna; 3.01.188
truly, my name is cinna. 3.03. 27 P
i am cinna the poet, i am cinna the poet. 3.03. 29 P
i am cinna the poet, i am cinna the poet. 3.03. 29 P
i am not cinna the conspirator. 3.03. 32 P
it is no matter, his name's cinna. 3.03. 33 P
CINQUEPACE *(also sink–a–pace)*
CINQUEPACE 2 FR 0.0002 REL FR 0 V 2 P
is as a scotch jig, a measure, and a cinquepace; ADO 2.01. 74 P
falls into the cinquepace faster and faster, 2.01. 79 P
CINQUE–PORTS 1 FR 0.0001 REL FR 1 V 0 P
over her, are four barons | of the cinque–ports. H8 4.01. 49
CINQUE–SPOTTED 1 FR 0.0001 REL FR 1 V 0 P
on her left breast | a mole cinque–spotted, like CYM 2.02. 38
CIPHER 6 FR 0.0006 REL FR 4 V 2 P
mine were the very cipher of a function, | to MM 2.02. 39
to prove you a cipher. LLL 1.02. 56 P
which i take to be either a fool or a cipher. AYL 3.02.290 P
and therefore, like a cipher | (yet standing in WT 1.02. 6
contrive, | to cipher me how fondly i did dote; LUC 207
how | to cipher what is writ in learned books, 811
CIPHER'D 1 FR 0.0001 REL FR 1 V 0 P
the face of either cipher'd either's heart, LUC 1396
CIPHERS 1 FR 0.0001 REL FR 1 V 0 P
and let us, ciphers to this great accompt, | on H5 pr 17
CIRCE 1 FR 0.0001 REL FR 1 V 0 P
as if, with circe, she would change my shape! 1H6 5.03. 35
CIRCE'S 1 FR 0.0001 REL FR 1 V 0 P
i think you all have drunk of circe's cup. ERR 5.01.271
CIRCLE 11 FR 0.0012 REL FR 9 V 2 P
a greek invocation, to call fools into a circle. AYL 2.05. 60 P
obscured in the circle of this forest. 5.04. 34
up into your hand | the circle of my glory. JN 5.01. 2
arms, | from out the circle of his territories. 5.02.136
would conjure in her, you must make a circle; H5 5.02.293 P
glory is like a circle in the water, | which 1H6 1.02.133
with henry's death the english circle ends, 1.02.136
you heavy people, circle me about, | that i may TIT 3.01.276
him | to raise a spirit in his mistress' circle, ROM 2.01. 24
the wheel is come full circle, i am here. LR 5.03.175
the circle of the ptolomies for her heirs, | now ANT 3.12. 18

/CIRCLED 1 FR 0.0001 REL FR 1 V 0 P
that monthly changes in her /circled orb, | lest ROM 2.02.110
CIRCLED 4 FR 0.0004 REL FR 4 V 0 P
face, | until thy head be circled with the same. 2H6 1.02. 10
or modest dian, circled with her nymphs, | shall 3H6 4.08. 21
her breasts like ivory globes circled with blue, LUC 407
with swelling drops gan wet | her circled eyne, 1229
CIRCLES 3 FR 0.0003 REL FR 3 V 0 P
the circles of his eyes show /fire within him, TNK 4.02. 81
her tear–distained eye | blue circles stream'd, LUC 1587
blood | circles her body in on every side, | who 1739
CIRCLING 2 FR 0.0002 REL FR 2 V 0 P
th' imperial metal, circling now thy head, | had R3 4.04.382
whose circling shadows kings have sought to TIT 2.04. 19
CIRCUIT 4 FR 0.0004 REL FR 4 V 0 P
to rage | until the golden circuit on my head, 2H6 3.01.352
within whose circuit is elysium | and all that 3H6 1.02. 30
in | the circuit of my breast any gross stuff TNK 3.01. 46
here | within the circuit of this ivory pale, VEN 230
CIRCUMCISED 1 FR 0.0001 REL FR 1 V 0 P
i took by th' throat the circumcised dog, | and OTH 5.02.355
CIRCUMFERENCE 3 FR 0.0003 REL FR 1 V 2 P
a good bilbo, in the circumference of a peck, WIV 3.05.111 P
horns are invisible within the circumference. MND 5.01.243 P
were harbor'd in their rude circumference. JN 2.01.262
CIRCUMMUR'D 1 FR 0.0001 REL FR 1 V 0 P
he hath a garden circummur'd with brick, | whose MM 4.01. 28
CIRCUMSCRIB'D 1 FR 0.0001 REL FR 1 V 0 P
and therefore must his choice be circumscrib'd HAM 1.03. 22
CIRCUMSCRIBED 1 FR 0.0001 REL FR 1 V 0 P
from where he circumscribed with his sword, TIT 1.01. 68
CIRCUMSCRIPTION 1 FR 0.0001 REL FR 1 V 0 P
condition | put into circumscription and confine OTH 1.02. 27
CIRCUMSPECT 2 FR 0.0002 REL FR 2 V 0 P
be wise and circumspect. 2H6 1.01.157
high–reaching buckingham grows circumspect. R3 4.02. 31
CIRCUMSTANC'D 1 FR 0.0001 REL FR 1 V 0 P
'tis very good; i must be circumstanc'd. OTH 3.04.201
CIRCUMSTANCE 35 FR 0.0039 REL FR 29 V 6 P
so, by your circumstance, you call me fool. TGV 1.01. 36
so, by your circumstance, i fear you'll prove. 1.01. 37
nay, that i can deny by a circumstance. 1.01. 84 P
therefore it must with circumstance be spoken 3.02. 36
neither in time, matter, or other circumstance. MM 4.02.105 P
with circumstance and oaths so to deny | this ERR 5.01. 16
time | to wind about my love with circumstance, MV 1.01.154
the sixt, the lie with circumstance; AYL 5.04. 96 P
no incredulous or unsafe circumstance — what TN 3.04. 80 P
but nothing of the circumstance more. 3.04.262 P
do not embrace me till each circumstance | of 5.01.251
so out of circumstance and sudden, tells us WT 5.01. 90
if ever truth were pregnant by circumstance. 5.02. 31 P
churlish drums | cuts off more circumstance. JN 2.01. 77
the circumstance considered, good my lord, 1H4 1.03. 70
the circumstance i'll tell you more at large. 1H6 1.01.109
and if your grace mark every circumstance, | you 3.01.152
this peroration with such circumstance? 2H6 1.01.105
good fellow, tell us here the circumstance, 2.01. 72
hath not essentially but by circumstance | the 5.02. 39
me leave | by circumstance but to acquit myself. R3 1.02. 77
by circumstance /t' /accuse thy cursed self. 1.02. 80
who, in his circumstance, expressly proves TRO 3.03.114
and tell them both the circumstance of all, TIT 4.02.156
say either, and i'll stay the circumstance. ROM 2.05. 36
woes | we cannot without circumstance descry. 5.03.181
girl, | unsifted in such perilous circumstance. HAM 1.03.102
and so, without more circumstance at all, | i 1.05.127
one scene of it comes near the circumstance 3.02. 76
but in our circumstance and course of thought 3.03. 83
other — | you do remember all the circumstance? 5.02. 2
evades them with a bumbast circumstance OTH 1.01. 13
pride, pomp, and circumstance of glorious war! 3.03.354
they think delight | in such–like circumstance, VEN 844
being constrain'd with dreadful circumstance? LUC 1703
CIRCUMSTANCES 12 FR 0.0013 REL FR 9 V 3 P
and, circumstances short'ned (for she has been ADO 3.02.102 P
in all these circumstances i'll instruct you; SHR 4.02.120
to leave frivolous circumstances, i pray you 5.01. 27 P
all other circumstances | made up to th' deed), WT 2.01.178
whereof being by circumstances partly laid open, 3.02. 18 P
trivial, | all circumstances well considered. R3 3.07.176
(induc'd by potent circumstances) that | you are H8 2.04. 76
if circumstances lead me, i will find | where HAM 2.02.157
diet, | or breed itself so out of circumstances, OTH 3.03. 16
if imputation and strong circumstances | which 3.03.406
sir, my circumstances, | being so near the truth CYM 2.04. 61
assail'd by night with circumstances strong | of LUC 1262
CIRCUMSTANTIAL 3 FR 0.0003 REL FR 1 V 2 P
and so to lie circumstantial and the lie direct. AYL 5.04. 81 P
durst go no further than the lie circumstantial, 5.04. 85 P
abridgment | hath to it circumstantial branches, CYM 5.05.383
CIRCUMVENT 1 FR 0.0001 REL FR 0 V 1 P
now o'erreaches, one that would circumvent god, HAM 5.01. 79 P
CIRCUMVENTION 2 FR 0.0002 REL FR 1 V 1 P
it will not in circumvention deliver a fly from TRO 2.03. 15 P
to bodily act ere rome | had circumvention? COR 1.02. 6
CIRENCESTER *(see ciceter)*
CISTERN *(see cestern, etc., cestron)*
CITA 1 FR 0.0001 REL FR 0 V 1 P
and i will whip about your infamy, /manu cita — LLL 5.01. 69 P
CITADEL 7 FR 0.0008 REL FR 5 V 2 P
swore i leapt from the window of the citadel — AWW 4.01. 56 P
they give /their greeting to the citadel. OTH 2.01. 94
bring thou the master to the citadel; 2.01.209
meet me by and by at the citadel. 2.01.284 P
i meet the captains at the citadel. 3.03. 59
emilia, run you to the citadel, | and tell my 5.01.126
a /tower'd citadel, a pendant rock, | a forked ANT 4.14. 4
CITAL 1 FR 0.0001 REL FR 1 V 0 P
indeed, | he made a blushing cital of himself, 1H4 5.02. 61
CITE 4 FR 0.0004 REL FR 4 V 0 P
for valentine, i need not cite him to it. TGV 2.04. 85
for we cite our faults | that they may hold 4.01. 51
the devil can cite scripture for his purpose. MV 1.03. 98
doth cite each moving sense from idle rest, PP 14.15
CITED 6 FR 0.0006 REL FR 6 V 0 P
to th' imperfections | which you have cited, you H5 5.02. 70
and had i not been cited so by them, | yet did i 2H6 3.02.281
england, | and cited up a thousand heavy times, R3 1.04. 14
to which | she was often cited by them, but H8 4.01. 29
(as truth's authentic author to be cited), | "as TRO 3.02.181
shalt have thy trespass cited up in rhymes, LUC 524
CITES 2 FR 0.0002 REL FR 2 V 0 P
whose aged honor cites a virtuous youth, | did AWW 1.03.210
i think it cites us, brother, to the field, 3H6 2.01. 34
CITIES 16 FR 0.0018 REL FR 12 V 4 P
knee, | met him in boroughs, cities, villages, 1H4 4.03. 69
the cities turn'd into a maid; H5 5.02.321 P
so the maiden cities you talk of may wait on her 5.02.326 P
razeth your cities, and subverts your towns, 1H6 2.03. 65
and see the cities and the towns defac'd | by 3.03. 45
twelve cities, and seven walled towns of 3.04. 7
and are the cities that i got with wounds 2H6 1.01.121
out of towns and cities for a dangerous thing, R3 1.04.142 P
degrees in schools, and brotherhoods in cities, TRO 1.03.104
troy, | and blind oblivion swallow'd cities up, 3.02.187
let courts and cities be | made all of COR 1.09. 43
in cities, mutinies; LR 1.02.107 P
the fire | is spied in populous cities. OTH 1.01. 77
green neptune's back | with ships made cities, ANT 4.14. 59
let those cities that of plenty's cup | and her PER 1.04. 52
and break'st | the stony girths of cities: TNK 5.01. 56
CITING 1 FR 0.0001 REL FR 1 V 0 P
digress too much, | citing my worthless praise. TIT 5.03.117
CITIZEN 6 FR 0.0006 REL FR 6 V 0 P
attempts | he seek the life of any citizen, MV 4.01.351
tell them how edward put to death a citizen R3 3.05. 76
that when he speaks not like a citizen, | you COR 3.03. 53
to every roman citizen he gives, | to every JC 3.02.241
but not so citizen a wanton as | to seem to die CYM 4.02. 8
may feel her heart (poor citizen!) LUC 465
CITIZENS 39 FR 0.0044 REL FR 37 V 2 P
the generous and gravest citizens | have hent MM 4.06. 13
doing displeasure to the citizens | by rushing ERR 5.01.142
"sweep on, you fat and greasy citizens, | 'tis AYL 2.01. 55
pisa, renowned for grave citizens, | gave me my SHR 1.01. 10
often been, | pisa renowned for grave citizens. 4.02. 95
which trust accordingly, kind citizens, | and JN 2.01.231
speak, citizens, for england. who's your king? 2.01.362
now, citizens of angiers, ope your gates, | let 2.01.536
the civil citizens kneading up the honey, | the H5 1.02.199
how london doth pour out her citizens! 5.pr. 24
here's gloucester, a foe to citizens, | one that 1H6 1.03. 62
dolphin, command the citizens make bonfires, 1.06. 12
years | wasted our country, slain our citizens, 2.03. 41
the citizens fly and forsake their houses; 2H6 4.04. 50
my sovereign, with the loving citizens, | like 3H6 4.08. 19
have signified the same | unto the citizens, who R3 3.05. 60
that i'll acquaint our duteous citizens | with 3.05. 65
how now, how now, what say the citizens? 3.07. 1
lord, | the citizens are mum, say not a word. 3.07. 3
"thanks, gentle citizens and friends," quoth i, 3.07. 38
such troops of citizens to come to him, | his 3.07. 85
for this, consorted with the citizens, | your 3.07.137
do, good my lord, your citizens entreat you. 3.07.201
come, citizens. 3.07.219
the citizens | i am sure have shown at full H8 4.01. 7
one word, good citizens. COR 1.01. 14 P
we are accounted poor citizens, the patricians 1.01. 15 P
the citizens of corioles have issued, | and 1.06. 10
help, ye citizens! 3.01.179
citizens! 3.01.185
citizens! 3.01.186
lo, citizens, he says he is content. 3.03. 48
whose fortunes rome's best citizens applaud! TIT 1.01.164
ay, but the citizens favor lucius, | and will 4.04. 79
and made verona's ancient citizens | cast by ROM 1.01. 92
the citizens are up, and tybalt slain. 3.01.133
throw, | as if they came from several citizens, JC 1.02.317
awake the snorting citizens with the bell, | or OTH 1.01. 90
civil streets, | and citizens to their dens. ANT 5.01. 17
CITTERN–HEAD 1 FR 0.0001 REL FR 0 V 1 P
a cittern–head. LLL 5.02.610 P
/CITY 1 FR 0.0001 REL FR 1 V 0 P
/priam's //six–gated /city, | /dardan /and TRO pr 15
CITY 130 FR 0.0147 REL FR 104 V 26 P
let us into the city presently | to sort some TGV 3.02. 90
and what shall become of those in the city? MM 1.02. 98 P
to geld and splay all the youth of the city? 2.01.231 P
consecrated fount, | a league below the city; 4.03. 99
proclaim it, provost, round about the city, | if 5.01.508
and wander up and down to view the city. ERR 1.02. 31
how is the man esteem'd here in the city? 5.01. 4
second to none that lives here in the city: 5.01. 7
the duke, and all that know me in the city, 5.01.324
on your worship as of any man in the city, and ADO 3.05. 26 P
for if we meet in the city, we shall be dogg'd MND 1.02.103 P
to leave the city and commit yourself | into the 2.01.215
since that the trade and profit of the city MV 3.03. 30
being native burghers of this desert city, AYL 2.01. 23
through | the body of /the country, city, court, 2.01. 59
what woman in the city do i name, | when that i 2.07. 74
own, | that, being a stranger in this city here, SHR 2.01. 89
my house within the city | is richly furnished 2.01.346
till you have done your business in the city. 4.02.111
somebody in this city under my countenance. 5.01. 39 P
the breach yourselves made, you lose your city. AWW 1.01.126 P
for if they do approach the city, we shall lose 3.05. 1 P
the things of fame | that do renown this city. TN 3.03. 24
which for traffic's sake | most of our city did. 3.03. 35
at several posterns | clear them o' th' city. WT 1.02.439
here, in your city; 5.01.186
craves harborage within your city walls. JN 2.01.234
then tell us, shall your city call us lord, | in 2.01.263
the flinty ribs of this contemptuous city. 2.01.384
win you this city without stroke or wound, 2.01.418
half so peremptory, | as we to keep this city. 2.01.455
been forward first | to speak unto this city: 2.01.483
the sea | (except this city now by us besieg'd) 2.01.489
there's that will sack a city. 1H4 5.03. 54 P
a city on th' inconstant billows dancing; H5 3.pr. 15
his bended sword | before him through the city. 5.pr. 19
sword, | how many would the peaceful city quit, 5.pr. 33
many a fair french city for one fair french maid 5.02.318 P
bars | in yonder tower to overpeer the city, 1H6 1.04. 11
for aught i see, this city must be famish'd, 1.04. 68
henry, | pity the city of london, pity us! 3.01. 77
our sacks shall be a mean to sack the city, 3.02. 10
so, in the famous ancient city tours, | in 2H6 1.01. 5
when in the city tours | thou ran'st a–tilt in 1.03. 50
and therefore in this city will i stay | and 4.04. 47
swear | to spoil the city and your royal court. 4.04. 53
the tower to defend the city from the rebels. 4.05. 5 P
now is mortimer lord of this city. 4.06. 1 P
defer the spoil of the city until night; 4.07.134 P
ah, know you not the city favors them, | and 3H6 1.01. 67
march'd through the city to the palace gates. 1.01. 92
if not, the city being but of small defense, 5.01. 64
desire, | and his enforcement of the city wives, R3 3.07. 8
others, to hear the city | abus'd extremely, and H8 ep 5
i wonder now how yonder city stands | when we TRO 4.05.211
the other side a' th' city is risen; COR 1.01. 47 P
that in these several places of the city | you 1.01.185
whereof they say | the city is well stor'd. 1.01.190
the rabble should have first /unroof'd the city 1.01.218
lartius are set down before their city corioles; 1.03. 99 P
they fear us not, but issue forth their city. 1.04. 23
he is himself alone, | to answer all the city. 1.04. 52
take | convenient numbers to make good the city, 1.05. 12
the treasure in this field achiev'd and city, 1.09. 33
go you to th' city, | learn how 'tis held, and 1.10. 27
i pray you | ('tis south the city mills) bring 1.10. 31
two know how you are censur'd here in the city, 2.01. 22 P
alone he ent'red | the mortal gate of th' city, 2.02.111
and till we call'd | both field and city ours, 2.02.121
to unbuild the city, and to lay all flat. 3.01.197
what is the city but the people? 3.01.198
true, | the people are the city. 3.01.199
that is the way to lay the city flat, | to bring 3.01.203
is this viper | that would depopulate the city, 3.01.263
our good city | cleave in the midst and perish. 3.02. 27
even from this instant, banish him our city, 3.03.101
for you, the city, thus i turn my back; 3.03.134
let a guard | attend us through the city. 3.03.141
a goodly city is this antium. 4.04. 1
city, | 'tis i that made thy widows; 4.04. 1
i' th' city of kites and crows. 4.05. 42 P
i' th' city of kites and crows? 4.05. 43 P
and | to melt the city leads upon your pates, 4.06. 82
clusters, | who did hoot him out o' th' city. 4.06.123
intended fire your city is ready to flame in, 5.02. 46 P
i am hush'd until our city be afire, | and then 5.03.181
in a male tiger, that shall our poor city find. 5.04. 29 P
of consuls, senators, patricians, | a city full; 5.04. 54
they are near the city? 5.04. 60
go tell the lords a' th' city i am here. 5.06. 1
i accuse | the city ports by this hath enter'd, 5.06. 6
up, | for certain drops of salt, your city rome, 5.06. 92
i say "your city," to his wife and mother, 5.06. 93
though in this city he | hath widowed and 5.06.150
lives not this day within the city walls. TIT 1.01. 26
why should you fear? is not your city strong? 4.04. 78
that westward rooteth from this city side, | so ROM 1.01.122
all our whole city is much bound to him. 4.02. 32
me, | here in this city visiting the sick, | and 5.02. 7
banish'd the new–made bridegroom from this city, 5.03.235
make not a city feast of it, to let the meat TIM 3.06. 67 P
will o'er some high–vic'd city hang his poison 4.03.110
broke the wall, that thou art out of the city? 4.03.350 P
his fellowship i' th' cause against your city, 5.02. 12
lord, | into our city with thy banners spread; 5.04. 30
bring me into your city, | and i will use the 5.04. 81
such delight in, the tragedians of the city. HAM 2.02.328 P
same estimation they did when i was in the city? 2.02.335 P
three great ones of the city, | in personal suit OTH 1.01. 8
there's many a beast then in a populous city, 4.01. 63
the city cast | her people out upon her; ANT 2.02.213
enter the city, clip your wives, your friends, 4.08. 8
upon the hills adjoining to the city | shall 4.10. 5
built up this city for his chiefest seat, | the PER 1.ch. 18
a city on whom plenty held full hand, | for 1.04. 22
i doubt not but this populous city will | yield 4.06.186
the city striv'd | god neptune's annual feast to 5.ch. 16
name | of pericles to rage the city turn, | that 5.03. 97
let us leave the city | thebes and the temptings TNK 1.02. 3
lead into the city, | where, having bound things 1.04. 47
this world's a city full of straying streets, 1.05. 15
away, and to the city made | with such a cry and 4.01. 97
'tis enough to infect the city with the palsy. STM II.C 11 P
it is our infection will make the city shake, II.C 14 P
much advantage the poor handicrafts of the city. II.C 71 P
to make the breach and enter this sweet city. LUC 469
greece, | for helen's rape the city to destroy, 1369
are balls of quenchless fire to burn thy city. 1554
that the ruffle knew | of court, of city, and LC 59
"and long upon these terms i held my city, 176
CITY–GATE 1 FR 0.0001 REL FR 1 V 0 P
come, i'll convey thee through the city–gate; TGV 3.01.254
CITY–GATES 3 FR 0.0003 REL FR 3 V 0 P
these are the city–gates, the gates of roan, 1H6 3.02. 1
open your city–gates, | be humble to us, call my 4.02. 5
now, warwick, wilt thou ope the city–gates, 3H6 5.01. 21
CITY'S 11 FR 0.0012 REL FR 10 V 1 P
our city's institutions, and the terms | for MM 1.01. 10
upon your charter and your city's freedom! MV 4.01. 39
by these french | /confronts /your city's eyes, JN 2.01.215
save unscratch'd your city's threat'ned cheeks, 2.01.225
will send destruction | into this city's bosom. 2.01.410
i charge and command that, of the city's cost, 2H6 4.06. 3 P
that seems disgracious in the city's eye, | and R3 3.07.112
transformed timon to our city's love | by humble TIM 5.04. 19
of regular justice in your city's bounds, | but 5.04. 61
with brazen din blast you the city's ear, | make ANT 4.08. 36
did you but know the city's usuries, | and felt CYM 3.03. 45
CITY–WIFE 1 FR 0.0001 REL FR 0 V 1 P
proud lady and a proud city–wife howl together! TNK 4.03. 52 P
CITY–WOMAN 1 FR 0.0001 REL FR 1 V 0 P
when that i say the city–woman bears | the cost AYL 2.07. 75
CIVET 4 FR 0.0004 REL FR 1 V 3 P
nay, 'a rubs himself with civet. ADO 3.02. 50 P
the courtier's hands are perfum'd with civet. AYL 3.02. 64 P
civet is of a baser birth than tar, the very 3.02. 67 P
give me an ounce of civet; LR 4.06.130
CIVIL 52 FR 0.0058 REL FR 42 V 10 P

they are reformed, civil, full of good, | and TGV 5.04.156
live again, but in honest, civil, godly company, WIV 1.01.182 P
your ear, she's as fartuous a civil modest wife, 2.02. 97 P
but civil count, civil as an orange, and ADO 2.01.294 P
but civil count, civil as an orange, and 2.01.294 P
this civil war of wits were much better used LLL 2.01.226
that the rude sea grew civil at her song, | and MND 2.01.152
if you were civil and knew courtesy, | you would 3.02.147
my soul, | no woman had it, but a civil doctor, MV 5.01.210
on every tree, | that shall civil sayings show: AYL 3.02.128
be clamorous and leap all civil bounds, | rather TN 1.04. 21
he is sad and civil, | and suits well for a 3.04. 5
and like a civil war set'st oath to oath, | thy JN 3.01.264
hostility and civil tumult reigns | between my 4.02.247
of civil wounds plough'd up with neighbors' R2 1.03.128
the king | should so with civil and uncivil arms 3.03.102
shock | and furious close of civil butchery, 1H4 1.01. 13
come a hot june and this civil buffeting hold, 2.04.362 P
you conjure from the breast of civil peace 4.03. 43
says he, "receive those that are civil, for," 2H4 2.04. 90 P
before this honest, virtuous, civil gentlewoman! 2.04.302 P
whose see is by a civil peace maintain'd, 4.01. 42
o my poor kingdom, sick with civil blows! 4.05.133
we bear our civil swords and native fire | as 5.05.106
the civil citizens kneading up the honey, | the H5 1.02.199
he was thinking of civil wars when he got me; 5.02.226 P
prosper this realm, keep it from civil broils, 1H6 1.01. 53
civil dissension is a viperous worm | that gnaws 3.01. 72
ireland, | in bringing them to civil discipline, 2H6 1.01.195
methinks already in this civil broil | i see 4.08. 44
thou take an oath | to cease this civil war, and 3H6 1.01.197
and let our hearts and eyes, like civil war, 2.05. 77
brittany, | till storms be past of civil enmity. 4.06. 98
now civil wounds are stopp'd, peace lives again; R3 5.05. 40
that gives our troy, our rome, the civil wound. TIT 5.03. 87
where civil blood makes civil hands unclean. ROM pr 4
where civil blood makes civil hands unclean. pr 4
with the men, i will be civil with the maids; 1.01. 22 P
three civil brawls, bred of an airy word, | by 1.01. 89
come, civil night, | thou sober–suited matron 3.02. 10
religious canons, civil laws are cruel; TIM 4.03. 61
either there is a civil strife in heaven, | or JC 1.03. 11
domestic fury and fierce civil strife | shall 3.01.263
on the mere form of civil and humane seeming, OTH 2.01.239 P
worthy montano, you were wont to be civil; 2.03.190
in a populous city, | and many a civil monster. 4.01. 64
our italy | shines o'er with civil swords; ANT 1.03. 45
should have shook lions into civil streets, 5.01. 16
if any thing that's civil, speak; CYM 3.06. 23
a mischief worse than civil home–bred strife, VEN 764
such civil war is in my love and hate, | that i SON 35.12
shook off my sober guards and civil fears; LC 298
CIVILITY 6 FR 0.0006 REL FR 5 V 1 P
i ever yet beheld seem'd but tameness, civility, WIV 4.02. 27 P
say amen, | use all the observance of civility, MV 2.02.195
that in civility thou seem'st so empty? AYL 2.07. 93
ta'en from me the show | of smooth civility; 2.07. 96
believe | that, from the sense of all civility, OTH 1.01.131
honor untaught, | civility not seen from other; CYM 4.02.179
CIVILL'ST 1 FR 0.0001 REL FR 1 V 0 P
is term'd the civill'st place of all this isle: 2H6 4.07. 61
CIVILLY 1 FR 0.0001 REL FR 1 V 0 P
and to proclaim it civilly were like | a ANT 3.13.129
CLACK–DISH 1 FR 0.0001 REL FR 0 V 1 P
his use was to put a ducat in her clack–dish. MM 3.02.126 P
CLAD *(also yclad)*
CLAD 5 FR 0.0005 REL FR 5 V 0 P
but am in that dimension grossly clad | which TN 5.01.237
and why thou comest thus knightly clad in arms, R2 1.03. 12
a woman clad in armor chaseth them. 1H6 1.05. 3
but look the morn in russet mantle clad | walks HAM 1.01.166
who finds his lucrece clad in mourning black, LUC 1585
CLAIM 64 FR 0.0072 REL FR 59 V 5 P
i claim the promise for her heavenly picture. TGV 4.04. 87
i claim her not, and therefore she is thine. 5.04.135
my sole earth's heaven, and my heaven's claim. ERR 3.02. 64
what claim lays she to thee? 3.02. 84 P
sir, such claim as you would lay to your horse, 3.02. 85 P
being a very beastly creature, lays claim to me. 3.02. 88 P
this drudge or diviner laid claim to me, call'd 3.02.140 P
where dowsabel did claim me for her husband: 4.01.110
lady is, | and claim her with a loving kiss." MV 3.02.138
and lawfully by this the jew may claim | a pound 4.01.231
is a youth here in the forest lays claim to you. AYL 5.01. 7 P
lays most lawful claim | to this fair island and JN 1.01. 9
born, | doth he lay claim to thine inheritance? 1.01. 72
what doth move you to claim your brother's land? 1.01. 91
my brother might not claim him, nor your father, 1.01.126
maine, | in right of arthur do i claim of thee. 2.01.153
stand in his face to contradict his claim. 2.01.280
may then make all the claim that arthur did. 3.04.143
after young arthur, claim this land for mine, 5.02. 94
but i, | and such as to my claim are liable, 5.02.101
and therefore personally i lay my claim | to my R2 2.03.135
nor claim no further than your new–fall'n right, 1H4 5.01. 44
or should, or should not, bar us in our claim; H5 1.02. 12
to make against your highness' claim to france 1.02. 36
make claim and title to the crown of france. 1.02. 68
king pepin's title and hugh capet's claim, 1.02. 87
may i with right and conscience make this claim? 1.02. 96
great–grandsire's tomb, | from whom you claim; 1.02.104
did claim some certain dukedoms, in the right 1.02.247
in answer of which claim, the prince our master 1.02.249
desires you let the dukedoms that you claim 1.02.256
know | 'tis no sinister nor no awkward claim, 2.04. 85
this is his claim, his threat'ning, and my 2.04.110
you claim no interest | in any of our towns of 1H6 5.04.167
a day will come when york shall claim his own, 2H6 1.01.239
and, when i spy advantage, claim the crown, 1.01.242
and if thy claim be good, | the nevils are thy 2.02. 7
from whose line | i claim the crown, had issue, 2.02. 35
as i have read, laid claim unto the crown, | and 2.02. 40
by her i claim the kingdom. 2.02. 47
henry doth claim the crown from john of gaunt, 2.02. 54
how they affect the house and claim of york. 3.01.375
from ireland thus comes york to claim his right, 5.01. 1
resolve thee, richard, claim the english crown. 3H6 1.01. 49
plantagenet, for all the claim thou lay'st, 1.01.152
i shall be, if i claim by open war. 1.02. 19
king, | had slipp'd our claim until another age. 2.02.162
our title to the crown and only claim | our 4.07. 46
we grow stronger, then we'll make our claim; 4.07. 59
and those who have the wit to claim the place. R3 3.01. 50
king, claim thou of me | the earldom of herford, 3.01.194
i'll claim that promise at your grace's hand. 3.01.197
my lord, i claim the gift, my due by promise, 4.02. 88
he makes for england, here to claim the crown. 4.04.468
of those that claim their offices this day | by H8 4.01. 15
and by those claim their greatness, not by blood 5.04. 38
i am your debtor, claim it when 'tis due. TRO 4.05. 51
that as his worthy deeds did claim no less COR 2.03.186
were fit for thee to use as they to claim, | in 3.02. 83
that most may claim this argument for ours? MAC 2.03.120
which now to claim my vantage doth invite me. HAM 5.02.390
for your claim, fair /sister, | i bar it in the LR 5.03. 84
by my excuse shall claim excuse's giving." LUC 1715
yet neither may possess the claim they lay. 1794
CLAIM'D 2 FR 0.0002 REL FR 2 V 0 P
had of your father claim'd this son for his? JN 1.01.122
prince hath neither claim'd it nor deserv'd it, R3 3.01. 51
CLAIMING 1 FR 0.0001 REL FR 1 V 0 P
to bar your highness claiming from the female, H5 1.02. 92
CLAIMS 9 FR 0.0010 REL FR 7 V 2 P
one that claims me, one that haunts me, one that ERR 3.02. 82 P
of mad flesh that claims marriage of me, i could 4.04.154 P
which both thy duty owes and our power claims, AWW 2.03.161
as your due, time claims, he does acknowledge, 2.04. 42
all the honor | that good convenience claims. 3.02. 72
the fourth son, york claims it from the third; 2H6 2.02. 55
is the first, and claims | to be high steward; H8 4.01. 17
whose beauty claims | no worse a husband than ANT 2.02.127
then virtue claims from beauty beauty's red, LUC 59
CLAMBER 1 FR 0.0001 REL FR 1 V 0 P
clamber not you up to the casements then, | nor MV 2.05. 31
CLAMB'RING 2 FR 0.0002 REL FR 2 V 0 P
reechy neck, | clamb'ring the walls to eye him; COR 2.01.210
boughs her crownet weeds | clamb'ring to hang, HAM 4.07.173
/CLAMOR* 1 FR 0.0001 REL FR 1 V 0 P
/whilst /i | /was /big /in /clamor, /came /there LR 5.03.209
CLAMOR* 16 FR 0.0018 REL FR 14 V 2 P
why, an hour in clamor and a quarter in rheum; ADO 5.02. 82 P
and with the clamor keep her still awake. SHR 4.01.207
contempt and clamor | will be my knell. WT 1.02.189
a savage clamor! 3.03. 56
clamor your tongues, and not a word more. 4.04.247 P
but start | an echo with the clamor of thy drum, JN 5.02.168
war, | the bitter clamor of two eager tongues, R2 1.01. 49
with deafing clamor in the slippery clouds, 2H4 3.01. 24
why, what tumultuous clamor have we here? 2H6 3.02.239
shall dizzy with more clamor neptune's ear | in TRO 5.02.174
with all th' applause and clamor of the host, COR 1.09. 64
as we shall make our griefs and clamor roar MAC 1.07. 78
the instant burst of clamor that she made, HAM 2.02.515
or, whilst i can vent clamor from my throat, LR 1.01.165
lest by his clamor (as it so fell out) | the OTH 2.03.231
this burst of clamor | is sure th' end o' th' TNK 5.03. 77
CLAMOR'D 1 FR 0.0001 REL FR 1 V 0 P
the obscure bird | clamor'd the livelong night. MAC 2.03. 60
//CLAMOR–MOISTENED 1 FR 0.0001 REL FR 1 V 0 P
/and, //clamor–moistened, /then /away /she LR 4.03. 31
/CLAMOROUS 1 FR 0.0001 REL FR 0 V 1 P
one whom i will beat into /clamorous whining, if LR 2.02. 23 P
CLAMOROUS 11 FR 0.0012 REL FR 10 V 1 P
and some keep back | the clamorous owl, that MND 2.02. 6
hen, more clamorous than a parrot against rain, AYL 4.01.151 P
and kiss'd her lips with such a clamorous smack SHR 3.02.178
be clamorous and leap all civil bounds, | rather TN 1.04. 21
tells what hour it is | are clamorous groans, R2 5.05. 56
were strangely clamorous to the frighted fields. 1H4 3.01. 39
with this immodest clamorous outrage | to 1H6 4.01.126
or with the clamorous report of war | thus will R3 4.04.153
encount'red | with clamorous demands of debt, TIM 2.02. 37
those clamorous harbingers of blood and death. MAC 5.06. 10
ceasing their clamorous cry till they have VEN 693
CLAMORS 12 FR 0.0013 REL FR 12 V 0 P
the venom clamors of a jealous woman | poisons ERR 5.01. 69
deaf'd with the clamors of their own dear groans LLL 5.02.864
their soul–fearing clamors have brawl'd down JN 2.01.383
clamors of hell, be measures to our pomp? 3.01.304
peace, you ungracious clamors! TRO 1.01. 89
that nothing canst but cry, | add to my clamors! 2.02.106
him to his house | with shouts and clamors. JC 3.02. 53
th' immortal jove's dread clamors counterfeit, OTH 3.03.356
and clamors through the wild air flying! TNK 1.05. 6
wears | he pens her piteous clamors in her head, LUC 681
with clamors fill'd | the dispers'd air, who, 1804
in clamors of all size, both high and low. LC 21
CLANG 1 FR 0.0001 REL FR 1 V 0 P
'larums, neighing steeds, and trumpets' clang? SHR 1.02.206
CLANGOR 1 FR 0.0001 REL FR 1 V 0 P
like to a dismal clangor heard from far, 3H6 2.03. 18
CLAP 19 FR 0.0021 REL FR 12 V 7 P
clap on more sails, pursue; WIV 2.02.136
i would desire you to clap into your prayers; MM 4.03. 41 P
clap 's into "light a' love"; ADO 3.04. 44 P
shall we clap into't roundly, without hawking or AYL 5.03. 11 P
with an invention and clap upon you two or three AWW 3.06. 98 P
open thy white hand | /and clap thyself my love; WT 1.02.104
hands | to clap this royal bargain up of peace, JN 3.01.235
and clap their female joints | in stiff unwieldy R2 3.02.114
hostess, clap to the doors! 1H4 2.04.276 P
i' faith, do, and so clap hands and a bargain. H5 5.02.129 P
on your heads | clap round fines for neglect. H8 5.03. 80
if they hold when their ladies bid 'em clap. ep 14
they clap the lubber ajax on the shoulder, | as TRO 3.03.139
tag–rag people did not clap him and hiss him, JC 1.02.259 P
what, fifty of my followers at a clap? LR 1.04.294
are dangerous, | i'll clap more irons on you. TNK 2.02.271
clap her aboard to–morrow night and stow her, 2.03. 32
methought i heard a dreadful clap of thunder 3.06. 83
should clap their wings and sing | to all the 4.02. 23
/CLAPP'D 1 FR 0.0001 REL FR 0 V 1 P
/and /are /most /tyrannically /clapp'd /for't. HAM 2.02.341 P
CLAPP'D 16 FR 0.0018 REL FR 11 V 5 P
and (how we know not) all clapp'd under hatches, TMP 5.01.231
hits me, let him be clapp'd on the shoulder, and ADO 1.01.258 P
all laugh'd, and clapp'd him on the shoulder, LLL 5.02.107
him that cupid hath clapp'd him o' th' shoulder, AYL 4.01. 48 P
was ever match clapp'd up so suddenly? SHR 2.01.325
clapp'd on the outward eye of fickle france, JN 2.01.583
of sugar, clapp'd even now into my hand by an 1H4 2.04. 23 P
'a would have clapp'd i' th' clout at twelve 2H4 3.02. 46 P
away with them, let them be clapp'd up close, 2H6 1.04. 50
hath clapp'd his tail between his legs and cried 5.01.154
that's clapp'd upon the court gate. H8 1.03. 18
of this fair company | clapp'd wings to me. 1.04. 9
you must needs, for you all clapp'd your hands, TRO 2.02. 87
who upon the sudden | clapp'd to their gates. COR 1.04. 51
howted, and clapp'd their chopp'd hands, and JC 1.02.245 P
and all of you clapp'd up together in | an ANT 4.02. 17
CLAPPER 1 FR 0.0001 REL FR 0 V 1 P
and his tongue is the clapper, for what his ADO 3.02. 13 P
CLAPPER–CLAW 1 FR 0.0001 REL FR 0 V 1 P
he will clapper–claw thee tightly, bully. WIV 2.03. 65 P
CLAPPER–CLAWING 1 FR 0.0001 REL FR 0 V 1 P
now they are clapper–clawing one another; TRO 5.04. 1 P
CLAPPER–DE–CLAW 2 FR 0.0002 REL FR 0 V 2 P
clapper–de–claw? vat is dat? WIV 2.03. 66 P
me do look he shall clapper–de–claw me, for, by 2.03. 68 P
CLAPPING 4 FR 0.0004 REL FR 4 V 0 P
this hand hath made him proud with clapping him. R2 5.05. 86
clapping their hands, and crying with loud voice 2H6 1.01.160
her pale cheek, till clapping makes it red; VEN 468
clapping their proud tails to the ground below, 923
CLAPS 5 FR 0.0005 REL FR 4 V 1 P
and boys, | whose shouts and claps out–voice the H5 5.pr. 11
of a tavern, claps me his sword upon the table, ROM 3.01. 6 P
claps on his sea–wing, and (like a doting ANT 3.10. 19
round, | and every one with claps can sound, PER 3.ch. 36
claps her pale cheek, till clapping makes it red VEN 468
CLARE 1 FR 0.0001 REL FR 1 V 0 P
the sisterhood, the votarists of saint clare. MM 1.04. 5
CLARENCE' 6 FR 0.0006 REL FR 6 V 0 P
married the duke of clarence' daughter, did he 2H6 4.02.137
descended from the duke of clarence' house, 4.04. 29
the bitter sentence of poor clarence' death? R3 1.04.186
pale when they did hear of clarence' death? 2.01.137
marry, my uncle clarence' angry ghost. 3.01.144
i will marry straight to clarence' daughter; 4.02. 54
CLARENCE 89 FR 0.0100 REL FR 88 V 1 P
is not his brother thomas of clarence with him? 2H4 4.04. 16
nothing but well to thee, thomas of clarence. 4.04. 19
who saw the duke of clarence? 4.05. 7
warwick! gloucester! clarence! 4.05. 48
exeter, | and brother clarence, and you, brother H5 5.02. 84
his grandfather was lionel duke of clarence, 1H6 2.04. 83
i derived am | from lionel duke of clarence, 2.05. 75
and the third, | lionel duke of clarence; 2H6 2.02. 13
the third son, duke of clarence, from whose line 2.02. 34
sole daughter unto lionel duke of clarence; 2.02. 50
duke of gloucester, | and george, of clarence. 3H6 2.06.104
let me be duke of clarence, george of gloucester 2.06.106
why, clarence, to myself. 3.02.112
is clarence, henry, and his son young edward, 3.02.130
and as for clarence, as my letters tell me, 3.03.208
now tell me, brother clarence, what think you 4.01. 1
now, brother of clarence, how like you our 4.01. 9
she better would have fitted me or clarence; 4.01. 54
alas, poor clarence! 4.01. 59
clarence will have the younger. 4.01.118
clarence and somerset both gone to warwick? 4.01.127
but see where somerset and clarence comes! 4.02. 3
then, gentle clarence, welcome unto warwick, 4.02. 6
else might i think that clarence, edward's 4.02. 10
but welcome, sweet clarence, my daughter shall 4.02. 12
yea, brother of clarence, art thou here too? 4.03. 41
for choosing me when clarence is in place. 4.06. 31
and i choose clarence only for protector. 4.06. 37
warwick and clarence, give me both your hands. 4.06. 38
what answers clarence to his sovereign's will? 4.06. 45
and, clarence, now then it is more than needful 4.06. 53
ay, therein clarence shall not want his part. 4.06. 57
ah, froward clarence, how evil it beseems thee 4.07. 84
and thou, son clarence, | shalt stir up in 4.08. 11
well–minded clarence, be thou fortunate! 4.08. 27
and, by thy guess, how nigh is clarence now? 5.01. 8
then clarence is at hand, i hear his drum. 5.01. 11
and lo, where george of clarence sweeps along, 5.01. 76
come, clarence, come; 5.01. 80
that clarence is so harsh, so blunt, unnatural, 5.01. 86
welcome, good clarence, this is brother–like. 5.01.105
what clarence but a quicksand of deceit? 5.04. 26
clarence, excuse me to the king my brother; 5.05. 46
then, clarence, do it thou. 5.05. 71
good clarence, do; 5.05. 73
sweet clarence, do thou do it. 5.05. 73
clarence, beware! 5.06. 84
clarence, thy turn is next, and then the rest, 5.06. 90
clarence and gloucester, love my lovely queen, 5.07. 26
/thanks, noble clarence, worthy brother, thanks. 5.07. 30
to set my brother clarence and the king | in R3 1.01. 34
this day should clarence closely be mew'd up 1.01. 38
down to my soul — here clarence comes! 1.01. 41
but what's the matter, clarence, may i know? 1.01. 51
my lady grey his wife, clarence, 'tis she | that 1.01. 64
we are not safe, clarence, we are not safe. 1.01. 70
simple plain clarence, i do love thee so | that 1.01.118
no doubt, no doubt, and so shall clarence too, 1.01.129
to urge his hatred more to clarence | with lies 1.01.147
intent, | clarence hath not another day to live: 1.01.150
clarence still breathes, edward still lives and 1.01.161
his majesty | against the duke of clarence, but 1.03. 85
poor clarence did forsake his father, warwick, 1.03.134
marry, as for clarence, he is well repaid; 1.03.312
clarence, who i indeed have cast in darkness, 1.03.326
for clarence is well–spoken, and perhaps | may 1.03.347
can this dark monarchy afford false clarence?" 1.04. 51
"clarence is come — false, fleeting, perjur'd 1.04. 55
is come — false, fleeting, perjur'd clarence, 1.04. 55
i would speak with clarence, and i came hither 1.04. 86 P
the noble duke of clarence to your hands. 1.04. 92

to take our brother clarence to your grace. 2.01. 77
is clarence dead? the order was revers'd. 2.01. 87
deserve not worse than wretched clarence did, 2.01. 94
ah, poor clarence! 2.01.134
and cry, "o clarence, my unhappy son!"? 2.02. 4
from my feeble hands, | clarence and edward. 2.02. 59
ah for our father, for our dear lord clarence! 2.02. 72
alas for both, both mine, edward and clarence! 2.02. 73
what stay had we but clarence? and he's gone. 2.02. 75
i for a clarence /weep, so doth not she; 2.02. 83
these babes for clarence weep, /and /so /do /i; 2.02. 84
to draw the brats of clarence out of sight, 3.05.107
the son of clarence have i pent up close, | his 4.03. 36
thou hadst a clarence too, and richard kill'd 4.04. 46
thy clarence he is dead that stabb'd my edward, 4.04. 67
toad, thou toad, where is thy brother clarence? 4.04.145
tell her thou mad'st away her uncle clarence, 4.04.281
poor clarence, by thy guile betray'd to death! 5.03.133

CLARET 1 FR 0.0001 REL FR 0 V 1 P
run nothing but claret wine this first year of 2H6 4.06. 4 P

CLARIBEL 4 FR 0.0004 REL FR 3 V 1 P
fair daughter claribel to the king of tunis. TMP 2.01. 71 P
claribel. 2.01.245
"how shall that claribel | measure us back to 2.01.258
voyage | did claribel her husband find at tunis, 5.01.209

CLASP 4 FR 0.0004 REL FR 4 V 0 P
most reverend nestor, i am glad to clasp thee. TRO 4.05.204
in prison, yet | you clasp young cupid's tables. CYM 3.02. 39
then you love us, we you, and we'll clasp hands: PER 2.04. 57
thousand cupids, | shall never clasp our necks; TNK 2.02. 32

CLASP'D 1 FR 0.0001 REL FR 1 V 0 P
fortune's tender arm | with favor never clasp'd, TIM 4.03.251

CLASPING 1 FR 0.0001 REL FR 1 V 0 P
and, clasping to the mast, endur'd a sea | that PER 4.01. 55

CLASPINGS 1 FR 0.0001 REL FR 1 V 0 P
son | by your untimely claspings with your child PER 1.01.128

CLASPS 3 FR 0.0003 REL FR 3 V 0 P
that in gold clasps locks in the golden story; ROM 1.03. 92
to the gross clasps of a lascivious moor — | if OTH 1.01.126
ivy buds, | with coral clasps and amber studs: PP 19.14

CLATPOLES *(also clodpole, clotpole)*

CLATPOLES 1 FR 0.0001 REL FR 0 V 1 P
see you hang'd like clatpoles ere i come any TRO 2.01.117 P

CLATTER 1 FR 0.0001 REL FR 1 V 0 P
by this great clatter, one of greatest note MAC 5.07. 21

CLAUDIO 103 FR 0.0116 REL FR 54 V 49 P
marry, sir, that's claudio, signior claudio. MM 1.02. 64 P
marry, sir, that's claudio, signior claudio. 1.02. 65 P
claudio to prison? 'tis not so. 1.02. 66 P
here comes signior claudio, led by the provost 1.02.114 P
why, how now, claudio? 1.02.124
what's thy offense, claudio? 1.02.135 P
fair sister | to her unhappy brother claudio? 1.04. 20
see that claudio | be executed by nine to–morrow 2.01. 33
it grieves me for the death of claudio — | but 2.01.280
but yet, poor claudio! 2.01.285
is it your will claudio shall die to–morrow? 2.02. 7
my business is a word or two with claudio. 3.01. 48
o, i do fear thee, claudio, and i quake, | lest 3.01. 73
dost thou think, claudio, | if i would yield him 3.01. 96
be ready, claudio, for your death to–morrow. 3.01.106
canst thou tell if claudio die to–morrow, or no? 3.02.169 P
marry, this claudio is condemn'd for untrussing. 3.02.179 P
will not be alter'd, claudio must die to–morrow. 3.02.208 P
me desire to know how you find claudio prepar'd. 3.02.239 P
morning are to die claudio and barnardine. 4.02. 8 P
call hither barnardine and claudio. 4.02. 60 P
here's the warrant, claudio, for thy death. 4.02. 63
or reprieve | for the most gentle claudio. 4.02. 72
what comfort is for claudio? 4.02. 77
have you no countermand for claudio yet, | but 4.02. 92
let claudio be executed by four of the clock, 4.02.121 P
claudio, whom here you have warrant to execute, 4.02.156 P
the visage | of ragozine, more like to claudio? 4.03. 76
and how shall we continue claudio, | to save me 4.03. 84
in secret holds, both barnardine and claudio. 4.03. 87
unhappy claudio! 4.03.121
i am the sister of one claudio, | condemn'd upon 5.01. 69
i came to her from claudio, and desir'd her | to 5.01. 75
"an angelo for claudio, death for death!" 5.01.409
the very block | where claudio stoop'd to death, 5.01.415
how came it claudio was beheaded | at an unusual 5.01.457
i would thou hadst done so by claudio. 5.01.468
should have died when claudio lost his head — 5.01.488
head — | as like almost to claudio as himself. 5.01.489
she, claudio, that you wrong'd, look you restore 5.01.525
much honor on a young florentine call'd claudio. ADO 1.01. 11 P
most in the company of the right noble claudio. 1.01. 85 P
god help the noble claudio! 1.01. 89 P
signior claudio and signior benedick — my dear 1.01.147 P
you hear, count claudio, i can be secret as a 1.01.209 P
dost thou affect her, claudio? 1.01.296
disguise, | and tell fair hero i am claudio, 1.01.322
the prince and count claudio, walking in a 1.02. 9 P
prince discover'd to claudio that he lov'd my 1.02. 12 P
who, the most exquisite claudio? 1.03. 50 P
comes me the prince and claudio, hand in hand in 1.03. 60 P
having obtain'd her, give her to count claudio. 1.03. 64 P
and that is claudio. i know him by his bearing. 2.01.159 P
hear these ill news with the ears of claudio. 2.01.173
count claudio? 2.01.183 P
i have brought count claudio, whom you sent me 2.01.287 P
here, claudio, i have woo'd in thy name, and 2.01.298 P
county claudio, when mean you to go to church? 2.01.355 P
but i warrant thee, claudio, the time shall not 2.01.363 P
the count claudio shall marry the daughter of 2.02. 1 P
his honor in marrying the renown'd claudio — 2.02. 24 P
enough to misuse the prince, to vex claudio, to 2.02. 29 P
to draw don pedro and the count claudio alone, 2.02. 34 P
a kind of zeal both to the prince and claudio — 2.02. 36 P
margaret hero, hear margaret term me claudio; 2.02. 44 P
by falling in love — and such a man is claudio. 2.03. 12 P
proposing with the prince and claudio. 3.01. 3
man of italy, | always excepted my dear claudio. 3.01. 93
if it please you — yet count claudio may hear, 3.02. 85 P
should first tell thee how the prince, claudio, 3.03.149 P
two of them did, the prince and claudio, but the 3.03.154 P
don john had made, away went claudio enrag'd; 3.03.159 P
would the two princes lie, and claudio lie, 4.01.152
so will it fare with claudio: 4.01.222
love | is very much unto the prince and claudio, 4.01.246
kill claudio. 4.01.289 P
is claudio thine enemy? 4.01.300 P
your soul the count claudio hath wrong'd hero? 4.01.328 P
hand, claudio shall render me a dear account. 4.01.333 P
and that count claudio did mean, upon his words, 4.02. 53 P
hero is belied, | and that shall claudio know; 5.01. 43
here comes the prince and claudio hastily. 5.01. 45
know, claudio, to thy head, | thou hast so 5.01. 62
thine, claudio, thine, i say. 5.01. 72
and dispose | for henceforth of poor claudio. 5.01.295
what hath pass'd between you and claudio. 5.02. 49 P
thee plainly, claudio undergoes my challenge, 5.02. 57 P
accus'd, the prince and claudio mightily abus'd, 5.02. 98 P
so are the prince and claudio, who accus'd her 5.04. 2
to call young claudio to a reckoning for it. 5.04. 9
the prince and claudio promis'd by this hour 5.04. 13
daughter, | and give her to young claudio. 5.04. 16
you had from me, | from claudio, and the prince. 5.04. 26
here comes the prince and claudio. 5.04. 33
good morrow, claudio; 5.04. 35
why then your uncle and the prince and claudio 5.04. 75
for thy part, claudio, i did think to have 5.04.109 P
call claudio and some other of my men, | i'll JC 4.03.242
varrus and claudio! 4.03.244
claudio! 4.03.289
claudio! 4.03.290
sirrah claudio! 4.03.299
they were given me by claudio. HAM 4.07. 40

CLAUDIO'S 6 FR 0.0006 REL FR 4 V 2 P
and here comes claudio's pardon. MM 4.02.101
let me have claudio's head sent me by five. 4.02.123 P
i may make my case as claudio's, to cross this 4.02.168 P
notorious pirate, | a man of claudio's years; 4.03. 72
he dies for claudio's death. 5.01.443
you home | the head of ragozine for claudio's, 5.01.533

CLAUSE 1 FR 0.0001 REL FR 1 V 0 P
do not extort thy reasons from this clause, TN 3.01.153

CLAW 2 FR 0.0002 REL FR 0 V 2 P
when i am merry, and claw no man in his humor. ADO 1.03. 17 P
if a talent be a claw, look how he claws him LLL 4.02. 63 P

CLAW'D 1 FR 0.0001 REL FR 0 V 1 P
elder hath not his pole claw'd like a parrot. 2H4 2.04.259 P

CLAWED 1 FR 0.0001 REL FR 1 V 0 P
stealing steps | hath clawed me in his clutch, HAM 5.01. 72

CLAWS 4 FR 0.0004 REL FR 1 V 3 P
be a claw, look how he claws him with a talent. LLL 4.02. 64 P
for they shall hang out for the lion's claws. MND 4.02. 42 P
heart had been wounded with the claws of a lion. AYL 5.02. 23 P
like a white hind under the gripe's sharp claws, LUC 543

CLAY 16 FR 0.0018 REL FR 15 V 1 P
which was embounded in this beauteous clay, JN 4.03.137
when this was now a king, and now is clay? 5.07. 69
away, | men are but gilded loam or painted clay. R2 1.01.179
the brain of this foolish–compounded clay, man, 2H4 1.02. 7 P
deum, | the dead with charity enclos'd in clay; H5 4.08.124
is numb | (unable to support this lump of clay), 1H6 2.05. 14
and temper clay with blood of englishmen. 2H6 3.01.311
a pit of clay for to be made | for such a guest HAM 5.01. 96
a pit of clay for to be made | /for /such /a 5.01.120
imperious caesar, dead and turn'd to clay, 5.01.213
the waters that you loose, | to temper clay. LR 1.04.304
here is my space, | kingdoms are clay; ANT 1.01. 35
be, | but clay and clay differs in dignity, CYM 4.02. 4
be, | but clay and clay differs in dignity, 4.02. 4
then kings' misdeeds cannot be hid in clay. LUC 609
when i (perhaps) compounded am with clay, | do SON 71.10

CLAY–BRAIN'D 1 FR 0.0001 REL FR 0 V 1 P
why, thou clay–brain'd guts, thou knotty–pated 1H4 2.04.227 P

CLEAN 24 FR 0.0027 REL FR 15 V 9 P
you, a sweet virtue in a maid with clean hands. TGV 3.01.279 P
roaming clean through the bounds of asia, | and, ERR 1.01.133
shoe, but her face nothing like so clean kept: 3.02.103 P
hath drops too few to wash her clean again, ADO 4.01.141
in any case, let thisby have clean linen; MND 4.02. 40 P
to wash your liver as clean as a sound sheep's AYL 3.02.422 P
trust a man again for keeping his sword clean, AWW 4.03.145 P
by you unhappied and disfigured clean; R2 3.01. 10
your lordship, though not clean past your youth, 2H4 1.02. 97 P
and therefore will he wipe his tables clean 4.01.199
must sweep the court clean of such filth as thou 2H6 4.07. 31 P
seated, and domestic broils | clean overblown, R3 2.04. 61
renouncing clean | the faith they have in tennis H8 1.03. 29
wash their faces, | and keep their teeth clean. COR 2.03. 61
this is clean kam. 3.01.302
let's hew his limbs till they be clean consum'd. TIT 1.01.129
would thou wert clean enough to spit upon! TIM 4.03.359
clean from the purpose of the things themselves. JC 1.03. 35
ocean wash this blood | clean from my hand? MAC 2.02. 58
what, will these hands ne'er be clean? 5.01. 43 P
of drowning thyself, it is clean out of the way. OTH 1.03.359 P
ere clean it o'erthrow nature, makes it valiant. CYM 3.06. 20
are as a man would wish 'em, strong and clean. TNK 4.02.114
sight, | and by and by clean starved for a look; SON 75.10

CLEANLIEST 1 FR 0.0001 REL FR 0 V 1 P
matter, the cleanliest shift is to kiss. AYL 4.01. 77 P

CLEANLY 6 FR 0.0006 REL FR 4 V 2 P
not neat, but cleanly, captain: WT 1.02.123
wherein neat and cleanly, but to carve a capon 1H4 2.04.456 P
sack, and live cleanly as a nobleman should do. 5.04.165 P
and borne her cleanly by the keeper's nose? TIT 2.01. 94
with much ado the cold fault cleanly out; VEN 694
nor fold my fault in cleanly coin'd excuses; LUC 1073

CLEANS'D 1 FR 0.0001 REL FR 1 V 0 P
priest–like, thou | hast cleans'd my bosom: WT 1.02.238

CLEANSE 2 FR 0.0002 REL FR 2 V 0 P
cleanse the foul body of th' infected world, AYL 2.07. 60
cleanse the stuff'd bosom of that perilous stuff MAC 5.03. 44

CLEANSING 1 FR 0.0001 REL FR 1 V 0 P
is pointing still, in cleansing them from tears. R2 5.05. 54

CLEAN–TIMBER'D 1 FR 0.0001 REL FR 0 V 1 P
i think hector was not so clean–timber'd. LLL 5.02.638 P

/CLEAR 1 FR 0.0001 REL FR 1 V 0 P
/understand /more /clear, | /what's /past /and TRO 4.05.165

CLEAR 74 FR 0.0083 REL FR 65 V 9 P
but heart's sorrow, | and a clear life ensuing. TMP 3.03. 82
if you know yourself clear, why, i am glad of it WIV 3.03.116 P
come away, it is almost clear dawn. MM 4.02.210 P
he in time may come to clear himself; 5.01.150
and all probation will make up full clear, 5.01.157
when you should, and that will clear your sight. ERR 3.02. 57
mine eye's clear eye, my dear heart's dearer 3.02. 62
by fountain clear, or spangled starlight sheen, MND 2.01. 29
you, the murtherer, look as bright, as clear, 3.02. 60
how to get clear of all the debts i owe. MV 1.01.134
and that clear honor | were purchas'd by the 2.09. 42
not be so long, this wrastler shall clear all. AYL 1.01.172 P
i'll say she looks as clear | as morning roses SHR 2.01.172
is very free and clear from any image of offense TN 3.04.227 P
art a foolish fellow, | let me be clear of thee. 4.01. 4
you have given me such clear lights of favor, 5.01.336
and with a countenance as clear | as friendship WT 1.02.343
at several posterns | clear them o' th' city. 1.02.439
fellows, if they please, | can clear me in't. 2.03.144
carriage of it | will clear or end the business. 3.01. 18
so soon as you arrive, shall clear that doubt. 4.04.620
quit all offenses with as clear excuse | as well 1H4 3.02. 19
and i in the clear sky of fame o'ershine you as 2H4 4.03. 51 P
so that, as clear as is the summer's sun, | king H5 1.02. 86
go, clear thy crystals. 2.03. 54
with those clear rays which she infus'd on me 1H6 1.02. 85
so clear, so shining, and so evident, | that it 2.04. 23
father's charge shall clear thee from that stain 4.05. 42
yes, master, clear as day, i thank god and saint 2H6 2.01.105 P
as i am clear from treason to my sovereign. 3.01.102
that you will clear yourself from all suspense. 3.01.140
burn bonfires clear and bright | to entertain 5.01. 3
that i am clear from this misdeed of edward's; 3H6 3.03.183
and proofs as clear as founts in july when | we H8 1.01.154
cloud puts on | by dark'ning my clear sun. 1.01.226
to this point, | and thus far clear him. 2.04.168
this candle burns not clear, 'tis i must snuff 3.02. 96
that i shall clear myself, | lay all the weight 5.02.100
so, 'tis clear, | they'll say 'tis naught; ep 4
the fountain of your mind were clear again, that TRO 3.03.310 P
crack my clear voice with sobs and break my 4.02.108
clear up, fair queen, that cloudy countenance; TIT 1.01.263
a while, | till we can clear these ambiguities, ROM 5.03.217
end, the villainies of man will set him clear. TIM 3.03. 30 P
his debts, | and make a clear way to the gods. 3.04. 76
you cannot make gross sins look clear; 3.05. 38
roots, you clear heavens! 4.03. 28
only look up clear: MAC 1.05. 71
hath been | so clear in his great office, that 1.07. 18
keep | my bosom franchis'd and allegiance clear, 2.01. 28
were i from dunsinane away and clear, | profit 5.03. 61
on the instant they got clear of our ship, so i HAM 4.06. 19 P
cyprus to him, | hath puddled his clear spirit; OTH 3.04.143
in our own filth drop our clear judgments, make ANT 3.13.113
mine own cause so well | to make it clear, but 5.02.122
and the sore eyes see clear | to stop the air PER 1.01. 99
then, lest my life be cropp'd to keep you clear, 1.01.141
persever in that clear way thou goest, | and the 4.06.106
where, by her own most clear remembrance, she 5.03. 12
bed, and for the sake | of clear virginity, be TNK 1.01. 31
begging in our eyes | to make petition clear. 1.01.157
to clear his own way with the mind and sword 3.01. 56
with 'em, | for we are more clear spirits. 5.04. 13
"o thou clear god, and patron of all light, VEN 860
to praise the clear unmatched red and white LUC 11
in his clear bed might have reposed still! 382
that is as clear from this attaint of mine | as 825
to clear this spot by death, at least, i give 1053
the better so to clear her | from that suspicion 1320
those round clear pearls of his, that move thy 1553
clear wells spring not, sweet birds sing not, PP 17.25
to the clear day with thy much clearer light, SON 43. 7
the clear eye's moiety and the dear heart's part 46.12
not making worse what nature made so clear, 84.10

CLEAR'D 9 FR 0.0010 REL FR 7 V 2 P
live, all debts are clear'd between you and i, MV 3.02.319 P
the imposition clear'd, | hereditary ours. WT 1.02. 74
let us be clear'd | of being tyrannous, since we 3.02. 4
see the coast clear'd, and then we will depart. 1H6 1.03. 89
of friends, | i clear'd him with five talents. TIM 2.02.226
all other doubts, by time let them be clear'd, CYM 4.03. 45
not lie till the ship be clear'd of the dead. PER 3.01. 49 P
palamon has clear'd you, | and got your pardon, TNK 4.01. 18
the blackest sin is clear'd with absolution; LUC 354

CLEARER 5 FR 0.0005 REL FR 4 V 1 P
fumes that mantle | their clearer reason. TMP 5.01. 68
when you shall come to clearer knowledge, that WT 2.01. 97
your mind is the clearer, /ajax, and your TRO 2.03.153 P
to the clear day with thy much clearer light, SON 43. 7
most full flame should afterwards burn clearer. 115. 4

CLEAREST 1 FR 0.0001 REL FR 1 V 0 P
think that the clearest gods, who make them LR 4.06. 73

CLEARLY 5 FR 0.0005 REL FR 5 V 0 P
if she, my liege, can make me know this clearly, AWW 5.03.315
own | from my remembrance clearly banish'd his. TN 5.01.282
lost | in this which he accounts so clearly won. JN 3.04.122
and wound our tott'ring colors clearly up, 5.05. 7
you do not understand yourself so clearly | as HAM 1.03. 96

CLEARNESS 3 FR 0.0003 REL FR 2 V 1 P
and make foul the clearness of our deservings, AWW 1.03. 6 P
the fresh taste be taken from that clearness, TIT 3.01.128
always thought | that i require a clearness: MAC 3.01.132

CLEARS 7 FR 0.0008 REL FR 7 V 0 P
so foul a sky clears not without a storm, | pour JN 4.02.108
the sun not yet thy sighs from heaven clears, ROM 2.03. 73
a little water clears us of this deed; MAC 2.02. 64
wholesome end | as clears her from all blame. LR 2.04.145
the poisoned fountain clears itself again, | and LUC 1707
her body's stain her mind untainted clears, 1710
the sun itself sees not till heaven clears. SON 148.12

CLEAR–SHINING 1 FR 0.0001 REL FR 1 V 0 P
but sever'd in a pale clear–shining sky. 3H6 2.01. 28

CLEAR–SPIRITED 1 FR 0.0001 REL FR 1 V 0 P
clear–spirited cousin, | let's leave his court, TNK 1.02. 74

CLEAVE* 11 FR 0.0012 REL FR 11 V 0 P
thy thoughts i cleave to. what's thy pleasure? TMP 4.01.165
to save a head, | to cleave a heart in twain. MM 3.01. 62
my tongue cleave to my roof within my mouth, R2 5.03. 31
our good city | cleave in the midst and perish. COR 3.02. 28

again, | and cleave to no revenge but lucius. TIT 5.02.136
knock me down with 'em, cleave me to the girdle! TIM 3.04. 90
cleave not to their mould | but with the aid of MAC 1.03.145
if you shall cleave to my consent, when 'tis, 2.01. 25
and cleave the general ear with horrid speech, HAM 2.02.563
twain would be | as if the world should cleave, ANT 3.04. 31
o, cleave, my sides! 4.14. 39
CLEAVES 1 FR 0.0001 REL FR 1 V 0 P
mistakes that aim and cleaves an infant's heart. VEN 942
CLEAVING* 3 FR 0.0003 REL FR 3 V 0 P
will she get the upshoot by cleaving the /pin. LLL 4.01.136
and this thy son's blood cleaving to my blade 3H6 1.03. 50
cleaving his conscience into twain and doing TNK 1.03. 46
CLEEP *(also clip*)*
CLEEP 2 FR 0.0002 REL FR 2 V 0 P
and flagging wings | cleep dead men's graves, 2H6 4.01. 6
here i cleep | the anvil of my sword, and do COR 4.05.109
CLEF *(see cliff*)*
CLEFT 9 FR 0.0010 REL FR 6 V 3 P
how oft hast thou with perjury cleft the root? TGV 5.04.103
and have cleft his club to make the fire too. ADO 2.01.254 P
an apple, cleft in two, is not more twin | than TN 5.01.223
cleft the heart | that could conceive a gross WT 3.02.196
my brain-pan had been cleft with a brown bill; 2H6 4.10. 12 P
i cleft his beaver with a downright blow. 3H6 1.01. 12
the very pin of his heart cleft with the blind ROM 2.04. 16 P
o hamlet, thou hast cleft my heart in twain. HAM 3.04.156
/o cleft effect! LC 293
CLEITUS *(see clytus)*
CLEMENCY 1 FR 0.0001 REL FR 1 V 0 P
our tragedy, | here stooping to your clemency, HAM 3.02.150
CLEMENT 3 FR 0.0003 REL FR 2 V 1 P
of woncote against clement perkes a' th' hill. 2H4 5.01. 39 P
i know you are more clement than vild men, | who CYM 5.04. 18
king, | as he is clement if th' offender mourn, STM II.C 123
CLEMENT'S 4 FR 0.0004 REL FR 0 V 4 P
i was once of clement's inn, where i think they 2H4 3.02. 14 P
by old nightwork before i came to clement's inn. 3.02.209 P
mile–end green, when i lay at clement's inn — i 3.02.280 P
i do remember him at clement's inn, like a man 3.02.308 P
CLEOMINES 4 FR 0.0004 REL FR 4 V 0 P
cleomines and dion, whom you know | of stuff'd WT 2.01.184
cleomines and dion, | being well arriv'd from 2.03.195
that you, cleomines and dion, have | been both 3.02.125
go, cleomines; 5.01.112
CLEON 9 FR 0.0010 REL FR 9 V 0 P
there will i visit cleon, for the babe | cannot PER 3.01. 78
most honor'd cleon, i must needs be gone. 3.03. 1
and by cleon train'd | in music's letters, who 4.ch. 7
our cleon hath | one daughter, and a full–grown 4.ch. 15
till cruel cleon, with his wicked wife, | did 5.01.171
as she should have been, | by savage cleon. 5.01.216
there to strike | the inhospitable cleon, but i 5.01.253
she at tharsus | was nurs'd with cleon, who at 5.03. 8
for wicked cleon and his wife, when fame | had 5.03. 95
CLEON'S 1 FR 0.0001 REL FR 1 V 0 P
that cleon's wife, with envy rare, | a present PER 4.ch. 37
CLEOPATRA 30 FR 0.0034 REL FR 27 V 3 P
dido a dowdy, cleopatra a gipsy, helen and hero ROM 2.04. 41 P
but stirr'd by cleopatra. ANT 1.01. 43
name cleopatra as she is call'd in rome. 1.02.106
cleopatra, catching but the least noise of this, 1.02.140 P
cleopatra — 1.03. 26
idleness so near the heart | as cleopatra this. 1.03. 95
is not more manlike | than cleopatra; 1.04. 6
of love, | salt cleopatra, soften thy wan'd lip! 2.01. 21
if cleopatra heard you, your /reproof | were 2.02.121
vacancy, | had gone to gaze on cleopatra too, 2.02.217
pray you, is he married to cleopatra? 2.06.108 P
cleopatra and himself in chairs of gold | were 3.06. 4
sister, cleopatra | hath nodded him to her. 3.06. 65
next, cleopatra does confess thy greatness, 3.12. 16
from antony win cleopatra, promise, | and in our 3.12. 27
what's her name, | since she was cleopatra? 3.13. 99
my lord | is antony again, i will be cleopatra. 3.13.186
i will o'ertake thee, cleopatra, and | weep for 4.14. 44
since cleopatra died | i have liv'd in such 4.14. 55
lord, | my mistress cleopatra sent me to thee. 4.14.118
bear me, good friends, where cleopatra bides, 4.14.131
o cleopatra! thou art taken, queen. 5.02. 38
cleopatra, | do not abuse my master's bounty by 5.02. 42
cleopatra! 5.02. 92
cleopatra, know | we will extenuate rather than 5.02.124
you shall advise me in all for cleopatra. 5.02.137
blush not, cleopatra, i approve | your wisdom in 5.02.149
cleopatra, | not what you have reserv'd, nor 5.02.179
see | some squeaking cleopatra boy my greatness 5.02.220
the story | proud cleopatra, when she met her CYM 2.04. 70
CLEOPATRA'S 4 FR 0.0004 REL FR 3 V 1 P
but not /her heart, | cleopatra's majesty, AYL 3.02.146
wine enough, | cleopatra's health to drink. ANT 1.02. 13
especially that of cleopatra's, which wholly 1.02.174 P
have built | in cleopatra's sails their nests. 4.12. 4
CLEPES *(also clepeth, clip*, clipt*, ycliped)*
CLEPES 1 FR 0.0001 REL FR 1 V 0 P
she clepes him king of graves and grave for VEN 995
CLEPETH 1 FR 0.0001 REL FR 0 V 1 P
he clepeth a calf, "cauf"; LLL 5.01. 22 P
/CLERESTORIES 1 FR 0.0001 REL FR 0 V 1 P
and the /clerestories toward the south north are TN 4.02. 37 P
CLERGY 3 FR 0.0003 REL FR 3 V 0 P
than ever at one time the clergy yet | did to H5 1.01. 80
mighty sum | as never did the clergy at one time 1.02.134
he was ill, and gave | the clergy ill example. H8 4.02. 44
CLERGYMAN 1 FR 0.0001 REL FR 1 V 0 P
scroop, besides a clergyman | of holy reverence, R2 3.03. 28
CLERGYMEN 3 FR 0.0003 REL FR 3 V 0 P
how i have sped among the clergymen | the sums i JN 4.02.141
you holy clergymen, is there no plot | to rid R2 4.01.324
where his grace stands, 'tween two clergymen! R3 3.07. 95
CLERGY'S 1 FR 0.0001 REL FR 1 V 0 P
the clergy's bags | are lank and lean with thy 2H6 1.03.128
/CLERK 1 FR 0.0001 REL FR 1 V 0 P
/am /i /both /priest /and /clerk? R2 4.01.173
CLERK 18 FR 0.0020 REL FR 14 V 4 P
answer, clerk. ADO 2.01.110 P
no more words; the clerk is answer'd. 2.01.111 P
clerk, draw a deed of gift. MV 4.01.394
in faith, i gave it to the judge's clerk. 5.01.143
gave it a judge's clerk! 5.01.157
the clerk will ne'er wear hair on 's face that 5.01.158
no higher than thyself, the judge's clerk, | a 5.01.163
and then the boy, his clerk, | that took some 5.01.181
and i his clerk; 5.01.234
for that same scrubbed boy, the doctor's clerk, 5.01.261
was the doctor, | nerissa there her clerk. 5.01.270
were you the clerk that is to make me cuckold? 5.01.281
ay, but the clerk that never means to do it, 5.01.282
my clerk hath some good comforts too for you. 5.01.289
till i were couching with the doctor's clerk. 5.01.305
to th' church take the priest, clerk, and some SHR 4.04. 94 P
the clerk of chartam. 2H6 4.02. 85 P
and, like unlettered clerk, still cry "amen" SON 85. 6
CLERK–LIKE 1 FR 0.0001 REL FR 1 V 0 P
thereto | clerk–like experienc'd, which no less WT 1.02.392
CLERKLY 4 FR 0.0004 REL FR 2 V 2 P
you, gentle servant — 'tis very clerkly done. TGV 2.01.108
thou /art clerkly, thou art clerkly, sir john. WIV 4.05. 57 P
thou /art clerkly, thou art clerkly, sir john. 4.05. 57 P
with ignominious words, though clerkly couch'd, 2H6 3.01.179
CLERK'S 1 FR 0.0001 REL FR 1 V 0 P
for if i do, i'll mar the young clerk's pen. MV 5.01.237
CLERKS 5 FR 0.0005 REL FR 4 V 1 P
great clerks have purposed | to greet me with MND 5.01. 93
if they meet not with saint nicholas' clerks, 1H4 2.01. 62 P
large gifts have i bestow'd on learned clerks, 2H6 4.07. 71
all the clerks | (i mean the learned ones in H8 2.02. 91
deep clerks she dumbs, and with her neele PER 5.ch. 5
CLEW 1 FR 0.0001 REL FR 1 V 0 P
if it be so, you have wound a goodly clew; AWW 1.03.182
CLIENT 1 FR 0.0001 REL FR 1 V 0 P
the client breaks, as desperate in his suit. VEN 336
CLIENT'S 1 FR 0.0001 REL FR 1 V 0 P
windy attorneys to their client's woes, | aery R3 4.04.127
CLIENTS 3 FR 0.0003 REL FR 1 V 2 P
good counsellors lack no clients. MM 1.02.107 P
when she should do for clients her fitment, and PER 4.06. 6 P
to trembling clients be you mediators: LUC 1020
CLIFF* 5 FR 0.0005 REL FR 4 V 1 P
d sol re, one cliff, two notes have i; SHR 3.01. 77
any man may sing her, if he can take her cliff; TRO 5.02. 11 P
or to the dreadful summit of the cliff | that HAM 1.04. 70
there is a cliff, whose high and bending head LR 4.01. 73
upon the crown o' th' cliff, what thing was that 4.06. 67
CLIFFORD 59 FR 0.0066 REL FR 55 V 4 P
what, buckingham and clifford, are ye so brave? 2H6 4.08. 20 P
a clifford! 4.08. 53 P
a clifford! 4.08. 53 P
we'll follow the king and clifford. 4.08. 54 P
call hither clifford, bid him come amain, | to 5.01.114
and here comes clifford to deny their bail. 5.01.123
i thank thee, clifford. 5.01.125
we are thy sovereign, clifford, kneel again; 5.01.127
ay, clifford, a bedlam and ambitious humor 5.01.132
clifford of cumberland, 'tis warwick calls! 5.02. 1
clifford, i say, come forth and fight with me. 5.02. 5
proud northern lord, clifford of cumberland, 5.02. 6
the deadly–handed clifford slew my steed; 5.02. 9
as i intend, clifford, to thrive to–day, | it 5.02. 17
lord clifford, and lord stafford, all abreast, 3H6 1.01. 7
and thine, lord clifford, and you both have 1.01. 55
the hope thereof makes clifford mourn in steel. 1.01. 58
true, clifford, that's richard duke of york. 1.01. 83
poor clifford, how i scorn his worthless threats 1.01.101
lord clifford vows to fight in thy defense. 1.01.160
o clifford, how thy words revive my heart! 1.01.163
ah, tutor, look where bloody clifford comes! 1.03. 2
ah, clifford, murther not this innocent child, 1.03. 8
ah, gentle clifford, kill me with thy sword 1.03. 16
sweet clifford, hear me speak before i die: 1.03. 18
he is a man, and, clifford, cope with him. 1.03. 24
sweet clifford, pity me! 1.03. 36
come, bloody clifford, rough northumberland, | i 1.04. 27
o clifford, but bethink thee once again, | and 1.04. 44
hold, valiant clifford! 1.04. 51
hold, clifford, do not honor him so much | to 1.04. 54
brave warriors, clifford and northumberland, 1.04. 66
that valiant clifford with his rapier's point 1.04. 80
for his death | 'gainst thee, fell clifford, and 1.04.149
hard–hearted clifford, take me from the world, 1.04.167
and watch'd him how he singled clifford forth. 2.01. 12
arm | of unrelenting clifford and the queen; 2.01. 58
of sweet young rutland, by rough clifford slain. 2.01. 63
o clifford, boist'rous clifford, thou hast slain 2.01. 70
o clifford, boist'rous clifford, thou hast slain 2.01. 70
is by the stern lord clifford done to death. 2.01.103
with clifford and the haught northumberland, 2.01.169
then, clifford, were thy heart as hard as steel, 2.01.201
full well hath clifford play'd the orator, 2.02. 43
but, clifford, tell me, didst thou never hear 2.02. 45
'twas not your valor, clifford, drove me thence. 2.02.107
of my big–swoll'n heart | upon that clifford, 2.02.112
now, clifford, i have singled thee alone: 2.04. 1
for margaret my queen, and clifford too, | have 2.05. 16
think you, lords, that clifford fled with them? 2.06. 37
revoke that doom of mercy, for 'tis clifford, 2.06. 46
your father's head, which clifford placed there; 2.06. 53
speak, clifford, dost thou know who speaks to 2.06. 61
clifford, ask mercy and obtain no grace. 2.06. 69
clifford, repent in bootless penitence. 2.06. 70
clifford, devise excuses for thy faults. 2.06. 71
they mock thee, clifford, swear as thou wast 2.06. 76
when clifford cannot spare his friends an oath. 2.06. 78
when black–fac'd clifford shook his sword at him R3 1.02.158
CLIFFORD'S 5 FR 0.0005 REL FR 5 V 0 P
come, thou new ruin of old clifford's house: 2H6 5.02. 61
from clifford's and northumberland's pursuit. 3H6 2.01. 3
or more than common fear of clifford's rigor, 2.01.126
that clifford's manhood lies upon his tongue. 2.02.125
with the steely point of clifford's lance; 2.03. 16
CLIFFORDS 1 FR 0.0001 REL FR 1 V 0 P
two cliffords, as the father and the son, | and 3H6 5.07. 7
CLIFFS 2 FR 0.0002 REL FR 1 V 1 P
i look'd for the chalky cliffs, but i could find ERR 3.02.126 P
as far as i could ken thy chalky cliffs, | when 2H6 3.02.101
CLIFTON 3 FR 0.0003 REL FR 3 V 0 P
hath for succor sent, | and so hath clifton. 1H4 5.04. 46
i'll to clifton straight. 5.04. 46
make up to clifton, i'll to sir nicholas gawsey. 5.04. 58
CLIMATE 8 FR 0.0009 REL FR 8 V 0 P
it is the quality o' th' climate. TMP 2.01.200
to it own protection | and favor of the climate. WT 2.03.179
from our air whilest you | do climate here! 5.01.170
that sways the earth this climate overlooks, JN 2.01.344
god, | that in a christian climate souls refin'd R2 4.01.130
is not their climate foggy, raw, and dull, | on H5 3.05. 16
things | unto the climate that they point upon. JC 1.03. 32
and, though he in a fertile climate dwell, OTH 1.01. 70
CLIMATE'S 1 FR 0.0001 REL FR 1 V 0 P
the climate's delicate, the air most sweet, WT 3.01. 1
CLIMATURES 1 FR 0.0001 REL FR 1 V 0 P
unto our climatures and countrymen. HAM 1.01.125
CLIMB 23 FR 0.0026 REL FR 21 V 2 P
determin'd of — how i must climb her window, TGV 2.04.181
to climb celestial silvia's chamber–window, 2.06. 34
and built so shelving that one cannot climb it 3.01.115
climb o'er the house to unlock the little gate. LLL 1.01.109
shall give us cause to climb in the merriness. 1.01.200 P
to marriage, which they will climb incontinent, AYL 5.02. 38 P
what, and wouldst climb a tree? 2H6 2.01. 96
and made me climb, with danger of my life. 2.01.101
and fearless minds climb soonest unto crowns. 3H6 4.07. 62
to climb steep hills | requires slow pace at H8 1.01.131
goes backward with a purpose | it hath to climb. TRO 1.03.129
or climb my palace, till from forth this place TIT 1.01.327
chase, | and climb the highest promontory top. 2.02. 22
nor i no strength to climb without thy help. 2.03.242
the orchard walls are high and hard to climb, ROM 2.02. 63
must climb a bird's nest soon when it is dark. 2.05. 74
the steepy mount | to climb his happiness, would TIM 1.01. 76
or else climb upward | to what they were before. MAC 4.02. 24
you do climb it up now. look how we labor. LR 4.06. 2
and let the laboring bark climb hills of seas OTH 2.01.187
whose top to climb | is certain falling, or so CYM 3.03. 47
let our crooked smokes climb to their nostrils 5.05.477
or if thou wilt permit the sun to climb | his LUC 775
CLIMB'D 4 FR 0.0004 REL FR 3 V 1 P
on a brick wall have i climb'd into this garden, 2H6 4.10. 7 P
make war with him that climb'd unto their nest, 3H6 2.02. 31
have you climb'd up to walls and battlements, JC 1.01. 38
and having climb'd the steep–up heavenly hill, SON 7. 5
CLIMBER–UPWARD 1 FR 0.0001 REL FR 1 V 0 P
whereto the climber–upward turns his face; JC 2.01. 23
CLIMBETH 1 FR 0.0001 REL FR 1 V 0 P
now climbeth tamora olympus' top, | safe out of TIT 2.01. 1
CLIMBING 7 FR 0.0008 REL FR 7 V 0 P
still climbing trees in the hesperides? LLL 4.03.338
upon the hempen tackle ship–boys climbing; H5 3.pr. 8
famine, quartering steel, and climbing fire, 1H6 4.02. 11
yea, man and birds are fain of climbing high. 2H6 2.01. 8
too true, and bought his climbing very dear. 2.01. 98
climbing my walls in spite of me the owner, 4.10. 35
/hysterica passio, down, thou climbing sorrow, LR 2.04. 57
CLIME 8 FR 0.0009 REL FR 8 V 0 P
the best–regarded virgins of our clime | have MV 2.01. 10
air, | and thou art flying to a fresher clime. R2 1.03.285
shivering cold and sickness pines the clime; 5.01. 77
leaving their earthly parts to choke your clime, H5 4.03.102
bank | drove back again unto my native clime? 2H6 3.02. 84
amongst the fair–fac'd breeders of our clime. TIT 4.02. 68
affect many proposed matches | of her own clime, OTH 3.03.230
to use one language in each several clime PER 4.04. 6
CLING 2 FR 0.0002 REL FR 2 V 0 P
as two spent swimmers that do cling together MAC 1.02. 8
shall thou hang alive, | till famine cling thee; 5.05. 39
CLINK 4 FR 0.0004 REL FR 4 V 0 P
"and let me the canakin clink, clink; OTH 2.03. 69
"and let me the canakin clink, clink; 2.03. 69
and let me the canakin clink. 2.03. 70
for that i heard the clink and fall of swords, 2.03.234
CLINKING 1 FR 0.0001 REL FR 0 V 1 P
lady, a long lease for the clinking of pewter. 1H4 2.04. 46 P
CLINQUANT 1 FR 0.0001 REL FR 1 V 0 P
all clinquant, all in gold, like heathen gods, H8 1.01. 19
CLIP* *(also cleep, clepes, etc., clipt*, ycliped)*
CLIP* 9 FR 0.0010 REL FR 9 V 0 P
let me clip ye | in arms as sound as when i COR 1.06. 29
they clip us drunkards, and with swinish phrase HAM 1.04. 19
above, | you elements that clip us round about, OTH 3.03.464
enter the city, clip your wives, your friends, ANT 4.08. 8
no grave upon the earth shall clip in it | a 5.02.359
makes me look dismal will i clip to form, | and PER 5.03. 74
and i'll clip my yellow locks an inch below mine TNK 3.04. 20
annoy, | to clip elysium and to lack her joy. VEN 600
to kiss and clip me till i run away! PP 11.14
CLIPPER 1 FR 0.0001 REL FR 0 V 1 P
to–morrow the king himself will be a clipper. H5 4.01.229 P
CLIPPETH 1 FR 0.0001 REL FR 1 V 0 P
that neptune's arms, who clippeth thee about, JN 5.02. 34
CLIPPING 1 FR 0.0001 REL FR 0 V 1 P
again worries he his daughter with clipping her. WT 5.02. 54 P
CLIPT* 7 FR 0.0008 REL FR 6 V 1 P
judas machabeus clipt is plain judas. LLL 5.02.599 P
clipt in with the sea | that chides the banks of 1H4 3.01. 43
and demi–wolves are clipt | all by the name of MAC 3.01. 93
the modest truth, | nor more nor clipt, but so. LR 4.07. 6
garment | that ever hath but clipt his body, is CYM 2.03.134
were clipt about | with this most tender air. 5.05.451
me," | and then she clipt adonis in her arms; PP 11. 6
CLIP–WING'D 1 FR 0.0001 REL FR 1 V 0 P
a clip–wing'd griffin and a moulten raven, | a 1H4 3.01.150
CLITUS 4 FR 0.0004 REL FR 4 V 0 P
sit thee down, clitus; JC 5.05. 4
hark thee, clitus. 5.05. 5
o clitus! 5.05. 10
to kill him, clitus. look, he meditates. 5.05. 12
CLOAK 28 FR 0.0031 REL FR 20 V 8 P
bear it | under a cloak that is of any length. TGV 3.01.130
a cloak as long as thine will serve the turn? 3.01.131
then let me see thy cloak — | i'll get me one 3.01.132
why, any cloak will serve the turn, my lord. 3.01.134

how shall i fashion me to wear a cloak? 3.01.135
i pray thee let me feel thy cloak upon me. 3.01.136
an old cloak makes a new jerkin; WIV 1.03. 17 P
or a hat, or a cloak, is nothing to a man. ADO 3.03.119 P
take my color'd hat and cloak. SHR 1.01.207
a velvet hose, a scarlet cloak, and a copatain 5.01. 67 P
we will not line his thin bestained cloak | with JN 4.03. 24
now happy he whose cloak and center can | hold 4.03.155
the cloak of night being pluck'd from off their R2 3.02. 45
about the satin for my short cloak and my slops? 2H4 1.02. 30 P
give me my sword and cloak. 2.04.366
till his face be like a wet cloak ill laid up. 5.01. 85 P
lend me thy cloak, sir thomas. H5 4.01. 24
say'st thou me so? what color is this cloak of? 2H6 2.01.107
thou oughtst not to let thy horse wear a cloak, 4.07. 50 P
i have night's cloak to hide me from their eyes, ROM 2.02. 75
get on your cloak and haste you to lord timon; TIM 2.01. 15
and what hast thou there under thy cloak, pretty 3.01. 14 P
you pull'd me by the cloak, would you speak with JC 1.02.215 P
'tis not alone my inky cloak, /good mother, HAM 1.02. 77
down, | /then take thy auld cloak about thee." OTH 2.03. 96
how | to cloak offenses with a cunning brow. LUC 749
which underneath thy black all–hiding cloak 801
and make me travel forth without my cloak, | to SON 34. 2

CLOAK–BAG 2 FR 0.0002 REL FR 1 V 1 P
bombard of sack, that stuff'd cloak–bag of guts, 1H4 2.04.452 P
i have already fit | ('tis in my cloak–bag) CYM 3.04.169

CLOAKS 4 FR 0.0004 REL FR 4 V 0 P
but cloaks and gowns, before this day, a many. 2H6 2.01.113
clouds are seen, wise men put on their cloaks; R3 2.03. 32
hats, cloaks | (doublets, i think) flew up, and H8 4.01. 73
and half their faces buried in their cloaks, JC 2.01. 74

/CLOCK 4 FR 0.0004 REL FR 4 V 0 P
your maw, like mine, should be your /clock, ERR 1.02. 66
wife — | a woman, that is like a german /clock, LLL 3.01.190
/ay, /what's /a' /clock? R3 4.02.109
/well, /but /what's /a' /clock? 4.02.111

CLOCK 76 FR 0.0086 REL FR 48 V 28 P
they'll tell the clock to any business that | we TMP 2.01.289
by seven a' clock i'll get you such a ladder. TGV 3.01.126
eleven o' clock the hour. WIV 2.02.309 P
vat is the clock, jack? 2.03. 3 P
the clock gives me my cue, and my assurance bids 3.02. 45 P
let him be sent for to–morrow, eight a' clock, 3.03.198 P
it hath strook ten a' clock. 5.02. 10 P
but till 'tis one a' clock, | our dance of 5.05. 74
what's a' clock, think you? MM 2.01.276 P
block and your axe to–morrow, four a' clock. 4.02. 53 P
let claudio be executed by four of the clock, 4.02.121 P
soon at five a' clock, | please you, i'll meet ERR 1.02. 26
the clock hath strucken twelve upon the bell: 1.02. 45
sure, luciana, it is two a' clock. 2.01. 3
at five a' clock | i shall receive the money for 4.01. 10
ere i left him, and now the clock strikes one. 4.02. 54
'tis almost five a' clock, cousin, 'tis time you ADO 3.04. 52 P
be ready at the farthest by five of the clock. MV 2.02.116 P
'tis now but four of clock, we have two hours 2.04. 8
monday last at six a' clock i' th' morning, 2.05. 25 P
hour, | for lovers ever run before the clock. 2.06. 4
'tis nine a' clock — our friends all stay for 2.06. 63
eye, | says very wisely, "it is ten a' clock. AYL 2.07. 22
i pray you, what is't a' clock? 3.02.299 P
there's no clock in the forest. 3.02.301 P
detect the lazy foot of time as well as a clock. 3.02.305 P
by two a' clock i will be with thee again. 4.01.181 P
two a' clock is your hour? 4.01.186 P
is it not past two a' clock? 4.03. 2 P
let's see, i think 'tis now some seven a' clock, SHR 4.03.187
i do, | it shall be what a' clock i say it is. 4.03.195
clock to itself, knew the true minute when AWW 1.02. 39
ten a' clock: 4.01. 24 P
the clock upbraids me with the waste of time. TN 3.01.130
i love thee not a jar o' th' clock behind | what WT 1.02. 43
for now hath time made me his numb'ring clock: R2 5.05. 50
i stand fooling here, his jack of the clock. 5.05. 60
to–morrow morning by four a' clock early, at 1H4 1.02.125 P
good morrow, carriers, what's a' clock? 2.01. 32 P
i think it be two a' clock. 2.01. 33 P
age of this present twelve a' clock at midnight. 2.04. 94 P
what's a' clock, francis? 2.04. 96 P
indeed, my lord, i think it be two a' clock. 2.04.525
temple hall | at two /a' clock in the afternoon; 3.03.200
and fought a long hour by shrewsbury clock. 5.04.148 P
born about three of the clock in the afternoon, 2H4 1.02.187 P
'tis one a' clock, and past. 3.01. 34
'twill be two a' clock ere they come from the 5.05. 3 P
is it four a' clock? H5 1.01. 93
it is now two a' clock; 3.07.156
sirs, what's a' clock? 2H6 2.04. 5
what is't a' clock? R3 3.02. 4
and towards three or four a' clock | look for 3.05.101
what is't a' clock? 5.03. 47
supper–time, my lord, | it's /nine a' clock. 5.03. 48
tell the clock there. 5.03.276
it's one a' clock, boy, is't not? H8 5.01. 1
by aleven of the clock it will go one way or TRO 3.03.296 P
what a' clock to–morrow | shall i send to thee? ROM 2.02.167
the clock strook nine when i did send the nurse; 2.05. 1
the curfew–bell hath rung, 'tis three a' clock. 4.04. 4
peace, count the clock. JC 2.01.192
the clock hath stricken three. 2.01.192
what is't a' clock? 2.02.114
what is't a' clock? 2.04. 23
'tis three a' clock, and, romans, yet ere night 5.03.109
the moon is down; i have not heard the clock. MAC 2.01. 2
by th' clock 'tis day, | and yet dark night 2.04. 6
'tis not yet ten o' th' clock. OTH 2.03. 14 P
and if thou canst awake by four o' th' clock, CYM 2.02. 6
to weep 'twixt clock and clock? 3.04. 42
to weep 'twixt clock and clock? 3.04. 42
unhappy was the clock | that strook the hour! 5.05.153
hear nothing but the clock that tells our woes; TNK 2.02. 42
when i do count the clock that tells the time, SON 12. 1
whilst i, my sovereign, watch the clock for you, 57. 6

CLOCK'S 1 FR 0.0001 REL FR 1 V 0 P
than the sands | that run i' th' clock's behalf. CYM 3.02. 73

CLOCKS 5 FR 0.0005 REL FR 4 V 1 P
straws | and merry larks are ploughmen's clocks; LLL 5.02.904
wishing clocks more swift? WT 1.02.289
minutes capons, and clocks the tongues of bawds, 1H4 1.02. 8 P
the country cocks do crow, the clocks do toll, H5 4.pr. 15
or device | their arms are set, like clocks, 1H6 1.02. 42

CLOCK–SETTER 1 FR 0.0001 REL FR 1 V 0 P
old time the clock–setter, that bald sexton time JN 3.01.324

CLOD 3 FR 0.0003 REL FR 2 V 1 P
sensible warm motion to become | a kneaded clod; MM 3.01.120
account of her life to a clod of wayward marl? ADO 2.01. 62 P
and then all this thou seest is but a clod | and JN 5.07. 57

CLODDY 1 FR 0.0001 REL FR 1 V 0 P
the meagre cloddy earth to glittering gold. JN 3.01. 80

CLODPOLE 1 FR 0.0001 REL FR 0 V 1 P
he will find it comes from a clodpole. TN 3.04.190 P

CLODPOLL *(see clatpoles, clodpole, clotpole)*

CLO'ES *(also clothes)*

CLO'ES 1 FR 0.0001 REL FR 1 V 0 P
"then up he rose and donn'd his clo'es, | and HAM 4.05. 52

CLOG 5 FR 0.0005 REL FR 2 V 3 P
with a muzzle and enfranchis'd with a clog, ADO 1.03. 33 P
here comes my clog. AWW 2.05. 53
in his liver as will clog the foot of a flea, TN 3.02. 62 P
away from his father with his clog at his heels. WT 4.04.679 P
with clog of conscience and sour melancholy R2 5.06. 20

CLOGGING 1 FR 0.0001 REL FR 1 V 0 P
along | the clogging burthen of a guilty soul. R2 1.03.200

CLOGS 2 FR 0.0002 REL FR 2 V 0 P
rue the time | that clogs me with this answer." MAC 3.06. 43
would teach me tyranny, | to hang clogs on them. OTH 1.03.198

CLOISTER 6 FR 0.0006 REL FR 5 V 1 P
wherewith my brother held you in the cloister? TGV 1.03. 2
this day my sister should the cloister enter, MM 1.02.177
a nun, | for aye to be in shady cloister mew'd, MND 1.01. 71
he will steal, sir, an egg out of a cloister. AWW 4.03.250 P
and cloister thee in some religious house. R2 5.01. 23
and now she would the caged cloister fly: LC 249

CLOISTER'D 1 FR 0.0001 REL FR 1 V 0 P
ere the bat hath flown | his cloister'd flight, MAC 3.02. 41

CLOIST'RED 1 FR 0.0001 REL FR 1 V 0 P
therefore still in night would cloist'red be. LUC 1085

CLOISTRESS 1 FR 0.0001 REL FR 1 V 0 P
but like a cloistress she will veiled walk, TN 1.01. 27

CLOS'D 8 FR 0.0009 REL FR 7 V 1 P
marry, after they clos'd in earnest, they parted TGV 2.05. 12 P
till either death hath clos'd these eyes of mine 3H6 2.03. 31
term | of a despised life clos'd in my breast ROM 1.04.110
poor living corse, clos'd in a dead man's tomb! 5.02. 30
a cup clos'd in my true love's hand? 5.03.161
which bounteous nature | hath in him clos'd; MAC 3.01. 98
i have not clos'd mine eyes | save when my lids TNK 3.02. 27
when heavy sleep had clos'd up mortal eyes. LUC 163

CLOSE 116 FR 0.0131 REL FR 95 V 21 P
close by, my master. TMP 1.02.216
that to close prison he commanded her, | with TGV 3.01.237
close at the heels of her virtues. 3.01.322 P
let me be blest to make this happy close; 5.04.117
it in the muddy ditch close by the thames side. WIV 3.03. 16 P
and follows close the rigor of the statute, | to MM 1.04. 67
your wisdom, daughter, in your close patience. 4.03.118
hark how the villain would close now, after his 5.01.342 P
lapwing, runs | close by the ground, to hear our ADO 3.01. 25
stand thee close then under this penthouse, for 3.03.103 P
some treason, masters; yet stand close. 3.03.107 P
i thought to close mine eyes some half an hour; LLL 5.02. 90
the sudden hand of death close up mine eye! 5.02.815
near to her close and consecrated bower, | while MND 3.02. 7
stand close; this is the same athenian. 3.02. 41
for the close night doth play the runaway, | and MV 2.06. 47
vesture of decay | doth grossly close it in, we 5.01. 65
which in a napkin (being close convey'd) | shall SHR in.1. 127
my banket is to close our stomachs up | after 5.02. 9
which nothing but to close | her eyes myself AWW 5.03.118
a beauteous wall | doth oft close in pollution, TN 1.02. 49
close, in the name of jesting! 2.05. 20 P
hands, | attested by the holy close of lips, 5.01.158
up with't, keep it close. WT 3.03.124 P
father died, | to lie close by his honest bones; 4.04.456
or | the close earth wombs, or the profound seas 4.04.490
close with him, give him gold; 4.04.800 P
close your hands. JN 2.01.533
that close aspect of his | /doth show the mood 4.02. 72
the setting sun, and music at the close, | as R2 2.01. 12
shock | and furious close of civil butchery, 1H4 1.01. 13
stand close. 2.02. 3 P
lay thine ear close to the ground, and list if 2.02. 32 P
here, hard by. stand close. 2.02. 75 P
stand close, i hear them coming. 2.02. 97 P
but i follow'd me close, came in, foot and hand, 2.04.217 P
what there is else, keep close, we'll read it at 2.04.542 P
wait close, i will not see him. 2H4 1.02. 57 P
if i can close with him, i care not for his 2.01. 18 P
this virtuous gentlewoman to close with us. 2.04.327 P
congreeing in a full and natural close, | like H5 1.02.182
as many lines close in the dial's centre; 1.02.210
keep close, i thee command. 2.03. 62
or close the wall up with our english dead. 3.01. 2
the english, in the suburbs close intrench'd, 1H6 1.04. 9
when death doth close his tender–dying eyes, 3.03. 48
my masters, let's stand close. 2H6 1.03. 1 P
away with them, let them be clapp'd up close, 1.04. 50
me leave | in this close walk to satisfy myself 2.02. 3
this is close dealing. 2.04. 73
and cry out for thee to close up mine eyes, | to 3.02.395
close up his eyes, and draw the curtain close, 3.03. 32
close up his eyes, and draw the curtain close, 3.03. 32
i vow by heaven these eyes shall never close. 3H6 1.01. 24
or is it fear | that makes him close his eyes? 1.03. 11
defy them then, or else hold close thy lips. 2.02.118
stand you thus close to steal the bishop's deer? 4.05. 17
as for another secret close intent | by marrying R3 1.01.158
no sleep close up that deadly eye of thine, 1.03.224
gold | will tempt unto a close exploit of death? 4.02. 35
i will take order for her keeping close. 4.02. 52
the son of clarence have i pent up close, | his 4.03. 36
let's stand close and behold him. H8 2.01. 55
stand close, the queen is coming. 4.01. 36
let 'em alone, and draw the curtain close; 5.02. 34
keep the door close, sirrah. 5.03. 30 P
stand close up, or i'll make your head ache. 5.03. 88
and 'twere dark you'd close sooner. TRO 3.02. 49 P
to close the day up, hector's life is done. 5.08. 8
the close enacts and counsels of thy heart! TIT 4.02.118
stop close their mouths, let them not speak a 5.02.164
and yours, close fighting ere i did approach. ROM 1.01.107
true) | but to himself so secret and so close, 1.01.149
hence will i to my ghostly /sire's close cell, 2.02.188
do thou but close our hands with holy words, 2.06. 6
follow me close, for i will speak to them. 3.01. 37
spread thy close curtain, love–performing night, 3.02. 5
holding thy ear close to the hollow ground, | so 5.03. 4
pray'd you | to hold your hand more close. TIM 2.02.139
up, | let your close fire predominate his smoke, 4.03.143
god, | that sold'rest close impossibilities, 4.03.387
i have a tree, which grows here in my close, 5.01.205
stand close a while, for here comes one in haste JC 1.03.131
it would become me better than to close | in 3.01.202
now sit we close about this taper here, | and 4.03.164
she'll close and be herself, whilest our poor MAC 3.02. 14
your charms, | the close contriver of all harms, 3.05. 7
observe her, stand close. 5.01. 20 P
which, being kept close, might move | more grief HAM 2.01.115
follow her close, give her good watch, i pray 4.05. 74
you do this, keep close within your chamber. 4.07.129
close pent–up guilts, | rive your concealing LR 3.02. 57
whose power | will close the eye of anguish. 4.04. 15
i found them close together | at blow and thrust OTH 2.03.237
in a man that's just | they're close dilations, 3.03.123
to seel her father's eyes up, close as oak, | he 3.03.210
you shall close prisoner rest, | till that the 5.02.335
fight, | follow me close, i'll bring you to't. ANT 4.04. 34
stand close, and list him. 4.09. 6
downy windows, close, | and golden phoebus never 5.02.316
fast to your affection, | still close as sure. CYM 1.06.139
she pray'd me to excuse her keeping close, 3.05. 46
close villain, | i'll have this secret from thy 3.05. 85
close by the battle, ditch'd, and wall'd with 5.03. 14
how close 'tis caulk'd and /bitum'd! PER 3.02. 56
without your noble hand to close mine eyes, | or TNK 2.02. 93
and there he shall keep close | till i provide 2.06. 6
there are you, | close in the thicket. 3.05. 13
i'll buckle't close. 3.06. 57
yet i keep close for all this, | close as a 4.01.130
i keep close for all this, | close as a cockle. 4.01.131
him i do not love that tells close offices | the 5.01.122
i'll close thine eyes, prince; 5.04. 96
she lifts the coffer–lids that close his eyes, VEN 1127
the curtains being close, about he walks, LUC 367
find | some purer chest to close so pure a mind. 761

CLOSED 2 FR 0.0002 REL FR 2 V 0 P
body | might in the ground be closed up in rest! 3H6 2.01. 76
be closed in our household's monument. TIT 5.03.194

CLOSELY 8 FR 0.0009 REL FR 8 V 0 P
i have been closely shrouded in this bush | and LLL 4.03.135
and therefore has he closely mew'd her up, SHR 1.01.183
go closely in with me; JN 4.01.132
follow fluellen closely at the heels. H5 4.07.171
this day should clarence closely be mew'd up R3 1.01. 38
intend | as closely to conceal what we impart. 3.01.159
vault, | meaning to keep her closely at my cell, ROM 5.03.255
for we have closely sent for hamlet hither, HAM 3.01. 29

CLOSENESS 1 FR 0.0001 REL FR 1 V 0 P
to closeness and the bettering of my mind | with TMP 1.02. 90

CLOSER 2 FR 0.0002 REL FR 2 V 0 P
no lady closer, for i well believe | thou wilt 1H4 2.03.110
fight closer or, good faith, you'll catch a blow 3H6 3.02. 23

CLOSES 5 FR 0.0005 REL FR 5 V 0 P
he closes with you in this consequence: HAM 2.01. 45
at "closes in the consequence." 2.01. 51
at "closes in the consequence," ay, marry. 2.01. 52
he closes thus: 2.01. 53
the marble pavement closes, he is enter'd | his CYM 5.04.120

CLOSEST 1 FR 0.0001 REL FR 1 V 0 P
fire that's closest kept burns most of all. TGV 1.02. 30

CLOSE–STOOL 2 FR 0.0002 REL FR 0 V 2 P
holds his poll–axe sitting on a close–stool, LLL 5.02.577 P
from fortune's close–stool to give to a nobleman AWW 5.02. 17 P

/CLOSET 1 FR 0.0001 REL FR 1 V 0 P
/i'll /to /thy /closet, /and /go /read /with TIT 3.02. 82

CLOSET 25 FR 0.0028 REL FR 14 V 11 P
go into this closet. WIV 1.04. 38 P
and vetch me in my closet /une /boite /en verd, 1.04. 45 P
dere is some simples in my closet, dat i vill 1.04. 63 P
vat is in my closet? 1.04. 67 P
what shall de honest man do in my closet? 1.04. 73 P
is no honest man dat shall come in my closet. 1.04. 74 P
but to my closet bring | the angry lords with JN 4.02.267
when you come into your closet, you'll question H5 5.02.198 P
and, in thy closet pent up, rue my shame, | and 2H6 2.04. 24
come, hastings, help me to my closet. R3 2.01.134
will you go with me into my closet | to help me ROM 4.02. 33
the taper burneth in your closet, sir. JC 2.01. 35
i found it in his closet, 'tis his will. 3.02.129
her night–gown upon her, unlock her closet, take MAC 5.01. 6 P
my lord, as i was sewing in my closet, | lord HAM 2.01. 74
speak with you in her closet ere you go to bed. 3.02.331 P
my lord, he's going to his mother's closet. 3.03. 27
from his mother's closet hath he dragg'd him. 4.01. 35
found it thrown in at the casement of my closet. LR 1.02. 61 P
i have lock'd the letter in my closet. 3.03. 11 P
a closet lock and key of villainous secrets; OTH 4.02. 22
and the primeroses, | bear to my closet. CYM 1.05. 84
fetch hither all my boxes in my closet. PER 3.02. 81
pure | doth in her poison'd closet yet endure." LUC 1659
lie | (a closet never pierc'd with crystal eyes) SON 46. 6

CLOSE–TONGU'D 1 FR 0.0001 REL FR 1 V 0 P
with close–tongu'd treason and the ravisher! LUC 770

CLOSET–WAR 1 FR 0.0001 REL FR 1 V 0 P
they call this bed–work, mapp'ry, closet–war, TRO 1.03.205

CLOSING 4 FR 0.0004 REL FR 4 V 0 P
and in the closing of some glorious day | be 1H4 3.02.133
knights, | with busy hammers closing rivets up, H5 4.pr. 13
the closing up of our most wretched eyes. TIT 3.01.262
this closing with him fits his lunacy. 5.02. 70

CLOSURE 4 FR 0.0004 REL FR 4 V 0 P
within the guilty closure of thy walls | richard R3 3.03. 11

souls, | and make a mutual closure of our house. TIT 5.03.134
run | into the quiet closure of my breast, | and VEN 782
art, | within the gentle closure of my breast, SON 48.11
CLOTEN 15 FR 0.0017 REL FR 15 V 0 P
that cloten, whose love–suit hath been to me CYM 3.04.133
know him, 'tis | cloten, the son o' th' queen. 4.02. 65
cloten, thou villain. 4.02. 88
cloten, thou double villain, be thy name, | i 4.02. 89
i am absolute | 'twas very cloten. 4.02.107
this cloten was a fool, an empty purse, | there 4.02.113
tell the fishes he's the queen's son, cloten. 4.02.153
for cloten | is quite forgot. 4.02.243
conspir'd with that irregulous devil cloten, 4.02.315
'tis he and cloten. 4.02.324
this is pisanio's deed, and cloten. 4.02.329
for cloten, | there wants no diligence in 4.03. 19
neither know i | what is betide to cloten, but 4.03. 40
though cloten then but young, you see, not wore 4.04. 23
lord cloten, | upon my lady's missing, came to 5.05.274
CLOTEN'S 4 FR 0.0004 REL FR 4 V 0 P
cut off one cloten's head, | son to the queen CYM 4.02.118
what cloten's being here to us portends, | or 4.02.182
i have sent cloten's clotpole down the stream 4.02.184
newness | of cloten's death (we being not known, 4.04. 10
CLOTENS 2 FR 0.0002 REL FR 2 V 0 P
color | i'ld let a parish of such clotens blood, CYM 4.02.168
more of thee merited than a band of clotens 5.05.304
CLOTH 13 FR 0.0014 REL FR 9 V 4 P
cloth a' gold and cuts, and lac'd with silver, ADO 3.04. 19 P
be scrap'd out of the painted cloth for this. LLL 5.02.576 P
but i answer you right painted cloth, from AYL 3.02.274 P
as ragged as lazarus in the painted cloth, where 1H4 4.02. 26 P
spoil his coat with scanting | a little cloth. H5 2.04. 48
this cloth thou dipp'dst in blood of my sweet 3H6 1.04.157
they that bear | the cloth of honor over her, H8 4.01. 48
this must be patch'd | with cloth of any color. COR 3.01.252
she did lie | in her pavilion — cloth of gold, ANT 2.02.199
a hilding for a livery, a squire's cloth, | a CYM 2.03.123
yea, bloody cloth, i'll keep thee, for i wish'd 5.01. 1
shrouded in cloth of state, balm'd and PER 3.02. 65
saw | shall by a painted cloth be kept in awe." LUC 245
CLOTHAIR 1 FR 0.0001 REL FR 1 V 0 P
blithild, which was daughter to king clothair, H5 1.02. 67
CLOTHARIUS 1 FR 0.0001 REL FR 1 V 0 P
had been councillors | to pepin or clotharius, H8 1.03. 10
CLOTH'D 2 FR 0.0002 REL FR 2 V 0 P
by your furtherance i am cloth'd in steel, | and PER 2.01.154
and you in ruff of your opinions cloth'd, | what STM II.C 79
CLOTHE 8 FR 0.0009 REL FR 8 V 0 P
to clothe mine age with angel–like perfection, TGV 2.04. 66
what 'tis to cram a maw or clothe a back | from MM 3.02. 22
go with me to clothe you as becomes you. SHR 4.02.121
and thus i clothe my naked villainy | with odd R3 1.03.335
but thy good spirits | to feed and clothe thee? HAM 3.02. 59
so shall i clothe me in a forc'd content, | and OTH 3.04.120
care no more to clothe and eat, | to thee the CYM 4.02.266
began to clothe his wit in state and pride, LUC 1809
CLOTHED 1 FR 0.0001 REL FR 1 V 0 P
clothed like a bride | for embracements even of PER 1.01. 6
CLOTHES *(also clo'es)*
/CLOTHES 1 FR 0.0001 REL FR 1 V 0 P
her desires | buys herself bread and /clothes. OTH 4.01. 95
CLOTHES 31 FR 0.0035 REL FR 12 V 19 P
go take up these clothes here quickly. WIV 3.03.146 P
me in the name of foul clothes to datchet–lane. 3.05. 99 P
for a search, and away went i for foul clothes. 3.05.106 P
with stinking clothes that fretted in their own 3.05.113 P
behold what honest clothes you send forth to 4.02.120 P
are you not asham'd? let the clothes alone. 4.02.139 P
will you take up your wive's clothes? 4.02.142 P
honest in nothing but in his clothes, and one MM 5.01.263 P
wrapp'd in sweet clothes, rings put upon his SHR in.1. 38
has my fellow tranio stol'n your clothes? 1.01.224 P
go to my chamber, put on clothes of mine. 3.02.113
to me she's married, not unto my clothes. 3.02.117
the soul of this man is his clothes. AWW 2.05. 44 P
or to drown my clothes, and say i was stripp'd. 4.01. 52 P
i have held familiarity with fresher clothes; 5.02. 3 P
these clothes are good enough to drink in, and TN 1.03. 11 P
see you these clothes? WT 5.02.130 P
hath this hotspur, mars in swathling clothes, 1H4 3.02.112
so 'a bade me lay more clothes on his feet. H5 2.03. 22 P
their clothes are after such a pagan cut to't, H8 1.03. 14
my mind gave me his clothes made a false report COR 4.05.151 P
dress'd, and in your clothes, and down again? ROM 4.05. 12
a fool in good clothes, and something like thee. TIM 2.02.108 P
her clothes spread wide, | and, mermaid–like, HAM 4.07.175
thorough tatter'd clothes /small vices do appear LR 4.06.164
i' th' swathing clothes the other, from their CYM 1.01. 59
will execute in the clothes that she so prais'd) 3.05.143 P
villain base, | know'st me not by my clothes? 4.02. 81
he made those clothes, | which, as it seems, 4.02. 82
speaks well, and has excellent good clothes; PER 4.02. 48 P
provide him necessaries and pack my clothes up, TNK 2.06. 32
CLOTHIER 1 FR 0.0001 REL FR 0 V 1 P
thee, jack cade the clothier means to dress the 2H6 4.02. 4 P
CLOTHIER'S 1 FR 0.0001 REL FR 0 V 1 P
draw me a clothier's yard. LR 4.06. 88 P
CLOTHIERS 1 FR 0.0001 REL FR 1 V 0 P
the clothiers all, not able to maintain | the H8 1.02. 31
CLOTHING 1 FR 0.0001 REL FR 1 V 0 P
for clothing me in these grave ornaments. 1H6 5.01. 54
CLOTHS 2 FR 0.0002 REL FR 1 V 1 P
in the flesh, set this in your painted cloths: TRO 5.10. 46 P
the fire and cloths. PER 3.02. 87
CLOTPOLE *(also clatpoles, clodpole)*
CLOTPOLE 2 FR 0.0002 REL FR 1 V 1 P
call the clotpole back. LR 1.04. 46 P
i have sent cloten's clotpole down the stream CYM 4.02.184
CLOUD 30 FR 0.0034 REL FR 26 V 4 P
yond same black cloud, yond huge one, looks like TMP 2.02. 20 P
yond same cloud cannot choose but fall by 2.02. 23 P
the sun, | and by and by a cloud takes all away. TGV 1.03. 87
worthies, away! the scene begins to cloud. LLL 5.02.721
let not the cloud of sorrow justle it | from 5.02.748
for my cloud of dignity | is held from falling 2H4 4.05. 98
thus sometimes hath the brightest day a cloud, 2H6 2.04. 1
doth cloud my joys with danger and with sorrow. 3H6 4.01. 74
i spy a black, suspicious, threat'ning cloud, 5.03. 4
a little gale will soon disperse that cloud, 5.03. 10
up, | for every cloud engenders not a storm. 5.03. 13
whose figure even this instant cloud puts on H8 1.01.225
shall call her from this cloud of darkness) 5.04. 44
o yes, and 'twere a cloud in autumn. TRO 1.02.126 P
should from yond cloud speak divine things, COR 4.05.104
face | blushing to be encount'red with a cloud. TIT 2.04. 32
one cloud of winter show'rs, | these flies are TIM 2.02.171
he goes away in a cloud; 3.04. 42
be, | and overcome us like a summer's cloud, MAC 3.04.110
see, | sits in a foggy cloud, and stays for me. 3.05. 35
do you see yonder cloud that's almost in shape HAM 3.02.376 P
he has a cloud in 's face. ANT 3.02. 51
sometime we see a cloud that's dragonish, | a 4.14. 2
dissolve, thick cloud, and rain, that i may say 5.02.299
why cloud they not their sights perpetually, PER 1.01. 74
to draw the cloud that hides the silver moon. LUC 371
rushing from forth a cloud, bereaves our sight, 373
when a black–fac'd cloud the world doth threat, 547
the region cloud hath mask'd him from me now. SON 33.12
not enough that through the cloud thou break, 34. 5
CLOUD–CAPP'D 1 FR 0.0001 REL FR 1 V 0 P
the cloud–capp'd tow'rs, the gorgeous palaces, TMP 4.01.152
CLOUD–ECLIPSED 1 FR 0.0001 REL FR 1 V 0 P
why her two suns were cloud–eclipsed so, | nor LUC 1224
CLOUDED 6 FR 0.0006 REL FR 6 V 0 P
my face is but a moon, and clouded too. LLL 5.02.203
to hear | my sovereign mistress clouded so, WT 1.02.280
hath clouded all thy happy days on earth. R2 3.02. 68
this world frowns, and edward's sun is clouded. 3H6 2.03. 7
had not his clouded with his brow's repine; VEN 490
the moon being clouded presently is miss'd, LUC 1007
CLOUDINESS 1 FR 0.0001 REL FR 1 V 0 P
so full of frost, of storm, and cloudiness? ADO 5.04. 42
CLOUD–KISSING 1 FR 0.0001 REL FR 1 V 0 P
threat'ning cloud–kissing ilion with annoy, LUC 1370
CLOUDS 69 FR 0.0078 REL FR 68 V 1 P
into the fire, to ride | on the curl'd clouds. TMP 1.02.192
the clouds methought would open and show riches 3.02.141
her deity | cutting the clouds towards paphos; 4.01. 93
blessed are clouds, to do as such clouds do! LLL 5.02.204
blessed are clouds, to do as such clouds do! 5.02.204
to shine | (those clouds removed) upon our 5.02.206
are angels /vailing clouds, or roses blown. 5.02.297
night's swift dragons cut the clouds full fast, MND 3.02.379
like far–off mountains turned into clouds. 4.01.188
as thunder when the clouds in autumn crack. SHR 1.02. 96
as the sun breaks through the darkest clouds, 4.03.173
brightest beams | distracted clouds give way, so AWW 5.03. 35
against th' /invulnerable clouds of heaven, JN 2.01.252
the uglier seem the clouds that in it fly. R2 1.01. 42
and sigh'd my english breath in foreign clouds, 3.01. 20
when he perceives the envious clouds are bent 3.03. 65
is mustering in his clouds on our behalf 3.03. 86
who doth permit the base contagious clouds | to 1H4 1.02.198
as if an angel /dropp'd down from the clouds 4.01.108
a naked subject to the weeping clouds | and 2H4 1.03. 61
of the wise sit in the clouds and mock us. 2.02.143 P
with deafing clamor in the slippery clouds, 3.01. 24
o'erblows the filthy and contagious clouds | of H5 3.03. 31
with their howls confus'd | do break the clouds, 3.03. 40
spirt up so suddenly into the clouds | and 3.05. 8
i thought as much, he would be above the clouds. 2H6 2.01. 15
and with the southern clouds contend in tears, 3.02.384
sun, | not separated with the racking clouds, 3H6 2.01. 27
when dying clouds contend with growing light, 2.05. 2
and all the clouds that low'r'd upon our house R3 1.01. 3
can curses pierce the clouds and enter heaven? 1.03.194
why then give way, dull clouds, to my quick 1.03.195
when clouds are seen, wise men put on their 2.03. 32
do through the clouds behold this present hour, 5.01. 8
towers, whose wanton tops do buss the clouds, TRO 4.05.220
by yond clouds, | let me deserve so ill as you, COR 3.01. 50
as sometime clouds | when they do hug him in TIT 3.01.212
adding to clouds more clouds with his deep sighs ROM 1.01.133
to clouds more clouds with his deep sighs, | but 1.01.133
when he bestrides the lazy puffing clouds, | and 2.02. 31
the eastern clouds with streaks of light, | and 2.03. 2
that gallant spirit hath aspir'd the clouds, 3.01.117
do lace the severing clouds in yonder east. 3.05. 8
is there no pity sitting in the clouds, | that 3.05.196
seeing she is advanc'd | above the clouds, as 4.05. 74
to be exalted with the threat'ning clouds; JC 1.03. 8
looks in the clouds, scorning the base degrees 2.01. 26
that fret the clouds are messengers of day. 2.01.104
fierce fiery warriors fight upon the clouds | in 2.02. 19
day is gone, | clouds, dews, and dangers come; 5.03. 64
how is it that the clouds still hang on you? HAM 1.02. 66
but the great cannon to the clouds shall tell, 1.02.126
feeds on this wonder, keeps himself in clouds, 4.05. 89
hands, and tongues applaud it to the clouds, 4.05.108
the chidden billow seems to pelt the clouds, OTH 2.01. 12
bore heads so high they kiss'd the clouds, | and PER 1.04. 24
the fift, an hand environed with clouds, 2.02. 36
leave 'em all behind us | like lazy clouds, TNK 2.02. 14
in hallowed clouds commend their swelling 5.01. 4
with hand armipotent from forth blue clouds 5.01. 54
and coal–black clouds that shadow heaven's light VEN 533
whose ridges with the meeting clouds contend: 820
like many clouds consulting for foul weather. 972
knit poisonous clouds about his golden head. LUC 777
her contrite sighs unto the clouds bequeathed 1727
dost him grace when clouds do blot the heaven; SON 28.10
anon permit the basest clouds to ride | with 33. 5
to let base clouds o'ertake me in my way, 34. 3
clouds and eclipses stain both moon and sun, 35. 3
CLOUDY 16 FR 0.0018 REL FR 15 V 1 P
in us all, good sir, | when you are cloudy. TMP 2.01.143
at meeting tears the cloudy cheeks of heaven. R2 3.03. 57
aspect | as cloudy men use to their adversaries, 1H4 3.02. 83
and suffolk's cloudy brow his stormy hate; 2H6 3.01.155
dark cloudy death o'ershades his beams of life, 3H6 2.06. 62
whose bright out–shining beams thy cloudy wrath R3 1.03.267
you cloudy princes and heart–sorrowing peers 2.02.112
clear up, fair queen, that cloudy countenance; TIT 1.01.263
eye, | my silence, an' my cloudy melancholy, 2.03. 33
west, | and bring in cloudy night immediately. ROM 3.02. 4
i," | the cloudy messenger turns me his back, MAC 3.06. 41
and the brine and cloudy billow kiss the moon, i PER 3.01. 45 P
thy lips | make modest dian cloudy and forlorn, VEN 725
no cloudy show of stormy blust'ring weather LUC 115
but cloudy lucrece shames herself to see, | and 1084
be bent, | her cloudy looks will calm yer night, PP 18.26
CLOUT 7 FR 0.0008 REL FR 3 V 4 P
must shoot nearer, or he'll ne'er hit the clout. LLL 4.01.134
would have clapp'd i' th' clout at twelve score, 2H4 3.02. 46 P
them, gav'st the duke a clout | steep'd in the R3 1.03.176
looks as pale as any clout in the versal world. ROM 2.04.206 P
a clout upon that head | where late the diadem HAM 2.02.506
i' th' clout, i' th' clout — hewgh! LR 4.06. 92 P
i' th' clout, i' th' clout — hewgh! 4.06. 92 P
CLOUTED 2 FR 0.0002 REL FR 2 V 0 P
spare none but such as go in clouted shoon, 2H6 4.02.185
and put | my clouted brogues from off my feet, CYM 4.02.214
CLOUTS 2 FR 0.0002 REL FR 2 V 0 P
son, | or madly think a babe of clouts were he. JN 3.04. 58
them home | with clouts about their heads. ANT 4.07. 6
CLOVEN 6 FR 0.0006 REL FR 3 V 3 P
her most unmitigable rage, | into a cloven pine; TMP 1.02.277
who with cloven tongues | do hiss me into 2.02. 13
no, cloven. LLL 5.02.649 P
and puts me her white hand to his cloven chin — TRO 1.02.119 P
juno have mercy! how came it cloven? 1.02.120 P
what work he makes | amongst your cloven army. COR 1.04. 21
CLOVER 1 FR 0.0001 REL FR 1 V 0 P
the freckled cowslip, burnet, and green clover, H5 5.02. 49
CLOVES 1 FR 0.0001 REL FR 0 V 1 P
stuck with cloves. LLL 5.02.648 P
CLOVEST 1 FR 0.0001 REL FR 0 V 1 P
when thou clovest thy /crown i' th' middle and LR 1.04.160 P
CLOWDER 1 FR 0.0001 REL FR 1 V 0 P
and couple clowder with the deep–mouth'd brach. SHR in.1. 18
/CLOWN 1 FR 0.0001 REL FR 0 V 1 P
/the /clown /shall /make /those /laugh /whose HAM 2.02.323 P
CLOWN 12 FR 0.0013 REL FR 5 V 7 P
by my soul, a swain, a most simple clown! LLL 4.01.140
the clown bore it, the fool sent it, and the 4.03. 15 P
sweet clown, sweeter fool, sweetest lady! 4.03. 17 P
my lord, the roynish clown, at whom so oft AYL 2.02. 8
holla! you clown! 2.04. 66
it is meat and drink to me to see a clown. 5.01. 10 P
therefore, you clown, abandon — which is in the 5.01. 47 P
of this female, or, clown, thou perishest; 5.01. 51 P
my clown (who wants but something to be a WT 4.04.604 P
out the burly–bon'd clown in chines of beef ere 2H6 4.10. 57 P
then the beast–eating clown, and next the fool, TNK 3.05.131
and a down, | say the schoolmaster's no clown. 3.05.141
CLOWNISH 1 FR 0.0001 REL FR 1 V 0 P
the clownish fool out of your father's court? AYL 1.03.130
CLOWNS 1 FR 0.0001 REL FR 0 V 1 P
those that play your clowns speak no more than HAM 3.02. 39 P
CLOY 4 FR 0.0004 REL FR 4 V 0 P
or cloy the hungry edge of appetite | by bare R2 1.03.296
revenge, | and now i cloy me with beholding it. R3 4.04. 62
other women cloy | the appetites they feed, but ANT 2.02.235
"and yet not cloy thy lips with loath'd saciety, VEN 19
/CLOY'D 1 FR 0.0001 REL FR 1 V 0 P
/mine /eyes /are /cloy'd /with /view /of TIT 3.02. 55
CLOY'D 5 FR 0.0005 REL FR 4 V 1 P
if you be not too much cloy'd with fat meat, our 2H4 ep 27 P
he hath dull'd and cloy'd with gracious favors H5 2.02. 9
when they are cloy'd | with long continuance in 1H6 2.05.105
eyes | and ears so cloy'd importantly as now, CYM 4.04. 19
that cloy'd with much, he pineth still for more. LUC 98
CLOYED 1 FR 0.0001 REL FR 1 V 0 P
the cloyed will — | that satiate yet CYM 1.06. 47
CLOYLESS 1 FR 0.0001 REL FR 1 V 0 P
sharpen with cloyless sauce his appetite, | that ANT 2.01. 25
CLOYMENT 1 FR 0.0001 REL FR 1 V 0 P
that suffer surfeit, cloyment, and revolt, | but TN 2.04. 99
CLOYS 1 FR 0.0001 REL FR 1 V 0 P
prunes the immortal wing and cloys his beak, CYM 5.04.118
CLUB 9 FR 0.0010 REL FR 4 V 5 P
and have cleft his club to make the fire too. ADO 2.01.254 P
where his codpiece seems as massy as his club? 3.03.138 P
butt–shaft is too hard for hercules' club, and LLL 1.02.176 P
thumb, he is not so big as the end of his club. 5.01.132 P
whose club kill'd cerberus, that three–headed 5.02.589
had his brains dash'd out with a grecian club, AYL 4.01. 98 P
as with a club, dash out my desp'rate brains? ROM 4.03. 54
those hands, that grasp'd the heaviest club, ANT 4.12. 46
(then weaker than your eyes) laid by his club; TNK 1.01. 67
CLUBS 8 FR 0.0009 REL FR 6 V 2 P
clubs cannot part them. AYL 5.02. 41 P
i'll call for clubs, if you will not away. 1H6 1.03. 84
and hit that woman, who cried out "clubs!", H8 5.03. 51 P
where go you | with bats and clubs? COR 1.01. 56
but make you ready your stiff bats and clubs, 1.01.161
clubs, clubs! TIT 2.01. 37
clubs, clubs! 2.01. 37
clubs, bills, and partisans! ROM 1.01. 73
CLUCK'D 1 FR 0.0001 REL FR 1 V 0 P
has cluck'd thee to the wars, and safely home COR 5.03.163
CLUNG 1 FR 0.0001 REL FR 1 V 0 P
lighted, how they clung | in their embracement, H8 1.01. 9
CLUSTERS 2 FR 0.0002 REL FR 2 V 0 P
and cowardly nobles gave way unto your clusters, COR 4.06.122
here come the clusters. 4.06.128
CLUST'RING 3 FR 0.0003 REL FR 3 V 0 P
i'll bring thee | to clust'ring filberts, and TMP 2.02.171
vines with clust'ring bunches growing, | plants 4.01.112
into the clust'ring battle of the french; 1H6 4.07. 13
CLUTCH 3 FR 0.0003 REL FR 3 V 0 P
not that i have the power to clutch my hand JN 2.01.589
come, let me clutch thee: MAC 2.01. 34
stealing steps | hath clawed me in his clutch, HAM 5.01. 72
CLUTCH'D 2 FR 0.0002 REL FR 1 V 1 P
hand in the pocket and extracting /it clutch'd? MM 3.02. 47 P
in thy hands clutch'd as many millions, in | thy COR 3.03. 71
CLYSTER–PIPES 1 FR 0.0001 REL FR 0 V 1 P
would they were clyster–pipes for your sake! OTH 2.01.177 P
CLYTUS 2 FR 0.0002 REL FR 0 V 2 P
angers, look you, kill his best friend, clytus. H5 4.07. 39 P

as alexander kill'd his friend clytus, being in 4.07. 45 P
CNEIUS 1 FR 0.0001 REL FR 1 V 0 P
nay, you were a fragment | of cneius pompey's — ANT 3.13.118
COACH 6 FR 0.0006 REL FR 3 V 3 P
i warrant you, coach after coach, letter after WIV 2.02. 65 P
i warrant you, coach after coach, letter after 2.02. 65 P
weep, | no drop but as a coach doth carry thee; LLL 4.03. 33
all my whole device | when i am in my coach, MV 3.04. 82
gallops the zodiac in his glistering coach, TIT 2.01. 7
come, my coach! HAM 4.05. 72 P
/COACHES 1 FR 0.0001 REL FR 1 V 0 P
your eyes do make no /coaches; LLL 4.03.153
COACHES 1 FR 0.0001 REL FR 0 V 1 P
and lords, and gentlemen, with their coaches; WIV 2.02. 64 P
COACH–FELLOW 1 FR 0.0001 REL FR 0 V 1 P
reprieves for you and your coach–fellow nym; WIV 2.02. 8 P
COACHMAKERS 1 FR 0.0001 REL FR 1 V 0 P
time out a' mind the fairies' coachmakers. ROM 1.04. 61
//CO–ACT 1 FR 0.0001 REL FR 1 V 0 P
but if i tell how these two did //co–act, TRO 5.02.118
CO–ACTIVE 1 FR 0.0001 REL FR 1 V 0 P
with what's unreal thou co–active art, | and WT 1.02.141
COAGULATE 1 FR 0.0001 REL FR 1 V 0 P
fire, | and thus o'er–sized with coagulate gore, HAM 2.02.462
COAL 11 FR 0.0012 REL FR 10 V 1 P
there is no malice in this burning coal; JN 4.01.108
your breath first kindled the dead coal of wars 5.02. 83
at his nose, and it is like a coal of fire, H5 3.06.104 P
have blown this coal betwixt my lord and me — H8 2.04. 79
you charge me | that i have blown this coal. 2.04. 94
no, | than is the coal of fire upon the ice, COR 1.01.173
if he could burn us all into one coal, | we have 4.06.137
the cat, with eyne of burning coal, | now PER 3.ch. 5
glow, | even as a dying coal revives with wind, VEN 338
affection is a coal that must be cool'd, | else, 387
to quench the coal which in his liver glows. LUC 47
//COAL–BLACK 1 FR 0.0001 REL FR 1 V 0 P
/comes /in /likeness /of /a //coal–black /moor. TIT 3.02. 78
COAL–BLACK 7 FR 0.0008 REL FR 7 V 0 P
and some will mourn in ashes, some coal–black, R2 5.01. 49
black, forsooth, coal–black as jet. 2H6 2.01.110
this hand, fast wound about thy coal–black hair, 3H6 5.01. 54
coal–black is better than another hue, | in that TIT 4.02. 99
they never do beget a coal–black calf. 5.01. 32
and coal–black clouds that shadow heaven's light VEN 533
"the crow may bathe his coal–black wings in mire LUC 1009
COALS 10 FR 0.0011 REL FR 7 V 3 P
shortly have a rasher on the coals for money. MV 3.05. 25 P
stars, stars, | and all eyes else dead coals! WT 5.01. 68
that piece of service the men would carry coals. H5 3.02. 47 P
bosoms of our part | hot coals of vengeance! 2H6 5.02. 36
is kindling coals that fires all my breast, 3H6 2.01. 83
and add more coals to cancer when he burns TRO 2.03.196
have wrack'd for rome | to make coals cheap! COR 5.01. 17
gregory, on my word, we'll not carry coals. ROM 1.01. 1 P
she red and hot as coals of glowing fire, | he VEN 35
like dying coals burnt out in tedious nights. LUC 1379
COARSE 3 FR 0.0003 REL FR 3 V 0 P
i feel | of what coarse metal ye are moulded, H8 3.02.239
you most coarse frieze capacities, ye /jane TNK 3.05. 8
but this poor petticoat and two coarse smocks. 5.02. 84
COARSELY 1 FR 0.0001 REL FR 1 V 0 P
serves the count | reports but coarsely of her. AWW 3.05. 57
COAST 21 FR 0.0023 REL FR 20 V 1 P
and travelling along this coast, i here am come LLL 5.02.554
for the four winds blow in from every coast MV 1.01.168
that appear'd upon the coast on we'nsday the WT 4.04.276 P
with some few private friends upon this coast. R2 3.03. 4
see the coast clear'd, and then we will depart. 1H6 1.03. 89
yet have i gold flies from another coast — | i 2H6 1.02. 93
for losing ken of albion's wished coast. 3.02.113
spare england, for it is your native coast. 4.08. 50
i'll undertake to land them on our coast, | and 3H6 3.03.205
hath rais'd in gallia have arriv'd our coast, 5.03. 8
on the western coast | rideth a puissant navy; R3 4.04.433
him) he was carried | from off our coast, twice CYM 3.01. 26
to show what coast thy sluggish /crare | mightst 4.02.205
are landed on your coast, with a supply | of 4.03. 25
lost, | by waves from coast to coast is toss'd. PER 2.ch. 34
lost, | by waves from coast to coast is toss'd. 2.ch. 34
may see the sea hath cast upon your coast — 2.01. 56
i thank thee. mariner, say, what coast is this? 3.01. 72
and on this coast | suppose him now at anchor. 5.ch. 15
upon this coast, i warrant you. 5.03. 20
from the south, | from the coast of barbary–a; TNK 3.05. 60
COASTETH 1 FR 0.0001 REL FR 1 V 0 P
and all in haste she coasteth to the cry. VEN 870
COASTING 2 FR 0.0002 REL FR 2 V 0 P
asia, | and, coasting homeward, came to ephesus; ERR 1.01.134
that give a coasting welcome ere it comes, | and TRO 4.05. 59
COASTS 3 FR 0.0003 REL FR 3 V 0 P
him, how he coasts | and hedges his own way. H8 3.02. 38
sky–planted, batters all rebelling coasts? CYM 5.04. 96
to th' ports and coasts for transportation, STM II.C 76
COAT 33 FR 0.0037 REL FR 20 V 13 P
may give the dozen white luces in their coat. WIV 1.01. 17 P
it is an old coat. 1.01. 18 P
dozen white louses do become an old coat well; 1.01. 20 P
is the fresh fish, the salt fish is an old coat. 1.01. 23 P
if he has a quarter of your coat, there is but 1.01. 29 P
there's a hole made in your best coat, master 3.05.141 P
each fair installment, coat, and sev'ral crest, 5.05. 63
since i see you fearful, that neither my coat, MM 4.02.189 P
show a child his new coat and forbid him to wear ADO 3.02. 7 P
i could shake them off my coat; AYL 1.03. 16 P
their discharge did stretch his leathern coat 2.01. 37
i am ambitious for a motley coat. 2.07. 43
nathaniel's coat, sir, was not fully made, | and SHR 4.01.132
saw myself unbreech'd | in my green velvet coat, WT 1.02.156
if this be a horseman's coat, it hath seen very 4.03. 68 P
point, | that it may enter mowbray's waxen coat, R2 1.03. 75
from my own windows torn my household coat, 3.01. 24
shoulders like a herald's coat without sleeves; 1H4 4.02. 44 P
covering discretion with a coat of folly, | as H5 2.04. 38
doth like a miser spoil his coat with scanting 2.04. 47
if i find a hole in his coat, i will tell him my 3.06. 84 P
arms, | of england's coat one half is cut away. 1H6 1.01. 81
give me my steeled coat, i'll fight for france. 1.01. 85
or tear the lions out of england's coat; 1.05. 28
not fear the sword, for his coat is of proof. 2H6 4.02. 61 P
but thou shalt wear it as a herald's coat, | to 4.10. 70
in a long motley coat guarded with yellow, H8 pr 16
your long coat, priest, protects you, thou 3.02.276
but that my coat is better than thou know'st. OTH 5.01. 25
to beg of you, kind friends, this coat of worth, PER 2.01.136
i'll cut my green coat a foot above my knee, TNK 3.04. 19
survive, | and be an eye–sore in my golden coat; LUC 205
for she was sought by spirits of richest coat, LC 236
COATS 17 FR 0.0019 REL FR 14 V 3 P
be, | in their gold coats spots you see: MND 2.01. 11
leathren wings | to make my small elves coats, 2.02. 5
two of the first, /like coats in heraldry, | due 3.02.213
be slickly comb'd, their blue coats brush'd, and SHR 4.01. 91 P
with silken coats and caps, and golden rings, 4.03. 55
would not be in some of your coats for twopence. TN 4.01. 31 P
the lining of his coffers shall make coats | to R2 1.04. 61
glittering in golden coats like images, | as 1H4 4.01.100
the king hath many marching in his coats. 5.03. 25
now, by my sword, i will kill all his coats; 5.03. 26
bardolph, give the soldiers coats. 2H4 3.02.291 P
investing lank–lean cheeks and war–worn coats, H5 4.pr. 26
the gay new coats o'er the french soldiers' 4.03.118
privileged place — | blue coats to tawny coats! 1H6 1.03. 47
privileged place — | blue coats to tawny coats! 1.03. 47
shall we go throw away our coats of steel, | and 3H6 2.01.160
and when they have lin'd their coats, | do OTH 1.01. 53
COBBLE 1 FR 0.0001 REL FR 0 V 1 P
why, sir, cobble you. JC 1.01. 19 P
COBBLED 1 FR 0.0001 REL FR 1 V 0 P
not in their liking | below their cobbled shoes. COR 1.01.196
COBBLER 2 FR 0.0002 REL FR 1 V 1 P
workman, i am but, as you would say, a cobbler. JC 1.01. 11 P
thou art a cobbler, art thou? 1.01. 20
COBHAM 4 FR 0.0004 REL FR 4 V 0 P
that harry duke of herford, rainold lord cobham, R2 2.01.279
stand forth, dame eleanor cobham, gloucester's 2H6 2.03. 1
you, edward, shall unto my lord cobham, | with 3H6 1.02. 40
let noble warwick, cobham, and the rest, | whom 1.02. 56
COBLOAF 1 FR 0.0001 REL FR 0 V 1 P
cobloaf! TRO 2.01. 38 P
COBWEB 6 FR 0.0006 REL FR 2 V 4 P
cobweb! MND 3.01.162
cobweb. 3.01.181
you of more acquaintance, good master cobweb. 3.01.183 P
where's mounsieur cobweb? 4.01. 8 P
mounsieur cobweb, good mounsieur, get you your 4.01. 10 P
but to help cavalery cobweb to scratch. 4.01. 23 P
COBWEBS 2 FR 0.0002 REL FR 1 V 1 P
hearts of men | faster than gnats in cobwebs. MV 3.02.123
rushes strew'd, cobwebs swept, the servingmen in SHR 4.01. 46 P
COCK* 28 FR 0.0031 REL FR 17 V 11 P
the old cock. TMP 2.01. 30 P
wont, when you laugh'd, to crow like a cock; TGV 2.01. 27 P
by cock and pie, you shall not choose, sir! WIV 1.01.303 P
and look thou meet me ere the first cock crow. MND 2.01.267
the woosel cock so black of hue, | with 3.01.125
of what kind should this cock come of? AYL 2.07. 90
a combless cock, so kate will be my hen. SHR 2.01.226
no cock of mine, you crow too like a craven. 2.01.227
none, sir; i have no pheasant cock, nor hen. WT 4.04.744 P
bit than i have been since the first cock. 1H4 2.01. 18 P
by cock and pie, sir, you shall not away 2H4 5.01. 1 P
for i can take, and pistol's cock is up, | and H5 2.01. 52
the early village cock | hath twice done R3 5.03.209
the second cock hath crowed, | the curfew–bell ROM 4.04. 3
i have retir'd me to a wasteful cock | and set TIM 2.02.162
sir, we were carousing till the second cock; MAC 2.03. 25 P
it was about to speak, when the cock crew. HAM 1.01.147
i have heard | the cock, that is the trumpet to 1.01.150
it faded on the crowing of the cock. 1.01.157
but even then the morning cock crew loud, | and 1.02.218
if they come to't, | by cock, they are to blame. 4.05. 61
at curfew, and walks /till /the first cock; LR 3.04.116 P
tall anchoring bark, | diminish'd to her cock; 4.06. 19
her cock, a buoy | almost too small for sight. 4.06. 19
go up and down like a cock that nobody can match CYM 2.01. 21 P
you are cock and capon too, and you crow, cock, 2.01. 23 P
too, and you crow, cock, with your comb on. 2.01. 24 P
the cock that treads them shall not know. PP 18.40
COCK–A–DIDDLE–DOW 1 FR 0.0001 REL FR 1 V 0 P
cock–a–diddle–dow. TMP 1.02.387
COCK–A–HOOP 1 FR 0.0001 REL FR 1 V 0 P
you will set cock–a–hoop! ROM 1.05. 81
COCKATRICE' 1 FR 0.0001 REL FR 1 V 0 P
here with a cockatrice' dead–killing eye | he LUC 540
COCKATRICE 2 FR 0.0002 REL FR 2 V 0 P
a cockatrice hast thou hatch'd to the world, R3 4.01. 54
than the death/–darting eye of cockatrice. ROM 3.02. 47
COCKATRICES 1 FR 0.0001 REL FR 0 V 1 P
kill one another by the look, like cockatrices. TN 3.04.196 P
COCKLE* 5 FR 0.0005 REL FR 5 V 0 P
sow'd cockle reap'd no corn, | and justice LLL 4.03.380
why, 'tis a cockle or a walnut–shell, | a knack, SHR 4.03. 66
'gainst our senate | the cockle of rebellion, COR 3.01. 70
by his cockle hat and staff, | and his sandal HAM 4.05. 25
i keep close for all this, | close as a cockle. TNK 4.01.131
COCKLED 1 FR 0.0001 REL FR 1 V 0 P
than are the tender horns of cockled snails. LLL 4.03.335
COCKLES 1 FR 0.0001 REL FR 1 V 0 P
sail seas in cockles, have and wish but for't, PER 4.04. 2
COCKLESHELL 1 FR 0.0001 REL FR 1 V 0 P
then would i make | a carreck of a cockleshell, TNK 3.04. 14
COCKLIGHT 1 FR 0.0001 REL FR 1 V 0 P
for i must lose my maidenhead by cocklight, TNK 4.01.112
COCKNEY 2 FR 0.0002 REL FR 0 V 2 P
great lubber, the world, will prove a cockney. TN 4.01. 15 P
as the cockney did to the eels when she put 'em LR 2.04.122 P
COCK–PIGEON 1 FR 0.0001 REL FR 0 V 1 P
of thee than a barbary cock–pigeon over his hen, AYL 4.01.150 P
COCKPIT 1 FR 0.0001 REL FR 1 V 0 P
can this cockpit hold | the vasty fields of H5 pr 11
COCK'RED 1 FR 0.0001 REL FR 1 V 0 P
a cock'red silken wanton, brave our fields, JN 5.01. 70
COCK'REL 1 FR 0.0001 REL FR 0 V 1 P
the cock'rel. TMP 2.01. 31 P
COCK'REL'S 1 FR 0.0001 REL FR 1 V 0 P
a bump as big as a young cock'rel's stone — | a ROM 1.03. 53
COCK'S* 2 FR 0.0002 REL FR 0 V 2 P
and therefore be not — cock's passion, silence! SHR 4.01.118 P
if the springe hold, the cock's mine. WT 4.03. 35 P
COCKS 3 FR 0.0003 REL FR 3 V 0 P
the country cocks do crow, the clocks do toll, H5 4.pr. 15
have drench'd our steeples, /drown'd the cocks! LR 3.02. 3
his cocks do win the battle still of mine, ANT 2.03. 37
COCK–SHUT 1 FR 0.0001 REL FR 1 V 0 P
much about cock–shut time, from troop to troop R3 5.03. 70
COCK–SURE 1 FR 0.0001 REL FR 0 V 1 P
we steal as in a castle, cock–sure; 1H4 2.01. 86 P
COCTUS 1 FR 0.0001 REL FR 0 V 1 P
twice sod simplicity, bis coctus! LLL 4.02. 22 P
/COCYTUS' 1 FR 0.0001 REL FR 1 V 0 P
as hateful as /cocytus' misty mouth. TIT 2.03.236
CODDING 1 FR 0.0001 REL FR 1 V 0 P
that codding spirit had they from their mother, TIT 5.01. 99
CODLING 1 FR 0.0001 REL FR 0 V 1 P
peascod, or a codling when 'tis almost an apple. TN 1.05.158 P
CODPIECE 7 FR 0.0008 REL FR 3 V 4 P
you must needs have them with a codpiece, madam. TGV 2.07. 53
unless you have a codpiece to stick pins on. 2.07. 56
for the rebellion of a codpiece to take away the MM 3.02.115 P
where his codpiece seems as massy as his club? ADO 3.03.137 P
'twas nothing to geld a codpiece of a purse; WT 4.04.611 P
the codpiece that will house | before the head LR 3.02. 27
here's grace and a codpiece — that's a wise man 3.02. 40 P
CODPIECES 1 FR 0.0001 REL FR 1 V 0 P
dread prince of plackets, king of codpieces, LLL 3.01.184
COD'S 1 FR 0.0001 REL FR 1 V 0 P
to change the cod's head for the salmon's tail; OTH 2.01.155
CODS 1 FR 0.0001 REL FR 0 V 1 P
from whom i took two cods and, giving her them AYL 2.04. 52 P
CO–EQUAL 1 FR 0.0001 REL FR 1 V 0 P
he'll make his cap co–equal with the crown." 1H6 5.01. 33
COEUR–DE–LION *(see cordelion, etc.)*
COFFER 8 FR 0.0009 REL FR 6 V 2 P
her as the key of the cuckoldly rogue's coffer, WIV 2.02.274 P
neither press, coffer, chest, trunk, well, vault 4.02. 61 P
dow'r | remaining in the coffer of her friends, MM 1.02.151
half | comes to the privy coffer of the state, MV 4.01.354
hold, there's half my coffer. TN 3.04.347
than the rich–jewell'd coffer of darius, 1H6 1.06. 25
great gifts, | and all out of an empty coffer; TIM 1.02.193
certain jewels | lay with you in your coffer, PER 3.04. 2
COFFER–LIDS 1 FR 0.0001 REL FR 1 V 0 P
she lifts the coffer–lids that close his eyes, VEN 1127
COFFERS 13 FR 0.0014 REL FR 11 V 2 P
my bed shall be abus'd, my coffers ransack'd, my WIV 2.02.293 P
and in the chambers, and in the coffers, and in 3.03.211 P
in ivory coffers i have stuff'd my crowns; SHR 2.01.350
and, for our coffers, with too great a court R2 1.04. 43
the lining of his coffers shall make coats | to 1.04. 61
shall our coffers then | be emptied to redeem a 1H4 1.03. 85
and his coffers sound | with hollow poverty and 2H4 1.03. 74
and to the coffers of the king beside, | a H5 1.01. 18
and from his coffers | receiv'd the golden 2.02.168
whose ransoms did the general coffers fill; JC 3.02. 89
iago, | go to the bay and disembark my coffers. OTH 2.01.208
self exhibition | which your own coffers yield; CYM 1.06.123
"the aged man that coffers up his gold | is LUC 855
COFFIN 11 FR 0.0012 REL FR 10 V 1 P
at my foot, and the ducats in her coffin! MV 3.01. 90 P
sweet, | on my black coffin let there be strown. TN 2.04. 60
within this coffin i present | thy buried fear. R2 5.06. 30
upon a wooden coffin we attend, | and death's 1H6 1.01. 19
my lord, stand back, and let the coffin pass. R3 1.02. 38
paste, | and of the paste a coffin i will rear, TIT 5.02.188
my heart is in the coffin there with caesar, JC 3.02.106
and bid nicander | bring me the satin coffin. PER 3.01. 67
'tis like a coffin, sir. 3.02. 52
understand, | if e'er this coffin drives a–land, 3.02. 69
i op'd the coffin, | found there rich jewels, 5.03. 23
COFFIN'D 2 FR 0.0002 REL FR 2 V 0 P
thou have laugh'd had i come coffin'd home, COR 2.01.176
straight | must cast thee, scarcely coffin'd, in PER 3.01. 60
COFFINS 2 FR 0.0002 REL FR 2 V 0 P
and hung their rotten coffins up in chains, | it 3H6 1.03. 28
his valiant sons | in coffins from the field, TIT 1.01. 35
CO'FIL' 1 FR 0.0001 REL FR 0 V 1 P
we'll to sutton co'fil' to–night. 1H4 4.02. 3 P
COG 7 FR 0.0008 REL FR 5 V 2 P
mistress ford, i cannot cog, i cannot prate, WIV 3.03. 48 P
i cannot cog and say thou art this and that, 3.03. 70 P
that lie and cog and flout, deprave and slander, ADO 5.01. 95
since you can cog, i'll play no more with you. LLL 5.02.235
smile in men's faces, smooth, deceive, and cog, R3 1.03. 48
cog their hearts from them, and come home COR 3.02.133
ay, and you hear him cog, see him dissemble, TIM 5.01. 95
COGGING 3 FR 0.0003 REL FR 2 V 1 P
scurvy, cogging companion, the host of the WIV 3.01.120 P
come both you cogging greeks, have at you both! TRO 5.06. 11
some cogging, cozening slave, to get some office OTH 4.02.132
COGITATION 1 FR 0.0001 REL FR 1 V 0 P
(for cogitation | resides not in that man that WT 1.02.271
COGITATIONS 1 FR 0.0001 REL FR 1 V 0 P
thoughts of great value, worthy cogitations. JC 1.02. 50
COGNITION 1 FR 0.0001 REL FR 1 V 0 P
be myself, nor have cognition | of what i feel; TRO 5.02. 63
COGNIZANCE 3 FR 0.0003 REL FR 3 V 0 P
rose, | as cognizance of my blood–drinking hate, 1H6 2.04.108
for tinctures, stains, relics, and cognizance. JC 2.02. 89
the cognizance of her incontinency | is this. CYM 2.04.127
COGSCOMB *(also coxcomb)*
COGSCOMB 1 FR 0.0001 REL FR 0 V 1 P
about your knave's cogscomb /for /missing /your WIV 3.01. 89 P
CO–HEIRS 1 FR 0.0001 REL FR 1 V 0 P
they are co–heirs, | and i had rather glib WT 2.01.148
COHER'D 1 FR 0.0001 REL FR 1 V 0 P
had time coher'd with place, or place with MM 2.01. 11
COHERE 1 FR 0.0001 REL FR 1 V 0 P
fortune, do cohere and jump | that i am viola — TN 5.01.252
COHERENCE 1 FR 0.0001 REL FR 0 V 1 P

see the semblable coherence of his men's spirits 2H4 5.01. 65 P
COHERENT 1 FR 0.0001 REL FR 1 V 0 P
with this deceit so lawful | may prove coherent. AWW 3.07. 39
/COHORTS 1 FR 0.0001 REL FR 0 V 1 P
/of /friends, /dissipation /of /cohorts, LR 1.02.148 P
COIF *(also quoifs)*
COIF 1 FR 0.0001 REL FR 1 V 0 P
and hence, thou sickly coif! 2H4 1.01.147
COIGN 2 FR 0.0002 REL FR 1 V 1 P
see you yond coign a' th' capitol, yond COR 5.04. 1 P
buttress, nor coign of vantage, but this bird MAC 1.06. 7
/COIGNS 1 FR 0.0001 REL FR 1 V 0 P
by the four opposing /coigns | which the world PER 3.ch. 17
COIL 12 FR 0.0013 REL FR 10 V 2 P
that this coil | would not infect his reason? TMP 1.02.207
here is a coil with protestation! TGV 1.02. 96
what a coil is there, dromio? ERR 3.01. 48
there to–morrow, there is a great coil to–night. ADO 3.03. 94 P
come to your uncle, yonder's old coil at home. 5.02. 96 P
you, mistress, all this coil is long of you. MND 3.02.339
and kept a coil with | "too young" and "the next AWW 2.01. 27
i am not worth this coil that's made for me. JN 2.01.165
and wilt thou have a reason for this coil? TIT 3.01.224
here's such a coil! come, what says romeo? ROM 2.05. 65
when we have shuffled off this mortal coil, HAM 3.01. 66
and there, | lord, what a coil he keeps! TNK 2.04. 18
COIL'S 1 FR 0.0001 REL FR 1 V 0 P
what a coil's here! TIM 1.02.230
COIN 20 FR 0.0022 REL FR 14 V 6 P
saucy sweetness that do coin heaven's image | in MM 2.04. 45
the face of an old roman coin, scarce seen. LLL 5.02.613 P
a coin that bears the figure of an angel MV 2.07. 56
but we pay them for it with stamped coin, not WT 4.04.725 P
full thirty thousand marks of english coin. JN 2.01.530
assistance we do seize to us | the plate, coin, R2 2.01.161
and elsewhere, so far as my coin would stretch, 1H4 1.02. 54 P
again for all the coin in thy father's exchequer 2.02. 36 P
let them coin his nose, let them coin his cheeks 3.03. 78 P
them coin his nose, let them coin his cheeks. 3.03. 78 P
his valor, coin, and people, in the wars? 2H6 1.01. 79
ever casts | such doubts, as false coin, from it H8 3.01.171
your holy hat to be stamp'd on the king's coin. 3.02.325
coin words till their decay against those COR 3.01. 78
know that this gold must coin a stratagem, TIT 2.03. 5
let molten coin be thy damnation, | thou disease TIM 3.01. 52
who bates mine honor shall not know my coin. 3.03. 26
and let out | their coin upon large interest — 3.05.107
i had rather coin my heart | and drop my blood JC 4.03. 72
his coin, ships, legions, | may be a coward's, ANT 3.13. 22
COINAGE 3 FR 0.0003 REL FR 2 V 1 P
twenty, take them all, i'll answer the coinage. 1H4 4.02. 8 P
this is the very coinage of your brain, | this HAM 3.04.137
at adventure humm'd /one | from musical coinage,
TNK 1.03. 76
COIN'D 3 FR 0.0003 REL FR 3 V 0 P
that (almost) mightst have coin'd me into gold, H5 2.02. 98
you coin'd it. CYM 5.04. 23
nor fold my fault in cleanly coin'd excuses; LUC 1073
COINED 1 FR 0.0001 REL FR 1 V 0 P
how many tales to please me hath she coined, PP 7. 9
COINER 1 FR 0.0001 REL FR 1 V 0 P
some coiner with his tools | made me a CYM 2.05. 5
/COINING 1 FR 0.0001 REL FR 0 V 1 P
no, they cannot touch me for /coining; LR 4.06. 83 P
COINING 1 FR 0.0001 REL FR 1 V 0 P
a mother hourly coining plots, a wooer | more CYM 2.01. 59
COINS 3 FR 0.0003 REL FR 2 V 1 P
a slave whose gall coins slanders like a mint, TRO 1.03.193
and give it timon, why, the dog coins gold. TIM 2.01. 6
how her brain coins! TNK 4.03. 40 P
/COINT 1 FR 0.0001 REL FR 1 V 0 P
sir robert waterton, and francis /coint — | all R2 2.01.284
CO–JOIN 1 FR 0.0001 REL FR 1 V 0 P
credent | thou mayst co–join with something, and WT 1.02.143
COL 2 FR 0.0002 REL FR 0 V 2 P
comment appelez–vous le col? H5 3.04. 32 P
de sin. le col, de nick; le menton, de sin. 3.04. 36 P
COLBRAND 2 FR 0.0002 REL FR 2 V 0 P
colbrand the giant, that same mighty man? JN 1.01.225
i am not sampson, nor sir guy, nor colbrand, H8 5.03. 22
COLCHIS' 1 FR 0.0001 REL FR 1 V 0 P
which makes her seat of belmont colchis' strond, MV 1.01.171
/COLD 2 FR 0.0002 REL FR 1 V 1 P
i rather will suspect the sun with /cold | than WIV 4.04. 7
the sharp hawthorn blow the /cold winds." LR 3.04. 47 P
COLD 217 FR 0.0245 REL FR 171 V 46 P
what, must our mouths be cold? TMP 1.01. 53 P
he receives comfort like cold porridge. 2.01. 10 P
sir, | the white cold virgin snow upon my heart 4.01. 55
betrims, | to make cold nymphs chaste crowns; 4.01. 66
yet here they shall not lie, for catching cold. TGV 1.02.133
methinks my zeal to valentine is cold, | and 2.04.203
i hope my master's suit will be but cold, 4.04.181
thy impatience, throw cold water on thy choler. WIV 2.03. 85 P
for my belly's as cold as if i had swallow'd 3.05. 22 P
old, cold, wither'd, and of intolerable entrails 5.05.153 P
you are too cold. MM 2.02. 45
you are too cold. 2.02. 56
to lie in cold obstruction, and to rot; 3.01.118
by cold gradation and weal–balanc'd form, | we 4.03.100
she is so hot, because the meat is cold: ERR 1.02. 47
the meat is cold, because you come not home: 1.02. 48
whence he came, lest he catch cold on 's feet. 3.01. 37
you stand here in the cold. 3.01. 71
when i am cold, he heats me with beating; 4.04. 32 P
i thank god and my cold blood, i am of your ADO 1.01.130 P
there's goodly catching of cold. 3.04. 66 P
faint hymns to the cold fruitless moon. MND 1.01. 73
flying between the cold moon and the earth, 2.01.156
me | to measure out my length on this cold bed. 3.02.429
but a hot temper leaps o'er a cold decree — MV 1.02. 19 P
pain | to allay with some cold drops of modesty 2.02.186
fare you well, your suit is cold." 2.07. 73
cold indeed, and labor lost: 2.07. 74
upon my body | even till i shrink with cold, i AYL 2.01. 9
go to thy cold bed, and warm thee. SHR in.1. 10 P
this were a bed but cold to sleep so soundly. in.1. 33
the weather, a taller man than i will take cold. 4.01. 11 P
thou shalt soon feel, to thy cold comfort, for 4.01. 31 P
a cold world, curtis, in every office but thine, 4.01. 35 P
therefore fire, for i have caught extreme cold. 4.01. 45 P
faith, as cold as can be. 4.03. 37
to watch the night in storms, the day in cold, 5.02.150
steely bones | looks bleak i' th' cold wind. AWW 1.01.104
see | cold wisdom waiting on superfluous folly. 1.01.105
'tis too cold a companion; 1.01.132 P
yourself within the list of too cold an adieu. 2.01. 52 P
that barefoot plod i the cold ground upon, 3.04. 6
with her but once | and found her wondrous cold, 3.06.113
for you are cold and stern, | and now you should 4.02. 8
o ay, make up that. he is now at a cold scent. TN 2.05.121 P
you smell this business with a sense as cold WT 2.01.151
the men are not yet cold under water, nor the 3.03.105 P
and was turn'd into a cold fish for she would 4.04.279 P
of war | is cold in amity and painted peace, JN 3.01.105
i muse your majesty doth seem so cold, | when 3.01.317
lo, by my troth, the instrument is cold, | and 4.01.103
kiss my parched lips | and comfort me with cold. 5.07. 41
i do not ask you much, | i beg cold comfort; 5.07. 42
let not my cold words here accuse my zeal. R2 1.01. 47
is pale cold cowardice in noble breasts. 1.02. 34
nobles they are fled, the commons they are cold, 2.02. 88
where shivering cold and sickness pines the 5.01. 77
for a cup of madeira and a cold capon's leg? 1H4 1.02.116 P
my blood hath been too cold and temperate, 1.03. 1
i then, all smarting with my wounds being cold, 1.03. 49
'tis dangerous to take a cold, to sleep, to 2.03. 8 P
sincerity of fear and cold heart will he to the 2.03. 30 P
hot livers and cold purses. 2.04.323 P
well, | you speak it out of fear and cold heart. 4.03. 7
but that the earthy and cold hand of death 5.04. 84
and that young harry percy's spur was cold. 2H4 1.01. 42
said he young harry percy's spur was cold? 1.01. 49
to sit under, he's like to be a cold soldier. 3.02.123 P
a whoreson cold, sir, a cough, sir, which i 3.02.181 P
we will have away thy cold, and i will take such 3.02.185 P
their cold intent, tenure, and substance thus: 4.01. 9
which before (cold and settled) left the liver 4.03.104 P
for the cold blood he did naturally inherit of 4.03.118 P
grace | by seeming cold or careless of his will, 4.04. 29
your majesty, | how cold it strook my heart! 4.05.151
after this cold considerance, sentence me, | and 5.02. 98
by, | all out of work and cold for action! H5 1.02.114
and it will endure cold as another man's sword 2.01. 9 P
felt them, and they were as cold as any stone; 2.03. 24 P
and up'ard, and all was as cold as any stone. 2.03. 25 P
decoct their cold blood to such valiant heat? 3.05. 20
thawing cold fear, that mean and gentle all 4.pr. 45
but i believe, as cold a night as 'tis, he could 4.01.114 P
to watch in darkness, rain, and cold. 1H6 2.01. 7
in winter's cold and summer's parching heat, 2H6 1.01. 81
cold news for me; 1.01.237
barren winter, with his wrathful nipping cold; 2.04. 3
cold news, lord somerset; 3.01. 86
cold news for me; 3.01. 87
lords, cold snow melts with the sun's hot beams: 3.01.223
henry my lord is cold in great affairs, | too 3.01.224
where biting cold would never let grass grow, 3.02.337
in whose cold blood no spark of honor bides. 3H6 1.01.184
ere my knee rise from the earth's cold face, | i 2.03. 35
his cold thin drink out of his leather bottle, 2.05. 48
a cold premeditation for my purpose! 3.02.133
him, | while he himself keeps in the cold field? 4.03. 14
cold biting winter mars our hop'd–for hay. 4.08. 61
thy tears would wash this cold congealed blood 5.02. 37
from cold and empty veins where no blood dwells.
R3 1.02. 59
good | that is too cold in thinking of it now. 1.03.311
/god, | when i am cold in love to you or yours. 2.01. 40
(all thin and naked) to the numb cold night? 2.01.118
if he be leaden, icy, cold, unwilling, | be thou 3.01.176
cold friends to me! 4.04.484
in to my tent, the dew is raw and cold. 5.03. 46
cold fearful drops stand on my trembling flesh. 5.03.181
shall be this cold corpse on the earth's cold 5.03.266
be this cold corpse on the earth's cold face; 5.03.266
life | felt so much cold as over shoes in snow? 5.03.326
and cold hearts freeze | allegiance in them; H8 1.02. 61
two women plac'd together makes cold weather. 1.04. 22
and sleep in dull cold marble where no mention 3.02.433
how pale she looks, | and of an earthy cold! 4.02. 98
dear, trouble not yourself, the morn is cold. TRO 4.02. 1
you will catch cold and curse me. 4.02. 15
which | cold lips blow to their deities, take 4.04. 27
in the back, lethargies, cold palsies, raw eyes, 5.01. 19 P
cold statues of the youth, and, in a word, 5.10. 20
sir, those cold ways, | that seem like prudent COR 3.01.219
your function, go, and batten on cold bits. 4.05. 32 P
the veins unfill'd, our blood is cold, and then 5.01. 51
i, | even like a stony image, cold and numb. TIT 3.01.258
o, take this warm kiss on thy pale cold lips, 5.03.153
of lead, bright smoke, cold fire, sick health, ROM 1.01.180
this field–bed is too cold for me to sleep. 2.01. 40
with one hand beats | cold death aside, and with 3.01.162
thy veins shall run | a cold and drowsy humor; 4.01. 96
shall, stiff and stark and cold, appear like 4.01.103
i have a faint cold fear thrills through my 4.03. 15
out, alas, she's cold, | her blood is settled, 4.05. 25
their blood is cak'd, 'tis cold, it seldom flows TIM 2.02.216
who cannot condemn rashness in cold blood? 3.05. 53
thou cold sciatica, | cripple our senators, that 4.01. 23
will the cold brook, | candied with ice, caudle 4.03.225
if thou didst put this sour cold habit on | to 4.03.239
can you eat roots and drink cold water? 5.01. 74
both | endure the winter's cold as well as he; JC 1.02. 99
your weak condition to the raw cold morning. 2.01.236
then, in a friend, it is cold modesty. 3.01.213
a hasty spark, | and straight is cold again. 4.03.113
that mak'st my blood cold, and my hair to stare? 4.03.280
perceive | but cold demeanor in octavio's wing, 5.02. 4
banners flout the sky | and fan our people cold. MAC 1.02. 50
to the heat of deeds too cold breath gives. 2.01. 61
but this place is too cold for hell. 2.03. 17 P
thy bones are marrowless, thy blood is cold; 3.04. 93
that under cold stone | days and nights has 4.01. 6
and yet seem cold, the time you may so hoodwink. 4.03. 72
'tis bitter cold, | and i am sick at heart. HAM 1.01. 8
the air bites shrowdly, it is very cold. 1.04. 1
to think they would lay him i' th' cold ground. 4.05. 70 P
no, believe me, 'tis very cold, the wind is 5.02. 95 P
it is indifferent cold, my lord, indeed. 5.02. 97 P
as the wind sits, thou'lt catch cold shortly. LR 1.04.101 P
the leisure of their answer, gave me cold looks: 2.04. 37
art cold? 3.02. 68
i am cold myself. 3.02. 69
this cold night will turn us all to fools and 3.04. 78 P
still through the hawthorn blows the cold wind: 3.04. 98 P
a small spark, all the rest on 's body cold. 3.04.113 P
cold, cold, my girl? OTH 5.02.275
cold, cold, my girl? 5.02.275
th' year between the extremes | of hot and cold, ANT 1.05. 52
when i was green in judgment, cold in blood, 1.05. 74
octavia is of a holy, cold, and still 2.06.122 P
of honor, cold and sickly | he vented /them, 3.04. 7
as a morsel, cold upon | dead caesar's trencher; 3.13.116
from my cold heart let heaven engender hail, 3.13.159
this case of that huge spirit now is cold. 4.15. 89
lest the bargain should catch cold and starve. CYM 1.04.166 P
live, like diana's priest, betwixt cold sheets, 1.06.133
it would make any man cold to lose. 2.03. 3 P
one bred of alms and foster'd with cold dishes, 2.03.114
which not to read would show the britains cold. 3.01. 75
there is cold meat i' th' cave, we'll browse on 3.06. 38
herbs that have on them cold dew o' th' night 4.02.284
take this life, | and cancel these cold bonds. 5.04. 28
dian had hot dreams, | and she alone were cold; 5.05.181
a man throng'd up with cold, my veins are chill, PER 2.01. 73
which is but cold in flaming, thy /lone bosom 4.01. 5
and she sent him away as cold as a snowball, 4.06.139 P
and if he lose her then, he's a cold coward. TNK 2.02.253
better have endur'd cold iron than done it. 2.06. 10
come between, | and chop on some cold thought! 3.01. 13
quit me of these cold gyves, give me a sword, 3.01. 72
i am very cold, and all the stars are out too, 3.04. 1
this is a cold beginning. 3.05.101
the huntress | all moist and cold, some say, 5.01. 93
o sacred, shadowy, cold, and constant queen, 5.01.137
cold as old saturn, and like him possess'd 5.04. 62
o'erworn, despised, rheumatic, and cold, VEN 135
liveless picture, cold and senseless stone, 211
to touch the fire, the weather being cold? 402
with much ado the cold fault cleanly out; 694
which with cold terror doth men's minds confound 1048
she takes him by the hand, and that is cold, 1124
o rash false heat, wrapp'd in repentant cold, LUC 48
that from the cold stone sparks of fire do fly, 177
"as from this cold flint i enforc'd this fire, 181
this hot desire converts to cold disdain; 691
that knows not parching heat nor freezing cold, 1145
for sinon in his fire doth quake with cold, 1556
and in that cold, hot burning fire doth dwell; 1557
youth is hot and bold, age is weak and cold, PP 12. 7
see thy blood warm when thou feel'st it cold. SON 2.14
without this, folly, age, and cold decay. 11. 6
day | and barren rage of death's eternal cold? 13.12
upon those boughs which shake against the cold, 73. 3
unmoved, cold, and to temptation slow, | they 94. 4
three winters cold | have from the forests shook 104. 3
in a cold valley–fountain of that ground; 153. 4
but kept cold distance, and did thence remove LC 237
as compound love to physic your cold breast. 259
what breast so cold that is not warmed here? 292
cold modesty, hot wrath, | both fire from hence 293
preach'd pure maid, and prais'd cold chastity. 315
COLD–BLOODED 1 FR 0.0001 REL FR 1 V 0 P
thou cold–blooded slave, | hast thou not spoke JN 3.01.123
COLDER 6 FR 0.0006 REL FR 6 V 0 P
your writing now | is colder than that theme, WT 5.01.100
power landed at milford | is colder /tidings, R3 4.04.534
or brew it to a weak and colder palate, | the TRO 4.04. 7
rages and revenges with | your colder reasons. COR 5.03. 86
and let his knights have colder looks among you; LR 1.03. 22
being oil to fire, snow to the colder moods; 2.02. 77
COLDEST 4 FR 0.0004 REL FR 3 V 1 P
at the hedge–corner, in the coldest fault? SHR in.1. 20
where hope is coldest and despair most /fits. AWW 2.01.144
to find, | you stand in coldest expectation. 2H4 5.02. 31
loss, the most coldest that ever turn'd up ace. CYM 2.03. 2 P
COLDFIELD *(see co'fil')*
COLD–HEARTED 1 FR 0.0001 REL FR 1 V 0 P
cold–hearted toward me? ANT 3.13.158
COLDLY 16 FR 0.0018 REL FR 13 V 3 P
yet will i woo for him, but yet so coldly | as, TGV 4.04.106
if he were mad, he would not plead so coldly. ERR 5.01.273
bear it coldly but till midnight, and let the ADO 3.02.129 P
who is that calls so coldly? SHR 4.01. 13 P
you, sir, | charge him too coldly. WT 1.02. 30
as now it coldly stands), when first i woo'd her 5.03. 36
gentle lord, | we coldly pause for thee; JN 2.01. 53
lies, | coldly embracing the discolored earth, 2.01.306
the french fight coldly, and retire themselves. 5.03. 13
modest as morning when she coldly eyes | the TRO 1.03.229
but it lies as coldly in him as fire in a flint, 3.03.256 P
place, | or reason coldly of your grievances, ROM 3.01. 52
did coldly furnish forth the marriage tables. HAM 1.02.181
us — thou mayst not coldly set | our sovereign 4.03. 62
let me deal coldly with you: TNK 2.02.184
how coldly those impediments stand forth | of LC 269
COLD–MOVING 1 FR 0.0001 REL FR 1 V 0 P
with certain half–caps and cold–moving nods, TIM 2.02.212
COLDNESS 2 FR 0.0002 REL FR 2 V 0 P
but whether 'twas the coldness of the king, 3H6 2.01.122
dull not device by coldness and delay. OTH 2.03.388
COLD–PALE 1 FR 0.0001 REL FR 1 V 0 P
with cold–pale weakness numbs each feeling part:
VEN 892
COLDSPUR 1 FR 0.0001 REL FR 1 V 0 P
of hotspur, coldspur? 2H4 1.01. 50
COLD'ST 1 FR 0.0001 REL FR 1 V 0 P
'tis strange that from their cold'st neglect LR 1.01.254
CO–LEAGUED 1 FR 0.0001 REL FR 1 V 0 P
co–leagued with this dream of his advantage, HAM 1.02. 21
COLEBROOK 1 FR 0.0001 REL FR 0 V 1 P
of maidenhead, of colebrook, of horses and money

WIV 4.05. 78 P
COLEVILE 9 FR 0.0010 REL FR 3 V 6 P
sir, and my name is colevile of the dale. 2H4 4.03. 3 P
well then, colevile is your name, a knight is 4.03. 5 P
colevile shall be still your name, a traitor 4.03. 6 P
so shall you be still colevile of the dale. 4.03. 9 P
valor, taken sir john colevile of the dale, a 4.03. 38 P
on the top on't (colevile kissing my foot), to 4.03. 49 P
is thy name colevile? 4.03. 61
a famous rebel art thou, colevile. 4.03. 63
send colevile with his confederates | to york, 4.03. 73
COLIC 3 FR 0.0003 REL FR 2 V 1 P
is with a kind of colic pinch'd and vex'd | by 1H4 3.01. 28
cheek | outswell the colic of puff'd aquilon; TRO 4.05. 9
if you chance to be pinch'd with the colic, you COR 2.01. 74 P
COLLAR 1 FR 0.0001 REL FR 0 V 1 P
while you live, draw your neck out of collar. ROM 1.01. 5 P
COLLARS 1 FR 0.0001 REL FR 1 V 0 P
her collars of the moonshine's wat'ry beams, ROM 1.04. 65
COLLATERAL 2 FR 0.0002 REL FR 2 V 0 P
in his bright radiance and collateral light AWW 1.01. 88
if by direct or by collateral hand | they find HAM 4.05.207
COLLATINE 21 FR 0.0023 REL FR 21 V 0 P
when collatine unwisely did not let | to praise LUC 10
or why is collatine the publisher | of that rich 33
therefore that praise which collatine doth owe 82
and in the self–same seat sits collatine. 289
then collatine again by lucrece' side | in his 381
line, | how tarquin wronged me, i collatine. 819
of mine | as i ere this was pure to collatine. 826
"if, collatine, thine honor lay in me, | from me 834
my collatine would else have come to me | when 916
well, dear collatine, thou shalt not know | the 1058
when both were kept for heaven and collatine? 1166
"yet die i will not till my collatine | have 1177
"thou, collatine, shalt oversee this will; 1205
by this short schedule collatine may know | her 1312
while collatine and his consorted lords | with 1609
(speaking to those that came with collatine), 1689
deed, | stood collatine and all his lordly crew, 1731
by this starts collatine as from a dream, | and 1772
mine, | and only must be wail'd by collatine." 1799
"woe, woe," quoth collatine, "she was my wife, 1802
"why, collatine, is woe the cure for woe? 1821
COLLATINE'S 3 FR 0.0003 REL FR 3 V 0 P
flames the waist | of collatine's fair love, LUC 7
and decks with praises collatine's high name, 108
for collatine's dear love be kept unspotted: 821
COLLATINUS' 2 FR 0.0002 REL FR 2 V 0 P
reproach is stamp'd in collatinus' face, | and LUC 829
to check the tears in collatinus' eyes. 1817
COLLATINUS 3 FR 0.0003 REL FR 3 V 0 P
"if collatinus dream of my intent, | will he not LUC 218
"had collatinus kill'd my son or sire, | or lain 232
band | where her beloved collatinus lies. 256
COLLATIUM 2 FR 0.0002 REL FR 2 V 0 P
and to collatium bears the lightless fire, LUC 4
when at collatium this false lord arrived, 50
COLLEAGUED *(see co–leagued)*
COLLECT 3 FR 0.0003 REL FR 3 V 0 P
i did in time collect myself and thought | this WT 3.03. 38
knight, | collect them all together at my tent. H5 4.01.287
made me collect these dangers in the duke. 2H6 3.01. 35
COLLECTED 14 FR 0.0015 REL FR 14 V 0 P
be collected, | no more amazement. TMP 1.02. 13
and manifest experience had collected | for AWW 1.03.223
the sums i have collected shall express. JN 4.02.142
our navy is address'd, our power collected, 2H4 4.04. 5
proportions for these wars | be soon collected, H5 1.02.305
should be maintain'd, assembled, and collected, 2.04. 19
levied host, | collected for this expedition. 1H6 4.04. 32
collected choicely, from each county some, | and 2H6 3.01.313
have collected | out of the duke of buckingham. H8 1.02.130
sins, the articles | collected from his life. 3.02.294
have you collected them by tribes? COR 3.03. 11
thou mixture rank, of midnight weeds collected, HAM 3.02.257
collected from all simples that have virtue 4.07.144
we are a few of those collected here | that TNK 3.05.103
COLLECTION 3 FR 0.0003 REL FR 2 V 1 P
use of it doth move | the hearers to collection. HAM 4.05. 9
habit of encounter, a kind of /yesty collection, 5.02.191 P
hardness, that i can | make no collection of it. CYM 5.05.432
COLLEGE 3 FR 0.0003 REL FR 2 V 1 P
a college of wit–crackers cannot flout me out of ADO 5.04.100 P
us, and | the congregated college have concluded AWW 2.01.117
i would the college of the cardinals | would 2H6 1.03. 61
COLLEGES 1 FR 0.0001 REL FR 1 V 0 P
together with all famous colleges | almost in H8 3.02. 66
COLLIED 2 FR 0.0002 REL FR 2 V 0 P
brief as the lightning in the collied night, MND 1.01.145
and passion, having my best judgment collied, OTH 2.03.206
COLLIER 1 FR 0.0001 REL FR 0 V 1 P
hang him, foul collier! TN 3.04.117 P
COLLIERS 2 FR 0.0002 REL FR 1 V 1 P
and since her time are colliers counted bright. LLL 4.03.263
no, for then we should be colliers. ROM 1.01. 2 P
COLLOP 2 FR 0.0002 REL FR 2 V 0 P
my collop! WT 1.02.137
god knows thou art a collop of my flesh, | and 1H6 5.04. 18
COLLUSION 1 FR 0.0001 REL FR 0 V 1 P
indeed, the collusion holds in the exchange. LLL 4.02. 42 P
COLMEKILL 1 FR 0.0001 REL FR 1 V 0 P
carried to colmekill, | the sacred store–house MAC 2.04. 33
COLME'S 1 FR 0.0001 REL FR 1 V 0 P
till he disbursed at saint colme's inch | ten MAC 1.02. 61
COLOQUINTIDA 1 FR 0.0001 REL FR 0 V 1 P
to him shortly as /acerb as /the coloquintida. OTH 1.03.349 P
COLOR 90 FR 0.0101 REL FR 57 V 33 P
what, angry, sir thurio? do you change color? TGV 2.04. 24 P
under the color of commending him, | i have 4.02. 3
not what i seek, show no color for my extremity; WIV 4.02.161 P
howsoever you color it in being a tapster, are MM 2.01.220 P
his beard and head | just of his color. 4.03. 73
her hair shall be of what color it please god. ADO 2.03. 35 P
green indeed is the color of lovers; LLL 1.02. 86 P
but to have a love of that color, methinks 1.02. 87 P
of color like the red rose on triumphant brier, MND 3.01. 94
that steals the color from bassanio's cheek — MV 3.02.244
sport! of what color? AYL 1.02.101 P
what color, madam? how shall i answer you? 1.02.102 P
change you color? 3.02.182 P
are for the most part cattle of this color; 3.02.415 P
his very hair is of the dissembling color. 3.04. 7 P
i' faith, his hair is of a good color. 3.04. 10 P
an excellent color. 3.04. 11 P
your chestnut was ever the only color. 3.04. 12 P
there was no link to color peter's hat, | and SHR 4.01.134
of color, weight, and heat, pour'd all together, AWW 2.03.119
which holds not color with the time, nor does 2.05. 59
and doughy youth of a nation in his color. 4.05. 4 P
scorn'd a fair color, or express'd it stol'n, 5.03. 50
wherein, by the color of his beard, the shape of TN 2.03.156 P
my purpose is indeed a horse of that color. 2.03.167 P
yellow stockings, and 'tis a color she abhors, 2.05.199 P
and he went | still in this fashion, color, 3.04.382
pray now | what color are your eyebrows? WT 2.01. 13
i must have saffron to color the warden pies; 4.03. 45 P
what color for my visitation shall i | hold up 4.04.555
who was most marble there chang'd color; 5.02. 90 P
the color of the king doth come and go | between JN 4.02. 76
color her working with such deadly wounds, | nor 1H4 1.03.109
for of no right, nor color like to right, | he 3.02.100
with some fine color that may please the eye 5.01. 75
i have the wars for my color, and my pension 2H4 1.02.246 P
as heart would desire, and your color, i warrant 2.04. 24 P
this that you heard was but a color. 5.05. 86 P
a color that i fear you will die in, sir john. 5.05. 87 P
abide carnation — 'twas a color he never lik'd. H5 2.03. 34 P
he's of the color of the nutmeg. 3.07. 19 P
nor doth he dedicate one jot of color | unto the 4.pr. 37
and without all color | of base insinuating 1H6 2.04. 34
saying the sanguine color of the leaves | did 4.01. 92
say'st thou me so? what color is this cloak of? 2H6 2.01.107
why, that's well said. what color is my gown of? 2.01.109
why then, thou know'st what color jet is of? 2.01.111
policy, | but yet we want a color for his death. 3.01.236
this way, | under the color of his usual game, 3H6 4.05. 11
but his red color hath forsook his cheeks. R3 2.01. 86
cousin, canst thou quake and change thy color, 3.05. 1
queen his aunt | (for 'twas indeed his color, H8 1.01.178
why, paris hath color enough. TRO 1.02. 99 P
he having color enough, and the other higher, is 1.02.103 P
this must be patch'd | with cloth of any color. COR 3.01.252
his coward lips did from their color fly, | and JC 1.02.122
will bear no color for the thing he is, 2.01. 29
my hands are of your color; MAC 2.02. 61
good hamlet, cast thy nighted color off, | and HAM 1.02. 68
your modesties have not craft enough to color. 2.02.280 P
he has not turn'd his color and has tears in 's 2.02.519 P
that show of such an exercise may color | your 3.01. 44
then what i have to do | will want true color — 3.04.130
this is a fellow of the self–same color | our LR 2.02.138
of vexation on't, | as it may lose some color. OTH 1.01. 73
nay, pray you, seek no color for your going, ANT 1.03. 32
let him not leave out | the color of her hair. 2.05.114
what color is it of? 2.07. 46 P
of it own color too. 2.07. 47 P
her hair, what color? 3.03. 32
put color in thy cheek. 4.14. 69
against all color here | did put the yoke upon CYM 3.01. 50
to gain his color | i'ld let a parish of such 4.02.167
give color to my pale cheek with thy blood, 4.02.330
you the marks of her, the color of her hair, PER 4.02. 57 P
where every evil | hath a good color; TNK 1.02. 39
this is a pretty color, will't not do | rarely 2.02.129
but such a manly color | next to an aborn; 4.02.124
in shape, in courage, color, pace, and bone. VEN 294
of either's color was the other queen, | proving LUC 66
o, how her fear did make her color rise! 257
"why hunt i then for color or excuses? 267
still | under what color he commits this ill. 476
"the color in thy face, | that even for anger 477
under that color am i come to scale | thy 481
her lively color kill'd with deadly cares. 1593
love, what spite hath thy fair color spent? 1600
but sweet or color it had stol'n from thee. SON 99.15
"truth needs no color with his color fix'd, 101. 6
"truth needs no color with his color fix'd, 101. 6
COLORABLE 1 FR 0.0001 REL FR 0 V 1 P
me of the father, i do fear colorable colors. LLL 4.02.149 P
COLOR'D 8 FR 0.0009 REL FR 7 V 1 P
his love, | i'll get me such a color'd periwig. TGV 4.04.191
take my color'd hat and cloak. SHR 1.01.207
but that our wits are so diversely color'd; COR 2.03. 21 P
for i wish'd | thou shouldst be color'd thus. CYM 5.01. 2
for that he color'd with his high estate, LUC 92
to pencill'd pensiveness and color'd sorrow; 1497
fair), | my worser spirit a woman (color'd ill). PP 2. 4
fair, | the worser spirit a woman color'd ill. SON 144. 4
COLORED 1 FR 0.0001 REL FR 1 V 0 P
these eyes, that see thee now well colored, 1H6 4.02. 37
COLORING 1 FR 0.0001 REL FR 1 V 0 P
to make no stain a stain | as passes coloring. WT 2.02. 18
COLOR'S 1 FR 0.0001 REL FR 1 V 0 P
the color's | not dry. WT 5.03. 47
COLORS 47 FR 0.0053 REL FR 38 V 9 P
with colors fairer painted their foul ends. TMP 1.02.143
manners, | i must advance the colors of my love, WIV 3.04. 81
myself into all the colors of the rainbow; 4.05.115 P
thoughts, master, are mask'd under such colors. LLL 1.02. 93 P
and wear his colors like a tumbler's hoop! 3.01.188
me of the father, i do fear colorable colors. 4.02.150 P
for fear their colors should be wash'd away. 4.03.267
hang'd in this world needs to fear no colors. TN 1.05. 6 P
that saying was born, of "i fear no colors." 1.05. 10 P
mind too, 'mongst all colors | no yellow in't, WT 2.03.106
hath ribbons of all the colors i' th' rainbow; 4.04.204 P
hither is he come | to spread his colors, boy, JN 2.01. 8
our colors do return in those same hands | that 2.01.319
and part your mingled colors once again, | turn 2.01.389
mocking the air with colors idlely spread, | and 5.01. 72
remote, | and follow unacquainted colors here? 5.02. 32
therefore thy threat'ning colors now wind up, 5.02. 73
and wound our tott'ring colors clearly up, 5.05. 7
under whose colors he had fought so long. R2 4.01.100
to all those | that wear those colors on them. 1H4 5.04. 27
bestow himself to–night in his true colors, and 2H4 2.02.170 P
fear no colors, go with me to dinner. 5.05. 88 P
suits not in native colors with the truth; H5 1.02. 17
and bungle up damnation | with patches, colors, 2.02.116
advance our waving colors on the walls, 1H6 1.06. 1
i love no colors; 2.04. 34
and know us by these colors for thy foes, | for 2.04.105
there goes the talbot, with his colors spread, 3.03. 31
disgracing of these colors that i wear | in 3.04. 29
prosper our colors in this dangerous fight! 4.02. 56
then call our captains and our colors forth, 5.03.128
as thus | to name the several colors we do wear. 2H6 2.01.126
sight may distinguish colors; 2.01.127
whose hopeful colors | advance our half–fac'd 4.01. 97
and with colors spread | march'd through the 3H6 1.01. 91
ay, and their colors, often borne in france, 1.01.127
the northern lords that have forsworn thy colors 1.01.251
let our bloody colors wave! 2.02.173
face, | the fatal colors of our striving houses; 2.05. 98
i can add colors to the chameleon, | change 3.02.191
o cheerful colors! see where oxford comes! 5.01. 58
unless i have mista'en his colors much | (which R3 5.03. 35
steep'd in the colors of their trade, their MAC 2.03.115
divorce under her colors are wonderfully to CYM 1.04. 20 P
see how near art can come near their colors. TNK 2.02.149
thousand fresh water–flowers of several colors, 4.01. 85
flowers are sweet, their colors fresh and trim, VEN 1079
COLOSSUS 2 FR 0.0002 REL FR 1 V 1 P
nothing but a colossus can do thee that 1H4 5.01.123 P
bestride the narrow world | like a colossus, and JC 1.02.136
COLOSSUS–WISE 1 FR 0.0001 REL FR 1 V 0 P
and stands colossus–wise, waving his beam, TRO 5.05. 9
COLT 5 FR 0.0005 REL FR 1 V 4 P
the hobby–horse is but a colt, and your love LLL 3.01. 31 P
he hath rid his prologue like a rough colt; MND 5.01.119 P
ay, that's a colt indeed, for he doth nothing MV 1.02. 40 P
what a plague mean ye to colt me thus? 1H4 2.02. 37 P
the colt that's back'd and burthen'd being young VEN 419
COLTED 2 FR 0.0002 REL FR 1 V 1 P
thou liest, thou art not colted, thou art 1H4 2.02. 38 P
never talk on't: | she hath been colted by him. CYM 2.04.133
COLT'S 1 FR 0.0001 REL FR 1 V 0 P
lord sands, | your colt's tooth is not cast yet? H8 1.03. 48
COLTS 3 FR 0.0003 REL FR 3 V 0 P
at which, like unback'd colts, they prick'd TMP 4.01.176
herd, | or race of youthful and unhandled colts, MV 5.01. 72
for young hot colts being rag'd do rage the more R2 2.01. 70
COLUMBINE 1 FR 0.0001 REL FR 1 V 0 P
that columbine. LLL 5.02.655
COLUMBINES 1 FR 0.0001 REL FR 0 V 1 P
there's fennel for you, and columbines. HAM 4.05.181 P
COM' *(also come)*
COM' 1 FR 0.0001 REL FR 1 V 0 P
com' on then, i will swear to study so, | to LLL 1.01. 59
COMAGENA 1 FR 0.0001 REL FR 1 V 0 P
mithridates, king | of comagena; ANT 3.06. 74
COMART 1 FR 0.0001 REL FR 1 V 0 P
by the same comart | and carriage of the article HAM 1.01. 93
CO–MATES 1 FR 0.0001 REL FR 1 V 0 P
now, my co–mates and brothers in exile, | hath AYL 2.01. 1
COMB 4 FR 0.0004 REL FR 3 V 1 P
to comb your noddle with a three–legg'd stool, SHR 1.01. 64
'tis seldom when the bee doth leave her comb 2H4 4.04. 79
comb down his hair; 2H6 3.03. 15
too, and you crow, cock, with your comb on. CYM 2.01. 24 P
COMBAT 30 FR 0.0034 REL FR 25 V 5 P
mine, | i combat challenge of this latten bilbo. WIV 1.01.162
you not see pompey is uncasing for the combat? LLL 5.02.702 P
pardon me, i will not combat in my shirt. 5.02.705 P
and would by combat make her good, so were i | a WT 2.03. 61
the noble combat that 'twixt joy and sorrow was 5.02. 73 P
what a noble combat hast /thou fought | between JN 5.02. 43
combat with adverse planets in the heavens! 1H6 1.01. 54
my courage try by combat, if thou dar'st, | and 1.02. 89
in single combat thou shalt buckle with me; 1.02. 95
grant me the combat, gracious sovereign. 4.01. 78
and me, my lord, grant me the combat too. 4.01. 79
and wherefore crave you combat? 4.01. 84
to us, | else ruin combat with their palaces! 5.02. 7
them | for single combat in convenient place, 2H6 1.03.208
and i accept the combat willingly. 1.03.212
and the day of combat shall be the last of the 1.03.219 P
this is the day appointed for the combat, | and 2.03. 48
kent, | took odds to combat a poor famish'd man. 4.10. 44
head, | the head of cade, whom i in combat slew. 5.01. 67
forc'd by the tide to combat with the wind; 3H6 2.05. 6
though't be a sportful combat, | yet in the TRO 1.03.335
t' invite the troyan lords after the combat | to 3.03.236
for if hector break not his neck i' th' combat, 3.03.259 P
by a most emulate pride, | dar'd to the combat; HAM 1.01. 84
whipt with rods, dares me to personal combat, ANT 4.01. 3
but say that one | had rather combat me? TNK 2.02.197
burst of clamor | is sure th' end o' th' combat. 5.03. 78
this beauteous combat, willful and unwilling, VEN 365
conceit and grief an eager combat fight, | what LUC 1298
long was the combat doubtful, that love with PP 15. 5
COMBATANT 1 FR 0.0001 REL FR 1 V 0 P
may pierce the head of the great combatant | and TRO 4.05. 5
COMBATANTS 5 FR 0.0005 REL FR 5 V 0 P
sound, trumpets, and set forward, combatants. R2 1.03.117
blood–stained with these valiant combatants. 1H4 1.03.107
come hither, you that would be combatants: 1H6 4.01.134
sound, trumpets, alarum to the combatants! 2H6 2.03. 92
the combatants being kin | half stints their TRO 4.05. 92
COMBATED 2 FR 0.0002 REL FR 1 V 1 P
had on | when he the ambitious norway combated. HAM 1.01. 61
is in, which is with falsehoods to be combated. TNK 4.03. 94 P
COMBATING 3 FR 0.0003 REL FR 2 V 1 P
wisdom and blood combating in so tender a body, ADO 2.03.163 P
his face still combating with tears and smiles, R2 5.02. 32
wisdom and fortune combating together, | if that ANT 3.13. 79
COMBAT'S 1 FR 0.0001 REL FR 1 V 0 P
the combat's consummation is proclaim'd | by the TNK 5.03. 94
COMB'D 1 FR 0.0001 REL FR 0 V 1 P
let their heads be slickly comb'd, their blue SHR 4.01. 91 P

COMBINATE–HUSBAND 1 FR 0.0001 REL FR 0 V 1 P
with both, her combinate–husband, this MM 3.01.222 P
COMBINATION 3 FR 0.0003 REL FR 3 V 0 P
a solemn combination shall be made | of our dear TN 5.01.383
the articles o' th' combination drew | as H8 1.01.169
hill, | a combination and a form indeed, | where HAM 3.04. 60
COMBIN'D 4 FR 0.0004 REL FR 4 V 0 P
and all combin'd, save what thou must combine ROM 2.03. 60
therefore let our alliance be combin'd, | our JC 4.01. 43
whether he was combin'd | with those of norway, MAC 1.03.111
that which combin'd us was most great, and let ANT 2.02. 18
COMBINE 7 FR 0.0008 REL FR 7 V 0 P
mine, | thy faith my fancy to thee doth combine. AYL 5.04.150
where these two christian armies might combine JN 5.02. 37
and friendship shall combine, and brotherhood. H5 2.01.109
combine your hearts in one, your realms in one! 5.02.360
by th' other lose | that they combine not there. COR 3.02. 45
save what thou must combine | by holy marriage. ROM 2.03. 60
combine together 'gainst the enemy; LR 5.01. 29
COMBINED 3 FR 0.0003 REL FR 3 V 0 P
my poor self, | i am combined by a sacred vow, MM 4.03.144
thy knotted and combined locks to part, | and HAM 1.05. 18
comes | their distract parcels in combined sums. LC 231
COMBLESS 1 FR 0.0001 REL FR 1 V 0 P
a combless cock, so kate will be my hen. SHR 2.01.226
COMBUSTION 2 FR 0.0002 REL FR 1 V 1 P
for kindling such a combustion in the state. H8 5.03. 49 P
of dire combustion and confus'd events | new MAC 2.03. 58
COMBUSTIOUS 1 FR 0.0001 REL FR 1 V 0 P
as dry combustious matter is to fire. VEN 1162
COME *(also com')*
/COME 32 FR 0.0036 REL FR 28 V 4 P
/this /paper /while /the /glass /doth /come. R2 4.01.269
/thou /torments /me /ere /i /come /to /hell! 4.01.270
/past /and /to /come /seems /best; 2H4 1.03.108
here /come the /lords of buckingham and derby. R3 1.03. 17
/come, /bring /forth /the /prisoners. 3.03. 1
/to /tenedos /they /come, | /and /the TRO pr 11
/all /on /hazard — /and /hither /am /i /come, pr 22
through the sight i bear in things to /come, | i 3.03. 4
cries "/come" to him that instantly must die. 4.04. 51
/and /what's /to /come /is /strew'd /with /husks 4.05.166
/come, /let's /fall /to, /and, /gentle /girl, TIT 3.02. 34
/come /hither /purposely /to /poison /me. 3.02. 73
/come, /take /away. 3.02. 81
/come, /boy, /and /go /with /me, /thy /sight /is 3.02. 84
/come, shall we in | and taste lord timon's TIM 1.01.273
/and /dare /scarce /come /thither. HAM 2.02.344 P
/to /let /this /canker /of /our /nature /come 5.02. 69
/come /on. 5.02.254
/come, /come, when saw you my father last? LR 1.02.152 P
/come, /come, when saw you my father last? 1.02.152 P
/thy /land, | /come /place /him /here /by /me, 1.04.142
/o, /sir, /are /you /come? 1.04.257
/yea, /is't /come /to /this? 1.04.304
/come /sit /thou /here, /most /learned /justicer 3.06. 21
"/come /o'er /the /bourn, /bessy, /to /me" — 3.06. 25
/why /she /dares /not /come /over /to /thee." 3.06. 28
/come /hither, /mistress. 3.06. 49 P
/come /help /to /bear /thy /master; 3.06.100
/i /do, | /if /this /man /come /to /good. 3.07.100
/must /wither, | /and /come /to /deadly /use. 4.02. 36
/tame /these /vild /offenses, | /it /will /come, 4.02. 48
/remembers | /what /we /are /come /about, /and 4.03. 40
COME 2606 FR 0.2945 REL FR 1802 V 804 P
the hour's now come, | the very minute bids thee TMP 1.02. 36
come away, servant, come; 1.02.187
come away, servant, come; 1.02.187
come. 1.02.188
i come | to answer thy best pleasure; 1.02.189
go take this shape | and hither come in't. 1.02.304
come on, | we'll visit caliban my slave, who 1.02.307
come forth, i say, there's other business for 1.02.315
come, thou tortoise, when? 1.02.316
devil himself | upon thy wicked dam, come forth! 1.02.320
come unto these yellow sands, | and then take 1.02.375
come, | i'll manacle thy neck and feet together. 1.02.461
come, from thy ward, | for i can here disarm 1.02.472
come on, obey: 1.02.484
come on. 1.02.494
come, follow. speak not for him. 1.02.502
what to come | in yours and my discharge. 2.01.253
as thou got'st milan, | i'll come by naples. 2.01.292
alas, the storm is come again! 2.02. 37 P
come on your ways. 2.02. 82 P
come. 2.02. 93 P
if thou beest trinculo, come forth. 2.02.103 P
come, swear to that; 2.02.142 P
come on then; down, and swear. 2.02.153 P
come, kiss. 2.02.157 P
stand farther. — come, proceed. 3.02. 86
come on, trinculo, let us sing. 3.02.120 P
wilt come? i'll follow stephano. 3.02.152 P
and what does else want credit, come to me, 3.03. 25
before you can say "come" and "go," | and 4.01. 44
now come, my ariel! 4.01. 57
in this very place, | to come and sport. 4.01. 74
spring come to you at the farthest | in the very 4.01.114
come, temperate nymphs, and help to celebrate 4.01.132
come hither from the furrow and be merry. 4.01.135
the minute of their plot | is almost come. 4.01.142
come with a thought. i thank thee. ariel! come. 4.01.164
come with a thought. i thank thee. ariel! come. 4.01.164
come, hang /them /on this line. 4.01.193
monster, come put some lime upon your fingers, 4.01.245 P
come hither, spirit. 5.01.251
come, come, open the matter in brief: TGV 1.01.127 P
come, come, open the matter in brief: 1.01.127 P
come, come, will't please you go? 1.02.137
come, come, will't please you go? 1.02.137
come on, panthino; 1.03. 76
i come, i come. 2.02. 19
i come, i come. 2.02. 19
now come i to my father: 2.03. 23 P
now come i to my mother. 2.03. 26 P
now come i to my sister; 2.03. 29 P
come; come away, man — i was sent to call thee. 2.03. 55 P
come; come away, man — i was sent to call thee. 2.03. 55 P
this gentleman is come to me | with commendation 2.04. 78
i told your ladyship | had come along with me, 2.04. 88
come, sir thurio, | go with me. 2.04.117
come on, you madcap, i'll to the alehouse with 2.05. 8 P
if proteus like your journey when you come, | no 2.07. 65
pray heav'n he prove so when you come to him! 2.07. 79
come, answer not, but to it presently, | i am 2.07. 89
that longs for every thing that he can come by. 3.01.125
o, could their master come and go as lightly, 3.01.142
come, i'll convey thee through the city–gate; 3.01.254
go, sirrah, find him out. come, valentine. 3.01.261
come, fool, come; try me in thy paper. 3.01.299 P
come, fool, come; try me in thy paper. 3.01.299 P
come, go with us, we'll bring thee to our crews, 4.01. 72
come, we'll have you merry: 4.02. 30 P
i am thus early come to know what service | it 4.03. 9
say | no grief did ever come so near thy heart 4.03. 19
come, shadow, come, and take this shadow up, 4.04.197
come, shadow, come, and take this shadow up, 4.04.197
hours, | unless it be to come before their time, 5.01. 5
come, come, | be patient; 5.03. 1
come, come, | be patient; 5.03. 1
come, bring her away. 5.03. 5
come, i must bring you to our captain's cave. 5.03. 12
come, come, a hand from either. 5.04.116
come, come, a hand from either. 5.04.116
come not within the measure of my wrath. 5.04.127
come, let us go, we will include all jars | with 5.04.160
come, proteus, 'tis your penance but to hear 5.04.170
and all his ancestors (that come after him) may. WIV 1.01. 15 P
or i would i might never come in mine own great 1.01.154 P
come, we have a hot venison pasty to dinner. 1.01.195 P
come, gentlemen, i hope we shall drink down all 1.01.196 P
come, coz, come, coz, we stay for you. 1.01.206 P
come, coz, come, coz, we stay for you. 1.01.206 P
will't please your worship to come in, sir? 1.01.266 P
they will not sit till you come. 1.01.278 P
come, gentle master slender, come; 1.01.300 P
come, gentle master slender, come; 1.01.300 P
come, come. 1.01.304 P
come, come. 1.01.304 P
come on, sir. 1.01.306 P
there's pippins and cheese to come. 1.02. 13 P
as ever servant shall come in house withal; 1.04. 11 P
come, take–a your rapier, and come after my heel 1.04. 59 P
rapier, and come after my heel to the court. 1.04. 59 P
is no honest man dat shall come in my closet. 1.04. 74 P
a great charge to come under one body's hand. 1.04. 99 P
rugby, come to the court with me. 1.04.123 P
come near the house, i pray you. 1.04.132 P
trifling respect, i could come to such honor! 2.01. 45 P
if he come under my hatches, i'll never to sea 2.01. 92 P
come hither. 2.01.108 P
you'll come to dinner, george. 2.01.156 P
you are come to see my daughter anne? 2.01.162 P
sir — i pray come a little nearer this ways. 2.02. 45 P
i pray your worship come a little nearer this 2.02. 49 P
mistress ford; come, mistress ford — 2.02. 58 P
and then you may come and see the picture, she 2.02. 86 P
from home, but she hopes there will come a time. 2.02.102 P
look you, he may come and go between you both; 2.02.125 P
could i come to her with any detection in my 2.02.245 P
come you to me at night, you shall know how i 2.02.266 P
come to me soon at night. 2.02.283 P
come to me soon at night. 2.02.286 P
by gar, he has save his soul, dat he is no come; 2.03. 7 P
he has pray his pible well, dat he is no come. 2.03. 7 P
jack rugby, he is dead already, if he be come. 2.03. 9 P
vat be all you, one, two, tree, four, come for? 2.03. 22 P
two, tree hours for him, and he is no come. 2.03. 37 P
doctor caius, i am come to fetch you home. 2.03. 52 P
come at my heels, jack rugby. 2.03. 98 P
we are come to you to do a good office, master 3.01. 49 P
come, lay their swords to pawn. 3.01.110 P
go home, john rugby, i come anon. 3.02. 86 P
come, come, come. 3.03. 5 P
come, come, come. 3.03. 5 P
come, come, come. 3.03. 5 P
and when i suddenly call you, come forth, and 3.03. 11 P
be gone, and come when you are call'd. 3.03. 19 P
sir john, is come in at your back door, mistress 3.03. 24 P
come, thou canst not hide it. 3.03. 66 P
come, i cannot cog and say thou art this and 3.03. 70 P
buds, that come like women in men's apparel, and 3.03. 71 P
i come before to tell you. 3.03.115 P
quickly, come. 3.03.148 P
pray you come near. 3.03.149 P
come, come, walk in the park. 3.03.223 P
come, come, walk in the park. 3.03.224 P
come, wife, come, mistress page, i pray you 3.03.226 P
come, wife, come, mistress page, i pray you 3.03.226 P
no, heaven so speed me in my time to come! 3.04. 12
i come to him. 3.04. 31
that i will, come cut and long–tail, under the 3.04. 46 P
good master fenton, come not to my child. 3.04. 72
come, master shallow; 3.04. 75
come, son slender, in. 3.04. 75
come, trouble not yourself. 3.04. 88
come, let me pour in some sack to the thames 3.05. 21 P
come in, woman! 3.05. 25 P
sir, i come to your worship from mistress ford. 3.05. 33 P
she desires you once more to come to her, 3.05. 46 P
you come to me to know what hath pass'd between me and 3.05. 61 P
come to me at your convenient leisure, and you 3.05.134 P
mistress ford desires you to come suddenly. 4.01. 6 P
come hither, william; hold up your head; come. 4.01. 17 P
come hither, william; hold up your head; come. 4.01. 18 P
come on, sirrah; 4.01. 19 P
come, we stay too long. 4.01. 85 P
no, i'll come no more i' th' basket. 4.02. 49 P
may i not go out ere he come? 4.02. 50 P
we'll come dress you straight. 4.02. 82 P
come, come, take it up. 4.02.111 P
come, come, take it up. 4.02.111 P
come, come forth! 4.02.120 P
come, come forth! 4.02.120 P
come hither, mistress ford, mistress ford, the 4.02.129 P
come forth, sirrah! 4.02.135 P
come away. 4.02.142 P
come you and the old woman down; 4.02.166 P
my husband will come into the chamber. 4.02.167 P
come down, you witch, you hag you, come down, i 4.02.178 P
down, you witch, you hag you, come down, i say! 4.02.179 P
come, mother prat, come give me your hand. 4.02.182 P
come, mother prat, come give me your hand. 4.02.182 P
come, gentlemen. 4.02.200 P
come, to the forge with it, then shape it. 4.02.223 P
they must come off. 4.03. 11 P
i'll sauce them, come. 4.03. 11 P
fie, fie, he'll never come. 4.04. 19 P
be terrors in him that he should not come; 4.04. 23 P
well, let it not be doubted but he'll come, 4.04. 44
sure he'll come. 4.04. 77
twenty thousand worthier come to crave her. 4.04. 90
sir, i come to speak with sir john falstaff from 4.05. 4 P
be so bold as stay, sir, till she come down. 4.05. 13 P
i come to speak with her indeed. 4.05. 13 P
ay; come; quick. 4.05. 43 P
there is a friend of mine come to town, tells me 4.05. 76 P
dere is no duke that the court is know to come. 4.05. 89 P
if it should come to the ear of the court, how i 4.05. 95 P
whence come you? 4.05.104 P
come up into my chamber. 4.05.127 P
come, come; 5.02. 1 P
come, come; 5.02. 1 P
i come to her in white, and cry "mum"; 5.02. 5 P
come, and remember your parts. 5.04. 1 P
come, come, trib, trib. 5.04. 4 P
come, come, trib, trib. 5.04. 4 P
let there come a tempest of provocation, i will 5.05. 21 P
mistress page is come with me, sweet heart. 5.05. 22 P
a trial, come. 5.05. 88
come, will this wood take fire? 5.05. 88
i pray you, come, hold up the jest no higher. 5.05.105
call hither, | i say, bid come before us angelo. MM 1.01. 15
grace's will, | i come to know your pleasure. 1.01. 26
with the other dukes come not to composition 1.02. 1 P
as many diseases under her roof as come to — 1.02. 47 P
come; 1.02.106 P
come, officer, away! 1.02.193
out my death, | and nothing come in partial. 2.01. 31
come, bring them away. 2.01. 41 P
come; 2.01.115 P
come me to what was done to her. 2.01.117 P
sir, your honor cannot come to that yet. 2.01.119 P
sir, but you shall come to it, by your honor's 2.01.121 P
now, sir, come on. 2.01.139 P
the time is yet to come that she was ever 2.01.168 P
thou wicked varlet, now, what's come upon thee. 2.01.190 P
come hither to me, master froth. 2.01.203 P
part, i never come into any room in a tap–house, 2.01.209 P
come you hither to me, master tapster. 2.01.212 P
come, tell me true, it shall be the better for 2.01.221 P
if you live to see this come to pass, say pompey 2.01.242 P
come hither to me, master elbow; 2.01.257 P
come hither, master constable. 2.01.257 P
come, sir. 2.01.286
he will come straight. 2.02. 1
i will bethink me. come again to–morrow. 2.02.144
well; come to me to–morrow. 2.02.155
i come to visit the afflicted spirits | here in 2.03. 4
come all to help him, and so stop the air | by 2.04. 25
i am come to know your pleasure. 2.04. 31
let it come on. 3.01. 43
come in, the wish deserves a welcome. 3.01. 45
that now you are come, you will be gone. 3.01.176 P
come your way, sir. 3.02. 11 P
his neck will come to your waist — a cord, sir. 3.02. 40 P
come your ways, sir, come. 3.02. 80 P
come your ways, sir, come. 3.02. 80 P
come your ways, sir, come. 3.02. 84 P
come your ways, sir, come. 3.02. 84 P
come, sir, i know what i know. 3.02.152 P
a year and a quarter old come philip and jacob. 3.02.201 P
of gracious order, late come from the /see, | in 3.02.219
the time is come even now. 4.01. 22 P
very well met, and well come. 4.01. 26
whose persuasion is | i come about my brother. 4.01. 47
come forth! 4.01. 49
come, let us go, | our corn's to reap, for yet 4.01. 74
come hither, sirrah; 4.02. 1 P
come, sir, leave me your snatches, and yield me 4.02. 6 P
come on, bawd, i will instruct thee in my trade; 4.02. 54 P
now are they come. 4.02. 85
fearless of what's past, present, or to come; 4.02.144 P
come away, it is almost clear dawn. 4.02.209 P
for look you, the warrant's come. 4.03. 42 P
you are to depart, i am come to advise you, 4.03. 51 P
have any thing to say to me, come to my ward; 4.03. 63 P
to save me from the danger that might come | if 4.03. 85
she's come to know | if yet her brother's pardon 4.03.107
if yet her brother's pardon be come hither. 4.03.108
might in the times to come have ta'en revenge, 4.04. 30
come, we will walk. 4.05. 12
o, peace, the friar is come. 4.06. 9
come, i have found you out a stand most fit, 4.06. 10
come, escalus, | you must walk by us on our 5.01. 16
he in time may come to clear himself; 5.01.150
being come to knowledge that there was complaint 5.01.153
come, cousin angelo, | in this i'll be impartial 5.01.165
now i come to't, my lord. 5.01.194
you to abide here till he come and enforce them 5.01.266 P
come on, mistress. 5.01.281 P
come, sir, did you set these women on to slander 5.01.288 P
come you to seek the lamb here of the fox, 5.01.298
villain's mouth | which here you come to accuse. 5.01.303
come hither, goodman bald–pate, do you know me? 5.01.326
come, sir, come, sir, come, sir; 5.01.351 P
come, sir, come, sir, come, sir; 5.01.351 P
come, sir, come, sir, come, sir; 5.01.351 P
come hither, mariana. 5.01.374
come hither, isabel, | your friar is now your 5.01.381
your life, | and choke your good to come. 5.01.422
and all my life to come | i'll lend you all my 5.01.431
mercy to provide | for better times to come. 5.01.485

syracusian born | come to the bay of ephesus, he ERR 1.01. 19
weeping before for what she saw must come, | and 1.01. 71
and stay there, dromio, till i come to thee. 1.02. 10
the meat is cold, because you come not home: 1.02. 48
you come not home, because you have no stomach: 1.02. 49
i from my mistress come to you in post: 1.02. 63
come, dromio, come, these jests are out of 1.02. 68
dromio, come, these jests are out of season, 1.02. 68
come on, sir knave, have done your foolishness, 1.02. 72
she that doth fast till you come home to dinner; 1.02. 89
and when they see time, | they'll go or come; 2.01. 9
till he come home again, i would forbear. 2.01. 31
when i desir'd him to come home to dinner, | he 2.01. 60
"will you come?" 2.01. 64
come, i will fasten on this sleeve of thine: 2.02.173
come, come, no longer will i be a fool, | to put 2.02.203
come, come, no longer will i be a fool, | to put 2.02.203
come, sir, to dinner. 2.02.206
come, sister. 2.02.211
come, come, antipholus, we dine too late. 2.02.219
come, come, antipholus, we dine too late. 2.02.219
here you must not, come again when you may. 3.01. 41
so, come, help: 3.01. 56
are you there, wife? you might have come before. 3.01. 63
and about evening come yourself alone | to know 3.01. 96
if any bark put forth, come to the mart, | where 3.02.150
bear it with you, lest i come not time enough. 4.01. 41
nay, come, i pray you, sir, give me the chain: 4.01. 45
come, come, you know i gave it you even now. 4.01. 55
come, come, you know i gave it you even now. 4.01. 55
come, where's the chain? 4.01. 58
on, officer, to prison till it come. 4.01.108
the hours come back! that did i never /hear. 4.02. 55
come, sister, i am press'd down with conceit — 4.02. 65
come not near her. 4.03. 57 P
avaunt, thou witch! come, dromio, let us go. 4.03. 79
come go along, my wife is coming yonder. 4.04. 40
o, bind him, bind him! let him not come near me. 4.04.106
come, jailer, bring me where the goldsmith is, 4.04.142
and come with naked swords: 4.04.145
come to the centaur, fetch our stuff from thence 4.04.149
let us come in, that we may bind him fast, | and 5.01. 40
come go: 5.01.114
have won his grace to come in person hither, 5.01.116
see where they come, we will behold his death. 5.01.128
and bid the lady abbess come to me: 5.01.166
come, stand by me, fear nothing. 5.01.185
from whence, i think, you are come by miracle. 5.01.265
come go with us, we'll look to that anon. 5.01.413
leonato, are you come to meet your trouble? ADO 1.01. 96 P
convert to disdain, if you come in her presence. 1.01.122 P
come, in what key shall a man take you to go in 1.01.185 P
is't come to this? 1.01.197 P
come thronging soft and delicate desires, | all 1.01.303
come, come, let us thither, this may prove food 1.03. 65 P
come, come, let us thither, this may prove food 1.03. 65 P
come, come, do you think i do not know you by 2.01.121 P
come, come, do you think i do not know you by 2.01.121 P
come let us to the banquet. 2.01.171 P
come, will you go with me? 2.01.185 P
come, talk not of her; 2.01.255 P
come, lady, come, you have lost the heart of 2.01.276 P
lady, come, you have lost the heart of signior 2.01.276 P
husbands, if a maid could come by them. 2.01.325 P
come, you shake the head at so long a breathing, 2.01.362 P
one woman, one woman shall not come in my grace. 2.03. 29 P
mild, or come not near me; 2.03. 32 P
come, shall we hear this music? 2.03. 37
come, balthasar, we'll hear that song again. 2.03. 43
nay, pray thee come, | or, if thou wilt hold 2.03. 52
come what plague could have come after it. 2.03. 82 P
come what plague could have come after it. 2.03. 83 P
come hither, leonato. 2.03. 89 P
proudly, if i perceive the love come from her; 2.03.226 P
my will i am sent to bid you come in to dinner. 2.03.247 P
if it had been painful, i would not have come. 2.03.252 P
will i am sent to bid you come in to dinner" — 2.03.258 P
i'll make her come, i warrant you, presently. 3.01. 14
now, ursula, when beatrice doth come, | as we do 3.01. 15
come go in, | i'll show thee some attires, and 3.01.101
come hither, neighbor seacole. 3.03. 13 P
come, neighbor. 3.03. 87 P
come, we'll obey you. 3.03.180 P
and bid her come hither. 3.04. 4 P
of the town are come to fetch you to church. 3.04. 97 P
come, friar francis, be brief — only to the 4.01. 1 P
you come hither, my lord, to marry this lady. 4.01. 4 P
friar, you come to marry her. 4.01. 7 P
you come hither to be married to this count. 4.01. 9 P
come, let us go. 4.01.111
these things, come thus to light, | smother her 4.01.111
shall come apparell'd in more precious habit, 4.01.227
come, lady, die to live; 4.01.253
come, bid me do any thing for thee. 4.01.288 P
bear her in hand until they come to take hands, 4.01.304 P
let them come before master constable. 4.02. 8 P
yea, marry, let them come before me. 4.02. 9 P
come you hither, sirrah; 4.02. 26 P
let the watch come forth. 4.02. 37 P
come let them be opinion'd. 4.02. 67 P
come, bind them. 4.02. 71 P
come follow me, boy; 5.01. 83
come, sir boy, come follow me. 5.01. 83
come, sir boy, come follow me. 5.01. 83
come, 'tis no matter; 5.01.100
no? come, brother, away! i will be heard. 5.01.108
you are almost come to part almost a fray. 5.01.113 P
come you, sir. 5.01.206 P
come, bring away the plaintiffs. 5.01.253 P
to-morrow morning come you to my house, | and 5.01.286
come, neighbor. 5.01.326 P
that no man living shall come over it, for in 5.02. 7 P
to have no man come over me? 5.02. 9 P
and therefore will come. 5.02. 25 P
beatrice, wouldst thou come when i call'd thee? 5.02. 42 P
madam, you must come to your uncle, yonder's old 5.02. 95 P
will you come presently? 5.02. 99 P
come let us hence, and put on other weeds, | and 5.03. 30

and when i send for you, come hither masked. 5.04. 12
come, cousin, i am sure you love the gentleman. 5.04. 84
come, i will have thee, but, by this light, i 5.04. 92 P
come, come, we are friends. 5.04.117 P
come, come, we are friends. 5.04.117 P
that no woman shall come within a mile of my LLL 1.01.119 P
sirrah, come on. 1.01.310 P
come, jaquenetta, away. 1.02.145 P
come, you transgressing slave, away. 1.02.154 P
it should none spare that come within his power. 2.01. 51
the packet is not come | where that and other 2.01.163
you may not come, fair princess, within my gates 2.01.171
come to our pavilion — boyet is dispos'd. 2.01.250
love her, because your heart cannot come by her; 3.01. 42 P
some enigma, some riddle — come, thy l'envoy — 3.01. 71
come hither, come hither. 3.01.105
come hither, come hither. 3.01.105
i will come to your worship to-morrow morning. 3.01.160 P
but come, the bow: 4.01. 24
why did he come? 4.01. 71 P
come, lords, away. 4.01.106
we choose by the horns, yourself come not near. 4.01.115
shall i come upon thee with an old saying, that 4.01.119 P
come, come, you talk greasily, your lips grow 4.01.137
come, come, you talk greasily, your lips grow 4.01.137
come, sir, you blush; 4.03.129
your mistresses dare never come in rain, | for 4.03.266
depart, | if fairings come thus plentifully in. 5.02. 2
we will do't, come what will come." 5.02.112
we will do't, come what will come." 5.02.112
but what, but what, come they to visit us? 5.02.119
come on then, wear the favors most in sight. 5.02.136
i make no doubt | the rest will /ne'er come in, 5.02.152
the trumpet sounds, be mask'd; the maskers come. 5.02.157
if to come hither you have measur'd miles, | and 5.02.191
will you not dance? how come you thus estranged? 5.02.213
since you are strangers and come here by chance, 5.02.218
tongue, | nor never come in vizard to my friend, 5.02.404
whether the three worthies shall come in or no. 5.02.486
i say they shall not come. 5.02.514
along this coast, i here am come by chance, 5.02.554
in minority, | ergo i come with this apology." 5.02.593
though my mocks come home by me, i will now be 5.02.634 P
come challenge me, challenge me by these deserts 5.02.805
come when the king doth to my lady come; 5.02.829
come when the king doth to my lady come; 5.02.829
come, sir, it wants a twelvemonth an' a day, 5.02.877
full of vexation come i, with complaint MND 1.01. 22
but, demetrius, come, | and come, egeus, you 1.01.114
come, | and come, egeus, you shall go with me; 1.01.115
come, my hippolyta; 1.01.122
so quick bright things come to confusion. 1.01.149
our queen and all her elves come here anon. 2.01. 17
take heed the queen come not within his sight; 2.01. 19
here | come from the farthest steep of india? 2.01. 69
wedded, and you come | to give their bed joy and 2.01. 72
my gentle puck, come hither. 2.01.148
come, now a roundel and a fairy song; 2.02. 1
do no wrong, | come not near our fairy queen. 2.02. 12
spell, nor charm, | come our lovely lady nigh. 2.02. 18
weaving spiders, come not here; 2.02. 20
and never mayst thou come lysander near! 2.02.136
if you think i come hither as a lion, it were 3.01. 42 P
or else one must come in with a bush of thorns 3.01. 59 P
come, sit down, every mother's son, and rehearse 3.01. 72 P
see a noise that he heard, and is to come again. 3.01. 92 P
come wait upon him; 3.01.197
scorn and derision never come in tears. 3.02.123
quick, come! 3.02.256
take on as you would follow, | but yet come not. 3.02.259
have you come by night | and stol'n my love's 3.02.283
let me come to her. 3.02.328
astray | as one come not within another's way. 3.02.359
that thou look'st for wars, | and wilt not come? 3.02.409
come, recreant, come, thou child, | i'll whip 3.02.409
come, recreant, come, thou child, | i'll whip 3.02.409
when i come where he calls, then he is gone. 3.02.414
come, thou gentle day! 3.02.418
come hither; i am here. 3.02.425
come one more; 3.02.437
come sit thee down upon this flow'ry bed, 4.01. 1
i have an exposition of sleep come upon me. 4.01. 39 P
come, my queen, take hands with me, | and rock 4.01. 85
come, my lord, and in our flight | tell me how 4.01. 99
but, as in health, come to my natural taste, 4.01.174
come, hippolyta. 4.01.186
is he come home yet? 4.02. 2 P
if he come not, then the play is marr'd. 4.02. 5 P
here come the lovers, full of joy and mirth. 5.01. 28
come now; 5.01. 32
where i have come, great clerks have purposed 5.01. 93
that you should think, we come not to offend, 5.01.109
consider then, we come but in despite. 5.01.112
we do not come, as minding to content you, | our 5.01.113
'tide life, 'tide death, i come without delay. 5.01.203
here come two noble beasts in, a man and a lion. 5.01.217 P
if i should as lion come in strife | into this 5.01.225
he dares not come there for the candle; 5.01.249 P
o fates, come, come, | cut thread and thrum, 5.01.285
o fates, come, come, | cut thread and thrum, 5.01.285
come, tears, confound, | out, sword, and wound 5.01.295
come, come to me, | with hands as pale as milk; 5.01.337
o sisters three, | come, come to me, | with 5.01.337
come, trusty sword, | come, blade, my breast 5.01.343
trusty sword, | come, blade, my breast imbrue! 5.01.344
but come, your bergomask; 5.01.361 P
with mirth and laughter let old wrinkles come, MV 1.01. 80
come, good lorenzo. 1.01.103
is to come fairly off from the great debts 1.01.128
strond, | and many jasons come in quest of her. 1.01.172
of these princely suitors that are already come? 1.02. 35 P
and you will come into the court and swear that 1.02. 70 P
and there is a forerunner come from a fift, the 1.02.124 P
come, nerissa. 1.02.132
go to then, you come to me, and you say, 1.03.115
come on, in this there can be no dismay, | my 1.03.180
my ships come home a month before the day. 1.03.181
nor will not. come bring me unto my chance. 2.01. 43

truth will come to light; 2.02. 79 P
father, i am glad you are come; 2.02.108 P
and desire gratiano to come anon to my lodging. 2.02.117 P
father, come, i'll take my leave of the jew in 2.02.167 P
if e'er the jew her father come to heaven, | it 2.04. 33
come go with me, peruse this as thou goest. 2.04. 38
go you before me, sirrah, | say i will come. 2.05. 39
for all this — there will come a christian by, 2.05. 42
but come at once, | for the close night doth 2.06. 46
what, art thou come? 2.06. 58
no masque to-night, the wind is come about, 2.06. 64
from the four corners of the earth they come 2.07. 39
now | for princes to come view fair portia. 2.07. 43
but they come | as o'er a brook to see fair 2.07. 46
come draw the curtain, nerissa. 2.09. 84
come, come, nerissa, for i long to see | quick 2.09. 99
come, come, nerissa, for i long to see | quick 2.09. 99
come, the full stop. 3.01. 15 P
that was us'd to come so smug upon the mart: 3.01. 46 P
come forth to view | the issue of th' exploit. 3.02. 59
what demigod | hath come so near creation? 3.02.116
leave, | i come by note, to give and to receive. 3.02.140
past all saying nay, | to come with him along. 3.02.230
come away! 3.02.310
if your love do not persuade you to come, let 3.02.321 P
but, till i come again, | no bed shall e'er be 3.02.325
fond | to come abroad with him at his request. 3.03. 10
pray god bassanio come | to see me pay his debt, 3.03. 35
come on, nerissa, i have work in hand | that you 3.04. 57
but come, i'll tell thee all my whole device 3.04. 81
in the meat, and we will come in to dinner. 3.05. 59 P
it, | in reason he should never come to heaven! 3.05. 78
thou art come to answer | a stony adversary, an 4.01. 3
sent for to determine this, | come here to-day. 4.01.107
letters from the doctor, | new come from padua. 4.01.109
and here, i take it, is the doctor come. 4.01.168
come you from old bellario? 4.01.169
a daniel come to judgment! 4.01.223
most learned judge! a sentence! come, prepare! 4.01.304
come, you and i will thither presently, | and in 4.01.455
come, antonio. 4.01.457
come, good sir, will you show me to this house? 4.02. 19
and waft her love | to come again to carthage. 5.01. 12
i would out-night you, did nobody come; 5.01. 23
tell him there's a post come from my master, 5.01. 46 P
come ho, and wake diana with a hymn, | with 5.01. 66
but there is come a messenger before, | to 5.01.117
i will ne'er come in your bed | until i see the 5.01.190
let not that doctor e'er come near my house. 5.01.223
argosies | are richly come to harbor suddenly. 5.01.277
certain that my ships | are safely come to road. 5.01.288
but were the day come, i should wish it dark 5.01.304
have i spent, that i should come to such penury? AYL 1.01. 39 P
come, come, elder brother, you are too young in 1.01. 53 P
come, come, elder brother, you are too young in 1.01. 53 P
hath a disposition to come in disguis'd against 1.01.125 P
him, as i must for my own honor if he come in; 1.01.131 P
if he come to-morrow, i'll give him his payment. 1.01.160 P
a pure blush thou mayst in honor come off again. 1.02. 29 P
mistress, you must come away to your father. 1.02. 57 P
by mine honor, but i was bid to come for you. 1.02. 61 P
come on. 1.02.149 P
i come but in, as others do, to try with him the 1.02.171 P
come, where is this young gallant that is so 1.02.200 P
but come your ways. 1.02.209 P
come, lame me with reasons. 1.03. 5 P
come, come, wrastle with thy affections. 1.03. 21 P
come, come, wrastle with thy affections. 1.03. 21 P
come, shall we go and kill us venison? 2.01. 21
aim had ta'en a hurt, | did come to languish; 2.01. 35
your praise is come too swiftly home before you. 2.03. 9
o unhappy youth, | come not within these doors! 2.03. 17
no matter whither, so you come not here. 2.03. 30
but come thy ways, we'll go along together, 2.03. 66
but what is, come see, | and in my voice most 2.04. 86
throat, | come hither, come hither, come hither! 2.05. 5
throat, | come hither, come hither, come hither! 2.05. 5
throat, | come hither, come hither, come hither! 2.05. 5
come, more, another stanzo. 2.05. 18 P
come, sing; 2.05. 29 P
come, warble, come. 2.05. 37 P
come, warble, come. 2.05. 37 P
gets, | come hither, come hither, come hither! 2.05. 42
gets, | come hither, come hither, come hither! 2.05. 42
gets, | come hither, come hither, come hither! 2.05. 42
if it do come to pass | that any man turn ass, 2.05. 50
gross fools as he, | and if he will come to me. 2.05. 57
but if thou diest before i come, thou art a 2.06. 13 P
come, i will bear thee to some shelter, and thou 2.06. 15 P
who can come in and say that i mean her, | when 2.07. 77
of what kind should this cock come of? 2.07. 90
instance, briefly; come, instance. 3.02. 52 P
come. 3.02. 58 P
a more sounder instance, come. 3.02. 61 P
come, shepherd, let us make an honorable retreat 3.02.160 P
call me rosalind and come every day to my cote 3.02.427 P
come, sister, will you go? 3.02.434 P
come apace, good audrey; 3.03. 1 P
sluttishness may come hereafter. 3.03. 41 P
come, sweet audrey, | we must be married, or we 3.03. 96
but why did he swear he would come this morning, 3.04. 18 P
o, come, let us remove, | the sight of lovers 3.04. 56
but till that time | come not thou near me; 3.05. 32
come, sister. 3.05. 77
come, to our flock. 3.05. 80
such another trick, never come in my sight more. 4.01. 41 P
rosalind, i come within an hour of my promise. 4.01. 42 P
and you be so tardy, come no more in my sight. 4.01. 51 P
come, woo me, woo me; 4.01. 68 P
but come, now i will be your rosalind in a more 4.01.112 P
come, sister, you shall be the priest, and marry 4.01.124 P
'tis but one cast away, and so, come death! 4.01.186 P
promise, or come one minute behind your hour, i 4.01.191 P
i'll go find a shadow, and sigh till he come. 4.01.217 P
come, come, you are a fool, | and turn'd into 4.03. 22
come, come, you are a fool, | and turn'd into 4.03. 22
come, you look paler and paler. 4.03.177 P
come, away, away! 5.01. 60 P

here come two of the banish'd duke's pages. 5.03. 5 P
come, sit, sit, and a song. 5.03. 8 P
come, audrey. 5.03. 41 P
let him come, and kindly. SHR in.1. 14 P
bid them come near. in.1. 79
well, you are come to me in happy time, | the in.1. 90
madam, undress you and come now to bed. in.2. 117
amendment, | are come to play a pleasant comedy, in.2. 130
come, madam wife, sit by my side, and let the in.2. 142 P
the world, | vincentio, come of the bentivolii; 1.01. 13
for i have pisa left | and am to padua come, as 1.01. 22
if, biondello, thou wert come ashore, | we could 1.01. 42
but come, since this bar in law makes us friends 1.01.135 P
come on. 1.01.145 P
sirrah, come hither, 'tis no time to jest, | and 1.01.226
signior hortensio, come you to part the fray? 1.02. 23
first, | then had not grumio come by the worst. 1.02. 35
and come you now with "knocking at the gate"? 1.02. 42 P
home, | and so am come abroad to see the world. 1.02. 58
petruchio, shall i then come roundly to thee, 1.02. 59
seas, | i come to wive it wealthily in padua; 1.02. 75
haste, | and every day i cannot come to woo. 2.01.115
thou hast hit it; come sit on me. 2.01.198
come, come, you wasp, i' faith you are too angry 2.01.209
come, come, you wasp, i' faith you are too angry 2.01.209
nay, come again, | good kate; 2.01.218
nay, come, kate, come; 2.01.228
nay, come, kate, come; 2.01.228
if it would please him come and marry her!" 3.02. 20
is he come? 3.02. 35 P
i am glad he's come, howsoe'er he comes. 3.02. 74 P
come, where be these gallants? who's at home? 3.02. 87
and yet i come not well. 3.02. 88
first were we sad, fearing you would not come, 3.02. 98
come, | now sadder, that you come so unprovided. 3.02. 99
hear — | sufficeth i am come to keep my word, 3.02.106
i must away to–day, before night come. 3.02.190
she shall, lucentio. come, gentlemen, let's go. 3.02.252
belly, ere i should come by a fire to thaw me. 4.01. 8 P
come, you are so full of cony–catching! 4.01. 43 P
and walter's dagger was not come from sheathing; 4.01.135
as they are, here are they come to meet you. 4.01.138
and bid my cousin ferdinand come hither; 4.01.151
come, kate, and wash, and welcome heartily. 4.01.154
come, kate, sit down, i know you have a stomach. 4.01.158
come, i will bring thee to thy bridal chamber. 4.01.178
to make her come and know her keeper's call, 4.01.194
and come to padua, careless of your life? 4.02. 79
death for any one in mantua | to come to padua. 4.02. 82
'tis marvel, but that you are but newly come, 4.02. 86
beggars that come unto my father's door | upon 4.03. 4
come, mistress kate, i'll bear you company. 4.03. 49
come, tailor, let us see these ornaments; 4.03. 61
come let me have a bigger. 4.03. 68
come, tailor, let us see't. 4.03. 86
well, come, my kate, we will unto your father's 4.03.169
and well we may come there by dinner–time. 4.03.188
and 'twill be supper–time ere you come there. 4.03.190
having come to padua | to gather in some debts, 4.04. 24
come, sir, we will better it in pisa. 4.04. 71
priest be ready to come against you come with 4.04.103 P
to come against you come with your appendix. 4.04.104 P
come on a' god's name! 4.05. 1
forward, i pray, since we have come so far, 4.05. 12
come go along and see the truth hereof, | for 4.05. 75
and then come back to my /master's as soon as i 5.01. 5 P
lucentio that his father is come from pisa, and 5.01. 28 P
his father is come from padua and here looking 5.01. 30 P
come hither, crack–hemp. 5.01. 45 P
come hither, you rogue. 5.01. 48 P
come, sirrah, let's away. 5.01.147
come, my sweet kate: 5.01.149
to come at first when he doth send for her, 5.02. 68
go, biondello, bid your mistress come to me. 5.02. 76
word | that she is busy, and she cannot come. 5.02. 81
she is busy, and she cannot come! 5.02. 82
and entreat my wife | to come to me forthwith. 5.02. 87
nay then she must needs come. 5.02. 88
she will not come; 5.02. 92
she bids you come to her. 5.02. 92
she will not come! 5.02. 93
your mistress, | say i command her come to me. 5.02. 96
if they deny to come, | swinge me them soundly 5.02.103
come, come, you're mocking; 5.02.132
come, come, you're mocking; 5.02.132
come on, i say, and first begin with her. 5.02.133
come, come, you froward and unable worms! 5.02.169
come, come, you froward and unable worms! 5.02.169
come on, and kiss me, kate. 5.02.180
come, kate, we'll to bed. 5.02.184
for the knaves come to do that for me which i am AWW 1.03. 43 P
you, madam, that he bid helen come to you. 1.03. 67 P
the business is for helen to come hither. 1.03. 96 P
come, come, disclose | the state of your 1.03.189
come, come, disclose | the state of your 1.03.189
monarchy) see that you come | not to woo honor, 2.01. 14
farewell. — come hither to me. 2.01. 23
nay, come your ways. 2.01. 93
nay, come your ways; 2.01. 94
i come to tender it, and my appliance, | with 2.01.113
come on, sir, i shall now put you to the height 2.02. 1 P
cheek for ever, | we'll ne'er come there again." 2.03. 72
i pray you. come, sirrah. 2.04. 55
come, come, no more of that. 2.05. 73
come, come, no more of that. 2.05. 73
where i will never come | whilst i can shake my 2.05. 90
ease, will day by day | come here for physic. 3.01. 19
see what he writes, and when he means to come. 3.02. 11 P
know it before the report come. 3.02. 23 P
here they come will tell you more; 3.02. 43 P
ring upon my finger, which never shall come off, 3.02. 58 P
no, come thou home, rossillion, | whence honor 3.02.120
come night, end day! 3.02.128
nay, come, for if they do approach the city, we 3.05. 1 P
come, let's return again and suffice ourselves 3.05. 10 P
hark you, they come this way. 3.05. 38
holy pilgrim, | but till the troops come by, | i 3.05. 40
so, now they come. 3.05. 75
come, pilgrim, i will bring you | where you 3.05. 93
he can come no other way but by this 4.01. 1 P
come on, thou /art granted space. 4.01. 88
we will not meddle with him till he come; 4.03. 36 P
which could not be her office to say is come, 4.03. 58 P
come, bring forth this counterfeit module, h'as 4.03. 98 P
come, headsman, off with his head. 4.03.308 P
for it will come to pass | that every braggart 4.03.335
of power you have | to come into his presence. 5.01. 21
i will come after you with what good speed | our 5.01. 34
come, you shall ha't; 5.02. 37 P
come on, my son, in whom my house's name | must 5.03. 73
of my daughter, | that she may quickly come. 5.03. 76
where you have never come, or sent it us | upon 5.03.111
and mak'st /conjectural fears to come into me, 5.03.114
who hath for four or five removes come short 5.03.131
come hither, count, do you know these women? 5.03.165
come, come, to th' purpose. 5.03.241 P
come, come, to th' purpose. 5.03.241 P
sir toby, you must come in earlier a' nights. TN 1.03. 4 P
church in a galliard and come home in a coranto? 1.03.128 P
how have you come so early by this lethargy? 1.05.123 P
come, throw it o'er my face. 1.05.165
come to what is important in't. 1.05.192 P
you come to me again | to tell me how he takes 1.05.281
if that the youth will come this way to–morrow, 1.05.305
but, come what may, i do adore thee so | that 2.01. 47
be never so hardy to come again in his affairs, 2.02. 10 P
come, sir, you peevishly threw it to her; 2.02. 13 P
come on, there is sixpence for you. 2.03. 31 P
what's to come is still unsure. 2.03. 49
plenty, | then come kiss me, sweet and twenty; 2.03. 51
good, i' faith. come, begin. 2.03. 71 P
thou wilt drop, that they come from my niece, 2.03.165 P
come, come, i'll go burn some sack, 'tis too 2.03.190 P
come, come, i'll go burn some sack, 'tis too 2.03.190 P
come, knight, come, knight. 2.03.191 P
come, knight, come, knight. 2.03.191 P
come, but one verse. 2.04. 7
come hither, boy. 2.04. 15
o fellow, come, the song we had last night. 2.04. 42
come away, come away, death, | and in sad 2.04. 51
come away, come away, death, | and in sad 2.04. 51
come thy ways, signior fabian. 2.05. 1 P
nay, i'll come. 2.05. 2 P
rascally sheep–biter come by some notable shame? 2.05. 5 P
and i have heard herself come thus near, that, 2.05. 25 P
having come from a day–bed, where i have left 2.05. 48 P
he will come to her in yellow stockings, and 2.05.198 P
i will conster to them whence you come; 3.01. 57 P
i come to whet your gentle thoughts | on his 3.01.105
and yet, when wit and youth is come to harvest, 3.01.132
yet come again; 3.01.163
come bring us, bring us where he is. 3.02. 84 P
he says he'll come. 3.04. 1
best to have some guard about you, if he come, 3.04. 13 P
it did come to his hands, and commands shall be 3.04. 27 P
to bed? ay, sweet heart, and i'll come to thee. 3.04. 30 P
i'll come to him. 3.04. 60 P
o ho, do you come near me now? 3.04. 64 P
that can be can come between me and the full 3.04. 81 P
ay, biddy, come with me. 3.04.115 P
come, we'll have him in a dark room and bound. 3.04.135 P
and i beseech you come again to–morrow. 3.04.210
well, come again to–morrow. 3.04.216
come, sir andrew, there's no remedy, the 3.04.305 P
come on, to't. 3.04.309 P
o good sir toby, hold! here come the officers. 3.04.319 P
come, sir, away. 3.04.339
come, sir, i pray you go. 3.04.358
come, come, sir. 3.04.371
come, come, sir. 3.04.371
come hither, knight; 3.04.377 P
come hither, fabian; 3.04.377 P
come, let's see the event. 3.04.395 P
you by my lady, to bid you come speak with her, 4.01. 6 P
come on, sir, hold! 4.01. 32 P
come, sir, i will not let you go. 4.01. 38 P
come, my young soldier, put up your iron; 4.01. 38 P
come on. 4.01. 40 P
nay, come, i prithee. 4.01. 64
come by and by to my chamber. 4.02. 71 P
whiles you are willing it shall come to note, 4.03. 29
sir, lullaby to your bounty till i come again. 5.01. 45 P
come, boy, with me, my thoughts are ripe in 5.01.129
come, away! 5.01.142
both form and suit, | you come to fright us. 5.01.236
bade me come smiling and cross–garter'd to you, 5.01.337
and let no quarrel nor no brawl to come | taint 5.01.356
cesario, come — | for so you shall be while you 5.01.385
come, i'll question you | of my lord's tricks WT 1.02. 60
come, captain, | we must be neat; 1.02.122
come, sir page, | look on me with your welkin 1.02.135
come, camillo, | i will respect thee as a father 1.02.460
come, sir, away. 1.02.465
come, my gracious lord, | shall i be your 2.01. 2
come, sir, now | i am for you again. 2.01. 21
come on, sit down, come on, and do your best 2.01. 27
sit down, come on, and do your best | to fright 2.01. 27
nay, come sit down; then on. 2.01. 29
come on then, | and give't me in mine ear. 2.01. 31
bear the boy hence, he shall not come about her. 2.01. 59
come between | ere you can say she's honest: 2.01. 75
when you shall come to clearer knowledge, that 2.01. 97
prison, then abound in tears | as i come out; 2.01.121
my women, come, you have leave. 2.01.124
credulity will not | come up to th' truth. 2.01.193
come follow us, | we are to speak in public; 2.01.196
please you, come something nearer. 2.02. 53
a moi'ty of my rest | might come to me again. 2.03. 9
to–night, commanded | none should come at him. 2.03. 32
so hot, good sir, | i come to bring him sleep. 2.03. 33
i | do come with words as medicinal as true, 2.03. 37
charg'd thee that she should not come about me: 2.03. 43
good my liege, i come; 2.03. 52
i say, i come | from your good queen. 2.03. 57
of our dear services | past and to come) that 2.03.151
you, sir, come you hither: 2.03.158
come on, poor babe. 2.03.185
from those you sent to th' oracle are come | an 2.03.194
and honor 'fore | who please to come and hear. 3.02. 42
faults i make, when i shall come to know them, 3.02.219
come, and lead me | to these sorrows. 3.02.242
come, poor babe. 3.03. 15
up for pity — yet i'll tarry till my son come; 3.03. 77 P
on when thou art dead and rotten, come hither. 3.03. 81 P
come, good boy, the next way home. 3.03.126 P
for the life to come, i sleep out the thought of 4.03. 30 P
a million of beating may come to a great matter. 4.03. 59 P
come, lend me thy hand. 4.03. 69 P
nuptial, which | we two have sworn shall come. 4.04. 51
come, quench your blushes, and present yourself 4.04. 67
come on, | and bid us welcome to your 4.04. 68
that come before the swallow dares, and take 4.04.119
come, take your flow'rs. 4.04.132
but come, our dance, i pray. 4.04.153
come on. strike up. 4.04.161
come, strike up. 4.04.165
he could never come better; 4.04.187 P
he shall come in. 4.04.187 P
handle, though they come to him by th' gross; 4.04.206 P
come buy of me, come; 4.04.228
come buy of me, come; 4.04.228
come buy, come buy, | buy, lads, or else your 4.04.228
come buy, come buy, | buy, lads, or else your 4.04.228
come buy. 4.04.230
the feast, but they come not too late now. 4.04.236 P
come, you promis'd me a tawdry–lace and a pair 4.04.249 P
come on, lay it by; 4.04.273 P
come bring away thy pack after me. 4.04.311 P
come to the pedlar, | money's a meddler, | that 4.04.321
these good men are pleas'd, let them come in; 4.04.341 P
but come on, | contract us 'fore these witnesses 4.04.389
come, your hand; | and, daughter, yours. 4.04.390
come, come, he must not. | mark our contract. 4.04.416
come, come, he must not. | mark our contract. 4.04.416
i told you what would come of this. 4.04.447
of his highness settle, | come not before him. 4.04.472
myself and fortune | tug for the time to come. 4.04.497
and had not the old man come in with a whoobub 4.04.615 P
mistress (let my prophecy | come home to ye!), 4.04.649
come, lady, come. 4.04.659
come, lady, come. 4.04.659
this hour, if i may come to th' speech of him. 4.04.758 P
fifty times) shall all come under the hangman; 4.04.774 P
to offer to have his daughter come into grace! 4.04.777 P
to break his grave | and come again to me; 5.01. 43
they are come. 5.01.123
good father's speed, | will come on very slowly. 5.01.211
come, good my lord. 5.01.233
here come those i have done good to against my 5.02.124 P
come, boy, i am past moe children, but thy sons 5.02.126 P
come, follow us; 5.02.174 P
come; 5.03.100
nay, come away; 5.03.101
come, camillo, | and take her by the hand, whose 5.03.143
come from the country to be judg'd by you | that JN 1.01. 45
come, madam, and come, richard, we must speed 1.01.178
come, madam, and come, richard, we must speed 1.01.178
brother, adieu, good fortune come to thee! 1.01.180
come, lady, i will show thee to my kin, | and 1.01.273
at our importance hither is he come | to spread 2.01. 7
with him along is come the mother–queen, | an 2.01. 62
come to thy grandame, child. 2.01.159
and like a jolly troop of huntsmen come | our 2.01.321
come, away, away! 2.01.415
beds, | that here come sacrifices for the field. 2.01.420
here is my throne, bid kings come bow to it. 3.01. 74
this day all things begun come to ill end, | yea 3.01. 94
upon which better part our pray'rs come in, | if 3.01.293
when gold and silver becks me to come on. 3.03. 13
come hither, little kinsman, hark, a word. 3.03. 18
come hither, hubert. 3.03. 19
yet it shall come for me to do thee good. 3.03. 32
come, grin on me, and i will think thou smil'st, 3.04. 34
misery's love, | o, come to me! 3.04. 36
young lad, come forth; 4.01. 8
and if an angel should have come to me | and 4.01. 68
come forth. do as i bid you do. 4.01. 71
let him come back, that his compassion may 4.01. 88
come, boy, prepare yourself. 4.01. 89
the color of the king doth come and go | between 4.02. 76
shame, | this murther had not come into my mind; 4.02.223
you shall think the devil is come from hell. 4.03.100
and grapple with him ere he come so nigh. 5.01. 61
come, come; 5.02. 60
come, come; 5.02. 60
himself to rome, his spirit is come in, | that 5.02. 70
and come ye now to tell me john hath made | his 5.02. 91
i come to learn how you have dealt for him; 5.02.121
maids | like amazons come tripping after drums, 5.02.155
to think | i come one way of the plantagenets. 5.06. 11
come, come; sans compliment, what news abroad? 5.06. 16
come, come; sans compliment, what news abroad? 5.06. 16
the lords are all come back, | and brought 5.06. 33
i doubt he will be dead or e'er i come. 5.06. 44
and none of you will bid the winter come | to 5.07. 36
o cousin, thou art come to set mine eye. 5.07. 51
now these her princes are come home again, 5.07.115
come the three corners of the world in arms, 5.07.116
us, | as well appeareth by the cause you come: R2 1.01. 26
come i appellant to this princely presence. 1.01. 34
let him not come there | to seek out sorrow that 1.02. 71
who hither come engaged by my oath | (which god 1.03. 17
come, come, my son, i'll bring thee on thy way; 1.03.304
come, come, my son, i'll bring thee on thy way; 1.03.304
whether our kinsman come to see his friends. 1.04. 22
if that come short, | our substitutes at home 1.04. 47
come, gentlemen, let's all go visit him. 1.04. 63
pray god we may make haste and come too late! 1.04. 64
will the king come, that i may breathe my last 2.01. 1
the king is come. 2.01. 69
come on, our queen, to–morrow must we part. 2.01.222
whilst others come to make him lose at home. 2.02. 81
come, sister — cousin, i would say — pray 2.02.105
come, cousin, i'll dispose of you. 2.02.117

here come the lords of ross and willoughby, 2.03. 57
and i am come to seek that name in england, 2.03. 71
to you, my lord, i come, what lord you will, 2.03. 76
and here art come | before the expiration of thy 2.03.110
herford, | but as i come, i come for lancaster. 2.03.114
herford, | but as i come, i come for lancaster. 2.03.114
but in this kind to come, in braving arms, | be 2.03.143
witnessing storms to come, woe, and unrest. 2.04. 22
come, lords, away, | to fight with glendower and 3.01. 42
and, till so much blood thither come again, 3.02. 78
and be slain — no worse can come to fight, 3.02.183
i come | to change blows with thee for our day 3.02.188
hither come | even at his feet to lay my arms 3.03. 38
he is come to open | the purple testament of 3.03. 93
speak with you, may it please you to come down. 3.03.177
down, down i come, like glist'ring phaeton, 3.03.178
to come at traitors' calls and do them grace. 3.03.181
in the base court, come down? 3.03.182
fondly like a frantic man, | yet he is come. 3.03.186
my gracious lord, i come but for mine own. 3.03.196
but stay, here come the gardeners. 3.04. 24
come, ladies, go | to; 3.04. 96
i come to thee | from plume–pluck'd richard, who 4.01.107
the woe's to come; 4.01.322
come home with me to supper, i'll lay | a plot 4.01.333
this way the king will come, this is the way 5.01. 1
come, come, in wooing sorrow let's be brief, 5.01. 93
come, come, in wooing sorrow let's be brief, 5.01. 93
lest you be cropp'd before you come to prime. 5.02. 51
never more come in my sight. 5.02. 86
i know she is come to pray for your foul sin. 5.03. 82
his words come from his mouth, ours from our 5.03.102
come, my old son, i pray god make thee new. 5.03.146
come, let's go. 5.04. 10
"come, little ones," and then again, | "it is as 5.05. 15
"it is as hard to come as for a camel | to 5.05. 16
come mourn with me for what i do lament, | and 5.06. 47
but come yourself with speed to us again, | for 1H4 1.01.105
indeed you come near me now, hal, for we that 1.02. 13 P
well, how then? come, roundly, roundly. 1.02. 22 P
well, come what will, i'll tarry at home. 1.02.145 P
but when they seldom come, they wish'd for come, 1.02.206
but when they seldom come, they wish'd for come, 1.02.206
not his report | come current for an accusation 1.03. 68
and if the devil come and roar for them, | i 1.03.125
days, | or fill up chronicles in time to come, 1.03.171
come away and be hang'd! 2.01. 22 P
come away. 2.01. 23 P
come, and be hang'd! 2.01. 30 P
what time do you mean to come to london? 2.01. 42 P
come, neighbor mugs, we'll call up the gentlemen 2.01. 44 P
come, shelter, shelter! 2.02. 1 P
come, neighbor, the boy shall lead our horses 2.02. 78 P
come, my masters, let us share, and then to 2.02. 98 P
come, come, you paraquito, answer me | directly 2.03. 85
come, come, you paraquito, answer me | directly 2.03. 85
come, wilt thou see me ride? 2.03.100
ned, prithee come out of that fat room, and lend 2.04. 1 P
to drive away the time till falstaff come, i 2.04. 29 P
come hither, francis. 2.04. 39 P
in barbary, sir, it cannot come to so much. 2.04. 75 P
come, what's the issue? 2.04. 91 P
unbound the rest, and then come in the other. 2.04.182 P
come, tell us your reason; 2.04.233 P
come, your reason, jack, your reason. 2.04.235 P
come, let's hear, jack, what trick hast thou now 2.04.265 P
all the titles of good fellowship come to you! 2.04.279 P
is like, if there come a hot june and this civil 2.04.361 P
now, harry, whence come you? 2.04.440 P
at the door, they are come to search the house. 2.04.490 P
but will they come when you do call for them? 3.01. 54
come, come, no more of this unprofitable chat. 3.01. 62
come, come, no more of this unprofitable chat. 3.01. 62
come, here is the map. 3.01. 69
and in my conduct shall your ladies come, | from 3.01. 91
come, you shall have trent turn'd. 3.01.134
natural scope | when you come 'cross his humor, 3.01.170
here come our wives, and let us take our leave. 3.01.189
come, kate, thou art perfect in lying down. 3.01.226 P
come, quick, quick, that i may lay my head in 3.01.227 P
come, kate, i'll have your song too. 3.01.245 P
come sing. 3.01.257 P
these two hours, and so come in when ye will. 3.01.261 P
come, come, lord mortimer, you are as slow | as 3.01.263
come, come, lord mortimer, you are as slow | as 3.01.263
for the time will come | that i shall make this 3.02.144
so hath the business that i come to speak of. 3.02.163
come sing me a bawdy song, make me merry. 3.03. 13 P
hostess, my breakfast, come! 3.03.205
these letters come from your father. 4.01. 14
he cannot come, my lord, he is grievous sick. 4.01. 16
under whose government come they along? 4.01. 19
spend upon the hope of what | /is to come in. 4.01. 55
let them come! 4.01.112
they come like sacrifices in their trim, | and 4.01.113
come let me taste my horse, | who is to bear me 4.01.119
o that glendower were come! 4.01.124
come let us take a muster speedily. 4.01.133
prodigals lately come from swine–keeping, from 4.02. 34 P
jack, whose fellows are these that come after? 4.02. 62 P
come, come, it may not be. 4.03. 16
come, come, it may not be. 4.03. 16
of my cousin vernon's are not yet come up. 4.03. 20
for god's sake, cousin, stay till all come in. 4.03. 29
i come with gracious offers from the king, | if 4.03. 30
even our love durst not come near your sight 5.01. 63
but how if honor prick me off when i come on? 5.01.131 P
if he do come in my way, so; 5.03. 57 P
if he do not, if i come in his willingly, let 5.03. 57 P
come, my lord, i'll lead you to your tent. 5.04. 9
come, cousin westmerland, | our duty this way 5.04. 15
for god's sake come. 5.04. 16
for the hour is come | to end the one of us, and 5.04. 68
new wound in your thigh, come you along with me. 5.04.128 P
come, brother john, full bravely hast thou 5.04.130
come bring your luggage nobly on your back. 5.04.156
come, brother, let us to the highest of the 5.04.160
the posts come tiring on, | and not a man of 2H4 in 37
say, morton, didst thou come from shrewsbury? 1.01. 64
come, we will all put forth, body and goods. 1.01.186
you would not come when i sent for you. 1.02.106 P
you for your life, to come speak with me. 1.02.133 P
the laws of this land–service, i did not come. 1.02.135 P
and come against us in full puissance, | need 1.03. 77
him once, and 'a come but within my /vice — 2.01. 21 P
widow to so rough a course to come by her own? 2.01. 83 P
wife, come in then and call me gossip quickly? 2.01. 94 P
throng of words that come with such more than 2.01.112 P
come hither, hostess. 2.01.132 P
as i am a gentleman! come, no more words of it. 2.01.138 P
come, and 'twere not for thy humors, there's not 2.01.148 P
come, thou must not be in this humor with me, 2.01.150 P
come, come, i know thou wast set on to this. 2.01.151 P
come, come, i know thou wast set on to this. 2.01.151 P
i hope you'll come to supper. 2.01.159 P
come all his forces back? 2.01.172
come, go along with me, good master gower. 2.01.179
is't come to that? 2.02. 2 P
come, you virtuous ass, you bashful fool, must 2.02. 75 P
word to your master that i am yet come to town. 2.02.161 P
come, come, go in with me. 2.03. 62
come, come, go in with me. 2.03. 62
supp'd is too hot, they'll come in straight. 2.04. 14 P
for to serve bravely is to come halting off, you 2.04. 49 P
to come off the breach with his pike bent 2.04. 50 P
come, i'll be friends with thee, jack. 2.04. 65 P
let him not come hither. 2.04. 72 P
if he swagger, let him not come here. 2.04. 73 P
come, i'll drink no proofs nor no bullets. 2.04.118 P
come give 's some sack. 2.04.180 P
come we to full points here? 2.04.184
come, get you down stairs. 2.04.195 P
come, atropos, i say! 2.04.199
come let me wipe thy face. 2.04.217 P
come on, you whoreson chops. 2.04.218 P
the music is come, sir. 2.04.226 P
come, it grows late, we'll to bed. 2.04.276 P
sir, and i come to draw you out by the ears. 2.04.289 P
o jesu, are you come from wales? 2.04.293 P
weak and wearied posts | come from the north, 2.04.357
thee these twenty–nine years, come peascod–time, 2.04.383 P
bid mistress tearsheet come to my master. 2.04.387 P
come. 2.04.389 P
will you come, doll? 2.04.391 P
but, ere they come, bid them o'er–read these 3.01. 2
"the time shall come," thus did he follow it, 3.01. 75
"the time will come, that foul sin, gathering 3.01. 76
main chance of things | as yet not come to life, 3.01. 84
come on, come on, come on, give me your hand, 3.02. 1 P
come on, come on, come on, give me your hand, 3.02. 1 P
come on, come on, come on, give me your hand, 3.02. 1 P
here come two of sir john falstaff's men, as i 3.02. 53 P
come prick bullcalf till he roar again. 3.02.175 P
come, thou shalt go to the wars in a gown. 3.02.184 P
come, i will go drink with you, but i cannot 3.02.191 P
come let's to dinner, come let's to dinner. 3.02.218 P
come let's to dinner, come let's to dinner. 3.02.218 P
come, come. 3.02.219 P
come, come. 3.02.219 P
come, sir, which men shall i have? 3.02.241 P
come, sir john, which four will you have? 3.02.246 P
your part, bullcalf, grow till you come unto it. 3.02.252 P
come off and on swifter than he that gibbets on 3.02.263 P
come manage me your caliver. 3.02.273 P
and about, and come you in and come you in. 3.02.283 P
and about, and come you in and come you in. 3.02.283 P
away again would 'a go, and again would 'a come. 3.02.285 P
here come i from our princely general | to know 4.01.139
we come within our aweful banks again, | and 4.01.174
my lord, we come. 4.01.226
when every thing is ended, then you come. 4.03. 27
and, when you come to court, stand my good lord 4.03. 82 P
none of these demure boys come to any proof, for 4.03. 90 P
come away. 4.03.131 P
afoot, | come underneath the yoke of government. 4.04. 10
fall | as those that i am come to tell you of! 4.04. 96
will fortune never come with both hands full, 4.04.103
come near me, now i am much ill. 4.04.111
come hither to me, harry. 4.05. 89
for now a time is come to mock at form. 4.05.118
come hither, harry, sit thou by my bed, | and 4.05.181
yea, marry, william cook, bid him come hither. 5.01. 11 P
come, come, come, off with your boots. 5.01. 54 P
come, come, come, off with your boots. 5.01. 54 P
come, come, come, off with your boots. 5.01. 54 P
come, sir john. 5.01. 59 P
i come, master shallow, i come, master shallow. 5.01. 87 P
i come, master shallow, i come, master shallow. 5.01. 87 P
here come the heavy issue of dead harry. 5.02. 14
come, cousin silence — and then to bed. 5.03. 3 P
come, cousin. 5.03. 15 P
"fill the cup, and let it come, | i'll pledge 5.03. 53
there's one pistol come from the court with news 5.03. 81 P
let him come in. 5.03. 82 P
sir, you come with news from the court, i take 5.03.109 P
come, pistol, utter more to me, and withal 5.03.133 P
come on! 5.04. 7 P
o the lord, that sir john were come! 5.04. 11 P
come, i charge you both go with me, for the man 5.04. 15 P
come, come, you she knight–arrant, come. 5.04. 22 P
come, come, you she knight–arrant, come. 5.04. 22 P
come, come, you she knight–arrant, come. 5.04. 23 P
come, you rogue, come bring me to a justice. 5.04. 26 P
come, you rogue, come bring me to a justice. 5.04. 26 P
ay, come, you starv'd bloodhound. 5.04. 27 P
come, you thin thing, come, you rascal. 5.04. 30 P
come, you thin thing, come, you rascal. 5.04. 30 P
two a' clock ere they come from the coronation. 5.05. 3 P
come here, pistol, stand behind me. 5.05. 10 P
not to come near our person by ten mile. 5.05. 65
come, lieutenant pistol, come, bardolph. 5.05. 88 P
come, lieutenant pistol, come, bardolph. 5.05. 89 P
come, will you hence? 5.05.109
if like an ill venture it come unluckily home, i ep 11 P
hour, i think, is come | to give him hearing. H5 1.01. 92
arrows loosed several ways | come to one mark; 1.02.208
but till the king come forth, and not till then, 2.pr. 41
mine host pistol, you must come to my master, 2.01. 81 P
good husband, come home presently. 2.01. 89 P
come, shall i make you two friends? 2.01. 90 P
as ever you come of women, come in quickly to 2.01.117 P
you come of women, come in quickly to sir john. 2.01.117 P
sweet men, come to him. 2.01.120 P
come they of noble family? 2.02.129
come, let's away. 2.03. 47
king | come here himself to question our delay; 2.04.142
"knocks go and come; 3.02. 8
fluellen, you must come presently to the mines; 3.02. 54 P
duke, it is not so good to come to the mines; 3.02. 58 P
send precepts to the leviathan | to come ashore. 3.03. 27
come, uncle exeter, | go you and enter harflew; 3.03. 51
now, captain fluellen, come you from the bridge? 3.06. 1 P
yet, god before, tell him we will come on, 3.06.156
i hope they will not come upon us now. 3.06.168
come, shall we about it? 3.07.155 P
if it come to the arbitrement of swords, can try 4.01.160 P
come, 'tis a foolish saying. 4.01.202 P
if ever thou come to me and say, after to–morrow 4.01.214 P
come, come away! 4.02. 62
come, come away! 4.02. 62
once more i come to know of thee, king harry, 4.03. 79
come thou no more for ransom, gentle herald, 4.03.122
thou wilt once more come again for a ransom. 4.03.128 P
come hither, boy, ask me this slave in french 4.04. 23
of monmouth's life is come after it indifferent 4.07. 32 P
if they will fight with us, bid them come down, 4.07. 58
if they'll do neither, we will come to them, 4.07. 60
i come to thee for charitable license, | that we 4.07. 71
soldier, you must come to the king. 4.07.119 P
i beseech you now, come apace to the king. 4.08. 3 P
a most contagious treason come to light, look 4.08. 21 P
all offenses, my lord, come from the heart. 4.08. 46 P
come, wherefore should you be so pashful? 4.08. 69 P
come, go /we in procession to the village; 4.08.113
of no merits, he is come to me, and prings me 5.01. 8 P
come, there is sauce for it. 5.01. 34 P
come, i know thou lovest me; 5.02.197 P
and at night, when you come into your closet, 5.02.198 P
that, when i come to woo ladies, i fright them. 5.02.228 P
come, your answer in broken music; 5.02.243 P
what's past and what's to come she can descry. 1H6 1.02. 57
come, come from behind, | i know thee well, 1.02. 66
come, come from behind, | i know thee well, 1.02. 66
then come a' god's name, i fear no woman. 1.02.102
come, let's away about it. 1.02.149
i am come to survey the tower this day; 1.03. 1
burst them open, if that you come not quickly. 1.03. 28
come, officer, as loud as e'er thou canst, | cry 1.03. 72
none durst come near for fear of sudden death. 1.04. 48
is come with a great power to raise the siege. 1.04.103
come, come, 'tis only i that must disgrace thee. 1.05. 8
come, come, 'tis only i that must disgrace thee. 1.05. 8
talbot, farewell, thy hour is not yet come. 1.05. 13
come in, and let us banquet royally, | after 1.06. 30
come hither, captain. 2.02. 59
by message crav'd, so is lord talbot come. 2.03. 13
well, well, come on, who else? 2.04. 55
come, let us four to dinner. 2.04.132
but tell me, keeper, will my nephew come? 2.05. 17
richard plantagenet, my lord, will come. 2.05. 18
and answer was return'd that he will come. 2.05. 20
my lord, your loving nephew now is come. 2.05. 33
richard plantagenet, my friend, is he come? 2.05. 34
men | that come to gather money for their corn. 3.02. 5
poor market folks that come to sell their corn. 3.02. 15
dare ye come forth and meet us in the field? 3.02. 61
will ye, like soldiers, come and fight it out? 3.02. 66
come, my lord, | we will bestow you in some 3.02. 87
come, come, return; 3.03. 76
come, come, return; 3.03. 76
come hither, you that would be combatants: 4.01.134
come go, i will dispatch the horsemen straight; 4.04. 40
now thou art come unto a feast of death, | a 4.05. 7
come, dally not, be gone. 4.05. 11
come, side by side, together live and die, | and 4.05. 54
come, come, and lay him in his father's arms, 4.07. 29
come, come, and lay him in his father's arms, 4.07. 29
i come to know what prisoners thou hast ta'en, 4.07. 56
"if once he come to be a cardinal, | he'll make 5.01. 32
now the time is come | that france must vail her 5.03. 24
is all your strict preciseness come to this? 5.04. 67
we come to be informed by yourselves | what the 5.04.118
that lady margaret do vouchsafe to come | to 5.05. 89
come, let us in, and with all speed provide | to 2H6 1.01. 73
a day will come when york shall claim his own, 1.01.239
i go. come, nell, thou wilt ride with us? 1.02. 59
gold cannot come amiss, were she a devil. 1.02. 92
my lord protector will come this way by and by, 1.03. 2 P
come back, fool. 1.03. 8 P
come, let's be gone. 1.03. 41 P
could i come near your beauty with my nails, | i 1.03.141
i come to talk of commonwealth affairs. 1.03.154
come, somerset, we'll see thee sent away. 1.03.219 P
come, my masters, the duchess, i tell you, 1.04. 1 P
come, come, my lords, these oracles | are hardly 1.04. 70
come, come, my lords, these oracles | are hardly 1.04. 70
faith, holy uncle, would't were come to that! 2.01. 37
come with thy two–hand sword. 2.01. 45
come to the king and tell him what miracle. 2.01. 60
by good saint albon, who said, "simon, come; 2.01. 89
come offer at my shrine, and i will help thee." 2.01. 90
come on, sirrah, off with your doublet quickly. 2.01.147 P
till they come to berwick, from whence they came 2.01.156
let it come, i' faith, and i'll pledge you all, 2.03. 66 P
come, leave your drinking, and fall to blows. 2.03. 79 P
masters, i am come hither, as it were, upon my 2.03. 85 P
come, fellow, follow us for thy reward. 2.03.105
come you, my lord, to see my open shame? 2.04. 19
come, stanley, shall we go? 2.04.104
i muse my lord of gloucester is not come; 3.01. 1
that he should come about your royal person, 3.01. 26
gloucester, know that thou art come too soon, 3.01. 95
is the hour to come | that e'er i prov'd thee 3.01.204
great lords, from ireland am i come amain, | to 3.01.282

the enemy, | and undiscover'd come to me again, 3.01.369
why, then from ireland come i with my strength, 3.01.380
come, basilisk, | and kill the innocent gazer 3.02. 52
come hither, gracious sovereign, view this body. 3.02.149
come, warwick, come, good warwick, go with me, 3.02.298
come, warwick, come, good warwick, go with me, 3.02.298
come, suffolk, i must waft thee to thy death. 4.01.116
come, soldiers, show what cruelty ye can, | that 4.01.132
therefore come you with us and let him go. 4.01.141
come and get thee a sword, though made of a lath 4.02. 1 P
come, come, let's fall in with them. 4.02. 30 P
come, come, let's fall in with them. 4.02. 30 P
come hither, sirrah, i must examine thee. 4.02. 97 P
over whom, in time to come, i hope to reign, 4.02.130
come, march forward. 4.02.190 P
at my horse heels till i do come to london, 4.03. 13 P
come, let's march towards london. 4.03. 17 P
come, margaret, god, our hope, will succor us. 4.04. 55
come, then, let's go fight with them. 4.06. 13 P
come, let's away. 4.06. 15 P
the laws of england may come out of your mouth. 4.07. 6 P
o monstrous coward! what, to come behind folks? 4.07. 83 P
we come ambassadors from the king | unto the 4.08. 7
the duke of york is newly come from ireland, 4.09. 24
come, wife, let's in, and learn to govern better 4.09. 48
the lord of the soil come to seize me for a 4.10. 24 P
and like a thief to come to rob my grounds, 4.10. 34
yet, come thou and thy five men, and if i do not 4.10. 39 P
let ten thousand devils come against me, and 4.10. 61 P
art thou a messenger, or come of pleasure? 5.01. 16
call hither clifford, bid him come amain, | to 5.01.114
see where they come, i'll warrant they'll make 5.01.122
bid salisbury and warwick come to me. 5.01.147
clifford, i say, come forth and fight with me. 5.02. 5
of one or both of us the time is come. 5.02. 13
come, thou new ruin of old clifford's house: 5.02. 61
york | shall be eterniz'd in all age to come. 5.03. 31
for shame, come down. he made thee duke of york.
3H6 1.01. 77
come, cousin, let us tell the queen these news. 1.01.182
come, son, let's away. 1.01.255
come, we'll after them. 1.01.256
come, son, away, we may not linger thus. 1.01.263
come, cousin, you shall be the messenger. 1.01.272
you are come to sandal in a happy hour; 1.02. 63
plantagenet, i come, plantagenet! 1.03. 49
come, bloody clifford, rough northumberland, | i 1.04. 27
why come you not? 1.04. 39
come make him stand upon this molehill here 1.04. 67
and in thy need such comfort come to thee | as 1.04.165
i come to tell you things sith then befall'n. 2.01.106
in haste, post–haste, are come to join with you; 2.01.139
i come to pierce it, or to give thee mine. 2.01.203
expostulate, make speed, | or else come after. 2.05.136
come, york and richard, warwick and the rest, 2.06. 29
for through this laund anon the deer will come, 3.01. 2
ay, but she's come to beg; 3.01. 42
and come some other time to know our mind. 3.02. 17
am come to crave thy just and lawful aid; 3.03. 32
i come, in kindness and unfeigned love, | first, 3.03. 51
come on, my masters, each man take his stand, 4.03. 1
king, | and come now to create you duke of york. 4.03. 34
come therefore let us fly while we may fly, | if 4.04. 34
come then, away, let's ha' no more ado. 4.05. 27
come hither, england's hope. 4.06. 68
come therefore, let's about it speedily. 4.06.102
welcome, sir john! but why come you in arms? 4.07. 42
to keep them back that come to succor you. 4.07. 56
come, fellow soldier, make thou proclamation. 4.07. 70
come on, brave soldiers; 4.07. 87
the knights and gentlemen to come with thee. 4.08. 13
shall rest in london till we come to him. 4.08. 22
o unbid spite, is sportful edward come? 5.01. 18
come, warwick, take the time, kneel down, kneel 5.01. 48
come, clarence, come; 5.01. 80
come, clarence, come; 5.01. 80
come to me, friend or foe, | and tell me who is 5.02. 5
come quickly, montague, or i am dead. 5.02. 39
ere ye come there, be sure to hear some news. 5.05. 48
so come to you, and yours, as to this prince! 5.05. 82
but wherefore dost thou come? 5.06. 29
come hither, bess, and let me kiss my boy. 5.07. 15
come now towards chertsey with your holy load, R3 1.02. 29
he is in heaven, where thou shalt never come. 1.02.106
and i | are come from visiting his majesty. 1.03. 32
come, come, we know your meaning, brother 1.03. 73
come, come, we know your meaning, brother 1.03. 73
the day will come that thou shalt wish for me 1.03.244
catesby, i come. lords, will you go with me? 1.03.321
but soft, here come my executioners. 1.03.338
we are, my lord, and come to have the warrant, 1.03.341
"clarence is come — false, fleeting, perjur'd 1.04. 55
what if it come to thee again? 1.04.133 P
come, shall we fall to work? 1.04.153 P
wherefore do you come? 1.04.171
come, you deceive yourself, | 'tis he that sends 1.04.242
come thou on my side, and entreat for me, | as 1.04.265
come, hastings, help me to my closet. 2.01.134
come, lords, will you go | to comfort edward 2.01.139
come, come, we fear the worst; all will be well. 2.03. 31
come, come, we fear the worst; all will be well. 2.03. 31
come, come, my boy, we will to sanctuary. 2.04. 66
come, come, my boy, we will to sanctuary. 2.04. 66
not | to tell us whether they will come or no! 3.01. 23
welcome, my lord. what, will our mother come? 3.01. 25
would fain have come with me to meet your grace, 3.01. 29
come on, lord hastings, will you go with me? 3.01. 58
say, uncle gloucester, if our brother come, 3.01. 61
but come, my lord; 3.01.149
come hither, catesby. 3.01.157
come, let us sup betimes, that afterwards | we 3.01.199
go, bid thy master rise and come to me, | and we 3.02. 31
come on, come on, where is your boar–spear, man? 3.02. 72
come on, come on, where is your boar–spear, man? 3.02. 72
come, come, have with you. 3.02. 90
come, come, have with you. 3.02. 90
but come, my lord, let's away. 3.02. 94
come the next sabbath, and i will content you. 3.02.111
come, will you go? 3.02.123
come, grey, come, vaughan, let us here embrace. 3.03. 25
come, grey, come, vaughan, let us here embrace. 3.03. 25
had you not come upon your cue, my lord, 3.04. 26
come, come, dispatch, the duke would be at 3.04. 94
come, come, dispatch, the duke would be at 3.04. 94
come, come, dispatch, 'tis bootless to exclaim. 3.04.102
come, come, dispatch, 'tis bootless to exclaim. 3.04.102
come, lead me to the block; 3.04.106
come, cousin, canst thou quake and change thy 3.05. 1
which since you come too late of our intent, 3.05. 69
nay, for a need, thus far come near my person: 3.05. 85
bad is the world, and all will come to nought, 3.06. 13
will not the mayor then and his brethren come? 3.07. 44
are come to have some conference with his grace. 3.07. 69
such troops of citizens to come to him, | his 3.07. 85
by heaven, we come to him in perfit love, | and 3.07. 90
and that you come to reprehend my ignorance. 3.07.113
in this just cause come i to move your grace. 3.07.140
come, citizens. 3.07.219
come, let us to our holy work again. 3.07.246
come, madam, you must straight to westminster, 4.01. 31
come, madam, come, i in all haste was sent. 4.01. 56
come, madam, come, i in all haste was sent. 4.01. 56
come hither, catesby. 4.02. 50
let me have open means to come to them, | and 4.02. 76
hark, come hither, tyrrel. 4.02. 78
come to me, tyrrel, soon, /at after–supper, 4.03. 31
come, i have learn'd that fearful commenting 4.03. 51
thou didst prophesy the time would come | that i 4.04. 79
of tears that you have shed | shall come again, 4.04.322
bound with triumphant garlands will i come | and 4.04.333
the time to come. 4.04.387
swear not by time to come, for that thou hast 4.04.395
/ratcliffe, come hither. 4.04.444
come lead me, officers, to the block of shame; 5.01. 28
come, noble gentlemen, | let us survey the 5.03. 14
come, gentlemen, | let us consult upon 5.03. 44
about the mid of night come to my tent | and 5.03. 77
come, go with me, | under our tents i'll play 5.03.220
one that made means to come by what he hath, 5.03.248
come, bustle, bustle! 5.03.289
my lord, he doth deny to come. 5.03.343
enrich the time to come with smooth–fac'd peace, 5.05. 33
i come no more to make you laugh; H8 pr 1
those that come to see | only a show or two, and pr 9
only they | that come to hear a merry, bawdy pr 14
and it's come to pass | this tractable obedience 1.02. 63
salisbury, | made suit to come in 's presence; 1.02.197
come, good sir thomas, | we shall be late else, 1.03. 64
my lord chamberlain, | prithee come hither. 1.04. 91
you that thus far have come to pity me, | hear 2.01. 56
hour | of my long weary life is come upon me. 2.01.133
in which we come | to know your royal pleasure. 2.02. 69
be acquainted | forthwith for what you come. 2.02.108
come hither, gardiner. 2.02.120
could | come pat betwixt too early and too late 2.03. 84
come, you are pleasant. 2.03. 93
say, henry king of england, come into the court. 2.04. 6 P
katherine queen of england, come into the court. 2.04. 10 P
katherine queen of england, come into the court. 2.04.126 P
to wear our mortal state to come with her, 2.04.229
pray their graces | to come near. 3.01. 19
we come not by the way of accusation | to taint 3.01. 54
come, reverend fathers, | bestow your counsels 3.01.181
no, he's settled | (not to come off) in his 3.02. 23
is he ready | to come abroad? 3.02. 83
employ'd you where high profits might come home, 3.02.158
have ever come too short of my desires, | yet 3.02.170
you come to take your stand here, and behold 4.01. 2
come, gentlemen, ye shall go my way, which | is 4.01.114
is come to lay his weary bones among ye; 4.02. 22
i am happily come hither. 5.01. 85
come, you and i must walk a turn together; 5.01. 93
come, come, give me your hand. 5.01. 94
come, come, give me your hand. 5.01. 94
that you shall | this morning come before us, 5.01.101
or else no witness | would come against you. 5.01.108
come back! what mean you? 5.01.157
i'll not come back, the tidings that i bring 5.01.158
let him come in. 5.02. 42
but know i come not | to hear such flattery now, 5.02.158
come, come, my lord, you'd spare your spoons. 5.02.201
come, come, my lord, you'd spare your spoons. 5.02.201
come, lords, we trifle time away; 5.02.212
indian with the great tool come to court, the 5.03. 34 P
running banquet of two beadles that is to come. 5.03. 66 P
th' are come already from the christening. 5.03. 83
some come to take their ease, | and sleep an act ep 2
i cannot come to cressid but by pandar, | and TRO 1.01. 95
come go we then together. 1.01.116
there's troilus will not come far behind him. 1.02. 57 P
th' other's not come to't. 1.02. 84 P
tell me another tale when th' other's come to't. 1.02. 85 P
and the devil come to him, it's all one. 1.02.211 P
good boy, tell him i come. 1.02.275 P
to us | that we come short of our suppose so far 1.03. 11
nor i from troy come not to whisper with him. 1.03.250
if any come, hector shall honor him; 1.03.280
of the giant mass | of things to come at large. 1.03.346
if the dull brainless ajax come safe off, 1.03.380
then would come some matter from him; 2.01. 8 P
like clatpoles ere i come any more to your tents 2.01.118 P
betimes | a moi'ty of that mass of moan to come. 2.02.107
foes, | and fame in time to come canonize us, 2.02.202
good thersites, come in and rail. 2.03. 24 P
from a tutor, and discipline come not near thee! 2.03. 30 P
art thou come? 2.03. 40 P
come, what's agamemnon? 2.03. 42 P
derive this; come. 2.03. 61 P
come, patroclus, i'll speak with nobody. 2.03. 69 P
come in with me, thersites. 2.03. 70 P
go and tell him | we come to speak with him, and 2.03.122
not be satisfied, | we come to speak with him. 2.03.141
fresh kings are come to troy; 2.03.261
here's a lord — come knights from east to west, 2.03.263
i come to speak with paris from the prince 3.01. 38 P
come, your disposer is sick. 3.01. 88 P
come, give me an instrument. 3.01. 94 P
come, come, i'll hear no more of this, i'll sing 3.01.105 P
come, come, i'll hear no more of this, i'll sing 3.01.105 P
they're come from the field. 3.01.148
she's making her ready, she'll come straight. 3.02. 30 P
come, come, what need you blush? 3.02. 40 P
come, come, what need you blush? 3.02. 40 P
come your ways, come your ways; 3.02. 44 P
come your ways, come your ways; 3.02. 44 P
come, draw this curtain and let's see your 3.02. 46 P
whereof the parties interchangeably" — come in, 3.02. 59 P
come in, come in, i'll go get a fire. 3.02. 59 P
true swains in love shall in the world to come 3.02.173
which you say live to come in my behalf. 3.03. 16
i will come last; 3.03. 42
to come as humbly as they us'd to creep | to 3.03. 73
valorous hector to come unarm'd to my tent, and 3.03.275 P
i come from the worthy achilles — 3.03.282 P
come, thou shalt bear a letter to him straight. 3.03.305
come, come, beshrew your heart, you'll ne'er be 4.02. 29
come, come, beshrew your heart, you'll ne'er be 4.02. 29
my lord, come you again into my chamber. 4.02. 36
come, you are deceived, i think of no such thing 4.02. 39
pray you come in. 4.02. 40
come, he is here, my lord, do not deny him. 4.02. 49
come, come, you'll do him wrong ere you are ware 4.02. 54 P
come, come, you'll do him wrong ere you are ware 4.02. 54 P
bid them have patience, she shall come anon. 4.04. 52
come kiss, and let us part. 4.04. 98
good brother, come you hither, | and bring 4.04. 99
come, to the port. 4.04.136
come, come, to field with him. 4.04.143
come, come, to field with him. 4.04.143
come, stretch thy chest, and let thy eyes spout 4.05. 10
come, come, thersites, help to trim my tent; 5.01. 45
come, come, thersites, help to trim my tent; 5.01. 45
come, come, enter my tent. 5.01. 87
come, come, enter my tent. 5.01. 87
it is prodigious, there will come some change; 5.01. 93 P
fo, fo, come, tell a pin. you are forsworn. 5.02. 22
come, my lord. 5.02. 41
you have not patience, come. 5.02. 42
in faith, i do not. come hither once again. 5.02. 49
come, come. 5.02. 51
come, come. 5.02. 51
come, tell me whose it was. 5.02. 88
what, shall i come? the hour — 5.02.104
ay, come — o jove! 5.02.105
do come. 5.02.105
i prithee come. 5.02.106
come, hector, come, go back. 5.03. 62
come, hector, come, go back. 5.03. 62
therefore come back. 5.03. 67
i come to lose my arm, or win my sleeve. 5.03. 96
here's a letter come from yond poor girl. 5.03. 99 P
handless, hack'd and chipp'd, come to him, 5.05. 34
come, come, thou boy–queller, show thy face, 5.05. 45
come, come, thou boy–queller, show thy face, 5.05. 45
come both you cogging greeks, have at you both! 5.06. 11
come here about me, you my myrmidons, | mark 5.07. 1
come, troy, sink down! 5.08. 11
come, tie his body to my horse's tail, | along 5.08. 21
come, come. COR 1.01. 49 P
come, come. 1.01. 49 P
come. 1.01.272
madam, the lady valeria is come to visit you. 1.03. 26
"come on, you cowards, you were got in fear, 1.03. 33
come, lay aside your stitchery, i must have you 1.03. 69 P
come, you must go visit the good lady that lies 1.03. 77 P
come, i would your cambric were sensible as your 1.03. 84 P
come, you shall go with us. 1.03. 86 P
come, good sweet lady. 1.03.107 P
come, blow thy blast. 1.04. 12
come on, my fellows! 1.04. 27
come on! 1.04. 40
we are come off | like romans, neither foolish 1.06. 1
come i too late? 1.06. 24
come i too late? 1.06. 27
ay, if you come not in the blood of others, 1.06. 28
our guider, come, to th' roman camp conduct us. 1.07. 7
come. 1.09. 94
come, sir, come, we know you well enough. 2.01. 66 P
come, sir, come, we know you well enough. 2.01. 66 P
come, come, you are well understood to be a 2.01. 81 P
come, come, yoou are well understood to be a 2.01. 81 P
he was wont to come home wounded. 2.01.119 P
thou have laugh'd had i come coffin'd home, 2.01.176
come, come, they are almost here. 2.02. 1 P
come, come, they are almost here. 2.02. 1 P
to coriolanus come all joy and honor! 2.02.154
come, we'll inform them | of our proceedings 2.02.158
together, but to come by him where he stands, by 2.03. 41 P
here come moe voices. 2.03.125
to th' capitol, come. 2.03.260
come, enough. 3.01.139
come, try upon yourselves what you have seen me. 3.01.224
come, sir, along with us. 3.01.236
nay, come away. 3.01.252
come. 3.01.317
he must come, | or what is worst will follow. 3.01.333
come, come, you have been too rough, something 3.02. 25
come, come, you have been too rough, something 3.02. 25
come, go with us, speak fair. 3.02. 70
come, come, we'll prompt you. 3.02.106
come, come, we'll prompt you. 3.02.106
come all to ruin, let | thy mother rather feel 3.02.125
and come home belov'd | of all the trades in 3.02.133
what, will he come? 3.03. 5
come, come, let's see him out at gates, come. 3.03.142
come, come, let's see him out at gates, come. 3.03.142
come, come, let's see him out at gates, come. 3.03.142
come. 3.03.143
come leave your tears: 4.01. 1
come, my sweet wife, my dearest mother, and | my 4.01. 48
i pray you come. 4.01. 50
come, let's not weep. 4.01. 54
give me thy hand. | come. 4.01. 58
come, come, peace. 4.02. 29

come, come, peace. 4.02. 29
come, let's go. 4.02. 51
come, come, come. 4.02. 53
come, come, come. 4.02. 53
come, come, come. 4.02. 53
and hope to come upon them in the heat of their 4.03. 18 P
come. 4.05. 31 P
o, come, go in, | and take our friendly senators 4.05.131
but come in, | let me commend thee first to 4.05.143
come, we are fellows and friends: 4.05.183 P
come, what talk you | of martius? 4.06. 46
here come the clusters. 4.06.128
come, masters, let's home. 4.06.153 P
so did we all. but come, let's home. 4.06.156 P
when he shall come to his account, he knows not 4.07. 18
hazard mine, | when e'er we come to our account. 4.07. 26
come, let's away. 4.07. 56
of state, and come | to speak with coriolanus. 5.02. 3
come, my captain knows you not. 5.02. 53 P
and swound for what's to come upon thee. 5.02. 67 P
i was hardly mov'd to come to thee; 5.02. 73 P
than all living women | are we come hither; 5.03. 98
come, let us go. 5.03.177
but let it come. 5.03.189
come enter with us. 5.03.206
say no more. | here come the lords. 5.06. 59
come, come, sweet emperor — come, andronicus —
TIT 1.01.456
come, come, sweet emperor — come, andronicus — 1.01.456
come, come, sweet emperor — come, andronicus — 1.01.456
come, if the emperor's court can feast two 1.01.489
come, come, our empress, with her sacred wit 2.01.120
come, come, our empress, with her sacred wit 2.01.120
come on then, horse and chariots let us have, 2.02. 18
and had you not by wondrous fortune come, | this 2.03.112
ay, come, semiramis, nay, barbarous tamora, 2.03.118
come, mistress, now perforce we will enjoy 2.03.134
come on, my lords, the better foot before. 2.03.192
thou canst not come to me — i come to thee. 2.03.245
thou canst not come to me — i come to thee. 2.03.245
come, lucius, come, stay not to talk with them. 2.03.306
come, lucius, come, stay not to talk with them. 2.03.306
come let us go, and make thy father blind, | for 2.04. 52
to make us wonder'd at in time to come. 3.01.135
nay, come, agree whose hand shall go along, 3.01.174
for fear they die before their pardon come. 3.01.175
come hither, aaron. 3.01.186
and threat me i shall never come to bliss | till 3.01.272
come let me see what task i have to do. 3.01.275
come, brother, take a head, | and in this hand 3.01.279
farewell, proud rome, till lucius come again; 3.01.290
come and take choice of all my library, | and so 4.01. 34
and come, i will go get a leaf of brass, | and 4.01.102
come go with me into mine armory; 4.01.113
come, come, thou'lt do my message, wilt thou not 4.01.117
come, come, thou'lt do my message, wilt thou not 4.01.117
lavinia, come. 4.01.120
come let us go and pray to all the gods | for 4.02. 46
were | he is enfranchised and come to light. 4.02.125
come on, you thick-lipp'd slave, i'll bear you 4.02.175
come, marcus, come; 4.03. 1
come, marcus, come; 4.03. 1
then, when you come to pluto's region, | i pray 4.03. 13
come, to this gear. 4.03. 53
marcus, the post is come. 4.03. 78
why, didst thou not come from heaven? 4.03. 89
sirrah, come hither, make no more ado, | but 4.03.102
and when you come to him, at the first approach 4.03.110 P
come let me see it. 4.03.115
come, marcus, let us go. publius, follow me. 4.03.121
come, sirrah, you must be hang'd. 4.04. 47
few come within the compass of my curse — 5.01.126
let him come near. 5.01.154
father and my uncle marcus, | and we will come. 5.01.165
tell him revenge is come to join with him, | and 5.02. 7
titus, i am come to talk with thee. 5.02. 16
come down and welcome me to this world's light; 5.02. 33
i am, therefore come down and welcome me. 5.02. 43
do me some service ere i come to thee. 5.02. 44
and then i'll come and be thy waggoner, | and 5.02. 48
these are my ministers, and come with me. 5.02. 60
o sweet revenge, now do i come to thee, | and, 5.02. 67
and bid him come and banquet at thy house, 5.02.114
publius, come hither! 5.02.151
come, come, lavinia, look, thy foes are bound. 5.02.166
come, come, lavinia, look, thy foes are bound. 5.02.166
lavinia, come, | receive the blood, and when 5.02.196
come, come, be every one officious | to make 5.02.201
come, come, be every one officious | to make 5.02.201
come, come, thou reverent man of rome, | and 5.03.137
come, come, thou reverent man of rome, | and 5.03.137
come hither, boy, come, come, and learn of us 5.03.160
come hither, boy, come, come, and learn of us 5.03.160
come, come, and learn of us | to melt in showers 5.03.160
old montague is come, | and flourishes his blade ROM 1.01. 77
me, | and, montague, come you this afternoon, 1.01.100
come, madam, let's away. 1.01.159
come go with me. 1.02. 34
whither should they come? 1.02. 71
montagues, i pray, come and crush a cup of wine. 1.02. 80 P
at twelve year old, | i bade her come. 1.03. 3
nurse, come back again, | i have rememb'red me, 1.03. 8
come lammas-eve at night shall she be fourteen. 1.03. 17
to see now how a jest shall come about! 1.03. 45
madam, the guests are come, supper serv'd up, 1.03.100 P
come knock and enter, and no sooner in, | but 1.04. 33
come, we burn daylight, ho! 1.04. 43
supper is done, and we shall come too late. 1.04.105
am i come near ye now? 1.05. 20
come, musicians, play. 1.05. 25
come pentecost as quickly as it will, | some 1.05. 36
what dares the slave | come hither, cover'd with 1.05. 56
a villain that is hither come in spite | to 1.05. 62
come on, then let's to bed. 1.05.125
come hither, nurse. what is yond gentleman? 1.05.128
come let's away, the strangers all are gone. 1.05.144
come, he hath hid himself among these trees | to 2.01. 30
come, shall we go? 2.01. 41
come to thy heart as that within my breast! 2.02.124
stay but a little, i will come again. 2.02.138
by one that i'll procure to come to thee, 2.02.145
i come, anon. 2.02.150
by and by, i come — | to cease thy /suit, and 2.02.151
but come, young waverer, come go with me, | in 2.03. 89
but come, young waverer, come go with me, | in 2.03. 89
come between us, good benvolio, my wits faints. 2.04. 67 P
for i was come to the whole depth of my tale, 2.04. 99 P
romeo, will you come to your father's? 2.04.140 P
some means to come to shrift this afternoon, 2.04.180
is /three long hours, yet she is not come. 2.05. 11
nay, come, i pray thee speak, good, good nurse, 2.05. 28
marry come up, i trow; 2.05. 62
here's such a coil! come, what says romeo? 2.05. 65
but come what sorrow can, | it cannot 2.06. 3
come, come with me, and we will make short work, 2.06. 35
come, come with me, and we will make short work, 2.06. 35
come, come, thou art as hot a jack in thy mood 3.01. 11 P
come, come, thou art as hot a jack in thy mood 3.01. 11 P
come, sir, your passado. 3.01. 85 P
come, civil night, | thou sober-suited matron 3.02. 10
come, night, come, romeo, come, thou day in 3.02. 17
come, night, come, romeo, come, thou day in 3.02. 17
night, come, romeo, come, thou day in night, 3.02. 17
come, gentle night, come, loving, black-brow'd 3.02. 20
come, gentle night, come, loving, black-brow'd 3.02. 20
shame come to romeo! 3.02. 90
come, cords, come, nurse, i'll to my wedding-bed 3.02.136
come, cords, come, nurse, i'll to my wedding-bed 3.02.136
and bid him come to take his last farewell. 3.02.143
romeo, come forth, come forth, thou fearful man: 3.03. 1
romeo, come forth, come forth, thou fearful man: 3.03. 1
i come, i come! 3.03. 77
i come, i come! 3.03. 77
whence come you? 3.03. 78
let me come in, and you shall know my errant. 3.03. 79
i come from lady juliet. 3.03. 80
my lord, i'll tell my lady you will come. 3.03.161
'tis very late, she'll not come down to-night. 3.04. 5
come, death, and welcome! 3.05. 24
for sweet discourses in our times to come. 3.05. 53
and cannot come to him | to wreak the love i 3.05.100
that he dares ne'er come back to challenge you; 3.05.214
come you to make confession to this father? 4.01. 22
now, | or shall i come to you at evening mass? 4.01. 38
come weep with me, past hope, past /cure, past 4.01. 45
and hither shall he come, an' he and i | will 4.01.115
come, vial. 4.03. 20
before the time that romeo | come to redeem me? 4.03. 32
come, stir, stir, stir! 4.04. 3
make haste, the bridegroom he is come already, 4.04. 27
for shame, bring juliet forth, her lord is come. 4.05. 22
come, is the bride ready to go to church? 4.05. 33
come, we'll in here, tarry for the mourners, and 4.05.145 P
come hither, man. 5.01. 58
come, cordial and not poison, go with me | to 5.01. 85
and keep her at my cell till romeo come — 5.02. 29
and here is come to do some villainous shame 5.03. 52
for i come hither arm'd against myself. 5.03. 65
come, bitter conduct, come, unsavory guide! 5.03.116
come, bitter conduct, come, unsavory guide! 5.03.116
come from that nest | of death, contagion, and 5.03.151
come, come away. 5.03.154
come, come away. 5.03.154
come, i'll dispose of thee | among a sisterhood 5.03.156
come go, good juliet, i dare no longer stay. 5.03.159
hold him in safety till the prince come hither. 5.03.183
come, montague, for thou art early up | to see 5.03.208
that he should hither come as this dire night 5.03.247
and i entreated her come forth | and bear this 5.03.260
and being enfranchis'd, bid him come to me; TIM 1.01.106
so they come by great bellies. 1.01.206 P
i come to have thee thrust me out of doors. 1.02. 25
i come to observe, i give thee warning on't. 1.02. 34
myself poorer, that i might come nearer to you. 1.02.101 P
and come freely | to gratulate thy plenteous 1.02.124
they only now come but to feast thine eyes. 1.02.127
senate | newly alighted, and come to visit you. 1.02.175
what will this come to? 1.02.191
farewell, and come with better music. 1.02.246 P
come! 2.01. 35
good even, varro. what, | you come for money? 2.02. 10
come hither. 2.02. 35
no, 'tis to thyself. come away. 2.02. 53 P
when men come to borrow of your masters, they 2.02.100 P
come with me, fool, come. 2.02.120 P
come with me, fool, come. 2.02.120 P
come, sermon me no further. 2.02.172
behalf, i come to entreat your honor to supply; 3.01. 17 P
and come again to supper to him of purpose to 3.01. 24 P
pray is my lord ready to come forth? 3.04. 35 P
come, bring in all together! 3.06. 47 P
come, damn'd earth, | thou common whore of 4.03. 42
come nearer. 4.03.482
when we may profit meet, and come too late. 5.01. 42
come. 5.01. 46
we are hither come to offer you our service. 5.01. 72
confound them by some course, and come to me, 5.01.103
two villains shall not be, | come not near him. 5.01.110
come hither, ere my tree hath felt the axe, 5.01.211
come not to me again, but say to athens, | timon 5.01.214
thither come, | and let my grave-stone be your 5.01.218
here come our brothers. 5.02. 13
fellow, come from the throng, look upon caesar. JC 1.02. 21
come on my right hand, for this ear is deaf, 1.02.213
to speak with me, | i will come home to you; 1.02.305
come home to me, and i will wait for you. 1.02.306
come, casca, you and i will yet, ere day, | see 1.03.153
when it is lighted, come and call me here. 2.01. 8
know i these men that come along with you? 2.01. 89
o, that we then could come by caesar's spirit, 2.01.169
whether caesar will come forth to-day or no; 2.01.194
he would embrace the means to come by it. 2.01.259
a necessary end, | will come when it will come. 2.02. 37
a necessary end, | will come when it will come. 2.02. 37
i come to fetch you to the senate-house. 2.02. 59
and you are come in very happy time | to bear my 2.02. 60
and tell them that i will not come to-day. 2.02. 62
i will not come to-day. 2.02. 64
decius, go tell them caesar will not come. 2.02. 68
the cause is in my will, i will not come: 2.02. 71
if you shall send them word you will not come, 2.02. 95
and look where publius is come to fetch me. 2.02.108
come not near casca; 2.03. 2 P
come hither, fellow; which way hast thou been? 2.04. 21
come to me again, | and bring me word what he 2.04. 45
the ides of march are come. 3.01. 1
come to the capitol. 3.01. 12
vouchsafe that antony | may safely come to him, 3.01.131
tell him, so please him come unto this place, 3.01.140
with ate by his side come hot from hell, | shall 3.01.271
caesar did write for him to come to rome. 3.01.278
i come to bury caesar, not to praise him. 3.02. 74
men), | come i to speak in caesar's funeral. 3.02. 84
and i must pause till it come back to me. 3.02.107
i fear there will a worse come in his place. 3.02.111
for if you should, o, what would come of it? 3.02.146
come down. 3.02.161 P
i come not, friends, to steal away your hearts. 3.02.216
away then, come, seek the conspirators. 3.02.232
come, away, away! 3.02.253
sir, octavius is already come to rome. 3.02.262
come, brands ho, fire-brands! 3.03. 35 P
and pindarus is come | to do you salutation from 4.02. 4
the horse in general, | are come with cassius. 4.02. 30
no man | come to our tent till we have done our 4.02. 51
is it come to this? 4.03. 50
come, antony, and young octavius, come, 4.03. 93
come, antony, and young octavius, come, 4.03. 93
you shall not come to them. 4.03.127
and come yourselves, and bring messala with you 4.03.141
come in, titinius. 4.03.163
antony | come down upon us with a mighty power, 4.03.169
come on refresh'd, new-added, and encourag'd; 4.03.209
never come such division 'tween our souls! 4.03.235
you said the enemy would not come down, | but 5.01. 2
places, and come down | with fearful bravery, 5.01. 9
come, come, the cause. 5.01. 48
come, come, the cause. 5.01. 48
come, antony; 5.01. 63
if you dare fight to-day, come to the field; 5.01. 65
the end of this day's business ere it come! 5.01.123
come ho, away! 5.01.125
ride, ride, messala, let them all come down. 5.02. 6
time is come round, | and where i did begin, 5.03. 23
come down, behold no more. 5.03. 33
come hither, sirrah. 5.03. 36
come now, keep thine oath; 5.03. 40
day is gone, | clouds, dews, and dangers come; 5.03. 64
brutus, come apace, | and see how i regarded 5.03. 87
come, cassius' sword, and find titinius' heart. 5.03. 90
come therefore, and to /thasos send his body; 5.03.104
lucilius, come, | and come, young cato, let us 5.03.106
and come, young cato, let us to the field. 5.03.107
come, poor remains of friends, rest on this rock 5.05. 1
come hither, good volumnius; list a word. 5.05. 15
i know my hour is come. 5.05. 20
i come, graymalkin! MAC 1.01. 8
from that spring whence comfort seem'd to come 1.02. 27
thumb, | wrack'd as homeward he did come. 1.03. 29
a drum, a drum! | macbeth doth come. 1.03. 31
new honors come upon him, | like our strange 1.03.144
come what come may, | time and the hour runs 1.03.146
come what come may, | time and the hour runs 1.03.146
till then, enough. come, friends. 1.03.156
my liege, | they are not yet come back. 1.04. 3
come, you spirits | that tend on mortal thoughts 1.05. 40
come to my woman's breasts, | and take my milk 1.05. 47
come, thick night, | and pall thee in the 1.05. 50
which shall to all our nights and days to come 1.05. 69
/shoal of time, | we'ld jump the life to come. 1.07. 7
come, let me clutch thee: 2.01. 34
come in time! 2.03. 5 P
o, come in, equivocator. 2.03. 11 P
an english tailor come hither for stealing out 2.03. 13 P
come in, tailor, here you may roast your goose. 2.03. 14 P
if there come truth from them — | as upon thee, 3.01. 6
rather than so, come fate into the list, | and 3.01. 70
yourselves apart, | i'll come to you anon. 3.01.138
come on; 3.02. 26
come, seeling night, | scarf up the tender eye 3.02. 46
let it come down. 3.03. 16
come, love and health to all, | then i'll sit 3.04. 86
come, we'll to sleep. 3.04.141
thither he | will come to know his destiny. 3.05. 17
profound, | i'll catch it ere it come to ground; 3.05. 25
come, let's make haste, she'll soon be back 3.05. 36
and unfold | his message ere he come, that a 3.06. 47
you profess | (how e'er you come to know it), 4.01. 51
come high or low; 4.01. 67
to high dunsinane hill | shall come against him. 4.01. 94
come like shadows, so depart. 4.01.111
come, sisters, cheer we up his sprites, | and 4.01.127
come in, without there! 4.01.135
come bring me where they are. 4.01.156
of horrid hell can come a devil more damn'd | in 4.03. 56
come go we to the king, our power is ready, 4.03.236
he cannot come out on 's grave. 5.01. 64 P
come, come, come, come, give me your hand. 5.01. 67 P
come, come, come, come, give me your hand. 5.01. 67 P
come, come, come, come, give me your hand. 5.01. 67 P
come, come, come, come, give me your hand. 5.01. 67 P
come, put mine armor on; 5.03. 48
come, sir, dispatch. 5.03. 50
bane, | till birnan forest come to dunsinane. 5.03. 60
outward walls, | the cry is still, "they come!" 5.05. 2
till birnan wood | do come to dunsinane," and 5.05. 44
blow wind, come wrack, | at least we'll die with 5.05. 50
though birnan wood be come to dunsinane, | and 5.08. 30
you come most carefully upon your hour. HAM 1.01. 6
night, | that, if again this apparition come, 1.01. 28
madam, come, | this gentle and unforc'd accord 1.02.122
come away. 1.02.128
that it should come /to /this! 1.02.137
it is not, nor it cannot come to good, | but 1.02.158

would the night were come! 1.02.255
come your ways. 1.03.135
have after. to what issue will this come? 1.04. 89
my hour is almost come, | when i to sulph'rous 1.05. 2
hillo, ho, ho, boy! come, /bird, come. 1.05.116
hillo, ho, ho, boy! come, /bird, come. 1.05.116
my lord, come from the grave | to tell us this. 1.05.125
come on, you hear this fellow in the cellarage, 1.05.151
come hither, gentlemen, | and lay your hands 1.05.157
but come — | here, as before, never, so help 1.05.168
nay, come, let's go together. 1.05.190
son, come you more nearer | than your particular 2.01. 11
come, go with me. 2.01. 98
come, go we to the king. 2.01.114
come. 2.01.117
come, come, deal justly with me. 2.02.275 P
come, come, deal justly with me. 2.02.275 P
come, come — nay, speak. 2.02.276 P
come, come — nay, speak. 2.02.276 P
come then, th' appurtenance of welcome is 2.02.371 P
happily he is the second time come to them, for 2.02.384 P
the actors are come hither, my lord. 2.02.392 P
come give us a taste of your quality, come, a 2.02.431 P
come give us a taste of your quality, come, a 2.02.432 P
say on, come to hecuba. 2.02.501 P
come, sirs. 2.02.534 P
for in that sleep of death what dreams may come, 3.01. 65
now this overdone, or come tardy off, though it 3.02. 25 P
come hither, my dear hamlet, sit by me. 3.02.108 P
and never come mischance between us twain! 3.02.228
come, the croaking raven doth bellow for revenge 3.02.253 P
come, some music! 3.02.291 P
come, the recorders! 3.02.291 P
come, some music! 3.02.295 P
then i will come to my mother by and by. 3.02.383 P
i will come by and by. 3.02.385 P
force, | to be forestalled ere we come to fall, 3.03. 49
'a will come straight. 3.04. 1
come, come, you answer with an idle tongue. 3.04. 11
come, come, you answer with an idle tongue. 3.04. 11
come, come, and sit you down, you shall not 3.04. 18
come, come, and sit you down, you shall not 3.04. 18
do you not come your tardy son to chide, | that, 3.04.106
repent what's past, avoid what is to come, | and 3.04.150
come, sir, to draw toward an end with you. 3.04.216
o gertrude, come away! 4.01. 28
come, gertrude, we'll call up our wisest friends 4.01. 38
o, come away! 4.01. 44
o, here they come. 4.02. 4 P
'a will stay till you come. 4.03. 39 P
but come, for england! 4.03. 48 P
come, for england! 4.03. 53 P
let her come in. 4.05. 16
young men will do't, if they come to't, | by 4.05. 60
sun, | and thou hadst not come to my bed.'" 4.05. 66
come, my coach! 4.05. 71 P
when sorrows come, they come not single spies, 4.05. 78
when sorrows come, they come not single spies, 4.05. 78
her brother is in secret come from france, 4.05. 88
no, let 's come in. 4.05.114
let come what comes, only i'll be reveng'd 4.05.136
"and will 'a not come again? 4.05.190
and will 'a not come again? 4.05.191
go to thy death–bed, | he never will come again. 4.05.194
let them come in. 4.06. 4 P
come, i will /give you way for these your 4.06. 32
for her perfections — but my revenge will come. 4.07. 29
are all the rest come back? 4.07. 49
but let him come, | it warms the very sickness 4.07. 54
shapes and tricks, | come short of what he did. 4.07. 90
hamlet return'd shall know you are come home. 4.07.130
but if the water come to him and drown him, he 5.01. 18 P
come, my spade. 5.01. 29 P
to't again, come. 5.01. 49 P
an inch thick, to this favor she must come. 5.01.194 P
dost /thou come here to whine? 5.01.277
sir, here is newly come to court laertes, 5.02.106 P
for nine, and it would come to immediate trial, 5.02.168 P
if it be /now, 'tis not to come; 5.02.221 P
if it be not to come, it will be now; 5.02.221 P
if it be not now, yet it /will come — the 5.02.222 P
come, hamlet, come, and take this hand from me. 5.02.225
come, hamlet, come, and take this hand from me. 5.02.225
come, one for me. 5.02.254
come begin; 5.02.278
come on, sir. 5.02.280
come, my lord. 5.02.280
come. 5.02.285
come, let me wipe thy face. 5.02.294
come, for the third, laertes, you do but dally. 5.02.297
say you so? come on. 5.02.300
nay, come again. 5.02.303
mine and my father's death come not upon thee, 5.02.330
fortinbras, with conquest come from poland, | to 5.02.350
why does the drum come hither? 5.02.361
and our affairs from england come too late. 5.02.368
nothing will come of nothing, speak again. LR 1.01. 90
come not between the dragon and his wrath; 1.01.122
to come betwixt our sentence and our power, 1.01.170
come, noble burgundy. 1.01.266
come, my fair cordelia. 1.01.282
come, if it be nothing, i shall not need 1.02. 34 P
come to me, that of this i may speak more. 1.02. 51 P
if you come slack of former services, | you 1.03. 9
i'd have it come to question. 1.03. 13
so may it come, thy master, whom thou lov'st, 1.04. 6
o, you, sir, you, come you hither, sir. 1.04. 78 P
come, sir, arise, away! 1.04. 89 P
come, boy. 1.05. 50 P
come before my father. 2.01. 31
that if they come to sojourn at my house, | i'll 2.01.103
you come with letters against the king, and take 2.02. 35 P
come your ways. 2.02. 39 P
come, i'll flesh ye, come on, young master. 2.02. 46 P
come, i'll flesh ye, come on, young master. 2.02. 46 P
come, bring away the stocks! 2.02.139
come, my /good lord, away. 2.02.151
bid them come forth and hear me, | or at their 2.04.117
is your lady come? 2.04.184
dismissing half your train, come then to me. 2.04.204
let shame come when it will, i do not call it. 2.04.226
if you will come to me | (for now i spy a danger 2.04.246
what, must i come to you | with five and twenty? 2.04.253
come out o' th' storm. 2.04.309
denied me to come in) return, and force | their 3.02. 66
come on, my boy. 3.02. 68
come, your hovel. 3.02. 71
true, boy. come bring us to this hovel. 3.02. 78
the realm of albion | come to great confusion. 3.02. 86
nor cutpurses come not to throngs; 3.02. 90
come not in here, nuncle, here's a spirit. 3.04. 39 P
come forth. 3.04. 45 P
and art thou come to this? 3.04. 50 P
come, unbutton here. 3.04.108 P
you, | yet have i ventured to come seek you out, 3.04.152
come, let's in all. 3.04.175
sirrah, come on; go along with us. 3.04.179 P
come, good athenian. 3.04.180
red burning spits | come hizzing in upon 'em — 3.06. 16
come, march to wakes and fairs and market towns. 3.06. 74 P
come hither, friend; 3.06. 86
come, come, away. 3.06.101
come, come, away. 3.06.101
come, sir, what letters had you late from france 3.07. 42
nay then come on, and take the chance of anger. 3.07. 79
best 'parel that i have, | come on't what will. 4.01. 50
come hither, fellow. 4.01. 53
come with my lady hither. 4.02. 89
come hither, friend, | tell me what more thou 4.02. 96
when shall i come to th' top of that same hill? 4.06. 1
come on, sir, here's the place; 4.06. 11
we cry that we are come | to this great stage of 4.06.182
come, come, i am a king, | masters, know you 4.06.199
come, come, i am a king, | masters, know you 4.06.199
come, and you get it, you shall get it by 4.06.202 P
nay, come not near th' old man; 4.06.240 P
come, no matter vor your foins. 4.06.244 P
come, father, i'll bestow you with a friend. 4.06.286
the king is come to his daughter, | with others 5.01. 21
come on. 5.02. 7
come on. 5.02. 11
come let's away to prison: 5.03. 8
come. 5.03. 26
come hither, captain; 5.03. 26
come hither, herald. 5.03.107
am i noble as the adversary | i come to cope. 5.03.124
the wheel is come full circle, i am here. 5.03.175
i am come | to bid my king and master aye good 5.03.235
what comfort to this great decay may come 5.03.298
thou'lt come no more, | never, never, never, 5.03.308
upon malicious /bravery dost thou come | to OTH 1.01.100
in simple and pure soul i come to you. 1.01.107
because we come to do you service and you think 1.01.109 P
and what's to come of my despised time | is 1.01.161
but look, what lights come yond? 1.02. 28
marry, to — come, captain, will you go? 1.02. 53
you, roderigo! come, sir, i am for you. 1.02. 58
and, /till she come, as truly as to heaven | i 1.03.122
she'ld come again, and with a greedy ear 1.03.149
come hither, gentle mistress. 1.03.178
come hither, moor: 1.03.192
come, desdemona, i have but an hour | of love, 1.03.298
come, be a man! 1.03.335 P
to the warlike moor othello, | is come on shore; 2.01. 28
as well to see the vessel that's come in | as to 2.01. 37
come, let's do so; 2.01. 40
the riches of the ship is come on shore! 2.01. 83
come on, come on; 2.01.109
come on, come on; 2.01.109
come on, assay. 2.01.120
come, how wouldst thou praise me? 2.01.124
if after every tempest come such calms, | may 2.01.185
come; 2.01.201
come, desdemona, | once more, well met at cyprus 2.01.211
come /hither. 2.01.214 P
qualification shall come into no true taste 2.01.275 P
come, my dear love, | the purchase made, the 2.03. 8
that profit's yet to come 'tween me and you. 2.03. 10
come, lieutenant, i have a stope of wine, and 2.03. 29 P
but here they come. 2.03. 61
platform, masters, come, let's set the watch. 2.03.120
come, come — you're drunk. 2.03.155 P
come, come — you're drunk. 2.03.155 P
come away to bed. 2.03.253
come, desdemona, 'tis the soldiers' life | to 2.03.257
come, you are too severe a moraler. 2.03.299 P
come, come; 2.03.309 P
come, come; 2.03.309 P
pray you come in. 3.01. 53
when shall he come? 3.03. 67
let him come when he will; 3.03. 75
my desdemona, i'll come to thee straight. 3.03. 87
emilia, come. 3.03. 88
and when i love thee not, | chaos is come again. 3.03. 92
come, i'll go in with you. 3.03.288
is't come to this? 3.03.363
come go with me apart, i will withdraw | to 3.03.477
seek him, bid him come hither. 3.04. 18 P
i cannot speak of this. come now, your promise. 3.04. 48
i have sent to bid cassio come speak with you. 3.04. 50
come, come; 3.04. 90
come, come; 3.04. 90
is't come to this? 3.04.183
/an' you'll come to supper to–night, you may; 4.01.159 P
will not, come when you are next prepar'd for. 4.01.160 P
prithee come; will you? 4.01.168 P
bid her come hither; 4.02. 19
pray you, chuck, come hither. 4.02. 24
cough, or cry "hem," if anybody come. 4.02. 29
come swear it, damn thyself, | lest, being like 4.02. 35
especial commission come from venice to depute 4.02.220 P
come, stand not amaz'd at it, but go along with 4.02.239 P
come, come; you talk. 4.03. 25
come, come; you talk. 4.03. 25
he'll come anon — "sing all a green willow must 4.03. 50 P
stand behind this /bulk, straight will he come. 5.01. 1
strumpet, i come. 5.01. 34
to come in to the cry without more help. 5.01. 44
nobody come? then shall i bleed to death. 5.01. 45
come in, and give some help. 5.01. 59
come, come; 5.01. 87
come, come; 5.01. 87
come, mistress, you must tell 's another tale. 5.01.125
will you come to bed, my lord? 5.02. 24
shall she come in? 5.02. 94
if she come in, she'll sure speak to my wife. 5.02. 96
o, come in, emilia. 5.02.103
o, are you come, iago? 5.02.169
come guard the door without; 5.02.241
so come my soul to bliss, as i speak true; 5.02.250
uncle, i must come forth. 5.02.254
come, bring away. 5.02.337
look where they come! ANT 1.01. 10
your dismission | is come from caesar, therefore 1.01. 27
come, my queen, | last night you did desire it. 1.01. 54
nay, come, tell iras hers. 1.02. 43 P
alexas — come, his fortune, his fortune! 1.02. 63 P
would she had never given you leave to come! 1.03. 21
cut my lace, charmian, come! 1.03. 71
come; 1.03.101
but come, away, | get me ink and paper. 1.05. 75
auguring hope | says it will come to th' full. 2.01. 11
come, menas. 2.01. 52
not if the small come first. 2.02. 12
but that to come | shall all be done by th' rule 2.03. 6
would i had never come from thence, nor you 2.03. 11 P
o, come, ventidius, | you must to parthia. 2.03. 41
let it alone, let's to billards. come, charmian. 2.05. 3
come, you'll play with me, sir? 2.05. 6
good will is show'd, though't come too short, 2.05. 8
thou shouldst come like a fury crown'd with 2.05. 40
he is afeard to come. 2.05. 81
come hither, sir. 2.05. 84
most meet | that first we come to words, and 2.06. 3
my face, | but in my bosom shall she never come, 2.06. 55
come. 2.06. 81
come, sir, will you aboard? 2.06.132 P
come, let's away. 2.06.136 P
come. 2.07. 95
come, let's all take hands, | till that the 2.07.106
come, thou monarch of the vine, | plumpy bacchus 2.07.113
come down into the boat. 2.07.129
ho, noble captain, come. 2.07.135
come, sir, come, | i'll wrastle with you in my 3.02. 61
come, sir, come, | i'll wrastle with you in my 3.02. 61
half afeard to come. 3.03. 1
go to, go to. come hither, sir. 3.03. 2
come thou near. 3.03. 6
there's strange news come, sir. 3.05. 2 P
come, sir. 3.05. 24
you come not | like caesar's sister. 3.06. 42
but you are come | a market–maid to rome, and 3.06. 50
to come thus was i not constrain'd, but did it 3.06. 56
him, | and his affairs come to me on the wind. 3.06. 63
friends, come hither: 3.11. 2
we sent our schoolmaster, | is 'a come back? 3.11. 72
let him appear that's come from antony. 3.12. 1
such as i am, i come from antony. 3.12. 7
o, is't come to this? 3.13.115
come, | let's have one other gaudy night. 3.13.181
come on, my queen, | there's sap in't yet. 3.13.190
well said, come on. 4.02. 8
let's to supper, come, | and drown consideration 4.02. 44
eros, come, mine armor, eros! 4.04. 2
come, good fellow, put thine iron on. 4.04. 3
come. 4.04. 5
come give me that: 4.04. 28
antony | is come into the field. 4.06. 7
come thee on. 4.07. 16
come on then, he may recover yet. 4.09. 33
all come to this? 4.12. 20
i come, my queen! 4.14. 50
come, eros, eros! 4.14. 54
that when the exigent should come, which now 4.14. 63
which now | is come indeed, when i should see 4.14. 64
do't, the time is come. 4.14. 67
come then; 4.14. 78
draw, and come. 4.14. 84
come then; 4.14.101
a prophesying fear | of what hath come to pass; 4.14.121
sent | me to proclaim the truth, and i am come, 4.14.126
come, your lord calls! 4.14.130
but come, come, antony — | help me, my women — 4.15. 29
but come, come, antony — | help me, my women — 4.15. 29
yet come a little — | wishers were ever fools 4.15. 36
wishers were ever fools — o, come, come, come, 4.15. 37
wishers were ever fools — o, come, come, come, 4.15. 37
wishers were ever fools — o, come, come, come, 4.15. 37
house of death | ere death dare come to us? 4.15. 82
come, away, | this case of that huge spirit now 4.15. 88
come, we have no friend | but resolution and the 4.15. 90
come hither, proculeius. 5.01. 61
guard her till caesar come. 5.02. 36
which your death | will never let come forth. 5.02. 46
come hither, come! 5.02. 47
come hither, come! 5.02. 47
come, come, and take a queen | worth many babes 5.02. 47
come, come, and take a queen | worth many babes 5.02. 47
let him come in. 5.02.236
husband, i come! 5.02.287
come then, and take the last warmth of my lips. 5.02.291
come, thou mortal wretch, | with thy sharp teeth 5.02.303
o, come apace, dispatch! 5.02.322
come, dolabella, see | high order in this great 5.02.365
if the king come, i shall incur i know not | how CYM 1.01.102
i would they had not come between us. 1.02. 22 P
come, i'll to my chamber. 1.02. 34 P
nay, come, let's go together. 1.02. 40 P
if i come off and leave her in such honor as you 1.04.151 P
of a stranger that's come to court /to–night? 2.01. 32 P
there's an italian come, and, 'tis thought, one 2.01. 37 P
come, i'll go see this italian. 2.01. 48 P
come; 2.01. 49 P
come off, come off; 2.02. 33

come off, come off; 2.02. 33
i would this music would come. 2.03. 11 P
come on, tune. 2.03. 14 P
come, our queen. 2.03. 63
he never can meet more mischance than come | to 2.03.132
state, and wish | that warmer days would come. 2.04. 6
the stone's too hard to come by. 2.04. 46
come, there's no more tribute to be paid. 3.01. 34 P
come, fellow, be thou honest, | do thou thy 3.04. 64
come, here's my heart: 3.04. 78
the king, he rages, none | dare come about him. 3.05. 68
come hither. 3.05. 81
come nearer. 3.05. 91
i would these garments were come. 3.05.133 P
come, and be true. 3.05.156 P
come, our stomachs | will make what's homely 3.06. 32
stay, come not in. 3.06. 39
fair youth, come in. 3.06. 89
in the cave, | we'll come to you after hunting. 4.02. 2
it is great morning. come away! — who's there? 4.02. 61
yet is't not probable | to come alone, either he 4.02.142
let ord'nance | come as the gods foresay it; 4.02.146
be haunted, | and worms will not come to thee. 4.02.218
come on then, and remove him. 4.02.257
all must, | as chimney–sweepers, come to dust. 4.02.263
physic, must | all follow this and come to dust. 4.02.269
lovers must | consign to thee and come to dust. 4.02.275
nothing ill come near thee! 4.02.279
we have done our obsequies. come lay him down. 4.02.282
come on, away, apart upon our knees. 4.02.288
and they come | under the conduct of bold 4.02.339
come, arm him. 4.02.400
come more, for more you're ready; 4.03. 30
so i'll fight | against the part i come with; 5.01. 25
though you, it seems, come from the fliers? 5.03. 2
on either side i come to spend my breath; 5.03. 81
come, sir, are you ready for death? 5.04.151 P
you come in faint for want of meat, depart 5.04.160 P
of what's past, is, and to come, the discharge. 5.04.169 P
our lives | may be call'd ransom, let it come. 5.05. 80
come, stand thou by our side, | make thy demand 5.05.129
i stand on fire: | come to the matter. 5.05.169
to all the villains past, in being, | to come! 5.05.213
was sung, | from ashes ancient gower is come, PER 1.ch. 2
from him i come | with message unto princely 1.03. 31
and come to us as favorers, not as foes. 1.04. 73
nor come we to add sorrow to your tears, | but 1.04. 90
ha, come and bring away the nets! 2.01. 13 P
come away, or i'll fetch th' with a wanton. 2.01. 16 P
them, they ne'er come but i look to be wash'd. 2.01. 26 P
come put it on, keep thee warm. 2.01. 79 P
come, thou shalt go home, and we'll have flesh 2.01. 80 P
princes and knights come from all parts of the 2.01.109 P
'twill hardly come out. 2.01.118 P
bots on't, 'tis come at last, and 'tis turn'd to 2.01.118 P
come, queen a' th' feast — | for, daughter, so 2.03. 17
who freely give to every one that come | to 2.03. 60
come, gentlemen, we sit too long on trifles, 2.03. 92
come, sir, here's a lady that wants breathing 2.03.100
nay, come, your hands and lips must seal it too; 2.05. 85
pericles | come not home in twice six moons, 3.ch. 31
come, come; 3.02.109
come, come; 3.02.109
come, dearest madam. 3.03. 38
come, my lord. 3.03. 41
come | give me your flowers, ere the sea mar it. 4.01. 25
come, | leonine, take her by the arm, walk with 4.01. 28
come, come, | i love the king your father, and 4.01. 31
come, come, | i love the king your father, and 4.01. 31
when he shall come and find | our paragon to all 4.01. 34
come, come, i know 'tis good for you. 4.01. 44
come, come, i know 'tis good for you. 4.01. 44
come say your prayers. 4.01. 65
your lady seeks my life, come you between, | and 4.01. 89
come, let's have her aboard suddenly. 4.01. 94 P
come, other sorts offend as well as we. 4.02. 36 P
come your ways, my masters. 4.02. 40 P
come, the gods have done their part in you. 4.02. 70 P
come, you're a young foolish sapling, and must 4.02. 87 P
i know he will come in our shadow, to scatter 4.02.111 P
pray you come hither a while. 4.02.115 P
come, young one, i like the manner of your 4.02.133 P
come your ways, follow me. 4.02.145 P
come, i am for no more bawdy–houses. 4.05. 6 P
twice the worth of her she had ne'er come here. 4.06. 2 P
come, we will leave his honor and her together. 4.06. 64 P
be a place of such resort, and will come into't? 4.06. 80 P
come bring me to some private place. 4.06. 90 P
come, come. 4.06. 90 P
come, come. 4.06. 91 P
come your ways. 4.06.125 P
come your /ways. 4.06.128 P
come your ways, i say. 4.06.130 P
would she had never come within my doors. 4.06.148 P
marry, come up, my dish of chastity with 4.06.150 P
come, mistress, come your /ways with me. 4.06.152 P
come, mistress, come your /ways with me. 4.06.152 P
come now, your one thing. 4.06.157 P
come, i'll do for thee what i can; 4.06.199 P
come your ways. 4.06.200 P
the governor, | who craves to come aboard. 5.01. 5
there is some of worth would come aboard; 5.01. 9
companion maid | be suffered to come near him. 5.01. 78
come, let us leave her, | and the gods make her 5.01. 78
falseness cannot come from thee, for thou 5.01.120
come sit by me. 5.01.141
o, come hither, | thou that beget'st him that 5.01.194
of your melancholy state, | did come to see you. 5.01.221
with all my heart, and, when you come ashore, 5.01.260
come, my marina. 5.01.264
that he can hither come so soon | is by your 5.02. 19
o, come, be buried | a second time within these 5.03. 43
we come unseasonably; TNK 1.01.168
carrier of that honor which | his enemy come in, 1.02.109
come all sad and solemn shows, | that are 1.05. 7
it be for great ones, yet they seldom come: 2.01. 4 P
have patiently | laid up my hour to come. 2.02. 6
summer shall come, and with her all delights, 2.02. 44
see how near art can come near their colors. 2.02.149
come; 2.02.277
twenty to one, he'll come to speak to her, | and 2.03. 14
come what can come, | the worst is death: 2.03. 17
come what can come, | the worst is death: 2.03. 17
do sweetly, | and god knows what may come on't. 2.03. 58
well, sir, | take your own time. come, boys. 2.03. 69
come, let's be gone, lads. 2.03. 73
when i come in | to bring him water in a morning 2.04. 21
that i, poor man, might eftsoons come between, 3.01. 12
come up to me! 3.01. 71
of one meal lend me — come before me then, | a 3.01. 74
come forth and fear not, here's no theseus. 3.03. 3
come, take courage, | you shall not die thus 3.03. 5
i'll come again some two hours hence and bring 3.03. 49
have your company | till /i come to the sound–a! 3.05. 66
come, lass, let's trip it. 3.05. 89
come forth, and foot it. 3.05.137
come, we are all made. 3.05.158
i spurr'd hard to come up, and under me | i had 3.06. 76
more | come near thee with such friendship. 3.06.103
and what to come shall threaten me | i fear less 3.06.124
then come what can come, | thou shalt know, 3.06.127
then come what can come, | thou shalt know, 3.06.127
come shake hands again then, | and take heed, as 3.06.302
come, i'll give ye | now usage like to princes 3.06.305
they come from all parts of the dukedom to him. 4.01.136
come hither, you are a wise man. 4.01.141
come weigh, my hearts, cheerly! 4.01.146
now, come ask me, brother — | alas, i know not! 4.02. 50
the knights are come. 4.02. 56
from whence come you, sir? 4.02. 71
come, i'll go visit 'em. 4.02.152
if it be your chance to come where the blessed 4.03. 22 P
to pieces with love, we shall come there, and do 4.03. 24 P
say you come to eat with her and to commune of 4.03. 77 P
come to her, stuck in as sweet flowers as the 4.03. 82 P
of this project, come in with my appliance. 4.03. 99 P
that this day come | to blow that nearness out 5.01. 9
come, your love palamon stays for you, child, 5.02. 41
and, for a jig, come cut and long tail to him! 5.02. 49
come, sweet, we'll go to dinner, | and then 5.02.107
we come towards the gods, | young and unwapper'd 5.04. 9
come! who begins? 5.04. 21
have at the worst can come, then! ep 10
it will come to that pass if strangers be STM II.C 4 P
should so much come too short of your great II.C 124
here come and sit, where never serpent hisses, VEN 17
come not within his danger by thy will, | they 639
now is he come unto the chamber door | that LUC 337
under that color am i come to scale | thy 481
my collatine would else have come to me | when 916
to all sins past, and all that are to come, 923
dread night, wouldst thou one hour come back, 965
this bastard graff shall never come to growth. 1062
"come, philomele, that sing'st of ravishment, 1128
see) | some present speed to come and visit me. 1307
to this well–painted piece is lucrece come, | to 1443
but now the mindful messenger, come back, 1583
words, so thick come in his poor heart's aid, 1784
quoth she, "and come again to–morrow." PP 14. 5
for why, she sight, and bade me come to–morrow. 14.24
fever's end, | to this troop come thou not near. PHT 8
who will believe my verse in time to come | if SON 17. 1
the age to come would say, "this poet lies, 17. 7
who even but now come back again, assured | of 45.11
whence at pleasure thou mayst come and part, 48.12
against that time (if ever that time come) 49. 1
two contracted new | come daily to the banks, 56.11
that time will come and take my love away. 64.12
how far a modern quill doth come too short, 83. 7
whose love to you | (though words come hindmost) 85.12
come in the rearward of a conquer'd woe; 90. 6
but in the onset come, so /shall i taste | at 90.11
of the wide world, dreaming on things to come, 107. 2
within his bending sickle's compass come, | love 116.10
if thy soul check thee that i come so near, 136. 1
state, | straight in her heart did mercy come, 145. 5

CO–MEDDLED 1 FR 0.0001 REL FR 1 V 0 P
whose blood and judgment are so well co–meddled, HAM 3.02. 69

COMEDIAN 1 FR 0.0001 REL FR 0 V 1 P
are you a comedian? TN 1.05.182 P

COMEDIANS 1 FR 0.0001 REL FR 1 V 0 P
the quick comedians | extemporally will stage us ANT 5.02.216

COMEDY 10 FR 0.0011 REL FR 4 V 6 P
as it were, spoke the prologue of our comedy; WIV 3.05. 75 P
merriment, | to dash it like a christmas comedy. LLL 5.02.462
might well have made our sport a comedy. 5.02.876
the most lamentable comedy and most cruel death MND 1.02. 12 P
are things in this comedy of pyramus and thisby 3.01. 9 P
but to hear them say, it is a sweet comedy. 4.02. 44 P
amendment, | are come to play a pleasant comedy, SHR in.2. 130
the world, either for tragedy, comedy, history, HAM 2.02.397 P
for if the king like not the comedy, | why then 3.02.293
he comes like the catastrophe of the old comedy. LR 1.02.134 P

COMELINESS 1 FR 0.0001 REL FR 0 V 1 P
when youth with comeliness pluck'd all gaze his COR 1.03. 7 P

COMELY 8 FR 0.0009 REL FR 7 V 1 P
show'd | bashful sincerity and comely love. ADO 4.01. 54
it, for in most comely truth thou deservest it. 5.02. 7 P
when what is comely | envenoms him that bears it AYL 2.03. 14
this is a happier and more comely time | than COR 4.06. 27
(setting his fate aside) | of comely virtues; TIM 3.05. 15
and the boar, | break comely out before him; TNK 3.05. 19
he dances very finely, very comely, | and, for a 5.02. 48
bat, | and comely distant sits he by her side; LC 65

COMER 2 FR 0.0002 REL FR 2 V 0 P
as fair | as any comer i have look'd on yet MV 2.01. 21
as he would fly | grasps in the comer. TRO 3.03.168

/COMES 6 FR 0.0006 REL FR 4 V 2 P
here he /comes. MV 3.05. 28 P
/comes hunting this way to disport himself. 3H6 4.05. 8
/that /comes /in /likeness /of /a //coal–black TIT 3.02. 78
/how /comes /it? /do /they /grow /rusty? HAM 2.02.337 P
/peace, /who /comes /here? 5.02. 80
/from /france /there /comes /a /power | /into LR 3.01. 30

COMES 634 FR 0.0716 REL FR 421 V 213 P
that's offer'd, | comes to th' entertainer — TMP 2.01. 17
dolor comes to him indeed; 2.01. 19 P
here comes a spirit of his, and to torment me 2.02. 15
great juno, comes, i know her by her gait. 4.01.102
neptune, and do fly him | when he comes back; 5.01. 36
peace, here she comes. TGV 2.01. 93 P
here comes my father. 2.04. 47 P
worth | comes all the praises that i now bestow) 2.04. 72
have done, have done; here comes the gentleman. 2.04. 99
gone, | and this way comes he with it presently, 3.01. 42
and thereof comes the proverb: 3.01.304 P
but here comes thurio. 4.02. 16
see where she comes. 5.01. 7
here comes the duke. 5.02. 30
who's this comes here? 5.04. 18
here comes sir john. WIV 1.01.108 P
here comes fair mistress anne. 1.01.259 P
out alas! here comes my master. 1.04. 36 P
i doubt he be not well, that he comes not home. 1.04. 41 P
why, look where he comes; 2.01.102 P
heed, ere summer comes or cuckoo–birds do sing. 2.01.123
look who comes yonder. 2.01.158 P
look where my ranting host of the garter comes. 2.01.190 P
there comes my master, master shallow, and 3.01. 31 P
here comes doctor caius. 3.01. 72 P
here comes little robin. 3.03. 21 P
you may ask your father, here he comes. 3.04. 66 P
o, here he comes. 3.05. 59 P
comes me in the instant of our encounter, after 3.05. 72 P
luck would have it, comes in one mistress page; 3.05. 84 P
look where his master comes; 4.01. 9 P
she comes of errands, does she? 4.02.173 P
what duke should that be comes so secretly? 4.03. 4 P
devise but how you'll use him when he comes, 4.04. 26
who comes here? 5.05. 15 P
here comes master fenton. 5.05.213 P
look where he comes. MM 1.01. 24
behold, behold, where madam mitigation comes! 1.02. 45 P
here comes signior claudio, led by the provost 1.02.114 P
whence comes this restraint? 1.02.124
this comes off well. here's a wise officer. 2.01. 57 P
look, here comes one; 2.03. 10
if he be a whoremonger, and comes before him, he 3.02. 36 P
but who comes here? 3.02.189
here comes a man of comfort, whose advice | hath 4.01. 8
him know | i have a servant comes with me along, 4.01. 45
with this maid, | she comes to do you good. 4.01. 51
yet i believe there comes | no countermand; 4.02. 96
and here comes claudio's pardon. 4.02.101
look you, sir, here comes your ghostly father. 4.03. 48 P
the duke comes home to–morrow — nay, dry your 4.03.127
as there comes light from heaven, and words from 5.01.225
my lord, here comes the rascal i spoke of, here 5.01.283 P
here comes the almanac of my true date: ERR 1.02. 41
here comes your man, now is your husband nigh. 2.01. 43
see, here he comes. 2.02. 6
how comes it now, my husband, o, how comes it, 2.02.119
how comes it now, my husband, o, how comes it, 2.02.119
faith, no, he comes too late, | and so tell your 3.01. 49
that labor may you save; see where he comes. 4.01. 14
that stays but till her owner comes aboard, 4.01. 86
that time comes stealing on by night and day? 4.02. 60
and here she comes in the habit of a light wench 4.03. 52 P
and thereof comes that the wenches say, "god 4.03. 53 P
here comes my man: 4.04. 8
and thereof comes it that his head is light. 5.01. 72
person | comes this way to the melancholy vale, 5.01.120
that don /pedro of arragon comes this night to ADO 1.01. 2 P
who comes here? 1.03. 40 P
a musty room, comes me the prince and claudio, 1.03. 59 P
and then comes repentance, and with his bad legs 2.01. 78 P
look here she comes. 2.01.262 P
him, and whatsoever comes athwart his affection 2.02. 6 P
here comes beatrice. 2.03.244 P
fortune, but to write and read comes by nature. 3.03. 15 P
ask my lady beatrice else, here she comes. 3.04. 38 P
indeed, neighbor, he comes too short of you. 3.05. 41 P
comes not that blood as modest evidence | to 4.01. 37
here comes the prince and claudio hastily. 5.01. 45
see, see, here comes the man we went to seek. 5.01.110
here, here comes master signior leonato, and the 5.01.257 P
i leave you too, for here comes one in haste. 5.02. 94 P
here comes the prince and claudio. 5.04. 33
here comes other reck'nings. 5.04. 52
for well you know here comes in embassy | the LLL 1.01.134
or vainly comes th' admired princess hither. 1.01.140
here comes boyet. 2.01. 80
like one that comes here to besiege his court, 2.01. 86
here comes navarre. 2.01. 89
the princess comes to hunt here in the park, 3.01.164
here comes a member of the commonwealth. 4.01. 41
when it comes so smoothly off, so obscenely as 4.01.143
here comes one with a paper, god give him grace 4.03. 19 P
who is he comes here? 4.03. 42
why, he comes in like a perjure, wearing papers. 4.03. 46
here comes boyet, and mirth is in his face. 5.02. 79
see where it comes! 5.02.337
ship is under sail, and here she comes amain. 5.02.546
thy head, achilles — here comes hector in arms. 5.02.632 P
the hall | and milk comes frozen home in pail; 5.02.915
keep promise, love. look, here comes helena. MND 1.01.179
here comes oberon. 2.01. 58
and this same progeny of evils comes | from our 2.01.115
but who comes here? 2.01.186
and a lantern, and say he comes to disfigure, or 3.01. 60 P
here comes my messenger. 3.02. 4
must be answered, | and forth my mimic comes. 3.02. 19
look where thy love comes; 3.02.176
here comes one. 3.02.400
here she comes, curst and sad. 3.02.439
how comes this gentle concord in the world, 4.01.143
when my cue comes, call me, and i will answer. 4.01.200 P
anon comes pyramus, sweet youth and tall, | and 5.01.144
yonder she comes. 5.01.187 P
here comes thisby. 5.01.261 P
is gone before thisby comes back and finds her 5.01.313 P

here she comes, and her passion ends the play. 5.01.315 P
here comes bassanio, your most noble kinsman, MV 1.01. 57
superfluity comes sooner by white hairs, but 1.02. 8 P
who is he comes here? 1.03. 38 P
here comes the man. 2.02.111 P
here comes lorenzo, more of this hereafter. 2.06. 20
his oath, | and comes to his election presently. 2.09. 3
that comes to hazard for my worthless self. 2.09. 18
venetian, one that comes before | to signify th' 2.09. 87
as this fore–spurrer comes before his lord. 2.09. 95
see | quick cupid's post that comes so mannerly. 2.09.100
for here he comes in the likeness of a jew. 3.01. 20 P
here comes another of the tribe; 3.01. 77 P
but who comes here? 3.02.218
this comes too near the praising of myself, 3.04. 22
he is ready at the door; he comes, my lord. 4.01. 15
whereof i cannot enough commend, comes with him, 4.01.159 P
half | comes to the privy coffer of the state, 4.01.354
the other half comes to the general state, 4.01.371
who comes so fast in silence of the night? 5.01. 25
who comes with her? 5.01. 32
it comes from padua, from bellario. 5.01.268
yonder comes my master, your brother. AYL 1.01. 26 P
here comes monsieur /le beau. 1.02. 91 P
there comes an old man and his three sons — 1.02.118 P
look, here comes the duke. 1.03. 39 P
look you, who comes here, a young man and an old 2.04. 20 P
but who comes here? 2.07. 87
of good breeding or comes of a very dull kindred 3.02. 30 P
here comes young master ganymed, my new 3.02. 86 P
here comes my sister reading, stand aside. 3.02.124
as wine comes out of a narrow–mouth'd bottle, 3.02.200 P
o, ominous! he comes to kill my heart. 3.02.246 P
you bring me out. soft, comes he not here? 3.02.251 P
here comes sir oliver. 3.03. 64 P
swear he would come this morning, and comes not? 3.04. 19 P
who comes here? 3.04. 46 P
and when that time comes, | afflict me with thy 3.05. 32
for though he comes slowly, he carries his house 4.01. 54 P
but he comes arm'd in his fortune, and prevents 4.01. 60 P
look who comes here. 4.03. 5 P
for here comes more company. 4.03. 74 P
here comes the man you mean. 5.01. 9 P
for look you, here comes my rosalind. 5.02. 16 P
here comes a lover of mine and a lover of hers. 5.02. 75 P
here comes a pair of very strange beasts, which 5.04. 36 P
hence comes it that your kindred shuns your SHR in.2. 28
when biondello comes, he waits on thee, | but i 1.01.208
here comes the rogue. 1.01.221
comes there any more of it? 1.01.251 P
and then i know after who comes by the worst. 1.02. 14
why, nothing comes amiss, so money comes withal. 1.02. 81 P
why, nothing comes amiss, so money comes withal. 1.02. 82 P
but who comes here? 2.01. 38
and woo her with some spirit when she comes. 2.01.169
but here she comes, and now, petruchio, speak. 2.01.181
here comes your father. 2.01.279
i will to venice, sunday comes apace. 2.01.322
and that lucentio that comes a–wooing, "priami," 3.01. 34 P
who comes with him? 3.02. 64 P
i am glad he's come, howsoe'er he comes. 3.02. 74 P
why, sir, he comes not. 3.02. 75 P
didst thou not say he comes? 3.02. 76 P
sir, i say his horse comes, with him on his back 3.02. 79 P
of you all shall find when he comes home. 4.01. 88 P
why, she comes to borrow nothing of them. 4.01.105 P
but, sir, here comes your boy; 4.04. 8
here comes baptista; 4.04. 18
i marvel cambio comes not all this while. 5.01. 7
son, i'll be your half, bianca comes. 5.02. 78
now, by my holidam, here comes katherina! 5.02. 99
see where she comes, and brings your froward 5.02.119
who comes here? AWW 1.01. 98
and florence is denied before he comes. 1.02. 12
what's he comes here? 1.02. 17
your marriage comes by destiny, | your cuckoo 1.03. 62
here comes the king. 2.03. 40 P
here he comes. 2.05. 13 P
here comes my clog. 2.05. 53
had it, save that he comes not along with her. 3.02. 2 P
look, here comes a pilgrim. 3.05. 30 P
here he comes. 3.06. 40 P
every night he comes | with musics of all sorts, 3.07. 39
but couch ho, here he comes, to beguile two 4.01. 22 P
when midnight comes, knock at my chamber–window; 4.02. 54
hush, hush! hoodman comes! portotartarossa. 4.03.118 P
his highness comes post from marsellis, of as 4.05. 80 P
look, here he comes himself. 5.02. 18 P
but love that comes too late, | like a 5.03. 57
your reputation comes too short for my daughter, 5.03.176 P
for here comes sir andrew agueface. TN 1.03. 43 P
i thank you. here comes the count. 1.04. 9 P
here comes my lady. 1.05. 30 P
for — here he comes — one of thy kin has a 1.05.114 P
so much, and therefore comes to speak with you. 1.05.141 P
that too, and therefore comes to speak with you. 1.05.144 P
here comes the fool, i' faith. 2.03. 15 P
here comes the little villain. 2.05. 13 P
for here comes the trout that must be caught 2.05. 22 P
and then i comes behind. 2.05.135 P
here comes my noble gull–catcher. 2.05.187 P
at every feather | that comes before his eye. 3.01. 65
look where the youngest wren of /nine comes. 3.02. 67 P
for it comes to pass oft that a terrible oath, 3.04.179 P
he will find it comes from a clodpole. 3.04.189 P
here he comes with your niece. 3.04.197 P
this comes with seeking you; 3.04.332
curate, who comes to visit malvolio the lunatic. 4.02. 21 P
but here the lady comes. 4.03. 21
here comes the man, sir, that did rescue me. 5.01. 50
here comes the countess, now heaven walks on 5.01. 97
here comes sir toby halting — you shall hear 5.01.192 P
so comes it, lady, you have been mistook; 5.01.259
here comes bohemia. WT 1.02.364
my part no other | but what comes from myself, 3.02. 25
of | which comes to me in name of fault, i must 3.02. 60
to me comes a creature, | sometimes her head on 3.03. 19
why, then comes in the sweet o' the year, | for 4.03. 3
fifteen hundred shorn, what comes the wool to? 4.03. 34 P
he comes not | like to his father's greatness. 5.01. 88
here comes a gentleman that happily knows more. 5.02. 20 P
here comes the lady paulina's steward, he can 5.02. 26 P
comes it not something near? 5.03. 23
still methinks | there is an air comes from her. 5.03. 78
and then comes answer like an absey book: JN 1.01.196
but who comes in such haste in riding–robes? 1.01.217
how comes it then that thou art call'd a king, 2.01.107
here comes the holy legate of the pope. 3.01.135
look who comes here! 3.04. 17
the tidings comes that they are all arriv'd. 4.02.115
look where the holy legate comes apace, | to 5.02. 65
to souse annoyance that comes near his nest; 5.02.150
after our sentence plaining comes too late. R2 1.03.175
for all in vain comes counsel to his ear. 2.01. 4
then all too late comes counsel to be heard, 2.01. 27
here comes the duke of york. 2.02. 73
now comes the sick hour that his surfeit made, 2.02. 84
comes rushing on this woeful land at once! 2.02. 99
but who comes here? 2.03. 20
which, till my infant fortune comes to years, 2.03. 66
but who comes here? 2.03. 67
words by you, | here comes his grace in person. 2.03. 82
but who comes here? 3.02. 90
comes at the last and with a little pin | bores 3.02.169
but who comes here? 3.03. 19
northumberland comes back from bullingbrook. 3.03.142
here comes my son aumerle. 5.02. 41
but who comes here? 5.03. 22
where no man never comes, but that sad dog 5.05. 70
here comes your uncle. 1H4 1.03.130
he says he comes from your father. 2.04.289 P
here comes lean jack, here comes bare–bone. 2.04.325 P
here comes lean jack, here comes bare–bone. 2.04.326 P
see how this river comes me cranking in, | and 3.01. 97
letters from him! why comes he not himself? 4.01. 15
and comes not in, overrul'd by prophecies, | i 4.04. 18
you have not sought it, how comes it then? 5.01. 27
here comes your cousin. 5.02. 27
my lord, prepare, the king comes on apace. 5.02. 89
but who comes here? 5.03. 38 P
if not, honor comes unlook'd for, and there's an 5.03. 60 P
here comes the earl. 2H4 1.01. 6
here comes my servant travers, who i sent | on 1.01. 28
now, travers, what good tidings comes with you? 1.01. 33
look, here comes more news. 1.01. 59
sir, here comes the nobleman that committed the 1.02. 55 P
'a comes /continuantly to pie–corner (saving 2.01. 26 P
yonder he comes, and that arrant malmsey–nose 2.01. 39 P
how comes this, sir john? 2.01. 80 P
comes the king back from wales, my noble lord? 2.01.176 P
by the mass, here comes bardolph. 2.02. 69 P
"how comes that?" 2.02.114 P
lo here comes sir john. 2.04. 32 P
shut the door, there comes no swaggerers here; 2.04. 76 P
there comes no swaggerers here. 2.04. 81 P
ancient /swagger, /'a comes not in my doors. 2.04. 84 P
there comes none here. 2.04. 94 P
now comes in the sweetest morsel of the night, 2.04.367 P
she comes blubber'd. 2.04.390 P
cousin, that comes hither anon about soldiers? 3.02. 27 P
it comes of accommodo, very good, a good phrase. 3.02. 71 P
look, here comes good sir john. 3.02. 81 P
off a mile, | in goodly form comes on the enemy, 4.01. 20
this offer comes from mercy, not from fear. 4.01.148
to say thus, some good thing comes to–morrow. 4.02. 84
here comes our general. 4.03. 23 P
and this valor comes of sherris. 4.03.113 P
hereof comes it that prince harry is valiant, 4.03.117 P
comes to no further use | but to be known and 4.04. 72
lo where he comes. 4.05. 89
look, look, here comes my john of lancaster. 4.05.225
here comes the prince. 5.02. 42
be merry, now comes in the sweet a' th' night. 5.03. 50 P
well, of sufferance comes ease. 5.04. 25 P
i will leer upon him as 'a comes by, and do but 5.05. 6 P
comes sneaking, and so sucks her princely eggs, H5 1.02.171
how he comes o'er us with our wilder days, | not 1.02.267
here comes ancient pistol and his wife. 2.01. 26 P
thus comes the english with full power upon us, 2.04. 1
th' embassador from the french comes back, 3.pr. 28
here 'a comes, and the scots captain, captain 3.02. 74 P
since that my penitence comes after all, 4.01.304
he that outlives this day, and comes safe home, 4.03. 41
comes to him where in gore he lay insteeped, 4.06. 12
here comes his majesty. 4.07. 54 P
here comes the herald of the french, my liege. 4.07. 66
why, here he comes, swelling like a turkey–cock. 5.01. 14 P
here comes your father. 5.02.279 P
here, here she comes. 1H6 1.05. 4
your nephew, late–despised richard, comes. 2.05. 36
now in the rearward comes the duke and his. 3.03. 33
there comes the ruin, there begins confusion. 4.01.194
too late comes rescue, he is ta'en or slain; 4.04. 42
here 'a comes, methinks, and the queen with him. 2H6 1.03. 6 P
here comes the townsmen on procession, | to 2.01. 66
but soft, i think she comes, and i'll prepare 2.04. 15
spring–time show'rs comes thought on thought, 3.01.337
here comes my lord. 3.02. 5
and still proclaimeth, as he comes along, | his 4.09. 28
from ireland thus comes york to claim his right, 5.01. 1
see, buckingham, somerset comes with th' queen. 5.01. 83
and here comes clifford to deny their bail. 5.01.123
but, noble as he is, look where he comes. 5.03. 14
and when the king comes, offer him no violence, 3H6 1.01. 33
here comes the queen, whose looks bewray her 1.01.211
ah, tutor, look where bloody clifford comes! 1.03. 2
and so he comes, to rend his limbs asunder. 1.03. 15
out, | and therefore comes my brother montague. 2.01.167
a band of thirty thousand men | comes warwick, 2.02. 69
for vengeance comes along with them. 2.05.134
here comes a man, let's stay till he be past. 3.01. 12
no, not a man comes for redress of thee; 3.01. 20
and see where comes the breeder of my sorrow! 3.03. 43
here comes the king. 4.01. 6
but see where somerset and clarence comes! 4.02. 3
i am inform'd that he comes towards london | to 4.04. 26
o cheerful colors! see where oxford comes! 5.01. 58
it is, and lo where youthful edward comes! 5.05. 11
he's sudden, if a thing comes in his head. 5.05. 86
down to my soul — here clarence comes! R3 1.01. 41
but who comes here? 1.01.121
here comes sir richard ratcliffe and the duke. 2.01. 46
ill news, by'r lady — seldom comes the better. 2.03. 4
here comes a messenger. what news? 2.04. 38
my lord, the mayor of london comes to greet you. 3.01. 17
that he comes not | to tell us whether they will 3.01. 22
and in good time, here comes the sweating lord. 3.01. 24
now in good time, here comes the duke of york. 3.01. 95
in happy time, here comes the duke himself. 3.04. 21
here catesby comes again. 3.07. 82
and in good time, here the lieutenant comes. 4.01. 12
and here he comes. 4.03. 23
who comes here? 4.04. 8
unless for that he comes to be your liege, | you 4.04.475
you cannot guess wherefore the welshman comes. 4.04.476
lo, where comes that rock | that i advise your H8 1.01.113
the subject's grief | comes through commissions, 1.02. 57
intercession this revokement | and pardon comes. 1.02.107
in your way | for more than blushing comes to. 2.03. 42
lo, who comes here? 2.03. 49
thy approach, i know, | my comfort comes along. 2.04.241
the third day comes a frost, a killing frost, 3.02.355
when it comes, | cranmer will find a friend will 4.01.106
o my good lord, that comfort comes too late, 4.02.120
his royal self in judgment comes to hear | the 5.02.155
and when fair cressid comes into my thoughts — TRO 1.01. 30
so, traitor, then she comes when she is thence. 1.01. 31
who comes here? 1.02. 37 P
when comes troilus? 1.02.193 P
yonder comes paris, yonder comes paris. 1.02.212 P
yonder comes paris, yonder comes paris. 1.02.212 P
what sneaking fellow comes yonder? 1.02.226 P
here comes more. 1.02.240 P
he hears nought privately that comes from troy. 1.03.249
of helen's needle, for whom he comes to fight. 2.01. 81 P
look you, who comes here? 2.03. 68 P
here comes patroclus. 2.03.103 P
o, here he comes! how now, how now? 3.02. 5 P
boldness comes to me now, and brings me heart. 3.02.113
what comes the general to speak with me? 3.03. 55
to this valiant greek | comes fast upon. 4.03. 3
here, here, here he comes. /ah, sweet ducks! 4.04. 11 P
that give a coasting welcome ere it comes, | and 4.05. 59
yonder comes the troop. 4.05. 64
half hector comes to seek | this blended knight, 4.05. 85
great agamemnon comes to meet us here. 4.05.159
here comes thersites. 5.01. 4
here comes himself to guide you. 5.01. 69
she comes to you. 5.02. 4
cressid comes forth to him. 5.02. 6
soft, here comes sleeve and t' other. 5.04. 18 P
how ugly night comes breathing at his heels; 5.08. 6
soft, who comes here? COR 1.01. 50 P
but it proceeds or comes from them to you, | and 1.01.153
again, and over and over he comes, and up again; 1.03. 62 P
yonder comes news: a wager they have met. 1.04. 1
he comes the third time home with the oaken 2.01.124 P
here he comes, and in the gown of humility, mark 2.03. 40 P
so, here comes a brace. 2.03. 61
well, here he comes. 3.03. 30
dismiss them home. | here comes his mother. 4.02. 8
my wife comes foremost; 5.03. 22
bury him where you can, he comes not here. TIT 1.01.354
how comes it that the subtile queen of goths 1.01.392
here comes a parcel of our hopeful booty, 2.03. 49
no more, great empress, bassianus comes. 2.03. 52
but who comes with our brother marcus here? 3.01. 58
good uncle marcus, see how swift she comes. 4.01. 3
soft, who comes here? 4.02. 51
aid, | and that it comes from old andronicus, 4.03. 16
but who comes here, led by a lusty goth? 5.01. 19
see here he comes, and i must ply my theme. 5.02. 80
and see them ready against their mother comes. 5.02.205
tool, here comes /two of the house of montagues. ROM 1.01. 31 P
"better," here comes one of my master's kinsmen. 1.01. 58 P
see where he comes! 1.01.156
and she comes | in shape no bigger than an 1.04. 54
and sometime comes she with a tithe–pig's tail 1.04. 79
ah, sirrah, this unlook'd–for sport comes well. 1.05. 29
here comes romeo, here comes romeo. 2.04. 36 P
here comes romeo, here comes romeo. 2.04. 36 P
o god, she comes! 2.05. 18
now comes the wanton blood up in your cheeks, 2.05. 70
here comes the lady. 2.06. 16
by my head, here comes the capulets. 3.01. 35 P
well, peace be with you, sir, here comes my man. 3.01. 56
here comes the furious tybalt back again. 3.01.121
but by and by comes back to romeo, | who had but 3.01.170
o, here comes my nurse, | and she brings news; 3.02. 31
and joy comes well in such a needy time. 3.05.105
ere he that should be husband comes to woo. 3.05.119
here comes your father, tell him so yourself; 3.05.124
look, sir, here comes the lady toward my cell. 4.01. 17
when the bridegroom in the morning comes | to 4.01.107
see where she comes from shrift with merry look. 4.02. 15
and there die strangled ere my romeo comes? 4.03. 35
fear comes upon me. 5.03.135
seek, and know how this foul murder comes. 5.03.198
then comes she to me, | and with wild looks bid 5.03.239
anon comes one with light to ope the tomb, | and 5.03.283
a picture, sir. when comes your book forth? TIM 1.01. 26
so 'tis. this comes off well and excellent. 1.01. 29
look who comes here; will you be chid? 1.01.176
there comes with them a forerunner, my lord, 1.02.119 P
what a sweep of vanity comes this way! 1.02.132
seldom rich, | it comes in charity to thee; 1.02.223
be round with him, now he comes from hunting. 2.02. 8
here comes the lord. 2.02. 13
stay, here comes the fool with apemantus, let's 2.02. 46 P
look you, here comes my master's page. 2.02. 72 P
aside, aside, here comes lord timon. 2.02.119 P
the future comes apace; 2.02.148
it comes not ill; 3.05.111

he sent to me, sir — here he comes. 3.06. 24 P
yonder comes a poet and a painter; 4.03.351 P
suspect still comes where an estate is least. 4.03.514
that comes in triumph over pompey's blood? JC 1.01. 51
comes caesar to the capitol to–morrow? 1.03. 36
close a while, for here comes one in haste. 1.03.131
the morning comes upon 's. 2.01.221
there | speak to great caesar as he comes along. 2.04. 38
soft, who comes here? a friend of antony's. 3.01.122
but here comes antony. welcome, mark antony! 3.01.147
here comes his body, mourn'd by mark antony, who 3.02. 41 P
when comes such another? 3.02.252
he comes upon a wish. 3.02.266
comes his army on? 4.02. 27
who comes here? 4.03.275
it comes upon me. 4.03.278
the enemy comes on in gallant show; 5.01. 13
here comes the general. 5.04. 17
who comes here? MAC 1.02. 45
the king comes here to–night. 1.05. 31
my dearest love, | duncan comes here to–night. 1.05. 59
here he comes. 2.03. 43
here comes the good macduff. 2.04. 20
then comes my fit again. 3.04. 20
of my thumbs, | something wicked this way comes. 4.01. 45
comes the king forth, i pray you? 4.03.140
see who comes here. 4.03.159
lo you, here she comes! 5.01. 19 P
i will set down what comes from her, to satisfy 5.01. 33 P
and now a wood | comes toward dunsinane. 5.05. 45
here comes newer comfort. 5.09. 19
look where it comes again! HAM 1.01. 40
figure | comes armed through our watch, so like 1.01.110
lo where it comes again! 1.01.126
some say that ever 'gainst that season comes 1.01.158
word made true and good, | the apparition comes. 1.02.211
i stay too long — but here my father comes. 1.03. 52
look, my lord, it comes! 1.04. 38
to speak of horrors — he comes before me. 2.01. 81
for this effect defective comes by cause: 2.02.103
look where sadly the poor wretch comes reading. 2.02.168
their inhibition comes by the means of the late 2.02.332 P
prophesy, he comes to tell me of the players, 2.02.386 P
you more, for look where my abridgment comes. 2.02.420 P
one scene of it comes near the circumstance 3.02. 76
let come what comes, only i'll be reveng'd 4.05.136
hamlet comes back. 4.07.124
toe of the peasant comes so near the heel of the 5.01.141 P
here comes the king, | the queen, the courtiers. 5.01.217
'tis dangerous when the baser nature comes 5.02. 60
only she comes too short, that i profess LR 1.01. 72
this villain of mine comes under the prediction; 1.02.109 P
he comes like the catastrophe of the old comedy. 1.02.134 P
tell him, so much the rent of his land comes to. 1.04.135 P
here comes one o' the parings. 1.04.188 P
now, gods that we adore, whereof comes this? 1.04.290
thing you know than comes from her demand out of 1.05. 3 P
how comes that? 2.01. 5 P
my worthy arch and patron, comes to–night. 2.01. 59
i know not /why he comes. 2.01. 79
all vengeance comes too short | which can pursue 2.01. 88
how chance the king comes with so small a number 2.04. 63
who comes here? 2.04.189
alack, the night comes on, and the /bleak winds 2.04.300
then comes the time, who lives to see't, | that 3.02. 93
look, here comes a walking fire. 3.04.114 P
i bleed apace, | untimely comes this hurt. 3.07. 98
but who comes here? 4.01. 9
madam, here comes my lord. 4.02. 28
but who comes here? 4.06. 80
here comes kent. 5.03.230
that comes to tell you your daughter and the OTH 1.01.115 P
here comes another troop to seek for you. 1.02. 54
general, be advis'd, | he comes to bad intent. 1.02. 56
here comes brabantio and the valiant moor. 1.03. 47
here comes the lady; 1.03.170
comes from my pate as birdlime does from frieze, 2.01.126
lo, where he comes! 2.01.181
hard at hand comes the master and main exercise, 2.01.262 P
how comes it, michael, you are thus forgot? 2.03.188
there comes a fellow crying out for help, | and 2.03.226
madam, here comes my lord. 3.03. 29
consider what is spoke | comes from /my love. 3.03.217
look where she comes: 3.03.277
look where he comes! 3.03.330
look where he comes. 3.04. 31
thou saidst (o, it comes o'er my memory, | as 4.01. 20
here he comes. 4.01. 99
certain venetians, and thither comes the bauble, 4.01.134 P
before me! look where she comes. 4.01.145 P
for if it touch not you, it comes near nobody. 4.01.198 P
'tis lodovico — | this comes from the duke. 4.01.215
how comes this trick upon him? 4.02.129
here's one comes in his shirt, with light and 5.01. 47
'tis like she comes to speak of cassio's death; 5.02. 92
she comes more nearer earth than she was wont, 5.02.110
he comes too short of that great property ANT 1.01. 58
hush, here comes antony. 1.02. 79
but here comes antony. 1.03. 13
worth love, | comes /dear'd by being lack'd. 1.04. 44
here comes | the noble antony. 2.02. 13
his grain, | and shortly comes to harvest. 2.07. 23
nay, i have done, | here comes the emperor. 3.07. 20
and there i will attend | what further comes. 3.10. 32
bid that welcome | which comes to punish us, and 4.14.137
here comes the gentleman, | the queen, and CYM 1.01. 68
where air comes out, air comes in; 1.02. 3 P
where air comes out, air comes in; 1.02. 3 P
betwixt two charming words, comes in my father, 1.03. 35
but how comes it he is to sojourn with you? 1.04. 24 P
here comes the britain. 1.04. 28 P
here comes a flattering rascal, upon him | will 1.05. 27
and every day that comes comes to decay | a 1.05. 56
and every day that comes comes to decay | a 1.05. 56
of rome, | comes from my lord with letters. 1.06. 11
here comes the king. 2.03. 32 P
fellow, | albeit he comes on angry purpose now; 2.03. 56
lack humanity | so much as this fact comes to? 3.02. 17
lo here she comes. 3.02. 22
the roman, comes to milford–haven | to–morrow. 3.04.142
for 'tis said a woman's fitness comes by fits. 4.01. 6 P
look, here he comes, | and brings the dire 4.02.195
how comes these staggers on me? 5.05.233
see where she comes, apparelled like the spring, PER 1.01. 12
here comes the lords of tyre. 1.03. 9 P
one sorrow never comes but brings an heir | that 1.04. 63
to know for what he comes, and whence he comes, 1.04. 80
to know for what he comes, and whence he comes, 1.04. 80
and here he comes. 2.ch. 39
for he comes | to an honor'd triumph strangely 2.02. 52
soft, here he comes, i must dissemble it. 2.05. 23
here comes my daughter, she can witness it. 2.05. 66
here she comes weeping for her only mistress' 4.01. 11
o, our credit comes not in like the commodity, 4.02. 30 P
but here comes boult. 4.02. 39 P
here comes the lord lysimachus disguis'd. 4.06. 16 P
here comes that which grows to the stalk, never 4.06. 41 P
custrel that comes inquiring for his tib. 4.06.166
well, comes in | like old importment's bastard) TNK 1.03. 79
i have, sir. here she comes. 2.01. 15 P
when the north comes near her, | rude and 2.02.140
here the duke comes; 3.05. 12
comes i' th' nick, as mad as a march hare. 3.05. 73
—is — now comes in, which being glu'd together 3.05.119
make the world think, when it comes to hearing, 3.06. 11
look where she comes, you shall perceive her 4.03. 9 P
time comes on. 5.01.136
so, | and when your fit comes, fit her home, and 5.02. 11
you'll find it so. she comes. pray /humor her. 5.02. 40
make curtsy, here your love comes. 5.02. 69
power could give his will, bounds, comes on end, 5.04. 67
and presently | backward the jade comes o'er, 5.04. 81
shake, which partly comes through the eating of STM II.C 14 P
bow, | who conquers where he comes in every jar, VEN 100
of thy face excelling | comes breath perfum'd, 444
lust's winter comes ere summer half be done; 802
and, beauty dead, black chaos comes again. 1020
how comes it then, vile opportunity, | being so LUC 895
he gratis comes, and thou art well apaid, | as 914
that thou shalt lend me | comes all too late, 1686
anon he comes, and throws his mantle by, | and PP 6. 9
anon adonis comes with horn and hounds; 9. 6
comes home again, on better judgment making. SON 87.12
thence comes it that my name receives a brand, 111. 5
and to your audit comes | their distract parcels LC 230

COMES'T 1 FR 0.0001 REL FR 1 V 0 P
how comes't that you | have holp to make this COR 3.01.274

COMEST 4 FR 0.0004 REL FR 3 V 1 P
and why thou comest thus knightly clad in arms, R2 1.03. 12
and how comest thou hither, | where no man never 5.05. 69
chid to–morrow when thou comest to thy father. 1H4 2.04.374 P
thou wilt fall backward when thou comest to age, ROM 1.03. 56

COMET 4 FR 0.0004 REL FR 4 V 0 P
monument, | some comet or unusual prodigy? SHR 3.02. 96
not stir | but like a comet i was wond'red at, 1H4 3.02. 47
now shine it like a comet of revenge, | a 1H6 3.02. 31
eyes, | but have been gaz'd on like a comet. PER 5.01. 86

COMETH 4 FR 0.0004 REL FR 4 V 0 P
both who he is and why he cometh hither | thus R2 1.03. 27
whence cometh this alarum, and the noise? 1H6 1.04. 99
here cometh charles, i marvel how he sped. 2.01. 48
cometh andronicus, bound with laurel boughs, TIT 1.01. 74

COMETS 3 FR 0.0003 REL FR 3 V 0 P
comets, importing change of times and states, 1H6 1.01. 2
when beggars die there are no comets seen; JC 2.02. 30
/... | comets prewarn, whose havoc in vast field TNK 5.01. 51

COMFECT 1 FR 0.0001 REL FR 0 V 1 P
a goodly count, count comfect, a sweet gallant ADO 4.01.316 P

COMFIT–MAKER'S 1 FR 0.0001 REL FR 0 V 1 P
heart, you swear like a comfit–maker's wife: 1H4 3.01.248 P

/COMFORT 1 FR 0.0001 REL FR 1 V 0 P
spirits, | /and /bring /all /cyprus /comfort! OTH 2.01. 82

COMFORT 202 FR 0.0228 REL FR 168 V 34 P
i have great comfort from this fellow. TMP 1.01. 28 P
wipe thou thine eyes, have comfort. 1.02. 25
be of comfort, | my father's of a better nature, 1.02.496
good sir, weigh | our sorrow with our comfort. 2.01. 9
he receives comfort like cold porridge. 2.01. 10 P
making | than we bring men to comfort them. 2.01.135
well, here's my comfort. 2.02. 45 P
but here's my comfort. 2.02. 55 P
much weaker | than you may call to comfort you; 5.01.147
to thy great comfort in this mystery of ill WIV 2.01. 71 P
meeting, give him a show of comfort in his suit, 2.01. 94 P
i thank you for that good comfort. 3.04. 53 P
that respites me a life whose very comfort | is MM 2.03. 41
now, sister, what's the comfort? 3.01. 54
and dried not one of them with his comfort; 3.01.226 P
i thank you for this comfort. 3.01.268 P
i spy comfort, i cry bail. 3.02. 41 P
here comes a man of comfort, whose advice | hath 4.01. 8
heaven give your spirits comfort! 4.02. 70
what comfort is for claudio? 4.02. 77
i am come to advise you, comfort you, and pray 4.03. 52 P
there is another comfort than this world, | that 5.01. 49
make it your comfort, | so happy is your brother 5.01.398
yet this my comfort, when your words are done, ERR 1.01. 26
comfort my sister, cheer her, call her /wife: 3.02. 26
conceit — | conceit, my comfort and my injury. 4.02. 66
for trouble being gone, comfort should remain; ADO 1.01.101 P
have comfort, lady. 4.01.118
go comfort your cousin. 4.01.334 P
can counsel and speak comfort to that grief 5.01. 21
comfort me, boy: LLL 1.02. 64 P
god comfort thy capacity! 4.02. 44 P
i could put thee in comfort: 4.03. 50
take comfort; MND 1.01.202
it good, | and tarry for the comfort of the day. 2.02. 38
would he not be a comfort to our travel? AYL 1.03.131
caters for the sparrow, | be comfort to my age! 2.03. 45
but i must comfort the weaker vessel, as doublet 2.04. 6 P
live a little, comfort a little, cheer thyself a 2.06. 5 P
i thank ye, and be blest for your good comfort! 2.07.135
the rest will comfort, for thy counsel 's sound. SHR 1.01.164
thou shalt soon feel, to thy cold comfort, for 4.01. 31 P
nay, there is some comfort in the news, some AWW 3.02. 36 P
there is some comfort in the news, some comfort. 3.02. 37 P
in my /similes of comfort and leave him to your 5.02. 25 P
true, madam, and, to comfort you with chance, TN 1.02. 8
god comfort thee! 3.04. 32 P
you stand amaz'd, | but be of comfort. 3.04.338
have an unspeakable comfort of your young prince WT 1.01. 34 P
nay, there's comfort in't, | whiles other men 1.02.196
why, that's some comfort. | what? camillo there? 1.02.208
be my friend, and comfort | the gracious queen, 1.02.458
the queen receives | much comfort in't; 2.02. 26
the crown and comfort of my life, your favor, 3.02. 94
my third comfort | (starr'd most unluckily) is 3.02. 98
comfort, good comfort! 4.04.818 P
comfort, good comfort! 4.04.818 P
for present comfort, and for future good, | to 5.01. 32
the great comfort | that i have had of thee! 5.03. 1
so much to my good comfort as it is | now 5.03. 33
has a taste as sweet | as any cordial comfort. 5.03. 77
courage and comfort! all shall yet go well. JN 3.04. 4
patience, good lady, comfort, gentle constance! 3.04. 22
as i, | i could give better comfort than you do. 3.04.100
being create for comfort, to be us'd | in 4.01.106
be of good comfort; 5.03. 9
be of good comfort, prince, for you are born 5.07. 25
kiss my parched lips | and comfort me with cold. 5.07. 41
i do not ask you much, | i beg cold comfort; 5.07. 42
this must my comfort be, | that sun that warms R2 1.03.144
what comfort, man? how is't with aged gaunt? 2.01. 72
say | how near the tidings of our comfort is. 2.01.272
my comfort is, that heaven will take our souls, 3.01. 33
nor with thy sweets comfort his ravenous sense, 3.02. 13
comfort, my liege, why looks your grace so pale? 3.02. 75
comfort, my liege, remember who you are. 3.02. 82
no matter where — of comfort no man speak: 3.02.144
what comfort have we now? 3.02.206
that bids me be of comfort any more. 3.02.208
a comfort of retirement lives in this. 1H4 4.01. 56
rascal, is that all the comfort you give me? 2H4 2.04. 40 P
to comfort you the more, i have received | a 3.01.102
which, cousin, you shall bear to comfort him, 4.03. 79
comfort, your majesty! 4.04.112
now i, to comfort him, bid him 'a should not H5 2.03. 20 P
beholding him, plucks comfort from his looks. 4.pr. 42
my comfort is, that old age, that ill layer–up 5.02.230 P
salisbury, cheer thy spirit with this comfort, 1H6 1.04. 90
a grave, | as witting i no other comfort have. 2.05. 16
god comfort him in this necessity! 4.03. 15
warwick, my son, the comfort of my age, | thy 2H6 1.01.190
gives light in darkness, comfort in despair! 2.01. 65
great is his comfort in this earthly vale, 2.01. 68
all comfort go with thee, | for none abides with 2.04. 87
comfort, my sovereign! gracious henry, comfort! 3.02. 38
comfort, my sovereign! gracious henry, comfort! 3.02. 38
what, doth my lord of suffolk comfort me? 3.02. 39
wren, | by crying comfort from a hollow breast, 3.02. 43
is all thy comfort shut in gloucester's tomb? 3.02. 78
and in thy need such comfort come to thee | as 3H6 1.04.165
comfort, my lord! and so i take my leave. 4.08. 28
therefore for god's sake entertain good comfort, R3 1.03. 4
you go | to comfort edward with our company. 2.01.140
and i for comfort have but one false glass, 2.02. 53
and hast the comfort of thy children left; 2.02. 56
comfort, dear mother, god is much displeas'd 2.02. 89
let him be crown'd, in him your comfort lives. 2.02. 98
sister, have comfort. 2.02.101
and came i not at last to comfort you? 4.04.165
and by their uncle cozen'd | of comfort, kingdom 4.04.224
but mine shall be a comfort to your age. 4.04.306
but this good comfort bring i to your highness: 4.04.520
lines of fair comfort and encouragement. 5.02. 6
all comfort that the dark night can afford | be 5.03. 80
be king, | doth comfort thee in thy sleep. 5.03.130
thy approach, i know, | my comfort comes along. H8 2.04.241
is this your comfort? 3.01.105
our ends are honest, | you'ld feel more comfort. 3.01.155
heaven comfort her! 4.02. 99
and heartily entreats you take good comfort. 4.02.119
o my good lord, that comfort comes too late, 4.02.120
keep comfort to you, and this morning see | you 5.01.144
partners and myself thus pray | all comfort, joy 5.04. 6
this oracle of comfort has so pleas'd me | that 5.04. 66
to troy with comfort go; TRO 5.10. 30
in that there's comfort. COR 2.01.226
which is a comfort | that all but we enjoy. 5.03.105
else thy person, | our comfort in the country. 5.03.111
if | the roman ladies bring not comfort home, 5.04. 38
but dawning day new comfort hath inspir'd. TIT 2.02. 10
why dost not comfort me and help me out | from 2.03.209
and rather comfort his distressed plight | than 4.04. 32
whose name was once our terror, now our comfort, 5.01. 10
such comfort as do lusty young men feel | when ROM 1.02. 26
all this is comfort, wherefore weep i then? 3.02.107
i'll find romeo | to comfort you, i wot well 3.02.139
to comfort thee though thou art banished. 3.03. 56
ascend her chamber, hence and comfort her. 3.03.147
how well my comfort is reviv'd by this! 3.03.165
comfort me, counsel me! 3.05.208
some comfort, nurse. 3.05.212
i'll call them back again to comfort me. 4.03. 17
o, play me some merry dump to comfort me. 4.05.108 P
him up, which failing, | periods his comfort. TIM 1.01. 99
o, what a precious comfort 'tis to have so many 1.02.104 P
o, let me stay, | and comfort you, my master. 4.03.534
to keep with you at meals, comfort your bed, JC 2.01.284
these tidings will well comfort cassius. 5.03. 54
from that spring whence comfort seem'd to come MAC 1.02. 27
there's comfort yet, they are assailable. 3.02. 39
be't their comfort | we are coming thither. 4.03.188
i could answer | this comfort with the like! 4.03.193
here comes newer comfort. 5.09. 19
here in the cheer and comfort of our eye, | our HAM 1.02.116
fierce, but thine | do comfort, and not burn. LR 2.04.173
i will piece out the comfort with what addition 3.06. 2 P
'twas yet some comfort, | when misery could 4.06. 62
i return to you again, | i'll bring you comfort. 5.02. 4
what comfort to this great decay may come 5.03.298

but the free comfort which from thence he hears; OTH 1.03.213
though he speak of comfort | touching the 2.01. 31
absolute | that not another comfort like to this 2.01.192
love him dearly, | comfort forswear me! 4.02.159
to thee, and make | thy spirits all of comfort. ANT 3.02. 41
best of comfort, | and ever welcome to us. 3.06. 89
nay, gentle madam, to him, comfort him. 3.11. 25
seize her, but | your comfort makes the rescue. 3.11. 48
for i spake to you for your comfort, did desire 4.02. 40
reward thee | once for thy sprightly comfort, 4.07. 15
have comfort, for i know your plight is pitied 5.02. 33
and make yourself some comfort | out of your CYM 1.01.155
their honest wills, | which seasons comfort. 1.06. 9
and often, to our comfort, shall we find | the 3.03. 19
or in my life what comfort, when i am | dead to 3.04.129
thou art all the comfort | the gods will diet me 3.04.179
i'll make't my comfort | he is a man, i'll love 3.06. 70
society is no comfort | to one not sociable. 4.02. 12
imogen, | the great part of my comfort, gone; 4.03. 5
it strikes me, past | the hope of comfort. 4.03. 9
but the comfort is, you shall be call'd to no 5.04.158 P
joyful too, | for they shall taste our comfort. 5.05.403
nor yet the other's distance comfort me. PER 1.02. 10
joy and all comfort in your sacred breast! 1.02. 34
and finding little comfort to relieve them, | i 1.02. 99
they may awake their helpers to comfort them. 1.04. 17
for comfort is too far for us to expect. 1.04. 59
for the sake of it | be manly, and take comfort. 3.01. 22
to defend you by men, then men must comfort you, 4.02. 91 P
pray have good comfort. TNK 1.01.129
and i will give you comfort | to give your dead 1.01.148
i pray you | take comfort and be strong. 3.01.100
be of good comfort, man; 4.01. 17
the gods comfort her! 4.01. 45
which doubt not will bring forth comfort. 4.03.101 P
and charge me live to comfort this unfriended, 5.03.141
some comfort | we have by so considering: 5.04. 3
whose lives (for this poor comfort) are laid 5.04. 14
two loves i have, of comfort and despair, | that PP 2. 1
take all my comfort of thy worth and truth. SON 37. 4
most worthy comfort, now my greatest grief, 48. 6
mine | thou wilt restore to be my comfort still: 134. 4
two loves i have of comfort and despair, | which 144. 1
COMFORTABLE 13 FR 0.0014 REL FR 9 V 4 P
for my sake be comfortable, hold death a while AYL 2.06. 9 P
be comfortable to my mother, your mistress, AWW 1.01. 76
a comfortable doctrine, and much may be said of TN 1.05.222 P
uncle, for god's sake speak comfortable words. R2 2.02. 76
what comfortable hour canst thou name | that R3 4.04.174
or express yourself in a more comfortable sort. COR 1.03. 2 P
o comfortable friar! ROM 5.03.148
his comfortable temper has forsook him, he's TIM 3.04. 71 P
so true, so just, and now so comfortable? 4.03.491
who i am sure is kind and comfortable. LR 1.04.306
that by thy comfortable beams i may | peruse 2.02.164
you return to us, | peaceful and comfortable! PER 1.02. 36
no comfortable star did lend his light, | no LUC 164
COMFORTED 7 FR 0.0008 REL FR 6 V 1 P
and collateral light | must i be comforted, not AWW 1.01. 89
well, thou hast comforted me marvellous much. ROM 3.05.230
be comforted. MAC 4.03.213
be comforted, good madam, the great rage, | you LR 4.07. 77
be comforted, dear madam. ANT 4.15. 2
shot | of angry eyes, not comforted to live, CYM 1.01. 90
so chid, or at least a sigher to be comforted. TNK 2.01. 44 P
COMFORTER 5 FR 0.0005 REL FR 5 V 0 P
when it doth, | it is a comforter. TMP 2.01.196
and the best comforter | to an unsettled fancy, 5.01. 58
nor let no comforter delight mine ear, | but ADO 5.01. 6
son | to be your comforter when he is gone. R3 1.03. 10
"look, the world's comforter, with weary gait, VEN 529
COMFORTETH 1 FR 0.0001 REL FR 1 V 0 P
"love comforteth like sunshine after rain, | but VEN 799
COMFORTING 4 FR 0.0004 REL FR 2 V 2 P
less appear so, in comforting your evils, | than WT 2.03. 56
to repair our nature | with comforting repose, H8 5.01. 4
if i find him comforting the king, it will stuff LR 3.05. 20 P
comforting therein, that when old robes are worn ANT 1.02.163 P
COMFORT-KILLING 1 FR 0.0001 REL FR 1 V 0 P
"o comfort-killing night, image of hell! LUC 764
COMFORTLESS 5 FR 0.0005 REL FR 5 V 0 P
kinsman to grim and comfortless despair, | and ERR 5.01. 80
black, fearful, comfortless, and horrible. JN 5.06. 20
the queen is comfortless, and we forgetful | in H8 2.03.105
that kiss is comfortless | as frozen water to a TIT 3.01.250
all dark and comfortless! LR 3.07. 85
COMFORT'S 1 FR 0.0001 REL FR 1 V 0 P
comfort's in heaven, and we are on the earth, R2 2.02. 78
COMFORTS 28 FR 0.0031 REL FR 25 V 3 P
why, | as all comforts are: MM 3.01. 55
to make her heavenly comforts of despair, | when 4.03.110
shine, comforts, from the east, | that i may MND 3.02.432
my clerk hath some good comforts too for you. MV 5.01.289
he that comforts my wife is the cherisher of my AWW 1.03. 46 P
sometimes we make us comforts of our losses! 4.03. 66 P
father | to greet him and to give him comforts. WT 4.04.557
tongues | they bring smooth comforts false, 2H4 in 40
king henry's issue, richmond, comforts thee. R3 5.03.123
our just opinions | and comforts to /your cause. H8 3.01. 61
they are (as all my other comforts) far hence 3.01. 90
but now i am past all comforts here but prayers. 4.02.123
eyes flow with joy, hearts dance with comforts, COR 5.03. 99
he comforts you | can make you greater than the TIT 1.01.268
thou sun that comforts, burn! TIM 5.01.131
and i'll beweep these comforts, worthy senators. 5.01.158
lay comforts to your bosom, and bestow | your LR 2.01.126
gone, | thy comforts can do me no good at all; 4.01. 16
but that our loves and comforts should increase OTH 2.01.194
of fashion, and i dote | in mine own comforts. 2.01.207
me expectations and comforts of sudden respect 4.02.189 P
events are welcome, | but comforts we despise; ANT 4.15. 4
give her what comforts | the quality of her 5.01. 62
his comforts thrive, his trials well are spent. CYM 5.04.104
now turn we towards your comforts. TNK 1.01.234
never more | must we behold those comforts, 2.02. 9
i see two comforts rising, two mere blessings, 2.02. 58
were not all appropriate to your comforts, | but STM II.C 137
COMIC 2 FR 0.0002 REL FR 2 V 0 P
wars | will turn unto a peaceful comic sport, 1H6 2.02. 45
with stately triumphs, mirthful comic shows, 3H6 5.07. 43
/COMING 1 FR 0.0001 REL FR 0 V 1 P
/which /since /his /coming /forth /is /thought LR 4.03. 4 P
COMING 153 FR 0.0173 REL FR 104 V 49 P
for, coming thence, | my son is lost and (in my TMP 2.01.109
my father at the road | expects my coming, there TGV 1.01. 54
my father stays my coming; 2.02. 13
adieu, my lord, sir valentine is coming. 3.01. 50
this evening coming. 4.03. 42
but, by my coming, i have made you happy. 5.04. 30
can see my master, master doctor caius, coming. WIV 1.04. 3 P
and, trust me, i was coming to you. 2.01. 35 P
yonder he is coming, this way, sir hugh. 3.01. 27 P
your husband's coming hither, woman, with all 3.03.106 P
but 'tis most certain your husband's coming, 3.03.114 P
she's coming; 3.04. 36 P
but is my husband coming? 4.02. 90 P
tarries the coming down of thy fat woman. 4.05. 20 P
he's coming; MM 2.02.125
he is coming, sir, he is coming. 4.03. 35 P
he is coming, sir, he is coming. 4.03. 35 P
who knew of your intent and coming hither? 5.01.124
but say, | i prithee, is he coming home? ERR 2.01. 55
come go along, my wife is coming yonder. 4.04. 40
our dinner done, and he not coming thither, | i 5.01.224
to-morrow then i will expect your coming, ADO 5.01.296
vouchsafe to read the purpose of my coming, LLL 2.01.109
sea-sick, i think, coming from muscovy. 5.02.393
coming too short of thanks | for my great suit 5.02.738
i have a beard coming. MND 1.02. 48 P
masters, the duke is coming from the temple, and 4.02. 15 P
the trusty thisby, coming first by night, | did 5.01.140
i fear we shall outsleep the coming morn | as 5.01.365
hath an argosy cast away, coming from tripolis. MV 3.01.100 P
for your coming in to dinner, sir, why, let it 3.05. 62 P
soul, let's in, and there expect their coming. 5.01. 49
a messenger before, | to signify their coming. 5.01.118
i confess your coming before me is nearer to his AYL 1.01. 50 P
where you are, they are coming to perform it. 1.02.116 P
yonder sure they are coming. 1.02.147 P
him take that for coming a-night to jane smile; 2.04. 48 P
toward, and these couples are coming to the ark. 5.04. 36 P
i be so bold to know the cause of your coming? SHR 2.01. 87 P
is it not news to /hear of petruchio's coming? 3.02. 34 P
he is coming. 3.02. 38 P
why, petruchio is coming in a new hat and an old 3.02. 43 P
and is the bride and bridegroom coming home? 3.02.151
and after me, i know, the rout is coming. 3.02.181
a fire, and they are coming after to warm them. 4.01. 4 P
is my master and his wife coming, grumio? 4.01. 18 P
away, away, for he is coming hither. 4.01.187
i spied | an ancient angel coming down the hill, 4.02. 61
but soft, company is coming here. 4.05. 26
feast | shall more attend upon the coming space, AWW 2.03.181
to make the coming hour o'erflow with joy | and 2.04. 46
marry, in coming on he has the cramp. 4.03.290 P
the king's coming, i know by his trumpets. 5.02. 51 P
o, stay and hear, your true-love's coming, TN 2.03. 40
malvolio's coming down this walk. 2.05. 16 P
he's coming, madam, but in very strange manner. 3.04. 8 P
shall i vent to her that thou art coming? 4.01. 17 P
i think, this coming summer, the king of sicilia WT 1.01. 5 P
liege, | he is not guilty of her coming hither. 2.03.145
your guests are coming: 4.04. 48
and ere our coming see thou shake the bags | of JN 3.03. 7
is coming towards me, and my inward soul | with R2 2.02. 11
the noble duke hath sworn his coming is | but 2.03.148
his coming hither hath no further scope | than 3.03.112
coming, | of our two cousins coming into london. 5.02. 3
money of the king's coming down the hill, 'tis 1H4 2.02. 54 P
stand close, i hear them coming. 2.02. 97 P
and since your coming hither have done enough 3.01.176
coming in to borrow a mess of vinegar, telling 2H4 2.01. 95 P
he heard of your grace's coming to town. 2.02.100 P
in peace, | what doth concern your coming. 4.01. 30
he is coming hither. 4.05. 87
coming to look on you, thinking you dead, | and 4.05.155
tell you the dolphin i am coming on | to venge H5 1.02.291
therefore in fierce tempest is he coming, | in 2.04. 99
the winter coming on, and sickness growing 3.03. 55
hark you, the king is coming, and i must speak 3.06. 86 P
the mastiffs in robustious and rough coming on, 3.07.148 P
as in good time he may, from ireland coming, 5.pr. 31
the emperor's coming in behalf of france, | to 5.pr. 38
and here i will expect thy coming. 1H6 5.03.145
me | to watch the coming of my punish'd duchess. 2H6 2.04. 7
thee hence, the king, thou know'st, is coming. 3.02.386
stood | and duly waited for my coming forth? 4.01. 62
that she was coming with a full intent | to dash 3H6 2.01.117
me | the queen is coming with a puissant host, 2.01.207
before thy coming, lewis was henry's friend. 3.03.143
my lords, we were forewarned of your coming, 4.07. 17
to white-friars, there attend my coming. R3 1.02.226
prepare there, | the duke is coming. H8 2.01. 98
i do not like their coming. 3.01. 21
shall give you | the full cause of our coming. 3.01. 29
i am not such a truant since my coming, | as not 3.01. 43
stand close, the queen is coming. 4.01. 36
from all parts they are coming, | as if we kept 5.03. 68
hark, they are coming from the field. TRO 1.02.177 P
ha? martius coming home? COR 2.01.102 P
martius coming home! 2.01.106 P
martius is coming home; 2.01.145 P
make way, they are coming. 2.02. 36 P
he's coming. 3.03. 6
some news is coming | that turns their 4.06. 59
now he's coming, | and not a hair upon a 4.06.132
lips, | coming and going with thy honey breath. TIT 2.04. 25
is not thy coming for my other hand? 5.02. 27
romeo is coming. ROM 3.03.158
your lady mother is coming to your chamber. 3.05. 39
stay not to question, for the watch is coming. 5.03.158
as he was coming from this churchyard's side. 5.03.186
told my lord of you, he is coming down to you. TIM 3.01. 1 P
no counsel, take no warning by my coming. 3.01. 27 P
him of an intent | that's coming toward him. 5.01. 21
he did receive his letters, and is coming, | and JC 3.01.279
is thy master coming? 3.01.285
coming from sardis, on our former ensign | two 5.01. 79
referr'd me to the coming on of time with 'hail, MAC 1.05. 9 P
our thane is coming. 1.05. 34
he that's coming | must be provided for; 1.05. 66
be't their comfort | we are coming thither. 4.03.189
that way are they coming. 5.02. 6
within this three mile may you see it coming; 5.05. 36
the fates | and prologue to the omen coming on, HAM 1.01.123
and hither are they coming to offer you service. 2.02.318 P
i hear him coming. withdraw, my lord. 3.01. 54
they are coming to the play. 3.02. 90
withdraw, | i hear him coming. 3.04. 7
beg | your sudden coming o'er to play with you. 4.07.105
the king and queen and all are coming down. 5.02.203 P
the king is coming. LR 1.01. 33 P
he's coming, madam, i hear him. 1.03. 11
he's coming hither, now i' th' night, i' th' 2.01. 24
i hear my father coming. 2.01. 28
or they impose, this usage, | coming from us. 2.04. 27
to oppose the bolt | against my coming in. 2.04.177
i told him you were coming; 4.02. 5
their going hence even as their coming hither, 5.02. 10
steal away so guilty-like, | seeing your coming. OTH 3.03. 40
indeed, sweet love, i was coming to your house. 3.04.171
i /hear him coming. 5.01. 22
yet, coming from him, that great med'cine hath ANT 1.05. 36
thyself art coming | to see perform'd the 5.02.330
this night forestall him of the coming day! CYM 3.05. 69
and stay your coming to present themselves. PER 2.02. 3
but stay, the knights are coming, we will 2.02. 58
you have fortunes coming upon you. 4.02.116 P
the keeper's coming. TNK 2.02.218
they are coming off. 5.03.103
he sees her coming, and begins to glow, | even VEN 337
far from the purpose of his coming thither, | he LUC 113
coming from thee, i could not put him back, 843
"the baser is he, coming from a king, | to shame 1002
against this coming end you should prepare, SON 13. 3
since, seldom coming, in the long year set, 52. 6
COMING-IN 1 FR 0.0001 REL FR 0 V 1 P
nine maids is a simple coming-in for one man. MV 2.02.163 P
COMING-ON 1 FR 0.0001 REL FR 0 V 1 P
your rosalind in a more coming-on disposition; AYL 4.01.112 P
COMINGS-IN 1 FR 0.0001 REL FR 1 V 0 P
what are thy comings-in? H5 4.01.243
COMINIUS' 1 FR 0.0001 REL FR 1 V 0 P
half all cominius' honors are to martius, COR 1.01.273
COMINIUS 18 FR 0.0020 REL FR 17 V 1 P
martius, | attend upon cominius to these wars. COR 1.01.237
follow cominius; 1.01.246
can brook to be commanded | under cominius. 1.01.263
on martius shall | of his demerits rob cominius. 1.01.272
cominius, martius your old enemy | (who is of 1.02. 12
against whom cominius the general is gone, with 1.03. 97 P
have the spirit, will haste | to help cominius. 1.05. 14
speak, good cominius: 2.02. 48
please you | to hear cominius speak? 2.02. 62
worthy cominius, speak. 2.02. 66
proceed, cominius. 2.02. 81
cominius, no. 3.01. 30
here is cominius. 3.02. 92
cominius, | droop not, adieu. 4.01. 19
take good cominius | with thee a while. 4.01. 34
if he coy'd | to hear cominius speak, i'll keep 5.01. 7
martius | return me, as cominius is return'd, 5.01. 42
lip | and hum at good cominius much unhearts me. 5.01. 49
COMMA 2 FR 0.0002 REL FR 2 V 0 P
malice | infects one comma in the course i hold, TIM 1.01. 48
wear | and stand a comma 'tween their amities, HAM 5.02. 42
/COMMAND 2 FR 0.0002 REL FR 2 V 0 P
/let /it /command /a /mirror /hither /straight, R2 4.01.265
may the passive drugs of it | freely /command, TIM 4.03.255
COMMAND 183 FR 0.0206 REL FR 142 V 41 P
if you can command these elements to silence, TMP 1.01. 21 P
i will be correspondent to command | and do my 1.02.297
neglect'st or dost unwillingly | what i command, 1.02.369
but then exactly do | all points of my command. 1.02.501
nor hath not | one spirit to command: 3.02. 94
juno does command. 4.01.131
graves at my command | have wak'd their sleepers 5.01. 48
and deal in her command without her power. 5.01.271
i will write | (please you command) a thousand TGV 2.01.114
which to requite, command me while i live. 3.01. 23
which to-morrow, by his master's command, he 4.02. 79 P
one that attends your ladyship's command. 4.03. 5
service | it is your pleasure to command me in. 4.03. 10
let us command to know that of your mouth, or of WIV 1.01.228 P
they have had my /house a week at command. 4.03. 10 P
a commandement to command the captain and all MM 1.02. 12 P
seat, that it may know | he can command, lets it 1.02.162
this other doth command a little door, | which 4.01. 32
having the hour limited, and an express command, 4.02.166 P
done, | and sent according to command, whiles i 4.03. 80
command these fretting waters from your eyes 4.03.146
with thy command | let him be brought forth, and ERR 5.01.159
i, sir, am dromio, command him away. 5.01.336
will your grace command me any service to the ADO 2.01.263 P
shall i command thy love? LLL 4.01. 80 P
by our /assistance, the king's command, and this 5.01.121 P
majesty | command me any service to her thither? 5.02.312
how many be commanded that command? MV 2.09. 45
and take upon command what help we have | that AYL 2.07.125
say, "what is it your honor will command?" SHR in.1. 54
and say, "what is't your honor will command," in.1. 115
or what you will command me will i do, | so well 2.01. 6
go, fool, and whom thou keep'st command. 2.01.257
they shall go forward, kate, at thy command. 3.02.222
why so: this gallant will command the sun. 4.03.196
luke's church is at your command at all hours. 4.04. 89 P
i think i shall command your welcome here; 5.01. 12
your mistress, | say i command her come to me. 5.02. 96
but i must attend his majesty's command, to whom AWW 1.01. 4 P
be gone, sir knave, and do as i command you. 1.03. 90 P
that man should be at woman's command, and yet 1.03. 92 P

hand | what husband in thy power i will command. 2.01.194
there was excellent command — to charge in with 3.06. 48 P
not to be blam'd in the command of the service; 3.06. 51 P
have prevented, if he had been there to command. 3.06. 54 P
i am a poor man, and at your majesty's command. 5.03.251 P
"i may command where i adore, | but silence, TN 2.05.104
"i may command where i adore." 2.05.115 P
why, she may command me: 2.05.116 P
could not sway her house, command her followers, 4.03. 17
it is in mine authority to command | the keys of WT 1.02.463
no less prevail'd than so | on your command. 2.01. 55
good mind of camillo tardied | my swift command, 3.02.163
i willingly obey your command. 4.02. 53 P
whereupon i command thee to open thy affair. 4.04.738 P
by his command | have i here touch'd sicilia, 5.01.138
"o sir," says answer, "at your best command, JN 1.01.197
at the other hill | command the rest to stand. 2.01.299
command thy son and daughter to join hands. 2.01.532
my life thou shalt command, but not my shame: R2 1.01.166
we were not born to sue, but to command, | which 1.01.196
command our officers–at–arms | be ready to 1.01.204
of england i shall command all the good lads in 1H4 2.04. 14 P
i can teach you, cousin, to command | the devil. 3.01. 55
dear men | of estimation and command in arms. 4.04. 32
and a word of exceeding good command, by heaven.
2H4 3.02. 76 P
that no man could better command his servants. 5.01. 74 P
acquit me, will you command me to use my legs? ep 19 P
keep close, i thee command. H5 2.03. 62
we may as bootless spend our vain command | upon 3.03. 24
whiles yet my soldiers are in my command, 3.03. 29
under his master's command transporting a sum of 4.01.151 P
the beggar's knee, | command the health of it? 4.01.257
virtue he had, deserving to command; 1H6 1.01. 9
and lookest to command the prince and realm. 1.01. 38
priest, dost thou command me to be shut out? 1.03. 30
peace and the king's, we charge and command you, 1.03. 76 P
dolphin, command the citizens make bonfires, 1.06. 12
and then your highness shall command a peace. 4.01.117
upon my blessing i command thee go. 4.05. 36
command the conquest, charles, it shall be thine 5.02. 19
command in anjou what your honor pleases. 5.03.147
mind | she is content to be at your command — 5.05. 19
command, i mean, of virtuous chaste intents, 5.05. 20
hast thou not worldly pleasure at command 2H6 1.02. 45
good, | the nevils are thy subjects to command. 2.02. 8
us'd to command, untaught to plead for favor. 4.01.122
down kings and princes — command silence. 4.02. 37 P
such aid as i can spare you shall command, | but 4.05. 6
upon london stone, i charge and command that, of 4.06. 2 P
away with him, and do as i command ye. 4.07.118 P
and we charge and command that their wives be as 4.07.124 P
retreat or parley when i command them kill? 4.08. 5 P
and could command no more content than i? 4.09. 2
command my eldest son, nay, all my sons, | as 5.01. 49
gust, | command an argosy to stem the waves. 3H6 2.06. 36
command, and i'll obey. 3.01. 93
what you command that rests in me to do. 3.02. 45
earth affords no joy to me | but to command, to 3.02.166
learn a while to serve | where kings command. 3.03. 6
let me entreat (for i command no more) | that 4.06. 59
/stand thou when i command. R3 1.02. 39
what we will do, we do upon command. 1.04.193
he may command me as my sovereign, | but you 3.01.108
tell her the king, that may command, entreats. 4.04.345
he sent command to the lord mayor straight | to H8 2.01.151
if i command him, follows my appointment; 2.02.133
something i can command. 4.01.116
you may command us, sir. 4.01.117
achievement is command; TRO 1.02.293
is a fool to offer to command achilles, achilles 2.03. 62 P
disguise the holy strength of their command, 2.03.127
command, i mean, /friend. 3.01. 25 P
who shall i command, sir? 3.01. 26 P
you shall be mistress, and command him wholly. 4.04.120
you shall command me, sir. 4.05.286
and four shall quickly draw out my command, COR 1.06. 84
appearance, and thy face | bears a command in't; 4.05. 61
but still subsisting | under your great command. 5.06. 73
you up | to be a warrior and command a camp. TIT 4.02.180
and i think | one business does command us all; TIM 3.04. 4
supply his life, or that which can command it. 4.02. 47
he did command me to call timely on him, | i MAC 2.03. 46
let your highness | command upon me, to the 3.01. 16
shall, my lord, | perform what you command us. 3.01.126
is thine and my poor country's to command: 4.03.132
has light by her continually, 'tis her command. 5.01. 23 P
those he commands move only in command, 5.02. 19
at a higher rate | than a command to parle. HAM 1.03.123
no, my good lord, but, as you did command, | i 2.01.105
us, | put your dread pleasures more into command 2.02. 28
lies where it falls, | repugnant to command. 2.02.471
such answer as i can make, you shall command, or 3.02.323 P
but these cannot i command to any utt'rance of 3.02.361 P
an eye like mars, to threaten and command, | a 3.04. 57
by | th' important acting of your dread command? 3.04.108
and, but that great command o'ersways the order, 5.01.228
an exact command, | larded with many several 5.02. 19
twice so many | have a command to tend you? LR 2.04.263
in your own behalf) | a mistress's command. 4.02. 21
lances in our eyes | which do command them. 5.03. 51
every house i'll call | (i may command at most). OTH 1.01.181
you shall more command with years | than with 1.02. 60
for the command, i'll lay't upon you. 2.01.265 P
let him command, | and to obey shall be in me 3.03.467
lie by an emperor's side and command him tasks. 4.01.185 P
for, as i think, they do command him home, 4.01.236
your power and your command is taken off, | and 5.02.331
is gone, | through whom i might command it? ANT 3.03. 6
and command what cost | your heart /has mind to. 3.04. 37
for indeed i have lost command, | therefore i 3.11. 23
might from the bidding of the gods | command me. 3.11. 61
a child as soon | as i' th' command of caesar. 3.13. 25
man, and worthiest | to have command obey'd. 3.13. 88
was your fellow too, | and suffer'd my command. 4.02. 23
of | disgrace and horror, that, on my command, 4.14. 66
'tis the last service that i shall command you. 4.14.132
madam, as thereto sworn by your command | (which 5.02.198
if after this command thou fraught the court CYM 1.01.126
you have done | not after our command. 1.01.152
on his command. 1.01.170
save when command to your dismission tends, 2.03. 52
and vows which i | have made to thy command? 3.02. 13
by her own command | shall give thee opportunity 3.02. 18
since i receiv'd command to do this business | i 3.04. 99
change | command into obedience; 3.04.155
command our present numbers | be muster'd; 4.02.343
and thou that hast | upon the winds command, PER 3.01. 3
you in your coffer, which are | at your command. 3.04. 3
get this done as i command you. 4.02. 62 P
since they do better thee in their command. 4.06.162
to perform thy just command, | i here confess 5.03. 1
there | that does command my rapier from my hip,
TNK 1.02. 56
but offends you, | command him die, he shall. 2.05. 41
and why her eyes command me | stay here to love 3.06.169
of beauty, that command | and threaten love, and 4.02. 39
yours to command i' th' way of honesty. 5.02. 71
have among yourselves, | command still audience. STM II.C 47
with the number, | command them to a stillness. II.C 52
lent | of dread, of justice, power and command, II.C 99
"hast thou command? LUC 624
from a pure heart command thy rebel will; 625
take all these similes to your own command, LC 227

COMMANDE 1 FR 0.0001 REL FR 0 V 1 P
il me commande a vous dire que vous faites vous H5 4.04. 34 P

COMMANDED 41 FR 0.0046 REL FR 37 V 4 P
that to close prison he commanded her, | with TGV 3.01.237
her father hath commanded her to slip | away WIV 4.06. 23
it was commanded so. MM 5.01.458
how many be commanded that command? MV 2.09. 45
gift | to rain a shower of commanded tears, | an SHR in.1. 125
i commanded the sleeves should be cut out, and 4.03.145 P
i am commanded here, and kept a coil with | "too AWW 2.01. 27
i have, sir, as i was commanded from you, 2.05. 54
to–night, commanded | none should come at him. WT 2.03. 31
such, | so and no other, as yourself commanded; 3.02. 66
we were all commanded out of the chamber; 5.02. 6 P
only convey me where thou art commanded. 2H6 2.04. 93
we have dispatch'd the duke, as he commanded. 3.02. 2
blows, | commanded always by the greater gust, 3H6 3.01. 88
go where you will, the king shall be commanded; 3.01. 92
in our king's behalf | i am commanded, with your 3.03. 60
i am in this commanded to deliver | the noble R3 1.04. 91
and he that hath commanded is our king. 1.04.194
hath in the table of his law commanded | that 1.04.196
they have not been commanded, mighty king. 4.04.486
but to be commanded | for ever by your grace, H8 2.02.118
from rome is read, | let silence be commanded. 2.04. 2
who had | commanded nature, that my lady's womb, 2.04.189
him, 'hath commanded | to–morrow morning to the 5.01. 50
deliver to her | what you commanded me, but by 5.01. 63
my lord the archbishop, | as you commanded me. 5.01. 81
is a fool to be commanded /of /agamemnon, TRO 2.03. 63 P
his insolence can brook to be commanded | under COR 1.01.262
and therefore do we what we are commanded. TIT 5.02.163
he will not be commanded. MAC 4.01. 75
service freely at your feet, | to be commanded. HAM 2.02. 32
commanded me to follow, and attend | the leisure LR 2.04. 36
i am commanded home. OTH 4.01.258
and hath commanded me to go to bed, | and bid me 4.03. 13
and commanded | by such poor passion as the maid
ANT 4.15. 73
commanded of me these most poisonous compounds,
CYM 1.05. 8
i am ignorant in what i am commanded. 3.02. 23
for 'tis commanded | i should do so. 3.04.125
is the second thing that i have commanded thee. 3.05.152 P
dispers'd as you commanded. TNK 3.05. 32
defect, | commanded by the motion of thine eyes?
SON 149.12

COMMANDEMENT 11 FR 0.0012 REL FR 6 V 5 P
'twas a commandement to command the captain and
MM 1.02. 12 P
my heels are at your commandement, i will run. MV 2.02. 32 P
be valued 'gainst your wive's commandement. 4.01.451
have i commandement on the pulse of life? JN 4.02. 92
and had the best of them all at commandement. 2H4 3.02. 24 P
the laws of england are at my commandement. 5.03.137 P
from him i have express commandement | that thou
1H6 1.03. 20
and thy commandement all alone shall live HAM 1.05.102
answer, i will do your mother's commandement; 3.02.316 P
he never gave commandement for their death. 5.02.374
women he be bent, | they have at commandement.
PP 20.44

COMMANDEMENTS 2 FR 0.0002 REL FR 1 V 1 P
that went to sea with the ten commandements, but
MM 1.02. 8 P
i could set my ten commandements in your face. 2H6 1.03.142

COMMANDER 13 FR 0.0014 REL FR 9 V 4 P
ay, my commander. TMP 4.01.167
thee, | love thee as our commander and our king. TGV 4.01. 65
the world i liv'd, i was the world's commander; LLL 5.02.562
world i liv'd, i was the world's commander" — 5.02.568
that he has taken their great'st commander, and AWW 3.05. 6 P
approach, | commander of this hot malicious day. JN 2.01.314
a good old commander and a most kind gentleman.
H5 4.01. 95 P
thou great commander, nerves and bone of greece,
TRO 1.03. 55
thy commander, achilles. 2.03. 44 P
king and commander of our commonweal, | the wide
TIT 1.01.247
lord of my life, commander of my thoughts, 4.04. 28
to deceive so good a commander with so slight, OTH 2.03.278 P
be wreak'd on him, invisible commander; VEN 1004

COMMANDERS' 1 FR 0.0001 REL FR 0 V 1 P
are perfit in the great commanders' names, and H5 3.06. 70 P

COMMANDERS 6 FR 0.0006 REL FR 5 V 1 P
scatter'd, and the commanders very poor rogues, AWW 4.03.132 P
feeds in the bosom of such great commanders, 1H6 4.03. 48
royal commanders, be in readiness, | for with a 3H6 2.02. 67
bid our commanders lead their charges off | a JC 4.02. 48
bid the commanders | prepare to lodge their 4.03.139
in great commanders, grace and majesty | you LUC 1387

COMMANDING 10 FR 0.0011 REL FR 9 V 1 P
dispose, | subjected tribute to commanding love, JN 1.01.264
he speaks with such a proud commanding spirit. 1H6 4.07. 88
the great commanding warwick | /is thither gone 3H6 3.01. 29
where every horse bears his commanding rein R3 2.02.128
for she commanding all, obey'd of none. 4.04.104
the court of rome commanding, you, my lord H8 2.02.104
obeying in commanding, and thy parts | sovereign 2.04.140
but commanding peace | even with the same COR 4.07. 43
so many like brothers commanding one another's TIM 1.02.105 P
free, | and reign'd commanding in his monarchy. LC 196

COMMAND'MENT 1 FR 0.0001 REL FR 1 V 0 P
i on the countenance | of stern command'ment. AYL 2.07.109

COMMANDMENT *(also commandement, etc., command'ment)*

COMMANDMENT 4 FR 0.0004 REL FR 4 V 0 P
to the contrary i have express commandment. WT 2.02. 8
and posts, like the commandment of a king, TRO 1.03. 93
him | more after our commandment than as guided
COR 2.03.230
to tell him his commandment is fulfill'd, | that HAM 5.02.370

COMMANDS 32 FR 0.0036 REL FR 29 V 3 P
to act her earthy and abhorr'd commands, TMP 1.02.273
heart, | i shall obey you in all fair commands. MV 3.04. 36
i have left you commands. AYL 5.02.121 P
what more commands he? AWW 2.04. 51
to his hands, and commands shall be executed. TN 3.04. 27 P
came from the king, commands the contrary. R2 5.05.101
priest, this place commands my patience, | or 1H6 3.01. 8
compassion on the king commands me stoop, | or i 3.01.119
stern falconbridge commands the narrow seas, 3H6 1.01.239
why then i will do what your grace commands. 3.02. 49
but why commands the king | that his chief 4.03. 12
who commands you | to render up the great seal H8 3.02.228
whose height commands as subject all the vale, TRO 1.02. 3
agamemnon commands achilles, achilles is my lord 2.03. 53 P
shall be done | to him that victory commands? 4.05. 66
ajax commands the guard to tend on you. 5.01. 72
man i am, necessity | commands me name myself. COR 4.05. 57
he commands us to provide, and give great gifts, TIM 1.02.192
those he commands move only in command, MAC 5.02. 19
who commands them, sir? HAM 4.04. 13
would with his daughter speak, commands, tends LR 2.04.102
commands the mind | to suffer with the body. 2.04.108
should many people under two commands | hold 2.04.241
t' obey in all your daughters' hard commands. 3.04.149
him, and the man commands | like a full soldier. OTH 2.01. 35
to caesar, and commands | the empire of the sea. ANT 1.02.184
the strong necessity of time commands | our 1.03. 42
notes | of what commands i should be subject to, CYM 1.01.172
levy, he commands | his absolute commission. 3.07. 9
every good servant does not all commands; 5.01. 6
commands men service, | and what they win in't, TNK 1.02. 69
for my sick heart commands mine eyes to watch. VEN 584

COMMAND'ST 2 FR 0.0002 REL FR 2 V 0 P
thou, when thou command'st the beggar's knee, H5 4.01.256
men well inclin'd to hear what thou command'st; 3H6 4.08. 16

COMME 1 FR 0.0001 REL FR 0 V 1 P
il est trop difficile, madame, comme je pense. H5 3.04. 27 P

COMMENC'D 2 FR 0.0002 REL FR 2 V 0 P
broils | to be commenc'd in stronds afar remote. 1H4 1.01. 4
his father's acts commenc'd in burning troy! 2H6 3.02.118

COMMENCE 7 FR 0.0008 REL FR 7 V 0 P
since many a wooer doth commence his suit | to ADO 2.03. 50
most shallowly did you these arms commence, 2H4 4.02.118
and like a hungry lion did commence | rough 1H6 4.07. 7
thy nature did commence in sufferance, time TIM 4.03.268
nor never did my actions yet commence | a deed PER 2.05. 53
here the anthem doth commence: PHT 21
and 'gainst myself a lawful plea commence. SON 35.11

COMMENCED 1 FR 0.0001 REL FR 1 V 0 P
the acts commenced on this ball of earth. 2H4 in 5

COMMENCEMENT 2 FR 0.0002 REL FR 1 V 1 P
the origin and commencement of his grief HAM 3.01.177
it was a violent commencement in her, and thou OTH 1.03.344 P

COMMENCES 1 FR 0.0001 REL FR 0 V 1 P
till sack commences it and sets it in act and 2H4 4.03.116 P

COMMENCING 1 FR 0.0001 REL FR 1 V 0 P
me earnest of success, | commencing in a truth? MAC 1.03.133

COMMEND 101 FR 0.0114 REL FR 73 V 28 P
commend thy grievance to my holy prayers, | for TGV 1.01. 17
and so, sir, i'll commend you to my master. 1.01.146 P
and to commend their service to his will. 1.03. 42
flatter and praise, commend, extol their graces; 3.01.102
when to her beauty i commend my vows, | she bids 4.02. 9
what is she, | that all our swains commend her? 4.02. 40
if thou seest her before me, commend me. WIV 1.04.157 P
woman, commend me to her, i will not fail her. 2.02. 92 P
fare thee well, commend me to them both. 2.02.131 P
had instance and argument to commend themselves. 2.02.247 P
commend me to my brother. MM 1.04. 88
commend me to the prison, pompey. 3.02. 69 P
sir, i commend you to your own content. ERR 1.02. 32
repair to leonato's, commend me to him, and tell ADO 1.01.276 P
i did commend the black oppressing humor to the
LLL 1.01.232 P
lady, i will commend you to /mine /own heart. 2.01.179 P
and to her white hand see thou do commend | this 3.01.168
is that tongue that well can thee commend, | all 4.02.112
i pray you commend me to mistress squash, your MND 3.01.186 P
this letter from bellario doth commend | a young MV 4.01.143
the greatness whereof i cannot enough commend, 4.01.159 P
commend me to your honorable wife, | tell her 4.01.273
your daughter and her cousin much commend | the
AYL 2.02. 12
orlando doth commend him to you both, | and to 4.03. 91
but i pray you commend my counterfeiting to him. 4.03.182 P
a word, | then i'll commend her volubility, SHR 2.01.175
away, i say, commend me to thy master. 4.03.168
commend me to my kinsmen and my son. AWW 2.02. 65
there, if they were more than they can commend. 4.03. 81 P
me, | commend the paper to his gracious hand, 5.01. 31
she did commend my yellow stockings of late, she
TN 2.05.166 P
commend my best obedience to the queen. WT 2.02. 34
that thou commend it strangely to some place 2.03.182
commend them and condemn them to her service, 4.04.377
commend these waters to those baby eyes | that JN 5.02. 56
commend me to one hubert with your king; 5.04. 40

commend me to thy brother, edmund york. R2 1.02. 62
therefore commend me; 1.02. 71
his glittering arms he will commend to rust, 3.03.116
commend me to my cousin westmerland. 2H4 1.02.226 P
"i commend me to thee, i commend thee, and i 2.02.126 P
"i commend me to thee, i commend thee, and i 2.02.126 P
do it, sir, you can do it, i commend you well. 3.02.147 P
both, | commend me to the princes in our camp; H5 4.01. 25
my lord, | commend my service to my sovereign." 4.06. 23
york, i commend this kind submission; 2H6 5.01. 54
and said, "commend me to my valiant brother." 3H6 5.02. 42
commend me to lord william. R3 3.01.181
commend me to thy lord. 4.05. 6
to thee i do commend my watchful soul | ere i 5.03.115
commend me to his grace; H8 2.01. 86
and durst commend a secret to your ear | much 5.01. 17
commend me to your niece. TRO 3.01.146 P
we'll not commend what we intend to sell. 4.01. 79
she's well, but bade me not commend her to you. 4.05.180
fellow, commend my service to her beauty; 5.05. 3
in place, we did commend | to your remembrances; COR 2.03.247
commend me to my wife. 3.02.135
let me commend thee first to those that shall 4.05.144
nurse, commend me to thy lady and mistress. ROM 2.04.171 P
farewell, commend me to thy mistress. 2.04.193
commend me to thy lady. 2.04.213 P
commend me to thy lady, | and bid her hasten all 3.03.155
madam, good night, commend me to your daughter. 3.04. 9
commend me to him. TIM 1.01.105
when | "commend me to your master" and the cap 2.01. 18
commend me to their loves; 2.02.190 P
well, commend me to thy honorable virtuous lord, 3.02. 28 P
commend me bountifully to his good lordship, and 3.02. 52 P
commend me to my loving countrymen — 5.01.194
commend me to them, | and tell them that, to 5.01.197
and buy men's voices to commend our deeds. JC 2.01.146
run, lucius, and commend me to my lord, | say i 2.04. 44
go and commend me to my brother cassius; 4.03.306
and so i do commend you to their backs. MAC 3.01. 38
i commend your pains, | and every one shall 4.01. 39
farewell, and let your haste commend your duty. HAM 1.02. 39
with all my love i do commend me to you, | and 1.05.183
i commend my duty to your lordship. 5.02.182 P
/'a does well to commend it himself, there are 5.02.183 P
doth this instant | so much commend itself, you LR 2.01.114
i did commend your highness' letters to them, 2.04. 28
of my note | commend a dear thing to you. 3.01. 19
commend me to my kind lord. OTH 5.02.125
to this great fairy i'll commend thy acts, ANT 4.08. 12
man, | commend unto his lips thy /favoring hand. 4.08. 23
whom i commend to you as a noble friend of mine. CYM 1.04. 31 P
commend me to the court where your lady is, with 1.04.128 P
to your protection i commend me, gods, | from 2.02. 8
show | can any way speak in his just commend; PER 2.02. 49
well, i do commend her choice, | and will no 2.05. 21
it is your grace's pleasure to commend, | not my 2.05. 29
the unborn event | i do commend to your content; 4.ch. 46
i commend thee. TNK 3.06.103
in hallowed clouds commend their swelling 5.01. 4
the goddess venus | commend we our proceeding, 5.01. 75
commend me to her, and, to piece her portion, 5.04. 31
commend us to her. 5.04. 35
so i commend me from our house in grief, | my LUC 1308
is that tongue that well can thee commend, | all PP 5. 8
utt'ring bare truth, even so as foes commend. SON 69. 4

COMMENDABLE 9 FR 0.0010 REL FR 7 V 2 P
sure, sure, such carping is not commendable. ADO 3.01. 71
as beatrice is, cannot be commendable. 3.01. 73
for silence is only commendable | in a neat's MV 1.01.111
and discourse grow commendable in none only but 3.05. 45 P
quaint, more pleasing, nor more commendable. SHR 4.03.102
are surely, and ever were, very commendable. 2H4 3.02. 71 P
and, commendable prov'd, let's die in pride. 1H6 4.06. 57
time, | and power, unto itself most commendable, COR 4.07. 51
'tis sweet and commendable in your nature, HAM 1.02. 87

COMMENDATION 9 FR 0.0010 REL FR 3 V 6 P
to me | with commendation from great potentates, TGV 2.04. 79
only this commendation i can afford her, that ADO 1.01.173 P
and the commendation is not in his wit but in 2.01.139 P
trial shall better publish his commendation." MV 4.01.165 P
albeit you have deserv'd | high commendation, AYL 1.02.263
not much commendation to them. AWW 2.02. 67 P
prevail in man's commendation with woman than TN 3.02. 38 P
parts besides, | beguiling them of commendation. 1H4 3.01.187
i have your commendation for my more free CYM 1.04.154 P

COMMENDATIONS 14 FR 0.0015 REL FR 8 V 6 P
or two | of commendations sent from valentine, TGV 1.03. 53
page hath her hearty commendations to you too; WIV 2.02. 96 P
pray you, do my commendations — i would be glad LLL 2.01.181 P
qualities, there commendations go with pity: AWW 1.01. 42 P
your commendations, madam, get from her tears. 1.01. 46 P
him letters of commendations to the king. 4.03. 79 P
no princely commendations to my king? 1H6 5.03.176
such commendations as becomes a maid, | a virgin 5.03.177
by me | sends you his princely commendations, H8 4.02.118
you were ever good at sudden commendations, 5.02.157
a mere saciety of commendations; TIM 1.01.166
so valiant, | and in his commendations i am fed; MAC 1.04. 55
testiness, shall turn all into my commendations. CYM 4.01. 22 P
to express | my commendations great, whose PER 2.02. 9

COMMENDED 11 FR 0.0012 REL FR 6 V 5 P
friends are well and have them much commended. TGV 2.04.123
priest o' th' town commended him for a true man. WIV 2.01.145 P
remember who commended thy yellow stockings, and TN 2.05.153 P
"remember who commended thy yellow stockings" — 3.04. 47 P
hazard of | all incertainties himself commended, WT 3.02.169
in which i have commended to his goodness | the H8 4.02.131
golden tongue had commended troilus for a copper TRO 1.02.105 P
i charm you, by my once commended beauty, | by JC 2.01.271
his majesty commended him to you by young osric, HAM 5.02.195 P
desire it, | commended to our master, not to us; PER 1.03. 37
o, one by nature's outwards so commended | that LC 80

COMMENDING 1 FR 0.0001 REL FR 1 V 0 P
under the color of commending him, | i have TGV 4.02. 3

COMMENDS 21 FR 0.0023 REL FR 17 V 4 P
he that commends me to mine own content, ERR 1.02. 33
commends me to the thing i cannot get: 1.02. 34
signior arme — arme — commends you. LLL 1.01.187 P
to wit (besides commends and courteous breath), MV 2.09. 90
signior antonio | commends him to you. 3.02.232
here 'tis — commends it to your blessing. WT 2.03. 67
liege, old gaunt commends him to your majesty. R2 2.01.147
tell her i send to her my kind commends; 3.01. 38
speak to his gentle hearing kind commends. 3.03.126
why, my lord of york commends the plot and the 1H4 2.03. 21 P
captain, sir, commends him to you, my captain, 2H4 3.02. 60 P
the duke of york commends him to your majesty. H5 4.06. 3
first, he commends him to your noble self. R3 3.02. 8
commends his good opinion of you to you, and H8 2.03. 61
but what the repining enemy commends, | that TRO 1.03.243
commends himself most affectionately to you — 3.01. 66 P
not, but commends itself | to others' eyes; 3.03.104
commends th' ingredience of our poison'd chalice MAC 1.07. 11
since every worth in show commends itself. PER 2.03. 6
delay | commends us to a famishing hope. TNK 1.01.167
eye, | his eye commends the leading to his hand; LUC 436

COMMENT* 15 FR 0.0017 REL FR 9 V 6 P
but is a physician to comment on your malady. TGV 2.01. 41 P
the day, | a vulgar comment will be made of it; ERR 3.01.100
forgive the comment that my passion made | upon JN 4.02.263
comment appelez–vous la main en anglois? H5 3.04. 5 P
comment appelez–vous les ongles? 3.04. 14 P
comment appelez–vous le col? 3.04. 32 P
comment appelez–vous le pied et la robe? 3.04. 50 P
ecoutez: comment etes–vous appele? 4.04. 25 P
and comment then upon his sudden death. 2H6 3.02.133
that every nice offense should bear his comment. JC 4.03. 8
even with the very comment of thy soul | observe HAM 3.02. 79
i comment not — the hot horse, hot as fire, TNK 5.04. 65
so to so, | for love can comment upon every woe. VEN 714
whereon the stars in secret influence comment; SON 15. 4
fault, | and i will comment upon that offense; 89. 2

COMMENTARIES 1 FR 0.0001 REL FR 1 V 0 P
kent, in the commentaries caesar writ, | is 2H6 4.07. 60

COMMENTING 2 FR 0.0002 REL FR 2 V 0 P
weeping and commenting | upon the sobbing deer. AYL 2.01. 65
i have learn'd that fearful commenting | is R3 4.03. 51

COMMENTS 3 FR 0.0003 REL FR 3 V 0 P
doth by the idle comments that it makes JN 5.07. 4
while comments of your praise, richly compil'd, SON 85. 2
days | (making lascivious comments on thy sport) 95. 6

COMMERCE 4 FR 0.0004 REL FR 2 V 2 P
he is now in some commerce with my lady, and TN 3.04.174 P
peaceful commerce from dividable shores, | the TRO 1.03.105
all the commerce that you have had with troy 3.03.205
my lord, have better commerce than with honesty? HAM 3.01.108 P

COMMISERATION 3 FR 0.0003 REL FR 2 V 1 P
have commiseration on thy heroical vassal! LLL 4.01. 64 P
and pluck commiseration of /his /state | from MV 4.01. 30
me most, | and force you to commiseration. TIT 5.03. 93

/COMMISSION 1 FR 0.0001 REL FR 1 V 0 P
/you /are /o' /th' /commission, | /sit /you /too LR 3.06. 38

COMMISSION 48 FR 0.0054 REL FR 39 V 9 P
there is our commission, | from which we would MM 1.01. 13
take thy commission. 1.01. 47
be glad to give out a commission for more heads. 2.01.240 P
i might ask you for your commission, but i do AYL 4.01.138 P
than the commission of your birth and virtue AWW 2.03.261 P
but this is from my commission; TN 1.05.189 P
have you any commission from your lord to 1.05.231 P
i'll give him my commission | to let him there a WT 1.02. 40
and thou dost | (and that beyond commission), 1.02.144
from whom hast thou this great commission, JN 2.01.110
use our commission in his utmost force. 3.03. 11
it is my cousin silence, in commission with me. 2H4 3.02. 88 P
hath the prince john a full commission, | in 4.01.160
with letters of commission from the king. 1H6 5.04. 95
not her penance exceed the king's commission. 2H6 2.04. 75
please your grace, here my commission stays; 2.04. 76
let him see our commission, and talk no more. R3 1.04. 90 P
have you a president | of this commission? H8 1.02. 92
that has denied | the force of this commission. 1.02.101
lord cardinal's, by commission and main power, 2.02. 6 P
to your highness' hand | i tender my commission; 2.02.103
whilst our commission from rome is read, | let 2.04. 1
warranted | by a commission from the consistory, 2.04. 92
where's your commission, lords? 3.02.233
you sent a large commission | to gregory de 3.02.320
did my commission | bid ye so far forget 5.02.176
seals a commission to a blank of danger, | and TRO 3.03.231
take your commission, hie you to your bands, COR 1.02. 26
take | th' one half of my commission, and set 4.05.138
you had not | join'd in commission with him; 4.07. 14
that | which the commission of thy years and art ROM 4.01. 64
/are not | those in commission yet return'd? MAC 1.04. 2
and his commission to employ those soldiers, HAM 2.02. 74
i your commission will forthwith dispatch, | and 3.03. 3
manners, to /unseal | their grand commission; 5.02. 18
here's the commission, read it at more leisure. 5.02. 26
down, | devis'd a new commission, wrote it fair. 5.02. 32
bore the commission of my place and person, LR 5.03. 64
he hath commission from thy wife and me | to 5.03.253
and he shall our commission bring to you; OTH 1.03.281
and is in full commission here for cyprus. 2.01. 29
there is especial commission come from venice to 4.02.220 P
caius lucius | will do 's commission throughly. CYM 2.04. 12
levy, he commands | his absolute commission. 3.07. 10
the words of your commission | will tie you to 3.07. 14
his seal'd commission, left in trust with me, PER 1.03. 12
my commission | is not to reason of the deed, 4.01. 82
chiefly in love, whose leave exceeds commission: VEN 568

COMMISSIONERS 1 FR 0.0001 REL FR 1 V 0 P
who are the late commissioners? H5 2.02. 61

COMMISSION'S 1 FR 0.0001 REL FR 1 V 0 P
your commission's ready; ANT 2.03. 42

COMMISSIONS 3 FR 0.0003 REL FR 3 V 0 P
execution do i leave you | of your commissions. MM 1.01. 60
there have been commissions | sent down among H8 1.02. 20
the subject's grief | comes through commissions, 1.02. 57

COMMIT 42 FR 0.0047 REL FR 35 V 7 P
i do as truly suffer | as e'er i did commit. TGV 5.04. 77
me for such an embassage, and so i commit you — ADO 1.01.280 P
to leave the city and commit yourself | into the MND 2.01.215
see | the pretty follies that themselves commit, MV 2.06. 37
i commit into your hands | the husbandry and 3.04. 24
for i know you lack not folly to commit them, AWW 1.03. 11 P
commit it, count. 2.01. 34
what else may hap, to time i will commit, | only TN 1.02. 60
which is for me less easy to commit | than you WT 1.02. 58
commit me for committing honor — trust it, | he 2.03. 49
together with the dam | commit them to the fire! 2.03. 96
and will again commit them to their bonds, JN 3.04. 74
i do commit his youth | to your direction. 4.02. 67
and commit | the oldest sins the newest kind of 2H4 4.05.125
bold way to my authority, | and did commit you. 5.02. 83
you did commit me; 5.02.112
for which i do commit into your hand | th' 5.02.113
be, and here i commit my body to your mercies. ep 13 P
commit them to the fortune of the sea. 1H6 5.01. 50
fact | did never traitor in the land commit. 2H6 1.03.174
and here commit you to my lord cardinal | to 3.01.137
and, somerset, we will commit thee thither, 4.09. 39
he should for that commit your godfathers. R3 1.01. 48
hath mov'd his highness to commit me now. 1.01. 61
in charging you with matters, to commit you, H8 5.01.146
uncle, what folly i commit, i dedicate to you. TRO 3.02.102 P
dames | commit the war of white and damask in COR 2.01.216
commit my cause in balance to be weigh'd. TIT 1.01. 55
love and favor of my country | commit myself, my 1.01. 59
bid him farewell, commit him to the grave, | do 5.03.170
he has been known to commit outrages | and TIM 3.05. 71
it is not for your health thus to commit | your JC 2.01.235
trice of time | commit a thing so monstrous, to LR 1.01.217
to your professed bosoms i commit him, | but yet 1.01.272
swear not, commit not with man's sworn spouse, 3.04. 81 P
loud, we do commit | murther in healing wounds. ANT 2.02. 21
but it is fit i should commit offense to my CYM 2.01. 28 P
the country base than to commit such slaughter, 5.03. 20
to do that fearfully which you commit willingly, PER 4.02.117 P
we commit no crime | to use one language in each 4.04. 5
and commit it | to the like innocent cradle, TNK 1.03. 69
cannot contain | commit to these waste /blanks, SON 77.10

COMMITS 6 FR 0.0006 REL FR 5 V 1 P
spirit | commits itself to yours to be directed, MV 3.02.164
commits his body | to painful labor, both by sea SHR 5.02.148
death, which commits some loving act upon her, ANT 1.02.143 P
still | under what color he commits this ill. LUC 476
that on himself such murd'rous shame commits. SON 9.14
those pretty wrongs that liberty commits | when 41. 1

COMMIT'ST 2 FR 0.0002 REL FR 2 V 0 P
or else commit'st thy knaveries willfully. MND 3.02.346
commit'st thy anointed body to the cure | of R2 2.01. 98

/COMMITTED 1 FR 0.0001 REL FR 1 V 0 P
/committed /by /your /person /and /your R2 4.01.224

COMMITTED 38 FR 0.0043 REL FR 29 V 9 P
forgive them what they have committed here | and TGV 5.04.154
john falstaff have committed disparagements unto WIV 1.01. 31 P
th' offense is holy that she hath committed, 5.05.225
bear me to prison, where i am committed. MM 1.02.117
there's many have committed it. 2.02. 89
most offenseful act | was mutually committed? 2.03. 27
that here and there his fury had committed. ERR 5.01.147
flat burglary as ever was committed. ADO 4.02. 50 P
marry, sir, they have committed false report; 5.01.215 P
sixt and lastly, why they are committed; 5.01.222 P
all the faults i have committed to your worship, WT 5.02.150 P
intended, or committed, was this fault? R2 5.03. 33
broke oath on oath, committed wrong on wrong, 1H4 4.03.101
comes the nobleman that committed the prince for 2H4 1.02. 55 P
see willful adultery and murther committed. H5 2.01. 38 P
exeter, | enlarge the man committed yesterday, 2.02. 40
very excellent services committed at the bridge. 3.06. 4 P
is new committed to the bishop of york, | fell 3H6 4.04. 11
have aught committed that is hardly borne | /by R3 2.01. 58
who hath committed them? 2.04. 44
the nobles were committed | is all unknown to me 2.04. 47
myself | for hateful deeds committed by myself. 5.03.190
quoth he, "i for this had been committed — | as H8 1.02.193
that i committed | the daring'st counsel which i 2.04.215
the willing'st sin i ever yet committed | may be 3.01. 49
you, | from hence you be committed to the tower, 5.02. 89
even in their throats that hath committed them. TIT 3.01.274
who committed treason enough for god's sake, yet MAC 2.03. 9 P
alas, what ignorant sin have i committed? OTH 4.02. 70
what committed? 4.02. 72
committed? 4.02. 73
what committed? 4.02. 76
what committed? 4.02. 80
the act of shame | a thousand times committed. 5.02.212
what sins have i committed, chaste diana, | that TNK 4.02. 58
and the dire thought of his committed evil LUC 972
let sin, alone committed, light alone | upon his 1480
what wretched errors hath my heart committed, SON 119. 5

COMMITTING 4 FR 0.0004 REL FR 3 V 1 P
committing me unto my brother's love, | who led AYL 4.03.144
commit me for committing honor — trust it, | he WT 2.03. 49
treason, in committing adultery with polixenes, 3.02. 14 P
in committing freely | your scruple to the voice H8 2.02. 86

COMMIX 1 FR 0.0001 REL FR 1 V 0 P
from so divine a temple to commix | with winds CYM 4.02. 55

COMMIX'D 1 FR 0.0001 REL FR 1 V 0 P
the mind and sight distractedly commix'd. LC 28

COMMIXTION 1 FR 0.0001 REL FR 1 V 0 P
were thy commixtion greek and troyan so | that TRO 4.05.124

COMMIXTURE 1 FR 0.0001 REL FR 1 V 0 P
dismask'd, their damask sweet commixture shown, LLL 5.02.296

COMMIXTURES 1 FR 0.0001 REL FR 1 V 0 P
and, now i fall, thy tough commixtures melts, 3H6 2.06. 6
COMMODIOUS 1 FR 0.0001 REL FR 0 V 1 P
for an almond than he for a commodious drab. TRO 5.02.194 P
COMMODITIES 3 FR 0.0003 REL FR 2 V 1 P
some offer me commodities to buy. ERR 4.03. 6
and take up commodities upon our bills? 2H6 4.07.127 P
and our mere defects | prove our commodities. LR 4.01. 21
COMMODITY 20 FR 0.0022 REL FR 10 V 10 P
he's in for a commodity of brown paper and old MM 4.03. 5 P
we are like to prove a goodly commodity, being ADO 3.03.177 P
a commodity in question, i warrant you. 3.03.179 P
neither have i money nor commodity | to raise a MV 1.01.178
for the commodity that strangers have | with us 3.03. 27
'twas a commodity lay fretting by you; SHR 2.01.328
'tis a commodity will lose the gloss with lying: AWW 1.01.153 P
now jove, in his next commodity of hair, send TN 3.01. 44 P
to me can life be no commodity; WT 3.02. 93
that smooth–fac'd gentleman, tickling commodity, JN 2.01.573
commodity, the bias of the world — | the world, 2.01.574
bias, | this sway of motion, this commodity, 2.01.578
intent — | and this same bias, this commodity, 2.01.581
and why rail i on this commodity? 2.01.587
since kings break faith upon commodity, | gain, 2.01.597
and i knew where a commodity of good names were 1H4 1.02. 83 P
on the banes, such a commodity of warm slaves, 4.02. 17 P
i will turn diseases to commodity. 2H4 1.02.248 P
our credit comes not in like the commodity, nor PER 4.02. 30 P
nor the commodity wages not with the danger; 4.02. 31 P
/COMMON 6 FR 0.0006 REL FR 4 V 2 P
/that /in /common /view | /he /may /surrender; R2 4.01.155
/so, /thou /common /dog, /didst /thou /disgorge 2H4 1.03. 97
/the /common /people /swarm /like /summer /flies 3H6 2.06. 8
/and /so /berattle /the /common /stages — /so HAM 2.02.342 P
/should /grow /themselves /to /common /players 2.02.349 P
/for /pilf'rings /and /most /common /trespasses LR 2.02.144
COMMON 151 FR 0.0170 REL FR 130 V 21 P
our hint of woe | is common: TMP 2.01. 4
all things in common nature should produce 2.01.160
rejoice | beyond a common joy, and set it down 5.01.207
thou common friend, that's without faith or love TGV 5.04. 62
had set me i' th' stocks, i' th' common stocks, WIV 4.05.120 P
and the terms | for common justice, y' are as MM 1.01. 11
for so i have strew'd it in the common ear, 1.03. 15
nothing but use their abuses in common houses, i 2.01. 43 P
do me the common right | to let me see them, and 2.03. 5
here is in our prison a common executioner, who 4.02. 9 P
you know the course is common. 4.02.177 P
love, | and make a common of my serious hours. ERR 2.02. 29
good meat, sir, is common; 3.01. 24
and welcome more common, for that's nothing but 3.01. 25
and that supposed by the common rout | against 3.01.101
to link my dear friend to a common stale. ADO 4.01. 65
hid and barr'd, you mean, from common sense. LLL 1.01. 57
when mistresses from common sense are hid; 1.01. 64
my lips are no common, though several they be. 2.01.223
i am a spirit of no common rate; MND 3.01.154
than common sleep of all these /five the sense. 4.01. 82
because i will not jump with common spirits, MV 2.09. 32
thou pale and common drudge | 'tween man and man 3.02.103
to the common ferry | which trades to venice. 3.04. 53
because that i am more than common tall, | that AYL 1.03.115
enforce | a thievish living on the common road? 2.03. 33
the common executioner, | whose heart th' 3.05. 3
of this female — which in the common is woman; 5.01. 49 P
and practice rhetoric in your common talk, SHR 1.01. 35
what impossibility would slay | in common sense, AWW 2.01.178
and common speech | gives him a worthy pass. 2.05. 52
but like a common and an outward man | that the 3.01. 11
and as in the common course of all treasons, we 4.03. 22 P
lord, | and was a common gamester to the camp. 5.03.188
so, | he might have bought me at a common price. 5.03.190
i think thee now some common customer. 5.03.286
an ayword, and make him a common recreation, do TN 2.03.135 P
will draw in | more than the common blocks. WT 1.02.225
much surpassing | the common praise it bears. 3.01. 3
word | is but the vain breath of a common man. JN 3.01. 8
no common wind, no customed event, | but they 3.04.155
young arthur's death is common in their mouths, 4.02.187
a maim | as to be cast forth in the common air, R2 1.03.157
observ'd his courtship to the common people, 1.04. 24
some way of common trade, where subjects' feet 3.03.156
go to, homo is a common name to all men. 1H4 2.01. 95 P
do show | i am not in the roll of common men. 3.01. 42
grew a companion to the common streets, 3.02. 68
not an eye | but is a–weary of thy common sight, 3.02. 88
they have a good thing, to make it too common. 2H4 1.02.216 P
as common as the way between saint albons and 2.02.167 P
couch | a watch–case or a common 'larum–bell? 3.01. 17
the time misord'red doth, in common sense, 4.02. 33
be, | which i with more than with a common pain 4.05.223
as 'tis ever common | that men are merriest when H5 1.02.271
or art thou base, common, and popular? 4.01. 38
to sort our nobles from our common men. 4.07. 74
you appear'd to me but as a common man; 4.08. 51 P
full fifteen hundred, besides common men. 4.08. 79
was infamous | and ill beseeming any common man, 1H6 4.01. 31
your grief, the common grief of all the land. 2H6 1.01. 77
what though the common people favor him, 1.01.158
the land | and common profit of his country! 1.01.206
all the realm shall be in common, and in 4.02. 68 P
and henceforward all things shall be in common. 4.07. 19 P
were by the swords of common soldiers slain. 3H6 1.01. 9
or more than common fear of clifford's rigor, 2.01.126
grief more than common grief! 2.05. 94
gust, | such is the lightness of you common men. 3.01. 89
the common people by numbers swarm to us. 4.02. 2
discharge the common sort | with pay and thanks, 5.05. 87
in common worldly things 'tis call'd ungrateful R3 2.02. 91
as you respect the common good, the state | of H8 3.02.290
the common voice, i see, is verified | of thee, 5.02.209
dread father's, in a scale | of common ounces? TRO 2.02. 28
the common curse of mankind, folly and ignorance 2.03. 28 P
and that old common arbitrator, time, | will one 4.05.225
unto the appetite and affection common | of the COR 1.01.104
rightly | touching the weal a' th' common, you 1.01.151
for our gentlemen, | the common file (a plague! 1.06. 43
before the common distribution, at | your only 1.09. 35
and stand upon my common part with those | that 1.09. 39
proud, and loves not the common people. 2.02. 6 P
your loving motion toward the common body | to 2.02. 53
as they were | the common muck of the world. 2.02.126
you have not indeed lov'd the common people. 2.03. 93 P
virtuous that i have not been common in my love. 2.03. 95 P
the people, | the tongues o' th' common mouth. 3.01. 22
hath he not pass'd the noble and the common? 3.01. 29
if you are learn'd, | be not as common fools; 3.01.100
hear me, my masters, and my common friends — 3.03.108
you common cry of curs, whose breath i hate | as 3.03.120
that common chances common men could bear, 4.01. 5
that common chances common men could bear, 4.01. 5
son | will or exceed the common or be caught 4.01. 32
more impression show | than that of common sons. 5.03. 52
stand | a special party, have by common voice, TIT 1.01. 21
'tis he the common people love so much; 4.04. 73
i know | the common voice do cry it shall be so. 5.03.140
to old free–town, our common judgment–place. ROM 1.01.102
and soar with them above a common bound. 1.04. 18
'tis common: TIM 1.01. 89
he speaks the common tongue | which all men 1.01.174
with more than common thanks i will receive it. 1.02.208
and which i hear from common rumors, now lord 3.02. 5 P
base | to sue and be denied such common grace. 3.05. 94
together with the common /lag of people — what 3.06. 80 P
thou common whore of mankind, that puts odds 4.03. 43
common mother, thou | whose womb unmeasurable 4.03.177
am not | one that rejoices in the common wrack, 5.01.192
the common wrack, | as common bruit doth put it. 5.01.193
nor all deserve | the common stroke of war. 5.04. 22
were i a common laughter, or did use | to stale JC 1.02. 72
he perceiv'd the common herd was glad he refus'd 1.02.264 P
a common slave — you know him well by sight — 1.03. 15
but 'tis a common proof | that lowliness is 2.01. 21
which so appearing to the common eyes, | we 2.01.179
of senators, of praetors, common suitors, | will 2.04. 35
some to the common pulpits, and cry out, 3.01. 80
and to your heirs for ever — common pleasures, 3.02.250
general honest thought | and common good to all, 5.05. 72
jewel | given to the common enemy of man, | to MAC 3.01. 68
masking the business from the common eye | for 3.01.124
thou know'st 'tis common, all that lives must HAM 1.02. 72
ay, madam, it is common. 1.02. 74
and is as common | as any the most vulgar thing 1.02. 98
whose common theme | is death of fathers, and 1.02.103
as it is common for the younger sort | to lack 2.01.113
good king, that must approve the common saw, LR 2.02.160
more, | to pluck the common bosom on his side, 5.03. 49
better guard | but with a knave of common hire, OTH 1.01.125
and yet his trespass, in our common reason 3.03. 64
you have a thing for me? it is a common thing — 3.03.302
full sorry | that he approves the common liar, ANT 1.01. 60
this common body, | like to a vagabond flag upon 1.04. 44
i' th' common show–place, where they exercise. 3.06. 12
slaver with lips as common as the stairs | that CYM 1.06.105
hereafter find | it is no act of common passage, 3.04. 91
that since the common men are now in action 3.07. 2
should therein make me vile, the common body, PER 3.03. 21
off, or the common hangman shall execute it. 4.06.128 P
empty | old receptacles, or common shores, of 4.06.175
serve by indenture to the common hangman: 4.06.176
and to follow | the common stream, 'twould bring TNK 1.02. 10
honor, | that liberty and common conversation, 2.02. 74
so did this horse excel a common one, | in shape VEN 293
love, | by holy human law, and common troth, LUC 571
the /soil is this, that thou dost common grow. SON 69.14
the earth can yield me but a common grave, 81. 7
and sweets grown common lose their dear delight. 102.12
my heart knows the wide world's common place? 137.10
COMMONALTY 2 FR 0.0002 REL FR 1 V 1 P
bid him strive | to the love o' th' commonalty; H8 1.02.170
he's a very dog to the commonalty. COR 1.01. 29 P
COMMONER 2 FR 0.0002 REL FR 2 V 0 P
all that | he gave it to a commoner a' th' camp, AWW 5.03.194
o thou public commoner, | i should make very OTH 4.02. 73
COMMONERS 2 FR 0.0002 REL FR 1 V 1 P
and then the vital commoners and inland petty 2H4 4.03.110 P
doubt not | the commoners, for whom we stand, COR 2.01.227
COMMON–HACKNEY'D 1 FR 0.0001 REL FR 1 V 0 P
been, | so common–hackney'd in the eyes of men, 1H4 3.02. 40
COMMON–KISSING 1 FR 0.0001 REL FR 1 V 0 P
to the greedy touch | of common–kissing titan, CYM 3.04.163
COMMONLY 4 FR 0.0004 REL FR 4 V 0 P
fathers commonly | do get their children; SHR 2.01.409
as our sex | commonly are, the want of which WT 2.01.109
spirit | (more than in women commonly is seen) 1H6 5.05. 71
and sweating devil here | that commonly rebels. OTH 3.04. 43
/COMMONS' 1 FR 0.0001 REL FR 1 V 0 P
/you, /lords, /to /grant /the /commons' /suit? R2 4.01.154
COMMONS' 3 FR 0.0003 REL FR 3 V 0 P
by flattery hath he won the commons' hearts; 2H6 3.01. 28
by this i shall perceive the commons' mind, 3.01.374
i, | even in theirs and in the commons' ears, COR 5.06. 4
/COMMONS 1 FR 0.0001 REL FR 1 V 0 P
/the /commons /will /not /then /be /satisfied. R2 4.01.272
COMMONS 23 FR 0.0026 REL FR 22 V 1 P
the commons hath he pill'd with grievous taxes, R2 2.01.246
nobles they are fled, the commons they are cold, 2.02. 88
and that is the wavering commons, for their love 2.02.129
will the hateful commons perform for us, 2.02.138
till that the nobles and the armed commons 2H4 2.03. 51
mitigation of this bill | urg'd by the commons? H5 1.01. 71
hath won the greatest favor of the commons, 2H6 1.01.192
suffolk, for enclosing the commons of melford." 1.03. 21 P
the commons hast thou rack'd, the clergy's bags 1.03.128
because i would not tax the needy commons, 3.01.116
the commons haply rise, to save his life; 3.01.240
the commons, like an angry hive of bees | that 3.02.125
dread lord, the commons send you word by me, 3.02.243
'tis like the commons, rude unpolish'd hinds, 3.02.271
the commons here in kent are up in arms, | and 4.01.100
and you that love the commons, follow me. 4.02.182
ambassadors from the king | unto the commons, 4.08. 8
the grieved commons | hardly conceive of me; H8 1.02.104
all the commons | hate him perniciously, and, o' 2.01. 49
and the commons made | a shower and thunder with COR 2.01.266
so | i' th' right and strength a' th' commons," 3.03. 14
let but the commons hear this testament — JC 3.02.130
ass) to shake his ears | and graze in commons. 4.01. 27
COMMON'ST 1 FR 0.0001 REL FR 1 V 0 P
and from the common'st creature pluck a glove R2 5.03. 17
COMMONWEAL 9 FR 0.0010 REL FR 8 V 1 P
good people in a commonweal that do nothing but MM 2.01. 42 P
a prince, | so kind a father of the commonweal, 1H6 3.01. 98
himself | unlike the ruler of a commonweal. 2H6 1.01.189
the king and commonweal | are deeply indebted 1.04. 43
that smooth'st it so with king and commonweal! 2.01. 22
how i have lov'd my king and commonweal; 2.01.187
if to fight for king and commonweal | were piety TIT 1.01.114
earth, | and ripen justice in this commonweal. 1.01.227
king and commander of our commonweal, | the wide 1.01.247
COMMONWEAL'S 1 FR 0.0001 REL FR 1 V 0 P
and see his shipwrack and his commonweal's. TIT 2.01. 24
/COMMONWEALTH 1 FR 0.0001 REL FR 1 V 0 P
/the /commonwealth /is /sick /of /their /own 2H4 1.03. 87
COMMONWEALTH 27 FR 0.0030 REL FR 14 V 13 P
i' th' commonwealth i would, by contraries, TMP 2.01.148
the latter end of his commonwealth forgets the 2.01.158 P
why, here's a change indeed in the commonwealth! MM 1.02.105 P
lechery that ever was known in the commonwealth. ADO 3.03.168 P
here comes a member of the commonwealth. LLL 4.01. 41
you are a good member of the commonwealth. 4.02. 76 P
says you are no good member of the commonwealth, MV 3.05. 34 P
that better to the commonwealth than you can the 3.05. 37 P
is not politic in the commonwealth of nature to AWW 1.01.126 P
the caterpillars of the commonwealth, | which i R2 2.03.166
that look too lofty in our commonwealth: 3.04. 35
continually to their saint, the commonwealth, or 1H4 2.01. 80 P
what, the commonwealth their boots? 2.01. 83 P
that lie too heavy on the commonwealth, | cries 4.03. 80
my brother general, the commonwealth, | i make 2H4 4.01. 93
law, | whiles i was busy for the commonwealth, 5.02. 76
hear him debate of commonwealth affairs, | you H5 1.01. 41
that gnaws the bowels of the commonwealth. 1H6 3.01. 73
the commonwealth hath daily run to wrack, | the 2H6 1.03.124
i come to talk of commonwealth affairs. 1.03.154
the clothier means to dress the commonwealth, 4.02. 5 P
that that lord say hath gelded the commonwealth, 4.02.165 P
more have strength'ned this our commonwealth 3H6 4.01. 37
the commonwealth doth stand, and so would do, COR 4.06. 14
sons, | to ruffle in the commonwealth of rome. TIT 1.01.313
the commonwealth of athens is become a forest of TIM 4.03.347 P
of his dying, a place in the commonwealth, as JC 3.02. 43 P
COMMOTION 7 FR 0.0008 REL FR 7 V 0 P
when tempest of commotion, like the south 2H4 2.04.363
if damn'd commotion so /appear'd | in his true, 4.01. 36
and when he please to make commotion, | 'tis to 2H6 3.01. 29
to make commotion, as full well he can, | under 3.01.358
some strange commotion | is in his brain; H8 3.02.112
commotion in the winds! TRO 1.03. 98
parts | kingdom'd achilles in commotion rages, 2.03.175
COMMOTIONS 1 FR 0.0001 REL FR 1 V 0 P
commotions, uproars, with a general taint | of H8 5.02. 63
COMMUNE 5 FR 0.0005 REL FR 4 V 1 P
for i would commune with you of such things MM 4.03.104
stay, | for i have more to commune with bianca. SHR 1.01.101
what need we | commune with you of this, but WT 2.01.162
laertes, i must commune with your grief, | or HAM 4.05.203
you come to eat with her and to commune of love. TNK 4.03. 77 P
COMMUNICATE 3 FR 0.0003 REL FR 2 V 1 P
makes me with thy strength to communicate: ERR 2.02.176
and did communicate to herself her own words to AWW 1.03.107 P
till he communicate his parts to others; TRO 3.03.117
COMMUNICATION 2 FR 0.0002 REL FR 1 V 1 P
argument, look you, and friendly communication; H5 3.02. 98 P
did this vanity | but minister communication of H8 1.01. 86
COMMUNICAT'ST 1 FR 0.0001 REL FR 1 V 0 P
communicat'st with dreams (how can this be?), WT 1.02.140
COMMUNITIES 1 FR 0.0001 REL FR 1 V 0 P
how could communities, | degrees in schools, and TRO 1.03.103
COMMUNITY 1 FR 0.0001 REL FR 1 V 0 P
such eyes | as, sick and blunted with community, 1H4 3.02. 77
COMMUTUAL *(see comutual)*
COMONTY 1 FR 0.0001 REL FR 0 V 1 P
is not a comonty a christmas gambold, or a SHR in.2. 138 P
COMPACT* 17 FR 0.0019 REL FR 17 V 0 P
compact with her that's gone, think'st thou thy MM 5.01.242
what is the course and drift of your compact? ERR 2.02.161
make us /but believe | (being compact of credit) 3.02. 22
and the poet | are of imagination all compact. MND 5.01. 8
if he, compact of jars, grow musical, | we shall AYL 2.07. 5
patience once more, whiles our compact is urg'd: 5.04. 5
and all the ceremony of this compact | seal'd in TN 5.01.160
and therefore take this compact of a truce, 1H6 5.04.163
of us, | and the compact is firm and true in me. R3 2.02.133
my heart is not compact of flint nor steel, TIT 5.03. 88
so, | but what compact mean you to have with us? JC 3.01.215
by a seal'd compact | well ratified by law and HAM 1.01. 86
when my dimensions are as well compact, | my LR 1.02. 7
reasons of your own | as may compact it more. 1.04.339
when he, compact, and flattering his displeasure 2.02.118
love is a spirit all compact of fire, | not VEN 149
conceit deceitful, so compact, so kind, | that LUC 1423
COMPACTED 1 FR 0.0001 REL FR 1 V 0 P
the poisonous simple sometime is compacted | in LUC 530
/COMPANIES 1 FR 0.0001 REL FR 1 V 0 P
to seek new friends and /stranger /companies. MND 1.01.219
COMPANIES 9 FR 0.0010 REL FR 7 V 2 P
when a cur cannot keep himself in all companies! TGV 4.04. 11 P
manners discreetly in all kind of companies. SHR 1.01.242
go | and thrust thyself into their companies; JN 4.02.167

lieutenants, gentlemen of companies — slaves as 1H4 4.02. 24 P
his companies unletter'd, rude, and shallow, H5 1.01. 55
rid me these villains from your companies; TIM 5.01.101
prepare to lodge their companies to-night. JC 4.03.140
time, so by your companies | to draw him on to HAM 2.02. 14
and my brother search | what companies are near.
CYM 4.02. 69

COMPANION 41 FR 0.0046 REL FR 24 V 17 P
not wish | any companion in the world but you; TMP 3.01. 55
lordship is not ignorant | how his companion, TGV 1.03. 26
scurvy, cogging companion, the host of the WIV 3.01.120 P
take then this your companion by the hand, | who MM 4.01. 54
too, and with the other confederate companion! 5.01.348 P
did this companion with the saffron face | revel ERR 4.04. 61
who is his companion now? ADO 1.01. 72 P
but i pray you, who is his companion? 1.01. 81 P
finding a bird's nest, shows it his companion, 2.01.224 P
this quondam day with a companion of the king's,
LLL 5.01. 7 P
the pale companion is not for our pomp. MND 1.01. 15
'tis too cold a companion; AWW 1.01.132 P
are you companion to the count rossillion? 2.03.192 P
been solicited by a gentleman his companion. 3.05. 15 P
what an equivocal companion is this! 5.03.250 P
destroy'd the sweet'st companion that e'er man WT 5.01. 11
sometimes brother's wife | with her companion, R2 1.02. 55
most mighty liege, and my companion peers, 1.03. 93
an old fat man, a tun of man is thy companion. 1H4 2.04.448 P
grew a companion to the common streets, 3.02. 68
well, god send the prince a better companion! 2H4 1.02.199 P
god send the companion a better prince! 1.02.201 P
i scorn you, scurvy companion. 2.04.123 P
a child, | fit to be made companion with a king. 1H6 5.03.149
affects, | must be companion of his nuptial bed. 5.05. 58
why, rude companion, whatsoe'er thou be, | i 2H6 4.10. 31
and am /glad | to have you therein my companion.
H8 3.02.143
now, you companion! COR 5.02. 60 P
from our companion thrown into his grave, | so TIM 4.02. 9
companion, hence! JC 4.03.138
was he not companion with the riotous knights LR 2.01. 94
caesar, and companion me with my mistress. ANT 1.02. 30 P
friend and companion in the front of war, | the 5.01. 44
there is a frenchman his companion, one | an CYM 1.06. 64
undertake every companion that you give offense 2.01. 27 P
i'ld change my sex to be companion with them, 3.06. 87
testy wrath | could never be her mild companion. PER 1.01. 18
the sad companion, dull-ey'd melancholy, | /be 1.02. 2
that none but i and my companion maid | be 5.01. 77
well, my companion friends, | if this but answer 5.01.237
to those that prate and have done, no companion;
TNK 5.01.119

COMPANIONS 19 FR 0.0021 REL FR 13 V 6 P
set caliban and his companions free; TMP 5.01.252
take with you your companions. 5.01.293
and at his heels a rabble of his companions, WIV 3.05. 75 P
such insociable and point-devise companions, LLL 5.01. 19 P
behold address'd | the king and his companions. 5.02. 93
for in companions | that do converse and waste MV 3.04. 11
now, my spruce companions, is all ready, and all SHR 4.01.113 P
frequent, | with unrestrained loose companions, R2 5.03. 7
receive," says he, "no swaggering companions." 2H4 2.04. 94 P
the prince but studies his companions | like a 4.04. 68
head, that he gives entrance to such companions? COR 4.05. 12 P
of sorriest fancies your companions making, MAC 3.02. 9
slips | as are companions noted and most known HAM 2.01. 23
o /heaven, that such companions thou'dst unfold, OTH 4.02.141
i create you | companions to our person, and CYM 5.05. 21
two of the sweet'st companions in the world. 5.05.349
and, sweet companions, let's rehearse by any TNK 2.03. 56
maids have been her companions and play-feres, 4.03. 90 P
nor laugh with his companions at thy state, LUC 1066

COMPANIONSHIP 2 FR 0.0002 REL FR 2 V 0 P
that it shall hold companionship in peace | with COR 3.02. 49
and some twenty horse, | all of companionship. TIM 1.01.242

/COMPANY 2 FR 0.0002 REL FR 2 V 0 P
she hath abjur'd the /company | and /sight of TN 1.02. 40
/i /see /thou /art /not /for /my /company. TIT 3.02. 58

COMPANY 207 FR 0.0234 REL FR 138 V 69 P
the king and all our company else being drown'd, TMP 2.02.174 P
her and her blind boy's scandall'd company | i 4.01. 90
and to thee and thy company i bid | a hearty 5.01.110
we have safely found | our king and company; 5.01.222
there are yet missing of your company | some few 5.01.254
i rather would entreat thy company | to see the TGV 1.01. 5
good company; 1.03. 43
spends what he borrows kindly in your company. 2.04. 39 P
forbid | sir valentine her company and my court; 3.01. 27
forsworn my company, and rail'd at me, | that i 3.02. 4
youth | thrust from the company of aweful men. 4.01. 44
peace, stand aside, the company parts. 4.02. 81
to pass, | i do desire thy worthy company, 4.03. 25
of sands, | to bear me company, and go with me; 4.03. 34
me himself into the company of three or four 4.04. 17 P
and eglamour is in her company. 5.02. 36
in honest, civil, godly company, for this trick. WIV 1.01.182 P
my father desires your worships' company. 1.01.262 P
i shall never laugh but in that maid's company! 1.04.153 P
why, he hath not been thrice in my company! 2.01. 26 P
she was in his company at page's house; 2.01.235 P
forbear; here's company. 2.03. 17 P
as she may hang together, for want of company. 3.02. 14 P
he kept company with the wild prince and poins; 3.02. 72 P
door, mistress ford, and requests your company. 3.03. 25 P
there is one, i shall make two in the company. 3.03.235 P
and the rest of their company from their sport, 4.02. 34 P
what ho! peace here; grace and good company! MM 3.01. 44
my habit, no loss shall touch her by my company. 3.01.178 P
token, i desire his company | at mariana's house 4.03.139
sir, your company is fairer than honest. 4.03.175 P
might bear him company in the quest of him: ERR 1.01.129
his company must do his minions grace, | whilst 2.01. 87
more company! the fiend is strong within him. 4.04.107
in company i often glanced it; 5.01. 66
i met him, | and in his company that gentleman. 5.01.226
error | have suffer'd wrong, go keep us company, 5.01.399
he is most in the company of the right noble ADO 1.01. 84 P
with me in your company? 2.01. 91 P
and i off'red him my company to a willow-tree, 2.01.217 P
none, but to desire your good company. 2.01.272 P
will only be bold with benedick for his company, 3.02. 8 P
what he is and steal out of your company. 3.03. 59 P
i must discontinue your company. 5.01.189 P
forbear till this company be past. LLL 1.02.126 P
by whom shall i send this? — company? stay. 4.03. 75
i am betrayed by keeping company | with men like 4.03.177
price you yourselves; what buys your company? 5.02.224
one show worse than the king's and his company. 5.02.513
is all our company here? MND 1.02. 1 P
we shall be dogg'd with company, and our devices 1.02.104 P
hence — | i have forsworn his bed and company. 2.01. 62
nor doth this wood lack worlds of company, | for 2.01.223
and love keep little company together now-a-days 3.01.144 P
you, i, | nor longer stay in your curst company. 3.02.341
from these that my poor company detest. 3.02.434
eye, | steal me a while from mine own company. 3.02.436
a bergomask dance between two of our company? 5.01.354 P
ye well, | we leave you now with better company. MV 1.01. 59
well, keep me company but two years moe, | thou 1.01.108
that came hither in company of the marquis of 1.02.114 P
a title good enough to keep his name company! 3.01. 14 P
creditors in my company to venice that swear he 3.01.114 P
for in choosing wrong | i lose your company; 3.02. 3
ring, and doth entreat | your company at dinner. 4.02. 8
usurping uncle | to keep his daughter company, AYL 1.02.275
my liege, | i cannot live out of her company. 1.03. 86
"thus misery doth part | the flux of company." 2.01. 52
gone, | that youth is surely in their company. 2.02. 16
or if thou hast not broke from company 2.04. 40
he is too disputable for my company. 2.05. 35 P
that your poor friends must woo your company? 2.07. 10
i thank you for your company, but, good faith, i 3.02.253 P
god 'ild you for your last company. 3.03. 75 P
thy company, which erst was irksome to me, | i 3.05. 95
for here comes more company. 4.03. 74 P
which in the boorish is company — of this 5.01. 49 P
arm'd | with his good will and thy good company, SHR 1.01. 6
but stay a while, what company is this? 1.01. 46
my books and instruments shall be my company, 1.01. 82
with her, | or else you like not of my company. 2.01. 65
that she shall still be curst in company. 2.01.305
frown, | and wherefore gaze this goodly company, 3.02. 94
and, honest company, i thank you all | that have 3.02.193
that calls for company to countenance her. 4.01.102 P
and for this night we'll fast for company. 4.01.177
come, mistress kate, i'll bear you company. 4.03. 49
but soft, company is coming here. 4.05. 26
with us, | we shall be joyful of thy company. 4.05. 52
to break a jest | upon the company you overtake? 4.05. 73
we shall not then have his company to-night? AWW 4.03. 28 P
gladly have him see his company anatomiz'd, that 4.03. 32 P
mine own company, chitopher, vaumond, bentii, 4.03.164 P
moreov'r, he's drunk nightly in your company. TN 1.03. 37 P
i would not undertake her in this company. 1.03. 59 P
for i myself am best | when least in company. 1.04. 38
both day and night did we keep company. 5.01. 96
in whose company | i shall re-view sicilia, for WT 4.04.665
and with our company piece the rejoicing? 5.02.107 P
and brought prince henry in their company, | at JN 5.06. 34
in ross and willoughby, wanting your company, R2 2.03. 10
by sight of what i have, your noble company. 2.03. 18
of much less value is my company | than your 2.03. 19
they will along with company, for they have 1H4 2.01. 45 P
it to one of his company last night at supper, a 2.01. 57 P
i am accurs'd to rob in that thieve's company. 2.02. 10 P
i have forsworn his company hourly any time this 2.02. 16 P
and yet i am bewitch'd with the rogue's company. 2.02. 17 P
doth defile, so doth the company thou keepest; 2.04.414 P
man whom i have often noted in thy company, but 2.04.418 P
banish not him thy harry's company, banish not 2.04.478 P
banish not him thy harry's company — banish 2.04.479 P
of men, | so stale and cheap to vulgar company, 3.02. 41
company, villainous company, hath been the spoil 3.03. 9 P
company, villainous company, hath been the spoil 3.03. 10 P
not a shirt and a half in all my company, and 4.02. 42 P
keeping such vile company as thou art hath in 2H4 2.02. 49 P
what company? 2.02.149 P
am i, | till time and vantage crave my company. 2.03. 68
discharge yourself of our company, pistol. 2.04.137 P
therefore let men take heed of their company. 5.01. 77 P
so will i those that kept me company. 5.05. 59
take all his company along with him. 5.05. 92
a while, | and then i would no other company. H5 4.01. 32
i am a gentleman of a company. 4.01. 39 P
any where so contented as in the king's company, 4.01.127 P
do it, though i take thee in the king's company. 4.01.220 P
we would not die in that man's company | that 4.03. 38
my soul shall thine keep company to heaven; 4.06. 16
traitors have never other company. 1H6 2.01. 19
will not your honors bear me company? 2.02. 53
grief | that such a valiant company are fled. 3.02.125
and so conduct me where, from company, | i may 5.05.100
in courtly company, or at my beads, | with you, 2H6 1.01. 27
nobility, | i banish her my bed and company, 2.01.193
affliction | be playfellows to keep you company! 3.02.302
enough, | so suffolk had thy heavenly company: 3.02.361
and i, my lord, will bear him company. 3H6 1.03. 6
and craves your company for speedy counsel. 2.01.208
that warwick's bones may keep thine company. 5.02. 4
and in my company my brother gloucester, | who R3 1.04. 11
you go | to comfort edward with our company. 2.01.140
which haply by much company might be urg'd; 2.02.137
and so was i. i'll bear you company. 2.03. 47
name | that ever grac'd me with thy company? 4.04.175
grace | to breakfast once, forth of my company. 4.04.177
nay, he must bear you company. H8 1.01.212
as merry | as, first, good company, good wine, 1.04. 6
the very thought of this fair company | clapp'd 1.04. 8
a noble company! 1.04. 64
my lord, you'll bear us company? 2.02. 58
for i must think of that which company | would 5.01. 75
to you, my lord, and to all this fair company! TRO 3.01. 44 P
sir, mine own company. 3.02.145
business | should rob my bed-mate of my company. 4.01. 6
let's have your company, or, if you please, 4.01. 40
diomed, | keep hector company an hour or two. 5.01. 81
i'll keep you company. 5.01. 86
your company to th' capitol, where i know | our COR 1.01.244
i'll keep you company. will you along? 2.03.149
let me desire your company. 3.01.333
well met, and most glad of your company. 4.03. 49 P
fire, | so i might have your company in hell, TIT 5.01.149
never wags | but in her company there is a moor; 5.02. 88
there, | rememb'ring how i love thy company. ROM 2.02.173
heads, | staying for thine to keep him company. 3.01.128
is my dear son with such sour company! 3.03. 7
i promise you, but for your company, | i would 3.04. 6
dram | that he shall soon keep tybalt company; 3.05. 91
alone, in company, still my care hath been | to 3.05.177
i'll keep you company. TIM 1.01.283
himself, | for he does neither affect company, 1.02. 31
entreats your company to-morrow to hunt with him 1.02.187 P
now, captain, what do you in this wise company? 2.02. 74 P
first mend /my company, take away thyself. 4.03.283
the plague of company light upon thee! 4.03.352 P
but two in company; 5.01.106
alone, | yet an arch-villain keeps him company. 5.01.108
to sports, to wildness, and much company. JC 2.01.189
fleance his son, that keeps him company, | whose MAC 3.01.134
highness | to grace us with your royal company? 3.04. 44
they keep, | what company, at what expense; HAM 2.01. 9
take you some company, and away to horse. LR 1.04.336
what, hath your grace no better company? 3.04.142
noble philosopher, your company. 3.04.172
edmund, keep you our sister company; 3.07. 7 P
do you perceive in all this noble company OTH 1.03.179
o, but i fear — how lost you company? 2.01. 91
say my wife is fair, feeds well, loves company, 3.03.184
well, i must leave her company. 4.01.144 P
who keeps her company? 4.02.137
let us, lepidus, | not lack your company. ANT 2.02.169
choose your own company, and command what cost 3.04. 37
queen, madam, | desires your highness' company. CYM 1.03. 38
your very goodness and your company | o'erpays 2.04. 9
what company | discover you abroad? 4.02.129
the soldier that did company these three | in 5.05.408
the temple see, | our king and all his company. PER 5.02. 18
bereave you | of your fair cousin's company. TNK 2.02.224
draw up the company. where's the taborer? 3.05. 23
let me have your company | till /i come to the 3.05. 65
or company, or by a figure, choris, | that 'fore 3.05.107
the maids that kept her company | have half 5.02. 2
annoy, | sad souls are slain in merry company, LUC 1110
the other takes in hand | no cause, but company, 1236
back, | brings home his lord and other company, 1584
fawn'd on him before | use his company no more. PP 20.48

COMPANY'S 1 FR 0.0001 REL FR 1 V 0 P
no company's abroad? CYM 4.02.101

COMPARATIVE 3 FR 0.0003 REL FR 2 V 1 P
/similes and art indeed the most comparative, 1H4 1.02. 80 P
the push | of every beardless vain comparative, 3.02. 67
if 'twere made | comparative for your virtues, CYM 2.03.129

COMPAR'D 3 FR 0.0003 REL FR 3 V 0 P
i am compar'd to twenty thousand fairs. LLL 5.02. 37
being compar'd | with my confineless harms. MAC 4.03. 54
compar'd with loss of thee will not seem so. SON 90.14

COMPARE 30 FR 0.0034 REL FR 25 V 5 P
made me compare with hermia's sphery eyne! MND 2.02. 99
to what, my love, shall i compare thine eyne? 3.02.138
now i perceive that she hath made compare 3.02.290
our strength as weak, our weakness past compare,
SHR 5.02.174
and yet i will not compare with an old man. TN 1.03.118 P
make no compare | between that love a woman can 2.04.101
compare our faces, and be judge yourself. JN 1.01. 79
grief, | or else he never would compare between. R2 2.01.185
i have been studying how i may compare | this 5.05. 1
compare with caesars and with cannibals | and 2H4 2.04.166
compare dead happiness with living woe; R3 4.04.119
full of protest, of oath and big compare, TRO 3.02.175
compare her face with some that i shall show, ROM 1.02. 86
not to be talk'd on, yet they are past compare. 2.05. 43 P
which she hath prais'd him with above compare 3.05.238
canst thou nearest compare to thy flatterers? TIM 4.03.319 P
i will hear cassius, and compare their reasons, JC 3.02. 9
lest i should compare with him in excellence, HAM 5.02.138 P
something failing | in him that should compare. CYM 1.01. 22
i can compare our rich misers to nothing so PER 2.01. 29 P
crown a' th' earth | i' th' justice of compare! 4.03. 9
"the field's chief flower, sweet above compare, VEN 8
braving compare, disdainfully did sting | his LUC 40
views, | and to herself all sorrow doth compare; 1102
shall i compare thee to a summer's day? SON 18. 1
making a couplement of proud compare | with sun 21. 5
compare them with the bett'ring of the time, 32. 5
this, | authorizing thy trespass with compare, 35. 6
as rare | as any she belied with false compare. 130.14
o, but with mine compare thou thine own state, 142. 3

COMPARED 2 FR 0.0002 REL FR 2 V 0 P
thy leg a stick compared with this truncheon; 2H6 4.10. 49
and now his grief may be compared well | to one VEN 701

COMPARES 1 FR 0.0001 REL FR 1 V 0 P
green-dropping sap, which she compares to tears.
VEN 1176

COMPARING 3 FR 0.0003 REL FR 2 V 1 P
such-like trifles — nothing comparing to his — TIM 3.02. 22 P
to smell, | comparing it to her adonis' breath, VEN 1172
comparing him to that unhappy guest | whose deed
LUC 1565

COMPARISON 8 FR 0.0009 REL FR 3 V 5 P
he'll but break a comparison or two on me, which
ADO 2.01.146 P
i am the king, for so stands the comparison; LLL 4.01. 79 P
that the comparison | may stand more proper, my MV 3.02. 45
stand'st thou aloof upon comparison? 1H6 5.04.150
there were no more comparison between the women!
TRO 1.01. 42 P
in whose comparison all whites are ink | writing 1.01. 56
o jupiter, there's no comparison. 1.02. 62 P
a kind of hand-in-hand comparison — had been CYM 1.04. 71 P

COMPARISONS 8 FR 0.0009 REL FR 4 V 4 P
comparisons are odorous — palabras, neighbor ADO 3.05. 16 P
full of comparisons and wounding flouts, | which LLL 5.02.844
thou hast tir'd thyself in base comparisons, 1H4 2.04.250 P

in the comparisons between macedon and monmouth, H5 4.07. 24 P
speak but in the figures and comparisons of it: 4.07. 44 P
a mint, | to match us in comparisons with dirt, TRO 1.03.194
/yet, after all comparisons of truth | (as 3.02.180
therefore | to lay his gay comparisons apart, ANT 3.13. 26
COMPASS 35 FR 0.0039 REL FR 25 V 10 P
blessings | of a glad father compass thee about! TMP 5.01.180
if not, to compass her i'll use my skill. TGV 2.04.214
what compass will you wear your farthingale?" 2.07. 51
that i may compass yours. 4.02. 92
the knave bragg'd of that he could not compass. WIV 3.03.200 P
sing, | like to the garter's compass, in a ring. 5.05. 66
and draw within the compass of suspect | th' ERR 3.01. 87
she is too big, i hope, for me to compass. 4.01.111
we the globe can compass soon, | swifter than MND 4.01. 97
that were hard to compass, | because she will TN 1.02. 44
whose compass is no bigger than thy head, | and R2 2.01.101
why should we in the compass of a pale | keep 3.04. 40
liv'd well and in good compass, and now i live 1H4 3.03. 19 P
now i live out of all order, out of all compass. 3.03. 20 P
that you must needs be out of all compass, out 3.03. 22 P
out of all reasonable compass, sir john. 3.03. 23 P
alanson, /reignier, compass him about, | and 1H6 4.04. 27
to compass wonders but by help of devils. 5.04. 48
above the reach or compass of thy thought? 2H6 1.02. 46
my mind exceeds the compass of her wheel. 3H6 4.03. 47
nor thou within the compass of my curse. R3 1.03.283
they did perform | beyond thought's compass, H8 1.01. 36
fall into th' compass of a praemunire — | that 3.02.340
be at once to all the points a' th' compass. COR 2.03. 24 P
few come within the compass of my curse — TIT 5.01.126
it strains me past the compass of my wits. ROM 4.01. 47
my life is run his compass. JC 5.03. 25
from my lowest note to /the /top /of my compass; HAM 3.02.367 P
for the better compass of his salt and most OTH 2.01.240 P
to do this is within the compass of man's wit, 3.04. 21 P
is it within reason and compass? 4.02.219 P
will, | to compass such a /boundless happiness! PER 1.01. 24
where's your compass? TNK 4.01.143
his foul thoughts might compass his fair fair, LUC 346
within his bending sickle's compass come, | love SON 116.10
COMPASS'D 8 FR 0.0009 REL FR 3 V 5 P
how now shall this be compass'd? TMP 3.02. 58 P
next, to be compass'd, like a good bilbo, in the WIV 3.05.110 P
"with a small compass'd cape" — SHR 4.03.139 P
then he compass'd a motion of the prodigal son, WT 4.03. 96 P
him th' other day into the compass'd window — TRO 1.02.111 P
i see thee compass'd with thy kingdom's pearl, MAC 5.09. 22
upon his compass'd crest now stand on end, | his VEN 272
out of hope are compass'd oft with vent'ring, 567
COMPASSES 1 FR 0.0001 REL FR 1 V 0 P
world | the sun to course two hundred compasses, OTH 3.04. 71
COMPASSING 2 FR 0.0002 REL FR 1 V 1 P
fault | my father made in compassing the crown! H5 4.01.294
to be hang'd in compassing thy joy than to be OTH 1.03.360 P
COMPASSION 15 FR 0.0017 REL FR 15 V 0 P
touch'd | the very virtue of compassion in thee, TMP 1.02. 27
that his compassion may | give life to yours. JN 4.01. 88
tongue, | and in compassion weep the fire out, R2 5.01. 48
compassion on the king commands me stoop, | or i 1H6 3.01.119
mov'd with compassion of my country's wrack, 4.01. 56
consent, | of mere compassion and of lenity, 5.04.125
melted with tenderness and /kind compassion, R3 4.03. 7
thing to make | mine eyes to sweat compassion. COR 5.03.196
groan | and not relent, or not compassion him? TIT 4.01.124
honor, health, and compassion to the senate! TIM 3.05. 5
say i felt | compassion to 'em both, how would TNK 3.06.213
sir, i am deaf | to all but your compassion), 3.06.239
what may be done? for now i feel compassion. 3.06.271
or the sweet compassion | of those two ladies; 4.01. 11
which yields compassion where he conquers; 4.02.132
COMPASSIONATE 3 FR 0.0003 REL FR 3 V 0 P
it boots thee not to be compassionate, | after R2 1.03.174
and my compassionate heart | will not permit TIT 2.03.217
art, | melt at my tears and be compassionate! LUC 594
COMPEERS 2 FR 0.0002 REL FR 2 V 0 P
rights, | by me invested, he compeers the best. LR 5.03. 69
he, nor his compeers by night | giving him aid, SON 86. 7
COMPEL 9 FR 0.0010 REL FR 6 V 3 P
hereafter, it may compel him to her recompense; MM 3.01.252 P
if she cannot entreat, i can compel. MND 3.02.248
thou canst compel no more than she entreat. 3.02.249
i were not a very coward, i'd compel it of you, AWW 4.03.321 P
but he hath forc'd us to compel this offer, 2H4 4.01.145
a jove, | that if requiring fail he will compel; H5 2.04.101
you will compel me then to read the will? JC 3.02.157
her in it and compel her to some second choice. OTH 2.01.234 P
it is | that nature must compel us to lament ANT 5.01. 29
/COMPELL'D 1 FR 0.0001 REL FR 1 V 0 P
/force /perforce /compell'd /to /banish /him; 2H4 4.01.114
COMPELL'D 17 FR 0.0019 REL FR 15 V 2 P
our compell'd sins | stand more for number than MM 2.04. 57
but puts it off to a compell'd restraint; AWW 2.04. 43
i was compell'd to her, but i love thee | by 4.02. 15
it is a curse | he cannot be compell'd to't) WT 2.03. 89
and, like a dog that is compell'd to fight, JN 4.01.115
that i and greatness were compell'd to kiss), 2H4 3.01. 74
say you not then our offer is compell'd. 4.01.156
there be nothing compell'd from the villages; H5 3.06.109 P
and we, for fear, compell'd to shut our shops. 1H6 3.01. 85
the son, compell'd, been butcher to the sire. R3 5.05. 26
compell'd by hunger | and lack of other means, H8 1.02. 34
fie, fie, fie upon | this compell'd fortune! 2.03. 87
am i compell'd to set | upon one battle all our JC 5.01. 74
compell'd these skipping kerns to trust their MAC 1.02. 30
in his true nature, and we ourselves compell'd, HAM 3.03. 62
too slow of sail, we put on a compell'd valor, 4.06. 18 P
and then they fight like compell'd bears, would TNK 3.01. 68
COMPELLED 2 FR 0.0002 REL FR 2 V 0 P
with pain, | being thereto not compelled. PER 3.02. 26
and why not i from this compelled stain?" LUC 1708
COMPELLING 1 FR 0.0001 REL FR 0 V 1 P
under a compelling occasion, let women die. ANT 1.02.137 P
COMPELS 1 FR 0.0001 REL FR 1 V 0 P
which compels from each | the sixt part of his H8 1.02. 57

COMPENSATION 1 FR 0.0001 REL FR 1 V 0 P
your compensation makes amends, for i | have TMP 4.01. 2
COMPETENCE 1 FR 0.0001 REL FR 1 V 0 P
for competence of life i will allow you, | that 2H4 5.05. 66
COMPETENCY 2 FR 0.0002 REL FR 1 V 1 P
by white hairs, but competency lives longer. MV 1.02. 9 P
veins | from me receive that natural competency COR 1.01.139
/COMPETENT 1 FR 0.0001 REL FR 0 V 1 P
derives itself out of a very /competent injury; TN 3.04.247 P
COMPETENT 1 FR 0.0001 REL FR 1 V 0 P
a moi'ty competent | was gaged by our king, HAM 1.01. 90
COMPETITOR 4 FR 0.0004 REL FR 4 V 0 P
myself in counsel his competitor. TGV 2.06. 35
tribunes, and me, a poor competitor. TIT 1.01. 63
natural vice to hate | /our great competitor. ANT 1.04. 3
brother, my competitor | in top of all design, 5.01. 42
COMPETITORS 5 FR 0.0005 REL FR 4 V 1 P
and he and his competitors in oath | were all LLL 2.01. 82
the competitors enter. TN 4.02. 10 P
and every hour more competitors | flock to the R3 4.04.504
they be, | and cannot brook competitors in love? TIT 2.01. 77
these three world–sharers, these competitors, ANT 2.07. 70
COMPIL'D 1 FR 0.0001 REL FR 1 V 0 P
while comments of your praise, richly compil'd, SON 85. 2
COMPILE 2 FR 0.0002 REL FR 2 V 0 P
did never sonnet for her sake compile, | nor LLL 4.03.132
yet be most proud of that which i compile, SON 78. 9
COMPILED 2 FR 0.0002 REL FR 1 V 1 P
vildly compiled, profound simplicity. LLL 5.02. 52
learned men have compiled in praise of the owl 5.02.886 P
COMPLAIN *(also plain*, etc.)*
COMPLAIN 21 FR 0.0023 REL FR 17 V 4 P
shallow, you'll complain of me to the king? WIV 1.01.109 P
elbow's wife, that he hath cause to complain of? MM 2.01.117 P
to whom should i complain? 2.04.171
by whose advice | thou cam'st here to complain. 5.01.114
as much, or more, we should ourselves complain: ERR 2.01. 37
complain unto the duke of this indignity. 5.01.113
let us complain to them what fools were here, LLL 5.02.302
nature nor art may complain of good breeding or AYL 3.02. 30 P
or shall i complain on thee to our mistress, SHR 4.01. 29 P
where then, alas, may i complain myself? R2 1.02. 42
and what i want it boots not to complain. 3.04. 18
same grievances | whereof you did complain, 2H4 4.02.114
what is that wrong whereof you both complain? 1H6 4.01. 87
the former agents, if they did complain, | what COR 1.01.123
but to his foe suppos'd he must complain, | and ROM 2.pr. 7
steal thine own freedom, and complain on theft. VEN 160
whereon they surfeit, yet complain on drouth: 544
to all the host of heaven i complain me: LUC 598
besides, of weariness he did complain him, | and 845
that to hear her so complain, | scarce i could PP 20.15
by toil, the other to complain | how far i toil, SON 28. 7
/COMPLAINANT 1 FR 0.0001 REL FR 1 V 0 P
/speechless /complainant, /i /will /learn /thy TIT 3.02. 39
COMPLAIN'D 1 FR 0.0001 REL FR 1 V 0 P
after the shepherd that complain'd of love, AYL 3.04. 48
COMPLAINED 1 FR 0.0001 REL FR 1 V 0 P
and by chaste lucrece' soul that late complained LUC 1839
COMPLAINEST 1 FR 0.0001 REL FR 0 V 1 P
and yet complainest thou of obstruction? TN 4.02. 38 P
COMPLAINING 7 FR 0.0008 REL FR 7 V 0 P
he couples it to his complaining names. TGV 1.02.124
and to the nightingale's complaining notes 5.04. 5
humbly complaining to her deity | got my lord R3 1.01. 76
poor heart, adieu, i pity thy complaining. 4.01. 87
thou mov'st no less with thy complaining than CYM 4.02.375
to the poor counterfeit of her complaining: LUC 1269
and time doth weary time with her complaining; 1570
COMPLAININGS 1 FR 0.0001 REL FR 1 V 0 P
these shreds | they vented their complainings, COR 1.01.209
COMPLAINS 1 FR 0.0001 REL FR 1 V 0 P
who is it that complains unto the king | that i, R3 1.03. 43
COMPLAINT 14 FR 0.0015 REL FR 10 V 4 P
before me again upon any complaint whatsoever; MM 2.01.246 P
till you have heard me in my true complaint 5.01. 24
being come to knowledge that there was complaint 5.01.153
hath set the women on to this complaint. 5.01.251
come i, with complaint | against my child, my MND 1.01. 22
both suffer under this complaint we bring, | and AWW 5.03.163
impediment this complaint may be to the flight WT 4.04.710 P
and that the complaint they have to the king 4.04.838 P
drops | are every one a woe, a sore complaint, H5 1.02. 26
this late complaint | will make but little for 2H6 1.03. 97
your office | on the complaint o' th' tenants. H8 1.02.173
who hath so far | given ear to our complaint, of 5.01. 48
imperfect in favoring the first complaint, hasty COR 2.01. 50 P
each buzz, each fancy, each complaint, dislike, LR 1.04.325
COMPLAINTS 10 FR 0.0011 REL FR 6 V 4 P
to have a dispatch of complaints, and to deliver MM 4.04. 12 P
the complaints i have heard of you i do not all AWW 1.03. 9 P
the complaints i hear of thee are grievous. 1H4 2.04.442 P
there is many complaints, davy, against that 2H4 5.01. 40 P
together with the pitiful complaints | of such 1H6 4.01. 57
but you must trouble him with lewd complaints. R3 1.03. 61
i am not barren to bring forth complaints. 2.02. 67
if you will now unite in your complaints, | and H8 3.02. 1
say, my lord, | grievous — complaints of you; 5.01. 99
the signiory | shall out–tongue his complaints. OTH 1.02. 19
COMPLEMENT 3 FR 0.0003 REL FR 2 V 1 P
but in all the accoustrement, complement, and WIV 4.02. 5 P
garnish'd and deck'd in modest complement, | not H5 2.02.134
and figure of my heart | in complement extern, OTH 1.01. 63
COMPLEMENTS 3 FR 0.0003 REL FR 1 V 2 P
a man of complements, whom right and wrong LLL 1.01.168
in all complements of devoted and heart–burning 1.01.276 P
these are complements, these are humors, these 3.01. 22 P
COMPLETE 19 FR 0.0021 REL FR 14 V 5 P
he is complete in feature and in mind | with all TGV 2.04. 73
dart of love | can pierce a complete bosom. MM 1.03. 3
a maid of grace and complete majesty — | about LLL 1.01.136
they are both the varnish of a complete man. 1.02. 44 P
no, my complete master, but to jig off a tune at 3.01. 11 P
is the young dolphin every way complete: JN 2.01.433
if not complete of, say he is not she, | and she 2.01.434
in complete glory she reveal'd herself; 1H6 1.02. 83
the most complete champion that ever i heard! 2H6 4.10. 55 P

how many makes the hour full complete, | how 3H6 2.05. 26
than all the complete armor that thou wear'st! R3 4.04.190
this man so complete, | who was enroll'd 'mongst H8 1.02.118
creature, and complete | in mind and feature. 3.02. 49
then marvel not, thou great and complete man, TRO 3.03.181
glory, | a thousand complete courses of the sun! 4.01. 28
and how does that honorable, complete, TIM 3.01. 10 P
the one is filling still, never complete; 4.03.244
again in complete steel | revisits thus the HAM 1.04. 52
a pestilent complete knave, and the woman hath OTH 2.01.247 P
COMPLEXION 46 FR 0.0052 REL FR 26 V 20 P
upon him, his complexion is perfect gallows. TMP 1.01. 29 P
all eve's daughters, of what complexion soever; WIV 4.02. 24 P
near the god drew to the complexion of a goose! 5.05. 8 P
for thy complexion shifts to strange effects, MM 3.01. 24
being the soul of your complexion, shall keep 3.01.183 P
what complexion is she of? ERR 3.02.101 P
that know love's grief by his complexion! ADO 1.01.313
and something of that jealous complexion. 2.01.295 P
of what complexion? LLL 1.02. 78 P
tell me precisely of what complexion. 1.02. 81 P
and ethiops of their sweet complexion crack. 4.03.264
of a saint and the complexion of a devil, i had MV 1.02.130 P
mislike me not for my complexion, | the shadowed 2.01. 1
let all of his complexion choose me so. 2.07. 79
and then it is the complexion of them all to 3.01. 29 P
good my complexion! AYL 3.02.194 P
between the pale complexion of true love | and 3.04. 53
the best thing in him | is his complexion; 3.05.116
great testimony in your complexion that it was a 4.03.170 P
forehead, and complexion, he shall find himself TN 2.03.158 P
of your complexion. 2.04. 26
she fancy, it should be one of my complexion. 2.05. 26 P
whose fresh complexion and whose heart together WT 4.04.574
men judge by the complexion of the sky | the R2 3.02.194
change the complexion of her maid–pale peace 3.03. 98
it discolors the complexion of my greatness to 2H4 2.02. 5 P
those papers that you lose | so much complexion? H5 2.02. 73
do with his smirch'd complexion all fell feats 3.03. 17
she prais'd his complexion above paris. TRO 1.02. 98 P
him above, his complexion is higher than his. 1.02.102 P
is too flaming a praise for a good complexion. 1.02.104 P
and the complexion of the element | /in favor's JC 1.03.128
by their o'ergrowth of some complexion | oft HAM 1.04. 27
hath now this dread and black complexion smear'd 2.02.455
it is very /sultry and hot /for my complexion. 5.02. 99 P
proposed matches | of her own clime, complexion, OTH 3.03.230
turn thy complexion there, | patience, thou 4.02. 62
reserve | that excellent complexion, which did PER 4.01. 40
her, the color of her hair, complexion, height, 4.02. 58 P
love, this only | from this hour is complexion. TNK 4.02. 43
his complexion | nearer a brown than black; 4.02. 78
his complexion | is, as a ripe grape, ruddy. 4.02. 95
though of a man's complexion, | for men will VEN 215
and often is his gold complexion dimm'd, | and SON 18. 6
which on thy soft cheek for complexion dwells 99. 4
and all they foul that thy complexion lack. 132.14
COMPLEXIONS 7 FR 0.0008 REL FR 4 V 3 P
frail, | for we are soft as our complexions are, MM 2.04.129
is that one of the four complexions? LLL 1.02. 83 P
of all complexions the cull'd sovereignty | do 4.03.230
that pleas'd me, complexions that lik'd me, and AYL ep 19 P
your chang'd complexions are to me a mirror WT 1.02.381
and ridges hors'd | with variable complexions, COR 2.01.212
shall have the difference of all complexions. PER 4.02. 80 P
COMPLICES *(also accomplices)*
COMPLICES 5 FR 0.0005 REL FR 5 V 0 P
is held | by bushy, bagot, and their complices, R2 2.03.165
to fight with glendower and his complices. 3.01. 43
the lives of all your loving complices | /lean 2H4 1.01.163
to quell the rebels and their complices. 2H6 5.01.212
of thee thyself and all thy complices, | edward 3H6 4.03. 44
COMPLIMENT 11 FR 0.0012 REL FR 7 V 4 P
is melted into cur'sies, valor into compliment, ADO 4.01.319 P
stay not thy compliment; LLL 4.02.142 P
but that they call compliment is like th' AYL 2.05. 26 P
since lowly feigning was call'd compliment. TN 3.01. 99
even now i met him | with customary compliment, WT 1.02.371
would, | saving in dialogue of compliment, | and JN 1.01.201
come, come; sans compliment, what news abroad? 5.06. 16
what i have spoke, but farewell compliment! ROM 2.02. 89
there is further compliment of leave–taking LR 1.01.302 P
the time will not allow the compliment | which 5.03.234
it were, to stand | on more mechanic compliment. ANT 4.04. 32
COMPLIMENTAL 1 FR 0.0001 REL FR 0 V 1 P
i will make a complimental assault upon him, for TRO 3.01. 39 P
COMPLIMENTS 1 FR 0.0001 REL FR 0 V 1 P
o, he's the courageous captain of compliments. ROM 2.04. 20 P
COMPLOT 4 FR 0.0004 REL FR 4 V 0 P
contrive, or complot any ill | 'gainst us, our R2 1.03.189
i know their complot is to have my life; 2H6 3.01.147
writ, | the complot of this timeless tragedy, TIT 2.03.265
now goes | to lay a complot to betray thy foes. 5.02.147
COMPLOTS 3 FR 0.0003 REL FR 3 V 0 P
lord hastings will not yield to our complots? R3 3.01.192
we may digest our complots in some form. 3.01.200
complots of mischief, treason, villainies, TIT 5.01. 65
COMPLOTTED 1 FR 0.0001 REL FR 1 V 0 P
years, | complotted and contrived in this land, R2 1.01. 96
/COMPLY 1 FR 0.0001 REL FR 0 V 1 P
'a did /comply, sir, with his dug before 'a HAM 5.02.187 P
COMPLY 2 FR 0.0002 REL FR 1 V 1 P
let me comply with you in this garb, /lest /my HAM 2.02.372 P
nor to comply with heat (the young affects | in OTH 1.03.263
/COMPOS'D 1 FR 0.0001 REL FR 1 V 0 P
/loving /well /compos'd /with /gift /of /nature, TRO 4.04. 77
COMPOS'D 9 FR 0.0010 REL FR 8 V 1 P
and he's compos'd of harshness. TMP 3.01. 9
he is compos'd and fram'd of treachery, | and ADO 5.01.249
one that compos'd your beauties; MND 1.01. 48
than in haste, | hath well compos'd thee. AWW 1.02. 21
sorts, and songs compos'd | to her unworthiness. 3.07. 40
imitate that which i compos'd to my courser, for H5 3.07. 43 P
were it a casque compos'd by vulcan's skill, TRO 5.02.170
words of so sweet breath compos'd | as made HAM 3.01. 97

there were no woman | worth so compos'd a man! TNK 5.03. 86
COMPOSE 2 FR 0.0002 REL FR 2 V 0 P
for thy undaunted mettle should compose MAC 1.07. 73
if we compose well here, to parthia. ANT 2.02. 15
COMPOSED 2 FR 0.0002 REL FR 2 V 0 P
whose composed rhymes | should be full–fraught TGV 3.02. 69
say | to this composed wonder of your frame, SON 59.10
COMPOSES 1 FR 0.0001 REL FR 1 V 0 P
and with her neele composes | nature's own shape PER 5.ch. 5
COMPOSITION 16 FR 0.0018 REL FR 11 V 5 P
dukes come not to composition with the king of MM 1.02. 2 P
proportions | came short of composition, but in 5.01.220
but the composition that your valor and fear AWW 1.01.203 P
thinks himself made in the unchaste composition. 4.03. 18 P
my son | in the large composition of this man? JN 1.01. 88
mad world, mad kings, mad composition! 2.01.561
o, how that name befits my composition! R2 2.01. 73
studied as to remember so weak a composition. 2H4 2.02. 8 P
mistake | the outward composition of his body. 1H6 2.03. 75
it was which caus'd | our swifter composition. COR 3.01. 3
sweno, the norways' king, craves composition; MAC 1.02. 59
take | more composition and fierce quality LR 1.02. 12
and art nothing but the composition of a knave, 2.02. 21 P
there's no composition in /these news | that OTH 1.03. 1
i crave our composition may be written | and ANT 2.06. 58
until live's composition be recured | by those SON 45. 9
COMPOST 1 FR 0.0001 REL FR 1 V 0 P
and do not spread the compost on the weeds | to HAM 3.04.151
COMPOSTURE 1 FR 0.0001 REL FR 1 V 0 P
that feeds and breeds by a composture stol'n TIM 4.03.441
COMPOSURE 3 FR 0.0003 REL FR 2 V 1 P
but it was a strong composure a fool could TRO 2.03. 99 P
the heavens, lord, thou art of sweet composure. 2.03.240
(as his composure must be rare indeed | whom ANT 1.04. 22
COMPOUND 19 FR 0.0021 REL FR 13 V 6 P
was the rankest compound of villainous smell WIV 3.05. 92 P
think it meet, compound with him by the year, MM 4.02. 24 P
grumio, rise, we will compound this quarrel. SHR 1.02. 27
you, gentlemen, i will compound this strife. 2.01.341
till you compound whose right is worthiest, | we JN 2.01.281
if thou didst, then behold that compound. 1H4 2.04.123 P
thou whoreson mad compound of majesty, by this 2H4 2.04.294 P
only compound me with forgotten dust; 4.05.115
as manhood shall compound. push home. H5 2.01. 98
if for thy ransom thou wilt now compound, 4.03. 80
i must perforce compound | with /mistful eyes, 4.06. 33
saint denis and saint george, compound a boy, 5.02.207 P
i pray, my lords, let me compound this strife. 2H6 2.01. 56
i find the ass in compound with the major part COR 2.01. 58 P
glow | o'er this solidity and compound mass, HAM 3.04. 49
danger, did compound for her | a certain stuff, CYM 5.05.254
sometime is compacted | in a pure compound; LUC 531
for compound sweet forgoing simple savor, SON 125. 7
as compound love to physic your cold breast. LC 259
/COMPOUNDED 1 FR 0.0001 REL FR 1 V 0 P
/compounded it with dust, whereto 'tis kin. HAM 4.02. 6
COMPOUNDED 10 FR 0.0011 REL FR 7 V 3 P
of mine own, compounded of many simples, AYL 4.01. 16 P
i would to god all strifes were well compounded. R3 2.01. 75
ones could have weigh'd | such a compounded one? H8 1.01. 12
a' th' senate, what | we have compounded on. COR 5.06. 83
to some she–beggar and compounded thee | poor TIM 4.03.273
my father compounded with my mother under the LR 1.02.128 P
the best she hath, and she, of all compounded, CYM 3.05. 73
of some other compounded odors which are TNK 4.03. 84 P
neither, | simple were so well compounded: PHT 44
when i (perhaps) compounded am with clay, | do SON 71.10
COMPOUNDS 6 FR 0.0006 REL FR 6 V 0 P
than these poor compounds that thou mayest not ROM 5.01. 82
to have his pomp, and all what state compounds, TIM 4.02. 35
commanded of me these most poisonous compounds, CYM 1.05. 8
of these thy compounds on such creatures as | we 1.05. 19
to new–found methods and to compounds strange? SON 76. 4
keen, | with eager compounds we our palate urge, 118. 2
COMPREHEND 4 FR 0.0004 REL FR 3 V 1 P
you shall comprehend all vagrom men; ADO 3.03. 25 P
those pleasures live that art would comprehend. LLL 4.02.110
conceit | can comprehend in still imagination! LUC 702
those pleasures live that art can comprehend. PP 5. 6
COMPREHENDED 1 FR 0.0001 REL FR 0 V 1 P
have indeed comprehended two aspicious persons, ADO 3.05. 46 P
COMPREHENDS 3 FR 0.0003 REL FR 3 V 0 P
more than cool reason ever comprehends. MND 5.01. 6
joy, | it comprehends some bringer of that joy; 5.01. 20
all this beforehand counsel comprehends. LUC 494
COMPREMIS'D 1 FR 0.0001 REL FR 1 V 0 P
when laban and himself were compremis'd | that MV 1.03. 78
COMPREMISE *(also compromise)*
COMPREMISE 2 FR 0.0002 REL FR 2 V 0 P
send fair–play orders and make compremise, JN 5.01. 67
and, now the matter grows to compremise, 1H6 5.04.149
COMPREMISES 1 FR 0.0001 REL FR 0 V 1 P
to make atonements and compremises between you. WIV 1.01. 33 P
COMPRIS'D 1 FR 0.0001 REL FR 1 V 0 P
compris'd | within the fore–rank of our articles H5 5.02. 96
COMPRISING 1 FR 0.0001 REL FR 1 V 0 P
comprising all that may be sworn or said, | his R2 3.03.111
COMPROMISE *(also compremise, etc.)*
COMPROMISE 1 FR 0.0001 REL FR 1 V 0 P
but basely yielded upon compromise | that which R2 2.01.253
COMPT *(also count*)*
COMPT 3 FR 0.0003 REL FR 3 V 0 P
strikes some scores away | from the great compt; AWW 5.03. 57
themselves, and what is theirs, in compt, | to MAC 1.06. 26
when we shall meet at compt, | this look of OTH 5.02.273
COMPTERS *(also counters)*
COMPTERS 2 FR 0.0002 REL FR 1 V 1 P
i cannot do't without compters. WT 4.03. 36 P
will you with compters sum | the past–proportion TRO 2.02. 28
COMPTIBLE 1 FR 0.0001 REL FR 0 V 1 P
i am very comptible, even to the least sinister TN 1.05.175 P
COMPTLESS *(also countless)*
COMPTLESS 1 FR 0.0001 REL FR 1 V 0 P
one sweet kiss shall pay this comptless debt. VEN 84
COMPTROLLERS *(also controller)*
COMPTROLLERS 1 FR 0.0001 REL FR 1 V 0 P
henry guilford | this night to be comptrollers. H8 1.03. 67
COMPULSATORY 1 FR 0.0001 REL FR 1 V 0 P
by strong hand | and terms compulsatory, those HAM 1.01.103
COMPULSION 10 FR 0.0011 REL FR 4 V 6 P
on what compulsion must i? tell me that. MV 4.01.183
life and in the highest compulsion of base fear, AWW 3.06. 29 P
by the compulsion of their ordinance | by this JN 2.01.218
fought | between compulsion and a brave respect! 5.02. 44
what, upon compulsion? 1H4 2.04.236 P
the world, i would not tell you on compulsion. 2.04.238 P
give you a reason on compulsion? 2.04.238 P
i would give no man a reason upon compulsion, i. 2.04.240 P
her possession up | on terms of base compulsion! TRO 2.02.153
necessity, fools by heavenly compulsion, knaves, LR 1.02.122 P
COMPULSIVE 2 FR 0.0002 REL FR 2 V 0 P
when the compulsive ardure gives the charge, HAM 3.04. 86
whose icy current and compulsive course | nev'r OTH 3.03.454
COMPUNCTIOUS 1 FR 0.0001 REL FR 1 V 0 P
that no compunctious visitings of nature | shake MAC 1.05. 45
COMPUTATION 2 FR 0.0002 REL FR 2 V 0 P
by computation and mine host's report, | i could ERR 2.02. 4
france, | and, by true computation of the time, R3 3.05. 89
COMRADE 1 FR 0.0001 REL FR 1 V 0 P
air, | to be a comrade with the wolf and owl — LR 2.04.210
COMRADES 1 FR 0.0001 REL FR 1 V 0 P
and his comrades, that daff'd the world aside 1H4 4.01. 96
/COM'ST 1 FR 0.0001 REL FR 1 V 0 P
against whom /com'st thou? R2 1.03. 33
COM'ST 26 FR 0.0029 REL FR 23 V 3 P
ho, ho, ho! coward, why com'st thou not? MND 3.02.421
"thou com'st to the lady olivia, and in my sight TN 3.04.155 P
against what man thou com'st, and what thy R2 1.03. 13
and wherefore com'st thou hither | before king 1.03. 31
lie that way thou goest, not whence thou com'st. 1.03.287
com'st thou because the anointed king is hence? 2.03. 96
com'st thou again for ransom? H5 4.07. 70
com'st thou with deep premeditated lines, | with 1H6 3.01. 1
curse, miscreant, when thou com'st to the stake. 5.03. 44
that, when thou com'st to kneel at henry's feet, 5.03.194
why com'st thou in such haste? 2H6 4.04. 26
why com'st thou in such post? 3H6 1.02. 48
or bad news, that thou com'st in so bluntly? R3 4.03. 45
when thou com'st thither — dull unmindful 4.04.445
whence com'st thou? COR 4.05. 53
thou com'st not to be made a scorn in rome; TIT 1.01.265
know'st well enough (although thou com'st to me) TIM 3.01. 41 P
why com'st thou? JC 4.03.282
thou never com'st unto a happy birth, | but 5.03. 70
thou com'st to use thy tongue; MAC 5.05. 28
thou com'st in such a questionable shape | that HAM 1.04. 43
com'st thou to beard me in denmark? 2.02.423 P
thou out of heaven's benediction com'st | to the LR 2.02.161
com'st thou smiling from | the world's great ANT 4.08. 17
thou com'st not, caius, now for tribute; CYM 5.05. 69
and when thou com'st thy tale to tell, | smooth PP 18. 7
COMUTUAL 1 FR 0.0001 REL FR 1 V 0 P
our hands | unite comutual in most sacred bands. HAM 3.02.160
CON* 7 FR 0.0008 REL FR 2 V 5 P
and desire you, to con them by to–morrow night; MND 1.02.100 P
con tutto /il core, ben trovato, may i say. SHR 1.02. 24
but i con him no thanks for't, in the nature he AWW 4.03.152 P
well penn'd, i have taken great pains to con it. TN 1.05.174 P
and this they con perfitly in the phrase of war, H5 3.06. 75 P
thy horse will sooner con an oration without TRO 2.01. 17 P
yet thanks i must you con | that you are thieves TIM 4.03.425
CONCAVE 3 FR 0.0003 REL FR 2 V 1 P
i do think him as concave as a cover'd goblet or AYL 3.04. 24 P
of your sounds | made in her concave shores? JC 1.01. 47
from off a hill whose concave womb reworded | a LC 1
CONCAVITIES 1 FR 0.0001 REL FR 0 V 1 P
the concavities of it is not sufficient. H5 3.02. 59 P
CONCEAL 15 FR 0.0017 REL FR 11 V 4 P
the law of friendship bids me to conceal, | but TGV 3.01. 5
i may not conceal them, sir. WIV 4.05. 44 P
conceal them, or thou diest. 4.05. 45 P
and if it sort not well, you may conceal her, ADO 4.01.240
(a time that lovers' flights doth still conceal) MND 1.01.212
conceal me what i am, and be my aid | for such TN 1.02. 53
he shall conceal it | whiles you are willing it 4.03. 28
i hold it the more knavery to conceal it; WT 4.04.682 P
woman, | wilt thou conceal this dark conspiracy? R2 5.02. 96
two ways, either to utter them, or conceal them. 2H4 5.03.111 P
till then, 'tis wisdom to conceal our meaning. 3H6 4.07. 60
intend | as closely to conceal what we impart. R3 3.01.159
'twill require | a strong faith to conceal it. H8 2.01.145
to utter that | which torments me to conceal. CYM 5.05.142
it, | or can conceal his hunger till he famish? PER 1.04. 12
CONCEAL'D 6 FR 0.0006 REL FR 3 V 3 P
to hear /them speak, where i may be conceal'd. MM 3.01. 53 P
mightst pour this conceal'd man out of thy mouth AYL 3.02.199 P
good, very good, let it be conceal'd awhile. AWW 2.03.266 P
says | my conceal'd lady to our cancell'd love? ROM 3.03. 98
if you have hitherto conceal'd this sight, | let HAM 1.02.246
i can set down a story | of faults conceal'd, SON 88. 7
CONCEALED 4 FR 0.0004 REL FR 4 V 0 P
to dive like buckets in concealed wells, | to JN 5.02.139
sorrow concealed, like an oven stopp'd, | doth TIT 2.04. 36
so of concealed sorrow may be said, | free vent VEN 333
the naked and concealed fiend he cover'd, | that LC 317
CONCEALING 4 FR 0.0004 REL FR 4 V 0 P
than, by concealing it, heap on your head | a TGV 3.01. 19
or else my heart concealing it will break, | and SHR 4.03. 78
rive your concealing continents, and cry | these LR 3.02. 58
shame folded up in blind concealing night, LUC 675
/CONCEALMENT 1 FR 0.0001 REL FR 1 V 0 P
/will /in /concealment /wrap /me /up /awhile; LR 4.03. 52
CONCEALMENT 3 FR 0.0003 REL FR 3 V 0 P
but let concealment, like a worm i' th' bud, TN 2.04.111
imprison't not | in ignorant concealment. WT 1.02.397
'twere a concealment | worse than a theft, no COR 1.09. 21
CONCEALMENTS 2 FR 0.0002 REL FR 2 V 0 P
and profited | in strange concealments, valiant 1H4 3.01.165
nor names concealments in | the boldest language TNK 5.01.123
CONCEALS 1 FR 0.0001 REL FR 1 V 0 P
he that conceals him, death. LR 2.01. 63
CONCEIT 48 FR 0.0054 REL FR 42 V 6 P
proteus, the good conceit i hold of thee | (for TGV 3.02. 17
lay open to my earthy, gross conceit, ERR 3.02. 34
come, sister, i am press'd down with conceit — 4.02. 65
conceit — | conceit, my comfort and my injury. 4.02. 66
be sworn, if he be so, his conceit is false. ADO 2.01.297 P
a good lustre of conceit in a turf of earth; LLL 4.02. 88 P
cut me to pieces with thy keen conceit; 5.02.399
opinion | of wisdom, gravity, profound conceit, MV 1.01. 92
you have a noble and a true conceit | of godlike 3.04. 2
thy conceit is nearer death than thy powers. AYL 2.06. 8 P
that i know you are a gentleman of good conceit. 5.02. 54 P
why, sir, what's your conceit in that? SHR 4.03.160
sir, the conceit is deeper than you think for: 4.03.161
for thy conceit is soaking, will draw in | more WT 1.02.224
son, with mere conceit and fear | of the queen's 3.02.144
reply | without a tongue, using conceit alone, JN 3.03. 50
'tis nothing but conceit, my gracious lady. R2 2.02. 33
conceit is still deriv'd | from some forefather 2.02. 34
infusing him with self and vain conceit, | as if 3.02.166
there's no more conceit in him than is in a 2H4 2.04.241 P
for though he seem with forged quaint conceit 1H6 4.01.102
lines, | able to ravish any dull conceit; 5.05. 15
there's some conceit or other likes him well, R3 3.04. 49
i shall not fail t' approve the fair conceit H8 2.03. 74
player, whose conceit | lies in his hamstring, TRO 1.03.153
afoot, | she would applaud andronicus' conceit, TIT 4.02. 30
conceit, more rich in matter than in words, ROM 2.06. 30
like | the horrible conceit of death and night, 4.03. 37
when thy first griefs were but a mere conceit, TIM 5.04. 14
yet rich conceit | taught thee to make vast 5.04. 77
that one of two bad ways you must conceit me, JC 3.01.192
could force his soul so to his own conceit HAM 2.02.553
function suiting | with forms to his conceit? 2.02.557
conceit in weakest bodies strongest works, 3.04.114
conceit upon her father. 4.05. 45
delicate carriages, and of very liberal conceit. 5.02.153 P
and yet i know not how conceit may rob | the LR 4.06. 42
shut up in thy brain | some horrible conceit. OTH 3.03.115
who, if it had conceit, would die, as i | am PER 3.01. 16
o, deeper sin than bottomless conceit | can LUC 701
conceit and grief an eager combat fight, | what 1298
conceit deceitful, so compact, so kind, | that 1423
but whether unripe years did want conceit, | or PP 4. 9
spenser to me, whose deep conceit is such | as, 8. 7
deep conceit is such | as, passing all conceit, 8. 8
then the conceit of this inconstant stay | sets SON 15. 9
but that i hope some good conceit of thine | in 26. 7
finding the first conceit of love there bred, 108.13
CONCEITED 8 FR 0.0009 REL FR 3 V 5 P
is not the humor conceited? WIV 1.03. 23 P
he is as horribly conceited of him; TN 3.04.294 P
thou talkest of an admirable conceited fellow. WT 4.04.202 P
well conceited, davy. about thy business, davy. 2H4 5.01. 36 P
need of him, | you have right well conceited. JC 1.03.162
first, a very excellent good conceited thing; CYM 2.03. 17 P
which the conceited painter drew so proud, | as LUC 1371
eyne, | which on it had conceited characters, LC 16
CONCEITLESS 1 FR 0.0001 REL FR 1 V 0 P
think'st thou i am so shallow, so conceitless, TGV 4.02. 96
CONCEIT'S 1 FR 0.0001 REL FR 1 V 0 P
which his fair tongue, conceit's expositor, LLL 2.01. 72
CONCEITS 4 FR 0.0004 REL FR 3 V 1 P
their conceits have wings | fleeter than arrows, LLL 5.02.260
bracelets of thy hair, rings, gawds, conceits, MND 1.01. 33
let it be as humors and conceits shall govern. MV 3.05. 63 P
dangerous conceits are in their natures poisons, OTH 3.03.326
CONCEIV'D 11 FR 0.0012 REL FR 8 V 3 P
either now, or by remissness new conceiv'd, MM 2.02. 96
that a woman conceiv'd me, i thank her; ADO 1.01.238 P
that was begot of thought, conceiv'd of spleen, AYL 4.01.212 P
it shall become to serve all hopes conceiv'd, SHR 1.01. 15
displeasure he hath conceiv'd against your son, AWW 4.05. 75 P
parts | we had conceiv'd against him. TN 5.01.362
if it conceiv'd a male–child by me, should | do H8 2.04.190
'tis conceiv'd to scope. TIM 1.01. 72
o error, soon conceiv'd, | thou never com'st JC 5.03. 69
by mine own | i may be reasonably conceiv'd; TNK 1.02. 48
gently they swell, like women new conceiv'd, 4.02.128
CONCEIVE 27 FR 0.0030 REL FR 18 V 9 P
well! i conceive. TMP 4.01. 50
nay, conceive me, conceive me, sweet coz; WIV 1.01.242 P
nay, conceive me, conceive me, sweet coz; 1.01.242 P
plainly conceive, i love you. MM 2.04.141
"fair" in "all hail" is foul, as i conceive. LLL 5.02.340
when we have laugh'd to see the sails conceive MND 2.01.128
is not able to taste, his tongue to conceive, 4.01.213 P
and would conceive for what i gave the ring, MV 5.01.195
more suits you to conceive than i to speak of. AYL 1.02.267
sir, you say well, and well you do conceive, SHR 1.02.269
thus i conceive by him. 5.02. 22
and as he does conceive | he is dishonor'd by a WT 1.02.454
that could conceive a gross and foolish sire 3.02.197
and make conceive a bark of baser kind | by bud 4.04. 94
says he, that takes upon him not to conceive. 2H4 2.02.115 P
ay, such a pleasure as incaged birds | conceive, 3H6 4.06. 13
the grieved commons | hardly conceive of me; H8 1.02.105
the slip, sir, the slip, can you not conceive? ROM 2.04. 48 P
hope his honor will conceive the fairest of me, TIM 3.02. 53 P
i do conceive. 3.06. 64 P
nor heart | cannot conceive nor name thee! MAC 2.03. 65
but as your daughter may conceive, friend, look HAM 2.02.185 P
i cannot conceive you. LR 1.01. 12 P
conceive, and fare thee well. 4.02. 24
alas, what does this gentleman conceive? OTH 4.02. 95
as i conceive the journey, be at /the mount ANT 2.04. 6
she's my good lady, and will conceive, i hope, CYM 2.03.153
CONCEIVES 4 FR 0.0004 REL FR 4 V 0 P
conceives by me! how likes hortensio that? SHR 5.02. 23
my widow says, thus she conceives her tale. 5.02. 24
conceives by idleness, and nothing teems | but H5 5.02. 51
i see one eye of yours conceives a tear, | the TNK 5.03.137
CONCEIVING 4 FR 0.0004 REL FR 4 V 0 P

who then conceiving did in eaning time | fall MV 1.03. 87
conceiving the dishonor of his mother! WT 2.03. 13
print your royal father off, | conceiving you. 5.01.126
speech and shows much more | his own conceiving. CYM 3.03. 98
CONCEPTION 10 FR 0.0011 REL FR 8 V 2 P
the strong and swelling evil | of my conception. MM 2.04. 7
note | this dangerous conception in this point, H8 1.02.139
i have a young conception in my brain, | be you TRO 1.03.312
joy had the like conception in our eyes, | and TIM 1.02.110
conception is a blessing, but as your daughter HAM 2.02.184 P
thou but rememb'rest me of mine own conception. LR 1.04. 67 P
think, | and no conception nor no jealious toy OTH 3.04.156
cannot remove nor choke the strong conception 5.02. 55
at whose conception, till lucina reigned, PER 1.01. 8
that have their first conception by misdread, 1.02. 12
CONCEPTIONS 1 FR 0.0001 REL FR 1 V 0 P
difference, | conceptions only proper to myself, JC 1.02. 41
CONCEPTIOUS 1 FR 0.0001 REL FR 1 V 0 P
ensear thy fertile and conceptious womb, | let TIM 4.03.187
CONCERN 12 FR 0.0013 REL FR 11 V 1 P
of all that may concern thy love–affairs. TGV 3.01.256
it may concern much. LLL 4.02.142 P
made bold, | nor how it may concern my modesty, MND 1.01. 60
it did concern | your highness with herself. AWW 5.03.137
your knowledge, nor | concern me the reporting. WT 4.04.504
in peace, | what doth concern your coming. 2H4 4.01. 30
me they concern, regent i am of france. 1H6 1.01. 84
vouchsafe me a word, it does concern you near. TIM 1.02.177
what concern they? MAC 4.03.195
which are not so — | or being, concern you not. ANT 2.02. 30
for the things he speaks | may concern caesar. 4.09. 25
their lives concern us | much more than thebes TNK 1.04. 32
CONCERNANCY 1 FR 0.0001 REL FR 0 V 1 P
the concernancy, sir? HAM 5.02.122 P
CONCERN'D 1 FR 0.0001 REL FR 1 V 0 P
when to sound your name | it not concern'd me. ANT 2.02. 35
CONCERNETH 1 FR 0.0001 REL FR 1 V 0 P
love concerneth us to add | her father's liking, SHR 3.02.128
CONCERNING 13 FR 0.0014 REL FR 8 V 5 P
nothing concerning me. TGV 1.02. 72
the question is concerning your marriage. WIV 1.01.221 P
between you 'greed concerning her observance? MM 4.01. 41
matter is to me, sir, as concerning jaquenetta: LLL 1.01.201 P
as concerning some entertainment of time, some 5.01.118 P
the opinion of pythagoras concerning wild–fowl? TN 4.02. 50 P
task our thoughts, concerning us and france. H5 1.02. 6
partly touching or concerning the disciplines of 3.02. 96 P
the londoners | concerning the french journey. H8 1.02.155
concerning his imprisonment was rather | (if 5.02.185
conception nor no jealious toy | concerning you. OTH 3.04.157
concerning this, sir — o well–painted passion! 4.01.257
said of me | concerning the escape of palamon? TNK 4.01. 2
CONCERNINGS 2 FR 0.0002 REL FR 2 V 0 P
as time and our concernings shall importune, MM 1.01. 56
from a bat, a gib, | such dear concernings hide? HAM 3.04.191
CONCERNS *(also 'cerns)*
CONCERNS 23 FR 0.0026 REL FR 19 V 4 P
then let it lie for those that it concerns. TGV 1.02. 73
it will not lie where it concerns | unless it 1.02. 74
and it concerns me | to look into the bottom of MM 1.01. 77
whom it concerns to hear this matter forth, | do 5.01.255
hear, for what i would speak of concerns him. ADO 3.02. 86 P
of something nearly that concerns yourselves. MND 1.01.126
happen, it concerns you something to know it. AWW 1.03.120 P
it alone concerns your ear. TN 1.05.208 P
which to deny concerns more than avails; WT 3.02. 86
they have to the king concerns him nothing, let 4.04.838 P
and more than carefully it us concerns | to H5 2.04. 2
why, what concerns his freedom unto me? 1H6 5.03.116
about that which concerns your grace and us: 3H6 1.02. 8
the chief cause concerns his grace of canterbury H8 5.02. 38
the cause were known to them it most concerns, TIT 2.01. 50
it highly us concerns | by day and night t' 4.03. 27
that, as it more concerns the turk than rhodes, OTH 1.03. 22
to leave that latest which concerns him first, 1.03. 28
when it concerns the fool or coward. ANT 1.02. 96
to know | something of me, or what concerns me: CYM 1.06. 94
and yet of moment too, for it concerns: 1.06.182
till thou art worthy, arcite, it concerns me, TNK 2.02.201
it concerns your credit | and my oath equally. 3.06.223
CONCERT *(see consort*)*
CONCLAVE 1 FR 0.0001 REL FR 1 V 0 P
and thank the holy conclave for their loves; H8 2.02. 99
CONCLUDE 29 FR 0.0032 REL FR 21 V 8 P
you conclude that my master is a shepherd then, TGV 1.01. 76 P
why, thou didst conclude hairy men plain dealers ERR 2.02. 86 P
to conclude, this drudge or diviner laid claim 3.02.139 P
conclude, conclude, he is in love. ADO 3.02. 62 P
conclude, conclude, he is in love. 3.02. 62 P
and, to conclude, they are lying knaves. 5.01.219 P
and, to conclude, what you lay to their charge. 5.01.222 P
and thrum, | quail, crush, conclude, and quell! MND 5.01.287
and to conclude, we have 'greed so well together SHR 2.01.297
forget, forgive, conclude and be agreed, | our R2 1.01.156
whither i must, i must, and, to conclude, | this 1H4 2.03.105
to conclude, i am so good a proficient in one 2.04. 17 P
till you conclude that he upon whose side | the 1H6 2.04. 40
shall we at last conclude effeminate peace? 5.04.107
if we conclude a peace, | it shall be with such 5.04.113
and here conclude with me | that margaret shall 5.05. 77
you can, | or else conclude my words effectual. 2H6 3.01. 41
will not conclude their plotted tragedy. 3.01.153
and to conclude, reproach and beggary | is crept 4.01.101
but, to conclude with truth, | their weapons 3H6 2.01.128
and to conclude, the shepherd's homely curds, 2.05. 47
then you conclude, my grandam, he is dead. R3 2.02. 12
us not values | the cost that did conclude it. H8 1.01. 89
commission | to gregory de cassado, to conclude, 3.02.321
then conclude | minds sway'd by eyes are full of TRO 5.02.111
cannot conclude but by the yea and no | of COR 3.01.145
and, to conclude, | the victory fell on us. MAC 1.02. 57
and in that point | i will conclude to hate her, CYM 3.05. 78
they did conclude to bear dead lucrece thence, LUC 1850
CONCLUDED 16 FR 0.0018 REL FR 14 V 2 P
virtues, yet at last she concluded with a sigh, ADO 5.01.171 P
the congregated college have concluded | that AWW 2.01.117
nay, i assure you a peace concluded. 4.03. 40 P
be it concluded, | no barricado for a belly. WT 1.02.203
to have a godly peace concluded of | between the 1H6 5.01. 5
for eighteen months concluded by consent. 2H6 1.01. 42
suffolk concluded on the articles, | the peers 1.01.217
is it concluded he shall be protector? R3 1.03. 14
it is determin'd, not concluded yet; 1.03. 15
which by my presence might have been concluded. 3.04. 25
is it so concluded? TRO 4.02. 66
the senate have concluded | to give this day a JC 2.02. 93
it is concluded: MAC 3.01.140
alack, | i had forgot. 'tis so concluded on. HAM 3.04.201
life and wits at once | had not concluded all. LR 4.07. 41
to the world, concluded | most cruel to herself. CYM 5.05. 32
CONCLUDES 8 FR 0.0009 REL FR 6 V 2 P
certes the text most infallibly concludes it. LLL 4.02.163 P
the sheep: the other two concludes it — o,u. 5.01. 56 P
this concludes: JN 1.01.127
and concludes in hearty prayers | that your 2H4 4.01. 14
wicked and vile, and so her death concludes. 1H6 5.04. 16
his fault concludes but what the law should end, ROM 3.01.185
her heavy anthem still concludes in woe, | and VEN 839
that she concludes the picture was belied. LUC 1533
CONCLUDING 1 FR 0.0001 REL FR 1 V 0 P
to a bootless inquisition, | concluding, "stay: TMP 1.02. 36
CONCLUD'ST 1 FR 0.0001 REL FR 0 V 1 P
thou conclud'st like the sanctimonious pirate, MM 1.02. 7 P
/CONCLUSION 1 FR 0.0001 REL FR 1 V 0 P
with epithites of war, | /and, /in /conclusion, OTH 1.01. 15
CONCLUSION 29 FR 0.0032 REL FR 18 V 11 P
in conclusion, i stand affected to her. TGV 2.01. 84 P
the conclusion is then, that it will. 2.05. 38 P
and the conclusion shall be crown'd with your WIV 3.05.135 P
the vild conclusion | i now begin with grief and MM 5.01. 95
for, in conclusion, he did beat me there. ERR 2.01. 74
i knew 'twould be a bald conclusion. 2.02.108 P
and the conclusion is, she shall be thine. ADO 1.01.327
man is a giddy thing, and this is my conclusion. 5.04.109 P
the conclusion is victory; LLL 4.01. 74 P
beauteous as ink — a good conclusion. 5.02. 41
and in conclusion dumbly have broke off, | not MND 5.01. 98
'tis i must make conclusion | of these most AYL 5.04.126
and, in conclusion, she shall watch all night, SHR 4.01.205
a false conclusion. TN 2.03. 6 P
but in conclusion put strange speech upon me. 5.01. 67
of this make no conclusion, lest you say | your WT 1.02. 81
po, | it draws toward supper in conclusion so. JN 1.01.204
and in conclusion drove us to seek out | this 1H4 4.03.102
and tell him, for conclusion, he hath betray'd H5 3.06.134 P
and in conclusion wins the king from her | with 3H6 3.01. 50
a virtuous and a christian–like conclusion — R3 1.03.315
in conclusion, equivocates him in a sleep, and, MAC 2.03. 35 P
and in conclusion to oppose the bolt | against LR 2.04.176
o most lame and impotent conclusion! OTH 2.01.161 P
and main exercise, th' incorporate conclusion. 2.01.263 P
but this denoted a foregone conclusion. 3.03.428
with her modest eyes | and still conclusion, ANT 4.15. 28
scorning advice, read the conclusion then; PER 1.01. 56
that mother tries a merciless conclusion | who, LUC 1160
CONCLUSIONS 7 FR 0.0008 REL FR 3 V 4 P
and so conclusions pass'd the careers. WIV 1.01.179 P
so that, conclusions to be as kisses, if your TN 5.01. 20 P
she will plod — there must be conclusions — H5 2.01. 24 P
ape, | to try conclusions in the basket creep, HAM 3.04.195
conduct us to most prepost'rous conclusions. OTH 1.03.329 P
tells me | she hath pursu'd conclusions infinite ANT 5.02.355
did amplify my judgment in | other conclusions? CYM 1.05. 18
CONCOLINEL 1 FR 0.0001 REL FR 0 V 1 P
"concolinel." LLL 3.01. 3 P
CONCORD 9 FR 0.0010 REL FR 9 V 0 P
and mar the concord with too harsh a descant: TGV 1.02. 91
how comes this gentle concord in the world, MND 4.01.143
how shall we find the concord of this discord? 5.01. 60
nor is not moved with concord of sweet sounds, MV 5.01. 84
his jarring, concord, and his discord, dulcet; AWW 1.01.172
but for the concord of my state and time | had R2 5.05. 47
pour the sweet milk of concord into hell, MAC 4.03. 98
if the true concord of well–tuned sounds, | by SON 8. 5
the wiry concord that mine ear confounds, | do i 128. 4
CONCORDANT 1 FR 0.0001 REL FR 1 V 0 P
"how true a twain | seemeth this concordant one! PHT 46
CONCUBINE 1 FR 0.0001 REL FR 1 V 0 P
queen, | and yet too good to be your concubine. 3H6 3.02. 98
CONCUPISCIBLE 1 FR 0.0001 REL FR 1 V 0 P
body | to his concupiscible intemperate lust, MM 5.01. 98
CONCUPY 1 FR 0.0001 REL FR 0 V 1 P
he'll tickle it for his concupy. TRO 5.02.177 P
CONCUR 1 FR 0.0001 REL FR 1 V 0 P
and your bounties shall | concur together, TRO 4.05.274
CONCURRING 1 FR 0.0001 REL FR 1 V 0 P
indeed, | concurring both in name and quality. 2H4 4.01. 87
CONCURS 1 FR 0.0001 REL FR 0 V 1 P
this concurs directly with the letter: TN 3.04. 65 P
CONDEMN 18 FR 0.0020 REL FR 16 V 2 P
did lie, | though fools at home condemn 'em. TMP 3.03. 27
condemn the fault, and not the actor of it? MM 2.02. 37
it is the law, not i, condemn your brother. 2.02. 80
we do condemn thee to the very block | where 5.01.414
well, we cannot greatly condemn our success. AWW 3.06. 55 P
i could condemn it as an improbable fiction. TN 3.04.128 P
commend them and condemn them to her service, WT 4.04.377
strumpet, thy words condemn thy brat and thee. 1H6 5.04. 84
i shall not want false witness to condemn me, 2H6 3.01.168
that faultless may condemn a nobleman! 3.02. 24
volsces whom you serve, you might condemn us, COR 5.03.134
who cannot condemn rashness in cold blood? TIM 3.05. 53
when all that is within him does condemn MAC 5.02. 24
and course of yours | though i condemn not, yet, LR 1.04.342
afterwards well done, | but must condemn it now. ANT 2.07. 80
condemn myself to lack | the courage of a woman 4.14. 59
away, i do condemn mine ears that have | so long CYM 1.06.141
if the law | find me, and then condemn me for't, TNK 2.06. 14
CONDEMNATION 3 FR 0.0003 REL FR 2 V 1 P
tongue, | either of condemnation or approof, MM 2.04.174
his followers, whose condemnation is pronounc'd. H5 3.06.135 P
the instant is | thy condemnation and thy death. CYM 3.05. 98
CONDEMN'D 34 FR 0.0038 REL FR 30 V 4 P
here is the sister of the man condemn'd MM 2.02. 18
i have a brother is condemn'd to die; 2.02. 34
why, every fault's condemn'd ere it be done. 2.02. 38
marry, this claudio is condemn'd for untrussing. 3.02.179 P
condemn'd upon the act of fornication | to lose 5.01. 70
to lose his head, condemn'd by angelo. 5.01. 71
on this man condemn'd | as if my brother liv'd. 5.01.444
thou'rt condemn'd, | but, for those earthly 5.01.482
therefore by law thou art condemn'd to die. ERR 1.01. 25
stand i condemn'd for pride and scorn so much? ADO 3.01.108
thou wilt be condemn'd into everlasting 4.02. 56 P
than one condemn'd by the king's own mouth — WT 1.02.445
on thy side, | poor thing, condemn'd to loss! 2.03.192
free — if i shall be condemn'd | upon surmises 3.02.111
wherein the king stands generally condemn'd. R2 2.02.132
will you permit that i shall stand condemn'd | a 2.03.119
condemn'd to die for treason, but no traitor; 1H6 2.04. 97
bring forth that sorceress condemn'd to burn. 5.04. 1
first let me tell you whom you have condemn'd: 5.04. 36
'tis meet he be condemn'd by course of law. 2H6 3.01.237
even thus two friends condemn'd | embrace, and 3.02.353
yes, truly is he, and condemn'd upon't. H8 2.01. 8
i stand condemn'd for this. TRO 3.03.219
i had as live be a condemn'd man. COR 4.05.176 P
you are condemn'd; 5.02. 49 P
and for his death | thy brothers are condemn'd, TIT 3.01.109
two of her brothers were condemn'd to death, 5.02.173
you have condemn'd and noted lucius pella | for JC 4.03. 2
are much condemn'd to have an itching palm, | to 4.03. 10
canst serve where thou dost stand condemn'd, LR 1.04. 5
the condemn'd pompey, | rich in his father's ANT 1.03. 49
by thine own tongue thou art condemn'd, and must CYM 5.05.298
was then of me approv'd, what not, condemn'd, TNK 1.03. 65
till forging nature be condemn'd of treason, VEN 729
CONDEMNED 9 FR 0.0010 REL FR 9 V 0 P
none, | and some condemned for a fault alone. MM 2.01. 40
to tyrannize | on unreprievable condemned blood. JN 5.07. 48
to whose flint bosom my condemned lord | is R2 5.01. 3
the poor condemned english, | like sacrifices, H5 4.pr. 22
you have sham'd me | in your condemned seconds. COR 1.08. 15
in my cheeks, | be pitiful to my condemned sons, TIT 3.01. 8
condemned villain, i do apprehend thee. ROM 5.03. 56
and purge | myself condemned and myself excus'd. 5.03.227
the lily i condemned for thy hand, | and buds of SON 99. 6
CONDEMNING 2 FR 0.0002 REL FR 2 V 0 P
condemning some to death, and some to exile; COR 1.06. 35
piece 'gainst fancy, | condemning shadows quite. ANT 5.02.100
CONDEMNS 3 FR 0.0003 REL FR 3 V 0 P
twice all this, | condemns you to the death. R2 3.01. 29
i cannot justify whom the law condemns. 2H6 2.03. 16
and every tale condemns me for a villain. R3 5.03.195
CONDESCEND 2 FR 0.0002 REL FR 2 V 0 P
benefit, | so you do condescend to help me now. 1H6 5.03. 17
thy head, | if thou wilt condescend to be my — 5.03.120
CONDIGN 2 FR 0.0002 REL FR 1 V 1 P
in thy condign praise. LLL 1.02. 25 P
i never gave them condign punishment. 2H6 3.01.130
CONDITION 58 FR 0.0065 REL FR 40 V 18 P
mark his condition, and th' event, then tell me TMP 1.02.117
now the condition. 1.02.120
i am, in my condition, | a prince, miranda; 3.01. 59
here is the cate–log of her condition. TGV 3.01.274 P
our haste from hence is of so quick condition MM 1.01. 53
a light condition in a beauty dark. LLL 5.02. 20
if he have the condition of a saint and the MV 1.02.129 P
sum or sums as are | express'd in the condition, 1.03.148
which is the hot condition of their blood, | if 5.01. 74
and in the gentle condition of blood you should AYL 1.01. 45 P
well, i will forget the condition of my estate, 1.02. 15 P
yet such is now the duke's condition | that he 1.02.264
as lief take her dowry with this condition — to SHR 1.01.132 P
demand of him my condition, and what credit i AWW 4.03.172 P
come | taint the condition of this present hour, TN 5.01.357
the condition of that farthel? WT 4.04.718 P
wrath, | a rage whose heat hath this condition, JN 3.01.341
on what condition stands it and wherein? R2 2.03.107
even in condition of the worst degree, | in 2.03.108
mighty and to be fear'd, than my condition, 1H4 1.03. 6
foretelling this same time's condition | and the 2H4 3.01. 78
and suffer the condition of these times | to lay 4.01. 99
of what condition are you, and of what place? 4.03. 1 P
i, in my condition, | shall better speak of you 4.03. 84
myself | to welcome the condition of the time, 5.02. 11
o hard condition, | twin–born with greatness, H5 4.01.233
so vile, | this day shall gentle his condition; 4.03. 63
correction teach you a good english condition. 5.01. 79 P
is rough, coz, and my condition is not smooth; 5.02.286 P
lord, a hard condition for a maid to consign to. 5.02.298 P
upon condition i may quietly | enjoy mine own, 1H6 5.03.153
upon condition thou wilt swear | to pay him 5.04.129
shall our condition stand? 5.04.165
if one so rude and of so mean condition | may 2H6 5.01. 64
maid | than a great queen with this condition, R3 1.03.107
best fitteth my degree or your condition. 3.07.143
madam, i have a touch of your condition, | that 4.04.158
and those of true condition, that your subjects H8 1.02. 19
condition i had gone barefoot to india. TRO 1.02. 74 P
and condition | made tame and most familiar to 3.03. 9
'twill be deliver'd back on good condition. COR 1.10. 2
condition? 1.10. 3
condition? 1.10. 5
what good condition can a treaty find | i' th' 1.10. 6
'tis a condition they account gentle. 2.03. 97 P
short a time can alter the condition of a man? 5.04. 10 P
would be well express'd | in our condition. TIM 1.01. 77
your weak condition to the raw cold morning. JC 2.01.236
as it hath much prevail'd on your condition, | i 2.01.254
upon condition publius shall not live, | who is 4.01. 4
the imperfections of long–engraff'd condition, LR 1.01.297 P
would i were assur'd | of my condition! 4.07. 56
i would not my unhoused free condition | put OTH 1.02. 26
in her, she's full of most bless'd condition. 2.01.250 P
place, and the condition of this country stands, 2.03.300 P

and then, of so gentle a condition! 4.01.193 P
for condition, | a shop of all the qualities CYM 5.05.165
or it shall be, | on fail of some condition? TNK 1.02.105
CONDITIONALLY 1 FR 0.0001 REL FR 1 V 0 P
conditionally that here thou take an oath | to 3H6 1.01.196
CONDITION'D 1 FR 0.0001 REL FR 1 V 0 P
go, live rich and happy, | but thus condition'd: TIM 4.03.526
/CONDITIONS 2 FR 0.0002 REL FR 2 V 0 P
/in /like /conditions /as /our /argument, | /to TRO pr 25
/stars /above /us, /govern /our /conditions, LR 4.03. 33
CONDITIONS 28 FR 0.0031 REL FR 24 V 4 P
done, | and leave her on such slight conditions. TGV 5.04.138
yes, and his ill conditions, and, in despite of ADO 3.02. 66 P
but that our soft conditions and our hearts SHR 5.02.167
your oaths | are words and poor conditions, but AWW 4.02. 30
but they know his conditions and lay him in 4.03.257 P
of what conditions we shall stand upon? 2H4 4.01.163
me | that no conditions of our peace can stand. 4.01.182
absolute | as our conditions shall consist upon, 4.01.185
shall be soon dispatch'd, with fair conditions. H5 2.04.144
all his senses have but human conditions. 4.01.104 P
to draw conditions of a friendly peace, | which 1H6 5.01. 38
what the conditions of that league must be. 5.04.119
they must either | (for so run the conditions) H8 1.03. 24
he cares not, he'll obey conditions. TRO 4.05. 72
bound with an oath to yield to his conditions; COR 5.01. 69
once more offer'd | the first conditions, which 5.03. 14
on like conditions, will have counter-seal'd. 5.03.205
you see how all conditions, how all minds, | as TIM 1.01. 52
i'll trust to your conditions, be whores still. 4.03.140
rome | under these hard conditions as this time JC 1.02.174
abler than yourself | to make conditions. 4.03. 32
sir, | election makes not up in such conditions. LR 1.01.206
our conditions | so diff'ring in their acts. ANT 2.02.113
i embrace these conditions, let us have articles CYM 1.04.156 P
quiet and gentle thy conditions! PER 3.01. 29
on what conditions? TNK 3.06.252
will you, arcite, | take these conditions? 3.06.264
but there be new conditions, which you'll hear 4.01. 29
CONDOLE 2 FR 0.0002 REL FR 1 V 1 P
i will condole in some measure. MND 1.02. 27 P
let us condole the knight, for, lambkins, we H5 2.01.127
CONDOLEMENT 1 FR 0.0001 REL FR 1 V 0 P
persever | in obstinate condolement is a course HAM 1.02. 93
CONDOLEMENTS 1 FR 0.0001 REL FR 0 V 1 P
there are certain condolements, certain vails. PER 2.01.150 P
CONDOLING 1 FR 0.0001 REL FR 0 V 1 P
a lover is more condoling. MND 1.02. 41 P
CONDUCE 2 FR 0.0002 REL FR 2 V 0 P
the reasons you allege do more conduce | to the TRO 2.02.168
within my soul there doth conduce a fight | of 5.02.147
/CONDUCT 1 FR 0.0001 REL FR 1 V 0 P
/i /will /be /his /conduct. R2 4.01.157
CONDUCT 47 FR 0.0053 REL FR 44 V 3 P
business more than nature | was ever conduct of. TMP 5.01.244
i will be welcome then — conduct me thither. LLL 2.01. 96
from the park let us conduct them thither; 4.03.371
go give him courteous conduct to this place. MV 4.01.148
go hence a little, and i shall conduct you, | if AYL 3.04. 55
power, which were on foot | in his own conduct, 5.04.157
done, conduct him to the drunkard's chamber, SHR in.1. 107
i will conduct you where you shall be lodg'd, AWW 3.05. 41
the house and desire some conduct of the lady. TN 3.04.242 P
pray you then, | conduct me to the queen. WT 2.02. 7
an honorable conduct let him have. JN 1.01. 29
under whose conduct came those pow'rs of france 4.02.129
conduct me to the king; 5.06. 43
sweet peace conduct his sweet soul to the bosom R2 4.01.103
and in my conduct shall your ladies come, | from 1H4 3.01. 91
percy | shall follow in your conduct speedily. 3.01.195
under the conduct of young lancaster | and 2H4 1.01.134
led by th' impartial conduct of my soul; 5.02. 36
convey them with safe conduct. H5 1.02.297
herald, conduct me to the dolphin's tent, | to 1H6 4.07. 51
and so conduct me where, from company, | i may 5.05.100
although thou hast been conduct of my shame. 2H6 2.04.101
will he conduct you through the heart of france, 4.08. 36
this conduct to convey me to the tower. R3 1.01. 45
go, i'll conduct you to the sanctuary. 2.04. 73
good lords, conduct him to his regiment. 5.03.103
and pray receive 'em nobly and conduct 'em H8 1.04. 58
and under your fair conduct | crave leave to 1.04. 70
to th' water side i must conduct your grace; 2.01. 95
election | is led on in the conduct of my will, TRO 2.02. 62
sir, /he stays for you to conduct him thither. 3.02. 3 P
ajax, your guard, stays to conduct you home. 5.02.184
our guider, come, to th' roman camp conduct us. COR 1.07. 7
hither march amain, under conduct | of lucius, TIT 4.04. 65
lenity, | and fire/–ey'd fury be my conduct now! ROM 3.01.124
love, | misshapen in the conduct of them both, 3.03.131
come, bitter conduct, come, unsavory guide! 5.03.116
conduct me to mine host, we love him highly, MAC 1.06. 29
to some provision | give thee quick conduct. LR 3.06. 97
hasten his musters and conduct his pow'rs. 4.02. 16
ancient, conduct them; OTH 1.03.121
baseness of our natures would conduct us to most 1.03.329 P
captain, | left in the conduct of the bold iago, 2.01. 75
of you | a conduct overland to milford–haven. CYM 3.05. 8
they come | under the conduct of bold jachimo, 4.02.340
to conduct | these knights unto their several PER 2.03.108
face, | extinguishing his conduct in this case; LUC 313
CONDUCTED 3 FR 0.0003 REL FR 3 V 0 P
stay a while, | and you shall be conducted. MM 2.03. 18
could wish | you were conducted to a gentle bath COR 1.06. 63
moor, | if foul desire had not conducted you? TIT 2.03. 79
/CONDUCTOR 1 FR 0.0001 REL FR 0 V 1 P
/who /is /conductor /of /his /people? LR 4.07. 87 P
CONDUIT 3 FR 0.0003 REL FR 2 V 1 P
a weather–bitten conduit of many kings' reigns. WT 5.02. 56 P
as from a conduit with /three issuing spouts, TIT 2.04. 30
how now, a conduit, girl? ROM 3.05.129
CONDUITS 3 FR 0.0003 REL FR 3 V 0 P
and all the conduits of my blood froze up, | yet ERR 5.01.314
that our best water brought by conduits hither, COR 2.03.242
like ivory conduits coral cesterns filling: LUC 1234
CONFECT *(see comfect, comfit–maker's)*
CONFECTION 1 FR 0.0001 REL FR 1 V 0 P
"given his mistress that confection | which i CYM 5.05.246
CONFECTIONARY 1 FR 0.0001 REL FR 1 V 0 P
myself, | who had the world as my confectionary, TIM 4.03.260
CONFECTIONS 1 FR 0.0001 REL FR 1 V 0 P
himself doth woo me oft | for my confections? CYM 1.05. 15
CONFEDERACY 5 FR 0.0005 REL FR 5 V 0 P
she is one of this confederacy. MND 3.02.192
us, | for he hath heard of our confederacy, 1H4 4.04. 38
under the countenance and confederacy | of lady 2H6 2.01.164
i' th' level | of a full–charg'd confederacy, H8 1.02. 3
and what confederacy have you with the traitors LR 3.07. 44
/CONFEDERATE 1 FR 0.0001 REL FR 1 V 0 P
/confederate season, else no creature seeing, HAM 3.02.256
CONFEDERATE 7 FR 0.0008 REL FR 6 V 1 P
too, and with the other confederate companion! MM 5.01.348 P
and art confederate with a damned pack | to make ERR 4.04.102
my heart is not confederate with my hand. R2 5.03. 53
the swords | in italy, and her confederate arms, COR 5.03.208
were more than one | confederate in the fact; TIT 4.01. 39
confederate with the queen and her two sons; 5.01.108
cymbeline | i was confederate with the romans. CYM 3.03. 68
CONFEDERATES 10 FR 0.0011 REL FR 10 V 0 P
confederates | (so dry he was for sway) wi' th' TMP 1.02.111
of the beast caliban and his confederates 4.01.140
i bestow | among my wife and /her confederates, ERR 4.01. 17
and a rabble more | of vild confederates. 5.01.237
send colevile with his confederates | to york, 2H4 4.03. 73
of /aire, | nor any of his false confederates. 1H6 2.02. 21
with thy confederates in this weighty cause. 2H6 1.02. 86
with many moe confederates, are in arms. R3 4.04.502
sons, | confederates all thus to dishonor me. TIT 1.01.303
confederates in the deed | that hath dishonored 1.01.344
CONFER 15 FR 0.0017 REL FR 13 V 2 P
and confer fair milan | with all the honors on TMP 1.02.126
i'll leave you to confer of home affairs; TGV 2.04.119
a while, | we have some secrets to confer about. 3.01. 2
confer at large | of all that may concern thy 3.01.255
makes me the better to confer with thee. 3.02. 19
where you with silvia may confer at large — 3.02. 61
and confer with you | of something nearly that MND 1.01.125
we'll crave a parley, to confer with him. 1H6 5.03.130
approacheth, to confer about some matter. 5.04.101
sirrah, leave us to ourselves, we must confer. 3H6 5.06. 6
god grant him health! did you confer with him? R3 1.03. 35
confer with me of murder and of death. TIT 5.02. 34
else, | on whom i may confer what i have got. TIM 1.01.122
you where you shall hear us confer of this, and LR 1.02. 91 P
man and his glass to confer in his own chamber CYM 4.01. 8 P
CONFERENCE 33 FR 0.0037 REL FR 29 V 4 P
it was the copy of our conference: ERR 5.01. 62
and claudio, hand in hand in sad conference. ADO 1.03. 60 P
hold three words' conference with this harpy. 2.01.270 P
the conference was sadly borne; 2.03.221 P
close by the ground, to hear our conference. 3.01. 25
/importunes personal conference with his grace. LLL 2.01. 32
so sensible | seemeth their conference, their 5.02.260
and i will overhear their conference. MND 2.01.187
love takes the meaning in love's conference: 2.02. 46
i cannot speak to her, yet she urg'd conference. AYL 1.02.258
with gentle conference, soft, and affable. SHR 2.01.251
madam, i must | be present at your conference. WT 2.02. 16
but needful conference | about some gossips for 2.03. 40
women and fools, break off your conference. JN 2.01.150
to have some conference with your grace alone. R2 5.03. 27
wales and i | must have some private conference, 1H4 3.02. 2
the mutual conference that my mind hath had, 2H6 1.01. 25
defy thee, | not willing any longer conference, 3H6 2.02.171
while i use further conference with warwick. 3.03.111
that no man shall have private conference | (of R3 1.01. 86
forbear your conference with the noble duke. 1.01.104
are come to have some conference with his grace. 3.07. 69
give us but an hour | of private conference. H8 2.02. 80
worth to know | the secret of your conference? 2.03. 51
being cross'd in conference by some senators. JC 1.02.188
nor with such free and friendly conference, | as 4.02. 17
to our tent till we have done our conference. 4.02. 51
i made good to you | in our last conference, MAC 3.01. 79
an' can you by no drift of conference | get from HAM 3.01. 1
you) in the ear | of all their conference. 3.01.185
not confound the time with conference harsh; ANT 1.01. 45
than the opportunity of a second conference, and CYM 1.04.130 P
not a man in private conference | or council has PER 2.04. 17
CONFERR'D 3 FR 0.0003 REL FR 3 V 0 P
conferr'd by testament to th' sequent issue, AWW 5.03.197
hast thou as yet conferr'd | with margery jordan 2H6 1.02. 74
and pleasure, | than that conferr'd on goneril. LR 1.01. 82
CONFERRING 2 FR 0.0002 REL FR 2 V 0 P
they sit conferring by the parlor fire. SHR 5.02.102
conferring them on younger strengths, while we LR 1.01. 40
CONFESS 129 FR 0.0145 REL FR 90 V 39 P
and hath so humbled me as i confess | there is TGV 2.04.137
you'll not confess, you'll not confess. WIV 1.01. 92 P
you'll not confess, you'll not confess. 1.01. 92 P
sir, he doth in some sort confess it. 1.01.103 P
albeit i will confess thy father's wealth | was 3.04. 13
if it confess | a natural guiltiness such as is MM 2.02.138
i do confess it, and repent it, father. 2.03. 29
confess the truth, and say by whose advice 5.01.113
to her eyes, | till she herself confess it. 5.01.162
my lord, i do confess i ne'er was married, | and 5.01.184
married, | and i confess besides i am no maid. 5.01.185
my lord, i must confess i know this woman, | and 5.01.216
handled her privately, she would sooner confess; 5.01.276 P
but i confess, sir, that we were lock'd out. ERR 4.04. 99
heard you confess you had the chain of him, 5.01.261
trust that you see, confess not that you know. ADO 3.02.120 P
i confess nothing, nor i deny nothing. 4.01.272 P
sir, i confess the wench. LLL 1.01.283 P
i do confess much of the hearing it, but little 1.01.285 P
i confess both, they are both the varnish of a 1.02. 43 P
i will hereupon confess i am in love; 1.02. 57 P
in so unseeming to confess receipt | of that 2.01.155
i confess, i confess. 4.03.201
i confess, i confess. 4.03.201
let us confess and turn it to a jest. 5.02.390
i must confess that i have heard so much, | and MND 1.01.111
perforce i must confess | i thought you lord of 2.02.131
which, when i saw rehears'd, i must confess, 5.01. 68
then confess | what treason there is mingled MV 3.02. 26
promise me life, and i'll confess the truth. 3.02. 34
well then, confess and live. 3.02. 35
confess and love | had been the very sum of my 3.02. 35
do you confess the bond? 4.01.181
albeit i confess your coming before me is nearer AYL 1.01. 50 P
wherein i confess me much guilty to deny so fair 1.02.184 P
she is apter to do than to confess she does. 3.02.389 P
i do so, i confess it. 4.03.165 P
and now in plainness do confess to thee, | that SHR 1.01.152
myself am strook in years, i must confess, | and 2.01.360
i must confess your offer is the best, | and let 2.01.386
i confess the cape. 4.03.140 P
i confess two sleeves. 4.03.142 P
confess, confess, hath he not hit you here? 5.02. 59
confess, confess, hath he not hit you here? 5.02. 59
'a has a little gall'd me, i confess; 5.02. 60
thy cheeks | confess it, /t' /one to th' other, AWW 1.03.177
then i confess | here on my knee, before high 1.03.191
my heart | will not confess he owes the malady 2.01. 9
i will confess what i know without constraint. 4.03.122 P
see what may be done, so you confess freely; 4.03.246 P
confess 'twas hers, and by what rough 5.03.107
my lord, i do confess the ring was hers. 5.03.231
though i confess, on base and ground enough, TN 5.01. 75
though, i confess, much like the character; 5.01.346
most freely i confess, myself and toby | set 5.01.359
if thou wilt confess, | or else be impudently WT 1.02.273
i do confess | i lov'd him as in honor he 3.02. 62
i must confess to you, sir, i am no fighter. 4.03.107 P
sir robert could do well — marry, to confess — JN 1.01.236
and though thou now confess thou didst but jest, 3.01. 16
awakes my conscience to confess all this. 5.04. 43
last receiv'd the sacrament | i did confess it, R2 1.01.140
confess thy treasons ere thou fly the realm; 1.03.198
i cannot mend it, i must needs confess, 2.03.153
you confess then you pick'd my pocket? 1H4 3.03.168 P
are in the vaward of our youth, i must confess, 2H4 1.02.177 P
and those two things i confess i cannot help. 2.02. 68 P
drive you then to confess the willful abuse, and 2.04.311 P
i do confess my fault, | and do submit me to H5 2.02. 76
though 'tis no wisdom to confess so much | unto 3.06.143
i will confess it to all the orld. 4.07.112 P
be glad to hear you confess it brokenly with 5.02.106 P
and yet thy tongue will not confess thy error. 1H6 2.04. 67
hold, peter, hold! i confess, i confess treason. 2H6 2.03. 93 P
hold, peter, hold! i confess, i confess treason. 2.03. 93 P
o, torture me no more, i will confess. 3.03. 11
i was, i must confess, | great albion's queen in 3H6 3.03. 6
yet i confess that often ere this day, | when i 3.03.131
right, and you must all confess | that i was not 4.01. 69
these news i must confess are full of grief, 4.04. 13
confess who set thee up and pluck'd thee down, 5.01. 26
and timorously confess | the manner and the R3 3.05. 57
i will confess she was not edward's daughter. 4.04.211
such a one, they all confess, | there is indeed, H8 1.04. 82
must now confess, if they have any goodness, 2.02. 90
and, if you may confess it, say withal | if you 3.02.164
i confess your royal graces | show'r'd on me 3.02.166
a brown favor (for so 'tis, i must confess) — TRO 1.02. 94 P
a marvell's white hand, i must needs confess. 1.02.137 P
if you'll confess /he brought home worthy prize 2.02. 86
if i confess much, you will play the tyrant. 3.02.119
must | confess yourselves wondrous malicious, COR 1.01. 88
to be silent and not confess so much were a kind 2.02. 31 P
hast not the soft way which, thou dost confess, 3.02. 82
i should have been more strange, i must confess, ROM 2.02.102
to answer that, i should confess to you. 4.01. 23
i will confess to you that i love him. 4.01. 25
for my own part, i must needs confess, i have TIM 3.02. 20 P
they confess | toward thee forgetfulness too 5.01.143
you shall confess that you are both deceiv'd. JC 2.01.105
do you confess so much? give me your hand. 4.03.117
yet now, i must confess, that duty done, | my HAM 1.02. 54
he does confess he feels himself distracted, 3.01. 5
confess yourself to heaven, | repent what's past 3.04.149
me not to the purpose, confess thyself — 5.01. 39 P
i dare not confess that, lest i should compare 5.02.138 P
"dear daughter, i confess that i am old; LR 2.04.154
that will confess perfection so could err OTH 1.03.100
to heaven | i do confess the vices of my blood, 1.03.123
if she confess that she was half the wooer, 1.03.176
i confess it is my shame to be so fond, but it 1.03.317 P
and i confess me knit to thy deserving with 1.03.337 P
confess yourself freely to her; 2.03.318 P
(as i confess it is my nature's plague | to spy 3.03.146
to confess, and be hang'd for his labor — first 4.01. 38 P
first to be hang'd, and then to confess. 4.01. 39 P
confess? 4.01. 43 P
did he confess it? 4.01. 65
therefore confess thee freely of thy sin; 5.02. 53
let him confess a truth. 5.02. 68
next, cleopatra does confess thy greatness, ANT 3.12. 16
but do confess i have | been laden with like 5.02.122
her bedchamber | (where i confess i slept not, CYM 2.04. 67
she did confess | was as a scorpion to her sight 5.05. 44
she did confess she had | for you a mortal 5.05. 49
i here confess myself the king of tyre, | who, PER 5.03. 2
then, gentle shadow (truth i must confess), | i VEN 1001
"had i been tooth'd like him, i must confess, 1117
let me confess that we two must be twain, SON 36. 1
CONFESS'D 22 FR 0.0024 REL FR 16 V 6 P
if it be confess'd, it is not redress'd. WIV 1.01.104 P
they have confess'd you did. MM 5.01.289 P
i have confess'd her, and i know her virtue. 5.01.527
confess'd the vile encounters they have had | a ADO 4.01. 93
he hath confess'd himself to morgan, whom he AWW 4.03.108 P
and what think you he hath confess'd? 4.03.111 P
came to't bravely confess'd and lamented by the WT 5.02. 86 P
he hath confess'd! 2H6 4.02.107 P
my lord, we always have confess'd it. TIM 1.02. 21
ho, ho, confess'd it? hang'd it, have you not? 1.02. 22
but treasons capital, confess'd and prov'd, MAC 1.03.115
that very frankly he confess'd his treasons, 1.04. 5
he hath confess'd. OTH 5.02. 68
cassio confess'd it, | and she did gratify his 5.02.212
this wretch hath part confess'd his villainy. 5.02.296
and he himself confess'd it but even now, | that 5.02.321

what she confess'd | i will report, so please CYM 5.05. 33
first, she confess'd she never lov'd you; 5.05. 37
i left out one thing which the queen confess'd, 5.05.244
my love, would make thee | a confess'd traitor! TNK 3.01. 35
your kinsman hath confess'd the right o' th' 5.04.116
so now i have confess'd that he is thine, | and SON 134. 1
CONFESSES 3 FR 0.0003 REL FR 3 V 0 P
scarce confesses | that his blood flows; MM 1.03. 51
confesses that she secretly o'erheard | your AYL 2.02. 11
she confesses it. LR 5.03.228
CONFESSETH 1 FR 0.0001 REL FR 1 V 0 P
forgot, | which he confesseth to be manifold, 1H4 4.03. 47
/CONFESSING 1 FR 0.0001 REL FR 1 V 0 P
/that, /by /confessing /them, /the /souls /of R2 4.01.226
CONFESSING 2 FR 0.0002 REL FR 1 V 1 P
night overheard me confessing to this man how ADO 5.01.235 P
ireland, not confessing | their cruel parricide, MAC 3.01. 30
CONFESSION 17 FR 0.0019 REL FR 13 V 4 P
cell, | where i intend holy confession. TGV 4.03. 44
she did intend confession | at patrick's cell 5.02. 41
i will, out of thine own confession, learn to MM 1.02. 38 P
but let my trial be mine own confession. 5.01.372
it appears not in this confession; ADO 5.02. 73 P
the fairest is confession. LLL 5.02.432
love | had been the very sum of my confession. MV 3.02. 36
his confession is taken, and it shall be read to AWW 4.03.113 P
i see a strange confession in thine eye. 2H4 1.01. 94
that loves his mistress more than in confession TRO 1.03.269
and fell so roundly to a large confession, | to 3.02.154
riddling confession finds but riddling shrift. ROM 2.03. 56
cell, | to make confession and to be absolv'd. 3.05.233
come you to make confession to this father? 4.01. 22
and there is a kind of confession in your looks, HAM 2.02.279 P
when we would bring him on to some confession 3.01. 9
he made confession of you, | and gave you such a 4.07. 95
/CONFESSION'S 1 FR 0.0001 REL FR 1 V 0 P
whom after under the /confession's seal | he H8 1.02.164
CONFESSIONS 3 FR 0.0003 REL FR 2 V 1 P
person | i'll hear him his confessions justify, H8 1.02. 6
proofs, confessions | of divers witnesses, which 2.01. 16
handkerchief — confessions — handkerchief! OTH 4.01. 37 P
CONFESSOR 9 FR 0.0010 REL FR 8 V 1 P
bring him his confessor, let him be prepar'd, MM 2.01. 35
i am confessor to angelo, and i know this to be 3.01.166 P
eyes — | one of our covent, and his confessor, 4.03.128
and the bodies | of the duke's confessor, john H8 1.01.218
his confessor, who fed him every minute | with 1.02.149
o that your lordship were but now confessor | to 1.04. 15
car, | confessor to him, with that devil monk, 2.01. 21
good even to my ghostly confessor. ROM 2.06. 21
heart, | being a divine, a ghostly confessor, 3.03. 49
CONFESSOR'S 1 FR 0.0001 REL FR 1 V 0 P
queen, | as holy oil, edward confessor's crown, H8 4.01. 88
CONFESSORS 1 FR 0.0001 REL FR 1 V 0 P
i have been harsh | to large confessors, and TNK 5.01.105
CONFESS'T 1 FR 0.0001 REL FR 1 V 0 P
/a /touch, /a /touch, i do confess't. HAM 5.02.286
/CONFIDENCE 1 FR 0.0001 REL FR 1 V 0 P
/but /not /in /confidence | /of /author's /pen TRO pr 23
CONFIDENCE 15 FR 0.0017 REL FR 11 V 4 P
had indeed no limit, | a confidence sans bound. TMP 1.02. 97
of the wart the next time we have confidence, WIV 1.04.160 P
sir, i would have some confidence with you that ADO 3.05. 2 P
upon thy certainty and confidence | what dar'st AWW 2.01.169
he thinks, nay, with all confidence he swears, WT 1.02.414
show boldness and aspiring confidence. JN 5.01. 56
the king reposeth all his confidence in thee. R2 2.04. 6
are true, | otherwise i renounce all confidence. 1H6 1.02. 97
with demure confidence | this pausingly ensu'd: H8 1.02.167
against us brats with no less confidence | than COR 4.06. 93
be he, sir, i desire some confidence with you. ROM 2.04.127 P
sum | your master's confidence was above mine, TIM 3.04. 31
lord, | your wisdom is consum'd in confidence. JC 2.02. 49
nay, in all confidence, he's not for rhodes. OTH 1.03. 31
against your confidence than her reputation; CYM 1.04.111 P
/CONFIDENT 1 FR 0.0001 REL FR 1 V 0 P
/divide /thy /lips, /than /we /are /confident, TRO 1.03. 72
CONFIDENT 18 FR 0.0020 REL FR 16 V 2 P
a man may be too confident. WIV 2.01.187 P
yet, confident, i'll keep what i have sworn, LLL 1.01.114
art thou so confident? AWW 2.01.159
secure | and confident from foreign purposes, JN 2.01. 28
his forces strong, his soldiers confident. 2.01. 61
lions more confident, mountains and rocks | more 2.01.452
as confident as is the falcon's flight | against R2 1.03. 61
be confident to speak, northumberland: 2.01.274
are confident against the world in arms. 1H4 5.01.117
it is not a confident brow, nor the throng of 2H4 2.01.111 P
all too confident | to give admittance to a 4.01.150
the confident and overlusty french | do the H5 4.pr. 18
i am confident; H8 2.01.146
unto me | as i am confident and kind to thee. TIT 1.01. 61
we learn no other but the confident tyrant MAC 5.04. 8
confident i am. CYM 2.03.145
three thousand confident, in act as many — 5.03. 29
no lesser of her honor confident | than i did 5.05.187
CONFIDENTLY 2 FR 0.0002 REL FR 0 V 2 P
you hear him so confidently undertake to do. AWW 3.06. 20 P
that so confidently seems to undertake this 3.06. 86 P
CONFIN'D 19 FR 0.0021 REL FR 17 V 2 P
wast thou | deservedly confin'd into this rock, TMP 1.02.361
confin'd together | in the same fashion as you 5.01. 7
whose honor cannot | be measur'd or confin'd. 5.01.122
now 'tis true, | i must be here confin'd by you, ep 4
from our free person she should be confin'd, WT 2.01.194
the poison | is as a fiend confin'd to tyrannize JN 5.07. 47
nature's hand | keep the wild flood confin'd! 2H4 1.01.154
to us and /to our purposes confin'd | we come 4.01.173
walls | are now confin'd two mighty monarchies, H5 pr 20
you and i cannot be confin'd within the weak 5.02.269 P
the will is infinite and the execution confin'd, TRO 3.02. 82 P
you stood, confin'd | into an auger's bore. COR 4.06. 86
cribb'd, confin'd, bound in | to saucy doubts MAC 3.04. 23
and for the day confin'd to fast in fires, HAM 1.05. 11
prescrib'd his pow'r, | confin'd to exhibition? LR 1.02. 25
confin'd in all she has, her monument, | of thy ANT 5.01. 53
therefore my verse, to constancy confin'd, | one SON 105. 7
suppos'd as forfeit to a confin'd doom. 107. 4

friend, | a god in love, to whom i am confin'd. 110.12
CONFINE 18 FR 0.0020 REL FR 12 V 6 P
refusing her grand hests, she did confine thee, TMP 1.02.274
but you must confine yourself within the modest TN 1.03. 8 P
confine? 1.03. 10 P
i'll confine myself no finer than i am. 1.03. 10 P
this kingdom, this confine of blood and breath, JN 4.02.246
hath wrought the mure that should confine it in 2H4 4.04.119
hands, and to confine yourself | to asher–house, H8 3.02.230
fie, you confine yourself most unreasonably. COR 1.03. 76 P
and erring spirit hies | to his confine; HAM 1.01.155
or confine him where | your wisdom best shall 3.01.186
you stands on the very verge | of his confine. LR 2.04.148
put into circumscription and confine | for the OTH 1.02. 27
apart, | confine yourself but in a patient list. 4.01. 75
third is up, till death enlarge his confine. ANT 3.05. 12 P
our pleasure his full fortune doth confine, CYM 5.04.110
confine her to a place where the light may TNK 4.03. 74 P
in whose confine immured is the store | which SON 84. 3
in thee hath neither sting, knot, nor confine, LC 265
CONFINED 1 FR 0.0001 REL FR 1 V 0 P
head | looks fearfully in the confined deep. LR 4.01. 74
CONFINELESS 1 FR 0.0001 REL FR 1 V 0 P
being compar'd | with my confineless harms. MAC 4.03. 55
CONFINERS 1 FR 0.0001 REL FR 1 V 0 P
the senate hath stirr'd up the confiners | and CYM 4.02.337
/CONFINES 1 FR 0.0001 REL FR 0 V 1 P
/in /which /there /are /many /confines, /wards, HAM 2.02.245 P
CONFINES 9 FR 0.0010 REL FR 8 V 1 P
art | i have from their confines call'd to enact TMP 4.01.121
should in their own confines with forked heads AYL 2.01. 24
might from our quiet confines fright fair peace, R2 1.03.137
measure our confines with such peaceful steps? 3.02.125
now, neighbor confines, purge you of your scum! 2H4 4.05.123
here in these confines slily have i lurk'd, | to R3 4.04. 3
confines | /thy spacious and dilated parts. TRO 2.03.249
when he enters the confines of a tavern, claps ROM 3.01. 6 P
shall in these confines with a monarch's voice JC 3.01.272
CONFINING 2 FR 0.0002 REL FR 2 V 0 P
with course disturb'd even thy confining shores, JN 2.01.338
story, | in little room confining mighty men, H5 ep 3
CONFIRM 29 FR 0.0032 REL FR 26 V 3 P
confirm his welcome with some special favor. TGV 2.04.101
these likelihoods confirm her flight from hence: 5.02. 43
which did confirm any slander that don john had ADO 3.03.158 P
and to confirm it plain, | you gave me this: LLL 5.02.452
and jump | that i am viola — which to confirm, TN 5.01.253
then let confusion of one part confirm | the JN 2.01.359
our souls religiously confirm thy words. 4.03. 73
which elder days shall ripen and confirm | to R2 2.03. 43
what she says i'll confirm. we'll fight it out. 1H6 1.02.128
confirm it so, mine honorable lord. 4.01.122
confirm it so? 4.01.123
france | as his alliance will confirm our peace, 5.05. 42
confirm the crown to me and to mine heirs, | and 3H6 1.01.172
to confirm that amity | with nuptial knot, if 3.03. 54
thou dost confirm his happiness for ever. R3 1.02.208
this, to confirm my welcome, | and to you all H8 1.04. 37
to confirm this too, | cardinal campeius is 2.01.159
and, to confirm his goodness, | tied it by 3.02.249
let me confirm my princely brother's greeting: TRO 4.05.174
nothing else to do | but to confirm my curses! COR 4.02. 46
and thus far i confirm you. TIM 1.02. 94 P
any one, having no witness to confirm my speech. MAC 5.01. 18 P
beloved sons, be yours, which to confirm, | this LR 1.01.138
yet do they all confirm | a turkish fleet, and OTH 1.03. 7
whose strength | i will confirm with oath, which CYM 2.04. 64
ay, and it doth confirm | another stain, as big 2.04.139
at court, | and that will well confirm it. 3.04.127
as i have brought my life here to confirm it, TNK 3.06.164
i have no voice, sir, to confirm her that way! 5.02. 15
CONFIRMATION 7 FR 0.0008 REL FR 7 V 0 P
receive | the confirmation of my promis'd gift, AWW 2.03. 50
yet, for a greater confirmation | (for in an act WT 2.01.180
quiet, | better opinion, better confirmation, 2H4 4.05.188
witness how dear i hold this confirmation. H8 5.02.207
for confirmation that i am much more | than my LR 3.01. 44
honor'd with confirmation your great judgment CYM 1.06.174
still confirmation! PER 5.03. 54
CONFIRMATIONS 2 FR 0.0002 REL FR 1 V 1 P
ay, and the particular confirmations, point from AWW 4.03. 61 P
are to the jealious confirmations strong | as OTH 3.03.323
CONFIRM'D 15 FR 0.0017 REL FR 12 V 3 P
of approv'd valor, and confirm'd honesty. ADO 2.01.379 P
confirm'd, confirm'd! 4.01.150
confirm'd, confirm'd! 4.01.150
which i will do with confirm'd countenance. 5.04. 17
until confirm'd, sign'd, ratified by you. MV 3.02.148
was faithfully confirm'd by the rector of the AWW 4.03. 58 P
confirm'd by mutual joinder of your hands, TN 5.01.157
confirm'd conspiracy with fearful france, | and H5 2.pr. 27
thy age confirm'd, proud, subtle, sly, and R3 4.04.172
h'as such a confirm'd countenance. COR 1.03. 59 P
he's not confirm'd, we may deny him yet. 2.03.209
all is confirm'd, my lord, which was reported. MAC 5.03. 31
the which no sooner had his prowess confirm'd 5.09. 7
that, | for truth can never be confirm'd enough, PER 5.01.201
in vain i spurn at my confirm'd despite: LUC 1026
CONFIRMED 2 FR 0.0002 REL FR 2 V 0 P
i am my master's true confirmed love; TGV 4.04.103
but like a constant and confirmed devil, | he LUC 1513
CONFIRMER 1 FR 0.0001 REL FR 0 V 1 P
they are both the confirmer of false reckonings. AYL 3.04. 32 P
CONFIRMERS 1 FR 0.0001 REL FR 1 V 0 P
be these sad signs confirmers of thy words? JN 3.01. 24
CONFIRMITIES 1 FR 0.0001 REL FR 0 V 1 P
you cannot one bear with another's confirmities. 2H4 2.04. 58 P
CONFIRMS 4 FR 0.0004 REL FR 3 V 1 P
his incivility confirms no less. ERR 4.04. 46
between his lord and my niece confirms no less. TN 3.04.187 P
consent, | and what we do establish he confirms. 2H6 3.01.317
that confirms it home. CYM 4.02.328
CONFISCATE 6 FR 0.0006 REL FR 6 V 0 P
his goods confiscate to the duke's dispose, ERR 1.01. 20
lest that your goods too soon be confiscate: 1.02. 2
venice, confiscate | unto the state of venice. MV 4.01.311
thou diest, and all thy goods are confiscate. 4.01.332
and all his lands and goods confiscate. 3H6 4.06. 55

and let it be confiscate all, so soon | as i CYM 5.05.323
/CONFISCATION 1 FR 0.0001 REL FR 1 V 0 P
although by /confiscation they are ours, | we do MM 5.01.423
CONFIXED 1 FR 0.0001 REL FR 1 V 0 P
my knees, | or else for ever be confixed here, MM 5.01.232
CONFLICT 10 FR 0.0011 REL FR 8 V 2 P
in our last conflict four of his five wits went ADO 1.01. 66 P
in conflict that you get the sun of them. LLL 4.03.366
who, in the conflict that it holds with death, 2H6 3.02.164
whom in this conflict i, unwares, have kill'd. 3H6 2.05. 62
and after conflict such as was suppos'd | the TIT 2.03. 21
did he bear himself | in the last conflict, and TIM 3.05. 65
the thane of cawdor, began a dismal conflict, MAC 1.02. 53
though the conflict be sore between that and my LR 3.05. 22 P
(alack, too weak the conflict to support!) 5.03.198
to note the fighting conflict of her hue, | how VEN 345
CONFLICTING 1 FR 0.0001 REL FR 1 V 0 P
trunks, | to the conflicting elements expos'd, TIM 4.03.230
CONFLICTS 1 FR 0.0001 REL FR 1 V 0 P
me, in these conflicts | what may befall him, to 3H6 4.06. 94
CONFLUENCE 1 FR 0.0001 REL FR 1 V 0 P
you see this confluence, this great flood of TIM 1.01. 42
CONFLUX 1 FR 0.0001 REL FR 1 V 0 P
as knots, by the conflux of meeting sap, TRO 1.03. 7
CONFORM 1 FR 0.0001 REL FR 1 V 0 P
fortune, | and to my humble seat conform myself. 3H6 3.03. 11
CONFORMABLE 2 FR 0.0002 REL FR 2 V 0 P
a kate | conformable as other household kates. SHR 2.01.278
wife, | at all times to your will conformable; H8 2.04. 24
/CONFOUND 1 FR 0.0001 REL FR 0 V 1 P
/and /war /and /lechery /confound /all! TRO 2.03. 75 P
CONFOUND 40 FR 0.0045 REL FR 36 V 4 P
bruise me with scorn, confound me with a flout, LLL 5.02.397
come, tears, confound, | out, sword, and wound MND 5.01.295
of man | so keen and greedy to confound a man. MV 3.02.276
would quite confound distinction, yet stands off AWW 2.03.120
they do confound their skill in covetousness, JN 4.02. 29
press to that last hold, | confound themselves. 5.07. 20
with too much riches it confound itself; R2 3.04. 60
shall kin with kin and kind with kind confound. 4.01.141
this let alone will all the rest confound. 5.03. 86
he did confound the best part of an hour | in 1H4 1.03.100
on ground, | confound themselves with working. 2H4 4.04. 41
kings | confound your hidden falsehood and award R3 2.01. 14
be not so hasty to confound my meaning: 4.04.262
myself myself confound! 4.04.399
how couldst thou in a mile confound an hour, COR 1.06. 17
and pray the roman gods confound you both! TIT 4.02. 6
traffic confound thee, if the gods will not! TIM 1.01.237 P
traffic's thy god, and thy god confound thee! 1.01.239 P
the gods confound (hear me, you good gods all) 4.01. 37
if thou dost perform, confound thee, for thou 4.03. 75 P
the gods confound them all in thy conquest, 4.03.104
and wrath would confound thee and make thine own 4.03.336 P
i give you, | and gold confound you howsoe'er! 4.03.449
confound them by some course, and come to me, 5.01.103
waves | confound and swallow navigation up; MAC 4.01. 54
universal peace, confound | all unity on earth. 4.03. 99
confound the ignorant, and amaze indeed | the HAM 2.02.565
o, confound the rest! 3.02.177
let's not confound the time with conference ANT 1.01. 45
but to confound such time | that drums him from 1.04. 28
the gods confound thee, dost thou hold there 2.05. 92
what willingly he did confound he wail'd, 3.02. 58
bound, | the interim, pray you, all confound. PER 5.02. 14
place | to seat something i would confound. TNK 5.01. 28
this battle shall confound | both these brave 5.01.166
with cold terror doth men's minds confound. VEN 1048
which in a moment doth confound and kill | all LUC 250
my shame be his that did my fame confound; 1202
and time that gave doth now his gift confound. SON 60. 8
in other accents do this praise confound | by 69. 7
CONFOUNDED 12 FR 0.0013 REL FR 11 V 1 P
their form confounded makes most form in mirth, LLL 5.02.519
but a clod | and module of confounded royalty. JN 5.07. 58
rock | o'erhang and jutty his confounded base, H5 3.01. 13
all is confounded, all! 4.05. 3
confounded be your strife, | and perish ye, with 1H6 4.01.123
and, thy fury spent, | confounded be thyself! TIM 4.03.129
here, quite confounded with this mutiny. JC 3.01. 86
by all likelihood have confounded one the other, CYM 1.04. 51 P
wood, | even so confounded in the dark she lay, VEN 827
wrapp'd and confounded in a thousand fears, LUC 456
reason, in itself confounded, | saw division PHT 41
of state, | or state itself confounded to decay, SON 64.10
CONFOUNDING 4 FR 0.0004 REL FR 4 V 0 P
a million fail, confounding oath on oath. MND 3.02. 93
laws, | decline to your confounding contraries; TIM 4.01. 20
by thy virtue | set them into confounding odds, 4.03.391
fortify | against confounding age's cruel knife, SON 63.10
'CONFOUNDS 1 FR 0.0001 REL FR 1 V 0 P
'confounds the tongue and makes the senses rough 1H6 5.03. 71
/CONFOUNDS 1 FR 0.0001 REL FR 1 V 0 P
the /shaft /confounds | not that it wounds, TRO 3.01.118
CONFOUNDS 13 FR 0.0014 REL FR 13 V 0 P
my shame and guilt confounds me. TGV 5.04. 73
once can touch | but it confounds the breather. MM 4.04. 28
(unseen, inquisitive), confounds himself. ERR 1.02. 38
confounds thy fame, as whirlwinds shake fair SHR 5.02.140
and in the taste confounds the appetite. ROM 2.06. 13
th' attempt, and not the deed, | confounds us. MAC 2.02. 11
appalls her senses and her spirit confounds. VEN 882
just | when he himself himself confounds, LUC 160
that eye which looks on her confounds his wits; 290
and one man's lust these many lives confounds. 1489
on | to hideous winter and confounds him there, SON 5. 6
who confounds | in singleness the parts that 8. 7
the wiry concord that mine ear confounds, | do i 128. 4
CONFRONT 2 FR 0.0002 REL FR 2 V 0 P
shall dunghill curs confront the helicons? 2H4 5.03.104
mercy | but to confront the visage of offense? HAM 3.03. 47
CONFRONTED 4 FR 0.0004 REL FR 4 V 0 P
we four indeed confronted were with four | in LLL 5.02.367
with strength, and power confronted power: JN 2.01.330
troubled, confronted thus, and, for the extent TIT 4.04. 3

proof, | confronted him with self–comparisons, MAC 1.02. 55
/CONFRONTS 1 FR 0.0001 REL FR 1 V 0 P
by these french | /confronts /your city's eyes, JN 2.01.215
CONFUS'D 6 FR 0.0006 REL FR 6 V 0 P
i never heard a passion so confus'd, | so MV 2.08. 12
which doth order give | to sounds confus'd; H5 3.pr. 10
whiles the mad mothers with their howls confus'd 3.03. 39
but with a din confus'd | enforce the present COR 3.03. 20
of dire combustion and confus'd events | new MAC 2.03. 58
but yet confus'd, | knavery's plain face is OTH 2.01.311
CONFUSED 2 FR 0.0002 REL FR 2 V 0 P
hand | of stern injustice and confused wrong. JN 5.02. 23
would make such fearful and confused cries, | as TIT 2.03.102
CONFUSEDLY 1 FR 0.0001 REL FR 1 V 0 P
hedges | they pitched in the ground confusedly, 1H6 1.01.118
CONFUSION 33 FR 0.0037 REL FR 32 V 1 P
infect thy sap, and live on thy confusion. ERR 2.02.180
so quick bright things come to confusion. MND 1.01.149
and mark the musical confusion | of hounds and 4.01.110
and there is such confusion in my powers, | as, MV 3.02.177
i bar confusion, | 'tis i must make conclusion AYL 5.04.125
then let confusion of one part confirm | the JN 2.01.359
and vast confusion waits, | as doth a raven on a 4.03.152
rightly gaz'd upon | show nothing but confusion; R2 2.02. 19
for a time | of pell–mell havoc and confusion. 1H4 5.01. 82
still | you may behold confusion of your foes. 1H6 4.01. 77
there comes the ruin, there begins confusion. 4.01.194
heaping confusion on their own heads thereby! 2H6 2.01.183
shame and confusion! 5.02. 31
how soon confusion | may enter 'twixt the gap of COR 3.01.110
ran about the streets, | crying confusion. 4.06. 29
confusion fall — TIT 2.03.184
with him, | and work confusion on his enemies. 5.02. 8
and yet confusion live! TIM 4.01. 21
to pay thy soldiers, | make large confusion; 4.03.128
thou have thyself fall in the confusion of men, 4.03.324 P
wars as thy redress | and not as our confusion, 5.04. 52
confusion now hath made his masterpiece! MAC 2.03. 66
illusion | shall draw him on to his confusion. 3.05. 29
get from him why he puts on this confusion, HAM 3.01. 2
confusion! LR 2.04. 95
the realm of albion | come to great confusion. 3.02. 86
laugh at 's while we strut | to our confusion. ANT 3.13.115
war and confusion | in caesar's name pronounce i CYM 3.01. 65
nay, to thy mere confusion, thou shalt know | i 4.02. 92
anon | a rout, confusion thick. 5.03. 41
the master calls, and trebles their confusion. PER 4.01. 64
and fright her with confusion of their cries. LUC 445
than they whose whole is swallowed in confusion. 1159
CONFUSION'S 2 FR 0.0002 REL FR 2 V 0 P
of breath, | confusion's near, i cannot speak. COR 3.01.189
confusion's /cure lives not | in these ROM 4.05. 65
CONFUSIONS 2 FR 0.0002 REL FR 1 V 1 P
i will try confusions with him. MV 2.02. 37 P
/cure lives not | in these confusions. ROM 4.05. 66
CONFUTATION 1 FR 0.0001 REL FR 1 V 0 P
in confutation of which rude reproach, | and in 1H6 4.01. 98
CONFUTES 2 FR 0.0002 REL FR 1 V 1 P
my sisterly remorse confutes mine honor, | and i MM 5.01.100
nothing confutes me but eyes, and nobody sees me
1H4 5.04.126 P
CONGEAL 1 FR 0.0001 REL FR 1 V 0 P
cool and congeal again to what it was. JN 2.01.479
CONGEAL'D 4 FR 0.0004 REL FR 3 V 1 P
when he makes water his urine is congeal'd ice, MM 3.02.110 P
too much sadness hath congeal'd your blood, SHR in.2. 132
congeal'd with this, do make me wipe off both. 3H6 1.03. 52
open their congeal'd mouths and bleed afresh! R3 1.02. 56
CONGEALED 5 FR 0.0005 REL FR 5 V 0 P
that pure congealed white, high taurus' snow, MND 3.02.141
as flaws congealed in the spring of day. 2H4 4.04. 35
thy tears would wash this cold congealed blood 3H6 5.02. 37
and stains her face with his congealed blood. VEN 1122
about the mourning and congealed face | of that LUC 1744
CONGEALMENT 1 FR 0.0001 REL FR 1 V 0 P
tears | wash the congealment from your wounds, ANT 4.08. 10
CONGEED *(see congied)*
CONGER *(see cunger)*
CONGEST 1 FR 0.0001 REL FR 1 V 0 P
strong, | must for your victory us all congest, LC 258
CONGIED 1 FR 0.0001 REL FR 0 V 1 P
i have congied with the duke, done my adieu with
AWW 4.03. 87 P
CONGRATULATE *(also gratulate)*
CONGRATULATE 1 FR 0.0001 REL FR 0 V 1 P
and affection to congratulate the princess at LLL 5.01. 88 P
CONGREEING 1 FR 0.0001 REL FR 1 V 0 P
congreeing in a full and natural close, | like H5 1.02.182
CONGREETED 1 FR 0.0001 REL FR 1 V 0 P
you have congreeted, let it not disgrace me, H5 5.02. 31
CONGREGATE 1 FR 0.0001 REL FR 1 V 0 P
even there where merchants most do congregate, MV 1.03. 49
CONGREGATED 2 FR 0.0002 REL FR 2 V 0 P
us, and | the congregated college have concluded AWW 2.01.117
the gutter'd rocks and congregated sands, OTH 2.01. 69
CONGREGATION 3 FR 0.0003 REL FR 0 V 3 P
to–morrow in the congregation, where i should ADO 3.02.124 P
before the whole congregation, shame her with 3.03.162 P
but a foul and pestilent congregation of vapors. HAM 2.02.303 P
CONGREGATIONS 1 FR 0.0001 REL FR 1 V 0 P
to show bare heads | in congregations, to yawn, COR 3.02. 11
CONGRUENT 2 FR 0.0002 REL FR 0 V 2 P
spoke it tender juvenal as a congruent epitheton LLL 1.02. 13 P
is liable, congruent, and measurable for the 5.01. 92 P
CONGRUING 1 FR 0.0001 REL FR 1 V 0 P
at full, | by letters congruing to that effect, HAM 4.03. 64
CONIES 2 FR 0.0002 REL FR 1 V 1 P
out of their burrows, like conies after rain, COR 4.05.212 P
and sometime where earth–delving conies keep, VEN 687
/CONJECTS 1 FR 0.0001 REL FR 1 V 0 P
/then, | from one that so imperfectly /conjects, OTH 3.03.149
/CONJECTURAL 1 FR 0.0001 REL FR 1 V 0 P
and mak'st /conjectural fears to come into me, AWW 5.03.114
CONJECTURAL 1 FR 0.0001 REL FR 1 V 0 P
and give out | conjectural marriages, making COR 1.01.194
/CONJECTURE 1 FR 0.0001 REL FR 1 V 0 P
/conjecture, /expectation, /and /surmise | /of 2H4 1.03. 23
CONJECTURE 4 FR 0.0004 REL FR 4 V 0 P
love, | and on my eyelids shall conjecture hang, ADO 4.01.106
(which was as gross as ever touch'd conjecture, WT 2.01.176
now entertain conjecture of a time | when H5 4.pr. 1
as to prenominate in nice conjecture | where TRO 4.05.250
CONJECTURES 4 FR 0.0004 REL FR 3 V 1 P
skirts for yourself, in my simple conjectures. WIV 1.01. 30 P
blown by surmises, jealousies, conjectures, 2H4 in 16
'tis likely, | by all conjectures: H8 2.01. 41
dangerous conjectures in ill–breeding minds. HAM 4.05. 15
CONJOIN 1 FR 0.0001 REL FR 1 V 0 P
by god's fair ordinance conjoin together! R3 5.05. 31
CONJOIN'D 5 FR 0.0005 REL FR 4 V 1 P
impediment why you should not be conjoin'd, i ADO 4.01. 13 P
ours, this day to be conjoin'd | in the state of 5.04. 29
now i perceive they have conjoin'd all three MND 3.02.193
was | into two parties, is now conjoin'd in one, 1H6 5.02. 12
his form and cause conjoin'd, preaching to HAM 3.04.126
CONJOINS 1 FR 0.0001 REL FR 1 V 0 P
this part of his conjoins with my disease, | and 2H4 4.05. 63
CONJOINTLY 2 FR 0.0002 REL FR 2 V 0 P
and both conjointly bend | your sharpest deeds JN 2.01.379
when these prodigies | do so conjointly meet, JC 1.03. 29
/CONJUNCT 1 FR 0.0001 REL FR 1 V 0 P
/am /doubtful /that /you /have /been /conjunct LR 5.01. 12
CONJUNCTION 9 FR 0.0010 REL FR 7 V 2 P
confusion | of hounds and echo in conjunction. MND 4.01.111
son, list to this conjunction, make this match, JN 2.01.468
knit, | and the conjunction of our inward souls 3.01.227
that with our small conjunction we should on, 1H4 4.01. 37
saturn and venus this year in conjunction! 2H4 2.04.263 P
spirits are so married in conjunction with the 5.01. 69 P
and this dear conjunction | plant neighborhood H5 5.02.352
smile heaven upon this fair conjunction, | that R3 5.05. 20
now all my joy | trace the conjunction! H8 3.02. 45
/CONJUNCTIVE 1 FR 0.0001 REL FR 1 V 0 P
she is so /conjunctive to my life and soul, HAM 4.07. 14
CONJUNCTIVE 1 FR 0.0001 REL FR 0 V 1 P
let us be conjunctive in our revenge against him OTH 1.03.367 P
/CONJURATION 1 FR 0.0001 REL FR 1 V 0 P
i do defy thy /conjuration, | and apprehend thee ROM 5.03. 68
CONJURATION 4 FR 0.0004 REL FR 4 V 0 P
mock not my senseless conjuration, lords, | this R2 3.02. 23
under this conjuration speak, my lord; H5 1.02. 29
an earnest conjuration from the king, | as HAM 5.02. 38
what conjuration, and what mighty magic | (for OTH 1.03. 92
CONJURATIONS 1 FR 0.0001 REL FR 1 V 0 P
and buzz these conjurations in her brain. 2H6 1.02. 99
CONJUR'D 8 FR 0.0009 REL FR 6 V 2 P
prophet the nazarite conjur'd the devil into. MV 1.03. 34 P
which has | my evils conjur'd to remembrance, WT 5.03. 40
till she had laid it and conjur'd it down. ROM 2.01. 26
spirits thy power | hath conjur'd to attend. TIM 1.01. 7
but he hath conjur'd me beyond them, and i must 3.06. 11 P
hast conjur'd up | my mortified spirit. JC 2.01.323
or with some dram, conjur'd to this effect, | he OTH 1.03.105
(for he conjur'd her she should ever keep it) 3.03.294
/CONJURE 1 FR 0.0001 REL FR 1 V 0 P
stiffen the sinews, /conjure up the blood, H5 3.01. 7
CONJURE 28 FR 0.0031 REL FR 18 V 10 P
and ev'n in kind love i do conjure thee, | who TGV 2.07. 2
i'll conjure you, i'll fortune–tell you! WIV 4.02.186 P
o prince, i conjure thee, as thou believ'st MM 5.01. 48
dost thou conjure for wenches, that thou call'st ERR 3.01. 34
i conjure thee to leave me and be gone. 4.03. 67
i conjure thee by all the saints in heaven! 4.04. 57
i would to god some scholar would conjure her, ADO 2.01.257 P
to conjure tears up in a poor maid's eyes | with MND 3.02.158
my way is to conjure you, and i'll begin with AYL ep 11 P
i conjure thee, by all the parts of man | which WT 1.02.400
i conjure thee but slowly; JN 4.02.269
you conjure from the breast of civil peace 1H4 4.03. 43
i am not barbason, you cannot conjure me. H5 2.01. 54 P
i cannot so conjure up the spirit of love in her 5.02.288 P
if you would conjure in her, you must make a 5.02.292 P
if conjure up love in her in his true likeness, 5.02.293 P
devil or devil's dam, i'll conjure thee. 1H6 1.05. 5
storm | than any thou canst conjure up to–day; 2H6 5.01.199
'sfoot, i'll learn to conjure and raise devils, TRO 2.03. 6 P
i cannot conjure, troyan. 5.02.125
sighs, and conjure thee to pardon rome and thy COR 5.02. 75 P
nay, i'll conjure too. ROM 2.01. 6
not, | the ape is dead, and i must conjure him. 2.01. 16
i conjure thee by rosaline's bright eyes, | by 2.01. 17
name | i conjure only but to raise up him. 2.01. 29
conjure with 'em, | "brutus" will start a spirit JC 1.02.146
i conjure you, by that which you profess | (how MAC 4.01. 50
but let me conjure you, by the rights of our HAM 2.02.283 P
CONJURER 6 FR 0.0006 REL FR 5 V 1 P
good doctor pinch, you are a conjurer, ERR 4.04. 47
between them they will kill the conjurer. 5.01.177
slave, | forsooth, took on him as a conjurer, 5.01.243
witch, | with roger bolingbrook, the conjurer? 2H6 1.02. 76
nay, then he is a conjurer. 4.02. 92 P
or a conjurer. TNK 3.05. 84
CONJURERS 2 FR 0.0002 REL FR 2 V 0 P
subtile–witted french | conjurers and sorcerers, 1H6 1.01. 26
dealing with witches and with conjurers, | whom 2H6 2.01.168
CONJURES 4 FR 0.0004 REL FR 3 V 1 P
what black magician conjures up this fiend | to R3 1.02. 34
conjures the wand'ring stars and makes them HAM 5.01.256
she conjures, away with her! PER 4.06.147 P
she conjures him by high almighty jove, | by LUC 568
CONJURING 1 FR 0.0001 REL FR 1 V 0 P
conjuring the moon | to stand /'s auspicious LR 2.01. 39
CONJURINGS 1 FR 0.0001 REL FR 1 V 0 P
these are strange conjurings. TNK 3.06.201
CONN'D 5 FR 0.0005 REL FR 4 V 1 P
that well by heart hath conn'd his embassage. LLL 5.02. 98
extremely stretch'd and conn'd with cruel pain, MND 5.01. 80
goldsmiths' wives, and conn'd them out of rings? AYL 3.02.271 P
make invincible | the heart that conn'd them. COR 4.01. 11
set in a note–book, learn'd, and conn'd by rote, JC 4.03. 98
CONNIVE 1 FR 0.0001 REL FR 0 V 1 P
sure the gods do this year connive at us, and we WT 4.04.677 P
CONQUER 21 FR 0.0023 REL FR 20 V 1 P
that england, that was wont to conquer others, R2 2.01. 65
to conquer the kingdom as to speak so much more
H5 5.02.185 P
heat, | to conquer france, his true inheritance? 2H6 1.01. 82
for, were there hope to conquer them again, | my 1.01.117
those provinces these arms of mine did conquer, 1.01.120
that i may conquer fortune's spite | by living 3H6 4.06. 19
wrongs in richard's bosom | /will conquer him! R3 5.03.145
arm, fight, and conquer for fair england's sake! 5.03.158
if we be conquered, let men conquer us, | and 5.03.332
he hath been us'd | ever to conquer, and to have COR 3.03. 26
that, if thou conquer rome, the benefit | which 5.03.142
thou wast born to conquer my country. TIM 4.03.107
we | have us'd to conquer standing on the earth, ANT 3.07. 65
does conquer him that did his master conquer, 3.13. 45
does conquer him that did his master conquer, 3.13. 45
that none but antony | should conquer antony, 4.15. 17
and to conquer | their most absurd intents. 5.02.225
"remember what your fathers were, and conquer!"
TNK 2.02. 36
which i to conquer sought with all my might; LUC 488
yield to my hand, my hand shall conquer thee: 1210
touches so soft still conquer chastity. PP 4. 8
CONQUER'D 13 FR 0.0014 REL FR 13 V 0 P
when you have conquer'd my yet maiden bed, AWW 4.02. 57
and, now it is half conquer'd, must i back JN 5.02. 95
defacing monuments of conquer'd france, 2H6 1.01.102
so triumph thieves upon their conquer'd booty, 3H6 1.04. 63
thou art not conquer'd, beauty's ensign yet | is ROM 5.03. 94
and thee after, when thou hast conquer'd! TIM 4.03.105
for what i have conquer'd, | i grant him part; ANT 3.06. 34
armenia | and other of his conquer'd kingdoms, i 3.06. 36
honor was not yielded, | but conquer'd merely. 3.13. 62
please | to give me conquer'd egypt for my son, 5.02. 19
and conquer'd it, cassibelan, thine uncle CYM 3.01. 5
the conquer'd triumphs, | the victor has the TNK 5.04.113
come in the rearward of a conquer'd woe; SON 90. 6
CONQUERED 7 FR 0.0008 REL FR 7 V 0 P
he ne'er lift up his hand but conquered. 1H6 1.01. 16
our great progenitors had conquered? 5.04.110
breast, | yet neither conqueror nor conquered; 3H6 2.05. 12
fift, | who by his prowess conquered all france: 3.03. 86
if we be conquered, let men conquer us, | and R3 5.03.332
whose wisdom hath her fortune conquered. TIT 1.01.336
is an armed knight that's conquered by a lady; PER 2.02. 26
CONQUERING 6 FR 0.0006 REL FR 6 V 0 P
north, and south, i spread my conquering might. LLL 5.02.563
in whose conquering name | let us resolve to 1H6 2.01. 26
and now to paris in this conquering vein, | all 4.07. 95
what heart receives from hence a conquering part TRO 1.03.352
from euphrates | his conquering banner shook, ANT 1.02.102
till that the conquering wine hath steep'd our 2.07.107
CONQUEROR 22 FR 0.0024 REL FR 16 V 6 P
the conqueror is dismay'd. LLL 5.02.567
take away the conqueror, take away alisander. 5.02.572 P
you have overthrown alisander the conqueror! 5.02.575 P
a conqueror, and afeard to speak! 5.02.578 P
when i from thebes came last a conqueror. MND 5.01. 51
present him to the duke like a roman conqueror, AYL 4.02. 4 P
we came in with richard conqueror. SHR in.1. 5 P
shall, | lie at the proud foot of a conqueror, JN 5.07.113
lives | and as his father here was conqueror, 1H6 3.02. 81
the conquest of our scarce–cold conqueror, 4.03. 50
for henry, son unto a conqueror, | is likely to 5.05. 73
breast, | yet neither conqueror nor conquered; 3H6 2.05. 12
his land then seiz'd on by the conqueror. 3.02. 3
death makes no conquest of this conqueror, | for R3 3.01. 87
ere from this war thou turn a conqueror, | or i 4.04.185
virtuous and holy, be thou conqueror! 5.03.128
gracious conqueror, | victorious titus, rue the TIT 1.01.104
which he stood seiz'd of, to the conqueror; HAM 1.01. 89
is nothing done, if he return the conqueror; LR 4.06.266 P
you did know | how much you were my conqueror,
ANT 3.11. 66
our caesar tells, | "i am conqueror of myself." 4.14. 62
a conqueror that will pray in aid for kindness 5.02. 27
CONQUEROR'S 1 FR 0.0001 REL FR 1 V 0 P
and lead thy daughter to a conqueror's bed; R3 4.04.334
CONQUERORS 7 FR 0.0008 REL FR 7 V 0 P
therefore, brave conquerors — for so you are, LLL 1.01. 8
to enter conquerors, and to proclaim | arthur of JN 2.01.310
conqueror, | is likely to beget more conquerors, 1H6 5.05. 74
clean overblown, themselves, the conquerors, R3 2.04. 61
your wives shall welcome home the conquerors; 5.03.260
the conquerors can but make a fire of him; JC 5.05. 55
her lips are conquerors, his lips obey, | paying VEN 549
CONQUERS 5 FR 0.0005 REL FR 5 V 0 P
the sweet breath of flattery conquers strife. ERR 3.02. 28
back our troops and conquers as she lists: 1H6 1.05. 22
the regent conquers, and the frenchmen fly. 5.03. 1
which yields compassion where he conquers; TNK 4.02.132
bow, | who conquers where he comes in every jar,
VEN 100
CONQUEST 34 FR 0.0038 REL FR 33 V 1 P
and better conquest never canst thou make | than JN 3.01.290
to outlook conquest and to win renown | even in 5.02.115
hath made a shameful conquest of itself. R2 2.01. 66
it is a conquest for a prince to boast of. 1H4 1.01. 77
the head | which princes, flesh'd with conquest, 2H4 1.01.149
a peace is of the nature of a conquest, | for 4.02. 89
not wish | success and conquest to attend on us. H5 2.02. 24
here had the conquest fully been seal'd up, | if 1H6 1.01.130
ascribes the glory of his conquest got | first 3.04. 11
o, think upon the conquest of my father, | my 4.01.148
the conquest of our scarce–cold conqueror, 4.03. 50
command the conquest, charles, it shall be thine 5.02. 19
shall henry's conquest, bedford's vigilance, 2H6 1.01. 96
henry the fourth by conquest got the crown. 3H6 1.01.132
my mind presageth happy gain and conquest. 5.01. 71
and, by my fall, the conquest to my foe. 5.02. 10
death makes no conquest of this conqueror, | for R3 3.01. 87
to whom i will retail my conquest won, | and she 4.04.335
the gods confound them all in thy conquest, TIM 4.03.104
make thine own self the conquest of thy fury; 4.03.337 P
what conquest brings he home? JC 1.01. 32
have i in conquest stretch'd mine arm so far, 2.02. 66
by this vile conquest shall attain unto. 5.05. 38
fortinbras, with conquest come from poland, | to HAM 5.02.350
your scutcheons and your signs of conquest, ANT 5.02.135
acknowledg'd, | put we i' th' roll of conquest. 5.02.181
a kind of conquest | caesar made here, but made CYM 3.01. 22

already, | and make a conquest of unhappy me, PER 1.04. 69
the foul boar's conquest on her fair delight, VEN 1030
prey, | sharp hunger by the conquest satisfied, LUC 422
rotten death make conquest of the stronger, 1767
to be death's conquest and make worms thine heir SON 6.14
war, | how to divide the conquest of thy sight: 46. 2
dead, | the coward conquest of a wretch's knife, 74.11
CONQUESTS 1 FR 0.0001 REL FR 1 V 0 P
are all thy conquests, glories, triumphs, spoils JC 3.01.149
CONQU'RING 2 FR 0.0002 REL FR 2 V 0 P
go forth and fetch their conqu'ring caesar in; H5 5.pr. 28
i kiss his conqu'ring hand. ANT 3.13. 75
CONRADE 4 FR 0.0004 REL FR 0 V 4 P
what, conrade! ADO 3.03. 95 P
conrade, i say! 3.03. 97 P
i am a gentleman, sir, and my name is conrade. 4.02. 14 P
write down master gentleman conrade. 4.02. 15 P
CONS 1 FR 0.0001 REL FR 0 V 1 P
that cons state without book and utters it by TN 2.03.149 P
CONSANGUINEOUS 1 FR 0.0001 REL FR 0 V 1 P
am not i consanguineous? TN 2.03. 77 P
CONSANGUINITY 1 FR 0.0001 REL FR 1 V 0 P
my father, | i know no touch of consanguinity; TRO 4.02. 97
CONSCIENCE' 1 FR 0.0001 REL FR 0 V 1 P
would return for conscience' sake to help to get COR 2.03. 33 P
CONSCIENCE 129 FR 0.0145 REL FR 90 V 39 P
thy conscience | is so possess'd with guilt. TMP 1.02.471
but, for your conscience? 2.01.275
you suffer for a pad conscience. WIV 3.03.219 P
womanhood and the witness of a good conscience, 4.02.208 P
now is cupid a child of conscience, he makes 5.05. 28 P
teach you how you shall arraign your conscience, MM 2.03. 21
old ends any further, examine your conscience, ADO 1.01.289 P
if don worm (his conscience) find no impediment 5.02. 84 P
and done in the testimony of a good conscience. LLL 4.02. 2 P
a very gentle beast, and of a good conscience. MND 5.01.227 P
certainly my conscience will serve me to run MV 2.02. 1 P
my conscience says, "no; 2.02. 6 P
well, my conscience, hanging about the neck of 2.02. 13 P
taste — well, my conscience says, "launcelot, 2.02. 18 P
"bouge not," says my conscience. 2.02. 20 P
"conscience," say i, "you counsel well." 2.02. 21 P
to be rul'd by my conscience, i should stay with 2.02. 23 P
and, in my conscience, my conscience is but a 2.02. 28 P
my conscience is but a kind of hard conscience, 2.02. 28 P
my conscience is but a kind of hard conscience, 2.02. 29 P
but in my conscience, sir, i do not care for you TN 3.01. 29 P
but, were my worth as is my conscience firm, 3.03. 17
i appeal | to your own conscience, sir, before WT 3.02. 46
in my conscience, | the heavens with that we 3.03. 4
earnest, but i cannot with conscience take it. 4.04.646 P
so much my conscience whispers in your ear, JN 1.01. 42
and france, whose armor conscience buckled on, 2.01.564
and go | between his purpose and his conscience, 4.02. 77
made it no conscience to destroy a prince. 4.02.229
between my conscience and my cousin's death. 4.02.248
awakes my conscience to confess all this. 5.04. 43
whom conscience and my kinred bids to right. R2 2.02.115
with clog of conscience and sour melancholy 5.06. 20
the guilt of conscience take thou for thy labor, 5.06. 41
my masters, for a true face and good conscience. 1H4 2.04.502 P
but a good conscience will make any possible 2H4 ep 21 P
that what you speak is in your conscience wash'd H5 1.02. 31
capet, | could not keep quiet in his conscience, 1.02. 79
may i with right and conscience make this claim? 1.02. 96
with conscience wide as hell, mowing like grass 3.03. 13
i think in my very conscience he is as valiant a 3.06. 13 P
a prating coxcomb, in your own conscience now? 4.01. 80 P
troth, i will speak my conscience of the king: 4.01.118 P
his bed, wash every mote out of his conscience; 4.01.179 P
in your conscience, now, is it not? 4.07. 4 P
and't please your majesty, in my conscience. 4.07.134 P
ground and his earth, in my conscience law! 4.07.143 P
your majesty is give me, in your conscience now. 4.08. 38 P
yes, my conscience, he did us great good. 4.08.121 P
but shall i speak my conscience, | our kinsman 2H6 3.01. 68
my conscience tells me you are innocent. 3.01.141
whose conscience with injustice is corrupted. 3.02.235
and in my conscience do repute his grace | the 5.01.177
my conscience tells me he is lawful king. 3H6 1.01.150
now, warwick, tell me, even upon thy conscience, 3.03.113
by, | having god, her conscience, and these bars R3 1.02.234
the worm of conscience still begnaw thy soul! 1.03.221
certain dregs of conscience are yet within me. 1.04.121 P
where's thy conscience now? 1.04.127 P
to give us our reward, thy conscience flies out. 1.04.130 P
my lord, this argues conscience in your grace, 3.07.174
albeit against my conscience and my soul. 3.07.226
hence both are gone with conscience and remorse 4.03. 20
every man's conscience is a thousand men, | to 5.02. 17
o coward conscience, how dost thou afflict me! 5.03.179
my conscience hath a thousand several tongues, 5.03.193
conscience is but a word that cowards use, 5.03.309
our strong arms be our conscience, swords our 5.03.311
hate him perniciously, and, o' my conscience, H8 2.01. 50
and if i have a conscience, let it sink me, 2.01. 60
wife | has crept too near his conscience. 2.02. 17
his conscience | has crept too near another lady 2.02. 17
dangers, doubts, wringing of the conscience, 2.02. 27
my wolsey, | the quiet of my wounded conscience, 2.02. 74
but conscience, conscience! 2.02.142
but conscience, conscience! 2.02.142
of your soft cheveril conscience would receive 2.03. 32
my conscience first receiv'd a tenderness, 2.04.171
this respite shook | the bosom of my conscience, 2.04.183
thus hulling in | the wild sea of my conscience, 2.04.201
i meant to rectify my conscience — which | i 2.04.204
nothing i have done yet, o' my conscience, 3.01. 30
wot you what i found | there (on my conscience, 3.02.123
what means got, i leave to your own conscience) 3.02.327
dignities, | a still and quiet conscience. 3.02.380
justice | for truth's sake and his conscience, 3.02.397
i cannot blame his conscience. 4.01. 47
amen, and yet my conscience says | she's a good 5.01. 24
both in his private conscience and his place, 5.02. 75
i make as little doubt as you do conscience | in 5.02.102
on my christian conscience, this one christening 5.03. 36 P
for, o' my conscience, twenty of the dog–days 5.03. 41 P
i'll haunt thee like a wicked conscience still, TRO 5.10. 28
and hast a thing within thee called conscience, TIT 5.01. 75
canst thou the conscience lack | to think i TIM 2.02.175
to dispense, | for policy sits above conscience. 3.02. 87
for, in my conscience, i was the first man 3.03. 16
that i hope i may use with a safe conscience, JC 1.01. 14 P
wherein i'll catch the conscience of the king. HAM 2.02.605
a lash that speech doth give my conscience! 3.01. 49
thus conscience does make cowards /of /us /all, 3.01. 82
conscience and grace, to the profoundest pit! 4.05.133
now must your conscience my acquittance seal, 4.07. 1
/employment, | they are not near my conscience. 5.02. 58
such coz'nage — is't not perfect conscience, 5.02. 67
and yet it is almost against my conscience. 5.02.296
yet do i hold it very stuff o' th' conscience OTH 1.02. 2
their best conscience | is not to leave't undone 3.03.203
dost thou in conscience think — tell me, emilia 4.03. 61
without offense | (my conscience bids me ask), CYM 1.05. 7
that from my mutest conscience to my tongue 1.06.116
as strongly as the conscience does within, | to 2.02. 36
heaven and my conscience knows | thou didst 3.03. 99
thy conscience witness! 3.04. 46
virtue | which their own conscience seal'd them, 3.06. 84
my conscience, thou art fetter'd | more than my 5.04. 8
yet, on my conscience, there are verier knaves 5.04.200 P
but now my heavy conscience sinks my knee, | as 5.05.413
let not conscience, | which is but cold in PER 4.01. 4
if there be not a conscience to be us'd in every 4.02. 11 P
true, there's two unwholesome, a' conscience. 4.02. 22 P
cleaving his conscience into twain and doing TNK 1.03. 46
and so would any young wench, o' my conscience, 2.04. 12
better, o' my conscience, | was never soldier's 4.02. 87
if he will | against his conscience, let him ep 8
'tween frozen conscience and hot burning will, LUC 247
love is too young to know what conscience is, SON 151. 1
yet who knows not conscience is born of love? 151. 2
no want of conscience hold it that i call | her 151.13
CONSCIENCES 6 FR 0.0006 REL FR 5 V 1 P
twenty consciences, | that stand 'twixt me and TMP 2.01.278
and consciences that will not die in debt | pay LLL 5.02.333
women still give the lie to their consciences. AYL 3.02.391 P
now, for our consciences, the arms are fair 1H4 5.02. 87
they are our outward consciences | and preachers H5 4.01. 8
yes, for /them | that have wild consciences. TNK 3.03. 24
CONSCIONABLE 1 FR 0.0001 REL FR 0 V 1 P
no further conscionable than in putting on the OTH 2.01.238 P
CONSECRATE 8 FR 0.0009 REL FR 8 V 0 P
and that this body, consecrate to thee, | by ERR 2.02.132
with this field–dew consecrate, | every fairy MND 5.01.415
we'll consecrate the steps that ajax makes TRO 2.03.183
the imperial seat, to virtue consecrate, | to TIT 1.01. 14
world's emperor, do i consecrate | my sword, my 1.01.248
wit | to villainy and vengeance consecrate, 2.01.121
parts | did i my soul and fortunes consecrate. OTH 1.03.254
review | the very part was consecrate to thee: SON 74. 6
CONSECRATED 5 FR 0.0005 REL FR 5 V 0 P
desire | to meet me at the consecrated fount, MM 4.03. 98
near to her close and consecrated bower, | while MND 3.02. 7
him, | and underneath that consecrated roof, TN 4.03. 25
whose blush doth thaw the consecrated snow TIM 4.03.385
have batter'd down her consecrated wall, | and LUC 723
CONSECRATIONS 1 FR 0.0001 REL FR 1 V 0 P
all vows and consecrations giving place. LC 263
/CONSENT 2 FR 0.0002 REL FR 2 V 0 P
/for /i /have /given /here /my /soul's /consent R2 4.01.249
/model, | /consent /upon /a /sure /foundation, 2H4 1.03. 52
CONSENT 98 FR 0.0110 REL FR 81 V 17 P
they fell together all, as by consent; TMP 2.01.203
plac'd, | i give consent to go along with you, TGV 4.03. 39
i will consent to act any villainy against him, WIV 2.01. 98 P
win her to consent to you; 2.02.236 P
not by my consent, i promise you. 3.02. 71 P
the wealth i have waits on my consent, and my 3.02. 77 P
on my consent, and my consent goes not that way. 3.02. 77 P
says is here now in the house, by your consent, 3.03.109 P
the maid hath given consent to go with him. 4.06. 45
fit thy consent to my sharp appetite, | lay by MM 2.04.161
it is not my consent, | but my entreaty too. 4.01. 66
i will not consent to die this day, that's 4.03. 56 P
either consent to pay this sum for me | or i ERR 4.01. 72
consent to pay thee that i never had! 4.01. 74
here was a consent, | knowing aforehand of our LLL 5.02.460
lord, | this man hath my consent to marry her. MND 1.01. 25
your grace | consent to marry with demetrius, 1.01. 40
but by your setting on, by your consent? 3.02.231
you of your wife, and me of my consent, | of my 4.01.158
of my consent that she should be your wife. 4.01.159
court | are of consent and sufferance in this. AYL 2.02. 3
in a holiday humor, and like enough to consent. 4.01. 69 P
for all your writers do consent that ipse is he: 5.01. 43 P
consent with both that we may enjoy each other. 5.02. 8 P
you have my consent. 5.02. 13 P
hope, | and marry sweet bianca with consent. SHR 3.02.137
with one consent to have her so bestowed; 4.04. 35
your son shall have my daughter with consent. 4.04. 47
dear sir, to my endeavors give consent, | of AWW 2.01.153
let her in fine consent, | as we'll direct her 3.07. 19
thou shouldst a husband take by my consent, | as WT 5.03.136
yea, without stop, didst let thy heart consent, JN 4.02.239
if thou didst but consent | to this most cruel 4.03.125
if i in act, consent, or sin of thought | be 4.03.135
the other part reserv'd i by consent, | for that R2 1.01.128
thou dost consent | in some large measure to thy 1.02. 25
of society that they flock together in consent, 2H4 5.01. 70 P
put into parts, doth keep in one consent, H5 1.02.181
having full reference | to one consent, may work 1.02.206
that grows not in a fair consent with ours; 2.02. 22
my lord, teach your cousin to consent winking. 5.02.305 P
i will wink on her to consent, my lord, if you 5.02.306 P
by my consent, we'll even let them alone. 1H6 1.02. 44
consent, and for thy honor give consent, | thy 5.03.136
consent, and for thy honor give consent, | thy 5.03.136
that, in regard king henry gives consent, | of 5.04.124
give consent | that marg'ret may be england's 5.05. 23
so should i give consent to flatter sin. 5.05. 25
for eighteen months concluded by consent. 2H6 1.01. 42
and my consent ne'er ask'd herein before? 2.04. 72
say you consent, and censure well the deed, 3.01.275
why, our authority is his consent, | and what we 3.01.316
he swore consent to your succession, | his oath 3H6 2.01.172
son, | didst yield consent to disinherit him, 2.02. 24
i was adopted heir by his consent. 2.02. 88
hadst thou never given consent | that phaeton 2.06. 11
wherein thy counsel and consent is wanting. 2.06.102
and therefore i yield thee my free consent. 4.06. 36
that he consents, if warwick yield consent, 4.06. 46
that he will lose his head ere give consent R3 3.04. 38
say, have i thy consent that they shall die? 4.02. 23
but by particular consent proceeded | under your H8 2.04.222
'tis his highness' pleasure | and our consent, 5.02. 88
do not consent | that ever hector and achilles TRO 1.03.361
your breath with full consent bellied his sails; 2.02. 74
your full consent | gave wings to my propension, 2.02.132
that all, with one consent, praise new–born 3.03.176
aeneas | consent upon the order of their fight, 4.05. 90
to take that course by your consent and voice, 5.03. 74
but cannot make my heart consent to take | a COR 1.09. 37
and their consent of one direct way should be at 2.03. 23 P
by the consent of all, we were establish'd | the 3.01.200
with the consent of supreme jove, inform | thy 5.03. 71
heart, | my will to her consent is but a part; ROM 1.02. 17
lies my consent and fair according voice. 1.02. 19
than your consent gives strength to make /it fly 1.03. 99
i pray, | that thou consent to marry us to–day. 2.03. 64
home, be merry, give consent | to marry paris. 4.01. 89
if in her marriage my consent be missing, | i TIM 1.01.136
the senators with one consent of love | entreat 5.01.140
do not consent | that antony speak in his JC 3.01.232
your brother too must die; consent you, lepidus? 4.01. 2
i do consent — 4.01. 3
if you shall cleave to my consent, when 'tis, MAC 2.01. 25
do you consent we shall acquaint him with it, HAM 1.01.172
last | upon his will i seal'd my hard consent. 1.02. 60
fellow in the cellarage, | consent to swear. 1.05.152
to give them seals never my soul consent! 3.02.399
if't be your pleasure and most wise consent OTH 1.01.121
i did consent, | and often did beguile her of 1.03.155
did you and he consent in cassio's death? 5.02.297
will you, not having my consent, | bestow your PER 2.05. 76
though not his /prime consent, he did not flow 4.03. 27
you, there's no going but by their consent. 4.06.197 P
when that shall be seen, i tender my consent. TNK 2.01. 14 P
i give consent. 3.06.279
the romans plausibly did give consent | to LUC 1854
do in consent shake hands to torture me, | the SON 28. 6
CONSENTED 8 FR 0.0009 REL FR 6 V 2 P
she hath consented. WIV 4.06. 25
'tis well consented; ADO 4.01.251
your father hath consented | that you shall be SHR 2.01.269
we have consented to all terms of reason. H5 5.02.329 P
stars | that have consented unto henry's death: 1H6 1.01. 5
you all consented unto salisbury's death, | for 1.05. 34
say that the queen hath heartily consented | he R3 4.05. 7
though we willingly consented to his banishment, COR 4.06.144 P
CONSENTING 4 FR 0.0004 REL FR 3 V 1 P
in such a one as, you consenting to't, | would MM 3.01. 70
consenting to the safeguard of your honor, | i 5.01.419
my sudden wooing, nor /her sudden consenting; AYL 5.02. 7 P
haply, | which his heart was not consenting to. AWW 3.02. 78
CONSENTS 6 FR 0.0006 REL FR 6 V 0 P
to seal our happiness with their consents! TGV 1.03. 49
yoke | my soul consents not to give sovereignty. MND 1.01. 82
the main consents are had, and here we'll stay AWW 5.03. 69
that he consents, if warwick yield consent, 3H6 4.06. 46
my poverty, but not my will, consents. ROM 5.01. 75
consents bewitch'd, ere he desire, have granted, LC 131
CONSEQUENCE 19 FR 0.0021 REL FR 17 V 2 P
your powder'd bawd, an unshunn'd consequence; MM 3.02. 60 P
the consequence is then, thy jealous fits | hath ERR 5.01. 85
joy be the consequence! MV 3.02.107
trust him not in matter of heavy consequence; AWW 2.05. 45 P
it is a matter of small consequence, | which for R2 5.02. 61
pause, | to answer matters of this consequence. H5 2.04.146
o bitter consequence, | that edward still should R3 4.02. 15
hoping the consequence | will prove as bitter, 4.04. 6
mighty moment in't | and consequence of dread, H8 2.04.215
some consequence yet hanging in the stars ROM 1.04.107
enterprise | of honorable–dangerous consequence; JC 1.03.124
trifles, to betray 's | in deepest consequence. MAC 1.03.126
could trammel up the consequence, and catch 1.07. 3
he closes with you in this consequence: HAM 2.01. 45
at "closes in the consequence." 2.01. 51
at "closes in the consequence," ay, marry. 2.01. 52
each small annexment, petty consequence, 3.03. 21
if consequence do but approve my dream, | my OTH 2.03. 62
enlargement by | the consequence o' th' crown, CYM 2.03.121
CONSEQUENCES 1 FR 0.0001 REL FR 1 V 0 P
all mortal consequences have pronounc'd me thus: MAC 5.03. 5
CONSEQUENTLY 3 FR 0.0003 REL FR 2 V 1 P
and consequently sets down the manner how: TN 3.04. 71 P
and consequently thy rude hand to act | the deed JN 4.02.240
and consequently, like a traitor coward, R2 1.01.102
CONSERV'D 1 FR 0.0001 REL FR 1 V 0 P
the skillful | conserv'd of maidens' hearts. OTH 3.04. 75
CONSERVE 1 FR 0.0001 REL FR 1 V 0 P
thou art too noble to conserve a life | in base MM 3.01. 87
CONSERVES 3 FR 0.0003 REL FR 1 V 2 P
please your honor taste of these conserves? SHR in.2. 3
and if you give me any conserves, give me in.2. 7 P
me any conserves, give me conserves of beef. in.2. 7 P
CONSIDER 51 FR 0.0057 REL FR 39 V 12 P
and that most deeply to consider is | the beauty TMP 3.02. 98
let her consider his frailty, and then judge of WIV 3.05. 50 P
consider how it stands upon my credit. ERR 4.01. 68
consider who the king your father sends, | to LLL 2.01. 2
consider what you first did swear unto: 4.03.287
masters, you ought to consider with /yourselves, MND 3.01. 29 P
consider then, we come but in despite. 5.01.112
though justice be thy plea, consider this, MV 4.01.198
yet have the grace to consider that tears do not AYL 3.04. 3 P
when i consider | what great creation and what AWW 2.03.168
consider, he's an enemy to mankind. TN 3.04. 98 P
and | so leaves me to consider what is breeding WT 1.02.374

consider little | what dangers, by his highness' 5.01. 26
will bring me to consider that which may 5.01.122
better consider what you have to do | than i, 1H4 5.02. 76
you that are old consider not the capacities of 2H4 1.02.174 P
these letters | and well consider of them. 3.01. 3
we consider | it was excess of wine that set him H5 2.02. 41
for us, we will consider of this further. 2.04.113
bid him therefore consider of his ransom, which 3.06.126 P
consider, lords, he is the next of blood, | and 2H6 1.01.151
widow, we will consider of your suit, | and come 3H6 3.02. 16
o, sirs, consider, they that set you on | to do R3 1.04.254
to consider further, that | what his high hatred H8 1.01.106
for goodness sake, consider what you do, | how 3.01.159
consider you what services he has done for his COR 1.01. 30 P
consider of it." 1.02. 17
consider this: 3.01.318
the warlike service he has done, consider; 3.03. 49
consider further: 3.03. 52
you must consider that a prodigal course | is TIM 3.04. 12
what you have said | i will consider; JC 1.02.168
but if you would consider the true cause | why 1.03. 62
if thou consider rightly of the matter, | caesar 3.02.109
consider it not so deeply. MAC 2.02. 27
'twere to consider too curiously, to consider so HAM 5.01.205 P
to consider too curiously, to consider so. 5.01.205 P
consider him well. LR 3.04.103 P
good my friends, consider | you are my guests. 3.07. 30
when we consider | th' importancy of cyprus to OTH 1.03. 19
i hope you will consider what is spoke | comes 3.03.216
not to consider in what case thou stand'st ANT 3.13. 54
rich words to it — and then let her consider. CYM 2.03. 19 P
i will consider your music the better; 2.03. 28 P
madam, you're best consider. 3.02. 77
consider, | when you above perceive me like a 3.03. 11
but i consider, | by med'cine life may be 5.05. 28
consider, sir, the chance of war, the day | was 5.05. 75
let him consider. TNK 1.01.105
nor gain | made him regard, or loss consider, 1.03. 30
when i consider every thing that grows | holds SON 15. 1
CONSIDERANCE 1 FR 0.0001 REL FR 1 V 0 P
after this cold considerance, sentence me, | and 2H4 5.02. 98
CONSIDERATE 2 FR 0.0002 REL FR 1 V 1 P
me | that look into me with considerate eyes. R3 4.02. 30
go to then — your considerate stone. ANT 2.02.110 P
CONSIDERATION 8 FR 0.0009 REL FR 6 V 2 P
unhatch'd rapier and on carpet consideration, TN 3.04.236 P
about, | startles and frights consideration, JN 4.02. 25
you, can thrust me from a level consideration. 2H4 2.01.113 P
consideration like an angel came | and whipt th' H5 1.01. 28
highness | would give it quick consideration, H8 1.02. 66
mind, | that from it all consideration slips — TIM 4.03.196
and in thy best consideration check | this LR 1.01.150
to supper, come, | and drown consideration. ANT 4.02. 45
CONSIDERATIONS 2 FR 0.0002 REL FR 1 V 1 P
albeit considerations infinite | do make against 1H4 5.01.102
these humble considerations make me out of love 2H4 2.02. 11 P
CONSIDER'D 12 FR 0.0013 REL FR 7 V 5 P
i have consider'd well his loss of time, | and TGV 1.03. 19
out in the service, you will be consider'd. MM 1.02.111 P
which if i have not enough consider'd (as too WT 4.02. 17 P
i have consider'd so much, camillo, and with 4.02. 34 P
being something gently consider'd, i'll bring 4.04.795 P
suits | have been consider'd and debated on. 1H6 5.01. 35
i have consider'd in my mind | the late request R3 4.02. 83
which, being consider'd, | have mov'd us and our H8 5.01. 99
then, now | have you consider'd of my speeches? MAC 3.01. 75
question of the play be then to be consider'd. HAM 3.02. 43 P
in the which | i have consider'd of a course. CYM 3.04.111
prithee away, | there's more to be consider'd; 3.04.181
CONSIDERED 6 FR 0.0006 REL FR 6 V 0 P
the circumstance considered, good my lord, 1H4 1.03. 70
i have considered with myself | the title of 2H6 5.01.175
trivial, | all circumstances well considered. R3 3.07.176
and at our more considered time we'll read, HAM 2.02. 81
which if thou hast considered, let us know | if ANT 2.06. 5
if thine, considered, prove the thousand part PER 5.01.135
CONSIDERING 5 FR 0.0005 REL FR 3 V 2 P
for, considering the weather, a taller man than SHR 4.01. 10 P
the moon, not worth | his serious considering. H8 3.02.135
considering how honor would become such a person COR 1.03. 9 P
and the place death, considering who thou art, ROM 2.02. 64
some comfort | we have by so considering: TNK 5.04. 4
CONSIDERINGS 1 FR 0.0001 REL FR 1 V 0 P
that many maz'd considerings did throng | and H8 2.04.186
CONSIDERS 2 FR 0.0002 REL FR 2 V 0 P
considers she my possessions? TGV 5.02. 25
when he considers more, this love of mine | will TNK 2.06. 27
CONSIGN 3 FR 0.0003 REL FR 2 V 1 P
out of our demands, | and we'll consign thereto. H5 5.02. 90
lord, a hard condition for a maid to consign to. 5.02.299 P
lovers must | consign to thee and come to dust. CYM 4.02.275
CONSIGN'D 1 FR 0.0001 REL FR 1 V 0 P
distinct breath and consign'd kisses to them, TRO 4.04. 45
CONSIGNING 1 FR 0.0001 REL FR 1 V 0 P
state, | and (god consigning to my good intents) 2H4 5.02.143
CONSIST 5 FR 0.0005 REL FR 4 V 1 P
if their purgation did consist in words, | they AYL 1.03. 53
does not our lives consist of the four elements? TN 2.03. 9 P
absolute | as our conditions shall consist upon, 2H4 4.01.185
which doth most consist | of war-mark'd footmen, ANT 3.07. 43
welcome is peace, if he on peace consist; PER 1.04. 83
CONSISTETH 1 FR 0.0001 REL FR 1 V 0 P
profit of the city | consisteth of all nations. MV 3.03. 31
CONSISTING 2 FR 0.0002 REL FR 2 V 0 P
length, | consisting equally of horse and foot; R3 5.03.294
though in and of him there be much consisting, TRO 3.03.116
CONSISTORY 3 FR 0.0003 REL FR 3 V 0 P
my other self, my counsel's consistory, | my R3 2.02.151
warranted | by a commission from the consistory, H8 2.04. 92
consistory, | yea, the whole consistory of rome. 2.04. 93
CONSISTS 4 FR 0.0004 REL FR 2 V 2 P
but i think it rather consists of eating and TN 2.03. 12 P
and now my whole charge consists of ancients, 1H4 4.02. 23 P
in her consists my happiness and thine; R3 4.04.406
fair /one, all goodness that consists in beauty, PER 5.01. 70
CONSOLATE 1 FR 0.0001 REL FR 1 V 0 P
may report my flight | to consolate thine ear. AWW 3.02.128
CONSOLATION 2 FR 0.0002 REL FR 1 V 1 P
take this of me, kate of my consolation — SHR 2.01.190
this grief is crown'd with consolation: ANT 1.02.168 P
CONSONANCY 2 FR 0.0002 REL FR 0 V 2 P
but then there is no consonancy in the sequel; TN 2.05.129 P
our fellowship, by the consonancy of our youth, HAM 2.02.284 P
CONSONANT 1 FR 0.0001 REL FR 0 V 1 P
quis, quis, thou consonant? LLL 5.01. 52 P
CONSORT* 13 FR 0.0014 REL FR 11 V 2 P
lady's chamber-window | with some sweet consort; TGV 3.02. 83
wilt thou be of our consort? 4.01. 62
mart, | and afterward consort you till bed-time: ERR 1.02. 28
health and fair desires consort your grace! LLL 2.01.177
and must for aye consort with black-brow'd night MND 3.02.387
and boding screech-owls make the consort full! 2H6 3.02.327
consort with me in loud and dear petition, TRO 5.03. 9
consort! ROM 3.01. 46 P
'zounds, consort! 3.01. 49 P
thou wretched boy, that didst consort him here, 3.01.130
let's not consort with them; MAC 2.03.135
yes, madam, he was of that consort. LR 2.01. 97
who bids them still consort with ugly night, VEN 1041
CONSORTED 8 FR 0.0009 REL FR 7 V 1 P
"sorted and consorted, contrary to thy LLL 1.01.258 P
with all the rest of that consorted crew, R2 5.03.138
two of the dangerous consorted traitors | that 5.06. 15
consorted with that harlot, strumpet shore, R3 3.04. 71
for this, consorted with the citizens, | your 3.07.137
trees | to be consorted with the humorous night. ROM 2.01. 31
hands, | who to philippi here consorted us. JC 5.01. 82
while collatine and his consorted lords | with LUC 1609
CONSORTEST 1 FR 0.0001 REL FR 0 V 1 P
mercutio, thou consortest with romeo — ROM 3.01. 45 P
CONSPECTUITIES 1 FR 0.0001 REL FR 0 V 1 P
can your beesom conspectuities glean out of this COR 2.01. 64 P
CONSPIRACY 11 FR 0.0012 REL FR 8 V 3 P
open-ey'd conspiracy | his time doth take. TMP 2.01.301
i had forgot that foul conspiracy | of the beast 4.01.139
knot, a /ging, a pack, a conspiracy against me. WIV 4.02.118 P
now for conspiracy, | i know not how it tastes, WT 3.02. 71
woman, | wilt thou conceal this dark conspiracy? R2 5.02. 96
o heinous, strong, and bold conspiracy! 5.03. 59
confirm'd conspiracy with fearful france, | and H5 2.pr. 27
o conspiracy, | sham'st thou to show thy JC 2.01. 77
seek none, conspiracy! 2.01. 81
security gives way to conspiracy. 2.03. 7 P
conspiracy? LR 1.02. 55 P
CONSPIRANT 1 FR 0.0001 REL FR 1 V 0 P
conspirant 'gainst this high illustrious prince, LR 5.03.136
CONSPIRATOR 6 FR 0.0006 REL FR 4 V 2 P
the grand conspirator, abbot of westminster, R2 5.06. 19
stand back, thou manifest conspirator, | thou 1H6 1.03. 33
cut off the proud'st conspirator that lives. TIT 4.04. 26
tear him to pieces, he's a conspirator. JC 3.03. 28 P
i am not cinna the conspirator. 3.03. 32 P
whisp'ring conspirator | with close-tongu'd LUC 769
CONSPIRATORS 3 FR 0.0003 REL FR 3 V 0 P
away then, come, seek the conspirators. JC 3.02.232
look, | i draw a sword against conspirators; 5.01. 51
all the conspirators, save only he, | did that 5.05. 69
CONSPIR'D 5 FR 0.0005 REL FR 4 V 1 P
have you conspir'd, have you with these MND 3.02.196
and they have conspir'd together. MV 2.05. 22 P
lightly conspir'd | and sworn unto the practices H5 2.02. 89
you have conspir'd against our royal person, 2.02.167
conspir'd with that irregulous devil cloten, CYM 4.02.315
CONSPIRE 8 FR 0.0009 REL FR 7 V 1 P
to whisper and conspire against my youth? TGV 1.02. 43
the times conspire with you, | for he that JN 3.04.146
what mutter you, or what conspire you, lords? 3H6 1.01.165
that do conspire my death with devilish plots R3 3.04. 60
be menelaus, i would conspire against destiny. TRO 5.01. 63 P
thou dost conspire against thy friend, iago, OTH 3.03.142
was't | that mov'd pale cassius to conspire? ANT 2.06. 15
'gainst thyself thou stick'st not to conspire, SON 10. 6
CONSPIRED 1 FR 0.0001 REL FR 1 V 0 P
hast thou conspired with thy brother too, | that JN 1.01.241
CONSPIRERS 1 FR 0.0001 REL FR 1 V 0 P
who chafes, who frets, or where conspirers are: MAC 4.01. 91
CONSPIRES 1 FR 0.0001 REL FR 1 V 0 P
what further woe conspires against mine age? ROM 5.03.212
CONSPIRING 1 FR 0.0001 REL FR 0 V 1 P
and conspiring with camillo to take away the WT 3.02. 15 P
CONSTABLE 34 FR 0.0038 REL FR 12 V 22 P
monster, i am in case to justle a constable. TMP 3.02. 26 P
the knave constable had set me i' th' stocks, i' WIV 4.05.119 P
i am the poor duke's constable, and my name is MM 2.01. 48 P
how dost thou know that, constable? 2.01. 78 P
he's in the right, constable. 2.01.160 P
come hither, master constable. 2.01.258 P
long have you been in this place of constable? 2.01.259 P
you the most desartless man to be constable? ADO 3.03. 10 P
both which, master constable — 3.03. 17 P
and fit man for the constable of the watch; 3.03. 23 P
you, constable, are to present the prince's own 3.03. 74 P
call up the right master constable. 3.03.166 P
let them come before master constable. 4.02. 8 P
master constable, you go not the way to examine; 4.02. 33 P
master constable — 4.02. 43 P
master constable, let these men be bound, and 4.02. 64 P
this learned constable is too cunning to be 5.01.228 P
sigh, | a critic, nay, a night-watch constable, LLL 3.01.176
from below your duke to beneath your constable, AWW 2.02. 31 P
well, 'tis not so, my lord high constable; H5 2.04. 41
charles delabreth, high constable of france, 3.05. 40
therefore, lord constable, haste on montjoy, 3.05. 61
now forth, lord constable and princes all, | and 3.05. 67
my lord of orleance, and my lord high constable, 3.07. 8 P
i tell thee, constable, my mistress wears his 3.07. 60 P
my lord constable, the armor that i saw in your 3.07. 69 P
my lord high constable, the english lie within 3.07.125 P
now, my lord constable? 4.02. 7
the constable desires thee thou wilt mind | thy 4.03. 84
the constable of france. 4.03. 89
tell the constable | we are but warriors for the 4.03.108
shall yield them little, tell the constable. 4.03.125
charles delabreth, high constable of france, 4.08. 92
hither, i was lord high constable | and duke of H8 2.01.102
CONSTABLE'S 2 FR 0.0002 REL FR 1 V 1 P
master froth do the constable's wife any harm? MM 2.01.158 P
tut, dun's the mouse, the constable's own word. ROM 1.04. 40
CONSTABLES 1 FR 0.0001 REL FR 0 V 1 P
the constables have deliver'd her over to me, 2H4 5.04. 4 P
CONSTANCE 8 FR 0.0009 REL FR 8 V 0 P
how that ambitious constance would not cease JN 1.01. 32
is not the lady constance in this troop? 2.01.540
call the lady constance; 2.01.553
lady constance, peace! 3.01.112
the lady constance speaks not from her faith, 3.01.210
patience, good lady, comfort, gentle constance! 3.04. 22
my name is constance, i was geffrey's wife, 3.04. 46
the lady constance in a frenzy died | three days 4.02.122
CONSTANCIES 1 FR 0.0001 REL FR 1 V 0 P
whose constancies | expire before their fashions AWW 1.02. 62
CONSTANCY 18 FR 0.0020 REL FR 14 V 4 P
here is my hand for my true constancy; TGV 2.02. 8
in your brow, provost, honesty and constancy; MM 4.02.154 P
and grows to something of great constancy; MND 5.01. 26
wisdom, and constancy, hath amaz'd me more AWW 2.01. 84
i would have men of such constancy put to sea, TN 2.04. 76 P
take a fellow of plain and uncoin'd constancy, H5 5.02.153 P
and force them with a constancy, the cardinal H8 3.02. 2
jove | to find persistive constancy in men? TRO 1.03. 21
to keep her constancy in plight and youth, 3.02.161
do, | with untir'd spirits and formal constancy. JC 2.01.227
i have made strong proof of my constancy, 2.01.299
o constancy, be strong upon my side, | set a 2.04. 6
your constancy | hath left you unattended. MAC 2.02. 65
whom in constancy you think stands so safe. CYM 1.04.126 P
love and constancy is dead, | phoenix and the PHT 22
therefore my verse, to constancy confin'd, | one SON 105. 7
prove | the constancy and virtue of your love. 117.14
oaths of thy love, thy truth, thy constancy, 152.10
CONSTANT 55 FR 0.0062 REL FR 43 V 12 P
who was so firm, so constant, that this coil TMP 1.02.207
not turn me about, my stomach is not constant. 2.02.115 P
i cannot now prove constant to myself, | without TGV 2.06. 31
were man | but constant, he were perfect; 5.04.111
spy | more fresh in julia's with a constant eye? 5.04.115
is virtuous to be constant in any undertaking. MM 3.02.226 P
friendship is constant in all other things ADO 2.01.175
be you constant in the accusation, and my 2.02. 54 P
and one on shore, | to one thing constant never. 2.03. 65
true, | shall she be placed in my constant soul. MV 2.06. 57
so much the constitution | of any constant man. 3.02.247
the constant service of the antique world, AYL 2.03. 57
betwixt the constant red and mingled damask. 3.05.123
save in the constant image of the creature TN 2.04. 19
make the trial of it in any constant question. 4.02. 48 P
still so constant, lord. 5.01.111
to this i am most constant, | though destiny say WT 4.04. 45
and therein am i constant to my profession. 4.04.682 P
than arm thy constant and thy nobler parts JN 3.01.291
as ever was laid, our friends true and constant: 1H4 2.03. 18 P
constant you are, | but yet a woman, and for 2.03.108
troth, i kiss thee with a most constant heart. 2H4 2.04.269 P
sate | crowned with faith and constant loyalty. H5 2.02. 5
constant in spirit, not swerving with the blood, 2.02.133
withal | how terrible in constant resolution, 2.04. 35
this shall assure my constant loyalty, | that if 3H6 3.03.240
so long as edward is thy constant friend | and 4.01. 77
bring me a constant woman to her husband, | one H8 3.01.134
ere they be woo'd, they are constant being won. TRO 3.02.111 P
let all constant men be troiluses, all false 3.02.202 P
sir, it is, | and i am constant. COR 1.01.239
valiant ignorance, | and perish constant fools. 4.06.105
you keep a constant temper. 5.02. 94
cassius, be constant; JC 3.01. 22
but i am constant as the northern star, | of 3.01. 60
that i was constant cimber should be banish'd, 3.01. 72
and constant do remain to keep him so. 3.01. 73
i am constant to my purposes, they follow the HAM 5.02.200 P
we have this hour a constant will to publish LR 1.01. 43
self-reproving — bring his constant pleasure. 5.01. 4
is of a constant, loving, noble nature, | and i OTH 2.01.289
wise, chaste, constant, qualified, and less CYM 1.04. 60 P
a sly and constant knave, | not to be shak'd; 1.05. 75
for even to vice | they are not constant, but 2.05. 30
mulier i divine | is this most constant wife, 5.05.449
she would with rich and constant pen | vail to PER 4.ch. 28
there constant to eternity it lives. TNK pr 14
that with such a constant nobility enforce a 2.01. 33 P
o sacred, shadowy, cold, and constant queen, 5.01.137
variable passions throng her constant woe, | as VEN 967
but like a constant and confirmed devil, | he LUC 1513
to myself forsworn, to thee i'll constant prove; PP 5. 3
and, constant stars, in them i read such art SON 14.10
but you like none, none you, for constant heart. 53.14
kind, | still constant in a wondrous excellence, 105. 6
CONSTANTINE 1 FR 0.0001 REL FR 1 V 0 P
helen, the mother of great constantine, | nor 1H6 1.02.142
CONSTANTINOPLE 1 FR 0.0001 REL FR 0 V 1 P
that shall go to constantinople and take the H5 5.02.208 P
CONSTANTLY 7 FR 0.0008 REL FR 4 V 3 P
i do constantly believe you. MM 4.01. 21 P
is, or any thing constantly but a time-pleaser, TN 2.03.148 P
i constantly believe | (or rather call my TRO 4.01. 41
resolv'd | to meet all perils very constantly. JC 5.01. 91
most constantly. HAM 1.02.234
patiently and constantly thou hast stuck to the CYM 3.05.118 P
i fix'd my note | constantly on them; TNK 1.04. 20
CONSTELLATION 2 FR 0.0002 REL FR 2 V 0 P
i know thy constellation is right apt | for this TN 1.04. 35
and set him by him, | a shining constellation. TNK 4.02. 18
CONSTER *(also construe)*
/CONSTER 1 FR 0.0001 REL FR 1 V 0 P
and his unbookish jealousy must /conster | poor OTH 4.01.101
CONSTER 5 FR 0.0005 REL FR 4 V 1 P
conster my speeches better, if you may. LLL 5.02.341
conster them. SHR 3.01. 30
now let me see if i can conster it: 3.01. 41
i will conster to them whence you come; TN 3.01. 56 P
in scorn or friendship, nill i conster whether. PP 14. 8

CONSTERS 1 FR 0.0001 REL FR 1 V 0 P
he in the worst sense consters their denial: LUC 324
CONSTITUTION 2 FR 0.0002 REL FR 1 V 1 P
could turn so much the constitution | of any MV 3.02.246
by the excellent constitution of thy leg, it was TN 1.03.132 P
CONSTRAIN 2 FR 0.0002 REL FR 1 V 1 P
i would your grace would constrain me to tell. ADO 1.01.206 P
i must | constrain you then; TNK 2.02.270
/CONSTRAIN'D 1 FR 0.0001 REL FR 1 V 0 P
/constrain'd | /as /men /drink /potions, /that 2H4 1.01.196
CONSTRAIN'D 9 FR 0.0010 REL FR 7 V 2 P
i shall be constrain'd in't to call thee knave, TN 2.03. 66 P
the first time i have constrain'd one to call me 2.03. 67 P
constrain'd to watch in darkness, rain, and cold 1H6 2.01. 7
inhuman traitors, you constrain'd and forc'd. TIT 5.02.177
to come thus was i not constrain'd, but did it ANT 3.06. 56
close, | whereto constrain'd by her infirmity, CYM 3.05. 47
than in gyves, | desir'd more than constrain'd. 5.04. 15
i am glad to be constrain'd to utter that 5.05.141
being constrain'd with dreadful circumstance? LUC 1703
CONSTRAINED 2 FR 0.0002 REL FR 2 V 0 P
and none serve with him but constrained things, MAC 5.04. 13
he | does pity, as constrained blemishes, | not ANT 3.13. 59
CONSTRAINETH 1 FR 0.0001 REL FR 1 V 0 P
faintness constraineth me | to measure out my MND 3.02.428
CONSTRAINS 3 FR 0.0003 REL FR 2 V 1 P
constrains them weep and shake with fear and COR 5.03.100
a case as yours constrains a man to bow in the ROM 2.04. 53 P
and constrains the garb | quite from his nature. LR 2.02. 97
CONSTRAINT 7 FR 0.0008 REL FR 6 V 1 P
he roar'd | with sharp constraint of hunger; AWW 3.02.118
i love thee | by love's own sweet constraint, 4.02. 16
i will confess what i know without constraint. 4.03.122 P
to you | than the constraint of hospitable zeal JN 2.01.244
i did suppose it should be on constraint, | but, 5.01. 28
bloody constraint; H5 2.04. 97
'tis a good constraint of fortune it belches PER 3.02. 55
CONSTRING'D 1 FR 0.0001 REL FR 1 V 0 P
call, | constring'd in mass by the almighty sun, TRO 5.02.173
CONSTRUCTION 9 FR 0.0010 REL FR 6 V 3 P
that there is shrewd construction made of her. WIV 2.02.223 P
o illegitimate construction! ADO 3.04. 50 P
observe his construction of it. TN 2.03.175 P
under your hard construction must i sit, | to 3.01.115
in | the merciful construction of good women, H8 ep 10
to strike at him admits | a good construction. COR 5.06. 20
to find the mind's construction in the face: MAC 1.04. 12
let him show | his skill in the construction. CYM 5.05.433
the fit and apt construction of thy name, 5.05.444
CONSTRUE *(also conster, etc.)*
/CONSTRUE 1 FR 0.0001 REL FR 1 V 0 P
/construe /the /times /to /their /necessities, 2H4 4.01.102
CONSTRUE 5 FR 0.0005 REL FR 4 V 1 P
they would have the profferer construe "ay." TGV 1.02. 56
i can construe the action of her familiar style, WIV 1.03. 46 P
you one), | nor construe any further my neglect, JC 1.02. 45
but men may construe things after their fashion, 1.03. 34
all my engagements i will construe to thee, 2.01.307
CONSUL 29 FR 0.0032 REL FR 25 V 4 P
on the sudden, | i warrant him consul. COR 2.01.222
were he to stand for consul, never would he 2.01.232
'tis thought | that martius shall be consul. 2.01.261
to desire | the present consul and last general 2.02. 43
are well pleas'd | to make thee consul. 2.02.133
and to our noble consul | wish we all joy and 2.02.152
the tune of your voices that i may be consul, i 2.03. 86 P
therefore, beseech you, i may be consul. 2.03.103 P
indeed i would be consul. 2.03.131
therefore let him be consul. 2.03.134 P
amen, amen. god save thee, noble consul! 2.03.136 P
it in scorn, | "i would be consul," says he; 2.03.168
they have chose a consul that will from them 2.03.214
you against the grain | to voice him consul. 2.03.234
they are worn, lord consul, so | that we shall 3.01. 6
why then should i be consul? 3.01. 50
spirit, | or never be so noble as a consul, 3.01. 56
this a consul? no! 3.01.171
martius, | whom late you have nam'd for consul. 3.01.195
consul? what consul? 3.01.277
consul? what consul? 3.01.277
the consul coriolanus. 3.01.278
he consul! 3.01.278
i'll return consul, | or never trust to what my 3.02.135
that being pass'd for consul with full voice, 3.03. 59
i have been consul, and can show /for rome | her 3.03.110
if he had gone forth consul, found it so. 4.06. 35
his stoutness | when he did stand for consul, 5.06. 27
sent by a consul to me, should not sooner | than CYM 4.02.385
CONSUL'S 2 FR 0.0002 REL FR 2 V 0 P
and i' th' consul's view | slew three opposers. COR 2.02. 93
as i do know the consul's worthiness, | so can i 3.01.276
CONSULS 6 FR 0.0006 REL FR 6 V 0 P
by jove himself, | it makes the consuls base; COR 3.01.108
this volumnia | is worth of consuls, senators, 5.04. 53
subscrib'd by th' consuls and patricians, 5.06. 81
wherein the /toged consuls can propose | as OTH 1.01. 25
and many of the consuls, rais'd and met, | are 1.02. 43
where thou slew'st | hirtius and pansa, consuls, ANT 1.04. 58
CONSULSHIP 1 FR 0.0001 REL FR 0 V 1 P
well then, i pray, your price a' th' consulship? COR 2.03. 73 P
CONSULSHIPS 1 FR 0.0001 REL FR 0 V 1 P
how many stand for consulships? COR 2.02. 2 P
CONSULT 4 FR 0.0004 REL FR 2 V 2 P
let's consult together against this greasy WIV 2.01.107 P
lest they consult about the giving up of some 2H6 4.07.132 P
let us consult upon to–morrow's business. R3 5.03. 45
then sit we down and let us all consult. TIT 4.02.132
CONSULTING 2 FR 0.0002 REL FR 2 V 0 P
and, not consulting, broke | into a general H8 1.01. 91
like many clouds consulting for foul weather. VEN 972
CONSUM'D 8 FR 0.0009 REL FR 8 V 0 P
and see it instantly consum'd with fire. WT 2.03.134
is that the rebels have consum'd with fire | our R2 5.06. 2
long, | and overmuch consum'd his royal person: R3 1.01.140
and what else dear that is consum'd | in hot TRO 2.02. 5
o'erborne their way, consum'd with fire, and COR 4.06. 78
let's hew his limbs till they be clean consum'd. TIT 1.01.129
lord, | your wisdom is consum'd in confidence. JC 2.02. 49
consum'd with that which it was nourish'd by. SON 73.12
CONSUME 11 FR 0.0012 REL FR 11 V 0 P
fire, | consume away in sighs, waste inwardly. ADO 3.01. 78
they do consume the thing that feeds their fury. SHR 2.01.133
nay, after that, consume away in rust, | but for JN 4.01. 65
break thou in pieces and consume to ashes, 1H6 5.04. 92
to my house the brand | that should consume it, COR 4.06.116
will it consume me? let me see it then. TIT 3.01. 62
fire and powder, | which as they kiss consume. ROM 2.06. 11
a plague consume you, wicked caitiffs left! TIM 5.04. 71
do not | consume your blood with sorrowing; PER 4.01. 23
quarrels consume us, envy of ill men | crave our TNK 2.02. 90
rot, and consume themselves in little time. VEN 132
CONSUMED 1 FR 0.0001 REL FR 1 V 0 P
whole, | not one word more of the consumed time. AWW 5.03. 38
CONSUMERS 1 FR 0.0001 REL FR 1 V 0 P
time, | fearful consumers, you will all devour! TNK 1.01. 70
CONSUMES 2 FR 0.0002 REL FR 1 V 1 P
a cheese, consumes itself to the very paring, AWW 1.01.142 P
as smoke from aetna, that in air consumes, | or LUC 1042
CONSUMING 4 FR 0.0004 REL FR 4 V 0 P
consuming means, soon preys upon itself. R2 2.01. 39
whiles thy consuming canker eats his falsehood. 1H6 2.04. 71
i bring consuming sorrow to thine age. TIT 3.01. 61
o' th' tongue, | consuming it with speaking! TIM 5.01.134
CONSUMMATE 4 FR 0.0004 REL FR 3 V 1 P
do you the office, friar, which consummate, MM 5.01.378
i do but stay till your marriage be consummate, ADO 3.02. 2 P
will post | to consummate this business happily. JN 5.07. 95
there shall we consummate our spousal rites. TIT 1.01.337
CONSUMMATION 3 FR 0.0003 REL FR 3 V 0 P
'tis a consummation | devoutly to be wish'd. HAM 3.01. 62
quiet consummation have, | and renowned be thy CYM 4.02.280
the combat's consummation is proclaim'd | by the TNK 5.03. 94
CONSUMPTION 4 FR 0.0004 REL FR 2 V 2 P
life, for i was told you were in a consumption. ADO 5.04. 96 P
no remedy against this consumption of the purse; 2H4 1.02.236 P
consumption catch thee! TIM 4.03.201
pit, burning, scalding, | stench, consumption. LR 4.06.129
CONSUMPTIONS 1 FR 0.0001 REL FR 1 V 0 P
consumptions sow | in hollow bones of man, TIM 4.03.151
CONSUM'ST 1 FR 0.0001 REL FR 1 V 0 P
that thou consum'st thyself in single life? SON 9. 2
CONTAGION 7 FR 0.0008 REL FR 6 V 1 P
thy flesh, | being strumpeted by thy contagion. ERR 2.02.144
to hear by the nose, it is dulcet in contagion. TN 2.03. 56 P
all the contagion of the south light on you, COR 1.04. 30
come from that nest | of death, contagion, and ROM 5.03.152
bed | to dare the vile contagion of the night, JC 2.01.265
itself /breathes out | contagion to this world. HAM 3.02.390
i'll touch my point | with this contagion, that, 4.07.147
CONTAGIOUS 11 FR 0.0012 REL FR 8 V 3 P
have suck'd up from the sea | contagious fogs; MND 2.01. 90
a contagious breath. TN 2.03. 54 P
very sweet and contagious, i' faith. 2.03. 55 P
whose black contagious breath | already smokes JN 5.04. 33
who doth permit the base contagious clouds | to 1H4 1.02.198
is in base durance and contagious prison, 2H4 5.05. 34
o'erblows the filthy and contagious clouds | of H5 3.03. 31
a most contagious treason come to light, look 4.08. 21 P
breathe foul contagious darkness in the air. 2H6 4.01. 7
to one man's honor, this contagious sickness, H8 5.02. 61
youth | contagious blastments are most imminent. HAM 1.03. 42
CONTAIN 14 FR 0.0015 REL FR 14 V 0 P
that show, contain, and nourish all the world, LLL 4.03.350
sings i' th' nose, | cannot contain their urine: MV 4.01. 50
ring, | or your own honor to contain the ring, 5.01.201
fear not, my lord, we can contain ourselves, SHR in.1. 100
this little abstract doth contain that large JN 2.01.101
yes, my good lord, | it doth contain a king. R2 3.03. 25
when that this body did contain a spirit, | a 1H4 5.04. 89
t' envelop and contain celestial spirits. H5 1.01. 31
is that the worst this letter doth contain? 1H6 4.01. 66
cask | that ever did contain a thing of worth. 2H6 3.02.410
o, contain yourself; TRO 5.02.180
contain thyself, good friend. TIM 2.02. 26
if after two days' shine athens contain thee, 3.05.100
look what thy memory cannot contain | commit to SON 77. 9
CONTAIN'D 3 FR 0.0003 REL FR 3 V 0 P
if you choose that wherein i am contain'd, MV 2.09. 5
which contain'd the name | of her that threw it. AWW 5.03. 94
let what is here contain'd relish of love, | of CYM 3.02. 30
/CONTAINING 1 FR 0.0001 REL FR 1 V 0 P
/containing /the /deposing /of /a /king, | /and R2 4.01.234
CONTAINING 5 FR 0.0005 REL FR 5 V 0 P
containing her affection unto benedick. ADO 5.04. 90
but for containing fire to harm mine eye. JN 4.01. 66
was ever book containing such vile matter | so ROM 3.02. 83
last, and as much containing as all these, | her HAM 4.05. 87
whose containing | is so from sense in hardness, CYM 5.05.430
CONTAINS 12 FR 0.0013 REL FR 11 V 1 P
the one of them contains my picture, prince: MV 2.07. 11
one of these three contains her heavenly picture 2.07. 48
is't like that lead contains her? 2.07. 49
royally! | why, it contains no king? R2 3.03. 24
for this contains our general grievances: 2H4 4.01.167
this packet, please it you, contains at large. 4.04.101
may i be bold to ask what that contains, | that H8 4.01. 13
made my heart | too great for what contains it. COR 5.06.103
open this purse and take | what it contains. LR 3.01. 46
your italy contains none so accomplish'd a CYM 1.04. 94 P
the worth of that is that which it contains, SON 74.13
by how much of me their reproach contains. LC 189
CONTAIN'T 1 FR 0.0001 REL FR 1 V 0 P
your roof were not sufficient to contain't. 1H6 2.03. 56
CONTAMINATE 2 FR 0.0002 REL FR 2 V 0 P
thee, | by ruffian lust should be contaminate? ERR 2.02.133
now | contaminate our fingers with base bribes? JC 4.03. 24
CONTAMINATED 5 FR 0.0005 REL FR 3 V 2 P
you mightily hold up — to a contaminated stale, ADO 2.02. 25 P
my dog, | his fairest daughter is contaminated. H5 4.05. 16
"contaminated, base, | and misbegotten blood i 1H6 4.06. 21
scruple | of her contaminated carrion weight, TRO 4.01. 72
in her bed, even the bed she hath contaminated. OTH 4.01.208 P
CONTEMN 3 FR 0.0003 REL FR 3 V 0 P
them | as if he did contemn what he requested COR 2.02.157
this way, and | contemn with mows the other; CYM 1.06. 41
"what am i, that thou shouldst contemn me this? VEN 205
CONTEMN'D 3 FR 0.0003 REL FR 3 V 0 P
should seek a plaster by contemn'd revolt, | and JN 5.02. 13
yet better thus, and known to be contemn'd, LR 4.01. 1
contemn'd, | than still contemn'd and flatter'd. 4.01. 2
CONTEMNED 1 FR 0.0001 REL FR 1 V 0 P
write loyal cantons of contemned love, | and TN 1.05.270
/CONTEMNED'ST 1 FR 0.0001 REL FR 1 V 0 P
/such /as /basest /and /contemned'st /wretches LR 2.02.143
/CONTEMNING 1 FR 0.0001 REL FR 1 V 0 P
forth blood | at grecian sword, /contemning. COR 1.03. 43
CONTEMNING 2 FR 0.0002 REL FR 2 V 0 P
i have done penance for contemning love, | whose TGV 2.04.129
contemning rome, he has done all this and more ANT 3.06. 1
/CONTEMNS 1 FR 0.0001 REL FR 1 V 0 P
/that /nature /which /contemns /it /origin LR 4.02. 32
CONTEMNS 1 FR 0.0001 REL FR 1 V 0 P
this is he contemns thee | and what thou dar'st TNK 3.06.143
CONTEMPLATE 1 FR 0.0001 REL FR 1 V 0 P
my rest, | so many hours must i contemplate, 3H6 2.05. 33
CONTEMPLATION 13 FR 0.0014 REL FR 8 V 5 P
in leaden contemplation have found out | such LLL 4.03.318
vow | to live in prayer and contemplation, MV 3.04. 28
and did you leave him in this contemplation? AYL 2.01. 64
indeed the sundry contemplation of my travels, 4.01. 18 P
contemplation makes a rare turkey–cock of him. TN 2.05. 30 P
my soul | with contemplation and devout desires. JN 5.04. 48
and so the prince obscur'd his contemplation H5 1.01. 63
thence, | so sweet is zealous contemplation. R3 3.07. 94
think | his contemplation were above the earth, H8 3.02.131
not have slipp'd out of my contemplation. TRO 2.03. 26 P
who doth molest my contemplation? TIT 5.02. 9
edmund, what serious contemplation are you in? LR 1.02.139 P
and given up himself to the contemplation, mark, OTH 2.03.317 P
CONTEMPLATIVE 4 FR 0.0004 REL FR 3 V 1 P
still and contemplative in living art. LLL 1.01. 14
that fools should be so deep contemplative; AYL 2.07. 31
letter will make a contemplative idiot of him. TN 2.05. 19 P
abandoner of revels, mute, contemplative, TNK 5.01.138
CONTEMPT 46 FR 0.0052 REL FR 41 V 5 P
sighs, | for, in revenge of my contempt of love, TGV 2.04.133
but wrong not that wrong with a more contempt. ERR 2.02.172
contempt, farewell, and maiden pride, adieu! ADO 3.01.109
that contempt will kill the speaker's heart, LLL 5.02.149
contempt nor bitterness | were in his pride or AWW 1.02. 36
when you put off that with such contempt? 2.02. 6 P
check thy contempt; 2.03.157
maid too virtuous | for the contempt of empire. 3.02. 32
contempt his scornful perspective did lend me, 5.03. 48
like my master's, be | plac'd in contempt! TN 1.05.288
my lady's favor at any thing more than contempt, 2.03.122 P
it is, in contempt of question, her hand. 2.05. 88 P
it cannot but turn him into a notable contempt. 2.05.203 P
in the contempt and anger of his lip! 3.01.146
contempt and clamor | will be my knell. WT 1.02.189
contrary and falling | a lip of much contempt, 1.02.373
their proud contempt that beats his peace to JN 2.01. 88
even so, or with much more contempt, men's eyes R2 5.02. 27
revenge the jeering and disdain'd contempt | of 1H4 1.03.183
seem'd it in contempt? 5.02. 50
his subjects to oppression and contempt, | and H5 2.02.172
scorn and defiance, slight regard, contempt, 2.04.117
once in contempt they would have barter'd me; 1H6 1.04. 31
who in contempt shall hiss at thee again; 2H6 4.01. 78
and tread it under foot with all contempt, 5.01.209
made | for kissing, lady, not for such contempt. R3 1.02.172
and the nobility | held in contempt, while great 1.03. 79
repays he my deep service | with such contempt? 4.02.120
and let the foul'st contempt | shut door upon me H8 2.04. 42
he did solicit you in free contempt | when he COR 2.03.200
that his contempt shall not be bruising to you 2.03.202
with what contempt he wore the humble weed, 2.03.221
of egall justice, us'd in such contempt? TIT 4.04. 4
ingrateful rome requites with foul contempt, 5.01. 12
contempt and beggary hangs upon thy back; ROM 5.01. 71
poverty, | walks, like contempt, alone. TIM 4.02. 15
since riches point to misery and contempt? 4.02. 32
bear great fortune | but by contempt of nature. 4.03. 8
the /senator shall bear contempt hereditary, 4.03. 10
pains and benefits | to laughter and contempt, LR 1.04.287
shape | that ever penury, in contempt of man, 2.03. 8
and /make me put into contempt the suits | of CYM 3.04. 89
how | can her contempt be answer'd? 3.05. 42
which will then be a torment to her contempt. 3.05.140 P
nature hath meal and bran, contempt and grace. 4.02. 27
and i, if you reveal me, | for my contempt. TNK 3.06.115
CONTEMPTIBLE 2 FR 0.0002 REL FR 1 V 1 P
(as you know all) hath a contemptible spirit. ADO 2.03.180 P
it pleas'd | to shine on my contemptible estate. 1H6 1.02. 75
CONTEMPTS 3 FR 0.0003 REL FR 2 V 1 P
sir, the contempts thereof are as touching me. LLL 1.01.190 P
the meanest or the best | for these contempts. TIT 4.04. 34
what our contempts doth often hurl from us, | we ANT 1.02.123
CONTEMPTUOUS 2 FR 0.0002 REL FR 2 V 0 P
the flinty ribs of this contemptuous city. JN 2.01.384
contemptuous base–born callot as she is, | she 2H6 1.03. 83
CONTEMPTUOUSLY 1 FR 0.0001 REL FR 1 V 0 P
trampling contemptuously on thy disdain. TGV 1.02.109
/CONTEND 1 FR 0.0001 REL FR 1 V 0 P
/as /they /contend /with /thee /in /courtesy. TRO 4.05.206
CONTEND 17 FR 0.0019 REL FR 17 V 0 P
now kiss, embrace, contend, do what you will. TGV 1.02.126
blood and virtue | contend for empire in thee, AWW 1.01. 63
for never two such kingdoms did contend H5 1.02. 24
and with the southern clouds contend in tears, 2H6 3.02.384
when dying clouds contend with growing light, 3H6 2.05. 2
if you contend, a thousand lives must wither. 2.05.102
strength i did | contend against thy valor. COR 4.05.113
his wonders and his praises do contend | which MAC 1.03. 92
were poor and single business to contend 1.06. 16
that death and nature do contend about them, 2.02. 7
wind, when both contend | which is the mightier. HAM 4.01. 7
if we contend, | out of our question wipe him. ANT 2.02. 80
for i will contend | even with his pestilent 3.13.192
'gainst whom i am too little to contend, | since PER 1.02. 17

contend not, sir, for we are gentlemen | have 2.03. 24
whose ridges with the meeting clouds contend: VEN 820
in sequent toil all forwards do contend. SON 60. 4
CONTENDED 1 FR 0.0001 REL FR 0 V 1 P
strifes, contended especially to know himself. MM 3.02.232 P
CONTENDING 10 FR 0.0011 REL FR 10 V 0 P
like one of two contending in a prize, | that MV 3.02.141
will, | what is she but a foul contending rebel, SHR 5.02.159
me, that the contending kingdoms | of france and H5 5.02.349
contending 'gainst obedience, as they would make MAC 2.04. 17
contending with the fretful elements; LR 3.01. 4
peril and want contending, they have skiff'd TNK 1.03. 37
your two contending lovers are return'd, | and 4.02. 66
till he take truce with her contending tears, VEN 82
"time's glory is to calm contending kings, | to LUC 939
thus art with arms contending was victor of the PP 15.13
CONTENDS 1 FR 0.0001 REL FR 1 V 0 P
still | this philoten contends in skill | with PER 4.ch. 30
CONTENT* 177 FR 0.0200 REL FR 148 V 29 P
and how does your content | tender your own good TMP 2.01.269
her sovereign aid, | and rest myself content. 5.01.144
to content ye | as much as me my dukedom. 5.01.170
are you content to be our general? TGV 4.01. 59
i hope, upon familiarity will grow more content. WIV 1.01.250 P
good master, be content. 1.04. 70 P
i have been content, sir, you should lay my 2.02. 5 P
how things go, and, i warrant, to your content. 4.05.123 P
be you content, fair maid, | it is the law, not MM 2.02. 79
be content. 2.02.105
how will you do to content this substitute, and 3.01.187 P
the image of it gives me content already, and i 3.01.259 P
but yet i will be content to be a lawful hangman 4.02. 16 P
sir, i commend you to your own content. ERR 1.02. 32
he that commends me to mine own content, 1.02. 33
content yourself. ADO 5.01. 87
hold you content. 5.01. 92
where zeal strives to content, and the contents LLL 5.02.517
then be content. MND 2.02.110
content with hermia? 2.02.111
we do not come, as minding to content you, | our 5.01.113
poor souls, they are content | to whisper. 5.01.133
content, in faith, i'll seal to such a bond, MV 1.03.152
falls to you, | be content, and seek no new. 3.02.134
i wish your ladyship all heart's content. 3.04. 42
fine for one half of his goods, | i am content; 4.01.382
i am content. 4.01.394
now go /we /in content | to liberty, and not to AYL 1.03.137
we'll light upon some settled low content. 2.03. 68
a better place, but travellers must be content. 2.04. 18 P
and content is without three good friends; 3.02. 25 P
glad of other men's good, content with my harm, 3.02. 75 P
doth my simple feature content you? 3.03. 3 P
i will content you, if what pleases you contents 5.02.116 P
sister, content you in my discontent. SHR 1.01. 80
gentlemen, content ye; 1.01. 90
basta, content thee; 1.01.198
another sense — | i am content to be lucentio, 1.01.216
content you, gentlemen, i will compound this 2.01.341
i am content. 3.02.201
are you content to stay? 3.02.201
i am content you shall entreat me stay, | but 3.02.202
o kate, content thee, prithee be not angry. 3.02.215
i am content, in a good father's care, | to have 4.04. 31
fear not, baptista, we will content you, go to; 5.01.135 P
content. what's the wager? 5.02. 70
content. 5.02. 74
the care i have had to even your content, i wish AWW 1.03. 4 P
the general is content to spare thee yet, | and, 4.01. 80
with very much content, my lord, and i wish it 4.05. 78 P
if this suit be won, | that you express content; ep 3
prithee be content. TN 5.01.351
would they else be content to die? WT 1.01. 42 P
and more it would content me | to have her honor 2.01.159
not without much content | in many singularities 5.03. 11
you can make her do, | i am content to look on; 5.03. 92
what to speak, | i am content to hear; 5.03. 93
england, how may we content | this widow lady? JN 2.01.547
i do beseech you, madam, be content. 3.01. 42
if thou that bid'st me be content wert grim, 3.01. 43
i would not care, i then would be content, | for 3.01. 48
pleas'd | not to be pardoned, am content withal. R2 2.01.188
good mother, be content, it is no more | than my 5.02. 82
thoughts tending to content flatter themselves 5.05. 23
for sport sake are content to do the profession 1H4 2.01. 71 P
will this content you, kate? 2.03.117
content, and the argument shall be thy running 2.04.281 P
content. 2.04.378 P
content. 4.03. 14
i could be well content | to entertain the lag 5.01. 23
i am content that he shall take the odds | of 5.01. 97
il est content a vous donner la liberte, le H5 4.04. 52 P
den it sall also content me. 5.02.250 P
i am content, so the maiden cities you talk of 5.02.326 P
content, i'll to the surgeon's. 1H6 3.01.146
are you not content? 4.01. 70
content, my liege? 4.01. 71
i shall be well content with any choice | tends 5.01. 26
how say you, madam, are ye so content? 5.03.126
and if my father please, i am content. 5.03.127
and yet methinks i could be well content | to be 5.03.165
mind | she is content to be at your command — 5.05. 19
such is the fullness of my heart's content. 2H6 1.01. 35
i | in england work your grace's full content. 1.03. 67
i am content. 3.01.319
i thank thee, /meg, these words content me much. 3.02. 26
i am content he shall reign, but i'll be 4.02.158 P
and could command no more content than i? 4.09. 2
it must and shall be so. content thyself. 3H6 1.01. 85
i am content: 1.01.174
my crown is call'd content, | a crown it is that 3.01. 64
well, if you be a king crown'd with content, 3.01. 66
your crown content and you must be contented 3.01. 67
and cry "content" to that which grieves my heart 3.02.183
why then, though loath, yet must i be content. 4.06. 48
as being well content with that alone. 4.07. 24
god hold it, to your honor's good content! R3 3.02.105
come the next sabbath, and i will content you. 3.02.111
times | repair'd with double riches of content. 4.04.319
night he dedicates | to fair content and you. H8 1.04. 3
born, | and range with humble livers in content, 2.03. 20
our content | is our best having. 2.03. 22
almost forgot my pray'rs to content him? 3.01.132
though my heart's content firm love doth bear, TRO 1.02.294
pray you content you. 3.02.143
and could be content to give him good report COR 1.01. 32 P
men can be content to say it was for his country 1.01. 38 P
and though i must be content to bear with those 2.01. 60 P
and is content | to spend the time to end it. 2.02.128
content, content. 2.03. 47 P
content, content. 2.03. 47 P
pray be content. 3.02.130
and are content | to suffer lawful censure for 3.03. 45
i am content. 3.03. 47
lo, citizens, he says he is content. 3.03. 48
content thee, prince, i will restore to thee TIT 1.01.210
and, if one arm's embracement will content thee, 5.02. 68
mind | that i repair to rome, i am content. 5.03. 2
and see how one another lends content; ROM 1.03. 84
content thee, gentle coz, let him alone, | 'a 1.05. 65
death, | i am content, so thou wilt have it so. 3.05. 18
wretched being, | worse than the worst, content. TIM 4.03.247
peace and content be here! 5.01.127
be you content. JC 1.03.142
cassius, be content, | speak your griefs softly; 4.02. 41
they could be content | to visit other places, 5.01. 8
hostess, and shut up | in measureless content. MAC 2.01. 17
where our desire is got without content; 3.02. 5
and it doth much content me | to hear him so HAM 3.01. 24
be you content to lend your patience to us, 4.05.211
labor with your soul | to give it due content. 4.05.213
let your study | be to content your lord, who LR 1.01.277
pray you, content. 1.04.313
your passion | must be content to think you old, 2.04.235
must make content with his fortunes fit, 3.02. 76
o, sir, content you; OTH 1.01. 41
must therefore be content to slubber the gloss 1.03.226 P
it gives me wonder great as my content | to see 2.01.183
i fear | my soul hath her content so absolute 2.01.191
i cannot speak enough of this content, | it 2.01.196
and nothing can or shall content my soul | till 2.01.298
content thyself a while. 2.03.378
masters, play here, i will content your pains; 3.01. 1
poor and content is rich, and rich enough, | but 3.03.172
farewell content! 3.03.348
yet be content. 3.03.450
so shall i clothe me in a forc'd content, | and 3.04.120
i pray you be content; 4.02.165
o'er your content these strong necessities, ANT 3.06. 83
content. 'tis strange. 4.03. 22
so, dolabella, | it shall content me best. 5.02. 68
o, content thee. CYM 1.05. 26
of my lord's health, of his content — yet not 3.02. 31
for it doth physic love — of his content, | all 3.02. 34
be content, | your low–laid son our godhead will 5.04.102
air | were all too little to content and please, PER 1.04. 35
me | a more content in course of true delight 3.02. 39
the unborn event | i do commend to your content; 4.ch. 46
the gods for murder seemed so content | to 5.03. 99
content to you! TNK pr 30
here, | i am sure, a more content, and all those 2.02.100
content. 2.03. 58
be content, | again betake you to your hawthorn 3.01. 81
content and anger | in me have but one face. 3.01.107
you | content to take th' other to your husband? 3.06.274
are you content too, princes? 3.06.279
will this content ye? 3.06.299
are you content, sister? 3.06.301
i am content, | if we shall keep our wedding 5.02. 75
what ending could be | of more content? 5.04. 16
(for 'tis no other) any way content ye | (for to ep 13
forc'd to content, but never to obey, | panting VEN 61
face, though full of cares, yet show'd content; LUC 1503
thy like ne'er was | for a sweet content, the PP 17.34
within thine own bud buriest thy content, | and, SON 1.11
so i return rebuk'd to my content, | and gain by 119.13
or forc'd examples, 'gainst her own content, LC 157
CONTENT–A 1 FR 0.0001 REL FR 0 V 1 P
wherefore shall i be content–a? WIV 1.04. 71 P
CONTENTA 1 FR 0.0001 REL FR 1 V 0 P
si fortuna me tormenta, spero contenta. 2H4 5.05. 96
/CONTENTED 1 FR 0.0001 REL FR 1 V 0 P
/are /you /contented /to /resign /the /crown? R2 4.01.200
CONTENTED 28 FR 0.0031 REL FR 21 V 7 P
good master ford, be contented. WIV 3.03.166 P
art thou contented, jew? what dost thou say? MV 4.01.393
invite the duke and all 's contented followers. AYL 5.02. 15 P
the meat was well, if you were so contented. SHR 4.01.169
i will with you, if you be so contented, 4.02. 25
i may and will, if she be so contented. 4.04.105
if men could be contented to be what they are, AWW 1.03. 50 P
the king shall be contented. R2 3.03.145
for no thought is contented. 5.05. 11
in one person many people, | and none contented. 5.05. 32
my lord, i could be well contented to be there, 1H4 2.03. 2 P
he could be contented: 2.03. 3 P
be you contented, wearing now the garland, | to 2H4 5.02. 84
not die any where so contented as in the king's H5 4.01.127 P
not contented that he lopp'd the branch | in 3H6 2.06. 47
your crown content and you must be contented 3.01. 67
nor how to be contented with one wife, | nor how 4.03. 37
from that contented hap which i enjoy'd, | i R3 1.03. 83
we are contented | to wear our mortal state to H8 2.04.228
and be well contented | to make your house our 5.01.105
and that we are contented caesar shall | have JC 3.01.240
battle, | you are contented to be led in triumph 5.01.108
well contented. MAC 2.03.134
nuncle, be contented, 'tis a naughty night to LR 3.04.110 P
to sell myself i can be well contented, | so VEN 513
scope, | with what i most enjoy contented least; SON 29. 8
but be contented: 74. 1
pride, | he is contented thy poor drudge to be, 151.11
CONTENTETH 1 FR 0.0001 REL FR 1 V 0 P
inheritance my father left me | contenteth me, 2H6 4.10. 19
CONTENTING 1 FR 0.0001 REL FR 1 V 0 P
and dead, | statue contenting but the eye alone, VEN 213
CONTENTION 11 FR 0.0012 REL FR 9 V 2 P
and pride of their contention did take horse, 1H4 1.01. 60
the times are wild, contention, like a horse 2H4 1.01. 9
a stage | to feed contention in a ling'ring act; 1.01.156
where i could not breed no contention with him; H5 5.01. 11 P
no quarrel, but a slight contention. 3H6 1.02. 6
/but when contention and occasion meet, | by TRO 4.01. 17
i would my arms could match thee in contention, 4.05.205
the great contention of /the sea and skies OTH 2.01. 92
'twas a contention in public, which may, without CYM 1.04. 54 P
'em never more | to make me their contention, or TNK 3.06.253
to arcite gave | the grace of the contention. 5.04.108
CONTENTIOUS 3 FR 0.0003 REL FR 3 V 0 P
bold head | 'bove the contentious waves he kept, TMP 2.01.119
think'st 'tis much that this contentious storm LR 3.04. 6
o' th' night | with their contentious throats, TNK 5.03.125
CONTENTLESS 1 FR 0.0001 REL FR 1 V 0 P
best state, contentless, | hath a distracted and TIM 4.03.245
CONTENTO 1 FR 0.0001 REL FR 1 V 0 P
"si fortune me tormente, sperato me contento." 2H4 2.04.181
CONTENTS' 1 FR 0.0001 REL FR 1 V 0 P
and for the contents' sake are sorry for our AWW 3.02. 63
CONTENTS* 27 FR 0.0030 REL FR 21 V 6 P
i will furnish it anon with new contents. TMP 2.02.143 P
that the contents will show. TGV 1.02. 36
a woman sometime scorns what best contents her. 3.01. 93
her | of such contents as you will wonder at; WIV 4.06. 13
the contents of this is the return of the duke. MM 4.02.196 P
whose contents | shall witness to him i am near 4.03. 94
under pardon, sir, what are the contents? LLL 4.02.101 P
and the contents | dies in the zeal of that 5.02.517
are some shrowd contents in yond same paper MV 3.02.243
i know not the contents, but, as i guess | by AYL 4.03. 8
no, i protest, i know not the contents, | phebe 4.03. 21
if what pleases you contents you, and you shall 5.02.117 P
hymen's bands, | if truth holds true contents. 5.04.130
go forward, this contents; SHR 1.01.163
because his painted skin contents the eye? 4.03.178
shall the contents discover, something rare WT 3.01. 20
to whose high will we bound our calm contents. R2 5.02. 38
these are the whole contents, and, good my lord, H8 4.02.154
that, on the view and knowing of these contents, HAM 5.02. 44
the contents, as in part i understand them, are LR 1.02. 42 P
but i hope his heart is not in the contents. 1.02. 68 P
on those contents | they summon'd up their meiny 2.04. 34
and the contents o' th' story. CYM 2.02. 27
to blot old books and alter their contents, | to LUC 948
you shall shine more bright in these contents SON 55. 3
and often reading what contents it bears; LC 19
big discontent so breaking their contents. 56
CONTEST 1 FR 0.0001 REL FR 1 V 0 P
and do contest | as hotly and as nobly with thy COR 4.05.110
CONTESTATION 1 FR 0.0001 REL FR 1 V 0 P
and their contestation | was theme for you — ANT 2.02. 43
CONTINENCE 1 FR 0.0001 REL FR 1 V 0 P
to justice, continence, and nobility; TIT 1.01. 15
CONTINENCY 2 FR 0.0002 REL FR 0 V 2 P
will unpeople the province with continency. MM 3.02.175 P
making a sermon of continency to her, and rails, SHR 4.01.182 P
CONTINENT 12 FR 0.0013 REL FR 9 V 3 P
proclaimed edict and continent canon; LLL 1.01.259 P
ay, my continent of beauty. 4.01.109
the continent and summary of my fortune. MV 3.02.130
as doth that orbed continent the fire | that TN 5.01.271
my past life | hath been as continent, as chaste WT 3.02. 34
gelding the opposed continent as much | as on 1H4 3.01.109
times | make mountains level, and the continent, 2H4 3.01. 47
all continent impediments would o'erbear | that MAC 4.03. 64
which is not tomb enough and continent | to hide HAM 4.04. 64
shall find in him the continent of what part a 5.02.110 P
i pray you have a continent forbearance till the LR 1.02.166 P
heart, once be stronger than thy continent, ANT 4.14. 40
CONTINENTS 3 FR 0.0003 REL FR 2 V 1 P
that they have overborne their continents. MND 2.01. 92
thou globe of sinful continents, what a life 2H4 2.04.285 P
rive your concealing continents, and cry | these LR 3.02. 58
CONTINUAL 15 FR 0.0017 REL FR 10 V 5 P
dwelling in a continual 'larum of jealousy, WIV 3.05. 71 P
a man of continual dissolution and thaw. 3.05.116 P
small have continual plodders ever won, | save LLL 1.01. 86
upon my tongues continual slanders ride, | the 2H4 in 6
with poins, and other his continual followers. 4.04. 53
prince harry in continual laughter the wearing 5.01. 79 P
setting endeavor in continual motion; H5 1.02.185
hell, | an age of discord and continual strife? 1H6 5.05. 63
continual meditations, tears, and sorrows, | he H8 4.02. 28
then must my earth with her continual tears TIT 3.01.228
into france i have been in continual practice. HAM 5.02.211 P
and they with continual action are even as good PER 4.02. 8 P
she seeks to kindle with continual kissing. VEN 606
to soften it with their continual motion; LUC 591
lie, | made more or less by thy continual haste. SON 123.12
CONTINUALLY 5 FR 0.0005 REL FR 2 V 3 P
i lie, for they pray continually to their saint, 1H4 2.01. 80 P
who prays continually for richmond's good. R3 5.03. 84
she has light by her continually, 'tis her MAC 5.01. 23 P
bring'st such pelting scurvy news continually, TNK 2.02.266
she is continually in a harmless distemper, 4.03. 3 P
CONTINUANCE 10 FR 0.0011 REL FR 7 V 3 P
long continuance, and increasing, | hourly joys TMP 4.01.107
hath yet in her the continuance of her first MM 3.01.240 P
a bawd of eleven years' continuance, may it 3.02.196 P
than my faint means would grant continuance. MV 1.01.125
call in question the continuance of his love. TN 1.04. 6 P
in their continuance will not feel themselves. JN 5.07. 14
we find | too indirect for long continuance. 1H4 4.03.105
with long continuance in a settled place. 1H6 2.05.106
and the continuance of their parents' rage, ROM pr 10
continuance tames the one, the other wild, LUC 1097
/CONTINUANTLY 1 FR 0.0001 REL FR 0 V 1 P
'a comes /continuantly to pie–corner (saving 2H4 2.01. 26 P
CONTINUATE 2 FR 0.0002 REL FR 2 V 0 P
were, | to an untirable and continuate goodness; TIM 1.01. 11
but i shall, in a more continuate time, | strike OTH 3.04.178
CONTINU'D 2 FR 0.0002 REL FR 1 V 1 P
the office, you had continu'd in it some time. MM 2.01.262 P
lov'd, | continu'd so, until we thought he died. CYM 5.05.380

CONTINUE 34 FR 0.0038 REL FR 24 V 10 P
so you may continue, and laugh at nothing still. TMP 2.01.178 P
if she would continue in it five weeks without 2.01.183 P
she shall not long continue love to him. TGV 3.02. 48
let him continue in his courses till thou MM 2.01.187 P
thou art to continue now, thou varlet, thou art 2.01.191 P
continue now, thou varlet, thou art to continue. 2.01.192 P
and how shall we continue claudio, | to save me 4.03. 84
will hear your idle scorns, continue then, | and LLL 5.02.865
glad that you thus continue your resolve | to SHR 1.01. 27
in, | i will continue that i broach'd in jest. 1.02. 84
equal fortune, and continue | a braving war. AWW 1.02. 2
for the which | i shall continue thankful. 5.01. 17
if the duke continue these favors towards you, TN 1.04. 1 P
the heavens continue their loves! WT 1.01. 32 P
and that with us | you did continue fault, and 1.02. 85
and will continue | the standing of his body. 1.02.430
to do your pleasure and continue friends. JN 3.01.252
our humble author will continue the story, with 2H4 ep 27 P
so let us still continue peace, and love. 1H6 4.01.161
continue still in this so good a mind, | and 2H6 4.09. 17
you peers, continue this united league. R3 2.01. 2
but this cannot continue. H8 2.02. 83
your anger did i | continue in my liking? 2.04. 33
may he continue | long in his highness' favor, 3.02.395
death | thou shalt continue two and forty hours, ROM 4.01.105
nor /resumes no care | of what is to continue. TIM 2.02. 5
and shall continue our graces towards him. MAC 1.06. 30
i have known her continue in this a quarter of 5.01. 29 P
desdemona should continue her love to the moor OTH 1.03.342 P
return he cannot, nor | continue where he is. CYM 1.05. 54
bed, | and will continue fast to your affection, 1.06.138
you know that we | must not continue friends. 2.04. 49
not | against your faith, yet i continue mine. TNK 1.03. 97
and quality | hold i may | continue in thy band. 5.01.162
CONTINUED 3 FR 0.0003 REL FR 3 V 0 P
more than three hours the fight continued, 1H6 1.01.120
how long continued, and what stock he springs of COR 2.03.237
i would he had continued to his country | as he 4.02. 30
CONTINUER 1 FR 0.0001 REL FR 0 V 1 P
speed of your tongue, and so good a continuer. ADO 1.01.142 P
CONTINUES 4 FR 0.0004 REL FR 3 V 1 P
do but go after, | and mark how he continues. OTH 4.01.281
your emperor | continues still a jove. ANT 4.06. 28
continues well my lord? his health, beseech you? CYM 1.06. 56
how she continues this fancy! TNK 4.03. 48 P
CONTINUING 1 FR 0.0001 REL FR 0 V 1 P
extremity of weather continuing, this mystery WT 5.02.120 P
CONTRACT 26 FR 0.0029 REL FR 24 V 2 P
contract, succession, | bourn, bound of land, TMP 2.01.152
heavens let fall | to make this contract grow; 4.01. 19
a contract of true love to celebrate, | and some 4.01. 84
and help to celebrate | a contract of true love; 4.01.133
upon a true contract | i got possession of MM 1.02.145
which time of the contract and limit of the 3.01.215 P
this is the hand which, with a vow'd contract, 5.01.209
maid between the contract of her marriage and AYL 3.02.314 P
favor of the king | smile upon this contract, AWW 2.03.178
a contract of eternal bond of love, | confirm'd TN 5.01.156
come on, | contract us 'fore these witnesses. WT 4.04.390
come, come, he must not. | mark our contract. 4.04.417
us, will not have | our contract celebrated. 5.01.204
how joyful am i made by this contract! 1H6 3.01.143
in argument and proof of which contract, | bear 5.01. 46
to cavil in the course of this contract. 5.04.156
how shall we then dispense with that contract, 5.05. 28
i did, with his contract with lady lucy, | and R3 3.07. 5
lucy, | and his contract by deputy in france, 3.07. 6
for first was he contract to lady lucy — | your 3.07.179
thee, | i have no joy of this contract to–night, ROM 2.02.117
aches contract and starve your supple joints! TIM 1.01.248
to contract — o — the time for — a — my HAM 5.01. 63
and didst contract and purse thy brow together, OTH 3.03.113
the contract you pretend with that base wretch, CYM 2.03.113
with scraps o' th' court, it is no contract, 2.03.115
CONTRACTED 11 FR 0.0012 REL FR 10 V 1 P
the truth is, she and i (long since contracted) WIV 5.05.223
wast thou e'er contracted to this woman? MM 5.01.375
extended or contracted all proportions | to a AWW 5.03. 51
you would have been contracted to a maid, | nor TN 5.01.261
your crown'd brother and these your contracted WT 5.03. 5
sons, inquire me out contracted bachelors, such 1H4 4.02. 16 P
here are the articles of contracted peace 2H6 1.01. 40
kingdom | to be contracted in one brow of woe, HAM 1.02. 4
i was contracted to them both; LR 5.03.229
but thou, contracted to thine own bright eyes, SON 1. 5
which parts the shore where two contracted new 56.10
CONTRACTING 1 FR 0.0001 REL FR 1 V 0 P
exacting, | and perform an old contracting. MM 3.02.282
CONTRACTION 1 FR 0.0001 REL FR 1 V 0 P
as from the body of contraction plucks | the HAM 3.04. 46
CONTRADICT 6 FR 0.0006 REL FR 6 V 0 P
stand in his face to contradict his claim. JN 2.01.280
as being thought to contradict your liking, 2H6 3.02.252
a greater power than we can contradict | hath ROM 5.03.153
dear duff, i prithee contradict thyself, | and MAC 2.03. 89
and i, her husband, contradict your banes. LR 5.03. 87
if thou my love's desire do contradict. LUC 1631
CONTRADICTED 1 FR 0.0001 REL FR 1 V 0 P
was the hour | i ever contradicted your desire? H8 2.04. 28
CONTRADICTION 5 FR 0.0005 REL FR 2 V 3 P
shall be accomplish'd without contradiction. R2 3.03.124
and to have his worth | of contradiction. COR 3.03. 27
without contradiction, i have heard that. ANT 2.07. 35 P
which may, without contradiction, suffer the CYM 1.04. 55 P
o, of this contradiction you shall now be quit. 5.04.166 P
CONTRADICTS 1 FR 0.0001 REL FR 1 V 0 P
be but that | which contradicts my accusation, WT 3.02. 23
CONTRARIES 5 FR 0.0005 REL FR 5 V 0 P
i' th' commonwealth i would, by contraries, TMP 2.01.148
is't good to soothe him in these contraries? ERR 4.04. 79
laws, | decline to your confounding contraries; TIM 4.01. 20
no contraries hold more antipathy | than i and LR 2.02. 87
these contraries such unity do hold | only to LUC 1558
CONTRARIETIES 1 FR 0.0001 REL FR 1 V 0 P
how can these contrarieties agree? 1H6 2.03. 59
CONTRARIETY 1 FR 0.0001 REL FR 1 V 0 P
can | no more atone than violent'st contrariety. COR 4.06. 73
CONTRARIOUS 2 FR 0.0002 REL FR 2 V 0 P
with these false and most contrarious /quests MM 4.01. 61
and the contrarious winds that held the king 1H4 5.01. 52
CONTRARIOUSLY 1 FR 0.0001 REL FR 1 V 0 P
to one consent, may work contrariously, | as H5 1.02.206
CONTRARY 49 FR 0.0055 REL FR 30 V 19 P
did beget of him | a falsehood in its contrary, TMP 1.02. 95
what instance of the contrary? TGV 2.04. 16 P
'tis pity love should be so contrary; 4.04. 83
i have to show to the contrary. WIV 2.01. 38 P
yet i say i could show you to the contrary. 2.01. 41 P
i think, hath appointed them contrary places; 2.01.208 P
hath to the public ear | profess'd the contrary. MM 4.02.100
"whatsoever you may hear to the contrary, let 4.02.120 P
though i had sworn the contrary, if hero would ADO 1.01.196 P
find no impediment to the contrary, to be the 5.02. 85 P
contrary to thy established proclaimed edict and LLL 1.01.258 P
he speaks the mere contrary, crosses love not 1.02. 33 P
so shall your loves | woo contrary, deceiv'd by 5.02.135
glass of rhenish wine on the contrary casket, MV 1.02. 96 P
have you heard any imputation to the contrary? 1.03. 13 P
thou hast to pull at a smack a' th' contrary. AWW 2.03.225 P
lost our labor, they are gone a contrary way. 3.05. 8 P
just the contrary: the better for thy friends. TN 5.01. 14 P
wafting his eyes to th' contrary and falling | a WT 1.02.372
to the contrary i have express commandment. 2.02. 8
contrary to the faith and allegiance of a true 3.02. 19 P
my lord should to the heavens be contrary, 5.01. 45
man, | i have a king's oath to the contrary. JN 3.01. 10
haste | had falsely thrust upon contrary feet, 4.02.198
came from the king, commands the contrary. R2 5.05.101
and wouldst thou turn our offers contrary? 1H4 5.05. 4
to be eaten in thy house, contrary to the law, 2H4 2.04.344 P
and, banding themselves in contrary parts, | do 1H6 3.01. 81
whereas the contrary bringeth bliss, | and is a 5.05. 64
did he not, contrary to form of law, | devise 2H6 3.01. 58
be us'd, and, contrary to the king, his crown, 4.07. 36 P
i'll prove the contrary, if you'll hear me speak 3H6 1.02. 20
the contrary doth make thee wond'red at. 1.04.131
the king hath strictly charg'd the contrary. R3 4.01. 17
no, to their lives ill friends were contrary. 4.04.217
the king's attorney on the contrary | urg'd on H8 2.01. 15
in the divorce his contrary proceedings | are 3.02. 26
of it, as i' th' contrary | the foulness is the 3.02.182
the best persuasions to the contrary | fail not 5.01.147
you must contrary me! ROM 1.05. 85
what storm is this that blows so contrary? 3.02. 64
and all things change them to the contrary. 4.05. 90
may your pains six months | be quite contrary. TIM 4.03.145
know'st none, but art despis'd for the contrary. 4.03.304 P
our wills and fates do so contrary run | that HAM 3.02.211
what in the contrary? OTH 4.02.174 P
but tidings to the contrary | are brought your PER 2.ch. 15
i know, | may be (nor can i think the contrary) 2.05. 79
mine own self–love quite contrary i read; SON 62.11
CONTRE 1 FR 0.0001 REL FR 0 V 1 P
encore qu'il est contre son jurement de H5 4.04. 50 P
CONTRIBUTION 2 FR 0.0002 REL FR 2 V 0 P
a trembling contribution! H8 1.02. 95
for they have grudg'd us contribution. JC 4.03.206
CONTRIBUTORS 1 FR 0.0001 REL FR 1 V 0 P
i promis'd we would be contributors | and bear SHR 1.02.214
CONTRITE 2 FR 0.0002 REL FR 2 V 0 P
and on it have bestowed more contrite tears, H5 4.01.296
her contrite sighs unto the clouds bequeathed LUC 1727
CONTRIV'D 8 FR 0.0009 REL FR 7 V 1 P
have you with these contriv'd | to bait me with MND 3.02.196
the guilt of premeditated and contriv'd murther; H5 4.01.162 P
by whom this great assembly is contriv'd, | we 5.02. 6
him, | by magic verses have contriv'd his end? 1H6 1.01. 27
hand | that hath contriv'd this woeful tragedy! 1.04. 77
deceit | contriv'd by art and baleful sorcery. 2.01. 15
that you have contriv'd to take | from rome all COR 3.03. 63
o' th' conscience | to do no contriv'd murder. OTH 1.02. 3
/CONTRIVE* 1 FR 0.0001 REL FR 0 V 1 P
him, /and /suddenly /contrive /the /means /of HAM 2.02.212 P
CONTRIVE* 8 FR 0.0009 REL FR 8 V 0 P
the party 'gainst the which he doth contrive MV 4.01.352
was't you that did so oft contrive to kill him? AYL 4.03.134
please ye we may contrive this afternoon | and SHR 1.02.274
by advised purpose meet | to plot, contrive, or R2 1.03.189
that do contrive how many hands shall strike TRO 1.03.201
if not, the fates with traitors do contrive. JC 2.03. 16
nor let thy soul contrive | against thy mother HAM 1.05. 85
some loathsome dash the herald will contrive, LUC 206
CONTRIVED 2 FR 0.0002 REL FR 2 V 0 P
thou hast contrived against the very life | of MV 4.01.360
years, | complotted and contrived in this land, R2 1.01. 96
CONTRIVEDST 1 FR 0.0001 REL FR 1 V 0 P
thou that contrivedst to murther our dead lord, 1H6 1.03. 34
CONTRIVER 4 FR 0.0004 REL FR 3 V 1 P
and villainous contriver against me his natural AYL 1.01.145 P
reveal the damn'd contriver of this deed. TIT 4.01. 36
we shall find of him | a shrewd contriver; JC 2.01.158
your charms, | the close contriver of all harms, MAC 3.05. 7
CONTRIVES 2 FR 0.0002 REL FR 1 V 1 P
he that in this action contrives against his own AWW 4.03. 24 P
she that her fame so to herself contrives, | the LC 243
CONTRIVING 3 FR 0.0003 REL FR 2 V 1 P
most generous, and free from all contriving, HAM 4.07.135
one that slept in the contriving of lust, and LR 3.04. 90 P
too | of many our contriving friends in rome ANT 1.02.182
CONTROL 17 FR 0.0019 REL FR 16 V 1 P
it would control my dam's god, setebos, | and TMP 1.02.373
and his more braver daughter could control thee, 1.02.440
and one so strong | that could control the moon, 5.01.270
smile with an austere regard of control — TN 2.05. 66 P
the proud control of fierce and bloody war, | to JN 1.01. 17
be propertied, | to be a secondary at control, 5.02. 80
heart, | without control, lusted to make a prey. R3 3.05. 84
age, | but not a sceptre to control the world. TIT 1.01.199
ah, now no more will i control thy griefs. 3.01.259
chanc'd to slack ye, | we could control them. LR 2.04.246
wrath, which men | may blame, but not control. 3.07. 27
who can control his fate? OTH 5.02.265
but nothing can affection's course control, | or LUC 500
who, mad that sorrow should his use control, 1781
i should in thought control your times of SON 58. 2
can yet the lease of my true love control, 107. 3
when most impeach'd stands least in thy control. 125.14
CONTROLL'D 5 FR 0.0005 REL FR 5 V 0 P
austerity and garb | as he controll'd the war; COR 4.07. 45
to be controll'd in that he frankly gave. TIT 1.01.420
the crying babe controll'd with this discourse: 5.01. 26
are by his flaming torch dimm'd and controll'd. LUC 448
with her own white fleece her voice controll'd 678
CONTROLLED 2 FR 0.0002 REL FR 2 V 0 P
controlling what he was controlled with. VEN 270
which in her prescience she controlled still, LUC 727
CONTROLLER *(also comptrollers)*
CONTROLLER 2 FR 0.0002 REL FR 2 V 0 P
nor cease to be an arrogant controller, | though 2H6 3.02.205
saucy controller of my private steps! TIT 2.03. 60
CONTROLLING 6 FR 0.0006 REL FR 6 V 0 P
two such controlling bounds shall you be, kings, JN 2.01.444
eagle's, lightens forth | controlling majesty. R2 3.03. 70
up, | and with the same to act controlling laws. 2H6 5.01.103
controlling what he was controlled with. VEN 270
a man in hue all hues in his controlling, SON 20. 7
and folly (doctor–like) controlling skill, | and 66.10
CONTROLMENT 4 FR 0.0004 REL FR 3 V 1 P
of this till you may do it without controlment. ADO 1.03. 20 P
blood for blood, | controlment for controlment: JN 1.01. 20
blood for blood, | controlment for controlment: 1.01. 20
without controlment, justice, or revenge? TIT 2.01. 68
CONTROLS 2 FR 0.0002 REL FR 2 V 0 P
are their males' subjects and at their controls: ERR 2.01. 19
and justly thus controls his thoughts unjust: LUC 189
CONTROL'T 1 FR 0.0001 REL FR 1 V 0 P
it would, | for th' ill which doth control't. COR 3.01.161
/CONTROVERSY 1 FR 0.0001 REL FR 0 V 1 P
/it /no /sin /to /tarre /them /to /controversy. HAM 2.02.354 P
CONTROVERSY 10 FR 0.0011 REL FR 5 V 5 P
grace is grace, despite of all controversy; MM 1.02. 25 P
who, but for staying on our controversy, | had ERR 5.01. 20
with the cause in controversy between the jew MV 4.01.155 P
stand aside and see the end of this controversy. SHR 5.01. 62 P
here is the strangest controversy | come from JN 1.01. 44
that shall be swallowed in this controversy. H5 2.04.109
then rejourn the controversy of threepence to a COR 2.01. 71 P
a chamber–pot, dismiss the controversy bleeding, 2.01. 77 P
and stemming it with hearts of controversy; JC 1.02.109
and controversy hence a question takes, LC 110
CONTUMELIOUS 3 FR 0.0003 REL FR 3 V 0 P
with scoffs and scorns and contumelious taunts. 1H6 1.04. 39
he dares not calm his contumelious spirit, | nor 2H6 3.02.204
our holy virgins to the stain | of contumelious, TIM 5.01.174
CONTUMELIOUSLY 1 FR 0.0001 REL FR 1 V 0 P
thus contumeliously should break the peace! 1H6 1.03. 58
CONTUMELY 1 FR 0.0001 REL FR 1 V 0 P
oppressor's wrong, the proud man's contumely, HAM 3.01. 70
CONTUSIONS 1 FR 0.0001 REL FR 1 V 0 P
forgets | aged contusions and all brush of time, 2H6 5.03. 3
/CONVENIENCE 1 FR 0.0001 REL FR 1 V 0 P
/which, /if /convenience /will /not /allow, LR 3.06. 99
CONVENIENCE 4 FR 0.0004 REL FR 2 V 2 P
and the place answer to convenience. MM 3.01.248 P
if i can meet him with any convenience, and he AWW 2.03.238 P
all the honor | that good convenience claims. 3.02. 72
weigh what convenience both of time and means HAM 4.07.149
CONVENIENCES 2 FR 0.0002 REL FR 1 V 1 P
from certain and possess'd conveniences | to TRO 3.03. 7
now for want of these requir'd conveniences, her OTH 2.01.231 P
CONVENIENCY 2 FR 0.0002 REL FR 1 V 1 P
but with all brief and plain conveniency | let MV 4.01. 82
from me all conveniency than suppliest me with OTH 4.02.177 P
CONVENIENT 20 FR 0.0022 REL FR 15 V 5 P
come to me at your convenient leisure, and you WIV 3.05.134 P
and 'tis not convenient you should be cozen'd. 4.05. 81 P
convenient is it. MM 4.03.103
and here's a marvail's convenient place for our MND 3.01. 2 P
madam, i go with all convenient speed. MV 3.04. 56
dispatch the most convenient messenger. AWW 3.04. 34
to which place | we have convenient convoy. 4.04. 10
be angry with you, if the time were convenient. H5 4.01.204 P
too loud, | the garden here is more convenient. 1H6 2.04. 4
them | for single combat in convenient place, 2H6 1.03.208
but it shall be convenient, master hume, that 1.04. 7 P
i will, my lord, with all convenient haste. R3 4.04.443
the most convenient place that i can think of H8 2.02.137
take | convenient numbers to make good the city, COR 1.05. 12
make true wars, | i'll frame convenient peace. 5.03.191
it were convenient you had such a devil. TIT 5.02. 90
know | where we shall find him most convenient. HAM 1.01.175
that under covert and convenient seeming | has LR 3.02. 56
and more convenient is he for my hand | than for 4.05. 31
'tis most convenient, pray go with us. 5.01. 36
CONVENIENTLY 4 FR 0.0004 REL FR 3 V 1 P
love | as shall conveniently become you there." MV 2.08. 45
if he may be conveniently deliver'd, i would he TN 4.02. 68 P
cell, | till i conveniently could send to romeo. ROM 5.03.256
action may | conveniently the rest convey, PER 3.ch. 56
CONVENT *(also covent)*
CONVENT 3 FR 0.0003 REL FR 3 V 0 P
all our surgeons | convent in their behoof, our TNK 1.04. 31
we convent nought else but woes: 1.05. 9
we convent, etc. 1.05. 10
CONVENTED 3 FR 0.0003 REL FR 3 V 0 P
make up full clear, | whensoever he's convented. MM 5.01.158
morning to the council–board | he be convented. H8 5.01. 52
we are convented | upon a pleasing treaty, and COR 2.02. 54
CONVENTICLES 1 FR 0.0001 REL FR 1 V 0 P
myself had notice of your conventicles — | and 2H6 3.01.166
CONVENTS 1 FR 0.0001 REL FR 1 V 0 P
when that is known and golden time convents, | a TN 5.01.382
CONVERSANT 3 FR 0.0003 REL FR 2 V 1 P
nor conversant with ease and idleness, | till i JN 4.03. 70
in birth, alike conversant in general services, CYM 4.01. 12 P
nature should be so conversant with pain, PER 3.02. 25
CONVERSATION 10 FR 0.0011 REL FR 6 V 4 P
out of my conversation, that he dares in this WIV 2.01. 24 P
king, | had from the conversation of my thoughts AWW 1.03.234
i mean, his conversation with shore's wife — R3 3.05. 31
more of your conversation would infect my brain, COR 2.01. 94 P
a man | as e'er my conversation cop'd withal. HAM 3.02. 55
and have not those soft parts of conversation OTH 3.03.264

is of a holy, cold, and still conversation. ANT 2.06.123 P
with five times so much conversation, i should CYM 1.04.103 P
the good in conversation, | to whom i give my PER 2.ch. 9
honor, | that liberty and common conversation, TNK 2.02. 74
CONVERSATIONS 1 FR 0.0001 REL FR 1 V 0 P
but all are banish'd till their conversations 2H4 5.05.100
CONVERS'D 4 FR 0.0004 REL FR 3 V 1 P
we have convers'd and spent our hours together, TGV 2.04. 63
prove you that any man with me convers'd | at ADO 4.01.181
i was three year old, convers'd with a magician, AYL 5.02. 60 P
honor and virtue, and convers'd with such | as, 2H6 2.01.191
CONVERSE 13 FR 0.0014 REL FR 9 V 4 P
hear sweet discourse, converse with noblemen, TGV 1.03. 31
did you converse, sir, with this gentlewoman? ERR 2.02.160
i did converse this quondam day with a companion
LLL 5.01. 6 P
borne ourselves | in the converse of breath — 5.02.735
visit the speechless sick and still converse 5.02.851
but, alas, who can converse with a dumb show? MV 1.02. 73 P
that do converse and waste the time together, 3.04. 12
why dost thou converse with that trunk of humors
1H4 2.04.449 P
let them practice and converse with spirits. 1H6 2.01. 25
i will converse with iron–witted fools | and R3 4.02. 28
your party in converse, him you would sound, HAM 2.01. 42
to converse with him that is wise and says LR 1.04. 15 P
that your converse and business | may be more OTH 3.01. 38
CONVERSED 1 FR 0.0001 REL FR 1 V 0 P
crafty kern, | hath he conversed with the enemy, 2H6 3.01.368
CONVERSES 1 FR 0.0001 REL FR 0 V 1 P
one that converses more with the buttock of the COR 2.01. 51 P
CONVERSING 2 FR 0.0002 REL FR 1 V 1 P
he, by conversing with them, is turn'd into a 2H4 5.01. 67 P
we grace the yeoman by conversing with him. 1H6 2.04. 81
CONVERSION 2 FR 0.0002 REL FR 2 V 0 P
i was, since my conversion | so sweetly tastes, AYL 4.03.136
and too sociable | for your conversion. JN 1.01.189
CONVERT 10 FR 0.0011 REL FR 9 V 1 P
courtesy itself must convert to disdain, if you ADO 1.01.122 P
that shall convert those tears | by number into 2H4 5.02. 60
now seeming sweet, convert to bitt'rest gall. ROM 1.05. 92
to general filths | convert o' th' instant, TIM 4.01. 7
and he whose pious breath seeks to convert you, 4.03.141
of your sword, let grief | convert to anger; MAC 4.03.229
lest with this piteous action you convert | my HAM 3.04.128
convert his gyves to graces, so that my arrows, 4.07. 21
for stones dissolv'd to water do convert. LUC 592
if from thyself to store thou wouldst convert; SON 14.12
CONVERTED 7 FR 0.0008 REL FR 4 V 3 P
may i be so converted and see with these eyes? ADO 2.03. 22 P
and how you may be converted i know not, but 3.04. 90 P
is mine, to you and yours | is now converted. MV 3.02.167
was converted | both from his enterprise and AYL 5.04.161
loam whereto he was converted might they not HAM 5.01.211 P
now converted are | from his low tract and look SON 7.11
eye, | when love converted from the thing it was 49. 7
CONVERTEST 1 FR 0.0001 REL FR 1 V 0 P
call thine, when thou from youth convertest. SON 11. 4
CONVERTING 3 FR 0.0003 REL FR 2 V 1 P
converting all your sounds of woe | into hey ADO 2.03. 68
for in converting jews to christians, you raise MV 3.05. 35 P
going, | for sure there's no converting of 'em. H8 1.03. 43
CONVERTITE 2 FR 0.0002 REL FR 2 V 0 P
but since you are a gentle convertite, | my JN 5.01. 19
he thence departs a heavy convertite, | she LUC 743
CONVERTITES 1 FR 0.0001 REL FR 1 V 0 P
out of these convertites | there is much matter AYL 5.04.184
CONVERTS 3 FR 0.0003 REL FR 3 V 0 P
the love of wicked men converts to fear, | that R2 5.01. 66
thy overflow of good converts to bad, | and thy 5.03. 64
this hot desire converts to cold disdain; LUC 691
/CONVEY 2 FR 0.0002 REL FR 2 V 0 P
/some /of /you, /convey /him /to /the /tower. R2 4.01.316
/convey! 4.01.317
CONVEY 36 FR 0.0040 REL FR 31 V 5 P
how shall i best convey the ladder thither? TGV 3.01.128
come, i'll convey thee through the city–gate; 3.01.254
"convey," the wise it call. WIV 1.03. 29 P
but if you have a friend here, convey, convey 3.03.117 P
you have a friend here, convey, convey him out. 3.03.117 P
grant | did but convey unto our fearful minds ERR 1.01. 67
if seriously i may convey my thoughts | in this AWW 2.01. 81
and convey what i will set down to my lady. TN 4.02.110 P
convey me to my bed, then to my grave; R2 2.01.137
god's sake, lords, convey my /tristful queen, 1H4 2.04.393
convey them with safe conduct. H5 1.02.297
and thence to france shall we convey you safe, 2.pr. 37
convey me salisbury into his tent, | and then 1H6 1.04.110
keepers, convey him hence, and i myself | will 2.05.120
only convey me where thou art commanded. 2H6 2.04. 93
convey him hence, and on our longboat's side 4.01. 68
away, convey him hence. 4.01.103
this conduct to convey me to the tower. R3 1.01. 45
if she convey | letters to richmond, you shall 4.02. 92
brothers, help to convey her hence away, | and TIT 1.01.287
whither wouldst thou convey | this growing image 5.01. 44
sirs, help our uncle to convey him in. 5.03. 15
some loving friends convey the emperor hence, 5.03.191
no opportunity | that may convey my greetings, ROM 3.05. 50
convey your pleasures in a spacious plenty, MAC 4.03. 71
winds give benefit | and convey /is assistant, HAM 1.03. 3
behind the arras i'll convey myself | to hear 3.03. 28
convey the business as i shall find means, and LR 1.02.101 P
into her womb convey sterility, | dry up in her 1.04.278
she is not well, convey her to my tent. 5.03.106
the weight we must convey with 's will permit, ANT 3.01. 36
see | how i convey my shame out of thine eyes 3.11. 52
action may | conveniently the rest convey, PER 3.ch. 56
convey thy deity | aboard our dancing boat, make 3.01. 12
of my rhyme, | which never could i so convey, 4.ch. 49
through which i may convey this troubled soul. LUC 1176
CONVEYANCE 7 FR 0.0008 REL FR 5 V 2 P
here at hand, bethink you of some conveyance. WIV 3.03.127 P
such impossible conveyance upon me that i stood ADO 2.01.245 P
henry's death, i fear, there is conveyance. 1H6 1.03. 2
thy sly conveyance and thy lord's false love, 3H6 3.03.160
mad'st quick conveyance with her good aunt anne.
R3 4.04.283
craves the conveyance of a promis'd march | over HAM 4.04. 3
to his conveyance i assign my wife, | with what OTH 1.03.285
CONVEYANCES 2 FR 0.0002 REL FR 1 V 1 P
these pipes and these conveyances of our blood COR 5.01. 54
the very conveyances of his lands will scarcely HAM 5.01.110 P
CONVEY'D 17 FR 0.0019 REL FR 14 V 3 P
and thence she cannot be convey'd away. TGV 3.01. 37
they convey'd me into a buck–basket. WIV 3.05. 86 P
there was one convey'd out of my house yesterday 4.02.146 P
you, fortune hath convey'd to my understanding; MM 3.01.185 P
i have convey'd aboard, and i have bought | the ERR 4.01. 88
see him safe convey'd | home to my house. 4.04.122
what think you, if he were convey'd to bed, SHR in.1. 37
which in a napkin (being close convey'd) | shall in.1. 127
convey'd himself as th' heir to th' lady lingare H5 1.02. 74
see that he be convey'd unto the tower; 3H6 3.02.120
see that forthwith duke edward be convey'd 4.03. 52
he was convey'd by richard, duke of gloucester, 4.06. 81
to have him suddenly convey'd from hence. R3 4.04. 76
you be convey'd to th' tower a prisoner; H8 5.02.124
my lord of gloucester hath convey'd him hence. LR 3.07. 15
that a king's children should be so convey'd, CYM 1.01. 63
in her light chariot, quickly is convey'd, VEN 1192
/CONVEYERS 1 FR 0.0001 REL FR 1 V 0 P
/conveyers /are /you /all, | /that /rise /thus R2 4.01.317
CONVEYING 1 FR 0.0001 REL FR 1 V 0 P
by interims and conveying gusts we have heard COR 1.06. 5
CONVICT 1 FR 0.0001 REL FR 1 V 0 P
before i be convict by course of law, | to R3 1.04.187
CONVICTED 1 FR 0.0001 REL FR 1 V 0 P
a whole armado of convicted sail | is scattered JN 3.04. 2
CONVINCE 6 FR 0.0006 REL FR 5 V 1 P
the holy suit which fain it would convince, LLL 5.02.746
else might the world convince of levity | as TRO 2.02.130
or that persuasion could but thus convince me 3.02.164
will i with wine and wassail so convince, | that MAC 1.07. 64
a courtier to convince the honor of my mistress, CYM 1.04. 95 P
time of both this truth shall ne'er convince, PER 1.02.123
CONVINCED 1 FR 0.0001 REL FR 1 V 0 P
convinced or supplied them, cannot choose | but OTH 4.01. 28
CONVINCES 1 FR 0.0001 REL FR 1 V 0 P
their malady convinces | the great assay of art; MAC 4.03.142
CONVIVE 1 FR 0.0001 REL FR 1 V 0 P
there in the full convive we. TRO 4.05.272
CONVOCATION 2 FR 0.0002 REL FR 1 V 1 P
upon our spiritual convocation | and in regard H5 1.01. 76
a certain convocation of politic worms are e'en HAM 4.03. 20 P
CONVOY 6 FR 0.0006 REL FR 4 V 2 P
mother i am returning, entertain'd my convoy, AWW 4.03. 89 P
to which place | we have convenient convoy. 4.04. 10
a sconce, at such a breach, at such a convoy; H5 3.06. 73 P
and crowns for convoy put into his purse. 4.03. 37
sailing pandar | our doubtful hope, our convoy, TRO 1.01.104
my joy | must be my convoy in the secret night. ROM 2.04.191
CONVULSIONS 2 FR 0.0002 REL FR 2 V 0 P
they grind their joints | with dry convulsions, TMP 4.01.259
torturing convulsions from his globy eyes | had TNK 5.01.113
CONY 2 FR 0.0002 REL FR 1 V 1 P
as the cony that you see dwell where she is AYL 3.02.339 P
so doth the cony struggle in the net. 3H6 1.04. 62
CONY–CATCH 1 FR 0.0001 REL FR 0 V 1 P
i must cony–catch, i must shift. WIV 1.03. 33 P
CONY–CATCH'D 1 FR 0.0001 REL FR 0 V 1 P
lest you be cony–catch'd in this business. SHR 5.01. 99 P
CONY–CATCHING 2 FR 0.0002 REL FR 0 V 2 P
and against your cony–catching rascals, bardolph WIV 1.01.124 P
come, you are so full of cony–catching! SHR 4.01. 43 P
COOK 16 FR 0.0018 REL FR 7 V 9 P
or his dry nurse — or his cook — or his WIV 1.02. 4 P
would the cook were a' my mind! ADO 1.03. 72 P
where's the cook? SHR 4.01. 45 P
where is the rascal cook? 4.01.162
this day she was both pantler, butler, cook, WT 4.04. 56
if the cook help to make the gluttony, you help 2H4 2.04. 44 P
yea, marry, william cook, bid him come hither. 5.01. 11 P
but for william cook — are there no young 5.01. 16 P
pretty little tiny kickshaws, tell william cook. 5.01. 28 P
thing he sees there, let thine eye be thy cook. H5 5.02.149 P
so, now bring them in, for i'll play the cook, TIT 5.02.204
sir, 'tis an ill cook that cannot lick his own ROM 4.02. 6 P
things for the cook, sir, but i know not what. 4.04. 15
my cook and i'll provide. TIM 3.04.117
cadwal and i | will play the cook and servant, CYM 3.06. 30
a cave–keeper, | and cook to honest creatures. 4.02.299
COOK'D 2 FR 0.0002 REL FR 1 V 1 P
on that | whilst what we have kill'd be cook'd. CYM 3.06. 39
if you be ready for that, you are well cook'd. 5.04.154 P
COOKERY 2 FR 0.0002 REL FR 2 V 0 P
your fine egyptian cookery | shall have the fame ANT 2.06. 63
but his neat cookery! CYM 4.02. 49
COOKS 3 FR 0.0003 REL FR 3 V 0 P
sirrah, go hire me twenty cunning cooks. ROM 4.02. 2
epicurean cooks | sharpen with cloyless sauce ANT 2.01. 24
to our rock, | you and fidele play the cooks. CYM 4.02.164
COOL *(also keel*)*
COOL 36 FR 0.0040 REL FR 27 V 9 P
my humor shall not cool. WIV 1.03.100 P
swallow'd snowballs for pills to cool the reins. 3.05. 23 P
i would not have things cool. 4.02.224 P
send me a cool rut–time, jove, or who can blame 5.05. 14 P
of it by your daughter, let it cool the while. ADO 2.03.206 P
under the cool shade of a sycamore | i thought LLL 5.02. 89
more than cool reason ever comprehends. MND 5.01. 6
than my heart cool with mortifying groans. MV 1.01. 82
"will't please your lordship cool your hands?" SHR in.1. 58
cool, blushes! AWW 4.03.337
cool and congeal again to what it was. JN 2.01.479
this act so evilly borne shall cool the hearts 3.04.149
the whilst his iron did on the anvil cool, 4.02.194
whiles yet the cool and temperate wind of grace H5 3.03. 30
'twill make them cool in zeal unto your grace. 2H6 3.01.177
which is not amiss to cool a man's stomach this 4.10. 9 P
which with my scimitar i'll cool to–morrow. TRO 5.01. 2
which doth ever cool | i' th' absence of the COR 4.01. 43
till i find the stream | to cool this heat, a TIT 2.01.134
now let hot aetna cool in sicily, | and be my 3.01.241
to let the meat cool ere we can agree upon the TIM 3.06. 68 P
cool it with a baboon's blood, | then the charm MAC 4.01. 37
this deed i'll do before this purpose cool. 4.01.154
flame of thy distemper | sprinkle cool patience. HAM 3.04.124
this is a brave night to cool a courtezan. LR 3.02. 79 P
but we have reason to cool our raging motions, OTH 1.03.330 P
bellows and the fan | to cool a gipsy's lust. ANT 1.01. 10
/glow the delicate cheeks which they did cool, 2.02.204
we should not, when the blood was cool, have CYM 5.05. 77
let your breath cool yourself, telling your PER 1.01.159
under the shadow of his sword may cool us; TNK 1.01. 92
honorable toil, | are paid with ice to cool 'em. 1.02. 34
shall cool the heat of this descending sun: VEN 190
cool shadow to his melting buttock lent; 315
a brook where adon us'd to cool his spleen. PP 6. 6
this brand she quenched in a cool well by, SON 154. 9
COOL'D 7 FR 0.0008 REL FR 4 V 3 P
dish) to be thrown into the thames, and cool'd, WIV 3.05.120 P
thwarted my bargains, cool'd my friends, heated MV 3.01. 57 P
warm'd and cool'd by the same winter and summer, 3.01. 63 P
the blood is hot that must be cool'd for this. R2 1.01. 51
my lord northumberland will soon be cool'd. 2H4 3.01. 44
been, my senses would have cool'd | to hear a MAC 5.05. 10
affection is a coal that must be cool'd, | else, VEN 387
COOLING 7 FR 0.0008 REL FR 6 V 1 P
whom i left cooling of the air with sighs, | in TMP 1.02.222
my wind cooling my broth | would blow me to an MV 1.01. 22
there all is marr'd; there lies a cooling card. 1H6 5.03. 84
nay, you must stay the cooling too, or ye may TRO 1.01. 26 P
the green leaves quiver with the cooling wind TIT 2.03. 14
thou hast describ'd | a hot friend cooling. JC 4.02. 19
cooling his hot face in the chastest tears LUC 682
COOLS 6 FR 0.0006 REL FR 4 V 2 P
when i am warm, he cools me with beating. ERR 4.04. 33 P
as fire cools fire | within the scorched veins JN 3.01.277
with the heart there cools and ne'er returneth 2H6 3.02.166
strike now, or else the iron cools. 3H6 5.01. 49
love cools, friendship falls off, brothers LR 1.02.106 P
love's fire heats water, water cools not love. SON 154.14
COOP'D 1 FR 0.0001 REL FR 1 V 0 P
alas, i am not coop'd here for defense! 3H6 5.01.109
COOPS 1 FR 0.0001 REL FR 1 V 0 P
and coops from other lands her islanders, | even JN 2.01. 25
CO–PARTNERS 1 FR 0.0001 REL FR 1 V 0 P
so should i have co–partners in my pain, | and LUC 789
COPATAIN 1 FR 0.0001 REL FR 0 V 1 P
hose, a scarlet cloak, and a copatain hat! SHR 5.01. 67 P
COP'D 4 FR 0.0004 REL FR 3 V 1 P
peruse the men | we should have cop'd withal. 2H4 4.02. 95
they say he yesterday cop'd hector in the battle TRO 1.02. 33 P
a man | as e'er my conversation cop'd withal. HAM 3.02. 55
but she, that never cop'd with stranger eyes, LUC 99
COPE* 12 FR 0.0013 REL FR 11 V 1 P
we freely cope your courteous pains withal. MV 4.01.412
i love to cope him in these sullen fits, | for AYL 2.01. 67
unworthy though thou art, i'll cope with thee, 2H6 3.02.230
he is a man, and, clifford, cope with him. 3H6 1.03. 24
remember whom you are to cope withal — | a sort
R3 5.03.315
in the fear | to cope malicious censurers, which H8 1.02. 78
/cull their flower, ajax shall cope the best. TRO 2.03.264
am i noble as the adversary | i come to cope. LR 5.03.124
when | he hath, and is again to cope your wife. OTH 4.01. 86
in the cheapest country under the cope, shall PER 4.06.123 P
that i have foregone | or futurely can cope. TNK 1.01.174
all strain court'sy who shall cope him first. VEN 888
COPESMATE 1 FR 0.0001 REL FR 1 V 0 P
"misshapen time, copesmate of ugly night, LUC 925
COPHETUA 3 FR 0.0003 REL FR 2 V 1 P
most illustrate king cophetua set eye upon the LLL 4.01. 65 P
let king cophetua know the truth thereof. 2H4 5.03.102
when king cophetua lov'd the beggar–maid! ROM 2.01. 14
COPIED 3 FR 0.0003 REL FR 3 V 0 P
my lord melune, let this be copied out, | and JN 5.02. 1
past | that youth and observation copied there, HAM 1.05.101
(as like enough it will) i would have it copied. OTH 3.04.190
COPIES 2 FR 0.0002 REL FR 0 V 2 P
we took him setting of boys' copies. 2H6 4.02. 88 P
takes virtuous copies to be wicked; TIM 3.03. 32 P
COPIOUS 2 FR 0.0002 REL FR 2 V 0 P
the trumpet sounds, be copious in exclaims. R3 4.04.135
their copious stories, oftentimes begun, | end VEN 845
COPP'D 1 FR 0.0001 REL FR 1 V 0 P
blind mole casts | copp'd hills towards heaven, PER 1.01.101
COPPER 6 FR 0.0006 REL FR 2 V 4 P
if so, our copper buys no better treasure. LLL 4.03.383
i know not how oft, that that ring was copper! 1H4 3.03. 84 P
yea, if he said my ring was copper. 3.03.142 P
i say 'tis copper. 3.03.143 P
tongue had commended troilus for a copper nose.
TRO 1.02.106 P
some with cunning gild their copper crowns, 4.04.105
COPPER–SPUR 1 FR 0.0001 REL FR 0 V 1 P
young master deep–vow, and master copper–spur,
MM 4.03. 13 P
COPPICE 1 FR 0.0001 REL FR 1 V 0 P
hereby, upon the edge of yonder coppice, | a LLL 4.01. 9
COPSE 1 FR 0.0001 REL FR 1 V 0 P
but lo from forth a copse that neighbors by, | a VEN 259
COP'ST 2 FR 0.0002 REL FR 2 V 0 P
must know | the royal fool thou cop'st with — WT 4.04.424
that cop'st with death himself to scape from it; ROM 4.01. 75
COPULATION 2 FR 0.0002 REL FR 1 V 1 P
to get your living by the copulation of cattle; AYL 3.02. 80 P
let copulation thrive; LR 4.06.114
COPULATIVES 1 FR 0.0001 REL FR 0 V 1 P
amongst the rest of the country copulatives, to AYL 5.04. 56 P
/COPY 1 FR 0.0001 REL FR 1 V 0 P
/was /the /mark /and /glass, /copy /and /book, 2H4 2.03. 31
COPY 11 FR 0.0012 REL FR 10 V 1 P
it was the copy of our conference: ERR 5.01. 62
almost the copy of my child that's dead, | and ADO 5.01.289
a man | might be a copy to these younger times; AWW 1.02. 46
will you give me a copy of the sonnet you writ 4.03.319 P
to the grave | and leave the world no copy. TN 1.05.243
they say it is a copy out of mine. WT 1.02.122
the whole matter | and copy of the father — eye 2.03.100
the copy of your speed is learn'd by them; JN 4.02.113
be copy now to /men of grosser blood, | and H5 3.01. 24
thou shouldst print more, not let that copy die. SON 11.14

let him but copy what in you is writ, | not 84. 9
COPY–BOOK 1 FR 0.0001 REL FR 1 V 0 P
fair as a text b in a copy–book. LLL 5.02. 42
COPY'S 1 FR 0.0001 REL FR 1 V 0 P
but in them nature's copy's not eterne. MAC 3.02. 38
CORAGGIO 3 FR 0.0003 REL FR 1 V 2 P
coraggio, bully–monster, coraggio! TMP 5.01.257 P
coraggio, bully–monster, coraggio! 5.01.258 P
bravely, coraggio! AWW 2.05. 92
CORAL 7 FR 0.0008 REL FR 7 V 0 P
thy father lies, | of his bones are coral made: TMP 1.02.398
tranio, i saw her coral lips to move, | and with SHR 1.01.174
the heavenly moisture, that sweet coral mouth, VEN 542
her coral lips, her snow–white dimpled chin. LUC 420
like ivory conduits coral cesterns filling: 1234
ivy buds, | with coral clasps and amber studs: PP 19.14
coral is far more red than her lips' red; SON 130. 2
CORAM 1 FR 0.0001 REL FR 0 V 1 P
of gloucester, justice of peace and coram. WIV 1.01. 6 P
CORAMBUS 1 FR 0.0001 REL FR 0 V 1 P
corambus, so many; AWW 4.03.162 P
CORANTO 2 FR 0.0002 REL FR 0 V 2 P
why, he's able to lead her a coranto. AWW 2.03. 43 P
church in a galliard and come home in a coranto? TN 1.03.129 P
CORANTOS 1 FR 0.0001 REL FR 1 V 0 P
and teach lavoltas high and swift corantos, H5 3.05. 33
CORBO 1 FR 0.0001 REL FR 0 V 1 P
cargo, cargo, cargo, villianda par corbo, cargo. AWW 4.01. 66 P
CORD 7 FR 0.0008 REL FR 5 V 2 P
his neck will come to your waist — a cord, sir. MM 3.02. 40 P
state, | thou hast not left the value of a cord; MV 4.01.366
and if thou want'st a cord, the smallest thread JN 4.03.127
cut | with edge of penny cord and vile reproach. H5 3.06. 48
if thou hadst hands to help thee knit the cord. TIT 2.04. 10
o, the charity of a penny cord! CYM 5.04.167 P
o, give me cord, or knife, or poison, | some 5.05.213
CORDED 2 FR 0.0002 REL FR 2 V 0 P
this night he meaneth with a corded ladder | to TGV 2.06. 33
and with a corded ladder fetch her down; 3.01. 40
/CORDELIA 2 FR 0.0002 REL FR 2 V 0 P
/burning /shame | /detains /him /from /cordelia. LR 4.03. 47
/the /question /of /cordelia /and /her /father 5.03. 58
CORDELIA 19 FR 0.0021 REL FR 19 V 0 P
what shall cordelia speak? love, and be silent. LR 1.01. 62
then poor cordelia! 1.01. 76
how, how, cordelia? 1.01. 94
and here i take cordelia by the hand, | duchess 1.01.243
fairest cordelia, that art most rich being poor, 1.01.250
bid them farewell, cordelia, though unkind, 1.01.260
father, with wash'd eyes | cordelia leaves you. 1.01.269
come, my fair cordelia. 1.01.282
fault, | how ugly didst thou in cordelia show! 1.04.267
i know 'tis from cordelia, | who hath most 2.02.166
if you shall see cordelia | (as fear not but you 3.01. 46
i think this lady | to be my child cordelia. 4.07. 69
which he intends to lear and to cordelia, | the 5.01. 66
upon such sacrifices, my cordelia, | the gods 5.03. 20
and where's cordelia? 5.03.238
writ | is on the life of lear and on cordelia. 5.03.247
wife and me | to hang cordelia in the prison, 5.03.254
cordelia, cordelia, stay a little. 5.03.272
cordelia, cordelia, stay a little. 5.03.272
CORDELION 3 FR 0.0003 REL FR 3 V 0 P
hand | of cordelion knighted in the field. JN 1.01. 54
or the reputed son of cordelion, | lord of thy 1.01.136
king richard cordelion was thy father. 1.01.253
CORDELION'S 3 FR 0.0003 REL FR 3 V 0 P
he hath a trick of cordelion's face, | the JN 1.01. 85
god shall forgive you cordelion's death | the 2.01. 12
town | great cordelion's heart was buried, | so 1H6 3.02. 83
CORDIAL 9 FR 0.0010 REL FR 9 V 0 P
which draught to me were cordial. WT 1.02.318
has a taste as sweet | as any cordial comfort. 5.03. 77
a pleasing cordial, princely buckingham, | is R3 2.01. 41
the cordial that ye bring a wretched lady, | a H8 3.01.106
the cordial of mine age to glad my heart! TIT 1.01.166
come, cordial and not poison, go with me | to ROM 5.01. 85
i do not know | what is more cordial. CYM 1.05. 64
which he said was precious | and cordial to me, 4.02.327
that confection | which i gave him for cordial, 5.05.247
CORDIS 1 FR 0.0001 REL FR 1 V 0 P
i have tremor cordis on me; WT 1.02.110
CORDS 12 FR 0.0013 REL FR 12 V 0 P
the ladder made of cords, and all the means TGV 2.04.182
why then a ladder, quaintly made of cords, | to 3.01.117
but he, i thank him, gnaw'd in two my cords: ERR 5.01.290
the cords, the ladder, or the hangman rather? 1H4 1.03.166
and bring thee cords made like a tackled stair, ROM 2.04.189
the cords | that romeo bid thee fetch? 3.02. 34
ay, ay, the cords. 3.02. 35
take up those cords. 3.02.132
come, cords, come, nurse, i'll to my wedding–bed 3.02.136
oft bite the holy cords a–twain | which are t' LR 2.02. 74
if there be cords, or knives, | poison, or fire, OTH 3.03.388
those that with cords, knives, drams, TNK 1.01.142
/CORE* 1 FR 0.0001 REL FR 1 V 0 P
how now, thou /core of envy? TRO 5.01. 4
CORE* 4 FR 0.0004 REL FR 3 V 1 P
con tutto /il core, ben trovato, may i say. SHR 1.02. 24
were not that a botchy core? TRO 2.01. 6 P
most putrefied core, so fair without, | thy 5.08. 1
and i will wear him | in my heart's core, ay, in HAM 3.02. 73
CORIN 3 FR 0.0003 REL FR 3 V 0 P
land, | and in the shape of corin sat all day, MND 2.01. 66
o corin, that thou knew'st how i do love her! AYL 2.04. 23
no, corin, being old, thou canst not guess, 2.04. 25
CORINTH 7 FR 0.0008 REL FR 6 V 1 P
was carried towards corinth, as we thought. ERR 1.01. 87
to us, | of corinth that, of epidaurus this. 1.01. 93
three were taken up | by fishermen of corinth, 1.01.111
but by and by rude fishermen of corinth | by 5.01.352
antipholus, thou cam'st from corinth first? 5.01.363
i came from corinth, my most gracious lord — 5.01.366
would we could see you at corinth! TIM 2.02. 70 P
CORINTHIAN 1 FR 0.0001 REL FR 0 V 1 P
no proud jack like falstaff, but a corinthian, a 1H4 2.04. 12 P
CORIOLANUS' 1 FR 0.0001 REL FR 1 V 0 P
greasy caps in hooting at | coriolanus' exile. COR 4.06.132
CORIOLANUS 33 FR 0.0037 REL FR 27 V 6 P
clamor of the host, | martius caius coriolanus! COR 1.09. 65
martius caius coriolanus! 1.09. 67
these | in honor follows coriolanus. 2.01.165
welcome to rome, renowned coriolanus! 2.01.166
welcome to rome, renowned coriolanus! 2.01.167
coriolanus must i call thee? 2.01.174
thought of every one coriolanus will carry it. 2.02. 4 P
for coriolanus neither to care whether they love 2.02. 12 P
work perform'd | by martius caius coriolanus, 2.02. 46
sit, coriolanus; 2.02. 67
the deeds of coriolanus | should not be utter'd 2.02. 82
call coriolanus. 2.02.130
the senate, coriolanus, are well pleas'd | to 2.02.132
to coriolanus come all joy and honor! 2.02.154
there, coriolanus. 2.03.145
nor has coriolanus | deserv'd this so dishonor'd 3.01. 59
coriolanus! 3.01.186
coriolanus, patience! 3.01.190
the consul coriolanus. 3.01.278
heart the banishment of that worthy coriolanus, 4.03. 22 P
coriolanus banish'd? 4.03. 27 P
his great opposer, coriolanus, being now in no 4.03. 35 P
no better entertainment | in being coriolanus. 4.05. 10
thereto witness may | my surname, coriolanus. 4.05. 68
your coriolanus | is not much miss'd but with 4.06. 12
we wish'd coriolanus | had lov'd you as we did. 4.06. 24
coriolanus | he would not answer to; 5.01. 11
of state, and come | to speak with coriolanus. 5.02. 4
with fire before | you'll speak with coriolanus. 5.02. 8
cannot office me from my son coriolanus. 5.02. 63 P
to his surname coriolanus 'longs more pride 5.03.170
thy stol'n name | coriolanus, in corioles? 5.06. 89
revenge, to do | as much as ever coriolanus did. TIT 4.04. 68
CORIOLES 17 FR 0.0019 REL FR 14 V 3 P
to your bands, | let us alone to guard corioles. COR 1.02. 27
lartius are set down before their city corioles; 1.03. 99 P
the citizens of corioles have issued, | and 1.06. 10
and holding corioles in the name of rome, | even 1.06. 37
tullus, | alone i fought in your corioles walls, 1.08. 8
for what he did before corioles, call him, 1.09. 63
you, titus lartius, | must to corioles back. 1.09. 76
i sometime lay here in corioles | at a poor 1.09. 82
been so fidius'd for all the chests in corioles, 2.01.131 P
alone martius did fight | within corioles gates; 2.01.163
dear, | such eyes the widows in corioles wear, 2.01.178
before and in corioles, let me say, | i cannot 2.02.102
reinforcement struck | corioles like a planet. 2.02.114
directly to say the troth on't, before corioles; 4.05.186 P
his wife is in corioles, and his child | like 5.03.179
thy stol'n name | coriolanus, in corioles? 5.06. 89
i | /flutter'd your volscians in corioles. 5.06.115
CORK 2 FR 0.0002 REL FR 0 V 2 P
i prithee take the cork out of thy mouth that i AYL 3.02.202 P
froth, as you'ld thrust a cork into a hogshead. WT 3.03. 94 P
CORKY 1 FR 0.0001 REL FR 1 V 0 P
bind fast his corky arms. LR 3.07. 29
CORMORANT 4 FR 0.0004 REL FR 4 V 0 P
when, spite of cormorant devouring time, | th' LLL 1.01. 4
light vanity, insatiate cormorant, | consuming R2 2.01. 38
in hot digestion of this cormorant war — TRO 2.02. 6
should by the cormorant belly be restrain'd, COR 1.01.121
/CORN* 1 FR 0.0001 REL FR 1 V 0 P
/thy /sheep /be /in /the /corn, | /and /for /one LR 3.06. 42
CORN* 35 FR 0.0039 REL FR 33 V 2 P
no use of metal, corn, or wine, or oil; TMP 2.01.154
he weeds the corn and still lets grow the LLL 1.01. 96
sow'd cockle reap'd no corn, | and justice 4.03.380
playing on pipes of corn and versing love | to MND 2.01. 67
and the green corn | hath rotted ere his youth 2.01. 94
our sighs and they shall lodge the summer corn, R2 3.03.162
that even our corn shall seem as light as chaff, 2H4 4.01.193
men | that come to gather money for their corn. 1H6 3.02. 5
poor market folks that come to sell their corn. 3.02. 15
good morrow, gallants, want ye corn for bread? 3.02. 41
and make thee curse the harvest of that corn. 3.02. 47
like over–ripen'd corn | hanging the head at 2H6 1.02. 1
like to the summer's corn by tempest lodged. 3.02.176
what valiant foemen, like to autumn's corn, 3H6 5.07. 3
where my chaff | and corn shall fly asunder; H8 5.01.111
her foes shake like a field of beaten corn, 5.04. 31
kill him, and we'll have corn at our own price. COR 1.01. 10 P
for corn at their own rates, whereof they say 1.01.189
the gods sent not | corn for the rich men only. 1.01.208
the volsces have much corn; 1.01.249
for once we stood up about the corn, he himself 2.03. 16 P
when corn was given them gratis, you repin'd, 3.01. 43
tell me of corn! 3.01. 61
give forth | the corn a' th' store–house gratis, 3.01.114
they know the corn | was not our recompense, 3.01.120
kind of service | did not deserve corn gratis. 3.01.125
first thrash the corn, then after burn the straw TIT 2.03.123
this scattered corn into one mutual sheaf, 5.03. 71
though bladed corn be lodg'd, and trees blown MAC 4.01. 55
his heart should make | shall of a corn cry woe, LR 3.02. 33
idle weeds that grow | in our sustaining corn. 4.04. 6
are stor'd with corn to make your needy bread, PER 1.04. 95
your grace, that fed my country with your corn, 3.03. 18
run | swifter than wind upon a field of corn, TNK 2.03. 77
as corn o'ergrown by weeds, so heedful fear | is LUC 281
CORNELIA 2 FR 0.0002 REL FR 2 V 0 P
cornelia never with more care | read to her sons TIT 4.01. 12
cornelia the midwife, and myself, | and no one 4.02.141
CORNELIUS 2 FR 0.0002 REL FR 2 V 0 P
and we here dispatch | you, good cornelius, and HAM 1.02. 34
what's this, cornelius? CYM 5.05.248
CORNER 13 FR 0.0014 REL FR 6 V 7 P
i may sit in a corner and cry "heigh–ho for a ADO 2.01.320 P
is't possible? sits the wind in that corner? 2.03. 98 P
east from the west corner of thy curious–knotted LLL 1.01.246 P
me for him at the corner of the orchard like a TN 3.04.177 P
even till that utmost corner of the west JN 2.01. 29
agreed. i'll to yond corner. 1H6 2.01. 33
the streets, and at every corner have them kiss. 2H6 4.07.136 P
down saint magnus' corner! 4.08. 2 P
done yet, o' my conscience, | deserves a corner. H8 3.01. 31
upon the corner of the moon | there hangs a MAC 3.05. 23
/an /ape an apple, in the corner of his jaw, HAM 4.02. 18 P
dungeon | than keep a corner in the thing i love OTH 3.03.272
cabin'd | in many as dangerous as poor a corner, TNK 1.03. 36
CORNER–CAP 1 FR 0.0001 REL FR 1 V 0 P
the triumphery, the corner–cap of society, | the LLL 4.03. 51
CORNERS 9 FR 0.0010 REL FR 7 V 2 P
all corners else o' th' earth | let liberty make TMP 1.02.492
duke of dark corners had been at home, he had MM 4.03.157 P
from the four corners of the earth they come MV 2.07. 39
launcelot, if you thus get my wife into corners! 3.05. 30 P
lame, | and unregarded age in corners thrown. AYL 2.03. 42
skulking in corners? WT 1.02.289
come the three corners of the world in arms, JN 5.07.116
and winds of all the corners kiss'd your sails, CYM 2.04. 28
winds and doth belie | all corners of the world. 3.04. 37
CORNERSTONE 1 FR 0.0001 REL FR 0 V 1 P
you yond coign a' th' capitol, yond cornerstone? COR 5.04. 2 P
CORNETS 1 FR 0.0001 REL FR 1 V 0 P
who in proud heart | doth stop my cornets, were 1H6 4.03. 25
CORN–FIELD 1 FR 0.0001 REL FR 1 V 0 P
that o'er the green corn–field did pass, | in AYL 5.03. 18
CORNISH 2 FR 0.0002 REL FR 2 V 0 P
a cornish name. H5 4.01. 50
art thou of cornish crew? 4.01. 50
CORN'S 1 FR 0.0001 REL FR 1 V 0 P
our corn's to reap, for yet our tithe's to sow. MM 4.01. 75
CORNS 2 FR 0.0002 REL FR 2 V 0 P
unplagu'd with corns will walk /a /bout with you ROM 1.05. 17
that makes dainty, | she i'll swear hath corns. 1.05. 20
CORNUTO 1 FR 0.0001 REL FR 0 V 1 P
/brook, but the peaking cornuto her husband, WIV 3.05. 70 P
/CORNWALL 1 FR 0.0001 REL FR 0 V 1 P
/that /the /duke /of /cornwall /was /so /slain? LR 4.07. 84 P
CORNWALL 10 FR 0.0011 REL FR 7 V 3 P
more affected the duke of albany than cornwall. LR 1.01. 2 P
our son of cornwall, | and you, our no less 1.01. 41
daughter, | our dearest regan, wife of cornwall? 1.01. 68
cornwall and albany, | with my two daughters' 1.01.127
that the duke of cornwall and regan his duchess 2.01. 3 P
toward, 'twixt the dukes of cornwall and albany? 2.01. 11 P
you not spoken 'gainst the duke of cornwall? 2.01. 23
speak with the duke of cornwall and his wife. 2.04. 97
the king would speak with cornwall, the dear 2.04.101
with mutual cunning) 'twixt albany and cornwall; 3.01. 21
/CORNWALL'S 1 FR 0.0001 REL FR 1 V 0 P
/of /albany's /and /cornwall's /powers /you LR 4.03. 48
CORNWALL'S 1 FR 0.0001 REL FR 1 V 0 P
o my good lord, the duke of cornwall's dead, LR 4.02. 70
COROLLARY 1 FR 0.0001 REL FR 1 V 0 P
bring a corollary, | rather than want a spirit. TMP 4.01. 57
CORONATION 18 FR 0.0020 REL FR 17 V 1 P
some reasons of this double coronation | i have JN 4.02. 40
next we solemnly proclaim | our coronation. R2 4.01.320
our coronation done, we will accite | (as i 2H4 5.02.141
two a' clock ere they come from the coronation. 5.05. 4 P
and in our coronation take your place. 1H6 3.04. 27
from callice, | to haste unto your coronation, 4.01. 10
provide | to see her coronation be perform'd. 2H6 1.01. 74
first will i see the coronation, | and then to 3H6 2.06. 96
where shall we sojourn till our coronation? R3 3.01. 62
to the tower | to sit about the coronation. 3.01.173
we are met | is to determine of the coronation. 3.04. 2
but for his purpose in the coronation, | i have 3.04. 15
there's order given for her coronation. H8 3.02. 46
shall be publish'd, and | her coronation. 3.02. 69
the voice is now | only about her coronation. 3.02.406
behold | the lady anne pass from her coronation? 4.01. 3
offices this day | by custom of the coronation. 4.01. 16
to denmark | to show my duty in your coronation, HAM 1.02. 53
CORONATION–DAY 2 FR 0.0002 REL FR 1 V 1 P
beheld | in london streets, that coronation–day, R2 5.05. 77
in the king's affairs upon his coronation–day, 2H4 3.02.183 P
CORONER *(see crowner, etc.)*
CORONET *(also crownet, etc.)*
CORONET 5 FR 0.0005 REL FR 5 V 0 P
subject his coronet to his crown, and bend | the TMP 1.02.114
with coronet of fresh and fragrant flowers; MND 4.01. 52
in this, | and doth deserve a coronet of gold. 1H6 3.03. 89
adorn his temples with a coronet, | and yet, in 5.04.134
to confirm, | this coronet part between you. LR 1.01.139
CORONETS 3 FR 0.0003 REL FR 2 V 1 P
with crowns imperial, crowns and coronets, H5 2.pr. 10
their coronets say so. these are stars indeed. H8 4.01. 54
neither, 'twas one of these coronets — and, as JC 1.02.238 P
CORPORAL* 21 FR 0.0023 REL FR 10 V 11 P
away, sir corporal nym! WIV 2.01.124
my name is corporal nym; 2.01.133 P
in corporal sufferance finds a pang as great MM 3.01. 79
and i to be a corporal of his field, | and wear LLL 3.01.187
by earth, she is not, corporal, there you lie. 4.03. 84
i would i had that corporal soundness now | as AWW 1.02. 24
i tell thee what, corporal bardolph, i could 2H4 2.04.153 P
and, good master corporal captain, for my old 3.02.229 P
of indignant faint souls past corporal toil, | a H5 1.01. 16
well met, corporal nym. 2.01. 1 P
let't be so, good corporal nym. 2.01. 13 P
it is certain, corporal, that he is married to 2.01. 17 P
good corporal, be patient here. 2.01. 27 P
good corporal! 2.01. 39 P
good corporal nym, show thy valor, and put up 2.01. 43 P
corporal nym, and thou wilt be friends, be 2.01.102 P
pray thee, corporal, stay. 3.02. 3 P
on, | his corporal motion govern'd by my spirit; JC 4.01. 33
and what seem'd corporal melted, | as breath MAC 1.03. 81
up | each corporal agent to this terrible feat. 1.07. 80
render to me some corporal sign about her, CYM 2.04.119
CORPORALS 1 FR 0.0001 REL FR 0 V 1 P
my whole charge consists of ancients, corporals, 1H4 4.02. 24 P
CORPORATE 2 FR 0.0002 REL FR 1 V 1 P
good master corporate bardolph, stand my friend, 2H4 3.02.220 P
they answer, in a joint and corporate voice, TIM 2.02.204
/CORPSE' 1 FR 0.0001 REL FR 1 V 0 P
/lord /your /son /had /only /but /the /corpse', 2H4 1.01.192
CORPSE' 1 FR 0.0001 REL FR 1 V 0 P
upon whose dead corpse' there was such misuse, 1H4 1.01. 43
CORPSE *(also corse, etc.)*
CORPSE 9 FR 0.0010 REL FR 9 V 0 P
not a friend greet | my poor corpse, where my TN 2.04. 62

her sainted spirit | again possess her corpse, WT 5.01. 58
a tomb, wherein his corpse shall be interr'd; 1H6 2.02. 13
enter his chamber, view his breathless corpse, 2H6 3.02.132
shall be this cold corpse on the earth's cold R3 5.03.266
hole, | where the dead corpse of bassianus lay; TIT 5.01.105
do grace to caesar's corpse, and grace his JC 3.02. 57
then make a ring about the corpse of caesar, 3.02.158
and humming water must o'erwhelm thy corpse, PER 3.01. 63
CORPULENT 1 FR 0.0001 REL FR 0 V 1 P
i' faith, and a corpulent, of a cheerful look, a 1H4 2.04.422 P
CORRECT 9 FR 0.0010 REL FR 7 V 2 P
i beseech your worship to correct yourself, for ADO 5.01.322 P
do correct | their proud contempt that beats his JN 2.01. 87
which made the fault that we cannot correct, R2 1.02. 5
where some, like magistrates, correct at home; H5 1.02.191
and when i did correct him for his fault the 2H6 1.03.199 P
to the laws, let them, | not you, correct him. H8 3.02.335
i would correct him. TRO 5.06. 3
to show his sorrow, he'd correct himself; PER 1.03. 22
nor double penance, to correct correction. SON 111.12
CORRECTED 1 FR 0.0001 REL FR 1 V 0 P
to your corrected son? COR 5.03. 57
CORRECTING 1 FR 0.0001 REL FR 1 V 0 P
which often thus correcting thy stout heart, COR 3.02. 78
/CORRECTION 1 FR 0.0001 REL FR 1 V 0 P
/your /purpos'd /low /correction | /is /such /as LR 2.02.142
CORRECTION 20 FR 0.0022 REL FR 14 V 6 P
i confess | there is no woe to his correction, TGV 2.04.138
i'll after, to rejoice in the boy's correction. 3.01.384 P
under your good correction, i have seen | when, MM 2.02. 10
correction and instruction must both work | ere 3.02. 32
as it shall follow in my correction, and god LLL 1.01.213 P
not so, sir, under correction, sir, i hope it is 5.02.489
under correction, sir, we know whereuntil it 5.02.493 P
but since correction lieth in those hands R2 1.02. 4
thee, | and minister correction to thy fault! 2.03.105
of faith, | to tie thee to my strong correction. 4.01. 77
take the correction, mildly kiss the rod, | and 5.01. 32
yield, | rebuke and dread correction wait on us, 1H4 5.01.111
and hangs resolv'd correction in the arm | that 2H4 4.01.211
are brought to the correction of your law. 4.04. 85
him life | after the taste of much correction. H5 2.02. 51
look you, under your correction, there is not 3.02.121 P
let a welsh correction teach you a good english 5.01. 78 P
under the correction of bragging be it spoken, i 5.02.138 P
shouldst have my office | ere that correction. TRO 5.06. 5
nor double penance, to correct correction. SON 111.12
CORRECTIONER 1 FR 0.0001 REL FR 0 V 1 P
you filthy famish'd correctioner, if you be not 2H4 5.04. 20 P
CORRECTOR 1 FR 0.0001 REL FR 1 V 0 P
o great corrector of enormous times, | shaker of TNK 5.01. 62
CORRECTS 2 FR 0.0002 REL FR 2 V 0 P
were he meal'd with that | which he corrects, MM 4.02. 84
corrects the /ill /aspects /of /planets /evil, TRO 1.03. 92
CORRESPONDENCE 1 FR 0.0001 REL FR 1 V 0 P
which have no correspondence with true sight, SON 148. 2
CORRESPONDENT 1 FR 0.0001 REL FR 1 V 0 P
i will be correspondent to command | and do my TMP 1.02.297
CORRESPONDING 1 FR 0.0001 REL FR 1 V 0 P
well corresponding | with your stiff age; CYM 3.03. 31
/CORRESPONSIVE 1 FR 0.0001 REL FR 1 V 0 P
/and /corresponsive /and /fulfilling /bolts TRO pr 18
CORRIGIBLE 2 FR 0.0002 REL FR 1 V 1 P
the power and corrigible authority of this lies OTH 1.03.325 P
bending down | his corrigible neck, his face ANT 4.14. 74
CORRIVAL 1 FR 0.0001 REL FR 1 V 0 P
might wear | without corrival all her dignities; 1H4 1.03.207
CORRIVALL'D 1 FR 0.0001 REL FR 1 V 0 P
sides but even now | corrivall'd greatness? TRO 1.03. 44
CORRIVALS 1 FR 0.0001 REL FR 1 V 0 P
and many moe corrivals and dear men | of 1H4 4.04. 31
CORROBORATE 1 FR 0.0001 REL FR 1 V 0 P
his heart is fracted and corroborate. H5 2.01.124
CORROSIVE 2 FR 0.0002 REL FR 2 V 0 P
care is no cure, but rather corrosive, | for 1H6 3.03. 3
though parting be a fretful corrosive, | it is 2H6 3.02.403
CORRUPT 30 FR 0.0034 REL FR 22 V 8 P
corrupt, corrupt, and tainted in desire! WIV 5.05. 90
corrupt, corrupt, and tainted in desire! 5.05. 90
as the flow'r, | corrupt with virtuous season. MM 2.02.167
angelo had never the purpose to corrupt her; 3.01.162 P
advantag'd, and the corrupt deputy scal'd. 3.01.255 P
in law, what plea so tainted and corrupt | but, MV 3.02. 75
you corrupt the song, sirrah. AWW 1.03. 80 P
so stain our judgment, or corrupt our hope, | to 2.01.120
disdain | rather corrupt me ever! 2.03.116
a suit | corrupt the tender honor of a maid. 3.05. 72
sums of gold to corrupt him to a revolt." 4.03.180 P
to ask you if gold will corrupt him to revolt. 4.03.277 P
and art indeed able to corrupt a saint. 1H4 1.02. 91 P
by this light flesh and corrupt blood, thou art 2H4 2.04.295 P
though in pure truth it was corrupt and naught, H5 1.02. 73
corrupt and tainted with a thousand vices, 1H6 5.04. 45
she did corrupt frail nature with some bribe, 3H6 3.02.155
and i'll corrupt her manners, stain her beauty, R3 4.04.207
i do know | to be corrupt and treasonous. H8 1.01.156
well dispos'd, the mind growing once corrupt, 1.02.116
there sits a judge | that no king can corrupt. 3.01.101
might corrupt minds procure knaves as corrupt 5.01.132
might corrupt minds procure knaves as corrupt 5.01.132
i will corrupt the grecian sentinels, | to give TRO 4.04. 72
of unburied men | that do corrupt my air — i COR 3.03.123
the fittest time to corrupt a man's wife is when 4.03. 32 P
that my disports corrupt and taint my business, OTH 1.03.271
and would corrupt my saint to be a devil, PP 2. 7
if eyes, corrupt by over–partial looks, | be SON 137. 5
and would corrupt my saint to be a devil, 144. 7
CORRUPTED 21 FR 0.0023 REL FR 19 V 2 P
holy, | to be corrupted with my worthless gifts. TGV 4.02. 6
start, | it is the flesh of a corrupted heart. WIV 5.05. 87
she is corrupted, chang'd, and won from thee; JN 3.01. 55
purchase corrupted pardon of a man | who in that 3.01.166
and three corrupted men, | one, richard earl of H5 2.pr. 22
corrupted, and exempt from ancient gentry? 1H6 2.04. 93
whose conscience with injustice is corrupted. 2H6 3.02.235
most traitorously corrupted the youth of the 4.07. 33 P
by underhand corrupted foul injustice, | if that R3 5.01. 6
law | of nature be corrupted through affection, TRO 2.02.177
whose souls is not corrupted as 'tis thought. TIT 3.01. 9
in the corrupted currents of this world HAM 3.03. 57
or embossed carbuncle, | in my corrupted blood. LR 2.04.225
and corrupted | by spells and medicines bought OTH 1.03. 60
desdemona would half have corrupted a votarist. 4.02.187 P
o, my fortunes have | corrupted honest men! ANT 4.05. 17
who knows if one her women, being corrupted, CYM 2.04.116
had i brought hither a corrupted mind, | thy PER 4.06.104
which once corrupted takes the worser part; LUC 294
her sacred temple spotted, spoil'd, corrupted, 1172
woes, | corrupted blood some watery token shows, 1748
CORRUPTER 2 FR 0.0002 REL FR 1 V 1 P
indeed not her fool, but her corrupter of words. TN 3.01. 36 P
harbor more craft and more corrupter ends | than LR 2.02.102
CORRUPTERS 1 FR 0.0001 REL FR 1 V 0 P
away, away, | corrupters of my faith! CYM 3.04. 83
CORRUPTIBLE 1 FR 0.0001 REL FR 0 V 1 P
ils sont les mots de son mauvais, corruptible, H5 3.04. 53 P
CORRUPTIBLY 1 FR 0.0001 REL FR 1 V 0 P
life of all his blood | is touch'd corruptibly; JN 5.07. 2
CORRUPTING 3 FR 0.0003 REL FR 3 V 0 P
lie on heaps, | corrupting in it own fertility. H5 5.02. 40
know'st thou not any whom corrupting gold | will R3 4.02. 34
myself corrupting, salving thy amiss, | excusing SON 35. 7
/CORRUPTION 1 FR 0.0001 REL FR 1 V 0 P
/corruption /in /the /place! LR 3.06. 55
CORRUPTION 19 FR 0.0021 REL FR 18 V 1 P
what corruption in this life, that it will let MM 3.01.232 P
where i have seen corruption boil and bubble, 5.01.318
by falsehood and corruption doth it shame. ERR 2.01.113
or any taint of vice whose strong corruption TN 3.04.356
the foul corruption of a sweet child's death. JN 4.02. 81
gathering head | shall break into corruption. R2 5.01. 59
on, | and, his corruption being ta'en from us, 1H4 5.02. 22
gathering head, | shall break into corruption": 2H4 3.01. 77
house, | to the corruption of a blemish'd stock; R3 3.07.122
ancestry | from the corruption of abusing times 3.07.199
corruption wins not more than honesty. H8 3.02.444
actions | to keep mine honor from corruption, 4.02. 71
the name of cassius honors this corruption, JC 4.03. 15
shall in the general censure take corruption HAM 1.04. 35
stew'd in corruption, honeying and making love 3.04. 93
whiles rank corruption, mining all within, 3.04.148
break and fall | off me with that corruption! TNK 1.02. 74
to keep us from corruption of worse men. 2.02. 72
might turn our blood | to much corruption. STM III 14
CORRUPTLY 1 FR 0.0001 REL FR 1 V 0 P
and offices | were not deriv'd corruptly, and MV 2.09. 42
CORRUPTS 1 FR 0.0001 REL FR 1 V 0 P
my son corrupts a well–derived nature | with his AWW 3.02. 88
CORSE *(also corpse)*
/CORSE 1 FR 0.0001 REL FR 1 V 0 P
/sirs, /take /up /the /corse. R3 1.02.225
CORSE 28 FR 0.0031 REL FR 27 V 1 P
what? like a corse? WT 4.04.129
not like a corse; 4.04.131
to bring a slovenly unhandsome corse | betwixt 1H4 1.03. 44
meet and ne'er part till one drop down a corse. 4.01.123
say'st thou, man, before dead henry's corse? 1H6 1.01. 62
rest you, whiles i lament king henry's corse. R3 1.02. 32
stay, you that bear the corse, and set it down. 1.02. 33
villains, set down the corse, or, by saint paul, 1.02. 36
paul, | i'll make a corse of him that disobeys. 1.02. 37
you do him injury to scorn his corse. 2.01. 81
now | came to me as i follow'd henry's corse, 4.01. 66
that lays thee out says thou art a fair corse, TRO 2.03. 32 P
as the most noble corse that ever herald | did COR 5.06.143
a piteous corse, a bloody piteous corse, | pale, ROM 3.02. 54
a piteous corse, a bloody piteous corse, | pale, 3.02. 54
weeping and wailing over tybalt's corse. 3.02.128
and stick your rosemary | on this fair corse, 4.05. 80
our bridal flowers serve for a buried corse; 4.05. 89
to follow this fair corse unto her grave. 4.05. 93
poor living corse, clos'd in a dead man's tomb! 5.02. 30
"here lies a wretched corse, of wretched soul TIM 5.04. 70
in the presence of thy corse? JC 3.01.199
thou shalt not back till i have borne this corse 3.01.291
from the first corse till he that died to–day, HAM 1.02.105
that thou, dead corse, again in complete steel 1.04. 52
the corse they follow did with desp'rate hand 5.01.220
are none, | to winter–ground thy corse — CYM 4.02.229
a corse? PER 3.02. 63
CORSES 2 FR 0.0002 REL FR 1 V 1 P
his beam, | upon the pashed corses of the kings TRO 5.05. 10
as we have many pocky corses, that will scarce HAM 5.01.166 P
CORSLET 2 FR 0.0002 REL FR 1 V 1 P
he is able to pierce a corslet with his eye, COR 5.04. 20 P
shall | by warranting moonlight corslet thee — TNK 1.01.177
CORYDON 1 FR 0.0001 REL FR 1 V 0 P
poor corydon must live alone, | other help for PP 17.35
COSMO 1 FR 0.0001 REL FR 0 V 1 P
guiltian, cosmo, lodowick, and gratii, two AWW 4.03.163 P
/COST 1 FR 0.0001 REL FR 1 V 0 P
/must /we /rate /the /cost /of /the /erection, 2H4 1.03. 44
COST 50 FR 0.0056 REL FR 38 V 12 P
that cost me two shilling and two pence a–piece WIV 1.01.156 P
to haunt assemblies | where youth, and cost, MM 1.03. 10
do so. this jest shall cost me some expense. ERR 3.01.123
it will cost him a thousand pound ere 'a be ADO 1.01. 90 P
the fashion of the world is to avoid cost, and 1.01. 98 P
you, though it cost me ten nights' watchings. 2.01.371 P
gone, cost me two thousand ducats in frankford! MV 3.01. 84 P
how little is the cost i have bestowed | in 3.04. 19
the cost of princes on unworthy shoulders? AYL 2.07. 76
that says his bravery is not on my cost, 2.07. 80
hath cost me /a hundred crowns since supper–time
SHR 5.02.128
and cost me the dearest groans of a mother, i AWW 4.05. 11 P
you, | here at my house and at my proper cost. TN 5.01.319
whose tongue shall ask me for one penny cost 1H4 1.03. 91
o'er, and leaves his part–created cost | a naked 2H4 1.03. 60
it may chance cost some of us our lives, for he 2.01. 11 P
indeed, sir, to my cost. 3.02. 12 P
gold, | nor care i who doth feed upon my cost; H5 4.03. 25
one would have ling'ring wars with little cost; 1H6 1.01. 74
gloucester, we'll meet to thy cost, be sure: 1.03. 82
when thou shalt see i'll meet thee to thy cost. 3.04. 43
king of england's own proper cost and charges, 2H6 1.01. 61 P
attire | have cost a mass of public treasury. 1.03.131
i charge and command that, of the city's cost, 4.06. 3 P
will cost my crown, and like an empty eagle 3H6 1.01.268
these words will cost ten thousand lives this 2.02.177
i will maintain it with some little cost. R3 1.02.259
long kept in britain at our mother's cost? 5.03.324
us not values | the cost that did conclude it. H8 1.01. 89
she is not worth what she doth cost | the TRO 2.02. 51
the fall of every phrygian stone will cost | a 4.05.223
thy goodly armor thus hath cost thy life. 5.08. 2
meats, good angelica, | spare not for cost. ROM 4.04. 6
and i have bred her at my dearest cost | in TIM 1.01.124
it would cost you a groaning to take off mine HAM 3.02.249 P
did these bones cost no more the breeding, but 5.01. 91 P
place where thee he got | cost him his eyes. LR 5.03.174
peer, | his breeches cost him but a crown; OTH 2.03. 90
if thou attempt it, it will cost thee dear: 5.02.255
and command what cost | your heart /has mind to.
ANT 3.04. 37
e'er it be, | what pain it cost, what danger. CYM 3.06. 80
lost | this queen, worth all our mundane cost. PER 3.02. 71
spouse, that welcomes to their cost | the galled TNK 3.05.128
that we should things desire which do cost us 5.04.110
and oft that wealth doth cost | the death of all LUC 146
in spite of physic, painting, pain, and cost. PP 13.12
the rich proud cost of outworn buried age; SON 64. 2
richer than wealth, prouder than garments' cost, 91.10
why so large cost, having so short a lease, 146. 5
yet showed his visage by that cost more dear, LC 96
COSTARD 19 FR 0.0021 REL FR 6 V 13 P
about his knave's costard when i have good WIV 3.01. 14 P
costard the swain and he shall be our sport, LLL 1.01.179
not a word of costard yet. 1.01.222 P
"which, as i remember, hight costard" — 1.01.256 P
took in the park with the rational hind costard. 1.02.118 P
duke's pleasure is that you keep costard safe, 1.02.128 P
here's a costard broken in a shin. 3.01. 70
by saying that a costard was broken in a shin. 3.01.106
me, how was there a costard broken in a shin? 3.01.111 P
i, costard, running out, that was safely within, 3.01.116
sirrah costard, i will enfranchise thee. 3.01.120 P
like the sequel, i. signior costard, adieu. 3.01.134
o, my good knave costard, exceedingly well met! 3.01.143 P
it was given me by costard, and sent me from don 4.02. 91 P
good costard, go with me. 4.02.144 P
of costard. 4.03.194
your servant, and costard. 5.02.571 P
take him on the costard with the hilts of thy R3 1.04.154 P
ice try whither your costard or my ballow be the LR 4.06.241 P
COSTERMONGERS' 1 FR 0.0001 REL FR 0 V 1 P
regard in these costermongers' times that true 2H4 1.02.169 P
COSTLIER 1 FR 0.0001 REL FR 1 V 0 P
no costlier than would fit | a franklin's CYM 3.02. 76
COSTLINESS 1 FR 0.0001 REL FR 1 V 0 P
and costliness of spirit look'd through him, it TNK 5.03. 97
COSTLY 12 FR 0.0013 REL FR 11 V 1 P
your grace is too costly to wear every day. ADO 2.01.328 P
sweet, | to show how costly summer was at hand, MV 2.09. 94
some one be ready with a costly suit, | and ask SHR in.1. 59
costly apparel, tents, and canopies, | fine 2.01.352
the great, | under the canopies of costly state, 2H4 3.01. 13
view, | i took a costly jewel from my neck, | a 2H6 3.02.106
king our master | to this last costly treaty — H8 1.01.165
with such a costly loss of wealth and friends. TRO 4.01. 61
woe to the hand that shed this costly blood! JC 3.01.258
costly thy habit as thy purse can buy, | but not HAM 1.03. 70
will long last and be more costly than | your TNK 1.01.132
painting thy outward walls so costly gay? SON 146. 4
COSTS 2 FR 0.0002 REL FR 2 V 0 P
sighs of love, that costs the fresh blood dear. MND 3.02. 97
for costs and charges in transporting her! 2H6 1.01.134
CO–SUPREMES 1 FR 0.0001 REL FR 1 V 0 P
and the dove, | co–supremes and stars of love, PHT 51
COTE* *(also quote, etc.)*
COTE* 6 FR 0.0006 REL FR 5 V 1 P
his face's own margent did cote such amazes LLL 2.01.246
we did not cote them so. 5.02.786
besides, his cote, his flocks, and bounds of AYL 2.04. 83
and come every day to my cote and woo me. 3.02.427 P
care i | what curious eye doth cote deformities? ROM 1.04. 31
will cote my loathsome trespass in my looks. LUC 812
COTED* 3 FR 0.0003 REL FR 2 V 1 P
her amber hairs for foul hath amber coted. LLL 4.03. 85
better heed and judgment | i had not coted him. HAM 2.01.109
we coted them on the way, and hither are they 2.02.317 P
COTES 1 FR 0.0001 REL FR 1 V 0 P
brother, see, note how she cotes the leaves. TIT 4.01. 50
COT–QUEAN 1 FR 0.0001 REL FR 1 V 0 P
go, you cot–quean, go, | get you to bed. ROM 4.04. 6
COTSALL 1 FR 0.0001 REL FR 0 V 1 P
i heard say he was outrun on cotsall. WIV 1.01. 90 P
COTSHALL 1 FR 0.0001 REL FR 1 V 0 P
from ravenspurgh to cotshall will be found | in R2 2.03. 9
COTSOLE 1 FR 0.0001 REL FR 0 V 1 P
pickbone, and will squele, a cotsole man. 2H4 3.02. 21 P
COTTAGE 4 FR 0.0004 REL FR 3 V 1 P
buy thou the cottage, pasture, and the flock, AYL 2.04. 92
and he hath bought the cottage and the bounds 3.05.107
can be thought to begin from such a cottage. WT 4.02. 44 P
court | hides not his visage from our cottage, 4.04.445
COTTAGES 2 FR 0.0002 REL FR 1 V 1 P
and poor men's cottages princes' palaces. MV 1.02. 14 P
home to your cottages, forsake this groom: 2H6 4.02.124
COTUS 2 FR 0.0002 REL FR 0 V 2 P
where's cotus? my master calls for him. cotus! COR 4.05. 3 P
where's cotus? my master calls for him. cotus! 4.05. 4 P
/COUCH 2 FR 0.0002 REL FR 2 V 0 P
/wherein /the //cub–drawn /bear /would /couch, LR 3.01. 12
hath made the flinty and steel /couch of war OTH 1.03.230
COUCH 18 FR 0.0020 REL FR 16 V 2 P
there i couch when owls do cry. TMP 5.01. 90
his gold will hold, | and his soft couch defile. WIV 1.03. 99
we'll couch i' th' castle–ditch till we see the 5.02. 1 P
i'll wink and couch; 5.05. 48
a bed | as ever beatrice shall couch upon? ADO 3.01. 46
we'll have thee to a couch, | softer and sweeter SHR in.2. 37
but couch ho, here he comes, to beguile two AWW 4.01. 21 P
arise forth from the couch of lasting night, JN 3.04. 27

and leavest the kingly couch | a watch–case or a 2H4 3.01. 16
murther or detested rape | can couch for fear, TIT 5.02. 38
with unstuff'd brain | doth couch his limbs, ROM 2.03. 38
be | a couch for luxury and damned incest. HAM 1.05. 83
couch we a while and mark. 5.01.222
arch–mock, | to lip a wanton in a secure couch, OTH 4.01. 71
i court moe women, you'll couch with moe men." 4.03. 57
where souls do couch on flowers, we'll hand in ANT 4.14. 51
o, if thou couch | but one night with her, every TNK 1.01.182
said, from her betumbled couch she starteth, LUC 1037

COUCH'D 4 FR 0.0004 REL FR 3 V 1 P
they are all couch'd in a pit hard by herne's WIV 5.03. 13 P
with ignominious words, though clerkly couch'd, 2H6 3.01.179
but sorrow that is couch'd in seeming gladness TRO 1.01. 39
of winter show'rs, | these flies are couch'd. TIM 2.02.172

COUCHED 5 FR 0.0005 REL FR 5 V 0 P
even now | is couched in the woodbine coverture. ADO 3.01. 30
i espy | virtue with valor couched in thine eye. R2 1.03. 98
a braver soldier never couched lance, | a 1H6 3.02.134
golden cup, | his body couched in a curious bed, 3H6 2.05. 53
when he lay couched in th' ominous horse, | hath HAM 2.02.454

COUCHES 1 FR 0.0001 REL FR 1 V 0 P
coal, | now couches from the mouse's hole; PER 3.ch. 6

COUCHETH 1 FR 0.0001 REL FR 1 V 0 P
coucheth the fowl below with his wings' shade, LUC 507

COUCHING 3 FR 0.0003 REL FR 3 V 0 P
till i were couching with the doctor's clerk. MV 5.01.305
lay couching, head on ground, with cat–like AYL 4.03.115
raven, | a couching lion and a ramping cat, 1H4 3.01.151

COUCHINGS 1 FR 0.0001 REL FR 1 V 0 P
these couchings and these lowly courtesies JC 3.01. 36

COUDE 1 FR 0.0001 REL FR 0 V 1 P
et le coude? H5 3.04. 23 P

COUGH 5 FR 0.0005 REL FR 4 V 1 P
and "tailor" cries, and falls into a cough; MND 2.01. 54
a whoreson cold, sir, a cough, sir, which i 2H4 3.02.181 P
to cough and spit, | and, with a palsy fumbling TRO 1.03.173
cough, or cry "hem," if anybody come. OTH 4.02. 29
the gilded puddle | which beasts would cough at; ANT 1.04. 63

COUGHING 2 FR 0.0002 REL FR 1 V 1 P
doth blow | and coughing drowns the parson's saw LLL 5.02.922
with a man for coughing in the street, because ROM 3.01. 25 P

/COULD 10 FR 0.0011 REL FR 8 V 2 P
/could /restrain | /the //stiff–borne /action. 2H4 1.01.176
/for /those /that /could /speak /low /and 2.03. 26
/when /there /was /nothing /could /have /stay'd 4.01.121
/the /prophet /could /not /at /that /time R3 4.02.100
/god, /i /could /be /bounded /in /a /nutshell, HAM 2.02.254 P
/could /he /dig /without /arms? 5.01. 37 P
/could /my /good /brother /suffer /you /to /do LR 4.02. 44
/beloved, | /if /all /could /so /become /it. 4.03. 24
/one /self /mate /and /make /could /not /beget 4.03. 34
/where /i /could /not /be /honest, | /i /never 5.01. 23

COULD 679 FR 0.0767 REL FR 480 V 199 P
damn'd, which sycorax | could not again undo. TMP 1.02.291
which good natures | could not abide to be with; 1.02.360
and his more braver daughter could control thee, 1.02.440
he could not miss't. 2.01. 41 P
if but one of his pockets could speak, would it 2.01. 66 P
i myself could make | a chough of as deep chat. 2.01.265
i could find in my heart to beat him — 2.02.155 P
i swam, ere i could recover the shore, five and 3.02. 14 P
i would i could see this taborer; 3.02.150 P
if you could hurt, | your swords are now too 3.03. 66
i here could pluck his highness' frown upon you 5.01.127
i chose her when i could not ask my father | for 5.01.190
were on land, | this fellow could not drown. 5.01.218
and one so strong | that could control the moon, 5.01.270
sir, i could perceive nothing at all from her; TGV 1.01.136 P
being in love, could not see to garter his hose; 2.01. 76 P
for last morning you could not see to wipe my 2.01. 80 P
for want of idle time, could not again reply; 2.01.166
o, that she could speak now like a /wood woman! 2.03. 27 P
were down, i could drive the boat with my sighs. 2.03. 53 P
how could he see his way to seek out you? 2.04. 94
o, could their master come and go as lightly, 3.01.142
could penetrate her uncompassionate sire; 3.01.233
whose golden touch could soften steel and stones 3.02. 78
nought but mine eye | could have persuaded me; 5.04. 65
it could not be judg'd, sir. WIV 1.01. 91 P
and i would i could do a good office between you 1.01. 99 P
yet i say i could show you to the contrary. 2.01. 40 P
trifling respect, i could come to such honor! 2.01. 45 P
an eternal moment or so, i could be knighted. 2.01. 50 P
i could have told you more. 2.01.224 P
could never have brought her to such a canary. 2.02. 62 P
you, they could never get an eye–wink of her. 2.02. 71 P
they could never get her so much as sip on a cup 2.02. 75 P
slight occasion that could but niggardly give me 2.02.197 P
could i come to her with any detection in my 2.02.245 P
i could drive her then from the ward of her 2.02.248 P
or else i could not be in that mind. 3.03. 84 P
i would i could wash myself of the buck! 3.03.157 P
the knave bragg'd of that he could not compass. 3.03.200 P
did he search for you, and could not find you? 3.05. 81 P
i would i could have spoken with the woman 4.05. 39 P
we could never meet. 5.05.117 P
that ever the devil could have made you our 5.05.149 P
if i could speak so wisely under an arrest, i MM 1.02.131 P
could have attain'd th' effect of your own 2.01. 13
froth, i could not give you threepence again. 2.01.103 P
how could master froth do the constable's wife 2.01.157 P
you could not with more tame a tongue desire it; 2.02. 46
could great men thunder | as jove himself does, 2.02.110
never could the strumpet, | with all her double 2.02.182
could i, with boot, change for an idle plume, 2.04. 11
beauty ten times louder | than beauty could, 2.04. 81
could fetch your brother from the manacles | of 2.04. 93
and well could wish | you had not found me here 4.01. 10
wife as strongly | as words could make up vows; 5.01.228
a heavier task could not have been impos'd ERR 1.01. 31
as could not be distinguish'd but by names. 1.01. 52
ere the ships could meet by twice five leagues, 1.01.100
could all my travels warrant me they live. 1.01.139
beshrew his hand, i scarce could understand it. 2.01. 49
so plainly, i could too well feel his blows; 2.01. 52 P
doubtfully, that i could scarce understand them. 2.01. 54 P
i could not speak with dromio since at first | i 2.02. 5
else it could never be | but i should know her 2.02.201
'tis in grain, noah's flood could not do it. 3.02.106 P
i could find out countries in her. 3.02.114 P
cliffs, but i could find no whiteness in them. 3.02.126 P
me, i could find in my heart to stay here still, 4.04.155 P
bed, | to do him all the grace and good i could. 5.01.164
could witness it, for he was with me then, | who 5.01.220
him, even so much that joy could not show itself ADO 1.01. 22 P
and i would i could find in my heart that i had 1.01.126 P
scratching could not make it worse, and 'twere 1.01.136 P
and never could maintain his part but in the 1.01.236 P
in the world, if 'a could get her good will. 2.01. 16 P
i could not endure a husband with a beard on his 2.01. 29 P
you could never do him so ill–well, unless you 2.01.117 P
were but little happy, if i could say how much! 2.01.307 P
husbands, if a maid could come by them. 2.01.324 P
come what plague could have come after it. 2.03. 83 P
well, and i could wish he would modestly examine 2.03.207 P
i could say she were worse; 3.02.110 P
i could find in my heart to bestow it all of 3.05. 21 P
could she here deny | the story that is printed 4.01.121
that could endure the toothache patiently, 5.01. 36
if he could right himself with quarrelling, 5.01. 51
what your wisdoms could not discover, these 5.01.233 P
and since you could not be my son–in–law, | be 5.01.287
i could. LLL 4.01. 81 P
ah, never faith could hold, if not to beauty 4.02.106
i could put thee in comfort: 4.03. 50
that which long process could not arbitrate. 5.02.743
which i could well | beteem them from the MND 1.01.130
for aught that i could ever read, | could ever 1.01.132
ever read, | could ever hear by tale or history, 1.01.133
o that my prayers could such affection move! 1.01.197
i could play ercles rarely, or a part to tear a 1.02. 29 P
make an ass of me, to fright me, if they could; 3.01.121 P
this falls out better than i could devise. 3.02. 35
could not a worm, an adder, do so much? 3.02. 71
and if i could, what should i get therefore? 3.02. 78
what love could press lysander from my side? 3.02.185
could not this make thee know, | the hate i bare 3.02.189
i could munch your good dry oats. 4.01. 31 P
he could not have scap'd sixpence a day. 4.02. 20 P
if i could bid the fift welcome with so good MV 1.02.127 P
was wont to tell me i could do nothing without 2.05. 8 P
for if they could, cupid himself would blush 2.06. 38
i could teach you | how to choose right, but 3.02. 10
but her eyes — | how could he see to do them? 3.02.124
the world | could turn so much the constitution 3.02.246
i could not do withal. 3.04. 72
e'en as many as could well live one by another. 3.05. 22 P
so she could | entreat some power to change this 4.01.291
i could not for my heart deny it him. 5.01.165
if i could add a lie unto a fault, | i would 5.01.186
unless you could teach me to forget a banish'd AYL 1.02. 5 P
i could have taught my love to take thy father 1.02. 11 P
i would we could do so; 1.02. 34 P
i could match this beginning with an old tale. 1.02.120 P
that could give more, but that her hand lacks 1.02.247
i could shake them off my coat; 1.03. 16 P
i would try, if i could cry "hem" and have him. 1.03. 19 P
i could find in my heart to disgrace my man's 2.04. 4 P
and willingly could waste my time in it. 2.04. 95
the feet were lame and could not bear themselves 3.02.169 P
finer than you could purchase in so remov'd a 3.02.342 P
if i could meet that fancy–monger, i would give 3.02.363 P
youth, i would i could make thee believe i love. 3.02.385 P
though all the world could see, | none could be 3.05. 78
see, | none could be so abus'd in sight as he. 3.05. 79
who could be out, being before his belov'd 4.01. 81 P
club, yet he did what he could to die before, 4.01. 99 P
or else she could not have the wit to do this; 4.01.160 P
and what wit could wit have to excuse that? 4.01.170 P
and that she could not love me | were man as 4.03. 16
could not drop forth such giant–rude invention, 4.03. 34
did woo me, | that could do no vengeance to me." 4.03. 48
i would love you if i could. 5.02.112 P
when seven justices could not take up a quarrel, 5.04. 99 P
ashore, | we could at once put us in readiness, SHR 1.01. 43
in the world, and a man could light on them, 1.01.128 P
so could i, faith, boy, to have the next wish 1.01.239
and could not get him for my heart to do it. 1.02. 38
face | which i could fancy more than any other. 2.01. 12
ay, if the fool could find it where it lies. 2.01.212
could i repair what she will wear in me, | as i 3.02.118
i could not forget you, for i never saw you 5.01. 50 P
if knowledge could be set up against mortality. AWW 1.01. 31 P
if men could be contented to be what they are, 1.03. 50 P
in the balance that i could neither believe nor 1.03.125 P
and that at my bidding you could so stand up. 2.01. 65
grapes, and if my royal fox | could reach them. 2.01. 72
though more to know could not be more to trust 2.01.206
to be young again, if we could, i will be a fool 2.02. 38 P
beat him, and if i could but meet him again. 2.03.241 P
her, | i could have well diverted her intents, 3.04. 21
that caesar himself could not have prevented, if 3.06. 53 P
which could not be her office to say is come, 4.03. 57 P
a dumb innocent, that could not say him nay. 4.03.187 P
i could endure any thing before but a cat, and 4.03.237 P
if you could find out a country where but women 4.03.326 P
i could not have ow'd her a more rooted love. 4.05. 12 P
i could not answer in that course of honor | as 5.03. 98
close | her eyes myself could win me to believe, 5.03.119
you saw one here in court could witness it. 5.03.200
of all these ways, | how could you give it him? 5.03.276
with the waves | so long as i could see. TN 1.02. 17
such love | could be but recompens'd, though you 1.05.253
though i could not with such estimable wonder 2.01. 27 P
bore a mind that envy could not but call fair. 2.01. 29 P
'slight, i could so beat the rogue! 2.05. 33 P
if i could make that resemble something in me! 2.05.119 P
i could marry this wench for this device — 2.05.182 P
so could i too. 2.05.183 P
i could not stay behind you. 3.03. 4
i could be sad. 3.04. 20 P
i could hardly entreat him back. 3.04. 58 P
i could condemn it as an improbable fiction. 3.04.127 P
opposite that you could possibly have found in 3.04.267 P
i could not find him at the elephant, | yet 4.03. 5
so, | she could not sway her house, command her 4.03. 17
sir, i would you could make it another. 5.01. 30 P
by swaggering could i never thrive, | for the 5.01.399
i' th' world, | so soon as yours could win me. WT 1.02. 21
ere i could make thee open thy white hand | /and 1.02.103
i could do this, and that with no rash potion, 1.02.319
could man so blench? 1.02.333
if i could find example | of thousands that had 1.02.357
how could that be? 2.01.172
they should not laugh if i could reach them, nor 2.03. 25
even since it could speak, from an infant, 3.02. 70
that could conceive a gross and foolish sire 3.02.197
could not move the gods | to look that way thou 3.02.213
no, the bagpipe could not move you. 4.04.183 P
he could never come better; 4.04.187 P
if | his going i could frame to serve my turn, 4.04.509
was the farthest off you could have been to him, 4.04.704 P
no fault could you make | which you have not 5.01. 2
could not say if th' importance were joy or 5.02. 17 P
if all the world could have seen't, the woe had 5.02. 91 P
himself eternity and could put breath into his 5.02. 98 P
but | i could afflict you farther. 5.03. 75
what fine chisel | could ever yet cut breath? 5.03. 79
so long could i | stand by, a looker–on. 5.03. 84
sir robert could do well — marry, to confess — JN 1.01.236
well — marry, to confess — | could /he get me. 1.01.237
sir robert could not do it; 1.01.237
the aweless lion could not wage the fight, | nor 1.01.266
no longer than we well could wash our hands | to 3.01.234
i could be merry now. 3.03. 67
well could i bear that england had this praise, 3.04. 15
so we could find some pattern of our shame. 3.04. 16
o, if i could, what grief should i forget! 3.04. 50
"o that these hands could so redeem my son | as 3.04. 71
as i, | i could give better comfort than you do. 3.04.100
that such an army could be drawn in france, 4.02.118
or have you read, or heard, or could you think? 4.03. 42
could thought, without this object, | form such 4.03. 44
as near as i could sift him on that argument, R2 1.01. 12
and labor'd all i could to do him right; 2.03.142
but if i could, by him that gave me life, | i 2.03.155
or that i could forget what i have been! 3.03.138
i could weep, madam, would it do you good. 3.04. 21
and i could sing, would weeping do me good, 3.04. 22
o that it could be prov'd | that some 1H4 1.01. 86
nor never could the noble mortimer | receive so 1.03.110
where fadom–line could never touch the ground, 1.03.204
ne'er a king christen could be better bit than i 2.01. 17 P
it could not be else, i have drunk medicines. 2.02. 19 P
could thou and i rob the thieves and go merrily 2.02. 94 P
my lord, i could be well contented to be there, 2.03. 1 P
he could be contented: 2.03. 3 P
rascal, i could brain him with his lady's fan. 2.03. 23 P
o, i could divide myself and go to buffets, for 2.03. 32 P
books in england, i could find in my heart — 2.04. 50 P
i would i were a weaver, i could sing psalms, or 2.04.133 P
a thousand pound i could run as fast as thou 2.04.148 P
waist, i could have crept into any alderman's 2.04.330 P
could the world pick thee out three such enemies 2.04.367 P
else, | could such inordinate and low desires, 3.02. 12
i would i could | quit all offenses with as 3.02. 18
seen, i could not stir | but like a comet i was 3.02. 46
o, i could wish this tavern were my drum! 3.03.206
and that his friends by deputation could not 4.01. 32
i could be well content | to entertain the lag 5.01. 23
though i could scape shot–free at london, i fear 5.03. 30 P
o, i could prophesy, | but that the earthy and 5.04. 83
could not all this flesh | keep in a little life 5.04.102
i could have better spar'd a better man. 5.04.104
and i could get me but a wife in the stews, i 2H4 1.02. 53 P
father is sick, albeit i could tell to thee — 2.02. 40 P
to call my friend — i could be sad, and sad 2.02. 42 P
and i could discern no part of his face from the 2.02. 80 P
o that this blossom could be kept from cankers! 2.02. 94 P
thee what, corporal bardolph, i could tear her. 2.04.154 P
enough before, and you could have let me alone. 3.02.112 P
she never could away with me. 3.02.201 P
she would always say she could not abide master 3.02.202 P
by the mass, i could anger her to th' heart. 3.02.204 P
with his quality, | the which he could not levy; 4.01. 12
when that my care could not withhold thy riots, 4.05.134
though thou stand'st more sure than i could do, 4.05.202
shallow that no man could better command his 5.01. 74 P
which i could with a ready guess declare, H5 1.01. 96
capet, | could not keep quiet in his conscience, 1.02. 79
that could entertain | with half their forces 1.02.111
could out of thee extract one spark of evil 2.02.101
'a could never abide carnation — 'twas a color 2.03. 33 P
they would serve me, could not be man to me; 3.02. 30 P
tell him we could have rebuk'd him at harflew, 3.06.121 P
but could be willing to march on to callice 3.06.141
i could make as true a boast as that, if i had a 3.07. 62 P
they could never wear such heavy head–pieces. 3.07.138 P
he could wish himself in thames up to the neck; 4.01.114 P
methinks i could not die any where so contented 4.01.126 P
quarrels enow, if you could tell how to reckon. 4.01.223 P
more help, could fight this royal battle! 4.03. 75
in a place where i could not breed no contention 5.01. 10 P
because he could not speak english in the native 5.01. 75 P
he could not therefore handle an english cudgel. 5.01. 76 P
if i could win a lady at leap–frog, or by 5.02.136 P
i could lay on like a butcher and sit like a 5.02.141 P
else ne'er could they hold out so as they do. 1H6 1.02. 43
else ne'er could he so long protract his speech. 1.02.120
henry, our late sovereign, ne'er could brook? 1.03. 24
three days have i watch'd | if i could see them. 1.04. 17
that they suppos'd i could rend bars of steel, 1.04. 51
in spite of us, or aught that we could do. 1.05. 37
this sudden mischief never could have fall'n. 2.01. 59
as far as i could well discern | for smoke and 2.02. 26
that could not live asunder day or night. 2.02. 31
men | i could not prevail with all their oratory, 2.02. 49
law, | and never yet could frame my will to it, 2.04. 8
ay, marry, sweeting, if we could do that, 3.03. 21
for fly he could not, if he would have fled; 4.04. 43
o, that i could but call these dead to life, 4.07. 81
and yet methinks i could be well content | to be 5.03.165

could i come near your beauty with my nails, | i 2H6 1.03.141
i could set my ten commandments in your face. 1.03.142
were it not good your grace could fly to heaven? 2.01. 17
that could restore this cripple to his legs 2.01.131
o master, that you could! 2.01.132
all these could not procure me any scathe | so 2.04. 62
the duke was dumb and could not speak a word. 3.02. 32
as far as i could ken thy chalky cliffs, | when 3.02.101
could send such message to their sovereign. 3.02.272
well could i curse away a winter's night, 3.02.335
o, could this kiss be printed in thy hand, 3.02.343
here could i breathe my soul into the air, | as 3.02.391
me, | and could it not enforce them to relent, 4.04. 17
them in prison, and because they could not read, 4.07. 44 P
and tears have mov'd me, gifts could never. 4.07. 68
and could command no more content than i? 4.09. 2
for a thousand years, i could stay no longer. 4.10. 6 P
o, i could hew up rocks and fight with flint, 5.01. 24
on sheep or oxen could i spend my fury. 5.01. 27
whose warlike ears could never brook retreat, 3H6 1.01. 5
for he could not so resign his crown | but that 1.01.145
it could not slake mine ire nor ease my heart. 1.03. 29
tidings, as swiftly as the posts could run, 2.01.109
york and young rutland could not satisfy. 2.06. 84
unless my hand and strength could equal them. 3.02.145
nestor, | deceive more slily than ulysses could, 3.02.189
but most himself if he could see his shame. 3.03.185
how could he stay till warwick made return? 4.01. 5
she could say little less; 4.01.101
that we could hear no news of his repair? 5.01. 20
for who liv'd king, but i could dig his grave? 5.02. 21
these eyes could not endure that beauty's wrack; R3 1.02.127
he lives, that loves thee better than he could. 1.02.141
and what these sorrows could not thence exhale, 1.02.165
my tongue could never learn sweet smoothing word 1.02.168
o that your young nobility could judge | what 1.03.256
could not believe but that i was in hell, | such 1.04. 62
i could have given my uncle's grace a flout, 2.04. 24
that he could gnaw a crust at two hours old; 2.04. 28
'twas full two years ere i could get a tooth. 2.04. 29
more bitterly could i expostulate, | save that, 3.07.192
conscience and remorse | they could not speak; 4.03. 21
i died for hope ere i could lend thee aid, | but 5.03.173
what four thron'd ones could have weigh'd | such H8 1.01. 11
and could wish he were | something mistaken in't 1.01.194
could not find | his hour of speech a minute — 1.02.120
this night to meet here, they could do no less 1.04. 68
but indeed he could not. 2.01. 25
that sought it i could wish more christians. 2.01. 64
she | so good a lady that no tongue could ever 2.03. 3
nor could | come pat betwixt too early and too 2.03. 83
with your theme, i could | o'ermount the lark. 2.03. 93
sovereign and pious else, could speak thee out) 2.04.141
could speak this with as free a soul as i do! 3.01. 32
could but be brought to know our ends are honest 3.01.154
show'r'd on me daily have been more than could 3.02.167
abound, as thick as thought could make 'em, and 3.02.195
how much, methinks, i could despise this man, 3.02.297
where a finger | could not be wedg'd in more. 4.01. 58
no man living | could say, "this is my wife" 4.01. 80
and grew so ill | he could not sit his mule. 4.02. 16
honors to his age | than man could give him, he 4.02. 68
but poverty could never draw 'em from me), 4.02.149
methinks i could | cry the amen, and yet my 5.01. 23
i could not personally deliver to her | what you 5.01. 62
i could say more, | but reverence to your 5.02.103
(you see the poor remainder) could distribute, 5.03. 20
would i could see troilus now! TRO 1.02.216 P
i could live and die in the eyes of troilus. 1.02.242 P
how could communities, | degrees in schools, and 1.03.103
that i could beat him, whilst he rail'd at me. 2.03. 4 P
if i could 'a' rememb'red a gilt counterfeit, 2.03. 25 P
it was a strong composure a fool could disunite. 2.03.100 P
could not you find out that by her attributes? 3.01. 35 P
o that i thought it could be in a woman — | as, 3.02.158
or that persuasion could but thus convince me 3.02.164
since she could speak, | she hath not given so 4.01. 73
and would, as i shall pity, i could help! 4.03. 11
if i could temporize with my affections, | or 4.04. 6
the like allayment could i give my grief: 4.04. 8
could promise to himself | a thought of added 4.05.144
i would my arms could match thee in contention, 4.05.205
i would they could. 4.05.207
a proof of strength she could not publish more, 5.02.113
would i could meet that rogue diomed! 5.02.190 P
and could be content to give him good report COR 1.01. 32 P
did complain, | what could the belly answer? 1.01.124
slaves, as high | as i could pick my lance. 1.01.200
that could be brought to bodily act ere rome 1.02. 5
though i could wish | you were conducted to a 1.06. 62
o that you could turn your eyes toward the napes 2.01. 38 P
o that you could! 2.01. 41 P
i could weep, | and i could laugh; 2.01.183
i could weep, | and i could laugh; 2.01.184
he had wounds, which he could show in private; 2.03.166
could you not have told him | as you were 2.03.176
could never be the native | of our so frank 3.01.129
on fair ground | i could beat forty of them. 3.01.242
i could myself | take up a brace o' th' best of 3.01.242
the vengeance, | could he not speak 'em fair? 3.01.262
bred i' th' wars | since 'a could draw a sword, 3.01.319
that common chances common men could bear, 4.01. 5
if i could shake off but one seven years | from 4.01. 55
if that i could for weeping, you should hear — 4.02. 13
could i meet 'em | but once a day, it would 4.02. 46
there was more in him than i could think. 4.05.159 P
been much better, if | he could have temporiz'd. 4.06. 17
if he could burn us all into one coal, | we have 4.06.137
them, but he could not | carry his honors even. 4.07. 36
very well. | could he say less? 5.01. 22
he could not stay to pick them in a pile | of 5.01. 25
being assur'd none but myself could move thee, i 5.02. 74 P
grace him only | that thought he could do more: 5.03. 16
arms, | could not have made this peace. 5.03.209
yet have i heard — o, could i find it now! TIT 2.03.150
well could i leave our sport to sleep a while. 2.03.197
that could have better sew'd than philomel. 2.04. 43
o, could our mourning ease thy misery! 2.04. 57

rome could afford no tribunes like to these. 3.01. 44
then into limits could i bind my woes: 3.01.220
sir, i could never say grace in all my life. 4.03.100 P
could not all hell afford you such a devil? 5.02. 86
villains, for shame you could not beg for grace. 5.02.179
or more than any living man could bear. 5.03.127
but their children's end, nought could remove, ROM pr 11
could we but learn from whence his sorrows grow, 1.01.154
and these, who, often drown'd, could never die, 1.02. 90
years, | for then she could stand high–lone; 1.03. 36
she could have run and waddled all about; 1.03. 37
that i have worn a visor and could tell | a 1.05. 22
thy love did read by rote that could not spell. 2.03. 88
could you not take some occasion without giving? 3.01. 43 P
could not take truce with the unruly spleen | of 3.01.157
for, ere i | could draw to part them, was stout 3.01.173
and all those twenty could but kill one life. 3.01.179
i could have stay'd here all the night | to hear 3.03.159
if you could find out but a man | to bear a 3.05. 96
and art | could to no issue of true honor bring. 4.01. 65
your part in her you could not keep from death, 4.05. 69
i could not send it — here it is again — | nor 5.02. 14
cell, | till i conveniently could send to romeo. 5.03.256
i could wish my best friend at such a feast. TIM 1.02. 79 P
spent, he'd be cross'd then, and he could. 1.02.162
methinks, i could deal kingdoms to my friends, 1.02.220
would we could see you at corinth! 2.02. 70 P
i could render one. 2.02.103 P
men and men's fortunes could i frankly use | as 2.02.179
but yet they could have wish'd — they know not 2.02.207
i would i could not think it! 2.02.232
told him on't, but i could ne'er get him from't. 3.01. 28 P
then they could smile, and fawn upon his debts, 3.04. 51
it could not else be i should prove so base | to 3.05. 93
but then renew i could not, like the moon; 4.03. 69
at duty, more than i could frame employment; 4.03.262
i would my tongue could rot them off! 4.03.365
the plague, | could i but catch it for them. 5.01.138
but ere we could arrive the point propos'd, JC 1.02.110
when could they say, till now, that talk'd of 1.02.154
that could be mov'd to smile at any thing. 1.02.207
i could tell you more news too. 1.02.284 P
was more foolery yet, if i could remember it. 1.02.287 P
now could i, casca, name to thee a man | most 1.03. 72
if you could | but win the noble brutus to our 1.03.140
o, that we then could come by caesar's spirit, 2.01.169
and could it work so much upon your shape | as 2.01.253
they could not find a heart within the beast. 2.02. 40
i could be well mov'd, if i were as you; 3.01. 58
if i could pray to move, prayers would move me; 3.01. 59
a friendly eye could never see such faults. 4.03. 90
o, i could weep | my spirit from mine eyes! 4.03. 99
i did not think you could have been so angry. 4.03.143
you, | but yet my nature could not bear it so. 4.03.195
they could be content | to visit other places, 5.01. 8
could trammel up the consequence, and catch MAC 1.07. 3
their daggers ready, | he could not miss 'em. 2.02. 12
list'ning their fear, i could not say "amen," 2.02. 26
but wherefore could not i pronounce "amen"? 2.02. 28
that could swear in both the scales against 2.03. 8 P
god's sake, yet could not equivocate to heaven. 2.03. 10 P
who could refrain, | that had a heart to love, 2.03.116
alas the day, | what good could they pretend? 2.04. 24
and though i could | with barefac'd power sweep 3.01.117
and your maids could not fill up | the cestern 4.03. 62
would i could answer | this comfort with the 4.03.192
children, servants, all | that could be found. 4.03.212
o, i could play the woman with mine eyes, | and 4.03.230
the devil himself could not pronounce a title 5.07. 8
i could a tale unfold whose lightest word HAM 1.05. 15
well, we know," or "we could, and if we would," 1.05.176
as i am, if like a crab you could go backward. 2.02.203 P
reason and /sanity could not so prosperously be 2.02.211 P
than natural, if philosophy could find it out. 2.02.368 P
you could, for need, study a speech of some 2.02.540 P
i would set down and insert in't, could you not? 2.02.542 P
could force his soul so to his own conceit 2.02.553
could beauty, my lord, have better commerce than 3.01.108 P
but yet i could accuse me of such things that it 3.01.122 P
and could of men distinguish her election, | sh' 3.02. 64
i could interpret between you and your love, if 3.02.246 P
your love, if i could see the puppets dallying. 3.02.247 P
now could i drink hot blood, | and do such 3.02.390
could you on this fair mountain leave to feed, 3.04. 66
else could you not have motion, but sure that 3.04. 72
part of one true sense | could not so mope. 3.04. 81
persuade revenge, | it could not move thus. 4.05.170
not but in his sphere, | i could not but by her. 4.07. 16
if you could devise it so | that i might be the 4.07. 69
be a sight indeed | if one could match you. 4.07.100
envy | that he could nothing do but wish and beg 4.07.104
but long it could not be | till that her 4.07.180
skull had a tongue in it, and could sing once. 5.01. 75 P
or of a courtier, which could say, "good morrow, 5.01. 82 P
could not with all their quantity of love | make 5.01.270
or i could make a prologue to my brains, | they 5.02. 30
matter, if we could carry a cannon by our sides; 5.02.159 P
strict in his arrest — o, i could tell you — 5.02.337
sir, this young fellow's mother could; LR 1.01. 13 P
fled this way, sir, when by no means he could — 2.01. 42
or a painter could not have made him so ill, 2.02. 59 P
they could not, would not do't. 2.04. 23
i could as well be brought | to knee his throne, 2.04.213
chanc'd to slack ye, | we could control them. 2.04.246
there could i have him now — and there — and 3.04. 61 P
nothing could have subdu'd nature | to such a 3.04. 70
he has some reason, else he could not beg. 4.01. 31
would i could meet /him, madam! 4.05. 39
if i could bear it longer, and not fall | to 4.06. 37
when misery could beguile the tyrant's rage, 4.06. 63
were all thy letters suns, i could not see. 4.06.140
myself could else out–frown false fortune's 5.03. 6
or lame of sense), | sans witchcraft could not. OTH 1.03. 64
that will confess perfection so could err 1.03.100
which ever as she could with haste dispatch, 1.03.148
and since i could distinguish betwixt a benefit 1.03.312 P
i could never better stead thee than now. 1.03.338 P
she that could think, and nev'r disclose her 2.01.156

i could well wish courtesy would invent some 2.03. 34 P
indignity | which patience could not pass. 2.03.246
i could heartily wish this had not befall'n; 2.03.301 P
/by'r /lady, i could do much — 3.03. 74
she that so young could give out such a seeming 3.03.209
with a raging tooth, | i could not sleep. 3.03.415
and could almost read | the thoughts of people. 3.04. 57
such perdition | as nothing else could match. 3.04. 68
if that the earth could teem with woman's tears, 4.01.245
this the nature | whom passion could not shake? 4.01.266
dart of chance | could neither graze nor pierce? 4.01.268
yet could i bear that too, well, very well; 4.02. 56
could not have laid such terms upon his callet. 4.02.121
not the world's mass of vanity could make me. 4.02.164
the hand could pluck her back that shov'd her on ANT 1.02.127
though age from folly could not give me freedom, 1.03. 57
name strikes more | than could his war resisted. 1.04. 55
with patience more | than savages could suffer. 1.04. 61
i could have given less matter | a better ear. 2.01. 31
i know you could not lack, i am certain on't, 2.02. 57
could not with graceful eyes attend those wars 2.02. 60
for that you must | but say i could not help it. 2.02. 71
me no service as a partisan i could not heave. 2.07. 13 P
i could well forbear't. 2.07. 98
i could do more to do antonius good, | but 3.01. 25
when perforce he could not | but pay me terms of 3.04. 6
well, i could reply: 3.07. 6
he could so quickly cut the ionian sea, | and 3.07. 22
mine eyes did sicken at the sight and could not 3.10. 16
i wish i could be made so many men, | and all of 4.02. 16
darts, | though enemy, lost aim and could not? 4.14. 71
we could not stall together | in the whole world 5.01. 39
that his time | could make him the receiver of, CYM 1.01. 44
the search so slow, | that could not trace them! 1.01. 65
long | as he could make me with /this eye or ear 1.03. 9
could best express how slow his soul sail'd on, 1.03. 13
ere i could tell him | how i would think on him 1.03. 26
or i could make him swear | the shes of italy 1.03. 28
or ere i could | give him that parting kiss 1.03. 33
but i could then have look'd on him without the 1.04. 4 P
had very many there could behold the sun with as 1.04. 12 P
i could not /but believe she excell'd many. 1.04. 74 P
a voucher, | stronger than ever law could make; 2.02. 40
if i could get this foolish imogen, i should 2.03. 8 P
could be so rarely and exactly wrought, | since 2.04. 75
could i find out | the woman's part in me — for 2.05. 19
dominion, could not be so cruel to me as you, o 3.02. 41 P
to 's execution, man, | could never go so slow. 3.02. 71
if you could wear a mind | dark as your fortune 3.04.143
two beggars told me | i could not miss my way. 3.06. 9
would i could free't! 3.06. 79
multitudes, | could not outpeer these twain. 3.06. 86
i could not stir him. 4.02. 38
hercules | could have knock'd out his brains, 4.02.115
not | absolute madness could so far have rav'd 4.02.135
who ever yet could sound thy bottom? 4.02.204
revengingly enfeebles me, or could this carl, 5.02. 4
which could have turn'd | a distaff to a lance, 5.03. 33
could not find death where i did hear him groan, 5.03. 69
where was he | that could stand up his parallel, 5.04. 54
of imogen, that best | could deem his dignity? 5.04. 57
swell'd boast | of him that best could speak; 5.05.163
that he could not | but think her bond of 5.05.206
me spurn the sea | if it could so roar to me. 5.05.295
those arts they have as i | could put into them. 5.05.339
testy wrath | could never be her mild companion. PER 1.01. 18
glass of light, i lov'd you, and could still, 1.01. 76
well–a–day, we could scarce help ourselves. 2.01. 22 P
hark you, my friend. you said you could not beg? 2.01. 85 P
to my desires, i could wish to make one there. 2.01.111 P
now, by the gods, he could not please me better. 2.03. 72
could i rage and roar | as doth the sea she lies 3.03. 10
of my rhyme, | which never could i so convey, 4.ch. 49
if in our youths we could pick up some pretty 4.02. 32 P
why, i could wish him to be my master, or rather 4.06.159 P
what thou professest, a baboon, could he speak, 4.06.178
but when could grief | cull forth, as unpang'c TNK 1.01.168
hard, and harsher | than strife or war could be. 1.02. 26
'hath set a mark which nature could not reach to 1.04. 43
sweet a rebuke that i could wish myself a sigh 2.01. 43 P
they must not, say they could; 2.02. 67
they could not be to one so fair. 2.02.123
i am wondrous merry–hearted, i could laugh now. 2.02.150
i could lie down, i am sure. 2.02.151
wicked, all my sins | could never pluck upon me. 2.03. 7
well i could have wrestled, | the best men 2.03. 75
i could have kept a hawk, and well have hollow'd 2.05. 11
could i persuade him to become a freeman, | he 2.06. 24
i could for each word give a cuff, my stomach 3.01.104
would i could find a fine frog! 3.04. 12
i did not think a week could have restor'd | my 3.06. 5
i could wish ye | as kind a kinsman as you force 3.06. 20
and i could wish i had not said i lov'd her, 3.06. 40
you outwent me, | nor could my wishes reach you. 3.06. 80
are equal precious — | i could doom neither; 5.01.156
that neither could find other, get herself 5.03. 26
that remain with you could wish their office 5.03. 35
it could | no more be hid in him than fire in 5.03. 97
if i could praise | each part of him to th' all 5.03.120
that the sense | could not be judge between 'em. 5.03.128
what ending could be | of more content? 5.04. 15
what disorder | his power could give his will, 5.04. 67
that nought could buy | dear love but loss of 5.04.111
that could have topp'd the peace, as now you STM II.C 64
could not have brought you to the state of men. II.C 67
there love liv'd, and there he could not die. VEN 246
and that i could not see, nor hear, nor touch, 440
"more i could tell, but more i dare not say, 805
could rule them both without ten women's wit." 1008
she thinks he could not die, he is not dead; 1060
eye, | which having all, all could not satisfy; LUC 96
could pick no meaning from their parling looks, 100
nor could she moralize his wanton sight, | more 104
all these poor forbiddings could not stay him, 323
what could he see but mightily he noted? 414
the spots whereof could weeping purify, | her 685
but her foresight could not forestall their will 728
coming from thee, i could not put him back, 843

i could prevent this storm, and shun thy wrack! 966
if tears could help, mine own would do me good. 1274
that jealousy itself could not mistrust | false 1516
more than "he" her poor tongue could not speak, 1718
that no man could distinguish what he said. 1785
'gainst whom the world could not hold argument, PP 3. 2
such looks as none could look but beauty's queen 4. 4
o, never faith could hold, if not to beauty 5. 2
fare well i could not, for i supp'd with sorrow. 14. 6
an englishman, the fairest that eye could see, 15. 3
that nothing could be used to turn them both to 15.10
alas, she could not help it! 15.12
complain, | scarce i could from tears refrain; 20.16
then what could death do if thou shouldst depart SON 6.11
if i could write the beauty of your eyes, | and 17. 5
o, that record could with a backward look, 59. 5
that i might see what the old world could say 59. 9
if like a lamb he could his looks translate! 96.10
in hue, | could make me any summer's story tell, 98. 7
yet i none could see | but sweet or color it had 99.14
that it could so preposterously be stain'd, | to 109.11
those that said i could not love you dearer, 115. 2
that poor retention could not so much hold, 122. 9
"well could he ride, and often men would say, LC 106
"for further i could say, 'this man's untrue,' 169
could scape the hail of his all-hurting aim, 310
COULDEST 1 FR 0.0001 REL FR 0 V 1 P
dark, hal, that thou couldest not see thy hand. 1H4 2.04.224 P
COULDST 33 FR 0.0037 REL FR 23 V 10 P
why? couldst thou perceive so much from her? TGV 1.01.134 P
him that thou wouldst discover if thou couldst, MM 2.01.186 P
doubtfully, thou couldst not feel his meaning? ERR 2.01. 50 P
that very time i saw (but thou couldst not) MND 2.01.155
i would thou couldst stammer, that thou mightst AYL 3.02.198 P
or if that thou couldst see me without eyes, JN 3.03. 48
o nation, that thou couldst remove! 5.02. 33
how couldst thou know these men in kendal green 1H4 2.04.231 P
it was so dark thou couldst not see thy hand? 2.04.232 P
for, if thou couldst, thou wouldst find me such H5 5.02.124 P
been his mother, thou couldst have better told. 2H6 2.01. 79
how couldst thou drain the life-blood of the 3H6 1.04.138
ah, couldst thou fly! 5.02. 32
unless thou couldst put on some other shape R3 4.04.286
greek and troyan so | that thou couldst say, TRO 4.05.125
how couldst thou in a mile confound an hour, COR 1.06. 17
and if thou couldst, thou couldst not make him ROM 3.05. 71
if thou couldst, thou couldst not make him live; 3.05. 71
what beast couldst thou be, that were not TIM 4.03.343 P
if thou couldst please me with speaking to me, 4.03.346 P
young man, thou couldst not die more honorable. JC 5.01. 60
i would thou couldst! MAC 2.02. 71
if thou couldst, doctor, cast | the water of my 5.03. 50
couldst thou save nothing? LR 3.04. 64
but what praise couldst thou bestow on a OTH 2.01.144 P
that thou couldst see my wars to-day, and ANT 4.04. 16
eros, what | i should, and thou couldst not. 4.14. 97
o, couldst thou speak, | that i might hear thee 5.02.306
did not think | thou couldst have spoke so well, PER 4.06.103
have spoke so well, ne'er dreamt thou couldst. 4.06.103
unless thou couldst return to make amends? LUC 961
since thou couldst not defend thy loyal dame, 1034
if thou couldst answer, "this fair child of mine SON 2.10
COULTER 1 FR 0.0001 REL FR 1 V 0 P
upon, while that the coulter rusts | that should H5 5.02. 46
COUNCIL 37 FR 0.0041 REL FR 30 V 7 P
the council shall hear it, it is a riot. WIV 1.01. 35 P
it is not meet the council hear a riot; 1.01. 36 P
the council, look you, shall desire to hear the 1.01. 37 P
the council shall know this. 1.01.117 P
and in our maiden council rated them | at LLL 5.02.779
that the great figure of a council frames | by AWW 3.01. 12
and list what with our council we have done: R2 1.03.124
what yesternight our council did decree | in 1H4 1.01. 32
on wednesday next our council we | will hold at 1.01.103
an old lord of the council rated me the other 1.02. 84 P
thy place in council thou hast rudely lost, 3.02. 32
to appoint some of your council presently | to H5 5.02. 79
them than in the tongues of the french council; 5.02.277 P
with all the learned council of the realm, 2H6 1.01. 89
and other of your highness' privy council, | as 2.01.172
or be admitted to your highness' council. 3.01. 27
more, the king's council are no good workmen. 4.02. 14 P
but little thinks we shall be of her council. 3H6 1.01. 36
which, in his nonage, council under him, | and, R3 2.03. 13
lord, | bid him not fear the separated council: 3.02. 20
letter, | the honorable board of council out, H8 1.01. 79
that they had gather'd a wise council to them 2.04. 51
the knowledge | either of king or council, when 3.02.317
house, | and one, already, of the privy council. 4.01.112
incens'd the lords o' th' council that he is 5.01. 43
have mov'd us and our council, that you shall 5.01.100
that was sent to me from the council pray'd me 5.02. 2
why are we met in council? 5.02. 37
some understanding | and wisdom of my council; 5.02.171
go we to council. TRO 2.03.265
the mortal instruments | are then in council; JC 2.01. 67
and let us presently go sit in council, | how 4.01. 45
grave and prosperous) | in this day's council; MAC 3.01. 22
the duke's in council, and your noble self | i OTH 1.02. 92
the duke in council? 1.02. 93
to that end | assemble /we immediate council. ANT 1.04. 75
or council has respect with him but he. PER 2.04. 18
COUNCIL-BOARD 2 FR 0.0002 REL FR 2 V 0 P
rated mine uncle from the council-board, | in 1H4 4.03. 99
to-morrow morning to the council-board | he be H8 5.01. 51
COUNCIL-HOUSE 2 FR 0.0002 REL FR 2 V 0 P
long, sat in the council-house | early and late, 2H6 1.01. 90
this day had plotted, in the council-house, | to R3 3.05. 38
COUNCILLOR 3 FR 0.0003 REL FR 3 V 0 P
me | wait else at door, a fellow councillor, H8 5.02. 17
you are a councillor, | and, by that virtue, no 5.02. 84
ye | power as he was a councillor to try him, 5.02.178
COUNCILLORS 1 FR 0.0001 REL FR 1 V 0 P
their very noses had been councillors | to pepin H8 1.03. 9
COUNCILS 3 FR 0.0003 REL FR 3 V 0 P
for we to-morrow hold divided councils, R3 3.01.179
besides, he says there are two councils kept; 3.02. 12
rood, | i do not like these several councils, i. 3.02. 76
/COUNSEL 1 FR 0.0001 REL FR 0 V 1 P
the players cannot keep /counsel, they'll tell HAM 3.02.142 P
COUNSEL 134 FR 0.0151 REL FR 107 V 27 P
but wherefore waste i time to counsel thee TGV 1.01. 51
war with good counsel, set the world at nought; 1.01. 68
wouldst thou then counsel me to fall in love? 1.02. 2
i like thy counsel; 1.03. 34
in these affairs to aid me with thy counsel. 2.04.185
myself in counsel his competitor. 2.06. 35
counsel, lucetta; 2.07. 1
better for you if it were known in counsel. WIV 1.01.119 P
o mistress page, give me some counsel! 2.01. 42 P
follow your friend's counsel. 3.03.138 P
and i will (at the least) keep your counsel. 4.06. 7 P
i thank your worship for your good counsel; MM 2.01.252 P
let her wear it out with good counsel. ADO 2.03.202 P
and counsel him to fight against his passion, 3.01. 83
and have thy counsel | which is the best to 3.01.102
and let my counsel sway you in this case. 4.01.201
i pray thee cease thy counsel, | which falls 5.01. 3
give not me counsel, | nor let no comforter 5.01. 5
can counsel and speak comfort to that grief 5.01. 21
their counsel turns to passion, which before 5.01. 23
therefore give me no counsel, | my griefs cry 5.01. 31
see thou do commend | this seal'd-up counsel. LLL 3.01.169
emptying our bosoms of their counsel /sweet, MND 1.01.216
of night | and the ill counsel of a desert place 2.01.218
is all the counsel that we two have shar'd, 3.02.198
o'er the meshes of good counsel the cripple. MV 1.02. 21 P
"conscience," say i, "you counsel well." 2.02. 21 P
"fiend," say i, "you counsel well." 2.02. 22 P
to offer to counsel me to stay with the jew. 2.02. 29 P
the fiend gives the more friendly counsel: 2.02. 31 P
your adventure would counsel you to a more equal AYL 1.02.177 P
i do in friendship counsel you | to leave this 1.02.261
i would give him some good counsel, for he seems 3.02.364 P
yet i profess curing it by counsel. 3.02.405 P
go thou with me, and let me counsel thee. 3.03. 95 P
i'll in to counsel them; SHR in.1. 136
counsel me, tranio, for i know thou canst; 1.01.157
the rest will comfort, for thy counsel 's sound. 1.01.164
thou'dst thank me but a little for my counsel; 1.02. 61
of a courtier's counsel and understand what AWW 1.01.209 P
and what to your sworn counsel i have spoken 3.07. 9
demand, you are not altogether of his counsel. 4.03. 44 P
madonna, that drink and good counsel will amend; TN 1.05. 44 P
his counsel now might do me golden service, 4.03. 8
o, you give me ill counsel. 5.01. 31 P
therefore mark my counsel, | which must be ev'n WT 1.02.408
as or by oath remove or counsel shake | the 1.02.428
will bring all, whose spiritual counsel had, 2.01.186
of a true subject, didst counsel and aid them, 3.02. 20 P
should hold some counsel | in such a business. 4.04.409
'tis your counsel | my lord should to the 5.01. 44
o that ever i | had squar'd me to thy counsel! 5.01. 52
how like you this wild counsel, mighty states? JN 2.01.395
no, i defy all counsel, all redress, | but that 3.04. 23
but that which ends all counsel, true redress: 3.04. 24
you were new crown'd, | we breath'd our counsel; 4.02. 36
in wholesome counsel to his unstayed youth? R2 2.01. 2
for all in vain comes counsel to his ear. 2.01. 4
though richard my live's counsel would not hear, 2.01. 15
then all too late comes counsel to be heard, 2.01. 27
again | to alter this, for counsel is but vain. 3.02.214
when we need | your use and counsel, we shall 1H4 1.03. 21
you do not counsel well, | you speak it out of 4.03. 6
i hold as little counsel with weak fear | as you 4.03. 11
me, and counsel every man | the aptest way for 2H4 1.01.212
by my learned counsel in the laws of this 1.02.134 P
i will take your counsel, | and were these 3.01.106
the very latest counsel | that ever i shall 4.05.182
and let us choose such limbs of noble counsel 5.02.135
by your own counsel is suppress'd and kill'd. H5 2.02. 80
well, i will lock his counsel in my breast, 1H6 2.05.118
goes, | for friendly counsel cuts off many foes. 3.01.184
your deeds of war, and all our counsel die? 2H6 1.01. 97
to me, | for i am bold to counsel you in this. 1.03. 93
what counsel give you in this weighty cause? 3.01.289
and craves your company for speedy counsel. 3H6 2.01.208
what counsel give you? 2.03. 11
wherein thy counsel and consent is wanting. 2.06.102
what counsel, lords? 4.08. 1
good counsel, marry! R3 1.03.260
what, dost thou scorn me for my gentle counsel? 1.03.296
souls | to counsel me to make my peace with god, 1.04.251
famously enrich'd | with politic grave counsel; 2.03. 20
if i may counsel you, some day or two | your 3.01. 64
full of wise care is this your counsel, madam; 4.01. 47
my counsel is my shield; 4.03. 56
bosom up my counsel, | you'll find it wholesome. H8 1.01.112
heaven keep me from such counsel! 2.02. 37
spain advis'd, whose counsel | i will implore. 2.04. 55
the daring'st counsel which i had to doubt, 2.04.216
a sign of peace, | his service and his counsel. 3.01. 67
let me have time and counsel for my cause. 3.01. 79
that any englishman dare give me counsel? 3.01. 84
would leave your griefs, and take my counsel. 3.01. 92
is this your christian counsel? 3.01. 99
holy and heavenly thoughts still counsel her. 5.04. 29
my weakness draws | my very soul of counsel! TRO 3.02.133
and very courtly counsel. 4.05. 22
whoever gave that counsel, to give forth | the COR 3.01.113
silk, never admitting | counsel a' th' war; 5.06. 96
thy counsel, lad, smells of no cowardice. TIT 2.01.132
two may keep counsel when the third's away. 4.02.144
unless good counsel may the cause remove. ROM 1.01.142
i have rememb'red me, thou s' hear our counsel. 1.03. 9
in night | so stumblest on my counsel? 2.02. 53
he lent me counsel, and i lent him eyes. 2.02. 81
say, | "two may keep counsel, putting one away"? 2.04.197
here all the night | to hear good counsel. 3.03.160
comfort me, counsel me! 3.05.208
give me some present counsel, or, behold, 4.01. 61
that men's ears should be | to counsel deaf, but TIM 1.02.250
and yet he would embrace no counsel, take no 3.01. 26 P
the gold thou givest me, | not all thy counsel. 4.03.131
more counsel with more money, bounteous timon. 4.03.167
how hard it is for women to keep counsel! JC 2.04. 9
that i can keep your counsel and not mine own. HAM 4.02. 11 P
of it, and so i thank you for your good counsel. 4.05. 71 P
i can keep honest counsel, ride, run, mar a LR 1.04. 32 P
this man hath had good counsel — a hundred 1.04.322
bestow | your needful counsel to our businesses, 2.01.127
when a wise man gives thee better counsel, give 2.04. 75 P
we lack'd your counsel and your help to-night. OTH 1.03. 51
to counsel cassio to this parallel course, 2.03.349
and when i told thee he was of my counsel | /in 3.03.111
i pray you turn the key and keep our counsel. 4.02. 94
dispose you as | yourself shall give us counsel. ANT 5.02.187
have these things set down by lawful counsel, CYM 1.04.165 P
be | you bees that make these locks of counsel! 3.02. 36
now for the counsel of my son and queen! 4.03. 27
with counsel of the night, i will be here | with TNK 3.01. 83
that thrive well take counsel of their friends. VEN 640
all this beforehand counsel comprehends. LUC 494
take counsel of some wiser head, | neither too PP 18. 5
counsel may stop a while what will not stay; LC 159
COUNSEL-KEEPER 1 FR 0.0001 REL FR 0 V 1 P
old tables, his note-book, his counsel-keeper. 2H4 2.04.267 P
COUNSEL-KEEPING 1 FR 0.0001 REL FR 1 V 0 P
and curtain'd with a counsel-keeping cave, | we TIT 2.03. 24
/COUNSELL'D 1 FR 0.0001 REL FR 1 V 0 P
/that /lord /that /counsell'd /thee | /to /give LR 1.04.140
COUNSELL'D 2 FR 0.0002 REL FR 2 V 0 P
pray be counsell'd. COR 3.02. 28
and allegiance clear, | i shall be counsell'd. MAC 2.01. 29
COUNSELLOR 15 FR 0.0017 REL FR 11 V 4 P
you are a counsellor; TMP 1.01. 21 P
love | as meet to be an emperor's counsellor. TGV 2.04. 77
precisian, he admits him not for his counsellor. WIV 2.01. 6 P
a counsellor, a traitress, and a dear: AWW 1.01.170
your physician, | your most obedient counsellor; WT 2.03. 55
therefore caveto be thy counsellor. H5 2.03. 53
the tongue of an enemy be a good counsellor, or 2H6 4.02.172 P
the counsellor heart, the arm our soldier, | our COR 1.01.116
but he, /his own affections' counsellor, | is to ROM 1.01.147
go, counsellor, | thou and my bosom henceforth 3.05.239
this counsellor | is now most still, most secret HAM 3.04.213
is he not a most profane and liberal counsellor? OTH 2.01.164 P
(love's counsellor should fill the bores of CYM 3.02. 57
fit counsellor and servant for a prince, | who PER 1.02. 63
thou art a grave and noble counsellor, | most 5.01.182
COUNSELLORS 6 FR 0.0006 REL FR 5 V 1 P
good counsellors lack no clients. MM 1.02.106 P
these are counsellors | that feelingly persuade AYL 2.01. 10
when rage and hot blood are his counsellors, 2H4 4.04. 63
all you sage counsellors, hence! 4.05.120
how well supplied with noble counsellors, | how H5 2.04. 33
linen cheeks of thine | are counsellors to fear. MAC 5.03. 17
COUNSEL'S 1 FR 0.0001 REL FR 1 V 0 P
my other self, my counsel's consistory, | my R3 2.02.151
COUNSELS 18 FR 0.0020 REL FR 17 V 1 P
keep your fellows' counsels and your own, and ADO 3.03. 86 P
about thy thoughts and counsels of thy heart! 4.01.102
their several counsels they unbosom shall | to LLL 5.02.141
did ever keep your counsels, never wrong'd you; MND 3.02.308
yourself, | hate counsels not in such a quality. MV 3.02. 6
our prerogative | calls not your counsels, but WT 2.01.164
cast your good counsels | upon his passion. 4.04.495
thou that didst bear the key of all my counsels, H5 2.02. 96
no more shall be the neighbor to my counsels. R3 4.02. 43
you are liberal of your loves and counsels, | be H8 2.01.126
he counsels a divorce, a loss of her | that, 2.02. 30
reverend fathers, | bestow your counsels on me. 3.01.182
as well my undertakings as your counsels, | but TRO 2.02.131
for examine | their counsels and their cares; COR 1.01.150
that they of rome are ent'red in our counsels, 1.02. 2
the close enacts and counsels of thy heart! TIT 4.02.118
tell me your counsels, i will not disclose 'em. JC 2.01.298
'tis a wild night, | my regan counsels well. LR 2.04.309
COUNT* *(also compt)*
/COUNT* 1 FR 0.0001 REL FR 0 V 1 P
/and /count /myself /a /king /of /infinite HAM 2.02.255 P
COUNT* 107 FR 0.0121 REL FR 49 V 58 P
one is painted, and the other out of all count. TGV 2.01. 57 P
how painted? and how out of count? 2.01. 58 P
but count the world a stranger for thy sake. 5.04. 70
love again, but i will always count you my deer. WIV 5.05.118 P
you hear, count claudio, i can be secret as a ADO 1.01.209 P
the prince and count claudio, walking in a 1.02. 9 P
having obtain'd her, give her to count claudio. 1.03. 63 P
was not count john here at supper? 2.01. 1 P
signior benedick's tongue in count john's mouth, 2.01. 12 P
and half count john's melancholy in signior 2.01. 12 P
count claudio? 2.01.183 P
now, signior, where's the count? 2.01.211 P
i have brought count claudio, whom you sent me 2.01.287 P
why, how now, count, wherefore are you sad? 2.01.288 P
the count is neither sad, nor sick, nor merry, 2.01.293 P
but civil count, civil as an orange, and 2.01.294 P
count, take of me my daughter, and with her my 2.01.302 P
speak, count, 'tis your cue. 2.01.305 P
the count claudio shall marry the daughter of 2.02. 1 P
to draw don pedro and the count claudio alone, 2.02. 34 P
if it please you — yet count claudio may hear, 3.02. 85 P
these gloves the count sent me — they are an 3.04. 62 P
the prince, the count, signior benedick, don 3.04. 95 P
you come hither to be married to this count. 4.01. 10 P
know you any, count? 4.01. 17 P
brother, and this grieved count | did see her, 4.01. 89
surely a princely testimony, a goodly count, 4.01.316 P
a goodly count, count comfect, a sweet gallant 4.01.316 P
you in your soul the count claudio hath wrong'd 4.01.328 P
and that count claudio did mean, upon his words, 4.02. 53 P
do you hear me, and let this count kill me. 5.01.231 P
bad habit of frowning than the count palentine; MV 1.02. 59 P
it is as easy to count atomies as to resolve the AYL 3.02.232 P
i count it but time lost to hear such a foolish 5.03. 39 P
it is the count /rossillion, my good lord, AWW 1.02. 18
how long is't, count, | since the physician at 1.02. 69
welcome, count, | my son's no dearer. 1.02. 75
the count rossillion cannot be my brother: 1.03.155
commit it, count. 2.01. 34

the help of heaven we count the act of men. 2.01.152
are you companion to the count rossillion? 2.03.192 P
to any count, to all counts: to what is man. 2.03.193 P
they say the french count has done most 3.05. 3 P
the count rossillion. know you such a one? 3.05. 49
there is a gentleman that serves the count 3.05. 56
or to the worth | of the great count himself, 3.05. 60
may be the amorous count solicits her | in the 3.05. 69
give me trust, the count he is my husband, | and 3.07. 8
the count he woos your daughter, | lays down his 3.07. 17
go tell the count rossillion, and my brother, 4.01. 89
what will count rossillion do then? 4.03. 41 P
hath the count all this intelligence? 4.03. 60 P
heed of the allurement of one count rossillion, 4.03.214 P
for i knew the young count to be a dangerous and 4.03.219 P
for count of this, the count's a fool, i know it 4.03.229
and the captain of his horse, count rossillion. 4.03.294 P
of that lascivious young boy the count, have i 4.03.301 P
writ to diana in behalf of the count rossillion? 4.03.320 P
now is the count rossillion a widower, his vows 5.03.141 P
go speedily and bring again the count. 5.03.152
come hither, count, do you know these women? 5.03.165
maid, the daughter of a count | that died some TN 1.02. 36
the count himself here hard by woos her. 1.03.107 P
she'll none o' th' count. 1.03.109 P
i thank you. here comes the count. 1.04. 9 P
from the count orsino, is it? 1.05.101 P
if it be a suit from the count, i am sick, or 1.05.108 P
i am bound to the count orsino's court. 2.01. 42 P
to be count malvolio! 2.05. 35 P
i saw thee late at the count orsino's. 3.01. 37 P
y' are servant to the count orsino, youth. 3.01.100
in a sea-fight 'gainst the count his galleys | i 3.03. 26
gentleman of the count orsino's is return'd. 3.04. 57 P
i arrest thee at the suit of count orsino. 3.04.326 P
i was preserv'd to serve this noble count. 5.01.256
against the pope, and count his friends my foes. JN 3.01.171
the count melune, a noble lord of france, 4.03. 15
it is the count melune. 5.04. 9
the count melune is slain; 5.05. 10
sure | i count myself in nothing else so happy R2 2.03. 46
go count thy way with sighs, i mine with groans. 5.01. 89
le foot, madame, et le count. H5 3.04. 51 P
le foot et le count! 3.04. 52 P
le foot et le count! 3.04. 56 P
d' elbow, de nick, de sin, de foot, le count. 3.04. 59 P
here, through this grate, i count each one, 1H6 1.04. 60
or count them happy that enjoys the sun? 2H6 2.04. 39
when they are gone, then must i count my gains. R3 1.01.162
i would not be a young count in your way | for H8 2.03. 41
count wisdom as no member of the war, TRO 1.03.198
do not count it holy | /to /hurt /by /being 5.03. 19
by my count, | i was your mother much upon these
ROM 1.03. 71
they are but beggars that can count their worth, 2.06. 32
by this count i shall be much in years | ere i 3.05. 46
doth she not count her blest, | unworthy as she 3.05.143
me, i count it one of my greatest afflictions, TIM 3.02. 55 P
peace, count the clock. JC 2.01.192
make us again count o'er ere love be done! HAM 3.02.162
motive, | why to a public count i might not go, 4.07. 17
creatures as | we count not worth the hanging CYM 1.05. 20
spare your arithmetic, never count the turns. 2.04.142
at parting) when our count | was each aleven. TNK 1.03. 53
yet these that we count errors may become him: 4.02. 31
"this fair child of mine | shall sum my count, SON 2.11
when i do count the clock that tells the time, 12. 1
which in their wills count bad what i think good 121. 8
only my plague thus far i count my gain, | that 141.13
COUNTABLE *(see comptible)*
COUNT-CARDINAL 1 FR 0.0001 REL FR 1 V 0 P
but our count-cardinal | has done this, and 'tis H8 1.01.172
COUNTED 9 FR 0.0010 REL FR 9 V 0 P
than you much willing to be counted wise | in LLL 2.01. 18
for native blood is counted painting now; 4.03.259
and since her time are colliers counted bright. 4.03.263
or else thou must be counted | a servant grafted WT 1.02.245
being counted falsehood, shall (as i express it) 3.02. 27
for the babe | is counted lost for ever, perdita 3.03. 33
nor mother, wife, nor england's counted queen. R3 4.01. 46
service, never | let me be counted serviceable. CYM 3.02. 15
in the old age black was not counted fair, | or SON 127. 1
COUNTENANC'D 3 FR 0.0003 REL FR 2 V 1 P
but faults so countenanc'd, that the strong MM 5.01.320
rage, | and countenanc'd by boys and beggary — 2H4 4.01. 35
therefore i beseech you let him be countenanc'd. 5.01. 51 P
COUNTENANCE 57 FR 0.0064 REL FR 34 V 23 P
sir, you should lay my countenance to pawn. WIV 2.02. 6 P
evil which is here wrapp'd up | in countenance! MM 5.01.118
which i will do with confirm'd countenance. ADO 5.04. 17
i will not be put out of countenance. LLL 5.02.607 P
forward, for we have put thee in countenance. 5.02.619 P
you have put me out of countenance. 5.02.621 P
nature gave me his countenance seems to take AYL 1.01. 18 P
and therefore put i on the countenance | of 2.07.108
god for making you that countenance you are; 4.01. 37 P
in their effect | than in their countenance. 4.03. 36
must meet my master to countenance my mistress.
SHR 4.01. 99 P
that calls for company to countenance her. 4.01.103 P
in gait and countenance surely like a father. 4.02. 65
set your countenance, sir. 4.04. 18
somebody in this city under my countenance. 5.01. 39 P
while he did bear my countenance in the town, 5.01.126
and with a countenance as clear | as friendship WT 1.02.343
the king hath on him such a countenance | as he 1.02.368
lift up your countenance, as it were the day 4.04. 49
with countenance of such distraction that they 5.02. 47 P
the moon, under whose countenance we steal. 1H4 1.02. 29 P
the poor abuses of the time want countenance. 1.02.156 P
o, the father, how he holds his countenance! 2.04.392 P
and gave his countenance, against his name, | to 3.02. 65
by unkind usage, dangerous countenance, | and 5.01. 69
would he abuse the countenance of the king, 2H4 4.02. 13
/employ the countenance and grace of heav'n, 4.02. 24
to countenance william visor of woncote against 5.01. 38 P
should have some countenance at his friend's 5.01. 45 P
do but mark the countenance that he will give me 5.05. 7 P
a monarch, and his countenance enforces homage.
H5 3.07. 28 P
my grisly countenance made others fly, | none 1H6 1.04. 47
under the countenance and confederacy | of lady 2H6 2.01.164
the strangeness of his alter'd countenance? 3.01. 5
nor change my countenance for this arrest; 3.01. 99
yea, subject to your countenance — glad, or H8 2.04. 26
a heed | was in his countenance. 3.02. 81
there's a countenance! TRO 1.02.202 P
but this thy countenance, still lock'd in steel, 4.05.195
h'as such a confirm'd countenance. COR 1.03. 60 P
he wag'd me with his countenance as if | i had 5.06. 39
clear up, fair queen, that cloudy countenance; TIT 1.01.263
i turn the trouble of my countenance | merely JC 1.02. 38
his countenance, like richest alchymy, | will 1.03.159
walk like sprites, | to countenance this horror! MAC 2.03. 80
a countenance more | in sorrow than in anger. HAM 1.02.231
and hath given countenance to his speech, my 1.03.113
majesty and skill | both countenance and excuse. 4.01. 32
sir, that soaks up the king's countenance, his 4.02. 15 P
no displeasure in him by word nor countenance? LR 1.02.157 P
have that in your countenance which i would fain 1.04. 27 P
his countenance likes me not. 2.02. 90
we'll use | his countenance for the battle, 5.01. 63
we did sleep day out of countenance, and made ANT 2.02.177 P
turn from me then that noble countenance, 4.14. 85
as if the heavens should countenance his sin. LUC 343
but when your countenance fill'd up his line, SON 86.13
COUNTENANCES 1 FR 0.0001 REL FR 1 V 0 P
news is coming | that turns their countenances. COR 4.06. 60
COUNTER* 4 FR 0.0004 REL FR 3 V 1 P
a hound that runs counter, and yet draws ERR 4.02. 39
what, for a counter, would i do but good? AYL 2.07. 63
you hunt counter, hence, avaunt! 2H4 1.02. 90 P
o, this is counter, you false danish dogs! HAM 4.05.111
COUNTER-CASTER 1 FR 0.0001 REL FR 1 V 0 P
by debitor and creditor — this counter-caster, OTH 1.01. 31
COUNTERCHANGE 1 FR 0.0001 REL FR 1 V 0 P
the counterchange | is severally in all. CYM 5.05.396
COUNTERCHECK 3 FR 0.0003 REL FR 1 V 2 P
this is call'd the countercheck quarrelsome; AYL 5.04. 80 P
the fift, the countercheck quarrelsome; 5.04. 95 P
have brought a countercheck before your gates, JN 2.01.224
COUNTERFEIT 54 FR 0.0061 REL FR 24 V 30 P
thou counterfeit to thy true friend! TGV 5.04. 53
to counterfeit thus grossly with your slave, ERR 2.02.169
to tell you true, i counterfeit him. ADO 2.01.116 P
may be she doth but counterfeit. 2.03.102 P
counterfeit? 2.03.104 P
there was never counterfeit of passion came so 2.03.105 P
persever, counterfeit sad looks, | make mouths MND 3.02.237
fie, fie, you counterfeit, you puppet, you! 3.02.288
fair portia's counterfeit! MV 3.02.115
now counterfeit to swound; AYL 3.05. 17
this was not counterfeit, there is too great 4.03.169 P
counterfeit, i assure you. 4.03.172 P
take a good heart and counterfeit to be a man. 4.03.173 P
they are busied about a counterfeit assurance. SHR 4.04. 92 P
while counterfeit supposes blear'd thine eyne. 5.01.117
to what metal this counterfeit lump of /ore will AWW 3.06. 37 P
so curiously he had set this counterfeit. 4.03. 34 P
come, bring forth this counterfeit module, h'as 4.03. 99 P
you not mad indeed, or do you but counterfeit? TN 4.02.114 P
not a counterfeit stone, not a ribbon, glass, WT 4.04.597 P
you have beguil'd me with a counterfeit JN 3.01. 99
craft | to counterfeit oppression of such grief R2 1.04. 14
never call a true piece of gold a counterfeit. 1H4 2.04.492 P
i fear thou art another counterfeit, | and yet, 5.04. 35
'sblood, 'twas time to counterfeit, or that hot 5.04.113 P
counterfeit? 5.04.114 P
i lie, i am no counterfeit. 5.04.115 P
to die is to be a counterfeit, for he is but the 5.04.116 P
for he is but the counterfeit of a man who hath 5.04.116 P
but to counterfeit dying, when a man thereby 5.04.117 P
a man thereby liveth, is to be no counterfeit, 5.04.118 P
how if he should counterfeit too and rise? 5.04.123 P
am afraid he would prove the better counterfeit. 5.04.124 P
this is an arrant counterfeit rascal, i remember H5 3.06. 61 P
go, go, you are a counterfeit cowardly knave. 5.01. 69 P
mean time your cheeks do counterfeit our roses; 1H6 2.04. 62
blush for pure shame to counterfeit our roses, 2.04. 66
'tis but his policy to counterfeit, | because he 3H6 2.06. 65
tut, i can counterfeit the deep tragedian, R3 3.05. 5
'tis no counterfeit. H8 5.02.137
if i could 'a' rememb'red a gilt counterfeit, TRO 2.03. 25 P
sir, i will counterfeit the bewitchment of some COR 2.03.101 P
you gave us the counterfeit fairly last night. ROM 2.04. 45 P
what counterfeit did i give you? 2.04. 46 P
strike me the counterfeit matron, | it is her TIM 4.03.113
thou draw'st a counterfeit | best in all athens; 5.01. 80
shake off this downy sleep, death's counterfeit, MAC 2.03. 76
the counterfeit presentment of two brothers. HAM 3.04. 54
an eye can stamp and counterfeit advantages, OTH 2.01.243 P
th' immortal jove's dread clamors counterfeit, 3.03.356
coiner with his tools | made me a counterfeit; CYM 2.05. 6
to the poor counterfeit of her complaining: LUC 1269
much liker than your painted counterfeit: SON 16. 8
and the counterfeit | is poorly imitated after 53. 5
COUNTERFEITED 5 FR 0.0005 REL FR 2 V 3 P
a body would think this was well counterfeited! AYL 4.03.166 P
you tell your brother how well i counterfeited. 4.03.167 P
tell you how i counterfeited to sound when he 5.02. 25 P
ta'en up, | under the counterfeited zeal of god, 2H4 4.02. 27
streams, | twinkling another counterfeited beam, 1H6 5.03. 63
COUNTERFEITING 4 FR 0.0004 REL FR 2 V 2 P
my counterfeiting the action of an old woman, WIV 4.05.118 P
but i pray you commend my counterfeiting to him.
AYL 4.03.182 P
were play'd in jest by counterfeiting actors? 3H6 2.03. 28
his part so much, | they mar my counterfeiting. LR 3.06. 61
COUNTERFEITLY 1 FR 0.0001 REL FR 0 V 1 P
nod and be off to them most counterfeitly; COR 2.03.100 P
COUNTERFEITS 5 FR 0.0005 REL FR 3 V 2 P
so do counterfeits. TGV 2.04. 12 P
the knave counterfeits well; a good knave. TN 4.02. 19 P
in one little body | thou counterfeits a bark, a ROM 3.05.131
these may be counterfeits; OTH 5.01. 43
and counterfeits to die with her a space, | till LUC 1776
COUNTERFEIT'ST 2 FR 0.0002 REL FR 2 V 0 P
thou | that counterfeit'st the person of a king? 1H4 5.04. 28
the best, | thou counterfeit'st most lively. TIM 5.01. 82
COUNTER-GATE 1 FR 0.0001 REL FR 0 V 1 P
as well say i love to walk by the counter-gate, WIV 3.03. 78 P
COUNTERMAND 4 FR 0.0004 REL FR 4 V 0 P
have you no countermand for claudio yet, | but MM 4.02. 92
yet i believe there comes | no countermand; 4.02. 97
some tardy cripple bare the countermand, | that R3 2.01. 90
my heart shall never countermand mine eye. LUC 276
COUNTERMANDS 1 FR 0.0001 REL FR 1 V 0 P
one that countermands | the passages of alleys, ERR 4.02. 37
COUNTERMINES 1 FR 0.0001 REL FR 0 V 1 P
digt himself four yard under the countermines. H5 3.02. 62 P
COUNTERPART 1 FR 0.0001 REL FR 1 V 0 P
and such a counterpart shall fame his wit, SON 84.11
COUNTERPOINTS 1 FR 0.0001 REL FR 1 V 0 P
in cypress chests my arras counterpoints, SHR 2.01.351
COUNTERPOIS'D 3 FR 0.0003 REL FR 3 V 0 P
fight | be counterpois'd with such a petty sum! 2H6 4.01. 22
which with her dowry shall be counterpois'd. 3H6 3.03.137
cannot in the world | be singly counterpois'd. COR 2.02. 87
COUNTERPOISE 5 FR 0.0005 REL FR 4 V 1 P
may counterpoise this rich and precious gift? ADO 4.01. 28
to whom i promise | a counterpoise; AWW 2.03.175
too light for the counterpoise of so great an 1H4 2.03. 13 P
doth more than counterpoise a full third part COR 5.06. 77
what you bestow, in him i'll counterpoise, | and TIM 1.01.145
COUNTER-REFLECT 1 FR 0.0001 REL FR 1 V 0 P
that it shall make a counter-reflect 'gainst TNK 1.01.127
COUNTERS *(also compters)*
COUNTERS 2 FR 0.0002 REL FR 1 V 1 P
to lock such rascal counters from his friends, JC 4.03. 80
your neck, sir, is pen, book, and counters; CYM 5.04.170 P
COUNTER-SEAL'D 1 FR 0.0001 REL FR 1 V 0 P
on like conditions, will have counter-seal'd. COR 5.03.205
COUNTERVAIL 2 FR 0.0002 REL FR 2 V 0 P
it cannot countervail the exchange of joy | that ROM 2.06. 4
had not a show might countervail his worth. PER 2.03. 56
COUNTESS 4 FR 0.0004 REL FR 3 V 1 P
were you not ev'n now with the countess olivia? TN 2.02. 1 P
here comes the countess, now heaven walks on 5.01. 97
the virtuous lady, countess of auvergne, | with 1H6 2.02. 38
the countess richmond, good my lord of derby, R3 1.03. 20
COUNTESSES 1 FR 0.0001 REL FR 1 V 0 P
it is, and all the rest are countesses. H8 4.01. 53
COUNTIES 6 FR 0.0006 REL FR 4 V 2 P
princes and counties! ADO 4.01.315 P
our discontented counties do revolt; JN 5.01. 8
are to take soldiers up in counties as you go. 2H4 2.01.187 P
your powers unto their several counties, | as we 4.02. 61
and those two counties i will undertake | your 1H6 5.03.158
all, | these counties were the keys of normandy. 2H6 1.01.114
COUNTING 4 FR 0.0004 REL FR 4 V 0 P
rest, | counting myself but bad till i be best. 3H6 5.06. 91
as he thus went counting | the flinty pavement, TNK 5.04. 58
now counting best to be with you alone, | then SON 75. 7
counting no old thing old, thou mine, i thine, 108. 7
COUNTLESS *(also comptless)*
COUNTLESS 3 FR 0.0003 REL FR 3 V 0 P
that i should pay | countless and infinite, yet TIT 5.03.159
enticeth thee to view | her countless glory, PER 1.01. 31
that gives heaven countless eyes to view men's 1.01. 73
COUNT'NANCE 5 FR 0.0005 REL FR 4 V 1 P
this pert berowne was out of count'nance quite. LLL 5.02.272
life, | puts my apparel and my count'nance on, SHR 1.01.229
in count'nance somewhat doth resemble you. 4.02.100
folk should have count'nance in this world to HAM 5.01. 27 P
thou need'st | but keep that count'nance still. CYM 3.04. 14
COUNTRIES 7 FR 0.0008 REL FR 3 V 4 P
i could find out countries in her. ERR 3.02.115 P
or in the shape of two countries at once, as a ADO 3.02. 34 P
and catechize | my picked man of countries. JN 1.01.193
the rest of the low countries have /made /a 2H4 2.02. 22 P
i do dismiss you to your several countries. 2H6 4.09. 21
haply the seas and countries different | with HAM 3.01.171
in countries, discord; LR 1.02.107 P
/COUNTRY 1 FR 0.0001 REL FR 1 V 0 P
/for /all /the /country /in /a /general /voice 2H4 4.01.134
COUNTRY 142 FR 0.0160 REL FR 105 V 37 P
nymphs encounter every one | in country footing. TMP 4.01.138
go unrewarded while i am king of this country. 4.01.243 P
power guide us | out of this fearful country! 5.01.106
he's a justice of peace in his country, simple WIV 1.01.219 P
and laugh this sport o'er by a country fire — 5.05.242
not of this country, though my chance is now MM 3.02.217
i do love that country girl that i took in the LLL 1.02.117 P
this significant to the country maid jaquenetta. 3.01.131 P
and the country proverb known, | that every man MND 3.02.458
a vessel of our country richly fraught. MV 2.08. 30
he pierceth through | the body of /the country, AYL 2.01. 59
as ridiculous in the country as the behavior of 3.02. 47 P
the behavior of the country is most mockable at 3.02. 47 P
it will be the earliest fruit i' th' country; 3.02.119 P
disable all the benefits of your own country; 4.01. 35 P
nonino, | these pretty country folks would lie, 5.03. 24
amongst the rest of the country copulatives, to 5.04. 55 P
our isbels a' th' country are nothing like your AWW 3.02. 13 P
is't i | that chase thee from thy country, and 3.02.103
except in that country he had the honor to be 4.03.268 P
if you could find out a country where but women 4.03.326 P
and i follow him to his country for justice. 5.03.144 P
what country, friends, is this? TN 1.02. 1
know'st thou this country? 1.02. 21
it is fifteen years since i saw my country; WT 4.02. 4 P
of that fatal country sicilia, prithee speak no 4.02. 20 P
having both their country quitted | with this 5.01.192
come from the country to be judg'd by you | that JN 1.01. 45
our country manners give our betters way. 1.01.156
the bay-trees in our country are all wither'd, R2 2.04. 8
in our marches through the country, there be H5 3.06.109 P
the country cocks do crow, the clocks do toll, 4.pr. 15
to die, we are enow | to do our country loss; 4.03. 21
the sciences that should become our country, 5.02. 58
the nice fashion of your country in denying me a 5.02.274 P
vocation | and free my country from calamity. 1H6 1.02. 81
tyranny these many years | wasted our country, 2.03. 41
look on thy country, look on fertile france, 3.03. 44

forgive me, country, and sweet countrymen, | and 3.03. 81
thy knee, | or sack this country with a mutiny. 5.01. 62
enjoy mine own, the country maine and anjou, 5.03.154
have i sought every country far and near, | and, 5.04. 3
beams | upon the country where you make abode; 5.04. 88
to ease your country of distressful war | and 5.04.126
the land | and common profit of his country! 2H6 1.01.206
my soul | as i in duty love my king and country! 1.03.158
done, | live in your country here in banishment, 2.03. 12
fight for your king, your country, and your 4.05. 11
sweet is the country, because full of riches, 4.07. 62
how well you love your prince and country: 4.09. 16
or unto death, to do my country good. 4.09. 43
peep out, for all the country is laid for me; 4.10. 4 P
how will the country for these woeful chances 3H6 2.05.107
here in this country where we now remain. 3.01. 75
or than for strength and safety of our country. 3.03.211
i had rather be a country servant maid | than a R3 1.03.106
whom their o'ercloyed country vomits forth | to 5.03.318
now | an honest country lord, as i am, beaten H8 1.03. 44
far hence | in mine own country, lords. 3.01. 91
that in their country did them that disgrace TRO 2.02. 95
she's bitter to her country. 4.01. 69
you what services he has done for his country? COR 1.01. 31 P
can be content to say it was for his country, he 1.01. 38 P
had eleven die nobly for their country than one 1.03. 25 P
as you have been — that's for my country: 1.09. 17
he hath deserv'd worthily of his country, and 2.02. 24 P
service that | hath thus stood for his country; 2.02. 41
you have deserv'd nobly of your country, and you 2.03. 88 P
you have receiv'd many wounds for your country. 2.03.107 P
marks of merit, wounds receiv'd for 's country. 2.03.164
how youngly he began to serve his country, | how 2.03.236
as for my country i have shed my blood, | not 3.01. 76
by many an ounce) he dropp'd it for his country; 3.01.299
to lose it by his country | were to us all that 3.01.300
when he did love his country, | it honor'd him. 3.01.303
as enemy to the people and his country. 3.03.118
i would he had continued to his country | as he 4.02. 30
being now in no request of his country. 4.03. 36 P
he give me way, | i'll do his country service. 4.04. 26
shed for my thankless country are requited | but 4.05. 70
those maims | of shame seen through thy country, 4.05. 87
against my cank'red country with the spleen | of 4.05. 91
mean to solicit him | for mercy to his country. 5.01. 73
how can we, for our country pray, | whereto we 5.03.107
or we must lose | the country, our dear nurse, 5.03.110
else thy person, | our comfort in the country. 5.03.111
march to assault thy country than to tread 5.03.123
destroy'd his country, and his name remains | to 5.03.147
and to the love and favor of my country | commit TIT 1.01. 58
to re–salute his country with his tears, | tears 1.01. 75
in right and service of their noble country. 1.01.197
oft | for his ungrateful country done the like. 4.01.111
then, as the manner of our country is, | /in thy ROM 4.01.109
thou wast born to conquer my country. TIM 4.03.107
but yet i love my country, and am not | one that 5.01.191
the men that gave their country liberty. JC 3.01.118
is here so vile that will not love his country? 3.02. 33 P
it shall please my country to need my death. 3.02. 47 P
far from this country pindarus shall run, 5.03. 49
may soon return to this our suffering country MAC 3.06. 48
bleed, bleed, poor country! 4.03. 31
i think our country sinks beneath the yoke: 4.03. 39
yet my poor country | shall have more vices than 4.03. 46
alas, poor country, | almost afraid to know 4.03.164
send out moe horses, skirr the country round, 5.03. 35
the phrase or the addition | of man and country. HAM 2.01. 48
the undiscover'd country, from whose bourn | no 3.01. 78
do you think i meant country matters? 3.02.116 P
he'll shape his old course in a country new. LR 1.01.187
the country gives me proof and president | of 2.03. 13
of years, of country, credit, every thing, | to OTH 1.03. 97
'tis pride that pulls the country down, | /then 2.03. 95
and the condition of this country stands, i 2.03.300 P
i know our country disposition well: 3.03.201
may fall to match you with her country forms, 3.03.237
and her country? 4.02.126
thou hast worn | most useful for thy country. ANT 4.14. 80
of us fell in praise of our country mistresses; CYM 1.04. 57 P
worthiest sir that ever | country call'd his; 1.06.161
these present wars shall find i love my country, 4.03. 43
if in your country wars you chance to die, 4.04. 51
belied a lady, | the princess of this country; 5.02. 3
beard came to, | in doing this for 's country. 5.03. 18
the country base than to commit such slaughter, 5.03. 20
here's them in our country of greece gets more PER 2.01. 64 P
he's but a country gentleman: 2.03. 33
your grace, that fed my country with your corn, 3.03. 18
he's the governor of this country, and a man 4.06. 53 P
if he govern the country, you are bound to him 4.06. 55 P
in the cheapest country under the cope, shall 4.06.123 P
who, frighted from my country, did wed | at 5.03. 3
where is our noble country? TNK 2.02. 7
be as that cursed man that hates his country, 2.02.199
what country bred you? 2.05. 5
some country sport, upon my life, sir. 3.05. 97
if you but favor, our country pastime made is. 3.05.102
you shall both to your country, | and each 3.06.290
our country is a great eating country, argo they STM II.C 5 P
our country is a great eating country, argo they II.C 5 P
they eat more in our country than they do in II.C 6 P
what country by the nature of your error II.C 126
by all our country rights in rome maintained, LUC 1838

/COUNTRYMAN 1 FR 0.0001 REL FR 1 V 0 P
thanks, good my /countryman. H5 4.07.110

COUNTRYMAN 18 FR 0.0020 REL FR 16 V 2 P
know ye don antonio, your countryman? TGV 2.04. 54
is your countryman, | according to our 3.02. 11
no, say'st me so, friend? what countryman? SHR 1.02.189
what countryman, i pray? 4.02. 77
here you shall see a countryman of yours | that AWW 3.05. 47
what countryman? TN 5.01.231
for i am welsh, you know, good countryman. H5 4.07.105
i am your majesty's countryman, i care not who 4.07.111 P
froissard, a countryman of ours, records 1H6 1.02. 29
the princely charles of france, thy countryman. 3.03. 38
army we can make, | might stop our countryman. COR 5.01. 38
far, one muliteus my countryman | his wife but TIT 4.02.152
then, dear countryman, | bring in thy ranks, but TIM 5.04. 38
my countryman; but yet i know him not. MAC 4.03.160
my friend and my dear countryman | roderigo! OTH 5.01. 89
cowardly put off my helmet to | my countryman — ANT 4.15. 57
a simple countryman, that brought her figs. 5.02.339
i was glad i did atone my countryman and you. CYM 1.04. 39 P

COUNTRYMEN 42 FR 0.0047 REL FR 40 V 2 P
to merchants, our well–dealing countrymen, | who ERR 1.01. 7
jars | 'twixt thy seditious countrymen and us, 1.01. 12
leave, | i bid my very friends and countrymen, MV 3.02.223
swear | to tubal and to chus, his countrymen, 3.02.285
visit his countrymen, and banquet them? SHR 1.01.197
with "thanks, my countrymen, my loving friends," R2 1.04. 34
days, | and hardly kept our countrymen together, 2.04. 2
our countrymen are gone and fled, | as well 2.04. 16
"i thank you, countrymen." 5.02. 20
then forth, dear countrymen! H5 2.02.189
calls them brothers, friends, and countrymen. 4.pr. 34
well have we done, thrice–valiant countrymen, 4.06. 1
hark, countrymen, either renew the fight, | or 1H6 1.05. 27
see here, my friends and loving countrymen, 3.01.137
torch | that joineth roan unto her countrymen, 3.02. 27
then, thou fight'st against thy countrymen | and 3.03. 74
forgive me, country, and sweet countrymen, | and 3.03. 81
stain to thy countrymen, thou hear'st thy doom! 4.01. 45
ah, countrymen! 2H6 4.07.114
what say ye, countrymen? 4.08. 11
more than i have said, loving countrymen, | the R3 5.03.237
what work's, my countrymen, in hand? COR 1.01. 55
to pardon rome and thy petitionary countrymen. 5.02. 76 P
and, countrymen, my loving followers, | plead my TIT 1.01. 3
if alcibiades kill my countrymen, | let TIM 5.01.169
commend me to my loving countrymen — 5.01.194
go, go, good countrymen, and for this fault JC 1.01. 56
the melting spirits of women, then, countrymen, 2.01.122
romans, countrymen, and lovers, hear me for my 3.02. 13 P
my countrymen — 3.02. 53
good countrymen, let me depart alone, | and, for 3.02. 55
friends, romans, countrymen, lend me your ears! 3.02. 73
o, what a fall was there, my countrymen! 3.02.190
stay, countrymen. 3.02.206
yet hear me, countrymen, yet hear me speak. 3.02.233
words before blows; is it so, countrymen? 5.01. 27
yet, countrymen! o, yet, hold up your heads! 5.04. 1
countrymen, | my heart doth joy that yet in all 5.05. 33
unto our climatures and countrymen. HAM 1.01.125
our countrymen | are men more order'd than when CYM 2.04. 20
friends, masters, countrymen — STM II.C 27
my masters, countrymen — II.C 29

/COUNTRY'S 1 FR 0.0001 REL FR 1 V 0 P
seems to weep | over his /country's wrongs, and 1H4 4.03. 82

COUNTRY'S 45 FR 0.0050 REL FR 44 V 1 P
which in our country's cradle | draws the sweet R2 1.03.132
then thus i turn me from my country's light, 1.03.176
imp out our drooping country's broken wing, 2.01.292
for i am loath to break our country's laws. 2.03.169
his body to that pleasant country's earth, | and 4.01. 98
the slave, a member of the country's peace, H5 4.01.281
within the weak list of a country's fashion. 5.02.270 P
one drop of blood drawn from thy country's bosom 1H6 3.03. 54
and wash away thy country's stained spots. 3.03. 57
mov'd with compassion of my country's wrack, 4.01. 56
tends to god's glory and my country's weal. 5.01. 27
sold their bodies for their country's benefit, 5.04.106
this pretty lad will prove our country's bliss. 3H6 4.06. 70
having my country's peace and brothers' loves. 5.07. 36
should enjoy, were you this country's king — R3 1.03.151
i bid them that did love their country's good 3.07. 21
which here we waken to our country's good, | the 3.07.124
if you do fight against your country's foes, 5.03.257
your country's fat shall pay your pains the hire 5.03.258
all the ends thou aim'st at be thy country's, H8 3.02.447
and that his country's dearer than himself; COR 1.06. 72
i got them in my country's service, when | some 2.03. 52
be that you seem, truly your country's friend, 3.01.217
my country's good with a respect more tender, 3.03.112
drawn tuns of blood out of thy country's breast, 4.05. 99
know'st | thy country's strength and weakness — 4.05.140
sure if you | would be your country's pleader, 5.01. 36
the father tearing | his country's bowels out. 5.03.103
else | triumphantly tread on thy country's ruin, 5.03.116
no more infected with my country's love | than 5.06. 71
sleep in peace, slain in your country's wars! TIT 1.01. 91
for valiant doings in their country's cause? 1.01.113
that in your country's service drew your swords, 1.01.175
and led my country's strength successfully, 1.01.194
too savage, doth root up | his country's peace. TIM 5.01.166
a foe to tyrants, and my country's friend. JC 5.04. 5
marcus brutus, i, | brutus, my country's friend; 5.04. 8
with both | he labor'd in his country's wrack, i MAC 1.03.114
here had we now our country's honor roof'd, 3.04. 39
is thine and my poor country's to command: 4.03.132
and with him pour we, in our country's purge, 5.02. 28
if thou art privy to thy country's fate, | which HAM 1.01.133
make | my country's high pyramides my gibbet, ANT 5.02. 61
that striking in our country's cause | fell CYM 5.04. 71
should step as 'twere up to my country's head STM III 7

COUNTRY/–WOMAN 1 FR 0.0001 REL FR 1 V 0 P
like something that — what country/–woman? PER 5.01.102

COUNTRY–WOMAN 1 FR 0.0001 REL FR 1 V 0 P
you are too bitter to your country–woman. TRO 4.01. 68

COUNT'S 8 FR 0.0009 REL FR 2 V 6 P
to what is count's man. AWW 2.03.194 P
count's master is of another style. 2.03.194 P
"dian, the count's a fool, and full of gold" — 4.03.211
for count of this, the count's a fool, i know it 4.03.229
the youth of the count's was to–day with my lady TN 2.03.132 P
more favors to the count's servingman than ever 3.02. 6 P
challenge me the count's youth to fight with him 3.02. 34 P
the count's gentleman, one cesario. 5.01.180 P

COUNTS* 7 FR 0.0008 REL FR 5 V 2 P
make her fair, that no man counts of her beauty. TGV 2.01. 60 P
to any count, to all counts: to what is man. AWW 2.03.193 P
mistress, | which he counts but a trifle. WT 5.01.224
there is a soul counts thee her creditor, | and JN 3.03. 21
counts it your weal he have his liberty. 4.02. 66
her father counts it dangerous | that she do ROM 4.01. 9
what counts harsh fortune casts upon my face, ANT 2.06. 54

/COUNTY 1 FR 0.0001 REL FR 0 V 1 P
of anjou and /the /county /of maine shall be 2H6 1.01. 58 P

COUNTY 26 FR 0.0029 REL FR 19 V 7 P
in the county of gloucester, justice of peace WIV 1.01. 5 P
next willow, about your own business, county. ADO 2.01.188 P
county claudio, when mean you to go to church? 2.01.355 P
then is there the county palentine. MV 1.02. 45 P
a ring the county wears, | that downward hath AWW 3.07. 22
a poor esquire of this county, and one of the 2H4 3.02. 58 P
duchy of anjou and the county of maine shall be 2H6 1.01. 51 P
collected choicely, from each county some, | and 3.01.313
be augmented | in every county as we go along. 3H6 5.03. 23
to every county | where this is question'd send H8 1.02. 98
county anselme and his beauteous sisters; ROM 1.02. 65 P
we follow thee. juliet, the county stays. 1.03.104
the county paris, at saint peter's church, 3.05.114
i think it best you married with the county. 3.05.217
on thursday next be married to this county. 4.01. 49
if, rather than to marry county paris, | thou 4.01. 71
send for the county, go tell him of this. 4.02. 23
let me see the county; 4.02. 29
i will walk myself | to county paris, to prepare 4.02. 45
the county will be here with music straight, 4.04. 22
the county paris hath set up his rest | that you 4.05. 6
ay, let the county take you in your bed, | he'll 4.05. 10
mercutio's kinsman, noble county paris! 5.03. 75
here lies the county slain, | and juliet 5.03.174
sovereign, here lies the county paris slain, 5.03.195
have married her perforce | to county paris. 5.03.239

/COUNTY'S 1 FR 0.0001 REL FR 1 V 0 P
same peevish messenger, | the /county's man. TN 1.05.301

COUNTY'S 1 FR 0.0001 REL FR 1 V 0 P
where is the county's page that rais'd the watch ROM 5.03.279

COUPER 1 FR 0.0001 REL FR 0 V 1 P
tout /a /cette /heure de couper votre gorge. H5 4.04. 36 P

COUPLE* 19 FR 0.0021 REL FR 13 V 6 P
bestow upon the eyes of this young couple | some TMP 4.01. 40
gods, | and on this couple drop a blessed crown! 5.01.202
in the basket, a couple of ford's knaves, his WIV 3.05. 97 P
ha' ta'en a couple of as arrant knaves as any in ADO 3.05. 31 P
begin these wood–birds but to couple now? MND 4.01.140
me in this place of the forest and to couple us. AYL 3.03. 45 P
and couple clowder with the deep–mouth'd brach. SHR in.1. 18
nay, let them go, a couple of quiet ones. 3.02.240
i lost a couple, that 'twixt heaven and earth WT 5.01.132
begetting wonder, as | you, gracious couple, do; 5.01.134
of this fair couple), meets he on the way | the 5.01.190
davy, a couple of short–legg'd hens, a joint of 2H4 5.01. 27 P
couple a gorge! H5 2.01. 71
truer, | than ever greek did couple in his arms, TRO 1.03.276
you a letter and a couple of pigeons here. TIT 4.04. 43 P
couple it with something, make it a word and a ROM 3.01. 39 P
and shall i couple hell? HAM 1.05. 93
couple then, | and see what's wanting. TNK 3.05. 32
will couple my reproach to tarquin's shame; LUC 816

COUPLED 7 FR 0.0008 REL FR 6 V 1 P
swans, | still we went coupled and inseparable. AYL 1.03. 76
for honesty coupled to beauty is to have honey a 3.03. 30 P
with slaughter coupled to the name of kings. JN 2.01.349
our inward souls | married in league, coupled, 3.01.228
tyranny, | coupled in bonds of perpetuity, | two 1H6 4.07. 20
and let your mind be coupled with your words. TRO 5.02. 15
discontents are unremovably | coupled to nature. TIM 5.01.225

COUPLEMENT 2 FR 0.0002 REL FR 1 V 1 P
you the peace of mind, most royal couplement. LLL 5.02.532 P
making a couplement of proud compare | with sun SON 21. 5

COUPLES 5 FR 0.0005 REL FR 4 V 1 P
he couples it to his complaining names. TGV 1.02.124
with us | these couples shall eternally be knit. MND 4.01.181
so shall all the couples three | ever true in 5.01.407
toward, and these couples are coming to the ark. AYL 5.04. 36 P
i'll go in couples with her; WT 2.01.135

COUPLET 1 FR 0.0001 REL FR 0 V 1 P
we'll whisper o'er a couplet or two of most sage TN 3.04.378 P

COUPLETS 1 FR 0.0001 REL FR 1 V 0 P
when that her golden couplets are disclosed, HAM 5.01.287

COUR 1 FR 0.0001 REL FR 0 V 1 P
/o, /je /m'en vois a la cour — la grande WIV 1.04. 52 P

COURAGE 78 FR 0.0088 REL FR 66 V 12 P
courage! MM 1.02.108 P
you have spoke, you have courage to maintain it. 3.02.157 P
what, courage, man! ADO 5.01.132 P
what, man, courage yet! MV 4.01.111
therefore courage, good aliena. AYL 2.04. 8 P
courage! 3.03. 51 P
wisdom, courage — all | that happiness and AWW 2.01.181
(courage and hope both teaching him the practice TN 1.02. 13
defense, | for courage mounteth with occasion. JN 2.01. 82
courage and comfort! all shall yet go well. 3.04. 4
away then with good courage! 5.01. 78
of manage to thy bounding steed, | cry "courage! 1H4 2.03. 50
though sometimes it show greatness, courage, 3.01.179
their courage with hard labor tame and dull, 4.03. 23
from the best–temper'd courage in his troops, 2H4 1.01.115
up with this retinue, doth any deed of courage; 4.03.112 P
the blood and courage that renowned them | runs H5 1.02.118
boy, bristle thy courage up; 2.03. 5
with men of courage and with means defendant; 2.04. 8
their mastiffs are of unmatchable courage. 3.07.141 P
the greater therefore should our courage be. 4.01. 2
he may show what outward courage he will; 4.01.113 P
and dout them with superfluous courage, ha! 4.02. 11
suppose | they had such courage and audacity? 1H6 1.02. 36
my courage try by combat, if thou dar'st, | and 1.02. 89
breast i'll burst with straining of my courage, 1.05. 10
and doth beget new courage in our breasts. 3.03. 87
valiant and virtuous, full of haughty courage, 4.01. 35
her valiant courage and undaunted spirit | (more 5.05. 70
king henry had resembled thee | in courage, 2H6 1.03. 54

ay, what else? fear you not her courage. 1.04. 5 P
hath given them heart and courage to proceed. 4.04. 35
to me, | and thrice cried, "courage, father! 3H6 1.04. 10
and this soft courage makes your followers faint 2.02. 57
this may plant courage in their quailing breasts 2.03. 54
which are so weak of courage and in judgment 4.01. 12
courage, my masters! 4.03. 24
strike up the drum, cry "courage!" 5.03. 24
which industry and courage might have sav'd? 5.04. 11
why, courage then! 5.04. 37
women and children of so high a courage, | and 5.04. 50
our ancient word of courage, fair saint george, R3 5.03.349
fled under shade, why then the thing of courage, TRO 1.03. 51
it, | nor once deject the courage of our minds, 2.02.121
whose present courage may beat down our foes, 2.02.201
as heart can think or courage execute. 4.01. 14
with starting courage, | give with thy trumpet a 4.05. 2
o, courage, courage, princes! 5.05. 30
o, courage, courage, princes! 5.05. 30
nor check my courage for what they can give, COR 3.03. 92
nay, mother, | where is your ancient courage? 4.01. 3
courage, man, the hurt cannot be much. ROM 3.01. 95
i'd such a courage to do him good. TIM 3.03. 24
fasten in our thoughts that they have courage; JC 5.01. 11
but screw your courage to the sticking place, MAC 1.07. 60
in that heart | courage to make 's love known? 2.03.118
devotion, patience, courage, fortitude, | i have 4.03. 94
of each new–hatch'd, unfledg'd courage. HAM 1.03. 65
than ever (i mean purpose, courage, and valor), OTH 4.02.214 P
myself to lack | the courage of a woman — less ANT 4.14. 60
with the courage which the heart did lend it, 5.01. 23
now to that name my courage prove my title! 5.02.288
winning will put any man into courage. CYM 2.03. 7 P
but found their courage | worthy his frowning at 2.04. 22
fires bright, | and britains strut with courage. 3.01. 33
woman it pretty self) into a waggish courage, 3.04.157
to, and will abide it with | a prince's courage. 3.04.184
other thought | but faithfulness and courage. PER 1.01. 63
amazement shall drive courage from the state, 1.02. 26
now, by the gods, i do applaud his courage. 2.05. 58
what courage, sir? god save you! 3.01. 38 P
courage enough. 3.01. 39
come, take courage, | you shall not die thus TNK 3.03. 5
mercy and manly courage | are bedfellows in his 5.03. 43
shows his hot courage and his high desire. VEN 276
in shape, in courage, color, pace, and bone. 294
and careless lust stirs up a desperate courage, 556
put fear to valor, courage to the coward. 1158

COURAGEOUS 12 FR 0.0013 REL FR 6 V 6 P
but truly he is very courageous mad about his WIV 4.01. 4 P
o most courageous day! MND 4.02. 27 P
well, the most courageous fiend bids me pack. MV 2.02. 10 P
ought to show itself courageous to petticoat; AYL 2.04. 7 P
well said, courageous feeble! 2H4 3.02.159 P
courageous bedford, let us now persuade you. 1H6 3.02. 93
in god's name cheerly on, courageous friends, R3 5.02. 14
courageous richmond, well hast thou acquit thee. 5.05. 3
o, he's the courageous captain of compliments. ROM 2.04. 20 P
thee, is | noble, courageous, high unmatchable, ANT 2.03. 21
lead, courageous cousin. TNK 5.04. 38
"courageous roman, do not steep thy heart | in LUC 1828

COURAGEOUSLY 3 FR 0.0003 REL FR 2 V 1 P
we may rehearse most obscenely and courageously.
MND 1.02.108 P
courageously, and with a free desire, R2 1.03.115
courageously to pluck him from his horse. VEN 30

COURAGES 1 FR 0.0001 REL FR 1 V 0 P
(now wing–led with their courages) will make CYM 2.04. 24

COURIER 1 FR 0.0001 REL FR 1 V 0 P
i met a courier, one mine ancient friend, | whom TIM 5.02. 6

COURIERS 1 FR 0.0001 REL FR 1 V 0 P
hors'd | upon the sightless couriers of the air, MAC 1.07. 23

COURONNE 1 FR 0.0001 REL FR 1 V 0 P
la fin couronne les /oeuvres. 2H6 5.02. 28

COURS'D 2 FR 0.0002 REL FR 2 V 0 P
cours'd one another down his innocent nose | in AYL 2.01. 39
we cours'd him at the heels, and had a purpose MAC 1.06. 21

/COURSE 1 FR 0.0001 REL FR 1 V 0 P
/the /end /meet /the /old /course /of /death, LR 3.07.101

COURSE 171 FR 0.0193 REL FR 154 V 17 P
prudence, who | should not upbraid our course. TMP 2.01.287
and perfected by the swift course of time. TGV 1.03. 23
but when his fair course is not hindered, | he 2.07. 27
then let me go, and hinder not my course: 2.07. 33
she did so course o'er my exteriors with such a WIV 1.03. 65 P
this being granted in course — and now follows MM 3.01.249 P
as dangerous to be ag'd in any kind of course, 3.02.225 P
you know the course is common. 4.02.177 P
not my holy order | if i pervert your course. 4.03.148
her brother, | cut off by course of justice — 5.01. 35
by course of justice! 5.01. 35
therefore homeward did they bend their course. ERR 1.01.117
what is the course and drift of your compact? 2.02.161
this course i fittest choose, | for forty ducats 4.03. 95
and given way unto this course of fortune, | by ADO 4.01.157
but not for that dream i on this strange course, 4.01.212
in the true course of all the question. 5.04. 6
therefore to 's seemeth it a needful course, LLL 2.01. 25
the course of true love never did run smooth; MND 1.01.134
the duke cannot deny the course of law; MV 3.03. 26
great pains to qualify | his rigorous course; 4.01. 8
that, in the course of justice, none of us 4.01.199
say thou wilt course, thy greyhounds are as SHR in.2. 47
a course of learning and ingenious studies. 1.01. 9
you must not marvel, helen, at my course, AWW 2.05. 58
that from the bloody course of war | my dearest 3.04. 8
and as in the common course of all treasons, we 4.03. 22 P
what e'er the course, the end is the renown. 4.04. 36
i could not answer in that course of honor | as 5.03. 98
as all impediments in fancy's course | are 5.03.214
behind, restraining | from course requir'd; WT 1.02.245
me | even so as i mine own course have set down. 1.02.340
unless he take the course that you have done — 2.03. 48
proceed in justice, which shall have due course, 3.02. 6
what course i mean to hold | shall nothing 4.04.502
a course more promising | than a wild dedication 4.04.565
full fourteen weeks before the course of time. JN 1.01.113
with course disturb'd even thy confining shores, 2.01.338
from all direction, purpose, course, intent — 2.01.580
stays in his course and plays the alchymist, 3.01. 78
the yearly course that brings this day about 3.01. 81
that takes away by any secret course | thy 3.01.178
it makes the course of thoughts to fetch about, 4.02. 24
leaving our rankness and irregular course, 5.04. 54
nor let my kingdom's rivers take their course 5.07. 38
of those seven are dried by nature's course, R2 1.02. 14
with slow but stately pace kept on his course, 5.02. 10
than i by letters shall direct your course. 1H4 1.03.293
the plot and the general course of the action. 2.03. 22 P
but | mark how he bears his course, and runs me 3.01.107
widow to so rough a course to come by her own? 2H4 2.01. 83 P
to the which course if i be enforc'd, if you do 4.03. 50 P
it, and makes it course from the inwards to the 4.03.106 P
read, | with every course in his particular. 4.04. 90
spoke and i had heard | the course of it so far. 4.05.142
in, | and found no course of breath within your 4.05.150
be it thy course to busy giddy minds | with 4.05.213
to trip the course of law and blunt the sword 5.02. 87
is an oath, and oaths must have their course. H5 2.01.101
majestical, | holding due course to harflew. 3.pr. 17
break out into a second course of mischief, 4.03.106
of time, of numbers, and due course of things, 5.pr. 4
and never changes, but keeps his course truly. 5.02.164 P
by starts the full course of their glory. ep 4
let me persuade you take a better course. 1H6 4.01.132
to cavil in the course of this contract. 5.04.156
'tis meet he be condemn'd by course of law. 2H6 3.01.237
for wise men say it is the wisest course. 3H6 3.01. 25
and, lords, towards coventry bend we our course, 4.08. 58
thus far our fortune keeps an upward course, 5.03. 1
that they do hold their course toward tewksbury. 5.03. 19
but keep our course (though the rough wind say 5.04. 22
thy father, minos, that denied our course; 5.06. 22
before i be convict by course of law, | to R3 1.04.187
he needs no indirect or lawless course | to cut 1.04.218
and may direct his course as please himself, 2.02.129
what an indirect and peevish course | is this of 3.01. 31
times | unto a lineal true–derived course. 3.07.200
thus hath the course of justice whirl'd about, 4.04.105
sail, and made his course again for britain. 4.04.527
that he would please to alter the king's course, H8 1.01.189
and is not this course pious? 2.02. 36
if, in the course | and process of this time, 2.04. 37
and did entreat your highness to this course 2.04.217
when he has run his course and sleeps in 3.02.398
teaching | and the strong course of my authority 5.02. 70
tortive and errant from his course of growth. TRO 1.03. 9
insisture, course, proportion, season, form, 1.03. 87
to take that course by your consent and voice, 5.03. 74
state, whose course will on | the way it takes, COR 1.01. 69
been too violent for | a second course of fight. 1.05. 16
the other course | will prove too bloody; 3.01.325
determine on some course | more than a wild 4.01. 35
a speedier course /than ling'ring languishment TIT 2.01.110
no, boy, not so, i'll teach thee another course. 4.01.119
who threats, in course of this revenge, to do 4.04. 67
but he that hath the steerage of my course ROM 1.04.112
uneven is the course, i like it not. 4.01. 5
aloof, | and do not interrupt me in my course. 5.03. 27
their course of love, the tidings of her death; 5.03.287
malice | infects one comma in the course i hold, TIM 1.01. 48
and this is all a liberal course allows: 3.03. 40
you must consider that a prodigal course | is 3.04. 12
confound them by some course, and come to me, 5.01.103
in antonio's way | when he doth run his course. JC 1.02. 4
will you go see the order of the course? 1.02. 25
our course will seem too bloody, caius cassius, 2.01.162
art afoot, | take thou what course thou wilt! 3.02.261
of hurt minds, great nature's second course, MAC 2.02. 36
fly, | but bear–like i must fight the course. 5.07. 2
had made his course t' illume that part of HAM 1.01. 37
in obstinate condolement is a course | of 1.02. 93
if 'a do blench, | i know my course. 2.02.598
but in our circumstance and course of thought 3.03. 83
and guildenstern hold their course for england, 4.06. 28 P
ourself, by monthly course, | with reservation LR 1.01.132
he'll shape his old course in a country new. 1.01.187
of his intent, you should run a certain course; 1.02. 82 P
straight to my sister | to hold my /very course. 1.03. 26
that you protect this course and put it on | by 1.04.208
this milky gentleness and course of yours 1.04.341
been inform'd | of my obscured course; 2.02.168
unremovable and fix'd he is | in his own course. 2.04. 94
bridges, to course his own shadow for a traitor. 3.04. 57 P
i will persever in my course of loyalty, though 3.05. 22 P
tied to th' stake, and i must stand the course. 3.07. 54
their punishment | might have the freer course. 4.02. 94
he is advis'd by aught | to change the course. 5.01. 3
fit time | of law and course of direct session OTH 1.02. 86
steering with due course toward the isle of 1.03. 34
and now they do restem | their backward course, 1.03. 38
tale deliver | of my whole course of love — 1.03. 91
or from what other course you please, which the 2.01.269 P
and indeed the course | to win the moor again? 2.03.338
to counsel cassio to this parallel course, 2.03.349
of my counsel | /in my whole course of wooing, 3.03.112
whose icy current and compulsive course | nev'r 3.03.454
world | the sun to course two hundred compasses, 3.04. 71
and shut myself up in some other course, | to 3.04.121
the lethargy must have his quiet course; 4.01. 53
we have done our course; 4.02. 93
i have myself resolv'd upon a course | which has ANT 3.11. 9
than was his loss, to course your flying flags, 3.13. 11
'tis your noblest course. 3.13. 78
stuck | a sun and moon, which kept their course, 5.02. 80
by taking | antony's course, you shall bereave 5.02.130
in the which | i have consider'd of a course. CYM 3.04.111
you should tread a course | pretty and full of 3.04.146
thou canst not, in the course of gratitude, but 3.05.119 P
you, leave me, | stick to your journal course: 4.02. 10
if each of you should take this course, how many 5.01. 3
will /'schew no course to keep them from the PER 1.01.136
he'll stop the course by which it might be known 1.02. 23
gentle mariner, | alter thy course for tyre. 3.01. 75
me | a more content in course of true delight 3.02. 39
and though you call my course unnatural, | you 4.03. 36
we must take another course with you! 4.06.121 P
up with a course or two, and tack about, boys! TNK 3.04. 10
till the hour prefix'd, and hold your course. 3.06.304
is't not a wise course? 4.01.127
and now direct your course to th' wood, where 4.01.144
and with his strong course opens them again. VEN 960
holding their course to paphos, where their 1193
who with a ling'ring stay his course doth let, LUC 328
but nothing can affection's course control, | or 500
make war against proportion'd course of time; 774
time, cease thou thy course and last no longer, 1765
by chance or nature's changing course untrimm'd:
SON 18. 8
him in thy course untainted do allow | for 19.11
strong minds to th' course of alt'ring things: 115. 8
what bounds, what course, what stop he makes!' LC 109

COURSER 5 FR 0.0005 REL FR 4 V 1 P
imitate that which i compos'd to my courser, for H5 3.07. 44 P
good words the other day of a bay courser | i TIM 1.02.211
thy value i will mount myself | upon a courser, PER 2.01.158
proud, | adonis' trampling courser doth espy; VEN 261
"let me excuse thy courser, gentle boy, | and 403

COURSER'S 3 FR 0.0003 REL FR 3 V 0 P
that they may break his foaming courser's back, R2 1.02. 51
which, like the courser's hair, hath yet but ANT 1.02.193
over one arm the lusty courser's rein, | under VEN 31

/COURSERS 1 FR 0.0001 REL FR 1 V 0 P
/their /neighing /coursers /daring /of /the 2H4 4.01.117

COURSERS 2 FR 0.0002 REL FR 1 V 1 P
ne'er spurr'd their coursers at the trumpet's 3H6 5.07. 9
you'll have coursers for cousins, and gennets OTH 1.01.113 P

COURSES 19 FR 0.0021 REL FR 17 V 2 P
set her two courses off to sea again! TMP 1.01. 49 P
him continue in his courses till thou know'st MM 2.01.187 P
courses as swift as thought in every power, LLL 4.03.327
but by bad courses may be understood | that R2 2.01.213
and all the courses of my life do show | i am 1H4 3.01. 41
each heart being set | on bloody courses, the 2H4 1.01.159
steers unyok'd, they take their courses | east, 4.02.103
the courses of his youth promis'd it not. H5 1.01. 24
it, | since his addiction was to courses vain, 1.01. 54
after | so many courses of the sun enthroned, H8 2.03. 6
follow your envious courses, men of malice! 3.02.243
glory, | a thousand complete courses of the sun! TRO 4.01. 28
that swift as quicksilver it courses through HAM 1.05. 66
did you by indirect and forced courses | subdue OTH 1.03.111
and his own courses will denote him so | that i 4.01.279
we have taken | no care to your best courses. PER 4.01. 38
he did not flow | from honorable courses. 4.03. 28
and bear his courses to be ordered | by lady 4.04. 47
even of five hundreth courses of the sun, | show SON 59. 6

COURSING 2 FR 0.0002 REL FR 1 V 1 P
i am coursing myself. LLL 4.03. 1 P
we do not mean the coursing snatchers only, H5 1.02.143

/COURT 2 FR 0.0002 REL FR 1 V 1 P
/shall /we /to /th' /court? HAM 2.02.265 P
/i'll /court /his /favors. 5.02. 78

COURT 248 FR 0.0280 REL FR 176 V 72 P
whose influence | if now i court not, but omit, TMP 1.02.183
this cell's my court. 5.01.166
attends the emperor in his royal court. TGV 1.03. 27
i will dispatch him to the emperor's court. 1.03. 38
time | with valentinus in the emperor's court; 1.03. 67
going with sir proteus to the imperial's court. 2.03. 5 P
forbid | sir valentine her company and my court; 3.01. 27
my health and happy being at your court. 3.01. 57
tutor | (for long agone i have forgot to court; 3.01. 85
will give thee time to leave our royal court, 3.01.165
rapier, and come after my heel to the court. WIV 1.04. 60 P
rugby, come to the court with me. 1.04.123 P
of them all (when the court lay at windsor) 2.02. 62 P
let the court of france show me such another. 3.03. 54 P
the duke himself will be to–morrow at court, and 4.03. 3 P
i hear not of him in the court. 4.03. 5 P
well money'd, and his friends | potent at court. 4.04. 89
dere is no duke that the court is know to come. 4.05. 88 P
if it should come to the ear of the court, how i 4.05. 95 P
the orchard and saw me court margaret in hero's ADO 5.01.238 P
our court shall be a little academe, | still and LLL 1.01. 13
and stay here in your court for three years' 1.01. 52
woman shall come within a mile of my court" — 1.01.120 P
as the rest of the court can possible devise." 1.01.131 P
our court you know is haunted | with a refined 1.01.162
years, | no woman may approach his silent court; 2.01. 24
like one that comes here to besiege his court, 2.01. 86
fair princess, welcome to the court of navarre. 2.01. 90
the roof of this court is too high to be yours, 2.01. 92 P
you shall be welcome, madam, to my court. 2.01. 95
did make their retire | to the court of his eye, 2.01.235
armado is a spaniard that keeps here in court, 4.01. 98
their purpose is to parley, to court, and dance, 5.02.122
and then the king will court thee for his dear. 5.02.131
you, and purpose now | to lead you to our court; 5.02.344
will come into the court and swear that i have a MV 1.02. 71 P
go one, and call the jew into the court. 4.01. 14
upon my power i may dismiss this court, | unless 4.01.104
a young and learned doctor to our court. 4.01.144
mean time the court shall hear bellario's letter 4.01.149
that holds this present question in the court? 4.01.172
this strict court of venice | must needs give 4.01.204
yes, here i tender it for him in the court, 4.01.209
most heartily i do beseech the court | to give 4.01.243
the court awards it, and the law doth give it. 4.01.300
the law allows it, and the court awards it. 4.01.303
he hath refus'd it in the open court; 4.01.338
so please my lord the duke and all the court 4.01.380
here in the court, of all he dies possess'd 4.01.389
charles, what's the new news at the new court? AYL 1.01. 97 P
there's no news at the court, sir, but the old 1.01. 98 P
she is at the court, and no less belov'd of her 1.01.110 P
your safest haste, | and get you from our court. 1.03. 42
so near our public court as twenty miles, | thou 1.03. 44
the clownish fool out of your father's court? 1.03.130
more free from peril than the envious court? 2.01. 4
through | the body of /the country, city, court, 2.01. 59
some villains of my court | are of consent and 2.02. 2
but in respect it is not in the court, it is 3.02. 18 P
wast ever in court, shepherd? 3.02. 33 P

for not being at court? your reason. 3.02. 39 P
if thou never wast at court, thou never saw'st 3.02. 40 P
good manners at the court are as ridiculous in 3.02. 46 P
of the country is most mockable at the court. 3.02. 48 P
me you salute not at the court but you kiss your 3.02. 49 P
and thrown into neglect the pompous court? 5.04.182
shall you have to court her at your pleasure. SHR 1.01. 54
to her, | and unsuspected court her by herself. 1.02.137
now, for my life, the knave doth court my love: 3.01. 49
see how they kiss and court! 4.02. 27
see how beastly she doth court him! 4.02. 34
remember thee, i will think of thee at court. AWW 1.01.189 P
my loving greetings | to those of mine in court. 1.03.253
i know my business is but to the court. 2.02. 4 P
to the court! 2.02. 5 P
but to the court! 2.02. 7 P
any manners, he may easily put it off at court. 2.02. 9 P
to say precisely, were not for the court; 2.02. 13 P
go call before me all the lords in court. 2.03. 46
i have no mind to isbel since i was at court. 3.02. 12 P
like your old ling and your isbels a' th' court. 3.02. 14 P
and, after some dispatch in hand at court, 3.02. 54
it i | that drive thee from the sportive court, 3.02.106
let his nobility remain in 's court. 4.05. 50 P
sir, i have seen you in the court of france. 5.01. 10
the last that e'er i took her leave at court, 5.03. 79
you saw one here in court could witness it. 5.03.200
i am bound to the count orsino's court. TN 2.01. 43 P
i have many enemies in orsino's court, | else 2.01. 45
i must | forsake the court. WT 1.02.362
what is the news i' th' court? 1.02.367
lady, | no court in europe is too good for thee, 2.02. 3
are both landed, | hasting to th' court. 2.03.197
that the queen | appear in person here in court. 3.02. 10
before polixenes | came to your court, how i was 3.02. 47
and why he left your court, the gods themselves 3.02. 75
much retir'd from court and is less frequent to 4.02. 32 P
but he was certainly whipt out of the court. 4.03. 90 P
there's no virtue whipt out of the court. 4.03. 92 P
follow us to the court. 4.04.432
the self–same sun that shines upon his court 4.04.444
not the air of the court in these enfoldings? 4.04.731 P
hath not my gait in it the measure of the court? 4.04.732 P
to your court | whiles he was hast'ning (in the 5.01.188
are they return'd to the court? 5.02. 93 P
how found | thy father's court? 5.03.125
what brings you here to court so hastily? JN 1.01.221
when i shall meet him in the court of heaven | i 3.04. 87
with too great a court | and liberal largess, R2 1.04. 43
no, my good lord, he hath forsook the court, 2.03. 26
temples of a king | keeps death his court, and 3.02.162
in the base court he doth attend | to speak with 3.03.176
in the base court? 3.03.180
base court, where kings grow base, | to come at 3.03.180
in the base court, come down? 3.03.182
down court! 3.03.182
that reacheth from the restful english court 4.01. 12
with my humor as well as waiting in the court, i 1H4 1.02. 70 P
is a nobleman of the court at door would speak 2.04.288 P
you must to the court in the morning. 2.04.335 P
i'll to the court in the morning. 2.04.543 P
for i was train'd up in the english court, 3.01.120
of all the court and princes of my blood; 3.02. 35
hal, to the news at court for the robbery, lad, 3.03.175 P
in rage dismiss'd my father from the court, 4.03.100
"when arthur first in court" — empty the jordan 2H4 2.04. 33 P
you must away to court, sir, presently, | a 2.04.371
'a must then to the inns a' court shortly. 3.02. 13 P
swingebucklers in all the inns a' court again; 3.02. 22 P
peradventure i will with ye to the court. 3.02.295 P
a treble hoboy was a mansion for him, a court, 3.02.327 P
hath been with scorn shov'd from the court, 4.02. 37
and now dispatch we toward the court, my lords, 4.03. 76
and, when you come to court, stand my good lord 4.03. 82 P
and to the english court assemble now, | from 4.05.121
a friend i' th' court is better than a penny in 5.01. 31 P
this is the english, not the turkish court, 5.02. 47
now call we our high court of parliament, | and 5.02.134
one pistol come from the court with news. 5.03. 81 P
from the court? 5.03. 82 P
you come with news from the court, i take it 5.03.110 P
were it the mistress court of mighty europe; H5 2.04.133
let us have knowledge at the court of guard. 1H6 2.01. 4
a gentler heart did never sway in court; 3.02.135
this shouldering of each other in the court, 4.01.189
this staff, mine office–badge in court, | was 2H6 1.02. 25
is this the fashions in the court of england? 1.03. 43
she sweeps it through the court with troops of 1.03. 77
strangers in court do take her for the queen. 1.03. 79
for purposely therefore | left i the court, to 2.03. 53
that all the court admir'd him for submission; 3.01. 12
swear | to spoil the city and your royal court. 4.04. 53
others to th' inns of court; 4.07. 2 P
that must sweep the court clean of such filth as 4.07. 31 P
who would live turmoiled in the court | and may 4.10. 16
or dare to bring thy force so near the court. 5.01. 22
london, | to call a present court of parliament. 5.03. 25
and i with grief and sorrow to the court. 3H6 1.01.210
such as befits the pleasure of the court? 5.07. 44
nor made to court an amorous looking–glass; R3 1.01. 15
that's clapp'd upon the court gate. H8 1.03. 18
that fill the court with quarrels, talk, and 1.03. 20
employment, | and far enough from court too. 2.01. 49
the court of rome commanding, you, my lord 2.02.104
i have been begging sixteen years in court | (am 2.03. 82
say, henry king of england, come into the court. 2.04. 7 P
katherine queen of england, come into the court. 2.04. 11 P
bootless | that longer you desire the court, as 2.04. 62
katherine queen of england, come into the court. 2.04.127 P
i left no reverend person in this court; 2.04.221
that we adjourn this court till further day. 2.04.233
break up the court! 2.04.241
farewell | the hopes of court! 3.02.459
held a late court at dunstable — six miles off 4.01. 27
which | is to th' court, and there ye shall be 4.01.115
do you take the court for parish garden? 5.03. 2 P
indian with the great tool come to court, the 5.03. 35 P
even to the court, the heart, to th' seat o' th' COR 1.01.136
if the emperor's court can feast two brides, TIT 1.01.489
more | be so dishonored in the court of rome. 2.01. 52
why should he despair that knows to court it, 2.01. 91
the emperor's court is like the house of fame, 2.01.126
that all the court may echo with the noise. 2.02. 6
lucius and i'll go brave it at the court. 4.01.121
to calm this tempest whirling in the court; 4.02.160
kinsmen, shoot all your shafts into the court, 4.03. 62
down fell both the ram's horns in the court, 4.03. 73
and in the emperor's court | there is a queen, 5.02.104
is banquo gone from court? MAC 3.02. 1
note of expectation | already are i' th' court. 3.03. 11
lives in the english court, and is receiv'd | of 3.06. 26
some holy angel | fly to the court of england, 3.06. 46
though lewdness court it in a shape of heaven, HAM 1.05. 54
that you voutsafe your rest here in our court 2.02. 13
they are here about the court, | and, as i think 3.01. 19
here is newly come to court laertes, believe me, 5.02.106 P
long in our court have made their amorous LR 1.01. 47
that this our court, infected with their manners 1.04.243
court holy–water in a dry house is better than 3.02. 10 P
and hear poor rogues | talk of court news; 5.03. 14
to–night watches on the court of guard. OTH 2.01.218 P
in night, and on the court and guard of safety? 2.03.216
if i court moe women, you'll couch with moe men. 4.03. 57
hour, | we must return to th' court of guard. ANT 4.09. 2
let us bear him | to th' court of guard; 4.09. 31
will not wait pinion'd at your master's court, 5.02. 53
liv'd in court | (which rare it is to do) most CYM 1.01. 46
if after this command thou fraught the court 1.01.126
and bless the good remainders of the court! 1.01.129
commend me to the court where your lady is, with 1.04.128 P
a saucy stranger in his court to mart | as in a 1.06.151
us, he hath a court | he little cares for and a 1.06.153
take my pow'r i' th' court for yours. 1.06.179
of a stranger that's come to court /to–night? 2.01. 33 P
with scraps o' th' court, it is no contract, 2.03.115
was caius lucius in the britain court | when you 2.04. 37
i will go there and do't, i' th' court, before 2.04.148
the art o' th' court, | as hard to leave as keep 3.03. 46
the perturb'd court | for my being absent? 3.04.105
you shall be miss'd at court, | and that will 3.04.126
if you'll back to th' court — 3.04.130
no court, no father, nor no more ado | with that 3.04.131
if not at court, | then not in britain must you 3.04.134
be suspected of | your carriage from the court. 3.04.187
but our great court | made me to blame in memory 3.05. 50
to the court i'll knock her back, foot her home 3.05.143 P
that had a court no bigger than this cave, 3.06. 82
our courtiers say all's savage but at court. 4.02. 33
it may be heard at court that such as we | cave 4.02.137
like romans, | and not o' th' court of britain. 5.05. 25
remember me at court, where i was taught | of 5.05.193
why fled you from the court? 5.05.387
here pleasures court mine eyes, and mine eyes PER 1.02. 6
so this is tyre, and this the court. 1.03. 1 P
how far is his court distant from this shore? 2.01.106 P
that you'd guide me to your sovereign's court, 2.01.140
and i'll bring thee to the court myself. 2.01.164 P
as if the entertainment in our court | had not a 2.03. 55
i came unto your court for honor's cause, | and 2.05. 61
to th' court of king simonides | are letters 3.ch. 23
let's leave his court, that we may nothing share TNK 1.02. 75
so soon as the court hurry is over, we will have 2.01. 18 P
i find the court here, | i am sure, a more 2.02. 99
what had we been, old in the court of creon, 2.02.105
for only in thy court, of all the world, 2.05. 28
did court the lad with many a lovely look, PP 4. 3
a blusterer that the ruffle knew | of court, of LC 59
which late her noble suit in court did shun, 234

COURT–CONTEMPT 1 FR 0.0001 REL FR 0 V 1 P
reflect i not on thy baseness court–contempt? WT 4.04.734 P

COURT–CUPBOARD 1 FR 0.0001 REL FR 0 V 1 P
with the join–stools, remove the court–cupboard, ROM 1.05. 7 P

COURTED 1 FR 0.0001 REL FR 0 V 1 P
i am courted now with a double occasion — gold WT 4.04.833 P

COURTEOUS 22 FR 0.0024 REL FR 16 V 6 P
be kind and courteous to this gentleman. MND 3.01.164
thanks, courteous wall; 5.01.178
to wit (besides commends and courteous breath), MV 2.09. 90
go give him courteous conduct to this place. 4.01.148
we freely cope your courteous pains withal. 4.01.412
this is call'd the retort courteous. AYL 5.04. 72 P
the first, the retort courteous; 5.04. 92 P
minola, | an affable and courteous gentleman. SHR 1.02. 98
thou art pleasant, gamesome, passing courteous, 2.01.245
delicate fine hats, and most courteous feathers, AWW 4.05.105 P
i beseech you do me this courteous office, as to TN 3.04.254 P
witty, courteous, liberal, full of spirit. 3H6 1.02. 43
my courteous lord, adieu. TRO 5.02.185
having been supple and courteous to the people, COR 2.02. 26 P
a most courteous exposition. ROM 2.04. 56 P
an' a courteous, and a kind, and a handsome, 2.05. 56
o courteous tybalt, honest gentleman, | that 3.02. 62
courteous destroyers, affable wolves, meek bears TIM 3.06. 95
look with what courteous action | it waves you HAM 1.04. 60
courteous lord, one word: ANT 1.03. 86
our courteous antony, | whom ne'er the word of 2.02.222
you are right courteous knights. PER 2.03. 27

COURTEOUSLY 1 FR 0.0001 REL FR 1 V 0 P
grecian, thou dost not use me courteously, | to TRO 4.04.121

COURTESIES 9 FR 0.0010 REL FR 7 V 2 P
that outward courtesies would fain proclaim MM 5.01. 15
my lord, for your many courtesies i thank you. ADO 5.01.189 P
nod to him, elves, and do him courtesies. MND 3.01.174
and for these courtesies | i'll lend you thus MV 1.03.128
and unwearied spirit | in doing courtesies, and 3.02.294
not so, but as we change our courtesies. AWW 3.02. 97
these couchings and these lowly courtesies JC 3.01. 36
for he hath laid strange courtesies and great ANT 2.02.154
when i have been debtor to you for courtesies, CYM 1.04. 37 P

COURTESY *(also court'sy)*

/COURTESY 3 FR 0.0003 REL FR 2 V 1 P
/the /mayor /in /courtesy /show'd /me /the R3 4.02.104
/as /they /contend /with /thee /in /courtesy. TRO 4.05.206
/an excellent /courtesy! OTH 2.01.175 P

COURTESY 64 FR 0.0072 REL FR 45 V 19 P
but if thou scorn our courtesy, thou diest. TGV 4.01. 66
do me both a present and a dangerous courtesy. MM 4.02.162 P
courtesy itself must convert to disdain, if you ADO 1.01.122 P
then is courtesy a turncoat. 1.01.124 P
i do beseech thee remember thy courtesy; LLL 5.01. 98 P
is he | that kiss'd his hand away in courtesy; 5.02.324
days) | in courtesy gives undeserving praise. 5.02.366
forbid the smiling courtesy of love | the holy 5.02.745
at courtship, pleasant jest, and courtesy, | as 5.02.780
these ladies' courtesy | might well have made 5.02.875
friend, for love and courtesy | lie further off, MND 2.02. 56
if you were civil and knew courtesy, | you would 3.02.147
but yet in courtesy, in all reason, we must stay 5.01.254 P
never train'd | to offices of tender courtesy. MV 4.01. 33
therefore i scant this breathing courtesy. 5.01.141
him, | i was beset with shame and courtesy, | my 5.01.217
the courtesy of nations allows you my better, in AYL 1.01. 46 P
that courtesy would be uncleanly if courtiers 3.02. 50 P
do, | with soft low tongue and lowly courtesy, SHR in.1. 114
well, sir, to do you courtesy, | this will i do, 4.02. 91
and your courtesy, for a ring–carrier! AWW 3.05. 92 P
deliver, when the courtesy of it is so fearful. TN 1.05.207 P
that will use the devil himself with courtesy. 4.02. 33 P
hearts | with humble and familiar courtesy, R2 1.04. 26
love | than my unpleased eye see your courtesy. 3.03.193
what a candy deal of courtesy | this fawning 1H4 1.03.251
yet i am the king of courtesy, and tell me 2.04. 11 P
and then i stole all courtesy from heaven, | and 3.02. 50
arm | that he shall shrink under my courtesy. 5.02. 74
never shall | a second time do such a courtesy. 5.02.100
if thou wert sensible of courtesy, | i should 5.04. 94
i thank your grace for this high courtesy, 5.05. 32
it was more of his courtesy than your deserving. 2H4 4.03. 43 P
remedy) | i mean to prove this lady's courtesy. 1H6 2.02. 58
and then i need not crave his courtesy. 5.03.105
cog, | duck with french nods and apish courtesy, R3 1.03. 49
buckingham, | the mirror of all courtesy — H8 2.01. 53
the elephant hath joints, but none for courtesy; TRO 2.03.105 P
and that which looks like pride is courtesy. 4.05. 82
i do disdain thy courtesy, proud troyan. 5.06. 15
bosom multiplied digest | the senate's courtesy? COR 3.01.132
thy life | show'd thy dear mother any courtesy, 5.03.161
warrants these words in princely courtesy. TIT 1.01.272
such a case as mine a man may strain courtesy. ROM 2.04. 51 P
nay, i am the very pink of courtesy. 2.04. 57 P
he is not the flower of courtesy, but, i'll 2.05. 43 P
these sweet knaves, | and all this courtesy! TIM 1.01.250
i thank you for your pains and courtesy. JC 2.02.115
with courtesy and with respect enough, | but not 4.02. 15
lord, this courtesy is not of the right breed. HAM 3.02.314 P
effects of courtesy, dues of gratitude: LR 2.04.179
in) return, and force | their scanted courtesy. 3.02. 67
this courtesy, forbid thee, shall the duke 3.03. 21
they do discharge their shot of courtesy; OTH 2.01. 56
that gives me this bold show of courtesy. 2.01. 99
yes, that i did; but that was but courtesy. 2.01.256 P
i could well wish courtesy would invent some 2.03. 35 P
the queen shall then have courtesy, so she ANT 3.13. 15
o | dissembling courtesy! CYM 1.01. 84
to have the courtesy your cradle promis'd, | but 4.04. 28
how courtesy would seem to cover sin, | when PER 1.01.121
with such a graceful courtesy delivered? 2.02. 41
as you would be denied | of your fair courtesy. 2.03.106
o sir, a courtesy | which if we should deny, the 5.01. 58

COURTEZAN 3 FR 0.0003 REL FR 2 V 1 P
scoff on, vile fiend and shameless courtezan! 1H6 3.02. 45
this is a brave night to cool a courtezan. LR 3.02. 79 P
some roman courtezan? CYM 3.04.123

COURTEZANS 2 FR 0.0002 REL FR 2 V 0 P
and purchase friends and give to courtezans, 2H6 1.01.223
not dallying with a brace of courtezans, | but R3 3.07. 74

COURT–GATE 1 FR 0.0001 REL FR 0 V 1 P
see him break scoggin's head at the court–gate, 2H4 3.02. 30 P

COURT–HAND 1 FR 0.0001 REL FR 0 V 1 P
he can make obligations, and write court–hand. 2H6 4.02. 94 P

COURTIER 27 FR 0.0030 REL FR 8 V 19 P
the best courtier of them all (when the court WIV 2.02. 61 P
flattering boy, now i see you'll be a courtier. 3.02. 8 P
thou wouldst make an absolute courtier, and the 3.03. 62 P
him to any french courtier for a new devis'd LLL 1.02. 62 P
one that hath been a courtier, | and says, if AYL 2.07. 36
he hath been a courtier, he swears. 5.04. 42 P
my lord, | 'tis an unseason'd courtier; AWW 1.01. 71
virginity, like an old courtier, wears her cap 1.01.156 P
i will return perfect courtier, in the which my 1.01.207 P
so like a courtier, contempt nor bitterness 1.02. 36
ask me if i am a courtier: 2.02. 36 P
i pray you, sir, are you a courtier? 2.02. 40 P
that youth's a rare courtier — "rain odors," TN 3.01. 86 P
are you a courtier, and't like you, sir? WT 4.04.729 P
whether it like me or no, i am a courtier. 4.04.730 P
thee thy business, i am therefore no courtier? 4.04.736 P
i am courtier cap–a–pe, and one that will either 4.04.736 P
this cannot be but a great courtier. 4.04.748 P
to think an english courtier may be wise | and H8 1.03. 22
years in court | (am yet a courtier beggarly) 2.03. 83
thou'dst courtier be again, | wert thou not TIM 4.03.241
our chiefest courtier, cousin, and our son. HAM 1.02.117
or of a courtier, which could say, "good morrow, 5.01. 82 P
peasant comes so near the heel of the courtier, 5.01.141 P
but not a courtier, | although they wear their CYM 1.01. 12
a (that way) accomplish'd courtier, would hazard 1.04. 92 P
so accomplish'd a courtier to convince the honor 1.04. 95 P

COURTIER'S 7 FR 0.0008 REL FR 2 V 5 P
why, do not your courtier's hands sweat? AYL 3.02. 55 P
the courtier's hands are perfum'd with civet. 3.02. 64 P
nor the courtier's, which is proud; 4.01. 12 P
dislike the cut of a certain courtier's beard. 5.04. 70 P
thou wilt be capable of a courtier's counsel and AWW 1.01.209 P
sometime she gallops o'er a courtier's nose, ROM 1.04. 77
the courtier's, soldier's, scholar's, eye, HAM 3.01.151

COURTIERS' 2 FR 0.0002 REL FR 2 V 0 P
/o'er courtiers' knees, that dream on cur'sies ROM 1.04. 72
no more obey the heavens than our courtiers' CYM 1.01. 2

COURTIERS 9 FR 0.0010 REL FR 7 V 2 P
would be uncleanly if courtiers were shepherds. AYL 3.02. 50 P
all scholars, lawyers, courtiers, gentlemen, 2H6 4.04. 36
or the men of troy | are ceremonious courtiers. TRO 1.03.234
courtiers as free, as debonair, unarm'd, | as 1.03.235

here comes the king, | the queen, the courtiers. HAM 5.01.218
the arm'd rest, courtiers of beauteous freedom, ANT 2.06. 17
our courtiers say all's savage but at court. CYM 4.02. 33
so follow, to be most unlike our courtiers, | as 5.04.136
lords and courtiers that have got maids with TNK 4.03. 41 P
COURT–LIKE 1 FR 0.0001 REL FR 0 V 1 P
allow'd for your many war–like, court–like, and WIV 2.02.228 P
COURTLY 7 FR 0.0008 REL FR 5 V 2 P
you have too courtly a wit for me, i'll rest. AYL 3.02. 70 P
sent him forth | from courtly friends, with AWW 3.04. 14
in courtly company, or at my beads, | with you, 2H6 1.01. 27
i am too courtly and thou too cunning. TRO 3.01. 28 P
and very courtly counsel. 4.05. 22
to promise is most courtly and fashionable; TIM 5.01. 27
that she hath all courtly parts more exquisite CYM 3.05. 71
COURTNEY 1 FR 0.0001 REL FR 1 V 0 P
sir edward courtney and the haughty prelate, R3 4.04.500
COURT–ODOR 1 FR 0.0001 REL FR 0 V 1 P
receives not thy nose court–odor from me? WT 4.04.733 P
COURT'S 1 FR 0.0001 REL FR 1 V 0 P
the court's a learning place, and he is one — AWW 1.01.177
COURTS 9 FR 0.0010 REL FR 9 V 0 P
the injury of tongues in courts and kingdoms WT 1.02.338
that all the courts of france will be disturb'd H5 1.02.265
as princes do their courts, when they are cloy'd 1H6 2.05.105
and princes' courts be fill'd with my reproach. 2H6 3.02. 69
my appearance make | in any of their courts. H8 2.04.134
let courts and cities be | made all of COR 1.09. 43
back, | happiness courts thee in her best array, ROM 3.03.142
revolve what tales i have told you | of courts, CYM 3.03. 15
for when the west wind courts her gently, | how TNK 2.02.138
COURTSHIP 8 FR 0.0009 REL FR 6 V 2 P
trim gallants, full of courtship and of state. LLL 5.02.363
in our maiden council rated them | at courtship, 5.02.780
employ your chiefest thoughts | to courtship, MV 2.08. 44
an inland man, one that knew courtship too well, AYL 3.02.346 P
observ'd his courtship to the common people, R2 1.04. 24
had resembled thee | in courage, courtship, and 2H6 1.03. 54
more courtship lives | in carrion flies than ROM 3.03. 34
i will gyve thee in thine own courtship. OTH 2.01.170 P
COURT'SY *(also courtesy)*
COURT'SY 3 FR 0.0003 REL FR 3 V 0 P
if this be court'sy, sir, accept of it. SHR 4.02.112
our power | shall do a court'sy to our wrath, LR 3.07. 26
they all strain court'sy who shall cope him VEN 888
COURT–WORD 1 FR 0.0001 REL FR 0 V 1 P
advocate's the court–word for a pheasant. WT 4.04.742 P
/COUSIN 5 FR 0.0005 REL FR 5 V 0 P
/here, /cousin, /seize /the /crown; R2 4.01.181
/here, /cousin, | /on /this /side /my /hand, 4.01.182
/name /it, /fair /cousin. 4.01.304
"/fair /cousin"? 4.01.305
farewell, my /cousin, farewell, gentle friends. R3 3.07.247
COUSIN 305 FR 0.0344 REL FR 230 V 75 P
ay, cousin slender, and custa–lorum. WIV 1.01. 7 P
where's simple, my man? can you tell, cousin? 1.01.135 P
nay, i will do as my cousin shallow says. 1.01.217 P
cousin abraham slender, can you love her? 1.01.232 P
that, upon your request, cousin, in any reason. 1.01.241 P
ay — i think my cousin meant well. 1.01.257 P
you are my man, go wait upon my cousin shallow. 1.01.272 P
a match between anne page and my cousin slender, 3.02. 58 P
mistress anne, my cousin loves you. 3.04. 42 P
some one with child by him? my cousin juliet? MM 1.04. 45
is she your cousin? 1.04. 46
my very worthy cousin, fairly met! 5.01. 1
come, cousin angelo, | in this i'll be impartial 5.01.165
you, lord escalus, | sit with my cousin; 5.01.246
and you, my noble and well–warranted cousin, 5.01.254
my cousin means signior benedick of padua. ADO 1.01. 35 P
there's her cousin, and she were not possess'd 1.01.190 P
how now, brother, where is my cousin, your son? 1.02. 1 P
good cousin, have a care this busy time. 1.02. 27 P
but yet for all that, cousin, let him be a 2.01. 54 P
the fault will be in the music, cousin, if you 2.01. 69 P
cousin, you apprehend passing shrewdly. 2.01. 81 P
speak, cousin, or, if you cannot, stop his mouth 2.01.310 P
my cousin tells him in his ear that he is in her 2.01.315 P
and so she doth, cousin. 2.01.317 P
my lord, to help my cousin to a good husband. 2.01.376 P
i will teach you how to humor your cousin, that 2.01.381 P
there shalt thou find my cousin beatrice 3.01. 2
some honest slanders | to stain my cousin with. 3.01. 85
o, do not do your cousin such a wrong. 3.01. 87
good ursula, wake my cousin beatrice, and desire 3.04. 1 P
so good, and i warrant your cousin will say so. 3.04. 10 P
'tis almost five a' clock, cousin, 'tis time you 3.04. 52 P
i am stuff'd, cousin, i cannot smell. 3.04. 64 P
why, how now, cousin, wherefore sink you down? 4.01.110
how now, cousin hero? 4.01.117
o, on my soul, my cousin is belied! 4.01.146
surely i do believe your fair cousin is wrong'd. 4.01.259 P
i am sorry for my cousin. 4.01.273 P
go comfort your cousin. 4.01.335 P
her the right you should have giv'n her cousin, 5.01.291
and now tell me, how doth your cousin? 5.02. 89 P
why then my cousin, margaret, and ursula | are 5.04. 78
come, cousin, i am sure you love the gentleman. 5.04. 84
my kinsman, live unbruis'd and love my cousin. 5.04.111 P
if my cousin do not look exceeding narrowly to 5.04.115 P
for the duke's daughter, her cousin, so loves AYL 1.01.107 P
shall we see this wrastling, cousin? 1.02.143 P
how now, daughter and cousin? 1.02.155 P
gentle cousin, | let us go thank him, and 1.02.239
why, cousin, why, rosalind! 1.03. 1 P
they are but burs, cousin, thrown upon thee in 1.03. 13 P
you, cousin. 1.03. 42
thou hast not, cousin, | prithee be cheerful. 1.03. 93
but, cousin, what if we assay'd to steal | the 1.03.129
your daughter and her cousin much commend | the 2.02. 12
give us some music, and, good cousin, sing. 2.07.173
there is more in it. cousin ganymed! 4.03.159
and bid my cousin ferdinand come hither; SHR 4.01.151
a certainty, vouch'd from our cousin austria, AWW 1.02. 5
therefore we marvel much our cousin france 3.01. 7
your cousin, my lady, takes great exceptions to TN 1.03. 5 P
what is he at the gate, cousin? 1.05.117 P
cousin, cousin, how have you come so early by 1.05.123 P

cousin, cousin, how have you come so early by 1.05.123 P
saying, "cousin toby, my fortunes, having cast 2.05. 69 P
where's my cousin toby? 3.04. 61 P
and given your drunken cousin rule over me, yet 5.01.304 P
cousin, go draw our puissance together. JN 3.01.339
cousin, look not sad, | thy grandame loves thee, 3.03. 2
cousin, away for england! 3.03. 6
farewell, gentle cousin. 3.03. 17
for england, cousin, go. 3.03. 71
bear with me, cousin, for i was amaz'd | under 4.02.137
o my gentle cousin, | hear'st thou the news 4.02.159
o cousin, thou art come to set mine eye. 5.07. 51
cousin of herford, what dost thou object R2 1.01. 28
what doth our cousin lay to mowbray's charge? 1.01. 84
cousin, throw up your gage, do you begin. 1.01.186
our cousin herford and fell mowbray fight. 1.02. 46
a caitive recreant to my cousin herford! 1.02. 53
cousin of herford, as thy cause is right, | so 1.03. 55
of you, my noble cousin, lord aumerle; 1.03. 64
you, cousin herford, upon pain of life, | till 1.03.140
cousin, farewell; 1.03.247
cousin, farewell! 1.03.249
cousin aumerle, | how far brought you high 1.04. 1
what said our cousin when you parted with him? 1.04. 10
he is our cousin's cousin, but 'tis doubt, 1.04. 20
why, cousin, wert thou regent of the world, | it 2.01.109
come, sister — cousin, i would say — pray 2.02.105
come, cousin, i'll dispose of you. 2.02.117
if that my cousin king be king in england, | it 2.03.123
you have a son, aumerle, my noble cousin, | had 2.03.125
discomfortable cousin, know'st thou not | that 3.02. 36
beshrew thee, cousin, which didst lead me forth 3.02.204
take not, good cousin, further than you should, 3.03. 16
thy thrice–noble cousin, | harry bullingbrook, 3.03.103
his noble cousin is right welcome hither, | and 3.03.122
we do debase ourselves, cousin, do we not, | to 3.03.127
aumerle, thou weep'st, my tender–hearted cousin! 3.03.160
fair cousin, you debase your princely knee | to 3.03.190
up, cousin, up, your heart is up, i know, | thus 3.03.194
cousin, i am too young to be your father, 3.03.204
set on towards london, cousin, is it so? 3.03.208
cousin, stand forth, and look upon that man. 4.01. 7
what means our cousin, that he stares and looks 5.03. 24
what is the matter with our cousin now? 5.03. 29
my dangerous cousin, let your mother in, | i 5.03. 81
uncle, farewell, and, cousin, adieu! 5.03.144
me hear | of you, my gentle cousin westmerland, 1H4 1.01. 31
ha, cousin, is it not? 1.01. 75
cousin, on wednesday next our council we | will 1.01.103
nay, then i cannot blame his cousin king, | that 1.03.158
peace, cousin, say no more. 1.03.187
good cousin, give me audience for a while. 1.03.211
hear you, cousin, a word. 1.03.227
and "gentle harry percy" and "kind cousin" — 1.03.254
cousin, farewell! 1.03.292
lord mortimer, and cousin glendower, | will you 3.01. 3
sit, cousin percy, sit, good cousin hotspur, 3.01. 7
sit, cousin percy, sit, good cousin hotspur, 3.01. 7
cousin, of many men | i do not bear these 3.01. 34
peace, cousin percy, you will make him mad. 3.01. 51
i can teach you, cousin, to command | the devil. 3.01. 55
to–morrow, cousin percy, you and i | and my good 3.01. 82
fie, cousin percy, how you cross my father! 3.01.145
shall i tell you, cousin? 3.01.167
my cousin vernon, welcome, by my soul! 4.01. 86
good cousin, be advis'd, stir not to–night. 4.03. 5
of my cousin vernon's are not yet come up. 4.03. 20
for god's sake, cousin, stay till all come in. 4.03. 29
this to my cousin scroop, and all the rest | to 4.04. 3
so tell your cousin, and bring me word | what he 5.01.109
therefore, good cousin, let not harry know, | in 5.02. 24
here comes your cousin. 5.02. 27
cousin, i think thou art enamored | on his 5.02. 69
come, cousin westmerland, | our duty this way 5.04. 15
and my cousin westmerland | towards york shall 5.05. 35
commend me to my cousin westmerland. 2H4 1.02.227 P
cap, "i am the king's poor cousin, sir." 2.02.116 P
you, cousin nevil, as i may remember — | when 3.01. 66
my cousin bullingbrook ascends my throne" 3.01. 71
and how doth my good cousin silence? 3.02. 3 P
good morrow, good cousin shallow. 3.02. 4 P
and how doth my cousin, your bedfellow? 3.02. 5 P
alas, a black woosel, cousin shallow! 3.02. 8 P
i dare say my cousin william is become a good 3.02. 9 P
you were call'd lusty shallow then, cousin. 3.02. 16 P
this sir john, cousin, that comes hither anon 3.02. 27 P
we shall all follow, cousin. 3.02. 35 P
sir john, it is my cousin silence, in commission 3.02. 87 P
ha, cousin silence, that thou hadst seen that 3.02.211 P
are well encount'red here, my cousin mowbray, 4.02. 1
health to my lord, and gentle cousin, mowbray. 4.02. 78
now, cousin, wherefore stands our army still? 4.02. 98
call in the powers, good cousin westmerland. 4.03. 25
fellow of rome, "there, cousin, i came, saw, and 4.03. 41 P
which, cousin, you shall bear to comfort him, 4.03. 79
good morrow, cousin warwick, good morrow. 5.02. 20
good morrow, cousin. 5.02. 21
come, cousin silence — and then to bed. 5.03. 4 P
come, cousin. 5.03. 15 P
not yet, my cousin. H5 1.02. 4
know the pleasure | of our fair cousin dolphin; 1.02.235
no more, cousin. 3.07. 30 P
cousin orleance. 4.02. 6
my cousin westmerland? 4.03. 19
no, my fair cousin. 4.03. 19
he cries aloud, "tarry, my cousin suffolk! 4.06. 15
follow, good cousin warwick. 4.07.175
to our most fair and princely cousin katherine; 5.02. 4
yet leave our cousin katherine here with us: 5.02. 95
my royal cousin, teach you our princess english? 5.02.281 P
i would have her learn, my fair cousin, how 5.02.283 P
my lord, teach your cousin to consent winking. 5.02.304 P
and so i shall catch the fly, your cousin, in 5.02.313 P
cousin of york, we institute your grace | to be 1H6 4.01.162
cousin of york, | we here discharge your grace 2H6 1.01. 65
cousin of somerset, join you with me, | and all 1.01.167
cousin of buckingham, though humphrey's pride 1.01.172
believe me, cousin gloucester, | had not your 2.01. 43

what tidings with our cousin buckingham? 2.01.161
well hast thou spoken, cousin, be it so. 3H6 1.01. 66
cousin of exeter, frowns, words, and threats 1.01. 72
come, cousin, let us tell the queen these news. 1.01.182
come, cousin, you shall be the messenger. 1.01.272
ah, cousin york, would thy best friends did know 2.02. 54
cousin of exeter, what thinks your lordship? 4.08. 34
of you, my noble cousin buckingham, | if ever R3 2.01. 65
my oracle, my prophet, my dear cousin, | i, as a 2.02.152
why, my good cousin, it is good to grow. 2.04. 9
welcome, dear cousin, my thoughts' sovereign, 3.01. 2
i'll tell you what, my cousin buckingham — 3.01. 89
how fares our cousin, noble lord of york? 3.01.101
o my fair cousin, i must not say so. 3.01.106
my dagger, little cousin? with all my heart. 3.01.111
a greater gift than that i'll give my cousin. 3.01.115
ay, gentle cousin, were it light enough. 3.01.117
myself and my good cousin buckingham | will to 3.01.137
cousin of buckingham, a word with you. 3.04. 35
come, cousin, canst thou quake and change thy 3.05. 1
go after, after, cousin buckingham. 3.05. 72
sorry i am my noble cousin should | suspect me 3.07. 88
cousin of buckingham, and sage grave men, 3.07.227
stand all apart. cousin of buckingham — 4.02. 1
cousin, thou wast not wont to be so dull. 4.02. 17
good morrow, cousin cressid. TRO 1.02. 43 P
how do you, cousin? 1.02. 45 P
well, cousin, i told you a thing yesterday, 1.02.170 P
who? my cousin cressida? 3.01. 34 P
you have broke it, cousin; 3.01. 50 P
my cousin will fall out with you. 3.01. 84 P
at my cousin cressida's? 3.02. 2 P
have you seen my cousin? 3.02. 7 P
where's my cousin cressid? 4.02. 24 P
cousin, all honor to thee! 4.05.138
i came to kill thee, cousin, and bear hence | a 4.05.140
desire | my famous cousin to our grecian tents. 4.05.151
give me thy hand, my cousin. 4.05.157
do not chafe thee, cousin, | and you, achilles, 4.05.260
he kill'd my cousin marcus! COR 5.06.122 P
cousin, a word; TIT 2.04. 12
a craftier tereus, cousin, hast thou met, | and 2.04. 41
good morrow, cousin. ROM 1.01.160
in sadness, cousin, i do love a woman. 1.01.204
signior valentio and his cousin tybalt; 1.02. 70 P
nay, sit, nay, sit, good cousin capulet, | for 1.05. 30
romeo! my cousin romeo! romeo! 2.01. 3
tybalt, that an hour | hath been my cousin! 3.01.113
tybalt, my cousin! 3.01.146
o cousin, cousin! 3.01.150
o cousin, cousin! 3.01.150
my dearest cousin, and my dearer lord? 3.02. 66
you speak well of him that kill'd your cousin? 3.02. 96
wherefore, villain, didst thou kill my cousin? 3.02.100
that villain cousin would have kill'd my husband 3.02.101
to wreak the love i bore my cousin | upon his 3.05.101
that murd'red my love's cousin, with which grief 5.03. 50
forgive me, cousin! 5.03.101
o valiant cousin, worthy gentleman! MAC 1.02. 24
o worthiest cousin! 1.04. 14
no, cousin, i'll to fife. 2.04. 36
my pretty cousin, | blessing upon you! 4.02. 25
my ever gentle cousin, welcome hither. 4.03.161
shall with my cousin, your right noble son, 5.06. 3
but now, my cousin hamlet, and my son — HAM 1.02. 64
our chiefest courtier, cousin, and our son. 1.02.117
how fares our cousin hamlet? 3.02. 92 P
cousin hamlet, you know the wager? 5.02.259
and what's the news, good cousin lodovico? OTH 4.01.219
cousin, there's fall'n between him and my lord 4.01.224
cousin, i charge you | bougde not from athens. TNK 1.01.222
and our prime cousin, yet unhard'ned in | the 1.02. 2
clear–spirited cousin, | let's leave his court, 1.02. 74
how do you, noble cousin? 2.02. 1
we are prisoners | i fear for ever, cousin. 2.02. 4
o cousin arcite, | where is thebes now? 2.02. 6
yet, cousin, | even from the bottom of these 2.02. 55
certainly | 'tis a main goodness, cousin, that 2.02. 63
how, gentle cousin? 2.02. 70
i might sicken, cousin, | where you should never 2.02. 91
me | (i thank you, cousin arcite) almost wanton 2.02. 96
cousin arcite, | had not the loving gods found 2.02.107
will ye go forward, cousin? 2.02.126
cousin, cousin! how do you, sir? why, palamon! 2.02.131
cousin, cousin! how do you, sir? why, palamon! 2.02.131
and yet he had a cousin, fair as he too; 2.04. 16
alas, | poor cousin palamon, poor prisoner! 3.01. 23
falsest cousin | that ever blood made kin! 3.01. 37
dear cousin palamon — 3.01. 43
i should be near the place. ho, cousin palamon! 3.03. 1
mad lodging | here in the wild woods, cousin? 3.03. 23
but if it did, yours is too tart, sweet cousin. 3.03. 26
had her share too, as i remember, cousin, | else 3.03. 37
base cousin, | dar'st thou break first? 3.03. 44
about this hour my cousin gave his faith | to 3.06. 1
that too much, fair cousin, | is but a debt to 3.06. 18
with your old strength, i'll stay, cousin, | and 3.06. 37
if you think so, cousin, | you are deceived, for 3.06. 47
pray thee tell me, cousin, | where got'st thou 3.06. 53
good cousin, thrust the buckle | through far 3.06. 61
prithee take mine, good cousin. 3.06. 65
i'll give you cause, sweet cousin. 3.06. 69
day, | i well remember, you outdid me, cousin; 3.06. 73
more by virtue. | you are modest, cousin. 3.06. 82
fight bravely, cousin. 3.06.101
once more farewell, my cousin. 3.06.106
lo, cousin, lo, our folly has undone us. 3.06.107
find | too many hours to die in, gentle cousin. 3.06.112
no, no, cousin! 3.06.117
know, weak cousin, | i love emilia, and in that 3.06.125
as i dare kill this cousin that denies it, | so 3.06.166
true, your cousin | has ten times more offended, 3.06.180
for that love must and dare kill this cousin, 3.06.262
can force his cousin | by fair and knightly 3.06.294
here, cousin arcite, | i am friends again till 3.06.299
wins | loses a noble cousin for thy sins. 4.02.156
before i turn, let me embrace thee, cousin; 5.01. 31
is not this your cousin arcite? 5.02. 90

and i am glad my cousin palamon | has made so 5.02. 91
lead, courageous cousin. 5.04. 38
your cousin, | mounted upon a steed that emily 5.04. 48
forgive me, cousin. 5.04. 93
o cousin, | that we should things desire which 5.04.109
COUSIN–GERMAN 1 FR 0.0001 REL FR 1 V 0 P
son, | a cousin–german to great priam's seed; TRO 4.05.121
/COUSIN'S 1 FR 0.0001 REL FR 1 V 0 P
see thou render this | into my /cousin's hands, MV 3.04. 50
COUSIN'S 15 FR 0.0017 REL FR 12 V 3 P
it is my cousin's duty to make cur'sy and say, ADO 2.01. 52 P
my cousin's a fool, and thou art another. 3.04. 11 P
and here's another | writ in my cousin's hand, 5.04. 89
between my conscience and my cousin's death. JN 4.02.248
he is our cousin's cousin, but 'tis doubt, R2 1.04. 20
i have had feeling of my cousin's wrongs, | and 2.03.141
land would be | in this your cousin's death. 4.01. 19
love | that are misled upon your cousin's part, 1H4 5.01.105
here i hold your hand, here my cousin's. TRO 3.02.198 P
evermore weeping for your cousin's death? ROM 3.05. 69
would none but i might venge my cousin's death! 3.05. 86
methinks i see my cousin's ghost | seeking out 4.03. 55
bereave you | of your fair cousin's company. TNK 2.02.224
that no man but thy cousin's fit to kill thee. 3.06. 44
as thou art valiant, for thy cousin's soul, 3.06.175
COUSINS 17 FR 0.0019 REL FR 13 V 4 P
cousins, you know what you have to do. ADO 1.02. 24 P
cousins, god give you joy! 2.01.336 P
then there were two cousins laid up, when the AYL 1.03. 7 P
off, | of our two cousins coming into london. R2 5.02. 3
good cousins both, of york and somerset, | quiet 1H6 4.01.114
my pretty cousins, you mistake me both: R3 2.02. 8
my noble lords and cousins all, good morrow. 3.04. 22
you speak as if that i had slain my cousins! 4.04.222
cousins indeed, and by their uncle cozen'd | of 4.04.223
dream on thy cousins smothered in the tower. 5.03.146
you, cousins, shall | go sound the ocean, and TIT 4.03. 6
cousins, a word, i pray you. MAC 1.03.127
we hear our bloody cousins are bestow'd | in 3.01. 29
cousins, i hope the days are near at hand | that 5.04. 1
you'll have coursers for cousins, and gennets OTH 1.01.113 P
else of after–ages | for these lost cousins. TNK 3.06.188
and in their funeral songs for these two cousins 3.06.248
COUTUME 1 FR 0.0001 REL FR 0 V 1 P
leur noces, il n'est pas la coutume de france. H5 5.02.259 P
COVENANT 3 FR 0.0003 REL FR 2 V 1 P
my heart this covenant makes, my hand thus seals
R2 2.03. 50
your hand — a covenant. CYM 1.04.164 P
good sir, we must, | if you keep covenant. 2.04. 50
COVENANTS 4 FR 0.0004 REL FR 3 V 1 P
us, | that covenants may be kept on either hand. SHR 2.01.127
shall be with such strict and severe covenants 1H6 5.04.114
agree to any covenants, and procure | that lady 5.05. 88
let there be covenants drawn between 's. CYM 1.04.143 P
COVENT *(also convent)*
COVENT 2 FR 0.0002 REL FR 2 V 0 P
one of our covent, and his confessor, | gives me MM 4.03.128
with all his covent honorably receiv'd him; H8 4.02. 19
/COVENTRY 1 FR 0.0001 REL FR 1 V 0 P
/he /ne'er /had /borne /it /out /of /coventry; 2H4 4.01.133
COVENTRY 8 FR 0.0009 REL FR 6 V 2 P
it, | at coventry upon saint lambert's day. R2 1.01.199
thou goest to coventry, there to behold | our 1.02. 45
sister, farewell, i must to coventry. 1.02. 56
bardolph, get thee before to coventry; 1H4 4.02. 1 P
i'll not march through coventry with them, 4.02. 39 P
farewell, sweet lords, let's meet at coventry. 3H6 4.08. 32
and, lords, towards coventry bend we our course, 4.08. 58
brave warriors, march amain towards coventry. 4.08. 64
COVER 30 FR 0.0034 REL FR 20 V 10 P
the cover of the salt hides the salt, and TGV 3.01.360 P
help to cover your master, boy. WIV 3.03.143 P
the damned'st body to invest and cover | in MM 3.01. 95
/event stamps them, but they have a good cover; ADO 1.02. 8 P
of truth | can cunning sin cover itself withal! 4.01. 36
death is the fairest cover for her shame | that 4.01.116
why seek'st thou then to cover with excuse 4.01.174
the starry welkin cover thou anon | with MND 3.02.356
a tomb | must cover thy sweet eyes. 5.01.329
how many then should cover that stand bare? MV 2.09. 44
that is done too, sir, only "cover" is the word. 3.05. 51 P
will you cover then, sir? 3.05. 53 P
go to thy fellows, bid them cover the table, 3.05. 58 P
sirs, cover the while; AYL 2.05. 31 P
cover thy head, cover thy head; 5.01. 16 P
cover thy head, cover thy head; 5.01. 17 P
is yet the cover of a fairer mind | than to be JN 4.02.258
which serves as paste and cover to our bones. R2 3.02.154
cover your heads, and mock not flesh and blood 3.02.171
why then cover and set them down, and see if 2H4 2.04. 10 P
lover, | to beautify him, only lacks a cover. ROM 1.03. 88
legs, | the cover of the wings of grasshoppers, 1.04. 63
i am rapt and cannot cover | the monstrous bulk TIM 5.01. 64
froth | the turbulent surge shall cover; 5.01.218
even so. cover their faces. LR 5.03.243
how courtesy would seem to cover sin, | when PER 1.01.121
though men can cover crimes with bold stern LUC 1252
for all that beauty that doth cover thee | is SON 22. 5
that churl death my bones with dust shall cover, 32. 2
where beauty's veil doth cover every blot, | and 95.11
COVER'D 14 FR 0.0015 REL FR 8 V 6 P
desk | that's cover'd o'er with turkish tapestry ERR 4.01.104
therefore let benedick, like cover'd fire, ADO 3.01. 77
for the meat, sir, it shall be cover'd; MV 3.05. 62 P
nay, pray be cover'd. AYL 3.03. 77 P
do think him as concave as a cover'd goblet or a 3.04. 24 P
nay, prithee be cover'd. 5.01. 17 P
we, well cover'd with the night's black mantle, 3H6 4.02. 22
what good is cover'd with the face of heaven, R3 4.04.240
slave | come hither, cover'd with an antic face, ROM 1.05. 56
all cover'd dishes! TIM 3.06. 48 P
and when my face is cover'd, as 'tis now, JC 5.03. 44
(although as yet the face of it is cover'd LR 3.01. 20
have your daughter cover'd with a barbary horse, OTH 1.01.111 P
the naked and concealed fiend he cover'd, | that LC 317
COVERED 1 FR 0.0001 REL FR 1 V 0 P
whose mouth is covered with rude–growing briers,
TIT 2.03.199
COVERING 7 FR 0.0008 REL FR 7 V 0 P
the covering sky is nothing, bohemia nothing, WT 1.02.294
covering your fearful land | with hard bright R2 3.02.110
covering discretion with a coat of folly, | as H5 2.04. 38
and bring some covering for this naked soul, LR 4.01. 44
the benediction of these covering heavens | fall CYM 5.05.350
that without covering, save yon field of stars, PER 1.01. 37
fled, | under the covering of a careful night, 1.02. 81
COVERLET 2 FR 0.0002 REL FR 2 V 0 P
this way the coverlet, another way the sheets. SHR 4.01.202
on the green coverlet, whose perfect white LUC 394
COVERS 5 FR 0.0005 REL FR 4 V 1 P
the hair that covers the wit is more than the TGV 3.01.361 P
fair fall the face it covers! LLL 2.01.124
who covers faults, at last with shame derides. LR 1.01.281
world, a garment | nobler than that it covers! CYM 5.04.135
covers the shame that follows sweet delight." LUC 357
COVERT 7 FR 0.0008 REL FR 7 V 0 P
it | to lock it in the wards of covert bosom, MM 5.01. 10
you must retire yourself | into some covert. WT 4.04.650
while covert enmity | under the smile of safety 2H4 in 9
and in this covert will we make our stand, 3H6 3.01. 3
of me, | and stole into the covert of the wood. ROM 1.01.125
how covert matters may be best disclos'd, | and JC 4.01. 46
that under covert and convenient seeming | has LR 3.02. 56
COVERTLY 1 FR 0.0001 REL FR 0 V 1 P
but so covertly that no dishonesty shall appear ADO 2.02. 9 P
COVERT'ST 1 FR 0.0001 REL FR 1 V 0 P
he was the covert'st shelt'red traitor | that R3 3.05. 33
COVERTURE 2 FR 0.0002 REL FR 2 V 0 P
even now | is couched in the woodbine coverture. ADO 3.01. 30
and now what rests but, in night's coverture, 3H6 4.02. 13
COVET 3 FR 0.0003 REL FR 3 V 0 P
but if it be a sin to covet honor, | i am the H5 4.03. 28
than in my greatness covet to be hid | and in R3 3.07.163
those that much covet are with gain so fond, LUC 134
COVETED 1 FR 0.0001 REL FR 1 V 0 P
scarcely have coveted what was mine own, | at no MAC 4.03.127
COVETING 1 FR 0.0001 REL FR 1 V 0 P
that which i have than, coveting for more, | be 1H6 5.04.145
COVETINGS 1 FR 0.0001 REL FR 1 V 0 P
ambitions, covetings, change of prides, disdain, CYM 2.05. 25
COVETOUS 9 FR 0.0010 REL FR 8 V 1 P
but she, more covetous, would have a chain. ERR 4.03. 74
by jove, i am not covetous for gold, | nor care H5 4.03. 24
if i were covetous, ambitious, or perverse, | as 1H6 3.01. 29
never | more covetous of wisdom and fair virtue H8 5.04. 24
or covetous of praise — TRO 2.03.237
you must in no way say he is covetous. COR 1.01. 43 P
sure), | is not thy kindness subtle, covetous, TIM 4.03.508
when marcus brutus grows so covetous | to lock JC 4.03. 79
free, | for thou art covetous, and he is kind; SON 134. 6
COVETOUSLY 1 FR 0.0001 REL FR 0 V 1 P
if he covetously reserve it, how shall 's get it TIM 4.03.404 P
COVETOUSNESS 4 FR 0.0004 REL FR 2 V 2 P
why, that were covetousness. AYL 3.05. 91
my desire of having is the sin of covetousness; TN 5.01. 47 P
they do confound their skill in covetousness, JN 4.02. 29
separate age and covetousness than 'a can part 2H4 1.02.229 P
COVETS 1 FR 0.0001 REL FR 1 V 0 P
he covets less | than misery itself would give, COR 2.02.126
COW 7 FR 0.0008 REL FR 5 V 2 P
is said, "god sends a curst cow short horns" — ADO 2.01. 23 P
horns" — but to a cow too curst he sends none. 2.01. 23 P
some such strange bull leapt your father's cow, 5.04. 49
might have kept | this calf, bred from his cow, JN 1.01.124
and that i would not for a cow, god save her! H8 5.03. 27
but where the bull and cow are both milk–white, TIT 5.01. 31
the breeze upon her, like a cow in /june — ANT 3.10. 14
COWARD 94 FR 0.0106 REL FR 63 V 31 P
was there ever man a coward that hath drunk so TMP 3.02. 27 P
by gar, he is de coward jack priest of de vorld; WIV 2.03. 31 P
by gar, you are de coward, de jack dog, john ape 3.01. 83 P
o faithless coward! MM 3.01.136
a fool, and a coward, as you then reported him 5.01.334 P
you, sirrah, that knew me for a fool, a coward, 5.01.500
hear from him, or i will subscribe him a coward. ADO 5.02. 59 P
thou runaway, thou coward, art thou fled? MND 3.02.405
thou coward, art thou bragging to the stars, 3.02.407
ho, ho, ho! coward, why com'st thou not? 3.02.421
who shut their coward gates on atomies, | should AYL 3.05. 13
think him a great way fool, soly a coward; AWW 1.01.101
he's a most notable coward, an infinite and 3.06. 9 P
he excels his brother for a coward, yet his 4.03.288 P
and i were not a very coward, i'd compel it of 4.03.321 P
hath the gift of a coward to allay the gust he TN 1.03. 31 P
he's a coward and a coystrill that will not 1.03. 40 P
paltry boy, and more a coward than a hare. 3.04.386 P
a coward, a most devout coward, religious in it. 3.04.389 P
a coward, a most devout coward, religious in it. 3.04.389 P
we took him for a coward, but he's the very 5.01.181 P
if thou inclin'st that way, thou art a coward, WT 1.02.243
than e'er the coward hand of france can win. JN 2.01.158
thou slave, thou wretch, thou coward! 3.01.115
call him a slanderous coward, and a villain, R2 1.01. 61
pale trembling coward, there i throw my gage, 1.01. 69
and consequently, like a traitor coward, 1.01.102
awake, thou coward majesty! 3.02. 84
thou dar'st not, coward, live to see that day. 4.01. 41
what, a coward, sir john paunch? 1H4 2.02. 66 P
gaunt, your grandfather, but yet no coward, hal. 2.02. 68 P
as to play the coward with thy indenture, and 2.04. 47 P
yet a coward is worse than a cup of sack with 2.04.126 P
a villainous coward! 2.04.127 P
are not you a coward? 2.04.142 P
ye fat paunch, and ye call me coward, by the 2.04.145 P
i call thee coward! 2.04.146 P
i'll see thee damn'd ere i call thee coward, but 2.04.147 P
this sanguine coward, this bed–presser, this 2.04.242 P
i was now a coward on instinct. 2.04.273 P
and thou a natural coward, without instinct. 2.04.494 P
foundation of the earth | shak'd like a coward. 3.01. 17
puff i' thy teeth, most recreant coward base! 2H4 5.03. 92
for coward dogs | most spend their mouths when H5 2.04. 69
his prayers, lest 'a should be thought a coward; 3.02. 38 P
if sir john falstaff had not play'd the coward. 1H6 1.01.131
coward of france, how much he wrongs his fame, 2.01. 16
let him that is no coward nor no flatterer, 2.04. 31
by forfeiting a traitor and a coward. 4.03. 27
the coward horse that bears me fall and die! 4.06. 47
i would, false murd'rous coward, on thy knee 2H6 3.02.220
fie, coward woman and soft–hearted wretch! 3.02.307
and i proclaim'd a coward through the world! 4.01. 43
o monstrous coward! what, to come behind folks? 4.07. 83 P
ay, like a dastard and a treacherous coward, 3H6 2.02.114
should, if a coward heard her speak these words, 5.04. 40
not meddle with it, it makes a man a coward. R3 1.04.135 P
go, coward as thou art. 1.04.279
pray god, i say, i prove a needless coward! 3.02. 88
o coward conscience, how dost thou afflict me! 5.03.179
for then the bold and coward, | the wise and TRO 1.03. 23
troilus, thou coward troilus! 5.05. 43
troilus, thou coward troilus, show thy head! 5.06. 1
the devil take thee, coward! 5.07. 23 P
and, thou great–siz'd coward, | no space of 5.10. 26
and by his rare example made the coward | turn COR 2.02.104
foul–spoken coward, that thund'rest with thy TIT 2.01. 58
have at thee, coward! ROM 1.01. 72
right, | base noble, old young, coward valiant. TIM 4.03. 30
sound to this coward and lascivious town | our 5.04. 1
his coward lips did from their color fly, | and JC 1.02.122
conceit me, | either a coward or a flatterer. 3.01.193
i slew the coward, and did take it from him. 5.03. 4
o, coward that i am, to live so long, | to see 5.03. 34
life, | and live a coward in thine own esteem, MAC 1.07. 43
then yield thee, coward, | and live to be the 5.08. 23
am i a coward? HAM 2.02.571
one part wisdom | and ever three parts coward — 4.04. 43
bringing the murderous coward to the stake; LR 2.01. 62
composition of a knave, beggar, coward, pandar, 2.02. 22 P
he rais'd the house with loud and coward cries. 2.04. 43
when it concerns the fool or coward. ANT 1.02. 96
a better cause, | but now thou seem'st a coward. CYM 3.04. 73
but that of coward hares, hot goats, and venison 4.04. 37
that some, turn'd coward | but by example (o, a 5.03. 35
strain you are, | and of how coward a spirit. PER 4.03. 25
and if he lose her then, he's a cold coward. TNK 2.02.253
if i fall, curse me, and say i was a coward, 3.06.104
affection faints not like a pale–fac'd coward, VEN 569
thy coward heart with false bethinking grieves." 1024
put fear to valor, courage to the coward. 1158
the coward captive vanquished doth yield | to LUC 75
the coward fights, and will not be dismay'd. 273
dead, | the coward conquest of a wretch's knife, SON 74.11
COWARDED 1 FR 0.0001 REL FR 1 V 0 P
that have so cowarded and chas'd your blood H5 2.02. 75
COWARDICE 16 FR 0.0018 REL FR 13 V 3 P
slander valentine | with falsehood, cowardice, TGV 3.02. 32
she needs not, when she knows it cowardice. 5.02. 21
do me right, or i will protest your cowardice. ADO 5.01.148 P
speed, | when cowardice pursues and valor flies. MND 2.01.234
i am a right maid for my cowardice. 3.02.302
is pale cold cowardice in noble breasts. R2 1.02. 34
fear and entire cowardice doth not make thee 2H4 2.04.326 P
is the badge of pusillanimity and cowardice; 4.03.105 P
age, | and twit with cowardice a man half dead? 1H6 3.02. 55
whose cowardice | hath made us by–words to our 3H6 1.01. 41
that slanders him with cowardice | whose frown 1.04. 47
i hold it cowardice | to rest mistrustful where 4.02. 7
they tax our policy, and call it cowardice, TRO 1.03.197
thy counsel, lad, smells of no cowardice. TIT 2.01.132
nor did he soil the fact with cowardice | (/an TIM 3.05. 16
the gods do this in shame of cowardice; JC 2.02. 41
COWARD–LIKE 1 FR 0.0001 REL FR 1 V 0 P
but coward–like with trembling terror die. LUC 231
COWARDLY 17 FR 0.0019 REL FR 9 V 8 P
a cowardly knave as you would desires to be WIV 3.01. 66 P
that same cowardly, giant–like ox–beef hath MND 3.01.192 P
not a more cowardly rogue in all bohemia. WT 4.03.105 P
a good tall fellow had destroyed | so cowardly, 1H4 1.03. 63
you are a shallow, cowardly hind, and you lie. 2.03. 15 P
and the cowardly rascals that ran from the H5 4.07. 6 P
go, go, you are a counterfeit cowardly knave. 5.01. 69 P
cowardly fled, not having struck one stroke. 1H6 1.01.134
cowardly knight, ill fortune follow thee! 3.02.109
no, he'll say 'twas done cowardly when he wakes. R3 1.04.101 P
relent? no: 'tis cowardly and womanish. 1.04.261
discretion, | yet are they passing cowardly. COR 1.01.203
foolish in our stands | nor cowardly in retire. 1.06. 3
and cowardly nobles gave way unto your clusters, 4.06.122
not how, | but i do find it cowardly and vile, JC 5.01.103
you cowardly rascal, nature disclaims in thee: LR 2.02. 54 P
die, | not cowardly put off my helmet to | my ANT 4.15. 56
COWARD'S 1 FR 0.0001 REL FR 1 V 0 P
may be a coward's, whose ministers would prevail
ANT 3.13. 23
COWARDS 31 FR 0.0035 REL FR 22 V 9 P
or hide your heads like cowards, and fly hence. LLL 5.02. 86
how many cowards, whose hearts are all as false MV 3.02. 83
as many other mannish cowards have | that do AYL 1.03.121
to be as true–bred cowards as ever turn'd back; 1H4 1.02.184 P
the prince and poins be not two arrant cowards, 2.02.100 P
a plague of all cowards, i say, and a vengeance 2.04.114 P
a plague of all cowards! 2.04.118 P
a plague of all cowards, i say still. 2.04.134 P
a plague of all cowards, still say i. 2.04.156 P
a plague of all cowards! 2.04.170 P
they are generally fools and cowards, which some 2H4 4.03. 95 P
cowards! 1H6 1.02. 23
or whether that such cowards ought to wear 4.01. 28
and make the cowards stand aloof at bay. 4.02. 52
man, and exhort all the world to be cowards; 2H6 4.10. 74 P
so cowards fight when they can fly no further, 3H6 1.04. 40
conscience is but a word that cowards use, R3 5.03.309
"come on, you cowards, you were got in fear, COR 1.03. 33
do) bear fire enough | to kindle cowards, and to JC 2.01.121
swear priests and cowards, and men cautelous, 2.01.129
cowards die many times before their deaths, 2.02. 32
thus conscience does make cowards /of /us /all, HAM 3.01. 82
none of these rogues and cowards | but ajax is LR 2.02.124
and have instructed cowards | to run and show ANT 3.11. 7
plenty and peace breeds cowards; CYM 3.06. 21
cowards father cowards and base things sire base 4.02. 26
cowards father cowards and base things sire base 4.02. 26
and cowards living | to die with length'ned 5.03. 12

and now our cowards, | like fragments in hard 5.03. 43
with us, | make talk for fools and cowards. TNK 3.03. 12
and there the painter interlaces | pale cowards, LUC 1391
COWARDSHIP 1 FR 0.0001 REL FR 0 V 1 P
and for his cowardship, ask fabian. TN 3.04.388 P
COW'D 1 FR 0.0001 REL FR 1 V 0 P
so, | for it hath cow'd my better part of man! MAC 5.08. 18
COW-DUNG 1 FR 0.0001 REL FR 0 V 1 P
the foul fiend rages, eats cow-dung for sallets; LR 3.04.132 P
COWISH 1 FR 0.0001 REL FR 1 V 0 P
it is the cowish terror of his spirit | that LR 4.02. 12
COWL-STAFF 1 FR 0.0001 REL FR 0 V 1 P
where's the cowl-staff? WIV 3.03.147 P
COW'R'D 1 FR 0.0001 REL FR 1 V 0 P
the splitting rocks cow'r'd in the sinking sands 2H6 3.02. 97
COW'RS 1 FR 0.0001 REL FR 0 V 1 P
know the french knight that cow'rs i' the hams? PER 4.02.105 P
COW'S 1 FR 0.0001 REL FR 0 V 1 P
of her batler and the cow's dugs that her pretty AYL 2.04. 49 P
COWS *(see kine)*
COWSLIP 3 FR 0.0003 REL FR 3 V 0 P
this cherry nose, | these yellow cowslip cheeks, MND 5.01.332
brought sweetly forth | the freckled cowslip, H5 5.02. 49
the crimson drops | i' th' bottom of a cowslip. CYM 2.02. 39
COWSLIP'S 2 FR 0.0002 REL FR 2 V 0 P
there suck i, | in a cowslip's bell i lie; TMP 5.01. 89
here, | and hang a pearl in every cowslip's ear. MND 2.01. 15
COWSLIPS 2 FR 0.0002 REL FR 2 V 0 P
the cowslips tall her pensioners be, | in their MND 2.01. 10
the violets, cowslips, and the primeroses, CYM 1.05. 83
COX 1 FR 0.0001 REL FR 0 V 1 P
cox my passion! AWW 5.02. 40 P
COXCOMB *(also cogscomb)*
COXCOMB 20 FR 0.0022 REL FR 5 V 15 P
shall i have a coxcomb of frieze? WIV 5.05.138 P
mome, malt-horse, capon, coxcomb, idiot, patch! ERR 3.01. 32
/off, coxcomb! ADO 4.02. 69 P
let him write down the prince's officer coxcomb. 4.02. 71 P
o most profane coxcomb! LLL 4.03. 82
what is your crest? a coxcomb? SHR 2.01.225
by this same coxcomb that we have i' th' wind, AWW 3.06.114
and has given sir toby a bloody coxcomb too. TN 5.01.176 P
if a bloody coxcomb be a hurt, you have hurt me. 5.01.190 P
i think you set nothing by a bloody coxcomb. 5.01.191 P
an ass-head and a coxcomb and a knave, a 5.01.206 P
is an ass and a fool, and a prating coxcomb, is H5 4.01. 78 P
be an ass and a fool, and a prating coxcomb, in 4.01. 79 P
for your green wound and your ploody coxcomb. 5.01. 43 P
away, the skin is good for your broken coxcomb. 5.01. 55 P
let me hire him too, here's my coxcomb. LR 1.04. 95 P
sirrah, you were best take my coxcomb. 1.04. 97 P
there, take my coxcomb. 1.04.101 P
follow him, thou must needs wear my coxcomb. 1.04.104 P
o murd'rous coxcomb, what should such a fool OTH 5.02.233
COXCOMBS 4 FR 0.0004 REL FR 1 V 3 P
as many coxcombs | as you threw caps up will he COR 4.06.134
would i had two coxcombs and two daughters! LR 1.04.105 P
all my living, i'ld keep my coxcombs myself. 1.04.108 P
she knapp'd 'em o' th' coxcombs with a stick, 2.04.124 P
COY 10 FR 0.0011 REL FR 10 V 0 P
coy looks with heart-sore sighs; TGV 1.01. 30
but she is nice and coy, | and nought esteems my 3.01. 82
i know her spirits are as coy and wild | as ADO 3.01. 35
bed, | while i thy amiable cheeks do coy, | and MND 4.01. 2
'twas told me you were rough and coy and sullen, SHR 2.01.243
and had in her | the coy denials of young maids, TNK 4.02. 11
but he is like his master, coy and scornful. 5.02. 63
boy, | 'tis but a kiss i beg, why art thou coy? VEN 96
obeyed, | yet was he servile to my coy disdain. 112
in stead of love's coy touch, shall rudely tear LUC 669
COY'D 1 FR 0.0001 REL FR 1 V 0 P
nay, if he coy'd | to hear cominius speak, i'll COR 5.01. 6
COYING 1 FR 0.0001 REL FR 1 V 0 P
than those that have /more coying to be strange. ROM 2.02.101
COYSTRILL *(also custrel)*
COYSTRILL 1 FR 0.0001 REL FR 0 V 1 P
he's a coward and a coystrill that will not TN 1.03. 40 P
COZ 44 FR 0.0049 REL FR 24 V 20 P
i may quarter, coz. WIV 1.01. 24 P
come, coz, come, coz, we stay for you. 1.01.206 P
come, coz, come, coz, we stay for you. 1.01.206 P
a word with you, coz; 1.01.207 P
marry, this, coz: 1.01.207 P
nay, conceive me, conceive me, sweet coz; 1.01.242 P
what i do is to pleasure you, coz. 1.01.243 P
to her, coz. 3.04. 36 P
she calls you, coz. 3.04. 53 P
good morrow, coz. ADO 3.04. 39 P
help to dress me, good coz, good meg, good 3.04. 98 P
i pray thee, rosalind, sweet my coz, be merry. AYL 1.02. 1 P
from henceforth i will, coz, and devise sports. 1.02. 24 P
were i my father, coz, would i do this? 1.02.231
shall we go, coz? 1.02.248
will you go, coz? 1.02.255
i' faith, coz, 'tis he. 3.02.216 P
o coz, coz, coz, my pretty little coz, that thou 4.01.205 P
o coz, coz, coz, my pretty little coz, that thou 4.01.205 P
o coz, coz, coz, my pretty little coz, that thou 4.01.205 P
coz, my pretty little coz, that thou didst know 4.01.205 P
and seek the crowner, and let him sit o' my coz; TN 1.05.135 P
coz, farewell. JN 3.03. 17
what think you, coz, | of this young percy's 1H4 1.01. 91
and i can teach thee, coz, to shame the devil 3.01. 57
and, dear coz, to you | the remnant northward 3.01. 77
therefore be merry, coz, since sudden sorrow 2H4 4.02. 83
no, faith, my coz, wish not a man from england. H5 4.03. 30
thou dost not wish more help from england, coz? 4.03. 73
our tongue is rough, coz, and my condition is 5.02.286 P
no, coz, i rather weep. ROM 1.01.183
farewell, my coz. 1.01.195
a right fair mark, fair coz, is soonest hit. 1.01.207
content thee, gentle coz, let him alone, | 'a 1.05. 65
my dearest coz, | i pray you school yourself. MAC 4.02. 14
i ear'd her language, liv'd in her eye, o coz, TNK 3.01. 29
you skip them in me, and with them, fair coz, 3.01. 52
my coz, my coz, you have been well advertis'd 3.01. 58
my coz, my coz, you have been well advertis'd 3.01. 58
spare it not, | the duke has more, coz. eat now. 3.03. 20
after you, coz. 3.03. 30
what did she there, coz? 3.03. 34
i would destroy th' offender, coz, i would, 5.01. 23
why, let it be so; farewell, coz! 5.01. 33
COZEN 5 FR 0.0005 REL FR 3 V 2 P
for who shall go about | to cozen fortune, and MV 2.09. 38
and swore | as if the vicar meant to cozen him. SHR 3.02.168
i believe 'a means to cozen somebody in this 5.01. 39 P
no sin | to cozen him that would unjustly win. AWW 4.02. 76
i would cozen the man of his wife and do his 4.05. 27 P
COZENAGE 3 FR 0.0003 REL FR 1 V 2 P
out, alas, sir, cozenage! mere cozenage. WIV 4.05. 63 P
out, alas, sir, cozenage! mere cozenage. 4.05. 63 P
they say this town is full of cozenage: ERR 1.02. 97
COZEN'D 15 FR 0.0017 REL FR 5 V 10 P
master slender of his chain cozen'd him of it. WIV 4.05. 37 P
that has cozen'd all the hosts of readins, of 4.05. 77 P
and 'tis not convenient you should be cozen'd. 4.05. 82 P
i would all the world might be cozen'd, for i 4.05. 93 P
cozen'd, for i have been cozen'd and beaten too. 4.05. 94 P
master /brook that you have cozen'd of money, to 5.05.166 P
by gar, i am cozen'd. 5.05.205 P
by gar, i am cozen'd. 5.05.207 P
is thus like to be cozen'd with the semblance of ADO 2.02. 39 P
when saucy trusting of the cozen'd thoughts AWW 4.04. 23
told thee how i was cozen'd by the way and lost WT 4.04.251 P
indeed, and by their uncle cozen'd | of comfort, R3 4.04.223
and basely cozen'd | of that true hand that TIT 5.03.101
that thus hath cozen'd you at hoodman-blind? HAM 3.04. 77
art not vanquish'd, | but cozen'd and beguil'd. LR 5.03.155
COZENER 2 FR 0.0002 REL FR 2 V 0 P
the usurer hangs the cozener. LR 4.06.163
cozener arcite — give me language such | as TNK 3.01. 44
COZENERS 3 FR 0.0003 REL FR 1 V 2 P
run away with the cozeners; WIV 4.05. 66 P
sir, there are cozeners abroad, therefore it WT 4.04.253 P
cousin" — | o, the devil take such cozeners! 1H4 1.03.255
COZEN-GERMANS 1 FR 0.0001 REL FR 0 V 1 P
me there is three cozen-germans that has cozen'd
WIV 4.05. 77 P
COZENING 4 FR 0.0004 REL FR 2 V 2 P
a witch, a quean, an old cozening quean! WIV 4.02.172 P
despair, and be at enmity | with cozening hope. R2 2.02. 69
else he had been damn'd for cozening the devil. 1H4 1.02.122 P
some cogging, cozening slave, to get some office OTH 4.02.132
COZENS 1 FR 0.0001 REL FR 1 V 0 P
that hostler | must rise betime that cozens him. TNK 5.02. 60
COZIERS' 1 FR 0.0001 REL FR 0 V 1 P
ye squeak out your coziers' catches without any TN 2.03. 90 P
COZ'NAGE 1 FR 0.0001 REL FR 1 V 0 P
and with such coz'nage — is't not perfect HAM 5.02. 67
COZ'NING 1 FR 0.0001 REL FR 1 V 0 P
under, | coz'ning the pillow of a lawful kiss; LUC 387
CRAB* 10 FR 0.0011 REL FR 3 V 7 P
i think crab my dog be the sourest-natur'd dog TGV 2.03. 5 P
why, he that's tied here, crab, my dog. 2.03. 40 P
with the smell before, knew it was crab, and 4.04. 24 P
anon falleth like a crab on the face of terra, LLL 4.02. 6 P
bowl, | in very likeness of a roasted crab, MND 2.01. 48
it is my fashion when i see a crab. SHR 2.01.229
why, here's no crab, and therefore look not sour 2.01.230
as i am, if like a crab you could go backward. HAM 2.02.203 P
taste as like this as a crab does to a crab. LR 1.05. 18 P
taste as like this as a crab does to a crab. 1.05. 19 P
CRABBED 4 FR 0.0004 REL FR 3 V 1 P
ten times more gentle than her father's crabbed; TMP 3.01. 8
something too crabbed that way, friar. MM 3.02. 98 P
three crabbed months had sour'd themselves to WT 1.02.102
crabbed age and youth cannot live together: PP 12. 1
CRAB'S 1 FR 0.0001 REL FR 0 V 1 P
she's as like this as a crab's like an apple, LR 1.05. 15 P
CRABS 2 FR 0.0002 REL FR 2 V 0 P
i prithee let me bring thee where crabs grow; TMP 2.02.167
when roasted crabs hiss in the bowl, | then LLL 5.02.925
CRAB-TREE 2 FR 0.0002 REL FR 1 V 1 P
and noble stock | was graft with crab-tree slip, 2H6 3.02.214
fetch me a dozen crab-tree staves, and strong H8 5.03. 8 P
CRAB-TREES 1 FR 0.0001 REL FR 1 V 0 P
we have some old crab-trees here at home that COR 2.01.188
/CRACK 1 FR 0.0001 REL FR 1 V 0 P
/the /strings /of /life | /began /to /crack. LR 5.03.218
CRACK 31 FR 0.0035 REL FR 24 V 7 P
i had rather crack my sinews, break my back, TMP 3.01. 26
my charms crack not; 5.01. 2
my heart is ready to crack with impatience. WIV 2.02.288 P
and ethiops of their sweet complexion crack. LLL 4.03.264
my love to thee is sound, sans crack or flaw. 5.02.415
as thunder when the clouds in autumn crack. SHR 1.02. 96
believe this crack to be in my dread mistress WT 1.02.322
or lay on that shall make your shoulders crack. JN 2.01.146
court-gate, when 'a was a crack not thus high; 2H4 3.02. 31 P
by the mass, you'll crack a quart together, ha, 5.03. 62 P
and from my shoulders crack my arms asunder, 1H6 1.05. 11
all the world should crack their duty to you H8 3.02.193
divert and crack, rend and deracinate | the TRO 1.03. 99
'a were as good crack a fusty nut with no kernel 2.01.101 P
crack my clear voice with sobs and break my 4.02.108
now crack thy lungs, and split thy brazen pipe. 4.05. 7
a crack, madam. COR 1.03. 68 P
secure of thunder's crack or lightning flash, TIT 2.01. 3
crack the lawyer's voice, | that he may never TIM 4.03.153
will the line stretch out to th' crack of doom? MAC 4.01.117
or (not to crack the wind of the poor phrase, HAM 1.03.108
blow, winds, and crack your cheeks! LR 3.02. 1
crack nature's moulds, all germains spill at 3.02. 8
use them so | that heaven's vault should crack. 5.03.260
this crack of your love shall grow stronger than OTH 2.03.324 P
than thy continent, | crack thy frail case! ANT 4.14. 41
so great a thing should make | a greater crack. 5.01. 15
now our voices | have got the mannish crack, CYM 4.02.236
shuns not to break one will crack /them both; PER 1.02.121
crack the glass of her virginity, and make the 4.06.142 P
when neither curb would crack, girth break, nor TNK 5.04. 74
CRACK'D *(also crak'd)*
/CRACK'D 1 FR 0.0001 REL FR 1 V 0 P
/it /is, /crack'd /in /an /hundred /shivers. R2 4.01.289
CRACK'D 18 FR 0.0020 REL FR 15 V 3 P
hast thou so crack'd and splitted my poor tongue ERR 5.01.309
the tackle of my heart is crack'd and burn'd, JN 5.07. 52
is crack'd, and all the precious liquor spilt, R2 1.02. 19
we must have bloody noses and crack'd crowns, 1H4 2.03. 93
are crack'd in pieces by malignant death, | and R3 2.02. 52
now he has crack'd the league | between us and H8 2.02. 24
do prize their hours | at a crack'd drachme! COR 1.05. 5
whom with a crack'd heart i have sent to rome, 5.03. 9
uncurrent gold, be not crack'd within the ring. HAM 2.02.428 P
and the bond crack'd 'twixt son and father. LR 1.02.108 P
o madam, my old heart is crack'd, it's crack'd! 2.01. 90
o madam, my old heart is crack'd, it's crack'd! 2.01. 90
would have broke mine eye-strings, crack'd them,
CYM 1.03. 17
surges, crack'd | as easily 'gainst our rocks. 3.01. 28
should reserve | my crack'd one to more care. 4.04. 50
but think her bond of chastity quite crack'd, 5.05.207
livers perish'd, crack'd to pieces with love, we TNK 4.03. 23 P
crack'd many a ring of posied gold and bone, LC 45
CRACKER 1 FR 0.0001 REL FR 1 V 0 P
what cracker is this same that deafs our ears JN 2.01.147
CRACK-HEMP 1 FR 0.0001 REL FR 0 V 1 P
come hither, crack-hemp. SHR 5.01. 45 P
/CRACKING 1 FR 0.0001 REL FR 1 V 0 P
/and /cracking /the /strong /warrant /of /an R2 4.01.235
CRACKING 4 FR 0.0004 REL FR 2 V 2 P
cracking the stones of the foresaid pruins — MM 2.01.107 P
o, cut my lace, lest my heart, cracking it, WT 3.02.173
cracking ten thousand curbs | of more strong COR 1.01. 70
thou wilt quarrel with a man for cracking nuts, ROM 3.01. 19 P
CRACKS 5 FR 0.0005 REL FR 5 V 0 P
the fire and cracks | of sulphurous roaring the TMP 1.02.203
known | how he hath drunk, he cracks his gorge, WT 2.01. 44
as cannons overcharg'd with double cracks, so MAC 1.02. 37
now cracks a noble heart. HAM 5.02.359
thou hast a heart | that ever cracks for woe! PER 3.02. 77
CRADLE 15 FR 0.0017 REL FR 14 V 1 P
here, | so near the cradle of the fairy queen? MND 3.01. 78
and fancy dies | in the cradle where it lies. MV 3.02. 69
which in our country's cradle | draws the sweet R2 1.03.132
brains | in cradle of the rude imperious surge, 2H4 3.01. 20
no sooner was i crept out of my cradle | but i 2H6 4.09. 3
rough cradle for such little pretty ones! R3 4.01.100
from his cradle | he was a scholar, and a ripe H8 4.02. 50
though in her cradle, yet now promises | upon 5.04. 18
spare thy athenian cradle and those kin | which TIM 5.04. 40
hath made his pendant bed and procreant cradle. MAC 1.06. 8
a son for her cradle ere she had a husband for LR 1.01. 15 P
a double set | if drink rock not his cradle. OTH 2.03.131
to have the courtesy your cradle promis'd, | but CYM 4.04. 28
and commit it | to the like innocent cradle, TNK 1.03. 70
lo in this hollow cradle take thy rest, | my VEN 1185
CRADLE-BABE 1 FR 0.0001 REL FR 1 V 0 P
as mild and gentle as the cradle-babe | dying 2H6 3.02.392
CRADLE-CLOTHES 1 FR 0.0001 REL FR 1 V 0 P
in cradle-clothes our children where they lay, 1H4 1.01. 88
CRADLED 1 FR 0.0001 REL FR 1 V 0 P
roots, and husks | wherein the acorn cradled. TMP 1.02.465
CRADLE'S 1 FR 0.0001 REL FR 1 V 0 P
and gives the crutch the cradle's infancy. LLL 4.03.241
CRADLES 3 FR 0.0003 REL FR 2 V 1 P
being ever from their cradles bred together, AYL 1.01.108 P
do thoughts unveil in their dumb cradles. TRO 3.03.200
oxlips in their cradles growing, | marigolds on TNK 1.01. 10
CRAFT 21 FR 0.0023 REL FR 17 V 4 P
and this deceit loses the name of craft, | of WIV 5.05.226
fox and lambskins too, to signify that craft, MM 3.02. 9 P
craft against vice i must apply. 3.02.277
had you that craft to reave her | of what should AWW 5.03. 86
or will not else thy craft so quickly grow, TN 5.01.166
that taught me craft | to counterfeit oppression R2 1.04. 13
wooing poor craftsmen with the craft of smiles 1.04. 28
wherein cunning, but in craft? 1H4 2.04.457 P
so much | unto an enemy of craft and vantage, H5 3.06.144
lose all the serpentine craft of thy caduceus, TRO 2.03. 12 P
perchance, my lord, i show more craft than love, 3.02.153
whiles others fish with craft for great opinion, 4.04.103
him some way, | or wrath or craft may get him. COR 1.10. 16
your modesties have not craft enough to color. HAM 2.02.280 P
am not in madness, | but mad in craft. 3.04.188
harbor more craft and more corrupter ends | than LR 2.02.102
time | (when she had fitted you with her craft), CYM 5.05. 55
false creeping craft and perjury should thrust LUC 1517
when craft hath taught her thus to say: PP 18.34
catching all passions in his craft of will, LC 126
"for lo his passion, but an art of craft, | even 295
CRAFTED 1 FR 0.0001 REL FR 1 V 0 P
you have crafted fair! COR 4.06.118
CRAFTIER 1 FR 0.0001 REL FR 1 V 0 P
a craftier tereus, cousin, hast thou met, | and TIT 2.04. 41
/CRAFTILY 1 FR 0.0001 REL FR 1 V 0 P
either you are ignorant, | or seem so /craftily; MM 2.04. 75
CRAFTILY 1 FR 0.0001 REL FR 0 V 1 P
and that was craftily qualified too — and OTH 2.03. 40 P
CRAFT'S 1 FR 0.0001 REL FR 0 V 1 P
he is not his craft's master, he doth not do it 2H4 3.02.278 P
CRAFTS 3 FR 0.0003 REL FR 3 V 0 P
and my integrity ne'er knew the crafts | that AWW 4.02. 33
you have made fair hands, | you and your crafts! COR 4.06.118
when in one line two crafts directly meet. HAM 3.04.210
CRAFTSMEN 1 FR 0.0001 REL FR 1 V 0 P
wooing poor craftsmen with the craft of smiles R2 1.04. 28
CRAFTY 11 FR 0.0012 REL FR 9 V 2 P
matter | is little cupid's crafty arrow made, ADO 3.01. 22
a vengeance on your crafty withered hide! SHR 2.01.404
nay, you may think my love was crafty love, JN 4.01. 53
wherein crafty, but in villainy? 1H4 2.04.457 P
they say, "a crafty knave does need no broker," 2H6 1.02.100
to call them both a pair of crafty knaves. 1.02.103
who being accus'd a crafty murtherer, | his 3.01.254
full often, like a shag-hair'd crafty kern, 3.01.367
the policy of those crafty swearing rascals, TRO 5.04. 9 P
but with a crafty madness keeps aloof | when we HAM 3.01. 8
that such a crafty devil as is his mother CYM 2.01. 52
CRAFTY-SICK 1 FR 0.0001 REL FR 1 V 0 P
father, old northumberland, | lies crafty-sick. 2H4 in 37
CRAGGY 1 FR 0.0001 REL FR 1 V 0 P
fields, | and all the craggy mountains yield. PP 19. 4
CRAK'D *(also crack'd)*

CRAK'D 1 FR 0.0001 REL FR 1 V 0 P
our brags | were crak'd of kitchen trulls, or CYM 5.05.177
CRAM 6 FR 0.0006 REL FR 5 V 1 P
you cram these words into mine ears against TMP 2.01.107
think | what 'tis to cram a maw or clothe a back MM 3.02. 22
whose skull jove cram with brains! TN 1.05.113 P
cram 's with praise, and make 's | as fat as WT 1.02. 91
or may we cram | within this wooden o the very H5 pr 12
and in despite i'll cram thee with more food. ROM 5.03. 48
CRAMM'D 8 FR 0.0009 REL FR 5 V 3 P
being thus cramm'd in the basket, a couple of WIV 3.05. 97 P
as would be cramm'd up in a sheet of paper, LLL 5.02. 7
a voyage, he hath strange places cramm'd | with AYL 2.07. 40
the best persuaded of himself, so cramm'd (as he TN 2.03.150 P
him to rest, cramm'd with distressful bread, H5 4.01.270
but your heart | is cramm'd with arrogancy, H8 2.04.110
fat their thoughts | with this cramm'd reason: TRO 2.02. 49
and their store–houses cramm'd with grain; COR 1.01. 81 P
CRAMP 4 FR 0.0004 REL FR 1 V 3 P
o, touch me not, i am not stephano, but a cramp. TMP 5.01.287 P
and being taken with the cramp was drown'd; AYL 4.01.104 P
marry, in coming on he has the cramp. AWW 4.03.291 P
the aged cramp | had screw'd his square foot TNK 5.01.110
CRAMPS 4 FR 0.0004 REL FR 4 V 0 P
this, be sure, to–night thou shalt have cramps, TMP 1.02.325
what i command, i'll rack thee with old cramps, 1.02.369
shorten up their sinews | with aged cramps, and 4.01.260
is plagu'd with cramps and gouts and painful LUC 856
CRAMS 1 FR 0.0001 REL FR 1 V 0 P
a robber's haste | crams his rich thiev'ry up, TRO 4.04. 43
CRANKING 1 FR 0.0001 REL FR 1 V 0 P
see how this river comes me cranking in, | and 1H4 3.01. 97
CRANKS 3 FR 0.0003 REL FR 3 V 0 P
and, through the cranks and offices of man, COR 1.01.137
the soldier in | the cranks and turns of thebes? TNK 1.02. 28
he cranks and crosses with a thousand doubles: VEN 682
CRANMER 7 FR 0.0008 REL FR 7 V 0 P
my learn'd and well–beloved servant, cranmer, H8 2.04.239
but, my lord, | when returns cranmer? 3.02. 63
is sprung up | an heretic, an arch–one, cranmer; 3.02.102
that cranmer is return'd with welcome, 3.02.400
of the archbishop's, | the virtuous cranmer. 4.01.105
cranmer will find a friend will not shrink from 4.01.107
till cranmer, cromwell, her two hands, and she 5.01. 31
CRANMER'S 1 FR 0.0001 REL FR 1 V 0 P
this same cranmer's | a worthy fellow, and hath H8 3.02. 71
CRANNIED 1 FR 0.0001 REL FR 1 V 0 P
that had in it a crannied hole or chink, MND 5.01.158
CRANNIES 2 FR 0.0002 REL FR 2 V 0 P
but creep in crannies, when he hides his beams: ERR 2.02. 31
through little vents and crannies of the place LUC 310
CRANNY 3 FR 0.0003 REL FR 2 V 1 P
and through that cranny shall pyramus and thisby MND 3.01. 70 P
and this the cranny is, right and sinister, 5.01.163
revealing day through every cranny spies, | and LUC 1086
CRANTS 1 FR 0.0001 REL FR 1 V 0 P
yet here she is allow'd her virgin crants, | her HAM 5.01.232
/CRARE 1 FR 0.0001 REL FR 1 V 0 P
to show what coast thy sluggish /crare | mightst CYM 4.02.205
CRASH 1 FR 0.0001 REL FR 1 V 0 P
base, and with a hideous crash | takes prisoner HAM 2.02.476
CRASING *(also grazing)*
CRASING 1 FR 0.0001 REL FR 1 V 0 P
that being dead, like to the bullet's crasing, H5 4.03.105
CRASSUS' 1 FR 0.0001 REL FR 1 V 0 P
pleas'd fortune does of marcus crassus' death ANT 3.01. 2
CRASSUS 2 FR 0.0002 REL FR 2 V 0 P
notice | to valentius, rowland, and to crassus, MM 4.05. 8
pacorus, orodes, | pays this for marcus crassus. ANT 3.01. 5
CRAV'D 3 FR 0.0003 REL FR 3 V 0 P
embassador upon that instant | crav'd audience; H5 1.01. 92
by message crav'd, so is lord talbot come. 1H6 2.03. 13
an offense, | which crav'd that very time. TNK 5.03. 64
CRAVE 51 FR 0.0057 REL FR 45 V 6 P
this must crave | (and if this be at all) a most TMP 5.01.116
twenty thousand worthier come to crave her. WIV 4.04. 90
i crave your honor's pardon. MM 2.02. 14
i shall crave your forbearance a little. 4.01. 22 P
effect, i crave but four days' respite; 4.02.160 P
that if any crave redress of injustice, they 4.04. 9 P
lord, | i crave no other, nor no better man. 5.01.426
never crave him, we are definitive. 5.01.427
that i crave death more willingly than mercy: 5.01.476
i crave your pardon. ERR 1.02. 26
you withal, to the end to crave your assistance. LLL 5.01.116 P
i crave the law, | the penalty and forfeit of my MV 4.01.206
i'll crave the day | when i shall ask the banes, SHR 2.01.179
therefore i shall crave of you your leave, that TN 2.01. 5 P
for his designs crave haste, his haste good hope R2 2.02. 44
am i, | till time and vantage crave my company. 2H4 2.03. 68
england | do crave admittance to your majesty. H5 2.04. 66
when ladies crave to be encount'red with. 1H6 2.02. 46
nor other satisfaction do i crave, | but only, 2.03. 77
and crave | i may have liberty to venge this 3.04. 41
and wherefore crave you combat? 4.01. 84
i crave the benefit of law of arms. 4.01.100
and then i need not crave his courtesy. 5.03.105
father's castle walls | we'll crave a parley, to 5.03.130
/is thither gone to crave the french king's 3H6 3.01. 30
am come to crave thy just and lawful aid; 3.03. 32
person, | and then to crave a league of amity, 3.03. 53
prevail, | i then crave pardon of your majesty. 4.06. 8
humbly on my knee | i crave your blessing. R3 2.02.106
fair conduct | crave leave to view these ladies, H8 1.04. 71
than crave the hire which first we do deserve. COR 2.03.114
my nobler friends, i crave their pardons. 3.01. 65
i may be heard, i would crave a word or two, 3.01.281
his help to crave, and my dear hap to tell. ROM 2.02.189
immortal gods, i crave no pelf, | i pray for no TIM 1.02. 62
but i shall crave your pardon; MAC 4.03. 20
i crave no more than hath your highness offer'd, LR 1.01.194
state, | i crave fit disposition for my wife, OTH 1.03.236
i crave your highness' pardon. ANT 2.05. 98
i crave our composition may be written | and 2.06. 58
for it seems | they crave to be demanded. CYM 4.02.362
here to have death in peace is all he'll crave. PER 2.01. 11
i did but crave. 2.01. 87
but crave? 2.01. 88 P
gives them what he will, not what they crave. 2.03. 47
us, envy of ill men | crave our acquaintance; TNK 2.02. 91
so offers he to give what she did crave, | but VEN 88
let him have time a beggar's orts to crave, LUC 985
and yet thou lefts me more than i did crave, PP 10. 9
o yes, dear friend, i pardon crave of thee, 10.11
or at your hand th' account of hours to crave, SON 58. 3
CRAVED 2 FR 0.0002 REL FR 2 V 0 P
and craved death | rather than i would be so 1H6 1.04. 32
crave, | for why i craved nothing of thee still. PP 10.10
CRAVEN 4 FR 0.0004 REL FR 3 V 1 P
no cock of mine, you crow too like a craven. SHR 2.01.227
he is a craven and a villain else, and't please H5 4.07.133 P
or durst not for his craven heart say thus. 1H6 2.04. 87
or some craven scruple | of thinking too HAM 4.04. 40
CRAVEN'S 1 FR 0.0001 REL FR 1 V 0 P
to tear the garter from thy craven's leg, 1H6 4.01. 15
CRAVENS 1 FR 0.0001 REL FR 1 V 0 P
so divine | that cravens my weak hand. CYM 3.04. 78
CRAVER 1 FR 0.0001 REL FR 0 V 1 P
then i'll turn craver too, and so i shall scape PER 2.01. 88 P
CRAVES 27 FR 0.0030 REL FR 26 V 1 P
and craves no other tribute at thy hands | but SHR 5.02.152
and to do that well craves a kind of wit. TN 3.01. 61
craves harborage within your city walls. JN 2.01.234
and craves to kiss your hand and take his leave. R2 1.03. 53
for my lady craves | to know the cause of your 1H6 2.03. 29
who craves a parley with the burgundy? 3.03. 37
a breach that craves a quick expedient stop! 2H6 3.01.288
the lord mayor craves aid of your honor from the 4.05. 4 P
and craves your company for speedy counsel. 3H6 2.01.208
nature craves | all dues be rend'red to their TRO 2.02.173
the violent fit a' th' time craves it as physic COR 3.02. 33
being gentle wounded, craves | a noble cunning. 4.01. 8
he craves a parley at your father's house, TIT 5.01.159
madam, your mother craves a word with you. ROM 1.05.111
what sorrow craves acquaintance at my hand, 3.03. 5
which craves as desperate an execution | as that 4.01. 69
which craves to be rememb'red | with those five TIM 2.02.228
forth the adder, | and that craves wary walking. JC 2.01. 15
sweno, the norways' king, craves composition; MAC 1.02. 59
craves the conveyance of a promis'd march | over HAM 4.04. 3
our businesses, | which craves the instant use. LR 2.01.128
this letter, madam, craves a speedy answer; 4.02. 82
and of thee craves | the circle of the ptolomies ANT 3.12. 17
and whence he comes, | and what he craves. PER 1.04. 81
the governor, | who craves to come aboard. 5.01. 5
their surfeit | that craves a present med'cine, TNK 1.01.191
the cause craves haste, and it will soon be writ LUC 1295
CRAVETH 1 FR 0.0001 REL FR 1 V 0 P
the earl of salisbury craveth supply, | and 1H6 1.01.159
CRAVING 5 FR 0.0005 REL FR 5 V 0 P
on serious business craving quick dispatch, LLL 2.01. 31
myself | craving your opinion of my title, 2H6 2.02. 4
she, on his left side, craving aid for henry; 3H6 3.01. 43
shall have cause of state | craving us jointly. MAC 3.01. 34
though craving seriousness and skill, pass'd TNK 1.03. 28
CRAWL 2 FR 0.0002 REL FR 2 V 0 P
briers, | i can no further crawl, no further go; MND 3.02.444
while we | unburthen'd crawl toward death. LR 1.01. 41
CRAWL'D 1 FR 0.0001 REL FR 1 V 0 P
one | hath crawl'd into the favor of the king, H8 3.02.103
CRAWLING 2 FR 0.0002 REL FR 1 V 1 P
to pluck this crawling serpent from my breast! MND 2.02.146
such fellows as i do crawling between earth and HAM 3.01.127 P
CRAWLS 1 FR 0.0001 REL FR 1 V 0 P
crawls to maturity, wherewith being crown'd, SON 60. 6
CRAYER *(see crare)*
CRAZ'D 3 FR 0.0003 REL FR 3 V 0 P
so many miseries have craz'd my voice | that my R3 4.04. 17
to half a soul and to a notion craz'd | say, MAC 3.01. 82
to tell thee, | the grief hath craz'd my wits. LR 3.04.170
CRAZED 1 FR 0.0001 REL FR 1 V 0 P
yield | thy crazed title to my certain right. MND 1.01. 92
CRAZY 1 FR 0.0001 REL FR 1 V 0 P
place, | fitter for sickness and for crazy age. 1H6 3.02. 89
CREAKING 2 FR 0.0002 REL FR 1 V 1 P
smock, | creaking my shoes on the plain masonry, AWW 2.01. 31
let not the creaking of shoes nor the rustling LR 3.04. 94 P
CREAM 5 FR 0.0005 REL FR 3 V 2 P
do cream and mantle like a standing pond, | and MV 1.01. 89
nor your cheek of cream | that can entame my AYL 3.05. 47
sooth, she is | the queen of curds and cream. WT 4.04.161
me, i am as vigilant as a cat to steal cream. 1H4 4.02. 59 P
i think, to steal cream indeed, for thy theft 4.02. 60 P
CREAM–FAC'D 1 FR 0.0001 REL FR 1 V 0 P
devil damn thee black, thou cream–fac'd loon! MAC 5.03. 11
/CREATE 1 FR 0.0001 REL FR 1 V 0 P
o any thing, of nothing first /create! ROM 1.01.177
CREATE 20 FR 0.0022 REL FR 20 V 0 P
would you create me new? ERR 3.02. 39
and the issue, there create, | ever shall be MND 5.01.405
creature as a maid, | i can create the rest. AWW 2.03.143
for we'll create young arthur duke of britain JN 2.01.551
being create for comfort, to be us'd | in 4.01.106
and we create, in absence of ourself, | our R2 2.01.219
this | king richard might create a perfect guess 2H4 3.01. 88
you | with hearts create of duty and of zeal. H5 2.02. 31
deserts | we here create you earl of shrewsbury, 1H6 3.04. 26
we here create thee the first duke of suffolk, 2H6 1.01. 64
richard, i will create thee duke of gloucester, 3H6 2.06.103
king, | and come now to create you duke of york. 4.03. 34
her ashes new create another heir | as great in H8 5.04. 41
that you create our emperor's eldest son, | lord TIT 1.01.224
we create | lord saturninus rome's great emperor 1.01.231
bride, | and will create thee empress of rome. 1.01.320
your eye in scotland | would create soldiers, MAC 4.03.187
create her child of spleen, that it may live LR 1.04.282
that i create thee here | my lord and master. 5.03. 77
i create you | companions to our person, and CYM 5.05. 20
CREATED 17 FR 0.0019 REL FR 15 V 2 P
new created | the creatures that were mine, i TMP 1.02. 81
are created | of every creature's best! 3.01. 47
have with our needles created both one flower, MND 3.02.204
i think thou wast created for men to breathe AWW 2.03.255 P
thee, | since thou, created to be aw'd by man, R2 5.05. 91
therefore was i created with a stubborn outside, H5 5.02.226 P
and if thou be not then created york, | i will 1H6 2.04.119
and rise created princely duke of york. 3.01.172
created, for his rare success in arms, | great 4.07. 62
he were created knight for his good service. 2H6 5.01. 77
o'er him whom heaven created for thy ruler. 5.01.105
pass'd over to the end they were created, 3H6 2.05. 39
functions, | created only to calumniate. TRO 5.02.124
things created | to buy and sell with groats, to COR 3.02. 9
and thou hast created | a mother and two CYM 5.04.124
and for a woman wert thou first created, | till SON 20. 9
which eyes not yet created shall o'er–read, 81.10
CREATES 1 FR 0.0001 REL FR 1 V 0 P
he creates | lucius proconsul; CYM 3.07. 7
CREATING 5 FR 0.0005 REL FR 4 V 1 P
that ever nature had praise for creating. AWW 4.05. 10 P
piedness shares | with great creating nature. WT 4.04. 88
and form, | creating awe and fear in other men? H5 4.01.247
bed, | go to th' creating a whole tribe of fops, LR 1.02. 14
creating every bad a perfect best | as fast as SON 114. 7
CREATION 12 FR 0.0013 REL FR 11 V 1 P
men their creation mar | in profiting by them. MM 2.04.127
and woman after this downright way of creation. 3.02.105 P
what demigod | hath come so near creation? MV 3.02.116
what great creation and what dole of honor AWW 2.03.169
that from the prime creation e'er she framed." R3 4.03. 19
but | a dagger of the mind, a false creation, MAC 2.01. 38
this bodiless creation ecstasy | is very cunning HAM 3.04.138
and in th' essential vesture of creation | does OTH 2.01. 64
born to uphold creation in that honor | first TNK 1.01. 82
come, | from the creation to the general doom. LUC 924
but heaven in thy creation did decree | that in SON 93. 9
lack, | sland'ring creation with a false esteem: 127.12
CREATOR'S 1 FR 0.0001 REL FR 1 V 0 P
days, | to sin's rebuke and my creator's praise. 3H6 4.06. 44
CREATURE 78 FR 0.0088 REL FR 59 V 19 P
(who had, no doubt, some noble creature in her) TMP 1.02. 7
as an hair | betid to any creature in the vessel 1.02. 31
no, precious creature, | i had rather crack my 3.01. 25
why, sir, she's a good creature. WIV 2.02. 55 P
i am not such a sickly creature, i give heaven 3.04. 59 P
the modest wife, the virtuous creature, that 4.02.131 P
a creature unprepar'd, unmeet for death; MM 4.03. 67
say he dines forth, and let no creature enter. ERR 2.02.210
teach me, dear creature, how to think and speak: 3.02. 33
being a very beastly creature, lays claim to me. 3.02. 88 P
no, not a creature enters in my house. 5.01. 92
he hath left to be known a reasonable creature. ADO 1.01. 71 P
the change of words with any creature, | refuse 4.01.183
dote | upon the next live creature that it sees. MND 2.01.172
bring me the fairest creature northward born, MV 2.01. 4
know | a creature that did bear the shape of man 3.02.275
when nature hath made a fair creature, may she AYL 1.02. 43 P
she was the fairest creature in the world, | and SHR in.2. 66
madam, a wicked creature, as you and all flesh AWW 1.03. 35 P
if thou canst like this creature as a maid, | i 2.03.142
i /warr'nt, good creature, wheresoe'er she is, 3.05. 66
she's a fair creature; 3.06.116
helen, that's dead, | was a sweet creature; 5.03. 78
my lord, this is a fond and desp'rate creature, 5.03.178
save in the constant image of the creature TN 2.04. 19
this jealousy | is for a precious creature: WT 1.02.452
which i'll not call a creature of thy place, 2.01. 83
to me comes a creature, | sometimes her head on 3.03. 19
this is a creature, | would she begin a sect, 5.01.106
the majesty of the creature in resemblance of 5.02. 35 P
there was not such a gracious creature born. JN 3.04. 81
and from the common'st creature pluck a glove R2 5.03. 17
and here is not a creature but myself, | i 5.05. 4
poor old jack, then am i no two–legg'd creature. 1H4 2.04.188 P
how now, my sweet creature of bumbast, how long 2.04.327 P
and many a creature else | had been alive this 5.05. 7
i do now remember the poor creature, small beer. 2H4 2.02. 11 P
ingrateful, savage, and inhuman creature? H5 2.02. 95
divinest creature, astraea's daughter, | how 1H6 1.06. 4
curse not thyself, fair creature — thou art R3 1.02.132
i took him for the plainest harmless creature 3.05. 25
there is no creature loves me, | and if i die no 5.03.200
he spoke | my chaplain to no creature living but H8 1.02.166
before the primest creature | that's paragon'd 2.04.230
in affection to | a creature of the queen's, 3.02. 36
she is a gallant creature, and complete | in 3.02. 49
yet my conscience says | she's a good creature, 5.01. 25
his horse, for that's the more capable creature. TRO 3.03.307 P
ah, beastly creature, | the blot and enemy to TIT 2.03.182
grief | it is supposed the fair creature died, ROM 5.03. 51
this fellow here, lord timon, this thy creature, TIM 1.01.116
and cassius is | a wretched creature, and must JC 1.02.117
it is a creature that i teach to fight, | to 4.01. 31
/confederate season, else no creature seeing, HAM 3.02.256
or like a creature native and indued | unto that 4.07.179
didst intend | to make this creature fruitful. LR 1.04.277
wheat, and hurts the poor creature of earth. 3.04.119 P
and the creature run from the cur? 4.06.157 P
indeed she's a most fresh and delicate creature. OTH 2.03. 20 P
good wine is a good familiar creature, if it be 2.03.310 P
this honest creature, doubtless, | sees and 3.03.242
cry, "o sweet creature!" 3.03.422
it is a creature | that dotes on cassio (as 'tis 4.01. 95
o, the world hath not a sweeter creature! 4.01.184 P
most sovereign creature — ANT 5.02. 81
and therefore banish'd) is a creature such | as, CYM 1.01. 19
make | us weep to hear your fate, fair creature, PER 3.02.103
i will do't, but yet she is a goodly creature. 4.01. 9
word, nor did ill turn | to any living creature. 4.01. 76
is she not a fair creature? 4.06. 43 P
dwell in proclaims you to be a creature of sale. 4.06. 78 P
your servant | (your most unworthy creature) but TNK 2.05. 40
a right good creature, more to me deserving 5.04. 34
'tis he, foul creature, that hath done thee VEN 1005
"bonnet nor veil henceforth no creature wear! 1081
in my chamber came | a creeping creature, with a LUC 1627
fair creature, kill'd too soon by death's sharp PP 10. 4
the most sweet favor or deformed'st creature, SON 113.10
CREATURE'S 3 FR 0.0003 REL FR 3 V 0 P
are created | of every creature's best! TMP 3.01. 48
the sweet'st, dear'st creature's dead, and WT 3.02.201
by him, | this creature's no such thing. ANT 3.03. 41
/CREATURES 1 FR 0.0001 REL FR 1 V 0 P

/thy /niece /and /i, /poor /creatures, /want TIT 3.02. 5
CREATURES 45 FR 0.0050 REL FR 37 V 8 P
new created | the creatures that were mine, i TMP 1.02. 82
the seas and shores — yea, all the creatures, 3.03. 74
how many goodly creatures are there here! 5.01.182
sovereign to all the creatures on the earth. TGV 2.04.153
foolish christian creatures as i would desires. WIV 4.01. 71 P
him | he us'd as creatures of another place, AWW 1.02. 42
fear of mars before it, and of his creatures, 4.01. 30 P
is not more twin | than these two creatures. TN 5.01.224
this place is famous for the creatures | of prey WT 3.03. 12
creatures of note for mercy–lacking uses. JN 4.01.120
creatures that by a rule in nature teach | the H5 1.02.188
island of england breeds very valiant creatures; 3.07.141 P
to see how god in all his creatures works! 2H6 2.01. 7
unreasonable creatures feed their young, | and 3H6 2.02. 26
kings it makes gods, and meaner creatures kings. R3 5.02. 24
and heav'nly blessings | follow such creatures. H8 2.03. 58
as well of glib and slipp'ry creatures as | of TIM 1.01. 53
they were the most needless creatures living, 1.02. 97 P
call the creatures | whose naked natures live in 4.03.227
home, you idle creatures, get you home! JC 1.01. 1
bad causes swear | such creatures as men doubt; 2.01.132
heard | that guilty creatures sitting at a play HAM 2.02.589
you nickname god's creatures and make your 3.01.145 P
we fat all creatures else to fat us, and we fat 4.03. 22 P
those wicked creatures yet do look well–favor'd LR 2.04.256
that we can call these delicate creatures ours, OTH 3.03.269
of no such baseness | as jealious creatures are, 3.04. 28
and kindly creatures | turn all to serpents! ANT 2.05. 78
of these thy compounds on such creatures as | we CYM 1.05. 19
two creatures heartily. 1.06. 83
cruel to me as you, o the dearest of creatures, 3.02. 42 P
these are kind creatures. 4.02. 32
a cave–keeper, | and cook to honest creatures. 4.02.299
creatures may be alike; 5.05.125
her knowledge only | in killing creatures vild, 5.05.252
if heaven slumber while their creatures want, PER 1.04. 16
although they gave their creatures in abundance, 1.04. 36
and hundreds call themselves | your creatures, 3.02. 45
we were never so much out of creatures. 4.02. 6 P
pursue these fearful creatures o'er the downs, VEN 677
and there we will unfold | to creatures stern, LUC 1147
a pretty while these pretty creatures stand, 1233
such harmless creatures have a true respect | to 1347
from fairest creatures we desire increase, SON 1. 1
one of her feathered creatures broke away, 143. 2
CREDENCE 3 FR 0.0003 REL FR 3 V 0 P
your majesty, may plead | for amplest credence. AWW 1.02. 11
hope, lay our best love and credence | upon thy 3.03. 2
sith yet there is a credence in my heart, | an TRO 5.02.120
CREDENT 4 FR 0.0004 REL FR 4 V 0 P
no, | for my authority bears of a credent bulk, MM 4.04. 26
then 'tis very credent | thou mayst co–join with WT 1.02.142
if with too credent ear you list his songs, | or HAM 1.03. 30
and credent soul to that strong–bonded oath LC 279
CREDIBLE 1 FR 0.0001 REL FR 1 V 0 P
nay, 'tis most credible; AWW 1.02. 4
/CREDIT 1 FR 0.0001 REL FR 1 V 0 P
/if /on /my /credit /you /dare /build /so /far LR 3.01. 35
CREDIT 57 FR 0.0064 REL FR 43 V 14 P
sinner of his memory | to credit his own lie — TMP 1.02.102
it is — which is indeed almost beyond credit — 2.01. 60 P
and what does else want credit, come to me, 3.03. 25
'tis a goodly credit for you. WIV 4.02.190 P
whose credit with the judge, or own great place, MM 2.04. 92
were testimonies against his worth and credit 5.01.244
the one ne'er got me credit, the other mickle ERR 3.01. 45
make us /but believe | (being compact of credit) 3.02. 22
consider how it stands upon my credit. 4.01. 68
of credit infinite, highly belov'd, | second to 5.01. 6
thus will i save my credit in the shoot: LLL 4.01. 26
titania, | glance at my credit with hippolyta, MND 2.01. 75
go forth, | try what my credit can in venice do. MV 1.01.180
double self, | and there's an oath of credit. 5.01.246
sir, i wrastle for my credit, and he that AYL 1.01.127 P
i call them forth to credit her. SHR 4.01.104 P
his name and credit shall you undertake, | and 4.02.107
lady, | you must hold the credit of your father. AWW 1.01. 78
how shall they credit | a poor unlearned virgin, 1.03.239
to dissever so | our great self and our credit, 2.01.123
my reputation and credit and as i hope to live. 4.03.134 P
condition, and what credit i have with the duke. 4.03.172 P
yet i was in that credit with them at that time 5.03.262 P
this is much credit to you. TN 2.03.108 P
yet there he was, and there i found this credit, 4.03. 6
what? lack i credit? WT 2.01.157
beseech your highness, give us better credit. 2.03.147
that which i shall report will bear no credit, 5.01.179
though credit be asleep and not an ear open: 5.02. 62 P
just, | and, as i am a gentleman, i credit him. R2 3.03.120
and where it would not, i have us'd my credit. 1H4 1.02. 56 P
into) for their own credit sake make all whole. 2.01. 72 P
man, i have little credit with your worship. 2H4 5.01. 49 P
such as were grown to credit by the wars; 1H6 4.01. 36
fight for credit of the prentices. 2H6 2.03. 71 P
and will you credit this base drudge's words, 4.02.151
thereon i pawn my credit and mine honor. 3H6 3.03.116
being now seen possible enough, got credit, H8 1.01. 37
else | this talking lord can lay upon my credit, 3.02.265
on his fracted dates | have smit my credit. TIM 2.01. 23
father, | and kept his credit with his purse; 3.02. 68
my credit now stands on such slippery ground JC 3.01.191
and partly credit things that do presage. 5.01. 78
in /these news | that gives them credit. OTH 1.03. 2
of years, of country, credit, every thing, | to 1.03. 97
she loves him, 'tis apt and of great credit. 2.01.287
good, | she shall undo her credit with the moor. 2.03.359
the credit that thy lady hath of thee | deserves CYM 1.06.157
thy most perfect goodness | her assur'd credit. 1.06.159
o, our credit comes not in like the commodity, PER 4.02. 30 P
and make /my senses credit thy relation | to 5.01.123
lord cerimon hath letters of good credit, sir, 5.03. 77
now, when the credit of our town lay on it, TNK 3.05. 56
it concerns your credit | and my oath equally. 3.06.223
you that have voice and credit with the number, STM II.C 51
i smiling credit her false–speaking tongue, PP 1. 7
simply i credit her false–speaking tongue; SON 138. 7
CREDITOR 6 FR 0.0006 REL FR 5 V 1 P
determines | herself the glory of a creditor, MM 1.01. 39
bear me forthwith unto his creditor, | and, ERR 4.04.120
of flesh | to–morrow to my bloody creditor. MV 3.03. 34
there is a soul counts thee her creditor, | and JN 3.03. 21
belee'd and calm'd | by debitor and creditor — OTH 1.01. 31
you have no true debitor and creditor but it; CYM 5.04.168 P
CREDITORS 6 FR 0.0006 REL FR 2 V 4 P
i would send for certain of my creditors; MM 1.02.132 P
divers of antonio's creditors in my company to MV 3.01.113 P
have all miscarried, my creditors grow cruel, my 3.02.316 P
i break, and you, my gentle creditors, lose. 2H4 ep 12 P
his means most short, his creditors most strait. TIM 1.01. 96
creditors? 3.04.104
CREDO 4 FR 0.0004 REL FR 0 V 4 P
sir nathaniel, haud credo. LLL 4.02. 11 P
'twas not a haud credo, 'twas a pricket. 4.02. 12 P
to insert again my haud credo for a deer. 4.02. 19 P
i said the deer was not a haud credo, 'twas a 4.02. 20 P
CREDULITY 1 FR 0.0001 REL FR 1 V 0 P
whose ignorant credulity will not | come up to WT 2.01.192
CREDULOUS 10 FR 0.0011 REL FR 9 V 1 P
a most poor credulous monster! TMP 2.02.146 P
are, | and credulous to false prints. MM 2.04.130
if he be credulous, and trust my tale, | i'll SHR 4.02. 67
maiden, | but may not be so credulous of cure, AWW 2.01.115
and, being credulous in this mad thought, | i'll TIT 5.02. 74
a credulous father and a brother noble, | whose LR 1.02.179
thus credulous fools are caught, | and many OTH 4.01. 45
ay me, most credulous fool, | egregious CYM 5.05.210
not to believe, and yet too credulous: VEN 986
story | the credulous old priam after slew; LUC 1522
CREED 1 FR 0.0001 REL FR 1 V 0 P
there's my creed. H8 2.02. 50
CREEK 1 FR 0.0001 REL FR 1 V 0 P
i'll throw't into the creek | behind our rock, CYM 4.02.151
CREEKS 1 FR 0.0001 REL FR 1 V 0 P
countermands | the passages of alleys, creeks, ERR 4.02. 38
CREEP 29 FR 0.0032 REL FR 22 V 7 P
my best way is to creep under his gaberdine; TMP 2.02. 38 P
love | will creep in service where it cannot go. TGV 4.02. 20
of any reasonable stature, he may creep in here, WIV 3.03.130 P
let me creep in here. 3.03.142 P
he cannot creep into a halfpenny purse, nor into 3.05.146 P
what shall i do? i'll creep up into the chimney. 4.02. 55 P
creep into the kill–hole. 4.02. 58 P
but creep in crannies, when he hides his beams: ERR 2.02. 31
now will he creep into sedges. ADO 2.01.202 P
th' idea of her life shall sweetly creep | into 4.01.224
creep into acorn–cups and hide them there. MND 2.01. 31
that the moon | may through the centre creep, 3.02. 54
with leaden legs and batty wings doth creep. 3.02.365
and creep into the jaundies | by being peevish? MV 1.01. 85
that creep into the dreaming bridegroom's ear, 3.02. 52
and let the sounds of music | creep in our ears. 5.01. 56
and subtle stealth | to creep in at mine eyes. TN 1.05.298
that creep like shadows by him and do sigh | at WT 2.03. 34
and creep time ne'er so slow, | yet it shall JN 3.03. 31
shall secretly into the bosom creep | of that 1H4 1.03.266
and creep into it far before thy time? 3H6 1.01.237
to come as humbly as they us'd to creep | to TRO 3.03. 73
how some men creep in skittish fortune's hall, 3.03.134
creep in the minds and marrows of our youth, TIM 4.01. 26
ape, | to try conclusions in the basket creep, HAM 3.04.195
sit, | long after fearing to creep forth again; VEN 1036
lame, blind, halt, creep, cry out for thee, LUC 902
lays open all the little worms that creep; 1248
million'd accidents | creep in 'twixt vows, and SON 115. 6
CREEPING 11 FR 0.0012 REL FR 10 V 1 P
as wild geese that the creeping fowler eye, | or MND 3.02. 20
lose and neglect the creeping hours of time; AYL 2.07.112
creeping like snail | unwillingly to school. 2.07.146
thou dost guess of harm | is creeping toward me; WT 1.02.404
borne with th' invisible and creeping wind, H5 3.pr. 11
time | when creeping murmur and the poring dark 4.pr. 2
or any creeping venom'd thing that lives! R3 1.02. 20
he has wings, he's more than a creeping thing. COR 5.04. 14 P
which drives the creeping thief to some regard; LUC 305
false creeping craft and perjury should thrust 1517
in my chamber came | a creeping creature, with a 1627
CREEPS 7 FR 0.0008 REL FR 6 V 1 P
smallest monstrous mouse that creeps on floor, MND 5.01.220
creeps in this petty pace from day to day, | to MAC 5.05. 20
creeps apace | into the hearts of such as have ANT 1.03. 50
she creeps; 3.03. 18
how creeps acquaintance? CYM 1.04. 24 P
he like a thievish dog creeps sadly thence, LUC 736
and they that watch see time how slow it creeps. 1575
CREON 5 FR 0.0005 REL FR 5 V 0 P
fell before | the wrath of cruel creon; TNK 1.01. 40
which to do | must make some work with creon. 1.01.150
our uncle creon. 1.02. 62
our services stand now for thebes, not creon. 1.02. 99
what had we been, old in the court of creon, 2.02.105
CREPT 17 FR 0.0019 REL FR 14 V 3 P
wrack, | this music crept by me upon the waters, TMP 1.02.392
how now, sir proteus, are you crept before us? TGV 4.02. 18
which is now crept into a lute–string and now ADO 3.02. 60 P
are you crept hither to see the wrastling? AYL 1.02.156 P
waist, i could have crept into any alderman's 1H4 2.04.331 P
day | is crept into the bosom of the sea; 2H6 4.01. 2
beggary | is crept into the palace of our king, 4.01.102
no sooner was i crept out of my cradle | but i 4.09. 3
since i am crept in favor with myself, | i will R3 1.02.258
where eyes did once inhabit, there were crept 1.04. 30
from forth the kennel of thy womb hath crept | a 4.04. 47
wife | has crept too near his conscience. H8 2.02. 17
conscience | has crept too near another lady. 2.02. 18
slept, | whilst emulation in the army crept: TRO 2.02.212
him | were slily crept into his human powers, COR 2.01.220
the deep of night is crept upon our talk, | and JC 4.03.226
in thy weak hive a wand'ring wasp hath crept, LUC 839
CRESCENT 4 FR 0.0004 REL FR 2 V 2 P
he is no crescent, and his horns are invisible MND 5.01.242 P
for nature crescent does not grow alone | in HAM 1.03. 11
my powers are crescent, and my auguring hope ANT 2.01. 10
he was then of a crescent note, expected to CYM 1.04. 2 P
CRESCIVE 1 FR 0.0001 REL FR 1 V 0 P
by night, | unseen, yet crescive in his faculty. H5 1.01. 66
CRESSETS 1 FR 0.0001 REL FR 1 V 0 P
was full of fiery shapes | of burning cressets, 1H4 3.01. 15
CRESSID 34 FR 0.0038 REL FR 29 V 5 P
grecian tents, | where cressid lay that night. MV 5.01. 6
and when fair cressid comes into my thoughts — TRO 1.01. 30
i cannot come to cressid but by pandar, | and 1.01. 95
what cressid is, what pandar, and what we: 1.01. 99
good morrow, cousin cressid. 1.02. 43 P
fellow, thou hast not seen the lady cressid. 3.01. 38 P
his painted wings, | and fly with me to cressid! 3.02. 15
o cressid, how often have i wish'd me thus! 3.02. 61 P
shall be such to cressid as what envy can say 3.02. 96 P
why was my cressid then so hard to win? 3.02.116
your leave, sweet cressid! 3.02.140
the heart of falsehood, | "as false as cressid." 3.02.196
desir'd my cressid in right great exchange, 3.03. 21
bear him, | and bring us cressid hither; 3.03. 31
for the enfreed antenor, the fair cressid. 4.01. 39
borne to greece | than cressid borne from troy. 4.01. 48
o foolish cressid! 4.02. 17
where's my cousin cressid? 4.02. 24 P
cressid, i love thee in so strain'd a purity 4.04. 24
a woeful cressid 'mongst the merry greeks! 4.04. 56
name cressid, and thy life shall be as safe | as 4.04.115
fair lady cressid, | so please you, save the 4.04.116
is this the lady cressid? 4.05. 17
and bent of amorous view | on the fair cressid. 4.05.283
cressid comes forth to him. 5.02. 6
was cressid here? 5.02.125
nor mine, my lord; cressid was here but now. 5.02.128
rather think this not cressid. 5.02.133
this is, and is not, cressid! 5.02.146
cressid is mine, tied with the bonds of heaven. 5.02.154
as much /as i do cressid love, | so much by 5.02.167
o cressid! 5.02.178
o false cressid! 5.02.178
present the fair steed to my lady cressid. 5.05. 2
CRESSIDA 10 FR 0.0011 REL FR 4 V 6 P
sir, to bring a cressida to this troilus. TN 3.01. 52 P
cressida was a beggar. 3.01. 55 P
good niece, do, sweet niece cressida. TRO 1.02.179 P
who? my cousin cressida? 3.01. 34 P
i'll lay my life, with my disposer cressida. 3.01. 87 P
why should you say cressida? 3.01. 92 P
o cressida! 4.02. 8
give up to diomedes' hand | the lady cressida. 4.02. 66
me, of what honor was | this cressida in troy? 4.05.288
no, this is diomed's cressida. 5.02.137
CRESSIDA'S 1 FR 0.0001 REL FR 0 V 1 P
at my cousin cressida's? TRO 3.02. 2 P
CRESSID'S 5 FR 0.0005 REL FR 5 V 0 P
i am cressid's uncle, | that dare leave two AWW 2.01. 97
fetch forth the lazar kite of cressid's kind, H5 2.01. 76
i tell thee i am mad | in cressid's love; TRO 1.01. 52
make cressid's name the very crown of falsehood, 4.02.100
to square the general sex | by cressid's rule. 5.02.133
CRESSIDS 1 FR 0.0001 REL FR 0 V 1 P
men be troiluses, all false women cressids, and TRO 3.02.203 P
CRESSY 1 FR 0.0001 REL FR 1 V 0 P
shame | when cressy battle fatally was struck, H5 2.04. 54
CREST 25 FR 0.0028 REL FR 24 V 1 P
each fair installment, coat, and sev'ral crest, WIV 5.05. 63
the devil's horn, | 'tis not the devil's crest. MM 2.04. 17
and beauty's crest becomes the heavens well. LLL 4.03.252
due but to one, and crowned with one crest. MND 3.02.214
the horn, | it was a crest ere thou wast born; AYL 4.02. 14
what is your crest? a coxcomb? SHR 2.01.225
there stuck no plume in any english crest | that JN 2.01.317
the heighth, the crest, or crest unto the crest, 4.03. 46
the heighth, the crest, or crest unto the crest, 4.03. 46
the heighth, the crest, or crest unto the crest, 4.03. 46
doth dogged war bristle his angry crest, | and 4.03.149
already smokes about the burning crest | of the 5.04. 34
up | the crest of youth against your dignity. 1H4 1.01. 99
and all the budding honors on thy crest | i'll 5.04. 72
from the dolphin's crest thy sword struck fire, 1H6 4.06. 10
that france must vail her lofty–plumed crest 5.03. 25
now, by my father's badge, old nevil's crest, 2H6 5.01.202
his crest that prouder than blue iris bends. TRO 1.03.379
on whose bright crest fame with her loud'st oyes 4.05.143
sir, his crest up again and the man in blood, COR 4.05.210 P
even thou hast strook upon my crest, | and with TIT 1.01.364
his batt'red shield, his uncontrolled crest, VEN 104
upon his compass'd crest now stand on end, | his 272
high crest, short ears, straight legs and 297
throwing the base thong from his bending crest, 395
CRESTED 1 FR 0.0001 REL FR 1 V 0 P
his rear'd arm | crested the world, his voice ANT 5.02. 83
CRESTFALLEN 1 FR 0.0001 REL FR 1 V 0 P
shall i seem crestfallen in my father's sight? R2 1.01.188
CRESTFALL'N 3 FR 0.0003 REL FR 2 V 1 P
wits till i were as crestfall'n as a dried pear. WIV 4.05.100 P
remember it, and let it make thee crestfall'n, 2H6 4.01. 59
grown so low | and crestfall'n with my wants. TNK 3.06. 7
CRESTLESS 1 FR 0.0001 REL FR 1 V 0 P
spring crestless yeomen from so deep a root? 1H6 2.04. 85
CRESTS 4 FR 0.0004 REL FR 4 V 0 P
his valors shown upon our crests to–day | have 1H4 5.05. 29
they fall their crests, and like deceitful jades JC 4.02. 26
let fall thy blade on vulnerable crests, | i MAC 5.08. 11
when tyrants' crests and tombs of brass are SON 107.14
CREST–WOUNDING 1 FR 0.0001 REL FR 1 V 0 P
o unfelt sore, crest–wounding private scar! LUC 828
CRETAN 1 FR 0.0001 REL FR 1 V 0 P
when with his knees he kiss'd the cretan strond. SHR 1.01.170
CRETE 5 FR 0.0005 REL FR 5 V 0 P
when in a wood of crete they bay'd the bear MND 4.01.113
horn, | in crete, in sparta, nor in thessaly. 4.01.126
o hound of crete, think'st thou my spouse to get H5 2.01. 73
then follow thou thy desp'rate sire of crete, 1H6 4.06. 54
what a peevish fool was that of crete | that 3H6 5.06. 18
CREVICE 1 FR 0.0001 REL FR 1 V 0 P
i pried me through the crevice of a wall, | when TIT 5.01.114
CREW* *(also crowed)*
CREW* 12 FR 0.0013 REL FR 12 V 0 P
a crew of patches, rude mechanicals, | that work MND 3.02. 9
point of honor to support | so dissolute a crew. R2 5.03. 12

with all the rest of that consorted crew, 5.03.138
art thou of cornish crew? H5 4.01. 50
at buckingham, and all the crew of them, | till 2H6 2.02. 72
and now to london all the crew are gone | to 3H6 2.01.174
and rice ap thomas, with a valiant crew, | and R3 4.05. 15
there are a crew of wretched souls | that stay MAC 4.03.141
it was about to speak, when the cock crew. HAM 1.01.147
but even then the morning cock crew loud, | and 1.02.218
do't, | a crew of pirates came and rescued me; PER 5.01.174
deed, | stood collatine and all his lordly crew, LUC 1731

CREWS 1 FR 0.0001 REL FR 1 V 0 P
come, go with us, we'll bring thee to our crews, TGV 4.01. 72

CRIB 1 FR 0.0001 REL FR 0 V 1 P
and his crib shall stand at the king's mess. HAM 5.02. 86 P

CRIBB'D 1 FR 0.0001 REL FR 1 V 0 P
but now i am cabin'd, cribb'd, confin'd, bound MAC 3.04. 23

CRIBS 1 FR 0.0001 REL FR 1 V 0 P
why rather, sleep, liest thou in smoky cribs, 2H4 3.01. 9

CRICKET 1 FR 0.0001 REL FR 1 V 0 P
cricket, to windsor chimneys shalt thou leap; WIV 5.05. 43

CRICKET'S 1 FR 0.0001 REL FR 1 V 0 P
her whip of cricket's bone, the lash of film, ROM 1.04. 66

/CRICKETS 1 FR 0.0001 REL FR 1 V 0 P
and /crickets sing at the oven's mouth, | are PER 3.ch. 7

CRICKETS 5 FR 0.0005 REL FR 4 V 1 P
it softly, | yond crickets shall not hear it. WT 2.01. 31
as merry as crickets, my lad. 1H4 2.04. 89 P
i heard the owl scream and the crickets cry. MAC 2.02. 15
the crickets sing, and man's o'erlabor'd sense CYM 2.02. 11
lo | the moon is down, the crickets chirp, the TNK 3.02. 35

/CRIED 3 FR 0.0003 REL FR 3 V 0 P
/a /general /voice | /cried /hate /upon /him; 2H4 4.01.135
/cried, "/sisters, /sisters! LR 4.03. 27
and then | /cried, "cursed fate that gave thee OTH 3.03.426

CRIED 72 FR 0.0081 REL FR 55 V 17 P
i, not rememb'ring how i cried out then, | will TMP 1.02.133
cried, "hell is empty, | and all the devils are 1.02.214
i shak'd you, sir, and cried. 2.01.319
me, that when i wak'd | i cried to dream again. 3.02.143
you, the women have so cried and shriek'd at it, WIV 1.01.297 P
cried game? 2.03. 88 P
i went to her in /white and cried "mum," and she 5.05.197 P
/white and cried "mum," and she cried "budget," 5.05.198 P
my lord, my mother cried, but then there was a ADO 2.01.334 P
with his finger and his thumb, | cried, "via! LLL 5.02.112
the third he caper'd, and cried, "all goes well. 5.02.113
your parishioners withal, and never cried, "have AYL 3.02.157 P
and cried, in fainting, upon rosalind. 4.03.149
he cried upon it at the merest loss, | and twice SHR in.1. 23
how i cried, how the horses ran away, how her 4.01. 80 P
tongue of loss | cried fame and honor on him. TN 5.01. 59
how he cried to me for help and said his name WT 3.03. 96 P
i tore them from their bonds, and cried aloud, JN 3.04. 70
whilst all tongues cried, "god save /thee, R2 5.02. 11
no man cried "god save him!" 5.02. 28
most omnipotent villain that ever cried "stand!" 1H4 1.02.109 P
i cried "hum," and "well, go to," | but mark'd 3.01.156
so 'a cried out, "god, god, god!" H5 2.03. 18 P
they say he cried out of sack. 2.03. 27 P
cried out amain, | and rush'd into the bowels of 1H6 1.01.128
clapp'd his tail between his legs and cried; 2H6 5.01.154
to me, | and thrice cried, "courage, father! 3H6 1.04. 10
warriors did retire, | richard cried, "charge! 1.04. 15
and cried, "a crown, or else a glorious tomb! 1.04. 16
and in the very pangs of death he cried, | like 2.03. 17
and to the latest gasp cried out for warwick, 5.02. 41
the night-crow cried, aboding luckless time; 5.06. 45
the midwife wonder'd and the women cried, | "o, 5.06. 74
judas kiss'd his master, | and cried "all hail!" 5.07. 34
and some ten voices cried, "god save king R3 3.07. 36
came to my tent and cried on victory. 5.03.231
now this masque | was cried incomparable; H8 1.01. 27
and they were ratified | as he cried, "thus let 1.01.171
grosser quality, is cried up | for our best act. 1.02. 84
i do assure you | the king cried "ha!" 3.02. 61
and hit that woman, who cried out "clubs!", 5.03. 50 P
as you must needs, for you all cried "go, go" — TRO 2.02. 85
clapp'd your hands, | and cried "inestimable!" 2.02. 88
he cried to me; COR 1.09. 84
a perilous knock — and it cried bitterly. ROM 1.03. 54
caesar cried, "help me, cassius, or i sink!" JC 1.02.111
alas, it cried, "give me some drink, titinius," 1.02.127
or four wenches, where i stood, cried, "alas, 1.02.272 P
thrice hath calphurnia in her sleep cried out, 2.02. 2
when that the poor have cried, caesar hath wept; 3.02. 91
one did laugh in 's sleep, and one cried, MAC 2.02. 20
one cried, "god bless us!" 2.02. 24
still it cried, "sleep no more!" 2.02. 38
who was it that thus cried? 2.02. 41
is death of fathers, and who still hath cried, HAM 1.02.104
in such matters cried in the top of mine — an 2.02.438 P
that he cried out 'twould be a sight indeed | if 4.07. 99
'em o' th' coxcombs with a stick, and cried, LR 2.04.124 P
what is the matter ho? who is't that cried? OTH 5.01. 74
who is't that cried? 5.01. 75
caesar dead, | he cried almost to roaring; ANT 3.02. 55
of late, when i cried "ho!" 3.13. 90
cried he? and begg'd 'a pardon? 3.13.132
a full-acorn'd boar, a german /one, | cried "o!" CYM 2.05. 17
made good the passage, cried to those that fled, 5.03. 23
says, did never fear, | but cried "good seamen!" PER 4.01. 53
sir, hast thou cried her through the market? 4.02. 93 P
i have cried her almost to the number of her 4.02. 94 P
your advice | is cried up with example. TNK 1.02. 13
and softly cried, 'awake, thou roman dame, | and LUC 1628
that it cried, "how true a twain | seemeth this PHT 45
cried, "o false blood, thou register of lies, LC 52

CRIEDST 2 FR 0.0002 REL FR 2 V 0 P
thou dream, lucius, that thou so criedst out? JC 4.03.295
/in my whole course of wooing, thou criedst, OTH 3.03.112

CRIER 2 FR 0.0002 REL FR 2 V 0 P
crier hobgoblin, make the fairy oyes. WIV 5.05. 41
hear the crier. JN 2.01.134

/CRIES 2 FR 0.0002 REL FR 1 V 1 P
/hoppedance /cries /in /tom's /belly /for /two LR 3.06. 30 P
/a /moral /fool, /sits /still /and /cries, 4.02. 58

CRIES 76 FR 0.0086 REL FR 68 V 8 P
she cries "budget"; WIV 5.02. 6 P
the very mercy of the law cries out | most MM 5.01.407
far from her nest the lapwing cries away; ERR 4.02. 27
he cries for you, and vows, if he can take you, 5.01.182
outfacing me, | cries out, i was possess'd. 5.01.246
the other cries; LLL 4.03.139
and "tailor" cries, and falls into a cough; MND 2.01. 54
he murther cries, and help from athens calls. 3.02. 26
who cries out on pride | that can therein tax AYL 2.07. 70
so near the heart as your gesture cries it out, 5.02. 63 P
our own love waking cries to see what's done, AWW 5.03. 65
in his rage and his wrath, | cries, ah, ha! TN 4.02.128
as if that joy were now become a loss, cries, "o WT 5.02. 51 P
a widow cries; JN 3.01.108
defense | cries out upon the name of salisbury! 5.02. 19
which blood, like sacrificing abel's, cries, R2 1.01.104
didst well, for wisdom cries out in the streets, 1H4 1.02. 88 P
cries out upon abuses, seems to weep | over his 4.03. 81
and that same word even now cries out on us. 2H4 3.01. 94
turning the widows' tears, the orphans' cries, H5 2.04.106
he cries aloud, "tarry, my cousin suffolk! 4.06. 15
cries out for noble york and somerset | to beat 1H6 4.04. 15
majesty | that ever even now he cries aloud for him. 2H6 3.02.378
and dead men's cries do fill the empty air, 5.02. 4
and every drop cries vengeance for his death 3H6 1.04.148
to see a sunshine day | that cries "retire!" 2.01.188
fill'd it with cursing cries and deep exclaims. R3 1.02. 52
such hideous cries that with the very noise | i, 1.04. 60
moan) | to overgo thy woes and drown thy cries! 2.02. 61
laughs out a loud applause, | cries, "excellent! TRO 1.03.164
yet god achilles still cries, "excellent! 1.03.169
cries, "o, enough, patroclus, | or give me ribs 1.03.176
cries "/come" to him that instantly must die. 4.04. 51
bright crest fame with her loud'st oyes | cries, 4.05.144
how hecuba cries out! 5.03. 83
whose every motion | was tim'd with dying cries. COR 2.02.110
of intercession which | great nature cries, 5.03. 33
would make such fearful and confused cries, | as TIT 2.03.102
so cries a pig prepared to the spit. 4.02.146
romeo he cries aloud, | "hold, friends! ROM 3.01.164
up, | and tybalt calls, and then on romeo cries, 3.03.101
thy form cries out thou art; 3.03.109
crouching marrow in the bearer strong | cries TIM 5.04. 10
the rump-fed ronyon cries. MAC 1.03. 6
that which cries, "thus thou must do," if thou 1.05. 23
harpier cries, "'tis time, 'tis time." 4.01. 3
and damn'd be him that first cries, "hold, 5.08. 34
my fate cries out, | and makes each petty artere HAM 1.04. 81
whips out his rapier, cries, "a rat, a rat!" 4.01. 10
cries cuckold to my father, brands the harlot 4.05.119
this quarry cries on havoc. 5.02.364
he rais'd the house with loud and coward cries. LR 2.04. 43
th' affair cries haste, | and speed must answer OTH 1.03.276
whose noise is this that cries on murther? 5.01. 48
one another by the disposition, he cries out, ANT 2.07. 7 P
cries, "fool lepidus!" 3.05. 17
cries "o, | can my sides hold, to think that man CYM 1.06. 68
to hear what pitiful cries they made to us to PER 2.01. 21 P
o, help now! | our cause cries for your knee. TNK 1.01.200
widows' cries | descend again into their throats 1.02. 81
and nods, and hums, | and then cries, "rare!" 3.05. 16
one cries, "o, this smoke!" 4.03. 53 P
one cries, "o, that ever i did it behind the 4.03. 54 P
souring his cheeks, cries, "fie, no more of love VEN 185
"pity," she cries, "some favor, some remorse!" 257
"for shame," he cries, "let go, and let me go, 379
she cries, and twenty times, "woe, woe!" 833
noise but owls' and wolves' death-boding cries; LUC 165
and fright her with confusion of their cries. 445
wolf hath seiz'd his prey, the poor lamb cries, 677
who nothing wants to answer her but cries, | and 1459
"daughter, dear daughter," old lucretius cries, 1751
life, | answer'd their cries, "my daughter!" 1806
and trouble deaf heaven with my bootless cries, SON 29. 3
cries to catch her whose busy care is bent | to 143. 6
lets not bounty fall | where want cries some LC 42

CRIME 17 FR 0.0019 REL FR 16 V 1 P
my blood is mingled with the crime of lust: ERR 2.02.141
impute it not a crime | to me, or my swift WT 4.01. 4
to the king wipes the crime of it out of us. H5 4.01.133 P
weigh but the crime with this. TIM 3.05. 58
if by this crime he owes the law his life, | why 3.05. 82
abound | in the division of each several crime, MAC 4.03. 96
he flashes into one gross crime or other | that LR 1.03. 4
if you bethink yourself of any crime OTH 5.02. 26
we commit no crime | to use one language in each PER 4.04. 5
whose crime will bear an ever-during blame. LUC 224
since thou art guilty of my cureless crime, 772
be guilty of my death, since of my crime. 931
and ever let his unrecalling crime | have time 993
but i forbid thee one most heinous crime, | o, SON 19. 8
belong | yourself to pardon of self-doing crime. 58.12
to weigh how once i suffered in your crime. 120. 8
die for goodness, who have liv'd for crime. 124.14

CRIMEFUL 1 FR 0.0001 REL FR 1 V 0 P
to make him curse this cursed crimeful night. LUC 970

CRIMELESS 1 FR 0.0001 REL FR 1 V 0 P
so long as i am loyal, true, and crimeless. 2H6 2.04. 63

/CRIMES 1 FR 0.0001 REL FR 1 V 0 P
/and /these /grievous /crimes | /committed /by R2 4.01.223

CRIMES 19 FR 0.0021 REL FR 18 V 1 P
as you from crimes would pardon'd be, | let your TMP ep 19
and i for such like petty crimes as these. TGV 4.01. 50
to make me know | the nature of their crimes, MM 2.03. 7
how may likeness made in crimes, | making 3.02.273
glory grows guilty of detested crimes, | when, LLL 4.01. 31
whipt them not, and our crimes would despair, if AWW 4.03. 73 P
shall we stretch our eye | when capital crimes, H5 2.02. 56
the manner of thy vile outrageous crimes, | that 1H6 3.01. 11
but mightier crimes are laid unto your charge, 2H6 3.01.134
of these supposed crimes, to give me leave | by R3 1.02. 76
crimes, like lands, | are not inherited. TIM 5.04. 37
till the foul crimes done in my days of nature HAM 1.05. 12
having ever seen in the prenominate crimes | the 2.01. 43
with all his crimes broad blown, as flush as may 3.03. 81
wretch | that hast within thee undivulged crimes LR 3.02. 52
that these our nether crimes | so speedily can 4.02. 79
yet unhard'ned in | the crimes of nature — let TNK 1.02. 3
not halting under crimes | many and stale. 5.04. 10
though men can cover crimes with bold stern LUC 1252

CRIMINAL 4 FR 0.0004 REL FR 4 V 0 P
being criminal, in double violation | of sacred MM 5.01.404
is indeed | more criminal in thee than it), so WT 3.02. 89
even this | so criminal, and in such capital COR 3.03. 81
feats, | so criminal and so capital in nature, HAM 4.07. 7

CRIMSON 14 FR 0.0015 REL FR 13 V 1 P
fall in the fresh lap of the crimson rose, | and MND 2.01.108
not painted with the crimson spots of blood. JN 4.02.253
such crimson tempest should bedrench | the fresh R2 3.03. 46
out at thy throat | in drops of crimson blood. H5 4.04. 15
ros'd over with the virgin crimson of modesty, 5.02.296 P
before his chaps be stain'd with crimson blood, 2H6 3.01.259
that slanders me with murther's crimson badge. 3.02.200
alas, a crimson river of warm blood, | like to a TIT 2.04. 22
wretched stump, witness these crimson lines, 5.02. 22
yet | is crimson in thy lips and in thy cheeks, ROM 5.03. 95
like the crimson drops | i' th' bottom of a CYM 2.02. 38
'twixt crimson shame and anger ashy-pale. VEN 76
o, never let their crimson liveries wear! 506
that the crimson blood | circles her body in on LUC 1738

CRIMSON'D 1 FR 0.0001 REL FR 1 V 0 P
sign'd in thy spoil, and crimson'd in thy lethe. JC 3.01.206

CRINGE 1 FR 0.0001 REL FR 1 V 0 P
till like a boy you see him cringe his face, ANT 3.13.100

CRIPPLE 7 FR 0.0008 REL FR 6 V 1 P
o'er the meshes of good counsel the cripple. MV 1.02. 21 P
and chide the cripple tardy-gaited night, | who H5 4.pr. 20
could restore this cripple to his legs again? 2H6 2.01.131
some tardy cripple bare the countermand, | that R3 2.01. 90
cripple our senators, that their limbs may halt TIM 4.01. 24
canst make | a cripple flourish with his crutch, TNK 5.01. 82
smell — | a cripple soon can find a halt — PP 18.10

CRISP 3 FR 0.0003 REL FR 3 V 0 P
leave your crisp channels, and on this green TMP 4.01.130
and hid his crisp head in the hollow bank 1H4 1.03.106
with all th' abhorred births below crisp heaven TIM 4.03.183

CRISPED 1 FR 0.0001 REL FR 1 V 0 P
so are those crisped snaky golden locks, | which MV 3.02. 92

CRISPIAN 4 FR 0.0004 REL FR 4 V 0 P
this day is call'd the feast of crispian: H5 4.03. 40
named, | and rouse him at the name of crispian. 4.03. 43
and say, "to-morrow is saint crispian." 4.03. 46
and crispin crispian shall ne'er go by, | from 4.03. 57

CRISPIANUS 1 FR 0.0001 REL FR 1 V 0 P
fought on the day of crispin crispianus. H5 4.07. 91

CRISPIN 2 FR 0.0002 REL FR 2 V 0 P
and crispin crispian shall ne'er go by, | from H5 4.03. 57
fought on the day of crispin crispianus. 4.07. 91

/CRISPIN'S 1 FR 0.0001 REL FR 1 V 0 P
"/these /wounds /i /had /on /crispin's /day." H5 4.03. 48

CRISPIN'S 1 FR 0.0001 REL FR 1 V 0 P
that fought with us upon saint crispin's day. H5 4.03. 67

/CRI'ST 1 FR 0.0001 REL FR 1 V 0 P
/cri'st /now, "/o /earth, /yield /us /that /king 2H4 1.03.106

CRITIC 3 FR 0.0003 REL FR 3 V 0 P
a critic, nay, a night-watch constable, | a LLL 3.01.176
the boys, | and critic timon laugh at idle toys! 4.03.168
sense | to critic and to flatterer stopped are. SON 112.11

CRITICAL 2 FR 0.0002 REL FR 2 V 0 P
that is some satire, keen and critical, | not MND 5.01. 54
put me to't, | for i am nothing if not critical. OTH 2.01.119

CRITICS 1 FR 0.0001 REL FR 1 V 0 P
do not give advantage | to stubborn critics, apt TRO 5.02.131

/CROAK 1 FR 0.0001 REL FR 0 V 1 P
/croak /not, /black /angel, /i /have /no /food LR 3.06. 31 P

CROAK 1 FR 0.0001 REL FR 0 V 1 P
i would croak like a raven, i would bode, i TRO 5.02.191 P

CROAKING 1 FR 0.0001 REL FR 0 V 1 P
the croaking raven doth bellow for revenge. HAM 3.02.254 P

CROAKS 1 FR 0.0001 REL FR 1 V 0 P
that croaks the fatal entrance of duncan | under MAC 1.05. 39

CROCADILE 1 FR 0.0001 REL FR 1 V 0 P
woo't drink up eisel, eat a crocadile? HAM 5.01.276

CROCODILE 4 FR 0.0004 REL FR 2 V 2 P
beguiles him as the mournful crocodile | with 2H6 3.01.226
each drop she falls would prove a crocodile. OTH 4.01.246
so is your crocodile. ANT 2.07. 27 P
what manner o' thing is your crocodile? 2.07. 41 P

CROMER 1 FR 0.0001 REL FR 0 V 1 P
into his son-in-law's house, sir james cromer, 2H6 4.07.111 P

CROMWELL 18 FR 0.0020 REL FR 18 V 0 P
lord cromwell of wingfield, lord furnival of 1H6 4.07. 66
the packet, cromwell, gave't you the king? H8 3.02. 76
why, how now, cromwell? 3.02.372
never so truly happy, my good cromwell; 3.02.377
o, 'tis a burden, cromwell, 'tis a burden | too 3.02.384
o, cromwell, | the king has gone beyond me! 3.02.407
go get thee from me, cromwell! 3.02.412
good cromwell, | neglect him not; 3.02.419
with what a sorrow cromwell leaves his lord. 3.02.425
cromwell, i did not think to shed a tear | in 3.02.428
and thus far hear me, cromwell, | and when i am 3.02.431
cromwell, i charge thee, fling away ambition! 3.02.440
then if thou fall'st, o cromwell, | thou fall'st 3.02.448
o cromwell, cromwell, | had i but serv'd my god 3.02.454
o cromwell, cromwell, | had i but serv'd my god 3.02.454
thomas cromwell, | a man in much esteem with th' 4.01.108
till cranmer, cromwell, her two hands, and she 5.01. 31
as for cromwell, | beside that of the jewel 5.01. 33

CRONE 1 FR 0.0001 REL FR 1 V 0 P
give't to thy crone. WT 2.03. 77

CROOK 1 FR 0.0001 REL FR 1 V 0 P
and crook the pregnant hinges of the knee HAM 3.02. 61

CROOK-BACK 3 FR 0.0003 REL FR 3 V 0 P
and where's that valiant crook-back prodigy, 3H6 1.04. 75
ay, crook-back, here i stand to answer thee, 2.02. 96
nay, take away this scolding crook-back, rather. 5.05. 30

CROOK'D 3 FR 0.0003 REL FR 2 V 1 P
by what by-paths and indirect crook'd ways | i 2H4 4.05.184
let hell make crook'd my mind to answer it. 3H6 5.06. 79
other of them may have crook'd noses, but to owe CYM 3.01. 37 P

CROOKED 16 FR 0.0018 REL FR 15 V 1 P
if crooked fortune had not thwarted me. TGV 4.01. 22
he is deformed, crooked, old, and sere, ERR 4.02. 19
lame, foolish, crooked, swart, prodigious, JN 3.01. 46
have, | and thy unkindness be like crooked age, R2 2.01.133

since a crooked figure may | attest in little H5 pr 15
a net | than amply to imbar their crooked titles 1.02. 94
lump, | as crooked in thy manners as thy shape! 2H6 5.01.158
that make | envy and crooked malice nourishment H8 5.02. 79
palate adversely, i make a crooked face at it. COR 2.01. 56 P
and let our crooked smokes climb to their CYM 5.05.477
ill–nurtur'd, crooked, churlish, harsh in voice, VEN 134
and whom he strikes his crooked tushes slay. 624
whose crooked beak threats, if he mount, he dies LUC 508
crooked eclipses 'gainst his glory fight, | and SON 60. 7
so thou prevent'st his scythe and crooked knife. 100.14
"his browny locks did hang in crooked curls, LC 85
CROOKED–PATED 1 FR 0.0001 REL FR 0 V 1 P
a she–lamb of a twelvemonth to a crooked–pated, AYL 3.02. 82 P
CROOK–KNEE'D 1 FR 0.0001 REL FR 1 V 0 P
crook–knee'd, and dewlapp'd like thessalian MND 4.01.122
CROP 10 FR 0.0011 REL FR 8 V 2 P
and for night–tapers crop their waxen thighs MND 3.01.169
that i shall think it a most plenteous crop | to AYL 3.05.101
my team and gives me leave to inn the crop. AWW 1.03. 45 P
to crop at once a too long withered flower. R2 2.01.134
all the budding honors on thy crest | i'll crop, 1H4 5.04. 73
bosoms, and their crop | be general leprosy! TIM 4.01. 29
to see this vaulted arch and the rich crop | of CYM 1.06. 33
no, my lord; nor crop the ears of them. 2.01. 12 P
that wildly grows in them but yields a crop | as 4.02.180
they bid thee crop a weed, thou pluck'st a VEN 946
CROP–EAR 1 FR 0.0001 REL FR 1 V 0 P
what horse? roan? a crop–ear, is it not? 1H4 2.03. 69
CROPP'D 8 FR 0.0009 REL FR 8 V 0 P
lest you be cropp'd before you come to prime. R2 5.02. 51
cropp'd are the flower–de–luces in your arms, 1H6 1.01. 80
the fewest roses are cropp'd from the tree 2.04. 41
how sweet a plant have you untimely cropp'd! 3H6 5.05. 62
that cropp'd the golden prime of this sweet R3 1.02.247
in rank achilles must or now be cropp'd | or, TRO 1.03.318
he ploughed her, and she cropp'd. ANT 2.02.228
then, lest my life be cropp'd to keep you clear, PER 1.01.141
CROPS 2 FR 0.0002 REL FR 2 V 0 P
she crops the stalk, and in the breach appears VEN 1175
to cheer the ploughman with increaseful crops, LUC 958
CROSBY 3 FR 0.0003 REL FR 3 V 0 P
mourner, | and presently repair to crosby house; R3 1.02.212
when you have done, repair to crosby place. 1.03.344
at crosby house, there shall you find us both. 3.01.190
'CROSS *(also across)*
'CROSS 1 FR 0.0001 REL FR 1 V 0 P
natural scope | when you come 'cross his humor, 1H4 3.01.170
/CROSS 3 FR 0.0003 REL FR 3 V 0 P
/have /here /deliver'd /me /to /my /sour /cross, R2 4.01.241
/nimble /stroke | /of /quick /cross /lightning? LR 4.07. 34
to him that bears the strong offense's /cross. SON 34.12
CROSS 67 FR 0.0075 REL FR 56 V 11 P
i'll quickly cross | by some sly trick blunt TGV 2.06. 40
to cross my friend in his intended drift, | than 3.01. 18
more to cross that love | than hate for silvia, 5.02. 55
he would never else cross me thus. WIV 5.05. 36 P
way going to temptation, | where prayers cross. MM 2.02.159
as claudio's, to cross this in the smallest. 4.02.168 P
and he will bless that cross with other beating: ERR 2.01. 79
i cross me for a sinner. 2.02.188
if i can cross him any way, i bless myself every ADO 1.03. 67 P
yea, my lord, but i can cross it. 2.02. 3 P
any bar, any cross, any impediment will be 2.02. 4 P
how canst thou cross this marriage? 2.02. 7 P
him another staff, this last was broke cross. 5.01.139 P
we cannot cross the cause why we were born; LLL 4.03.214
the effect of my intent is to cross theirs: 5.02.138
o cross! too high to be enthrall'd to /low. MND 1.01.136
patience, | because it is a customary cross, 1.01.153
why should titania cross her oberon? 2.01.119
and never dare misfortune cross her foot, MV 2.04. 35
amen betimes, lest the devil cross my prayer, 3.01. 20 P
yet i should bear no cross if i did bear you, AYL 2.04. 12 P
so you and you no cross shall part; 5.04.131
to be whipt at the high cross every morning. SHR 1.01.133 P
when did she cross thee with a bitter word? 2.01. 28
nor hast thou pleasure to be cross in talk; 2.01.249
streaming the ensign of the christian cross R2 4.01. 94
under whose blessed cross | we are impressed and 1H4 1.01. 20
nail'd | for our advantage on the bitter cross. 1.01. 27
so honor cross it from the north to south, | and 1.03.196
true liegeman upon the cross of a welsh hook — 2.04.338 P
fie, cousin percy, how you cross my father! 3.01.145
to cross the seas and to be crown'd in france. 1H6 3.01.179
whiles they each other cross, | lives, honors, 4.03. 52
to cross the seas to england and be crown'd 5.05. 90
i charge thee waft me safely cross the channel. 2H6 4.01.115
and then to brittany i'll cross the sea | to 3H6 2.06. 97
to cross me from the golden time i look for! 3.02.127
shall cross the seas and bid false edward battle 3.03.235
and bear with mildness my misfortune's cross; 4.04. 20
tower | and was embark'd to cross to burgundy, R3 1.04. 10
my lord of york will still be cross in talk. 3.01.126
if thou wilt outstrip death, go cross the seas, 4.01. 41
what cross devil | made me put this main secret H8 3.02.214
who dare cross 'em, | bearing the king's will 3.02.234
dispos'd | ere they lack'd power to cross you. COR 3.02. 23
be cross with him, and i'll go fetch thy sons TIT 2.03. 53
well thou knowest, is cross and full of sin. ROM 4.03. 5
to cross my obsequies and true love's rite? 5.03. 20
and when the cross blue lightning seem'd to open JC 1.03. 50
why do you cross me in this exigent? 5.01. 19
i do not cross you; but i will do so. 5.01. 20
i'll cross it, though it blast me. HAM 1.01.127
each thing give him way, cross him in nothing. ANT 1.03. 9
whom best i love, i cross; CYM 5.04.101
makes her desire — | which who shall cross? PER 3.ch. 41
who can cross it? 4.03. 16
it is not good to cross him, give him way. 5.01.230
three or four | i saw from far off cross her — TNK 4.01.100
by no mean cross her, she is then distemper'd 4.01.119
love, and what young maid dare cross 'em? 4.02. 40
to cross the curious workmanship of nature, | to VEN 734
so cross him with their opposite persuasion, LUC 286
to cross their arms and hang their heads with 793

with some mischance cross tarquin in his flight. 968
one silly cross wrought all my loss, | o PP 17. 9
and both for my sake lay on me this cross. SON 42.12
now while the world is bent my deeds to cross, 90. 2
CROSS–BOW 1 FR 0.0001 REL FR 1 V 0 P
the noise of thy cross–bow | will scare the herd 3H6 3.01. 6
CROSS–BOWS 1 FR 0.0001 REL FR 1 V 0 P
the master of the cross–bows, lord rambures, H5 4.08. 94
CROSS'D 25 FR 0.0028 REL FR 20 V 5 P
how young leander cross'd the hellespont. TGV 1.01. 22
a man i am cross'd with adversity; 4.01. 12
not serve heaven well, that you are so cross'd. WIV 4.05.126 P
i love not to be cross'd. LLL 1.02. 32 P
with your arms cross'd on your thin/–bellied 3.01. 18 P
if then true lovers have been ever cross'd, | it MND 1.01.150
farewell, and if my fortune be not cross'd, | i MV 2.05. 56
but hadst thou not cross'd me, thou shouldst SHR 4.01. 73 P
evermore cross'd and cross'd, nothing but 4.05. 10
evermore cross'd and cross'd, nothing but 4.05. 10
cross'd and cross'd, nothing but cross'd! 4.05. 10
your precious self had then not cross'd the eyes WT 1.02. 79
prosperous south–wind friendly) we have cross'd, 5.01.161
lest that their hopes prodigiously be cross'd; JN 3.01. 91
chance is this that suddenly hath cross'd us? 1H6 1.04. 72
when all's spent, he'ld be cross'd then, and he TIM 1.02.162
he cross'd himself by't; 3.03. 29 P
being cross'd in conference by some senators. JC 1.02.188
how scap'd i killing when i cross'd you so? 4.03.150
how you were borne in hand, how cross'd, the MAC 3.01. 80
i cross'd the seas on purpose and on promise CYM 1.06.202
my lords, | till he have cross'd the severn. 3.05. 17
this fool's speed | be cross'd with slowness; 3.05.162
after your will, have cross'd the sea, attending 4.02.334
lest this match between 's | be cross'd ere met. TNK 3.01. 98
CROSSED 1 FR 0.0001 REL FR 1 V 0 P
a torment thrice threefold thus to be crossed. SON 133. 8
CROSSES 13 FR 0.0014 REL FR 11 V 2 P
speaks the mere contrary, crosses love not him. LLL 1.02. 34 P
she doth stray about | by holy crosses, where MV 5.01. 31
where nothing lives but crosses, cares, and R2 2.02. 79
a penny, you are too impatient to bear crosses. 2H4 1.02.226 P
what perils past, what crosses to ensue, | would 3.01. 55
uncle, but our crosses on the way | have made it R3 3.01. 4
i am old now, | and these same crosses spoil me. LR 5.03.279
fortune, yet, that, after all /thy crosses, PER 2.01.121
to mourn thy crosses, with thy daughter's, call 5.01.245
in that i'll bury | thee and all crosses else. TNK 3.06.127
he cranks and crosses with a thousand doubles: VEN 682
"i see what crosses my attempt will bring, | i LUC 491
a thousand crosses keep them from thy aid: 912
CROSSEST 1 FR 0.0001 REL FR 1 V 0 P
name, that in battle thus | thou crossest me? 1H4 5.03. 2
CROSS–GARTER'D 8 FR 0.0009 REL FR 1 V 7 P
and wish'd to see thee ever cross–garter'd: TN 2.05.154 P
she did praise my leg being cross–garter'd, and 2.05.167 P
in yellow stockings, and cross–garter'd, even 2.05.171 P
and 'tis a color she abhors, and cross–garter'd, 2.05.200 P
and cross–garter'd? 3.02. 74 P
"and wish'd to see thee cross–garter'd." 3.04. 50 P
cross–garter'd? 3.04. 51 P
bade me come smiling and cross–garter'd to you, 5.01.337
CROSS–GARTERING 1 FR 0.0001 REL FR 0 V 1 P
obstruction in the blood, this cross–gartering, TN 3.04. 21 P
CROSSING 5 FR 0.0005 REL FR 4 V 1 P
of prolixity or crossing the plain highway of MV 3.01. 11 P
do, or think to do, | you are still crossing it. SHR 4.03.193
crossing the sea from england into france, 1H6 4.01. 89
move them no more by crossing their high will. ROM 4.05. 95
there is no crossing him in 's humor, | else i TIM 1.02.160
CROSSINGS 1 FR 0.0001 REL FR 1 V 0 P
of many men | i do not bear these crossings. 1H4 3.01. 35
CROSSLY 1 FR 0.0001 REL FR 1 V 0 P
and crossly to thy good all fortune goes. R2 2.04. 24
CROSSNESS 1 FR 0.0001 REL FR 0 V 1 P
bate one breath of her accustom'd crossness. ADO 2.03.177 P
CROSS–ROW 1 FR 0.0001 REL FR 1 V 0 P
and from the cross–row plucks the letter g, R3 1.01. 55
CROSSWAYS 1 FR 0.0001 REL FR 1 V 0 P
all, | that in crossways and floods have burial, MND 3.02.383
CROTCHETS 4 FR 0.0004 REL FR 1 V 3 P
faith, thou hast some crotchets in thy head now. WIV 2.01.154 P
the duke had crotchets in him. MM 3.02.127 P
why, these are very crotchets that he speaks — ADO 2.03. 56
i will carry no crotchets, i'll re you, i'll fa ROM 4.05.118 P
CROUCH 4 FR 0.0004 REL FR 4 V 0 P
to crouch in litter of your stable planks, | to JN 5.02.140
famine, sword, and fire | crouch for employment. H5 pr 8
that england shall crouch down in fear, and 4.02. 37
must i stand and crouch | under your testy humor JC 4.03. 45
CROUCHING 1 FR 0.0001 REL FR 1 V 0 P
when crouching marrow in the bearer strong TIM 5.04. 9
CROW* 31 FR 0.0035 REL FR 24 V 7 P
adrian, for a good wager, first begins to crow? TMP 2.01. 29 P
wont, when you laugh'd, to crow like a cock; TGV 2.01. 27 P
well, i'll break in: go borrow me a crow. ERR 3.01. 80
a crow without feather? 3.01. 81
if a crow help us in, sirrah, we'll pluck a crow 3.01. 83
help us in, sirrah, we'll pluck a crow together. 3.01. 83
go, get thee gone, fetch me an iron crow. 3.01. 84
hear my dog bark at a crow than a man swear he ADO 1.01.132 P
and look thou meet me ere the first cock crow. MND 2.01.267
turns to a crow | when thou hold'st up thy hand. 3.02.142
the crow doth sing as sweetly as the lark | when MV 5.01.102
time, | my lungs began to crow like chanticleer, AYL 2.07. 30
no cock of mine, you crow too like a craven. SHR 2.01.227
e'en a crow a' th' same nest; AWW 4.03.286 P
these wise men that crow so at these set kind of TN 1.05. 88 P
driven snow, | cypress black as e'er was crow, WT 4.04.219
even at the crying of your nation's crow, JN 5.02.144
he'll yield the crow a pudding one of these days H5 2.01. 87 P
the country cocks do crow, the clocks do toll, 4.pr. 15
and i will make thee think thy swan a crow. ROM 1.02. 87
get me an iron crow, and bring it straight 5.02. 21
and the crow | makes wing to th' rooky wood; MAC 3.02. 50
shouldst have made him | as little as a crow, or CYM 1.03. 15
you are cock and capon too, and you crow, cock, 2.01. 24 P
when you above perceive me like a crow, | that 3.03. 12
the dove of paphos might with the crow | vie PER 4.ch. 32

the crow, the sland'rous cuckoo, nor | the TNK 1.01. 19
"the crow may bathe his coal–black wings in mire LUC 1009
and thou treble–dated crow, | that thy sable PHT 17
a crow that flies in heaven's sweetest air. SON 70. 4
the crow or dove, it shapes them to your feature 113.12
CROWD 4 FR 0.0004 REL FR 4 V 0 P
in obsequious fondness | crowd to his presence, MM 2.04. 29
crowd us and crush us to this monstrous form 2H4 4.02. 34
among the crowd i' th' abbey, where a finger H8 4.01. 57
will crowd a feeble man almost to death. JC 2.04. 36
CROWDED 1 FR 0.0001 REL FR 0 V 1 P
into whom nature hath so crowded humors that his TRO 1.02. 22 P
CROWDING 2 FR 0.0002 REL FR 1 V 1 P
burst his head for crowding among the marshal's 2H4 3.02.323 P
the poor mechanic porters crowding in | their H5 1.02.200
CROWED *(also crew*)*
CROWED 1 FR 0.0001 REL FR 1 V 0 P
the second cock hath crowed, | the curfew–bell ROM 4.04. 3
CROW–FLOWERS 1 FR 0.0001 REL FR 1 V 0 P
garlands did she make | of crow–flowers, nettles HAM 4.07.169
CROWING 2 FR 0.0002 REL FR 1 V 1 P
and yet he'll be crowing as if he had writ man 2H4 1.02. 26 P
it faded on the crowing of the cock. HAM 1.01.157
CROW–KEEPER 2 FR 0.0002 REL FR 1 V 1 P
lath, | scaring the ladies like a crow–keeper, ROM 1.04. 6
that fellow handles his bow like a crow–keeper; LR 4.06. 88 P
/CROWN 12 FR 0.0013 REL FR 10 V 2 P
/the /resignation /of /thy /state /and /crown R2 4.01.179
/give /me /the /crown. 4.01.181
/here, /cousin, /seize /the /crown; 4.01.181
/is /this /golden /crown /like /a /deep /well 4.01.184
/my /crown /i /am, /but /still /my /griefs /are 4.01.191
/your /cares /you /give /me /with /your /crown. 4.01.194
/they /tend /the /crown, /yet /still /with /me 4.01.199
/are /you /contented /to /resign /the /crown? 4.01.200
/mine /own /hands /i /give /away /my /crown, 4.01.208
our head shall go bare till merit /crown /it. TRO 3.02. 92 P
thou clovest thy /crown i' th' middle and gav'st LR 1.04.160 P
as if she ever meant to /crown his valor. TNK 4.02.109
CROWN 248 FR 0.0280 REL FR 228 V 20 P
subject his coronet to his crown, and bend | the TMP 1.02.114
my strong imagination sees a crown | dropping 2.01.208
and crown what i profess with kind event | if i 3.01. 69
and with each end of thy blue bow dost crown 4.01. 80
from toe to crown he'll fill our skins with 4.01.233
gods, | and on this couple drop a blessed crown! 5.01.202
a french crown more. MM 1.02. 52 P
not the king's crown, nor the deputed sword, 2.02. 60
against my crown, my oath, my dignity, | which ERR 1.01.143
from the crown of his head to the sole of his ADO 3.02. 9 P
why, it is a fairer name than french crown! LLL 3.01.141 P
and on old hiems' /thin and icy crown | an MND 2.01.109
the throned monarch better than his crown. MV 4.01.189
wedding is great juno's crown, | o blessed bond AYL 5.04.141
his crown bequeathing to his banish'd brother, 5.04.163
as your french crown for your taffety punk, as AWW 2.02. 22 P
still the fine's the crown; 4.04. 35
device to the bar and crown thee for a finder of TN 3.04.140 P
one day shall crown th' alliance on't, so please 5.01.318
there is a plot against my life, my crown; WT 2.01. 47
the crown and comfort of my life, your favor, 3.02. 94
bold oxlips, and | the crown imperial; 4.04.126
not for issue, | the crown will find an heir. 5.01. 47
might you have beheld one joy crown another, so 5.02. 44 P
a rape | upon the maiden virtue of the crown. JN 2.01. 98
which owe the crown that thou o'ermasterest? 2.01.109
doth not the crown of england prove the king? 2.01.273
tie | thy now unsur'd assurance to the crown, 2.01.471
find liable to our crown and dignity, | shall 2.01.490
become thy great birth nor deserve a crown. 3.01. 50
your highness should deliver up your crown. 4.02.152
whereon he says | i shall yield up my crown, let 4.02.157
at noon | my crown i should give off? 5.01. 27
to win this easy match play'd for a crown? 5.02.106
good hap, | add an immortal title to your crown! R2 1.01. 24
a thousand flatterers sit within thy crown, 2.01.100
redeem from broking pawn the blemish'd crown, 2.01.293
to lift shrewd steel against our golden crown, 3.02. 59
in stiff unwieldy arms against thy crown; 3.02.115
for within the hollow crown | that rounds the 3.02.160
and threat the glory of my precious crown. 3.03. 90
but ere the crown he looks for live in peace, 3.03. 95
had he done so, himself had borne the crown, 3.04. 65
and if you crown him, let me prophesy, | the 4.01.136
our holy lives must win a new world's crown, 5.01. 24
a twofold marriage — 'twixt my crown and me, 5.01. 72
my brother edmund mortimer | heir to the crown? 1H4 1.03.157
you, that set the crown | upon the head of this 1.03.160
dagger my sceptre, and this cushion my crown. 2.04.379 P
and thy precious rich crown for a pitiful bald 2.04.382 P
precious rich crown for a pitiful bald crown! 2.04.382 P
and on your eyelids crown the god of sleep, 3.01.214
opinion, that did help me to the crown, | had 3.02. 42
uneasy lies the head that wears a crown. 2H4 3.01. 31
set me the crown upon my pillow here. 4.05. 5
why doth the crown lie there upon his pillow, 4.05. 21
my due from thee is this imperial crown, | which 4.05. 41
where is the crown? who took it from my pillow? 4.05. 57
but wherefore did he take away the crown? 4.05. 88
there is your crown; 4.05.142
and he that wears the crown immortally | long 4.05.143
were, | i spake unto this crown as having sense, 4.05.157
and indirect crook'd ways | i met this crown, 4.05.185
how i came by the crown, o god forgive, | and 4.05.218
and generally to the crown and seat of france, H5 1.01. 88
make claim and title to the crown of france. 1.02. 68
who usurp'd the crown | of charles the duke of 1.02. 69
wearing the crown of france, till satisfied 1.02. 80
great | was re–united to the crown of france. 1.02. 85
shall strike his father's crown into the hazard. 1.02.263
to him and to his heirs, namely, the crown, 2.04. 81
ordinance of times, | unto the crown of france. 2.04. 84
bids you then resign | your crown and kingdom, 2.04. 94
for if you hide the crown | even in your hearts, 2.04. 97
deliver up the crown, and to take mercy | on the 2.04.103

ball, | the sword, the mace, the crown imperial, 4.01.261
fault | my father made in compassing the crown! 4.01.294
think i had sold my farm to buy my crown. 5.02.126 P
his crown shall be the ransom of my friend; 1H6 1.01.150
to crown himself king and suppress the prince. 1.03. 68
for which i will divide my crown with her, | and 1.06. 18
o, what a scandal is it to our crown | that two 3.01. 69
lord bishop, set the crown upon his head. 4.01. 1
as well they may upbraid me with my crown, 4.01.156
he'll make his cap co–equal with the crown." 5.01. 33
hand, | and set a precious crown upon thy head, 5.03.119
you shall become true liegemen to his crown. 5.04.128
nor be rebellious to the crown of england, 5.04.171
thou, nor thy nobles, to the crown of england. 5.04.172
and crown her queen of england ere the thirtieth 2H6 1.01. 48 P
blood, | and heir–apparent to the english crown. 1.01.152
and, when i spy advantage, claim the crown, 1.01.242
whose church–like humors fits not for a crown. 1.01.247
force perforce i'll make him yield the crown, 1.01.258
the duke of york was rightful heir to the crown. 1.03. 27 P
of york say he was rightful heir to the crown? 1.03. 29 P
and set the triple crown upon his head — | that 1.03. 63
was rightful heir unto the english crown | and 1.03.184
thine eyes and thoughts | beat on a crown, the 2.01. 20
mother, priest, i'll shave your crown for this, 2.01. 50
which is infallible, to england's crown. 2.02. 5
thus got the house of lancaster the crown. 2.02. 29
from whose line | i claim the crown, had issue, 2.02. 35
as i have read, laid claim unto the crown, | and 2.02. 40
anne, | my mother, being heir unto the crown, 2.02. 44
henry doth claim the crown from john of gaunt, 2.02. 54
with honor of his birthright to the crown. 2.02. 62
thrust from the crown | by shameful murther of a 4.01. 94
reign, | for i am rightful heir unto the crown. 4.02.131
and vows to crown himself in westminster. 4.04. 31
contrary to the king, his crown, and dignity, 4.07. 37 P
and pluck the crown from feeble henry's head. 5.01. 2
that head of thine doth not become a crown: 5.01. 96
of capital treason 'gainst the king and crown. 5.01.107
nobly, york, 'tis for a crown thou fight'st. 5.02. 16
resolve thee, richard, claim the english crown. 3H6 1.01. 49
to aspire unto the crown and reign as king. 1.01. 53
thy father was a traitor to the crown. 1.01. 79
exeter, thou art a traitor to the crown, | in 1.01. 80
will you we show our title to the crown? 1.01.102
what title hast thou, traitor, to the crown? 1.01.104
father, tear the crown from the usurper's head. 1.01.114
henry the fourth by conquest got the crown. 1.01.132
lords, | resign'd the crown to henry the fourth, 1.01.139
and made him to resign his crown perforce. 1.01.142
think you 'twere prejudicial to his crown? 1.01.144
for he could not so resign his crown | but that 1.01.145
henry of lancaster, resign thy crown. 1.01.164
confirm the crown to me and to mine heirs, | and 1.01.172
the crown to thee and to thine heirs for ever, 1.01.195
to entail him and his heirs unto the crown, 1.01.235
will cost my crown, and like an empty eagle 1.01.268
the crown of england, father, which is yours. 1.02. 9
think | how sweet a thing it is to wear a crown, 1.02. 29
and cried, "a crown, or else a glorious tomb! 1.04. 16
york cannot speak unless he wear a crown. 1.04. 93
a crown for york! 1.04. 94
off with the crown; 1.04.107
and, with the crown, his head, | and, whilest we 1.04.107
there, take the crown, and, with the crown, my 1.04.164
take the crown, and, with the crown, my curse, 1.04.164
that sought to be encompass'd with your crown. 2.02. 3
ambitious york did level at thy crown, | thou 2.02. 19
leave, | i'll draw it as apparent to the crown, 2.02. 64
you that are king, though he do wear the crown, 2.02. 90
say'st thou, henry, wilt thou yield the crown? 2.02.101
ne'er shall dine unless thou yield the crown. 2.02.128
and heap'd sedition on his crown at home. 2.02.158
but, if thou be a king, where is thy crown? 3.01. 61
my crown is in my heart, not on my head; 3.01. 62
my crown is call'd content, | a crown it is that 3.01. 64
a crown it is that seldom kings enjoy. 3.01. 65
your crown content and you must be contented 3.01. 67
so do i wish the crown, being so far off, | and 3.02.140
i'll make my heaven to dream upon the crown, 3.02.168
head | be round impaled with a glorious crown. 3.02.171
and yet i know not how to get the crown, | for 3.02.172
torment myself to catch the english crown; 3.02.179
can i do this, and cannot get a crown? 3.02.194
but if your title to the crown be weak, | as may 3.03.145
did i impale him with the regal crown? 3.03.189
i was the chief that rais'd him to the crown, 3.03.262
stay not for the love of edward, but the crown. 4.01.126
but henry now shall wear the english crown, 4.03. 49
edward's fruit, true heir to th' english crown. 4.04. 24
to set the crown once more on henry's head. 4.04. 27
and pray that i may repossess the crown. 4.05. 29
warwick, although my head still wear the crown, 4.06. 23
adjudg'd an olive branch and laurel crown, | as 4.06. 34
his head by nature fram'd to wear a crown, | his 4.06. 72
for if edward repossess the crown, | 'tis like 4.06. 99
my waned state for henry's regal crown. 4.07. 4
forget | our title to the crown and only claim 4.07. 46
by what safe means the crown may be recover'd. 4.07. 52
that thou mightst repossess the crown in peace, 5.07. 19
to fight on edward's party for the crown, | and R3 1.03.137
when thou didst crown his warlike brows with 1.03.174
my husband lost his life to get the crown, | and 2.04. 57
how? wear the garland? dost thou mean the crown? 3.02. 41
i'll have this crown of mine cut from my 3.02. 43
before i'll see the crown so foul misplac'd. 3.02. 44
he would make his son | heir to the crown — 3.05. 78
away, | and that my path were even to the crown, 3.07.157
and by that knot looks proudly on the crown, 4.03. 42
hid'st thou that forehead with a golden crown 4.04.140
slaughter of the prince that ow'd that crown, 4.04.142
now, by my george, my garter, and my crown — 4.04.366
thy crown, usurp'd, disgrac'd his kingly glory. 4.04.371
he makes for england, here to claim the crown. 4.04.468
the first was i that help'd thee to the crown; 5.03.167
call'd upon | for high feats done to th' crown, H8 1.01. 61
how grounded he his title to the crown | upon 1.02.144
there 'long'd | no more to th' crown but that. 2.03. 49
and with his deed did crown | his word upon you. 3.02.155
queen, | as holy oil, edward confessor's crown, 4.01. 88
and yet no day without a deed to crown it. 5.04. 58
"as true as troilus" shall crown up the verse, TRO 3.02.182
make cressid's name the very crown of falsehood, 4.02.100
now the gods crown thee! COR 2.01.179
crown him and say, "long live our emperor!" TIT 1.01.229
why, there was a crown offer'd him; JC 1.02.221 P
was the crown offer'd him thrice? 1.02.228
who offer'd him the crown? 1.02.232
i saw mark antony offer him a crown — yet 'twas 1.02.237 P
him a crown — yet 'twas not a crown neither, 1.02.237 P
breath because caesar refus'd the crown, that it 1.02.247 P
the common herd was glad he refus'd the crown, 1.02.264 P
and he shall wear his crown by sea and land, 1.03. 87
crown him that, | and then i grant we put a 2.01. 15
to give this day a crown to mighty caesar. 2.02. 94
i thrice presented him a kingly crown, | which 3.02. 96
he would not take the crown, | therefore 'tis 3.02.112
home, | might yet enkindle you unto the crown, MAC 1.03.121
why, chance may crown me | without my stir. 1.03.143
and fill me from the crown to the toe topful 1.05. 42
upon my head they plac'd a fruitless crown, 3.01. 60
thy crown does sear mine eyeballs. 4.01.113
to crown my thoughts with acts, be it thought 4.01.149
sting thy father's life | now wears his crown. HAM 1.05. 40
by a brother's hand | of life, of crown, of 1.05. 75
my crown, mine own ambition, and my queen. 3.03. 55
our crown, our life, and all that we call ours, 4.05.209
successive kings | in denmark's crown have worn. 5.02.274
wit in thy bald crown when thou gav'st thy LR 1.04.163 P
upon the crown o' th' cliff, what thing was that 4.06. 67
peer, | his breeches cost him but a crown; OTH 2.03. 90
thy crown and hearted throne | to tyrannous hate 3.03.448
i am prompt | to lay my crown at 's feet, and ANT 3.13. 76
my turpitude | thou dost so crown with gold! 4.06. 33
the crown o' th' earth doth melt. 4.15. 63
bring our crown and all. 5.02.232
give me my robe, put on my crown, i have 5.02.280
my supreme crown of grief, and those repeated CYM 1.06. 4
enlargement by | the consequence o' th' crown, 2.03.121
put | his brows within a golden crown and call'd 3.01. 60
down, | i have the placing of the british crown. 3.05. 65
work | her son into th' adoption of the crown; 5.05. 56
and crown you king of this day's happiness. PER 2.03. 11
you shall like diamonds sit about his crown. 2.04. 53
of helicanus would set on | the crown of tyre, 3.ch. 28
obedient to their dooms, | will take the crown. 3.ch. 33
to equal any single crown a' th' earth | i' th' 4.03. 8
whose twelve strong labors crown his memory, TNK 3.06.176
to crown all this, by your most noble soul, 3.06.208
honor crown the worthiest! 5.01. 17
and garland | to crown the question's title. 5.03. 17
or what fond beggar, but to touch the crown, LUC 216
incertainties now crown themselves assur'd, SON 107. 7

CROWN'D 45 FR 0.0050 REL FR 43 V 2 P
conclusion shall be crown'd with your enjoying WIV 3.05.136 P
though you were crown'd | the nonpareil of TN 1.05.253
that, were i crown'd the most imperial monarch, WT 4.04.372
with your crown'd brother and these your 5.03. 5
once /again crown'd, | and look'd upon, i hope, JN 4.02. 1
you were crown'd before, | and that high royalty 4.02. 4
to this effect, before you were new crown'd, 4.02. 35
harry the fift is crown'd! 2H4 4.05.119
up in the air, crown'd with the golden sun, H5 2.04. 58
in infant bands crown'd king | of france and ep 9
to cross the seas and to be crown'd in france. 1H6 3.01.179
because, forsooth, the king of scots is crown'd. 4.01.157
to cross the seas to england and be crown'd 5.05. 90
that chair where kings and queens were crown'd, 2H6 1.02. 38
crown'd by the name of henry the fourth, 2.02. 23
but i am not your king | till i be crown'd, and 2.02. 65
to be a queen, and crown'd with infamy! 3.02. 71
when i was crown'd i was but nine months old. 3H6 1.01.112
it that great plantagenet | is crown'd so soon, 1.04.100
who crown'd the gracious duke in high despite, 2.01. 59
well, if you be a king crown'd with content, 3.01. 66
let him be crown'd, in him your comfort lives. R3 2.02. 98
fet | hither to london, to be crown'd our king. 2.02.122
was crown'd in paris but at nine months old. 2.03. 17
to–morrow may it please you to be crown'd? 3.07.242
for queen, a very caitiff crown'd with care; 4.04.101
ships, | and turn'd crown'd kings to merchants. TRO 2.02. 83
for 'tis a throne where honor may be crown'd ROM 3.02. 93
in some sort these wants of mine are crown'd, TIM 2.02.181
outlives incertain pomp, is crown'd before: 4.03.243
thy saints for aye | be crown'd with plagues, 5.01. 53
he would be crown'd: JC 2.01. 12
better parts | shall be crown'd in brutus. 3.02. 52
look whe'er he have not crown'd dead cassius! 5.03. 97
aid doth seem | to have thee crown'd withal. MAC 1.05. 30
whom we invite to see us crown'd at scone. 5.09. 41
crown'd with rank /femiter and furrow–weeds, LR 4.04. 3
this grief is crown'd with consolation: ANT 1.02.167 P
shouldst come like a fury crown'd with snakes, 2.05. 40
drown'd, | with thy grapes our hairs be crown'd! 2.07.116
a /palace | for the crown'd truth to dwell in. PER 5.01.122
led on by heaven, and crown'd with joy at last. 5.03. 90
crawls to maturity, wherewith being crown'd, SON 60. 6
outward thus with outward praise is crown'd, 69. 5
or whether doth my mind, being crown'd with you, 114. 1

CROWNED 14 FR 0.0015 REL FR 14 V 0 P
due but to one, and crowned with one crest. MND 3.02.214
nonino, | for love is crowned with the prime, AYL 5.03. 32
where he sits crowned in his master's spite. TN 5.01.128
anointed, crowned, planted many years, | be R2 4.01.127
even in the presence of the crowned king. 1H4 3.02. 54
bells ring to thine ear | that thou art crowned, 2H4 4.05.112
sate | crowned with faith and constant loyalty. H5 2.02. 5
the dolphin charles is crowned king in rheims; 1H6 1.01. 92
the dolphin crowned king? 1.01. 96
infancy | crowned in paris in despite of foes? 2H6 1.01. 94
there to be crowned england's royal king; 3H6 2.06. 88
there to be crowned richard's royal queen. R3 4.01. 32
that for our crowned heads we have no roof TNK 1.01. 52
more, | entitled in /thy parts do crowned sit, SON 37. 7

CROWNER 2 FR 0.0002 REL FR 0 V 2 P
go thou and seek the crowner, and let him sit o' TN 1.05.134 P
the crowner hath sate on her, and finds it HAM 5.01. 4 P

CROWNER'S 1 FR 0.0001 REL FR 0 V 1 P
ay, marry, is't — crowner's quest law. HAM 5.01. 22 P

CROWNET *(also coronet, etc.)*

CROWNET 2 FR 0.0002 REL FR 2 V 0 P
there, on the pendant boughs her crownet weeds HAM 4.07.172
whose bosom was my crownet, my chief end, | like ANT 4.12. 27

/CROWNETS 1 FR 0.0001 REL FR 1 V 0 P
/that /wore | /their /crownets /regal, /from TRO pr 6

CROWNETS 1 FR 0.0001 REL FR 1 V 0 P
in his livery | walk'd crowns and crownets; ANT 5.02. 91

CROWNING 2 FR 0.0002 REL FR 2 V 0 P
i mean, your voice for crowning of the king. R3 3.04. 28
crowning the present, doubting of the rest? SON 115.12

CROWN'S 2 FR 0.0002 REL FR 1 V 1 P
a crown's worth of good interpretation. 2H4 2.02. 92 P
your crown's /awry, | i'll mend it, and then ANT 5.02.318

CROWNS' 1 FR 0.0001 REL FR 1 V 0 P
in a field | that their crowns' titles tried. TNK 3.01. 22

CROWNS 63 FR 0.0071 REL FR 47 V 16 P
betrims, | to make cold nymphs chaste crowns; TMP 4.01. 66
with your sedg'd crowns and ever–harmless looks, 4.01.129
the payment of a hundred thousand crowns, LLL 2.01.129
to have repaid | a hundred thousand crowns, and 2.01.143
/on payment of a hundred thousand crowns, | to 2.01.144
some of your french crowns have no hair at all; MND 1.02. 97 P
crowns him with flowers, and makes him all her 2.01. 27
me by will but poor a thousand crowns, and, as AYL 1.01. 3 P
and yet give no thousand crowns neither. 1.01. 87 P
i have five hundred crowns, | the thrifty hire i 2.03. 38
crowns in my purse i have, and goods at home, SHR 1.02. 57
and in possession twenty thousand crowns. 2.01.122
in ivory coffers i have stuff'd my crowns; 2.01.350
twenty crowns. 5.02. 70
twenty crowns! 5.02. 71
add | unto their losses twenty thousand crowns, 5.02.113
cost me /a hundred crowns since supper–time. 5.02.128
her, i'll add three thousand crowns | to what is AWW 3.07. 35
crowns what you are doing in the present deeds, WT 4.04.145
ten thousand bloody crowns of mothers' sons R2 3.03. 96
the offer of an hundred thousand crowns | than 4.01. 16
go, i will stuff your purses full of crowns; 1H4 1.02.132 P
we must have bloody noses and crack'd crowns, 2.03. 93
give crowns like pins! 2H4 2.04.174 P
harry ten shillings in french crowns for you. 3.02.222 P
with crowns imperial, crowns and coronets, H5 2.pr. 10
with crowns imperial, crowns and coronets, 2.pr. 10
which he fills | with treacherous crowns; 2.pr. 22
and this man | hath, for a few light crowns, 2.02. 89
lay twenty french crowns to one they will beat 4.01.226 P
it is no english treason to cut french crowns, 4.01.228 P
and crowns for convoy put into his purse. 4.03. 37
unless thou give me crowns, brave crowns; 4.04. 38
unless thou give me crowns, brave crowns; 4.04. 38
his ransom he will give you two hundred crowns. 4.04. 46 P
fury shall abate, and i | the crowns will take. 4.04. 48
here, uncle exeter, fill this glove with crowns, 4.08. 57
give him the crowns; 4.08. 60
a thousand crowns, or else lay down your head. 2H6 4.01. 16
what, think you much to pay two thousand crowns, 4.01. 18
boys went to span–counter for french crowns), i 4.02.158 P
shall have a thousand crowns for his reward. 4.08. 67
me, and get a thousand crowns of the king by 4.10. 27 P
a wisp of straw were worth a thousand crowns 3H6 2.02.144
may be possessed with some store of crowns, 2.05. 57
than to accomplish twenty golden crowns! 3.02.152
and fearless minds climb soonest unto crowns. 4.07. 62
prerogative of age, crowns, sceptres, laurels, TRO 1.03.107
whom opinion crowns | the sinow and the forehand 1.03.142
says, opinion crowns | with an imperial voice — 1.03.186
some with cunning gild their copper crowns, 4.04.105
the end crowns all, | and that old common 4.05.224
yes, mine's three thousand crowns; what's yours? TIM 3.04. 28
five thousand crowns, my lord. 3.04. 95 P
with twenty mortal murthers on their crowns, MAC 3.04. 80
him threescore thousand crowns in annual fee, HAM 2.02. 73
give me an egg, and i'll give thee two crowns. LR 1.04.156 P
what two crowns shall they be? 1.04.157 P
and eat up the meat, the two crowns of the egg. 1.04.159 P
in his livery | walk'd crowns and crownets; ANT 5.02. 91
did vail their crowns to his supremacy; PER 2.03. 42
in our shadow, to scatter his crowns in the sun. 4.02.112 P
but if store of crowns be scant, | no man will PP 20.35

CROWS 18 FR 0.0020 REL FR 13 V 5 P
and crows are fatted with the murrion flock; MND 2.01. 97
the casting forth to crows thy baby–daughter WT 3.02.191
and their executors, the knavish crows, | fly H5 4.02. 51
leaving thy trunk for crows to feed upon. 2H6 4.10. 84
and made a prey for carrion kites and crows 5.02. 11
crows and daws, crows and daws! TRO 1.02.244 P
crows and daws, crows and daws! 1.02.244 P
wak'd by the lark, hath rous'd the ribald crows, 4.02. 9
and bring in | the crows to peck the eagles. COR 3.01.139
i' th' city of kites and crows. 4.05. 42 P
i' th' city of kites and crows? 4.05. 43 P
so shows a snowy dove trooping with crows, | as ROM 1.05. 48
and in their steads do ravens, crows, and kites JC 5.01. 84
the crows and choughs that wing the midway air LR 4.06. 13
our crows shall fare the better for you; CYM 3.01. 81 P
to tell | what crows have peck'd them here. 5.03. 93
and pecks of crows in the foul fields of thebes. TNK 1.01. 42
outstripping crows that strive to overfly them. VEN 324

CRUDY 1 FR 0.0001 REL FR 0 V 1 P
foolish and dull and crudy vapors which environ 2H4 4.03. 98 P

/CRUEL 1 FR 0.0001 REL FR 1 V 0 P
/ministers /and /instruments | /of /cruel /war. TRO pr 5

CRUEL 75 FR 0.0084 REL FR 69 V 6 P
were not you then as cruel as the sentence MM 2.04.109
shame to him whose cruel striking | kills for 3.02.267
there died this morning of a cruel fever | one 4.03. 70
this is that face, thou cruel angelo, | which 5.01.207
comedy and most cruel death of pyramus and MND 1.02. 12 P
away, | and you sat smiling at his cruel prey. 2.02.150
extremely stretch'd and conn'd with cruel pain, 5.01. 80
have all miscarried, my creditors grow cruel, my MV 3.02.316 P
wrong, | and curb this cruel devil of his will. 4.01.217
you have seen cruel proof of this man's strength AYL 1.02.174 P

why, 'tis a boisterous and a cruel style, | a 4.03. 31
ah, tranio, what a cruel father's he! SHR 1.01.185
and my desires, like fell and cruel hounds, TN 1.01. 21
away, breath, | i am slain by a fair cruel maid. 2.04. 54
still so cruel? 5.01.110
dearly, | him will i tear out of that cruel eye, 5.01.127
but this most cruel usage of your queen | (not WT 2.03.117
i will devise a death as cruel for thee | as 4.04.440
thou didst but consent | to this most cruel act, JN 4.03.126
for i do see the cruel pangs of death | right in 5.04. 59
shall i say to thee, lord scroop, thou cruel, H5 2.02. 94
and of buxom valor, hath, by cruel fate, | and 3.06. 26
defac'd | by wasting ruin of the cruel foe. 1H6 3.03. 46
out, | must i behold thy timeless cruel death? 5.04. 5
and not with such a cruel threat'ning look. 3H6 1.03. 17
to thee | as now i reap at thy too cruel hand! 1.04.166
upon that clifford, that cruel child–killer. 2.02.112
but is't not cruel | that she should feel the H8 2.01.165
take my cause | out of the gripes of cruel men, 5.02.135
sure | thou hast a cruel nature and a bloody. 5.02.164
troy, | that find such cruel battle here within? TRO 1.01. 3
make cruel way | through ranks of greekish youth 4.05.184
to a cruel war i sent him, from whence he COR 1.03. 13 P
more cruel to your good report than grateful 1.09. 54
o cruel, irreligious piety! TIT 1.01.130
the cruel father and his traitorous sons, | to 1.01.452
and cruel death hath catch'd it from my sight! ROM 4.05. 48
by cruel cruel thee quite overthrown! 4.05. 57
by cruel cruel thee quite overthrown! 4.05. 57
religious canons, civil laws are cruel; TIM 4.03. 61
o you hard hearts, you cruel men of rome, | knew JC 1.01. 36
though now we must appear bloody and cruel, | as 3.01.165
take | the cruel issue of these bloody men, 3.01.294
too cruel any where. MAC 2.03. 88
not confessing | their cruel parricide, filling 3.01. 31
but cruel are the times when we are traitors, 4.02. 18
producing forth the cruel ministers | of this 5.09. 34
firm bosom, | let me be cruel, not unnatural; HAM 3.02.395
i must be cruel, only to be kind. 3.04.178
hah, ha, he wears cruel garters. LR 2.04. 7 P
because i would not see thy cruel nails | pluck 3.07. 56
o cruel! 3.07. 70
i must weep, | but they are cruel tears. OTH 5.02. 21
i that am cruel am yet merciful, | i would not 5.02. 87
she lov'd thee, cruel moor; 5.02.249
i have told him lepidus was grown too cruel, ANT 3.06. 32
a father cruel, and a step–dame false, | a CYM 1.06. 1
dominion, could not be so cruel to me as you, o 3.02. 41 P
which, being cruel to the world, concluded 5.05. 32
to the world, concluded | most cruel to herself. 5.05. 33
till cruel cleon, with his wicked wife, | did PER 5.01.171
fell before | the wrath of cruel creon; TNK 1.01. 40
that were too cruel. 2.05. 41
that were a cruel wisdom! 3.06.242
i am cruel fearful. ep 3
cries, | and bitter words to ban her cruel foes; LUC 1460
o cruel speeding, fraughted with gall. PP 17.16
thyself thy foe, to thy sweet self too cruel. SON 1. 8
praising thy worth, despite his cruel hand. 60.14
fortify | against confounding age's cruel knife, 63.10
savage, extreme, rude, cruel, not to trust, 129. 4
as those whose beauties proudly make them cruel; 131. 2
me from myself thy cruel eye hath taken, | and 133. 5
be wise as thou art cruel, do not press | my 140. 1
canst thou, o cruel, say i love thee not, | when 149. 1

CRUEL–HEARTED 1 FR 0.0001 REL FR 0 V 1 P
yet did not this cruel–hearted cur shed one tear TGV 2.03. 9 P

CRUELLER 1 FR 0.0001 REL FR 0 V 1 P
long in spectatorship and crueller in suffering; COR 5.02. 66 P

CRUELL'ST 1 FR 0.0001 REL FR 1 V 0 P
you are the cruell'st she alive | if you will TN 1.05.241

CRUELLY 4 FR 0.0004 REL FR 2 V 2 P
most cruelly | didst thou, alonso, use me and my TMP 5.01. 71
i am a man whom fortune hath cruelly scratch'd. AWW 5.02. 27 P
gentle princess, because i love thee cruelly. H5 5.02.203 P
the law, | and none but tyrants use it cruelly. TIM 3.05. 9

CRUELS 1 FR 0.0001 REL FR 1 V 0 P
all cruels else subscribe; LR 3.07. 65

CRUELTY 22 FR 0.0024 REL FR 20 V 2 P
through the heart with your stern cruelty. MND 3.02. 59
soul, | from out the state of hellish cruelty! MV 3.04. 21
strange | than is thy strange apparent cruelty; 4.01. 21
man, | to excuse the current of thy cruelty. 4.01. 64
yet heard too much of phebe's cruelty. AYL 4.03. 38
farewell, fair cruelty. TN 1.05.288
get thee to yond same sovereign cruelty. 2.04. 80
bears in his visage no great presage of cruelty. 3.02. 65 P
against this cruelty fight on thy side, | poor WT 2.03.191
teaching his duteous land | audacious cruelty. 1H4 4.03. 45
for when /lenity and cruelty play for a kingdom, H5 3.06.112 P
thy cruelty in execution | upon offenders hath 2H6 1.03.132
come, soldiers, show what cruelty ye can, | that 4.01.132
in cruelty will i seek out my fame. 5.02. 60
'tis a cruelty | to load a falling man. H8 5.02.111
the cruelty and envy of the people, | permitted COR 4.05. 74
the crown to the toe topful | of direst cruelty! MAC 1.05. 43
to do worse to you were fell cruelty, | which is 4.02. 71
if there be any cunning cruelty | that can OTH 5.02.333
but if you seek | to lay on me a cruelty, by ANT 5.02.129
for these two cousins | despise my cruelty, and TNK 3.06.249
of their sons, | shall never curse my cruelty. 4.02. 6

CRUMB 1 FR 0.0001 REL FR 1 V 0 P
he that keeps nor crust /nor crumb, | weary of LR 1.04.198

CRUMBLE 1 FR 0.0001 REL FR 1 V 0 P
bosom | that all my bowels crumble up to dust. JN 5.07. 31

CRUMBS 1 FR 0.0001 REL FR 0 V 1 P
go, sir, rub your chain with crumbs. TN 2.03.120 P

CRUPPER 3 FR 0.0003 REL FR 1 V 2 P
to pay the saddler for my mistress' crupper? ERR 1.02. 56
times piec'd, and a woman's crupper of velure, SHR 3.02. 60 P
how i lost my crupper, with many things of 4.01. 81 P

CRUSADOES 1 FR 0.0001 REL FR 1 V 0 P
rather have lost my purse | full of crusadoes; OTH 3.04. 26

CRUSH 13 FR 0.0014 REL FR 11 V 2 P
then crush this herb into lysander's eye; MND 3.02.366
and thrum, | quail, crush, conclude, and quell! 5.01.287
and yet, to crush this a little, it would bow to TN 2.05.140 P
let nature crush the sides o' th' earth together WT 4.04.478
to crush our old limbs in ungentle steel. 1H4 5.01. 13
crowd us and crush us to this monstrous form 2H4 4.02. 34
that they may crush down with a heavy fall | the R3 5.03.111
why then we do our main opinion crush | in taint TRO 1.03.372
i thought to crush him in an equal force, | true COR 1.10. 14
bruising to you | when he hath power to crush? 2.03.203
montagues, i pray, come and crush a cup of wine. ROM 1.02. 80 P
crush him together rather than unfold | his CYM 1.01. 26
"fie, fie," he says, "you crush me, let me go, VEN 611

CRUSH'D 5 FR 0.0005 REL FR 2 V 3 P
who cannot be crush'd with a plot? AWW 4.03.325 P
at home, | yet that is but a crush'd necessity, H5 1.02.175
and have their heads crush'd like rotten apples! 3.07.144 P
humors that his valor is crush'd into folly, his TRO 1.02. 23 P
with time's injurious hand crush'd and o'erworn, SON 63. 2

CRUSHEST 1 FR 0.0001 REL FR 0 V 1 P
done, hercules, now thou crushest the snake!" LLL 5.01.139 P

CRUSHETH 1 FR 0.0001 REL FR 1 V 0 P
the iron bit he crusheth 'tween his teeth, VEN 269

CRUSHING 1 FR 0.0001 REL FR 1 V 0 P
then crushing penury | persuades me i was better R2 5.05. 34

CRUST 4 FR 0.0004 REL FR 4 V 0 P
that he could gnaw a crust at two hours old; R3 2.04. 28
the infinite malady | crust you quite o'er! TIM 3.06. 99
most lazar–like, with vile and loathsome crust, HAM 1.05. 72
he that keeps nor crust /nor crumb, | weary of LR 1.04.198

CRUSTS 1 FR 0.0001 REL FR 0 V 1 P
not for that neither, because i love crusts. TGV 3.01.342 P

CRUSTY 1 FR 0.0001 REL FR 1 V 0 P
thou crusty batch of nature, what's the news? TRO 5.01. 5

CRUTCH 12 FR 0.0013 REL FR 12 V 0 P
and gives the crutch the cradle's infancy. LLL 4.03.241
hence therefore, thou nice crutch! 2H4 1.01.145
thus king henry throws away his crutch | before 2H6 3.01.189
youth take leave and leave you to the crutch. 3H6 3.02. 35
to as much end | as give a crutch to th' dead. H8 1.01.172
him, priam, hold him fast, | he is thy crutch. TRO 5.03. 60
i'll lean upon one crutch, and fight with t' COR 1.01.242
a crutch, a crutch! why call you for a sword? ROM 1.01. 76
a crutch, a crutch! why call you for a sword? 1.01. 76
pluck the lin'd crutch from thy old limping sire TIM 4.01. 14
to have turn'd my leaping time into a crutch, CYM 4.02.200
canst make | a cripple flourish with his crutch, TNK 5.01. 82

CRUTCHES 4 FR 0.0004 REL FR 1 V 3 P
time goes on crutches till love have all his ADO 2.01.358 P
they that went on crutches ere he was born WT 1.01. 40 P
desire to live on crutches till he had one. 1.01. 46 P
and pluck'd two crutches from my feeble hands, R3 2.02. 58

/CRY 3 FR 0.0003 REL FR 1 V 2 P
/did /they /not /sometimes /cry "/all /hail!" R2 4.01.169
/that /cry /out /on /the /top /of /question, HAM 2.02.340 P
/cry /you /mercy, /i /took /you /for /a LR 3.06. 52 P

CRY 225 FR 0.0254 REL FR 190 V 35 P
o, the cry did knock | against my very heart. TMP 1.02. 8
creature in the vessel | which thou heardst cry, 1.02. 32
how i cried out then, | will cry it o'er again. 1.02.134
us, | to cry to th' sea, that roar'd to us; 1.02.149
a space whose ev'ry cubit | seems to cry out, 2.01.258
with a tang, | would cry to a sailor, 'go hang!' 2.02. 51
and "go," | and breathe twice, and cry "so, so," 4.01. 45
there i couch when owls do cry. 5.01. 90
such another proof will make me cry "baa." TGV 1.01. 93 P
why dost thou cry "alas"? 4.04. 77
and thinking on it makes me cry "alas!" 4.04. 84
o, cry you mercy, sir, i have mistook; 5.04. 94
i have a great dispositions to cry. WIV 3.01. 22 P
proceedings all my neighbors shall cry aim. 3.02. 44 P
i cry you mercy! 3.05. 26 P
if i cry out thus upon no trail, never trust me 4.02.196 P
hue and cry, villain, go! 4.05. 90 P
fly, run, hue and cry, villain! 4.05. 91 P
i come to her in white, and cry "mum"; 5.02. 6 P
i spy comfort, i cry bail. MM 3.02. 41 P
i cry you mercy, sir, and well could wish | you 4.01. 10
we bid be quiet when we hear it cry; ERR 2.01. 35
you'll cry for this, minion, if i beat the door 3.01. 59
be mad, good master, | cry "the devil!" 4.04.128
o, i cry you mercy, friend, go you with me, and ADO 1.02. 25 P
i love you the better; the hearers may cry amen. 2.01.106 P
sit in a corner and cry "heigh–ho for a husband! 2.01.320 P
i cry you mercy, uncle. by your grace's pardon. 2.01.339 P
if you hear a child cry in the night, you must 3.03. 65 P
not every earthly thing | cry shame upon her? 4.01.121
stroke his beard, | and, sorrow wag, cry "hem!" 5.01. 16
my griefs cry louder than advertisement. 5.01. 32
if any of the audience hiss, you may cry, "well LLL 5.01.138 P
bleat softly then, the butcher hears you cry. 5.02.255
a bird the lie, though he cry "cuckoo" never so? MND 3.01.135 P
i cry your worships mercy, heartily. 3.01.179 P
every region near | seem all one mutual cry. 4.01.117
a cry more tuneable | was never hollow'd to, nor 4.01.124
and seen our wishes prosper, | to cry good joy. MV 3.02.188
i would cry, if i could cry "hem" and have him. AYL 1.03. 19 P
my man's apparel and to cry like a woman; 2.04. 5 P
cry "holla" to /thy tongue, i prithee; 3.02.244 P
cry the man mercy, love him, take his offer; 3.05. 61
what you seek, | that fame may cry you loud. AWW 2.01. 17
do you cry, "o lord, sir!" 2.02. 52 P
babbling gossip of the air | cry out "olivia!" TN 1.05.274
sowter will cry upon't for all this, though it 2.05.123 P
ay, or i'll cudgel him, and make him cry o! 2.05.134 P
whereof the execution did cry out | against the WT 1.02.260
or both yourself and me | cry lost, and so good 1.02.411
and my near'st of kin | cry fie upon my grave! 3.02. 54
last — o lords, | when i have said, cry "woe!" 3.02.200
o, the most piteous cry of the poor souls! 3.03. 90 P
come buy, | buy, lads, or else your lasses cry: 4.04.229
it ill beseems this presence to cry aim | to JN 2.01.196
cry "havoc," kings! 2.01.357
cardinal, cry thou amen | to my keen curses; 3.01.181
no, no, i will not, having breath to cry. 3.04. 37
indeed your drums, being beaten, will cry out; 5.02.166
strong as a tower in hope, i cry amen. R2 1.03.102
cry woe, destruction, ruin, and decay: 3.02.102
child, child's children, cry against you "woe!" 4.01.149
shrill/–voic'd suppliant makes this eager cry? 5.03. 75
i cry you mercy. 1H4 1.03.212
of manage to thy bounding steed, | cry "courage! 2.03. 50
you breathe in your watering, they cry "hem!" 2.04. 16 P
a hue and cry | hath followed certain men unto 2.04.507
i had rather be a kitten and cry mew | than one 3.01.127
my good lord of westmerland, i cry you mercy! 4.02. 52 P
and upon this charge | cry, "god for harry, H5 3.01. 34
let him cry, "praise and glory on his head!" 4.pr. 31
join together at the latter day and cry all, "we 4.01.137 P
to cry amen to that, thus we appear. 5.02. 21
winchester goose, i cry, "a rope! 1H6 1.03. 53
officer, as loud as e'er thou canst, | cry. 1.03. 73
no longer on saint denis will we cry, | but joan 1.06. 28
the cry of talbot serves me for a sword, | for i 2.01. 79
dangerous ends, | enter and cry "the dolphin!" 3.02. 34
i cry you mercy, 'tis but quid for quo. 5.03.109
will cry for vengeance at the gates of heaven. 5.04. 53
i cry you mercy, madam; 2H6 1.03.139
time when screech–owls cry and ban–dogs howl, 1.04. 18
and therefore do they cry, though you forbid, 3.02.264
and cry out for thee to close up mine eyes, | to 3.02.395
who having pinch'd a few and made them cry, 3H6 2.01. 16
foaming steeds, | and once again cry "charge!" 2.01.184
cry "saint george!" 2.02. 80
and cry "content" to that which grieves my heart 3.02.183
strike up the drum, cry "courage!" 5.03. 24
i cry thee mercy then; R3 1.03.234
and cry, "o clarence, my unhappy son!"? 2.02. 4
madam, my mother, i do cry you mercy, | i did 2.02.104
you live that shall cry woe for this hereafter. 3.03. 7
them that did love their country's good | cry, 3.07. 22
i cry thee mercy; 4.04.513
cry mercy, lords and watchful gentlemen, | that 5.03.224
and from a mouth of honor quite cry down | this H8 1.01.137
then my guiltless blood must cry against 'em. 2.01. 68
soul forsake, | shall cry for blessings on him. 2.01. 90
now god incense him, | and let him cry "ha!" 3.02. 62
if you can blush, and cry "guilty," cardinal, 3.02.305
methinks i could | cry the amen, and yet my 5.01. 24
good master secretary, | i cry your honor mercy; 5.02.113
to hear the city | abus'd extremely, and to cry, ep 6
hark, do you not hear the people cry "troilus"? TRO 1.02.225 P
more ready to cry out, "who knows what follows?" 2.02. 13
cry, troyans, cry! 2.02. 97
cry, troyans, cry! 2.02. 97
cry, troyans! 2.02. 99
cry, troyans, cry! 2.02.101
cry, troyans, cry! 2.02.101
soft infancy, that nothing canst but cry, | add 2.02.105
cry, troyans, cry! 2.02.108
cry, troyans, cry! 2.02.108
cry, troyans, cry! 2.02.111
cry, troyans, cry! 2.02.111
cry, cry! 2.02.112
cry, cry! 2.02.112
that the death–tokens of it | cry "no recovery." 2.03.178
these lovers cry, o ho, they die! 3.01.121
the cry went once on thee, | and still it might, 3.03.184
antics, one another meet, | and all cry, hector! 5.03. 87
on, myrmidons, and cry you all amain, 5.08. 13
of the city | you cry against the noble senate, COR 1.01.186
giddy censure | will then cry out of martius, "o 1.01.269
into a rapture lets her baby cry | while she 2.01.207
or had you tongues to cry | against the 2.03.204
the people cry you mock'd them; 3.01. 42
do not cry havoc where you should but hunt 3.01.273
then let them, | if i say fine, cry "fine!" 3.03. 16
if death, cry "death!" 3.03. 16
and when such time they have begun to cry, | let 3.03. 19
you common cry of curs, whose breath i hate | as 3.03.120
you have made | good work, you and your cry! 4.06.147
side | give the all–hail to thee, and cry, "be 5.03.139
cry, "welcome, ladies, welcome!" 5.05. 6
i heard a child cry underneath a wall. TIT 5.01. 24
and stop their mouths if they begin to cry. 5.02.161
i know | the common voice do cry it shall be so. 5.03.140
there let him stand and rave and cry for food. 5.03.180
cry but "ay me!" ROM 2.01. 10
and spurs, swits and spurs, or i'll cry a match. 2.04. 69 P
o, i cry you mercy, you are the singer; 4.05.139 P
o, the people in the street cry "romeo," | some 5.03.191
hand, thus — but tell him | my uses cry to me; TIM 2.01. 20
shriller than all the music | cry "caesar!" JC 1.02. 17
they shouted thrice; what was the last cry for? 1.02.226
run hence, proclaim, cry it about the streets. 3.01. 79
some to the common pulpits, and cry out, 3.01. 80
wives, and children stare, cry out, and run, 3.01. 97
let's all cry, "peace, freedom, and liberty!" 3.01.110
confines with a monarch's voice | cry "havoc," 3.01.273
my lord, i do not know that i did cry. 4.03.296
why did you so cry out, sirs, in your sleep? 4.03.303
but i am faint, my gashes cry for help. MAC 1.02. 42
peep through the blanket of the dark | to cry, 1.05. 54
i heard the owl scream and the crickets cry. 2.02. 15
methought i heard a voice cry, "sleep no more! 2.02. 32
new morn | new widows howl, new orphans cry, new 4.03. 5
outward walls, | the cry is still, "they come!" 5.05. 2
it is the cry of women, my good lord. 5.05. 8
wherefore was that cry? 5.05. 15
shoes, get me a fellowship in a cry of players? HAM 3.02.278 P
/they cry, "choose we, laertes shall be king!" 4.05.107
how cheerfully on the false trail they cry! 4.05.110
cry to be heard, as 'twere from heaven to earth, 4.05.217
i'll beat the drum | till it cry sleep to death. LR 2.04.119
cry to it, nuncle, as the cockney did to the 2.04.122 P
his heart should make | shall of a corn cry woe, 3.02. 33
and cry | these dreadful summoners grace. 3.02. 58
o, cry you mercy, sir. 3.04.171
affliction till it do cry out itself | "enough, 4.06. 76
time that we smell the air | we wawl and cry. 4.06.180
we cry that we are come | to this great stage of 4.06.182
whom the rigor of our state | forc'd to cry out. 5.01. 23
when time shall serve, let but the herald cry, 5.01. 48
th' sea | stand ranks of people, and they cry, OTH 2.01. 54
go out and cry a mutiny. 2.03.157
hound that hunts, but one that fills up the cry. 2.03.364 P
cry, "o sweet creature!" 3.03.422
/faith, the cry goes that you marry her. 4.01.123 P
cough, or cry "hem," if anybody come. 4.02. 29
i cry you mercy then. 4.02. 88

to come in to the cry without more help. 5.01. 44
/did not you hear a cry? 5.01. 49
what are you here that cry so grievously? 5.01. 53
i cry you mercy. here's cassio hurt by villains. 5.01. 69
i cry your gentle pardon; 5.01. 93
/o /lord, what cry is that? 5.02.117
all, all, cry shame against me, yet i'll speak. 5.02.222
kings would start forth | and cry, "your will?" ANT 3.13. 92
i'll strike, and cry, "take all!" 4.02. 8
a fearful dream of him, | and cry myself awake? CYM 3.04. 44
from east to occident, cry out for service, 4.02.372
or we poor ghosts will cry | to th' shining 5.04. 88
/midwife gentle | to those that cry by night, PER 3.01. 12
with warrant of her virginity, and cry, "he that 4.02. 59 P
innocent | and for an honest attribute cry out, 4.03. 18
and make him cry from under ground, "o, fan TNK pr 18
may | be wish'd upon thy head, i cry amen to't! 1.04. 3
him to th' plains, his learning makes no cry. 2.03. 54
and well have hollow'd | to a deep cry of dogs; 2.05. 12
how they cry! 3.04. 8
laid upon ye, | and do you still cry, "where?" 3.05. 7
despise my cruelty, and cry woe worth me, | till 3.06.249
city made | with such a cry and swiftness that, 4.01. 98
cannot distinguish, but must cry for both! 4.02. 54
if you do, love, i'll cry. 5.02.112
that the cry | was general "a palamon!"; 5.03. 80
i prithee lay attention to the cry; 5.03. 91
the cry is | "arcite!" 5.03. 92
look what you do offend you cry upon, | that is STM II.C 61
"o, pity," gan she cry, "flint–hearted boy, VEN 95
and in a peaceful hour doth cry, 'kill, kill!' 652
their clamorous cry till they have singled 693
and twenty echoes twenty times cry so. 834
and all in haste she coasteth to the cry. 870
proud, | because the cry remaineth in one place, 885
this dismal cry rings sadly in her ear, 889
lame, blind, halt, creep, cry out for thee, LUC 902
"with this i did begin to start and cry, | and 1639
"fie, fie, fie," now would she cry, | "tereu, PP 20.13
tir'd with all these, for restful death i cry: SON 66. 1
still cry "amen" | to every hymn that able 85. 6
though reason weep and cry, 'it is thy last.' LC 168
CRYING 30 FR 0.0034 REL FR 24 V 6 P
purpose hurried thence | me and thy crying self. TMP 1.02.132
my father wailing, my sister crying, our maid TGV 2.03. 7 P
and so buffets himself on the forehead, crying, WIV 4.02. 26 P
and let the child wake her with crying, for the ADO 3.03. 70 P
crying, his stones, his daughter, and his ducats MV 2.08. 24
offense, | crying, "that's good that's gone." AWW 5.03. 60
in bohemia, | there weep and leave it crying; WT 3.03. 32
even at the crying of your nation's crow, JN 5.02.144
"lay by," and spent with crying "bring in"; 1H4 1.02. 36 P
some swearing, some crying for a surgeon, some H5 4.01.138 P
dogs, | now, like to whelps, we crying run away. 1H6 1.05. 26
their hands, and crying with loud voice, | "jesu 2H6 1.01.160
wren, | by crying comfort from a hollow breast, 3.02. 43
it in london streets, | crying "villiago!" 4.08. 46
throng to the bar, crying all, "guilty! R3 5.03.199
what, is she crying out? H8 5.01. 67
and chipp'd, come to him, | crying on hector. TRO 5.05. 35
ran about the streets, | crying confusion. COR 4.06. 29
the crying babe controll'd with this discourse: TIT 5.01. 26
the pretty wretch left crying and said, "ay." ROM 1.03. 44
laugh | to think it should leave crying and say, 1.03. 51
made in caesar's heart, | crying, "long live! JC 5.01. 32
we came crying hither. LR 4.06.178
there comes a fellow crying out for help, | and OTH 2.03.226
myself the crying fellow did pursue, | lest by 2.03.230
crying, "o dear cassio!" 4.01.137 P
undo that prayer, by crying out as loud, | "o, ANT 3.04. 17
ripp'd, | came crying 'mongst his foes, | a CYM 5.04. 46
and fright her crying babe with tarquin's name; LUC 814
if thou turn back and my loud crying still. SON 143.14
CRY'S 1 FR 0.0001 REL FR 1 V 0 P
the cry's "a palamon!" TNK 5.03. 67
CRYSTAL 16 FR 0.0018 REL FR 16 V 0 P
did hold his eyes lock'd in her crystal looks. TGV 2.04. 89
as jewels in crystal for some prince to buy, LLL 2.01.243
her hairs were gold, crystal the other's eyes. 4.03.140
crystal is muddy. MND 3.02.139
with these crystal beads heaven shall be brib'd JN 2.01.171
since the more fair and crystal is the sky, R2 1.01. 41
brandish your crystal tresses in the sky, | and 1H6 1.01. 3
but in that crystal scales let there be weigh'd ROM 1.02. 96
thy crystal window ope; CYM 5.04. 81
which through the crystal tears gave light, VEN 491
thy soft hands, sweet lips, and crystal eyne, 633
the crystal tide that from her two cheeks fair 957
through crystal walls each little mote will peep LUC 1251
(a closet never pierc'd with crystal eyes), SON 46. 6
of amber, crystal, and of beaded jet, | which LC 37
who glaz'd with crystal gate the glowing roses 286
CRYSTAL–BUTTON 1 FR 0.0001 REL FR 0 V 1 P
thou rob this leathern–jerkin, crystal–button, 1H4 2.04. 69 P
CRYSTALLINE 1 FR 0.0001 REL FR 1 V 0 P
mount, eagle, to my palace crystalline. CYM 5.04.113
CRYSTALS 2 FR 0.0002 REL FR 2 V 0 P
go, clear thy crystals. H5 2.03. 54
both crystals, where they view'd each other's VEN 963
C'S 2 FR 0.0002 REL FR 0 V 2 P
these be her very c's, her u's, and her t's, and TN 2.05. 87 P
her c's, her u's, and her t's: why that? 2.05. 89 P
CUB 1 FR 0.0001 REL FR 1 V 0 P
o thou dissembling cub! TN 5.01.164
//CUB–DRAWN 1 FR 0.0001 REL FR 1 V 0 P
/wherein /the //cub–drawn /bear /would /couch, LR 3.01. 12
CUBICULO 1 FR 0.0001 REL FR 0 V 1 P
we'll call thee at the cubiculo. go. TN 3.02. 52 P
CUBIT 1 FR 0.0001 REL FR 1 V 0 P
a space whose ev'ry cubit | seems to cry out, TMP 2.01.257
CUBS 1 FR 0.0001 REL FR 1 V 0 P
pluck the young sucking cubs from the she–bear, MV 2.01. 29
CUCKOLD 29 FR 0.0032 REL FR 7 V 22 P
/brook, shalt know him for knave, and cuckold. WIV 2.02.285 P
but cuckold! 2.02.299 P
cuckold! 2.02.299 P
cuckold! 2.02.313 P
cuckold! 2.02.313 P
cuckold! 2.02.314 P
(ordaining he should be a cuckold) held his hand 3.05.105 P
master /brook, you shall cuckold ford. 3.05.138 P
now, sir, who's a cuckold now? 5.05.109 P
do not recompense me in making me a cuckold. MM 5.01.517 P
meet me like an old cuckold with horns on his ADO 2.01. 44 P
were you the clerk that is to make me cuckold? MV 5.01.281
if i be his cuckold, he's my drudge. AWW 1.03. 45 P
the nail to his hole, the cuckold to his horn, 2.02. 25 P
as there is no true cuckold but calamity, so TN 1.05. 51 P
and made lucifer cuckold and swore the devil his 1H4 2.04.337 P
or old, | he or she, cuckold or cuckold–maker, H8 5.03. 25
all the argument is a whore and a cuckold, a TRO 2.03. 73 P
what, does the cuckold scorn me? 3.03. 64
he, like a puling cuckold, would drink up | the 4.01. 62
the cuckold and the cuckold–maker are at it. 5.07. 9 P
cries cuckold to my father, brands the harlot HAM 4.05.119
if thou canst cuckold him, thou dost thyself a OTH 1.03.368 P
that cuckold lives in bliss | who, certain of 3.03.167
i will chop her into messes. cuckold me! 4.01.200 P
make her husband a cuckold to make him a monarch 4.03. 76 P
him laughing to his grave, fiftyfold a cuckold! ANT 1.02. 67 P
if it lay in their hands to make me a cuckold, 1.02. 77 P
if thou dost deny | thou'st made me cuckold. CYM 2.04.146
CUCKOLDLY 4 FR 0.0004 REL FR 0 V 4 P
hang him, poor cuckoldly knave! WIV 2.02.270 P
her as the key of the cuckoldly rogue's coffer, 2.02.274 P
/brook, falstaff's a knave, a cuckoldly knave; 5.05.110 P
old, cuckoldly ram, out of all reasonable match. AYL 3.02. 82 P
CUCKOLD–MAD 1 FR 0.0001 REL FR 1 V 0 P
i mean not cuckold–mad — | but sure he is stark ERR 2.01. 58
CUCKOLD–MAKER 2 FR 0.0002 REL FR 1 V 1 P
or old, | he or she, cuckold or cuckold–maker, H8 5.03. 25
the cuckold and the cuckold–maker are at it. TRO 5.07. 9 P
CUCKOLD'S 3 FR 0.0003 REL FR 1 V 2 P
hang like a meteor o'er the cuckold's horns. WIV 2.02.280 P
infamy, /manu cita — a gig of a cuckold's horn. LLL 5.01. 70 P
eye–glass | is thicker than a cuckold's horn), WT 1.02.269
CUCKOLDS 4 FR 0.0004 REL FR 2 V 2 P
what, are we cuckolds ere we have deserv'd it? MV 5.01.265
been | (or i am much deceiv'd) cuckolds ere now, WT 1.02.191
statue and oblique memorial of cuckolds, a TRO 5.01. 55 P
denied but peace is a great maker of cuckolds. COR 4.05.229 P
CUCKOO 19 FR 0.0021 REL FR 15 V 4 P
compiled in praise of the owl and the cuckoo? LLL 5.02.887 P
maintained by the owl, th' other by the cuckoo. 5.02.893 P
the cuckoo then on every tree | mocks married 5.02.898
for thus sings he, | "cuckoo; 5.02.900
cuckoo, cuckoo" — o word of fear, | unpleasing 5.02.901
cuckoo, cuckoo" — o word of fear, | unpleasing 5.02.901
the cuckoo then on every tree | mocks married 5.02.907
for thus sings he, | "cuckoo; 5.02.909
cuckoo, cuckoo" — o word of fear, | unpleasing 5.02.910
cuckoo, cuckoo" — o word of fear, | unpleasing 5.02.910
and the lark, | the plain–song cuckoo grey, MND 3.01.131
a bird the lie, though he cry "cuckoo" never so? 3.01.135 P
he knows me as the blind man knows the cuckoo, MV 5.01.112
comes by destiny, | your cuckoo sings by kind. AWW 1.03. 63
a' horseback, ye cuckoo, but afoot he will not 1H4 2.04.353 P
be seen, | he was but as the cuckoo is in june, 3.02. 75
"the hedge–sparrow fed the cuckoo so long, LR 1.04.215
but since the cuckoo builds not for himself, ANT 2.06. 28
the crow, the sland'rous cuckoo, nor | the TNK 1.01. 19
CUCKOO–BIRDS 1 FR 0.0001 REL FR 1 V 0 P
heed, ere summer comes or cuckoo–birds do sing. WIV 2.01.123
CUCKOO–BUDS 1 FR 0.0001 REL FR 1 V 0 P
all silver–white | and cuckoo–buds of yellow hue LLL 5.02.896
CUCKOO–FLOW'RS 1 FR 0.0001 REL FR 1 V 0 P
with hardocks, hemlock, nettles, cuckoo–flow'rs, LR 4.04. 4
CUCKOO'S 1 FR 0.0001 REL FR 1 V 0 P
so | as that ungentle gull, the cuckoo's bird, 1H4 5.01. 60
CUCKOOS 1 FR 0.0001 REL FR 1 V 0 P
or hateful cuckoos hatch in sparrows' nests? LUC 849
CUCULLUS 2 FR 0.0002 REL FR 0 V 2 P
cucullus non facit monachum: MM 5.01.262 P
lady, "cucullus non facit monachum": TN 1.05. 56 P
CUDGEL 16 FR 0.0018 REL FR 2 V 14 P
i will awe him with my cudgel; WIV 2.02.280 P
heaven guide him to thy husband's cudgel; 4.02. 89 P
and the devil guide his cudgel afterwards! 4.02. 89 P
i'll have the cudgel hallow'd and hung o'er the 4.02.204 P
of ford's but his buck–basket, his cudgel, and 5.05.113 P
do i look like a cudgel or a hovel–post, a staff MV 2.02. 68 P
ay, or i'll cudgel him, and make him cry o! TN 2.05.133 P
to cudgel you and make you take the hatch, | to JN 5.02.138
i would cudgel him like a dog if he would say so 1H4 3.03. 86 P
man as he is, and said he would cudgel you. 3.03.108 P
call'd you jack, and said he would cudgel you. 3.03.139 P
quiet thy cudgel, thou dost see i eat. H5 5.01. 52 P
he could not therefore handle an english cudgel. 5.01. 77 P
as much as one sound cudgel of four foot | (you H8 5.03. 19
had thought to have strooken him with a cudgel, COR 4.05.150 P
cudgel thy brains no more about it, for your HAM 5.01. 56 P
CUDGELL'D 6 FR 0.0006 REL FR 3 V 3 P
transformation hath been wash'd and cudgell'd, WIV 4.05. 97 P
that i might have cudgell'd thee out of thy ADO 5.04.113 P
our ears are cudgell'd — not a word of his JN 2.01.464
and from my weary limbs | honor is cudgell'd. H5 5.01. 85
patches will i get unto these cudgell'd scars, 5.01. 88
i have been to–night exceedingly well cudgell'd; OTH 2.03.366 P
CUDGELLING 1 FR 0.0001 REL FR 0 V 1 P
proud of an heroical cudgelling that he raves in TRO 3.03.249 P
CUDGELS 2 FR 0.0002 REL FR 0 V 2 P
i owe you any thing, i will pay you in cudgels; H5 5.01. 65 P
a woodmonger, and buy nothing of me but cudgels. 5.01. 66 P
/CUE 1 FR 0.0001 REL FR 1 V 0 P
had he the motive and /the /cue for passion HAM 2.02.561
CUE 12 FR 0.0013 REL FR 3 V 9 P
the clock gives me my cue, and my assurance bids WIV 3.02. 45 P
mistress page, remember you your cue. 3.03. 37 P
speak, count, 'tis your cue. ADO 2.01.305 P
and so every one according to his cue. MND 3.01. 76 P
your cue is past; 3.01.101 P
when my cue comes, call me, and i will answer. 4.01.200 P
"deceiving me" is thisby's cue. 5.01.185 P
now we speak upon our cue, and our voice is H5 3.06.123 P
had you not come upon your cue, my lord, R3 3.04. 26
my cue is villainous melancholy, with a sigh LR 1.02.135 P
were it my cue to fight, i should have known it OTH 1.02. 83
give me some meditation, | and mark your cue. TNK 3.05. 94
CUES 1 FR 0.0001 REL FR 0 V 1 P
you speak all your part at once, cues and all. MND 3.01.100 P
CUFF 6 FR 0.0006 REL FR 4 V 2 P
i swear i'll cuff you, if you strike again. SHR 2.01.220
this mad–brain'd bridegroom took him such a cuff 3.02.163
and this cuff was but to knock at your ear, and 4.01. 65 P
do, cuff him soundly, but never draw thy sword. TN 3.04.392 P
i mean to tug it and to cuff you soundly. 1H6 1.03. 48
i could for each word give a cuff, my stomach TNK 3.01.104
/CUFFS* 1 FR 0.0001 REL FR 0 V 1 P
/player /went /to /cuffs /in /the /question. HAM 2.02.355 P
CUFFS* 1 FR 0.0001 REL FR 1 V 0 P
with ruffs and cuffs, and fardingales, and SHR 4.03. 56
/CUIQUE 1 FR 0.0001 REL FR 1 V 0 P
suum /cuique is our roman justice: TIT 1.01.280
CUISSES *(see cushes)*
/CULL 1 FR 0.0001 REL FR 1 V 0 P
and /cull their flower, ajax shall cope the best TRO 2.03.264
CULL 5 FR 0.0005 REL FR 5 V 0 P
to cull the plots of best advantages. JN 2.01. 40
fortune shall cull forth | out of one side her 2.01.391
approach the fold and cull th' infected forth, TIM 5.04. 43
and do you now cull out a holiday? JC 1.01. 49
but when could grief | cull forth, as unpang'd TNK 1.01.169
CULL–COLD 1 FR 0.0001 REL FR 1 V 0 P
but our cull–cold maids do dead men's fingers HAM 4.07.171
CULL'D 7 FR 0.0008 REL FR 6 V 1 P
of all complexions the cull'd sovereignty | do LLL 4.03.230
the word is well cull'd, chose, sweet, and apt, 5.01. 93 P
and cull'd these fiery spirits from the world, JN 5.02.114
these cull'd and choice–drawn cavaliers to H5 3.pr. 24
that are cull'd | out of the powerful regions 1H6 5.03. 10
perhaps, she cull'd it from among the rest. TIT 4.01. 44
madam, we have cull'd such necessaries | as are ROM 4.03. 7
CULLING 2 FR 0.0002 REL FR 2 V 0 P
stand, | culling the principal of all the deer. 3H6 3.01. 4
with overwhelming brows, | culling of simples; ROM 5.01. 40
CULLION 1 FR 0.0001 REL FR 1 V 0 P
a gentleman | and makes a god of such a cullion. SHR 4.02. 20
CULLIONLY 1 FR 0.0001 REL FR 0 V 1 P
of you, you whoreson cullionly barber–monger, LR 2.02. 33 P
CULLIONS 2 FR 0.0002 REL FR 1 V 1 P
avaunt, you cullions! H5 3.02. 21 P
away, base cullions! 2H6 1.03. 40
CULPABLE 1 FR 0.0001 REL FR 1 V 0 P
esteem | he be approv'd in practice culpable. 2H6 3.02. 22
CULVERIN 1 FR 0.0001 REL FR 1 V 0 P
parapets, | of basilisks, of cannon, culverin, 1H4 2.03. 53
CUM 3 FR 0.0003 REL FR 2 V 1 P
of her, cum privilegio ad imprimendum solum; SHR 4.04. 93 P
they may, cum privilegio, "/oui" away | the lag H8 1.03. 34
long tool, | cum multis aliis that make a dance. TNK 3.05.133
CUMBER 2 FR 0.0002 REL FR 1 V 1 P
let it not cumber your better remembrance. TIM 3.06. 46 P
strife | shall cumber all the parts of italy; JC 3.01.264
CUMBERLAND 4 FR 0.0004 REL FR 4 V 0 P
clifford of cumberland, 'tis warwick calls! 2H6 5.02. 1
proud northern lord, clifford of cumberland, 5.02. 6
we name hereafter | the prince of cumberland; MAC 1.04. 39
the prince of cumberland! 1.04. 48
CUNGER 2 FR 0.0002 REL FR 0 V 2 P
hang yourself, you muddy cunger, hang yourself! 2H4 2.04. 53 P
at quoits well, and eats cunger and fennel, and 2.04.245 P
/CUNNING 2 FR 0.0002 REL FR 2 V 0 P
her /inf'nite /cunning, with her modern grace, AWW 5.03.216
/cunning in dumbness, from my weakness draws TRO 3.02.132
CUNNING 78 FR 0.0088 REL FR 64 V 14 P
hence, bashful cunning, | and prompt me, plain TMP 3.01. 81
that by his cunning hath | cheated me of the 3.02. 43
with all the cunning manner of our flight, TGV 2.04.180
that you shall say my cunning drift excels. 4.02. 83
o cunning enemy, that, to catch a saint, | with MM 2.02.179
o, 'tis the cunning livery of hell, | the 3.01. 94
in the boldness of my cunning, i will lay myself 4.02.156 P
be cunning in the working this, and thy fee is a ADO 2.02. 52 P
accusation, and my cunning shall not shame me. 2.02. 55 P
of truth | can cunning sin cover itself withal! 4.01. 36
constable is too cunning to be understood. 5.01.228 P
a bargain well is as cunning as fast and loose: LLL 3.01.103
with cunning hast thou filch'd my daughter's MND 1.01. 36
you do advance your cunning more and more; 3.02.128
the seeming truth which cunning times put on MV 3.02.100
hand, | wherein your cunning can assist me much. SHR in.1. 92
for to cunning men | i will be very kind, and 1.01. 97
to get her cunning schoolmasters to instruct her 1.01.187
of mine, | cunning in music and the mathematics, 2.01. 56
long studying at rheims, as cunning in greek, 2.01. 81 P
shall get a sire, if i fail not of my cunning. 2.01.411
nature's own sweet and cunning hand laid on. TN 1.05.240
the cunning of her passion | invites me in this 2.02. 22
to force that on you in a shameful cunning 3.01.116
he had been valiant, and so cunning in fence, 3.04.284 P
where being apprehended, his false cunning 5.01. 86
my love was crafty love, | and call it cunning. JN 4.01. 54
trust not those cunning waters of his eyes, 4.03.107
a harp, | or like a cunning instrument cas'd up, R2 1.03.163
what cunning match have you made with this jest 1H4 2.04. 90 P
wherein cunning, but in craft? 2.04.457 P
and whatsoever cunning fiend it was | that H5 2.02.111
nor i have no cunning in protestation; 5.02.144 P
is this thy cunning, thou deceitful dame? 1H6 2.01. 50
and of thy cunning had no diffidence; 3.03. 10
with margery jordan, the cunning witch, | with 2H6 1.02. 75
and would ye not think /his cunning to be great, 2.01.130
a cunning man did calculate my birth | and told 4.01. 34
so cunning and so young is wonderful. R3 3.01.135
this cunning cardinal | the articles o' th' H8 1.01.168
woman, much too weak | t' oppose your cunning. 2.04.107
i am too courtly and thou too cunning. TRO 3.01. 28 P
whilst some with cunning gild their copper 4.04.105
as if that /luck, in very spite of cunning, 5.05. 41
being gentle wounded, craves | a noble cunning. COR 4.01. 9
i'll find some cunning practice out of hand, TIT 5.02. 77
sirrah, go hire me twenty cunning cooks. ROM 4.02. 2

woods | by putting on the cunning of a carper. TIM 4.03.209
shame, that they wanted cunning in excess, 5.04. 28
set down with as much modesty as cunning. HAM 2.02.440 P
a play | have by the very cunning of the scene 2.02.590
bodiless creation ecstasy | is very cunning in. 3.04.139
of deaths put on by cunning and /forc'd cause, 5.02.383
time shall unfold what plighted cunning hides, LR 1.01.280
there's the cunning of it. 1.02. 60 P
in cunning i must draw my sword upon you. 2.01. 29
the face of it is cover'd | with mutual cunning) 3.01. 21
cunning. 3.07. 49
to find out practices of cunning hell | why this OTH 1.03.102
that errs in ignorance and not in cunning, | i 3.03. 49
i will be found most cunning in my patience; 4.01. 90
i took you for that cunning whore of venice 4.02. 89
if there be any cunning cruelty | that can 5.02.333
she is cunning past man's thought. ANT 1.02.145
this cannot be cunning in her; 1.02.150 P
and in our sports my better cunning faints 2.03. 35
try thy cunning, thidias, | make thine own edict 3.12. 31
a cunning thief, or a (that way) accomplish'd CYM 1.04. 92 P
this her bracelet | (o cunning, how i got/'t!), 5.05.205
virtue and cunning were endowments greater PER 3.02. 27
long, | and with a finger of so deep a cunning, TNK 1.03. 43
i know your cunning, and i know your cause. 3.06.120
her, | which cunning love did wittily prevent: VEN 471
to make the cunning hounds mistake their smell, 686
how | to cloak offenses with a cunning brow. LUC 749
yet eyes this cunning want to grace their art, SON 24.13
need'st thou wound with cunning when thy might 139. 7
o cunning love, with tears thou keep'st me blind 148.13
CUNNINGLY 6 FR 0.0006 REL FR 6 V 0 P
do it so cunningly | that my discovery be not TGV 3.01. 44
out, | though ne'er so cunningly you smother it. 1H6 4.01.110
devil | that tempts most cunningly, but be not TRO 4.04. 91
which, cunningly effected, will beget | a very TIT 2.03. 6
why then would you deal so cunningly, | so TNK 2.02.189
persuasively and cunningly. 3.05. 92
CUNNINGS 1 FR 0.0001 REL FR 1 V 0 P
we'll make a solemn wager on your cunnings — HAM 4.07.155
CUNNING'ST 1 FR 0.0001 REL FR 1 V 0 P
thou cunning'st pattern of excelling nature, | i OTH 5.02. 11
CUORE *(see core*)*
CUP 49 FR 0.0055 REL FR 27 V 22 P
her so much as sip on a cup with the proudest of WIV 2.02. 75 P
i think you all have drunk of circe's cup. ERR 5.01.271
therefore welcome the sour cup of prosperity! LLL 1.01.313 P
being pour'd out of a cup into a glass, by AYL 5.01. 42 P
please your /lordship drink a cup of sack? SHR in.2. 2
o knight, thou lack'st a cup of canary. TN 1.03. 80 P
how i am gall'd — mightst bespice a cup, | to WT 1.02.316
there may be in the cup | a spider steep'd, and 2.01. 39
for a cup of madeira and a cold capon's leg? 1H4 1.02.116 P
to filthy tunes, let a cup of sack be my poison. 2.02. 46 P
give me a cup of sack, boy. 2.04.115 P
give me a cup of sack, rogue. 2.04.118 P
coward is worse than a cup of sack with lime in 2.04.126 P
give me a cup of sack. 2.04.152 P
thou stolest a cup of sack eighteen years ago, 2.04.314 P
give me a cup of sack to make my eyes look red, 2.04.384 P
pistol, i charge you with a cup of sack, do you 2H4 2.04.112 P
mocks | and changes fill the cup of alteration 3.01. 52
a cup of wine, sir? 5.03. 45 P
"a cup of wine that's brisk and fine, | and 5.03. 46
"fill the cup, and let it come, | i'll pledge 5.03. 53
'twould drink the cup and all. H5 1.01. 20
horner, i drink to you in a cup of sack; 2H6 2.03. 60 P
and here, neighbor, here's a cup of charneco. 2.03. 62 P
how often hast thou waited at my cup, | fed from 4.01. 56
his viands sparkling in a golden cup, | his body 3H6 2.05. 52
where art thou, keeper? give me a cup of wine. R3 1.04.161
and one that loves a cup of hot wine with not a COR 2.01. 48 P
montagues, i pray, come and crush a cup of wine. ROM 1.02. 80 P
of the second cup draws him on the drawer, when 3.01. 8 P
a cup clos'd in my true love's hand? 5.03.161
fill, lucius, till the wine o'erswell the cup; JC 4.03.161
and in the cup an /union shall he throw, HAM 5.02.272
give him the cup. 5.02.283
it is the pois'ned cup, it is too late. 5.02.292
as th' art a man, | give me the cup. 5.02.343
and all foes | the cup of their deservings. LR 5.03.305
they are our friends — but one cup, i'll drink OTH 2.03. 37 P
i have drunk but one cup to-night — and that 2.03. 39 P
if i can fasten but one cup upon him, | with 2.03. 48
every inordinate cup is unbless'd, and the 2.03.307 P
where's this cup i call'd for? ANT 2.07. 54
no, pompey, i have kept me from the cup. 2.07. 66
fill till the cup be hid. 2.07. 87
cup us till the world go round, | cup us till 2.07.117
go round, | cup us till the world go round! 2.07.118
let those cities that of plenty's cup | and her PER 1.04. 52
here, with a cup that's /stor'd unto the brim — 2.03. 50
and to his palate doth prepare the cup. SON 114.12
CUPBEARER 2 FR 0.0002 REL FR 2 V 0 P
his cupbearer — whom i from meaner form | have WT 1.02.313
i am his cupbearer: 1.02.345
CUPBOARDING 1 FR 0.0001 REL FR 1 V 0 P
still cupboarding the viand, never bearing COR 1.01.100
CUPID 34 FR 0.0038 REL FR 19 V 15 P
why, now is cupid a child of conscience, he WIV 5.05. 28 P
in messina, and challeng'd cupid at the flight, ADO 1.01. 40 P
reading the challenge, subscrib'd for cupid, and 1.01. 41 P
jack, to tell us cupid is a good hare-finder and 1.01.184 P
of a brothel-house for the sign of blind cupid. 1.01.254 P
if cupid have not spent all his quiver in venice 1.01.271 P
if we can do this, cupid is no longer an archer; 2.01.385 P
some cupid kills with arrows, some with traps. 3.01.106
methinks i should outswear cupid. LLL 1.02. 64 P
this senior/-junior, giant-dwarf, dan cupid, 3.01.180
a plague | that cupid will impose for my neglect 3.01.202
proceed, sweet cupid, thou hast thump'd him with 4.03. 23 P
saint cupid, then! and, soldiers, to the field! 4.03.363
saint denis to saint cupid! 5.02. 87
and therefore is wing'd cupid painted blind. MND 1.01.235
the cold moon and the earth, | cupid all arm'd. 2.01.157
yet mark'd i where the bolt of cupid fell. 2.01.165
cupid is a knavish lad, | thus to make poor 3.02.440
cupid himself would blush | to see me thus MV 2.06. 38
cupid have mercy, not a word? AYL 1.03. 1 P
be said of him that cupid hath clapp'd him o' 4.01. 48 P
christendoms | that blinking cupid gossips. AWW 1.01.175
o cupid, cupid, cupid! TRO 3.01.111 P
o cupid, cupid, cupid! 3.01.111 P
o cupid, cupid, cupid! 3.01.111 P
and cupid grant all tongue-tied maidens here 3.02.210
and the weak wanton cupid | shall from your neck 3.03.222
we'll have no cupid hoodwink'd with a scarf, ROM 1.04. 4
young abraham cupid, he that shot so /trim, 2.01. 13
and therefore hath the wind-swift cupid wings. 2.05. 8
no, do thy worst, blind cupid, i'll not love. LR 4.06.137 P
of feather'd cupid seel with wanton dullness OTH 1.03.269
cupid laid by his brand and fell asleep: SON 153. 1
for my help lies | where cupid got new fire — 153.14
CUPID'S 20 FR 0.0022 REL FR 16 V 4 P
this punk is one of cupid's carriers. WIV 2.02.135
matter | is little cupid's crafty arrow made, ADO 3.01. 22
he hath twice or thrice cut cupid's bow-string, 3.02. 10 P
cupid's butt-shaft is too hard for hercules' LLL 1.02.175 P
he is cupid's grandfather, and learns news of 2.01.255
o, rhymes are guards on wanton cupid's hose: 4.03. 56
all, | that he was fain to seal on cupid's name. 5.02. 9
i swear to thee, by cupid's strongest bow, | by MND 1.01.169
but i might see young cupid's fiery shaft 2.01.161
of this purple dye, | hit with cupid's archery, 3.02.103
dian's bud o'er cupid's flower | hath such force 4.01. 73
see | quick cupid's post that comes so mannerly. MV 2.09.100
the brains of my cupid's knock'd out, and i AWW 3.02. 15 P
from cupid's shoulder pluck his painted wings, TRO 3.02. 14
in all cupid's pageant there is presented no 3.02. 75 P
she'll not be hit | with cupid's arrow, she hath ROM 1.01.209
you are a lover, borrow cupid's wings, | and 1.04. 17
in prison, yet | you clasp young cupid's tables. CYM 3.02. 39
here they stand martyrs, slain in cupid's wars; PER 1.01. 38
the which, by cupid's bow she doth protest, | he VEN 581
CUPIDS 3 FR 0.0003 REL FR 3 V 0 P
stood pretty dimpled boys, like smiling cupids, ANT 2.02.202
them) were two winking cupids | of silver, each CYM 2.04. 89
loaden with kisses, arm'd with thousand cupids, TNK 2.02. 31
CUPPELE 1 FR 0.0001 REL FR 1 V 0 P
owy, cuppele gorge, permafoy, | peasant, unless H5 4.04. 37
CUPS 8 FR 0.0009 REL FR 6 V 2 P
there, take it to you, trenchers, cups, and all. SHR 4.01.165
unless hours were cups of sack, and minutes 1H4 1.02. 7 P
be in their flowing cups freshly rememb'red. H5 4.03. 55
friend clytus, being in his ales and his cups; 4.07. 46 P
give me the cups, | and let the kettle to the HAM 5.02.274
have i to-night fluster'd with flowing cups, OTH 2.03. 58
scant not my cups, and make as much of me | as ANT 4.02. 21
'tis strange he hides him in fresh cups, soft CYM 5.03. 71
CUR 32 FR 0.0036 REL FR 14 V 18 P
hang, cur! TMP 1.01. 43 P
did not this cruel-hearted cur shed one tear. TGV 2.03. 9 P
a man's servant shall play the cur with him, 4.04. 1 P
a foul thing when a cur cannot keep himself in 4.04. 10 P
"what cur is that?" 4.04. 21 P
she says your dog was a cur, and tells you 4.04. 48 P
a cur, sir. WIV 1.01. 95 P
out, cur! MND 3.02. 65
and foot me as you spurn a stranger cur | over MV 1.03.118
a cur can lend three thousand ducats?" 1.03.122
it is the most impenetrable cur | that ever kept 3.03. 18
(brach merriman, the poor cur, is emboss'd), SHR in.1. 17
the cur is excellent at faults. TN 2.05.127 P
thou prick-ear'd cur of iceland! H5 2.01. 42
yield, cur! 4.04. 1 P
brass, cur! 4.04. 18
oft have i seen a hot o'erweening cur | run back 2H6 5.01.151
what valor were it, when a cur doth grin, | for 3H6 1.04. 56
how do i thank thee that this carnal cur | preys R3 4.04. 56
this butcher's cur is venom'd-mouth'd, and i H8 1.01.120
you whoreson cur! TRO 2.01. 41 P
you cur! 2.01. 52 P
o thou damn'd cur! i shall — 2.01. 85 P
butt, you whoreson indistinguishable cur, no. 5.01. 29 P
set me up, in policy, that mongril cur, ajax, 5.04. 13 P
and now is the cur ajax prouder than the cur 5.04. 14 P
is the cur ajax prouder than the cur achilles, 5.04. 15 P
my grave lords, | must give this cur the lie; COR 5.06.106
him, | i spurn thee like a cur out of my way. JC 3.01. 46
whilst damned casca, like a cur, behind | strook 5.01. 43
you whoreson dog, you slave, you cur! LR 1.04. 81 P
and the creature run from the cur? 4.06.157 P
CURAN 1 FR 0.0001 REL FR 0 V 1 P
'save thee, curan. LR 2.01. 1 P
CURATE 4 FR 0.0004 REL FR 0 V 4 P
that the curate and your sweet self are good at LLL 5.01.113 P
the parish curate, alexander; 5.02.535 P
make him believe thou art sir topas the curate, TN 4.02. 2 P
sir topas the curate, who comes to visit 4.02. 21 P
CURB 14 FR 0.0015 REL FR 12 V 2 P
wrong, | and curb this cruel devil of his will. MV 4.01.217
bow, sir, the horse his curb, and the falcon her AYL 3.03. 80 P
and thus i'll curb her mad and headstrong humor. SHR 4.01.209
as it is with the rusty curb of old father antic 1H4 1.02. 61 P
for when his headstrong riot hath no curb, 2H4 4.04. 62
nation | to curb those raging appetites that are TRO 2.02.181
by plot, | to curb the will of the nobility. COR 3.01. 39
the laws, your curb and whip, in their rough TIM 4.03.443
yea, curb and woo for leave to do him good. HAM 3.04.155
licentious ear, | but curb it, spite of seeing. PER 5.03. 31
when neither curb would crack, girth break, nor TNK 5.04. 74
what cares he now for curb or pricking spur, VEN 285
no exclamation | can curb his heat, or rein his LUC 706
blood | that we must curb it upon others' proof, LC 163
CURB'D 3 FR 0.0003 REL FR 2 V 1 P
of a living daughter curb'd by the will of a MV 1.02. 25 P
for the fift harry from curb'd license plucks 2H4 4.05.130
yet you are curb'd from that enlargement by CYM 2.03.120
CURBED 1 FR 0.0001 REL FR 1 V 0 P
which they distill now in the curbed time, | to AWW 2.04. 45
CURBING 1 FR 0.0001 REL FR 1 V 0 P
arm 'gainst arm, | curbing his lavish spirit; MAC 1.02. 57
CURBS 4 FR 0.0004 REL FR 4 V 0 P
(the needful bits and curbs to headstrong weeds) MM 1.03. 20
the fair reverence of your highness curbs me R2 1.01. 54
and curbs himself even of his natural scope 1H4 3.01.169
cracking ten thousand curbs | of more strong COR 1.01. 70
CUR'D 12 FR 0.0013 REL FR 8 V 4 P
will cost him a thousand pound ere 'a be cur'd. ADO 1.01. 90 P
why they are not so punish'd and cur'd is, that AYL 3.02.403 P
and thus i cur'd him, and this way will i take 3.02.421 P
i would not be cur'd, youth. 3.02.425 P
will you be cur'd | of your infirmity? AWW 2.01. 68
my lord, be cur'd | of this diseas'd opinion, WT 1.02.296
this meeting here | cannot be cur'd by words; 3H6 2.02.122
the king has cur'd me, | i humbly thank his H8 3.02.380
that gentle physic given in time had cur'd me; 4.02.122
for with a wound i must be cur'd. ANT 4.14. 78
groan so in perpetuity than be cur'd | by th' CYM 5.04. 6
sick between 's, | by bleeding must be cur'd. TNK 3.01.114
CURD 2 FR 0.0002 REL FR 2 V 0 P
does it curd thy blood | to say i am thy mother? AWW 1.03.149
with a sudden vigor it doth /posset | and curd, HAM 1.05. 69
CURDIED 1 FR 0.0001 REL FR 1 V 0 P
that's curdied by the frost from purest snow COR 5.03. 66
CURDS 3 FR 0.0003 REL FR 3 V 0 P
sooth, she is | the queen of curds and cream. WT 4.04.161
and to conclude, the shepherd's homely curds, 3H6 2.05. 47
and feed on curds and whey, and suck the goat, TIT 4.02.178
CURDY *(see crudy)*
/CURE 3 FR 0.0003 REL FR 3 V 0 P
weep with me, past hope, past /cure, past help! ROM 4.01. 45
confusion's /cure lives not | in these 4.05. 65
/will /not /allow, | /stand /in /hard /cure. LR 3.06.100
CURE 63 FR 0.0071 REL FR 56 V 7 P
your tale, sir, would cure deafness. TMP 1.02.106
to an unsettled fancy, cure thy brains, | now 5.01. 59
loss, and patience | says, it is past her cure. 5.01.141
such a one were past cure of the thing you wot MM 2.01.111 P
and the cure of it not only saves your brother, 3.01.236 P
too general a vice, and severity must cure it. 3.02.100 P
that the dissolution of it must cure it. 3.02.223 P
to strange sores strangely they strain the cure. ADO 4.01.252
great reason: for past care is still past cure. LLL 5.02. 28
did you ever cure any so? AYL 3.02.406 P
i would cure you, if you would but call me 3.02.426 P
ray'd with the yellows, past cure of the fives, SHR 3.02. 53 P
to cure the desperate languishings whereof | the AWW 1.03.229
the well-lost life of mine on his grace's cure 1.03.248
maiden, | but may not be so credulous of cure, 2.01.115
my art is not past power, nor you past cure. 2.01.158
within what space | hop'st thou my cure? 2.01.160
made | will give her sadness very little cure. JN 2.01.546
my widow-comfort, and my sorrows' cure! 3.04.105
indeed we fear'd his sickness was past cure. 4.02. 86
the which no balm can cure but his heart-blood R2 1.01.172
commit'st thy anointed body to the cure | of 2.01. 98
and bid thy ceremony give thee cure! H5 4.01.252
care is no cure, but rather corrosive, | for 1H6 3.03. 3
is able with the change to kill and cure. 2H6 5.01.101
there is my purse to cure that blow of thine. R3 4.04.514
for my little cure, | let me alone. H8 1.04. 33
conscience, | thou art a cure fit for a king. 2.02. 75
therefore in him | it lies to cure me, and the 2.04.101
and the cure is to | remove these thoughts from 2.04.101
we are to cure such sorrows, not to sow 'em. 3.01.158
is there no way to cure this? 3.02.216
leave us to cure this cause. COR 3.01.234
to cure it, easy. 3.01.295
grow, | we would as willingly give cure as know. ROM 1.01.155
must i take th' cure upon me? TIM 3.03. 12
morning taste | to cure thy o'ernight's surfeit? 4.03.227
a crew of wretched souls | that stay his cure. MAC 4.03.142
our great revenge | to cure this deadly grief. 4.03.215
cure /her of that. 5.03. 39
in my blood he rages, | and thou must cure me. HAM 4.03. 67
thus with his despair | is done to cure it. LR 4.06. 34
cure this great breach in his abused nature, 4.07. 14
(not surfeited to death) | stand in bold cure. OTH 2.01. 51
jealousy so strong | that judgment cannot cure. 2.01.302
and would do much | to cure him of this evil. 2.03.144
the cure whereof, my lord, | 'tis time must do. CYM 3.05. 37
cure their surfeit | that craves a present TNK 1.01.190
she's lost | past all cure. 4.01.140
with his crutch, and cure him | before apollo; 5.01. 82
far better, | for there the cure lies mainly. 5.02. 8
yes, in the way of cure. 5.02. 19
cure her first this way; 5.02. 22
nothing but my body's bane would cure thee." VEN 372
"long may they kiss each other for this cure! 505
the scar that will despite of cure remain, LUC 732
gain | but torment that it cannot cure his pain. 861
"why, collatine, is woe the cure for woe? 1821
ye | even that your pity is enough to cure me. SON 111.14
past cure i am, now reason is past care, | and 147. 9
against strange maladies a sovereign cure. 153. 8
but found no cure: 153.13
came there for cure, and this by that i prove: 154.13
CURED 3 FR 0.0003 REL FR 3 V 0 P
and true obedience, of this madness cured, 2H4 4.02. 41
it easeth some, though none it ever cured, | to LUC 1581
which, rank of goodness, would by ill be cured. SON 118.12
CURELESS 3 FR 0.0003 REL FR 3 V 0 P
good youth, or it will fall | to cureless ruin. MV 4.01.142
are plaints, and cureless are my wounds; 3H6 2.06. 23
since thou art guilty of my cureless crime, LUC 772
CURER 3 FR 0.0003 REL FR 0 V 3 P
he is a curer of souls, and you a curer of WIV 2.03. 39 P
is a curer of souls, and you a curer of bodies. 2.03. 39 P
little blood they do, i'll be a curer of madmen. TRO 5.01. 50 P
CURES 11 FR 0.0012 REL FR 10 V 1 P
thy grace being gain'd cures all disgrace in me. LLL 4.03. 65
and with his varying childness cures in me WT 1.02.170
and falsehood falsehood cures, as fire cools JN 3.01.277
to fear the worst oft cures the worse. TRO 3.02. 73 P
one desperate grief cures with another's ROM 1.02. 48
eye, | the mere despair of surgery, he cures, MAC 4.03.152
that cures us both. CYM 2.03.104
that nature works, and of her cures; PER 3.02. 38
it cures her ipso facto | the melancholy humor TNK 5.02. 37
thy grace being gain'd cures all disgrace in me. PP 3. 8
heals the wound, and cures not the disgrace; SON 34. 8
CURFEW 3 FR 0.0003 REL FR 2 V 1 P

that rejoice | to hear the solemn curfew: TMP 5.01. 40
none since the curfew rung. MM 4.02. 75
he begins at curfew, and walks /till /the first LR 3.04.116 P
CURFEW–BELL 1 FR 0.0001 REL FR 1 V 0 P
the curfew–bell hath rung, 'tis three a' clock. ROM 4.04. 4
CURING 2 FR 0.0002 REL FR 1 V 1 P
yet i profess curing it by counsel. AYL 3.02.404 P
before the curing of a strong disease, | even in JN 3.04.112
CURIO 1 FR 0.0001 REL FR 1 V 0 P
what, curio? TN 1.01. 16
CURIOSITY 4 FR 0.0004 REL FR 1 V 3 P
they mock'd thee for too much curiosity; TIM 4.03.303 P
that curiosity in neither can make choice of LR 1.01. 6 P
permit | the curiosity of nations to deprive me, 1.02. 4
as mine own jealous curiosity than as a very 1.04. 70 P
CURIOUS 16 FR 0.0018 REL FR 14 V 2 P
for curious i cannot be with you, | signior SHR 4.04. 36
frank nature, rather curious than in haste, AWW 1.02. 20
i am so fraught with curious business that | i WT 4.04.514
golden cup, | his body couched in a curious bed, 3H6 2.05. 53
what too curious dreg espies my sweet lady in TRO 3.02. 65 P
care i | what curious eye doth cote deformities? ROM 1.04. 31
ride, run, mar a curious tale in telling it, and LR 1.04. 33 P
though you be therein curious, the least cause ANT 3.02. 35
and i am something curious, being strange, | to CYM 1.06.191
was lapp'd | in a most curious mantle, wrought 5.05.361
where is read | nothing but curious pleasures, PER 1.01. 16
thought nought too curious, are ready now | to 1.04. 43
his thigh a sword | hung by a curious baldrick, TNK 4.02. 86
to cross the curious workmanship of nature, | to VEN 734
if my slight muse do please these curious days, SON 38.13
enswath'd, and seal'd to curious secrecy. LC 49
CURIOUS–GOOD 1 FR 0.0001 REL FR 1 V 0 P
this is too curious–good, this blunt and ill: LUC 1300
CURIOUS–KNOTTED 1 FR 0.0001 REL FR 0 V 1 P
the west corner of thy curious–knotted garden. LLL 1.01.246 P
CURIOUSLY 4 FR 0.0004 REL FR 0 V 4 P
the which if i do not carve most curiously, say ADO 5.01.156 P
"the sleeves curiously cut." SHR 4.03.143 P
wherein so curiously he had set this counterfeit AWW 4.03. 34 P
'twere to consider too curiously, to consider so HAM 5.01.205 P
/CURL 1 FR 0.0001 REL FR 0 V 1 P
for thou seest it will not /curl /by nature. TN 1.03. 99 P
CURL'D 4 FR 0.0004 REL FR 2 V 2 P
into the fire, to ride | on the curl'd clouds. TMP 1.02.192
will turn white, a curl'd pate will grow bald, a H5 5.02.160 P
that curl'd my hair; LR 3.04. 86 P
hard–hair'd, and curl'd, thick twin'd like TNK 4.02.104
CURL'D–PATE 1 FR 0.0001 REL FR 1 V 0 P
make curl'd–pate ruffians bald, | and let the TIM 4.03.160
CURLED 4 FR 0.0004 REL FR 4 V 0 P
or swell the curled waters 'bove the main, LR 3.01. 6
the wealthy curled /darlings of our nation, OTH 1.02. 68
if she first meet the curled antony, | he'll ANT 5.02.301
"let him have time to tear his curled hair, LUC 981
CURLING 2 FR 0.0002 REL FR 2 V 0 P
curling their monstrous heads and hanging them 2H4 3.01. 23
of corn, | curling the wealthy ears, never flew. TNK 2.03. 78
CURLS 4 FR 0.0004 REL FR 4 V 0 P
his arched brows, his hawking eye, his curls, AWW 1.01. 94
hyperion's curls, the front of jove himself, HAM 3.04. 56
and sable curls /all silver'd o'er with white; SON 12. 4
"his browny locks did hang in crooked curls, LC 85
CURRANCE 1 FR 0.0001 REL FR 1 V 0 P
in a flood | with such a heady currance, H5 1.01. 34
CURRANT 1 FR 0.0001 REL FR 1 V 0 P
haste, | i stamp this kiss upon thy currant lip. TNK 1.01.216
CURRANTS 1 FR 0.0001 REL FR 0 V 1 P
three pound of sugar, five pound of currants, WT 4.03. 38 P
CURRENT 27 FR 0.0030 REL FR 24 V 3 P
the current that with gentle murmur glides, TGV 2.07. 25
(like an impediment in the current) made it more MM 3.01.242 P
man, | to excuse the current of thy cruelty. MV 4.01. 64
say, shall the current of our right roam on? JN 2.01.335
thy word is current with him for my death, | but R2 1.03.231
hath held his current and defil'd himself! 5.03. 63
speak "pardon" as 'tis current in our land, 5.03.123
not his report | come current for an accusation 1H4 1.03. 68
spirit | as to o'erwalk a current roaring loud 1.03.192
it holds current that i told you yesternight: 2.01. 54 P
and crack'd crowns, | and pass them current too. 2.03. 94
i'll have the current in this place damm'd up, 3.01.100
should go so general current through the world. 4.01. 5
money, and the other with current repentance. 2H4 2.01.121 P
make | no excuse current but to hang thyself. R3 1.02. 84
your fire–new stamp of honor is scarce current. 1.03.255
did, | and yet go current from suspicion! 2.01. 95
touch, | to try if thou be current gold indeed. 4.02. 9
and, by'r lady, | held current music too. H8 1.03. 47
to say he'll turn your current in a ditch, | and COR 3.01. 96
provokes itself and like the current flies TIM 1.01. 24
and we must take the current when it serves, JC 4.03.223
whose icy current and compulsive course | nev'r OTH 3.03.454
the fountain from the which my current runs | or 4.02. 59
i' th' aid o' th' current were almost to sink, TNK 1.02. 8
thus ebbs and flows the current of her sorrow, LUC 1569
with brinish current downward flow'd apace: LC 284
CURRENTS 6 FR 0.0006 REL FR 6 V 0 P
o, two such silver currents when they join | do JN 2.01.441
currents that spring from one most gracious head R2 3.03.108
slain, | and all the currents of a heady fight; 1H4 2.03. 55
all springs reduce their currents to mine eyes, R3 2.02. 68
with this regard their currents turn awry, | and HAM 3.01. 86
in the corrupted currents of this world 3.03. 57
CURRISH 5 FR 0.0005 REL FR 4 V 1 P
and tells you currish thanks is good enough for TGV 4.04. 49 P
thy currish spirit | govern'd a wolf, who, MV 4.01.133
entreat some power to change this currish jew. 4.01.292
a good swift simile, but something currish. SHR 5.02. 54
his currish riddles sorts not with this place. 3H6 5.05. 26
CURRY 1 FR 0.0001 REL FR 0 V 1 P
i would curry with master shallow that no man 2H4 5.01. 73 P
CURS 14 FR 0.0015 REL FR 11 V 3 P
are too precious to be cast away upon curs, AYL 1.03. 5 P
us, | except like curs to tear us all to pieces. R2 2.02.139
shall dunghill curs confront the helicons? 2H4 5.03.104
foolish curs, that run winking into the mouth of H5 3.07.143 P
maz'd with a yelping kennel of french curs! 1H6 4.02. 47
small curs are not regarded when they grin, 2H6 3.01. 18
they may astonish these fell–lurking curs. 5.01.146
why they are so, but, like to village curs, H8 2.04.160
two curs shall tame each other; TRO 1.03.389
what would you have, you curs, | that like nor COR 1.01.168
you common cry of curs, whose breath i hate | as 3.03.120
two of thy whelps, fell curs of bloody kind, TIT 2.03.281
hounds and greyhounds, mungrels, spaniels, curs, MAC 3.01. 92
avaunt, you curs! LR 3.06. 65 P
/CURS'D 1 FR 0.0001 REL FR 1 V 0 P
/are /curs'd | /by /those /that /feel /their LR 5.03. 56
CURS'D 15 FR 0.0017 REL FR 13 V 2 P
curs'd be i that did so! TMP 1.02.339
merciful, | i have curs'd them without cause. 5.01.179
curs'd be thy stones for thus deceiving me! MND 5.01.181
thou shalt stand curs'd and excommunicate, | and JN 3.01.173
more, | if thou stand excommunicate and curs'd? 3.01.223
what did i then, but curs'd the gentle gusts, 2H6 3.02. 88
for had i curs'd now, i had curs'd myself. R3 1.03.318
for had i curs'd now, i had curs'd myself. 1.03.318
then curs'd she richard, then curs'd she 3.03. 18
curs'd she richard, then curs'd she buckingham, 3.03. 18
she buckingham, | then curs'd she hastings. 3.03. 19
ache in my bones that, unless a man were curs'd, TRO 5.03.106 P
curs'd be that heart that forc'd us to this TIT 4.01. 72
lady ask'd for, the nurse curs'd in the pantry, ROM 1.03.102 P
and curs'd be he that will not second it. PER 2.04. 20
CURSE 111 FR 0.0125 REL FR 104 V 7 P
and my profit on't | is, i know how to curse. TMP 1.02.364
spirits hear me, | and yet i needs must curse. 2.02. 4
do curse the grace that with such grace hath TGV 3.01.146
i curse myself, for they are sent by me, | that 3.01.148
o, 'tis the curse in love, and still approv'd, 5.04. 43
do curse the gout, sapego, and the rheum | for MM 3.01. 31
heart prays for him, though my tongue do curse. ERR 4.02. 28
for thou, i fear, hast given me cause to curse. MND 3.02. 46
methinks, being sensible, should curse again. 5.01.183 P
the curse never fell upon our nation till now, i MV 3.01. 85 P
but you will curse your wooing. SHR 2.01. 75
it is a curse | he cannot be compell'd to't) WT 2.03. 88
better burn it now | than curse it then. 2.03.157
to curse the fair proceedings of this day. JN 3.01. 97
dreading the curse that money may buy out, | and 3.01.164
that i have room with rome to curse a while! 3.01.180
is no tongue hath power to curse him right. 3.01.183
there's law and warrant, lady, for my curse. 3.01.184
how can the law forbid my tongue to curse? 3.01.190
philip of france, on peril of a curse, | let go 3.01.191
is purchase of a heavy curse from rome, | or the 3.01.205
that's the curse of rome. 3.01.207
let the church, our mother, breathe her curse, 3.01.256
curse, | a mother's curse, on her revolting son. 3.01.257
i will denounce a curse upon his head. 3.01.319
it is the curse of kings to be attended | by 4.02.208
those whom you curse | have felt the worst of R2 3.02.138
i would my skill were subject to thy curse. 3.04.103
shall have cause to curse the dolphin's scorn. H5 1.02.288
shall we curse the planets of mishap | that 1H6 1.01. 23
and make thee curse the harvest of that corn. 3.02. 47
can, | but curse the cause i cannot aid the man. 4.03. 44
i prithee give me leave to curse a while. 5.03. 43
curse, miscreant, when thou com'st to the stake. 5.03. 44
with whom i leave my curse: 5.04. 86
to free us from his father's wrathful curse, | i 2H6 3.02.155
hast thou not spirit to curse thine enemy? 3.02.308
wherefore should i curse them? 3.02.309
ay, every joint should seem to curse and ban; 3.02.319
heart would break, | should i not curse them. 3.02.321
well could i curse away a winter's night, 3.02.335
and seeing ignorance is the curse of god, 4.07. 73
and so god's curse light upon you all! 4.08. 32 P
for yet may england curse my wretched reign. 4.09. 49
damned wretch, the curse of her that bare thee; 4.10. 77
take the crown, and, with the crown, my curse, 3H6 1.04.164
but ere sunset i'll make thee curse the deed. 2.02.116
curse not thyself, fair creature — thou art R3 1.02.132
the curse my noble father laid on thee | when 1.03.173
did york's dread curse prevail so much with 1.03.190
o, let me make the period to my curse! 1.03.237
have you breath'd your curse against yourself. 1.03.239
to help thee curse this poisonous bunch–back'd 1.03.245
false–boding woman, end thy frantic curse, 1.03.246
nor thou within the compass of my curse. 1.03.283
now margaret's curse is fall'n upon our heads, 3.03. 15
now thy heavy curse | is lighted on poor 3.04. 92
and make me die the thrall of margaret's curse, 4.01. 45
lo, ere i can repeat this curse again, | within 4.01. 77
and prov'd the subject of mine own soul's curse, 4.01. 80
that i should wish for thee to help me curse 4.04. 80
and teach me how to curse mine enemies! 4.04.117
revolving this will teach thee how to curse. 4.04.123
therefore take with thee my most grievous curse, 4.04.188
yet much less spirit to curse | abides in me; 4.04.197
thus margaret's curse falls heavy on my neck: 5.01. 25
all your studies | make me a curse like this! H8 3.01.124
that methinks is the curse depending on those TRO 2.03. 19 P
the common curse of mankind, folly and ignorance 2.03. 28 P
you will catch cold and curse me. 4.02. 15
of envy, thou, what means thou to curse thus? 5.01. 26 P
do i curse thee? 5.01. 27 P
like fathers, | when you curse them as enemies. COR 1.01. 78
subdues him, | and curse that justice did it. 1.01.176
a curse begin at very root on 's heart, | that 2.01.185
and did curse | against the volsces for they had 3.01. 9
even now i curse the day — and yet i think TIT 5.01.125
few come within the compass of my curse — 5.01.126
much, | and that we have a curse in having her. ROM 3.05.167
or dost thou not, heaven's curse upon thee! TIM 4.03.132
if thou wilt curse, thy father (that poor rag) 4.03.271
a plague on thee, thou art too bad to curse! 4.03.360
hate all, curse all, show charity to none, | but 4.03.527
pass by and curse thy fill, but pass and stay 5.04. 73
holy chase, | shake off their sterile curse. JC 1.02. 9
a curse shall light upon the limbs of men; 3.01.262
me this, | and an eternal curse fall on you! MAC 4.01.105
and to be baited with the rabble's curse. 5.08. 29
it hath the primal eldest curse upon't, | a HAM 3.03. 37
dow'r'd with our curse, and stranger'd with our LR 1.01.204
th' untented woundings of a father's curse 1.04.300
no, regan, thou shalt never have my curse. 2.04.170
who redeems nature from the general curse 4.06.206
'tis the curse of service; OTH 1.01. 35
o curse of marriage! 3.03.268
let heaven requite it with the serpent's curse! 4.02. 16
yea, curse his better angel from his side, | and 5.02.208
write against them, | detest them, curse them; CYM 2.05. 33
the curse of heaven and men succeed their evils! PER 1.04.104
a curse upon him, die he like a thief, | that 4.06.114
and in their songs curse ever–blinded fortune TNK 2.02. 38
we shall die | (which is the curse of honor) 2.02. 54
if i fall, curse me, and say i was a coward, 3.06.104
if your vow stand, shall curse me and my beauty, 3.06.247
of their sons, | shall never curse my cruelty. 4.02. 6
the destinies will curse thee for this stroke: VEN 945
shall curse my bones, and hold it for no sin LUC 209
to make him curse this cursed crimeful night. 970
teach me to curse him that thou taught'st this 996
cries, | and look upon myself and curse my fate, SON 29. 4
you to your beauteous blessings add a curse, 84.13
CURSED 38 FR 0.0043 REL FR 38 V 0 P
a thousand irreligious cursed hours | which WIV 5.05.229
cursed be my tribe | if i forgive him! MV 1.03. 51
o cursed wretch, | that knew'st this was the WT 4.04.458
thee | to make a second fall of cursed man? R2 3.04. 76
prove | that ever fell upon this cursed earth. 4.01.147
this be damascus, be thou cursed cain, | to slay 1H6 1.03. 39
the middle centure of this cursed town. 2.02. 6
to pine, | was cursed instrument of his decease. 2.05. 58
now cursed be the time | of thy nativity! 5.04. 26
dost thou deny thy father, cursed drab? 5.04. 32
o, cursed be the hand that made these holes! R3 1.02. 14
cursed the heart that had the heart to do it! 1.02. 15
cursed the blood that let this blood from hence! 1.02. 16
by circumstance /t' /accuse thy cursed self. 1.02. 80
fields, | and be adveng'd on cursed tamora. TIT 5.01. 16
a pair of cursed hell–hounds and their dame. 5.02.144
her, as that name's cursed hand | murder'd her ROM 3.03.104
what cursed foot wanders this way to–night, | to 5.03. 19
there's nothing level in our cursed natures TIM 4.03. 19
how cursed athens, mindless of thy worth, 4.03. 94
and as he pluck'd his cursed steel away, | mark JC 3.02.177
restrain in me the cursed thoughts that nature MAC 2.01. 8
behold where stands | th' usurper's cursed head: 5.09. 21
stole, | with juice of cursed hebona in a vial, HAM 1.05. 62
the time is out of joint — o cursed spite, 1.05.188
what if this cursed hand | were thicker than 3.03. 43
woe | fall ten times /treble on that cursed head 5.01.247
"cursed fate that gave thee to the moor!" OTH 3.03.426
o cursed, cursed slave! 5.02.276
o cursed, cursed slave! 5.02.276
art, hath done you both | this cursed injury. CYM 3.04.122
dead, | and cursed dionyza hath | the pregnant PER 4.ch. 43
and her gain | she gives the cursed bawd. 5.ch. 11
when fame | had spread his cursed deed, the 5.03. 96
be as that cursed man that hates his country, TNK 2.02.199
it is a cursed haste you made | if you have done 5.04. 41
to make him curse this cursed crimeful night. LUC 970
loss, | o frowning fortune, cursed, fickle dame! PP 17.10
CURSED–BLESSED 1 FR 0.0001 REL FR 1 V 0 P
to hold their cursed–blessed fortune long. LUC 866
CURSED'ST 1 FR 0.0001 REL FR 1 V 0 P
to make me blest or cursed'st among men. MV 2.01. 46
CURSES 33 FR 0.0037 REL FR 28 V 5 P
so curses all eve's daughters, of what WIV 4.02. 24 P
beats her heart, tears her hair, prays, curses: ADO 2.03.148 P
i give him curses; yet he gives me love. MND 1.01.196
the curses he shall have, the tortures he shall WT 4.04.769 P
cardinal, cry thou amen | to my keen curses; JN 3.01.182
know | the peril of our curses light on thee 3.01.295
it be | that you a world of curses undergo, 1H4 1.03.164
and so both the degrees prevent my curses. 2H4 1.02.232 P
would curses kill, as doth the mandrake's groan, 2H6 3.02.310
and these dread curses, like the sun 'gainst 3.02.330
renders good for bad, blessings for curses. R3 1.02. 69
with curses in her mouth, tears in her eyes, 1.02.232
his curses then, from bitterness of soul 1.03.178
can curses pierce the clouds and enter heaven? 1.03.194
then give way, dull clouds, to my quick curses! 1.03.195
for curses never pass | the lips of those that 1.03.284
my hair doth stand an end to hear her curses. 1.03.303
o thou well skill'd in curses, stay awhile, 4.04.116
their curses now | live where their prayers did; H8 1.02. 62
too many curses on their heads | that were the 2.01.138
his curses and his blessings | touch me alike; 2.02. 52
your voices might | be curses to yourselves? COR 2.03.185
nothing else to do | but to confirm my curses! 4.02. 46
whose repetition will be dogg'd with curses, 5.03.144
some devil whisper curses in my ear, | and TIT 5.03. 11
but all, save thee, | i fell with curses. TIM 4.03.501
if thou hat'st curses, | stay not; 4.03.534
curses, not loud but deep, mouth–honor, breath, MAC 5.03. 27
my curses on her! LR 2.04.146
all curses madded hecuba gave the greeks, | and CYM 4.02.313
and had their epitaphs, the people's curses. TNK 2.02.110
yours | will bear the curses else of after–ages 3.06.187
th' other curses a suing fellow and her 4.03. 55 P
CUR'SIES 3 FR 0.0003 REL FR 2 V 1 P
but manhood is melted into cur'sies, valor into ADO 4.01.319 P
knees, that dream on cur'sies straight; ROM 1.04. 72
the homely villain cur'sies to her low, | and, LUC 1338
CURSING 6 FR 0.0006 REL FR 4 V 2 P
nay, and you be a cursing hypocrite once, you ADO 5.01.208 P
air, | blaspheming god and cursing men on earth. 2H6 3.02.372
fill'd it with cursing cries and deep exclaims. R3 1.02. 52
is arming, weeping, cursing, vowing vengeance. TRO 5.05. 31
beating your officers, cursing yourselves, COR 3.03. 78
boiling, hissing, howling, chatt'ring, cursing! TNK 4.03. 33 P
/CURSITORY 1 FR 0.0001 REL FR 1 V 0 P
i have but with a /cursitory eye | o'erglanc'd H5 5.02. 77
CUR'ST 1 FR 0.0001 REL FR 1 V 0 P
and cur'st the world | o' th' plurisy of people! TNK 5.01. 65
CURST 28 FR 0.0031 REL FR 19 V 9 P
"item, she is curst." TGV 3.01.343 P
in faith, she's too curst. ADO 2.01. 20 P
too curst is more than curst. 2.01. 21 P
too curst is more than curst. 2.01. 21 P

is said, "god sends a curst cow short horns" — 2.01. 23 P
horns" — but to a cow too curst he sends none. 2.01. 23 P
so, by being too curst, god will send you no 2.01. 25 P
do not curst wives hold that self–sovereignty LLL 4.01. 36
i was never curst; MND 3.02.300
you, i, | nor longer stay in your curst company. 3.02.341
here she comes, curst and sad. 3.02.439
her elder sister is so curst and shrewd | that SHR 1.01.180
and as curst and shrowd | as socrates' xantippe, 1.02. 70
is that she is intolerable curst | and shrowd 1.02. 89
till katherine the curst have got a husband. 1.02.128
katherine the curst! 1.02.129
liking, | will undertake to woo curst katherine, 1.02.183
and bonny kate, and sometimes kate the curst; 2.01.186
if she be curst, it is for policy, | for she's 2.01.292
that she shall still be curst in company. 2.01.305
now go thy ways, thou hast tam'd a curst shrow. 5.02.188
write it in a martial hand, be curst and brief. TN 3.02. 42 P
they are never curst but when they are hungry. WT 3.03.130 P
to thick–ey'd musing and curst melancholy? 1H4 2.03. 46
as curst, as harsh, and horrible to hear, 2H6 3.02.312
sweet saint, for charity, be not so curst. R3 1.02. 49
with curst speech | i threaten'd to discover him LR 2.01. 65
finding their enemy to be so curst, | they all VEN 887
CURSTER 1 FR 0.0001 REL FR 1 V 0 P
curster than she? why, 'tis impossible. SHR 3.02.154
CURSTEST 1 FR 0.0001 REL FR 1 V 0 P
a meacock wretch can make the curstest shrew. SHR 2.01.313
CURSTNESS 1 FR 0.0001 REL FR 1 V 0 P
terms, | nor curstness grow to th' matter. ANT 2.02. 25
CUR'SY *(also curtsy, etc.)*
CUR'SY 11 FR 0.0012 REL FR 3 V 8 P
it is my cousin's duty to make cur'sy and say, ADO 2.01. 53 P
or else make another cur'sy and say, "father, as 2.01. 55 P
to any french courtier for a new devis'd cur'sy. LLL 1.02. 63 P
the petty traffickers | that cur'sy to them, do MV 1.01. 13
was wont to lend money for a christian cur'sy, 3.01. 49 P
first my fear, then my cur'sy, last my speech. 2H4 ep 1 P
fear, is your displeasure, my cur'sy, my duty, ep 2 P
o kate, nice customs cur'sy to great kings. H5 5.02.268 P
the match is made, she seals it with a cur'sy. 3H6 3.02. 57
and she whom mighty kingdoms cur'sy to, | like a TIT 5.03. 74
meaning to cur'sy. ROM 2.04. 54 P
CURTAIL'D 1 FR 0.0001 REL FR 1 V 0 P
i, that am curtail'd of this fair proportion, R3 1.01. 18
CURTAIN 14 FR 0.0015 REL FR 11 V 3 P
quick, i pray thee, draw the curtain straight; MV 2.09. 1
come draw the curtain, nerissa. 2.09. 84
wherefore have these gifts a curtain before 'em? TN 1.03.126 P
but we will draw the curtain and show you the 1.05.233 P
do not draw the curtain. WT 5.03. 59
i'll draw the curtain. 5.03. 68
shall i draw the curtain? 5.03. 83
this absence of your father's draws a curtain 1H4 4.01. 73
drew priam's curtain in the dead of night, | and 2H4 1.01. 72
close up his eyes, and draw the curtain close, 2H6 3.03. 32
let 'em alone, and draw the curtain close; H8 5.02. 34
draw this curtain and let's see your picture. TRO 3.02. 47 P
spread thy close curtain, love–performing night, ROM 3.02. 5
even so, the curtain drawn, his eyes begun | to LUC 374
CURTAIN'D 2 FR 0.0002 REL FR 2 V 0 P
and curtain'd with a counsel–keeping cave, | we TIT 2.03. 24
and wicked dreams abuse | the curtain'd sleep; MAC 2.01. 51
CURTAINS 8 FR 0.0009 REL FR 7 V 1 P
the fringed curtains of thine eye advance | and TMP 1.02.409
go, draw aside the curtains and discover | the MV 2.07. 1
draw the curtains, go. 2.07. 78
their ragged curtains poorly are let loose, H5 4.02. 41
to draw | the shady curtains from aurora's bed, ROM 1.01.136
make no noise, make no noise, draw the curtains. LR 3.06. 84 P
soft, by and by, let me the curtains draw. OTH 5.02.104
the curtains being close, about he walks, LUC 367
CURTAL 5 FR 0.0005 REL FR 4 V 1 P
hope is a curtal dog in some affairs. WIV 2.01.110
she had transform'd me to a curtal dog, and made
ERR 3.02.146
i'd give bay curtal and his furniture, | my AWW 2.03. 59
is not for any standers–by to curtal his oaths. CYM 2.01. 11 P
my curtal dog, that wont to have play'd, | plays PP 17.19
CURTAL–AXE *(see curtle–axe)*
CURTIS 6 FR 0.0006 REL FR 0 V 6 P
holla, ho, curtis! SHR 4.01. 12 P
a fire, good curtis. 4.01. 17 P
o, ay, curtis, ay, and therefore fire, fire; 4.01. 19 P
she was, good curtis, before this frost; 4.01. 22 P
and my new mistress and myself, fellow curtis. 4.01. 25 P
a cold world, curtis, in every office but thine, 4.01. 35 P
CURTLE–AXE 2 FR 0.0002 REL FR 2 V 0 P
a gallant curtle–axe upon my thigh, | a AYL 1.03.117
veins | to give each naked curtle–axe a stain, H5 4.02. 21
CURTSIED 1 FR 0.0001 REL FR 1 V 0 P
curtsied when you have, and kiss'd, | the wild TMP 1.02.377
CURTSIES 4 FR 0.0004 REL FR 2 V 2 P
let thy curtsies alone, they are scurvy ones. AWW 5.03.323 P
curtsies there to me — TN 2.05. 61 P
honest fools lay out their wealth on curtsies. TIM 1.02.235
low–crooked curtsies, and base spaniel fawning. JC 3.01. 43
CURTSY *(also cur'sy, etc.)*
CURTSY 11 FR 0.0012 REL FR 7 V 4 P
bidding the law make curtsy to their will, MM 2.04.175
curtsy, sweet hearts — and so the measure ends. LLL 5.02.221
pray you, leave your curtsy, good mounsieur. MND 4.01. 20 P
for my kind offer, when i make curtsy, bid me AYL ep 23 P
let them curtsy with their left legs and not SHR 4.01. 92 P
to dog his heels and curtsy at his frowns, | to 1H4 3.02.127
if a man will make curtsy and say nothing, he is 2H4 2.01.124 P
what is that curtsy worth? COR 5.03. 27
what's worse, | must curtsy at the censure. CYM 3.03. 55
make curtsy, here your love comes. TNK 5.02. 69
there's a curtsy! 5.02. 70
CURVET 1 FR 0.0001 REL FR 1 V 0 P
which should sustain the bound and high curvet AWW 2.03.282
CURVETS 2 FR 0.0002 REL FR 1 V 1 P
it curvets unseasonably. AYL 3.02.244 P
anon he rears upright, curvets, and leaps, | as VEN 279
CUSHES 1 FR 0.0001 REL FR 1 V 0 P
on, | his cushes on his thighs, gallantly arm'd, 1H4 4.01.105
CUSHION 7 FR 0.0008 REL FR 4 V 3 P
o, a stool and a cushion for the sexton. ADO 4.02. 2 P
both on one sampler, sitting on one cushion, MND 3.02.205
dagger my sceptre, and this cushion my crown. 1H4 2.04.379 P
a grave as to stuff a botcher's cushion, or to COR 2.01. 89 P
not moving | from th' casque to th' cushion, but 4.07. 43
whilst with no softer cushion than the flint | i 5.03. 53
his right cheek | reposing on a cushion. CYM 4.02.212
/CUSHIONS 1 FR 0.0001 REL FR 1 V 0 P
/you /lie /down /and /rest /upon /the /cushions? LR 3.06. 34
CUSHIONS 5 FR 0.0005 REL FR 4 V 1 P
fine linen, turkey cushions boss'd with pearl, SHR 2.01.353
it do, you shall have a dozen of cushions again; 2H4 5.04. 14 P
cushions, leaden spoons, | irons of a doit, COR 1.05. 5
if you are not, | let them have cushions by you. 3.01.101
i'll have them sleep on cushions in my tent. JC 4.03.243
CUSTA–LORUM 1 FR 0.0001 REL FR 0 V 1 P
ay, cousin slender, and custa–lorum. WIV 1.01. 7 P
CUSTARD 1 FR 0.0001 REL FR 0 V 1 P
and all, like him that leapt into the custard; AWW 2.05. 37 P
CUSTARD–COFFIN 1 FR 0.0001 REL FR 1 V 0 P
cap, | a custard–coffin, a bauble, a silken pie. SHR 4.03. 82
CUSTODY 3 FR 0.0003 REL FR 3 V 0 P
jailer, take him to thy custody. ERR 1.01.155
so great a charge from thine own custody? 1.02. 61
nor shall not, whilst 'tis in my custody. OTH 3.03.164
/CUSTOM 1 FR 0.0001 REL FR 0 V 1 P
still observ'd, and we are strong in /custom; PER 3.01. 52 P
CUSTOM 45 FR 0.0050 REL FR 38 V 7 P
i am more serious than my custom; TMP 2.01.219
'tis a custom with him | i' th' afternoon to 3.02. 87
our dance of custom, round about the oak | of WIV 5.05. 75
till custom make it | their perch and not their MM 2.01. 3
or would you have me speak after my custom, as ADO 1.01.168 P
ripe wants of my friend, | i'll break a custom. MV 1.03. 64
shows herself more kind | than is her custom. 4.01.268
hath not old custom made this life more sweet AYL 2.01. 2
for you shall hop without my custom, sir. SHR 4.03. 99
self–born hour | to plant and o'erwhelm custom. WT 4.01. 9
and the feeders | digest/'t with a custom, i 4.04. 12
would beguile nature of her custom, so perfectly 5.02. 99 P
wide–stretched honors that pertain | by custom, H5 2.04. 83
offices this day | by custom of the coronation. H8 4.01. 16
office, and custom, in all line of order; TRO 1.03. 88
acquaintance, custom, and condition | made tame 3.03. 9
their rotten privilege and custom 'gainst | my COR 1.10. 23
i do beseech you, | let me o'erleap that custom; 2.02.136
pray you go fit you to the custom, and | take to 2.02.142
custom calls me to't. 2.03.117
what custom wills, in all things should we do't, 2.03.118
the custom of request you have discharg'd. 2.03.142
"aged custom, | but by your voices, will not so 2.03.168
on this fair corse, and as the custom is, | and ROM 4.05. 80
all pity chok'd with custom of fell deeds; JC 3.01.269
of this, good peers, | but as a thing of custom. MAC 3.04. 96
pay his breath | to time and mortal custom. 4.01.100
is it a custom? HAM 1.04. 12
it is a custom | more honor'd in the breach than 1.04. 15
my orchard, | my custom always of the afternoon, 1.05. 60
all my mirth, forgone all custom of exercises; 2.02.297 P
if damned custom have not brass'd it so | that 3.04. 37
that monster custom, who all sense doth eat, 3.04.161
to begin, | antiquity forgot, custom not known, 4.05.105
nature her custom holds, | let shame say what it 4.07.187
custom hath made it in him a property of 5.01. 67 P
should i | stand in the plague of custom, and LR 1.02. 3
the tyrant custom, most grave senators, | hath OTH 1.03.229
would invent some other custom of entertainment. 2.03. 35 P
a false disloyal knave | are tricks of custom; 3.03.122
her, nor custom stale | her infinite variety. ANT 2.02.234
this is but a custom in your tongue; CYM 1.04.138 P
the breach of custom | is breach of all. 4.02. 10
but custom what they did begin | was with long PER 1.ch. 29
you'll lose nothing by custom. 4.02.138 P
CUSTOMARY 6 FR 0.0006 REL FR 5 V 1 P
patience, | because it is a customary cross, MND 1.01.153
work | than customary bounty can enforce you. MV 3.04. 9
even now i met him | with customary compliment,
WT 1.02.371
time | his charters and his customary rights; R2 2.01.196
i may be consul, i have here the customary gown. COR 2.03. 87 P
mother, | nor customary suits of solemn black, HAM 1.02. 78
CUSTOM'D 1 FR 0.0001 REL FR 1 V 0 P
to wring the widow from her custom'd right, 2H6 5.01.188
CUSTOMED 1 FR 0.0001 REL FR 1 V 0 P
day, | no common wind, no customed event, | but JN 3.04.155
CUSTOMER 2 FR 0.0002 REL FR 1 V 1 P
i think thee now some common customer. AWW 5.03.286
a customer! OTH 4.01.119 P
CUSTOMERS 4 FR 0.0004 REL FR 1 V 3 P
house, for here be many of her old customers. MM 4.03. 4 P
you minion, you, are these your customers? ERR 4.04. 60
milliner can so fit his customers with gloves. WT 4.04.192 P
peevish baggage would but give way to customers.
PER 4.06. 19 P
CUSTOMS 4 FR 0.0004 REL FR 3 V 1 P
o kate, nice customs cur'sy to great kings. H5 5.02.268 P
new customs, | though they be never so H8 1.03. 2
had i not known those customs | i should have 4.01. 20
degrees, observances, customs, and laws, TIM 4.01. 19
CUSTOM–SHRUNK 1 FR 0.0001 REL FR 0 V 1 P
and what with poverty, i am custom–shrunk. MM 1.02. 84 P
CUSTREL *(also coystrill)*
CUSTREL 1 FR 0.0001 REL FR 1 V 0 P
custrel that comes inquiring for his tib. PER 4.06.166
CUSTURE 1 FR 0.0001 REL FR 0 V 1 P
/calen /o custure me! H5 4.04. 4 P
CUT 181 FR 0.0204 REL FR 128 V 53 P
a stake, | or cut his wezand with thy knife. TMP 3.02. 91
why then your ladyship must cut your hair. TGV 2.07. 44
i will cut his troat in de park; WIV 1.04.108 P
by gar, i will cut all his two stones; 1.04.111 P
by gar, me vill cut his ears. 2.03. 64 P
that i will, come cut and long–tail, under the 3.04. 46 P
yet | let us be keen, and rather cut a little, MM 2.01. 5
can you cut off a man's head? 4.02. 1 P
head, and i can never cut off a woman's head. 4.02. 5 P
her brother, | cut off by course of justice — 5.01. 35
brother by himself, | and not have cut him off. 5.01.112
and from my false hand cut the wedding–ring, ERR 2.02.137
cut with her golden oars the silver stream, ADO 3.01. 27
if low, an agot very vildly cut; 3.01. 65
he hath twice or thrice cut cupid's bow–string, 3.02. 10 P
whose edge hath power to cut, whose will still LLL 2.01. 50
cut me to pieces with thy keen conceit; 5.02.399
enough; hold, or cut bow–strings. MND 1.02.111 P
if i cut my finger, i shall make bold with you. 3.01.183 P
night's swift dragons cut the clouds full fast, 3.02.379
o fates, come, come, | cut thread and thrum, 5.01.286
sit like his grandsire cut in alablaster? MV 1.01. 84
to be cut off and taken | in what part of your 1.03.150
to cut the forfeiture from that bankrout there. 4.01.122
to be by him cut off | nearest the merchant's 4.01.232
penance | of such misery doth she cut me off. 4.01.272
for if the jew do cut but deep enough, | i'll 4.01.280
and you must cut this flesh from off his breast, 4.01.302
therefore prepare thee to cut off the flesh. 4.01.324
nor cut thou less nor more | but just a pound of 4.01.325
why, i were best to cut my left hand off, | and 5.01.177
sent in this fool to cut off the argument? AYL 1.02. 46 P
that, | he will have other means to cut you off; 2.03. 25
with eyes severe and beard of formal cut, | full 2.07.155
i did dislike the cut of a certain courtier's 5.04. 70 P
if i said his beard was not cut well, he was in 5.04. 71 P
if i sent him word again, it was not well cut, 5.04. 73 P
would send me word he cut it to please himself: 5.04. 74 P
if again, it was not well cut, he disabled my 5.04. 76 P
if again, it was not well cut, he would answer i 5.04. 77 P
if again, it was not well cut, he would say i 5.04. 79 P
how oft did you say his beard was not well cut? 5.04. 84 P
and to cut off all strife, here sit we down: SHR 3.01. 21
here's snip and nip and cut and slish and slash, 4.03. 90
but did you not request to have it cut? 4.03.121
unto thee, i bid thy master cut out the gown, 4.03.126 P
gown, but i did not bid him cut it to pieces. 4.03.127 P
"the sleeves curiously cut." 4.03.143 P
i commanded the sleeves should be cut out, and 4.03.146 P
of it, and cut th' entail from all remainders, AWW 4.03.279 P
faith, i can cut a caper. TN 1.03.121 P
and i can cut the mutton to't. 1.03.122 P
if thou hast her not i' th' end, call me cut. 2.03.187 P
o, cut my lace, lest my heart, cracking it, WT 3.02.173
by th' pattern of mine own thoughts i cut out 4.04.382
lethargy i pick'd and cut most of their festival 4.04.614 P
what fine chisel | could ever yet cut breath? 5.03. 79
king, | cut off the sequence of posterity, JN 2.01. 96
or, hubert, if you will, cut out my tongue, | so 4.01.100
cut him to pieces. 4.03. 93
some of those branches by the destinies cut; R2 1.02. 15
the king had cut off my head with my brother's. 2.02.102
arms, | be his own carver and cut out his way, 2.03.144
cut off the heads of /too fast growing sprays, 3.04. 34
this fest'red joint cut off, the rest rest sound 5.03. 85
knife, | no more shall cut his master. 1H4 1.01. 18
rob them, cut this head off from my shoulders. 1.02.165 P
cut the villains' throats! 2.02. 83 P
the hose, my buckler cut through and through, my 2.04.167 P
cut me off the heads | of all the favorites that 4.03. 85
bardolph, cut me off the villain's head, throw 2H4 2.01. 46 P
not this nave of a wheel have his ears cut off. 2.04.256 P
i cut them off, and had a purpose now | to lead 4.05.209
i will cut thy throat one time or other in fair H5 2.01. 69 P
we keep knives to cut one another's throats? 2.01. 92 P
us | will cut their passage through the force of 2.02. 16
and there is throats to be cut, and works to be 3.02.112 P
so chrish save me, i will cut off your head. 3.02.133 P
and let not bardolph's vital thread be cut 3.06. 47
beard of the general's cut and a horrid suit of 3.06. 77 P
we would have all such offenders so cut off; 3.06.107 P
but when our throats are cut, he may be ransom'd 4.01.193 P
it is no english treason to cut french crowns, 4.01.228 P
bid him prepare, for i will cut his throat. 4.04. 32
every soldier to cut his prisoner's throat. 4.07. 9 P
besides, we'll cut the throats of those we have, 4.07. 63
and there my rendezvous is quite cut off. 5.01. 83
arms, | of england's coat one half is cut away. 1H6 1.01. 81
the ruthless flint doth cut my tender feet, 2H6 2.04. 34
cut both the villains' throats; 4.01. 20
an ox, and iniquity's throat cut like a calf. 4.02. 27 P
rather than bloody war shall cut them short, 4.04. 12
or cut not out the burly–bon'd clown in chines 4.10. 56 P
and there cut off thy most ungracious head, 4.10. 82
into as many gobbets will i cut it | as wild 5.02. 58
that winter should cut off our spring–time so. 3H6 2.03. 47
from whence shall warwick cut the sea to france, 2.06. 89
it, | and so, i say, i'll cut the causes off, 3.02.142
shall, whiles thy head is warm and new cut off, 5.01. 55
look in his youth to have him so cut off | as, 5.05. 66
age, | but by some unlook'd accident cut off! R3 1.03.213
to cut off those that have offended him. 1.04.219
have this crown of mine cut from my shoulders 3.02. 43
first, if all obstacles were cut away, | and 3.07.156
ah, cut my lace asunder, | that my pent heart 4.01. 33
their clothes are after such a pagan cut to't, H8 1.03. 14
strong–ribb'd bark through liquid mountains cut, TRO 1.03. 40
i shall cut out your tongue. 2.01.110 P
and cut off | all fears attending on so dire a 2.02.133
achilles be thy guard, | i'll cut thy throat. 4.04.129
he's a disease that must be cut away. COR 3.01.293
mortal, to cut it off; 3.01.295
which not to cut would show thee but a fool, 4.05. 97
the news is, our general is cut i' th' middle, 4.05.197 P
cut me to pieces, volsces, men and lads, | stain 5.06.111
you, you'll rejoice | that he is thus cut off. 5.06.138
and easy it is | of a cut loaf to steal a shive, TIT 2.01. 87
who 'twas that cut thy tongue and ravish'd thee. 2.04. 2
lest thou shouldst detect /him, cut thy tongue. 2.04. 27
but, lovely niece, that mean is cut from thee. 2.04. 40
and he hath cut those pretty fingers off | that 2.04. 42
is that the one will help to cut the other. 3.01. 78
or shall we cut away our hands like thine? 3.01.130
cut off the proud'st conspirator that lives. 4.04. 26
they cut thy sister's tongue, and ravish'd her, 5.01. 92
and cut her hands, and trimm'd her as thou 5.01. 93
why, she was wash'd, and cut, and trimm'd, and 5.01. 95
death, | my hand cut off and made a merry jest; 5.02.174
this one hand yet is left to cut your throats, 5.02.181

they ravish'd her, and cut away her tongue, 5.03. 57
i will cut off their heads. ROM 1.01. 23 P
he swung about his head and cut the winds, | who 1.01.111
die, | take him and cut him out in little stars, 3.02. 22
than with that hand that cut thy youth in twain 5.03. 99
cut my heart in sums. TIM 3.04. 92
and let the foes quietly cut their throats 3.05. 44
your knives, | and cut your trusters' throats! 4.01. 10
hath doubtfully pronounc'd the throat shall cut, 4.03.122
cut throats, | all that you meet are thieves. 4.03.445
that mine own use invites me to cut down, | and 5.01.206
his doublet, and offer'd them his throat to cut. JC 1.02.266 P
to cut the head off and then hack the limbs — 2.01.163
death, | as here by caesar, and by you cut off, 3.01.162
this was the most unkindest cut of all; 3.02.183
how to cut off some charge in legacies. 4.01. 9
from which advantage shall we cut him off | if 4.03.210
my lord, his throat is cut; MAC 3.04. 15
i should cut off the nobles for their lands, 4.03. 79
gentle heavens, | cut short all intermission. 4.03.232
cut off even in the blossoms of my sin, HAM 1.05. 76
to cut his throat i' th' church. 4.07.126
after i have cut the egg i' th' middle and eat LR 1.04.158 P
be a maid long, unless things be cut shorter. 1.05. 52
to grudge my pleasures, to cut off my train, 2.04.174
let me have surgeons, | i am cut to th' brains. 4.06.193
you have many opportunities to cut him off; 4.06.263 P
i had rather have this tongue cut from my mouth OTH 2.03.221
my leg is cut in two. 5.01. 72
then had you indeed a cut, and the case to be ANT 1.02.166 P
cut my lace, charmian, come! 1.03. 71
let me cut the cable, | and, when we are put off 2.07. 71
he could so quickly cut the ionian sea, | and 3.07. 22
sword, the paper | hath cut her throat already! CYM 3.04. 33
thy garments cut to pieces before /her face: 4.01. 18 P
he cut our roots in characters, | and sauc'd our 4.02. 49
cut off one cloten's head, | son to the queen 4.02.118
devil cloten, | hath here cut off my lord. 4.02.316
i cut off 's head, | and am right glad he is not 5.05.295
or till the destinies do cut his thread of life. PER 1.02.108
half the flood | hath their keel cut. 3.ch. 46
he offer'd to cut a caper at the proclamation, 4.02.107 P
thou mayst cut a morsel off the spit. 4.02.131 P
never to wash his face, nor cut his hairs; 4.04. 28
"for i'll cut my green coat a foot above my knee TNK 3.04. 19
"he s' buy me a white cut, forth for to ride, 3.04. 22
it was a hawk, | and her bells were cut away." 3.05. 71
i'll be cut a–pieces | before i take this oath. 3.06.256
through a small glade cut by the fishermen, | i 4.01. 64
and, for a jig, come cut and long tail to him! 5.02. 49
kill them, cut their throats, possess their STM II.C 120
that he shall never cut from memory | my sweet SON 63.11
CUTLER'S 1 FR 0.0001 REL FR 1 V 0 P
for all the world like cutler's poetry | upon a MV 5.01.149
CUTPURSE 6 FR 0.0006 REL FR 3 V 3 P
and a nimble hand, is necessary for a cutpurse; WT 4.04.672 P
away, you cutpurse rascal! 2H4 2.04.128 P
a bawd, a cutpurse. H5 3.06. 62 P
and something lean to cutpurse of quick hand. 5.01. 86
kings, | a cutpurse of the empire and the rule, HAM 3.04. 99
thou art baser in it than a cutpurse. TNK 2.02.211
CUTPURSES 2 FR 0.0002 REL FR 1 V 1 P
nor cutpurses come not to throngs; LR 3.02. 90
amongst a whole million of cutpurses, and there TNK 4.03. 38 P
CUT'S 1 FR 0.0001 REL FR 0 V 1 P
tom, beat cut's saddle, put a few flocks in the 1H4 2.01. 5 P
CUTS* 13 FR 0.0014 REL FR 12 V 1 P
we'll draw cuts for the senior, till then, lead ERR 5.01.423
cloth a' gold and cuts, and lac'd with silver, ADO 3.04. 19 P
churlish drums | cuts off more circumstance. JN 2.01. 77
cuts off his tale and talks of arthur's death. 4.02.202
and cuts me from the best of all my land | a 1H4 3.01. 98
i thank him that he cuts me from my tale, | for 5.02. 90
goes, | for friendly counsel cuts off many foes. 1H6 3.01.184
time | cuts off the ceremonious vows of love R3 5.03. 98
severity | cuts beauty off from all posterity. ROM 1.01.220
he that cuts off twenty years of life | cuts off JC 3.01.101
life | cuts off so many years of fearing death. 3.01.102
preferment falls on him that cuts him off. LR 4.05. 38
that cuts away | a life more worthy from him TNK 5.03.142
CUT'ST 1 FR 0.0001 REL FR 1 V 0 P
thou cut'st my head off with a golden axe, | and ROM 3.03. 22
CUTTER 1 FR 0.0001 REL FR 1 V 0 P
the cutter | was as another nature, dumb; CYM 2.04. 83
CUTTER–OFF 1 FR 0.0001 REL FR 0 V 1 P
nature's natural the cutter–off of nature's wit. AYL 1.02. 49 P
CUT–THROAT 1 FR 0.0001 REL FR 1 V 0 P
you call me misbeliever, cut–throat dog, | and MV 1.03.111
CUT–THROATS 1 FR 0.0001 REL FR 1 V 0 P
thou art the best o' th' cut–throats, | yet he's MAC 3.04. 16
CUTTING 8 FR 0.0009 REL FR 6 V 2 P
her deity | cutting the clouds towards paphos; TMP 4.01. 93
cutting a smaller hair than may be seen; LLL 5.02.258
but, in the cutting it, if thou dost shed | one MV 4.01.309
i would the cutting of my garments would serve AWW 4.01. 46 P
the pains you take | by cutting off your heads. JN 5.04. 16
hangs on the cutting short that fraudful man. 2H6 3.01. 81
drawing their massy irons and cutting the web! TRO 2.03. 17 P
and then dreams he of cutting foreign throats, ROM 1.04. 83
CUTTLE 1 FR 0.0001 REL FR 0 V 1 P
chaps, and you play the saucy cuttle with me. 2H4 2.04.130 P
CYCLOPS' 2 FR 0.0002 REL FR 2 V 0 P
no big–bon'd men fram'd of the cyclops' size, TIT 4.03. 47
and never did the cyclops' hammers fall | on HAM 2.02.489
CYDNUS 3 FR 0.0003 REL FR 2 V 1 P
purs'd up his heart upon the river of cydnus. ANT 2.02.187 P
i am again for cydnus | to meet mark antony. 5.02.228
and cydnus swell'd above the banks, or for | the CYM 2.04. 71
/CYGNET 1 FR 0.0001 REL FR 1 V 0 P
i am the /cygnet to this pale faint swan | who JN 5.07. 21
CYGNET'S 1 FR 0.0001 REL FR 1 V 0 P
the cygnet's down is harsh and spirit of sense TRO 1.01. 58
CYGNETS 1 FR 0.0001 REL FR 1 V 0 P
so doth the swan her downy cygnets save, 1H6 5.03. 56
CYMBALS 1 FR 0.0001 REL FR 1 V 0 P
tabors and cymbals, and the shouting romans, COR 5.04. 50
CYMBELINE 10 FR 0.0011 REL FR 10 V 0 P
i am sorry, cymbeline, | that i am to pronounce CYM 3.01. 61
cymbeline lov'd me, | and when a soldier was the 3.03. 58
swore to cymbeline | i was confederate with the 3.03. 67
nor cymbeline dreams that they are alive. 3.03. 81
the heir of cymbeline and britain, who | the 3.03. 87
o cymbeline, heaven and my conscience knows 3.03. 99
posthumus hath | to cymbeline perform'd. 5.04. 76
and ask of cymbeline what boon thou wilt, 5.05. 97
the lofty cedar, royal cymbeline, | personates 5.05.453
unite | his favor with the radiant cymbeline, 5.05.475
CYME 1 FR 0.0001 REL FR 1 V 0 P
what rhubarb, cyme, or what purgative drug, MAC 5.03. 55
CYNIC 1 FR 0.0001 REL FR 1 V 0 P
ha, ha! how vildly doth this cynic rhyme! JC 4.03.133
CYNTHIA 3 FR 0.0003 REL FR 3 V 0 P
this by the eye of cynthia hath she vowed, | and PER 2.05. 11
"when cynthia with her borrowed light," etc. TNK 4.01.153
cynthia for shame obscures her silver shine, VEN 728
CYNTHIA'S 1 FR 0.0001 REL FR 1 V 0 P
'tis but the pale reflex of cynthia's brow; ROM 3.05. 20
CYPRESS* 6 FR 0.0006 REL FR 6 V 0 P
in cypress chests my arras counterpoints, SHR 2.01.351
death, | and in sad cypress let me be laid. TN 2.04. 52
a cypress, not a bosom, | hides my heart. 3.01.121
driven snow, | cypress black as e'er was crow, WT 4.04.219
their sweetest shade a grove of cypress trees! 2H6 3.02.323
i am attended at the cypress grove. COR 1.10. 30
/CYPRUS 1 FR 0.0001 REL FR 1 V 0 P
spirits, | /and /bring /all /cyprus /comfort! OTH 2.01. 82
CYPRUS 23 FR 0.0026 REL FR 19 V 4 P
eyes had seen the proof | at rhodes, at cyprus, OTH 1.01. 29
with such loud reason to the cyprus wars 1.01.150
something from cyprus, as i may divine; 1.02. 39
a turkish fleet, and bearing up to cyprus. 1.03. 8
consider | th' importancy of cyprus to the turk, 1.03. 20
frank appearance | their purposes toward cyprus. 1.03. 39
'tis certain then for cyprus. 1.03. 43
so let the turk of cyprus us beguile, | we lose 1.03.210
with a most mighty preparation makes for cyprus. 1.03.222 P
and is in full commission here for cyprus. 2.01. 29
you men of cyprus, let her have your knees. 2.01. 84
honey, you shall be well desir'd in cyprus, | i 2.01.204
desdemona, | once more, well met at cyprus. 2.01.212
of that will i cause these of cyprus to mutiny, 2.01.274 P
bless the isle of cyprus and our noble general 2.02. 11 P
are a brace of cyprus gallants that would fain 2.03. 31 P
three else of cyprus, noble swelling spirits 2.03. 55
that he you hurt is of great fame in cyprus, 3.01. 45
made demonstrable here in cyprus to him, | hath 3.04.142
welcome to cyprus. 4.01.221
you are welcome, sir, to cyprus. 4.01.263
is taken off, | and cassio rules in cyprus. 5.02.332
egypt, made her | of lower syria, cyprus, lydia, ANT 3.06. 10
CYRUS' 1 FR 0.0001 REL FR 1 V 0 P
exploit | as scythian tomyris by cyrus' death. 1H6 2.03. 6
CYTHEREA 4 FR 0.0004 REL FR 4 V 0 P
running brook, | and cytherea all in sedges hid, SHR in.2. 51
cytherea, | how bravely thou becom'st thy bed! CYM 2.02. 14
sweet cytherea, sitting by a brook | with young PP 4. 1
when cytherea (all in love forlorn) | a longing 6. 3
CYTHEREA'S 1 FR 0.0001 REL FR 1 V 0 P
the lids of juno's eyes | or cytherea's breath; WT 4.04.122
D'* *(also de*, do*, the)*
D'* 13 FR 0.0014 REL FR 0 V 13 P
d' elbow. H5 3.04. 24 P
d' elbow. 3.04. 25 P
d' hand, de fingre, de nailes, d' arma, de 3.04. 28 P
hand, de fingre, de nailes, d' arma, de bilbow. 3.04. 29 P
d' elbow, madame. 3.04. 30 P
o seigneur dieu, je m'en oublie d' elbow. 3.04. 31 P
d' hand, de fingre, de mailes — 3.04. 45 P
sauf votre honneur, d' elbow. 3.04. 48 P
d' elbow, de nick, et de sin. 3.04. 49 P
d' hand, de fingre, de nailes, d' arma, d' elbow 3.04. 58 P
de fingre, de nailes, d' arma, d' elbow, de nick 3.04. 58 P
de nailes, d' arma, d' elbow, de nick, de sin, 3.04. 58 P
why, d' ye take it, and the gods give thee good PER 2.01.146 P
D 1 FR 0.0001 REL FR 1 V 0 P
d sol re, one cliff, two notes have i; SHR 3.01. 77
DABBLED 1 FR 0.0001 REL FR 1 V 0 P
with bright hair | dabbled in blood, and he R3 1.04. 54
DACE 1 FR 0.0001 REL FR 0 V 1 P
if the young dace be a bait for the old pike, i 2H4 3.02.330 P
DAD 3 FR 0.0003 REL FR 3 V 0 P
like a mad lad, | pare thy nails, dad. TN 4.02.130
since i first call'd my brother's father dad. JN 2.01.467
voice | was wont to cheer his dad in mutinies? 3H6 1.04. 77
DAEDALUS 2 FR 0.0002 REL FR 2 V 0 P
i, daedalus; 3H6 5.06. 21
doughty dismal fame | from dis to daedalus, from TNK 3.05.115
DAEMON *(also demon)*
DAEMON 1 FR 0.0001 REL FR 1 V 0 P
thy daemon, that thy spirit which keeps thee, is ANT 2.03. 20
DAFF *(also doff)*
DAFF 1 FR 0.0001 REL FR 1 V 0 P
canst thou so daff me? ADO 5.01. 78
DAFFADILLIES 1 FR 0.0001 REL FR 1 V 0 P
with chaplets on their heads of daffadillies, TNK 4.01. 73
DAFFADILS 2 FR 0.0002 REL FR 2 V 0 P
when daffadils begin to peer, | with heigh, the WT 4.03. 1
daffadils, | that come before the swallow dares, 4.04.118
DAFF'D 4 FR 0.0004 REL FR 3 V 1 P
on me, i would have daff'd all other respects, ADO 2.03.169 P
that daff'd the world aside | and bid it pass? 1H4 4.01. 96
and daff'd me to a cabin hang'd with care, | to PP 14. 3
there my white stole of chastity i daff'd, LC 297
DAFFODILS *(see daffadillies, etc.)*
DAFF'ST 1 FR 0.0001 REL FR 0 V 1 P
every day thou daff'st me with some device, iago OTH 4.02.175 P
DAFF'T 1 FR 0.0001 REL FR 1 V 0 P
till we do please | to daff't for our repose, ANT 4.04. 13
DAGGER 38 FR 0.0043 REL FR 20 V 18 P
playing at sword and dagger with a master of WIV 1.01.284 P
master starve–lackey the rapier and dagger man, MM 4.03. 14 P
hath no man's dagger here a point for me? ADO 4.01.109
in mulberry shade, | his dagger drew, and died. MND 5.01.149
thou stick'st a dagger in me. MV 3.01.110 P
two, | and wear my dagger with the braver grace, 3.04. 65
and walter's dagger was not come from sheathing;
and the practice in the chape of his dagger. SHR 4.01.135
sir, or i'll throw your dagger o'er the house. AWW 4.03.143 P
who, with dagger of lath, | in his rage and his TN 4.01. 28 P
my dagger muzzled | lest it should bite its 4.02.126
thee out of thy kingdom with a dagger of lath, WT 1.02.156
he hack'd it with his dagger, and said he would 1H4 2.04.137 P
chair shall be my state, this dagger my sceptre, 2.04.305 P
thy golden sceptre for a leaden dagger, and thy 2.04.379 P
and now is this vice's dagger become a squire, 2.04.381 P
do not you wear your dagger in your cap that day 2H4 3.02.319 P
one may pare his nails with a wooden dagger, and H5 4.01. 56 P
use any sword, weapon, or dagger, henceforward, 4.04. 72 P
i pray you, uncle, give me this dagger. 1H6 1.03. 78 P
my dagger, little cousin? with all my heart. R3 3.01.110
stretch'd him, and, with one hand on his dagger, 3.01.111
ay, with my dagger in their bosoms, grandsire. H8 1.02.204
lay the serving–creature's dagger on your pate. TIT 4.01.118
pray you put up your dagger, and put out your ROM 4.05.117 P
you with an iron wit, and put up my iron dagger. 4.05.121 P
o happy dagger, | this is thy sheath; 4.05.124 P
this dagger hath mista'en, for lo his house | is 5.03.169
i know where i will wear this dagger then; 5.03.203
good of rome, i have the same dagger for myself, JC 1.03. 89
look, in this place ran cassius' dagger through; 3.02. 46 P
there is my dagger, | and here my naked breast; 3.02.174
sheathe your dagger. 4.03.100
is this a dagger which i see before me, | the 4.03.107
or art thou but | a dagger of the mind, a false MAC 2.01. 33
this is the air–drawn dagger which you said 2.01. 38
rapier and dagger. 3.04. 61
for i wear not | my dagger in my mouth. HAM 5.02.145 P
CYM 4.02. 79
DAGGER'S 2 FR 0.0002 REL FR 2 V 0 P
my breast can better brook thy dagger's point 3H6 5.06. 27
bids thee christen it with thy dagger's point. TIT 4.02. 70
/DAGGERS 1 FR 0.0001 REL FR 1 V 0 P
i will speak /daggers to her, but use none. HAM 3.02.396
DAGGERS 12 FR 0.0013 REL FR 12 V 0 P
thou hid'st a thousand daggers in thy thoughts, 2H4 4.05.106
when my son | was stabb'd with bloody daggers: R3 1.03.211
men | whose daggers have stabb'd caesar; JC 3.02.152
when your vile daggers | hack'd one another in 5.01. 39
of his own chamber, and us'd their very daggers, MAC 1.07. 76
i laid their daggers ready, | he could not miss 2.02. 11
why did you bring these daggers from the place? 2.02. 45
give me the daggers. 2.02. 50
so were their daggers, which unwip'd we found 2.03.103
their daggers | unmannerly breech'd with gore. 2.03.115
where we are, | there's daggers in men's smiles; 2.03.140
these words like daggers enter in my ears. HAM 3.04. 95
DAGONET 1 FR 0.0001 REL FR 0 V 1 P
i was then sir dagonet in arthur's show — there 2H4 3.02.280 P
DAILY 33 FR 0.0037 REL FR 30 V 3 P
well–belov'd | and daily graced by the emperor; TGV 1.03. 58
with nightly tears, and daily heart–sore sighs, 2.04.132
boys, | made daily motions for our home return: ERR 1.01. 59
what men daily do, not knowing what they do! ADO 4.01. 20 P
this exercise, so long | i daily vow to use it. WT 3.02.242
that daily break–vow, he that wins of all, | of JN 2.01.569
and daily new exactions are devis'd, | as blanks R2 2.01.249
for there, they say, he daily doth frequent, 5.03. 6
that, being daily swallowed by men's eyes, 1H4 3.02. 70
which daily grew to quarrel and to bloodshed, 2H4 4.05.194
we lose, they daily get; 1H6 4.03. 32
and ruthless slaughters as are daily seen | by 5.04.161
the commonwealth hath daily run to wrack, | the 2H6 1.03.124
this deadly quarrel daily doth beget! 3H6 2.05. 91
for hunting was his daily exercise. 4.06. 85
promotions | are daily given to ennoble those R3 1.03. 80
show'r'd on me daily have been more than could H8 3.02.167
as you do conscience | in doing daily wrongs. 5.02.103
much are we bound to heaven | in daily thanks, 5.02.150
when with your blood you daily paint her thus. TRO 1.01. 91
repeal daily any wholesome act establish'd COR 1.01. 82 P
piercing statutes daily to chain up and restrain 1.01. 84 P
which out of daily fortune ever taints | the 4.07. 38
the want whereof doth daily make revolt | in my TIM 4.03. 92
men daily find it. 4.03.174
of the sea may beat | thy grave–stone daily; 4.03.379
and /why such daily /cast of brazen cannon, HAM 1.01. 73
he hath a daily beauty in his life | that makes OTH 5.01. 19
to you | which daily she was bound to proffer. CYM 3.05. 49
the petty streams that pay a daily debt | to LUC 649
but day doth daily draw my sorrows longer, | and SON 28.13
two contracted new | come daily to the banks, 56.11
for as the sun is daily new and old, | so is my 76.13
DAINTIER 1 FR 0.0001 REL FR 0 V 1 P
of little employment hath the daintier sense. HAM 5.01. 70 P
DAINTIES 4 FR 0.0004 REL FR 4 V 0 P
i hold your dainties cheap, sir, and your ERR 3.01. 21
never fed of the dainties that are bred in a LLL 4.02. 24
for dainties are all kates, and therefore, kate, SHR 2.01.189
dainties to taste, fresh beauty for the use, VEN 164
DAINTIEST 2 FR 0.0002 REL FR 2 V 0 P
so i regreet | the daintiest last, to make the R2 1.03. 68
worse than gall, the daintiest that they taste! 2H6 3.02.322
DAINTILY 2 FR 0.0002 REL FR 2 V 0 P
whereof their mother daintily hath fed, | eating TIT 5.03. 61
fought'st against | (though daintily brought up) ANT 1.04. 60
DAINTINESS 1 FR 0.0001 REL FR 1 V 0 P
and here have i the daintiness of ear | to check R2 5.05. 45
DAINTRY *(also daventry)*
DAINTRY 1 FR 0.0001 REL FR 1 V 0 P
by this at daintry, with a puissant troop. 3H6 5.01. 6
DAINTY 24 FR 0.0027 REL FR 24 V 0 P
why, that's my dainty ariel! TMP 5.01. 95
full of welcome makes scarce one dainty dish. ERR 3.01. 23
and dainty bits | make rich the ribs, but LLL 1.01. 26
/a' /th' /one side — o, a most dainty man! 4.01.144
her feet were much too dainty for such tread! 4.03.275
love's tongue proves dainty bacchus gross in 4.03.336
o dainty duck! MND 5.01.281
basins and ewers to lave her dainty hands; SHR 2.01.348
lace for your cape, | my dainty duck, my dear–a? WT 4.04.317
weary | of dainty and such picking grievances, 2H4 4.01.196
no shape but his can please your dainty eye. 1H6 5.03. 38
by heaven, she is a dainty one. H8 1.04. 94
grows dainty of his worth, and in his tent TRO 1.03.145

glove, | and gives memorial dainty kisses to it, 5.02. 80
pleas'd with this dainty bait, thus goes to bed. 5.08. 20
single you thither then this dainty doe, | and TIT 2.01.117
but hope to pluck a dainty doe to ground. 2.02. 26
she that makes dainty, | she i'll swear hath ROM 1.05. 19
and let us not be dainty of leave–taking, | but MAC 2.03.144
and forget | your laborsome and dainty trims, CYM 3.04.164
dainty, madam. TNK 2.02.130
but will the dainty domine, the schoolmaster, 2.03. 40
there's a dainty mad woman, master, | comes i' 3.05. 72
and, dainty duke, whose doughty dismal fame 3.05.114

DAISIED 1 FR 0.0001 REL FR 1 V 0 P
us | find out the prettiest daisied plot we can, CYM 4.02.398

DAISIES 3 FR 0.0003 REL FR 3 V 0 P
when daisies pied and violets blue | and LLL 5.02.894
nettles, daisies, and long purples | that HAM 4.07.169
daisies smell–less, yet most quaint, | and sweet TNK 1.01. 5

DAISY 2 FR 0.0002 REL FR 1 V 1 P
there's a daisy. HAM 4.05.184 P
white | show'd like an april daisy on the grass, LUC 395

DALE 9 FR 0.0010 REL FR 5 V 4 P
over hill, over dale, | thorough bush, thorough MND 2.01. 2
met we on hill, in dale, forest, or mead, | by 2.01. 83
to peer, | with heigh, the doxy over the dale! WT 4.03. 2
sir, and my name is colevile of the dale. 2H4 4.03. 4 P
knight is your degree, and your place the dale. 4.03. 6 P
so shall you be still colevile of the dale. 4.03. 9 P
taken sir john colevile of the dale, a most 4.03. 38 P
feed where thou wilt, on mountain or in dale; VEN 232
as from a mountain spring that feeds a dale, LUC 1077

DALES 1 FR 0.0001 REL FR 1 V 0 P
that hills and valleys, dales and fields, | and PP 19. 3

DALLIANCE 7 FR 0.0008 REL FR 7 V 0 P
do not give dalliance | too much the rein. TMP 4.01. 51
you use this dalliance to excuse | your breach ERR 4.01. 48
my business cannot brook this dalliance. 4.01. 59
and silken dalliance in the wardrobe lies; H5 2.pr. 2
books | than wanton dalliance with a paramour. 1H6 5.01. 23
and keep not back your powers in dalliance. 5.02. 5
himself the primrose path of dalliance treads, HAM 1.03. 50

DALLIED 2 FR 0.0002 REL FR 2 V 0 P
that high all–seer, which i dallied with, | hath R3 5.01. 20
grief dallied with nor law nor limit knows. LUC 1120

DALLIES 2 FR 0.0002 REL FR 2 V 0 P
sooth, | and dallies with the innocence of love, TN 2.04. 47
and dallies with the wind and scorns the sun. R3 1.03.264

DALLY 12 FR 0.0013 REL FR 8 V 4 P
tell me, and dally not, where is the money? ERR 1.02. 59
thus, dally with my excrement, with my mustachio LLL 5.01.104 P
dally not with the gods, but get thee gone. SHR 4.04. 68
they that dally nicely with words may quickly TN 3.01. 14 P
and to dally with that word might make my sister 3.01. 19 P
what, is it a time to jest and dally now? 1H4 5.03. 55 P
come, dally not, be gone. 1H6 4.05. 11
take heed you dally not before your king, | lest R3 2.01. 12
come, for the third, laertes, you do but dally. HAM 5.02.297
if thou shouldst dally half an hour, his life, LR 3.06. 93
to toy, to wanton, dally, smile, and jest, VEN 106
yet, foul night–waking cat, he doth but dally, LUC 554

DALLYING 2 FR 0.0002 REL FR 1 V 1 P
not dallying with a brace of courtezans, | but R3 3.07. 74
your love, if i could see the puppets dallying. HAM 3.02.247 P

DALMATIANS 2 FR 0.0002 REL FR 2 V 0 P
that the pannonians and dalmatians for | their CYM 3.01. 73
action | 'gainst the pannonians and dalmatians, 3.07. 3

DAM* *(also tam*)*

DAM* 27 FR 0.0030 REL FR 22 V 5 P
got by the devil himself | upon thy wicked dam, TMP 1.02.320
saw a woman | but only sycorax my dam and she; 3.02.101
the devil take one party and his dam the other! WIV 4.05.106 P
she is worse, she is the devil's dam, and here ERR 4.03. 51 P
joiner am | a lion fell, nor else no lion's dam, MND 5.01.224
is the complexion of them all to leave the dam. MV 3.01. 30 P
and, whilst thou layest in thy unhallowed dam, 4.01.136
you may go to the devil's dam; SHR 1.01.105 P
why, she's a devil, a devil, the devil's dam. 3.02.156
can thy dam? WT 1.02.137
and together with the dam | commit them to the 2.03. 95
and foolish sire | blemish'd his gracious dam; 3.02.198
as like | as rain to water, or devil to his dam. JN 2.01.128
devil or devil's dam, i'll conjure thee. 1H6 1.05. 5
and as the dam runs lowing up and down, 2H6 3.01.214
now will i dam up this thy yawning mouth | for 4.01. 73
but thou art neither like thy sire nor dam, 3H6 2.02.135
that carries no impression like the dam. 3.02.162
is a kind of puppy | to th' old dam, treason), H8 1.01.176
like an unnatural dam | should now eat up her COR 3.01.291
when did the tiger's young ones teach the dam? TIT 2.03.142
the dam will wake and if she wind ye once; 4.01. 97
why, then she is the devil's dam: 4.02. 65
and bid that strumpet, your unhallowed dam, 5.02.190
what, all my pretty chickens, and their dam, MAC 4.03.218
let the devil and his dam haunt you! OTH 4.01.148 P
which ever was | the dam of horror, who does TNK 5.03. 23

DAMAGE 4 FR 0.0004 REL FR 4 V 0 P
to stop all hopes whose growth may damage me. R3 4.02. 59
he answer'd, "tush, | it can do me no damage"; H8 1.02.183
"deliver helen, and all damage else — | as TRO 2.02. 3
what will | the fall o' th' stroke do damage? TNK 1.02.113

DAMASCUS 1 FR 0.0001 REL FR 1 V 0 P
this be damascus, be thou cursed cain, | to slay 1H6 1.03. 39

DAMASK 7 FR 0.0008 REL FR 7 V 0 P
dismask'd, their damask sweet commixture shown, LLL 5.02.296
betwixt the constant red and mingled damask. AYL 3.05.123
a worm i' th' bud, | feed on her damask cheek. TN 2.04.112
was crow, | gloves as sweet as damask roses, WT 4.04.220
commit the war of white and damask in | their COR 2.01.216
with cherry lips and cheeks of damask roses, TNK 4.01. 74
a lily pale, with damask dye to grace her, PP 7. 5

DAMASK'D 1 FR 0.0001 REL FR 1 V 0 P
i have seen roses damask'd, red and white, | but SON 130. 5

DAME 36 FR 0.0040 REL FR 33 V 3 P
plead you to me, fair dame? ERR 2.02.147
no — which was the fairest dame | that liv'd, MND 5.01.293
why, how now, dame, whence grows this insolence? SHR 2.01. 23
unroosted | by thy dame partlet here. WT 2.03. 76
pantler, butler, cook, | both dame and servant; 4.04. 57
damn'd brawn shall play dame mortimer his wife. 1H4 2.04.110 P
how now, dame partlet the hen? 3.03. 52 P
my old dame will be undone now for one to do her 2H4 3.02.112 P
is this thy cunning, thou deceitful dame? 1H6 2.01. 50
am | to woo so fair a dame to be his wife | and 5.03.124
the chief perfections of that lovely dame | (had 5.05. 12
where henry and dame margaret kneel'd to me, 2H6 1.02. 39
presumptuous dame, ill–nurtur'd eleanor, | art 1.02. 42
dame eleanor gives gold to bring the witch; 1.02. 91
they, knowing dame eleanor's aspiring humor, 1.02. 97
do vex me half so much | as that proud dame, the 1.03. 76
she shall not strike dame eleanor unreveng'd. 1.03.147
stand forth, dame eleanor cobham, gloucester's 2.03. 1
why then dame /margaret was ne'er thy joy. 3.02. 79
for mocking marriage with a dame of france. 3H6 3.03.255
and father of that chaste dishonored dame, TIT 4.01. 90
"peace, tawny slave, half me and half thy dame. 5.01. 27
a pair of cursed hell–hounds and their dame. 5.02.144
bless you, fair dame! MAC 4.02. 65
behold yond simp'ring dame, | whose face between LR 4.06.118
shut your mouth, dame, | or with this paper 5.03.155
fare thee well, dame, what e'er becomes of me. ANT 4.04. 29
the beauty of this sinful dame | made many PER 1.ch. 31
but king nor peer to such a peerless dame. LUC 21
well was he welcom'd by the roman dame, | within 51
since thou couldst not defend thy loyal dame, 1034
the sire, the son, the dame, and daughter die. 1477
and softly cried, 'awake, thou roman dame, | and 1628
"no dame hereafter living | by my excuse shall 1714
loss, | o frowning fortune, cursed, fickle dame! PP 17.10
when as thine eye hath chose the dame, | and 18. 1

DAME'S 1 FR 0.0001 REL FR 0 V 1 P
master corporal captain, for my old dame's sake, 2H4 3.02.230 P

DAMES 10 FR 0.0011 REL FR 8 V 2 P
"a holy parcel of the fairest dames | that ever LLL 5.02.160
et non pour les dames de honneur d'user. H5 3.04. 54 P
les dames et demoiselles pour etre baisees 5.02.258 P
the grecian dames are sunburnt, and not worth TRO 1.03.282
our veil'd dames | commit the war of white and COR 2.01.215
dost overshine the gallant'st dames of rome, TIT 1.01.317
i would we had a thousand roman dames | at such 4.02. 41
we have willing dames enough; MAC 4.03. 73
and many worthy and chaste dames even thus, OTH 4.01. 46
whose men and dames so jetted and adorn'd, PER 1.04. 26

DAMM'D 3 FR 0.0003 REL FR 3 V 0 P
i'll have the current in this place damm'd up, 1H4 3.01.100
that the strait pass was damm'd | with dead men CYM 5.03. 11
head declin'd, and voice damm'd up with woe, LUC 1661

DAMN 18 FR 0.0020 REL FR 15 V 3 P
comes that the wenches say, "god damn me," ERR 4.03. 53 P
speak, would almost damn those ears | which, MV 1.01. 98
if i do not, damn me. AWW 4.01. 87
a pox damn you, you muddy rascal, is that all 2H4 2.04. 39 P
nay, rather damn them with | king cerberus, and 2.04.167
do you damn others, and let this damn you, | and TIM 4.03.165
do you damn others, and let this damn you, | and 4.03.165
look, with a spot i damn him. JC 4.01. 6
the devil damn thee black, thou cream–fac'd loon MAC 5.03. 11
with such spirits, | abuses me to damn me. HAM 2.02.603
if thou wilt needs damn thyself, do it a more OTH 1.03.353 P
damn them then, | if ever mortal eyes do see 3.03.398
damn her, lewd minx! 3.03.476
o, damn her, damn her! 3.03.476
o, damn her, damn her! 3.03.476
come swear it, damn thyself, | lest, being like 4.02. 35
perform't, or else we damn thee." ANT 1.01. 24
thou shalt not damn my hand. CYM 3.04. 74

DAMNABLE 11 FR 0.0012 REL FR 4 V 7 P
if it were damnable, he being so wise, | why MM 3.01.112
transport him in the mind he is | were damnable. 4.03. 69
o thou damnable fellow! 5.01.339 P
most profound in his art, and yet not damnable. AYL 5.02. 61 P
is it not meant damnable in us, to be trumpeters AWW 4.03. 26 P
damnable both–sides rogue! 4.03.222 P
of a fool, inconstant | and damnable ingrateful; WT 3.02.187
o, thou hast damnable iteration, and art indeed 1H4 1.02. 90 P
the deed you undertake is damnable. R3 1.04.192
why, thou damnable box of envy, thou, what means TRO 5.01. 25 P
murtherer, leave thy damnable faces and begin. HAM 3.02.253 P

DAMNABLY 1 FR 0.0001 REL FR 0 V 1 P
i have misus'd the king's press damnably. 1H4 4.02. 13 P

DAMNATION 14 FR 0.0015 REL FR 10 V 4 P
and our revolted wives share damnation together. WIV 3.02. 39 P
is that she will not add to her damnation | a ADO 4.01.172
'twere damnation | to think so base a thought; MV 2.07. 49
and wickedness is sin, and sin is damnation. AYL 3.02. 43 P
hand and seal | witness against us to damnation! JN 4.02.218
do botch and bungle up damnation | with patches, H5 2.02.115
master the author of the servant's damnation. 4.01.154 P
guilty of their damnation than he was before 4.01.174 P
ancient damnation! ROM 3.05.235
let molten coin be thy damnation, | thou disease TIM 3.01. 52
against | the deep damnation of his taking–off; MAC 1.07. 20
i dare damnation. HAM 4.05.134
for nothing canst thou to damnation add OTH 3.03.372
death and damnation! o! 3.03.396

/DAMN'D 2 FR 0.0002 REL FR 2 V 0 P
/a /blot, /damn'd /in /the /book /of /heaven. R2 4.01.236
/and /is't /not /to /be /damn'd, | /to /let HAM 5.02. 68

DAMN'D 66 FR 0.0074 REL FR 37 V 29 P
this damn'd witch sycorax, | for mischiefs TMP 1.02.263
it was a torment | to lay upon the damn'd, which 1.02.290
i am damn'd in hell for swearing to gentlemen my WIV 2.02. 10 P
what a damn'd epicurean rascal is this! 2.02.287 P
i think the devil will not have me damn'd, lest 5.05. 34 P
she is damn'd for it. MV 3.01. 31 P
a' good cheer, for truly i think you are damn'd. 3.05. 6 P
then i fear you are damn'd both by father and 3.05. 15 P
o, be thou damn'd, inexecrable dog! 4.01.128
then thou art damn'd. AYL 3.02. 35 P
truly, thou art damn'd, like an ill–roasted egg 3.02. 37 P
wilt thou rest damn'd? 3.02. 71 P
if thou beest not damn'd for this, the devil 3.02. 83 P
poor, though many of the rich are damn'd, but, AWW 1.03. 17 P
where dust and damn'd oblivion is the tomb | of 2.03.140
to do, and dares better be damn'd than to do't? 3.06. 89 P
i'd have seen him damn'd ere i'd have challeng'd TN 3.04.285 P
by some putter–on | that will be damn'd for't. WT 2.01.142
this deed of death, | art thou damn'd, hubert. JN 4.03.119
thou'rt damn'd as black — nay, nothing is so 4.03.121
thou art more deep damn'd than prince lucifer. 4.03.122
by some damn'd hand was robb'd and ta'en away. 5.01. 41
o villains, vipers, damn'd without redemption! R2 3.02.129
fitzwater, thou art damn'd to hell for this. 4.01. 43
i'll be damn'd for never a king's son in 1H4 1.02. 97 P
then art thou damn'd for keeping thy word with 1.02.120 P
else he had been damn'd for cozening the devil. 1.02.122 P
against that great magician, damn'd glendower, 1.03. 83
and that damn'd brawn shall play dame mortimer 2.04.110 P
i'll see thee damn'd ere i call thee coward, but 2.04.146 P
then many an old host that i know is damn'd. 2.04.472 P
let him be damn'd like the glutton! 2H4 1.02. 34 P
thou abominable damn'd cheater, art thou not 2.04.140 P
i'll see her damn'd first, to pluto's damned 2.04.156 P
her money, and whether she be damn'd for that, i 2.04.340 P
if damn'd commotion so /appear'd | in his true, 4.01. 36
thee what, thou damn'd tripe–visag'd rascal, and 5.04. 8 P
die and be damn'd! and figo for thy friendship! H5 3.06. 57
a warrant, but to be damn'd for killing him, R3 1.04.111 P
o thou damn'd cur! i shall — TRO 2.01. 85 P
reveal the damn'd contriver of this deed. TIT 4.01. 36
to her chance, and damn'd her loathed choice! 4.02. 78
that chiron and the damn'd demetrius | were they 5.03. 97
come, damn'd earth, | thou common whore of TIM 4.03. 42
ride, | and damn'd all those that trust them! MAC 4.01.139
of horrid hell can come a devil more damn'd | in 4.03. 56
out, damn'd spot! 5.01. 35 P
and damn'd be him that first cries, "hold, 5.08. 34
be thou a spirit of health, or goblin damn'd, HAM 1.04. 40
and most dear life | a damn'd defeat was made. 2.02.571
and that his soul may be as damn'd and black 3.03. 94
paddling in your neck with his damn'd fingers, 3.04.185
(a fellow almost damn'd in a fair wife), | that OTH 1.01. 21
damn'd as thou art, thou hast enchanted her, 1.02. 63
rot, and perish, and be damn'd to–night, for she 4.01.181 P
therefore be double damn'd: 4.02. 37
o damn'd iago! o inhuman dog! 5.01. 62
o, i were damn'd beneath all depth in hell | but 5.02.137
be a sin to make a true election, she is damn'd. CYM 1.02. 28 P
her malice with | a drug of such damn'd nature. 1.05. 36
should i (damn'd then) | slaver with lips as 1.06.104
o damn'd paper, | black as the ink that's on 3.02. 19
damn'd pisanio | hath with his forged letters 4.02.317
hath with his forged letters (damn'd pisanio!) 4.02.318
a sin in war, | damn'd in the first beginners!), 5.03. 37
and damn'd despair | swear nature's death for VEN 743

/DAMNED 2 FR 0.0002 REL FR 2 V 0 P
a /damned saint, an honorable villain! ROM 3.02. 79
fall'n in the practice of a /damned slave, OTH 5.02.292

DAMNED 42 FR 0.0047 REL FR 41 V 1 P
most damned angelo! MM 4.03.122
and art confederate with a damned pack | to make ERR 4.04.102
damned spirits all, | that in crossways and MND 3.02.382
what damned error but some sober brow | will MV 3.02. 78
where is that damned villain tranio, | that SHR 5.01.120
it is a damned and a bloody work, | the JN 4.03. 57
we will untread the steps of damned flight, 5.04. 52
see her damn'd first, to pluto's damned lake, by 2H4 2.04.156 P
o braggard vile and damned furious wight! H5 2.01. 60
myself, | prevented from a damned enterprise. 2.02.164
pax, and hanged must 'a be — | a damned death! 3.06. 41
thou damned and luxurious mountain goat, 4.04. 19
pucelle, that witch, that damned sorceress, 1H6 3.02. 38
die, damned wretch, the curse of her that bare 2H6 4.10. 77
too | thou mayst be damned for that wicked deed! R3 1.02.103
and frantic outrage, end thy damned spleen, | or 2.04. 64
a knot you are of damned blood–suckers. 3.03. 6
with devilish plots | of damned witchcraft, and 3.04. 61
thou protector of this damned strumpet, 3.04. 74
my damned son that thy two sweet sons smother'd. 4.04.134
here grow no damned drugs, here are no storms, TIT 1.01.154
like damned guilty deeds to sinners' minds: ROM 3.02.111
o friar, the damned use that word in hell; 3.03. 47
/lives, | by doing damned hate upon thyself? 3.03.118
fly, damned baseness, | to him that worships TIM 3.01. 47
whilst damned casca, like a cur, behind | strook JC 5.01. 43
and fortune, on his damned /quarrel smiling, MAC 1.02. 14
damned fact! 3.06. 10
be | a couch for luxury and damned incest. HAM 1.05. 83
o villain, villain, smiling, damned villain! 1.05.106
that lend a tyrannous and a damned light | to 2.02.460
it is a damned ghost that we have seen, | and my 3.02. 82
if damned custom have not brass'd it so | that 3.04. 37
here, thou incestious /murd'rous, damned dane, 5.02.325
to thy suggestion, plot, and damned practice; LR 2.01. 73
what damned minutes tells he o'er | who dotes, OTH 3.03.169
you told a lie, an odious, damned lie; 5.02.180
that same villain, | for 'tis a damned slave. 5.02.243
roderigo meant t' have sent this damned villain; 5.02.316
avaunt, thou damned door–keeper! PER 4.06.118
thou art the damned door–keeper to every 4.06.165
would have seem'd more black and damned here!" LC 54

DAMNED'ST 1 FR 0.0001 REL FR 1 V 0 P
the damned'st body to invest and cover | in MM 3.01. 95

DAMNS 1 FR 0.0001 REL FR 0 V 1 P
he knows is not to be done, damns himself to do, AWW 3.06. 88 P

DAMON 1 FR 0.0001 REL FR 1 V 0 P
for thou dost know, o damon dear, | this realm HAM 3.02.281

DAMOSELLA *(also damsel)*

DAMOSELLA 1 FR 0.0001 REL FR 0 V 1 P
but, damosella virgin, was this directed to you? LLL 4.02.127 P

DAMP 2 FR 0.0002 REL FR 2 V 0 P
ere twice in murk and occidental damp | moist AWW 2.01.163
the poisonous damp of night dispunge upon me, ANT 4.09. 13

DAMPS 1 FR 0.0001 REL FR 1 V 0 P

"with rotten damps ravish the morning air; LUC 778
DAM'S 1 FR 0.0001 REL FR 1 V 0 P
it would control my dam's god, setebos, | and TMP 1.02.373
DAMS 1 FR 0.0001 REL FR 1 V 0 P
no more dams i'll make for fish, | nor fetch in TMP 2.02.180
DAMSEL *(also damosella)*
DAMSEL 8 FR 0.0009 REL FR 4 V 4 P
taken with none, sir, i was taken with a damsel. LLL 1.01.290 P
well, it was proclaim'd damsel. 1.01.291 P
this was no damsel neither, sir, she was a 1.01.292 P
for this damsel, i must keep her at the park; 1.02.130 P
damsel, i'll have a bout with you again, | or 1H6 3.02. 56
damsel of france, i think i have you fast: 5.03. 30
dii boni! | a tinker, damsel? TNK 3.05. 84
alas, it was a spite | unto the silly damsel! PP 15. 8
DAMSONS 1 FR 0.0001 REL FR 1 V 0 P
alas, good master, my wife desired some damsons, 2H6 2.01.100
DAM'ST 1 FR 0.0001 REL FR 1 V 0 P
the more thou dam'st it up, the more it burns: TGV 2.07. 24
DAN 1 FR 0.0001 REL FR 1 V 0 P
this senior/–junior, giant–dwarf, dan cupid, LLL 3.01.180
DANC'D 8 FR 0.0009 REL FR 5 V 3 P
the gentleman that danc'd with her told her she ADO 2.01.237 P
but then there was a star danc'd, and under that 2.01.335 P
own report, sir, hath danc'd before the king; WT 4.04.338 P
i danc'd attendance on his will | till paris was 2H6 1.03.171
many a time he danc'd thee on his knee, | sung TIT 5.03.162
i learnt even now | of one i danc'd withal. ROM 1.05.143
and three better lads nev'r danc'd | under green TNK 2.03. 38
ye have danc'd rarely, wenches. 3.05.159
DANCE 69 FR 0.0078 REL FR 54 V 15 P
forsake unsounded deeps to dance on sands. TGV 3.02. 80
i'll make him dance. WIV 3.02. 90 P
our dance of custom, round about the oak | of 5.05. 75
meant to acknowledge it this night in a dance; ADO 1.02. 13 P
in every thing, and so dance out the answer. 2.01. 72 P
keep him out of my sight when the dance is done! 2.01.110 P
do you sing it, and i'll dance it. 3.04. 45 P
let's have a dance ere we are married, that we 5.04.118 P
did not i dance with you in brabant once? LLL 2.01.114
did not i dance with you in brabant once? 2.01.115
i'll make one in a dance, or so; 5.01.153
to the worthies, and let them dance the hay. 5.01.154
their purpose is to parley, to court, and dance, 5.02.122
but shall we dance, if they desire us to't? 5.02.145
no dance! 5.02.212
will you not dance? how come you thus estranged? 5.02.213
we will not dance. 5.02.219
if you deny to dance, let's hold more chat. 5.02.228
and i will wish thee never more to dance, | nor 5.02.400
to dance our ringlets to the whistling wind, MND 2.01. 86
if you will patiently dance in our round | and 2.01.140
dance in duke theseus' house triumphantly, | and 4.01. 89
or to hear a bergomask dance between two of our 5.01.353 P
after me, | sing, and dance it trippingly. 5.01.396
(as wealth is burthen of my wooing dance), | be SHR 1.02. 68
i must dance barefoot on her wedding–day, | and 2.01. 33
up, and no sword worn | but one to dance with! AWW 2.01. 33
and make you dance canary | with spritely fire 2.01. 74
but shall we make the welkin dance indeed? TN 2.03. 57 P
would sing her song and dance her turn; WT 4.04. 58
when you do dance, i wish you | a wave o' th' 4.04.140
but come, our dance, i pray. 4.04.153
you would never dance again after a tabor and 4.04.182 P
and they have a dance which the wenches say is a 4.04.327 P
no more | than a delightful measure or a dance, R2 1.03.291
rich men look sad, and ruffians dance and leap, 2.04. 12
madam, we'll dance. 3.04. 6
have you a ruffin that will swear, drink, dance, 2H4 4.05.124
but light payment, to dance out of your debt. ep 20 P
put me to verses, or to dance for your sake, H5 5.02.133 P
and sooner dance upon a bloody pole | than stand 2H6 4.01.127
rave, and fret, that i may sing and dance. 3H6 1.04. 91
i dance attendance here; R3 3.07. 56
favor, | to dance attendance on their lordships' H8 5.02. 31
there they are like to dance these three days; 5.03. 65 P
eyes flow with joy, hearts dance with comforts, COR 5.03. 99
and the shouting romans, | make the sun dance. 5.04. 51
nay, gentle romeo, we must have you dance. ROM 1.04. 13
which of you all | will now deny to dance? 1.05. 19
he that follows here, that would not dance? 1.05.132
fiddlestick, here's that shall make you dance. 3.01. 49 P
they dance? TIM 1.02.133
i should fear those that dance before me now 1.02.143
some to dance, some to make bonfires, each man OTH 2.02. 4 P
shall we dance now the egyptian bacchanals | and ANT 2.07.104
address'd, | will well become a soldier's dance. PER 2.03. 95
proclaim that i can sing, weave, sew, and dance, 4.06.183
she must see the duke, and she must dance too. TNK 2.03. 45
if we can get her dance, we are made again. 3.05. 74
shall we dance ho? 3.05. 81
that 'fore thy dignity will dance a morris. 3.05.108
long tool, | cum multis aliis that make a dance. 3.05.133
'twas an excellent dance, and for a preface, | i 3.05.150
and all we'll dance an antic 'fore the duke, 4.01. 75
vassal, and induce | stale gravity to dance; 5.01. 85
you never saw him dance? 5.02. 47
he'll dance the morris twenty mile an hour, 5.02. 51
and for my sake hath learn'd to sport and dance, VEN 105
dance on the sands, and yet no footing seen. 148
DANCER 2 FR 0.0002 REL FR 1 V 1 P
god match me with a good dancer! ADO 2.01.107 P
at philippi kept | his sword e'en like a dancer, ANT 3.11. 36
DANCES 11 FR 0.0012 REL FR 10 V 1 P
he capers, he dances, he has eyes of youth; WIV 3.02. 67 P
for revels, dances, masks, and merry hours LLL 4.03.376
lull'd in these flowers with dances and delight; MND 2.01.254
what masques, what dances shall we have, | to 5.01. 32
my heart dances, | but not for joy; WT 1.02.110
swain is this | which dances with your daughter? 4.04.167
she dances featly. 4.04.176
more dances my rapt heart | than when i first my COR 4.05.116
free of speech, sings, plays, and dances /well; OTH 3.03.185
and she dances | as goddess–like to her admired PER 5.ch. 3
he dances very finely, very comely, | and, for a TNK 5.02. 48
DANCETH 1 FR 0.0001 REL FR 1 V 0 P
time, | hell only danceth at so harsh a chime. PER 1.01. 85
/DANCING 1 FR 0.0001 REL FR 1 V 0 P
/the /emptier /ever /dancing /in /the /air, R2 4.01.186
DANCING 16 FR 0.0018 REL FR 13 V 3 P
there dancing up to th' chins, that the foul TMP 4.01.183
we'll have dancing afterward. ADO 5.04.120 P
in two words, the dancing horse will tell you. LLL 1.02. 53 P
i am for other than for dancing measures. AYL 5.04.193
in the tongues that i have in fencing, dancing, TN 1.03. 93 P
play | upon the dancing banners of the french, JN 2.01.308
more than my dancing soul doth celebrate | this R2 1.03. 91
therefore no dancing, girl, some other sport. 3.04. 9
a city on th' inconstant billows dancing; H5 3.pr. 15
i fear, with dancing is a little heated. H8 1.04.100
you have dancing shoes | with nimble soles, i ROM 1.04. 14
for you and i are past our dancing days. 1.05. 31
if you find him sad, | say i am dancing; ANT 1.03. 4
convey thy deity | aboard our dancing boat, make PER 3.01. 13
dancing as 'twere to th' music | his own hoofs TNK 5.04. 59
state | and situation with those dancing chips, SON 128.10
DANCING–RAPIER 1 FR 0.0001 REL FR 1 V 0 P
gave you a dancing–rapier by your side, | are TIT 2.01. 39
DANCING–SCHOOLS 1 FR 0.0001 REL FR 1 V 0 P
they bid us to the english dancing–schools, H5 3.05. 32
DANDLE 2 FR 0.0002 REL FR 2 V 0 P
she'll hamper thee, and dandle thee like a baby. 2H6 1.03.145
and let the emperor dandle him for his own. TIT 4.02.161
DANDLING 1 FR 0.0001 REL FR 1 V 0 P
like the froward infant still'd with dandling, VEN 562
DANE 9 FR 0.0010 REL FR 7 V 2 P
if there be here german, or dane, low dutch, AWW 4.01. 71
and liegemen to the dane. HAM 1.01. 15
you cannot speak of reason to the dane | and 1.02. 44
call thee hamlet, | king, father, royal dane. 1.04. 45
this is i, | hamlet the dane! 5.01.258
here, thou incestious /murd'rous, damned dane, 5.02.325
i am more an antique roman than a dane. 5.02.341
your dane, your german, and your swag–bellied OTH 2.03. 77 P
drinks you, with facility, your dane dead drunk; 2.03. 82 P
/DANGER 3 FR 0.0003 REL FR 2 V 1 P
/him /where /most /trade /of /danger /rang'd; 2H4 1.01.174
/kingdom /so /much /fear /and /danger /that /his LR 4.03. 5 P
/and /yet /it /is /danger | /to /make /him /even 4.07. 78
DANGER 106 FR 0.0119 REL FR 93 V 13 P
my master through his art foresees the danger TMP 2.01.297
trinculo, run into no further danger. 3.02. 68 P
and in thy danger | (if ever danger do environ TGV 1.01. 15
in thy danger | (if ever danger do environ thee) 1.01. 16
thyself) | regard thy danger, and along with me. 3.01.258
acquaint her with the danger of my state; MM 1.02.179
to save me from the danger that might come | if 4.03. 85
it, let the danger light | upon your charter and MV 4.01. 38
you stand within his danger, do you not? 4.01.180
incurr'd | the danger formerly by me rehears'd. 4.01.362
alas, what danger will it be to us, | maids as AYL 1.03.108
human as she is, and without any danger. 5.02. 68 P
doctrine, have left off | the danger to itself? AWW 1.03.242
the danger is in standing to't. 3.02. 41 P
whence honor but of danger wins a scar, | as oft 3.02.121
where death and danger dogs the heels of worth. 3.04. 15
were no further danger known but the modesty 3.05. 27 P
and trusty business in a main danger fail you. 3.06. 15 P
boy the count, have i run into this danger. 4.03.301 P
do adore thee so | that danger shall seem sport, TN 2.01. 48
i do not without danger walk these streets. 3.03. 25
love) | into the danger of this adverse town, 5.01. 84
(not meaning to partake with me in danger) 5.01. 87
honor, i | will stand betwixt you and danger. WT 2.02. 64
save him from danger, do him love and honor, 4.04.510
that she might no more be in danger of losing. 5.02. 78 P
much danger do i undergo for thee. JN 4.01.133
apt, liable to be employ'd in danger, | i 4.02.226
nor tempt the danger of my true defense, | lest 4.03. 84
even in the jaws of danger and of death. 5.02.116
strike up our drums, to find this danger out. 5.02.179
on some apparent danger seen in him | aim'd at R2 1.01. 13
must suffer, | and unavoided is the danger now, 2.01.268
or both | to worthy danger and deserved death. 5.01. 68
tell us how near is danger | that we may arm us 5.03. 47
i do see | danger and disobedience in thine eye. 1H4 1.03. 16
send danger from the east unto the west, | so 1.03.195
out of this nettle, danger, we pluck this flower 2.03. 10 P
done, | without the taste of danger and reproof. 3.01.173
but i must go and meet with danger there, | or 2H4 2.03. 48
and with what danger, near the heart of it. 3.01. 40
and inly ruminate | the morning's danger; H5 4.pr. 25
'tis true that we are in great danger, | the 4.01. 1
of death, | a terrible and unavoided danger; 1H6 4.05. 8
and made me climb, with danger of my life. 2H6 2.01.101
away, | but i in danger for the breach of law. 2.04. 66
so might your grace's person be in danger. 4.04. 45
but still, where danger was, still there i met 5.03. 11
thou draw not on thy danger and dishonor; 3H6 3.03. 75
doth cloud my joys with danger and with sorrow. 4.01. 74
what danger or what sorrow can befall thee | so 4.01. 76
are well foretold that danger lurks within. 4.07. 12
o, full of danger is the duke of gloucester, R3 2.03. 27
instinct men's minds mistrust | ensuing danger; 2.03. 43
to shun the danger that his soul divines. 3.02. 18
a man, | daring an opposite to every danger. 5.04. 3
all in uproar, | and danger serves among them. H8 1.02. 37
would prove perfidious, | to the king's danger. 1.02.157
i weigh'd the danger which my realms stood in 2.04.198
you take a precipit for no leap of danger, | and 5.01.139
how rank soever rounded in with danger. TRO 1.03.196
seals a commission to a blank of danger, | and 3.03.231
and danger, like an ague, subtly taints | even 3.03.232
and i'll grow friend with danger. 4.04. 70
to let him seek danger where he was like to find COR 1.03. 13 P
to eject him hence | were but one danger, and to 3.01.286
we'll deliver you | of your great danger. 5.06. 14
the great danger | which this man's life did owe 5.06.136
and the neglecting it | may do much danger. ROM 5.02. 20
to his heart, | to bring it into danger. TIM 3.05. 35
when they are in great danger, i recover them. JC 1.01. 24 P
in him | that at his will he may do danger with. 2.01. 17
danger knows full well | that caesar is more 2.02. 44
malice | remains in danger of her former tooth. MAC 3.02. 15
i doubt some danger does approach you nearly. 4.02. 67
out of the shot and danger of desire. HAM 1.03. 35
hatch and the disclose | will be some danger: 3.01.167
thou find'st to be too busy is some danger. 3.04. 33
to all that fortune, death, and danger dare, 4.04. 52
that we can let our beard be shook with danger 4.07. 32
your honor, and to no other pretense of danger. LR 1.02. 88 P
were in 's heels, were't not in danger of kibes? 1.05. 9 P
sith that both charge and danger | speak 'gainst 2.04.239
you will come to me | (for now i spy a danger), 2.04.247
and gain | to wake and wage a danger profitless. OTH 1.03. 30
worthy othello, i am hurt to danger. 2.03.197
going on, | the sides o' th' world may danger. ANT 1.02.192
you were wrong led | and we in negligent danger. 3.06. 81
is | no danger in what show of death it makes, CYM 1.05. 40
a pain that only seems to seek out danger | i' 3.03. 50
by this | may prove his travel, not her danger. 3.05.103
e'er it be, | what pain it cost, what danger. 3.06. 80
nor seek for danger | where there's no profit. 4.02.162
a madness, of which her life's in danger. 4.03. 3
dreading that her purpose | was of more danger, 5.05.254
received | the danger of the task you undertake. PER 1.01. 2
by flight i'll shun the danger which i fear. 1.01.142
and danger, which i fear'd, is at antioch, 1.02. 7
any profit, | or my life imply her any danger? 4.01. 81
nor the commodity wages not with the danger; 4.02. 31 P
able once again | to out–dure danger. TNK 3.06. 10
or what great danger dwells upon my suit? VEN 206
come not within his danger by thy will, | they 639
danger deviseth shifts, wit waits on fear. 690
the path is smooth that leadeth on to danger. 788
such danger to resistance did belong | that LUC 1265
DANGEROUS 105 FR 0.0118 REL FR 88 V 17 P
and, for the ways are dangerous to pass, | i do TGV 4.03. 24
what dangerous action, stood it next to death, 5.04. 41
for the revolt of mine is dangerous — that is WIV 1.03.102 P
most dangerous | is that temptation that doth MM 2.02.180
as dangerous to be ag'd in any kind of course, 3.02.224 P
do me both a present and a dangerous courtesy. 4.02.161 P
save that his riotous youth with dangerous sense 4.04. 29
recover'd the most dangerous piece of lechery ADO 3.03.167 P
vice, and they are dangerous weapons for maids. 5.02. 21 P
a dangerous law against gentility. LLL 1.01.128
a dangerous rhyme, master, against the reason of 1.02.107 P
and not bethink me straight of dangerous rocks, MV 1.01. 31
they call the place, a very dangerous flat, and 3.01. 5 P
but the guiled shore | to a most dangerous sea; 3.02. 98
and by all pretty oaths that are not dangerous, AYL 4.01.190 P
and my state that way is dangerous, since i AWW 2.05. 12 P
young count to be a dangerous and lascivious boy 4.03.220 P
prove | (as /ornament oft does) too dangerous. WT 1.02.158
opinion, and betimes, | for 'tis most dangerous. 1.02.298
these dangerous, unsafe lunes i' th' king, 2.02. 28
to break into this dangerous argument: JN 4.02. 54
to know the meaning | of dangerous majesty, when 4.02.213
that he is a traitor, foul and dangerous, | to R2 1.03. 39
that they have let the dangerous enemy | measure 3.02.124
he makes upon my land | is dangerous treason. 3.03. 93
my dangerous cousin, let your mother in, | i 5.03. 81
two of the dangerous consorted traitors | that 5.06. 15
i'll read you matter deep and dangerous, | as 1H4 1.03.190
"the purpose you undertake is dangerous" — why, 2.03. 7 P
'tis dangerous to take a cold, to sleep, to 2.03. 8 P
"the purpose you undertake is dangerous, the 2.03. 11 P
it meet | to lay so dangerous and dear a trust 4.01. 34
by unkind usage, dangerous countenance, | and 5.01. 69
knew that we ventured on such dangerous seas 2H4 1.01.181
there is not a dangerous action can peep out his 1.02.212 P
whose dangerous eyes may well be charm'd asleep 4.02. 39
at the discovery of most dangerous treason H5 2.02.162
this dangerous treason lurking in our way | to 2.02.186
defer no time, delays have dangerous ends, 1H6 3.02. 33
sacrament | to rive their dangerous artillery 4.02. 29
prosper our colors in this dangerous fight! 4.02. 56
gloss, | he will be found a dangerous protector. 2H6 1.01.164
heart, | pernicious protector, dangerous peer, 2.01. 21
do you as i do in these dangerous days: 2.02. 69
what's more dangerous than this fond affiance! 3.01. 74
ah, gracious lord, these days are dangerous: 3.01.142
is either slain or wounded dangerous; 3H6 1.01. 11
'tis the more honor, because more dangerous. 4.03. 15
i like it better than a dangerous honor. 4.03. 17
plots have i laid, inductions dangerous, | by R3 1.01. 32
out of towns and cities for a dangerous thing, 1.04.142 P
which would be so much the more dangerous, | by 2.02.126
those uncles which you want were dangerous; 3.01. 12
his ancient knot of dangerous adversaries 3.01.182
the dangerous and unsuspected hastings. 3.05. 23
flag | to be the aim of every dangerous shot; 4.04. 89
and dangerous success of bloody wars, | as i 4.04.237
so thrive i in my dangerous affairs | of hostile 4.04.398
note | this dangerous conception in this point, H8 1.02.139
and that 'twas dangerous for /him | to ruminate 1.02.179
with new opinions, | divers and dangerous; 5.02. 53
we first put this dangerous stone a–rolling, 5.02.139
two traded pilots 'twixt the dangerous /shores TRO 2.02. 64
manly as hector, but more dangerous, | for 4.05.104
this place is dangerous, | the time right deadly 5.02. 38
drop is rather physical | than dangerous to me. COR 1.05. 19
it will be dangerous to go on — no further. 3.01. 26
if none, awake | your dangerous lenity. 3.01. 99
to jump a body with a dangerous physic | that's 3.01.154
not what is dangerous present, but the loss | of 3.02. 71
thy pride than fear | thy dangerous stoutness; 3.02.127
and think you not how dangerous | it is to jet TIT 2.01. 63
in dangerous wars whilst you securely slept; 3.01. 3
with words more sweet, and yet more dangerous, 4.04. 90
her father counts it dangerous | that she do ROM 4.01. 9
they should spy my windpipe's dangerous notes: TIM 1.02. 51
us, | his days are foul and his drink dangerous. 3.05. 73
it almost turns my dangerous nature wild. 4.03.492
to all the rout, then hold me dangerous. JC 1.02. 78
such men are dangerous. 1.02.195
fear him not, caesar, he's not dangerous, | he 1.02.196
and therefore are they very dangerous. 1.02.210
well | that caesar is more dangerous than he. 2.02. 45
why, and wherein, caesar was dangerous. 3.01.222
here is a mourning rome, a dangerous rome, | no 3.01.288
to do good sometime | accounted dangerous folly. MAC 4.02. 77

of quiet | with turbulent and dangerous lunacy? HAM 3.01. 4
how dangerous is it that this man goes loose! 4.03. 2
dangerous conjectures in ill–breeding minds. 4.05. 15
rash, | yet have i in me something dangerous, 5.01.262
'tis dangerous when the baser nature comes 5.02. 60
this night — 'tis dangerous to be spoken; LR 3.03. 10 P
the ways are dangerous. 4.05. 17
for i have lost him on a dangerous sea. OTH 2.01. 46
dangerous conceits are in their natures poisons, 3.03.326
and men in dangerous bonds pray not alike; CYM 3.02. 37
dangerous fellow, hence! 5.05.237
for mine own part unfold a dangerous speech, 5.05.313
with golden fruit, but dangerous to be touch'd; PER 1.01. 28
within our law, | as dangerous as the rest. 1.01. 89
'tis dangerous. 1.03. 3 P
how dangerous, if we will keep our honors, | it TNK 1.02. 37
cabin'd | in many as dangerous as poor a corner, 1.03. 36
and, for you are dangerous, | i'll clap more 2.02.270
to drive infection from the dangerous year! VEN 508
DANGEROUSLY 3 FR 0.0003 REL FR 3 V 0 P
the streets | do prophesy upon it dangerously. JN 4.02.186
have practic'd dangerously against your state, 2H6 2.01.167
most dangerously you have with him prevail'd, COR 5.03.188
DANGER'S 1 FR 0.0001 REL FR 1 V 0 P
your danger's ours. CYM 5.05.314
DANGERS 22 FR 0.0024 REL FR 22 V 0 P
i see thy age and dangers make thee dote. ERR 5.01.330
consider little | what dangers, by his highness' WT 5.01. 27
among the thorns and dangers of this world. JN 4.03.141
you pluck a thousand dangers on your head, | you R2 2.01.205
boldly did outdare | the dangers of the time. 1H4 5.01. 41
the dangers of the days but newly gone, | whose 2H4 4.01. 80
made me collect these dangers in the duke. 2H6 3.01. 35
soul, and there scatters | dangers, doubts, H8 2.02. 27
my lord, to dangers | as infinite as imminent! TRO 4.04. 68
that gods and men | address their dangers in. 5.10. 14
the extreme dangers, and the drops of blood COR 4.05. 69
a hand that warded him | from thousand dangers, TIT 3.01.195
into what dangers would you lead me, cassius, JC 1.02. 63
i am arm'd, | and dangers are to me indifferent. 1.03.115
day is gone, | clouds, dews, and dangers come; 5.03. 64
she lov'd me for the dangers i had pass'd, | and OTH 1.03.167
on your love, | shar'd dangers with you — 3.04. 95
all great fears, which now import their dangers, ANT 2.02.132
by all our friendship, sir, by all our dangers, TNK 3.06.202
shows him hardy, fearless, proud of dangers. 4.02. 80
the sundry dangers of his will's obtaining; LUC 128
the dangers of his loathsome enterprise; 184
DANGLE'T 1 FR 0.0001 REL FR 1 V 0 P
to dangle't in my hand, or to go tiptoe | before TNK 1.02. 57
D'ANGLETERRE 3 FR 0.0003 REL FR 0 V 3 P
mots aussi droit que les natifs d'angleterre. H5 3.04. 38 P
et tres /distingue seigneur d'angleterre. 4.04. 57 P
notre tres cher fils henri, roi d'angleterre, 5.02.340 P
DANGLING 1 FR 0.0001 REL FR 1 V 0 P
go bind thou up young dangling apricocks, R2 3.04. 29
D'ANGLOIS 1 FR 0.0001 REL FR 0 V 1 P
j'ai gagne deux mots d'anglois vitement. H5 3.04. 14 P
DANG'ROUS 2 FR 0.0002 REL FR 2 V 0 P
and speak /off half a dozen dang'rous words, ADO 5.01. 97
thou to show thy dang'rous brow by night, | when JC 2.01. 78
DANIEL 6 FR 0.0006 REL FR 6 V 0 P
a daniel come to judgment! MV 4.01.223
yea, a daniel! 4.01.223
a second daniel! 4.01.333
a daniel, jew! 4.01.333
a daniel, still say i, a second daniel! 4.01.340
a daniel, still say i, a second daniel! 4.01.340
DANISH 5 FR 0.0005 REL FR 4 V 1 P
looks raw and red | after the danish sword, and HAM 4.03. 61
go, captain, from me greet the danish king. 4.04. 1
o, this is counter, you false danish dogs! 4.05.111
which was the model of that danish seal; 5.02. 50
that's the french bet against the danish. 5.02.163 P
DANK* *(also tank, thank)*
DANK* 6 FR 0.0006 REL FR 4 V 2 P
by gar, me dank you vor dat. WIV 2.03. 90 P
sleeping sound, | on the dank and dirty ground. MND 2.02. 75
peas and beans are as dank here as a dog, and 1H4 2.01. 8 P
the day to cheer and night's dank dew to dry, ROM 2.03. 6
and suck up the humors | of the dank morning? JC 2.01.263
as the dank earth weeps at thy languishment, LUC 1130
DANKISH 1 FR 0.0001 REL FR 1 V 0 P
and in a dark and dankish vault at home | there ERR 5.01.248
DANSKERS 1 FR 0.0001 REL FR 1 V 0 P
inquire me first what danskers are in paris, HAM 2.01. 7
DAPHNE 2 FR 0.0002 REL FR 2 V 0 P
apollo flies, and daphne holds the chase; MND 2.01.231
or daphne roaming through a thorny wood, SHR in.2. 57
DAPHNE'S 1 FR 0.0001 REL FR 1 V 0 P
tell me, apollo, for thy daphne's love, | what TRO 1.01. 98
DAPPLED 1 FR 0.0001 REL FR 1 V 0 P
and yet it irks me the poor dappled fools, AYL 2.01. 22
DAPPLES 1 FR 0.0001 REL FR 1 V 0 P
dapples the drowsy east with spots of grey. ADO 5.03. 27
D'APPRENDRE 1 FR 0.0001 REL FR 0 V 1 P
je ne doute point d'apprendre, par la grace de H5 3.04. 40 P
DAR'D 9 FR 0.0010 REL FR 8 V 1 P
those many had not dar'd to do that evil | if MM 2.02. 91
then | you have not dar'd to break the holy seal WT 3.02.129
dar'd once to touch a dust of england's ground? R2 2.03. 91
why have they dar'd to march | so many miles 2.03. 92
the flat unraised spirits that hath dar'd | on H5 pr 9
am i dar'd and bearded to my face? 1H6 1.03. 45
the letter's master, how he dares, being dar'd. ROM 2.04. 12 P
by a most emulate pride, | dar'd to the combat; HAM 1.01. 84
so hath my lord dar'd him to single fight. ANT 3.07. 30
/DARDAN 2 FR 0.0002 REL FR 2 V 0 P
/now /on /dardan /plains | /the /fresh /and /yet TRO pr 13
/dardan /and /timbria, /helias, /chetas, /troien pr 16
DARDAN 1 FR 0.0001 REL FR 1 V 0 P
and from the strond of dardan, where they fought LUC 1436
DARDANIAN 1 FR 0.0001 REL FR 1 V 0 P
the rest aloof are the dardanian wives, | with MV 3.02. 58
DARDANIUS 2 FR 0.0002 REL FR 2 V 0 P
hark thee, dardanius. JC 5.05. 8
o dardanius! 5.05. 9

DARE* *(also dure)*
/DARE* 2 FR 0.0002 REL FR 1 V 1 P
//goose–quills /and /dare /scarce /come /thither HAM 2.02.344 P
/if /on /my /credit /you /dare /build /so /far LR 3.01. 35
DARE* 226 FR 0.0255 REL FR 187 V 39 P
that dare not offer | what i desire to give; TMP 3.01. 77
i know thou dar'st, | but this thing dare not — 3.02. 55
dare you presume to harbor wanton lines? TGV 1.02. 42
and, proteus, we dare trust you in this kind, 3.02. 56
now i dare not say | i have one friend alive; 5.04. 65
i dare thee but to breathe upon my love. 5.04.131
i dare be bold | with our discourse to make your 5.04.162
i dare not for my head fill my belly; MM 4.03.153 P
dare no more stretch this finger of mine than he 5.01.314
this finger of mine than he | dare rack his own. 5.01.315
i dare, and do defy thee for a villain. ERR 5.01. 32
i dare swear he is no hypocrite, but prays from ADO 1.01.151 P
but who dare tell her so? 3.01. 74
and the little hangman dare not shoot at him. 3.02. 11 P
if you dare not trust that you see, confess not 3.02.119 P
i dare make his answer, none. 4.01. 18 P
o, what men dare do! 4.01. 19 P
you dare easier be friends with me than fight 4.01.298 P
lord, | i'll prove it on his body, if he dare, 5.01. 74
that dare as well answer a man indeed | as i 5.01. 89
indeed | as i dare take a serpent by the tongue. 5.01. 90
i will make it good how you dare, with what you 5.01.146 P
make it good how you dare, with what you dare, 5.01.147 P
you dare, with what you dare, and when you dare. 5.01.147 P
your mistresses dare never come in rain, | for LLL 4.03.266
i dare not call them fools; 5.02.371
and never dare misfortune cross her foot, MV 2.04. 35
who dare scarce show his head on the rialto; 3.01. 45 P
i dare be sworn for him he would not leave it, 5.01.172
i dare be bound again, | my soul upon the 5.01.251
and here she stands, touch her whoever dare, SHR 3.02.233
no, no, forsooth, i dare not for my life. 4.03. 1
i dare assure you, sir, 'tis almost two, | and 4.03.189
i dare swear this is the right vincentio. 5.01. 99 P
nay, i dare not swear it. 5.01.102 P
she thought, i dare vow for her, they touch'd AWW 1.03.109 P
amaz'd me more | than i dare blame my weakness. 2.01. 85
that dare leave two together, fare you well. 2.01. 98
i dare not say i take you, but i give | me and 2.03.102
what i dare too well do, i dare not do. 2.03.200 P
what i dare too well do, i dare not do. 2.03.200 P
of the wealth i owe, | nor dare i say 'tis mine; 2.05. 80
therefore dare not | say what i think of it, 3.01. 13
and great ones i dare not give; 4.01. 40 P
half of the which dare not shake the snow from 4.03.168 P
"o no, no, no, no, you dare not." TN 2.03.112
i dare lay any money 'twill be nothing yet. 3.04.396 P
i dare not know, my lord. WT 1.02.376
how, dare not? 1.02.377
do you know, and dare not? 1.02.377
know, you must, | and cannot say you dare not. 1.02.380
if therefore you dare trust my honesty, | that 1.02.434
if you seek to prove, | i dare not stand by; 1.02.444
i dare my life lay down — and will do't, sir, 2.01.130
i dare be sworn. 2.02. 27
divorce, young sir, | whom son i dare not call. 4.04.418
nor think, | nor dare to know that which i know. 4.04.452
but yet i dare defend | my innocent life against JN 4.03. 88
but i dare not say | how near the tidings of our R2 2.01.271
how dare thy joints forget | to pay their aweful 3.03. 75
if i dare eat, or drink, or breathe, or live, 4.01. 73
or live, | i dare meet surrey in a wilderness, 4.01. 74
my lord, i dare not. 5.05.100
so strongly that they dare not meet each other; 1H4 2.02.106
as thou art but man, i dare, but as thou art 3.03.146 P
a larger dare to our great enterprise, | than if 4.01. 78
and i dare well maintain it with my life, | if 4.03. 9
and, prince of wales, so dare we venture thee, 5.01.101
unless a brother should a brother dare | to 5.02. 53
ragged'st hour that time and spite dare bring 2H4 1.01.151
i hear for certain and dare speak the truth, 1.01.188
i dare say my cousin william is become a good 3.02. 9 P
and i dare swear you borrow not that face | of 5.02. 28
i dare not fight, but i will wink and hold out H5 2.01. 7 P
you must not dare, for shame, to talk of mercy, 2.02. 81
a valiant flea that dare eat his breakfast on 3.07.146 P
i dare say you love him not so ill to wish him 4.01.124 P
for our approach shall so much dare the field, 4.02. 36
if alive and ever dare to challenge this glove, 4.07.127 P
and dare not avouch in your deeds any of your 5.01. 72 P
by which honor i dare not swear thou lovest me, 5.02.222 P
we'll try what these dastard frenchmen dare. 1H6 1.04.111
dare no man answer in a case of truth? 2.04. 2
but dare maintain the party of the truth, 2.04. 32
where false plantagenet dare not be seen. 2.04. 74
i dare say | this quarrel will drink blood 2.04.132
an uproar, i dare warrant, | begun through 3.01. 74
do what ye dare, we are as resolute. 3.01. 91
dare ye come forth and meet us in the field? 3.02. 61
and dare not take up arms like gentlemen. 3.02. 70
sir, as well as you dare patronage | the envious 3.04. 32
i dare presume, sweet prince, he thought no harm 4.01.179
fain would i woo her, yet i dare not speak: 5.03. 65
ready to starve, and dare not touch his own. 2H6 1.01.229
i dare not say from the rich cardinal | and from 1.02. 94
dares not warwick, if false suffolk dare him? 3.02.203
though suffolk dare him twenty thousand times. 3.02.206
dare you be so bold? 3.02.238
more can i bear than you dare execute. 4.01.130
and such | as would (but that they dare not) 4.02.187
dare any be so bold to sound retreat or parley 4.08. 4 P
here they be that dare and will disturb thee. 4.08. 6
or dare to bring thy force so near the court. 5.01. 22
i dare your quenchless fury to more rage. 3H6 1.04. 28
how now, long–tongu'd warwick, dare you speak? 2.02.102
dare he presume to scorn us in this manner? 3.03.178
(without your special pardon) | dare not relate. 4.01. 88
wrens make prey where eagles dare not perch. R3 1.03. 70
i dare adventure to be sent to th' tow'r. 1.03.115
have mercies | more than i dare make faults. H8 2.01. 71
me | and dare be bold to weep for buckingham, 2.01. 72
all that dare | look into these affairs see this 2.02. 39
how dare you thrust yourselves | into my private 2.02. 64

that any englishman dare give me counsel? 3.01. 84
a woman (i dare say without vainglory) | never 3.01.127
i dare not make myself so guilty | to give up 3.01.139
who dare cross 'em, | bearing the king's will 3.02.234
officious lords, | i dare and must deny it. 3.02.238
dare mate a sounder man than surrey can be, 3.02.274
forward, | and dare us with his cap, like larks. 3.02.282
speak on, sir, | i dare your worst objections. 3.02.307
far | than my weak–hearted enemies dare offer. 3.02.390
to heaven, is all | i dare now call mine own. 3.02.454
of which there is not one, i dare avow | (and 4.02.142
and who dare speak | one syllable against him? 5.01. 38
there are that dare, and i myself have ventur'd 5.01. 40
crooked malice nourishment | dare bite the best. 5.02. 80
and, by that virtue, no man dare accuse you. 5.02. 85
you shall know many dare accuse you boldly, 5.02. 91
how many shallow bauble boats dare sail | upon TRO 1.03. 35
and dare avow her beauty and her worth | in 1.03.271
stomach, and such a one that dare | maintain — 2.01.125
spirit on our party | without a heart to dare, 2.02.157
we dare not move the question of our place, | or 2.03. 82
but dare all imminence that gods and men 5.10. 13
plains, | let titan rise as early as he dare, 5.10. 25
to you, yet dare i never | deny your asking. COR 1.06. 64
(which, i dare vouch, is more than that he hath, 3.01.298
it cannot be | the volsces dare break with us. 4.06. 49
for i dare so far free him — made him fear'd, 4.07. 47
i dare be sworn you were; 5.03.194
but on mine honor dare i undertake | for good TIT 1.01.436
full well shalt thou perceive how much i dare. 2.01. 44
so near the emperor's palace dare ye draw, | and 2.01. 46
nay, as they dare. ROM 1.01. 42 P
warrant you, i dare draw as soon as another man, 2.04.159 P
then love–devouring death do what he dare, | it 2.06. 7
i dare not, sir. 5.03.131
come go, good juliet, i dare no longer stay. 5.03.159
that game, we must not dare | to imitate them; TIM 1.02. 12
i wonder men dare trust themselves with men. 1.02. 43
do you dare our anger? 3.05. 95
bed | to dare the vile contagion of the night, JC 2.01.265
and that i dare not, falser: 2.02. 63
if you dare fight to–day, come to the field; 5.01. 65
i dare assure thee that no enemy | shall ever 5.04. 21
letting "i dare not" wait upon "i would," | like MAC 1.07. 44
i dare do all that may become a man; 1.07. 46
look on't again i dare not. 2.02. 49
that dare look on that | which might appall the 3.04. 58
what man dare, i dare. 3.04. 98
what man dare, i dare. 3.04. 98
and dare me to the desert with thy sword; 3.04.103
how did you dare | to trade and traffic with 3.05. 3
i dare not speak much further, | but cruel are 4.02. 17
i dare abide no longer. 4.02. 73
basis sure, | for goodness dare not check thee; 4.03. 33
i think, but dare not speak. 5.01. 79
the poor heart would fain deny, and dare not. 5.03. 28
and then they say no spirit dare stir abroad, HAM 1.01.161
to all that fortune, death, and danger dare, 4.04. 52
i dare damnation. 4.05.134
i dare not confess that, lest i should compare 5.02.138 P
i dare not drink yet, madam; by and by. 5.02.293
i dare pawn down my life for him that he hath LR 1.02. 85 P
i dare avouch it, sir. 2.04.237
and dare upon the warrant of my note | commend a 3.01. 18
hear | (if you dare venture in your own behalf) 4.02. 20
and i dare think he'll prove to desdemona | a OTH 2.01.290
and dare not task my weakness with any more. 2.03. 42 P
i dare be sworn i think that he is honest. 3.03.125
the pranks | they dare not show their husbands; 3.03.203
i dare not say he lies any where. 3.04. 3 P
and more i will | than for myself i dare. 3.04.131
unproper beds | which they dare swear peculiar; 4.01. 69
if you dare do yourself a profit and a right. 4.02.232 P
pompeius | /hath given the dare to caesar, and ANT 1.02.184
herod of jewry dare not look upon you | but when 3.03. 3
i dare him therefore | to lay his gay 3.13. 25
if that the former dare but what it can, | no 3.13. 80
grimly, | and dare not speak their knowledge. 4.12. 6
i dare not, dear — | dear my lord, pardon — i 4.15. 21
dear — | dear my lord, pardon — i dare not, 4.15. 22
house of death | ere death dare come to us? 4.15. 82
i dare lay mine honor | he will remain so. CYM 1.01.174
i dare thereupon pawn the moi'ty of my estate to 1.04.108 P
i dare you to this match: 1.04.145 P
they dare not fight with me because of the queen 2.01. 19 P
the king, he rages, none | dare come about him. 3.05. 68
i dare not call; 3.06. 19
i dare speak it to myself, for it is not 4.01. 7 P
i dare be bound he's true and shall perform 4.03. 18
how dare you ghosts | accuse the thunderer, 5.04. 94
from henceforth i'll not dare | to ask you any TNK 1.01.203
of whose success i dare not | make any timorous 1.03. 2
no hard oppressor | dare take this from us; 2.02. 85
her, | i must, i ought to do so, and i dare — 2.02.205
if he dare make himself a worthy lover, | yet in 2.02.251
i'll be hang'd though, | if he dare venture. 2.03. 72
i dare not praise | my feat in horsemanship, yet 2.05. 12
i dare assure you | you'll find a loving 2.05. 56
you have been well advertis'd | how much i dare; 3.01. 59
for none but such dare die in these just trials. 3.06.105
i dare as well | die as discourse or sleep. 3.06.128
as i dare kill this cousin that denies it, | so 3.06.166
for that love must and dare kill this cousin, 3.06.262
we dare not fail thee, theseus. 3.06.305
love, and what young maid dare cross 'em? 4.02. 40
i dare say, many a better, to prolong | your old ep 16
or at the roe which no encounter dare; VEN 676
"more i could tell, but more i dare not say, 805
they basely fly, and dare not stay the field. 894
then may i dare to boast how i do love thee, SON 26.13
nor dare i chide the world–without–end hour, 57. 5
nor dare i question with my jealious thought 57. 9
to say they err i dare not be so bold, 131. 7
DAREFUL 1 FR 0.0001 REL FR 1 V 0 P
we might have met them dareful, beard to beard, MAC 5.05. 6
/DARES 1 FR 0.0001 REL FR 1 V 0 P
/why /she /dares /not /come /over /to /thee." LR 3.06. 28
DARES 52 FR 0.0058 REL FR 45 V 7 P

that he dares in this manner assay me? WIV 2.01. 25 P
the folly of my soul dares not present itself; 2.02.244 P
in their so sacred paths he dares to tread | in 4.04. 60
yet reason dares her no, | for my authority MM 4.04. 25
— be to me, and every man that dares not fight! LLL 1.01.227 P
eye | dares look upon the heaven of her brow, 4.03.223
a man doth mark, | and dares not answer nay — MND 3.01.133
he goes before me and still dares me on. 3.02.413
he dares not come there for the candle; 5.01.249 P
to do, and dares better be damn'd than to do't? AWW 3.06. 88 P
that for his love dares yet do more | than you TN 3.04.316
if she dares trust me with her little babe, WT 2.02. 35
yet that dares | less appear so, in comforting 2.03. 55
that come before the swallow dares, and take 4.04.119
who dares not stir by day must walk by night, JN 1.01.172
who lives and dares but say thou didst not well 1.01.271
and dares him to set forward to the fight. R2 1.03.109
how dares thy harsh rude tongue sound this 3.04. 74
what my tongue dares not, that my heart shall 5.05. 97
bold, | that dares do justice on my proper son; 2H4 5.02.109
what dares not warwick, if false suffolk dare 2H6 3.02.203
he dares not calm his contumelious spirit, | nor 3.02.204
dares stir a wing if warwick shake his bells. 3H6 1.01. 47
i'll plant plantagenet, root him up who dares. 1.01. 48
yes, warwick, edward dares, and leads the way. 5.01.112
let me see the proudest | he, that dares most, H8 5.02.166
grieve his spirit that dares not challenge it. TRO 5.02. 94
what dares the slave | come hither, cover'd with ROM 1.05. 55
and what love can do, that dares love attempt; 2.02. 68
will answer the letter's master, how he dares, 2.04. 12 P
that he dares ne'er come back to challenge you; 3.05.214
who then dares to be half so kind again? TIM 4.02. 40
who dares? 4.03. 13
who dares | in purity of manhood stand upright 4.03. 13
who dares /do more is none. MAC 1.07. 47
who dares receive it other, | as we shall make 1.07. 77
'tis much he dares, | and, to that dauntless 3.01. 50
terror of his spirit | that dares not undertake; LR 4.02. 13
he that dares approach: 5.03. 99
for that he dares us to't. ANT 3.07. 29
whipt with rods, dares me to personal combat, 4.01. 3
or a debtor that not dares | to stride a limit. CYM 3.03. 34
and the fellow dares not deceive me. 4.01. 25 P
who dares not stand his foe, i'll be his friend; 5.03. 60
and if jove stray, who dares say jove doth ill? PER 1.01.104
how dares the plants look up to heaven, from 1.02. 55
good dares not. TNK 1.02. 71
dares any | so noble bear a guilty business? 3.01. 89
i am, and, which is more, dares think her his. 3.06.149
who is so faint that dares not be so bold | to VEN 401
she dares not look, yet, winking, there appears LUC 458
she dares not thereof make discovery, | lest he 1314

DAREST 6 FR 0.0006 REL FR 3 V 3 P
darest with thy frozen admonition | make pale R2 2.01.117
pawn, | engage it to the trial, if thou darest. 4.01. 56
if thou darest not stand for ten shillings. 1H4 1.02.141 P
darest thou be so valiant as to play the coward 2.04. 46 P
darest thou be as good as thy word now? 3.03.143 P
and if thou darest, i'll give thee remedy. ROM 4.01. 76

/DARING 1 FR 0.0001 REL FR 1 V 0 P
/neighing /coursers /daring /of /the /spur, 2H4 4.01.117

DARING 14 FR 0.0015 REL FR 13 V 1 P
car, | and with thy daring folly burn the world? TGV 3.01.155
outbrave the heart most daring on the earth, MV 2.01. 28
creatures, not daring the reports of my tongue. AWW 4.01. 30 P
i know your daring tongue | scorns to unsay what R2 4.01. 8
more daring or more bold, is now alive | to 1H4 5.01. 91
they that of late were daring with their scoffs 1H6 3.02.113
for daring to affy a mighty lord | unto the 2H6 4.01. 80
thy prime of manhood daring, bold, and venturous R3 4.04.171
a man, | daring an opposite to every danger. 5.04. 3
manner | daring th' event to th' teeth, are all H8 1.02. 36
upon the daring huntsman that has gall'd him; 3.02.207
our life, this daring deed | of fate in wedlock. TNK 1.01.164
corrupted, | grossly engirt with daring infamy: LUC 1173
not daring trust the office of mine eyes. PP 14.16

DARING–HARDY 1 FR 0.0001 REL FR 1 V 0 P
so bold | or daring–hardy as to touch the lists, R2 1.03. 43

DARING'ST 1 FR 0.0001 REL FR 1 V 0 P
the daring'st counsel which i had to doubt, H8 2.04.216

DARIUS 1 FR 0.0001 REL FR 1 V 0 P
than the rich–jewell'd coffer of darius, 1H6 1.06. 25

DARK 90 FR 0.0101 REL FR 77 V 13 P
else | in the dark backward and abysm of time? TMP 1.02. 50
like a fire–brand, in the dark | out of my way, 2.02. 6
the night is dark, light and spirits will become WIV 5.02. 11 P
duke yet would have dark deeds darkly answer'd, MM 3.02.177 P
none but only a repair i' th' dark, | and that i 4.01. 42
old fantastical duke of dark corners had been at 4.03.157 P
they must be bound and laid in some dark room. ERR 4.04. 94
and in a dark and dankish vault at home | there 5.01.248
first possess'd them, partly by the dark night, ADO 3.03.157 P
and make a dark night too of half the day — LLL 1.01. 45
your light grows dark by losing of your eyes. 1.01. 79
dark needs no candles now, for dark is light. 4.03.265
dark needs no candles now, for dark is light. 4.03.265
what's your dark meaning, mouse, of this light 5.02. 19
a light condition in a beauty dark. 5.02. 20
look what you do, you do it still i' th' dark. 5.02. 24
it grows dark, he may stumble. 5.02.630
dark night, that from the eye his function takes MND 3.02.177
did fly, | that fallen am i in dark uneven way, 3.02.417
as night, | and his affections dark as /erebus: MV 5.01. 87
i should wish it dark | till i were couching 5.01.304
you, deserves as well a dark house and a whip as AYL 3.02.401 P
you | than without candle may go dark to bed — 3.05. 39
to the dark house and the /detested wife. AWW 2.03.292
for with the dark, poor thief, i'll steal away. 3.02.129
till then i'll keep him dark and safely lock'd. 4.01. 94
come, we'll have him in a dark room and bound. TN 3.04.135 P
say'st thou that house is dark? 4.02. 34 P
mad, sir topas, i say to you this house is dark. 4.02. 41 P
i say this house is as dark as ignorance, though 4.02. 45 P
though ignorance were as dark as hell; 4.02. 46 P
kept in a dark house, visited by the priest, 5.01.342
to dark dishonor's use thou shalt not have. R2 1.01.169
woman, | wilt thou conceal this dark conspiracy? 5.02. 96
my back and let drive at me, for it was so dark, 1H4 2.04.223 P
green when it was so dark thou couldst not see 2.04.232 P
when creeping murmur and the poring dark | fills H5 4.pr. 2
deep night, dark night, the silent of the night, 2H6 1.04. 16
dark shall be my light, and night my day; 2.04. 40
dark cloudy death o'ershades his beams of life, 3H6 2.06. 62
can this dark monarchy afford false clarence?" R3 1.04. 51
gulf | of dark forgetfulness and deep oblivion. 3.07.129
all comfort that the dark night can afford | be 5.03. 80
and 'twere dark you'd close sooner. TRO 3.02. 49 P
death, that dark spirit, in 's nervy arm doth COR 2.01.160
in this detested, dark, blood–drinking pit. TIT 2.03.224
if it be dark, how dost thou know 'tis he? 2.03.225
stars that make dark heaven light. ROM 1.02. 25
blind is his love and best befits the dark. 2.01. 32
love, | which the dark night hath so discovered. 2.02.106
must climb a bird's nest soon when it is dark. 2.05. 74
light and light, more dark and dark our woes! 3.05. 36
light and light, more dark and dark our woes! 3.05. 36
keeps | thee here in dark to be his paramour? 5.03.105
where wilt thou find a cavern dark enough | to JC 2.01. 80
nor heaven peep through the blanket of the dark MAC 1.05. 53
and yet dark night strangles the travelling lamp 2.04. 7
of the night | for a dark hour or twain. 3.01. 27
must embrace the fate | of that dark hour. 3.01.137
shark, | root of hemlock digg'd i' th' dark, 4.01. 25
me, in the dark | grop'd i to find out them, had HAM 5.02. 13
here stood he in the dark, his sharp sword out, LR 2.01. 38
skies | gallow the very wanderers of the dark, 3.02. 44
"child rowland to the dark tower came, | his 3.04.182
all dark and comfortless! 3.07. 85
the dark and vicious place where thee he got 5.03.173
all's cheerless, dark, and deadly. 5.03.291
i might do't as well i' th' dark. OTH 4.03. 67
kill men i' th' dark? 5.01. 63
cassio hath here been set on in the dark | by 5.01.112
bright day is done, | and we are for the dark. ANT 5.02.194
hear | the rain and wind beat dark december, how CYM 3.03. 37
you could wear a mind | dark as your fortune is, 3.04.144
to thee no star be dark! TNK 1.04. 1
and with a heavy, dark, disliking eye, | his VEN 182
and now 'tis dark, and going i shall fall." 719
"now of this dark night i perceive the reason: 727
if thou destroy them not in dark obscurity? 760
and homeward through the dark laund runs apace, 813
wood, | even so confounded in the dark she lay, 827
that from their dark beds once more leap her 1050
from earth's dark womb some gentle gust doth get LUC 549
this thought through the dark night he stealeth, 729
dark harbor for defame! 768
some dark deep desert, seated from the way, 1144
"for in the dreadful dead of dark midnight, 1625
ditty, | and drives away dark dreaming night. PP 14.20
and, darkly bright, are bright in dark directed. SON 43. 4
what freezings have i felt, what dark days seen! 97. 3
who art as black as hell, as dark as night. 147.14

DARKEN 6 FR 0.0006 REL FR 6 V 0 P
i prithee darken not | the mirth o' th' feast. WT 4.04. 41
and their blaze | shall darken him for ever. COR 2.01.259
are | evils enow to darken all his goodness: ANT 1.04. 11
heirs | may the two latter darken and expend; PER 3.02. 29
bring away, | vapors, sighs, darken the day; TNK 1.05. 2
not | to darken her whose light excelleth thine; LUC 191

DARKENS 1 FR 0.0001 REL FR 1 V 0 P
choice of loss | than gain which darkens him. ANT 3.01. 24

DARKER 3 FR 0.0003 REL FR 2 V 1 P
hair were not somewhat darker than helen's — TRO 1.01. 41 P
mean time we shall express our darker purpose. LR 1.01. 36
those darker humors that | stick misbecomingly TNK 5.03. 53

DARKEST 2 FR 0.0002 REL FR 2 V 0 P
as the sun breaks through the darkest clouds, SHR 4.03.173
skill shall, like a star i' th' darkest night, HAM 5.02.256

DARK–EY'D 1 FR 0.0001 REL FR 1 V 0 P
thus out of season, threading dark–ey'd night: LR 2.01.119

DARKLING 3 FR 0.0003 REL FR 2 V 1 P
o, wilt thou darkling leave me? do not so. MND 2.02. 86
out went the candle, and we were left darkling. LR 1.04.217 P
darkling stand | the varying shore o' th' world! ANT 4.15. 10

DARKLY 8 FR 0.0009 REL FR 4 V 4 P
duke yet would have dark deeds darkly answer'd, MM 3.02.177 P
i will go darkly to work with her. 5.01.278 P
therefore i'll darkly end the argument. LLL 5.02. 23
but you shall let it dwell darkly with you. AWW 4.03. 11 P
my stars shine darkly over me. TN 2.01. 3 P
a pause | when i spake darkly what i purposed, JN 4.02.232
how darkly and how deadly dost thou speak! R3 1.04.169
and, darkly bright, are bright in dark directed. SON 43. 4

DARK'NED 2 FR 0.0002 REL FR 1 V 1 P
be more, it is much dark'ned in your malice. MM 3.02.148 P
and you are dark'ned in this action, sir, | even COR 4.07. 5

DARKNESS 48 FR 0.0054 REL FR 36 V 12 P
gates of milan, and, i' th' dead of darkness, TMP 1.02.130
melting the darkness, so their rising senses 5.01. 66
this thing of darkness i | acknowledge mine. 5.01.275
die, | i will encounter darkness as a bride, MM 3.01. 83
and to thy state of darkness hie thee straight: ERR 4.04. 56
so, ere you find where light in darkness lies, LLL 1.01. 78
the jaws of darkness do devour it up: MND 1.01.148
of the sun, | following darkness like a dream, 5.01.386
alias the prince of darkness, alias the devil. AWW 4.05. 43 P
they have laid me here in hideous darkness. TN 4.02. 30 P
i say there is no darkness but ignorance, in 4.02. 42 P
remain thou still in darkness. 4.02. 57 P
have here propertied me, keep me in darkness, 4.02. 92 P
intended | to keep in darkness what occasion now 5.01.153
though you have put me into darkness, and given 5.01.304 P
they are villains and the sons of darkness. 1H4 2.04.172 P
light in thy face, the son of utter darkness. 3.03. 37 P
end, | and darkness be the burier of the dead! 2H4 1.01.160
constrain'd to watch in darkness, rain, and cold 1H6 2.01. 7
but darkness and the gloomy shade of death 5.04. 89
descend to darkness and the burning lake! 2H6 1.04. 39
to believing souls | gives light in darkness, 2.01. 65
breathe foul contagious darkness in the air. 4.01. 7
wrath | hath in eternal darkness folded up. R3 1.03.268
clarence, who i indeed have cast in darkness, 1.03.326
on, | and flaky darkness breaks within the east. 5.03. 86
shall call her from this cloud of darkness) H8 5.04. 44
and fleckled darkness like a drunkard reels ROM 2.03. 3
who did hide their faces | even from darkness. JC 2.01.278
the instruments of darkness tell us truths, MAC 1.03.124
that darkness does the face of earth entomb, 2.04. 9
darkness and devils! LR 1.04.252
heart and did the act of darkness with her; 3.04. 87 P
the prince of darkness is a gentleman. 3.04.143 P
me nero is an angler in the lake of darkness. 3.06. 7 P
there's hell, there's darkness, | there is the 4.06.127
teeth, | and send to darkness all that stop me. ANT 3.13.181
to darkness fleet souls that fly backwards. CYM 5.03. 25
the which hath fire in darkness, none in light: PER 2.03. 44
if she'd do the deeds of darkness, thou wouldst 4.06. 29 P
night, | and darkness lord o' th' world! TNK 3.02. 4
darkness, which ever was | the dam of horror, 5.03. 22
where lo, two lamps burnt out in darkness lies; VEN 1128
upon the world dim darkness doth display, | and LUC 118
light, | and canopied in darkness sweetly lay, 398
in darkness daunts them with more dreadful 462
and therefore would they still in darkness be, 752
looking on darkness which the blind do see; SON 27. 8

DARK'NING 3 FR 0.0003 REL FR 3 V 0 P
cloud puts on | by dark'ning my clear sun. H8 1.01.226
even with the vail and dark'ning of the sun, TRO 5.08. 7
dark'ning thy pow'r to lend base subjects light? SON 100. 4

DARKS 1 FR 0.0001 REL FR 1 V 0 P
this so darks | in philoten all graceful marks, PER 4.ch. 35

DARK–SEATED 1 FR 0.0001 REL FR 1 V 0 P
all the foul terrors in dark–seated hell — 2H6 3.02.328

DARKSOME 1 FR 0.0001 REL FR 1 V 0 P
o, had they in that darksome prison died, | then LUC 379

DARK–WORKING 1 FR 0.0001 REL FR 1 V 0 P
dark–working sorcerers that change the mind, ERR 1.02. 99

DARLING 5 FR 0.0005 REL FR 5 V 0 P
is drown'd, | and his and mine lov'd darling. TMP 3.03. 93
and of his old experience th' only darling, | he AWW 2.01.107
with the rest, where is your darling, rutland? 3H6 1.04. 78
make it a darling like your precious eye. OTH 3.04. 66
rough winds do shake the darling buds of may, SON 18. 3

DARLING'S 1 FR 0.0001 REL FR 1 V 0 P
and can do nought but wail her darling's loss, 2H6 3.01.216

/DARLINGS 1 FR 0.0001 REL FR 1 V 0 P
the wealthy curled /darlings of our nation, OTH 1.02. 68

DARLINGS 1 FR 0.0001 REL FR 1 V 0 P
to eat those little darlings whom they lov'd. PER 1.04. 44

DARNEL 3 FR 0.0003 REL FR 3 V 0 P
her fallow leas | the darnel, hemlock, and rank H5 5.02. 45
'twas full of darnel; 1H6 3.02. 44
darnel, and all the idle weeds that grow | in LR 4.04. 5

DARRAIGN 1 FR 0.0001 REL FR 1 V 0 P
darraign your battle, for they are at hand. 3H6 2.02. 72

DAR'ST 47 FR 0.0053 REL FR 41 V 6 P
who mak'st a show but dar'st not strike, thy TMP 1.02.471
revenge it on him — for i know thou dar'st, 3.02. 54
sir — call me what thou dar'st. TGV 2.03. 57 P
dar'st thou die? MM 3.01. 76
how dar'st thou trust | so great a charge from ERR 1.02. 60
arrest me, foolish fellow, if thou dar'st. 4.01. 75
against thee presently, if thou dar'st stand. 5.01. 31
now follow, if thou dar'st, to try whose right, MND 3.02.336
abide me, if thou dar'st; 3.02.422
and dar'st not stand, nor look me in the face. 3.02.424
swear, if thou dar'st. SHR 5.01.101 P
and confidence | what dar'st thou venter? AWW 2.01.170
if thou dar'st tempt me further, draw thy sword. TN 4.01. 42
not wonder how thou dar'st venture to be drunk, WT 5.02.171 P
thou dar'st not say so, villain, for thy life. JN 3.01.132
out, dunghill! dar'st thou brave a nobleman? 4.03. 87
dar'st thou, thou little better thing than earth R2 3.04. 78
thou dar'st not, coward, live to see that day. 4.01. 41
seize it, if thou dar'st. 4.01. 48
pawn, | engage it to the trial, if thou dar'st. 4.01. 71
do, and thou dar'st for thy heart. 2H4 2.04.224 P
then, if ever thou dar'st acknowledge it, i will H5 4.01.209 P
thou dar'st as well be hang'd. 4.01.218 P
my courage try by combat, if thou dar'st, | and 1H6 1.02. 89
do what thou dar'st, i beard thee to thy face. 1.03. 44
dar'st thou maintain the former words thou 3.04. 31
marry, when thou dar'st. 2H6 2.01. 38
ay, where thou dar'st not peep. 2.01. 41
and if thou dar'st, | this evening, on the east 2.01. 41
say, if thou dar'st, proud lord of warwickshire, 3.02.201
if from this presence thou dar'st go with me. 3.02.228
thou dar'st not, for thy own. 4.01. 69
which dar'st not, no, nor canst not rule a 5.01. 95
if thou dar'st bring them to the baiting–place. 5.01.150
and bid thee battle, edward, if thou dar'st. 3H6 5.01.111
dar'st thou resolve to kill a friend of mine? R3 4.02. 69
but if so be | thou dar'st not this, and that to COR 4.05. 93
and with thy weapon nothing dar'st perform! TIT 2.01. 59
caesar said to me, "dar'st thou, cassius, now JC 1.02.102
that thou dar'st wag thy tongue | in noise so HAM 3.04. 39
thou art, if thou dar'st be, the earthly jove. ANT 2.07. 67
and what art thou that dar'st | appear thus to 5.01. 4
thou dar'st not, fool, thou canst not, thou art TNK 2.02.214
base cousin, | dar'st thou break first? 3.03. 45
is he contemns thee | and what thou dar'st do; 3.06.144
if in thy hope thou dar'st do such outrage, LUC 605
what dar'st thou not when once thou art a king? 606

DART 10 FR 0.0011 REL FR 10 V 0 P
believe not that the dribbling dart of love MM 1.03. 2
here stand i, lady, dart thy skill at me, LLL 5.02.396
and dart not scornful glances from those eyes, SHR 5.02.137
dart your blinding flames | into her scornful LR 2.04.165
the shot of accident nor dart of chance | could OTH 4.01.267
slumber, | not as death's dart being laugh'd at; CYM 4.02.211
if there be such a dart in princes' frowns, PER 1.02. 53
age, but thy false dart | mistakes that aim and VEN 941
and not death's ebon dart to strike him dead. 948
that they elsewhere might dart their injuries: SON 139.12

DARTED 4 FR 0.0004 REL FR 4 V 0 P
which i have darted at thee, hurt thee not, AYL 3.05. 25
through casements darted their desiring eyes R2 5.02. 14
greeks, | and mine to boot, be darted on thee! CYM 4.02.314
with fire malevolent, darted a spark, | or what TNK 5.04. 63

DARTING 1 FR 0.0001 REL FR 1 V 0 P

now, darting parthia, art thou strook, and now ANT 3.01. 1
DARTS 10 FR 0.0011 REL FR 10 V 0 P
and darts his light through every guilty hole, R2 3.02. 43
till that his thighs with darts | were almost 2H6 3.01.362
shaking the bloody darts as he his bells. 3.01.366
where 'twill not extend, | thither he darts it. H8 1.01.112
filling the air with swords advanc'd and darts, COR 1.06. 61
for piercing steel, and darts envenomed, | shall JC 5.03. 76
shall i do that which all the parthian darts, ANT 4.14. 70
our rages, | struck with our well-steel'd darts. TNK 2.02. 51
thine eye darts forth the fire that burneth me, VEN 196
which after him she darts, as one on shore 817
DASH 11 FR 0.0012 REL FR 10 V 1 P
merriment, | to dash it like a christmas comedy. LLL 5.02.462
with these my proper hands | shall i dash out. WT 2.03.141
now, had i not the dash of my former life in me, 5.02.113 P
touch ground | and dash themselves to pieces. 2H4 4.01. 18
she takes upon her bravely at first dash. 1H6 1.02. 71
and would not dash me with their ragged sides, 2H6 3.02. 98
intent | to dash our late decree in parliament 3H6 2.01.118
if they fall, they dash themselves to pieces. R3 1.03.259
as with a club, dash out my desp'rate brains? ROM 4.03. 54
all your thunderbolts, | dash him to pieces! JC 4.03. 82
some loathsome dash the herald will contrive, LUC 206
DASH'D 7 FR 0.0008 REL FR 5 V 2 P
noble creature in her) | dash'd all to pieces! TMP 1.02. 8
man, an honest man, look you, and soon dash'd. LLL 5.02.582 P
had his brains dash'd out with a grecian club, AYL 4.01. 98 P
and when that we have dash'd them to the ground, JN 2.01.405
their most reverend heads dash'd to the walls; H5 3.03. 37
and dash'd the brains out, and | so sworn as you MAC 1.07. 58
i see this hath a little dash'd your spirits. OTH 3.03.214
DASHES 1 FR 0.0001 REL FR 1 V 0 P
to th' welkin's cheek, | dashes the fire out. TMP 1.02. 5
DASHING 2 FR 0.0002 REL FR 2 V 0 P
dashing the garment of this peace, aboded | the H8 1.01. 93
on | the dashing rocks thy sea-sick weary bark! ROM 5.03.118
DASTARD 6 FR 0.0006 REL FR 6 V 0 P
my height | before this outdar'd dastard? R2 1.01.190
aid, | unto his dastard foemen is betray'd. 1H6 1.01.144
we'll try what these dastard frenchmen dare. 1.04.111
this dastard, at the battle of poictiers, | when 4.01. 19
ay, like a dastard and a treacherous coward, 3H6 2.02.114
permitted by our dastard nobles, who | have all COR 4.05. 75
DASTARDS 2 FR 0.0002 REL FR 1 V 1 P
dastards! 1H6 1.02. 23
but you are all recreants and dastards, and 2H6 4.08. 27 P
DAT *(also that)*
DAT 24 FR 0.0027 REL FR 0 V 24 P
vere is dat knave rugby? WIV 1.04. 55 P
dat i vill not for the varld i shall leave 1.04. 64 P
dere is no honest man dat shall come in my 1.04. 74 P
it is no matter-a ver dat. 1.04.115 P
do not you tell-a me dat i shall have anne page 1.04.116 P
by gar, he has save his soul, dat he is no come; 2.03. 6 P
he has pray his pible well, dat he is no come. 2.03. 7 P
mock-vater? vat is dat? 2.03. 59 P
clapper-de-claw? vat is dat? 2.03. 66 P
me tank you for dat. 2.03. 72 P
by gar, me dank you vor dat. 2.03. 90 P
ay, dat is very good, excellant. 3.01. 99 P
ha, do i perceive dat? 3.01.115 P
dat is good, by gar; with all my heart! 3.03.241 P
i cannot tell vat is dat; 4.05. 86 P
but it is tell-a me dat you make grand 4.05. 87 P
dat de tongeus of de mans is be full of deceits: H5 5.02.119 P
dat is de princess. 5.02.120 P
is it possible dat i sould love de enemy of 5.02.169 P
i cannot tell wat is dat. 5.02.177 P
i do not know dat. 5.02.211 P
de most sage demoiselle dat is en france. 5.02.219 P
dat is as it shall please de roi mon pere. 5.02.247 P
dat it is not be de fashon pour les ladies of 5.02.261 P
DATCHET-LANE 1 FR 0.0001 REL FR 0 V 1 P
me in the name of foul clothes to datchet-lane. WIV 3.05.100 P
DATCHET-MEAD 3 FR 0.0003 REL FR 0 V 3 P
carry it among the whitsters in datchet-mead, WIV 3.03. 15 P
send him by your two men to datchet-mead. 3.03.133 P
carry them to the laundress in datchet-mead; 3.03.148 P
DATE* 23 FR 0.0026 REL FR 19 V 4 P
here comes the almanac of my true date: ERR 1.02. 41
with league whose date till death shall never MND 3.02.373
your date is better in your pie and your AWW 1.01.159 P
my date of life out for his sweet live's loss. JN 4.03.106
is not my teeming date drunk up with time? R2 5.02. 91
both which i have had, but their date is out, 1H4 2.04.503 P
to my determin'd time thou gav'st new date. 1H6 4.06. 9
last longer telling than thy kindness' date. R3 4.04.255
and then to be bak'd with no date in the pie, TRO 1.02.257 P
date in the pie, for then the man's date is out. 1.02.257 P
and fame's eternal date, for virtue's praise! TIT 1.01.168
the date is out of such prolixity: ROM 1.04. 3
shall bitterly begin his fearful date | with 1.04.108
for my short date of breath | is not so long as 5.03.229
where you may abide till your date expire. PER 3.04. 14
an expir'd date, cancell'd ere well begun: LUC 26
me | to endless date of never-ending woes? 935
live's lasting date from cancell'd destiny. 1729
thy end is truth's and beauty's doom and date. SON 14.14
and summer's lease hath all too short a date; 18. 4
so long as youth and thou are of one date, | but 22. 2
forth | eternal numbers to outlive long date. 38.12
above that idle rank remain | beyond all date, 122. 4
DATELESS 4 FR 0.0004 REL FR 4 V 0 P
the dateless limit of thy dear exile; R2 1.03.151
kiss | a dateless bargain to engrossing death! ROM 5.03.115
precious friends hid in death's dateless night, SON 30. 6
this holy fire of love | a dateless lively heat, 153. 6
DATES* 5 FR 0.0005 REL FR 4 V 1 P
dates, none — that's out of my note; WT 4.03. 46 P
they call for dates and quinces in the pastry. ROM 4.04. 2
and my reliances on his fracted dates | have TIM 2.01. 22
bonds along with you, | and have the dates in. 2.01. 35
our dates are brief, and therefore we admire SON 123. 5
DAUB 3 FR 0.0003 REL FR 2 V 1 P
shall daub her lips with her own children's 1H4 1.01. 6
mortar, and daub the wall of a jakes with him. LR 2.02. 66 P
poor tom's a-cold. i cannot daub it further. 4.01. 52
DAUB'D 1 FR 0.0001 REL FR 1 V 0 P
so smooth he daub'd his vice with show of virtue R3 3.05. 29
DAUB'RY 1 FR 0.0001 REL FR 0 V 1 P
by th' figure, and such daub'ry as this is, WIV 4.02.177 P
/DAUGHTER 3 FR 0.0003 REL FR 1 V 2 P
remember, son slender, my /daughter. WIV 5.02. 3 P
he says, my lord, your /daughter is not well. LR 1.04. 50 P
/means | /will /yield /to /see /his /daughter. 4.03. 41
DAUGHTER 429 FR 0.0485 REL FR 340 V 89 P
thee | (of thee my dear one, thee my daughter), TMP 1.02. 17
of virtue, and | she said thou wast my daughter; 1.02. 57
and his more braver daughter could control thee, 1.02.440
of the king's fair daughter claribel to the king 2.01. 71 P
were at tunis at the marriage of your daughter, 2.01. 99 P
would i had never | married my daughter there! 2.01.109
would not bless our europe with your daughter, 2.01.125
true, my brother's daughter 's queen of tunis, 2.01.255
to consider is | the beauty of his daughter. 3.02. 99
his daughter and i will be king and queen — 3.02.106 P
worthily purchas'd, take my daughter. 4.01. 14
plot | the means that dusky dis my daughter got, 4.01. 89
didst thou, alonso, use me and my daughter; 5.01. 72
for i | have lost my daughter. 5.01.148
a daughter? 5.01.148
when did you lose your daughter? 5.01.152
she | is daughter to this famous duke of milan, 5.01.192
now, daughter silvia, you are hard beset. TGV 2.04. 49
for thurio, he intends, shall wed his daughter; 2.06. 39
this night intends to steal away your daughter; 3.01. 11
on thurio, whom your gentle daughter hates, 3.01. 14
to match my friend sir thurio to my daughter. 3.01. 62
beseeming such a wife as your fair daughter. 3.01. 66
far exceed the love | i ever bore my daughter, 3.01.167
my daughter takes his going grievously. 3.02. 14
the match between sir thurio and my daughter? 3.02. 23
saw you my daughter? 5.02. 33
page, which is daughter to master /george page, WIV 1.01. 45 P
but not kiss'd your keeper's daughter? 1.01.113 P
nay, daughter, carry the wine in, we'll drink 1.01.188 P
you are come to see my daughter anne? 2.01.162 P
love him, daughter anne. 3.04. 67
i told you, sir, my daughter is dispos'd of. 3.04. 70
page, for that i love your daughter | in such a 3.04. 78
my daughter will i question how she loves you, 3.04. 90
nan page (my daughter) and my little son, | and 4.04. 48
master doctor, my daughter is in green. 5.03. 1 P
will chafe at the doctor's marrying my daughter. 5.03. 9 P
her master slender hath married her daughter. 5.05.173 P
if anne page be my daughter, she is, by this, 5.05.175 P
how you should know my daughter by her garments? 5.05.195 P
turn'd my daughter into /green; 5.05.201 P
'tis meet so, daughter, but lest you do repent MM 2.03. 30
nor, gentle daughter, fear you not at all. 4.01. 70
good morning to you, fair and gracious daughter. 4.03.112
show your wisdom, daughter, in your close 4.03.118
i think this is your daughter. ADO 1.01.104 P
didst thou note the daughter of signior leonato? 1.01.162 P
with hero, leonato's short daughter. 1.01.214 P
he lov'd my niece your daughter and meant to 1.02. 12 P
but i will acquaint my daughter withal, that she 1.02. 21 P
one hero, the daughter and heir of leonato. 1.03. 54 P
daughter, remember what i told you. 2.01. 66 P
count, take of me my daughter, and with her my 2.01.302 P
for i have heard my daughter say, she hath often 2.01.344 P
claudio shall marry the daughter of leonato. 2.02. 2 P
sit you — you heard my daughter tell you how. 2.03.111 P
'tis true indeed, so your daughter says. 2.03.127 P
my daughter tells us all. 2.03.133 P
a pretty jest your daughter told /us /of. 2.03.135 P
she doth indeed, my daughter says so; 2.03.150 P
her that my daughter is sometime afeard she will 2.03.152 P
we will hear further of it by your daughter, let 2.03.206 P
and that must your daughter and her gentlewomen 2.03.214 P
for you to give your daughter to her husband. 3.05. 55 P
soul | give me this maid, your daughter? 4.01. 25
let me but move one question to your daughter, 4.01. 73
your daughter here the /princes left for dead, 4.01.202
the old man's daughter told us all. 5.01.178 P
i cannot bid you bid my daughter live — | that 5.01.279
my brother hath a daughter, | almost the copy of 5.01.288
well, daughter, and you gentlewomen all, 5.04. 10
you must be father to your brother's daughter, 5.04. 15
that eye my daughter lent her, 'tis most true. 5.04. 23
to-day to marry with my brother's daughter? 5.04. 37
the french king's daughter with yourself to LLL 1.01.135
tell him, the daughter of the king of france, 2.01. 30
pray you, sir, whose daughter? 2.01.201
against my child, my daughter hermia. MND 1.01. 23
made love to nedar's daughter, helena, | and won 1.01.107
my lord, this' my daughter here asleep, | and 4.01.128
nothing undervalu'd | to cato's daughter, MV 1.01.166
will of a living daughter curb'd by the will of 1.02. 24 P
but though i am a daughter to his blood, | i am 2.03. 18
i have a father, you a daughter, lost. 2.05. 57
"my daughter! 2.08. 15
o my daughter! 2.08. 15
my ducats, and my daughter! 2.08. 17
of double ducats, stol'n from me by my daughter! 2.08. 19
and precious stones, | stol'n by my daughter! 2.08. 21
his stones, his daughter, and his ducats. 2.08. 24
i say, my daughter is my flesh and my blood. 3.01. 37 P
hast thou found my daughter? 3.01. 80 P
i would my daughter were dead at my foot, and 3.01. 88 P
your daughter spent in genoa, as i heard, one 3.01.108 P
ring that he had of your daughter for a monkey. 3.01.119 P
you not, that you are not the jew's daughter. 3.05. 12 P
for me in heaven because i am a jew's daughter; 3.05. 33 P
i have a daughter — | would any of the stock of 4.01.295
the gentleman | that lately stole his daughter. 4.01.385
unto his son lorenzo and his daughter. 4.01.390
can you tell if rosalind, the duke's daughter, AYL 1.01.105 P
for the duke's daughter, her cousin, so loves 1.01.107 P
less belov'd of her uncle than his own daughter, 1.01.111 P
how now, daughter and cousin? 1.02.155 P
which of the two was daughter of the duke, 1.02.269
neither his daughter, if we judge by manners, 1.02.271
but yet indeed the /smaller is his daughter. 1.02.272
the other is daughter to the banish'd duke, 1.02.273
usurping uncle | to keep his daughter company, 1.02.275
thou art thy father's daughter, there's enough. 1.03. 58
not the duke | hath banish'd me, his daughter? 1.03. 95
your daughter and her cousin much commend | the 2.02. 12
you your word, o duke, to give your daughter; 5.04. 19
you, yours, orlando, to receive his daughter; 5.04. 20
methought he was a brother to your daughter. 5.04. 29
good duke, receive thy daughter, | hymen from 5.04.111
if there be truth in sight, you are my daughter. 5.04.118
even daughter, welcome, in no less degree. 5.04.148
not to bestow my youngest daughter | before i SHR 1.01. 50
baptista's eldest daughter to a husband we set 1.01.137 P
her face, | such as the daughter of agenor had, 1.01.168
indeed had baptista's youngest daughter. 1.01.240
his youngest daughter, beautiful bianca, | and 1.02.120
and were his daughter fairer than she is, | she 1.02.240
fair leda's daughter had a thousand wooers, 1.02.242
you, | did you yet ever see baptista's daughter? 1.02.250
the youngest daughter, whom you hearken for, 1.02.258
pray have you not a daughter | call'd katherina, 2.01. 42
i have a daughter, sir, call'd katherina. 2.01. 44
but for my daughter katherine, this i know, 2.01. 62
do make myself a suitor to your daughter, | unto 2.01. 90
what, will my daughter prove a good musician? 2.01.144
proceed in practice with my younger daughter; 2.01.164
us, | or shall i send my daughter kate to you? 2.01.167
petruchio, how speed you with my daughter? 2.01.281
why, how now, daughter katherine, in your dumps? 2.01.284
call you me daughter? 2.01.285
but now, baptista, to your younger daughter — 2.01.332
that can assure my daughter greatest dower 2.01.343
if i may have your daughter to my wife, | i'll 2.01.365
know | my daughter katherine is to be married. 2.01.394
'twixt me and one baptista's daughter here. 4.02.119
of love between your daughter and himself; 4.04. 27
and for the love he beareth to your daughter 4.04. 29
your son lucentio here | doth love my daughter, 4.04. 41
him, | and pass my daughter a sufficient dower, 4.04. 45
your son shall have my daughter with consent. 4.04. 47
send for your daughter by your servant here; 4.04. 58
his daughter is to be brought by you to the 4.04. 85 P
that have by marriage made thy daughter mine, 5.01.116
have you married my daughter without asking my 5.01.134 P
crowns, | another dowry to another daughter, 5.02.114
gentlewoman the daughter of gerard de narbon? AWW 1.01. 37 P
why — that you are my daughter? 1.03.153
but, i your daughter, he must be my brother? 1.03.166
daughter and mother | so strive upon your pulse. 1.03.168
charge — | a poor physician's daughter my wife! 2.03.115
a poor physician's daughter — thou dislik'st 2.03.123
the count he woos your daughter, | lays down his 3.07. 17
it is no more | but that your daughter, ere she 3.07. 31
instruct my daughter how she shall persever, 3.07. 37
my master to speak in the behalf of my daughter, 4.05. 72 P
what says he to your daughter? have you spoke? 5.03. 28
you remember | the daughter of this lord? 5.03. 43
you | to sparkle in the spirits of my daughter, 5.03. 75
your reputation comes too short for my daughter, 5.03.177 P
maid, the daughter of a count | that died some TN 1.02. 36
my father had a daughter lov'd a man, | as it 2.04.107
a daughter, and a goodly babe, | lusty and like WT 2.02. 24
is good) hath brought you forth a daughter — 2.03. 66
the daughter of a king, our wife, and one | of 3.02. 3
a moi'ty of the throne, a great king's daughter, 3.02. 39
a shepherd's daughter, | and what to her adheres 4.01. 27
a man, who hath a daughter of most rare note. 4.02. 42 P
fie, daughter, when my old wife liv'd, upon 4.04. 55
swain is this | which dances with your daughter? 4.04.167
he says he loves my daughter. 4.04.171
but, my daughter, | say you the like to him? 4.04.379
i give my daughter to him, and will make | her 4.04.385
that must be | i' th' virtue of your daughter. 4.04.387
come, your hand; | and, daughter, yours. 4.04.391
whoobub against his daughter and the king's son, 4.04.616 P
that should have married a shepherd's daughter. 4.04.767 P
to offer to have his daughter come into grace! 4.04.777 P
know 'tis none of your daughter nor my sister; 4.04.820 P
him, whose daughter | his tears proclaim'd his, 5.01.159
might i a son and daughter now have look'd on, 5.01.177
his hopes, and with | a shepherd's daughter. 5.01.185
my lord, | is this the daughter of a king? 5.01.208
the king's daughter is found. 5.02. 23 P
with all certainty, to be the king's daughter. 5.02. 39 P
out of himself for joy of his found daughter, as 5.02. 50 P
again worries he his daughter with clipping her. 5.02. 54 P
how attentiveness wounded his daughter, till, 5.02. 87 P
overfond of the shepherd's daughter (so he then 5.02.117 P
not | that which my daughter came to look upon, 5.03. 13
from thy admiring daughter took the spirits, 5.03. 41
directing, | is troth-plight to your daughter. 5.03.151
that daughter there of spain, the lady blanch, JN 2.01.423
command thy son and daughter to join hands. 2.01.532
'tis true, fair daughter, and this blessed day 3.01. 75
whose daughter, as we hear, that earl of march 1H4 1.03. 84
i am afraid my daughter will run mad, | so much 3.01.143
my daughter weeps, she'll not part with you, 3.01.192
i pray thee, loving wife, and gentle daughter, 2H4 2.03. 1
fair daughter, you do draw my spirits from me 2.03. 46
and your fairest daughter and mine, my 3.02. 6 P
blithild, which was daughter to king clothair, H5 1.02. 67
daughter to charlemain, who was the son | to 1.02. 75
daughter to charles, the foresaid duke of 1.02. 83
let the inheritance | descend unto the daughter. 1.02.100
king doth offer him | katherine his daughter, 3.pr. 30
my dog, | his fairest daughter is contaminated. 4.05. 16
his daughter first; 5.02.333
the rest, | and thereupon give me your daughter. 5.02.347
dolphin, i am by birth a shepherd's daughter, 1H6 1.02. 72
divinest creature, astraea's daughter, | how 1.06. 4
proffers his only daughter to your grace | in 5.01. 19
margaret my name, and daughter to a king, | the 5.03. 51
see, reignier, see, thy daughter prisoner! 5.03.131
thy daughter shall be wedded to my king, | whom 5.03.137
hath gain'd thy daughter princely liberty. 5.03.140
my daughter shall be henry's, if he please. 5.03.156
joan, sweet daughter joan, i'll die with thee! 5.04. 6
a poor earl's daughter is unequal odds, | and 5.05. 34

but margaret, that is daughter to a king? 5.05. 67
margaret, daughter unto reignier king of naples, 2H6 1.01. 47 P
change two dukedoms for a duke's fair daughter. 1.01.219
till suffolk gave two dukedoms for his daughter. 1.03. 87
the crown, had issue, philippe, a daughter, 2.02. 35
sole daughter unto lionel duke of clarence; 2.02. 50
lord | unto the daughter of a worthless king, 4.01. 81
she was indeed a pedlar's daughter, and sold 4.02. 45 P
married the duke of clarence' daughter, did he 4.02.137
i'll join mine eldest daughter, and my joy, | to 3H6 3.03.242
that only warwick's daughter shall be thine. 3.03.248
to give the heir and daughter of lord scales 4.01. 52
young prince edward marries warwick's daughter. 4.01.117
for i will hence to warwick's other daughter, 4.01.120
sweet clarence, my daughter shall be thine. 4.02. 12
than jephthah when he sacrific'd his daughter. 5.01. 91
for then i'll marry warwick's youngest daughter. R3 1.01.153
daughter, well met. 4.01. 5
i will marry straight to clarence' daughter; 4.02. 54
i must be married to my brother's daughter, | or 4.02. 60
his daughter meanly have i match'd in marriage, 4.03. 37
at young elizabeth, my brother's daughter, | and 4.03. 41
you have a daughter call'd elizabeth, | virtuous 4.04.204
i will confess she was not edward's daughter. 4.04.211
then know that from my soul i love thy daughter. 4.04.256
that thou dost love my daughter from thy soul; 4.04.259
i mean that with my soul i love thy daughter, 4.04.263
this /is not the way | to win your daughter. 4.04.285
to make amends i'll give it to your daughter; 4.04.295
mine issue of your blood upon your daughter. 4.04.298
and by that loss your daughter is made queen. 4.04.308
king, that calls your beauteous daughter wife, 4.04.315
go then, my mother, to thy daughter go, | make 4.04.325
and lead thy daughter to a conqueror's bed; 4.04.334
i tender not thy beauteous princely daughter! 4.04.405
shall i go win my daughter to thy will? 4.04.426
he should espouse elizabeth her daughter. 4.05. 8
your grace, sir thomas bullen's daughter — H8 1.04. 92
certain | the daughter of a king, my drops of 2.04. 72
the duke of orleance and | our daughter mary. 2.04.176
whether our daughter were legitimate, 2.04.180
a knight's daughter, | to be her mistress' 3.02. 94
model of our chaste loves, his young daughter — 4.02.132
yet like | a queen, and daughter to a king, 4.02.172
a sister were a grace, or a daughter a goddess, TRO 1.02.237 P
great princes, | and he shall buy my daughter? 3.03. 28
is not yond diomed, with calchas' daughter? 4.05. 13
a token from her daughter, my fair love, | both 5.01. 40
diomed. calchas, i think. where's your daughter? 5.02. 3
i pray you, daughter, sing, or express yourself COR 1.03. 1 P
i tell thee, daughter, i sprang not more in joy 1.03. 15 P
daughter, speak you; 5.03.155
my daughter! 5.06.121 P
this was thy daughter. TIT 3.01. 63
thy warlike hand, thy mangled daughter here, 3.01.255
did you not use his daughter very friendly? 4.02. 40
for worse than philomel you us'd my daughter, 5.02.194
to slay his daughter with his own right hand, 5.03. 37
why hast thou slain thine only daughter thus? 5.03. 55
nurse, where's my daughter? ROM 1.03. 1
tell me, daughter juliet, | how stands your 1.03. 64
i nurs'd her daughter that you talk'd withal; 1.05.115
is set | on the fair daughter of rich capulet. 2.03. 58
romeo shall thank thee, daughter, for us both. 2.06. 22
that we have had no time to move our daughter. 3.04. 2
madam, good night, commend me to your daughter. 3.04. 9
ho, daughter, are you up? 3.05. 64
my leisure serves me, pensive daughter, now. 4.01. 39
hold, daughter! 4.01. 68
what, is my daughter gone to friar lawrence? 4.02. 11
death is my heir, | my daughter he hath wedded. 4.05. 39
o wife, look how our daughter bleeds! 5.03.202
one only daughter have i, no kin else, | on whom TIM 1.01.121
him in itself, | it must not bear my daughter. 1.01.131
give him thy daughter; 1.01.144
withal | a woman well reputed, cato's daughter. JC 2.01.295
as it behooves my daughter and your honor. HAM 1.03. 97
these blazes, daughter, | giving more light than 1.03.117
i have a daughter — have while she is mine — 2.02.106
this in obedience hath my daughter shown me, 2.02.125
before my daughter told me — what might you, 2.02.134
at such a time i'll loose my daughter to him. 2.02.162
a good kissing carrion — have you a daughter? 2.02.182 P
a blessing, but as your daughter may conceive, 2.02.185 P
still harping on my daughter. 2.02.188 P
/of /meeting /between /him and my daughter. 2.02.213 P
why — "one fair daughter, and no more, | the 2.02.407
still on my daughter. 2.02.409 P
i have a daughter that i love passing well. 2.02.412 P
they say the owl was a baker's daughter. 4.05. 43 P
false steward, that stole his master's daughter. 4.05.173 P
what says our second daughter, | our dearest LR 1.01. 67
and reliev'd, | as thou my sometime daughter. 1.01.120
thy youngest daughter does not love thee least, 1.01.152
with this king | hath rivall'd for our daughter. 1.01.191
thy dow'rless daughter, king, thrown to my 1.01.256
for we | have no such daughter, nor shall ever 1.01.263
you, you, sirrah, where's my daughter? 1.04. 44 P
as in the duke himself also, and your daughter. 1.04. 62 P
go you and tell my daughter i would speak with 1.04. 76 P
how now, daughter? 1.04.189 P
are you our daughter? 1.04.218
yet have i left a daughter. 1.04.255
i have another daughter, | who i am sure is kind 1.04.305
when one has caught her, | and such a daughter, 1.04.318
acquaint my daughter no further with any thing 1.05. 2 P
shalt see thy other daughter will use thee 1.05. 14 P
it is both he and she, | your son and daughter. 2.04. 14
your son and daughter found this trespass worth 2.04. 44
where is this daughter? 2.04. 58
the dear father | would with his daughter speak, 2.04.102
"dear daughter, i confess that i am old; 2.04.154
i prithee, daughter, do not make me mad. 2.04.218
yet thou art my flesh, my blood, my daughter — 2.04.221
sir, | your most dear daughter — 4.06.189
thou hast /one daughter | who redeems nature 4.06.205
the king is come to his daughter, | with others 5.01. 21
king lear hath lost, he and his daughter ta'en. 5.02. 6
look to your house, your daughter, and your bags OTH 1.01. 80
hast heard me say | my daughter is not for thee; 1.01. 98
you'll have your daughter cover'd with a barbary 1.01.111 P
to tell you your daughter and the moor are /now 1.01.116 P
partly i find it is) that your fair daughter, 1.01.122
your daughter (if you have not given her leave), 1.01.133
foul thief, where hast thou stow'd my daughter? 1.02. 62
my daughter! o, my daughter! 1.03. 59
my daughter! o, my daughter! 1.03. 59
hath thus beguil'd your daughter of herself, 1.03. 66
that i have ta'en away this old man's daughter, 1.03. 78
i am charg'd withal) | i won his daughter. 1.03. 94
i think this tale would win my daughter too. 1.03.171
i am hitherto your daughter. 1.03.185
him repent | thou wast not made his daughter, ANT 3.13.135
his daughter, and the heir of 's kingdom (whom CYM 1.01. 4
no, be assur'd you shall not find me, daughter, 1.01. 70
would i were | a neat–herd's daughter, and my 1.01.149
peace, | dear lady daughter, peace! 1.01.154
this matter of marrying his king's daughter, 1.04. 14 P
he little cares for and a daughter who | he not 1.06.154
attend you here the door of our stern daughter? 2.03. 37
vantages that may | prefer you to his daughter. 2.03. 46
but, my gentle queen, | where is our daughter? 3.05. 30
your daughter, whom she bore in hand to love 5.05. 43
yet, o my daughter, | that it was folly in me, 5.05. 66
that paragon, thy daughter, | for whom my heart 5.05.147
my daughter? 5.05.150
of your chaste daughter the wide difference 5.05.194
that kill'd thy daughter — villain–like, i lie 5.05.218
the piece of tender air, thy virtuous daughter, 5.05.446
bring in our daughter, clothed like a bride PER 1.01. 6
and i'll tell you, he hath a fair daughter, and 2.01.108 P
and our daughter here, | in honor of whose birth 2.02. 4
'tis now your honor, daughter, to entertain 2.02. 14
for, daughter, so you are — here take your 2.03. 18
o, attend, my daughter: 2.03. 58
an inestimable value, and his daughter with him, 2.04. 8
knights, from my daughter this i let you know, 2.05. 2
what do you think of my daughter, sir? 2.05. 33
sir, my daughter thinks very well of you, | ay, 2.05. 37
that never aim'd so high to love your daughter, 2.05. 47
thou hast bewitch'd my daughter, and thou art 2.05. 49
here comes my daughter, she can witness it. 2.05. 66
antiochus and his daughter dead, | the men of 3.ch. 25
a little daughter. 3.01. 21
her burying, | she was the daughter of a king. 3.02. 73
our cleon hath | one daughter, and a full–grown 4.ch. 16
that her daughter | might stand peerless by this 4.ch. 39
how chance my daughter is not with you? 4.01. 22
of kindness | perform'd to your sole daughter. 4.03. 39
to see his daughter, all his live's delight. 4.04. 12
to fetch his daughter home, who first is gone. 4.04. 20
she was of tyrus the king's daughter, | on whom 4.04. 36
he is arriv'd | here where his daughter dwells, 5.ch. 15
the loss | of a beloved daughter and a wife. 5.01. 30
and such a one | my daughter might have been. 5.01.108
how, a king's daughter? | and call'd marina? 5.01.149
my mother was the daughter of a king, | who died 5.01.157
this cannot be | my daughter — buried! 5.01.163
i am the daughter to king pericles, | if good 5.01.178
is it no more to be your daughter than | to say 5.01.209
seems to dote, | how sure you are my daughter. 5.01.226
were it to woo my daughter, for it seems | you 5.01.262
she | made known herself my daughter. 5.03. 13
prince, the fair–betrothed of your daughter, 5.03. 71
our son and daughter shall in tyrus reign. 5.03. 82
in antiochus and his daughter you have heard 5.03. 85
in pericles, his queen and daughter, seen, 5.03. 87
i will assure upon my daughter at the day of my TNK 2.01. 8 P
and i will estate your daughter in what i have 2.01. 11 P
him | and the tanner's daughter to let slip now; 2.03. 44
the lord steward's daughter — | do you remember 3.03. 29
would | be here, cicely the sempster's daughter. 3.05. 44
alas, sir, where's your daughter? 4.01. 32
by the fishermen, | i saw it was your daughter. 4.01. 65
your gentle daughter gave me freedom once; 5.04. 24
"to show the beldame daughters of her daughter, LUC 953
the sire, the son, the dame, and daughter die. 1477
"daughter, dear daughter," old lucretius cries, 1751
"daughter, dear daughter," old lucretius cries, 1751
who should weep most, for daughter or for wife. 1792
"my daughter!" 1804
life, | answer'd their cries, "my daughter!" 1806
it was a lording's daughter, the fairest one of PP 15. 1

DAUGHTER–BEAMED 1 FR 0.0001 REL FR 1 V 0 P
you were best call it "daughter–beamed eyes." LLL 5.02.172

DAUGHTER–IN–LAW 3 FR 0.0003 REL FR 1 V 2 P
yes, helen, you might be my daughter–in–law. AWW 1.03.167
"i have sent you a daughter–in–law; 3.02. 19 P
your daughter–in–law had been alive at this hour 4.05. 4 P

DAUGHTER'S 26 FR 0.0029 REL FR 24 V 2 P
when i wore it at your daughter's marriage? TMP 2.01.106 P
i now beseech you (for your daughter's sake) TGV 5.04.149
my heart is sorry for your daughter's death; ADO 5.01.103
i thank you, princes, for my daughter's death; 5.01.268
cunning hast thou filch'd my daughter's heart, MND 1.01. 36
it will be for his gentle daughter's sake, | and MV 2.04. 34
none so well as you, of my daughter's flight. 3.01. 25 P
some lively touches of my daughter's favor. AYL 5.04. 27
then tell me, if i get your daughter's love, SHR 2.01.119
hath brought me up to be your daughter's dower, AWW 4.04. 19
and here beholding | his daughter's trial! WT 3.02.121
stand and read | as 'twere my daughter's eyes; 4.04.174
pour your graces | upon my daughter's head! 5.03.123
my daughter's mother thinks it with her soul. R3 4.04.257
but in your daughter's womb i bury them; 4.04.423
that ancus martius, numa's daughter's son, | who COR 2.03.239
thou knowest my daughter's of a pretty age. ROM 1.03. 10
and it mis–sheathed in my daughter's bosom! 5.03.205
this is my daughter's jointure, for no more 5.03.297
great rivals in our youngest daughter's love, LR 1.01. 46
your daughter's chastity — there it begins. CYM 5.05.179
now to my daughter's letter. PER 2.05. 15
let pericles believe his daughter's dead, | and 4.04. 46
play | his daughter's woe and heavy well–a–day 4.04. 49
to mourn thy crosses, with thy daughter's, call 5.01.245
means he escap'd, which was your daughter's, TNK 4.01. 20

DAUGHTERS' 5 FR 0.0005 REL FR 5 V 0 P
will to publish | our daughters' several dowers, LR 1.01. 44
with my two daughters' dow'rs digest the third; 1.01.128
if it be you that stirs these daughters' hearts 2.04.274
t' obey in all your daughters' hard commands. 3.04.149
from hence trust not your daughters' minds | by OTH 1.01.170

/DAUGHTERS 3 FR 0.0003 REL FR 3 V 0 P
/be /false /persuaded | /i /had /daughters. LR 1.04.234
/tigers, /not /daughters, /what /have /you 4.02. 40
/rights | /to /his //dog–hearted /daughters — 4.03. 45

DAUGHTERS 49 FR 0.0055 REL FR 32 V 17 P
so curses all eve's daughters, of what WIV 4.02. 24 P
and their daughters profit very greatly under LLL 4.02. 75 P
if their daughters be capable, i will put it to 4.02. 79 P
he that has the two fair daughters? SHR 1.02.221
and toward the education of your daughters, | i 2.01. 98
lead these gentlemen | to my daughters, and tell 2.01.109
i am all the daughters of my father's house, TN 2.04.120
be she honor–flaw'd, | i have three daughters: WT 2.01.144
but thy sons and daughters will be all gentlemen 5.02.127 P
the locks of your shrill–shriking daughters; H5 3.03. 35
nor yet saint philip's daughters, were like thee 1H6 1.02.143
your wives and daughters before your faces. 2H6 4.08. 30 P
nay, bear three daughters; 3H6 2.01. 41
no more than when my daughters call thee mother. 3.02.101
which stretch'd unto their servants, daughters, R3 3.05. 82
for my daughters, richard, | they shall be 4.04.201
ravish our daughters? 5.03.337
you are in love | with one of priam's daughters. TRO 3.03.194
of opportunity, | and daughters of the game. 4.05. 63
you have holp to ravish your own daughters, and COR 4.06. 81
the virginal palms of your daughters, or with 5.02. 43 P
"signior martino and his wife and daughters; ROM 1.02. 65 P
mine uncle capulet, his wife, and daughters; 1.02. 68 P
your wives, your daughters, | your matrons, and MAC 4.03. 61
with blood of fathers, mothers, daughters, sons, HAM 2.02.458
tell me, my daughters | (since now we will LR 1.01. 48
this fellow has banish'd two on 's daughters, 1.04.102 P
would i had two coxcombs and two daughters! 1.04.105 P
there's mine, beg another of thy daughters. 1.04.109 P
since thou mad'st thy daughters thy mothers, for 1.04.173 P
i marvel what kin thou and thy daughters are. 1.04.182 P
not to give it away to his daughters, and leave 1.05. 31 P
many dolors for thy daughters as thou canst tell 2.04. 55 P
good nuncle, in, ask thy daughters blessing. 3.02. 12 P
nor rain, wind, thunder, fire are my daughters. 3.02. 15
that will with two pernicious daughters join 3.02. 22
didst thou give all to thy daughters? 3.04. 49 P
has his daughters brought him to this pass? 3.04. 63
fated o'er men's faults light on thy daughters! 3.04. 68
he hath no daughters, sir. 3.04. 69
to such a lowness but his unkind daughters. 3.04. 71
this flesh begot | those pelican daughters. 3.04. 75
his daughters seek his death. 3.04.163
was kinder to his father than my daughters | got 4.06.115
we not see these daughters and these sisters? 5.03. 7
your eldest daughters have foredone themselves, 5.03.292
get many more such prisoners and such daughters, TNK 2.06. 38
and barren dearth of daughters and of sons, | be VEN 754
"to show the beldame daughters of her daughter, LUC 953

DAUNT 2 FR 0.0002 REL FR 2 V 0 P
think you a little din can daunt mine ears? SHR 1.02.199
and let not discontent | daunt all your hopes. TIT 1.01.268

DAUNTED 3 FR 0.0003 REL FR 3 V 0 P
wilt thou be daunted at a woman's sight? 1H6 5.03. 69
a heart unspotted is not easily daunted. 2H6 3.01.100
what, are ye daunted now? 4.01.119

DAUNTLESS 4 FR 0.0004 REL FR 4 V 0 P
a braver choice of dauntless spirits | than now JN 2.01. 72
and put on | the dauntless spirit of resolution. 5.01. 53
yoke, but let thy dauntless mind | still ride in 3H6 3.03. 17
and, to that dauntless temper of his mind, | he MAC 3.01. 51

DAUNTS 1 FR 0.0001 REL FR 1 V 0 P
in darkness daunts them with more dreadful LUC 462

DAUPHIN *(see dolphin*, etc.)*

DAVENTRY *(also daintry)*

DAVENTRY 1 FR 0.0001 REL FR 0 V 1 P
albons, or the red–nose innkeeper of daventry. 1H4 4.02. 47 P

DAVY 24 FR 0.0027 REL FR 1 V 23 P
what, davy, i say! 2H4 5.01. 2 P
why, davy! 5.01. 7 P
davy, davy, davy, davy, let me see, davy, let me 5.01. 9 P
davy, davy, davy, davy, let me see, davy, let me 5.01. 9 P
davy, davy, davy, davy, let me see, davy, let me 5.01. 9 P
davy, davy, davy, davy, let me see, davy, let me 5.01. 9 P
davy, davy, let me see, davy, let me see, davy, 5.01. 9 P
let me see, davy, let me see, davy, let me see. 5.01. 10 P
with red wheat, davy. 5.01. 16 P
some pigeons, davy, a couple of short–legg'd 5.01. 26 P
yea, davy, i will use him well. 5.01. 30 P
use his men well, davy, for they are arrant 5.01. 32 P
well conceited, davy. about thy business, davy. 5.01. 36 P
well conceited, davy. about thy business, davy. 5.01. 37 P
there is many complaints, davy, against that 5.01. 40 P
look about, davy. 5.01. 53 P
spread, davy, spread, davy. 5.03. 8 P
spread, davy, spread, davy. 5.03. 9 P
well said, davy. 5.03. 9 P
this davy serves you for good uses, he is your 5.03. 10 P
give master bardolph some wine, davy. 5.03. 25 P
davy! 5.03. 43 P
and i might see you there, davy! 5.03. 61 P
suffolk, | sir richard ketly, davy gam, esquire; H5 4.08.104

DAVY'S *(also tavy's)*

DAVY'S 2 FR 0.0002 REL FR 1 V 1 P
his leek about his pate | upon saint davy's day. H5 4.01. 55
saint davy's day is past. 5.01. 2 P

DAW 2 FR 0.0002 REL FR 1 V 1 P
upon a knive's point and choke a daw withal. ADO 2.03.255 P
the law, | good faith, i am no wiser than a daw. 1H6 2.04. 18

DAWN 3 FR 0.0003 REL FR 2 V 1 P
come away, it is almost clear dawn. MM 4.02.210 P
next day after dawn, | doth rise and help H5 4.01.274
chirp, the screech–owl | calls in the dawn! TNK 3.02. 36

DAWNING 6 FR 0.0006 REL FR 4 V 2 P
as near the dawning, provost, as it is, | you MM 4.02. 94

he longs not for the dawning as we do. H5 3.07.131 P
but dawning day new comfort hath inspir'd. TIT 2.02. 10
this bird of dawning singeth all night long, HAM 1.01.160
good dawning to thee, friend. art of this house? LR 2.02. 1 P
night, that dawning | may bare the raven's eye! CYM 2.02. 48

DAWS 6 FR 0.0006 REL FR 2 V 4 P

when turtles tread, and rooks and daws, | and LLL 5.02.905
at your request! yes, nightingales answer daws. TN 3.04. 36 P
crows and daws, crows and daws! TRO 1.02.244 P
crows and daws, crows and daws! 1.02.244 P
then thou dwell'st with daws too? COR 4.05. 44 P
my heart upon my sleeve | for daws to peck at: OTH 1.01. 65

/DAY 5 FR 0.0005 REL FR 5 V 0 P

this ungodly day | wear out the /day in peace; JN 3.01.110
/alack /the /heavy /day, | /that /i /have /worn R2 4.01.257
/that /every /day /under /his /household /roof 4.01.282
"/these /wounds /i /had /on /crispin's /day." H5 4.03. 48
/the /glory /of /our /troy /doth /this /day /lie TRO 4.04.147

DAY 766 FR 0.0865 REL FR 625 V 141 P

o, woe the day! TMP 1.02. 15
what is the time o' th' day? 1.02.239
and how the less, | that burn by day and night; 1.02.336
me, | might i but through my prison once a day 1.02.491
every day some sailor's wife, | the masters of 2.01. 4
my doublet as fresh as the first day i wore it? 2.01.104 P
never till this day | saw i him touch'd with 4.01.144
how's the day? 5.01. 3
of this, | for 'tis a chronicle of day by day, 5.01.163
of this, | for 'tis a chronicle of day by day, 5.01.163
that every day with parle encounter me, | in thy TGV 1.02. 5
please you deliberate a day or two. 1.03. 73
the uncertain glory of an april day, | which now 1.03. 85
and when that hour o'erslips me in the day 2.02. 9
of men, | that no man hath access by day to her. 3.01.109
unless i look on silvia in the day, | there is 3.01.180
the day, | there is no day for me to look upon. 3.01.181
trust me, i think 'tis almost day. 4.02.138 P
gentlewoman, good day; 4.04.108
that done, our day of marriage shall be yours — 5.04.172
my shin th' other day with playing at sword and WIV 1.01.283 P
by me, thine own true knight, | by day or night, 2.01. 15
your doublet and hose, this raw rheumatic day? 3.01. 47 P
slender, and this day we shall have our answer. 3.02. 58 P
how i love you, and you shall one day find it. 3.03. 81 P
heaven forgive my sins at the day of judgment! 3.03.212 P
alas the day! 3.05. 38 P
alas the day, i know not! 4.02. 69 P
this day my sister should the cloister enter, MM 1.02.177
forsworn, | and those eyes, the break of day, 4.01. 3
i have sat here all day. 4.01. 20 P
for, as i take it, it is almost day. 4.02.106 P
drunk many times a day, if not many days 4.02.149 P
for he this very day receives letters of strange 4.02.200 P
morning, may sleep the sounder all the next day. 4.03. 47 P
i will not consent to die this day, that's 4.03. 56 P
well; you'll answer this one day. fare ye well. 4.03.163 P
i'll limit thee this day | to seek thy /health ERR 1.01.150
this very day a syracusian merchant | is 1.02. 3
well, i will marry one day, but to try. 2.01. 42
in | now in the stirring passage of the day, | a 3.01. 99
for locking me out of my doors by day. 4.01. 18
that time comes stealing on by night and day? 4.02. 60
he not reason to turn back an hour in a day? 4.02. 62
o most unhappy day! 4.04.123
this ill day | a most outrageous fit of madness 5.01.138
that she this day hath shameless thrown on me. 5.01.202
this day, great duke, she shut the doors upon me 5.01.204
ne'er may i look on day, nor sleep on night, 5.01.210
this woman lock'd me out this day from dinner; 5.01.218
that i this day of him receiv'd the chain, 5.01.228
and there live we as merry as the day is long. ADO 2.01. 49 P
i hope to see you one day fitted with a husband. 2.01. 57 P
name the day of marriage, and god give thee joy! 2.01.300 P
your grace is too costly to wear every day. 2.01.329 P
i will presently go learn their day of marriage. 2.02. 56 P
by this day! 2.03.245 P
why, every day to–morrow. 3.01.101
o day untowardly turn'd! 3.02.131 P
good day to both of you. 5.01. 46
good day, my lord. 5.01.112 P
thee how beatrice prais'd thy wit the other day. 5.01.160 P
wolves have preyed, and look, the gentle day, 5.03. 25
ours, this day to be conjoin'd | in the state of 5.04. 29
you, but, by this good day, i yield upon great 5.04. 95 P
and one day in a week to touch no food, | and LLL 1.01. 39
no food, | and but one meal on every day beside, 1.01. 40
and not be seen to wink of all the day — | when 1.01. 43
and make a dark night too of half the day — 1.01. 45
and bide the penance of each three years' day. 1.01.115
affliction may one day smile again, and till 1.01.314 P
what time a' day? 2.01.121
put up this — 'twill be thine another day. 4.01.107
as fair as day. 4.03. 88
"on a day — alack the day! 4.03. 99
"on a day — alack the day! 4.03. 99
o, but for my love, day would turn to night! 4.03.229
converse this quondam day with a companion of 5.01. 7 P
at her pavilion in the posteriors of this day, 5.01. 89 P
the posterior of the day, most generous sir, is 5.01. 91 P
some show in the posterior of this day, to be 5.01.120 P
all hail, sweet madam, and fair time of day! 5.02.339
i have seen the day of wrong through the little 5.02.723 P
a twelvemonth and a day | i'll mark no words 5.02.827
you shall this twelvemonth term from day to day 5.02.850
you shall this twelvemonth term from day to day 5.02.850
come, sir, it wants a twelvemonth an' a day, 5.02.877
upon that day either prepare to die | for MND 1.01. 86
a proper man as one shall see in a summer's day; 1.02. 87 P
land, | and in the shape of corin sat all day, 2.01. 66
it good, | and tarry for the comfort of the day. 2.02. 38
play | intended for great theseus' nuptial day. 3.02. 12
the sun was not so true unto the day | as he to 3.02. 50
for fear lest day should look their shames upon, 3.02.385
we may effect this business yet ere day. 3.02.395
come, thou gentle day! 3.02.418
here will i rest me till the break of day. 3.02.446
and since we have the vaward of the day, | my 4.01.105
is not this the day | that hermia should give 4.01.135
hath he lost sixpence a day during his life; 4.02. 20 P
he could not have scap'd sixpence a day. 4.02. 21 P
given him sixpence a day for playing pyramus, 4.02. 22 P
sixpence a day in pyramus, or nothing. 4.02. 23 P
o most courageous day! 4.02. 27 P
o night, which ever art when day is not! 5.01.171
now, until the break of day, | through this 5.01.401
meet me all by break of day. 5.01.422
you shall seek all day ere you find them, and MV 1.01.117 P
you spurn'd me such a day, another time | you 1.03.127
sport, | if you repay me not on such a day, | in 1.03.146
if he should break his day, what should i gain 1.03.163
my ships come home a month before the day. 1.03.181
alack the day, i know you not, young gentleman, 2.02. 70 P
shylock thy master spoke with me this day, | and 2.02.145
and he sleeps by day | more than the wild–cat. 2.05. 47
let good antonio look he keep his day, | or he 2.08. 25
a day in april never came so sweet, | to show 2.09. 93
tarry, pause a day or two | before you hazard, 3.02. 1
is | as are those dulcet sounds in break of day 3.02. 51
have by your wisdom been this day acquitted | of 4.01.409
and be a day before our husbands home. 4.02. 3
my mistress will before the break of day | be 5.01. 29
methinks it sounds much sweeter than by day. 5.01.100
the nightingale, if she should sing by day, 5.01.104
'tis a day, | such as the day is when the sun is 5.01.125
a day, | such as the day is when the sun is hid. 5.01.126
we should hold day with the antipodes, | if you 5.01.127
or go to bed now, being two hours to day. 5.01.303
but were the day come, i should wish it dark 5.01.304
say many young gentlemen flock to him every day, AYL 1.01.117 P
one so young and so villainous this day living. 1.01.155 P
thus men may grow wiser every day. 1.02.137 P
he hath been all this day to look you. 2.05. 33 P
and i have been all this day to avoid him. 2.05. 34 P
alas the day, what shall i do with my doublet 3.02.219 P
he as freshly as he did the day he wrastled? 3.02.231 P
you should ask me what time o' day; 3.02.300 P
of her marriage and the day it is solemniz'd. 3.02.314 P
and i set him every day to woo me. 3.02.409 P
and come every day to my cote and woo me. 3.02.427 P
good day and happiness, dear rosalind! 4.01. 30 P
for ever and a day. 4.01.145 P
say "a day," without the "ever." 4.01.146 P
to–morrow is the joyful day, audrey, to–morrow 5.03. 1 P
hearing how that every day | men of great worth 5.04.154
haste, | and every day i cannot come to woo. SHR 2.01.115
i'll crave the day | when i shall ask the banes, 2.01.179
now is the day we long have looked for. 2.01.333
signior lucentio, this is the 'pointed day, 3.02. 1
woo a thousand, 'point the day of marriage, 3.02. 15
now, | that shall be woo'd and wedded in a day. 4.02. 51
my father is here look'd for every day, | to 4.02.117
and that you look'd for him this day in padua. 4.04. 16
but bid bianca farewell for ever and a day. 4.04. 97
fair lovely maid, once more good day to thee. 4.05. 33
to watch the night in storms, the day in cold, 5.02.150
on his grace's cure | by such a day an' hour. AWW 1.03.249
nay, i'll fit you, | and not be all day neither. 2.01. 91
ease, will day by day | come here for physic. 3.01. 18
ease, will day by day | come here for physic. 3.01. 18
come night, end day! 3.02.128
this very day, | great mars, i put myself into 3.03. 8
writ to me this other day to turn him out a' th' 4.03.199 P
but this exceeding posting day and night | must 5.01. 1
i am not a day of season, | for thou mayst see a 5.03. 32
with strife to please you, day exceeding day. ep 4
with strife to please you, day exceeding day. ep 4
and water once a day her chamber round | with TN 1.01. 28
him put down the other day with an ordinary fool 1.05. 84 P
alas the day! 2.01. 24 P
as i am woman (now alas the day!), 2.02. 38
"o' the twelf day of december" — 2.03. 84
both day and night did we keep company. 5.01. 96
and died that day when viola from her birth 5.01.244
that day that made my sister thirteen years. 5.01.248
continent the fire | that severs day from night. 5.01.272
one day shall crown th' alliance on't, so please 5.01.318
but a toy, | for the rain it raineth every day. 5.01.392
and we'll strive to please you every day. 5.01.408
this satisfaction | the by–gone day proclaim'd. WT 1.02. 32
behind | but such a day to–morrow as to–day, 1.02. 64
he makes a july's day short as december, | and 1.02.169
good day, camillo. 1.02.366
nor night, nor day, no rest. 2.03. 1
once a day i'll visit | the chapel where they 3.02.238
the day frowns more and more; 3.03. 54
i never saw | the heavens so dim by day. 3.03. 56
'tis a lucky day, boy, and we'll do good deeds 3.03.138 P
a merry heart goes all the day, | your sad tires 4.03.125
as it were the day | of celebration of that 4.04. 49
upon | this day she was both pantler, butler, 4.04. 56
should take on me | the hostess–ship o' th' day. 4.04. 72
spring that might | become your time of day — 4.04.114
as he is (and in the hottest day prognostication 4.04.788 P
for she hath privately twice or thrice a day, 5.02.106 P
you denied to fight with me this other day, 5.02.129 P
now blessed be the hour by night or day | when i JN 1.01.165
who dares not stir by day must walk by night, 1.01.172
who by the hand of france this day hath made 2.01.302
approach, | commander of this hot malicious day. 2.01.314
to whom in favor she shall give the day, | and 2.01.393
but they will quake and tremble all this day. 3.01. 18
and this blessed day | ever in france shall be 3.01. 75
to solemnize this day the glorious sun | stays 3.01. 77
the yearly course that brings this day about 3.01. 81
day about | shall never see it but a holy day. 3.01. 82
a wicked day, and not a holy day! 3.01. 83
a wicked day, and not a holy day! 3.01. 83
what hath this day deserv'd? 3.01. 84
nay, rather turn this day out of the week, 3.01. 87
week, | this day of shame, oppression, perjury. 3.01. 88
pray that their burthens may not fall this day, 3.01. 90
but on this day let seamen fear no wrack; 3.01. 92
no bargains break that are not this day made: 3.01. 93
this day all things begun come to ill end, | yea 3.01. 94
to curse the fair proceedings of this day. 3.01. 97
let not the hours of this ungodly day | wear out 3.01.109
fair day, adieu! 3.01.326
now, by my life, this day grows wondrous hot; 3.02. 1
the sun is in the heaven, and the proud day, 3.03. 34
then, in despite of brooded watchful day, | i 3.03. 52
what have you lost by losing of this day? 3.04.116
sky, | no scope of nature, no distemper'd day, 3.04.154
i should be as merry as the day is long; 4.01. 18
and on that day at noon, whereon he says | i 4.02.156
whose office is this day | to feast upon whole 5.02.177
how goes the day with us? o, tell me, hubert. 5.03. 1
in spite of spite, alone upholds the day. 5.04. 5
for if the french be lords of this loud day, 5.04. 14
i say again, if lewis do win the day, | he is 5.04. 30
of yours | behold another day break in the east; 5.04. 32
if lewis by your assistance win the day. 5.04. 39
the day shall not be up so soon as i, | to try 5.05. 21
each day still better other's happiness | until R2 1.01. 22
i pray | your highness to assign our trial day. 1.01.151
it, | at coventry upon saint lambert's day. 1.01.199
stay yet another day, thou trusty welshman. 2.04. 5
his face, | not able to endure the sight of day, 3.02. 52
one day too late, i fear me, noble lord, | hath 3.02. 67
to–day, to–day, unhappy day, too late, 3.02. 71
the worst is death, and death will have his day. 3.02.103
like an unseasonable stormy day, | which makes 3.02.106
to change blows with thee for our day of doom. 3.02.189
the sky | the state and inclination of the day; 3.02.195
from richard's night to bullingbrook's fair day. 3.02.218
alack the heavy day | when such a sacred king 3.03. 8
thou dar'st not, coward, live to see that day. 4.01. 41
that honorable day shall never be seen. 4.01. 91
to keep him safely till his day of trial. 4.01.153
shall feel this day as sharp to them as thorn. 4.01.323
i'll lay | a plot shall show us all a merry day. 4.01.334
sent back like hollowmas or short'st of day. 5.01. 80
into | for gay apparel 'gainst the triumph day. 5.02. 66
knees, | and never see day that the happy sees, 5.03. 94
and never show thy head by day nor light. 5.06. 44
on holy–rood day, the gallant hotspur there, 1H4 1.01. 52
now, hal, what time of day is it, lad? 1.02. 1 P
devil hast thou to do with the time of the day? 1.02. 6 P
be so superfluous to demand the time of the day. 1.02. 12 P
rated me the other day in the street about you, 1.02. 84 P
who studies day and night | to answer all the 1.03.184
an' it be not four by the day, i'll be hang'd. 2.01. 1 P
let us share, and then to horse before day. 2.02. 99 P
have ta'en a thousand pound this day morning. 2.04.159 P
there let him sleep till day. 2.04.543 P
as is the difference betwixt day and night | the 3.01.217
"as god shall mend me," and "as sure as day"; 3.01.250 P
and in the closing of some glorious day | be 3.02.133
and that shall be the day, when e'er it lights, 3.02.138
and said this other day you ought him a thousand 3.03.134 P
the powers of us may serve so great a day. 4.01.132
you, my lord, or any scot that this day lives. 4.03. 12
is a day | wherein the fortune of ten thousand 4.04. 8
the day looks pale | at his distemp'rature. 5.01. 2
foretells a tempest and a blust'ring day. 5.01. 6
i have not sought the day of this dislike. 5.01. 26
and posted day and night | to meet you on the 5.01. 35
yet, i would be loath to pay him before his day. 5.01.128 P
the world, | if he outlive the envy of this day, 5.02. 66
withal | in the adventure of this perilous day. 5.02. 95
our soldiers stand full fairly for the day. 5.03. 29
did such deeds in arms as i have done this day. 5.03. 46 P
the trumpet sounds retrait, the day is our. 5.04.159
the fortune of the day quite turn'd from him, 5.05. 18
sway, | meeting the check of such another day, 5.05. 42
o, such a day! 2H4 1.01. 20
if my young lord your son have not the day, 1.01. 52
god give your lordship good time of day. 1.02. 94 P
at home, that our armies join not in a hot day! 1.02.208 P
if it be a hot day, and i brandish any thing but 1.02.210 P
alas the day, take heed of him! 2.01. 13 P
and fubb'd off, from this day to that day, that 2.01. 35 P
from this day to that day, that it is a shame to 2.01. 35 P
master tisick, the debuty, t' other day, and, as 2.04. 85 P
asia, | which cannot go but thirty mile a day, 2.04.165
and the very same day did i fight with one 3.02. 31 P
by this day, i know not the phrase, but i will 3.02. 74 P
good day to you, gentle lord archbishop, | and 4.02. 2
and a hand | open as day for /meting charity; 4.04. 32
as flaws congealed in the spring of day. 4.04. 35
haunch of winter sings | the lifting up of day. 4.04. 93
sit | like a rich armor worn in heat of day, 4.05. 30
my day is dim. 4.05.100
say, | god shorten harry's happy life one day! 5.02.145
o joyful day! 5.03.126 P
i would make this a bloody day to somebody. 5.04. 12 P
as it were, to ride day and night, and not to 5.05. 20 P
sala, | as is at this day in germany call'd meisen. H5 1.02. 53
so do the kings of france unto this day. 1.02. 90
i say gud day, captain fluellen. 3.02. 83 P
the day is hot, and the weather, and the wars, 3.02.106 P
our expectation hath this day an end. 3.03. 44
the pridge as you shall see in a summer's day. 3.06. 64 P
would it were day! 3.07. 2 P
will it never be day? 3.07. 80 P
would it were day! 3.07.130 P
his leek about his pate | upon saint davy's day. 4.01. 55
not you wear your dagger in your cap that day, 4.01. 57 P
no great cause to desire the approach of day. 4.01. 88 P
we see yonder the beginning of the day, but i 4.01. 89 P
join together at the latter day and cry all, "we 4.01.137 P
he let him outlive that day to see his greatness 4.01.184 P
next day after dawn, | doth rise and help 4.01.274
who twice a day their wither'd hands hold up 4.01.299
the day, my /friends, and all things stay for me 4.01.309
the sun is high, and we outwear the day. 4.02. 63
this day is call'd the feast of crispian: 4.03. 40
he that outlives this day, and comes safe home, 4.03. 41
will stand a' tiptoe when this day is named, 4.03. 42
he that shall see this day, and live old age, 4.03. 44
with advantages | what feats he did that day. 4.03. 51
by, | from this day to the ending of the world, 4.03. 58
so vile, | this day shall gentle his condition; 4.03. 63
that fought with us upon saint crispin's day. 4.03. 67

and how thou pleasest, god, dispose the day! 4.03.133
herald, | i know not if the day be ours or no, 4.07. 84
the day is yours. 4.07. 86
fought on the day of crispin crispianus. 4.07. 91
no scorn to wear the leek upon saint tavy's day. 4.07.103 P
look you, as you shall desire in a summer's day. 4.08. 22 P
by this day and this light, the fellow has 4.08. 62 P
saint davy's day is past. 5.01. 2 P
to our sister, | health and fair time of day; 5.02. 3
of this good day and of this gracious meeting, 5.02. 13
and that this day | shall change all griefs and 5.02. 19
on which day, | my lord of burgundy, we'll take 5.02.370
be the heavens with black, yield day to night! 1H6 1.01. 1
unto the french the dreadful judgment day | so 1.01. 29
so in the earth, to this day is not known. 1.02. 2
i am come to survey the tower this day; 1.03. 1
here in arms this day against god's peace and 1.03. 75 P
this day is ours, as many more shall be. 1.05. 18
that one day bloom'd and fruitful were the next. 1.06. 7
'tis joan, not we, by whom the day is won; 1.06. 17
royally, | after this golden day of victory. 1.06. 31
secure, | having all day carous'd and banqueted: 2.01. 12
the day begins to break, and night is fled, 2.02. 1
that could not live asunder day or night. 2.02. 31
say | this quarrel will drink blood another day. 2.04.133
this day, in argument upon a case, | some words 2.05. 45
lost, and recovered in a day again! 3.02.115
'tis but the short'ning of my life one day. 4.06. 37
in, | we should have found a bloody day of this. 4.07. 34
to know who hath obtain'd the glory of the day. 4.07. 52
by day, by night, waking and in my dreams, | in 2H6 1.01. 26
a day will come when york shall claim his own, 1.01.239
she vaunted 'mongst her minions t' other day, 1.03. 84
i did correct him for his fault the other day, 1.03.199 P
and let these have a day appointed them | for 1.03.207
and the day of combat shall be the last of the 1.03.218 P
i saw not better sport these seven years' day; 2.01. 2
let never day nor night unhallowed pass, | but 2.01. 83
yes, master, clear as day, i thank god and saint 2.01.105 P
but cloaks and gowns, before this day, a many. 2.01.113
never, before this day, in all his life. 2.01.114
you made in a day, my lord, whole towns to fly. 2.01.160
shall one day make the duke of york a king. 2.02. 79
this is the day appointed for the combat, | and 2.03. 48
thus sometimes hath the brightest day a cloud, 2.04. 1
dark shall be my light, and night my day; 2.04. 40
when every one will give the time of day, | he 3.01. 14
by means whereof the towns each day revolted? 3.01. 63
my use, | be brought against me at my trial day! 3.01.114
he'll wrest the sense and hold us here all day. 3.01.186
and so break off, the day is almost spent; 3.01.325
and remorseful day | is crept into the bosom of 4.01. 1
the bricks are alive at this day to testify it; 4.02.149 P
soldiers, this day have you redeem'd your lives, 4.09. 15
staff, | this day i'll wear aloft my burgonet, 5.01.204
and the premised flames of the last day | knit 5.02. 41
and we will live | to see their day, and them 5.02. 89
this happy day | is not itself, nor have we won 5.03. 5
now, by my /faith, lords, 'twas a glorious day. 5.03. 29
the queen this day here holds her parliament, 3H6 1.01. 35
and we, in them, no hope to win the day, | so 2.01.136
ne'er may he live to see a sunshine day | that 2.01.187
he might have kept that glory to this day. 2.02.153
and grac'd thy poor sire with his bridal day, 2.02.155
words will cost ten thousand lives this day. 2.02.177
can neither call it perfect day nor night. 2.05. 4
complete, | how many hours brings about the day, 2.05. 27
and thou this day hadst kept thy chair in peace. 2.06. 20
i'll tell thee what befell me on a day | in this 3.01. 10
that's a day longer than a wonder lasts. 3.02.114
yet i confess that often ere this day, | when i 3.03.131
to–morrow then belike shall be the day, | if 4.03. 7
warwick may lose, that now hath won the day. 4.04. 15
doubt not of the day, | and, that once gotten, 4.07. 87
but, in the midst of this bright–shining day, 5.03. 3
hope | go home to bed, and like the owl by day, 5.04. 56
good day, my lord. what, at your book so hard? 5.06. 1
light, | but i will sort a pitchy day for thee; 5.06. 85
room, | and triumph, henry, in thy day of doom. 5.06. 93
this day should clarence closely be mew'd up R3 1.01. 38
brother, good day. 1.01. 42
from whence this present day he is delivered? 1.01. 69
good time of day unto my gracious lord! 1.01.122
intent, | clarence hath not another day to live: 1.01.150
it is my day, my life. 1.02.130
black night o'ershade thy day, and death thy 1.02.131
good time of day unto your royal grace! 1.03. 18
the day will come that thou shalt wish for me 1.03.244
o, but remember this another day, | when he 1.03.298
shall never wake until the great judgment day. 1.04.104 P
i every day expect an embassage | from my 2.01. 3
and, princely peers, a happy time of day! 2.01. 48
happy indeed, as we have spent the day. 2.01. 49
a holy day shall this be kept hereafter. 2.01. 74
to–morrow, or next day, they will be here. 2.04. 3
some day or two | your highness shall repose you 3.01. 64
posterity, | even to the general all–ending day. 3.01. 78
news, | that this same very day your enemies, 3.02. 49
but yet you see how soon the day o'ercast. 3.02. 86
the day is spent. 3.02. 89
this day those enemies are put to death, | and i 3.02.103
in god's name speak, when is the royal day? 3.04. 3
to–morrow then i judge a happy day. 3.04. 6
we have not yet set down this day of triumph. 3.04. 42
as else i would be, were the day prolong'd. 3.04. 45
that the subtile traitor | this day had plotted, 3.05. 38
lord, | to visit him to–morrow or next day. 3.07. 60
graces both | a happy and a joyful time of day! 4.01. 6
but shall we wear these glories for a day? 4.02. 5
which in the day of battle tire thee more | than 4.04.189
day, yield me not thy light, nor, night, thy 4.04.401
this is all–souls' day, fellow, is it not? 5.01. 10
why then all–souls' day is my body's doomsday. 5.01. 12
this is the day which, in king edward's time, 5.01. 13
this is the day wherein i wish'd to fall | by 5.01. 16
this, this all–souls' day to my fearful soul, 5.01. 18
no delay, | for, lords, to–morrow is a busy day. 5.03. 18
car | gives token of a goodly day to–morrow. 5.03. 21
awake and win the day! 5.03.145
'tis not yet near day. 5.03.220
a black day will it be to somebody. 5.03.280
rescue, fair lord, or else the day is lost! 5.04. 6
the day is ours, the bloody dog is dead. 5.05. 2
each following day | became the next day's H8 1.01. 16
him — every day | it would infect his speech — 1.02.132
by day and night, | he's traitor to th' height. 1.02.213
i have this day receiv'd a traitor's judgment, 2.01. 58
that blood will make 'em one day groan for't. 2.01.106
good day to both your graces. 2.02. 13
the king will know him one day. 2.02. 21
heaven will one day open | the king's eyes, that 2.02. 41
that we adjourn this court till further day. 2.04.233
the third day comes a frost, a killing frost, 3.02.355
this day was view'd in open as his queen, 3.02.404
forward | in celebration of this day with shows, 4.01. 10
of those that claim their offices this day | by 4.01. 15
faces | been loose, this day they had been lost. 4.01. 75
than the business | that seeks dispatch by day. 5.01. 16
and indeed this day, | sir (i may tell it you), 5.01. 41
i think your highness saw this many a day. 5.02. 21
and yet no day without a deed to crown it. 5.04. 58
this day, no man think | h'as business at his 5.04. 74
helen herself swore th' other day that troilus, TRO 1.02. 93 P
she came to him th' other day into the compass'd 1.02.111 P
upon a lazy bed the livelong day | breaks 1.03.147
alas the day, how loath you are to offend 3.02. 47 P
i have lov'd you night and day | for many weary 3.02.114
as sun to day, as turtle to her mate, | as iron 3.02.178
good day, good day. 3.03. 62
good day, good day. 3.03. 62
ay, and good next day too. 3.03. 69
if to–morrow be a fair day, by aleven of the 3.03.295 P
but that the busy day, | wak'd by the lark, hath 4.02. 8
never's my day, and then a kiss of you. 4.05. 52
common arbitrator, time, | will one day end it. 4.05.226
you may have every day enough of hector, | if 4.05.263
my dreams will sure prove ominous to the day. 5.03. 6
enrapt | to tell thee that this day is ominous: 5.03. 66
to close the day up, hector's life is done. 5.08. 8
when for a day of kings' entreaties a mother COR 1.03. 8 P
my ladies both, good day to you. 1.03. 48 P
as merry as when our nuptial day was done | and 1.06. 31
of threepence to a second day of audience. 2.01. 72 P
pent to linger | but with a grain a day, i would 3.03. 90
could i meet 'em | but once a day, it would 4.02. 47
the day serves well for them now. 4.03. 31 P
i, it exceeds peace as far as day does night; 4.05.222 P
a merrier day did never yet greet rome, | no, 5.04. 42
lives not this day within the city walls. TIT 1.01. 26
favors done | to us in our election this day, 1.01.235
the dismall'st day is this that e'er i saw, | to 1.01.384
alone, | i'll find a day to massacre them all, 1.01.450
this day all quarrels die, andronicus. 1.01.465
this day shall be a love–day, tamora. 1.01.491
but dawning day new comfort hath inspir'd. 2.02. 10
thee, | this is the day of doom for bassianus: 2.03. 42
by day and night t' attend him carefully, | and 4.03. 28
like stinging bees in hottest summer's day, 5.01. 14
even now i curse the day — and yet i think 5.01.125
care, | witness the tiring day and heavy night, 5.02. 24
trot like a servile footman all day long, | even 5.02. 55
and day by day i'll do this heavy task, | so 5.02. 58
and day by day i'll do this heavy task, | so 5.02. 58
is the day so young? ROM 1.01.160
of all the days of the year, upon that day; 1.03. 25
for even the day before, she broke her brow, 1.03. 38
waste our lights in vain, /like lights by day! 1.04. 45
i have seen the day | that i have worn a visor 1.05. 21
the day to cheer and night's dank dew to dry, 2.03. 6
the day is hot, the capels /are abroad, | and if 3.01. 2
night, come, romeo, come, thou day in night, 3.02. 17
so tedious is this day | as is the night before 3.02. 28
alack the day, he's gone, he's kill'd, he's dead 3.02. 39
it did, it did, alas the day, it did! 3.02. 72
or by the break of day /disguis'd from hence. 3.03.168
we'nsday next — | but soft, what day is this? 3.04. 18
it is not yet near day. 3.05. 1
out, and jocund day | stands tiptoe on the misty 3.05. 9
let's talk, it is not day. 3.05. 25
hunting thee hence with hunt's–up to the day. 3.05. 34
the day is broke, be wary, look about. 3.05. 40
then, window, let day in, and let life out. 3.05. 41
i must hear from thee every day in the hour, 3.05. 44
hath sorted out a sudden day of joy, | that thou 3.05.109
madam, in happy time, what day is that? 3.05.111
day, night, work, play, | alone, in company, 3.05.176
like death when he shuts up the day of life; 4.01.101
good /faith, 'tis day. 4.04. 21
o lamentable day! 4.05. 17
look, look! o heavy day! 4.05. 18
she's dead, deceas'd, she's dead, alack the day! 4.05. 23
alack the day, she's dead, she's dead, she's 4.05. 24
o lamentable day! 4.05. 30
accurs'd, unhappy, wretched, hateful day! 4.05. 43
o woeful, woeful, woeful day! 4.05. 49
most lamentable day, most woeful day | that ever 4.05. 50
lamentable day, most woeful day | that ever, 4.05. 50
o day, o day, o day, o hateful day! 4.05. 52
o day, o day, o day, o hateful day! 4.05. 52
o day, o day, o day, o hateful day! 4.05. 52
o day, o day, o day, o hateful day! 4.05. 52
never was seen so black a day as this. 4.05. 53
o woeful day, o woeful day! 4.05. 54
o woeful day, o woeful day! 4.05. 54
and all this day an unaccustom'd spirit | lifts 5.01. 4
good day, sir. TIM 1.01. 1
what time a' day is't, apemantus? 1.01.256
before me now | would one day stamp upon me. 1.02.144
gave | good words the other day of a bay courser 1.02.211
learning die then that day thou art hang'd. 2.02. 82 P
i should purchase the day before for a little 3.02. 47 P
good day at once. 3.04. 7
the good time of day to you, sir. 3.06. 1 P
honorable lord did but try us this other day. 3.06. 3 P
when your lordship this other day sent to me, i 3.06. 42 P
he gave me a jewel th' other day, and now he has 3.06.112 P
one day he gives us diamonds, next day stones. 3.06.120
one day he gives us diamonds, next day stones. 3.06.120
embalms and spices | to th' april day again. 4.03. 42
when the day serves, before black–corner'd night 5.01. 44
who once a day with his embossed froth | the 5.01.217
not walk | upon a laboring day without the sign JC 1.01. 4
and there have sate | the livelong day, with 1.01. 41
for once, upon a raw and gusty day, | the 1.02.100
come, casca, you and i will yet, ere day, | see 1.03.153
and ere day | we will awake him and be sure of 1.03.163
of the stars | give guess how near to day. 2.01. 3
it is the bright day that brings forth the adder 2.01. 14
get you to bed again, it is not day. 2.01. 39
by day | where wilt thou find a cavern dark 2.01. 79
here lies the east; doth not the day break here? 2.01.101
that fret the clouds are messengers of day. 2.01.104
we /are two lions litter'd in one day, | and i 2.02. 46
to give this day a crown to mighty caesar. 2.02. 94
in his tent, | that day he overcame the nervii. 3.02.173
o woeful day! 3.02.200 P
for, from this day forth, | i'll use you for my 4.03. 48
the enemy increaseth every day; 4.03.216
as this very day | was cassius born. 5.01. 71
but this same day | must end that work the ides 5.01.112
but it sufficeth that the day will end, | and 5.01.124
this day i breathed first: 5.03. 23
so in his red blood cassius' day is set! 5.03. 62
our day is gone, | clouds, dews, and dangers 5.03. 63
i shall have glory by this losing day | more 5.05. 36
away, | to part the glories of this happy day. 5.05. 81
sleep shall neither night nor day | hang upon MAC 1.03. 19
so foul and fair a day i have not seen. 1.03. 38
in viewing o'er the rest o' th' self–same day, 1.03. 94
time and the hour runs through the roughest day. 1.03.147
are regist'red where every day i turn | the leaf 1.03.151
"they met me in the day of success; 1.05. 1 P
by th' clock 'tis day, | and yet dark night 2.04. 6
alas the day, | what good could they pretend? 2.04. 23
night, | scarf up the tender eye of pitiful day, 3.02. 47
good things of day begin to droop and drowse, 3.02. 52
the west yet glimmers with some streaks of day; 3.03. 5
and each new day a gash | is added to her wounds 4.03. 40
than on her feet, | died every day she liv'd. 4.03.111
the night is long that never finds the day. 4.03.240
creeps in this petty pace from day to day, | to 5.05. 20
creeps in this petty pace from day to day, | to 5.05. 20
war, | the day almost itself professes yours, 5.07. 27
see, | so great a day as this is cheaply bought. 5.09. 3
doth make the night joint–laborer with the day: HAM 1.01. 78
shrill–sounding throat | awake the god of day, 1.01.152
foe in heaven | or ever i had seen that day, 1.02.183
and it must follow, as the night the day, | thou 1.03. 79
and for the day confin'd to fast in fires, 1.05. 11
o day and night, but this is wondrous strange! 1.05.164
i saw him yesterday, or th' other day, | or then 2.01. 54
why day is day, night night, and time is time, 2.02. 88
why day is day, night night, and time is time, 2.02. 88
were nothing but to waste night, day, and time; 2.02. 89
lord, | how does your honor for this many a day? 3.01. 90
sport and repose lock from me day and night, 3.02.217
i would beguile | the tedious day with sleep. 3.02.227
and do such /bitter /business /as /the day 3.02.391
"to–morrow is saint valentine's day, | all in 4.05. 48
your judgment 'pear | as day does to your eye. 4.05.153
i came to't that day that our last king hamlet 5.01.144 P
it was that very day that young hamlet was born 5.01.147 P
the cat will mew, and dog will have his day. 5.01.292
now, the next day | was our sea–fight, and what 5.02. 53
it is the breathing time of day with me. 5.02.174 P
if, on the tenth day following, | thy banish'd LR 1.01.176
of a prediction i read this other day, what 1.02.141 P
by day and night he wrongs me, every hour | he 1.03. 3
fit, | though the rain it raineth every day." 3.02. 77
alack, alack the day! 4.06.181
i have seen the day, with my good biting 5.03.277
the day had broke | before we parted. OTH 3.01. 32
alas the day, i never gave him cause. 3.04.158
i was the other day talking on the sea–bank with 4.01.133 P
alas the heavy day! 4.02. 42
do not weep, do not weep. alas the day! 4.02.124
every day thou daff'st me with some device, iago 4.02.175 P
his pernicious soul | rot half a grain a day! 5.02.156
i have seen the day | that, with this little arm 5.02.261
who's born that day | when i forget to send to ANT 1.05. 63
he shall have every day a several greeting, | or 1.05. 77
but next day | i told him of myself, which was 2.02. 77
sir, we did sleep day out of countenance, and 2.02.177 P
pompey doth this day laugh away his fortune. 2.06.104 P
of the goddess isis | that day appear'd, and oft 3.06. 18
brother, good night; to–morrow is the day. 4.03. 1
the gods make this a happy day to antony! 4.05. 1
prove this a prosp'rous day, the three–nook'd 4.06. 5
o thou day o' th' world, | chain mine arm'd neck 4.08. 13
this last day was | a shrewd one to 's. 4.09. 4
most heavy day! 4.14.134
have shown to thee such a declining day, | or 5.01. 38
finish, good lady, the bright day is done, | and 5.02.193
let her languish | a drop of blood a day, and, CYM 1.01.157
and every day that comes comes to decay | a 1.05. 56
day, my lord. 2.03. 10 P
make pastime with us a day or two, or longer. 3.01. 78 P
a week, why may not i | glide thither in a day? 3.02. 52
a goodly day not to keep house with such | whose 3.03. 1
mother, | and every day do honor to her grave. 3.03.105
day? 3.04.136
nor to us hath tender'd | the duty of the day. 3.05. 32
this night forestall him of the coming day! 3.05. 69
i had no mind | to hunt this day; 4.02.148
the day that she was missing he was here; 4.03. 17
it is a day turn'd strangely. 5.02. 17
chance of war, the day | was yours by accident. 5.05. 75
day serves not light more faithful than i'll be. PER 1.02.110
i would have been that day in the belfry. 2.01. 37 P
if it be a day fits you, search out of the 2.01. 54 P
this day i'll rise, or else add ill to ill. 2.01.166
set purpose let his armor rust | until this day, 2.02. 55
call it by what you will, the day is /yours, 2.03. 13
with me? and welcome. happy day, my lords. 2.04. 22

or never more to view nor day nor light. 2.05. 17
as a fair day in summer; wondrous fair. 2.05. 36
by break of day, if the wind cease. 3.01. 76 P
we every day | expect him here: 4.01. 33
and held a mawkin | not worth the time of day. 4.03. 35
the day | that he should marry you, at such a TNK 1.01. 59
bring away, | vapors, sighs, darken the day; 1.05. 2
assure upon my daughter at the day of my death. 2.01. 9 P
would he would do so ev'ry day! 2.04. 27
the whole week's not fair | if any day it rain. 3.01. 66
and ev'ry day discourse you into health, | as i 3.06. 38
thou wor'st that day the three kings fell, but 3.06. 71
that was a very good one, and that day, | i well 3.06. 72
every day | they'ld fight about you; 3.06.220
her, but this very day | i ask'd her questions, 4.01. 37
ev'n thus all day long. 4.03. 18 P
and do nothing all day long but pick flowers 4.03. 25 P
that this day come | to blow that nearness out 5.01. 9
drum, instruct this day | with military skill, 5.01. 57
and by thee | be styl'd the lord o' th' day. 5.01. 60
and while i live, | this day i give to tears. 5.04. 98
your day is length'ned, and | the blissful dew 5.04.103
a day or two | let us look sadly, and give grace 5.04.124
by a halfpenny loaf a day, troy weight. STM II.C 7 P
a summer's day will seem an hour but short, VEN 23
and i will wink, so shall the day seem night. 122
the night of sorrow now is turn'd to day: 481
to shame the sun by day and her by night. 732
but like a stormy day, now wind, now rain, 965
like stars asham'd of day, themselves withdrew. 1032
and never fright the silly lamb that day. 1098
thou being dead, the day should yet be light. 1134
throbbing heart shall rock thee day and night; 1186
and in her vaulty prison stows the day. LUC 119
lay, | till they might open to adorn the day. 399
light, | she prays she never may behold the day: 746
"for day," quoth she, "night's scapes doth open 747
let not the jealous day behold that face, 800
"make me not object to the tell-tale day, | the 806
grooms are sightless night, kings glorious day; 1013
revealing day through every cranny spies, | and 1086
for day hath nought to do what's done by night." 1092
for, poor bird, thou sing'st not in the day, 1142
myself was stirring ere the break of day, | and 1280
into so bright a day such black-fac'd storms, 1518
hot was the day, she hotter that did look | for PP 6. 7
pack night, peep day; 14.29
good day, of night now borrow: 14.29
art with arms contending was victor of the day, 15.13
on a day (alack the day!) 16. 1
on a day (alack the day!) 16. 1
and twice desire, yer it be day, | that which 18.29
as it fell upon a day, | in the merry month of 20. 1
car, | like feeble age he reeleth from the day, SON 7.10
and see the brave day sunk in hideous night; 12. 2
against the stormy gusts of winter's day | and 13.11
to change your day of youth to sullied night, 15.12
shall i compare thee to a summer's day? 18. 1
lo thus by day my limbs, by night my mind, | for 27.13
but day by night, and night by day, oppress'd; 28. 4
but day by night, and night by day, oppress'd; 28. 4
i tell the day, to please him, thou art bright, 28. 9
but day doth daily draw my sorrows longer, | and 28.13
(like to the lark at break of day arising | from 29.11
if thou survive my well-contented day, | when 32. 1
why didst thou promise such a beauteous day, 34. 1
for all the day they view things unrespected, 43. 2
to the clear day with thy much clearer light, 43. 7
made | by looking on thee in the living day, 43.10
in me thou seest the twilight of such day | as 73. 5
thus do i pine and surfeit day by day, | or 75.13
thus do i pine and surfeit day by day, | or 75.13
i must each day say o'er the very same, 108. 6
the mountain or the sea, the day or night, | the 113.11
call, | whereto all bonds do tie me day by day; 117. 4
call, | whereto all bonds do tie me day by day; 117. 4
that follow'd it as gentle day | doth follow 145.10
swear that brightness doth not grace the day? 150. 4

DAY-BED 1 FR 0.0001 REL FR 0 V 1 P
having come from a day-bed, where i have left TN 2.05. 48 P

DAY-LIGHT 1 FR 0.0001 REL FR 1 V 0 P
yond light is not day-light, i know it, i; ROM 3.05. 12

DAYLIGHT 12 FR 0.0013 REL FR 8 V 4 P
we burn daylight. WIV 2.01. 54 P
good eye, uncle, i can see a church by daylight. ADO 2.01. 83 P
this dear, | if ever i thy face by daylight see. MND 3.02.427
east, | that i may back to athens by daylight, 3.02.433
this night methinks is but the daylight sick, MV 5.01.124
daylight and champian discovers not more. TN 2.05.160 P
the day, how loath you are to offend daylight! TRO 3.02. 48 P
shuts up his windows, locks fair daylight out, ROM 1.01.139
come, we burn daylight, ho! 1.04. 43
shame those stars, | as daylight doth a lamp; 2.02. 20
fair daylight? LR 4.07. 51
for she doth welcome daylight with her ditty, PP 14.19

/DAY'S 1 FR 0.0001 REL FR 1 V 0 P
/or /ill, /as /this /day's /battle's /fought. LR 4.07. 96

DAY'S 35 FR 0.0039 REL FR 29 V 6 P
take away | the edge of that day's celebration, TMP 4.01. 29
news is old enough, yet it is every day's news. MM 3.02.230 P
that by this sympathized one day's error | have ERR 5.01.398
by day's approach look to be visited. MND 3.02.430
body be call'd thieves of the day's beauty. 1H4 1.02. 25 P
your day's service at shrewsbury hath a little 2H4 1.02.148 P
it be book'd with the rest of this day's deeds, 4.03. 47 P
shall witness live in brass of this day's work. H5 4.03. 97
thy heart-blood i will have for this day's work. 1H6 1.03. 83
now have i done a good day's work. R3 2.01. 1
from tamworth thither is but one day's march. 5.02. 13
following day | became the next day's master, H8 1.01. 17
now is my day's work done, i'll take /good TRO 5.08. 3
if i should tell thee o'er this thy day's work, COR 1.09. 1
in that day's feats, | when he might act the 2.02. 95
you have well sav'd me a day's journey. 4.03. 12 P
from forth day's path and titan's /fiery wheels. ROM 2.03. 4
upon the highmost hill | of this day's journey, 2.05. 10
this day's black fate on moe days doth depend, 3.01.119
the end of this day's business ere it come! JC 5.01.123
(whereto the rather shall his day's hard journey MAC 1.07. 62
the death of each day's life, sore labor's bath, 2.02. 35
is't night's predominance, or the day's shame, 2.04. 8
grave and prosperous) | in this day's council; 3.01. 22
who were the opposites of this day's strife; LR 5.03. 42
and drink carouses to the next day's fate, ANT 4.08. 34
unarm, eros, the long day's task is done, | and 4.14. 35
that comes comes to decay | a day's work in him. CYM 1.05. 57
in the day's glorious walk or peaceful night, PER 1.02. 4
marry, sir, half a day's journey. 2.01.107 P
and crown you king of this day's happiness. 2.03. 11
why, a day's journey, wench. TNK 5.02. 73
my day's delight is past, my horse is gone, VEN 380
his day's hot task hath ended in the west; 530
when day's oppression is not eas'd by night, SON 28. 3

DAYS' 7 FR 0.0008 REL FR 6 V 1 P
effect, i crave but four days' respite; MM 4.02.160 P
for 'twill be | two long days' journey, lords, JN 4.03. 20
shall, after three days' open penance done, 2H6 2.03. 11
these few days' wonder will be quickly worn. 2.04. 69
if after three days' space thou here be'st found 3.02.295
that would be ten days' wonder at the least. 3H6 3.02.113
if after two days' shine athens contain thee, TIM 3.05.100

/DAYS 3 FR 0.0003 REL FR 3 V 0 P
/your /sureties /for /your /days /of /answer. R2 4.01.159
/send /him /many /years /of /sunshine /days! 4.01.221
to sleep the /nights, and fast the /days; R3 4.04.118

DAYS 198 FR 0.0223 REL FR 169 V 29 P
and after two days | i will discharge thee. TMP 1.02.298
i'll free thee | within two days for this. 1.02.422
as i hope | for quiet days, fair issue, and long 4.01. 24
were't not affection chains thy tender days | to TGV 1.01. 3
name) | made use and fair advantage of his days; 2.04. 68
where have you been these two days loitering? 4.04. 44
fenton, | heaven give you many, many merry days! WIV 5.05.240
within these three days his head to be chopp'd MM 1.02. 69 P
times a day, if not many days entirely drunk. 4.02.150 P
find, within these two days he will be here. 4.02.198 P
and, with grey hairs and bruise of many days, ADO 5.01. 65
four days ago. LLL 1.01.122
epitheton appertaining to thy young days, which 1.02. 14 P
no penance, but 'a must fast three days a week. 1.02.129 P
i do see the merry days of desolation that i 1.02.159 P
o heresy in fair, fit for these days! 4.01. 22
ay, as some days, but then no sun must shine. 4.03. 89
her favor turns the fashion of the days, | for 4.03.258
my lady (to the manner of the days) | in 5.02.365
four happy days bring in | another moon; MND 1.01. 2
four days will quickly steep themselves in night 1.01. 7
joy and fresh days of love | accompany your 5.01. 29
you'll be whipt for taxation one of these days. AYL 1.02. 85 P
within these ten days if that thou beest found 1.03. 43
if ever you have look'd on better days, | if 2.07.113
true is it that we have seen better days, | and 2.07.120
i was seven of the nine days out of the wonder 3.02.174 P
have endur'd shrewd days and nights with us, 5.04.173
me, | and i do hope good days and long to see. SHR 1.02.192
ere three days pass, which hath as long lov'd me 4.02. 38
by our remembrances of days foregone, | such AWW 1.03.134
'twill be two days ere i shall see you, so | i 2.05. 70
since you have made the days and nights as one, 5.01. 3
he hath known you but three days, and already TN 1.04. 3 P
"his eyes do show his days are almost done." 2.03.104
in those unfledg'd days was my wife a girl; WT 1.02. 78
did expect my hence departure | two days ago. 1.02.451
to a fine new prince | one of these days, and 2.01. 18
twenty-three days | they have been absent. 2.03.198
sir, it is three days since i saw the prince. 4.02. 29 P
all days of glory, joy, and happiness. JN 3.04.117
and to choke his days | with barbarous ignorance 4.02. 58
constance in a frenzy died | three days before; 4.02.123
many years of happy days befall | my gracious R2 1.01. 20
shorten my days thou canst with sullen sorrow, 1.03.227
which elder days shall ripen and confirm | to 2.03. 43
my lord of salisbury, we have stay'd ten days, 2.04. 1
hath clouded all thy happy days on earth. 3.02. 68
gage | till we assign you to your days of trial. 4.01.106
my lord, some two days since i saw the prince, 5.03. 13
well then, once in my days i'll be a madcap. 1H4 1.02.142 P
shall it for shame be spoken in these days, | or 1.03.170
humors since the old days of goodman adam to the 2.04. 93 P
nor shall we need his help these fourteen days. 3.01. 87
for this advertisement is five days old. 3.02.172
some twelve days hence | our general forces at 3.02.177
poor jack falstaff do in the days of villainy? 3.03.166 P
why, my lord, four days ere i set forth, 4.01. 22
he /cannot draw his power this fourteen days. 4.01.126
death rock me asleep, abridge my doleful days! 2H4 2.04.197
leave fighting a' days and foining a' nights, 2.04.232 P
jesu, jesu, the mad days that i have spent! 3.02. 33 P
jesus, the days that we have seen! 3.02.219 P
the dangers of the days but newly gone, | whose 4.01. 80
all | that feel the bruises of the days before, 4.01. 98
th' unguided days | and rotten times that you 4.04. 59
out, | may waste the memory of the former days. 4.05.215
why, here it is, welcome these pleasant days! 5.03.141
how he comes o'er us with our wilder days, | not H5 1.02.267
yield the crow a pudding one of these days. 2.01. 88 P
from the worm-holes of long-vanish'd days, | nor 2.04. 86
between the promise of his greener days | and 2.04.136
winding up days with toil, and nights with sleep 4.01.279
of my leek, or i will peat his pate four days. 5.01. 41 P
expect saint martin's summer, halcyons' days, 1H6 1.02.131
and even these three days have i watch'd | if i 1.04. 16
for treason executed in our late king's days? 2.04. 91
and like a hermit overpass'd thy days. 2.05.117
his days may finish ere that hapless time. 3.01.200
do you as i do in these dangerous days: 2H6 2.02. 69
thus eleanor's pride dies in her youngest days. 2.03. 46
ah, gracious lord, these days are dangerous: 3.01.142
within fourteen days | at bristow i expect my 3.01.327
infection in this air | but three days longer, 3.02.288
they have been up these two days. 4.02. 2 P
these five days have i hid me in these woods and 4.10. 2 P
i have eat no meat these five days, yet, come 4.10. 39 P
all, | and more such days as these to us befall! 5.03. 33
ah, let me live in prison all my days, | and 3H6 1.03. 43
ten days ago i drown'd these news in tears; 2.01.104
day, | how many days will finish up the year, 2.05. 28
so many days my ewes have been with young, | so 2.05. 35
so minutes, hours, days, months, and years, 2.05. 38
great albion's queen in former golden days; 3.03. 7
life, | and in devotion spend my latter days, 4.06. 43
to entertain these fair well-spoken days, | i am R3 1.01. 29
and hate the idle pleasures of these days. 1.01. 31
that scarce some two days since were worth a 1.03. 81
my lord of gloucester, in those busy days, 1.03.144
long die thy happy days before thy death, | and, 1.03.206
though 'twere to buy a world of happy days — 1.04. 6
before the days of change, still is it so. 2.03. 41
accursed and unquiet wrangling days, | how many 2.04. 55
god bless your grace with health and happy days! 3.01. 18
and never in my days, i do protest, | was it so 3.02. 79
widow, | even in the afternoon of her best days, 3.07.186
brief abstract and record of tedious days, 4.04. 28
we have many goodly days to see: 4.04.320
awake, | and in a bloody battle end thy days! 5.03.155
with smiling plenty, and fair prosperous days! 5.05. 34
that would reduce these bloody days again, | and 5.05. 36
did you not of late days hear | a buzzing of a H8 2.01.147
as of late days our neighbors, | the upper 5.02. 64
there they are like to dance these three days; 5.03. 65 P
in her days every man shall eat in safety 5.04. 33
many days shall see her, | and yet no day 5.04. 57
nestor, were your days | as green as ajax', and TRO 2.03.253
you told how diomed, a whole week by days, | did 4.01. 10
'tis but early days. 4.05. 12
that i shall leave you one a' th's days; 5.03.104 P
'tis not four days gone | since i heard thence; COR 1.02. 6
lavinia, live, outlive thy father's days, | and TIT 1.01.167
shows | pass the remainder of our hateful days? 3.01.132
this done, see that you take no longer days, 4.02.165
be so bold to press to heaven in my young days. 4.03. 92 P
a fortnight and odd days. ROM 1.03. 15
even or odd, of all days in the year, | come 1.03. 16
of all the days of the year, upon that day; 1.03. 25
go, girl, seek happy nights to happy days. 1.03.105
for you and i are past our dancing days. 1.05. 31
for now, these hot days, is the mad blood 3.01. 4
this day's black fate on moe days doth depend, 3.01.119
the hour, | for in a minute there are many days. 3.05. 45
dead, | who here hath lain this two days buried. 5.03.176
his days and times are past, | and my reliances TIM 2.01. 21
off | to the succession of new days this month. 2.02. 20
ay, but the days are wax'd shorter with him. 3.04. 11
us, | his days are foul and his drink dangerous. 3.05. 73
master's fortunes, | "we have seen better days." 4.02. 27
where feed'st thou a' days, apemantus? 4.03.293 P
offering the fortunes of his former days, | the 5.01.124
an ag'd interpreter, though young in days. 5.03. 8
for we will shake him, or worse days endure. JC 1.02.322
sir, march is wasted fifteen days. 2.01. 59
and drawing days out, that men stand upon. 3.01.100
octavius, i have seen more days than you, | and 4.01. 18
may, | lovers in peace, lead on our days to age! 5.01. 94
which shall to all our nights and days to come MAC 1.05. 69
cold stone | days and nights has thirty-one 4.01. 7
when shalt thou see thy wholesome days again, 4.03.105
i hope the days are near at hand | that chambers 5.04. 1
till the foul crimes done in my days of nature HAM 1.05. 12
being of so young days brought up with him, 2.02. 11
grating so harshly all his days of quiet | with 3.01. 3
this physic but prolongs thy sickly days. 3.03. 96
ere we were two days old at sea, a pirate of 4.06. 16 P
of /all the days i' th' year, i came to't that 5.01.143 P
five days we do allot thee, for provision | to LR 1.01.173
i have not seen him this two days. 1.04. 72 P
is it two days since i tripp'd up thy heels, and 2.02. 29 P
even from my boyish days | to th' very moment OTH 1.03.132
should increase | even as our days do grow! 2.01.195
the time, but let it not | exceed three days. 3.03. 63
within these three days let me hear thee say 3.03.472
seven days and nights? 3.04.173
my salad days, | when i was green in judgment, ANT 1.05. 73
you'll win two days upon me. 2.04. 9
but i had rather fast from all, four days, 2.07.102
and within three days | you with your children 5.02.201
state, and wish | that warmer days would come. CYM 2.04. 6
old servant, | i have not seen these two days. 3.05. 55
we might proceed to /cancel of your days; PER 1.01.113
forty days longer we do respite you; 1.01.116
your presence glads our days. 2.03. 21
upon thy grave | while summer days doth last. 4.01. 17
will in that kingdom spend our following days. 5.03. 81
i lov'd my lips the better ten days after. TNK 2.04. 26
food took i none these two days — | sipp'd some 3.02. 26
to the wenches | we have known in our days! 3.03. 29
i'll warrant you within these three or four days 5.02.104
to sland'rous tongues and wretched hateful days? LUC 161
where all the treasure of thy lusty days, | to SON 2. 6
then look i death my days should expiate. 22. 4
if my slight muse do please these curious days, 38.13
all days are nights to see till i see thee, 43.13
and nights bright days when dreams do show thee 43.14
sure i am the wits of former days | to subjects 59.13
painting my age with beauty of thy days. 62.14
against the wrackful siege of batt'ring days, 65. 6
show what wealth she had | in days long since, 67.14
thus is his cheek the map of days outworn, 68. 1
thou hast pass'd by the ambush of young days, 70. 9
some fresher stamp of the time-bettering days. 82. 8
that tongue that tells the story of thy days 95. 5
what freezings have i felt, what dark days seen! 97. 3
and stops /her pipe in growth of riper days: 102. 8
for we, which now behold these present days, 106.13
although she knows my days are past the best, 138. 6

DAY-WEARIED 1 FR 0.0001 REL FR 1 V 0 P
crest | of the old, feeble, and day-wearied sun, JN 5.04. 35

/DAZZLE 1 FR 0.0001 REL FR 1 V 0 P
/shalt /read /when /mine /begin /to /dazzle. TIT 3.02. 85

DAZZLE 2 FR 0.0002 REL FR 2 V 0 P
that i will dazzle all the eyes of france, | yea H5 1.02.279
dazzle mine eyes, or do i see three suns? 3H6 2.01. 25

DAZZLED 2 FR 0.0002 REL FR 2 V 0 P
and that hath dazzled my reason's light; TGV 2.04.210

more dazzled and drove back his enemies | than 1H6 1.01. 13
DAZZLETH 1 FR 0.0001 REL FR 1 V 0 P
she reflects so bright | that dazzleth them, or LUC 377
DAZZLING 2 FR 0.0002 REL FR 2 V 0 P
who dazzling so, that eye shall be his heed, LLL 1.01. 82
that her sight dazzling makes the wound seem VEN 1064
DE* *(also d'*, do*, the)*
DE* 112 FR 0.0126 REL FR 14 V 98 P
what shall de honest man do in my closet? WIV 1.04. 73 P
i will cut his troat in de park; 1.04.109 P
by gar, i vill kill de jack priest; 1.04.117 P
appointed mine host of de jarteer to measure our 1.04.118 P
de herring is no dead so as i vill kill him. 2.03. 12 P
by gar, he is de coward jack priest of de vorld; 2.03. 31 P
by gar, he is de coward jack priest of de vorld; 2.03. 31 P
then i have as much mock–vater as de englishman. 2.03. 63 P
by gar, me vill kill de priest, for he speak for 2.03. 82 P
and i shall procure–a you de good guest: 2.03. 91 P
de earl, de knight, de lords, de gentlemen, my 2.03. 92 P
de earl, de knight, de lords, de gentlemen, my 2.03. 92 P
de earl, de knight, de lords, de gentlemen, my 2.03. 92 P
de knight, de lords, de gentlemen, my patients. 2.03. 92 P
by gar, you are de coward, de jack dog, john ape 3.01. 83 P
gar, you are de coward, de jack dog, john ape. 3.01. 83 P
jack rugby — mine host de jarteer — have i not 3.01. 91 P
have i not, at de place i did appoint? 3.01. 93 P
have you make–a de sot of us, ha, ha? 3.01.116 P
ay, be–gar, and de maid is love–a me. 3.02. 64 P
vere is mine host de jarteer? 4.05. 83 P
you make grand preparation for a duke de jamany. 4.05. 87 P
heat of duty, don adriano de armado." LLL 1.01.278 P
design of industry, don adriano de armado. 4.01. 87 P
nominated, or called, don adriano de armado. 5.01. 8 P
put it, as they say, to fortuna de la /guerra. 5.02.530 P
i am the youngest son of sir rowland de boys. AYL 1.01. 57 P
liege, the youngest son of sir rowland de boys. 1.02.223 P
his great right to be so — gerard de narbon. AWW 1.01. 27 P
gentlewoman the daughter of gerard de narbon? 1.01. 37 P
gerard de narbon was my father, | in what he did 2.01.101
themselves to slomber, ay'll de gud service, or H5 3.02.115 P
la main? elle est appelee de hand. 3.04. 7 P
de hand. et les doigts? 3.04. 8 P
je pense qu'ils sont appeles de fingres, oui, de 3.04. 11 P
qu'ils sont appeles de fingres, oui, de fingres. 3.04. 11 P
la main, de hand; 3.04. 12 P
les doigts, de fingres. 3.04. 12 P
les ongles? /nous les appelons de nailes. 3.04. 16 P
de nailes. 3.04. 17 P
de hand, de fingres, et de nailes. 3.04. 18 P
de hand, de fingres, et de nailes. 3.04. 18 P
de hand, de fingres, et de nailes. 3.04. 18 P
de arma, madame. 3.04. 22 P
fais la repetition de tous les mots que vous 3.04. 25 P
d' hand, de fingre, de nailes, d' arma, de 3.04. 28 P
d' hand, de fingre, de nailes, d' arma, de 3.04. 29 P
hand, de fingre, de nailes, d' arma, de bilbow. 3.04. 29 P
de nick, madame. 3.04. 33 P
de nick. et le menton? 3.04. 34 P
de chin. 3.04. 35 P
de sin. le col, de nick; le menton, de sin. 3.04. 36 P
de sin. le col, de nick; le menton, de sin. 3.04. 36 P
de sin. le col, de nick; le menton, de sin. 3.04. 36 P
doute point d'apprendre, par la grace de dieu, 3.04. 41 P
par la grace de dieu, et en peu de temps. 3.04. 41 P
d' hand, de fingre, de mailes — 3.04. 45 P
d' hand, de fingre, de mailes — 3.04. 45 P
de nailes, madame. 3.04. 46 P
de nailes, de arma, de ilbow. 3.04. 47 P
de nailes, de arma, de ilbow. 3.04. 47 P
de nailes, de arma, de ilbow. 3.04. 47 P
d' elbow, de nick, et de sin. 3.04. 49 P
d' elbow, de nick, et de sin. 3.04. 49 P
ils sont les mots de son mauvais, corruptible, 3.04. 53 P
et non pour les dames de honneur d'user. 3.04. 54 P
mots devant les seigneurs de france pour tout le 3.04. 56 P
d' hand, de fingre, de nailes, d' arma, d' elbow 3.04. 58 P
d' hand, de fingre, de nailes, d' arma, d' elbow 3.04. 58 P
d' arma, d' elbow, de nick, de sin, de foot, le 3.04. 59 P
d' elbow, de nick, de sin, de foot, le count. 3.04. 59 P
d' elbow, de nick, de sin, de foot, le count. 3.04. 59 P
dieu de batailles! 3.05. 15
volant, the pegasus, chez les narines de feu! 3.07. 14 P
que vous etes le gentilhomme de bonne qualite. 4.04. 2 P
o, prenez misericorde! ayez pitie de moi! 4.04. 12 P
impossible d'echapper la force de ton bras? 4.04. 16 P
tout /a /cette /heure de couper votre gorge. 4.04. 35 P
o, je vous supplie, pour l'amour de dieu, me 4.04. 40 P
je suis le gentilhomme de bonne maison; 4.04. 41 P
qu'il est contre son jurement de pardonner aucun 4.04. 50 P
langues des hommes sont pleines de tromperies. 5.02.116 P
dat de tongeus of de mans is be full of deceits: 5.02.119 P
dat de tongeus of de mans is be full of deceits: 5.02.119 P
dat is de princess. 5.02.120 P
it possible dat i sould love de enemy of france? 5.02.169 P
je quand sur le possession de france, et quand 5.02.181 P
et quand vous avez le possession de moi — let 5.02.182 P
enough to deceive de most sage demoiselle dat is 5.02.219 P
dat is as it shall please de roi mon pere. 5.02.247 P
leur noces, il n'est pas la coutume de france. 5.02.259 P
dat it is not be de fashon pour les ladies of 5.02.261 P
henri, roi d'angleterre, heritier de france; 5.02.340 P
call'd the brave lord ponton de santrailles, 1H6 1.04. 28
the dolphin, with one joan de pucelle join'd, 1.04.101
thus joan de pucelle hath perform'd her word. 1.06. 3
but joan de pucelle shall be france's saint. 1.06. 29
away, away, good william de la pole! 2.04. 80
paysans, la pauvre gens de france, | poor market 3.02. 14
fie, de la pole, disable not thyself. 5.03. 67
the french king charles, and william de la pole, 2H6 1.01. 44 P
and william de la pole, first duke of suffolk. 1.02. 30
the duke of suffolk, william de la pole. 4.01. 45
of the duke's confessor, john de la car, | one H8 1.01.218
to me, wishing me to permit | john de la car, my 1.02.162
sent a large commission | to gregory de cassado, 3.02.321
tom's a–cold — o, do de, do de, do de. LR 3.04. 58 P
tom's a–cold — o, do de, do de, do de. 3.04. 59 P
tom's a–cold — o, do de, do de, do de. 3.04. 59 P
do de, de, de. 3.06. 74 P
do de, de, de. 3.06. 74 P
do de, de, de. 3.06. 74 P
/DEAD 2 FR 0.0002 REL FR 2 V 0 P
/now /thou /wouldst /eat /thy /dead /vomit /up, 2H4 1.03. 99
/hector /is /dead; TRO 5.10. 22
DEAD 581 FR 0.0656 REL FR 519 V 62 P
gates of milan, and, i' th' dead of darkness, TMP 1.02.130
he were that which now he's like — that's dead, 2.01.282
dead or alive? 2.02. 25 P
they will lay out ten to see a dead indian. 2.02. 33 P
i hid me under the dead moon–calf's gaberdine 2.02.111 P
the mistress which i serve quickens what's dead, 3.01. 6
we were dead of sleep, | and (how we know not) 5.01.230
rememb'ring that my love to her is dead; TGV 2.06. 28
is silvia dead? 3.01.210
the night's dead silence | will well become such 3.02. 84
but she is dead. 4.02.106
i likewise hear that valentine is dead. 4.02.112
she is dead, belike? 4.04. 75
and would i might be dead | if i in thought felt 4.04.171
three men and a boy yet, till my mother be dead. WIV 1.01.275 P
jack rugby, he is dead already, if he be come. 2.03. 8 P
de herring is no dead so as i vill kill him. 2.03. 12 P
is he dead, my ethiopian? 2.03. 27 P
is he dead, my francisco? 2.03. 28 P
is he dead, bully–stale? 2.03. 30 P
is he dead? 2.03. 30 P
if your husbands were dead, you two would marry. 3.02. 15 P
i would thy husband were dead. 3.03. 50 P
you are utterly sham'd, and he's but a dead man. 4.02. 43 P
dead to infliction, to themselves are dead, MM 1.03. 28
dead to infliction, to themselves are dead, 1.03. 28
the law hath not been dead, though it hath slept 2.02. 90
'tis now dead midnight, and by eight to–morrow 4.02. 64
in request, for the old women were all dead. 4.03. 8 P
and dwell upon your grave when you are dead; ERR 3.01.104
sharp–looking wretch, | a living dead man. 5.01.242
dead, i think. ADO 4.01.113
your daughter here the /princes left for dead, 4.01.202
in, | and publish it that she is dead indeed. 4.01.204
i must say she is dead; 4.01.335 P
and she is dead, slander'd to death by villains, 5.01. 88
the lady is dead upon mine and my master's false 5.01.242 P
almost the copy of my child that's dead, | and 5.01.289
graves, yawn and yield your dead, | till death 5.03. 19
the former hero! hero that is dead! 5.04. 65
they swore that you were well–nigh dead for me. 5.04. 81
the sweet war–man is dead and rotten, sweet LLL 5.02.660 P
him and hang'd for pompey that is dead by him. 5.02.682 P
dead, for my life! 5.02.720
dead, or asleep? MND 2.02.101
so should a murtherer look — so dead, so grim. 3.02. 57
nor is he dead, for aught that i can tell. 3.02. 76
see me no more, whether he be dead or no. 3.02. 81
should i hurt her, strike her, kill her dead? 3.02.269
and strike more dead | than common sleep of all 4.01. 81
now am i dead, | now am i fled; 5.01.301
for he is dead, he is nothing. 5.01.308 P
what, dead, my dove? 5.01.325
dead, dead? 5.01.328
dead, dead? 5.01.328
moonshine and lion are left to bury the dead. 5.01.349 P
for when the players are all dead, there need 5.01.357 P
glimmering light | by the dead and drowsy fire, 5.01.392
daughter curb'd by the will of a dead father. MV 1.02. 25 P
me, is my boy, god rest his soul, alive or dead? 2.02. 72 P
i would my daughter were dead at my foot, and 3.01. 88 P
o, then be bold to say bassanio's dead! 3.02.185
some dear friend dead, else nothing in the world 3.02.245
well, the beginning, that is dead and buried. AYL 1.02.117 P
kill'd, but one dead that is willing to be so. 1.02.188 P
bring him dead or living | within this 3.01. 6
it strikes a man more dead than a great 3.03. 15 P
dead shepherd, now i find thy saw of might, 3.05. 81
to prey on nothing that doth seem as dead. 4.03.118
one dead, or drunk? SHR in.1. 31
my father dead, my fortune lives for me, | and i 1.02.191
moderate lamentation is the right of the dead, AWW 1.01. 55 P
when you are dead, you should be such a one | as 4.02. 7
he had sworn to marry me | when his wife's dead; 4.02. 72
when you have spoken it, 'tis dead, and i am the 4.03. 12 P
you must know | i am supposed dead. 4.04. 11
the nature of his great offense is dead, | and 5.03. 23
and ev'ry hair that's on't, helen, that's dead, 5.03. 77
and she is dead, which nothing but to close 5.03.118
to marry me when his wife was dead, i blush to 5.03.140 P
dead though she be, she feels her young one kick 5.03.302
one that's dead is quick — | and now behold the 5.03.303
all this to season | a brother's dead love, TN 1.01. 30
and sing them loud even in the dead of night; 1.05.271
with a sense as cold | as is a dead man's nose; WT 2.01.152
is dead. 3.02.145
the sweet'st, dear'st creature's dead, and 3.02.201
i say she's dead; 3.02.203
me | to the dead bodies of my queen and son. 3.02.235
the spirits o' th' dead | may walk again. 3.03. 16
thing to talk on when thou art dead and rotten, 3.03. 81 P
one being dead, | i shall have more than you can 4.04.387
yet we free thee | from the dead blow of it. 4.04.434
stand till he be three quarters and a dram dead; 4.04.786 P
stars, stars, | and all eyes else dead coals! 5.01. 68
so her dead likeness, i do well believe, 5.03. 15
would i were dead but that methinks already — 5.03. 62
she has liv'd, | or how stol'n from the dead. 5.03.115
for i saw her, | as i thought, dead; 5.03.140
whose valor plucks dead lions by the beard; JN 2.01.138
we bear, | or add a royal number to the dead, 2.01.347
now doth death line his dead chaps with steel, 2.01.352
prate | he will awake my mercy, which lies dead; 4.01. 26
the fire is dead with grief, | being create for 4.01.105
your uncle must not know but you are dead. 4.01.127
the suit which you demand is gone and dead. 4.02. 84
mother dead? 4.02.127
my mother dead! 4.02.181
i had a mighty cause | to wish him dead, but 4.02.206
spleen to do me shame, | i'll strike thee dead. 4.03. 98
up | from forth this morsel of dead royalty! 4.03.143
they found him dead and cast into the streets, 5.01. 39
your breath first kindled the dead coal of wars 5.02. 83
i doubt he will be dead or e'er i come. 5.06. 44
dead, forsook, cast off, | and none of you will 5.07. 35
you breathe these dead news in as dead an ear. 5.07. 65
you breathe these dead news in as dead an ear. 5.07. 65
lament we may, but not revenge /thee dead. R2 1.03. 58
but dead, thy kingdom cannot buy my breath. 1.03.232
is not gaunt dead? 2.01.191
well, lords, the duke of lancaster is dead. 2.01.224
'tis thought the king is dead; 2.04. 7
as well assured richard their king is dead. 2.04. 17
for all the welshmen, hearing thou wert dead, 3.02. 73
have i not reason to look pale and dead? 3.02. 79
is bushy, green, and the earl of wiltshire dead? 3.02.141
what, are they dead? 3.04. 54
in that dead time when gloucester's death was 4.01. 10
why, bishop, is norfolk dead? 4.01.101
the field of golgotha and dead men's skulls. 4.01.144
think i am dead, and that even here thou takest, 5.01. 38
this dead king to the living king i'll bear; 5.05.117
though i did wish him dead, | i hate the 5.06. 39
upon whose dead corpse' there was such misuse, 1H4 1.01. 43
and as the soldiers bore dead bodies by, | he 1.03. 42
not he proclaim'd | by richard, that dead is, 1.03.146
all the gibbets and press'd the dead bodies. 4.02. 37 P
wars | that all in england did repute him dead; 5.01. 54
yea, to the dead. 5.01.138 P
this earth that bears /thee dead | bears not 5.04. 92
of this gunpowder percy though he be dead. 5.04.122 P
did you not tell me this fat man was dead? 5.04.132
i did, i saw him dead, | breathless and bleeding 5.04.133
why, percy i kill'd myself, and saw thee dead. 5.04.144
to see what friends are living, who are dead. 5.04.161
so dull, so dead in look, so woe–begone, | drew 2H4 1.01. 71
drew priam's curtain in the dead of night, | and 1.01. 72
ending with "brother, son, and all are dead." 1.01. 81
why, he is dead. 1.01. 83
yet, for all this, say not that percy's dead. 1.01. 93
and he doth sin that doth belie the dead, | not 1.01. 98
dead, | not he which says the dead is not alive. 1.01. 99
i cannot think, my lord, your son is dead. 1.01.104
end, | and darkness be the burier of the dead! 1.01.160
how now, whose mare's dead? what's the matter? 2.01. 43 P
answer, thou dead elm, answer. 2.04.331 P
a certain instance that glendower is dead. 3.01.103
to see how many of my old acquaintance are dead! 3.02. 34 P
dead, sir. 3.02. 42 P
jesu, jesu, dead! 3.02. 43 P
'a drew a good bow, and dead! 3.02. 44 P
dead! 3.02. 45 P
and is old double dead? 3.02. 52 P
mayst effect | of mediation, after i am dead, 4.04. 25
bee doth leave her comb | in the dead carrion. 4.04. 80
ear | that thou art crowned, not that i am dead. 4.05.112
coming to look on you, thinking you dead, | and 4.05.155
and dead almost, my liege, to think you were, 4.05.156
i hope, not dead. 5.02. 4
here come the heavy issue of dead harry. 5.02. 14
me, | i'll to the king my master that is dead, 5.02. 40
yet weep that harry's dead, and so will i, | but 5.02. 59
what, is the old king dead? 5.03.120 P
me, for the man is dead that you and pistol beat 5.04. 16 P
awake remembrance of these valiant dead, | and H5 1.02.115
for falstaff he is dead, | and we must ern 2.03. 5
the dead men's blood, the privy maidens' groans, 2.04.107
and leave your england as dead midnight, still, 3.pr. 19
or close the wall up with our english dead. 3.01. 2
thou to harry of england, though we seem'd dead, 3.06.119 P
the organs, though defunct and dead before, 4.01. 21
that being dead, like to the bullet's crasing, 4.03.105
o'er this bloody field | to book our dead, and 4.07. 73
out their armed heels at their dead masters, 4.07. 80
in safety, and dispose | of their dead bodies! 4.07. 83
bring me just notice of the numbers dead | on 4.07.117
now, herald, are the dead numb'red? 4.08. 73
there lie dead | one hundred twenty–six; 4.08. 82
the names of those their nobles that lie dead: 4.08. 91
where is the number of our english dead? 4.08.102
deum, | the dead with charity enclos'd in clay; 4.08.124
news have i that my doll is dead i' th' spittle 5.01. 81
henry is dead, and never shall revive. 1H6 1.01. 18
since arms avail not now that henry's dead. 1.01. 47
and none but women left to wail the dead. 1.01. 51
say'st thou, man, before dead henry's corse? 1.01. 62
thou that contrivedst to murther our dead lord, 1.03. 34
as who should say, "when i am dead and gone, 1.04. 93
in memory of her when she is dead, | her ashes, 1.06. 23
nails | shall pitch a field when we are dead. 3.01.103
age, | and twit with cowardice a man half dead? 3.02. 55
shall see thee withered, bloody, pale, and dead. 4.02. 38
that, talbot dead, great york might bear the 4.04. 9
if he be dead, brave talbot, then adieu! 4.04. 45
fly, to revenge my death when i am dead; 4.06. 30
during the life, let us not wrong it dead. 4.07. 50
ta'en, | and to survey the bodies of the dead. 4.07. 57
o, that i could but call these dead to life, 4.07. 81
for richard, the first son's heir, being dead, 2H6 2.02. 31
when i am dead and gone, | may honorable peace 2.03. 37
or waking, 'tis no matter how, | so he be dead; 3.01.264
but i would have him dead, my lord of suffolk, 3.01.273
for that john mortimer, which now is dead, | in 3.01.372
for humphrey being dead, as he shall be, | and 3.01.382
ay, my good lord, he's dead. 3.02. 7
dead in his bed, my lord; gloucester is dead. 3.02. 29
dead in his bed, my lord; gloucester is dead. 3.02. 29
help, lords, the king is dead. 3.02. 33
in life but double death, now gloucester's dead. 3.02. 55
that he is dead, good warwick, 'tis too true, 3.02.130
and to survey his dead and earthy image, | what 3.02.147
who finds the heifer dead and bleeding fresh, 3.02.188
nest | but may imagine how the bird was dead, 3.02.192
if thou be found by me, thou art but dead. 3.02.387
and flagging wings | cleep dead men's graves, 4.01. 6
i fear me, love, if that i had been dead, | thou 4.04. 23
those that i never saw, and struck them dead. 4.07. 82
if i do not leave you all as dead as a doornail, 4.10. 40 P
and hang thee o'er my tomb when i am dead. 4.10. 68
o, let me view his visage, being dead, | that 5.01. 69

and dead men's cries do fill the empty air, 5.02. 4
but is your grace dead, my lord of somerset? 3H6 1.01. 18
mine, boys? not till king henry be dead. 1.02. 10
is he dead already? 1.03. 10
whilest we breathe, take time to do him dead. 1.04.108
would i were dead, if god's good will were so; 2.05. 19
to some man else, as this dead man doth me. 2.05. 60
and wheresoe'er he is, he's surely dead. 2.06. 41
i know by that he's dead, and, by my soul, | if 2.06. 79
ay, but he's dead. 2.06. 85
am i dead? 3.01. 82
but were he dead, | yet here prince edward 3.03. 72
come quickly, montague, or i am dead. 5.02. 39
see dead henry's wounds | open their congeal'd R3 1.02. 55
heav'n with lightning strike the murth'rer dead; 1.02. 64
but dead they are, and, devilish slave, by thee. 1.02. 90
nay, he is dead, and slain by edward's hands. 1.02. 92
would they were basilisks, to strike thee dead! 1.02.150
if he were dead, what would betide on me? 1.03. 6
some lay in dead men's skulls, and, in the holes 1.04. 29
and mock'd the dead bones that lay scatt'red by. 1.04. 33
that princely novice, was struck dead by thee? 1.04.222
who knows not that the gentle duke is dead? 2.01. 80
who knows not he is dead? who knows he is? 2.01. 82
is clarence dead? the order was revers'd. 2.01. 87
good grandam, tell us, is our father dead? 2.02. 1
then you conclude, my grandam, he is dead. 2.02. 12
edward, my lord, thy son, our king, is dead! 2.02. 40
drown desperate sorrow in dead edward's grave, 2.02. 99
yes, that the king is dead. 2.03. 3
his nurse? why, she was dead ere thou wast born. 2.04. 33
i fear no uncles dead. 3.01.146
they smile at me who shortly shall be dead. 3.04.107
lest thou increase the number of the dead, | and 4.01. 44
i wish the bastards dead, | and i would have it 4.02. 18
but didst thou see them dead? 4.03. 27
edward plantagenet, why art thou dead? 4.04. 19
dead life, blind sight, poor mortal–living ghost 4.04. 26
thy edward he is dead, that kill'd my edward; 4.04. 63
/thy other edward dead, to quit my edward; 4.04. 64
thy clarence he is dead that stabb'd my edward, 4.04. 67
that i may live to say, "the dog is dead." 4.04. 78
compare dead happiness with living woe; 4.04.119
o no, my reasons are too deep and dead — | too 4.04.362
too deep and dead, poor infants, in their graves 4.04.363
is the king dead? 4.04.470
it is now dead midnight. 5.03.180
the day is ours, the bloody dog is dead. 5.05. 2
from the dead temples of this bloody wretch 5.05. 5
to as much end | as give a crutch to th' dead. H8 1.01.172
of life to't than | the grave does to th' dead; 2.04.192
child of honor, cardinal wolsey, | was dead? 4.02. 7
when i am dead, good wench, | let me be us'd 4.02.167
and the rude son should strike his father dead; TRO 1.03.115
there's many a greek and troyan dead | since 4.05.214
nice conjecture | where thou wilt hit me dead? 4.05.251
hector's dead! 5.03. 87
he's dead, and at the murtherer's horse's tail, 5.10. 4
go in to troy and say /there, "hector's dead!" 5.10. 17
i prize | as the dead carcasses of unburied men COR 3.03.122
throat, | and wak'd half dead with nothing. 4.05.126
had, | behold the poor remains, alive and dead! TIT 1.01. 81
there greet in silence, as the dead are wont, 1.01. 90
whom your goths beheld | alive and dead, and for 1.01.123
dead, if you will, but not to be his wife, 1.01.297
they told me, here. at dead time of the night, 2.03. 99
and make his dead trunk pillow to our lust. 2.03.130
doth shine upon the dead man's earthy cheeks, 2.03.229
hour, | to find thy brother bassianus dead. 2.03.252
my brother dead! 2.03.253
but out alas, here have we found him dead. 2.03.258
hath hurt me more than had he kill'd me dead: 3.01. 92
thy husband he is dead, and for his death | thy 3.01.108
thy brothers are condemn'd, and dead by this. 3.01.109
hole, | where the dead corpse of bassianus lay; 5.01.105
oft have i digg'd up dead men from their graves, 5.01.135
"let not your sorrow die, though i am dead." 5.01.140
receive the blood, and when that they are dead, 5.02.197
and talk of them when he was dead and gone. 5.03.166
ev'n with all my heart | would i were dead, so 5.03.173
and, being dead, let birds on her take pity. 5.03.200
vow | do i live dead that live to tell it now. ROM 1.01.224
kin, | to strike him dead i hold it not a sin. 1.05. 59
not, | the ape is dead, and i must conjure him. 2.01. 16
poor romeo, he is already dead, stabb'd with a 2.04. 13 P
but old folks — many feign as they were dead, 2.05. 16
o romeo, romeo, brave mercutio is dead! 3.01.116
ah, weraday, he's dead, he's dead, he's dead! 3.02. 37
ah, weraday, he's dead, he's dead, he's dead! 3.02. 37
ah, weraday, he's dead, he's dead, he's dead! 3.02. 37
the day, he's gone, he's kill'd, he's dead! 3.02. 39
that ever i should live to see thee dead! 3.02. 63
and is tybalt dead? 3.02. 65
and tybalt's dead that would have slain my 3.02.106
"tybalt is dead, and romeo banished." 3.02.112
when she said, "tybalt's dead," | thy father or 3.02.118
tybalt, romeo, juliet, | all slain, all dead: 3.02.124
for whose dear sake thou wast but lately dead: 3.03.136
so low, | as one dead in the bottom of a tomb. 3.05. 56
with romeo, till i behold him — dead — | is my 3.05. 94
your first is dead, or 'twere as good he were 3.05.224
quite with dead men's rattling bones, | with 4.01. 82
and hide me with a dead man in his /shroud — 4.01. 85
to rouse thee from thy bed, there art thou dead. 4.01.108
subtilly hath minist'red to have me dead, | lest 4.03. 25
my lady's dead! 4.05. 14
she's dead, deceas'd, she's dead, alack the day! 4.05. 23
she's dead, deceas'd, she's dead, alack the day! 4.05. 23
alack the day, she's dead, she's dead, she's 4.05. 24
the day, she's dead, she's dead, she's dead! 4.05. 24
the day, she's dead, she's dead, she's dead! 4.05. 24
dead art thou! 4.05. 63
alack, my child is dead, | and with my child my 4.05. 63
i dreamt my lady came and found me dead — 5.01. 6
dream, that gives a dead man leave to think! 5.01. 7
veins | that the life–weary taker may fall dead, 5.01. 62
poor living corse, clos'd in a dead man's tomb! 5.02. 30
but chiefly to take thence from her dead finger 5.03. 30

do some villainous shame | to the dead bodies. 5.03. 53
death, lie thou there, by a dead man interr'd. 5.03. 87
thy husband in thy bosom there lies dead; 5.03.155
and juliet bleeding, warm, and newly dead, | who 5.03.175
and romeo dead, and juliet, dead before, | warm 5.03.196
and romeo dead, and juliet, dead before, | warm 5.03.196
upon them, fit to open | these dead men's tombs. 5.03.201
alas, my liege, my wife is dead to–night; 5.03.210
romeo, there dead, was husband to that juliet, 5.03.231
and she, there dead, /that romeo's faithful wife 5.03.232
lay | the noble paris and true romeo dead. 5.03.259
for all thy living | is 'mongst the dead, and TIM 1.02.224
now his friends are dead, | doors, that were 3.03. 36
poor thin roofs | with burthens of the dead — 4.03.146
but not till i am dead. 4.03.393
our hope in him is dead. 5.01.226
"timon is dead, who hath outstretch'd his span: 5.03. 3
dead, sure, and this his grave. 5.03. 5
my noble general, timon is dead, | entomb'd upon 5.04. 65
dead | is noble timon, of whose memory 5.04. 79
but, woe the while, our fathers' minds are dead, JC 1.03. 82
graves have yawn'd and yielded up their dead; 2.02. 18
tyranny is dead! 3.01. 78
mark antony shall not love caesar dead | so well 3.01.133
than that caesar were dead, to live all freemen? 3.02. 24 P
i rather choose | to wrong the dead, to wrong 3.02.126
and they would go and kiss dead caesar's wounds, 3.02.132
no man bears sorrow better. portia is dead. 4.03.147
she is dead. 4.03.149
cicero is dead, | and by that order of 4.03.179
for certain she is dead, and by strange manner. 4.03.189
look whe'er he have not crown'd dead cassius! 5.03. 97
to this dead man than you shall see me pay. 5.03.102
when you do find him, or alive or dead, | he 5.04. 24
go on, | and see whe'er brutus be alive or dead, 5.04. 30
who, almost dead for breath, had scarcely more MAC 1.05. 36
now o'er the one half world | nature seems dead, 2.01. 50
the sleeping and the dead | are but as pictures; 2.02. 50
renown and grace is dead, | the wine of life is 2.03. 94
better be with the dead, | whom we, to gain our 3.02. 19
marry, he was dead. 3.06. 4
rebellious dead, rise never till the wood | of 4.01. 97
sirrah, your father's dead, | and what will you 4.02. 30
my father is not dead, for all your saying. 4.02. 37
yes, he is dead. how wilt thou do for a father? 4.02. 38
if he were dead, you'ld weep for him; 4.02. 61 P
the dead man's knell | is there scarce ask'd for 4.03.170
the queen, my lord, is dead. 5.05. 16
then he is dead? 5.09. 9
of this dead butcher and his fiend–like queen, 5.09. 35
in the same figure, like the king that's dead. HAM 1.01. 41
thus twice before, and jump at this dead hour, 1.01. 65
graves stood /tenantless and the sheeted dead 1.01.115
a fault against the dead, a fault to nature, 1.02.102
but two months dead! 1.02.138
in the dead waste and middle of the night, 1.02.198
that thou, dead corse, again in complete steel 1.04. 52
for if the sun breed maggots in a dead dog, 2.02.181 P
a second time i kill my husband dead, | when 3.02.184
die thy thoughts when thy first lord is dead. 3.02.215
how now? a rat? dead, for a ducat, dead! 3.04. 24
how now? a rat? dead, for a ducat, dead! 3.04. 24
what have you done, my lord, with the dead body? 4.02. 5
where the dead body is bestow'd, my lord, | we 4.03. 12
"he is dead and gone, lady, | he is dead and 4.05. 29
is dead and gone, lady, | he is dead and gone, 4.05. 30
dead. 4.05.129
how came he dead? 4.05.131
no, no, he is dead, | go to thy death–bed, | he 4.05.192
cull–cold maids do dead men's fingers call them. 4.07.171
'tis for the dead, not for the quick, therefore 5.01.126 P
a woman, sir, but, rest her soul, she's dead. 5.01.136 P
is a sore decayer of your whoreson dead body. 5.01.172 P
imperious caesar, dead and turn'd to clay, 5.01.213
we should profane the service of the dead | to 5.01.236
now pile your dust upon the quick and dead, 5.01.251
i am dead, horatio. 5.02.333
horatio, i am dead, | thou livest. 5.02.338
that rosencrantz and guildenstern are dead. 5.02.371
o my good lord, the duke of cornwall's dead, LR 4.02. 70
flew on him, and amongst them fell'd him dead, 4.02. 76
my lord is dead; 4.05. 30
alive or dead? 4.06. 45
what, is he dead? 4.06.254
he's dead; 4.06.257
it came even from the heart of — o, she's dead! 5.03.225
who dead? speak, man. 5.03.226
produce the bodies, be they alive or dead. 5.03.231
i know when one is dead, and when one lives; 5.03.261
she's dead as earth. 5.03.262
he's dead and rotten. 5.03.286
foredone themselves, | and desperately are dead. 5.03.293
edmund is dead, my lord. 5.03.296
dead? OTH 1.03. 59
drinks you, with facility, your dane dead drunk; 2.03. 83 P
honest iago, that looks dead with grieving, 2.03.177
my friend is dead; 3.03.474
minion, your dear lies dead, | and your unblest 5.01. 33
he's almost slain, and roderigo quite dead. 5.01.114
be thus when thou art dead, and i will kill thee 5.02. 18
o, my fear interprets. what, is he dead? 5.02. 73
not dead? 5.02. 86
not yet quite dead? 5.02. 86
she's dead. 5.02. 91
i am glad thy father's dead. 5.02.204
dead, desdemon! 5.02.281
dead! 5.02.281
but now he spake | (after long seeming dead) 5.02.328
fulvia thy wife is dead. ANT 1.02.118
fulvia is dead. 1.02.156
fulvia is dead. 1.02.158
dead. 1.02.160
she's dead, my queen. 1.03. 59
his wife that's dead did trespasses to caesar; 2.01. 40
antonio's dead! 2.05. 26
sirrah, mark, we use | to say the dead are well. 2.05. 33
when antony found julius caesar dead, | he cried 3.02. 54
as a morsel, cold upon | dead caesar's trencher; 3.13.117

lock yourself, and send him word you are dead. 4.13. 4
dead then? 4.14. 34
dead. 4.14. 34
how, not dead? 4.14.103
not dead? 4.14.103
let him that loves me strike me dead. 4.14.108
not be purg'd, she sent you word she was dead; 4.14.124
is he dead? 4.15. 6
his death's upon him, but not dead. 4.15. 7
she's dead too, our sovereign. 4.15. 69
i say, o caesar, antony is dead. 5.01. 13
he is dead, caesar, | not by a public minister 5.01. 19
all dead. 5.02.329
trimming up the diadem | on her dead mistress; 5.02.343
you woo another wife, | when imogen is dead. CYM 1.01.114
either your unparagon'd mistress is dead, or 1.04. 80 P
i'll give but notice you are dead, and send him 3.04.124
what comfort, when i am | dead to my husband? 3.04.130
i'll write to my lord she's dead. 3.05.104
my speech of insultment ended on his dead body, 3.05.141 P
the bird is dead | that we have made so much on. 4.02.197
or dead, or sleeping on him? 4.02.356
but dead rather; 4.02.356
bed | with the defunct, or sleep upon the dead. 4.02.358
pass was damm'd | with dead men hurt behind, and 5.03. 12
which, being dead many years, shall after revive 5.04.141 P
no bolts for the dead. 5.04.197 P
he hath been search'd among the dead and living; 5.05. 11
happiness, i must report | the queen is dead. 5.05. 27
the same dead thing alive. 5.05.123
but we /saw him dead. 5.05.126
most like i did, for i was dead. 5.05.259
imogen, | thy mother's dead. 5.05.270
thou'rt dead. 5.05.299
which, being dead many years, shall after revive 5.05.439 P
for many years thought dead, are now reviv'd, 5.05.456
and with dead cheeks advise thee to desist | for PER 1.01. 39
unless thou say prince pericles is dead. 1.01.164
till pericles be dead, | my heart can lend no 1.01.168
give them life whom hunger starv'd half dead. 1.04. 96
which if you shall refuse, when i am dead, | for 2.01. 76
which my dead father did bequeath to me, | with 2.01.124
or, dead, give 's cause to mourn his funeral, 2.04. 32
antiochus and his daughter dead, | the men of 3.ch. 25
in your arms this piece | of your dead queen. 3.01. 18
not lie till the ship be clear'd of the dead. 3.01. 49 P
your master will be dead ere you return, 3.02. 7
of an egyptian | that had nine hours lien dead, 3.02. 85
to stead, | lychorida, our nurse, is dead, | and 4.ch. 42
i'll swear she's dead, | and thrown into the sea 4.01. 98
the poor transylvanian is dead that lay with the 4.02. 22 P
that she is dead. 4.03. 14
yet none does know but you how she came dead, 4.03. 29
let pericles believe his daughter's dead, | and 4.04. 46
she is not dead at tharsus, as she should have 5.01.215
the voice of dead thaisa! 5.03. 34
that thaisa am i, supposed dead | and drown'd. 5.03. 35
will you deliver | how this dead queen relives? 5.03. 64
letters of good credit, sir, | my father's dead. 5.03. 78
give us the bones | of our dead kings, that we TNK 1.01. 50
i have heard the fortunes | of your dead lords, 1.01. 57
none fit for th' dead! 1.01.141
you comfort | to give your dead lords graves; 1.01.149
go and find out | the bones of your dead lords, 1.04. 7
'tis right — those, those. | they are not dead? 1.04. 24
(sound and at liberty), i would 'em dead; 1.04. 35
if one of them were dead, as one must, are you 3.06.273
that thine may live, when thou thyself art dead; VEN 172
stone, | well–painted idol, image dull and dead, 212
struck dead at first, what needs a second 250
as if the dead the living should exceed; 292
the silly boy, believing she is dead, | claps 467
"if he be dead — o no, it cannot be, | seeing 937
and not death's ebon dart to strike him dead. 948
for he being dead, with him is beauty slain, 1019
and, beauty dead, black chaos comes again. 1020
she thinks he could not die, he is not dead; 1060
and yet," quoth she, "behold two adons dead! 1070
but he is dead, and never did he bless | my 1119
that thou being dead, the day should yet be 1134
"since thou art dead, lo here i prophesy, 1135
now stole upon the time the dead of night, LUC 162
pure thoughts are dead and still, | while lust 167
imagine her as one in dead of night | from forth 449
but as reproof and reason beat it dead, | by thy 489
and in thy dead arms do i mean to place him, 517
life, | the one will live, the other being dead: 1187
my shame so dead, mine honor is new born. 1190
thou dead, both die, and both shall victors be." 1211
body spread, | and who cannot abuse a body dead? 1267
fed, | show'd life imprison'd in a body dead. 1456
"for in the dreadful dead of dark midnight, 1625
they did conclude to bear dead lucrece thence, 1850
lost, vaded, broken, dead within an hour. PP 13. 6
as flowers dead lie withered on the ground, | as 13. 9
fled, | all our love is lost, for love is dead. 17.32
king pandion, he is dead: 20.23
love and constancy is dead, | phoenix and the PHT 22
for these dead birds sigh a prayer. 67
hearts, | which i by lacking have supposed dead, SON 31. 2
stol'n from mine eye | as interest of the dead, 31. 7
when in dead night /thy fair imperfect shade 43.11
and steal dead seeing of his living hue? 67. 6
before the golden tresses of the dead, | the 68. 5
ere beauty's dead fleece made another gay: 68. 8
no longer mourn for me when i am dead | than you 71. 1
life, | the prey of worms, my body being dead, 74.10
when all the breathers of this world are dead; 81.12
above a mortal pitch, that struck me dead? 86. 6
ere you were born was beauty's summer dead. 104.14
in praise of ladies dead and lovely knights, 106. 4
where time and outward form would show it dead. 108.14
that all the world besides methinks are dead. 112.14
making dead wood more blest than living lips: 128.12
and death once dead, there's no more dying then. 146.14

DEAD–COLD 2 FR 0.0002 REL FR 2 V 0 P
but dead–cold winter must inhabit here still. TNK 2.02. 45
following the dead–cold ashes of their sons, 4.02. 5

DEAD–KILLING 2 FR 0.0002 REL FR 2 V 0 P
or else i swoon with this dead–killing news! R3 4.01. 35
here with a cockatrice' dead–killing eye | he LUC 540
/DEADLY 1 FR 0.0001 REL FR 1 V 0 P
/must /wither, | /and /come /to /deadly /use. LR 4.02. 36
DEADLY 56 FR 0.0063 REL FR 52 V 4 P
her | is self from self, a deadly banishment. TGV 3.01.173
i fly not death, to fly his deadly doom: 3.01.185
sin, | or of the deadly seven it is the least. MM 3.01.110
i know it by their pale and deadly looks. ERR 4.04. 93
poisons more deadly than a mad dog's tooth. 5.01. 70
and if she did not hate him deadly, she would ADO 5.01.177 P
'tis deadly sin to keep that oath, my lord, LLL 2.01.105
'twere deadly sickness or else present death. SHR 4.03. 14
thou didst hate her deadly, | and she is dead, AWW 5.03.117
deadly divorce step between me and you! 5.03.318
with such a suff'ring, such a deadly life, | in TN 1.05.265
thy assailant is quick, skillful, and deadly. 3.04.225 P
and prove a deadly bloodshed but a jest, JN 4.03. 55
by so much fills their hearts with deadly hate. R2 2.02.131
turns to the sourest and most deadly hate. 3.02.136
excuse | this deadly blot in thy digressing son. 5.03. 66
color her working with such deadly wounds, | nor 1H4 1.03.109
this is the deadly spite that angers me: 3.01.190
a thousand souls to death and deadly night. 1H6 2.04.127
teeth, | with full as many signs of deadly hate, 2H6 3.02.314
alas, poor york, but that i hate thee deadly, 3H6 1.04. 84
this deadly quarrel daily doth beget! 2.05. 91
the air hath got into my deadly wounds, | and 2.06. 27
a deadly groan, like life and death's departing. 2.06. 43
king | in deadly hate the one against the other; R3 1.01. 35
thee, | i lay it naked to the deadly stroke, 1.02.177
no sleep close up that deadly eye of thine, 1.03.224
spider | whose deadly web ensnareth thee about? 1.03.242
how darkly and how deadly dost thou speak! 1.04.169
star'd each on other, and look'd deadly pale; 3.07. 26
anointed let me be with deadly venom, | and die 4.01. 61
that in the sty of the most deadly boar | my son 4.05. 2
body | by thee was punched full of deadly holes. 5.03.125
o deadly gall, and theme of all our scorns, TRO 4.05. 30
name her not now, sir, she's a deadly theme. 4.05.181
place is dangerous, | the time right deadly. 5.02. 39
is slain, | amphimachus and thoas deadly hurt, 5.05. 12
men, yet they lie deadly that tell you have good COR 2.01. 61 P
myself, | set deadly enmity between two friends, TIT 5.01.131
there's meed for meed, death for a deadly deed! 5.03. 66
who, all as hot, turns deadly point to point, ROM 3.01.160
o deadly sin! 3.03. 24
name, | shot from the deadly level of a gun, 3.03.103
our great revenge | to cure this deadly grief. MAC 4.03.215
all's cheerless, dark, and deadly. LR 5.03.291
scapes i' th' imminent deadly breach, | of being OTH 1.03.136
so it is a deadly sorrow to behold a foul knave ANT 1.02. 72 P
a languishing death, | but though slow, deadly. CYM 1.05. 10
appalls) hath sent | deadly defiance to him, and TNK 1.02. 91
our dole more deadly looks than dying; 1.05. 3
staineth, | or like the deadly bullet of a gun, VEN 461
by their suggestion gives a deadly groan. 1044
deed, | reproach, disdain, and deadly enmity, LUC 503
light, | for light and lust are deadly enemies; 674
her lively color kill'd with deadly cares. 1593
stone–still, astonish'd with this deadly deed, 1730
DEADLY–HANDED 1 FR 0.0001 REL FR 1 V 0 P
the deadly–handed clifford slew my steed; 2H6 5.02. 9
DEADLY–STANDING 1 FR 0.0001 REL FR 1 V 0 P
what signifies my deadly–standing eye, | my TIT 2.03. 32
DEAEQUE 1 FR 0.0001 REL FR 1 V 0 P
dii deaeque omnes! TNK 3.05.158
DEAF 27 FR 0.0030 REL FR 23 V 4 P
ay, i would i were deaf; TGV 4.02. 64 P
left, | my dull deaf ears a little use to hear: ERR 5.01.317
match, | the sea enraged is not half so deaf, JN 2.01.451
ire, | in rage, deaf as the sea, hasty as fire. R2 1.01. 19
face, | and bid his ears a little while be deaf, 1.01.112
boy, tell him i am deaf. 2H4 1.02. 66 P
you must speak louder, my master is deaf. 1.02. 67 P
art thou like the adder waxen deaf? 2H6 3.02. 76
to tell my love unto his dumb deaf trunk, | and 3.02.144
wrath makes him deaf; 3H6 1.04. 53
have ears more deaf than adders to the voice TRO 2.02.172
the gods are deaf to hot and peevish vows; 5.03. 16
lethargy, mull'd, deaf, /sleepy, insensible, a COR 4.05.224 P
woods are ruthless, dreadful, deaf, and dull. TIT 2.01.128
thee, | be not obdurate, open thy deaf ears. 2.03.160
heart | almost impregnable, his old ears deaf, 4.04. 98
what, deaf? 5.01. 46
the unruly spleen | of tybalt deaf to peace, but ROM 3.01.158
/i will be deaf to pleading and excuses, | nor 3.01.192
that men's ears should be | to counsel deaf, but TIM 1.02.250
come on my right hand, for this ear is deaf, JC 1.02.213
to their deaf pillows will discharge their MAC 5.01. 73
hence, | be deaf to my unpitied folly, ANT 1.03. 98
sir, i am deaf | to all but your compassion), TNK 3.06.238
or were i deaf, thy outward parts would move VEN 435
but will is deaf and hears no heedful friends; LUC 495
and trouble deaf heaven with my bootless cries, SON 29. 3
DEAF'D 2 FR 0.0002 REL FR 2 V 0 P
deaf'd with the clamors of their own dear groans LLL 5.02.864
i think the echoes of his shames have deaf'd TNK 1.02. 80
/DEAFEN'D 1 FR 0.0001 REL FR 1 V 0 P
and make a batt'ry through his /deafen'd parts, PER 5.01. 47
DEAFING 2 FR 0.0002 REL FR 2 V 0 P
with deafing clamor in the slippery clouds, 2H4 3.01. 24
'gainst the which there is | no deafing — but TNK 5.03. 9
DEAFNESS 2 FR 0.0002 REL FR 1 V 1 P
your tale, sir, would cure deafness. TMP 1.02.106
his effects in galen, it is a kind of deafness. 2H4 1.02.117 P
DEAF'NING 1 FR 0.0001 REL FR 1 V 0 P
o, still | thy deaf'ning, dreadful thunders, PER 3.01. 5
DEAFS 1 FR 0.0001 REL FR 1 V 0 P
what cracker is this same that deafs our ears JN 2.01.147
/DEAL 2 FR 0.0002 REL FR 1 V 1 P
/let /us /deal /justly. LR 3.06. 40 P
/she /started | /to /deal /with /grief /alone. 4.03. 32
DEAL 58 FR 0.0065 REL FR 36 V 22 P
and deal in her command without her power. TMP 5.01.271
i will incense /page to deal with poison; WIV 1.03.101 P
little chiding than a great deal of heart–break. 5.03. 10 P
i will deal in this | as secretly and justly as ADO 4.01.247
do not you meddle, let me deal in this. 5.01.101
gratiano speaks an infinite deal of nothing, MV 1.01.114 P
i will deal in poison with thee, or in bastinado AYL 5.01. 54 P
that like a father you will deal with him, | and SHR 4.04. 44
lady, | the fellow has a deal of that too much, AWW 3.02. 90
for a week escape a great deal of discoveries, 3.06. 92 P
sir, so should i be a great deal of his act. 4.03. 46 P
in goodness, but greater a great deal in evil. 4.03.287 P
o, what a deal of scorn looks beautiful | in the TN 3.01.145
peace, peace, we must deal gently with him. 3.04. 95 P
you pay a great deal too dear for what's given WT 1.01. 17 P
such a deal of wonder is broken out within this 5.02. 23 P
we cannot deal but with the very hand | of stern JN 5.02. 22
will but remember me what a deal of world | i R2 1.03.269
deal mildly with his youth, | for young hot 2.01. 69
what a candy deal of courtesy | this fawning 1H4 1.03.251
a weasel hath not such a deal of spleen | as you 2.03. 78
of bread to this intolerable deal of sack! 2.04.541 P
and such a deal of skimble–skamble stuff | as 3.01.152
out of a great deal of old iron i chose forth. 1H6 1.02.101
but god in mercy so deal with my soul | as i in 2H6 1.03.157
for i am never able to deal with my master, he 2.03. 77 P
for i will deal with him | that henceforth he 3.01.323
and doubt not so to deal | as all things shall 4.09. 46
and, for i should not deal in her soft laws, 3H6 3.02.154
are they that i would have thee deal upon: R3 4.02. 74
men shall deal unadvisedly sometimes, | which 4.04.292
so deal with him as i prove true to you. 4.04.497
a great deal of your wit, too, lies in your TRO 2.01. 98 P
and great deal misprising | the knight oppos'd. 4.05. 74
will rob you of a great deal of patience. COR 2.01. 29 P
to weep with them that weep doth ease some deal, TIT 3.01.244
show me a murtherer, i'll deal with him. 5.02. 93
what a deal of brine | hath wash'd thy sallow ROM 2.03. 69
therefore, if you should deal double with her, 2.04.168 P
methinks, i could deal kingdoms to my friends, TIM 1.02.220
a little part, and undo a great deal of honor! 3.02. 48 P
a usuring kindness, and, as rich men deal gifts, 4.03.509
and utter'd such a deal of stinking breath JC 1.02.246 P
but god above | deal between thee and me! MAC 4.03.121
come, come, deal justly with me. HAM 2.02.276 P
and put upon him such a deal of man | that LR 2.02.120
heavens, deal so still! 4.01. 66
and, to deal plainly, | i fear i am not in my 4.07. 61
him, i doubt not, a great deal from the matter. CYM 1.04. 16 P
you are a great deal abus'd in too bold a 1.04.114 P
you, live, | and deal with others better. 5.05.420
get, he may lawfully deal for his wive's soul. PER 2.01.114 P
that a man may deal withal and defy the surgeon? 4.06. 25 P
let me deal coldly with you: TNK 2.02.184
why then would you deal so cunningly, | so 2.02.189
thee | and take thy life, i deal but truly. 2.02.203
yet a great deal short, | methinks, of him 4.02. 89
my shepherd's pipe can sound no deal, | my PP 17.17
DEALER 1 FR 0.0001 REL FR 0 V 1 P
the plainer dealer, the sooner lost; ERR 2.02. 88 P
DEALERS 1 FR 0.0001 REL FR 0 V 1 P
conclude hairy men plain dealers without wit. ERR 2.02. 87 P
DEALING 11 FR 0.0012 REL FR 7 V 4 P
if the duke avouch the justice of your dealing? MM 4.02.186 P
firm, | you should find better dealing. TN 3.03. 18
there is no honesty in such dealing, unless a 2H4 2.01. 37 P
dealing with witches and with conjurers, | whom 2H6 2.01.168
this is close dealing. 2.04. 73
when such ill dealing must be seen in thought. R3 3.06. 14
truth loves open dealing. H8 3.01. 39
"lo jupiter is yonder, dealing life!" TRO 4.05.191
to any gentlewoman, and very weak dealing. ROM 2.04.170 P
edmund, i like not this unnatural dealing. LR 3.03. 2 P
so thou wilt buy, and pay, and use good dealing, VEN 514
DEALINGS 3 FR 0.0003 REL FR 3 V 0 P
whose own hard dealings teaches them suspect MV 1.03.161
to those whose dealings have deserv'd the place R3 3.01. 49
with a learned spirit, | of human dealings. OTH 3.03.260
DEALS 1 FR 0.0001 REL FR 1 V 0 P
him — privily | deals with our cardinal, and, H8 1.01.184
DEAL'ST 1 FR 0.0001 REL FR 0 V 1 P
i do not find that thou deal'st justly with me. OTH 4.02.173 P
DEALT 8 FR 0.0009 REL FR 4 V 4 P
i come to learn how you have dealt for him; JN 5.02.121
i never dealt better since i was a man; 1H4 2.04.169 P
worth | than to be dealt in by attorneyship. 1H6 5.05. 56
uncharitably with me have you dealt, | and R3 1.03.274
they have dealt with me like thieves of mercy, HAM 4.06. 20 P
yet i protest i have dealt most directly in thy OTH 4.02.208 P
he alone | dealt on lieutenantry, and no ANT 3.11. 39
the nobleman would have dealt with her like a PER 4.06.138 P
DEANERY 1 FR 0.0001 REL FR 0 V 1 P
away with her to the deanery, and dispatch it WIV 5.03. 3 P
DEAN'RY 2 FR 0.0002 REL FR 1 V 1 P
and at the dean'ry, where a priest attends, WIV 4.06. 31
she is now with the doctor at the dean'ry, and 5.05.202 P
/DEAR* 3 FR 0.0003 REL FR 3 V 0 P
/by /christ's /dear /blood /shed /for /our R3 1.04.190
/casualties, /gave /her /dear /rights | /to /his LR 4.03. 44
/some /dear /cause | /will /in /concealment 4.03. 51
DEAR* 479 FR 0.0541 REL FR 421 V 58 P
but in care of thee | (of thee my dear one, thee TMP 1.02. 17
dear, they durst not, | so dear the love my 1.02.140
durst not, | so dear the love my people bore me; 1.02.141
bountiful fortune | (now my dear lady) hath mine 1.02.179
awake, dear heart, awake! 1.02.305
o dear father, | make not too rash a trial of 1.02.467
thy case, dear friend, | shall be my president: 2.01.290
o most dear mistress, | the sun will set before 3.01. 21
men than you, good friend, | and my dear father. 3.01. 52
my dear son ferdinand. 5.01.139
and, supportable | to make the dear loss, have i 5.01.146
the island, one dear son | shall i twice lose. 5.01.176
pardon, dear madam, 'tis a passing shame | that TGV 1.02. 17
welcome, dear proteus! 2.04.100
and when the flight is made to one so dear, | of 2.07. 12
o my dear silvia! hapless valentine! 3.01.262
thou art not ignorant what dear good will | i 4.03. 14
for whose dear sake thou didst then rend thy 5.04. 47
there is a gentleman, my dear friend; WIV 3.03.122 P
with the dear love i bear to fair anne page, 4.06. 9
dear sir, ere long i'll visit you again. MM 3.01. 46
thanks, dear isabel. 3.01.105
how doth my dear morsel, thy mistress? 3.02. 54 P
and now, dear maid, be you as free to us. 5.01.388
o my dear lord, | i crave no other, nor no 5.01.425
dear isabel, | i have a motion much imports your 5.01.534
am better than thy dear self's better part. ERR 2.02.123
your dainties cheap, sir, and your welcome dear. 3.01. 21
teach me, dear creature, how to think and speak: 3.02. 33
eye's clear eye, my dear heart's dearer heart, 3.02. 62
you shall buy this sport as dear | as all the 4.01. 81
buried some dear friend? 5.01. 50
what, my dear lady disdain! are you yet living? ADO 1.01.118 P
a dear happiness to women, they would else have 1.01.128 P
my dear friend leonato hath invited you all. 1.01.147 P
not till monday, my dear son, which is hence a 2.01.359 P
man of italy, | always excepted my dear claudio. 3.01. 93
it possible that any villainy should be so dear? 3.03.111 P
dear my lord, if you, in your own proof, | have 4.01. 45
to link my dear friend to a common stale. 4.01. 65
hand, claudio shall render me a dear account. 4.01.333 P
so much, dear liege, i have already sworn, LLL 1.01. 34
is one and the self–same thing, dear imp. 1.02. 5 P
more authority, dear boy, name more; 1.02. 68 P
who was sampson's love, my dear moth? 1.02. 76 P
be now as prodigal of all dear grace | as nature 2.01. 9
grace | as nature was in making graces dear, 2.01. 10
hear me, dear lady: i have sworn an oath. 2.01. 97
dear princess, were not his requests so far 2.01.149
i never knew man hold vile stuff so dear. 4.03.272
and then the king will court thee for his dear. 5.02.131
he swore that he did hold me dear | as precious 5.02.444
and lord berowne (i thank him) is my dear. 5.02.457
full of dear guiltiness, and therefore this: 5.02.791
with the clamors of their own dear groans, 5.02.864
if i have thanks, it is a dear expense. MND 1.01.249
ah pyramus, my lover dear! 1.02. 53 P
thy thisby dear, and lady dear!" 1.02. 54 P
thy thisby dear, and lady dear!" 1.02. 54 P
shall appear | when thou wak'st, it is thy dear: 2.02. 33
for my sake, my dear, | lie further off yet; 2.02. 43
so hath thy breath, my dearest thisby dear. 3.01. 85
sighs of love, that costs the fresh blood dear. 3.02. 97
know, | lest, to thy peril, thou aby it dear. 3.02.175
yonder is thy dear. 3.02.176
thou shalt buy this dear, | if ever i thy face 3.02.426
and, most dear actors, eat no onions nor garlic, 4.02. 42 P
o dear! 5.01.281
this passion, and the death of a dear friend, 5.01.288 P
since lion vild hath here deflow'r'd my dear; 5.01.292
your worth is very dear in my regard. MV 1.01. 62
some dear friend dead, else nothing in the world 3.02.245
and yet, dear lady, | rating myself at nothing, 3.02.256
indeed | i have engag'd myself to a dear friend, 3.02.261
is it your dear friend that is thus in trouble? 3.02.291
since you are dear bought, i will love you dear. 3.02.313
since you are dear bought, i will love you dear. 3.02.313
how dear a lover of my lord your husband, | i 3.04. 7
o dear discretion, how his words are suited! 3.05. 65
a wife | which is as dear to me as life itself, 4.01.283
dear sir, of force i must attempt you further. 4.01.421
dear lady, welcome home! 5.01.113
had held up the very life | of my dear friend. 5.01.215
dear celia — i show more mirth than i am AYL 1.02. 3 P
my sweet rose, my dear rose, be merry. 1.02. 23 P
(as i do trust i am not), then, dear uncle, 1.03. 50
dear sovereign, hear me speak. 1.03. 66
dear master, i can go no further. 2.06. 1 P
o dear phebe, | if ever (as that ever may be 3.05. 27
good day and happiness, dear rosalind! 4.01. 30 P
pardon me, dear rosalind. 4.01. 50 P
alas, dear love, i cannot lack thee two hours! 4.01.179 P
o my dear orlando, how it grieves me to see thee 5.02. 19 P
o my dear niece, welcome thou art to me! 5.04.147
that art to me as secret and as dear | as anna SHR 1.01.153
youngling, thou canst not love so dear as i. 2.01.337
while you, sweet dear, prove mistress of my 4.02. 10
pardon, dear father. 5.01.113
a counsellor, a traitress, and a dear: AWW 1.01.170
my master, my dear lord he is, and i | his 1.03.158
eye, | safer than mine own two, more dear. 2.01.109
of my dear father's gift stands chief in power, 2.01.112
dear sir, to my endeavors give consent, | of 2.01.153
thy life is dear, for all that life can rate 2.01.179
of war | my dearest master, your dear son, may 3.04. 9
to buy his will, it would not seem too dear, 3.07. 27
i'll lend it thee, my dear; 4.02. 40
dear almost as his life, which gratitude 4.04. 6
whose dear perfection hearts that scorn'd to 5.03. 18
what is lost | makes the remembrance dear. 5.03. 20
blames, | dear sovereign, pardon to me. 5.03. 37
which better than the first, o dear heaven, 5.03. 71
o my dear mother, do i see you living? 5.03.319
for whose dear love, | they say, she hath TN 1.02. 39
pourquoi, my dear knight? 1.03. 90 P
surprise her with discourse of my dear faith; 1.04. 25
dear lad, believe it; 1.04. 29
"farewell, dear heart, since i must needs be 2.03.102
thy exquisite reason, dear knight? 2.03.144 P
in my presence still smile, dear my sweet, i 2.05.177 P
dear lady — 3.01.110
thy reason, dear venom, give thy reason. 3.02. 2 P
this is a dear manikin to you, sir toby. 3.02. 53 P
i have been dear to him, lad, some two thousand 3.02. 54 P
i be lapsed in this place, | i shall pay dear. 3.03. 37
that i, dear brother, be now ta'en for you! 3.04.376
be not offended, dear cesario. 4.01. 50
whom thou, in terms so bloody and so dear, 5.01. 71
antonio, o my dear antonio! 5.01.218
combination shall be made | of our dear souls. 5.01.384
you pay a great deal too dear for what's given WT 1.01. 17 P
let what is dear in sicily be cheap. 1.02.175
dear gentlewoman, | how fares our gracious lady? 2.02. 18
(as recompense of our dear services | past and 2.03.150
but shall i go mourn for that, my dear? 4.03. 15
softly, dear sir; 4.03. 75 P
purchase the sight again of dear sicilia | and 4.04.511

dear, look up. 5.01.215
chide me, dear stone, that i may say indeed 5.03. 24
dear queen, that ended when i but began, | give 5.03. 45
dear my brother, | let him that was the cause of 5.03. 53
for from him | dear life redeems you. 5.03.103
yet sell your face for five pence and 'tis dear. JN 1.01.153
"my dear sir," | thus, leaning on mine elbow, i 1.01.193
charge | that art the issue of my dear offense, 1.01.257
and out of my dear love i'll give thee more 2.01.157
but thou art fair, and at thy birth, dear boy, 3.01. 51
will | as dear be to thee as thy father was. 3.03. 4
divers dear friends slain? 3.04. 7
up the womb | of your dear mother england, blush 5.02.153
swore to you | dear amity and everlasting love. 5.04. 20
in my debt, | upon remainder of a dear account, R2 1.01.130
my dear dear lord, | the purest treasure mortal 1.01.176
my dear dear lord, | the purest treasure mortal 1.01.176
then, dear my liege, mine honor let me try; 1.01.184
but thomas, my dear lord, my life, my gloucester 1.02. 16
with that dear blood which it hath fostered; 1.03.126
the dateless limit of thy dear exile; 1.03.151
look what thy soul holds dear, imagine it | to 1.03.286
this land of such dear souls, this dear dear 2.01. 57
land of such dear souls, this dear dear land, 2.01. 57
land of such dear souls, this dear dear land, 2.01. 57
dear for her reputation through the world, | is 2.01. 58
and holds you dear | as harry duke of herford, 2.01.143
dear earth, i do salute thee with my hand, 3.02. 6
to a dear friend of the good duke of york's 3.04. 70
the cheapest of us is ten groats too dear. 5.05. 68
did decree | in forwarding this dear expedience. 1H4 1.01. 33
here is /a dear, a true industrious friend, 1.01. 62
and shed my dear blood drop by drop in the dust, 1.03.134
and, dear coz, to you | the remnant northward 3.01. 77
to lay so dangerous and dear a trust | on any 4.01. 34
and many moe corrivals and dear men | of 4.04. 31
the lord of stafford dear to–day hath bought 5.03. 7
a borrowed title hast thou bought too dear. 5.03. 23
i should not make so dear a show of zeal; 5.04. 95
when your own percy, when my heart's dear harry, 2H4 2.03. 12
we would, dear lords, unto the holy land. 3.01.108
and filial tenderness | shall, o dear father, 4.05. 40
i had forestall'd this dear and deep rebuke 4.05.140
year, | when flesh is cheap and females dear, 5.03. 19
and god forbid, my dear and faithful lord, H5 1.02. 13
o, let their bodies follow, my dear liege, 1.02.130
this his mock mock out of their dear husbands; 1.02.285
in their dear care | and tender preservation of 2.02. 58
and true repentance | of all your dear offenses! 2.02.181
then forth, dear countrymen! 2.02.189
once more unto the breach, dear friends, once 3.01. 1
use mercy to them all for us, dear uncle. 3.03. 54
my dear lord gloucester, and my good lord exeter 4.03. 9
and, with a feeble gripe, says, "dear my lord, 4.06. 22
he is my dear friend, and please you. 4.07.166 P
dear nurse of arts, plenties, and joyful births, 5.02. 35
i said so, dear katherine, and i must not blush 5.02.113 P
and while thou liv'st, dear kate, take a fellow 5.02.153 P
dear kate, you and i cannot be confin'd within 5.02.269 P
i pray you then, in love and dear alliance, 5.02.345
and this dear conjunction | plant neighborhood 5.02.352
sell every man his life as dear as mine, | and 1H6 4.02. 53
and they shall find dear deer of us, my friends. 4.02. 54
therefore, dear boy, mount on my swiftest horse, 4.05. 9
o my dear lord, lo where your son is borne! 4.07. 17
too true, and bought his climbing very dear. 2H6 2.01. 98
so will the queen, that living held him dear. 4.01.147
who would not buy thee dear? 5.01. 5
wast thou ordain'd, dear father, | to lose thy 5.02. 45
withhold revenge, dear god! 3H6 2.02. 7
dear brother, how shall bona be reveng'd | but 3.03.212
when thou hast broke it in such dear degree? R3 1.04.210
he loves me and he holds me dear. 1.04.233
and said, "dear brother, live, and be a king"? 2.01.114
the precious image of our dear redeemer, | you 2.01.124
ah for my husband, for my dear lord edward! 2.02. 71
ah for our father, for our dear lord clarence! 2.02. 72
was never widow had so dear a loss. 2.02. 77
were never orphans had so dear a loss. 2.02. 78
was never mother had so dear a loss. 2.02. 79
comfort, dear mother, god is much displeas'd 2.02. 89
my oracle, my prophet, my dear cousin, | i, as a 2.02.152
welcome, dear cousin, my thoughts' sovereign, 3.01. 2
are dear | to princely richard and to buckingham 3.02. 67
i hold my life as dear as /you /do yours, | and 3.02. 78
be satisfied, dear god, with our true blood, 3.03. 22
so dear i lov'd the man that i must weep. 3.05. 24
right well, dear madam. 4.01. 15
and that dear saint which then i weeping 4.01. 69
than thou hast made me by my dear lord's death!" 4.01. 76
me some little breath, some pause, dear lord, 4.02. 24
cancel his bond of life, dear god, i pray, 4.04. 77
to my proceeding, if with dear heart's love, 4.04.403
therefore, dear mother — i must call you so — 4.04.412
her | so dear in heart not to deny her that | a H8 2.02.110
she should have bought her dignities so dear. 3.01.184
that holy duty, out of dear respect, | his royal 5.02.154
witness how dear i hold this confirmation. 5.02.207
or the limbs of limehouse, their dear brothers, 5.03. 63 P
and what else dear that is consum'd | in hot TRO 2.02. 5
thousand dismes, | hath been as dear as helen; 2.02. 20
dear lord, go you and greet him in his tent. 2.03.179
dear lord, you are full of fair words. 3.01. 47 P
i have business to my lord, dear queen. 3.01. 58 P
my dear lord and most esteem'd friend, your 3.01. 63 P
troy holds him very dear. 3.03. 19
are | most /abject in regard, and dear in use! 3.03.128
what things again most dear in the esteem, | and 3.03.129
perseverance, dear my lord, | keeps honor bright 3.03.150
dear, trouble not yourself, the morn is cold. 4.02. 1
strangles our dear vows | even in the birth of 4.04. 37
consort with me in loud and dear petition, 5.03. 9
life every man holds dear, but the dear man 5.03. 27
dear, but the dear man | holds honor far more 5.03. 27
you know me dutiful, therefore, dear sir, | let 5.03. 72
do not, dear father. 5.03. 76
o, farewell, dear hector! 5.03. 80
but they think we are too dear. COR 1.01. 19 P
alike, and none less dear than thine and my good 1.03. 23 P
ah, my dear, | such eyes the widows in corioles 2.01.177
my dear wive's estimate, her womb's increase 3.03.114
shall grow dear friends | and interjoin their 4.04. 21
who loved him | in a most dear particular. 5.01. 3
heaven, that kiss | i carried from thee, dear; 5.03. 47
and hangs on dian's temple — dear valeria! 5.03. 67
or we must lose | the country, our dear nurse, 5.03.110
thy life | show'd thy dear mother any courtesy, 5.03.161
and if thy sons were ever dear to thee, | o, TIT 1.01.107
to thee, | o, think my son to be as dear to me! 1.01.108
dear father, soul and substance of us all — 1.01.374
sons, | to whom i sued for my dear son's life; 1.01.453
how now, dear sovereign and our gracious mother? 2.03. 89
so thou refuse to drink my dear sons' blood. 3.01. 22
it was my dear, and he that wounded her | hath 3.01. 91
my soul the greatest spurn | is dear lavinia, 3.01.102
patience, dear niece. 3.01.138
and yet dear too, because i bought mine own. 3.01.199
do then, dear heart, for heaven shall hear our 3.01.210
thy other banish'd son with this dear sight 3.01.256
aunt | loves me as dear as e'er my mother did, 4.01. 23
set them upright at their dear friends' door, 5.01.136
and that more dear | than hands or tongue, her 5.02.175
speak, rome's dear friend, as erst our ancestor, 5.03. 80
beauty too rich for use, for earth too dear! ROM 1.05. 47
o then, dear saint, let lips do what hands do, 1.05.103
o dear account! 1.05.118
retain that dear perfection which he owes 2.02. 46
my name, dear saint, is hateful to myself, 2.02. 55
if my heart's dear love — 2.02.115
dear love, adieu! 2.02.136
three words, dear romeo, and good night indeed. 2.02.142
his help to crave, and my dear hap to tell. 2.02.189
then plainly know my heart's dear love is set 2.03. 57
is rosaline, that thou didst love so dear, | so 2.03. 66
what say'st thou, my dear nurse? 2.04.195
o god's lady dear! 2.05. 61
both | receive in either by this dear encounter. 2.06. 29
o, the blood is spill'd | of my dear kinsman! 3.01.148
who now the price of his dear blood doth owe? 3.01.183
is my dear son with such sour company! 3.03. 7
this is dear mercy, and thou seest it not. 3.03. 28
on the white wonder of dear juliet's hand, | and 3.03. 36
thy dear love sworn but hollow perjury, 3.03.128
for whose dear sake thou wast but lately dead: 3.03.136
farewell, dear father! 4.01.126
of dear import, and the neglecting it | may do 5.02. 19
a ring that i must use | in dear employment — 5.03. 32
ah, dear juliet, | why art thou yet so fair? 5.03.101
believe't, dear lord, | you mend the jewel by TIM 1.01.171
my dear lord — 3.04.105
i am thy friend, and pity thee, dear timon. 4.03. 98
o, a root, dear thanks! 4.03.192
and dear divorce | 'twixt natural /son and /sire 4.03.381
other means is left unto us | in our dear peril. 5.01.228
then, dear countryman, | bring in thy ranks, but 5.04. 38
the fault, dear brutus, is not in our stars, JC 1.02.140
dear my lord, | make me acquainted with your 2.01.255
as dear to me as are the ruddy drops | that 2.01.289
for my dear dear love | to your proceeding bids 2.02.102
for my dear dear love | to your proceeding bids 2.02.102
in this assembly, any dear friend of caesar's, 3.02. 18 P
if it be found so, some will dear abide it. 3.02.114
o my dear brother! 4.03.233
dear duff, i prithee contradict thyself, | and MAC 2.03. 89
o, full of scorpions is my mind, dear wife! 3.02. 36
and to our dear friend banquo, whom we miss; 3.04. 89
for their dear causes | would to the bleeding 5.02. 3
though yet of hamlet our dear brother's death HAM 1.02. 1
or thinking by our late dear brother's death 1.02. 19
fear it, ophelia, fear it, my dear sister, | and 1.03. 33
if thou didst ever thy dear father love — 1.05. 23
welcome, dear rosencrantz and guildenstern! 2.02. 1
he tells me, my dear gertrude, he hath found 2.02. 54
o dear ophelia, i am ill at these numbers. 2.02.120 P
thine evermore, most dear lady, whilst this 2.02.123 P
or my dear majesty your queen here, think, | if 2.02.135
my most dear lord! 2.02.223 P
and sure, dear friends, my thanks are too dear a 2.02.273 P
friends, my thanks are too dear a halfpenny. 2.02.274 P
and by what more dear a better proposer can 2.02.286 P
in what, my dear lord? 2.02.377 P
upon whose property and most dear life | a 2.02.570
that i, the son of a dear /father murthered, 2.02.583
o my dear lord — 3.02. 56
since my dear soul was mistress of her choice 3.02. 63
come hither, my dear hamlet, sit by me. 3.02.108 P
for thou dost know, o damon dear, | this realm 3.02.281
thanks, dear my lord. 3.03. 35
from a bat, a gib, | such dear concernings hide? 3.04.191
farewell, dear mother. 4.03. 49 P
o my dear gertrude, this, | like to a 4.05. 94
to know the certainty | of your dear father, 4.05.142
dear maid, kind sister, sweet ophelia! 4.05.159
laertes, was your father dear to you? 4.07.107
in faith, are very dear to fancy, very 5.02.151 P
no, the drink, the drink — o my dear hamlet — 5.02.309
alone felicitate | in your dear highness' love. LR 1.01. 76
dear sir, forbear. 1.01.162
the gods to their dear shelter take thee, maid, 1.01.182
when she was dear to us, we did hold her so, 1.01.196
let thy folly in | and thy dear judgment out! 1.04.272
hear, nature, hear, dear goddess, hear! 1.04.275
my dear lord, | you know the fiery quality of 2.04. 91
the dear father | would with his daughter speak, 2.04.101
"dear daughter, i confess that i am old; 2.04.154
of my note | commend a dear thing to you. 3.01. 19
farewell, dear sister, farewell, my lord of 3.07. 12 P
o dear son edgar, | the food of thy abused 4.01. 21
my most dear gloucester! 4.02. 25
o dear father, | it is thy business that i go 4.04. 23
but love, dear love, and our ag'd father's right 4.04. 28
sir, | your most dear daughter — 4.06.189
pardon, dear madam, | yet to be known shortens 4.07. 8
o my dear father, restoration hang | thy 4.07. 25
kind and dear princess! 4.07. 28
dear my lord, | be not familiar with her. 5.01. 15
so that, dear lords, if i be left behind, | a OTH 1.03.255
interim shall support | by his dear absence. 1.03.259
my dear othello! 2.01.182
he'll prove to desdemona | a most dear husband. 2.01.291
come, my dear love, | the purchase made, the 2.03. 8
he held them sixpence all too dear, | with that 2.03. 91
what is the matter, dear? 2.03.252
good name in man and woman, dear my lord, | is 3.03.155
that her jesses were my dear heart–strings, 3.03.261
how now, my dear othello? 3.03.279
crying, "o dear cassio!" 4.01.137 P
minion, your dear lies dead, | and your unblest 5.01. 33
o my dear cassio, my sweet cassio! 5.01. 76
my friend and my dear countryman | roderigo! 5.01. 89
lies slain here, cassio, | was my dear friend. 5.01.102
if thou attempt it, it will cost thee dear: 5.02.255
dear general, i never gave you cause. 5.02.299
dear goddess, hear that prayer of the people! ANT 1.02. 70 P
therefore, dear isis, keep decorum, and fortune 1.02. 73 P
help me away, dear charmian, i shall fall. 1.03. 15
last thing he did, dear queen, | he kiss'd — 1.05. 39
good night, dear lady. 2.03. 7
brought from rome | are all too dear for me. 2.05.105
hail, most dear caesar! 3.06. 39
welcome to rome, | nothing more dear to me. 3.06. 86
welcome, dear madam. 3.06. 91
do, most dear queen. 3.11. 26
ah, dear, if i be so, | from my cold heart let 3.13.158
my dear master, | my captain, and my emperor: 4.14. 89
be comforted, dear madam. 4.15. 2
i dare not, dear — | dear my lord, pardon — i 4.15. 21
dear my lord, pardon — i dare not, | lest i be 4.15. 22
this i'll report, dear lady. 5.02. 32
no, dear queen, | for we intend so to dispose 5.02.185
pays dear for my offenses. CYM 1.01.106
peace, | dear lady daughter, peace! 1.01.154
my ring i hold dear as my finger, 'tis part of 1.04.133 P
what, dear sir, | thus raps you? are you well? 1.06. 50
the foul expulsion is | of thy dear husband, 2.01. 61
heavens hold firm | the walls of thy dear honor; 2.01. 63
our dear son, | when you have given good morning 2.03. 60
than some, whose tailors are as dear as yours, 2.03. 79
my dear lord, | thou art one o' th' false ones. 3.06. 14
for imogen's dear life take mine, and though 5.04. 22
and though | 'tis not so dear, yet 'tis a life; 5.04. 23
their dear loss, | the more of you 'twas felt, 5.05.345
and yet the end of all is bought thus dear, PER 1.01. 98
a terrible child–bed past thou had, my dear, 3.01. 56
o dear diana, | where am i? 3.02.104
who shall not be more dear to my respect | than 3.03. 33
to take from you the jewel you hold so dear. 4.06.155 P
could he speak, | would own a name too dear. 4.06.179
embrace him, dear thaisa, this is he. 5.03. 55
all dear nature's children sweet, | lie 'fore TNK 1.01. 13
dear glass of ladies, | bid him that we, whom 1.01. 90
think, dear duke, think | what beds our slain 1.01.139
our beds, | that our dear lords have none! 1.01.141
dear palamon, dearer in love than blood, | and 1.02. 1
pieces, keep enthron'd | in your dear heart! 1.03. 11
than a gap | should be in their dear rites, we 1.04. 9
dear cousin palamon — 3.01. 43
ay, ay, by any means, dear domine. 3.05.135
in my face, dear sister, | i find no anger to 3.06.188
help me, dear sister, in a deed so virtuous 3.06.193
my dear kinsmen, | whose lives (for this poor 5.04. 13
could buy | dear love but loss of dear love! 5.04.112
could buy | dear love but loss of dear love! 5.04.112
or were he not my dear friend, this desire LUC 234
but as he is my kinsman, my dear friend, | the 237
where their dear governess and lady lies, | do 443
for collatine's dear love be kept unspotted: 821
well, dear collatine, thou shalt not know | the 1058
"dear lord of that dear jewel i have lost, 1191
"dear lord of that dear jewel i have lost, 1191
to bear | a letter to my lord, my love, my dear. 1293
unmask, dear dear, this moody heaviness, | and 1602
unmask, dear dear, this moody heaviness, | and 1602
dear husband, in the interest of thy bed | a 1619
"dear lord, thy sorrow to my sorrow lendeth 1676
"daughter, dear daughter," old lucretius cries, 1751
dowland to thee is dear, whose heavenly touch PP 8. 5
o yes, dear friend, i pardon crave of thee, 10.11
dear my love, you know | you had a father, let SON 13.13
the dear repose for limbs with travel tired, 27. 2
and with old woes new wail my dear time's waste; 30. 4
but if the while i think on thee, dear friend, 30.13
hath dear religious love stol'n from mine eye 31. 6
and our dear love lose name of single one, 39. 6
clear eye's moiety and the dear heart's part — 46.12
for truth proves thievish for a prize so dear. 48.14
you should love | after my death, dear love, 72. 3
farewell, thou art too dear for my possessing, 87. 1
take heed, dear heart, of this large privilege, 95.13
and sweets grown common lose their dear delight. 102.12
that may express my love, or thy dear merit? 108. 4
mine own thoughts, sold cheap what is most dear, 110. 3
pity me then, dear friend, and i assure ye 111.13
nor need i tallies thy dear love to score; 122.10
if my dear love were but the child of state, 124. 1
for well thou know'st to my dear doting heart 131. 3
dear heart, forbear to glance thine eye aside; 139. 6
love is my sin, and thy dear virtue hate, | hate 142. 1
her "love" for whose dear love i rise and fall. 151.14
yet showed his visage by that cost more dear, LC 96
mood, | effects of terror and dear modesty, 202
that did amplify | each stone's dear nature, 210

DEAR–A 1 FR 0.0001 REL FR 1 V 0 P
lace for your cape, | my dainty duck, my dear–a? WT 4.04.317

DEAR–BELOV'D 1 FR 0.0001 REL FR 1 V 0 P
nuptial | of these our dear–belov'd solemnized, TMP 5.01.310

DEAR–BOUGHT 1 FR 0.0001 REL FR 1 V 0 P
his new bride and england's dear–bought queen, 2H6 1.01.252

/DEAR'D 1 FR 0.0001 REL FR 1 V 0 P
worth love, | comes /dear'd by being lack'd. ANT 1.04. 44

/DEARER 2 FR 0.0002 REL FR 0 V 2 P
knowledge, and knowledge with /dearer love. MM 3.02.151 P
and thou shalt find a /dearer father in my love. LR 3.05. 25 P

DEARER 25 FR 0.0028 REL FR 22 V 3 P
i to myself am dearer than a friend, | for love TGV 2.06. 23
eye's clear eye, my dear heart's dearer heart, ERR 3.02. 62
are dearer than the natural bond of sisters. AYL 1.02.276
welcome, count, | my son's no dearer. AWW 1.02. 76
blood had been the dearer by i know how much an
WT 4.04.705 P
a dearer merit, not so deep a maim | as to be R2 1.03.156
though many dearer, in this bloody fray. 1H4 5.04.108
you should have won them dearer than you have. 2H4 4.03. 67
and that his country's dearer than himself; COR 1.06. 72
the people, to earn a dearer estimation of them; 2.03. 96 P
spurn | is dear lavinia, dearer than my soul. TIT 3.01.102
he loves his pledges dearer than his life. 3.01.291
my dearest cousin, and my dearer lord? ROM 3.02. 66
shall it not grieve thee dearer than thy death, JC 3.01.196
a heart | dearer than pluto's mine, richer than 4.03.102
than this, who yet is no dearer in my account. LR 1.01. 20 P
dearer than eyesight, space, and liberty, 1.01. 56
i lov'd him, friend, | no father his son dearer; 3.04.169
is dearer | in my respect than all the hairs CYM 2.03.134
diseases have been sold dearer than physic — PER 4.06. 98
dear palamon, dearer in love than blood, | and TNK 1.02. 1
but she hath lost a dearer thing than life, LUC 687
"my body or my soul, which was the dearer, 1163
a dearer birth than this his love had brought SON 32.11
those that said i could not love you dearer, 115. 2
DEAREST* 59 FR 0.0066 REL FR 53 V 6 P
if by your art, my dearest father, you have TMP 1.02. 1
worth | what's dearest to the world! 3.01. 39
my mistress, dearest, | and i thus humble ever. 3.01. 86
no, my dearest love, | i would not for the world 5.01.172
now, madam, summon up your dearest spirits; LLL 2.01. 1
thine, in the dearest design of industry, don 4.01. 86 P
so hath thy breath, my dearest thisby dear. MND 3.01. 85
the dearest friend to me, the kindest man, | the MV 3.02.292
the dearest ring in venice will i give you, 4.01.435
hearts, | to have the touches dearest priz'd. AYL 3.02.152
wherein our dearest friend | prejudicates the AWW 1.02. 7
my dearest madam, | let not your hate encounter 1.03.207
which, as the dearest issue of his practice, 2.01.106
the bloody course of war | my dearest master, 3.04. 9
which of them both | is dearest to me, i have no 3.04. 39
and cost me the dearest groans of a mother, i 4.05. 11 P
hermione, my dearest, thou never spok'st | to WT 1.02. 88
and that's the dearest grace it renders you — 1H4 3.01.180
foes, | which art my nearest and dearest enemy? 3.02.123
as good cheap at the dearest chandler's in 3.03. 46 P
we were the first and dearest of your friends. 5.01. 33
york shall bend you with your dearest speed, 5.05. 36
else this blow should broach thy dearest blood. 1H6 3.04. 40
wouldst have left thy dearest heart-blood there 3H6 1.01.223
even with the dearest blood your bodies bear. 5.01. 69
and take deep traitors for thy dearest friends! R3 1.03.223
which in his dearest need will fly from him. 5.02. 21
by that you love the dearest in this world, | as H8 4.02.155
come, my sweet wife, my dearest mother, and | my
COR 4.01. 48
my dearest cousin, and my dearer lord? ROM 3.02. 66
gorg'd with the dearest morsel of the earth, 5.03. 46
and i have bred her at my dearest cost | in TIM 1.01.124
my dearest lord, blest to be most accurs'd, 4.02. 42
my dearest master! 4.03.471
to throw away the dearest thing he ow'd, | as MAC 1.04. 10
deliver thee, my dearest partner of greatness, 1.05. 11 P
my dearest love, | duncan comes here to-night. 1.05. 58
be innocent of the knowledge, dearest chuck, 3.02. 45
my dearest coz, | i pray you school yourself. 4.02. 14
than that which dearest father bears his son HAM 1.02.111
would i had met my dearest foe in heaven | or 1.02.182
daughter, | our dearest regan, wife of cornwall? LR 1.01. 68
the best, the dearest, should in this trice of 1.01.216
us'd | their dearest action in the tented field; OTH 1.03. 85
now, my dearest queen — ANT 1.03. 17
farewell, my dearest sister, fare thee well! 3.02. 39
to thy sinking, for | thy dearest quit thee. 3.13. 65
my dearest husband, | i something fear my CYM 1.01. 85
i have enjoy'd the dearest bodily part of your 1.04.149 P
o dearest soul! 1.06.118
cruel to me as you, o the dearest of creatures, 3.02. 42 P
seat, and cast | from her his dearest one, 5.04. 61
come, dearest madam. PER 3.03. 38
my dearest wife was like this maid, and such a 5.01.107
dearest beauty, | thus let me seal my vow'd TNK 2.05. 38
to buy you i have lost what's dearest to me 5.03.112
so i, made lame by fortune's dearest spite, SON 37. 3
thou, best of dearest and mine only care, | art 48. 7
repay, | forgot upon your dearest love to call, 117. 3
DEAREST-VALUED 1 FR 0.0001 REL FR 1 V 0 P
the blood and dearest-valued blood of france. JN 3.01.343
/DEARLY 1 FR 0.0001 REL FR 1 V 0 P
ear | that are most /dearly sweet and bitter. TNK 5.04. 47
DEARLY 45 FR 0.0050 REL FR 37 V 8 P
dearly, my delicate ariel. TMP 4.01. 49
i hate, | for his advantage that i dearly love. MM 2.04.120
how dearly would it touch thee to the quick, ERR 2.02.130
not hate him deadly, she would love him dearly. ADO 5.01.178 P
i demand of him | is dearly bought as mine, and MV 4.01.100
manage, and to that end riders dearly hir'd; AYL 1.01. 13 P
the duke my father lov'd his father dearly. 1.03. 30 P
ensue that you should love his son dearly? 1.03. 32 P
hate him, for my father hated his father dearly; 1.03. 33 P
i do, which i tender dearly, though i say i am a 5.02. 70 P
flame of liking | wish chastely and love dearly, AWW 1.03.212
by jove's great attributes | i lov'd you dearly, 4.02. 26
i'll love her dearly, ever, ever dearly. 5.03.316
i'll love her dearly, ever, ever dearly. 5.03.316
my master loves her dearly, | and i (poor TN 2.02. 33
and whom, by heaven i swear, i tender dearly, 5.01.126
most dearly welcome! WT 5.01.130
oath | lives in this bosom, dearly cherished. JN 3.03. 24
soul | shall pay full dearly for this encounter, 1H4 5.01. 84
which held thee dearly as his soul's redemption, 3H6 2.01.102
ay, full as dearly as i love myself. 3.02. 37
and he would love me dearly as a child. R3 2.02. 26
sake that lov'd him | heaven knows how dearly. H8 4.02.138
the upper germany, can dearly witness, | yet 5.02. 65
writes me that man, how dearly ever parted, TRO 3.03. 96
most dearly welcome to the greeks, sweet lady. 4.05. 18
he lov'd his mother dearly. COR 5.04. 15 P
will hold thee dearly for thy mother's sake." TIT 5.01. 36
which name i tender | as dearly as mine own — ROM 3.01. 72
look you, she lov'd her kinsman tybalt dearly, 3.04. 3
judge, o you gods, how dearly caesar lov'd him! JC 3.02.182
tender yourself more dearly, | or (not to crack HAM 1.03.107
as we dearly grieve | for that which thou hast 4.03. 41
wine lov'd i /deeply, dice dearly; LR 3.04. 91 P
off | to beggarly divorcement) love him dearly, OTH 4.02.158
madam, methinks, if you did love him dearly, ANT 1.03. 6
you, whom no brother | did ever love so dearly. 2.02.150
nay, but how dearly he adores mark antony! 3.02. 8
is in safety | and greets your highness dearly. CYM 1.06. 13
rubies unparagon'd, | how dearly they do't! 2.02. 18
she hath bought the name of whore thus dearly. 2.04.128
it kept where i kept, i so dearly lov'd it, PER 2.01.130
he loved me dearly, | and for his sake i wish 2.01.138
i was as dearly sorry | as glad of arcite; TNK 5.04.129
and yet it may be said i lov'd her dearly; SON 42. 2
DEARN *(also dern)*
/DEARN 1 FR 0.0001 REL FR 1 V 0 P
wolves had at thy gate howl'd that /dearn time, LR 3.07. 63
DEARNESS 1 FR 0.0001 REL FR 0 V 1 P
and in dearness of heart hath holp to effect ADO 3.02. 98 P
DEAR-PURCHAS'D 1 FR 0.0001 REL FR 1 V 0 P
and given to time your own dear-purchas'd right; SON 117. 6
DEARS 1 FR 0.0001 REL FR 1 V 0 P
stomachers | for my lads to give their dears; WT 4.04.225
DEAR'ST 7 FR 0.0008 REL FR 7 V 0 P
so is the dear'st o' th' loss. TMP 2.01.136
most dear'st! WT 1.02.137
the sweet'st, dear'st creature's dead, and 3.02.201
thou dear'st perdita, | with these forc'd 4.04. 40
for here the troyans taste our dear'st repute TRO 1.03.337
my dear'st sister! ANT 3.06. 98
since death of my dear'st mother | it did not CYM 4.02.190
/DEARTH 1 FR 0.0001 REL FR 0 V 1 P
/death, /dearth, /dissolutions /of /ancient LR 1.02.145 P
DEARTH 11 FR 0.0012 REL FR 10 V 1 P
pity the dearth that i have pined in, | by TGV 2.07. 16
and make a dearth in this revolting land. R2 3.03.163
untimely storms makes men expect a dearth. R3 2.03. 35
your suffering in this dearth, you may as well COR 1.01. 67
for the dearth, | the gods, not the patricians, 1.01. 72
the dearth is great, | the people mutinous; 1.02. 10
and his infusion of such dearth and rareness as, HAM 5.02.117 P
or the mean, if dearth | or foison follow. ANT 2.07. 19
with her plenty press'd, she faint with dearth, VEN 545
and barren dearth of daughters and of sons, | be 754
why dost thou pine within and suffer dearth, SON 146. 3
DEARTHS 1 FR 0.0001 REL FR 1 V 0 P
of plagues, of dearths, or seasons' quality; SON 14. 4
/DEATH 5 FR 0.0005 REL FR 4 V 1 P
vale, | the place of /death and sorry execution, ERR 5.01.121
or let me die, to look on /death no more! R3 2.04. 65
/a /deed /of /death /done /on /the /innocent TIT 3.02. 56
/between /the /child /and /the /parent, /death, LR 1.02.145 P
/the /end /meet /the /old /course /of /death, 3.07.101
DEATH 921 FR 0.1041 REL FR 825 V 96 P
but i would fain die a dry death. TMP 1.01. 68 P
say this were death | that now hath seiz'd them, 2.01.260
shall laugh myself to death at this puppy-headed 2.02.154 P
lo, lo, again! bite him to death, i prithee. 3.02. 34 P
(worse than any death | can be at once) shall 3.03. 77
i shall be pinch'd to death. 5.01.276
being destin'd to a drier death on shore. TGV 1.01.150
and why not death, rather than living torment? 3.01.170
i fly not death, to fly his deadly doom: 3.01.185
tarry i here, i but attend on death, | but, fly 3.01.186
i kill'd a man, whose death i much repent, | but 4.01. 27
what dangerous action, stood it next to death, 5.04. 41
thurio, give back, or else embrace thy death; 5.04.126
th' earth, | and bowl'd to death with turnips! WIV 3.04. 87
was shelvy and shallow — a death that i abhor; 3.05. 15 P
find a man there, he shall die a flea's death. 4.02.151 P
numbers, either in nativity, chance, or death. 5.01. 4 P
cut a little, | than fall, and bruise to death. MM 2.01. 6
let mine own judgment pattern out my death, 2.01. 30
it grieves me for the death of claudio — | but 2.01.280
he's not prepar'd for death. 2.02. 84
that is, were i under the terms of death, | th' 2.04.100
and strip myself to death, as to a bed | that, 2.04.102
will, | or else he must not only die the death, 2.04.165
but thy unkindness shall his death draw out | to 2.04.166
and fit his mind to death, for his soul's rest. 2.04.187
be absolute for death: 3.01. 5
either death or life | shall thereby be the 3.01. 5
yet grossly fear'st | thy death, which is no 3.01. 19
riches but a journey, | and death unloads thee. 3.01. 28
yet death we fear | that makes these odds all 3.01. 40
i seek to die, | and, seeking death, find life. 3.01. 43
free your life, | but fetter you till death. 3.01. 66
the sense of death is most in apprehension, 3.01. 77
be ready, claudio, for your death to-morrow. 3.01.106
death is a fearful thing. 3.01.115
nature is a paradise | to what we fear of death. 3.01.131
i'll pray a thousand prayers for thy death, | no 3.01.145
therefore prepare yourself to death. 3.01.167 P
a merit were it in death to take this poor maid 3.01.231 P
and advis'd him for th' entertainment of death. 3.02.213 P
here's the warrant, claudio, for thy death. 4.02. 63
a man that apprehends death no more dreadfully 4.02.142 P
in the delaying death. 4.02.164 P
of the penitent to be so bar'd before his death. 4.02.177 P
perchance of the duke's death, perchance 4.02.201 P
be so good, sir, to rise and be put to death. 4.03. 27 P
a creature unprepar'd, unmeet for death; 4.03. 67
immediate sentence then, and sequent death, | is 5.01.373
your brother's death i know sits at your heart; 5.01.389
maid, | it was the swift celerity of his death, 5.01.394
that life is better life, past fearing death, 5.01.397
"an angelo for claudio, death for death!" 5.01.409
"an angelo for claudio, death for death!" 5.01.409
the very block | where claudio stoop'd to death, 5.01.415
away with him to death! 5.01.429
he dies for claudio's death. 5.01.443
that i crave death more willingly than mercy: 5.01.476
a punk, my lord, is pressing to death, whipping, 5.01.523 P
and by the doom of death end woes and all. ERR 1.01. 2
made | to epidamium, till my factor's death, 1.01. 41
minds | a doubtful warrant of immediate death, 1.01. 68
my life, | and happy were i in my timely death, 1.01.138
but, though thou art adjudged to the death, 1.01.146
he gains by death that hath such means to die: 3.02. 51
see where they come, we will behold his death. 5.01.128
unless the fear of death doth make me dote, | i 5.01.195
to the death, my lord. ADO 1.03. 70 P
is in that, to be the death of this marriage? 2.02. 19 P
me | out of myself, press me to death with wit. 3.01. 76
it were a better death than die with mocks, 3.01. 79
death is the fairest cover for her shame | that 4.01.116
refuse me, hate me, torture me to death! 4.01.184
the supposition of the lady's death | will 4.01.238
and she is dead, slander'd to death by villains, 5.01. 88
my heart is sorry for your daughter's death; 5.01.103
lady, and her death shall fall heavy on you. 5.01.149 P
rather seal with my death than repeat over to my 5.01.241 P
i thank you, princes, for my daughter's death; 5.01.268
"done to death by slanderous tongues | was the 5.03. 3
death, in guerdon of her wrongs, | gives her 5.03. 5
with shame | lives in death with glorious fame." 5.03. 8
and yield your dead, | till death be uttered, 5.03. 20
i'll tell you largely of fair hero's death. 5.04. 69
and then grace us in the disgrace of death; LLL 1.01. 3
an extemporal epitaph on the death of the deer? 4.02. 51 P
that the lover, sick to death, | /wish'd himself 4.03.105
no, to the death we will not move a foot, | nor 5.02.146
for the remembrance of my father's death. 5.02.810
the sudden hand of death close up mine eye! 5.02.815
to move wild laughter in the throat of death? 5.02.855
or to her death, according to our law MND 1.01. 44
either to die the death, or to abjure | for ever 1.01. 65
to death, or to a vow of single life. 1.01.121
war, death, or sickness did lay siege to it, 1.01.142
comedy and most cruel death of pyramus and 1.02. 12 P
either death, or you, i'll find immediately. 2.02.156
whom i do love and will do till my death. 3.02.167
which death, or absence, soon shall remedy. 3.02.244
league whose date till death shall never end. 3.02.373
the more gracious, i shall sing it at her death. 4.01.219 P
"the thrice three muses mourning for the death 5.01. 52
'tide life, 'tide death, i come without delay. 5.01.203
this passion, and the death of a dear friend, 5.01.288 P
virtuous, and holy men at their death have good MV 1.02. 28 P
a carrion death, within whose empty eye | there 2.07. 63
she wept for the death of a third husband. 3.01. 10 P
you and i, if i might but see you at my death. 3.02.320 P
wether of the flock, | meetest for death; 4.01.115
to stop his wounds, lest he do bleed to death. 4.01.258
say how i lov'd you, speak me fair in death; 4.01.275
to render it | upon his death unto the gentleman 4.01.384
that you would wear it till your hour of death, 5.01.153
after his death, of all he dies possess'd of. 5.01.293
i faint almost to death. AYL 2.04. 66
thy conceit is nearer death than thy powers. 2.06. 8 P
hold death a while at the arm's end. 2.06. 10 P
heart th' accustom'd sight of death makes hard, 3.05. 4
'tis but one cast away, and so, come death! 4.01.186 P
translate thy life into death, thy liberty into 5.01. 53 P
to have her and death were both one thing. 5.04. 17
grim death, how foul and loathsome is thine SHR in.1. 35
after my death the one half of my lands, | and 2.01.121
master and mistress are almost frozen to death. 4.01. 38 P
'tis death for any one in mantua | to come to 4.02. 81
'twere deadly sickness or else present death. 4.03. 14
it, and beat me to death with a bottom of brown 4.03.136 P
going, madam, weep o'er my father's death anew;
AWW 1.01. 4 P
and death should have play for lack of work. 1.01. 20 P
i think it would be the death of the king's 1.01. 23 P
on 's bed of death | many receipts he gave me; 2.01.104
as one near death to those that wish him live. 2.01.131
try, | that ministers thine own death if i die. 2.01.186
uncertain life, and sure death. 2.03. 18 P
let the white death sit on thy cheek for ever, 2.03. 71
not, i am the cause | his death was so effected. 3.02.116
where death and danger dogs the heels of worth. 3.04. 15
he is too good and fair for death and me, | whom 3.04. 16
her story true, even to the point of her death. 4.03. 57 P
her death itself, which could not be her office 4.03. 57 P
lord, sir, let me live, or let me see my death! 4.03.310 P
let death and honesty | go with your impositions 4.04. 28
it was the death of the most virtuous 4.05. 9 P
of the good lady's death and that my lord your 4.05. 70 P
my niece to take the death of her brother thus? TN 1.03. 2 P
good fool, for my brother's death. 1.05. 67 P
and shall do till the pangs of death shake him. 1.05. 75 P
come away, come away, death, | and in sad 2.04. 51
my part of death, no one so true | did share it. 2.04. 57
let me be boil'd to death with melancholy. 2.05. 3 P
can be none but by pangs of death and sepulchre. 3.04.239 P
i snatch'd one half out of the jaws of death, 3.04.360
like to th' egyptian thief at point of death, 5.01.118
crabbed months had sour'd themselves to death, WT 1.02.102
death to thyself but to thy lewd-tongu'd wife, 2.03.172
though a present death | had been more merciful. 2.03.184
easiest passage | look for no less than death. 3.02. 91
look down | and see what death is doing. 3.02.149
though i with death and with | reward did 3.02.163
laid to thee, the death | of the young prince, 3.02.194
them shall | the causes of their death appear 3.02.237
i do believe | hermione hath suffer'd death, and 3.03. 42
either for life or death, upon the earth | of 3.03. 45
a death to grant this. 4.02. 3 P
and then, death, death! 4.03. 53 P
and then, death, death! 4.03. 53 P
not yet on summer's death, nor on the birth | of 4.04. 80
i will devise a death as cruel for thee | as 4.04.440
but that death is too soft for him, say i. 4.04.778 P
he is to behold him with flies blown to death. 4.04.791 P
threatens them | with divers deaths in death. 5.01.202
of their master's death and in the view of the 5.02. 70 P
at the relation of the queen's death (with the 5.02. 85 P
thrice a day, ever since the death of hermione, 5.02.106 P
mock'd as ever | still sleep mock'd death. 5.03. 20

bequeath to death your numbness; 5.03.102
and took it on his death | that this my mother's JN 1.01.110
madam, i'll follow you unto the death. 1.01.154
god shall forgive you cordelion's death | the 2.01. 12
now doth death line his dead chaps with steel, 2.01.352
till then, blows, blood, and death! 2.01.360
at your industrious scenes and acts of death. 2.01.376
no, not death himself | in mortal fury half so 2.01.453
that shakes the rotten carcass of old death 2.01.456
that spits forth death and mountains, rocks and 2.01.458
which only lives but by the death of faith, 3.01.212
that faith would live again by death of need. 3.01.214
though that my death were adjunct to my act, 3.03. 57
death. 3.03. 65
death, death. 3.04. 25
death, death. 3.04. 25
o amiable lovely death! 3.04. 25
the foul corruption of a sweet child's death. 4.02. 81
indeed we heard how near his death he was 4.02. 87
no certain life achiev'd by others' death. 4.02.105
young arthur's death is common in their mouths, 4.02.187
cuts off his tale and talks of arthur's death. 4.02.202
why urgest thou so oft young arthur's death? 4.02.204
i faintly broke with thee of arthur's death; 4.02.227
between my conscience and my cousin's death. 4.02.248
o death, made proud with pure and princely 4.03. 35
o, he is bold, and blushes not at death. 4.03. 76
of mercy, if thou didst this deed of death, 4.03.118
even in the jaws of danger and of death. 5.02.116
and in his forehead sits | a bare–ribb'd death, 5.02.177
wounded to death. 5.04. 9
have i not hideous death within my view, 5.04. 22
for i do see the cruel pangs of death | right in 5.04. 59
death, having prey'd upon the outward parts, 5.07. 15
'tis strange that death should sing. 5.07. 20
who chaunts a doleful hymn to his own death, 5.07. 22
that he did plot the duke of gloucester's death, R2 1.01.100
for gloucester's death, | i slew him not, but to 1.01.132
despite of death that lives upon my grave, | to 1.01.168
in some large measure to thy father's death, 1.02. 26
the best way is to venge my gloucester's death. 1.02. 36
hath caus'd his death, the which if wrongfully, 1.02. 39
on pain of death, no person be so bold | or 1.03. 42
not sick, although i have to do with death, 1.03. 65
what is thy sentence /then but speechless death, 1.03.172
and blindfold death not let me see my son. 1.03.224
thy word is current with him for my death, | but 1.03.231
my life, | how happy then were my ensuing death! 2.01. 68
though death be poor, it ends a mortal woe. 2.01.152
not gloucester's death, nor herford's banishment 2.01.165
even through the hollow eyes of death | i spy 2.01.270
flatterer, | a parasite, a keeper–back of death, 2.02. 70
these signs forerun the death or fall of kings. 2.04. 15
twice all this, | condemns you to the death. 3.01. 29
over | to execution and the hand of death. 3.01. 30
more welcome is the stroke of death to me | than 3.01. 31
throw death upon thy sovereign's enemies. 3.02. 22
the worst is death, and death will have his day. 3.02.103
the worst is death, and death will have his day. 3.02.103
and nothing can we call our own but death, | and 3.02.152
and tell sad stories of the death of kings: 3.02.156
temples of a king | keeps death his court, and 3.02.162
and fight and die is death destroying death, 3.02.184
and fight and die is death destroying death, 3.02.184
where fearing dying pays death servile breath. 3.02.185
i am press'd to death through want of speaking! 3.04. 72
what thou dost know of noble gloucester's death, 4.01. 3
dead time when gloucester's death was plotted, 4.01. 10
land would be | in this your cousin's death. 4.01. 19
there is my gage, the manual seal of death, 4.01. 25
thou wert cause of noble gloucester's death. 4.01. 37
and he and i | will keep a league till death. 5.01. 22
or both | to worthy danger and deserved death. 5.01. 68
the traitor lives, the true man's put to death. 5.03. 73
how now, what means death in this rude assault? 5.05.105
and on my face he turn'd an eye of death, 1H4 1.03.143
and for whose death we in the world's wide mouth 1.03.153
who bears hard | his brother's death at bristow, 1.03.271
the price of oats rose, it was the death of him. 2.01. 13 P
doubt not but to die a fair death for all this, 2.02. 14 P
falstaff sweats to death, | and lards the lean 2.02.108
and i know his death will be a march of twelve 2.04.546 P
of death or death's hand for this one half year. 4.01.136
why, thou owest god a death. 5.01.126 P
the better cherish'd, still the nearer death. 5.02. 15
if die, brave death, when princes die with us! 5.02. 86
king that will revenge | lord stafford's death. 5.03. 13
that ever said i heark'ned for your death. 5.04. 52
but that the earthy and cold hand of death 5.04. 84
death hath not strook so fat a deer to–day, 5.04.107
i'll take it upon my death, i gave him this 5.04.151 P
bear worcester to the death and vernon too. 5.05. 14
stoop'd his anointed head as low as death. 2H4 in 32
the king is almost wounded to the death, | and, 1.01. 14
where hateful death put on his ugliest mask | to 1.01. 66
and i my percy's death ere thou report'st it. 1.01. 75
the tongue offends not that reports his death, 1.01. 97
in few, his death, whose spirit lent a fire 1.01.112
better to be eaten to death with a rust than to 1.02.219 P
proper to madmen, led his powers to death, | and 1.03. 32
then death rock me asleep, abridge my doleful 2.04.197
that, with the hurly, death itself awakes? 3.01. 25
death, as the psalmist saith, is certain to all, 3.02. 37 P
death is certain. 3.02. 40 P
a man can die but once, we owe god a death. 3.02.235 P
for he hath found to end one doubt by death 4.01.197
turning the word to sword and life to death. 4.02. 10
guard /these /traitors to the block of death, 4.02.122
of thy lovers, and they weep for thy death; 4.03. 14 P
stretches itself beyond the hour of death. 4.04. 57
hasty that he doth suppose | my sleep my death? 4.05. 61
and at my death | thou hast seal'd up my 4.05.102
and now my death | changes the mood, for what in 4.05.198
goodman death, goodman bones! 5.04. 28 P
till then i banish thee, on pain of death, | as 5.05. 63
the grave doth gape, and doting death is near, H5 2.01. 61
his sovereign's life to death and treachery. 2.02. 11
and i repent my fault more than my death, 2.02.152

receiv'd the golden earnest of our death; 2.02.169
hence, | poor miserable wretches, to your death; 2.02.178
ay, or go to death; 3.02.116 P
pax, and hanged must 'a be — | a damned death! 3.06. 41
but exeter hath given the doom of death | for 3.06. 44
purpose not their death when they purpose their 4.01.158 P
where they fear'd the death, they have borne 4.01.172 P
and dying so, death is to him advantage; 4.01.180 P
said their prayers, and they stay for death. 4.02. 56
and so espous'd to death, with blood he seal'd 4.06. 26
here was a royal fellowship of death! 4.08.101
and be it death proclaimed through our host | to 4.08.114
stars | that have consented unto henry's death: 1H6 1.01. 5
make him burst his lead and rise from death. 1.01. 64
him i forgive my death that killeth me, | when 1.02. 20
with henry's death the english circle ends, 1.02.136
since henry's death, i fear, there is conveyance 1.03. 2
or dagger, henceforward, upon pain of death. 1.03. 79 P
and craved death | rather than i would be so 1.04. 32
none durst come near for fear of sudden death. 1.04. 48
you all consented unto salisbury's death, | for 1.05. 34
the treacherous manner of his mournful death, 2.02. 16
exploit | as scythian tomyris by cyrus' death. 2.03. 6
a thousand souls to death and deadly night. 2.04.127
and these grey locks, the pursuivants of death, 2.05. 5
just death, kind umpire of men's miseries, 2.05. 29
and did upbraid me with my father's death; 2.05. 48
and death approach not ere my tale be done. 2.05. 62
and that my fainting words do warrant death. 2.05. 95
and humble service till the point of death. 3.01.167
lance, | and run a–tilt at death within a chair? 3.02. 51
when death doth close his tender–dying eyes, 3.03. 48
that whoso draws a sword, 'tis present death, 3.04. 39
not fearing death, nor shrinking for distress, 4.01. 37
henceforth we banish thee, on pain of death. 4.01. 47
thou ominous and fearful owl of death, | our 4.02. 15
on us thou canst not enter but by death; 4.02. 18
but death doth front thee with apparent spoil, 4.02. 26
sund'red friends greet in the hour of death. 4.03. 42
to beat assailing death from his weak /legions; 4.04. 16
now thou art come unto a feast of death, | a 4.05. 7
fly, to revenge my death, if i be slain. 4.05. 18
upon my death the french can little boast; 4.05. 24
if death be so apparent, then both fly. 4.05. 44
i gave thee life, and rescu'd thee from death. 4.06. 5
fly, to revenge my death when i am dead; 4.06. 30
triumphant death, smear'd with captivity, 4.07. 3
thou antic death, which laugh'st us here to 4.07. 18
o thou whose wounds become hard–favored death, 4.07. 23
brave death by speaking, whether he will or no; 4.07. 25
had death been french, then death had died 4.07. 28
death been french, then death had died to–day. 4.07. 28
out, | must i behold thy timeless cruel death? 5.04. 5
wicked and vile, and so her death concludes. 5.04. 16
womb, | although ye hale me to a violent death. 5.04. 64
but darkness and the gloomy shade of death 5.04. 89
now, by the death of him that died for all, 2H6 1.01.113
but him out–live, and die a violent death. 1.04. 31
but him out–live, and die a violent death." 1.04. 60
demanding of king henry's life and death, | and 2.01.171
after edward the third's death reign'd as king 2.02. 20
such as by god's book are adjudg'd to death. 2.03. 4
welcome is banishment, welcome were my death. 2.03. 14
touching the duke of york, i will take my death, 2.03. 88 P
for by his death we do perceive his guilt, | and 2.03.101
nothing, till the axe of death | hang over thee, 2.04. 49
my joy is death; 2.04. 88
death, at whose name i oft have been afeard, 2.04. 89
and if my death might make this island happy, 3.01.148
policy, | but yet we want a color for his death. 3.01.236
more than mistrust, that shows him worthy death. 3.01.242
'tis york that hath more reason for his death. 3.01.245
so the poor chicken should be sure of death. 3.01.251
to be, or what thou art | resign to death; 3.01.334
for in the shade of death i shall find joy; 3.02. 54
in life but double death, now gloucester's dead. 3.02. 55
yet he most christian–like laments his death; 3.02. 58
this get i by his death. 3.02. 70
until they hear the order of his death. 3.02.129
and comment then upon his sudden death. 3.02.133
for, seeing him, i see my life in death. 3.02.152
who, in the conflict that it holds with death, 3.02.164
why, warwick, who should do the duke to death? 3.02.179
as guilty of duke humphrey's timeless death. 3.02.187
that i am faulty in duke humphrey's death. 3.02.202
unless lord suffolk straight be done to death, 3.02.244
and torture him with grievous ling'ring death. 3.02.247
they say, in him they fear your highness' death; 3.02.249
in pain of your dislike, or pain of death, | yet 3.02.257
but three days longer, on the pain of death. 3.02.288
that cardinal beauford is at point of death; 3.02.369
from thee to die were torture more than death. 3.02.401
this way fall i to death. 3.02.412
if thou beest death, i'll give thee england's 3.03. 2
see how the pangs of death do make him grin! 3.03. 24
so bad a death argues a monstrous life. 3.03. 30
what, doth death affright? 4.01. 32
thy name affrights me, in whose sound is death. 4.01. 33
thou that smil'dst at good duke humphrey's death 4.01. 76
come, suffolk, i must waft thee to thy death. 4.01.116
can, | that this my death may never be forgot! 4.01.133
lamenting and mourning for suffolk's death? 4.04. 22
sir humphrey stafford and his brother's death 4.04. 34
call false caterpillars, and intend their death. 4.04. 37
whom have i injur'd that ye seek my death? 4.07.101
expect your highness' doom, of life or death. 4.09. 12
or unto death, to do my country good. 4.09. 43
we'll bait thy bears to death, | and manacle the 5.01.148
hast, | i am resolv'd for death /or dignity. 5.01.194
for i myself must hunt this deer to death. 5.02. 15
hath made the wizard famous in his death. 5.02. 69
you have defended me from imminent death. 5.03. 19
as shall revenge his death before i stir. 3H6 1.01.100
your right depends not on his life or death. 1.02. 11
o, let me pray before i take my death! 1.03. 35
like men born to renown by life or death. 1.04. 8
and if thine eyes can water for his death, | i 1.04. 82
that not a tear can fall for rutland's death? 1.04. 88

till our king henry had shook hands with death. 1.04.102
that beggars mounted run their horse to death. 1.04.127
and every drop cries vengeance for his death 1.04.148
for my oath, here's for my father's death. 1.04.175
richard, i bear thy name, i'll venge thy death, 2.01. 87
is by the stern lord clifford done to death. 2.01.103
who thunders to his captives blood and death, 2.01.127
and in that quarrel use it to the death. 2.02. 65
or strike, ungentle death! 2.03. 6
and in the very pangs of death he cried, | like 2.03. 17
brother, revenge my death!" 2.03. 19
till either death hath clos'd these eyes of mine 2.03. 31
here's the heart that triumphs in their death, 2.04. 8
for i myself will hunt this wolf to death. 2.04. 13
o that my death would stay these ruthful deeds! 2.05. 95
how will my mother for a father's death | take 2.05.103
was ever son so ru'd a father's death? 2.05.109
for death doth hold us in pursuit. 2.05.127
had left no mourning widows for our death, | and 2.06. 19
that nothing sung but death to us and ours. 2.06. 57
now death shall stop his dismal threat'ning 2.06. 58
dark cloudy death o'ershades his beams of life, 2.06. 62
which in the time of death he gave our father. 2.06. 67
my love till death, my humble thanks, my prayers 3.02. 62
the lord aubrey vere, | was done to death? 3.03.103
when nature brought him to the door of death? 3.03.105
of york | my father came untimely to his death? 3.03.187
or else you famish — that's a threefold death. 5.04. 32
sheathe thy sword, i'll pardon thee my death. 5.05. 70
what scene of death hath roscius now to act? 5.06. 10
orphans for their parents' timeless death — 5.06. 42
how my sword weeps for the poor king's death! 5.06. 63
and then, to purge his fear, i'll be thy death. 5.06. 88
that makes us wretched by the death of thee R3 1.02. 18
which this blood mad'st, revenge his death! 1.02. 62
which this blood drink'st, revenge his death! 1.02. 63
sleep | to undertake the death of all the world, 1.02.123
night o'ershade thy day, and death thy life! 1.02.131
for now they kill me with a living death. 1.02.152
told the sad story of my father's death, | and 1.02.160
stroke, | and humbly beg the death upon my knee. 1.02.178
though i wish thy death, | i will not be thy 1.02.184
wert thou not banished on pain of death? 1.03.166
than death can yield me here by my abode. 1.03.168
so much with heaven | that henry's death, my 1.03.191
that henry's death, my lovely edward's death, 1.03.191
mayst thou live to wail thy children's death, 1.03.203
long die thy happy days before thy death, | and, 1.03.206
witness my son, now in the shade of death, 1.03.266
his venom tooth will rankle to the death. 1.03.290
sin, death, and hell have set their marks on him 1.03.292
what sights of ugly death within /my eyes! 1.04. 23
had you such leisure in the time of death | to 1.04. 34
the bitter sentence of poor clarence' death? 1.04.186
to threaten me with death is most unlawful. 1.04.188
life | than edward will for tidings of my death. 1.04.231
'tis death to me to be at enmity; 2.01. 61
have i a tongue to doom my brother's death, 2.01.103
and yet his punishment was bitter death. 2.01.106
(almost) to death, how he did lap me | even in 2.01.116
pale when they did hear of clarence' death? 2.01.137
as loath to lose him, not your father's death; 2.02. 10
you cannot guess who caus'd your father's death. 2.02. 19
i have bewept a worthy husband's death, | and 2.02. 49
are crack'd in pieces by malignant death, | and 2.02. 52
but death hath snatch'd my husband from my arms, 2.02. 57
you wept not for our father's death; 2.02. 62
doth the news hold of good king edward's death? 2.03. 7
death makes no conquest of this conqueror, | for 3.01. 87
which by his death hath lost much majesty. 3.01.100
god knows i will not do it, to the death! 3.02. 55
this day those enemies are put to death, | and i 3.02.103
richard the second here was hack'd to death; 3.03. 12
make haste, the hour of death is expiate. 3.03. 24
that do conspire my death with devilish plots 3.04. 60
i say, my lord, they have deserved death. 3.04. 66
proceed thus rashly in the villain's death, 3.05. 43
he deserv'd his death, | and your good graces 3.05. 47
may | misconster us in him and wail his death. 3.05. 61
tell them how edward put to death a citizen 3.05. 76
death and destruction dogs thee at thy heels; 4.01. 39
if thou wilt outstrip death, go cross the seas, 4.01. 41
o my accursed womb, the bed of death! 4.01. 53
than thou hast made me by my dear lord's death!" 4.01. 76
gold | will tempt unto a close exploit of death? 4.02. 35
when thou shalt tell the process of their death. 4.03. 32
and drop into the rotten mouth of death. 4.04. 2
a hell–hound that doth hunt us all to death: 4.04. 48
and the dire death of my poor sons and brothers? 4.04.143
shame serves thy life and doth thy death attend. 4.04.196
my babes were destin'd to a fairer death, | if 4.04.220
and i, in such a desp'rate bay of death, | like 4.04.233
my father's death — 4.04.376
soul, | death, desolation, ruin, and decay. 4.04.409
nothing but songs of death? 4.04.507
i that was wash'd to death with fulsome wine, 5.03.132
poor clarence, by thy guile betray'd to death! 5.03.133
and weigh thee down to ruin, shame, and death! 5.03.148
dream on, dream on, of bloody deeds and death; 5.03.171
seeking for richmond in the throat of death. 5.04. 5
death, my lord, | their clothes are after such a H8 1.03. 13
i do not think he fears death. 2.01. 37
the law i bear no malice for my death; 2.01. 62
nothing but death | shall e'er divorce my 3.01.141
brings his physic | after his patient's death. 3.02. 41
be growing, | till death, that winter, kill it. 3.02.179
o griffith, sick to death! 4.02. 1
after my death i wish no other herald, | no 4.02. 69
tell him, in death i blest him, | for so i will. 4.02.163
her suff'rance made | almost each pang a death. 5.01. 69
whose life were ill bestow'd, or death unfam'd, TRO 2.02.159
let thy blood be thy direction till thy death; 2.03. 31 P
draw emulous factions and bleed to death upon. 2.03. 74 P
death, i fear me, | sounding destruction, or 3.02. 22
of your pretty encounters, press it to death. 3.02.209 P
as for her greeks and troyans suff'red death. 4.01. 75
i knew thou wouldest be his death. 4.02. 86 P
'twill be his death, 'twill be his bane, he 4.02. 92 P

time, force, and death, | do to this body what 4.02.101
for i will throw my glove to death himself 4.04. 63
hence | a great addition earned in thy death. 4.05.141
to–morrow do i meet thee, fell as death; 4.05.269
sword, thou hast thy fill of blood and death. 5.08. 4
if in his death the gods have us befriended, 5.09. 9
i do not speak of flight, of fear, of death, 5.10. 12
condemning some to death, and some to exile; COR 1.06. 35
if any think brave death outweighs bad life, 1.06. 71
ingratitude, | and tent themselves with death. 1.09. 31
death, that dark spirit, in 's nervy arm doth 2.01.160
physic | that's sure of death without it — at 3.01.155
this deserves death. 3.01.206
theirs, martius is worthy | of present death. 3.01.211
forget that ever | he heard the name of death. 3.01.259
and to keep him here | our certain death; 3.01.287
what has he done to rome that's worthy death? 3.01.296
present me | death on the wheel, or at wild 3.02. 2
for i mock at death | with as big heart as thou. 3.02.127
commons," be it either | for death, for fine, or 3.03. 15
if death, cry "death!" 3.03. 16
if death, cry "death!" 3.03. 16
capital kind, | deserves th' extremest death. 3.03. 82
let them pronounce the steep tarpeian death, 3.03. 88
for if | i had fear'd death, of all the men i' 4.05. 81
or of some death more long in spectatorship and 5.02. 65 P
home, | they'll give him death by inches. 5.04. 39
and sure as death i swore | i would not part a TIT 1.01.487
vengeance is in my heart, death in my hand, 2.03. 38
yew, | and leave me to this miserable death. 2.03.108
'tis present death i beg, and one thing more 2.03.173
and see a fearful sight of blood and death. 2.03.216
by my soul, were there worse end than death, 2.03.302
unbind my sons, reverse the doom of death, | and 3.01. 24
tribunes with their tongues doom men to death. 3.01. 47
to rescue my two brothers from their death, 3.01. 49
this way to death my wretched sons are gone, 3.01. 98
and for his death | thy brothers are condemn'd, 3.01.108
to ransom my two nephews from their death; 3.01.172
let me redeem my brothers both from death. 3.01.180
more than remembrance of my father's death. 3.01.240
deal, | but sorrow flouted at is double death. 3.01.245
that ever death should let life bear his name, 3.01.248
the emperor in his rage will doom her death. 4.02.114
and this shall all be buried in my death, 5.01. 67
as kill a man, or else devise his death, 5.01.128
not die | so sweet a death as hanging presently. 5.01.146
confer with me of murder and of death. 5.02. 34
i pray thee do on them some violent death, 5.02.108
two of her brothers were condemn'd to death, 5.02.173
there's meed for meed, death for a deadly deed! 5.03. 66
to be /adjudg'd some direful slaught'ring death, 5.03.144
doth with their death bury their parents' strife ROM pr 8
turn thee, benvolio, look upon thy death. 1.01. 67
once more, on pain of death, all men depart. 1.01.103
breast | by some vile forfeit of untimely death. 1.04.111
and the place death, considering who thou art, 2.02. 64
than death prorogued, wanting of thy love. 2.02. 78
full soon the canker death eats up that plant. 2.03. 30
to catch my death with jauncing up and down! 2.05. 52
then love–devouring death do what he dare, | it 2.06. 7
rat, a mouse, a cat, to scratch a man to death! 3.01.101 P
the prince will doom thee death | if thou art 3.01.134
with one hand beats | cold death aside, and with 3.01.162
some word there was, worser than tybalt's death, 3.02.108
tybalt's death | was woe enough if it had ended 3.02.114
but with a rearward following tybalt's death, 3.02.121
in that word's death, no words can that woe 3.02.126
and death, not romeo, take my maidenhead! 3.02.137
not body's death, but body's banishment. 3.03. 11
be merciful, say "death"; 3.03. 12
more terror in his look, | much more than death. 3.03. 14
from the world, | and world's exile is death; 3.03. 20
then "banished" | is death misterm'd. 3.03. 21
calling death "banished," | thou cut'st my head 3.03. 21
thy fault our law calls death, but the kind 3.03. 25
turn'd that black word "death" to "banishment." 3.03. 27
and sayest thou yet that exile is not death? 3.03. 43
no sudden mean of death, though ne'er so mean, 3.03. 45
law that threat'ned death becomes thy friend, 3.03.139
let me be ta'en, let me be put to death, | i am 3.05. 17
come, death, and welcome! 3.05. 24
evermore weeping for your cousin's death? 3.05. 69
girl, thou weep'st not so much for his death, 3.05. 78
would none but i might venge my cousin's death! 3.05. 86
immoderately she weeps for tybalt's death, | and 4.01. 6
a thing like death to chide away this shame, 4.01. 74
that cop'st with death himself to scape from it; 4.01. 75
like death when he shuts up the day of life; 4.01.101
stiff and stark and cold, appear like death, 4.01.103
and in this borrowed likeness of shrunk death 4.01.104
like | the horrible conceit of death and night, 4.03. 37
death lies on her like an untimely frost | upon 4.05. 28
death, that hath ta'en her hence to make me wail 4.05. 31
thy wedding–day | hath death lain with thy wife. 4.05. 36
death is my son–in–law, death is my heir, | my 4.05. 38
death is my son–in–law, death is my heir, | my 4.05. 38
and cruel death hath catch'd it from my sight! 4.05. 48
most detestable death, by thee beguil'd, | by 4.05. 56
not life, but love in death! 4.05. 58
your part in her you could not keep from death, 4.05. 69
now, | whose sale is present death in mantua, 5.01. 51
law | is death to any he that utters them. 5.01. 67
why i descend into this bed of death | is partly 5.03. 28
thou detestable maw, thou womb of death, 5.03. 45
can vengeance be pursued further than death? 5.03. 55
death, lie thou there, by a dead man interr'd. 5.03. 87
how oft when men are at the point of death 5.03. 88
their keepers call | a lightning before death! 5.03. 90
death, that hath suck'd the honey of thy breath, 5.03. 92
i believe | that unsubstantial death is amorous, 5.03.103
kiss | a dateless bargain to engrossing death! 5.03.115
and fearfully did menace me with death | if i 5.03.133
come from that nest | of death, contagion, and 5.03.152
this sight of death is as a bell | that warns my 5.03.206
of your woes, | and lead you even to death. 5.03.220
whose untimely death | banish'd the new–made 5.03.234
for it wrought on her | the form of death. 5.03.246
i brought my master news of juliet's death, 5.03.272
and threat'ned me with death, going in the vault 5.03.276
their course of love, the tidings of her death; 5.03.287
right, if doing nothing be death by th' law. TIM 1.01.194 P
a dog, and thou shalt famish a dog's death. 2.02. 87 P
by whose death he's stepp'd | into a great 2.02.223
and, when he's sick to death, let not that part 3.01. 61
seeing his reputation touch'd to death, | he did 3.05. 19
that death in me at others' lives may laugh. 4.03.380
only be men's works, and death their gain! 5.01.222
by decimation, and a tithed death, | if thy 5.04. 31
set honor in one eye and death i' th' other, JC 1.02. 86
love | the name of honor more than i fear death. 1.02. 89
it must be by his death; 2.01. 10
like wrath in death and envy afterwards; 2.01.164
themselves blaze forth the death of princes. 2.02. 31
the valiant never taste of death but once. 2.02. 33
seeing that death, a necessary end, | will come 2.02. 36
will crowd a feeble man almost to death. 2.04. 36
life | cuts off so many years of fearing death. 3.01.102
grant that, and then is death a benefit; 3.01.103
that have abridg'd | his time of fearing death. 3.01.105
how caesar hath deserv'd to lie in death, | mark 3.01.132
no place will please me so, no mean of death, 3.01.161
beg not your death of us. 3.01.164
shall it not grieve thee dearer than thy death, 3.01.196
and show the reason of our caesar's death. 3.01.237
reasons shall be rendered | of caesar's death. 3.02. 8
and death for his ambition. 3.02. 28 P
the question of his death is enroll'd in the 3.02. 38 P
offenses enforc'd, for which he suffer'd death. 3.02. 40 P
who, though he had no hand in his death, shall 3.02. 42 P
it shall please my country to need my death. 3.02. 47 P
most noble caesar! we'll revenge his death. 3.02.243
nothing but death shall stay me. 4.03.128
for with her death | that tidings came. 4.03.154
lepidus | have put to death an hundred senators. 4.03.175
by which i did blame cato for the death | which 5.01.101
kill brutus, and be honor'd in his death. 5.04. 14
and no man else hath honor by his death. 5.05. 57
go pronounce his present death, | and with his MAC 1.02. 64
by sinel's death i know i am thane of glamis, 1.03. 71
thyself didst make | strange images of death. 1.03. 97
as one that had been studied in his death, | to 1.04. 9
their drenched natures lies as in a death, 1.07. 68
our griefs and clamor roar | upon his death? 1.07. 79
that death and nature do contend about them, 2.02. 7
the death of each day's life, sore labor's bath, 2.02. 35
strange screams of death, | and prophesying, 2.03. 56
death's counterfeit, | and look on death itself! 2.03. 77
in his life, | which in his death were perfect. 3.01.107
on his head, | the least a death to nature. 3.04. 27
with macbeth | in riddles and affairs of death; 3.05. 5
he shall spurn fate, scorn death, and bear | his 3.05. 30
these murther'd deer | to add the death of you. 4.03.207
death of thy soul! 5.03. 16
i will not be afraid of death and bane, | till 5.03. 59
have lighted fools | the way to dusty death. 5.05. 23
those clamorous harbingers of blood and death. 5.06. 10
i would not wish them to a fairer death. 5.09. 15
which, they say, your spirits oft walk in death, HAM 1.01.138
though yet of hamlet our dear brother's death 1.02. 1
or thinking by our late dear brother's death 1.02. 19
whose common theme | is death of fathers, and 1.02.104
why thy canoniz'd bones, hearsed in death, 1.04. 47
is by a forged process of my death | rankly 1.05. 37
more than his father's death, that thus hath put 2.02. 8
his father's death and our /o'erhasty marriage. 2.02. 57
and the orb below | as hush as death, anon the 2.02.486
after your death you were better have a bad 2.02.525 P
for in that sleep of death what dreams may come, 3.01. 65
but that the dread of something after death, 3.01. 77
which i have told thee of my father's death. 3.02. 77
o bosom black as death! 3.03. 67
and will answer well | the death i gave him. 3.04.177
to that effect, | the present death of hamlet. 4.03. 65
mortal and unsure | to all that fortune, death, 4.04. 52
see | the imminent death of twenty thousand men, 4.04. 60
it springs | all from her father's death — and 4.05. 76
and whispers | for good polonius' death; 4.05. 83
with pestilent speeches of his father's death, 4.05. 91
in many places | gives me superfluous death. 4.05. 96
that i am guiltless of your father's death, 4.05.150
his means of death, his obscure funeral — | no 4.05.214
with as much speed as thou wouldest fly death. 4.06. 24 P
and for his death no wind of blame shall breathe 4.07. 66
can save the thing from death | that is but 4.07.145
that, if i gall him slightly, | it may be death. 4.07.148
wretch from her melodious lay | to muddy death. 4.07.183
not guilty of his own death shortens not his own 5.01. 20 P
her death was doubtful, | and, but that great 5.01.227
he should those bearers put to sudden death, 5.02. 46
mine and my father's death come not upon thee, 5.02.330
had i but time — as this fell sergeant, death, 5.02.336
o proud death, | what feast is toward in thine 5.02.364
he never gave commandement for their death. 5.02.374
while we | unburthen'd crawl toward death. LR 1.01. 41
in our dominions, | the moment is thy death. 1.01.178
life and death! 1.04.296
he that conceals him, death. 2.01. 63
if they not thought the profits of my death 2.01. 75
'tis they have put him on the old man's death, 2.01. 99
death! 2.04. 95
death on my state! 2.04.112
i'll beat the drum | till it cry sleep to death. 2.04.119
death, traitor! 3.04. 70
his daughters seek his death. 3.04.163
evil disposition made him seek his death; 3.05. 6 P
i have o'erheard a plot of death upon him. 3.06. 89
yours in the ranks of death. 4.02. 25
depriv'd that benefit, | to end itself by death? 4.06. 62
o untimely death! 4.06.250
death! 4.06.251
that of thy death and business i can tell. 4.06.278
that we the pain of death would hourly die 5.03.186
to die, when death is our physician. OTH 1.03.309 P
therefore my hopes (not surfeited to death) 2.01. 50
may the winds blow till they have waken'd death! 2.01.186
i bleed still, | i am hurt to th' death. 2.03.165
'tis destiny unshunnable, like death. 3.03.275
death and damnation! o! 3.03.396
to furnish me with some swift means of death 3.03.478
a necessity in his death that you shall think 4.02.240 P
nobody come? then shall i bleed to death. 5.01. 45
'tis like she comes to speak of cassio's death; 5.02. 92
a guiltless death i die. 5.02.122
did you and he consent in cassio's death? 5.02.297
imports | the death of cassio to be undertook 5.02.311
who tells me true, though in his tale lie death, ANT 1.02. 98
i do think there is mettle in death, which 1.02.143 P
for not alone | the death of fulvia, with more 1.02.180
you should safe my going, | is fulvia's death. 1.03. 56
in fulvia's death, how mine receiv'd shall be. 1.03. 65
pleas'd fortune does of marcus crassus' death 3.01. 2
third is up, till death enlarge his confine. 3.05. 12 P
the token'd pestilence, | where death is sure. 3.10. 10
her head's declin'd, and death will seize her, 3.11. 47
next time i do fight, | i'll make death love me; 3.13.192
married to your good service, stay till death. 4.02. 31
expect victorious life | than death and honor. 4.02. 44
the hand of death hath raught him. 4.09. 29
fury, for one death | might have prevented many. 4.12. 41
mardian, | and bring me how he takes my death. 4.13. 10
she hath betray'd me, and shall die the death. 4.14. 26
death of one person can be paid but once, | and 4.14. 27
than she which by her death our caesar tells, 4.14. 61
thus i do escape the sorrow | of antony's death. 4.14. 95
but i will be | a bridegroom in my death, and 4.14.100
thy death and fortunes bid thy followers fly. 4.14.111
and give me | sufficing strokes for death. 4.14.117
only | i here importune death awhile, until | of 4.15. 19
to rush into the secret house of death | ere 4.15. 81
house of death | ere death dare come to us? 4.15. 82
fashion, | and make death proud to take us. 4.15. 88
the death of antony | is not a single doom, in 5.01. 17
what, of death too, | that rids our dogs of 5.02. 41
which your death | will never let come forth. 5.02. 45
where art thou, death? 5.02. 46
the stroke of death is as a lover's pinch, 5.02.295
now boast thee, death, in thy possession lies 5.02.315
embracements from a next | with bonds of death! CYM 1.01.117
there cannot be a pinch in death | more sharp 1.01.130
which are the movers of a languishing death, 1.05. 9
is | no danger in what show of death it makes, 1.05. 40
hath the king | five times redeem'd from death. 1.05. 63
o sleep, thou ape of death, lie dull upon her, 2.02. 31
though peril to my modesty, not death on't, | i 3.04.152
words are /strokes, | and strokes death to her. 3.05. 41
gone she is | to death or to dishonor, and my 3.05. 63
the instant is | thy condemnation and thy death. 3.05. 98
die the death! 4.02. 96
us portends, | or what his death will bring us. 4.02.183
since death of my dear'st mother | it did not 4.02.190
newness | of cloten's death (we being not known, 4.04. 10
whose answer would be death | drawn on with 4.04. 13
even for whom my life | is every breath a death; 5.01. 27
could not find death where i did hear him groan, 5.03. 69
for me, my ransom's death. 5.03. 80
than be cur'd | by th' sure physician, death, 5.04. 7
come, sir, are you ready for death? 5.04.151 P
your death has eyes in 's head then; 5.04.178 P
yet death | will seize the doctor too. 5.05. 29
i see a thing | bitter to me as death; 5.05.104
is not this boy reviv'd from death? 5.05.120
do mean to strike me | to death with mortal joy. 5.05.235
way she was gone, | it was my instant death. 5.05.278
think death no hazard in this enterprise. PER 1.01. 5
for death remembered should be like a mirror, 1.01. 45
thus ready for the way of life or death, | i 1.01. 54
against the face of death | i sought the 1.02. 71
with whom each minute threatens life or death. 1.03. 24
breath | nothing to think on but ensuing death. 2.01. 7
here to have death in peace is all he'll crave. 2.01. 11
it hath been a shield | 'twixt me and death" — 2.01.127
whose death indeed the strongest in our censure, 2.04. 34
whistle | is as a whisper in the ears of death, 3.01. 9
in silken bags, | to please the fool and death. 3.02. 42
death may usurp on nature many hours, | and yet 3.02. 82
she comes weeping for her only mistress' death. 4.01. 11
wherein my death might yield her any profit, 4.01. 80
on whom foul death hath made this slaughter. 4.04. 37
you not name a tempest, | a birth, and death? 5.03. 34
rather have 'em | prisoners to us than death. TNK 1.04. 37
assure upon my daughter at the day of my death. 2.01. 9 P
and after death our spirits shall be led | to 2.02.116
punishment, a death | beyond imagination! 2.03. 4
come what can come, | the worst is death: 2.03. 18
dirge, | and tell to memory my death was noble, 2.06. 16
i would not, | should i try death by dozens. 3.02. 25
and die for her, | make death a devil. 3.06.270
any death thou canst invent, duke. 3.06.281
must open | and bleed to death for my sake else. 4.02. 2
a miller's mare, he'll be the death of her. 5.02. 67
is as momentary | as to us death is certain. 5.04. 18
and call your lovers from the stage of death, 5.04.123
and so in spite of death thou dost survive, | in VEN 173
it, | for i have heard it is a life in death, 413
but now i died, and death was lively joy. 498
that the star–gazers, having writ on death, 509
that if i love thee, i thy death should fear. 660
i prophesy thy death, my living sorrow, | if 671
swear nature's death for framing thee so fair. 744
and sighing it again, exclaims on death. 930
divorce of love" — thus chides she death — 932
adonis lives, and death is not to blame; 992
no," quoth she, "sweet death, i did but jest, 997
thrive, | with death she humbly doth insinuate; 1012
to wail his death who lives and must not die 1017
sith in his prime death doth my love destroy, 1163
since he himself is reft from her by death. 1174
though death be adjunct, there's no death LUC 133
death be adjunct, there's no death supposed. 133
oft that wealth doth cost | the death of all, 147
showing life's triumph in the map of death, 402
but that life liv'd in death, and death in life. 406
but that life liv'd in death, and death in life. 406

in bloody death and ravishment delighting, | nor 430
wounding itself to death, rise up and fall, 466
her thrall | to living death and pain perpetual; 726
grim cave of death! 769
be guilty of my death, since of my crime. 931
to find some desp'rate instrument of death, 1038
to clear this spot by death, at least, i give 1053
till life to death acquit my forc'd offense. 1071
'tis double death to drown in ken of shore, | he 1114
when life is sham'd and death reproach's debtor. 1155
having two sweet babes, when death takes one, 1161
have heard the cause of my untimely death, 1178
for in my death i murther shameful scorn: 1189
this plot of death when sadly she had laid, 1212
with circumstances strong | of present death, 1263
and shame that might ensue | by that her death, 1264
th' adulterate death of lucrece and her groom. 1645
shows me a bare-bon'd death by time outworn. 1761
shall rotten death make conquest of the stronger 1767
breath, | and live to be revenged on her death. 1778
we will revenge the death of this true wife." 1841
passage find, | that the lover, sick to death, PP 16. 7
death is now the phoenix' nest, | and the PHT 56
then what could death do if thou shouldst depart SON 6.11
nor shall death brag thou wand'rest in his shade 18.11
then look i death my days should expiate. 22. 4
when that churl death my bones with dust shall 32. 2
with two alone | sinks down to death, oppress'd 45. 8
'gainst death and all-oblivious enmity | shall 55. 9
this thought is as a death, which cannot choose 64.13
tir'd with all these, for restful death i cry: 66. 1
in me that you should love | after my death, 72. 3
from hence your memory death cannot take, 81. 3
growth | a vengeful canker eat him up to death. 99.13
my love looks fresh, and death to me subscribes, 107.10
so shalt thou feed on death, that feeds on men, 146.13
and death once dead, there's no more dying then. 146.14
and i desperate now approve | desire is death, 147. 8

DEATH-BED 9 FR 0.0010 REL FR 9 V 0 P
be the stream | and wat'ry death-bed for him. MV 3.02. 47
upon his death-bed he by will bequeath'd | his JN 1.01.109
thy death-bed is no lesser than thy land, R2 2.01. 95
as from my death-bed, thy last living leave. 5.01. 39
wilt thou on thy death-bed play the ruffian, 2H6 5.01.164
now old desire doth in his death-bed lie, | and ROM 2.pr. 1
no, no, he is dead, | go to thy death-bed, | he HAM 4.05.193
take heed of perjury, thou art on thy death-bed. OTH 5.02. 51
lie, | as the death-bed whereon it must expire, SON 73.11

DEATH-BEDS 1 FR 0.0001 REL FR 1 V 0 P
growing, | marigolds on death-beds blowing, TNK 1.01. 11

DEATH-BODING 1 FR 0.0001 REL FR 1 V 0 P
noise but owls' and wolves' death-boding cries; LUC 165

DEATH-COUNTERFEITING
1 FR 0.0001 REL FR 1 V 0 P
till o'er their brows death-counterfeiting sleep MND 3.02.364

DEATH/-DARTING 1 FR 0.0001 REL FR 1 V 0 P
than the death/-darting eye of cockatrice. ROM 3.02. 47

DEATH-DIVINING 1 FR 0.0001 REL FR 1 V 0 P
music can, | be the death-divining swan, | lest PHT 15

DEATHFUL 1 FR 0.0001 REL FR 1 V 0 P
corrosive, | it is applied to a deathful wound. 2H6 3.02.404

DEATH-LIKE 1 FR 0.0001 REL FR 1 V 0 P
for death-like dragons here affright thee hard. PER 1.01. 29

DEATH-MARK'D 1 FR 0.0001 REL FR 1 V 0 P
the fearful passage of their death-mark'd love, ROM pr 9

DEATH-PRACTIC'D 1 FR 0.0001 REL FR 1 V 0 P
strike the sight | of the death-practic'd duke. LR 4.06.277

DEATH'S 35 FR 0.0039 REL FR 32 V 3 P
merely, thou art death's fool, | for him thou MM 3.01. 11
o, death's a great disguiser, and you may add to 4.02.174 P
a death's face in a ring. LLL 5.02.612 P
not helping, death's my fee, | but, if i help, AWW 2.01.189
my death's sad tale may yet undeaf his ear. R2 2.01. 16
have felt the worst of death's destroying wound, 3.02.139
thy own hand yields thy death's instrument, | go 5.05.106
of death or death's hand for this one half year. 1H4 4.01.136
and death's dishonorable victory | we with our 1H6 1.01. 20
my death's revenge, thy youth, and england's 4.06. 39
where death's approach is seen so terrible! 2H6 3.03. 6
a deadly groan, like life and death's departing. 3H6 2.06. 43
that now are dimm'd with death's black veil, 5.02. 16
his sword, death's stamp, | where it did mark, COR 2.02.107
ah sir, ah sir, death's the end of all! ROM 3.03. 92
life, living, all is death's. 4.05. 40
and death's pale flag is not advanced there. 5.03. 96
is no hour so fit | as caesar's death's hour, JC 3.01.154
shake off this downy sleep, death's counterfeit, MAC 2.03. 76
that death's unnatural that kills for loving. OTH 5.02. 42
if they suffer our departure, death's the word. ANT 1.02.135 P
his death's upon him, but not dead. 4.15. 7
slumber, | not as death's dart being laugh'd at; CYM 4.02.211
thee to desist | for going on death's net, whom PER 1.01. 40
to themselves | been death's most horrid agents, TNK 1.01.144
out together where death's self was lodg'd; 1.03. 40
and death's the market-place, where each one 1.05. 16
but now i liv'd, and life was death's annoy, VEN 497
and not death's ebon dart to strike him dead. 948
and death's dim look in life's mortality. LUC 403
kill'd too soon by death's sharp sting! PP 10. 4
to be death's conquest and make worms thine heir
SON 6.14
day | and barren rage of death's eternal cold? 13.12
precious friends hid in death's dateless night, 30. 6
death's second self, that seals up all in rest. 73. 8

DEATHS' 1 FR 0.0001 REL FR 1 V 0 P
like /two children in their deaths' sad story. R3 4.03. 8

DEATHS 23 FR 0.0026 REL FR 21 V 2 P
i suffer'd the pangs of three several deaths: WIV 3.05.108 P
yet in this life | lie hid moe thousand deaths; MM 3.01. 40
to do you rest, a thousand deaths would die. TN 5.01.133
all deaths are too few, the sharpest too easy. WT 4.04.780 P
threatens them | with divers deaths in death. 5.01.202
men | i will unfold some causes of your deaths: R2 3.01. 7
even with the bloody payment of your deaths. 1H4 1.03.186
and i will die a hundred thousand deaths | ere 3.02.158
enemies, | whose deaths are yet unreveng'd. 5.03. 43
they in seeking that | shall find their deaths. 2H6 2.02. 76
devise strange deaths for small offenses done? 3.01. 59
you, | or let a /rebel lead you to your deaths? 4.08. 13
is not the causer of the timeless deaths | of R3 1.02.117
to both their deaths shalt thou be accessary. 1.02.191
within thine eyes sate twenty thousand deaths, COR 3.03. 70
you do but plot your deaths | by this device. TIT 2.01. 78
a thousand deaths | would i propose to achieve 2.01. 79
cowards die many times before their deaths, JC 2.02. 32
of deaths put on by cunning and /forc'd cause, HAM 5.02.383
the manner of their deaths? ANT 5.02.337
till our deaths it cannot, | and after death our TNK 2.02.115
of their sweet deaths are sweetest odors made: SON 54.12
as testy sick men, when their deaths be near, 140. 7

DEATH'S-BED 1 FR 0.0001 REL FR 0 V 1 P
is her grandsire upon his death's-bed (got WIV 1.01. 52 P

DEATH'S-HEAD 3 FR 0.0003 REL FR 0 V 3 P
be married to a death's-head with a bone in his MV 1.02. 51 P
a man doth of a death's-head or a memento mori.
1H4 3.03. 30 P
do not speak like a death's-head, do not bid me 2H4 2.04.234 P

DEATHSMAN 3 FR 0.0003 REL FR 3 V 0 P
and i should rob the deathsman of his fee, 2H6 3.02.217
i am only sorry | he had no other deathsman. LR 4.06.258
as sland'rous deathsman to so base a slave? LUC 1001

DEATHSMEN 1 FR 0.0001 REL FR 1 V 0 P
youth to have him so cut off | as, deathsmen, 3H6 5.05. 67

DEATH-TOKENS 1 FR 0.0001 REL FR 1 V 0 P
is so plaguy proud that the death-tokens of it TRO 2.03.177

DEATH-WORTHY 1 FR 0.0001 REL FR 1 V 0 P
guilt would seem death-worthy in thy brother. LUC 635

DEBARR'D 1 FR 0.0001 REL FR 1 V 0 P
plight | that am debarr'd the benefit of rest? SON 28. 2

DEBASE 3 FR 0.0003 REL FR 3 V 0 P
we do debase ourselves, cousin, do we not, | to R2 3.03.127
you debase your princely knee | to make the base 3.03.190
thus we debase | the nature of our seats and COR 3.01.135

DEBATE 17 FR 0.0019 REL FR 16 V 1 P
i will debate this matter at more leisure, | and ERR 4.01.100
from tawny spain, lost in the world's debate. LLL 1.01.173
same progeny of evils comes | from our debate, MND 2.01.116
and sickness | debate it at their leisure. AWW 1.02. 75
end | to this debate that bleedeth at our doors, 2H4 4.04. 2
hear him debate of commonwealth affairs, | you H5 1.01. 41
i and my bosom must debate a while, | and then i 4.01. 31
and we'll debate | by what safe means the crown 3H6 4.07. 51
of every realm, that did debate this business, H8 2.04. 52
will not debate the question of this straw. HAM 4.04. 26
state | stands on me to defend, not to debate. LR 5.01. 69
when we debate | our trivial difference loud, we ANT 2.02. 20
she is not worth our debate. CYM 1.04.160 P
and in his inward mind he doth debate | what LUC 185
debate where leisure serves with dull debaters; 1019
it seem'd they would debate with angry swords. 1421
for thee, against myself i'll vow debate, | for SON 89.13

DEBATED 4 FR 0.0004 REL FR 4 V 0 P
her | upon the error that you heard debated. ADO 5.04. 3
suits | have been consider'd and debated on. 1H6 5.01. 35
parle, | these quarrels must be quietly debated. TIT 5.03. 20
"i have debated, even in my soul, | what wrong, LUC 498

DEBATEMENT 2 FR 0.0002 REL FR 2 V 0 P
and, after much debatement, | my sisterly MM 5.01. 99
without debatement further, more or less, | he HAM 5.02. 45

DEBATERS 1 FR 0.0001 REL FR 1 V 0 P
debate where leisure serves with dull debaters; LUC 1019

DEBATETH 1 FR 0.0001 REL FR 1 V 0 P
where wasteful time debateth with decay | to SON 15.11

DEBATING 6 FR 0.0006 REL FR 6 V 0 P
in debating which was best, we shall part with ERR 3.01. 67
i am debating of my present store, | and, by the MV 1.03. 53
debating to and fro | how france and frenchmen 2H6 1.01. 91
what talk you of debating? 3H6 4.07. 53
who had been hither sent on the debating | /a H8 2.04.174
"then childish fear, avaunt, debating, die! LUC 274

DEBAUCH'D *(see debosh'd)*

DEBILE 2 FR 0.0002 REL FR 1 V 1 P
and debile minister, great power, great AWW 2.03. 34 P
nose that bled, or foil'd some debile wretch — COR 1.09. 48

DEBILITY 1 FR 0.0001 REL FR 1 V 0 P
woo | the means of weakness and debility; AYL 2.03. 51

DEBITOR 2 FR 0.0002 REL FR 1 V 1 P
belee'd and calm'd | by debitor and creditor — OTH 1.01. 31
you have no true debitor and creditor but it; CYM 5.04.168 P

DEBONAIR 1 FR 0.0001 REL FR 1 V 0 P
courtiers as free, as debonair, unarm'd, | as TRO 1.03.235

DEBORAH 1 FR 0.0001 REL FR 1 V 0 P
and fightest with the sword of deborah. 1H6 1.02.105

DEBOSH'D 4 FR 0.0004 REL FR 3 V 1 P
why, thou debosh'd fish thou, was there ever man
TMP 3.02. 26 P
mere word's a slave | debosh'd on every tomb, on AWW 2.03.138
all the spots a' th' world tax'd and debosh'd, 5.03.206
men so disorder'd, so debosh'd and bold, | that LR 1.04.242

D,E,B,T 1 FR 0.0001 REL FR 0 V 1 P
when he should pronounce "debt" — d,e,b,t, not LLL 5.01. 21 P

DEBT *(also det)*

DEBT 48 FR 0.0054 REL FR 41 V 7 P
for debt, pompey? MM 3.02. 64 P
and the prisoner the very debt of your calling. 3.02.250 P
/that he, unknown to me, should be in debt. ERR 4.02. 48
as if time were in debt! 4.02. 57
if /'a be in debt and theft, and a sergeant in 4.02. 61
go, | the debt he owes will be requir'd of me. 4.04.118
and, knowing how the debt grows, i will pay it. 4.04.121
when he should pronounce "debt" — d,e,b,t, not LLL 5.01. 21 P
and consciences that will not die in debt | pay 5.02.333
for debt that bankrout /sleep doth sorrow owe; MND 3.02. 85
gold | to pay the petty debt twenty times over. MV 3.02.307
pray god bassanio come | to see me pay his debt, 3.03. 36
and he repents not that he pays your debt; 4.01.279
too little payment for so great a debt. SHR 5.02.154
to pay this debt of love but to a brother, | how TN 1.01. 33
we should, for perpetuity, | go hence in debt. WT 1.02. 6
for that my sovereign liege was in my debt, R2 1.01.129
i throw off | and pay the debt i never promised, 1H4 1.02.209
night | to answer all the debt he owes to you 1.03.185
the king will always think him in our debt, 1.03.286
and, being no more in debt to years than thou, 3.02.103
pay her the debt you owe her, and unpay the 2H4 2.01.118 P
but light payment, to dance out of your debt. ep 20 P
with dull unwillingness to repay a debt, | which R3 2.02. 92
for it requires the royal debt it lent you. 2.02. 95
i am in your debt for your last exercise; 3.02.110
edward for edward pays a dying debt. 4.04. 21
what nearer debt in all humanity | than wife is TRO 2.02.175
i'll pay that doctrine, or else die in debt. ROM 1.01.238
my life is my foe's debt. 1.05.118
ay, my good lord, five talents is his debt, TIM 1.01. 95
i'll pay the debt and free him. 1.01.103
his state | that what he speaks is all in debt: 1.02.198
encount'red | with clamorous demands of debt, 2.02. 37
his own time | and be in debt to none — yet 3.05. 77
in like manner was i in debt to my importunate 3.06. 13 P
ambition's debt is paid. JC 3.01. 83
your son, my lord, has paid a soldier's debt. MAC 5.09. 5
to pay ourselves what to ourselves is debt. HAM 3.02.193
no squire in debt, nor no poor knight; LR 3.02. 88
his steel was in debt, it went o' th' backside CYM 1.02. 12 P
protract with admiration what | is now due debt. 4.02.233
cousin, | is but a debt to honor, and my duty. TNK 3.06. 19
one sweet kiss shall pay this comptless debt. VEN 84
say for non-payment that the debt should double, 521
let, | till every minute pays the hour his debt. LUC 329
the petty streams that pay a daily debt | to 649
did exceed | the barren tender of a poet's debt; SON 83. 4

DEBTED 1 FR 0.0001 REL FR 1 V 0 P
more | than i stand debted to this gentleman. ERR 4.01. 31

DEBTOR 12 FR 0.0013 REL FR 10 V 2 P
there's my purse, i am yet thy debtor. WIV 2.02.132 P
let me not die your debtor, | my red dominical, LLL 5.02. 43
and thankfully rest debtor for the first. MV 1.01.152
than to die well, and not my master's debtor. AYL 2.03. 76
i am your debtor, claim it when 'tis due. TRO 4.05. 51
dolabella, | i shall remain your debtor. ANT 5.02.205
when i have been debtor to you for courtesies, CYM 1.04. 36 P
they failing, | i must die much your debtor. 2.04. 8
or a debtor that not dares | to stride a limit. 3.03. 34
till then, rest your debtor. PER 2.01.143
when life is sham'd and death reproach's debtor. LUC 1155
use, | and sue a friend came debtor for my sake, SON 134.11

DEBTORS 3 FR 0.0003 REL FR 2 V 1 P
and (as most debtors do) promise you infinitely; 2H4 ep 15 P
men, | who of their broken debtors take a third, CYM 5.04. 19
lending him wit that to bad debtors lends: LUC 964

DEBTS 17 FR 0.0019 REL FR 12 V 5 P
he that dies pays all debts. TMP 3.02.131 P
is to come fairly off from the great debts MV 1.01.128
how to get clear of all the debts i owe. 1.01.134
live, all debts are clear'd between you and i, 3.02.318 P
having come to padua | to gather in some debts, SHR 4.04. 25
poor behind them, some upon the debts they owe,
H5 4.01.140 P
our debts, our careful wives, | our children, 4.01.231
words pay no debts, give her deeds; TRO 3.02. 55 P
and the detention of long since due debts, TIM 2.02. 38
of your estate | and your great flow of debts. 2.02.142
having lacks a half | to pay your present debts. 2.02.145
then they could smile, and fawn upon his debts, 3.04. 51
methinks he should the sooner pay his debts, 3.04. 75
these debts may well be call'd desperate ones, 3.04.101 P
swallow 'em, | debts wither 'em to nothing; 4.03.531
paid | more pious debts to heaven than in all CYM 3.03. 72
gets | all praises, which are paid as debts, PER 4.ch. 34

DEBUTY *(also deputy)*

DEBUTY 1 FR 0.0001 REL FR 0 V 1 P
i was before master tisick, the debuty, t' other 2H4 2.04. 85 P

DECAY 31 FR 0.0035 REL FR 30 V 1 P
this is enough to be the decay of lust and WIV 5.05.144 P
but whilst this muddy vesture of decay | doth MV 5.01. 64
wrath, | and sullen presage of your own decay. JN 1.01. 28
beast, | the imminent decay of wrested pomp. 4.03.154
cry woe, destruction, ruin, and decay: R2 3.02.102
o'er | to stormy passion, must perforce decay. 2H4 1.01.165
fly | towards fronting peril and oppos'd decay! 4.04. 66
for, good king henry, thy decay i fear. 2H6 3.01.194
till then fair hope must hinder live's decay; 3H6 4.04. 16
soul, | death, desolation, ruin, and decay. R3 4.04.409
coin words till their decay against those COR 3.01. 78
full of decay and failing? TIM 4.03.460
when love begins to sicken and decay | it useth JC 4.02. 20
that, from your first of difference and decay, LR 5.03.289
what comfort to this great decay may come 5.03.298
and every day that comes comes to decay | a CYM 1.05. 56
plighted with | a love that grows as you decay. TNK 5.03.111
to kill thine honor with thy live's decay; LUC 516
my brow, | the story of sweet chastity's decay, 808
to feed oblivion with decay of things, | to blot 947
his leaves will wither and his sap decay; 1168
care, | to descant on the doubts of my decay. PP 14. 4
without this, folly, age, and cold decay. SON 11. 6
who lets so fair a house fall to decay, | which 13. 9
where wasteful time debateth with decay | to 15.11
and fortify yourself in your decay | with means 16. 3
and in mine own love's strength seem to decay, 23. 7
of state, | or state itself confounded to decay, 64.10
but let your love even with my life decay; 71.12
my love was my decay. 80.14
if any, be a satire to decay, | and make time's 100.11

DECAY'D 6 FR 0.0006 REL FR 3 V 3 P
that takes pity on decay'd men and gives them ERR 4.03. 26 P
for he looks like a poor, decay'd, ingenious, AWW 5.02. 23 P
his thread of life had not so soon decay'd. 1H6 1.01. 34
of such a decay'd dotant as you seem to be? COR 5.02. 44 P
and, if possess'd, as soon decay'd and done, LUC 23
but now my gracious numbers are decay'd, | and SON 79. 3

DECAYED 1 FR 0.0001 REL FR 1 V 0 P
my decayed fair | a sunny look of his would soon ERR 2.01. 98

DECAYER 1 FR 0.0001 REL FR 0 V 1 P
your water is a sore decayer of your whoreson HAM 5.01.172 P

DECAYING 1 FR 0.0001 REL FR 1 V 0 P
kind keepers of my weak decaying age, | let 1H6 2.05. 1

DECAYS 7 FR 0.0008 REL FR 6 V 1 P
infirmity, that decays the wise, doth ever make TN 1.05. 76 P
that doth renew swifter than blood decays! TRO 3.02.163
to their throne, decays | the thing we sue for. ANT 2.01. 4
did begin | as if you met decays of many kinds. TNK 1.02. 29
i pity | decays where e'er i find them, but such 1.02. 32
for there it revels, and when that decays, | the LUC 713

nor gates of steel so strong, but time decays? SON 65. 8
DECEAS'D 10 FR 0.0011 REL FR 9 V 1 P
death | of learning, late deceas'd in beggary." MND 5.01. 53
such branches of learning, is indeed deceas'd, MV 2.02. 64 P
antonio, my father, is deceas'd, | and i have SHR 1.02. 54
with them a bastard of the king's deceas'd, JN 2.01. 65
he tells us arthur is deceas'd to–night. 4.02. 85
figuring the natures /of the times deceas'd, 2H4 3.01. 81
the noble duke of bedford late deceas'd, | but 1H6 3.02.132
my hope is gone, now suffolk is deceas'd. 2H6 4.04. 56
she's dead, deceas'd, she's dead, alack the day! ROM 4.05. 23
gentleman, our theme, deceas'd | as he was born. CYM 1.01. 39
DECEASE *(also decesse)*
DECEASE 6 FR 0.0006 REL FR 6 V 0 P
to pine, | was cursed instrument of his decease. 1H6 2.05. 58
and his advantage following your decease, | that 2H6 3.01. 25
enjoy the kingdom after my decease. 3H6 1.01.175
die, | but as the riper should by time decease, SON 1. 3
were | /yourself again after yourself's decease, 13. 7
like widowed wombs after their lords' decease: 97. 8
DECEASED 4 FR 0.0004 REL FR 4 V 0 P
not her, | and he knew my deceased father well. SHR 1.02.102
behalf | of thy deceased brother geffrey's son, JN 1.01. 8
these poor rude lines of thy deceased lover, SON 32. 4
and hang more praise upon deceased i | than 72. 7
DECEIT 22 FR 0.0024 REL FR 21 V 1 P
and this deceit loses the name of craft, | of WIV 5.05.226
of the benefit defends the deceit from reproof. MM 3.01.258 P
of your title to him | doth flourish the deceit. 4.01. 74
the folded meaning of your words' deceit. ERR 3.02. 36
that time and place with this deceit so lawful AWW 3.07. 38
yet, to avoid deceit, i mean to learn; JN 1.01.215
since i must lose the use of all deceit? 5.04. 27
as fitting best to quittance their deceit 1H6 2.01. 14
a man | unsounded yet and full of deep deceit. 2H6 3.01. 57
who cannot steal a shape that means deceit? 3.01. 79
for that is good deceit | which mates him first 3.01.264
which mates him first that first intends deceit. 3.01.265
love, | but from deceit bred by necessity; 3H6 3.03. 68
what clarence but a quicksand of deceit? 5.04. 26
that deceit should steal such gentle shape, R3 2.02. 27
yet from my dugs he drew not this deceit. 2.02. 30
hath not yet div'd into the world's deceit; 3.01. 8
if that be call'd deceit, i will be honest, TIT 3.01.188
o that deceit should dwell | in such a gorgeous ROM 3.02. 84
who makes the fairest show means most deceit. PER 1.04. 75
thou look'st not like deceit, do not deceive me. LUC 585
painter labor'd with his skill | to hide deceit, 1507
DECEITFUL 8 FR 0.0009 REL FR 7 V 1 P
all these are servants to deceitful men. TGV 2.07. 72
with the deceiving father of a deceitful son. SHR 4.04. 83 P
is this thy cunning, thou deceitful dame? 1H6 2.01. 50
breast from harboring foul deceitful thoughts. 2H6 4.07.103
deceitful warwick, it was thy device | by this 3H6 3.03.141
and like deceitful jades | sink in the trial. JC 4.02. 26
luxurious, avaricious, false, deceitful, MAC 4.03. 58
conceit deceitful, so compact, so kind, | that LUC 1423
DECEITS 3 FR 0.0003 REL FR 1 V 2 P
that the tongues of men are full of deceits? H5 5.02.118 P
dat de tongeus of de mans is be full of deceits: 5.02.120 P
saw how deceits were gilded in his smiling, LC 172
DECEIVABLE 2 FR 0.0002 REL FR 2 V 0 P
there's something in't | that is deceivable. TN 4.03. 21
thy knee, | whose duty is deceivable and false. R2 2.03. 84
DECEIV'D 52 FR 0.0058 REL FR 33 V 19 P
that hast deceiv'd so many with thy vows? TGV 4.02. 98
i shall be glad if he have deceiv'd me. WIV 3.01. 13 P
boys of art, i have deceiv'd you both; 3.01.107 P
o, how have you deceiv'd me! 3.03.128 P
that my husband is deceiv'd, or sir john. 3.03.179 P
o, how much is the good duke deceiv'd in angelo! MM 3.01.192 P
o, sir, you are deceiv'd. 3.02.123 P
thou art deceiv'd in me, friar. 3.02.168 P
i have deceiv'd even your very eyes. ADO 5.01.232 P
and ursula | are much deceiv'd, for they did 5.04. 79
loves | woo contrary, deceiv'd by these removes. LLL 5.02.135
play the knave and get thee, i am much deceiv'd. MV 2.03. 12 P
the world is still deceiv'd with ornament. 3.02. 74
the voice, | or i am much deceiv'd, of portia. 5.01.111
fare you well! pray heaven i be deceiv'd in you! AYL 1.02.197 P
you are deceiv'd, sir, we kept time, we lost not 5.03. 37 P
and watch withal, for, but i be deceiv'd, | our SHR 3.01. 62
your worship is deceiv'd, the gown is made 4.03.115
do you think i am so far deceiv'd in him? AWW 3.06. 6 P
module, h'as deceiv'd me like a double–meaning 4.03. 99 P
y' are deceiv'd, my lord, this is monsieur 4.03.140 P
to–morrow, or i am deceiv'd by him that in such 4.05. 82 P
you are deceiv'd, my lord, she never saw it. 5.03. 92
nor are you therein, by my life, deceiv'd, | you TN 5.01.262
there have been | (or i am much deceiv'd) WT 1.02.191
but we have been | deceiv'd in thy integrity, 1.02.240
integrity, deceiv'd | in that which seems so. 1.02.240
you have deceiv'd our trust, | and made us doff 1H4 5.01. 11
by god, thou hast deceiv'd me, lancaster, | i 5.04. 17
you are deceiv'd, my substance is not here; 1H6 2.03. 51
you are deceiv'd, my child is none of his, | it 5.04. 72
thou art deceiv'd. 3H6 1.01.155
our trusty friend, unless i be deceiv'd. 4.07. 41
but he's deceiv'd, we are in readiness. 5.04. 64
you are deceiv'd, your brother gloucester hates R3 1.04.232
coat guarded with yellow, | will be deceiv'd. H8 pr 17
devil's illusions | the monk might be deceiv'd, 1.02.179
no, you are deceiv'd; COR 5.02. 47 P
you are deceiv'd, for what i mean to do | see TIT 5.02. 13
fie, publius, fie, thou art too much deceiv'd. 5.02.155
o, thou art deceiv'd; ROM 2.04. 98 P
tush, thou art deceiv'd. 5.01. 29
cassius, | be not deceiv'd. JC 1.02. 37
you shall confess that you are both deceiv'd. 2.01.105
my uncle–father and aunt–mother are deceiv'd. HAM 2.02.376 P
i was the more deceiv'd. 3.01.119 P
y' are much deceiv'd. LR 4.06. 9
she has deceiv'd her father, and may thee. OTH 1.03.293
i am sorry that i am deceiv'd in him. 4.01.282
you, but | i do not greatly care to be deceiv'd, ANT 5.02. 14
so poor birds, deceiv'd with painted grapes, VEN 601
hath motion, and mine eye may be deceiv'd; SON 104.12
DECEIVE 29 FR 0.0032 REL FR 23 V 6 P
'twere a substance, you would sure deceive it, TGV 4.02.126
behavior, | which, if my augury deceive me not, 4.04. 68
by gar, he deceive me too. WIV 3.01.123 P
which means she to deceive, father or mother? 4.06. 46
as, nimble jugglers that deceive the eye, ERR 1.02. 98
i see two husbands, or mine eyes deceive me. 5.01.332
by the dark night, which did deceive them, but ADO 3.03.157 P
eyes, | deceive me not now, navarre is infected. LLL 2.01.230
are hated most of those they did deceive, | so MND 2.02.140
packing, with a witness, to deceive us all! SHR 5.01.118 P
the king's disease — my project may deceive me, AWW 1.01.228
which, though i will not practice to deceive, JN 1.01.214
what in the world should make me now deceive, 5.04. 26
french enough to deceive de most sage demoiselle H5 5.02.219 P
nestor, | deceive more slily than ulysses could, 3H6 3.02.189
smile in men's faces, smooth, deceive, and cog, R3 1.03. 48
come, you deceive yourself, | 'tis he that sends 1.04.242
with best advantage will deceive the time, | and 5.03. 92
thou dost thyself and all our troy deceive. TRO 5.03. 90
i'll deceive them both; TIT 3.01.186
and never whilst i live deceive men so; 3.01.189
but i'll deceive you in another sort, | and that 3.01.190
no more that thane of cawdor shall deceive | our MAC 1.02. 63
be despis'd than to deceive so good a commander OTH 2.03.277 P
she did deceive her father, marrying you, | and 3.03.206
and the fellow dares not deceive me. CYM 4.01. 25 P
thou look'st not like deceit, do not deceive me. LUC 585
thou of thyself thy sweet self dost deceive, SON 4.10
which time and thoughts so sweetly dost deceive, 39.12
DECEIVED 7 FR 0.0008 REL FR 7 V 0 P
and the prince and claudio | have been deceived. ADO 5.04. 76
i am much deceived but i remember the style. LLL 4.01. 96
you are deceived, 'tis not so. 5.02.541
and, but i be deceived, | signior baptista may SHR 4.04. 2
come, you are deceived, i think of no such thing TRO 4.02. 39
you are deceived, for, as i am a soldier, | i TNK 3.06. 48
like a deceived husband, so love's face | may SON 93. 2
DECEIVER 1 FR 0.0001 REL FR 1 V 0 P
and pardon'd the deceiver, dwell | in this bare TMP ep 7
DECEIVERS 1 FR 0.0001 REL FR 1 V 0 P
ladies, sigh no more, | men were deceivers ever, ADO 2.03. 63
DECEIVES 3 FR 0.0003 REL FR 3 V 0 P
but trusts a knave | that mightily deceives you. TIM 5.01. 94
o, she deceives me | past thought! OTH 1.01.165
in either's aptness, as it best deceives, | to LC 306
DECEIVEST 1 FR 0.0001 REL FR 1 V 0 P
if thou this self deceivest | by willful taste SON 40. 7
DECEIVETH 1 FR 0.0001 REL FR 0 V 1 P
man should be lewdly given, he deceiveth me; 1H4 2.04.427 P
DECEIVING 8 FR 0.0009 REL FR 4 V 4 P
of his frailty) many deceiving promises of life, MM 3.02.246 P
curs'd be thy stones for thus deceiving me! MND 5.01.181
"deceiving me" is thisby's cue. 5.01.184 P
talking with the deceiving father of a deceitful SHR 4.04. 83 P
deceiving, hers; CYM 2.05. 23
part burns, and the deceiving part freezes: TNK 4.03. 44 P
"lest the deceiving harmony should run | into VEN 781
and most deceiving when it seems most just; 1156
DECEMBER 6 FR 0.0006 REL FR 4 V 2 P
as the first of may doth the last of december. ADO 1.01.192 P
are april when they woo, december when they wed; AYL 4.01.147 P
"o' the twelf day of december" — TN 2.03. 84
he makes a july's day short as december, | and WT 1.02.169
or wallow naked in december snow | by thinking R2 1.03.298
hear | the rain and wind beat dark december, how CYM 3.03. 37
DECEMBER'S 1 FR 0.0001 REL FR 1 V 0 P
what old december's bareness every where! SON 97. 4
DECENT 1 FR 0.0001 REL FR 1 V 0 P
of the soul, | for honesty and decent carriage, H8 4.02.145
DECENTLY 1 FR 0.0001 REL FR 1 V 0 P
lovers, | cast yourselves in a body decently, TNK 3.05. 20
/DECEPTIOUS 1 FR 0.0001 REL FR 1 V 0 P
as if those organs /had /deceptious functions, TRO 5.02.123
DECERNS 1 FR 0.0001 REL FR 0 V 1 P
confidence with you that decerns you nearly. ADO 3.05. 3 P
DECESSE *(also decease)*
DECESSE 1 FR 0.0001 REL FR 1 V 0 P
i rail'd on thee, fearing my love's decesse. VEN 1002
D'ECHAPPER 1 FR 0.0001 REL FR 0 V 1 P
est–il impossible d'echapper la force de ton H5 4.04. 16 P
DECIDE *(also 'cide)*
DECIDE 2 FR 0.0002 REL FR 2 V 0 P
call the swords | which must decide it. 2H4 4.01.180
betwixt ourselves let us decide it then. 1H6 4.01.119
DECIDER 2 FR 0.0002 REL FR 2 V 0 P
virtuous, | the true decider of all injuries, TNK 3.06.153
thou grand decider | of dusty and old titles, 5.01. 63
DECIDES 1 FR 0.0001 REL FR 1 V 0 P
decides | that which long process could not LLL 5.02.742
DECIMATION 1 FR 0.0001 REL FR 1 V 0 P
by decimation, and a tithed death, | if thy TIM 5.04. 31
DECIPHER 1 FR 0.0001 REL FR 0 V 1 P
the white will decipher her well enough. WIV 5.02. 9 P
DECIPHER'D 2 FR 0.0002 REL FR 2 V 0 P
i fear we should have seen decipher'd there 1H6 4.01.184
that you are both decipher'd, that's the news, TIT 4.02. 8
DECIPHERS 1 FR 0.0001 REL FR 1 V 0 P
who deciphers them? ERR 5.01.335
DECISION 4 FR 0.0004 REL FR 4 V 0 P
whose great decision hath much blood let forth AWW 3.01. 3
than adders to the voice | of any true decision. TRO 2.02.173
that will with due decision make us know | what MAC 5.04. 17
see a wren hawk at a fly | than this decision. TNK 5.03. 3
DECIUS' 1 FR 0.0001 REL FR 0 V 1 P
some to decius' house, and some to casca's; JC 3.03. 37 P
DECIUS 8 FR 0.0009 REL FR 7 V 1 P
is decius brutus and trebonius there? JC 1.03.148
this, decius brutus. 2.01. 95
decius, well urg'd. 2.01.155
here's decius brutus, he shall tell them so. 2.02. 57
tell them so, decius. 2.02. 64
decius, go tell them caesar will not come. 2.02. 68
decius brutus loves thee not; 2.03. 4 P
now, decius brutus, yours; 3.01.187
DECK 17 FR 0.0019 REL FR 16 V 1 P
now in the waist, the deck, in every cabin, | i TMP 1.02.197
which, when he has a house, he'll deck withal. 3.02. 97
i'll be sure to keep him above deck. WIV 2.01. 91 P
to deck his fortune with his virtuous deeds. SHR 1.01. 16
to deck thy body with his ruffling treasure. 4.03. 60
to deck our soldiers for these irish wars. R2 1.04. 62
'tis your thoughts that now must deck our kings, H5 pr 28
lady's lap, | and deck my body in gay ornaments, 3H6 3.02.149
the king was slily finger'd from the deck! 5.01. 44
go thou to juliet, help to deck up her. ROM 4.02. 41
and we, poor mates, stand on the dying deck, TIM 4.02. 20
he did keep | the deck, with glove or hat or CYM 1.03. 11
ship, upon whose deck | the seas–toss'd pericles PER 3.ch. 59
endur'd a sea | that almost burst the deck. 4.01. 56
from the deck | you may discern the place. 5.01.114
and deck the temples of those gods that hate us; TNK 2.02. 23
the orator, to deck his oratory, | will couple LUC 815
DECK'D 8 FR 0.0009 REL FR 8 V 0 P
when i have deck'd the sea with drops full salt, TMP 1.02.155
o, if in black my lady's brows be deck'd, | it LLL 4.03.254
garnish'd and deck'd in modest complement, | not H5 2.02.134
deck'd with /five flower–de–luces on each side, 1H6 1.02. 99
not deck'd with diamonds and indian stones, 3H6 3.01. 63
deck'd in thy rights as thou art stall'd in mine R3 1.03.205
if you do find them deck'd with ceremonies. JC 1.01. 65
i thought thy bride–bed to have deck'd, sweet HAM 5.01.245
DECKING 2 FR 0.0002 REL FR 2 V 0 P
decking with liquid pearl the bladed grass | (a MND 1.01.211
/wear) i followed | for my most serious decking. TNK 1.03. 74
DECKS 2 FR 0.0002 REL FR 2 V 0 P
sweet ornament that decks a thing divine — | ah TGV 2.01. 4
and decks with praises collatine's high name, LUC 108
DECLARE 7 FR 0.0008 REL FR 7 V 0 P
that thou declare | what incidency thou dost WT 1.02.402
which i could with a ready guess declare, H5 1.01. 96
and now declare, sweet stem from york's great 1H6 2.05. 41
alliance sake, declare the cause | my father, 2.05. 53
highness | that it shall please you to declare, H8 2.04.146
be't so, declare thine office. ANT 3.12. 10
read, and declare the meaning. CYM 5.05.434
DECLARES 1 FR 0.0001 REL FR 1 V 0 P
my scutcheon plain declares that i am alisander" LLL 5.02.564
DECLENSION 2 FR 0.0002 REL FR 2 V 0 P
degree | to base declension and loath'd bigamy. R3 3.07.189
thence to /a lightness, and, by this declension, HAM 2.02.149
DECLENSIONS 1 FR 0.0001 REL FR 0 V 1 P
now, william, some declensions of your pronouns. WIV 4.01. 74 P
DECLIN'D 9 FR 0.0010 REL FR 6 V 3 P
borrow'd of the pronoun, and be thus declin'd, WIV 4.01. 41 P
he straight declin'd, droop'd, took it deeply, WT 2.03. 14
she had one eye declin'd for the loss of her 5.02. 74 P
what the declin'd is | he shall as soon read in TRO 3.03. 76
sons at perfect age and fathers declin'd, the LR 1.02. 73 P
or for i am declin'd | into the vale of years OTH 3.03.265
her head's declin'd, and death will seize her, ANT 3.11. 47
and answer me declin'd, sword against sword, 3.13. 27
with head declin'd, and voice damm'd up with woe LUC 1661
DECLINE 9 FR 0.0010 REL FR 8 V 1 P
far more, far more, to you do i decline. ERR 3.02. 44
decline all this, and see what now thou art: R3 4.04. 97
thy spirit wonder | a great man should decline? H8 3.02.375
i'll decline the whole question: TRO 2.03. 52 P
air, | not letting it decline on the declined, 4.05.189
laws, | decline to your confounding contraries; TIM 4.01. 20
we, at the height, are ready to decline. JC 4.03.217
and to decline | upon a wretch whose natural HAM 1.05. 50
decline your head: LR 4.02. 22
DECLINED 1 FR 0.0001 REL FR 1 V 0 P
air, | not letting it decline on the declined, TRO 4.05.189
DECLINES 3 FR 0.0003 REL FR 3 V 0 P
like to rise, | who thrives, and who declines; COR 1.01.193
being advanc'd, declines, and then men die. 2.01.161
and every fair from fair sometime declines, | by SON 18. 7
DECLINING 6 FR 0.0006 REL FR 5 V 1 P
declining their rich aspect to the hot breath of ERR 3.02.135 P
and with declining head into his bosom, | bid SHR in.1. 119
moe | of noble blood in this declining land. R2 2.01.240
down, | not one accompanying his declining foot. TIM 1.01. 88
which was declining on the milky head | of HAM 2.02.478
have shown to thee such a declining day, | or ANT 5.01. 38
DECOCT 1 FR 0.0001 REL FR 1 V 0 P
decoct their cold blood to such valiant heat? H5 3.05. 20
DECORUM 3 FR 0.0003 REL FR 2 V 1 P
the nurse, and quite athwart | goes all decorum. MM 1.03. 31
dear isis, keep decorum, and fortune him ANT 1.02. 74 P
must tell him | that majesty, to keep decorum, 5.02. 17
DECREAS'D 1 FR 0.0001 REL FR 1 V 0 P
which i have bettered rather than decreas'd. SHR 2.01.118
DECREASE 3 FR 0.0003 REL FR 2 V 1 P
yet heaven may decrease it upon better WIV 1.01.247 P
and tyrants' /fears | decrease not, but grow PER 1.02. 85
vaunt in their youthful sap, at height decrease, SON 15. 7
DECREASING 1 FR 0.0001 REL FR 0 V 1 P
a white beard, a decreasing leg, an increasing 2H4 1.02.181 P
DECREE 12 FR 0.0013 REL FR 11 V 1 P
we must of force dispense with this decree, LLL 1.01.147
young blood doth not obey an old decree. 4.03.213
but a hot temper leaps o'er a cold decree — MV 1.02. 19 P
in venice | can alter a decree established. 4.01.219
while we return these dukes what we decree. R2 1.03.122
what yesternight our council did decree | in 1H4 1.01. 32
intent | to dash our late decree in parliament 3H6 2.01.118
have you delivered to her our decree? ROM 3.05.138
and turn preordinance and first decree | into JC 3.01. 38
thy brother by decree is banished; 3.01. 44
"poor hand, why quiver'st thou at this decree? LUC 1030
but heaven in thy creation did decree | that in SON 93. 9
DECREED 9 FR 0.0010 REL FR 8 V 1 P
and us, | it hath in solemn synods been decreed, ERR 1.01. 13
therefore i have decreed not to sing in my cage. ADO 1.03. 34 P
what is decreed must be; TN 1.05.311
eye, | it is decreed hector the great must die. TRO 5.07. 8
therefore it is decreed | he dies to–night. COR 3.01.287
same pit | where we decreed to bury bassianus. TIT 2.03.274
go get thee to thy love as was decreed, | ascend ROM 3.03.146

which read and not expounded, 'tis decreed, | as PER 1.01. 57
in framing an artist, art hath thus decreed, 2.03. 15
/DECREES 1 FR 0.0001 REL FR 1 V 0 P
/my /acts, /decrees, /and /statutes /i /deny; R2 4.01.213
DECREES 11 FR 0.0012 REL FR 10 V 1 P
so our decrees, | dead to infliction, to MM 1.03. 27
and to the strictest decrees i'll write my name. LLL 1.01.117
there is no force in the decrees of venice. MV 4.01.102
or as the destinies decrees. AYL 1.02.105 P
and on our quick'st decrees | th' inaudible and AWW 5.03. 40
some certain edicts and some strait decrees 1H4 4.03. 79
pluck down my officers, break my decrees, | for 2H4 4.05.117
to have a son set your decrees at nought? 5.02. 85
as with a man busied about decrees: COR 1.06. 34
the door | that so my sad decrees may fly away, TIT 5.02. 11
in 'twixt vows, and change decrees of kings, SON 115. 6
DECREPIT 4 FR 0.0004 REL FR 4 V 0 P
surrender up of aquitaine | to her decrepit, LLL 1.01.138
decrepit miser! 1H6 5.04. 7
teaching decrepit age to tread the measures; VEN 1148
as a decrepit father takes delight | to see his SON 37. 1
DECRETAS 1 FR 0.0001 REL FR 1 V 0 P
i am call'd decretas; ANT 5.01. 5
DEDICATE 8 FR 0.0009 REL FR 7 V 1 P
from fasting maids whose minds are dedicate | to MM 2.02.154
nor doth he dedicate one jot of color | unto the H5 4.pr. 37
h§ that is truly dedicate to war | hath no 2H6 5.02. 37
uncle, what folly i commit, i dedicate to you. TRO 3.02.102 P
to the air | or dedicate his beauty to the /sun. ROM 1.01.153
many | as will to greatness dedicate themselves, MAC 4.03. 75
i dedicate myself to your sweet pleasure, | more CYM 1.06.136
to the face of peril | myself i'll dedicate. 5.01. 29
DEDICATED 3 FR 0.0003 REL FR 3 V 0 P
all dedicated | to closeness and the bettering TMP 1.02. 89
his poor self, | a dedicated beggar to the air, TIM 4.02. 13
o'erlook | the dedicated words which writers use SON 82. 3
DEDICATES 2 FR 0.0002 REL FR 1 V 1 P
man is a fool when he dedicates his behaviors to ADO 2.03. 9 P
this night he dedicates | to fair content and H8 1.04. 2
DEDICATION 3 FR 0.0003 REL FR 3 V 0 P
retention or restraint, | all his in dedication. TN 5.01. 82
promising | than a wild dedication of yourselves WT 4.04.566
some work, some dedication | to the great lord. TIM 1.01. 19
/DEED 2 FR 0.0002 REL FR 2 V 0 P
/a /deed /of /death /done /on /the /innocent TIT 3.02. 56
/for /thou /hast /done /a /charitable /deed. 3.02. 70
DEED 163 FR 0.0184 REL FR 152 V 11 P
for which foul deed | the pow'rs, delaying (not TMP 3.03. 72
pay thy graces | home both in word and deed. 5.01. 71
th' edict infringe | had answer'd for his deed. MM 2.02. 93
life, | nature dispenses with the deed so far, 3.01.134
this deed unshapes me quite, makes me unpregnant 4.04. 20
had you a special warrant for the deed? 5.01.459
one that will do the deed | though argus were LLL 3.01.198
wands, | and, in the doing of the deed of kind, MV 1.03. 85
clerk, draw a deed of gift. 4.01.394
send the deed after me, | and i will sign it. 4.01.396
inquire the jew's house out, give him this deed, 4.02. 1
this deed will be well welcome to lorenzo. 4.02. 4
so shines a good deed in a naughty world. 5.01. 91
from the rich jew, a special deed of gift, 5.01.292
shouldst have better pleas'd me with this deed AYL 1.02.227
is it honest in deed and word? 3.03. 18 P
as lively painted as the deed was done. SHR in.2. 56
as high as word, my deed shall match thy deed. AWW 2.01.210
as high as word, my deed shall match thy deed. 2.01.210
the place is dignified by th' doer's deed. 2.03.126
think he will make no deed at all of this that 3.06. 94 P
it speed, | is wicked meaning in a lawful deed, 3.07. 45
'twere as good a deed as to drink when a man's TN 2.03.126 P
yet, good deed, leontes, | i love thee not a jar WT 1.02. 42
one good deed dying tongueless | slaughters a 1.02. 92
my last good deed was to entreat his stay; 1.02. 97
to do this deed, | promotion follows. 1.02.356
all other circumstances | made up to th' deed), 2.01.179
in more than this deed does require! 2.03.190
that's a good deed. 3.03.133 P
i hope your warrant will bear out the deed. JN 4.01. 6
i am best pleas'd to be from such a deed. 4.01. 85
this is the man should do the bloody deed; 4.02. 69
quoted, and sign'd to do a deed of shame, | this 4.02.222
consequently thy rude hand to act | the deed, 4.02.241
the earth had not a hole to hide this deed. 4.03. 36
of mercy, if thou didst this deed of death, 4.03.118
should show so heinous, black, obscene a deed! R2 4.01.131
o would the deed were good! 5.05.114
says that this deed is chronicled in hell. 5.05.116
wrought | a deed of slander with thy fatal hand 5.06. 35
from your own mouth, my lord, did i this deed. 5.06. 37
'twere not as good deed as drink to break the 1H4 2.01. 29 P
'twere not as good a deed as drink to turn true 2.02. 22 P
up with this retinue, doth any deed of courage; 2H4 4.03.112 P
if the deed were ill, | be you contented, 5.02. 83
my tongue, | seeing the deed is meritorious, 2H6 3.01.270
say you consent, and censure well the deed, 3.01.275
here is my hand, the deed is worthy doing. 3.01.278
i will reward you for this venturous deed. 3.02. 9
sword, i will hallow thee for this thy deed, 4.10. 67
by any solemn vow | to do a murd'rous deed, to 5.01.185
york, | and die in bands for this unmanly deed! 3H6 1.01.186
tears, | and say, "alas, it was a piteous deed!" 1.04.163
but ere sunset i'll make thee curse the deed. 2.02.116
blame, | if this foul deed were by to equal it. 5.05. 55
too | thou mayst be damned for that wicked deed! R3 1.02.103
and god, not we, hath plagu'd thy bloody deed. 1.03.180
o, 'twas the foulest deed to slay that babe, 1.03.182
the deed you undertake is damnable. 1.04.192
for whose sake did i that ill deed? 1.04.211
if god will be avenged for the deed, | o, know 1.04.215
on | to do this deed will hate you for the deed. 1.04.255
on | to do this deed will hate you for the deed. 1.04.255
a bloody deed, and desperately dispatch'd! 1.04.271
if they have done this deed, my noble lord — 3.04. 73
the most arch deed of piteous massacre | that 4.03. 2
when didst thou sleep when such a deed was done? 4.04. 24
and be a happy mother by the deed. 4.04.427
if it be known to him | that i gainsay my deed, H8 2.04. 96
and 'tis a kind of good deed to say well, | and 3.02.153
and with his deed did crown | his word upon you. 3.02.155
and yet no day without a deed to crown it. 5.04. 58
rate, | and do a deed that never fortune did, TRO 2.02. 90
and whatever praises itself but in the deed, 2.03.156 P
but in the deed, devours the deed in the praise. 2.03.157 P
without any further deed to have them at all COR 2.02. 27 P
you have done a brave deed. 4.02. 38
thou hast done a deed whereat valor will weep. 5.06.132
confederates in the deed | that hath dishonored TIT 1.01.344
o, say thou for her, who hath done this deed? 3.01. 87
no, no, they would not do so foul a deed; 3.01.118
reveal the damn'd contriver of this deed. 4.01. 36
what roman lord it was durst do the deed; 4.01. 62
performers of this heinous, bloody deed? 4.01. 80
o lord, sir, 'tis a deed of policy. 4.02.148
this was but a deed of charity | to that which 5.01. 89
what, was she ravish'd? tell who did the deed. 5.03. 53
die, frantic wretch, for this accursed deed! 5.03. 64
there's meed for meed, death for a deadly deed! 5.03. 66
if one good deed in all my life i did, | i do 5.03.189
seal'd, | shall be the label to another deed, ROM 4.01. 57
that's a deed thou't die for. TIM 1.01.193 P
striving to make an ugly deed look fair. 3.05. 25
people | the deed of saying is quite out of use. 5.01. 26
do so, and let no man abide this deed, | but we JC 3.01. 94
so pity pity — | hath done this deed on caesar. 3.01.172
that this foul deed shall smell above the earth 3.01.274
they that have done this deed are honorable. 3.02.212
mistrust of my success hath done this deed. 5.03. 65
mistrust of good success hath done this deed. 5.03. 66
slaying is the word, | it is a deed in fashion. 5.05. 5
shall i do such a deed? 5.05. 8
and his subject, | strong both against the deed; MAC 1.07. 14
air, | shall blow the horrid deed in every eye, 1.07. 24
th' attempt, and not the deed, | confounds us. 2.02. 10
i have done the deed. 2.02. 14
a little water clears us of this deed; 2.02. 64
to know my deed, 'twere best not know myself. 2.02. 70
unnatural, | even like the deed that's done. 2.04. 11
is't known who did this more than bloody deed? 2.04. 22
which puts upon them | suspicion of the deed. 2.04. 27
there shall be done | a deed of dreadful note. 3.02. 44
dearest chuck, | till thou applaud the deed. 3.02. 46
we are yet but young in deed. 3.04.143
a deed without a name. 4.01. 49
never is o'ertook | unless the deed go with it. 4.01.146
this deed i'll do before this purpose cool. 4.01.154
act and place | may give his saying deed, which HAM 1.03. 27
it | than is my deed to my most painted word. 3.01. 52
o, what a rash and bloody deed is this! 3.04. 27
a bloody deed! 3.04. 28
o, such a deed | as from the body of contraction 3.04. 45
o heavy deed! 4.01. 12
alas, how shall this bloody deed be answer'd? 4.01. 16
hence, and this vile deed | we must with all our 4.01. 30
hamlet, this deed, for thine especial safety — 4.03. 40
whose wicked deed thy most ingenious sense 5.01.248
heart | i find she names my very deed of love; LR 1.01. 71
either in discourse of thought or actual deed, OTH 4.02.153
wouldst thou do such a deed for all the world? 4.03. 64
wouldst thou do such a deed for all the world? 4.03. 68
i have no great devotion to the deed, | and yet 5.01. 8
o, who hath done this deed? 5.02.123
this deed of thine is no more worthy heaven 5.02.160
thou hast done a deed — | i care not for thy 5.02.164
not in deed, madam, for i can do nothing | but ANT 1.05. 15
good enobarbus, 'tis a worthy deed, | and shall 2.02. 1
than by our deed | acquire too high a fame when 3.01. 14
cleopatra, i approve | your wisdom in the deed. 5.02.150
what poor an instrument | may do a noble deed! 5.02.237
shall, by the power we hold, be our good deed, CYM 3.01. 57
envy much | thou hast robb'd me of this deed. 4.02.159
this is pisanio's deed, and cloten. 4.02.329
that will prove aweful both in deed and word. PER 2.ch. 4
a deed might gain her love or your displeasure. 2.05. 54
my commission | is not to reason of the deed, 4.01. 83
spacious world, | i'd give it to undo the deed. 4.03. 6
when fame | had spread his cursed deed, the 5.03. 96
this good deed | shall raze you out o' th' book TNK 1.01. 32
our life, this daring deed | of fate in wedlock. 1.01.164
and do the deed with a bent brow. 3.01.101
in a deed so virtuous | the powers of all women 3.06.193
let fair humanity abhor the deed | that spots LUC 195
when thou shalt charge me with so black a deed? 226
that what is vile shows like a virtuous deed. 252
i know repentant tears ensue the deed, 502
"this deed will make thee only lov'd for fear, 610
my live's foul deed, my life's fair end shall 1208
whose deed hath made herself herself detest. 1566
and so did kill | the lechers in their deed. 1637
stone–still, astonish'd with this deadly deed, 1730
whether the horse by him became his deed, | or LC 111
DEED–ACHIEVING 1 FR 0.0001 REL FR 1 V 0 P
and | by deed–achieving honor newly nam'd — COR 2.01.173
DEEDLESS 1 FR 0.0001 REL FR 1 V 0 P
speaking /in deeds, and deedless in his tongue, TRO 4.05. 98
DEED'S 1 FR 0.0001 REL FR 0 V 1 P
remember our reward when the deed's done. R3 1.04.123 P
/DEEDS 1 FR 0.0001 REL FR 1 V 0 P
/but /my /deeds /shall /stay /thy /fury /soon. 2H6 4.01.113
DEEDS 125 FR 0.0141 REL FR 109 V 16 P
for truth hath better deeds than words to grace TGV 2.02. 18
when evil deeds have their permissive pass, MM 1.03. 38
duke yet would have dark deeds darkly answer'd, 3.02.177 P
think | a due sincerity governed his deeds, 5.01.446
ill deeds is doubled with an evil word. ERR 3.02. 20
record it with your high and worthy deeds. ADO 5.01.269
teach us all to render | the deeds of mercy. MV 4.01.202
my deeds upon my head! 4.01.206
way to heaven | by doing deeds of hospitality. AYL 2.04. 82
to deck his fortune with his virtuous deeds. SHR 1.01. 16
beloved of me, and that my deeds shall prove. 1.02.176
'tis deeds must win the prize, and he of both 2.01.342
may token to the future our past deeds. AWW 4.02. 63
them ill to friend | till your deeds gain them; 5.03.183
how his piety | does my deeds make the blacker! WT 3.02.172
a lucky day, boy, and we'll do good deeds on't. 3.03.139 P
crowns what you are doing in the present deeds, 4.04.145
it is my father's music | to speak your deeds; 4.04.519
your sharpest deeds of malice on this town. JN 2.01.380
how oft the sight of means to do ill deeds 4.02.219
of means to do ill deeds | make deeds ill done! 4.02.220
renowned for their deeds as far from home, | for R2 2.01. 53
whose high deeds, | whose hot incursions and 1H4 3.02.107
his glorious deeds for my indignities. 3.02.146
to engross up glorious deeds on my behalf; 3.02.148
to grace this latter age with noble deeds. 5.01. 92
never did such deeds in arms as i have done this 5.03. 45 P
have taught us how to cherish such high deeds 5.05. 30
stopping my greedy ear with their bold deeds, 2H4 1.01. 78
doth his prince's name, | in deeds dishonorable? 4.02. 26
it be book'd with the rest of this day's deeds, 4.03. 47 P
bad words are match'd with as few good deeds; H5 3.02. 39 P
dare not avouch in your deeds any of your words? 5.01. 73 P
his deeds exceed all speech: 1H6 1.01. 15
whose bloody deeds shall make all europe quake. 1.01.156
let no words, but deeds, revenge this treason! 3.02. 49
erects | thy noble deeds as valor's monuments. 3.02.120
rough deeds of rage and stern impatience; 4.07. 8
your deeds of war, and all our counsel die? 2H6 1.01. 97
thy deeds, thy plainness, and thy house–keeping, 1.01.191
cherish duke humphrey's deeds | while they do 1.01.203
made impudent with use of evil deeds, | i would 3H6 1.04.117
as thou hast shown it flinty by thy deeds, | i 2.01.202
i'll leave my son my virtuous deeds behind, 2.02. 49
o that my death would stay these ruthful deeds! 2.05. 95
thee, | for thou art fortunate in all thy deeds. 4.06. 25
this fiend | to stop devoted charitable deeds? R3 1.02. 35
if thou delight to view thy heinous deeds, 1.02. 53
thy deeds inhuman and unnatural | provokes this 1.02. 60
gloucester, we have done deeds of charity, 2.01. 50
to love, | send her a letter of thy noble deeds: 4.04.280
dream on, dream on, of bloody deeds and death; 5.03.171
myself | for hateful deeds committed by myself. 5.03.190
deed to say well, | and yet words are no deeds. H8 3.02.154
a spur to valiant and magnanimous deeds, | whose TRO 2.02.200
and hot thoughts beget hot deeds, and hot deeds 3.01.130 P
thoughts beget hot deeds, and hot deeds is love. 3.01.130 P
love — hot blood, hot thoughts, and hot deeds? 3.01.132 P
words pay no debts, give her deeds; 3.02. 55 P
but she'll bereave you a' th' deeds too, if she 3.02. 56 P
what, are my deeds forgot? 3.03.144
those scraps are good deeds past, which are 3.03.148
whose glorious deeds, but in these fields of 3.03.188
speaking /in deeds, and deedless in his tongue, 4.05. 98
but i'll endeavor deeds to match these words, 4.05.259
do deeds worth praise, and tell you them at 5.03. 93
she feeds, | but edifies another with her deeds. 5.03.112
intend to do, which now we'll show 'em in deeds. COR 1.01. 59 P
thy day's work, | thou't not believe thy deeds: 1.09. 2
in this action outdone his former deeds doubly. 2.01.136 P
the deeds of coriolanus | should not be utter'd 2.02. 82
rewards | his deeds with doing them, and is 2.02.128
if he show us his wounds and tell us his deeds, 2.03. 6 P
if he tell us his noble deeds, we must also tell 2.03. 8 P
that as his worthy deeds did claim no less 2.03.186
let deeds express | what's like to be their 3.01.132
and will with deeds requite thy gentleness; TIT 1.01.237
agree these deeds with that proud brag of thine, 1.01.306
my nephew mutius' deeds do plead for him, | he 1.01.356
that hath express'd himself in all his deeds | a 1.01.422
prince bassianus, leave to plead my deeds, 1.01.424
whose high exploits and honorable deeds 5.01. 11
acts of black night, abominable deeds, 5.01. 64
well, let my deeds be witness of my worth: 5.01.103
art thou not sorry for these heinous deeds? 5.01.123
like damned guilty deeds to sinners' minds: ROM 3.02.111
at first | to set a gloss on faint deeds, hollow TIM 1.02. 16
forgetting thy great deeds when neighbor states, 4.03. 95
and wonder of good deeds evilly bestow'd! 4.03.461
and he looks | quite through the deeds of men. JC 1.02.203
and buy men's voices to commend our deeds. 2.01.146
all pity chok'd with custom of fell deeds; 3.01.269
our deeds are done! 5.03. 64
words to the heat of deeds too cold breath gives MAC 2.01. 61
these deeds must not be thought | after these 2.02. 30
unnatural deeds | do breed unnatural troubles; 5.01. 71
/foul deeds will rise, | though all the earth HAM 1.02.256
and your large speeches may your deeds approve, LR 1.01.184
do deeds to make heaven weep, all earth amaz'd; OTH 3.03.371
burn up modesty, | did i but speak thy deeds. 4.02. 76
hates the slime | that sticks on filthy deeds. 5.02.149
when you shall these unlucky deeds relate, 5.02.341
but i will hope | of better deeds to–morrow. ANT 1.01. 62
they shall assist | the deeds of justest men. 2.01. 2
compel us to lament | our most persisted deeds. 5.01. 30
to do that thing that ends all other deeds, 5.02. 5
such precious deeds in one that promis'd nought CYM 5.05. 9
i would not thy good deeds should from my lips 5.05.288
/to place upon the volume of your deeds, | as in PER 2.03. 3
if she'd do the deeds of darkness, thou wouldst 4.06. 29 P
she shall see deeds of honor in their kind TNK 5.03. 12
thou grant'st no time for charitable deeds: LUC 908
king, | to shame his hope with deeds degenerate; 1003
have a true respect | to talk in deeds, while 1348
help wounds, or grief help grievous deeds? 1822
and they are rich, and ransom all ill deeds. SON 34.14
to see his active child do deeds of youth, | so 37. 2
thee | so far from home into my deeds to pry, 61. 6
and that, in guess, they measure by thy deeds, 69.10
now while the world is bent my deeds to cross, 90. 2
for sweetest things turn sourest by their deeds; 94.13
chide, | the guilty goddess of my harmful deeds, 111. 2
their rank thoughts my deeds must not be shown, 121.12
in nothing art thou black save in thy deeds, 131.13
that in the very refuse of thy deeds | there is 150. 6
/DEEM 1 FR 0.0001 REL FR 1 V 0 P
/may /deem /that /you /are /worthily /depos'd. R2 4.01.227
DEEM 9 FR 0.0010 REL FR 8 V 1 P
as you shall deem yourself lodg'd in my heart, LLL 2.01.173
a senseless help when help past sense we deem. AWW 2.01.124
for bird–bolts that you deem cannon–bullets. TN 1.05. 93 P
see, my lord, | would you not deem it breath'd? WT 5.03. 64

what know i how the world may deem of me, | for 2H6 3.02. 65
sure in that | i deem you an ill husband, and am H8 3.02.142
i true? how now? what wicked deem is this? TRO 4.04. 59
of imogen, that best | could deem his dignity? CYM 5.04. 57
but fairer we it deem | for that sweet odor SON 54. 3
DEEM'D 3 FR 0.0003 REL FR 3 V 0 P
in iron walls they deem'd me not secure; 1H6 1.04. 49
this business, | who deem'd our marriage lawful; H8 2.04. 53
truths translated, and for true things deem'd. SON 96. 8
DEEMED 1 FR 0.0001 REL FR 1 V 0 P
lost, which is so deemed | not by our feeling, SON 121. 3
DEEMS 1 FR 0.0001 REL FR 1 V 0 P
more than speed but dull and slow she deems: LUC 1336
DEEM'ST 1 FR 0.0001 REL FR 1 V 0 P
me thou deem'st at thebes, | and therein TNK 3.01. 26
/DEEP 5 FR 0.0005 REL FR 5 V 0 P
/is /this /golden /crown /like /a /deep /well R2 4.01.184
/leave /these /bitter /deep /laments, | /make TIT 3.02. 46
we'll teach you to drink /deep ere you depart. HAM 1.02.175
/on /itself, | /like /monsters /of /the /deep. LR 4.02. 50
/to /stand /against /the /deep //dread–bolted 4.07. 32
DEEP 161 FR 0.0182 REL FR 149 V 12 P
harbor | is the king's ship, in the deep nook, TMP 1.02.227
it much to tread the ooze | of the salt deep, 1.02.253
i myself could make | a chough of as deep chat. 2.01.266
that deep and dreadful organ–pipe, pronounc'd 3.03. 98
that's on some shallow story of deep love, | how TGV 1.01. 21
that's a deep story of a deeper love, | for he 1.01. 23
sad sighs, deep groans, nor silver–shedding 3.01.232
the anchor is deep. will that humor pass? WIV 1.03. 51 P
/and the bottom were as deep as hell, i should 3.05. 13 P
in deep of night to walk by this herne's oak. 4.04. 40
cast, he would appear | a pond as deep as hell. MM 3.01. 93
and so deep sticks it in my penitent heart 5.01.475
before the always–wind–obeying deep | gave any ERR 1.01. 63
wars, and took | deep scars to save thy life; 5.01.193
for these deep shames and great indignities. 5.01.254
subscribe to your deep oaths, and keep it too. LLL 1.01. 23
that will not be deep search'd with saucy looks; 1.01. 85
through the transparent bosom of the deep, | as 4.03. 30
from lovers' food till morrow deep midnight. MND 1.01.223
and they shall fetch thee jewels from the deep, 3.01.158
being o'er shoes in blood, plunge in the deep, 3.02. 48
i pray thee set a deep glass of rhenish wine on MV 1.02. 96 P
for if the jew do cut but deep enough, | i'll 4.01.280
that fools should be so deep contemplative; AYL 2.07. 31
didst know how many fathom deep i am in love! 4.01.206 P
are out, let him be judge how deep i am in love. 4.01.215 P
a shallow plash to plunge him in the deep, | and SHR 1.01. 23
how deep? AWW 4.01. 57 P
which to reiterate were sin | as deep as that, WT 1.02.284
deep shame had struck me dumb, made me break off JN 4.02.235
thou art more deep damn'd than prince lucifer. 4.03.122
for thou shalt thrust thy hand as deep | into 5.02. 60
deep malice makes too deep incision. R2 1.01.155
deep malice makes too deep incision. 1.01.155
o, god defend my soul from such deep sin! 1.01.187
not so deep a maim | as to be cast forth in the 1.03.156
dying men | enforce attention like deep harmony. 2.01. 6
ours of true zeal and deep integrity; 5.03.108
i'll read you matter deep and dangerous, | as 1H4 1.03.190
moon, | or dive into the bottom of the deep, 1.03.203
they call drinking deep, dyeing scarlet, and 2.04. 15 P
of art, | and hold me pace in deep experiments. 3.01. 48
i can call spirits from the vasty deep. 3.01. 52
it shall not wind with such a deep indent, | to 3.01.103
of him, | to fill the mouth of deep defiance up, 3.02.116
by this hand, to th' infernal deep, with erebus 2H4 2.04.157 P
well, master shallow, deep, master shallow. 3.02.161 P
how deep you were within the books of god? 4.02. 17
and the dungeon your place, a place deep enough; 4.03. 8 P
with such a deep demeanor in great sorrow | that 4.05. 84
i had forestall'd this dear and deep rebuke 4.05.140
this would drink deep. H5 1.01. 20
wounded steeds | fret fetlock deep in gore, and 4.07. 79
the spirit of deep prophecy she hath, 1H6 1.02. 55
spring crestless yeomen from so deep a root? 2.04. 85
com'st thou with deep premeditated lines, | with 3.01. 1
receiv'd deep scars in france and normandy? 2H6 1.01. 87
deep night, dark night, the silent of the night, 1.04. 16
smooth runs the water where the brook is deep, 3.01. 53
a man | unsounded yet and full of deep deceit. 3.01. 57
that is to see how deep my grave is made, | for 3.02.150
my mind was troubled with deep melancholy. 5.01. 34
fair queen, whence springs this deep despair? 3H6 3.03. 12
house | in the deep bosom of the ocean buried. R3 1.01. 4
this deep disgrace in brotherhood | touches me 1.01.111
and, if i fail not in my deep intent, | clarence 1.01.149
fill'd it with cursing cries and deep exclaims. 1.02. 52
and take deep traitors for thy dearest friends! 1.03.223
gems, | that woo'd the slimy bottom of the deep, 1.04. 32
death | to gaze upon these secrets of the deep? 1.04. 35
if my deep pray'rs cannot appease thee, | but 1.04. 69
for this, | for in that sin he is as deep as i. 1.04.214
deep, hollow, treacherous, and full of guile 2.01. 38
and with a virtuous visor hide deep vice! 2.02. 28
this land | would i be guilty of so deep a sin. 3.01. 43
tumble down | into the fatal bowels of the deep. 3.04.101
tut, i can counterfeit the deep tragedian, 3.05. 5
intending deep suspicion, ghastly looks | are at 3.05. 8
in deep designs, in matter of great moment, | no 3.07. 67
but meditating with two deep divines; 3.07. 75
gulf | of dark forgetfulness and deep oblivion. 3.07.129
two deep enemies, | foes to my rest and my sweet 4.02. 72
repays he my deep service | with such contempt? 4.02.119
o no, my reasons are too deep and dead — | too 4.04.362
too deep and dead, poor infants, in their graves 4.04.363
that trick of state | was a deep envious one. H8 2.01. 45
o' my conscience, | i wish him ten fadom deep. 2.01. 51
so deep suspicion, where all faith was meant. 3.01. 53
reply not in how many fadoms deep | they lie TRO 1.01. 50
from his deep chest laughs out a loud applause, 1.03.163
sail swift, though greater hulks draw deep. 2.03.266
would i were as deep under the earth as i am 4.02. 82 P
goddess fortune | fall deep in love with thee, COR 1.05. 21
of thy deep duty more impression show | than 5.03. 51
into the swallowing womb | of this deep pit, TIT 2.03.240
in the dust i write | my heart's deep languor, 3.01. 13
and do not break into these deep extremes. 3.01.215
is not my sorrow deep, having no bottom? 3.01.216
ah, that this sight should make so deep a wound, 3.01.246
loss hath pierc'd him deep and scarr'd his heart 4.04. 31
to clouds more clouds with his deep sighs, | but ROM 1.01.133
but no more deep will i endart mine eye | than 1.03. 98
spanish blades, | of healths five fadom deep; 1.04. 85
is as boundless as the sea, | my love as deep; 2.02.134
no, 'tis not so deep as a well, nor so wide as a 3.01. 96 P
why should you fall into so deep an o? 3.03. 90
one may reach deep enough and yet | find little. TIM 3.04. 15
'tis much deep, and it should seem by th' sum 3.04. 30
the deep of night is crept upon our talk, | and JC 4.03.226
pardon, and set forth | a deep repentance. MAC 1.04. 7
let not light see my black and deep desires; 1.04. 51
against those honors deep and broad wherewith 1.06. 17
against | the deep damnation of his taking–off; 1.07. 20
our fears in banquo | stick deep, and in his 3.01. 49
curses, not loud but deep, mouth–honor, breath, 5.03. 27
the lie i' th' throat | as deep as to the lungs? HAM 2.02.575
o, this is the poison of deep grief, it springs 4.05. 75
serves us well | when our deep plots do pall, 5.02. 9
natures of such deep trust we shall much need; LR 2.01.115
head | looks fearfully in the confined deep. 4.01. 74
pinches black, | and wrinkled deep in time? ANT 1.05. 29
if you but said so, 'twere as deep with me. CYM 2.03. 91
flies, as deep | as these poor pickaxes can dig; 4.02.388
our tongues and sorrows to sound deep our woes PER 1.04. 13
in brass, | having call'd them from the deep! 3.01. 4
if fires be hot, knives sharp, or waters deep, 4.02.146
deep clerks she dumbs, and with her neele 5.ch. 5
and almost breathless swim | in this deep water. TNK pr 25
long, | and with a finger of so deep a cunning, 1.03. 43
and well have hollow'd | to a deep cry of dogs; 2.05. 12
then love's deep groans i never shall regard, VEN 377
the sea hath bounds, but deep desire hath none, 389
ears' deep sweet music, and heart's deep sore 432
sweet music, and heart's deep sore wounding. 432
sad pause and deep regard beseems the sage; LUC 277
so she, deep drenched in a sea of care, | holds 1100
deep woes roll forward like a gentle flood, 1118
tear, | and with deep groans the diapason bear; 1132
some dark deep desert, seated from the way, 1144
(and there she stay'd | till after a deep groan) 1276
and that deep torture may be call'd a hell, 1287
deep sounds make lesser noise than shallow fords 1329
showed deep regard and smiling government. 1400
brought | by deep surmise of others' detriment, 1579
that map which deep impression bears | of hard 1712
that blow did bail it from the deep unrest | of 1725
the deep vexation of his inward soul | hath 1779
by, | wherein deep policy did him disguise, 1815
and that deep vow which brutus made before, | he 1847
spenser to me, whose deep conceit is such | as, PP 8. 7
and i in deep delight am chiefly drown'd | when 8.11
boar, | deep in the thigh, a spectacle of ruth! 9.11
with sighs so deep procures to weep, | in 17.21
and dig deep trenches in thy beauty's field, SON 2. 2
the canker–blooms have full as deep a dye | as 54. 5
whilst he upon your soundless deep doth ride, 80.10
nor praise the deep vermilion in the rose, 98.10
for that deep wound it gives my friend and me! 133. 2
for i have sworn deep oaths of thy deep kindness 152. 9
i have sworn deep oaths of thy deep kindness, 152. 9
all kind of arguments and question deep, | all LC 121
DEEP–BRAIN'D 1 FR 0.0001 REL FR 1 V 0 P
and deep–brain'd sonnets that did amplify | each LC 209
DEEP–DARK 1 FR 0.0001 REL FR 1 V 0 P
fled | into the deep–dark cabins of her head, VEN 1038
DEEP–DIVORCING 1 FR 0.0001 REL FR 1 V 0 P
and break it with a deep–divorcing vow? ERR 2.02.138
//DEEP–DRAWING 1 FR 0.0001 REL FR 1 V 0 P
/and /the //deep–drawing /barks /do /there TRO pr 12
/DEEPER 2 FR 0.0002 REL FR 2 V 0 P
/no /deeper /wrinkles /yet? R2 4.01.277
/of /mine, | /and /made /no /deeper /wounds? 4.01.279
DEEPER 13 FR 0.0014 REL FR 13 V 0 P
i'll seek him deeper than e'er plummet sounded, TMP 3.03.101
and deeper than did ever plummet sound | i'll 5.01. 56
that's a deep story of a deeper love, | for he TGV 1.01. 23
sir, the conceit is deeper than you think for: SHR 4.03.161
and deeper than oblivion we do bury | th' AWW 5.03. 24
between two dogs, which hath the deeper mouth, 1H6 2.04. 12
touches me deeper than you can imagine. R3 1.01.112
but thou art deeper read, and better skill'd; TIT 4.01. 33
this avarice | sticks deeper, grows with more MAC 4.03. 85
or something deeper, | whereof, perchance, these LR 3.01. 28
wanting form, | is press'd with deeper matter. TNK 1.01.109
joy, | which breeds a deeper longing, cure their 1.01.190
o, deeper sin than bottomless conceit | can LUC 701
DEEPEST 6 FR 0.0006 REL FR 6 V 0 P
the private wound is deepest: TGV 5.04. 71
the deepest loathing to the stomach brings, | or MND 2.02.138
and with the deepest malice of the war | destroy COR 4.06. 41
'tis deepest winter in lord timon's purse; TIM 3.04. 14
trifles, to betray 's | in deepest consequence. MAC 1.03.126
of woe might have rememb'red | my deepest sense, SON 120.10
DEEP–FET 1 FR 0.0001 REL FR 1 V 0 P
to see my tears and hear my deep–fet groans. 2H6 2.04. 33
DEEP–GREEN 1 FR 0.0001 REL FR 1 V 0 P
the deep–green em'rald, in whose fresh regard LC 213
/DEEPLY 1 FR 0.0001 REL FR 0 V 1 P
wine lov'd i /deeply, dice dearly; LR 3.04. 91 P
DEEPLY 17 FR 0.0019 REL FR 16 V 1 P
and that most deeply to consider is | the beauty TMP 3.02. 98
and entertain'd 'em deeply in her heart. TGV 5.04.102
sounded, | yet not so deeply as to thee belongs, SHR 2.01.193
or both dissemble deeply their affections; 4.04. 42
now he's deeply in. TN 2.05. 42 P
he straight declin'd, droop'd, took it deeply, WT 2.03. 14
yet not so sound, and half so deeply sweet, | as 2H4 4.05. 26
appears | that i will deeply put the fashion on 5.02. 52
are deeply indebted for this piece of pains. 2H6 1.04. 44
thou art sworn as deeply to effect what we R3 3.01.158
she's with the lion deeply still in league, TIT 4.01. 98
consider it not so deeply. MAC 2.02. 27
'tis deeply sworn. HAM 3.02.225
to know if your affiance | were deeply rooted, CYM 1.06.164
heavens, | how deeply you at once do touch me! 4.03. 4
leaves love upon her back, deeply distress'd. VEN 814
passion on passion deeply is redoubled: 832
DEEP–MOUTH'D 3 FR 0.0003 REL FR 3 V 0 P
and couple clowder with the deep–mouth'd brach. SHR in.1. 18
ear, | and mock the deep–mouth'd thunder; JN 5.02.173
shouts and claps out–voice the deep–mouth'd sea, H5 5.pr. 11
DEEP–REVOLVING 1 FR 0.0001 REL FR 1 V 0 P
the deep–revolving witty buckingham | no more R3 4.02. 42
DEEPS 2 FR 0.0002 REL FR 2 V 0 P
forsake unsounded deeps to dance on sands. TGV 3.02. 80
thunder above, and deeps below, | makes such PER 2.ch. 30
DEEP–SUNKEN 1 FR 0.0001 REL FR 1 V 0 P
to say within thine own deep–sunken eyes | were SON 2. 7
DEEP–SWORN 1 FR 0.0001 REL FR 1 V 0 P
gave the sound of words | was deep–sworn faith, JN 3.01.231
DEEP–VOW 1 FR 0.0001 REL FR 0 V 1 P
we here young dizzy, and young master deep–vow, MM 4.03. 13 P
DEEP–WOUNDED 1 FR 0.0001 REL FR 1 V 0 P
here in these brakes deep–wounded with a boar, PP 9.10
DEER 42 FR 0.0047 REL FR 29 V 13 P
you have beaten my men, kill'd my deer, and WIV 1.01.112 P
sir john? art thou there, my deer? my male deer? 5.05. 16 P
sir john? art thou there, my deer? my male deer? 5.05. 17 P
love again, but i will always count you my deer. 5.05.118 P
night–dogs run, all sorts of deer are chas'd. 5.05.238
but, too unruly deer, he breaks the pale, | and ERR 2.01.100
and who is your deer? LLL 4.01.114
the deer was, as you know, sanguis, in blood, 4.02. 3 P
to insert again my haud credo for a deer. 4.02. 19 P
i said the deer was not a haud credo, 'twas a 4.02. 20 P
an extemporal epitaph on the death of the deer? 4.02. 51 P
/call /i the deer the princess kill'd a pricket. 4.02. 52 P
the king he is hunting the deer: 4.03. 1 P
"poor deer," quoth he, "thou mak'st a testament AYL 2.01. 47
weeping and commenting | upon the sobbing deer. 2.01. 66
the noblest deer hath them as huge as the rascal 3.03. 57 P
which is he that kill'd the deer? 4.02. 1 P
what shall he have that kill'd the deer? 4.02. 10
'tis thought your deer does hold you at a bay. SHR 5.02. 56
jowl horns together like any deer i' th' herd. AWW 1.03. 55 P
to sigh, as 'twere | the mort o' th' deer — o, WT 1.02.118
death hath not strook so fat a deer to–day, 1H4 5.04.107
a little herd of england's timorous deer, 1H6 4.02. 46
if we be english deer, be then in blood, | not 4.02. 48
and they shall find dear deer of us, my friends. 4.02. 54
for i myself must hunt this deer to death. 2H6 5.02. 15
for through this laund anon the deer will come, 3H6 3.01. 2
stand, | culling the principal of all the deer. 3.01. 4
ay, here's a deer whose skin's a keeper's fee: 3.01. 22
stand you thus close to steal the bishop's deer? 4.05. 17
as doth the deer | that hath receiv'd some TIT 3.01. 89
how like a deer, strooken by many princes, JC 3.01.209
were on the quarry of these murther'd deer | to MAC 4.03.206
why, let the strooken deer go weep, | the hart HAM 3.02.271
but mice and rats, and such small deer, | have LR 3.04.138
up | their deer to th' stand o' th' stealer; CYM 2.03. 70
ta'en thy stand, | th' elected deer before thee? 3.04.109
i'll be a park, and thou shalt be my deer: VEN 231
then be my deer, since i am such a park, | no 239
and sometime sorteth with a herd of deer: 689
as the poor frighted deer that stands at gaze, LUC 1149
and stall'd the deer that thou shouldst strike, PP 18. 2
DEER'S 2 FR 0.0002 REL FR 1 V 1 P
alone now seek to spill | the poor deer's blood, LLL 4.01. 35
do well to set the deer's horns upon his head, AYL 4.02. 4 P
DEESSE 1 FR 0.0001 REL FR 0 V 1 P
du monde, mon tres cher et devin deesse? H5 5.02.217 P
DEFAC'D 4 FR 0.0004 REL FR 4 V 0 P
and see the cities and the towns defac'd | by 1H6 3.03. 45
broke be my sword, my arms torn and defac'd, 2H6 4.01. 42
and defac'd | the precious image of our dear R3 2.01.123
/her face defac'd with scars of infamy, | /her 3.07.126
DEFACE 5 FR 0.0005 REL FR 5 V 0 P
pay him six thousand, and deface the bond; MV 3.02.299
and deface | the patterns that by god and by H5 2.04. 60
and not deface your honor with reproach? 1H6 5.05. 29
none fairer, nor none falser to deface her. PP 7. 6
then let not winter's ragged hand deface | in SON 6. 1
DEFACED 2 FR 0.0002 REL FR 2 V 0 P
besides, his soul's fair temple is defaced, | to LUC 719
when i have seen by time's fell hand defaced SON 64. 1
DEFACER 1 FR 0.0001 REL FR 1 V 0 P
blood, | that foul defacer of god's handiwork, R3 4.04. 51
DEFACERS 1 FR 0.0001 REL FR 1 V 0 P
place, | defacers of a public peace than i do. H8 5.02. 76
DEFACING 1 FR 0.0001 REL FR 1 V 0 P
defacing monuments of conquer'd france, 2H6 1.01.102
DEFAM'D 1 FR 0.0001 REL FR 1 V 0 P
heard of, | that england was defam'd by tyranny. 2H6 3.01.123
DEFAME 3 FR 0.0003 REL FR 3 V 0 P
dark harbor for defame! LUC 768
feast–finding minstrels, tuning my defame, 817
thee, | but if i live, thou liv'st in my defame. 1033
DEFAULT 4 FR 0.0004 REL FR 3 V 1 P
pray, | are penitent for your default to–day. ERR 1.02. 52
that i may say in the default, "he is a man i AWW 2.03.229 P
duke of alanson, this was your default, | that, 1H6 2.01. 60
about, | and talbot perisheth by your default. 4.04. 28
DEFEAT 13 FR 0.0014 REL FR 12 V 1 P
her youth, | and made defeat of her virginity — ADO 4.01. 47
my honor's at the stake, which to defeat, | i AWW 2.03.149
making defeat on the full power of france, H5 1.02.107
purpose, and be all well borne | without defeat. 1.02.213
alleged | many sharp reasons to defeat the law. H8 2.01. 14
that your activity may defeat and quell | the TIM 4.03.163
therein, ye gods, you tyrants do defeat; JC 1.03. 92
and most dear life | a damn'd defeat was made. HAM 2.02.571
their defeat | does by their own insinuation 5.02. 58
defeat thy favor with an usurp'd beard. OTH 1.03.340 P
much, | and his unkindness may defeat my life, 4.02.160
by some mortal stroke | she do defeat us; ANT 5.01. 65

mine own true love that doth my rest defeat, SON 61.11
DEFEATED 4 FR 0.0004 REL FR 3 V 1 P
thereby to have defeated you and me: MND 4.01.157
if these men have defeated the law and outrun H5 4.01.166 P
state, | have we, as 'twere with a defeated joy, HAM 1.02. 10
a–doting, | and by addition me of thee defeated, SON 20.11
DEFEATS 1 FR 0.0001 REL FR 1 V 0 P
my stronger guilt defeats my strong intent, HAM 3.03. 40
DEFEAT'ST 1 FR 0.0001 REL FR 1 V 0 P
strik'st not me, 'tis caesar thou defeat'st. ANT 4.14. 68
DEFEATURE 1 FR 0.0001 REL FR 1 V 0 P
and pure perfection with impure defeature, VEN 736
DEFEATURES 2 FR 0.0002 REL FR 2 V 0 P
then is he the ground | of my defeatures. ERR 2.01. 98
have written strange defeatures in my face: 5.01.300
/DEFECT 1 FR 0.0001 REL FR 1 V 0 P
whether /defect of judgment, | to fail in the COR 4.07. 39
DEFECT 13 FR 0.0014 REL FR 11 V 2 P
with so full soul but some defect in her | did TMP 3.01. 44
through, saying thus, or to the same defect: MND 3.01. 39 P
that is the very defect of the matter, sir. MV 2.02.143 P
defect of manners, want of government, | pride, 1H4 3.01.182
our will became the servant to defect, | which MAC 2.01. 18
men, | carrying, i say, the stamp of one defect, HAM 1.04. 31
or rather say, the cause of this defect, | for 2.02.102
panted, | that she did make defect perfection, ANT 2.02.231
for defect of judgment | is oft the cause of CYM 4.02.111
much, torments us with defect | of that we have: LUC 151
groom, god wot, it was defect | of spirit, life, 1345
that thou are blam'd shall not be thy defect, SON 70. 1
when all my best doth worship thy defect, 149.11
DEFECTIVE 5 FR 0.0005 REL FR 4 V 1 P
dream | we, poising us in her defective scale, AWW 2.03.154
defective in their natures, grow to wildness. H5 5.02. 55
rather our state's defective for requital | than COR 2.02. 50
for this effect defective comes by cause: HAM 2.02.103
beauties — all which the moor is defective in. OTH 2.01.230 P
DEFECTS 7 FR 0.0008 REL FR 7 V 0 P
for those defects i have before rehears'd, SHR 1.02.124
of spirit, | so mighty and so many my defects, R3 3.07.160
the faint defects of age | must be the scene of TRO 1.03.172
and our mere defects | prove our commodities. LR 4.01. 20
yourself | by laying defects of judgment to me; ANT 2.02. 55
but having no defects, why dost abhor me? VEN 138
when i shall see thee frown on my defects, SON 49. 2
DEFEND 72 FR 0.0081 REL FR 55 V 17 P
o, defend me! TMP 2.02. 88 P
all your senses to you, defend your reputation, WIV 3.03.119 P
heavens defend me from that welsh fairy, lest he 5.05. 81 P
for god defend the lute should be like the case! ADO 2.01. 94 P
o, god defend me, how am i beset! 4.01. 77
for god defend but god should go before such 4.02. 19 P
in my correction, and god defend the right! LLL 1.01.214 P
god defend me from these two! MV 1.02. 52 P
pray god defend me! TN 3.04.302 P
town, | drew to defend him when he was beset; 5.01. 85
for thine own gain shouldst defend mine honor? JN 1.01.242
but yet i dare defend | my innocent life against 4.03. 88
mean time, let this defend my loyalty: R2 1.01. 67
traitor, | which in myself i boldly will defend, 1.01.145
o, god defend my soul from such deep sin! 1.01.187
oath, | as so defend thee heaven and thy valor! 1.03. 15
(which god defend a knight should violate!) 1.03. 18
both to defend my loyalty and truth | to god, my 1.03. 19
me — | and as i truly fight, defend me heaven! 1.03. 25
speak like a true knight, so defend thee heaven! 1.03. 34
me — | and as i truly fight, defend me heaven! 1.03. 41
receive thy lance, and god defend the right! 1.03.101
both to defend himself and to approve | henry of 1.03.112
whom both my oath | and duty bids defend; 2.02.113
and god defend but still i should stand so, | so 1H4 4.03. 38
i will assay thee, and defend thyself. 5.04. 34
but lay down our proportions to defend | against H5 1.02.137
shall be a wall sufficient to defend | our 1.02.141
cannot defend our own doors from the dog, | let 1.02.218
here let them end it, and god defend the right! 2H6 2.03. 55
honor from the tower to defend the city from the 4.05. 5 P
and with their helps only defend ourselves: 3H6 4.01. 45
tent | but to defend his person from night–foes? 4.03. 22
for edward will defend the town and thee, | and 4.07. 38
him, from the which no warrant can defend me. R3 1.04.112 P
whom thou wast sworn to cherish and defend. 1.04.208
look back, defend thee, here are enemies! 3.05. 19
god and our /innocence defend and guard us! 3.05. 20
marry, god defend his grace should say us nay! 3.07. 81
which god defend that i should wring from him! 3.07.173
sleeping and waking, o, defend me still! 5.03.117
upon my back, to defend my belly, upon my wit, TRO 1.02.260 P
upon my wit, to defend my wiles, upon my secrecy 1.02.261 P
upon my secrecy, to defend mine honesty, my mask 1.02.261 P
honesty, my mask, to defend my beauty, and you, 1.02.262 P
defend my beauty, and you, to defend all these; 1.02.263 P
and you as well to keep her, that defend her, 4.01. 59
five tribunes to defend their vulgar wisdoms, COR 1.01.215
or defend yourself | by calmness or by absence. 3.02. 94
defend the justice of my cause with arms; TIT 1.01. 2
what shall defend the interim? TIM 2.02.149
the mighty gods defend thee! JC 2.03. 8 P
the gods defend him from so great a shame! 5.04. 23
angels and ministers of grace defend us! HAM 1.04. 39
why then the polack never will defend it. 4.04. 23
o, yet defend me, friends, i am but hurt. 5.02.324
draw, seem to defend yourself; LR 2.01. 30
defend you | from seasons such as these? 3.04. 31
with thine and all that offer to defend him, 3.06. 94
for my state | stands on me to defend, not to 5.01. 69
the gods defend her! bear him hence awhile. 5.03.257
and heaven defend your good souls, that you OTH 1.03.266
and to defend ourselves it be a sin | when 2.03.203
the souls of all my tribe defend | from jealousy 3.03.175
isis else defend! ANT 3.03. 43
fence the roots they grow by and defend them — PER 1.02. 31
may defend thee." 2.01.129
the gods defend me! 4.02. 89
if it please the gods to defend you by men, then 4.02. 90 P
fair fall the wit that can so well defend her! VEN 472
since thou couldst not defend thy loyal dame, LUC 1034
suppose thou dost defend me | from what is past: 1684

DEFENDANT 4 FR 0.0004 REL FR 4 V 0 P
against the very life | of the defendant; MV 4.01.361
with men of courage and with means defendant; H5 2.04. 8
and ready are the appellant and defendant, | the 2H6 2.03. 49
eyes), | but the defendant doth that plea deny, SON 46. 7
DEFENDED 5 FR 0.0005 REL FR 5 V 0 P
if you had pleas'd to have defended it | with MV 5.01.204
she hath herself not only well defended | but H5 1.02.159
you have defended me from imminent death. 2H6 5.03. 19
or sword to draw, | when helen is defended; TRO 2.02.158
which of your hands hath not defended rome, TIT 3.01.167
DEFENDER 2 FR 0.0002 REL FR 1 V 1 P
push'd out your gates the very defender of them, COR 5.02. 40 P
thou great defender of this capitol, | stand TIT 1.01. 77
DEFENDERS 1 FR 0.0001 REL FR 1 V 0 P
have the power still | to banish your defenders, COR 3.03.128
DEFENDING 2 FR 0.0002 REL FR 2 V 0 P
off, | and swear i lost the ring defending it. MV 5.01.178
arm, | to prove him, in defending of myself, | a R2 1.03. 23
DEFENDS 3 FR 0.0003 REL FR 2 V 1 P
of the benefit defends the deceit from reproof. MM 3.01.257 P
th' advised head defends itself at home; H5 1.02.179
i know what thorns the growing rose defends, | i LUC 492
DEFENSE 42 FR 0.0047 REL FR 35 V 7 P
muster your wits, stand in your own defense, LLL 5.02. 85
and by how much defense is better than no skill, AYL 3.03. 62 P
though valiant in the defense, yet is weak. AWW 1.01.116 P
him and keeps her guard | in honestest defense. 3.05. 74
that defense thou hast, betake thee to't. TN 3.04.220 P
which was so strongly urg'd past my defense. JN 1.01.258
by so much | we must awake endeavor for defense, 2.01. 81
nor tempt the danger of my true defense, | lest 4.03. 84
be said, | they saw we had a purpose of defense. 5.01. 76
where honorable rescue and defense | cries out 5.02. 18
he sees | ourselves well sinewed to our defense. 5.07. 88
to god, the widow's champion and defense. R2 1.02. 43
i, | make fearful musters and prepar'd defense, 2H4 in 12
that england, being empty of defense, | hath H5 1.02.153
in cases of defense 'tis best to weigh | the 2.04. 43
so the proportions of defense are fill'd; 2.04. 45
or, guilty in defense, be thus destroy'd? 3.03. 43
and in defense of my lord's worthiness, | i 1H6 4.01. 99
wisdom, and defense | to give the enemy way, and 2H6 5.02. 75
lord clifford vows to fight in thy defense. 3H6 1.01.160
their own lives in their young's defense? 2.02. 32
and hearten those that fight in your defense. 2.02. 79
if not, the city being but of small defense, 5.01. 64
alas, i am not coop'd here for defense! 5.01.109
of troyan blood | spent more in her defense. TRO 2.02.198
for the defense of a town, our general is COR 4.05.170 P
and defense | that rome can make against them. 4.06.127
and thou dismemb'red with thine own defense. ROM 3.03.134
but in defense, by mercy, 'tis most just. TIM 3.05. 55
safety were remotion and thy defense absence. 4.03.342 P
are full of rest, defense, and nimbleness. JC 4.03.202
thy praises in his kingdom's great defense, MAC 1.03. 99
then, alas, | do i put up that womanly defense, 4.02. 78
report | for art and exercise in your defense, HAM 4.07. 97
unless she drown'd herself in her own defense? 5.01. 7 P
he is bold in his defense." LR 5.03.114 P
heavens | give him defense against the elements, OTH 2.01. 45
soft, soft, we'll no defense, | obedient as the CYM 3.04. 79
as, passing all conceit, needs no defense. PP 8. 8
nothing 'gainst time's scythe can make defense SON 12.13
halt, | against thy reasons making no defense. 89. 4
is more than my o'erpress'd defense can bide? 139. 8
DEFENSES 4 FR 0.0004 REL FR 3 V 1 P
and a thousand other her defenses, which now are WIV 2.02.250 P
us concerns | to answer royally in our defenses. H5 2.04. 3
but that defenses, musters, preparations, 2.04. 18
go, put on thy defenses. ANT 4.04. 10
/DEFENSIBLE 1 FR 0.0001 REL FR 1 V 0 P
/of /hotspur's /name | /did /seem /defensible: 2H4 2.03. 38
DEFENSIBLE 1 FR 0.0001 REL FR 1 V 0 P
us and ours, | for we no longer are defensible. H5 3.03. 50
DEFENSIVE 2 FR 0.0002 REL FR 2 V 0 P
of a wall, | or as /a moat defensive to a house, R2 2.01. 48
tut, holy joan was his defensive guard. 1H6 2.01. 49
DEFER 2 FR 0.0002 REL FR 1 V 1 P
defer no time, delays have dangerous ends, 1H6 3.02. 33
defer the spoil of the city until night; 2H6 4.07.133 P
DEFERR'D 1 FR 0.0001 REL FR 1 V 0 P
my god, | deferr'd the visitation of my friends. R3 3.07.107
DEFIANCE 13 FR 0.0014 REL FR 12 V 1 P
take my defiance! MM 3.01.142
then take my king's defiance from my mouth, JN 1.01. 21
and send | defiance to the traitor, and so die? R2 3.03.130
of him, | to fill the mouth of deep defiance up, 1H4 3.02.116
thrown | a brave defiance in king henry's teeth, 5.02. 42
even to the eyes of richard | gave him defiance. 2H4 3.01. 65
scorn and defiance, slight regard, contempt, H5 2.04.117
let him greet england with our sharp defiance. 3.05. 37
to this add defiance; 3.06.134 P
arm'd, as black defiance | as heart can think or TRO 4.01. 13
which, as he breath'd defiance to my ears, | he ROM 1.01.110
defiance, traitors, hurl we in your teeth. JC 5.01. 64
appalls) hath sent | deadly defiance to him, and TNK 1.02. 91
DEFICIENT 2 FR 0.0002 REL FR 2 V 0 P
and the deficient sight | topple down headlong. LR 4.06. 23
so prepost'rously to err | (being not deficient, OTH 1.03. 63
DEFIED 4 FR 0.0004 REL FR 1 V 3 P
but as she spit in his face, so she defied him. MM 2.01. 84 P
that lik'd me, and breaths that i defied not; AYL ep 20 P
to th' broom–staff to me, i defied 'em still, H8 5.03. 55 P
thus defied, | i thank thee for myself. CYM 3.01. 67
DEFIER 2 FR 0.0002 REL FR 2 V 0 P
of state came in the instant | with the defier. TNK 1.02.107
to those that boast and have not, a defier; 5.01.120
DEFIES 1 FR 0.0001 REL FR 1 V 0 P
why, she defies me, | like turk to christian. AYL 4.03. 32
DEFIL'D 9 FR 0.0010 REL FR 8 V 1 P
i think they that touch pitch will be defil'd. ADO 3.03. 57 P
one hero died defil'd, but i do live, | and 5.04. 63
he is defil'd | that draws a sword on thee. MND 3.02.410
he knows himself my bed he hath defil'd, | and AWW 5.03.300
hath held his current and defil'd himself! R2 5.03. 63

ay, defil'd land, my lord. TIM 1.02.225
as houses are defil'd for want of use, | they PER 1.04. 37
her twinkling handmaids too (by him defil'd) LUC 787
honesty, but yet defil'd | with inward vice: 1545
/DEFILE 2 FR 0.0002 REL FR 2 V 0 P
hand | /defile the locks of your shrill–shriking H5 3.03. 35
/opinion, /whose /wrong /thoughts /defile /thee, LR 3.06.112
DEFILE 4 FR 0.0004 REL FR 2 V 2 P
his gold will hold, | and his soft couch defile. WIV 1.03. 99
in a pitch — pitch that defiles — defile! LLL 4.03. 3 P
(as ancient writers do report) doth defile, so 1H4 2.04.413 P
with such | as, like to pitch, defile nobility, 2H6 2.01.192
DEFILED 1 FR 0.0001 REL FR 1 V 0 P
me good | is to let forth my foul defiled blood. LUC 1029
DEFILER 1 FR 0.0001 REL FR 1 V 0 P
thou bright defiler | of hymen's purest bed! TIM 4.03.382
DEFILES 2 FR 0.0002 REL FR 1 V 1 P
i am toiling in a pitch — pitch that defiles — LLL 4.03. 3 P
the cozen'd thoughts | defiles the pitchy night; AWW 4.04. 24
DEFILING 2 FR 0.0002 REL FR 2 V 0 P
flesh | by the defiling of her parent's bed; PER 1.01.131
knew vows were ever brokers to defiling, LC 173
DEFINE 5 FR 0.0005 REL FR 3 V 2 P
define, define, well–educated infant. LLL 1.02. 94 P
define, define, well–educated infant. 1.02. 94 P
gentle all | behold, as may unworthiness define, H5 4.pr. 46
mad call i it, for, to define true madness, HAM 2.02. 93
and for myself mine own worth do define, | as i SON 62. 7
DEFINEMENT 1 FR 0.0001 REL FR 0 V 1 P
sir, his definement suffers no perdition in you, HAM 5.02.112 P
DEFINITE 1 FR 0.0001 REL FR 1 V 0 P
this case of favor would | be wisely definite; CYM 1.06. 43
DEFINITIVE 1 FR 0.0001 REL FR 1 V 0 P
never crave him, we are definitive. MM 5.01.427
DEFINITIVELY 1 FR 0.0001 REL FR 1 V 0 P
the last — | definitively thus i answer you: R3 3.07.153
DEFLOWERED 1 FR 0.0001 REL FR 1 V 0 P
lies, | flower as she was, deflowered by him. ROM 4.05. 37
DEFLOW'R 2 FR 0.0002 REL FR 2 V 0 P
and let my spleenful sons this trull deflow'r. TIT 2.03.191
quoth he, "i must deflow'r: LUC 348
DEFLOW'R'D 2 FR 0.0002 REL FR 2 V 0 P
since lion vild hath here deflow'r'd my dear; MND 5.01.292
she was enforc'd, stain'd, and deflow'r'd? TIT 5.03. 38
DEFLOW'RED 2 FR 0.0002 REL FR 2 V 0 P
a deflow'red maid! MM 4.04. 21
but sure some tereus hath deflow'red thee, | and TIT 2.04. 26
DEFORM 1 FR 0.0001 REL FR 1 V 0 P
soul–killing witches that deform the body, ERR 1.02.100
DEFORM'D 4 FR 0.0004 REL FR 2 V 2 P
you never saw her since she was deform'd. TGV 2.01. 63 P
how long hath she been deform'd? 2.01. 64 P
none can be call'd deform'd but the unkind. TN 3.04.368
deform'd, unfinish'd, sent before my time | into R3 1.01. 20
DEFORMED 11 FR 0.0012 REL FR 5 V 6 P
he is deformed, crooked, old, and sere, ERR 4.02. 19
and careful hours with time's deformed hand 5.01.299
thou not what a deformed thief this fashion is? ADO 3.03.124 P
i know that deformed; 3.03.125 P
i say, what a deformed thief this fashion is, 3.03.130 P
and one deformed is one of them; 3.03.169 P
you'll be made bring deformed forth, i warrant 3.03.172 P
also, the watch heard them talk of one deformed. 5.01.308 P
monster ignorance, how deformed dost thou look! LLL 4.02. 23
hath much deformed us, fashioning our humors 5.02.757
hope, | to wit, an indigested and deformed lump, 3H6 5.06. 51
DEFORMED'ST 1 FR 0.0001 REL FR 1 V 0 P
the most sweet favor or deformed'st creature, SON 113.10
DEFORMITIES 1 FR 0.0001 REL FR 1 V 0 P
care i | what curious eye doth cote deformities? ROM 1.04. 31
DEFORMITY 5 FR 0.0005 REL FR 4 V 1 P
own present folly, and her passing deformity: TGV 2.01. 76 P
my back, | where sits deformity to mock my body; 3H6 3.02.158
in the sun | and descant on mine own deformity. R3 1.01. 27
blush, blush, thou lump of foul deformity; 1.02. 57
proper deformity /shows not in the fiend | so LR 4.02. 60
DEFTLY 1 FR 0.0001 REL FR 1 V 0 P
thyself and office deftly show! MAC 4.01. 68
DEFUNCT 3 FR 0.0003 REL FR 3 V 0 P
the organs, though defunct and dead before, H5 4.01. 21
(the young affects | in /me defunct) and proper OTH 1.03.264
doth abhor to make his bed | with the defunct, CYM 4.02.358
DEFUNCTION 1 FR 0.0001 REL FR 1 V 0 P
years | after defunction of king pharamond, H5 1.02. 58
DEFUNCTIVE 1 FR 0.0001 REL FR 1 V 0 P
in surplice white, | that defunctive music can, PHT 14
DEFUS'D 2 FR 0.0002 REL FR 2 V 0 P
to swearing and stern looks, defus'd attire, H5 5.02. 61
vouchsafe, defus'd infection of /a man, | of R3 1.02. 78
DEFUSE *(also diffused)*
DEFUSE 1 FR 0.0001 REL FR 1 V 0 P
that can my speech defuse, my good intent | may LR 1.04. 2
/DEFY 2 FR 0.0002 REL FR 2 V 0 P
i /thee /defy again. H5 2.01. 72
then i /defy you, stars! ROM 5.01. 24
DEFY 29 FR 0.0032 REL FR 20 V 9 P
i defy thee. TMP 3.02.131 P
given me this morning, but i defy all angels (in WIV 2.02. 73 P
i dare, and do defy thee for a villain. ERR 5.01. 32
him, that for a tricksy word | defy the matter. MV 3.05. 70
i defy lechery. TN 1.05.125 P
what, man, defy the devil! 3.04. 97 P
if you offend him, i for him defy you. 3.04.314
i do defy thee, france. JN 2.01.155
why then defy each other, and pell–mell | make 2.01.406
no, i defy all counsel, all redress, | but that 3.04. 23
i do defy him, and i spit at him, | call him a R2 1.01. 60
all studies here i solemnly defy, | save how to 1H4 1.03.228
no, i defy thee. 3.03. 62 P
flatter, i do defy | the tongues of soothers, 4.01. 6
defy him by the lord of westmerland. 5.02. 31
proud of destruction, | defy us to our worst; H5 3.03. 5
gloucester, i do defy thee. 1H6 3.01. 27
ten meals i have lost, and i'd defy them all. 2H6 4.10. 62 P
defy them then, or else hold close thy lips. 3H6 2.02.118
and in this resolution, i defy thee, | not 2.02.170

and so, proud–hearted warwick, i defy thee, 5.01. 98
i do defy thy /conjuration, | and apprehend thee ROM 5.03. 68
not a whit, we defy augury. HAM 5.02.219 P
from lenders' books, and defy the foul fiend. LR 3.04. 97 P
at heel of that, defy him. ANT 2.02.157
that a man may deal withal and defy the surgeon? PER 4.06. 26 P
defy me in these fair terms, and you show | more TNK 3.06. 25
age, i do defy thee. PP 12.11
thy registers and thee i both defy, | not SON 123. 9
DEFYING 2 FR 0.0002 REL FR 2 V 0 P
and here defying | those whose great power must COR 3.03. 79
love is dying, faith's defying, | heart's PP 17. 3
/DEGENERATE 1 FR 0.0001 REL FR 1 V 0 P
/most /barbarous, /most /degenerate, /have /you LR 4.02. 43
DEGENERATE 11 FR 0.0012 REL FR 11 V 0 P
the more degenerate and base art thou | to make TGV 5.04.136
and you degenerate, you ingrate revolts, | you JN 5.02.151
a recreant and most degenerate traitor, | which R2 1.01.144
his noble kinsman — most degenerate king! 2.01.262
frowns, | to show how much thou art degenerate. 1H4 3.02.128
the mind, | and makes it fearful and degenerate; 2H6 4.04. 2
farewell, faint–hearted and degenerate king, 3H6 1.01.183
can it be | that so degenerate a strain as this TRO 2.02.154
become so loose, | or bassianus so degenerate, TIT 2.01. 66
degenerate bastard, i'll not trouble thee; LR 1.04.254
king, | to shame his hope with deeds degenerate; LUC 1003
DEGRADED 2 FR 0.0002 REL FR 2 V 0 P
be quite degraded, like a hedge–born swain 1H6 4.01. 43
embassade | then i degraded you from being king, 3H6 4.03. 33
DEGREE 47 FR 0.0053 REL FR 33 V 14 P
cut and long–tail, under the degree of a squire. WIV 3.04. 47 P
and he that breaks them in the least degree LLL 1.01.156
own part, i know not the degree of the worthy, 5.02.507 P
even daughter, welcome, in no less degree. AYL 5.04.148
she'll not match above her degree, neither in TN 1.03.110 P
he be, under the degree of my betters, and yet i 1.03.118 P
misprision in the highest degree! 1.05. 55 P
for he's in the third degree of drink, he's 1.05.135 P
that's a degree to love. 3.01.123
not "malvolio," nor after my degree, but "fellow 3.04. 77 P
fool, i'll requite it in the highest degree. 4.02.118 P
i'll answer thee in any fair degree | or R2 1.01. 80
his, | and he our subjects' next degree in hope. 1.04. 36
even in condition of the worst degree, | in 2.03.108
colevile is your name, a knight is your degree, 2H4 4.03. 6 P
shall be still your name, a traitor your degree, 4.03. 7 P
art thou aught else but place, degree, and form, H5 4.01.246
great sort, quite from the answer of his degree. 4.07.136 P
i will make you to–day a squire of low degree. 5.01. 36 P
grave, | or flourish to the height of my degree. 1H6 2.04.111
beseems | a man of thy profession and degree; 3.01. 20
as fest'red members rot but by degree, | till 3.01.191
thou wast installed in that high degree. 4.01. 17
and call'd unto a cardinal's degree? 5.01. 29
how art thou call'd? and what is thy degree? 2H6 5.01. 73
the next degree is england's royal throne; 3H6 2.01.193
private conference | (of what degree soever) R3 1.01. 87
when thou hast broke it in such dear degree? 1.04.210
best fitteth my degree or your condition. 3.07.143
seduc'd the pitch and height of his degree | to 3.07.188
perjury, perjury, in the highest degree; 5.03.196
murther, stern murther, in the direst degree; 5.03.197
all several sins, all us'd in each degree, 5.03.198
degree being vizarded, | th' unworthiest shows TRO 1.03. 83
and this centre | observe degree, priority, and 1.03. 86
o, when degree is shak'd, | which is the ladder 1.03.101
but by degree, stand in authentic place? 1.03.108
take but degree away, untune that string, | and 1.03.109
this chaos, when degree is suffocate, | follows 1.03.125
and this neglection of degree it is | that by a 1.03.127
in the highest degree | he hath abus'd your COR 5.06. 84
tell athens, in the sequence of degree, | from TIM 5.01.208
must be of such unnatural degree | that monsters LR 1.01.219
man of quality or degree within the lists of the 5.03.110 P
so eminent in the degree of this fortune as OTH 2.01.237 P
high renown, | and thou art but of low degree. 2.03. 94
of her own clime, complexion, and degree, 3.03.230
DEGREES 18 FR 0.0020 REL FR 12 V 6 P
born, | are now to have no successive degrees, MM 2.02. 98
i'll leave it by degrees. LLL 5.02.418
o, that estates, degrees, and offices | were not MV 2.09. 41
and in these degrees have they made a pair of AYL 5.02. 37 P
nominate in order now the degrees of the lie? 5.04. 88 P
i will name you the degrees. 5.04. 92 P
that by degrees we mean to look into, | and SHR 3.02.143
should a like language use to all degrees, | and WT 2.01. 85
and so both the degrees prevent my curses. 2H4 1.02.232 P
no, nor hector is not troilus in some degrees. TRO 1.02. 69 P
degrees in schools, and brotherhoods in cities, 1.03.104
ascent is not by such easy degrees as those who, COR 2.02. 25 P
degrees, observances, customs, and laws, TIM 4.01. 19
the sweet degrees that this brief world affords 4.03.253
scorning the base degrees | by which he did JC 2.01. 26
you know your own degrees, sit down. MAC 3.04. 1
what wound did ever heal but by degrees? OTH 2.03.371
/smite, | till by degrees the memory of my womb, ANT 3.13.163
DEIFIED 1 FR 0.0001 REL FR 1 V 0 P
abide, | she was new lodg'd and newly deified. LC 84
DEIFIES 1 FR 0.0001 REL FR 1 V 0 P
in a fever, and deifies alone | voluble chance; TNK 1.02. 66
/DEIFYING 1 FR 0.0001 REL FR 0 V 1 P
all, forsooth, /deifying the name of rosalind. AYL 3.02.363 P
DEIGN 7 FR 0.0008 REL FR 7 V 0 P
i fear my julia would not deign my lines, TGV 1.01.152
will deign to sip or touch one drop of it. SHR 5.02.145
since thou dost deign to woo her little worth 1H6 5.03.151
and all those friends that deign to follow me. 3H6 4.07. 39
nor would we deign him burial of his men | till MAC 1.02. 60
thy palate then did deign | the roughest berry ANT 1.04. 63
if thou wilt deign this favor, for thy meed | a VEN 15
DEIGNED 1 FR 0.0001 REL FR 1 V 0 P
cheeks, | god's mother deigned to appear to me, 1H6 1.02. 78
DEIPHOBUS 3 FR 0.0003 REL FR 1 V 2 P
that's deiphobus. TRO 1.02.227 P
hector, deiphobus, helenus, antenor, and all the 3.01.135 P
is at hand | paris your brother, and deiphobus, 4.02. 61
DEITIES 5 FR 0.0005 REL FR 3 V 2 P
themselves | (humbling their deities to love) WT 4.04. 26
which | cold lips blow to their deities, take TRO 4.04. 27
still to give, lest your deities be despis'd. TIM 3.06. 72 P
it pleaseth their deities to take the wife of a ANT 1.02.162 P
so the deities | have show'd due justice. TNK 5.04.108
DEITY 9 FR 0.0010 REL FR 9 V 0 P
but i feel not | this deity in my bosom. TMP 2.01.278
i met her deity | cutting the clouds towards 4.01. 92
is the liver–vein, which makes flesh a deity, LLL 4.03. 72
nor can there be that deity in my nature | of TN 5.01.227
humbly complaining to her deity | got my lord R3 1.01. 76
a thing | made by some other deity than nature, COR 4.06. 91
shining synod of the rest | against thy deity. CYM 5.04. 90
convey thy deity | aboard our dancing boat, make PER 3.01. 12
and earn'st a deity | equal with mars. TNK 1.01.227
DEJA 1 FR 0.0001 REL FR 0 V 1 P
n'avez vous deja oublie ce que je vous ai H5 3.04. 42 P
DEJECT 3 FR 0.0003 REL FR 3 V 0 P
respect | make livers pale and lustihood deject. TRO 2.02. 50
it, | nor once deject the courage of our minds, 2.02.121
and i, of ladies most deject and wretched, HAM 3.01.155
DEJECTED 6 FR 0.0006 REL FR 4 V 2 P
you have the start of me, i am dejected. WIV 5.05.162 P
moated grange, resides this dejected mariana. MM 3.01.265 P
eye, | nor the dejected havior of the visage, HAM 1.02. 81
the lowest and most dejected thing of fortune, LR 4.01. 3
antony | is valiant, and dejected, and by starts ANT 4.12. 7
from the dejected state wherein he is, | he PER 2.02. 46
DELABRETH 2 FR 0.0002 REL FR 2 V 0 P
charles delabreth, high constable of france, H5 3.05. 40
charles delabreth, high constable of france, 4.08. 92
DELATED 1 FR 0.0001 REL FR 1 V 0 P
the scope | of these delated articles allow. HAM 1.02. 38
DELAY 38 FR 0.0043 REL FR 31 V 7 P
and lead him on with a fine–baited delay, till WIV 2.01. 96 P
by the sergeant to tarry for the hoy delay. ERR 4.03. 40 P
but, notwithstanding, haste, make no delay; MND 3.02.394
'tide life, 'tide death, i come without delay. 5.01.203
one inch of delay more is a south–sea of AYL 3.02.196 P
if thou delay me not the knowledge of his chin. 3.02.211 P
whose want, and whose delay, is strew'd with AWW 2.04. 44
now, god delay our rebellion! 4.03. 19 P
who of my people hold him in delay? TN 1.05.104 P
in delay there lies no plenty, | then come kiss 2.03. 50
we make woe wanton with this fond delay, | once R2 5.01.101
away, | advantage feeds him fat while men delay. 1H4 3.02.180
king | come here himself to question our delay; H5 2.04.142
won away, | long all of somerset and his delay. 1H6 4.03. 46
this weighty business will not brook delay, 2H6 1.01.170
right gracious lord, i cannot brook delay. 3H6 3.02. 18
therefore delay not, give thy hand to warwick, 3.03.246
the sun shines hot, and, if we use delay, | cold 4.08. 60
be not ta'en tardy by unwise delay. R3 4.01. 51
commenting | is leaden servitor to dull delay; 4.03. 52
delay /leads impotent and snail–pac'd beggary. 4.03. 53
let's lack no discipline, make no delay, | for, 5.03. 17
of his substance, to be levied | without delay; H8 1.02. 59
and that, without delay, their arguments | be 2.04. 67
and that you not delay the present, but, COR 1.06. 60
sir, in delay | we waste our lights in vain, ROM 1.04. 44
the excuse that thou dost make in this delay 2.05. 33
delay this marriage for a month, a week, | or, 3.05.199
delay not, caesar, read it instantly. JC 3.01. 9
the pangs of despis'd love, the law's delay, HAM 3.01. 71
delay it not, i'll have him hence to–night. 4.03. 55
without any further delay than this very evening LR 1.02. 93 P
what safe and nicely i might well delay | by 5.03.145
dull not device by coldness and delay. OTH 2.03.388
that what they do delay, they not deny. ANT 2.01. 3
delay | commends us to a famishing hope. TNK 1.01.166
to delay it longer | would make the world think, 3.06. 10
doors, the wind, the glove that did delay him, LUC 325
DELAY'D 4 FR 0.0004 REL FR 4 V 0 P
delay'd, | but nothing alt'red. WT 4.04.463
i would not be delay'd. OTH 3.04.114
to make my gift, | the more delay'd, delighted. CYM 5.04.102
her audit (though delay'd) answer'd must be, SON 126.11
DELAYED 1 FR 0.0001 REL FR 1 V 0 P
choice, | and will no longer have it be delayed. PER 2.05. 22
DELAYING 2 FR 0.0002 REL FR 1 V 1 P
for which foul deed | the pow'rs, delaying (not TMP 3.03. 73
in the delaying death. MM 4.02.164 P
DELAYS 10 FR 0.0011 REL FR 10 V 0 P
forc'd me to seek delays for them and me. ERR 1.01. 74
leave off delays, and let us raise the siege. 1H6 1.02.146
defer no time, delays have dangerous ends, 3.02. 33
that thus delays my promised supply | of 4.03. 10
nor posted off their suits with slow delays; 3H6 4.08. 40
he doth me wrong to feed me with delays. TIT 4.03. 43
and hath abatements and delays as many | as HAM 4.07.120
her more than haste is mated with delays, | like VEN 909
so his unhallowed haste her words delays, | and LUC 552
not speak, | till after many accents and delays, 1719
DELECTABLE 2 FR 0.0002 REL FR 1 V 1 P
making the hard way sweet and delectable. R2 2.03. 7
of nimble, fiery, and delectable shapes, which, 2H4 4.03.100 P
DELIBERATE 6 FR 0.0006 REL FR 5 V 1 P
please you deliberate a day or two. TGV 1.03. 73
whose settled visage and deliberate word | nips MM 3.01. 89
o, these deliberate fools! MV 2.09. 80
to ride day and night, and not to deliberate, 2H4 5.05. 21 P
your most grave belly was deliberate, | not rash COR 1.01.128
sending him away must seem | deliberate pause. HAM 4.03. 9
/DELICATE 1 FR 0.0001 REL FR 1 V 0 P
/tear /trill'd /down | /her /delicate /cheek. LR 4.03. 13
DELICATE 29 FR 0.0032 REL FR 19 V 10 P
for thou wast a spirit too delicate | to act her TMP 1.02.272
delicate ariel, | i'll set thee free for this. 1.02.442
be of subtle, tender, and delicate temperance. 2.01. 42 P
"temperance" was a delicate wench. 2.01. 44 P
a most delicate monster! 2.02. 89 P
dearly, my delicate ariel. 4.01. 49
come thronging soft and delicate desires, | all ADO 1.01.303
more moving, delicate, and full of life, | into 4.01.228
there's a dozen of 'em, with delicate fine hats, AWW 4.05.104 P
the climate's delicate, the air most sweet, WT 3.01. 1
with such delicate burthens of dildos and 4.04.194 P
that shall first spring and be most delicate. H5 2.04. 40
ever young, fresh, lov'd, and delicate wooer, TIM 4.03.384
haunt, i have observ'd | the air is delicate. MAC 1.06. 10
charge | led by a delicate and tender prince, HAM 4.04. 48
to the hilts, most delicate carriages, and of 5.02.152 P
when the mind's free, | the body's delicate; LR 3.04. 12
it were a delicate stratagem, to shoe | a troop 4.06.184
abus'd her delicate youth with drugs or minerals OTH 1.02. 74
do it a more delicate way than drowning. 1.03.353 P
her delicate tenderness will find itself abus'd, 2.01.232 P
indeed she's a most fresh and delicate creature. 2.03. 20 P
that we can call these delicate creatures ours, 3.03.269
so delicate with her needle! 4.01.187 P
to /glow the delicate cheeks which they did cool ANT 2.02.204
steep'd our sense | in soft and delicate lethe. 2.07.108
right proud | of that most delicate lodging. CYM 2.04.136
o most delicate fiend! 5.05. 47
a delicate odor. PER 3.02. 61
DELICATES 1 FR 0.0001 REL FR 1 V 0 P
enjoys, | is far beyond a prince's delicates — 3H6 2.05. 51
DELICIOUS 4 FR 0.0004 REL FR 4 V 0 P
fingers, | a most delicious banquet by his bed, SHR in.1. 39
bait, | the other rotted with delicious /feed. TIT 4.04. 93
now i feed myself | with most delicious poison. ANT 1.05. 27
his taste delicious, in digestion souring, LUC 699
DELICIOUSNESS 1 FR 0.0001 REL FR 1 V 0 P
honey | is loathsome in his own deliciousness, ROM 2.06. 12
DELICULO 1 FR 0.0001 REL FR 0 V 1 P
is to be up betimes, and "deliculo surgere," TN 2.03. 2 P
/DELIGHT 1 FR 0.0001 REL FR 1 V 0 P
/in /diet, /in /affections /of /delight, | /in 2H4 2.03. 29
DELIGHT 75 FR 0.0084 REL FR 62 V 13 P
and their labor | delight in them /sets off; TMP 3.01. 2
and sweet airs, that give delight and hurt not. 3.02.136
i perceive you delight not in music. TGV 4.02. 66 P
when all our pageants of delight were play'd, 4.04.159
ever the devil could have made you our delight? WIV 5.05.150 P
where indeed you have a delight to sit, have you MM 2.01.129 P
left to both of us alike | what to delight in, ERR 1.01.106
hast thou delight to see a wretched man | do 4.04.115
none but libertines delight in him, and the ADO 2.01.139 P
nor let no comforter delight mine ear, | but 5.01. 6
and train our intellects to vain delight. LLL 1.01. 71
how you delight, my lords, i know not, i, | but 1.01.174
suffer him to take no delight nor no penance, 1.02.129 P
yellow hue | do paint the meadows with delight, 5.02.897
lull'd in these flowers with dances and delight; MND 2.01.254
thou tak'st | true delight | in the sight | of 3.02.455
the lazy time, if not with some delight? 5.01. 41
all for your delight | we are not here. 5.01.114
i desire no more delight | than to be under sail MV 2.06. 67
embraced heaviness | with some delight or other. 2.08. 53
you will take little delight in it, i can tell AYL 1.02.158 P
and for i know she taketh most delight | in SHR 1.01. 92
i delight in masques and revels sometimes TN 1.03.113 P
your ladyship takes delight in such a barren 1.05. 83 P
the lady olivia's father took much delight in. 2.04. 12 P
the world, | never to be infected with delight, JN 4.03. 69
my legs can keep no measure in delight, | when R2 3.04. 7
us look in, the sight will much delight thee. 1H6 1.04. 62
if holy churchmen take delight in broils? 3.01.111
and delight to live in slavery to the nobility. 2H6 4.08. 28 P
peace, | have no delight to pass away the time, R3 1.01. 25
if thou delight to view thy heinous deeds, 1.02. 53
if sanctimony be the gods' delight, | if there TRO 5.02.140
make the silken strings delight to kiss them, TIT 2.04. 46
a den, | unless the gods delight in tragedies? 4.01. 60
even such delight | among fresh fennel buds ROM 1.02. 28
and find delight writ there with beauty's pen; 1.03. 82
i am the drudge, and toil in your delight; 2.05. 75
the labor we delight in physics pain. MAC 2.03. 50
and delight | no less in truth than life. 4.03.129
in equal scale weighing delight and dole, HAM 1.02. 13
my lord, if you delight not in man, what lenten 2.02.315 P
those you were wont to take such delight in, the 2.02.327 P
rouse him, make after him, poison his delight, OTH 1.01. 68
such a thing as thou — to fear, not to delight! 1.02. 71
and what delight shall she have to look on the 2.01.225 P
love we rise betime, | and go to't with delight. ANT 4.04. 21
sight, | and not so much to feed on as delight; PER 1.04. 29
must have inventions to delight the taste, 1.04. 40
a more content in course of true delight | than 3.02. 39
to see his daughter, all his live's delight. 4.04. 12
her best is better'd with a more delight. VEN 78
my day's delight is past, my horse is gone, 380
fed, | his other agents aim at like delight? 400
do i delight to die, or life desire? 496
others they think delight | in such–like 843
the foul boar's conquest on her fair delight, 1030
which triumph'd in that sky of his delight; LUC 12
covers the shame that follows sweet delight." 357
sell her joy, her life, her world's delight. 385
my will that marks thee for my earth's delight, 487
balk | the prey wherein by nature they delight, 697
runs, and chides his vanish'd loath'd delight. 742
eater of youth, false slave to false delight, 927
she told him stories to delight his /ear; PP 4. 5
and i in deep delight am chiefly drown'd | when 8.11
will repent | that thus dissembled her delight; 18.28
doth it steal sweet hours from love's delight. SON 36. 8
as a decrepit father takes delight | to see his 37. 1
awakes my heart to heart's and eye's delight. 47.14
possessing or pursuing no delight | save what is 75.11
cost, | of more delight than hawks or horses be; 91.11
they were but sweet, but figures of delight, 98.11
and sweets grown common lose their dear delight. 102.12
and in some perfumes is there more delight 130. 7
DELIGHTED 6 FR 0.0006 REL FR 5 V 1 P
and the delighted spirit | to bathe in fiery MM 3.01.120
speak, brave hector, we are much delighted. LLL 5.02.665 P
signior, | if virtue no delighted beauty lack, OTH 1.03.289
any sense | delighted them /in any other form; 4.02.155
to make my gift, | the mgre delay'd, delighted. CYM 5.04.102
are mine ears with thy tongue's tune delighted, SON 141. 5
/DELIGHTFUL 1 FR 0.0001 REL FR 1 V 0 P
whose /delightful steps | shall make the gazer PER 2.01.158
DELIGHTFUL 6 FR 0.0006 REL FR 5 V 1 P
(sweet chuck) with some delightful ostentation, LLL 5.01.111 P
no more | than a delightful measure or a dance, R2 1.03.291

our dreadful marches to delightful measures. R3 1.01. 8
o, that delightful engine of her thoughts, TIT 3.01. 82
fed | with such delightful pleasing harmony. PER 2.05. 28
sweet bottom grass and high delightful plain, VEN 236
DELIGHTING 1 FR 0.0001 REL FR 1 V 0 P
in bloody death and ravishment delighting, | nor LUC 430
DELIGHTS 21 FR 0.0023 REL FR 18 V 3 P
o, flatter me; for love delights in praises. TGV 2.04.148
the grosser manner of these world's delights LLL 1.01. 29
all delights are vain, but that most vain 1.01. 72
nor god, nor i, delights in perjur'd men. 5.02.346
as we do trust they'll end, in true delights. AYL 5.04.198
fit man to teach her that wherein she delights, SHR 1.01.111 P
whom heaven delights to hear | and loves to AWW 3.04. 27
so full replete with choice of all delights, 1H6 5.05. 17
now am i seated as my soul delights, | having my 3H6 5.07. 35
be hours for necessities, | not for delights; H8 5.01. 3
like one besotted on your sweet delights. TRO 2.02.143
these violent delights have violent ends, | and ROM 2.06. 9
if sour woe delights in fellowship | and needly 3.02.116
sprites, | and show the best of our delights. MAC 4.01.128
man delights not me — nor women neither, though HAM 2.02.309 P
laugh then, when i said, "man delights not me"? 2.02.314 P
and drive his purpose into these delights. 3.01. 27
his delights | were dolphin-like, they show'd ANT 5.02. 88
summer shall come, and with her all delights, TNK 2.02. 44
sweets with sweets war not, joy delights in joy. SON 8. 2
wherethrough the sun | delights to peep, to gaze 24.12
DELINQUENTS 1 FR 0.0001 REL FR 1 V 0 P
in pious rage the two delinquents tear, | that MAC 3.06. 12
DELIVER 105 FR 0.0118 REL FR 72 V 33 P
i'll deliver all, | and promise you calm seas, TMP 5.01.314
to my friends, | and i am going to deliver them. TGV 3.01. 54
ay, if his enemy deliver it; 3.02. 35
i was sent to deliver him as a present to 4.04. 6 P
ring with thee, | deliver it to madam silvia — 4.04. 72
my master charg'd me to deliver a ring to madam 5.04. 88 P
(got deliver to a joyful resurrections!) WIV 1.01. 52 P
eld | receiv'd and did deliver to our age | this 4.04. 37
and i will deliver his wife into your hand. 5.01. 28 P
more depends on it than we must yet deliver. MM 4.02.125 P
to deliver his head in the view of angelo? 4.02.167 P
and to deliver us from devices hereafter, which 4.04. 12 P
these letters at fit time deliver me. 4.05. 1
words | didst thou deliver to me on the mart. ERR 2.02.164
are the angels that you sent for to deliver you. 4.03. 41 P
some blessed power deliver us from hence! 4.03. 44
my life, | and pay the sum that may deliver me. 5.01.285
so deliver i up my apes, and away to saint peter ADO 2.01. 47 P
of affection would deliver me from the reprobate LLL 1.02. 60 P
deliver this paper into the royal hand of the 4.02.141 P
deliver me the key. MV 2.07. 59
them all | here to this devil, to deliver you. 4.01.287
from all such devils, good lord deliver us! SHR 1.01. 66
from florence, and must here deliver them. 4.02. 90
to betray you and deliver all the intelligence AWW 3.06. 30 P
pray you, sir, deliver me this paper. 5.02. 15 P
sure you have some hideous matter to deliver, TN 1.05.206 P
or i'll deliver thy indignation to him by word 2.03.130 P
now will not i deliver his letter; 3.04.184 P
i will deliver his challenge by word of mouth, 3.04.190 P
this you may know, | and so deliver: WT 4.04.498
what you (as from your father) shall deliver, 4.04.559
the old shepherd deliver the manner how he found 5.02. 4 P
lady paulina's steward, he can deliver you more. 5.02. 26 P
but from the inward motion to deliver | sweet, JN 1.01.212
your highness should deliver up your crown. 4.02.152
deliver him to safety, and return, | for i must 4.02.158
than can my care-tun'd tongue deliver him! R2 3.02. 92
parley | into his ruin'd ears, and thus deliver: 3.03. 34
deliver them up without their ransom straight, 1H4 1.03.260
deliver what you will, i'll say 'tis so. 5.02. 26
return'd, | deliver up my lord of westmerland. 5.02. 28
douglas, and deliver him | up to his pleasure, 5.05. 27
and deliver to the army | this news of peace. 2H4 4.02. 69
happiness | added to that that i am to deliver! 4.04. 82
a son | that would deliver up his greatness so 5.02.111
i pray thee now deliver them like a man of this 5.03. 97 P
i will deliver her. 5.05. 39 P
sought, that to her laws | we do deliver you. H5 2.02.177
let us deliver | our puissance into the hand of • 2.02.189
deliver up the crown, and to take mercy | on the 2.04.103
i shall deliver so. thanks to your highness. 3.06.167
i deliver her, | and those two counties i will 1H6 5.03.157
deliver up my title in the queen | to your most 2H6 1.01. 12
and then we may deliver our supplications in the 1.03. 3 P
long, | i will deliver you, or else lie for you. R3 1.01.115
i am in this commanded to deliver | the noble 1.04. 91
what from your grace i shall deliver to him. 4.04.448
lord cardinal, | deliver all with charity. H8 1.02.143
deliver this with modesty to th' queen. 2.02.136
pray do not deliver | what here y' have heard to 2.03.106
between the king and you, and to deliver | (like 3.01. 59
i most humbly pray you to deliver | this to my 4.02.129
i could not personally deliver to her | what you 5.01. 62
this ring | deliver them, and your appeal to us 5.01.151
"deliver helen, and all damage else — | as TRO 2.02. 3
now to deliver her possession up | on terms of 2.02.152
not in circumvention deliver a fly from a spider 2.03. 16 P
and to his hand when i deliver her, | think it 4.03. 7
is the lady | which for antenor we deliver you. 4.04.110
but, and't please you, deliver. COR 1.01. 95 P
once cannot | see what i do deliver out to each, 1.01.143
deliver him, titus. 1.09. 89
deliver you as most | abated captives to some 3.03.131
deliver them this paper. 5.06. 2
we'll deliver you | of your great danger. 5.06. 13
and we here deliver, | subscrib'd by th' consuls 5.06. 80
i'll deliver | myself your loyal servant, or 5.06.139
of lucius, | he hath some message to deliver us. TIT 4.02. 2
region, | i pray you deliver him this petition. 4.03. 14
and let him deliver the pigeons to the emperor 4.03. 96 P
can you deliver an oration to the emperor with a 4.03. 98 P
can you with a grace deliver up a supplication? 4.03.107 P
kiss his foot, then deliver up your pigeons, and 4.03.111 P
see thou deliver it to my lord and father. ROM 5.03. 24
cassius from bondage will deliver cassius. JC 1.03. 90

and then we will deliver you the cause | why i, 3.01.181
this have i thought good to deliver thee, my MAC 1.05. 10 P
while | with an attent ear, till i may deliver, HAM 1.02.193
shall i deliver you so? 5.02.179 P
all this can i | truly deliver. 5.02.386
telling it, and deliver a plain message bluntly. LR 1.04. 33 P
from the loath'd warmth whereof deliver me, and 4.06.267 P
i will a round unvarnish'd tale deliver | of my OTH 1.03. 90
thou dost deliver more or less than truth, 2.03.219
have had from me to deliver desdemona would half 4.02.187 P
this is most certain that i shall deliver: ANT 2.01. 28
but | your jailer shall deliver you the keys CYM 1.01. 73
deliver with more openness your answers | to my 1.06. 88
gods | would safely deliver me from this place! PER 4.06.180
i am great with woe, and shall deliver weeping. 5.01.106
you by the syllable | of what you shall deliver. 5.01.168
will you deliver | how this dead queen relives? 5.03. 63
what's your request? deliver you for all. TNK 1.01. 38
conceives a tear, | the which it will deliver. 5.03.138
DELIVERANCE 10 FR 0.0011 REL FR 6 V 4 P
i'd throw it down for your deliverance | as MM 3.01.104
and your deliverance with an unpitied whipping, 4.02. 12 P
doth teach me answers for deliverance! MV 3.02. 38
my thoughts | in this my light deliverance, i AWW 2.01. 82
you have it from his own deliverance. 2.05. 4 P
i do desire deliverance from these officers, 2H4 2.01.127 P
and at each word's deliverance | stab poniards 3H6 2.01. 97
need pray, | and heartily, for our deliverance, H8 2.02. 45
ne'er mother | rejoic'd deliverance more. CYM 5.05.370
martyr'd as 'twere i' th' deliverance, will TNK 2.01. 41 P
/DELIVER'D 1 FR 0.0001 REL FR 1 V 0 P
/have /here /deliver'd /me /to /my /sour /cross, R2 4.01.241
DELIVER'D 47 FR 0.0053 REL FR 24 V 23 P
and a subtle, as he most learnedly deliver'd. TMP 2.01. 45 P
and the matter may be both at once deliver'd. TGV 1.01.130 P
deliver'd by a friend that came from him. 1.03. 54
and that letter hath she deliver'd, and there an 2.01.161 P
me, shall be deliver'd | even in the milk-white 3.01.251
she lov'd me well deliver'd it to me. 4.04. 73
deliver'd you a paper that i should not: 4.04.123
the action of an old woman, deliver'd me, the WIV 4.05.119 P
i have deliver'd to lord angelo | (a man of MM 1.03. 11
duke had not either deliver'd him to his liberty 4.02.133 P
he came to me, and i deliver'd it. ERR 4.04. 88
i have already deliver'd him letters, and there ADO 1.01. 20 P
see these letters deliver'd, put the liveries to MV 2.02.116 P
i oft deliver'd from his forfeitures | many that 3.03. 22
this she deliver'd in the most bitter touch of AWW 1.03.117 P
when back again this ring shall be deliver'd; 4.02. 60
if he may be conveniently deliver'd, i would he TN 4.02. 68 P
so it skills not much when they are deliver'd. 5.01.288 P
see him deliver'd, fabian, bring him hither. 5.01.315
she is, something before her time, deliver'd. WT 2.02. 23
by the hand deliver'd | of great apollo's priest 3.02.127
which i have given already, | but not deliver'd. 4.04.360
reason | how i may be deliver'd of these woes, JN 3.04. 55
ginger, to be deliver'd as far as charing-cross. 1H4 2.01. 25 P
dreamt she was deliver'd of a fire-brand, and 2H4 2.02. 90 P
deliver'd with good respect. 2.02.101 P
which, deliver'd o'er to the voice, the tongue, 4.03.100 P
the constables have deliver'd her over to me, 5.04. 4 P
a letter was deliver'd to my hands, | writ to 1H6 4.01. 11
be releas'd and deliver'd /over to the king her 2H6 1.01. 52 P
be releas'd and deliver'd over to the king her 1.01. 59 P
wounds | deliver'd up again with peaceful words? 1.01.122
deliver'd strongly through my fixed teeth, 3.02.313
nor he deliver'd | his gracious pleasure any way R3 3.04. 16
is the queen deliver'd? H8 5.01.162
loose shot, deliver'd such a show'r of pibbles, 5.03. 56 P
diomed, and our antenor | deliver'd to /us; TRO 4.02. 63
'twill be deliver'd back on good condition. COR 1.10. 2
your worships have deliver'd the matter well, 2.01. 57 P
and more, | more fearful, is deliver'd. 4.06. 64
could not so prosperously be deliver'd of. HAM 2.02.211 P
my lord, till i have deliver'd your letter. LR 1.05. 6 P
deliver'd letters, spite of intermission, 2.04. 33
in the womb of time which will be deliver'd. OTH 1.03.370 P
but my muse labors, | and thus she is deliver'd: 2.01.128
i would i were really that i am deliver'd to be. TNK 2.01. 7 P
those children nurs'd, deliver'd from thy brain, SON 77.11
DELIVERED 22 FR 0.0024 REL FR 21 V 1 P
a mean woman was delivered | of such a burthen ERR 1.01. 54
hour | my heavy burthen /ne'er delivered. 5.01.403
my lord berowne, see him delivered o'er, | and LLL 1.01.305
and delivered upon the mellowing of occasion. 4.02. 69 P
and might not be delivered to the world | till i TN 1.02. 42
see them delivered over | to execution and the R2 3.01. 29
take special care my greetings be delivered. 3.01. 39
scorns to unsay what once it hath delivered. 4.01. 9
denied | as is delivered to your majesty. 1H4 1.03. 26
i promised | should be delivered to his holiness 1H6 5.01. 53
i well might hear, delivered with a groan, | "o, 3H6 5.02. 46
from whence this present day he is delivered? R3 1.01. 69
she is delivered, lords, she is delivered. TIT 4.02. 61
she is delivered, lords, she is delivered. 4.02. 61
and no one else but the delivered empress. 4.02.142
and they shall be immediately delivered. 5.01.161
of this was tamora delivered, | the issue of an 5.03.120
have you delivered to her our decree? ROM 3.05.138
where, as they had delivered, both in time, HAM 1.02.209
with such a graceful courtesy delivered? PER 2.02. 41
but whether there | delivered, by the holy gods 3.04. 7
nurse lychorida hath oft | delivered weeping. 5.01.160
DELIVERING 4 FR 0.0004 REL FR 2 V 2 P
so much as a ducat for delivering your letter: TGV 1.01.137 P
and i, delivering you, am satisfied, | and MV 4.01.416
in delivering my son from me, i bury a second AWW 1.01. 1 P
delivering o'er to executors pale | the lazy H5 1.02.203
DELIVERLY 1 FR 0.0001 REL FR 1 V 0 P
bodies, | and carry it sweetly and deliverly, TNK 3.05. 29
DELIVERS 9 FR 0.0010 REL FR 7 V 2 P
delivers in such apt and gracious words | that LLL 2.01. 73
in fine, delivers me to fill the time, | herself AWW 3.07. 33
no thanks for't, in the nature he delivers it. 4.03.153 P
well edified when the fool delivers the madman. TN 5.01.291 P
doth, when he delivers you | from this earth's R3 1.04.247
the sorrow that delivers us thus chang'd | makes COR 5.03. 39
our mistrust, since he delivers | our offices, MAC 3.03. 2

the post attends, and she delivers it, LUC 1333
for it no form delivers to the heart | of bird, SON 113. 5
DELIVER'T 1 FR 0.0001 REL FR 0 V 1 P
but you'll not deliver't? TN 3.02. 57 P
DELIVERY 4 FR 0.0004 REL FR 3 V 1 P
i make a broken delivery of the business; WT 5.02. 9 P
lord hastings was /to /her /for /his delivery? R3 1.01. 75
with sobs | that he would labor my delivery. 1.04.246
for her delivery to this valiant greek | comes TRO 4.03. 2
DELIV'RED 1 FR 0.0001 REL FR 0 V 1 P
i have deliv'red it an hour since. AWW 4.03. 3 P
DELPHOS 3 FR 0.0003 REL FR 3 V 0 P
i have dispatch'd in post | to sacred delphos, WT 2.01.183
being well arriv'd from delphos, are both landed 2.03.196
have | been both at delphos, and from thence 3.02.126
DELUDED 1 FR 0.0001 REL FR 1 V 0 P
o, give me leave, i have deluded you, | 'twas 1H6 5.04. 76
DELUDING 2 FR 0.0002 REL FR 2 V 0 P
go get thee gone, thou false deluding slave, SHR 4.03. 31
justice of the state | for thus deluding you. OTH 1.01.140
DELUGE 2 FR 0.0002 REL FR 2 V 0 P
unnatural | provokes this deluge most unnatural. R3 1.02. 61
with her continual tears | become a deluge, TIT 3.01.229
DELVE 2 FR 0.0002 REL FR 2 V 0 P
but i will delve one yard below their mines, HAM 3.04.208
i cannot delve him to the root: CYM 1.01. 28
DELVER 1 FR 0.0001 REL FR 0 V 1 P
nay, but hear you, goodman delver — HAM 5.01. 14 P
DELVES 1 FR 0.0001 REL FR 1 V 0 P
and delves the parallels in beauty's brow, SON 60.10
DEMAND 62 FR 0.0070 REL FR 49 V 13 P
how now? moody? | what is't thou canst demand? TMP 1.02.245
sir, | you will demand of me why i do this. MM 1.03. 17
better please me | than to demand what 'tis. 2.04. 33
and i will please you what you will demand. ERR 4.04. 49
for here he doth demand to have repaid | a LLL 2.01.142
where? when? what vizard? why demand you this? 5.02.386
the pound of flesh which i demand of him | is MV 4.01. 99
and more shall be paid her than she'll demand. AWW 1.03.105 P
french lack language to deny | if they demand. 2.01. 21
for that is her demand — and know her business? 2.01. 86
make thy demand. 2.01.191
blood will nought deny | that she'll demand. 3.07. 22
i perceive, by this demand, you are not 4.03. 43 P
"first demand of him, how many horse the duke is 4.03.129 P
"demand of him, of what strength they are afoot. 4.03.158 P
demand of him my condition, and what credit i 4.03.171 P
"you shall demand of him, whether one captain 4.03.175 P
demand them singly. 4.03.183 P
where we may leisurely | each one demand, and WT 5.03.153
do in his name religiously demand | why thou JN 3.01.140
name, | pope innocent, i do demand of thee. 3.01.146
the suit which you demand is gone and dead. 4.02. 84
why may not i demand | of thine affairs, as well 5.06. 4
demand of yonder champion | the cause of his R2 1.03. 7
hast forgotten to demand that truly which thou 1H4 1.02. 5 P
be so superfluous to demand the time of the day. 1.02. 11 P
of him | i did demand what news from shrewsbury. 2H4 1.01. 40
if i demand, before this royal view, | what rub H5 5.02. 32
she is our capital demand, compris'd | within 5.02. 96
to give thee answer of thy just demand. 1H6 5.03.144
that suffolk should demand a whole fifteenth 2H6 1.01.133
end, | the king hath yielded unto thy demand: 5.01. 40
no, if thou dost say no to my demand. 3H6 3.02. 80
his demand | springs not from edward's 3.03. 66
me, | but dreadful war shall answer his demand. 3.03.259
did of me demand | what was the speech among the H8 1.02.153
my good lord, | not your demand; 2.03. 52
make that demand of the prover, it suffices me TRO 2.03. 67 P
what wouldst thou of us, troyan? make demand. 3.03. 17
a good demand. COR 3.02. 45
i do demand | if you submit you to the people's 3.03. 43
bid him demand what pledge will please him best. TIT 4.04.106
house, | willing you to demand your hostages, 5.01.160
daughter's jointure, for no more | can i demand. ROM 5.03.298
a most importunate aspect, | a visage of demand; TIM 2.01. 29
if then that friend demand why brutus rose JC 3.02. 20 P
here, | answering before we do demand of them. 5.01. 6
demand. MAC 4.01. 61
for the demand of our neglected tribute. HAM 3.01.170
let him demand his fill. 4.05.130
than comes from her demand out of the letter. LR 1.05. 3 P
pray, demand that demi-devil | why he hath thus OTH 5.02.301
demand me nothing; 5.02.303
of his conquer'd kingdoms, i | demand the like. ANT 3.06. 37
he'll make demand of her, and spend that kiss 5.02.302
we'll mannerly demand thee of thy story, | so CYM 3.06. 91
and a demand who is't shall die, i'ld say | "my 4.02. 23
yea, though thou do demand a prisoner, | the 5.05. 99
stand thou by our side, | make thy demand aloud. 5.05.130
when noble pericles shall demand his child? PER 4.03. 13
sir, i demand no more than your own offer, and i TNK 2.01. 10 P
did, | demand of him, nor being desired yielded; LC 149
DEMANDED 9 FR 0.0010 REL FR 8 V 1 P
well demanded, wench; TMP 1.02.139
those prisoners in your highness' name demanded, 1H4 1.03. 23
amongst the rest demanded | my prisoners in your 1.03. 47
besides, to be demanded of a spunge, what HAM 4.02. 12 P
methinks our pleasure might have been demanded LR 5.03. 62
ere it be demanded | (as like enough it will) i OTH 3.04.189
for it seems | they crave to be demanded. CYM 4.02.362
i know not how much more, should be demanded, 5.05.389
being demanded that, | she would sit still and PER 5.01.188
DEMANDING 2 FR 0.0002 REL FR 2 V 0 P
demanding of king henry's life and death, | and 2H6 2.01.171
which even but now, demanding after you, LR 3.02. 65
DEMANDS 19 FR 0.0021 REL FR 14 V 5 P
i will marry her upon any reasonable demands. WIV 1.01.226 P
obedience, agree with his demands to the point; MM 3.01.245 P
a hundred thousand crowns, and not demands, LLL 2.01.143
most monstrous size that must fit all demands. AWW 2.02. 33 P
england, impatient of your just demands, | hath JN 2.01. 56
and all the number of his fair demands | shall R2 3.03.123

it shall appear that your demands are just, 2H4 4.01.142
do not, in grant of all demands at large, H5 2.04.121
with full accord to all our just demands, 5.02. 71
dignity, | any thing in or out of our demands, 5.02. 89
where your majesty demands, that the king of 5.02.336 P
i have not stopp'd mine ears to their demands, 3H6 4.08. 39
his presence, let patroclus make demands to me; TRO 3.03.271 P
and in true fear | they gave us our demands." COR 3.01.135
encount'red | with clamorous demands of debt, TIM 2.02. 37
than your particular demands will touch it. HAM 2.01. 12
but of our demands | most free in his reply. 3.01. 13
and bids thee study on what fair demands | thou ANT 5.02. 10
with more openness your answers | to my demands. CYM 1.06. 89
DEMEAN 2 FR 0.0002 REL FR 2 V 0 P
is mad, | else would he never so demean himself. ERR 4.03. 82
and demean himself | unlike the ruler of a 2H6 1.01.188
DEMEAN'D 3 FR 0.0003 REL FR 3 V 0 P
when he demean'd himself rough, rude, and wildly ERR 5.01. 88
if york have ill demean'd himself in france, 2H6 1.03.103
they have demean'd themselves | like men born to 3H6 1.04. 7
DEMEANOR 5 FR 0.0005 REL FR 5 V 0 P
aspect, | and fashion your demeanor to my looks, ERR 2.02. 33
with such a deep demeanor in great sorrow | that 2H4 4.05. 84
blunt-witted lord, ignoble in demeanor! 2H6 3.02.210
perceive | but cold demeanor in octavio's wing, JC 5.02. 4
know, | which he by dumb demeanor seeks to show; LUC 474
DEMERITS 3 FR 0.0003 REL FR 3 V 0 P
on martius shall | of his demerits rob cominius. COR 1.01.272
not for their own demerits, but for mine, | fell MAC 4.03.226
men of royal siege, and my demerits | may speak, OTH 1.02. 22
DEMESNES 3 FR 0.0003 REL FR 3 V 0 P
and the demesnes that there adjacent lie, | that ROM 2.01. 20
of fair demesnes, youthful and nobly /lien'd, 3.05.180
this rock and these demesnes have been my world, CYM 3.03. 70
DEMETRIUS' 3 FR 0.0003 REL FR 3 V 0 P
rank'd | (if not with vantage) as demetrius'; MND 1.01.102
art | you sway the motion of demetrius' heart. 1.01.193
can, | deserve a sweet look from demetrius' eye, 2.02.127
DEMETRIUS 45 FR 0.0050 REL FR 45 V 0 P
stand forth, demetrius. MND 1.01. 24
your grace | consent to marry with demetrius, 1.01. 40
demetrius is a worthy gentleman. 1.01. 52
me in this case, | if i refuse to wed demetrius. 1.01. 64
or else to wed demetrius, as he would, | or on 1.01. 88
you have her father's love, demetrius, | let me 1.01. 93
my right of her | i do estate unto demetrius. 1.01. 98
demetrius, i'll avouch it to his head, | made 1.01.106
and with demetrius thought to have spoke thereof 1.01.112
but, demetrius, come, | and come, egeus, you 1.01.114
demetrius and egeus, go along; 1.01.123
demetrius loves your fair, o happy fair! 1.01.182
were the world mine, demetrius being bated, 1.01.190
and good luck grant thee thy demetrius! 1.01.221
as you on him, demetrius dote on you! 1.01.225
demetrius thinks not so; 1.01.228
for ere demetrius look'd on hermia's eyne, | he 1.01.242
and, demetrius, | the more you beat me, i will 2.01.203
fie, demetrius! 2.01.239
stay, though thou kill me, sweet demetrius. 2.02. 84
therefore no marvel though demetrius | do, as a 2.02. 96
where is demetrius? 2.02.106
ah, good demetrius, wilt thou give him me? 3.02. 63
noise they make | will cause demetrius to awake. 3.02.117
demetrius loves her; and he loves not you. 3.02.136
you are unkind, demetrius; 3.02.162
and made your other love, demetrius | (who even 3.02.224
demetrius, i will keep my word with thee. 3.02.266
save that, in love unto demetrius, | i told him 3.02.309
with demetrius. 3.02.320
then stir demetrius up with bitter wrong; 3.02.361
and sometime rail thou like demetrius; 3.02.362
where art thou, proud demetrius? speak thou now. 3.02.401
i'll find demetrius and revenge this spite. 3.02.420
asleep, | and this lysander, this demetrius is, 4.01.129
would have stol'n away, they would, demetrius, 4.01.156
and i have found demetrius like a jewel, | mine 4.01.191
demetrius, thou dost overween in all, | and so TIT 2.01. 29
"stuprum — chiron — demetrius." 4.01. 78
demetrius, here's the son of lucius, | he hath 4.02. 1
had he not reason, lord demetrius? 4.02. 39
empress' sons i take them, chiron, demetrius. 5.02.154
o villains, chiron and demetrius! 5.02.169
not i, 'twas chiron and demetrius: 5.03. 56
that chiron and the damn'd demetrius | were they 5.03. 97
DEMI-ATLAS 1 FR 0.0001 REL FR 1 V 0 P
the demi-atlas of this earth, the arm | and ANT 1.05. 23
DEMI-CANNON 1 FR 0.0001 REL FR 1 V 0 P
'tis like /a demi-cannon. SHR 4.03. 88
DEMI-DEVIL 2 FR 0.0002 REL FR 2 V 0 P
these three have robb'd me, and this demi-devil TMP 5.01.272
pray, demand that demi-devil | why he hath thus OTH 5.02.301
DEMIGOD 3 FR 0.0003 REL FR 3 V 0 P
thus can the demigod, authority, | make us pay MM 1.02.120
like a demigod here sit i in the sky, | and LLL 4.03. 77
what demigod | hath come so near creation? MV 3.02.115
DEMI-NATUR'D 1 FR 0.0001 REL FR 1 V 0 P
as had he been incorps'd and demi-natur'd | with HAM 4.07. 87
DEMI-PARADISE 1 FR 0.0001 REL FR 1 V 0 P
seat of mars, | this other eden, demi-paradise, R2 2.01. 42
DEMI-PUPPETS 1 FR 0.0001 REL FR 1 V 0 P
you demi-puppets that | by moonshine do the TMP 5.01. 36
DEMISE 1 FR 0.0001 REL FR 1 V 0 P
honor, | canst thou demise to any child of mine? R3 4.04.248
DEMI-WOLVES 1 FR 0.0001 REL FR 1 V 0 P
and demi-wolves are clipt | all by the name of MAC 3.01. 93
DEMOISELLE 1 FR 0.0001 REL FR 0 V 1 P
de most sage demoiselle dat is en france. H5 5.02.219 P
DEMOISELLES 1 FR 0.0001 REL FR 0 V 1 P
les dames et demoiselles pour etre baisees H5 5.02.258 P
DEMON *(also daemon)*
DEMON 1 FR 0.0001 REL FR 1 V 0 P
if that same demon that hath gull'd thee thus H5 2.02.121
DEMONSTRABLE 1 FR 0.0001 REL FR 1 V 0 P
made demonstrable here in cyprus to him, | hath OTH 3.04.142
DEMONSTRATE 5 FR 0.0005 REL FR 5 V 0 P
would demonstrate them now | but goers backward. AWW 1.02. 47
to demonstrate the life of such a battle, | in H5 4.02. 54
that shall demonstrate these quick blows of TIM 1.01. 91
for when my outward action doth demonstrate OTH 1.01. 61
other proofs | that do demonstrate thinly. 3.03.431
DEMONSTRATED 1 FR 0.0001 REL FR 1 V 0 P
have heaven and earth together demonstrated HAM 1.01.124
DEMONSTRATING 1 FR 0.0001 REL FR 0 V 1 P
every thing about you demonstrating a careless AYL 3.02.380 P
/DEMONSTRATION 1 FR 0.0001 REL FR 0 V 1 P
/the /queen /to /any /demonstration /of /grief? LR 4.03. 10 P
DEMONSTRATION 2 FR 0.0002 REL FR 1 V 1 P
by a familiar demonstration of the working, my LLL 1.02. 9 P
indeed — | such heart-pierc'd demonstration! TNK 1.01.124
DEMONSTRATIVE 1 FR 0.0001 REL FR 1 V 0 P
line, | in every branch truly demonstrative; H5 2.04. 89
DEMURE 4 FR 0.0004 REL FR 2 V 2 P
and after a demure travel of regard — telling TN 2.05. 53 P
never none of these demure boys come to any 2H4 4.03. 90 P
with demure confidence | this pausingly ensu'd: H8 1.02.167
her mistress she doth give demure good morrow, LUC 1219
DEMURELY 2 FR 0.0002 REL FR 2 V 0 P
wear prayer-books in my pocket, look demurely, MV 2.02.192
hark, the drums | demurely wake the sleepers. ANT 4.09. 30
DEMURING 1 FR 0.0001 REL FR 1 V 0 P
shall acquire no honor | demuring upon me. ANT 4.15. 29
DEN* *(also then)*
DEN* 16 FR 0.0018 REL FR 12 V 4 P
with such love as 'tis now, the murkiest den, TMP 4.01. 25
good den, brother. ADO 3.02. 81 P
good den, good den. 5.01. 46
good den, good den. 5.01. 46
food for his rage, repasture for his den." LLL 4.01. 93
"good den, sir richard!" JN 1.01.185
at your den, sirrah, with your lioness, | i 2.01.291
what, shall they seek the lion in his den, | and 5.01. 57
up revenge from ebon den with fell alecto's 2H4 5.05. 37
den it sall also content me. H5 5.02.250 P
not to the beast that would usurp their den. 3H6 2.02. 12
heart, | aaron and thou look down into this den, TIT 2.03.215
o, why should nature build so foul a den, 4.01. 59
god ye good den, fair gentlewoman. ROM 2.04.110 P
is it good den? 2.04.111 P
gentlemen, good den, a word with one of you. 3.01. 38
DENAY *(also deny, etc.)*
DENAY 1 FR 0.0001 REL FR 1 V 0 P
say | my love can give no place, bide no denay. TN 2.04.124
DENAY'D 1 FR 0.0001 REL FR 1 V 0 P
then let him be denay'd the regentship. 2H6 1.03.104
DENIAL 11 FR 0.0012 REL FR 9 V 2 P
word of denial in thy labras here! WIV 1.01.163
word of denial! 1.01.164
him that gracious denial which he is most glad MM 3.01.165 P
never make denial; SHR 2.01.279
and would seem | to have us make denial. AWW 1.02. 9
he's fortified against any denial. TN 1.05.145 P
life, | in your denial i would find no sense. 1.05.266
your grant, or your denial, shall be mine. 3H6 3.03.130
my moneys, be not ceas'd | with slight denial; TIM 2.01. 17
the worst is but denial and reproving. LUC 242
he in the worst sense consters their denial: 324
DENIALS 3 FR 0.0003 REL FR 3 V 0 P
to grant may never | be held by you denials. COR 5.03. 81
make denials | increase your services; CYM 2.03. 48
and had in her | the coy denials of young maids, TNK 4.02. 11
/DENIED 1 FR 0.0001 REL FR 1 V 0 P
/we /are /denied /access /unto /his /person 2H4 4.01. 78
DENIED 57 FR 0.0064 REL FR 42 V 15 P
you hear all these matters denied, gentlemen; WIV 1.01.186 P
most manifest, and not denied by himself. MM 4.02.139 P
i durst have denied that before you were so ERR 2.02. 66 P
denied my house for his, me for his wife. 2.02.159
first he denied you had in him no right. 4.02. 7
were shut, | and i denied to enter in my house? 4.04. 64
it must not be denied but i am a plain-dealing ADO 1.03. 32 P
well hop'd thou wouldst have denied beatrice, 5.04.112 P
though so denied fair harbor in my house. LLL 2.01.174
have | with us in venice, if it be denied, MV 3.03. 28
how if the kiss be denied? AYL 4.01. 78 P
and florence is denied before he comes. AWW 1.02. 12
when miracles have by the great'st been denied. 2.01.141
be not denied access, stand at her doors, | and TN 1.04. 16
denied me mine own purse, | which i had 5.01. 90
request, although | 'twere needful i denied it. WT 1.02. 23
minister of honor, | lest she should be denied. 2.02. 49
hatred | the child-bed privilege denied, which 3.02.103
you denied to fight with me this other day, 5.02.128 P
hast thou denied thyself a faulconbridge? JN 1.01.251
i am denied to sue my livery here, | and yet my R2 2.03.129
attorneys are denied me, | and therefore 2.03.134
he prays but faintly, and would be denied, | we 5.03.103
not with such strength denied | as is delivered 1H4 1.03. 25
when ever yet was your appeal denied? 2H4 4.01. 88
that strength of speech is utterly denied me. 4.05.217
brother, so denied, | but your request shall H5 5.02.343
thy father, minos, that denied our course; 3H6 5.06. 22
free pardon to each man that has denied | the H8 1.02.100
whom troy hath still denied, but this antenor, TRO 3.03. 22
have you | ere now denied the asker; COR 2.03.206
so it cannot be denied but peace is a great 4.05.228 P
who like a block hath denied my access to thee. 5.02. 78 P
nephews kneel for grace, | i will not be denied. TIT 1.01.481
i'll know his grievance, or be much denied. ROM 1.01.157
necessity belong'd to't, and yet was denied. TIM 3.02. 14 P
i tell you, denied, my lord. 3.02. 16 P
denied that honorable man? 3.02. 18 P
i should ne'er have denied his occasion so many 3.02. 24 P
and he that's once denied will hardly speed. 3.02. 62
base metal, | for they have all denied him. 3.03. 7
have they denied him? 3.03. 7
has ventidius and lucullus denied him, | and 3.03. 8
base | to sue and be denied such common grace. 3.05. 94
for certain sums of gold, which you denied me; JC 4.03. 70
gold to pay my legions, | which you denied me. 4.03. 77
i denied you not. 4.03. 82
i, that denied thee gold, will give my heart: 4.03.104
his letters, and denied | his access to me. HAM 2.01.106
denied me to come in) return, and force | their LR 3.02. 66
i requir'd them, | the which you both denied. ANT 2.02. 89
though it cannot be denied what i have done by 2.06. 89 P
'gainst pompey, presently denied him rivality, 3.05. 8 P
that will not be denied your highness' presence. 5.02.234
that's as much as you would be denied | of your PER 2.03.105
now or never, sister, | speak, not to be denied. TNK 3.06.186
hide, | by self-example mayst thou be denied. SON 142.14
DENIEDST 1 FR 0.0001 REL FR 1 V 0 P
since thou deniedst the gentle king to speak. 3H6 2.02.172
DENIER 3 FR 0.0003 REL FR 1 V 2 P
no, not a denier. SHR in.1. 9 P
i'll not pay a denier. 1H4 3.03. 79 P
my dukedom to a beggarly denier, | i do mistake R3 1.02.251
DENIES 13 FR 0.0014 REL FR 11 V 2 P
here's a gentlewoman denies all that you have MM 5.01.282 P
though thou wouldst deny, denies thee vantage. 5.01.413
both one and other he denies me now. ERR 4.03. 85
the goldsmith here | denies that saying. 5.01.275
and whatsoever a man denies, you are now bound 5.01.306 P
she not denies it. ADO 4.01.173
a greater pow'r than we denies all this, | and JN 2.01.368
what merit's in that reason which denies | the TRO 2.02. 24
more | that womanhood denies my tongue to tell. TIT 2.03.174
that macduff denies his person | at our great MAC 3.04.127
then hamlet does it not, hamlet denies it. HAM 5.02.236
now he denies it faintly, and laughs it out. OTH 4.01.112
as i dare kill this cousin that denies it, | so TNK 3.06.166
DENIEST 2 FR 0.0002 REL FR 2 V 0 P
if thou deniest it twenty times, thou liest, R2 4.01. 38
give to dogs | what thou deniest to men. TIM 4.03.530
DENIS 5 FR 0.0005 REL FR 3 V 2 P
saint denis to saint cupid! LLL 5.02. 87
saint denis be my speed! H5 5.02.183 P
and i, between saint denis and saint george, 5.02.207 P
no longer on saint denis will we cry, | but joan 1H6 1.06. 28
saint denis bless this happy stratagem! 3.02. 18
DENI'ST 1 FR 0.0001 REL FR 0 V 1 P
if thou deni'st the least syllable of thy LR 2.02. 24 P
/DENMARK 1 FR 0.0001 REL FR 0 V 1 P
/dungeons, /denmark /being /one /o' /th' /worst. HAM 2.02.246 P
DENMARK 18 FR 0.0020 REL FR 14 V 4 P
in which the majesty of buried denmark | did HAM 1.01. 48
than is the throne of denmark to thy father. 1.02. 49
from whence though willingly i came to denmark 1.02. 52
and let thine eye look like a friend on denmark. 1.02. 69
be as ourself in denmark. 1.02.122
no jocund health that denmark drinks to-day, 1.02.125
than the main voice of denmark goes withal. 1.03. 28
something is rotten in the state of denmark. 1.04. 90
me, so the whole ear of denmark | is by a forged 1.05. 36
let not the royal bed of denmark be | a couch 1.05. 82
at least i am sure it may be so in denmark. 1.05.109
never a villain dwelling in all denmark — | but 1.05.123
for my uncle is king of denmark, and those that 2.02.364 P
com'st thou to beard me in denmark? 2.02.424 P
the king himself for your succession in denmark? 3.02.342 P
where is the beauteous majesty of denmark? 4.05. 21
why, here in denmark. 5.01.161 P
your lordship is right welcome back to denmark. 5.02. 81
/DENMARK'S 1 FR 0.0001 REL FR 0 V 1 P
/denmark's /a /prison. HAM 2.02.243 P
DENMARK'S 2 FR 0.0002 REL FR 2 V 0 P
importing denmark's health and england's too, HAM 5.02. 21
successive kings | in denmark's crown have worn. 5.02.274
DENNIS 1 FR 0.0001 REL FR 0 V 1 P
holla, dennis! AYL 1.01. 87 P
DENNY 1 FR 0.0001 REL FR 1 V 0 P
'tis true; where is he, denny? H8 5.01. 82
/DENOTE 3 FR 0.0003 REL FR 3 V 0 P
(the better to /denote her to the doctor, | for WIV 4.06. 39
thy wild acts /denote | the unreasonable fury of ROM 3.03.110
/shapes of grief, | that can /denote me truly. HAM 1.02. 83
DENOTE 2 FR 0.0002 REL FR 2 V 0 P
and his own courses will denote him so | that i OTH 4.01.279
then love doth well denote | love's eye is not SON 148. 7
DENOTED 1 FR 0.0001 REL FR 1 V 0 P
but this denoted a foregone conclusion. OTH 3.03.428
/DENOTEMENT 1 FR 0.0001 REL FR 0 V 1 P
mark, and /denotement of her parts and graces. OTH 2.03.317 P
DENOUNC'D 2 FR 0.0002 REL FR 2 V 0 P
bitterness of soul | denounc'd against thee, are R3 1.03.179
if not denounc'd against us, why should not we ANT 3.07. 5
DENOUNCE 1 FR 0.0001 REL FR 1 V 0 P
i will denounce a curse upon his head. JN 3.01.319
DENOUNCING 1 FR 0.0001 REL FR 1 V 0 P
plainly denouncing vengeance upon john. JN 3.04.159
DENS 2 FR 0.0002 REL FR 2 V 0 P
whiles lions war and battle for their dens, 3H6 2.05. 74
civil streets, | and citizens to their dens. ANT 5.01. 17
DENUNCIATION 1 FR 0.0001 REL FR 1 V 0 P
save that we do the denunciation lack | of MM 1.02.148
DENY *(also denay, etc.)*
/DENY 3 FR 0.0003 REL FR 3 V 0 P
/mine /own /tongue /deny /my /sacred /state, R2 4.01.209
/my /acts, /decrees, /and /statutes /i /deny; 4.01.213
/she /cannot /deny /it. LR 3.06. 51
DENY 137 FR 0.0154 REL FR 110 V 27 P
how to deny them, who t' advance, and who | to TMP 1.02. 80
to be your fellow | you may deny me, but i'll be 3.01. 85
nay, that i can deny by a circumstance. TGV 1.01. 84 P
i not deny | the jury, passing on the prisoner's MM 2.01. 18
which, though thou wouldst deny, denies thee 5.01.413
villain, thou didst deny the gold's receipt, ERR 2.02. 17
gold, | and that i did deny my wife and house. 3.01. 9
and why dost thou deny the bag of gold? 4.04. 96
me, | though most dishonestly he doth deny it. 5.01. 3
with circumstance and oaths so to deny | this 5.01. 16
this chain you had of me, can you deny it? 5.01. 22
i think i had, i never did deny it. 5.01. 23
who heard me to deny it or forswear it? 5.01. 25
i think it be, sir, i deny it not. 5.01.379
i think i did, sir, i deny it not. 5.01.381
could she here deny | the story that is printed ADO 4.01.121
i confess nothing, nor i deny nothing. 4.01.272 P
you kill me to deny it. farewell. 4.01.291 P

and this is more, masters, than you can deny. 4.02. 60 P
i would not deny you, but, by this good day, i 5.04. 94 P
if it were, i deny her virginity; LLL 1.01.296 P
but an ethiop were, | and deny himself for jove, 4.03.117
if you deny to dance, let's hold more chat. 5.02.228
you may not deny it; 5.02.706 P
if this thou do deny, let our hands part, 5.02.811
if this, or more than this, i would deny, | to 5.02.813
then by your side no bed–room me deny; MND 2.02. 51
and wherefore doth lysander | deny your love (so 3.02.229
you must not deny me; MV 2.02.178 P
of the state, | if they deny him justice. 3.02.279
lord, | if law, authority, and power deny not, 3.02.289
the duke cannot deny the course of law; 3.03. 26
i do desire you | not to deny this imposition, 3.04. 33
if you deny it, let the danger light | upon your 4.01. 38
if you deny me, fie upon your law! 4.01.101
i pray you, | not to deny me, and to pardon me. 4.01.424
more, | and you in love shall not deny me this! 4.01.429
i could not for my heart deny it him. 5.01.165
could add a lie unto a fault, | i would deny it; 5.01.187
and begg'd the ring, the which i did deny him, 5.01.212
as you, | i'll not deny him any thing i have, 5.01.227
me much guilty to deny so fair and excellent AYL 1.02.184 P
that i can make, | or else by him my love deny, 4.03. 62
if she deny to wed, i'll crave the day | when i SHR 2.01.179
deny him, forswear him, or else we are all 5.01.110 P
if they deny to come, | swinge me them soundly 5.02.103
they say our french lack language to deny | if AWW 2.01. 20
do all they deny her? 2.03. 86 P
now his important blood will nought deny | that 3.07. 21
i neither can nor will deny | but that i know 5.03.166
what shall you ask of me that i'll deny, | that TN 3.04.211
will you deny me now? 3.04.347
do not deny. 4.01. 58
ay, husband. can he that deny? 5.01.144
you must not now deny it is your hand; 5.01.331
if i then deny it, | 'tis none of mine. WT 1.02.266
which to deny concerns more than avails; 3.02. 86
as faithfully as i deny the devil. JN 1.01.252
should use to do me wrong | deny their office; 4.01.118
and deny his youth | the rich advantage of good 4.02. 59
so strait | and so ingrateful, you deny me that. 5.07. 43
sue | his livery, and deny his off'red homage, R2 2.01.204
my liege, i did deny no prisoners, | but i 1H4 1.03. 29
why, yet he doth deny his prisoners, | but with 1.03. 77
reverence, a whoremaster, that i utterly deny. 2.04.470 P
i deny your major. 2.04.495 P
if you will deny the sheriff, so, if not, let 2.04.495 P
thou speak'st as if i would deny my name. 5.04. 60
if the man were alive and would deny it, 'zounds 5.04.152 P
canst thou deny it? 2H4 2.01. 93 P
deny it if thou canst. 2.01.103 P
the good–year, do you think i would deny her? 2.04.177 P
and means to boot, | deny it to a king? 3.01. 30
if she deny the appearance of a naked blind boy H5 5.02.296 P
how canst thou tell she will deny thy suit, 1H6 5.03. 75
graceless, wilt thou deny thy parentage? 5.04. 14
deny me not, i prithee, gentle joan. 5.04. 20
dost thou deny thy father, cursed drab? 5.04. 32
his son am i, deny it if you can. 2H6 4.02.146
therefore deny it not. 4.02.150 P
and here comes clifford to deny their bail. 5.01.123
if thou deny, their blood upon thy head, | for 3H6 2.02.129
lands, | which we in justice cannot well deny, 3.02. 5
it were dishonor to deny it her. 3.02. 9
can you deny all this? R3 1.01. 96
you may deny that you were not the mean | of my 1.03. 89
and then deny her aiding hand therein | and lay 1.03. 95
if she deny, lord hastings, go with him, | and 3.01. 35
if you deny them, all the land will rue it. 3.07.222
my lord, he doth deny to come. 5.03.343
so dear in heart not to deny her that | a woman H8 2.02.110
i do deny it. 2.04. 94
officious lords, | i dare and must deny it. 3.02.238
i have a suit which you must not deny me: 5.02.195
come, he is here, my lord, do not deny him. TRO 4.02. 49
to you, yet dare i never | deny your asking. COR 1.06. 65
do require our voices, we ought not to deny him. 2.03. 2 P
he's not confirm'd, we may deny him yet. 2.03.209
and will deny him. 2.03.210
which | great nature cries, "deny not." 5.03. 33
else to ask but that | which you deny already. 5.03. 89
which of you all | will now deny to dance? ROM 1.05. 19
deny thy father and refuse thy name; 2.02. 34
form, fain, fain deny | what i have spoke, but 2.02. 88
do not deny to him that you love me. 4.01. 24
he does deny him (in respect of his) | what TIM 3.02. 74
deny me this, | and an eternal curse fall on you MAC 4.01.104
which the poor heart would fain deny, and dare 5.03. 28
your own liberty if you deny your griefs to your HAM 3.02.339 P
commune with your grief, | or you deny me right. 4.05.204
what /i /should deny | (as this i would, /ay, LR 2.01. 70
would he deny his letter, said he? 2.01. 78
varlet art thou, to deny thou knowest me? 2.02. 28 P
deny to speak with me? 2.04. 88
soul | what you would ask me that i should deny, OTH 3.03. 69
i will deny thee nothing. 3.03. 76
i will deny thee nothing; 3.03. 83
shall i deny you? no. farewell, my lord. 3.03. 86
for to deny each article with oath | cannot 5.02. 54
though thou deny me a matter of more weight; ANT 1.02. 68 P
that what they do delay, they not deny. 2.01. 3
which the wise pow'rs | deny us for our good; 2.01. 7
yes, something you can deny for your own safety: 2.06. 91 P
there i deny my land service. 2.06. 94 P
and i will kill thee if thou dost deny | thou'st CYM 2.04.145
i'll deny nothing. 2.04.146
i'll make bold your highness | cannot deny. 5.05. 90
who should deny it? PER 4.02.133 P
a courtesy | which if we should deny, the most 5.01. 59
not love at all! who shall deny me? TNK 2.02.166
if i priz'd life so much | as to deny my act; 3.02. 24
by that you would have trembled to deny | a 3.06.204
that you would nev'r deny me any thing | fit for 3.06.234
if thou deny, then force must work my way, | for LUC 513
an ethiope were, | and deny himself for jove, PP 16.17
for shame deny that thou bear'st love to any, SON 10. 1
eyes), | but the defendant doth that plea deny, 46. 7

DENYING 7 FR 0.0008 REL FR 4 V 3 P
you wrong me more, sir, in denying it. ERR 4.01. 67
which i denying, they fell sick and died. MV 3.04. 71
his friend here in necessity and denying him; TN 3.04.387 P
'tis a sickness denying thee any thing; WT 4.02. 2 P
fashion of your country in denying me a kiss; H5 5.02.274 P
she may do more, sir, than denying that: R3 1.03. 93
defying, | heart's denying, causer of this. PP 17. 4

DENY'T 4 FR 0.0004 REL FR 4 V 0 P
with more strength | than thou hast to deny't. COR 5.03.177
raise me this beggar, and deny't that lord, TIM 4.03. 9
any heart alive | to hear the men deny't. MAC 3.06. 16
prithee, valiant youth, | deny't again. CYM 5.05.290

DEO 1 FR 0.0001 REL FR 0 V 1 P
laus deo, /bone intelligo. LLL 5.01. 27 P

DEPART 68 FR 0.0076 REL FR 56 V 12 P
to thee, | that i may venture to depart alone. TGV 4.03. 36
at my depart | i gave this unto julia. 5.04. 96
have you to say | when you depart from him, but, MM 4.01. 68
and hearing how hastily you are to depart, i am 4.03. 51 P
be rul'd by me, depart in patience, | and let us ERR 3.01. 94
i will depart in quiet, | and in despite of 3.01.107
and did not i in rage depart from thence? 4.04. 76
therefore depart, and leave him here with me. 5.01.108
be quiet and depart, thou shalt not have him. 5.01.112
but when you depart from me, sorrow abides and ADO 1.01.101 P
why then depart in peace, and let the child wake 3.03. 69 P
i humbly give you leave to depart, and if a 5.01.325 P
yea, signior, and depart when you bid me. 5.02. 44 P
therefore i will depart unkiss'd. 5.02. 54 P
which we much rather had depart withal, | and LLL 2.01.146
sweet hearts, we shall be rich ere we depart, 5.02. 1
and they, well mock'd, depart away with shame. 5.02.156
you, | and you embrace th' occasion to depart. MV 1.01. 64
therefore tremble and depart. AYL 5.01. 57 P
with my lady, and will by and by depart. TN 3.04.175 P
i prithee, foolish greek, depart from me. 4.01. 18
so you shall pay your fees | when you depart, WT 1.02. 54
depart, | and yet partake no venom (for his 2.01. 40
unlawful business | i am about, let them depart. 5.03. 97
bear mine to him, and so depart in peace. JN 1.01. 23
lo this is all — nay, yet depart not so; R2 1.02. 63
depart the chamber, leave us here alone. 2H4 4.05. 90
let him depart, his passport shall be made, H5 4.03. 36
see the coast clear'd, and then we will depart. 1H6 1.03. 89
now, quiet soul, depart when heaven please, 3.02.110
and then depart to paris to the king, | for 3.02.128
i had in charge at my depart for france, | as 2H6 1.01. 2
if i depart from thee, i cannot live, | and in 3.02.388
set, | it is our pleasure one of them depart; 4.01.140
were brought me of your loss and his depart. 3H6 2.01.110
i would your highness would depart the field, 2.02. 73
at my depart, these were his very words: 4.01. 92
if it be so, then both depart to him; 4.01.138
let him depart before we need his help. 5.04. 49
that you depart, and lay no hands on me. R3 1.04.191
i cannot tell if to depart in silence, | or 3.07.141
you are moved, prince, let us depart, i pray, TRO 5.02. 36
madam, depart at pleasure, leave us here. TIT 5.02.145
for this time all the rest depart away. ROM 1.01. 98
once more, on pain of death, all men depart. 1.01.103
coldly of your grievances, | or else depart; 3.01. 53
from this /palace of dim night | depart again. 5.03.108
ere we depart, we'll share a bounteous time | in TIM 1.01.254
a fool of thee. depart. 4.03.232
and, by my honor, | depart untouch'd. JC 3.01.142
with this i depart, that, as i slew my best 3.02. 44 P
good countrymen, let me depart alone, | and, for 3.02. 55
i do entreat you, not a man depart, | save i 3.02. 60
come like shadows, so depart. MAC 4.01.111
we'll teach you to drink /deep ere you depart. HAM 1.02.175
strange that they should so depart from home, LR 2.04. 1
i will have my revenge ere i depart his house. 3.05. 1 P
to live, | the loathness to depart would grow. CYM 1.01.108
you shall have better cheer | ere you depart, 3.06. 67
of meat, depart reeling with too much drink; 5.04.161 P
he would depart, i'll give some light unto you. PER 1.03. 17
yet, ere you shall depart, this we desire, | as 1.03. 38
brief, he must hence depart to tyre: 3.ch. 39
since his depart, his sports, | though craving TNK 1.03. 27
i may depart with little, while i live; 2.01. 1 P
the poor fool prays her that he may depart. VEN 578
what could death do if thou shouldst depart, SON 6.11
as easy might i from myself depart | as from my 109. 3

DEPARTED 8 FR 0.0009 REL FR 8 V 0 P
i from thee departed | thy penitent reform'd. WT 1.02.238
whole, | hath willingly departed with a part, JN 2.01.563
how would it fare with your departed souls? 2H6 4.07.116
as you wish christian peace to souls departed, H8 4.02.156
vault, | if i departed not and left him there. ROM 5.03.277
maid, that out a maid | never departed more." HAM 4.05. 55
observ'd him | since our great lord departed? TNK 1.03. 34
ere i departed, a great likelihood | of both 4.01. 6

DEPARTEDST 1 FR 0.0001 REL FR 1 V 0 P
why thou departedst from thy native home, | and ERR 1.01. 29

DEPARTEST 1 FR 0.0001 REL FR 1 V 0 P
in one of thine, from that which thou departest, SON 11. 2

DEPARTING 4 FR 0.0004 REL FR 4 V 0 P
praise in departing. TMP 3.03. 39
the first departing of the king for ireland. R2 2.01.290
bell, | rememb'red tolling a departing friend. 2H4 1.01.103
a deadly groan, like life and death's departing. 3H6 2.06. 43

DEPARTS 1 FR 0.0001 REL FR 1 V 0 P
he thence departs a heavy convertite, | she LUC 743

DEPART'ST 1 FR 0.0001 REL FR 1 V 0 P
that thou depart'st hence safe | does pay thy ANT 4.14. 36

DEPARTURE 21 FR 0.0023 REL FR 16 V 5 P
desert, | is privilege for thy departure hence. TGV 3.01.160
times | his julia gave it him at his departure: 4.04.135
and i pray god grant them a fair departure. MV 1.02.111 P
i am glad of your departure. AYL 3.02.293 P
and this morning your departure hence, it AWW 4.03. 94 P
my people did expect my hence departure | two WT 1.02.450
you knew of his departure, as you know | what 3.02. 77
so), which is another spur to my departure. 4.02. 9 P
on their departure most of all show evil. JN 3.04.115
looking awry upon your lord's departure, | find R2 2.02. 21
more than your lord's departure weep not — more 2.02. 25
we license your departure with your son. 1H4 1.03.123
break with your wives of your departure hence. 3.01.142
and at the time of my departure thence | he was 4.01. 23
to know the cause of your abrupt departure. 1H6 2.03. 30
and mine shall ring thy dire departure out. 4.02. 41
a drowsy head | have i since your departure had, R3 5.03.229
that's a maid now, and laughs at my departure, LR 1.05. 51
if they suffer our departure, death's the word. ANT 1.02.135 P
who needs must know of her departure and | dost CYM 4.03. 10
further to question me of your king's departure. PER 1.03. 11

DEPECHE 1 FR 0.0001 REL FR 0 V 1 P
depeche, quickly. WIV 1.04. 54 P

DEPEND 15 FR 0.0017 REL FR 11 V 4 P
i find my zenith doth depend upon | a most TMP 1.02.181
my soldier, bidding me depend | upon thy stars, JN 3.01.125
you depend upon him, i mean. TRO 3.01. 4 P
sir, i do depend upon the lord. 3.01. 5 P
you depend upon a notable gentleman; 3.01. 6 P
this day's black fate on moe days doth depend, ROM 3.01.119
or shall we on, and not depend on you? JC 3.01.217
and the remainders that shall still depend, | to LR 1.04.250
be fast to my hopes, if i depend on the issue? OTH 1.03.362 P
a season, but our jealousy | does yet depend. CYM 4.03. 23
poor wretches that depend | on greatness' favor 5.04.127
on whose grace | you may depend hereafter. PER 3.03. 41
honor and honesty | i cherish and depend on, TNK 3.01. 51
than that which on thy humor doth depend. SON 92. 8
"'now all these hearts that do on mine depend, LC 274

DEPENDANCE 1 FR 0.0001 REL FR 1 V 0 P
for 'tis a cause that hath no mean dependance TRO 2.02.192

DEPENDANCY 3 FR 0.0003 REL FR 3 V 0 P
of sense, | such a dependancy of thing on thing, MM 5.01. 62
let me report to him | your sweet dependancy, ANT 5.02. 26
(on whom there is no more dependancy | but brats CYM 2.03.118

DEPENDANT 2 FR 0.0002 REL FR 2 V 0 P
i am your free dependant. MM 4.03. 91
thereon dependant, for your brother's life — 5.01.406

DEPENDANTS 4 FR 0.0004 REL FR 2 V 2 P
ward of mine honor is rewarding my dependants. LLL 3.01.133 P
all his dependants | which labor'd after him to TIM 1.01. 85
in the general dependants as in the duke himself LR 1.04. 61 P
who, with some other of the lord's dependants, 3.07. 18

DEPENDED 1 FR 0.0001 REL FR 1 V 0 P
seeing the worst, which late on hopes depended. OTH 1.03.203

DEPENDER 1 FR 0.0001 REL FR 1 V 0 P
expect | to be depender on a thing that leans? CYM 1.05. 58

DEPENDING 9 FR 0.0010 REL FR 7 V 2 P
will, | and not depending on his friendly wish. TGV 1.03. 62
thy living is a life, | so stinkingly depending? MM 3.02. 27
father's imposition depending on the caskets. MV 1.02.105 P
ask | than whereupon our weal, on you depending, JN 4.02. 65
"the care on thee depending | hath fed upon the 2H4 4.05.158
is the curse depending on those that war for a TRO 2.03. 19 P
on whom depending, their obedience fails | to COR 3.01.165
standing, nicely | depending on their brands. CYM 2.04. 91
in me moe woes than words are now depending, LUC 1615

DEPENDS 11 FR 0.0012 REL FR 9 V 2 P
a thought that more depends on it than we must MM 4.02.124 P
there's more depends on this than on the value. MV 4.01.434
tell me whereon the /likelihood depends. AYL 1.03. 57
your right depends not on his life or death. 3H6 1.02. 11
he that depends | upon your favors swims with COR 1.01.179
for on his choice depends | the safety and HAM 1.03. 20
that spirit upon whose weal depends and rests 3.03. 14
witchcraft, | and wit depends on dilatory time. OTH 2.03.373
cleopatra's, which wholly depends on your abode. ANT 1.02.175 P
stay, | for it depends upon that love of thine. SON 92. 4
both truth and beauty on my love depends; 101. 3

DEPLORE 1 FR 0.0001 REL FR 1 V 0 P
more | will i my master's tears to you deplore. TN 3.01.162

DEPLORING 1 FR 0.0001 REL FR 1 V 0 P
to their instruments | tune a deploring dump — TGV 3.02. 84

DEPOPULATE 1 FR 0.0001 REL FR 1 V 0 P
is this viper | that would depopulate the city, COR 3.01.263

/DEPOS'D 1 FR 0.0001 REL FR 1 V 0 P
/may /deem /that /you /are /worthily /depos'd. R2 4.01.227

DEPOS'D 17 FR 0.0019 REL FR 17 V 0 P
be by some certain king purg'd and depos'd. JN 2.01.372
how some have been depos'd, some slain in war, R2 3.02.157
must he be depos'd? 3.03.144
is already, and depos'd | 'tis doubt he will be. 3.04. 68
why dost thou say king richard is depos'd? 3.04. 77
hath bullingbrook depos'd | thine intellect? 5.01. 27
he intercepted did return | to be depos'd, and 1H4 1.03.152
in short time after, he depos'd the king, | soon 4.03. 90
depos'd his nephew richard, edward's son, | the 1H6 2.05. 64
seiz'd on the realm, depos'd the rightful king, 2H6 2.02. 24
and bashful henry depos'd, whose cowardice 3H6 1.01. 41
think not that henry shall be so depos'd. 1.01.153
depos'd he shall be, in despite of all. 1.01.154
she weeps, and says her henry is depos'd; 3.01. 45
you are the king king edward hath depos'd; 3.01. 69
yet that, by you depos'd, you quake like rebels? R3 1.03.161
lepidus of the triumpherate | should be depos'd; ANT 3.06. 29

/DEPOSE 1 FR 0.0001 REL FR 1 V 0 P
/you /may /my /glories /and /my /state /depose, R2 4.01.192

DEPOSE 9 FR 0.0010 REL FR 8 V 1 P
a time | when i'll depose i had him in mine arms MM 5.01.198
law, | depose him in the justice of his cause. R2 1.03. 30
which art possess'd now to depose thyself. 2.01.108
the breath of worldly men cannot depose | the 3.02. 56
depose me? 1H4 2.04.435 P
the duke yet lives that henry shall depose; 2H6 1.04. 30
"the duke yet lives that henry shall depose; 1.04. 59
then, seeing 'twas he that made you to depose, 3H6 1.02. 26
loath to depose the child, your brother's son; R3 3.07.209

DEPOSED 4 FR 0.0004 REL FR 4 V 0 P
save our deposed bodies to the ground? R2 3.02.150
some haunted by the ghosts they have deposed, 3.02.158
what, think you the king shall be deposed? 3.04. 67
say, | king pepin, which deposed childeric, H5 1.02. 65

/DEPOSING 1 FR 0.0001 REL FR 1 V 0 P
/containing /the /deposing /of /a /king, | /and R2 4.01.234

DEPOSING 2 FR 0.0002 REL FR 2 V 0 P

deposing thee before thou wert possess'd, R2 2.01.107
for the deposing of a rightful king. 5.01. 50
DEPOSITARIES 1 FR 0.0001 REL FR 1 V 0 P
made you my guardians, my depositaries, | but LR 2.04.251
DEPRAVATION 1 FR 0.0001 REL FR 1 V 0 P
without a theme | for depravation, to square the TRO 5.02.132
DEPRAV'D 1 FR 0.0001 REL FR 1 V 0 P
not believe | with how deprav'd a quality — o LR 2.04.137
DEPRAVE 1 FR 0.0001 REL FR 1 V 0 P
that lie and cog and flout, deprave and slander, ADO 5.01. 95
DEPRAVED 1 FR 0.0001 REL FR 1 V 0 P
who lives that's not depraved or depraves? TIM 1.02.140
DEPRAVES 1 FR 0.0001 REL FR 1 V 0 P
who lives that's not depraved or depraves? TIM 1.02.140
DEPRESS'D 1 FR 0.0001 REL FR 1 V 0 P
depress'd he is already, and depos'd | 'tis R2 3.04. 68
DEPRIV'D 6 FR 0.0006 REL FR 6 V 0 P
soon after that, depriv'd him of his life, | and 1H4 4.03. 91
obscur'd, | depriv'd of honor and inheritance. 1H6 2.05. 27
each part, depriv'd of supple government, ROM 4.01.102
thy most ingenious sense | depriv'd thee of! HAM 5.01.249
that hath depriv'd me of your grace and favor, LR 1.01.229
is wretchedness depriv'd that benefit, | to end 4.06. 61
DEPRIVE 3 FR 0.0003 REL FR 3 V 0 P
which might deprive your sovereignty of reason, HAM 1.04. 73
permit | the curiosity of nations to deprive me, LR 1.02. 4
'tis honor to deprive dishonor'd life, | the one LUC 1186
DEPRIVED 1 FR 0.0001 REL FR 1 V 0 P
life was mine which thou hast here deprived. LUC 1752
DEPTH 8 FR 0.0009 REL FR 6 V 2 P
and i, to sound the depth of this knavery. SHR 5.01.137 P
a spirit rais'd from depth of under ground, 2H6 1.02. 79
to weep is to make less the depth of grief: 3H6 2.01. 85
in a sea of glory, | but far beyond my depth. H8 3.02.361
finds bottom in th' uncomprehensive depth, TRO 3.03.198
for i was come to the whole depth of my tale, ROM 2.04. 99 P
the law, which is past depth | to those that, TIM 3.05. 12
o, i were damn'd beneath all depth in hell | but OTH 5.02.137
DEPTHS 1 FR 0.0001 REL FR 1 V 0 P
and sounded all the depths and shoals of honor, H8 3.02.436
/DEPUTATION 1 FR 0.0001 REL FR 1 V 0 P
say to great caesar this in /deputation: ANT 3.13. 74
DEPUTATION 4 FR 0.0004 REL FR 4 V 0 P
and given his deputation all the organs | of our MM 1.01. 20
and that his friends by deputation could not 1H4 4.01. 32
king | in deputation left behind him here, 4.03. 87
agamemnon, | thy topless deputation he puts on, TRO 1.03.152
DEPUTE 2 FR 0.0002 REL FR 1 V 1 P
come from venice to depute cassio in othello's OTH 4.02.221 P
but those we will depute which shall invest TNK 1.04. 10
DEPUTED 1 FR 0.0001 REL FR 1 V 0 P
not the king's crown, nor the deputed sword, MM 2.02. 60
DEPUTIES 1 FR 0.0001 REL FR 1 V 0 P
hail, you anointed deputies of heaven! JN 3.01.136
DEPUTING 1 FR 0.0001 REL FR 1 V 0 P
him home, | deputing cassio in his government. OTH 4.01.237
DEPUTY *(also debuty)*
DEPUTY 23 FR 0.0026 REL FR 17 V 6 P
and the new deputy now for the duke — | whether
MM 1.02.157
that she make friends | to the strict deputy; 1.02.181
this outward–sainted deputy, | whose settled 3.01. 88
advantag'd, and the corrupt deputy scal'd. 3.01.255 P
picklock, which we have sent to the deputy. 3.02. 18 P
he must before the deputy, sir, he has given him 3.02. 34 P
the deputy cannot abide a whoremaster. 3.02. 35 P
what is the news from this good deputy? 4.01. 27
it is a bitter deputy. 4.02. 78
were you sworn to the duke, or to the deputy? 4.02.183 P
and satisfy the deputy with the visage | of 4.03. 75
hath yet the deputy sent my brother's pardon? 4.03.114
i went | to this pernicious caitiff deputy — 5.01. 88
"great deputy, the welkin's vicegerent, and sole LLL 1.01.219 P
in us, that are our own great deputy, | and bear JN 2.01.365
substitute, | his deputy anointed in his sight, R2 1.02. 38
cannot depose | the deputy elected by the lord; 3.02. 57
majesty, | his captain, steward, deputy, elect, 4.01.126
royal name, | as deputy unto that gracious king, 1H6 5.03.161
i swear, | whose far–unworthy deputy i am, | he 2H6 3.02.286
lucy, | and his contract by deputy in france, R3 3.07. 6
then deputy of ireland, who remov'd, | earl H8 2.01. 42
you sent me deputy for ireland, | far from his 3.02.260
DEPUTY'S 1 FR 0.0001 REL FR 0 V 1 P
marian may be the deputy's wife of the ward to 1H4 3.03.114 P
DERACINATE 2 FR 0.0002 REL FR 2 V 0 P
rusts | that should deracinate such savagery; H5 5.02. 47
rend and deracinate | the unity and married calm TRO 1.03. 99
DERAIGN *(see darraign)*
DERBY 9 FR 0.0010 REL FR 9 V 0 P
lancaster, and derby | am i, who ready here do R2 1.03. 35
harry of herford, lancaster, and derby, 1.03.100
lancaster, and derby | stands here for god, his 1.03.104
henry of herford, lancaster, and derby, | to god 1.03.113
here /come the /lords of buckingham and derby. R3 1.03. 17
the countess richmond, good my lord of derby, 1.03. 20
yet, derby, notwithstanding she's your wife 1.03. 22
saw you the king to–day, my lord of derby? 1.03. 30
namely, to derby, hastings, buckingham — | and 1.03.328
DERCETAS *(see decretas)*
DERE *(also there)*
DERE 3 FR 0.0003 REL FR 0 V 3 P
dere is some simples in my closet, dat i vill WIV 1.04. 63 P
dere is no honest man dat shall come in my 1.04. 74 P
dere is no duke that the court is know to come. 4.05. 88 P
DERIDES 1 FR 0.0001 REL FR 1 V 0 P
who covers faults, at last with shame derides. LR 1.01.281
DERISION 5 FR 0.0005 REL FR 5 V 0 P
scorn and derision never come in tears. MND 3.02.123
up in a poor maid's eyes | with your derision! 3.02.159
contriv'd | to bait me with this foul derision? 3.02.197
wake, all this derision | shall seem a dream and 3.02.370
so, i have derision medicinable | to use between TRO 3.03. 44
DERIVATION 2 FR 0.0002 REL FR 1 V 1 P
of war, and in the derivation of my birth, and H5 3.02.130 P
my derivation was from ancestors | who stood PER 5.01. 90
DERIVATIVE 1 FR 0.0001 REL FR 1 V 0 P
for honor, | 'tis a derivative from me to mine, WT 3.02. 44
DERIV'D 14 FR 0.0015 REL FR 14 V 0 P
that you are well deriv'd. TGV 5.02. 23
thou art a gentleman and well deriv'd, | take 5.04.146
to find out this abuse, whence 'tis deriv'd. MM 5.01.247
i am, my lord, as well deriv'd as he, | as well MND 1.01. 99
and offices | were not deriv'd corruptly, and MV 2.09. 42
conceit is still deriv'd | from some forefather R2 2.02. 34
how is this deriv'd? 2H4 1.01. 23
deriv'd from edward, his great–grandfather. H5 1.01. 89
and when you find him evenly deriv'd | from his 2.04. 91
then, deriv'd | from famous edmund langley, duke
1H6 2.05. 84
tell thee whence thou cam'st, of whom deriv'd, 3H6 1.04.119
mine | that had to him deriv'd your anger did i H8 2.04. 32
service, from whose help | i deriv'd liberty. TIM 1.02. 8
brave son, deriv'd from honorable loins! JC 2.01.322
DERIVE 11 FR 0.0012 REL FR 7 V 4 P
from women's eyes this doctrine i derive: LLL 4.03.298
from women's eyes this doctrine i derive: 4.03.347
or, if we did derive it from our friends, AYL 1.03. 62
when rather from our acts we them derive | than AWW 2.03.136
things which would derive me ill will to speak 5.03.265 P
face put on, derive a liberty | from heartiness, WT 1.02.112
derive this; come. TRO 2.03. 61 P
some other hour, i should derive much from't; TIM 3.04. 69 P
of the war | derive some pain from you. 4.03.162
my brother till you can derive from him better LR 1.02. 81 P
but from thine eyes my knowledge i derive, | and SON 14. 9
DERIVED 3 FR 0.0003 REL FR 3 V 0 P
florentine, | derived from the ancient capilet. AWW 5.03.159
for by my mother i derived am | from lionel duke 1H6 2.05. 74
thou wast not to this end from me derived. LUC 1755
/DERIVES 1 FR 0.0001 REL FR 1 V 0 P
/derives /from /heaven /his /quarrel /and /his 2H4 1.01.206
DERIVES 4 FR 0.0004 REL FR 2 V 2 P
this shame derives itself from unknown loins"? ADO 4.01.135
she derives her honesty and achieves her AWW 1.01. 45 P
his indignation derives itself out of a very TN 3.04.246 P
thy place and blood, | derives itself to me. 2H4 4.05. 43
DERN *(also dearn)*
DERN 1 FR 0.0001 REL FR 1 V 0 P
by many a dern and painful perch, | of pericles PER 3.ch. 15
DEROGATE 3 FR 0.0003 REL FR 1 V 2 P
and from her derogate body never spring | a babe LR 1.04.280
you cannot derogate, my lord. CYM 2.01. 44 P
your issues, being foolish, do not derogate. 2.01. 47 P
DEROGATELY 1 FR 0.0001 REL FR 1 V 0 P
that i should | once name you derogately, when ANT 2.02. 34
DEROGATION 1 FR 0.0001 REL FR 0 V 1 P
is there no derogation in't? CYM 2.01. 43 P
DERRY 2 FR 0.0002 REL FR 2 V 0 P
been merry, | and have pleas'd /ye with a derry, TNK 3.05.139
/ye with a derry, | and a derry and a down, 3.05.140
DES 3 FR 0.0003 REL FR 0 V 3 P
i do not like des toys. WIV 1.04. 44 P
les mots que vous m'avez appris des a present. H5 3.04. 26 P
les langues des hommes sont pleines de 5.02.115 P
DESARTLESS 1 FR 0.0001 REL FR 0 V 1 P
who think you the most desartless man to be ADO 3.03. 9 P
DESCANT 4 FR 0.0004 REL FR 4 V 0 P
and mar the concord with too harsh a descant: TGV 1.02. 91
in the sun | and descant on mine own deformity. R3 1.01. 27
for on that ground i'll make a holy descant — 3.07. 49
care, | to descant on the doubts of my decay. PP 14. 4
DESCANTS 1 FR 0.0001 REL FR 1 V 0 P
while thou on tereus descants better skill. LUC 1134
/DESCEND 1 FR 0.0001 REL FR 1 V 0 P
/descend, and open your uncharged ports. TIM 5.04. 55
DESCEND 21 FR 0.0023 REL FR 18 V 3 P
let her descend, bully, let her descend; WIV 4.05. 21 P
let her descend, bully, let her descend; 4.05. 22 P
the flame will back descend | and turn him to no 5.05. 85
descend, for you must be my torch–bearer. MV 2.06. 40
it, | i'll make the statue move indeed, descend, WT 5.03. 88
descend; 5.03. 99
we will descend and fold him in our arms. R2 1.03. 54
o, pardon me that i descend so low | to show the 1H4 1.03.167
to thee it shall descend with better quiet, 2H4 4.05.187
let the inheritance | descend unto the daughter. H5 1.02.100
i descend | to give thee answer of thy just 1H6 5.03.143
descend to darkness and the burning lake! 2H6 1.04. 39
thou factious duke of york, descend my throne, 3H6 1.01. 74
who art thou that lately didst descend | into TIT 2.03.248
farewell, farewell! one kiss, and i'll descend. ROM 3.05. 42
why i descend into this bed of death | is partly 5.03. 28
descend, and keep your words. TIM 5.04. 64
shall i descend? JC 3.02.160
descend. 3.02.162 P
descend. LR 2.01. 19
descend again into their throats and have not TNK 1.02. 82
/DESCENDED 1 FR 0.0001 REL FR 1 V 0 P
he sits 'mongst men like a /descended god; CYM 1.06.169
DESCENDED 13 FR 0.0014 REL FR 12 V 1 P
and all those oaths | descended into perjury, to TGV 5.04. 49
deed | hadst thou descended from another house. AYL 1.02.228
as heir general, being descended | of blithild, H5 1.02. 66
i am descended of a gentler blood. 1H6 5.04. 8
being all descended to the laboring heart, | who 2H6 3.02.163
my wife descended of the lacies — 4.02. 44 P
descended from the duke of clarence' house. 4.04. 29
one thus descended, | that hath beside well in COR 2.03.245
as i descended? MAC 2.02. 16
a princess | descended of so many royal kings. ANT 5.02.327
as well descended as thyself, and hath | more of CYM 5.05.303
and solemn night with slow sad gait descended LUC 1081
for some, untuck'd, descended her sheav'd hat, LC 31
DESCENDING 3 FR 0.0003 REL FR 3 V 0 P
ascend his throne, descending now from him, R2 4.01.111
thee — that thou cam'st | from good descending? PER 5.01.128
shall cool the heat of this descending sun: VEN 190
DESCENDS 2 FR 0.0002 REL FR 2 V 0 P
from these our henry lineally descends. 3H6 3.03. 87
the flow'r is fall'n, the tree descends. TNK 5.01.169
DESCENSION 1 FR 0.0001 REL FR 0 V 1 P
a heavy descension! 2H4 2.02.173 P
DESCENT 17 FR 0.0019 REL FR 17 V 0 P
with falsehood, cowardice, and poor descent, TGV 3.02. 32
o, that a mighty man of such descent, | of such SHR in.2. 14
and, by the glorious worth of my descent, | this R2 1.01.107
my claim | to my inheritance of free descent. 2.03.136
of edward king, the third of that descent; 1H6 2.05. 66
from whence you spring by lineal descent. 3.01.165
first note that he is near you in descent, | and 2H6 3.01. 21
faults, | yet, by reputing of his high descent, 3.01. 48
and made a preachment of your high descent? 3H6 1.04. 72
show thy descent by gazing 'gainst the sun; 2.01. 92
all confess | that i was not ignoble of descent, 4.01. 70
to bar my master's heirs in true descent — R3 3.02. 54
in his descent than shall my prompted sword TRO 5.02.175
their spring, their head, their true descent, ROM 5.03.218
head | to the descent and dust below thy foot, LR 5.03.138
how of descent | as good as we? CYM 5.05.308
that never relish'd of a base descent. PER 2.05. 60
DESCENTS 1 FR 0.0001 REL FR 1 V 0 P
some four or five descents | since the first AWW 3.07. 24
DESCRIB'D 2 FR 0.0002 REL FR 2 V 0 P
thou hast describ'd | a hot friend cooling. JC 4.02. 18
thou hast well describ'd him. TNK 4.02. 89
DESCRIBE 2 FR 0.0002 REL FR 1 V 1 P
and as thou namest them, i will describe them; MV 1.02. 37 P
describe adonis, and the counterfeit | is poorly SON 53. 5
DESCRIBES 2 FR 0.0002 REL FR 1 V 1 P
how he describes himself! TRO 2.03.209 P
pattern'd by that the poet here describes, | by TIT 4.01. 57
DESCRIED 6 FR 0.0006 REL FR 6 V 0 P
we were descried, they'll mock us now downright.
LLL 5.02.389
ashore | i kill'd a man and fear i was descried. SHR 1.01.232
who hath descried the number of the traitors? R3 5.03. 9
he is descried; ANT 3.07. 54
we have descried, upon our neighboring shore, PER 1.04. 60
for marks descried in men's nativity | are LUC 538
DESCRIPTION 19 FR 0.0021 REL FR 10 V 9 P
slender, i will description the matter to you, WIV 1.01.215 P
a right description of our sport, my lord. LLL 5.02.521
and according to my description level at my MV 1.02. 38 P
before a friend of this description | shall lose 3.02.301
then should i know you by description — | such AYL 4.03. 84
for this description of thine honesty? AWW 4.03.263 P
to follow it and undoes description to do it. WT 5.02. 58 P
poet makes a most excellent description of it. H5 3.06. 38 P
description cannot suit itself in words | to 4.02. 53
your wondrous rare description, noble earl, | of 1H6 5.05. 1
'tis his description. TIM 4.03.409 P
by all description this should be the place. 5.03. 1
maid | that paragons description and wild fame; OTH 2.01. 62
her own person, | it beggar'd all description: ANT 2.02.198
will this description satisfy him? 2.07. 50 P
the description | of what is in her chamber CYM 2.04. 93
this is the very description of their 4.01. 24 P
or his description | prov'd us unspeaking sots. 5.05.177
and he went to bed to her very description. PER 4.02.101 P
DESCRIPTIONS 1 FR 0.0001 REL FR 1 V 0 P
time | i see descriptions of the fairest wights, SON 106. 2
DESCRY 6 FR 0.0006 REL FR 6 V 0 P
what's past and what's to come she can descry. 1H6 1.02. 57
woes | we cannot without circumstance descry. ROM 5.03.181
moreover, to descry | the strength o' th' enemy. LR 4.05. 13
the main descry | stands on the hourly thought. 4.06.213
'twixt the heaven and the main, | descry a sail. OTH 2.01. 4
in helicanus may you well descry | a figure of PER 5.03. 91
DESDEMON 7 FR 0.0008 REL FR 7 V 0 P
of some brief discourse | with desdemon alone. OTH 3.01. 53
not now, sweet desdemon, some other time. 3.03. 55
ah, desdemon! away, away, away! 4.02. 41
have you pray'd to–night, desdemon? 5.02. 25
poor desdemon! 5.02.204
o desdemon! 5.02.281
dead, desdemon! 5.02.281
DESDEMONA 33 FR 0.0037 REL FR 23 V 10 P
iago, | but that i love the gentle desdemona, OTH 1.02. 25
fetch desdemona hither. 1.03.120
to hear | would desdemona seriously incline; 1.03.146
what would you, desdemona? 1.03.247
adieu, brave moor, use desdemona well. 1.03.291
iago, | my desdemona must i leave to thee. 1.03.295
come, desdemona, i have but an hour | of love, 1.03.298
it cannot be long that desdemona should continue 1.03.342 P
letting go safely by | the divine desdemona. 2.01. 73
come, desdemona, | once more, well met at cyprus 2.01.211
desdemona is directly in love with him. 2.01.219 P
and i dare think he'll prove to desdemona | a 2.01.290
us thus early for the love of his desdemona; 2.03. 15 P
to desdemona hath to–night carous'd | potations 2.03. 53
come, desdemona, 'tis the soldiers' life | to 2.03.257
the virtuous desdemona to undertake for me. 2.03.330 P
most easy | th' inclining desdemona to subdue 2.03.340
fool | plies desdemona to repair his fortune, 2.03.354
is that she will to virtuous desdemona | procure 3.01. 35
farewell, my desdemona, i'll come to thee 3.03. 87
why, that the moor first gave to desdemona, 3.03.308
in sleep i heard him say, "sweet desdemona, 3.03.419
how do you, desdemona? 3.04. 35
ply desdemona well, and you are sure on't. 4.01.106
had from me to deliver desdemona would half have 4.02.187 P
i will make myself known to desdemona. 4.02.197 P
the next night following enjoy not desdemona, 4.02.215 P
why, then othello and desdemona return again to 4.02.223 P
and taketh away with him the fair desdemona, 4.02.225 P
will you walk, sir? | o, desdemona! 4.03. 5 P
that i bobb'd from him | as gifts to desdemona; 5.01. 17
ay, desdemona. 5.02. 23
sweet desdemona, o sweet mistress, speak! 5.02.121
DESDEMONA'S 2 FR 0.0002 REL FR 2 V 0 P
make love's quick pants in desdemona's arms, OTH 2.01. 80
i do not think but desdemona's honest. 3.03.225
DESERT* 48 FR 0.0054 REL FR 39 V 9 P
though this island seem to be desert — TMP 2.01. 35 P
and not without desert so well reputed. TGV 2.04. 57
and think my patience, more than thy desert, 3.01.159
(for thou hast shown some sign of good desert) 3.02. 18
this shadowy desert, unfrequented woods, | i 5.04. 2
o, your desert speaks loud, and i should wrong MM 5.01. 9
mean, | my wife (but, i protest, without desert) ERR 3.01.112
and the ill counsel of a desert place | with the MND 2.01.218
i will assume desert. MV 2.09. 51
being native burghers of this desert city, AYL 2.01. 23

can in this desert place buy entertainment, 2.04. 72
a dinner if there live any thing in this desert. 2.06. 18 P
e'er you are | that in this desert inaccessible, 2.07.110
"why should this /a desert be? 3.02.125
as how i came into that desert place — | /in 4.03.141
him, | yet never know how that desert should be. AWW 1.03.200
misprision shackle up | my love and her desert; 2.03.153
it | to some remote and desert place quite out WT 2.03.176
confirm | to more approved service and desert. R2 2.03. 44
let me have right, and let desert mount. 2H4 4.03. 55 P
sooner than quittance of desert and merit, H5 2.02. 34
would i were able to load him with his desert! 3.07. 79 P
our king, | and not of any challenge of desert, 1H6 5.04.153
when i have heard your king's desert recounted, 3H6 3.03.132
for my desert is honor; 3.03.192
and lay those honors on your high desert. R3 1.03. 96
that all without desert have frown'd on me; 2.01. 68
but my desert | unmeritable shuns your high 3.07.154
we will not name desert before his birth, and, TRO 3.02. 94 P
high birth, vigor of bone, desert in service, 3.03.172
mine own desert. COR 2.03. 65 P
your own desert! 2.03. 66 P
but let desert in pure election shine, | and, TIT 1.01. 16
o, none of both but are of high desert. 3.01.170
and dare me to the desert with thy sword; MAC 3.04.103
that would be howl'd out in the desert air, 4.03.194
lord, i will use them according to their desert. HAM 2.02.528 P
use every man after his desert, and who shall 2.02.530 P
you less know how to value her desert | than she LR 2.04.139
that set thee on to this desert, am bound | to CYM 1.05. 73
her countless glory, which desert must gain; PER 1.01. 31
and which, without desert, because thine eye 1.01. 32
grace's pleasure to commend, | not my desert. 2.05. 30
some dark deep desert, seated from the way, LUC 1144
there | where thy desert may merit praise, | by PP 18.15
here | within the knowledge of mine own desert, SON 49.10
as, to behold desert a beggar born, | and needy 66. 2
lie, | to do more for me than mine own desert, 72. 6

DESERTS* 21 FR 0.0023 REL FR 21 V 0 P
dispose of them as thou know'st their deserts. TGV 5.04.159
challenge me, challenge me by these deserts, LLL 5.02.805
the hyrcanian deserts and the vasty wilds | of MV 2.07. 41
are my deserts no better? 2.09. 60
is't possible that my deserts to you | can lack TN 3.04.348
ship hath touch'd upon | the deserts of bohemia? WT 3.03. 2
king | have any way your good deserts forgot, 1H4 4.03. 46
and for these good deserts | we here create you 1H6 3.04. 25
see you well guerdon'd for these good deserts. 2H6 1.04. 46
not my deserts, but what i will deserve. R3 4.04.415
the duke by law | found his deserts. H8 3.02.267
pius | for many good and great deserts to rome. TIT 1.01. 24
plead your deserts in peace and humbleness. 1.01. 45
i give thee thanks in part of thy deserts, | and 1.01.236
forget | the least of these unspeakable deserts, 1.01.256
base o' th' mount | is rank'd with all deserts, TIM 1.01. 65
take my deserts to his, and join 'em both; 3.05. 78
wherein of antres vast and deserts idle, | rough OTH 1.03.140
to the deserver | till his deserts are past, ANT 1.02.187
if it were fill'd with your most high deserts? SON 17. 2
all | wherein i should your great deserts repay, 117. 2

/DESERV'D 1 FR 0.0001 REL FR 0 V 1 P
/deserv'd /at /the /hands /of /fortune, /that HAM 2.02.240 P

DESERV'D 53 FR 0.0060 REL FR 42 V 11 P
rock, | who hadst deserv'd more than a prison. TMP 1.02.362
thou thy silvia, for thou hast deserv'd her. TGV 5.04.147
a madman, | wherein have i so deserv'd of you, MM 5.01.502
much deserv'd on his part, and equally ADO 1.01. 12 P
he would have deserv'd it. MND 4.02. 23 P
and know how well i have deserv'd this ring, MV 4.01.446
that begg'd it, and indeed | deserv'd it too; 5.01.181
what, are we cuckolds ere we have deserv'd it? 5.01.265
sir, you have well deserv'd. AYL 1.02.242
albeit you have deserv'd | high commendation, 1.02.262
spoke, unpitied let me die, | and well deserv'd. AWW 2.01.189
i have not, my lord, deserv'd it. 2.03.220 P
i know not how i have deserv'd to run into my 2.05. 34 P
no matter, his heels have deserv'd it, in 4.03.103 P
shall know your mistress | has deserv'd prison, WT 2.01.120
i have deserv'd | all tongues to talk their 3.02.215
very nobly | have you deserv'd. 4.04.518
what hath this day deserv'd? JN 3.01. 84
of the lamb, vary deserv'd praise on my palfrey. H5 3.07. 33 P
richard hath best deserv'd of all my sons. 3H6 1.01. 17
hath he deserv'd to lose his birthright thus? 1.01.219
for at their hands i have deserv'd no pity. 2.06. 26
than if thou never hadst deserv'd our hate. 5.01.104
to those whose dealings have deserv'd the place R3 3.01. 49
prince hath neither claim'd it nor deserv'd it, 3.01. 51
i know they do, and i have well deserv'd it. 3.02. 71
he deserv'd his death, | and your good graces 3.05. 47
he hath deserv'd worthily of his country, and COR 2.02. 24 P
you have deserv'd nobly of your country, and you 2.03. 88 P
your country, and you have not deserv'd nobly. 2.03. 89 P
coriolanus | deserv'd this so dishonor'd rub, 3.01. 60
give him deserv'd vexation. 3.03.140
i have deserv'd no better entertainment | in 4.05. 9
as those should do that had deserv'd his hate, 4.06.113
us all into one coal, | we have deserv'd it. 4.06.138
i have not deserv'd it. 5.06. 60
i have | deserv'd this hearing — bid 'em send TIM 2.02.198
how caesar hath deserv'd to lie in death, | mark JC 3.01.132
wherein hath caesar thus deserv'd your loves? 3.02.236
would thou hadst less deserv'd, | that the MAC 1.04. 18
that hast no less deserv'd, nor must be known 1.04. 30
for that question, thou'dst well deserv'd it. LR 2.04. 65 P
own disorders | deserv'd much less advancement. 2.04.200
i have not deserv'd this. OTH 4.01.241
your /reproof | were well deserv'd of rashness. ANT 2.02.122
matter of feast, which worthily deserv'd noting. 2.02.183 P
when you have well deserv'd ten times as much 2.06. 77
he has deserv'd it, were it carbuncled | like 4.08. 28
hath not deserv'd my service nor your loves, CYM 4.04. 25
who deserv'd | so long a breeding as his white 5.03. 16
that he deserv'd the praise o' th' world, | as 5.04. 50
her pleading hath deserv'd a greater fee; VEN 609
how much more praise deserv'd thy beauty's use, SON 2. 9

DESERVE 67 FR 0.0075 REL FR 55 V 12 P
only deserve my love by loving him, | and TGV 2.07. 82
i know not how i may deserve to be your porter. WIV 2.02.174 P
keep in that mind, i'll deserve it. 3.03. 82 P
at me, then let me be your jest, i deserve it. 3.03.151 P
gentleman | deserve as full as fortunate a bed ADO 3.01. 45
i know he doth deserve | as much as may be 3.01. 47
for others say thou dost deserve, and i 3.01.115
how much might the man deserve of me that would 4.01.261 P
deserve well at my hands by helping me to the 5.02. 1 P
me, and knows me, | how pitiful i deserve" — 5.02. 29
vows for thee broke deserve not punishment. LLL 4.03. 61
are pick–purses in love, and we deserve to die. 4.03.205
when at your hands did i deserve this scorn? MND 2.02.124
can, | deserve a sweet look from demetrius' eye, 2.02.127
thou dost deserve enough, and yet enough | may MV 2.07. 27
as much as i deserve! 2.07. 31
i do in birth deserve her, and in fortunes, | in 2.07. 32
but more than these, in love i do deserve. 2.07. 34
did i deserve no more than a fool's head? 2.09. 59
why should i not? doth he not deserve well? AYL 1.03. 36 P
nor would i have him till i do deserve him, AWW 1.03.199
you than you have or will to deserve at my hand, 2.05. 47 P
only to seem to deserve well, and to beguile the 4.03.299 P
fool, as ever thou wilt deserve well at my hand, TN 4.02. 80 P
become thy great birth nor deserve a crown. JN 3.01. 50
did not the one deserve to have an heir? R2 2.01.193
as my true service shall deserve your love. 3.03.199
well you deserve; 3.03.200
they well deserve to have | that know the 3.03.200
shall better speak of you than you deserve. 2H4 4.03. 85
in this, | and doth deserve a coronet of gold. 1H6 3.03. 89
that, to deserve well at my brother's hands, | i 3H6 5.01. 93
'tis more than you deserve; R3 1.02.222
deserve not worse than wretched clarence did, 2.01. 94
it so, | 'tis more than we deserve or i expect. 2.03. 37
tell me what they deserve | that do conspire my 3.04. 59
not my deserts, but what i will deserve. 4.04.415
the subject will deserve it. H8 pr 7
grace must needs deserve all strangers' loves, 2.02.101
he will deserve more. 4.01.113
a saucy fellow, | deserve we no more reverence? 4.02.101
i hope she will deserve well — and a little 4.02.136
(and now i should not lie), but will deserve, 4.02.143
sweet lady, does | deserve our better wishes. 5.01. 26
this good man (few of you deserve that title), 5.02.173
how may i deserve it, | that am a poor and 5.02.199
and your beards deserve not so honorable a grave COR 2.01. 88 P
than crave the hire which first we do deserve. 2.03.114
we pray the gods he may deserve your loves. 2.03.157
let me deserve so ill as you, and make me | your 3.01. 51
kind of service | did not deserve corn gratis. 3.01.125
people | deserve such pity of him as the wolf 4.06.110
you deserve | to have a temple built you. 5.03.206
to serve, and to deserve my mistress' grace, TIT 2.01. 34
nor all deserve | the common stroke of war. TIM 5.04. 21
own honor and dignity — the less they deserve, HAM 2.02.532 P
he which finds him shall deserve our thanks, LR 2.01. 61
modest haste which way | thou mightst deserve, 2.04. 26
on, good roderigo, i will deserve your pains. OTH 1.01.183
authority abus'd, | and did deserve his change. ANT 3.06. 34
(as you call it) deserve more — a punishment CYM 1.04.119 P
many times | doth ill deserve by doing well; 3.03. 54
many dream not to find, neither deserve, | and 5.04.130
marshal, the rest, as they deserve their grace. PER 2.03. 19
if you deserve well, sir, i shall soon see't. TNK 2.05. 42
vows for thee broke deserve not punishment. PP 3. 4
it grows, | thy pity may deserve to pitied be. SON 142.12

DESERVED 5 FR 0.0005 REL FR 5 V 0 P
air, | have i deserved at your highness' hands. R2 1.03.158
or both | to worthy danger and deserved death. 5.01. 68
i say, my lord, they have deserved death. R3 3.04. 66
towards her deserved children is enroll'd | in COR 3.01.290
as constrained blemishes, | not as deserved. ANT 3.13. 60

DESERVEDLY 1 FR 0.0001 REL FR 1 V 0 P
wast thou | deservedly confin'd into this rock, TMP 1.02.361

DESERVER 2 FR 0.0002 REL FR 2 V 0 P
in the lily–beds | propos'd for the deserver! TRO 3.02. 13
whose love is never link'd to the deserver ANT 1.02.186

DESERVERS 1 FR 0.0001 REL FR 1 V 0 P
like stars, shall shine | on all deservers. MAC 1.04. 42

DESERVES 40 FR 0.0045 REL FR 35 V 5 P
to plead for love deserves more fee than hate. TGV 1.02. 48
a son that well deserves it, | the honor and regard 2.04. 59
and truly she deserves it, for if there be a WIV 2.02.120 P
come in, the wish deserves a welcome. MM 3.01. 45
when it deserves, with characters of brass, | a 5.01. 11
slandering a prince deserves it. 5.01.524
she deserves well. LLL 1.02.119 P
chooseth me shall get as much as he deserves"; MV 2.07. 7
chooseth me shall get as much as he deserves." 2.07. 23
as much as he deserves! 2.07. 24
chooseth me shall get as much as he deserves." 2.09. 36
chooseth me shall get as much as he deserves." 2.09. 50
chooseth me shall have as much as he deserves"! 2.09. 58
you, deserves as well a dark house and a whip as AYL 3.02.401 P
no, he deserves no pity. 4.03. 66 P
your patience and your virtue well deserves it; 5.04.187
and she deserves a lord | that twenty such rude AWW 3.02. 81
deserves a name | as rank as any flax–wench that WT 1.02.276
form | (which on my faith deserves high speech) 2.01. 70
whose every word deserves | to taste of thy most 3.02.178
little deserves | the scourge of greatness to be 1H4 1.03. 10
yes, i accept her, for she well deserves it, 3H6 3.03.249
for this one speech lord hastings well deserves 4.01. 47
your love deserves my thanks, but my desert R3 3.07.154
done yet, o' my conscience, | deserves a corner. H8 3.01. 31
what he deserves of you and me i know; 3.02. 14
who, in your thoughts, deserves fair helen best, TRO 4.01. 54
who deserves greatness | deserves your hate; COR 1.01.176
who deserves greatness | deserves your hate; 1.01.177
this deserves death. 3.01.206
capital kind, | deserves th' extremest death. 3.03. 82
him | a gentleman that well deserves a help, TIM 1.01.102
and my estate deserves an heir more rais'd 1.01.119
for brave macbeth (well he deserves that name), MAC 1.02. 16
bears that life | which he deserves to lose. 1.03.111
wrack discern you in me | deserves your pity? CYM 1.06. 85
that thy lady hath of thee | deserves thy trust, 1.06.158
ay, sir, and he deserves so to be call'd for his PER 2.01.102 P
thy prison — | think well what that deserves; TNK 3.06.140
deserves the travail of a worthier pen, | yet SON 79. 6

DESERVEST 1 FR 0.0001 REL FR 0 V 1 P
it, for in most comely truth thou deservest it. ADO 5.02. 8 P

DESERVING 17 FR 0.0019 REL FR 11 V 6 P
'tis my deserving, and i do entreat it. MM 5.01.477
look'd upon, was the best deserving a fair lady. MV 1.02.118 P
and yet to be afeard of my deserving | were but 2.07. 29
all her deserving | is a reserved honesty, and AWW 3.05. 61
it was more of his courtesy than your deserving. 2H4 4.03. 43 P
virtue he had, deserving to command; 1H6 1.01. 9
though i know her virtuous | and well deserving? H8 3.02. 98
you shall not be | the grave of your deserving; COR 1.09. 20
sir, i shall study deserving. LR 1.01. 31 P
this seems a fair deserving, and must draw me 3.03. 23
confess me knit to thy deserving with cables of OTH 1.03.338 P
thou bestow on a deserving woman indeed — one 2.01.145 P
got without merit, and lost without deserving. 2.03.270 P
vanish, or i shall give thee thy deserving, ANT 4.12. 32
no whit less | than in his feats deserving it), CYM 3.01. 7
more to me deserving | than i can quite or speak TNK 5.04. 34
and for that riches where is my deserving? SON 87. 6

DESERVINGS 6 FR 0.0006 REL FR 5 V 1 P
how much unlike my hopes and my deservings! MV 2.09. 57
let his deservings and my love withal | be 4.01.450
and make foul the clearness of our deservings, AWW 1.03. 6 P
some | envy your great deservings and good name, 1H4 4.03. 35
spoke your deservings like a chronicle, | making 5.02. 57
and all foes | the cup of their deservings. LR 5.03.305

DESERV'ST 3 FR 0.0003 REL FR 1 V 2 P
and thou deserv'st it. WIV 3.03. 74 P
and, to speak truth, thou deserv'st no less. 2H6 4.03. 10 P
that due to thee which thou deserv'st alone. SON 39. 8

DESIGN 21 FR 0.0023 REL FR 18 V 3 P
being then appointed | master of this design, TMP 1.02.163
infinite distance | from his true–meant design. MM 1.04. 55
thine, in the dearest design of industry, don LLL 4.01. 86 P
of laughter, hinder not the honor of his design. AWW 3.06. 42 P
he has discover'd my design, and i | remain a WT 2.01. 50
offer, | who but to–day hammered of this design, 2.02. 47
fast by, but not prepar'd | for this design. 4.04.502
degree | or chivalrous design of knightly trial; R2 1.01. 81
see | justice design the victor's chivalry. 1.01.203
trust | my absence doth neglect no great design, R3 3.04. 24
far, until | it forg'd him some design, which, H8 1.02.181
why, there you touch'd the life of our design: TRO 2.02.194
by using means i lame the foot | of our design. COR 4.07. 8
towards his design | moves like a ghost. MAC 2.01. 55
my competitor | in top of all design, my mate in ANT 5.01. 43
but my design! CYM 2.02. 23
that thou wilt be a voluntary mute to my design. 3.05.153 P
away to britain | post i in this design. 5.05.192
and in thy name | to my design march boldly. TNK 5.01. 68
for 'tis a meritorious fair design | to chase LUC 1692
lending soft audience to my sweet design, | and LC 278

/DESIGN'D 1 FR 0.0001 REL FR 1 V 0 P
comart | and carriage of the article /design'd, HAM 1.01. 94

DESIGNMENT 1 FR 0.0001 REL FR 1 V 0 P
bang'd the turks, | that their designment halts. OTH 2.01. 22

DESIGNMENTS 1 FR 0.0001 REL FR 1 V 0 P
serv'd his designments | in mine own person; COR 5.06. 34

DESIGNS 11 FR 0.0012 REL FR 10 V 1 P
other /importunate and most serious designs, and LLL 5.01.100 P
our slow designs when we ourselves are dull. AWW 1.01.219
appointed to direct these fair designs. R2 1.03. 45
for his designs crave haste, his haste good hope 2.02. 44
that it may please you leave these sad designs R3 1.02.210
in deep designs, in matter of great moment, | no 3.07. 67
and be not peevish–fond in great designs. 4.04.417
hope makes | in all designs begun on earth below TRO 1.03. 4
which is the ladder of all high designs, | the 1.03.102
and in his tent | lies mocking our designs. 1.03.146
in our loves, | and sway our great designs! ANT 2.02.148

DESIR'D 27 FR 0.0030 REL FR 22 V 5 P
it is a life that i have desir'd. i will thrive. WIV 1.03. 19 P
finding yourself desir'd of such a person, MM 2.04. 91
and desir'd her | to try her gracious fortune 5.01. 75
when i desir'd him to come home to dinner, | he ERR 2.01. 60
under which lorenzo | desir'd us to make stand. MV 2.06. 2
save mine, which hath desir'd to see thee more, 1H4 3.02. 89
honors as can be desir'd in the hearts of his H5 4.07.161 P
in fine, redeem'd i was as i desir'd. 1H6 1.04. 34
madam, | according as your ladyship desir'd, 2.03. 12
and pav'd with gold, the emperor thus desir'd, H8 1.01.188
which the duke desir'd | to him brought viva 2.01. 17
this business, never desir'd | it to be stirr'd; 2.04.164
and desir'd your highness | most heartily to 5.01. 65
he touch'd the ports desir'd, | and for an old TRO 2.02. 76
desir'd my cressid in right great exchange, 3.03. 21
he desir'd their worships to think it was his JC 1.02.270 P
we should have else desir'd your good advice MAC 3.01. 20
be then desir'd | by her, that else will take LR 1.04.247
when i desir'd their leave that i might pity him 3.03. 2 P
honey, you shall be well desir'd in cyprus, | i OTH 2.01.204
for he partly begs | to be desir'd to give. ANT 3.13. 67
a lover's pinch, | which hurts, and is desir'd. 5.02.296
so is the queen, | that most desir'd the match. CYM 1.01. 12
love, she's flown | to her desir'd posthumus. 3.05. 62
than in gyves, | desir'd more than constrain'd. 5.04. 15
king, desir'd he might know none of his secrets. PER 1.03. 5 P
and desir'd your spirit | to send him hence TNK 5.04.119

/DESIRE 2 FR 0.0002 REL FR 1 V 1 P
sir, the /germans /desire to have three of your WIV 4.03. 1 P
most miserable | is the /desire that's glorious. CYM 1.06. 7

DESIRE 267 FR 0.0301 REL FR 179 V 88 P
that dare not offer | what i desire to give; TMP 3.01. 78
counsel thee | that art a votary to fond desire? TGV 1.01. 52
to pass, | i do desire thy worthy company, 4.03. 25
i do desire thee, even from a heart | as full of 4.03. 32
i'll force thee yield to my desire. 5.04. 59
look you, shall desire to hear the fear of got, WIV 1.01. 38 P
as just as you will desire, and seven hundred 1.01. 50 P
and desire a marriage between master abraham and 1.01. 55 P
and the letter is to desire and require her to 1.02. 9 P
ay, forsooth; to desire her to — 1.04. 79 P
to desire this honest gentlewoman, your maid, to 1.04. 82 P

would you desire better sympathy? 2.01. 9 P
mistress page would desire you to send her your 2.02.113 P
/brook, i desire more acquaintance of you. 2.02.162 P
had never so good means as desire to make myself 2.02.182 P
i most fehemently desire you you will also look 3.01. 8 P
i desire you in friendship, and i will one way 3.01. 86 P
i desire you that we may be friends; 3.01.118 P
corrupt, corrupt, and tainted in desire! 5.05. 90
a bloody fire, | kindled with unchaste desire, 5.05. 96
where i will desire thee to laugh at my wife, 5.05.171 P
i shall desire you, sir, to give me leave | to MM 1.01. 76
why i desire thee | to give me secret harbor, 1.03. 3
and most desire should meet the blow of justice; 2.02. 30
you could not with more tame a tongue desire it; 2.02. 46
shall we desire to raze the sanctuary | and 2.02.170
dost thou desire her foully for those things 2.02.173
her, | that i desire to hear her speak again? 2.02.177
let me desire you to make your answer before him 3.02.155 P
and let me desire to know how you find claudio 3.02.239 P
i do desire the like. 4.01. 51
i do desire to learn, sir; 4.02. 56 P
and say it was the desire of the penitent to be 4.02.176 P
i would desire you to clap into your prayers; 4.03. 41 P
him i'll desire | to meet me at the consecrated 4.03. 97
token, i desire his company | at mariana's house 4.03.139
none, but to desire your good company. ADO 2.01.272 P
wake my cousin beatrice, and desire her to rise. 3.04. 2 P
i, but god send every one their heart's desire! 3.04. 61 P
as, god help, i would desire they were, but, in 3.05. 11 P
i will not desire that. 4.01.257 P
i desire nothing but the reward of a villain. 5.01.243 P
in which, good friar, i shall desire your help. 5.04. 31
at christmas i no more desire a rose | than wish LLL 1.01.105
thought of it, i would take desire prisoner, and 1.02. 61 P
perchance light in the light. i desire her name. 2.01.199
one for herself, to desire that were a shame. 2.01.200
the court of his eye, peeping thorough desire: 2.01.235
would you desire more? 3.01.100 P
but shall we dance, if they desire us to't? 5.02.145
with duty and desire we follow you. MND 1.01.127
you, request you, and desire you, to con them by 1.02.100 P
out of this wood do not desire to go; 3.01.152
i shall desire you of more acquaintance, good 3.01.182 P
i shall desire you of more acquaintance too. 3.01.188 P
i desire you /of more acquaintance, good master 3.01.195 P
and never did desire to see thee more. 3.02.278
i have a great desire to a bottle of hay. 4.01. 32 P
would you desire lime and hair to speak better? 5.01.165 P
but soft, how many months | do you desire? MV 1.03. 59
and desire gratiano to come anon to my lodging. 2.02.117 P
i serve the jew, and have a desire, as my father 2.02.128 P
i desire no more delight | than to be under sail 2.06. 67
chooseth me shall gain what many men desire"; 2.07. 5
chooseth me shall gain what many men desire." 2.07. 37
chooseth me shall gain what many men desire." 2.09. 24
what many men desire! 2.09. 25
i will not choose what many men desire, 2.09. 31
i do desire you | not to deny this imposition, 3.04. 32
i humbly do desire your grace of pardon, | i 4.01.402
i shall desire more love and knowledge of you. AYL 1.02.285
i do not desire you to please me, i do desire 2.05. 17 P
you to please me, i do desire you to sing. 2.05. 17 P
i do desire we may be better strangers. 3.02.258 P
as good cause as one would desire, therefore 3.04. 5 P
then, can one desire too much of a good thing? 4.01.123 P
when he had a desire to eat a grape, would open 5.01. 33 P
i do desire it with all my heart; 5.03. 3 P
hope it is no dishonest desire to desire to be a 5.03. 4 P
dishonest desire to desire to be a woman of the 5.03. 4 P
god 'ild you, sir, i desire you of the like. 5.04. 54 P
since for the great desire i had | to see fair SHR 1.01. 1
but how did you desire it should be made? 4.03.119
madam, i desire your holy wishes. AWW 1.01. 59 P
i have a desire to hold my acquaintance with 2.03.227 P
swear them lordship, | yet you desire to marry. 5.03.157
mistress accost, i desire better acquaintance. TN 1.03. 52 P
desire him not to flatter with his lord, | nor 1.05.303
kill him whom you have recover'd, desire it not. 2.01. 38 P
if you desire the spleen, and will laugh 3.02. 68 P
my desire, | more sharp than filed steel, did 3.03. 4
upon some toy | you have desire to purchase; 3.03. 45
into the house and desire some conduct of the 3.04.241 P
therefore get you on, and give him his desire. 3.04.248 P
do not desire to see this letter. 5.01. 5 P
a dog and in recompense desire my dog again. 5.01. 7 P
you to think that my desire of having is the sin 5.01. 47 P
ere he was born desire yet their life to see him WT 1.01. 40 P
no other excuse why they should desire to live. 1.01. 44 P
they would desire to live on crutches till he 1.01. 45 P
air'd abroad, i desire to lay my bones there. 4.02. 6 P
and only therefore | desire to breed by me. 4.04.103
this hour, i have liv'd | to die when i desire. 4.04.462
i desire my life | once more to look on him. 5.01.137
least they desire (upon this push) to trouble 5.03.129
go, faulconbridge, now hast thou thy desire, | a JN 1.01.176
courageously, and with a free desire, R2 1.03.115
have thy desire. 5.03. 38
prawns, whereby thou didst desire to eat some, 2H4 2.01. 97 P
desire me to be no more so familiarity with such 2.01. 99 P
i do desire deliverance from these officers, 2.01.127 P
it not show vildly in me to desire small beer? 2.02. 6 P
beats as extraordinarily as heart would desire, 2.04. 24 P
it not strange that desire should so many years 2.04.260 P
own part, have a desire to stay with my friends, 3.02.225 P
travel, and sweating with desire to see him, 5.05. 25 P
you would desire the king were made a prelate; H5 1.01. 40
for i desire | nothing but odds with england. 2.04.128
i would desire the duke to use his good pleasure 3.06. 55 P
them, and anon | desire them all to my pavilion. 4.01. 27
no great cause to desire the approach of day. 4.01. 88 P
i do not desire he should answer for me, and yet 4.01.188 P
look you, as you shall desire in a summer's day. 4.08. 22 P
where that his lords desire him to have borne 5.pr. 17
not agree with it, i would desire you to eat it. 5.01. 27 P
i will desire you to live in the mean time, and 5.01. 33 P
impatiently i burn with thy desire; 1H6 1.02.108
swift-winged with desire to get a grave, | as 2.05. 15
it warm'd thy father's heart with proud desire 4.06. 11
i desire no more. 2H6 4.03. 9 P
whose haughty spirit, winged with desire, | will 3H6 1.01.267
and yet, between my soul's desire and me — 3.02.128
mine ear hath tempted judgment to desire. 3.03.133
i desire | to reconcile me to his friendly peace R3 2.01. 59
i hate it, and desire all good men's love. 2.01. 62
th' unsatiate greediness of his desire, | and 3.07. 7
see, | how far i am from the desire of this. 3.07.236
do thee good, | and be inheritor of thy desire. 4.03. 34
morning | desire the earl to see me in my tent. 5.03. 32
sir, i desire you do me right and justice, | and H8 2.04. 13
was the hour | i ever contradicted your desire? 2.04. 28
bootless | that longer you desire the court, as 2.04. 62
you do desire to know | wherefore i sent for you 5.01. 89
that when i am in heaven i shall desire | to see 5.04. 67
knew | love got so sweet as when desire did sue. TRO 1.02.291
i do desire it. 3.01. 14 P
that the desire is boundless and the act a slave 3.02. 83 P
which his own will shall have desire to drink. 3.03. 46
i'll send the fool to ajax and desire him | t' 3.03.235
tell him i humbly desire the valiant ajax to 3.03.274 P
dispraise the thing that they desire to buy, 4.01. 77
i do desire it. 4.05. 48
i would desire | my famous cousin to our grecian 4.05.150
desire them home. 4.05.157
gentry to him | and the desire of the nobles. COR 2.01.239
to desire | the present consul and last general 2.02. 42
you must desire them | to think upon you. 2.03. 55
ay, /not mine own desire. 2.03. 67 P
how, not your own desire? 2.03. 68 P
'twas never my desire yet to trouble the poor 2.03. 69 P
let me desire your company. 3.01.333
desire not | t' allay my rages and revenges with 5.03. 84
moor, | if foul desire had not conducted you? TIT 2.03. 79
but when ye have the honey we desire, | let not 2.03.131
now old desire doth in his death-bed lie, | and ROM 2.pr. 1
be he, sir, i desire some confidence with you. 2.04.127 P
than that i know thee | i not desire to know. TIM 4.03. 59
thou shouldst desire to die, being miserable. 4.03.248
our town till we | have seal'd thy full desire. 5.04. 54
at the door, | who doth desire to see you. JC 2.01. 71
trebonius doth desire you to o'er-read | (at 3.01. 4
be it so; | i do desire no more. 3.01.252
when i burnt in desire to question them further, MAC 1.05. 4 P
thine own act and valor | as thou art in desire? 1.07. 41
it provokes the desire, but it takes away the 2.03. 30 P
where our desire is got without content; 3.02. 5
and my desire | all continent impediments would 4.03. 63
desire his jewels, and this other's house, | and 4.03. 80
whose voices i desire aloud with mine: 5.09. 24
it is most retrograde to our desire, | and we HAM 1.02.114
out of the shot and danger of desire. 1.03. 35
as if it some impartment did desire | to you 1.04. 59
as your business and desire shall point you, 1.05.129
you, | for every man hath business and desire, 1.05.130
for your desire to know what is between us, 1.05.139
if you desire to know the certainty | of your 4.05.141
dark | grop'd i to find out them, had my desire, 5.02. 14
you, | i pray desire her call her wisdom to her. LR 4.05. 35
vices of thy mistress | as badness would desire. 4.06.254
desire him to go in, trouble him no more | till 4.07. 80
'tis a night of revels, the gallants desire it. OTH 2.03. 44 P
a special purpose | which wrought to his desire. 5.02.323
come, my queen, | last night you did desire it. ANT 1.01. 55
thus did i desire it. 1.02.122
the queen | of audience nor desire shall fail, 3.12. 21
did desire you | to burn this night with torches 4.02. 40
the party that should desire you to touch him, 5.02.246 P
of thy preferment, such | as thou'lt desire; CYM 1.05. 72
oppos'd, | should make desire vomit emptiness, 1.06. 45
that satiate yet unsatisfied desire, that tub 1.06. 48
desire my man's abode where i did leave him: 1.06. 53
do thy master's bidding | when i desire it too. 3.04. 98
lucius | present yourself, desire his service, 3.04.173
i desire of you | a conduct overland to 3.05. 7
that's not my desire. 5.04. 21
there are verier knaves desire to live, for all 5.04.200 P
that have inflam'd desire in my breast | to PER 1.01. 20
drawn by report, advent'rous by desire, | tell 1.01. 35
we have no reason to desire it, | commended to 1.03. 36
yet, ere you shall depart, this we desire, | as 1.03. 38
good alive, | and to fulfill his prince' desire, 2.ch. 21
him, we desire to know of him | of whence he is, 2.03. 73
his queen, with child, makes her desire — 3.ch. 40
tyre, | welcom'd and settled to his own desire. 4.ch. 2
i will go, | but yet i have no desire to it. 4.01. 43
i desire to find him so, that i may worthily 4.06. 51 P
desire of liberty, a fever, madness, | 'hath set TNK 1.04. 42
we are young and yet desire the ways of honor, 2.02. 73
and desire her? 2.02.158
and that blood we desire to shed is mutual — 3.06. 95
if you desire their lives, invent a way | safer 3.06.217
desire to eat with her, /carve her, drink to her 4.03. 87 P
that we should things desire which do cost us 5.04.110
which do cost us | the loss of our desire! 5.04.111
desire doth lend her force | courageously to VEN 29
fire, | he red for shame, but frosty in desire. 36
shows his hot courage and his high desire. 276
welcomes the warm approach of sweet desire; 386
the sea hath bounds, but deep desire hath none, 389
do i delight to die, or life desire? 496
now quick desire hath caught the yielding prey, 547
distemp'ring gentle love in his desire, | as air 653
"in night," quoth she, "desire sees best of all. 720
so shall i die by drops of hot desire. 1074
to grow unto himself was his desire, | and so 1180
borne by the trustless wings of false desire, LUC 2
arm, | is madly toss'd between desire and dread; 171
retire, | beaten away by brain-sick rude desire. 175
fire, | so lucrece must i force to my desire." 182
this desire | might have excuse to work upon his 234
desire my pilot is, beauty my prize, | then who 279
by reprobate desire thus madly led, | the roman 300
his hot heart, which fond desire doth scorch, 314
and stoop to honor, not to foul desire. 574
his true respect will prison false desire, | and 642
this hot desire converts to cold disdain; 691
drunken desire must vomit his receipt | ere he 703
can curb his heat, or rein his rash desire, 706
feeble desire, all recreant, poor, and meek, 710
flesh being proud, desire doth fight with grace, 712
but if the like the snow-white swan desire, 1011
had doting priam check'd his son's desire, 1490
at length address'd to answer his desire, | she 1606
if thou my love's desire do contradict. 1631
and twice desire, yer it be day, | that which PP 18.29
from fairest creatures we desire increase, SON 1. 1
which to repair should be thy chief desire. 10. 8
the first my thought, the other my desire, 45. 3
then can no horse with my desire keep pace; 51. 9
therefore desire (of /perfect'st love being made 51.10
tend | upon the hours and times of your desire? 57. 2
dost thou desire my slumbers should be broken 61. 3
and rather make them born to our desire | than 123. 7
desire to be invited | to any sensual feast with 141. 7
and i desperate now approve | desire is death, 147. 8
and so the general of hot desire | was sleeping 154. 7
consents bewitch'd, ere he desire, have granted, LC 131

DESIRED 8 FR 0.0009 REL FR 7 V 1 P

"your ladyship's in all desired employment, LLL 4.02.136 P
time was, i did him a desired office, | dear AWW 4.04. 5
alas, good master, my wife desired some damsons, 2H6 2.01.100
seas, | and brought desired help from burgundy. 3H6 4.07. 6
what did he note but strongly he desired? LUC 415
so ill, | to set a form upon desired change, SON 89. 6
i, sick withal, the help of bath desired, | and 153.11
did, | demand of him, nor being desired yielded; LC 149

DESIRERS 1 FR 0.0001 REL FR 0 V 1 P

man, and give it bountiful to the desirers. COR 2.03.102 P

DESIRE'S 1 FR 0.0001 REL FR 1 V 0 P

by this black-fac'd night, desire's foul nurse, VEN 773

/DESIRES 1 FR 0.0001 REL FR 1 V 0 P

/being /now /trimm'd /in /thine /own /desires, 2H4 1.03. 94

DESIRES 81 FR 0.0091 REL FR 55 V 26 P

you must lay lime to tangle her desires | by TGV 3.02. 68
if you can carry her your desires towards her. WIV 1.01.236 P
my father desires your worships' company. 1.01.262 P
your master's desires to mistress anne page. 1.02. 10 P
my desires had instance and argument to commend 2.02.246 P
knave as you would desires to be acquainted 3.01. 67 P
a omans as i will desires among five thousand, 3.03.220 P
she desires you once more to come to her, 3.05. 45 P
mistress ford desires you to come suddenly. 4.01. 5 P
foolish christian creatures as i would desires. 4.01. 72 P
his flesh is punish'd, he shall have no desires. 4.04. 24 P
serve got, and leave your desires, and fairies 5.05.130 P
of the man condemn'd | desires access to you. MM 2.02. 19
one isabel, a sister, desires access to you. 2.04. 18
come thronging soft and delicate desires, | all ADO 1.01.303
and the huge army of the world's desires — LLL 1.01. 10
health and fair desires consort your grace! 2.01.177
she lingers my desires, | like to a step-dame, MND 1.01. 4
therefore, fair hermia, question your desires, 1.01. 67
my legs can keep no pace with my desires. 3.02.445
why, that's the lady, all the world desires her. MV 2.07. 38
is at his house and desires to speak with you 3.01. 75 P
for thy desires | are wolvish, bloody, starv'd, 4.01.137
your heart's desires be with you! AYL 1.02.199 P
or have acquaintance with mine own desires; 1.03. 48
the falcon her bells, so man hath his desires; 3.03. 81 P
an ape, more giddy in my desires than a monkey. 4.01.153 P
only he desires | some private speech with you. AWW 2.05. 56
ere she seems as won, | desires this ring; 3.07. 32
off, | but give thyself unto my sick desires, 4.02. 35
and my desires, like fell and cruel hounds, TN 1.01. 21
young gentleman much desires to speak with you. 1.05.100 P
since my desires | run not before mine honor, WT 4.04. 33
beheld), desires access | to your high presence. 5.01. 87
desires you to attach his son, who has | (his 5.01.182
your honor not o'erthrown by your desires, | i 5.01.230
desires your majesty to leave the field, | and JN 5.03. 6
my soul | with contemplation and devout desires. 5.04. 48
else, | could such inordinate and low desires, 1H4 3.02. 12
you shall have your desires with interest | and 4.03. 49
with grant of our most just and right desires, 2H4 4.02. 40
desires you let the dukedoms that you claim H5 1.02.256
such outward things dwell not in my desires. 4.03. 27
the constable desires thee thou wilt mind | thy 4.03. 84
i will tell him a little piece of my desires. 5.01. 13 P
lousy knave, at my desires, and my requests, and 5.01. 23 P
he desires to make atonement | between the duke R3 1.03. 36
have ever come too short of my desires, | yet H8 3.02.170
your queen | desires your visitation, and to be 5.01.167
fair desires, in all fair measure, fairly guide TRO 3.01. 44 P
my lord, he desires you, that if the king call 3.01. 76 P
who most humbly desires you to invite hector to 3.03.284 P
who desires most that | which would increase his COR 1.01.178
to those that shall | say yea to thy desires. 4.05.145
gave him way | in all his own desires; 5.06. 32
goths, | she will a handmaid be to his desires, TIT 1.01.331
madam, though venus govern your desires, 2.03. 30
some book there is that she desires to see. 4.01. 31
rome | desires to be admitted to your presence. 5.01.153
your honorable letter he desires | to those have TIM 1.01. 97
let me not hinder, cassius, your desires; JC 1.02. 30
let not light see my black and deep desires; MAC 1.04. 51
most fair return of greetings and desires. HAM 2.02. 60
she desires to speak with you in her closet ere 3.02.331 P
the queen desires you to use some gentle 5.02.206 P
journey to your desires by the means i shall OTH 2.01.277 P
so likes your music, that he desires you, for 3.01. 12 P
a huswife that by selling her desires | buys 4.01. 94
desires for sport, and frailty, as men have? 4.03.101
so your desires are yours. ANT 3.04. 28
more, domitius, | my lord desires you presently; 3.05. 21
monument, | of thy intents desires instruction, 5.01. 54
queen, madam, | desires your highness' company. CYM 1.03. 38
were my fortunes equal to my desires, i could PER 2.01.111 P
he desires to know of you | of whence you are, 2.03. 79
receive such pay | as thy desires can wish. 5.01. 75
he much desires | to have some speech with you. TNK 5.04. 84
and that you sit as kings in your desires, STM II.C 77
age, desires to know | in brief the grounds and LC 62
when he again desires her, being sat, | her 66
of pensiv'd and subdu'd desires the tender, 219

DESIREST 2 FR 0.0002 REL FR 1 V 1 P
or say, sweet love, what thou desirest to eat. MND 4.01. 30
thou desirest me to stop in my tale against the ROM 2.04. 95 P
DESIRING 6 FR 0.0006 REL FR 6 V 0 P
i speak not as desiring more, | but rather MM 1.04. 3
desiring thee to lay aside the sword | which JN 1.01. 12
through casements darted their desiring eyes R2 5.02. 14
lord, in heart desiring still | you may behold 1H6 4.01. 76
desiring thee that publius cimber may | have an JC 3.01. 53
desiring this man's art, and that man's scope, SON 29. 7
DESIROUS 6 FR 0.0006 REL FR 3 V 3 P
gallant that is so desirous to lie with his AYL 1.02.201 P
my niece is desirous you should enter, if your TN 3.01. 75 P
i have not been desirous of their wealth, | nor 3H6 4.08. 44
and how desirous of our sight they are. TIT 5.01. 4
are certain ladies most desirous of admittance. TIM 1.02.117 P
night, | and when you are desirous to be blest, HAM 3.04.171
DESIR'ST 4 FR 0.0004 REL FR 2 V 2 P
that in love's grief desir'st society: LLL 4.03.126
thou shalt have justice more than thou desir'st. MV 4.01.316
go to, thou art made if thou desir'st to be so; TN 2.05.155 P
to, thou art made, if thou desir'st to be so" — 3.04. 52 P
/DESIST 1 FR 0.0001 REL FR 1 V 0 P
/or /at /least /desist | /to /build /at /all? 2H4 1.03. 47
DESIST 3 FR 0.0003 REL FR 3 V 0 P
desist, and drink. ANT 2.07. 80
and with dead cheeks advise thee to desist | for PER 1.01. 39
i will desist, | but there is something glows 5.01. 94
DESK 4 FR 0.0004 REL FR 4 V 0 P
in the desk | that's cover'd o'er with turkish ERR 4.01.103
the desk, the purse! 4.02. 29
mistress, redemption, the money in his desk? 4.02. 46
think, | if i had play'd the desk or table–book, HAM 2.02.136
DESOLATE 7 FR 0.0008 REL FR 6 V 1 P
which here, in this most desolate isle, else TMP 3.03. 80
alas, poor lady, desolate and left! TGV 4.04.174
desolate, desolate, will i hence and die: R2 1.02. 73
desolate, desolate, will i hence and die: 1.02. 73
towns, | and in a moment makes them desolate. 1H6 2.03. 66
mischiefs, and makes them leave me desolate. 2H6 4.08. 58 P
let us seek out some desolate shade, and there MAC 4.03. 1
DESOLATION 11 FR 0.0012 REL FR 8 V 3 P
the merry days of desolation that i have seen, LLL 1.02.160 P
o, you have liv'd in desolation here, | unseen, 5.02.357
about you demonstrating a careless desolation. AYL 3.02.381 P
even till unfenced desolation | leave them as JN 2.01.386
and his whole kingdom into desolation. H5 2.02.173
fell feats | enlink'd to waste and desolation? 3.03. 18
and where thou art not, desolation. 2H6 3.02.364
soul, | death, desolation, ruin, and decay. R3 4.04.409
my desolation does begin to make | a better life ANT 5.02. 1
there were desolation of jailers and gallowses! CYM 5.04.204 P
tyre, | and seen the desolation of your streets; PER 1.04. 89
/DESPAIR 1 FR 0.0001 REL FR 1 V 0 P
/as /despair | /that /frosts /will /bite /them. 2H4 1.03. 40
DESPAIR 59 FR 0.0066 REL FR 57 V 2 P
art to enchant, | and my ending is despair, TMP ep 15
to make her heavenly comforts of despair, | when MM 4.03.110
kinsman to grim and comfortless despair, | and ERR 5.01. 80
as doubtful thoughts, and rash–embrac'd despair, MV 3.02.109
presume not, "celsa senis," despair not. SHR 3.01. 45 P
where hope is coldest and despair most /fits. AWW 2.01.144
and our crimes would despair, if they were not 4.03. 74 P
should all despair | that have revolted wives, WT 1.02.198
therefore betake thee | to nothing but despair. 3.02.210
but in despair die under their black weight. JN 3.01.297
to this most cruel act, do but despair, | and if 4.03.126
call it not patience, gaunt, it is despair. R2 1.02. 29
and driven into despair an enemy's hope, | who 2.02. 47
despair not, madam. 2.02. 67
i will despair, and be at enmity | with cozening 2.02. 68
and bids me speak of nothing but despair. 3.02. 66
forth | of that sweet way i was in to despair! 3.02.205
till mischief and despair | drive you to break 1H6 5.04. 90
gives light in darkness, comfort in despair! 2H6 2.01. 65
and from his bosom purge this black despair! 3.03. 23
our hap is loss, our hope but sad despair, | our 3H6 2.03. 9
fair queen, whence springs this deep despair? 3.03. 12
unless thou rescue him from foul despair? 3.03.215
and i the rather wain me from despair | for love 4.04. 17
by such despair i should accuse myself. R3 1.02. 85
i'll join with black despair against my soul, 2.02. 36
despair therefore and die! 5.03.120
despair and die! 5.03.126
harry the sixt bids thee despair and die. 5.03.127
despair and die! 5.03.135
despair and die! 5.03.140
think upon grey, and let thy soul despair! 5.03.141
despair and die! 5.03.143
thy nephews' souls bid thee despair and die! 5.03.149
despair and die! 5.03.156
despair and die! 5.03.163
fainting, despair; 5.03.172
i shall despair; 5.03.200
nodding of their plumes, | fan you into despair! COR 3.03.127
then why should he despair that knows to court TIT 2.01. 91
too fair, | to merit bliss by making me despair. ROM 1.01.222
pray — grant thou, lest faith turn to despair. 1.05.104
the mere despair of surgery, he cures, | hanging MAC 4.03.152
despair thy charm, | and let the angel whom thou 5.08. 13
why i do trifle thus with his despair | is done LR 4.06. 33
led him, begg'd for him, sav'd him from despair; 5.03.192
and | to lay the blame upon her own despair, 5.03.255
take the hint | which my despair proclaims: ANT 3.11. 19
past hope, and in despair, that way past grace. CYM 1.01.137
haply despair hath seiz'd her; 3.05. 60
and damn'd despair | swear nature's death for VEN 743
here overcome, as one full of despair, | she 955
despair and hope makes thee ridiculous: 988
despair to gain doth traffic oft for gaining, LUC 131
let him have time of time's help to despair, 983
two loves i have, of comfort and despair, | that PP 2. 1
/one blushing shame, another white despair; SON 99. 9
for if i should despair, i should grow mad, 140. 9
two loves i have of comfort and despair, | which 144. 1
DESPAIRING 7 FR 0.0008 REL FR 7 V 0 P
and manage it against despairing thoughts. TGV 3.01.249
fame, | despairing of his own arm's fortitude, 1H6 2.01. 17
base, fearful, and despairing henry! 3H6 1.01.178
and by despairing shalt thou stand excused | for R3 1.02. 86
despairing, yield thy breath! 5.03.172
so | despairing died. CYM 5.05. 61
dwell'd, | till she despairing hecuba beheld, LUC 1447
DESPAIRS 2 FR 0.0002 REL FR 2 V 0 P
but now, the arbitrator of despairs, | just 1H6 2.05. 28
fears, and despairs, and all these for his H8 2.02. 28
DESPERATE 56 FR 0.0063 REL FR 50 V 6 P
all three of them are desperate: TMP 3.03.104
at me, | that i am desperate of obtaining her. TGV 3.02. 5
my suit then is desperate; WIV 3.05.125 P
she will do a desperate outrage to herself. ADO 2.03.152 P
of many desperate studies by his uncle, | whom AYL 5.04. 32
part, | and venture madly on a desperate mart. SHR 2.01.327
limit, as a desperate offendress against nature. AWW 1.01.140 P
to cure the desperate languishings whereof | the 1.03.229
skill infinite or monstrous desperate. 2.01.184
your lord into a desperate assurance she will TN 2.02. 8 P
my state is desperate for my master's love; 2.02. 37
in the streets, desperate of shame and state, 5.01. 64
this is desperate, sir. WT 4.04.485
so | as doth the fury of two desperate men, JN 3.01. 32
as dissolute as desperate, yet through both | i R2 5.03. 20
she is desperate here, a peevish self–will'd 1H4 3.01.196
yond island carrions, desperate of their bones, H5 4.02. 39
salisbury is a desperate homicide, | he fighteth 1H6 1.02. 25
more venturous or desperate than this. 2.01. 45
and, desperate stags, | turn on the bloody 4.02. 50
of former honor | by this unheedful, desperate, 4.04. 7
so desperate thieves, all hopeless of their 3H6 1.04. 42
drown desperate sorrow in dead edward's grave, R3 2.02. 99
to desperate adventures and assur'd destruction. 5.03.319
in desperate manner | daring th' event to th' H8 1.02. 35
(though he be grown so desperate to be honest), 3.01. 86
are you so desperate grown to threat your TIT 2.01. 40
to, | like a forlorn and desperate castaway, 5.03. 75
one desperate grief cures with another's ROM 1.02. 48
hold thy desperate hand! 3.03.108
i will make a desperate tender | of my child's 3.04. 12
which craves as desperate an execution | as that 4.01. 69
as that is desperate which we would prevent. 4.01. 70
to enter in the thoughts of desperate men! 5.01. 36
thou desperate pilot, now at once run on | the 5.03.117
and she, too desperate, would not go with me, 5.03.263
these debts may well be call'd desperate ones, TIM 3.04.102 P
he waxes desperate with /imagination. HAM 1.04. 87
and leads the will to desperate undertakings 2.01.101
diseases desperate grown | by desperate 4.03. 9
grown | by desperate appliance are reliev'd, 4.03. 10
he is attended with a desperate train, | and LR 2.04.305
go after her; she's desperate, govern her. 5.03.162
the desperate tempest hath so bang'd the turks, OTH 2.01. 21
i am desperate of my fortunes if they check me 2.03.331 P
this sight would make him do a desperate turn, 5.02.207
of rest, would purge | by any desperate change. ANT 1.03. 54
my queen | upon a desperate bed, and in a time CYM 4.03. 6
his strange absence, | grew shameless desperate; 5.05. 58
i care not, i am desperate. TNK 2.06. 13
souls | in doing this, o desperate as you are? STM II.C 107
the client breaks, as desperate in his suit. VEN 336
and careless lust stirs up a desperate courage, 556
or theirs whose desperate hands themselves do 765
she, desperate, with her nails her flesh doth LUC 739
and i desperate now approve | desire is death, SON 147. 7
DESPERATELY 4 FR 0.0004 REL FR 3 V 1 P
insensible of mortality, and desperately mortal. MM 4.02.145 P
air | but toiling desperately to find it out — 3H6 3.02.178
a bloody deed, and desperately dispatch'd! R3 1.04.271
foredone themselves, | and desperately are dead. LR 5.03.293
DESPERATION 4 FR 0.0004 REL FR 4 V 0 P
mad, and play'd | some tricks of desperation. TMP 1.02.210
desperation | is all the policy, strength, and COR 4.06.126
the very place puts toys of desperation, HAM 1.04. 75
night, | to desperation turn my trust and hope, 3.02.218
DESPIS'D 16 FR 0.0018 REL FR 11 V 5 P
since his exile she hath despis'd me most, TGV 3.02. 3
why didst thou say, of late thou wert despis'd? 1H6 2.05. 42
or live in peace abandon'd and despis'd! 3H6 1.01.188
the state | of our despis'd nobility, our issues H8 3.02.291
thus is the poor agent despis'd! TRO 5.10. 37 P
our father's tears despis'd, and basely cozen'd TIT 5.03.101
despis'd, distressed, hated, martyr'd, kill'd! ROM 4.05. 59
still to give, lest your deities be despis'd. TIM 3.06. 73 P
know'st none, but art despis'd for the contrary. 4.03.304 P
is yond despis'd and ruinous man my lord? 4.03.459
the pangs of despis'd love, the law's delay, HAM 3.01. 71
most choice forsaken, and most lov'd despis'd, LR 1.01.251
a poor, infirm, weak, and despis'd old man; 3.02. 20
rather sue to be despis'd than to deceive so OTH 2.03.277 P
she hath despis'd me rejoicingly, and i'll be CYM 3.05.144 P
so then i am not lame, poor, nor despis'd, SON 37. 9
DESPISE 23 FR 0.0026 REL FR 17 V 6 P
that i despise thee for thy wrongful suit, | and TGV 4.02.102
i do despise a liar as i do despise one that is WIV 1.01. 68 P
a liar as i do despise one that is false, or as 1.01. 69 P
is false, or as i despise one that is not true. 1.01. 69 P
despise me when i break this oath of mine. LLL 5.02.441
this you should pity rather than despise. MND 3.02.235
if he would despise me, i would forgive him, for MV 1.02. 63 P
but, being awak'd, i do despise my dream. 2H4 5.05. 51
you may not, my lord, despise her gentle suit. 1H6 2.02. 47
how much, methinks, i could despise this man, H8 3.02.297
i do despise them! COR 3.01. 22
rome will despise her for this foul escape. TIT 4.02.113
let not your ears despise my tongue for ever, MAC 4.03.201
despise me if i do not. OTH 1.01. 8
me another, to make me frankly despise myself. 2.03.298 P
events are welcome, | but comforts we despise; ANT 4.15. 4
/envied the great, nor shall the low despise. PER 2.03. 26
despise profit where you have most gain. 4.02.118 P
for these two cousins | despise my cruelty, and TNK 3.06.249
o all ye gods, despise me then. 3.06.258
scornfully, he doth despise | his naked armor of LUC 187
but 'tis my heart that loves what they despise, SON 141. 3
that is so proud thy service to despise, | when 149.10
DESPISED 11 FR 0.0012 REL FR 11 V 0 P
shall lie | his old betrothed (but despised); MM 3.02.279
my master said, | despised the athenian maid; MND 2.02. 73
prodigious, such as are | despised in nativity, 5.01.413
with war | and ostentation of despised arms? R2 2.03. 95
we'll make foul weather with despised tears; 3.03.161
term | of a despised life clos'd in my breast ROM 1.04.110
despised substance of divinest show! 3.02. 77
and what's to come of my despised time | is OTH 1.01.161
o'erworn, despised, rheumatic, and cold, VEN 135
and make time's spoils despised every where. SON 100.12
enjoy'd no sooner but despised straight, | past 129. 5
DESPISER 1 FR 0.0001 REL FR 1 V 0 P
or else a rude despiser of good manners, | that AYL 2.07. 92
DESPISERS 1 FR 0.0001 REL FR 1 V 0 P
both despisers | of thee and of thy goodness. TNK 3.06.137
DESPISETH 2 FR 0.0002 REL FR 2 V 0 P
him | that with his very heart despiseth me? TGV 4.04. 94
because he loves her, he despiseth me; 4.04. 95
DESPISING 3 FR 0.0003 REL FR 3 V 0 P
despising many forfeits and subduements, | when TRO 4.05.187
despising, | for you, the city, thus i turn my COR 3.03.133
yet in these thoughts myself almost despising, SON 29. 9
DESPISINGS 1 FR 0.0001 REL FR 1 V 0 P
despisings of our persons, and such poutings, TNK 3.06. 33
/DESPITE 1 FR 0.0001 REL FR 1 V 0 P
/despite thy victor–sword and fire–new fortune, LR 5.03.133
DESPITE 56 FR 0.0063 REL FR 42 V 14 P
in despite of the teeth of all rhyme and reason, WIV 5.05.125 P
grace is grace, despite of all controversy; MM 1.02. 24 P
art a wicked villain, despite of all grace. 1.02. 26 P
and in despite of mirth mean to be merry. ERR 3.01.108
an obstinate heretic in the despite of beauty. ADO 1.01.235 P
that, in despite of his quick wit and his queasy 2.01.383 P
only to despite them, i will endeavor any thing. 2.02. 31 P
and, in despite of all, dies for him. 3.02. 66 P
and yet now in despite of his heart he eats his 3.04. 89 P
despite his nice fence and his active practice, 5.01. 75
grace, | despite of suit, to see a lady's face. LLL 5.02.129
consider then, we come but in despite. MND 5.01.112
you will try in time, in despite of a fall. AYL 1.03. 25 P
i made yesterday in despite of my invention. 2.05. 47 P
shall in despite enforce a watery eye. SHR in.1. 128
therefore tarry in despite of the flesh and the in.2. 127 P
i'll keep mine own, despite of all the world. 3.02.142
but thy intercepter, full of despite, bloody as TN 3.04.222 P
then, in despite of brooded watchful day, | i JN 3.03. 52
despite of death that lives upon my grave, | to R2 1.01.168
on whom, as in despite, the sun looks pale, H5 3.05. 17
foul fiend of france, and hag of all despite, 1H6 3.02. 52
till with thy warlike sword, despite of fate, 4.06. 8
sky, | in thy despite shall scape mortality. 4.07. 22
infancy | crowned in paris in despite of foes? 2H6 1.01. 94
despite duke humphrey or the cardinal. 1.01.179
in despite of the devils and hell, have through 4.08. 60 P
despite the bearard that protects the bear. 5.01.210
depos'd he shall be, in despite of all. 3H6 1.01.154
proud, | can set the duke up in despite of me. 1.01.158
who crown'd the gracious duke in high despite, 2.01. 59
buy two hours' life | that i, in all despite, 2.06. 81
ay, in despite of all that shall withstand you. 4.01.146
yet, warwick, in despite of all mischance, | of 4.03. 43
thou wretch, despite o'erwhelm thee! COR 3.01.163
as he hath follow'd you, with all despite; 3.03.139
what, would you bury him in my despite? TIT 1.01.361
and in despite i'll cram thee with more food. ROM 5.03. 48
no, in despite of sense and secrecy, | unpeg the HAM 3.04.192
good i mean to do, | despite of mine own nature. LR 5.03.245
thrown such despite and heavy terms upon her, OTH 4.02.116
us, | or scant our former having in despite: 4.03. 91
in your despite, upon your purse — revenge it. CYM 1.06.135
imperceiverant thing loves him in my despite. 4.01. 15 P
open'd (in despite | of heaven and men) her 5.05. 58
she fram'd thee in high heaven's despite, | to VEN 731
"therefore, despite of fruitless chastity, 751
in despite | virtue would stain that o'er with LUC 55
the scar that will despite of cure remain, 732
in vain i spurn at my confirm'd despite: 1026
despite of wrinkles, this thy golden time. SON 3.12
despite thy wrong, | my love shall in my verse 19.13
for then, despite of space, i would be brought, 44. 3
praising thy worth, despite his cruel hand. 60.14
i will be true, despite thy scythe and thee. 123.14
who in despite of view is pleas'd to dote; 141. 4
DESPITEFUL 7 FR 0.0008 REL FR 7 V 0 P
study | to seem despiteful and ungentle to you. AYL 5.02. 80
o despiteful love! SHR 4.02. 14
i, his despiteful juno, sent him forth | from AWW 3.04. 13
despiteful tidings, o unpleasing news! R3 4.01. 36
this is the most despiteful gentle greeting, TRO 4.01. 33
despiteful and intolerable wrongs! TIT 4.04. 50
to scourge th' ingratitude that despiteful rome ANT 2.06. 22
DESPITEFULLY 1 FR 0.0001 REL FR 1 V 0 P
despitefully i mean to bear thee | unto the base LUC 670
DESPOILED 1 FR 0.0001 REL FR 1 V 0 P
born, | despoiled of your honor in your life, 2H6 2.03. 10
DESP'RATE 12 FR 0.0013 REL FR 12 V 0 P
my lord, this is a fond and desp'rate creature, AWW 5.03.178
then follow thou thy desp'rate sire of crete, 1H6 4.06. 54
and haste is needful in this desp'rate case. 3H6 4.01.129
thy school–days frightful, desp'rate, wild, and R3 4.04.170
and i, in such a desp'rate bay of death, | like 4.04.233
as with a club, dash out my desp'rate brains? ROM 4.03. 54
good gentle youth, tempt not a desp'rate man. 5.03. 59
an alteration of honor has desp'rate want made! TIM 4.03.462
lost, | a sister driven into desp'rate terms, HAM 4.07. 26
the corse they follow did with desp'rate hand 5.01.220
not wake, and in a desp'rate rage | post hither, LUC 219
to find some desp'rate instrument of death, 1038
DESP'RATELY 1 FR 0.0001 REL FR 1 V 0 P
that desp'rately he hurried through the street ERR 5.01.140
DESTIN'D 5 FR 0.0005 REL FR 5 V 0 P
being destin'd to a drier death on shore. TGV 1.01.150
it now, | by putting on the destin'd livery. MM 2.04.138
my babes were destin'd to a fairer death, | if R3 4.04.220
nature loathes, take thou the destin'd tenth, TIM 5.04. 33
the destin'd ill she must herself assay? LC 156
DESTINIES 7 FR 0.0008 REL FR 5 V 2 P
according to fates and destinies, and such odd MV 2.02. 62 P
or as the destinies decrees. AYL 1.02.105 P

some of those branches by the destinies cut; R2 1.02. 15
mark'd by the destinies to be avoided, | as 3H6 2.02.137
or till the destinies do cut his thread of life. PER 1.02.108
"and therefore hath she brib'd the destinies VEN 733
the destinies will curse thee for this stroke: 945
DESTINY *(also dest'ny)*
DESTINY 21 FR 0.0023 REL FR 18 V 3 P
make the rope of his destiny our cable, for our TMP 1.01. 31 P
and by that destiny, to perform an act | whereof 2.01.252
you are three men of sin, whom destiny, | that 3.03. 53
of night, | you orphan heirs of fixed destiny, WIV 5.05. 39
cross'd, | it stands as an edict in destiny. MND 1.01.151
the lott'ry of my destiny | bars me the right of MV 2.01. 15
no heresy, | hanging and wiving goes by destiny. 2.09. 83
besides, he brings his destiny with him. AYL 4.01. 57 P
your marriage comes by destiny, | your cuckoo AWW 1.03. 62
i am most constant, | though destiny say no. WT 4.04. 46
think you i bear the shears of destiny? JN 4.02. 91
all unavoided is the doom of destiny. R3 4.04.218
true — when avoided grace makes destiny: 4.04.219
laboring for destiny, make cruel way | through TRO 4.05.184
be menelaus, i would conspire against destiny. 5.01. 64 P
city, which he painted | with shunless destiny; COR 2.02.112
thither he | will come to know his destiny. MAC 3.05. 17
'tis destiny unshunnable, like death. OTH 3.03.275
but let determin'd things to destiny | hold ANT 3.06. 84
and to that destiny have patiently | laid up my TNK 2.02. 5
live's lasting date from cancell'd destiny. LUC 1729
DESTITUTE 3 FR 0.0003 REL FR 3 V 0 P
the king himself | of his wings destitute, the CYM 5.03. 5
have, | wherein we are not destitute for want, PER 5.01. 57
left their round turrets destitute and pale. LUC 441
DEST'NY *(also destiny)*
DEST'NY 1 FR 0.0001 REL FR 0 V 1 P
and't be my dest'ny, so; 2H4 3.02.236 P
DESTROY 28 FR 0.0031 REL FR 28 V 0 P
wherefore did they not | that hour destroy us? TMP 1.02.139
i would my valiant master would destroy thee. 3.02. 46
wilt thou destroy him then? 3.02.114
destroy our friends and after weep their dust; AWW 5.03. 64
made it no conscience to destroy a prince. JN 4.02.229
seen how his son's son should destroy his sons, R2 2.01.105
dost thou teach pardon pardon to destroy? 5.03.120
to slay your sovereign and destroy the realm. 1H6 3.01.114
here, purposing the bastard to destroy, | came 4.06. 25
'tis he that sends us to destroy you here. R3 1.04.243
which part of his body | shall i destroy him — TRO 4.05.243
in parts remote, | to fright them, ere destroy. COR 4.05.143
of the war | destroy what lies before 'em. 4.06. 42
thereby to destroy | the volsces whom you serve, 5.03.133
task, | so thou destroy rapine and murder there. TIT 5.02. 59
and destroy your sight | with a new gorgon. MAC 2.03. 71
'tis safer to be that which we destroy | than by 3.02. 6
their own enactures with themselves destroy. HAM 3.02.197
meet what i would have well and it destroy! 3.02.221
the sword is out | that must destroy thee. LR 4.06.230
and being join'd, i'll thus your hopes destroy, PER 2.05. 86
i would destroy th' offender, coz, i would, TNK 5.01. 23
hue, | how white and red each other did destroy! VEN 346
if thou destroy them not in dark obscurity? 760
sith in his prime death doth my love destroy, 1163
for one sweet grape who will the vine destroy? LUC 215
way, | for in thy bed i purpose to destroy thee. 514
greece, | for helen's rape the city to destroy, 1369
DESTROY'D *(also 'stroy'd)*
/DESTROY'D 2 FR 0.0002 REL FR 2 V 0 P
/soon /my /sorrow /hath /destroy'd /my /face. R2 4.01.291
/the /shadow /of /your /sorrow /hath /destroy'd 4.01.292
DESTROY'D 6 FR 0.0006 REL FR 5 V 1 P
when prospero is destroy'd. TMP 3.02.146
destroy'd the sweet'st companion that e'er man WT 5.01. 11
had heard of a world ransom'd, or one destroy'd. 5.02. 15 P
or, guilty in defense, be thus destroy'd? H5 3.03. 43
peers and chief nobility | destroy'd themselves, 1H6 4.01.147
destroy'd his country, and his name remains | to COR 5.03.147
DESTROYED 3 FR 0.0003 REL FR 3 V 0 P
and in the sentence my own life destroyed. R2 1.03.242
which many a good tall fellow had destroyed | so 1H4 1.03. 62
of mankind, had | destroyed in such a shape. ANT 4.08. 26
DESTROYER 1 FR 0.0001 REL FR 0 V 1 P
bastard children than war's a destroyer of men. COR 4.05.225 P
DESTROYERS 1 FR 0.0001 REL FR 1 V 0 P
courteous destroyers, affable wolves, meek bears TIM 3.06. 95
DESTROYING 3 FR 0.0003 REL FR 3 V 0 P
have felt the worst of death's destroying wound, R2 3.02.139
and fight and die is death destroying death, 3.02.184
good and loyal, | destroying them for wealth. MAC 4.03. 84
DESTROYS 2 FR 0.0002 REL FR 2 V 0 P
prays, and destroys the prayer, no midway ANT 3.04. 19
end, | and kept unus'd, the user so destroys it: SON 9.12
DESTRUCTION 28 FR 0.0031 REL FR 27 V 1 P
we from the west will send destruction | into JN 2.01.409
again | to push destruction and perpetual shame 5.07. 77
cry woe, destruction, ruin, and decay: R2 3.02.102
destruction straight shall dog them at the heels 5.03.139
death, | and, winking, leapt into destruction. 2H4 1.03. 33
or, like to men proud of destruction, | defy us H5 3.03. 4
and pale destruction meets thee in the face. 1H6 4.02. 27
iron | and hemm'd about with grim destruction. 4.03. 21
she'll gallop far enough to her destruction. 2H6 1.03.151
welcome destruction, blood, and massacre! R3 2.04. 53
death and destruction dogs thee at thy heels; 4.01. 39
hour, | even for revenge mock my destruction! 5.01. 9
to desperate adventures and assur'd destruction. 5.03.319
leap of danger, | and woo your own destruction. H8 5.01.140
sounding destruction, or some joy too fine, TRO 3.02. 23
a sure destruction. COR 2.01.243
and from thence | into destruction cast him. 3.01.213
which dreads not yet their lives' destruction. TIT 2.03. 50
writing destruction on the enemy's castle? 3.01.169
them, you gods, make suitable for destruction. TIM 3.06. 82 P
destruction fang mankind! 4.03. 23
hath in her more destruction than thy sword, 4.03. 63
the gods, | incenses them to send destruction. JC 1.03. 13
blood and destruction shall be so in use, | and 3.01.265
than by destruction dwell in doubtful joy. MAC 3.02. 7
all together, | even till destruction sicken; 4.01. 60
destruction on my head if my bad blame | light OTH 1.03.177
to that destruction which i'll guard them from ANT 5.02.132
DESTRUCTION'S 1 FR 0.0001 REL FR 1 V 0 P
virtue /preserv'd from fell destruction's blast, PER 5.03. 89
DESTRUCTIONS 1 FR 0.0001 REL FR 1 V 0 P
and linger not our sure destructions on! TRO 5.10. 9
D,E,T 1 FR 0.0001 REL FR 0 V 1 P
should pronounce "debt" — d,e,b,t, not d,e,t: LLL 5.01. 22 P
DET *(also debt)*
DET 1 FR 0.0001 REL FR 0 V 1 P
"det," when he should pronounce "debt" — LLL 5.01. 21 P
DETAIN 9 FR 0.0010 REL FR 7 V 2 P
would that alone a' love he would detain, | so ERR 2.01.107
prays some occasion may detain us longer. ADO 1.01.150 P
i would detain you here some month or two MV 3.02. 9
i shall offend either to detain or give it: LR 1.02. 41 P
noble antony, | not sickness should detain me. ANT 2.02.170
and, being, that we detain | all his revenue. 3.06. 29
do it, | detain no jot, i charge thee. 4.05. 13
for pity now she can no more detain him; VEN 577
she may detain, but not still keep, her treasure SON 126.10
DETAIN'D 4 FR 0.0004 REL FR 4 V 0 P
and here detain'd by her usurping uncle | to AYL 1.02.274
hath all so long detain'd you from your wife, SHR 3.02.103
the which he hath detain'd for lewd employments,
R2 1.01. 90
me | and hath detain'd me all my flow'ring youth 1H6 2.05. 56
/DETAINS 1 FR 0.0001 REL FR 1 V 0 P
/burning /shame | /detains /him /from /cordelia. LR 4.03. 47
DETECT 5 FR 0.0005 REL FR 3 V 2 P
i will prevent this, detect my wife, be reveng'd WIV 2.02.310 P
every hour would detect the lazy foot of time as AYL 3.02.304 P
to let thy tongue detect thy base–born heart? 3H6 2.02.143
and, lest thou shouldst detect /him, cut thy TIT 2.04. 27
all that may men approve or men detect! PER 2.01. 51
DETECTED 2 FR 0.0002 REL FR 0 V 2 P
fright, to be detected with a jealious rotten WIV 3.05.109 P
heard the absent duke much detected for women, MM 3.02.121 P
/DETECTING 1 FR 0.0001 REL FR 1 V 0 P
and scape /detecting, i will pay the theft. HAM 3.02. 89
DETECTION 1 FR 0.0001 REL FR 0 V 1 P
i come to her with any detection in my hand, my WIV 2.02.246 P
DETECTOR 1 FR 0.0001 REL FR 0 V 1 P
this treason were not — or not i the detector! LR 3.05. 13 P
DETECTS 1 FR 0.0001 REL FR 0 V 1 P
with his neighbor's wife, but it detects him. R3 1.04.137 P
DETENTION 1 FR 0.0001 REL FR 1 V 0 P
and the detention of long since due debts, TIM 2.02. 38
DETERMINATE 5 FR 0.0005 REL FR 3 V 2 P
my determinate voyage is mere extravagancy. TN 2.01. 11 P
slow hours shall not determinate | the dateless R2 1.03.150
ere a determinate resolution, he | (i mean the H8 2.04.177
none can be so determinate as the removing of OTH 4.02.227 P
my bonds in thee are all determinate. SON 87. 4
DETERMINATION 6 FR 0.0006 REL FR 4 V 2 P
how so, sir? did she change her determination? WIV 3.05. 68 P
humbles himself to the determination of justice; MM 3.02.244 P
would to god | you were of our determination! 1H4 4.03. 33
than to make up a free determination | 'twixt TRO 2.02.170
i have in quick determination | thus set it down HAM 3.01.168
which you hold in lease | find no determination; SON 13. 6
DETERMINATIONS 1 FR 0.0001 REL FR 0 V 1 P
have acquainted me with their determinations, MV 1.02.102 P
DETERMIN'D 15 FR 0.0017 REL FR 15 V 0 P
determin'd of — how i must climb her window, TGV 2.04.181
i know you have determin'd to bestow her | on 3.01. 13
vastidity you had, | to a determin'd scope. MM 3.01. 69
but stir not you till you have well determin'd 5.01.258
hath drawn him from his own determin'd aid, JN 2.01.584
till his friend sickness /have determin'd me? 2H4 4.05. 81
to my determin'd time thou gav'st new date. 1H6 4.06. 9
it is determin'd, not concluded yet; R3 1.03. 15
and that may be determin'd at the one | which 3.02. 13
yet had we not determin'd he should die | until 3.05. 52
soul, | is the determin'd respite of my wrongs. 5.01. 19
having determin'd of the volsces and | to send COR 2.02. 37
how i have govern'd our determin'd jest? TIT 5.02.139
and cassio following him with determin'd sword OTH 2.03.227
but let determin'd things to destiny | hold ANT 3.06. 84
DETERMINE 26 FR 0.0029 REL FR 24 V 2 P
and afterward determine our proceedings. TGV 3.02. 96
as the flesh and fortune shall better determine. MM 2.01.254 P
i will determine this before i stir. ERR 5.01.167
whom i have sent for to determine this, | come MV 4.01.106
/philip, determine what we shall do straight. JN 2.01.149
to hear and absolutely to determine | of what 2H4 4.01.162
and yet i determine to fight lustily for him. H5 4.01.189 P
long sitting to determine poor men's causes 2H6 4.07. 88
and go we to determine | who they shall be that R3 2.02.141
something we will determine. 3.01.193
we are met | is to determine of the coronation. 3.04. 2
must all determine here? COR 3.03. 43
determine on some course | more than a wild 4.01. 35
to wait on fortune till | these wars determine. 5.03.120
but let the laws of rome determine all, | mean TIT 1.01.407
this shall determine that. ROM 3.01.131
brief sounds determine my weal or woe. 3.02. 51
and we shall determine | how to cut off some JC 4.01. 8
speak, | but what we do determine, oft we break. HAM 3.02.187
let's then determine | with th' ancient of war LR 5.01. 31
merits and our safety | may equally determine. 5.03. 45
be it as you shall privately determine, | either OTH 1.03.275
it will determine one way; ANT 4.03. 2
determine this great war in single fight! 4.04. 37
honorable and how kindly we | determine for her; 5.01. 59
what | shall we determine, sir? TNK 3.05. 53
DETERMINED 5 FR 0.0005 REL FR 5 V 0 P
are you yet determined | to–day to marry with my
ADO 5.04. 36
what else? and that succession be determined. 3H6 4.06. 56
i am determined to prove a villain | and hate R3 1.01. 30
what are you then determined to do? JC 5.01. 99
and by their verdict is determined | the clear SON 46.11
DETERMINES 3 FR 0.0003 REL FR 3 V 0 P
she determines | herself the glory of a creditor MM 1.01. 38
till you know | how he determines further. H8 1.01.214
as it determines, so | dissolve my life! ANT 3.13.161
DETERMINING 1 FR 0.0001 REL FR 1 V 0 P
at gaze, | wildly determining which way to fly, LUC 1150
DETEST 10 FR 0.0011 REL FR 6 V 4 P
no, we detest such vile base practices. TGV 4.01. 71
cannot be) | i do detest false perjur'd proteus. 5.04. 39
but, i detest, an honest maid as ever broke WIV 1.04.150 P
whom i detest before heaven and your honor — MM 2.01. 69 P
dost thou detest her therefore? 2.01. 74 P
sir, i will detest myself also, as well as she, 2.01. 75 P
from these that my poor company detest. MND 3.02.434
dishonor that the gods | detest my baseness. ANT 4.14. 57
write against them, | detest them, curse them; CYM 2.05. 33
whose deed hath made herself herself detest. LUC 1566
DETESTABLE 6 FR 0.0006 REL FR 5 V 1 P
me, and these detestable things put upon me. WT 4.03. 62 P
and i will kiss thy detestable bones, | and put JN 3.04. 29
o detestable villain, call'st thou that trimming TIT 5.01. 94
most detestable death, by thee beguil'd, | by ROM 4.05. 56
thou detestable maw, thou womb of death, 5.03. 45
from thee | but nakedness, thou detestable town! TIM 4.01. 33
/DETESTED 1 FR 0.0001 REL FR 1 V 0 P
to the dark house and the /detested wife. AWW 2.03.292
DETESTED 16 FR 0.0018 REL FR 15 V 1 P
glory grows guilty of detested crimes, | when, LLL 4.01. 31
ay me, detested! how am i beguil'd! TN 5.01.139
in gross rebellion and detested treason. R2 2.03.109
then murthers, treasons, and detested sins, 3.02. 44
and for his sake wear the detested blot | of 1H4 1.03.162
thou detested — R3 1.03.232
body's hue, | spotted, detested, and abominable. TIT 2.03. 74
a barren detested vale you see it is; 2.03. 93
in this detested, dark, blood–drinking pit. 2.03.224
and yet detested life not shrink thereat! 3.01.247
where bloody murther or detested rape | can 5.02. 37
most smiling, smooth, detested parasites, TIM 3.06. 94
unnatural, detested, brutish villain! LR 1.02. 76 P
detested kite, thou liest. 1.04.262
be slave and sumpter | to this detested groom. 2.04.217
whet their detested knives against your throats, STM II.C 134
DETESTING 1 FR 0.0001 REL FR 1 V 0 P
to become the wife | of a detesting lord. AWW 3.05. 65
DETESTS 2 FR 0.0002 REL FR 1 V 1 P
and cross–garter'd, a fashion she detests; TN 2.05.200 P
a man that more detests, more stirs against, H8 5.02. 74
DETRACT 2 FR 0.0002 REL FR 1 V 1 P
voice is to utter foul speeches and to detract. TMP 2.02. 92 P
detract so much from that prerogative | as to be 1H6 5.04.142
DETRACTION 3 FR 0.0003 REL FR 1 V 2 P
you might see more detraction at your heels than TN 2.05.137 P
detraction will not suffer it. 1H4 5.01.139 P
direction, and | unspeak mine own detraction; MAC 4.03.123
DETRACTIONS 1 FR 0.0001 REL FR 0 V 1 P
that hear their detractions and can put them to ADO 2.03.229 P
DETRIMENT 1 FR 0.0001 REL FR 1 V 0 P
brought | by deep surmise of others' detriment, LUC 1579
DEUCALION 2 FR 0.0002 REL FR 1 V 1 P
no, not our kin, | farre than deucalion off. WT 4.04.431
is worth all your predecessors since deucalion, COR 2.01. 92 P
DEUCE–ACE 1 FR 0.0001 REL FR 0 V 1 P
how much the gross sum of deuce–ace amounts to.
LLL 1.02. 46 P
DEUM 3 FR 0.0003 REL FR 3 V 0 P
let there be sung non nobis and te deum, | the H5 4.08.123
music of the kingdom, | together sung te deum. H8 4.01. 92
proh deum, medius fidius, ye are all dunces! TNK 3.05. 11
DEUX 2 FR 0.0002 REL FR 0 V 2 P
j'ai gagne deux mots d'anglois vitement. H5 3.04. 13 P
ma vie, et je vous donnerai deux cents ecus. 4.04. 42 P
DEVANT 2 FR 0.0002 REL FR 0 V 2 P
prononcer ces mots devant les seigneurs de H5 3.04. 55 P
demoiselles pour etre baisees devant leur noces, 5.02.258 P
DEVESTING *(also divest)*
DEVESTING 1 FR 0.0001 REL FR 1 V 0 P
like bride and groom | devesting them for bed; OTH 2.03.181
DEVICE 48 FR 0.0054 REL FR 34 V 14 P
o excellent device, was thare ever heard a TGV 2.01.139
and there is also another device in my prain, WIV 1.01. 43 P
marry, this is our device: 4.04. 41
well, husband your device; 4.06. 52
life, by some device or other | the villain is ERR 1.02. 95
an excellent device! LLL 5.01.137 P
and shape his service wholly to my device, | and 5.02. 65
but i will forward with my device. 5.02.663 P
i have a device to make all well. MND 3.01. 16 P
that is an old device; 5.01. 50
i'll tell thee all my whole device | when i am MV 3.04. 81
entrap thee by some treacherous device, and AYL 1.01.151 P
school'd and yet learned, full of noble device, 1.01.167 P
well, | this is a letter of your own device. 4.03. 20
that's your device. SHR 1.01.193
that so i may, by this device, at least | have 1.02.135
excellent! i smell a device. TN 2.03.162 P
i could marry this wench for this device — 2.05.182 P
genius hath taken the infection of the device, 3.04.130 P
him now, lest the device take air and taint. 3.04.131 P
we will bring the device to the bar and crown 3.04.140 P
toby | set this device against malvolio here, 5.01.360
and not alone in habit and device, | exterior JN 1.01.210
what device? 1H4 2.04.263 P
i think by some odd gimmors or device | their 1H6 1.02. 41
it was thy device | by this alliance to make 3H6 3.03.141
o excellent device! and make a sop of him. R3 1.04.157 P
so gross | that cannot see this palpable device? 3.06. 11
i shall perish | under device and practice. H8 1.01.204
no new device to beat this from his brains? 3.02.217
and by device let blockish ajax draw | the sort TRO 1.03.374
but i know it is | (whether by device or no, the TIT 1.01.395
you do but plot your deaths | by this device. 2.01. 79
tongues | plot some device of further misery, 3.01.134
i know from whence this same device proceeds. 4.04. 52
what says andronicus to this device? 5.02.120
and entertain'd me with mine own device. TIM 1.02.150
work him | to an exploit, now ripe in my device, HAM 4.07. 64
dull not device by coldness and delay. OTH 2.03.388
every day thou daff'st me with some device, iago 4.02:175 P
'tis plate of rare device, and jewels | of rich CYM 1.06.189
the labor of each knight in his device. PER 2.02. 15
and the device he bears upon his shield | is a 2.02. 19
and the device he bears upon his shield | is an 2.02. 25
and his device, a wreath of chivalry; 2.02. 29

i hate not love, but your device in love, | that VEN 789
the shame that from them no device can take, LUC 535
"'lo this device was sent me from a nun, | or LC 232
DEVICES 6 FR 0.0006 REL FR 3 V 3 P
and to deliver us from devices hereafter, which MM 4.04. 12 P
be dogg'd with company, and our devices known. MND 1.02.104 P
before, i blush'd to hear his monstrous devices. 1H4 2.04.313 P
again, | and bury all thy fear in my devices. TIT 4.04.112
and will o'erreach them in their own devices, 5.02.143
run | that our devices still are overthrown, HAM 3.02.212
DEVIL *(also dev'l, etc., tevil)*
DEVIL 222 FR 0.0251 REL FR 129 V 93 P
got by the devil himself | upon thy wicked dam, TMP 1.02.319
where the devil should he learn our language? 2.02. 66 P
this is a devil, and no monster. 2.02. 98 P
your monster, and the devil take your fingers! 3.02. 81 P
if thou beest a devil, take't as thou list. 3.02.129 P
a devil, a born devil, on whose nature | nurture 4.01.188
a devil, a born devil, on whose nature | nurture 4.01.188
the devil speaks in him. 5.01.129
the devil himself hath not such a name. WIV 2.02.299 P
spirit, what devil suggests this imagination? 3.03.215 P
lest the devil that guides him should aid him, i 3.05.147 P
and the devil guide his cudgel afterwards! 4.02. 89 P
now shall the devil be sham'd. 4.02.119 P
if the devil have him not in fee-simple, with 4.02.210 P
the devil take one party and his dam the other! 4.05.106 P
hath the finest mad devil of jealousy in him, 5.01. 18 P
no man means evil but the devil, and we shall 5.02. 13 P
her troop of fairies, and the welsh devil /hugh? 5.03. 12 P
i think the devil will not have me damn'd, lest 5.05. 34 P
that ever the devil could have made you our 5.05.149 P
/enew | as falcon doth the fowl, is yet a devil; MM 3.01. 91
if the devil have given thee proofs for sin, 3.02. 30
duke, | you bid me seek redemption of the devil. 5.01. 29
and let the devil | be sometime honor'd for his 5.01.292
a devil in an everlasting garment hath him; ERR 4.02. 33
it is the devil. 4.03. 50 P
have a long spoon that must eat with the devil. 4.03. 64 P
the devil will shake her chain, and fright us 4.03. 76
be mad, good master, | cry "the devil!" 4.04.128
that will make a voyage with him to the devil? ADO 1.01. 83 P
and there will the devil meet me like an old 2.01. 44 P
but the devil my master knew she was margaret; 3.03.155 P
love is a devil; LLL 1.02.172 P
no devil will fright thee then so much as she. 4.03.271
tricks, some quillets, how to cheat the devil. 4.03.284
i should have fear'd her had she been a devil." 5.02.106
the contrary casket, for if the devil be within, MV 1.02. 97 P
of a saint and the complexion of a devil, i had 1.02.130 P
prophet the nazarite conjur'd the devil into. 1.03. 34 P
the devil can cite scripture for his purpose. 1.03. 98
who, god bless the mark, is a kind of devil; 2.02. 24 P
saving your reverence, is the devil himself. 2.02. 26 P
certainly the jew is the very devil incarnation, 2.02. 27 P
our house is hell, and thou, a merry devil, 2.03. 2
amen betimes, lest the devil cross my prayer, 3.01. 19 P
that's certain, if the devil may be her judge. 3.01. 32 P
be match'd, unless the devil himself turn jew. 3.01. 78 P
wrong, | and curb this cruel devil of his will. 4.01.217
ay, sacrifice them all | here to this devil, to 4.01.287
why then the devil give him good of it! 4.01.345
this, the devil himself will have no shepherds. AYL 3.02. 84 P
nay, but the devil take mocking. 3.02.214 P
a husband! a devil. SHR 1.01.121 P
i say, a devil. 1.01.123 P
why, he's a devil, a devil, a very fiend. 3.02.155
why, he's a devil, a devil, a very fiend. 3.02.155
why, she's a devil, a devil, the devil's dam. 3.02.156
why, she's a devil, a devil, the devil's dam. 3.02.156
and he must needs go that the devil drives. AWW 1.03. 30 P
star, and though the devil lead the measure, 2.01. 56 P
the devil it is that's thy master. 2.03.249 P
what the devil should move me to undertake the 4.01. 34 P
alias the prince of darkness, alias the devil. 4.05. 43 P
me at once both the office of god and the devil? 5.02. 49 P
let him be the devil, and he will, i care not; TN 1.05.128 P
but, if you were the devil, you are fair. 1.05.251
of tartar, thou most excellent devil of wit! 2.05.206 P
what, man, defy the devil! 3.04. 98 P
and you speak ill of the devil, how he takes it 3.04.100 P
but he is a devil in private brawl. 3.04.236 P
man, he's a very devil, i have not seen such a 3.04.273 P
i have persuaded him the youth's a devil. 3.04.293 P
are empty trunks o'erflourish'd by the devil. 3.04.370
that will use the devil himself with courtesy. 4.02. 33 P
to the devil; 4.02.128
adieu, goodman devil. 4.02.131
a coward, but he's the very devil incardinate. 5.01.181 P
though a devil | would have shed water out of WT 3.02.192
as faithfully as i deny the devil. JN 1.01.252
as like | as rain to water, or devil to his dam. 2.01.128
what the devil art thou? 2.01.134
one that will play the devil, sir, with you, 2.01.135
with that same purpose-changer, that sly devil, 2.01.567
look to that, devil, lest that france repent, 3.01.196
the devil tempts thee here | in likeness of a 3.01.208
some aery devil hovers in the sky | and pours 3.02. 2
thou wert better gall the devil, salisbury. 4.03. 95
you shall think the devil is come from hell. 4.03.100
that misbegotten devil faulconbridge, | in spite 5.04. 4
the devil take henry of lancaster and thee! R2 5.05.102
for now the devil that told me i did well | says 5.05.115
what a devil hast thou to do with the time of 1H4 1.02. 6 P
how agrees the devil and thee about thy soul 1.02.114 P
to his word, the devil shall have his bargain, 1.02.117 P
he will give the devil his due. 1.02.119 P
thou damn'd for keeping thy word with the devil. 1.02.121 P
else he had been damn'd for cozening the devil. 1.02.123 P
he durst as well have met the devil alone | as 1.03.116
and if the devil come and roar for them, | i 1.03.125
cousin" — | o, the devil take such cozeners! 1.03.255
but, as the devil would have it, three 2.04.221 P
cuckold and swore the devil his true liegeman 2.04.338 P
that spirit percy, and that devil glendower? 2.04.369 P
there is a devil haunts thee in the likeness of 2.04.447 P
the devil rides upon a fiddlestick. 2.04.487 P
i can teach you, cousin, to command | the devil. 3.01. 56
coz, to shame the devil | by telling truth: 3.01. 57
tell truth and shame the devil. 3.01. 58
while you live, tell truth and shame the devil! 3.01. 61
now i perceive the devil understands welsh, 3.01.229
if that the devil and mischance look big | upon 4.01. 58
as had as lieve hear the devil as a drum, such 4.02. 18 P
what a devil dost thou in warwickshire? 4.02. 51 P
he will foin like any devil, he will spare 2H4 2.01. 16 P
what the devil hast thou brought there? 2.04. 1 P
angel about him, but the devil blinds him too. 2.04.336 P
learning a mere hoard of gold kept by a devil, 4.03.115 P
why the devil should we keep knives to cut one H5 2.01. 91 P
will take up that with "give the devil his due." 3.07.116 P
there stands your friend for the devil; 3.07.119 P
eye of that proverb with "a pox of the devil." 3.07.120 P
weed, | and make a moral of the devil himself. 4.01. 12
valor than this roaring devil i' th' old play, 4.04. 71 P
the devil take order now! 4.05. 22
he be as good a gentleman as the devil is, as 4.07.137 P
the french exclaim'd, the devil was in arms; 1H6 1.01.125
this cardinal's more haughty than the devil. 1.03. 85
devil or devil's dam, i'll conjure thee. 1.05. 5
gold cannot come amiss, were she a devil. 2H6 1.02. 92
this devil here shall be my substitute; 3.01.371
there's two of you, the devil make a third, 3.02.303
"good gloucester" and "good devil" were alike, 3H6 5.06. 4
and mortal eyes cannot endure the devil. R3 1.02. 45
foul devil, for god's sake hence, and trouble us 1.02. 50
but the plain devil and dissembling looks? 1.02.236
out, devil! 1.03.117
and soothe the devil that i warn thee from? 1.03.297
and seem a saint, when most i play the devil. 1.03.337
take the devil in thy mind, and believe him not; 1.04.147 P
my brother's love, the devil, and my rage. 1.04.223
the devil" — there the villain stopp'd; 4.03. 16
shall i be tempted of the devil thus? 4.04.418
ay, if the devil tempt you to do good. 4.04.419
the devil speed him! H8 1.01. 52
if not from hell, the devil is a niggard, | or 1.01. 70
why the devil, | upon this french going out, 1.01. 72
the devil fiddle 'em! 1.03. 42
car, | confessor to him, with that devil monk, 2.01. 21
what cross devil | made me put this main secret 3.02.214
whose honesty the devil | and his disciples only 5.02.146
the devil was amongst 'em, i think, surely. 5.03. 58 P
and the devil come to him, it's all one. TRO 1.02.210 P
i have said my prayers, and devil envy say amen. 2.03. 21 P
the devil take antenor! 4.02. 75 P
there lurks a still and dumb-discoursive devil 4.04. 90
how the devil luxury, with his fat rump and 5.02. 55 P
wert thou the devil, and wor'st it on thy horn, 5.02. 95
a burning devil take them! 5.02.196 P
the devil take thee, coward! 5.07. 23 P
he's the devil. COR 1.10. 16
a devil. TIT 4.02. 64
goth, this is the incarnate devil | that robb'd 5.01. 40
bring down the devil, for he must not die | so 5.01.145
if there be devils, would i were a devil, | to 5.01.147
could not all hell afford you such a devil? 5.02. 86
it were convenient you had such a devil. 5.02. 90
this ravenous tiger, this accursed devil; 5.03. 5
some devil whisper curses in my ear, | and 5.03. 11
what devil art thou that dost torment me thus? ROM 3.02. 43
the devil knew not what he did when he made man TIM 3.03. 28 P
th' eternal devil to keep his state in rome | as JC 1.02.160
art thou some god, some angel, or some devil, 4.03.279
what, can the devil speak true? MAC 1.03.107
eye of childhood | that fears a painted devil. 2.02. 52
look on that | which might appall the devil. 3.04. 59
of horrid hell can come a devil more damn'd | in 4.03. 56
would not betray | the devil to his fellow, and 4.03.129
the devil damn thee black, thou cream-fac'd loon 5.03. 11
the devil himself could not pronounce a title 5.07. 8
action we do sugar o'er | the devil himself. HAM 3.01. 48
what devil was't | that thus hath cozen'd you at 3.04. 76
of habits devil, is angel yet in this, | that to 3.04.162
and either /... the devil or throw him out, 3.04.169
vows, to the blackest devil! 4.05.132
the devil take thy soul! 5.01.259
see thyself, devil! LR 4.02. 59
or else the devil will make a grandsire of you. OTH 1.01. 91
that will not serve god, if the devil bid you. 1.01.109 P
delight shall she have to look on the devil? 2.01.226 P
no name to be known by, let us call thee devil! 2.03.283 P
it hath pleas'd the devil drunkenness to give 2.03.296 P
drunkenness to give place to the devil wrath: 2.03.297 P
cup is unbless'd, and the ingredient is a devil. 2.03.308 P
some swift means of death | for the fair devil. 3.03.479
for here's a young and sweating devil here 3.04. 42
and, like the devil, from his very arm | puff'd 3.04.136
it is hypocrisy against the devil. 4.01. 6
the devil their virtue tempts, and they tempt 4.01. 8
o devil! 4.01. 43 P
let the devil and his dam haunt you! 4.01.148 P
devil! 4.01.240
o devil, devil! 4.01.244
o devil, devil! 4.01.244
the more angel she, | and you the blacker devil! 5.02.131
thou dost belie her, and thou art a devil. 5.02.133
if that thou be'st a devil, i cannot kill thee. 5.02.287
simple but i know the devil himself will not eat ANT 5.02.273 P
a dish for the gods, if the devil dress her not. 5.02.274 P
a lady that disdains | thee and the devil alike. CYM 1.06.148
that such a crafty devil as is his mother 2.01. 52
"his garments"! now the devil — 2.03.137
conspir'd with that irregulous devil cloten, 4.02.315
that she would make a puritan of the devil, if PER 4.06. 9 P
raise me a devil now, and let him play | qui TNK 3.05. 85
and die for her, | make death a devil. 3.06.270
this earthly saint, adored by this devil, LUC 85
evil, | when virtue is profan'd in such a devil! 847
shape every bush a hideous shapeless devil. 973
wherein is stamp'd the semblance of a devil. 1246
but like a constant and confirmed devil, | he 1513
and would corrupt my saint to be a devil, PP 2. 7
and would corrupt my saint to be a devil, SON 144. 7
DEVILISH 13 FR 0.0014 REL FR 12 V 1 P
there is a devilish mercy in the judge, | if MM 3.01. 64
for shame, thou hilding of a devilish spirit, SHR 2.01. 26
when, with a most impatient devilish spirit, 2.01.151
with linstock now the devilish cannon touches, H5 3.pr. 33
upon my life, began her devilish practices; 2H6 3.01. 46
by devilish policy art thou grown great | and, 4.01. 83
unless you be possess'd with devilish spirits 4.07. 75
but dead they are, and, devilish slave, by thee. R3 1.02. 90
not to relent is beastly, savage, devilish. 1.04.262
that do conspire my death with devilish plots 3.04. 60
devilish macbeth | by many of these trains hath MAC 4.03.117
a devilish knave. OTH 2.01.244 P
proceeded | (unless thou think'st me devilish), CYM 1.05. 16
DEVILISH-HOLY 1 FR 0.0001 REL FR 1 V 0 P
when truth kills truth, o devilish-holy fray! MND 3.02.129
DEVIL-PORTER 1 FR 0.0001 REL FR 0 V 1 P
i'll devil-porter it no further. MAC 2.03. 17 P
DEVIL'S 17 FR 0.0019 REL FR 12 V 5 P
flemish drunkard pick'd (with the devil's name!) WIV 2.01. 24 P
let's write "good angel" on the devil's horn, MM 2.04. 16
the devil's horn, | 'tis not the devil's crest. 2.04. 17
she is worse, she is the devil's dam, and here ERR 4.03. 51 P
you may go to the devil's dam; SHR 1.01.105 P
why, she's a devil, a devil, the devil's dam. 3.02.156
why, what a' devil's name, tailor, call'st thou 4.03. 92
how scapes he agues, in the devil's name? 1H4 3.01. 68
me as far in the devil's book as thou and 2H4 2.02. 46 P
devil or devil's dam, i'll conjure thee. 1H6 1.05. 5
a goodly prize, fit for the devil's grace! 5.03. 33
now pray, my lord, let's see the devil's writ. 2H6 1.04. 57
where is that devil's butcher, | hard-favor'd 3H6 5.05. 77
by th' devil's illusions | the monk might be H8 1.02.178
why, then she is the devil's dam: TIT 4.02. 65
who's there, in th' other devil's name? MAC 2.03. 8 P
throw your vild guesses in the devil's teeth, OTH 3.04.184
DEVILS' 2 FR 0.0002 REL FR 1 V 1 P
yet they are devils' additions, the names of WIV 2.02.298 P
in reckoning up the several devils' names | that 1H4 3.01.155
DEVILS 39 FR 0.0044 REL FR 27 V 12 P
"hell is empty, | and all the devils are here." TMP 1.02.215
have we devils here? 2.02. 57 P
and these are devils. 2.02. 88 P
of you three present | are worse than devils. 3.03. 36
as many devils entertain; WIV 1.03. 54 P
set spurs and away, like three german devils, 4.05. 69 P
some devils ask but the parings of one's nail, ERR 4.03. 71
devils soonest tempt, resembling spirits of LLL 4.03.253
one sees more devils than vast hell can hold; MND 5.01. 9
from all such devils, good lord deliver us! SHR 1.01. 66
if all the devils of hell be drawn in little, TN 3.04. 85 P
lest you say | your queen and i are devils. WT 1.02. 82
and other devils that suggest by treasons | do H5 2.02.114
they will eat like wolves and fight like devils. 3.07.151 P
to compass wonders but by help of devils. 1H6 5.04. 48
in despite of the devils and hell, have through 2H6 4.08. 60 P
let ten thousand devils come against me, and 4.10. 61 P
o wonderful, when devils tell the /troth! R3 1.02. 73
affrights thee with a hell of ugly devils! 1.03.226
i'll learn to conjure and raise devils, but i'll TRO 2.03. 6 P
fears make devils of cherubins, they never see 3.02. 69 P
not, | and sometimes we are devils to ourselves, 4.04. 95
pray to the devils, the gods have given us over. TIT 4.02. 48
if there be devils, would i were a devil, | to 5.01.147
devils! TIM 3.04.104
darkness and devils! LR 1.04.252
saints in your injuries, devils being offended, OTH 2.01.111
when devils will the blackest sins put on, 2.03.351
the devils themselves | should fear to seize 4.02. 36
let heaven and men and devils, let them all, 5.02.221
whip me, ye devils, | from the possession of 5.02.277
now, gods and devils! ANT 3.13. 89
these same whoreson devils do the gods great 5.02.275 P
every ten that they make, the devils mar five. 5.02.277 P
o, all the devils! CYM 2.05. 13
the very devils cannot plague them better. 2.05. 35
devils take 'em | that are so envious to me! TNK 2.02.262
let all the dukes and all the devils roar, | he 2.06. 1
"such devils steal effects from lightless hell, LUC 1555
DEVIN 1 FR 0.0001 REL FR 0 V 1 P
du monde, mon tres cher et devin deesse? H5 5.02.217 P
DEVIS'D 20 FR 0.0022 REL FR 15 V 5 P
lord, they have devis'd a mean | how he her TGV 3.01. 38
with no sauce that can be devis'd to it. ADO 4.01.279 P
who devis'd this penalty? LLL 1.01.124 P
to any french courtier for a new devis'd cur'sy. 1.02. 63 P
through athens gates have we devis'd to steal. MND 1.01.213
the lott'ry that he hath devis'd in these three MV 1.02. 29 P
of many parts | by heavenly synod was devis'd, AYL 3.02.150
though devis'd | and play'd to take spectators. WT 3.02. 36
and daily new exactions are devis'd, | as blanks R2 2.01.249
me beg | as, in reproof of many tales devis'd, 1H4 3.02. 23
with written pamphlets studiously devis'd? 1H6 3.01. 2
queen, | devis'd impeachments to imprison him; R3 2.02. 22
devis'd at first to keep the strong in awe: 5.03.310
they say | they are devis'd by you, or else you H8 1.02. 51
there let them bide until we have devis'd | some TIT 2.03.284
ceremony was but devis'd at first | to set a TIM 1.02. 15
down, | devis'd a new commission, wrote it fair. HAM 5.02. 32
some office, | have not devis'd this slander. OTH 4.02.133
or my reporter devis'd well for her. ANT 2.02.189 P
yet when they have devis'd | what strained SON 82. 9
DEVISE 50 FR 0.0056 REL FR 37 V 13 P
good hearts, devise something; WIV 4.02. 73 P
devise but how you'll use him when he comes, 4.04. 26
and let us two devise to bring him thither. 4.04. 27
the antipodes that you can devise to send me on; ADO 2.01.265 P
and truly i'll devise some honest slanders | to 3.01. 84
i'll devise thee brave punishments for him. 5.04.128 P
as the rest of the court can possible devise." LLL 1.01.132 P
devise, wit, write, pen, for i am for whole 1.02.184 P
therefore let us devise | some entertainment for 4.03.369
this falls out better than i could devise. MND 3.02. 35
the brain may devise laws for the blood, but a MV 1.02. 18 P
from henceforth i will, coz, and devise sports. AYL 1.02. 24 P
therefore devise with me how we may fly, 1.03.100
devise the fittest time and safest way | to hide 1.03.135
i shall devise something; 4.03.181 P
i will devise a death as cruel for thee | as WT 4.04.440

cardinal, devise a name | so slight, unworthy, JN 3.01.149
out of your grace devise, ordain, impose | some 3.01.250
what i have spoke, or thou canst worse devise. R2 1.01. 77
what sport shall we devise here in this garden 3.04. 1
to effect | what ever i shall happen to devise. 4.01.330
i will devise matter enough out of this shallow 2H4 5.01. 78 P
and withal devise something to do thyself good. 5.03.133 P
and for his safety there i'll best devise. 1H6 1.01.172
what devise you on? 1.02.124
then thus it must be, this doth joan devise: 3.03. 17
devise strange deaths for small offenses done? 2H6 3.01. 59
in your protectorship you did devise | strange 3.01.121
we'll devise a mean | to reconcile you all unto 4.08. 68
clifford, devise excuses for thy faults. 3H6 2.06. 71
while we devise fell tortures for thy faults. 2.06. 72
be appeas'd | by such invention as i can devise? 4.01. 35
for our mistress to devise imposition enough TRO 3.02. 79 P
other instruments | did see and hear, devise, COR 1.01.102
measure fit the honors | which we devise him. 2.02.124
month, devise with thee | where thou shalt rest, 4.01. 38
as kill a man, or else devise his death, TIT 5.01.128
bid her devise | some means to come to shrift ROM 2.04.179
but love thee better than thou canst devise, 3.01. 69
and with wild looks bid me devise some mean | to 5.03.240
but speak all good you can devise of caesar, JC 3.01.246
can you devise me? HAM 4.07. 53
if you could devise it so | that i might be the 4.07. 69
let her who would be rid of him devise | his LR 5.01. 64
and i'll devise a mean to draw the moor | out of OTH 3.01. 37
and for me to devise a lodging and say he lies 3.04. 11 P
with treachery and devise engines for my life. 4.02.216 P
devise extremes beyond extremity, | to make him LUC 969
unless you would devise some virtuous lie, | to SON 72. 5
than both your poets can in praise devise. 83.14
DEVISED 2 FR 0.0002 REL FR 2 V 0 P
law | was not devised for the realm of france; H5 1.02. 55
a thing devised by the enemy. R3 5.03.306
DEVISES 1 FR 0.0001 REL FR 0 V 1 P
she plots, then she ruminates, then she devises; WIV 2.02.306 P
DEVISETH 1 FR 0.0001 REL FR 1 V 0 P
danger deviseth shifts, wit waits on fear. VEN 690
DEVISING 1 FR 0.0001 REL FR 0 V 1 P
only his gift is in devising impossible slanders ADO 2.01.138 P
DEV'L *(also devil, etc., tevil)*
/DEV'L 2 FR 0.0002 REL FR 2 V 0 P
the spirit that i have seen | may be a /dev'l, HAM 2.02.599
and the /dev'l hath power | t' assume a pleasing 2.02.599
DEV'L 7 FR 0.0008 REL FR 2 V 5 P
the dev'l a puritan that he is, or any thing TN 2.03.147 P
said once, the dev'l would have him about women. H5 2.03. 35 P
where the dev'l should this romeo be? ROM 2.04. 1
why the dev'l came you between us? 3.01.103 P
nay then let the dev'l wear black, for i'll have HAM 3.02.129 P
the dev'l cannot rule them. STM II.C 53 P
you | to lead those that the dev'l cannot rule. II.C 56
DEV'LS 1 FR 0.0001 REL FR 0 V 1 P
'a did, and said they were dev'ls incarnate. H5 2.03. 31 P
DEVOID 1 FR 0.0001 REL FR 1 V 0 P
her life was beastly and devoid of pity, | and, TIT 5.03.199
DEVONSHIRE 1 FR 0.0001 REL FR 1 V 0 P
my gracious sovereign, now in devonshire, | as i R3 4.04.498
DEVOTE 1 FR 0.0001 REL FR 1 V 0 P
or so devote to aristotle's checks | as ovid be SHR 1.01. 32
DEVOTED 6 FR 0.0006 REL FR 3 V 3 P
of your perfect self | is else devoted, i am but TGV 4.02.124
in all complements of devoted and heart-burning LLL 1.01.276 P
this is your devoted friend, sir, the manifold AWW 4.03.235 P
this fiend | to stop devoted charitable deeds? R3 1.02. 35
and if thy poor devoted servant may | but beg 1.02.206
for that he hath devoted and given up himself to OTH 2.03.316 P
DEVOTION 18 FR 0.0020 REL FR 16 V 2 P
promise | most venerable worth, did i devotion. TN 3.04.363
have breath'd out | that e'er devotion tender'd! 5.01.115
speech, | in the devotion of a subject's love, R2 1.01. 31
my devotion — 2H4 5.05. 18 P
cam'st thou here by chance | or of devotion, to 2H6 2.01. 86
god knows, of pure devotion, being call'd | a 2.01. 87
foes | tell our devotion with revengeful arms? 3H6 2.01.164
life, | and in devotion spend my latter days, 4.06. 43
of thy devotion and right christian zeal. R3 3.07.103
i guess, | upon the like devotion as yourselves, 4.01. 9
immaculate devotion, holy thoughts, | i tender 4.04.404
more bright in zeal than the devotion which TRO 4.04. 26
hate with greater devotion than they can render COR 2.02. 19 P
much, | which mannerly devotion shows in this: ROM 1.05. 98
god shield i should disturb devotion! 4.01. 41
devotion, patience, courage, fortitude, | i have MAC 4.03. 94
i have no great devotion to the deed, | and yet OTH 5.01. 8
now turn | the office and devotion of their view ANT 1.01. 5
DEVOTION'S 1 FR 0.0001 REL FR 1 V 0 P
that with devotion's visage | and pious action HAM 3.01. 46
DEVOUR 14 FR 0.0015 REL FR 12 V 2 P
so much admire | that they devour their reason, TMP 5.01.155
and greedily devour the treacherous bait; ADO 3.01. 28
the jaws of darkness do devour it up: MND 1.01.148
may drop upon his kingdom and devour | incertain WT 5.01. 28
so | he seem'd in running to devour the way, 2H4 1.01. 47
the present wars devour him! COR 1.01.258
ay, to devour him, as the hungry plebeians would 2.01. 9 P
that vulture in you to devour so many | as will MAC 4.03. 74
the good-years shall devour them, flesh and fell LR 5.03. 24
and with a greedy ear | devour up my discourse. OTH 1.03.150
him, and at last devour them all at a mouthful. PER 2.01. 31 P
time, | fearful consumers, you will all devour! TNK 1.01. 70
not that devour'd, but that which doth devour, LUC 1256
and make the earth devour her own sweet brood; SON 19. 2
DEVOUR'D 6 FR 0.0006 REL FR 5 V 1 P
ox-beef hath devour'd many a gentleman of your MND 3.01.193 P
whom the blind waves and surges have devour'd. TN 5.01.229
which are devour'd | as fast as they are made, TRO 3.03.148
have all forsook me, hath devour'd the rest, COR 4.05. 76
and pericles, in sorrow all devour'd, | with PER 4.04. 25
not that devour'd, but that which doth devour, LUC 1256
DEVOURED 2 FR 0.0002 REL FR 2 V 0 P
these lincoln washes have devoured them; JN 5.06. 41
all unwarily | devoured by the unexpected flood. 5.07. 64
DEVOURERS 1 FR 0.0001 REL FR 1 V 0 P
then, | from these devourers to be banished! TIT 3.01. 57
DEVOURING 8 FR 0.0009 REL FR 8 V 0 P
a grace it had, devouring. TMP 3.03. 84
when, spite of cormorant devouring time, | th' LLL 1.01. 4
suppose | devouring pestilence hangs in our air, R2 1.03.284
wretch | that trembles under his devouring paws; 3H6 1.03. 13
hath — | out of this fell devouring receptacle, TIT 2.03.235
shaking her wings, devouring all in haste, VEN 57
devours his will, that liv'd by foul devouring. LUC 700
devouring time, blunt thou the lion's paws, SON 19. 1
DEVOURS 4 FR 0.0004 REL FR 2 V 2 P
to virginity and devours up all the fry it finds AWW 4.03.221 P
but in the deed, devours the deed in the praise. TRO 2.03.157 P
devours his will, that liv'd by foul devouring. LUC 700
sing, | what virtue breeds iniquity devours: 872
DEVOUT 8 FR 0.0009 REL FR 6 V 2 P
but more devout than this /in our respects LLL 5.02.782
a coward, a most devout coward, religious in it. TN 3.04.389 P
my soul | with contemplation and devout desires. JN 5.04. 48
which men devout | by testament have given to H5 1.01. 9
when holy and devout religious men | are at R3 3.07. 92
what, art thou devout? wast thou in prayer? TRO 2.03. 35 P
when the devout religion of mine eye | maintains ROM 1.02. 88
and prayer, | much castigation, exercise devout, OTH 3.04. 41
DEVOUTLY 3 FR 0.0003 REL FR 3 V 0 P
devoutly dotes, dotes in idolatry, | upon this MND 1.01.109
her fair eyes to heaven, and pray'd devoutly; H8 4.01. 84
'tis a consummation | devoutly to be wish'd. HAM 3.01. 63
DEW* 38 FR 0.0043 REL FR 38 V 0 P
thou call'dst me up at midnight to fetch dew TMP 1.02.228
as wicked dew as e'er my mother brush'd | with 1.02.321
the night of dew that on my cheeks down flows; LLL 4.03. 28
fairy queen, | to dew her orbs upon the green. MND 2.01. 9
bedabbled with the dew and torn with briers, | i 3.02.443
and that same dew, which sometime on the buds 4.01. 53
with ears that sweep away the morning dew; 4.01.121
a night | did thisby fearfully o'ertrip the dew, MV 5.01. 7
clear | as morning roses newly wash'd with dew; SHR 2.01.173
the want of which vain dew | perchance shall dry WT 2.01.109
before the dew of evening fall, shall fleet | in JN 2.01.285
let me wipe off this honorable dew, | that 5.02. 45
that you in pity may dissolve to dew | and wash R2 5.01. 9
o signieur dew should be a gentleman. H5 4.04. 7
perpend my words, o signieur dew, and mark: 4.04. 8
o signieur dew, thou diest on point of fox, 4.04. 9
that i may dew it with my mournful tears; 2H6 3.02.340
shall be to me even as the dew to fire, | and 5.02. 53
his bed | did i enjoy the golden dew of sleep, R3 4.01. 83
in to my tent, the dew is raw and cold. 5.03. 46
my lord and me — | which god's dew quench! H8 2.04. 80
as fresh as morning dew distill'd on flowers? TIT 2.03.201
with tears augmenting the fresh morning's dew, ROM 1.01.132
the day to cheer and night's dank dew to dry, 2.03. 6
when the sun sets, the earth doth drizzle dew, 3.05.126
which with sweet water nightly i will dew, | or, 5.03. 14
matter, | enjoy the honey-heavy dew of slumber. JC 2.01.230
to dew the sovereign flower and drown the weeds. MAC 5.02. 30
walks o'er the dew of yon high eastward hill. HAM 1.01.167
melt, | thaw, and resolve itself into a dew! 1.02.130
and in the morn and liquid dew of youth 1.03. 41
your bright swords, for the dew will rust them. OTH 1.02. 59
herbs that have on them cold dew o' th' night CYM 4.02.284
covering heavens | fall on their heads like dew! 5.05.351
the blissful dew of heaven does arrouse you. TNK 5.04.104
as is the morning's silver melting dew | against LUC 24
with pearly sweat resembling dew of night. 396
heart | in such relenting dew of lamentations, 1829
DEW-BEDABBLED 1 FR 0.0001 REL FR 1 V 0 P
"then shalt thou see the dew-bedabbled wretch VEN 703
DEWBERRIES 1 FR 0.0001 REL FR 1 V 0 P
feed him with apricocks and dewberries, | with MND 3.01.166
DEW'D 1 FR 0.0001 REL FR 1 V 0 P
so they were dew'd with such distilling showers. VEN 66
DEWDROP 1 FR 0.0001 REL FR 1 V 0 P
and, like /a dewdrop from the lion's mane, | be TRO 3.03.224
DEW-DROPPING 1 FR 0.0001 REL FR 1 V 0 P
turning his side to the dew-dropping south. ROM 1.04.103
DEWDROPS 1 FR 0.0001 REL FR 1 V 0 P
i must go seek some dewdrops here, | and hang a MND 2.01. 14
DEW-LAPP'D 1 FR 0.0001 REL FR 1 V 0 P
dew-lapp'd, like bulls, whose throats had TMP 3.03. 45
DEWLAPP'D 1 FR 0.0001 REL FR 1 V 0 P
and dewlapp'd like thessalian bulls; MND 4.01.122
DEWLOP 1 FR 0.0001 REL FR 1 V 0 P
bob, | and on her withered dewlop pour the ale. MND 2.01. 50
DEW'S 1 FR 0.0001 REL FR 1 V 0 P
whiles yet the dew's on ground, gather those CYM 1.05. 1
DEWS 6 FR 0.0006 REL FR 5 V 1 P
his dews fall every where. H8 1.03. 57
the dews of heaven fall thick in blessings on 4.02.133
being three parts melted away with rotten dews, COR 2.03. 32 P
he watered his new plants with dews of flattery, 5.06. 22
day is gone, | clouds, dews, and dangers come; JC 5.03. 64
as stars with trains of fire and dews of blood, HAM 1.01.117
DEWY 3 FR 0.0003 REL FR 3 V 0 P
i would these dewy tears were from the ground. R3 5.03.284
which makes the maid weep like the dewy night. LUC 1232
scarce had the sun dried up the dewy morn, | and PP 6. 1
DEXTER 2 FR 0.0002 REL FR 2 V 0 P
my mother's blood | runs on the dexter cheek, TRO 4.05.128
to give the smooth and dexter way to me | that STM III 11
DEXTERIOUSLY 1 FR 0.0001 REL FR 0 V 1 P
dexteriously, good madonna. TN 1.05. 60 P
DEXTERITY 6 FR 0.0006 REL FR 4 V 2 P
but that my admirable dexterity of wit, my WIV 4.05.117 P
guts away as nimbly, with as quick dexterity, 1H4 2.04.259 P
dexterity so obeying appetite | that what he TRO 5.05. 27
it back to tybalt, whose dexterity | retorts it. ROM 3.01.163
post | with such dexterity to incestious sheets! HAM 1.02.157
in youth, quick bearing and dexterity; LUC 1389
DEY-WOMAN 1 FR 0.0001 REL FR 0 V 1 P
she is allow'd for the dey-woman. LLL 1.02.131 P
DIABLE 4 FR 0.0004 REL FR 1 V 3 P
o diable, diable! WIV 1.04. 67 P
o diable, diable! 1.04. 67 P
diable! 3.01. 91 P
o diable! H5 4.05. 1
DIABLO 1 FR 0.0001 REL FR 1 V 0 P
diablo, ho! OTH 2.03.161
DIADEM 13 FR 0.0014 REL FR 13 V 0 P
to redeem | and have install'd me in the diadem. 1H6 2.05. 89
fist, | nor wear the diadem upon his head, 2H6 1.01.246
king henry's diadem, | enchas'd with all the 1.02. 7
to me, | and on my head did set the diadem. 1.02. 40
having neither subject, wealth, nor diadem. 4.01. 82
glory, | and rob his temples of the diadem, 3H6 1.04.104
can pluck the diadem from faint henry's head, 2.01.153
for grace, | and set thy diadem upon my head, 2.02. 82
my right, | and henry but usurps the diadem. 4.07. 66
last | that ware the imperial diadem of rome, TIT 1.01. 6
upon that head | where late the diadem stood, HAM 2.02.507
that from a shelf the precious diadem stole, 3.04.100
i found her trimming up the diadem | on her dead ANT 5.02.342
DIAL 9 FR 0.0010 REL FR 7 V 2 P
by this i think the dial points at five. ERR 5.01.118
and then he drew a dial from his poke, | and, AYL 2.07. 20
laugh sans intermission | an hour by his dial. 2.07. 33
then my dial goes not true. AWW 2.05. 6 P
the bawdy hand of the dial is now upon the prick ROM 2.04.113 P
more tedious than the dial eightscore times? OTH 3.04.175
or as those bars which stop the hourly dial, LUC 327
thy dial how thy precious minutes waste; SON 77. 2
ah, yet doth beauty, like a dial hand, | steal 104. 9
DIALECT 3 FR 0.0003 REL FR 2 V 1 P
youth | there is a prone and speechless dialect, MM 1.02.183
to go out of my dialect, which you discommend so LR 2.02.109 P
weep, | he had the dialect and different skill, LC 125
DIALOGU'D 1 FR 0.0001 REL FR 1 V 0 P
and dialogu'd for him what he would say, | ask'd LC 132
DIALOGUE 7 FR 0.0008 REL FR 3 V 4 P
fear you not my part of the dialogue. ADO 3.01. 31
will you hear the dialogue that the two learned LLL 5.02.885 P
shall we have this dialogue between the fool and AWW 4.03. 97 P
with me to make one in so skipping a dialogue. TN 1.05.201 P
would, | saving in dialogue of compliment, | and JN 1.01.201
to hear the wooden dialogue and sound | 'twixt TRO 1.03.155
dost dialogue with thy shadow? TIM 2.02. 51 P
DIAL'S 4 FR 0.0004 REL FR 4 V 0 P
watch, | whereto my finger, like a dial's point, R2 5.05. 53
too long | if life did ride upon a dial's point, 1H4 5.02. 83
as many lines close in the dial's centre; H5 1.02.210
thou by thy dial's shady stealth mayst know SON 77. 7
DIALS 2 FR 0.0002 REL FR 1 V 1 P
of bawds, and dials the signs of leaping-houses, 1H4 1.02. 8 P
to carve out dials quaintly, point by point, 3H6 2.05. 24
DIAMETER 1 FR 0.0001 REL FR 1 V 0 P
/... | whose whisper o'er the world's diameter, HAM 4.01. 41
DIAMOND 15 FR 0.0017 REL FR 9 V 6 P
i see how thine eye would emulate the diamond. WIV 3.03. 55 P
or, for my diamond, the chain you promis'd, ERR 4.03. 69
sir, i must have that diamond from you. 5.01.392
a diamond gone, cost me two thousand ducats in MV 3.01. 83 P
set this diamond safe | in golden palaces, as it 1H6 5.03.169
this diamond he greets your wife withal, | by MAC 2.01. 15
look here, love, | this diamond was my mother's. CYM 1.01.112
as that diamond of yours outlustres many i have 1.04. 73 P
have not seen the most precious diamond that is, 1.04. 75 P
i shall but lend my diamond till your return. 1.04.142 P
ducats are yours, so is your diamond too. 1.04.151 P
it must be married | to that your diamond, i'll 2.04. 98
that diamond upon your finger, say | how came it 5.05.137
to me he seems like diamond to glass. PER 2.03. 36
"'the diamond? LC 211
/DIAMONDS 1 FR 0.0001 REL FR 1 V 0 P
/thence, | /as /pearls /from /diamonds /dropp'd. LR 4.03. 22
DIAMONDS 6 FR 0.0006 REL FR 6 V 0 P
a lady wall'd about with diamonds! LLL 5.02. 3
neck, | a heart it was, bound in with diamonds, 2H6 3.02.107
not deck'd with diamonds and indian stones, 3H6 3.01. 63
one day he gives us diamonds, next day stones. TIM 3.06.120
you shall like diamonds sit about his crown. PER 2.04. 53
the diamonds | of a most praised water doth 3.02.100
DIAN 21 FR 0.0023 REL FR 21 V 0 P
you seem to me as dian in her orb, | as chaste ADO 4.01. 57
did ever dian so become a grove | as kate this SHR 2.01.258
o, be thou dian, and let her be kate, | and then 2.01.260
and then let kate be chaste and dian sportful! 2.01.261
that your dian | was both herself and love, o, AWW 1.03.212
now, dian, from thy altar do i fly, | and to 2.03. 74
"dian, the count's a fool, and full of gold" — 4.03.211
and say a soldier, dian, told thee this: 4.03.227
or modest dian, circled with her nymphs, | shall 3H6 4.08. 21
or is it dian habited like her, | who hath TIT 2.03. 57
had i the pow'r that some say dian had, | thy 2.03. 61
and the chimney-piece | chaste dian bathing. CYM 2.04. 82
yet my mother seem'd | the dian of that time. 2.05. 7
he spake of her, as dian had hot dreams, | and 5.05.180
and constant pen | vail to her mistress dian; PER 4.ch. 29
celestial dian, goddess argentine, | i will obey 5.01.250
till he had done his sacrifice, | as dian bade; 5.02. 13
hail, dian! 5.03. 1
immortal dian! 5.03. 37
pure dian, | /i bless thee for thy vision, and 5.03. 68
thy lips | make modest dian cloudy and forlorn, VEN 725
/DIANA 1 FR 0.0001 REL FR 0 V 1 P
/diana /no queen of virgins, that would suffer AWW 1.03.114 P
DIANA 17 FR 0.0019 REL FR 8 V 9 P
i will die as chaste as diana, unless i be MV 1.02.107 P
come ho, and wake diana with a hymn, | with 5.01. 66
he hath bought a pair of cast lips of diana. AYL 3.04. 15 P
weep for nothing, like diana in the fountain, 4.01.154 P
well, diana, take heed of this french earl. AWW 3.05. 11 P
beware of them, diana; 3.05. 18 P
no, my good lord, diana. 4.02. 2
to a proper maid in florence, one diana, to take 4.03.214 P
sonnet you writ to diana in behalf of the count 4.03.320 P
you, diana, | under my poor instructions yet 4.04. 26
diana capilet." 5.03.147 P
o dear diana, | where am i? PER 3.02.104
madam, | by bright diana, whom we honor, all 3.03. 28
at ephesus, | unto diana there 's a votaress. 4.ch. 4
diana aid my purpose! 4.02.148
what have we to do with diana? 4.02.149 P

what sins have i committed, chaste diana, | that TNK 4.02. 58
DIANA'S 10 FR 0.0011 REL FR 9 V 1 P
or on diana's altar to protest | for aye MND 1.01. 89
diana's lip | is not more smooth and rubious; TN 1.04. 31
let us be diana's foresters, gentlemen of the 1H4 1.02. 25 P
by all diana's waiting–women yond, | and by TRO 5.02. 91
should he make me | live, like diana's priest, CYM 1.06.133
and makes | diana's rangers false themselves, 2.03. 69
twelve moons more she'll wear diana's livery; PER 2.05. 10
ye speak, | diana's temple is not distant far, 3.04. 13
sir, | if you have told diana's altar true, 5.03. 17
her, and plac'd her | here in diana's temple. 5.03. 25
DIAN'S 7 FR 0.0008 REL FR 7 V 0 P
dian's bud o'er cupid's flower | hath such force MND 4.01. 73
from purest snow | and hangs on dian's temple — COR 5.03. 67
hit | with cupid's arrow, she hath dian's wit; ROM 1.01.209
the consecrated snow | that lies on dian's lap! TIM 4.03.386
that was as fresh | as dian's visage, is now OTH 3.03.387
do observance | to flow'ry may, in dian's wood. TNK 2.05. 51
a maid of dian's this advantage found, | and his SON 153. 2
DIAPASON 1 FR 0.0001 REL FR 1 V 0 P
tear, | and with deep groans the diapason bear; LUC 1132
DIAPER 1 FR 0.0001 REL FR 1 V 0 P
another bear the ewer, the third a diaper, | and SHR in.1. 57
DIBBLE 1 FR 0.0001 REL FR 1 V 0 P
the dibble in earth to set one slip of them; WT 4.04.100
DIC'D 1 FR 0.0001 REL FR 0 V 1 P
swore little, dic'd not above seven times — a 1H4 3.03. 16 P
DICE 10 FR 0.0011 REL FR 7 V 3 P
keep a gamester from the dice, and a good WIV 3.01. 38 P
once before he won it of me with false dice, ADO 2.01.281 P
well run, dice! LLL 5.02.233
at tables, chides the dice | in honorable terms; 5.02.326
if hercules and lichas play at dice | which is MV 2.01. 32
as dice are to be wish'd by one that fixes | no WT 1.02.133
french | do the low–rated english play at dice; H5 4.pr. 19
these the wretches that we play'd at dice for? 4.05. 8
wine lov'd i /deeply, dice dearly; LR 3.04. 91 P
the very dice obey him, | and in our sports my ANT 2.03. 34
DICERS' 1 FR 0.0001 REL FR 1 V 0 P
makes marriage vows | as false as dicers' oaths, HAM 3.04. 45
DICH 1 FR 0.0001 REL FR 0 V 1 P
much good dich thy good heart, apemantus! TIM 1.02. 72 P
DICK 8 FR 0.0009 REL FR 4 V 4 P
mumble–news, some trencher–knight, some dick, LLL 5.02.464
the wall | and dick the shepherd blows his nail 5.02.913
sot, didst see dick surgeon, sot? TN 5.01.197 P
their christen names, as tom, dick, and francis. 1H4 2.04. 8 P
and dick the butcher — 2H6 4.02. 25 P
where's dick, the butcher of ashford? 4.03. 1 P
and thou misshapen dick, i tell ye all | i am 3H6 5.05. 35
should i stand here | to beg of hob and dick, COR 2.03.116
DICKENS 1 FR 0.0001 REL FR 0 V 1 P
i cannot tell what the dickens his name is my WIV 3.02. 19 P
DICKON 1 FR 0.0001 REL FR 1 V 0 P
for dickon thy master is bought and sold." R3 5.03.305
DICKY 1 FR 0.0001 REL FR 1 V 0 P
dicky, your boy, that with his grumbling voice 3H6 1.04. 76
DICTATOR 1 FR 0.0001 REL FR 1 V 0 P
our then dictator, | whom with all praise i COR 2.02. 89
DICTION 1 FR 0.0001 REL FR 0 V 1 P
and rareness as, to make true diction of him, HAM 5.02.118 P
/DICTYNNA 3 FR 0.0003 REL FR 2 V 1 P
/dictynna, goodman dull, /dictynna, goodman dull
LLL 4.02. 36
goodman dull, /dictynna, goodman dull. 4.02. 36
what is /dictynna? 4.02. 37 P
/DID 20 FR 0.0022 REL FR 19 V 1 P
/did /they /not /sometimes /cry "/all /hail!" R2 4.01.169
/so /judas /did /to /christ; 4.01.170
/which /tired /majesty /did /make /thee /offer: 4.01.178
/roof | /did /keep /ten /thousand /men? 4.01.283
/like /the /sun, /did /make /beholders /wink? 4.01.284
/yet /did /you /say, "/go /forth!" 2H4 1.01.175
/did /divide | /the /action /of /their /bodies 1.01.194
/and /they /did /fight /with /queasiness, 1.01.196
/him /did /you /leave, | /second /to /none, 2.03. 33
/of /hotspur's /name | /did /seem /defensible: 2.03. 38
/when /the /king /did /throw /his /warder /down 4.01.123
/on | /and /bless'd /and /grac'd /and /did, 4.01.137
/if /marcus /did /not /name /the /word /of TIT 3.02. 33
horses /did neigh, and dying men did groan, JC 2.02. 23
/they /did /make /love /to /this /employment, HAM 5.02. 57
/the /bravery /of /his /grief /did /put /me 5.02. 79
/did /your /letters /pierce /the /queen /to /any LR 4.03. 9 P
/and /did /him /service | /improper /for /a 5.03.221
that i /did love the moor to live with him, | my OTH 1.03.248
/did not you hear a cry? 5.01. 49
DID 1774 FR 0.2005 REL FR 1536 V 238 P
o, the cry did knock | against my very heart. TMP 1.02. 8
to know | did never meddle with my thoughts. 1.02. 22
or blessed was't we did? 1.02. 61
did beget of him | a falsehood in its contrary, 1.02. 94
lie — he did believe | he was indeed the duke, 1.02.102
purpose, did antonio open | the gates of milan, 1.02.129
wherefore did they not | that hour destroy us? 1.02.138
sighing back again, | did us but loving wrong. 1.02.151
o, a cherubin | thou wast that did preserve me. 1.02.153
appointed | master of this design, did give us, 1.02.163
thou did promise | to bate me a full year. 1.02.249
forget | from what a torment i did free thee? 1.02.251
for one thing she did | they would not take her 1.02.266
refusing her grand hests, she did confine thee, 1.02.274
(save for the son that /she did litter here, | a 1.02.282
best know'st | what torment i did find thee in; 1.02.287
thy groans | did make wolves howl, and penetrate 1.02.288
curs'd be i that did so! 1.02.339
and did it to minister occasion to these 2.01.172 P
you did supplant your brother prospero. 2.01.271
(and that a strange one too) which did awake me. 2.01.318
if it should thunder as it did before, i know 2.02. 22 P
might scratch her where e'er she did itch. 2.02. 53
did quarrel with the noblest grace she ow'd, 3.01. 45
i saw you, did | my heart fly to your service, 3.01. 64
why, what did i? 3.02. 72 P
i did nothing. 3.02. 72 P
i did not give the lie. 3.02. 78 P
travellers ne'er did lie, | though fools at home 3.03. 26
three | from milan did supplant good prospero, 3.03. 70
the winds did sing it to me, and the thunder, 3.03. 97
it did base my trespass. 3.03. 99
your last service | did worthily perform; 4.01. 36
since they did plot | the means that dusky dis 4.01. 88
i did say so, | when first i rais'd the tempest. 5.01. 5
and deeper than did ever plummet sound | i'll 5.01. 56
when did you lose your daughter? 5.01.152
voyage | did claribel her husband find at tunis, 5.01.209
if i did think, sir, i were well awake, | i'ld 5.01.229
i say, she did nod; TGV 1.01.113 P
and you ask me if she did nod, and i say, "ay." 1.01.114 P
being in the way, | did in your name receive it; 1.02. 40
and did request me to importune you | to let him 1.03. 13
but did you perceive her earnest? 2.01.156 P
yet did not this cruel–hearted cur shed one tear 2.03. 9 P
did hold his eyes lock'd in her crystal looks. 2.04. 89
and duty never yet did want his meed. 2.04.112
that i did love, for now my love is thaw'd, 2.04.200
how did thy master part with madam julia? 2.05. 11 P
at first i did adore a twinkling star, | but now 2.06. 9
but truer stars did govern proteus' birth: 2.07. 74
but she did scorn a present that i sent her. 3.01. 92
she did, my lord, when valentine was here. 3.02. 27
the heaven such grace did lend her, | that she 4.02. 42
i grant, sweet love, that i did love a lady; 4.02.105
say | no grief did ever come so near thy heart 4.03. 19
he, to take a fault upon me that he did, i think 4.04. 14 P
quoth i, "'twas i did the thing you wot of." 4.04. 27 P
did not i bid thee still mark me and do as i do? 4.04. 36 P
no indeed did she not; 4.04. 52 P
when she did think my master lov'd her well, 4.04.150
but since she did neglect her looking–glass, 4.04.152
weep agood, | for i did play a lamentable part. 4.04.166
she did intend confession | at patrick's cell 5.02. 41
i do as truly suffer | as e'er i did commit. 5.04. 77
and julia herself did give it me — | and julia 5.04. 98
did her grandsire leave her seven hundred pound?
WIV 1.01. 58 P
pistol, did you pick master slender's purse? 1.01.151 P
ay, by these gloves, did he, or i would i might 1.01.153 P
i cannot remember what i did when you made me 1.01.171 P
why, did you not lend it to alice shortcake upon 1.01.203 P
i thank you as much as though i did. 1.01.280 P
then did the sun on dunghill shine. 1.03. 63 P
she did so course o'er my exteriors with such a 1.03. 65 P
the appetite of her eye did seem to scorch me up 1.03. 67 P
did you ever hear the like? 2.01. 68 P
you heard what this knave told me, did you not? 2.01.169 P
have i not, at de place i did appoint? 3.01. 93 P
so did i mine, to build upon a foolish woman's 3.05. 41 P
how so, sir? did she change her determination? 3.05. 68 P
and did he search for you, and could not find 3.05. 81 P
him at the door with it, as they did last time. 4.02. 96 P
nay, by th' mass, that he did not; 4.02.202 P
discretions of a oman as ever i did look upon. 4.04. 2 P
and did he send you both these letters at an 4.04. 3 P
eld | receiv'd and did deliver to our age | this 4.04. 37
if i did not think it had been anne page, would 5.05.186 P
did not i tell you how you should know my 5.05.194 P
why? did you take her in /green? 5.05.208 P
for if our virtues | did not go forth of us, MM 1.01. 34
ay, so i did indeed. 2.01.108 P
you, sir, ask him what this man did to my wife. 2.01.143 P
well, sir, what did this gentleman to her? 2.01.146 P
did not i tell thee yea? 2.02. 8
evil | if the first that did th' edict infringe 2.02. 92
my mouth, | as if i did but only chew his name, 2.04. 5
my brother did love juliet, | and you tell me 2.04.142
did i tell this, | who would believe me? 2.04.171
my father's grave | did utter forth a voice. 3.01. 86
can this be so? did angelo so leave her? 3.01.224 P
of precept, he did show me | the way twice o'er. 4.01. 39
did you such a thing? 4.03.171 P
yes, marry, did i; 4.03.172 P
confutes mine honor, | and i did yield to him; 5.01.101
we did believe no less. 5.01.142
a man that never yet | did, as he vouches, 5.01.148
and did supply thee at thy garden–house | in her 5.01.212
i did but smile till now. 5.01.233
did not you say you knew that friar lodowick to 5.01.260 P
sir, did you set these women on to slander lord 5.01.288 P
they have confess'd you did. 5.01.289 P
is this the man | that you did tell us of? 5.01.325
o, did you so? 5.01.330 P
did not i pluck thee by the nose for thy 5.01.339 P
which i did think with slower foot came on, 5.01.395
governed his deeds, | till he did look on me. 5.01.447
in that he did the thing for which he died; 5.01.449
his act did not o'ertake his bad intent, | and 5.01.451
yet did repent me, after more advice, | for 5.01.464
but longer did we not retain much hope; ERR 1.01. 65
for what obscured light the heavens did grant 1.01. 66
grant | did but convey unto our fearful minds 1.01. 67
and therefore homeward did they bend their 1.01.117
for, in conclusion, he did beat me there. 2.01. 74
i did not see you since you sent me hence | home 2.02. 15
marry, and did, sir: 2.02.102 P
that he did buffet thee, and, in his blows, 2.02.158
did you converse, sir, with this gentlewoman? 2.02.160
gold, | and that i did deny my wife and house. 3.01. 9
if you did wed my sister for her wealth, | then 3.02. 5
o, sir, i did not look so low. 3.02.139 P
where dowsabel did claim me for her husband: 4.01.110
ah, luciana, did he tempt thee so? 4.02. 1
in his eye | that he did plead in earnest? 4.02. 3
he meant he did me none: the more my spite. 4.02. 8
with what persuasion did he tempt thy love? 4.02. 13
first he did praise my beauty, then my speech. 4.02. 15
the hours come back! that did i never /hear. 4.02. 55
to what end did i bid thee hie thee home? 4.04. 15
did this companion with the saffron face | revel 4.04. 61
sir, sooth to say, you did not dine at home. 4.04. 69
and did not she herself revile me there? 4.04. 72
did not her kitchen maid rail, taunt, and scorn 4.04. 74
certes she did, the kitchen vestal scorn'd you. 4.04. 75
and did not i in rage depart from thence? 4.04. 76
in verity you did, my bones bears witness, 4.04. 77
and i am witness with her that she did. 4.04. 89
i did not, gentle husband, lock thee forth. 4.04. 97
he did bespeak a chain for me, but had it not. 4.04.136
straight after did i meet him with a chain. 4.04.140
it may be so, but i did never see it. 4.04.141
i think i had, i never did deny it. 5.01. 23
yes, that you did, sir, and forswore it too. 5.01. 24
these ears of mine thou know'st did hear thee; 5.01. 26
i am sorry now that i did draw on him. 5.01. 43
why, so i did. 5.01. 58
still did i tell him it was vild and bad. 5.01. 67
she did betray me to my own reproof. 5.01. 90
rings, jewels, any thing his rage did like. 5.01.144
once did i get him bound, and sent him home, 5.01.145
i have not breath'd almost since i did see it. 5.01.181
even for the service that long since i did thee, 5.01.191
he, and my sister | to–day did dine together: 5.01.208
where balthazar and i did dine together. 5.01.223
there did this perjur'd goldsmith swear me down 5.01.227
the which | he did arrest me with an officer. 5.01.230
i did obey, and sent my peasant home | for 5.01.231
he did, and from my finger snatch'd that ring. 5.01.277
which of you two did dine with me to–day? 5.01.370
and so do i, yet did she call me so; 5.01.373
her sister here, | did call me brother. 5.01.375
i think i did, sir, i deny it not. 5.01.381
from you, | and dromio my man did bring them me. 5.01.386
i see we still did meet each other's man, | and 5.01.387
did he break out into tears? ADO 1.01. 24 P
well, i would you did like me. 2.01.100 P
did he never make you laugh? 2.01.135 P
so did i too, and he swore he would marry her 2.01.169 P
but did you think the prince would have serv'd 2.01.195 P
did you see him? 2.01.211 P
i did never think that lady would have lov'd any 2.03. 93 P
she did indeed. 2.03.112 P
i did never think to marry. 2.03.228 P
i did not think i should live till i were 2.03.243 P
to praise him more than ever man did merit. 3.01. 19
and did they bid you tell her of it, madam? 3.01. 39
they did entreat me to acquaint her of it, | but 3.01. 40
why did you so? 3.01. 44
his excellence did earn it, ere he had it. 3.01. 99
indeed he looks younger than he did, by the loss 3.02. 48 P
two of them did, the prince and claudio, but the 3.03.154 P
by the dark night, which did deceive them, but 3.03.157 P
which did confirm any slander that don john had 3.03.158 P
as freely, son, as god did give her me. 4.01. 26
you will say, she did embrace me as a husband, 4.01. 49
and this grieved count | did see her, hear her, 4.01. 90
for, did i think thou wouldst not quickly die, 4.01.124
and that count claudio did mean, upon his words, 4.02. 53 P
never any did so, though very many have been 5.01.127 P
thus did she an hour together trans–shape thy 5.01.170 P
yea, that she did, but yet, for all that, and if 5.01.176 P
all that, and if she did not hate him deadly, 5.01.177 P
did he not say my brother was fled? 5.01.204 P
but did my brother set thee on to this? 5.01.247
nor knew not what she did when she spoke to me, 5.01.301
plaintiff here, the offender, did call me ass. 5.01.306 P
which of my good parts did you first suffer love 5.02. 65 P
did i not tell you she was innocent? 5.04. 1
at thee, | as once europa did at lusty jove, 5.04. 46
they swore you did. 5.04. 76
are much deceiv'd, for they did swear you did. 5.04. 79
are much deceiv'd, for they did swear you did. 5.04. 79
claudio, i did think to have beaten thee, but in 5.04.109 P
marry, that did i. LLL 1.01.125
i did commend the black oppressing humor to the 1.01.232 P
i mean, i did encounter that obscene and most 1.01.241 P
there did i see that low–spirited swain, that 1.01.247 P
did you hear the proclamation? 1.01.284 P
when she did starve the general world beside 2.01. 11
did not i dance with you in brabant once? 2.01.114
did not i dance with you in brabant once? 2.01.115
i know you did. 2.01.116
all his behaviors did make their retire | to the 2.01.234
did stumble with haste in his eyesight to be; 2.01.239
all senses to that sense did make their repair, 2.01.240
did point you to buy them, along as you pass'd; 2.01.245
his face's own margent did cote such amazes 2.01.246
how did this argument begin? 3.01.105
why did he come? 4.01. 71 P
why did he see? 4.01. 72 P
did you ever hear better? 4.01. 95
by my troth, most pleasant. how both did fit it! 4.01.129
marvellous well shot, for they both did hit /it. 4.01.130
the dogs did yell: 4.02. 58
did they please you, sir nathaniel? 4.02.150 P
"did not the heavenly rhetoric of thine eye, 4.03. 58
did never sonnet for her sake compile, | nor 4.03.132
and mark'd you both, and for you both did blush. 4.03.136
faith infringed, which such zeal did swear? 4.03.144
for all the wealth that ever i did see, | i 4.03.147
you found his mote, the king your mote did see; 4.03.159
it did move him to passion, and therefore let's 4.03.198
did these rent lines show some love of thine? 4.03.216
did they, quoth you? 4.03.217
'twere good yours did; 4.03.268
consider what you first did swear unto: 4.03.287
i did converse this quondam day with a companion 5.01. 6 P
did he not send you twain? 5.02. 48
action and accent did they teach him there: 5.02. 99
with that they all did tumble on the ground, 5.02.115
know | by favors several which they did bestow. 5.02.125
berowne did swear himself out of all suit. 5.02.275
they did not bless us with one happy word. 5.02.370
here, | what did you whisper in your lady's ear? 5.02.436
that more than all the world i did respect her. 5.02.437
what did the russian whisper in your ear? 5.02.443
he swore that he did hold me dear | as precious 5.02.444
eyesight, and did value me | above this world; 5.02.445
by heaven, you did; 5.02.452
my faith and this the princess i did give; 5.02.454
pardon me, sir, this jewel did she wear, | and 5.02.456
once disclos'd, | the ladies did change favors; 5.02.468
with targe and shield did make my foe to sweat, 5.02.553
thus did he strangle serpents in his manus. 5.02.591

so did our looks. 5.02.786
we did not cote them so. 5.02.786
of self–affairs, | my mind did lose it. MND 1.01.114
the course of true love never did run smooth; 1.01.134
war, death, or sickness did lay siege to it, 1.01.142
(where i did meet thee once with helena | to do 1.01.166
before the time i did lysander see, | seem'd 1.01.204
so he dissolv'd, and show'rs of oaths did melt. 1.01.245
but she, being mortal, of that boy did die, 2.01.135
when at your hands did i deserve this scorn? 2.02.124
that i did never, no, nor never can, | deserve a 2.02.126
are hated most of those they did deceive, | so 2.02.140
the story) did talk through the chink of a wall. 3.01. 64 P
when i did him at this advantage take, | an 3.02. 16
with the love–juice, as i did bid thee do? 3.02. 37
an adder did it! 3.02. 72
never did mockers waste more idle breath. 3.02.168
(who even but now did spurn me with his foot), 3.02.225
and never did desire to see thee more. 3.02.278
i evermore did love you, hermia, | did ever keep 3.02.307
did ever keep your counsels, never wrong'd you; 3.02.308
did not you tell me i should know the man | by 3.02.348
and so far am i glad it so did sort, | as this 3.02.352
i followed fast, but faster he did fly, | that 3.02.416
fool, | i did upbraid her and fall out with her. 4.01. 50
like tears that did their own disgrace bewail. 4.01. 56
i then did ask of her her changeling child; 4.01. 59
never did i hear | such gallant chiding; 4.01.114
gaud | which in my childhood i did dote upon; 4.01.168
but like a sickness did i loathe this food; 4.01.173
and he did bid us follow to the temple. 4.01.197
that vile wall, which did these lovers sunder; 5.01.132
by moonshine did these lovers think no scorn 5.01.137
night, | did scare away, or rather did affright; 5.01.141
night, | did scare away, or rather did affright; 5.01.141
and, as she fled, her mantle she did fall, 5.01.142
which lion vile with bloody mouth did stain. 5.01.143
and thisby, | did whisper often, very secretly. 5.01.160
slumb'red here | while these visions did appear. 5.01.426
that self way | which you did shoot the first, i MV 1.01.149
eyes | i did receive fair speechless messages. 1.01.164
and what of him? did he take interest? 1.03. 75
mark what jacob did: 1.03. 77
who then conceiving did in eaning time | fall 1.03. 87
that did void your rheum upon my beard | and 1.03.117
for when did friendship take | a breed for 1.03.133
son, for indeed my father did something smack, 2.02. 17 P
rest, | for i did dream of money–bags to–night. 2.05. 18
the unbated fire | that he did pace them first? 2.06. 12
as the dog jew did utter in the streets. 2.08. 14
did i deserve no more than a fool's head? 2.09. 59
that judgment is, | that did never choose amiss. 2.09. 65
i often came where i did hear of her, but cannot 3.01. 81 P
when he did redeem | the virgin tribute paid by 3.02. 55
and so did mine too, as the matter falls; 3.02.202
he did entreat me, past all saying nay, | to 3.02.229
i did, my lord, | and i have reason for it. 3.02.230
lady, | when i did first impart my love to you, 3.02.253
never did i know | a creature that did bear the 3.02.274
know | a creature that did bear the shape of man 3.02.275
the value of the sum | that he did owe him; 3.02.288
i never did repent for doing good, | nor shall 3.04. 10
even from the gallows did his fell soul fleet, 4.01.135
i did, my lord. 4.01.170
which i did make him swear to keep for ever. 4.02. 14
that they did give the rings away to men; 4.02. 16
when the sweet wind did gently kiss the trees 5.01. 2
kiss the trees | and they did make no noise, in 5.01. 3
a night | did thisby fearfully o'ertrip the dew, 5.01. 7
the enchanted herbs | that did renew old aeson. 5.01. 14
night | did jessica steal from the wealthy jew, 5.01. 15
and with an unthrift love did run from venice, 5.01. 16
did young lorenzo swear he lov'd her well, 5.01. 18
in such a night | did pretty jessica (like a 5.01. 21
i would out–night you, did nobody come; 5.01. 23
did you see master lorenzo? 5.01. 41 P
the poet | did feign that orpheus drew trees, 5.01. 80
when the moon shone, we did not see the candle. 5.01. 92
a paltry ring | that she did give me, whose posy 5.01.148
you swore to me, when i did give /it you, | that 5.01.152
if you did know to whom i gave the ring, | if 5.01.193
if you did know for whom i gave the ring, | and 5.01.194
which did refuse three thousand ducats of me, 5.01.211
and begg'd the ring, the which i did deny him, 5.01.212
and that which you did swear to keep for me, | i 5.01.225
i once did lend my body for his wealth, | which, 5.01.249
in lieu of this last night did lie with me. 5.01.262
carelessly, as they did in the golden world. AYL 1.01.118 P
but i did find him still mine enemy. 1.02.226
did you call, sir? 1.02.253
a thought unborn | did i offend your highness. 1.03. 52
if their purgation did consist in words, | they 1.03. 53
or, if we did derive it from our friends, 1.03. 62
i did not then entreat to have her stay, | it 1.03. 69
that i did suit me all points like a man? 1.03.116
myself | did steal behind him as he lay along 2.01. 30
aim had ta'en a hurt, | did come to languish; 2.01. 35
that their discharge did stretch his leathern 2.01. 37
did he not moralize this spectacle? 2.01. 44
and did you leave him in this contemplation? 2.01. 64
we did, my lord, weeping and commenting | upon 2.01. 65
i cannot hear of any that did see her. 2.02. 4
that did but lately foil the sinowy charles, 2.02. 14
which i did store to be my foster–nurse | when 2.03. 40
for in my youth i never did apply | hot and 2.03. 48
nor did not with unbashful forehead woo | the 2.03. 50
yet i should bear no cross if i did bear you, 2.04. 12 P
as sure i think did never man love so — | how 2.04. 29
folly | that ever love did make thee run into, 2.04. 35
when i did hear | the motley fool thus moral on 2.07. 28
and i did laugh sans intermission | an hour by 2.07. 32
what did he when thou saw'st him? 3.02.220 P
did he ask for me? 3.02.222 P
he as freshly as he did the day he wrastled? 3.02.230 P
did you ever cure any so? 3.02.406 P
but why did he swear he would come this morning, 3.04. 18 P
and faster than his tongue | did make offense, 3.05.117
did make offense, his eye did heal it up. 3.05.117

had they mark'd him | in parcels as i did, would 3.05.125
club, yet he did what he could to die before, 4.01. 98 P
my gentle phebe did bid me give you this. 4.03. 7
which she did use as she was writing of it, | it 4.03. 10
i know not the contents, | phebe did write it. 4.03. 22
i verily did think | that her old gloves were on 4.03. 25
i say she never did invent this letter, | this 4.03. 28
did you ever hear such railing? 4.03. 46 P
"whiles the eye of man did woo me, | that could 4.03. 47
whiles you chid me, i did love; 4.03. 54
you | the owner of the house i did inquire for? 4.03. 89
and mark what object did present itself | under 4.03.103
and with indented glides did slip away | into a 4.03.112
orlando did approach the man | and found it was 4.03.119
and he did render him the most unnatural | that 4.03.122
did he leave him there, | food to the suck'd and 4.03.125
twice did he turn his back, and purpos'd so; 4.03.127
was't you that did so oft contrive to kill him? 4.03.134
did your brother tell you how i counterfeited to 5.02. 25 P
that o'er the green corn–field did pass, | in 5.03. 18
how did you find the quarrel on the seventh 5.04. 66 P
i did dislike the cut of a certain courtier's 5.04. 69 P
and how oft did you say his beard was not well 5.04. 83 P
nap, | but did i never speak of all that time? SHR in.2. 82
and with her breath she did perfume the air. 1.01.175
you, | did you yet ever see baptista's daughter? 1.02.250
dost thou wrong her that did ne'er wrong thee? 2.01. 27
when did she cross thee with a bitter word? 2.01. 28
i did but tell her she mistook her frets, | and 2.01.149
while she did call me rascal fiddler | and 2.01.157
i love her ten times more than e'er i did. 2.01.161
did ever dian so become a grove | as kate this 2.01.258
where did you study all this goodly speech? 2.01.262
that at the parting all the church did echo. 3.02.179
did i not bid thee meet me in the park, | and 4.01.130
and better 'twere that both of us did fast, 4.01.173
what, did he marry me to famish me? 4.03. 3
here is the cap your worship did bespeak. 4.03. 63
marry, and did; 4.03. 96
i did not bid you mar it to the time. 4.03. 97
but how did you desire it should be made? 4.03.119
but did you not request to have it cut? 4.03.121
gown, but i did not bid him cut it to pieces. 4.03.127 P
while he did bear my countenance in the town, 5.01.126
what tranio did, myself enforc'd him to; 5.01.129
and, as the jest did glance away from me, | 'tis 5.02. 61
to show her merit, that did miss her love? AWW 1.01.227
he did look far | into the service of the time, 1.02. 26
long, | but on us both did haggish age steal on, 1.02. 29
and did communicate to herself her own words to 1.03.107 P
did ever in so true a flame of liking | wish 1.03.211
my father, | in what he did profess, well found. 2.01.102
your lord and master did well to make his 2.03.186 P
i did think thee, for two ordinaries, to be a 2.03.201 P
bannerets about thee did manifoldly dissuade me 2.03.204 P
and i her money, i would she did as you say. 2.04. 21 P
did you find me in yourself, sir, or were you 2.04. 33 P
although | the air of paradise did fan the house 3.02.125
you did never lack advice so much | as letting 3.04. 19
i did so. 3.05. 46
tokens and letters which she did re–send, | and 3.06.115
my mother did but duty, such, my lord, | as you 4.02. 12
you believe my oaths | when i did love you ill? 4.02. 27
time was, i did him a desired office, | dear 4.04. 5
a self–gracious remembrance, did first propose. 4.05. 74 P
me in some grace, for you did bring me out. 5.02. 47 P
the young lord | did to his majesty, his mother, 5.03. 13
a wife | whose beauty did astonish the survey 5.03. 16
contempt his scornful perspective did lend me, 5.03. 48
was in mine eye | the dust that did offend it. 5.03. 55
it did concern | your highness with herself. 5.03.137
respect and rich validity | did lack a parallel; 5.03.193
i did, my lord, but loath am to produce | so bad 5.03.201
she knew her distance and did angle for me, 5.03.212
did he love this woman? 5.03.241 P
faith, sir, he did love her, but how? 5.03.243 P
he did love her, sir, as a gentleman loves a 5.03.245 P
i did go between them, as i said, but more than 5.03.258 P
where did you buy it? or who gave it you? 5.03.271
it was not given me, nor i did not buy it. 5.03.272
where did you find it then? 5.03.274
o, when mine eyes did see olivia first, TN 1.01. 18
assure yourself, after our ship did split, 1.02. 9
of) | that he did seek the love of fair olivia. 1.02. 34
when did i see thee so put down? 1.03. 81 P
i did think, by the excellent constitution of 1.03.132 P
excellently done, if god did all. 1.05.236 P
if i did love you in my master's flame, | with 1.05.264
for she did speak in starts distractedly. 2.02. 21
did you never see the picture of "we three"? 2.03. 16 P
i did impeticos thy gratillity; 2.03. 26 P
we did keep time, sir, in our catches. sneck up! 2.03. 93 P
methought it did relieve my passion much, | more 2.04. 4
my part of death, no one so true | did share it. 2.04. 58
maria once told me she did affect me, and i have 2.05. 24 P
did not i say he would work it out? 2.05.127 P
she did commend my yellow stockings of late, she 2.05.166 P
she did praise my leg being cross–garter'd, and 2.05.166 P
i did send, | after the last enchantment you did 3.01.111
send, | after the last enchantment you did here, 3.01.112
so did i abuse | myself, my servant, and, i fear 3.01.113
did she see /thee the while, old boy? 3.02. 8 P
she did show favor to the youth in your sight 3.02. 18 P
more sharp than filed steel, did spur me forth, 3.03. 5
the count his galleys | i did some service, of 3.03. 27
which for traffic's sake | most of our city did. 3.03. 35
it did come to his hands, and commands shall be 3.04. 27 P
did not i tell you? 3.04. 92 P
which methought did promise | most venerable 3.04.362
promise | most venerable worth, did i devotion. 3.04.363
thee more than ever the bearing of letter did. 4.02.112 P
that he did range the town to seek me out. 4.03. 7
here comes the man, sir, that did rescue me. 5.01. 50
with which such scathful grapple did he make 5.01. 56
and this is he that did the tiger board, | when 5.01. 62
in private brabble did we apprehend him. 5.01. 65
he did me kindness, sir, drew on my side, | but 5.01. 66
sea's enrag'd and foamy mouth | did i redeem. 5.01. 79

life i gave him, and did thereto add | my love, 5.01. 80
for his sake | did i expose myself (pure for his 5.01. 83
both day and night did we keep company. 5.01. 96
broke my head for nothing, and that that i did, 5.01.185 P
would have tickled you othergates than he did. 5.01.194 P
clad | which from the womb i did participate. 5.01.238
the captain that did bring me first on shore 5.01.274
did he write this? 5.01.312 P
were as twinn'd lambs that did frisk i' th' sun, WT 1.02. 67
of ill–doing, nor dream'd | that any did. 1.02. 71
and that with us | you did continue fault, and 1.02. 85
methoughts i did recoil | twenty–three years, 1.02.154
how came't, camillo, | that he did stay? 1.02.220
whereof the execution did cry out | against the 1.02.260
you never spoke what did become you less | than 1.02.282
be yok'd with his that did betray the best! 1.02.419
and | my people did expect my hence departure 1.02.450
i am glad you did not nurse him. 2.01. 56
me throughly, then, to say | you did mistake. 2.01.100
i had rather you did lack than i, my lord, 2.01.158
so i would you did; 2.03. 81
durst not call me so, | if she did know me one. 2.03.124
i did not, sir. 2.03.142
less impudence to gainsay what they did | than 3.02. 56
that he did but see | the flatness of my misery, 3.02.121
with | reward did threaten and encourage him, 3.02.164
that did but show thee, of a fool, inconstant 3.02.186
she did approach | my cabin where i lay; 3.03. 23
the fury spent, anon | did this break from her: 3.03. 27
i did in time collect myself and thought | this 3.03. 38
i would you did but see how it chafes, how it 3.03. 88 P
accident, | should pass this way as you did. 4.04. 20
if you did but hear the pedlar at the door, you 4.04.181 P
does nothing | but what he did being childish? 4.04.402
and so still think of | the wrong i did myself; 5.01. 9
i did so; 5.01. 17
but thou strik'st me | sorely, to say i did. 5.01. 18
who, on my life, | did perish with the infant. 5.01. 44
for she did print your royal father off, 5.01.125
as i did him, and speak of something wildly | by 5.01.129
did you see the meeting of the two kings? 5.02. 39 P
from one sign of dolor to another, she did (with 5.02. 88 P
sovereign sir, | i did not well, i meant well. 5.03. 3
scarce any joy | did ever so long live; 5.03. 52
already — | what was he that did make it? 5.03. 63
and that those veins | did verily bear blood? 5.03. 65
if old sir robert did beget us both, | and were JN 1.01. 80
your brother did employ my father much — 1.01. 96
where how he did prevail i shame to speak. 1.01.104
your father's wife did after wedlock bear him; 1.01.117
and if she did play false, the fault was hers, 1.01.118
my mother's son did get your father's heir; 1.01.128
o'er | did never float upon the swelling tide 2.01. 74
o, well did he become that lion's robe, | that 2.01.141
robe, | that did disrobe the lion of that robe! 2.01.142
that did display them when we first march'd 2.01.320
that i did so when i was first assur'd. 2.01.535
where revenge did paint | the fearful difference 3.01.237
till this time my tongue did ne'er pronounce, 3.01.307
bell | did with his iron tongue and brazen mouth 3.03. 38
child, | to him that did but yesterday suspire, 3.04. 80
may then make all the claim that arthur did. 3.04.143
and lose it, life and all, as arthur did. 3.04.144
when your head did but ache, | i knit my 4.01. 41
it me) | and i did never ask it you again; 4.01. 44
these eyes that never did nor never shall | so 4.01. 57
yet am i sworn, and i did purpose, boy, | with 4.01.123
than did the fault before it was so patch'd. 4.02. 34
and the fift did whirl about | the other four in 4.02.183
the whilst his iron did on the anvil cool, 4.02.194
no had, my lord? why, did you not provoke me? 4.02.207
here is your hand and seal for what i did. 4.02.215
if they did, | this ship–boy's semblance hath 4.03. 3
did not the prophet | say that before 5.01. 25
i did suppose it should be on constraint, | but, 5.01. 28
that villain hubert told me he did live. 5.01. 42
so, on my soul, he did, for aught he knew. 5.01. 43
i did not think the king so stor'd with friends. 5.04. 1
i did not think to be so sad to–night | as this 5.05. 15
said | king john did fly an hour or two before 5.05. 17
the stumbling night did part our weary pow'rs? 5.05. 18
how did he take it? who did taste to him? 5.06. 28
how did he take it? who did taste to him? 5.06. 28
of my pow'r, | as i upon advantage did remove, 5.07. 62
this england never did, nor never shall, | lie 5.07.112
but when it first did help to wound itself. 5.07.114
that he did plot the duke of gloucester's death, R2 1.01.100
foe, | once did i lay an ambush for your life, 1.01.137
last receiv'd the sacrament | i did confess it, 1.01.140
never did captive with a freer heart | cast off 1.03. 88
think not the king did banish thee, | but thou 1.03.279
we did observe. 1.04. 1
did grace our hollow parting with a tear. 1.04. 9
how he did seem to dive into their hearts | with 1.04. 25
what reverence he did throw away on slaves, 1.04. 27
whereof our uncle gaunt did stand possess'd. 2.01.162
his noble hand | did win what he did spend, and 2.01.180
his noble hand | did win what he did spend, and 2.01.180
did not the one deserve to have an heir? 2.01.193
to please the king i did, to please myself | i 2.02. 5
that is not forgot | which ne'er i did remember. 2.03. 38
knowledge, | i never in my life did look on him. 2.03. 39
in love | till you did make him misinterpret me, 3.01. 18
of twenty thousand men | did triumph in my face, 3.02. 77
which his broad–spreading leaves did shelter, 3.04. 50
here did she fall a tear, here in this place 3.04.104
well | the very time aumerle and you did talk. 4.01. 61
ah, thou, the model where old troy did stand, 5.01. 11
where did i leave? 5.02. 4
men's eyes | did scowl on gentle richard. 5.02. 28
'tis full three months since i did see him last. 5.03. 2
it was, villain, ere thy hand did set it down. 5.03. 54
and urg'd it twice together, did he not? 5.04. 5
he did. 5.04. 6
of that proud man that did usurp his back? 5.05. 89
for now the devil that told me i did well | says 5.05.115
from your own mouth, my lord, did i this deed. 5.06. 37
though i did wish him dead, | i hate the 5.06. 39

did lately meet in the intestine shock | and 1H4 1.01. 12
what yesternight our council did decree | in 1.01. 32
this match'd with other did, my gracious lord, 1.01. 49
came from the north, and thus it did import: 1.01. 51
where they did spend a sad and bloody hour, | as 1.01. 56
and pride of their contention did take horse, 1.01. 60
did sir walter see | on holmedon's plains. 1.01. 69
did i ever call for thee to pay thy part? 1.02. 51 P
mists | of vapors that did seem to strangle him. 1.02.203
my liege, i did deny no prisoners, | but i 1.03. 29
the lives of those that he did lead to fight 1.03. 82
he never did fall off, my sovereign liege, | but 1.03. 94
he did confound the best part of an hour | in 1.03.100
they breath'd and three times did they drink, 1.03.102
never did bare and rotten policy | color her 1.03.108
he never did encounter with glendower. 1.03.114
did set forth | upon his irish expedition; 1.03.149
from whence he intercepted did return | to be 1.03.151
you, did king richard then | proclaim my brother 1.03.155
he did, myself did hear it. 1.03.157
he did, myself did hear it. 1.03.157
power | did gage them both in an unjust behalf 1.03.173
this fawning greyhound then did proffer me! 1.03.252
then did we two set on you four, and, with a 2.04.255 P
by'r lady, you fought fair, so did you, peto, so 2.04.299 P
fair, so did you, peto, so did you, bardolph. 2.04.299 P
i did that i did not this seven year before, i 2.04.312 P
i did that i did not this seven year before, i 2.04.312 P
so did he never the sparrow. 2.04.348 P
i say the earth did shake when i was born. 3.01. 20
heavens were all on fire, the earth did tremble. 3.01. 23
opinion, that did help me to the crown, | had 3.02. 42
that i did pluck allegiance from men's hearts, 3.02. 52
thus did i keep my person fresh and new, | my 3.02. 55
if i did not think thou hadst been an ignis 3.03. 39 P
what, he did not? 3.03.109 P
did i, bardolph? 3.03.140 P
he did, my lord, four days ere i set forth, 4.01. 22
nor did he think it meet | to lay so dangerous 4.01. 33
i did never see such pitiful rascals. 4.02. 64 P
did give him that same royalty he wears, | and 4.03. 55
perceiv'd northumberland did lean to him, | the 4.03. 67
did he win | the hearts of all that he did angle 4.03. 83
win | the hearts of all that he did angle for; 4.03. 84
where you did give a fair and natural light, 5.01. 18
for you my staff of office did i break | in 5.01. 34
and boldly did outdare | the dangers of the time 5.01. 40
us, | and you did swear that oath at doncaster, 5.01. 42
that you did nothing purpose 'gainst the state, 5.01. 43
wars | that all in england did repute him dead; 5.01. 54
did oppress our nest, | grew by our feeding to 5.01. 61
and never yet did insurrection want | such 5.01. 79
'twere best he did. 5.02. 3
we did train him on, | and, his corruption being 5.02. 21
did you beg any? god forbid! 5.02. 35
and westmerland, that was engag'd, did bear it, 5.02. 43
life | did hear a challenge urg'd more modestly, 5.02. 52
there did he pause, but let me tell the world, 5.02. 65
day, | england did never owe so sweet a hope, 5.02. 67
never did i hear | of any prince so wild a 5.02. 70
too long | if life did ride upon a dial's point, 5.02. 83
turk gregory never did such deeds in arms as i 5.03. 45 P
not i, my lord, unless i did bleed too. 5.04. 4
i did not think thee lord of such a spirit. 5.04. 18
with lustier maintenance than i did look for 5.04. 22
they did me too much injury | that ever said i 5.04. 51
when that this body did contain a spirit, | a 5.04. 89
did you not tell me this fat man was dead? 5.04.132
i did, i saw him dead, | breathless and bleeding 5.04.133
thus ever did rebellion find rebuke. 5.05. 1
ill-spirited worcester, did not we send grace, 5.05. 2
of him | i did demand what news from shrewsbury. 2H4 1.01. 40
thou wouldst say, "your son did thus and thus; 1.01. 76
so did our men, heavy in hotspur's loss, | lend 1.01.121
toward their aim | than did our soldiers, aiming 1.01.124
gan vail his stomach and did grace the shame 1.01.129
why, sir, did i say you were an honest man? 1.02. 80 P
the laws of this land-service, i did not come. 1.02.135 P
if i did say of wax, my growth would approve the 1.02.158 P
it never yet did hurt | to lay down likelihoods 1.03. 34
did not goodwife keech, the butcher's wife, come 2.01. 93 P
but he did long in vain. 2.03. 14
his light | did all the chevalry of england move 2.03. 20
wherein the noble youth did dress themselves: 2.03. 22
so did your son, | he was so suff'red; 2.03. 56
how vildly did you speak of me /even now before 2.04.301 P
me, as you did when you ran away by gadshill. 2.04.306 P
so, i did not think thou wast within hearing. 2.04.309 P
did feast together, and in two year after | were 3.01. 59
did speak these words, now prov'd a prophecy? 3.01. 69
"the time shall come," thus did he follow it, 3.01. 75
and the very same day did i fight with one 3.02. 31 P
else, sir, i did not care, for mine own part, so 3.02.226 P
same grievances | whereof you did complain, 4.02.114
most shallowly did you these arms commence, 4.02.118
for the cold blood he did naturally inherit of 4.03.118 P
say it did so a little time before | that our 4.04.127
did he suspire, that light and weightless down 4.05. 33
why did you leave me here alone, my lords? 4.05. 50
but wherefore did he take away the crown? 4.05. 88
thy life did manifest thou lov'dst me not, | and 4.05.104
but if it did infect my blood with joy, | or 4.05.169
mine | did with the least affection of a welcome 4.05.172
unto the lodging where i first did swound? 4.05.233
the service that i truly did his life | hath 5.02. 7
sweet princes, what i did, i did in honor, | led 5.02. 35
sweet princes, what i did, i did in honor, | led 5.02. 35
i then did use the person of your father, | the 5.02. 73
bold way to my authority, | and did commit you. 5.02. 83
son of mine | offend you and obey you, as i did. 5.02.106
you did commit me; 5.02.112
i did not think master silence had been a man of 5.03. 37 P
that did affright the air at agincourt? H5 pr 14
time | did push it out of farther question. 1.01. 5
willfulness | so soon did lose his seat (and all 1.01. 36
yet | did to his predecessors part withal. 1.01. 81
how did this offer seem receiv'd, my lord? 1.01. 82
for never two such kingdoms did contend 1.02. 24
nor did the french possess the salique land 1.02. 56
and did seat the french | beyond the river sala, 1.02. 62
did, as heir general, being descended | of 1.02. 66
as did the former lions of your blood. 1.02.124
mighty sum | as never did the clergy at one time 1.02.134
whom she did send to france | to fill king 1.02.161
did claim some certain dukedoms, in the right 1.02.247
hence, did give ourself | to barbarous license; 1.02.270
when thousands weep more than did laugh at it. 1.02.296
nell quickly, and certainly she did you wrong, 2.01. 18 P
so did you me, my liege. 2.02. 64
cause | that admiration did not hoop at them; 2.02.108
for me, the gold of france did not seduce, 2.02.155
although i did admit it as a motive | the sooner 2.02.156
never did faithful subject more rejoice | at the 2.02.161
ay, that 'a did. 2.03. 28 P
nay, that 'a did not. 2.03. 30 P
yes, that 'a did, and said they were dev'ls 2.03. 31 P
'a did in some sort, indeed, handle women; 2.03. 37 P
i did present him with the paris balls. 2.04.131
those whom you call'd fathers did beget you. 3.01. 23
clouds, as did the wives of jewry | at herod's 3.03. 40
world, but i did see him do as gallant service. 3.06. 15 P
though we seem'd dead, we did but sleep; 3.06.119 P
of english legs | did march three frenchmen. 3.06.150
then did they imitate that which i compos'd to 3.07. 43 P
so perhaps did yours. 3.07. 50 P
he never did harm, that i heard of. 3.07.100 P
with advantages | what feats he did that day. 4.03. 51
the man that once did sell the lion's skin 4.03. 93
i did never know so full a voice issue from so 4.04. 67 P
gashes | that bloodily did yawn upon his face. 4.06. 14
so did he turn and over suffolk's neck | he 4.06. 24
being a little intoxicates in his prains, did, 4.07. 37 P
they did, fluellen. 4.07. 96
the welshmen did good service in a garden where 4.07. 98 P
good service in a garden where leeks did grow, 4.07. 99 P
i promis'd to strike him, if he did. 4.08. 31 P
yes, my conscience, he did us great good. 4.08.121 P
and much more cause, | did they this harry. 5.pr. 35
of france and england, did this king succeed; ep 10
his brandish'd sword did blind men with his 1H6 1.01. 10
late did he shine upon the english side; 1.02. 3
during the time edward the third did reign. 1.02. 31
and if i did but stir out of my bed, | ready 1.04. 55
whilst any trump did sound, or drum struck up, 1.04. 80
his sword did ne'er leave striking in the field. 1.04. 81
more blessed hap did ne'er befall our state. 1.06. 10
did look no better to that weighty charge. 2.01. 62
they did amongst the troops of armed men | leap 2.02. 24
i did not entertain thee as thou art. 2.03. 72
as you did mistake | the outward composition of 2.03. 74
and did upbraid me with my father's death; 2.05. 48
(succeeding his father bullingbrook) did reign, 2.05. 83
a gentler heart did never sway in court; 3.02.135
i vow'd, base knight, when i did meet thee next, 4.01. 14
given, | like to a trusty squire did run away; 4.01. 23
did represent my master's blushing cheeks, 4.01. 93
when stubbornly he did repugn the truth | about 4.01. 94
king | prettily, methought, did play the orator. 4.01.175
and so he did, but yet i like it not, | in that 4.01.176
and if i /wist he did — but let it rest, 4.01.180
this seven years did not talbot see his son, 4.03. 37
talbot, i did send for thee | to tutor thee in 4.05. 1
and like a hungry lion did commence | rough 4.07. 7
and in that sea of blood my boy did drench | his 4.07. 14
did flesh his puny sword in frenchmen's blood! 4.07. 36
verified | henry the fift did sometime prophesy: 5.01. 31
not so, | i did beget her, all the parish knows. 5.04. 11
i did imagine what would be her refuge. 5.04. 69
as did the youthful paris once to greece, | with 5.05.104
love, | but prosper better than the troyan did. 5.05.106
of that great shadow i did represent: 2H6 1.01. 14
her sight did ravish, but her grace in speech, 1.01. 32
did my brother henry spend his youth, | his 1.01. 78
did he so often lodge in open field, | in 1.01. 80
and did my brother bedford toil his wits, | to 1.01. 83
myself did win them both. 1.01.119
those provinces these arms of mine did conquer, 1.01.120
did bear him like a noble gentleman. 1.01.184
that maine which by main force warwick did win, 1.01.210
and would have kept so long as breath did last! 1.01.211
and bloud | as did the fatal brand althaea burnt 1.01.234
to me, | and on my head did set the diadem. 1.02. 40
did the duke of york say he was rightful heir to 1.03. 28 P
fact | did never traitor in the land commit. 1.03.174
he did speak them to me in the garret one night, 1.03.191 P
and when i did correct him for his fault the 1.03.198 P
he did vow upon his knees he would be even with 1.03.199 P
and yet, i think, jet did he never see. 2.01.112
alas, sir, we did it for pure need. 2.01.154
that erst did follow thy proud chariot-wheels 2.04. 13
and if we did but glance a far-off look, 3.01. 10
did instigate the bedlam brain-sick duchess | by 3.01. 51
did he not, contrary to form of law, | devise 3.01. 58
and did he not, in his protectorship, | levy 3.01. 60
in your protectorship you did devise | strange 3.01.121
i did dream to-night | the duke was dumb and 3.02. 31
but well forewarning wind | did seem to say, 3.02. 86
what did i then, but curs'd the gentle gusts, 3.02. 88
as ascanius did | when he to madding dido would 3.02.116
by them, | yet did i purpose as they do entreat; 3.02.282
cask | that ever did contain a thing of worth. 3.02.410
a cunning man did calculate my birth | and told 4.01. 34
never yet did base dishonor blur our name | but 4.01. 39
for i did but seal once to a thing, and i was 4.02. 82 P
the duke of clarence' daughter, did he not? 4.02.137
king did i call thee? 5.01. 93
i cut it | as wild medea young absyrtus did; 5.02. 59
as did aeneas old anchises bear, | so bear i 5.02. 62
by th' mass, so did we all. 5.03. 16
speak thou for me and tell them what i did. 3H6 1.01. 16
suppose, my lords, he did it unconstrain'd, 1.01.143
i, | or felt that pain which i did for him once, 1.01.221
once, | or nourish'd him as i did with my blood, 1.01.222
henry had none, but did usurp the place. 1.02. 25
i never did thee harm; why wilt thou slay me? 1.03. 38
three times did richard make a lane to me, | and 1.04. 9
and when the hardiest warriors did retire, 1.04. 14
think but upon the wrong he did us all, | and 1.04.173
ambitious york did level at thy crown, | thou 2.02. 19
would thy best friends did know | how it doth 2.02. 54
your legs did better service than your hands. 2.02.104
i, that did never weep, now melt with woe | that 2.03. 46
pardon me, god, i knew not what i did! 2.05. 69
do, | or as thy father and his father did, 2.06. 15
whence that tender spray did sweetly spring, | i 2.06. 50
o, would he did! 2.06. 64
but did you never swear and break an oath? 3.01. 72
where did you dwell when i was king of england? 3.01. 74
york | the worthy gentleman did lose his life. 3.02. 7
no, by my troth, i did not mean such love. 3.02. 64
why then you mean not as i thought you did. 3.02. 65
you cavil, widow, i did mean my queen. 3.02. 99
she did corrupt frail nature with some bribe, 3.02.155
because thy father henry did usurp, | and thou 3.03. 79
which did subdue the greatest part of spain; 3.03. 82
can oxford, that did ever fence the right, | now 3.03. 98
did i forget that by the house of york | my 3.03.186
did i let pass th' abuse done to my niece? 3.03.188
did i impale him with the regal crown? 3.03.189
did i put henry from his native right? 3.03.190
unless our halberds did shut up his passage. 4.03. 20
did glad my heart with hope of this young 4.06. 93
at southam i did leave him with his forces, 5.01. 9
or did he make the jest against his will? 5.01. 30
for did i but suspect a fearful man, | he should 5.04. 44
did not offend, nor were not worthy blame, | if 5.05. 54
whose envious gulf did swallow up his life. 5.06. 25
i did not kill your husband. R3 1.02. 91
that did haunt me in my sleep | to undertake the 1.02.122
did it to help thee to a better husband. 1.02.139
time | my manly eyes did scorn an humble tear; 1.02.164
for i did kill king henry — | but 'twas thy 1.02.179
this hand, which for thy love did kill thy love, 1.02.189
god grant him health! did you confer with him? 1.03. 35
i never did incense his majesty | against the 1.03. 84
poor clarence did forsake his father, warwick, 1.03.134
did york's dread curse prevail so much with 1.03.190
for i did think | that thou hadst call'd me all 1.03.234
why, so i did, but look'd for no reply. 1.03.236
i never did her any to my knowledge. 1.03.308
and, in the holes | where eyes did once inhabit, 1.04. 30
and often did i strive | to yield the ghost; 1.04. 36
the first that there did greet my stranger soul 1.04. 48
for whose sake did i that ill deed? 1.04.211
died, | and that a winged mercury did bear; 2.01. 89
deserve not worse than wretched clarence did, 2.01. 94
who told me how the poor soul did forsake | the 2.01.110
the mighty warwick and did fight for me? 2.01.111
how he did lap me | even in his /own garments, 2.01.116
even in his /own garments, and did give himself 2.01.117
look'd pale when they did hear of clarence' 2.01.137
o, they did urge it still unto the king! 2.01.138
think you my uncle did dissemble, grandam? 2.02. 31
i do cry you mercy, | i did not see your grace. 2.02.105
i marvel that her grace did leave it out. 2.02.111
grandam, one night as we did sit at supper, | my 2.04. 10
my uncle rivers talk'd how i did grow | more 2.04. 11
the saying did not hold | in him that did object 2.04. 16
hold | in him that did object the same to thee: 2.04. 17
did julius caesar build that place, my lord? 3.01. 69
he did, my gracious lord, begin that place, 3.01. 70
with what his valor did enrich his wit, | his 3.01. 85
and make pursuit where he did mean no chase. 3.02. 30
stanley did dream the boar did /rase our helms, 3.04. 82
stanley did dream the boar did /rase our helms, 3.04. 82
helms, | and i did scorn it and disdain to fly. 3.04. 83
times to-day my foot-cloth horse did stumble, 3.04. 84
yet witness what you hear we did intend. 3.05. 70
i did, with his contract with lady lucy, | and 3.07. 5
withal i did infer your lineaments, | being the 3.07. 12
i bid them that did love their country's good 3.07. 21
and did they so? 3.07. 23
his bed | did i enjoy the golden dew of sleep, 4.01. 83
the late request that you did sound me in. 4.02. 84
did prophesy that richmond should be king, 4.02. 96
who i did suborn | to do this piece of /ruthless 4.03. 4
i did, my lord. 4.03. 28
as sometimes margaret | did to thy father, 4.04.275
her, did drain | the purple sap from her sweet 4.04.276
say that i did all this for love of her. 4.04.288
if i did take the kingdom from your sons, | to 4.04.294
soft, i did but dream. 5.03.178
and every one did threat | to-morrow's vengeance 5.03.205
did almost sweat to bear | the pride upon them, H8 1.01. 24
best, now worst, | as presence did present them: 1.01. 30
they did perform | beyond thought's compass, 1.01. 35
the office did | distinctly his full function. 1.01. 44
who did guide — | i mean, who set the body and 1.01. 45
what did this vanity | but minister 1.01. 85
us not values | the cost that did conclude it. 1.01. 89
and like a glass | did break i' th' wrenching. 1.01.167
faith, and so it did. 1.01.167
for worthy wolsey | (who cannot err), he did it. 1.01.174
their curses now | live where their prayers did; 1.02. 63
did of me demand | what was the speech among the 1.02.153
he did discharge a horrible oath, whose tenor 1.02.206
after all this, how did he bear himself? 2.01. 30
did you not of late days hear | a buzzing of a 2.01.147
mine | that had to him deriv'd your anger did i 2.04. 32
of every realm, that did debate this business, 2.04. 52
i | did broach this business to your highness, 2.04.150
he | (i mean the bishop) did require a respite, 2.04.178
that many maz'd considerings did throng | and 2.04.186
my conscience, i did steer | toward this remedy, 2.04.201
which | i then did feel full sick, and yet not 2.04.205
how under my oppression i did reek | when i 2.04.209
the question did at first so stagger me, 2.04.213
and did entreat your highness to this course 2.04.217
that freeze, | bow themselves when he did sing. 3.01. 5
when did he regard | the stamp of nobleness in 3.02. 11
how that the cardinal did entreat his holiness 3.02. 32
for if | it did take place, "i do," quoth he, 3.02. 34
presently | he did unseal them, and the first he 3.02. 79

he view'd, | he did it with a serious mind; 3.02. 80
if we did think | his contemplation were above 3.02.130
he said he did, and with his deed did crown 3.02.155
and with his deed did crown | his word upon you. 3.02.155
it from their soul, though perils did | abound, 3.02.194
i did not think to shed a tear | in all my 3.02.428
that i did. 4.01. 60
unwilling to outlive the good that did it; 4.02. 60
i did, sir thomas, and left him at primero 5.01. 7
sir, i did never win of you before. 5.01. 58
did my commission | bid ye so far forget 5.02.176
you did nothing, sir. 5.03. 21
that fire–drake did i hit three times on the 5.03. 44 P
before | this happy child, did i get any thing. 5.04. 65
somebody had heard her talk yesterday, as i did. TRO 1.01. 46 P
where every flower | did, as a prophet, weep 1.02. 10
did her eyes run o'er too? 1.02.147 P
knew | love got so sweet as when desire did sue. 1.02.291
have record, trial did draw | bias and thwart, 1.03. 14
truer, | than ever greek did couple in his arms, 1.03.276
and those biles did run — say so — did not the 2.01. 5 P
run — say so — did not the general run then? 2.01. 5 P
wranglers, took a truce, | and did him service; 2.02. 76
rate, | and do a deed that never fortune did, 2.02. 90
that in their country did them that disgrace 2.02. 95
did move your greatness and this noble state 2.03.109
enjoy | at ample point all that i did possess, 3.03. 89
sing, | "great hector's sister did achilles win, 3.03.212
week by days, | did haunt you in the field. 4.01. 11
did not i tell you? 4.02. 34
we met by chance, you did not find me here. 4.02. 71
so many thousand sighs | did buy each other, 4.04. 40
did in great ilion thus translate him to me. 4.05.112
what did you swear you would bestow on me? 5.02. 25
i did swear patience. 5.02. 84
but if i tell how these two did //co–act, 5.02.118
never did young man fancy | with so eternal and 5.02.165
he hath done famously, he did it to that end. COR 1.01. 37 P
for his country, he did it to please his mother, 1.01. 38 P
that only like a gulf it did remain | i' th' 1.01. 98
where th' other instruments | did see and hear, 1.01.102
did minister | unto the appetite and affection 1.01.103
the former agents, if they did complain, | what 1.01.123
subdues him, | and curse that justice did it. 1.01.176
nor did you think it folly | to keep your great 1.02. 19
when she did suckle hector, look'd not lovelier 1.03. 41
how 'twas, he did so set his teeth and tear it. 1.03. 64 P
in ulysses' absence did but fill /ithaca full of 1.03. 83 P
as if the world | were feverous and did tremble. 1.04. 61
let him alone, | he did inform the truth. 1.06. 42
mouse ne'er shunn'd the cat as they did budge 1.06. 44
fought, and did | retire to win our purpose. 1.06. 49
for what he did before corioles, call him, 1.09. 63
rome, that all alone martius did fight | within 2.01.162
if he did not care whether he had their love or 2.02. 16 P
death's stamp, | where it did mark, it took; 2.02.108
where he did | run reeking o'er the lives of men 2.02.118
to brag unto them, "thus i did, and thus!" 2.02.147
them | as if he did contemn what he requested 2.02.157
no, 'tis his kind of speech, he did not mock us. 2.03.161
why, so he did, i am sure. 2.03.165
that as his worthy deeds did claim no less 2.03.186
did you perceive | he did solicit you in free 2.03.199
perceive | he did solicit you in free contempt 2.03.200
in free contempt | when he did need your loves; 2.03.201
of him that did not ask but mock, bestow | your 2.03.207
he did fashion | after the inveterate hate he 2.03.225
in place, we did commend | to your remembrances; 2.03.247
and did curse | against the volsces for they had 3.01. 9
he did, my lord. 3.01. 12
well assur'd | they ne'er did service for't; 3.01.122
kind of service | did not deserve corn gratis. 3.01.125
"we did request it, | we are the greater pole, 3.01.133
when he did love his country, | it honor'd him. 3.01.303
why did you wish me milder? 3.02. 14
as ever in ambitious strength i did | contend 4.05.112
so did i, i'll be sworn. 4.05.160 P
though they themselves did suffer by't, behold 4.06. 6
we wish'd coriolanus | had lov'd you as we did. 4.06. 25
as hercules | did shake down mellow fruit. 4.06.100
clusters, | who did hoot him out o' th' city. 4.06.123
and so did i. 4.06.141 P
and so did i; 4.06.142 P
and, to say the truth, so did very many of us. 4.06.142 P
that we did, we did for the best, and though we 4.06.143 P
that we did, we did for the best, and though we 4.06.143 P
so did we all. but come, let's home. 4.06.156 P
thought he would | when first i did embrace him; 4.07. 10
yet one time he did call me by my name. 5.01. 9
which they did refuse | and cannot now accept, 5.03. 14
if it were so that our request did tend | to 5.03.132
so did he me; 5.04. 16 P
a merrier day did never yet greet rome, | no, 5.04. 42
his stoutness | when he did stand for consul, 5.06. 27
to reap the fame | which he did end all his, and 5.06. 36
so he did, my lord. 5.06. 40
alone i did it. 5.06.116
danger | which this man's life did owe you, 5.06.137
corse that ever herald | did follow to his urn. 5.06.144
the greeks upon advice did bury ajax | that slew TIT 1.01.379
son | did graciously plead for his funerals; 1.01.381
with his own hand did slay his youngest son, 1.01.418
that what we did was mildly as we might, 1.01.475
terms | that ever ear did hear to such effect, 2.03.111
when did the tiger's young ones teach the dam? 2.03.142
milk thou suck'st from her did turn to marble, 2.03.144
did endure | to have his princely paws par'd all 2.03.151
so pale did shine the moon on /pyramus | when he 2.03.231
andronicus himself did take it up. 2.03.294
i did, my lord, yet let me be their bail, | for 2.03.295
if they did hear, | they would not mark me; 3.01. 33
if they did mark, | they would not pity me; 3.01. 34
when i did name her brothers, then fresh tears 3.01.111
if they did kill thy husband, then be joyful, 3.01.116
did ever raven sing so like a lark | that gives 3.01.158
ay, when my father was in rome she did. 4.01. 7
aunt | loves me as dear as e'er my mother did, 4.01. 23
ay, such a place there is where we did hunt | (o 4.01. 55
it did me good, before the palace gate | to 4.02. 35
did you not use his daughter very friendly? 4.02. 40
o, tell me, did you see aaron the moor? 4.02. 52
revenge, to do | as much as ever coriolanus did. 4.04. 68
and, as i earnestly did fix mine eye | upon the 5.01. 22
did not thy hue bewray whose brat thou art, 5.01. 28
curse — | wherein i did not some notorious ill: 5.01.127
what, was she ravish'd? tell who did the deed. 5.03. 53
they, 'twas they, that did her all this wrong. 5.03. 58
when with his solemn tongue he did discourse 5.03. 81
would i were dead, so you did live again! 5.03.173
ten thousand worse than ever yet i did | would i 5.03.187
if one good deed in all my life i did, | i do 5.03.189
and yours, close fighting ere i did approach. ROM 1.01.107
side, | so early walking did i see your son. 1.01.123
when it did taste the wormwood on the nipple 1.03. 30
and so did i. 1.04. 50
did my heart love till now? 1.05. 52
love's light wings did i o'erperch these walls, 2.02. 66
by love, that first did prompt me to inquire; 2.02. 80
i have forgot why i did call thee back. 2.02.170
the other did not so. 2.03. 87
thy love did read by rote that could not spell. 2.03. 88
what counterfeit did i give you? 2.04. 47 P
did you ne'er hear say, | "two may keep counsel, 2.04.196
the clock strook nine when i did send the nurse; 2.05. 1
but all this did i know before. 2.05. 46
which too untimely here did scorn the earth. 3.01.118
tybalt, here slain, whom romeo's hand did slay! 3.01.152
and, as he fell, did romeo turn and fly. 3.01.174
o god, did romeo's hand shed tybalt's blood? 3.02. 71
it did, it did, alas the day, it did! 3.02. 72
it did, it did, alas the day, it did! 3.02. 72
it did, it did, alas the day, it did! 3.02. 72
did ever dragon keep so fair a cave? 3.02. 74
did murther her, as that name's cursed hand 3.03.104
lov'd her kinsman tybalt dearly, | and so did i. 3.04. 4
or if it did not, | your first is dead, or 3.05.223
that did spit his body | upon a rapier's point. 4.03. 56
woeful day | that ever, ever, i did yet behold! 4.05. 51
since you did leave it for my office, sir. 5.01. 23
i said, | "an' if a man did need a poison now, 5.01. 50
o, this same thought did but forerun my need, 5.01. 53
where the infectious pestilence did reign, 5.02. 10
betossed soul | did not attend him as we rode? 5.03. 77
or did i dream it so? 5.03. 79
and fearfully did menace me with death | if i 5.03.133
death | if i did stay to look on his intents. 5.03.134
as i did sleep under this /yew tree here, | i 5.03.137
but then a noise did scare me from the tomb, 5.03.262
me, | but, as it seems, did violence on herself. 5.03.264
grave, | and bid me stand aloof, and so i did. 5.03.282
and here he writes that he did buy a poison | of 5.03.288
did not you chiefly belong to my heart? TIM 1.02. 92 P
if you did know, my lord, my master's wants — 2.02. 29
i did endure | not seldom, nor no slight checks, 2.02.139
to lacedaemon did my land extend. 2.02.151
the devil knew not what he did when he made man 3.03. 28 P
nor did he soil the fact with cowardice | (/an 3.05. 16
touch'd to death, | he did oppose his foe; 3.05. 20
and unnoted passion | he did behoove his anger, 3.05. 22
how full of valor did he bear himself | in the 3.05. 64
this honorable lord did but try us this other 3.06. 3 P
many my near occasions did urge me to put off; 3.06. 10 P
push, did you see my cap? 3.06.109 P
did you see my jewel? 3.06.113 P
did you see my cap? 3.06.115 P
i never did thee harm. 4.03.172
i love thee better now than e'er i did. 4.03.233
thy nature did commence in sufferance, time 4.03.268
nev'r did poor steward wear a truer grief | for 4.03.480
have fear'd false times when you did feast: 4.03.513
so did we woo | transformed timon to our city's 5.04. 18
i, timon, who, alive, all living men did hate; 5.04. 72
or did use | to stale with ordinary oaths my JC 1.02. 72
so indeed he did. 1.02.106
and we did buffet it | with lusty sinews, 1.02.107
did from the flames of troy upon his shoulder 1.02.113
the waves of tiber | did i the tired caesar. 1.02.115
fit was on him, i did mark | how he did shake — 1.02.120
him, i did mark | how he did shake — 'tis true, 1.02.121
he did shake — 'tis true, this god did shake; 1.02.121
his coward lips did from their color fly, | and 1.02.122
bend doth awe the world | did lose his lustre; 1.02.124
i did hear him groan; 1.02.124
it was mere foolery, i did not mark it. 1.02.236 P
but soft, i pray you; what, did caesar swound? 1.02.251
if the tag–rag people did not clap him and hiss 1.02.258 P
did cicero say any thing? 1.02.278
now, | did i go through a tempest dropping fire. 1.03. 10
which did flame and burn | like twenty torches 1.03. 16
and yesterday the bird of night did sit | even 1.03. 26
for he did bid antonio | send word to you he 1.03. 37
i did present myself | even in the aim and very 1.03. 51
but wherefore did you so much tempt the heavens? 1.03. 53
the base degrees | by which he did ascend. 2.01. 27
sure | it did not lie there when i went to bed. 2.01. 38
my ancestors did from the streets of rome | the 2.01. 53
since cassius first did whet me against caesar, 2.01. 61
our cause or our performance | did need an oath; 2.01.136
so i did, | fearing to strengthen that 2.01.247
vow | which did incorporate and make us one, 2.01.273
who did hide their faces | even from darkness. 2.01.277
horses /did neigh, and dying men did groan, 2.02. 23
and ghosts did shriek and squeal about the 2.02. 24
with an hundred spouts, | did run pure blood; 2.02. 78
came smiling and did bathe their hands in it. 2.02. 79
i am ashamed i did yield to them. 2.02.106
thus, brutus, did my master bid me kneel; 3.01.123
thus did mark antony bid me fall down; 3.01.124
why i, that did love caesar when i strook him, 3.01.182
that i did love thee, caesar, o, 'tis true; 3.01.194
caesar did write for him to come to rome. 3.01.278
he did receive his letters, and is coming, | and 3.01.279
whose ransoms did the general coffers fill; 3.02. 89
did this in caesar seem ambitious? 3.02. 90
you all did see that on the lupercal | i thrice 3.02. 95
a kingly crown, | which he did thrice refuse. 3.02. 97
you all did love him once, not without cause; 3.02.102
i dreamt to–night that i did feast with caesar, 3.03. 1
did not great julius bleed for justice' sake? 4.03. 19
his body, that did stab | and not for justice? 4.03. 20
did i say "better"? 4.03. 57
if you did, i care not. 4.03. 57
i did send to you | for certain sums of gold, 4.03. 69
i did send | to you for gold to pay my legions, 4.03. 75
you did. 4.03. 83
i did not. 4.03. 84
i did not think you could have been so angry. 4.03.143
i was sure your lordship did not give it me. 4.03.254
my lord, i do not know that i did cry. 4.03.296
why did you so cry out, sirs, in your sleep? 4.03.303
did we, my lord? 4.03.304
you did not so, when your vile daggers | hack'd 5.01. 39
by which i did blame cato for the death | which 5.01.101
for the death | which he did give himself — i 5.01.102
i slew the coward, and did take it from him. 5.03. 4
and where i did begin, there shall i end; 5.03. 24
in parthia did i take thee prisoner, | and then 5.03. 37
thy life, | that whatsoever i did bid thee do, 5.03. 39
where did you leave him? 5.03. 55
did i not meet thy friends? 5.03. 81
and did not they | put on my brows this wreath 5.03. 81
what ill request did brutus make to thee? 5.05. 11
i held the sword, and he did run on it. 5.05. 65
that did the latest service to my master. 5.05. 67
he, | did that they did in envy of great caesar; 5.05. 70
he, | did that they did in envy of great caesar; 5.05. 70
thumb, | wrack'd as homeward he did come. MAC 1.03. 29
and every one did bear | thy praises in his 1.03. 98
or did line the rebel | with hidden help and 1.03.112
who did report | that very frankly he confess'd 1.04. 4
so green and pale | at what it did so freely? 1.07. 38
did then adhere, and yet you would make both: 1.07. 52
did not you speak? 2.02. 16
there's one did laugh in 's sleep, and one cried 2.02. 20
that they did wake each other. 2.02. 21
but they did say their prayers, and address'd 2.02. 22
say "amen," | when they did say "god bless us!" 2.02. 27
why did you bring these daggers from the place? 2.02. 45
that it did, sir, i' the very throat on me; 2.03. 38 P
he did command me to call timely on him, | i 2.03. 46
he does; he did appoint so. 2.03. 53
say, the earth | was feverous, and did shake. 2.03. 61
do repent me of my fury, | that i did kill them. 2.03.107
wherefore did you so? 2.03.107
they did so — to th' amazement of mine eyes 2.04. 19
is't known who did this more than bloody deed? 2.04. 22
and to a notion craz'd | say, "thus did banquo." 3.01. 83
i did so; 3.01. 84
but who did bid thee join with us? 3.03. 1
who did strike out the light? 3.03. 19
that i did for him. 3.04. 16
yet he's good that did the like for fleance. 3.04. 17
thou canst not say i did it; 3.04. 49
did you send to him, sir? 3.04.128
how did you dare | to trade and traffic with 3.05. 3
how it did grieve macbeth! 3.06. 11
did he not straight | in pious rage the two 3.06. 11
he did; 3.06. 40
may kindly say | our duties did his welcome pay. 4.01.132
i did hear | the galloping of horse. 4.01.139
perchance even there where i did find my doubts. 4.03. 25
would o'erbear | that did oppose my will. 4.03. 65
stands scotland where it did? 4.03.164
they were well at peace when i did leave 'em. 4.03.179
did you say all? 4.03.217
did heaven look on, | and would not take their 4.03.223
as i did stand my watch upon the hill, | i 5.05. 32
majesty of buried denmark | did sometimes march? HAM 1.01. 49
did slay this fortinbras, who, by a seal'd 1.01. 86
did forfeit (with his life) all /those his lands 1.01. 88
did squeak and gibber in the roman streets. 1.01.116
did coldly furnish forth the marriage tables. 1.02.181
to me | in dreadful secrecy impart they did, 1.02.207
did you not speak to it? 1.02.214
my lord, i did, | but answer made it none. 1.02.214
it lifted up it head and jid address | itself to 1.02.216
and we did think it writ down in our duty | to 1.02.222
as if it some impartment did desire | to you 1.04. 59
the serpent that did sting thy father's life 1.05. 39
and in the porches of my ears did pour | the 1.05. 63
so did it mine, | and a most instant tetter 1.05. 70
my lord, i did intend it. 2.01. 5
where did i leave? 2.01. 51
as it did seem to shatter all his bulk | and end 2.01. 92
no, my good lord, but, as you did command, | i 2.01.105
i did repel his letters, and denied | his access 2.01.106
i fear'd he did but trifle | and meant to wrack 2.01.109
moreover that we much did long to see you, | the 2.02. 2
the need we have to use you did provoke | our 2.02. 3
and my young mistress thus i did bespeak: 2.02.140
why did ye laugh then, when i said, "man 2.02.313 P
same estimation they did when i was in the city? 2.02.334 P
did the night resemble | when he lay couched in 2.02.453
a neutral to his will and matter, | did nothing. 2.02.482
and never did the cyclops' hammers fall | on 2.02.489
but if the gods themselves did see her then, 2.02.512
did he receive you well? 3.01. 10
did you assay him | to any pastime? 3.01. 14
and there did seem in him a kind of joy | to 3.01. 18
my honor'd lord, you know right well you did, 3.01. 96
i did love you once. 3.01.114 P
that did i, my lord, and was accounted a good 3.02.100 P
what did you enact? 3.02.102 P
i did enact julius caesar. 3.02.103 P
since love our hearts and hymen did our hands 3.02.159
i did very well note him. 3.02.290 P
my lord, you once did love me. 3.02.335 P
never alone | did the king sigh, but /with a 3.03. 23
of those effects for which i did the murther: 3.03. 54
where every god did seem to set his seal | to 3.04. 61
nor did you nothing hear? 3.04.133
which bewept to the ground did not go | with 4.05. 39
thieves of mercy, but they knew what they did: 4.06. 21 P

did not together pluck such envy from him | as 4.07. 74
pluck such envy from him | as did that one, and 4.07. 75
shapes and tricks, | come short of what he did. 4.07. 90
of his | did hamlet so envenom with his envy 4.07.103
not that i think you did not love your father, 4.07.110
that might hold | if this did blast in proof. 4.07.154
therewith fantastic garlands did she make | of 4.07.168
"in youth, when i did love, did love, 5.01. 61
"in youth, when i did love, did love, 5.01. 61
cain's jaw–bone, that did the first murder! 5.01. 77 P
did these bones cost no more the breeding, but 5.01. 91 P
the corse they follow did with desp'rate hand 5.01.220
but wilt thou hear now how i did proceed? 5.02. 27
i once did hold it, as our statists do, | a 5.02. 33
but, sir, now | it did me yeman's service. 5.02. 36
i would you did, sir, yet, in faith, if you did, 5.02.134 P
in faith, if you did, it would not much approve 5.02.134 P
'a did /comply, sir, with his dug before 'a 5.02.187 P
it did always seem so to us; LR 1.01. 3 P
when she was dear to us, we did hold her so, 1.01.196
did my father strike my gentleman for chiding of 1.03. 1
and did the third a blessing against his will; 1.04.103 P
breeches, "then they for sudden joy did weep, 1.04.175
i did her wrong. 1.05. 24 P
'gainst parricides did all the thunder bend, 2.01. 46
what, did my father's godson seek your life? 2.01. 91
he did bewray his practice, and receiv'd | this 2.01.107
i did commend your highness' letters to them, 2.04. 28
as the cockney did to the eels when she put 'em 2.04.122 P
you? did you? 2.04.200
my mistress' heart and did the act of darkness 3.04. 87 P
if you did wear a beard upon your chin, | i'ld 3.07. 76
where was his son when they did take his eyes? 4.02. 88
these white flakes | did challenge pity of them. 4.07. 30
you are a spirit, i know; /when did you die? 4.07. 48
nor i know not | where i did lodge last night. 4.07. 67
methought thy very gait did prophesy | a royal 5.03.176
heart, if ever i | did hate thee or thy father. 5.03.179
'tis true, my lords, he did. 5.03.276
did i not, fellow? 5.03.276
if ever i did dream of such a matter, | abhor me OTH 1.01. 5
godliness i have, | i did full hard forbear him. 1.02. 10
i did not see you; 1.03. 50
so did i yours. 1.03. 52
did you by indirect and forced courses | subdue 1.03.111
how i did thrive in this fair lady's love, | and 1.03.125
i did consent, | and often did beguile her of 1.03.155
and often did beguile her of her tears, | when i 1.03.156
when i did speak of some distressful stroke 1.03.157
and i lov'd her that she did pity them. 1.03.168
i never yet did hear | that the bruis'd heart 1.03.218
parts | did i my soul and fortunes consecrate. 1.03.254
i never did like molestation view | on the 2.01. 16
did justly put on the vouch of very malice 2.01.146 P
yes, that i did; but that was but courtesy. 2.01.256 P
myself the crying fellow did pursue, | lest by 2.03.230
they were | when you yourself did part them. 2.03.239
though cassio did some little wrong to him, | as 2.03.242
what wound did ever heal but by degrees? 2.03.371
did michael cassio, when /you woo'd my lady, 3.03. 94
he did, from first to last. why dost thou ask? 3.03. 96
i did not think he had been acquainted with her. 3.03. 99
she did deceive her father, marrying you, | and 3.03.206
and so she did. 3.03.208
why did i marry? 3.03.242
that which so often you did bid me steal. 3.03.309
i did say so. 3.03.329
did i to–day | see cassio wipe his beard with. 3.03.438
did an egyptian to my mother give; 3.04. 56
i did so; 3.04. 65
the worms were hallowed that did breed the silk, 3.04. 73
/faith, that he did — i know not what he did. 4.01. 32
/faith, that he did — i know not what he did. 4.01. 32
did he confess it? 4.01. 65
what did you mean by that same handkerchief you 4.01.149 P
did you perceive how he laugh'd at his vice? 4.01.171 P
and did you see the handkerchief? 4.01.173 P
he did not call; 4.01.230
ay, you did wish that i would make her turn. 4.01.252
or did the letters work upon his blood | and 4.01.275
nor ever heard — nor ever did suspect. 4.02. 2
what? did they never whisper? 4.02. 6
burn up modesty, | did i but speak thy deeds. 4.02. 76
such as she said my lord did say i was. 4.02.119
why did he so? 4.02.122
if e'er my will did trespass 'gainst his love, 4.02.152
or that i do not yet, and ever did, | and ever 4.02.156
how goes it now? he looks gentler than he did. 4.03. 11
he she lov'd prov'd mad, | and did forsake her. 4.03. 28
even he, sir; did you know him? 5.01. 92
o, did he so? i charge you go with me. 5.01.120
i never did | offend you in my life; 5.02. 58
th' affrighted globe | did yawn at alteration. 5.02.101
cassio did top her; 5.02.136
hell | but that i did proceed upon just grounds 5.02.138
but did you ever tell him she was false? 5.02.178
i did. 5.02.179
did you say with cassio? 5.02.182
sweetest innocent | that e'er did lift up eye. 5.02.200
i scarce did know you, uncle; 5.02.201
did he live now, | this sight would make him do 5.02.206
and she did gratify his amorous works | with 5.02.213
i found by fortune, and did give my husband; 5.02.226
alas, i found it, | and i did give't my husband. 5.02.231
what did thy song bode, lady? 5.02.246
a better never did itself sustain | upon a 5.02.260
for nought i did in hate, but all in honor. 5.02.295
did you and he consent in cassio's death? 5.02.297
this did i fear, but thought he had no weapon; 5.02.360
why did he marry fulvia, and not love her? ANT 1.01. 41
come, my queen, | last night you did desire it. 1.01. 55
thus did i desire it. 1.02.122
i did not see him since. 1.03. 1
i did not send you. 1.03. 3
madam, methinks, if you did love him dearly, 1.03. 6
at thy heel | did famine follow, whom thou 1.04. 59
thy palate then did deign | the roughest berry 1.04. 63
strange flesh, | which some did die to look on; 1.04. 68
time we twain | did show ourselves i' th' field, 1.04. 74
and think | what venus did with mars. 1.05. 18
last thing he did, dear queen, | he kiss'd — 1.05. 39
and soberly did mount an arm–gaunt steed, | who 1.05. 48
did i, charmian, | ever love caesar so? 1.05. 66
i did not think | this amorous surfeiter would 2.01. 32
his wife that's dead did trespasses to caesar; 2.01. 40
yet if you there | did practice on my state, 2.02. 39
at mine intent | by what did here befall me. 2.02. 42
my brother never | did urge me in his act. 2.02. 46
i did inquire it, | and have my learning from 2.02. 46
did he not rather | discredit my authority with 2.02. 48
of this my letters | before did satisfy you. 2.02. 52
i grieving grant | did you too much disquiet. 2.02. 70
in alexandria you | did pocket up my letters; 2.02. 73
taunts | did gibe my missive out of audience. 2.02. 74
and did want | of what i was i' th' morning; 2.02. 76
you, whom no brother | did ever love so dearly. 2.02.150
i did not think to draw my sword 'gainst pompey, 2.02.153
sir, we did sleep day out of countenance, and 2.02.177 P
she did lie | in her pavilion — cloth of gold, 2.02.198
whose wind did seem | to /glow the delicate 2.02.203
/glow the delicate cheeks which they did cool, 2.02.204
which they did cool, | and what they undid did. 2.02.205
enthron'd i' th' market–place, did sit alone, 2.02.215
panted, | that she did make defect perfection, 2.02.231
your diver | did hang a salt–fish on his hook, 2.05. 17
your mother came to sicily and did find | her 2.06. 45
i did not think, sir, to have met you here. 2.06. 49
no more /of that; he did so. 2.06. 69
ten times as much | as i have said you did. 2.06. 78
what willingly he did confound he wail'd, 3.02. 58
him, he not /took't, | or did it from his teeth. 3.04. 10
authority abus'd, | and did deserve his change. 3.06. 34
tell of her approach, | long ere she did appear; 3.06. 46
i not constrain'd, but did it | on my free will. 3.06. 56
your letters did withhold our breaking forth, 3.06. 79
mine eyes did sicken at the sight and could not 3.10. 16
honor, ne'er before | did violate so itself. 3.10. 23
you did know | how much you were my conqueror, 3.11. 65
does conquer him that did his master conquer, 3.13. 45
that you embrace not antony | as you did love, 3.13. 57
he did ask favor. 3.13.133
lucky, men did ransom lives | of me for jests; 3.13.179
did desire you | to burn this night with torches 4.02. 40
alexas did revolt, and went to jewry on 4.06. 11
there did dissuade | great herod to incline 4.06. 12
poor enobarbus did | before thy face repent! 4.09. 9
then in the midst a tearing groan did break 4.14. 31
when i did make thee free, swor'st thou not then 4.14. 81
when did she send thee? 4.14.119
you did suspect | she had dispos'd with caesar, 4.14.122
to tell them that this world did equal theirs 4.15. 77
which writ his honor in the acts it did | hath, 5.01. 22
with the courage which the heart did lend it, 5.01. 23
a rarer spirit never | did steer humanity; 5.01. 32
heart | where mine his thoughts did kindle — 5.01. 46
antony | did tell me of you, bade me trust you, 5.02. 13
the record of what injuries you did us, | though 5.02.118
that you did fear is done. 5.02.335
who did join his honor | against the romans with CYM 1.01. 29
loyall'st husband that did e'er plight troth. 1.01. 96
as i my poor self did exchange for you, | to 1.01.119
i chose an eagle, | and did avoid a puttock. 1.01.140
him from others, he did keep | the deck, with 1.03. 10
madam, so i did. 1.03. 16
i did not take my leave of him, but had | most 1.03. 25
i was glad i did atone my countryman and you. 1.04. 39 P
not meet | that i did amplify my judgment in 1.05. 17
desire my man's abode where i did leave him: 1.06. 53
he did incline to sadness, and oft–times | not 1.06. 62
did you hear of a stranger that's come to court 2.01. 32 P
did softly press the rushes ere he waken'd | the 2.02. 13
that it did strive | in workmanship and value, 2.04. 73
her pretty action did outsell her gift, | and 2.04.102
most venerable man which i | did call my father, 2.05. 4
did it with | a pudency so rosy the sweet view 2.05. 10
till the injurious romans did extort | this 3.01. 47
which swell'd so much that it did almost stretch 3.01. 49
all color here | did put the yoke upon 's; 3.01. 51
who was the first of britain which did put | his 3.01. 59
did you but know the city's usuries, | and felt 3.03. 45
i as a tree | whose boughs did bend with fruit; 3.03. 61
sinon's weeping | did scandal many a holy tear, 3.04. 60
that did attend themselves and had the virtue 3.06. 83
thus did he answer me; 4.02. 41
thing | more slavish did i ne'er than answering 4.02. 73
none in the world. you did mistake him sure. 4.02.102
fidele's sickness | did make my way long forth. 4.02.149
which he did wave against my throat, i have 4.02.150
of my dear'st mother | it did not speak before. 4.02.191
was he | that (otherwise than noble nature did) 4.02.364
who did promise | to yield me often tidings. 4.03. 38
what thing is't that i never | did see man die, 4.04. 36
i did, | though you, it seems, come from the 5.03. 1
i did. 5.03. 2
gan to look | the way that they did, and to grin 5.03. 38
could not find death where i did hear him groan, 5.03. 69
why did you suffer jachimo, | slight thing of 5.04. 63
she did confess | was as a scorpion to her sight 5.05. 44
she did confess she had | for you a mortal 5.05. 49
we did, so please your highness. 5.05. 62
her honor confident | than i did truly find her, 5.05.188
danger, did compound for her | a certain stuff, 5.05.254
most like i did, for i was dead. 5.05.259
why did you throw your wedded lady /from you? 5.05.261
though you did love this youth, i blame ye not, 5.05.267
i have spoke it, and i did it. 5.05.290
the wrongs he did me | were nothing prince–like; 5.05.292
for he did provoke me | with language that would 5.05.293
that i suffer'd | was all the harm i did. 5.05.336
punishment before | for that which i did then. 5.05.344
did you e'er meet? 5.05.378
and did relieve me | to see this gracious season 5.05.400
the soldier that did company these three | in 5.05.408
sinks my knee, | as then your force did. 5.05.414
sir, | as you did mean indeed to be our brother; 5.05.423
never was a war did cease | (ere bloody hands 5.05.484
liking took, | and her to incest did provoke — PER 1.ch. 26
but custom what they did begin | was with long 1.ch. 29
so for her many /a wight did die, | as yon grim 1.ch. 39
the senate–house of planets all did sit, | to 1.01. 10
gripe not at earthly joys as erst they did; 1.01. 49
i feed | on mother's flesh which did me breed. 1.01. 65
i did but crave. 2.01. 87
which my dead father did bequeath to me, | with 2.01.124
did vail their crowns to his supremacy; 2.03. 42
never did thought of mine levy offense; 2.05. 52
nor never did my actions yet commence | a deed 2.05. 53
angry father if my tongue | did e'er solicit, or 2.05. 69
upon the sea, | shook as the earth did quake; 3.02. 15
the very principals did seem to rend, | and all 3.02. 16
did the sea toss up upon our shore this chest. 3.02. 50
did the sea cast it up? 3.02. 57
which did steal | the eyes of young and old. 4.01. 40
my father, as nurse says, did never fear, | but 4.01. 52
my troth, | i never did her hurt in all my life. 4.01. 74
word, nor did ill turn | to any living creature. 4.01. 75
he did not flow | from honorable courses. 4.03. 27
she did /distain my child, and stood between 4.03. 31
did you ever hear the like? 4.05. 1 P
did you ever dream of such a thing? 4.05. 4 P
did you go to't so young? 4.06. 74 P
though they did change me to the meanest bird 4.06.101
i did not think | thou couldst have spoke so 4.06.102
though wayward fortune did malign my state, | my 5.01. 89
i said, my lord, if you did know my parentage, 5.01. 99
thou not /say, when i did push thee back — 5.01.126
so indeed i did. 5.01.128
what my thoughts | did warrant me was likely. 5.01.134
e'er dull'd sleep | did mock sad fools withal. 5.01.162
believe me, 'twere best i did give o'er. 5.01.166
the king my father did in tharsus leave me, 5.01.170
with his wicked wife, | did seek to murther me; 5.01.172
thou that beget'st him that did thee beget; 5.01.195
enough, | though doubts did ever sleep. 5.01.202
was my mother, who did end | the minute i began. 5.01.211
of your melancholy state, | did come to see you. 5.01.221
did wed | at pentapolis the fair thaisa. 5.03. 3
did you not name a tempest, | a birth, and death 5.03. 33
you have heard me say, when i did fly from tyre, 5.03. 50
think, | did i not by th' abstaining of my joy, TNK 1.01.189
who did propound | to his bold ends honor and 1.02. 16
you did begin | as if you met decays of many 1.02. 28
'tis not this | i did begin to speak of. 1.02. 35
and i did love him for't. 1.03. 35
lov'd for we did, and like the elements | that 1.03. 61
operance, our souls | did so to one another. 1.03. 64
came privately in the night, and so did they. 2.01. 47 P
he made such scruples of the wrong he did | to 2.06. 25
but if it did, yours is too tart, sweet cousin. 3.03. 26
she did so; well, sir? 3.03. 31
what did she there, coz? 3.03. 34
something she did, sir. 3.03. 35
do you, | as once did meleager and the boar, 3.05. 18
i did not think a week could have restor'd | my 3.06. 5
yet a little | i did by imitation. 3.06. 81
o sir, when did you see her? 4.01. 33
sir, when did she sleep? 4.01. 35
pray did you ever hear | of one young palamon? 4.01.116
no, would she did! 4.01.142
cries, "o, that ever i did it behind the arras!" 4.03. 54 P
i did think so too, and would account i had a 4.03. 66 P
the heavenly fires | did scorch his mortal son, 5.01. 92
but have blush'd | at simp'ring sirs that did. 5.01.104
you did so? 5.02. 13
did you nev'r see the horse he gave me? 5.02. 45
how did you like her? 5.02.103
so mingled as if mirth did make him sad, | and 5.03. 52
i did think | good palamon would miscarry, yet i 5.03.100
miscarry, yet i knew not | why i did think so. 5.03.102
brave a knight as e'er | did spur a noble steed. 5.03.116
i have spoke, your arcite | did not lose by't; 5.03.122
till heavens did | make hardly one the winner. 5.03.129
a steed that emily | did first bestow on him — 5.04. 50
the calkins | did rather tell than trample; 5.04. 56
and, though it were too short, | he did it well; 5.04.103
never fortune | did play a subtler game. 5.04.113
the right o' th' lady | did lie in you, for you 5.04.117
sin | which oft th' apostle did forewarn us of, STM II.C 94
upon this promise did he raise his chin, | like VEN 85
so offers he to give what she did crave, | but 88
never did passenger in summer's heat | more 91
whose sinowy neck in battle ne'er did bow, | who 99
with burning eye did hotly overlook them, 178
so did this horse excel a common one, | in shape 293
look what a horse should have he did not lack, 299
hue, | how white and red each other did destroy! 346
with tears which chorus–like her eyes did rain. 360
which to his speech did honey passage yield, 452
for sharply he did think to reprehend her, 470
her, | which cunning love did wittily prevent: 471
when he did frown, o, had she then gave over, 571
i fear'd thy fortune, and my joints did tremble. 642
"where did i leave?" 715
whereat th' impartial gazer late did wonder, 748
so did the merciless and pitchy night | fold in 821
fold in the object that did feed her sight. 822
o, how her eyes and tears did lend and borrow! 961
the dire imagination she did follow | this sound 975
no," quoth she, "sweet death, i did but jest, 997
i did but act, he's author of thy slander. 1006
if he did see his face, why then i know | he 1109
who did not whet his teeth at him again, | but 1113
and never did he bless | my youth with his, the 1119
when collatine unwisely did not let | to praise LUC 10
with pure aspects did him peculiar duties. 14
disdainfully did sting | his high–pitch'd 40
but some untimely thought did instigate | his 43
no comfortable star did lend his light, | no 164
contrive, | to cipher me how fondly i did dote; 207
o, how her fear did make her color rise! 257
until her husband's welfare she did hear; 263
doors, the wind, the glove that did delay him, 325
what did he note but strongly he desired? 415
ranks of blue veins, as his hand did scale, 440

"in tarquin's likeness i did entertain thee; 596
wrack, | yet for thy honor did i entertain him; 842
besides, of weariness he did complain him, | and 845
would else have come to me | when tarquin did, 917
he shall not boast who did thy stock pollute 1063
my shame be his that did my fame confound; 1202
such danger to resistance did belong | that 1265
her earnest eye did make him more amazed. 1356
which heartless peasants did so well resemble, 1392
and from his lips did fly | thin winding breath, 1406
as if some mermaid did their ears entice, | some 1411
of what she was, no semblance did remain. 1453
and therefore lucrece swears he did her wrong, 1462
did incur | this load of wrath that burning troy 1473
as priam him did cherish, | so did i tarquin, so 1546
so did i tarquin, so my troy did perish. 1547
so did i tarquin, so my troy did perish. 1547
and swear i found you where you did fulfill 1635
and so did kill | the lechers in their deed. 1636
"with this i did begin to start and cry, | and 1639
that blow did bail it from the deep unrest | of 1725
i often did behold | in thy sweet semblance my 1758
"i did give that life | which she too early and 1800
by, | wherein deep policy did him disguise, 1815
who, wond'ring at him, did his words allow. 1845
they did conclude to bear dead lucrece thence, 1850
the romans plausibly did give consent | to 1854
did not the heavenly rhetoric of thine eye, PP 3. 1
did court the lad with many a lovely look, 4. 3
but whether unripe years did want conceit, | or 4. 9
she hotter that did look | for his approach that 6. 7
"did i see a fair sweet youth | here in these 9. 9
and yet thou lefts me more than i did crave, 10. 9
she told the youngling how god mars did try her, 11. 3
and with her lips on his did act the seizure: 11.10
yet at my parting sweetly did she smile, | in 14. 7
combat doubtful, that love with love did fight, 15. 5
by a gift of learning did bear the maid away: 15.14
made, | beasts did leap and birds did sing, 20. 5
made, | beasts did leap and birds did sing, 20. 5
sing, | trees did grow and plants did spring; 20. 6
sing, | trees did grow and plants did spring; 20. 6
every thing did banish moan, | save the 20. 7
so between them love did shine, | that the PHT 33
those hours that with gentle work did frame SON 5. 1
which erst from heat did canopy the herd, | and 12. 6
who all their parts of me to thee did give: 31.11
even so my sun one early morn did shine | with 33. 9
no matter then although my foot did stand | upon 44. 5
as if by some instinct the wretch did know | his 50. 7
showing their birth and where they did proceed? 76. 8
whilst i alone did call upon thy aid, | my verse 79. 1
i never saw that you did painting need, | and 83. 1
you did exceed | the barren tender of a poet's 83. 3
this silence for my sin you did impute, | which 83. 9
that did my ripe thoughts in my brain inhearse, 86. 3
but heaven in thy creation did decree | that in 93. 9
nor did i wonder at the lily's white, | nor 98. 9
as with your shadow i with these did play. 98.14
the forward violet thus did i chide: 99. 1
the roses fearfully on thorns did stand, | /one 99. 8
than when her mournful hymns did hush the night, 102.10
that did not better for my life provide | than 111. 3
since my appeal says i did strive to prove | the 117.13
to bitter sauces did i frame my feeding, | and, 118. 6
now, | and for that sorrow which i then did feel 120. 2
those lips that love's own hand did make 145. 1
state, | straight in her heart did mercy come, 145. 5
desire is death, which physic did except. 147. 8
and his love–kindling fire did quickly steep 153. 3
oft did she heave her napkin to her eyne, LC 15
as they did batt'ry to the spheres intend; 23
some in her threaden fillet still did bide, 33
and when in his fair parts she did abide, | she 83
"his browny locks did hang in crooked curls, 85
each eye that saw him did enchant the mind, 89
did livery falseness in a pride of truth. 105
for his advantage still did wake and sleep. 123
"that he did in the general bosom reign | of 127
"many there were that did his picture get | to 134
self, that did in freedom stand | and was my own 143
"yet did i not, as some my equals did, | demand 148
"yet did i not, as some my equals did, | demand 148
till now did ne'er invite, nor never vow. 182
sought their shame that so their shame did find, 187
and deep–brain'd sonnets that did amplify | each 209
hard, | whereto his invis'd properties did tend; 212
with sighs that burning lungs did raise; 228
which late her noble suit in court did shun, 234
and did thence remove | to spend her living in 237
playing the place which did no form receive, 241
her eye | upon the moment did her force subdue, 248
"this said, his wat'ry eyes he did dismount, 281
his poison'd me, and mine did him restore. 301
and, veil'd in them, did win whom he would maim. 312
o, that forc'd thunder from his heart did fly, 325

DIDO 12 FR 0.0013 REL FR 4 V 8 P
widow dido! TMP 2.01. 79 P
"widow dido," said you? 2.01. 82 P
bate, i beseech you, widow dido. 2.01.101 P
o, widow dido? ay, widow dido. 2.01.102 P
o, widow dido? ay, widow dido. 2.01.102 P
a night | stood dido with a willow in her hand MV 5.01. 10
did | when he to madding dido would unfold | his 2H6 3.02.117
the wand'ring prince and dido once enjoyed, TIT 2.03. 22
berhyme her), dido a dowdy, cleopatra a gipsy, ROM 2.04. 41 P
'twas aeneas' /tale to dido, and thereabout of HAM 2.02.446 P
dido and her aeneas shall want troops, | and all ANT 4.14. 53
for in the next world will dido see palamon, and TNK 4.03. 15 P

DIDO'S 2 FR 0.0002 REL FR 1 V 1 P
not since widow dido's time. TMP 2.01. 77 P
to love–sick dido's sad attending ear | the TIT 5.03. 82

/DIDST 2 FR 0.0002 REL FR 2 V 0 P
/didst /thou /beat /heaven /with /blessing 2H4 1.03. 92
/didst /thou /disgorge | /thy /glutton /bosom 1.03. 97

DIDST 188 FR 0.0212 REL FR 147 V 41 P
thou didst smile, | infused with a fortitude TMP 1.02.153
thou didst painfully remain | a dozen years; 1.02.278
where thou didst vent thy groans | as fast as 1.02.280
till thou didst seek to violate | the honor of 1.02.347
thou didst prevent me; 1.02.350
when thou didst not, savage, | know thine own 1.02.355
but thy vild race | (though thou didst learn) 1.02.359
what is it thou didst say? 2.01.212
how didst thou scape? 2.02.119 P
didst thou not say he lied? 3.02. 74 P
say again, where didst thou leave these varlots? 4.01.170
most cruelly | didst thou, alonso, use me and my 5.01. 72
why didst thou stoop then? TGV 1.02. 70
didst thou but know the inly touch of love, 2.07. 18
why didst not tell me sooner? 3.01.380 P
when didst thou see me heave up my leg and make 4.04. 37 P
didst thou ever see me do such a trick? 4.04. 39 P
what, didst thou offer her this from me? 4.04. 54 P
whose dear sake thou didst then rend thy faith 5.04. 47
didst not thou share? WIV 2.02. 14
say, didst thou speak with him? ERR 2.01. 47
mad, | that thus so madly thou didst answer me? 2.02. 12
villain, thou didst deny the gold's receipt, 2.02. 17
why, thou didst conclude hairy men plain dealers 2.02. 86 P
by thee, and this thou didst return from him: 2.02.157
words | didst thou deliver to me on the mart. 2.02.164
drunkard, thou, what didst thou mean by this? 3.01. 10
didst speak him fair? 4.02. 16
say, wherefore didst thou lock me forth to–day? 4.04. 95
when thou didst make him master of thy bed, | to 5.01.163
a grievous fault! say, woman, didst thou so? 5.01.206
nor ever didst thou draw thy sword on me; 5.01.267
didst thou note the daughter of signior leonato? ADO 1.01.162 P
didst thou not hear somebody? 3.03.128 P
which of my bad parts didst thou first fall in 5.02. 60 P
as much as thou didst me in carrying gates. LLL 1.02. 75 P
didst not thou lead him through the glimmering MND 2.01. 77
but why unkindly didst thou leave me so? 3.02.183
o, wherefore, nature, didst thou lions frame? 5.01.291
didst rob it of some taste of tediousness. MV 2.03. 3
i had as lief thou didst break his neck as his AYL 1.01.146 P
o, thou didst then never love so heartily! 2.04. 33
didst thou hear these verses? 3.02.163 P
but didst thou hear without wondering how thy 3.02.172 P
a poet, i might have some hope thou didst feign. 3.03. 27 P
that thou didst know how many fathom deep i am 4.01.206 P
thou didst it excellent. SHR in.1. 89
didst thou not say he comes? 3.02. 76 P
peter, didst ever see the like? 4.01.179 P
didst thou never see thy /master's father, 5.01. 52 P
thou didst make tolerable vent of thy travel; AWW 2.03.202 P
that thou didst love her, strikes some scores 5.03. 56
thou didst hate her deadly, | and she is dead, 5.03.117
sot, didst see dick surgeon, sot? TN 5.01.197 P
then didst thou utter, | "i am yours for ever." WT 1.02.104
didst note it? 1.02.214
didst perceive it? 1.02.216
of a true subject, didst counsel and aid them, 3.02. 20 P
thou didst speak but well | when most the truth; 3.02.232
who lives and dares but say thou didst not well JN 1.01.271
and though thou now confess thou didst but jest, 3.01. 16
thou idle dreamer, wherefore didst thou so? 4.02.153
but thou didst understand me by my signs, | and 4.02.237
and didst in signs again parley with sin, | yea, 4.02.238
yea, without stop, didst let thy heart consent, 4.02.239
of mercy, if thou didst this deed of death, 4.03.118
as thou shalt be, if thou didst kill this child. 4.03.124
if thou didst but consent | to this most cruel 4.03.125
who didst thou leave to tend his majesty? 5.06. 32
which didst lead me forth | of that sweet way i R2 3.02.204
didst send two of thy men | to execute the noble 4.01. 81
didst thou not mark the king, what words he 5.04. 1
thou didst well, for wisdom cries out in the 1H4 1.02. 88 P
didst thou never see titan kiss a dish of butter 2.04.120 P
if thou didst, then behold that compound. 2.04.122 P
what didst thou lose, jack? 3.03.100 P
why didst thou tell me that thou wert a king? 5.03. 24
didst thou? 5.04.145 P
say, morton, didst thou come from shrewsbury? 2H4 1.01. 64
thou didst swear to me upon a parcel–gilt goblet 2.01. 86 P
of windsor, thou didst swear to me then, as i 2.01. 91 P
prawns, whereby thou didst desire to eat some, 2.01. 97 P
and didst thou not, when she was gone down 2.01. 98 P
and didst thou not kiss me, and bid me fetch 2.01.101 P
didst thou hear me? 2.04.305 P
thou that didst bear the key of all my counsels, H5 2.02. 96
didst bring in | wonder to wait on treason and 2.02.109
why, so didst thou. 2.02.128
why, so didst thou. 2.02.129
why, so didst thou. 2.02.130
why, so didst thou. 2.02.131
such and so finely bolted didst thou seem. 2.02.137
it was ourself thou didst abuse. 4.08. 49
didst thou at first, to flatter us withal, 1H6 2.01. 51
why didst thou say, of late thou wert despis'd? 2.05. 42
well didst thou, richard, to suppress thy voice; 4.01.182
of mine | which thou didst force from talbot, my 4.06. 24
or else, when thou didst keep my lambs a–field, 5.04. 30
when thou didst ride in triumph through the 2H6 2.04. 14
thou never didst them wrong, nor no man wrong; 3.01.209
didst ever hear a man so penitent? 3.02. 4
son, | didst yield consent to disinherit him, 3H6 2.02. 24
didst thou never hear | that things ill got had 2.02. 45
as thou didst kill our tender brother rutland, 2.02.115
thou didst love york, and i am son to york. 2.06. 73
for, brother, if thou didst, | thy tears would 5.02. 36
didst thou not hear me swear i would not do it? 5.05. 74
thou been kill'd when first thou didst presume, 5.06. 35
that didst unworthy slaughter upon others. R3 1.02. 88
the which thou once didst bend against her 1.02. 95
didst thou not kill this king? 1.02.101
when thou didst crown his warlike brows with 1.03.174
thou didst receive the sacrament to fight | in 1.04.203
to the name of god | didst break that vow, and 1.04.206
but didst thou see them dead? 4.03. 27
when didst thou sleep when such a deed was done? 4.04. 24
i had a richard too, and thou didst kill him; 4.04. 44
thou didst prophesy the time would come | that i 4.04. 79
thou didst usurp my place, and dost thou not 4.04.109
so from thy soul's love didst thou love her 4.04.260
if thou didst fear to break an oath with him, 4.04.378
yet thou didst kill my children. 4.04.422
didst thou not tell me, griffith, as thou ledst H8 4.02. 5
i would thou didst itch from head to foot; TRO 2.01. 27 P
who art thou that lately didst descend | into TIT 2.03.248
wherefore didst thou this? 4.02.147
why, didst thou not come from heaven? 4.03. 89
if thou didst know me, thou wouldst talk with me 5.02. 20
i gave thee mine before thou didst request it; ROM 2.02.128
is rosaline, that thou didst love so dear, | so 2.03. 66
didst thou not fall out with a tailor for 3.01. 27 P
thou wretched boy, that didst consort him here, 3.01.130
when thou didst bower the spirit of a fiend | in 3.02. 81
wherefore, villain, didst thou kill my cousin? 3.02.100
if thou didst put this sour cold habit on | to TIM 4.03.239
what man didst thou ever know unthrift that was 4.03.311 P
thou talk'st of, didst thou ever know belov'd? 4.03.314 P
here didst thou fall, and here thy hunters stand JC 3.01.205
strike as thou didst at caesar; 4.03.105
when thou didst hate him worst, thou lovedst him 4.03.106
didst thou dream, lucius, that thou so criedst 4.03.295
yes, that thou didst. didst thou see any thing? 4.03.297
yes, that thou didst. didst thou see any thing? 4.03.297
why didst thou send me forth, brave cassius? 5.03. 80
didst thou not hear their shouts? 5.03. 83
knowledge of the broil | as thou didst leave it. MAC 1.02. 7
nothing afeard of what thyself didst make 1.03. 96
didst thou not hear a noise? 2.02. 14
if thou didst it, thou art the nonpareil. 3.04. 18
if thou didst ever thy dear father love — HAM 1.05. 23
didst perceive? 3.02.287 P
hadst thou thy wits and didst persuade revenge, 4.05.169
and tell him to his teeth, | "thus didst thou." 4.07. 57
if thou didst ever hold me in thy heart, 5.02.346
fault, | how ugly didst thou in cordelia show! LR 1.04.267
if thou didst intend | to make this creature 1.04.276
though thou didst produce | my very character), 2.01. 71
i have good hope | thou didst not know on't. 2.04.189
didst thou give all to thy daughters? 3.04. 49 P
in better phrase and matter than thou didst. 4.06. 8
thou toldst me thou didst hold him in thy hate. OTH 1.01. 7
now, roderigo, | where didst thou see her? 1.01.163
how didst thou know 'twas she? 1.01.165
didst thou not see her paddle with the palm of 2.01.253 P
didst not mark that? 2.01.255 P
what didst not like? 3.03.110
and didst contract and purse thy brow together, 3.03.113
i know thou didst not; 5.02.174
thou didst drink | the stale of horses and the ANT 1.04. 61
it is reported thou didst eat strange flesh, 1.04. 67
o, i would thou didst; 2.05. 93
didst thou behold octavia? 3.03. 7
didst hear her speak? 3.03. 12
knows | thou didst unjustly banish me; CYM 3.03.100
thou didst accuse him of incontinency; 3.04. 47
that didst set up my disobedience 'gainst the 3.04. 88
wherefore then | didst undertake it? 3.04.102
'twas leonatus' jewel, | whom thou didst banish; 5.05.144
didst thou not /say, when i did push thee back PER 5.01.126
reveal how thou at sea didst lose thy wife. 5.01.244
"o, thou didst kill me, kill me once again. VEN 499
when thou didst name the boar, not to dissemble, 641
"didst thou not mark my face? 643
he learn'd to sin, and thou didst teach the way? LUC 630
thy discontent thou didst bequeath to me. PP 10.12
why didst thou promise such a beauteous day, SON 34. 1
say that thou didst forsake me for some fault, 89. 1
whence didst thou steal thy sweet that smells, 99. 2

DID'T 1 FR 0.0001 REL FR 1 V 0 P
did't not wake you? TMP 2.01.312

/DIE* 2 FR 0.0002 REL FR 1 V 1 P
/when /richard /liv'd, /would /have /him /die, 2H4 1.03.101
/die men like dogs! 2.04.174 P

DIE* 521 FR 0.0589 REL FR 436 V 85 P
but i would fain die a dry death. TMP 1.01. 68 P
thou let'st thy fortune sleep — die, rather; 2.01.216
here shall i die ashore —" | this is a very 2.02. 43
and much less take | what i shall die to want. 3.01. 79
if not, i'll die your maid. 3.01. 84
i'll die on him that says so but yourself. TGV 2.04.114
to die is to be banish'd from myself, | and 3.01.171
but valentine, if he be ta'en, must die. 3.01.234
let him die; WIV 2.03. 84 P
why, now let me die, for i have liv'd long 3.03. 44 P
if you go out in your own semblance, you die, 4.02. 67 P
find a man there, he shall die a flea's death. 4.02.150 P
are fairies, he that speaks to them shall die. 5.05. 47
a thirsty evil, and when we drink we die. MM 1.02.130
sir, he must die. 2.01. 31
ages smack of this vice, and he | to die for't! 2.02. 6
is it your will claudio shall die to–morrow? 2.02. 7
i have a brother is condemn'd to die; 2.02. 34
must he needs die? 2.02. 48
he must die to–morrow. 2.02. 82
to do another such offense | than die for this. 2.03. 15
when must he die? 2.03. 16
your partner, as i hear, must die to–morrow, 2.03. 37
must die to–morrow? 2.03. 40
yet he must die. 2.04. 36
your brother is to die. 2.04. 83
then must your brother die. 2.04.104
sister, by redeeming him, | should die for ever. 2.04.108
else let my brother die, | if not a fedary, but 2.04.121
and you tell me that he shall die for't. 2.04.143
will, | or else he must not only die the death, 2.04.165
then, isabel, live chaste, and, brother, die; 2.04.184
i have hope to live, and am prepar'd to die. 3.01. 4
to sue to live, i find i seek to die, | and, 3.01. 42
dar'st thou die? 3.01. 76
if i must die, | i will encounter darkness as a 3.01. 82
yes, thou must die: 3.01. 86
ay, but to die, and go we know not where; 3.01.117
die, perish! 3.01.143
hopes that are fallible, to–morrow you must die; 3.01.169 P
had rather my brother die by the law than my son 3.01.190 P
canst thou tell if claudio die to–morrow, or no? 3.02.170 P
wh; should he die, sir? 3.02.171 P
will not be alter'd, claudio must die to–morrow. 3.02.208 P

to him, and now is he resolv'd to die. 3.02.248 P
morning are to die claudio and barnardine. 4.02. 7 P
for claudio yet, | but he must die to-morrow? 4.02. 93
i will not consent to die this day, that's 4.03. 56 P
i swear i will not die to-day for any man's 4.03. 59 P
unfit to live, or die; 4.03. 64
i | persuade this rude wretch willingly to die. 4.03. 81
but barnardine must die this afternoon; 4.03. 83
since it is so, | let him not die. 5.01.448
therefore by law thou art condemn'd to die. ERR 1.01. 25
if no, then thou art doom'd to die. 1.01.154
i'll weep what's left away, and weeping die. 2.01.115
he gains by death that hath such means to die: 3.02. 51
him, | he shall not die, so much we tender him. 5.01.132
disdain should die while she hath such meet food ADO 1.01.120 P
i will die in it at the stake. 1.01.232 P
i shall see thee, ere i die, look pale with love 1.01.247 P
hero thinks surely she will die, for she says 2.03.173 P
for she says she will die if he love her not, 2.03.174 P
and she will die ere she make her love known, 2.03.174 P
her love known, and she will die if he woo her, 2.03.175 P
that she will rather die than give any sign of 2.03.227 P
when i said i would die a bachelor, i did not 2.03.243 P
it were a better death than die with mocks, 3.01. 79
mocks, | which is as bad as die with tickling. 3.01. 80
for, did i think thou wouldst not quickly die, 4.01.124
hence from her, let her die. 4.01.154
come, lady, die to live; 4.01.253
therefore i will die a woman with grieving. 4.01.323 P
i will live in thy heart, die in thy lap, and be 5.02.102 P
to love, to wealth, to pomp, i pine and die, LLL 1.01. 31
are pick-purses in love, and we deserve to die. 4.03.205
let me not die your debtor, | my red dominical, 5.02. 43
then die a calf, before your horns do grow. 5.02.253
one word in private with you ere i die. 5.02.254
and consciences that will not die in debt | pay 5.02.333
that he would wed me, or else die my lover. 5.02.447
die when you will, a smock shall be your shroud. 5.02.479
thou shalt die. 5.02.679 P
either to die the death, or to abjure | for ever MND 1.01. 65
so will i grow, so live, so die, my lord, | ere 1.01. 79
upon that day either prepare to die | for 1.01. 86
but she, being mortal, of that boy did die, 2.01.135
of hell, | to die upon the hand i love so well. 2.01.244
thus die i, thus, thus, thus. 5.01.300
take thy flight, | now die, die, die, die, die. 5.01.306
take thy flight, | now die, die, die, die, die. 5.01.306
take thy flight, | now die, die, die, die, die. 5.01.306
take thy flight, | now die, die, die, die, die. 5.01.306
take thy flight, | now die, die, die, die, die. 5.01.306
no die, but an ace, for him; for he is but one. 5.01.307 P
old as sibylla, i will die as chaste as diana, MV 1.02.106 P
unworthier may attain, | and die with grieving. 2.01. 38
if you poison us, do we not die? 3.01. 66 P
i'll die for't but some woman had the ring! 5.01.208
and in the greatness of my word, you die. AYL 1.03. 89
cannot recompense me better | than to die well, 2.03. 76
o, i die for food! 2.06. 1 P
something to eat, i will give thee leave to die: 2.06. 12 P
and thou shalt not die for lack of a dinner if 2.06. 17 P
will not be answer'd with reason, i must die. 2.07.101 P
i almost die for food, and let me have it. 2.07.104
should have, | and i to live and die her slave." 3.02.154
then, in mine own person, i die. 4.01. 93 P
no, faith, die by attorney. 4.01. 94 P
yet he did what he could to die before, and he 4.01. 99 P
my love deny, | and then i'll study how to die." 4.03. 63
upon you, and here live and die a shepherd. 5.02. 12 P
that will i, should i die the hour after. 5.04. 12
and if i die to-morrow, this is hers, | if SHR 2.01.361
if you should die before him, where's her dower? 2.01.389
and may not young men die as well as old? 2.01.391
e la mi, show pity, or i die." 3.01. 78
they not quickly, i should die with laughing. 3.02.241
which now shall die in oblivion and thou return 4.01. 83 P
would be mated by the lion | must die for love. AWW 1.01. 92
for't a little, though therefore i die a virgin. 1.01.134 P
i | his servant live, and will his vassal die. 1.03.159
whether i live or die, be you the sons | of 2.01. 11
health shall live free, and sickness freely die. 2.01.168
try, | that ministers thine own death if i die. 2.01.186
property | of what i spoke, unpitied let me die, 2.01.188
braid, | marry that will, i live and die a maid. 4.02. 74
not that i am afraid to die, but that, my 4.03.242 P
there is no remedy, sir, but you must die. 4.03.303 P
therefore you must die. 4.03.307 P
me, that i hope i shall see him ere i die. 4.05. 85 P
the appetite may sicken, and so die. TN 1.01. 3
"but i will never die." 2.03.106
to die, even when they to perfection grow! 2.04. 41
to do you rest, a thousand deaths would die. 5.01.133
would they else be content to die? WT 1.01. 42 P
i have here alive, | that i should fear to die? 3.02.108
with die and drab i purchas'd this caparison, 4.03. 26 P
that die unmarried, ere they can behold | bright 4.04.123
yea, | to die upon the bed my father died, | to 4.04.455
if i might die within this hour, i have liv'd 4.04.461
this hour, i have liv'd | to die when i desire. 4.04.462
do not shun her | until you see her die again, 5.03.106
rescue those breathing lives to die in beds, JN 2.01.419
teach thou this sorrow how to make me die, | and 3.01. 30
men, | which in the very meeting fall, and die. 3.01. 33
but in despair die under their black weight. 3.01.297
o, this will make my mother die with grief! 3.03. 5
and meagre as an ague's fit, | and so he'll die; 3.04. 86
as good to die and go, as die and stay. 4.03. 8
as good to die and go, as die and stay. 4.03. 8
that i must die here and live hence by truth? 5.04. 29
in that i live, and for that will i die. R2 1.01.185
in that thou seest thy wretched brother die, 1.02. 27
desolate, desolate, will i hence and die: 1.02. 73
is now leas'd out — i die pronouncing it — 2.01. 59
no, no, men living flatter those that die. 2.01. 89
live in thy shame, but die not shame with thee! 2.01.135
and let them die that age and sullens have, 2.01.139
and fight and die is death destroying death, 3.02.184
and send | defiance to the traitor, and so die? 3.03.130
give richard leave to live till richard die? 3.03.174

and, for they cannot, die in their own pride. 5.05. 22
my gross flesh sinks downward, here to die. 5.05.112
as thou liv'st in peace, die free from strife, 5.06. 27
may reasonably die, and never rise | to do him 1H4 1.03. 74
i doubt not but to die a fair death for all this 2.02. 14 P
go thy ways, old jack, die when thou wilt; 2.04.127 P
and i will die a hundred thousand deaths | ere 3.02.158
a hundred thousand rebels die in this. 3.02.160
doomsday is near, die all, die merrily. 4.01.134
doomsday is near, die all, die merrily. 4.01.134
if die, brave death, when princes die with us! 5.02. 86
if die, brave death, when princes die with us! 5.02. 86
to die is to be a counterfeit, for he is but the 5.04.115 P
let order die! 2H4 1.01.154
would shut the book, and sit him down and die. 3.01. 56
saith, is certain to all, all shall die. 3.02. 38 P
a man can die but once, we owe god a death. 3.02.234 P
not, | and thou wilt have me die assur'd of it. 4.05.105
feign, | o, let me in my present wildness die, 4.05.152
many years, | i should not die but in jerusalem, 4.05.237
i'll lie, | in that jerusalem shall harry die. 4.05.240
i hope to see london once ere i die. 5.03. 60 P
under which king, besonian? speak, or die. 5.03.113
i would to god that i might die, that i might 5.04. 2 P
a color that i fear you will die in, sir john. 5.05. 87 P
any thing i know) falstaff shall die of a sweat, ep 30 P
wildness, mortified in him, | seem'd to die too; H5 1.01. 27
and by their hands this grace of kings must die, 2.pr. 28
god's vassals drop and die; 3.02. 8
die and be damn'd! and figo for thy friendship! 3.06. 57
methinks i could not die any where so contented 4.01.126 P
i am afeard there are few die well that die in a 4.01.141 P
there are few die well that die in a battle; 4.01.142 P
now, if these men do not die well, it will be a 4.01.144 P
assail'd by robbers and die in many irreconcil'd 4.01.152 P
then if they die unprovided, no more is the king 4.01.173 P
if we are mark'd to die, we are enow | to do our 4.03. 20
we would not die in that man's company | that 4.03. 38
that fears his fellowship to die with us. 4.03. 39
let us die! 4.05. 11
base troyan, thou shalt die. 5.01. 31
not, to say to thee that i shall die, is true; 5.02.151 P
this comfort, | thou shalt not die whiles — 1H6 1.04. 91
o, would i were to die with salisbury! 1.05. 38
condemn'd to die for treason, but no traitor; 2.04. 97
france, | either to get the town again, or die: 3.02. 79
so sure i swear to get the town, or die. 3.02. 84
but kings and mightiest potentates must die, 3.02.136
that thus we die, while remiss traitors sleep. 4.03. 29
york set him on to fight and die in shame, 4.04. 8
if we both stay, we both are sure to die. 4.05. 20
and leave my followers here to fight and die? 4.05. 45
for live i will not if my father die. 4.05. 51
come, side by side, together live and die, | and 4.05. 54
if i to-day die not with frenchmen's rage, 4.06. 34
rage, | to-morrow i shall die with mickle age. 4.06. 35
the coward horse that bears me fall and die! 4.06. 47
if son to talbot, die at talbot's foot. 4.06. 53
and, commendable prov'd, let's die in pride. 4.06. 57
joan, sweet daughter joan, i'll die with thee! 5.04. 6
and shall these labors and these honors die? 2H6 1.01. 95
your deeds of war, and all our counsel die? 1.01. 97
but him out-live, and die a violent death. 1.04. 31
by water shall he die, and take his end. 1.04. 33
but him out-live, and die a violent death." 1.04. 60
"by water shall he die, and take his end." 1.04. 65
here, robin, and if i die, i give thee my aporn; 2.03. 74 P
that he should die is worthy policy, | but yet 3.01.235
so that, by this, you would not have him die. 3.01.243
let him die, in that he is a fox, | by nature 3.01.257
die, /margaret! 3.02.120
loather a hundred times to part than die. 3.02.355
and in thy sight to die, what were it else | but 3.02.389
to die by thee were but to die in jest, | from 3.02.400
to die by thee were but to die in jest, | from 3.02.400
from thee to die were torture more than death. 3.02.401
where should he die? 3.03. 9
for die you shall. 4.01. 20
and therefore to revenge it shalt thou die, 4.01. 26
birth | and told me that by water i should die: 4.01. 35
it is impossible that i should die | by such a 4.01.110
great men oft die by vild besonians: 4.01.134
unless i find him guilty, he shall not die. 4.02. 96 P
therefore yield, or die. 4.02.127
my love, i should not mourn, but die for thee. 4.04. 25
he shall die, and it be but for pleading so well 4.07.106 P
die, damned wretch, the curse of her that bare 4.10. 77
i have | is his to use, so somerset may die. 5.01. 53
thy chair-days, thus | to die in ruffian battle? 5.02. 49
we'll all assist you; he that flies shall die. 3H6 1.01. 30
york, | and die in bands for this unmanly deed! 1.01.186
i will be king, or die. 1.02. 35
whose father slew my father, he shall die. 1.03. 5
sweet clifford, hear me speak before i die: 1.03. 18
then let me die, for now thou hast no cause. 1.03. 45
therefore die. 1.03. 47
thy death, | or die renowned by attempting it. 2.01. 88
fly, | if warwick take us we are sure to die. 4.04. 35
die thou, and die our fear, | for warwick was a 5.02. 1
die thou, and die our fear, | for warwick was a 5.02. 1
and, live we how we can, yet die we must. 5.02. 28
die, prophet, in thy speech: 5.06. 57
and must not die | till george be pack'd with R3 1.01.145
i would they were, that i might die at once; 1.02.151
though not by war, by surfeit die your king, 1.03.196
die in his youth by like untimely violence! 1.03.200
long die thy happy days before thy death, | and, 1.03.206
die neither mother, wife, nor england's queen! 1.03.208
never, my lord, therefore prepare to die. 1.04.180
make peace with god, for you must die, my lord. 1.04.249
if die, be brief, | that our swift-winged souls 2.02. 43
and make me die a good old man! 2.02.109
or let me die, to look on /death no more! 2.04. 65
again, | or die a soldier as i liv'd a king. 3.01. 93
the kindred of the queen, must die at pomfret. 3.02. 50
'tis a vile thing to die, my gracious lord, 3.02. 62
to-day shalt thou behold a subject die | for 3.03. 3
yet had we not determin'd he should die | until 3.05. 52

and make me die the thrall of margaret's curse, 4.01. 45
and die ere men can say, "god save the queen!" 4.01. 62
say, have i thy consent that they shall die? 4.02. 23
that anne, my queen, is sick and like to die. 4.02. 57
either thou wilt die by god's just ordinance 4.04.184
and must she die for this? 4.04.206
despair therefore and die! 5.03.120
despair and die! 5.03.126
harry the sixt bids thee despair and die. 5.03.127
despair and die! 5.03.135
despair and die! 5.03.140
despair and die! 5.03.143
thy nephews' souls bid thee despair and die! 5.03.149
despair and die! 5.03.156
despair and die! 5.03.163
and die in terror of thy guiltiness! 5.03.170
loves me, | and if i die no soul will pity me. 5.03.201
after the battle let george stanley die. 5.03.346
cast, | and i will stand the hazard of the die. 5.04. 10
that if the king | should without issue die, H8 1.02.134
traitor's judgment, | and by that name must die; 2.01. 59
grief of heart | fall asleep, or hearing, die. 3.01. 14
but she must die, | she must, the saints must 5.04. 59
i could live and die in the eyes of troilus. TRO 1.02.242 P
these lovers cry, o ho, they die! 3.01.121
down another, and together | die in the fall. 3.03. 87
but in mine emulous honor let him die, | with 4.01. 29
cries "/come" to him that instantly must die. 4.04. 51
die i a villain then! 4.04. 83
and there they fly or die, like scaling sculls 5.05. 22
eye, | it is decreed hector the great must die. 5.07. 8
are all resolv'd rather to die than to famish? COR 1.01. 4 P
i had rather had eleven die nobly for their 1.03. 24 P
let the first budger die the other's slave, 1.08. 5
being advanc'd, declines, and then men die. 2.01.161
better it is to die, better to starve, | than 2.03.113
no, i'll die here. 3.01.222
he that hath a will to die by himself fears it 5.02.104 P
home to rome, | and die among our neighbors. 5.03.173
therefore shall he die, | and i'll renew me in 5.06. 47
let him die for't. 5.06.119
to this your son is mark'd, and die he must, TIT 1.01.125
thee, | but honor thee, and will do till i die. 1.01.213
this day all quarrels die, andronicus. 1.01.465
should straight fall mad, or else die suddenly. 2.03.104
for fear they die before their pardon come. 3.01.175
die, andronicus. 3.01.253
and see their blood or die with this reproach. 4.01. 94
it shall not die. 4.02. 81
"let not your sorrow die, though i am dead." 5.01.140
devil, for he must not die | so sweet a death as 5.01.145
die, die, lavinia, and thy shame with thee, 5.03. 46
die, die, lavinia, and thy shame with thee, 5.03. 46
and with thy shame thy father's sorrow die! 5.03. 47
die, frantic wretch, for this accursed deed! 5.03. 64
i'll pay that doctrine, or else die in debt. ROM 1.01.238
eye, | and the rank poison of the old will die. 1.02. 50
and these, who, often drown'd, could never die, 1.02. 90
fair for which love groan'd for and would die, 2.pr. 3
and in their triumph die, like fire and powder, 2.06. 10
this is the truth, or let benvolio die. 3.01.175
give me my romeo, and, when i shall die, | take 3.02. 21
to my bed, | but i, a maid, die maiden-widowed. 3.02.135
take heed, take heed, for such die miserable. 3.03.145
well, we were born to die. 3.04. 4
i must be gone and live, or stay and die. 3.05. 11
be not, hang, beg, starve, die in the streets, 3.05.192
if all else fail, myself have power to die. 3.05.242
be not so long to speak, i long to die, | if 4.01. 66
and there die strangled ere my romeo comes? 4.03. 35
revive, look up, or i will die with thee! 4.05. 20
i will die, | and leave him all; 4.05. 39
and full of wretchedness, | and fearest to die? 5.01. 69
obey and go with me, for thou must die. 5.03. 57
thus with a kiss i die. 5.03.120
on them, | to make me die with a restorative. 5.03.166
there rust, and let me die. 5.03.170
and therewithal | came to this vault to die, and 5.03.290
that's a deed thou't die for. TIM 1.01.193 P
will little learning die then that day thou art 2.02. 82 P
thou wast born a bastard, and thou't die a bawd. 2.02. 85 P
'tis necessary he should die. 3.05. 2
thou shouldst desire to die, being miserable. 4.03.248
long live so, and so die. i am quit. 4.03.396
and by the hazard of the spotted die | let die 5.04. 34
hazard of the spotted die | let die the spotted. 5.04. 35
to himself — take thought and die for caesar; JC 2.01.187
let him not die, | for he will live, and laugh 2.01.190
when beggars die there are no comets seen; 2.02. 30
cowards die many times before their deaths, 2.02. 32
that we shall die we know, 'tis but the time, 3.01. 99
years, | i shall not find myself so apt to die; 3.01.160
rather caesar were living, and die all slaves, 3.02. 23 P
hear him, we'll follow him, we'll die with him. 3.02.208 P
these many then shall die, their names are 4.01. 1
your brother too must die; consent you, lepidus? 4.01. 2
and took his voice who should be prick'd to die 4.01. 16
we must die, messala. 4.03.190
with meditating that she must die once, | i have 4.03.191
caesar, thou canst not die by traitors' hands, 5.01. 56
i was not born to die on brutus' sword. 5.01. 58
young man, thou couldst not die more honorable. 5.01. 60
only i yield to die: 5.04. 12
but i have spoke | with one that saw him die; MAC 1.04. 4
contend about them, | whether they live or die. 2.02. 8
when the brains were out, the man would die, 3.04. 78
at least we'll die with harness on our back. 5.05. 51
the roman fool, and die | on mine own sword? 5.08. 1
know'st 'tis common, all that lives must die, HAM 1.02. 72
to die, to sleep, | no more, and by a sleep to 3.01. 59
to die, to sleep, | to sleep, perchance to dream 3.01. 63
o heavens, die two months ago, and not forgotten 3.02.130 P
but die thy thoughts when thy first lord is dead 3.02.215
if 'a be not rotten before 'a die — as we have 5.01.165 P
o, i die, horatio, | the potent poison quite 5.02.352
if i die for/'t (as no less is threat'ned me), LR 3.03. 17 P
away, and let me die. 4.06. 48
do cry out itself | "enough, enough," and die. 4.06. 77

thou shalt not die. 4.06.111
die for adultery? 4.06.111
i will die bravely, like a smug bridegroom. 4.06.198
tempt me again | to die before you please! 4.06.219
you are a spirit, i know; /when did you die? 4.07. 48
i should ev'n die with pity | to see another 4.07. 52
that we the pain of death would hourly die 5.03.186
would hourly die | rather than die at once!), 5.03.187
and then have we a prescription to die, when OTH 1.03.309 P
if it were now to die, | 'twere now to be most 2.01.189
for thy solicitor shall rather die | than give 3.03. 27
if i do die before /thee, prithee shroud me | in 4.03. 24
no, he must die. 5.01. 22
yet she must die, else she'll betray more men. 5.02. 6
ay, but not yet to die. 5.02. 52
thou art to die. 5.02. 56
a guiltless death i die. 5.02.122
i will play the swan, | and die in music. 5.02.248
so speaking as i think, alas, i die. 5.02.251
for, in my sense, 'tis happiness to die. 5.02.290
but this, | killing myself, to die upon a kiss. 5.02.359
and let her die too, and give him a worse! ANT 1.02. 65 P
under a compelling occasion, let women die. 1.02.137 P
i have seen her die twenty times upon far poorer 1.02.141 P
can fulvia die? 1.03. 58
strange flesh, | which some did die to look on; 1.04. 68
his aspect, and die | with looking on his life. 1.05. 33
forget to send to antony, | shall die a beggar. 1.05. 65
think, and die. 3.13. 1
ruffian know | i have many other ways to die; 4.01. 5
no, i will go seek | some ditch wherein to die; 4.06. 37
the witch shall die. 4.12. 47
she hath betray'd me, and shall die the death. 4.14. 26
die when thou hast liv'd, | quicken with kissing 4.15. 38
and do now not basely die, | not cowardly put 4.15. 55
noblest of men, woo't die? 4.15. 59
say, i would die. 5.02. 70
those that do die of it do seldom or never 5.02.247 P
conclusions infinite | of easy ways to die. 5.02.356
a day, and, being aged, | die of this folly! CYM 1.01.158
came in too suddenly, let it die as it was born, 1.04.121 P
they failing, | i must die much your debtor. 2.04. 8
why, i must die; 3.04. 74
the sweat of industry would dry and die, | but 3.06. 31
citizen a wanton as | to seem to die ere sick. 4.02. 9
i'll rob none but myself, and let me die, 4.02. 15
and a demand who is't shall die, i'ld say | "my 4.02. 23
die the death! 4.02. 96
what thing is't that i never | did see man die, 4.04. 36
if in your country wars you chance to die, 4.04. 51
so i'll die | for thee, o imogen, even for whom 5.01. 25
cowards living | to die with length'ned shame. 5.03. 13
"our britain's harts die flying, not our men. 5.03. 24
those that would die or e'er resist are grown 5.03. 50
i am merrier to die than thou art to live. 5.04.171 P
some of them too that die against their wills. 5.04.202 P
briefly die their joys | that place them on the 5.05.106
while nature will | than die ere i hear more. 5.05.152
there like fruit, my soul, | till the tree die! 5.05.264
and thou shalt die for't. 5.05.310
we will die all three, | but i will prove that 5.05.310
so for her many /a wight did die, | as yon grim PER 1.ch. 39
yon celestial tree | (or die in th' adventure), 1.01. 22
presumes to reach, all the whole heap must die. 1.01. 33
oppression, and the poor worm doth die for't. 1.01.102
and therefore instantly this prince must die, 1.01.148
draw lots who first shall die to lengthen life. 1.04. 46
die, keth 'a? 2.01. 78 P
if it had conceit, would die, as i | am like to 3.01. 16
fault | to scape his hands where i was to die. 4.02. 75
a curse upon him, die he like a thief, | that 4.06.114
outlive the age i am, | and die as i would do. 5.01. 16
we shall die | (which is the curse of honor) TNK 2.02. 53
the free enjoying of that face i die for — | o, 2.03. 3
but offends you, | command him die, he shall. 2.05. 41
take courage, | you shall not die thus beastly. 3.03. 6
for none but such dare die in these just trials. 3.06.105
we shall find | too many hours to die in, gentle 3.06.112
i dare as well | die as discourse or sleep. 3.06.129
by castor, both shall die. 3.06.136
me | a thing as soon to die as thee to say it, 3.06.159
let 's die together, at one instant, duke. 3.06.177
i have said they die; 3.06.224
the honor of affection, and die for her, | make 3.06.269
he that she refuses | must die then. 3.06.281
once again it stands, | or both shall die: 3.06.290
must these men die too? 4.02.112
surely the gods | would have him die a bachelor, 5.03.117
than all women, | i should and would die too. 5.03.144
i die. 5.04. 95
there love liv'd, and there he could not die. VEN 246
do i delight to die, or life desire? 496
lest she should steal a kiss and die forsworn. 726
to wail his death who lives and must not die 1017
she thinks he could not die, he is not dead; 1060
so shall i die by drops of hot desire. 1074
and die, unhallowed thoughts, before you blot LUC 192
"yea, though i die, the scandal will survive, 204
but coward-like with trembling terror die. 231
"then childish fear, avaunt, debating, die! 274
for if i die, my honor lives in thee, | but if i 1032
and therefore now i need not fear to die. 1052
who, if it wink, shall thereon fall and die. 1139
to live or die which of the twain were better, 1154
"yet die i will not till my collatine | have 1177
thou dead, both die, and both shall victors be." 1211
the sire, the son, the dame, and daughter die. 1477
comes all too late, yet let the traitor die, 1686
the old bees die, the young possess their hive: 1769
live again and see | thy father die, and not thy 1771
and counterfeits to die with her a space, | till 1776
that thereby beauty's rose might never die, SON 1. 2
die single, and thine image dies with thee. 3.14
if thou issueless shalt hap to die, | the world 9. 3
thou shouldst print more, not let that copy die. 11.14
and die as fast as they see others grow, | and 12.12
for at a frown they in their glory die. 25. 8
and unrespected fade, | die to themselves. 54.11
gone, | save that to die, i leave my love alone. 66.14
though i (once gone) to all the world must die; 81. 6
i find, | happy to have thy love, happy to die! 92.12
sweet, | though to itself it only live and die, 94.10
which die for goodness, who have liv'd for crime 124.14

/DIED 1 FR 0.0001 REL FR 1 V 0 P
/late /king /richard (/being /infected) /died. 2H4 4.01. 58

DIED 117 FR 0.0132 REL FR 102 V 15 P
within which space she died, | and left thee TMP 1.02.279
heart | as when thy lady and thy true-love died, TGV 4.03. 20
whose father died at hallowmas. MM 2.01.124 P
who is it that hath died for this offense? 2.02. 88
better it were a brother died at once, | than 2.04.106
there died this morning of a cruel fever | one 4.03. 70
in that he did the thing for which he died; 5.01.449
that should by private order else have died, | i 5.01.466
who should have died when claudio lost his head 5.01.488
when he shall hear she died upon his words, ADO 4.01.223
and upon the grief of this suddenly died. 4.02. 63 P
people in messina here | how innocent she died, 5.01.282
so the life that died with shame | lives in 5.03. 7
one hero died defil'd, but i do live, | and 5.04. 63
she died, my lord, but whiles her slander liv'd. 5.04. 66
melancholy, sad, and heavy, | and so she died. LLL 5.02. 15
she might 'a' been /a grandam ere she died. 5.02. 17
in mulberry shade, | his dagger drew, and died. MND 5.01.149
which i denying, they fell sick and died. MV 3.04. 71
her exile, or have died to stay behind her. AYL 1.01.110 P
there was not any man died in his own person, 4.01. 96 P
men have died from time to time and worms have 4.01.106 P
since the physician at your father's died? AWW 1.02. 70
of a count | that died some twelvemonth since, TN 1.02. 37
his son, her brother, | who shortly also died; 1.02. 39
but died thy sister of her love, my boy? 2.04.119
and died that day when viola from her birth 5.01.244
yea, | to die upon the bed my father died, | to WT 4.04.455
not a month | 'fore your queen died, she was 5.01.226
doth contain that large | which died in geffrey; JN 2.01.102
the first of april died | your noble mother; 4.02.120
the lady constance in a frenzy died | three days 4.02.122
an hour before i came, the duchess died. R2 2.02. 97
had you first died, and he been thus trod down, 2.03.126
is turn'd upside down since robin ostler died. 1H4 2.01. 11 P
he that died a' wednesday. 5.01.136 P
our great-grandsire, edward, sick'd and died. 2H4 4.04.128
for oldcastle died /a martyr, and this is not ep 32 P
who died within the year of our redemption H5 1.02. 60
day and cry all, "we died at such a place" — 4.01.138 P
suffolk first died, and york, all haggled over, 4.06. 11
hath at least five frenchmen died to-night. 1H6 2.02. 9
and there died | my icarus, my blossom, in his 4.07. 15
death been french, then death had died to-day. 4.07. 28
now, by the death of him that died for all, 2H6 1.01.113
edward the black prince died before his father, 2.02. 18
but william of hatfield died without an heir. 2.02. 33
king, | who kept him in captivity till he died. 2.02. 42
true, | but how he died god knows, not henry. 3.02.131
they say, by him the good duke humphrey died; 3.02.248
died he not in his bed? 3.03. 9
would i had died a maid | and never seen thee, 3H6 1.01.216
say how he died, for i will hear it all. 2.01. 49
but he, poor man, by your first order died, R3 2.01. 88
too late he died that might have kept that title 3.01. 99
when holy harry died, and my sweet son. 4.04. 25
and only in that safety died her brothers. 4.04.215
thou hadst not broken, nor my brothers died. 4.04.380
soul to-morrow, | rivers, that died at pomfret! 5.03.140
i died for hope ere i could lend thee aid, | but 5.03.173
so griev'd him, | that he ran mad, and died. H8 2.02.129
her male issue | or died where they were made, 2.04.193
prithee, good griffith, tell me how he died. 4.02. 9
than man could give him, he died fearing god. 4.02. 68
but had he died in the business, madam, how then COR 1.03. 18 P
nest, | that died in honor and lavinia's cause. TIT 1.01.377
he lives in fame, that died in virtue's cause. 1.01.390
so long, | poor i was slain when bassianus died. 2.03.171
wept, | because they died in honor's lofty bed. 3.01. 11
that died by law for murther of our brother, 4.04. 54
grief | it is supposed the fair creature died, ROM 5.03. 51
he might have died in war. TIM 3.05. 74
and died so? JC 4.03.157
mine speak of seventy senators that died | by 4.03.177
how died my master, strato? 5.05. 64
he died | as one that had been studied in his MAC 1.04. 8
had i but died an hour before this chance, | i 2.03. 91
those thoughts which should indeed have died 3.02. 10
than on her feet, | died every day she liv'd. 4.03.111
their sleep who have died holily in their beds. 5.01. 61 P
she should have died hereafter; 5.05. 17
where he fought, | but like a man he died. 5.09. 9
from the first corse till he that died to-day, HAM 1.02.105
looks, and my father died within 's two hours. 3.02.127 P
but they wither'd all when my father died. 4.05.185 P
alexander died, alexander was buried, alexander 5.01.209 P
her fortune, | and she died singing it. OTH 4.03. 30
where died she? ANT 1.02.118
the last, best, | see when and where she died. 1.03. 62
since cleopatra died | i have liv'd in such 4.14. 55
remember'st thou any that have died on't? 5.02.249
of honesty — how she died of the biting of it, 5.02.254 P
most probable | that so she died; 5.02.354
o' th' time | died with their swords in hand; CYM 1.01. 36
fault, i should | have died had i not made it. 3.06. 57
took heel to do't, | and yet died too! 5.03. 68
i died whilst in the womb he stay'd | attending 5.04. 37
so | despairing died. 5.05. 61
more resembles that sweet rosy lad | who died, 5.05.122
lov'd, | continu'd so, until we thought he died. 5.05.380
took a peer, | who died and left a female heir, PER 1.ch. 22
maid, | born in a tempest when my mother died, 4.01. 18
she died at night; 4.03. 16
attribute cry out, | "she died by foul play." 4.03. 19
of a king, | who died the minute i was born, 5.01.158
at sea in child-bed died she, but brought forth 5.03. 5
where, phoenix-like, | they died in perfume. TNK 1.03. 71
we had died as they do, ill old men, unwept, 2.02.109
that have died manly, which will seek of me 3.01. 79
i had not said i lov'd her, | though i had died; 3.06. 41
and died to kiss his shadow in the brook. VEN 162
she had not brought forth thee, but died unkind. 204
but now i died, and death was lively joy. 498
but true sweet beauty liv'd and died with him. 1080
o, had they in that darksome prison died, | then LUC 379
but since he died and poets better prove, SON 32.13
when beauty liv'd and died as flowers do now, 68. 2

DIEDST 1 FR 0.0001 REL FR 1 V 0 P
thou diedst, a most rare boy, of melancholy. CYM 4.02.208

DIES* 76 FR 0.0086 REL FR 65 V 11 P
and sends me forth | (for else his project dies) TMP 2.01.299
he that dies pays all debts. 3.02.131 P
your brother dies to-morrow; MM 2.02.105
finds a pang as great | as when a giant dies. 3.01. 80
he dies for claudio's death. 5.01.443
born | come to the bay of ephesus, he dies, ERR 1.01. 19
town, | dies ere the weary sun set in the west. 1.02. 7
and, in despite of all, dies for him. ADO 3.02. 67 P
have giv'n her cousin, | and so dies my revenge. 5.01.292
not erect in this age his own tomb ere he dies, 5.02. 78 P
her wrongs, | gives her fame which never dies. 5.03. 6
dies in the zeal of that which it presents. LLL 5.02.518
grows, lives, and dies in single blessedness. MND 1.01. 78
and fancy dies | in the cradle where it lies. MV 3.02. 68
of all he dies possess'd | unto his son lorenzo 4.01.389
after his death, of all he dies possess'd of. 5.01.293
and truly, when he dies, thou shalt be his heir; AYL 1.02. 18 P
he dies that touches any of this fruit | till i 2.07. 98
than he that dies and lives by bloody drops? 3.05. 7
and so dies with feeding his own stomach. AWW 1.01.143 P
but riddle-like lives sweetly where she dies! 1.03.217
bonos dies, sir toby: TN 4.02. 12 P
know'st | he dies to me again when talk'd of. WT 5.01.120
where my fortune lives, there my life dies. JN 3.01.338
not gone already, | even at that news he dies; 3.04.164
there lives or dies, true to king richard's R2 1.03. 86
mine honor lives when his dishonor dies, | or my 5.03. 70
though that be sick, it dies not. 2H4 2.02.105 P
he that dies this year is quit for the next. 3.02.238 P
when the man dies, let the inheritance | descend H5 1.02. 99
'tis certain, every man that dies ill, the ill 4.01.186 P
the merry cheerer of the heart, | unpruned dies; 5.02. 42
here dies the dusky torch of mortimer, | chok'd 1H6 2.05.122
he dies, we lose; 4.03. 31
but dies, betray'd to fortune by your strife. 4.04. 39
in thee thy mother dies, our household's name, 4.06. 38
it dies, and if it had a thousand lives. 5.04. 75
thus eleanor's pride dies in her youngest days. 2H6 2.03. 46
he dies, and makes no sign. 3.03. 29
and suffolk dies by pirates. 4.01.138
ay, here it dies, | which, whiles it lasted, 3H6 2.06. 1
/'zounds, he dies! i had forgot the reward. R3 1.04.125 P
but as when | the bird of wonder dies, the H8 5.04. 40
and at this sport | sir valor dies; TRO 1.03.176
therefore it is decreed | he dies to-night. COR 3.01.288
heart | that dies in tempest of thy angry frown. TIT 1.01.458
got, | he dies upon my scimitar's sharp point, 4.02. 91
or pities him, | for the offense he dies. 5.03.182
only poor | that, when she dies, with beauty ROM 1.01.216
that, when she dies, with beauty dies her store. 1.01.216
but she's best married that dies married young. 4.05. 78
who dies that bears not one spurn to their TIM 1.02.141
he dies. 3.05. 74
we are for law, he dies, urge it no more | on 3.05. 85
the cess of majesty | dies not alone, but, like HAM 3.03. 16
and shows no cause without | why the man dies. 4.04. 29
to a plurisy, | dies in his own too much. 4.07.118
he dies that strikes again. LR 2.02. 49
he dies. OTH 2.03.165
he dies upon his motion. 2.03.174
he dies. 5.01. 10
but the least noise of this, dies instantly; ANT 1.02.141 P
she dies for't. 4.12. 49
and, eros, | thy master dies thy scholar: 4.14.102
name of fame and honor which dies i' th' search, CYM 3.03. 51
what means the /nun? she dies, help, gentlemen! PER 5.03. 15
a willing man dies sleeping, and all's done. TNK 2.02. 68
if he keep touch, he dies for't. 3.03. 53
nor think he dies with interest in this lady. 3.06.298
love surfeits not, lust like a glutton dies; VEN 803
crooked beak threats, if he mount, he dies: LUC 508
"the patient dies while the physician sleeps, 904
"lo here weeps hecuba, here priam dies, | here 1485
and when the judge is robb'd, the prisoner dies. 1652
a flower that dies when first it gins to bud, PP 13. 3
die single, and thine image dies with thee. SON 3.14

DIEST 21 FR 0.0023 REL FR 17 V 4 P
but if thou scorn our courtesy, thou diest. TGV 4.01. 66
conceal them, or thou diest. WIV 4.05. 45 P
i abhor to name, | or else thou diest to-morrow. MM 3.01.102
a bawd, | 'tis best that thou diest quickly. 3.01.150
thou diest, and all thy goods are confiscate. MV 4.01.332
court as twenty miles, | thou diest for it. AYL 1.03. 45
but if thou diest before i come, thou art a 2.06. 12 P
or, to thy better understanding, diest; 5.01. 52 P
thee, else thou diest in thine unthankfulness, AWW 1.01.210 P
hadst this ring, | thou diest within this hour. 5.03.284
why, how now, father? | speak ere thou diest. WT 4.04.451
o no, thou diest, though i the sicker be. R2 2.01. 91
o signieur dew, thou diest on point of fox, H5 4.04. 9
stay, or thou diest! 3H6 4.03. 27
look how thou diest! TRO 5.03. 81
why, now thou diest as bravely as titinius, JC 5.04. 10
yield, or thou diest. 5.04. 12
villain, thou diest! OTH 5.01. 23
ay, and for that thou diest. 5.02. 41
the court | with thy unworthiness, thou diest. CYM 1.01.127
noon, | unlook'd on diest unless thou get a son. SON 7.14

/DIET 2 FR 0.0002 REL FR 2 V 0 P
/in /diet, /in /affections /of /delight, | /in 2H4 2.03. 29
/to /diet /rank /minds /sick /of /happiness, 4.01. 64

DIET 16 FR 0.0018 REL FR 11 V 5 P
to fast, like one that takes diet; TGV 2.01. 24 P
unless they kept very good diet, as i told you MM 2.01.112 P
diet his sickness, for it is my office, | and ERR 5.01. 99
off a first so noble wife, | may justly diet me. AWW 5.03.221
i will bespeak our diet, | whiles you beguile TN 3.03. 40

sir john, for your diet and by–drinkings, and 1H4 3.03. 73 P
or are they spare in diet, | free from gross H5 2.02.131
o, he hath kept an evil diet long, | and R3 1.01.139
your diet shall be in all places alike. TIM 3.06. 66 P
youth | to the /tub–fast and the diet. 4.03. 88
for food and diet, to some enterprise | that HAM 1.01. 99
your worm is your only emperor for diet: 4.03. 21 P
a sin), | but partly led to diet my revenge, OTH 2.01.294
or feed upon such nice and waterish diet, | or 3.03. 15
rank of gross diet, shall we be enclouded, | and ANT 5.02.212
all the comfort | the gods will diet me with. CYM 3.04.180
DIETED 5 FR 0.0005 REL FR 4 V 1 P
for he is dieted to his hour. AWW 4.03. 29 P
either they must be dieted like mules | and have 1H6 1.02. 10
as if i lov'd my little should be dieted | in COR 1.09. 52
watch him | till he be dieted to my request, 5.01. 57
/nun, | who, disciplin'd, ay, dieted in grace, LC 261
DIETER 1 FR 0.0001 REL FR 1 V 0 P
as juno had been sick | and he her dieter. CYM 4.02. 51
/DIEU 1 FR 0.0001 REL FR 1 V 0 P
mort /dieu, ma vie! H5 3.05. 11
DIEU 11 FR 0.0012 REL FR 4 V 7 P
dieu vous garde, monsieur. TN 3.01. 71 P
o seigneur dieu, je m'en oublie d' elbow. H5 3.04. 31 P
doute point d'apprendre, par la grace de dieu, 3.04. 41 P
o seigneur dieu! 3.04. 52 P
o dieu vivant! 3.05. 5
dieu de batailles! 3.05. 15
o seigneur dieu! 4.04. 6 P
o, je vous supplie, pour l'amour de dieu, me 4.04. 40 P
mort dieu, ma vie! 4.05. 3
o bon dieu! 5.02.115 P
mort dieu! 2H6 1.01.123
DIFFER 2 FR 0.0002 REL FR 2 V 0 P
therein do men from children nothing differ. ADO 5.01. 33
is't possible the world should so much differ, TIM 3.01. 46
DIFFERENCE 40 FR 0.0045 REL FR 30 V 10 P
if that be all the difference in his love, TGV 4.04.190
have an eye to make difference of men's liking: WIV 2.01. 57 P
him bear it for a difference between himself and ADO 1.01. 69 P
the difference of old shylock and bassanio. MV 2.05. 2
there is more difference between thy flesh and 3.01. 39 P
are you acquainted with the difference | that 4.01.171
thou shalt see the difference of our spirit, | i 4.01.368
the seasons' difference, as the icy fang | and AYL 2.01. 6
'twas just the difference | betwixt the constant 3.05.122
that had put such difference betwixt their two AWW 1.03.112 P
great difference betwixt our bohemia and your WT 1.01. 3 P
to me the difference forges dread; 4.04. 17
for the difference | is purchase of a heavy JN 3.01.204
the fearful difference of incensed kings — 3.01.238
the swelling difference of your settled hate. R2 1.01.201
making such difference 'twixt wake and sleep 1H4 3.01.216
as is the difference betwixt day and night | the 3.01.217
and, be assur'd, you'll find a difference, | as H5 2.04.134
the state takes notice of the private difference H8 1.01.101
or proclaim | there's difference in no persons. 1.01.139
how you stand minded in the weighty difference 3.01. 58
thy mercy and thy honor | at difference in thee. COR 5.03.201
whilst | 'twixt you there's difference; 5.06. 17
'tis not the difference of a year or two | makes TIT 2.01. 31
i am | of late with passions of some difference, JC 1.02. 40
of choice, | to serve in such a difference. HAM 3.04. 76
you may wear your rue with a difference. 4.05.183 P
dost thou know the difference, my boy, between a LR 1.04.137 P
what is your difference? speak. 2.02. 51 P
o, the difference of man and man! 4.02. 26
that, from your first of difference and decay, 5.03.289
'tis oft with difference), yet do they all OTH 1.03. 7
and bind up | the petty difference, we yet not ANT 2.01. 49
when we debate | our trivial difference loud, we 2.02. 21
we, with manners, ask what was the difference? CYM 1.04. 53 P
of your chaste daughter the wide difference 5.05.194
you shall have the difference of all complexions PER 4.02. 80 P
scorn us, | and say we had a noble difference, TNK 3.06.116
and, if you can love, end this difference. 3.06.278
one thing expressing, leaves out difference. SON 105. 8
DIFFERENCES 7 FR 0.0008 REL FR 5 V 2 P
yet stands off | in differences so mighty. AWW 2.03.121
of men, | in undetermin'd differences of kings. JN 2.01.355
these differences shall all rest under gage R2 4.01. 86
your differences shall all rest under gage 4.01.105
full of most excellent differences, of very soft HAM 5.02.107 P
i'll teach you differences. LR 1.04. 90 P
of differences, which i best /thought it fit 2.01.123
DIFFERENCY 1 FR 0.0001 REL FR 0 V 1 P
there is differency between a grub and a COR 5.04. 11 P
/DIFFERENT 1 FR 0.0001 REL FR 1 V 0 P
/could /not /beget | /such /different /issues. LR 4.03. 35
DIFFERENT 11 FR 0.0012 REL FR 10 V 1 P
writ with blank space for different names (sure, WIV 2.01. 75 P
sad, | and much different from the man he was; ERR 5.01. 46
but either it was different in blood — MND 1.01.135
i feel | the different plague of each calamity. JN 3.04. 60
my flesh tremble in their different greeting. ROM 1.05. 90
none but for some, and yet all different. 2.03. 14
share a bounteous time | in different pleasures. TIM 1.01.255
down thy youth | in different beds of lust, and 4.03.257
haply the seas and countries different | with HAM 3.01.171
smell | of different flowers in odor and in hue, SON 98. 6
weep, | he had the dialect and different skill, LC 125
DIFFERING 3 FR 0.0003 REL FR 3 V 0 P
things of like value differing in the owners TIM 1.01.170
by | that nothing–gift of differing multitudes, CYM 3.06. 85
a thousand differing ways to one sure end. TNK 1.05. 14
DIFFERS 4 FR 0.0004 REL FR 2 V 2 P
but that the name of page and ford differs! WIV 2.01. 71 P
that differs not from the stalling of an ox? AYL 1.01. 10 P
there's nothing differs but the outward fame. R3 1.04. 83
be, | but clay and clay differs in dignity, CYM 4.02. 4
DIFFICILE 1 FR 0.0001 REL FR 0 V 1 P
il est trop difficile, madame, comme je pense. H5 3.04. 27 P
DIFFICULT 1 FR 0.0001 REL FR 1 V 0 P
it shall be full of poise and difficult weight, OTH 3.03. 82
DIFFICULTIES 2 FR 0.0002 REL FR 1 V 1 P
all difficulties are but easy when they are MM 4.02.205 P
were i alone to pass the difficulties, | and had TRO 2.02.139
DIFFICULTY 3 FR 0.0003 REL FR 1 V 2 P
if the business be of any difficulty, and this AWW 4.03. 93 P
than for us to undergo any difficulty impos'd. TRO 3.02. 80 P
it were a tedious difficulty, i think, | to OTH 3.03.397
DIFFIDENCE 2 FR 0.0002 REL FR 2 V 0 P
and wound her honor with this diffidence. JN 1.01. 65
and of thy cunning had no diffidence; 1H6 3.03. 10
/DIFFIDENCES 1 FR 0.0001 REL FR 0 V 1 P
/king /and /nobles, /needless /diffidences, LR 1.02.147 P
DIFF'RENCE 3 FR 0.0003 REL FR 2 V 1 P
or to the place of diff'rence call the swords 2H4 4.01.179
lord, the diff'rence of men! TNK 2.01. 54 P
melting, though our drops this diff'rence bore: LC 300
DIFF'RING 3 FR 0.0003 REL FR 3 V 0 P
our conditions | so diff'ring in their acts. ANT 2.02.114
mind nurse equal | to these so diff'ring twins. TNK 1.03. 33
nor diff'ring plunges | disroot his rider whence 5.04. 74
DIFFUSED *(also defuse, etc.)*
DIFFUSED 1 FR 0.0001 REL FR 1 V 0 P
a sawpit rush at once | with some diffused song. WIV 4.04. 55
DIFFUSEST 1 FR 0.0001 REL FR 1 V 0 P
wings upon my flow'rs | diffusest honey–drops, TMP 4.01. 79
/DIG 1 FR 0.0001 REL FR 0 V 1 P
/could /he /dig /without /arms? HAM 5.01. 37 P
DIG 9 FR 0.0010 REL FR 8 V 1 P
and i with my long nails will dig thee pig–nuts, TMP 2.02.168
then get thee gone, and dig my grave thyself, 2H4 4.05.110
wilt thou go dig a grave to find out war, | and 2H6 5.01.169
for who liv'd king, but i could dig his grave? 3H6 5.02. 21
do thou so much as dig the grave for him: TIT 2.03.270
'tis you must dig with mattock and with spade, 4.03. 11
what man dost thou dig it for? HAM 5.01.130 P
flies, as deep | as these poor pickaxes can dig; CYM 4.02.389
and dig deep trenches in thy beauty's field, SON 2. 2
DIGEST *(also disgest, etc.)*
DIGEST 10 FR 0.0011 REL FR 10 V 0 P
false, | i do digest the poison of thy flesh, ERR 2.02.143
be | they will digest this harsh indignity. LLL 5.02.289
as hungry as the sea, | and can digest as much. TN 2.04.101
on, and we'll digest | th' abuse of distance; H5 2.pr. 31
go cheerfully together and digest | your angry 1H6 4.01.167
we may digest our complots in some form. R3 3.01.200
the king | digest this letter of the cardinal's? H8 3.02. 53
how shall this bosom multiplied digest | the COR 3.01.131
you shall digest the venom of your spleen JC 4.03. 47
with my two daughters' dow'rs digest the third; LR 1.01.128
/DIGESTED 1 FR 0.0001 REL FR 1 V 0 P
/to /what /may /be /digested /in /a /play. TRO pr 29
DIGESTED 4 FR 0.0004 REL FR 2 V 2 P
son, in whom my house's name | must be digested; AWW 5.03. 74
capital crimes, chew'd, swallow'd, and digested, H5 2.02. 56
we have lost, the disgrace we have digested; 3.06.128 P
an excellent play, well digested in the scenes, HAM 2.02.439 P
DIGESTION 6 FR 0.0006 REL FR 5 V 1 P
things sweet to taste prove in digestion sour. R2 1.03.236
a good digestion to you all; H8 1.04. 62
in hot digestion of this cormorant war — TRO 2.02. 6
why, my cheese, my digestion, why hast thou not 2.03. 41 P
now good digestion wait on appetite, | and MAC 3.04. 37
his taste delicious, in digestion souring, LUC 699
DIGESTIONS 1 FR 0.0001 REL FR 1 V 0 P
unquiet meals make ill digestions, | thereof the ERR 5.01. 74
DIGEST/'T 1 FR 0.0001 REL FR 1 V 0 P
and the feeders | digest/'t with a custom, i WT 4.04. 12
DIGG'D *(also digt)*
/DIGG'D 1 FR 0.0001 REL FR 0 V 1 P
/the /scripture /says /adam /digg'd; HAM 5.01. 37 P
DIGG'D 7 FR 0.0008 REL FR 7 V 0 P
two kinsmen digg'd their graves with weeping R2 3.03.169
this villainous saltpetre should be digg'd | out 1H4 1.03. 60
me, | and with my nails digg'd stones out of the 1H6 1.04. 45
air, | thy grave is digg'd already in the earth. 2H6 4.10. 52
no, if i digg'd up thy forefathers' graves | and 3H6 1.03. 27
oft have i digg'd up dead men from their graves, TIT 5.01.135
shark, | root of hemlock digg'd i' th' dark, MAC 4.01. 25
DIGGING 1 FR 0.0001 REL FR 1 V 0 P
being loose, unfirm, with digging up of graves, ROM 5.03. 6
DIGHTON 3 FR 0.0003 REL FR 3 V 0 P
dighton and forrest, who i did suborn | to do R3 4.03. 4
thus," quoth dighton, "lay the gentle babes." 4.03. 9
when dighton thus told on, "we smothered | the 4.03. 17
DIGNIFIED 6 FR 0.0006 REL FR 6 V 0 P
she shall be dignified with this high honor — TGV 2.04.158
the place is dignified by th' doer's deed. AWW 2.03.126
and vice sometime by action dignified. ROM 2.03. 22
thou wert dignified enough, | even to the point CYM 2.03.127
thou nobly base, they basely dignified; LUC 660
so dost thou too, and therein dignified. SON 101. 4
/DIGNIFIES 1 FR 0.0001 REL FR 0 V 1 P
that /dignifies the renown of a bawd, no less PER 4.06. 39 P
DIGNIFIES 3 FR 0.0003 REL FR 3 V 0 P
nor dignifies an impare thought with breath; TRO 4.05.103
chiefest virtue, and | most dignifies the haver; COR 2.02. 85
tell | that you are you, so dignifies his story. SON 84. 8
DIGNIFY 2 FR 0.0002 REL FR 2 V 0 P
he leaves his friends to dignify them more; TGV 1.01. 64
won, | came not till now to dignify the times, 2H4 1.01. 22
DIGNITIES 15 FR 0.0017 REL FR 13 V 2 P
since their more mature dignities and royal WT 1.01. 25 P
might wear | without corrival all her dignities; 1H4 1.03.207
i will double–charge thee with dignities. 2H4 5.03.125 P
in spite of pope or dignities of church, | here 1H6 1.03. 50
but death | shall e'er divorce my dignities. H8 3.01.142
she should have bought her dignities so dear. 3.01.184
to prepare the ways | you have for dignities, to 3.02.329
within me | a peace above all earthly dignities, 3.02.379
upon our joint and several dignities. TRO 2.02.193
who have thought | on special dignities, which TIM 5.01.142
any man's | in the disposing of new dignities. JC 3.01.178
old, | and the late dignities heap'd up to them, MAC 1.06. 19
pompey the great and all his dignities | upon ANT 1.02.188
fit you | with dignities becoming your estates. CYM 5.05. 22
which shall invest | you in your dignities, and TNK 1.04. 11
DIGNITY 39 FR 0.0044 REL FR 34 V 5 P
duke, being so reputed | in dignity, and for the TMP 1.02. 73
laws, | against my crown, my oath, my dignity, ERR 1.01.143
where several worthies make one dignity, | where LLL 4.03.232
love can transpose to form and dignity. MND 1.01.233
none presume | to wear an undeserved dignity. MV 2.09. 40
mean time, forget this new–fall'n dignity, | and AYL 5.04.176
the great dignity that his valor hath here AWW 4.03. 68 P
how often said my dignity would last | but till WT 4.04.475
who has | (his dignity and duty both cast off) 5.01.183
the dignity of this act was worth the audience 5.02. 79 P
find liable to our crown and dignity, | shall JN 2.01.490
up | the crest of youth against your dignity. 1H4 1.01. 99
for my cloud of dignity | is held from falling 2H4 4.05. 98
a son, | hear your own dignity so much profan'd, 5.02. 93
best | shall see advantageable for our dignity, H5 5.02. 88
under him, | and still enjoy thy regal dignity. 1H6 5.04.132
and not a thought but thinks on dignity. 2H6 3.01.338
his behalf | is slander to your royal dignity. 3.02.209
king, his crown, and dignity, thou hast built a 4.07. 37 P
hast, | i am resolv'd for death /or dignity. 5.01.194
royal self | this proffer'd benefit of dignity; R3 3.07.196
a sign of dignity, a breath, a bubble; 4.04. 90
unto the dignity and height of fortune, | the 4.04.244
tell me, what state, what dignity, what honor, 4.04.247
home | to high promotions and great dignity. 4.04.314
your honor nor | the dignity of your office, is H8 1.02. 16
lawful, by my life | and kingly dignity, we are 2.04.228
why, this hath not a finger's dignity. TRO 1.03.204
it holds his estimate and dignity | as well 2.02. 54
two households, both alike in dignity, | in fair ROM pr 1
in my bosom for the dignity of the whole body. MAC 5.01. 56 P
whose love was of that dignity | that it went HAM 1.05. 48
use them after your own honor and dignity — the 2.02.531 P
things of such dignity | as we greet modern ANT 5.02.166
be, | but clay and clay differs in dignity, CYM 4.02. 4
of imogen, that best | could deem his dignity? 5.04. 57
that 'fore thy dignity will dance a morris. TNK 3.05.108
his hand, as proud of such a dignity, | smoking LUC 437
meet, | the basest weed outbraves his dignity: SON 94.12
DIGRESS 2 FR 0.0002 REL FR 2 V 0 P
word, | though in some part enforced to digress, SHR 3.02.107
but soft, methinks i do digress too much, TIT 5.03.116
DIGRESSING 2 FR 0.0002 REL FR 2 V 0 P
excuse | this deadly blot in thy digressing son. R2 5.03. 66
of wax, | digressing from the valor of a man; ROM 3.03.127
DIGRESSION 3 FR 0.0003 REL FR 2 V 1 P
that i may example my digression by some mighty LLL 1.02.116 P
but this is mere digression from my purpose. 2H4 4.01.138
then my digression is so vile, so base, | that LUC 202
DIGS 2 FR 0.0002 REL FR 2 V 0 P
it, | for who digs hills because they do aspire PER 1.04. 5
his snout digs sepulchres where e'er he goes; VEN 622
DIGT *(also digg'd)*
DIGT 1 FR 0.0001 REL FR 0 V 1 P
is digt himself four yard under the countermines H5 3.02. 62 P
DIG–YOU–DEN 1 FR 0.0001 REL FR 0 V 1 P
god dig–you–den all! LLL 4.01. 42 P
DII 3 FR 0.0003 REL FR 3 V 0 P
dii faciant laudis summa sit ista tuae! 3H6 1.03. 48
dii boni! | a tinker, damsel? TNK 3.05. 83
dii deaeque omnes! 3.05.158
DILATE 2 FR 0.0002 REL FR 2 V 0 P
do me the favor to dilate at full | what have ERR 1.01.122
heart | that i would all my pilgrimage dilate, OTH 1.03.153
DILATED 2 FR 0.0002 REL FR 1 V 1 P
after them, and take a more dilated farewell. AWW 2.01. 57 P
confines | /thy spacious and dilated parts. TRO 2.03.250
DILATIONS 1 FR 0.0001 REL FR 1 V 0 P
in a man that's just | they're close dilations, OTH 3.03.123
DILATORY 2 FR 0.0002 REL FR 2 V 0 P
abhor | this dilatory sloth and tricks of rome. H8 2.04.238
witchcraft, | and wit depends on dilatory time. OTH 2.03.373
DILD 1 FR 0.0001 REL FR 0 V 1 P
well, god dild you! HAM 4.05. 42 P
DILDOS 1 FR 0.0001 REL FR 0 V 1 P
such delicate burthens of dildo? and fadings, WT 4.04.195 P
DILEMMA 1 FR 0.0001 REL FR 0 V 1 P
doctor, in perplexity and doubtful dilemma. WIV 4.05. 85 P
DILEMMAS 1 FR 0.0001 REL FR 0 V 1 P
and i will presently pen down my dilemmas, AWW 3.06. 75 P
DILICULO *(see deliculo)*
DILIGENCE 11 FR 0.0012 REL FR 8 V 3 P
hence with diligence! TMP 1.02.304
bravely, my diligence. thou shalt be free. 5.01.241
with whispering and most guilty diligence, | in MM 4.01. 38
as he shall think by our true diligence | he is SHR in.1. 70
proof | of your accustom'd diligence to me. 1H6 5.03. 9
receive it, sir, with all diligence of spirit. HAM 5.02. 91 P
qualified in, and the best of me is diligence. LR 1.04. 35 P
if your diligence be not speedy, i shall be 1.05. 4 P
there wants no diligence in seeking him, | and CYM 4.03. 20
is made with all due diligence | that horse and PER 3.ch. 19
which being done with speedy diligence, | the LUC 1853
DILIGENT 6 FR 0.0006 REL FR 4 V 2 P
hath into bondage | brought my too diligent ear. TMP 3.01. 42
thou seest how diligent i am | to dress thy meat SHR 4.03. 39
tell him that, he knows you are too diligent. TIM 3.04. 40 P
by diligent discovery, but your haste | is now LR 5.01. 53
gratitude, but be a diligent follower of mine. CYM 3.05.120 P
had | a page so kind, so duteous, diligent, | so 5.05. 86
DIM 22 FR 0.0024 REL FR 22 V 0 P
so doth the greater glory dim the less: MV 5.01. 93
i never saw | the heavens so dim by day. WT 3.03. 56
violets, dim, | but sweeter than the lids of 4.04.120
a ghost, | as dim and meagre as an ague's fit, JN 3.04. 85
bent | to dim his glory and to stain the track R2 3.03. 66
my day is dim. 2H4 4.05.100
let not sloth dim your honors new begot. 1H6 1.01. 79
spent, | wax dim, as drawing to their exigent; 2.05. 9
gazing on that which seems to dim thy sight? 2H6 1.02. 6
mine eyes grow dim. H8 4.02.164
or with our sighs we'll breathe the welkin dim, TIT 3.01.211
bed | in that dim monument where tybalt lies. ROM 3.05.201
thee, | and never from this /palace of dim night 5.03.107
not erebus itself were dim enough | to hide thee JC 2.01. 84
spring–time's harbinger, | with her bells dim; TNK 1.01. 9
upon the world dim darkness doth display, | and LUC 118
and death's dim look in life's mortality. 403
in his dim mist th' aspiring mountains hiding, 548
and wipe the dim mist from thy doting eyne, 643

dim register and notary of shame! 765
these water–galls in her dim element | foretell 1588
but now that fair fresh mirror, dim and old, 1760
DIMENSION 2 FR 0.0002 REL FR 2 V 0 P
and in dimension and the shape of nature | a TN 1.05.261
but am in that dimension grossly clad | which 5.01.237
DIMENSIONS 3 FR 0.0003 REL FR 1 V 2 P
not a jew hands, organs, dimensions, senses, MV 3.01. 60 P
that his dimensions to any thick sight were 2H4 3.02.312 P
when my dimensions are as well compact, | my LR 1.02. 7
DIMINISH 2 FR 0.0002 REL FR 2 V 0 P
as diminish | one dowle that's in my plume. TMP 3.03. 64
that reason wonder may diminish | how thus we AYL 5.04.139
DIMINISH'D 2 FR 0.0002 REL FR 2 V 0 P
tall anchoring bark, | diminish'd to her cock; LR 4.06. 19
if springing things be any jot diminish'd, VEN 417
DIMINISHING 1 FR 0.0001 REL FR 1 V 0 P
drop again, | without addition or diminishing, ERR 2.02.128
DIMINUTION 2 FR 0.0002 REL FR 2 V 0 P
see still | a diminution in our captain's brain ANT 3.13.197
till the diminution | of space had pointed him CYM 1.03. 18
DIMINUTIVE 2 FR 0.0002 REL FR 2 V 0 P
with spans and inches so diminutive | as fears TRO 2.02. 31
the most diminutive of birds, will fight, | her MAC 4.02. 10
DIMINUTIVES 2 FR 0.0002 REL FR 1 V 1 P
with such water–flies, diminutives of nature! TRO 5.01. 34 P
be shown | for poor'st diminutives, for dolts, ANT 4.12. 37
DIMM'D 7 FR 0.0008 REL FR 7 V 0 P
and dimm'd mine eyes, that i can read no further 2H6 1.01. 55
tears, and with dimm'd eyes | look after him, 3.01.218
that now are dimm'd with death's black veil, 3H6 5.02. 16
hath dimm'd your infant morn to aged night. R3 4.04. 16
is the sun dimm'd, that gnats do fly in it? TIT 4.04. 82
are by his flaming torch dimm'd and controll'd. LUC 448
and often is his gold complexion dimm'd, | and SON 18. 6
DIMMING 1 FR 0.0001 REL FR 1 V 0 P
cause | to wail the dimming of our shining star; R3 2.02.102
DIMPLE 1 FR 0.0001 REL FR 1 V 0 P
that in each cheek appears a pretty dimple; VEN 242
DIMPLED 5 FR 0.0005 REL FR 4 V 1 P
why, you know 'tis dimpled. TRO 1.02.121 P
whose dimpled smiles from fools exhaust their TIM 4.03.120
on each side her | stood pretty dimpled boys, ANT 2.02.202
fortune at you | dimpled her cheek with smiles. TNK 1.01. 66
her coral lips, her snow–white dimpled chin. LUC 420
DIMPLES 1 FR 0.0001 REL FR 1 V 0 P
the pretty dimples of his chin and cheek, his WT 2.03.102
DIMS 1 FR 0.0001 REL FR 1 V 0 P
that dims the honor of this warlike isle! 2H6 1.01.125
DIN 10 FR 0.0011 REL FR 10 V 0 P
roar | that beasts shall tremble at thy din. TMP 1.02.371
o, 'twas a din to fright a monster's ear, | to 2.01.314
that mortal ears might hardly endure the din? SHR 1.01.173
think you a little din can daunt mine ears? 1.02.199
when by and by the din of war gan pierce | his COR 2.02.115
but with a din confus'd | enforce the present 3.03. 20
with brazen din blast you the city's ear, | make ANT 4.08. 36
no farther with your din | express impatience, CYM 5.04.111
rout, | no din but snores /the /house /about, PER 3.ch. 2
what shows, | what minstrelsy, and pretty din, 5.02. 7
DIN'D 17 FR 0.0019 REL FR 10 V 7 P
i have din'd. TGV 2.01.171 P
i have not din'd to–day. ERR 3.01. 40
that is where we din'd, | where dowsabel did 4.01.109
o husband, god doth know you din'd at home, 4.04. 65
din'd at home? thou villain, what sayest thou? 4.04. 68
that he din'd not at home, but was lock'd out. 5.01.256
you say he din'd at home; 5.01.274
sir, he din'd with her there, at the porpentine. 5.01.276
i will tell you is, that the duke hath din'd. MND 4.02. 35 P
what, hast thou din'd? SHR 4.03. 59
water, nor the bear half din'd on the gentleman. WT 3.03.106 P
of this feast, | having fully din'd before. COR 1.09. 11
he was not taken well, he had not din'd: 5.01. 50
has he din'd, canst thou tell? 5.02. 34 P
what, have you din'd at home? ROM 2.05. 45 P
many a time and often i ha' din'd with him, and TIM 3.01. 24 P
dead body, and when my lust hath din'd (which, CYM 3.05.142 P
DINE 25 FR 0.0028 REL FR 19 V 6 P
now can i break my fast, dine, sup, and sleep, TGV 2.04.141
we have appointed to dine with mistress anne, WIV 3.02. 55 P
i am fain to dine and sup with water and bran; MM 4.03.153 P
town, | and then go to my inn and dine with me? ERR 1.02. 23
good sister, let us dine, and never fret; 2.01. 6
husband, i'll dine above with you to–day, | and 2.02.207
come, come, antipholus, we dine too late. 2.02.219
there will we dine. 3.01.111
sir, sooth to say, you did not dine at home. 4.04. 69
he, and my sister | to–day did dine together: 5.01.208
where balthazar and i did dine together. 5.01.223
which of you two did dine with me to–day? 5.01.370
as thus — to study where i well may dine, LLL 1.01. 61
i do dine to–day at the father's of a certain 4.02.153 P
if it please you to dine with us. MV 1.03. 32 P
i know you think to dine with me to–day, | and SHR 3.02.185
dine with my father, drink a health to me, | for 3.02.196
that ne'er shall dine unless thou yield the 3H6 2.02.128
i swear | i will not dine until i see the same. R3 3.04. 77
where shall we dine? ROM 1.01.173
we must needs dine together. TIM 1.01.164
wilt dine with me, apemantus? 1.01.203 P
you must needs dine with me; 1.01.244
will you dine with me to–morrow? JC 1.02.290 P
i shall not dine at home; OTH 3.03. 58
DINER 1 FR 0.0001 REL FR 0 V 1 P
c'est assez pour une fois: allons–nous a diner. H5 3.04. 62 P
DINES 2 FR 0.0002 REL FR 2 V 0 P
say he dines forth, and let no creature enter. ERR 2.02.210
he is not there to–day, he dines in london. 2H4 4.04. 51
DING 5 FR 0.0005 REL FR 5 V 0 P
i'll begin it — ding, dong, bell. MV 3.02. 71
ding, dong, bell. 3.02. 72
when birds do sing, hey ding a ding, ding, AYL 5.03. 20
when birds do sing, hey ding a ding, ding, 5.03. 20
when birds do sing, hey ding a ding, ding, 5.03. 20
DING–DONG 2 FR 0.0002 REL FR 2 V 0 P
ding–dong. TMP 1.02.404
hark now i hear them — ding–dong bell. 1.02.405
DINING–CHAMBER 1 FR 0.0001 REL FR 0 V 1 P
sooner into the dining–chamber but he steps me TGV 4.04. 8 P
DINING–CHAMBERS 1 FR 0.0001 REL FR 0 V 1 P
my plate and the tapestry of my dining–chambers. 2H4 2.01.142 P
DINNER 83 FR 0.0093 REL FR 43 V 40 P
i must eat my dinner. TMP 1.02.330
madam, | dinner is ready, and your father stays. TGV 1.02.128
when you fasted, it was presently after dinner; 2.01. 29 P
come, we have a hot venison pasty to dinner. WIV 1.01.195 P
the dinner is on the table. 1.01.261 P
the dinner attends you, sir. 1.01.269 P
i will make an end of my dinner; 1.02. 12 P
you'll come to dinner, george. 2.01.157 P
heartily, some of you go home with me to dinner. 3.02. 80 P
well, i promis'd you a dinner. 3.03.223 P
i pray you home to dinner with me. MM 2.01.278 P
i pray you jest, sir, as you sit at dinner. ERR 1.02. 62
home to your house, the phoenix, sir, to dinner; 1.02. 75
she that doth fast till you come home to dinner; 1.02. 89
and prays that you will hie you home to dinner. 1.02. 90
and from the mart he's somewhere gone to dinner. 2.01. 5
when i desir'd him to come home to dinner, | he 2.01. 60
your mistress sent to have me home to dinner? 2.02. 10
and toldst me of a mistress, and a dinner, | for 2.02. 18
that at dinner they should not drop in his 2.02. 98 P
she sent for you by dromio home to dinner. 2.02.154
dromio, go bid the servants spread for dinner. 2.02.187
come, sir, to dinner. 2.02.206
for my dinner: 3.01. 40
and let us to the tiger all to dinner; 3.01. 95
to her will we to dinner. 3.01.114
we'll mend our dinner here. 4.03. 59
give me the ring of mine you had at dinner, | or 4.03. 68
rage, | is a mad tale he told to–day at dinner, 4.03. 88
this woman lock'd me out this day from dinner; 5.01.218
our dinner done, and he not coming thither, | i 5.01.224
that kitchen'd me for you to–day at dinner: 5.01.416
my lord, will you walk? dinner is ready. ADO 2.03.210 P
let us send her to call him in to dinner. 2.03.219 P
my will i am sent to bid you come in to dinner. 2.03.248 P
will i am sent to bid you come in to dinner" — 2.03.258 P
your reasons at dinner have been sharp and LLL 5.01. 3 P
a while, | i'll end my exhortation after dinner. MV 1.01.104
after dinner | your hazard shall be made. 2.01. 44
go in, sirrah, bid them prepare for dinner. 3.05. 47 P
then bid them prepare dinner! 3.05. 50 P
in the meat, and we will come in to dinner. 3.05. 60 P
for your coming in to dinner, sir, why, let it 3.05. 63 P
i will anon, first let us go to dinner. 3.05. 86
sir, i entreat you home with me to dinner. 4.01.401
ring, and doth entreat | your company at dinner. 4.02. 8
die for lack of a dinner if there live any thing AYL 2.06. 17 P
i must attend the duke at dinner. 4.01.180 P
i would i were as sure of a good dinner. SHR 1.02.217
a little in the orchard, | and then to dinner. 2.01.112
let us entreat you stay till after dinner. 3.02.198
gentlemen, forward to the bridal dinner. 3.02.219
is something at the latter end of a dinner, but AWW 2.05. 29 P
i'll to dinner. 1H4 3.01. 50
and he is indited to dinner to the lubber's head 2H4 2.01. 28 P
gower, shall i entreat you with me to dinner? 2.01.183 P
and so i pray you go in with me to dinner. 3.02.190 P
go drink with you, but i cannot tarry dinner. 3.02.192 P
come let's to dinner, come let's to dinner. 3.02.218 P
come let's to dinner, come let's to dinner. 3.02.219 P
fear no colors, go with me to dinner. 5.05. 88 P
come, let us four to dinner. 1H6 2.04.132
nay, like enough, for i stay dinner there. R3 3.02.121
come, dispatch, the duke would be at dinner. 3.04. 94
i would not speak with him till after dinner. COR 5.02. 35 P
we'll to dinner thither. ROM 2.04.141 P
go, i'll to dinner, hie you to the cell. 2.05. 77
here, tarry for the mourners, and stay dinner. 4.05.146 P
a breakfast of enemies than a dinner of friends. TIM 1.02. 77 P
your importunacy cease till after dinner, | that 2.02. 41
our dinner will not recompense this long stay; 3.06. 32 P
thou shouldst hazard thy life for thy dinner; 4.03.335 P
mind hold, and your dinner worth the eating. JC 1.02.292 P
prepare for dinner. LR 1.03. 26
let me not stay a jot for dinner, go get it 1.04. 8 P
if i like thee no worse after dinner, i will not 1.04. 41 P
dinner, ho, dinner! 1.04. 42 P
dinner, ho, dinner! 1.04. 42 P
to–morrow dinner then? OTH 3.03. 58
your dinner, and the generous islanders | by you 3.03.280
mark antony | in egypt sits at dinner, and will ANT 2.01. 12
return, and bring him | to dinner presently. CYM 4.02.166
come, sweet, we'll go to dinner, | and then TNK 5.02.107
DINNER'S 2 FR 0.0002 REL FR 2 V 0 P
when dinner's done, | show me this piece. TIM 1.01.245
so soon as dinner's done, we'll forth again, 2.02. 14
DINNERS 2 FR 0.0002 REL FR 1 V 1 P
dinners and suppers and sleeping–hours excepted. AYL 3.02. 97 P
shall we go send them dinners and fresh suits, H5 4.02. 57
DINNER–TIME 10 FR 0.0011 REL FR 8 V 2 P
is't near dinner–time? TGV 1.02. 67
'tis dinner–time. 2.01.170 P
within this hour it will be dinner–time; ERR 1.02. 11
"'tis dinner–time," quoth i: 2.01. 62
but say, sir, is it dinner–time? 2.02. 54 P
but at dinner–time | i pray you have in mind MV 1.01. 70
well, we will leave you then till dinner–time. 1.01.105
and well we may come there by dinner–time. SHR 4.03.188
that i will by to–morrow dinner–time | send him 1H4 2.04.515
have thirty miles to ride yet ere dinner–time. 3.03.198
/DINT 1 FR 0.0001 REL FR 1 V 0 P
/that /by /indictment /and /by /dint /of /sword 2H4 4.01.126
DINT 2 FR 0.0002 REL FR 2 V 0 P
and i perceive you feel | the dint of pity. JC 3.02.194
as apt as new–fall'n snow takes any dint. VEN 354
DIOMED 34 FR 0.0038 REL FR 31 V 3 P
good diomed, | furnish you fairly for this TRO 3.03. 32
wherein | you told how diomed, a whole week by 4.01. 10
the one and other diomed embraces. 4.01. 15
and tell me, noble diomed — faith, tell me true 4.01. 52
fair diomed, you do as chapmen do, | dispraise 4.01. 76
the grecian diomed, and our antenor | deliver'd 4.02. 62
welcome, sir diomed! 4.04.109
usage, and to diomed | you shall be mistress, 4.04.119
i'll tell thee, diomed, | this brave shall oft 4.04.136
is not yond diomed, with calchas' daughter? 4.05. 13
here is sir diomed. 4.05. 88
since first i saw yourself and diomed | in ilion 4.05.215
there diomed doth feast with him to–night, | who 4.05.280
and you too, diomed, | keep hector company an 5.01. 80
borrows of the moon when diomed keeps his word. 5.01. 94 P
diomed. calchas, i think. where's your daughter? 5.02. 3
diomed — 5.02. 31
here, diomed, keep this sleeve. 5.02. 66
i prithee, diomed, visit me no more. 5.02. 74
you shall not have it, diomed, faith, you shall 5.02. 85
farewell, | thou never shalt mock diomed again. 5.02. 99
of her o'er–eaten faith, are given to diomed. 5.02.160
love, | so much by weight hate i her diomed. 5.02.168
shall my prompted sword | falling on diomed. 5.02.176
and, diomed, | stand fast, and wear a castle on 5.02.186
would i could meet that rogue diomed! 5.02.190 P
proud diomed, believe, | i come to lose my arm, 5.03. 95
that dissembling abominable varlet, diomed, has 5.04. 3 P
haste we, diomed, | to reinforcement, or we 5.05. 15
o traitor diomed! 5.06. 6
i'll fight with him alone. stand, diomed. 5.06. 9
there, diomed, there. ANT 4.14.114
art thou there, diomed? 4.14.116
too late, good diomed. call my guard, i prithee. 4.14.128
DIOMEDE 1 FR 0.0001 REL FR 1 V 0 P
that as ulysses and stout diomede | with sleight 3H6 4.02. 19
DIOMEDES' 1 FR 0.0001 REL FR 1 V 0 P
we must give up to diomedes' hand | the lady TRO 4.02. 65
DIOMEDES 1 FR 0.0001 REL FR 1 V 0 P
let diomedes bear him, | and bring us cressid TRO 3.03. 30
DIOMED'S 2 FR 0.0002 REL FR 1 V 1 P
that same diomed's a false–hearted rogue, a most TRO 5.01. 88 P
no, this is diomed's cressida. 5.02.137
DION 3 FR 0.0003 REL FR 3 V 0 P
cleomines and dion, whom you know | of stuff'd WT 2.01.184
cleomines and dion, | being well arriv'd from 2.03.195
that you, cleomines and dion, have | been both 3.02.125
DIONYZA 6 FR 0.0006 REL FR 6 V 0 P
my dionyza, shall we rest us here, | and by PER 1.04. 1
o dionyza! 1.04. 10
dead, | and cursed dionyza hath | the pregnant 4.ch. 43
dionyza does appear, | with leonine, a murtherer 4.ch. 51
o dionyza, such a piece of slaughter | the sun 4.03. 2
epitaph is for marina writ | by wicked dionyza. 4.04. 33
DIP 3 FR 0.0003 REL FR 2 V 1 P
me to see so many dip their meat in one man's TIM 1.02. 41 P
and dip their napkins in his sacred blood; JC 3.02.133
so mortal that, but dip a knife in it, | where HAM 4.07.142
DIPP'DST 1 FR 0.0001 REL FR 1 V 0 P
this cloth thou dipp'dst in blood of my sweet 3H6 1.04.157
DIPPING 1 FR 0.0001 REL FR 1 V 0 P
who, dipping all his faults in their affection, HAM 4.07. 19
DIPS 1 FR 0.0001 REL FR 1 V 0 P
him | his friend that dips in the same dish? TIM 3.02. 66
DIRE* 20 FR 0.0022 REL FR 19 V 1 P
mark'd | to bear the extremity of dire mishap! ERR 1.01.141
and for our eyes do hate the dire aspect | of R2 1.03.127
that sought at oxfgrd thy dire overthrow. 5.06. 16
il me commande a vous dire que vous faites vous H5 4.04. 34 P
and mine shall ring thy dire departure out. 1H6 4.02. 41
a dire induction am i witness to, | and will to R3 4.04. 5
and the dire death of my poor sons and brothers? 4.04.143
and lancaster, | divided in their dire division, 5.05. 28
off | all fears attending on so dire a project. TRO 2.02.134
to ruminate strange plots of dire revenge; TIT 5.02. 6
that hath been breeder of these dire events. 5.03.178
that he should hither come as this dire night ROM 5.03.247
of dire combustion and confus'd events | new MAC 2.03. 58
women fight, | to doff their dire distresses. 4.03.188
thy natural magic and dire property | on HAM 3.02.259
do, with like timorous accent and dire yell | as OTH 1.01. 75
and brings the dire occasion in his arms | of CYM 4.02.196
the dire imagination she did follow | this sound VEN 975
"it shall be cause of war and dire events, | and 1159
and the dire thought of his committed evil LUC 972
DIRECT 36 FR 0.0040 REL FR 25 V 11 P
i'll first direct my men what they shall do with WIV 4.02. 99 P
me your snatches, and yield me a direct answer. MM 4.02. 7 P
some god direct my judgment! MV 2.07. 13
that by direct or indirect attempts | he seek 4.01.350
and so to lie circumstantial and the lie direct. AYL 5.04. 82 P
nor he durst not give me the lie direct; 5.04. 86 P
the seventh, the lie direct. 5.04. 96 P
all these you may avoid but the lie direct; 5.04. 97 P
my lord, in mine own direct knowledge, without AWW 3.06. 7 P
as we'll direct her how 'tis best to bear it. 3.07. 20
her, but direct thy feet | where thou and i, TN 5.01.168
yet indirection thereby grows direct, | and JN 3.01.276
be ready to direct these home alarms. R2 1.01.205
appointed to direct these fair designs. 1.03. 45
direct not him whose way himself will choose, 2.01. 29
than i by letters shall direct your course. 1H4 1.03.293
direct mine arms i may embrace his neck, | and 1H6 2.05. 37
and i'll direct thee how thou shalt escape | by 4.05. 10
and may direct his course as please himself, R3 2.02.129
more stronger to direct you than yourself, | if H8 1.01.147
or /hedge aside from the direct forthright, TRO 3.03.158
and their consent of one direct way should be at COR 2.03. 23 P
me, and i'll direct you how you shall go by him. 2.03. 46 P
direct me, if it be your will, | where great 4.04. 7
the steerage of my course | direct my /sail! ROM 1.04.113
in our cursed natures | but direct villainy. TIM 4.03. 20
heaven will direct it. HAM 1.04. 91
charge you withal, be even and direct with me, 2.02.287 P
if by direct or by collateral hand | they find 4.05.207
that you may direct me | to him from whom you 4.06. 33
of law and course of direct session | call thee OTH 1.02. 86
o world, | to be direct and honest is not safe. 3.03.378
may the gods | direct you to the best! CYM 3.04.193
none want eyes to direct them the way i am going 5.04.186 P
your rule direct to any; PER 1.02.109
and now direct your course to th' wood, where TNK 4.01.144
DIRECTED 13 FR 0.0014 REL FR 9 V 4 P

i have directed you to wrong places. WIV 3.01.107 P
i am directed by you. MM 4.03.136
but, damosella virgin, was this directed to you? LLL 4.02.128 P
she hath directed | how i shall take her from MV 2.04. 29
spirit | commits itself to yours to be directed, 3.02.164
and all the rest | to whom they are directed. 1H4 4.04. 4
is given, is altogether directed by an irishman, H5 3.02. 66 P
words sweetly plac'd and /modestly directed. 1H6 5.03.179
they thus directed, we will follow | in the main R3 5.03.298
i was directed hither. TIM 4.03.198
you must either be directed by some that take CYM 5.04.179 P
pocket, which directed him | to seek her on the 5.05.280
and, darkly bright, are bright in dark directed. SON 43. 4

DIRECTING 2 FR 0.0002 REL FR 2 V 0 P
and son unto the king, whom heavens directing, WT 5.03.150
another | directing in his head, his mind nurse TNK 1.03. 32

DIRECTION 23 FR 0.0026 REL FR 18 V 5 P
told them over and over, they lack no direction. WIV 3.03. 19 P
such assistance as i shall give you direction. ADO 2.01.370 P
give him direction for this merry bond, | and i MV 1.03.173
soly led | by nice direction of a maiden's eyes; 2.01. 14
gown is made | just as my master had direction. SHR 4.03.116
your gracious self, embrace but my direction, WT 4.04.523
from all direction, purpose, course, intent — JN 2.01.580
i do commit his youth | to your direction. 4.02. 68
purses than giving direction doth from laboring; 1H4 2.01. 51 P
as touching the direction of the military H5 3.02.100 P
i, as a child, will go by thy direction. R3 2.02.153
thy head (all indirectly) gave direction. 4.04.226
call for some men of sound direction: 5.03. 16
why, then 'tis time to arm and give direction. 5.03.236
a good direction, warlike sovereign. 5.03.302
let thy blood be thy direction till thy death; TRO 2.03. 31 P
by whose direction foundst thou out this place? ROM 2.02. 79
and what we have to do, | to the direction just. MAC 3.03. 4
for even now | i put myself to thy direction, 4.03.122
hour | of love, of wordly matter and direction, OTH 1.03.299
iago hath direction what to do; 2.03. 4
fit to stand by caesar | and give direction; 2.03.123
for men will kiss even by their own direction." VEN 216

DIRECTION-GIVER 1 FR 0.0001 REL FR 1 V 0 P
therefore, sweet proteus, my direction-giver, TGV 3.02. 89

DIRECTIONS 7 FR 0.0008 REL FR 4 V 3 P
then with directions to repair to ravenspurgh. R2 2.03. 35
to your well-practic'd wise directions. 2H4 5.02.121
plow up all, if there is not better directions. H5 3.02. 64 P
he has no more directions in the true 3.02. 71 P
upon my particular knowledge of his directions. 3.02. 79 P
things well, | according as i gave directions? 2H6 3.02. 12
of bias, | by indirections find directions out. HAM 2.01. 63

DIRECTITUDE 2 FR 0.0002 REL FR 0 V 2 P
it) his friends whilest he's in directitude. COR 4.05.208 P
directitude? what's that? 4.05.209 P

/DIRECTIVE 1 FR 0.0001 REL FR 1 V 0 P
/swords /and /bows | /directive /by /the /limbs. TRO 1.03.356

DIRECTLY 32 FR 0.0036 REL FR 19 V 13 P
not, as you would say, | directly int'rest. MV 1.03. 77
proceeding, | that indirectly, and directly too, 4.01.359
this concurs directly with the letter: TN 3.04. 66 P
nor is't directly laid to thee, the death | of WT 3.02.194
out of the path which shall directly lead | thy JN 3.04.129
me | directly unto this question that i ask. 1H4 2.03. 86
pleaseth your grace to answer them directly 2H4 4.02. 52
it in love, but directly to say "i love you"; H5 5.02.127 P
you would swear directly | their very noses had H8 1.03. 8
that you directly | set me against aufidius and COR 1.06. 58
hard for him, directly to say the troth on't, 4.05.185 P
but what trade art thou? answer me directly. JC 1.01. 12
stand you directly in antonio's way | when he 1.02. 3
east | stands, as the capitol, directly here. 2.01.111
answe› every man directly. 3.03. 9 P
then to answer every man directly and briefly, 3.03. 15 P
proceed directly. 3.03. 19 P
directly, i am going to caesar's funeral. 3.03. 20 P
that matter is answer'd directly. 3.03. 23 P
fight, | to wind, to stop, to run directly on, 4.01. 32
directly. MAC 5.01. 70 P
doth try, | directly seasons him his enemy. HAM 3.02.209
when in one line two crafts directly meet. 3.04.210
desdemona is directly in love with him. OTH 2.01.219 P
to this parallel course, | directly to his good? 2.03.350
which lead directly to the door of truth | will 3.03.407
i have dealt most directly in thy affair. 4.02.208 P
her and give me directly to understand you have CYM 1.04.158 P
i shall flying fight — | rather, directly fly. 1.06. 21
i bid thee do, to perform it directly and truly, 3.05.113 P
fiend, | suspect i may (yet not directly tell): PP 2.10
fiend | suspect i may, yet not directly tell, SON 144.10

DIRECTS 1 FR 0.0001 REL FR 1 V 0 P
i find, | the error of our eye directs our mind. TRO 5.02.110

DIREFUL 9 FR 0.0010 REL FR 9 V 0 P
the direful spectacle of the wrack, which TMP 1.02. 26
more direful hap betide that hated wretch | that R3 1.02. 17
the flattering index of a direful pageant; 4.04. 85
to be /adjudg'd some direful slaught'ring death, TIT 5.03.144
doth make against me, of this direful murther; ROM 5.03.225
shipwracking storms and direful thunders /break, MAC 1.02. 26
'tis some mischance, the voice is very direful. OTH 5.01. 38
now, | even by the stern and direful god of war, VEN 98
she stays, exclaiming on the direful night, | he LUC 741

DIRE-LAMENTING 1 FR 0.0001 REL FR 1 V 0 P
after your dire-lamenting elegies, | visit by TGV 3.02. 81

DIRENESS 1 FR 0.0001 REL FR 1 V 0 P
direness, familiar to my slaughterous thoughts, MAC 5.05. 14

DIREST 2 FR 0.0002 REL FR 2 V 0 P
murther, stern murther, in the direst degree; R3 5.03.197
the crown to the toe topful | of direst cruelty! MAC 1.05. 43

DIRGE 3 FR 0.0003 REL FR 3 V 0 P
mirth in funeral, and with dirge in marriage, HAM 1.02. 12
some honest-hearted maids, will sing my dirge, TNK 2.06. 15
begins the sad dirge of her certain ending: LUC 1612

DIRGES 1 FR 0.0001 REL FR 1 V 0 P
our solemn hymns to sullen dirges change; ROM 4.05. 88

DIRT 10 FR 0.0011 REL FR 4 V 6 P
out of their saddles into the dirt, and thereby SHR 4.01. 57 P
she waded through the dirt to pluck him off me; 4.01. 78 P
sink, whose filth and dirt | troubles the silver 2H6 4.01. 71
paris is dirt to him, and i warrant helen, to TRO 1.02.238 P
a mint, | to match us in comparisons with dirt, 1.03.194
to have his fine pate full of fine dirt? HAM 5.01.108 P
as i say, spacious in the possession of dirt. 5.02. 88 P
thou bor'st thine ass on thy back o'er the dirt. LR 1.04.162 P
o gull, o dolt, | as ignorant as dirt! OTH 5.02.164
all gold and silver rather turn to dirt, | as CYM 3.06. 53

DIRT-ROTTEN 1 FR 0.0001 REL FR 0 V 1 P
raw eyes, dirt-rotten livers, whissing lungs, TRO 5.01. 20 P

DIRTY 7 FR 0.0008 REL FR 6 V 1 P
sleeping sound, | on the dank and dirty ground. MND 2.02. 75
the world, | prizes not quantity of dirty lands; TN 2.04. 82
thither | by most mechanical and dirty hand. 2H4 5.05. 36
to buy a slobb'ry and a dirty farm | in that H5 3.05. 13
i kiss his dirty shoe, and from heart-string | i 4.01. 47
knock him about the sconce with a dirty shovel, HAM 5.01.102 P
reckon'd, but of those | who worship dirty gods. CYM 3.06. 55

DIS 2 FR 0.0002 REL FR 2 V 0 P
plot | the means that dusky dis my daughter got, TMP 4.01. 89
doughty dismal fame | from dis to daedalus, from TNK 3.05.115

DISABILITY 1 FR 0.0001 REL FR 1 V 0 P
leave off discourse of disability. TGV 2.04.109

DISABLE 2 FR 0.0002 REL FR 1 V 1 P
disable all the benefits of your own country; AYL 4.01. 34 P
fie, de la pole, disable not thyself. 1H6 5.03. 67

DISABLED 3 FR 0.0003 REL FR 2 V 1 P
antonio, | how much i have disabled mine estate, MV 1.01.123
it was not well cut, he disabled my judgment: AYL 5.04. 76 P
and strength by limping sway disabled, | and art SON 66. 8

DISABLING 1 FR 0.0001 REL FR 1 V 0 P
deserving | were but a weak disabling of myself. MV 2.07. 30

/DISADVANTAGE 1 FR 0.0001 REL FR 1 V 0 P
/the /hideous /god /of /war | /in /disadvantage, 2H4 2.03. 36

DISADVANTAGE 1 FR 0.0001 REL FR 1 V 0 P
we have at disadvantage fought, and did | retire COR 1.06. 49

DISAGREE 1 FR 0.0001 REL FR 1 V 0 P
looks, | and that within ourselves we disagree, 1H6 4.01.140

DISALLOW 1 FR 0.0001 REL FR 1 V 0 P
what follows if we disallow of this? JN 1.01. 16

DISANIMATES 1 FR 0.0001 REL FR 1 V 0 P
loyal friends, | as it disanimates his enemies. 1H6 3.01.182

DISANNUL 1 FR 0.0001 REL FR 1 V 0 P
which princes, would they, may not disannul, ERR 1.01.144

DISANNULS 1 FR 0.0001 REL FR 1 V 0 P
then warwick disannuls great john of gaunt, 3H6 3.03. 81

DISAPPOINTED 1 FR 0.0001 REL FR 1 V 0 P
sin, | unhous'led, disappointed, unanel'd, | no HAM 1.05. 77

DISARM 3 FR 0.0003 REL FR 2 V 1 P
for i can here disarm thee with this stick, TMP 1.02.473
disarm them, and let them question. WIV 3.01. 76 P
all the island kings — disarm great hector. TRO 3.01.154

DISARM'D 1 FR 0.0001 REL FR 1 V 0 P
desire | was sleeping by a virgin hand disarm'd. SON 154. 8

DISASTER 6 FR 0.0006 REL FR 3 V 3 P
his faith, his sweet disaster; AWW 1.01.173
it was a disaster of war that caesar himself 3.06. 52 P
this very instant disaster of his setting i' th' 4.03.110 P
come, or sent it us | upon her great disaster. 5.03.112
should be, which pitifully disaster the cheeks. ANT 2.07. 16 P
till the disaster that, one mortal /night, PER 5.01. 37

DISASTERS 6 FR 0.0006 REL FR 4 V 2 P
checks and disasters | grow in the veins of TRO 1.03. 5
so weary with disasters, tugg'd with fortune, MAC 3.01.111
fire and dews of blood, | disasters in the sun; HAM 1.01.118
to shield thee from disasters of the world, LR 1.01.174
we make guilty of our disasters the sun, the 1.02.120 P
nothing of their own restraint and disasters. TNK 2.01. 40 P

DISASTROUS 1 FR 0.0001 REL FR 1 V 0 P
wherein i spoke of most disastrous chances: OTH 1.03.134

DISAVOUCH'D *(see disvouch'd)*

DISBENCH'D 1 FR 0.0001 REL FR 1 V 0 P
sir, i hope | my words disbench'd you not? COR 2.02. 71

/DISBRANCH 1 FR 0.0001 REL FR 1 V 0 P
/that /herself /will /sliver /and /disbranch LR 4.02. 34

DISBURDENED 1 FR 0.0001 REL FR 1 V 0 P
ere't be disburdened with a liberal tongue. R2 2.01.229

DISBURS'D 1 FR 0.0001 REL FR 1 V 0 P
disburs'd i duly to his highness' soldiers; R2 1.01.127

DISBURSE 1 FR 0.0001 REL FR 1 V 0 P
wife | disburse the sum on the receipt thereof. ERR 4.01. 38

DISBURSED *(also dispersed)*

DISBURSED 3 FR 0.0003 REL FR 3 V 0 P
entire sum | disbursed by my father in his wars. LLL 2.01.131
men | till he disbursed at saint colme's inch MAC 1.02. 61
and all my fame that lives disbursed be | to LUC 1203

DISCANDY 1 FR 0.0001 REL FR 1 V 0 P
to whom i gave | their wishes, do discandy, melt ANT 4.12. 22

/DISCANDYING 1 FR 0.0001 REL FR 1 V 0 P
by the /discandying of this pelleted storm, ANT 3.13.165

DISCARD 3 FR 0.0003 REL FR 1 V 2 P
discard, bully hercules, cashier; WIV 1.03. 6 P
go off, i discard you. TN 3.04. 89 P
romans bow before, | i here discard my sickness! JC 2.01.321

DISCARDED 6 FR 0.0006 REL FR 4 V 2 P
our wives are a yoke of his discarded men — WIV 2.01.175 P
and welcome home again discarded faith. JN 5.04. 12
that you are fool'd, discarded, and shook off 1H4 1.03.178
never soldiers, but discarded unjust servingmen, 4.02. 27 P
that discarded fathers | should have thus little LR 3.04. 72
to be discarded thence! OTH 4.02. 60

DISCASE 2 FR 0.0002 REL FR 1 V 1 P
i will discase me, and myself present | as i was TMP 5.01. 85
therefore discase thee instantly (thou must WT 4.04.633 P

DISCERN 9 FR 0.0010 REL FR 7 V 2 P
if thou mayest discern by that which is left of WT 3.03.133 P
and i could discern no part of his face from the 2H4 2.02. 80 P
as far as i could well discern | for smoke and 1H6 2.02. 26
as i discern, | it burneth in the capels' ROM 5.03.126
something | you may discern of him through me, MAC 4.03. 15
what from the cape can you discern at sea? OTH 2.01. 1
what wrack discern you in me | deserves your CYM 1.06. 84
from the deck | you may discern the place. PER 5.01.115
wilt thou be glass wherein it shall discern LUC 619

DISCERN'D 1 FR 0.0001 REL FR 1 V 0 P
which, once discern'd, shows that her meaning is 1H6 3.02. 24

DISCERNER 1 FR 0.0001 REL FR 1 V 0 P
one, and no discerner | durst wag his tongue in H8 1.01. 32

DISCERNING 1 FR 0.0001 REL FR 1 V 0 P
who hast not in thy brows an eye discerning LR 4.02. 52

DISCERNINGS 1 FR 0.0001 REL FR 1 V 0 P
weakens, his discernings | are lethargied — ha! LR 1.04.228

DISCERNS 1 FR 0.0001 REL FR 1 V 0 P
by some discretion that discerns your state LR 2.04.149

DISCERN'ST 1 FR 0.0001 REL FR 1 V 0 P
discern'st thou aught in that? OTH 3.03.102

DISCHARG'D 13 FR 0.0014 REL FR 10 V 3 P
i pray you see him presently discharg'd, | for ERR 4.01. 32
so it is, truly, and very notably discharg'd. MND 5.01.361 P
you have discharg'd this honestly, keep it to AWW 1.03.122 P
'tis hop'd his sickness is discharg'd. WT 2.03. 11
ay, ay, farewell, thy office is discharg'd. 2H6 2.04.103
all the rest, discharg'd me with these words: 3H6 4.01.109
gave notice | he was from thence discharg'd? H8 2.04. 34
three times was his nose discharg'd against me; 5.03. 45 P
the custom of request you have discharg'd. COR 2.03.142
lo, as the bark that hath discharg'd his fraught TIT 1.01. 71
and that the trunk may be discharg'd of breath ROM 5.01. 63
would we were all discharg'd! TIM 2.02. 12
be paid but once, | and that she has discharg'd. ANT 4.14. 28

DISCHARGE 34 FR 0.0038 REL FR 25 V 9 P
and after two days | i will discharge thee. TMP 1.02.299
what to come | in yours and my discharge. 2.01.254
the sun will set before i shall discharge | what 3.01. 22
there they always use to discharge their WIV 4.02. 57 P
for which i do discharge you of your office; MM 5.01.461
i will discharge my bond, and thank you too. ERR 4.01. 13
i will discharge thee ere i go from thee: 4.04.119
go, i discharge thee of thy prisoner, and i ADO 5.01.319 P
i will discharge it in either your straw-color MND 1.02. 93 P
in all athens able to discharge pyramus but he. 4.02. 8 P
he had | the present money to discharge the jew, MV 3.02.273
is he not able to discharge the money? 4.01.208
that their discharge did stretch his leathern AYL 2.01. 37
that power i have, discharge, and let them go R2 3.02.211
discharge my followers, let them hence away, 3.02.217
as by discharge of their artillery | and shape 1H4 1.01. 57
cup of sack, do you discharge upon mine hostess. 2H4 2.04.112 P
i will discharge upon her, sir john, with two 2.04.114 P
discharge yourself of our company, pistol. 2.04.137 P
charge you and discharge you with the motion of 3.02.262 P
you, | discharge your powers unto their several 4.02. 61
we here discharge your grace from being regent 2H6 1.01. 66
somerset will keep me here | without discharge, 1.03.169
discharge the common sort | with pay and thanks, 3H6 5.05. 87
he did discharge a horrible oath, whose tenor H8 1.02.206
with the rude brevity and discharge of one. TRO 4.04. 41
which never | i shall discharge to th' life. COR 3.02.106
their deaf pillows will discharge their secrets. MAC 5.01. 73
my name, have in my name | took their discharge. LR 5.03.105
they do discharge their shot of courtesy; OTH 2.01. 56
we will discharge our duty. CYM 3.07. 16
of what's past, is, and to come, the discharge. 5.04.169 P
to discharge my life? TNK 2.02.260
ere once she can discharge one word of woe; LUC 1605

DISCHARGED 4 FR 0.0004 REL FR 4 V 0 P
thus have i, wall, my part discharged so; MND 5.01.204
my lord, | and let our army be discharged too. 2H4 4.02. 92
the army is discharged all and gone. 4.03.127
or that which from discharged cannon fumes. LUC 1043

DISCHARGEST 1 FR 0.0001 REL FR 1 V 0 P
o mistress, | thou here dischargest me. TNK 5.01.170

DISCHARGING 1 FR 0.0001 REL FR 0 V 1 P
and discharging less than the tenth part of one. TRO 3.02. 87 P

DISCIPLED 1 FR 0.0001 REL FR 1 V 0 P
of the time, and was | discipled of the bravest. AWW 1.02. 28

DISCIPLES 1 FR 0.0001 REL FR 1 V 0 P
the devil | and his disciples only envy at, | ye H8 5.02.147

DISCIPLIN'D 3 FR 0.0003 REL FR 2 V 1 P
but he the disciplin'd thine arms to fight, TRO 2.03.244
has he disciplin'd aufidius soundly? COR 2.01.126 P
/nun, | who, disciplin'd, ay, dieted in grace, LC 261

DISCIPLINE 16 FR 0.0018 REL FR 11 V 5 P
this discipline shows thou hast been in love. TGV 3.02. 87
admire | this virtue and this moral discipline, SHR 1.01. 30
call for our chiefest men of discipline | to JN 2.01. 39
though all these english and their discipline 2.01.261
o prudent discipline! 2.01.413
the direction of the military discipline, that H5 3.02.101 P
most valiantly, with excellent discipline. 3.06. 11 P
for discipline ought to be used. 3.06. 56 P
o, negligent and heedless discipline! 1H6 4.02. 44
ireland, | in bringing them to civil discipline, 2H6 1.01.195
your discipline in war, wisdom in peace, | your R3 3.07. 16
let's lack no discipline, make no delay, | for, 5.03. 17
from a tutor, and discipline come not near thee! TRO 2.03. 30 P
speaking too loud, or tainting his discipline, OTH 2.01.268 P
their discipline | (now wing-led with their CYM 2.04. 23
ever you can make, | whose discipline is riot. STM II.C 113

DISCIPLINES 7 FR 0.0008 REL FR 0 V 7 P
is not according to the disciplines of the war; H5 3.02. 59 P
directions in the true disciplines of the wars, 3.02. 72 P
look you, of the roman disciplines, than is a 3.02. 73 P
in the disciplines of the pristine wars of the 3.02. 81 P
or concerning the disciplines of the war, the 3.02. 96 P
man as yourself, both in the disciplines of war, 3.02.129 P
as to tell you i know the disciplines of war; 3.02.140 P

DISCLAIM 3 FR 0.0003 REL FR 3 V 0 P
them now, | and straight disclaim their tongues? COR 3.01. 35
here i disclaim all my paternal care, LR 1.01.113
us, i disclaim | if thou once think upon her! TNK 2.02.173

DISCLAIM'D 1 FR 0.0001 REL FR 1 V 0 P
son, | i have disclaim'd sir robert and my land, JN 1.01.247

DISCLAIMING 2 FR 0.0002 REL FR 2 V 0 P
gage, | disclaiming here the kinred of the king, R2 1.01. 70
let my disclaiming from a purpos'd evil | free HAM 5.02.241

DISCLAIMS 1 FR 0.0001 REL FR 0 V 1 P
you cowardly rascal, nature disclaims in thee: LR 2.02. 54 P

DISCLAIM'ST 1 FR 0.0001 REL FR 1 V 0 P
art a woman, and disclaim'st | flinty mankind, TIM 4.03.483

DISCLOS'D 6 FR 0.0006 REL FR 6 V 0 P
that which thyself hast now disclos'd to me. TGV 3.01. 32
that in words which his eye hath disclos'd. LLL 2.01.251
which once disclos'd, | the ladies did change 5.02.467
the sum of all i can i have disclos'd. R3 2.04. 46
how covert matters may be best disclos'd, | and JC 4.01. 46
too oft before their buttons be disclos'd, | and HAM 1.03. 40

DISCLOSE 4 FR 0.0004 REL FR 4 V 0 P
come, disclose | the state of your affection, AWW 1.03.189
tell me your counsels, i will not disclose 'em. JC 2.01.298
and i do doubt the hatch and the disclose | will HAM 3.01.166
that could think, and nev'r disclose her mind, OTH 2.01.156
DISCLOSED 2 FR 0.0002 REL FR 2 V 0 P
the heart's still rhetoric disclosed with eyes, LLL 2.01.229
when that her golden couplets are disclosed, HAM 5.01.287
DISCLOSES 1 FR 0.0001 REL FR 1 V 0 P
summer's breath their masked buds discloses; SON 54. 8
DISCOLOR 1 FR 0.0001 REL FR 1 V 0 P
tawny ground with your red blood | discolor; H5 3.06.162
DISCOLOR'D 2 FR 0.0002 REL FR 2 V 0 P
to lie discolor'd by this place of peace? ROM 5.03.143
and then with lank and lean discolor'd cheek, LUC 708
DISCOLORED 2 FR 0.0002 REL FR 2 V 0 P
lies, | coldly embracing the discolored earth, JN 2.01.306
or with their blood stain this discolored shore. 2H6 4.01. 11
DISCOLORS 1 FR 0.0001 REL FR 0 V 1 P
me, though it discolors the complexion of my 2H4 2.02. 4 P
DISCOMFIT 1 FR 0.0001 REL FR 1 V 0 P
uncurable discomfit | reigns in the hearts of 2H6 5.02. 86
DISCOMFITED 4 FR 0.0004 REL FR 4 V 0 P
well, go with me and be not so discomfited. SHR 2.01.163
the earl of douglas is discomfited: 1H4 1.01. 67
in his enterprises | discomfited great douglas, 3.02.114
cade, | who since i heard to be discomfited. 2H6 5.01. 63
DISCOMFITURE 1 FR 0.0001 REL FR 1 V 0 P
of loss, of slaughter, and discomfiture: 1H6 1.01. 59
DISCOMFORT 8 FR 0.0009 REL FR 7 V 1 P
discomfort guides my tongue | and bids me speak R2 3.02. 65
is return'd with some discomfort from wales. 2H4 1.02.104 P
my lord, you do discomfort all the host. TRO 5.10. 10
not be in our camp, | lest it discomfort us. JC 5.03.106
comfort seem'd to come | discomfort swells. MAC 1.02. 28
it would be my disgrace and your discomfort. 4.02. 29
discomfort you, my lord, it nothing must, | /for HAM 3.02.166
mean you, sir, | to give them this discomfort? ANT 4.02. 34
DISCOMFORTABLE 1 FR 0.0001 REL FR 1 V 0 P
discomfortable cousin, know'st thou not | that R2 3.02. 36
DISCOMMEND 1 FR 0.0001 REL FR 0 V 1 P
out of my dialect, which you discommend so much. LR 2.02.109 P
DISCONSOLATE 1 FR 0.0001 REL FR 1 V 0 P
all disconsolate, | with pindarus his bondman, JC 5.03. 55
DISCONTENT 19 FR 0.0021 REL FR 17 V 2 P
hath often still'd my brawling discontent. MM 4.01. 9
can you make no use of your discontent? ADO 1.03. 38 P
sister, content you in my discontent. SHR 1.01. 80
what may be wrought out of their discontent, JN 3.04.179
doth move the murmuring lips of discontent | to 4.02. 53
i see your brows are full of discontent, | your R2 4.01.331
for what's more miserable than discontent? 2H6 3.01.201
heart's discontent and sour affliction | be 3.02.301
mine full of sorrow and heart's discontent. 3H6 3.03.173
now is the winter of our discontent | made R3 1.01. 1
and let not discontent | daunt all your hopes. TIT 1.01.267
my soul, my lord leans wondrously to discontent. TIM 3.04. 70 P
i leave /you, sir, | to th' worst of discontent. CYM 2.03.155
losing her woes in shows of discontent. LUC 1580
why art thou thus attir'd in discontent? 1601
thy discontent thou didst bequeath to me. PP 10.12
falls | under the blow of thralled discontent, SON 124. 7
not prizing her poor infant's discontent; 143. 8
big discontent so breaking their contents. LC 56
DISCONTENTED 13 FR 0.0014 REL FR 13 V 0 P
me, till i have pleas'd | my discontented peers! JN 4.02.127
our discontented counties do revolt; 5.01. 8
as doth the blushing discontented sun | from out R2 3.03. 63
duke | hath banish'd moody discontented fury, 1H6 3.01.123
i know a discontented gentleman | whose humble R3 4.02. 36
soul | leads discontented steps in foreign soil, 4.04.312
if that your moody discontented souls | do 5.01. 7
he's discontented. H8 3.02. 91
replied | to th' discontented members, the COR 1.01.111
but as a discontented friend, grief–shot | with 5.01. 44
i'll cheer up | my discontented troops, and lay TIM 3.05.114
now here's another discontented paper, | found OTH 5.02.314
know | if 'twill tie up thy discontented sword, ANT 2.06. 6
DISCONTENTING 1 FR 0.0001 REL FR 1 V 0 P
your discontenting father strive to qualify, WT 4.04.532
DISCONTENTS 7 FR 0.0008 REL FR 7 V 0 P
now powers from home and discontents at home JN 4.03.151
and to your quick–conceiving discontents | i'll 1H4 1.03.189
of fickle changelings and poor discontents, 5.01. 76
dissemble all your griefs and discontents. TIT 1.01.443
his discontents are unremovably | coupled to TIM 5.01.224
to the ports | the discontents repair, and men's ANT 1.04. 39
sire, | subject and servile to all discontents, VEN 1161
DISCONTINUE 1 FR 0.0001 REL FR 0 V 1 P
i must discontinue your company. ADO 5.01.189 P
DISCONTINUED 1 FR 0.0001 REL FR 1 V 0 P
that men shall swear i have discontinued school MV 3.04. 75
DISCORD 19 FR 0.0021 REL FR 17 V 2 P
and discord shall bestrew | the union of your TMP 4.01. 20
the enmity and discord which of late | sprung ERR 1.01. 5
i never heard | so musical a discord, such sweet MND 4.01.118
how shall we find the concord of this discord? 5.01. 60
we shall have shortly discord in the spheres. AYL 2.07. 6
his jarring, concord, and his discord, dulcet; AWW 1.01.172
set armed discord 'twixt these perjur'd kings! JN 3.01.111
you two never meet but you fall to some discord. 2H4 2.04. 56 P
o, how this discord doth afflict my soul! 1H6 3.01.106
so will this base and envious discord breed. 3.01.193
that sees | this jarring discord of nobility, 4.01.188
let not your private discord keep away | the 4.04. 22
hell, | an age of discord and continual strife? 5.05. 63
that string, | and hark what discord follows. TRO 1.03.110
my soul is full of discord and dismay. HAM 4.01. 45
in countries, discord; LR 1.02.108 P
perch or sing, | or with them any discord bring, TNK 1.01. 23
melodious discord, heavenly tune harsh sounding, VEN 431
my restless discord loves no stops nor rests; LUC 1124
DISCORD'S 1 FR 0.0001 REL FR 1 V 0 P
should the empress know | this discord's ground, TIT 2.01. 70
DISCORDS 5 FR 0.0005 REL FR 4 V 1 P
and chatt'ring pies in dismal discords sung; 3H6 5.06. 48
of us, look to hear nothing but discords. ROM 3.01. 48 P
straining harsh discords and unpleasing sharps. 3.05. 28
and i for winking at your discords too | have 5.03.294
the greatest discords be | that e'er our hearts OTH 2.01.198
DISCOURSE 64 FR 0.0072 REL FR 48 V 16 P
of tongue) a kind | of excellent dumb discourse. TMP 3.03. 39
i'll waste | with such discourse as, i not doubt 5.01.304
hear sweet discourse, converse with noblemen, TGV 1.03. 31
leave off discourse of disability. 2.04.109
now no discourse, except it be of love; 2.04.140
how likes she my discourse? 5.02. 15
but well, when i discourse of love and peace. 5.02. 17
therefore i pray you stand not to discourse, 5.02. 44
with our discourse to make your grace to smile. 5.04.163
of excellent breeding, admirable discourse, of WIV 2.02.226 P
would seem in me t' affect speech and discourse, MM 1.01. 4
when she will play with reason and discourse, 1.02.185
if voluble and sharp discourse be marr'd, ERR 2.01. 92
i know a wench of excellent discourse, | pretty 3.01.109
of such enchanting presence and discourse, 3.02.161
the body of your discourse is sometime guarded ADO 1.01.286 P
of good discourse, an excellent musician, and 2.03. 34 P
and our whole discourse | is all of her. 3.01. 5
so sweet and voluble is his discourse. LLL 2.01. 76
it is an epilogue or discourse, to make plain 3.01. 81
his humor is lofty, his discourse peremptory, 5.01. 10 P
of this discourse we more will hear anon. MND 4.01.178
masters, i am to discourse wonders; 4.02. 29 P
and lovers twain | at large discourse, while 5.01.151
wittiest partition that ever i heard discourse, 5.01.168 P
and discourse grow commendable in none only but MV 3.05. 45 P
surprise her with discourse of my dear faith; TN 1.04. 25
so far exceed all instance, all discourse, 4.03. 12
and yet your fair discourse hath been as sugar, R2 2.03. 6
list his discourse of war, and you shall hear H5 1.01. 43
it is no time to discourse, so chrish save me. 3.02.105 P
it is no time to discourse. 3.02.107 P
discourse, i prithee, on this turret's top. 1H6 1.04. 26
nephew, what means this passionate discourse, 2H6 1.01.104
how haps it in this smooth discourse | you told 3H6 3.03. 88
untouch'd or slightly handled in discourse. R3 3.07. 19
and ample interchange of sweet discourse | which 5.03. 99
handlest in thy discourse, o, that her hand, TRO 1.01. 55
beauty, good shape, discourse, manhood, learning 1.02.253 P
so madly hot that no discourse of reason, | nor 2.02.116
in his blood such swoll'n and hot discourse 2.03.173
o madness of discourse, | that cause sets up, 5.02.142
turns up the white o' th' eye to his discourse. COR 4.05.196 P
the crying babe controll'd with this discourse: TIT 5.01. 26
when with his solemn tongue he did discourse 5.03. 81
according to the which thou shalt discourse | to JC 3.01.295
o god, a beast, that wants discourse of reason, HAM 1.02.150
should admit no discourse to your beauty. 3.01.107 P
my lord, put your discourse into some frame, and 3.02.308 P
and it will discourse most eloquent music. 3.02.359 P
and with th' incorporal air do hold discourse? 3.04.118
sure he that made us with such large discourse, 4.04. 36
and with a greedy ear | devour up my discourse. OTH 1.03.150
and discourse fustian with one's own shadow? 2.03.280 P
give me advantage of some brief discourse | with 3.01. 52
either in discourse of thought or actual deed, 4.02.153
shall we discourse | the freezing hours away? CYM 3.03. 38
discourse is heavy, fasting; 3.06. 90
i'll then discourse our woes, felt several years PER 1.04. 18
look merrily, discourse of many things, but TNK 2.01. 39 P
and ev'ry day discourse you into health, | as i 3.06. 38
i dare as well | die as discourse or sleep. 3.06.129
"bid me discourse, i will enchant thine ear, VEN 145
my thoughts and my discourse as madmen's are, SON 147.11
DISCOURSED 2 FR 0.0002 REL FR 2 V 0 P
and hear at large discoursed all our fortunes; ERR 5.01.396
appear | at large discoursed in this paper here. R2 5.06. 10
DISCOURSER 1 FR 0.0001 REL FR 1 V 0 P
would by a good discourser lose some life, H8 1.01. 41
DISCOURSES 4 FR 0.0004 REL FR 3 V 1 P
she discourses, she carves, she gives the leer WIV 1.03. 45 P
are my discourses dull? ERR 2.01. 91
her eye discourses, i will answer it. ROM 2.02. 13
for sweet discourses in our times to come. 3.05. 53
DISCOURTESY 1 FR 0.0001 REL FR 1 V 0 P
i shall unfold equal discourtesy | to your best CYM 2.03. 96
DISCOVER 34 FR 0.0038 REL FR 24 V 10 P
some to discover islands far away; TGV 1.03. 9
some messenger, that might her mind discover, 2.01.167
lord, that which i would discover | the law of 3.01. 4
feeling line | that may discover such integrity: 3.02. 76
i shall discover a thing to you, wherein i must WIV 2.02.183 P
him that thou wouldst discover if thou couldst, MM 2.01.186 P
my lips in vain, or discover his government. 3.01.193 P
seen them both, and will discover the favor. 4.02.172 P
discover how, and thou shalt find me just. ERR 5.01.203
it by some other, if she will not discover it. ADO 2.03.155 P
there be any impediment, i pray you discover it. 3.02. 94 P
what your wisdoms could not discover, these 5.01.233 P
go, draw aside the curtains and discover | the MV 2.07. 1
to me, | i'll discover that which shall undo the AWW 4.01. 73
shall the contents discover, something rare WT 3.01. 20
thing that is fitting to be known — discover. 4.04.720 P
to discover | what power the duke of york had R2 2.03. 33
and thence discover how with most advantage 1H6 1.04. 12
discover more at large what cause that was, 2.05. 59
then, joan, discover thine infirmity, | that 5.04. 60
stand where the torch may not discover us. TRO 5.02. 5
why then you should discover a brace of COR 2.01. 43 P
that may fully discover him their opposite. 2.02. 20 P
up, | or else i will discover nought to thee. TIT 5.01. 85
i can discover all | the unlucky manage of this ROM 3.01.142
will modestly discover to yourself | that of JC 1.02. 69
that by no means i may discover them | by any 2.01. 75
curst speech | i threaten'd to discover him; LR 2.01. 66
i think i can discover him, if you please | to OTH 1.01.178
where their appointment we may best discover, ANT 4.10. 8
yond pine does stand | i shall discover all; 4.12. 2
discover to me | what both you spur and stop. CYM 1.06. 98
discover where thy mistress is, at once, | at 3.05. 95
what company | discover you abroad? 4.02.130
DISCOVER'D 11 FR 0.0012 REL FR 8 V 3 P
the prince discover'd to claudio that he lov'd ADO 1.02. 11 P
of a maid — that you have discover'd thus. 2.02. 40 P
so traitorously discover'd the secrets of your AWW 4.03.304 P
he has discover'd my design, and i | remain a WT 2.01. 50
our purposes god justly hath discover'd, | and i H5 2.02.151
heaven, | to be discover'd, that can do me good? R3 4.04.241
most wisely hath ulysses here discover'd | the TRO 1.03.138
thou hast painfully discover'd; TIM 5.02. 1
if i discover'd not which way she was gone, | it CYM 5.05.277
shall be discover'd, please you sit and hark. PER 5.ch. 24
and discover'd how | and by whose means he TNK 4.01. 19
DISCOVERED 7 FR 0.0008 REL FR 7 V 0 P
to hear | the story of your loves discovered; TGV 5.04.171
calm, and we discovered | two ships from far, ERR 1.01. 91
by your espials were discovered | two mightier 1H6 4.03. 6
how easily murder is discovered! TIT 2.03.287
what god will have discovered for revenge. 4.01. 74
love, | which the dark night hath so discovered. ROM 2.02.106
i fear our purpose is discovered. JC 3.01. 17
DISCOVERERS 1 FR 0.0001 REL FR 1 V 0 P
and send discoverers forth | to know the numbers 2H4 4.01. 3
DISCOVERIES 3 FR 0.0003 REL FR 0 V 3 P
pretending in her discoveries of dishonor; MM 3.01.227 P
for a week escape a great deal of discoveries, AWW 3.06. 92 P
and take again such preposterous discoveries! TRO 5.01. 24 P
DISCOVERS 3 FR 0.0003 REL FR 1 V 2 P
so near the life of passion as she discovers it. ADO 2.03.106 P
daylight and champian discovers not more. TN 2.05.160 P
your painted gloss discovers, | to men that H8 5.02.106
DISCOVERY 14 FR 0.0015 REL FR 12 V 2 P
a wink beyond, | but doubt discovery there. TMP 2.01.243
cunningly | that my discovery be not aimed at: TGV 3.01. 45
why, 'tis an office of discovery, love, | and i MV 2.06. 43
inch of delay more is a south–sea of discovery. AYL 3.02.197 P
which are here | by this discovery lost. WT 1.02.441
at the discovery of most dangerous treason H5 2.02.162
by the discovery | we shall be short'ned in our COR 1.02. 22
so close, | so far from sounding and discovery, ROM 1.01.150
with a discovery of the infinite flatteries TIM 5.01. 36
host, and make discovery | err in report of us. MAC 5.04. 6
so shall my anticipation prevent your discovery, HAM 2.02.294 P
by diligent discovery, but your haste | is now LR 5.01. 53
having lost the fair discovery of her way. VEN 828
she dares not thereof make discovery, | lest he LUC 1314
DISCOV'RY 1 FR 0.0001 REL FR 1 V 0 P
on thee, lafew, | to bring forth this discov'ry. AWW 5.03.151
DISCREDIT 5 FR 0.0005 REL FR 4 V 1 P
fie upon him, he will discredit our mystery. MM 4.02. 28 P
breach | discredit more in hiding of the fault JN 4.02. 33
dirt, | to weaken /or discredit our exposure, TRO 1.03.195
it would discredit the blest gods, proud man, 4.05.247
not rather | discredit my authority with yours, ANT 2.02. 49
DISCREDITED 2 FR 0.0002 REL FR 0 V 2 P
i (by my good leisure) have discredited to him, MM 3.02.247 P
blest withal would have discredited your travel. ANT 1.02.155 P
DISCREDITS 1 FR 0.0001 REL FR 0 V 1 P
not have relish'd among my other discredits. WT 5.02.123 P
DISCREET 7 FR 0.0008 REL FR 4 V 3 P
nor no railing in a known discreet man, though TN 1.05. 95 P
their dispatch | with such a smooth, discreet, 4.03. 19
breeds no bate with telling of discreet stories; 2H4 2.04.250 P
you that will be less fearful than discreet; COR 3.01.150
a madness most discreet, | a choking gall, and a ROM 1.01.193
then necessity | will call discreet proceeding. LR 1.04.214
prating — let not thy discreet heart think it. OTH 2.01.224 P
DISCREETLY 2 FR 0.0002 REL FR 1 V 1 P
the cause with as great discreetly as we can. WIV 1.01.146 P
you use your manners discreetly in all kind of SHR 1.01.242
DISCRETION 33 FR 0.0037 REL FR 12 V 21 P
i will not adventure my discretion so weakly. TMP 2.01.188 P
that can with some discretion do my business — TGV 4.04. 65
it is a fery discretion answer, save the fall is WIV 1.01.253 P
folks, you know, have discretion, as they say, 2.02.130 P
nor do i think the man of safe discretion | that MM 1.01. 71
for either he avoids them with great discretion, ADO 2.03.191 P
purse of wit, thou pigeon–egg of discretion. LLL 5.01. 74 P
of wrong through the little hole of discretion, 5.02.724 P
would have no more discretion but to hang us; MND 1.02. 81 P
true; and a goose for his discretion. 5.01.232 P
for his valor cannot carry his discretion, and 5.01.234 P
his discretion, i am sure, cannot carry his 5.01.235 P
leave it to his discretion, and let us listen to 5.01.237 P
by his small light of discretion, that he is in 5.01.253 P
o dear discretion, how his words are suited! MV 3.05. 65
therefore use thy discretion — i had as lief AYL 1.01.146 P
the better part of valor is discretion, in the 1H4 5.04.120 P
covering discretion with a coat of folly, | as H5 2.04. 38
affability as in discretion you ought to use me, 3.02.127 P
all this was ord'red by the good discretion | of H8 1.01. 50
was it discretion, lords, to let this man, 5.02.172
into folly, his folly sauc'd with discretion. TRO 1.02. 23 P
why, have you any discretion? 1.02.251 P
for though abundantly they lack discretion, COR 1.01.202
yet so far hath discretion fought with nature HAM 1.02. 5
for the younger sort | to lack discretion. 2.01.114
spoken, with good accent and good discretion. 2.02.467 P
but let your own discretion be your tutor. 3.02. 17 P
by some discretion that discerns your state LR 2.04.149
honorable stop, | not to outsport discretion. OTH 2.03. 3
well, do your discretion. 3.03. 34
the greater war between him and his discretion. ANT 2.07. 10 P
was a wise fellow and had good discretion that, PER 1.03. 4 P
DISCRETIONS 3 FR 0.0003 REL FR 1 V 2 P
peradventure prings goot discretions with it: WIV 1.01. 44 P
one of the best discretions of a oman as ever i 4.04. 1 P
but your discretions better can persuade | than 1H6 4.01.158
DISCUSS 6 FR 0.0006 REL FR 1 V 5 P
i will discuss the humor of this love to /page. WIV 1.03. 95 P
speak, breathe, discuss; 4.05. 2 P
th' athversary — you may discuss unto the duke, H5 3.02. 61 P
discuss unto me, art thou officer, | or art thou 4.01. 37
discuss. 4.04. 5 P
discuss the same in french unto him. 4.04. 29 P
DISDAIN 42 FR 0.0047 REL FR 38 V 4 P
sour–ey'd disdain, and discord shall bestrew TMP 4.01. 20
trampling contemptuously on thy disdain. TGV 1.02.109
disdain to root the summer–swelling flow'r | and 2.04.162
knock elsewhere, to see if they'll disdain me. ERR 3.01.121

what, my dear lady disdain! are you yet living? ADO 1.01.118 P
is it possible disdain should die while she hath 1.01.120 P
courtesy itself must convert to disdain, if you 1.01.122 P
disdain and scorn ride sparkling in her eyes, 3.01. 51
and the red glow of scorn and proud disdain, AYL 3.04. 54
bondmaid and a slave of me — | that i disdain; SHR 2.01. 3
senses | all but new things disdain; AWW 1.02. 61
disdain | rather corrupt me ever! 2.03.115
believe not thy disdain, but presently | do 2.03.159
me as these are, | therefore i will not disdain. WT 4.04.747
pride, haughtiness, opinion, and disdain, | the 1H4 3.01.183
holding in disdain the german women | for some H5 1.02. 48
it shall be so, disdain they ne'er so much. 1H6 5.03. 98
normans thorough thee | disdain to call us lord, 2H6 4.01. 88
sun, | exempt from envy, but not from disdain, 3H6 3.03.127
these were her words, utt'red with mild disdain: 4.01. 98
helms, | and i did scorn it and disdain to fly. R3 3.04. 83
the disdain and shame whereof hath ever since TRO 1.02. 34 P
i do disdain thy courtesy, proud troyan. 5.06. 15
they do disdain us much beyond our thoughts, COR 1.04. 26
measles | which we disdain should tetter us, yet 3.01. 79
where /one part does disdain with cause, the 3.01.143
by rule of knighthood, i disdain and spurn. LR 5.03.146
ambitions, covetings, change of prides, disdain, CYM 2.05. 25
boy, | who blush'd and pouted in a dull disdain, VEN 33
obeyed, | yet was he servile to my coy disdain. 112
at this adonis smiles as in disdain, | that in 241
fee, | he held such petty bondage in disdain, 394
and such disdain | that they have murd'red this 501
if so, the world will hold thee in disdain, 761
reproach, disdain, and deadly enmity, | yet LUC 503
thy kinsmen hang their heads at this disdain, 521
this hot desire converts to cold disdain; 691
back, | for it had been dishonor to disdain him. 844
live | disdain to him disdained scraps to give. 987
two the trusty knight was wounded with disdain: PP 15.11
me, | knowing thy heart torment me with disdain, SON 132. 2
my tongue–tied patience with too much disdain, 140. 2

DISDAIN'D 8 FR 0.0009 REL FR 7 V 1 P
fits my blood to be disdain'd of all than to ADO 1.03. 29 P
so proudly as if he disdain'd the ground. R2 5.05. 83
revenge the jeering and disdain'd contempt | of 1H4 1.03.183
the general's disdain'd | by him one step below, TRO 1.03.129
assume a semblance | that very dogs disdain'd; LR 5.03.189
man, a thing | the most disdain'd of fortune. CYM 3.04. 20
seem | like lies disdain'd in the reporting. PER 5.01.119
eyes wooed still, his eyes disdain'd the wooing: VEN 358

DISDAINED 3 FR 0.0003 REL FR 3 V 0 P
for my heart disdained that my tongue | should R2 1.04. 12
behold yourself so by a son disdained; 2H4 5.02. 95
live | disdain to him disdained scraps to give. LUC 987

DISDAINETH 2 FR 0.0002 REL FR 2 V 0 P
and now like nilus it disdaineth bounds. TIT 3.01. 71
yet him for this my love no whit disdaineth: SON 33.13

DISDAINFUL 9 FR 0.0010 REL FR 7 V 2 P
that i was disdainful, and that i had my good ADO 2.01.129 P
no, truly, ursula, she is too disdainful, | i 3.01. 34
lady is in love | with a disdainful youth; MND 2.01.261
you do) | in such disdainful manner me to woo. 2.02.130
praising the proud disdainful shepherdess | that AYL 3.04. 50
as i have lov'd this proud disdainful haggard. SHR 4.02. 39
upbraided or abus'd in disdainful language; H5 3.06.111 P
to accuse it, and | disdainful to be tried by't: H8 2.04.123
for he seems | proud and disdainful, harping on ANT 3.13.142

DISDAINFULLY 2 FR 0.0002 REL FR 2 V 0 P
or else disdainfully, which shall shake him more TRO 3.03. 53
disdainfully did sting | his high–pitch'd LUC 40

DISDAINING 4 FR 0.0004 REL FR 4 V 0 P
which i, disdaining, scorn'd, and craved death 1H6 1.04. 32
knee, | disdaining duty that to us belongs. 2H6 3.01. 17
disdaining fortune, with his brandish'd steel, MAC 1.02. 17
but | disdaining me and throwing favors on | the CYM 3.05. 75

DISDAINS 7 FR 0.0008 REL FR 7 V 0 P
then he disdains to shine, for by the book | he R3 5.03.278
disdains the shadow | which he treads on at noon COR 1.01.260
his semblable, yea, himself, timon disdains; TIM 4.03. 22
solicits here a lady that disdains | thee and CYM 1.06.147
the boy disdains me, | he leaves me, scorns me. 5.05.105
glass, as to | his ear which now disdains you. TNK 3.01. 71
womb | disdains the tillage of thy husbandry? SON 3. 6

DISDAIN'ST 1 FR 0.0001 REL FR 1 V 0 P
'tis only title thou disdain'st in her, the AWW 2.03.117

DISEAS'D 9 FR 0.0010 REL FR 7 V 2 P
be cur'd | of this diseas'd opinion, and betimes WT 1.02.297
o lord, sir, i am a diseas'd man. 2H4 3.02.179 P
we are all diseas'd, | /and /with /our 4.01. 54
hug their diseas'd perfumes, and have forgot TIM 4.03.207
canst thou not minister to a mind diseas'd, MAC 5.03. 40
you a wholesome answer — my wit's diseas'd. HAM 3.02.322 P
with diseas'd ventures | that play with all CYM 1.06.123
to be diseas'd ere that there was true needing. SON 118. 8
a bath and healthful remedy | for men diseas'd, 154.12

/DISEASE 1 FR 0.0001 REL FR 1 V 0 P
/of /which /disease | /our /late /king /richard 2H4 4.01. 57

DISEASE 30 FR 0.0034 REL FR 20 V 10 P
fall and make him | by inch–meal a disease! TMP 2.02. 3
his dissolute disease will scarce obey this WIV 3.03.192 P
o lord, he will hang upon him like a disease; ADO 1.01. 86 P
and that his lady mourns at his disease. SHR in.1. 62
it would be the death of the king's disease. AWW 1.01. 23 P
the king's disease — my project may deceive me, 1.01.228
many thousand on 's | have the disease, and WT 1.02.207
but | i cannot name the disease, and it is 1.02.386
before the curing of a strong disease, | even in JN 3.04.112
i think you are fall'n into the disease, for you 2H4 1.02.118 P
please you, it is the disease of not list'ning, 1.02.121 P
lingers it out, but the disease is incurable. 1.02.238 P
what disease hast thou? 3.02.180 P
this part of his conjoins with my disease, | and 4.05. 63
and in that ease, i'll tell thee my disease. 1H6 2.05. 44
appliance only | which your disease requires. H8 1.01.125
is now, she will but disease our better mirth. COR 1.03.105 P
very poisonous | where the disease is violent. 3.01.221
he's a disease that must be cut away. 3.01.293
o, he's a limb that has but a disease: 3.01.294
thou disease of a friend, and not himself! TIM 3.01. 53
air, | with his disease of all–shunn'd poverty, 4.02. 14
what's the disease he means? MAC 4.03.146
this disease is beyond my practice; 5.01. 59 P
cast | the water of my land, find her disease, 5.03. 51
fit, | but, like the owner of a foul disease, HAM 4.01. 21
and /the fee bestow | upon the foul disease. LR 1.01.164
or rather a disease that's in my flesh, | which 2.04.222
well, as for him, he brought his disease hither; PER 4.02.110 P
for that which longer nurseth the disease, SON 147. 2

DISEASED 1 FR 0.0001 REL FR 1 V 0 P
diseased nature oftentimes breaks forth | in 1H4 3.01. 26

DISEASES 22 FR 0.0024 REL FR 11 V 11 P
purchas'd as many diseases under her roof as MM 1.02. 46 P
thou art always figuring diseases in me; 1.02. 53 P
the air, | that rheumatic diseases do abound. MND 2.01.105
subject to the same diseases, heal'd by the same MV 3.01. 62 P
the fool's bolt, sir, and such dulcet diseases. AYL 5.04. 65 P
she have as many diseases as two and fifty SHR 1.02. 81 P
it, he might have moe diseases than he knew for. 2H4 1.02. 5 P
i will turn diseases to commodity. 1.02.248 P
gluttony and diseases make, i make them not. 2.04. 42 P
gluttony, you help to make the diseases, doll. 2.04. 45 P
how foul it is, what rank diseases grow, | and 3.01. 39
carriage is caught, as men take diseases, one of 5.01. 76 P
hath made me full of sickness and diseases. 2H6 4.07. 89
physic, their diseases | are grown so catching. H8 1.03. 36
now the rotten diseases of the south, the TRO 5.01. 18 P
and at that time bequeath you my diseases. 5.10. 56
o, may diseases only work upon't! TIM 3.01. 60
give them diseases, leaving with thee their lust 4.03. 85
and may diseases lick up their false bloods! 4.03.532
diseases desperate grown | by desperate HAM 4.03. 9
but we do launch | diseases in our bodies. ANT 5.01. 37
diseases have been sold dearer than physic — PER 4.06. 98

DISEDG'D 1 FR 0.0001 REL FR 1 V 0 P
when thou shalt be disedg'd by her | that now CYM 3.04. 93

DISEMBARK 2 FR 0.0002 REL FR 2 V 0 P
to disembark | some necessaries that i needs TGV 2.04.187
iago, | go to the bay and disembark my coffers. OTH 2.01.208

DISENSANITY 1 FR 0.0001 REL FR 1 V 0 P
what tediosity and disensanity | is here among TNK 3.05. 2

DISFIGURE 5 FR 0.0005 REL FR 3 V 2 P
to scorch your face, and to disfigure you. ERR 5.01.183
disfigure not his shop. LLL 4.03. 57
his power | to leave the figure or disfigure it. MND 1.01. 51
and say he comes to disfigure, or to present, 3.01. 60 P
in her face, and so disfigure her with it, that SHR 1.02.114 P

DISFIGURED 2 FR 0.0002 REL FR 2 V 0 P
face | of plain old form is much disfigured, JN 4.02. 22
by you unhappied and disfigured clean; R2 3.01. 10

DISFURNISH 3 FR 0.0003 REL FR 1 V 2 P
of which if you should here disfurnish me, | you TGV 4.01. 14
beast was i to disfurnish myself against such a TIM 3.02. 44 P
or she'll disfurnish us of all our cavalleria, PER 4.06. 11 P

DISGEST *(also digest, etc.)*

DISGEST 3 FR 0.0003 REL FR 3 V 0 P
'mong other things | i shall disgest it. MV 3.05. 90
disgest things rightly | touching the weal a' COR 1.01.150
which gives men stomach to disgest his words JC 1.02.301

DISGESTED 1 FR 0.0001 REL FR 0 V 1 P
to be glad that matters are so well disgested. ANT 2.02.176 P

DISGESTION 1 FR 0.0001 REL FR 1 V 0 P
but for your health and your disgestion sake, TRO 2.03.111

DISGESTIONS 1 FR 0.0001 REL FR 0 V 1 P
appetites and your disgestions doo's not agree H5 5.01. 26 P

/DISGORGE 2 FR 0.0002 REL FR 2 V 0 P
/didst /thou /disgorge | /thy /glutton /bosom 2H4 1.03. 97
/the //deep–drawing /barks /do /there /disgorge TRO pr 12

DISGORGE 1 FR 0.0001 REL FR 1 V 0 P
wouldst thou disgorge into the general world. AYL 2.07. 69

DISGORGES 1 FR 0.0001 REL FR 1 V 0 P
grisled north | disgorges such a tempest forth, PER 3.ch. 48

DISGRAC'D 14 FR 0.0015 REL FR 10 V 4 P
your grace is welcome to a man disgrac'd, TGV 5.04.123
how you disgrac'd her when you should marry her. ADO 5.01.238 P
he hath disgrac'd me, and hind'red me half a MV 3.01. 54 P
are very rascals since bonds disgrac'd them. TN 3.01. 21 P
and i | play too, but so disgrac'd a part, whose WT 1.02.188
i am disgrac'd, impeach'd, and baffled here, R2 1.01.170
disgrac'd me in my happy victories, | sought to 1H4 4.03. 97
who was shot, who disgrac'd, what terms the H5 3.06. 74 P
when you disgrac'd me in my embassade | then i 3H6 4.03. 32
myself disgrac'd, and the nobility | held in R3 1.03. 78
thy crown, usurp'd, disgrac'd his kingly glory. 4.04.371
law o'ertake ye, | you'll part away disgrac'd. H8 3.01. 97
h'as much disgrac'd me in't, i'm angry at him, TIM 3.03. 13
and right perfection wrongfully disgrac'd, | and SON 66. 7

DISGRACE 56 FR 0.0063 REL FR 43 V 13 P
there is not only disgrace and dishonor in that, TMP 4.01.209 P
unworthily, disgrace the man | (a rashness that TGV 3.01. 29
where we may take him, and disgrace him for it. WIV 4.04. 15
her, i will join with thee to disgrace her. ADO 3.02.127 P
to disgrace hero before the whole assembly, and 4.02. 54 P
and then grace us in the disgrace of death; LLL 1.01. 3
his disgrace is to be called boy, but his glory 1.02.179 P
thy grace being gain'd cures all disgrace in me. 4.03. 65
like tears that did their own disgrace bewail. MND 4.01. 56
or brook such disgrace well as he shall run into AYL 1.01.134 P
for if thou dost him any slight disgrace, or if 1.01.148 P
find in my heart to disgrace my man's apparel 2.04. 4 P
thou hast a son shall take this disgrace off me, AWW 2.03.235 P
but to my own disgrace | neglected my sworn duty R2 1.01.133
and spit it bleeding in his high disgrace, 1.01.194
about his marriage, nor my own disgrace, | have 2.01.168
and i will take it as a sweet disgrace | and 2H4 1.01. 89
what a disgrace is it to me to remember thy name 2.02. 13 P
we have lost, the disgrace we have digested; H5 3.06.128 P
and for our disgrace, his own person kneeling at 3.06.132 P
we shall much disgrace | with four or five most 4.pr. 49
you have congreeted, let it not disgrace me, 5.02. 31
come, come, 'tis only i that must disgrace thee. 1H6 1.05. 8
blood, and in disgrace | bespoke him thus: 4.06. 20
disgrace not so your king, | that he should be 5.05. 48
till we have brought duke humphrey in disgrace. 2H6 1.03. 96
and spread they shall be, to thy foul disgrace, 3H6 1.01.253
this deep disgrace in brotherhood | touches me R3 1.01.111
to the disgrace and downfall of your house; 3.07.217
pray heaven he sound not my disgrace! H8 5.02. 13
that in their country did them that disgrace TRO 2.02. 95
disgrace to your great worths, and shame to me, 2.02.151
not think to fob off our disgrace with a tale. COR 1.01. 94 P
part, and i am out, | even to a full disgrace. 5.03. 42
our empress' shame, and stately rome's disgrace! TIT 4.02. 60
them, which is disgrace to them if they bear it. ROM 1.01. 43 P
feast, i hear | macduff lives in disgrace. MAC 3.06. 23
it would be my disgrace and your discomfort. 4.02. 29
no disgrace | shall fall you for refusing him at ANT 3.07. 38
inevitable prosecution of | disgrace and horror, 4.14. 66
my father ever hated — | disgrace and blows. TNK 2.05. 59
my love to love is love but to disgrace it, VEN 412
and the red rose blush at her own disgrace, LUC 479
the same disgrace which they themselves behold; 751
cloak | immodestly lies martyr'd with disgrace. 802
"o unseen shame, invisible disgrace! 827
tears may grace the fashion | of her disgrace, 1320
thy grace being gain'd cures all disgrace in me. PP 3. 8
when in disgrace with fortune and men's eyes, SON 29. 1
stealing unseen to west with this disgrace: 33. 8
heals the wound, and cures not the disgrace; 34. 8
thou canst not, love, disgrace me half so ill, 89. 5
as i'll myself disgrace, knowing thy will: 89. 7
dulling my lines, and doing me disgrace. 103. 8
may time disgrace and wretched /minutes kill. 126. 8
but is profan'd, if not lives in disgrace. 127. 8

DISGRACED 3 FR 0.0003 REL FR 3 V 0 P
to be disgraced by an inkhorn mate, | we and our 1H6 3.01. 99
through the length of times he stands disgraced; LUC 718
rome herself in them doth stand disgraced) | by 1833

DISGRACEFUL 1 FR 0.0001 REL FR 1 V 0 P
away with these disgraceful wailing robes! 1H6 1.01. 86

DISGRACE'S 1 FR 0.0001 REL FR 1 V 0 P
thyself | from top of honor to disgrace's feet? 2H6 1.02. 49

DISGRACES 5 FR 0.0005 REL FR 4 V 1 P
and disgraces have of late knock'd too often at AWW 4.01. 27 P
causeless have laid disgraces on my head, | and 2H6 3.01.162
but that you shall sustain moe new disgraces H8 3.02. 5
how eagerly ye follow my disgraces | as if it 3.02.240
parcel the sum of my disgraces by | addition of ANT 5.02.163

DISGRACING 1 FR 0.0001 REL FR 1 V 0 P
disgracing of these colors that i wear | in 1H6 3.04. 29

DISGRACIOUS 2 FR 0.0002 REL FR 2 V 0 P
that seems disgracious in the city's eye, | and R3 3.07.112
if i be so disgracious in your eye, | let me 4.04.178

/DISGUIS'D 3 FR 0.0003 REL FR 3 V 0 P
/disguis'd /like /herne, /with /huge /horns /on WIV 4.04. 43
/jove /sometime /went /disguis'd, /and /why /not 2H6 4.01. 48
or by the break of day /disguis'd from hence. ROM 3.03.168

DISGUIS'D 14 FR 0.0015 REL FR 10 V 4 P
die, sir john — unless you go out disguis'd. WIV 4.02. 67 P
known unto these, and to myself disguis'd? ERR 2.02.214
love doth approach disguis'd, | armed in LLL 5.02. 83
that by and by disguis'd /they will be here. 5.02. 96
mock them still, as well known as disguis'd. 5.02.301
disguis'd like muscovites, in shapeless gear; 5.02.303
were not you here but even now, disguis'd? 5.02.433
to come in disguis'd against me to try a fall. AYL 1.01.125 P
and offer me disguis'd in sober robes | to old SHR 1.02.132
tellus," disguis'd thus to get your love, "hic 3.01. 33 P
all this while | you were disguis'd. JN 4.01.126
ship–boy's semblance hath disguis'd me quite. 4.03. 4
here comes the lord lysimachus disguis'd. PER 4.06. 17 P
cheeks with chops and wrinkles were disguis'd, LUC 1452

/DISGUISE 1 FR 0.0001 REL FR 1 V 0 P
/who /in /disguise | /followed /his /enemy /king LR 5.03.220

DISGUISE 20 FR 0.0022 REL FR 16 V 4 P
if shame live | in a disguise of love! TGV 5.04.107
into't, and i have a disguise to sound falstaff. WIV 2.01.238 P
how might we disguise him? 4.02. 68 P
in which disguise, | while other jests are 4.06. 21
so disguise shall by th' disguised | pay with MM 3.02.280
i will assume thy part in some disguise, | and ADO 1.01.321
disguise us at my lodging, and return | all in MV 2.04. 2
but one that scorn to live in this disguise SHR 4.02. 18
when his disguise and he is parted, tell me what AWW 3.06.104 P
only in this disguise i think't no sin | to 4.02. 75
my aid | for such disguise as haply shall become TN 1.02. 54
disguise, i see thou art a wickedness | wherein 2.02. 27
my best camillo! we must disguise ourselves. WT 4.02. 54 P
disguise fair nature with hard–favor'd rage; H5 3.01. 8
disguise the holy strength of their command, TRO 2.03.127
the wild disguise hath almost | antick'd us all. ANT 2.07.124
your fortune is, and but disguise | that which, CYM 3.04.144
venture, | and in some poor disguise be there. TNK 2.03. 79
and in this disguise, | against /thy own edict, 3.06.144
by, | wherein deep policy did him disguise, LUC 1815

DISGUISED 2 FR 0.0002 REL FR 2 V 0 P
so disguise shall by th' disguised | pay with MM 3.02.280
disguised cheaters, prating mountebanks, | and ERR 1.02.101

DISGUISER 1 FR 0.0001 REL FR 0 V 1 P
o, death's a great disguiser, and you may add to MM 4.02.174 P

DISGUISES 2 FR 0.0002 REL FR 0 V 2 P
be a fancy that he hath to strange disguises — ADO 3.02. 33 P
ned, where are our disguises? 1H4 2.02. 74 P

DISGUISING 2 FR 0.0002 REL FR 2 V 0 P
of their disguising and pretended flight, | who, TGV 2.06. 37
to our hearts, | disguising what they are. MAC 3.02. 35

DISH 33 FR 0.0037 REL FR 12 V 21 P
nor scrape trenchering, nor wash dish. TMP 2.02.183
fence (three veneys for a dish of stew'd prunes) WIV 1.01.285 P
than half stew'd in grease, like a dutch dish) 3.05.119 P
in a fruit–dish, a dish of some threepence — MM 2.01. 92 P
go to, go to; no matter for the dish, sir. 2.01. 95 P
and having but two in the dish (as i said), 2.01.100 P
full of welcome makes scarce one dainty dish. ERR 3.01. 23
sir, here's a dish i love not, i cannot endure ADO 2.01.274 P
four woodcocks in a dish! LLL 4.03. 80
i have here a dish of doves that i would bestow MV 2.02.135 P
slut were to put good meat into an unclean dish. AYL 3.03. 37 P
a dish that i do love to feed upon. SHR 4.03. 24
here, take away this dish. 4.03. 44
was moulded on a porringer — | a velvet dish. 4.03. 65
what dish a' poison has she dress'd him! TN 2.05.112 P
edge, | for a quart of ale is a dish for a king. WT 4.03. 8
gown, | my figur'd goblets for a dish of wood, R2 3.03.150
for moving such a dish of skim–milk with so 1H4 2.03. 33 P
thou never see titan kiss a dish of butter, 2.04.120 P

telling us she had a good dish of prawns, 2H4 2.01. 96 P
the prince once set a dish of apple–johns before 2.04. 5 P
of mine own graffing, with a dish of caraways, 5.03. 3 P
there's a dish of leather–coats for you. 5.03. 41 P
yea, like fair fruit in an unwholesome dish, TRO 2.03.120
why, thou full dish of fool, from troy. 5.01. 9 P
him | his friend that dips in the same dish? TIM 3.02. 66
let's carve him as a dish fit for the gods, JC 2.01.173
i' faith — of the chameleon's dish, i eat the HAM 3.02. 93 P
he will to his egyptian dish again. ANT 2.06.126 P
i know that a woman is a dish for the gods, if 5.02.274 P
for the dish, | poor tributary rivers as sweet CYM 4.02. 35
to the spectators, the dish pays the shot. 5.04.156 P
up, my dish of chastity with rosemary and bays! PER 4.06.150 P
DISHABITED 1 FR 0.0001 REL FR 1 V 0 P
their fixed beds of lime | had been dishabited, JN 2.01.220
DISHCLOUT 2 FR 0.0002 REL FR 1 V 1 P
he wore none but a dishclout of jaquenetta's, LLL 5.02.714 P
romeo's a dishclout to him. ROM 3.05.219
DISH'D 1 FR 0.0001 REL FR 1 V 0 P
tastes, though it be dish'd | for me to try how. WT 3.02. 72
DISHEARTEN 1 FR 0.0001 REL FR 0 V 1 P
he, by showing it, should dishearten his army. H5 4.01.112 P
DISHEARTENS 1 FR 0.0001 REL FR 0 V 1 P
it persuades him, and disheartens him; MAC 2.03. 33 P
DISHES 9 FR 0.0010 REL FR 2 V 7 P
threepence — your honors have seen such dishes;
MM 2.01. 93 P
they are not china dishes, but very good dishes. 2.01. 94 P
they are not china dishes, but very good dishes. 2.01. 94 P
banquet, just so many strange dishes. ADO 2.03. 21 P
all cover'd dishes! TIM 3.06. 48 P
to sauce thy dishes. 4.03.299 P
lean beggar is but variable service, two dishes, HAM 4.03. 24 P
or feed on nourishing dishes, or keep you warm, OTH 3.03. 78
one bred of alms and foster'd with cold dishes, CYM 2.03.114
DISHEVELL'D 1 FR 0.0001 REL FR 1 V 0 P
make thy sad grove in my dishevell'd hair; LUC 1129
DISHEVELLED 1 FR 0.0001 REL FR 1 V 0 P
or like a nymph, with long dishevelled hair, VEN 147
DISHONEST 11 FR 0.0012 REL FR 2 V 9 P
hang him, dishonest rascal! WIV 3.03.185 P
hang him, dishonest varlet! 4.02.102 P
o dishonest wretch! MM 3.01.136
that friar lodowick to be a dishonest person? 5.01.261 P
and i hope it is no dishonest desire to desire AYL 5.03. 4 P
besides, you grow dishonest. TN 1.05. 42 P
bid the dishonest man mend himself: 1.05. 45 P
if he mend, he is no longer dishonest; 1.05. 46 P
a very dishonest paltry boy, and more a coward 3.04.385 P
fie, thou dishonest sathan! 4.02. 31 P
for some dishonest manners of their life, H5 1.02. 49
DISHONESTLY 2 FR 0.0002 REL FR 2 V 0 P
me, | though most dishonestly he doth deny it. ERR 5.01. 3
dishonestly afflicted, but yet honest. CYM 4.02. 40
DISHONESTY 4 FR 0.0004 REL FR 1 V 3 P
do, /and if you suspect me in any dishonesty. WIV 4.02.134 P
covertly that no dishonesty shall appear in me. ADO 2.02. 10 P
his dishonesty appears in leaving his friend TN 3.04.386 P
from all dishonesty he can. WT 2.03. 47
DISHONOR 47 FR 0.0053 REL FR 42 V 5 P
back, | than you should such dishonor undergo, TMP 3.01. 27
there is not only disgrace and dishonor in that, 4.01.209 P
pretending in her discoveries of dishonor; MM 3.01.227 P
but keeps you from dishonor in doing it. 3.01.237 P
dishonor not your eye | by throwing it on any 5.01. 22
i am more amaz'd at his dishonor | than at the 5.01.380
and all of them that thus dishonor her. ADO 5.01. 44
some dishonor we had in the loss of that drum, AWW 3.06. 56 P
conceiving the dishonor of his mother! WT 2.03. 13
shall i so much dishonor my fair stars | on R2 4.01. 21
mine honor lives when his dishonor dies, | or my 5.03. 70
dies, | or my sham'd life in his dishonor lies: 5.03. 71
see riot and dishonor stain the brow | of my 1H4 1.01. 85
dishonor not your mothers; H5 3.01. 22
lord talbot, do not so dishonor me: 1H6 3.02. 90
dishonor not her honorable name | to make a 4.05. 14
a knight, | and will not any way dishonor me. 5.03.102
this dishonor in thine age | will bring thy head 2H6 2.03. 18
than bring a burthen of dishonor home | by 3.01.298
never yet did base dishonor blur our name | but 4.01. 39
it were dishonor to deny it her. 3H6 3.02. 9
down, | and with dishonor laid me on the ground, 3.03. 9
thou draw not on thy danger and dishonor; 3.03. 75
tongue could ever | pronounce dishonor of her — H8 2.03. 4
her, | not palating the taste of her dishonor, TRO 4.01. 60
your dishonor | mangles true judgment, and COR 3.01.157
it is my more dishonor | than thou of them. 3.02.124
and suffer not dishonor to approach | the TIT 1.01. 13
of mine, | my sons would never so dishonor me. 1.01.295
sons, | confederates all thus to dishonor me. 1.01.303
forfend | i should be author to dishonor you! 1.01.435
that he hath breath'd in my dishonor here. 2.01. 56
for since dishonor traffics with man's nature, TIM 1.01.158
do what you will, dishonor shall be humor. JC 4.03.109
none so rank | as may dishonor him, take heed of HAM 2.01. 21
my lord, that would dishonor him. 2.01. 27
what i have left behind | 'stroy'd in dishonor. ANT 3.11. 54
i have liv'd in such dishonor that the gods 4.14. 56
art the pander to her dishonor and equally to me CYM 3.04. 31 P
gone she is | to death or to dishonor, and my 3.05. 63
honor /him, | if he suspect i may dishonor him; PER 1.02. 21
yet to be neutral to him were dishonor; TNK 1.02.100
thee but my sword, | a bruise would be dishonor. 3.06. 88
o foul dishonor to my household's grave! LUC 198
for blame, | to privilege dishonor in thy name? 621
into thy boundless flood | black lust, dishonor, 654
back, | for it had been dishonor to disdain him. 844
DISHONORABLE 6 FR 0.0006 REL FR 5 V 1 P
dishonorable boy! R2 4.01. 65
ten times more dishonorable ragged than an old 1H4 4.02. 31 P
doth his prince's name, | in deeds dishonorable? 2H4 4.02. 26
and death's dishonorable victory | we with our 1H6 1.01. 20
o calm, dishonorable, vile submission! ROM 3.01. 73
about | to find ourselves dishonorable graves. JC 1.02.138
DISHONOR'D 12 FR 0.0013 REL FR 11 V 1 P
by so receiving a dishonor'd life | with ransom MM 4.04. 31
i stand dishonor'd, that have gone about | to ADO 4.01. 64
slander'd, scorn'd, dishonor'd my kinswoman? 4.01.302 P
conceive | he is dishonor'd by a man which ever WT 1.02.455
or thou shouldst find thou hast dishonor'd me. 1H6 3.01. 9
profan'd, dishonor'd, and the third usurp'd. R3 4.04.367
thy life hath it dishonor'd. 4.04.376
coriolanus | deserv'd this so dishonor'd rub, COR 3.01. 60
i am so dishonor'd that the very hour | you take 3.03. 60
to see your wives dishonor'd to your noses — 4.06. 83
lest in this marriage he should be dishonor'd ROM 4.03. 26
'tis honor to deprive dishonor'd life, | the one LUC 1186
DISHONORED 12 FR 0.0013 REL FR 12 V 0 P
that hath abused and dishonored me, | even in ERR 5.01.199
that hath dishonored gloucester's honest name. 2H6 2.01.195
is now dishonored by this new marriage. 3H6 4.01. 33
dishonored thus and challenged of wrongs? TIT 1.01.340
the deed | that hath dishonored all our family: 1.01.345
i saw, | to be dishonored by my sons in rome! 1.01.385
'tis thou, and those, that have dishonored me. 1.01.425
what, madam, be dishonored openly, | and basely 1.01.432
more | be so dishonored in the court of rome. 2.01. 52
and father of that chaste dishonored dame, 4.01. 90
no unchaste action, or dishonored step, | that LR 1.01.228
the knife | that wounds my body so dishonored. LUC 1185
DISHONOR'S 1 FR 0.0001 REL FR 1 V 0 P
to dark dishonor's use thou shalt not have. R2 1.01.169
DISHONORS 3 FR 0.0003 REL FR 3 V 0 P
no more my king, for he dishonors me, | but most 3H6 3.03.184
this no more dishonors you at all | than to take COR 3.02. 58
you, | let not my jealousies be your dishonors, MAC 4.03. 29
DIS–HORN 1 FR 0.0001 REL FR 1 V 0 P
dis–horn the spirit, | and mock him home to WIV 4.04. 64
DISINHERIT 3 FR 0.0003 REL FR 3 V 0 P
my son, | whom i unnaturally shall disinherit. 3H6 1.01.193
father, you cannot disinherit me. 1.01.226
son, | didst yield consent to disinherit him, 2.02. 24
DISINHERITED 3 FR 0.0003 REL FR 3 V 0 P
thine heir, | and disinherited thine only son. 3H6 1.01.225
be repeal'd | whereby my son is disinherited. 1.01.250
that by g | his issue disinherited should be; R3 1.01. 57
DIS–JE 1 FR 0.0001 REL FR 0 V 1 P
ainsi dis–je; H5 3.04. 49 P
DISJOIN 1 FR 0.0001 REL FR 1 V 0 P
i may disjoin my hand, but not my faith. JN 3.01.262
DISJOIN'D 2 FR 0.0002 REL FR 2 V 0 P
is scattered and disjoin'd from fellowship. JN 3.04. 3
till breathless he disjoin'd, and backward drew VEN 541
DISJOINING 1 FR 0.0001 REL FR 1 V 0 P
and, by disjoining hands, hell lose a soul. JN 3.01.197
DISJOINS 1 FR 0.0001 REL FR 1 V 0 P
th' abuse of greatness is when it disjoins JC 2.01. 18
DISJOINT 2 FR 0.0002 REL FR 2 V 0 P
but let the frame of things disjoint, both the MAC 3.02. 16
our state to be disjoint and out of frame, HAM 1.02. 20
DISJUNCTION 1 FR 0.0001 REL FR 1 V 0 P
there's no disjunction to be made, but by | (as WT 4.04.529
DISLIKE 16 FR 0.0018 REL FR 11 V 5 P
i never heard any soldier dislike it. MM 1.02. 17 P
choose who i would, nor refuse who i dislike; MV 1.02. 24 P
i did dislike the cut of a certain courtier's AYL 5.04. 69 P
your fooling grows old, and people dislike it. TN 1.05.111 P
and mere dislike | of our proceedings kept the 1H4 4.01. 64
i have not sought the day of this dislike. 5.01. 26
disturb your rest | in pain of your dislike, or 2H6 3.02.257
ever in fear to kindle your dislike, | yea, H8 2.04. 25
for no dislike i' th' world against the person 2.04.224
my lord, you feed too much on this dislike. TRO 2.03.225
neither, fair maid, if either thee dislike. ROM 2.02. 61
if your mind dislike any thing, obey it. HAM 5.02.217 P
each buzz, each fancy, each complaint, dislike, LR 1.04.325
what most he should dislike seems pleasant to 4.02. 10
i do not much dislike the matter, but | the ANT 2.02.111
in't, | not minding whether i dislike or no! PER 2.05. 20
DISLIKEN 1 FR 0.0001 REL FR 1 V 0 P
can, disliken | the truth of your own seeming, WT 4.04.652
DISLIKES 3 FR 0.0003 REL FR 1 V 2 P
so your dislikes, to whom i would be pleasing, 3H6 4.01. 73
the people is as bad as that which he dislikes, COR 2.02. 22 P
i'll do't, but it dislikes me. OTH 2.03. 47 P
DISLIKING 1 FR 0.0001 REL FR 1 V 0 P
sprite, | and with a heavy, dark, disliking eye, VEN 182
DISLIK'ST 2 FR 0.0002 REL FR 2 V 0 P
that is virtuous — save what thou dislik'st, AWW 2.03.122
thou dislik'st | of virtue for the name. 2.03.123
DISLIMNS 1 FR 0.0001 REL FR 1 V 0 P
even with a thought | the rack dislimns, and ANT 4.14. 10
/DISLOCATE 1 FR 0.0001 REL FR 1 V 0 P
/are /apt /enough /to /dislocate /and /tear LR 4.02. 65
DISLODG'D 1 FR 0.0001 REL FR 1 V 0 P
the volscians are dislodg'd, and martius gone. COR 5.04. 41
DISLOYAL 12 FR 0.0013 REL FR 9 V 3 P
thou subtile, perjur'd, false, disloyal man, TGV 4.02. 95
too long a–talking of), the lady is disloyal. ADO 3.02.104 P
disloyal? 3.02.108 P
that we may arraign | our most disloyal lady; WT 2.03.203
to god, his sovereign, and to him disloyal, R2 1.03.114
suspect | that i have been disloyal to thy bed, 5.02.105
assisted by that most disloyal traitor, | the MAC 1.02. 52
for such things in a false disloyal knave | are OTH 3.03.121
give me a living reason she's disloyal. 3.03.409
o disloyal thing, | that shouldst repair my CYM 1.01.131
disloyal? 3.02. 6
to her dishonor and equally to me disloyal." 3.04. 31 P
DISLOYALTY 2 FR 0.0002 REL FR 1 V 1 P
look sweet, speak fair, become disloyalty; ERR 3.02. 11
appear such seeming truth of hero's disloyalty, ADO 2.02. 48 P
DISMAL 22 FR 0.0024 REL FR 22 V 0 P
i am wrapp'd in dismal thinkings. AWW 5.03.128
woe, | and bullingbrook my sorrow's dismal heir. R2 2.02. 63
i must inform you of a dismal fight | betwixt 1H6 1.01.105
whose dismal tune bereft my vital pow'rs; 2H6 3.02. 41
like to a dismal clangor heard from far, 3H6 2.03. 18
death shall stop his dismal threat'ning sound, 2.06. 58
and chatt'ring pies in dismal discords sung; 5.06. 48
days — | so full of dismal terror was the time. R3 1.04. 7
and, for more slander to thy dismal seat, | we 3.03. 13
bind me here | unto the body of a dismal yew, TIT 2.03.107
and be this dismal sight | the closing up of our 3.01.261
a joyless, dismal, black, and sorrowful issue! 4.02. 66
this torture should be roar'd in dismal hell. ROM 3.02. 44
my dismal scene i needs must act alone. 4.03. 19
the thane of cawdor, began a dismal conflict, MAC 1.02. 53
i'll spend | unto a dismal and a fatal end. 3.05. 21
hair | would at a dismal treatise rouse and stir 5.05. 12
complexion smear'd | with heraldy more dismal. HAM 2.02.456
the sight is dismal, | and our affairs from 5.02.367
makes me look dismal will i clip to form, | and PER 5.03. 74
whose doughty dismal fame | from dis to daedalus
TNK 3.05.114
this dismal cry rings sadly in her ear, VEN 889
DISMALL'ST 2 FR 0.0002 REL FR 2 V 0 P
the dismall'st day is this that e'er i saw, | to TIT 1.01.384
with the dismall'st object hurt | that ever eye 2.03.204
DISMANTLE 2 FR 0.0002 REL FR 2 V 0 P
dismantle you, and, as you can, disliken | the WT 4.04.652
to dismantle | so many folds of favor. LR 1.01.217
DISMANTLED 1 FR 0.0001 REL FR 1 V 0 P
this realm dismantled was | of jove himself, and HAM 3.02.282
DISMASK'D 1 FR 0.0001 REL FR 1 V 0 P
dismask'd, their damask sweet commixture shown,
LLL 5.02.296
DISMAY 6 FR 0.0006 REL FR 5 V 1 P
over them, | brimful of sorrow and dismay; TMP 5.01. 14
no, she shall not dismay me. WIV 3.04. 27 P
come on, in this there can be no dismay, | my MV 1.03.180
much more dismay | i view the fight than thou 3.02. 61
dismay not, princes, at this accident, | nor 1H6 3.03. 1
my soul is full of discord and dismay. HAM 4.01. 45
DISMAY'D 11 FR 0.0012 REL FR 10 V 1 P
son, in a mov'd sort, | as if you were dismay'd; TMP 4.01.147
be not dismay'd. WIV 3.04. 26 P
the conqueror is dismay'd. LLL 5.02.567
be not dismay'd, for succor is at hand: 1H6 1.02. 50
be not dismay'd, fair lady, nor misconster | the 2.03. 73
but cheer thy heart, and be thou not dismay'd. R3 5.03.174
go, masters, get you home, be not dismay'd. COR 4.06.149
dismay'd not this | our captains, macbeth and MAC 1.02. 33
do you go back dismay'd? OTH 5.02.269
till, cheering up her senses all dismay'd, | she VEN 896
the coward fights, and will not be dismay'd. LUC 273
DISMAYED 1 FR 0.0001 REL FR 1 V 0 P
shadow ere himself, | and ran dismayed away. MV 5.01. 9
DISMEMBER 2 FR 0.0002 REL FR 2 V 0 P
of both, | they whirl asunder and dismember me. JN 3.01.330
by caesar's spirit, | and not dismember caesar! JC 2.01.170
DISMEMB'RED 1 FR 0.0001 REL FR 1 V 0 P
and thou dismemb'red with thine own defense. ROM 3.03.134
DISMES 1 FR 0.0001 REL FR 1 V 0 P
every tithe soul, 'mongst many thousand dismes, TRO 2.02. 19
DISMISS 24 FR 0.0027 REL FR 20 V 4 P
if not, use him for the present and dismiss him. MM 4.02. 25 P
o, dismiss this audience, and i shall tell you LLL 4.03.206
upon my power i may dismiss this court, | unless MV 4.01.104
or not at home — what you will, to dismiss it. TN 1.05.109 P
and he hath promis'd to dismiss the powers | led JN 5.01. 64
king | dismiss his power he means to visit us, 1H4 4.04. 37
with sweet enlargement doth dismiss me hence. 1H6 2.05. 30
so, now dismiss your army when ye please; 5.04.173
i do dismiss you to your several countries. 2H6 4.09. 21
then, buckingham, i do dismiss my pow'rs. 5.01. 44
please you dismiss me, either with ay or no. 3H6 3.02. 78
a chamber–pot, dismiss the controversy bleeding, COR 2.01. 76 P
will you dismiss the people? 2.03.154
dismiss them home. | here comes his mother. 4.02. 7
do not bid me | dismiss my soldiers, or 5.03. 82
dismiss your followers, and, as suitors should, TIT 1.01. 44
that i will here dismiss my loving friends; 1.01. 53
i thank you all and here dismiss you all, | and 1.01. 57
bars, | never lacks power to dismiss itself. JC 1.03. 97
dismiss me. MAC 4.01. 72
dismiss your attendant there. OTH 4.03. 8 P
me to go to bed, | and bid me to dismiss you. 4.03. 14
dismiss me? 4.03. 14
dismiss your vows, your feigned tears, your VEN 425
DISMISS'D 8 FR 0.0009 REL FR 8 V 0 P
which a dismiss'd offense would after gall, MM 2.02.102
i have from your sicilian shores dismiss'd; WT 5.01.164
that hath dismiss'd us from our stewardship, R2 3.03. 78
in rage dismiss'd my father from the court, 1H4 4.03.100
and, ere they be dismiss'd, let them march by. 2H4 4.02. 96
thither, | until his army be dismiss'd from him. 2H6 4.09. 40
dismiss'd me | thus, with his speechless hand. COR 5.01. 66
and fifty men dismiss'd? LR 2.04.207
DISMISSED 1 FR 0.0001 REL FR 1 V 0 P
whose shadow the dismissed bachelor loves, TMP 4.01. 67
DISMISSING 1 FR 0.0001 REL FR 1 V 0 P
dismissing half your train, come then to me. LR 2.04.204
DISMISSION 2 FR 0.0002 REL FR 2 V 0 P
longer, your dismission | is come from caesar, ANT 1.01. 26
save when command to your dismission tends, CYM 2.03. 52
DISMOUNT 3 FR 0.0003 REL FR 2 V 1 P
dismount thy tuck, be yare in thy preparation, TN 3.04.224 P
i will dismount, and by thy waggon–wheel | trot TIT 5.02. 54
"this said, his wat'ry eyes he did dismount, LC 281
DISMOUNTED 2 FR 0.0002 REL FR 1 V 1 P
as well, were some of your brags dismounted. H5 3.07. 77 P
dismounted from your snow–white goodly steed, TIT 2.03. 76
DISNATUR'D 1 FR 0.0001 REL FR 1 V 0 P
and be a thwart disnatur'd torment to her. LR 1.04.283
DISOBEDIENCE 8 FR 0.0009 REL FR 7 V 1 P
of disobedience, or unduteous title, | since WIV 5.05.227
to die | for disobedience to your father's will, MND 1.01. 87
mothers, which is most infallible disobedience. AWW 1.01.138 P
been in me | both disobedience and ingratitude WT 3.02. 68
i do see | danger and disobedience in thine eye. 1H4 1.03. 16
stomachs be provok'd | to willful disobedience, 1H6 4.01.142
i say they nourish'd disobedience, fed | the COR 3.01.117
didst set up my disobedience 'gainst the king CYM 3.04. 88
DISOBEDIENT 5 FR 0.0005 REL FR 5 V 0 P
proud, disobedient, stubborn, lacking duty, TGV 3.01. 69
that are | most disobedient and refractory. TRO 2.02.182
disobedient wretch! ROM 3.05.160
me to repent the sin | of disobedient opposition 4.02. 18
and we must | be vile or disobedient — not his TNK 1.02. 78
DISOBEY 3 FR 0.0003 REL FR 2 V 1 P
that ne'er | dost disobey the wife of jupiter; TMP 4.01. 77
who to disobey were against all proportion of H5 4.01.145 P

never to disobey | nor be rebellious to the 1H6 5.04.170
DISOBEYS 1 FR 0.0001 REL FR 1 V 0 P
paul, | i'll make a corse of him that disobeys. R3 1.02. 37
DISORB'D 1 FR 0.0001 REL FR 1 V 0 P
mercury from jove, | or like a star disorb'd? TRO 2.02. 46
DISORDER 9 FR 0.0010 REL FR 9 V 0 P
my head | when there is such disorder in my wit. JN 3.04.102
disorder, horror, fear, and mutiny | shall here R2 4.01.142
disorder, that hath spoil'd us, friend us now! H5 4.05. 17
fear frames disorder, and disorder wounds 2H6 5.02. 32
and disorder wounds | where it should guard. 5.02. 32
planets | in evil mixture to disorder wander, TRO 1.03. 95
the good meeting, | with most admir'd disorder. MAC 3.04.109
and fell to what disorder | his power could give TNK 5.04. 66
disorder breeds by heating of the blood; VEN 742
DISORDER'D 4 FR 0.0004 REL FR 3 V 1 P
nothing impair'd, but all disorder'd. MND 5.01.126 P
with hair, | put forth disorder'd twigs; H5 5.02. 44
men so disorder'd, so debosh'd and bold, | that LR 1.04.242
and your disorder'd rabble make servants of 1.04.256
DISORDERED 3 FR 0.0003 REL FR 3 V 0 P
her knots disordered and her wholesome herbs R2 3.04. 46
he that hath suffered this disordered spring 3.04. 48
to check time broke in a disordered string; 5.05. 46
DISORDERLY 1 FR 0.0001 REL FR 1 V 0 P
affairs | thus disorderly thrust into my hands, R2 2.02.110
DISORDER'S 1 FR 0.0001 REL FR 1 V 0 P
and the disorder's such | as war were hoodwink'd CYM 5.02. 15
DISORDERS 3 FR 0.0003 REL FR 1 V 2 P
kinsman, she's nothing allied to your disorders. TN 2.03. 97 P
and all ruinous disorders follow us disquietly LR 1.02.113 P
but his own disorders | deserv'd much less 2.04.199
DISPARAGE 2 FR 0.0002 REL FR 1 V 1 P
i will disparage her no farther till you are my ADO 3.02.128 P
disparage not the faith thou dost not know, MND 3.02.174
DISPARAGEMENT 2 FR 0.0002 REL FR 2 V 0 P
but to our honor's great disparagement, | yet ERR 1.01.148
town | here in my house do him disparagement; ROM 1.05. 70
DISPARAGEMENTS 1 FR 0.0001 REL FR 0 V 1 P
falstaff have committed disparagements unto you,
WIV 1.01. 31 P
DISPARITY 1 FR 0.0001 REL FR 1 V 0 P
gives | the prejudice of disparity, value's TNK 5.03. 88
DISPARK'D 1 FR 0.0001 REL FR 1 V 0 P
dispark'd my parks and fell'd my forest woods, R2 3.01. 23
/DISPATCH 1 FR 0.0001 REL FR 1 V 0 P
/my /lord, /dispatch, /read /o'er /these R2 4.01.243
DISPATCH 75 FR 0.0084 REL FR 62 V 13 P
i will dispatch him to the emperor's court. TGV 1.03. 38
only, in lieu thereof, dispatch me hence. 2.07. 88
dispatch, sweet gentlemen, and follow me. 5.02. 48
quickly, dispatch. WIV 4.02.110 P
her to the deanery, and dispatch it quickly. 5.03. 3 P
place call upon me, and dispatch with angelo, MM 3.01.266 P
dispatch it presently, the hour draws on 4.03. 78
quick, dispatch, and send the head to angelo. 4.03. 92
to have a dispatch of complaints, and to deliver 4.04. 12 P
the hour steals on, i pray you, sir, dispatch. ERR 4.01. 52
on serious business craving quick dispatch, LLL 2.01. 31
well, lords, to–day we shall have our dispatch; 4.01. 5
dispatch, i say, and find the forester. MND 4.01.108
o love! dispatch all business, and be gone! MV 3.02.323
mistress, dispatch you with your safest haste, AYL 1.03. 41
will you dispatch us here under this tree, or 3.03. 65 P
and, after some dispatch in hand at court, AWW 3.02. 54
dispatch the most convenient messenger. 3.04. 34
main parcels of dispatch /effected many nicer 4.03. 90 P
take and give back affairs and their dispatch TN 4.03. 18
nay, prithee dispatch. WT 4.04.640 P
dispatch, i prithee. 4.04.644 P
therefore i will be sudden, and dispatch. JN 4.01. 27
dispatch. 2H4 2.04. 13 P
and now dispatch we toward the court, my lords, 4.03. 76
dispatch, dispatch. 5.05. 4 P
dispatch, dispatch. 5.05. 4 P
you, prince dolphin, with all swift dispatch, H5 2.04. 6
dispatch us with all speed, lest that our king 2.04.141
come go, i will dispatch the horsemen straight; 1H6 4.04. 40
dispatch. 2H6 2.03. 91
nay, never bear me hence, dispatch me here; 3H6 5.05. 69
nay, now dispatch: R3 1.02.181
are you now going to dispatch this thing? 1.03.340
go, go, dispatch. 1.03.354
dispatch, the limit of your lives is out. 3.03. 8
come, dispatch, the duke would be at dinner. 3.04. 94
come, come, dispatch, 'tis bootless to exclaim. 3.04.102
i will dispatch it straight. 4.02. 82
than the business | that seeks dispatch by day. H8 5.01. 16
and hear | how the dispatch is made, and in what COR 1.01.277
do send, dispatch | those centuries to our aid; 1.07. 2
then, | for we are peremptory to dispatch | this 3.01.284
yet give us our dispatch. 5.03.180
dispatch. 5.06. 8
give it me, my sword shall soon dispatch it. TIT 4.02. 86
of twenty men, it would dispatch you straight. ROM 5.01. 79
i will dispatch you severally: TIM 2.02.187 P
this night's great business into my dispatch, MAC 1.05. 68
come, sir, dispatch. 5.03. 50
and we here dispatch | you, good cornelius, and HAM 1.02. 33
i your commission will forthwith dispatch, | and 3.03. 3
then that terrible dispatch of it into your LR 1.02. 32 P
and found — dispatch. 2.01. 58
several messengers | from hence attend dispatch. 2.01.125
of his misery, to dispatch | his nighted life; 4.05. 12
write from us to him, post–post–haste. dispatch! OTH 1.03. 46
which ever as she could with haste dispatch, 1.03.148
/nay, dispatch. 4.02. 30
prithee dispatch. 4.03. 33
dispatch we | the business we have talk'd of. ANT 2.02.165
dispatch. 3.12. 26
dispatch. 4.04. 15
dispatch. 4.05. 17
o, dispatch me! 4.14.104
now, noble charmian, we'll dispatch indeed, 5.02.230
poor venomous fool, | be angry, and dispatch. 5.02.306
o, come apace, dispatch! 5.02.322
dispatch. CYM 1.05. 3
prithee dispatch, | the lamb entreats the 3.04. 95
to the numbers and the time | of their dispatch. 3.07. 16
i am sworn, | and will dispatch. PER 4.01. 91
whilst we dispatch | this grand act of our life, TNK 1.01.163
not so few last night | as twenty to dispatch. 4.01.138
sets down her babe and makes all swift dispatch SON 143. 3
DISPATCH'D 21 FR 0.0023 REL FR 18 V 3 P
son? how now? how now, son? have you dispatch'd?
WIV 5.05.179 P
dispatch'd! 5.05.180 P
see this dispatch'd with all the haste thou SHR in.1. 129
i have to–night dispatch'd sixteen businesses, a AWW 4.03. 85 P
i have dispatch'd in post | to sacred delphos, WT 2.01.182
and once dispatch'd him in an embassy | to JN 1.01. 99
for many carriages he hath dispatch'd | to the 5.07. 90
what, are there no posts dispatch'd for ireland? R2 2.02.103
my lord northumberland, see them dispatch'd. 3.01. 35
a gentleman of mine i have dispatch'd | with 3.01. 40
you shall be soon dispatch'd, with fair H5 2.04.144
whilst a field should be dispatch'd and fought, 1H6 1.01. 72
let him know | we have dispatch'd the duke, as 2H6 3.02. 2
now, sirs, have you dispatch'd this thing? 3.02. 6
a bloody deed, and desperately dispatch'd! R3 1.04.271
stay your strife, what shall be is dispatch'd. TIT 3.01.192
is he dispatch'd? MAC 3.04. 15
of life, of crown, of queen, at once dispatch'd, HAM 1.05. 75
they have dispatch'd with pompey, he is gone; ANT 3.02. 2
those things i bid you do, get them dispatch'd, CYM 1.03. 39
so, | they are well dispatch'd; PER 2.05. 15
DISPENSATION 3 FR 0.0003 REL FR 3 V 0 P
court, | than seek a dispensation for his oath, LLL 2.01. 87
and yet a dispensation may be had. 1H6 5.03. 86
and with good thoughts makes dispensation, LUC 248
DISPENSE 11 FR 0.0012 REL FR 9 V 2 P
dispense with trifles. WIV 2.01. 47 P
might you dispense with your leisure, i would by MM 3.01.153 P
unfeeling fools can with such wrongs dispense: ERR 2.01.103
we must of force dispense with this decree, LLL 1.01.147
how shall we then dispense with that contract, 1H6 5.05. 28
canst thou dispense with heaven for such an oath 2H6 5.01.181
men must learn now with pity to dispense, | for TIM 3.02. 86
and with my trespass never will dispense, | till LUC 1070
yet with the fault i thus far can dispense: 1279
may my pure mind with the foul act dispense, 1704
mark how with my neglect i do dispense: SON 112.12
DISPENSES 1 FR 0.0001 REL FR 1 V 0 P
life, | nature dispenses with the deed so far, MM 3.01.134
DISPERS'D 13 FR 0.0014 REL FR 13 V 0 P
in troops i have dispers'd them 'bout the isle. TMP 1.02.220
for the rest o' th' fleet | (which i dispers'd), 1.02.233
dispers'd those vapors that offended us, | and ERR 1.01. 89
and dispers'd | the household of the king. R2 2.03. 27
are gone to bullingbrook, dispers'd and fled. 3.02. 74
we learn | the welshmen are dispers'd, and 3.03. 2
my lord, our army is dispers'd already: 2H4 4.02.102
to gather our soldiers, scatter'd and dispers'd, 1H6 2.01. 76
but now is cade driven back, his men dispers'd, 2H6 4.09. 34
buckingham's army is dispers'd and scatter'd, R3 4.04.511
the britain navy is dispers'd by tempest. 4.04.521
dispers'd as you commanded. TNK 3.05. 32
with clamors fill'd | the dispers'd air, who, LUC 1805
DISPERSE 11 FR 0.0012 REL FR 11 V 0 P
away, disperse! WIV 5.05. 74
king, | therefore we will disperse ourselves. R2 2.04. 4
till by broad spreading it disperse to nought. 1H6 1.02.135
disperse yourselves. 2H6 5.01. 45
a little gale will soon disperse that cloud, 3H6 5.03. 10
allay those tongues | that durst disperse it. H8 2.01.153
sing, and disperse 'em if thou canst. 3.01. 2
hand, | to scatter and disperse the giddy goths, TIT 5.02. 78
as will disperse itself through all the veins ROM 5.01. 61
brutus, | and, friends, disperse yourselves; JC 2.01.222
my use, | and under thee their poesy disperse. SON 78. 4
DISPERSED *(also disbursed)*
DISPERSED 2 FR 0.0002 REL FR 2 V 0 P
ends, | dispersed are the glories it included. 1H6 1.02.137
and not the puddle in thy sea dispersed. LUC 658
DISPITEOUS 1 FR 0.0001 REL FR 1 V 0 P
turning dispiteous torture out of door? JN 4.01. 34
DISPLAC'D 3 FR 0.0003 REL FR 3 V 0 P
well might lodge a fear | to be again displac'd; 2H4 4.05.208
if gloucester be displac'd, he'll be protector. 2H6 1.01.177
you have displac'd the mirth, broke the good MAC 3.04.108
DISPLACE 2 FR 0.0002 REL FR 1 V 1 P
possible for you to displace it with your little COR 5.04. 4 P
displace our heads where (thanks, /ye gods!) CYM 4.02.122
DISPLACEST 1 FR 0.0001 REL FR 1 V 0 P
thou plantest scandal and displacest laud. LUC 887
DISPLANT 1 FR 0.0001 REL FR 1 V 0 P
displant a town, reverse a prince's doom, | it ROM 3.03. 59
DISPLANTING 1 FR 0.0001 REL FR 0 V 1 P
taste again but by the displanting of cassio. OTH 2.01.276 P
DISPLAY 4 FR 0.0004 REL FR 3 V 1 P
meeting, they will at once display to the night. WIV 5.03. 16 P
that did display them when we first march'd JN 2.01.320
and here display at last | what god will have TIT 4.01. 73
upon the world dim darkness doth display, | and LUC 118
DISPLAY'D 8 FR 0.0009 REL FR 8 V 0 P
with visages display'd, to talk and greet. LLL 5.02.144
whose fair flow'r | being once display'd, doth TN 2.04. 39
and to sun's parching heat display'd my cheeks, 1H6 1.02. 77
his hands abroad display'd, as one that grasp'd 2H6 3.02.172
and display'd th' effects | of disposition H8 2.04. 86
display'd so saucily against your highness — LR 2.04. 41
the semblance | of their white flags display'd, PER 1.04. 72
and when his gaudy banner is display'd, | the LUC 272
DISPLAYED 2 FR 0.0002 REL FR 2 V 0 P
ten times louder | than beauty could, displayed. MM 2.04. 81
who are at hand, triumphantly displayed, | to JN 2.01.309
DISPLEAS'D 9 FR 0.0010 REL FR 8 V 1 P
no matter who's displeas'd when you are gone: TGV 2.07. 66
my mirth it much displeas'd, but pleas'd my woe. MM 4.01. 13
which, i hope, thou felt'st i was displeas'd. ERR 2.02. 19
him, | and suffer'd him to go displeas'd away — MV 5.01.213
there's reason he should be displeas'd at it. 2H6 1.01.155
god is much displeas'd | that you take with R3 2.02. 89
lavinia, you are not displeas'd with this? TIT 1.01.270
having displeas'd my father, to lawrence' cell, ROM 3.05.232
according as he pleas'd and displeas'd them, as JC 1.02.259 P
DISPLEASE 4 FR 0.0004 REL FR 4 V 0 P
and so displease | her brother's noontide with MND 3.02. 54
and let it not displease thee, good bianca, SHR 1.01. 76
in such a kind from me | as will displease you. 1H4 1.03.122
we must not now displease him. OTH 4.03. 17
DISPLEASING 2 FR 0.0002 REL FR 1 V 1 P
so | for some displeasing service i have done, 1H4 3.02. 5
lately here in the end of a displeasing play, to 2H4 ep 8 P
DISPLEASURE 42 FR 0.0047 REL FR 25 V 17 P
if i should take a displeasure against you, look TMP 4.01.202 P
man | do outrage and displeasure to himself? ERR 4.04.116
doing displeasure to the citizens | by rushing 5.01.142
thither, this may prove food to my displeasure. ADO 1.03. 66 P
i am sick in displeasure to him, and whatsoever 2.02. 5 P
would abate the strength of your displeasure. MV 5.01.198
hath ta'en displeasure 'gainst his gentle niece, AYL 1.02.278
have deserv'd to run into my lord's displeasure. AWW 2.05. 35 P
the everlasting displeasure of the king, who had 4.03. 9 P
to stop up the displeasure he hath conceiv'd 4.05. 75 P
smell somewhat strong of her strong displeasure. 5.02. 5 P
fortune's displeasure is but sluttish if it 5.02. 6 P
into the unclean fishpond of her displeasure, 5.02. 21 P
not fearing the displeasure of your master, 5.03.235
though full of our displeasure, yet we free thee WT 4.04.433
to meet displeasure farther from the doors, JN 5.01. 60
my fear, is your displeasure, my cur'sy, my duty 2H4 ep 2 P
poor and a private displeasure can do against a H5 4.01.198 P
duke of buckingham | is run in your displeasure. H8 1.02.110
hath my behavior given to your displeasure, 2.04. 20
settled | (not to come off) in his displeasure. 3.02. 23
the worst | is your displeasure with the king. 3.02.392
lest your displeasure should enlarge itself | to TRO 5.02. 37
the malice and displeasure of the people is as COR 2.02. 21 P
and witness of the malice and displeasure 4.05. 72
was, and urg'd withal | your high displeasure; ROM 3.01.155
urge it no more | on height of our displeasure. TIM 3.05. 86
or all of it, with our displeasure piec'd, | and LR 1.01.199
found you no displeasure in him by word nor 1.02.157 P
time hath qualified the heat of his displeasure, 1.02.162 P
i should win your displeasure to entreat me to't 2.02.113 P
he, compact, and flattering his displeasure, 2.02.118
pain of perpetual displeasure neither to speak 3.03. 4 P
leave him to my displeasure. 3.07. 6 P
bade her wrong stay, and her displeasure fly; OTH 2.01.153
i am sorry | for your displeasure; 3.01. 42
a man that languishes in your displeasure. 3.03. 43
and stood within the blank of his displeasure 3.04.128
turn your displeasure that way, for our faults ANT 3.04. 34
incur i know not | how much of his displeasure. CYM 1.01.103
took some displeasure at him, at least he judg'd PER 1.03. 20
a deed might gain her love or your displeasure. 2.05. 54
DISPLEASURE'S 1 FR 0.0001 REL FR 1 V 0 P
lord, | on your displeasure's peril and on mine, WT 2.03. 45
DISPLEASURES 2 FR 0.0002 REL FR 1 V 1 P
oft our displeasures, to ourselves unjust, AWW 5.03. 63
and his moods, and his displeasures, and his H5 4.07. 36 P
DISPORT 2 FR 0.0002 REL FR 2 V 0 P
/comes hunting this way to disport himself. 3H6 4.05. 8
we make ourselves fools to disport ourselves, TIM 1.02.136
DISPORTS 1 FR 0.0001 REL FR 1 V 0 P
that my disports corrupt and taint my business, OTH 1.03.271
DISPOS'D 25 FR 0.0028 REL FR 22 V 3 P
the mariners, say how thou hast dispos'd, | and TMP 1.02.225
i find not | myself dispos'd to sleep. 2.01.202
i told you, sir, my daughter is dispos'd of. WIV 3.04. 70
the children thus dispos'd, my wife and i, ERR 1.01. 83
and tell me how thou hast dispos'd thy charge. 1.02. 73
come to our pavilion — boyet is dispos'd. LLL 2.01.250
to make my lady laugh when she's dispos'd, 5.02.466
will do that when you are dispos'd to be merry. AYL 4.01.155 P
he does well enough if he be dispos'd, and so do TN 2.03. 81 P
so hot a speed with such advice dispos'd, | such JN 3.04. 11
on, | to see how fortune is dispos'd to us, 1H4 4.01. 38
the king your father is dispos'd to sleep. 2H4 4.05. 17
vile and ragged foils | (right ill dispos'd, in H5 4.pr. 51
noble benefits shall prove | not well dispos'd, H8 1.02.116
within his tent, but ill dispos'd, my lord. TRO 2.03. 77
his blows are well dispos'd. there, ajax! 4.05.116
you had not show'd them how ye were dispos'd COR 3.02. 22
may be wrought | from that it is dispos'd; JC 1.02.310
if i were dispos'd to stir | your hearts and 3.02.121
he was dispos'd to mirth, but on the sudden | a ANT 1.02. 82
you did suspect | she had dispos'd with caesar, 4.14.123
is he dispos'd to mirth? i hope he is. CYM 1.06. 58
when a gentleman is dispos'd to swear, it is not 2.01. 10 P
being so few and well dispos'd, they show TNK 4.02.122
when thou shalt be dispos'd to set me light, SON 88. 1
DISPOSE 25 FR 0.0028 REL FR 23 V 2 P
all that is mine i leave at thy dispose, | my TGV 2.07. 86
which, with ourselves, all rest at thy dispose. 4.01. 74
dispose of them as thou know'st their deserts. 5.04.159
dispose of her | to some more fitter place; MM 2.02. 16
his goods confiscate to the duke's dispose, ERR 1.01. 20
and dispose | for henceforth of poor claudio. ADO 5.01.294
as she is mine, i may dispose of her; MND 1.01. 42
to your own bents dispose you; WT 1.02.179
needs must you lay your heart at his dispose, JN 1.01.263
come, cousin, i'll dispose of you. R2 2.02.117
and i beseech your grace | i may dispose of him. 1H4 5.05. 24
enter our gates, dispose of us and ours, | for H5 3.03. 49
how can they charitably dispose of any thing, 4.01.143 P
and how thou pleasest, god, dispose the day! 4.03.133
ce soldat ici est dispose tout /a /cette /heure 4.04. 35 P
in safety, and dispose | of their dead bodies! 4.07. 82
none, | but carries on the stream of his dispose TRO 2.03.164
there to dispose this treasure in mine arms, TIT 4.02.173
i'll dispose of thee | among a sisterhood of ROM 5.03.156
attends you, | please you to dispose yourselves. TIM 1.02.156
dispose of them, of me; LR 5.03. 76
he hath a person and a smooth dispose | to be OTH 1.03.397
for we intend so to dispose you as | yourself ANT 5.02.186
and by whose letters i'll dispose myself. PER 1.02.117
pirithous, | dispose of this fair gentleman. TNK 2.05. 32
DISPOSED 1 FR 0.0001 REL FR 1 V 0 P
for he's disposed as the hateful raven. 2H6 3.01. 76
DISPOSER 2 FR 0.0002 REL FR 0 V 2 P
i'll lay my life, with my disposer cressida. TRO 3.01. 87 P
come, your disposer is sick. 3.01. 89 P

DISPOSER'S 1 FR 0.0001 REL FR 0 V 1 P
no, your /poor disposer's sick. TRO 3.01. 92 P
DISPOSERS 1 FR 0.0001 REL FR 1 V 0 P
a noble difference, | but base disposers of it. TNK 3.06.117
DISPOSING 5 FR 0.0005 REL FR 5 V 0 P
and quarrel | to the disposing of the cardinal, JN 5.07. 92
to the disposing of it nought rebell'd, | order H8 1.01. 43
to fail in the disposing of those chances COR 4.07. 40
any man's | in the disposing of new dignities. JC 3.01.178
light | to the disposing of her troubled brain, VEN 1040
/DISPOSITION 1 FR 0.0001 REL FR 1 V 0 P
/i /fear /your /disposition; LR 4.02. 31
DISPOSITION 44 FR 0.0049 REL FR 25 V 19 P
have sworn his disposition would have gone to WIV 2.01. 60 P
of man's disposition is able to bear. 4.05.109 P
i do it not in evil disposition, | but from lord MM 1.02.118
his judgment with the disposition of natures. 3.01.163 P
pray you, sir, of what disposition was the duke? 3.02.231 P
he is of a very melancholy disposition. ADO 2.01. 5 P
disposition of beatrice that puts the world into 2.01.208 P
hath a disposition to come in disguis'd against AYL 1.01.125 P
my father's rough and envious disposition 1.02.241
my master is of churlish disposition, | and 2.04. 80
i have a doublet and hose in my disposition? 3.02.196 P
your rosalind in a more coming-on disposition; 4.01.113 P
for 'tis | the royal disposition of that beast 4.03.117
this drum sticks sorely in your disposition. AWW 3.06. 45 P
guiltless, and of free disposition, is to take TN 1.05. 92 P
will now be so unsuitable to her disposition, 2.05.202 P
grace and good disposition attend your ladyship! 3.01.135
since fate (against thy better disposition) WT 3.03. 28
this robe of mine | does change my disposition. 4.04.135
and entertain a cheerful disposition. R2 2.02. 4
the king, on his own royal disposition | (and R3 1.03. 63
display'd th' effects | of disposition gentle, H8 2.04. 87
the bitter disposition of the time | will have TRO 4.01. 49
minded, | wave thus to express his disposition, COR 1.06. 74
the true knowledge he has in their disposition, 2.02. 14 P
away, my disposition, and possess me | some 3.02.111
i thought thy disposition better temper'd. ROM 3.03.115
me strange | even to the disposition that i owe, MAC 3.04.112
a truant disposition, good my lord. HAM 1.02.169
so horridly to shake our disposition | with 1.04. 55
think meet | to put an antic disposition on — 1.05.172
indeed it goes so heavily with my disposition, 2.02.298 P
but with much forcing of his disposition. 3.01. 12
authority with such disposition as he bears, LR 1.01.304 P
to lay his goatish disposition on the charge of 1.02.127 P
but let his disposition have that scope | as 1.04.292
whose disposition, all the world well knows, 2.02.153
brother's evil disposition made him seek his 3.05. 6 P
state, | i crave fit disposition for my wife, OTH 1.03.236
so apt, so bless'd a disposition, she holds it a 2.03.320 P
i know our country disposition well: 3.03.201
o well-divided disposition! ANT 1.05. 53
as they pinch one another by the disposition, he 2.07. 6 P
with noble disposition | each present lord began LUC 1695
DISPOSITIONS 6 FR 0.0006 REL FR 3 V 3 P
i have a great dispositions to cry. WIV 3.01. 22 P
her dispositions she inherits, which makes fair AWW 1.01. 40 P
give your dispositions the reins and be angry at COR 2.01. 30 P
had been | the /thwartings of your dispositions, 3.02. 21
how stands your dispositions to be married? ROM 1.03. 65
these dispositions which of late transport you LR 1.04.221
DISPOSSESS 4 FR 0.0004 REL FR 3 V 1 P
a woodcock lest thou dispossess the soul of thy TN 4.02. 60 P
to dispossess that child which is not his? JN 1.01.131
of no more force to dispossess me, sir, | than 1.01.132
beggars of the world, | and dispossess her all. TIM 1.01.139
DISPOSSESS'D 1 FR 0.0001 REL FR 1 V 0 P
the king hath dispossess'd himself of us. JN 4.03. 23
DISPOSSESSING 1 FR 0.0001 REL FR 1 V 0 P
and dispossessing all my others parts | of MM 2.04. 22
DISPRAIS'D 3 FR 0.0003 REL FR 2 V 1 P
praise his faith which i would have disprais'd. TGV 4.04.102
i disprais'd him before the wicked, that the 2H4 2.04.319 P
in praising antony i have disprais'd caesar. ANT 2.05.107
DISPRAISE 10 FR 0.0011 REL FR 7 V 3 P
it | by aught that i can speak in his dispraise, TGV 3.02. 47
much | as you in worth dispraise sir valentine. 3.02. 55
and therefore red, that would avoid dispraise, LLL 4.03.260
not to dispraise me, and call me pantler and 2H4 2.04.314 P
you will to her dispraise those parts in me that H5 5.02.200 P
i will not dispraise your sister cassandra's wit TRO 1.01. 46 P
dispraise the thing that they desire to buy, 4.01. 77
or to dispraise my lord with that same tongue ROM 3.05.237
what, my lord, dispraise? TIM 1.01.165
cannot dispraise but in a kind of praise, SON 95. 7
DISPRAISING 2 FR 0.0002 REL FR 2 V 0 P
by still dispraising praise valued with you, 1H4 5.02. 59
hint, | and (not dispraising whom we prais'd; CYM 5.05.173
DISPRAISINGLY 1 FR 0.0001 REL FR 1 V 0 P
time, | when i have spoke of you dispraisingly, OTH 3.03. 72
DISPROPERTIED 1 FR 0.0001 REL FR 1 V 0 P
and | dispropertied their freedoms, holding them COR 2.01.248
DISPROPORTION 1 FR 0.0001 REL FR 1 V 0 P
size, | to disproportion me in every part, 3H6 3.02.160
DISPROPORTION'D 1 FR 0.0001 REL FR 1 V 0 P
he is as disproportion'd in his manners | as in TMP 5.01.291
DISPROPORTIONED 1 FR 0.0001 REL FR 1 V 0 P
indeed, they are disproportioned; OTH 1.03. 2
DISPROPORTIONS 1 FR 0.0001 REL FR 1 V 0 P
rank, | foul disproportions, thoughts unnatural. OTH 3.03.233
DISPROVE 4 FR 0.0004 REL FR 4 V 0 P
thou wouldst disprove me. TGV 5.04. 66
and warwick shall disprove it. 3H6 1.01. 89
i speak not to disprove what brutus spoke, | but JC 3.02.100
disprove this villain, if thou be'st a man. OTH 5.02.172
DISPROVED 1 FR 0.0001 REL FR 1 V 0 P
her shall you hear disproved to her eyes, | till MM 5.01.161
DISPROV'ST 1 FR 0.0001 REL FR 1 V 0 P
experience, o, thou disprov'st report! CYM 4.02. 34
DISPUNGE 1 FR 0.0001 REL FR 1 V 0 P
the poisonous damp of night dispunge upon me, ANT 4.09. 13
DISPURSED 1 FR 0.0001 REL FR 1 V 0 P
commons, | have i dispursed to the garrisons, 2H6 3.01.117
DISPUTABLE 1 FR 0.0001 REL FR 0 V 1 P
he is too disputable for my company. AYL 2.05. 35 P
DISPUTATION 4 FR 0.0004 REL FR 4 V 0 P
thou mine, | and that's a feeling disputation, 1H4 3.01.203
holds he disputation | 'tween frozen conscience LUC 246
if that be made a theme for disputation, | the 822
holds disputation with each thing she views, 1101
DISPUTATIONS 1 FR 0.0001 REL FR 0 V 1 P
look you, a few disputations with you, as partly H5 3.02. 95 P
DISPUTE 6 FR 0.0006 REL FR 6 V 0 P
dispute his own estate? WT 4.04.400
grace be worthy, yea or no, | dispute not that; 2H6 1.03.108
dispute not with her, she is lunatic. R3 1.03.253
let me dispute with thee of thy estate. ROM 3.03. 63
dispute it like a man. MAC 4.03.220
and with you leave dispute | that are above our TNK 5.04.135
DISPUTED 1 FR 0.0001 REL FR 1 V 0 P
i'll have't disputed on, | 'tis probable, and OTH 1.02. 75
DISPUTES 2 FR 0.0002 REL FR 1 V 1 P
thou disputes like an infant; go whip thy gig. LLL 5.01. 66 P
for though my soul disputes well with my sense, TN 4.03. 9
DISPUTING 1 FR 0.0001 REL FR 1 V 0 P
fought, | you are disputing of your generals. 1H6 1.01. 73
DISQUANTITY 1 FR 0.0001 REL FR 1 V 0 P
she begs, | a little to disquantity your train, LR 1.04.249
DISQUIET 3 FR 0.0003 REL FR 2 V 1 P
so indeed all disquiet, horror, and perturbation ADO 2.01.260 P
i pray you, husband, be not so disquiet. SHR 4.01.168
i grieving grant | did you too much disquiet. ANT 2.02. 70
DISQUIETLY 1 FR 0.0001 REL FR 0 V 1 P
disorders follow us disquietly to our graves. LR 1.02.114 P
DISRELISH 1 FR 0.0001 REL FR 0 V 1 P
heave the gorge, disrelish and abhor the moor; OTH 2.01.233 P
DISROBE 3 FR 0.0003 REL FR 3 V 0 P
robe, | that did disrobe the lion of that robe! JN 2.01.142
disrobe the images, | if you do find them deck'd JC 1.01. 64
i'll disrobe me | of these italian weeds and CYM 5.01. 22
DISROOT 1 FR 0.0001 REL FR 1 V 0 P
plunges | disroot his rider whence he grew, but TNK 5.04. 75
DIS'S 1 FR 0.0001 REL FR 1 V 0 P
frighted, thou let'st fall | from dis's waggon! WT 4.04.118
/DISSEAT 1 FR 0.0001 REL FR 1 V 0 P
push | will cheer me ever, or /disseat me now. MAC 5.03. 21
DISSEAT 1 FR 0.0001 REL FR 1 V 0 P
to disseat | his lord that kept it bravely. TNK 5.04. 72
DISSEMBLE 13 FR 0.0014 REL FR 12 V 1 P
see thou dissemble not. SHR 2.01. 9
or both dissemble deeply their affections; 4.04. 42
put it on, and i will dissemble myself in't, and TN 4.02. 4 P
so help me god, as i dissemble not! 1H6 3.01.140
i must dissemble. 2H6 5.01. 13
dissemble not your hatred, swear your love. R3 2.01. 8
think you my uncle did dissemble, grandam? 2.02. 31
i would dissemble with my nature where | my COR 3.02. 62
dissemble all your griefs and discontents. TIT 1.01.443
ay, and you hear him cog, see him dissemble, TIM 5.01. 95
o, hardness to dissemble! OTH 3.04. 34
soft, here he comes, i must dissemble it. PER 2.05. 23
when thou didst name the boar, not to dissemble, VEN 641
DISSEMBLED 4 FR 0.0004 REL FR 3 V 1 P
the first that ever dissembled in such a gown. TN 4.02. 5 P
whose fury not dissembled speaks his griefs. TIT 1.01.438
will repent | that thus dissembled her delight; PP 18.28
women work, | dissembled with an outward show, 18.38
DISSEMBLER 2 FR 0.0002 REL FR 2 V 0 P
thou dost wrong me, thou dissembler, thou — ADO 5.01. 53
arise, dissembler! R3 1.02.184
DISSEMBLERS 1 FR 0.0001 REL FR 1 V 0 P
all forsworn, all naught, all dissemblers. ROM 3.02. 87
DISSEMBLING 14 FR 0.0015 REL FR 10 V 4 P
you dissembling knight! WIV 3.03.144 P
dissembling villain, thou speak'st false in both ERR 4.04.100
dissembling harlot, thou art false in all, | and 4.04.101
what wicked and dissembling glass of mine | made MND 2.02. 98
his very hair is of the dissembling color. AYL 3.04. 7 P
o thou dissembling cub! TN 5.01.164
should be found such false dissembling guile? 1H6 4.01. 63
all dissembling set aside, | tell me for truth 3H6 3.03.119
cheated of feature by dissembling nature, R3 1.01. 19
but the plain devil and dissembling looks? 1.02.236
that dissembling abominable varlet, diomed, has TRO 5.04. 2 P
sleeve back to the dissembling luxurious drab, 5.04. 8 P
play one scene | of excellent dissembling, and ANT 1.03. 79
o | dissembling courtesy! CYM 1.01. 84
DISSEMBLY 1 FR 0.0001 REL FR 0 V 1 P
is our whole dissembly appear'd? ADO 4.02. 1 P
DISSENSION 10 FR 0.0011 REL FR 10 V 0 P
comes | from our debate, from our dissension; MND 2.01.116
and for dissension, who preferreth peace | more 1H6 3.01. 33
civil dissension is a viperous worm | that gnaws 3.01. 72
this late dissension grown betwixt the peers 3.01.188
let this dissension first be tried by fight, 4.01.116
if they perceive dissension in our looks, | and 4.01.139
i feel such sharp dissension in my breast, 5.05. 84
hearts, | that no dissension hinder government. 3H6 4.06. 40
on a dissension of a doit, break out | to COR 4.04. 17
and set dissension 'twixt the son and sire, VEN 1160
DISSENSIONS 1 FR 0.0001 REL FR 0 V 1 P
and prabbles, and quarrels and dissensions, and, H5 4.08. 65 P
DISSENTIOUS 5 FR 0.0005 REL FR 5 V 0 P
thy lewd, pestiferous, and dissentious pranks, 1H6 3.01. 15
that fill his ears with such dissentious rumors. R3 1.03. 46
what's the matter, you dissentious rogues, COR 1.01.164
behold | dissentious numbers pest'ring streets, 4.06. 7
spring, | this carry-tale, dissentious jealousy, VEN 657
DISSEVER 2 FR 0.0002 REL FR 2 V 0 P
or to dissever so | our great self and our AWW 2.01.122
that done, dissever your united strengths, | and JN 2.01.388
DISSEVER'D 1 FR 0.0001 REL FR 1 V 0 P
gap of time since first | we were dissever'd. WT 5.03.155
/DISSIPATION 1 FR 0.0001 REL FR 0 V 1 P
/of /friends, /dissipation /of /cohorts, LR 1.02.148 P
DISSOLUTE 3 FR 0.0003 REL FR 2 V 1 P
his dissolute disease will scarce obey this WIV 3.03.191 P
point of honor to support | so dissolute a crew. R2 5.03. 12
as dissolute as desperate, yet through both | i 5.03. 20
DISSOLUTELY 3 FR 0.0003 REL FR 0 V 3 P
that i am freely dissolv'd, and dissolutely. WIV 1.01.252 P
save the fall is in the ord "dissolutely." 1.01.254 P
night and most dissolutely spent on tuesday 1H4 1.02. 34 P
DISSOLUTION 4 FR 0.0004 REL FR 2 V 2 P
a man of continual dissolution and thaw. WIV 3.05.116 P
that the dissolution of it must cure it. MM 3.02.223 P
reproach and dissolution hangeth over him. R2 2.01.258
love's fire fear's frost hath dissolution. LUC 355
/DISSOLUTIONS 1 FR 0.0001 REL FR 0 V 1 P
/dearth, /dissolutions /of /ancient /amities, LR 1.02.145 P
DISSOLV'D 6 FR 0.0006 REL FR 5 V 1 P
that i am freely dissolv'd, and dissolutely. WIV 1.01.251 P
so he dissolv'd, and show'rs of oaths did melt. MND 1.01.245
as if the world were all dissolv'd to tears, R2 3.02.108
the bonds of heaven are slipp'd, dissolv'd, and TRO 5.02.156
they are dissolv'd. COR 1.01.204
for stones dissolv'd to water do convert. LUC 592
DISSOLVE 10 FR 0.0011 REL FR 10 V 0 P
yea, all which it inherit, shall dissolve, | and TMP 4.01.154
are now so sure that nothing can dissolve us. WIV 5.05.224
who gently would dissolve the bands of life, R2 2.02. 71
that you in pity may dissolve to dew | and wash 5.01. 9
lest his ungovern'd rage dissolve the life LR 4.04. 19
hold it in, | for i am almost ready to dissolve, 5.03.204
as it determines, so | dissolve my life! ANT 3.13.162
dissolve, thick cloud, and rain, that i may say 5.02.299
alas, | dissolve, my life! TNK 3.02. 29
would in thy palm dissolve, or seem to melt. VEN 144
DISSOLVED 1 FR 0.0001 REL FR 1 V 0 P
home, | i quickly were dissolved from my hive, AWW 1.02. 66
DISSOLVES 3 FR 0.0003 REL FR 3 V 0 P
the charm dissolves apace, | and as the morning TMP 5.01. 64
which with an hour's heat | dissolves to water, TGV 3.02. 8
what wax so frozen but dissolves with temp'ring, VEN 565
DIS-STAIN'D 1 FR 0.0001 REL FR 1 V 0 P
bed, | i live dis-stain'd, thou undishonored. ERR 2.02.146
DISSUADE 7 FR 0.0008 REL FR 2 V 5 P
i pray you dissuade him from her, she is no ADO 2.01.165 P
underhand means labor'd to dissuade him from it; AYL 1.01.141 P
challenger's youth i would fain dissuade him, 1.02.160 P
thee did manifoldly dissuade me from believing AWW 2.03.204 P
cannot for all that dissuade succession, but 3.05. 23 P
there did dissuade | great herod to incline ANT 4.06. 12
dissuade one foolish heart from serving thee, SON 141.10
DISSUADED 2 FR 0.0002 REL FR 2 V 0 P
when i dissuaded him from his intent, | and LR 2.01. 64
which | we were dissuaded by our wicked queen, CYM 5.05.463
DI'ST 1 FR 0.0001 REL FR 1 V 0 P
let go, slave, or thou di'st! LR 4.06.236
DISTAFF 3 FR 0.0003 REL FR 2 V 1 P
it hangs like flax on a distaff; TN 1.03.102 P
and give the distaff | into my husband's hands. LR 4.02. 17
which could have turn'd | a distaff to a lance, CYM 5.03. 34
DISTAFFS 1 FR 0.0001 REL FR 1 V 0 P
stay, | we'll thwack him hence with distaffs. WT 1.02. 37
DISTAFF-WOMEN 1 FR 0.0001 REL FR 1 V 0 P
distaff-women manage rusty bills | against thy R2 3.02.118
/DISTAIN 1 FR 0.0001 REL FR 1 V 0 P
she did /distain my child, and stood between PER 4.03. 31
DISTAIN 2 FR 0.0002 REL FR 2 V 0 P
they would restrain the one, distain the other. R3 5.03.322
the silver-shining queen he would distain; LUC 786
DISTAINS 1 FR 0.0001 REL FR 1 V 0 P
the worthiness of praise distains his worth, TRO 1.03.241
DISTANCE 19 FR 0.0021 REL FR 14 V 5 P
and that, i hope, is an unmeasurable distance. WIV 2.01.105 P
in these times you stand on distance: 2.01.225 P
stock, thy reverse, thy distance, thy montant. 2.03. 27 P
his /givings-out were of an infinite distance MM 1.04. 54
in the world, i will hold a long distance. AWW 3.02. 24 P
she knew her distance and did angle for me, 5.03.212
meet his grace just distance 'tween our armies. 2H4 4.01.224
on, and we'll digest | th' abuse of distance; H5 2.pr. 32
in the choir, fell off | a distance from her; H8 4.01. 65
keeps time, distance, and proportion; ROM 2.04. 21 P
and in such bloody distance, | that every minute MAC 3.01.115
t' hold what distance | his wisdom can provide. 3.06. 44
that hold their honors in a wary distance, | the OTH 2.03. 56
no farther off | than in a politic distance. 3.03. 13
nor yet the other's distance comfort me. PER 1.02. 10
distance and no space was seen | 'twixt this PHT 30
injurious distance should not stop my way, | for SON 44. 2
with safest distance i mine honor shielded. LC 151
but kept cold distance, and did thence remove 237
DISTANT 6 FR 0.0006 REL FR 4 V 2 P
house, which at that very distant time stood, as MM 2.01. 92 P
bachelor and a maid, | so far be distant; MND 2.02. 60
you, as 'twere, some distant knowledge of him, HAM 2.01. 13
how far is his court distant from this shore? PER 2.01.106 P
ye speak, | diana's temple is not distant far, 3.04. 13
bat, | and comely distant sits he by her side; LC 65
DISTASTE 4 FR 0.0004 REL FR 4 V 0 P
(although my will distaste what it elected) TRO 2.02. 66
cannot distaste the goodness of a quarrel 2.02.123
if he distaste it, let him to my sister, | whose LR 1.03. 14
which at the first are scarce found to distaste, OTH 3.03.327
DISTASTED 1 FR 0.0001 REL FR 1 V 0 P
kiss, | distasted with the salt of broken tears. TRO 4.04. 48
DISTASTEFUL 1 FR 0.0001 REL FR 1 V 0 P
after distasteful looks, and these hard TIM 2.02.211
DISTEMPER 11 FR 0.0012 REL FR 5 V 6 P
i would not ha' your distemper in this kind for WIV 3.03.216 P
provok'd and instigated by his distemper, and, 3.05. 76 P
and patience to this his distemper he is in now. 4.02. 28 P
of my fate might perhaps distemper yours; TN 2.01. 5 P
a sickness | which puts some of us in distemper, WT 1.02.385
if little faults, proceeding on distemper, H5 2.02. 54
the head and source of all your son's distemper. HAM 2.02. 55
good my lord, what is your cause of distemper? 3.02.337 P
son, | upon the heat and flame of thy distemper 3.04.123
a dram of this | will drive away distemper. CYM 3.04.191
she is continually in a harmless distemper, TNK 4.03. 3 P
DISTEMPERATURE 2 FR 0.0002 REL FR 2 V 0 P
and thorough this distemperature we see | the MND 2.01.106
upon what ground is his distemperature? PER 5.01. 27
DISTEMPERATURES 1 FR 0.0001 REL FR 1 V 0 P
of pale distemperatures and foes to life? ERR 5.01. 82
DISTEMPER'D 8 FR 0.0009 REL FR 6 V 2 P
saw i him touch'd with anger, so distemper'd. TMP 4.01.145

malvolio, and taste with a distemper'd appetite. TN 1.05. 91 P
sky, | no scope of nature, no distemper'd day, JN 3.04.154
once more to-day well met, distemper'd lords! 4.03. 21
he cannot buckle his distemper'd cause | within MAC 5.02. 15
she is then distemper'd | /far worse than now TNK 4.01.119
of her eye hath distemper'd the other senses. 4.03. 71 P
and thither hied, a sad distemper'd guest; SON 153.12
DISTEMPERED 3 FR 0.0003 REL FR 3 V 0 P
that this distempered messenger of wet, | the AWW 1.03.151
it is but as a body yet distempered, | which to 2H4 3.01. 41
it argues a distempered head | so soon to bid ROM 2.03. 33
DISTEMP'RATURE 3 FR 0.0003 REL FR 3 V 0 P
our grandam earth, having this distemp'rature, 1H4 3.01. 33
the day looks pale | at his distemp'rature. 5.01. 3
thou art up-rous'd with some distemp'rature; ROM 2.03. 40
DISTEMP'RED 2 FR 0.0002 REL FR 1 V 1 P
to the hot passion of distemp'red blood | than TRO 2.02.169
is in his retirement marvellous distemp'red. HAM 3.02.301 P
DISTEMP'RING* 2 FR 0.0002 REL FR 2 V 0 P
(being full of supper and distemp'ring draughts) OTH 1.01. 99
distemp'ring gentle love in his desire, | as air VEN 653
DISTILL 4 FR 0.0004 REL FR 4 V 0 P
which they distill now in the curbed time, | to AWW 2.04. 45
evil, | would men observingly distill it out; H5 4.01. 5
that shall distill from these two ancient /urns, TIT 3.01. 17
distill? CYM 1.05. 13
DISTILLATION 2 FR 0.0002 REL FR 1 V 1 P
to be stopp'd in, like a strong distillation, WIV 3.05.113 P
then were not summer's distillation left | a SON 5. 9
DISTILL'D 11 FR 0.0012 REL FR 10 V 1 P
you some of this distill'd carduus benedictus, ADO 3.04. 73 P
but earthlier happy is the rose distill'd, MND 1.01. 76
nature presently distill'd | helen's cheek, but AYL 3.02.144
us all) a man distill'd | out of our virtues, TRO 1.03.350
as fresh as morning dew distill'd on flowers? TIT 2.03.201
or, wanting that, with tears distill'd by moans. ROM 5.03. 15
and that, distill'd by magic sleights, | shall MAC 3.05. 26
distill'd | almost to jelly with the act of fear HAM 1.02.204
but flowers distill'd, though they with winter SON 5.13
in thee thy summer ere thou be distill'd: 6. 2
distill'd from limbecks foul as hell within, 119. 2
DISTILLED 1 FR 0.0001 REL FR 1 V 0 P
balm his foul head in warm distilled waters, SHR in.1. 48
DISTILLING 2 FR 0.0002 REL FR 2 V 0 P
and this distilling liquor drink thou off, ROM 4.01. 94
so they were dew'd with such distilling showers. VEN 66
DISTILLMENT 1 FR 0.0001 REL FR 1 V 0 P
of my ears did pour | the leprous distillment, HAM 1.05. 64
DISTILLS 1 FR 0.0001 REL FR 1 V 0 P
that shall vade, by verse distills your truth. SON 54.14
DISTINCT 3 FR 0.0003 REL FR 3 V 0 P
to offend and judge are distinct offices, | and MV 2.09. 61
with distinct breath and consign'd kisses to TRO 4.04. 45
and make distinct the very breach whereout 4.05.245
DISTINCTION 10 FR 0.0011 REL FR 8 V 2 P
would quite confound distinction, yet stands off AWW 2.03.120
i have no skill in sense | to make distinction. 3.04. 40
your distinction? 4.05. 26 P
we can hardly make distinction of our hands. TN 2.03.161 P
distinction, with a broad and powerful fan, TRO 1.03. 27
that i shall lose distinction in my joys, | as 3.02. 27
bran together | he throws without distinction. COR 3.01.321
and his sword | grants scarce distinction. ANT 3.01. 29
doth make distinction | of place 'tween high and CYM 4.02.248
branches, which | distinction should be rich in. 5.05.384
DISTINCTLY 7 FR 0.0008 REL FR 5 V 2 P
yards and boresprit, would i flame distinctly, TMP 1.02.200
thou dost snore distinctly, | there's meaning in 2.01.217
the office did | distinctly his full function. H8 1.01. 45
and bury all, which yet distinctly ranges, | in COR 3.01.205
and their charges, distinctly billeted, already 4.03. 44 P
a mass of things, but nothing distinctly; OTH 2.03.289 P
i do not in position | distinctly speak of her, 3.03.235
DISTINCTS 1 FR 0.0001 REL FR 1 V 0 P
but in one, | two distincts, division none: PHT 27
/DISTINGUE 1 FR 0.0001 REL FR 0 V 1 P
et tres /distingue seigneur d'angleterre. H5 4.04. 57 P
DISTINGUISH 11 FR 0.0012 REL FR 10 V 1 P
ey'd awry | distinguish form; R2 2.02. 20
sight may distinguish colors; 2H6 2.01.127
nor more can you distinguish of a man | than of R3 3.01. 9
and could of men distinguish her election, | sh' HAM 3.02. 64
one hears that, | which can distinguish sound. LR 4.06.211
and since i could distinguish betwixt a benefit OTH 1.03.312 P
/this eye or ear | distinguish him from others, CYM 1.03. 10
which can distinguish 'twixt | the fiery orbs 1.06. 34
here | that ruder tongues distinguish villager, TNK 3.05.104
cannot distinguish, but must cry for both! 4.02. 54
that no man could distinguish what he said. LUC 1785
DISTINGUISH'D 3 FR 0.0003 REL FR 3 V 0 P
as could not be distinguish'd but by names. ERR 1.01. 52
nor can we be distinguish'd by our faces | for SHR 1.01.200
in a vault, | that mought not be distinguish'd; 3H6 5.02. 45
DISTINGUISHES 1 FR 0.0001 REL FR 1 V 0 P
the valued file | distinguishes the swift, the MAC 3.01. 95
DISTINGUISHMENT 1 FR 0.0001 REL FR 1 V 0 P
and mannerly distinguishment leave out | betwixt WT 2.01. 86
DISTRACT 10 FR 0.0011 REL FR 9 V 1 P
the fellow is distract, and so am i, | and here ERR 4.03. 42
they say, poor gentleman, he's much distract. TN 5.01.280
mine hair be fix'd an end, as one distract; 2H6 3.02.318
case, | to see thy noble uncle thus distract? TIT 4.03. 26
with this she fell distract, | and, her JC 4.03.155
she is importunate, indeed distract. HAM 4.05. 2
better i were distract, | so should my thoughts LR 4.06.281
one gender of herbs or distract it with many, OTH 1.03.323 P
distract your army, which doth most consist | of ANT 3.07. 43
comes | their distract parcels in combined sums. LC 231
DISTRACTED *(also distraught)*
DISTRACTED 14 FR 0.0015 REL FR 12 V 2 P
brother, and yours, abide all three distracted, TMP 5.01. 12
in most uneven and distracted manner. MM 4.04. 3 P
to fetch my poor distracted husband hence. ERR 5.01. 39
i led them on in this distracted fear, | and MND 3.02. 31
brightest beams | distracted clouds give way, so AWW 5.03. 35
and the truth is, poverty hath distracted her. 2H4 2.01.107 P
accept distracted thanks. TRO 5.02.189
you only speak from your distracted soul; TIM 3.04.113
hath a distracted and most wretched being, 4.03.246
they star'd and were distracted; MAC 2.03.104
memory holds a seat | in this distracted globe. HAM 1.05. 97
he does confess he feels himself distracted, 3.01. 5
he's lov'd of the distracted multitude, | who 4.03. 4
silence those whom this vild brawl distracted. OTH 2.03.256
DISTRACTEDLY 2 FR 0.0002 REL FR 2 V 0 P
for she did speak in starts distractedly. TN 2.02. 21
the mind and sight distractedly commix'd. LC 28
/DISTRACTION 2 FR 0.0002 REL FR 2 V 0 P
you flow to great /distraction. TRO 5.02. 41
behold, /distraction, frenzy, and amazement, 5.03. 85
DISTRACTION 11 FR 0.0012 REL FR 8 V 3 P
in her invention and ford's wive's distraction, WIV 3.05. 86 P
i know not what 'twas but distraction. TN 5.01. 68
this savors not much of distraction. 5.01.314
as if you held a brow of much distraction. WT 1.02.149
of such distraction that they were to be known 5.02. 48 P
madam, this is a mere distraction, | you turn H8 3.01.112
tears in his eyes, distraction in his aspect, HAM 2.02.555
how i am punish'd | with a sore distraction. 5.02.230
breath, but now | make boot of his distraction: ANT 4.01. 9
her distraction is more at some time of the moon TNK 4.03. 1 P
in the distraction of this madding fever? SON 119. 8
DISTRACTIONS 2 FR 0.0002 REL FR 2 V 0 P
are all knit up | in their distractions. TMP 3.03. 90
his power went out in such distractions as ANT 3.07. 76
DISTRACTS 1 FR 0.0001 REL FR 0 V 1 P
this news distracts me! WIV 2.02.134 P
DISTRAIN'D 2 FR 0.0002 REL FR 2 V 0 P
my father's goods are all distrain'd and sold, R2 2.03.131
hath here distrain'd the tower to his use. 1H6 1.03. 61
DISTRAUGHT *(also distracted)*
DISTRAUGHT 2 FR 0.0002 REL FR 2 V 0 P
as if thou were distraught and mad with terror? R3 3.05. 4
o, if i /wake, shall i not be distraught, ROM 4.03. 49
/DISTRESS 1 FR 0.0001 REL FR 1 V 0 P
and remediate | in the good man's /distress! LR 4.04. 18
DISTRESS 17 FR 0.0019 REL FR 15 V 2 P
of the same strain were in the same distress. WIV 3.03.186 P
art thou thus bolden'd, man, by thy distress? AYL 2.07. 91
of bare distress hath ta'en from me the show 2.07. 95
i do pity his distress in my /similes of comfort AWW 5.02. 24 P
was, | again, in pity of my hard distress, 1H6 2.05. 87
not fearing death, nor shrinking for distress, 4.01. 37
me, | as you would beg, were you in my distress. R3 1.04.266
our fatherless distress was left unmoan'd, 2.02. 64
help, yet do not | upbraid 's with our distress. COR 5.01. 35
who, though they cannot answer my distress, TIT 3.01. 38
loves to him in this suppos'd | distress of his; TIM 5.01. 13
lauds, | as one incapable of her own distress, HAM 4.07.178
he wrings at some distress. CYM 3.06. 78
lord is taken | heart-deep with your distress. TNK 1.01.105
distress likes dumps when time is kept with LUC 1127
to find a face where all distress is stell'd. 1444
but none where all distress and dolor dwell'd, 1446
DISTRESS'D 8 FR 0.0009 REL FR 8 V 0 P
o, send some succor to the distress'd lord! 1H6 4.03. 30
my state, 'twixt cade and york distress'd, 2H6 4.09. 31
you three on me, threefold distress'd, | pour R3 2.02. 86
being distress'd, was by that wretch betray'd, H8 2.01.110
this youth, how e'er distress'd, appears he hath CYM 4.02. 47
what woman i may stead that is distress'd | does TNK 1.01. 36
leaves love upon her back, deeply distress'd. VEN 814
distress'd, | wounding itself to death, rise up LUC 465
/DISTRESSED 1 FR 0.0001 REL FR 1 V 0 P
/the /poor /distressed /lear's /i' /th' /town, LR 4.03. 38
DISTRESSED 9 FR 0.0010 REL FR 9 V 0 P
o that thou wert not, poor distressed soul! ERR 4.04. 59
but by thy help to this distressed queen? 3H6 3.03.213
sons, | a beauty-waning and distressed widow, R3 3.07.185
for happy wife, a most distressed widow; 4.04. 98
the eldest son of this distressed queen. TIT 1.01.103
and rather comfort his distressed plight | than 4.04. 32
despis'd, distressed, hated, martyr'd, kill'd! ROM 4.05. 59
o my distressed lord, even such our griefs are; PER 1.04. 7
lord, | a stranger and distressed gentleman, 2.05. 46
DISTRESSES 3 FR 0.0003 REL FR 3 V 0 P
notes | tune my distresses and record my woes. TGV 5.04. 6
women fight, | to doff their dire distresses. MAC 4.03.188
be advocate | for us and our distresses! TNK 1.01. 32
DISTRESSFUL 4 FR 0.0004 REL FR 4 V 0 P
him to rest, cramm'd with distressful bread, H5 4.01.270
to ease your country of distressful war | and 1H6 5.04.126
and all the ruins of distressful times R3 4.04.318
when i did speak of some distressful stroke OTH 1.03.157
DISTRIBUTE 2 FR 0.0002 REL FR 2 V 0 P
(you see the poor remainder) could distribute, H8 5.03. 20
on the ministers | that doth distribute it — in COR 3.03. 99
DISTRIBUTED 1 FR 0.0001 REL FR 1 V 0 P
got on the antiates | was ne'er distributed. COR 3.03. 5
DISTRIBUTION 2 FR 0.0002 REL FR 2 V 0 P
before the common distribution, at | your only COR 1.09. 35
so distribution should undo excess, | and each LR 4.01. 70
DISTRUST 6 FR 0.0006 REL FR 6 V 0 P
that i am ready to distrust mine eyes | and TN 4.03. 13
let not the world see fear and sad distrust JN 5.01. 46
one sudden foil shall never breed distrust. 1H6 3.03. 11
from /your former state, | that i distrust you. HAM 3.02.165
yet, though i distrust, | discomfort you, my 3.02.165
make me not offended | in your distrust. ANT 3.02. 34
DISTRUSTFUL 1 FR 0.0001 REL FR 1 V 0 P
distrustful recreants, | fight till the last 1H6 1.02.126
DISTURB 14 FR 0.0015 REL FR 14 V 0 P
not a mouse | shall disturb this hallowed house. MND 5.01.388
shall we disturb him, since he keeps no mean? 1H6 1.02.121
to trouble and disturb the king and us? 4.01.127
and charge that no man should disturb your rest 2H6 3.02.256
disturb him not, let him pass peaceably. 3.03. 25
here they be that dare and will disturb thee. 4.08. 6
buckingham, to disturb me? 5.01. 12
you'll find a most unfit time to disturb him. H8 2.02. 60
if ever you disturb our streets again | your ROM 1.01. 96
god shield i should disturb devotion! 4.01. 41
let none disturb us. PER 1.02. 1
'twill disturb us, | we shall have time enough. TNK 3.03. 15
should by his stealing in disturb the feast?" VEN 450
"disturb his hours of rest with restless trances LUC 974
DISTURBANCES 1 FR 0.0001 REL FR 1 V 0 P
and can speak of the disturbances | that nature PER 3.02. 37
DISTURB'D 7 FR 0.0008 REL FR 7 V 0 P
be not disturb'd with my infirmity. TMP 4.01.160
and life-preserving rest | to be disturb'd, ERR 5.01. 84
with thy brawls thou hast disturb'd our sport. MND 2.01. 87
with course disturb'd even thy confining shores, JN 2.01.338
that all the courts of france will be disturb'd H5 1.02.265
nor we disturb'd with prodigies on earth. TIT 1.01.101
have thrice disturb'd the quiet of our streets, ROM 1.01. 91
DISTURBED 4 FR 0.0004 REL FR 4 V 0 P
neither disturbed with the effect of wine, | nor ERR 5.01.215
this disturbed sky | is not to walk in. JC 1.03. 39
looks on the dull earth with disturbed mind, VEN 340
from sleep disturbed, heedfully doth view | the LUC 454
DISTURBERS 2 FR 0.0002 REL FR 2 V 0 P
foes to my rest and my sweet sleep's disturbers, R3 4.02. 73
however these disturbers of our peace | buzz in TIT 4.04. 6
DISTURBING 2 FR 0.0002 REL FR 1 V 1 P
like a dog, but for disturbing the lords within. COR 4.05. 52 P
reigns, disturbing jealousy | doth call himself VEN 649
DISUNITE 1 FR 0.0001 REL FR 0 V 1 P
it was a strong composure a fool could disunite. TRO 2.03.100 P
DISVALUED 1 FR 0.0001 REL FR 1 V 0 P
for that her reputation was disvalued | in MM 5.01.221
DISVOUCH'D 1 FR 0.0001 REL FR 0 V 1 P
every letter he hath writ hath disvouch'd other. MM 4.04. 1 P
DIT 1 FR 0.0001 REL FR 0 V 1 P
c'est bien dit, madame, il est fort bon anglois. H5 3.04. 19 P
DITCH 5 FR 0.0005 REL FR 4 V 1 P
empty it in the muddy ditch close by the thames WIV 3.03. 15 P
to say he'll turn your current in a ditch, | and COR 3.01. 96
safe in a ditch he bides, | with twenty trenched MAC 3.04. 25
no, i will go seek | some ditch wherein to die; ANT 4.06. 37
rather a ditch in egypt | be gentle grave unto 5.02. 57
DITCH'D 1 FR 0.0001 REL FR 1 V 0 P
close by the battle, ditch'd, and wall'd with CYM 5.03. 14
DITCH-DELIVER'D 1 FR 0.0001 REL FR 1 V 0 P
babe | ditch-deliver'd by a drab, | make the MAC 4.01. 31
DITCH-DOG 1 FR 0.0001 REL FR 0 V 1 P
swallows the old rat and the ditch-dog; LR 3.04.133 P
DITCHERS 1 FR 0.0001 REL FR 0 V 1 P
is no ancient gentlemen but gard'ners, ditchers, HAM 5.01. 30 P
DITCHES 2 FR 0.0002 REL FR 2 V 0 P
behind the ditches of the abbey here. ERR 5.01.122
let this damn you, | and ditches grave you all! TIM 4.03.166
DITES-MOI 2 FR 0.0002 REL FR 0 V 2 P
ecoutez, dites-moi si je parle bien: H5 3.04. 17 P
dites-moi l'anglois pour le bras. 3.04. 21 P
DIT-IL 4 FR 0.0004 REL FR 0 V 4 P
que dit-il, monsieur? H5 4.04. 33 P
petit monsieur, que dit-il? 4.04. 49 P
que dit-il? que je suis semblable a les anges? 5.02.111 P
oui, vraiment, sauf votre grace, ainsi dit-il. 5.02.112 P
DITTIES 2 FR 0.0002 REL FR 2 V 0 P
sing no more ditties, sing no moe, | of dumps so ADO 2.03. 70
makes welsh as sweet as ditties highly penn'd, 1H4 3.01.206
DITTY 7 FR 0.0008 REL FR 6 V 1 P
the ditty does remember my drown'd father. TMP 1.02.406
and this ditty, after me, | sing, and dance it MND 5.01.395
though there was no great matter in the ditty, AYL 5.03. 35 P
to the harp | many an english ditty lovely well, 1H4 3.01.122
note, | and sings extemporally a woeful ditty, VEN 836
for she doth welcome daylight with her ditty, PP 14.19
a thorn, | and there sung the dolefull'st ditty, 20.11
DIURNAL 1 FR 0.0001 REL FR 1 V 0 P
bring | their fiery torcher his diurnal ring, AWW 2.01.162
DIV'D 1 FR 0.0001 REL FR 1 V 0 P
hath not yet div'd into the world's deceit; R3 3.01. 8
DIVE 7 FR 0.0008 REL FR 7 V 0 P
to swim, to dive into the fire, to ride | on the TMP 1.02.191
to dive like buckets in concealed wells, | to JN 5.02.139
how he did seem to dive into their hearts | with R2 1.04. 25
moon, | or dive into the bottom of the deep, 1H4 1.03.203
dive, thoughts, down to my soul — here clarence R3 1.01. 41
i'll dive into the burning lake below, | and TIT 4.03. 44
that girdles in those wolves, dive in the earth, TIM 4.01. 2
DIVE-DAPPER 1 FR 0.0001 REL FR 1 V 0 P
like a dive-dapper peering through a wave, | who VEN 86
DIVER 1 FR 0.0001 REL FR 1 V 0 P
when your diver | did hang a salt-fish on his ANT 2.05. 16
DIVERS 16 FR 0.0018 REL FR 11 V 5 P
for divers philosophers hold that the lips is WIV 1.01.229 P
there came divers of antonio's creditors in my MV 3.01.113 P
time travels in divers paces with divers persons AYL 3.02.308 P
travels in divers paces with divers persons. 3.02.309 P
i will give out divers schedules of my beauty. TN 1.05.245 P
threatens them | with divers deaths in death. WT 5.01.202
divers dear friends slain? JN 3.04. 7
for divers reasons | which i shall send you 1H4 1.03.262
the cup of alteration | with divers liquors! 2H4 3.01. 53
divide | the state of man in divers functions, H5 1.02.184
myself and divers gentlemen beside | were there 1H6 4.01. 25
for divers unknown reasons, i beseech you, R3 1.02.217
confessions | of divers witnesses, which the H8 2.01. 17
with new opinions, | divers and dangerous; 5.02. 53
and from her womb children of divers kind | we ROM 2.03. 11
to ease ourselves of divers sland'rous loads, JC 4.01. 20
DIVERS-COLOR'D 1 FR 0.0001 REL FR 1 V 0 P
with divers-color'd fans, whose wind did seem ANT 2.02.203
DIVERSELY 1 FR 0.0001 REL FR 0 V 1 P
but that our wits are so diversely color'd; COR 2.03. 20 P
DIVERSITY 1 FR 0.0001 REL FR 1 V 0 P
and moe diversity of sounds, all horrible, | we TMP 5.01.234
DIVERT 3 FR 0.0003 REL FR 3 V 0 P
policy | seek to divert the english purposes. H5 2.pr. 15
divert and crack, rend and deracinate | the TRO 1.03. 99
divert strong minds to th' course of alt'ring SON 115. 8
DIVERTED 3 FR 0.0003 REL FR 3 V 0 P
malice | of a diverted blood and bloody brother. AYL 2.03. 37
her, | i could have well diverted her intents, AWW 3.04. 21
sometime diverted their poor balls are tied | to LC 24
DIVERTS 1 FR 0.0001 REL FR 1 V 0 P
infects the sound pine and diverts his grain TRO 1.03. 8
DIVES* 3 FR 0.0003 REL FR 2 V 1 P
upon hell-fire and dives that liv'd in purple; 1H4 3.03. 32 P
he dives into the king's soul, and there H8 2.02. 26
forth, | that, as a duck for life that dives, PER 3.ch. 49

DIVEST *(also devesting)*
DIVEST 2 FR 0.0002 REL FR 2 V 0 P
that you divest yourself, and lay apart | the H5 2.04. 78
(since now we will divest us both of rule, LR 1.01. 49
DIVIDABLE 1 FR 0.0001 REL FR 1 V 0 P
peaceful commerce from dividable shores, | the TRO 1.03.105
DIVIDANT 1 FR 0.0001 REL FR 1 V 0 P
and birth | scarce is dividant, touch them with TIM 4.03. 5
/DIVIDE 2 FR 0.0002 REL FR 2 V 0 P
/did /divide | /the /action /of /their /bodies 2H4 1.01.194
/divide /thy /lips, /than /we /are /confident, TRO 1.03. 72
DIVIDE 26 FR 0.0029 REL FR 21 V 5 P
sometime i'ld divide, | and burn in many places; TMP 1.02.198
divide me like a brib'd–buck, each a haunch. WIV 5.05. 24 P
he that will divide a minute into a thousand AYL 4.01. 45 P
though he divide the realm and give thee half, R2 5.01. 60
o, i could divide myself and go to buffets, for 1H4 2.03. 32 P
shall we divide our right | according to our 3.01. 69
then this remains, that we divide our power. 5.05. 34
into a thousand parts divide one man, | and make H5 pr 24
therefore doth heaven divide | the state of man 1.02.183
divide your happy england into four, | whereof 1.02.214
for which i will divide my crown with her, | and 1H6 1.06. 18
than can yourself yourself in twain divide. 4.05. 49
when this is known, then to divide the times: 3H6 2.05. 30
doth valor's show and valor's worth divide | in TRO 1.03. 46
to fight, | let mars divide eternity in twain, 2.03.245
and you shall | divide in all with us. COR 1.06. 87
task | does not divide the sunday from the week, HAM 1.01. 76
know, to divide him inventorially would dozy th' 5.02.113 P
cools, friendship falls off, brothers divide: LR 1.02.107 P
will sometimes | divide me from your bosom. ANT 2.03. 2
a ship | laden with gold, take that, divide it; 3.11. 5
should divide | our equalness to this. 5.01. 47
fiends of hell | divide themselves between you! CYM 2.04.130
her breast, it doth divide | in two slow rivers, LUC 1737
war, | how to divide the conquest of thy sight: SON 46. 2
sat, | her grievance with his hearing to divide: LC 67
DIVIDED 20 FR 0.0022 REL FR 18 V 2 P
even in a dream, were we divided from them, TMP 5.01.239
eyes, | they have o'erlook'd me and divided me: MV 3.02. 15
as she, | and she a fair divided excellence, JN 2.01.439
and must we be divided? must we part? R2 5.01. 81
the archdeacon hath divided it | into three 1H4 3.01. 71
so is the unfirm king | in three divided, and 2H4 1.03. 74
army, that divided was | into two parties, is 1H6 5.02. 11
he little thought of this divided friendship. R3 1.04.238
for we to–morrow hold divided councils, 3.01.179
all this divided york and lancaster, | divided 5.05. 27
and lancaster, | divided in their dire division, 5.05. 28
or shall they be divided | by any voice or order TRO 4.05. 69
pledges the breath of him in a divided draught, TIM 1.02. 48 P
the threefold world divided, he should stand JC 4.01. 14
divided from herself and her fair judgment, HAM 4.05. 85
know that we have divided | in three our kingdom
LR 1.01. 37
father, | i do perceive here a divided duty: OTH 1.03.181
it was divided | between her heart and lips. ANT 4.14. 32
yet sometime a divided sigh, martyr'd as 'twere TNK 2.01. 41 P
even for this, let us divided live, | and our SON 39. 5
DIVIDES 3 FR 0.0003 REL FR 3 V 0 P
o'er and o'er divides him | 'twixt his WT 4.04.551
divides one thing entire to many objects, | like R2 2.02. 17
divides more wider than the sky and earth, | and TRO 5.02.149
DIVIDETH 1 FR 0.0001 REL FR 1 V 0 P
this doth not so, for she divideth us. ROM 3.05. 30
DIVIDING 1 FR 0.0001 REL FR 1 V 0 P
hind'ring their present fall by this dividing; LUC 551
/DIVIDUAL 1 FR 0.0001 REL FR 1 V 0 P
and maid may be | more than in sex /dividual. TNK 1.03. 82
DIVINATION 4 FR 0.0004 REL FR 4 V 0 P
morton, | tell thou an earl his divination lies, 2H4 1.01. 88
high strains | of divination in our sister work TRO 2.02.114
portends | (unless my sins abuse my divination) CYM 4.02.351
bleed, | and fear doth teach it divination: VEN 670
/DIVINE 1 FR 0.0001 REL FR 1 V 0 P
/bids /thee, /with /most /divine /integrity, TRO 4.05.170
DIVINE 53 FR 0.0060 REL FR 48 V 5 P
by providence divine. TMP 1.02.159
i might call him | a thing divine, for nothing 1.02.419
sweet ornament that decks a thing divine — | ah TGV 2.01. 4
call her divine. 2.04.147
if not divine, | yet let her be a principality, 2.04.151
of such divine perfection, as sir proteus. 2.07. 13
i know him for a man divine and holy, | not MM 5.01.144
when i perceive your grace, like pow'r divine, 5.01.369
man, more divine, the master of all these, ERR 2.01. 20
than our earth's wonder, more than earth divine. 3.02. 32
now, divine air! ADO 2.03. 58 P
o most divine kate! LLL 4.03. 81
o /wood divine! 4.03.244
o helen, goddess, nymph, perfect, divine! MND 3.02.137
to call me goddess, nymph, divine and rare, 3.02.226
it is a good divine that follows his own MV 1.02. 14 P
and that with the divine forfeit of his soul AWW 3.06. 32 P
(thus by apollo's great divine seal'd up) WT 3.01. 19
if pow'rs divine | behold our human actions (as 3.02. 28
for has not the divine apollo said, | is't not 5.01. 37
earth, | or my divine soul answer it in heaven. R2 1.01. 38
better thing than earth, | divine his downfall? 3.04. 79
as thoughts of things divine, are intermix'd 5.05. 12
and your tongue divine | to a loud trumpet and a 2H4 4.01. 51
book | of forg'd rebellion with a seal divine. 4.01. 92
and, which is more, she is not so divine, | so 1H6 5.05. 16
'tis government that makes them seem divine, 3H6 1.04.132
this word "love," which greybeards call divine, 5.06. 81
vouchsafe, divine perfection of a woman, | of R3 1.02. 75
by a divine instinct men's minds mistrust 2.03. 42
which hath an operation more divine | than TRO 3.03.203
o you gods divine, | make cressid's name the 4.02. 99
what may be sworn by, both divine and human, COR 3.01.141
should from yond cloud speak divine things, 4.05.104
being a divine, a ghostly confessor, | a ROM 3.03. 49
more needs she the divine than the physician. MAC 5.01. 74
whose spirit with divine ambition puff'd | makes HAM 4.04. 49
that we are evil in, by a divine thrusting on. LR 1.02.126 P
something from cyprus, as i may divine; OTH 1.02. 39
letting go safely by | the divine desdemona. 2.01. 73
if i were bound to divine of this unity, i would ANT 2.06.116 P
thou divine imogen, what thou endur'st, CYM 2.01. 57
there is a prohibition so divine | that cravens 3.04. 77
it would fly | from so divine a temple to commix 4.02. 55
thou divine nature, thou thyself thou blazon'st 4.02.170
which mulier i divine | is this most constant 5.05.448
the gods by their divine arbitrement | have TNK 5.03.107
stealing moulds from heaven that were divine, VEN 730
with your uncleanness that which is divine; LUC 193
that eye which him beholds, as more divine, 291
when the one pure, the other made divine? 1164
sweet boy, but yet, like prayers divine, | i SON 108. 5
buy terms divine in selling hours of dross; 146.11
DIVINELY 2 FR 0.0002 REL FR 2 V 0 P
is most divinely vow'd upon the right | of him JN 2.01.237
reverend fathers, | divinely bent to meditation, R3 3.07. 62
DIVINENESS 1 FR 0.0001 REL FR 1 V 0 P
behold divineness | no elder than a boy! CYM 3.06. 43
DIVINER 1 FR 0.0001 REL FR 0 V 1 P
this drudge or diviner laid claim to me, call'd ERR 3.02.140 P
DIVINES 4 FR 0.0004 REL FR 3 V 1 P
let him be furnish'd with divines, and have all MM 3.02.209 P
to shun the danger that his soul divines. R3 3.02. 18
but meditating with two deep divines; 3.07. 75
the virtues | which our divines lose by 'em. COR 2.03. 58
DIVINEST 3 FR 0.0003 REL FR 3 V 0 P
divinest creature, astraea's daughter, | how 1H6 1.06. 4
despised substance of divinest show! ROM 3.02. 77
divinest patroness, and /midwife gentle | to PER 3.01. 11
DIVINING 2 FR 0.0002 REL FR 2 V 0 P
suggest but truth to my divining thoughts, 3H6 4.06. 69
and, for they look'd but with divining eyes, SON 106.11
DIVINITY 10 FR 0.0011 REL FR 5 V 5 P
they say there is divinity in odd numbers, WIV 5.01. 3 P
my age, | my reverence, calling, nor divinity, ADO 4.01.168
to your ears, divinity; TN 1.05.217 P
us the place alone, we will hear this divinity. 1.05.219 P
hear him but reason in divinity, | and, H5 1.01. 38
there's such divinity doth hedge a king | that HAM 4.05.124
us | there's a divinity that shapes our ends, 5.02. 10
"ay," and "no" too, was no good divinity. LR 4.06.100 P
divinity of hell! OTH 2.03.350
but to have divinity preach'd there! PER 4.05. 4 P
DIVISION 23 FR 0.0026 REL FR 19 V 4 P
rightly reason'd, and in his own division, and, ADO 5.01.224 P
substance | or the division of the twentith part MV 4.01.329
i'll make division of my present with you. TN 3.04.346
how have you made division of yourself? 5.01.222
it will the woefullest division prove | that R2 4.01.146
bow'r, | with ravishing division, to her lute. 1H4 3.01.208
and hair of our attempt | brooks no division. 4.01. 62
condition | and the division of our amity. 2H4 3.01. 79
but more, when envy breeds unkind division: 1H6 4.01.193
and lancaster, | divided in their dire division, R3 5.05. 28
and yet the spacious breadth of this division TRO 5.02.150
to come upon them in the heat of their division. COR 4.03. 19 P
some say the lark makes sweet division; ROM 3.05. 29
never come such division 'tween our souls! JC 4.03.235
abound | in the division of each several crime, MAC 4.03. 96
but now, in the division of the kingdom, it LR 1.01. 4 P
there is division | (although as yet the face of 3.01. 19
there is division between the dukes, and a worse 3.03. 8 P
nor the division of a battle knows | more than a OTH 1.01. 23
is there division 'twixt my lord and cassio? 4.01.231
if this division chance, ne'er stood between, ANT 3.04. 13
but in one, | two distincts, division none: PHT 27
itself confounded, | saw division grow together, 42
/DIVISIONS 1 FR 0.0001 REL FR 0 V 1 P
/of /ancient /amities, /divisions /in /state, LR 1.02.146 P
DIVISIONS 3 FR 0.0003 REL FR 2 V 1 P
for his divisions, as the times do brawl, | /are 2H4 1.03. 70
o, these eclipses do portend these divisions! LR 1.02.137 P
how the fear of us | may cement their divisions, ANT 2.01. 48
DIVORC'D 4 FR 0.0004 REL FR 3 V 1 P
souls and bodies hath he divorc'd three, and his TN 3.04.237 P
doubly divorc'd! R2 5.01. 71
that from this golden rigol hath divorc'd | so 2H4 4.05. 36
of all these learned men she was divorc'd, | and H8 4.01. 32
DIVORCE 22 FR 0.0024 REL FR 21 V 1 P
so that, in this unjust divorce of us, | fortune ERR 1.01.104
and quite divorce his memory from his part. LLL 5.02.150
deadly divorce step between me and you! AWW 5.03.318
mark your divorce, young sir, | whom son i dare WT 4.04.417
made a divorce betwixt his queen and him, R2 3.01. 12
that would divorce this terror from my heart" — 5.04. 9
sweet earl, divorce not wisdom from your honor, 2H4 1.01.162
to make divorce of their incorporate league; H5 5.02.366
i here divorce myself | both from thy table, 3H6 1.01.247
and, as the long divorce of steel falls on me, H8 2.01. 76
he counsels a divorce, a loss of her | that, 2.02. 30
fortune, do divorce | it from the bearer, 'tis a 2.03. 14
but death | shall e'er divorce my dignities. 3.01.142
in the divorce his contrary proceedings | are 3.02. 26
holiness | to stay the judgment o' th' divorce; 3.02. 33
which | have satisfied the king for his divorce, 3.02. 65
and dear divorce | 'twixt natural /son and /sire TIM 4.03.381
i would divorce me from thy /mother's tomb, LR 2.04.131
he will divorce you, | or put upon you what OTH 1.02. 14
weep this lamentable divorce under her colors CYM 1.04. 20 P
that horrid act | of the divorce he'ld make. 2.01. 62
hateful divorce of love" — thus chides she VEN 932
DIVORCED 1 FR 0.0001 REL FR 1 V 0 P
beguil'd, divorced, wronged, spited, slain! ROM 4.05. 55
DIVORCEMENT 1 FR 0.0001 REL FR 1 V 0 P
he do shake me off | to beggarly divorcement) OTH 4.02.158
DIVULG'D 1 FR 0.0001 REL FR 1 V 0 P
in voices well divulg'd, free, learn'd, and TN 1.05.260
DIVULGE 1 FR 0.0001 REL FR 0 V 1 P
divulge page himself for a secure and willful WIV 3.02. 42 P
DIVULGED 2 FR 0.0002 REL FR 2 V 0 P
a strumpet's boldness, a divulged shame, AWW 2.01.171
and that shall be divulged well | in characters TRO 5.02.163
DIVULGING 1 FR 0.0001 REL FR 1 V 0 P
to keep it from divulging, let it feed | even on HAM 4.01. 22
DIZZY 3 FR 0.0003 REL FR 2 V 1 P
then have we here young dizzy, and young master
MM 4.03. 12 P
shall dizzy with more clamor neptune's ear | in TRO 5.02.174
how fearful | and dizzy 'tis, to cast one's eyes LR 4.06. 12
DIZZY–EY'D 1 FR 0.0001 REL FR 1 V 0 P
none, | dizzy–ey'd fury and great rage of heart 1H6 4.07. 11
DO* *(also d'*, de*)*
/DO* 34 FR 0.0038 REL FR 28 V 6 P
DO* 3964 FR 0.4480 REL FR 3020 V 944 P
DOBBIN 1 FR 0.0001 REL FR 0 V 1 P
on thy chin than dobbin my fill–horse has on his MV 2.02. 95 P
DOBBIN'S 1 FR 0.0001 REL FR 0 V 1 P
seem then that dobbin's tail grows backward. MV 2.02. 96 P
/DOCK'D 1 FR 0.0001 REL FR 1 V 0 P
and see my wealthy andrew /dock'd in sand, MV 1.01. 27
DOCKS 2 FR 0.0002 REL FR 2 V 0 P
or docks, or mallows. TMP 2.01.145
and nothing teems | but hateful docks, rough H5 5.02. 52
DOCTOR 71 FR 0.0080 REL FR 42 V 29 P
and ask of doctor caius' house which is the way; WIV 1.02. 1 P
if you can see my master, master doctor caius, 1.04. 3 P
the very yea and the no is, the french doctor, 1.04. 94 P
the welsh priest and caius the french doctor. 2.01.202 P
i myself dwell with master doctor caius — 2.02. 46 P
/god save you, master doctor caius! 2.03. 19 P
now, good master doctor! 2.03. 20 P
he is the wiser man, master doctor: 2.03. 38 P
master doctor caius, i am come to fetch you home 2.03. 52 P
you must go with me, master doctor. 2.03. 56 P
and i will bring the doctor about by the fields. 2.03. 78 P
adieu, good master doctor. 2.03. 81 P
caius, that calls himself doctor of physic? 3.01. 4 P
master doctor caius, the renown'd french 3.01. 60 P
here comes doctor caius. 3.01. 72 P
so do you, good master doctor. 3.01. 75 P
shall i lose my doctor? 3.01.102 P
but my wife, master doctor, is for you 3.02. 62 P
master doctor, you shall go, so shall you, 3.02. 82 P
that's my master, master doctor. 3.04. 85 P
i'll to the doctor, he hath my good will, | and 4.04. 84
the doctor is well money'd, and his friends 4.04. 88
three german devils, three doctor faustuses. 4.05. 69 P
here, master doctor, in perplexity and doubtful 4.05. 84 P
against that match | and firm for doctor caius) 4.06. 28
likewise hath | made promise to the doctor, 4.06. 34
(the better to /denote her to the doctor, | for 4.06. 39
and when the doctor spies his vantage ripe, | to 4.06. 43
master doctor, my daughter is in green. 5.03. 1 P
daughter, she is, by this, doctor caius' wife. 5.05.175 P
she is now with the doctor at the dean'ry, and 5.05.202 P
why went you not with master doctor, maid? 5.05.219
good doctor pinch, you are a conjurer, ERR 4.04. 47
good master doctor, see him safe convey'd | home 4.04.122
beaten the maids a–row, and bound the doctor, 5.01.170
ape, but then is an ape a doctor to such a man. ADO 5.01.202 P
this | into my /cousin's hands, doctor bellario, MV 3.04. 50
this court, | unless bellario, a learned doctor, 4.01.105
a messenger with letters from the doctor, | new 4.01.108
a young and learned doctor to our court. 4.01.144
visitation was with me a young doctor of rome. 4.01.153 P
and here, i take it, is the doctor come. 4.01.168
here 'tis, most reverend doctor, here it is. 4.01.226
my soul, | no woman had it, but a civil doctor, 5.01.210
the ring of me to give the worthy doctor. 5.01.222
let not that doctor e'er come near my house. 5.01.223
own, | i'll have that doctor for /my bedfellow. 5.01.233
by heaven, it is the same i gave the doctor! 5.01.257
for, by this ring, the doctor lay with me. 5.01.259
there you shall find that portia was the doctor, 5.01.269
were you the doctor, and i knew you not? 5.01.280
sweet doctor, you shall be my bedfellow — 5.01.284
why, doctor she! AWW 2.01. 79
you giant, what says the doctor to my water? 2H4 1.02. 1 P
go, lovel, with all speed to doctor shaw; R3 3.05.103
was not one doctor pace | in this man's place H8 2.02.121
i thank you, doctor. MAC 4.03.145
good night, good doctor. 5.01. 79
how does your patient, doctor? 5.03. 37
doctor, the thanes fly from me. 5.03. 49
if thou couldst, doctor, cast | the water of my 5.03. 50
more richer to signify this to the doctor, for, HAM 3.02.305 P
now, master doctor, have you brought those drugs
CYM 1.05. 4
i wonder, doctor, | thou ask'st me such a 1.05. 10
doctor, your service for this time is ended, 1.05. 30
no further service, doctor, | until i send for 1.05. 44
yet death | will seize the doctor too. 5.05. 30
ho there, doctor! TNK 5.02. 18
thank ye, doctor. 5.02. 23
but, doctor, | methinks you are i' th' wrong 5.02. 26
i am of your mind, doctor. 5.02. 39
DOCTOR–LIKE 1 FR 0.0001 REL FR 1 V 0 P
and folly (doctor–like) controlling skill, | and SON 66.10
DOCTOR'S 3 FR 0.0003 REL FR 2 V 1 P
will chafe at the doctor's marrying my daughter. WIV 5.03. 8 P
for that same scrubbed boy, the doctor's clerk, MV 5.01.261
till i were couching witm the doctor's clerk. 5.01.305
DOCTORS 6 FR 0.0006 REL FR 4 V 2 P
we are justices and doctors and churchmen, WIV 2.03. 47 P
doctors doubt that. 5.05.174 P
comedy, | for so your doctors hold it very meet, SHR in.2. 131
when our most learned doctors leave us, and AWW 2.01.116
our doctors say this is no month to bleed. R2 1.01.157
fathers of the land | and doctors learn'd. H8 2.04.207
DOCTRINE 8 FR 0.0009 REL FR 7 V 1 P
from women's eyes this doctrine i derive: LLL 4.03.298
from women's eyes this doctrine i derive: 4.03.347
embowell'd of their doctrine, have left off AWW 1.03.241
a comfortable doctrine, and much may be said of TN 1.05.222 P
we knew not | the doctrine of ill–doing, nor WT 1.02. 70
would show a worse sin than ill doctrine. H8 1.03. 60
i'll pay that doctrine, or else die in debt. ROM 1.01.238
i hourly learn | a doctrine of obedience, and ANT 5.02. 31
DOCUMENT 1 FR 0.0001 REL FR 0 V 1 P
a document in madness, thoughts and remembrance
HAM 4.05.178 P
DODGE 1 FR 0.0001 REL FR 1 V 0 P
dodge | and palter in the shifts of lowness, who ANT 3.11. 62
DOE 9 FR 0.0010 REL FR 7 V 2 P
my doe? WIV 5.05. 15 P
my doe with the black scut? 5.05. 18 P

whiles, like a doe, i go to find my fawn | and AYL 2.07.128
for, o, love's bow | shoots buck and doe. TRO 3.01.117
what, hast not thou full often strook a doe, TIT 2.01. 93
single you thither then this dainty doe, | and 2.01.117
but hope to pluck a dainty doe to ground. 2.02. 26
like a milch doe, whose swelling dugs do ache, VEN 875
his bow | to strike a poor unseasonable doe. LUC 581
DOER 1 FR 0.0001 REL FR 0 V 1 P
not i, is the doer of this, and he is to be TN 3.04. 83 P
DOER'S 1 FR 0.0001 REL FR 1 V 0 P
the place is dignified by th' doer's deed. AWW 2.03.126
DOERS' 1 FR 0.0001 REL FR 1 V 0 P
and make them dread it, to the doers' thrift. CYM 5.01. 15
DOERS 5 FR 0.0005 REL FR 3 V 2 P
forty more — all great doers in our trade, and MM 4.03. 18 P
now, justice on the doers! AWW 5.03.154
talkers are no good doers. R3 1.03.350
let no man abide this deed, | but we the doers. JC 3.01. 95
reported in the battle to be the only doers. TNK 2.01. 30 P
DOES *(also doo's)*
/DOES 2 FR 0.0002 REL FR 2 V 0 P
/and /cries, | "/alack, /why /does /he /so?" LR 4.02. 59
him offense, | /and /he /does /chide /with /you. OTH 4.02.167
DOES 348 FR 0.0393 REL FR 262 V 86 P
he does make our fire, | fetch in our wood, and TMP 1.02.311
the ditty does remember my drown'd father. 1.02.406
he does hear me, | and that he does i weep. 1.02.434
he does hear me, | and that he does i weep. 1.02.435
and how does your content | tender your own good 2.01.269
his fit now, and does not talk after the wisest. 2.02. 73 P
how does thine ague? 2.02.136 P
it would become me | as well as it does you; 3.01. 29
how does thy honor? 3.02. 23 P
far surpasseth sycorax | as great'st does least. 3.02.103
and what does else want credit, come to me, 3.03. 25
how does my bounteous sister? 4.01.103
juno does command. 4.01.131
now does my project gather to a head: 5.01. 1
that a living prince | does now speak to thee, i 5.01.109
how does your lady, and how thrives your love? TGV 2.04.125
how does your fallow greyhound, sir? WIV 1.01. 89 P
does he not wear a great round beard, like a 1.04. 20 P
does he not hold up his head, as it were, and 1.04. 29 P
yes indeed does he. 1.04. 31 P
what news? how does pretty mistress anne? 1.04.137 P
for i know anne's mind as well as another does. 1.04.164 P
and i pray, how does good mistress anne? 2.01.164 P
does he lie at the garter? 2.01.179 P
ay, marry, does he. 2.01.181 P
in windsor leads a better life than she does: 2.02.117 P
terms, and by him that does me this wrong. 2.02.296 P
and how does good master fenton? 3.04. 34 P
what does master fenton here? 3.04. 68
she does so take on with her men; 3.05. 39 P
what is he, william, that does lend articles? 4.01. 39 P
why, does he talk of him? 4.02. 30 P
she comes of errands, does she? 4.02.174 P
sure, one of you does not serve heaven well, 4.05.125 P
man of safe discretion | that does affect it. MM 1.01. 72
does your worship mean to geld and splay all the 2.01.230 P
with one half so good a grace | as mercy does. 2.02. 63
could great men thunder | as jove himself does, 2.02.111
do as the carrion does, not as the flow'r, 2.02.166
why does my blood thus muster to my heart, 2.04. 20
indeed, it does stink in some sort, sir; 3.02. 28 P
does bridget paint still, pompey? ha? 3.02. 79 P
he does well in't. 3.02. 96 P
you know he does. ADO 3.02. 90 P
she is apter to do than to confess she does. AYL 3.02.389 P
who knows not where a wasp does wear his sting? SHR 2.01.213
why does the world report that kate doth limp? 2.01.252
how does my father? 3.02. 93
wants, | he does it under name of perfect love; 4.03. 12
a hundred marks, my kate does put her down. 5.02. 35
'tis thought your deer does hold you at a bay. 5.02. 56
what does this knave here? AWW 1.03. 8 P
does it curd thy blood | to say i am thy mother? 1.03.149
now, fair one, does your business follow us? 2.01. 99
oft does them by the weakest minister: 2.01.137
else, does err. 2.03.183
what does she ail that she's not very well? 2.04. 6 P
o, my knave, how does my old lady? 2.04. 18 P
as your due, time claims, he does acknowledge, 2.04. 42
nor does | the ministration and required office 2.05. 59
fain would steal | what law does vouch mine own. 2.05. 82
say i, madam, if he run away, as i hear he does. 3.02. 41 P
of her worth, | that he does weigh too light. 3.04. 32
he does indeed, | and brokes with all that can 3.05. 70
that so seriously he does address himself unto? 3.06. 95 P
how does he carry himself? 4.03.104 P
our interpreter does it well. 4.03.209 P
who pays before, but not when he does owe it. 4.03.230
and in his sleep he does little harm, save to 4.03.256 P
why does he ask him of me? 4.03.284 P
how does your ladyship like it? 4.05. 77 P
how does your drum? 5.02. 41 P
if he does think | he had not my virginity. 5.03.185
he does me wrong, my lord; 5.03.189
she does abuse our ears. to prison with her! 5.03.294
of beef and i believe that does harm to my wit. TN 1.03. 85 P
and it does indifferent well in a /dun–color'd 1.03.134 P
how does he love me? 1.05.254
your lord does know my mind, i cannot love him, 1.05.257
wherein the pregnant enemy does much. 2.02. 28
does not our lives consist of the four elements? 2.03. 9 P
ay, he does well enough if he be dispos'd, and 2.03. 81 P
he does it with a better grace, but i do it more 2.03. 82 P
and does not toby take you a blow o' the lips 2.05. 67 P
a should follow, but o does. 2.05.131 P
nay, but say true, does it work upon him? 2.05.195 P
sir, does walk about the orb like the sun, it 3.01. 38 P
he does obey every point of the letter that i 3.02. 77 P
he does smile his face into more lines than is 3.02. 78 P
why, what's the matter? does he rave? 3.04. 10
no, madam, he does nothing but smile. 3.04. 11 P
this does make some obstruction in the blood, 3.04. 20 P
ah ha, does she so? 3.04. 94 P
jolly robin, | tell me how thy lady does." 4.02. 73
and stable bearing | as i perceive she does. 4.03. 20
who does beguile you? who does you wrong? 5.01.140
who does beguile you? who does you wrong? 5.01.140
how does he, sirrah? 5.01.283 P
and so prove | (as /ornament oft does) too WT 1.02.158
resides not in that man that does not think) 1.02.272
who does infect her? 1.02.306
if you know aught which does behove my knowledge 1.02.395
the parts of man | which honor does acknowledge, 1.02.401
and as he does conceive | he is dishonor'd by a 1.02.454
though he does bear some signs of me, yet you 2.01. 57
that mercy does, for calumny will sear | virtue 2.01. 73
how does the boy? 2.03. 10
no yellow in't, lest she suspect, as he does, 2.03.107
in more than this deed does require! 2.03.190
how his piety | does my deeds make the blacker! 3.02.172
weeds to each part of you | does give a life; 4.04. 2
this is an art | which does mend nature — 4.04. 96
this robe of mine | does change my disposition. 4.04.135
nothing she does, or seems, | but smacks of 4.04.157
so she does any thing, though i report it | that 4.04.177
your heart is full of something that does take 4.04.346
he neither does nor shall. 4.04.393
and again does nothing | but what he did being 4.04.401
but it does fulfill my vow; 4.04.486
much as this old man does when the business is 4.04.821 P
does not the stone rebuke me | for being more 5.03. 37
now shame upon you, whe'er she does or no! JN 2.01.167
he does me double wrong | that wounds me with R2 3.02.215
he does, he does, we'll be reveng'd on him. 1H4 1.03.291
he does, he does, we'll be reveng'd on him. 1.03.291
when you come 'cross his humor, faith, he does. 3.01.170
why, sir john, my face does you no harm. 3.03. 28 P
'a cares not what mischief he does, if his 2H4 2.01. 15 P
faith, it does me, though it discolors the 2.02. 4 P
why does the prince love him so then? 2.04.243 P
they say, "a crafty knave does need no broker," 2H6 1.02.100
does buy and sell his honor as he pleases, | and H8 1.01.192
as a performance | does an irresolute purpose. 1.02.209
sure he does not, | he never was so womanish. 2.01. 37
and my favor | to him that does best, god forbid 2.02.114
and | does purpose honor to you no less flowing 2.03. 62
of life to't than | the grave does to th' dead; 2.04.192
he hears the king | does whet his anger to him. 3.02. 92
name of thrift, | does he rake this together? 3.02.110
and nature does require | her times of 3.02.146
the honor of it | does pay the act of it, as i' 3.02.182
how does your grace? 3.02.376
how does your grace? 4.02. 1
how does his highness? 4.02.124
sweet lady, does | deserve our better wishes. 5.01. 25
a pestilence | that does infect the land; 5.01. 46
no, sir, it does not please me. 5.02.169
i shall desire | to see what this child does, 5.04. 68
nay, i am sure she does. TRO 1.02.110 P
does he not? 1.02.125 P
it does a /man's heart good. 1.02.204 P
by god's lid, it does one's heart good. 1.02.211 P
why, 'tis this naming of him does him harm. 2.03.228
she does so blush, and fetches her wind so short 3.02. 31 P
what, does the cuckold scorn me? 3.03. 64
so obeying appetite | that what he will he does, 5.05. 28
he does, and does so much | that proof is call'd 5.05. 28
how does your little son? COR 1.03. 53 P
yonder, | that does appear as he were flea'd? 1.06. 22
her blood, | when she does praise me grieves me. 1.09. 15
pray you, who does the wolf love? 2.01. 7 P
no more of this, it does offend my heart; 2.01.168
here | to beg of hob and dick, that does appear, 2.03.116
where /one part does disdain with cause, the 3.01.143
does forget that ever | he heard the name of 3.01.258
i muse my mother | does not approve me further, 3.02. 8
good man, the wounds that he does bear for rome! 4.02. 28
whom you have banish'd — does exceed you all. 4.02. 42
if he slay me, | he does fair justice; 4.04. 25
i, it exceeds peace as far as day does night; 4.05.222 P
pity of him as the wolf | does of the shepherds. 4.06.111
and does achieve as soon | as draw his sword; 4.07. 23
i tell you, he does sit in gold, his eye | red 5.01. 63
then you should hate rome, as he does. 5.02. 38 P
thee no worse than thy old father menenius does! 5.02. 70 P
does reason our petition with more strength 5.03.176
does she love him? TIM 1.01.131
e'en as apemantus does now: 1.01.229 P
have got a humor there | does not become a man, 1.02. 27
himself, | for he does neither affect company, 1.02. 31
vouchsafe me a word, it does concern you near. 1.02.177
man | can justly praise but what he does affect. 1.02.215
gramercies, good fool; how does your mistress? 2.02. 67 P
and how does that honorable, complete, 3.01. 9 P
he does deny him (in respect of his) | what 3.02. 74
lucullus denied him, | and does he send to me? 3.03. 9
and does he think so backwardly of me now, 3.03. 18
and i think | one business does command us all; 3.04. 4
most true, he does. 3.04. 18
how? what does his cashier'd worship mutter? 3.04. 60 P
the place which i have feasted, does it now 3.04. 82
it does; but time will — and so — 3.06. 63 P
what does his lordship mean? 3.06. 86 P
when man's worst sin is, he does too much good! 4.02. 39
as the moon does, by wanting light to give: 4.03. 68
for here it sleeps, and does no hired harm. 4.03.291
choler does kill me that thou art alive; 4.03.367
how rarely does it meet with this time's guise, 4.03.465
does the rumor hold for true that he's | so full 5.01. 3
there does not live a man." 5.03. 4
tell him he hates flatterers | he says he does, JC 2.01.208
and these does she apply for warnings and 2.02. 80
what does he say of brutus? 3.02. 66
it does, my boy. 4.03.258
the temple–haunting /marlet does approve, | by MAC 1.06. 4
and that their fitness now | does unmake you. 1.07. 54
macbeth does murther sleep" — the innocent 2.02. 33
what three things does drink especially provoke? 2.03. 26 P
he does; he did appoint so. 2.03. 53
is an office | which the false man does easy. 2.03.137
that darkness does the face of earth entomb, 2.04. 9
ay, my good lord. our time does call upon 's. 3.01. 36
whereby he does receive | particular addition, 3.01. 98
but he does usually, | so all men do, from hence 3.03. 12
thy crown does sear mine eyeballs. 4.01.113
in a place | from whence himself does fly? 4.02. 8
every one that does so is a traitor, and must be 4.02. 49 P
i doubt some danger does approach you nearly. 4.02. 67
stands accus'd, | and does blaspheme his breed? 4.03.108
how does my wife? 4.03.176
the grief that does not speak | whispers the 4.03.209
what is it she does now? 5.01. 26 P
what does the tyrant? 5.02. 11
now does he feel | his secret murthers sticking 5.02. 16
now does he feel his title | hang loose about 5.02. 20
when all that is within him does condemn 5.02. 24
how does your patient, doctor? 5.03. 37
if this which he avouches does appear, | there 5.05. 46
task | does not divide the sunday from the week, HAM 1.01. 76
for nature crescent does not grow alone | in 1.03. 11
what does this mean, my lord? 1.04. 7
and then, sir, does 'a this — 'a does — what 2.01. 49
does 'a this — 'a does — what was i about to 2.01. 49
under heaven | that does afflict our natures. 2.01.103
so he does indeed. 2.02.161
give me leave, | how does my good lord hamlet? 2.02.171
who does me this? 2.02.575
he does confess he feels himself distracted, 3.01. 5
thus conscience does make cowards /of /us /all, 3.01. 82
lord, | how does your honor for this many a day? 3.01. 90
heaven's face does glow | o'er this solidity and 3.04. 48
what, gertrude? how does hamlet? 4.01. 6
your judgment 'pear | as day does to your eye. 4.05.153
the gallows does well; 5.01. 46 P
but how does it well? 5.01. 46 P
it does well to those that do ill. 5.01. 46 P
why does he suffer this mad knave now to knock 5.01.101 P
defeat | does by their own insinuation grow. 5.02. 59
does it not, think thee, stand me now upon — 5.02. 63
/'a does well to commend it himself, there are 5.02.183 P
and when he's not himself does wrong laertes, 5.02.235
then hamlet does it not, hamlet denies it. 5.02.236
who does it then? 5.02.237
how does the queen? 5.02.308
why does the drum come hither? 5.02.361
thy youngest daughter does not love thee least, LR 1.01.152
does any here know me? 1.04.226
does lear walk thus? 1.04.227
taste as like this as a crab does to a crab. 1.05. 18 P
no more, perchance, does mine, nor his, nor hers 2.02. 91
unusual vigilance | does not attend my taking. 2.03. 5
old, and so — | but she knows what she does. 2.04.236
that will not see | because he does not feel, 4.01. 69
i know your lady does not love her husband, | i 4.05. 23
the small gilded fly | does lecher in my sight. 4.06.113
and does shake the head | to hear of pleasure's 4.06.120
arm it in rags, a pigmy's straw does pierce it. 4.06.167
none does offend, none, i say none, i'll able 4.06.168
then be't so, my good lord. how does the king? 4.07. 12
how does my royal lord? how fares your majesty? 4.07. 43
to be tender–minded | does not become a sword. 5.03. 32
it is a chance which does redeem all sorrows 5.03.267
what a /full fortune does the thick–lips owe OTH 1.01. 66
the duke does greet you, general, | and he 1.02. 36
vesture of creation | does tire the /ingener. 2.01. 65
comes from my pate as birdlime does from frieze, 2.01.126
but does foul pranks which fair and wise ones do 2.01.142
how does my old acquaintance of this isle? 2.01.203
his worthiness | does challenge much respect. 2.01.211
in the degree of this fortune as cassio does? 2.01.238 P
be unworthy of his place that does those things. 2.03.102 P
to hear music the general does not greatly care. 3.01. 17 P
i'll intermingle every thing he does | with 3.03. 25
i thank you. how does lieutenant cassio? 4.01.222
alas, what does this gentleman conceive? 4.02. 95
it does abhor me now i speak the word; 4.02.162
the business of the state does him offense, 4.02.166
low'ring, does become | the opposite of itself. ANT 1.02.125
see where he is, who's with him, what he does. 1.03. 2
give me freedom, | it does from childishness. 1.03. 58
how this herculean roman does become | the 1.03. 84
or does he walk? 1.05. 20
either thee becomes, | so does it no man's else. 1.05. 61
"but yet," it does allay | the good precedence; 2.05. 50
'tis not my profit that does lead mine honor; 2.07. 76
pleas'd fortune does of marcus crassus' death 3.01. 2
who does i' th' wars more than his captain can 3.01. 21
who does he accuse? 3.06. 23
then does he say he lent me | some shipping 3.06. 26
two friends | that does afflict each other! 3.06. 78
each heart in rome does love and pity you; 3.06. 92
next, cleopatra does confess thy greatness, 3.12. 16
the loyalty well held to fools does make | our 3.13. 42
does conquer him that did his master conquer, 3.13. 45
he | does pity, as constrained blemishes, | not 3.13. 59
a halter'd neck which does the hangman thank 3.13.130
what does he mean? 4.02. 23
it signs well, does it not? 4.03. 14
where yond pine does stand | i shall discover 4.12. 1
it does, my lord. 4.14. 11
hence safe | does pay thy labor richly; 4.14. 37
now all labor | mars what it does; 4.14. 48
maid that milks | and does the meanest chares. 4.15. 75
and impatience does | become a dog that's mad. 4.15. 79
my desolation does begin to make | a better life 5.02. 1
the ingratitude of this seleucus does | even 5.02.153
our courtiers' | still seem as does the king's. CYM 1.01. 3
do him wrong | but he does buy my injuries, to 1.01.105
as strongly as the conscience does within, | to 2.02. 36
what does he mean? 4.02.190
a season, but our jealousy | does yet depend. 4.03. 23
every good servant does not all commands; 5.01. 6
and suit myself | as does a britain peasant; 5.01. 24
does the world go round? 5.05.232
when signior sooth here does proclaim peace, PER 1.02. 44
does speak sufficiently he's gone to travel. 1.03. 13
and, to remember what he does, | build his 2.ch. 13
does fall in travail with her fear; 3.ch. 52
how does my queen? 3.01. 7

a present murderer does prepare | for good 4.ch. 38
dionyza does appear, | with leonine, a murtherer 4.ch. 51
here he does but repair it. 4.02.111 P
yet none does know but you how she came dead, 4.03. 29
wherefore she does, and swears she'll never 4.04. 42
no visor does become black villainy | so well as 4.04. 44
stead that is distress'd | does bind me to her. TNK 1.01. 37
sword | that does good turns to th' world; 1.01. 49
there | that does command my rapier from my hip, 1.02. 56
each thing | our haste does leave imperfect. 1.04. 12
for he does all, ye know. 2.03. 41
a fire ill take her! does she flinch now? 3.05. 52
take twenty, domine. — how does my sweet heart? 3.05.148
does she know him? 4.01.141
he does no wrongs, | nor takes none. 4.02.134
horror, who does stand accurs'd | of many mortal 5.03. 23
so does arcite's mirth, | but palamon's sadness 5.03. 50
pray, how does she? 5.04. 25
the blissful dew of heaven does arrouse you. 5.04.104
DOES'T 2 FR 0.0002 REL FR 1 V 1 P
but it becomes /me well enough, does't not? TN 1.03.100 P
does't not go well? OTH 2.03.374
DOEST 2 FR 0.0002 REL FR 1 V 1 P
rob me the exchequer the first thing thou doest, 1H4 3.03.184 P
do any thing but this thou doest. PER 4.06.174
DOFF *(also daff, etc.)*
DOFF 6 FR 0.0006 REL FR 6 V 0 P
fie, doff this habit, shame to your estate, | an SHR 3.02.100
doff it for shame, | and hang a calve's–skin on JN 3.01.128
and made us doff our easy robes of peace, | to 1H4 5.01. 12
faith, young troilus, doff thy harness, youth, TRO 5.03. 31
romeo, doff thy name, | and for thy name, which ROM 2.02. 47
women fight, | to doff their dire distresses. MAC 4.03.188
/DOG 2 FR 0.0002 REL FR 1 V 1 P
/so, /thou /common /dog, /didst /thou /disgorge 2H4 1.03. 97
to be a /dog, a moile, a cat, a fitchook, a toad TRO 5.01. 61 P
DOG 140 FR 0.0158 REL FR 68 V 72 P
you bawling, blasphemous, incharitable dog! TMP 1.01. 41 P
my mistress show'd me thee, and thy dog, and thy 2.02.141
i think crab my dog be the sourest–natur'd dog TGV 2.03. 5 P
my dog be the sourest–natur'd dog that lives: 2.03. 6 P
stone, and has no more pity in him than a dog. 2.03. 11 P
i am the dog — no, the dog is himself, and i am 2.03. 22 P
no, the dog is himself, and i am the dog — o! 2.03. 22 P
no, the dog is himself, and i am the dog — o! 2.03. 22 P
the dog is me, and i am myself; 2.03. 23 P
now the dog all this while sheds not a tear, nor 2.03. 30 P
why, he that's tied here, crab, my dog. 2.03. 40 P
ask my dog. 2.05. 35 P
gone to seek his dog, which to–morrow, by his 4.02. 78 P
would say precisely, "thus i would teach a dog." 4.04. 6 P
one that takes upon him to be a dog indeed, to 4.04. 12 P
indeed, to be, as it were, a dog at all things. 4.04. 13 P
"out with the dog," says one. 4.04. 20 P
"friend," quoth i, "you mean to whip the dog?" 4.04. 25 P
i carried mistress silvia the dog you bade me. 4.04. 46 P
marry, she says your dog was a cur, and tells 4.04. 48 P
but she receiv'd my dog? 4.04. 51 P
mine own, who is a dog as big as ten of yours, 4.04. 57 P
go, get thee hence, and find my dog again, | or 4.04. 59
'tis a good dog. WIV 1.01. 94 P
he's a good dog, and a fair dog — can there be 1.01. 96 P
he's a good dog, and a fair dog — can there be 1.01. 96 P
he shall not have a stone to throw at his dog. 1.04.113 P
hope is a curtal dog in some affairs. 2.01.110
gar, you are de coward, de jack dog, john ape. 3.01. 83 P
and give them to a dog for a new–year's gift. 3.05. 8 P
why, this is lunatics! this is mad as a mad dog! 4.02.125 P
she had transform'd me to a curtal dog, and made
ERR 3.02.146
i had rather hear my dog bark at a crow than a ADO 1.01.131 P
and he had been a dog that should have howl'd 2.03. 79 P
truly, i would not hang a dog by my will, much 3.03. 63 P
with me) | than to be used as you use your dog? MND 2.01.210
out, dog! 3.02. 65
this man, with lantern, dog, and bush of thorn, 5.01.135
thorn–bush my thorn–bush, and this dog my dog. 5.01.259 P
thorn–bush my thorn–bush, and this dog my dog. 5.01.259 P
and when i ope my lips let no dog bark!" MV 1.01. 94
you call me misbeliever, cut–throat dog, | and 1.03.111
should i not say, | "hath a dog money? 1.03.121
me such a day, another time | you call'd me dog; 1.03.128
as the dog jew did utter in the streets. 2.08. 14
thou call'dst me dog before thou hadst a cause, 3.03. 6
cause, | but, since i am a dog, beware my fangs. 3.03. 7
o, be thou damn'd, inexecrable dog! 4.01.128
get you with him, you old dog. AYL 1.01. 81 P
is "old dog" my reward? 1.01. 82 P
not one to throw at a dog. 1.03. 3 P
i would not lose the dog for twenty pound. SHR in.1. 21
trust me, i take him for the better dog. in.1. 25
i am dog at a catch. TN 2.03. 60 P
o, if i thought that, i'd beat him like a dog! 2.03.142 P
this is to give a dog and in recompense desire 5.01. 6 P
a dog and in recompense desire my dog again. 5.01. 7 P
and, like a dog that is compell'd to fight, JN 4.01.115
straight shall dog them at the heels. R2 5.03.139
but that sad dog | that brings me food to make 5.05. 70
peas and beans are as dank here as a dog, and 1H4 2.01. 8 P
to dog his heels and curtsy at his frowns, | to 3.02.127
would cudgel him like a dog if he would say so. 3.03. 87 P
the fellow with the great belly, and he my dog. 2H4 1.02.146 P
this wen to be as familiar with me as my dog, 2.02.107 P
and the wild dog | shall flesh his tooth on 4.05.131
cannot defend our own doors from the dog, | let H5 1.02.218
pish for thee, iceland dog! 2.01. 42
"solus," egregious dog? 2.01. 46
and hold–fast is the only dog, my duck; 2.03. 52
let gallows gape for dog, let man go free, | and 3.06. 42
whilst /by /a slave, no gentler than my dog, 4.05. 15
"a staff is quickly found to beat a dog." 2H6 3.01.171
that i should snarl, and bite, and play the dog. 3H6 5.06. 77
unmanner'd dog! R3 1.02. 39
stay, dog, for thou shalt hear me. 1.03.215
o buckingham, take heed of yonder dog! 1.03.288
that dog, that had his teeth before his eyes 4.04. 49
that i may live to say, "the dog is dead." 4.04. 78
the day is ours, the bloody dog is dead. 5.05. 2
dog! TRO 2.01. 7 P
you dog! 2.01. 50 P
a whoreson dog, that shall palter with us thus! 2.03.233
rather leave to see hector than not to dog him. 5.01. 95 P
cur, ajax, against that dog of as bad a kind, 5.04. 13 P
now, dog! 5.07. 10 P
he's a very dog to the commonalty. COR 1.01. 28 P
i'd have beaten him like a dog, but for 4.05. 51 P
and therein, hellish dog, thou hast undone her. TIT 4.02. 77
of me, | as true a dog as ever fought at head. 5.01.102
ay, like a black dog, as the saying is. 5.01.122
away, inhuman dog, unhallowed slave! 5.03. 14
a dog of the house of montague moves me. ROM 1.01. 8 P
a dog of that house shall move me to stand! 1.01. 11 P
he hath waken'd thy dog that hath lain asleep in 3.01. 26 P
'zounds, a dog, a rat, a mouse, a cat, to 3.01.100 P
lives, and every cat and dog | and little mouse, 3.03. 30
when thou art timon's dog, and these knaves TIM 1.01.180
y' are a dog. 1.01.200 P
what's she, if i be a dog? 1.01.202 P
away, unpeaceable dog, or i'll spurn thee hence! 1.01.270 P
i will fly, like a dog, the heels a' th' ass. 1.01.272 P
her weeping, | or a dog that seems a–sleeping, 1.02. 67
steal but a beggar's dog | and give it timon, 2.01. 5
and give it timon, why, the dog coins gold. 2.01. 6
a plague upon him, dog! 2.02. 49 P
thou wast whelp'd a dog, and thou shalt famish a 2.02. 86 P
for thy part, i do wish thou wert a dog, | that 4.03. 55
'tis, then, because thou dost not keep a dog, 4.03.200
arm | with favor never clasp'd, but bred a dog. 4.03.251
thou hadst some means to keep a dog. 4.03.317 P
i had rather be a beggar's dog than apemantus. 4.03.356 P
away, thou issue of a mangy dog! 4.03.366
i had rather be a dog, and bay the moon, | than JC 4.03. 27
toe of frog, | wool of bat and tongue of dog, MAC 4.01. 15
for if the sun breed maggots in a dead dog, HAM 2.02.181 P
the cat will mew, and dog will have his day. 5.01.292
you whoreson dog, you slave, you cur! LR 1.04. 81 P
truth's a dog must to kennel, he must be whipt 1.04.111 P
why, madam, if i were your father's dog, | you 2.02.136
wolf in greediness, dog in madness, lion in prey 3.04. 93 P
how now, you dog? 3.07. 75
they flatter'd me like a dog, and told me i had 4.06. 97 P
thou hast seen a farmer's dog bark at a beggar? 4.06.155 P
mine enemy's dog, | though he had bit me, should 4.07. 35
why should a dog, a horse, a rat, have life, 5.03.307
quarrel and offense | as my young mistress' dog. OTH 2.03. 51
would beat his offenseless dog to affright an 2.03.275 P
thou hadst been better have been born a dog 3.03.362
of yours, but not that dog i shall throw it to. 4.01.142 P
o damn'd iago! o inhuman dog! 5.01. 62
i took by th' throat the circumcised dog, | and 5.02.355
o spartan dog, | more fell than anguish, hunger, 5.02.361
and impatience does | become a dog that's mad. ANT 4.15. 80
slave, soulless villain, dog! 5.02.157
whoreson dog! CYM 2.01. 14 P
a dog! 5.03. 91
no dog shall rouse thee, though a thousand bark. VEN 240
he like a thievish dog creeps sadly thence, LUC 736
my curtal dog, that wont to have play'd, | plays PP 17.19
DOG–APES 1 FR 0.0001 REL FR 0 V 1 P
is like th' encounter of two dog–apes; AYL 2.05. 27 P
DOGBERRY 1 FR 0.0001 REL FR 0 V 1 P
well, give them their charge, neighbor dogberry. ADO 3.03. 8 P
DOG–DAYS 1 FR 0.0001 REL FR 0 V 1 P
twenty of the dog–days now reign in 's nose; H8 5.03. 42 P
DOGFISH 1 FR 0.0001 REL FR 1 V 0 P
pucelle or puzzel, dolphin or dogfish, | your 1H6 1.04.107
DOG–FOX 1 FR 0.0001 REL FR 0 V 1 P
cheese, nestor, and that same dog–fox, ulysses, TRO 5.04. 11 P
DOGG'D 5 FR 0.0005 REL FR 3 V 2 P
in the city, we shall be dogg'd with company, MND 1.02.104 P
i have dogg'd him like his murtherer. TN 3.02. 76 P
that dogg'd the mighty army of the dolphin? 1H6 4.03. 2
in this | are dogg'd with two strange followers. TRO 1.03.364
whose repetition will be dogg'd with curses; COR 5.03.144
DOGGED 3 FR 0.0003 REL FR 3 V 0 P
i'll fill these dogged spies with false reports; JN 4.01.128
doth dogged war bristle his angry crest, | and 4.03.149
and dogged york, that reaches at the moon, 2H6 3.01.158
//DOG–HEARTED 1 FR 0.0001 REL FR 1 V 0 P
/rights | /to /his //dog–hearted /daughters — LR 4.03. 45
DOG–HOLE 1 FR 0.0001 REL FR 1 V 0 P
france is a dog–hole, and it no more merits AWW 2.03.274
/DOG'S 1 FR 0.0001 REL FR 0 V 1 P
ah, mocker, that's the /dog's name. ROM 2.04.209 P
DOG'S 3 FR 0.0003 REL FR 1 V 2 P
poisons more deadly than a mad dog's tooth. ERR 5.01. 70
a dog, and thou shalt famish a dog's death. TIM 2.02. 87 P
a dog's obey'd in office. LR 4.06.159 P
DOGS 48 FR 0.0054 REL FR 37 V 11 P
but you'll lie like dogs, and yet say nothing TMP 3.02. 19 P
company of three or four gentleman–like dogs, TGV 4.04. 17 P
and goes me to the fellow that whips the dogs: 4.04. 24 P
why do your dogs bark so? WIV 1.01.287 P
the dogs did yell: LLL 4.02. 58
which, like your asses, and your dogs and mules, MV 4.01. 91
what dogs are these? SHR 4.01.162
where death and danger dogs the heels of worth. AWW 3.04. 15
by'r lady, sir, and some dogs will catch well. TN 2.03. 62 P
dogs, easily won to fawn on any man! R2 3.02.130
where the glutton's dogs lick'd his sores, and 1H4 4.02. 26 P
down, down, dogs! 2H4 2.04.159 P
/die men like dogs! 2.04.174 P
as dogs upon their masters, worrying you. H5 2.02. 83
for coward dogs | most spend their mouths when 2.04. 69
up to the breach, you dogs! 3.02. 20 P
dogs! 1H6 1.02. 23
they call'd us for our fierceness english dogs, 1.05. 25
between two dogs, which hath the deeper mouth, 2.04. 12
or as a bear, encompass'd round with dogs, | who 3H6 2.01. 15
dogs howl'd, and hideous tempest shook down 5.06. 46
that dogs bark at me as i halt by them — | why, R3 1.01. 23
death and destruction dogs thee at thy heels; 4.01. 39
albeit they were flesh'd villains, bloody dogs, 4.03. 6
hunger broke stone walls, that dogs must eat, COR 1.01.206
and that's as easy | as to set dogs on sheep — 2.01.257
make them of no more voice | than dogs, that are 2.03.216
i have dogs, my lord, | will rouse the proudest TIT 2.02. 20
uncover, dogs, and lap! TIM 3.06. 85 P
give to dogs | what thou deniest to men. 4.03.529
out, rascal dogs! 5.01.115
cry "havoc," and let slip the dogs of war, JC 3.01.273
demi–wolves are clipt | all by the name of dogs; MAC 3.01. 94
throw physic to the dogs, i'll none of it. 5.03. 47
o, this is counter, you false danish dogs! HAM 4.05.111
knowing nought (like dogs) but following. LR 2.02. 80
tied by the heads, dogs and bears by th' neck, 2.04. 8 P
the little dogs and all, | trey, blanch, and 3.06. 62
head, | dogs leapt the hatch, and all are fled. 3.06. 73
assume a semblance | that very dogs disdain'd; 5.03.189
of death too, | that rids our dogs of languish? ANT 5.02. 42
first, perchance, she'll prove on cats and dogs, CYM 1.05. 38
upon me, set | the dogs o' th' street to bay me; 5.05.223
creatures vild, as cats and dogs | of no esteem. 5.05.252
and well have hollow'd | to a deep cry of dogs; TNK 2.05. 12
stand long, | and thy dogs be swift and strong! 3.05.155
spurn you like dogs, and like as if that god STM II.C 135
place, | where fearfully the dogs exclaim aloud: VEN 886
DOGSKIN 1 FR 0.0001 REL FR 1 V 0 P
next gloves that i give her shall be dogskin; TNK 3.05. 45
DOG'S–LEATHER 1 FR 0.0001 REL FR 0 V 1 P
skins of our enemies, to make dog's–leather of. 2H6 4.02. 24 P
DOG–WEARY 1 FR 0.0001 REL FR 1 V 0 P
i have watch'd so long | that i am dog–weary, SHR 4.02. 60
DOIGTS 5 FR 0.0005 REL FR 0 V 5 P
de hand. et les doigts? H5 3.04. 8 P
les doigts? 3.04. 9 P
ma foi, j'oublie les doigts, mais je me 3.04. 9 P
les doigts? 3.04. 10 P
le? doigts, de fingres. 3.04. 12 P
DOING 75 FR 0.0084 REL FR 58 V 17 P
whiles you, doing thus, | to the perpetual wink TMP 2.01.284
this is my doing, now. WIV 3.04. 95 P
this is my doing. 3.04. 98 P
to the love i have in doing good a remedy MM 3.01.198 P
but keeps you from dishonor in doing it. 3.01.237 P
doing displeasure to the citizens | by rushing ERR 5.01.142
himself beyond the promise of his age, doing, in ADO 1.01. 14 P
sword, | and won thy love doing thee injuries; MND 1.01. 17
wands, | and, in the doing of the deed of kind, MV 1.03. 85
and unwearied spirit | in doing courtesies, and 3.02.294
i never did repent for doing good, | nor shall 3.04. 10
what judgment shall i dread, doing no wrong? 4.01. 89
way to heaven | by doing deeds of hospitality. AYL 2.04. 82
me, signior gremio, i would fain be doing. SHR 2.01. 74
for thy sake, and my poor doing eternal; AWW 2.03.233 P
for doing i am past, as i will by thee, in what 2.03.233 P
i have lim'd her, but it is jove's doing, and TN 3.04. 75 P
would do that | which should undo more doing; WT 1.02.312
as you feel doing thus — and see withal | the 2.01.153
look down | and see what death is doing. 3.02.149
encourage him, | not doing it and being done. 3.02.165
each your doing | (so singular in each 4.04.143
crowns what you are doing in the present deeds, 4.04.145
a piece many years in doing and now newly 5.02. 96 P
and being not done, where doing tends to ill, JN 3.01.272
ill, | the truth is then most done not doing it. 3.01.273
way, | doing annoyance to the treacherous feet, R2 3.02. 16
and thus still doing, thus he pass'd along. 5.02. 21
for doing these fair rites of tenderness. 1H4 5.04. 98
and make thee rich for doing me such wrong. 2H4 1.01. 90
in which doing, i have done the part of a 2.04.321 P
doing the execution and the act | for which we H5 2.02. 17
doing is activity, and he will still be doing. 3.07. 99 P
doing is activity, and he will still be doing. 3.07. 99 P
here is my hand, the deed is worthy doing. 2H6 3.01.278
and warwick, doing what you gave in charge, | is 3H6 4.01. 32
excused | for doing worthy vengeance on thyself, R3 1.02. 87
that you take with unthankfulness his doing. 2.02. 90
yet will be | the chronicles of my doing, let me H8 1.02. 74
this is the cardinal's doing. 2.02. 19
you cause) my doing well | with my well saying! 3.02.151
as you do conscience | in doing daily wrongs. 5.02.103
won are done, joy's soul lies in the doing. TRO 1.02.287
persist | in doing wrong extenuates not wrong, 2.02.187
part with those | that have beheld the doing. COR 1.09. 40
are too infant–like for doing much alone. 2.01. 38 P
indifferently 'twixt doing them neither good nor 2.02. 17 P
rewards | his deeds with doing them, and is 2.02.128
please you | that i may pass this doing. 2.02.139
unless, by not so doing, our good city | cleave 3.02. 27
trim sport for them which had the doing of it. TIT 5.01. 96
/lives, | by doing damned hate upon thyself? ROM 3.03.118
doing more murther in this loathsome world, 5.01. 81
right, if doing nothing be death by th' law. TIM 1.01.194 P
doing himself offense, whilst we, lying still, JC 4.03.201
the loyalty i owe, | in doing it, pays itself. MAC 1.04. 23
by doing every thing | safe toward your love and 1.04. 26
and to such wondrous doing brought his horse, HAM 4.07. 86
whose nature is so far from doing harms | that LR 1.02.180
he shall never more | be fear'd of doing harm. 2.01.111
wit, and therefore i will attempt the doing it. OTH 3.04. 22 P
nothing but what i protest intendment of doing. 4.02.203 P
doing the honor of thy lordliness | to one so ANT 5.02.161
richer than doing nothing for a /bable; CYM 3.03. 23
many times | doth ill deserve by doing well; 3.03. 54
yet i not doing this, the fool had borne | my 4.02.116
beard came to, | in doing this for 's country. 5.03. 18
he, doing so, put forth to seas, | where when PER 2.ch. 27
till fortune, tir'd with doing bad, | threw him 2.ch. 37
and princes not doing so are like to gnats, 2.03. 62
and that work presents itself to th' doing: TNK 1.01.151
cleaving his conscience into twain and doing 1.03. 46
what do you to your souls | in doing this, o STM II.C 107
i do, | doing thee vantage, double–vantage me. SON 88.12
dulling my lines, and doing me disgrace. 103. 8
/DOINGS 1 FR 0.0001 REL FR 1 V 0 P
/and /buzz /lamenting /doings /in /the /air! TIT 3.02. 62
DOINGS 4 FR 0.0004 REL FR 4 V 0 P
and most contrarious /quests | upon thy doings; MM 4.01. 62
fear, | among the infinite doings of the world, WT 1.02.253
to hide your doings, and to silence that | which COR 1.09. 23
for valiant doings in their country's cause? TIT 1.01.113
DOIT 9 FR 0.0010 REL FR 5 V 4 P
when they will not give a doit to relieve a lame TMP 2.02. 32 P

and take no doit | of usance for my moneys, and MV 1.03.140
was i, and little john doit of staffordshire, 2H4 3.02. 19 P
that doit that e'er i wrested from the king, 2H6 3.01.112
irons of a doit, doublets that hangmen would COR 1.05. 6
on a dissension of a doit, break out | to 4.04. 17
of your throats | i'd not have given a doit. 5.04. 57
plain–dealing, which will not cast a man a doit. TIM 1.01.212 P
i cannot be bated one doit of a thousand pieces. PER 4.02. 51 P
DOLABELLA 8 FR 0.0009 REL FR 8 V 0 P
go to him, dolabella, bid him yield; ANT 5.01. 1
where's dolabella, | to second proculeius? 5.01. 69
dolabella! 5.01. 70
so, dolabella, | it shall content me best. 5.02. 67
dolabella! 5.02.197
dolabella, | i shall remain your debtor. 5.02.204
there's dolabella sent from caesar; call him. 5.02.324
come, dolabella, see | high order in this great 5.02.365
DOLCERA 1 FR 0.0001 REL FR 1 V 0 P
"piu per dolcera que per forca." PER 2.02. 27
/DOLE* 1 FR 0.0001 REL FR 1 V 0 P
/that /in /the /dole /of /blows /your /son 2H4 1.01.169
DOLE* 10 FR 0.0011 REL FR 6 V 4 P
if not, happy man be his dole! WIV 3.04. 65 P
mark, poor knight, | what dreadful dole is here! MND 5.01.278
making such pitiful dole over them that all the AYL 1.02.130 P
happy man be his dole! SHR 1.01.140 P
what great creation and what dole of honor AWW 2.03.169
why, happy man be 's dole! WT 1.02.163
now, my masters, happy man be his dole, say i, 1H4 2.02. 76 P
in equal scale weighing delight and dole, HAM 1.02. 13
omit we all their dole and woe. PER 3.ch. 42
our dole more deadly looks than dying; TNK 1.05. 3
/DOLEFUL 1 FR 0.0001 REL FR 1 V 0 P
/and /doleful /dumps /the /mind /oppress, | then ROM 4.05.127
DOLEFUL 7 FR 0.0008 REL FR 5 V 2 P
well, if it be doleful matter merrily set down, WT 4.04.188 P
here's one to a very doleful tune, how a 4.04.262 P
who chaunts a doleful hymn to his own death, JN 5.07. 22
death rock me asleep, abridge my doleful days! 2H4 2.04.197
little strength rings out the doleful knell: LUC 1495
no deal, | my wether's bell rings doleful knell, PP 17.18
in howling wise, to see my doleful plight. 17.22
DOLEFULL'ST 1 FR 0.0001 REL FR 1 V 0 P
a thorn, | and there sung the dolefull'st ditty, PP 20.11
DOLL 19 FR 0.0021 REL FR 4 V 15 P
will you have doll tearsheet meet you at supper? 2H4 2.01.163 P
mistress quickly and mistress doll tearsheet. 2.02.153 P
this doll tearsheet should be some road. 2.02.166 P
how now, mistress doll? 2.04. 35 P
you make fat rascals, mistress doll. 2.04. 41 P
gluttony, you help to make the diseases, doll. 2.04. 45 P
we catch of you, doll, we catch of you. 2.04. 45 P
hark thee hither, mistress doll. 2.04.152 P
sit on my knee, doll. 2.04.228 P
peace, good doll, do not speak like a 2.04.234 P
kiss me, doll. 2.04.262 P
farewell, hostess, farewell, doll. 2.04.374 P
o, run, doll, run, run, good doll. 2.04.389 P
o, run, doll, run, run, good doll. 2.04.389 P
will you come, doll? 2.04.391 P
thy doll, and helen of thy noble thoughts, | is 5.05. 33
den with fell alecto's snake, | for doll is in. 5.05. 38
doll tearsheet she by name, and her espouse. H5 2.01. 77
news have i that my doll is dead i' th' spittle 5.01. 81
DOLLAR 1 FR 0.0001 REL FR 0 V 1 P
a dollar. TMP 2.01. 18 P
DOLLARS 1 FR 0.0001 REL FR 1 V 0 P
inch | ten thousand dollars to our general use. MAC 1.02. 62
DOLOR 7 FR 0.0008 REL FR 5 V 2 P
dolor comes to him indeed; TMP 2.01. 19 P
ear, | as ending anthem of my endless dolor. TGV 3.01.242
till, from one sign of dolor to another, she did WT 5.02. 87 P
to breathe the abundant dolor of the heart. R2 1.03.257
and yell'd out | like syllable of dolor. MAC 4.03. 8
but none where all distress and dolor dwell'd, LUC 1446
to think their dolor others have endured. 1582
DOLOROUS 1 FR 0.0001 REL FR 1 V 0 P
you take me in too dolorous a sense, | for i ANT 4.02. 39
DOLORS 4 FR 0.0004 REL FR 2 V 2 P
to three thousand dolors a year. MM 1.02. 50 P
how poor andromache shrills her dolors forth! TRO 5.03. 84
shalt have as many dolors for thy daughters as LR 2.04. 54 P
his merits due, | being all to dolors turn'd? CYM 5.04. 80
DOLPHIN* 65 FR 0.0073 REL FR 60 V 5 P
why, your dolphin is not lustier. AWW 2.03. 26 P
of lewis the dolphin and that lovely maid. JN 2.01.425
is the young dolphin every way complete: 2.01.433
if that the dolphin there, thy princely son, 2.01.484
speak then, prince dolphin, can you love this 2.01.524
thou virtuous dolphin, alter not the doom 3.01.311
o noble dolphin, | go with me to the king. 3.04.177
under the dolphin. 4.02.131
away toward bury, to the dolphin there! 4.03.114
like a kind host, the dolphin and his powers. 5.01. 32
to dismiss the powers | led by the dolphin. 5.01. 65
and, noble dolphin, albeit we swear | a 5.02. 9
the dolphin is too willful–opposite, | and will 5.02.124
and thou shalt find it, dolphin, do not doubt. 5.02.180
supply, | that was expected by the dolphin here, 5.03. 10
where is my prince, the dolphin? 5.05. 9
the dolphin is preparing hitherward, | where 5.07. 59
the dolphin rages at our very heels. 5.07. 80
who half an hour since came from the dolphin, 5.07. 83
goblet, sitting in my dolphin chamber, at the 2H4 2.01. 87 P
call in the messengers sent from the dolphin. H5 1.02.221
know the pleasure | of our fair cousin dolphin; 1.02.235
this the dolphin speaks. 1.02.257
we are glad the dolphin is so pleasant with us, 1.02.259
but tell the dolphin i will keep my state, | be 1.02.273
yea, strike the dolphin blind to look on us. 1.02.280
whose name | tell you the dolphin i am coming on 1.02.291
and tell the dolphin | his jest will savor but 1.02.294
we'll chide this dolphin at his father's door. 1.02.308
and you, prince dolphin, with all swift dispatch 2.04. 6
o, peace, prince dolphin! 2.04. 29
unless the dolphin be in presence here, | to 2.04.111
for the dolphin, | i stand here for him. 2.04.115
the dolphin, whom of succors we entreated, 3.03. 45
prince dolphin, you shall stay with us in roan. 3.05. 64
the dolphin longs for morning. 3.07. 90 P
of france, the brave sir guichard dolphin, 4.08. 95
the dolphin charles is crowned king in rheims; 1H6 1.01. 92
the dolphin crowned king? 1.01. 96
i'll hale the dolphin headlong from his throne, 1.01.149
either to quell the dolphin utterly, | or bring 1.01.163
where's the prince dolphin? i have news for him. 1.02. 46
reignier, stand thou as dolphin in my place; 1.02. 61
where is the dolphin? 1.02. 66
dolphin, i am by birth a shepherd's daughter, 1.02. 72
'tis the french dolphin sueth to thee thus. 1.02.112
the dolphin, with one joan de pucelle join'd, 1.04.101
pucelle or puzzel, dolphin or dogfish, | your 1.04.107
dolphin, command the citizens make bonfires, 1.06. 12
am sure i scar'd the dolphin and his trull, 2.02. 28
that charles the dolphin may encounter them. 3.02. 9
dangerous ends, | enter and cry "the dolphin!" 3.02. 34
if dolphin and the rest will be but rul'd. 3.03. 8
if thou retire, the dolphin, well appointed, 4.02. 21
that dogg'd the mighty army of the dolphin? 4.03. 2
two mightier troops than that the dolphin led, 4.03. 7
submission, dolphin? 4.07. 54
o, charles the dolphin is a proper man, | no 5.03. 37
she and the dolphin have been juggling. 5.04. 68
and here at hand the dolphin and his train 5.04.100
the dolphin hath prevail'd beyond the seas, 2H6 1.03.125
unto mounsieur basimecu, the dolphin of france? 4.07. 29 P
who made the dolphin and the french to stoop, 3H6 1.01.108
and tam'd the king and made the dolphin stoop; 2.02.151
dolphin my boy, boy, sessa! LR 3.04. 99 P
DOLPHIN–LIKE 1 FR 0.0001 REL FR 1 V 0 P
his delights | were dolphin–like, they show'd ANT 5.02. 89
DOLPHIN'S* 12 FR 0.0013 REL FR 12 V 0 P
and heard a mermaid on a dolphin's back MND 2.01.150
where, like /arion on the dolphin's back, | i TN 1.02. 15
whose private with me of the dolphin's love | is JN 4.03. 16
far off | the dolphin's meaning and our embassy? H5 1.02.240
uncurbed plainness | tell us the dolphin's mind. 1.02.245
shall have cause to curse the dolphin's scorn. 1.02.288
a base wallon, to win the dolphin's grace, 1H6 1.01.137
i muse we met not with the dolphin's grace, 2.02. 19
hark, hark, the dolphin's drum, a warning bell, 4.02. 39
when from the dolphin's crest thy sword struck 4.06. 10
herald, conduct me to the dolphin's tent, | to 4.07. 51
till france be won into the dolphin's hands. 2H6 1.03.170
DOLT 1 FR 0.0001 REL FR 1 V 0 P
o gull, o dolt, | as ignorant as dirt! OTH 5.02.163
DOLTS 2 FR 0.0002 REL FR 1 V 1 P
asses, fools, dolts! TRO 1.02.241 P
be shown | for poor'st diminutives, for dolts, ANT 4.12. 37
DOMBLEDON *(see dommelton)*
DOMESTIC 8 FR 0.0009 REL FR 8 V 0 P
seated, and domestic broils | clean overblown, R3 2.04. 60
domestic awe, night–rest, and neighborhood, TIM 4.01. 17
domestic fury and fierce civil strife | shall JC 3.01.263
malice domestic, foreign levy, nothing, | can MAC 3.02. 25
for these domestic and particular broils | are LR 5.01. 30
fear, | to manage private and domestic quarrel? OTH 2.03.215
equality of two domestic powers | breed ANT 1.03. 47
his servants than | thyself domestic officers) CYM 3.01. 64
DOMESTICS 1 FR 0.0001 REL FR 1 V 0 P
and your words | (domestics to you) serve your H8 2.04.114
DOMINATIONS 1 FR 0.0001 REL FR 1 V 0 P
thou and thine usurp | the dominations, JN 2.01.176
DOMINATOR 3 FR 0.0003 REL FR 2 V 1 P
vicegerent, and sole dominator of navarre, my LLL 1.01.220 P
your desires, | saturn is dominator over mine: TIT 2.03. 31
magni dominator poli, | tam lentus audis scelera 4.01. 81
DOMINE 5 FR 0.0005 REL FR 4 V 1 P
lege, domine. LLL 4.02.104
ne intelligis, domine? 5.01. 26 P
but will the dainty domine, the schoolmaster, TNK 2.03. 40
ay, ay, by any means, dear domine. 3.05.135
take twenty, domine. — how does my sweet heart? 3.05.148
DOMINEER 1 FR 0.0001 REL FR 1 V 0 P
go to the feast, revel and domineer, | carouse SHR 3.02.224
DOMINEERING 1 FR 0.0001 REL FR 1 V 0 P
constable, | a domineering pedant o'er the boy, LLL 3.01.177
DOMINICAL 1 FR 0.0001 REL FR 1 V 0 P
debtor, | my red dominical, my golden letter: LLL 5.02. 44
DOMINION 1 FR 0.0001 REL FR 0 V 1 P
should he take me in his dominion, could not be CYM 3.02. 41 P
DOMINIONS 6 FR 0.0006 REL FR 6 V 0 P
and desert place quite out | of our dominions, WT 2.03.177
priest | shall tithe or toll in our dominions; JN 3.01.154
fields | shall not regreet our fair dominions, R2 1.03.142
and a stranger, | born out of your dominions; H8 2.04. 16
through your dominions for this enterprise, | on HAM 2.02. 78
thy banish'd trunk be found in our dominions, LR 1.01.177
DOMITIUS 2 FR 0.0002 REL FR 2 V 0 P
more, domitius, | my lord desires you presently; ANT 3.05. 20
he will not fight with me, domitius? 4.02. 1
DOMMELTON 1 FR 0.0001 REL FR 0 V 1 P
what said master dommelton about the satin for 2H4 1.02. 29 P
DON* *(also dun*)*
DON* 24 FR 0.0027 REL FR 4 V 20 P
you, don alphonso | with other gentlemen of good TGV 1.03. 39
know ye don antonio, your countryman? 2.04. 54
in this letter that don /pedro of arragon comes ADO 1.01. 1 P
i find here that don /pedro hath bestow'd much 1.01. 9 P
his part, and equally rememb'red by don pedro. 1.01. 13 P
don pedro is approach'd. 1.01. 95 P
look, don pedro is return'd to seek you. 1.01.202 P
me a meet hour to draw don pedro and the count 2.02. 34 P
know i have earn'd of don john a thousand ducats 3.03.108 P
and plac'd and possess'd by my master don john, 3.03.150 P
did confirm any slander that don john had made, 3.03.159 P
signior benedick, don john, and all the gallants 3.04. 96 P
said, sir, that don john, the prince's brother, 4.02. 39 P
a thousand ducats of don john for accusing the 4.02. 48 P
to this man how don john your brother incens'd 5.01.235 P
is it most expedient for the wise, if don worm 5.02. 84 P
abus'd, and don john is the author of all, who 5.02. 98 P
heat of duty, don adriano de armado." LLL 1.01.278 P
and don armado shall be your keeper. 1.01.304 P
design of industry, don adriano de armado. 4.01. 87 P
me by costard, and sent me from don armado. 4.02. 92 P
nominated, or called, don adriano de armado. 5.01. 8 P
what should i don this robe and trouble you? TIT 1.01.189
cannot weep | when our friends don their helms, TNK 1.03. 19
DONALBAIN 5 FR 0.0005 REL FR 5 V 0 P
donalbain. MAC 2.02. 18
banquo and donalbain! 2.03. 75
malcolm and donalbain, the king's two sons, 2.04. 25
it was for malcolm and for donalbain | to kill 3.06. 9
who knows if donalbain be with his brother? 5.02. 7
DONATION 4 FR 0.0004 REL FR 4 V 0 P
and some donation freely to estate | on the TMP 4.01. 85
never be the native | of our so frank donation. COR 3.01.130
me, | i would have put my wealth into donation, TIM 3.02. 83
it was wise nature's end in the donation, | to CYM 5.05.367
DONC 1 FR 0.0001 REL FR 0 V 1 P
donc votre est france et vous etes mienne. H5 5.02.183 P
DONCASTER 2 FR 0.0002 REL FR 2 V 0 P
us, | and you did swear that oath at doncaster, 1H4 5.01. 42
hand, | forgot your oath to us at doncaster, 5.01. 58
/DONE 10 FR 0.0011 REL FR 9 V 1 P
and time it is, when raging war is /done, | to SHR 5.02. 2
/care /is /loss /of /care, /by /old /care /done, R2 4.01.196
/those /men /that /most /have /done /us /wrong. 2H4 4.01. 79
/peace, /fool, /i /have /not /done. TRO 2.03. 56 P
/a /deed /of /death /done /on /the /innocent TIT 3.02. 56
/for /thou /hast /done /a /charitable /deed. 3.02. 70
the game was ne'er so fair, and i am /done. ROM 1.04. 39
/it /shall /be /done, /i /will /arraign /them LR 3.06. 20
/what /have /you /done? 4.02. 39
/ere /they /have /done /their /mischief, 4.02. 55
DONE 698 FR 0.0789 REL FR 571 V 127 P
the wills above be done! TMP 1.01. 67 P
tell your piteous heart | there's no harm done. 1.02. 15
i have done nothing, but in care of thee | (of 1.02. 16
remember i have done thee worthy service, | told 1.02.247
my lord, it shall be done. 1.02.318
would't had been done! 1.02.349
sir, | i fear you have done yourself some wrong; 1.02.444
thou hast done well, fine ariel! 1.02.495
well, i have done. but yet — 2.01. 26
done. the wager? 2.01. 32 P
prospero my lord shall know what i have done. 2.01.326
ministers | their several kinds have done. 3.03. 88
here thought they to have done | some wanton 4.01. 94
well done! 4.01.142
this was well done, my bird. 4.01.184
has done little better than play'd the jack with 4.01.197 P
all this service | have i done since i went. 5.01.226
was't well done? 5.01.240
you, gentle servant — 'tis very clerkly done. TGV 2.01.108
'twill be this hour ere i have done weeping; 2.03. 1 P
ay, sir, and done too — for this time. 2.04. 30 P
have done, have done; here comes the gentleman. 2.04. 99
have done, have done; here comes the gentleman. 2.04. 99
when you have done, we look to hear from you. 2.04.120
i have done penance for contemning love, | whose 2.04.129
i call to mind your gracious favors | done to me 3.01. 7
which must be done by praising me as much | as 3.02. 54
why, ne'er repent it, if it were done so. 4.01. 30
your message done, hie home unto my chamber, 4.04. 88
madam, this service i have done for you 5.04. 19
which, out of my neglect, was never done. 5.04. 90 P
to make such means for her as thou hast done, 5.04.137
that done, our day of marriage shall be yours — 5.04.172
and have done any time these three hundred years WIV 1.01. 12 P
i have done all this. 1.01.115 P
i'll make more of thy old body than i have done. 2.02.139 P
let them say 'tis grossly done, so it be fairly 2.02.143 P
say 'tis grossly done, so it be fairly done, no 2.02.143 P
that done, trudge with it in all haste, and 3.03. 13 P
o mistress ford, what have you done? 3.03. 94 P
make known to you why i have done this. 3.03.225 P
it hath done meritorious service. 4.02.205 P
him thither, | what shall be done with him? 4.04. 46
a fault done first in the form of a beast (o 5.05. 8 P
i think i have done myself wrong, have i not? MM 1.02. 40 P
well; what has he done? 1.02. 87 P
i have done so, but he's not to be found. 1.02.175
for we bid this be done, | when evil deeds have 1.03. 37
what was done to elbow's wife, that he hath 2.01.116 P
come me to what was done to her. 2.01.117 P
what was done to elbow's wife, once more? 2.01.139 P
once, sir? there was nothing done to her once. 2.01.141 P
what shall be done, sir, with the groaning 2.02. 15
why, every fault's condemn'd ere it be done. 2.02. 38
takes note of what is done, and like a prophet 2.02. 94
the evil that thou causest to be done, | that is 3.02. 20
would the duke that is absent have done this? 3.02.116 P
see this be done, | and sent according to 4.03. 79
this shall be done, good father, presently. 4.03. 82
let this be done: 4.03. 86
i would thou hadst done so by claudio. 5.01.468
yet this my comfort, when your words are done, ERR 1.01. 26
o, had the gods done so, i had not now 1.01. 98
come on, sir knave, have done your foolishness, 1.02. 72
you have done wrong to this my honest friend, 5.01. 19
it cannot be that she hath done thee wrong. 5.01.135
our dinner done, and he not coming thither, | i 5.01.224
he hath done good service, lady, in these wars. ADO 1.01. 48 P
but keep your way a' god's name, i have done. 1.01.143 P
shall we go prove what's to be done? 1.03. 74 P
keep him out of my sight when the dance is done! 2.01.110 P
well, a horn for my money, when all's done. 2.03. 61 P
of age to brag | what i have done being young, 5.01. 61
officers, what offense have these men done? 5.01.214 P
first, i ask thee what they have done; 5.01.221 P
'twas bravely done, if you bethink you of it. 5.01.270
"done to death by slanderous tongues | was the 5.03. 3
it was well done of you to take him at his word. LLL 2.01.217
when would you have it done, sir? 3.01.154 P
i shall know, sir, when i have done it. 3.01.158 P
it must be done this afternoon. 3.01.162 P
and done in the testimony of a good conscience. 4.02. 1 P
sir, you have done this in the fear of god, very 4.02.147 P
hiss, you may cry, "well done, hercules, now 5.01.138 P
peace, i have done. 5.02.483

would say, "thanks, pompey," i had done. 5.02.556
we must leave the killing out, when all is done. MND 3.01. 15 P
what hast thou done? 3.02. 88
my fairy lord, this must be done with haste, 3.02.378
and, being done, thus wall away doth go. 5.01.205
do | that in your knowledge may by me be done, MV 1.01.159
easier teach twenty what were good to be done, 1.02. 16 P
truth is that the jew, having done me wrong, 2.02.133 P
see it done. 2.02.155
my best endeavors shall be done herein. 2.02.173
as thou hast done with me — what, jessica! 2.05. 4
that thinks he hath done well in people's eyes, 3.02.142
that is done, sir, they have all stomachs! 3.05. 48 P
that is done too, sir, only "cover" is the word. 3.05. 51 P
that he misconsters all that you have done. AYL 1.02.265
trow you who hath done this? 3.02.179 P
world what the bird hath done to her own nest. 4.01.204 P
youth, you have done me much ungentleness, | to 5.02. 77
that done, conduct him to the drunkard's chamber SHR in.1. 107
as lively painted as the deed was done. in.2. 56
it is; may it be done? 1.01.193
would 'twere done! 1.01.254 P
so said, so done, is well. 1.02.185
his lecture will be done ere you have tun'd. 3.01. 23
therefore ha' done with words; 3.02.116
but after many ceremonies done, | he calls for 3.02.169
this done, he took the bride about the neck 3.02.177
that all is done in reverend care of her, | and, 4.01.204
till you have done your business in the city. 4.02.111
grumio gave order how it should be done. 4.03.117
but hast thou done thy errand to baptista? 4.04. 14
dower, | the match is made, and all is done: 4.04. 46
a match! 'tis done. 5.02. 74
fond done, done fond, | was this king priam's AWW 1.03. 72
fond done, done fond, | was this king priam's 1.03. 72
be at woman's command, and yet no hurt done! 1.03. 93 P
that done, laugh well at me. 2.01. 87
please it your majesty, i have done already. 2.03. 68
thou not, bertram, | what she has done for me? 2.03.109
the king has done you wrong; 2.03.300
these things shall be done, sir. 2.05. 15 P
might you not know she would do as she has done 3.04. 2
the french count has done most honorable service 3.05. 3 P
of yours | that has done worthy service. 3.05. 48
which he knows is not to be done, damns himself 3.06. 88 P
she did re–send, | and this is all i have done. 3.06.116
what shall i say i have done? 4.01. 26 P
a wife of me, though there my hope be done. 4.02. 65
with the duke, done my adieu with his nearest; 4.03. 87 P
what shall be done to him? 4.03.170 P
we'll see what may be done, so you confess 4.03.246 P
natural rebellion, done i' th' blade of youth, 5.03. 6
our own love waking cries to see what's done, 5.03. 65
this is done. 5.03.313
the king's a beggar, now the play is done; ep 1
is't not well done? TN 1.05.235 P
excellently done, if god did all. 1.05.236 P
if you will not undo what you have done, that is 2.01. 37 P
why, this is the best fooling, when all is done. 2.03. 30 P
"his eyes do show his days are almost done." 2.03.104
and it shall be done to–morrow morning if i live 3.04.103 P
what nature the wrongs are thou hast done him, i 3.04.221 P
clear from any image of offense done to any man. 3.04.228 P
if this young gentleman | have done offense, i 3.04.313
those kindnesses | that i have done for you. 3.04.352
thou hast, sebastian, done good feature shame. 3.04.366
thou mightst have done this without thy beard 4.02. 64 P
who has done this, sir andrew? 5.01.179 P
i must have done no less with wit and safety. 5.01.211
and for your service done him, | so much against 5.01.321
madam, you have done me wrong, | notorious wrong 5.01.328
but that's all one, our play is done, | and 5.01.407
have i done well? WT 2.01.187
well done, my lord. 2.01.188
unless he take the course that you have done — 2.03. 48
within this hour bring me word 'tis done | (and 2.03.136
aside, have done | like offices of pity. 2.03.188
which not to have done i think had been in me 3.02. 67
which had been done, | but that the good mind of 3.02.161
encourage him, | not doing it and being done. 3.02.165
girls of nine), o, think what they have done, 3.02.182
their sacred wills be done! 3.03. 7
away with thee the very services thou hast done; 4.02. 17 P
you ha' done me a charitable office. 4.03. 76 P
what you do | still betters what is done. 4.04.136
i have done. 4.04.249 P
camillo, | may this (almost a miracle) be done? 4.04.534
no remedy. | have you done there? 4.04.657
this being done, let the law go whistle; 4.04.697 P
after i have done what i promis'd? 4.04.810 P
sir, you have done enough, and have perform'd 5.01. 1
paid down | more penitence than done trespass. 5.01. 4
at the last | do as the heavens have done, 5.01. 5
have done the time more benefit and grac'd 5.01. 22
i have done. 5.01. 75
the wrongs i have done thee stir | afresh within 5.01.148
person | (so sacred as it is) i have done sin, 5.01.172
so near to hermione hath done hermione that they 5.02.100 P
come those i have done good to against my will, 5.02.124 P
yet you look'd upon | or hand of man hath done; 5.03. 17
as now she might have done, | so much to my good 5.03. 32
masterly done! 5.03. 65
and done a rape | upon the maiden virtue of the JN 2.01. 97
bedlam, have done. 2.01.183
that done, dissever your united strengths, | and 2.01.388
what other harm have i, good lady, done, | but 3.01. 38
but spoke the harm that is by others done? 3.01. 39
what hath it done, | that it in golden letters 3.01. 84
do amiss | is not amiss when it is truly done; 3.01.271
and being not done, where doing tends to ill, 3.01.272
ill, | the truth is then most done not doing it. 3.01.273
but that your royal pleasure must be done, 4.02. 17
breast, | and i do fearfully believe 'tis done, 4.02. 74
of means to do ill deeds | make deeds ill done! 4.02.220
murther, as hating what himself hath done, 4.03. 37
thou and endless night | have done me shame. 5.06. 13
nay, 'tis in a manner done already, | for many 5.07. 89

one, | take honor from me, and my life is done. R2 1.01.183
for sorrow ends not when it seemeth done. 1.02. 61
and list what with our council we have done: 1.03.124
your will be done. 1.03.144
my inch of taper will be burnt and done, | and 1.03.223
as mine hath done | by sight of what i have, 2.03. 17
and though you think that all, as you have done, 3.03. 82
had he done so to great and growing men, | they 3.04. 61
had he done so, himself had borne the crown, 3.04. 65
hadst thou groan'd for him | as i have done, 5.02.103
key, | that no man enter till my tale be done. 5.03. 37
by those welshwomen done as may not be | without 1H4 1.01. 45
for more is to be said and to be done | than out 1.01.106
thou hast done much harm upon me, hal, god 1.02. 91 P
but i remember, when the fight was done, | when 1.03. 30
have done) | to put down richard, that sweet 1.03.174
good uncle, tell your tale — i have done. 1.03.256
i have done, i' faith. 1.03.258
art thou to hack thy sword as thou hast done, 2.04.262 P
he would make you believe it was done in fight, 2.04.307 P
so it would have done | at the same season if 3.01. 17
might so have tempted him as you have done, 3.01.172
and since your coming hither have done enough 3.01.176
so | for some displeasing service i have done, 3.02. 5
all's done, all's won, here breathless lies the 5.03. 16
did such deeds in arms as i have done this day. 5.03. 46 P
what i have done my safety urg'd me to; 5.05. 11
day, | and since this business so fair is done, 5.05. 43
my lord, but he hath since done good service at 2H4 1.02. 61 P
and unpay the villainy you have done with her. 2.01.119 P
as thou hast not done a great while, because the 2.02. 21 P
i have done the part of a careful friend and a 2.04.321 P
and i would have done any thing indeed too, and 3.02. 18 P
that it would have done a man's heart good to 3.02. 48 P
battle as thou hast done in a woman's petticoat? 3.02.154 P
starv'd justice hath done nothing but prate to 3.02.304 P
and the feats he hath done about turnbull street 3.02.306 P
'tis well done. 4.01. 5
what i have done that misbecame my place, | my 5.02.100
impartial spirit | as you have done 'gainst me. 5.02.117
our coronation done, we will accite | (as i 5.02.141
why, now you have done me right. 5.03. 72 P
were nothing else to be done but to see him. 5.05. 27 P
as i have done the rest of my misleaders, | not 5.05. 64
as i perceiv'd his grace would fain have done, H5 1.01. 85
by chrish law, 'tish ill done! 3.02. 88 P
and my father's soul, the work ish ill done; 3.02. 91 P
o, 'tish ill done, 'tish ill done; 3.02. 93 P
o, 'tish ill done, 'tish ill done; 3.02. 93 P
by my hand, 'tish ill done! 3.02. 93 P
is throats to be cut, and works to be done, and 3.02.112 P
and there ish nothing done, so christ sa' me law 3.02.112 P
learn you by rote where services were done — at 3.06. 72 P
very little little let us do, | and all is done. 4.02. 34
well have we done, thrice–valiant countrymen, 4.06. 1
but all's not done — yet keep the french the 4.06. 2
ran from the battle ha' done this slaughter. 4.07. 6 P
it is not well done, mark you now, to take the 4.07. 42 P
and when you have done so, bring the keys to me. 1H6 2.03. 2
what you have done hath not offended me; 2.03. 76
and death approach not ere my tale be done. 2.05. 62
but join in friendship, as your lords have done. 3.01.145
my foot, | and, in reguerdon of that duty done, 3.01.169
done like a frenchman — turn and turn again! 3.03. 85
which i have done, because, unworthily, | thou 4.01. 16
then judge, great lords, if i have done amiss; 4.01. 27
with him, my lord, for he hath done me wrong. 4.01. 85
and i with him, for he hath done me wrong. 4.01. 86
now they meet where both their lives are done. 4.03. 38
but mine it will, that no exploit have done. 4.05. 27
the life thou gav'st me first was lost and done, 4.06. 7
we thank you all for this great favor done | in 2H6 1.01. 71
thy late exploits done in the heart of france 1.01.196
ask what thou wilt. that i had said, and done! 1.04. 28
have done, for more i hardly can endure. 1.04. 38
but still remember what the lord hath done. 2.01. 84
my lords, saint albon here hath done a miracle; 2.01.129
duke humphrey has done a miracle to–day. 2.01.157
but you have done more miracles than i: 2.01.159
shall, after three days' open penance done, 2.03. 11
madam, your penance done, throw off this sheet, 2.04.105
devise strange deaths for small offenses done? 3.01. 59
but god's will be done! 3.01. 86
not resolute, except so much were done, | for 3.01.267
no, not to lose it all, as thou hast done. 3.01.296
i'll see it truly done, my lord of york. 3.01.330
'tis politicly done, | to send me packing with 3.01.341
what have we done? 3.02. 3
and after all this fearful homage done, | give 3.02.224
unless lord suffolk straight be done to death, 3.02.244
justice with favor have i always done; 4.07. 67
it shall be done. 4.07.113 P
what would your grace have done unto him now? 3H6 1.04. 65
is by the stern lord clifford done to death. 2.01.103
but in this troublous time what's to be done? 2.01.159
have done with words, my lords, and hear me 2.02.117
'tis better said than done, my gracious lord. 3.02. 90
the ghostly father now hath done his shrift. 3.02.107
and if thou fail us, all our hope is done. 3.03. 33
if that go forward, henry's hope is done. 3.03. 58
the lord aubrey vere, | was done to death? 3.03.103
did i let pass th' abuse done to my niece? 3.03.188
tell him from me that he hath done me wrong, 3.03.231
and yet methinks your grace hath not done well 4.01. 51
him," quoth she, "my mourning weeds are done, 4.01.104
"tell him from me that he hath done me wrong, 4.01.110
it shall be done, my sovereign, with all speed. 4.06. 64
hold, richard, hold, for we have done too much. 5.05. 43
what will your grace have done with margaret? 5.07. 37
which done, god take king edward to his mercy, R3 1.01.151
when done thee wrong? 1.03. 56
have done thy charm, thou hateful with'red hag. 1.03.214
'tis done by me, and ends in "margaret." 1.03.238
have done, have done. 1.03.278
have done, have done. 1.03.278
my part thereof that i have done to her. 1.03.307

to pray for them that have done scath to us. 1.03.316
when you have done, repair to crosby place. 1.03.344
keeper, i have done these things | (that now 1.04. 66
no, he'll say 'twas done cowardly when he wakes. 1.04.101 P
remember our reward when the deed's done. 1.04.124 P
now have i done a good day's work. 2.01. 1
gloucester, we have done deeds of charity, 2.01. 50
a boon, my sovereign, for my service done! 2.01. 96
waiting vassals | have done a drunken slaughter, 2.01.123
if they have done this deed, my noble lord — 3.04. 73
lovel and ratcliffe, look that it be done: 3.04. 78
had he done so? 3.05. 40
when he had done, some followers of mine own, 3.07. 34
i do suspect i have done some offense | that 3.07.111
say it is done, | and i will love thee and 4.02. 80
the tyrannous and bloody act is done, | the most 4.03. 1
if to have done the thing you gave in charge 4.03. 25
your happiness, be happy then, | for it is done. 4.03. 27
when didst thou sleep when such a deed was done? 4.04. 24
all the slaughters, wretch, that thou hast done! 4.04.139
which thou supposest i have done to thee. 4.04.253
and not be richard that hath done all this. 4.04.287
look what is done cannot be now amended: 4.04.291
(which well i am assur'd i have not done), | his 5.03. 36
any good | that i myself have done unto myself? 5.03.188
cock | hath twice done salutation to the morn, 5.03.210
how have ye done | since last we saw in france? H8 1.01. 1
call'd upon | for high feats done to th' crown, 1.01. 61
but our count–cardinal | has done this, and 'tis 1.01.173
will of heav'n | be done in this and all things! 1.01.210
the will of heaven be done, and the king's 1.01.215
things done well | and with a care exempt 1.02. 88
things done without example, in their issue 1.02. 90
they have done my poor house grace; 1.04. 73
all's now done but the ceremony | of bringing 2.01. 4
't has done, upon the premises, but justice; 2.01. 63
i have done; 2.01.136
yea, as much | as you have done my truth. 2.04. 98
there's nothing i have done yet, o' my 3.01. 30
and to that woman (when she has done most) | yet 3.01.136
because all those things you have done of late 3.02.338
such things have been done. 5.01.133
and has done half an hour, to know your 5.02. 41
i have done. 5.02.121
may do, | not being torn a–pieces, we have done. 5.03. 76
which we have not done neither: ep 7
things won are done, joy's soul lies in the TRO 1.02.287
that's done, as near as the extremest ends | of 1.03.167
and jove forbid there should be done amongst us 2.02.127
paris should ne'er retract what he hath done, 2.02.141
why, this is kindly done. 3.01. 96 P
have you not done talking yet? 3.02.100 P
o heavens, what have i done! 3.02.138
now, princes, for the service i have done, | th' 3.03. 1
shall quite strike off all service i have done, 3.03. 29
fast as they are made, forgot as soon | as done. 3.03.150
to have done is to hang | quite out of fashion, 3.03.151
but something may be done that we will not, 4.04. 94
what shall be done | to him that victory 4.05. 65
'tis done like hector. 4.05. 73
but securely done, | a little proudly, and great 4.05. 73
nay, i have done already. 4.05.236
well, well, 'tis done, 'tis past. 5.02. 97
all's done, my lord. 5.02.115
what hath she done, prince, that can /soil our 5.02.134
who hath done to–day | mad and fantastic 5.05. 37
now is my day's work done, i'll take /good 5.08. 3
to close the day up, hector's life is done. 5.08. 8
let it be done. COR 1.01. 12 P
you what services he has done for his country? 1.01. 30 P
i say unto you, what he hath done famously, he 1.01. 36 P
presume to know | what's done i' th' capitol; 1.01.192
'tis done. 1.04. 2
slaves, | ere yet the fight be done, pack up. 1.05. 8
as merry as when our nuptial day was done | and 1.06. 31
i have done | as you have done — that's what i 1.09. 15
i have done | as you have done — that's what i 1.09. 16
not to reward | what you have done, before our 1.09. 27
without note, here's many else have done — 1.09. 49
never shame to hear | what you have nobly done. 2.02. 68
for your voices have | done many things, some 2.03.130
he has done nobly, and cannot go without any 2.03.132 P
is this done? 2.03.141
barr'd, it follows | nothing is done to purpose. 3.01.149
what has he done to rome that's worthy death? 3.01.296
this but done, | even as she speaks, why, their 3.02. 86
perform a part | thou hast not done before. 3.02.110
the warlike service he has done, consider; 3.03. 49
six of his labors you'ld have done, and sav'd 4.01. 18
let us seem humbler after it is done | than when 4.02. 4
you have done a brave deed. 4.02. 38
martius, who hath done | to thee particularly, 4.05. 65
evident as a chair | t' extol what it hath done. 4.07. 53
what have you done? 5.03.183
what he bids be done is finish'd with his 5.04. 23 P
thou hast done a deed whereat valor will weep. 5.06.132
for thy favors done | to us in our election this TIT 1.01.234
o, see what thou hast done! 1.01.341
my lord, what i have done, as best i may, 1.01.411
in the other's arms | (our pastimes done), 2.03. 26
o, say thou for her, who hath done this deed? 3.01. 87
oft | for his ungrateful country done the like. 4.01.111
villain, what hast thou done? 4.02. 73
villain, i have done thy mother. 4.02. 76
advise thee, aaron, what is to be done, | and we 4.02.129
this done, see that you take no longer days, 4.02.165
publius, publius, what hast thou done? 4.03. 69
and wherein rome hath done you any scath, | let 5.01. 7
and what not done, that thou hast cause to rue, 5.01.109
ay, that i had not done a thousand more. 5.01.124
but i have done a thousand dreadful things | as 5.01.141
show me a villain that hath done a rape, | and i 5.02. 94
show me a thousand that hath done thee wrong, 5.02. 96
was it well done of rash virginius | to slay his 5.03. 36
what hast thou done, unnatural and unkind? 5.03. 48
he | to do this outrage, and it now is done. 5.03. 52
have we done aught amiss, show us wherein, | and 5.03.129
you sad andronici, have done with woes. 5.03.176

prayers | i should repent the evils i have done. 5.03.186
peace, i have done. ROM 1.03. 59
supper is done, and we shall come too late. 1.04.105
the measure done, i'll watch her place of stand, 1.05. 50
if our wits run the wild–goose chase, i am done; 2.04. 72 P
excuse the injuries | that thou hast done me, 3.01. 67
therefore have done. 3.05. 72
do as thou wilt, for i have done with thee. 3.05.203
marry, i will, and this is wisely done. 3.05.234
o, shut the door, and when thou hast done so, 4.01. 44
when dinner's done, | show me this piece. TIM 1.01.245
't 'as been done; 1.02.144
you have done our pleasures much grace, fair 1.02.146
what shall be done, he will not hear, till feel. 2.02. 7
so soon as dinner's done, we'll forth again, 2.02. 14
now lord timon's happy hours are done and past, 3.02. 6 P
his service done | at lacedaemon and byzantium 3.05. 59
why, /i say, my lords, h'as done fair service, 3.05. 62
sun, hide thy beams, timon hath done his reign. 5.01.223
the games are done, and caesar is returning. JC 1.02.178
he said, if he had done or said any thing amiss, 1.02.269 P
their mothers, they would have done no less. 1.02.275 P
all this done, | repair to pompey's porch, where 1.03.146
that done, repair to pompey's theatre. 1.03.152
as we are going, | to whom it must be done. 2.01.331
brutus, what shall be done? 3.01. 20
and this the bleeding business they have done. 3.01.168
so pity pity — | hath done this deed on caesar. 3.01.172
i have done no more to caesar than you shall do 3.02. 36 P
they that have done this deed are honorable. 3.02.212
some worthy cause to wish | things done undone; 4.02. 9
most noble brother, you have done me wrong. 4.02. 37
to our tent till we have done our conference. 4.02. 51
you have done that you should be sorry for. 4.03. 65
was that done like cassius? 4.03. 77
it was well done, and thou shalt sleep again; 4.03.264
it shall be done, my lord. 4.03.308
out, | and something to be done immediatel;. 5.01. 15
not so have been, | durst i have done my will. 5.03. 48
our deeds are done! 5.03. 64
mistrust of my success hath done this deed. 5.03. 65
mistrust of good success hath done this deed. 5.03. 66
when the hurly–burly's done, | when the battle's MAC 1.01. 3
i'll see it done. 1.02. 66
is execution done on cawdor? 1.04. 1
nor must be known | no less to have done so, let 1.04. 31
that be | which the eye fears, when it is done, 1.04. 53
all our service | in every point twice done, and 1.06. 15
in every point twice done, and then done double, 1.06. 15
if it were done, when 'tis done, then 'twere 1.07. 1
if it were done, when 'tis done, then 'twere 1.07. 1
done, then 'twere well | it were done quickly. 1.07. 2
out, had i so sworn as you | have done to this. 1.07. 59
i go, and it is done; 2.01. 62
am afraid they have awak'd, | and 'tis not done; 2.02. 10
i have done the deed. 2.02. 14
i am afraid to think what i have done; 2.02. 48
unnatural, | even like the deed that's done. 2.04. 11
well, may you see things well done there: 2.04. 37
the moment on't, for't must be done to–night, 3.01.130
what's done, is done. 3.02. 12
what's done, is done. 3.02. 12
treason has done his worst; 3.02. 24
there shall be done | a deed of dreadful note. 3.02. 43
what's to be done? 3.02. 44
well, let's away, and say how much is done. 3.03. 22
which of you have done this? 3.04. 48
when all's done, | you look but on a stool. 3.04. 66
all you have done | hath been but for a wayward 3.05. 10
was not that nobly done? 3.06. 14
o, well done! 4.01. 39
my thoughts with acts, be it thought and done: 4.01.149
what had he done, to make him fly the land? 4.02. 1
i have done no harm. 4.02. 74
womanly defense, | to say i have done no harm? 4.02. 79
what's done cannot be undone. 5.01. 68 P
it shall be done. 5.04. 7
if there be any good thing to be done | that may HAM 1.01.130
yet now, i must confess, that duty done, | my 1.02. 54
till the foul crimes done in my days of nature 1.05. 12
that done, he lets me go, | and, with his head 2.01. 93
which done, she took the fruits of my advice; 2.02.145
make us again count o'er ere love be done! 3.02.162
play is the image of a murther done in vienna. 3.02.238 P
o me, what hast thou done? 3.04. 25
what have i done, that thou dar'st wag thy 3.04. 39
'a weeps for what is done. 4.01. 27
what we mean to do | and what's untimely done, 4.01. 40
what have you done, my lord, with the dead body? 4.02. 5
dearly grieve | for that which thou hast done — 4.03. 42
for every thing is seal'd and done | that else 4.03. 56
till i know 'tis done, | how e'er my haps, my 4.03. 67
"'so would i 'a' done, by yonder sun, | and thou 4.05. 65
and we have done but greenly | in hugger–mugger 4.05. 83
must there no more be done? 5.01.235
no more be done: 5.01.235
must be edified by the margent ere you had done. 5.02.156 P
i have done you wrong, | but pardon't, as you 5.02.226
what i have done | that might your nature, honor 5.02.230
all this done | upon the gad? LR 1.02. 25
some villain hath done me wrong. 1.02.165 P
by what yourself too late have spoke and done, 1.04.207
'tis most ignobly done | to pluck me by the 3.07. 35
but better service have i never done you | than 3.07. 74
thus with his despair | is done to cure it. 4.06. 34
there is nothing done, if he return the 4.06.265 P
sisters | have (as i do remember) done me wrong: 4.07. 73
countenance for the battle, which being done, 5.01. 63
the battle done, and they within our power, 5.01. 67
about it, and write happy when th' hast done. 5.03. 35
what you have charg'd me with, that have i done, 5.03.163
we then have done you bold and saucy wrongs; OTH 1.01.128
my services which i have done the signiory 1.02. 18
my story being done, | she gave me for my pains 1.03.158
i have done. 1.03.189
i have done, my lord. 1.03.198
that 'twixt my sheets | /h'as done my office. 1.03.388
our wars are done. 2.01. 20
our wars are done; 2.01.202
by me that's said or done amiss this night, 2.03.201
what had he done to you? 2.03.285 P
two things are to be done: 2.03.382
you, | if you think fit, or that it may be done, 3.01. 51
that done, i will be walking on the works; 3.02. 3
yet we see nothing done; 3.03.432
'tis done at your request. 3.03.474
we have done our course; 4.02. 93
look't be done. 4.03. 9 P
o me, lieutenant! what villains have done this? 5.01. 56
being done, there is no pause. 5.02. 82
o, my good lord, yonder's foul murthers done! 5.02.106
o, who hath done this deed? 5.02.123
thou hast done a deed — | i care not for thy 5.02.164
you have done well, | that men must lay their 5.02.169
i have done the state some service, and they 5.02.339
things that are past are done with me. ANT 1.02. 97
thy biddings have been done, and every hour, 1.04. 34
nothing | but what indeed is honest to be done; 1.05. 16
that to come | shall all be done by th' rule. 2.03. 7
i have done my duty. 2.05. 88
you have done well by water. 2.06. 86 P
it cannot be denied what i have done by land. 2.06. 89 P
nor what i have done by water. 2.06. 90 P
ah, this thou shouldst have done, | and not have 2.07. 73
being done unknown, | i should have found it 2.07. 78
i should have found it afterwards well done, 2.07. 79
o silius, silius, | i have done enough; 3.01. 12
he has done all this and more | in alexandria. 3.06. 1
'tis done already, and the messenger gone. 3.06. 31
nay, i have done, | here comes the emperor. 3.07. 19
provoke not battle | till we have done at sea. 3.08. 4
if he mislike | my speech and what is done, tell 3.13.148
have you done yet? 3.13.153
see it done, | and feast the army; 4.01. 14
might do you service | so good as you have done. 4.02. 19
hadst thou done so, | the kings that have 4.05. 3
i have done ill, | of which i do accuse myself 4.06. 17
had we done so at first, we had droven them home 4.07. 5
i am reveng'd upon my charm, | i have done all. 4.12. 17
what thou wouldst do | is done unto thy hand; 4.14. 29
unarm, eros, the long day's task is done, | and 4.14. 35
seal then, and all is done. 4.14. 49
i have done my work ill, friends. 4.14.105
what thou hast done thy master caesar knows, 5.02. 65
shall remember | as things but done by chance. 5.02.120
finish, good lady, the bright day is done, | and 5.02.193
and when thou hast done this chare, i'll give 5.02.231
so, have you done? 5.02.290
what work is here, charmian? is this well done? 5.02.325
it is well done, and fitting for a princess 5.02.326
that you did fear is done. 5.02.335
you have done | not after our command. CYM 1.01.151
hah? | no harm, i trust, is done? 1.01.161
would there had been some hurt done! 1.02. 35 P
well done, well done. 1.05. 82
well done, well done. 1.05. 82
(the factor for the rest) have done | in france. 1.06.188
but take this service i have done fatherly. 2.03. 35 P
a piece of work | so bravely done, so rich, that 2.04. 73
this service is not service, so being done, 3.03. 16
i sit and tell | the warlike feats i have done, 3.03. 90
to strike and to make me certain it is done, 3.04. 30 P
art, hath done you both | this cursed injury. 3.04.121
and all this done, spurn her home to her father, 4.01. 18 P
what hast thou done? 4.02.117
howsoe'er, | my brother hath done well. 4.02.147
well, 'tis done. 4.02.161
prithee have done, | and do not play in 4.02.229
rages, | thou thy worldly task hast done, | home 4.02.260
we have done our obsequies. come lay him down. 4.02.282
and so extort from 's that | which we have done, 4.04. 13
hath my poor boy done aught but well, | whose 5.04. 35
on greatness' favor dream as i have done, | wake 5.04.128
he hath done no britain harm, | though he have 5.05. 90
the service that you three have done is more 5.05.353
entice his own | to evil should be done by none. PER 1.ch. 28
sin, | when what is done is like an hypocrite, 1.01.122
say, is it done? 1.01.158
my lord, 'tis done. 1.01.158
and what was first but fear what might be done, 1.02. 14
grows elder now, and cares it be not done. 1.02. 15
and make pretense of wrong that i have done him; 1.02. 91
h'as done no more than other knights have done, 2.03. 34
h'as done no more than other knights have done, 2.03. 34
thanks, gentlemen, to all, all have done well; 2.03.107
fear the flaw, | it hath done to me the worst. 3.01. 40
get this done as i command you. 4.02. 61 P
come, the gods have done their part in you. 4.02. 70 P
and care in us | at whose expense 'tis done. 4.03. 46
me leave a word, and i'll have done presently. 4.06. 47 P
ha' you done? 4.06. 62 P
where what is done in action, more, if might, 5.ch. 23
but in no wise | till he had done his sacrifice, 5.02. 12
so content | to punish, although not done, but 5.03.100
what you do quickly | is not done rashly; TNK 1.01.135
till she for shame see what a wrong she has done 2.02. 39
a willing man dies sleeping, and all's done. 2.02. 68
i cannot tell what you have done; 2.02.156
this must be done i' th' woods. 2.03. 50
you have done worthily. 2.05. 1
better have endur'd cold iron than done it. 2.06. 10
he has not thank'd me | for what i have done; 2.06. 22
i will forgive | the trespass thou hast done me, 3.01. 77
all offices are done | save what i fail in. 3.02. 36
too | and have done as good boys should do, 3.05.143
think either, | well done, a noble recompense. 3.06. 24
what may be done? for now i feel compassion. 3.06.271
if she see him once, she's gone — she's done, 4.01.124
i am | to those that prate and have done, no 5.01.119
this advice i told you done any good upon her? 5.02. 1
'twas well done. 5.02. 7
'twas very ill done then. 5.02. 13
and has done this long hour, to visit you. 5.02. 42
let it here be done. 5.03.133
you'll see't done now for ever. 5.04. 25
haste you made | if you have done so quickly. 5.04. 42
'tis done. 5.04. 94
let's us do as we may be done by. STM II.C 141 P
me, | and were i not immortal, life were done, VEN 197
her words are done, her woes the more increasing 254
thy mermaid's voice hath done me double wrong: 429
are on the sudden wasted, thaw'd, and done, | as 749
lust's winter comes ere summer half be done; 802
end without audience and are never done. 846
he, foul creature, that hath done thee wrong, 1005
and, if possess'd, as soon decay'd and done, LUC 23
in that high task hath done her beauty wrong, 80
that done, some worthless slave of thine i'll 515
a little harm done to a great good end | for 528
"have done," quoth he, "my uncontrolled tide 645
that done, despitefully i mean to bear thee 670
for day hath nought to do what's done by night." 1092
and rail on pyrrhus that hath done him wrong, 1467
by foul enforcement might be done to me, | from 1623
which being done with speedy diligence, | the 1853
now see what good turns eyes for eyes have done: SON 24. 9
no more be griev'd at that which thou hast done: 35. 1
since mind at first in character was done! 59. 8
when other petty griefs have done their spite, 90.10
now all is done, have what shall have no end, 110. 9
it saw | the carcass of a beauty spent and done. LC 11
harm have i done to them, but ne'er was harmed, 194

/DONE'T 1 FR 0.0001 REL FR 0 V 1 P
i think i should, and undo't when i had /done't. OTH 4.03. 72 P

DONE'T 12 FR 0.0013 REL FR 10 V 2 P
his successors (gone before him) hath done't; WIV 1.01. 15 P
would have shed water out of fire ere done't. WT 3.02.193
you not known | the worthiest men have done't? COR 2.03. 49
say you ne'er had done't | (harp on that still) 2.03.251
not, for the wealth of athens, i had done't now. TIM 3.02. 52 P
their very daggers, | that they have done't? MAC 1.07. 77
resembled | my father as he slept, i had done't. 2.02. 13
those of his chamber, as it seem'd, had done't. 2.03.101
mine office, | or would have done't myself. ANT 4.06. 27
if you will swear you have not done't, you lie, CYM 2.04.144
would, polydore, thou hadst not done't! 4.02.155
would i had done't! 4.02.156

DONG 2 FR 0.0002 REL FR 2 V 0 P
i'll begin it — ding, dong, bell. MV 3.02. 71
ding, dong, bell. 3.02. 72

DONN'D 2 FR 0.0002 REL FR 2 V 0 P
"then up he rose and donn'd his clo'es, | and HAM 4.05. 52
amorous surfeiter would have donn'd his helm ANT 2.01. 33

DONNE 1 FR 0.0001 REL FR 0 V 1 P
mes genoux /je vous donne mille /remerciments; H5 4.04. 54 P

DONNER 1 FR 0.0001 REL FR 0 V 1 P
il est content a vous donner la liberte, le H5 4.04. 52 P

DONNERAI 1 FR 0.0001 REL FR 0 V 1 P
ma vie, et je vous donnerai deux cents ecus. H5 4.04. 42 P

DOOM 54 FR 0.0061 REL FR 54 V 0 P
i fly not death, to fly his deadly doom: TGV 3.01.185
and she hath offered to the doom | (which, 3.01.224
i was, and held me glad of such a doom. 4.01. 32
that it may stand till the perpetual doom | in WIV 5.05. 58
judgment hath | repented o'er his doom. MM 2.02. 12
and by the doom of death end woes and all. ERR 1.01. 2
firm and irrevocable is my doom | which i have AYL 1.03. 83
alter not the doom | forethought by heaven! JN 3.01.311
norfolk, for thee remains a heavier doom, R2 1.03.148
to change blows with thee for our day of doom. 3.02.189
thy kingly doom and sentence of his pride. 5.06. 23
carlisle, this is your doom: 5.06. 24
that, in his secret doom, out of my blood 1H4 3.02. 6
but exeter hath given the doom of death | for H5 3.06. 44
stain to thy countrymen, thou hear'st thy doom! 1H6 4.01. 45
this doom, my lord, if i may judge: 2H6 1.03.204
this is the law, and this duke humphrey's doom. 1.03.210
it skills not greatly who impugns our doom. 3.01.281
expect your highness' doom, of life or death. 4.09. 12
revoke that doom of mercy, for 'tis clifford, 3H6 2.06. 46
call him my king by whose injurious doom | my 3.03.101
room, | and triumph, henry, in thy day of doom. 5.06. 93
have i a tongue to doom my brother's death, R3 2.01.103
this princely presence | to doom th' offenders, 3.04. 65
in the air | and be not fix'd in doom perpetual, 4.04. 12
all unavoided is the doom of destiny. 4.04.218
other's slave, | and the gods doom him after! COR 1.08. 6
thee, | this is the day of doom for bassianus: TIT 2.03. 42
unbind my sons, reverse the doom of death, | and 3.01. 24
tribunes with their tongues doom men to death. 3.01. 47
pronounc'd | my everlasting doom of banishment. 3.01. 51
the emperor in his rage will doom her death. 4.02.114
this is our doom. 5.03.182
the prince will doom thee death | if thou art ROM 3.01.134
then, dreadful trumpet, sound the general doom, 3.02. 67
what is the prince's doom? 3.03. 4
i bring thee tidings of the prince's doom. 3.03. 8
what less than dooms–day is the prince's doom? 3.03. 9
displant a town, reverse a prince's doom, | it 3.03. 59
will the line stretch out to th' crack of doom? MAC 4.01.117
mass, | with heated visage, as against the doom; HAM 3.04. 50
all–obeying breath i hear | the doom of egypt. ANT 3.13. 78
the death of antony | is not a single doom, in 5.01. 18
so soon | is by your fancies' thankful doom. PER 5.02. 20
are equal precious — | i could doom neither; TNK 5.01.156
to be thy partner in this shameful doom." LUC 672
for now against himself he sounds this doom, 717
come, | from the creation to the general doom. 924
when they had sworn to this advised doom, | they 1849
thy end is truth's and beauty's doom and date. SON 14.14
that wear this world out to the ending doom. 55.12
suppos'd as forfeit to a confin'd doom. 107. 4
but bears it out even to the edge of doom. 116.12
ever sweet, | was us'd in giving gentle doom, 145. 7

DOOM'D 5 FR 0.0005 REL FR 5 V 0 P
if no, then thou art doom'd to die. ERR 1.01.154
or, when he doom'd this beauty to a grave, JN 4.03. 39
is doom'd a prisoner by proud bullingbrook. R2 5.01. 4
doom'd for a certain term to walk the night, HAM 1.05. 10
nobly doom'd! CYM 5.05.420

DOOM'S 1 FR 0.0001 REL FR 1 V 0 P
up, up, and see | the great doom's image! MAC 2.03. 78

DOOMS 1 FR 0.0001 REL FR 1 V 0 P

twice six moons, | he, obedient to their dooms, PER 3.ch. 32
DOOMS–DAY 2 FR 0.0002 REL FR 2 V 0 P
what less than dooms–day is the prince's doom? ROM 3.03. 9
stol'n marriage–day | was tybalt's dooms–day, 5.03.234
DOOMSDAY 9 FR 0.0010 REL FR 6 V 3 P
if she lives till doomsday, she'll burn a week ERR 3.02. 99 P
i'll prove her fair, or talk till doomsday here. LLL 4.03.270
doomsday is near, die all, die merrily. 1H4 4.01.134
why then all–souls' day is my body's doomsday. R3 5.01. 12
stare, cry out, and run, | as it were doomsday. JC 3.01. 98
was sick almost to doomsday with eclipse. HAM 1.01.120
then is doomsday near. 2.02.238 P
the houses he makes lasts till doomsday. 5.01. 59 P
i'll give thee leave | to play till doomsday. ANT 5.02.232
DOOR 112 FR 0.0126 REL FR 69 V 43 P
i will peat the door for master page. WIV 1.01. 72 P
page, i shall turn your head out of my door. 1.04.125 P
is come in at your back door, mistress ford, and 3.03. 25 P
here's mistress page at the door, sweating, and 3.03. 86 P
met the jealous knave their master in the door, 3.05.101 P
ford's brothers watch the door with pistols, 4.02. 52 P
basket again, to meet him at the door with it, 4.02. 96 P
your master is hard at door. 4.02.109 P
out of my door, you witch, you rag, you baggage, 4.02.184 P
this other doth command a little door, | which MM 4.01. 32
because their business still lies out a' door. ERR 2.01. 11
but soft, my door is lock'd; 3.01. 30
either get thee from the door, or sit down at 3.01. 33
go get thee from the door. 3.01. 35
who talks within there? ho, open the door! 3.01. 38
master, knock the door hard. 3.01. 58
cry for this, minion, if i beat the door down. 3.01. 59
who is that at the door that keeps all this 3.01. 61
your wife, sir knave! go get you from the door. 3.01. 64
they stand at the door, master, bid them welcome 3.01. 68
lam'd me, i shall beg with it from door to door. 4.04. 39 P
lam'd me, i shall beg with it from door to door. 4.04. 39 P
and hang me up at the door of a brothel–house ADO 1.01.253 P
i pray you watch about signior leonato's door, 3.03. 92 P
until the goose came out of door, | and stayed LLL 3.01. 91
until the goose came out of door, | staying the 3.01. 97
before, | to sweep the dust behind the door. MND 5.01.390
gate upon one wooer, another knocks at the door. MV 1.02.133
he is ready at the door; he comes, my lord. 4.01. 15
so please you, he is here at the door, and AYL 1.01. 91 P
yet would you say ye were beaten out of door, SHR in.2. 85
the door is open, sir, there lies your way; 3.02.210
no man at door | to hold my stirrup nor to take 4.01.120
beggars that come unto my father's door | upon 4.03. 4
sir, here's the door, this is lucentio's house. 5.01. 8
pisa, and is here at the door to speak with him. 5.01. 28 P
have of late knock'd too often at my door. AWW 4.01. 28 P
he'll stand at your door like a sheriff's post, TN 1.05.148 P
let the garden door be shut, and leave me to my 3.01. 92 P
hence with her, out o' door! WT 2.03. 68
if you did but hear the pedlar at the door, you 4.04.182 P
why, they stay at door, sir. 4.04.342 P
sits on 's horseback at mine hostess' door, JN 2.01.289
turning dispiteous torture out of door? 4.01. 34
hand which had the strength, even at your door, 5.02.137
out of the weak door of our fainting land. 5.07. 78
open the door, secure, foolhardy king! R2 5.03. 43
open the door, or i will break it open. 5.03. 45
speak with me, pity me, open the door! 5.03. 77
sir john with half a dozen more are at the door, 1H4 2.04. 83 P
let them alone awhile, and then open the door. 2.04. 85 P
and the rest of the thieves are at the door; 2.04. 88 P
of the court at door would speak with you. 2.04.288 P
with a most monstrous watch is at the door. 2.04.483 P
the sheriff and all the watch are at the door, 2.04.489 P
is the wind in that door, i' faith? 3.03. 88 P
shut the door, there comes no swaggerers here; 2H4 2.04. 76 P
shut the door, i pray you. 2.04. 78 P
who knocks so loud at door? 2.04.352 P
look to th' door there, francis. 2.04.353 P
more knocking at the door! 2.04.369 P
a dozen captains stay at door for you. 2.04.372
this door is open, he is gone this way. 4.05. 55
look who's at door there ho! 5.03. 70 P
as nail in door. the things i speak are just. 5.03.121
we'll chide this dolphin at his father's door. H5 1.02.308
when nature brought him to the door of death? 3H6 3.03.105
let the foul'st contempt | shut door upon me, H8 2.04. 43
they would shame to make me | wait else at door, 5.02. 17
who holds his state at door 'mongst pursuivants, 5.02. 24
and at the door too, like a post with packets. 5.02. 32
we sweep 'em from the door with cannons — | to 5.03. 13
keep the door close, sirrah. 5.03. 30 P
bless me, what a fry of fornication is at door! 5.03. 36 P
there is a fellow somewhat near the door, he 5.03. 40 P
no, pandarus, i stalk about her door, | like to TRO 3.02. 8
who's that at door? 4.02. 35
will you beat down the door? 4.02. 43 P
turn thy solemnness out a' door, and go along COR 1.03.108 P
pray go to the door. 4.05. 8 P
and with my sword i'll keep this door safe. TIT 1.01.288
knock at my door, and tell me what he says. 4.03.119
set them upright at their dear friends' door, 5.01.136
is it your trick to make me ope the door | that 5.02. 10
what's he that now is going out of door? ROM 1.05.130
o, shut the door, and when thou hast done so, 4.01. 44
sir, 'tis your brother cassius at the door, JC 2.01. 70
let /lucilius and titinius guard our door. 4.02. 52
who should against his murtherer shut the door, MAC 1.07. 15
this is the door. 2.03. 51
now go to the door, and stay there till we call. 3.01. 72
you do surely bar the door upon your own liberty HAM 3.02.338 P
let them guard the door. 4.05. 98
i thank you, keep the door. 4.05.116
ho, let the door be lock'd! 5.02.311
thy drink and thy whore, | and keep in a' door, LR 1.04.125
is better than this rain–water out o' door. 3.02. 11 P
here, at the door; i pray you call them in. OTH 2.03. 46 P
which lead directly to the door of truth | will 3.03.407
leave procreants alone, and shut the door; 4.02. 28
speak within door. 4.02.144
come guard the door without; 5.02.241
all of her that is out of door most rich! CYM 1.06. 15
attend you here the door of our stern daughter? 2.03. 37
the bier at door, | and a demand who is't shall 4.02. 22
having found the back door open | of the 5.03. 45
'twere not amiss to keep our door hatch'd. PER 4.02. 33 P
last, | and bid suspicion double–lock the door, VEN 448
the threshold grates the door to have him heard, LUC 306
now is he come unto the chamber door | that 337
and with his knee the door he opens wide. 359
much like a press of people at a door, | throng 1301
DOOR–KEEPER 2 FR 0.0002 REL FR 2 V 0 P
avaunt, thou damned door–keeper! PER 4.06.118
thou art the damned door–keeper to every 4.06.165
DOORNAIL 1 FR 0.0001 REL FR 0 V 1 P
if i do not leave you all as dead as a doornail, 2H6 4.10. 41 P
/DOORS 1 FR 0.0001 REL FR 1 V 0 P
you are pictures out /a' /doors, | bells in your OTH 2.01.109
DOORS 53 FR 0.0060 REL FR 41 V 12 P
i'll turn my mercy out o' doors, and make a TMP 3.02. 70 P
but the doors be lock'd and the keys kept safe, TGV 3.01.111
why at this time the doors are made against you. ERR 3.01. 93
since mine own doors refuse to entertain me, 3.01.120
for locking me out of my doors by day. 4.01. 18
of his own doors being shut against his entrance 4.03. 89
on purpose shut the doors against his way. 4.03. 91
driven out of doors with it when i go from home, 4.04. 35 P
whilst upon me the guilty doors were shut, | and 4.04. 63
and were not my doors lock'd up, and i shut out? 4.04. 70
perdie, your doors were lock'd, and you shut out 4.04. 71
day, great duke, she shut the doors upon me, 5.01.204
lock up my doors, and when you hear the drum MV 2.05. 29
do as i bid you, shut doors after you; 2.05. 53
i will make fast the doors, and gild myself 2.06. 49
o unhappy youth, | come not within these doors! AYL 2.03. 17
well, push him out of doors, | and let my 3.01. 15
make the doors upon a woman's wit, and it will 4.01.161 P
her, | be not denied access, stand at her doors, TN 1.04. 16
malvolio and bid him turn you out of doors, 2.03. 74 P
to meet displeasure farther from the doors, JN 5.01. 60
it would not out at windows nor at doors. 5.07. 29
hostess, clap to the doors! 1H4 2.04.276 P
ancient /swagger, /'a comes not in my doors. 2H4 2.04. 84 P
have you turn'd him out a' doors? 2.04.212 P
end | to this debate that bleedeth at our doors, 4.04. 2
how now, rain within doors, and none abroad? 4.05. 9
cannot defend our own doors from the dog, | let H5 1.02.218
be hang'd up for example at their doors. 2H6 4.02.180
what's all the doors open here? TRO 4.02. 19 P
no, good madam, i will not out of doors. COR 1.03. 71 P
not out of doors? 1.03. 72 P
seal'd up the doors and would not let us forth, ROM 5.02. 11
lips, o you | the doors of breath, seal with a 5.03.114
i come to have thee thrust me out of doors. TIM 1.02. 25
men shut their doors against a setting sun. 1.02.145
doors, that were ne'er acquainted with their 3.03. 37
what, are my doors oppos'd against my passage? 3.04. 79
as rushing out of doors to be resolv'd | if JC 3.02.179
i have no will to wander forth of doors, | yet 3.03. 3
the doors are open; MAC 2.02. 5
for out a' doors he went without their helps, HAM 2.01. 96
let the doors be shut upon him, that he may play 3.01.131 P
the doors are broke. 4.05.112
shut up your doors. LR 2.04.304
shut up your doors, my lord, 'tis a wild night, 2.04.308
though their injunction be to bar my doors, 3.04.150
are your doors lock'd? OTH 1.01. 85
i have charg'd thee not to haunt about my doors. 1.01. 96
her doors lock'd? CYM 3.05. 51
to me | the very doors and windows savor vilely. PER 4.06.110
would she had never come within my doors. 4.06.148 P
the doors, the wind, the glove that did delay LUC 325
DOO'S *(also does)*
DOO'S 2 FR 0.0002 REL FR 0 V 2 P
your grace doo's me as great honors as can be H5 4.07.160 P
and your digestions doo's not agree with it, i 5.01. 26 P
DORCAS 1 FR 0.0001 REL FR 1 V 0 P
give me those flow'rs there, dorcas. WT 4.04. 73
DOREUS 1 FR 0.0001 REL FR 1 V 0 P
bastard margarelon | hath doreus prisoner, | and TRO 5.05. 8
DORICLES 4 FR 0.0004 REL FR 4 V 0 P
o doricles, | your praises are too large. WT 4.04.146
with wisdom i might fear, my doricles, | you 4.04.150
they call him doricles, and boasts himself | to 4.04.168
if young doricles | do light upon her, she shall 4.04.178
DORMOUSE 1 FR 0.0001 REL FR 0 V 1 P
to exasperate you, to awake your dormouse valor, TN 3.02. 19 P
DOROTHY 3 FR 0.0003 REL FR 1 V 2 P
then to you, mistress dorothy, i will charge you 2H4 2.04.121 P
i know you, mistress dorothy. 2.04.127 P
to dorothy my woman hie thee presently, CYM 2.03.138
DORSET 15 FR 0.0017 REL FR 15 V 0 P
rivers and dorset, you were standers–by, | and R3 1.03.209
whet me | to be reveng'd on rivers, dorset, grey 1.03.332
nor you, son dorset; 2.01. 19
dorset, embrace him; 2.01. 25
of you, and you, lord rivers, and of dorset, 2.01. 67
look i so pale, lord dorset, as the rest? 2.01. 84
o dorset, speak not to me, get thee gone! 4.01. 38
the marquess dorset, as i hear, is fled | to 4.02. 48
well, let that rest. dorset is fled to richmond. 4.02. 85
dorset your son, that with a fearful soul 4.04.311
familiarly shall call thy dorset brother; 4.04.316
stirr'd up by dorset, buckingham, and morton, 4.04.467
sir thomas lovel and lord marquess dorset, 4.04.518
marquess dorset, | and that the earl of surrey, H8 4.01. 38
duchess of norfolk | and lady marquess dorset. 5.02.203
DORSETSHIRE 1 FR 0.0001 REL FR 1 V 0 P
richmond in dorsetshire sent out a boat | unto R3 4.04.522
/DOST 6 FR 0.0006 REL FR 4 V 2 P
/in /prosperity, | /thou /dost /beguile /me! R2 4.01.281
/of /woe, /that /thus /dost /talk /in /signs! TIT 3.02. 12
/ah, /wherefgre /dost /thou /urge /the /name /of 3.02. 26
/what /dost /thou /strike /at, /marcus, /with 3.02. 52
/how /dost /thou /understand /the /scripture? HAM 5.01. 35 P
/dost /thou /call /me /fool, /boy? LR 1.04.148 P
DOST 445 FR 0.0503 REL FR 347 V 98 P
thy false uncle — | dost thou attend me? TMP 1.02. 78
hence his ambition growing — | dost thou hear? 1.02.106
since thou dost give me pains, | let me remember 1.02.242
dost thou forget | from what a torment i did 1.02.250
thou dost; 1.02.252
if thou neglect'st or dost unwillingly | what i 1.02.368
thou dost here usurp | the name thou ow'st not, 1.02.454
prithee no more; thou dost talk nothing to me. 2.01.171
thou dost snore distinctly, | there's meaning in 2.01.217
thou dost me yet but little hurt; 2.02. 79 P
dost thou like the plot, trinculo? 3.02.108 P
but | if thou dost break her virgin–knot before 4.01. 15
do not approach | till thou dost hear me call. 4.01. 50
where thou thyself dost air — the queen o' th' 4.01. 70
that ne'er | dost disobey the wife of jupiter; 4.01. 77
and with each end of thy blue bow dost crown 4.01. 80
bow, | if venus or her son, as thou dost know, 4.01. 87
dost thou think so, spirit? 5.01. 19
in thy happiness | when thou dost meet good hap; TGV 1.01. 15
but dost thou hear? 1.01. 94 P
but tell me: dost thou know my lady silvia? 2.01. 42 P
dost thou know her by my gazing on her, and yet 2.01. 46 P
what dost thou know? 2.01. 51 P
thy service — why dost thou stop my mouth? 2.03. 44 P
why dost thou cry "alas"? 4.04. 77
dost thou know her? 4.04.142
o thou that dost inhabit in my breast, | leave 5.04. 7
how now, good woman, how dost thou? WIV 1.04.134 P
i think thou dost; MM 1.02. 36 P
fellow, why dost thou show me thus to th' world? 1.02.116
why dost thou not speak, elbow? 2.01. 59 P
dost thou detest her therefore? 2.01. 74 P
how dost thou know that, constable? 2.01. 78 P
why dost thou ask again? 2.02. 9
what dost thou? 2.02.172
dost thou desire her foully for those things 2.02.173
catch a saint, | with saints dost bait thy hook! 2.02.180
how often dost thou with thy case, thy habit, 2.04. 13
that dost this habitation where thou keep'st 3.01. 10
for thou dost fear the soft and tender fork | of 3.01. 16
dost thou think, claudio, | if i would yield him 3.01. 96
yea, dost thou jeer and flout me in the teeth? ERR 2.02. 22
dost thou not know? 2.02. 40 P
dost thou conjure for wenches, that thou call'st 3.01. 34
how dost thou mean a fat marriage? 3.02. 94 P
how fondly dost thou reason! 4.02. 57
what gold is this? what adam dost thou mean? 4.03. 15 P
and why dost thou deny the bag of gold? 4.04. 96
on thee, villain, wherefore dost thou mad me? 4.04.126
and that is false thou dost report to us. 5.01.179
but tell me yet, dost thou not know my voice? 5.01.301
i am sure thou dost! 5.01.304
well, if ever thou dost fall from this faith, ADO 1.01.255 P
dost thou affect her, claudio? 1.01.296
if thou dost love fair hero, cherish it, | and i 1.01.308
yea, marry, dost thou hear, balthasar? 2.03. 84 P
if thou dost love, my kindness shall incite thee 3.01.113
for others say thou dost deserve, and i 3.01.115
dost thou look up? 4.01.119
dost thou not suspect my place? 4.02. 74 P
dost thou not suspect my years? 4.02. 74 P
marry, thou dost wrong me, thou dissembler, thou 5.01. 53
dost thou wear thy wit by thy side? 5.01.126 P
how dost thou, benedick, the married man? 5.04. 99
dost thou think i care for a satire or an 5.04.102 P
thus dost thou hear the nemean lion roar LLL 4.01. 88
monster ignorance, how deformed dost thou look! 4.02. 23
how far dost thou excel | no thought can think, 4.03. 39
thou, fair sun, which on my earth dost shine, 4.03. 67
how now, what is in you? why dost thou tear it? 4.03.196
dost thou not wish in heart | the chain were 5.02. 55
nay, why dost thou stay? 5.02.626
dost thou infamonize me among potentates? 5.02.678 P
what thou seest when thou dost wake, | do it for MND 2.02. 27
sing while thou on pressed flowers dost sleep. 3.01.159
disparage not the faith thou dost not know, 3.02.174
if thou dost intend | never so little show of 3.02.333
where dost thou hide thy head? 3.02.406
how dost thou and thy master agree? MV 2.02. 99 P
thou dost deserve enough, and yet enough | may 2.07. 27
tell me once more what title thou dost bear: 2.09. 35
rather threaten'st than dost promise aught, 3.02.105
how dost thou like the lord bassanio's wife? 3.05. 72
why dost thou whet thy knife so earnestly? 4.01.121
if thou dost shed | one drop of christian blood, 4.01.309
art thou contented, jew? what dost thou say? 4.01.393
for if thou dost him any slight disgrace, or if AYL 1.01.148 P
how dost thou, charles? 1.02.219
that dost not bite so nigh | as benefits forgot; 2.07.185
lands and all things that thou dost call thine 3.01. 9
dost thou think, though i am caparison'd like a 3.02.194 P
dost thou believe, orlando, that the boy | can 5.04. 1
dost thou love hawking? SHR in.2. 43
dost thou love pictures? in.2. 49
gramercies, tranio, well dost thou advise. 1.01. 41
why dost thou wrong her that did ne'er wrong 2.01. 27
how now, my friend, why dost thou look so pale? 2.01.142
thou dost not halt. 2.01.256
of thy passion, | to say thou dost not: AWW 1.03.175
dost thou believe't? 1.03.249
that dost in vile misprision shackle up | my 2.03.152
why dost thou garter up thy arms a' this fashion 2.03.249 P
dost make hose of thy sleeves? 2.03.250 P
whether dost thou profess thyself — a knave or 4.05. 22 P
dost thou put upon me at once both the office of 5.02. 48 P
why dost thou not go to church in a galliard and TN 1.03.128 P
what dost thou mean? 1.03.131 P
dost thou think, because thou art virtuous, 2.03.114 P
how dost thou like this tune? 2.04. 20
thou dost speak masterly. 2.04. 22
what dost thou know? 2.04.104
dost thou live by thy tabor? 3.01. 1 P
why, how dost thou, man? 3.04. 24 P
why dost thou smile so, and kiss thy hand so oft 3.04. 32 P
why, how now, my bawcock? how dost thou, chuck? 3.04.112 P
i know thee well; how dost thou, my good fellow? 5.01. 10 P
what thou dost know | hath newly pass'd between 5.01.154
thou dost make possible things not so held, WT 1.02.139
thou mayst co–join with something, and thou dost 1.02.143

dost think i am so muddy, so unsettled, | to 1.02.325
thou dost advise me | even so as i mine own 1.02.339
dost thou hear, camillo, | i conjure thee, by 1.02.399
declare | what incidency thou dost guess of harm 1.02.403
good for thee, | what dost thou then in prison? 2.02. 4
dost lack any money? 4.03. 77 P
if to either, thou dost ill. 4.04.304
if i may ever know thou dost but sigh | that 4.04.427
on thee, rude man, thou dost shame thy mother, JN 1.01. 64
alack, thou dost usurp authority. 2.01.118
who is it thou dost call usurper, france? 2.01.120
it cannot be, thou dost but say 'tis so. 3.01. 6
what dost thou mean by shaking of thy head? 3.01. 19
why dost thou look so sadly on my son? 3.01. 20
thou dost shame | that bloody spoil. 3.01.114
thou fortune's champion that dost never fight 3.01.118
and dost thou now fall over to my foes? 3.01.127
we like not this, thou dost forget thyself. 3.01.134
our holy mother, | so willfully dost spurn; 3.01.142
keep in peace that hand which thou dost hold. 3.01.261
but thou dost swear only to be forsworn, | and 3.01.286
and most forsworn, to keep what thou dost swear; 3.01.287
dost thou understand me? 3.03. 63
how easy dost thou take all england up | from 4.03.142
a noble temper dost thou show in this, | and 5.02. 40
whither dost thou go? 5.06. 3
what dost thou object | against the duke of R2 1.01. 28
thou dost consent | in some large measure to thy 1.02. 25
o, to what purpose dost thou hoard thy words, 1.03.253
since thou dost seek to kill my name in me, | i 2.01. 86
let us share thy thoughts, as thou dost ours. 2.01.273
then wherefore dost thou hope he is not shipp'd? 2.02. 45
why dost thou say king richard is depos'd? 3.04. 77
what thou dost know of noble gloucester's death, 4.01. 3
how fondly dost thou spur a forward horse! 4.01. 72
thou dost suspect | that i have been disloyal to 5.02.104
thou frantic woman, what dost thou make here? 5.03. 89
dost thou teach pardon pardon to destroy? 5.03.120
thou dost belie him, percy, thou dost belie him; 1H4 1.03.113
thou dost belie him, percy, thou dost belie him; 1.03.113
what a brawling dost thou keep! 2.02. 6 P
why dost thou bend thine eyes upon the earth, 2.03. 42
thou wilt not utter what thou dost not know, 2.03.111
away, you rogue, dost thou not hear them call? 2.04. 78 P
dost thou hear me, hal? 2.04.209 P
dost thou speak like a king? 2.04.433 P
if thou dost it half so gravely, so majestically 2.04.435 P
why dost thou converse with that trunk of humors 2.04.449 P
i know thou dost. 2.04.465 P
dost thou hear, hal? 2.04.491 P
but thou dost in thy passages of life | make me 3.02. 8
dost thou think i'll fear thee as i fear thy 3.03.150 P
dost thou hear, hal? 3.03.164 P
what a devil dost thou in warwickshire? 4.02. 51 P
what honor dost thou seek | upon my head? 5.03. 2
not be in this humor with me, dost not know me? 2H4 2.01.151 P
dost thou hear, hostess? 2.04. 79 P
dost thou hear? it is mine ancient. 2.04. 82 P
and thou dost, i'll canvass thee between a pair 2.04.225 P
thou dost give me flattering busses. 2.04.268 P
sinful continents, what a life dost thou lead! 2.04.286 P
what, dost thou roar before thou art prick'd? 3.02.178 P
he loves thee, and thou dost neglect him, thomas 4.04. 21
when thou dost pinch thy bearer, thou dost sit 4.05. 29
thou dost sit | like a rich armor worn in heat 4.05. 29
dost thou so hunger for mine empty chair | that 4.05. 94
when thou dost hear i am as i have been, 5.05. 60
thou dost thy office fairly. H5 3.06.139
thou dost not wish more help from england, coz? 4.03. 73
any such, apprehend him, and thou dost me love. 4.07.158 P
dost thou thirst, base troyan, | to have me fold 5.01. 19
quiet thy cudgel, thou dost see i eat. 5.01. 52 P
kate, dost thou understand thus much english? 5.02.192 P
my blood begins to flatter me that thou dost — 5.02.223 P
priest, dost thou command me to be shut out? 1H6 1.03. 30
mayor, farewell; thou dost but what thou mayst. 1.03. 86
thou dost then wrong me, as that slaughterer 2.05.109
how dost thou fare? 4.06. 27
since thou dost deign to woo her little worth 5.03.151
dost thou deny thy father, cursed drab? 5.04. 32
o nell, sweet nell, if thou dost love thy lord, 2H6 1.02. 17
fellow, what miracle dost thou proclaim? 2.01. 58
now thou dost penance too. 2.04. 20
what, dost thou turn away and hide thy face? 3.02. 74
for henry weeps that thou dost live so long. 3.02.121
if thou dost plead for him, | thou wilt but add 3.02.291
dost thou use to write thy name? 4.02.102 P
thou dost ride in a foot–cloth, dost thou not? 4.07. 46 P
thou dost ride in a foot–cloth, dost thou not? 4.07. 47 P
why dost thou quiver, man? 4.07. 92 P
then what intends these forces thou dost bring? 5.01. 60
or wherefore dost abuse it if thou hast it? 5.01.172
and if thou dost not hide thee from the bear, 5.02. 2
why dost thou pause? 5.02. 19
and seeing thou dost, i here divorce myself 3H6 1.01.247
nor now my scandal, richard, dost thou hear; 2.01.151
clifford, dost thou know who speaks to thee? 2.06. 61
no, if thou dost say no to my demand. 3.02. 80
but wherefore dost thou come? 5.06. 29
as thou dost swallow up this good king's blood, R3 1.02. 66
dost grant me, hedgehog? 1.02.102
here. why dost thou spit at me? 1.02.144
out of my sight, thou dost infect mine eyes! 1.02.148
thou dost confirm his happiness for ever. 1.02.208
what, dost thou scorn me for my gentle counsel? 1.03.296
how dost thou feel thyself now? 1.04.120 P
how darkly and how deadly dost thou speak! 1.04.169
if thou dost find him tractable to us, 3.01.174
how? wear the garland? dost thou mean the crown? 3.02. 41
wherein dost thou joy? 4.04. 93
and dost thou not | usurp the just proportion of 4.04.109
that thou dost love my daughter from thy soul; 4.04.259
well then, who dost thou mean shall be her king? 4.04.265
o coward conscience, how dost thou afflict me! 5.03.179
thou dost not speak so much. TRO 1.01. 65
dost thou think i have no sense, thou strikest 2.01. 22 P
grecian, thou dost not use me courteously, | to 4.04.121
for, by the dreadful pluto, if thou dost not, 4.04.127

why dost thou so oppress me with thine eye? 4.05.241
dost thou entreat me, hector? 4.05.268
thou dost thyself and all our troy deceive. 5.03. 90
thou dost miscall retire. 5.04. 20
hast not the soft way which, thou dost confess, COR 3.02. 82
seeing me, dost not | think me for the man i am, 4.05. 55
why dost not speak? 5.03.153
dost thou think | i'll grace thee with that 5.06. 87
dost overshine the gallant'st dames of rome, TIT 1.01.317
queen of goths, dost thou applaud my choice? 1.01.321
demetrius, thou dost overween in all, | and so 2.01. 29
why dost not comfort me and help me out | from 2.03.209
if it be dark, how dost thou know 'tis he? 2.03.225
i know thou dost but jest. 2.03.253
now to the bottom dost thou search my wound; 2.03.262
why dost not speak to me? 2.04. 21
dost thou not perceive | that rome is but a 3.01. 53
thou dost not slumber; 3.01.254
why dost thou laugh? it fits not with this hour. 3.01.265
why, what a caterwauling dost thou keep! 4.02. 57
what dost thou wrap and fumble in thy arms? 4.02. 58
why dost not speak? 5.01. 46
i know thou dost, and, sweet revenge, farewell. 5.02.148
dost thou not laugh? ROM 1.01.183
"yea," quoth he, "dost thou fall upon thy face? 1.03. 41
dost thou love me? 2.02. 90
if thou dost love, pronounce it faithfully; 2.02. 94
thou dost not mark me. 2.04.175 P
the excuse that thou dost make in this delay 2.05. 33
is longer than the tale thou dost excuse. 2.05. 34
what, dost thou make us minstrels? 3.01. 46 P
why dost thou stay? 3.01.136
ay me, what news? why dost thou wring thy hands? 3.02. 36
what devil art thou that dost torment me thus? 3.02. 43
thou canst not speak of that thou dost not feel. 3.03. 64
what dost thou with him | that is renowm'd for 3.05. 61
dost thou not bring me letters from the friar? 5.01. 13
dost return to pry | in what i farther shall 5.03. 33
then say at once what thou dost know in this. 5.03.228
why dost thou call them knaves? TIM 1.01.181
how dost thou like this jewel, apemantus? 1.01.210 P
what dost thou think 'tis worth? 1.01.213 P
how dost, fool? 2.02. 50 P
dost dialogue with thy shadow? 2.02. 51 P
how dost thou, apemantus? 2.02. 74 P
why dost thou weep? 2.02.175
dost thou speak seriously, servilius? 3.02. 42
what, dost thou go? 3.06. 99
if thou dost perform, confound thee, for thou 4.03. 75 P
how dost thou pity him whom thou dost trouble? 4.03. 99
how dost thou pity him whom thou dost trouble? 4.03. 99
dost thou, or dost thou not, heaven's curse upon 4.03.132
dost thou, or dost thou not, heaven's curse upon 4.03.132
men report | thou dost affect my manners, and 4.03.199
thou dost affect my manners, and dost use them. 4.03.199
'tis, then, because thou dost not keep a dog, 4.03.200
why dost thou seek me out? 4.03.236
dost please thyself in't? 4.03.238
but thou | dost it enforcedly. 4.03.241
dost hate a medlar? 4.03.307 P
why dost ask that? 4.03.473
what, dost thou weep? 4.03.482
what dost thou with thy best apparel on? JC 1.01. 8
why dost thou lead these men about the streets? 1.01. 28
he loves no plays, | as thou dost, antony; 1.02.204
why dost thou stay? 2.04. 3
if thou dost bend, and pray, and fawn for him, 3.01. 45
dost thou lie so low? 3.01.148
strooken by many princes, | dost thou here lie! 3.01.210
if thou dost nod, thou break'st thy instrument, 4.03.271
as in thy red rays thou dost sink to–night, | so 5.03. 61
why dost thou show to the apt thoughts of men 5.03. 69
and that which rather thou dost fear to do MAC 1.05. 24
in those eyes | which thou dost glare with! 3.04. 95
sooth, | i care not if thou dost for me as much. 5.05. 40
how dost thou, guildenstern? HAM 2.02.224 P
dost thou hear me, old friend? 2.02.537 P
if thou dost marry, i'll give thee this plague 3.01.134 P
dost thou hear? 3.02. 62
for thou dost know, o damon dear, | this realm 3.02.281
what dost thou mean by this? 4.03. 29 P
now thou dost ill to say the gallows is built 5.01. 47 P
how dost thou, sweet lord?" 5.01. 83 P
thou dost lie in't, to be in't and say it is 5.01.125 P
what man dost thou dig it for? 5.01.130 P
dost thou think alexander look'd a' this fashion 5.01.197 P
dost /thou come here to whine? 5.01.277
dost know this water–fly? 5.02. 82
from my throat, | i'll tell thee thou dost evil. LR 1.01.166
canst serve where thou dost stand condemn'd, 1.04. 5
what dost thou profess? 1.04. 11 P
dost thou know me, fellow? 1.04. 26 P
how now, my pretty knave, how dost thou? 1.04. 96 P
dost thou know the difference, my boy, between a 1.04.137 P
that i'll resume the shape which thou dost think 1.04.309
"thou unpossessing bastard, dost thou think, 2.01. 67
how dost, my lord? 2.01. 89
why dost thou use me thus? i know thee not. 2.02. 11 P
what dost thou know me for? 2.02. 14 P
why dost thou call him knave? what is his fault? 2.02. 89
"inform'd" them? dost thou understand me, man? 2.04. 99
how dost, my boy? 3.02. 68
what art thou that dost grumble there i' th' 3.04. 44 P
these hairs which thou dost ravish from my chin 3.07. 38
dost thou know dover? 4.01. 71
and i'll repair the misery thou dost bear | with 4.01. 76
but thou dost breathe, | hast heavy substance, 4.06. 51
dost thou know me? 4.06.135
dost thou squiny at me? 4.06.136 P
why dost thou lash that whore? 4.06.161
seem | to see the things thou dost not. 4.06.172
when thou dost ask me blessing, i'll kneel down 5.03. 10
thee, if thou dost | as this instructs thee, 5.03. 28
thou dost make thy way | to noble fortunes. 5.03. 29
upon malicious /bravery dost thou come | to OTH 1.01.100
if thou dost, i shall never love thee after. 1.03.306 P
canst cuckold him, thou dost thyself a pleasure, 1.03.369 P
dost thou prate, rogue? 2.03.150 P

thou dost deliver more or less than truth, 2.03.219
dost thou hear, mine honest friend? 3.01. 21 P
what dost thou say? 3.03. 35
what dost thou say, iago? 3.03. 93
he did, from first to last. why dost thou ask? 3.03. 96
what dost thou think? 3.03.105
thou dost mean something. 3.03.108
if thou dost love me, | show me thy thought. 3.03.115
i think thou dost; 3.03.117
as thou dost ruminate, and give thy worst of 3.03.132
thou dost conspire against thy friend, iago, 3.03.142
/'zounds, what dost thou mean? 3.03.154
dost thou say so? 3.03.205
if more thou dost perceive, let me know more; 3.03.239
if thou dost slander her and torture me, | never 3.03.368
dost thou mock me? 4.01. 60
dost thou hear, iago, | i will be found most 4.01. 89
but (dost thou hear) most bloody. 4.01. 91
dost thou in conscience think — tell me, emilia 4.03. 61
that dost almost persuade | justice to break her 5.02. 16
o perjur'd woman, thou dost stone my heart, 5.02. 63
thou dost belie her, and thou art a devil. 5.02.133
dost understand the word? 5.02.153
now — how dost thou look now? 5.02.272
well, thou dost best. 5.02.306
if thou dost play with him at any game, | thou ANT 2.03. 26
gods confound thee, dost thou hold there still? 2.05. 92
thou dost o'er–count me of my father's house; 2.06. 27
dost thou hear, lady? 3.13.172
my turpitude | thou dost so crown with gold! 4.06. 33
dost fall? 5.02.293
dost thou lie still? 5.02.296
dost thou not see my baby at my breast, | that 5.02.309
dost thou think in time | she will not quench, CYM 1.05. 46
and i will kill thee if thou dost deny | thou'st 2.04.145
the first service thou dost me, fetch that suit 3.05.127 P
thou dost approve thyself the very same; 4.02.380
of her departure and | dost seem so ignorant, 4.03. 11
ay, so thou dost, | italian fiend! 5.05.209
how dost thou find the inclination of the people PER 4.02. 96 P
which, to betray, dost, with thine angel's face, 4.03. 47
if thou dost | hear from me, it shall be for thy 4.06.115
yet thou dost look | like patience gazing on 5.01.137
thou little know'st how thou dost startle me 5.01.146
thus dost thou still make good | the tongue o' TNK 1.01.226
(though in't i know thou dost believe thyself) 1.03. 88
all, or dost thou do it | to make me spare thee? 3.06. 46
who dost pluck | with hand armipotent from forth 5.01. 53
but having no defects, why dost abhor me? VEN 138
and so in spite of death thou dost survive, | in 173
me my hand," saith he, "why dost thou feel it?" 373
within my bosom, whereon thou dost lie, | my 646
lend thee light, as thou dost lend to other." 864
what dost thou mean | to stifle beauty and to 933
to see, | but hatefully at randon dost thou hit. 940
"dost thou drink tears, that thou provok'st such 949
if thou dost weep for grief of my sustaining, LUC 1272
thee befall'n, that thou dost trembling stand? 1599
suppose thou dost defend me | from what is past: 1684
thou dost beguile the world, unbless some mother SON 3. 4
why dost thou spend | upon thyself thy beauty's 4. 1
why dost thou abuse | the bounteous largess 4. 5
why dost thou use | so great a sum of sums, yet 4. 7
thou of thyself thy sweet self dost deceive, 4.10
and dost him grace when clouds do blot the 28.10
subject to invent | while thou dost breathe, 38. 2
when thou thyself dost give invention light? 38. 8
which time and thoughts so sweetly dost deceive, 39.12
thou dost love her because thou know'st i love 42. 6
from limits far remote, where thou dost stay. 44. 4
my heart doth plead that thou in him dost lie 46. 5
dost thou desire my slumbers should be broken 61. 3
thee watch i, whilst thou dost wake elsewhere, 61.13
the /soil is this, that thou dost common grow. 69.14
thou dost review | the very part was consecrate 74. 5
in others' works thou dost but mend the style, 78.11
and dost advance | as high as learning my rude 78.13
since what he owes thee thou thyself dost pay. 79.14
for i must ne'er love him whom thou dost hate. 89.14
how sweet and lovely dost thou make the shame 95. 1
o, in what sweets dost thou thy sins enclose! 95. 4
so dost thou too, and therein dignified. 101. 4
what thou dost foist upon us that is old, | and 123. 6
in thy power | dost hold time's fickle glass, 126. 2
what dost thou to mine eyes | that they behold 137. 1
if thou dost seek to have what thou dost hide, 142.13
if thou dost seek to have what thou dost hide, 142.13
why dost thou pine within and suffer dearth, 146. 3
dost thou upon thy fading mansion spend? 146. 6
lies, | what unapproved witness dost thou bear! LC 53

/DO'T 1 FR 0.0001 REL FR 1 V 0 P
/oats, | /if /it /be /man's /work, /i'll /do't. LR 5.03. 39

DO'T 86 FR 0.0097 REL FR 72 V 14 P
could control thee, | if now 'twere fit to do't. TMP 1.02.441
practic'd well to this, or they'll nev'r do't. WIV 4.04. 66
i will not do't. MM 2.02. 51
but might you do't, and do the world no wrong, 2.02. 53
please you to do't, | i'll take it as a peril to 2.04. 64
pleas'd you to do't at peril of your soul, 2.04. 67
thou shalt not do't. 3.01.102
not wounding, pity would not let me do't; LLL 4.01. 27
we will do't, come what will come." 5.02.112
i cannot love her, nor will strive to do't. AWW 2.03.145
shall i stay here to do't? 3.02.124
to do, and dares better be damn'd than to do't? 3.06. 89 P
and you love me, let's do't. TN 2.03. 60 P
do't, knight. 2.03.129 P
that i did, i was set on to do't by sir toby. 5.01.186 P
do't, and thou hast the one half of my heart; WT 1.02.348
do't not, thou split'st thine own. 1.02.349
i'll do't, my lord. 1.02.349
and my ground to do't | is the obedience to a 1.02.353
kings | and flourish'd after, i'ld not do't; 1.02.359
to do't, or no, is certain | to me a break–neck. 1.02.362
i dare my life lay down — and will do't, sir, 2.01.130
i cannot do't without compters. 4.03. 36 P
to acquaint the king withal, i would not do't. 4.04.681 P

i shall do't, my lord. H5 4.01.288
i as little question | as he is proud to do't. COR 2.01.231
what custom wills, in all things should we do't, 2.03.118
country | were to us all that do't and suffer it 3.01.301
do it to the gods, | must i then do't to them? 3.02. 39
well, i will do't; 3.02.101
well, i must do't. 3.02.110
i will not do't, | lest i surcease to honor mine 3.02.120
and he's as like to do't as any man i can 4.05.203 P
do't? 4.05.205 P
he will do't; 4.05.205 P
the tribunes cannot do't for shame; 4.06.109
do't in your parents' eyes! TIM 4.01. 8
do, /villains, do, since you protest to do't. 4.03.434
of caesar, | and say you do't by our permission; JC 3.01.247
one — two — why then 'tis time to do't. MAC 5.01. 36 P
which i say i saw, | but know not how to do't. 5.05. 31
let's do't, i pray, and i this morning know HAM 1.01.174
and now i'll do't — and so 'a goes to heaven, 3.03. 74
i will do't, my lord. 4.04. 7
and will, and strength, and means | to do't. 4.04. 46
young men will do't, if they come to't, | by 4.05. 60
and do't the speedier, that you may direct me 4.06. 33
i will do't, | and, for /that purpose, i'll 4.07.139
i'll do't. 5.01.277
i'll do't before i speak — that you make known LR 1.01.226
they durst not do't; 2.04. 22
they could not, would not do't. 2.04. 23
peace, this piece of toasted cheese will do't. 4.06. 90 P
either say thou'lt do't, | or thrive by other 5.03. 33
i'll do't, my lord. 5.03. 34
i'll do't, but it dislikes me. OTH 2.03. 47 P
well, my good lord, i'll do't. 3.02. 4
'tis she must do't; 3.04.107
take it, and do't, and leave me for this time. 3.04.191
i have seen her do't. 4.02. 23
i might do't as well i' th' dark. 4.03. 67
such a mutual pair | and such a twain can do't, ANT 1.01. 38
would make themselves whores but they'ld do't! 1.02. 78 P
i shall do't. 1.02.197 P
but if we fail, | we then can do't at land. 3.07. 53
and at this time most easy 'tis to do't: 3.13.144
we have store to do't, | and they have earn'd 4.01. 15
shall outstrike thought, but thought will do't, 4.06. 35
do't, the time is come. 4.14. 67
let's do't after the high roman fashion, | and 4.15. 87
do't as from thyself. CYM 1.05. 67
to greet your lord with writing, do't to–night. 1.06.206
rubies unparagon'd, | how dearly they do't! 2.02. 18
i will go there and do't, i' th' court, before 2.04.148
"do't; 3.02. 17
do't, and to bed then. 3.04.100
work | more plentiful than tools to do't — 5.03. 9
took heel to do't, | and yet died too! 5.03. 67
than myself, | a sacrilegious thief, to do't. 5.05.220
thy oath remember, thou hast sworn to do't. PER 4.01. 1
i will do't, but yet she is a goodly creature. 4.01. 9
is not to reason of the deed, but do't. 4.01. 83
you will not do't for all the world, i hope. 4.01. 84
villain to attempt it, who having drawn to do't, 5.01.173
do't, and happy, by my silver bow! 5.01.248
for | your offer do't i only, sir; TNK 3.01. 94

DOTAGE 10 FR 0.0011 REL FR 8 V 2 P
i would she had bestow'd this dotage on me, i ADO 2.03.168 P
they hold one an opinion of another's dotage, 2.03.216 P
her dotage now i do begin to pity. MND 4.01. 47
banish your dotage, banish usury, | that makes TIM 3.05. 98
have that scope | as dotage gives it. LR 1.04.293
he may enguard his dotage with their pow'rs, 1.04.326
that indiscretion finds | and dotage terms so. 2.04.197
suit, | or voluntary dotage of some mistress, OTH 4.01. 27
but this dotage of our general's | o'erflows the ANT 1.01. 1
i must break, | or lose myself in dotage. 1.02.117

DOTANT 1 FR 0.0001 REL FR 0 V 1 P
of such a decay'd dotant as you seem to be? COR 5.02. 44 P

DOTARD 3 FR 0.0003 REL FR 2 V 1 P
i speak not like a dotard nor a fool, | as under ADO 5.01. 59
away with the dotard! to the jail with him! SHR 5.01.106 P
bastard, | thou dotard, thou art woman–tir'd; WT 2.03. 75

DOTARDS 1 FR 0.0001 REL FR 1 V 0 P
and to the graver | a child that guided dotards. CYM 1.01. 50

/DOTE 1 FR 0.0001 REL FR 1 V 0 P
/has /sorrow /made /thee /dote /already? TIT 3.02. 23

DOTE 31 FR 0.0035 REL FR 24 V 7 P
what do you mean | to dote thus on such luggage? TMP 4.01.231
thee, | because thou seest me dote upon my love. TGV 2.04.173
how shall i dote on her with more advice, | that 2.04.207
you dote on her that cares not for your love. 4.04. 82
i never knew a woman so dote upon a man; WIV 2.02.103 P
sing, siren, for thyself, and i will dote; ERR 3.02. 47
unless the fear of death doth make me dote, | i 5.01.195
i see thy age and dangers make thee dote. 5.01.330
away myself for you, and dote upon the exchange. ADO 2.01.309 P
that she should so dote on signior benedick, 2.03. 96 P
if he do not dote on her upon this, i will never 2.03.211 P
for none offend where all alike do dote. LLL 4.03.124
as fool'ry in the wise, when wit doth dote, 5.02. 76
as you on him, demetrius dote on you! MND 1.01.225
will make or man or woman madly dote | upon the 2.01.171
her eye, | which she must dote on in extremity. 3.02. 3
how i dote on thee! 4.01. 45
gaud | which in my childhood i did dote upon; 4.01.168
one among them but i dote on his very absence, MV 1.02.110 P
mars dote on you for his novices! AWW 2.01. 47 P
and she (mistaken) seems to dote on me. TN 2.02. 35
this duke as much | they love and dote on; H8 2.01. 52
/you are three | that rome should dote on; COJ 2.01.187
nor so old to dote on her for any thing. LR 1.04. 38 P
of fashion, and i dote | in mine own comforts. OTH 2.01.206
o'er, point by point, for yet he seems to dote, PER 5.01.225
love makes young men thrall and old men dote, VEN 837
contrive, | to cipher me how fondly i did dote; LUC 207
who in despite of view is pleas'd to dote; SON 141. 4
if that be fair whereon my false eyes dote, 148. 5
whose rarest havings made the blossoms dote, LC 235

/DOTED 1 FR 0.0001 REL FR 1 V 0 P
/whom /they /doted /on | /and /bless'd /and 2H4 4.01.136

DOTED 1 FR 0.0001 REL FR 1 V 0 P
what he beheld, on that he firmly doted, | and LUC 416

DOTERS 1 FR 0.0001 REL FR 1 V 0 P
hair | should ravish doters with a false aspect: LLL 4.03.256

DOTES 9 FR 0.0010 REL FR 7 V 2 P
and she, sweet lady, dotes, | devoutly dotes, MND 1.01.108
devoutly dotes, dotes in idolatry, | upon this 1.01.109
dotes, | devoutly dotes, dotes in idolatry, 1.01.109
is there yet another dotes upon rib–breaking? AYL 1.02.142 P
and the will dotes that is attributive | to what TRO 2.02. 58
same breed that i know the drossy age dotes on, HAM 5.02.189 P
what damned minutes tells he o'er | who dotes, OTH 3.03.170
it is a creature | that dotes on cassio (as 'tis 4.01. 96
and dotes on what he looks, 'gainst law or duty. LUC 497

DOTETH 2 FR 0.0002 REL FR 2 V 0 P
run mad, | so much she doteth on her mortimer. 1H4 3.01.144
dumbly she passions, franticly she doteth, | she VEN 1059

/DOTH 12 FR 0.0013 REL FR 12 V 0 P
/doth show the mood of a much troubled breast, JN 4.02. 73
/that /my /wretchedness /doth /bait /myself, R2 4.01.238
/this /paper /while /the /glass /doth /come. 4.01.269
/or /what /doth /this /bold /enterprise /bring 2H4 1.01.178
/and /doth /enlarge /his /rising /with /the 1.01.204
/tells /them /he /doth /bestride /a /bleeding 1.01.207
/which /way /the /stream /of /time /doth /run, 4.01. 70
/not /the /king, /that /doth /you /injuries. 4.01.104
/the /glory /of /our /troy /doth /this /day /lie TRO 4.04.147
/mov'd, | /doth /weep /to /see /his /grandsire's TIT 3.02. 49
/the /mind /much /sufferance /doth /o'erskip, LR 3.06.106
/a /woman's /shape /doth /shield /thee. 4.02. 67

DOTH 1072 FR 0.1211 REL FR 974 V 98 P
our cable, for our own doth little advantage. TMP 1.01. 32 P
prescience | i find my zenith doth depend upon 1.02.181
nothing of him that doth fade, | but doth suffer 1.02.400
but doth suffer a sea–change | into something 1.02.401
no; he doth but mistake the truth totally. 2.01. 58 P
the truth you speak doth lack some gentleness, 2.01.138
when it doth, | it is a comforter. 2.01.195
why | doth it not then our eyelids sink? 2.01.201
open–ey'd conspiracy | his time doth take. 2.01.302
doth thy other mouth call me? 2.02. 97 P
on this island | where man doth not inhabit — 3.03. 57
the sole drift of my purpose doth extend | not a 5.01. 29
embrace his heart | that doth not wish you joy! 5.01.215
indeed a sheep doth very often stray, | and if TGV 1.01. 74
know'st, being stopp'd, impatiently doth rage; 2.07. 26
much turmoil | a blessed soul doth in elysium. 2.07. 38
the tenure of them doth but signify | my health 3.01. 56
take no repulse, what ever she doth say; 3.01.100
for "get you gone," she doth not mean "away!" 3.01.101
doth silvia know that i am banished? 3.01.223
"item, she doth talk in her sleep." 3.01.329 P
dissolves to water, and doth lose his form. 3.02. 8
love doth to her eyes repair, | to help him of 4.02. 46
doth this sir proteus that we talk on | often 4.02. 73
i think she doth; 4.04.147
how use doth breed a habit in a man! 5.04. 1
(though you respect not aught your servant doth) 5.04. 20
how doth good mistress page? WIV 1.01. 83 P
sir, he doth in some sort confess it. 1.01.103 P
what doth he think of us? 2.01. 83 P
he doth object i am too great of birth, | and 3.04. 4
now doth thy honor stand, | in him that was of 4.04. 8
doth all the winter–time, at still midnight, 4.04. 30
since therein she doth evitate and shun | a 5.05.228
that to th' observer doth thy history | fully MM 1.01. 28
heaven doth with us as we with torches do, | not 1.01. 32
and do look to know | what doth befall you here. 1.01. 58
be | a horse whereon the governor doth ride, 1.02.160
but doth rebate and blunt his natural edge 1.04. 60
doth he so seek his life? 1.04. 72
doth your honor mark his face? 2.01.149 P
doth your honor see any harm in his face? 2.01.153 P
and ask your heart what it doth know | that's 2.02.137
nor doth she tempt; 2.02.164
is that temptation that doth goad us on | to sin 2.02.181
to appear most bright | when it doth tax itself; 2.04. 79
as aged, and doth beg the alms | of palsied eld; 3.01. 35
and follies doth /enew | as falcon doth the fowl 3.01. 90
follies doth /enew | as falcon doth the fowl, is 3.01. 91
how doth my dear morsel, thy mistress? 3.02. 54 P
this other doth command a little door, | which 4.01. 32
of your title to him | doth flourish the deceit. 4.01. 74
your bawd — he doth oft'ner ask forgiveness. 4.02. 50 P
he doth with holy abstinence subdue | that in 4.02. 81
from this to that, | as cause doth minister. 4.05. 6
mouth, what he doth know | is true and false; 5.01.155
in self–same manner doth accuse my husband, 5.01.196
like doth quit like, and measure still for 5.01.411
hopeless and helpless doth egeon wend, | but to ERR 1.01.157
she that doth fast till you come home to dinner; 1.02. 89
"your meat doth burn," quoth i: 2.01. 63
i know his eye doth homage otherwhere, | or else 2.01.104
by falsehood and corruption doth it shame. 2.01.113
so it doth appear | by the wrongs i suffer, and 3.01. 15
she that doth call me husband, even my soul 3.02.158
husband, even my soul | doth for a wife abhor. 3.02.159
which doth amount to three odd ducats more 4.01. 30
there's not a man i meet but doth salute me | as 4.03. 1
friend, | and every one doth call me by my name: 4.03. 3
o husband, god doth know you din'd at home, 4.04. 65
me, | though most dishonestly he doth deny it. 5.01. 3
what doth ensue | but moody and dull melancholy, 5.01. 78
and ill it doth beseem your holiness | to 5.01.110
unless the fear of death doth make me dote, | i 5.01.195
as the first of may doth the last of december. ADO 1.01.192 P
"in time the savage bull doth bear the yoke." 1.01.261
and so she doth, cousin. 2.01.317 P
since many a wooer doth commence his suit | to 2.03. 50
may be she doth but counterfeit. 2.03.102 P
she doth indeed, my daughter says so; 2.03.150 P
she doth well. 2.03.178 P
he doth indeed show some sparks that are like 2.03.186 P
and so will he do, for the man doth fear god, 2.03.196 P
but doth not the appetite alter? 2.03.238 P
now, ursula, when beatrice doth come, | as we do 3.01. 15
doth not the gentleman | deserve as full as 3.01. 44
i know he doth deserve | as much as may be 3.01. 47
one doth not know | how much an ill word may 3.01. 85
doth not my wit become me rarely? 3.04. 69 P
is my lord well, that he doth speak so wide? 4.01. 62
how doth the lady? 4.01.113
doth not every earthly thing | cry shame upon 4.01.120
which with experimental seal doth warrant | the 4.01.166
than that which maiden modesty doth warrant, 4.01.179
my soul doth tell me hero is belied, | and that 5.01. 42
hero, now thy image doth appear | in the rare 5.01.251
your overkindness doth wring tears from me. 5.01.293
and now tell me, how doth your cousin? 5.02. 88 P
study knows that which yet it doth not know. LLL 1.01. 68
which, with pain purchas'd, doth inherit pain: 1.01. 73
doth falsely blind the eyesight of his look. 1.01. 76
seeking light, doth light of light beguile; 1.01. 77
while it doth study to have what it would, | it 1.01.143
it doth forget to do the thing it should; 1.01.144
tongue | doth ravish like enchanting harmony; 1.01.167
it doth amount to one more than two. 1.02. 47 P
possess the same | which native she doth owe. 1.02.106
guided by her foot (which is basest) doth tread. 1.02.169 P
all–telling fame | doth noise abroad, navarre 2.01. 22
for every object that the one doth catch | the 2.01. 70
your father here doth intimate | the payment of 2.01.128
for here he doth demand to have repaid | a 2.01.142
doth the inconsiderate take salve for l'envoy, 3.01. 78 P
speak of thee as the traveller doth of venice: 4.02. 95 P
so doth the hound his master, the ape his keeper 4.02.126 P
as doth thy face through tears of mine give 4.03. 31
weep, | no drop but as a coach doth carry thee; 4.03. 33
young blood doth not obey an old decree. 4.03.213
where nothing wants that want itself doth seek. 4.03.233
passes praise, then praise too short doth blot. 4.03.237
beauty doth varnish age, as if new born, | and 4.03.240
that i may swear beauty doth beauty lack, | if 4.03.247
from whence doth spring the true promethean fire 4.03.300
as fool'ry in the wise, when wit doth dote, 5.02. 76
since all the power thereof it doth apply | to 5.02. 77
love doth approach disguis'd, | armed in 5.02. 83
tell | how many inches doth fill up one mile. 5.02.193
and utters it again when god doth please. 5.02.316
and we that sell by gross, the lord doth know, 5.02.319
but that you take what doth to you belong, | it 5.02.381
lord | most honorably doth uphold his word. 5.02.449
sir, we know whereuntil it doth amount. 5.02.494 P
sir, will show whereuntil it doth amount. 5.02.500 P
sport best pleases that doth /least know how: 5.02.516
doth this man serve god? 5.02.524 P
varying in subjects as the eye doth roll | to 5.02.764
come when the king doth to my lady come; 5.02.829
our wooing doth not end like an old play: 5.02.874
note, | while greasy joan doth keel the pot. 5.02.920
when all aloud the wind doth blow | and coughing 5.02.921
note, | while greasy joan doth keel the pot. 5.02.929
when phoebe doth behold | her silver visage in MND 1.01.209
(a time that lovers' flights doth still conceal) 1.01.212
the king doth keep his revels here to–night; 2.01. 18
nor doth this wood lack worlds of company, | for 2.01.223
weeds of athens he doth wear: 2.02. 71
i throw | all the power this charm doth owe. 2.02. 79
doth the moon shine that night we play our play? 3.01. 51 P
yes; it doth shine that night. 3.01. 55 P
grey, | whose note full many a man doth mark, 3.01.132
doth move me | on the first view to say, to 3.01.140
the summer still doth tend upon my state; 3.01.155
so sorrow's heaviness doth heavier grow | for 3.02. 84
for debt that bankrout /sleep doth sorrow owe; 3.02. 85
when his love he doth espy, | let her shine as 3.02.105
wherein it doth impair the seeing sense, | it 3.02.179
why should he stay, whom love doth press to go? 3.02.184
and wherefore doth lysander | deny your love (so 3.02.228
with leaden legs and batty wings doth creep. 3.02.365
so doth the woodbine the sweet honeysuckle 4.01. 42
it goes not forward, doth it? 4.02. 6 P
doth glance from heaven to earth, from earth to 5.01. 13
for pyramus therein doth kill himself. 5.01. 67
this fellow doth not stand upon points. 5.01.118 P
with lime and rough–cast, doth present | wall, 5.01.131
in this same enterlude it doth befall | that i, 5.01.155
and this stone doth show | that i am that same 5.01.161
and, being done, thus wall away doth go. 5.01.205
when lion rough in wildest rage doth roar. 5.01.222
this lanthorn doth the horned moon present — 5.01.239
this lanthorn doth the horned moon present; 5.01.244
ay, that left pap, | where heart doth hop. 5.01.299
for he doth nothing but talk of his horse, and MV 1.02. 40 P
he doth nothing but frown, as who should say, 1.02. 46 P
jew, having done me wrong, doth cause me, as my 2.02.133 P
table, which doth offer to swear upon a book, i 2.02.159 P
my young master doth expect your reproach. 2.05. 20 P
where is the horse that doth untread again | his 2.06. 10
how like the prodigal doth she return, | with 2.06. 17
for the close night doth play the runaway, | and 2.06. 47
to these injunctions every one doth swear | that 2.09. 17
not learning more than the fond eye doth teach, 2.09. 27
doth teach me answers for deliverance! 3.02. 38
let music sound while he doth make his choice; 3.02. 43
substance of my praise doth wrong this shadow 3.02.127
this shadow | doth limp behind the substance. 3.02.129
there doth appear | among the buzzing pleased 3.02.179
i pray you tell me how my good friend doth. 3.02.233
how doth that royal merchant, good antonio? 3.02.239
and doth impeach the freedom of the state, | if 3.02.278
look what notes and garments he doth give thee, 3.04. 51
this letter from bellario doth commend | a young 4.01.143
wherein doth sit the dread and fear of kings; 4.01.192
and earthly power doth then show likest god's 4.01.196
and that same prayer doth teach us all to render 4.01.201
it doth appear you are a worthy judge; 4.01.236
so says the bond, doth it not, noble judge? 4.01.253
penance | of such misery doth she cut me off. 4.01.272
the court awards it, and the law doth give it. 4.01.300
this bond doth give thee here no jot of blood; 4.01.306
why doth the jew pause? take thy forfeiture. 4.01.335
the party 'gainst the which he doth contrive 4.01.352
do take the prop | that doth sustain my house; 4.01.376
ring, and doth entreat | your company at dinner. 4.02. 7

she doth stray about | by holy crosses, where 5.01. 30
vesture of decay | doth grossly close it in, we 5.01. 65
but music for the time doth change his nature. 5.01. 82
so doth the greater glory dim the less: 5.01. 93
as doth an inland brook | into the main of 5.01. 96
the crow doth sing as sweetly as the lark | when 5.01.102
for a light wife doth make a heavy husband, 5.01.130
bountiful blind woman doth most mistake in her AYL 1.02. 36 P
doth it therefore ensue that you should love his 1.03. 31 P
why should i not? doth he not deserve well? 1.03. 36 P
than doth your brother that hath banish'd you. 2.01. 28
"thus misery doth part | the flux of company." 2.01. 51
take that, and he that doth the ravens feed, 2.03. 43
who doth ambition shun, | and loves to live i' 2.05. 38
he that a fool doth very wisely hit | doth very 2.07. 53
fool doth very wisely hit | doth very foolishly, 2.07. 54
doth it not flow as hugely as the sea, | till 2.07. 72
and as mine eye doth his effigies witness | most 2.07.193
thy huntress' name that my full life doth sway. 3.02. 4
but doth he know that i am in this forest and in 3.02.229 P
i prithee, who doth he trot withal? 3.02.312 P
who doth he gallop withal? 3.02.326 P
doth my simple feature content you? 3.03. 3 P
but at this hour the house doth keep itself, 4.03. 81
orlando doth commend him to you both, | and to 4.03. 91
to prey on nothing that doth seem as dead. 4.03.118
youth | that he in sport doth call his rosalind. 4.03.156
a saying, "the fool doth think he is wise, but 5.01. 31 P
glass, by filling the one doth empty the other. 5.01. 42 P
to her that is not here, nor doth not hear. 5.02.108
mine, | thy faith my fancy to thee doth combine. 5.04.150
you to a love, that your true faith doth merit; 5.04.188
see, doth he breathe? SHR in.1. 31
why does the world report that kate doth limp? 2.01.252
thy beauty that doth make me like thee well, 2.01.274
greybeard, thy love doth freeze. 2.01.338
but thine doth fry. 2.01.338
now, for my life, the knave doth court my love: 3.01. 49
doth watch bianca's steps so narrowly, | 'twere 3.02.139
but so it is, my haste doth call me hence, | and 3.02.187
bianca | doth fancy any other but lucentio? 4.02. 2
see how beastly she doth court him! 4.02. 34
in count'nance somewhat doth resemble you. 4.02.100
as much as an apple doth an oyster, and all one. 4.02.101 P
i'll have no bigger, this doth fit the time, 4.03. 69
your son lucentio here | doth love my daughter, 4.04. 41
there doth my father lie; 4.04. 56
to come at first when he doth send for her, 5.02. 68
only doth backward pull | our slow designs when AWW 1.01.218
doth to our rose of youth rightly belong; 1.03.130
the gift doth stretch itself as 'tis receiv'd, 2.01. 4
he owes the malady | that doth my life besiege. 2.01. 10
methinks in thee some blessed spirit doth speak 2.01.175
so lust doth play | with what it loathes for 4.04. 24
a beauteous wall | doth oft close in pollution, TN 1.02. 49
doth he not mend? 1.05. 73 P
decays the wise, doth ever make the better fool. 1.05. 76 P
meeting, | every wise man's son doth know." 2.03. 44
being once display'd, doth fall that very hour. 2.04. 39
strong a passion | as love doth give my heart; 2.04. 95
with bloodless stroke my heart doth gore; 2.05.106
m.o.a.i. doth sway my life." 2.05.107
"m.o.a.i. doth sway my life." 2.05.110 P
my house, and my house doth stand by the church. 3.01. 6 P
it doth not fit me. 3.03. 38
yet doth this accident and flood of fortune | so 4.03. 11
in soul | as doth that orbed continent the fire 5.01.271
(these petty brands | that calumny doth use — o WT 2.01. 72
up to th' deed), doth push on this proceeding. 2.01.179
if never, yet that time himself doth say, | he 4.01. 31
doth set my pugging tooth an edge, | for a quart 4.03. 7
a meddler, | that doth utter all men's ware–a. 4.04.323
is the time that the unjust man doth thrive. 4.04.674 P
as every present time doth boast itself | above 5.01. 96
born, | doth he lay claim to thine inheritance? JN 1.01. 72
what doth move you to claim your brother's land? 1.01. 91
for new–made honor doth forget men's names; 1.01.187
time | that doth not /smack of observation — 1.01.208
their privilege on earth, | and so doth yours: 1.01.262
this little abstract doth contain that large 2.01.101
when living blood doth in these temples beat, 2.01.108
stones, | that as a waist doth girdle you about, 2.01.217
doth not the crown of england prove the king? 2.01.273
doth play | upon the dancing banners of the 2.01.307
john, your king and england's, doth approach, 2.01.313
now doth death line his dead chaps with steel, 2.01.352
he doth espy | himself love's traitor. 2.01.506
so | as doth the fury of two desperate men, 3.01. 32
and blessed shall he be that doth revolt | from 3.01.174
it is religion that doth make vows kept, | but 3.01.279
i muse your majesty doth seem so cold, | when 3.01.317
and wheresoe'er this foot of mine doth tread, 3.03. 62
order in so fierce a cause, | doth want example. 3.04. 13
snatch at his master that doth tarre him on. 4.01.116
doth make the fault the worse by th' excuse: 4.02. 31
doth make a stand at what your highness will. 4.02. 39
doth move the murmuring lips of discontent | to 4.02. 53
the color of the king doth come and go | between 4.02. 76
of all this isle, | three foot of it doth hold; 4.02.100
and he that speaks doth gripe the hearer's wrist 4.02.190
doth arthur live? 4.02.260
done, | doth lay it open to urge on revenge. 4.03. 38
arthur doth live, the king hath sent for you. 4.03. 75
doth dogged war bristle his angry crest, | and 4.03.149
waits, | as doth a raven on a sick–fall'n beast, 4.03.153
and heaven itself doth frown upon the land. 4.03.159
thy bosom | doth make an earthquake of nobility. 5.02. 42
that silverly doth progress on thy cheeks. 5.02. 46
what lusty trumpet thus doth summon us? 5.02.117
king, | for thus his royalty doth speak in me: 5.02.129
the king doth smile at, and is well prepar'd 5.02.134
doth by the idle comments that it makes 5.07. 4
his highness yet doth speak, and holds belief 5.07. 6
doth he still rage? 5.07. 11
by all my hopes, most falsely doth he lie. R2 1.01. 68
what doth our cousin lay to mowbray's charge? 1.01. 84
a trespass that doth vex my grieved soul; 1.01.138
where shame doth harbor, even in mowbray's face. 1.01.195
blood | doth more solicit me than your exclaims 1.02. 2
doth with a twofold vigor lift me up | to reach 1.03. 71
more than my dancing soul doth celebrate | this 1.03. 91
woe doth the heavier sit | where it perceives it 1.03.280
fell sorrow's tooth doth never rankle more 1.03.302
the open ear of youth doth always listen; 2.01. 20
where doth the world thrust forth a vanity — 2.01. 24
where will doth mutiny with wit's regard. 2.01. 28
with eager feeding food doth choke the feeder; 2.01. 37
the ripest fruit first falls, and so doth he; 2.01.153
and doth not herford live? 2.01.191
but what, a' god's name, doth become of this? 2.01.251
yes, my good lord, | it doth contain a king. 3.03. 25
on both his knees doth kiss king richard's hand, 3.03. 36
see, see, king richard doth himself appear, | as 3.03. 62
as doth the blushing discontented sun | from out 3.03. 63
harry bullingbrook, doth humbly kiss thy hand, 3.03.104
in the base court he doth attend | to speak with 3.03.176
it doth remember me the more of sorrow; 3.04. 14
state, for every one doth so | against a change; 3.04. 27
so, | i speak no more than every one doth know. 3.04. 91
of foot, | doth not thy embassage belong to me, 3.04. 93
what doth he with a bond | that he is bound to? 5.02. 67
for there, they say, he daily doth frequent, 5.03. 6
twice saying "pardon" doth not pardon twain, 5.03.134
i wasted time, and now doth time waste me; 5.05. 49
are the moon's men doth ebb and flow like the 1H4 1.02. 31 P
who doth permit the base contagious clouds | to 1.02.198
why, yet he doth deny his prisoners, | but with 1.03. 77
so he that doth redeem her thence might wear 1.03.206
and see already how he doth begin | to make us 1.03.289
purses than giving direction doth from laboring; 2.01. 51 P
i fear my brother mortimer doth stir | about his 2.03. 81
what doth gravity out of his bed at midnight? 2.04.294 P
doth not thy blood thrill at it? 2.04.370 P
he doth it as like one of these harlotry players 2.04.395 P
hanging of thy nether lip, that doth warrant me. 2.04.405 P
(as ancient writers do report) doth defile, so 2.04.413 P
doth defile, so doth the company thou keepest; 2.04.413 P
name as oft as lancaster | doth speak of you, 3.01. 9
not wind? it shall, it must, you see it doth. 3.01.105
yet oftentimes it doth present harsh rage, 3.01.181
which now doth that i would not have it do, 3.02. 90
he doth fill fields with harness in the realm, 3.02.101
of it as many a man doth of a death's–head or a 3.03. 30 P
how doth thy husband? 3.03. 93 P
so he doth you, my lord, and said this other day 3.03.133 P
i prithee tell me, doth he keep his bed? 4.01. 21
this sickness doth infect | the very life–blood 4.01. 28
yet doth he give us bold advertisement | that 4.01. 36
sun in march, | this praise doth nourish agues. 4.01.112
wind | doth play the trumpet to his purposes, 5.01. 4
the prince of wales doth join with all the world 5.01. 86
and so i hear he doth account me too; 5.01. 95
doth he feel it? 5.01.136 P
doth he hear it? 5.01.137 P
that the lord bardolph doth attend him here. 2H4 1.01. 3
how doth my son and brother? 1.01. 67
and he doth sin that doth belie the dead, | not 1.01. 98
and he doth sin that doth belie the dead, | not 1.01. 98
this strained passion doth you wrong, my lord. 1.01.161
doth not the king lack subjects? 1.02. 73 P
doth this become your place, your time, and 2.01. 66
doth it not show vildly in me to desire small 2.02. 5 P
and how doth thy master, bardolph? 2.02. 98 P
and how doth the martlemas, your master? 2.02.101 P
doth the old boar feed in the old frank? 2.02.146 P
and entire cowardice doth not make thee wrong 2.04.326 P
where he doth nothing but roast malt–worms. 2.04.334 P
doth begin to melt | and drop upon our bare 2.04.364
rumor doth double, like the voice and echo, 3.01. 97
and how doth my good cousin silence? 3.02. 3 P
and how doth my cousin, your bedfellow? 3.02. 5 P
how doth the good knight? 3.02. 64 P
may i ask how my lady his wife doth? 3.02. 65 P
doth she hold her own well? 3.02.205 P
not his craft's master, he doth not do it right. 3.02.278 P
here doth he wish his person, with such powers 4.01. 10
in peace, | what doth concern your coming. 4.01. 30
enemy, | he doth unfasten so and shake a friend, 4.01.207
that he now doth lack | the very instruments of 4.01.214
as a false favorite doth his prince's name, | in 4.02. 25
the time misord'red doth, in common sense, 4.02. 33
as much as the full moon doth the cinders of the 4.03. 52 P
same young sober–blooded boy doth not love me, 4.03. 88 P
for thin drink doth so over–cool their blood, 4.03. 91 P
up with this retinue, doth any deed of courage; 4.03.112 P
if god doth give successful end | to this debate 4.04. 1
'tis seldom when the bee doth leave her comb 4.04. 79
prince john your son doth kiss your grace's hand 4.04. 83
how doth the king? 4.05. 10
why doth the crown lie there upon his pillow, 4.05. 21
doth the king call? 4.05. 48
is he so hasty that he doth suppose | my sleep 4.05. 60
is | that doth with awe and terror kneel to it! 4.05.176
doth any name particular belong | unto the 4.05.232
doth the man of war stay all night, sir? 5.01. 29 P
how doth the king? 5.02. 2
i know he doth not, and do arm myself | to 5.02. 10
now doth it turn and ebb back to the sea, 5.02.131
but 'tis no matter, this poor show doth better, 5.05. 13 P
this doth infer the zeal i had to see him. 5.05. 13 P
it doth so. 5.05. 15 P
it doth so. 5.05. 17 P
it doth, it doth, it doth. 5.05. 19 P
it doth, it doth, it doth. 5.05. 19 P
it doth, it doth, it doth. 5.05. 19 P
know the grave doth gape | for thee thrice wider 5.05. 53
for god doth know, so shall the world perceive, 5.05. 57
doth his majesty | incline to it, or no? H5 1.01. 71
for god doth know how many now in health | shall 1.02. 18
then doth it well appear the salique law | was 1.02. 54
while that the armed hand doth fight abroad, 1.02.178
put into parts, doth keep in one consent, 1.02.181
therefore doth heaven divide | the state of man 1.02.183
the grave doth gape, and doting death is near, 2.01. 61
nor leave not one behind that doth not wish 2.02. 23
for my manly heart doth ern. 2.03. 3
doth like a miser spoil his coat with scanting 2.04. 47
the mighty sender, doth he prize you at. 2.04.119
hear the shrill whistle which doth order give 3.pr. 9
back, | tells harry that the king doth offer him 3.pr. 29
it | as fearfully as doth a galled rock 3.01. 12
in bloody field, | doth win immortal fame." 3.02. 11
but not as truly, | as bird doth sing on bough." 3.02. 19
as doth the melted snow | upon the valleys whose 3.05. 50
the alps doth spit and void his rheum upon. 3.05. 52
the duke of exeter doth love thee well. 3.06. 22
who like a foul and ugly witch doth limp | so 4.pr. 21
nor doth he dedicate one jot of color | unto the 4.pr. 37
sun, | his liberal eye doth give to every one, 4.pr. 44
the violet smells to him as it doth to me; 4.01.102 P
the element shows to him as it doth to me; 4.01.103 P
doth rise and help hyperion to his horse, | and 4.01.275
the sun doth gild our armor, up, my lords! 4.02. 1
gold, | nor care i who doth feed upon my cost; 4.03. 25
in which array, brave soldier, doth he lie, 4.06. 7
this note doth tell me of ten thousand french 4.08. 80
how london doth pour out her citizens! 5.pr. 24
doth fortune play the huswife with me now? 5.01. 80
and all her husbandry doth lie on heaps, 5.02. 39
and rank femetary | doth root upon, while that 5.02. 46
/reignier, duke of anjou, doth take his part; 1H6 1.01. 94
though thy speech doth fail, | one eye thou hast 1.04. 82
hear, hear how dying salisbury doth groan! 1.04.104
arm, arm! the enemy doth make assault! 2.01. 38
between two horses, which doth bear him best, 2.04. 14
poor gentleman, his wrong doth equal mine. 2.05. 22
with sweet enlargement doth dismiss me hence. 2.05. 30
he | from john of gaunt doth bring his pedigree, 2.05. 77
me, as that slaughterer doth | which giveth many 2.05.109
o, how this discord doth afflict my soul! 3.01.106
fury, | as by his smoothed brows it doth appear. 3.01.124
give | that doth belong unto the house of york, 3.01.164
which is so plain that exeter doth wish | his 3.01.199
then thus it must be, this doth joan devise: 3.03. 17
when death doth close his tender–dying eyes, 3.03. 48
and doth beget new courage in our breasts. 3.03. 87
in this, | and doth deserve a coronet of gold. 3.03. 89
doth but usurp the sacred name of knight, 4.01. 40
that doth presume to boast of gentle blood. 4.01. 44
or doth this churlish superscription | pretend 4.01. 53
what? doth my uncle burgundy revolt? 4.01. 64
he doth, my lord, and is become your foe. 4.01. 65
is that the worst this letter doth contain? 4.01. 66
but that it doth presage some ill event. 4.01.191
but death doth front thee with apparent spoil, 4.02. 26
renowned talbot doth expect my aid, | and i am 4.03. 12
who in proud heart | doth stop my cornets, were 4.03. 25
sleeping neglection doth betray to loss | the 4.03. 49
how doth your grace affect their motion? 5.01. 7
he doth intend she shall be england's queen. 5.01. 45
see how the ugly witch doth bend her brows, | as 5.03. 34
so doth the swan her downy cygnets save, 5.03. 56
margaret knows | that suffolk doth not flatter, 5.03.142
as doth a ruler with unlawful oaths, | or one 5.05. 30
beside, his wealth doth warrant a liberal dower, 5.05. 46
affords | and overjoy of heart doth minister. 2H6 1.01. 31
but 'tis my presence that doth trouble ye; 1.01.141
why doth the great duke humphrey knit his brows, 1.02. 3
my troublous dreams this night doth make me sad. 1.02. 22
this was my dream, what it doth bode god knows. 1.02. 31
doth any one accuse york for a traitor? 1.03.179
that doth accuse his master of high treason. 1.03.182
such as my heart doth tremble to unfold: 2.01.162
henry doth claim the crown from john of gaunt, 2.02. 54
the ruthless flint doth cut my tender feet, 2.04. 34
back, | by false accuse doth level at my life. 3.01.160
doth sting a child | that for the beauty thinks 3.01.229
in face, in gait, in speech, he doth resemble. 3.01.373
he doth revive again. madam, be patient. 3.02. 36
what, doth my lord of suffolk comfort me? 3.02. 39
god, | for judgment only doth belong to thee. 3.02.140
would curses kill, as doth the mandrake's groan, 3.02.310
what, doth death affright? 4.01. 32
doth york intend no harm to us | that thus he 5.01. 56
york doth present himself unto your highness. 5.01. 59
that head of thine doth not become a crown: 5.01. 96
what valor were it, when a cur doth grin, | for 3H6 1.04. 56
so doth the cony struggle in the net. 1.04. 62
'tis beauty that doth oft make women proud, 1.04.128
'tis virtue that doth make them most admir'd, 1.04.130
the contrary doth make thee wond'red at. 1.04.131
troop | as doth a lion in a herd of neat, | or 2.01. 14
they set the same, and there it doth remain, 2.01. 66
doth not the object cheer your heart, my lord? 2.02. 4
whose hand is that the forest bear doth lick? 2.02. 13
how it doth grieve me that thy head is here! 2.02. 55
wailing our losses, whiles the foe doth rage, 2.03. 26
sheep | than doth a rich embroider'd canopy | to 2.05. 44
o yes, it doth; 2.05. 46
a thousandfold it doth. 2.05. 46
to some man else, as this dead man doth me. 2.05. 60
this deadly quarrel daily doth beget! 2.05. 91
for death doth hold us in pursuit. 2.05.127
for what doth cherish weeds but gentle air? 2.06. 21
and much effuse of blood doth make me faint. 2.06. 28
as doth a sail, fill'd with a fretting gust, 2.06. 35
and so, perhaps, he doth; 2.06. 64
the tiger will be mild whiles she doth mourn; 3.01. 39
her looks doth argue her replete with modesty, 3.02. 84
her words doth show her wit incomparable, | all 3.02. 85
that thou shouldst stand while lewis doth sit. 3.03. 3
doth cloud my joys with danger and with sorrow. 4.01. 74
so doth my heart misgive me, in these conflicts 4.06. 94
and with his troops doth march amain to london, 4.08. 4
famous grandfather | doth live again in thee. 5.04. 53
doth she swoun? 5.05. 45
first the harmless sheep doth yield his fleece, 5.06. 8
the thief doth fear each bush an officer. 5.06. 12
he that doth naught with her (excepting one) R3 1.01. 99
his better doth not breathe upon the earth. 1.02.140
what doth she say, my lord of buckingham? 1.03.294
my hair doth stand an end to hear her curses. 1.03.303
and so doth mine. i muse why she's at liberty. 1.03.304
madam, his majesty doth call for you, | and for 1.03.319

where is the evidence that doth accuse me? 1.04.183
and that same vengeance doth he hurl on thee 1.04.201
the deed, | o, know you yet he doth it publicly. 1.04.216
why, so he doth, when he delivers you | from 1.04.247
when ever buckingham doth turn his hate | upon 2.01. 32
all duteous love | doth cherish you and yours, 2.01. 34
children, peace, the king doth love you well. 2.02. 17
i for a clarence /weep, so doth not she; 2.02. 83
doth the news hold of good king edward's death? 2.03. 7
when the sun sets, who doth not look for night? 2.03. 34
how doth the prince? 2.04. 40
he will do all in all as hastings doth. 3.01.168
how he doth stand affected to our purpose, | and 3.01.171
but canst thou guess that he doth aim at it? 3.02. 45
trust | my absence doth neglect no great design, 3.04. 24
he doth entreat your grace, my noble lord, | to 3.07. 59
the noble isle doth want /her proper limbs; 3.07.125
for god doth know, and you may partly see, | how 3.07.235
how doth the prince and my young son of york? 4.01. 14
plantagenet doth quit plantagenet, | edward for 4.04. 20
a hell–hound that doth hunt us all to death: 4.04. 48
shame serves thy life and doth thy death attend. 4.04.196
to vail the title, as her mother doth. 4.04.348
white–liver'd runagate, what doth he there? 4.04.464
thus doth he force the swords of wicked men | to 5.01. 23
be king, | doth comfort thee in thy sleep. 5.03.130
thy adversary's wife doth pray for thee. 5.03.166
the sky doth frown and low'r upon our army. 5.03.283
and who doth lead them but a paltry fellow, 5.03.323
my lord, he doth deny to come. 5.03.343
not almost appears, | it doth appear; H8 1.02. 30
as doth a rock against the chiding flood, 3.02.197
doth lesser blench at suff'rance than i do. TRO 1.01. 28
i have (as when the sun doth light a–scorn) 1.01. 37
though my heart's content firm love doth bear, 1.02.294
so | doth valor's show and valor's worth divide 1.03. 46
as rous'd with rage, with rage doth sympathize, 1.03. 52
and doth think it rich | to hear the wooden 1.03.154
makes merit her election, and doth boil | (as 1.03.349
she is not worth what she doth cost | the 2.02. 51
act | such and no other than event doth form it, 2.02.120
how doth pride grow? 2.03.151 P
he doth rely on none, | but carries on the 2.03.163
save such as doth revolve | and ruminate himself 2.03.187
which seems the wound to kill, | doth turn o ho! 3.01.123
as doth a battle, when they charge on heaps 3.02. 28
even such a passion doth embrace my bosom: 3.02. 35
that doth renew swifter than blood decays! 3.02.163
doth one pluck down another, and together | die 3.03. 86
nor doth the eye itself, | that most pure spirit 3.03.105
nor doth he of himself know them for aught, 3.03.118
an act that very chance doth throw upon him — 3.03.131
he merits well to have her that doth seek her, 4.01. 56
it doth import him much to speak with me. 4.02. 50
our general doth salute you with a kiss. 4.05. 19
doth long to see unarm'd the valiant hector. 4.05.153
in what place of the field doth calchas keep? 4.05.278
there diomed doth feast with him to–night, | who 4.05.280
she is, and doth: 4.05.292
doth that grieve thee? | o withered truth! 5.02. 45
he that takes that doth take my heart withal. 5.02. 82
but with my heart the other eye doth see. 5.02.108
that doth invert th' attest of eyes and ears, 5.02.122
within my soul there doth conduce a fight | of 5.02.147
with that which here his passion doth express? 5.02.162
cassandra doth foresee, and i myself | am like a 5.03. 64
th' effect doth operate another way. 5.03.109
full merrily the humble–bee doth sing, | till he 5.10. 41
that dark spirit, in 's nervy arm doth lie, COR 2.01.160
he doth appear. 2.02.131
it would, | for th' ill which doth control't. 3.01.161
whose rage doth rend | like interrupted waters, 3.01.247
on the ministers | that doth distribute it — in 3.03. 99
which doth ever cool | i' th' absence of the 4.01. 43
as far as doth the capitol exceed | the meanest 4.02. 39
the commonwealth doth stand, and so would do, 4.06. 14
doth more than counterpoise a full third part 5.06. 77
whose smoke like incense doth perfume the sky. TIT 1.01.145
me, andronicus, doth this motion please thee? 1.01.243
it doth, my worthy lord, and in this match | i 1.01.244
brother, for in that name doth nature plead — 1.01.370
father, and in that name doth nature speak — 1.01.371
upon her wit doth earthly honor wait, | and 2.01. 10
when every thing doth make a gleeful boast? 2.03. 11
even as an adder when she doth unroll | to do 2.03. 35
doth make your honor of his body's hue, 2.03. 73
why doth your highness look so pale and wan? 2.03. 90
'tis true, the raven doth not hatch a lark, 2.03.149
upon his bloody finger he doth wear | a precious 2.03.226
doth shine upon the dead man's earthy cheeks, 2.03.229
doth rise and fall between thy rosed lips, 2.04. 24
doth burn the heart to cinders where it is. 2.04. 37
as doth the deer | that hath receiv'd some 3.01. 89
as doth the honey–dew | upon a gath'red lily 3.01.112
doth fat me with the very thoughts of it! 3.01.203
when heaven doth weep, doth not the earth 3.01.221
heaven doth weep, doth not the earth o'erflow? 3.01.221
if the winds rage, doth not the sea wax mad, 3.01.222
hark how her sighs doth /blow! 3.01.225
to weep with them that weep doth ease some deal, 3.01.244
fear her not, lucius, somewhat doth she mean. 4.01. 9
on him that thus doth tyrannize o'er me. 4.03. 20
he doth me wrong to feed me with delays. 4.03. 43
who doth molest my contemplation? 5.02. 9
for up and down she doth resemble thee. 5.02.107
whiles that lavinia 'tween her stumps doth hold 5.02.182
doth with their death bury their parents' strife ROM pr 8
doth add more grief to too much of mine own. 1.01.189
what doth her beauty serve but as a note | where 1.01.235
that book in many's eyes doth share the glory, 1.03. 91
so shall you share all that he doth possess, 1.03. 93
care i | what curious eye doth cote deformities? 1.04. 31
what lady's that which doth enrich the hand | of 1.05. 41
o, she doth teach the torches to burn bright! 1.05. 44
now old desire doth in his death–bed lie, | and 2.pr. 1
shame those stars, | as daylight doth a lamp; 2.02. 20
which doth cease to be | ere one can say it 2.02.119
for nought so vile that on the earth doth live 2.03. 17
but to the earth some special good doth give; 2.03. 18
with unstuff'd brain | doth couch his limbs, 2.03. 38
couch his limbs, there golden sleep doth reign. 2.03. 38
therefore thy earliness doth me assure | thou 2.03. 39
to season love, that of it doth not taste! 2.03. 72
lo here upon thy cheek the stain doth sit | of 2.03. 75
doth grace for grace and love for love allow; 2.03. 86
doth not rosemary and romeo begin both with a 2.04.206 P
long love doth so; 2.06. 14
thee | doth much excuse the appertaining rage 3.01. 63
this day's black fate on moe days doth depend, 3.01.119
who now the price of his dear blood doth owe? 3.01.183
blood for your rude brawls doth lie a–bleeding; 3.01.189
doth not she think me an old murtherer, | now i 3.03. 94
and how doth she? 3.03. 97
vile part of this anatomy | doth my name lodge? 3.03.107
this doth not so, for she divideth us. 3.05. 30
since arm from arm that voice doth us affray, 3.05. 33
and yet no man like he doth grieve my heart. 3.05. 83
where that same banish'd runagate doth live, 3.05. 89
when the sun sets, the earth doth drizzle dew, 3.05.126
doth she not give us thanks? 3.05.142
doth she not count her blest, | unworthy as she 3.05.143
then, since the case so stands as now it doth, 3.05.216
and doth it give me such a sight as this? 4.05. 42
"when griping griefs the heart doth wound, 4.05.126
sound | with speedy help doth lend redress." 4.05.143
how doth my lady? 5.01. 14
how doth my juliet? 5.01. 15
fir'd | doth hurry from the fatal cannon's womb. 5.01. 65
the boy gives warning, something doth approach. 5.03. 18
it doth so, holy sir, and there's my master, 5.03.128
lips, | haply some poison yet doth hang on them, 5.03.165
is the place, there where the torch doth burn. 5.03.171
as the time and place | doth make against me, of 5.03.225
this letter doth make good the friar's words, 5.03.286
whom this beneath world doth embrace and hug TIM 1.01. 44
the want whereof doth daily make revolt | in my 4.03. 92
whereon hyperion's quick'ning fire doth shine: 4.03.184
whose blush doth thaw the consecrated snow 4.03.385
body, which doth seldom | play the recanter, 5.01.145
too savage, doth root up | his country's peace. 5.01.165
the common wrack, | as common bruit doth put it. 5.01.193
that nature's fragile vessel doth sustain | in 5.01.201
fearful scouring | doth choke the air with dust. 5.02. 16
in antonio's way | when he doth run his course. JC 1.02. 4
and that same eye whose bend doth awe the world 1.02.123
it doth amaze me | a man of such a feeble temper 1.02.128
man, he doth bestride the narrow world | like a 1.02.135
sound them, it doth become the mouth as well; 1.02.145
upon what meat doth this our caesar feed | that 1.02.149
the angry spot doth glow on caesar's brow, | and 1.02.183
caesar doth bear me hard, but he loves brutus. 1.02.313
he doth; 1.03. 37
and roars | as doth the lion in the capitol — 1.03. 75
at the door, | who doth desire to see you. 2.01. 71
and every one doth wish | you had but that 2.01. 91
here lies the east; doth not the day break here? 2.01.101
o, pardon, sir, it doth; 2.01.103
caius ligarius doth bear caesar hard, | who 2.01.215
and take good note | what caesar doth, what 2.04. 15
and bring me word what he doth say to thee. 2.04. 46
trebonius doth desire you to o'er–read | (at 3.01. 4
for look he smiles, and caesar doth not change. 3.01. 24
know, caesar doth not wrong, nor without cause 3.01. 47
as low as to thy foot doth cassius fall, | to 3.01. 56
they are all fire, and every one doth shine; 3.01. 64
but there's but one in all doth hold his place. 3.01. 65
doth not brutus bootless kneel? 3.01. 75
that you have wrong'd me doth appear in this: 4.03. 1
and chastisement doth therefore hide his head. 4.03. 16
ha, ha! how vildly doth this cynic rhyme! 4.03.133
where, where, messala, doth his body lie? 5.03. 91
what bastard doth not? 5.04. 2
my heart doth joy that yet in all my life | i 5.05. 34
a drum, a drum! | macbeth doth come. MAC 1.03. 31
whose horrid image doth unfix my hair | and make 1.03.135
which fate and metaphysical aid doth seem | to 1.05. 29
face must hide what the false heart doth know. 1.07. 82
he hath a wisdom that doth guide his valor | to 3.01. 52
that of an hour's age doth hiss the speaker; 4.03.175
doth make the night joint–laborer with the day: HAM 1.01. 78
other, | as it doth well appear unto our state, 1.01.101
doth with his lofty and shrill–sounding throat 1.01.151
and now no soil nor cautel doth besmirch | the 1.03. 15
the king doth wake to–night and takes his rouse, 1.04. 8
/ev'l | doth all the noble substance of a doubt 1.04. 37
and with a sudden vigor it doth /posset | and 1.05. 68
stars are fire, | doubt that the sun doth move, 2.02.117
the dreadful thunder | doth rend the region; 2.02.487
and it doth much content me | to hear him so 3.01. 24
a lash that speech doth give my conscience! 3.01. 49
the passion ending, doth the purpose lose. 3.02.195
where joy most revels, grief doth most lament; 3.02.198
and hitherto doth love on fortune tend, | for 3.02.206
and who in want a hollow friend doth try, 3.02.208
the lady doth protest too much, methinks. 3.02.230 P
the croaking raven doth bellow for revenge. 3.02.254 P
hazard so near 's as doth hourly grow | out of 3.03. 6
like a gulf, doth draw | what's near it with it. 3.03. 16
since frost itself as actively doth burn, | and 3.04. 87
my pulse, as yours, doth temperately keep time, 3.04.140
that monster custom, who all sense doth eat, 3.04.161
yet the unshaped use of it doth move | the 4.05. 8
there's such divinity doth hedge a king | that 4.05.124
one woe doth tread upon another's heel, | so 4.07.163
this doth betoken | the corse they follow did 5.01.219
which now to claim my vantage doth invite me. 5.02.390
which of you shall we say doth love us most, LR 1.01. 51
extend | where nature doth with merit challenge? 1.01. 53
more composition and fierce quality | than doth, 1.02. 13
the shame itself doth speak | for instant remedy 1.04.246
whose virtue and obedience doth this instant 2.01.113
for bluntness, doth affect | a saucy roughness, 2.02. 96
infirmity doth still neglect all office 2.04.106
thy fifty yet doth double five and twenty, | and 2.04.259
the younger rises when the old doth fall. 3.03. 25
doth from my senses take all feeling else, 3.04. 13
grown so vild | that it doth hate what gets it. 3.04.146
no blown ambition doth our arms incite, | but 4.04. 27
in his own grace he doth exalt himself, | more 5.03. 67
for when my outward action doth demonstrate OTH 1.01. 61
nor doth the general care | take hold on me; 1.03. 54
of quality and respect | as doth import you. 1.03.283
the thought whereof | doth, like a poisonous 2.01.297
thy honesty and love doth mince this matter, 2.03.247
it is the green–ey'd monster which doth mock 3.03.166
witness that here iago doth give up | the 3.03.465
as doth the raven o'er the infectious house, 4.01. 21
it doth abuse your bosom. 4.02. 14
upon my knee, what doth your speech import? 4.02. 31
heaven doth truly know it. 4.02. 38
nay, heaven doth know. 4.02.129
my love doth so approve him, | that even his 4.03. 19
doth that bode weeping? 4.03. 59
and doth affection breed it? 4.03. 98
i think it doth. 4.03. 99
heavenly, | it strikes where it doth love. 5.02. 22
what our contempts doth often hurl from us, | we ANT 1.02.123
than the ills i know, | my idleness doth hatch. 1.02.130
pompey doth this day laugh away his fortune. 2.06.104 P
which doth most consist | of war–mark'd footmen, 3.07. 43
the crown o' th' earth doth melt. 4.15. 63
of more tenderness | than doth become a man. CYM 1.01. 95
that our great king himself doth woo me oft 1.05. 14
she doth think she has | strange ling'ring 1.05. 33
your cause doth strike my heart | with pity that 1.06.118
my heart | with pity that doth make me sick. 1.06.119
'tis gold | which buys admittance (oft it doth), 2.03. 68
she writes so to you? doth she? 2.04.105
ay, and it doth confirm | another stain, as big 2.04.139
so doth my wife | the nonpareil of this. 2.05. 7
for it doth physic love — of his content, | all 3.02. 34
we make a choir, as doth the prison'd bird, 3.03. 43
many times | doth ill deserve by doing well; 3.03. 54
rides on the posting winds and doth belie | all 3.04. 36
yet who this should be | doth miracle itself, 4.02. 29
that by the top doth take the mountain pine 4.02.175
doth make distinction | of place 'tween high and 4.02.248
for nature doth abhor to make his bed | with the 4.02.357
our pleasure his full fortune doth confine, 5.04.110
as it doth me — a nobler sir ne'er liv'd 5.05.145
name, | being leo–natus, doth import so much. 5.05.445
oppression, and the poor worm doth die for't. PER 1.01.102
and if jove stray, who dares say jove doth ill? 1.01.104
as your fair self, doth tune us otherwise. 1.01.115
be | as doth befit our honor and your worth. 1.01.120
one sin, i know, another doth provoke: 1.01.137
nor tell the world antiochus doth sin | in such 1.01.146
doth your highness call? 1.01.150
archer hits the mark | his eye doth level at, so 1.01.163
and should he /doubt't, as no doubt he doth, 1.02. 86
who is the first that doth prefer himself? 2.02. 17
awhile, | yon knight doth sit too melancholy, 2.03. 54
doth my lord call? 3.02. 2
which doth give me | a more content in course of 3.02. 38
diamonds | of a most praised water doth appear, 3.02.101
i rage and roar | as doth the sea she lies in, 3.03. 11
upon thy grave | while summer days doth last. 4.01. 17
house, but for this virgin that doth prop it, 4.06.119
basest groom | that doth frequent your house. 4.06.191
doth your lordship call? 5.01. 8
bid him that we, whom flaming war doth scorch, TNK 1.01. 91
desire doth lend her force | courageously to VEN 29
now doth she stroke his cheek, now doth he frown 45
doth she stroke his cheek, now doth he frown, 45
doth quench the maiden burning of his cheeks; 50
chin, | and where she ends, she doth anew begin. 60
my beauty as the spring doth yearly grow, | my 141
the sun doth burn my face, i must remove." 186
the heat i have from thence doth little harm, 195
and swelling passion doth provoke a pause. 218
being mad before, how doth she now for wits? 249
and from her twining arms doth urge releasing. 256
proud, | adonis' trampling courser doth espy; 261
again | as from a furnace, vapors doth he send; 274
jealous of catching, swiftly doth forsake him, 321
free vent of words love's fire doth assuage, 334
or as the wolf doth grin before he barketh, | or 459
the mellow plum doth fall, the green sticks fast 527
whose vultur thought doth pitch the price so 551
her face doth reek and smoke, her blood doth 555
face doth reek and smoke, her blood doth boil, 555
the which, by cupid's bow she doth protest, | he 581
all is imaginary she doth prove, | he will not 597
eyes like glow–worms shine when he doth fret, 621
doth call himself affection's sentinel, | gives 650
and in a peaceful hour doth cry, 'kill, kill!' 652
sometime true news, sometime false doth bring, 658
under whose sharp fangs on his back doth lie 663
doth make them droop with grief and hang the 666
the thought of it doth make my faint heart bleed 669
bleed, | and fear doth teach it divination: 670
anon their loud alarums he doth hear, | and now 700
love's gentle spring doth always fresh remain, 801
who doth the world so gloriously behold | that 857
from whom each lamp and shining star doth borrow 861
the fear whereof doth make him shake and shudder 880
soldiers when their captain once doth yield, 893
follow | this sound of hope doth labor to expel, 976
the one doth flatter thee in thoughts unlikely, 989
is alive, | her rash suspect she doth extenuate, 1010
thrive, | and with death she humbly doth insinuate; 1012
and there, all smoth'red up, in shade doth sit, 1035
with cold terror doth men's minds confound. 1048
this mutiny each part doth so surprise | that 1049
over one shoulder doth she hang her head; 1058
the sun doth scorn you and the wind doth hiss 1084
sun doth scorn you and the wind doth hiss you. 1084
sith in his prime death doth my love destroy, 1163
beauty itself doth of itself persuade | the eyes LUC 29
venus' doves, doth challenge that fair field; 58
the coward captive vanquished doth yield | to 75
therefore that praise which collatine doth owe 82
her joy with heav'd–up hand she doth express, 111
doth yet in his fair welkin once appear, | till 116

upon the world dim darkness doth display, | and 118
leaden slumber with live's strength doth fight, 124
as one of which doth tarquin lie revolving | the 127
despair to gain doth traffic oft for gaining, 131
and oft that wealth doth cost | the death of all 146
charm, | doth too too oft betake him to retire, 174
here pale with fear he doth premeditate | the 183
and in his inward mind he doth debate | what 185
scornfully, he doth despise | his naked armor of 187
guilt being great, the fear doth still exceed; 229
which in a moment doth confound and kill | all 250
and doth so far proceed | that what is vile 251
and as their captain, so their pride doth grow, 298
his hot heart, which fond desire doth scorch, 314
who with a ling'ring stay his course doth let, 328
that for his prey to pray he doth begin, | as if 342
so o'er this sleeping soul doth tarquin stay, 423
heedfully doth view | the sight which makes 454
first like a trumpet doth his tongue begin | to 470
when a black–fac'd cloud the world doth threat, 547
earth's dark womb some gentle gust doth get, 549
yet, foul night–waking cat, he doth but dally, 554
that twice she doth begin ere once she speaks. 567
he is no woodman that doth bend his bow | to 580
when most unseen, then most doth tyrannize. 676
this forced league doth force a further strife, 689
till, like a jade, self–will himself doth tire. 707
flesh being proud, desire doth fight with grace, 712
desperate, with her nails her flesh doth tear; 739
day," quoth she, "night's scapes doth open lay, 747
and grave, like water that doth eat in steel, 755
pain, | and fellowship in woe doth woe assuage, 790
absolute, | that some impurity doth not pollute. 854
to slay the tiger that doth live by slaughter, 955
and time to see one that by alms doth live 986
this helpless smoke of words doth me no right. 1027
views, | and to herself all sorrow doth compare; 1102
for mirth doth search the bottom of annoy, | sad 1109
to see the salve doth make the wound ache more, 1116
as winter meads when sun doth melt their snow. 1218
her mistress she doth give demure good morrow, 1219
but as the earth doth weep, the sun being set, 1226
not that devour'd, but that which doth devour, 1256
the ear | the heavy motion that it doth behold, 1326
when every part a part of woe doth bear. 1327
no, | and forth with bashful innocence doth hie. 1341
that she her plaints a little while doth stay, 1364
this load of wrath that burning troy doth bear; 1474
sad tales doth tell | to pencill'd pensiveness 1496
them words, and she their looks doth borrow. 1498
and who she finds forlorn she doth lament. 1500
for sinon in his fire doth quake with cold, 1556
and in that cold, hot burning fire doth dwell; 1557
priam's trust false sinon's tears doth flatter, 1560
and time doth weary time with her complaining; 1570
pure | doth in her poison'd closet yet endure." 1659
outruns the eye that doth behold his haste, 1668
and through her wounds doth fly | live's lasting 1728
her breast, it doth divide | in two slow rivers, 1737
and blood untainted still doth red abide, 1749
the one doth call her his, the other his, | yet 1793
rome herself in them doth stand disgraced) | by 1833
he doth again repeat, and that they swore. 1848
thou, fair sun, that on this earth doth shine, PP 3.10
touch | upon the lute doth ravish human sense; 8. 6
my heart doth charge the watch; 14.14
doth cite each moving sense from idle rest, 14.15
for she doth welcome daylight with her ditty, 14.19
full oft, | a woman's nay doth stand for nought? 18.42
grief in heart | he with thee doth bear a part. 20.54
here the anthem doth commence: PHT 21
turtle's loyal breast | to eternity doth rest. 58
nature's bequest gives nothing, but doth lend, SON 4. 3
the lovely gaze where every eye doth dwell 5. 2
same, | and that unfair which fairly doth excel: 5. 4
eye | doth homage to his new–appearing sight, 7. 3
look what an unthrift in the world doth spend 9. 9
who heaven itself for ornament doth use, | and 21. 3
and every fair with his fair doth rehearse, 21. 4
for all that beauty that doth cover thee | is 22. 5
which in thy breast doth live, as thine in me: 22. 7
but day doth daily draw my sorrows longer, | and 28.13
and night doth nightly make grief's length seem 28.14
thou art the grave where buried love doth live, 31. 9
yet doth it steal sweet hours from love's 36. 8
that this shadow doth such substance give, 37.10
by praising him here who doth hence remain! 39.14
and for my sake even so doth she abuse me, 42. 7
thou, whose shadow shadows doth make bright, 43. 5
through heavy sleep on sightless eyes doth stay! 43.12
my heart doth plead that thou in him dost lie 46. 5
eyes), | but the defendant doth that plea deny, 46. 7
and each doth good turns now unto the other: 47. 2
heart in love with sighs himself doth smother, 47. 4
with my love's picture then my eye doth feast, 47. 5
and in his thoughts of love doth share a part. 47. 8
doth teach that ease and that repose to say, 50. 3
for that same groan doth put this in my mind: 50.13
or as the wardrobe which the robe doth hide, 52.10
year, | the one doth shadow of your beauty show, 53.10
show, | the other as your bounty doth appear, 53.11
o, how much more doth beauty beauteous seem | by 54. 1
by that sweet ornament which truth doth give! 54. 2
for that sweet odor which doth in it live. 54. 4
to you it doth belong | yourself to pardon of 58.11
and time that gave doth now his gift confound. 60. 8
time doth transfix the flourish set on youth, 60. 9
mine own true love that doth my rest defeat, 61.11
new, | and him as for a map doth nature store, 68.13
parts of thee that the world's eye doth view 69. 1
good, slander doth but approve | /thy worth the 70. 5
for canker vice the sweetest buds doth love, 70. 7
which by and by black night doth take away, 73. 7
fire | that on the ashes of his youth doth lie, 73.10
that every word doth almost /tell my name, 76. 7
and my sick muse doth give another place. 79. 4
yet what of thee thy poet doth invent | he robs 79. 7
beauty doth he give, | and found it in thy cheek 79.10
no praise to thee but what in thee doth live. 79.12
then thank him not for that which he doth say, 79.13
knowing a better spirit doth use your name, 80. 2
is) | the humble as the proudest sail doth bear, 80. 6
his) | on your broad main doth willfully appear. 80. 8
whilst he upon your soundless deep doth ride, 80.10
how far a modern quill doth come too short, 83. 7
speaking of worth, what worth in you doth grow. 83. 8
lean penury within that pen doth dwell | that to 84. 5
thus have i had thee as a dream doth flatter: 87.13
than that which on thy humor doth depend. 92. 8
since that my life on thy revolt doth lie; 92.10
how like eve's apple doth thy beauty grow, | if 93.13
doth spot the beauty of thy budding name! 95. 3
where beauty's veil doth cover every blot, | and 95.11
the hardest knife ill us'd doth lose his edge. 95.14
sing to the ear that doth thy lays esteem, | and 100. 7
the owner's tongue doth publish every where. 102. 4
lays, | as philomel in summer's front doth sing, 102. 7
ah, yet doth beauty, like a dial hand, | steal 104. 9
your sweet hue, which methinks still doth stand, 104.11
as from my soul, which in thy breast doth lie: 109. 4
your love and pity doth th' impression fill 112. 1
governs me to go about | doth part his function, 113. 3
bird, of flow'r, or shape, which it doth /latch, 113. 6
nor his own vision holds what it doth catch; 113. 8
or whether doth my mind, being crown'd with you, 114. 1
and to his palate doth prepare the cup. 114.12
that mine eye loves it and doth first begin. 114.14
give full growth to that which still doth grow. 115.14
for thy records and what we see doth lie, | made 123.11
even | doth half that glory to the sober west, 132. 8
to mourn for me, since mourning doth thee grace, 132.11
me | under that bond that him as fast doth bind. 134. 8
follow'd it as gentle day | doth follow night, 145.11
feeding on that which doth preserve the ill, 147. 3
then love doth well denote | love's eye is not 148. 7
when all my best doth.worship thy defect, 149.11
swear that brightness doth not grace the day? 150. 4
my soul doth tell my body that he may | triumph 151. 7
doth point out thee | as his triumphant prize. 151. 9
the true gouty landlord which doth owe them. LC 140

DOTING 17 FR 0.0019 REL FR 15 V 2 P
follow'd her with a doting observance; WIV 2.02.195 P
peace, doting wizard, peace! i am not mad. ERR 4.04. 58
and as he errs, doting on hermia's eyes, | so i, MND 1.01.230
and the old folk (time's doting chronicles) 2H4 4.04.126
the grave doth gape, and doting death is near, H5 2.01. 61
in love | than is the doting title of a mother; R3 4.04.300
has got that same scurvy doting foolish /young TRO 5.04. 3 P
for doting, not for loving, pupil mine. ROM 2.03. 82
doting like me, and like me banished, | then 3.03. 67
that, doting on his own obsequious bondage, OTH 1.01. 46
on his sea–wing, and (like a doting mallard), ANT 3.10. 19
rashness, and they them | for fear and doting. 3.11. 15
such hazard now must doting tarquin make, LUC 155
and wipe the dim mist from thy doting eyne, 643
that thou art doting father of his fruit. 1064
had doting priam check'd his son's desire, 1490
for well thou know'st to my dear doting heart SON 131. 3

/DOUBLE 2 FR 0.0002 REL FR 1 V 1 P
/man | /who /with /a /double /surety /binds /his 2H4 1.01.191
more of his purchases, and /double /ones /too, HAM 5.01.109 P

DOUBLE 83 FR 0.0093 REL FR 65 V 18 P
well then i'll double your folly. TGV 2.04. 21 P
is there not a double excellency in this? WIV 3.03.176 P
with all her double vigor, art and nature, MM 2.02.183
double and treble admonition, and still forfeit 3.02.193 P
in double violation | of sacred chastity and of 5.01.404
'tis double wrong, to truant with your bed, ERR 3.02. 17
use for it, a double heart for his single one. ADO 2.01.279 P
to dinner" — there's a double meaning in that. 2.03.258 P
there's a double tongue, there's two tongues." 5.01.169 P
and gives to every power a double power, | above LLL 4.03.328
you have a double tongue within your mask, | and 5.02.245
i understand you not, my griefs are double. 5.02.752
you spotted snakes with double tongue, | thorny MND 2.02. 9
sense, | it pays the hearing double recompense. 3.02.180
like to a double cherry, seeming parted, | but 3.02.209
parted eye, | when every thing seems double. 4.01.190
of double ducats, stol'n from me by my daughter! MV 2.08. 19
double six thousand, and then treble that, 3.02.300
swear by your double self, | and there's an oath 5.01.245
you do me double wrong | to strive for that SHR 3.01. 16
scarfs and fans, and double change of brav'ry, 4.03. 57
and he were double and double a lord. AWW 2.03.239 P
and he were double and double a lord. 2.03.239 P
the double gilt of this opportunity you let time TN 3.02. 25 P
i am courted now with a double occasion — gold WT 4.04.833 P
her die again, for then | you kill her double. 5.03.107
why answer not the double majesties | this JN 2.01.480
therefore, to be possess'd with double pomp, 4.02. 9
some reasons of this double coronation | i have 4.02. 40
whose double tongue may with a mortal touch R2 3.02. 21
he does me double wrong | that wounds me with 3.02.215
not like that paying back, 'tis a double labor. 1H4 3.03.179 P
as if he mast'red there a double spirit | of 5.02. 63
nor can one england brook a double reign | of 5.04. 66
no, that's certain, i am not a double man; 5.04.138 P
your wind short, your chin double, your wit 2H4 1.02.183 P
rumor doth double, like the voice and echo, 3.01. 97
is old double of your town living yet? 3.02. 40 P
and is old double dead? 3.02. 52 P
england shall double gild his treble guilt, 4.05.128
this is a double honor, burgundy; 1H6 3.02.116
and here's a pot of good double beer, neighbor. 2H6 2.03. 64 P
this knave's tongue begins to double. 2.03. 91
in life but double death, now gloucester's dead. 3.02. 55
we'll yoke together like a double shadow | to 3H6 4.06. 49
times | repair'd with double riches of content. R3 4.04.319
of ten times double gain of happiness. 4.04.324
and be ever double | both in his words and H8 4.02. 38
this double worship, | where /one part does COR 3.01.142
whose double bosoms seems to wear one heart, 4.04. 13
horns, | as if a double hunt were heard at once, TIT 2.03. 19
deal, | but sorrow flouted at is double death. 3.01.245
therefore, if you should deal double with her, ROM 2.04.168 P
as cannons overcharg'd with double cracks, so MAC 1.02. 37
in every point twice done, and then done double, 1.06. 15
he's here in double trust: 1.07. 12
double, double, toil and trouble; 4.01. 10
double, double, toil and trouble; 4.01. 10
double, double, toil and trouble; 4.01. 20
double, double, toil and trouble; 4.01. 20
double, double, toil and trouble; 4.01. 35
double, double, toil and trouble; 4.01. 35
but yet i'll make assurance double sure, | and 4.01. 83
that palter with us in a double sense, | that 5.08. 20
a double blessing is a double grace, | occasion HAM 1.03. 53
a double blessing is a double grace, | occasion 1.03. 53
and, like a man to double business bound, | i 3.03. 41
and set a double varnish on the fame | the 4.07.132
his fines, his double vouchers, his recoveries. 5.01.105 P
thy fifty yet doth double five and twenty, | and LR 2.04.259
a voice potential | as double as the duke's. OTH 1.02. 14
and to plume up my will | in double knavery — 1.03.394
he'll watch the horologe a double set | if drink 2.03.130
therefore be double damn'd: 4.02. 37
empery | would make the great'st king double — CYM 1.06.121
cloten, thou double villain, be thy name, | i 4.02. 89
thy mermaid's voice hath done me double wrong: VEN 429
say for non–payment that the debt should double, 521
'tis double death to drown in ken of shore, | he LUC 1114
single nature's double name | neither two nor PHT 39
wing, | and given grace a double majesty. SON 78. 8
nor double penance, to correct correction. 111.12
my spirits t' attend this double voice accorded, LC 3

DOUBLE–CHARGE 1 FR 0.0001 REL FR 0 V 1 P
i will double–charge thee with dignities. 2H4 5.03.124 P

DOUBLED 8 FR 0.0009 REL FR 8 V 0 P
ill deeds is doubled with an evil word. ERR 3.02. 20
these terms of treason doubled down his throat. R2 1.01. 57
the good, | shall still be doubled on her. H8 5.04. 28
then straight his doubled spirit | requick'ned COR 2.02.116
doubled with thanks and service, from whose help TIM 1.02. 7
he kiss'd — the last of many doubled kisses — ANT 1.05. 40
still as she tasted, should be doubled on her, TNK 2.02.240
face seems twain, each several limb is doubled, VEN 1067

DOUBLE–DEALER 2 FR 0.0002 REL FR 0 V 2 P
thy single life, to make thee a double–dealer, ADO 5.04.114 P
will be so much a sinner to be a double–dealer. TN 5.01. 35 P

DOUBLE–DEALING 1 FR 0.0001 REL FR 0 V 1 P
but that it would be double–dealing, sir, i TN 5.01. 29 P

DOUBLE–FATAL 1 FR 0.0001 REL FR 1 V 0 P
bows | of double–fatal yew against thy state; R2 3.02.117

DOUBLE–HENN'D 1 FR 0.0001 REL FR 0 V 1 P
now my double–henn'd spartan! TRO 5.07. 11 P

DOUBLE–LOCK 1 FR 0.0001 REL FR 1 V 0 P
last, | and bid suspicion double–lock the door, VEN 448

DOUBLE–MEANING 1 FR 0.0001 REL FR 0 V 1 P
deceiv'd me like a double–meaning prophesier. AWW 4.03. 99 P

DOUBLENESS 1 FR 0.0001 REL FR 0 V 1 P
the doubleness of the benefit defends the deceit MM 3.01.257 P

DOUBLER 1 FR 0.0001 REL FR 1 V 0 P
for with doubler tongue | than thine, thou MND 3.02. 72

DOUBLES 1 FR 0.0001 REL FR 1 V 0 P
he cranks and crosses with a thousand doubles: VEN 682

DOUBLET 25 FR 0.0028 REL FR 2 V 23 P
my doublet as fresh as the first day i wore it? TMP 2.01.103 P
my jerkin is a doublet. TGV 2.04. 20 P
and youthful still, in your doublet and hose, WIV 3.01. 46 P
thee and shall make thee a new doublet and hose. 3.03. 35 P
awake carving the fashion of a new doublet; ADO 2.03. 18 P
and a spaniard from the hip upward, no doublet. 3.02. 37 P
thou knowest that the fashion of a doublet, or a 3.03.118 P
when he goes in his doublet and hose and leaves 5.01.200 P
on your thin/–bellied doublet like a rabbit on a LLL 3.01. 19 P
i think he bought his doublet in italy, his MV 1.02. 74 P
vessel, as doublet and hose ought to show itself AYL 2.04. 6 P
i have a doublet and hose in my disposition? 3.02.195 P
day, what shall i do with my doublet and hose? 3.02.219 P
we must have your doublet and hose pluck'd over 4.01.202 P
a silken doublet, a velvet hose, a scarlet cloak SHR 5.01. 66 P
and the tailor make thy doublet of changeable TN 2.04. 74 P
francis, your white canvas doublet will sully. 1H4 2.04. 74 P
i am eight times thrust through the doublet, 2.04.166 P
you give me your doublet and stuff me out with 2H4 5.05. 82 P
the fat knight with the great belly doublet. H5 4.07. 48 P
come on, sirrah, off with your doublet quickly. 2H6 2.01.148 P
for wearing his new doublet before easter? ROM 3.01. 28 P
he pluck'd me ope his doublet, and offer'd them JC 1.02.265 P
lord hamlet, with his doublet all unbrac'd, | no HAM 2.01. 75
fit | ('tis in my cloak–bag) doublet, hat, hose, CYM 3.04.169

DOUBLETS 4 FR 0.0004 REL FR 2 V 2 P
for i have no more doublets than backs, no more SHR in.2. 9 P
men than thou go in their hose and doublets. 2H6 4.07. 51 P
hats, cloaks | (doublets, i think) flew up, and H8 4.01. 74
doublets that hangmen would | bury with those COR 1.05. 6

DOUBLE–VANTAGE 1 FR 0.0001 REL FR 1 V 0 P
i do, | doing thee vantage, double–vantage me. SON 88.12

DOUBLING 2 FR 0.0002 REL FR 1 V 1 P
mile–end, to instruct for the doubling of files. AWW 4.03.270 P
he's honorable, | and doubling that, most holy. CYM 3.04.177

DOUBLY 8 FR 0.0009 REL FR 7 V 1 P
in both my eyes he doubly sees himself, | in MV 5.01.244
will you be mine now you are doubly won? AWW 5.03.314
and let thy blows, doubly redoubled, | fall like R2 1.03. 80
doubly portcullis'd with my teeth and lips, 1.03.167
doubly divorc'd! 5.01. 71
wolf | (so doubly seconded with will and power), TRO 1.03.122
in this action outdone his former deeds doubly. COR 2.01.136 P
so they | doubly redoubled strokes upon the foe. MAC 1.02. 38

DOUBT *(also dout*)*

DOUBT 187 FR 0.0211 REL FR 155 V 32 P
(who had, no doubt, some noble creature in her) TMP 1.02. 7
i not doubt | he came alive to land. 2.01.122
a wink beyond, | but doubt discovery there. 2.01.243
them | is a plain fish, and no doubt marketable. 5.01.266
waste | with such discourse as, i not doubt, 5.01.304
o, sir, she makes no doubt of that. TGV 5.02. 20
i doubt he be not well, that he comes not home. WIV 1.04. 41 P
he will print them, out of doubt; 2.01. 77 P
doctors doubt that. 5.05.174 P
my power? alas, i doubt — MM 1.04. 77
you know the character, i doubt not, and the 4.02.193 P

and doubt not, sir, but she will well excuse ERR 3.01. 92
to your notorious shame, i doubt it not. 4.01. 84
now, out of doubt antipholus is mad, | else 4.03. 81
but he'll be meet with you, i doubt it not. ADO 1.01. 47 P
were you in doubt, sir, that you ask'd her? 1.01.106 P
it a match, and i doubt not but to fashion it, 2.01.368 P
so, and doubt not but success | will fashion the 4.01.234
i doubt we should have been too young for them. 5.01.118 P
speak "dout," fine, when he should say "doubt"; LLL 5.01. 20 P
and ever and anon they made a doubt | presence 5.02.101
and i make no doubt | the rest will /ne'er come 5.02.151
therefore be out of hope, of question, of doubt; MND 3.02.279
no doubt they rose up early to observe | the 4.01.132
out of doubt he is transported. 4.02. 3 P
and i do not doubt but to hear them say, it is a 4.02. 44 P
my ventures, out of doubt | would make me sad. MV 1.01. 21
which you did shoot the first, i do not doubt, 1.01.149
and out of doubt you do me now more wrong | in 1.01.155
will no doubt never be chosen by any rightly but 1.02. 31 P
still gazing in a doubt | whether those peals of 3.02.144
if any man doubt that, let him put me to my AYL 5.04. 43 P
doubt not her care should be | to comb your SHR 1.01. 63
i doubt it not, sir; 2.01. 75
no doubt but he hath got a quiet catch. 2.01.331
i should be arguing still upon that doubt. 3.01. 55
if thou doubt it, thou mayst slide from my 4.01. 14 P
will be pleas'd, then wherefore should i doubt? 4.04.106
doubt not but heaven | hath brought me up to be AWW 4.04. 18
ass, i doubt not. TN 2.03.170 P
with the which i doubt not but to do myself much 5.01.307 P
not you seen, camillo | (but that's past doubt; WT 1.02.268
then 'twere past all doubt | you'ld call your 2.03. 81
do), | i doubt not then but innocence shall make 3.02. 30
so soon as you arrive, shall clear that doubt. 4.04.620
of that i doubt, as all men's children may. JN 1.01. 63
do so, king philip, hang no more in doubt. 3.01.219
but that i doubt | my uncle practices more harm 4.01. 19
out | to all our sorrows, and ere long i doubt. 4.02.102
or turn'd an eye of doubt upon my face, | as bid 4.02.233
and thou shalt find it, dolphin, do not doubt. 5.02.180
i doubt he will be dead or e'er i come. 5.06. 44
he is our cousin's cousin, but 'tis doubt, R2 1.04. 20
is already, and depos'd | 'tis doubt he will be. 3.04. 69
old, | i doubt not but to ride as fast as york. 5.02.115
yea, but i doubt they will be too hard for us. 1H4 1.02.181 P
i doubt not but to die a fair death for all this 2.02. 13 P
doubt not, my lord, they shall be well oppos'd. 4.04. 33
for he hath found to end one doubt by death 2H4 4.01.197
i do not doubt you. 4.02. 77
both which we doubt not but your majesty | shall 4.04. 11
say) will (i doubt) prove mine own marring. ep 6 P
under the veil of wildness, which (no doubt) H5 1.01. 64
no doubt, my liege, if each man do his best. 2.02. 19
i doubt not that, since we are well persuaded 2.02. 20
we doubt not of a fair and lucky war, | since 2.02.184
we doubt not now | but every rub is smoothed on 2.02.187
you are worth your breeding, which i doubt not; 3.01. 28
and when the mind is quick'ned, out of doubt, 4.01. 20
his fears, out of doubt, be of the same relish 4.01.109 P
a many of our bodies shall no doubt | find 4.03. 95
and out of doubt and out of question too, and 5.01. 45 P
house, | i doubt not but with honor to redress. 1H6 2.05.126
my lord protector will, i doubt it not, | see 2H6 1.04. 45
god on our side, doubt not of victory. 4.08. 52
and doubt not so to deal | as all things shall 4.09. 46
be great, | i doubt not, uncle, of our victory. 3H6 1.02. 72
yet, ere thou go, but answer me one doubt: 3.03.238
i go, hastings and montague, | resolve my doubt. 4.01.135
why, master mayor, why stand you in a doubt? 4.07. 27
i doubt not, i, but we shall soon persuade 4.07. 33
doubt not of the day, | and, that once gotten, 4.07. 87
and, that once gotten, doubt not of large pay. 4.07. 88
the doubt is that he will seduce the rest. 4.08. 37
for they no doubt | will issue out again and bid 5.01. 62
no doubt, no doubt, and so shall clarence too, R3 1.01.129
no doubt, no doubt, and so shall clarence too, 1.01.129
valiant, wise, and (no doubt) right royal — 1.02.244
there's no doubt his majesty | will soon recover 1.03. 1
no doubt shall then, and till then, govern well. 2.03. 15
and so no doubt he is, my gracious madam. 2.04. 21
i hope he is, but yet let mothers doubt. 2.04. 22
no doubt, no doubt. 3.01.154
no doubt, no doubt. 3.01.154
and do not doubt, right noble princes both, 3.05. 64
doubt not, my lord, i'll play the orator | as if 3.05. 95
myself, | no doubt we bring it to a happy issue. 3.07. 54
and make (no doubt) us happy by his reign. 3.07.170
and will, no doubt, shortly be rid of me. 4.01. 86
and will, no doubt, tempt him to any thing. 4.02. 39
no doubt the murd'rous knife was dull and blunt 4.04.227
i doubt not but his friends will turn to us. 5.02. 19
no doubt, my lord. 5.03.214
no doubt he's noble; H8 1.03. 57
at his return | no doubt he will requite it. 2.01. 46
you do not doubt my faith, sir? 2.01.143
the daring'st counsel which i had to doubt, 2.04.216
'em, and no doubt | in time will find their fit 3.02.244
shall know it, and, no doubt, shall thank you. 3.02.348
yes, without all doubt. 4.01.113
i make as little doubt as you do conscience | in 5.02.102
we shall have | great store of room, no doubt, 5.03. 73
i doubt he be hurt. TRO 1.02.276 P
but modest doubt is call'd | the beacon of the 2.02. 15
unarm thee, go, and doubt thou not, brave boy, 5.03. 35
we never yet made doubt but rome was ready | to COR 1.02. 18
o, doubt not that, | i speak from certainties. 1.02. 30
they nothing doubt prevailing, and to make it 1.03. 99 P
if any such be here | (as it were sin to doubt) 1.06. 68
which i doubt not but | our rome will cast upon 2.01.201
doubt not | the commoners, for whom we stand, 2.01.226
better put in hazard | than stay, past doubt, 2.03.257
of state | more than you doubt the change on't; 3.01.152
have you lurk'd, that you make doubt of it? 5.04. 46
nay more, i doubt it not. ROM 3.04. 14
i doubt it not, and all these woes shall serve 3.05. 52
and i will do it without fear or doubt, | to 4.01. 87
his looks i fear, and his intents i doubt. 5.03. 44
o, no doubt, my good friends, but the gods TIM 1.02. 88 P
filthy, and would not hold taking, i doubt me. 1.02.154 P
i doubt whether their legs be worth the sums 1.02.232
doubt not that, if money and the season can 3.06. 50 P
but tell me true | (for i must ever doubt, 4.03.507
in whose breast | doubt and suspect, alas, are 4.03.512
doubt it not, worthy lord. 5.01. 92
bad causes swear | such creatures as men doubt; JC 2.01.132
i doubt not of your wisdom. 3.01.183
and will no doubt with reasons answer you. 3.02.215
i do not doubt | but that my noble master will 4.02. 10
i doubt some danger does approach you nearly. MAC 4.02. 67
shall never sag with doubt, nor shake with fear. 5.03. 10
we doubt it nothing. 5.04. 2
begin | to doubt th' equivocation of the fiend 5.05. 42
we doubt it nothing, heartily farewell. HAM 1.02. 41
all is not well, | i doubt some foul play. 1.02.255
do you doubt that? 1.03. 4
doth all the noble substance of a doubt | to his 1.04. 37
i doubt it is no other but the main, | his 2.02. 56
"doubt thou the stars are fire, | doubt that the 2.02.116
stars are fire, | doubt that the sun doth move, 2.02.117
the sun doth move, | doubt truth to be a liar, 2.02.118
truth to be a liar, | but never doubt i love. 2.02.119
and i do doubt the hatch and the disclose | will 3.01.166
speaks things in doubt | that carry but half 4.05. 6
do awake him, | i doubt /not of his temperance. LR 4.07. 23
do not doubt, cassio, | but i will have my lord OTH 3.03. 5
do not doubt that; 3.03. 19
to be once in doubt | is /once to be resolv'd. 3.03.179
draw | the smallest fear or doubt of her revolt, 3.03.188
no, iago, | i'll see before i doubt; 3.03.190
when i doubt, prove; 3.03.190
bear no hinge nor loop | to hang a doubt on; 3.03.366
'tis a shrewd doubt, though it be but a dream, 3.03.429
doubt not, sir, | i knew it for my bond. ANT 1.04. 83
i will be even with thee, doubt it not. 3.07. 1
words him, i doubt not, a great deal from the CYM 1.04. 16 P
i do nothing doubt you have store of thieves; 1.04. 97 P
and i doubt not you sustain what y' are worthy 1.04.115 P
which i doubt not | you'll give me leave to 2.04. 64
in seeking him, | and will, no doubt, be found. 4.03. 21
a doubt | in such a time nothing becoming you, 4.04. 14
and should he /doubt't, as no doubt he doth, PER 1.02. 86
to lop that doubt, he'll fill this land with 1.02. 90
i do not doubt thy faith; 1.02.111
o, sir, we doubt it not. 4.02. 42 P
i doubt not but thy training hath been noble. 4.06.112
i doubt not but this populous city will | yield 4.06.186
and i doubt not but i shall find them tractable 4.06.199 P
he has felt | without doubt what he fights for, TNK 4.02. 97
which doubt not will bring forth comfort. 4.03.101 P
yes, without doubt. 5.02. 93
and there's no doubt, but mercy may be found if STM II.C 147
hot scent–snuffing hounds are driven to doubt, VEN 692
who, overcome by doubt and bloodless fear, 891
the truth i shall not know, but live in doubt, PP 2.13
yet this shall i ne'er know, but live in doubt, SON 144.13
and nice affections wavering stood in doubt | if LC 97

DOUBTED 9 FR 0.0010 REL FR 9 V 0 P
well, let it not be doubted but he'll come, WIV 4.04. 44
to do a thing, where i the issue doubted, WT 1.02.259
bosom, let't not be doubted | i shall do good. 2.02. 51
stands, | 'tis to be doubted he would waken him. 3H6 4.03. 19
and that he doubted | 'twould prove the verity H8 1.02.158
and to be doubted that your moor and you | are TIT 2.03. 68
he is not doubted. JC 4.02. 13
'tis to be doubted, madam. LR 5.01. 6
of another | you would not hear me doubted, but TNK 3.01. 61

/DOUBTFUL 1 FR 0.0001 REL FR 1 V 0 P
/i /am /doubtful /that /you /have /been LR 5.01. 12

DOUBTFUL 25 FR 0.0028 REL FR 24 V 1 P
doctor, in perplexity and doubtful dilemma. WIV 4.05. 85 P
minds | a doubtful warrant of immediate death, ERR 1.01. 68
as doubtful thoughts, and rash–embrac'd despair, MV 3.02.109
so, | as doubtful whether what i see be true, 3.02.147
but i am doubtful of your modesties, | lest, SHR in.1. 94
that my most jealious and too doubtful soul TN 4.03. 27
the little number of your doubtful friends. JN 5.01. 36
main | on the nice hazard of one doubtful hour? 1H4 4.01. 48
his is certain, ours is doubtful. 4.03. 4
let me be umpeer in this doubtful strife. 1H6 4.01.151
by doubtful fear | my joy of liberty is half 3H6 4.06. 62
throng many doubtful hollow–hearted friends, R3 4.04.435
have no cause to hold my friendship doubtful. 4.04.492
and aid thee in this doubtful shock of arms; 5.03. 93
and this sailing pandar | our doubtful hope, our TRO 1.01.104
possess'd conveniences | to doubtful fortunes, 3.03. 8
but it is doubtful yet | whether caesar will JC 2.01.193
doubtful it stood, | as two spent swimmers that MAC 1.02. 7
than by destruction dwell in doubtful joy. 3.02. 7
or by pronouncing of some doubtful phrase, | as HAM 1.05.175
her death was doubtful, | and, but that great 5.01.227
you, and know this man, | yet i am doubtful: LR 4.07. 64
beauty is but a vain and doubtful good, | a PP 13. 1
a doubtful good, a gloss, a glass, a flower, 13. 5
long was the combat doubtful, that love with 15. 5

DOUBTFULLY 4 FR 0.0004 REL FR 2 V 2 P
it goes, | i writ at random, very doubtfully. TGV 2.01.111
spake he so doubtfully, thou couldst not feel ERR 2.01. 50 P
and withal so doubtfully, that i could scarce 2.01. 53 P
hath doubtfully pronounc'd the throat shall cut, TIM 4.03.122

DOUBTING 8 FR 0.0009 REL FR 6 V 2 P
thee, | doubting thy birth and lawful progeny. 1H6 3.03. 61
i speak not this as doubting any here; 3H6 5.04. 43
nothing doubting your present assistance therein TIM 3.01. 20 P
"nothing doubting," says he? 3.01. 21 P
since doubting things go ill often hurts more CYM 1.06. 95
and doubting lest he had err'd or sinn'd, | to PER 1.03. 21
anon | doubting the filching age will steal his SON 75. 6
crowning the present, doubting of the rest? 115.12

DOUBTLESS 12 FR 0.0013 REL FR 11 V 1 P
bawd is he doubtless, and of antiquity too; MM 3.02. 68 P
child, sleep doubtless and secure | that hubert, JN 4.01.129
excuse | as well as i am doubtless i can purge 1H4 3.02. 20
doubtless he shrives this woman to her smock, 1H6 1.02.119
doubtless he would have made a noble knight. 4.07. 44
for doubtless burgundy will yield him help, 3H6 4.06. 90
slain, sir, doubtless. COR 1.04. 48
this honest creature, doubtless, | sees and OTH 3.03.242
doubtless | with joy he will embrace you; CYM 3.04.175
doubtless | there is a best, and reason has no TNK 1.03. 47
yet doubtless | she would run mad for this man. 4.02. 11
and he is | doubtless the prim'st of men. 5.03. 70

DOUBTS 14 FR 0.0015 REL FR 14 V 0 P
our doubts are traitors, | and makes us lose the MM 1.04. 77
from hence i go | to make these doubts all even. AYL 5.04. 25
ay, who doubts that? JN 2.01.193
urge doubts to them that fear. R2 2.01.299
and there scatters | dangers, doubts, wringing H8 2.02. 27
you, ever casts | such doubts, as false coin, 3.01.171
confin'd, bound in | to saucy doubts and fears. MAC 3.04. 24
perchance even there where i did find my doubts. 4.03. 25
love is great, the littlest doubts are fear; HAM 3.02.171
minutes tells he o'er | who dotes, yet doubts; OTH 3.03.170
all other doubts, by time let them be clear'd, CYM 4.03. 45
with thousand doubts | how i might stop this PER 1.02. 97
enough, | though doubts did ever sleep. 5.01.202
care, | to descant on the doubts of my decay. PP 14. 4

DOUBT'ST 1 FR 0.0001 REL FR 1 V 0 P
gloucester, why doubt'st thou of my forwardness? 1H6 1.01.100

/DOUBT'T 1 FR 0.0001 REL FR 1 V 0 P
and should he /doubt't, as no doubt he doth, PER 1.02. 86

DOUCETS *(see dowsets)*

DOUGH 2 FR 0.0002 REL FR 1 V 1 P
our cake's dough on both sides. SHR 1.01.109 P
my cake is dough, but i'll in among the rest, 5.01.140

DOUGHTY 2 FR 0.0002 REL FR 2 V 0 P
thou doughty duke, all hail! TNK 3.05.100
whose doughty dismal fame | from dis to daedalus 3.05.114

DOUGHTY–HANDED 1 FR 0.0001 REL FR 1 V 0 P
for doughty–handed are you, and have fought ANT 4.08. 5

DOUGHY 1 FR 0.0001 REL FR 0 V 1 P
all the unbak'd and doughy youth of a nation in AWW 4.05. 3 P

DOUGLAS' 2 FR 0.0002 REL FR 2 V 0 P
and make the douglas' son your only mean | for 1H4 1.03.261
and that the king before the douglas' rage 2H4 in 31

DOUGLAS 28 FR 0.0031 REL FR 25 V 3 P
the earl of douglas is discomfited: 1H4 1.01. 67
earl of fife and eldest son | to beaten douglas, 1.01. 72
where you and douglas and our powers at once, 1.03.296
is there not besides the douglas? 2.03. 26 P
and that sprightly scot of scots, douglas, that 2.04.343 P
three such enemies again as that fiend douglas, 2.04.368 P
honor hath he got | against renowmed douglas! 3.02.107
in his enterprises | discomfited great douglas, 3.02.114
the archbishop's grace of york, douglas, 3.02.119
word | that douglas and the english rebels met 3.02.165
such attribution should the douglas have | as 4.01. 3
do me no slander, douglas. 4.03. 8
not fear, | there is douglas and lord mortimer. 4.04. 22
the douglas and the hotspur both together | are 5.01.116
lord douglas, go you and tell him so. 5.02. 32
know then, my name is douglas, | and i do haunt 5.03. 3
o douglas, hadst thou fought at holmedon thus, 5.03. 14
this, douglas? 5.03. 19
i am the douglas, fatal to all those | that wear 5.04. 26
who, douglas, grieves at heart | so many of his 5.04. 29
alone | the insulting hand of douglas over you, 5.04. 54
the noble scot, lord douglas, when he saw | the 5.05. 17
at my tent | the douglas is; 5.05. 23
go to the douglas, and deliver him | up to his 5.05. 27
both the blunts | kill'd by the hand of douglas, 2H4 1.01. 17
so fought the noble douglas" — | stopping my 1.01. 77
douglas is living, and your brother yet, | but, 1.01. 82
the bloody douglas, whose well–laboring sword 1.01.127

DOUT* *(also doubt)*

DOUT* 2 FR 0.0002 REL FR 1 V 1 P
such rackers of ortography, as to speak "dout," LLL 5.01. 20 P
and dout them with superfluous courage, ha! H5 4.02. 11

DOUTE 1 FR 0.0001 REL FR 0 V 1 P
je ne doute point d'apprendre, par la grace de H5 3.04. 40 P

/DOVE 1 FR 0.0001 REL FR 1 V 0 P
/pronounce but "love" and "/dove"; ROM 2.01. 10

DOVE 23 FR 0.0026 REL FR 20 V 3 P
his dove will prove, his gold will hold, | and WIV 1.03. 98
i will roar you as gently as any sucking dove; MND 1.02. 83 P
the dove pursues the griffin; 2.01.232
who will not change a raven for a dove? 2.02.114
what, dead, my dove? 5.01.325
for she's not froward, but modest as the dove; SHR 2.01.293
tut, she's a lamb, a dove, a fool to him! 3.02.157
love, | to spite a raven's heart within a dove. TN 5.01.131
as the wrathful dove or most magnanimous mouse. 2H4 3.02.160 P
the dove, and very blessed spirit of peace, 4.01. 46
was mahomet inspired with a dove? 1H6 1.02.140
as is the sucking lamb or harmless dove. 2H6 3.01. 71
seems he a dove? 3.01. 75
so shows a snowy dove trooping with crows, | as ROM 1.05. 48
rain'd many a tear" — | fare you well, my dove! HAM 4.05.168 P
anon, as patient as the female dove, | when that 5.01.286
in that mood | the dove will peck the estridge; ANT 3.13.196
so | the dove of paphos might with the crow PER 4.ch. 32
the dove sleeps fast that this night–owl will LUC 360
mild as a dove, but neither true nor trusty, PP 7. 2
paler for sorrow than her milk–white dove, | for 9. 3
made this threne | to the phoenix and the dove, PHT 50
the crow or dove, it shapes them to your feature SON 113.12

DOVE–COTE 1 FR 0.0001 REL FR 1 V 0 P
like an eagle in a dove–cote, i | /flutter'd COR 5.06.114

DOVE–DRAWN 1 FR 0.0001 REL FR 1 V 0 P
and her son | dove–drawn with her. TMP 4.01. 94

DOVE–FEATHER'D 1 FR 0.0001 REL FR 1 V 0 P
dove–feather'd raven! ROM 3.02. 76

DOVE–HOUSE 2 FR 0.0002 REL FR 2 V 0 P
sitting in the sun under the dove–house wall. ROM 1.03. 27
shake, quoth the dove–house; 1.03. 33

DOVE–LIKE 1 FR 0.0001 REL FR 1 V 0 P
lay by your anger for an hour, and dove–like, TNK 5.01. 11

/DOVER 1 FR 0.0001 REL FR 1 V 0 P
/so /far | /to /make /your /speed /to /dover, LR 3.01. 36

DOVER 12 FR 0.0013 REL FR 12 V 0 P
nothing there holds out | but dover castle. JN 5.01. 31
see them guarded | and safely brought to dover, 1H6 5.01. 49
and drive toward dover, friend, where thou shalt LR 3.06. 91

are gone with him toward dover, where they boast 3.07. 19
to dover. 3.07. 51
wherefore to dover? 3.07. 52
wherefore to dover? let him answer that. 3.07. 53
wherefore to dover? 3.07. 55
at gates, and let him smell | his way to dover. 3.07. 94
hence a mile or twain | i' th' way toward dover, 4.01. 43
know'st thou the way to dover? 4.01. 55
dost thou know dover? 4.01. 71

DOVE'S 2 FR 0.0002 REL FR 2 V 0 P
as soft as dove's down and as white as it, | or WT 4.04.363
than a dove's motion when the head's pluck'd off TNK 1.01. 98

DOVES' 1 FR 0.0001 REL FR 1 V 0 P
or those doves' eyes, | which can make gods COR 5.03. 27

DOVES 12 FR 0.0013 REL FR 10 V 2 P
head, | by the simplicity of venus' doves, | by MND 1.01.171
i have here a dish of doves that i would bestow MV 2.02.135 P
so bees with smoke and doves with noisome stench 1H6 1.05. 23
so doves do peck the falcon's piercing talons, 3H6 1.04. 41
and doves will peck in safeguard of their brood. 2.02. 18
he eats nothing but doves, love, and that breeds TRO 3.01.128 P
therefore do nimble–pinion'd doves draw love, ROM 2.05. 7
more white and red than doves or roses are: VEN 10
two strengthless doves will draw me through the 153
showed like two silver doves that sit a–billing. 366
and yokes her silver doves, by whose swift aid 1190
in that white intituled | from venus' doves, LUC 58

DOWAGER 5 FR 0.0005 REL FR 5 V 0 P
my desires, | like to a step–dame, or a dowager, MND 1.01. 5
i have a widow aunt, a dowager, | of great 1.01.157
respecting this our marriage with the dowager, H8 2.04.181
but princess dowager | and widow to prince 3.02. 70
become of katherine, | the princess dowager? 4.01. 23

DOWAGERS 1 FR 0.0001 REL FR 1 V 0 P
dowagers, take hands, | let us be widows to our TNK 1.01.165

DOWDY 1 FR 0.0001 REL FR 0 V 1 P
berhyme her), dido a dowdy, cleopatra a gipsy, ROM 2.04. 41 P

DOWER 11 FR 0.0012 REL FR 11 V 0 P
but, by my modesty | (the jewel in my dower), i TMP 3.01. 54
that can assure my daughter greatest dower SHR 2.01.343
if you should die before him, where's her dower? 2.01.389
him, | and pass my daughter a sufficient dower, 4.04. 45
virtue and she | is her own dower; AWW 2.03.144
hath brought me up to be your daughter's dower, 4.04. 19
choose thou thy husband, and i'll pay thy dower, 5.03.328
gifts, | her beauty, and the value of her dower, 1H6 5.01. 44
beside, his wealth doth warrant a liberal dower, 5.05. 46
why then mine honesty shall be my dower, | for 3H6 3.02. 72
will you require in present dower with her, | or LR 1.01.192

DOWERLESS 1 FR 0.0001 REL FR 1 V 0 P
france, that dowerless took | our youngest born, LR 2.04.212

DOWERS 1 FR 0.0001 REL FR 1 V 0 P
will to publish | our daughters' several dowers, LR 1.01. 44

DOWLAND 1 FR 0.0001 REL FR 1 V 0 P
dowland to thee is dear, whose heavenly touch PP 8. 5

DOWLAS 2 FR 0.0002 REL FR 0 V 2 P
dowlas, filthy dowlas. 1H4 3.03. 69 P
dowlas, filthy dowlas. 3.03. 69 P

DOWLE 1 FR 0.0001 REL FR 1 V 0 P
as diminish | one dowle that's in my plume. TMP 3.03. 65

/DOWN* 11 FR 0.0012 REL FR 11 V 0 P
/the /other /down, /unseen, /and /full /of R2 4.01.187
/that /bucket /down /and /full /of /tears /am /i 4.01.188
/set /up /do /not /pluck /my /cares /down: 4.01.195
/to /pluck /a /kingdom /down | /and /set 2H4 1.03. 49
/staves /in /charge, /their /beavers /down, 4.01.118
/when /the /king /did /throw /his /warder /down 4.01.123
/then /threw /he /down /himself /and /all /their 4.01.125
/my /flesh, | /then /thus /i /thump /it /down. TIT 3.02. 11
/will /you /lie /down /and /rest /upon /the LR 3.06. 34
/send /quickly /down /to /tame /these /vild 4.02. 47
/now /and /then /an /ample /tear /trill'd /down 4.03. 12

DOWN* 635 FR 0.0717 REL FR 478 V 157 P
down with the topmast! TMP 1.01. 34 P
sky, it seems, would pour down stinking pitch, 1.02. 3
sit down, | for thou must now know farther. 1.02. 32
come on then; down, and swear. 2.02.153 P
pray set it down, and rest you. 3.01. 18
if you'll sit down, | i'll bear your logs the 3.01. 23
sit down, and rest. 3.03. 6
crown | my bosky acres and my unshrubb'd down, 4.01. 81
his tears runs down his beard like winter's 5.01. 16
look down, you gods, | and on this couple drop a 5.01.201
and set it down | with gold on lasting pillars: 5.01.207
twice, or thrice, was "proteus" written down: TGV 1.02.114
nay, i was taken up for laying them down; 1.02.132
here's my mother's breath up and down. 2.03. 29 P
if the wind were down, i could drive the boat 2.03. 53 P
a pack of sorrows which would press you down, 3.01. 20
and with a corded ladder fetch her down; 3.01. 40
o villain, that set this down among her vices! 3.01.333 P
she cannot, for that's writ down she is slow of; 3.01.350 P
if there be ten, shrink not, but down with 'em. 4.01. 2
i hope we shall drink down all unkindness. WIV 1.01.196 P
and down, down, adown–a, etc. 1.04. 43
and down, down, adown–a, etc. 1.04. 43
and to be up early and down late; 1.04.102 P
in the parliament for the putting down of men. 2.01. 29 P
here, set it down. 3.03. 6 P
the bottom were as deep as hell, i should down. 3.05. 14 P
if he bid you set it down, obey him. 4.02.110 P
set down the basket, villain! 4.02.115 P
come you and the old woman down; 4.02.167 P
come down, you witch, you hag you, come down, i 4.02.178 P
down, you witch, you hag you, come down, i say! 4.02.179 P
be so bold as stay, sir, till she come down. 4.05. 13 P
tarries the coming down of thy fat woman. 4.05. 21 P
in the suburbs of vienna must be pluck'd down. MM 1.02. 96 P
they had gone down too, but that a wise burgher 1.02.100 P
houses of resort in the suburbs be pull'd down? 1.02.102 P
make us pay down for our offense by weight | the 1.02.121
like rats that ravin down their proper bane, | a 1.02.129
was (as they say) pluck'd down in the suburbs; 2.01. 65 P
kneel down before him, hang upon his gown; 2.02. 44
'tis set down so in heaven, but not in earth. 2.04. 50
you must lay down the treasures of your body 2.04. 96
had he twenty heads to tender down | on twenty 2.04.180
i'd throw it down for your deliverance | as 3.01.104
might but my bending down | reprieve thee from 3.01.143
the merriest was put down, and the worser 3.02. 6 P
friar, till eating and drinking be put down. 3.02.103 P
they would swear down each particular saint, 5.01.243
sit you down, | we'll borrow place of him. 5.01.361
should she kneel down in mercy of this fact, 5.01.434
and wander up and down to view the city. ERR 1.02. 31
but here's a villain that would face me down 3.01. 6
thee from the door, or sit down at the hatch: 3.01. 33
cry for this, minion, if i beat the door down. 3.01. 59
pleaseth you walk with me down to his house, | i 4.01. 12
come, sister, i am press'd down with conceit — 4.02. 65
there did this perjur'd goldsmith swear me down 5.01.227
here's his dry hand up and down. ADO 2.01.119 P
you have put him down, lady, you have put him 2.01.283 P
have put him down, lady, you have put him down. 2.01.284 P
then down upon her knees she falls, weeps, sobs, 2.03.146 P
come, | as we do trace this alley up and down, 3.01. 16
'a goes up and down like a gentleman. 3.03.127 P
set with pearls, down sleeves, side sleeves, and 3.04. 20 P
learned writer to set down our excommunication, 3.05. 63 P
why, how now, cousin, wherefore sink you down? 4.01.110
shape | than i can lay it down in likelihood. 4.01.236
pray write down borachio. yours, sirrah? 4.02. 12 P
write down master gentleman conrade. 4.02. 15 P
write down, that they hope they serve god; 4.02. 18 P
have you writ down, that they are none? 4.02. 31 P
write down prince john a villain. 4.02. 41 P
let him write down the prince's officer coxcomb. 4.02. 71 P
o that he were here to write me down as ass! 4.02. 76 P
though it be not written down, yet forget not 4.02. 77 P
o that i had been writ down an ass! 4.02. 87 P
we have been up and down to seek thee, for we 5.01.122 P
that his own hand may strike his honor down LLL 1.01. 20
and men sit down to that nourishment which is 1.01.237 P
again, and till then, sit thee down, sorrow! 1.01.315 P
lord, how the ladies and i have put him down! 4.01.141
well, "set thee down, sorrow!" 4.03. 4 P
the night of dew that on my cheeks down flows; 4.03. 28
his loving bosom to keep down his heart. 4.03.134
pell–mell, down with them! 4.03.365
the fourth turn'd on the toe, and down he fell. 5.02.114
thus pour the stars down plagues for perjury. 5.02.394
he hail'd down oaths that he was only mine; MND 1.01.243
you, nick bottom, are set down for pyramus. 1.02. 20 P
then slip i from her bum, down topples she, 2.01. 53
come, sit down, every mother's son, and rehearse 3.01. 73 P
i will walk up and down here, and i will sing, 3.01.123 P
up and down, up and down, | i will lead them up 3.02.396
up and down, up and down, | i will lead them up 3.02.396
up and down, | i will lead them up and down; 3.02.397
goblin, lead them up and down. 3.02.399
come sit thee down upon this flow'ry bed, 4.01. 1
you, the wall is down that parted their fathers. 5.01.352 P
and brings down | the rate of usance here with MV 1.03. 44
but turn down indirectly to the jew's house. 2.02. 44 P
with that keen appetite that he sits down? 2.06. 9
we have been up and down to seek him. 3.01. 76 P
what, and stake down? 3.02.215 P
shall ne'er win at that sport, and stake down. 3.02.217 P
his back, | enow to press a royal merchant down, 4.01. 29
it must appear | that malice bears down truth. 4.01.214
down therefore, and beg mercy of the duke. 4.01.363
in mine eye, i can tell who should down. AYL 1.02.215 P
my better parts | are all thrown down, and that 1.02.250
cours'd one another down his innocent nose | in 2.01. 39
here lie i down, and measure out my grave. 2.06. 2 P
who laid him down and bask'd him in the sun, 2.07. 15
sit down and feed, and welcome to our table. 2.07.105
and therefore sit you down in gentleness | and 2.07.124
set down your venerable burthen, | and let him 2.07.167
will you sit down with me? 3.02.277 P
why, now fall down, | or if thou canst not, o, 3.05. 17
mistress, know yourself, down on your knees, 3.05. 57
west of this place, down in the neighbor bottom, 4.03. 78
and to cut off all strife, here sit we down: SHR 3.01. 21
letters for her name fairly set down in studs, 3.02. 62 P
such a cuff | that down fell priest and book, 3.02.164
inprimis, we came down a foul hill, my master 4.01. 67 P
are those" — | sit down, kate, and welcome. 4.01.142
come, kate, sit down, i know you have a stomach. 4.01.158
i spied | an ancient angel coming down the hill, 4.02. 61
what, up and down carv'd like an apple–tart? 4.03. 89
he that knocks as he would beat down the gate? 5.01. 17 P
pray you sit down, | for now we sit to chat as 5.02. 10
a hundred marks, my kate does put her down. 5.02. 35
thee may furnish, and my prayers pluck down, AWW 1.01. 69
man, setting down before you, will undermine you 1.01.118 P
virginity being blown down, man will quicklier 1.01.123 P
marry, in blowing him down again, with the 1.01.124 P
rest, | there is a remedy, approv'd, set down, 1.03.228
to bring me down | must answer for your raising? 2.03.112
though little he do feel it, set down sharply. 3.04. 33
and i will presently pen down my dilemmas, 3.06. 75 P
lays down his wanton siege before her beauty, 3.07. 18
house, | bequeathed down from many ancestors, 4.02. 43
house, | bequeathed down from many ancestors, 4.02. 47
shall i set down your answer so? 4.03.135 P
well, that's set down. 4.03.147 P
"or thereabouts," set down, for i'll speak truth 4.03.149 P
well, that's set down. 4.03.155 P
well, that's set down. 4.03.174 P
when did i see thee so put down? TN 1.03. 81 P
i think, unless you see canary put me down. 1.03. 83 P
i saw him put down the other day with an 1.05. 84 P
malvolio's coming down this walk. 2.05. 16 P
for the bed of ware in england, set 'em down. 3.02. 48 P
and consequently sets down the manner how: 3.04. 72 P
and convey what i will set down to my lady. 4.02.110 P
me | even so as i mine own course have set down. WT 1.02.340
come on, sit down, come on, and do your best 2.01. 27
nay, come sit down; then on. 2.01. 29
i dare my life lay down — and will do't, sir, 2.01.130
the level of your dreams, | which i'll lay down. 3.02. 82
ay, my lord, even so | as it is here set down. 3.02.139
look down | and see what death is doing. 3.02.148
and vengeance for't | not dropp'd down yet. 3.02.202
if it be doleful matter merrily set down, or a 4.04.189 P
as soft as dove's down and as white as it, | or 4.04.363
known betwixt us three, i'll write you down, 4.04.560
indeed paid down | more penitence than done 5.01. 3
look down | and from your sacred vials pour your 5.03.121
kneel thou down philip, but rise more great, JN 1.01.161
that holds in chase mine honor up and down? 1.01.223
excuse it is to beat usurping down. 2.01.119
wilt thou resign them and lay down thy arms? 2.01.154
before we will lay down our just–borne arms 2.01.345
down our just–borne arms | we'll put thee down, 2.01.346
their soul–fearing clamors have brawl'd down 2.01.383
to tread down fair respect of sovereignty, | and 3.01. 58
o then tread down my need, and faith mounts up; 3.01.215
keep my need up, and faith is trodden down! 3.01.216
hovers in the sky | and pours down mischief. 3.02. 3
which else runs tickling up and down the veins, 3.03. 44
lies in his bed, walks up and down with me, 3.04. 94
not without a storm, | pour down thy weather. 4.02.109
the wall is high, and yet will i leap down. 4.03. 1
if i get down, and do not break my limbs, | i'll 4.03. 6
go i to make the french lay down their arms. 5.01. 24
and wild amazement hurries up and down | the 5.01. 35
that, having our fair order written down, | both 5.02. 4
he flatly says he'll not lay down his arms. 5.02.126
these terms of treason doubled down his throat. R2 1.01. 57
now swallow down that lie. 1.01.132
and interchangeably hurl down my gage | upon 1.01.146
throw down, my son, the duke of norfolk's gage. 1.01.161
and, norfolk, throw down his. 1.01.162
norfolk, throw down, we bid, there is no boot. 1.01.164
is hack'd down, and his summer leaves all faded, 1.02. 20
stay, the king hath thrown his warder down. 1.03.118
had you first died, and he been thus trod down, 2.03.126
speak with you, may it please you to come down. 3.03.177
down, down i come, like glist'ring phaeton, 3.03.178
down, down i come, like glist'ring phaeton, 3.03.178
in the base court, come down? 3.03.182
down court! 3.03.182
down king! 3.03.182
waste of idle hours hath quite thrown down. 3.04. 66
and with that odds he weighs king richard down. 3.04. 89
that norfolk lies, here do i throw down this, 4.01. 84
which our profane hours here have thrown down. 5.01. 25
and interchangeably set down their hands, | to 5.02. 98
it was, villain, ere thy hand did set it down. 5.03. 54
would he not fall down, | since pride must have 5.05. 87
and many limits of the charge set down | but 1H4 1.01. 35
alone, i will lay him down such reasons for this 1.02.150 P
hath been smooth as oil, soft as young down, 1.03. 7
to put down richard, that sweet lovely rose, 1.03.175
i know | is ruminated, plotted, and set down, 1.03.274
is turn'd upside down since robin ostler died. 2.01. 10 P
for they ride up and down on her, and make her 2.01. 82 P
peace, ye fat–guts, lie down. 2.02. 32 P
you any levers to lift me up again, being down? 2.02. 35 P
money of the king's coming down the hill, 'tis 2.02. 54 P
the boy shall lead our horses down the hill. 2.02. 79 P
down with them! 2.02. 83 P
down with them! 2.02. 85 P
look down into the pomgarnet, ralph. 2.04. 37 P
his industry is up stairs and down stairs, his 2.04.100 P
down fell their hose. 2.04.215 P
mark now how a plain tale shall put you down. 2.04.255 P
and cousin glendower, | will you sit down? 3.01. 4
and topples down | steeples and moss–grown 3.01. 31
which thou pourest down from these swelling 3.01.199
she bids you on the wanton rushes lay you down, 3.01.211
come, kate, thou art perfect in lying down. 3.01.226 P
the skipping king, he ambled up and down, | with 3.02. 60
but rather drows'd and hung their eyelids down, 3.02. 81
help | we shall o'erturn it topsy–turvy down. 4.01. 82
as if an angel /dropp'd down from the clouds 4.01.108
meet and ne'er part till one drop down a corse. 4.01.123
it rain'd down fortune show'ring on your head, 5.01. 47
if thou see me down in the battle and bestride 5.01.121 P
i grant you i was down and out of breath, and so 5.04.146 P
hath beaten down young hotspur and his troops, 2H4 in 25
broke loose, | and bears down all before him. 1.01. 11
whose swift wrath beat down | the never–daunted 1.01.109
you follow the young prince up and down, like 1.02.163 P
do you set down your name in the scroll of youth 1.02.178 P
of youth, that are written down old with all the 1.02.179 P
to lay down likelihoods and forms of hope. 1.03. 35
didst thou not, when she was gone down stairs, 2.01. 99 P
soul, and she says up and down the town that her 2.01.105 P
why then cover and set them down, and see if 2.04. 10 P
pray thee go down, good ancient. 2.04.151 P
pray thee go down. 2.04.155 P
down, down, dogs! 2.04.159 P
down, down, dogs! 2.04.159 P
down, faitors! 2.04.159 P
for god's sake thrust him down stairs. 2.04.188 P
thrust him down stairs! 2.04.190 P
quoit him down, bardolph, like a shove–groat 2.04.192 P
come, get you down stairs. 2.04.195 P
get you down stairs. 2.04.203 P
fiend hath prick'd down bardolph irrecoverable, 2.04.332 P
that thou no more wilt weigh my eyelids down, 3.01. 7
then (happy) low, lie down! 3.01. 30
would shut the book, and sit him down and die. 3.01. 56
and though we here fall down, | we have supplies 4.02. 44
that light and weightless down | perforce must 4.05. 33
pluck down my officers, break my decrees, | for 4.05.117
down, royal state! 4.05.120
to pluck down justice from your aweful bench? 5.02. 86
who hath writ me down | after my seeming. 5.02.128
now sit down, now sit down. 5.03. 14 P
now sit down, now sit down. 5.03. 15 P
and so i kneel down before you — but, indeed, ep 16 P
but lay down our proportions to defend | against H5 1.02.137
mock mothers from their sons, mock castles down; 1.02.286
cannon touches, | and down goes all before them. 3.pr. 34
when down the hill he holds his fierce career? 3.03. 23
go down upon him, you have power enough, | and 3.05. 53
that england shall crouch down in fear, and 4.02. 37
and their poor jades | lob down their heads, 4.02. 47
thrice within this hour | i saw him down; 4.06. 5

if they will fight with us, bid them come down, 4.07. 58
when alanson and myself were down together, i 4.07.155 P
walls they'll tear down than forsake the siege. 1H6 1.02. 40
bright star of venus, fall'n down on the earth, 1.02.144
here by the cheeks i'll drag thee up and down. 1.03. 51
our windows are broke down in every street, 3.01. 84
not rascal–like, to fall down with a pinch, 4.02. 49
beat down alanson, orleance, burgundy, | and 4.06. 14
kneel down and take my blessing, good my girl. 5.04. 25
lord marquess, kneel down. 2H6 1.01. 63
bookish rule hath pull'd fair england down. 1.01.259
to tumble down thy husband and thyself | from 1.02. 48
to mow down thorns that would annoy our foot 3.01. 67
and as the dam runs lowing up and down, 3.01.214
that want their leader, scatter up and down, 3.02.126
comb down his hair; 3.03. 15
a thousand crowns, or else lay down your head. 4.01. 16
fed from my trencher, kneel'd down at the board, 4.01. 57
then is sin struck down like an ox, and 4.02. 26 P
the spirit of putting down kings and princes — 4.02. 36 P
stand, villain, stand, or i'll fell thee down. 4.02.115 P
mark'd for the gallows, lay your weapons down, 4.02.123
until a power be rais'd to put them down. 4.04. 40
knock him down there. 4.06. 8 P
fire, and, if you can, burn down the tower too. 4.06. 15 P
now go some and pull down the savoy; 4.07. 1 P
down with them all. 4.07. 2 P
down saint magnus' corner! 4.08. 1 P
kill and knock down! 4.08. 2 P
iden, kneel down. 5.01. 78
let's pluck him down. 3H6 1.01. 59
for shame, come down. he made thee duke of york. 1.01. 77
to seek to put me down and reign thyself. 1.01.200
hews down and fells the hardest–timber'd oak. 2.01. 55
fell gently down, as if they struck their 2.01.132
edward, kneel down. 2.02. 60
we'll never leave till we have hewn thee down, 2.02.168
race, | i lay me down a little while to breathe; 2.03. 2
here on this molehill will i sit me down. 2.05. 14
from off the gates of york fetch down the head, 2.06. 52
tut, were it farther off, i'll pluck it down. 3.02.195
of england, worthy margaret, | sit down with us. 3.03. 2
but now mischance hath trod my title down, | and 3.03. 8
and i'll be chief to bring him down again; 3.03.263
at unawares may beat down edward's guard, | and 4.02. 23
the king by this is set him down to sleep. 4.03. 2
nay, then i see that edward needs must down. 4.03. 42
king edward's friends must down. 4.04. 28
like that richmond with the rest shall down. 4.06.100
confess who set thee up and pluck'd thee down, 5.01. 26
warwick, take the time, kneel down, kneel down. 5.01. 48
warwick, take the time, kneel down, kneel down. 5.01. 48
howl'd, and hideous tempest shook down trees; 5.06. 46
down, down to hell, and say i sent thee thither 5.06. 67
down, down to hell, and say i sent thee thither 5.06. 67
have we mow'd down in tops of all their pride! 5.07. 4
thoughts, down to my soul — here clarence comes R3 1.01. 41
set down, set down your honorable load — | if 1.02. 1
set down, set down your honorable load — | if 1.02. 1
stay, you that bear the corse, and set it down. 1.02. 33
villains, set down the corse, or, by saint paul, 1.02. 36
and then hurl down their indignation | on thee, 1.03.219
when oxford had me down, he rescued me, | and 2.01.113
and often up and down my sons were toss'd | for 2.04. 58
wit, | his wit set down to make his valure live. 3.01. 86
we have not yet set down this day of triumph. 3.04. 42
ready with every nod to tumble down | into the 3.04.100
one heav'd a–high, to be hurl'd down below; 4.04. 86
yet to beat down these rebels here at home. 4.04.530
set it down. 5.03. 75
lest leaden slumber peize me down to–morrow, 5.03.105
that they may crush down with a heavy fall | the 5.03.111
and weigh thee down to ruin, shame, and death! 5.03.148
if you do sweat to put a tyrant down, | you 5.03.255
like heathen gods, | shone down the english; H8 1.01. 20
and from a mouth of honor quite cry down | this 1.01.137
have been commissions | sent down among 'em, 1.02. 21
have got a speeding trick to lay down ladies. 1.03. 40
there was the weight that pull'd me down. 3.02.407
while her grace sate down | to rest a while, 4.01. 65
let's sit down quiet | for fear we wake her; 4.02. 81
good man, sit down. 5.02.165
guy, nor colbrand, | to mow 'em down before me; 5.03. 23
should you do, but knock 'em down by th' dozens? 5.03. 32 P
the cygnet's down is harsh and spirit of sense TRO 1.01. 58
cop'd hector in the battle and strook him down, 1.02. 34 P
troy, yet upon his bases, had been down, | and 1.03. 75
so that the ram that batters down the wall, 1.03.206
ajax employ'd plucks down achilles' plumes. 1.03.385
whose present courage may beat down our foes, 2.02.201
in commotion rages, | and batters down himself. 2.03.176
doth one pluck down another, and together | die 3.03. 86
much | to throw down hector than polyxena. 3.03.208
but our great ajax bravely beat down him." 3.03.213
ajax goes up and down the field, asking for 3.03.244 P
why, 'a stalks up and down like a peacock — a 3.03.251 P
but her brain to set down her reckoning; 3.03.253 P
then, sweet my lord, i'll call mine uncle down, 4.02. 2
will you beat down the door? 4.02. 43 P
set them down | for sluttish spoils of 4.05. 61
the fierce polydamas | hath beat down menon; 5.05. 7
fall down before him like a mower's swath. 5.05. 25
come, troy, sink down! 5.08. 11
fins of lead, | and hews down oaks with rushes. COR 1.01.181
if they set down before 's, for the remove 1.02. 28
see him pluck aufidius down by th' hair; 1.03. 30
and titus lartius are set down before their city 1.03. 99 P
down with them! 1.05. 8
keep your duties, | as i have set them down. 1.07. 2
pray now, sit down. 2.02. 74
down with him, down with him! 3.01.183
down with him, down with him! 3.01.183
down with that sword! 3.01.225
down with him, down with him! 3.01.228
down with him, down with him! 3.01.228
he shall be thrown down the tarpeian rock | with 3.01.265
masters, lay down your weapons. 3.01.329
that the precipitation might down stretch 3.02. 4
that we have procur'd | set down by th' pole? 3.03. 10
we have been down together in my sleep, 4.05.124
th' one half of my commission, and set down — 4.05.138
he will mow all down before him, and leave his 4.05.202 P
as hercules | did shake down mellow fruit. 4.06.100
as you threw caps up will he tumble down, | and 4.06.135
all places yields to him ere he sits down, | and 4.07. 28
him | a mile before his tent, fall down, and 5.01. 5
the walls of rome to–morrow | set down our host. 5.03. 2
down, ladies; 5.03.169
down! 5.03.171
the gods look down, and this unnatural scene 5.03.184
and hale him up and down, all swearing, if | the 5.04. 37
and so in this, to bear me down with braves. TIT 2.01. 30
those reproachful speeches down his throat, 2.01. 55
let us sit down and mark their yellowing noise; 2.03. 20
heart, | aaron and thou look down into this den, 2.03.215
write down thy mind, bewray thy meaning so, 2.04. 3
if i do wake, some planet strike me down, | that 2.04. 14
thine, | that hath thrown down so many enemies, 3.01.163
which made me down to throw my books, and fly — 4.01. 25
sit down, sweet niece; 4.01. 65
brother, sit down by me. 4.01. 65
my lord, kneel down with me, lavinia, kneel, 4.01. 87
then sit we down and let us all consult. 4.02.132
to send down justice for to wreak our wrongs. 4.03. 52
that down fell both the ram's horns in the court 4.03. 73
he says that he hath taken them down again, for 4.03. 82 P
with frost, or grass beat down with storms. 4.04. 71
bring down the devil, for he must not die | so 5.01.145
do | see here in bloody lines i have set down: 5.02. 14
come down and welcome me to this world's light; 5.02. 33
i am, therefore come down and welcome me. 5.02. 43
for up and down she doth resemble thee. 5.02.107
beat them down! ROM 1.01. 73
down with the capulets! 1.01. 74
down with the montagues! 1.01. 74
prick love for pricking, and you beat love down. 1.04. 28
till she had laid it and conjur'd it down. 2.01. 26
runs lolling up and down to hide his bable in a 2.04. 92 P
speak any thing against me, i'll take him down, 2.04.151 P
to catch my death with jauncing up and down! 2.05. 52
draw, benvolio, beat down their weapons. 3.01. 86
his /agile arm beats down their fatal points, 3.01.166
on romeo cries, | and then down falls again. 3.03.102
'tis very late, she'll not come down to–night. 3.04. 5
is she not down so late, or up so early? 3.05. 66
dress'd, and in your clothes, and down again? 4.05. 12
up | to see thy son and heir now /early down. 5.03.209
tender down | their services to lord timon. TIM 1.01. 54
even he drops down | the knee before him, and 1.01. 60
change of mood | spurns down her late beloved, 1.01. 85
on their knees and /hands, let him /slip down, 1.01. 87
that man goes up and down in from fourscore to 2.02.113 P
told my lord of you, he is coming down to you. 3.01. 2 P
and take down th' int'rest into their glutt'nous 3.04. 52
knock me down with 'em, cleave me to the girdle! 3.04. 90
bring down rose–cheek'd youth | to the /tub–fast 4.03. 87
writ, | but set them down horrible traitors. 4.03.119
down with the nose, | down with it flat; 4.03.157
down with the nose, | down with it flat; 4.03.158
melted down thy youth | in different beds of 4.03.256
than their offense can weigh down by the dram; 5.01.151
that mine own use invites me to cut down, | and 5.01.206
before proud athens he's set down by this, 5.03. 9
go you down that way towards the capitol, | this JC 1.01. 63
caesar, for he swounded, and fell down at it; 1.02.248 P
he fell down in the market–place, and foam'd at 1.02.252 P
mean by that, but i am sure caesar fell down. 1.02.258 P
marry, before he fell down, when he perceiv'd 1.02.263 P
men, all in fire, walk up and down the streets. 1.03. 25
thus did mark antony bid me fall down; 3.01.124
from the point, by looking down on caesar. 3.01.219
come down. 3.02.161 P
then i, and you, and all of us fell down, 3.02.191
pluck down benches. 3.02.258 P
pluck down forms, windows, any thing. 3.02.259 P
prick him down, antony. 4.01. 3
then take we down his load, and turn him off 4.01. 25
antony | come down upon us with a mighty power, 4.03.169
lie down, good sirs, | it may be i shall 4.03.250
is not the leaf turn'd down | where i left 4.03.273
you said the enemy would not come down, | but 5.01. 2
places, and come down | with fearful bravery, 5.01. 9
ride, ride, messala, let them all come down. 5.02. 6
come down, behold no more. 5.03. 33
o young and noble cato, art thou down? 5.04. 9
sit thee down, clitus; 5.05. 4
defense, | and pour'd them down before him. MAC 1.03.100
that is a step | on which i must fall down, or 1.04. 49
the moon is down; i have not heard the clock. 2.01. 2
and she goes down at twelve. 2.01. 3
our chimneys were blown down, and, as they say, 2.03. 55
but wail his fall | who i myself struck down. 3.01.122
let it come down. 3.03. 16
there's but one down; the son is fled. 3.03. 20
you know your own degrees, sit down. 3.04. 1
love and health to all, | then i'll sit down. 3.04. 87
bladed corn be lodg'd, and trees blown down; 4.01. 55
down! 4.01.112
i will set down what comes from her, to satisfy 5.01. 32 P
let every soldier hew him down a bough, | and 5.04. 4
and will endure | our setting down before't. 5.04. 10
your leavy screens throw down, | and show like 5.06. 1
sit down a while, | and let us once again assail HAM 1.01. 30
well, sit we down, | and let us hear barnardo 1.01. 33
good now, sit down, and tell me, he that knows, 1.01. 70
and we did think it writ down in our duty | to 1.02.222
and, as he drains his draughts of rhenish down, 1.04. 10
oft breaking down the pales and forts of reason, 1.04. 28
meet it is i set it down | that one may smile, 1.05.107
and thrice his head thus waving up and down, 2.01. 90
safety and allowance | as therein are set down. 2.02. 80
i hold it not honesty to have it thus set down, 2.02.202 P
set down with as much modesty as cunning. 2.02.440 P
and bowl the round nave down the hill of heaven 2.02.496
"run barefoot up and down, threat'ning the 2.02.505
lines, which i would set down and insert in't, 2.02.542 P
observ'd of all observers, quite, quite down! 3.01.154
have in quick determination | thus set it down: 3.01.169
clowns speak no more than is set down for them, 3.02. 39 P
the great man down, you mark his favorite flies, 3.02.204
ere we come to fall, | or /pardon'd being down? 3.03. 50
come, and sit you down, you shall not boudge; 3.04. 18
sit you down, | and let me wring your heart, for 3.04. 34
basket creep, | and break your own neck down. 3.04.196
when down her weedy trophies and herself | fell 4.07.174
i sat me down, | devis'd a new commission, wrote 5.02. 31
the king and queen and all are coming down. 5.02.204 P
i dare pawn down my life for him that he hath LR 1.02. 86 P
the rod, and put'st down thine own breeches, 1.04.174 P
being down, insulted, rail'd, | and put upon him 2.02.119
/hysterica passio, down, thou climbing sorrow, 2.04. 57
go thy hold when a great wheel runs down a hill, 2.04. 72 P
o me, my heart! my rising heart! but down! 2.04.121
with a stick, and cried, "down, wantons, down!" 2.04.124 P
with a stick, and cried, "down, wantons, down!" 2.04.125 P
send down, and take my part. 2.04.192
i have a letter guessingly set down, | which 3.07. 47
half way down | hangs one that gathers sampire, 4.06. 14
and the deficient sight | topple down headlong. 4.06. 24
air | (so many fathom down precipitating), 4.06. 50
down from the waist they are centaurs, | though 4.06.124
sit you down, father; 4.06.255
for thee, oppressed king, i am cast down, 5.03. 5
i'll kneel down | and ask of thee forgiveness. 5.03. 10
and carry it so | as i have set it down. 5.03. 37
down with him, thief! OTH 1.02. 57
/couch of war | my thrice–driven bed of down. 1.03.231
but i'll set down the pegs that make this music, 2.01.200
'tis pride that pulls the country down, | /then 2.03. 95
and let her down the wind | to prey at fortune. 3.03.262
lay down my soul at stake. 4.02. 13
down, strumpet! 5.02. 79
nay, lay thee down and roar; 5.02.198
i look down towards his feet; 5.02.286
extenuate, | nor set down aught in malice. 5.02.343
set you down this: 5.02.351
i melt and pour | down thy ill–uttering throat. ANT 2.05. 35
the least wind i' th' world will blow them down. 2.07. 3 P
come down into the boat. 2.07.129
caesar, | kneel down, kneel down, and wonder. 3.02. 19
caesar, | kneel down, kneel down, and wonder. 3.02. 19
inform her tongue — the swan's down feather, 3.02. 48
let me sit down. o juno! 3.11. 28
caesar sets down in alexandria, where | i will 3.13.168
torch is out, | lie down and stray no farther. 4.14. 47
arms, bending down | his corrigible neck, his 4.14. 73
have these things set down by lawful counsel, CYM 1.04.165 P
and i must go up and down like a cock that 2.01. 21 P
a woman that | bears all down with her brain, 2.01. 54
fold down the leaf where i have left. 2.02. 4
to note the chamber, i will write all down: 2.02. 24
why should i write this down, that's riveted, 2.02. 43
here the leaf's turn'd down | where philomele 2.02. 45
shook down my mellow hangings, nay, my leaves, 3.03. 63
she being down, | i have the placing of the 3.05. 64
when resty sloth | finds the down pillow hard. 3.06. 35
i have sent cloten's clotpole down the stream 4.02.184
we have done our obsequies. come lay him down. 4.02.282
faith, i'll lie down and sleep. 4.02.294
tools to do't — strook down | some mortally, 5.03. 9
i had you down and might | have made you finish. 5.05.411
i am down again; 5.05.412
would draw heaven down, and all the gods to PER 1.01. 83
sit down. 1.02. 60
throws down one mountain to cast up a higher. 1.04. 6
vessels with their power | to beat us down, the 1.04. 68
to beat us down, the which are down already, 1.04. 68
a burning torch that's turned upside down; 2.02. 32
dives, | so up and down the poor ship drives. 3.ch. 50
set't down, let's look upon't. 3.02. 51
ay, to eleven, and brought them down again. 4.02. 16 P
down on thy knees, thank the holy gods as loud 5.01.198
book of trespasses | all you are set down there. TNK 1.01. 34
he tumbled down upon his /nemean hide, | and 1.01. 68
o, my petition was | set down in ice, which, by 1.01.107
i could lie down, i am sure. 2.02.151
and let mine honor down, and never charge? 2.02.195
i'll set it down | he's torn to pieces. 3.02. 17
lo | the moon is down, the crickets chirp, the 3.02. 35
sit down, and, good now, | no more of these vain 3.03. 9
pray sit down then, and let me entreat you | by 3.03. 13
ladies, sit down, we'll stay it. 3.05. 99
/ye with a derry, | and a derry and a down, 3.05.140
i laid me down | and list'ned to the words she 4.01. 62
or as iris | newly dropp'd down from heaven. 4.01. 88
all–fear'd gods, bow down your stubborn bodies. 5.01. 13
whose breath blows down | the teeming ceres' 5.01. 52
he was kept down with hard meat and ill lodging, 5.02. 97
lives (for this poor comfort) are laid down, 5.04. 14
prentices simple, down with him! STM II.C 22 P
thus will they bear down all things. II.C 40
hath chid down all the majesty of england, II.C 73
you'll put down strangers, | kill them, cut II.C 119
so soon was she along as he was down, | each VEN 43
all swoll'n with chafing, down adonis sits, 325
sat, | and like a lowly lover down she kneels; 350
and at his look she flatly falleth down, | for 463
she sinketh down, still hanging by his neck, 593
pluck down the rich, enrich the poor with 1150
with the sceptre straight be strooken down? LUC 217
have batter'd down her consecrated wall, | and 723
the stain upon his silver down will stay. 1012
from thee, that down thy cheeks are raining? 1271
what wit sets down is blotted straight with will 1299
wagg'd up and down, and from his lips did fly 1406
and town, | the golden bullet beats it down. PP 18.18
with two alone | sinks down to death, oppress'd SON 45. 8
when sometime lofty towers i see down rased, 64. 3
upon thy part i can set down a story | of faults 88. 6
book both my willfulness and errors down, | and 117. 9
sets down her babe and makes all swift dispatch 143. 3
and down i laid to list the sad–tun'd tale, LC 4
so slides he down upon his grained bat, | and 64

his phoenix down began but to appear | like 93
whose white weighs down the airy scale of praise 226
DOWN–A 2 FR 0.0002 REL FR 0 V 2 P
the burden on't was "down–a, down–a," and penn'd TNK 4.03. 12 P
the burden on't was "down–a, down–a," and penn'd 4.03. 12 P
DOWN–BED 1 FR 0.0001 REL FR 1 V 0 P
as easy as a down–bed would afford it. H8 1.04. 18
DOWNFALL 7 FR 0.0008 REL FR 7 V 0 P
better thing than earth, | divine his downfall? R2 3.04. 79
given | to dream on evil or to work my downfall. 2H6 3.01. 73
even in the downfall of his mellow'd years, 3H6 3.03.104
from those that wish the downfall of our house! 5.06. 65
to the disgrace and downfall of your house; R3 3.07.217
the east, | until his very downfall in the sea; TIT 5.02. 57
like good men | bestride our downfall birthdom. MAC 4.03. 4
DOWN–GYVED 1 FR 0.0001 REL FR 1 V 0 P
ungart'red, and down–gyved to his ankle, | pale HAM 2.01. 77
DOWNRIGHT 13 FR 0.0014 REL FR 9 V 4 P
and woman after this downright way of creation. MM 3.02.105 P
we were descried, they'll mock us now downright. LLL 5.02.389
we shall chide downright, if i longer stay. MND 2.01.145
you have heard him swear downright he was. AYL 3.04. 29 P
appetite, his sleep, | and downright languish'd. WT 2.03. 17
only downright oaths, which i never use till H5 5.02.144 P
peter, have at thee with a downright blow! 2H6 2.03. 90 P
i cleft his beaver with a downright blow. 3H6 1.01. 12
with downright payment show'd unto my father. 1.04. 32
certainly, | he flouted us downright. COR 2.03.160
sunset of my brother's son | it rains downright. ROM 3.05.128
my downright violence and storm of fortunes OTH 1.03.249
and fell i not downright? VEN 645
DOWN–ROPING 1 FR 0.0001 REL FR 1 V 0 P
the gum down–roping from their pale–dead eyes, H5 4.02. 48
DOWNS 2 FR 0.0002 REL FR 2 V 0 P
for, whilst our pinnace anchors in the downs, 2H6 4.01. 9
pursue these fearful creatures o'er the downs, VEN 677
DOWN–TROD 1 FR 0.0001 REL FR 1 V 0 P
but i will lift the down–trod mortimer | as high 1H4 1.03.135
DOWN–TRODDEN 1 FR 0.0001 REL FR 1 V 0 P
for this down–trodden equity, we tread | in JN 2.01.241
DOWNWARD 6 FR 0.0006 REL FR 5 V 1 P
as a german from the waist downward, all slops, ADO 3.02. 35 P
that downward hath succeeded in his house | from AWW 3.07. 23
whilst my gross flesh sinks downward, here to R2 5.05.112
and downward look on us | as we were sickly prey JC 5.01. 85
whose downward eye still looketh for a grave, VEN 1106
with brinish current downward flow'd apace: LC 284
DOWNWARDS 1 FR 0.0001 REL FR 1 V 0 P
looking all downwards to behold our cheeks, TIT 3.01.124
DOWNY 4 FR 0.0004 REL FR 4 V 0 P
there lies a downy feather which stirs not. 2H4 4.05. 32
so doth the swan her downy cygnets save, 1H6 5.03. 56
shake off this downy sleep, death's counterfeit, MAC 2.03. 76
downy windows, close, | and golden phoebus never ANT 5.02.316
DOW'R 4 FR 0.0004 REL FR 4 V 0 P
only for propagation of a dow'r | remaining in MM 1.02.150
day, | to pass assurance of a dow'r in marriage SHR 4.02.118
a dow'r, my lords? 1H6 5.05. 48
thy truth then be thy dow'r! LR 1.01.108
DOW'R'D 1 FR 0.0001 REL FR 1 V 0 P
dow'r'd with our curse, and stranger'd with our LR 1.01.204
DOWRIES 1 FR 0.0001 REL FR 1 V 0 P
large sums of gold and dowries with their wives, 2H6 1.01.129
DOW'RLESS 1 FR 0.0001 REL FR 1 V 0 P
thy dow'rless daughter, king, thrown to my LR 1.01.256
DOW'RS 1 FR 0.0001 REL FR 1 V 0 P
with my two daughters' dow'rs digest the third; LR 1.01.128
DOWRY 25 FR 0.0028 REL FR 17 V 8 P
will you, upon good dowry, marry her? WIV 1.01.239 P
in that perish'd vessel the dowry of his sister. MM 3.01.217 P
weight | than aquitaine, a dowry for a queen. LLL 2.01. 8
often known | to be the dowry of a second head, MV 3.02. 95
well, that is the dowry of his wife, 'tis none AYL 3.03. 55 P
had as lief take her dowry with this condition SHR 1.01.132 P
yea, and to marry her, if her dowry please. 1.02.184
what dowry shall i have with her to wife? 2.01.120
and for that dowry, i'll assure her of | her 2.01.123
your dowry 'greed on; 2.01.270
her dowry wealthy, and of worthy birth; 4.05. 65
crowns, | another dowry to another daughter, 5.02.114
and ask no other dowry with her but such another TN 2.05.184 P
not have him miscarry for the half of my dowry. 3.04. 63 P
give with our niece a dowry large enough, | for JN 2.01.469
her dowry shall weigh equal with a queen; 2.01.486
katherine his daughter, and with her, to dowry, H5 3.pr. 30
in marriage, with a large and sumptuous dowry. 1H6 5.01. 20
cost and charges, without having any dowry." 2H6 1.01. 62 P
which with her dowry shall be counterpois'd. 3H6 3.03.137
marry, i'll give thee this plague for thy dowry: HAM 3.01.135 P
she is herself a dowry. LR 1.01.241
till lucina reigned, | nature this dowry gave: PER 1.01. 9
what dowry has she? TNK 5.02. 64
bred, | not spend the dowry of a lawful bed. LUC 938
DOWSABEL 1 FR 0.0001 REL FR 1 V 0 P
where dowsabel did claim me for her husband: ERR 4.01.110
DOWSETS 1 FR 0.0001 REL FR 1 V 0 P
without lets, | and the ladies eat his dowsets! TNK 3.05.157
DOXY 1 FR 0.0001 REL FR 1 V 0 P
to peer, | with heigh, the doxy over the dale! WT 4.03. 2
DOZEN 35 FR 0.0039 REL FR 14 V 21 P
thou didst painfully remain | a dozen years; TMP 1.02.279
they may give the dozen white luces in their WIV 1.01. 16 P
the dozen white louses do become an old coat 1.01. 19 P
no? a dozen times at least. MM 1.02. 20 P
and speak /off half a dozen dang'rous words, ADO 5.01. 97
there's half a dozen sweets. LLL 5.02.234
fleet, | i would esteem him worth a dozen such. SHR in.1. 27
faith, there's a dozen of 'em, with delicate AWW 4.05.104 P
if but a dozen french | were there in arms, they JN 3.04.173
a dozen of them here have ta'en the sacrament, R2 5.02. 97
sir john with half a dozen more are at the door, 1H4 2.04. 82 P
kills me some six or seven dozen of scots at a 2.04.103 P
not at half–sword with a dozen of them two hours 2.04.165 P
we four set upon some dozen — 2.04.174 P
i bought you a dozen of shirts to your back. 3.03. 68 P
along | i met and overtook a dozen captains, 2H4 2.04.358
a dozen captains stay at door for you. 2.04.372
provided me here half a dozen sufficient men? 3.02. 93 P
i must a dozen mile to–night. 3.02.290 P
i should make four dozen of such bearded 5.01. 63 P
it do, you shall have a dozen of cushions again; 5.04. 14 P
lodge and board a dozen or fourteen gentlewomen H5 2.01. 33 P
i have half a dozen healths | to drink to these H8 1.04.105
fetch me a dozen crab–tree staves, and strong 5.03. 7 P
had i a dozen sons, each in my love alike, and COR 1.03. 22 P
for your voices bear | of wounds two dozen odd; 2.03.128
therefore we'll have some half a dozen friends, ROM 3.04. 27
women at the table, let a dozen of them be — as TIM 3.06. 78 P
study a speech of some dozen lines, or sixteen HAM 2.02.541 P
and thirty dozen moons with borrowed sheen 3.02.157
that in a dozen passes between yourself and him, 5.02.165 P
galleys | have sent a dozen sequent messengers OTH 1.02. 41
yes, a dozen; 4.03. 84 P
some dozen romans of us and your lord | (the CYM 1.06.185
how now? how a dozen of virginities? PER 4.06. 20 P
DOZENS 2 FR 0.0002 REL FR 1 V 1 P
should you do, but knock 'em down by th' dozens? H8 5.03. 33 P
i would not, | should i try death by dozens. TNK 3.02. 25
DOZY 1 FR 0.0001 REL FR 0 V 1 P
him inventorially would dozy th' arithmetic of HAM 5.02.114 P
DRAB 8 FR 0.0009 REL FR 4 V 4 P
with die and drab i purchas'd this caparison, WT 4.03. 27 P
dost thou deny thy father, cursed drab? 1H6 5.04. 32
follow the knave, and take this drab away. 2H6 2.01.153
they say he keeps a troyan drab, and uses the TRO 5.01. 96 P
for an almond than he for a commodious drab. 5.02.194 P
sleeve back to the dissembling luxurious drab, 5.04. 8 P
babe | ditch–deliver'd by a drab, | make the MAC 4.01. 31
words, | and fall a–cursing, like a very drab, HAM 2.02.586
DRABBING 1 FR 0.0001 REL FR 1 V 0 P
quarrelling, | drabbing — you may go so far. HAM 2.01. 26
DRABS 1 FR 0.0001 REL FR 0 V 1 P
will take order for the drabs and the knaves, MM 2.01.234 P
DRACHMAES 2 FR 0.0002 REL FR 2 V 0 P
to every several man, seventy–five drachmaes. JC 3.02.242
and drop my blood for drachmaes than to wring 4.03. 73
DRACHME 1 FR 0.0001 REL FR 1 V 0 P
do prize their hours | at a crack'd drachme! COR 1.05. 5
DRAFF 2 FR 0.0002 REL FR 1 V 1 P
still swine eats all the draff. WIV 4.02.107
from swine–keeping, from eating draff and husks. 1H4 4.02. 35 P
DRAG 10 FR 0.0011 REL FR 10 V 0 P
my affairs | do even drag me homeward; WT 1.02. 24
not what impediments | drag back our expedition. 1H4 4.03. 19
here by the cheeks i'll drag thee up and down. 1H6 1.03. 51
away even now, or i will drag thee hence. 2H6 3.02.229
jades | that drag the tragic melancholy night; 4.01. 4
hence will i drag thee headlong by the heels 4.10. 80
drag hence her husband to some secret hole, TIT 2.03.129
sirs, drag them from the pit unto the prison, 2.03.283
go drag the villain hither by the hair, | nor 4.04. 56
or i will drag thee on a hurdle thither. ROM 3.05.155
DRAGG'D 4 FR 0.0004 REL FR 3 V 1 P
the bodies shall be dragg'd at my horse heels 2H6 4.03. 12 P
sort, dragg'd through the shameful field. TRO 5.10. 5
from his mother's closet hath he dragg'd him. HAM 4.01. 35
know my prize | must be dragg'd out of blood; TNK 5.01. 43
DRAGON 8 FR 0.0009 REL FR 7 V 1 P
saint george, that swing'd the dragon, and e'er JN 2.01.288
and of a dragon and a finless fish, | a 1H4 3.01.149
the dragon wing of night o'erspreads the earth, TRO 5.08. 17
like to a lonely dragon, that his fen | makes COR 4.01. 30
this martius is grown from man to dragon: 5.04. 13 P
did ever dragon keep so fair a cave? ROM 3.02. 74
scale of dragon, tooth of wolf, | witch's mummy, MAC 4.01. 22
come not between the dragon and his wrath; LR 1.01.122
DRAGONISH 1 FR 0.0001 REL FR 1 V 0 P
sometime we see a cloud that's dragonish, | a ANT 4.14. 2
DRAGON–LIKE 1 FR 0.0001 REL FR 1 V 0 P
fights dragon–like, and does achieve as soon COR 4.07. 23
DRAGON'S 2 FR 0.0002 REL FR 1 V 1 P
his arms spread wider than a dragon's wings; 1H6 1.01. 11
with my mother under the dragon's tail, and my LR 1.02.129 P
DRAGONS' 1 FR 0.0001 REL FR 1 V 0 P
with ladies' faces and fierce dragons' spleens, JN 2.01. 68
DRAGONS 5 FR 0.0005 REL FR 5 V 0 P
for night's swift dragons cut the clouds full MND 3.02.379
inspire us with the spleen of fiery dragons! R3 5.03.350
go great with tigers, dragons, wolves, and bears TIM 4.03.189
swift, you dragons of the night, that dawning CYM 2.02. 48
for death–like dragons here affright thee hard. PER 1.01. 29
DRAIN 4 FR 0.0004 REL FR 4 V 0 P
and to drain | upon his face an ocean of salt 2H6 3.02.142
how couldst thou drain the life–blood of the 3H6 1.04.138
her, did drain | the purple sap from her sweet R3 4.04.276
i'll drain him dry as hay: MAC 1.03. 18
DRAIN'D 1 FR 0.0001 REL FR 1 V 0 P
when hours have drain'd his blood and fill'd his SON 63. 3
DRAINED 1 FR 0.0001 REL FR 1 V 0 P
aunt, should by my mortal sword | be drained! TRO 4.05.135
DRAINS 1 FR 0.0001 REL FR 1 V 0 P
and, as he drains his draughts of rhenish down, HAM 1.04. 10
DRAM 16 FR 0.0018 REL FR 11 V 5 P
pity, void and empty | from any dram of mercy. MV 4.01. 6
good faith, ev'ry dram of it, and i will not AWW 2.03.221 P
adheres together, that no dram of a scruple, no TN 3.04. 79 P
but with a ling'ring dram that should not work WT 1.02.320
ay, every dram of woman's flesh is false, | if 2.01.138
stand till he be three quarters and a dram dead; 4.04.785 P
the wise may make some dram of a scruple, or 2H4 1.02.130 P
shall give him such an unaccustom'd dram | that ROM 3.05. 90
let me have | a dram of poison, such 5.01. 60
than their offense can weigh down by the dram; TIM 5.01.151
the dram of /ev'l | doth all the noble substance HAM 1.04. 36
or with some dram, conjur'd to this effect, | he OTH 1.03.105
if you buy ladies' flesh at a million a dram, CYM 1.04.135 P
a dram of this | will drive away distemper. 3.04.190
of baseness cannot | a dram of worth be drawn. 3.05. 89
by the queen's dram she swallow'd. 5.05.381
DRAMS 1 FR 0.0001 REL FR 1 V 0 P
that with cords, knives, drams, precipitance, TNK 1.01.142
DRANK 2 FR 0.0002 REL FR 0 V 2 P
i ne'er drank sack in my life; SHR in.2. 6 P
jubiter, i never drank with him in all my life. TIT 4.03. 85 P
DRAUGHT 10 FR 0.0011 REL FR 5 V 5 P
sent your worship a morning's draught of sack. WIV 2.02.147 P
one draught above heat makes him a fool, the TN 1.05.132 P
of, | for shallow draught and bulk unprizable, 5.01. 55
which draught to me were cordial. WT 1.02.318
i have taken my last draught in this world. 2H6 2.03. 73 P
sweet draught! TRO 5.01. 75 P
pledges the breath of him in a divided draught, TIM 1.02. 48 P
them, or stab them, drown them in a draught, 5.01.102
drink a good hearty draught, it breeds good TNK 3.03. 17
i'll tell you | after a draught or two more. 3.03. 19
DRAUGHT–OXEN 1 FR 0.0001 REL FR 0 V 1 P
/on /their /toes, yoke you like draught–oxen, TRO 2.01.106 P
DRAUGHTS 3 FR 0.0003 REL FR 3 V 0 P
with liquorish draughts | and morsels unctious, TIM 4.03.194
and, as he drains his draughts of rhenish down, HAM 1.04. 10
(being full of supper and distemp'ring draughts) OTH 1.01. 99
DRAVE *(also drove)*
DRAVE 3 FR 0.0003 REL FR 2 V 1 P
that i drave my suitor from his mad humor of AYL 3.02.418 P
themselves, | and drave great mars to faction. TRO 3.03.190
italy, | upon the first encounter, drave them. ANT 1.02. 94
/DRAW 4 FR 0.0004 REL FR 4 V 0 P
/survey /the /plot, /then /draw /the /model, 2H4 1.03. 42
/what /do /we /then /but /draw /anew /the /model 1.03. 46
/please /you, /draw /near. LR 4.07. 24
/i /cannot /draw /a /cart, /nor /eat /dried 5.03. 38
DRAW 208 FR 0.0235 REL FR 162 V 46 P
draw thy sword. TMP 2.01.292
draw together; 2.01.294
let's draw our weapons. 2.01.322
please you draw near. 5.01.319
else, no worldly good should draw from me. TGV 3.01. 9
he shall draw, he shall tap. WIV 1.03. 10 P
they will draw you, master froth, and you will MM 2.01.205 P
but thy unkindness shall his death draw out | to 2.04.166
to draw with idle spiders' strings | most 3.02.275
and draw within the compass of suspect | th' ERR 3.01. 87
good sir, draw near to me, i'll speak to him. 5.01. 12
i am sorry now that i did draw on him. 5.01. 43
nor ever didst thou draw thy sword on me; 5.01.267
we'll draw cuts for the senior, till then, lead 5.01.423
me a meet hour to draw don pedro and the count ADO 2.02. 33 P
draw it. 3.02. 22 P
you must hang it first, and draw it afterwards. 3.02. 24 P
it is in my scabbard, shall i draw it? 5.01.125 P
i will bid thee draw, as we do the minstrels, 5.01.128 P
as we do the minstrels, draw to pleasure us. 5.01.129 P
the mean time i will draw a bill of properties, MND 1.02.105 P
you draw me, you hard–hearted adamant; 2.01.195
but yet you draw not iron, for my heart | is 2.01.196
leave you your power to draw, | and i shall have 2.01.197
pyramus must draw a sword to kill himself; 3.01. 11 P
go, draw aside the curtains and discover | the MV 2.07. 1
draw the curtains, go. 2.07. 78
quick, i pray thee, draw the curtain straight; 2.09. 1
come draw the curtain, nerissa. 2.09. 84
time, | to eche it and to draw it out in length, 3.02. 23
i would not draw them, i would have my bond. 4.01. 87
clerk, draw a deed of gift. 4.01.394
do not draw back your hand, i'll take no more, 4.01.428
mistress' ear, | and draw her home with music. 5.01. 68
pray you draw homewards. AYL 4.03.178 P
in some little measure draw a belief from you, 5.02. 57 P
draw forth thy weapon, we are beset with thieves SHR 3.02.236
bush, | and then pursue me as you draw your bow. 5.02. 47
every hour, to sit and draw | his arched brows, AWW 1.01. 93
a man may draw his heart out ere 'a pluck one. 1.03. 88 P
will you draw near? 3.02. 98
would thou mightst never draw sword again. TN 1.03. 62 P
i would i might never draw sword again. 1.03. 64 P
but we will draw the curtain and show you the 1.05.233 P
in a catch that will draw three souls out of one 2.03. 58 P
so soon as ever thou seest him, draw, and, as 3.04.178 P
therefore draw, for the supportance of his vow. 3.04.299 P
do, cuff him soundly, but never draw thy sword. 3.04.392 P
if thou dar'st tempt me further, draw thy sword. 4.01. 42
will draw in | more than the common blocks. WT 1.02.224
draw our throne into a sheep–cote! 4.04.779 P
do not draw the curtain. 5.03. 59
i'll draw the curtain. 5.03. 68
shall i draw the curtain? 5.03. 83
shall draw this brief into as huge a volume. JN 2.01.103
france, | to draw my answer from thy articles? 2.01.111
cousin, go draw our puissance together. 3.01.339
that i must draw this metal from my side | to be 5.02. 16
draw near, | and list what with our council we R2 1.03.123
he /cannot draw his power this fourteen days. 1H4 4.01.126
and that no man might draw short breath to–day 5.02. 48
each man do his best, and here draw i | a sword, 5.02. 92
that he should draw his several strengths 2H4 1.03. 76
shall we go draw our numbers and set on? 1.03.109
draw, bardolph, cut me off the villain's head, 2.01. 46 P
go wash thy face, and draw the action. 2.01.149 P
you do draw my spirits from me | with new 2.03. 46
i pray thee, jack, i pray thee do not draw. 2.04.202 P
sir, and i come to draw you out by the ears. 2.04.289 P
and draw no swords but what are sanctified. 4.04. 4
draw the huge bottoms through the furrowed sea, H5 3.pr. 12
that our french gallants shall to–day draw out, 4.02. 22
and draw their honors reeking up to heaven, 4.03.101
draw, men, for all this privileged place — 1H6 1.03. 46
blood will i draw on thee — thou art a witch — 1.05. 6
these words of yours draw life–blood from my 4.06. 43
to draw conditions of a friendly peace, | which 5.01. 38
close up his eyes, and draw the curtain close, 2H6 3.03. 32
draw thy sword in right. 3H6 2.02. 62
leave, | i'll draw it as apparent to the crown, 2.02. 64
thou draw not on thy danger and dishonor; 3.03. 75
draw near, queen margaret, and be a witness 3.03.138
ay, ay, for this i draw in many a tear, | and 4.04. 21

nay rather, wilt thou draw thy forces hence, 5.01. 25
falsely to draw me in these vile suspects. R3 1.03. 88
to draw the brats of clarence out of sight, 3.05.107
be mov'd, | to draw him from his holy exercise. 3.07. 64
at their beads, 'tis much to draw them thence, 3.07. 93
yet to draw forth your noble ancestry | from the 3.07.198
i'll draw the form and model of our battle, 5.03. 24
your standards, draw your willing swords. 5.03.264
draw, archers, draw your arrows to the head! 5.03.339
draw, archers, draw your arrows to the head! 5.03.339
such noble scenes as draw the eye to flow, | we H8 pr 4
but poverty could never draw 'em from me), 4.02.149
let 'em alone, and draw the curtain close; 5.02. 34
far some forty truncheoners draw to her succor, 5.03. 52 P
pibbles, that i was fain to draw mine honor in, 5.03. 57 P
have record, trial did draw | bias and thwart, TRO 1.03. 14
and by device let blockish ajax draw | the sort 1.03.374
without a heart to dare, or sword to draw, 2.02.157
a good quarrel to draw emulous factions and 2.03. 73 P
sail swift, though greater hulks draw deep. 2.03.266
and you draw backward, we'll put you i' th' 3.02. 45 P
draw this curtain and let's see your picture. 3.02. 46 P
so, so, we draw together. 5.05. 44
and four shall quickly draw out my command, COR 1.06. 84
bred i' th' wars | since 'a could draw a sword, 3.01.319
draw near, ye people. 3.03. 39
and does achieve as soon | as draw his sword; 4.07. 24
wilt thou draw near the nature of the gods? TIT 1.01.117
draw near them then in being merciful: 1.01.118
patricians, draw your swords, and sheathe them 1.01.204
so near the emperor's palace dare ye draw, | and 2.01. 46
do not draw back, for we will mourn with thee. 2.04. 56
look ye draw home enough, and 'tis there 4.03. 3
now, masters, draw. 4.03. 64
you, therefore, draw nigh and take your places. 5.03. 24
draw you near | to shed obsequious tears upon 5.03.151
i mean, and we be in choler, we'll draw. ROM 1.01. 3 P
while you live, draw your neck out of collar. 1.01. 4 P
draw thy tool, here comes /two of the house of 1.01. 31 P
draw, if you be men. 1.01. 62 P
should in the farthest east begin to draw | the 1.01.135
dun, we'll draw thee from the mire | /of /this 1.04. 41
warrant you, i dare draw as soon as another man, 2.04.159 P
therefore do nimble–pinion'd doves draw love, 2.05. 7
that thou hast done me, therefore turn and draw. 3.01. 67
draw, benvolio, beat down their weapons. 3.01. 86
for, ere i | could draw to part them, was stout 3.01.173
pray draw near. TIM 2.02. 45
draw nearer, honest flaminius. 3.01. 39 P
my worthy friends, will you draw near? 3.06. 58 P
sun, draw from the earth | rotten humidity; 4.03. 1
draw them to tiber banks, and weep your tears JC 1.01. 58
look, | i draw a sword against conspirators; 5.01. 51
in form as palpable | as this which now i draw. MAC 2.01. 41
illusion | shall draw him on to his confusion. 3.05. 29
profit again should hardly draw me here. 5.03. 62
of reason, | and draw you into madness? HAM 1.04. 74
such perusal of my face | as 'a would draw it. 2.01. 88
by your companies | to draw him on to pleasures, 2.02. 15
like a gulf, doth draw | what's near it with it. 3.03. 16
come, sir, to draw toward an end with you. 3.04.216
to draw apart the body he hath kill'd, | o'er 4.01. 24
swoopstake, you will draw both friend and foe, 4.05.143
and in this harsh world draw thy breath in pain 5.02.348
from his mouth whose voice will draw /on more, 5.02.392
what can you say to draw | a third more opulent LR 1.01. 85
in cunning i must draw my sword upon you. 2.01. 29
draw, seem to defend yourself; 2.01. 30
draw, you rogue, for though it be night, yet the 2.02. 30 P
you, you whoreson cullionly barber–monger, draw! 2.02. 33 P
draw, you rascal! 2.02. 35 P
draw, you rogue, or i'll so carbonado your 2.02. 37 P
draw, you rascal! 2.02. 38 P
one that goes upward, let him draw thee after. 2.04. 74 P
and must draw me | that which my father loses: 3.03. 23
make no noise, make no noise, draw the curtains. 3.06. 83 P
draw me a clothier's yard. 4.06. 88 P
the enemy's in view, draw up your powers. 5.01. 51
draw thy sword, | that, if my speech offend a 5.03.126
still the house affairs would draw her /thence, OTH 1.03.147
to draw from her a prayer of earnest heart 1.03.152
gone | is the next way to draw new mischief on. 1.03.205
on — | myself a while to draw the moor apart, 2.03.385
and i'll devise a mean to draw the moor | out of 3.01. 37
nor from mine own weak merits will i draw | the 3.03.187
fellow that's but yok'd | may draw with you. 4.01. 67
soft, by and by, let me the curtains draw. 5.02.104
entertained cause enough | to draw their swords; ANT 2.01. 47
to other and all loves to both | draw after her. 2.02.136
i did not think to draw my sword 'gainst pompey, 2.02.153
if we draw lots, he speeds; 2.03. 36
is shorter, | my purposes do draw me much about. 2.04. 8
and, as i draw them up, | i'll think them every 2.05. 13
we part, and let's | draw lots who shall begin. 2.06. 61
let your best love draw to that point which 3.04. 21
outward | do draw the inward quality after them, 3.13. 33
draw that thy honest sword, which thou hast worn 4.14. 79
draw, and come. 4.14. 84
draw thy sword, and give me | sufficing strokes 4.14.116
help, friends below, let's draw him hither. 4.15. 13
help me, my women — we must draw thee up. 4.15. 30
he takes his part | to draw upon an exile. CYM 1.01.166
what shall i need to draw my sword, the paper 3.04. 32
look | i draw the sword myself, take it, and hit 3.04. 67
best draw my sword; 3.06. 25
pray draw near. 3.06. 92
i pray draw near. 3.06. 95
than we | that draw his knives i' th' war. 5.03. 73
would draw heaven down, and all the gods to PER 1.01. 83
draw lots who first shall die to lengthen life. 1.04. 46
but, master, i'll go draw up the net. 2.01. 93 P
can draw him but to answer thee in aught, | thy 5.01. 73
draw thy fear'd sword | that does good turns to TNK 1.01. 48
that best knowest | how to draw out, fit to this 1.01.160
or i am none | that draw i' th' sequent trace. 1.02. 60
hands shall never draw 'em out like lightning, 2.02. 24
draw up the company. where's the taborer? 3.05. 23
strengthless doves will draw me through the sky, VEN 153
that she will draw his lips' rich treasure dry. 552
to draw the cloud that hides the silver moon. LUC 371
draw not thy sword to guard iniquity, | for it 626
to push grief on, and back the same grief draw. 1673
nor draw no lines there with thine antique pen; SON 19.10
they draw but what they see, know not the heart. 24.14
but day doth daily draw my sorrows longer, | and 28.13

DRAWBRIDGE 1 FR 0.0001 REL FR 1 V 0 P
look to the drawbridge there! R3 3.05. 15

DRAWER 6 FR 0.0006 REL FR 0 V 6 P
give us leave, drawer. WIV 2.02.159 P
i question my puny drawer to what end he gave me 1H4 2.04. 30 P
have you made with this jest of the drawer? 2.04. 91 P
call him up, drawer. 2H4 2.04.101 P
i am a gentleman, thou art a drawer. 2.04.288 P
of the second cup draws him on the drawer, when ROM 3.01. 9 P

DRAWERS 2 FR 0.0002 REL FR 0 V 2 P
i am sworn brother to a leash of drawers, and 1H4 2.04. 7 P
and wait upon him at his table as drawers. 2H4 2.02.172 P

DRAWETH 2 FR 0.0002 REL FR 0 V 2 P
event that draweth from my snow–white pen the LLL 1.01.242 P
he draweth out the thread of his verbosity finer 5.01. 16 P

DRAWING 7 FR 0.0008 REL FR 5 V 2 P
if black, why, nature, drawing of an antic, ADO 3.01. 63
if drawing my sword against the humor of LLL 1.02. 59 P
but lusty, young, and cheerly drawing breath. R2 1.03. 66
spent, | wax dim, as drawing to their exigent; 1H6 2.05. 9
without drawing their massy irons and cutting TRO 2.03. 16 P
centre of the earth, | drawing all things to it. 4.02.105
and drawing days out, that men stand upon. JC 3.01.100

DRAWLING 1 FR 0.0001 REL FR 0 V 1 P
i never heard such a drawling, affecting rogue. WIV 2.01.141 P

DRAWN 86 FR 0.0097 REL FR 74 V 12 P
have follow'd it, | or it hath drawn me rather. TMP 1.02.395
why are you drawn? 2.01.308
mine eyes open'd, | i saw their weapons drawn. 2.01.320
well drawn, monster, in good sooth! 2.02.147 P
upon advice, hath drawn my love from her, | and, TGV 3.01. 73
and hath drawn him and the rest of their company WIV 4.02. 34 P
into any room in a tap–house, but i am drawn in. MM 2.01.210 P
each one with ireful passion, with drawn swords, ERR 5.01.151
o, he hath drawn my picture in his letter! LLL 5.02. 38
here, villain, drawn and ready. where art thou? MND 3.02.402
hast thou been drawn to by thy fantasy? AYL 2.04. 31
shade | a lioness, with udders all drawn dry, 4.03.114
so workmanly the blood and tears are drawn. SHR in.2. 60
let specialties be therefore drawn between us, 2.01.126
and there it is in writing, fairly drawn. 3.01. 70
though our silence be drawn from us with cars, TN 2.05. 63 P
as might have drawn one to a longer voyage) 3.03. 7
if all the devils of hell be drawn in little, 3.04. 85 P
you had drawn oaths from him not to stay. WT 1.02. 29
seest a game play'd home, the rich stake drawn, 1.02.248
drawn in the flattering table of her eye. JN 2.01.503
drawn in the flattering table of her eye! 2.01.504
that, hang'd and drawn and quarter'd, there 2.01.508
hath drawn him from his own determin'd aid, 2.01.584
that such an army could be drawn in france, 4.02.118
form, drawn with a pen | upon a parchment, and 5.07. 32
tongue speaks, my right drawn sword may prove. R2 1.01. 46
with tears drawn from her eyes by your foul 3.01. 15
and our indentures tripartite are drawn, | which 1H4 3.01. 79
within that space you may have drawn together 3.01. 88
are the indentures drawn? 3.01.139
by that time will our book, i think, be drawn. 3.01.221
and the indentures be drawn, i'll away within 3.01.260 P
by this our book is drawn, we'll but seal, | and 3.01.265
there's no more truth in thee than in a drawn fox, 3.03.113 P
by deputation could not | so soon be drawn, nor 4.01. 33
but yet the king hath drawn | the special head 4.04. 27
upon me | than i have drawn it in my fantasy. 2H4 5.02. 13
thou hast drawn my shoulder out of joint. 5.04. 3 P
for every drop of blood was drawn from him 1H6 2.02. 8
one drop of blood drawn from thy country's bosom 3.03. 54
your wrathful weapons drawn | here in our 2H6 3.02.237
whose dreadful swords were never drawn in vain, 4.01. 92
and now forthwith shall articles be drawn 3H6 3.03.135
eyes of thine from mine have drawn salt tears, R3 1.02.153
are you drawn forth among a world of men | to 1.04.181
my foreward shall be drawn out all in length, 5.03.293
all that world of wealth i have drawn together H8 3.02.211
how long her face is drawn! 4.02. 97
the first sword was drawn about this question, TRO 2.02. 18
nor you, my brother, with your true sword drawn, 5.03. 56
and presently, when you have drawn your number, COR 2.03.253
drawn tuns of blood out of thy country's breast, 4.05. 99
wherefore stand'st thou with thy weapon drawn? TIT 3.01. 48
with this, my weapon drawn, i rush'd upon him, 5.01. 37
art thou drawn among these heartless hinds? ROM 1.01. 66
what, drawn and talk of peace? 1.01. 70
drawn with a team of little atomi | over men's 1.04. 57
and there were drawn | upon a heap a hundred JC 1.03. 22
the wine of life is drawn, and the mere lees MAC 2.03. 95
the bow is bent and drawn, make from the shaft. LR 1.01.143
some blood drawn on me would beget opinion | of 2.01. 33
you fen–suck'd fogs, drawn by the pow'rful sun, 2.04.167
seat | of fortunate caesar, drawn before him, ANT 4.14. 76
my sword is drawn. 4.14. 88
do at once | the thing why thou hast drawn it. 4.14. 89
see | how hardly i was drawn into this war, 5.01. 74
let there be covenants drawn between 's. CYM 1.04.143 P
hath in gallia | will soon be drawn to head, 3.05. 25
of baseness cannot | a dram of worth be drawn. 3.05. 89
the lines of my body are as well drawn as his; 4.01. 10 P
the roman legions, all from gallia drawn, | are 4.03. 24
answer would be death | drawn on with torture. 4.04. 14
the purse too light, being drawn of heaviness. 5.04.165 P
came to me | with his sword drawn, foam'd at the 5.05.276
drawn by report, advent'rous by desire, | tell PER 1.01. 35
hairs, i have drawn her picture with my voice. 4.02. 95 P
villain to attempt it, who having drawn to do't, 5.01.173
his globy eyes | had almost drawn their spheres, TNK 5.01.114
even so, the curtain drawn, his eyes begun | to LUC 374
before the which is drawn the power of greece, 1368
and my laments would be drawn out too long | to 1616
and you must live drawn by your own sweet skill. SON 16.14
mine eyes have drawn thy shape, and thine for me 24.10
drawn after you, you pattern of all those. 98.12
for on his visage was in little drawn | what LC 90

DRAWS 29 FR 0.0032 REL FR 23 V 6 P
the hour draws on. to the oak, to the oak! WIV 5.03. 23 P
the minute draws on. 5.05. 2 P
it draws something near to the speech we had to MM 1.02. 77 P
wrong to th' appetite, | to follow as it draws! 2.04.177
the hour draws on | prefix'd by angelo. 4.03. 78
that runs counter, and yet draws dry–foot well; ERR 4.02. 39
hippolyta, our nuptial hour | draws on apace. MND 1.01. 2
he is defil'd | that draws a sword on thee. 3.02.411
pyramus draws near the wall. silence! 5.01.169 P
appears | than any that draws breath in italy. MV 3.02.296
po, | it draws toward supper in conclusion so. JN 1.01.204
draws those heaven–moving pearls from his poor 2.01.169
draws the sweet infant breath of gentle sleep; R2 1.03.133
draws out our miles and makes them wearisome, 2.03. 5
this absence of your father's draws a curtain 1H4 4.01. 73
like /one that draws the model of an house 2H4 1.03. 58
march to the bridge, it now draws toward night; H5 3.06.170
law of arms is such | that whoso draws a sword, 1H6 3.04. 39
from my weakness draws | my very soul of counsel TRO 3.02.132
his insolence draws folly from my lips, | but 4.05.258
your passion draws ears hither. 5.02.181
of the second cup draws him on the drawer, when ROM 3.01. 8 P
which busy care draws in the brains of men; JC 2.01.232
brutus, | he draws mark antony out of the way. 3.01. 26
it then draws near the season | wherein the HAM 1.04. 5
where it draws blood, no cataplasm so rare, 4.07.143
not an ass know when the cart draws the horse? LR 1.04.223 P
thus | draws us a profit from all things we see; CYM 3.03. 18
so she at these sad signs draws up her breath, VEN 929

DRAW'ST 2 FR 0.0002 REL FR 1 V 1 P
him, draw, and, as thou draw'st, swear horrible; TN 3.04.178 P
thou draw'st a counterfeit | best in all athens; TIM 5.01. 80

DRAYMAN 1 FR 0.0001 REL FR 0 V 1 P
achilles! a drayman, a porter, a very camel. TRO 1.02.249 P

DRAYMEN 1 FR 0.0001 REL FR 1 V 0 P
a brace of draymen bid god speed him well, | and R2 1.04. 32

/DREAD 1 FR 0.0001 REL FR 1 V 0 P
and, in the fleshment of this /dread exploit, LR 2.02.123

DREAD 53 FR 0.0060 REL FR 53 V 0 P
waves tremble, | yea, his dread trident shake. TMP 1.02.206
to the dread rattling thunder | have i given 5.01. 44
o my dread lord, | i should be guiltier than my MM 5.01.366
to fright them hence with that dread penalty. LLL 1.01.127
dread prince of plackets, king of codpieces, 3.01.184
what judgment shall i dread, doing no wrong? MV 4.01. 89
wherein doth sit the dread and fear of kings; 4.01.192
by your dread "verily," | one of them you shall WT 1.02. 55
believe this crack to be in my dread mistress 1.02.322
to me the difference forges dread; 4.04. 17
if guilty dread have left thee so much strength R2 1.01. 73
myself i throw, dread sovereign, at thy foot, 1.01.165
that laid the sentence of dread banishment | on 3.03.134
yield, | rebuke and dread correction wait on us, 1H4 5.01.111
the sin upon my head, dread sovereign! H5 1.02. 97
go, my dread lord, to your great–grandsire's 1.02.103
no note | how dread an army hath enrounded him; 4.pr. 36
with that dread king that took our state upon 2H6 3.02.154
dread lord, the commons send you word by me, 3.02.243
and these dread curses, like the sun 'gainst 3.02.330
a messenger from henry, our dread liege, | to 5.01. 17
thou shalt not dread | the scatt'red foe that 3H6 2.06. 92
be pitiful, dread lord, and grant it then. 3.02. 32
did york's dread curse prevail so much with R3 1.03.190
man | that looks not heavily and full of dread. 2.03. 40
well, my dread lord — so must i call you now. 3.01. 97
mighty moment in't | and consequence of dread, H8 2.04.215
most dread liege, | the good i stand on is my 5.01.121
dread sovereign, how much are we bound to heaven 5.02.149
my most dread sovereign, may it like your grace 5.02.183
as toucheth my particular, | yet, dread priam, TRO 2.02. 10
of a king | so great as our dread father's, in a 2.02. 27
welcome, dread fury, to my woeful house; TIT 5.02. 82
welcome, dread queen; 5.03. 26
time, thou anticipat'st my dread exploits: MAC 4.01.144
my dread lord, | your leave and favor to return HAM 1.02. 50
us, | put your dread pleasures more into command 2.02. 28
hath now this dread and black complexion smear'd 2.02.455
but that the dread of something after death, 3.01. 77
by | th' important acting of your dread command? 3.04.108
thou that duty shall have dread to speak | when LR 1.01.147
from the dread summit of this chalky bourn. 4.06. 57
th' immortal jove's dread clamors counterfeit, OTH 3.03.356
ay, dread queen. ANT 3.03. 8
the truth, and i am come, | i dread, too late. 4.14.127
and make them dread it, to the doers' thrift. CYM 5.01. 15
an angry brow, dread lord. PER 1.02. 52
taint mine eye | with dread sights it may shun. TNK 5.03. 10
to the king god hath his office lent | of dread, STM II.C 99
but having thee at vantage (wondrous dread!) VEN 635
till sable night, mother of dread and fear, LUC 117
arm, | is madly toss'd between desire and dread; 171
o, this dread night, wouldst thou one hour come 965

//DREAD–BOLTED 1 FR 0.0001 REL FR 1 V 0 P
/against /the /deep //dread–bolted /thunder? LR 4.07. 32

DREADED 6 FR 0.0006 REL FR 6 V 0 P
us in full puissance, | need not to be dreaded. 2H4 1.03. 78
that not in the presence | of dreaded justice, COR 3.03. 98
who bids beware | of what is to be dreaded. 4.06. 56
take hold of him | touching this dreaded sight, HAM 1.01. 25
to see perform'd the dreaded act which thou | so ANT 5.02.331
most dreaded amazonian, that hast slain | the TNK 1.01. 78

DREADETH 1 FR 0.0001 REL FR 1 V 0 P
thrives not in the heart that shadows dreadeth, LUC 270

DREADFUL 68 FR 0.0076 REL FR 67 V 1 P
the precursors | o' th' dreadful thunder–claps, TMP 1.02.202
that deep and dreadful organ–pipe, pronounc'd 3.03. 98
a chain | in a most hideous and dreadful manner. WIV 4.04. 34
and it in you more dreadful would have seem'd MM 1.03. 33
i do fear — too dreadful; 1.03. 34
neglect | of his almighty dreadful little might. LLL 3.01.203

lightning bears, thy voice his dreadful thunder, 4.02.115
a lion among ladies, is a most dreadful thing; MND 3.01. 31 P
mark, poor knight, | what dreadful dole is here! 5.01.278
and not one vessel scape the dreadful touch | of MV 3.02.270
this is a dreadful sentence. AWW 3.02. 61
(at least ungentle) of the dreadful neptune, WT 5.01.154
fleet | in dreadful trial of our kingdom's king! JN 2.01.286
like heralds 'twixt two dreadful battles set: 4.02. 78
withhold thy speed, dreadful occasion! 4.02.125
my towns | with dreadful pomp of stout invasion! 4.02.173
the dreadful motion of a murderous thought, 4.02.255
with harsh-resounding trumpets' dreadful bray, R2 1.03.135
see your most dreadful laws so loosely slighted, 2H4 5.02. 94
of this most dreadful preparation, | shake in H5 2.pr. 13
rivets up, | give dreadful note of preparation. 4.pr. 14
unto the french the dreadful judgment day | so 1H6 1.01. 29
day | so dreadful will not be as was his sight. 1.01. 30
the tenth of august last this dreadful lord, 1.01.110
great is the rumor of this dreadful knight, 2.03. 7
shore, | or turn our stern upon a dreadful rock? 2H6 3.02. 91
a dreadful oath, sworn with a solemn tongue! 3.02.158
whose dreadful swords were never drawn in vain, 4.01. 92
a dreadful lay! address thee instantly! 5.02. 27
in dreadful war mayst thou be overcome, | or 3H6 1.01.187
some dreadful story hanging on thy tongue? 2.01. 44
as venom toads, or lizards' dreadful stings. 2.02.138
me, | but dreadful war shall answer his demand. 3.03.259
our dreadful marches to delightful measures. R3 1.01. 8
avaunt, thou dreadful minister of hell! 1.02. 46
what dreadful noise of /waters in /my ears! 1.04. 22
how canst thou urge god's dreadful law to us, 1.04.209
for, by the dreadful pluto, if thou dost not, TRO 4.04.127
thou dreadful ajax, that the appalled air | may 4.05. 4
not the dreadful spout | which shipmen do the 5.02.171
the dreadful sagittary | appalls our numbers. 5.05. 14
yet, | to hover on the dreadful shore of styx? TIT 1.01. 88
the woods are ruthless, dreadful, deaf, and dull 2.01.128
but i have done a thousand dreadful things | as 5.01.141
and in their ears tell them my dreadful name, 5.02. 39
then, dreadful trumpet, sound the general doom, ROM 3.02. 67
send | such dreadful heralds to astonish us. JC 1.03. 56
to thee a man | most like this dreadful night, 1.03. 73
between the acting of a dreadful thing | and the 2.01. 63
so in use, | and dreadful objects so familiar, 3.01.266
i have seen | hours dreadful and things strange; MAC 2.04. 3
there shall be done | a deed of dreadful note. 3.02. 44
to me | in dreadful secrecy impart they did, HAM 1.02.207
or to the dreadful summit of the cliff | that 1.04. 70
anon the dreadful thunder | doth rend the region 2.02.486
that keep this dreadful pudder o'er our heads, LR 3.02. 50
and cry | these dreadful summoners grace. 3.02. 59
hangs one that gathers sampire, dreadful trade! 4.06. 15
silence that dreadful bell, it frights the isle OTH 2.03.175
still | thy deaf'ning, dreadful thunders, gently PER 3.01. 5
and power | i' th' least of these was dreadful, TNK 1.03. 39
methought i heard a dreadful clap of thunder 3.06. 83
gazed, | infusing them with dreadful prophecies: VEN 928
from forth dull sleep by dreadful fancy waking, LUC 450
darkness daunts them with more dreadful sights. 462
"for in the dreadful dead of dark midnight, 1625
being constrain'd with dreadful circumstance? 1703
lightning seems, thy voice his dreadful thunder, PP 5.11

/DREADFULLY 1 FR 0.0001 REL FR 0 V 1 P
/man, /i /am /most /dreadfully /attended. HAM 2.02.269 P

DREADFULLY 2 FR 0.0002 REL FR 1 V 1 P
death no more dreadfully but as a drunken sleep, MM 4.02.143 P
lies, | do tell her she is dreadfully beset, LUC 444

DREADING 4 FR 0.0004 REL FR 4 V 0 P
dreading the curse that money may buy out, | and JN 3.01.164
dreading that her purpose | was of more danger, CYM 5.05.253
dreading my love, the loss whereof still fearing PP 7.10
leaves look pale, dreading the winter's near. SON 97.14

DREADS 2 FR 0.0002 REL FR 2 V 0 P
he dreads his wife. WT 2.03. 80
which dreads not yet their lives' destruction. TIT 2.03. 50

/DREAM 2 FR 0.0002 REL FR 0 V 2 P
/is /merely /the /shadow /of /a /dream. HAM 2.02.259 P
/a /dream /itself /is /but /a /shadow. 2.02.260 P

DREAM 124 FR 0.0140 REL FR 108 V 16 P
and rather like a dream than an assurance | that TMP 1.02. 45
my spirits, as in a dream, are all bound up. 1.02.487
me, that when i wak'd | i cried to dream again. 3.02.143
even in a dream, were we divided from them, 5.01.239
forgive me, that i do not dream on thee, TGV 2.04.172
then never dream on infamy, but go. 2.07. 64
how like a dream is this! 5.04. 26
i'll tell you my dream. WIV 3.03.161 P
is this a dream? 3.05.139 P
alas, | he hath but as offended in a dream! MM 2.02. 4
what is't i dream on? 2.02.178
make thee the father of their idle dream | and 4.01. 63
what, was i married to her in my dream? ERR 2.02.182
if i dream not, thou art aemilia. 5.01.347
good, | if this be not a dream i see and hear. 5.01.377
we will hold it as a dream till it appear itself ADO 1.02. 20 P
are these things spoken, or do i but dream? 4.01. 66
but not for that dream i on this strange course, 4.01.212
can you still dream and pore and thereon look? LLL 4.03.294
four nights will quickly dream away the time; MND 1.01. 8
sound, | swift as a shadow, short as any dream, 1.01.144
what a dream was here! 2.02.147
shall seem a dream and fruitless vision, | and 3.02.371
but as the fierce vexation of a dream. 4.01. 69
it seems to me | that yet we sleep, we dream. 4.01.194
i have had a dream, past the wit of man to say 4.01.205 P
past the wit of man to say what dream it was. 4.01.206 P
an ass, if he go about /t' expound this dream. 4.01.207 P
nor his heart to report, what my dream was. 4.01.214 P
peter quince to write a ballet of this dream. 4.01.215 P
it shall be call'd "bottom's dream," because it 4.01.216 P
of the sun, | following darkness like a dream, 5.01.386
and idle theme, | no more yielding but a dream, 5.01.428
rest, | for i did dream of money-bags to-night. MV 2.05. 18
if that i do not dream, or be not frantic | (as AYL 1.03. 49
even as a flatt'ring dream or worthless fancy. SHR in.1. 44
or do i dream? in.2. 69
these fifteen years you have been in a dream, in.2. 79
speak, | and sits as one new risen from a dream. 4.01.186
that canst not dream | we, poising us in her AWW 2.03.153
'tis, | poor lady, she were better love a dream. TN 2.02. 26
for this night, to bed, and dream on the event. 2.03.176 P
thou hast put him in such a dream, that when the 2.05.193 P
or i am mad, or else this is a dream. 4.01. 61
if it be thus to dream, still let me sleep! 4.01. 63
for ne'er was dream | so like a waking. WT 3.03. 18
i shall have more than you can dream of yet, 4.04.388
this dream of mine — | being now awake, i'll 4.04.448
soul, | to think our former state a happy dream, R2 5.01. 18
away, you rascally althaea's dream, away! 2H4 2.02. 87 P
instruct us, boy, what dream, boy? 2.02. 88 P
fire-brand, and therefore i call him her dream. 2.02. 91 P
but, being awak'd, i do despise my dream. 5.05. 51
by interception which they dream not of. H5 2.02. 7
no, thou proud dream, | that play'st so subtilly 4.01.257
than is in your knowledge to dream of. 4.08. 5 P
it | with sweet rehearsal of my morning's dream. 2H6 1.02. 24
this was my dream, what it doth bode god knows. 1.02. 31
with eleanor, for telling but her dream? 1.02. 52
given | to dream on evil or to work my downfall. 3.01. 73
i did dream to-night | the duke was dumb and 3.02. 31
you were best to go to bed and dream again, | to 5.01.196
why then i do but dream on sovereignty, | like 3H6 3.02.134
i'll make my heaven to dream upon the crown, 3.02.168
unless it be while some tormenting dream R3 1.03.225
what was your dream, my lord? 1.04. 8
no, no, my dream was lengthen'd after life. 1.04. 43
hell, | such terrible impression made my dream. 1.04. 63
stanley did dream the boar did /rase our helms, 3.04. 82
a dream of what thou wast, a garish flag | to be 4.04. 88
dream on thy cousins smothered in the tower. 5.03.146
sleep, | dream of success and happy victory! 5.03.165
dream on, dream on, of bloody deeds and death; 5.03.171
dream on, dream on, of bloody deeds and death; 5.03.171
soft, i did but dream. 5.03.178
o ratcliffe, i have dream'd a fearful dream! 5.03.212
jocund | in the remembrance of so fair a dream. 5.03.233
and then let's dream | who's best in favor. H8 1.04.107
if i do dream, would all my wealth would wake me TIT 2.04. 13
it is an /honor that i dream not of. ROM 1.03. 66
i dreamt a dream to-night. 1.04. 50
in bed asleep, while they do dream things true. 1.04. 52
lovers' brains, and then they dream of love; 1.04. 71
knees, that dream on cur'sies straight; 1.04. 72
lawyers' fingers, who straight dream on fees; 1.04. 73
o'er ladies' lips, who straight on kisses dream, 1.04. 74
being in night, all this is but a dream, | too 2.02.140
strange dream, that gives a dead man leave to 5.01. 7
or did i dream it so? 5.03. 79
or to live | but in a dream of friendship, | to TIM 4.02. 34
is | like a phantasma or a hideous dream. JC 2.01. 65
this dream is all amiss interpreted, | it was a 2.02. 83
this by calphurnia's dream is signified. 2.02. 90
didst thou dream, lucius, that thou so criedst 4.03.295
co-leagued with this dream of his advantage, HAM 1.02. 21
understanding of himself, | i cannot dream of. 2.02. 10
here, | but in a fiction, in a dream of passion, 2.02.552
die, to sleep, | to sleep, perchance to dream! 3.01. 64
yes, that, on every dream, | each buzz, each LR 1.04.324
if ever i did dream of such a matter, | abhor me OTH 1.01. 5
this accident is not unlike my dream, | belief 1.01.142
if consequence do but approve my dream, | my 2.03. 62
nay, this was but his dream. 3.03.427
'tis a shrewd doubt, though it be but a dream, 3.03.429
that so fairly shows) | dream of impediment! ANT 2.02.145
that he should dream, | knowing all measures, 3.13. 34
if not, | let her lie still and dream. CYM 2.03. 65
to break it with a fearful dream of him, | and 3.04. 43
i hope i dream; 4.02.297
dream often so, | and never false. 4.02.352
on greatness' favor dream as i have done, | wake 5.04.128
many dream not to find, neither deserve, | and 5.04.130
'tis still a dream, or else such stuff as madmen 5.04.145
did you ever dream of such a thing? PER 4.05. 5 P
this is the rarest dream that e'er dull'd sleep 5.01.161
awake, and tell thy dream. 5.01.249
hast felt what sorrow was, | dream how i suffer! TNK 2.02.277
what | hath wak'd us from our dream? 5.04. 48
for unstain'd thoughts do seldom dream on evil; LUC 87
a dream, a breath, a froth of fleeting joy. 212
"if collatinus dream of my intent, | will he not 218
by this starts collatine as from a dream, | and 1772
thus have i had thee as a dream doth flatter: SON 87.13
woe, | before, a joy propos'd, behind, a dream. 129.12

DREAM'D 11 FR 0.0012 REL FR 10 V 1 P
gentlemen, i have dream'd to-night; WIV 3.03.161 P
or have i dream'd till now? SHR in.2. 69
they say that i have dream'd | and slept above in.2. 112
of ill-doing, nor dream'd | that any did. WT 1.02. 70
a bastard by polixenes, | and i but dream'd it. 3.02. 84
what dream'd my lord? 2H6 1.02. 23
o ratcliffe, i have dream'd a fearful dream! R3 5.03.212
that | we are a queen (or long have dream'd so), H8 2.04. 71
one that ne'er dream'd a joy beyond his pleasure 3.01.135
what have you dream'd of late of this war's CYM 4.02.345
that ever dream'd, or vow'd her maidenhead | to TNK 2.04. 13

DREAMER 3 FR 0.0003 REL FR 3 V 0 P
thou idle dreamer, wherefore didst thou so? JN 4.02.153
ant, | of the dreamer merlin and his prophecies, 1H4 3.01.148
he is a dreamer, let us leave him. pass. JC 1.02. 24

DREAMERS 1 FR 0.0001 REL FR 1 V 0 P
that dreamers often lie. ROM 1.04. 51

DREAMING 11 FR 0.0012 REL FR 10 V 1 P
and then, in dreaming, | the clouds methought TMP 3.02.140
dreaming on both, for all thy blessed youth MM 3.01. 34
that creep into the dreaming bridegroom's ear, MV 3.02. 52
stay we no longer, dreaming of renown, | but 3H6 2.01.199
who (but for dreaming on this fond exploit) R3 5.03.330
and dreaming night will hide our joys no longer, TRO 4.02. 10
this foolish, dreaming, superstitious girl 5.03. 79
were one such, | it's past the size of dreaming. ANT 5.02. 97
dreaming of another world and a better; TNK 4.03. 5 P
ditty, | and drives away dark dreaming night. PP 14.20
of the wide world, dreaming on things to come, SON 107. 2

DREAM'S 1 FR 0.0001 REL FR 1 V 0 P
the dream's here still; CYM 4.02.306

/DREAMS 2 FR 0.0002 REL FR 0 V 2 P
/were /it /not /that /i /have /bad /dreams. HAM 2.02.256 P
/which /dreams /indeed /are /ambition, /for /the 2.02.257 P

DREAMS 45 FR 0.0050 REL FR 44 V 1 P
we are such stuff | as dreams are made on; TMP 4.01.157
she dreams on him that has forgot her love; TGV 4.04. 81
as due to love as thoughts and dreams and sighs, MND 1.01.154
him, | and by the way let's recount our dreams. 4.01.199
and when he says he is, say that he dreams, SHR in.1. 64
and banish hence these abject lowly dreams. in.2. 32
i would be loath to fall into my dreams again. in.2. 126 P
communicat'st with dreams (how can this be?), WT 1.02.140
my life stands in the level of your dreams, 3.02. 81
your actions are my dreams. 3.02. 82
dreams are toys, | yet for this once, yea, 3.03. 39
shall bring him that | which he not dreams of. 4.04.180
possess'd with rumors, full of idle dreams, JN 4.02.145
by day, by night, waking and in my dreams, | in 2H6 1.01. 26
my troublous dreams this night doth make me sad. 1.02. 22
next time i'll keep my dreams unto myself, | and 1.02. 53
the first i warrant thee, if dreams prove true. 5.01.195
by drunken prophecies, libels, and dreams, | to R3 1.01. 33
he hearkens after prophecies and dreams, | and 1.01. 54
so full of fearful dreams, of ugly sights, 1.04. 3
and for his dreams, i wonder he's so simple | to 3.02. 26
but with his timorous dreams was still awak'd. 4.01. 84
the sweetest sleep and fairest-boding dreams 5.03.227
let not our babbling dreams affright our souls; 5.03.308
madam, such good dreams | possess your fancy. H8 4.02. 93
you are for dreams and slumbers, brother priest, TRO 2.02. 37
my dreams will sure prove ominous to the day. 5.03. 6
and then dreams he of smelling out a suit; ROM 1.04. 78
asleep, | then he dreams of another benefice. 1.04. 81
and then dreams he of cutting foreign throats, 1.04. 83
true, i talk of dreams, | which are the children 1.04. 96
my dreams presage some joyful news at hand. 5.01. 2
opinion he held once | of fantasy, of dreams, JC 2.01.197
caesar's wife shall meet with better dreams." 2.02. 99
and wicked dreams abuse | the curtain'd sleep; MAC 2.01. 50
in the affliction of these terrible dreams 3.02. 18
for in that sleep of death what dreams may come, HAM 3.01. 65
he dreams; ANT 2.01. 19
you laugh when boys or women tell their dreams; 5.02. 74
nor cymbeline dreams that they are alive. CYM 3.03. 81
he spake of her, as dian had hot dreams, | and 5.05.180
not dreams we stand before your puissance, TNK 1.01.155
thoughts are but dreams till their effects be LUC 353
but when i sleep, in dreams they look on thee, SON 43. 3
nights bright days when dreams do show thee me. 43.14

DREAM'ST 4 FR 0.0004 REL FR 3 V 1 P
are other troyans that thou dream'st not of, the 1H4 2.01. 70 P
that never dream'st on aught but butcheries. R3 1.02.100
look how thou dream'st! 4.02. 56
thou | so little dream'st upon my fortune that TNK 3.01. 24

DREAMT 21 FR 0.0023 REL FR 17 V 4 P
you strange news that you yet dreamt not of. ADO 1.02. 4 P
she hath often dreamt of unhappiness and wak'd 2.01.345 P
ignorant a kind of fear | before not dreamt of. 1H4 4.01. 75
althaea dreamt she was deliver'd of a fire-brand 2H4 2.02. 89 P
i have long dreamt of such a kind of man, | so 5.05. 49
he dreamt the boar had rased off his helm. R3 3.02. 11
for i have dreamt | of bloody turbulence, and TRO 5.03. 10
thy wife hath dreamt, thy mother hath had 5.03. 63
dreamt of encounters 'twixt thyself and me; COR 4.05.123
i dreamt a dream to-night. ROM 1.04. 50
i dreamt my lady came and found me dead — 5.01. 6
here, | i dreamt my master and another fought, 5.03.138
i dreamt of a silver basin and ew'r to-night. TIM 3.01. 6 P
she dreamt to-night she saw my statue, | which, JC 2.02. 76
i dreamt to-night that i did feast with caesar, 3.03. 1
i dreamt last night of the three weird sisters: MAC 2.01. 20
than are dreamt of in your philosophy. HAM 1.05.167
i dreamt there was an emperor antony. ANT 5.02. 76
or might be such a man | as this i dreamt of? 5.02. 94
who dreamt? PER 3.ch. 38
have spoke so well, ne'er dreamt thou couldst. 4.06.103

DREARY 1 FR 0.0001 REL FR 1 V 0 P
my lord, to step out of these dreary dumps, TIT 1.01.391

DREG 1 FR 0.0001 REL FR 0 V 1 P
what too curious dreg espies my sweet lady in TRO 3.02. 65 P

DREGG'D 1 FR 0.0001 REL FR 1 V 0 P
when that his action's dregg'd with mind assur'd TNK 1.02. 97

DREGS 7 FR 0.0008 REL FR 3 V 4 P
here shroud till the dregs of the storm be past. TMP 2.02. 40 P
some certain dregs of conscience are yet within R3 1.04.121 P
more dregs than water, if my /fears have eyes. TRO 3.02. 67 P
up | the lees and dregs of a flat tamed piece; 4.01. 63
and turn the dregs of it upon this varlet here COR 5.02. 77 P
friendship's full of dregs; TIM 1.02.233
so then thou hast but lost the dregs of life, SON 74. 9

DRENCH 5 FR 0.0005 REL FR 4 V 1 P
"give my roan horse a drench," says he, and 1H4 2.04.107 P
water, | a drench for sur-rein'd jades, their H5 3.05. 19
so do our vulgar drench their peasant limbs | in 4.07. 77
and in that sea of blood my boy did drench | his 1H6 4.07. 14
to drench the capitol, but that they would ANT 2.06. 18

DRENCH'D 5 FR 0.0005 REL FR 4 V 1 P
being, as they were, drench'd in the sea, hold TMP 2.01. 63 P
and drench'd me in the sea, where i am drown'd. TGV 1.03. 79
spout | till you have drench'd our steeples, LR 3.02. 3
or in the ocean drench'd, or in the fire? VEN 494
tears, that his wound wept, /was drench'd. 1054

DRENCHED 2 FR 0.0002 REL FR 2 V 0 P
their drenched natures lies as in a death, MAC 1.07. 68
so she, deep drenched in a sea of care, | holds LUC 1100

DRESS 20 FR 0.0022 REL FR 12 V 8 P
scour, dress meat and drink, make the beds, and WIV 1.04. 96 P
we'll come dress you straight. 4.02. 82 P
let's go dress him like the witch of brainford. 4.02. 98 P
of their growth, we'll dress | like urchins, 4.04. 49
dress him in my apparel and make him my ADO 2.01. 34 P
help to dress me, good coz, good meg, good 3.04. 98 P
and help to dress your sister's chamber up. SHR 3.01. 83
how diligent i am | to dress thy meat myself, 4.03. 40
old adam's likeness, set to dress this garden, R2 3.04. 73
wherein the noble youth did dress themselves: 2H4 2.03. 22
prove that ever i dress myself handsome till thy 2.04.279 P
had not been here to dress the ugly form | of 4.01. 39

that we should dress us fairly for our end. H5 4.01. 10
the clothier means to dress the commonwealth, 2H6 4.02. 5 P
come safe off, | we'll dress him up in voices; TRO 1.03.381
why do you dress me | in borrowed robes? MAC 1.03.108
till i shall see you in your soldier's dress, ANT 2.04. 4
a dish for the gods, if the devil dress her not. 5.02.274 P
boys, we'll go dress our hunt. CYM 3.06. 89
green, | robbing no old to dress his beauty new, SON 68.12
DRESS'D 16 FR 0.0018 REL FR 14 V 2 P
lent him our terror, dress'd him with our love, MM 1.01. 19
man, | dress'd in a little brief authority, 2.02.118
with purpose to be dress'd in an opinion | of MV 1.01. 91
and see him dress'd in all suits like a lady; SHR in.1. 106
what dish a' poison has she dress'd him! TN 2.05.112 P
sir toby, because we'll be dress'd together. 5.01.205 P
that he had not so trimm'd and dress'd his land R2 3.04. 56
that horse that i so carefully have dress'd! 5.05. 80
there a certain lord, neat, and trimly dress'd, 1H4 1.03. 33
and dress'd myself in such humility | that i did 3.02. 51
beard, | as he being dress'd to some oration." TRO 1.03.166
what, dress'd, and in your clothes, and down ROM 4.05. 12
the hope drunk | wherein you dress'd yourself? MAC 1.07. 36
th' abilities | that rhodes is dress'd in — if OTH 1.03. 26
gentlemen, let's go see poor cassio dress'd. 5.01.124
when proud-pied april (dress'd in all his trim) SON 98. 2
DRESSER 1 FR 0.0001 REL FR 1 V 0 P
bring it from the dresser | and serve it thus to SHR 4.01.163
DRESSING 1 FR 0.0001 REL FR 1 V 0 P
so all my best is dressing old words new, SON 76.11
DRESSINGS 2 FR 0.0002 REL FR 2 V 0 P
in all his dressings, caracts, titles, forms, MM 5.01. 56
they are but dressings of a former sight. SON 123. 4
DREW 39 FR 0.0044 REL FR 36 V 3 P
how near the god drew to the complexion of a WIV 5.05. 7 P
drew me from kind embracements of my spouse; ERR 1.01. 43
namely, some love that drew him oft from home. 5.01. 56
mart, | and thereupon i drew my sword on you; 5.01.263
in mulberry shade, | his dagger drew, and died. MND 5.01.149
the poet | did feign that orpheus drew trees, MV 5.01. 80
and then he drew a dial from his poke, | and, AYL 2.07. 20
he did me kindness, sir, drew on my side, | but TN 5.01. 66
a witchcraft drew me hither: 5.01. 76
town, | drew to defend him when he was beset; 5.01. 85
you drew your sword upon me without cause, | but 5.01.188
but nature to her bias drew in that. 5.01.260
which so drew the rest of the herd to me that WT 4.04.608 P
before i drew this gallant head of war, | and JN 5.02.113
drew priam's curtain in the dead of night, | and 2H4 1.01. 72
'a drew a good bow, and dead! 3.02. 43 P
bastard orleance, that drew blood | from thee, 1H6 4.06. 16
leave off to wonder why i drew you hither | into 3H6 4.05. 2
yet from my dugs he drew not this deceit. R3 2.02. 30
and when /mine oratory drew /to /an end, | i bid 3.07. 20
the articles o' th' combination drew | as H8 1.01.169
that in your country's service drew your swords, TIT 1.01.175
hand, | and when i had it, drew myself apart, 5.01.112
i drew to part them. ROM 1.01.108
the tomb, | and by and by my master drew on him, 5.03.284
drew from my heart all love, | and added to the LR 1.04.269
of this /dread exploit, | drew on me here again. 2.02.124
having more man than wit about me, drew. 2.04. 42
he was born | drew all such humors from him. OTH 3.04. 31
true reports | that drew their swords with you. ANT 2.02. 48
on his hook, which he | with fervency drew up. 2.05. 18
my lord your son drew on my master. CYM 1.01.160
drew sleep out of mine eyes, blood from my PER 1.02. 96
and backward drew | the heavenly moisture, that VEN 541
which the conceited painter drew so proud, | as LUC 1371
the well-skill'd workman this mild image drew 1520
and from the purple fountain brutus drew | the 1734
a thousand favors from a maund she drew, | of LC 36
towards this afflicted fancy fastly drew, | and, 61
DREW'ST 1 FR 0.0001 REL FR 1 V 0 P
and with thy scorns drew'st rivers from his eyes R3 1.03.175
DRIBBLING 1 FR 0.0001 REL FR 1 V 0 P
believe not that the dribbling dart of love MM 1.03. 2
/DRIED 1 FR 0.0001 REL FR 1 V 0 P
/cannot /draw /a /cart, /nor /eat /dried /oats, LR 5.03. 38
DRIED 15 FR 0.0017 REL FR 8 V 7 P
wits till i were as crestfall'n as a dried pear. WIV 4.05.100 P
have i laid my brain in the sun and dried it, 5.05.135 P
and dried not one of them with his comfort; MM 3.01.225 P
time hath not yet so dried this blood of mine, ADO 4.01.193
had rather have a handful or two of dried peas. MND 4.01. 37 P
in a neat's tongue dried and a maid not vendible MV 1.01.112
i tell thee, kate, 'twas burnt and dried away, SHR 4.01.170
and great seas have dried | when miracles have AWW 2.01.140
of those seven are dried by nature's course, R2 1.02. 14
you /eel-skin, you dried neat's tongue, you 1H4 2.04.245 P
lives upon mouldy stew'd pruins and dried cakes. 2H4 2.04.147 P
my mercy dried their water-flowing tears; 3H6 4.08. 43
without his roe, like a dried herring: ROM 2.04. 37 P
which, being dried with grief, will break to ANT 4.09. 17
scarce had the sun dried up the dewy morn, | and PP 6. 1
DRIER 2 FR 0.0002 REL FR 2 V 0 P
being destin'd to a drier death on shore. TGV 1.01.150
sirrah, fetch drier logs. ROM 4.04. 16
DRIES 4 FR 0.0004 REL FR 3 V 1 P
dries me there all the foolish and dull and 2H4 4.03. 97 P
the blood upon your visage dries, 'tis time | it COR 1.09. 93
the which my current runs | or else dries up: OTH 4.02. 60
dries up his oil to lend the world his light. VEN 756
DRIFT 19 FR 0.0021 REL FR 17 V 2 P
the sole drift of my purpose doth extend | not a TMP 5.01. 29
as thou hast lent me wit to plot this drift. TGV 2.06. 43
to cross my friend in his intended drift, | than 3.01. 18
that you shall say my cunning drift excels. 4.02. 83
o, understand my drift. WIV 2.02.242 P
and hold you ever to our special drift, | though MM 4.05. 4
what is the course and drift of your compact? ERR 2.02.161
go in with me, and i will tell you my drift. ADO 2.01.387 P
shall rain their drift of bullets on this town. JN 2.01.412
rise, | and yet the king not privy to my drift, 3H6 1.02. 46
it is familiar — but at the author's drift, TRO 3.03.113
we know your drift. speak what? COR 3.03.116
be plain, good son, and homely in thy drift, ROM 2.03. 55
shall romeo by my letters know our drift, | and 4.01.114
my free drift | halts not particularly, but TIM 1.01. 45
by this encompassment and drift of question HAM 2.01. 10
marry, sir, here's my drift, | and i believe it 2.01. 37
an' can you by no drift of conference | get from 3.01. 1
fail, | and that our drift look through our bad 4.07.151
DRIFT-WINDS 1 FR 0.0001 REL FR 1 V 0 P
with waters | that drift-winds force to raging. TNK 5.03.100
DRILY 1 FR 0.0001 REL FR 0 V 1 P
pears, it looks ill, it eats drily, marry, 'tis AWW 1.01.162 P
/DRINK 3 FR 0.0003 REL FR 3 V 0 P
/constrain'd | /as /men /drink /potions, /that 2H4 1.01.197
/here /is /no /drink! TIT 3.02. 35
/she /drinks /no /other /drink /but /tears, 3.02. 37
DRINK 161 FR 0.0182 REL FR 94 V 67 P
sea-water shalt thou drink; TMP 1.02.463
but that the poor monster's in drink. 2.02.158 P
when the butt is out, we will drink water — not 3.02. 2 P
servant-monster, drink to me. 3.02. 3 P
drink, servant-monster, when i bid thee. 3.02. 8 P
he shall drink nought but brine, for i'll not 3.02. 66
i drink the air before me, and return | or ere 5.01.102
daughter, carry the wine in, we'll drink within. WIV 1.01.189 P
i hope we shall drink down all unkindness. 1.01.196 P
that's meat and drink to me, now. 1.01.294 P
he was gotten in drink. 1.03. 22 P
scour, dress meat and drink, make the beds, and 1.04. 97 P
knight falstaff, and drink canary with him. 3.02. 88 P
i think i shall drink in pipe-wine first with 3.02. 89 P
but, whilst i live, forget to drink after thee. MM 1.02. 39 P
a thirsty evil, and when we drink we die. 1.02.130
have all the world drink brown and white bastard 3.02. 3 P
their abominable and beastly touches | i drink, 3.02. 25
drink some wine ere you go; fare you well. ADO 3.05. 53 P
they are thirsty, fools would fain have drink. LLL 5.02.372
and sometime make the drink to bear no barm, MND 2.01. 38
but i will not eat with you, drink with you, nor MV 1.03. 37 P
the duke will drink under this tree. AYL 2.05. 32 P
out of thy mouth that i may drink thy tidings. 3.02.203 P
it is meat and drink to me to see a clown. 5.01. 10 P
for it is a figure in rhetoric that drink, being 5.01. 41 P
please your /lordship drink a cup of sack? SHR in.2. 2
strive mightily, but eat and drink as friends. 1.02.277
dine with my father, drink a health to me, | for 3.02.196
hold thee that to drink. 4.04. 17
you shall not choose but drink before you go. 5.01. 11
but i will eat and drink, and sleep as soft | as AWW 4.03.332
these clothes are good enough to drink in, and TN 1.03. 11 P
i'll drink to her as long as there is a passage 1.03. 39 P
is a passage in my throat and drink in illyria. 1.03. 40 P
that will not drink to my niece till his brains 1.03. 41 P
your hand to th' butt'ry-bar, and let it drink. 1.03. 70 P
madonna, that drink and good counsel will amend; 1.05. 43 P
for give the dry fool drink, then is the fool 1.05. 44 P
for he's in the third degree of drink, he's 1.05.135 P
let us therefore eat and drink. 2.03. 14 P
as good a deed as to drink when a man's a-hungry 2.03.126 P
but if he had not been in drink, he would have 5.01.193 P
the cup | a spider steep'd, and one may drink; WT 2.01. 40
near these eyes, would drink my tears, | and JN 4.01. 62
if i dare eat, or drink, or breathe, or live, R2 4.01. 73
they breath'd and three times did they drink, 1H4 1.03.102
not as good deed as drink to break the pate on 2.01. 29 P
and speak sooner than drink, and drink sooner 2.01. 78 P
sooner than drink, and drink sooner than pray; 2.01. 78 P
not as good a deed as drink to turn true man and 2.02. 22 P
take a cold, to sleep, to drink, but i tell you, 2.03. 9 P
that i can drink with any tinker in his own 2.04. 19 P
why then your brown bastard is your only drink! 2.04. 74 P
i do not speak to thee in drink but in tears; 2.04.415 P
is he good, but to taste sack and drink it? 2.04.455 P
come, i'll drink no proofs nor no bullets. 2H4 2.04.118 P
i'll drink no more than will do me good, for no 2.04.119 P
come, i will go drink with you, but i cannot 3.02.191 P
let's drink together friendly and embrace, 4.02. 63
word, | and thereupon i drink unto your grace. 4.02. 68
this present peace, | you would drink freely. 4.02. 75
for thin drink doth so over-cool their blood, 4.03. 91 P
have you a ruffin that will swear, drink, dance, 4.05.124
what you want in meat, we'll have in drink, but 5.03. 28 P
and drink unto /thee, leman mine, | and a merry 5.03. 47
i'll drink to master bardolph, and to all the 5.03. 58 P
this would drink deep. H5 1.01. 20
'twould drink the cup and all. 1.01. 20
say | this quarrel will drink blood another day. 1H6 2.04.133
horner, i drink to you in a cup of sack; 2H6 2.03. 59 P
drink, and fear not your man. 2.03. 65 P
here, peter, i drink to thee, and be not afraid. 2.03. 68 P
drink, and pray for me, i pray you, for i think 2.03. 72 P
poison be their drink! 3.02.321
give me some drink, and bid the apothecary 3.03. 17
and i will make it felony to drink small beer. 4.02. 67 P
all shall eat and drink on my score, and i will 4.02. 73 P
serv'd me instead of a quart pot to drink in; 4.10. 14 P
his cold thin drink out of his leather bottle, 3H6 2.05. 48
i speak, | ye see i drink the water of my eye. 5.04. 75
gramercy, fellow. there, drink that for me. R3 3.02.106
we give to thee our guiltless blood to drink. 3.03. 14
root, thus hack'd, | the air will drink the sap. H8 1.02. 98
a dozen healths | to drink to these fair ladies, 1.04.106
which his own will shall have desire to drink. TRO 3.03. 46
would drink up | the lees and dregs of a flat 4.01. 62
if the drink you give me touch my palate COR 2.01. 55 P
but we will drink together; 5.03.203
so thou refuse to drink my dear sons' blood. TIT 3.01. 22
i wot, | thy napkin cannot drink a tear of mine, 3.01.140
and this distilling liquor drink thou off, ROM 4.01. 94
here's drink — i drink to thee. 4.03. 58
here's drink — i drink to thee. 4.03. 58
in any liquid thing you will | and drink it off, 5.01. 78
stirrup, and through him | drink the free air. TIM 1.01. 83
a huge man, i should fear to drink at meals, 1.02. 50 P
great men should drink with harness on their 1.02. 52
to forget their faults, i drink to you. 1.02.107 P
thou weep'st to make them drink, timon. 1.02.109 P
and spend our flatteries to drink those men 1.02.137
us, | his days are foul and his drink dangerous. 3.05. 73
thy flatterers yet wear silk, drink wine, lie 4.03.206
can you eat roots and drink cold water? 5.01. 74
alas, it cried, "give me some drink, titinius," JC 1.02.127
i cannot drink too much of brutus' love. 4.03.162
go bid thy mistress, when my drink is ready, MAC 2.01. 31
and drink, sir, is a great provoker of three 2.03. 25 P
what three things does drink especially provoke? 2.03. 26 P
therefore much drink may be said to be an 2.03. 31 P
i believe drink gave thee the lie last night. 2.03. 37 P
anon we'll drink a measure | the table round. 3.04. 11
i drink to th' general joy o' th' whole table, 3.04. 88
were the slaves of drink and thralls of sleep? 3.06. 13
we'll teach you to drink /deep ere you depart. HAM 1.02.175
with drink, sir? 3.02.302 P
now could i drink hot blood, | and do such 3.02.390
and that he calls for drink, i'll have preferr'd 4.07.159
till that her garments, heavy with their drink, 4.07.181
woo't drink up eisel, eat a crocadile? 5.01.276
the king shall drink to hamlet's better breath, 5.02.271
stay, give me drink. 5.02.282
gertrude, do not drink. 5.02.290
i dare not drink yet, madam; by and by. 5.02.293
no, no, the drink, the drink — o my dear hamlet 5.02.309
no, the drink, the drink — o my dear hamlet — 5.02.309
o my dear hamlet — | the drink, the drink! 5.02.310
o my dear hamlet — | the drink, the drink! 5.02.310
damned dane, | drink off this potion! 5.02.326
leave thy drink and thy whore, | and keep in a' LR 1.04.124
if you have poison for me, i will drink it. 4.07. 71
our friends — but one cup, i'll drink for you. OTH 2.03. 38 P
why then let a soldier drink." 2.03. 73
and your swag-bellied hollander — drink ho! 2.03. 78 P
a double set | if drink rock not his cradle. 2.03.131
a beggar in his drink | could not have laid such 4.02.120
wine enough, | cleopatra's health to drink. ANT 1.02. 13
thou didst drink | the stale of horses and the 1.04. 61
ha, ha! | give me to drink mandragora. 1.05. 4
they have made him drink alms-drink. 2.07. 5 P
them to his entreaty, and himself to th' drink. 2.07. 8 P
desist, and drink. 2.07. 80
drink thou; increase the reels. 2.07. 94
all, four days, | than drink so much in one. 2.07.103
egyptian bacchanals | and celebrate our drink? 2.07.105
and drink carouses to the next day's fate, 4.08. 34
sir, i will eat no meat, i'll not drink, sir; 5.02. 49
be enclouded, | and forc'd to drink their vapor. 5.02.213
with mine eyes i'll drink the words you send, CYM 1.01.100
of meat, depart reeling with too much drink; 5.04.162 P
mistress' lips — | we drink this health to you. PER 2.03. 52
say we drink this standing-bowl of wine to him. 2.03. 65
here, sir, drink — | i know you are faint — TNK 3.03. 6
drink a good hearty draught, it breeds good 3.03. 17
her, /carve her, drink to her, and still among 4.03. 88 P
more thirst for drink than she for this good VEN 92
his nostrils drink the air, and forth again | as 273
"dost thou drink tears, that thou provok'st such 949
mud not the fountain that gave drink to thee, LUC 577
whilst like a willing patient i will drink SON 111. 9
drink up the monarch's plague, this flattery? 114. 2
/DRINKING 1 FR 0.0001 REL FR 1 V 0 P
/drinking /my /griefs, /whilst /you /mount /up R2 4.01.189
DRINKING 24 FR 0.0027 REL FR 4 V 20 P
this can sack an- drinking do. TMP 3.02. 80 P
told you, sir, they were red-hot with drinking, 4.01.171
friar, till eating and drinking be put down. MM 3.02.103 P
you rogue, i have been drinking all night, i am 4.03. 43 P
i have been drinking hard all night, and i will 4.03. 53 P
with love than i will get again with drinking, ADO 1.01.251 P
and seem'd to ask him sops as he was drinking. SHR 3.02.176
that quaffing and drinking will undo you. TN 1.03. 14 P
with drinking healths to my niece. 1.03. 38 P
if sir toby would leave drinking, thou wert as 1.05. 27 P
think it rather consists of eating and drinking. 2.03. 12 P
is numb'ring sands and drinking oceans dry; R2 2.02.146
art so fat-witted with drinking of old sack, and 1H4 1.02. 2 P
they call drinking deep, dyeing scarlet, and 2.04. 15 P
glasses, is the only drinking, and for thy walls 2H4 2.01.143 P
endeavor of drinking good and good store of 4.03.121 P
come, leave your drinking, and fall to blows. 2H6 2.03. 79 P
ay, or drinking, fencing, swearing, quarrelling, HAM 2.01. 25
have very poor and unhappy brains for drinking. OTH 2.03. 34 P
your /englishman so exquisite in his drinking? 2.03. 81 P
i had rather heat my liver with drinking. ANT 1.02. 24 P
and made the night light with drinking. 2.02.178 P
my part, i am sorry it is turn'd to a drinking. 2.06.104 P
without appetite, save often drinking, dreaming TNK 4.03. 5 P
DRINKINGS 1 FR 0.0001 REL FR 0 V 1 P
and to drinkings and swearings and starings, WIV 5.05.159 P
/DRINKS 1 FR 0.0001 REL FR 1 V 0 P
/she /drinks /no /other /drink /but /tears, TIT 3.02. 37
DRINKS 17 FR 0.0019 REL FR 10 V 7 P
for he that drinks all night, and is hang'd MM 4.03. 45 P
and when she drinks, against her lips i bob, MND 2.01. 49
we will give you sleepy drinks, that your senses WT 1.01. 14 P
and drinks off candles' ends for flap-dragons, 2H4 2.04.246 P
laugh, but that's no marvel, he drinks no wine. 4.03. 89 P
troubles the silver spring where england drinks. 2H6 4.01. 72
and how his silence drinks up his applause! TRO 2.03.201
dry sorrow drinks our blood. ROM 3.05. 59
he ne'er drinks | but timon's silver treads upon TIM 3.02. 70
no jocund health that denmark drinks to-day, HAM 1.02.125
to earth, | "now the king drinks to hamlet." 5.02.278
drinks the green mantle of the standing pool; LR 3.04.133 P
the wine she drinks is made of grapes. OTH 2.01.251 P
why, he drinks you, with facility, your dane 2.03. 82 P
he fishes, drinks, and wastes | the lamps of ANT 1.04. 4
what he breathes out his breath drinks up again. LUC 1666
and my great mind most kingly drinks it up: SON 114.10
DRINK'ST 2 FR 0.0002 REL FR 2 V 0 P
what drink'st thou oft, in stead of homage sweet H5 4.01.250
which this blood drink'st, revenge his death! R3 1.02. 63
DRIVE 37 FR 0.0041 REL FR 26 V 11 P
were down, i could drive the boat with my sighs. TGV 2.03. 53 P
i could drive her then from the ward of her WIV 2.02.248 P
hand | than to drive liking to the name of love. ADO 1.01.300
here's that shall drive some of them to a 3.05. 62 P
but none can drive him from the envious plea MV 3.02.282
state, | which humbleness may drive unto a fine. 4.01.372
it i | that drive thee from the sportive court, AWW 3.02.106
notable report of valor, and drive the gentleman TN 3.04.192 P
bell, book, and candle shall not drive me back, JN 3.03. 12

nay, hear me, hubert, drive these men away, 4.01. 78
to drive away the heavy thought of care? R2 3.04. 2
ned, to drive away the time till falstaff come, 1H4 2.04. 28 P
and drive all thy subjects afore thee like a 2.04.137 P
four rogues in buckrom let drive at me — 2.04.196 P
green came at my back and let drive at me, for 2.04.223 P
and god forbid a shallow scratch should drive 5.04. 11
he will drive you out of your revenge and turn 2H4 2.04.297 P
i shall drive you then to confess the willful 2.04.311 P
and drive the english forth the bounds of france 1H6 1.02. 54
drive them from orleance and be immortaliz'd. 1.02.148
i will not slay thee, but i'll drive thee back. 1.03. 41
drive you to break your necks or hang yourselves 5.04. 91
should drive upon thy new–transformed limbs, TIT 2.03. 64
east, | a troubled mind drive me to walk abroad, ROM 1.01.120
so soon we shall drive back | of alcibiades th' TIM 5.01.163
and drive away the vulgar from the streets; JC 1.01. 70
the tarquin drive when he was call'd a king. 2.01. 54
and drive his purpose into these delights. HAM 3.01. 27
of me, as if you would drive me into a toil? 3.02.347 P
plain, | i'ld drive ye cackling home to camelot. LR 2.02. 84
and drive toward dover, friend, where thou shalt 3.06. 91
let his shames quickly | drive him to rome. ANT 1.04. 73
she | from egypt drive her all–disgraced friend, 3.12. 22
a dram of this | will drive away distemper. CYM 3.04.191
may drive us to a render | where we have liv'd, 4.04. 11
amazement shall drive courage from the state, PER 1.02. 26
to drive infection from the dangerous year! VEN 508
DRIVELLING 1 FR 0.0001 REL FR 0 V 1 P
for this drivelling love is like a great natural ROM 2.04. 91 P
DRIVEN *(also droven)*
DRIVEN 18 FR 0.0020 REL FR 14 V 4 P
driven out of doors with it when i go from home, ERR 4.04. 35 P
know into what straits of fortune she is driven, AYL 5.02. 65 P
i am driven on by the flesh, and he must needs AWW 1.03. 29 P
lawn as white as driven snow, | cypress black as WT 4.04.218
and driven into despair an enemy's hope, | who R2 2.02. 47
are from their hives and houses driven away. 1H6 1.05. 24
tide, | so am i driven by breath of her renown, 5.05. 7
but now is cade driven back, his men dispers'd, 2H6 4.09. 34
i saw our party to their trenches driven, | and COR 1.06. 12
either led or driven, as we point the way; JC 4.01. 23
lost, | a sister driven into desp'rate terms, HAM 4.07. 26
and must be driven | to find out practices of OTH 1.03.101
and after shipwrack driven upon this shore. PER 2.03. 85
we'll have no more gentlemen driven away. 4.06.129 P
where, driven before the winds, he is arriv'd 5.ch. 14
the matter's too far driven between him | and TNK 2.03. 43
what pushes are we wenches driven to | when 2.04. 6
hot scent–snuffing hounds are driven to doubt, VEN 692
DRIVES 16 FR 0.0018 REL FR 14 V 2 P
or as one nail by strength drives out another, TGV 2.04.193
what error drives our eyes and ears amiss? ERR 2.02.184
and he must needs go that the devil drives. AWW 1.03. 30 P
this drives me to entreat you | that presently 2.05. 63
a kind of injunction drives me to these habits TN 2.05.169 P
drives him beyond the bounds of patience. 1H4 1.03.200
drives back our troops and conquers as she lists 1H6 1.05. 22
of my alleged reasons, drives this forward. H8 2.04.226
one fire drives out one fire; COR 4.07. 54
as fire drives out fire, so pity pity — | hath JC 3.01.171
pyrrhus at priam drives, in rage strikes wide, HAM 2.02.472
which drives | o'er your content these strong ANT 3.06. 82
dives, | so up and down the poor ship drives. PER 3.ch. 50
understand, | if e'er this coffin drives a–land, 3.02. 69
which drives the creeping thief to some regard; LUC 305
ditty, | and drives away dark dreaming night. PP 14.20
DRIVETH 1 FR 0.0001 REL FR 1 V 0 P
sometime she driveth o'er a soldier's neck, ROM 1.04. 82
DRIVING 3 FR 0.0003 REL FR 2 V 1 P
hung on our driving boat, i saw your brother, TN 1.02. 11
driving back shadows over low'ring hills; ROM 2.05. 6
and tumbles, driving the poor fry before him, PER 2.01. 31 P
DRIV'ST 1 FR 0.0001 REL FR 1 V 0 P
thou driv'st me past the bounds | of maiden's MND 3.02. 65
DRIZZLE 1 FR 0.0001 REL FR 1 V 0 P
when the sun sets, the earth doth drizzle dew, ROM 3.05.126
DRIZZLED 2 FR 0.0002 REL FR 2 V 0 P
hid | in sap–consuming winter's drizzled snow, ERR 5.01.313
of war, | which drizzled blood upon the capitol; JC 2.02. 21
DRIZZLES 1 FR 0.0001 REL FR 0 V 1 P
then under this penthouse, for it drizzles rain, ADO 3.03.104 P
DROIT 1 FR 0.0001 REL FR 0 V 1 P
les mots aussi droit que les natifs d'angleterre H5 3.04. 38 P
DROLLERY 2 FR 0.0002 REL FR 1 V 1 P
a living drollery. TMP 3.03. 21
and for thy walls, a pretty slight drollery, or 2H4 2.01.144 P
DROMIO 36 FR 0.0040 REL FR 31 V 5 P
and stay there, dromio, till i come to thee. ERR 1.02. 10
come, dromio, come, these jests are out of 1.02. 68
the gold i gave to dromio is laid up | safe at 2.02. 1
i could not speak with dromio since at first | i 2.02. 5
she sent for you by dromio home to dinner. 2.02.154
by dromio? 2.02.155
dromio, go bid the servants spread for dinner. 2.02.187
dromio, thou /drumble, thou snail, thou slug, 2.02.194
dromio, keep the gate. 2.02.206
dromio, play the porter well. 2.02.211
for this time, sir, and my name is dromio. 3.01. 43
if thou hadst been dromio to–day in my place, 3.01. 46
what a coil is there, dromio? 3.01. 48
why, how now, dromio, where run'st thou so fast? 3.02. 71 P
am i dromio? 3.02. 73 P
thou art dromio, thou art my man, thou art 3.02. 75 P
or diviner laid claim to me, call'd me dromio, 3.02.141 P
i'll to the mart and there for dromio stay: 3.02.184
where is thy master, dromio? is he well? 4.02. 31
go, dromio, there's the money, bear it straight, 4.02. 63
why, dromio? 4.03. 62 P
avaunt, thou witch! come, dromio, let us go. 4.03. 79
you, | by dromio here, who came in haste for it. 4.04. 84
bind dromio too, and bear them to my house. 5.01. 35
me dote, | i see my son antipholus and dromio. 5.01.196
and is not that your bondman, dromio? 5.01.288
now am i dromio, and his man, unbound. 5.01.291
dromio, nor thou? 5.01.303
i, sir, am dromio, command him away. 5.01.336
i, sir, am dromio, pray let me stay. 5.01.337
and i, | and the twin dromio, all were taken up; 5.01.351
by force took dromio and my son from them, | and 5.01.353
by dromio, but i think he brought it not. 5.01.383
from you, | and dromio my man did bring them me. 5.01.386
dromio, what stuff of mine hast thou embark'd? 5.01.410
i am your master, dromio. 5.01.412
DROMIOS 1 FR 0.0001 REL FR 1 V 0 P
and these two dromios, one in semblance — ERR 5.01.359
DRONE* 3 FR 0.0003 REL FR 2 V 1 P
yea, or the drone of a lincolnshire bagpipe. 1H4 1.02. 76 P
o'er to executors pale | the lazy yawning drone. H5 1.02.204
not to eat honey like a drone | from others' PER 2.ch. 18
DRONE–LIKE 1 FR 0.0001 REL FR 1 V 0 P
my honey lost, and i, a drone–like bee, | have LUC 836
DRONES 3 FR 0.0003 REL FR 2 V 1 P
drones hive not with me, | therefore i part with MV 2.05. 48
drones suck not eagles' blood, but rob beehives. 2H6 4.01.109
we would purge the land of these drones, that PER 2.01. 46 P
DROOP 7 FR 0.0008 REL FR 7 V 0 P
but omit, my fortunes | will ever after droop. TMP 1.02.184
o, this is it that makes your servants droop! SHR in.2. 27
but wherefore do you droop? JN 5.01. 44
droop now? 1H4 4.01. 28
cominius, | droop not, adieu. COR 4.01. 20
good things of day begin to droop and drowse, MAC 3.02. 52
doth make them droop with grief and hang the VEN 666
DROOP'D 1 FR 0.0001 REL FR 1 V 0 P
he straight declin'd, droop'd, took it deeply, WT 2.03. 14
DROOPETH 1 FR 0.0001 REL FR 1 V 0 P
now, france, thy glory droopeth to the dust. 1H6 5.03. 29
DROOPING 10 FR 0.0011 REL FR 10 V 0 P
anon | with drooping fog as black as acheron, MND 3.02.357
imp out our drooping country's broken wing, R2 2.01.292
i, from the orient to the drooping west 2H4 in 3
should bring thy father to his drooping chair. 1H6 4.05. 5
news, my lords, may cheer our drooping spirits: 5.02. 1
cheer'd up the drooping army, and himself, 3H6 1.01. 6
those gracious words revive my drooping thoughts 3.03. 21
are disclosed, | his silence will sit drooping. HAM 5.01.288
who had not now been drooping here, if seconds CYM 5.03. 90
thee, | and keep my drooping eyelids open wide, SON 27. 7
DROOPS 3 FR 0.0003 REL FR 3 V 0 P
that droops his sapless branches to the ground. 1H6 2.05. 12
why droops my lord, like over–ripen'd corn 2H6 1.02. 1
thus droops this lofty pine and hangs his sprays 2.03. 45
/DROP 2 FR 0.0002 REL FR 2 V 0 P
/the /dole /of /blows /your /son /might /drop. 2H4 1.01.169
that any /drop thou borrow'dst from thy mother, TRO 4.05.133
DROP 77 FR 0.0087 REL FR 68 V 9 P
though every drop of water swear against it, TMP 1.01. 59
feather from unwholesome fen | drop on you both! 1.02.323
with this stick, | and make thy weapon drop. 1.02.474
out, we will drink water — not a drop before; 3.02. 2 P
open and show riches | ready to drop upon me, 3.02.142
gods, | and on this couple drop a blessed crown! 5.01.202
they would melt me out of my fat drop by drop, WIV 4.05. 98 P
they would melt me out of my fat drop by drop, 4.05. 98 P
i to the world am like a drop of water, | that ERR 1.02. 35
water, | that in the ocean seeks another drop, 1.02. 36
at dinner they should not drop in his porridge. 2.02. 99 P
fall | a drop of water in the breaking gulf, 2.02.126
and take unmingled thence that drop again, 2.02.127
nail, | a rush, a hair, a drop of blood, a pin, 4.03. 72
there's no true drop of blood in him to be truly ADO 3.02. 19 P
weep, | no drop but as a coach doth carry thee; LLL 4.03. 33
i'll drop the paper. 4.03. 41
asleep, | and drop the liquor of it in her eyes; MND 2.01.178
ere thou shalt lose for me one drop of blood. MV 4.01.113
if thou dost shed | one drop of christian blood, 4.01.310
you drop manna in the way | of starved people. 5.01.294
could not drop forth such giant–rude invention, AYL 4.03. 34
will deign to sip or touch one drop of it. SHR 5.02.145
"when he swears oaths, bid him drop gold, and AWW 4.03.223
i will drop in his way some obscure epistles of TN 2.03.155 P
by the letters that thou wilt drop, that they 2.03.165 P
may drop upon his kingdom and devour | incertain WT 5.01. 28
life in me, would preferment drop on my head. 5.02.114 P
and then we shall repent each drop of blood JN 2.01. 48
thou hast not sav'd one drop of blood | in this 2.01.341
where but by chance a silver drop hath fall'n, 3.04. 63
even to that drop ten thousand wiry /friends 3.04. 64
lest resolution drop | out at mine eyes in 4.01. 35
as thus to drop them still upon one place, R2 3.03.166
his eyes do drop no tears, his prayers are in 5.03.101
and shed my dear blood drop by drop in the dust, 1H4 1.03.134
and shed my dear blood drop by drop in the dust, 1.03.134
meet and ne'er part till one drop down a corse. 4.01.123
to melt | and drop upon our bare unarmed heads. 2H4 2.04.365
with so weak a wind | that it will quickly drop; 4.05.100
health | shall drop their blood in approbation H5 1.02. 19
god's vassals drop and die; 3.02. 8
he'll drop his heart into the sink of fear, 3.05. 59
for every drop of blood was drawn from him 1H6 2.02. 8
one drop of blood drawn from thy country's bosom 3.03. 54
and every drop cries vengeance for his death 3H6 1.04.148
your eyes drop millstones, when fools' eyes fall R3 1.03.352
and drop into the rotten mouth of death. 4.04. 2
so much the more | must pity drop upon her. H8 2.03. 18
i would not wish a drop of troyan blood | spent TRO 2.02.197
for every false drop in her bawdy veins, | a 4.01. 70
stone will cost | a drop of grecian blood. 4.05.224
the blood i drop is rather physical | than COR 1.05. 18
hot wine with not a drop of allaying tiber in't; 2.01. 48 P
'fore my wars | have i heard groan and drop. 4.04. 4
in summer's drought i'll drop upon thee still, TIT 3.01. 19
and left no friendly drop | to help me after? ROM 5.03.163
range on, | till each man drop by lottery. JC 2.01.119
when every drop of blood | that every roman 2.01.136
and drop my blood for drachmaes than to wring 4.03. 73
whose loves i may not drop, but wail his fall MAC 3.01.121
the moon | there hangs a vap'rous drop profound, 3.05. 24
we, in our country's purge, | each drop of us. 5.02. 29
that drop of blood that's calm proclaims me HAM 4.05.118
she let it drop by negligence, | and, to th' OTH 3.03.311
each drop she falls would prove a crocodile. 4.01.246
in some place of my soul | a drop of patience; 4.02. 53
in our own filth drop our clear judgments, make ANT 3.13.113
source, and the first stone | drop in my neck; 3.13.161
let her languish | a drop of blood a day, and, CYM 1.01.157
yet left in heaven as small a drop of pity | as 4.02.304
to drop on such a mistress, expectation | most TNK 3.01. 14
yet sometimes falls an orient drop beside, VEN 981
her tears should drop on them perpetually. LUC 686
many a dry drop seem'd a weeping tear, | shed 1375
and drop sweet balm in priam's painted wound, 1466
me bow, | and do not drop in for an after–loss. SON 90. 4
DROP–HEIR 1 FR 0.0001 REL FR 0 V 1 P
and young drop–heir that kill'd lusty pudding, MM 4.03. 15 P
DROPLETS 1 FR 0.0001 REL FR 1 V 0 P
and those our droplets which | from niggard TIM 5.04. 76
/DROPP'D 2 FR 0.0002 REL FR 2 V 0 P
as if an angel /dropp'd down from the clouds 1H4 4.01.108
/thence, | /as /pearls /from /diamonds /dropp'd. LR 4.03. 22
DROPP'D 16 FR 0.0018 REL FR 13 V 3 P
they dropp'd, as by a thunder–stroke. TMP 2.01.204
hast thou not dropp'd from heaven? 2.02.137 P
i found him under a tree, like a dropp'd acorn. AYL 3.02.235 P
of the letter that i dropp'd to betray him. TN 3.02. 78 P
and vengeance for't | not dropp'd down yet. WT 3.02.202
my heart dropp'd love, my pow'r rain'd honor, H8 3.02.185
from the tongue of roaring typhon dropp'd, TRO 1.03.160
by many an ounce) he dropp'd it for his country; COR 3.01.299
he would have dropp'd his knife, and fell asleep TIT 2.04. 50
such instigations have been often dropp'd JC 2.01. 49
that there he dropp'd it for a special purpose OTH 5.02.322
were | as plates dropp'd from his pocket. ANT 5.02. 92
she stood, | and on the sudden dropp'd. 5.02.344
or as iris | newly dropp'd down from heaven. TNK 4.01. 88
hath dropp'd a precious jewel in the flood, | or VEN 824
in the sweet channel of her bosom dropp'd; 958
DROPPETH 1 FR 0.0001 REL FR 1 V 0 P
it droppeth as the gentle rain from heaven MV 4.01.185
DROPPING 5 FR 0.0005 REL FR 5 V 0 P
sees a crown | dropping upon thy head. TMP 2.01.209
down their heads, dropping the hides and hips, H5 4.02. 47
now, | did i go through a tempest dropping fire. JC 1.03. 10
joy, | with an auspicious, and a dropping eye, HAM 1.02. 11
and with a dropping industry they skip | from PER 4.01. 62
DROPPINGS 1 FR 0.0001 REL FR 1 V 0 P
and curd, like eager droppings into milk, | the HAM 1.05. 69
DROPS 53 FR 0.0060 REL FR 49 V 4 P
when i have deck'd the sea with drops full salt, TMP 1.02.155
tears runs down his beard like winter's drops 5.01. 16
to the show of thine, | fall fellowly drops. 5.01. 64
hath drops too few to wash her clean again, ADO 4.01.141
to those fresh morning drops upon the rose, | as LLL 4.03. 26
to allay with some cold drops of modesty | thy MV 2.02.186
these foolish drops do something drown my manly 2.03. 13 P
kind of fruit | drops earliest to the ground, 4.01.116
of drops that sacred pity hath engend'red; AYL 2.07.123
call'd jove's tree, when it drops /such fruit. 3.02.237 P
than he that dies and lives by bloody drops? 3.05. 7
she drops booties in my mouth. WT 4.04.832 P
but this effusion of such manly drops, | this JN 5.02. 49
if i do sweat, they are the drops of thy lovers, 2H4 4.03. 13 P
hearse | be drops of balm to sanctify thy head; 4.05.114
whose guiltless drops | are every one a woe, a H5 1.02. 25
sweat drops of gallant youth in our rich fields! 3.05. 25
than from it issued forced drops of blood. 4.01.297
out at thy throat | in drops of crimson blood. 4.04. 15
drops bloody sweat from his war–wearied limbs, 1H6 4.04. 18
than drops of blood were in my father's veins. 3H6 1.01. 97
their aspects with store of childish drops: R3 1.02.154
the liquid drops of tears that you have shed 4.04.321
cold fearful drops stand on my trembling flesh. 5.03.181
my drops of tears | i'll turn to sparks of fire. H8 2.04. 72
prove this troth with my three drops of blood. TRO 1.03.301
and the drops of blood | shed for my thankless COR 4.05. 69
and the drops | that we have bled together. 5.01. 10
at a few drops of women's rheum, which are | as 5.06. 45
for certain drops of salt, your city rome, | i 5.06. 92
to them | as unrelenting flint to drops of rain. TIT 2.03.141
upon whose leaves are drops of new–shed blood 2.03.200
these sorrowful drops upon thy blood/–stain'd 5.03.154
spring, | your tributary drops belong to woe, ROM 3.02.103
ere he drops down | the knee before him, and TIM 1.01. 60
five thousand drops pays that. 3.04. 96
as dear to me as are the ruddy drops | that JC 2.01.289
these are gracious drops. 3.02.194
the proof of it will turn to redder drops. 5.01. 49
seek to hide themselves | in drops of sorrow. MAC 1.04. 35
drops tears as fast as the arabian trees | their OTH 5.02.350
grace grow where those drops fall, my hearty ANT 4.02. 38
like the crimson drops | i' th' bottom of a CYM 2.02. 38
for whom my heart drops blood, and my false 5.05.148
by hot grief uncandied, | melts into drops; TNK 1.01.108
i know | his ocean needs not my poor drops, yet 1.03. 7
so shall i die by drops of hot desire. VEN 1074
which in round drops upon their whiteness stood. 1170
even so the maid with swelling drops gan wet LUC 1228
no cause, but company, of her drops spilling. 1236
his eye drops fire, no water thence proceeds; 1552
now with the drops of this most balmy time | my SON 107. 9
melting, though our drops this diff'rence bore: LC 300
DROPSIED 1 FR 0.0001 REL FR 1 V 0 P
's, and virtue none, | it is a dropsied honor. AWW 2.03.128
DROPSIES 1 FR 0.0001 REL FR 0 V 1 P
that swoll'n parcel of dropsies, that huge 1H4 2.04.451 P
DROPSY 1 FR 0.0001 REL FR 1 V 0 P
the dropsy drown this fool! TMP 4.01.230
DROSS 5 FR 0.0005 REL FR 5 V 0 P
if aught possess thee from me, it is dross, ERR 2.02.177
a golden mind stoops not to shows of dross. MV 2.07. 20
and by the merit of vild gold, dross, dust, JN 3.01.165
my love admits no qualifying dross, | no more my TRO 4.04. 9
buy terms divine in selling hours of dross; SON 146.11
DROSSY 1 FR 0.0001 REL FR 0 V 1 P
same breed that i know the drossy age dotes on, HAM 5.02.189 P
DROUGHT 1 FR 0.0001 REL FR 1 V 0 P
in summer's drought i'll drop upon thee still, TIT 3.01. 19
DROUTH 2 FR 0.0002 REL FR 2 V 0 P
mouth, | are the blither for their drouth. PER 3.ch. 8
whereon they surfeit, yet complain on drouth: VEN 544
DROVE *(also drave)*
DROVE 8 FR 0.0009 REL FR 6 V 2 P

drove the grossness of the foppery into a WIV 5.05.124 P
and in conclusion drove us to seek out | this 1H4 4.03.102
more dazzled and drove back his enemies | than 1H6 1.01. 13
bank | drove back again unto my native clime? 2H6 3.02. 84
'twas not your valor, clifford, drove me thence. 3H6 2.02.107
when with his amazonian /chin he drove | the COR 2.02. 91
of his friends, drove him into this melancholy. TIM 4.03.401 P
that, one mortal /night, | drove him to this. PER 5.01. 38
DROVEN *(also driven)*
DROVEN 1 FR 0.0001 REL FR 1 V 0 P
we had droven them home | with clouts about ANT 4.07. 5
DROVIER 1 FR 0.0001 REL FR 0 V 1 P
why, that's spoken like an honest drovier; ADO 2.01.194 P
/DROWN 1 FR 0.0001 REL FR 1 V 0 P
/drown /the /lamenting /fool /in //sea–salt TIT 3.02. 20
DROWN 49 FR 0.0055 REL FR 34 V 15 P
shall we give o'er and drown? TMP 1.01. 39 P
for my part, the sea cannot drown me; 3.02. 13 P
and even with such–like valor men hang and drown 3.03. 59
the dropsy drown this fool! 4.01.230
did ever plummet sound | i'll drown my book. 5.01. 57
were on land, | this fellow could not drown. 5.01.218
to drown me in thy /sister's flood of tears. ERR 3.02. 46
drops do something drown my manly spirit. MV 2.03. 13 P
o'erflow with joy | and pleasure drown the brim. AWW 2.04. 47
or to drown my clothes, and say i was stripp'd. 4.01. 52 P
some other times we drown our gain in tears! 4.03. 68 P
though i seem to drown her remembrance again TN 2.01. 31 P
here which burns | worse than tears drown. WT 2.01.112
or wouldst thou drown thyself, | put but a JN 4.03.130
which makes the silver rivers drown their shores R2 3.02.107
the pretty vaulting sea refus'd to drown me, 2H6 3.02. 94
i'll drown more sailors than the mermaid shall, 3H6 3.02.186
lest with my sighs or tears i blast or drown 4.04. 23
o lord, methought what pain it was to drown! R3 1.04. 21
do, | i'll drown you in the malmsey–butt within. 1.04.270
moan) | to overgo thy woes and drown thy cries! 2.02. 61
send forth plenteous tears to drown the world! 2.02. 70
drown desperate sorrow in dead edward's grave, 2.02. 99
of war | thus will i drown your exclamations. 4.04.154
thou drown the sad remembrance of those wrongs 4.04.252
one hour's storm will drown the fragrant meads, TIT 2.04. 54
but floods of tears will drown my oratory, | and 5.03. 90
they may strive, | and drown themselves in riot! TIM 4.01. 28
them, or stab them, drown them in a draught, 5.01.102
in every eye, | that tears shall drown the wind. MAC 1.07. 25
to dew the sovereign flower and drown the weeds. 5.02. 30
he would drown the stage with tears, | and HAM 2.02.562
if i drown myself wittingly, it argues an act, 5.01. 10 P
if the man go to this water and drown himself, 5.01. 17 P
but if the water come to him and drown him, he 5.01. 18 P
in this world to drown or hang themselves, more 5.01. 28 P
i will incontinently drown myself. OTH 1.03.305 P
i would say i would drown myself for the love of 1.03.315 P
drown thyself? 1.03.335 P
drown cats and blind puppies! 1.03.336 P
to supper, come, | and drown consideration. ANT 4.02. 45
mortality, | and drown me with their sweetness. PER 5.01.194
us to an eddy | where we should turn or drown; TNK 1.02. 11
let not my sense unsettle | lest i should drown, 3.02. 30
if one be mad, or hang or drown themselves, 4.03. 35 P
'tis double death to drown in ken of shore, | he LUC 1114
and then they drown their eyes or break their 1239
let it then suffice | to drown /one woe, one 1680
then can i drown an eye (unus'd to flow) | for SON 30. 5
/DROWN'D 1 FR 0.0001 REL FR 1 V 0 P
have drench'd our steeples, /drown'd the cocks! L2 3.02. 3
DROWN'D 50 FR 0.0056 REL FR 32 V 18 P
we are less afraid to be drown'd than thou art. TMP 1.01. 44 P
the ditty does remember my drown'd father. 1.02.406
you grant with me | that ferdinand is drown'd? 2.01.244
it should be — but he is drown'd; 2.02. 88 P
but art thou not drown'd, stephano? 2.02.109 P
i hope now thou art not drown'd. 2.02.110 P
the king and all our company else being drown'd, 2.02.175 P
my man–monster hath drown'd his tongue in sack. 3.02. 12 P
he is drown'd | whom thus we stray to find, and 3.03. 8
young ferdinand, whom they suppose is drown'd, 3.03. 92
the mean is drown'd with /your unruly bass. TGV 1.02. 93
and drench'd me in the sea, where i am drown'd. 1.03. 79
as they would have drown'd a blind bitch's WIV 3.05. 10 P
i had been drown'd, but that the shore was 3.05. 14 P
is't not drown'd i' th' last rain? MM 3.02. 49 P
he is drown'd in the brook; AYL 3.02.287 P
and being taken with the cramp was drown'd; 4.01.104 P
perchance he is not drown'd — what think you, TN 1.02. 5
like a drown'd man, a fool, and a madman. 1.05.131 P
he's in the third degree of drink, he's drown'd. 1.05.136 P
the breach of the sea was my sister drown'd. 2.01. 23 P
she is drown'd already, sir, with salt water, 2.01. 30 P
lie drown'd and soak'd in mercenary blood; H5 4.07. 76
my heart is drown'd with grief, | whose flood 2H6 3.01.198
that thou wouldst have me drown'd on shore 3.02. 95
ten days ago i drown'd these news in tears; 3H6 2.01.104
my tongue, while heart is drown'd in cares. 3.03. 14
yet, for all his wings, the fool was drown'd. 5.06. 20
when i do tell thee there my hopes lie drown'd, TRO 1.01. 49
thou, poor man, hast drown'd it with thine own. TIT 3.01.141
tears | become a deluge, overflow'd and drown'd: 3.01.229
who drown'd their enmity in my true tears, | and 5.03.107
and these, who, often drown'd, could never die, ROM 1.02. 90
wits | are drown'd and lost in his calamities. TIM 4.03. 90
your sister's drown'd, laertes. HAM 4.07.164
drown'd! o, where? 4.07.165
alas, then she is drown'd? 4.07.183
drown'd, drown'd. 4.07.184
drown'd, drown'd. 4.07.184
unless she drown'd herself in her own defense? 5.01. 6 P
/argal, she drown'd herself wittingly. 5.01. 12 P
thy joy than to be drown'd and go without her. OTH 1.03.360 P
not enshelter'd and embay'd, they are drown'd; 2.01. 18
the turks are drown'd. 2.01.202
in thy fats our cares be drown'd, | with thy ANT 2.07.115
but tell me now | my drown'd queen's name, as in PER 5.01.205
that thaisa am i, supposed dead | and drown'd. 5.03. 36
who is but drunken when she seemeth drown'd. VEN 984
self–love had never drown'd him in the flood. LUC 266
and i in deep delight am chiefly drown'd | when PP 8.11

DROWNED 5 FR 0.0005 REL FR 5 V 0 P
let love, being light, be drowned if she sink! ERR 3.02. 52
the fold stands empty in the drowned field, MND 2.01. 96
and say, "thrice welcome, drowned viola!" TN 5.01.241
and pluck up drowned honor by the locks, | so he 1H4 1.03.205
or piteous they will look, like drowned mice. 1H6 1.02. 12
/DROWNING 1 FR 0.0001 REL FR 0 V 1 P
/no /more /of /drowning, /do /you /hear? OTH 1.03.378 P
DROWNING 8 FR 0.0009 REL FR 1 V 7 P
methinks he hath no drowning mark upon him, his
TMP 1.01. 29 P
i'll warrant him for drowning, though the ship 1.01. 46 P
would thou mightst lie drowning | the washing of 1.01. 57
i have not scap'd drowning to be afeard now of 2.02. 59 P
one that i sav'd from drowning, when three or TGV 4.04. 3 P
and then to scape drowning thrice, and to be in MV 2.02.164 P
do it a more delicate way than drowning. OTH 1.03.354 P
a pox of drowning thyself, it is clean out of 1.03.358 P
DROWNS 7 FR 0.0008 REL FR 5 V 2 P
doth blow | and coughing drowns the parson's saw
LLL 5.02.922
the second mads him, and a third drowns him. TN 1.05.133 P
often | drowns him and takes his valor prisoner. TIM 3.05. 68
would blaze, | but that this folly drowns it. HAM 4.07.191
to him and drown him, he drowns not himself; 5.01. 19 P
with too much labor drowns for want of skill. LUC 1099
it nor grows with heat nor drowns with show'rs. SON 124.12
DROWS'D 1 FR 0.0001 REL FR 1 V 0 P
but rather drows'd and hung their eyelids down, 1H4 3.02. 81
DROWSE 1 FR 0.0001 REL FR 1 V 0 P
good things of day begin to droop and drowse, MAC 3.02. 52
DROWSILY 1 FR 0.0001 REL FR 1 V 0 P
what, thou speak'st drowsily? JC 4.03.240
DROWSINESS 1 FR 0.0001 REL FR 1 V 0 P
what a strange drowsiness possesses them! TMP 2.01.199
DROWSY 17 FR 0.0019 REL FR 16 V 1 P
a name | now puts the drowsy and neglected act MM 1.02.170
sleep when i am drowsy, and tend on no man's ADO 1.03. 16 P
dapples the drowsy east with spots of grey. 5.03. 27
the gods | make heaven drowsy with the harmony.
LLL 4.03.342
glimmering light | by the dead and drowsy fire, MND 5.01.392
mouth | sound on into the drowsy race of night; JN 3.03. 39
tale | vexing the dull ear of a drowsy man; 3.04.109
and the third hour of drowsy morning /name. H5 4.pr. 16
break up their drowsy grave, and newly move 4.01. 22
rous'd on the sudden from their drowsy beds, 1H6 2.02. 23
who with their drowsy, slow, and flagging wings 2H6 4.01. 5
that ever ent'red in a drowsy head | have i R3 5.03.228
will /strike amazement to their drowsy spirits. TRO 2.02.210
patroclus' wounds have rous'd his drowsy blood, 5.05. 32
thy veins shall run | a cold and drowsy humor; ROM 4.01. 96
the shard–borne beetle with his drowsy hums MAC 3.02. 42
nor all the drowsy syrups of the world | shall OTH 3.03.331
DRUDGE 7 FR 0.0008 REL FR 5 V 2 P
this drudge or diviner laid claim to me, call'd ERR 3.02.140 P
thou pale and common drudge | 'tween man and man
MV 3.02.103
you whoreson malt–horse drudge! SHR 4.01.129
if i be his cuckold, he's my drudge. AWW 1.03. 46 P
i am the drudge, and toil in your delight; ROM 2.05. 75
a very drudge of nature's, have subdu'd me | in CYM 5.02. 5
pride, | he is contented thy poor drudge to be, SON 151.11
DRUDGERY 1 FR 0.0001 REL FR 0 V 1 P
for one to do her husbandry and her drudgery. 2H4 3.02.113 P
DRUDGE'S 1 FR 0.0001 REL FR 1 V 0 P
and will you credit this base drudge's words, 2H6 4.02.151
DRUDGES *(also drugs*)*
DRUDGES 1 FR 0.0001 REL FR 1 V 0 P
upon these paltry, servile, abject drudges! 2H6 4.01.105
DRUG 5 FR 0.0005 REL FR 5 V 0 P
what rhubarb, cyme, or what purgative drug, MAC 5.03. 55
her malice with | a drug of such damn'd nature. CYM 1.05. 36
he hath a drug of mine; 3.05. 57
pisanio, | i'll now taste of thy drug. 4.02. 38
the drug he gave me, which he said was precious 4.02.326
DRUG–DAMN'D 1 FR 0.0001 REL FR 1 V 0 P
that drug–damn'd italy hath outcraftied him, CYM 3.04. 15
DRUGG'D 1 FR 0.0001 REL FR 1 V 0 P
i have drugg'd their possets, | that death and MAC 2.02. 6
DRUGS* *(also drudges)*
DRUGS* 11 FR 0.0012 REL FR 11 V 0 P
with wholesome syrups, drugs, and holy prayers, ERR 5.01.104
here grow no damned drugs, here are no storms, TIT 1.01.154
such mortal drugs i have, but mantua's law | is ROM 5.01. 66
thy drugs are quick. 5.03.120
to such as may the passive drugs of it | freely TIM 4.03.254
black, hands apt, drugs fit, and time agreeing, HAM 3.02.255
abus'd her delicate youth with drugs or minerals OTH 1.02. 74
of my whole course of love — what drugs, what 1.03. 91
with me, if knife, drugs, serpents have | edge, ANT 4.15. 25
master doctor, have you brought those drugs? CYM 1.05. 4
drugs poison him that so fell sick of you. SON 118.14
/DRUM 1 FR 0.0001 REL FR 1 V 0 P
/done /their /mischief, /where's /thy /drum? LR 4.02. 55
DRUM 62 FR 0.0070 REL FR 39 V 23 P
was no music with him but the drum and the fife, ADO 2.03. 13 P
be still, drum, for your manager is in love; LLL 1.02.182 P
doors, and when you hear the drum | and the vile MV 2.05. 29
whilst i can shake my sword or hear the drum. AWW 2.05. 91
and i shall prove | a lover of thy drum, hater 3.03. 11
lose our drum! well. 3.05. 88 P
none better than to let him fetch off his drum, 3.06. 20 P
the love of laughter, let him fetch his drum; 3.06. 35 P
let him fetch off his drum in any hand. 3.06. 42 P
this drum sticks sorely in your disposition. 3.06. 44 P
a pox on't, let it go, 'tis but a drum. 3.06. 46 P
but a drum! 3.06. 47 P
is't but a drum? 3.06. 47 P
a drum so lost! 3.06. 47 P
some dishonor we had in the loss of that drum, 3.06. 56 P
performer, i would have that drum or another, or 3.06. 62 P
move me to undertake the recovery of this drum, 4.01. 35 P
i would i had any drum of the enemy's. 4.01. 61 P
a drum now of the enemy's — 4.01. 64 P
h'as led the drum before the english tragedians. 4.03.266 P
how does your drum? 5.02. 41 P
he's a good drum, my lord, but a naughty orator. 5.03.253 P

good tom drum, lend me a handkercher. 5.03.321 P
but start | an echo with the clamor of thy drum, JN 5.02.168
and even at hand a drum is ready brac'd | that 5.02.169
march without the noise of threat'ning drum, R2 3.03. 51
o, i could wish this tavern were my drum! 1H4 3.03.206
as had as lieve hear the devil as a drum, such 4.02. 18 P
cheering a rout of rebels with your drum, 2H4 4.02. 9
whilst any trump did sound, or drum struck up, 1H6 1.04. 80
by the sound of drum you may perceive | their 3.03. 29
hark, hark, the dolphin's drum, a warning bell, 4.02. 39
sound drum and trumpets, and to london all, 2H6 5.03. 32
then clarence is at hand, i hear his drum. 3H6 5.01. 11
the drum your honor hears marcheth from warwick. 5.01. 13
strike up the drum, cry "courage!" 5.03. 24
hark, a drum. R3 3.05. 16
strike up the drum. 4.04.180
hark, i hear their drum. 5.03.337
methinks i hear hither your husband's drum; COR 1.03. 29
the swords and hear a drum than look upon his 1.03. 55 P
which quier'd with my drum, into a pipe | small 3.02.113
you shall have the drum strook up this afternoon 4.05.215 P
beat thou the drum, that it speak mournfully; 5.06.149
proclaim our honors, lords, with trump and drum.
TIT 1.01.275
strike, drum. ROM 1.04.114
a drum? TIM 4.03. 45
follow thy drum, | with man's blood paint the 4.03. 59
i prithee beat thy drum and get thee gone. 4.03. 97
strike up the drum towards athens! 4.03.169
the enemy's drum is heard, and fearful scouring 5.02. 15
a drum, a drum! | macbeth doth come. MAC 1.03. 30
a drum, a drum! | macbeth doth come. 1.03. 30
why does the drum come hither? HAM 5.02.361
or at their chamber–door i'll beat the drum LR 2.04.118
far off methinks i hear the beaten drum. 4.06.285
let the drum strike, and prove my title thine. 5.03. 81
the spirit–stirring drum, th' ear–piercing fife, OTH 3.03.352
being able | to make mars spurn his drum. TNK 1.01.182
youngest follower of thy drum, instruct this day 5.01. 57
to choke mars's drum | and turn th' alarm to 5.01. 80
scorning his churlish drum and ensign red, VEN 107
/DRUMBLE 1 FR 0.0001 REL FR 1 V 0 P
dromio, thou /drumble, thou snail, thou slug, ERR 2.02.194
DRUMBLE 1 FR 0.0001 REL FR 0 V 1 P
look how you drumble! WIV 3.03.147 P
DRUMMER 1 FR 0.0001 REL FR 1 V 0 P
drummer, strike up, and let us march away. 3H6 4.07. 50
DRUMMING 2 FR 0.0002 REL FR 1 V 1 P
i'll no more drumming, a plague of all drums! AWW 4.03.298 P
his drumming heart cheers up his burning eye, LUC 435
DRUM'S 1 FR 0.0001 REL FR 0 V 1 P
if you give him not john drum's entertainment, AWW 3.06. 38 P
DRUMS 27 FR 0.0030 REL FR 26 V 1 P
i'll no more drumming, a plague of all drums! AWW 4.03.299 P
the interruption of their churlish drums | cuts JN 2.01. 76
shall braying trumpets and loud churlish drums, 3.01.303
maids | like amazons come tripping after drums, 5.02.155
strike up the drums, and let the tongue of war 5.02.164
indeed your drums, being beaten, will cry out; 5.02.166
strike up our drums, to find this danger out. 5.02.179
so rous'd up with boist'rous untun'd drums, R2 1.03.134
like a waiting–gentlewoman | of guns, and drums, 1H4 1.03. 56
strike up our drums, pursue the scatt'red stray; 2H4 4.02.120
hang up your ensigns, let your drums be still, 1H6 5.04.174
sound drums and trumpets, and the king will fly. 3H6 1.01.118
i hear their drums. 1.02. 69
then strike up drums. 2.01.204
sound drums and trumpets! 5.07. 45
strike alarum, drums! R3 4.04.149
sound drums and trumpets boldly and cheerfully. 5.03.269
peace, drums! TRO 5.09. 2
hark, our drums | are bringing forth our youth. COR 1.04. 15
briefly we heard their drums. 1.06. 16
when drums and trumpets shall | i' th' field 1.09. 42
and ran | from th' noise of our own drums." 2.03. 54
and then anon | drums in his ear, at which he ROM 1.04. 86
let our drums strike. TIM 5.04. 85
that drums him from his sport and speaks as loud ANT 1.04. 29
these drums, these trumpets, flutes! 2.07.131
hark, the drums | demurely wake the sleepers. 4.09. 29
/DRUNK 1 FR 0.0001 REL FR 0 V 1 P
/me /to /the /tavern /and /made /me /drunk, /and
WIV 1.01.126 P
DRUNK 68 FR 0.0076 REL FR 28 V 40 P
scape being drunk, for want of wine. TMP 2.01.147
if he have never drunk wine afore, it will go 2.02. 75 P
man a coward that hath drunk so much sack as i 3.02. 27 P
he is drunk now. where had he wine? 5.01.278
remember what i did when you made me drunk, yet
WIV 1.01.172 P
i say the gentleman had drunk himself out of his 1.01.175 P
i'll ne'er be drunk whilst i live again, but in 1.01.181 P
if i be drunk, i'll be drunk with those that 1.01.183 P
i'll be drunk with those that have the fear of 1.01.183 P
he would be drunk too, that let me inform you. MM 3.02.128 P
drunk many times a day, if not many days 4.02.149 P
times a day, if not many days entirely drunk. 4.02.150 P
he was drunk then, my lord, it can be no better. 5.01.188 P
i think you all have drunk of circe's cup. ERR 5.01.271
and bid those that are drunk get them to bed. ADO 3.03. 43 P
make misfortune drunk | with candle–wasters, 5.01. 17
i have drunk poison whiles he utter'd it. 5.01.246
he hath not drunk ink; LLL 4.02. 25 P
most vildly in the afternoon, when he is drunk. MV 1.02. 87 P
one dead, or drunk? SHR in.1. 31
i am sure thy father drunk wine — but if thou AWW 2.03.100 P
moreov'r, he's drunk nightly in your company. TN 1.03. 36 P
by mine honor, half drunk. 1.05.116 P
o, he's drunk, sir toby, an hour agone; 5.01.198 P
make known | how he hath drunk, he cracks his WT 2.01. 44
i have drunk, and seen the spider. 2.01. 45
of thy hands and that thou wilt not be drunk; 5.02.165 P
fellow of thy hands and that thou wilt be drunk; 5.02.166 P
not wonder how thou dar'st venture to be drunk, 5.02.171 P
o, where hath our intelligence been drunk? JN 4.02.116
is not my teeming date drunk up with time? R2 5.02. 91
drunk with choler? 1H4 1.03.129
it could not be else, i have drunk medicines. 2.02. 20 P

i am a rogue if i drunk to–day. 2.04.152 P
sack that thou hast drunk me would have bought 3.03. 44 P
i' faith, you have drunk too much canaries, and 2H4 2.04. 26 P
the rascal's drunk; 2.04.213 P
the mass, i have drunk too much sack at supper. 5.03. 13 P
and that was against a post when he was drunk. H5 3.02. 41 P
brother's blood the thirsty earth hath drunk, 3H6 2.03. 15
unlawfully made drunk with innocent blood! R3 4.04. 30
so do all men, unless th' are drunk, sick, or TRO 1.02. 17 P
my ears have yet not drunk a hundred words | of ROM 2.02. 58
on the ground, with his own tears made drunk. 3.03. 83
o churl, drunk all, and left no friendly drop 5.03.163
was the hope drunk | wherein you dress'd MAC 1.07. 35
which hath made them drunk hath made me bold; 2.02. 1
when he is drunk asleep, or in his rage, | or in HAM 3.03. 89
i have drunk but one cup to–night — and that OTH 2.03. 39 P
with that which he hath drunk to–night already, 2.03. 49
drinks you, with facility, your dane dead drunk; 2.03. 83 P
do not think, gentlemen, i am drunk: 2.03.113 P
i am not drunk now; 2.03.115 P
you must not think then that i am drunk. 2.03.119 P
come, come — you're drunk. 2.03.155 P
drunk? 2.03.156 P
drunk? 2.03.279 P
i have well approv'd it, sir. i drunk! 2.03.312 P
or any man living, may be drunk at a time, man. 2.03.313 P
and fools as gross | as ignorance made drunk. 3.03.405
our fortunes to–night, shall be — drunk to bed. ANT 1.02. 46 P
ere the ninth hour, i drunk him to his bed; 2.05. 21
hast thou drunk well? 2.07. 65
the third part then is drunk. 2.07. 92
the king my father, sir, has drunk to you — PER 2.03. 75
if thou hadst drunk to him, 't 'ad been a 4.03. 11
now you may take him | drunk with his victory. TNK 1.01.158
what potions have i drunk of siren tears SON 119. 1

DRUNKARD 12 FR 0.0013 REL FR 7 V 5 P
monster, to make a wonder of a poor drunkard! TMP 2.02.166 P
ass | was i to take this drunkard for a god, 5.01.297
behavior hath this flemish drunkard pick'd (with WIV 2.01. 23 P
thou drunkard, thou, what didst thou mean by ERR 3.01. 10
and i will, like a true drunkard, utter all to ADO 3.03.104 P
one drunkard loves another of the name. LLL 4.03. 48
such duty to the drunkard let him do, | with SHR in.1. 113
i long to hear him call the drunkard husband, in.1. 133
says the drunkard. 1H4 2.04.111 P
woes, | but like a drunkard must i vomit them. TIT 3.01.231
and fleckled darkness like a drunkard reels ROM 2.03. 3
place again, he shall tell me i am a drunkard! OTH 2.03.304 P

DRUNKARD'S 1 FR 0.0001 REL FR 1 V 0 P
done, conduct him to the drunkard's chamber, SHR in.1. 107

DRUNKARDS 6 FR 0.0006 REL FR 4 V 2 P
we are merely cheated of our lives by drunkards. TMP 1.01. 56
to every modern censure worse than drunkards. AYL 4.01. 7 P
they clip us drunkards, and with swinish phrase HAM 1.04. 19
drunkards, liars, and adulterers by an enforc'd LR 1.02.124 P
i have seen drunkards | do more than this in 2.01. 34
now 'mongst this flock of drunkards | am i to OTH 2.03. 59

DRUNKEN 22 FR 0.0024 REL FR 13 V 9 P
light, a most perfidious and drunken monster! TMP 2.02.150 P
a howling monster; a drunken monster! 2.02.179 P
is not this stephano, my drunken butler? 5.01.277
the fear of god, and not with drunken knaves. WIV 1.01.184 P
death no more dreadfully but as a drunken sleep, MM 4.02.143 P
thou drunken slave, i sent thee for a rope, ERR 4.01. 96
sirs, i will practice on this drunken man. SHR in.1. 36
what's a drunken man like, fool? TN 1.05.130 P
i hate a drunken rogue. 5.01.201 P
and given your drunken cousin rule over me, yet 5.01.304 P
with toss–pots still had drunken heads, | for 5.01.403
then let the earth be drunken with our blood! 3H6 2.03. 23
by drunken prophecies, libels, and dreams, | to R3 1.01. 33
waiting vassals | have done a drunken slaughter, 2.01.123
looks | lives like a drunken sailor on a mast, 3.04. 99
vaults have wept | with drunken spilth of wine, TIM 2.02.160
so good a commander with so slight, so drunken, OTH 2.03.278 P
antony | shall be brought drunken forth, and i ANT 5.02.219
what a drunken knave was the sea to cast thee in PER 2.01. 57 P
like the proceedings of a drunken brain, | full VEN 910
who is but drunken when she seemeth drown'd. 984
drunken desire must vomit his receipt | ere he LUC 703

DRUNKENLY 1 FR 0.0001 REL FR 1 V 0 P
hast thou tapp'd out and drunkenly carous'd. R2 2.01.127

DRUNKENNESS 4 FR 0.0004 REL FR 1 V 3 P
drunkenness is his best virtue, for he will be AWW 4.03.255 P
"you must amend your drunkenness." TN 2.05. 73 P
than lying, vainness, babbling, drunkenness, 3.04.355
pleas'd the devil drunkenness to give place to OTH 2.03.296 P

DRUNK'ST 1 FR 0.0001 REL FR 0 V 1 P
lips are scarce wip'd since thou drunk'st last. 1H4 2.04.154 P

/DRY 2 FR 0.0002 REL FR 1 V 1 P
/now, /the /dry /suppeago /on /the /subject, TRO 2.03. 74 P
//belly–pinched /wolf | /keep /their /fur /dry, LR 3.01. 14

DRY 73 FR 0.0082 REL FR 51 V 22 P
but i would fain die a dry death. TMP 1.01. 68 P
confederates | (so dry he was for sway) wi' th' 1.02.112
they grind their joints | with dry convulsions, 4.01.259
man, if the river were dry, i am able to fill it TGV 2.03. 52 P
write till your ink be dry, and with your tears 3.02. 74
the manner of his nurse — or his dry nurse — WIV 1.02. 4 P
comes home to–morrow — nay, dry your eyes — MM 4.03.127
well, sir, then 'twill be dry. ERR 2.02. 59 P
choleric, and purchase me another dry basting. 2.02. 63 P
here's his dry hand up and down. ADO 2.01.118 P
this jest is dry to me. LLL 5.02.373
i could munch your good dry oats. MND 4.01. 32 P
and swearing till my very /roof was dry | with MV 3.02.204
which is as dry as the remainder biscuit | after AYL 2.07. 39
with age | and high top bald with dry antiquity: 4.03.105
shade | a lioness, with udders all drawn dry, 4.03.114
none so dry or thirsty | will deign to sip or SHR 5.02.144
it's dry, sir. TN 1.03. 73 P
i am not such an ass but i can keep my hand dry. 1.03. 75 P
a dry jest, sir. 1.03. 76 P
go to, y' are a dry fool; 1.05. 41 P
for give the dry fool drink, then is the fool 1.05. 44 P
the dry fool drink, then is the fool not dry; 1.05. 45 P
vain dew | perchance shall dry your pities; WT 2.01.110
the color's | not dry. 5.03. 48
winters cannot blow away, | so many summers dry. 5.03. 51
is numb'ring sands and drinking oceans dry; R2 2.02.146
nay, dry your eyes — | tears show their love, 3.03.202
when i was dry with rage and extreme toil, 1H4 1.03. 31
turn'd, | or a dry wheel grate on the axle–tree, 3.01.130
have you not a moist eye, a dry hand, a yellow 2H4 1.02.181 P
"i will now take my leave of these six dry, 2.04. 7 P
i' good truth, as rheumatic as two dry toasts, 2.04. 57 P
time, when i have been dry and bravely marching, 2H6 4.10. 13 P
i give thee this to dry thy cheeks withal. 3H6 1.04. 83
and that will quickly dry thy melting tears. 1.04.174
the ruthless queen gave him to dry his cheeks 2.01. 61
saying, he'll lade it dry to have his way: 3.02.139
stops thy spring, my sea shall suck them dry, 4.08. 55
thy very beams will dry those vapors up, | for 5.03. 12
and then, to dry them, gav'st the duke a clout R3 1.03.176
let's dry our eyes; H8 3.02.431
'tis dry enough), will, with great speed of TRO 1.03.329
pour in, pour /in, his ambition is dry. 2.03.224 P
that stale old mouse–eaten dry cheese, nestor, 5.04. 10 P
will be his fire | to kindle their dry stubble; COR 2.01.258
let my tears staunch the earth's dry appetite, TIT 3.01. 14
how they are stain'd like meadows yet not dry, 3.01.125
good titus, dry thine eyes. 3.01.138
the day to cheer and night's dank dew to dry, ROM 2.03. 6
when theirs are dry, for romeo's banishment. 3.02.131
dry sorrow drinks our blood. 3.05. 59
dry up your tears, and stick your rosemary | on 4.05. 79
dry up thy marrows, vines, and plough–torn leas, TIM 4.03.193
i'll drain him dry as hay: MAC 1.03. 18
you, and, spunge, you shall be dry again. HAM 4.02. 21 P
o heat, dry up my brains! 4.05.155
when in your motion you are hot and dry — | as 4.07.157
dry up in her the organs of increase, | and from LR 1.04.279
court holy–water in a dry house is better than 3.02. 10 P
poor tom, thy horn is dry. 3.06. 75 P
the sweat of industry would dry and die, | but CYM 3.06. 31
rain, being in't, | knows neither wet nor dry. TNK 1.01.121
to fan and blow them dry again she seeks. VEN 52
graze on my lips, and if those hills be dry, 233
that she will draw his lips' rich treasure dry. 552
sorrow that friendly sighs sought still to dry; 964
sighs dry her cheeks, tears make them wet again. 966
would strive who first should dry his tears. 1092
as dry combustious matter is to fire. 1162
to dry the old oak's sap and cherish springs, LUC 950
many a dry drop seem'd a weeping tear, | shed 1375
to dry the rain on my storm–beaten face, | for SON 34. 6

DRY–BEAT 2 FR 0.0002 REL FR 0 V 2 P
me hereafter, dry–beat the rest of the eight. ROM 3.01. 79 P
i will dry–beat you with an iron wit, and put up 4.05.123 P

DRY–BEATEN 1 FR 0.0001 REL FR 1 V 0 P
by heaven, all dry–beaten with pure scoff! LLL 5.02.263

DRY–FOOT 1 FR 0.0001 REL FR 1 V 0 P
that runs counter, and yet draws dry–foot well; ERR 4.02. 39

DRYLY *(see drily)*

DRYNESS 1 FR 0.0001 REL FR 1 V 0 P
full surfeits and the dryness of his bones ANT 1.04. 27

DU 3 FR 0.0003 REL FR 1 V 2 P
mort du vinaigre! is not this helen? AWW 2.03. 44 P
la plus belle katherine du monde, mon tres cher H5 5.02.216 P
richard du champ. CYM 4.02.377

DUB 3 FR 0.0003 REL FR 3 V 0 P
"do me right, | and dub me knight, | samingo." 2H4 5.03. 74
unless to dub thee with the name of traitor. H5 2.02.120
unsheathe your sword, and dub him presently. 3H6 2.02. 59

DUBB'D 4 FR 0.0004 REL FR 3 V 1 P
dubb'd with unhatch'd rapier and on carpet TN 3.04.235 P
what, i am dubb'd! JN 1.01.245
five hundred were but yesterday dubb'd knights. H5 4.08. 86
since that our brother dubb'd them gentlewomen, R3 1.01. 82

DUCAT 6 FR 0.0006 REL FR 4 V 2 P
no, not so much as a ducat for delivering your TGV 1.01.137 P
his use was to put a ducat in her clack–dish. MM 3.02.126 P
but fare thee well, there is a ducat for thee, MV 2.03. 4
if every ducat in six thousand ducats | were in 4.01. 85
were in six parts, and every part a ducat, | i 4.01. 86
how now? a rat? dead, for a ducat, dead! HAM 3.04. 24

DUCATS 53 FR 0.0060 REL FR 35 V 18 P
which doth amount to three odd ducats more ERR 4.01. 30
turkish tapestry | there is a purse of ducats; 4.01.105
a ring he hath of mine worth forty ducats, | and 4.03. 83
choose, | for forty ducats is too much to lose. 4.03. 96
five hundred ducats, villain, for a rope? 4.04. 13
went'st not thou to her for a purse of ducats? 4.04. 87
two hundred ducats. 4.04.134
and sent my peasant home | for certain ducats; 5.01.232
this purse of ducats i receiv'd from you, | and 5.01.385
these ducats pawn i for my father here. 5.01.390
working this, and thy fee is a thousand ducats. ADO 2.02. 53 P
i have earn'd of don john a thousand ducats. 3.03.109 P
had receiv'd a thousand ducats of don john for 4.02. 48 P
three thousand ducats — well. MV 1.03. 1 P
three thousand ducats for three months, and 1.03. 9 P
three thousand ducats: 1.03. 26 P
up the gross | of full three thousand ducats. 1.03. 56
ay, ay, three thousand ducats. 1.03. 65
three thousand ducats — 'tis a good round sum. 1.03.103
a cur can lend three thousand ducats?" 1.03.122
and i will go and purse the ducats straight, 1.03.174
and gild myself | with some moe ducats, and be 2.06. 50
o my ducats! 2.08. 15
o my christian ducats! 2.08. 16
my ducats, and my daughter! 2.08. 17
a sealed bag, two sealed bags of ducats, | of 2.08. 18
of double ducats, stol'n from me by my daughter! 2.08. 19
she hath the stones upon her, and the ducats." 2.08. 22
his stones, his daughter, and his ducats. 2.08. 24
gone, cost me two thousand ducats in frankford! 3.01. 84 P
two thousand ducats in that, and other precious, 3.01. 86 P
at my foot, and the ducats in her coffin! 3.01. 90 P
genoa, as i heard, one night fourscore ducats. 3.01.109 P
fourscore ducats at a sitting! 3.01.111 P
fourscore ducats! 3.01.112 P
with them the first boy for a thousand ducats. 3.02.214 P
for me, three thousand ducats. 3.02.298
flesh than to receive | three thousand ducats. 4.01. 42
and i be pleas'd to give ten thousand ducats 4.01. 45
for thy three thousand ducats here is six. 4.01. 84
if every ducat in six thousand ducats | were in 4.01. 85
in lieu whereof | three thousand ducats, due 4.01.411
which did refuse three thousand ducats of me, 5.01.211
besides two thousand ducats by the year | of SHR 2.01.369
two thousand ducats by the year of land! 2.01.372
why, he has three thousand ducats a year. TN 1.03. 22 P
but he'll have but a year in all these ducats. 1.03. 24 P
hold, there is forty ducats; ROM 5.01. 59
a hundred ducats a–piece for his picture in HAM 2.02.366 P
to pay five ducats, five, i would not farm it; 4.04. 20
two thousand souls and twenty thousand ducats 4.04. 25
will lay you ten /thousand ducats to your ring, CYM 1.04.127 P
your mistress, my ten thousand ducats are yours, 1.04.151 P

DUCDAME 4 FR 0.0004 REL FR 3 V 1 P
will to please, | ducdame, ducdame, ducdame! AYL 2.05. 54
will to please, | ducdame, ducdame, ducdame! 2.05. 54
will to please, | ducdame, ducdame, ducdame! 2.05. 54
what's that "ducdame"? 2.05. 58 P

DUCHESS' 2 FR 0.0002 REL FR 2 V 0 P
hume must make merry with the duchess' gold; 2H6 1.02. 87
hume's knavery will be the duchess' wrack, | and 1.02.105

DUCHESS 20 FR 0.0022 REL FR 14 V 6 P
i saw the duchess of milan's gown that they ADO 3.04. 15 P
our enterlude before the duke and the duchess, MND 1.02. 6 P
you would fright the duchess and the ladies, 1.02. 75 P
an hour before i came, the duchess died. R2 2.02. 97
humor, | have hired me to undermine the duchess, 2H6 1.02. 98
come, my masters, the duchess, i tell you, 1.04. 1 P
me | to watch the coming of my punish'd duchess. 2.04. 7
as he stood by, whilest i, his forlorn duchess, 2.04. 45
like to a duchess, and duke humphrey's lady, 2.04. 98
the duchess by his subornation, | upon my life, 3.01. 45
did instigate the bedlam brain–sick duchess | by 3.01. 51
sent | from your kind aunt, duchess of burgundy. 3H6 2.01.146
but i pray you, | what think you of a duchess? H8 2.03. 38
time | i know your back will bear a duchess. 2.03. 99
it shall be to the duchess of alanson, | the 3.02. 85
is that old noble lady, duchess of norfolk. 4.01. 52
the old duchess of norfolk | and lady marquess 5.02.202
cordelia by the hand, | duchess of burgundy. LR 1.01.244
and regan his duchess will be here with him this 2.01. 4 P
go with me to the duchess. 3.05. 14 P

/DUCHY 1 FR 0.0001 REL FR 0 V 1 P
that the /duchy of anjou and /the /county /of 2H6 1.01. 58 P

DUCHY 2 FR 0.0002 REL FR 1 V 1 P
that the duchy of anjou and the county of maine 2H6 1.01. 50 P
hath given the duchy of anjou, and maine, | unto 1.01.110

DUCK* 11 FR 0.0012 REL FR 6 V 5 P
swom ashore, man, like a duck. TMP 2.02.128 P
i can swim like a duck, i'll be sworn. 2.02.129 P
though thou canst swim like a duck, thou art 2.02.131 P
o dainty duck! MND 5.01.281
lace for your cape, | my dainty duck, my dear–a? WT 4.04.317
no more valor in that poins than in a wild duck. 1H4 2.02.101 P
worse than a struck fowl or a hurt wild duck. 4.02. 20 P
and hold–fast is the only dog, my duck; H5 2.03. 52
cog, | duck with french nods and apish courtesy, R3 1.03. 49
and duck again as low | as hell's from heaven! OTH 2.01.188
forth, | that, as a duck for life that dives, PER 3.ch. 49

DUCKS* 4 FR 0.0004 REL FR 2 V 2 P
as the tercel, for all the ducks i' th' river. TRO 3.02. 53 P
here, here, here he comes. /ah, sweet ducks! 4.04. 12 P
the learned pate | ducks to the golden fool. TIM 4.03. 18
who, being look'd on, ducks as quickly in; VEN 87

DUDGEON 1 FR 0.0001 REL FR 1 V 0 P
and on thy blade and dudgeon gouts of blood, MAC 2.01. 46

DUE* *(also endow)*

/DUE* 1 FR 0.0001 REL FR 1 V 0 P
(the voice of souls) give thee that /due, SON 69. 3

DUE* 85 FR 0.0096 REL FR 76 V 9 P
if imprisonment be the due of a bawd, why, 'tis MM 3.02. 67 P
i have ta'en a due and wary note upon't. 4.01. 37
think | a due sincerity governed his deeds, 5.01.446
so that my arrant, due unto my tongue, | i thank ERR 2.01. 72
marry, sir, besides myself, i am due to a woman: 3.02. 81 P
you know since pentecost the sum is due, | and 4.01. 1
say, how grows it due? 4.04.134
due for a chain your husband had of him. 4.04.135
fair payment for foul words is more than due. LLL 4.01. 19
debt | pay him the due of honey–tongued boyet. 5.02.334
turn'd her obedience (which is due to me) | to MND 1.01. 37
as due to love as thoughts and dreams and sighs, 1.01.154
due but to one, and crowned with one crest. 3.02.214
sworn | to have the due and forfeit of my bond. MV 4.01. 37
which here appeareth due upon the bond. 4.01.249
three thousand ducats, due unto the jew, | we 4.01.411
love, | which, as your due, time claims, he does AWW 2.04. 42
there lies your way, due west. TN 3.01.134
proceed in justice, which shall have due course, WT 3.02. 6
though 'tis a saying, sir, not due to me. 3.02. 58
are making hither with all due expedience, | and R2 2.01.287
a pale | keep law and form and due proportion, 3.04. 41
no, i'll give thee thy due, thou hast paid all 1H4 1.02. 52 P
he will give the devil his due. 1.02.119 P
'tis not due yet, i would be loath to pay him 5.01.127 P
look to taste the due | meet for rebellion /and 2H4 4.02.116
thy due from me | is tears and heavy sorrows of 4.05. 37
my due from thee is this imperial crown, | which 4.05. 41
majestical, | holding due course to harflew. H5 3.pr. 17
but let my horse have his due. 3.07. 4 P
will take up that with "give the devil his due." 3.07.117 P
of time, of numbers, and due course of things, 5.pr. 4
thy praise | that i, thy enemy, due thee withal; 1H6 4.02. 34
ere you can take due orders for a priest. 2H6 3.01.274
i cannot give due action to my words, | except a 5.01. 8
at our enlargement what are thy due fees? 3H6 4.06. 5
thy honor, state, and seat is due to me. R3 1.03.111
your state of fortune, and your due of birth, 3.07.120
crown, | as the ripe revenue and due of birth, 3.07.158
my lord, i claim the gift, my due by promise, 4.02. 88
world's shame, grave's due by life usurp'd, 4.04. 27
hath but wrong, and blame the due of blame. 5.01. 29
carries | the due o' th' verdict with it. H8 5.01.131
with due observance of /thy godlike seat, TRO 1.03. 31

shores, | the primogenity and due of birth, 1.03.106
i am your debtor, claim it when 'tis due. 4.05. 51
as boasting show their scars | a mock is due. 4.05.291
'twas due on forfeiture, my lord, six weeks TIM 2.02. 30
and the detention of long since due debts, 2.02. 38
give't these fellows | to whom 'tis instant due. 2.02.230
a towardly prompt spirit — give thee thy due — 3.01. 35 P
more is thy due than more than all can pay. MAC 1.04. 21
(from whom this tyrant holds the due of birth) 3.06. 25
is it a fee–grief | due to some single breast? 4.03.197
that will with due decision make us know | what 5.04. 17
labor with your soul | to give it due content. HAM 4.05.213
shall our abode | make with you by due turn. LR 1.01.135
would unstate myself to be in a due resolution. 1.02.100 P
that all the kingdom | may have due note of him, 2.01. 83
to thee a woman's services are due, | /a fool 4.02. 27
steering with due course toward the isle of OTH 1.03. 34
challenge that i may profess | due to the moor, 1.03.189
wife, | due reference of place and exhibition, 1.03.237
ebb, but keeps due on | to the propontic and the 3.03.455
in the due reverence of a sacred vow | i here 3.03.461
the due of honor in no point omit. CYM 3.05. 11
protract with admiration what | is now due debt. 4.02.233
the hazard therefore due fall on me by | the 4.04. 46
thus adjourn'd | the graces for his merits due, 5.04. 79
any thing | that's due to all the villains past, 5.05.212
of nature should again | do their due functions. 5.05.258
in store, | due to this heinous capital offense, PER 2.04. 5
is made with all due diligence | that horse and 3.ch. 19
of monstrous lust the due and just reward. 5.03. 86
throats and have not | due audience of the gods. TNK 1.02. 83
your virtues, | and, as your due, y' are hers. 2.05. 37
which cannot want due mercy, i beg first. 3.06.209
let no due be wanting; 5.01. 5
so the deities | have show'd due justice. 5.04.109
be spent, | and as his due writ in my testament. LUC 1183
to eat the world's due, by the grave and thee. SON 1.14
that due of many, now is thine alone. 31.12
that due to thee which thou deserv'st alone. 39. 8
mine eye's due is /thy outward part, | and my 46.13
the earth can have but earth, which is his due. 74. 7

DUELLIST 2 FR 0.0002 REL FR 0 V 2 P
the very butcher of a silk button, a duellist, a ROM 2.04. 24 P
of a silk button, a duellist, a duellist; 2.04. 24 P

DUELLO 2 FR 0.0002 REL FR 0 V 2 P
he respects not, the duello he regards not: LLL 1.02.179 P
he cannot by the duello avoid it; TN 3.04.307 P

DUER 1 FR 0.0001 REL FR 0 V 1 P
duer paid to the hearer than the turk's tribute. 2H4 3.02.307 P

DUES 7 FR 0.0008 REL FR 6 V 1 P
craves | all dues be rend'red to their owners: TRO 2.02.174
my lord, here is a note of certain dues. TIM 2.02. 16
dues? whence are you? 2.02. 17
will hardly stop the mouth | of present dues. 2.02.148
mightst not lose the dues of rejoicing by being MAC 1.05. 12 P
effects of courtesy, dues of gratitude: LR 2.04.179
you shall receive all dues | fit for the honor TNK 2.05. 60

DUFF 1 FR 0.0001 REL FR 1 V 0 P
dear duff, i prithee contradict thyself, | and MAC 2.03. 89

DUG 5 FR 0.0005 REL FR 4 V 1 P
dying with mother's dug between its lips; 2H6 3.02.393
for i had then laid wormwood to my dug, ROM 1.03. 26
on the nipple | of my dug and felt it bitter, 1.03. 31
to see it techy and fall out wi' th' dug! 1.03. 32
/comply, sir, with his dug before 'a suck'd it. HAM 5.02.187 P

DUGS 4 FR 0.0004 REL FR 3 V 1 P
of her batler and the cow's dugs that her pretty AYL 2.04. 50 P
shall thy old dugs once more a traitor rear? R2 5.03. 90
yet from my dugs he drew not this deceit. R3 2.02. 30
like a milch doe, whose swelling dugs do ache, VEN 875

/DUKE 3 FR 0.0003 REL FR 2 V 1 P
/to /all /the /duke /of /norfolk's /signories, 2H4 4.01.109
/that /the /duke /of /cornwall /was /so /slain? LR 4.07. 84 P
the servants of the /duke? OTH 1.02. 34

DUKE 522 FR 0.0590 REL FR 415 V 107 P
thy father was the duke of milan and | a prince TMP 1.02. 54
and thy father | was duke of milan, and his only 1.02. 58
and prospero the prime duke, being so reputed 1.02. 72
he did believe | he was indeed the duke, out o' 1.02.103
the duke of milan | and his brave son being 1.02.438
the duke of milan | and his more braver daughter 1.02.439
brother, my lord the duke, | stand to, and do as 3.03. 51
sir king, | the wronged duke of milan, prospero. 5.01.107
that i am prospero and that very duke | which 5.01.159
she | is daughter to this famous duke of milan, 5.01.192
/an heir, and /near allied unto the duke. TGV 4.01. 47
"hang him up," says the duke. 4.04. 22 P
here comes the duke. 5.02. 30
it is my lord the duke. 5.04.122
the duke himself will be to–morrow at court, and WIV 4.03. 2 P
what duke should that be comes so secretly? 4.03. 4 P
they are gone but to meet the duke, villain, do 4.05. 71 P
you make grand preparation for a duke de jamany. 4.05. 87 P
dere is no duke that the court is know to come. 4.05. 88 P
if the duke with the other dukes come not to MM 1.02. 1 P
and the new deputy now for the duke — | whether 1.02.157
send after the duke and appeal to him. 1.02.174 P
the duke is very strangely gone from hence; 1.04. 50
o, how much is the good duke deceiv'd in angelo! 3.01.191 P
and much please the absent duke, if peradventure 3.01.203 P
what news, friar, of the duke? 3.02. 86 P
would the duke that is absent have done this? 3.02.116 P
heard the absent duke much detected for women, 3.02.121 P
not the duke? 3.02.125 P
the duke had crotchets in him. 3.02.127 P
a shy fellow was the duke, and i believe i know 3.02.131 P
file of the subject held the duke to be wise. 3.02.136 P
but if ever the duke return (as our prayers are 3.02.154 P
sir, my name is lucio, well known to the duke. 3.02.160 P
o, you hope the duke will return no more; 3.02.164 P
i would the duke we talk of were return'd again. 3.02.173 P
the duke yet would have dark deeds darkly 3.02.176 P
the duke (i say to thee again) would eat mutton 3.02.181 P
pray you, sir, of what disposition was the duke? 3.02.231 P
it that the absent duke had not either deliver'd 4.02.132 P
were you sworn to the duke, or to the deputy? 4.02.182 P
if the duke avouch the justice of your dealing? 4.02.186 P
you, sir, here is the hand and seal of the duke; 4.02.192 P
the contents of this is the return of the duke. 4.02.197 P
the duke comes home to–morrow — nay, dry your 4.03.127
grace of the duke, revenges to your heart, | and 4.03.135
and he shall bring you | before the duke; 4.03.142
but they say the duke will be here to–morrow. 4.03.155 P
if the old fantastical duke of dark corners had 4.03.157 P
the duke is marvellous little beholding to your 4.03.159 P
thou knowest not the duke so well as i do; 4.03.161 P
i can tell thee pretty tales of the duke. 4.03.166 P
where you may have such vantage on the duke, 4.06. 11
and very near upon | the duke is ent'ring; 4.06. 15
justice, o royal duke! 5.01. 20
o worthy duke, | you bid me seek redemption of 5.01. 28
o gracious duke, | harp not on that; 5.01. 63
hath spoke most villainous speeches of the duke. 5.01.264 P
where is the duke? 5.01.294
is the duke gone? 5.01.299
then to glance from him | to th' duke himself, 5.01.310
the duke | dare no more stretch this finger of 5.01.313
you at the prison, in the absence of the duke. 5.01.329 P
and do you remember what you said of the duke? 5.01.331 P
and was the duke a fleshmonger, a fool, and a 5.01.333 P
i protest i love the duke as i love myself. 5.01.341 P
art the first knave that e'er mad'st a duke. 5.01.356
your highness said even now i made you a duke; 5.01.516 P
sprung from the rancorous outrage of your duke ERR 1.01. 6
complain unto the duke of this indignity. 5.01.113
anon i'm sure the duke himself in person | comes 5.01.119
kneel to the duke before he pass the abbey. 5.01.129
justice, most sacred duke, against the abbess! 5.01.133
therefore, most gracious duke, with thy command 5.01.159
justice, most gracious duke, o, grant me justice 5.01.190
this day, great duke, she shut the doors upon me 5.01.204
most mighty duke, vouchsafe me speak a word: 5.01.283
the duke, and all that know me in the city, 5.01.324
most mighty duke, behold a man much wrong'd. 5.01.331
duke menaphon, your most renowned uncle. 5.01.369
renowned duke, vouchsafe to take the pains | to 5.01.394
the duke, my husband, and my children both, 5.01.404
promised to study three years with the duke. LLL 1.02. 36 P
that are vow–fellows with this virtuous duke? 2.01. 38
i saw him at the duke alanson's once, | and much 2.01. 61
happy be theseus, our renowned duke! MND 1.01. 20
and, my gracious duke, | this man hath bewitch'd 1.01. 26
and, my gracious duke, | be it so she will not 1.01. 38
our enterlude before the duke and the duchess, 1.02. 6 P
that i will make the duke say, "let him roar 1.02. 72 P
it in action as we will do it before the duke. 3.01. 6 P
dance in duke theseus' house triumphantly, | and 4.01. 89
do not you think | the duke was here, and bid us 4.01.195
it in the latter end of a play, before the duke. 4.01.217 P
masters, the duke is coming from the temple, and 4.02. 15 P
and the duke had not given him sixpence a day 4.02. 21 P
i will tell you is, that the duke hath din'd. 4.02. 35 P
the young german, the duke of saxony's nephew? MV 1.02. 84 P
the villain jew with outcries rais'd the duke, 2.08. 4
but there the duke was given to understand 2.08. 7
antonio certified the duke | they were not with 2.08. 10
he plies the duke at morning and at night, | and 3.02.277
the duke himself, and the magnificoes | of 3.02.280
the duke shall grant me justice. 3.03. 8
i am sure the duke | will never grant this 3.03. 24
the duke cannot deny the course of law; 3.03. 26
life lies in the mercy | of the duke only, 4.01.356
down therefore, and beg mercy of the duke. 4.01.363
so please my lord the duke and all the court 4.01.380
the old duke is banish'd by his younger brother AYL 1.01. 99 P
is banish'd by his younger brother the new duke, 1.01.100 P
whose lands and revenues enrich the new duke; 1.01.103 P
where will the old duke live? 1.01.113 P
what, you wrastle to–morrow before the new duke? 1.01.121 P
had banish'd thy uncle, the duke my father, so 1.02. 10 P
it our suit to the duke that the wrastling might 1.02.182 P
the duke is humorous — what he is indeed | more 1.02.266
which of the two was daughter of the duke, 1.02.269
the other is daughter to the banish'd duke, 1.02.273
but i can tell you that of late this duke | hath 1.02.277
from tyrant duke unto a tyrant brother. 1.02.288
the duke my father lov'd his father dearly. 1.03. 29 P
look, here comes the duke. 1.03. 39 P
know'st thou not the duke | hath banish'd me, 1.03. 94
the bonny priser of the humorous duke? 2.03. 8
the duke will drink under this tree. 2.05. 32 P
and i'll go seek the duke, his banket is 2.05. 62 P
i am the duke | that lov'd your father. 2.07.195
here in the forest on the duke your father. 3.04. 33 P
i met the duke yesterday, and had much question 3.04. 35 P
i must attend the duke at dinner. 4.01.180 P
present him to the duke like a roman conqueror, 4.02. 3 P
/in brief, he led me to the gentle duke, | who 4.03.142
will i invite the duke and all 's contented 5.02. 14 P
and i will bid the duke to the nuptial. 5.02. 43 P
keep you your word, o duke, to give your 5.04. 19
good duke, receive thy daughter, | hymen from 5.04.111
duke frederick, hearing how that every day | men 5.04.154
the duke hath put on a religious life, | and 5.04.181
your ships are stay'd at venice, and the duke, SHR 4.02. 83
for private quarrel 'twixt your duke and him, 4.02. 84
from below your duke to beneath your constable, AWW 2.02. 30 P
madam, he's gone to serve the duke of florence. 3.02. 52
the duke will lay upon him all the honor | that 3.02. 71
well in it, the duke shall both speak of it, and 3.06. 69 P
he met the duke in the street, sir, of whom he 4.03. 76 P
the duke hath offer'd him letters of 4.03. 78 P
i have congied with the duke, done my adieu with 4.03. 87 P
of him, how many horse the duke is strong." 4.03.130 P
condition, and what credit i have with the duke. 4.03.173 P
what his reputation is with the duke; 4.03.177 P
is this captain in the duke of florence's camp? 4.03.192 P
what is his reputation with the duke? 4.03.197 P
the duke knows him for no other but a poor 4.03.198 P
have answer'd to his reputation with the duke, 4.03.249 P
a noble duke, in nature as in name. TN 1.02. 25
i'll serve this duke; 1.02. 55
if the duke continue these favors towards you, 1.04. 1 P
by this brave duke came early to his grave; JN 2.01. 5
welcome before the gates of angiers, duke. 2.01. 17
and let young arthur, duke of britain, in, | who 2.01.301
for we'll create young arthur duke of britain 2.01.551
against the duke of norfolk, thomas mowbray? R2 1.01. 6
him, | if he appeal the duke on ancient malice, 1.01. 9
dost thou object | against the duke of norfolk, 1.01. 29
that he did plot the duke of gloucester's death, 1.01.100
we'll calm the duke of norfolk, you your son. 1.01.159
throw down, my son, the duke of norfolk's gage. 1.01.161
the duke of norfolk, sprightfully and bold, 1.03. 3
my name is thomas mowbray, duke of norfolk, 1.03. 16
against the duke of herford that appeals me, 1.03. 21
in lists, on thomas mowbray, duke of norfolk, 1.03. 38
go bear this lance to thomas duke of norfolk. 1.03.103
to prove the duke of norfolk, thomas mowbray, 1.03.107
here standeth thomas mowbray, duke of norfolk, 1.03.110
and holds you dear | as harry duke of herford, 2.01.144
well, lords, the duke of lancaster is dead. 2.01.224
and living too, for now his son is duke. 2.01.225
that thou wouldst speak to the duke of herford? 2.01.232
but by the robbing of the banish'd duke. 2.01.261
intelligence | that harry duke of herford, 2.01.279
that late broke from the duke of exeter, | his 2.01.281
well furnished by the duke of britain | with 2.01.285
here comes the duke of york. 2.02. 73
alas, poor duke, the task he undertakes | is 2.02.145
to offer service to the duke of herford, | and 2.03. 32
what power the duke of york had levied there, 2.03. 34
have you forgot the duke of /herford, boy? 2.03. 36
then learn to know him now, this is the duke. 2.03. 40
the duke of york, to know what pricks you on 2.03. 78
it must be granted i am duke of lancaster. 2.03.124
the noble duke hath been too much abused. 2.03.137
the noble duke hath sworn his coming is | but 2.03.148
where is the duke my father with his power? 3.02.143
to a dear friend of the good duke of york's 3.04. 70
thy men | to execute the noble duke at callice. 4.01. 82
great duke of lancaster, i come to thee | from 4.01.107
then, as i said, the duke, great bullingbrook, 5.02. 7
'twas where the madcap duke his uncle kept — 1H4 1.03.244
to god | he came but to be duke of lancaster, 4.03. 61
i look to be either earl or duke, i can assure 5.04.142 P
the duke of lancaster and westmerland; 2H4 1.03. 82
and page to thomas mowbray, duke of norfolk. 3.02. 26 P
the prince, lord john and duke of lancaster. 4.01. 28
who saw the duke of clarence? 4.05. 7
the crown | of charles the duke of lorraine, H5 1.02. 70
to charles, the foresaid duke of lorraine; 1.02. 83
be merciful, great duke, to men of mould. 3.02. 22
thy manly rage, | abate thy rage, great duke! 3.02. 24
the duke of gloucester would speak with you. 3.02. 55 P
tell you the duke, it is not so good to come to 3.02. 57 P
you may discuss unto the duke, look you — is 3.02. 61 P
the duke of gloucester, to whom the order of the 3.02. 65 P
is the duke of exeter safe? 3.06. 5 P
the duke of exeter is as magnanimous as 3.06. 6 P
the duke of exeter doth love thee well. 3.06. 22
go speak, the duke will hear thy voice; 3.06. 46
i would desire the duke to use his good pleasure 3.06. 55 P
the duke of exeter has very gallantly maintain'd 3.06. 90 P
and the duke of exeter is master of the pridge. 3.06. 95 P
can tell your majesty, the duke is a prave man. 3.06. 96 P
my part, i think the duke hath lost never a man, 3.06.100 P
the duke of york commends him to your majesty. 4.06. 3
him, he's a friend of the duke alanson's. 4.08. 18 P
charles duke of orleance, nephew to the king, 4.08. 76
john duke of bourbon, and lord bouciqualt: 4.08. 77
john duke of alanson, anthony duke of brabant, 4.08. 96
john duke of alanson, anthony duke of brabant, 4.08. 96
brabant, | the brother to the duke of burgundy, 4.08. 97
the duke of burgundy, | and edward duke of bar; 4.08. 98
edward the duke of york, the earl of suffolk, 4.08.103
contriv'd, | we do salute you, duke of burgundy, 5.02. 7
if, duke of burgundy, you would the peace, 5.02. 68
/reignier, duke of anjou, doth take his part; 1H6 1.01. 94
the duke of alanson flieth to his side. 1.01. 95
it is the noble duke of gloucester. 1.03. 6
have patience, noble duke, i may not open, | the 1.03. 18
duke of alanson, this was your default, | that, 2.01. 60
his grandfather was lionel duke of clarence, 2.04. 83
i derived am | from lionel duke of clarence, 2.05. 75
from famous edmund langley, duke of york, 2.05. 85
it is not that that hath incens'd the duke: 3.01. 36
the bishop and the duke of gloucester's men, 3.01. 78
the duke | hath banish'd moody discontented fury 3.01.122
well, duke of gloucester, i will yield to thee; 3.01.134
o loving uncle, kind duke of gloucester, | how 3.01.142
and rise created princely duke of york. 3.01.172
welcome, high prince, the mighty duke of york! 3.01.176
perish, base prince, ignoble duke of york! 3.01.177
i think the duke of burgundy will fast | before 3.02. 42
dying prince, | the valiant duke of bedford. 3.02. 87
thanks, gentle duke. 3.02.121
the noble duke of bedford late deceas'd, | but 3.02.132
we will entice the duke of burgundy | to leave 3.03. 19
now in the rearward comes the duke and his. 3.03. 33
a parley with the duke of burgundy! 3.03. 36
was not the duke of orleance thy foe? 3.03. 69
welcome, brave duke, thy friendship makes us 3.03. 86
tongue | against my lord the duke of somerset. 3.04. 34
writ to your grace from th' duke of burgundy. 4.01. 12
shame to the duke of burgundy and thee! 4.01. 13
letter | sent from our uncle duke of burgundy. 4.01. 49
law | argu'd betwixt the duke of york and him; 4.01. 96
to burdeaux, warlike duke! 4.03. 22
duke of anjou and maine, yet is he poor, | and 5.03. 95
'twas neither charles nor yet the duke i nam'd, 5.04. 77
we here create thee the first duke of suffolk, 2H6 1.01. 64
to you duke humphrey must unload his grief, 1.01. 76
suffolk, the new–made duke that rules the roast, 1.01.109
for suffolk's duke, may he be suffocate, | that 1.01.124
him "humphrey, the good duke of gloucester," 1.01.159
with "god preserve the good duke humphrey!" 1.01.162
and all together, with the duke of suffolk, 1.01.168
we'll quickly hoise duke humphrey from his seat. 1.01.169
delay, | i'll to the duke of suffolk presently. 1.01.171
despite duke humphrey or the cardinal. 1.01.179
i never saw but humphrey duke of gloucester 1.01.183
excepting none but good duke humphrey; 1.01.193
cherish duke humphrey's deeds | while they do 1.01.203

and make a show of love to proud duke humphrey, 1.01.241
why doth the great duke humphrey knit his brows, 1.02. 3
plac'd the heads of edmund duke of somerset, 1.02. 29
and william de la pole, first duke of suffolk. 1.02. 30
but list to me, my humphrey, my sweet duke: 1.02. 35
were i a man, a duke, and next of blood, | i 1.02. 63
and from the great and new–made duke of suffolk; 1.02. 95
this is the duke of suffolk and not my lord 1.03. 8 P
"against the duke of suffolk, for enclosing the 1.03. 21 P
for saying that the duke of york was rightful 1.03. 26 P
did the duke of york say he was rightful heir to 1.03. 28 P
style, | and must be made a subject to a duke? 1.03. 49
more like an empress than duke humphrey's wife. 1.03. 78
till we have brought duke humphrey in disgrace. 1.03. 96
as for the duke of york, this late complaint 1.03. 97
pray god the duke of york excuse himself! 1.03.178
that richard duke of york | was rightful heir 1.03.183
this is the law, and this duke humphrey's doom. 1.03.210
the duke yet lives that henry shall depose; 1.04. 30
/me what /fate /awaits the duke of suffolk?" 1.04. 32
"what shall /betide the duke of somerset?" 1.04. 34
injurious duke, that threatest where's no cause. 1.04. 48
"the duke yet lives that henry shall depose; 1.04. 59
"tell me what fate awaits the duke of suffolk?" 1.04. 64
"what shall betide the duke of somerset?" 1.04. 66
duke humphrey has done a miracle to–day. 2.01.157
and the third, | lionel duke of clarence; 2.02. 13
whom | was john of gaunt, the duke of lancaster; 2.02. 14
the fift was edmund langley, duke of york; 2.02. 15
was thomas of woodstock, duke of gloucester; 2.02. 16
till henry bullingbrook, duke of lancaster, 2.02. 21
father, the duke hath told the truth; 2.02. 28
the third son, duke of clarence, from whose line 2.02. 34
sole daughter unto lionel duke of clarence; 2.02. 50
wink at the duke of suffolk's insolence, | at 2.02. 70
that virtuous prince, the good duke humphrey. 2.02. 74
shall one day make the duke of york a king. 2.02. 79
stay, humphrey duke of gloucester! 2.03. 22
and humphrey duke of gloucester scarce himself, 2.03. 40
and touching the duke of york, i will take my 2.03. 87 P
sometime i'll say, i am duke humphrey's wife, 2.04. 42
like to a duchess, and duke humphrey's lady, 2.04. 98
made me collect these dangers in the duke. 3.01. 35
i will subscribe, and say i wrong'd the duke. 3.01. 38
well hath your highness seen into this duke; 3.01. 42
will bring to light in smooth duke humphrey. 3.01. 65
the duke is virtuous, mild, and too well given 3.01. 72
sirs, take away the duke, and guard him sure. 3.01.188
as place duke humphrey for the king's protector? 3.01.250
but now return we to the false duke humphrey. 3.01.322
let him know | we have dispatch'd the duke, as 3.02. 2
the duke was dumb and could not speak a word. 3.02. 32
although the duke was enemy to him, | yet he 3.02. 57
sighs, | and all to have the noble duke alive. 3.02. 64
it may be judg'd i made the duke away, | so 3.02. 67
that good duke humphrey traitorously is murd'red 3.02.123
laid | upon the life of this thrice–famed duke. 3.02.157
why, warwick, who should do the duke to death? 3.02.179
but both of you were vowed duke humphrey's foes, 3.02.182
and you, forsooth, had the good duke to keep. 3.02.183
as guilty of duke humphrey's timeless death. 3.02.187
that i am faulty in duke humphrey's death. 3.02.202
and do some service to duke humphrey's ghost. 3.02.231
they say, by him the good duke humphrey died; 3.02.248
sometime he talks as if duke humphrey's ghost 3.02.373
the duke of suffolk, william de la pole. 4.01. 45
the duke of suffolk muffled up in rags? 4.01. 46
ay, but these rags are no part of the duke; 4.01. 47
thou that smil'dst at good duke humphrey's death 4.01. 76
married the duke of clarence' daughter, did he 4.02.137
cade, the duke of york hath taught you this. 4.02.154
descended from the duke of clarence' house, 4.04. 29
ah, were the duke of suffolk now alive, | these 4.04. 41
the duke of york is newly come from ireland, 4.09. 24
only to remove from thee | the duke of somerset, 4.09. 30
tell him i'll send duke edmund to the tower; 4.09. 38
the duke of somerset is in the tower. 5.01. 41
go bid her hide him quickly from the duke. 5.01. 84
myself | the title of this most renowned duke, 5.01.176
lord stafford's father, duke of buckingham, | is 3H6 1.01. 10
unless plantagenet, duke of york, be king, | and 1.01. 40
but when the duke is slain, they'll quickly fly. 1.01. 69
thou factious duke of york, descend my throne, 1.01. 74
for shame, come down. he made thee duke of york. 1.01. 77
true, clifford, that's richard duke of york. 1.01. 83
be duke of lancaster, let him be king. 1.01. 86
he is both king and duke of lancaster, | and 1.01. 87
/thy father was, as thou art, duke of york, 1.01.105
art thou against us, duke of exeter? 1.01.147
proud, | can set the duke up in despite of me. 1.01.158
do right unto this princely duke of york, | or i 1.01.166
than have made that savage duke thine heir, 1.01.224
the earl of warwick and the duke enforc'd me. 1.01.229
seas, | the duke is made protector of the realm, 1.01.240
reveng'd may she be on that hateful duke, 1.01.266
thou, richard, shalt to the duke of norfolk, 1.02. 38
as for the brat of this accursed duke, | whose 1.03. 4
when as the noble duke of york was slain, | your 2.01. 46
who crown'd the gracious duke in high despite, 2.01. 59
sweet duke of york, our prop to lean upon, | now 2.01. 68
his name that valiant duke hath left with thee; 2.01. 89
o valiant lord, the duke of york is slain! 2.01.100
where is the duke of norfolk, gentle warwick? 2.01.142
six miles off the duke is with the soldiers, 2.01.144
no longer earl of march, but duke of york; 2.01.192
the duke of norfolk sends you word by me | the 2.01.206
he, but a duke, would have his son a king, | and 2.02. 21
comes warwick, backing of the duke of york, 2.02. 69
suppose this arm is for the duke of york, | and 2.04. 2
i mean our princely father, duke of york. 2.06. 51
richard, i will create thee duke of gloucester, 2.06.103
let me be duke of clarence, george of gloucester 2.06.106
richard, be duke of gloucester. 2.06.109
while proud ambitious edward, duke of york, 3.03. 27
let them go, here is | the duke. 4.03. 30
the duke? 4.03. 30
king, | and come now to create you duke of york. 4.03. 34
see that forthwith duke edward be convey'd 4.03. 52
now for awhile farewell, good duke of york. 4.03. 57
he was convey'd by richard, duke of gloucester, 4.06. 81
yet edward, at the least, is duke of york. 4.07. 21
again, | i came to serve a king and not a duke. 4.07. 49
and thou shalt still remain the duke of york. 5.01. 28
forbear your conference with the noble duke. R3 1.01.104
but now the duke of buckingham and i | are come 1.03. 31
between the duke of gloucester and your brothers 1.03. 37
his majesty | against the duke of clarence, but 1.03. 85
them, gav'st the duke a clout | steep'd in the 1.03.176
that stir the king against the duke my brother. 1.03.330
the noble duke of clarence to your hands. 1.04. 92
there lies the duke asleep, and there the keys. 1.04. 95
i'll back to the duke of gloucester and tell him 1.04.115 P
o, in the duke of gloucester's purse. 1.04.128 P
at my elbow, persuading me not to kill the duke. 1.04.146 P
the duke shall know how slack you have been! 1.04.275
i say, | for i repent me that the duke is slain. 1.04.278
till that the duke give order for his burial; 1.04.281
here comes sir richard ratcliffe and the duke. 2.01. 46
who knows not that the gentle duke is dead? 2.01. 80
lately attendant on the duke of norfolk. 2.01.102
o, full of danger is the duke of gloucester, 2.03. 27
persuade the queen to send the duke of york 3.01. 33
can from his mother win the duke of york, | anon 3.01. 38
now in good time, here comes the duke of york. 3.01. 95
for the installment of this noble duke | in the 3.01.163
who is most inward with the noble duke? 3.04. 8
in happy time, here comes the duke himself. 3.04. 21
where is my lord, the duke of gloucester? 3.04. 46
come, dispatch, the duke would be at dinner. 3.04. 94
being nothing like the noble duke my father. 3.05. 92
and his resemblance, being not like the duke. 3.07. 11
"thus saith the duke, thus hath the duke 3.07. 32
saith the duke, thus hath the duke inferr'd" — 3.07. 32
i think the duke will not be spoke withal. 3.07. 57
return, good catesby, to the gracious duke, 3.07. 65
light–foot friend post to the duke of norfolk; 4.04.440
catesby, fly to the duke. 4.04.442
stay'st thou here, and go'st not to the duke? 4.04.446
my liege, the duke of buckingham is taken — 4.04.531
john duke of norfolk, thomas earl of surrey, 5.03.296
john duke of norfolk, walter lord /ferrers, 5.05. 13
the duke of buckingham's surveyor? H8 1.01.115
my lord the duke of buckingham and earl | of 1.01.199
as the duke said, | the will of heaven be done, 1.01.214
i am sorry that the duke of buckingham | is run 1.02.109
have collected | out of the duke of buckingham. 1.02.131
the duke being at the rose, within the parish 1.02.152
presently the duke | said, 'twas the fear indeed 1.02.157
the king nor 's heirs | (tell you the duke) 1.02.169
the duke | shall govern england.'" 1.02.170
i told my lord the duke, by th' devil's 1.02.178
after your highness had reprov'd the duke 1.02.189
my sworn servant, | the duke retain'd him his. 1.02.192
after "the duke his father," with the "knife," 1.02.203
shall become | of the great duke of buckingham. 2.01. 3
the great duke | came to the bar; 2.01. 11
which the duke desir'd | to him brought viva 2.01. 17
this duke as much | they love and dote on; 2.01. 51
prepare there, | the duke is coming. 2.01. 98
lord high constable | and duke of buckingham; 2.01.103
if the duke be guiltless, | 'tis full of woe; 2.01.139
/a marriage 'twixt the duke of orleance and 2.04.175
me | remembrance of my father–in–law, the duke, 3.02. 8
the duke by law | found his deserts. 3.02.266
the duke of buckingham came from his trial. 4.01. 5
the duke of suffolk is the first, and claims 4.01. 17
next, the duke of norfolk, | he to be earl 4.01. 18
that should be | the duke of suffolk. 4.01. 41
left him at primero | with the duke of suffolk. 5.01. 8
king had more affected the duke of albany than LR 1.01. 2 P
general dependants as in the duke himself also, 1.04. 61 P
him notice that the duke of cornwall and regan 2.01. 3 P
the duke be here to–night? 2.01. 14
you not spoken 'gainst the duke of cornwall? 2.01. 23
upon his party 'gainst the duke of albany? 2.01. 26
the noble duke my master, | my worthy arch and 2.01. 58
the duke must grant me that. 2.01. 81
lord, | you know the fiery quality of the duke, 2.04. 92
i'ld speak with the duke of cornwall and his 2.04. 97
the fiery duke? 2.04.104
tell the hot duke that — | no, but not yet, may 2.04.104
me | that this remotion of the duke and her | is 2.04.114
go tell the duke, and 's wife, i'ld speak with 2.04.116
go you and maintain talk with the duke, that my 3.03. 15 P
forbid thee, shall the duke | instantly know, 3.03. 21
advise the duke, where you are going, to a most 3.07. 9 P
o my good lord, the duke of cornwall's dead, 4.02. 70
strike the sight | of the death–practic'd duke. 4.06.277
know of the duke if his last purpose hold, | or 5.01. 1
fear /me not. | she and the duke her husband! 5.01. 17
the duke does greet you, general, | and he OTH 1.02. 36
how may the duke be therewith satisfied, | whose 1.02. 88
the duke in council? 1.02. 93
the duke himself, | or any of my brothers of the 1.02. 95
most gracious duke, | to my unfolding lend your 1.03.243
'tis lodovico — | this comes from the duke. 4.01.215
the duke and the senators of venice greet you. 4.01.217
o, pity, duke! TNK 1.01. 47
think, dear duke, think | what beds our slain 1.01.139
the duke himself came privately in the night, 2.01. 46 P
lord arcite, you must presently to th' duke; 2.02.221
and like enough the duke hath taken notice 2.02.227
and she must see the duke, and she must dance 2.03. 45
where he himself will edify the duke | most 2.03. 52
the duke himself | will be in person there. 2.03. 65
the duke has lost hippolyta; 3.01. 1
spare it not, | the duke has more, coz. eat now. 3.03. 20
here the duke comes; 3.05. 12
the duke appears; 3.05. 13
thou doughty duke, all hail! 3.05.100
and, dainty duke, whose doughty dismal fame 3.05.114
duke, if we have pleas'd /thee too | and have 3.05.142
this is the duke, a–hunting as i told you. 3.06.108
for scorning thy edict, duke, ask that lady 3.06.168
let 's die together, at one instant, duke. 3.06.177
o duke theseus, | the goodly mothers that have 3.06.244
else, never trifle, | but take our lives, duke. 3.06.261
no, never, duke. 3.06.266
any death thou canst invent, duke. 3.06.281
pity, that the duke | methought stood staggering 4.01. 9
and all we'll dance an antic 'fore the duke, 4.01. 75
from the noble duke your brother, | madam, i 4.02. 55
you know | the chestnut mare the duke has? 5.02. 61

DUKEDOM 26 FR 0.0029 REL FR 24 V 2 P

man) my library | was dukedom large enough: TMP 1.02.110
crown, and bend | the dukedom yet unbow'd (alas, 1.02.115
extirpate me and mine | out of the dukedom, and 1.02.126
with volumes that | i prize above my dukedom. 1.02.168
thy dukedom i resign, and do entreat | thou 5.01.118
and require | my dukedom of thee, which perforce 5.01.133
my dukedom since you have given me again, | i 5.01.168
to content ye | as much as me my dukedom. 5.01.171
prospero, his dukedom | in a poor isle; 5.01.211
let me not, | since i have my dukedom got, | and ep 6
so was i when your highness took his dukedom, AYL 1.03. 59
a land itself at large, a potent dukedom. 5.04.169
the seat of gaunt, dukedom of lancaster. 1H4 5.01. 45
had the wit, 'twere better than your dukedom. 2H4 4.03. 87 P
unfought withal, but i will sell my dukedom, H5 3.05. 12
say's head for selling the dukedom of maine. 2H6 4.02.161 P
his dukedom and his chair with me is left. 3H6 2.01. 90
for chair and dukedom, throne and kingdom say, 2.01. 93
for gloucester's dukedom is too ominous. 2.06.107
york, | but that we enter as into our dukedom? 4.07. 9
why, and i challenge nothing but my dukedom, 4.07. 23
our dukedom till god please to send the rest. 4.07. 47
is not a dukedom, sir, a goodly gift? 5.01. 31
my dukedom to a beggarly denier, | i do mistake R3 1.02.251
to tread upon thy dukedom, and to be, | where TNK 3.06.254
they come from all parts of the dukedom to him. 4.01.136

DUKEDOMS 8 FR 0.0009 REL FR 8 V 0 P

of his true titles to some certain dukedoms, H5 1.01. 87
o'er france and all her almost kingly dukedoms, 1.02.227
did claim some certain dukedoms, in the right 1.02.247
you cannot revel into dukedoms there. 1.02.253
desires you let the dukedoms that you claim 1.02.256
dowry, | some petty and unprofitable dukedoms. 3.pr. 31
to change two dukedoms for a duke's fair 2H6 1.01.219
till suffolk gave two dukedoms for his daughter. 1.03. 87

/DUKE'S 1 FR 0.0001 REL FR 1 V 0 P

for thee, friend, 'tis the /duke's pleasure. LR 2.02.152

DUKE'S 38 FR 0.0043 REL FR 19 V 19 P

gentleman–like dogs, under the duke's table. TGV 4.04. 18 P
your honor, i am the poor duke's constable, and MM 2.01. 47 P
your worship think me the poor duke's officer. 2.01.177 P
was with child by him in the duke's time; 3.02.200 P
strange tenor — perchance of the duke's death, 4.02.201 P
'tis that he sent me of the duke's return. 4.03.138
the duke's in us; 5.01.295
the duke's unjust | thus to retort your manifest 5.01.300
his goods confiscate to the duke's dispose, ERR 1.01. 20
and charge you in the duke's name to obey me. 4.01. 70
to say so, but we are the poor duke's officers; ADO 3.05. 20 P
which is the duke's own person? LLL 1.01.181 P
the duke's pleasure is that you keep costard 1.02.127 P
at the duke's oak we meet. MND 1.02.110 P
was not charles, the duke's wrastler, here to AYL 1.01. 89 P
can you tell if rosalind, the duke's daughter, 1.01.105 P
for the duke's daughter, her cousin, so loves 1.01.107 P
wrastled with charles, the duke's wrastler, 1.02.126 P
yet such is now the duke's condition | that he 1.02.264
here come two of the banish'd duke's pages. 5.03. 5 P
hold on him, i charge you, in the duke's name. SHR 5.01. 88 P
with his own hand he slew the duke's brother. AWW 3.05. 7 P
that is antonio, the duke's eldest son, | that, 3.05. 76
upon a file with the duke's other letters in my 4.03.204 P
that is not the duke's letter, sir; 4.03.212 P
admit no kind of suit, | no, not the duke's. TN 1.02. 46
change two dukedoms for a duke's fair daughter. 2H6 1.01.219
she bears a duke's revenues on her back, | and 1.03. 80
and in the duke's behalf i'll give my voice, R3 3.04. 19
and the bodies | of the duke's confessor, john H8 1.01.218
you were the duke's surveyor, and lost your 1.02.172
gonzago is the duke's name, his wife, baptista. HAM 3.02.239 P
hark, the duke's trumpets! LR 2.01. 79
the duke's to blame in this, 'twill be ill taken 2.02.159
a voice potential | as double as the duke's. OTH 1.02. 14
rais'd and met, | are at the duke's already. 1.02. 44
the duke's in council, and your noble self | i 1.02. 92
'tis the duke's, | and, to say true, i stole it. TNK 3.06. 54

DUKES 20 FR 0.0022 REL FR 13 V 7 P

if the duke with the other dukes come not to MM 1.02. 1 P
why then all the dukes fall upon the king. 1.02. 3 P
lord angelo dukes it well in his absence; 3.02. 94 P
while we return these dukes what we decree. R2 1.03.122
therefore the dukes of berri and of britain, H5 2.04. 4
and the wars, and the king, and the dukes; 3.02.107 P
you dukes of orleance, bourbon, and of berri, 3.05. 41
high dukes, great princes, barons, lords, and 3.05. 46
the dukes of orleance, calaber, bretagne, and 2H6 1.01. 7
and make the meanest of you earls and dukes? 4.08. 37
two of thy name, both dukes of somerset, | have 3H6 5.01. 73
three dukes of somerset, threefold /renown'd 5.07. 5
dukes, earls, lords, gentlemen — indeed of all. R3 2.01. 69
the mighty dukes, | gloucester and buckingham. 2.04. 44
appears not which of the dukes he values most, LR 1.01. 5 P
not all the dukes of wat'rish burgundy | can buy 1.01.258
toward, 'twixt the dukes of cornwall and albany? 2.01. 11 P
either in snuffs and packings of the dukes, | or 3.01. 26
there is division between the dukes, and a worse 3.03. 9 P
let all the dukes and all the devils roar, | he TNK 2.06. 1

DULCET 6 FR 0.0006 REL FR 4 V 2 P

uttering such dulcet and harmonious breath MND 2.01.151
is | as are those dulcet sounds in break of day MV 3.02. 51
the fool's bolt, sir, and such dulcet diseases. AYL 5.04. 65 P
wakes, | to make a dulcet and a heavenly sound; SHR in.1. 51
his jarring, concord, and his discord, dulcet; AWW 1.01.172
to hear by the nose, it is dulcet in contagion. TN 2.03. 56 P

DULCHE 1 FR 0.0001 REL FR 0 V 1 P

o, pray, pray, pray! manka revania dulche. AWW 4.01. 78 P

DULL 97 FR 0.0109 REL FR 86 V 11 P

dull thing, i say so; TMP 1.02.285
for a god, | and worship this dull fool! 5.01.298
some sly trick blunt thurio's dull proceeding. TGV 2.06. 41

mortal thing | upon the dull earth dwelling. 4.02. 52
me unpregnant | and dull to all proceedings. MM 4.04. 21
oft, | when i am dull with care and melancholy, ERR 1.02. 20
are my discourses dull? 2.01. 91
what doth ensue | but moody and dull melancholy, 5.01. 79
left, | my dull deaf ears a little use to hear: 5.01.317
he is the prince's jester, a very dull fool; ADO 2.01.137 P
sing no moe, | of dumps so dull and heavy; 2.03. 71
by thy sweet grace's officer, anthony dull, a LLL 1.01.268 P
me, an't shall please you: i am anthony dull. 1.01.271 P
is not lead a metal heavy, dull, and slow? 3.01. 59
/dictynna, goodman dull, /dictynna, goodman dull 4.02. 36
goodman dull, /dictynna, goodman dull. 4.02. 36
via, goodman dull! 5.01.149 P
most dull, honest dull! to our sport; away! 5.01.155
most dull, honest dull! to our sport; away! 5.01.155
while she was in her dull and sleeping hour, | a MND 3.02. 8
this third, dull lead, with warning all as blunt MV 2.07. 8
she is not bred so dull but she can learn; 3.02.162
the motions of his spirit are dull as night, 5.01. 86
our natural wits too dull to reason of such AYL 1.02. 53 P
good breeding or comes of a very dull kindred. 3.02. 30 P
peace, you dull fool, i found them on a tree. 3.02.115 P
our slow designs when we ourselves are dull. AWW 1.01.219
and tell me for what dull part in't | you chose WT 5.01. 64
tale | vexing the dull ear of a drowsy man; JN 3.04.109
and dull unfeeling barren ignorance | is made my R2 1.03.168
so may you by my dull and heavy eye: 3.02.196
a feast | fits a dull fighter and a keen guest. 1H4 4.02. 80
their courage with hard labor tame and dull, 4.03. 23
so dull, so dead in look, so woe–begone, | drew 2H4 1.01. 71
turn'd on themselves, like dull and heavy lead. 1.01.118
o thou dull god, why li'st thou with the vile 3.01. 15
sanctities of heaven, | and our dull workings? 4.02. 22
all the foolish and dull and crudy vapors which 4.03. 98 P
unless some dull and favorable hand | will 4.05. 2
for peace itself should not so dull a kingdom H5 2.04. 16
is not their climate foggy, raw, and dull, | on 3.05. 16
and the dull elements of earth and water never 3.07. 21 P
boastful neighs | piercing the night's dull ear; 4.pr. 11
and in their pale dull mouths the /gimmal'd bit 4.02. 49
lines, | able to ravish any dull conceit; 1H6 5.05. 15
why then give way, dull clouds, to my quick R3 1.03.195
with dull unwillingness to repay a debt, | which 2.02. 92
cousin, thou wast not wont to be so dull. 4.02. 17
commenting | is leaden servitor to dull delay; 4.03. 52
my words are dull, o, quicken them with thine! 4.04.124
no doubt the murd'rous knife was dull and blunt 4.04.227
thou com'st thither — dull unmindful villain, 4.04.445
and sleep in dull cold marble where no mention H8 3.02.433
who in /this dull and long–continued truce | is TRO 1.03.262
if the dull brainless ajax come safe off, 1.03.380
the dull and factious nobles of the greeks 2.02.209
where the dull tribunes, | that with the fusty COR 1.09. 6
like a dull actor now | i have forgot my part, 5.03. 40
woods are ruthless, dreadful, deaf, and dull. TIT 2.01.128
my sight is very dull, what e'er it bodes. 2.03.195
bound | i cannot bound a pitch above dull woe; ROM 1.04. 21
turn back, dull earth, and find thy centre out. 2.01. 2
is fashion'd for the journey, dull and heavy. TIM 2.02.219
you are dull, casca; JC 1.03. 57
my dull brain was wrought | with things MAC 1.03.149
but do not dull thy palm with entertainment | of HAM 1.03. 64
a dull and muddy–mettled rascal, peak | like 2.02.567
my spirits grow dull, and fain i would beguile 3.02.226
inform against me, | and spur my dull revenge! 4.04. 33
that we are made of stuff so flat and dull 4.07. 31
for your dull ass will not mend his pace with 5.01. 57 P
and fierce quality | than doth, within a dull, LR 1.02. 13
this is a dull sight. are you not kent? 5.03.283
at this odd–even and dull watch o' th' night, OTH 1.01.123
the blood is made dull with the act of sport, 2.01.227 P
dull not device by coldness and delay. 2.03.388
o thou dull moor, that handkerchief thou 5.02.225
dull of tongue, and dwarfish. ANT 3.03. 16
shall i abide | in this dull world, which in thy 4.15. 61
chastis'd with the sober eye | of dull octavia. 5.02. 55
has | will stupefy and dull the sense awhile, CYM 1.05. 37
o sleep, thou ape of death, lie dull upon her, 2.02. 31
or is't not | too dull for your good wearing? 2.04. 41
play do not keep | a little dull time from us, TNK pr 31
is but his foil, to him, a mere dull shadow; 4.02. 26
boy, | who blush'd and pouted in a dull disdain, VEN 33
stone, | well–painted idol, image dull and dead, 212
looks on the dull earth with disturbed mind, 340
from forth dull sleep by dreadful fancy waking, LUC 450
debate where leisure serves with dull debaters; 1019
more than speed but dull and slow she deems: 1336
if the dull substance of my flesh were thought, SON 44. 1
excuse the slow offense | of my dull bearer, 51. 2
shall neigh (no dull flesh) in his fiery race, 51.11
'tis with so dull a cheer | that leaves look 97.13
because i would not dull you with my song. 102.14
while he insults o'er dull and speechless tribes 107.12
DULLARD 2 FR 0.0002 REL FR 2 V 0 P
and thou must make a dullard of the world | if LR 2.01. 74
what, mak'st thou me a dullard in this act? CYM 5.05.265
DULL–BRAIN'D 1 FR 0.0001 REL FR 1 V 0 P
the petty rebel, dull–brain'd buckingham, R3 4.04.332
DULL'D 2 FR 0.0002 REL FR 2 V 0 P
whom he hath dull'd and cloy'd with gracious H5 2.02. 9
this is the rarest dream that e'er dull'd sleep PER 5.01.161
DULLER 5 FR 0.0005 REL FR 3 V 2 P
jester, that i was duller than a great thaw, ADO 2.01.244 P
an animal, only sensible in the duller parts; LLL 4.02. 27 P
performance is ever the duller for his act, TIM 5.01. 24
and duller shouldst thou be than the fat weed HAM 1.05. 32
brain | gan in your duller britain operate CYM 5.05.197
DULLEST 3 FR 0.0003 REL FR 3 V 0 P
and twice to–day pick'd out the dullest scent. SHR in.1. 24
to | a savor that may strike the dullest nostril WT 1.02.421
fire | even to the dullest peasant in his camp, 2H4 1.01.113
DULLETH 1 FR 0.0001 REL FR 1 V 0 P
and borrowing dulleth /th' edge of husbandry. HAM 1.03. 77
DULL–EY'D 2 FR 0.0002 REL FR 2 V 0 P
i'll not be made a soft and dull–ey'd fool | to MV 3.03. 14
the sad companion, dull–ey'd melancholy, | /be PER 1.02. 2
DULLING 2 FR 0.0002 REL FR 2 V 0 P
with weariness | to th' dulling of my spirits. TMP 3.03. 6
dulling my lines, and doing me disgrace. SON 103. 8
DULLNESS 6 FR 0.0006 REL FR 4 V 2 P
'tis a good dullness, | and give it way. TMP 1.02.185
for always the dullness of the fool is the AYL 1.02. 55 P
wert the ass, thy dullness would torment thee, TIM 4.03.332 P
of feather'd cupid seel with wanton dullness OTH 1.03.269
his honor | even till a lethe'd dullness — how ANT 2.01. 27
the spirit of love with a perpetual dullness: SON 56. 8
/DULLY 1 FR 0.0001 REL FR 1 V 0 P
plods /dully on, to bear that weight in me, | as SON 50. 6
DULLY 2 FR 0.0002 REL FR 1 V 1 P
than (living dully sluggardiz'd at home) | wear TGV 1.01. 7
claudio, the time shall not go dully by us. ADO 2.01.364 P
DULY 8 FR 0.0009 REL FR 7 V 1 P
let this be duly perform'd, with a thought that MM 4.02.124 P
i duly am inform'd | his grace is at marsellis, AWW 4.04. 8
disburs'd i duly to his highness' soldiers; R2 1.01.127
"as duly, but not as truly, | as bird doth sing H5 3.02. 18
stood | and duly waited for my coming forth? 2H6 4.01. 62
nor my prayers | are not words duly hallowed, H8 2.03. 68
that they may have their wages duly paid 'em, 4.02.150
together rather than unfold | his measure duly. CYM 1.01. 27
DUMAINE 13 FR 0.0014 REL FR 9 V 4 P
you three, berowne, dumaine, and longaville, LLL 1.01. 15
my loving lord, dumaine is mortified: 1.01. 28
the young dumaine, a well–accomplish'd youth, 2.01. 56
dumaine transformed! 4.03. 80
dumaine, thy love is far from charity, | that in 4.03.125
where lies thy grief, o, tell me, good dumaine? 4.03.169
what was sent to you from fair dumaine? 5.02. 47
dumaine was at my service, and his sword: 5.02.276
dumaine is mine, as sure as bark on tree. 5.02.285
whether one captain dumaine be i' th' camp, a AWW 4.03.176 P
do you know this captain dumaine? 4.03.184 P
therefore once more to this captain dumaine. 4.03.248 P
what's his brother, the other captain dumaine? 4.03.283 P
/DUMB 2 FR 0.0002 REL FR 2 V 0 P
upon the tomb, | praising her when i am /dumb. ADO 5.03. 10
/in /thy /dumb /action /will /i /be /as /perfect TIT 3.02. 40
DUMB 47 FR 0.0053 REL FR 41 V 6 P
of tongue) a kind | of excellent dumb discourse. TMP 3.03. 39
this parting strikes poor lovers dumb. TGV 2.02. 20
dumb jewels often in their silent kind | more 3.01. 90
then in dumb silence will i bury mine, | for 3.01.208
count claudio, i can be secret as a dumb man; ADO 1.01.210 P
i would see, which will be merely a dumb show. 2.03.218 P
quite dumb? MND 5.01.327
i must be one of these same dumb wise men, | for MV 1.01.106
but, alas, who can converse with a dumb show? 1.02. 73 P
i am dumb. 5.01.279
and as oft is dumb | where dust and damn'd AWW 2.03.139
the shrieve's fool with child, a dumb innocent, 4.03.187 P
deep shame had struck me dumb, made me break off JN 4.02.235
in dumb significants proclaim your thoughts: 1H6 2.04. 26
the duke was dumb and could not speak a word. 2H6 3.02. 32
to tell my love unto his dumb deaf trunk, | and 3.02.144
but, like dumb statues or breathing stones, R3 3.07. 25
do thoughts unveil in their dumb cradles. TRO 3.03.200
i have seen the dumb men throng to see him, and COR 2.01.262
and in dumb shows | pass the remainder of our TIT 3.01.131
my scars can witness, dumb although they are, 5.03.114
ah, why should wrath be mute and fury dumb? 5.03.184
(which like dumb mouths do ope their ruby lips JC 3.01.260
sweet caesar's wounds, poor, poor, dumb mouths, 3.02.225
this spirit, dumb to us, will speak to him. HAM 1.01.171
act of fear, | stand dumb and speak not to him. 1.02.206
or given my heart a /winking, mute and dumb, 2.02.137
nothing but inexplicable dumb shows and noise. 3.02. 12 P
words to speak in thine ear will make thee dumb, 4.06. 25 P
the cutter | was as another nature, dumb; CYM 2.04. 84
what's dumb in show i'll plain with speech. PER 3.ch. 14
are almost run, | more a little, and then dumb. 5.02. 2
force, | or sentencing for aye their vigor dumb, TNK 1.01.195
and all this dumb play had his acts made plain VEN 359
though i were dumb, yet his proceedings teach 406
strike the wise dumb, and teach the fool to 1146
all orators are dumb when beauty pleadeth, LUC 268
know, | which he by dumb demeanor seeks to show; 474
sometime her grief is dumb and hath no words, 1105
and in my hearing be you mute and dumb, | my 1123
hath serv'd a dumb arrest upon his tongue, | who 1780
and dumb presagers of my speaking breast, | who SON 23.10
for who's so dumb that cannot write to thee, 38. 7
eyes, that taught the dumb on high to sing, 78. 5
which shall be most my glory, being dumb, | for 83.10
me for my dumb thoughts, speaking in effect. 85.14
because he needs no praise, wilt thou be dumb? 101. 9
/DUMB'D 1 FR 0.0001 REL FR 1 V 0 P
i would have spoke | was beastly /dumb'd by him. ANT 1.05. 50
DUMB–DISCOURSIVE 1 FR 0.0001 REL FR 1 V 0 P
there lurks a still and dumb–discoursive devil TRO 4.04. 90
DUMBE 1 FR 0.0001 REL FR 0 V 1 P
quickly," says he — master dumbe, our minister, 2H4 2.04. 88 P
DUMBLY 3 FR 0.0003 REL FR 3 V 0 P
and in conclusion dumbly have broke off, | not MND 5.01. 98
one kiss shall stop our mouths, and dumbly part; R2 5.01. 95
dumbly she passions, franticly she doteth, | she VEN 1059
/DUMBNESS 1 FR 0.0001 REL FR 0 V 1 P
/hobbididence, /prince /of /dumbness; LR 4.01. 60 P
DUMBNESS 4 FR 0.0004 REL FR 2 V 2 P
you should have bang'd the youth into dumbness. TN 3.02. 23 P
there was speech in their dumbness, language in WT 5.02. 13 P
/cunning in dumbness, from my weakness draws TRO 3.02.132
to th' dumbness of the gesture | one might TIM 1.01. 33
DUMBS 1 FR 0.0001 REL FR 1 V 0 P
deep clerks she dumbs, and with her neele PER 5.ch. 5
DUMP 3 FR 0.0003 REL FR 1 V 2 P
to their instruments | tune a deploring dump — TGV 3.02. 84
o, play me some merry dump to comfort me. ROM 4.05.107 P
not a dump we, 'tis no time to play now. 4.05.109 P
/DUMPS 1 FR 0.0001 REL FR 1 V 0 P
/and /doleful /dumps /the /mind /oppress, | then ROM 4.05.127
DUMPS 4 FR 0.0004 REL FR 4 V 0 P
sing no moe, | of dumps so dull and heavy; ADO 2.03. 71
why, how now, daughter katherine, in your dumps? SHR 2.01.284
my lord, to step out of these dreary dumps, TIT 1.01.391
distress likes dumps when time is kept with LUC 1127
D'UN 1 FR 0.0001 REL FR 0 V 1 P
que je tombe entre les mains d'un chevalier, je H5 4.04. 56 P
DUN* *(also don*)*
DUN* 4 FR 0.0004 REL FR 4 V 0 P
of dun adramadio, dun adramadio. LLL 4.03.195
of dun adramadio, dun adramadio. 4.03.195
if thou art dun, we'll draw thee from the mire ROM 1.04. 41
if snow be white, why then her breasts are dun; SON 130. 3
DUNCAN 13 FR 0.0014 REL FR 13 V 0 P
that croaks the fatal entrance of duncan | under MAC 1.05. 39
my dearest love, | duncan comes here to–night. 1.05. 59
this duncan | hath borne his faculties so meek, 1.07. 16
when duncan is asleep | (whereto the rather 1.07. 61
you and i perform upon | th' unguarded duncan? 1.07. 70
hear it not, duncan, for it is a knell, | that 2.01. 63
wake duncan with thy knocking! 2.02. 71
here lay duncan, | his silver skin lac'd with 2.03.111
for them the gracious duncan have i murther'd, 3.01. 65
duncan is in his grave; 3.02. 22
dagger which you said | led you to duncan. 3.04. 62
the gracious duncan | was pitied of macbeth; 3.06. 3
the /son of duncan | (from whom this tyrant 3.06. 24
DUNCAN'S 3 FR 0.0003 REL FR 3 V 0 P
and duncan's horses (a thing most strange and MAC 2.04. 14
where is duncan's body? 2.04. 32
think | that, had he duncan's sons under his key 3.06. 18
DUNCES 1 FR 0.0001 REL FR 1 V 0 P
proh deum, medius fidius, ye are all dunces! TNK 3.05. 11
/DUN–COLOR'D 1 FR 0.0001 REL FR 0 V 1 P
does indifferent well in a /dun–color'd stock. TN 1.03.135 P
D'UNE 1 FR 0.0001 REL FR 0 V 1 P
votre /grandeur en baisant la main d'une (notre H5 5.02.255 P
DUNG 3 FR 0.0003 REL FR 1 V 2 P
which sleeps, and never palates more the dung, ANT 5.02. 7
for these bastards of dung — as you know they STM II.C 12 P
as you know they grow in dung — have infected II.C 13 P
DUNGEON 7 FR 0.0008 REL FR 5 V 2 P
let me live, sir, in a dungeon, i' th' stocks, AWW 4.03.244 P
traitor your degree, and the dungeon your place, 2H4 4.03. 7 P
my flow'ring youth | within a loathsome dungeon, 1H6 2.05. 57
some dungeon. R3 1.02.111
nor airless dungeon, nor strong links of iron, JC 1.03. 94
and live upon the vapor of a dungeon | than keep OTH 3.03.271
sun, and solace | i' th' dungeon by a snuff! CYM 1.06. 87
/DUNGEONS 1 FR 0.0001 REL FR 0 V 1 P
/wards, /and /dungeons, /denmark /being /one /o' HAM 2.02.246 P
DUNGEONS 1 FR 0.0001 REL FR 1 V 0 P
the hue of dungeons, and the school of night; LLL 4.03.251
DUNGHILL 10 FR 0.0011 REL FR 7 V 3 P
then did the sun on dunghill shine. WIV 1.03. 63 P
go to, thou hast it ad dunghill, at the fingers' LLL 5.01. 77 P
o, i smell false latin, "dunghill" for unguem. 5.01. 79 P
out, dunghill! dar'st thou brave a nobleman? JN 4.03. 87
shall dunghill curs confront the helicons? 2H4 5.03.104
shall i be flouted thus by dunghill grooms? 1H6 1.03. 14
base dunghill villain and mechanical, | i'll 2H6 1.03.193
thee headlong by the heels | unto a dunghill, 4.10. 81
throw this slave | upon the dunghill. LR 3.07. 97
out, dunghill! 4.06.243
DUNGHILLS 2 FR 0.0002 REL FR 1 V 1 P
his animals on his dunghills are as much bound AYL 1.01. 15 P
dying like men, though buried in your dunghills, H5 4.03. 99
DUNGY 2 FR 0.0002 REL FR 2 V 0 P
the face to sweeten | of the whole dungy earth. WT 2.01.157
our dungy earth alike | feeds beast as man; ANT 1.01. 35
DUNNEST 1 FR 0.0001 REL FR 1 V 0 P
and pall thee in the dunnest smoke of hell, MAC 1.05. 51
DUN'S 1 FR 0.0001 REL FR 1 V 0 P
tut, dun's the mouse, the constable's own word. ROM 1.04. 40
DUNSINANE 9 FR 0.0010 REL FR 9 V 0 P
great birnan wood to high dunsinane hill | shall MAC 4.01. 93
great dunsinane he strongly fortifies. 5.02. 12
till birnan wood remove to dunsinane | i cannot 5.03. 2
bane, | till birnan forest come to dunsinane. 5.03. 60
were i from dunsinane away and clear, | profit 5.03. 61
the confident tyrant | keeps still in dunsinane, 5.04. 9
till birnan wood | do come to dunsinane," and 5.05. 44
and now a wood | comes toward dunsinane. 5.05. 45
though birnan wood be come to dunsinane, | and 5.08. 30
DUNSMORE 1 FR 0.0001 REL FR 1 V 0 P
by this at dunsmore, marching hitherward. 3H6 5.01. 3
DUNSTABLE 1 FR 0.0001 REL FR 1 V 0 P
held a late court at dunstable — six miles off H8 4.01. 27
DUPP'D 1 FR 0.0001 REL FR 1 V 0 P
his clo'es, | and dupp'd the chamber–door, | let HAM 4.05. 53
DURANCE 7 FR 0.0008 REL FR 4 V 3 P
perpetual durance? MM 3.01. 66
ay, just, perpetual durance — a restraint, 3.01. 67
on decay'd men and gives them suits of durance; ERR 4.03. 27 P
i give thee thy liberty, set thee from durance, LLL 3.01.128 P
he upon some action | is now in durance, at TN 5.01.276
not a buff jerkin a most sweet robe of durance? 1H4 1.02. 43 P
is in base durance and contagious prison, 2H4 5.05. 34
DURE *(also dare*)*
DURE 1 FR 0.0001 REL FR 1 V 0 P
and't might be, | to dure ill–dealing fortune. TNK 1.03. 5
DURING 14 FR 0.0015 REL FR 10 V 4 P
during which time he ne'er saw syracusa: ERR 5.01.329
hath he lost sixpence a day during his life; MND 4.02. 20 P
any tinker in his own language during my life. 1H4 2.04. 19 P
the better of myself, and thee, during my life; 2.04.274 P
they are for the town's end, to beg during life. 5.03. 38 P
during the time edward the third did reign. 1H6 1.02. 31
during whose reign the percies of the north, 2.05. 67
for that which we have fled | during the life, 4.07. 50
times, | during the wars of york and lancaster, R3 1.04. 15
it, with the place and honors, | during my life; H8 3.02.249
sir, | during all question of the gentle truce; TRO 4.01. 12
our office may, | during his power, go sleep. COR 2.01.223
resign, | during the life of this old majesty, LR 5.03.300
and unnatural revolts | during their use, and CYM 4.04. 7
/DURST 1 FR 0.0001 REL FR 1 V 0 P
/durst thou support a publish'd traitor? LR 4.06.232
DURST 58 FR 0.0065 REL FR 48 V 10 P
dear, they durst not, | so dear the love my TMP 1.02.140

i durst have denied that before you were so ERR 2.02. 66 P
might hurt their enemies — if they durst — ADO 5.01. 98
never durst poet touch a pen to write | until LLL 4.03.343
soul, she durst not lie | near this lack–love, MND 2.02. 76
durst thou have look'd upon him being awake? 3.02. 69
i durst go no further than the lie AYL 5.04. 85 P
nor he durst not give me the lie direct; 5.04. 86 P
how durst you, villains, bring it from the SHR 4.01.163
you that durst swear that your mistress bianca 4.02. 12
to the king | that which i durst not speak. AWW 2.03.289
durst make too bold a herald of my tongue; 5.03. 46
but durst not tempt a minister of honor, | lest WT 2.02. 48
she durst not call me so, | if she did know me 2.03.123
thin | that in mine ear i durst not stick a rose JN 1.01.142
where ever englishman durst set his foot. R2 1.01. 66
he durst as well have met the devil alone | as 1H4 1.03.116
that even our love durst not come near your 5.01. 63
i had thought weariness durst not have attach'd 2H4 2.02. 3 P
be, if he durst steal any thing adventurously. H5 4.04. 73 P
he sent to hell, and none durst stand him; 1H6 1.01.123
durst not presume to look once in the face. 1.01.140
none durst come near for fear of sudden death. 1.04. 48
or durst not for his craven heart say thus. 2.04. 87
i hid me in these woods and durst not peep out, 2H6 4.10. 3 P
he durst not sit there, had your father liv'd. 3H6 1.01. 63
no, nor your manhood that durst make you stay. 2.02.108
durst the traitor breathe out so proud words? 4.01.112
and who durst smile when warwick bent his brow? 5.02. 22
no discerner | durst wag his tongue in censure. H8 1.01. 33
allay those tongues | that durst disperse it. 2.01.153
within these forty hours surrey durst better 3.02.253
and durst commend a secret to your ear | much 5.01. 17
(with whom relation | durst never meddle) in the TRO 3.03.202
sir, as it were, durst not (look you, sir) show COR 4.05.207 P
stood for rome, | and durst not once peep out. 4.06. 46
what roman lord it was durst do the deed; TIT 4.01. 62
and for mine own part, i durst not laugh, for JC 1.02.249 P
caesar liv'd, he durst not thus have mov'd me. 4.03. 58
peace, peace, you durst not so have tempted him. 4.03. 59
i durst not? 4.03. 60
what? durst not tempt him? 4.03. 62
for your life you durst not. 4.03. 62
not so have been, | durst i have done my will. 5.03. 48
when you durst do it, then you were a man; MAC 1.07. 49
which we durst never yet — and with strain'd LR 1.01.169
were good, my lord, i durst swear it were his; 1.02. 63 P
they durst not do't; 2.04. 22
this kiss, if it durst speak, | would stretch 4.02. 22
i durst, my lord, to wager she is honest; OTH 4.02. 12
i durst attempt it against any lady in the world CYM 1.04.112 P
how durst thy tongue move anger to our face? PER 1.02. 54
we have a maid in meteline, i durst wager, 5.01. 43
an offer'd opportunity | i durst not wish for. TNK 2.03. 75
durst better have endur'd cold iron than done it 2.06. 10
that thou durst, arcite! 3.01. 57
but durst not ask of her audaciously | why her LUC 1223
were born, | or durst inhabit on a living brow; SON 68. 4

D'USER 1 FR 0.0001 REL FR 0 V 1 P
et non pour les dames de honneur d'user. H5 3.04. 54 P

DUSKY 6 FR 0.0006 REL FR 6 V 0 P
plot | the means that dusky dis my daughter got, TMP 4.01. 89
for smoke and dusky vapors of the night, | am 1H6 2.02. 27
here dies the dusky torch of mortimer, | chok'd 2.05.122
and when the dusky sky began to rob | my 2H6 3.02.104
and call'd them blind and dusky spectacles, 3.02.112
untimely smoth'red in their dusky graves. R3 4.04. 70

/DUST 2 FR 0.0002 REL FR 2 V 0 P
/that /threw'st /dust /upon /his /goodly /head 2H4 1.03.103
water–pots, | /ay, /and /laying /autumn's /dust. LR 4.06.197

DUST 63 FR 0.0071 REL FR 56 V 7 P
but see how i lay the dust with my tears. TGV 2.03. 32 P
many a thousand grains | that issue out of dust. MM 3.01. 21
to be overmaster'd with a piece of valiant dust? ADO 2.01. 61 P
before, | to sweep the dust behind the door. MND 5.01.390
where dust and damn'd oblivion is the tomb | of AWW 2.03.140
was in mine eye | the dust that did offend it. 5.03. 55
destroy our friends and after weep their dust; 5.03. 64
are they like to take dust, like mistress mall's TN 1.03.127 P
and lay me | where no priest shovels in dust. WT 4.04.458
and by the merit of vild gold, dross, dust, JN 3.01.165
and stop this gap of breath with fulsome dust, 3.04. 32
of what i mean to speak | shall blow each dust, 3.04.128
a grain, a dust, a gnat, a wandering hair, | any 4.01. 92
my liege, her ear | is stopp'd with dust: 4.02.120
bosom | that all my bowels crumble up to dust. 5.07. 31
wipe off the dust that hides our sceptre's gilt, R2 2.01.294
dar'd once to touch a dust of england's ground? 2.03. 91
make dust our paper, and with rainy eyes | write 3.02.146
and lay the summer's dust with show'rs of blood 3.03. 43
threw dust and rubbish on king richard's head. 5.02. 6
but dust was thrown upon his sacred head, 5.02. 30
and shed my dear blood drop by drop in the dust, 1H4 1.03.134
no, percy, thou art dust, | and food for — 5.04. 85
only compound me with forgotten dust; 2H4 4.05.115
days, | nor from the dust of old oblivion rak'd, H5 2.04. 87
now, france, thy glory droopeth to the dust. 1H6 5.03. 29
he hath no eyes, the dust hath blinded them. 2H6 3.03. 14
write in the dust this sentence with thy blood: 3H6 5.01. 56
lo, now my glory smear'd in dust and blood! 5.02. 23
what is pomp, rule, reign, but earth and dust? 5.02. 27
which now, two tender bedfellows for dust, | thy R3 4.04.385
and /give to dust, that is a little gilt, | more TRO 3.03.178
the dust on antique time would lie unswept, COR 2.03.119
be meet, | and throw their power i' th' dust. 3.01.170
they to dust should grind it | and throw't 3.02.103
in the dust i write | my heart's deep languor, TIT 3.01. 12
hark, villains, i will grind your bones to dust, 5.02.186
strew — | o woe, thy canopy is dust and stones! ROM 5.03. 13
fearful scouring | doth choke the air with dust. TIM 5.02. 16
basis /lies along | no worthier than the dust! JC 3.01.116
lids | seek for thy noble father in the dust. HAM 1.02. 71
yet, to me, what is this quintessence of dust? 2.02.308 P
/compounded it with dust, whereto 'tis kin. 4.02. 6
imagination trace the noble dust of alexander, 5.01.203 P
alexander returneth to dust, the dust is earth, 5.01.210 P
alexander returneth to dust, the dust is earth, 5.01.210 P
now pile your dust upon the quick and dead, 5.01.251
you are not worth the dust which the rude wind LR 4.02. 30
head | to the descent and dust below thy foot, 5.03.138
the dust | should have ascended to the roof of ANT 3.06. 48
differs in dignity, | whose dust is both alike. CYM 4.02. 5
rotting | together, have one dust, yet reverence 4.02.247
all must, | as chimney–sweepers, come to dust. 4.02.263
physic, must | all follow this and come to dust. 4.02.269
lovers must | consign to thee and come to dust. 4.02.275
blows dust in others' eyes, to spread itself; PER 1.01. 97
rust | until this day, to scour it in the dust. 2.02. 55
humane grace | affords them dust and shadow. TNK 1.01.145
'twas thy power | to put life into dust: 5.01.110
and smear with dust their glitt'ring golden LUC 945
begrim'd with sweat, and smeared all with dust, 1381
that churl death my bones with dust shall cover, SON 32. 2
case | weighs not the dust and injury of age, 108.10

DUSTY 3 FR 0.0003 REL FR 3 V 0 P
characterless are grated | to dusty nothing, yet TRO 3.02.189
have lighted fools | the way to dusty death. MAC 5.05. 23
thou grand decider | of dusty and old titles, TNK 5.01. 64

DUTCH 2 FR 0.0002 REL FR 1 V 1 P
than half stew'd in grease, like a dutch dish) WIV 3.05.119 P
if there be here german, or dane, low dutch, AWW 4.01. 71

DUTCHMAN 3 FR 0.0003 REL FR 1 V 2 P
strange disguises — as to be a dutchman to–day, ADO 3.02. 33 P
"veal," quoth the dutchman. is not veal a calf? LLL 5.02.247
lustick, as the dutchman says. AWW 2.03. 41 P

DUTCHMAN'S 1 FR 0.0001 REL FR 0 V 1 P
will hang like an icicle on a dutchman's beard, TN 3.02. 28 P

/DUTEOUS 1 FR 0.0001 REL FR 1 V 0 P
/own /breath /release /all /duteous /oaths; R2 4.01.210

DUTEOUS 11 FR 0.0012 REL FR 10 V 1 P
teaching his duteous land | audacious cruelty. 1H4 4.03. 44
which my most inward true and duteous spirit 2H4 4.05.147
but with all duteous love | doth cherish you and R3 2.01. 33
which i will purchase with my duteous service; 2.01. 64
that i'll acquaint our duteous citizens | with 3.05. 65
as duteous to the vices of thy mistress | as LR 4.06.253
mark | many a duteous and knee–crooking knave OTH 1.01. 45
be but duteous, and true preferment shall tender CYM 3.05.154 P
never master had | a page so kind, so duteous, 5.05. 86
and yet the duteous vassal scarce is gone; LUC 1360
the eyes ('fore duteous) now converted are SON 7.11

DUTIES 20 FR 0.0022 REL FR 19 V 1 P
recount their particular duties afterwards. ADO 4.01. 3 P
he gave you all the duties of a man, | trimm'd 1H4 5.02. 55
they know their duties. 2H4 4.02.101
tongues spit their duties out, and cold hearts H8 1.02. 61
keep your duties, | as i have set them down. COR 1.07. 1
by all the duties that i owe to rome, | this TIT 1.01.414
face, | the last true duties of thy noble son! 5.03.155
your highness' part | is to receive our duties; MAC 1.04. 24
and our duties | are to your throne and state, 1.04. 24
me, to the which my duties | are with a most 3.01. 16
our duties, and the pledge. 3.04. 91
may kindly say | our duties did his welcome pay. 4.01.132
to give these mourning duties to your father. HAM 1.02. 88
i | return those duties back as are right fit, LR 1.01. 97
observants | that stretch their duties nicely. 2.02.104
pilot, | and by him do my duties to the senate. OTH 3.02. 2
say that they slack their duties, | and pour our 4.03. 87
you were inspir'd to do those duties which | you CYM 2.03. 50
friends, | the boy hath taught us manly duties. 4.02.397
with pure aspects did him peculiar duties. LUC 14

DUTIFUL 2 FR 0.0002 REL FR 2 V 0 P
show men dutiful? H5 2.02.127
you know me dutiful, therefore, dear sir, | let TRO 5.03. 72

DUTY 158 FR 0.0178 REL FR 138 V 20 P
proceed in, | but for my duty to your ladyship. TGV 2.01.107
my duty will i boast of, nothing else. 2.04.111
and duty never yet did want his meed. 2.04.112
my duty pricks me on to utter that | which, else 3.01. 8
proud, disobedient, stubborn, lacking duty, 3.01. 69
have been cherish'd by her child–like duty, | i 3.01. 75
of mine oath, | a charitable duty of my order, ERR 5.01.107
i owe you all duty. ADO 1.01.156 P
it is my cousin's duty to make cur'sy and say, 2.01. 52 P
him i (as my ever–esteemed duty pricks me on) LLL 1.01.265 P
of devoted and heart–burning heat of duty, don 1.01.277 P
i forgive thy duty. 4.02.143 P
our duty is so rich, so infinite, | that we may 5.02.199
with duty and desire we follow you. MND 1.01.127
be amiss, | when simpleness and duty tender it. 5.01. 83
and duty in his service perishing. 5.01. 86
and what poor duty cannot do, noble respect 5.01. 91
and in the modesty of fearful duty | i read as 5.01.101
not so, sir, neither, i know my duty. MV 3.05. 54 P
i attend them with all respect and duty. AYL 1.02.167 P
when service sweat for duty, not for meed! 2.03. 58
all adoration, duty, and observance, | all 5.02. 96
so please your lordship to accept our duty. SHR in.1. 82
such duty to the drunkard let him do, | with in.1. 113
may show her duty and make known her love?" in.1. 117
so shall i no whit be behind in duty | to fair 1.02.174
i do, | so well i know my duty to my elders. 2.01. 7
do thy duty and have thy duty, for my master and 4.01. 36 P
do thy duty and have thy duty, for my master and 4.01. 37 P
no duty? 4.01.126
now do your duty throughly, i advise you. 4.04. 11
fie, what a foolish duty call you this? 5.02.125
i would your duty were as foolish too. 5.02.126
the wisdom of your duty, fair bianca, | hath 5.02.127
the more fool you for laying on my duty. 5.02.129
what duty they do owe their lords and husbands. 5.02.131
such duty as the subject owes the prince, | even 5.02.155
in token of which duty, if he please, | my hand 5.02.178
my thanks and duty are your majesty's. AWW 1.02. 23
which i held my duty speedily to acquaint you 1.03.118 P
my duty then shall pay me for my pains. 2.01.125
which both thy duty owes and our power claims, 2.03.161
my duty to you. 3.02. 25 P
my mother did but duty, such, my lord, | as you 4.02. 12
my duty, madam, and most humble service. TN 3.01. 95
my lord would speak, my duty hushes me. 5.01.107
i leave my duty a little unthought of, and speak 5.01.309 P
who has | (his dignity and duty both cast off) WT 5.01.183
from his liking, | where you were tied in duty; 5.01.213
then | to pay that duty which you truly owe | to JN 2.01.247
be your man, attend on you | with all true duty. 3.03. 73
disgrace | neglected my sworn duty in that case. R2 1.01.134
the one my duty owes, but my fair name, 1.01.167
the appellant in all duty greets your highness, 1.03. 52
swear by the duty that y' owe to god | (our part 1.03.180
long | shall tender duty make me suffer wrong? 2.01.164
whom both my oath | and duty bids defend; 2.02.113
thy knee, | whose duty is deceivable and false. 2.03. 84
tradition, form, and ceremonious duty, | for you 3.02.173
land, | my stooping duty tenderly shall show. 3.03. 48
to pay their aweful duty to our presence? 3.03. 76
all apart, | and show fair duty to his majesty. 3.03.188
to bear and he to taste | their fruits of duty. 3.04. 63
cousin westmerland, | our duty this way lies; 1H4 5.04. 16
my lord, my humble duty rememb'red, i will not 2H4 2.01.125 P
displeasure, my cur'sy, my duty, and my speech, ep 2 P
you | with hearts create of duty and of zeal. H5 2.02. 31
my soul, and my heart, and my duty, and my live, 3.06. 8 P
every subject's duty is the king's, but every 4.01.177 P
my duty to you both, on equal love. 5.02. 23
appear | how much in duty i am bound to both. 1H6 2.01. 37
my lord, it were your duty to forbear. 3.01. 52
my foot, | and, in reguerdon of that duty done, 3.01.169
and as my duty springs, so perish they | that 3.01.174
unto my wars, | to do my duty to my sovereign; 3.04. 4
i owe him little duty, and less love, | and take 4.04. 34
my soul | as i in duty love my king and country! 2H6 1.03.158
knee, | disdaining duty that to us belongs. 3.01. 17
in duty bend thy knee to me | that bows unto the 5.01.173
i know my duty, you are all undutiful. 3H6 5.05. 33
the duty that i owe unto your majesty | i seal 5.07. 28
tears) | i will with all expedient duty see you. R3 1.02.216
you well serv'd, you would be taught your duty. 1.03.249
to serve me well, you all should do me duty, 1.03.250
serve me well, and teach yourselves that duty! 1.03.252
thy brother's love, our duty, and thy faults 1.04.224
love, charity, obedience, and true duty! 2.02.108
thou behold a subject die | for truth, for duty, 3.03. 4
(as he made semblance of his duty) would | have H8 1.02.198
with my love and duty | i would surrender it. 1.04. 80
our breach of duty this way | is business of 2.02. 68
my bond to wedlock or my love and duty, 2.04. 40
should, notwithstanding that your bond of duty, 3.02.188
all the world should crack their duty to you 3.02.193
and | appear in forms more horrid), yet my duty, 3.02.196
it is my duty | t' attend your highness' 5.01. 90
and, to strengthen | that holy duty, out of dear 5.02.154
what he shall receive of us in duty | gives us TRO 3.01.156
of thy deep duty more impression show | than COR 5.03. 51
show duty as mistaken all this while | between 5.03. 55
that thou restrain'st from me the duty which 5.03.167
and hearts of men | at duty, more than i could TIM 4.03.262
duty, and zeal to your unmatched mind, | care of 4.03.516
it is my duty, sir. JC 4.03.260
i should not urge thy duty past thy might; 4.03.261
it, | as needful in our loves, fitting our duty? HAM 1.01.173
farewell, and let your haste commend your duty. 1.02. 39
in that, and all things, will we show our duty. 1.02. 40
to denmark | to show my duty in your coronation, 1.02. 53
yet now, i must confess, that duty done, | my 1.02. 54
and we did think it writ down in our duty | to 1.02.222
our duty to your honor. 1.02.252
good liege | i hold my duty as i hold my soul, 2.02. 44
what majesty should be, what duty is, | why day 2.02. 87
who in her duty and obedience, mark, | hath 2.02.107
o my lord, if my duty be too bold, my love is 3.02.348 P
with us, | we shall express our duty in his eye, 4.04. 6
i commend my duty to your lordship. 5.02.182 P
half my love with him, half my care and duty. LR 1.01.102
think'st thou that duty shall have dread to 1.01.147
prescribe not us our duty. 1.01.276
for my duty cannot be silent when i think your 1.04. 65 P
parts, | that all particulars of duty know, 1.04.264
it was my duty, sir. 2.01.106
from the place that showed | my duty kneeling, 2.04. 30
value her desert | than she to scant her duty. 2.04.140
my duty cannot suffer | t' obey in all your 3.04.148
my lady charg'd my duty in this business. 4.05. 18
are | who, trimm'd in forms and visages of duty, OTH 1.01. 50
heaven is my judge, not i for love and duty, 1.01. 59
tying her duty, beauty, wit, and fortunes | in 1.01.135
with his free duty recommends you thus, | and 1.03. 41
father, | i do perceive here a divided duty: 1.03.181
you are the lord of duty; 1.03.184
and so much duty as my mother show'd | to you, 1.03.186
a knave teach me my duty? 2.03.147 P
have you forgot all place of sense and duty? 2.03.167
though i am bound to every act of duty, | i am 3.03.134
to show the love and duty that i bear you | with 3.03.194
not a present thought, | by duty ruminated. ANT 2.02.138
i have done my duty. 2.05. 88
give me grace to lay | my duty on your hand. 3.13. 82
may be it is the period of your duty; 4.02. 25
(always reserv'd my holy duty) what | his rage CYM 1.01. 87
nor to us hath tender'd | the duty of the day. 3.05. 32
like | a thing more made of malice than of duty, 3.05. 33
she should that duty leave unpaid to you | which 3.05. 48
we will discharge our duty. 3.07. 16
by you reliev'd, would force me to my duty; PER 3.03. 22
cousin, | is but a debt to honor, and my duty. TNK 3.06. 19
thou wast begot, to get it is thy duty. VEN 168
and dotes on what he looks, 'gainst law or duty. LUC 497
for fleet–wing'd duty with thought's feathers 1216
his kindled duty kindled her mistrust, | that 1352
thy merit hath my duty strongly knit, | to thee SON 26. 2
i send this written ambassage | to witness duty, 26. 4
duty so great, which wit so poor as mine | may 26. 5
or to remain | in personal duty, following where LC 130

DUTY'S 1 FR 0.0001 REL FR 1 V 0 P
thus, for my duty's sake, i rather chose | to TGV 3.01. 17

DWARF 4 FR 0.0004 REL FR 3 V 1 P
you like a man than follow him like a dwarf. WIV 3.02. 6 P
get you gone, you dwarf; MND 3.02.328
alas, this is a child, a silly dwarf! 1H6 2.03. 22
a stirring dwarf we do allowance give | before a TRO 2.03.137

DWARFISH 5 FR 0.0005 REL FR 5 V 0 P
esteem, | because i am so dwarfish and so low? MND 3.02.295
is well prepar'd | to whip this dwarfish war, JN 5.02.135
their dwarfish pages were | as cherubins, all H8 1.01. 22

like a giant's robe | upon a dwarfish thief. MAC 5.02. 22
dull of tongue, and dwarfish. ANT 3.03. 16
DWELL 46 FR 0.0052 REL FR 36 V 10 P
there's nothing ill can dwell in such a temple. TMP 1.02.458
good things will strive to dwell with't. 1.02.460
dwell | in this bare island by your spell, | but ep 7
i myself dwell with master doctor caius — WIV 2.02. 45 P
and dwell upon your grave when you are dead; ERR 3.01.104
o then, what graces in my love do dwell, | that MND 1.01.206
for me, | i'll rather dwell in my necessity. MV 1.03.155
that dwells with him, dwell with him or no? 2.02. 47 P
where dwell you, pretty youth? AYL 3.02.334 P
the cony that you see dwell where she is kindled 3.02.339 P
france is a stable, we that dwell in't jades, AWW 2.03.284
but you shall let it dwell darkly with you. 4.03. 11 P
to dwell in solemn shades of endless night. R2 1.03.177
such outward things dwell not in my desires. H5 4.03. 27
to all that do dwell in this house, because the 2H6 4.10. 64 P
where did you dwell when i was king of england? 3H6 3.01. 74
so long sund'red friends should dwell upon. R3 5.03.100
enforcement of the time | forbids to dwell upon, 5.03.239
he should still | dwell in his musings, but i am H8 3.02.133
my hopes in heaven do dwell. 3.02.459
when i shall dwell with worms, and my poor name 4.02.126
fain would i dwell on form, fain, fain deny ROM 2.02. 88
sleep dwell upon thine eyes, peace in thy breast 2.02.186
o that deceit should dwell | in such a gorgeous 3.02. 84
dwell i but in the suburbs | of your good JC 2.01.285
where do you dwell? 3.03. 7 P
where do i dwell? 3.03. 14 P
briefly, i dwell by the capitol. 3.03. 25 P
than by destruction dwell in doubtful joy. MAC 3.02. 7
and, though he in a fertile climate dwell, OTH 1.01. 70
scorns | that dwell in every region of his face, 4.01. 83
the house you dwell in proclaims you to be a PER 4.06. 77 P
a /palace | for the crown'd truth to dwell in. 5.01.122
her spirits would sojourn (rather dwell on) TNK 1.03. 77
place | where i may ever dwell in sight of her? 2.03. 82
by him, like a shadow, | i'll ever dwell. 2.06. 35
long time his eye | will dwell upon his object; 5.03. 49
and says, within her bosom it shall dwell, VEN 1173
and in that cold, hot burning fire doth dwell; LUC 1557
the lovely gaze where every eye doth dwell SON 5. 2
you live in this, and dwell in lovers' eyes. 55.14
this vile world, with vildest worms to dwell: 71. 4
lean penury within that pen doth dwell | that to 84. 5
thy sweet beloved name no more shall dwell, 89.10
that in thy face sweet love should ever dwell; 93.10
to dwell with him in thoughts, or to remain | in LC 129
DWELL'D 1 FR 0.0001 REL FR 1 V 0 P
but none where all distress and dolor dwell'd, LUC 1446
DWELLERS 1 FR 0.0001 REL FR 1 V 0 P
have i not seen dwellers on form and favor SON 125. 5
DWELLING 11 FR 0.0012 REL FR 5 V 6 P
mortal thing | upon the dull earth dwelling. TGV 4.02. 52
dwelling in a continual 'larum of jealousy, WIV 3.05. 71 P
no, not for dwelling where you do. MM 2.01.247 P
you could purchase in so remov'd a dwelling. AYL 3.02.342 P
my name is call'd vincentio, my dwelling pisa, SHR 4.05. 55
the place of your dwelling? WT 4.04.718 P
god, you have here goodly dwelling and rich. 2H4 5.03. 5 P
for your dwelling — briefly. JC 3.03. 24 P
never a villain dwelling in all denmark — | but HAM 1.05.123
on others, on /him | live in fair dwelling. TNK 5.03. 55
love lack'd a dwelling and made him her place; LC 82
DWELLING-HOUSE 1 FR 0.0001 REL FR 1 V 0 P
some suppose the soul's frail dwelling-house) JN 5.07. 3
DWELLING-PLACE 1 FR 0.0001 REL FR 1 V 0 P
in their assign'd and native dwelling-place. AYL 2.01. 63
DWELLING-PLACES 1 FR 0.0001 REL FR 0 V 1 P
to repair to your several dwelling-places, and 1H6 1.03. 77 P
DWELLS 22 FR 0.0024 REL FR 16 V 6 P
she that dwells | ten leagues beyond man's life; TMP 2.01.246
in the sweetest bud | the eating canker dwells, TGV 1.01. 43
and there dwells one mistress quickly, which is WIV 1.02. 2 P
she dwells so securely on the excellency of her 2.02.242 P
"here dwells benedick the married man"? ADO 5.01.183 P
me whether one launcelot, that dwells with him, MV 2.02. 47 P
approach, | here dwells my father jew. 2.06. 25
rich honesty dwells like a miser, sir, in a poor AYL 5.04. 60 P
lies by a beggar, if a beggar dwells near him; TN 3.01. 9 P
to seek out sorrow that dwells every where. R2 1.02. 72
from cold and empty veins where no blood dwells.
R3 1.02. 59
tear-falling pity dwells not in this eye. 4.02. 65
combat, | yet in the trial much opinion dwells; TRO 1.03.336
but value dwells not in particular will, | it 2.02. 53
that dwells with gods above. 3.02.157
and hereabouts 'a dwells — which late i noted ROM 5.01. 38
dwells in the /fickle grace of her he follows. LR 2.04.186
the blest infusions | that dwells in vegetives, PER 3.02. 36
he is arriv'd | here where his daughter dwells, 5.ch. 15
of all the world, | dwells fair-ey'd honor. TNK 2.05. 29
or what great danger dwells upon my suit? VEN 206
which on thy soft cheek for complexion dwells SON 99. 4
DWELL'ST 2 FR 0.0002 REL FR 0 V 2 P
where dwell'st thou? COR 4.05. 37 P
then thou dwell'st with daws too? 4.05. 44 P
DWELT 2 FR 0.0002 REL FR 1 V 1 P
"there dwelt a man in babylon, lady, lady!" TN 2.03. 78 P
dwelt by a churchyard. WT 2.01. 30
DWINDLE 2 FR 0.0002 REL FR 1 V 1 P
do i not dwindle? 1H4 3.03. 2 P
times nine, | shall he dwindle, peak, and pine; MAC 1.03. 23
DY'D 7 FR 0.0008 REL FR 6 V 1 P
being rather new dy'd than stain'd with salt TMP 2.01. 64 P
dy'd in /his blood, unto the shepherd youth AYL 4.03.155
dy'd in the dying slaughter of their foes. JN 2.01.323
until the white rose that i wear be dy'd | even 3H6 1.02. 33
and it was dy'd in mummy which the skillful OTH 3.04. 74
in my love's veins thou hast too grossly dy'd. SON 99. 5
for thy neglect of truth in beauty dy'd? 101. 2
DYE 7 FR 0.0008 REL FR 7 V 0 P
flower of this purple dye, | hit with cupid's MND 3.02.102
shall dye your white rose in a bloody red. 1H6 2.04. 61
for that dye is on me | which makes my whit'st H8 1.01.208
not of that dye which their investments show, HAM 1.03.128
a lily pale, with damask dye to grace her, PP 7. 5
not, | green plants bring not forth their dye; 17.26
the canker-blooms have full as deep a dye | as SON 54. 5
DYEING 1 FR 0.0001 REL FR 0 V 1 P
they call drinking deep, dyeing scarlet, and 1H4 2.04. 15 P
DYER'S 1 FR 0.0001 REL FR 1 V 0 P
to what it works in, like the dyer's hand. SON 111. 7
DYING 54 FR 0.0061 REL FR 48 V 6 P
whose very comfort | is still a dying horror! MM 2.03. 42
she dying, as it must be so maintain'd, | upon ADO 4.01.214
that strain again, it had a dying fall; TN 1.01. 4
one good deed dying tongueless | slaughters a WT 1.02. 92
thou met'st with things dying, i with things 3.03.114 P
dy'd in the dying slaughter of their foes. JN 2.01.323
but they say the tongues of dying men | enforce R2 2.01. 5
should dying men flatter with those that live? 2.01. 88
where fearing dying pays death servile breath. 3.02.185
the lion dying thrusteth forth his paw, | and 5.01. 29
talk not of dying, i am out of fear | of death 1H4 4.01.135
but to counterfeit dying, when a man thereby 5.04.117 P
and dying so, death is to him advantage; H5 4.01.180 P
or not dying, the time was blessedly lost 4.01.181 P
dying like men, though buried in your dunghills, 4.03. 99
hear, hear how dying salisbury doth groan! 1H6 1.04.104
age, | let dying mortimer here rest himself. 2.05. 2
but ere we go, regard this dying prince, | the 3.02. 86
undaunted spirit in a dying breast! 3.02. 99
dying with mother's dug between its lips; 2H6 3.02.393
when dying clouds contend with growing light, 3H6 2.05. 2
edward for edward pays a dying debt. R3 4.04. 21
to leave | is only bitter to him, only dying, H8 2.01. 74
me, | this from a dying man receive as certain: 2.01.125
so dying love lives still. TRO 3.01.124
whose every motion | was tim'd with dying cries. COR 2.02.110
and we, poor mates, stand on the dying deck, TIM 4.02. 20
horses /did neigh, and dying men did groan, JC 2.02. 23
shall receive the benefit of his dying, a place 3.02. 43 P
and, dying, mention it within their wills, 3.02.135
in their caps, | dying or e'er they sicken. MAC 4.03.173
lights | on fortinbras, he has my dying voice. HAM 5.02.356
she, dying, gave it me, | and bid me, when my OTH 3.04. 63
act upon her, she hath such a celerity in dying. ANT 1.02.144 P
a lion's whelp | than with an old one dying. 3.13. 95
or bathe my dying honor in the blood | shall 4.02. 6
i am dying, egypt, dying; 4.15. 18
i am dying, egypt, dying; 4.15. 18
i am dying, egypt, dying. 4.15. 41
i am dying, egypt, dying. 4.15. 41
how they wound | some slain before, some dying, CYM 5.03. 47
with horror, madly dying, like her life, | which 5.05. 31
and, but she spoke it dying, i would not 5.05. 41
our dole more deadly looks than dying; TNK 1.05. 3
my death was noble, | dying almost a martyr. 2.06. 17
i am palamon, | one that yet loves thee dying. 5.04. 90
glow, | even as a dying coal revives with wind, VEN 338
this dying virtue, this surviving shame, | whose LUC 223
livery, | a dying life to living infamy. 1055
that dying fear through all her body spread, 1266
and dying eyes gleam'd forth their ashy lights, 1378
like dying coals burnt out in tedious nights. 1379
love is dying, faith's defying, | heart's PP 17. 3
and death once dead, there's no more dying then. SON 146.14
E 1 FR 0.0001 REL FR 1 V 0 P
e la mi, show pity, or i die." SHR 3.01. 78
/EACH 1 FR 0.0001 REL FR 1 V 0 P
/us /from /his /soul /to /love /each /other, R3 1.04.237
EACH 277 FR 0.0313 REL FR 263 V 14 P
each pinch more stinging | than bees that made TMP 1.02.329
taught thee each hour | one thing or other. 1.02.354
each putter-out of five for one will bring us 3.03. 48
cry "so, so," | each one, tripping on his toe, 4.01. 46
and with each end of thy blue bow dost crown 4.01. 80
be cheerful | and think of each thing well. 5.01.251
i'll kiss each several paper for amends. TGV 1.02.105
till i have found each letter in the letter, 1.02.116
stream, | and make a pastime of each weary step, 2.07. 35
she excels each mortal thing | upon the dull 4.02. 51
wife acquainted each other how they love me? WIV 2.02.109 P
divide me like a brib'd-buck, each a haunch. 5.05. 24 P
each fair installment, coat, and sev'ral crest, 5.05. 63
they would swear down each particular saint, MM 5.01.243
each one with ireful passion, with drawn swords, ERR 5.01.151
i see we still did meet each other's man, | and 5.01.387
good morrow, masters — each his several way. ADO 5.03. 29
but like of each thing that in season grows. LLL 1.01.107
and bide the penance of each three years' day. 1.01.115
which each to other hath so strongly sworn. 1.01.307
but i a beam do find in each of three. 4.03.160
in that each of you have forsworn his book, 4.03.293
but while 'tis spoke each turn away /her face. 5.02.148
pick out five such, take each one in his vein. 5.02.545
wink each at other, hold the sweet jest up; MND 3.02.239
and from each other look thou lead them thus, 3.02.363
match'd in mouth like bells, | each under each. 4.01.124
match'd in mbuth like bells, | each under each. 4.01.124
song by rote, | to each word a warbling note. 5.01.398
of day, | through this house each fairy stray. 5.01.402
take his gait, | and each several chamber bless, 5.01.417
eyes he doubly sees himself, | in each eye, one. MV 5.01.245
consent with both that we may enjoy each other. AYL 5.02. 9 P
him, | and each one to his office when he wakes. SHR in.1. 73
on thee, | each in his office ready at thy beck. in.2. 34
assurance | let's each one send unto his wife, 5.02. 66
to each of you one fair and virtuous mistress AWW 2.03. 57
marry, to each but one! 2.03. 58
lodowick, and gratii, two hundred fifty each; 4.03.164 P
vaumond, bentii, two hundred fifty each; 4.03.166 P
the vows | we made each other but so late ago. TN 5.01.215
do not embrace me till each circumstance | of 5.01.251
over | by each particular star in heaven and WT 1.02.425
him and do sigh | at each his needless heavings, 2.03. 35
i am a feather for each wind that blows. 2.03.154
these your unusual weeds to each part of you 4.04. 1
took to quench it | she would to each one sip. 4.04. 62
each your doing | (so singular in each 4.04.143
your doing | (so singular in each particular) 4.04.144
where we may leisurely | each one demand, and 5.03.153
and then we shall repent each drop of blood JN 2.01. 48
why then defy each other, and pell-mell | make 2.01.406
austria and france shoot in each other's mouth. 2.01.414
i am with both, each army hath a hand, | and in 3.01.328
i feel | the different plague of each calamity. 3.04. 60
of what i mean to speak | shall blow each dust, 3.04.128
to speak | shall blow each dust, each straw, 3.04.128
blow each dust, each straw, each little rub, 3.04.128
each day still better other's happiness | until R2 1.01. 22
namely, to appeal each other of high treason. 1.01. 27
god, | embrace each other's love in banishment, 1.03.184
nor never look upon each other's face, | nor 1.03.185
each substance of a grief hath twenty shadows, 2.02. 14
three judases, each one thrice worse than judas! 3.02.132
horse, | stain'd with the variation of each soil 1H4 1.01. 64
so strongly that they dare not meet each other; 2.02.106
each takes his fellow for an officer. 2.02.107
let each man do his best, and here draw i | a 5.02. 92
that, each heart being set | on bloody courses, 2H4 1.01.158
each several article herein redress'd, | all 4.01.168
each hurries toward his home and sporting-place. 4.02.105
no doubt, my liege, if each man do his best. H5 2.02. 19
gentlemen both, you will mistake each other. 3.02.134 P
ten | we shall have each a hundred englishmen. 3.07.157
the secret whispers of each other's watch. 4.pr. 7
each battle sees the other's umber'd face. 4.pr. 9
veins | to give each naked curtle-axe a stain, 4.02. 21
look pale | with envy of each other's happiness, 5.02.351
french, french englishmen, | receive each other. 5.02.368
each hath his place and function to attend: 1H6 1.01.173
deck'd with /five flower-de-luces on each side, 1.02. 99
here, through this grate, i count each one, 1.04. 60
this shouldering of each other in the court, 4.01.189
whiles they each other cross, | lives, honors, 4.03. 52
and each of them had twenty times their power, 2H6 2.04. 61
by means whereof the towns each day revolted? 3.01. 63
i will weep, and 'twixt each groan | say, "who's 3.01.221
collected choicely, from each county some, | and 3.01.313
three glorious suns, each one a perfect sun, 3H6 2.01. 26
each one already blazing by our meeds, | should 2.01. 36
and at each word's deliverance | stab poniards 2.01. 97
come on, my masters, each man take his stand, 4.03. 1
the thief doth fear each bush an officer. 5.06. 12
came, | ready to catch each other by the throat, R3 1.03.188
live each of you the subjects to his hate, | and 1.03.301
/hastings and rivers, take each other's hand, 2.01. 7
now cheer each other in each other's love. 2.02.114
now cheer each other in each other's love. 2.02.114
we know each other's faces; 3.04. 10
star'd each on other, and look'd deadly pale; 3.07. 26
and each hour's joy wrack'd with a week of teen. 4.01. 96
/which in their summer beauty kiss'd each other. 4.03. 13
limit each leader to his several charge, | and 5.03. 25
all several sins, all us'd in each degree, 5.03.198
the true succeeders of each royal house, | by 5.05. 30
each following day | became the next day's H8 1.01. 16
nought rebell'd, | order gave each thing view; 1.01. 44
see his pride | peep through each part of him. 1.01. 69
in july when | we see each grain of gravel, i do 1.01.155
which compels from each | the sixt part of his 1.02. 57
obedience is a slave | to each incensed will. 1.02. 65
sixt part of each? 1.02. 94
with | free pardon to each man that has denied 1.02.100
were those that went on each side of the queen? 4.01.100
her suff'rance made | almost each pang a death. 5.01. 69
each troyan that is master of his heart, | let TRO 1.01. 4
'tis just to each of them; he is himself. 1.02. 71 P
each thing /meets | in mere oppugnancy: 1.03.110
so shall each lord of greece, from tent to tent. 1.03.307
two curs shall tame each other; 1.03.389
we may not think the justness of each act | such 2.02.119
there is a law in each well-order'd nation | to 2.02.180
so do each lord, and either greet him not, | or 3.03. 52
salutes each other with each other's form; 3.03.108
salutes each other with each other's form; 3.03.108
we know each other well. 4.01. 31
we do, and long to know each other worse. 4.01. 32
merits pois'd, each weighs nor less nor more, 4.01. 66
so many thousand sighs | did buy each other, 4.04. 40
but i can tell that in each grace of these 4.04. 89
the edge of all extremity | pursue each other, 4.05. 69
once cannot | see what i do deliver out to each, COR 1.01.143
had i a dozen sons, each in my love alike, and 1.03. 22 P
not unlike, | each way, to better yours. 3.01. 49
in peace what each of them by th' other lose 3.02. 44
more than a wild exposture to each chance | that 4.01. 36
each word thou hast spoke hath weeded from my 4.05.102
unbuckling helms, fisting each other's throat, 4.05.125
and each in either side | give the all-hail to 5.03.138
men of heart | look'd wond'ring each at others. 5.06. 99
we may, each wreathed in the other's arms | (our TIT 2.03. 25
about, | that i may turn me to each one of you, 3.01.277
being smelt, with that part cheers each part, ROM 2.03. 25
each part, depriv'd of supple government, 4.01.102
like the current flies | each bound it chases. TIM 1.01. 25
each man to his stool, with that spur as he 3.06. 65 P
lend to each man enough, that one need not lend 3.06. 73 P
let each take some; 4.02. 27
the bounteous huswife nature on each bush | lays 4.03.420
each thing's a thief. 4.03.442
each man apart, all single and alone, | yet an 5.01.107
for each true word, a blister, and each false 5.01.132
and each false | be as a cantherizing to the 5.01.132
make each | prescribe to other as each other's 5.04. 83
each | prescribe to other as each other's leech. 5.04. 84
range on, | till each man drop by lottery. JC 2.01.119
let each man render me his bloody hand. 3.01.184
by each at once her choppy finger laying | upon MAC 1.03. 44
let us speak | our free hearts each to other. 1.03.155
up | each corporal agent to this terrible feat. 1.07. 80
that they did wake each other. 2.02. 21
the death of each day's life, sore labor's bath, 2.02. 35
'tis said, they eat each other. 2.04. 18
float upon a wild and violent sea | each way, 4.02. 22
each new morn | new widows howl, new orphans cry 4.03. 4
and each new day a gash | is added to her wounds 4.03. 40
abound | in the division of each several crime, 4.03. 96
each minute teems a new one. 4.03.176
we, in our country's purge, | each drop of us. 5.02. 29
so thanks to all at once and to each one, | whom 5.09. 40

form of the thing, each word made true and good, HAM 1.02.210
palm with entertainment | of each new–hatch'd, 1.03. 65
take each man's censure, but reserve thy 1.03. 69
and makes each petty artere in this body | as 1.04. 82
and each particular hair to stand an end, | like 1.05. 19
as his shirt, his knees knocking each other, 2.01. 78
and you too — at each ear a hearer — that 2.02.382 P
"then came each actor on his ass" — 2.02.395
each opposite that blanks the face of joy | meet 3.02.220
each small annexment, petty consequence, 3.03. 21
each toy seems prologue to some great amiss, 4.05. 18
each buzz, each fancy, each complaint, dislike, LR 1.04.325
each buzz, each fancy, each complaint, dislike, 1.04.325
each buzz, each fancy, each complaint, dislike, 1.04.325
should undo excess, | and each man have enough. 4.01. 71
ten masts at each make not the altitude | which 4.06. 53
each jealous of the other, as the stung | are of 5.01. 56
where each second | stood heir to th' first. OTH 1.01. 37
and of the cannibals that each /other eat, | the 1.03.143
each man to what sport and revels his /addiction 2.02. 5 P
each drop she falls would prove a crocodile. 4.01.246
each syllable that breath made up between them. 4.02. 5
or cassio him, or each do kill the other, 5.01. 13
for to deny each article with oath | cannot 5.02. 54
in each thing give him way, cross him in nothing ANT 1.03. 9
both | would each to other and all loves to both 2.02.135
on each side her | stood pretty dimpled boys, 2.02.201
we'll feast each other ere we part, and let's 2.06. 60
two friends | that does afflict each other! 3.06. 78
each heart in rome does love and pity you; 3.06. 92
with labor, and throes forth | each minute some. 3.07. 81
war, whose several ranges | frighted each other? 3.13. 6
cause, but as't had been | each man's like mine; 4.08. 7
with so mortal a purpose as then each bore, upon CYM 1.04. 41 P
where each of us fell in praise of our country 1.04. 57 P
cupids | of silver, each on one foot standing, 2.04. 90
if each of you should take this course, how many 5.01. 3
to second ills with ills, each elder worse, 5.01. 14
are now each one the slaughter–man of twenty. 5.03. 49
her master, hitting | each object with a joy; 5.05.396
with whom each minute threatens life or death. PER 1.03. 24
where each man | thinks all is writ he /speken 2.ch. 11
the labor of each knight in his device. 2.02. 15
therefore each one betake him to his rest; 2.03.114
to use one language in each several clime 4.04. 6
thirds his own worth (the case is each of ours), TNK 1.02. 96
into twain and doing | each side like justice, 1.03. 47
at parting) when our count | was each aleven. 1.03. 54
and even each thing | our haste does leave 1.04. 11
death's the market–place, where each one meets. 1.05. 16
her bright eyes break each morning 'gainst thy 2.03. 9
each took | a several land. 3.01. 1
i could for each word give a cuff, my stomach 3.01.104
each errant step beside is torment. 3.02. 34
and each within this month, accompanied | with 3.06.291
each stroke laments | the place whereon it falls 5.03. 4
each part of him to th' all i have spoke, your 5.03.121
each leaning on their elbows and their hips. VEN 44
that in each cheek appears a pretty dimple; 242
hue, | how white and red each other did destroy! 346
move | each part in me that were but sensible: 436
"long may they kiss each other for this cure! 505
each envious brier his weary legs do scratch, 705
each shadow makes him stop, each murmur stay, 706
each shadow makes him stop, each murmur stay, 706
from whom each lamp and shining star doth borrow 861
with cold–pale weakness numbs each feeling part: 892
crystals, where they view'd each other's sorrow, 963
all entertain'd, each passion labors so, | that 969
whereat each tributary subject quakes, | as when 1045
this mutiny each part doth so surprise | that 1049
face seems twain, each several limb is doubled, 1067
that oft they interchange each other's seat. LUC 70
each one by him enforc'd retires his ward; 303
as each unwilling portal yields him way, 309
pain pays the income of each precious thing: 334
each in her sleep themselves so beautify, | as 404
will tie the hearers to attend each line, | how 818
holds disputation with each thing she views, 1101
so i at each sad strain will strain a tear, 1131
set, | each flow'r moist'ned like a melting eye, 1227
through crystal walls each little mote will peep 1251
far from home, wond'ring each other's chance. 1596
each present lord began to promise aid, | as 1696
for being both to me, both to each friend, | i PP 2.11
between each kiss her oaths of true love 7. 8
doth cite each moving sense from idle rest, 14.15
to spite me now, each minute seems /a /moon, 14.27
head, each under eye | doth homage to his SON 7. 2
strikes each in each by mutual ordering; 8.10
strikes each in each by mutual ordering; 8.10
'pointing to each his thunder, rain, and wind, 14. 6
and each (though enemies to /either's reign) 28. 5
both find each other, and i lose both twain, 42.11
and each doth good turns now unto the other: 47. 2
way, | each trifle under truest bars to thrust, 48. 2
bide each check | without accusing you of injury 58. 7
each changing place with that which goes before, 60. 3
although in me each part will be forgotten. 81. 4
i must each day say o'er the very same, 108. 6
till each to raz'd oblivion yield his part | of 122. 7
for since each hand hath put on nature's power, 127. 5
but being both from me, both to each friend, | i 144.11
each eye that saw him did enchant the mind, LC 89
that did amplify | each stone's dear nature, 210
each several stone, | with wit well blazon'd, 216
each cheek a river running from a fount | with 283

EAGER 11 FR 0.0012 REL FR 11 V 0 P
war, | the bitter clamor of two eager tongues, R2 1.01. 49
with eager feeding food doth choke the feeder; 2.01. 37
shrill/–voic'd suppliant makes this eager cry? 5.03. 75
and hunger will enforce them to be more eager. 1H6 1.02. 38
and all my followers to the eager foe | turn 3H6 1.04. 3
if so thou think'st, vex him with eager words. 2.06. 68
it is /a nipping and an eager air. HAM 1.04. 2
and curd, like eager droppings into milk, | the 1.05. 69
hand, | and gaz'd for tidings in my eager eyes, LUC 254
conceit and grief an eager combat fight, | what 1298
keen, | with eager compounds we our palate urge, SON 118. 2

EAGERLY 3 FR 0.0003 REL FR 3 V 0 P
how eagerly ye follow my disgraces | as if it H8 3.02.240
where eagerly his sickness | pursu'd him still, 4.02. 24
advantage on octavius, | took it too eagerly. JC 5.03. 7

EAGERNESS 1 FR 0.0001 REL FR 1 V 0 P
me, | madding my eagerness with her restraint, AWW 5.03.213

EAGLE 23 FR 0.0026 REL FR 22 V 1 P
a lover's eyes will gaze an eagle blind. LLL 4.03.331
arms, | and like an eagle o'er his aery tow'rs, JN 5.02.149
for once the eagle (england) being in prey, | to H5 1.02.169
thou with an eagle art inspired then. 1H6 1.02.141
an empty eagle were set | to guard the chicken 2H6 3.01.248
and like an empty eagle | tire on the flesh of 3H6 1.01.268
whose arms gave shelter to the princely eagle, 5.02. 12
'tis there | that, like an eagle in a dove–cote, COR 5.06.114
the eagle suffers little birds to sing, | and is TIT 4.04. 83
an eagle, madam, | hath not so green, so quick, ROM 3.05.219
but flies an eagle flight, bold, and forth on, TIM 1.01. 49
that have outliv'd the eagle, page thy heels 4.03.224
this was but as a fly by an eagle; ANT 2.02.181 P
i chose an eagle, | and did avoid a puttock. CYM 1.01.139
in a safer hold | than is the full–wing'd eagle. 3.03. 21
i saw jove's bird, the roman eagle, wing'd 4.02.348
mount, eagle, to my palace crystalline. 5.04.113
the holy eagle | stoop'd, as to foot us. 5.04.115
great jupiter, upon his eagle back'd, | appear'd 5.05.427
for the roman eagle, | from south to west on 5.05.470
which foreshow'd our princely eagle, | th' 5.05.473
even as an empty eagle, sharp by fast, | tires VEN 55
tyrant wing, | save the eagle, feath'red king; PHT 11

EAGLE'S 4 FR 0.0004 REL FR 3 V 1 P
as bright as is the eagle's, lightens forth R2 3.03. 69
hal, i was not an eagle's talent in the waist, i 1H4 2.04.330 P
nay, if thou be that princely eagle's bird, 3H6 2.01. 91
face, | seize with thine eagle's talents. PER 4.03. 48

EAGLES' 1 FR 0.0001 REL FR 1 V 0 P
drones suck not eagles' blood, but rob beehives. 2H6 4.01.109

EAGLES 10 FR 0.0011 REL FR 9 V 1 P
wind | bated like eagles having lately bath'd, 1H4 4.01. 99
more pity that the eagles should be mew'd, R3 1.01.132
wrens make prey where eagles dare not perch. 1.03. 70
ne'er look, ne'er look, the eagles are gone; TRO 1.02.243 P
and bring in | the crows to peck the eagles. COR 3.01.139
on our former ensign | two mighty eagles fell, JC 5.01. 80
yes, | as sparrows eagles; MAC 1.02. 35
chickens, the way which they /stoop'd eagles; CYM 5.03. 42
and like young eagles teach 'em | boldly to gaze TNK 2.02. 34
fly, | but eagles gaz'd upon with every eye. LUC 1015

EAGLE–SIGHTED 1 FR 0.0001 REL FR 1 V 0 P
what peremptory eagle–sighted eye | dares look LLL 4.03.222

EAGLE–WINGED 1 FR 0.0001 REL FR 1 V 0 P
and for we think the eagle–winged pride | of R2 1.03.129

EAN 1 FR 0.0001 REL FR 1 V 0 P
so many weeks ere the poor fools will ean, | so 3H6 2.05. 36

/EANING 1 FR 0.0001 REL FR 1 V 0 P
even on my /eaning time, but whether there PER 3.04. 6

EANING 1 FR 0.0001 REL FR 1 V 0 P
who then conceiving did in eaning time | fall MV 1.03. 87

EANLINGS 1 FR 0.0001 REL FR 1 V 0 P
that all the eanlings which were streak'd and MV 1.03. 79

EAR* *(also year*)*

/EAR* 4 FR 0.0004 REL FR 4 V 0 P
/lear /and /him | /that /ever /ear /received, LR 5.03.216
the bruis'd heart was pierced through the /ear. OTH 1.03.219
time, to abuse othello's /ear | that he is too 1.03.395
she told him stories to delight his /ear; PP 4. 5

EAR* 218 FR 0.0246 REL FR 177 V 41 P
come, | the very minute bids thee ope thine ear. TMP 1.02. 37
i' th' state | to what tune pleas'd his ear, 1.02. 85
my quaint ariel, | hark in thine ear. 1.02.318
it strook mine ear most terribly. 2.01.313
o, 'twas a din to fright a monster's ear, | to 2.01.314
hath into bondage | brought my too diligent ear. 3.01. 42
your life, which must | take the ear strangely. 5.01.314
if so — i pray thee breathe it in mine ear, TGV 3.01.241
and give some evening music to her ear. 4.02. 17
you have a quick ear. 4.02. 63 P
"he hears with ear"? WIV 1.01.150 P
give ear to his motions: 1.01.214 P
but notwithstanding (to tell you in your ear, i 1.04.103 P
and let me tell you in your ear, she's as 2.02. 97 P
i pray you let–a me speak a word with your ear. 3.01. 80 P
if it should come to the ear of the court, how i 4.05. 95 P
for so i have strew'd it in the common ear, MM 1.03. 15
if he took you a box o' th' ear, you might have 2.01.180 P
therefore fasten your ear on my advisings: 3.01.197 P
the hand, | who hath a story ready for your ear. 4.01. 55
lord angelo hath to the public ear | profess'd 4.02. 99
you of such things | that want no ear but yours. 4.03.105
lord, and i have heard | your royal ear abus'd. 5.01.139
mouth, | and in the witness of his proper ear, 5.01.308
good, | whereto if you'll a willing ear incline, 5.01.536
ay, ay, he told his mind upon mine ear. ERR 2.01. 48
vow | that never words were music to thine ear, 2.02.114
there is my hand, and let it feel your ear. 4.04. 53
tells him in his ear that he is in her heart. ADO 2.01.316 P
whisper her ear, and tell her i and ursley 3.01. 4
that her ear lose nothing | of the false sweet 3.01. 32
a word in your ear, sir. 4.02. 27 P
nor let no comforter delight mine ear, | but 5.01. 6
shall i speak a word in your ear? 5.01.143 P
he wears a key in his ear and a lock hanging by 5.01.309 P
the neck of the wax, and every one give ear. LLL 4.01. 59
now hangeth like a jewel in the ear of caelo, 4.02. 5 P
listen, ear. 4.03. 43
a lover's ear will hear the lowest sound, | when 4.03.332
madam, and pretty mistresses, give ear: 5.02.286
here, | what did you whisper in your lady's ear? 5.02.436
what did the russian whisper in your ear? 5.02.443
honest plain words best pierce the ear of grief, 5.02.753
a jest's prosperity lies in the ear | of him 5.02.861
o word of fear, | unpleasing to a married ear! 5.02.902
o word of fear, | unpleasing to a married ear! 5.02.911
more tuneable than lark to shepherd's ear | when MND 1.01.184
my ear should catch your voice, my eye your eye, 1.01.188
here, | and hang a pearl in every cowslip's ear. 2.01. 15
mine ear is much enamored of thy note; 3.01.138
the ear more quick of apprehension makes; 3.02.178
mine ear, i thank it, brought me to thy sound. 3.02.182
i have a reasonable good ear in music. 4.01. 28 P
hath not heard, the ear of man hath not seen, 4.01.211 P
he borrow'd a box of the ear of the englishman, MV 1.02. 80 P
were dead at my foot, and the jewels in her ear! 3.01. 89 P
that creep into the dreaming bridegroom's ear, 3.02. 52
with sweetest touches pierce your mistress' ear, 5.01. 67
for i must tell you friendly in your ear, | sell AYL 3.05. 59
lend thine ear. SHR 4.01. 60 P
and this cuff was but to knock at your ear, and 4.01. 65 P
may report my flight | to consolate thine ear. AWW 3.02.128
but by the ear, that hears most nobly of him. 3.05. 50
as he vow'd to thee in thine ear, parolles." 4.03.231 P
this man may help me to his majesty's ear, | if 5.01. 7
it came o'er my ear like the sweet sound | that TN 1.01. 5
it alone concerns your ear. 1.05.208 P
to your own most pregnant and vouchsafed ear. 3.01. 89 P
it is as fat and fulsome to mine ear | as 5.01.109
therefore perpend, my princess, and give ear. 5.01.300 P
come on then, | and give't me in mine ear. WT 2.01. 32
to have an open ear, a quick eye, and a nimble 4.04.671 P
though credit be asleep and not an ear open: 5.02. 63 P
so much my conscience whispers in your ear, JN 1.01. 42
thin | that in mine ear i durst not stick a rose 1.01.142
own soldier, rounded in the ear | with that same 2.01.566
tale | vexing the dull ear of a drowsy man; 3.04.109
my liege, her ear | is stopp'd with dust: 4.02.119
heads, | and whisper one another in the ear; 4.02.189
(as loud as thine) rattle the welkin's ear, 5.02.172
should scape the true acquaintance of mine ear. 5.06. 15
you breathe these dead news in as dead an ear. 5.07. 65
for all in vain comes counsel to his ear. R2 2.01. 4
my death's sad tale may yet undeaf his ear. 2.01. 16
the open ear of youth doth always listen; 2.01. 20
quick is mine ear to hear of good towards him. 2.01.234
mine ear is open, and my heart prepar'd, | the 3.02. 93
to ear the land that hath some hope to grow, 3.02.212
as may be hollowed in thy treacherous ear | from 4.01. 54
or in thy piteous heart plant thou thine ear, 5.03.126
and here have i the daintiness of ear | to check 5.05. 45
had not an ear to hear my true time broke. 5.05. 48
start away, | and lend no ear unto my purposes. 1H4 1.03.217
asleep, | and in his ear i'll hollow "mortimer!" 1.03.222
tying thine ear to no tongue but thine own! 1.03.238
lay thine ear close to the ground, and list if 2.02. 32 P
which oft the ear of greatness needs must hear 3.02. 24
stopping my greedy ear with their bold deeds, 2H4 1.01. 78
deeds, | but in the end, to stop my ear indeed, 1.01. 79
and bid the merry bells ring to thine ear | that 4.05.111
my voice shall sound as you do prompt mine ear, 5.02.119
not working with the eye without the ear, | and H5 2.02.135
boastful neighs | piercing the night's dull ear; 4.pr. 11
by this hand i will take thee a box on the ear. 4.01.216 P
i have sworn to take him a box a' th' ear; 4.07.128 P
favor | may haply purchase him a box a' th' ear. 4.07.173
terms, | such as will enter at a lady's ear, 5.02.100
word thou shalt no sooner bless mine ear withal, 5.02.238 P
words as no christian ear can endure to hear. 2H6 4.07. 40 P
give him a box o' th' ear, and that will make 4.07. 86 P
mine ear hath tempted judgment to desire. 3H6 3.03.133
prince, | lend favorable ear to our requests, R3 3.07.101
rise, and lend thine ear. 4.02. 79
out of the pain you suffer'd, gave no ear to't. H8 4.02. 8
and durst commend a secret to your ear | much 5.01. 17
who hath so far | given ear to our complaint, of 5.01. 48
host, | having his ear full of his airy fame, TRO 1.03.144
i bring a trumpet to awake his ear, | to set his 1.03.251
hark a word in your ear. 5.02. 34
shall dizzy with more clamor neptune's ear | in 5.02.174
reproof and rebuke from every ear that heard it. COR 2.02. 33 P
that's worthily | as any ear can hear. 4.01. 54
private friends, hereafter | will i lend ear to. 5.03. 19
terms | that ever ear did hear to such effect, TIT 2.03.111
sung | sweet varied notes, enchanting every ear! 3.01. 86
yet should both ear and heart obey my tongue. 4.04. 99
some devil whisper curses in my ear, | and 5.03. 11
to love–sick dido's sad attending ear | the 5.03. 82
and then anon | drums in his ear, at which he ROM 1.04. 86
tell | a whispering tale in a fair lady's ear, 1.05. 23
of night | as a rich jewel in an ethiop's ear — 1.05. 46
black eye, run through the ear with a love–song, 2.04. 15 P
i will bite thee by the ear for that jest. 2.04. 77 P
that pierc'd the fearful hollow of thine ear; 3.05. 3
holding thy ear close to the hollow ground, | so 5.03. 4
rain sacrificial whisperings in his ear, | make TIM 1.01. 81
come on my right hand, for this ear is deaf, JC 1.02.213
your ear is good. cassius, what night is this! 1.03. 42
had you a healthful ear to hear of it. 2.01.319
to sound more sweetly in great caesar's ear 3.01. 50
that i may pour my spirits in thine ear, | and MAC 1.05. 26
the repetition in a woman's ear | would murther 2.03. 85
have been perform'd | too terrible for the ear. 3.04. 77
pronounce a title | more hateful to mine ear. 5.07. 9
that keep the word of promise to our ear, | and 5.08. 21
say so, | nor shall you do my ear that violence, HAM 1.02.171
admiration for a while | with an attent ear, 1.02.193
if with too credent ear you list his songs, | or 1.03. 30
give every man thy ear, but few thy voice, 1.03. 68
me, so the whole ear of denmark | is by a forged 1.05. 36
by means, and place, | all given to mine ear. 2.02.128
and you too — at each ear a hearer — that 2.02.382 P
a hideous crash | takes prisoner pyrrhus' ear; 2.02.477
and cleave the general ear with horrid speech, 2.02.563
you) in the ear | of all their conference. 3.01.184
here is your husband, like a mildewed ear, 3.04. 64
of it, a knavish speech sleeps in a foolish ear. 4.02. 24 P
and wants not buzzers to infect his ear | with 4.05. 90
stick our person to arraign | in ear and ear. 4.05. 94
stick our person to arraign | in ear and ear. 4.05. 94
words to speak in thine ear will make thee dumb, 4.06. 25 P
sith you have heard, and with a knowing ear, 4.07. 3
give ear, sir, to my sister, | for those that LR 2.04.233
being apt | to have his ear abus'd, wisdom bids 2.04.307
false of heart, light of ear, bloody of hand; 3.04. 92 P
hark in thine ear: 4.06.153 P
and with a greedy ear | devour up my discourse. OTH 1.03.149

to my unfolding lend your prosperous ear, | and 1.03.244
i'll pour this pestilence into his ear — | that 2.03.356
and mak'st his ear | a stranger to thy thoughts. 3.03.143
prognostication, i cannot scratch mine ear. ANT 1.02. 53 P
which they ear and wound | with keels of every 1.04. 49
mine ear must pluck it thence. 1.05. 42
i could have given less matter | a better ear. 2.01. 32
pour out the pack of matter to mine ear, | the 2.05. 54
say in mine ear, what is't. 2.07. 37
i'll tell you in your ear. 3.02. 46
made his will, and read it | to public ear; 3.04. 5
for war, acquainted | my grieved ear withal; 3.06. 59
with brazen din blast you the city's ear, | make 4.08. 36
long | as he could make me with /this eye or ear CYM 1.03. 9
a strange infection | is fall'n into thy ear! 3.02. 4
i have heard i am a strumpet, and mine ear, 3.04.113
report should render him hourly to your ear | as 3.04.150
him know | if that his head have ear in music; 3.04.175
to glad your ear and please your eyes. PER 1.ch. 4
the rest (hark in thine ear) as black as incest, 1.02. 76
for | the gods are quick of ear, and i am sworn 4.01. 69
fisting of every rogue | thy ear is liable; 4.06.168
hail, sir! my lord, lend ear. 5.01. 82
and whispers in mine ear, "go not till he speak. 5.01. 96
will to my sense bend no licentious ear, | but 5.03. 30
that your fame | knolls in the ear o' th' world. TNK 1.01.134
had mine ear | stol'n some new air, or at 1.03. 74
glass, as to | his ear which now disdains you. 3.01. 71
as thou art just, thy noble ear against us; 3.06.174
and attentive | i gave my ear, when i might well 4.01. 57
sacred silver mistress, lend thine ear | (which 5.01.146
the belief | both seal'd with eye and ear. 5.03. 15
two emulous philomels beat the ear o' th' night 5.03.124
and give the tidings ear | that are most /dearly 5.04. 46
for to a pretty ear she tunes her tale. VEN 74
"bid me discourse, i will enchant thine ear, 145
knocks at my heart, and whispers in mine ear, 659
stands on his hinder–legs with list'ning ear, 698
yet from mine ear the tempting tune is blown; 778
for know, my heart stands armed in mine ear, 779
this dismal cry rings sadly in her ear, 889
trifles, unwitnessed with eye or ear, | thy 1023
away he steals with open list'ning ear, | full LUC 283
his ear her prayers admits, but his heart 558
for then the eye interprets to the ear | the 1325
his nose being shadowed by his neighbor's ear; 1416
merit praise, | by ringing in thy lady's ear. PP 18.16
she will not stick to round me on th' ear, | to 18.51
by unions married, do offend thine ear, | they SON 8. 6
sing to the ear that doth thy lays esteem, | and 100. 7
the wiry concord that mine ear confounds, | do i 128. 4

EAR–/BUSSING 1 FR 0.0001 REL FR 0 V 1 P
for they are yet but ear–/bussing arguments? LR 2.01. 8 P

EAR'D 1 FR 0.0001 REL FR 1 V 0 P
and that | i ear'd her language, liv'd in her TNK 3.01. 29

EAR–DEAF'NING 1 FR 0.0001 REL FR 1 V 0 P
and the ear–deaf'ning voice o' th' oracle, | kin WT 3.01. 9

EARING 1 FR 0.0001 REL FR 1 V 0 P
still, and our ills told us | is as our earing. ANT 1.02.111

/EARL 4 FR 0.0004 REL FR 3 V 1 P
/son /and /heir /to /th' /earl /of /arundel, R2 2.01.280
/the /earl /of /herford /was /reputed /then 2H4 4.01.129
/let's /follow /the /old /earl, /and /get /the LR 3.07.103
/is /with /the /earl /of /kent /in /germany. 4.07. 90 P

EARL 92 FR 0.0104 REL FR 80 V 12 P
de earl, de knight, de lords, de gentlemen, my WIV 2.03. 92 P
well, diana, take heed of this french earl. AWW 3.05. 12 P
he is in those suggestions for the young earl. 3.05. 18 P
arthur duke of britain | and earl of richmond, JN 2.01.552
go, bushy, to the earl of wiltshire straight, R2 2.01.215
the earl of wiltshire hath the realm in farm. 2.01.256
whereupon the earl of worcester | hath broken 2.02. 58
the earl of wiltshire is already there. 2.02.136
where is the earl of wiltshire? 3.02.122
is bushy, green, and the earl of wiltshire dead? 3.02.141
i mean the earl of wiltshire, bushy, green. 3.04. 53
the earl of douglas is discomfited: 1H4 1.01. 67
took | mordake earl of fife and eldest son | to 1.01. 71
son | to beaten douglas, and the earl of athol, 1.01. 72
i shall have none but mordake earl of fife. 1.01. 95
hear, that earl of march | hath lately married. 1.03. 84
the earl of westmerland set forth to–day, | with 3.02.170
of our proceedings kept the earl from hence, 4.01. 65
than if the earl were here, for men must think, 4.01. 79
the earl of westmerland, seven thousand strong, 4.01. 88
i look to be either earl or duke, i can assure 5.04.142 P
a noble earl, and many a creature else | had 5.05. 7
to fight with glendower and the earl of march. 5.05. 40
who keeps the gate here ho? where is the earl? 2H4 1.01. 1
tell thou the earl | that the lord bardolph doth 1.01. 2
here comes the earl. 1.01. 6
noble earl, | i bring you certain news from 1.01. 11
morton, | tell thou an earl his divination lies, 1.01. 88
sweet earl, divorce not wisdom from your honor, 1.01.162
the archbishop and the earl of northumberland. 1.02.205 P
to the prince, this to the earl of westmerland, 1.02.239 P
the earl northumberland and the lord bardolph, 4.04. 97
one, richard earl of cambridge, and the second, H5 2.pr. 23
then, richard earl of cambridge, there is yours; 2.02. 66
by the name of richard earl of cambridge. 2.02.146 P
wounds) | the noble earl of suffolk also lies. 4.06. 10
edward the duke of york, the earl of suffolk, 4.08.103
the earl of salisbury craveth supply, | and 1H6 1.01.159
the earl of bedford had a prisoner | call'd the 1.04. 27
was not thy father, richard earl of cambridge, 2.04. 90
the cause | my father, earl of cambridge, lost 2.05. 54
thy father, earl of cambridge then, deriv'd 2.05. 84
so fell that noble earl | and was beheaded. 2.05. 90
deserts | we here create you earl of shrewsbury, 3.04. 26
valiant lord talbot, earl of shrewsbury, 4.07. 61
great earl of washford, waterford, and valence, 4.07. 63
pope, | the emperor, and the earl of arminack? 5.01. 2
the earl of arminack, near knit to charles, | a 5.01. 17
an earl i am, and suffolk am i call'd. 5.03. 53
say, earl of suffolk — if thy name be so — 5.03. 72
welcome, brave earl, into our territories! 5.03.146
your wondrous rare description, noble earl, | of 5.05. 1
her father is no better than an earl, | although 5.05. 37
and so the earl of arminack may do, | because he 5.05. 44
who married edmund mortimer, earl of march; 2H6 2.02. 36
edmund had issue, roger earl of march; 2.02. 37
married richard earl of cambridge, who was | to 2.02. 45
she was heir | to roger earl of march, who was 2.02. 48
my heart assures me that the earl of warwick 2.02. 78
richard shall live to make the earl of warwick 2.02. 81
edmund mortimer, earl of march, | married the 4.02.136
brother, here's the earl of wiltshire's blood, 3H6 1.01. 14
earl of northumberland, he slew thy father, 1.01. 54
be patient, gentle earl of westmerland. 1.01. 61
thy grandfather, roger mortimer, earl of march: 1.01.106
the earl of warwick and the duke enforc'd me. 1.01.229
all the friends that thou, brave earl of march, 2.01.179
no longer earl of march, but duke of york; 2.01.192
my father, being the earl of warwick's man, 2.05. 65
our earl of warwick, edward's greatest friend. 3.03. 45
well as lewis of france or the earl of warwick, 4.01. 11
my liege, it is young henry, earl of richmond. 4.06. 67
ay, by my faith, for a poor earl to give. 5.01. 32
that the earl of richmond | is with a mighty R3 4.04.532
the earl of pembroke keeps his regiment; 5.03. 29
morning | desire the earl to see me in my tent. 5.03. 32
thomas the earl of surrey and himself, | much 5.03. 69
john duke of norfolk, thomas earl of surrey, 5.03.296
my lord the duke of buckingham and earl | of H8 1.01.199
earl surrey was sent thither, and in haste too, 2.01. 43
the duke of norfolk, | he to be earl marshal. 4.01. 19
and that the earl of surrey, with the rod. 4.01. 39
for after the stout earl northumberland 4.02. 12
her, | she shall be married to this noble earl. ROM 3.04. 21
with the earl, sir, here within. LR 2.04. 59
or false, it hath made thee earl of gloucester. 3.05. 17 P
find'st about me | to edmund earl of gloucester; 4.06.249
upon edmund, supposed earl of gloucester, that 5.03.112 P
he that speaks for edmund earl of gloucester? 5.03.125
the noble earl of shrewsbury, let's hear him. STM II.C 30 P
we'll hear the earl of surrey. II.C 31 P
the earl of shrewsbury. II.C 32 P

/EARLDOM 1 FR 0.0001 REL FR 1 V 0 P
/my /lord, /your /promise /for /the /earldom — R3 4.02.102

EARLDOM 4 FR 0.0004 REL FR 4 V 0 P
france, | and not have title of an earldom here. 1H6 3.03. 26
it was my inheritance, as the earldom was. 3H6 1.01. 78
claim thou of me | the earldom of herford, and R3 3.01.195
th' earldom of /herford, and the moveables, 4.02. 90

EARLIER 2 FR 0.0002 REL FR 0 V 2 P
sir toby, you must come in earlier a' nights. TN 1.03. 5 P
earlier too, sir, if now i be one. PER 4.06. 76 P

EARLIEST 3 FR 0.0003 REL FR 2 V 1 P
kind of fruit | drops earliest to the ground, MV 4.01.116
then it will be the earliest fruit i' th' AYL 3.02.118 P
to–morrow with your earliest | let me have OTH 2.03. 7

EARLINESS 1 FR 0.0001 REL FR 1 V 0 P
therefore thy earliness doth me assure | thou ROM 2.03. 39

EARL'S 1 FR 0.0001 REL FR 1 V 0 P
a poor earl's daughter is unequal odds, | and 1H6 5.05. 34

EARLS 9 FR 0.0010 REL FR 8 V 1 P
of them all, and yet there has been earls, nay WIV 2.02. 76 P
go call the earls of surrey and of warwick; 2H4 3.01. 1
full fifteen earls and fifteen hundred knights, H5 1.01. 13
of lusty earls, | grandpre and roussi, 4.08. 98
seven earls, twelve barons, and twenty reverend 2H6 1.01. 8
and make the meanest of you earls and dukes? 4.08. 37
the queen with all the northern earls and lords 3H6 1.02. 49
dukes, earls, lords, gentlemen — indeed of all. R3 2.01. 69
henceforth be earls, the first that ever MAC 5.09. 29

/EARLY 2 FR 0.0002 REL FR 2 V 0 P
/as /in /an /early /spring | /we /see /th' 2H4 1.03. 38
up | to see thy son and heir now /early down. ROM 5.03.209

EARLY 53 FR 0.0060 REL FR 45 V 8 P
i am thus early come to know what service | it TGV 4.03. 9
and to be up early and down late; WIV 1.04.101 P
no doubt they rose up early to observe | the MND 4.01.132
and in the morning early will we both | fly MV 4.01.456
and in the morning early | they found the bed AYL 2.02. 6
young" and "the next year" and "'tis too early." AWW 2.01. 28
how have you come so early by this lethargy? TN 1.05.123 P
after midnight and to go to bed then, is early; 2.03. 8 P
by this brave duke came early to his grave; JN 2.01. 5
to–morrow morning by four a' clock early, at 1H4 1.02.125 P
and in the morning early shall mine uncle 4.03.110
an early stirrer, by the rood! 2H4 3.02. 2 P
for our bad neighbor makes us early stirrers, H5 4.01. 6
long, sat in the council–house | early and late, 2H6 1.01. 91
good morrow, catesby, you are early stirring. R3 3.02. 36
be — | prepare thy battle early in the morning, 5.03. 88
the early village cock | hath twice done 5.03.209
come pat betwixt too early and too late | for H8 2.03. 84
e'en so; hector was stirring early. TRO 1.02. 51 P
what business, lord, so early? 4.01. 35
what news with you so early? 4.02. 46
'tis but early days. 4.05. 12
plains, | let titan rise as early as he dare, 5.10. 25
somewhat too early for new–married ladies. TIT 2.02. 15
side, | so early walking did i see your son. ROM 1.01.123
and too soon marr'd are those so early made. 1.02. 13
i fear, too early, for my mind misgives | some 1.04.106
too early seen unknown, and known too late! 1.05.139
what early tongue so sweet saluteth me? 2.03. 32
i will, and know her mind early to–morrow; 3.04. 10
very late that we | may call it early by and by. 3.04. 35
is she not down so late, or up so early? 3.05. 66
marry, my child, early next thursday morn, | the 3.05.112
juliet, on thursday early will i rouse ye; 4.01. 42
so early waking — what with loathsome smells, 4.03. 46
early in the morning | see thou deliver it to my 5.03. 23
what misadventure is so early up, | that calls 5.03.188
for thou art early up | to see thy son and heir 5.03.208
this letter he early bid me give his father, 5.03.275
what, brutus, are you stirr'd so early too? JC 2.02.110
early to–morrow will we rise, and hence. 4.03.230
o cassius, brutus gave the word too early, | who 5.03. 5
general cast us thus early for the love of his OTH 2.03. 14 P
early though't be, have on their riveted trim, ANT 4.04. 22
late, for that's the reason i was up so early. CYM 2.03. 34 P
gentlemen, | why do you stir so early? PER 3.02. 12
that is the cause we trouble you so early, 3.02. 19
you, should at these early hours | shake off the 3.02. 22
early in blustering morn this lady was | thrown 5.03. 22
fast, | or being early pluck'd is sour to taste. VEN 528
which she too early and too late hath spill'd." LUC 1801
even so my sun one early morn did shine | with SON 33. 9
is me, too early i attended | a youthful suit — LC 78

EARN 6 FR 0.0006 REL FR 3 V 3 P
his excellence did earn it, ere he had it. ADO 3.01. 99
i earn that i eat, get that i wear, owe no man AYL 3.02. 73 P
a barber shall never earn sixpence out of it; 2H4 1.02. 25 P
the people, to earn a dearer estimation of them; COR 2.03. 96 P
to do the act that might the addition earn, OTH 4.02.163
i and my sword will earn our chronicle. ANT 3.13.175

EARN'D 6 FR 0.0006 REL FR 3 V 3 P
know i have earn'd of don john a thousand ducats ADO 3.03.108 P
than ever proof itself would have earn'd him. TN 3.04.182 P
the one for ever earn'd a royal husband; WT 1.02.107
names upon you before you have earn'd them. 2H4 2.04.143 P
to martius, | though martius earn'd them not; COR 1.01.274
store to do't, | and they have earn'd the waste. ANT 4.01. 16

EARNED 2 FR 0.0002 REL FR 2 V 0 P
hence | a great addition earned in thy death. TRO 4.05.141
oft the wrack | of earned praise, marina's life PER 4.ch. 13

EARNEST* 40 FR 0.0045 REL FR 24 V 16 P
but jid you perceive her earnest? TGV 2.01.157 P
after they clos'd in earnest, they parted very 2.05. 12 P
now your jest is earnest, | upon what bargain do ERR 2.02. 24
in his eye | that he did plead in earnest? 4.02. 3
even take sixpence in earnest of the berrord, ADO 2.01. 40 P
he is in earnest. 5.01.194 P
in most profound earnest, and, i'll warrant you, 5.01.195 P
in earnest, shall i say? MND 3.02.277
but love no man in good earnest, nor no further AYL 1.02. 27 P
out of service, let us talk in good earnest. 1.03. 26 P
by my troth, and in good earnest, and so god 4.01.188 P
complexion that it was a passion of earnest. 4.03.171 P
no, in good earnest. WT 1.02.150
are you in earnest, sir? i smell the trick on't. 4.04.642 P
indeed i have had earnest, but i cannot with 4.04.645 P
pleads he in earnest? R2 5.03.100
faith, tell me now in earnest, how came 1H4 2.04.303 P
receiv'd the golden earnest of our death; H5 2.02.169
i take thy groat in earnest of revenge. 5.01. 63
give it you | in earnest of a further benefit, 1H6 5.03. 16
my tongue should stumble in mine earnest words, 2H6 3.02.316
been | an earnest advocate to plead for him. R3 1.03. 86
with earnest prayers all to that effect. 2.02. 15
me, | who, earnest in the service of my god, 3.07.106
and given in earnest what i begg'd in jest. 5.01. 22
mean while must be an earnest motion | made to H8 2.04.234
in earnest, it's true; COR 1.03. 95 P
how, sir? are you in earnest then, my lord? TIT 1.01.277
he hath sent me an earnest inviting, which many TIM 3.06. 10 P
nay, stay thou out for earnest. 4.03. 48
i have given you earnest. 4.03.168
and for an earnest of a greater honor, | he bade MAC 1.03.104
ill, | why hath it given me earnest of success, 1.03.132
an earnest conjuration from the king, | as HAM 5.02. 38
i thank thee, there's earnest of thy service. LR 1.04. 94 P
to draw from her a prayer of earnest heart OTH 1.03.152
that you have been so earnest | to have me filch 3.03.314
it is an earnest of a farther good | that i mean CYM 1.05. 65
if not, i have lost my earnest. PER 4.02. 45 P
her earnest eye did make him more amazed. LUC 1356

EARNEST–GAPING 1 FR 0.0001 REL FR 1 V 0 P
my earnest–gaping sight of thy land's view, | i 2H6 3.02.105

EARNESTLY 9 FR 0.0010 REL FR 8 V 1 P
why dost thou whet thy knife so earnestly? MV 4.01.121
doth say, | he wishes earnestly you never may. WT 4.01. 32
have earnestly implor'd a general peace 1H6 5.04. 98
along, | how earnestly he cast his eyes upon me! H8 5.02. 12
how earnestly they knock! TRO 4.02. 40
and bawds, how earnestly are you set a–work, and 5.10. 37 P
and, as i earnestly did fix mine eye | upon the TIT 5.01. 22
why so earnestly seek you to put up that letter? LR 1.02. 28
partners, | the rather for i earnestly beseech, ANT 2.02. 23

EARNESTNESS 4 FR 0.0004 REL FR 3 V 1 P
it shows my earnestness of affection — 2H4 5.05. 16 P
all agreeing | in earnestness to see him. COR 2.01.213
the nobles in great earnestness are going | all 4.06. 58
for often, with a solemn earnestness | (more OTH 5.02.227

EARNS* *(also ern, etc., yearn, etc.)*

EARNS* 2 FR 0.0002 REL FR 2 V 0 P
the heart of brutus earns to think upon! JC 2.02.129
conquer, | and earns a place i' th' story. ANT 3.13. 46

EARN'ST 1 FR 0.0001 REL FR 1 V 0 P
and earn'st a deity | equal with mars. TNK 1.01.227

EAR–PIERCING 1 FR 0.0001 REL FR 1 V 0 P
the spirit–stirring drum, th' ear–piercing fife, OTH 3.03.352

EARS' 1 FR 0.0001 REL FR 1 V 0 P
ears' deep sweet music, and heart's deep sore VEN 432

EARS* 183 FR 0.0206 REL FR 156 V 27 P
you cram these words into mine ears against TMP 2.01.107
instruments | will hum about mine ears, and 3.02.138
like unback'd colts, they prick'd their ears, 4.01.176
so i charm'd their ears | that calf–like they my 4.01.178
my bottle, though i be o'er ears for my labor. 4.01.213 P
my ears are stopp'd and cannot hear good news, TGV 3.01.206
he hears with ears. WIV 1.01.148
by gar, me vill cut his ears. 2.03. 64 P
hands with me, and that my two ears can witness. ERR 2.01. 46 P
what error drives our eyes and ears amiss? 2.02.184
i'll stop mine ears against the mermaid's song. 3.02.164
and teach your ears to list me with more heed. 4.01.101
i tell you, 'twill sound harshly in her ears. 4.04. 7
you may prove it by my long ears. 4.04. 30 P
these ears of mine thou know'st did hear thee; 5.01. 26
i will be sworn these ears of mine | heard you 5.01.260
left, | my dull deaf ears a little use to hear: 5.01.317
hear these ill news with the ears of claudio. ADO 2.01.173
what fire is in mine ears? 3.01.107
which falls into mine ears as profitless | as 5.01. 4
words | that aged ears play truant at his tales, LLL 2.01. 74
o, then his lines would ravish savage ears | and 4.03.345
our ears vouchsafe it. 5.02.217
then, if sickly ears, | deaf'd with the clamors 5.02.863
and kiss thy fair large ears, my gentle joy. MND 4.01. 4

with ears that sweep away the morning dew; 4.01.121
speak, would almost damn those ears | which, MV 1.01. 98
but stop my house's ears, i mean my casements; 2.05. 34
and let the sounds of music | creep in our ears. 5.01. 56
sound, | or any air of music touch their ears, 5.01. 76
crop | to glean the broken ears after the man AYL 3.05.102
that mortal ears might hardly endure the din? SHR 1.01.173
think you a little din can daunt mine ears? 1.02.199
and if you cannot, best you stop your ears. 4.03. 76
for you know | pitchers have ears, and i have 4.04. 52
the florentines and senoys are by th' ears, AWW 1.02. 1
his plausive words | he scatter'd not in ears, 1.02. 54
he that ears my land spares my team and gives me 1.03. 44 P
to herself her own words to her own ears; 1.03.108 P
richest eyes, whose words all ears took captive, 5.03. 17
she does abuse our ears. to prison with her! 5.03.294
to your ears, divinity; TN 1.05.217 P
go shake your ears. 2.03.125 P
knee–deep, o'er head and ears a fork'd one! WT 1.02.186
to have nor eyes nor ears nor thought, then say 1.02.275
ballads and all men's ears grew to his tunes. 4.04.185 P
to me that all their other senses stuck in ears. 4.04.609 P
that even your ears | should rift to hear me, 5.01. 65
bohemia stops his ears, and threatens them 5.01.201
what cracker is this same that deafs our ears JN 2.01.147
smoke, | to make a faithless error in your ears; 2.01.230
our ears are cudgell'd — not a word of his 2.01.464
hear me without thine ears, and make reply 3.03. 49
without eyes, ears, and harmful sound of words 3.03. 51
face, | and bid his ears a little while be deaf, R2 1.01.112
mowbray, impartial are our eyes and ears. 1.01.115
that is not quickly buzz'd into his ears? 2.01. 26
the breath of parley | into his ruin'd ears, and 3.03. 34
of persuasion and him the ears of profiting, 1H4 1.02.153 P
on his /altar sit | up to the ears in blood. 4.01.117
we will not trust our eyes | without our ears: 5.04.137
open your ears; 2H4 in 1
stuffing the ears of men with false reports. in 8
heels would amend the attention of your ears, 1.02.124 P
well spoke on, i can hear it with mine own ears. 2.02. 66 P
not this nave of a wheel have his ears cut off? 2.04.256 P
sir, and i come to draw you out by the ears. 2.04.290 P
and the mute wonder lurketh in men's ears | to H5 1.01. 49
but when the blast of war blows in our ears, 3.01. 5
i would fain be about the ears of the english. 3.07. 84 P
fain would mine eyes be witness with mine ears 1H6 2.03. 9
whose warlike ears could never brook retreat, 3H6 1.01. 5
yet look to have them buzz to offend thine ears. 2.06. 95
where fame, late ent'ring at his heedful ears, 3.03. 63
i have not stopp'd mine ears to their demands, 4.08. 39
or shall we beat the stones about thine ears? 5.01.108
point | than can my ears that tragic history. 5.06. 28
that fill his ears with such dissentious rumors. R3 1.03. 46
what dreadful noise of /waters in /my ears! 1.04. 22
me, and howled in mine ears | such hideous cries 1.04. 59
pitchers have ears. 2.04. 37
my tongue should to thy ears not name my boys 4.04.231
prepare her ears to hear a wooer's tale; 4.04.327
to declare, in hearing | of all these ears (for, H8 2.04.147
and may be left | to some ears unrecounted. 3.02. 48
knit all the greekish ears | to his experienc'd TRO 1.03. 67
sir, pardon, 'tis for agamemnon's ears. 1.03.248
his evasions have ears thus long. 2.01. 69 P
will, | my will enkindled by mine eyes and ears, 2.02. 63
have ears more deaf than adders to the voice 2.02.172
that doth invert th' attest of eyes and ears, 5.02.122
your passion draws ears hither. 5.02.181
to stop his ears against admonishment? 5.03. 2
were half to half the world by th' ears, and he COR 1.01.233
and carry with us ears and eyes for th' time, 2.01.269
we do request your kindest ears, and after, 2.02. 52
for honor | than /one /on /'s ears to hear it? 2.02. 81
let them pull all about mine ears, present me 3.02. 1
of th' ignorant | more learned than the ears), 3.02. 77
a name unmusical to the volscians' ears, | and 4.05. 58
and sowl the porter of rome gates by th' ears. 4.05.201 P
he'll shake | your rome about your ears. 4.06. 99
lots to blanks | my name hath touch'd your ears: 5.02. 11
mine ears against your suits are stronger than 5.02. 88
stopp'd your ears against | the general suit of 5.03. 5
i, | even in theirs and in the commons' ears, 5.06. 4
unholy braggart, | 'fore your own eyes and ears? 5.06.119
the palace full of tongues, of eyes, and ears; TIT 2.01.127
thee, | be not obdurate, open thy deaf ears. 2.03.160
of our peace | buzz in the people's ears, there 4.04. 7
for i can smooth and fill his aged ears | with 4.04. 96
heart | almost impregnable, his old ears deaf, 4.04. 98
and in their ears tell them my dreadful name, 5.02. 39
tell us what sinon hath bewitch'd our ears, | or 5.03. 85
the which if you with patient ears attend, ROM pr 13
which, as he breath'd defiance to my ears, | he 1.01.110
love, wherein thou stickest | up to the ears. 1.04. 43
my ears have yet not drunk a hundred words | of 2.02. 58
night, | like softest music to attending ears! 2.02.166
thy old groans yet ringing in mine ancient ears; 2.03. 74
pluck your sword out of his pilcher by the ears? 3.01. 81 P
lest mine be about your ears ere it be out. 3.01. 81 P
o, then i see that /madmen have no ears. 3.03. 61
what fear is this which startles in your ears? 5.03.194
o, that men's ears should be | to counsel deaf, TIM 1.02.249
feast your ears with the music awhile, if they 3.06. 33 P
put armor on thine ears and on thine eyes, 4.03.124
thou gav'st thine ears (like tapsters that bade 4.03.215
and enter in our ears like great triumphers | in 5.01.196
sir, their hats are pluck'd about their ears, JC 2.01. 73
friends, romans, countrymen, lend me your ears! 3.02. 73
ass) to shake his ears | and graze in commons. 4.01. 26
brutus, thrusting this report | into his ears; 5.03. 75
shall be as welcome to the ears of brutus | as 5.03. 77
had i three ears, i'ld hear thee. MAC 4.01. 78
let not your ears despise my tongue for ever, 4.03.201
while, | and let us once again assail your ears, HAM 1.01. 31
blazon must not be | to ears of flesh and blood. 1.05. 22
and in the porches of my ears did pour | the 1.05. 63
indeed | the very faculties of eyes and ears. 2.02.566
rags, to spleet the ears of the groundlings, who 3.02. 10 P
ears without hands or eyes, smelling sans all, 3.04. 79
these words like daggers enter in my ears. 3.04. 95
the ears are senseless that should give us 5.02.369
look with thine ears; LR 4.06.151 P
so justly to your grave ears i'll present | how OTH 1.03.124
noses, ears, and lips. 4.01. 42 P
or that mine eyes, mine ears, or any sense 4.02.154
ram thou thy fruitful tidings in mine ears, ANT 2.05. 24
make battery to our ears with the loud music; 2.07.109
for antony, | i have no ears to his request. 3.12. 20
have you no ears? 3.13. 92
(as i have such a heart that both mine ears CYM 1.06.130
away, i do condemn mine ears that have | so long 1.06.141
no, my lord; nor crop the ears of them. 2.01. 12 P
it is a /vice in her ears, which horsehairs and 2.03. 29 P
and will to ears and tongues | be theme and 3.01. 3
eyes | and ears so cloy'd importantly as now, 4.04. 19
mine ears, that /heard her flattery, nor my 5.05. 64
should let their ears hear their faults hid! PER 1.02. 62
i do | protest my ears were never better fed 2.05. 27
whistle | is as a whisper in the ears of death, 3.01. 9
what do you stop your ears? 4.02. 81 P
your ears unto your eyes i'll reconcile. 4.04. 22
who starves the ears she feeds, and makes them 5.01.112
have deaf'd | the ears of heav'nly justice. TNK 1.02. 81
of corn, | curling the wealthy ears, never flew. 2.03. 78
set both thine ears to th' business. 5.03. 92
his ears up–prick'd, his braided hanging mane VEN 271
high crest, short ears, straight legs and 297
"had i no eyes but ears, my ears would love 433
my ears would love | that inward beauty and 433
though neither eyes nor ears to hear nor see, 437
mine ears, that to your wanton talk attended, 809
shaking their scratch'd ears, bleeding as they 924
cold, | she whispers in his ears a heavy tale, 1125
he should keep unknown | from thievish ears, LUC 35
for by our ears our hearts oft tainted be; 38
he stories to her ears her husband's fame, | won 106
relish your nimble notes to pleasing ears, 1126
as if some mermaid did their ears entice, | some 1411
bad, | mad slanderers by mad ears believed be. SON 140.12
nor are mine ears with thy tongue's tune 141. 5

/EARTH 2 FR 0.0002 REL FR 1 V 1 P
/cri'st /now, "/o /earth, /yield /us /that /king 2H4 1.03.106
/heaven /and /earth! LR 1.02. 97 P

EARTH 330 FR 0.0373 REL FR 305 V 25 P
have sunk the sea within the earth or ere | it TMP 1.02. 11
to do me business in the veins o' th' earth 1.02.255
thou earth, thou! 1.02.314
i' th' air, or th' earth? 1.02.388
business, nor no sound | that the earth owes. 1.02.408
all corners else o' th' earth | let liberty make 1.02.492
no better than the earth he lies upon, | if he 2.01.281
o heaven, o earth, bear witness to this sound, 3.01. 68
rich scarf to my proud earth — why hath thy 4.01. 82
my staff, | bury it certain fadoms in the earth, 5.01. 55
nor to his service no such joy on earth: TGV 2.04.139
sovereign to all the creatures on the earth. 2.04.153
lest the base earth | should from her vesture 2.04.159
heart as far from fraud as heaven from earth. 2.07. 78
mortal thing | upon the dull earth dwelling. 4.02. 52
sweet lady, let me rake it from the earth. 4.02.115
is not satisfied | is nor of heaven nor earth, 5.04. 80
for it is as positive as the earth is firm that WIV 3.02. 48 P
alas, i had rather be set quick i' th' earth, 3.04. 86
'tis set down so in heaven, but not in earth. MM 2.04. 50
at length the sun, gazing upon the earth, ERR 1.01. 88
heaven's eye | but hath his bound in earth, in 2.01. 17
am i in earth, in heaven, or in hell? 2.02.212
than our earth's wonder, more than earth divine. 3.02. 32
god make men of some other mettle than earth. ADO 2.01. 60 P
face of terra, the soil, the land, the earth. LLL 4.02. 7 P
a good lustre of conceit in a turf of earth; 4.02. 88 P
thou, fair sun, which on my earth dost shine, 4.03. 67
by earth, she is not, corporal, there you lie. 4.03. 84
"all hail, the richest beauties on the earth!" 5.02.158
in a spleen, unfolds both heaven and earth; MND 1.01.146
flying between the cold moon and the earth, 2.01.156
i'll put a girdle round about the earth | in 2.01.175
believe as soon | this whole earth may be bor'd, 3.02. 53
doth glance from heaven to earth, from earth to 5.01. 13
from heaven to earth, from earth to heaven; 5.01. 13
outbrave the heart most daring on the earth, MV 2.01. 28
from the four corners of the earth they come 2.07. 39
a kinder gentleman treads not the earth. 2.08. 35
he finds the joys of heaven here on earth; 3.05. 76
and if on earth he do not /merit it, | in reason 3.05. 77
is so desirous to lie with his mother earth? AYL 1.02.201 P
and fetch shrill echoes from the hollow earth. SHR in.2. 46
the other, that she's in earth, from whence god AWW 2.04. 12 P
a heaven on earth i have won by wooing thee. 4.02. 66
rest | between the elements of air and earth, TN 1.05.275
comes the countess, now heaven walks on earth. 5.01. 97
as heaven sees earth and earth sees heaven, WT 1.02.315
as heaven sees earth and earth sees heaven, 1.02.315
the face to sweeten | of the whole dungy earth. 2.01.157
or death, upon the earth | of its right father. 3.03. 45
the dibble in earth to set one slip of them; 4.04.100
than he, and men — the earth, the heavens, and 4.04.371
nature crush the sides o' th' earth together, 4.04.478
or | the close earth wombs, or the profound seas 4.04.490
the most peerless piece of earth, i think, 5.01. 94
that 'twixt heaven and earth | might thus have 5.01.132
welcome hither, | as is the spring to th' earth. 5.01.152
they kneel, they kiss the earth; 5.01.199
she lifted the princess from the earth, and so 5.02. 76 P
some sins do bear their privilege on earth, JN 1.01.261
thou monstrous slanderer of heaven and earth! 2.01.173
thou monstrous injurer of heaven and earth, 2.01.174
lies, | coldly embracing the discolored earth, 2.01.306
that sways the earth this climate overlooks, 2.01.344
that no supporter but the huge firm earth | can 3.01. 72
the meagre cloddy earth to glittering gold. 3.01. 80
o, when the last accompt 'twixt heaven and earth 4.02.216
the earth had not a hole to hide this deed. 4.03. 36
as it on earth hath been thy servant still. 5.07. 73
speak | my body shall make good upon this earth, R2 1.01. 37
even from the tongueless caverns of the earth, 1.01.105
who, when they see the hour's ripe on earth, 1.02. 7
that our kingdom's earth should not be soil'd 1.03.125
this earth of majesty, this seat of mars, | this 2.01. 41
this blessed plot, this earth, this realm, this 2.01. 50
comfort's in heaven, and we are on the earth, 2.02. 78
the pale–fac'd moon looks bloody on the earth, 2.04. 10
fall to the base earth from the firmament. 2.04. 20
dear earth, i do salute thee with my hand, 3.02. 6
so weeping, smiling, greet i thee, my earth, 3.02. 10
feed not thy sovereign's foe, my gentle earth, 3.02. 12
this earth shall have a feeling, and these 3.02. 24
hath clouded all thy happy days on earth. 3.02. 68
eyes | write sorrow on the bosom of the earth. 3.02.147
and that small model of the barren earth | which 3.02.153
his, whilst on the earth i rain | my waters — 3.03. 59
on the earth i rain | my waters — on the earth, 3.03. 60
fretted us a pair of graves | within the earth, 3.03.168
to make the base earth proud with kissing it. 3.03.191
thou, thou little better thing than earth, 3.04. 78
i task the earth to the like, forsworn aumerle, 4.01. 52
lie | in earth as quiet as thy father's skull; 4.01. 69
his body to that pleasant country's earth, | and 4.01. 98
prove | that ever fell upon this cursed earth. 4.01.147
if this rebellious earth | have any resting for 5.01. 5
and wounds the earth, if nothing else, with rage 5.01. 30
for ever may my knees grow to the earth, | my 5.03. 30
a god on earth thou art. 5.03.136
and telling me the sovereignest thing on earth 1H4 1.03. 57
out of the bowels of the harmless earth, | which 1.03. 61
and lards the lean earth as he walks along. 2.02.109
why dost thou bend thine eyes upon the earth, 2.03. 42
be not forgot upon the face of the earth, then 2.04.129 P
the frame and huge foundation of the earth 3.01. 16
i say the earth did shake when i was born. 3.01. 20
and i say the earth was not of my mind, | if you 3.01. 21
heavens were all on fire, the earth did tremble. 3.01. 23
then the earth shook to see the heavens on fire, 3.01. 24
oft the teeming earth | is with a kind of colic 3.01. 27
shakes the old beldame earth, and topples down 3.01. 31
at your birth | our grandam earth, having this 3.01. 33
for, heaven to earth, some of us never shall | a 5.02. 99
but now two paces of the vilest earth | is room 5.04. 91
this earth that bears /thee dead | bears not 5.04. 92
the acts commenced on this ball of earth. 2H4 in 5
down | the never–daunted percy to the earth, 1.01.110
let heaven kiss earth! 1.01.153
whose memory is written on the earth | with yet 4.01. 81
the achievement goes | with me into the earth. 4.05.190
their proud hoofs i' th' receiving earth; H5 pr 27
your brother kings and monarchs of the earth 1.02.122
he bounds from the earth, as if his entrails 3.07. 13 P
the earth sings when he touches it; 3.07. 16 P
and the dull elements of earth and water never 3.07. 22 P
black shoe trod upon god's ground and his earth, 4.07.142 P
so in the earth, to this day is not known. 1H6 1.02. 2
bright star of venus, fall'n down on the earth, 1.02.144
whose pitchy mantle over–veil'd the earth. 2.02. 2
who in a moment even with the earth | shall lay 4.02. 12
never so needful on the earth of france, | spur 4.03. 18
out of the powerful regions under earth, | help 5.03. 11
grace, | to work exceeding miracles on earth. 5.04. 41
why are thine eyes fix'd to the sullen earth, 2H6 1.02. 5
be you prostrate and grovel on the earth. 1.04. 11 P
thy heaven is on earth, thine eyes and thoughts 2.01. 19
for blessed are the peacemakers on earth. 2.01. 34
air, | blaspheming god and cursing men on earth. 3.02.372
air, | thy grave is digg'd already in the earth. 4.10. 52
where shall it find a harbor in the earth? 5.01.168
the last day | knit earth and heaven together! 5.02. 42
and over–shine the earth as this the world. 3H6 2.01. 38
brother's blood the thirsty earth hath drunk, 2.03. 15
then let the earth be drunken with our blood! 2.03. 23
where e'er it be, in heaven or in earth. 2.03. 43
thy burning car never had scorch'd the earth. 2.06. 13
since this earth affords no joy to me | but to 3.02.165
shows, | that i must yield my body to the earth, 5.02. 9
what is pomp, rule, reign, but earth and dust? 5.02. 27
for thou hast made the happy earth thy hell, R3 1.02. 51
o earth! 1.02. 63
or earth gape open wide and eat him quick, | as 1.02. 65
for he was fitter for that place than earth. 1.02.108
his bettar doth not breathe upon the earth. 1.02.140
since i have made my friends at peace on earth. 2.01. 6
that breath'd upon the earth a christian; 3.05. 26
rest thy unrest on england's lawful earth, 4.04. 29
that excellent grand tyrant of the earth | that 4.04. 52
earth gapes, hell burns, fiends roar, saints 4.04. 75
thou cam'st on earth to make the earth my hell. 4.04.167
thou cam'st on earth to make the earth my hell. 4.04.167
beneficial sun, | and keep it from the earth. H8 1.01. 57
would i had never trod this english earth, | or 3.01.143
think | his contemplation were above the earth, 3.02.131
my legs like loaden branches bow to th' earth, 4.02. 2
give him a little earth for charity!" 4.02. 23
whiles here he liv'd | upon this naughty earth? 5.01.138
in all designs begun on earth below | fails in TRO 1.03. 4
shaking of earth! 1.03. 97
as iron to adamant, as earth to th' centre, 3.02.179
false | as air, as water, wind, or sandy earth, 3.02.192
i were as deep under the earth as i am above! 4.02. 82 P
of my love | is as the very centre of the earth, 4.02.104
of his | in aspiration lifts him from the earth. 4.05. 16
who neither looks upon the heaven nor earth, 4.05.281
divides more wider than the sky and earth, | and 5.02.149
the dragon wing of night o'erspreads the earth, 5.08. 17
no space of earth shall sunder our two hates. 5.10. 27
that of all things upon the earth he hated COR 3.01. 14
which heaven | will not have earth to know. 4.02. 36
and am not | of stronger earth than others. 5.03. 29
sink, my knee, i' th' earth; 5.03. 50
and his fame folds in | this orb o' th' earth. 5.06.125
nor we disturb'd with prodigies on earth. TIT 1.01.101
joy | shed on this earth for thy return to rome. 1.01.162
reflect on rome as /titan's rays on earth, | and 1.01.226
descend | into this gaping hollow of the earth? 2.03.249
o earth, i will befriend thee more with rain, 3.01. 16
heaven, | and bow this feeble ruin to the earth; 3.01.207
heaven doth weep, doth not the earth o'erflow? 3.01.221
she is the weeping welkin, i the earth: 3.01.226
then must my earth with her continual tears 3.01.228

there is enough written upon this earth | to 4.01. 84
and pierce the inmost centre of the earth; 4.03. 12
and, sith there's no justice in earth nor hell, 4.03. 50
like to the earth swallow her own increase. 5.02.191
set him breast–deep in earth and famish him, 5.03.179
some stay to see him fast'ned in the earth. 5.03.183
earth hath swallowed all my hopes but she; ROM 1.02. 14
she's the hopeful lady of my earth. 1.02. 15
beauty too rich for use, for earth too dear! 1.05. 47
turn back, dull earth, and find thy centre out. 2.01. 2
the earth that's nature's mother is her tomb; 2.03. 9
for nought so vile that on the earth doth live 2.03. 17
but to the earth some special good doth give; 2.03. 18
which too untimely here did scorn the earth. 3.01.118
vile earth, to earth resign, end motion here, 3.02. 59
vile earth, to earth resign, end motion here, 3.02. 59
crown'd | sole monarch of the universal earth. 3.02. 94
the heaven and earth? 3.03.119
and heaven, and earth, all three do meet | in 3.03.120
when the sun sets, the earth doth drizzle dew, 3.05.126
my husband is on earth, my faith in heaven; 3.05.205
how shall that faith return again to earth, 3.05.206
send it me from heaven | by leaving earth? 3.05.208
where bloody tybalt, yet but green in earth, 4.03. 42
shrikes like mandrakes' torn out of the earth, 4.03. 47
gorg'd with the dearest morsel of the earth, 5.03. 46
and nature, as it grows again toward earth, | is TIM 2.02.218
that girdles in those wolves, dive in the earth, 4.01. 2
sun, draw from the earth | rotten humidity; 4.03. 1
earth, yield me roots! 4.03. 23
come, damn'd earth, | thou common whore of 4.03. 42
behold, the earth hath roots; 4.03.417
what vilder thing upon the earth than friends, 4.03.463
when all the sway of earth | shakes like a thing JC 1.03. 3
that have known the earth so full of faults. 1.03. 45
nor heaven nor earth have been at peace to–night 2.02. 1
o, pardon me, thou bleeding piece of earth, 3.01.254
that this foul deed shall smell above the earth 3.01.274
that look not like th' inhabitants o' th' earth, MAC 1.03. 41
the earth hath bubbles, as the water has, | and 1.03. 79
thou /sure and firm–set earth, | hear not my 2.01. 56
some say, the earth | was feverous, and did 2.03. 60
that darkness does the face of earth entomb, 2.04. 9
let the earth hide thee! 3.04. 92
universal peace, confound | all unity on earth. 4.03.100
have heaven and earth together demonstrated HAM 1.01.124
life | extorted treasure in the womb of earth, 1.01.137
whether in sea or fire, in earth or air, | th' 1.01.153
we pray you throw to earth | this unprevailing 1.02.106
heaven and earth, | must i remember? 1.02.142
though all the earth o'erwhelm them, to men's 1.02.257
o earth! 1.05. 92
said, old mole, canst work i' th' earth so fast? 1.05.162
there are more things in heaven and earth, 1.05.166
as the indifferent children of the earth. 2.02.227 P
that this goodly frame, the earth, seems to me a 2.02.298 P
as i do crawling between earth and heaven? 3.01.127 P
nor earth to me give food, nor heaven light, 3.02.216
examples gross as earth exhort me: 4.04. 46
cry to be heard, as 'twere from heaven to earth, 4.05.217
how long will a man lie i' th' earth ere he rot? 5.01.163 P
now hath lien you i' th' earth three and twenty 5.01.173 P
alexander look'd a' this fashion i' th' earth? 5.01.198 P
alexander returneth to dust, the dust is earth, 5.01.210 P
the dust is earth, of earth we make loam, and 5.01.210 P
o, that that earth which kept the world in awe 5.01.215
lay her i' th' earth, | and from her fair and 5.01.238
hold off the earth a while, | till i have caught 5.01.249
the cannons to the heavens, the heaven to earth, 5.02.277
but they shall be | the terrors of the earth! LR 2.04.282
bids the wind blow the earth into the sea, | or 3.01. 5
wheat, and hurts the poor creature of earth. 3.04.119 P
all you unpublish'd virtues of the earth, 4.04. 16
she's dead as earth. 5.03.262
do deeds to make heaven weep, all earth amaz'd; OTH 3.03.371
if that the earth could teem with woman's tears, 4.01.245
is hush'd within the hollow mine of earth | and 4.02. 79
she comes more nearer earth than she was wont, 5.02.110
must thou needs find out new heaven, new earth. ANT 1.01. 17
our dungy earth alike | feeds beast as man; 1.01. 35
him, it shows to man the tailors of the earth; 1.02.163 P
the demi–atlas of this earth, the arm | and 1.05. 23
are levying | the kings o' th' earth for war. 3.06. 68
we | have us'd to conquer standing on the earth, 3.07. 65
let him breathe between the heavens and earth, 3.12. 14
under the earth. 4.03. 13
i am alone the villain of the earth, | and feel 4.06. 29
that heaven and earth may strike their sounds 4.08. 38
the crown o' th' earth doth melt. 4.15. 63
course, and lighted | the little o, th' earth. 5.02. 81
no grave upon the earth shall clip in it | a 5.02.359
to seek through the regions of the earth | for CYM 1.01. 20
i am not vex'd more at any thing in th' earth; 2.01. 17 P
that all th' abhorred things o' th' earth amend 5.05.216
my riches to the earth from whence they came; PER 1.01. 52
heaven, to tell the earth is throng'd | by man's 1.01.101
we'll mingle our bloods together in the earth, 1.02.113
these mouths who, but of late, earth, sea, and 1.04. 34
water, earth, and heaven can make | to herald 3.01. 33
upon the sea, | shook as the earth did quake; 3.02. 15
to equal any single crown a' th' earth | i' th' 4.03. 8
being proud, swallowed some part a' th' earth. 4.04. 39
therefore the earth, fearing to be o'erflowed, 4.04. 40
thou purger of the earth, draw thy fear'd sword TNK 1.01. 48
he that will all the treasure know o' th' earth 1.01.114
both heaven and earth | friend thee for ever! 1.04. 1
which will seek of me | some news from earth, 3.01. 80
by heaven and earth, | there's nothing in thee 3.03. 45
kill this cousin, | on any piece the earth has. 3.06.263
heal'st with blood | the earth when it is sick, 5.01. 65
him his own name, | calls him a god on earth. STM II.C 104
would not afford you an abode on earth, | whet II.C 133
unless the earth with thy increase be fed? VEN 170
the bearing earth with his hard hoof he wounds, 267
looks on the dull earth with disturbed mind, 340
he cheers the morn, and all the earth relieveth; 484
quoth she, "in earth or heaven, | or in the 493
their lips together glued, fall to the earth. 546
the earth, in love with thee, thy footing trips, 722
that on the earth would breed a scarcity | and 753
since sweating lust on earth usurp'd his name, 794
by heaven and earth, and all the power of both, LUC 572
seasoning the earth with show'rs of silver brine 796
as the dank earth weeps at thy languishment, 1130
but as the earth doth weep, the sun being set, 1226
thou, fair sun, that on this earth doth shine, PP 3.10
and make the earth devour her own sweet brood; SON 19. 2
sun and moon, with earth and sea's rich gems, 21. 6
at break of day arising | from sullen earth) 29.12
upon the farthest earth remov'd from thee, | for 44. 6
but that, so much of earth and water wrought, 44.11
brass, nor stone, nor earth, nor boundless sea, 65. 1
the earth can have but earth, which is his due, 74. 7
the earth can have but earth, which is his due, 74. 7
or you survive when i in earth am rotten, | from 81. 2
the earth can yield me but a common grave, 81. 7
poor soul, the centre of my sinful earth, | /... 146. 1
their poor balls are tied | to th' orbed earth; LC 25

EARTH–BOUND 1 FR 0.0001 REL FR 1 V 0 P
bid the tree | unfix his earth–bound root? MAC 4.01. 96

EARTH'D 1 FR 0.0001 REL FR 1 V 0 P
be of as little memory | when he is earth'd, TMP 2.01.234

EARTH–DELVING 1 FR 0.0001 REL FR 1 V 0 P
and sometime where earth–delving conies keep, VEN 687

EARTHEN 1 FR 0.0001 REL FR 1 V 0 P
green earthen pots, bladders, and musty seeds, ROM 5.01. 46

EARTHLIER 1 FR 0.0001 REL FR 1 V 0 P
but earthlier happy is the rose distill'd, MND 1.01. 76

EARTHLY 36 FR 0.0040 REL FR 33 V 3 P
thy true subject, for the liquor is not earthly. TMP 2.02.126 P
no; but she is an earthly paragon. TGV 2.04.146
that there were | no earthly mean to save him, MM 2.04. 95
but, for those earthly faults, i quit them all, 5.01.483
doth not every earthly thing | cry shame upon ADO 4.01.120
these earthly godfathers of heaven's lights, LLL 1.01. 88
heaven's praise with such an earthly tongue." 4.02.118
my vow was earthly, thou a heavenly love; 4.03. 64
match, | and on the wager lay two earthly women, MV 3.05. 80
and earthly power doth then show likest god's 4.01.196
when earthly things made even | atone together. AYL 5.04.109
of a heavenly effect in an earthly actor." AWW 2.03. 24 P
o thou, the earthly author of my blood, | whose R2 1.03. 69
leaving their earthly parts to choke your clime, H5 4.03.102
face | a world of earthly blessings to my soul, 2H6 1.01. 22
great is his comfort in this earthly vale, 2.01. 68
was ever king that joy'd an earthly throne | and 4.09. 1
a sceptre, or an earthly sepulchre!" 3H6 1.04. 17
then you lost | the view of earthly glory. H8 1.01. 14
speak thee out) | the queen of earthly queens. 2.04.142
a brief span | to keep your earthly audit; 3.02.141
within me | a peace above all earthly dignities, 3.02.379
and the moon, were she earthly, no nobler — COR 2.01. 98 P
upon her wit doth earthly honor wait, | and TIT 2.01. 10
i remember now | i am in this earthly world — MAC 4.02. 75
shall bruit again, | respeaking earthly thunder. HAM 1.02.128
thou art, if thou dar'st be, the earthly jove. ANT 2.07. 67
or, if not, | an earthly paragon! CYM 3.06. 43
gripe not at earthly joys as erst they did; PER 1.01. 49
remember earthly man | is but a substance that 2.01. 2
done, | between this heavenly and earthly sun. VEN 198
there lives a son that suck'd an earthly mother, 863
this earthly saint, adored by this devil, LUC 85
my vow was earthly, thou a heavenly love; PP 3. 7
heaven's praise with such an earthly tongue. 5.14
heavenly touches ne'er touch'd earthly faces." SON 17. 8

EARTHQUAKE 7 FR 0.0008 REL FR 5 V 2 P
fright a monster's ear, | to make an earthquake! TMP 2.01.315
i look for an earthquake too then. ADO 1.01.273 P
but /or every blazing star or at an earthquake, AWW 1.03. 87 P
thy bosom | doth make an earthquake of nobility. JN 5.02. 42
in thunder and in earthquake, like a jove, H5 2.04.100
'tis since the earthquake now aleven years, ROM 1.03. 23
but, like an earthquake, shakes thee on my VEN 648

EARTHQUAKES 1 FR 0.0001 REL FR 0 V 1 P
but mountains may be remov'd with earthquakes, AYL 3.02.185 P

EARTH'S 20 FR 0.0022 REL FR 19 V 1 P
earth's increase, foison plenty, | barns and TMP 4.01.110
grace you show not | than our earth's wonder, ERR 3.02. 32
my sole earth's heaven, and my heaven's claim. 3.02. 64
dominator of navarre, my soul's earth's god, and LLL 1.01.221 P
until the heavens, envying earth's good hap, R2 1.01. 23
theirs for the earth's increase, mine for my 2H6 3.02.385
ere my knee rise from the earth's cold face, | i 3H6 2.03. 35
you | from this earth's thralldom to the joys of R3 1.04.248
the high imperial type of this earth's glory. 4.04.245
be this cold corpse on the earth's cold face; 5.03.266
let my tears staunch the earth's dry appetite, TIT 3.01. 14
the earth's a thief, | that feeds and breeds by TIM 4.03.440
kings are earth's gods; PER 1.01.103
earth's sovereign salve, to do a goddess good. VEN 28
"upon the earth's increase why shouldst thou 169
"grim–grinning ghost, earth's worm, what dost 933
for passage, earth's foundation shakes, | which 1047
my will that marks thee for my earth's delight, LUC 487
from earth's dark womb some gentle gust doth get 549
fair sun that breeds the fat earth's store, | by 1837

EARTH–TREADING 1 FR 0.0001 REL FR 1 V 0 P
earth–treading stars that make dark heaven light ROM 1.02. 25

EARTH–VEXING 1 FR 0.0001 REL FR 1 V 0 P
and shielded him | from this earth–vexing smart. CYM 5.04. 42

/EARTHY 1 FR 0.0001 REL FR 1 V 0 P
/and /soon /lie /richard /in /an /earthy /pit! R2 4.01.219

EARTHY 8 FR 0.0009 REL FR 8 V 0 P
to act her earthy and abhorr'd commands, TMP 1.02.273
lay open to my earthy, gross conceit, ERR 3.02. 34
what earthy name to interrogatories | can taste JN 3.01.147
but that the earthy and cold hand of death 1H4 5.04. 84
and to survey his dead and earthy image, | what 2H6 3.02.147
how pale she looks, | and of an earthy cold! H8 4.02. 98
before this earthy prison of their bones, | that TIT 1.01. 99
doth shine upon the dead man's earthy cheeks, 2.03.229

EAR–WAX 1 FR 0.0001 REL FR 0 V 1 P
quails, but he has not so much brain as ear–wax; TRO 5.01. 53 P

EAS'D 3 FR 0.0003 REL FR 3 V 0 P
pleas'd, till he be eas'd | with being nothing. R2 5.05. 40
it shall be eas'd if france can yield relief. 3H6 3.03. 20
when day's oppression is not eas'd by night, SON 28. 3

EASE 63 FR 0.0071 REL FR 52 V 11 P
and i should do it | with much more ease, for my TMP 3.01. 30
nor persuasion can with ease attempt you, i will MM 4.02.190 P
play | to ease the anguish of a torturing hour? MND 5.01. 37
leaving his wealth and ease | a stubborn will to AYL 2.05. 52
the more one sickens the worse at ease he is; 3.02. 24 P
please, | my hand is ready, may it do him ease. SHR 5.02.179
that surfeit on their ease, will day by day AWW 3.01. 18
i can with ease translate it to my will; JN 2.01.513
nor conversant with ease and idleness, | till i 4.03. 70
they whom youth and ease have taught to glose. R2 2.01. 10
and in this thought they find a kind of ease, 5.05. 28
and tell him so, for i will ease my heart, 1H4 1.03.127
we'll walk afoot a while, and ease our legs. 2.02. 80 P
got with much ease. 2.02.104
shall i not take mine ease in mine inn but i 3.03. 80 P
and vaulted with such ease into his seat | as if 4.01.107
well, of sufferance comes ease. 2H4 5.04. 25 P
myself | for living idly here in pomp and ease, 1H6 1.01.142
and in that ease, i'll tell thee my disease. 2.05. 44
to ease your country of distressful war | and 5.04.126
sorrow would solace, and mine age would ease. 2H6 2.03. 21
but here's a vengeful sword, rusted with ease, 3.02.198
it could not slake mine ire nor ease my heart. 3H6 1.03. 29
henry now lives in scotland at his ease; 3.03.151
while he enjoys the honor and his ease. 4.06. 52
by heaven, i will not do thee so much ease. 5.05. 72
help nothing else, yet do they ease the heart. R3 4.04.131
now, methinks, i feel a little ease. H8 4.02. 4
at what ease | might corrupt minds procure 5.01.131
some come to take their ease, | and sleep an act ep 2
that holds his honor higher than his ease, | and TRO 1.03.266
"because thou canst not ease thy smart | by 4.04. 19
never stood | to ease his breast with panting. COR 2.02.122
that i might rail at him to ease my mind! TIT 2.04. 35
o, could our mourning ease thy misery! 2.04. 57
or make some sign how i may do thee ease. 3.01.121
to ease their stomachs with their bitter tongues 3.01.233
to weep with them that weep doth ease some deal, 3.01.244
to ease the gnawing vulture of thy mind, | by 5.02. 31
and on them shalt thou ease thy angry heart. 5.02.119
that they cannot sit at ease on the old bench? ROM 2.04. 35 P
o, musicians, "heart's ease, heart's ease"! 4.05.102 P
o, musicians, "heart's ease, heart's ease"! 4.05.103 P
and you will have me live, play "heart's ease." 4.05.104 P
why "heart's ease"? 4.05.105 P
tell them that, to ease them of their griefs, TIM 5.01.198
shall sit and pant in your great chairs of ease, 5.04. 11
such men as he be never at heart's ease | whiles JC 1.02.208
to ease ourselves of divers sland'rous loads, 4.01. 20
thing to be done | that may to thee do ease, and HAM 1.01.131
weed | that roots itself in ease on lethe wharf, 1.05. 33
will not peruse the foils, so that, with ease, 4.07.136
nay, good my lord, for my ease, in good faith. 5.02.105 P
prithee go in thyself, seek thine own ease. LR 3.04. 23
neglecting an attempt of ease and gain | to wake OTH 1.03. 29
i am very ill at ease, | unfit for mine own 3.03. 32
for more probation | i can with ease produce. CYM 5.05.363
where when men been, there's seldom ease, | for PER 2.ch. 28
where's hourly trouble for a minute's ease. 2.04. 44
with honor, wealth, and ease, in waning age; LUC 142
give physic to the sick, ease to the pained? 901
doth teach that ease and that repose to say, SON 50. 3
in things of great receipt with ease we prove 136. 7

EASED 1 FR 0.0001 REL FR 1 V 0 P
so the spirit is eased; H5 4.01. 19

EASE–DROPPER 1 FR 0.0001 REL FR 1 V 0 P
under our tents i'll play the ease–dropper, | to R3 5.03.221

EASEFUL 1 FR 0.0001 REL FR 1 V 0 P
sun, | ere he attain his easeful western bed: 3H6 5.03. 6

EASES 1 FR 0.0001 REL FR 1 V 0 P
till then i'll sweat and seek about for eases, TRO 5.10. 55

EASETH 1 FR 0.0001 REL FR 1 V 0 P
it easeth some, though none it ever cured, | to LUC 1581

EASIER 9 FR 0.0010 REL FR 4 V 5 P
that i may pass with a reproof the easier, sith WIV 2.02.188 P
you dare easier be friends with me than fight ADO 4.01.298 P
thou art easier swallow'd than a flap–dragon. LLL 5.01. 41 P
i can easier teach twenty what were good to be MV 1.02. 15 P
i would your spirit were easier for advice, | or WT 4.04.505
forgo the easier. JN 3.01.207
is my beaver easier than it was? R3 5.03. 50
lest our old robes sit easier than our new! MAC 2.04. 38
do you think i am easier to be play'd on than a HAM 3.02.370 P

EASIEST 1 FR 0.0001 REL FR 1 V 0 P
in whose easiest passage | look for no less than WT 3.02. 90

EASIL'EST 1 FR 0.0001 REL FR 1 V 0 P
sluggish /crare | mightst easil'est harbor in? CYM 4.02.206

EASILY 30 FR 0.0034 REL FR 20 V 10 P
will break | as easily as i do tear his paper. TGV 4.04.131
yet i cannot put off my opinion so easily. WIV 2.01.235 P
it is a rupture that you may easily heal; MM 3.01.235 P
very easily possible. ADO 1.01. 75 P
sir, your wit ambles well, it goes easily. 5.01.158 P
thanks | for my great suit so easily obtain'd. LLL 5.02.739
for the one sleeps easily because he cannot AYL 3.02.320 P
any manners, he may easily put it off at court. AWW 2.02. 9 P
he will bear you easily, and reins well. TN 3.04.324 P
how came the posterns | so easily open? WT 2.01. 53
of their hearts | may easily win a woman's. JN 1.01.269
dogs, easily won to fawn on any man! R2 3.02.130
written, be assur'd | will easily be granted. 1H4 1.03.264
forth | shall bring this prize in very easily. 2H4 3.01.101
a heart unspotted is not easily daunted. 2H6 3.01.100
whereof you cannot easily purge yourself. 3.01.135
and be not easily won to our requests: R3 3.07. 50
that wisdom knits not, folly may easily untie. TRO 2.03.102 P
which easily endures not article | tying him to COR 2.03.196
how easily murder is discovered! TIT 2.03.287
if he care not for't, he will supply us easily; TIM 4.03.404 P
to keep his state in rome | as easily as a king. JC 1.02.161
"by and by" is easily said. HAM 3.02.387
o, for a chair, | to bear him easily hence! OTH 5.01. 83
of one not easily jealious, but, being wrought, 5.02.345
you see how easily she may be surpris'd. ANT 5.02. 35
not easily, i think. CYM 2.01. 45 P

surges, crack'd | as easily 'gainst our rocks. 3.01. 29
do, maids will not so easily | trust men again. TNK 2.06. 20
his short thick neck cannot be easily harmed; VEN 627
EASINESS 3 FR 0.0003 REL FR 2 V 1 P
out of our easiness and childish pity | to one H8 5.02. 60
and that shall lend a kind of easiness | to the HAM 3.04.166
hath made it in him a property of easiness. 5.01. 68 P
EASING 2 FR 0.0002 REL FR 1 V 1 P
all, or half, for easing me of the carriage. WIV 2.02.173 P
a spendthrift's sigh, | that hurts by easing. HAM 4.07.123
EAS'LY 2 FR 0.0002 REL FR 2 V 0 P
many, | the measure then of one is eas'ly told. LLL 5.02.190
properly, | i will enforce it eas'ly to my love. JN 2.01.515
EAST 42 FR 0.0047 REL FR 39 V 3 P
they shall be my east and west indies, and i WIV 1.03. 71 P
dapples the drowsy east with spots of grey. ADO 5.03. 27
and by east from the west corner of thy LLL 1.01.245 P
at the first op'ning of the gorgeous east, 4.03.219
by east, west, north, and south, i spread my 5.02.563
shine, comforts, from the east, | that i may MND 3.02.432
"from the east to western inde, | no jewel is AYL 3.02. 88
think it — | from east, west, north, and south. WT 1.02.203
by east and west let france and england mount JN 2.01.381
of yours | behold another day break in the east; 5.04. 32
shall see us rising in our throne, the east, R2 3.02. 50
sun | from out the fiery portal of the east, 3.03. 64
send danger from the east unto the west, | so 1H4 1.03.195
by south and east is to my part assign'd; 3.01. 74
team | begins his golden progress in the east. 3.01.219
unyok'd, they take their courses | east, west, 2H4 4.02.104
this evening, on the east side of the grove. 2H6 2.01. 42
are ye advis'd? the east side of the grove. 2.01. 47
on, | and flaky darkness breaks within the east. R3 5.03. 86
he should have brav'd the east an hour ago. 5.03.279
here's a lord — come knights from east to west, TRO 2.03.263
but it is not known | whether for east or west. COR 1.02. 10
to issue out of one skull, they would fly east, 2.03. 22 P
even from /hyperion's rising in the east, TIT 5.02. 56
peer'd forth the golden window of the east, | a ROM 1.01.119
should in the farthest east begin to draw | the 1.01.135
it is the east, and juliet is the sun. 2.02. 3
do lace the severing clouds in yonder east. 3.05. 8
here lies the east; doth not the day break here? JC 2.01.101
presents his fire, and the high east | stands, 2.01.110
the tyrant's grasp, | and the rich east to boot. MAC 4.03. 37
this heavy–headed revel east and west | makes us HAM 1.04. 17
the world | even from the east to th' west! OTH 4.02.144
all the east, | say thou, shall call her ANT 1.05. 46
for my peace, | i' th' east my pleasure lies. 2.03. 41
the beds i' th' east are soft, and thanks to you 2.06. 50
nay, cadwal, we must lay his head to th' east, CYM 4.02.255
i may wander | from east to occident, cry out 4.02.372
then start amongst 'em | and, as an east wind, TNK 2.02. 13
by east and north–east to the king of pigmies, 3.04. 15
lord, how mine eyes throw gazes to the east! PP 14.13
better becomes the grey cheeks of th' east, SON 132. 6
EASTCHEAP 7 FR 0.0008 REL FR 0 V 7 P
bespoke supper to–morrow night in eastcheap. 1H4 1.02.130 P
farewell, you shall find me in eastcheap. 1.02.157 P
and meet me to–morrow night in eastcheap, there 1.02.193 P
i shall command all the good lads in eastcheap. 2.04. 14 P
my noble lord, from eastcheap. 2.04.441 P
grace, i am a poor widow of eastcheap, and he is 2H4 2.01. 70 P
at the old place, my lord, in eastcheap. 2.02.148 P
EASTER 1 FR 0.0001 REL FR 0 V 1 P
for wearing his new doublet before easter? ROM 3.01. 28 P
EASTERN 7 FR 0.0008 REL FR 7 V 0 P
fann'd with the eastern wind, turns to a crow MND 3.02.142
groves may tread | even till the eastern gate, 3.02.391
he fires the proud tops of the eastern pines R2 3.02. 42
up to the eastern tower, | whose height commands
TRO 1.02. 2
check'ring the eastern clouds with streaks of ROM 2.03. 2
o eastern star! ANT 5.02.308
muster thy mists to meet the eastern light, LUC 773
EASTWARD 1 FR 0.0001 REL FR 1 V 0 P
walks o'er the dew of yon high eastward hill. HAM 1.01.167
EASY 62 FR 0.0070 REL FR 47 V 15 P
what impossible matter will he make easy next? TMP 2.01. 89 P
you yourself know how easy it is to be such an WIV 2.02.189 P
mile, as easy as a cannon will shoot point–blank 3.02. 33 P
'tis all as easy | falsely to take away a life MM 2.04. 46
which are as easy broke as they make forms. 2.04.126
difficulties are but easy when they are known. 4.02.205 P
as easy mayst thou fall | a drop of water in the ERR 2.02.125
pains that i take for you is as easy as thanks." ADO 2.03.261 P
and how easy it is to put "years" to the word LLL 1.02. 52 P
some fear, | how easy is a bush suppos'd a bear! MND 5.01. 22
and 'twere as easy | for you to laugh and leap, MV 1.01. 48
if to do were as easy as to know what were good 1.02. 12 P
it is as easy to count atomies as to resolve the AYL 3.02.232 P
you shall as easy | prove that i husbanded her AWW 5.03.125
this woman's an easy glove, my lord, she goes 5.03.277 P
how easy is it for the proper–false | in women's TN 2.02. 29
which is for me less easy to commit | than you WT 1.02. 58
all deaths are too few, the sharpest too easy. 4.04.780 P
for 'tis as easy | to make her speak as move. 5.03. 93
made whole | with very easy arguments of love, JN 1.01. 36
how easy dost thou take all england up | from 4.03.142
to win this easy match play'd for a crown? 5.02.106
overblown, | an easy task it is to win our own. R2 3.02.191
by heaven, methinks it were an easy leap, | to 1H4 1.03.201
and made us doff our easy robes of peace, | to 5.01. 12
and of so easy and so plain a stop | that the 2H4 in 17
majesty, | sits not so easy on me as you think. 5.02. 45
was this easy? 5.02. 71
win | a soul so easy as that englishman's." H5 2.02.125
it is as easy for me, kate, to conquer the 5.02.184 P
my lord, these faults are easy, quickly answer'd 2H6 3.01.133
an easy task, 'tis but to love a king. 3H6 3.02. 53
our scouts have found the adventure very easy; 4.02. 18
is it not an easy matter | to make william lord R3 3.01.161
i would i were, | they should find easy penance. H8 1.04. 17
faith, how easy? 1.04. 17
as easy as a down–bed would afford it. 1.04. 18
when he thinks, good easy man, full surely | his 3.02.356
at last, with easy roads, he came to leicester, 4.02. 17
and that's as easy | as to set dogs on sheep — COR 2.01.256
ascent is not by such easy degrees as those who, 2.02. 25 P
to cure it, easy. 3.01.295
his revenges with the easy groans of old women, 5.02. 42 P
the last, i think | might have found easy fines; 5.06. 64
and easy it is | of a cut loaf to steal a shive, TIT 2.01. 86
of them | as jewels purchas'd at an easy price, 3.01.198
how easy is it then! MAC 2.02. 65
is an office | which the false man does easy. 2.03.137
as easy mayst thou the intrenchant air | with 5.08. 9
it is as easy as lying. HAM 3.02.357 P
to the next abstinence, the next more easy; 3.04.167
whose foolish honesty | my practices ride easy. LR 1.02.182
for 'tis most easy | th' inclining desdemona to OTH 2.03.339
babes | do it with gentle means and easy tasks. 4.02.112
which with a snaffle | you may pace easy, but ANT 2.02. 64
'tis easy to't, and there i will attend | what 3.10. 31
and at this time most easy 'tis to do't: 3.13.144
conclusions infinite | of easy ways to die. 5.02.356
which else an easy battery might lay flat, for CYM 1.04. 22 P
not a whit, | your lady being so easy. 2.04. 47
words are easy, like the wind, | faithful PP 20.31
as easy might i from myself depart | as from my SON 109. 3
EASY–BORROWED 1 FR 0.0001 REL FR 1 V 0 P
this is a slave whose easy–borrowed pride LR 2.04.185
EASY–HELD 1 FR 0.0001 REL FR 1 V 0 P
and this her easy–held imprisonment | hath 1H6 5.03.139
EASY–MELTING 1 FR 0.0001 REL FR 1 V 0 P
have wrought the easy–melting king like wax. 3H6 2.01.171
EASY–YIELDING 1 FR 0.0001 REL FR 0 V 1 P
upon the easy–yielding spirit of this woman, and 2H4 2.01.115 P
/EAT 4 FR 0.0004 REL FR 4 V 0 P
/now /thou /wouldst /eat /thy /dead /vomit /up, 2H4 1.03. 99
/and /look /you /eat /no /more | /than /will TIT 3.02. 1
/fall /to, /and, /gentle /girl, /eat /this. 3.02. 34
/cannot /draw /a /cart, /nor /eat /dried /oats, LR 5.03. 38
EAT 156 FR 0.0176 REL FR 74 V 82 P
i must eat my dinner. TMP 1.02.330
i' faith, i'll eat nothing. WIV 1.01.279 P
i'll eat nothing, i thank you, sir. 1.01.302 P
thou shalt eat a posset to–night at my house, 5.05.170 P
abominable and beastly touches | i drink, i eat, MM 3.02. 25
say to thee again) would eat mutton on fridays. 3.02.181 P
if it be, sir, i pray you eat none of it. ERR 2.02. 60 P
have a long spoon that must eat with the devil. 4.03. 64 P
for indeed i promis'd to eat all of his killing. ADO 1.01. 44 P
had musty victual, and he hath holp to eat it. 1.01. 51 P
eat when i have stomach, and wait for no man's 1.03. 14 P
for the fool will eat no supper that night. 2.01.149 P
blood of mine, | nor age so eat up my invention, 4.01.194
do not swear and eat it. 4.01.275 P
and i will make him eat it that says i love not 4.01.277 P
will you not eat your word? 4.01.278 P
i would eat his heart in the market–place. 4.01.306 P
he hath not eat paper, as it were; LLL 4.02. 25 P
methought a serpent eat my heart away, | and you
MND 2.02.149
or say, sweet love, what thou desirest to eat. 4.01. 30
most dear actors, eat no onions nor garlic, for 4.02. 42 P
to eat of the habitation which your prophet the MV 1.03. 33 P
but i will not eat with you, drink with you, nor 1.03. 37 P
shall i keep your hogs and eat husks with them? AYL 1.01. 37 P
at an instant, learn'd, play'd, eat together, 1.03. 74
and if i bring thee not something to eat, i will 2.06. 12 P
forbear, and eat no more. 2.07. 88
why, i have eat none yet. 2.07. 88
i earn that i eat, get that i wear, owe no man 3.02. 73 P
when he had a desire to eat a grape, would open 5.01. 33 P
that grapes were made to eat and lips to open. 5.01. 36 P
i will not eat my word, now thou art mine, | thy 5.04.149
strive mightily, but eat and drink as friends. SHR 1.02.277
she eat no meat to–day, nor none shall eat; 4.01.197
she eat no meat to–day, nor none shall eat; 4.01.197
as who should say, if i should sleep or eat, 4.03. 13
eat it up all, hortensio, if thou lovest me. 4.03. 50
kate, eat apace. 4.03. 52
down, | for now we sit to chat as well as eat. 5.02. 11
nothing but sit and sit, and eat and eat! 5.02. 12
nothing but sit and sit, and eat and eat! 5.02. 12
there do muster true gait, eat, speak, and move AWW 2.01. 54 P
o, will you eat | no grapes, my royal fox? 2.01. 69
sir, you can eat none of this homely meat. 2.02. 46 P
and this gentle maid | to eat with us to–night, 3.05. 98
but i will eat and drink, and sleep as soft | as 4.03.332
i will henceforth eat no fish of fortune's 5.02. 8 P
you are a fool and a knave, you shall eat. 5.02. 54 P
let us therefore eat and drink. TN 2.03. 13 P
of a flea, i'll eat the rest of th' anatomy. 3.02. 62 P
and how she long'd to eat adders' heads, and WT 4.04.264 P
sir robert might have eat his part in me | upon JN 1.01.234
but now will canker–sorrow eat my bud, | and 3.04. 82
if i dare eat, or drink, or breathe, or live, R2 4.01. 73
that jade hath eat bread from my royal hand, 5.05. 85
of heaven prove a micher and eat blackberries? 1H4 2.04.408 P
and cleanly, but to carve a capon and eat it? 2.04.457 P
you leave to powder me and eat me too to–morrow. 5.04.112 P
i would make him eat a piece of my sword. 5.04.153 P
whereby thou didst desire to eat some, whereby i 2H4 2.01. 97 P
have /made /a /shift /to eat up thy holland. 2.02. 22 P
steep this letter in sack and make him eat it. 2.02.136 P
that's to make him eat twenty of his words. 2.02.137 P
most renown'd, | hast eat thy bearer up." 4.05.164
we will eat a last year's pippin of mine own 5.03. 2 P
'a, we shall "do nothing but eat, and make good 5.03. 17
cat, | to 'tame and havoc more than she can eat. H5 1.02.173
he longs to eat the english. 3.07. 91 P
i think he will eat all he kills. 3.07. 92 P
valiant flea that dare eat his breakfast on the 3.07.146 P
they will eat like wolves and fight like devils. 3.07.150 P
have only stomachs to eat and none to fight. 3.07.154 P
yesterday, look you, and bid me eat my leek. 5.01. 10 P
my requests, and my petitions, to eat, look you, 5.01. 24 P
not agree with it, i would desire you to eat it. 5.01. 27 P
will you be so good, scald knave, as eat it? 5.01. 30 P
to live in the mean time, and eat your victuals. 5.01. 34 P
if you can mock a leek, you can eat a leek. 5.01. 38 P
i say, i will make him eat some part of my leek, 5.01. 40 P
i will most horribly revenge — i eat and eat — 5.01. 48 P
i will most horribly revenge — i eat and eat — 5.01. 48 P
eat, i pray you. 5.01. 49 P
quiet thy cudgel, thou dost see i eat. 5.01. 52 P
another leek in my pocket, which you shall eat. 5.01. 62 P
the bud, | and caterpillars eat my leaves away; 2H6 3.01. 90
all shall eat and drink on my score, and i will 4.02. 73 P
into this garden, to see if i can eat grass, or 4.10. 8 P
but i'll make thee eat iron like an ostridge, 4.10. 28 P
i have eat no meat these five days, yet, come 4.10. 39 P
doornail, i pray god i may never eat grass more. 4.10. 41 P
or earth gape open wide and eat him quick, | as R3 1.02. 65
in her days every man shall eat in safety H8 5.04. 33
idle head, you would eat chickens i' th' shell. TRO 1.02.134 P
an universal prey, | and last eat up himself. 1.03.124
not bear it so, 'a should eat swords first. 2.03.217 P
weep seas, live in fire, eat rocks, tame tigers; 3.02. 78 P
i will go eat with thee and see your knights. 4.05.158
if the wars eat us not up, they will; COR 1.01. 85 P
hunger broke stone walls, that dogs must eat, 1.01.206
think, should we encounter | as often as we eat. 1.10. 10
an unnatural dam | should now eat up her own! 3.01.292
'twill fill your stomachs, please you eat of it. TIT 5.03. 29
will't please you eat? 5.03. 54
no; i eat not lords. TIM 1.01.204 P
o, they eat lords; 1.01.206 P
rich men sin, and i eat root. 1.02. 71
when your false masters eat of my lord's meat? 3.04. 50
keep it, i cannot eat it. 4.03.101
thus would i eat it. 4.03.282
stomach finds meat, or, rather, where i eat it. 4.03.295 P
there's a medlar for thee, eat it. 4.03.305 P
if thou wert the lamb, the fox would eat thee; 4.03.329 P
eat, timon, and abhor /them. 4.03.397
you must eat men. 4.03.425
can you eat roots and drink cold water? 5.01. 74
it will not let you eat, nor talk, nor sleep; JC 2.01.252
'tis said, they eat each other. MAC 2.04. 18
ere we will eat our meal in fear, and sleep | in 3.02. 17
them lie | till famine and the ague eat them up. 5.05. 4
faith — of the chameleon's dish, i eat the air, HAM 3.02. 94 P
that monster custom, who all sense doth eat, 3.04.161
may fish with the worm that hath eat of a king, 4.03. 27 P
and eat of the fish that hath fed of that worm. 4.03. 28 P
woo't drink up eisel, eat a crocadile? 5.01.276
fight when i cannot choose, and to eat no fish. LR 1.04. 17 P
cut the egg i' th' middle and eat up the meat, 1.04.159 P
and of the cannibals that each /other eat, | the OTH 1.03.143
they eat us hungerly, and when they are full 3.04.105
it is reported thou didst eat strange flesh, ANT 1.04. 67
pays his heart | for what his eyes eat only. 2.02.226
sir, i will eat no meat, i'll not drink, sir; 5.02. 49
will it eat me? 5.02.271
i know the devil himself will not eat a woman. 5.02.273 P
like warlike as the wolf for what we eat; CYM 3.03. 41
ere you depart, and thanks to stay and eat it. 3.06. 67
care no more to clothe and eat, | to thee the 4.02.266
to eat those little darlings whom they lov'd. PER 1.04. 44
not to eat honey like a drone | from others' 2.ch. 18
the great ones eat up the little ones. 2.01. 28 P
all viands that i eat do seem unsavory, 2.03. 31
have sod their infants in (and after eat them) TNK 1.03. 21
they eat well, look merrily, discourse of many 2.01. 38 P
he'll eat a horn–book ere he fail. 2.03. 42
spare it not, | the duke has more, coz. eat now. 3.03. 20
friend, you must eat no white bread; 3.05. 80
without lets, | and the ladies eat his dowsets! 3.05.157
say you come to eat with her and to commune of 4.03. 77 P
desire to eat with her, /carve her, drink to her 4.03. 87 P
this may bring her to eat, to sleep, and reduce 4.03. 94 P
smiling to me | and ask'd me what i would eat, 5.02. 5
argo they eat more in our country than they do STM II.C 5 P
and grave, like water that doth eat in steel, LUC 755
of foes, | to eat up errors by opinion bred, 937
to eat the world's due, by the grave and thee. SON 1.14
growth | a vengeful canker eat him up to death. 99.13
inheritors of this excess, | eat up thy charge? 146. 8
EATEN 19 FR 0.0021 REL FR 5 V 14 P
bud | is eaten by the canker ere it blow, | even TGV 1.01. 46
ford, your sorrow hath eaten up my sufferance. WIV 4.02. 1 P
this very man, having eaten the rest (as i said) MM 2.01.101 P
sir, she hath eaten up all her beef, and she is 3.02. 56 P
how many hath he kill'd and eaten in these wars? ADO 1.01. 43 P
thy master hath not eaten thee for a word, for LLL 5.01. 39 P
from time to time and worms have eaten them, but
AYL 4.01.107 P
the oats have eaten the horses. SHR 3.02.205 P
from the gentleman and how much he hath eaten.
WT 3.03.130 P
he utters them as he had eaten ballads and all 4.04.185 P
i were better to be eaten to death with a rust 2H4 1.02.219 P
he hath eaten me out of house and home, he hath 2.01. 74 P
for suffering flesh to be eaten in thy house, 2.04.344 P
i wish some ravenous wolf had eaten thee! 1H6 5.04. 31
given, he might have boil'd and eaten him too. COR 4.05.189 P
or have we eaten on the insane root | that takes MAC 1.03. 84
sow's blood, that hath eaten | her nine farrow; 4.01. 64
not where he eats, but where 'a is eaten; HAM 4.03. 19 P
i see, /sir, you are eaten up with passion; OTH 3.03.391
EATER 4 FR 0.0004 REL FR 2 V 2 P
but i am a great eater of beef and i believe TN 1.03. 85 P
a knave, a rascal, an eater of broken meats; LR 2.02. 15 P
and she an eater of her mother's flesh | by the PER 1.01.130
eater of youth, false slave to false delight, LUC 927
EATING 14 FR 0.0015 REL FR 7 V 7 P
in the sweetest bud | the eating canker dwells, TGV 1.01. 43
so eating love | inhabits in the finest wits of 1.01. 43
friar, till eating and drinking be put down. MM 3.02.103 P
think it rather consists of eating and drinking. TN 2.03. 12 P
be magic, let it be an art | lawful as eating. WT 5.03.111
clouds, | eating the bitter bread of banishment, R2 3.01. 21
that seem'd in eating him to hold him up, | are 3.04. 51
from swine–keeping, from eating draff and husks.
1H4 4.02. 35 P
hope, | eating the air, and promise of supply, 2H4 1.03. 28
his breath stinks with eating toasted cheese. 2H6 4.07. 12 P
eating the flesh that she herself hath bred. TIT 5.03. 62
mind hold, and your dinner worth the eating. JC 1.02.292 P
our country is a great eating country, argo they STM II.C 5 P
partly comes through the eating of parsnips. II.C 15 P

EATS 20 FR 0.0022 REL FR 10 V 10 P
it eats and sleeps and hath such senses | as we TMP 1.02.413
still swine eats all the draff. WIV 4.02.107
of his heart he eats his meat without grudging; ADO 3.04. 89 P
to live i' th' sun, | seeking the food he eats, AYL 2.05. 40
pears, it looks ill, it eats drily, marry, 'tis AWW 1.01.162 P
at quoits well, and eats cunger and fennel, and 2H4 2.04.245 P
whiles thy consuming canker eats his falsehood. 1H6 2.04. 71
he that is proud eats up himself. TRO 2.03.154 P
he eats nothing but doves, love, and that breeds 3.01.128 P
how one man eats into another's pride, | while 3.03.136
miracle — yet, in a sort, lechery eats itself. 5.04. 35 P
full soon the canker death eats up that plant. ROM 2.03. 30
what a number of men eats timon, and he sees 'em TIM 1.02. 40 P
not where he eats, but where 'a is eaten; HAM 4.03. 19 P
eats not the flats with more impiteous haste 4.05.101
poor tom, that eats the swimming frog, the toad, LR 3.04.129 P
the foul fiend rages, eats cow–dung for sallets; 3.04.132 P
/on reason, | it eats the sword it fights with. ANT 3.13.199
but that it eats our victuals, i should think CYM 3.06. 40
this canker that eats up love's tender spring, VEN 656
EAUX 1 FR 0.0001 REL FR 1 V 0 P
via! les eaux et terre. H5 4.02. 4
EAVES 2 FR 0.0002 REL FR 2 V 0 P
beard like winter's drops | from eaves of reeds. TMP 5.01. 17
nothing steads us | to chide him from our eaves, AWW 3.07. 42
EAVESDROPPER *(see ease–dropper)*
EBB 15 FR 0.0017 REL FR 12 V 3 P
who with mine eyes (never since at ebb) beheld TMP 1.02.436
do so. to ebb | hereditary sloth instructs me. 2.01.222
the sea will ebb and flow, heaven show his face; LLL 4.03.212
sea, | till that the weary very means do ebb? AYL 2.07. 73
the moon's men doth ebb and flow like the sea, 1H4 1.02. 31 P
now in as low an ebb as the foot of the ladder, 1.02. 37 P
for it is a low ebb of linen with thee when thou 2H4 2.02. 19 P
the river hath thrice flowed, no ebb between, 4.04.125
now doth it turn and ebb back to the sea, 5.02.131
and swell so much the higher by their ebb. 3H6 4.08. 56
may call the sea, | do ebb and flow with tears; ROM 3.05.133
i have | prompted you in the ebb of your estate TIM 2.02.141
of great ones, | that ebb and flow by th' moon. LR 5.03. 19
compulsive course | nev'r /feels retiring ebb, OTH 3.03.455
shall nev'r look back, nev'r ebb to humble love, 3.03.458
EBB'D 2 FR 0.0002 REL FR 2 V 0 P
'tis shrewdly ebb'd, | to say you have seen a WT 5.01.102
and the ebb'd man, ne'er lov'd till ne'er worth ANT 1.04. 43
EBBING 2 FR 0.0002 REL FR 2 V 0 P
ebbing men, indeed, | most often, do so near the TMP 2.01.226
printless foot | do chase the ebbing neptune, 5.01. 35
EBBS 6 FR 0.0006 REL FR 6 V 0 P
could control the moon, make flows and ebbs, TMP 5.01.270
yea, watch | his /pettish /lines, his ebbs, /his TRO 2.03.130
as it ebbs, the seedsman | upon the slime and ANT 2.07. 21
see what our general of ebbs and flows | out TNK 5.01.163
and sorrow ebbs, being blown with wind of words. LUC 1330
thus ebbs and flows the current of her sorrow, 1569
EBON 2 FR 0.0002 REL FR 2 V 0 P
rouse up revenge from ebon den with fell 2H4 5.05. 37
and not death's ebon dart to strike him dead. VEN 948
EBON–COLORED 1 FR 0.0001 REL FR 0 V 1 P
pen the ebon–colored ink which here thou viewest LLL 1.01.243 P
EBONY 3 FR 0.0003 REL FR 2 V 1 P
by heaven, thy love is black as ebony. LLL 4.03.243
is ebony like her? 4.03.244
toward the south north are as lustrous as ebony; TN 4.02. 38 P
EBREW *(also hebrew)*
EBREW 1 FR 0.0001 REL FR 0 V 1 P
man of them, or i am a jew else, an ebrew jew. 1H4 2.04.179 P
ECCE 1 FR 0.0001 REL FR 0 V 1 P
my sword hack'd like a hand–saw — ecce signum! 1H4 2.04.169 P
ECHE *(also eke*)*
/ECHE 1 FR 0.0001 REL FR 1 V 0 P
spent | with your fine fancies quaintly /eche: PER 3.ch. 13
ECHE 2 FR 0.0002 REL FR 2 V 0 P
time, | to eche it and to draw it out in length, MV 3.02. 23
and eche out our performance with your mind. H5 3.pr. 35
ECHO 11 FR 0.0012 REL FR 11 V 0 P
confusion | of hounds and echo in conjunction. MND 4.01.111
if echo were as fleet, | i would esteem him SHR in.1. 26
that at the parting all the church did echo. 3.02.179
it gives a very echo to the seat | where love is TN 2.04. 21
but start | an echo with the clamor of thy drum, JN 5.02.168
rumor doth double, like the voice and echo, 2H4 3.01. 97
that all the court may echo with the noise. TIT 2.02. 6
and whilst the babbling echo mocks the hounds, 2.03. 17
else would i tear the cave where echo lies, ROM 2.02.161
health, | i would applaud thee to the very echo, MAC 5.03. 53
echo replies, | as if another chase were in the VEN 695
ECHOES 5 FR 0.0005 REL FR 5 V 0 P
and fetch shrill echoes from the hollow earth. SHR in.2. 46
i think the echoes of his shames have deaf'd TNK 1.02. 80
that shook the aged forest with their echoes, 2.02. 47
and twenty echoes twenty times cry so. VEN 834
woe, | and still the choir of echoes answer so. 840
ECHO'ST 1 FR 0.0001 REL FR 1 V 0 P
/by /heaven, thou echo'st me, | as if there were OTH 3.03.106
ECLIPS'D 2 FR 0.0002 REL FR 2 V 0 P
fear | my joy of liberty is half eclips'd. 3H6 4.06. 63
our terrene moon | is now eclips'd, and it ANT 3.13.154
ECLIPSE 5 FR 0.0005 REL FR 5 V 0 P
son, | born to eclipse thy life this afternoon. 1H6 4.05. 53
slips of yew | sliver'd in the moon's eclipse, MAC 4.01. 28
was sick almost to doomsday with eclipse. HAM 1.01.120
methinks it should be now a huge eclipse | of OTH 5.02. 99
the mortal moon hath her eclipse endur'd, | and SON 107. 5
ECLIPSES 5 FR 0.0005 REL FR 2 V 3 P
these late eclipses in the sun and moon portend LR 1.02.103 P
o, these eclipses do portend these divisions! 1.02.136 P
other day, what should follow these eclipses. 1.02.141 P
clouds and eclipses stain both moon and sun, SON 35. 3
crooked eclipses 'gainst his glory fight, | and 60. 7
ECOLIER 1 FR 0.0001 REL FR 0 V 1 P
je pense que je suis le bon ecolier; H5 3.04. 13 P
ECOUTEZ 3 FR 0.0003 REL FR 0 V 3 P
ecoutez, dites–moi si je parle bien: H5 3.04. 17 P
ecoutez: 3.04. 28 P
ecoutez: comment etes–vous appele? 4.04. 25 P
ECSTASIES 1 FR 0.0001 REL FR 1 V 0 P
his feigned ecstasies | shall be no shelter to TIT 4.04. 21
/ECSTASY 1 FR 0.0001 REL FR 1 V 0 P
/ecstasy? HAM 3.04.139
ECSTASY 14 FR 0.0015 REL FR 13 V 1 P
and hinder them from what this ecstasy | may now TMP 3.03.108
mark, how he trembles in his ecstasy! ERR 4.04. 51
and the ecstasy hath so much overborne her that ADO 2.03.151 P
o love, be moderate, allay thy ecstasy, | in MV 3.02.111
marcus, attend him in his ecstasy, | that hath TIT 4.01.125
of the mind to lie | in restless ecstasy. MAC 3.02. 22
where violent sorrow seems | a modern ecstasy. 4.03.170
this is the very ecstasy of love, | whose HAM 2.01. 99
stature of blown youth | blasted with ecstasy. 3.01.160
nor sense to ecstasy was ne'er so thrall'd | but 3.04. 74
this bodiless creation ecstasy | is very cunning 3.04.138
away, | and laid good 'scuses upon your ecstasy; OTH 4.01. 79
thus stands she in a trembling ecstasy, | till, VEN 895
which may her suffering ecstasy assuage, | 'tis LC 69
ECUS 2 FR 0.0002 REL FR 0 V 2 P
ma vie, et je vous donnerai deux cents ecus. H5 4.04. 42 P
pour les ecus que vous /lui promettez, il est 4.04. 51 P
EDDY 2 FR 0.0002 REL FR 2 V 0 P
'twould bring us to an eddy | where we should TNK 1.02. 10
yet in the eddy boundeth in his pride | back to LUC 1669
EDEN 1 FR 0.0001 REL FR 1 V 0 P
this other eden, demi–paradise, | this fortress R2 2.01. 42
/EDGAR 2 FR 0.0002 REL FR 0 V 2 P
/edgar — pat! LR 1.02.133 P
/they /say /edgar, /his /banish'd /son, /is 4.07. 89 P
EDGAR 9 FR 0.0010 REL FR 7 V 2 P
then, | legitimate edgar, i must have your land. LR 1.02. 16
edgar." 1.02. 54 P
my son edgar! 1.02. 56 P
he whom my father nam'd, your edgar? 2.01. 92
edgar i nothing am. 2.03. 21
then edgar was abus'd. 3.07. 91
o dear son edgar, | the food of thy abused 4.01. 21
if edgar live, o bless him! 4.06. 40
my name is edgar, and thy father's son. 5.03.170
/EDGE 1 FR 0.0001 REL FR 1 V 0 P
/knew /he /walk'd /o'er /perils, /on /an /edge, 2H4 1.01.170
EDGE 42 FR 0.0047 REL FR 38 V 4 P
take away | the edge of that day's celebration, TMP 4.01. 29
but doth rebate and blunt his natural edge MM 1.04. 60
honor which shall bate his scythe's keen edge, LLL 1.01. 6
whose edge hath power to cut, whose will still 2.01. 50
hereby, upon the edge of yonder coppice, | a 4.01. 9
are as keen | as is the razor's edge invisible, 5.02.257
peril of my life with the edge of a feather–bed, MV 2.02.165 P
not removes, at least, | affection's edge in me. SHR 1.02. 73
worthy sake | to th' extreme edge of hazard. AWW 3.03. 6
doth set my pugging tooth an edge, | for a quart WT 4.03. 7
or cloy the hungry edge of appetite | by bare R2 1.03.296
the edge of war, like an ill–sheathed knife, 1H4 1.01. 17
and that would set my teeth nothing an edge, 3.01.131
as great aim level at the edge of a penknife. 2H4 3.02.267 P
him whose wrongs gives edge unto the swords H5 1.02. 27
cut | with edge of penny cord and vile reproach. 3.06. 48
news, i think, hath turn'd your weapon's edge; 2H6 2.01.176
steel, if thou turn the edge, or cut not out the 4.10. 56 P
and though the edge hath something hit ourselves 3H6 2.02.166
thus yields the cedar to the axe's edge, | whose 5.02. 11
abate the edge of traitors, gracious lord, R3 5.05. 35
and i know his sword | hath a sharp edge; H8 1.01.110
shall more obey than to the edge of steel | or TRO 3.01.152
the knights | shall to the edge of all extremity 4.05. 68
and there the strawy greeks, ripe for his edge, 5.05. 24
him for a volsce, | and he shall feel mine edge. COR 1.04. 29
thy years wants wit, thy wits wants edge, | and TIT 2.01. 26
fife, give to th' edge o' th' sword | his wife, MAC 4.01.151
or else my sword with an unbattered edge | i 5.07. 19
and borrowing dulleth /th' edge of husbandry. HAM 1.03. 77
good gentlemen, give him a further edge, | and 3.01. 26
would cost you a groaning to take off mine edge. 3.02.250 P
hoop should hold us staunch from edge to edge ANT 2.02.115
hoop should hold us staunch from edge to edge 2.02.115
drugs, serpents have | edge, sting, or operation 4.15. 26
whose edge is sharper than the sword, whose CYM 3.04. 34
bring your grace e'en to the edge a' th' shore, PER 3.03. 35
i may not wish | more than my sword's edge on't. TNK 3.01. 96
set | this bateless edge on his keen appetite; LUC 9
said | thy edge should blunter be than appetite, SON 56. 2
the hardest knife ill us'd doth lose his edge. 95.14
but bears it out even to the edge of doom. 116.12
EDGED 2 FR 0.0002 REL FR 2 V 0 P
with spirit of honor edged | more sharper than H5 3.05. 38
o, turn the edged sword another way, | strike 1H6 3.03. 52
EDGELESS 2 FR 0.0002 REL FR 2 V 0 P
think on me, | and fall thy edgeless sword. R3 5.03.135
think on me, | and fall thy edgeless sword. 5.03.163
EDGES 3 FR 0.0003 REL FR 2 V 1 P
at that time, and some say knives have edges. H5 2.01. 22 P
men and lads, | stain all your edges on me. COR 5.06.112
to part with unhack'd edges and bear back | our ANT 2.06. 38
EDICT 10 FR 0.0011 REL FR 9 V 1 P
if the first that did th' edict infringe | had MM 2.02. 92
our late edict shall strongly stand in force: LLL 1.01. 11
proclaimed edict and continent canon; 1.01.259 P
cross'd, | it stands as an edict in destiny. MND 1.01.151
yet, notwithstanding such a strait edict, | were 2H6 3.02.258
will you then | spurn at his edict, and fulfill R3 1.04.198
make thine own edict for thy pains, which we ANT 3.12. 32
though by the tenor of /our strict edict, | your PER 1.01.111
against /thy own edict, follows thy sister, TNK 3.06.145
for scorning thy edict, duke, ask that lady 3.06.168
EDICTS 2 FR 0.0002 REL FR 1 V 1 P
some certain edicts and some strait decrees 1H4 4.03. 79
make edicts for usury, to support usurers; COR 1.01. 81 P
EDIFICE 2 FR 0.0002 REL FR 1 V 1 P
so that i have lost my edifice by mistaking the WIV 2.02.216 P
to church | and see the holy edifice of stone, MV 1.01. 30
EDIFICES 1 FR 0.0001 REL FR 1 V 0 P
an heir | of these fair edifices 'fore my wars COR 4.04. 3
EDIFIED 3 FR 0.0003 REL FR 0 V 3 P
look then to be well edified when the fool TN 5.01.290 P
i knew you must be edified by the margent ere HAM 5.02.155 P
you inquire him out, and be edified by report? OTH 3.04. 14 P
EDIFIES 1 FR 0.0001 REL FR 1 V 0 P
she feeds, | but edifies another with her deeds. TRO 5.03.112
EDIFY 3 FR 0.0003 REL FR 3 V 0 P
where he himself will edify the duke | most TNK 2.03. 52
stay, and edify. 3.05. 95
well, sir, go forward, we will edify. 3.05. 98
EDITION 1 FR 0.0001 REL FR 0 V 1 P
and these are of the second edition. WIV 2.01. 77 P
EDMUND 46 FR 0.0052 REL FR 37 V 9 P
commend me to thy brother, edmund york. R2 1.02. 62
proclaim my brother edmund mortimer | heir to 1H4 1.03.156
lord edmund mortimer, my lord of york, and owen 2.03. 24 P
age of care, | argue the end of edmund mortimer. 1H6 2.05. 7
deriv'd | from famous edmund langley, duke of 2.05. 85
plac'd the heads of edmund duke of somerset, 2H6 1.02. 29
the fift was edmund langley, duke of york; 2.02. 15
who married edmund mortimer, earl of march; 2.02. 36
edmund had issue, roger earl of march; 2.02. 37
roger had issue, edmund, anne, and eleanor. 2.02. 38
this edmund, in the reign of bullingbrook, | as 2.02. 39
who was | to edmund langley, edward the third's 2.02. 46
march, who was the son | of edmund mortimer, who 2.02. 49
edmund mortimer, earl of march, | married the 4.02.136
tell him i'll send duke edmund to the tower; 4.09. 38
do you know this noble gentleman, edmund? LR 1.01. 25 P
our father's love is to the bastard edmund | as 1.02. 17
edmund the base | shall /top th' legitimate. 1.02. 20
edmund, how now? 1.02. 26
edmund, seek him out; 1.02. 97 P
find out this villain, edmund, it shall lose 1.02.115 P
how now, brother edmund, what serious 1.02.138 P
now, edmund, where's the villain? 2.01. 37
where is the villain, edmund? 2.01. 41
edmund, i hear that you have shown your father 2.01.105
for you, edmund, | whose virtue and obedience 2.01.112
alack, edmund, i like not this unnatural dealing 3.03. 1 P
there is strange things toward, edmund, pray you 3.03. 19 P
edmund, keep you our sister company; 3.07. 6 P
edmund, farewell. 3.07. 22
where's my son edmund? 3.07. 85
edmund, enkindle all the sparks of nature, | to 3.07. 86
back, edmund, to my brother, | hasten his 4.02. 15
lord edmund spake not with your lord at home? 4.05. 4
edmund, i think, is gone, | in pity of his 4.05. 11
why should she write to edmund? 4.05. 19
and most speaking looks | to noble edmund. 4.05. 26
edmund and i have talk'd, | and more convenient 4.05. 30
find'st about me | to edmund earl of gloucester; 4.06.249
edmund, i arrest thee | on capital treason, and, 5.03. 82
the lists of the army will maintain upon edmund, 5.03.111 P
he that speaks for edmund earl of gloucester? 5.03.125
i am no less in blood than thou art, edmund; 5.03.168
speak, edmund, where's the king? 5.03.238
yet edmund was belov'd! 5.03.240
edmund is dead, my lord. 5.03.296
EDMUNDSBURY 2 FR 0.0002 REL FR 2 V 0 P
lords, i will meet him at saint edmundsbury. JN 4.03. 11
with me, | upon the altar at saint edmundsbury, 5.04. 18
EDUCATE 1 FR 0.0001 REL FR 0 V 1 P
do you not educate youth at the charge–house on LLL 5.01. 82 P
EDUCATION 10 FR 0.0011 REL FR 6 V 4 P
him lies, mines my gentility with my education. AYL 1.01. 21 P
you in his will to give me good education. 1.01. 68 P
by birth a pedlar, by education a card–maker, by SHR in.2. 19 P
and toward the education of your daughters, | i 2.01. 98
hopes of her good that her education promises; AWW 1.01. 40 P
as she in beauty, education, blood, | holds hand JN 2.01.493
to you i am bound for life and education; OTH 1.03.182
my life and education both do learn me | how to 1.03.183
pericles, | my education been in arts and arms; PER 2.03. 82
who hath gain'd | of education all the grace, 4.ch. 9
EDWARD *(also yead, yedward)*
/EDWARD 1 FR 0.0001 REL FR 1 V 0 P
/i /for /an /edward /weep, so do not they. R3 2.02. 85
EDWARD 136 FR 0.0153 REL FR 133 V 3 P
in mill–sixpences, and two edward shovel–boards, WIV 1.01.156 P
time before | that our great–grandsire, edward, 2H4 4.04.128
deriv'd from edward, his great–grandfather. H5 1.01. 89
and your great–uncle's, edward the black prince, 1.02.105
your great predecessor, king edward the third. 1.02.248
by the hand | of that black name, edward, black 2.04. 56
edward the third, he bids you then resign | your 2.04. 93
and your great–uncle edward the plack prince of 4.07. 93 P
the duke of burgundy, | and edward duke of bar; 4.08. 98
edward the duke of york, the earl of suffolk, 4.08.103
during the time edward the third did reign. 1H6 1.02. 31
third son to the third edward, king of england. 2.04. 84
and the lawful heir | of edward king, the third 2.05. 66
clarence, third son | to king edward the third; 2.05. 76
edward the third, my lords, had seven sons: 2H6 2.02. 10
the first, edward the black prince, prince of 2.02. 11
edward the black prince died before his father, 2.02. 18
who after edward the third's death reign'd as 2.02. 20
to edmund langley, edward the third's fift /son, 2.02. 46
gentle son edward, thou wilt stay /with me? 3H6 1.01.259
you, edward, shall unto my lord cobham, | with 1.02. 40
edward and richard, you shall stay with me, | my 1.02. 54
and full as oft came edward to my side | with 1.04. 11
now, | the wanton edward, and the lusty george? 1.04. 74
must edward fall, which peril heaven forefend! 2.01.191
king edward, valiant richard, montague, | stay 2.01.198
edward, kneel down. 2.02. 60
edward plantagenet, arise a knight, | and learn 2.02. 61
stay, edward. 2.02.175
edward and richard, like a brace of greyhounds 2.05.129
the french king's sister | to wife for edward. 3.01. 31
he, on his right, asking a wife for edward. 3.01. 44
he smiles, and says his edward is install'd; 3.01. 46
you are the king king edward hath depos'd; 3.01. 69
we are true subjects to the king, king edward. 3.01. 94
to henry, | if he were seated as king edward is. 3.01. 96
say that king edward take thee for his queen? 3.02. 89

ay, edward will use women honorably. 3.02.124
is clarence, henry, and his son young edward, 3.02.130
while proud ambitious edward, duke of york, 3.03. 27
with this my son, prince edward, henry's heir, 3.03. 31
from worthy edward, king of albion, | my lord 3.03. 49
yet here prince edward stands, king henry's son. 3.03. 73
for shame, leave henry, and call edward king. 3.03.100
queen margaret, prince edward, and oxford, 3.03.109
upon thy conscience, | is edward your true king? 3.03.114
to edward, but not to the english king. 3.03.140
and tell false edward, thy supposed king, | that 3.03.223
cross the seas and bid false edward battle; 3.03.235
son edward, she is fair and virtuous, 3.03.245
i long till edward fall by war's mischance, 3.03.254
i came from edward as ambassador, | but i return 3.03.256
they are but lewis and warwick, i am edward, 4.01. 15
leave me, or tarry, edward will be king, | and 4.01. 65
thee | so long as edward is thy constant friend 4.01. 77
"go tell false edward, the supposed king, | that 4.01. 93
that young prince edward marries warwick's 4.01.117
i | stay not for the love of edward, but the 4.01.126
but follow me, and edward shall be ours. 4.03. 25
nay, then i see that edward needs must down. 4.03. 42
edward will always bear himself as king. 4.03. 45
then, for his mind, be edward england's king, 4.03. 48
see that forthwith duke edward be convey'd 4.03. 52
what late misfortune is befall'n king edward? 4.04. 3
have shaken edward from the regal seat, | and 4.06. 2
forthwith that edward be pronounc'd a traitor, 4.06. 54
that margaret your queen and my son edward | be 4.06. 60
that edward is escaped from your brother, | and 4.06. 78
for if edward repossess the crown, | 'tis like 4.06. 99
yet edward, at the least, is duke of york. 4.07. 21
for edward will defend the town and thee, | and 4.07. 38
to help king edward in his time of storm, | as 4.07. 43
sound trumpet, edward shall be here proclaim'd. 4.07. 69
"edward the fourth, by the grace of god, king of 4.07. 71 P
long live edward the fourth! 4.07. 76
edward from belgia, | with hasty germans and 4.08. 1
methinks the power that edward hath in field 4.08. 35
then why should they love edward more than me? 4.08. 47
o unbid spite, is sportful edward come? 5.01. 18
call edward king and at his hands beg mercy? 5.01. 23
pardon me, edward, i will make amends; 5.01.100
and bid thee battle, edward, if thou dar'st. 5.01.111
yes, warwick, edward dares, and leads the way. 5.01.112
and what is edward but a ruthless sea? 5.04. 25
prepare you, lords, for edward is at hand, 5.04. 60
that who finds edward | shall have a high reward 5.05. 9
it is, and lo where youthful edward comes! 5.05. 11
edward, what satisfaction canst thou make | for 5.05. 14
lascivious edward, and thou perjur'd george, 5.05. 34
the wings of my sweet boy, | thy brother edward; 5.06. 24
that edward shall be fearful of his life, | and 5.06. 87
and if king edward be as true and just | as i am R3 1.01. 36
which done, god take king edward to his mercy, 1.01.151
still breathes, edward still lives and reigns; 1.01.161
wife to thy edward, to thy slaught'red son, 1.02. 10
of these plantagenets, henry and edward, | as 1.02.118
when my father york and edward wept | to hear 1.02.156
'twas i that stabb'd young edward — | but 'twas 1.02.181
edward, her lord, whom i, some three months 1.02.240
tower, | and edward, my poor son, at tewksbury. 1.03.119
edward thy son, that now is prince of wales, 1.03.198
for edward our son, that was prince of wales, 1.03.199
for edward, for my brother, for his sake. 1.04.212
life | than edward will for tidings of my death. 1.04.231
you go | to comfort edward with our company. 2.01.140
edward, my lord, thy son, our king, is dead! 2.02. 40
from my feeble hands, | clarence and edward. 2.02. 59
ah for my husband, for my dear lord edward! 2.02. 71
alas for both, both mine, edward and clarence! 2.02. 73
what stay had i but edward? and he's gone. 2.02. 74
she for an edward weeps, and so do i; 2.02. 82
tell them how edward put to death a citizen 3.05. 76
went with child | of that insatiate edward, 3.05. 87
ah ha, my lord, this prince is not an edward! 3.07. 71
you say that edward is your brother's son: 3.07.177
he got | this edward, whom our manners call the 3.07.191
young edward lives: 4.02. 10
ha? am i king? 'tis so — but edward lives. 4.02. 14
that edward still should live true noble prince! 4.02. 16
the sons of edward sleep in abraham's bosom, 4.03. 38
edward plantagenet, why art thou dead? 4.04. 19
edward for edward pays a dying debt. 4.04. 21
edward for edward pays a dying debt. 4.04. 21
i had an edward, till a richard kill'd him; 4.04. 40
thou hadst an edward, till a richard kill'd him; 4.04. 42
thy edward he is dead, that kill'd my edward; 4.04. 63
thy edward he is dead, that kill'd my edward; 4.04. 63
/thy other edward dead, to quit my edward; 4.04. 64
/thy other edward dead, to quit my edward; 4.04. 64
thy clarence he is dead that stabb'd my edward, 4.04. 67
thereon engrave | "edward" and "york"é 4.04.273
sir edward courtney and the haughty prelate, 4.04.500
holy king henry and thy fair son edward, 5.01. 4
now, poor edward bohun. H8 2.01.103
queen, | as holy oil, edward confessor's crown, 4.01. 88
of the most pious edward with such grace | that MAC 3.06. 27

EDWARD'S 52 FR 0.0058 REL FR 52 V 0 P

edward's seven sons, whereof thy self art one, R2 1.02. 11
one vial full of edward's sacred blood, | one 1.02. 17
wert thou not brother to great edward's son, 2.01.121
o, spare me not, my /brother edward's son, | for 2.01.124
son, | for that i was his father edward's son, 2.01.125
thou respect'st not spilling edward's blood. 2.01.131
i am the last of noble edward's sons, | of whom 2.01.171
to fill king edward's fame with prisoner kings, H5 1.02.162
depos'd his nephew richard, edward's son, | the 1H6 2.05. 64
this world frowns, and edward's sun is clouded. 3H6 2.03. 7
to strengthen and support king edward's place. 3.01. 52
and me — | the lustful edward's title buried — 3.02.129
our earl of warwick, edward's greatest friend. 3.03. 45
springs not from edward's well–meant honest love 3.03. 67
our sister shall be edward's. 3.03.134
weak, | as may appear by edward's good success, 3.03.146
this proveth edward's love and warwick's honesty 3.03.180
that i am clear from this misdeed of edward's; 3.03.183
misery, | but seek revenge on edward's mockery. 3.03.265
and hastings as he favors edward's cause! 4.01.144
might i think that clarence, edward's brother, 4.02. 10
at unawares may beat down edward's guard, | and 4.02. 23
for love of edward's offspring in my womb. 4.04. 18
or tears i blast or drown | king edward's fruit, 4.04. 24
king edward's friends must down. 4.04. 28
to save, at least, the heir of edward's right; 4.04. 32
my lord, i like not of this flight of edward's; 4.06. 89
himself, | and now will i be edward's champion. 4.07. 68
and whosoe'er gainsays king edward's right, | by 4.07. 74
but warwick's king is edward's prisoner. 5.01. 39
g | of edward's heirs the murtherer shall be. R3 1.01. 40
were it to call king edward's widow sister, | i 1.01.109
nay, he is dead, and slain by edward's hands. 1.02. 92
on me, whose all not equals edward's moi'ty? 1.02.249
to fight on edward's party for the crown, | and 1.03.137
would to god my heart were flint, like edward's, 1.03.139
or edward's soft and pitiful, like mine: 1.03.140
that henry's death, my lovely edward's death, 1.03.191
for edward's sake, and see how he requites me! 1.04. 68
drown desperate sorrow in dead edward's grave, 2.02. 99
and plant your joys in living edward's throne. 2.02.100
doth the news hold of good king edward's death? 2.03. 7
and this is edward's wife, that monstrous witch, 3.04. 70
time, | infer the bastardy of edward's children. 3.05. 75
touch'd you the bastardy of edward's children? 3.07. 4
so say we too, but not by edward's wife; 3.07.178
and there the little souls of edward's children 4.04.192
slander myself as false to edward's bed, | throw 4.04.208
i will confess she was not edward's daughter. 4.04.211
hastings, and edward's children, grey and rivers 5.01. 3
this is the day which, in king edward's time, 5.01. 13
edward's unhappy sons do bid thee flourish. 5.03.153

E'E *(also eye)*

E'E 1 FR 0.0001 REL FR 1 V 0 P

clip my yellow locks an inch below mine e'e. TNK 3.04. 20

EEL 5 FR 0.0005 REL FR 2 V 3 P

i will praise an eel with the same praise. LLL 1.02. 26 P
what? that an eel is ingenious? 1.02. 27 P
that an eel is quick. 1.02. 28 P
or is the adder better than the eel, | because SHR 4.03.177
an eel and woman, | a learned poet says, unless TNK 3.05. 48

EELS 2 FR 0.0002 REL FR 0 V 2 P

cockney did to the eels when she put 'em i' th' LR 2.04.123 P
so awake the beds of eels as my giving out her PER 4.02.143 P

/EEL–SKIN 1 FR 0.0001 REL FR 0 V 1 P

you starveling, you /eel–skin, you dried neat's 1H4 2.04.244 P

EEL–SKIN 1 FR 0.0001 REL FR 0 V 1 P

thrust him and all his apparel into an eel–skin. 2H4 3.02.326 P

EEL–SKINS 1 FR 0.0001 REL FR 1 V 0 P

my arms such eel–skins stuff'd, my face so thin JN 1.01.141

E'EN *(also even, ev'n*, and compounds)*

/E'EN 6 FR 0.0006 REL FR 3 V 3 P

/e'en no time to recover hair lost by nature. ERR 2.02.102 P
/e'en that you have there. AWW 3.02. 18 P
'a calls me /e'en /now, my lord, through a red 2H4 2.02. 79 P
/e'en for the loss of thee, having no more, | as 3H6 2.05.119
is it /e'en so? ROM 5.01. 24
no more but /e'en a woman, and commanded | by ANT 4.15. 73

E'EN 30 FR 0.0034 REL FR 10 V 20 P

e'en as many as could well live one by another. MV 3.05. 22 P
e'en at hand, alighted by this; SHR 4.01.117 P
e'en such as you speak to me. AWW 4.01. 13 P
e'en a crow a' th' same nest; 4.03.286 P
e'en so; hector was stirring early. TRO 1.02. 51 P
e'en so; 2.01. 98 P
is it e'en so? ROM 1.05.123
e'en as apemantus does now: TIM 1.01.229 P
o, joy's e'en made away ere't can be born! 1.02.105 P
to feed | than such that do e'en enemies exceed. 1.02.204
she's e'en setting on water to scald such 2.02. 69 P
e'en so thou outrun'st grace. 2.02. 88 P
and e'en as if your lord should wear rich jewels 3.04. 23
they have e'en put my breath from me, the slaves 3.04.103
honorable lord, i am e'en sick of shame that, 3.06. 41 P
e'en so, sir, as i say. 5.01. 83
i think it be no other but e'en so. HAM 1.01.108
we'll e'en to't like /french falc'ners — fly at 2.02.429 P
thou art e'en as just a man | as e'er my 3.02. 54
convocation of politic worms are e'en at him. 4.03. 20 P
'tis e'en so, the hand of little employment hath 5.01. 69 P
why, e'en so, and now my lady worm's, chopless, 5.01. 88 P
faith, e'en with losing his wits. 5.01.159 P
e'en that. • 5.01.183 P
e'en so. 5.01.199 P
e'en so, my lord. 5.01.201 P
e'en as the o'erflowing nilus presageth famine. ANT 1.02. 49 P
mark antony | will e'en but kiss octavia, and 2.04. 3
at philippi kept | his sword e'en like a dancer, 3.11. 36
bring your grace e'en to the edge a' th' shore, PER 3.03. 35

E'ER *(also ever, ev'r, and compounds)*

E'ER 135 FR 0.0152 REL FR 126 V 9 P

as wicked dew as e'er my mother brush'd | with TMP 1.02.321
this | is the third man that e'er i saw; 1.02.446
the first | that e'er i sigh'd for. 1.02.447
and the rarest that e'er came there. 2.01.100 P
might scratch her where e'er she did itch. 2.02. 53
a heart as willing | as bondage e'er of freedom. 3.01. 89
i'll seek him deeper than e'er plummet sounded, 3.03.101
this is as strange a maze as e'er men trod, 5.01.242
this is a strange thing as e'er i look'd on. 5.01.290
been the longest night | that e'er i watch'd, TGV 4.02.140
she shall thank you for't, if e'er you know her. 4.04.179
i do as truly suffer | as e'er i did commit. 5.04. 77
i grant it, for thine own, what e'er it be. 5.04.151
of thing on thing, | as e'er i heard in madness. MM 5.01. 63
art the first knave that e'er mad'st a duke. 5.01.356
wast thou e'er contracted to this woman? 5.01.375
a stranger pyramus than e'er played here. MND 3.01. 88
if e'er i lov'd her, all that love is gone. 3.02.170
very best at a beast, my lord, that e'er i saw. 5.01.229 P
if e'er the jew her father come to heaven, | it MV 2.04. 33
again, | no bed shall e'er be guilty of my stay, 3.02.326
let not that doctor e'er come near my house. 5.01.223
but what e'er you are | that in this desert AYL 2.07.109
what e'er i read to her, i'll plead for you | as SHR 1.02.154
i love her ten times more than e'er i did. 2.01.161
and twice as much, what e'er thou off'rest next. 2.01.380
worship, | i am to get a man — what e'er he be, 3.02.131
as willingly as e'er i came from school. 3.02.150
touch of sorrow that e'er i heard virgin exclaim AWW 1.03.117 P
the first truth that e'er thine own tongue was 4.01. 32 P
what e'er the course, the end is the renown. 4.04. 36
to be well thank'd, | what e'er falls more. 5.01. 37
the last that e'er i took her leave at court, 5.03. 79
fell and cruel hounds, | e'er since pursue me. TN 1.01. 22
have breath'd out | that e'er devotion tender'd! 5.01.115
more, by all mores, than e'er i shall love wife. 5.01.136
geck and gull | that e'er invention play'd on? 5.01.344
infection | that e'er was heard or read! WT 1.02.424
driven snow, | cypress black as e'er was crow, 4.04.219
has the old man e'er a son, sir, do you hear, 4.04.781 P
destroy'd the sweet'st companion that e'er man 5.01. 11
i think, | that e'er the sun shone bright on. 5.01. 95
that e'er i put between your holy looks | my ill 5.03.148
country to be judg'd by you | that e'er i heard. JN 1.01. 46
than e'er the coward hand of france can win. 2.01.158
and e'er since | sits on 's horseback at mine 2.01.288
two long days' journey, lords, or e'er we meet. 4.03. 20
leaves the print of blood where e'er it walks. 4.03. 26
what e'er you think, good words, i think, were 4.03. 28
he is forsworn if e'er those eyes of yours 5.04. 31
i doubt he will be dead or e'er i come. 5.06. 44
where e'er i wander, boast of this i can, R2 1.03.308
that e'er this tongue of mine | that laid the 3.03.133
if on the first, how heinous e'er it be, | to 5.03. 34
to oxford, or where e'er these traitors are. 5.03.141
but what e'er i be, | nor i, nor any man that 5.05. 38
what e'er lord harry percy then had said | to 1H4 1.03. 71
and that shall be the day, when e'er it lights, 3.02.138
better than i love e'er a scurvy young boy of 2H4 2.04.272 P
gloucester, what e'er we like, thou art 1H6 1.01. 37
who would e'er suppose | they had such courage 1.02. 35
come, officer, as loud as e'er thou canst, | cry 1.03. 72
the greatest miracle that e'er ye wrought! 5.04. 66
trowest thou that e'er i'll look upon the world, 2H6 2.04. 38
man, | what e'er occasion keeps him from us now. 3.01. 3
that doit that e'er i wrested from the king, 3.01.112
that e'er i prov'd thee false or fear'd thy 3.01.205
scorning what e'er you can afflict me with. 3H6 1.04. 38
what e'er it bodes, henceforward will i bear 2.01. 39
the saddest spectacle that e'er i view'd. 2.01. 67
where e'er it be, in heaven or in earth. 2.03. 43
what e'er it be, be thou still like thyself, 3.03. 15
and the most merciless, that e'er was heard of! R3 1.03.183
death, | and i in better state than e'er i was. 3.02.104
that from the prime creation e'er she framed." 4.03. 19
for it grows again | fresher than e'er it was, H8 2.01.155
but death | shall e'er divorce my dignities. 3.01.142
patience herself, what goddess e'er she be, TRO 1.01. 27
the noblest hateful love, that e'er i heard of. 4.01. 34
if e'er thou stand at mercy of my sword, | name 4.04.114
therefore achilles, but what e'er, know this: 4.05. 77
if e'er again i meet him beard to beard, | he's COR 1.10. 11
and more a friend than e'er an enemy; 4.05.146
hazard mine, | when e'er we come to our account. 4.07. 26
and my true lip | hath virgin'd it e'er since. 5.03. 48
the dismall'st day is this that e'er i saw, | to TIT 1.01.384
my sight is very dull, what e'er it bodes. 2.03.195
aunt | loves me as dear as e'er my mother did, 4.01. 23
what e'er i forge to feed his brain–sick humors, 5.02. 71
thou wast the prettiest babe that e'er i nurs'd. ROM 1.03. 60
if e'er thou wast thyself and these woes thine, 2.03. 77
most miserable hour that e'er time saw | in 4.05. 44
what e'er thou hearest or seest, stand all aloof 5.03. 26
first man | that e'er received gift from him; TIM 3.03. 17
i love thee better now than e'er i did. 4.03.233
you profess | (how e'er you come to know it), MAC 4.01. 51
what e'er thou art, for thy good caution, thanks 4.01. 73
in their caps, | dying or e'er they sicken. 4.03.173
of woman | shall e'er have power upon thee." 5.03. 7
a man | as e'er my conversation cop'd withal. HAM 3.02. 55
how e'er my haps, my joys /were ne'er /begun. 4.03. 68
as much as child e'er lov'd, or father found; LR 1.01. 59
e'er since thou mad'st thy daughters thy mothers 1.04.172 P
i am worse than e'er i was. 4.01. 26
if e'er your grace had speech with man so poor, 5.01. 38
who e'er he be that in this foul proceeding OTH 1.03. 65
discords be | that e'er our hearts shall make! 2.01.199
what e'er you be, i am obedient. 3.03. 89
if e'er my will did trespass 'gainst his love, 4.02.152
sweetest innocent | that e'er did lift up eye. 5.02.200
what e'er the ocean pales, or sky inclips, | is ANT 2.07. 68
repent that e'er thy tongue | hath so betray'd 2.07. 77
remember, | if e'er thou look'st on majesty. 3.03. 18
fare thee well, dame, what e'er becomes of me. 4.04. 29
loyall'st husband that did e'er plight troth. CYM 1.01. 96
why should excuse be born or e'er begot? 3.02. 65
or i, what e'er it be, | what pain it cost, what 3.06. 79
this youth, how e'er distress'd, appears he hath 4.02. 47
those that would die or e'er resist are grown 5.03. 50
did you e'er meet? 5.05.378
angry father if my tongue | did e'er solicit, or PER 2.05. 69
what e'er it be, | 'tis wondrous heavy. 3.02. 52
understand, | if e'er this coffin drives a–land, 3.02. 69
have fresh ones, what e'er we pay for them. 4.02. 10 P
e'er since i can remember. 4.06. 73 P
this is the rarest dream that e'er dull'd sleep 5.01.161
i pity | decays where e'er i find them, but such TNK 1.02. 32
what e'er you are, you run the best, and wrastle 2.05. 3
what e'er you are, y' are mine, and i shall give 2.05. 33
what e'er her father says, if you perceive | her 5.02. 33
he speaks now of as brave a knight as e'er | did 5.03.115
his snout digs sepulchres where e'er he goes; VEN 622
mov'd, he strikes, what e'er is in his way, 623
and do what e'er thou wilt, swift–footed time, SON 19. 6
what e'er thy thoughts or thy heart's workings 93.11

/E'ER–REMAINING 1 FR 0.0001 REL FR 1 V 0 F

the /e'er–remaining lamps, the belching whale PER 3.01. 62

EFFECT 75 FR 0.0084 REL FR 62 V 13 P

forgo the purpose | that you resolv'd t' effect. TMP 3.03. 13
base men, that use them to so base effect! TGV 2.07. 73
thou know'st how willingly i would effect | the 3.02. 22
as much as i can do, i will effect. 3.02. 66
what they think in their hearts they may effect, WIV 2.02.307 P

will break their hearts but they will effect. 2.02.308 P
have attain'd th' effect of your own purpose, MM 2.01. 13
make you understand this in a manifested effect, 4.02.160 P
him in mine arms | with all th' effect of love. 5.01.199
angels of light, light is an effect of fire, and ERR 4.03. 56 P
neither disturbed with the effect of wine, | nor 5.01.215
heart hath holp to effect your ensuing marriage ADO 3.02. 98 P
the effect of my intent is to cross theirs: LLL 5.02.138
effect it with some care, that he may prove MND 2.01.265
we may effect this business yet ere day. 3.02.395
words, blacker in their effect | than in their AYL 4.03. 35
in me what strange effect | would they work in 4.03. 52
love, to labor and effect one thing specially. SHR 1.01.118 P
on, | i found the effect of love in idleness, 1.01.151
thou know'st not gold's effect. 1.02. 93
of a heavenly effect in an earthly actor." AWW 2.03. 24 P
foot of time | steals ere we can effect them. 5.03. 42
be in man besides the king to effect your suits, WT 4.04.798 P
too fairly, hubert, for so foul effect. JN 4.01. 38
to this effect, before you were new crown'd, 4.02. 35
but also to effect | what ever i shall happen to R2 4.01.329
your face but should have his effect of gravity. 2H4 1.02.161 P
his effect of gravy, gravy, gravy. 1.02.162 P
but answer in th' effect of your reputation, and 2.01.130 P
and noble offices thou mayst effect | of 4.04. 24
a motive | the sooner to effect what i intended. H5 2.02.157
the poor and untempering effect of my visage. 5.02.224 P
the sooner to effect | and surer bind this knot 1H6 5.01. 15
is all our travail turn'd to this effect? 5.04.102
i'll cross the sea | to effect this marriage, so 3H6 2.06. 98
thou wast the cause, and most accurs'd effect. R3 1.02.120
your beauty was the cause of that effect — 1.02.121
with earnest prayers all to that effect. 2.02. 15
art sworn as deeply to effect what we intend 3.01.158
good catesby, go effect this business soundly. 3.01.186
what his high hatred would effect wants not | a H8 1.01.107
and the late marriage made of none effect; 4.01. 33
to this effect, achilles, have i mov'd you. TRO 3.03.216
they are at hand and ready to effect it. 4.02. 68
th' effect doth operate another way. 5.03.109
on, you heavens, effect your rage with speed! 5.10. 6
terms | that ever ear did hear to such effect, TIT 2.03.111
of my word, i have written to effect, | there's 4.03. 60
fly away, | and all my study be to no effect? 5.02. 12
then move not while my prayer's effect i take. ROM 1.05.106
potion, which so took effect | as i intended, 5.03.244
'tis in few words, but spacious in effect: TIM 3.05. 96
to what effect? JC 1.02.280
withal | hoping it was but an effect of humor, 2.01.250
nor keep peace between | th' effect and /it! MAC 1.05. 47
i shall the effect of this good lesson keep | as HAM 1.03. 45
whose effect | holds such an enmity with blood 1.05. 64
that we find out the cause of this effect, | or 2.02.101
for this effect defective comes by cause: 2.02.103
at full, | by letters congruing to that effect, 4.03. 64
wilt thou know | th' effect of what i wrote? 5.02. 37
to this effect, sir — after what flourish your 5.02.180 P
few words, but, to effect, more than all yet: LR 3.01. 52
and hath in his effect a voice potential | as OTH 1.02. 13
or with some dram, conjur'd to this effect, | he 1.03.105
suit | and seek to effect it to my uttermost. 3.04.167
she is fool'd | with a most false effect; CYM 1.05. 43
yet do effect | rare issues by their operance, TNK 1.03. 62
rain, | but lust's effect is tempest after sun; VEN 800
and every beauty robb'd of his effect. 1132
so applied, | his venom in effect is purified. LUC 532
beauty's effect with beauty were bereft, | nor SON 5.11
which though it alter not love's sole effect, 36. 7
me for my dumb thoughts, speaking in effect. 85.14
/o cleft effect! LC 293
/EFFECTED 1 FR 0.0001 REL FR 0 V 1 P
parcels of dispatch /effected many nicer needs. AWW 4.03. 91 P
EFFECTED 8 FR 0.0009 REL FR 7 V 1 P
not, i am the cause | his death was so effected. AWW 3.02.116
my lord, and i wish it happily effected. 4.05. 79 P
we'll see these things effected to the full. 2H6 1.02. 84
the ancient proverb will be well effected: 3.01.170
he that has but effected his good will | hath COR 1.09. 18
which, cunningly effected, will beget | a very TIT 2.03. 6
that magical word of war, we have effected; ANT 3.01. 31
the evils she hatch'd were not effected; CYM 5.05. 60
EFFECTING 2 FR 0.0002 REL FR 2 V 0 P
hand with all things, nought at all effecting. VEN 912
obdurate vassals fell exploits effecting, | in LUC 429
EFFECTLESS 2 FR 0.0002 REL FR 2 V 0 P
up, | and they have serv'd me to effectless use. TIT 3.01. 76
sure all effectless; PER 5.01. 53
EFFECTS 31 FR 0.0035 REL FR 24 V 7 P
and all the fair effects of future hopes. TGV 1.01. 50
for thy complexion shifts to strange effects, MM 3.01. 24
why, what effects of passion shows she? ADO 2.03.107 P
what effects, my lord? 2.03.110 P
sorry am i that our good will effects | bianca's SHR 1.01. 86
might with effects of them follow our friends, AWW 1.01.184
some prescriptions | of rare and prov'd effects, 1.03.222
th' effects of his fond jealousies so grieving WT 4.01. 18
i have read the cause of his effects in galen, 2H4 1.02.117 P
whose tenures and particular effects | you have H5 5.02. 72
and display'd th' effects | of disposition H8 2.04. 86
th' effects of sorrow for his valiant sons, TIT 4.04. 30
benefit of sleep and do the effects of watching! MAC 5.01. 10 P
of those effects for which i did the murther: HAM 3.03. 54
piteous action you convert | my stern effects, 3.04.129
and all the large effects | that troop with LR 1.01.131
that good effects may spring from words of love. 1.01.185
finds itself scourg'd by the sequent effects. 1.02.106 P
you, the effects he writes of succeed unhappily, 1.02.143 P
effects of courtesy, dues of gratitude: 2.04.179
our wishes on the way | may prove effects. 4.02. 15
a sovereign mistress of effects, throws a more OTH 1.03.225 P
thy thoughts | touch their effects in this: ANT 5.02.330
them gather | their several virtues and effects. CYM 1.05. 23
the seeing these effects will be | both noisome 1.05. 25
let thy effects | so follow, to be most unlike 5.04.135
the warm effects which she in him finds missing VEN 605
doth confound and kill | all pure effects, and LUC 251
are but dreams till their effects be tried, 353
"such devils steal effects from lightless hell, 1555
mood, | effects of terror and dear modesty, LC 202
EFFECTUAL 4 FR 0.0004 REL FR 4 V 0 P
(which, unrevers'd, stands in effectual force) TGV 3.01.225
sort, | more pleasant, pithy, and effectual, SHR 3.01. 68
you can, | or else conclude my words effectual. 2H6 3.01. 41
a reason mighty, strong, and effectual, | a TIT 5.03. 43
EFFECTUALLY 2 FR 0.0002 REL FR 2 V 0 P
your bidding shall i do effectually. TIT 4.04.107
blind, | seems seeing, but effectually is out; SON 113. 4
EFFEMINATE 7 FR 0.0008 REL FR 6 V 1 P
youth, grieve, be effeminate, changeable, AYL 3.02.410 P
which he, young wanton and effeminate boy, R2 5.03. 10
none do you like but an effeminate prince, 1H6 1.01. 35
shall we at last conclude effeminate peace? 5.04.107
of heart | and gentle, kind, effeminate remorse, R3 3.07.211
is not more loath'd than an effeminate man | in TRO 3.03.218
juliet, | thy beauty hath made me effeminate, ROM 3.01.114
EFFIGIES 1 FR 0.0001 REL FR 1 V 0 P
and as mine eye doth his effigies witness | most AYL 2.07.193
EFFUS'D 1 FR 0.0001 REL FR 1 V 0 P
whose maiden blood, thus rigorously effus'd, 1H6 5.04. 52
EFFUSE 1 FR 0.0001 REL FR 1 V 0 P
and much effuse of blood doth make me faint. 3H6 2.06. 28
EFFUSION 4 FR 0.0004 REL FR 3 V 1 P
/sire, | the mere effusion of thy proper loins, MM 3.01. 30
but this effusion of such manly drops, | this JN 5.02. 49
for th' effusion of our blood, the muster of his H5 3.06.130 P
means | to stop effusion of our christian blood, 1H6 5.01. 9
EFTEST 1 FR 0.0001 REL FR 0 V 1 P
yea, marry, that's the eftest way; ADO 4.02. 36 P
EFTSOONS 2 FR 0.0002 REL FR 2 V 0 P
eftsoons i'll tell thee why. PER 5.01.255
that i, poor man, might eftsoons come between, TNK 3.01. 12
EGALL *(also equal, etc.)*
EGALL 2 FR 0.0002 REL FR 2 V 0 P
whose souls do bear an egall yoke of love, MV 3.04. 13
for the extent | of egall justice, us'd in such TIT 4.04. 4
EGALLY 1 FR 0.0001 REL FR 1 V 0 P
kindred | and egally indeed to all estates — R3 3.07.213
EGEON 5 FR 0.0005 REL FR 5 V 0 P
hapless egeon, whom the fates have mark'd | to ERR 1.01.140
hopeless and helpless doth egeon wend, | but to 1.01.157
egeon art thou not? or else his ghost? 5.01.338
speak, old egeon, if thou be'st the man | that 5.01.342
o, if thou be'st the same egeon, speak, | and 5.01.345
EGET 1 FR 0.0001 REL FR 1 V 0 P
purus, | non eget mauri jaculis, nec arcu." TIT 4.02. 21
EGEUS 5 FR 0.0005 REL FR 5 V 0 P
thanks, good egeus. what's the news with thee? MND 1.01. 21
come, | and come, egeus, you shall go with me; 1.01.115
demetrius and egeus, go along; 1.01.123
but speak, egeus, is not this the day | that 4.01.135
egeus, i will overbear your will; 4.01.179
EGG 14 FR 0.0015 REL FR 4 V 10 P
damn'd, like an ill-roasted egg all on one side. AYL 3.02. 38 P
he will steal, sir, an egg out of a cloister. AWW 4.03.250 P
will serve to be prologue to an egg and butter. 1H4 1.02. 21 P
esteems her no more than i esteem an addle egg. TRO 1.02.132 P
if you love an addle egg as well as you love an 1.02.133 P
some trick not worth an egg, shall grow dear COR 4.04. 21
as full of quarrels as an egg is full of meat, ROM 3.01. 22 P
been beaten as addle as an egg for quarrelling. 3.01. 24 P
and therefore think him as a serpent's egg, JC 2.01. 32
what, you egg! | young fry of treachery! MAC 4.02. 83
nuncle, give me an egg, and i'll give thee two LR 1.04.156 P
after i have cut the egg i' th' middle and eat 1.04.158 P
and eat up the meat, the two crowns of the egg. 1.04.159 P
precipitating), | thou'dst shiver'd like an egg: 4.06. 51
/EGGS 1 FR 0.0001 REL FR 1 V 0 P
/i'll /fetch /some /flax /and /whites /of /eggs LR 3.07.106
EGGS 7 FR 0.0008 REL FR 4 V 3 P
with eggs, sir? WIV 3.05. 30 P
out of a song, as a weasel sucks eggs. AYL 2.05. 13 P
yet they say we are | almost as like as eggs; WT 1.02.130
honest friend, | will you take eggs for money? 1.02.161
are up already, and call for eggs and butter. 1H4 2.01. 59 P
comes sneaking, and so sucks her princely eggs, H5 1.02.171
he roast eggs! TNK 2.03. 73
EGG-SHELL 1 FR 0.0001 REL FR 1 V 0 P
death, and danger dare, | even for an egg-shell. HAM 4.04. 53
EGG-SHELLS 1 FR 0.0001 REL FR 1 V 0 P
like egg-shells mov'd upon their surges, crack'd CYM 3.01. 28
EGLAMOUR 11 FR 0.0012 REL FR 11 V 0 P
what think'st thou of the fair sir eglamour? TGV 1.02. 9
sir eglamour, a thousand times good morrow. 4.03. 6
o eglamour, thou art a gentleman — | think not 4.03. 11
sir eglamour, i would to valentine, | to mantua, 4.03. 22
urge not my father's anger, eglamour, | but 4.03. 27
good morrow, kind sir eglamour. 4.03. 46
go on, good eglamour, | out at the postern by 5.01. 8
which of you saw eglamour of late? 5.02. 32
and eglamour is in her company. 5.02. 36
more to be reveng'd on eglamour | than for the 5.02. 51
love | than hate of eglamour that goes with her. 5.02. 54
EGLANTINE 2 FR 0.0002 REL FR 2 V 0 P
with sweet musk-roses and with eglantine; MND 2.01.252
nor | the leaf of eglantine, whom not to slander CYM 4.02.223
EGMA 1 FR 0.0001 REL FR 0 V 1 P
no egma, no riddle, no l'envoy, no salve in the LLL 3.01. 72 P
EGO 1 FR 0.0001 REL FR 1 V 0 P
"ego et rex meus" | was still inscrib'd; H8 3.02.314
EGREGIOUS 4 FR 0.0004 REL FR 3 V 1 P
my lord, you give me most egregious indignity. AWW 2.03.216 P
"solus," egregious dog? H5 2.01. 46
signieur, thou do give to me | egregious ransom. 4.04. 11
egregious murtherer, thief, any thing | that's CYM 5.05.211
EGREGIOUSLY 1 FR 0.0001 REL FR 1 V 0 P
reward me, | for making him egregiously an ass, OTH 2.01.309
EGRESS 1 FR 0.0001 REL FR 0 V 1 P
thou shalt have egress and regress — said i WIV 2.01.217 P
EGYPT 44 FR 0.0049 REL FR 39 V 5 P
sees helen's beauty in a brow of egypt. MND 5.01. 11
i'll rail against all the first-born of egypt. AYL 2.05. 61 P
that would she not, | for all the mud in egypt. H8 2.03. 92
shouldst know | there were a heart in egypt. ANT 1.03. 41
to me, and say the tears | belong to egypt. 1.03. 78
thy freer thoughts | may not fly forth of egypt. 1.05. 12
sovereign of egypt, hail! 1.05. 34
"say the firm roman to great egypt sends | this 1.05. 43
his remembrance lay | in egypt with his joy; 1.05. 58
a several greeting, | or i'll unpeople egypt. 1.05. 78
mark antony | in egypt sits at dinner, and will 2.01. 12
since he went from egypt, 'tis | a space for 2.01. 30
my being in egypt, caesar, | what was't to you? 2.02. 35
here at rome | might be to you in egypt; 2.02. 38
your being in egypt | might be my question. 2.02. 39
to have me out of egypt, made wars here; 2.02. 95
welcome from egypt, sir. 2.02.171 P
you stay'd well by't in egypt. 2.02.176 P
now, sirrah; you do wish yourself in egypt? 2.03. 10
but yet hie you to egypt again. 2.03. 15
i will to egypt; 2.03. 39
melt egypt into nile! 2.05. 78
so half my egypt were submerg'd and made | a 2.05. 94
we have us'd our throats in egypt. 2.06.135 P
your serpent of egypt is bred now of your mud by 2.07. 26 P
three in egypt | cannot make better note. 3.03. 22
unto her | he gave the stablishment of egypt, 3.06. 9
yon ribaudred nag of egypt | (whom leprosy 3.10. 10
o, whither hast thou led me, egypt? 3.11. 51
egypt, thou knew'st too well | my heart was to 3.11. 56
thee, and | requires to live in egypt, which not 3.12. 12
she | from egypt drive her all-disgraced friend, 3.12. 22
all-obeying breath i hear | the doom of egypt. 3.13. 78
as he had power | to beat me out of egypt. 4.01. 2
o this false soul of egypt! 4.12. 25
i made these wars for egypt, and the queen, 4.14. 15
i am dying, egypt, dying; 4.15. 18
i am dying, egypt, dying. 4.15. 41
royal egypt! | empress! 4.15. 70
caesar sends greeting to the queen of egypt, 5.02. 9
please | to give me conquer'd egypt for my son, 5.02. 19
rather a ditch in egypt | be gentle grave unto 5.02. 57
which is the queen of egypt? 5.02.112
i pray you rise, rise, egypt. 5.02.115
EGYPTIAN 12 FR 0.0013 REL FR 11 V 1 P
like to th' egyptian thief at point of death, TN 5.01.118
did an egyptian to my mother give; OTH 3.04. 56
these strong egyptian fetters i must break, | or ANT 1.02.116
rare egyptian! 2.02.218
your fine egyptian cookery | shall have the fame 2.06. 63
he will to his egyptian dish again. 2.06.126 P
shall we dance now the egyptian bacchanals | and 2.07.104
th' antoniad, the egyptian admiral, | with all 3.10. 2
this foul egyptian hath betrayed me. 4.12. 10
a poor egyptian yet; 5.01. 52
thou, an egyptian puppet, shall be shown | in 5.02.208
i heard of an egyptian | that had nine hours PER 3.02. 84
EGYPTIANS 3 FR 0.0003 REL FR 2 V 1 P
more puzzled than the egyptians in their fog. TN 4.02. 44 P
let th' egyptians | and the phoenicians go ANT 3.07. 63
my womb, | together with my brave egyptians all, 3.13.164
EGYPT'S 3 FR 0.0003 REL FR 3 V 0 P
as i am egypt's queen, | thou blushest, antony, ANT 1.01. 29
can from the lap of egypt's widow pluck | the 2.01. 37
the juice of egypt's grape shall moist this lip. 5.02.282
/EIGHT 1 FR 0.0001 REL FR 0 V 1 P
/i /shall /have /my /eight /shillings /i /won H5 2.01.105 P
EIGHT 35 FR 0.0039 REL FR 13 V 22 P
let him be sent for to-morrow, eight a' clock, WIV 3.03.198 P
more to come to her, between eight and nine. 3.05. 46 P
eight and nine, sir. 3.05. 54 P
'twixt eight and nine is the hour, master /brook 3.05.130 P
'tis past eight already, sir. 3.05.132 P
and by eight to-morrow | thou must be made MM 4.02. 64
i have studied eight or nine wise words to speak ADO 3.02. 72 P
and it shall be written in eight and six. MND 3.01. 24 P
let it be written in eight and eight. 3.01. 26 P
let it be written in eight and eight. 3.01. 26 P
i'll rhyme you so eight years together, dinners AYL 3.02. 96 P
here's eight that must take hands | to join in 5.04.128
his eyes were set at eight i' th' morning. TN 5.01.199 P
that mowbray hath receiv'd eight thousand nobles R2 1.01. 88
by the duke of britain | with eight tall ships, 2.01.286
eight yards of uneven ground is threescore and 1H4 2.02. 24 P
some eight or ten. 2.02. 64 P
in his life than "eight shillings and sixpence," 2.04. 25 P
i am eight times thrust through the doublet, 2.04.166 P
a true woman, holland of eight shillings an ell. 3.03. 71 P
it is but eight years since | this percy was the 2H4 3.01. 60
your worship truly, sir, this eight years; 5.01. 47 P
river sala, in the year | eight hundred five. H5 1.02. 64
you'll pay me the eight shillings i won of you 2.01. 94 P
gentlemen, | eight thousand and four hundred; 4.08. 85
henry the eight, life, honor, name, and all H8 2.01.116
about the hour of eight, which he himself 4.02. 26
me hereafter, dry-beat the rest of the eight. ROM 3.01. 79 P
by the eight hour; is that the uttermost? JC 2.01.213
caesar, 'tis strucken eight. 2.02.114
and yet the eight appears, who bears a glass MAC 4.01.119
'a will last you some eight year or nine year. HAM 5.01.167 P
because they are not eight. LR 1.05. 37 P
eightscore eight hours? OTH 3.04.174
eight wild-boars roasted whole at a breakfast, ANT 2.02.179 P
EIGHTEEN 7 FR 0.0008 REL FR 6 V 1 P
at eighteen years became inquisitive | after his ERR 1.01.125
that all the treasons for these eighteen years, R2 1.01. 95
thou stolest a cup of sack eighteen years ago, 1H4 2.04.314 P
for eighteen months concluded by consent. 2H6 1.01. 42
till term of eighteen months | be full expir'd. 1.01. 67
twenty, for his heart, | and leave eighteen. CYM 2.01. 56
she's eighteen. TNK 5.02. 31
EIGHTH *(see eight)*
EIGHT-PENNY 1 FR 0.0001 REL FR 0 V 1 P
a trifle, some eight-penny matter. 1H4 3.03.104 P
EIGHTSCORE 2 FR 0.0002 REL FR 2 V 0 P
eightscore eight hours? OTH 3.04.174
more tedious than the dial eightscore times? 3.04.175
EIGHTY 2 FR 0.0002 REL FR 2 V 0 P
eighty odd years of sorrow have i seen, | and R3 4.01. 95
i knew a man | of eighty winters — this i told TNK 5.01.108
EIGHT-YEAR-OLD 1 FR 0.0001 REL FR 0 V 1 P
his mother now than an eight-year-old horse. COR 5.04. 17 P
EISEL 2 FR 0.0002 REL FR 2 V 0 P
woo't drink up eisel, eat a crocadile? HAM 5.01.276

potions of eisel 'gainst my strong infection, SON 111.10
/EITHER 2 FR 0.0002 REL FR 1 V 1 P
/either /from /the /king /or /in /the /present 2H4 4.01.106
/for /there /is /nothing /either /good /or /bad, HAM 2.02.250 P
EITHER 184 FR 0.0208 REL FR 142 V 42 P
come, come, a hand from either. TGV 5.04.116
there is either liquor in his pate, or money in WIV 2.01.190 P
have merited, either in my mind or in my means, 2.02.203 P
is divinity in odd numbers, either in nativity, 5.01. 4 P
but what needs either your "mum" or her "budget" 5.02. 8 P
either now, or by remissness new conceiv'd, MM 2.02. 96
whose rate are either rich or poor | as fancy 2.02.150
either you are ignorant, | or seem so /craftily; 2.04. 74
him, but that either | you must lay down the 2.04. 95
tongue, | either of condemnation or approof, 2.04.174
either death or life | shall thereby be the 3.01. 5
either this is envy in you, folly, or mistaking. 3.02.141 P
absent duke had not either deliver'd him to his 4.02.133 P
that which i must speak | must either punish me, 5.01. 31
fast'ned ourselves at either end the mast, | and ERR 1.01. 85
o, signior balthazar, either at flesh or fish, 3.01. 22
either get thee from the door, or sit down at 3.01. 33
we would fain have either. 3.01. 66
either send the chain, or send me by some token. 4.01. 56
either consent to pay this sum for me | or i 4.01. 72
to a willow–tree, either to make him a garland, ADO 2.01.218 P
for either he avoids them with great discretion, 2.03.191 P
if either of you know any inward impediment why 4.01. 12 P
and either i must shortly hear from him, or i 5.02. 58 P
neither of either; LLL 5.02.459
which shall be either to this gentleman, | or to MND 1.01. 43
either to die the death, or to abjure | for ever 1.01. 65
upon that day either prepare to die | for 1.01. 86
but either it was different in blood — 1.01.135
i will discharge it in either your straw–color 1.02. 93 P
either i mistake your shape and making quite, 2.01. 32
either death, or you, i'll find immediately. 2.02.156
a bone in his mouth than to either of these. MV 1.02. 52 P
and either not attempt to choose at all, | or 2.01. 39
withal, that either you might stay him from his AYL 1.01.132 P
i will either be food for it or bring it for 2.06. 7 P
narrow–mouth'd bottle, either too much at once, 3.02.201 P
which i take to be either a fool or a cipher. 3.02.290 P
that are in extremity of either are abominable 4.01. 5 P
if either of you both love katherina, | because SHR 1.01. 52
i'll tell you news indifferent good for either. 1.02.180
us, | that covenants may be kept on either hand. 2.01.127
as shall with either part's agreement stand? 4.04. 50
have they leave | to stand on either part. AWW 1.02. 15
either it is there, or it is upon a file with 4.03.203 P
you must marry me, | either both or none. 5.03.175
i am either maid, or else this old man's wife. 5.03.293
you either fear his humor or my negligence, that TN 1.04. 5 P
nay, either tell me where thou hast been, or i 1.05. 1 P
or o' mine either? 2.05.189 P
i' faith, or i either? 2.05.192 P
some laudable attempt either of valor or policy. 3.02. 29 P
will either of you bear me a challenge to him? 3.02. 40 P
is not in the world either malice or matter to WT 1.01. 33 P
either thou art most ignorant by age, | or thou 2.01.173
honest as either, to purge him of that humor 2.03. 38
either for life or death, upon the earth | of 3.03. 45
must either stay to execute them thyself, or 4.02. 15 P
if to either, thou dost ill. 4.04.304
and one that will either push on or pluck back 4.04.737 P
either forbear, | quit presently the chapel, or 5.03. 85
this must be answer'd either here or hence. JN 4.02. 89
of either, madam. R2 3.04. 11
either i must, or have mine honor soil'd | with 4.01. 23
either envy, therefore, or misprision | is 1H4 1.03. 27
on high, | and either we or they must lower lie. 3.03.204
and will, to save the blood on either side, 5.01. 99
i look to be either earl or duke, i can assure 5.04.142 P
/and either end in peace, which god so frame! 2H4 4.01.178
she either gives a stomach and no food — | such 4.04.105
it is certain that either wise bearing or 5.01. 75 P
it there's but two ways, either to utter them, 5.03.111 P
either our history shall with full mouth | speak H5 1.02.230
wheresome'er he is, either in heaven or in hell! 2.03. 8 P
either past or not arriv'd to pith and puissance 3.pr. 21
night, | the hum of either army stilly sounds, 4.pr. 5
either to quell the dolphin utterly, | or bring 1H6 1.01.163
either they must be dieted like mules | and have 1.02. 10
hark, countrymen, either renew the fight, | or 1.05. 27
parliament, | either to be restored to my blood, 2.05.128
france, | either to get the town again, or die: 3.02. 79
either she hath bewitch'd me with her words, 3.03. 58
on either hand thee there are squadrons pitch'd, 4.02. 23
i'll either make thee stoop and bend thy knee, 5.01. 61
either accept the title thou usurp'st, | of 5.04.151
either to suffer shipwrack, or arrive | where i 5.05. 8
so shouldst thou either turn my flying soul, 2H6 3.02.397
is either slain or wounded dangerous; 3H6 1.01. 11
either that is thine, or else thou wert not his. 2.01. 94
and either victory, or else a grave. 2.02.174
till either death hath clos'd these eyes of mine 2.03. 31
please you dismiss me, either with ay or no. 3.02. 78
either betray'd by falsehood of his guard | or 4.04. 8
either heav'n with lightning strike the R3 1.02. 64
either not believe | the envious slanders of her 1.03. 25
and award | either of you to be the other's end. 2.01. 15
either be patient and entreat me fair, | or with 4.04.152
either thou wilt die by god's just ordinance 4.04.184
whose puissance on either side | shall be well 5.03.299
what men of name are slain on either side? 5.05. 12
they must either | (for so run the conditions) H8 1.03. 23
but all | was either pitied in him or forgotten. 2.01. 29
either the cardinal, | or some about him near, 2.01.156
looking | either for such men or such business. 3.01. 76
the knowledge | either of king or council, when 3.02.317
that had a head to hit, either young or old, 5.03. 24
either to harbor fled, | or made a toast for TRO 1.03. 44
catch, and /'a knock /out either of your brains; 2.01.100 P
so do each lord, and either greet him not, | or 3.03. 52
fight, | so be it, either to the uttermost, | or 4.05. 91
either you must | confess yourselves wondrous COR 1.01. 87
why either were you ignorant to see't, | or, 2.03.174
from him pluck'd | either his gracious promise, 2.03.193
a' th' commons," be it either | for death, for 3.03. 14
but either | have borne the action of yourself, 4.07. 14
for either thou | must as a foreign recreant be 5.03.113
and each in either side | give the all–hail to 5.03.138
but the fall of either | makes the survivor heir 5.06. 17
till the prince came, who parted either part. ROM 1.01.115
by, | herself pois'd with herself in either eye; 1.02. 95
neither, fair maid, if either thee dislike. 2.02. 61
say either, and i'll stay the circumstance. 2.05. 36
both | receive in either by this dear encounter. 2.06. 29
either withdraw unto some private place, | or 3.01. 51
either thou or i, or both, must go with him. 3.01.129
either be gone before the watch be set, | or by 3.03.167
either my eyesight fails, or thou lookest pale. 3.05. 57
either in hope or present, i'd exchange | for TIM 4.03.520
either there is a civil strife in heaven, | or JC 1.03. 11
conceit me, | either a coward or a flatterer. 3.01.193
either led or driven, as we point the way; 4.01. 23
swear in both the scales against either scale, MAC 2.03. 9 P
either thou, macbeth, | or else my sword with an 5.07. 18
best actors in the world, either for tragedy, HAM 2.02.396 P
the violence of either grief or joy | their own 3.02.196
and either /... the devil or throw him out, 3.04.169
my virtue or my plague, be it either which — 4.07. 13
he that builds stronger than either the mason, 5.01. 41 P
i shall offend either to detain or give it: LR 1.02. 41 P
either his notion weakens, his discernings | are 1.04.228
to keep one's eyes of either side 's nose, that 1.05. 22 P
either in snuffs and packings of the dukes, | or 3.01. 26
either say thou'lt do't, | or thrive by other 5.03. 33
determine, | either for her stay or going; OTH 1.03.276
many, either to have it sterile with idleness or 1.03.324 P
to anger cassio, either by speaking too loud, or 2.01.267 P
lady, | that policy may either last so long, 3.03. 14
either from venice, or some unhatch'd practice 3.04.141
where either i must live or bear no life; 4.02. 58
either in discourse of thought or actual deed, 4.02.153
this is the night | that either makes me, or 5.01.129
or merry, | the violence of either thee becomes, ANT 1.05. 60
he neither loves, | nor either cares for him. 2.01. 16
either your unparagon'd mistress is dead, or CYM 1.04. 80 P
for certainties | either are past remedies, or, 1.06. 97
and my end | can make good use of either. 3.05. 64
to come alone, either he so undertaking, | or 4.02.142
on either side i come to spend my breath; 5.03. 81
either both or nothing, | or senseless speaking, 5.04.146
you must either be directed by some that take 5.04.179 P
either our brags | were crak'd of kitchen trulls 5.05.176
either expound now, or receive your sentence. PER 1.01. 90
who either by public war or private treason 1.02.104
mistress, either frame | your will to mine — 2.05. 81
either be rul'd by me, or i'll make you — | man 2.05. 83
we must either get her ravish'd or be rid of her 4.06. 5 P
either presuming them to have some force, | or TNK 1.01.194
either i am | the forehorse in the team, or i am 1.02. 58
either way, i am happy: 2.03. 22
and with thy teeth thou hold, will either fail. 3.05. 50
i shall think either, | well done, a noble 3.06. 23
either this was her love to palamon, | or fear 4.01. 49
the more thou hast | either of honor, office, STM III 15
till either gorge be stuff'd, or prey be gone; VEN 58
the sovereignty of either being so great | that LUC 69
swelling on either side to want his bliss; 389
whose love of either to myself was nearer, 1165
the face of either cipher'd either's heart, 1396
to put in practice either, alas, it was a spite PP 15. 7
either was the other's mine. PHT 36
together, | to themselves yet either neither, 43
let those repair | that are either true or fair; 66
so, either by thy picture or my love, | thyself SON 47. 9
either not assail'd, or victor being charg'd, 70.10
/EITHER'S 1 FR 0.0001 REL FR 1 V 0 P
and each (though enemies to /either's reign) SON 28. 5
EITHER'S 7 FR 0.0008 REL FR 6 V 1 P
they are both in either's pow'rs; TMP 1.02.451
as two yoke–devils sworn to either's purpose, H5 2.02.106
in neither can make choice of either's moi'ty. LR 1.01. 7 P
of either's color was the other queen, | proving LUC 66
the face of either cipher'd either's heart, 1396
slow | but heavy tears, badges of either's woe. SON 44.14
in either's aptness, as it best deceives, | to LC 306
EJECT 1 FR 0.0001 REL FR 1 V 0 P
to eject him hence | were but one danger, and to COR 3.01.285
EKE* *(also eche)*
EKE* 6 FR 0.0006 REL FR 4 V 2 P
and i to /ford shall eke unfold | how falstaff, WIV 1.03. 96
and master page, and eke cavaleiro slender, go 2.03. 74 P
most brisky juvenal and eke most lovely jew, MND 3.01. 95
and mine, to eke out hers. AYL 1.02.196 P
the tithe observance seek to eke out that AWW 2.05. 74
the bavian, with long tail and eke long tool, TNK 3.05.132
/ELBE 2 FR 0.0002 REL FR 2 V 0 P
between the floods of sala and of /elbe; H5 1.02. 45
which salique, as i said, 'twixt /elbe and sala, 1.02. 52
ELBOW *(also bilbow, ilbow)*
ELBOW 23 FR 0.0026 REL FR 4 V 19 P
the poor duke's constable, and my name is elbow.
MM 2.01. 48 P
elbow is your name? 2.01. 58 P
why dost thou not speak, elbow? 2.01. 60 P
he cannot, sir; he's out at elbow. 2.01. 61 P
as i say, this mistress elbow, being (as i say) 2.01. 98 P
come hither to me, master elbow; 2.01.257 P
here, man, i am at thy elbow. ADO 3.03. 98 P
mass, and my elbow itch'd; 3.03. 99 P
one rubb'd his elbow thus, and fleer'd, and LLL 5.02.109
the fiend is at mine elbow and tempts me, saying MV 2.02. 3 P
sir," | thus, leaning on mine elbow, i begin, JN 1.01.194
which gape and rub the elbow at the news | of 1H4 5.01. 77
go pluck him by the elbow, i must speak with him 2H4 1.02. 69 P
no, nor i neither, i'll be at your elbow. 2.01. 20 P
d' elbow. H5 3.04. 24 P
d' elbow. 3.04. 25 P
d' elbow, madame. 3.04. 30 P
o seigneur dieu, je m'en oublie d' elbow. 3.04. 31 P
sauf votre honneur, d' elbow. 3.04. 48 P
d' elbow, de nick, et de sin. 3.04. 49 P
de nailes, d' arma, d' elbow, de nick, de sin, 3.04. 59 P
/'zounds, 'tis even now at my elbow, persuading R3 1.04.145 P
i'll be at thy elbow. OTH 5.01. 3
ELBOW–ROOM 1 FR 0.0001 REL FR 1 V 0 P
ay, marry, now my soul hath elbow–room; JN 5.07. 28
ELBOW'S 2 FR 0.0002 REL FR 0 V 2 P
what was done to elbow's wife, that he hath MM 2.01.116 P
what was done to elbow's wife, once more? 2.01.139 P
/ELBOWS 1 FR 0.0001 REL FR 1 V 0 P
/a /sovereign /shame /so /elbows /him: LR 4.03. 42
ELBOWS 3 FR 0.0003 REL FR 2 V 1 P
hast no more brain than i have in mine elbows, TRO 2.01. 44 P
our hands in caesar's blood | up to the elbows, JC 3.01.107
each leaning on their elbows and their hips. VEN 44
/ELD 1 FR 0.0001 REL FR 1 V 0 P
virgins and boys, mid–age and wrinkled /eld, TRO 2.02.104
ELD 2 FR 0.0002 REL FR 2 V 0 P
the superstitious idle–headed eld | receiv'd and WIV 4.04. 36
as aged, and doth beg the alms | of palsied eld; MM 3.01. 36
ELDER* 40 FR 0.0045 REL FR 31 V 9 P
my heart of elder? WIV 2.03. 29 P
not i, sir, you are my elder. ERR 5.01.421
begin, sir, you are my elder. LLL 5.02.605 P
well follow'd: judas was hang'd on an elder. 5.02.606 P
how much more elder art thou than thy looks! MV 4.01.251
come, elder brother, you are too young in this. AYL 1.01. 53 P
and found it was his brother, his elder brother. 4.03.120
before i have a husband for the elder. SHR 1.01. 51
her elder sister is so curst and shrewd | that 1.01.180
any man, | until the elder sister first be wed. 1.02.261
achieve the elder, set the younger free | for 1.02.266
still the woman take | an elder than herself, so TN 2.04. 30
it has an elder sister, | or i mistake you. WT 1.02. 98
is that the elder, and art thou the heir? JN 1.01. 57
that geffrey was thy elder brother born, | and 2.01.104
son to the elder brother of this man, | and king 2.01.239
which elder days shall ripen and confirm | to R2 2.03. 43
which elder years | may happily bring forth. 5.03. 21
look whe'er the wither'd elder hath not his pole 2H4 2.04.258 P
kate, the elder i wax, the better i shall appear H5 5.02.229 P
if the issue of the elder son | succeed before 2H6 2.02. 51
the elder of them, being put to nurse, | was by 4.02.142
king by whose injurious doom | my elder brother, 3H6 3.03.102
belike the elder; 4.01.118
prelate, | bishop of exeter, his elder brother, R3 4.04.501
he is elder. TRO 1.02. 82 P
choice, | lavinia is thine elder brother's hope. TIT 2.01. 74
his son is elder, sir; ROM 1.05. 38
i do not always follow lover, elder brother, and TIM 2.02.121 P
in one day, | and i the elder and more terrible; JC 2.02. 47
i said an elder soldier, not a better. 4.03. 56
till by some elder masters of known honor | i HAM 5.02.248
by order of law, some year elder than this, who LR 1.01. 20 P
both as the same, or rather ours the elder — ANT 3.10. 13
behold divineness | no elder than a boy! CYM 3.06. 44
and let the stinking elder, grief, untwine | his 4.02. 59
to second ills with ills, each elder worse, 5.01. 14
grows elder now, and cares it be not done. PER 1.02. 15
and tithe of knees | from elder kinsmen, and him STM III 10
how can i then be elder than thou art? SON 22. 8
ELDER–GUN 1 FR 0.0001 REL FR 0 V 1 P
that's a perilous shot out of an elder–gun, that H5 4.01.198 P
ELDERS 4 FR 0.0004 REL FR 4 V 0 P
i do, | so well i know my duty to my elders. SHR 2.01. 7
see, our best elders. COR 1.01.226
most reverend and grave elders, to desire | the 2.02. 42
for our elders say, | the barren, touched in JC 1.02. 7
ELDER–TREE 2 FR 0.0002 REL FR 2 V 0 P
reward | among the nettles at the elder–tree, TIT 2.03.272
this is the pit, and this the elder–tree. 2.03.277
ELDEST 26 FR 0.0029 REL FR 20 V 6 P
my youngest boy, and yet my eldest care, | at ERR 1.01.124
and the other too like my lady's eldest son, ADO 2.01. 9 P
i know you are my eldest brother, and in the AYL 1.01. 44 P
the eldest of the three wrastled with charles, 1.02.125 P
since once he play'd a farmer's eldest son. SHR in.1. 84
helping baptista's eldest daughter to a husband 1.01.137 P
to me, | in the preferment of the eldest sister. 2.01. 93
that is antonio, the duke's eldest son, | that, AWW 3.05. 76
madonna, as if thy eldest son should be a fool; TN 1.05.113 P
the eldest is eleven; WT 2.01.144
born in northamptonshire, and eldest son, | as i JN 1.01. 51
philip, good old sir robert's wive's eldest son. 1.01.159
this is thy eldest son's son, | infortunate in 2.01.177
mordake earl of fife and eldest son | to beaten 1H4 1.01. 71
down the town that her eldest son is like you. 2H4 2.01.105 P
the eldest son and heir of john of gaunt, 2H6 2.02. 22
his eldest sister, anne, | my mother, being heir 2.02. 43
command my eldest son, nay, all my sons, | as 5.01. 49
i'll join mine eldest daughter, and my joy, | to 3H6 3.03.242
blind priest, like the eldest son of fortune, H8 2.02. 20
the eldest son of this distressed queen. TIT 1.01.103
that you create our emperor's eldest son, | lord 1.01.224
we will establish our estate upon | our eldest, MAC 1.04. 38
it hath the primal eldest curse upon't, | a HAM 3.03. 37
your eldest daughters have foredone themselves, LR 5.03.292
mark it), the eldest of them at three years old, CYM 1.01. 58
ELDEST–BORN 1 FR 0.0001 REL FR 1 V 0 P
goneril, | our eldest–born, speak first. LR 1.01. 54
ELD'ST 1 FR 0.0001 REL FR 1 V 0 P
your eld'st acquaintance cannot be three hours. TMP 5.01.186
ELEANOR 10 FR 0.0011 REL FR 10 V 0 P
nay, eleanor, then must i chide outright. 2H6 1.02. 41
presumptuous dame, ill–nurtur'd eleanor, | art 1.02. 42
are you so choleric | with eleanor, for telling 1.02. 52
dame eleanor gives gold to bring the witch; 1.02. 91
she shall not strike dame eleanor unreveng'd. 1.03.147
lord cardinal, i will follow eleanor, | and 1.03.148
countenance and confederacy | of lady eleanor, 2.01.165
roger had issue, edmund, anne, and eleanor. 2.02. 38
stand forth, dame eleanor cobham, gloucester's 2.03. 1
eleanor, the law, thou seest, hath judged thee; 2.03. 15
ELEANOR'S 2 FR 0.0002 REL FR 2 V 0 P
they, knowing dame eleanor's aspiring humor, 2H6 1.02. 97
thus eleanor's pride dies in her youngest days. 2.03. 46
ELECT 4 FR 0.0004 REL FR 4 V 0 P
majesty, | his captain, steward, deputy, elect, R2 4.01.126
that you elect no other king but him; 1H6 4.01. 4
yea, the elect o' th' land, who are assembled H8 2.04. 60

then, if you will elect by my advice, | crown TIT 1.01.228
ELECTED 5 FR 0.0005 REL FR 5 V 0 P
soul | elected him our absence to supply, | lent MM 1.01. 18
cannot depose | the deputy elected by the lord; R2 3.02. 57
(although my will distaste what it elected) TRO 2.02. 66
in whose power | we were elected theirs, martius COR 3.01.210
ta'en thy stand, | th' elected deer before thee? CYM 3.04.109
ELECTION 23 FR 0.0026 REL FR 22 V 1 P
his oath, | and comes to his election presently. MV 2.09. 3
it out in length, | to stay you from election. 3.02. 24
thy frank election make; AWW 2.03. 55
before we make election, give me leave | to show 2H6 1.03.162
makes merit her election, and doth boil | (as TRO 1.03.349
and my election | is led on in the conduct of my 2.02. 61
judgment all revoke | your ignorant election. COR 2.03.219
but that you must | cast your election on him. 2.03.229
almost all | repent in their election. 2.03.255
but let desert in pure election shine, | and, TIT 1.01. 16
voice, | in election for the roman empery, 1.01. 22
hue, | and name thee in election for the empire, 1.01.183
favors done | to us in our election this day, 1.01.235
and could of men distinguish her election, | sh' HAM 3.02. 64
popp'd in between th' election and my hopes, 5.02. 65
but i do prophesy th' election lights | on 5.02.355
sir, | election makes not up in such conditions. LR 1.01.206
but he, sir, had th' election; OTH 1.01. 27
his virtue | by her election may be truly read, CYM 1.01. 53
if it be a sin to make a true election, she is 1.02. 28 P
judgment | in the election of a sir so rare, 1.06.175
funeral, | and leave us to our free election. PER 2.04. 33
his success, but i | am guiltless of election. TNK 5.01.154
ELEGANCY *(also alligant)*
ELEGANCY 1 FR 0.0001 REL FR 0 V 1 P
ratified, but, for the elegancy, facility, and LLL 4.02.122 P
ELEGIES 2 FR 0.0002 REL FR 1 V 1 P
after your dire-lamenting elegies, | visit by TGV 3.02. 81
odes upon hawthorns and elegies on brambles; AYL 3.02.362 P
ELEMENT 12 FR 0.0013 REL FR 6 V 6 P
and such daub'ry as this is, beyond our element; WIV 4.02.178 P
there's little of the melancholy element in her, ADO 2.01.342 P
the element itself, till seven years' heat, TN 1.01. 25
are out of my welkin — i might say "element," 3.01. 58 P
idle shallow things, i am not of your element. 3.04.124 P
as the full moon doth the cinders of the element 2H4 4.03. 53 P
the element shows to him as it doth to me; H5 4.01.103 P
that promises no element | in such a business. H8 1.01. 48
and the complexion of the element | /in favor's JC 1.03.128
creature native and indued | unto that element. HAM 4.07.180
his back above | the element they liv'd in. ANT 5.02. 90
these water-galls in her dim element | foretell LUC 1588
ELEMENT'S 1 FR 0.0001 REL FR 1 V 0 P
thou climbing sorrow, | thy element's below. LR 2.04. 58
ELEMENTS 26 FR 0.0029 REL FR 22 V 4 P
if you can command these elements to silence, TMP 1.01. 21 P
the elements, | of whom your swords are temper'd 3.03. 61
then to the elements | be free, and fare thou 5.01.318
brain, | but, with the motion of all elements, LLL 4.03.326
rest | between the elements of air and earth, TN 1.05.275
does not our lives consist of the four elements? 2.03. 10 P
with no less terror than the elements | of fire R2 3.03. 55
and the dull elements of earth and water never H5 3.07. 21 P
cut, | bounding between the two moist elements, TRO 1.03. 41
by th' elements, | if e'er again i meet him COR 1.10. 10
trunks, | to the conflicting elements expos'd, TIM 4.03.230
and the elements | so mix'd in him that nature JC 5.05. 73
contending with the fretful elements; LR 3.01. 4
i tax not you, you elements, with unkindness; 3.02. 16
heavens | give him defense against the elements, OTH 2.01. 45
the very elements of this warlike isle, | have i 2.03. 57
she's fram'd as fruitful | as the free elements. 2.03.342
above, | you elements that clip us round about, 3.03.464
nourisheth it, and the elements once out of it, ANT 2.07. 45 P
the elements be kind to thee, and make | thy 3.02. 40
my other elements | i give to baser life. 5.02.289
th' unfriendly elements | forgot thee utterly, PER 3.01. 57
and like the elements | that know not what nor TNK 1.03. 61
nor that the elements | were not all appropriate STM II.C 136
receiving /nought by elements so slow | but SON 44.13
for when these quicker elements are gone | in 45. 5
ELEPHANT 6 FR 0.0006 REL FR 3 V 3 P
in the south suburbs at the elephant | is best TN 3.03. 39
to th' elephant. 3.03. 48
i could not find him at the elephant, | yet 4.03. 5
churlish as the bear, slow as the elephant; TRO 1.02. 21 P
shall the elephant ajax carry it thus? 2.03. 2 P
the elephant hath joints, but none for courtesy; 2.03.105 P
ELEPHANTS 1 FR 0.0001 REL FR 1 V 0 P
and bears with glasses, elephants with holes, JC 2.01.205
ELEVATED 1 FR 0.0001 REL FR 0 V 1 P
another elevated that the oracle was fulfill'd. WT 5.02. 75 P
ELEVEN *(also aleven, etc., 'leven)*
ELEVEN 20 FR 0.0022 REL FR 5 V 15 P
absence from his house between ten and eleven. WIV 2.02. 84 P
ten and eleven? 2.02. 85 P
ten and eleven. 2.02. 92 P
say i shall be with her between ten and eleven; 2.02.264 P
eleven o' clock the hour. 2.02.309 P
eleven, sir. MM 2.01.277 P
a bawd of eleven years' continuance, may it 3.02.196 P
and after one hour more 'twill be eleven, | and AYL 2.07. 25
that teacheth tricks eleven and twenty long, SHR 4.02. 57
to fight with him, hurt him in eleven places — TN 3.02. 35 P
the eldest is eleven; WT 2.01.144
and with a thought seven of the eleven i paid. 1H4 2.04.218 P
eleven buckram men grown out of two. 2.04.219 P
you have but eleven now. 2H4 5.04. 15 P
eleven hours i have spent to write it over, R3 3.06. 5
i had rather had eleven die nobly for their COR 1.03. 24 P
hour of five till the bell have told eleven. OTH 2.02. 10 P
as i think, i have brought up some eleven — PER 4.02. 15 P
ay, to eleven, and brought them down again. 4.02. 16 P
o thou that from eleven to ninety reign'st | in TNK 5.01.130
ELEVENTH 2 FR 0.0002 REL FR 2 V 0 P
met | the eleventh of this month at shrewsbury. 1H4 3.02.166
which in th' eleventh year of the last king's H5 1.01. 2
ELF 2 FR 0.0002 REL FR 2 V 0 P
every elf and fairy sprite | hop as light as MND 5.01.393
blanket my loins, elf all my hairs in knots, LR 2.03. 10

/ELF-LOCKS 1 FR 0.0001 REL FR 1 V 0 P
and bakes the /elf-locks in foul sluttish hairs, ROM 1.04. 90
ELIADS *(also iliads)*
ELIADS 1 FR 0.0001 REL FR 1 V 0 P
she gave strange eliads and most speaking looks LR 4.05. 25
ELIZABETH 6 FR 0.0006 REL FR 5 V 1 P
the britain richmond aims | at young elizabeth, R3 4.03. 40
you have a daughter call'd elizabeth, | virtuous 4.04.204
he should espouse elizabeth her daughter. 4.05. 8
division, | o, now let richmond and elizabeth, 5.05. 29
high and mighty princess of england, elizabeth! H8 5.04. 3 P
elizabeth. 5.04. 9
ELL 3 FR 0.0003 REL FR 0 V 3 P
quarters, that's an ell and three quarters, will ERR 3.02.110 P
a true woman, holland of eight shillings an ell. 1H4 3.03. 72 P
stretches from an inch narrow to an ell broad! ROM 2.04. 84 P
ELLE 1 FR 0.0001 REL FR 0 V 1 P
la main? elle est appelee de hand. H5 3.04. 7 P
ELLEN 1 FR 0.0001 REL FR 0 V 1 P
fairest daughter and mine, my goddaughter ellen?
2H4 3.02. 7 P
ELM 3 FR 0.0003 REL FR 2 V 1 P
thou art an elm, my husband, i a vine, | whose ERR 2.02.174
ivy so | enrings the barky fingers of the elm. MND 4.01. 44
answer, thou dead elm, answer. 2H4 2.04.331 P
ELOQUENCE 13 FR 0.0014 REL FR 10 V 3 P
and coy, | and nought esteems my aged eloquence.
TGV 3.01. 83
tongue | of saucy and audacious eloquence. MND 5.01.103
thy paleness moves me more than eloquence, | and
MV 3.02.106
and say she uttereth piercing eloquence; SHR 2.01.176
stairs, his eloquence the parcel of a reckoning. 1H4 2.04.100 P
cannot look greenly, nor gasp out my eloquence, H5 5.02.143 P
there is more eloquence in a sugar touch of them 5.02.276 P
(for in such business | action is eloquence, and COR 3.02. 76
that blabb'd them with such pleasing eloquence, TIT 3.01. 83
but romeo's name speaks heavenly eloquence. ROM 3.02. 33
to try thy eloquence, now 'tis time; ANT 3.12. 26
her modest eloquence with sighs is mixed, LUC 563
o, let my books be then the eloquence | and dumb
SON 23. 9
ELOQUENT 4 FR 0.0004 REL FR 1 V 3 P
witty, so it be eloquent and full of invention. TN 3.02. 43 P
turn the sands into eloquent tongues, and my H5 3.07. 34 P
be eloquent in my behalf to her. R3 4.04.357
and it will discourse most eloquent music. HAM 3.02.359 P
/ELSE 3 FR 0.0003 REL FR 3 V 0 P
/or /else | we fortify in paper and in figures, 2H4 1.03. 55
who /should /be /else? R3 4.04.266
/else /one /self /mate /and /make /could /not LR 4.03. 34
ELSE 448 FR 0.0506 REL FR 369 V 79 P
what seest thou else | in the dark backward and TMP 1.02. 49
i say, or chang'd 'em, | or else new form'd 'em; 1.02. 83
but what my power might else exact — like one 1.02. 99
and mine, invisible | to every eyeball else. 1.02.303
i had peopled else | this isle with calibans. 1.02.350
all corners else o' th' earth | let liberty make 1.02.492
hark what thou else shalt do me. 1.02.496
and sends me forth | (for else his project dies) 2.01.299
the king and all our company else being drown'd, 2.02.174 P
i, | beyond all limit of what else i' th' world, 3.01. 72
where should they be set else? 3.02. 10 P
and what does else want credit, come to me, 3.03. 25
desolate isle, else falls | upon your heads — 3.03. 80
more abstenious, | or else good night your vow! 4.01. 54
there's something else to do. 4.01.126
hush and be mute, | or else our spell is marr'd. 4.01.127
my sails | must fill, or else my project fails, ep 12
with wit, | or else a wit by folly vanquished. TGV 1.01. 35
and what news else | betideth here in absence of 1.01. 58
or else return no more into my sight. 1.02. 47
your worship, sir, or else i mistook. 2.01. 10 P
without you were so simple, none else would: 2.01. 37 P
or else for want of idle time, could not again 2.01.166
or fearing else some messenger, that might her 2.01.167
my duty will i boast of, nothing else. 2.04.111
duty pricks me on to utter that | which, else, 3.01. 9
this, or else nothing, will inherit her. 3.02. 86
me happy, | or else i often had been miserable. 4.01. 35
sir, but i do; or else i would be hence. 4.02. 22
of your perfect self | is else devoted, i am but 4.02.124
or else, by jove i vow, | i should have 4.04.203
thurio, give back, or else embrace thy death; 5.04.126
never come in mine own great chamber again else,
WIV 1.01.155 P
ay, or else i would i might be hang'd, la! 1.01.258 P
or else you had look'd through the grate, like a 2.02. 8 P
give me my gown, or else keep it in your arms. 3.01. 34 P
my brows become nothing else, nor that well 3.03. 60 P
or else i could not be in that mind. 3.03. 84 P
no, nor no where else but in your brain. 4.02.159 P
he would never else cross me thus. 5.05. 36 P
would i were hang'd la, else! 5.05.181 P
which else would stand under grievous imposition
MM 1.02.188 P
what else? 2.01.215 P
you had marr'd all else. 2.02.148
to this supposed, or else to let him suffer — 2.04. 97
else let my brother die, | if not a fedary, but 2.04.121
will, | or else he must not only die the death, 2.04.165
i abhor to name, | or else thou diest to-morrow. 3.01.102
they would else have married me to the rotten 4.03.173 P
or else thou art suborn'd against his honor | in 5.01.106
my knees, | or else for ever be confixed here, 5.01.232
else imputation, | for that he knew you, might 5.01.420
that should by private order else have died, | i 5.01.466
or else what lets it but he would be here? ERR 2.01.105
or else i shall seek my wit in my shoulders. 2.02. 38 P
else it could never be | but i should know her 2.02.201
sweet mistress — what your name is else, i know 3.02. 29
all this my sister is, or else should be. 3.02. 65
or else you may return without your money. 4.01. 44
i pray you, sir, my ring, or else the chain; 4.03. 77
is mad, | else would he never so demean himself. 4.03. 82
hath not else his eye | stray'd his affection in 5.01. 50
egeon art thou not? or else his ghost? 5.01.338
women, they would else have been troubled with a

ADO 1.01.129 P
fellow, or else make another cur'sy and say, 2.01. 55 P
highly that to her | all matter else seems weak. 3.01. 54
yea, or else it were pity but they should suffer 3.03. 2 P
ask my lady beatrice else, here she comes. 3.04. 38 P
what heard you him say else? 4.02. 46 P
what else, fellow? 4.02. 52 P
what else? 4.02. 58 P
i, being else by faith enforc'd | to call young 5.04. 8
why, that to know which else we should not know.
LLL 1.01. 56
will shall break it, will, and nothing else. 2.01.100
else your memory is bad, going o'er it erewhile. 4.01. 97
from thicket, | or pricket sore, or else sorel; 4.02. 59
this will i send and something else more plain 4.03.119
else none at all in aught proves excellent. 4.03.351
or else we lose ourselves to keep our oaths. 4.03.359
madam, came nothing else along with that? 5.02. 5
that he would wed me, or else die my lover. 5.02.447
or else to wed demetrius, as he would, | or on MND 1.01. 88
or else the law of athens yields you up | (which 1.01.119
or else misgraffed in respect of years — 1.01.137
or else it stood upon the choice of friends — 1.01.139
or else you are that shrewd and knavish sprite 2.01. 33
or else one must come in with a bush of thorns 3.01. 59 P
or else commit'st thy knaveries willfully. 3.02.346
joiner am | a lion fell, nor else no lion's dam, 5.01.224
how is it else the man i' th' moon? 5.01.248 P
else the puck a liar call. 5.01.435
nothing else. MV 2.05. 45
if it will feed nothing else, it will feed my 3.01. 54 P
else nothing in the world | could turn so much 3.02.245
there must be something else | pawn'd with the 3.05. 81
the wish would make else an unquiet house. 4.01.294
tarry a little, there is something else. 4.01.305
a halter gratis — nothing else, for god sake. 4.01.379
or else i do recant | the pardon that i late 4.01.391
i will have nothing else but only this, | and 4.01.432
but is there any else longs to see this broken AYL 1.02.141 P
i would thou hadst been son to some man else: 1.02.224
else had she with her father rang'd along. 1.03. 68
else are they very wretched. 2.04. 68
or else a rude despiser of good manners, | that 2.07. 92
i cannot see else how thou shouldst scape. 3.02. 85 P
else sighing every minute and groaning every 3.02.303 P
or else she could not have the wit to do this; 4.01.160 P
that i can make, | or else by him my love deny, 4.03. 62
or else be incontinent before marriage. 5.02. 39 P
or else, refusing me, to wed this shepherd; 5.04. 22
mine, sir, to take that no man else will. 5.04. 59 P
madam, and nothing else — so lordy call ladies. SHR in.2. 111
but in all places else /your master lucentio. 1.01.244
accept of him, or else you do me wrong. 2.01. 59
with her, | or else you like not of my company. 2.01. 65
a witty mother! witless else her son. 2.01.264
she is your own, else you must pardon me; 2.01.388
i must believe my master, else, i promise you, 3.01. 54
you give thanks, sweet kate, or else shall i? 4.01.159
you might have heard it else proclaim'd about. 4.02. 87
'twere deadly sickness or else present death. 4.03. 14
mustard, | or else you get no beef of grumio. 4.03. 28
or else my heart concealing it will break, | and 4.03. 78
ay, what else? 4.04. 2
but is this true, or is it else your pleasure, 4.05. 71
him, forswear him, or else we are all undone. 5.01.111 P
thee, else thou diest in thine unthankfulness, AWW 1.01.210 P
else paris, and the medicine, and the king, 1.03.233
else, does err. 2.03.183
not worth another word, else i'd call you knave. 2.03.263 P
what's his will else? 2.04. 47
the gods forbid else! 3.05. 74
i am either maid, or else this old man's wife. 5.03.293
hath kill'd the flock of all affections else TN 1.01. 35
what else may hap, to time i will commit, | only 1.02. 60
what shall we do else? 1.03.137 P
else would i very shortly see thee there. 2.01. 46
are, | unstaid and skittish in all motions else, 2.04. 18
respect than any one else that follows her. 2.05. 27 P
i prithee vent thy folly somewhere else, | thou 4.01. 10
or i am mad, or else this is a dream. 4.01. 61
but that i am mad | or else the lady's mad; 4.03. 16
or will not else thy craft so quickly grow, 5.01.166
would they else be content to die? WT 1.01. 42 P
or else thou must be counted | a servant grafted 1.02.245
or else a fool | that seest a game play'd home, 1.02.247
wilt confess, | or else be impudently negative, 1.02.274
or else a hovering temporizer, that | canst with 1.02.302
thy life, | with what thou else call'st thine. 2.03.138
(all proofs sleeping else | but what your 3.02.112
come buy, | buy, lads, or else your lasses cry: 4.04.229
father (all whose joy is nothing else | but fair 4.04.408
we are gone else. 4.04.820 P
that title and what shame else belongs to't. 4.04.840 P
stars, stars, | and all eyes else dead coals! 5.01. 68
might quench the zeal | of all professors else, 5.01.108
or else 'twere hard luck, being in so 5.02.147 P
or else it must go wrong with you and me; JN 1.01. 41
in at the window, or else o'er the hatch. 1.01.171
bastards, and else. 2.01.276
else what a mockery should it be to swear! 3.01.285
which else runs tickling up and down the veins, 3.03. 44
see else yourself, | there is no malice in this 4.01.107
'tis true — to hurt his master, no /man else. 4.03. 33
who else but i, | and such as to my claim are 5.02.100
which else would post until it had return'd R2 1.01. 56
by that, and all the rites of knighthood else, 1.01. 75
boast of nothing else | but that i was a 1.03.273
which live like venom where no venom else | but 2.01.157
grief, | or else he never would compare between. 2.01.185
i count myself in nothing else so happy | as in 2.03. 46
seymour, | none else of name and noble estimate. 2.03. 56
else heaven would, | and we will not. 3.02. 30
who sets me else? 4.01. 57
and wounds the earth, if nothing else, with rage 5.01. 30
else he had been damn'd for cozening the devil. 1H4 1.02.122 P
it could not be else, i have drunk medicines. 2.02. 19 P
and i must know it, else he loves me not. 2.03. 64
every man of them, or i am a jew else, an ebrew 2.04.179 P

seven, by these hilts, or i am a villain else. 2.04.206 P
what there is else, keep close, we'll read it at 2.04.542 P
tell me else, | could such inordinate and low 3.02. 11
neither faith, truth, nor womanhood in me else. 3.03.111 P
and many a creature else | had been alive this 5.05. 7
have a desire to stay with my friends, else, sir 2H4 3.02.226 P
i will have it in a particular ballad else, with 4.03. 48 P
or else a feast | and takes away the stomach — 4.04.106
desire to see him, thinking of nothing else, 5.05. 25 P
else, putting all affairs else in oblivion, as 5.05. 26 P
if there were nothing else to be done but to see 5.05. 27 P
speak freely of our acts, or else our grave, H5 1.02.231
or else what follows? 2.04. 96
age, or else you may be marvellously mistook. 3.06. 80 P
art thou aught else but place, degree, and form, 4.01.246
let life be short, else shame will be too long. 4.05. 23
he is a craven and a villain else, and't please 4.07.133 P
none else of name; 4.08.105
else ne'er could they hold out so as they do. 1H6 1.02. 43
christ's mother helps me, else i were too weak. 1.02.106
else ne'er could he so long protract his speech. 1.02.120
or else was wrangling somerset in th' error? 2.04. 6
well, well, come on, who else? 2.04. 55
tongue, | else with the like i had requited him. 2.05. 50
else would i have a fling at winchester. 3.01. 64
or else let talbot perish with this shame. 3.02. 57
or else reproach be talbot's greatest fame! 3.02. 76
or else this blow should broach thy dearest 3.04. 40
else farewell talbot, france, and england's 4.03. 23
to us, | else ruin combat with their palaces! 5.02. 7
or else, when thou didst keep my lambs a-field, 5.04. 30
which i will win from france, or else be slain. 2H6 1.01.213
sirrah, or you must fight, or else be hang'd. 1.03.217
ay, what else? fear you not her courage. 1.04. 5 P
nothing else, my lord. 2.01. 49
you can, | or else conclude my words effectual. 3.01. 41
above the felon or what trespass else. 3.01.132
what were it else | but like a pleasant slumber 3.02.389
a thousand crowns, or else lay down your head. 4.01. 16
and cried, "a crown, or else a glorious tomb! 3H6 1.04. 16
either that is thine, or else thou wert not his. 2.01. 94
defy them then, or else hold close thy lips. 2.02.118
and either victory, or else a grave. 2.02.174
yield both my life and them | to some man else, 2.05. 60
expostulate, make speed, | or else come after. 2.05.136
her | with promise of his sister and what else, 3.01. 51
and she shall be my love or else my queen. 3.02. 88
had he none else to make a stale but me? 3.03.260
or else you would not have bestow'd the heir 4.01. 56
else might i think that clarence, edward's 4.02. 10
wherefore else guard we his royal tent | but to 4.03. 21
what else? and that succession be determined. 4.06. 56
strike now, or else the iron cools. 5.01. 49
or else you famish — that's a threefold death. 5.04. 32
and take his thanks that yet hath nothing else. 5.04. 59
long, | i will deliver you, or else lie for you. R3 1.01.115
yes, one place else, if you will hear me name it 1.02.110
(and not provok'd by any suitor else), | aiming, 1.03. 64
or else reported | successively from age to age, 3.01. 72
and so 'twill do | with some men else, that 3.02. 66
am not so well provided | as else i would be, 3.04. 45
else wherefore breathe i in a christian land? 3.07.116
or else i swoon with this dead-killing news! 4.01. 35
or else my kingdom stands on brittle glass. 4.02. 61
what they will impart | help nothing else, yet 4.04.131
or else his head's assurance is but frail. 4.04.496
there's none else by. 5.03.182
rescue, fair lord, or else the day is lost! 5.04. 6
or else you suffer | too hard an exclamation. H8 1.02. 51
we shall be late else, which i would not be, 1.03. 65
pray god he do, he'll never know himself else. 2.02. 22
favor | to him that does best, god forbid else. 2.02.114
i will have none so near else. 2.02.134
and thy parts | sovereign and pious else, could 2.04.141
and all else | this talking lord can lay upon my 3.02.264
feel | my sword i' th' life-blood of thee else. 3.02.277
you writ to rome, or else | to foreign princes, 3.02.313
yes, good griffith, | i were malicious else. 4.02. 48
or else no witness | would come against you. 5.01.107
i'll have more, or else unsay't; 5.01.175
they would shame to make me | wait else at door, 5.02. 17
th' rail, | i'll peck you o'er the pales else. 5.03. 90
and she must thank ye, | she will be sick else. 5.04. 74
than ever i saw her look, or any woman else. TRO 1.01. 33 P
call them shames which are indeed nought else 1.03. 19
if none else, i am he. 1.03.290
who may you else oppose | that can from hector 1.03.333
lies in your sinews, or else there be liars. 2.01. 99 P
"deliver helen, and all damage else — | as 2.02. 3
and what else dear that is consum'd | in hot 2.02. 5
troy burns, or else let helen go. 2.02.112
else might the world convince of levity | as 2.02.130
but you are wise, | or else you love not; 3.02.156
or else disdainfully, which shall shake him more 3.03. 53
it, either to the uttermost, | or else a breath. 4.05. 92
in faith i will lo, never trust me else. 5.02. 59
i'll give you something else. 5.02. 86
wars and lechery, nothing else holds fashion. 5.02.195 P
in awe, which else | would feed on one another? COR 1.01.187
wheel | three or four miles about, else had i, 1.06. 20
without note, here's many else have done — 1.09. 49
or else your actions would grow wondrous single; 2.01. 36 P
or else it would have gall'd his surly nature, 2.03.195
all will be naught else. 3.01.230
which else would put you to your fortune and 3.02. 60
i would the gods had nothing else to do | but to 4.02. 45
had we no other quarrel else to rome but that 4.05.127
o, ay, what else? 4.06.148
of yourself, or else | to him had left it soly. 4.07. 15
for we have nothing else to ask but that | which 5.03. 88
the country, our dear nurse, or else thy person, 5.03.110
or else | triumphantly tread on thy country's 5.03.115
should straight fall mad, or else die suddenly. TIT 2.03.104
or else to heaven she heaves them for revenge. 4.01. 40
and no one else but the delivered empress. 4.02.142
thinks, with jove in heaven, or some where else, 4.03. 41
ay, of my pigeons, sir, nothing else. 4.03. 88 P
up, | or else i will discover nought to thee. 5.01. 85
as kill a man, or else devise his death, 5.01.128
me, | or else i'll call my brother back again, 5.02.135
what is it else? ROM 1.01.193
i'll pay that doctrine, or else die in debt. 1.01.238
tut, you saw her fair, none else being by, 1.02. 94
else would a maiden blush bepaint my cheek | for 2.02. 86
so thou wilt woo, but else not for the world. 2.02. 97
else would i tear the cave where echo lies, 2.02.161
thou wouldst else have made thy tale large. 2.04. 97 P
as much to him, else is his thanks too much. 2.06. 23
coldly of your grievances, | or else depart; 3.01. 53
else, when he is found, that hour is his last. 3.01.195
and from my soul too, else beshrew them both. 3.05.227
if all else fail, myself have power to die. 3.05.242
who else? 5.03.144
one only daughter have i, no kin else, | on whom TIM 1.01.121
how had you been my friends else? 1.02. 90 P
else i should tell him well (i' faith, i should) 1.02.161
was above mine, | else surely his had equall'd. 3.04. 32
it could not else be i should prove so base | to 3.05. 93
when i know not what else to do, i'll see thee 4.03.353 P
nothing else. 5.01. 9
thy glove, | or any token of thine honor else, 5.04. 50
who else would soar above the view of men, | and JC 1.01. 74
or else the world, too saucy with the gods, 1.03. 12
in a roman you do want, | or else you use not. 1.03. 59
shall no man else be touch'd but only caesar? 2.01.154
run to the capitol, and nothing else? 2.04. 11
and so return to you, and nothing else? 2.04. 12
intended to your person, | nor to no roman else. 3.01. 91
who else must be let blood, who else is rank; 3.01.152
who else must be let blood, who else is rank; 3.01.152
or else were this a savage spectacle. 3.01.223
else shall you not have any hand at all | about 3.01.248
by the gods, this speech were else your last. 4.03. 14
and no man else hath honor by his death. 5.05. 57
on which i must fall down, or else o'erleap, MAC 1.04. 49
defect, | which else should free have wrought. 2.01. 19
th' other senses, | or else worth all the rest. 2.01. 45
we should have else desir'd your good advice 3.01. 20
and all things else that might | to half a soul 3.01. 81
i had else been perfect, | whole as the marble, 3.04. 20
or else climb upward | to what they were before. 4.02. 24
we | shall take upon 's what else remains to do, 5.06. 5
or else my sword with an unbattered edge | i 5.07. 19
of all men else i have avoided thee. 5.08. 4
and what needful else | that calls upon us, by 5.09. 37
and whatsomever else shall hap to-night, | give HAM 1.02.248
youth to itself rebels, though none else near. 1.03. 44
his virtues else, be they as pure as grace, | as 1.04. 33
what else? 1.05. 92
or else this brain of mine | hunts not the trail 2.02. 46
what is't but to be nothing else but mad? 2.02. 94
then, or else shall 'a suffer not thinking on, 3.02.133 P
whether love lead fortune, or else fortune love. 3.02.203
/confederate season, else no creature seeing, 3.02.256
else could you not have motion, but sure that 3.04. 72
we fat all creatures else to fat us, and we fat 4.03. 22 P
seal'd and done | that else leans on th' affair. 4.03. 57
all things else | you mainly were stirr'd up. 4.07. 8
it must be /se /offendendo, it cannot be else. 5.01. 9 P
what ceremony else? 5.01.223
what ceremony else? 5.01.225
is his mirror, and who else would trace him, his 5.02.119 P
himself, there are no tongues else for 's turn. 5.02.184 P
which else were shame, that then necessity LR 1.04.213
by her, that else will take the thing she begs, 1.04.248
i shall serve you, sir, | truly, however else. 2.01.117
doth from my senses take all feeling else, 3.04. 13
reserv'd a blanket, else we had been all sham'd. 3.04. 65 P
all cruels else subscribe; 3.07. 65
he has some reason, else he could not beg. 4.01. 31
myself could else out-frown false fortune's 5.03. 6
well, else i should answer | from a full-flowing 5.03. 73
nor no man else. 5.03.291
or else the devil will make a grandsire of you. OTH 1.01. 91
and such things else of quality and respect | as 1.03.282
with what else needful your good grace shall 1.03.286
nay, it is true, or else i am a turk: 2.01.114
three else of cyprus, noble swelling spirits 2.03. 55
such perdition | as nothing else could match. 3.04. 68
i am a very villain else. 4.01.125 P
/faith, i must, she'll rail in the streets else. 4.01.163 P
the which my current runs | or else dries up: 4.02. 60
i will be hang'd else. 4.02.133
or else break out in peevish jealousies, 4.03. 89
else let them know, | the ills we do, their ills 4.03.102
yet she must die, else she'll betray more men. 5.02. 6
ask thy husband else. 5.02.136
perform't, or else we damn thee." ANT 1.01. 24
else so thy cheek pays shame | when 1.01. 31
a palm presages chastity, if nothing else. 1.02. 48 P
with what else more serious | importeth thee to 1.02.120
either thee becomes, | so does it no man's else. 1.05. 61
to wrangle in when you have nothing else to do. 2.02.106 P
graces speak | that which none else can utter. 2.02.130
presently be sought, | or else he seeks out us. 2.02.159
much tall youth | that else must perish here. 2.06. 8
pompey gives him, else he is a very epicure. 2.07. 51 P
what's else to say? 2.07. 58
isis else defend! 3.03. 43
by sea, what else? 3.07. 28
do? why, what else? 3.11. 27
which else an easy battery might lay flat, for CYM 1.04. 22 P
else, sir, no more tribute, pray you now. 3.01. 45 P
her judgment | that what's else rare is chok'd; 3.05. 77
or else | thou art straightway with the fiends. 3.05. 82
or else such stuff as madmen | tongue and brain 5.04.145
all leave us else; PER 1.02. 48
this day i'll rise, or else add ill to ill. 2.01.166
how? | do as i bid you, or you'll move me else. 2.03. 71
she thinks not so; peruse this writing else. 2.05. 41
what else, man? 4.02. 18 P
not see thee, or else look friendly upon thee. 4.06. 89 P
we convent nought else but woes: TNK 1.05. 9
else, if thou pursuest her, | be as that cursed 2.02.198
'twere wrong else. 2.05. 61
remember, cousin, | else there be tales abroad. 3.03. 38
you'll lose all else. 3.04. 9
i shall sleep like a top else. 3.04. 26
i would be sorry else. | give me your hand. 3.05. 77
fable, | we are a merry rout, or else a rable, 3.05.106
and me my love! is there aught else to say? 3.06. 93
in that i'll bury | thee and all crosses else. 3.06.127
will bear the curses else of after-ages | for 3.06.187
else, never trifle, | but take our lives, duke. 3.06.260
yes, i must, sir, | else both miscarry. 3.06.302
do, very /rearly, i must be abroad else, | to 4.01.110
by cocklight, | 'twill never thrive else. 4.01.113
must open | and bleed to death for my sake else. 4.02. 2
to go on, i mean, | else wish we to be snails. 5.01. 42
or else grant | the file and quality i hold i 5.01.160
what is there else to do? 5.02. 75
i had no end in't else; 5.03. 75
or what fierce sulphur else, to this end made, 5.04. 64
fair, but speak fair words, or else be mute. VEN 208
he sees his love, and nothing else he sees, 287
for nothing else with his proud sight agrees. 288
else, suffer'd, it will set the heart on fire: 388
that dazzleth them, or else some shame supposed, LUC 377
or kills his life or else his quality. 875
my collatine would else have come to me | when 916
and what wrong else may be imagined | by foul 1622
else lasting shame | on thee and thine this 1629
pity the world, or else this glutton be, | to SON 1.13
or else receiv'st with pleasure thine annoy? 8. 4
or else of thee this i prognosticate: 14.13
or me, to whom thou gav'st it, else mistaking, 87.10
none else to me, nor i to none alive, | that my 112. 7
for thou art all, and all things else are thine. LC 266

ELSEWHERE 10 FR 0.0011 REL FR 9 V 1 P
i'll knock elsewhere, to see if they'll disdain ERR 3.01.121
or if you like elsewhere, do it by stealth, 3.02. 7
if not, elsewhere they meet with charity; SHR 4.03. 6
or here or elsewhere to the furthest verge R2 1.01. 93
yea, and elsewhere, so far as my coin would 1H4 1.02. 54 P
and leave your brothers to go speed elsewhere. 3H6 4.01. 58
there is a world elsewhere. COR 3.03.135
thee watch i, whilst thou dost wake elsewhere, SON 61.13
tell me thou lov'st elsewhere, but in my sight, 139. 5
that they elsewhere might dart their injuries: 139.12

ELSINORE 4 FR 0.0004 REL FR 1 V 3 P
but what is your affair in elsinore? HAM 1.02.174
way of friendship, what make you at elsinore? 2.02.270 P
gentlemen, you are welcome to elsinore. 2.02.370 P
you are welcome to elsinore. 2.02.547 P

ELTAM 3 FR 0.0003 REL FR 3 V 0 P
to eltam will i, where the young king is, 1H6 1.01.170
the king from eltam i intend to send, | and sit 1.01.176
occasions | at eltam place i told your majesty. 3.01.155

ELVES 8 FR 0.0009 REL FR 8 V 0 P
ye elves of hills, brooks, standing lakes, and TMP 5.01. 33
elves, list your names; WIV 5.05. 42
search windsor castle, elves, within and out. 5.05. 56
our queen and all her elves come here anon. MND 2.01. 17
that all their elves for fear | creep into 2.01. 30
leathren wings | to make my small elves coats, 2.02. 5
nod to him, elves, and do him courtesies. 3.01.174
sing, | like elves and fairies in a ring, MAC 4.01. 42

ELVISH-MARK'D 1 FR 0.0001 REL FR 1 V 0 P
thou elvish-mark'd, abortive, rooting hog! R3 1.03.227

ELY 4 FR 0.0004 REL FR 4 V 0 P
at ely house. R2 1.04. 58
bid him repair to us to ely house | to see this 2.01.216
my lord of ely, when i was last in holborn, | i R3 3.04. 31
ely with richmond troubles me more near | than 4.03. 49

ELYSIUM 8 FR 0.0009 REL FR 8 V 0 P
much turmoil | a blessed soul doth in elysium. TGV 2.07. 38
my brother he is in elysium. TN 1.02. 4
of phoebus, and all night | sleeps in elysium; H5 4.01.274
thy body, | and then it liv'd in sweet elysium. 2H6 3.02.399
within whose circuit is elysium | and all that 3H6 1.02. 30
poor shadows of elysium, hence, and rest | upon CYM 5.04. 97
thy brave soul seek elysium! TNK 5.04. 95
annoy, | to clip elysium and to lack her joy. VEN 600

'EM *(also them, 'um)*

/'EM 4 FR 0.0004 REL FR 3 V 1 P
for god's sake let him have /'em; 1H6 4.07. 89
we be rid of them, do with /'em what thou wilt. 4.07. 94
he has made too much plenty with /'em. TIM 3.05. 66
/who /maintains /'em? HAM 2.02.346 P

'EM 222 FR 0.0251 REL FR 171 V 51 P
creatures that were mine, i say, or chang'd 'em, TMP 1.02. 82
i say, or chang'd 'em, | or else new form'd 'em; 1.02. 83
pinch more stinging | than bees that made 'em. 1.02.330
his fellows, | and strays about to find 'em. 1.02.418
in the dark | out of my way, unless he bid 'em; 2.02. 7
rain grace | on that which breeds between 'em! 3.01. 76
therefore bear up and board 'em. 3.02. 3 P
"flout 'em and /scout 'em, | and scout 'em and 3.02.121
"flout 'em and /scout 'em, | and scout 'em and 3.02.121
and /scout 'em, | and scout 'em and flout 'em! 3.02.122
and /scout 'em, | and scout 'em and flout 'em! 3.02.122
did lie, | though fools at home condemn 'em. 3.03. 27
whose throats had hanging at 'em | wallets of 3.03. 45
your charm so strongly works 'em | that if you 5.01. 17
op'd, and let 'em forth | by my so potent art. 5.01. 49
will money buy 'em? 5.01.265
find this grand liquor that hath gilded 'em? 5.01.280
if there be ten, shrink not, but down with 'em. TGV 4.01. 2
ay; but peace, let's hear 'em. 4.02. 38 P
and entertain'd 'em deeply in her heart. 5.04.102
women, indeed, cannot abide 'em, they are very WIV 1.01.298 P
hang 'em, slaves! 2.01.173 P
call you 'em stanzos? AYL 2.05. 19 P
the church together, god send 'em good shipping! SHR 5.01. 42 P
to the english, the french ne'er got 'em. AWW 2.03. 95 P
what will you say without 'em? 4.03.121 P
in breaking 'em he is stronger than hercules. 4.03.252 P
if i put any tricks upon 'em, sir, they shall be 4.05. 60 P
faith, there's a dozen of 'em, with delicate 4.05.104 P
wherefore have these gifts a curtain before 'em? TN 1.03.126 P
and some have greatness thrust upon 'em. 2.05.146 P
i'll get 'em all three all ready. 3.01. 91 P
for the bed of ware in england, set 'em down. 3.02. 48 P

by mine honor, | i'll geld 'em all; WT 2.01.147
sometimes to see 'em, and not to see 'em; 3.03. 91 P
sometimes to see 'em, and not to see 'em; 3.03. 91 P
i'll swear for 'em. 4.04.155
he sings 'em over as they were gods or goddesses 4.04.208 P
and you shall pay well for 'em. 4.04.314 P
to see leeks hereafter, i pray you mock at 'em, H5 5.01. 56 P
o' th' ear, and that will make 'em red again. 2H6 4.07. 87 P
when these suns | (for so they phrase 'em) by H8 1.01. 34
have broke their backs with laying manors on 'em 1.01. 84
have been commissions | sent down among 'em, 1.02. 21
most pestilent to th' hearing, and, to bear 'em, 1.02. 49
never so ridiculous | (nay, let 'em be unmanly), 1.03. 4
for when they hold 'em, you would swear directly 1.03. 8
it, | that never see 'em pace before, the spavin 1.03. 12
the spavin | /and springhalt reign'd among 'em. 1.03. 13
'tis time to give 'em physic, their diseases 1.03. 36
the devil fiddle 'em! 1.03. 42
going, | for sure there's no converting of 'em. 1.03. 43
they rested, | i think would better please 'em. 1.04. 13
my lord sands, you are one will keep 'em waking; 1.04. 23
then we shall have 'em | talk us to silence. 1.04. 44
good lord chamberlain, | go, give 'em welcome: 1.04. 57
and pray receive 'em nobly and conduct 'em 1.04. 58
and pray receive 'em nobly and conduct 'em 1.04. 58
and entreat | an hour of revels with 'em. 1.04. 72
for which i pay 'em | a thousand thanks, and 1.04. 73
thanks, and pray 'em take their pleasures. 1.04. 74
pray tell 'em thus much from me: 1.04. 77
there should be one amongst 'em, by his person 1.04. 78
and a measure | to lead 'em once again, and then 1.04.107
be what they will, i heartily forgive 'em; 2.01. 65
yet let 'em look they glory not in mischief, 2.01. 66
then my guiltless blood must cry against 'em. 2.01. 68
that blood will make 'em one day groan for't. 2.01.106
by commission and main power, took 'em from me, 2.02. 6 P
every tongue speaks 'em, | and every true heart 2.02. 38
sing, and disperse 'em if thou canst. 3.01. 2
were tried by ev'ry tongue, ev'ry eye saw 'em, 3.01. 35
'em, | envy and base opinion set against 'em, 3.01. 36
mend 'em for shame, my lords! 3.01.105
we are to cure such sorrows, not to sow 'em. 3.01.158
as thick as thought could make 'em, and | appear 3.02.195
who dare cross 'em, | bearing the king's will 3.02.234
you have christian warrant for 'em, and no doubt 3.02.244
as, let 'em have their rights, they are ever 4.01. 9
shake the press | and make 'em reel before 'em. 4.01. 79
shake the press | and make 'em reel before 'em. 4.01. 79
sure those men are happy that shall have 'em. 4.02.147
but poverty could never draw 'em from me), 4.02.149
that they may have their wages duly paid 'em, 4.02.150
'tis well thare's one above 'em yet. 5.02. 27
they had parted so much honesty among 'em — 5.02. 28
let 'em alone, and draw the curtain close; 5.02. 34
pace 'em not in their hands to make 'em gentle, 5.02. 57
pace 'em not in their hands to make 'em gentle, 5.02. 57
their mouths with stubborn bits and spur 'em 5.02. 58
these are but switches to 'em. 5.03. 9 P
unless we sweep 'em from the door with cannons 5.03. 13
to scatter 'em, as 'tis to make 'em sleep | on 5.03. 14
as 'tis to make 'em sleep | on may–day morning, 5.03. 14
we may as well push against powle's as stir 'em. 5.03. 16
guy, nor colbrand, | to mow 'em down before me; 5.03. 23
should you do, but knock 'em down by th' dozens? 5.03. 32 P
to th' broom–staff to me, i defied 'em still, 5.03. 55 P
when suddenly a file of boys behind 'em, loose 5.03. 56 P
to draw mine honor in, and let 'em win the work. 5.03. 58 P
the devil was amongst 'em, i think, surely. 5.03. 58 P
i have some of 'em in limbo patrum, and there 5.03. 64 P
an army cannot rule 'em. 5.03. 77
none think flattery, for they'll find 'em truth. 5.04. 16
of good women, | for such a one we show'd 'em. ep 11
if they hold when their ladies bid 'em clap. ep 14
intend to do, which now we'll show 'em in deeds. COR 1.01. 59 P
hang 'em! 1.01.190
hang 'em! 1.01.204
some of the best of 'em were hereditary hangmen. 2.01. 92 P
hang 'em, | i would they would forget me, like 2.03. 56
the virtues | which our divines lose by 'em. 2.03. 58
pray you speak to 'em, i pray you, | in 2.03. 59
no, no; no man saw 'em. 2.03.165
five hundred, and their friends to piece 'em. 2.03.212
the vengeance, | could he not speak 'em fair? 3.01.262
than spend a fawn upon 'em | for the inheritance 3.02. 67
inevitable strokes, | as 'tis to laugh at 'em. 4.01. 27
could i meet 'em | but once a day, it would 4.02. 46
and my services are, as you are, against 'em. 4.03. 5 P
of the war | destroy what lies before 'em. 4.06. 42
a number of men eats timon, and he sees 'em not!
TIM 1.02. 40 P
freedom, | or my friends, if i should need 'em. 1.02. 69
bleeding new, my lord, there's no meat like 'em; 1.02. 79 P
that then thou mightst kill 'em — and bid me to 1.02. 82 P
then thou mightst kill 'em — and bid me to 'em! 1.02. 83 P
friends, if we should ne'er have need of 'em? 1.02. 96 P
living, should we ne'er have use for 'em; 1.02. 98 P
welcome all, let 'em have kind admittance. 1.02.128
legs be worth the sums | that are given for 'em. 1.02.233
with apemantus, let's ha' some sport with 'em. 2.02. 47 P
speak to 'em, fool. 2.02. 65 P
have found time to use 'em toward a supply of 2.02.192 P
bid 'em send o' th' instant | a thousand talents 2.02.198
wear rich jewels | and send for money for 'em. 3.04. 24
knock me down with 'em, cleave me to the girdle! 3.04. 90
be call'd desperate ones, for a madman owes 'em. 3.04.102 P
most true; the law shall bruise 'em. 3.05. 4
take my deserts to his, and join 'em both; 3.05. 78
let prisons swallow 'em, | debts wither 'em to 4.03.530
swallow 'em, | debts wither 'em to nothing; 4.03.531
conjure with 'em, | "brutus" will start a spirit JC 1.02.146
let 'em enter. 2.01. 76
an act of rage, | and after seem to chide 'em. 2.01.177
tell me your counsels, i will not disclose 'em. 2.01.298
that will hear me speak, let 'em stay here; 3.02. 5
there is some grudge between 'em; 4.03.125
their daggers ready, | he could not miss 'em. MAC 2.02. 12
call 'em; let me see 'em. 4.01. 63
call 'em; let me see 'em. 4.01. 63

then you'll buy 'em to sell again. 4.02. 41
they were well at peace when i did leave 'em. 4.03.179
thy asses are gone about 'em. LR 1.05. 34 P
to the eels when she put 'em i' th' paste alive; 2.04.123 P
she knapp'd 'em o' th' coxcombs with a stick, 2.04.123 P
wouldst thou give 'em all? 3.04. 64
red burning spits | come hizzing in upon 'em — 3.06. 16
not peace at my bidding, there i found 'em, 4.06.103 P
there i found 'em, there i smelt 'em out. 4.06.103 P
does offend, none, i say none, i'll able 'em. 4.06.168
we'll see 'em starv'd first. 5.03. 25
lie they upon thy hand, | and be undone by 'em! ANT 2.05.106
we'll beat 'em into bench–holes. 4.07. 9
and snatch 'em up, as we take hares, behind: 4.07. 13
pray let us follow 'em. CYM 1.04.172 P
but none of 'em can be found. 5.03. 88
says to 'em, if king pericles | come not home in PER 3.ch. 30
as wakes my vengeance and revenge for 'em. TNK 1.01. 58
in a /glassy stream, | you may behold 'em. 1.01.113
honorable toil, | are paid with ice to cool 'em. 1.02. 34
eat them) | the brine they wept at killing 'em. 1.03. 22
then like men use 'em. 1.04. 28
rather than have 'em | freed of this plight, and 1.04. 33
(sound and at liberty), i would 'em dead; 1.04. 35
but forty thousand fold we had rather have 'em 1.04. 36
bear 'em speedily | from our kind air, to them 1.04. 37
the prison itself is proud of 'em; 2.01. 24 P
i think fame but stammers 'em, they stand a 2.01. 28 P
i never saw 'em. 2.01. 45 P
then start amongst 'em | and, as an east wind, 2.02. 12
leave 'em all behind us | like lazy clouds, 2.02. 13
garlands, | ere they have time to wish 'em ours. 2.02. 17
hands shall never draw 'em out like lightning, 2.02. 24
and like young eagles teach 'em | boldly to gaze 2.02. 34
bodies, let 'em suffer | the gall of hazard, so 2.02. 65
i'll have a gown full of 'em — and of these: 2.02.128
bold young men that, when he bids 'em charge, 2.02.249
devils take 'em | that are so envious to me! 2.02.262
i'll shake 'em so, ye shall not sleep, | i'll 2.02.272
'tis a benefit, | a mercy i must thank 'em for; 2.03. 2
one see 'em all rewarded. 3.05.152
none here speak for 'em, | for, ere the sun set, 3.06.183
sister, | i find no anger to 'em, nor no ruin: 3.06.189
the misadventure of their owen eyes kill 'em; 3.06.190
say i felt | compassion to 'em both, how would 3.06.213
live, | and have the agony of love about 'em, 3.06.219
be wise then | and here forget 'em; 3.06.223
heaven's sake save their lives, and banish 'em. 3.06.251
swear 'em never more | to make me their 3.06.252
look upon 'em, | and, if you can love, end this 3.06.277
what will become of 'em? 3.06.288
by, and to 'em spoke | the prettiest posies — 4.01. 89
her — one of 'em | i knew to be your brother; 4.01.100
him, but i laugh at 'em | and let 'em all alone. 4.01.126
him, but i laugh at 'em | and let 'em all alone. 4.01.127
and fights | of gods and such men near 'em. 4.02. 25
love, and what young maid dare cross 'em? 4.02. 40
bring 'em in | quickly, by any means, i long to 4.02. 64
in | quickly, by any means, i long to see 'em. 4.02. 65
who saw 'em? 4.02. 70
his lineaments | are as a man would wish 'em, 4.02.114
to spy advantages, and where he finds 'em, 4.02.133
he finds 'em, | he's swift to make 'em his. 4.02.134
now, as i have a soul, i long to see 'em. 4.02.142
you have steel'd 'em with your beauty. 4.02.149
come, i'll go visit 'em. 4.02.152
now let 'em enter, and before the gods | tender 5.01. 1
hand will honor | the very powers that love 'em. 5.01. 7
that the sense | could not be judge between 'em. 5.03.128
since i know | their lives but pinch 'em. 5.03.133
sooner than such, to give us nectar with 'em, 5.04. 12
laid down, | you have sold 'em too too cheap. 5.04. 15
EMBALLING 1 FR 0.0001 REL FR 1 V 0 P
little england | you'ld venture an emballing. H8 2.03. 47
EMBALM 1 FR 0.0001 REL FR 1 V 0 P
embalm me, | then lay me forth. H8 4.02.170
EMBALMS 1 FR 0.0001 REL FR 1 V 0 P
this embalms and spices | to th' april day again TIM 4.03. 41
EMBAR *(see imbar)*
EMBARK 2 FR 0.0002 REL FR 2 V 0 P
but now he parted hence to embark for milan. TGV 1.01. 71
king at /hampton pier | embark his royalty; H5 3.pr. 5
EMBARK'D *(also inbark'd)*
EMBARK'D 4 FR 0.0004 REL FR 4 V 0 P
dromio, what stuff of mine hast thou embark'd? ERR 5.01.410
tower | and was embark'd to cross to burgundy, R3 1.04. 10
for he's embark'd | with such loud reason to the OTH 1.01.149
he embark'd at milford; CYM 3.06. 61
EMBARKED 2 FR 0.0002 REL FR 2 V 0 P
marking th' embarked traders on the flood; MND 2.01.127
on shore | gazing upon a late embarked friend, VEN 818
EMBARKS 1 FR 0.0001 REL FR 1 V 0 P
leaves tharsus and again embarks. PER 4.04. 27
EMBARQUEMENTS 1 FR 0.0001 REL FR 1 V 0 P
embarquements all of fury, shall lift up | their COR 1.10. 22
EMBASSADE 1 FR 0.0001 REL FR 1 V 0 P
when you disgrac'd me in my embassade | then i 3H6 4.03. 32
EMBASSADOR *(also ambassador, etc.)*
EMBASSADOR 7 FR 0.0008 REL FR 5 V 2 P
a horse to be embassador for an ass. LLL 3.01. 52 P
have not seen | so likely an embassador of love. MV 2.09. 92
the french embassador upon that instant | crav'd H5 1.01. 91
suppose th' embassador from the french comes 3.pr. 28
that he was the lord embassador | sent from a 2H6 3.02.276
th' bishop of bayonne, then french embassador, H8 2.04.173
it came from th' embassador that was bound for HAM 4.06. 10 P
EMBASSADORS 9 FR 0.0010 REL FR 9 V 0 P
your favors, embassadors of love; LLL 5.02.778
question your grace the late embassadors, | with H5 2.04. 31
embassadors from harry king of england | do 2.04. 65
yet call th' embassadors, and as you please, 1H6 5.01. 24
kingdom, | that know not how to use embassadors,
3H6 4.03. 36
as great embassadors | from foreign princes. H8 1.04. 55
th' embassadors from norway, my good lord, | are HAM 2.02. 40
give first admittance to th' embassadors; 2.02. 51
to th' embassadors of england gives | this 5.02.351
EMBASSAGE *(also ambassage)*

EMBASSAGE 5 FR 0.0005 REL FR 3 V 2 P
matter enough in me for such an embassage, and ADO 1.01.280 P
beard, do you any embassage to the pigmies, 2.01.269 P
that well by heart hath conn'd his embassage. LLL 5.02. 98
of foot, | doth not thy embassage belong to me, R2 3.04. 93
i every day expect an embassage | from my R3 2.01. 3
EMBASSIES 2 FR 0.0002 REL FR 1 V 1 P
letters, loving embassies, that they have seem'd WT 1.01. 28 P
fresh embassies and suits, | nor from the state COR 5.03. 17
EMBASSY *(also ambassy)*
EMBASSY 13 FR 0.0014 REL FR 13 V 0 P
for well you know here comes in embassy | the LLL 1.01.134
to whom he sends, and what's his embassy: 2.01. 3
we'll once more hear orsino's embassy. TN 1.05.166
silence, good mother, hear the embassy. JN 1.01. 6
my mouth, | the farthest limit of my embassy. 1.01. 22
and once dispatch'd him in an embassy | to 1.01. 99
stay for an answer to your embassy, | lest 2.01. 44
then go we in, to know his embassy; H5 1.01. 95
far off | the dolphin's meaning and our embassy? 1.02.240
with what great state he heard their embassy, 2.04. 32
and diomed | in ilion, on your greekish embassy. TRO 4.05.216
down the stream | in embassy to his mother. CYM 4.02.185
are gone | in tender embassy of love to thee, SON 45. 6
EMBATTAILED 1 FR 0.0001 REL FR 1 V 0 P
that were embattailed and rank'd in kent. JN 4.02.200
EMBATTLE 1 FR 0.0001 REL FR 1 V 0 P
and they say we shall embattle | by th' second ANT 4.09. 3
EMBATTLED 2 FR 0.0002 REL FR 1 V 1 P
now are too too strongly embattled against me. WIV 2.02.251 P
the english are embattled, you french peers. H5 4.02. 14
EMBAY'D 1 FR 0.0001 REL FR 1 V 0 P
turkish fleet | be not enshelter'd and embay'd, OTH 2.01. 18
EMBELLISH'D 1 FR 0.0001 REL FR 0 V 1 P
upon her nose, all o'er embellish'd with rubies, ERR 3.02.134 P
EMBER–EVES 1 FR 0.0001 REL FR 1 V 0 P
at festivals, | on ember–eves and holy/–ales; PER 1.ch. 6
EMBERS 2 FR 0.0002 REL FR 2 V 0 P
but pray you stir no embers up. ANT 2.02. 13
which, in pale embers hid, lurks to aspire | and LUC 5
EMBLAZE 1 FR 0.0001 REL FR 1 V 0 P
to emblaze the honor that thy master got. 2H6 4.10. 71
EMBLEM 2 FR 0.0002 REL FR 1 V 1 P
/with his cicatrice, an emblem of war, here on AWW 2.01. 43 P
it is the very emblem of a maid; TNK 2.02.137
EMBLEMS 1 FR 0.0001 REL FR 1 V 0 P
peace, and all such emblems | laid nobly on her; H8 4.01. 89
EMBODIED 1 FR 0.0001 REL FR 1 V 0 P
for i by vow am so embodied yours, | that she AWW 5.03.173
EMBOLDENS 1 FR 0.0001 REL FR 1 V 0 P
nothing emboldens sin so much as mercy. TIM 3.05. 3
EMBOLD'NED 2 FR 0.0002 REL FR 1 V 1 P
hath something embold'ned me to this unseason'd
WIV 2.02.167 P
soul | embold'ned with the glory of her praise, PER 1.01. 4
EMBOSS'D* 5 FR 0.0005 REL FR 3 V 2 P
(brach merriman, the poor cur, is emboss'd), SHR in.1. 17
but we have almost emboss'd him, you shall see AWW 3.06. 99 P
impudent, emboss'd rascal, if there were any 1H4 3.03.157 P
the boar of thessaly | was never so emboss'd. ANT 4.13. 3
he bears a charging–staff emboss'd with silver. TNK 4.02.140
EMBOSSED 3 FR 0.0003 REL FR 3 V 0 P
and all th' embossed sores and headed evils, AYL 2.07. 67
who once a day with his embossed froth | the TIM 5.01.217
a bile, | a plague–sore, or embossed carbuncle, LR 2.04.224
EMBOUNDED 1 FR 0.0001 REL FR 1 V 0 P
which was embounded in this beauteous clay, JN 4.03.137
EMBOWEL 1 FR 0.0001 REL FR 0 V 1 P
if thou embowel me to–day, i'll give you leave 1H4 5.04.111 P
EMBOWELL'D 4 FR 0.0004 REL FR 3 V 1 P
embowell'd of their doctrine, have left off AWW 1.03.241
embowell'd will i see thee by and by, | till 1H4 5.04.109
embowell'd! 5.04.111 P
makes his trough | in your embowell'd bosoms — R3 5.02. 10
EMBRAC'D 12 FR 0.0013 REL FR 7 V 5 P
instant of our encounter, after we had embrac'd, WIV 3.05. 73 P
what cannot be eschew'd must be embrac'd. 5.05.237
your brother and his lover have embrac'd. MM 1.04. 40
which though myself would gladly have embrac'd,
ERR 1.01. 69
and embrac'd, as it were, from the ends of WT 1.01. 30 P
the means that heavens yield must be embrac'd, R2 3.02. 29
you'll see your rome embrac'd with fire before COR 5.02. 7
their lips that their breaths embrac'd together. OTH 2.01.260 P
to, but weigh | what it is worth embrac'd. ANT 2.06. 33
find, and be embrac'd by a piece of tender air; CYM 5.04.139 P
find, and be embrac'd by a piece of tender air; 5.05.437 P
quoth she, "the warlike god embrac'd me," | and PP 11. 5
EMBRACE 76 FR 0.0086 REL FR 69 V 7 P
does now speak to thee, i embrace thy body, TMP 5.01.109
let me embrace thine age, whose honor cannot 5.01.121
let grief and sorrow still embrace his heart 5.01.214
now kiss, embrace, contend, do what you will. TGV 1.02.126
thurio, give back, or else embrace thy death; 5.04.126
embrace thy brother there, rejoice with him. ERR 5.01.414
you embrace your charge too willingly. ADO 1.01.103 P
you will say, she did embrace me as a husband, 4.01. 49
i do embrace your offer, and dispose | for 5.01.294
sweet lords, sweet lovers, o, let us embrace! LLL 4.03.210
you, | and you embrace th' occasion to depart. MV 1.01. 64
for your own sake to embrace your own safety, AYL 1.02.179 P
sweet kate, embrace her for her beauty's sake. SHR 4.05. 34
let me embrace with old vincentio, | and wander 4.05. 68
me, | whom i myself embrace to set him free." AWW 3.04. 17
let thy blood and spirit embrace them, and, to TN 2.05.147 P
do not embrace me till each circumstance | of 5.01.251
madam, i am most apt t' embrace your offer. 5.01.320
your gracious self, embrace but my direction, WT 4.04.523
embrace him, love him, give him welcome hither. JN 2.01. 11
and we must embrace | this gentle offer of the 4.03. 12
bondage, and embrace | his golden uncontroll'd R2 1.03. 89
god, | embrace each other's love in banishment, 1.03.184
night | i will embrace him with a soldier's arm 1H4 5.02. 73
of war, | and by that music let us all embrace, 5.02. 98
and i embrace this fortune patiently, | since 5.05. 12
let's drink together friendly and embrace, 2H4 4.02. 63
i embrace it. H5 4.01.206 P
embrace we then this opportunity | as fitting 1H6 2.01. 13

direct mine arms i may embrace his neck, | and 2.05. 37
and, lords, accept this hearty kind embrace. 3.03. 82
i do embrace thee, as i would embrace | the 5.03.171
thee, as i would embrace | the christian prince, 5.03.171
even thus two friends condemn'd | embrace, and 2H6 3.02.354
but where's the body that i should embrace? 4.04. 6
who loves the king, and will embrace his pardon, 4.08. 14
long live king henry! plantagenet, embrace him. 3H6 1.01.202
see, see, they join, embrace, and seem to kiss, 2.01. 29
warwick, | let me embrace thee in my weary arms. 2.03. 45
let me embrace /thee, sour /adversities, | for 3.01. 24
dorset, embrace him; R3 2.01. 25
come, grey, come, vaughan, let us here embrace. 3.03. 25
make me no more ado, but all embrace him. H8 5.02.193
i charge you, | embrace and love this man. 5.02.205
even such a passion doth embrace my bosom: TRO 3.02. 35
let me embrace too. 4.04. 15 P
let me embrace thee, ajax. 4.05.135
o, let an old man embrace thee, | and, worthy 4.05.199
let me embrace thee, good old chronicle, | that 4.05.202
thought he would | when first i did embrace him; COR 4.07. 10
thee, | i will embrace thee in it by and by. TIT 5.02. 69
and op'd their arms to embrace me as a friend. 5.03.108
arms, take your last embrace! ROM 5.03.113
whom this beneath world doth embrace and hug TIM 1.01. 44
spend less, and yet he would embrace no counsel, 3.01. 26 P
he would embrace the means to come by it. JC 2.01.259
must embrace the fate | of that dark hour. MAC 3.01.136
i embrace it freely, | and will this brother's HAM 5.02.252
for me, with sorrow i embrace my fortune. 5.02.388
then, | thou unsubstantial air that i embrace: LR 4.01. 7
i must embrace thee. 5.03.177
he knows that you embrace not antony | as you ANT 3.13. 56
i embrace these conditions, let us have articles CYM 1.04.156 P
doubtless | with joy he will embrace you; 3.04.176
i will embrace | your offer. PER 3.03. 37
i embrace you. 5.01.221
embrace him, dear thaisa, this is he. 5.03. 55
i do embrace you and your offer. TNK 3.01. 93
i embrace ye. 3.06.300
before i turn, let me embrace thee, cousin; 5.01. 31
which might accite thee to embrace and hug them,
STM III 16
her arms do lend his neck a sweet embrace; VEN 539
with this he breaketh from the sweet embrace 811
she wildly breaketh from their strict embrace, 874
enmity, | yet strive i to embrace mine infamy." LUC 504
swearing i slew him, seeing thee embrace him. 518

EMBRACED 2 FR 0.0002 REL FR 2 V 0 P
bay, | hugg'd and embraced by the strumpet wind!
MV 2.06. 16
him out | and quicken his embraced heaviness 2.08. 52

EMBRACEMENT 4 FR 0.0004 REL FR 4 V 0 P
friends, | bring them to our embracement. WT 5.01.114
how they clung | in their embracement, as they H8 1.01. 10
the issue is embracement. TRO 4.05.148
and, if one arm's embracement will content thee, TIT 5.02. 68

EMBRACEMENTS 8 FR 0.0009 REL FR 7 V 1 P
drew me from kind embracements of my spouse; ERR 1.01. 43
and then with kind embracements, tempting kisses
SHR in.1. 118
with thy embracements to my wive's allies, | and R3 2.01. 30
honor than in the embracements of his bed where
COR 1.03. 4 P
and cere up my embracements from a next | with CYM 1.01.116
a bride | for embracements even of jove himself; PER 1.01. 7
beating his kind embracements with her heels. VEN 312
that lends embracements unto every stranger. 790

EMBRACES 6 FR 0.0006 REL FR 5 V 1 P
or /hoop his body more with thy embraces, | i WT 4.04.439
then embraces his son–in–law; 5.02. 52 P
she embraces him. 5.03.111
the one and other diomed embraces. TRO 4.01. 15
the sweet embraces of a loving wife, | loaden TNK 2.02. 30
foe, that my embraces | might thank ye, not my 3.06. 22

EMBRACING 5 FR 0.0005 REL FR 4 V 1 P
and so locks her in embracing, as if she would WT 5.02. 77 P
lies, | coldly embracing the discolored earth, JN 2.01.306
hot, faint, and weary, with her hard embracing, VEN 559
the thorny brambles and embracing bushes, | as 629
and girdle with embracing flames the waist | of LUC 6

EMBRASURES 1 FR 0.0001 REL FR 1 V 0 P
forcibly prevents | our lock'd embrasures, TRO 4.04. 37

EMBROIDER'D 1 FR 0.0001 REL FR 1 V 0 P
sheep | than doth a rich embroider'd canopy | to 3H6 2.05. 44

EMBROIDERED 1 FR 0.0001 REL FR 1 V 0 P
kirtle | embroidered all with leaves of myrtle; PP 19.12

EMBROIDERY 1 FR 0.0001 REL FR 1 V 0 P
like sapphire, pearl, and rich embroidery, WIV 5.05. 71

EMERALD *(see em'rald)*

EMILIA 24 FR 0.0027 REL FR 23 V 1 P
emilia? WT 2.02. 12
your attendants, i | shall bring emilia forth. 2.02. 14
pray you, emilia; 2.02. 33
tell her, emilia, | i'll use that tongue i have. 2.02. 49
do not learn of him, emilia, though he be thy OTH 2.01.162 P
before emilia here, | i give thee warrant of thy 3.03. 19
emilia, come. 3.03. 88
where should i lose the handkerchief, emilia? 3.04. 23
beshrew me much, emilia, | i was (unhandsome 3.04.150
do not talk to me, emilia; 4.02.102
therefore, good emilia, | give me my nightly 4.03. 15
thou in conscience think — tell me, emilia — 4.03. 61
prithee, emilia, | go know of cassio where he 5.01.116
emilia, run you to the citadel, | and tell my 5.01.126
'tis emilia. 5.02. 91
o, come in, emilia. 5.02.103
and you, emilia — and you, friend — and all — TNK 2.05. 49
o queen emilia, | fresher than may, sweeter 3.01. 4
the happier thing to be | so near emilia. 3.01. 26
i love emilia, and in that i'll bury | thee and 3.06.126
that fortunate bright star, the fair emilia, 3.06.146
say, emilia, | if one of them were dead, as one 3.06.272
take emilia, | and with her all the world's joy. 5.04. 90
one kiss from fair emilia. 5.04. 94

EMILIA'S 1 FR 0.0001 REL FR 0 V 1 P
worse man than giraldo, emilia's schoolmaster. TNK 4.03. 13 P

EMILY 9 FR 0.0010 REL FR 9 V 0 P
emily, i hope | he shall not go afoot. TNK 2.05. 52
o lady fortune | (next after emily my sovereign) 3.01. 16
and do but say | that emily is thine, i will 3.01. 76
for emily, upon my life! 3.03. 42
i say again, | that sigh was breath'd for emily. 3.03. 44
and fair–ey'd emily, upon their knees | begg'd 4.01. 8
fairest emily, | the gods by their divine 5.03.106
emily, | to buy you i have lost what's dearest 5.03.111
mounted upon a steed that emily | did first 5.04. 49

EMINENCE 6 FR 0.0006 REL FR 6 V 0 P
place, | or in his eminence that fills it up, MM 1.02.164
which ever yet | affected eminence, wealth, H8 2.03. 29
sol | in noble eminence enthron'd and spher'd TRO 1.03. 90
you should not have the eminence of him, | but 2.03.255
present him eminence both with eye and tongue: MAC 3.02. 31
maugre thy strength, place, youth, and eminence, LR 5.03.132

EMINENT 6 FR 0.0006 REL FR 5 V 1 P
and by an eminent body that enforc'd | the law MM 4.04. 22
and bow'd his eminent top to their low ranks, AWW 1.02. 43
neither allied | to eminent assistants, but H8 1.01. 62
who stands so eminent in the degree of this OTH 2.01.237 P
one | an eminent monsieur that, it seems, much CYM 1.06. 65
a squire's cloth, | a pantler — not so eminent. 2.03.124

EMMANUEL 1 FR 0.0001 REL FR 0 V 1 P
emmanuel. 2H6 4.02. 99 P

EMPALE *(also impale)*

EMPALE 1 FR 0.0001 REL FR 1 V 0 P
empale him with your weapons round about, | in TRO 5.07. 5

EMPANELLED *(see impanelled)*

EMPATRON *(see enpatron)*

EMPERAL'S 1 FR 0.0001 REL FR 0 V 1 P
betwixt my uncle and one of the emperal's men. TIT 4.03. 94 P

EMPERESS *(also empress)*

EMPERESS 8 FR 0.0009 REL FR 8 V 0 P
family, | lavinia will i make my emperess, TIT 1.01.240
bride, | and will create thee emperess of rome. 1.01.320
and gold, | to wait upon this new–made emperess. 2.01. 20
rome's royal emperess, | unfurnish'd of her 2.03. 55
under your patience, gentle emperess, | 'tis 2.03. 66
and make proud saturnine and his emperess | beg 3.01.297
the emperess, the midwife, and yourself. 4.02.143
the child | and bear it from me to the emperess. 5.01. 54

EMPERIAL *(also imperial)*

EMPERIAL 1 FR 0.0001 REL FR 0 V 1 P
yea forsooth, and your mistriship be emperial. TIT 4.04. 40 P

EMPEROR 83 FR 0.0093 REL FR 77 V 6 P
he's a present for any emperor that ever trod on TMP 2.02. 70 P
attends the emperor in his royal court. TGV 1.03. 27
esteem | are journeying to salute the emperor, 1.03. 41
well–belov'd | and daily graced by the emperor; 1.03. 58
thou'rt an emperor — caesar, keiser, and WIV 1.03. 9 P
some say he is with the emperor of russia; MM 3.02. 88 P
the emperor of russia was my father. WT 3.02.119
there with the emperor | to treat of high JN 1.01.100
defend | my innocent life against an emperor. 4.03. 89
who was the son | to lewis the emperor, and H5 1.02. 76
bring home | to the tent–royal of their emperor. 1.02.196
as good a gentleman as the emperor. 4.01. 42
pope, | the emperor, and the earl of arminack? 1H6 5.01. 2
to th' old dam, treason), charles the emperor, H8 1.01.176
for i am sure the emperor | paid ere he promis'd 1.01.185
and pav'd with gold, the emperor thus desir'd, 1.01.188
and merely to revenge him on the emperor | for 2.01.162
crack'd the league | between us and the emperor 2.02. 25
when you went | ambassador to the emperor, you 3.02.318
you should be lord ambassador from the emperor, 4.02.109
them not | till saturninus be rome's emperor. TIT 1.01.205
crown him and say, "long live our emperor!" 1.01.229
create | lord saturninus rome's great emperor, 1.01.232
and say, "long live our emperor saturnine!" 1.01.233
the wide world's emperor, do i consecrate | my 1.01.248
now, madam, are you prisoner to an emperor; 1.01.258
traitor, restore lavinia to the emperor. 1.01.296
no, titus, no, the emperor needs her not, | nor 1.01.299
your noble emperor and his lovely bride, | sent 1.01.334
come, come, sweet emperor — come, andronicus — 1.01.456
and must advise the emperor for his good. 1.01.464
my word and promise to the emperor | that you 1.01.469
nay, nay, sweet emperor, we must all be friends. 1.01.479
and wake the emperor and his lovely bride, | and 2.02. 4
high emperor, upon my feeble knee | i beg this 2.03.288
my lord the emperor | sends thee this word — 3.01.150
o gracious emperor! 3.01.157
with all my heart i'll send the emperor my hand. 3.01.160
for that good hand thou sent'st the emperor. 3.01.235
belike for joy the emperor hath a son. 4.02. 50
the emperor in his rage will doom her death. 4.02.114
and let the emperor dandle him for his own. 4.02.161
this wicked emperor may have shipp'd her hence, 4.03. 23
we will afflict the emperor in his pride. 4.03. 63
him deliver the pigeons to the emperor from you. 4.03. 97 P
deliver an oration to the emperor with a grace? 4.03. 99 P
ado, | but give your pigeons to the emperor. 4.03.103
and when thou hast given it the emperor, | knock 4.03.118
ever seen | an emperor in rome thus overborne, 4.04. 2
empress i am, but yonder sits the emperor. 4.04. 41
they have wish'd that lucius were their emperor. 4.04. 77
then cheer thy spirit, for know thou, emperor, 4.04. 88
say that the emperor requests a parley | of 4.04.101
and now, sweet emperor, be blithe again, | and 4.04.111
signifies what hate they bear their emperor, 5.01. 3
villain, thou mightst have been an emperor. 5.01. 30
goths, | the roman emperor greets you all by me, 5.01.157
let the emperor give his pledges | unto my 5.01.163
sons, | the emperor himself and all thy foes, 5.02.117
tell him the emperor and the empress too | feast 5.02.127
whiles i go tell my lord the emperor | how i 5.02.138
i fear the emperor means no good to us. 5.03. 10
the trumpets show the emperor is at hand. 5.03. 16
rome's emperor, and nephew, break the parle, 5.03. 19
my lord the emperor, resolve me this: 5.03. 35
and bring our emperor gently in thy hand, 5.03.138
lucius our emperor, for well i know | the common 5.03.139
lucius, all hail, rome's royal emperor! 5.03.141
some loving friends convey the emperor hence, 5.03.191
in my lips | that i reviv'd and was an emperor. ROM 5.01. 9
your worm is your only emperor for diet: HAM 4.03. 21 P
ha, my brave emperor! ANT 2.07.103
nay, i have done, | here comes the emperor. 3.07. 20
o noble emperor, do not fight by sea, | trust 3.07. 61
the emperor calls canidius. 3.07. 79
your emperor | continues still a jove. 4.06. 27
o my brave emperor, this is fought indeed! 4.07. 4
my dear master, | my captain, and my emperor: 4.14. 90
i dreamt there was an emperor antony. 5.02. 76
it is the emperor, madam. 5.02.113
mingled sums | to buy a present for the emperor; CYM 1.06.187
my emperor hath wrote i must from hence, | and 3.05. 2
lucius hath wrote already to the emperor | how 3.05. 21

EMPEROR'S 20 FR 0.0022 REL FR 19 V 1 P
i will dispatch him to the emperor's court. TGV 1.03. 38
time | with valentinus in the emperor's court; 1.03. 67
love | as meet to be an emperor's counsellor. 2.04. 77
the emperor's coming in behalf of france, | to H5 5.pr. 38
with these our late–deceased emperor's sons. TIT 1.01.184
that you create our emperor's eldest son, | lord 1.01.224
where is the emperor's guard? 1.01.283
if the emperor's court can feast two brides, 1.01.489
so near the emperor's palace dare ye draw, | and 2.01. 46
though bassianus be the emperor's brother, 2.01. 88
the emperor's court is like the house of fame, 2.01.126
to attend the emperor's person carefully. 2.02. 8
why do the emperor's trumpets flourish thus? 4.02. 49
and be received for the emperor's heir, | and 4.02.158
and in the emperor's court | there is a queen, 5.02.104
were they that murd'red our emperor's brother, 5.03. 98
she might lie by an emperor's side and command OTH 4.01.185 P
the emperor's guard! ANT 4.14.129
this is the tenor of the emperor's writ: CYM 3.07. 1
the roman emperor's letters, | sent by a consul 4.02.384

EMPERY 6 FR 0.0006 REL FR 6 V 0 P
ruling in large and ample empery | o'er france H5 1.02.226
your right of birth, your empery, your own. R3 3.07.136
by friends | ambitiously for rule and empery, TIT 1.01. 19
voice, | in election for the roman empery, 1.01. 22
titus, thou shalt obtain and ask the empery. 1.01.201
fair, and fasten'd to an empery | would make the CYM 1.06.120

EMPHASIS 2 FR 0.0002 REL FR 2 V 0 P
what is he whose grief | bears such an emphasis, HAM 5.01.255
be chok'd with such another emphasis! ANT 1.05. 68

EMPIERCED *(see enpierced)*

EMPIRE 16 FR 0.0018 REL FR 16 V 0 P
blood and virtue | contend for empire in thee, AWW 1.01. 63
maid too virtuous | for the contempt of empire. 3.02. 32
had henry got an empire by his marriage, | and 2H6 1.01.153
the empire unpossess'd? R3 4.04.470
hue, | and name thee in election for the empire, TIT 1.01.183
that saidst i begg'd the empire at thy hands. 1.01.307
that beasts | may have the world in empire! TIM 4.03.392
upon whose influence neptune's empire stands HAM 1.01.119
kings, | a cutpurse of the empire and the rule, 3.04. 99
and the wide arch | of the rang'd empire fall! ANT 1.01. 34
to caesar, and commands | the empire of the sea. 1.02.185
he hath given his empire | up to a whore, who 3.06. 66
of me | as when mine empire was your fellow too, 4.02. 22
in top of all design, my mate in empire, 5.01. 43
and to the roman empire, promising | to pay our CYM 5.05.461
and from their wat'ry empire recollect | all PER 2.01. 50

EMPIRICS 1 FR 0.0001 REL FR 1 V 0 P
prostitute our past–cure malady | to empirics, AWW 2.01.122

EMPIRICUTIC 1 FR 0.0001 REL FR 0 V 1 P
prescription in galen is but empiricutic, and, COR 2.01.117 P

/EMPLOY 1 FR 0.0001 REL FR 1 V 0 P
/employ the countenance and grace of heav'n, 2H4 4.02. 24

EMPLOY 21 FR 0.0023 REL FR 18 V 3 P
there's some great matter she'ld employ me in. TGV 4.03. 3
and will employ thee in some service presently. 4.04. 41
we shall employ thee in a worthier place. MM 5.01.531
i must employ him in a letter to my love. LLL 3.01. 6 P
i must employ thee. 3.01.151 P
/allons! we will employ thee. 5.01.152 P
i must employ you in some business | against our MND 1.01.124
whiles i in this affair do thee employ, | i'll 3.02.374
and employ your chiefest thoughts | to courtship MV 2.08. 43
and i'll employ thee too. AYL 3.05. 96
for her, employ them all, | commend them and WT 4.04.376
your brother did employ my father much — JN 1.01. 96
employ thee then, sweet virgin, for our good. 1H6 3.03. 16
king, | and whatsoe'er you will employ me in, R3 1.01.108
when i have most need to employ a friend, | and 2.01. 36
and his commission to employ those soldiers, HAM 2.02. 74
we must straight employ you | against the OTH 1.03. 48
i will employ thee back again; ANT 3.03. 36
you shall please, | if you'll employ me to him. 5.02. 70
subject to, | when't pleas'd you to employ me. CYM 1.01.173
have need | t' employ you towards this roman. 2.03. 63

EMPLOY'D 24 FR 0.0027 REL FR 23 V 1 P
you shall be employ'd | to hasten on his TGV 1.03. 76
vassal, have employ'd and pain'd | your unknown MM 5.01.386
you cannot better be employ'd, bassanio, | than MV 4.01.117
sir, be better employ'd and be naught a while. AYL 1.01. 35 P
than thine own gladness that thou art employ'd. 3.05. 98
whom i employ'd was pre–employ'd by him: WT 2.01. 49
your tale must be how he employ'd my mother. JN 1.01. 98
apt, liable to be employ'd in danger, | i 4.02.226
for i myself at this time have employ'd him. 1H4 2.04.513
precinct | i was employ'd in passing to and fro, 1H6 2.01. 69
i should have begg'd i might have been employ'd. 4.01. 72
'tis meet that lucky ruler be employ'd — 2H6 3.01.291
but you, my lord, were glad to be employ'd, | to 3.02.273
while you are thus employ'd, what resteth more, 3H6 1.02. 44
wherein thyself shalt highly be employ'd. R3 3.01.180
how is the king employ'd? H8 2.02. 14
employ'd you where high profits might come home, 3.02.158
ajax employ'd plucks down achilles' plumes. TRO 1.03.385
you know a sword employ'd is perilous, | and 2.02. 40
and, lavinia, thou shalt be employ'd; TIT 3.01.281
marry, for justice, she is so employ'd, | he 4.03. 40
tell us, old man, how shall we be employ'd? 5.02.149
year, must be employ'd | now to guard sure their TIM 3.03. 38
for i remember now | how he's employ'd; ANT 5.01. 72

EMPLOYED 3 FR 0.0003 REL FR 3 V 0 P
and these, and all, are all amiss employed. R2 2.03.132
you thus employed, i will go root away | the 3.04. 37
your son in scotland being thus employed, 1H4 1.03.265

EMPLOYER 1 FR 0.0001 REL FR 0 V 1 P

swimmer, troilus the first employer of pandars, ADO 5.02. 31 P
/EMPLOYMENT 1 FR 0.0001 REL FR 1 V 0 P
/they /did /make /love /to /this /employment, HAM 5.02. 57
EMPLOYMENT 19 FR 0.0021 REL FR 10 V 9 P
and fit for great employment, worthy lord. TGV 5.04.157
a jack–a–lent, when 'tis upon ill employment! WIV 5.05.127 P
you have no employment for me? ADO 2.01.271 P
proud of employment, willingly i go. LLL 2.01. 35
"your ladyship's in all desired employment, 4.02.136 P
not much employment for you. you understand me? AWW 2.02. 68 P
what employment have we here? TN 2.05. 82 P
his employment between his lord and my niece 3.04.186 P
at your employment, at your service, sir." JN 1.01.198
is there not employment? 2H4 1.02. 73 P
being upon hasty employment in the king's 2.01.128 P
famine, sword, and fire | crouch for employment. H5 pr 8
the card'nal instantly will find employment, H8 2.01. 48
a ring that i must use | in dear employment — ROM 5.03. 32
at duty, more than i could frame employment; TIM 4.03.262
the hand of little employment hath the daintier HAM 5.01. 69 P
king, | on whose employment i was sent to you. LR 2.02.129
thy great employment | will not bear question; 5.03. 32
but to win time | to lose so bad employment, in CYM 3.04.110
EMPLOYMENTS 2 FR 0.0002 REL FR 1 V 1 P
the which he hath detain'd for lewd employments, R2 1.01. 90
undergo those employments wherein i should have CYM 3.05.110 P
EMPOISON 1 FR 0.0001 REL FR 1 V 0 P
know | how much an ill word may empoison liking. ADO 3.01. 86
EMPOISON'D 1 FR 0.0001 REL FR 1 V 0 P
so | as with a man by his own alms empoison'd, COR 5.06. 10
/EMPRESS' 1 FR 0.0001 REL FR 1 V 0 P
/like /to /the /empress' /moor, /therefore /i TIT 3.02. 67
EMPRESS' 13 FR 0.0014 REL FR 13 V 0 P
he is as worthy for an empress' love | as meet TGV 2.04. 76
and think thee worthy of an empress' love. 5.04.141
that have their alms out of the empress' chest. TIT 2.03. 9
boy | shall carry from me to the empress' sons 4.01.115
our empress' shame, and stately rome's disgrace! 4.02. 60
and secretly to greet the empress' friends. 4.02.174
who should find them but the empress' villain? 4.03. 74
who, when he knows thou art the empress' babe, 5.01. 35
is the pearl that pleas'd your empress' eye, 5.01. 42
good lord, how like the empress' sons they are! 5.02. 64
the empress' sons i take them, chiron, demetrius 5.02.154
villains, forbear, we are the empress' sons. 5.02.162
till he be brought unto the empress' face | for 5.03. 7
EMPRESS *(also emperess)*
EMPRESS 28 FR 0.0031 REL FR 27 V 1 P
o sweet maria, empress of my love, | these LLL 4.03. 54
were now the general of our gracious empress, H5 5.pr. 30
of your heart with the looks of an empress, take 5.02.236 P
more like an empress than duke humphrey's wife. 2H6 1.03. 78
rise, titus, rise, my empress hath prevail'd. TIT 1.01.459
and should the empress know | this discord's 2.01. 69
come, our empress, with her sacred wit | to 2.01.120
hark, tamora, the empress of my soul, | which 2.03. 40
no more, great empress, bassianus comes. 2.03. 52
but were our witty empress well afoot, | she 4.02. 29
the empress sends it thee, thy stamp, thy seal, 4.02. 69
tell the empress from me, i am of age | to keep 4.02.104
aaron, what shall i say unto the empress? 4.02.128
and no one else but the delivered empress. 4.02.142
go to the empress, tell her this i said. 4.02.145
empress i am, but yonder sits the emperor. 4.04. 41
first know thou, i begot him on the empress. 5.01. 87
and when i told the empress of this sport, | she 5.01.118
that i know thee well | for our proud empress, 5.02. 26
and you, the empress! 5.02. 65
how like the empress and her sons you are! 5.02. 84
for well i wot the empress never wags | but in 5.02. 87
i will bring in the empress and her sons, | the 5.02.116
tell him the emperor and the empress too | feast 5.02.127
to entertain your highness and your empress. 5.03. 32
madam, o good empress! ANT 3.11. 33
royal egypt! | empress! 4.15. 71
most noble empress, you have heard of me? 5.02. 71
EMPTIED 2 FR 0.0002 REL FR 2 V 0 P
then | be emptied to redeem a traitor home? 1H4 1.03. 86
have emptied all their fountains in my well, LC 255
/EMPTIER 1 FR 0.0001 REL FR 1 V 0 P
/the /emptier /ever /dancing /in /the /air, R2 4.01.186
EMPTIER 1 FR 0.0001 REL FR 0 V 1 P
weaker vessel, as they say, the emptier vessel. 2H4 2.04. 60 P
EMPTIES 2 FR 0.0002 REL FR 2 V 0 P
and then his state | empties itself, as doth an MV 5.01. 96
and whoso empties them | by so much fills their R2 2.02.130
EMPTINESS 3 FR 0.0003 REL FR 3 V 0 P
sound | with hollow poverty and emptiness. 2H4 1.03. 75
the full caesar will | answer his emptiness! ANT 3.13. 36
oppos'd, | should make desire vomit emptiness, CYM 1.06. 45
EMPTY 53 FR 0.0060 REL FR 41 V 12 P
cried, "hell is empty, | and all the devils are TMP 1.02.214
foison plenty, | barns and garners never empty; 4.01.111
and there empty it in the muddy ditch close by WIV 3.03. 15 P
empty the basket, i say! 4.02.143 P
heaven hath my empty words, | whilst my MM 2.04. 2
and i shall find you empty of that fault, LLL 5.02.868
the fold stands empty in the drowned field, MND 2.01. 96
within whose empty eye | there is a written MV 2.07. 63
pity, void and empty | from any dram of mercy. 4.01. 5
be better supplied when i have made it empty. AYL 1.02.193 P
that in civility thou seem'st so empty? 2.07. 93
glass, by filling the one doth empty the other. 5.01. 42 P
my falcon now is sharp and passing empty, | and SHR 4.01.190
are empty trunks o'erflourish'd by the devil. TN 3.04.370
an empty casket, where the jewel of life | by JN 5.01. 40
not with the empty hollowness, but weight. R2 1.02. 59
see | but empty lodgings and unfurnish'd walls, 1.02. 68
yea, on his part i'll empty all these veins, 1H4 1.03.133
arthur first in court" — empty the jordan. 2H4 2.04. 34 P
can a weak empty vessel bear such a huge full 2.04. 62 P
dost thou so hunger for mine empty chair | that 4.05. 94
that england, being empty of defense, | hath H5 1.02.153
so full a voice issue from so empty a heart; 4.04. 68 P
"the empty vessel makes the greatest sound." 4.04. 69 P
an empty eagle were set | to guard the chicken 2H6 3.01.248
and dead men's cries do fill the empty air, 5.02. 4
and like an empty eagle | tire on the flesh of 3H6 1.01.268
from cold and empty veins where no blood dwells. R3 1.02. 59
and would not let it forth | to find the empty, 1.04. 39
is the chair empty? 4.04.469
nor my wishes | more worth than empty vanities; H8 2.03. 69
present, and behold | that chair stand empty; 5.02. 45
sharp /at reasons, | you are so empty of them. TRO 2.02. 34
to thy senses | as infants empty of all thought! 4.02. 6
her chariot is an empty hazel–nut, | made by the ROM 1.04. 59
his shelves | a beggarly account of empty boxes, 5.01. 45
far | than empty tigers or the roaring sea. 5.03. 39
lo his house | is empty on the back of montague, 5.03.204
great gifts, | and all out of an empty coffer; TIM 1.02.193
faith, nothing but an empty box, sir, which, in 3.01. 16 P
lordship that i return'd you an empty messenger. 3.06. 37 P
false vows with him, | like empty purses pick'd; 4.02. 12
and turn him off | (like to the empty ass) to JC 4.01. 26
shade, and there | weep our sad bosoms empty. MAC 4.03. 2
his purse is empty already: HAM 5.02.130 P
the town is empty; OTH 2.01. 53
have empty left their orbs, and shot their fires ANT 3.13.146
fear not, 'tis empty of all things but grief. CYM 3.04. 69
this cloten was a fool, an empty purse, | there 4.02.113
purse and brain both empty; 5.04.164 P
empty | old receptacles, or common shores, of PER 4.06.174
even as an empty eagle, sharp by fast, | tires VEN 55
their mistress mounted through the empty skies, 1191
EMPTY–HEARTED 1 FR 0.0001 REL FR 1 V 0 P
nor are those empty–hearted whose low sounds LR 1.01.153
EMPTYING 3 FR 0.0003 REL FR 3 V 0 P
emptying our bosoms of their counsel /sweet, MND 1.01.216
of us, | the emptying of our fathers' luxury, H5 3.05. 6
th' untimely emptying of the happy throne, | and MAC 4.03. 68
EM'RALD 2 FR 0.0002 REL FR 2 V 0 P
soit qui mal y pense" write | in em'rald tuffs, WIV 5.05. 70
the deep–green em'rald, in whose fresh regard LC 213
EMULATE 2 FR 0.0002 REL FR 1 V 1 P
i see how thine eye would emulate the diamond. WIV 3.03. 55 P
thereto prick'd on by a most emulate pride, HAM 1.01. 83
EMULATION 11 FR 0.0012 REL FR 10 V 1 P
the scholar's melancholy, which is emulation; AYL 4.01. 11 P
keep off aloof with worthless emulation. 1H6 4.04. 21
for emulation who shall now be nearest | will R3 2.03. 25
envious fever | of pale and bloodless emulation, TRO 1.03.134
slept, | whilst emulation in the army crept: 2.02.212
for emulation hath a thousand sons | that one by 3.03.156
forbids | a gory emulation 'twixt us twain. 4.05.123
horns a' th' moon, | /shouting their emulation. COR 1.01.214
mine emulation | hath not that honor in't it had 1.10. 12
cannot live | out of the teeth of emulation. JC 2.03. 14
side, | seeing such emulation in their woe, LUC 1808
EMULATIONS 1 FR 0.0001 REL FR 1 V 0 P
a cause | such factious emulations shall arise! 1H6 4.01.113
EMULATOR 1 FR 0.0001 REL FR 0 V 1 P
an envious emulator of every man's good parts, a AYL 1.01.143 P
EMULOUS 5 FR 0.0005 REL FR 4 V 1 P
good quarrel to draw emulous factions and bleed TRO 2.03. 73 P
he is not emulous, as achilles is. 2.03.231
late, | made emulous missions 'mongst the gods 3.03.189
but in mine emulous honor let him die, | with 4.01. 29
two emulous philomels beat the ear o' th' night TNK 5.03.124
EN *(also in)*
/EN 1 FR 0.0001 REL FR 0 V 1 P
and vetch me in my closet /une /boite /en verd, WIV 1.04. 46 P
EN 7 FR 0.0008 REL FR 0 V 7 P
alice, tu as ete en angleterre, et tu bien H5 3.04. 1 P
comment appelez–vous la main en anglois? 3.04. 5 P
sauf votre honneur, en verite, vous prononcez 3.04. 37 P
par la grace de dieu, et en peu de temps. 3.04. 41 P
de most sage demoiselle dat is en france. 5.02.219 P
votre /grandeur en baisant la main d'une (notre 5.02.254 P
i cannot tell wat is /baiser en anglish. 5.02.262 P
ENACT 3 FR 0.0003 REL FR 1 V 2 P
i have from their confines call'd to enact | my TMP 4.01.121
what did you enact? HAM 3.02.102 P
i did enact julius caesar. 3.02.103 P
ENACTED 5 FR 0.0005 REL FR 5 V 0 P
it is enacted in the laws of venice, | if it be MV 4.01.348
enacted wonders with his sword and lance: 1H6 1.01.122
too, | hath been enacted through your enmity. 3.01.116
charles, and the rest, it is enacted thus: 5.04.123
good end | for lawful policy remains enacted. LUC 529
ENACTS 2 FR 0.0002 REL FR 2 V 0 P
the king enacts more wonders than a man, R3 5.04. 2
the close enacts and counsels of thy heart! TIT 4.02.118
ENACTURES 1 FR 0.0001 REL FR 1 V 0 P
their own enactures with themselves destroy. HAM 3.02.197
ENAMELL'D 3 FR 0.0003 REL FR 3 V 0 P
he makes sweet music with th' enamell'd stones, TGV 2.07. 28
and there the snake throws her enamell'd skin, MND 2.01.255
th' enamell'd knacks o' th' mead or garden! TNK 3.01. 7
ENAMELLED 1 FR 0.0001 REL FR 1 V 0 P
i see the jewel best enamelled | will lose his ERR 2.01.109
/ENAMOR'D 1 FR 0.0001 REL FR 1 V 0 P
/are /now /become /enamor'd /on /his /grave. 2H4 1.03.102
ENAMOR'D 3 FR 0.0003 REL FR 2 V 1 P
he is enamor'd on hero. ADO 2.01.164 P
methought i was enamor'd of an ass. MND 4.01. 77
affliction is enamor'd of thy parts, | and thou ROM 3.03. 2
ENAMORED 2 FR 0.0002 REL FR 2 V 0 P
mine ear is much enamored of thy note; MND 3.01.138
i think thou art enamored | on his follies. 1H4 5.02. 69
ENCAGED *(see incaged)*
ENCAMP 3 FR 0.0003 REL FR 3 V 0 P
beyond the river we'll encamp ourselves, | and H5 3.06.171
bid him encamp his soldiers where they are. TIT 5.02.126
two such opposed kings encamp them still | in ROM 2.03. 27
ENCAMP'D 3 FR 0.0003 REL FR 2 V 1 P
what, is the king encamp'd? 1H4 4.02. 76 P
thy brother being carelessly encamp'd, | his 3H6 4.02. 14
encamp'd in hearts, but fighting outwardly. LC 203
ENCAVE 1 FR 0.0001 REL FR 1 V 0 P
do but encave yourself, | and mark the fleers, OTH 4.01. 81
ENCELADUS 1 FR 0.0001 REL FR 1 V 0 P
i tell you, younglings, not enceladus, | with TIT 4.02. 93
ENCHAF'D 1 FR 0.0001 REL FR 1 V 0 P
their royal blood enchaf'd, as the rud'st wind CYM 4.02.174
ENCHAFED 1 FR 0.0001 REL FR 1 V 0 P
like molestation view | on the enchafed flood. OTH 2.01. 17
ENCHAINED 1 FR 0.0001 REL FR 1 V 0 P
fortunes, and enchained me | to endless date of LUC 934
ENCHANT 5 FR 0.0005 REL FR 5 V 0 P
now i want | spirits to enforce, art to enchant, TMP ep 14
speak, pucelle, and enchant him with thy words. 1H6 3.03. 40
i will enchant the old andronicus | with words TIT 4.04. 89
"bid me discourse, i will enchant thine ear, VEN 145
each eye that saw him did enchant the mind, LC 89
ENCHANTED 6 FR 0.0006 REL FR 6 V 0 P
or some enchanted trifle to abuse me | (as late TMP 5.01.112
that all eyes saw his eyes enchanted with gazes. LLL 2.01.247
medea gathered the enchanted herbs | that did MV 5.01. 13
damn'd as thou art, thou hast enchanted her, OTH 1.02. 63
owe | enchanted tarquin answers with surmise, LUC 83
of young, of old, and sexes both enchanted, | to LC 128
ENCHANTING 8 FR 0.0009 REL FR 8 V 0 P
of such enchanting presence and discourse, ERR 3.02.161
tongue | doth ravish like enchanting harmony; LLL 1.01.167
/these your white enchanting fingers touch'd, TRO 3.01.151
sung | sweet varied notes, enchanting every ear! TIT 3.01. 86
in a ring, | enchanting all that you put in. MAC 4.01. 43
i must from this enchanting queen break off; ANT 1.02.128
these lovely caves, these round enchanting pits, VEN 247
whose enchanting story | the credulous old priam LUC 1521
ENCHANTINGLY 1 FR 0.0001 REL FR 0 V 1 P
noble device, of all sorts enchantingly belov'd, AYL 1.01.168 P
ENCHANTMENT 2 FR 0.0002 REL FR 2 V 0 P
send, | after the last enchantment you did here, TN 3.01.112
and you, enchantment — | worthy enough a WT 4.04.434
ENCHANTRESS 1 FR 0.0001 REL FR 1 V 0 P
fell banning hag, enchantress, hold thy tongue! 1H6 5.03. 42
ENCHANTS 2 FR 0.0002 REL FR 2 V 0 P
relish is so sweet | that it enchants my sense; TRO 3.02. 20
witch | that he enchants societies into him; CYM 1.06.167
ENCHAS'D 1 FR 0.0001 REL FR 1 V 0 P
enchas'd with all the honors of the world? 2H6 1.02. 8
ENCIRCLE 1 FR 0.0001 REL FR 1 V 0 P
then let them all encircle him about, | and, WIV 4.04. 57
ENCIRCLED 1 FR 0.0001 REL FR 1 V 0 P
encircled you to hear with reverence | your 2H4 4.02. 6
ENCLOG 1 FR 0.0001 REL FR 1 V 0 P
traitors ensteep'd to enclog the guiltless keel, OTH 2.01. 70
ENCLOS'D 3 FR 0.0003 REL FR 3 V 0 P
deum, | the dead with charity enclos'd in clay; H5 4.08.124
spoil, | whilst we by antony are all enclos'd. JC 5.03. 8
all simplicity, | here enclos'd, in cinders lie. PHT 55
ENCLOSE 2 FR 0.0002 REL FR 2 V 0 P
eye, o coz, | what passion would enclose thee! TNK 3.01. 30
o, in what sweets dost thou thy sins enclose! SON 95. 4
ENCLOSED 5 FR 0.0005 REL FR 5 V 0 P
that lies enclosed in this trunk which you WT 1.02.435
enclosed were they with their enemies. 1H6 1.01.136
titinius is enclosed round about | with horsemen JC 5.03. 28
to see th' enclosed lights, now canopied | under CYM 2.02. 21
blind they are, and keep themselves enclosed. LUC 378
ENCLOSES 2 FR 0.0002 REL FR 2 V 0 P
in their pure ranks his traitor eye encloses, LUC 73
flame through water which their hue encloses. LC 287
ENCLOSETH 1 FR 0.0001 REL FR 1 V 0 P
even so thy breast encloseth my poor heart: R3 1.02.204
ENCLOSING 1 FR 0.0001 REL FR 0 V 1 P
suffolk, for enclosing the commons of melford." 2H6 1.03. 21 P
ENCLOUDED 1 FR 0.0001 REL FR 1 V 0 P
rank of gross diet, shall we be enclouded, | and ANT 5.02.212
ENCOMPASS'D 7 FR 0.0008 REL FR 6 V 1 P
ford and mistress page, have i encompass'd you? WIV 2.02.153 P
encompass'd with thy lustful paramours! 1H6 3.02. 53
or as a bear, encompass'd round with dogs, | who 3H6 2.01. 15
that sought to be encompass'd with your crown. 2.02. 3
that her wide walks encompass'd but one man? JC 1.02.155
rushes and the reeds | had so encompass'd it. TNK 4.01. 62
fly, | or one encompass'd with a winding maze, LUC 1151
ENCOMPASSED 1 FR 0.0001 REL FR 1 V 0 P
thousand of the french | was round encompassed, 1H6 1.01.114
ENCOMPASSETH 1 FR 0.0001 REL FR 1 V 0 P
look how my ring encompasseth thy finger, | even R3 1.02.203
ENCOMPASSMENT 1 FR 0.0001 REL FR 1 V 0 P
by this encompassment and drift of question HAM 2.01. 10
ENCORE 1 FR 0.0001 REL FR 0 V 1 P
encore qu'il est contre son jurement de H5 4.04. 50 P
ENCOUNTER 55 FR 0.0062 REL FR 40 V 15 P
fair encounter | of two most rare affections! TMP 3.01. 74
and these fresh nymphs encounter every one | in 4.01.137
lords | at this encounter do so much admire 5.01.154
that every day with parle encounter me, | in thy TGV 1.02. 5
comes me in the instant of our encounter, after WIV 3.05. 73 P
die, | i will encounter darkness as a bride, MM 3.01. 83
if the encounter acknowledge itself hereafter, 3.01.251 P
world is to avoid cost, and you encounter it. ADO 1.01. 98 P
force | and strong encounter of my amorous tale; 1.01.325
afar off in the orchard this amiable encounter. 3.03.151 P
i mean, i did encounter that obscene and most LLL 1.01.241 P
is like th' encounter of two dog–apes; AYL 2.05. 27 P
be remov'd with earthquakes, and so encounter. 3.02.186 P
you | to give you over at this first encounter, SHR 1.02.105
that with your strange encounter much amaz'd me, 4.05. 54
let not your hate encounter with my love | for AWW 1.03.208
appoints him an encounter; 3.07. 32
will you encounter the house? TN 3.01. 74 P
good time encounter her! WT 2.01. 20
thou refuse | and wilt encounter with my wrath, 2.03.139
with what encounter so uncurrent i | have 3.02. 49
i never heard of such another encounter, which 5.02. 57 P
and let belief and life encounter so | as doth JN 3.01. 31
is danger | that we may arm us to encounter it. R2 5.03. 48
he never did encounter with glendower. 1H4 1.03.114
if they scape from your encounter, then they 2.02. 62 P
soul | shall pay full dearly for this encounter, 5.01. 84
hath sent out | a speedy power to encounter you, 2H4 1.01.133
if thou encounter any such, apprehend him, and H5 4.07.157 P
that charles the dolphin may encounter them. 1H6 3.02. 9
in field | should not be able to encounter mine. 3H6 4.08. 36

that will encounter with our glorious sun, | ere 5.03. 5
to leave this keen encounter of our wits | and R3 1.02.115
at our last encounter, | the duke of buckingham H8 4.01. 4
think, should we encounter | as often as we eat. COR 1.10. 9
if they shall encounter such ridiculous subjects 2.01. 85 P
fortunate thus accidentally to encounter you. 4.03. 38 P
habiliment, | i will encounter with andronicus, TIT 5.02. 2
nor bide th' encounter of assailing eyes, | nor ROM 1.01.213
and is he a man to encounter tybalt? 2.04. 17 P
both | receive in either by this dear encounter. 2.06. 29
upon the next encounter yields him ours. JC 1.03.156
they encounter thee with their hearts' thanks. MAC 3.04. 9
i behind an arras then, | mark the encounter: HAM 2.02.164
we may of their encounter frankly judge, | and 3.01. 33
out of an habit of encounter, a kind of /yesty 5.02.190 P
in the quarrel's right, rous'd to th' encounter, LR 2.01. 54
italy, | upon the first encounter, drave them. ANT 1.02. 94
till which encounter, | it is my business too. 1.04. 79
t' encounter me with orisons, for then | i am in CYM 1.03. 32
hell should at one time | encounter such revolt. 1.06.112
oppose and she | should from encounter guard. 2.05. 19
her champion mounted for the hot encounter: VEN 596
if thou encounter with the boar to–morrow. 672
or at the roe which no encounter dare; 676

ENCOUNTER'D 1 FR 0.0001 REL FR 1 V 0 P
well encounter'd! CYM 3.06. 65

ENCOUNTERED 1 FR 0.0001 REL FR 1 V 0 P
of thy first fight, i soon encountered, | and 1H6 4.06. 18

ENCOUNTERERS 1 FR 0.0001 REL FR 1 V 0 P
o, these encounterers, so glib of tongue, | that TRO 4.05. 58

ENCOUNTERS 6 FR 0.0006 REL FR 4 V 2 P
the loose encounters of lascivious men: TGV 2.07. 41
confess'd the vile encounters they have had | a ADO 4.01. 93
encounters mounted are | against your peace. LLL 5.02. 82
separation of their society, their encounters WT 1.01. 26 P
it shall not speak of your pretty encounters, TRO 3.02.209 P
dreamt of encounters 'twixt thyself and me; COR 4.05.123

ENCOUNT'RED 16 FR 0.0018 REL FR 11 V 5 P
leagues, | we were encount'red by a mighty rock, ERR 1.01.101
"that have so oft encount'red him with scorn, ADO 2.03.128 P
men of peace, well encount'red. LLL 5.01. 34 P
him shall at home be encount'red with a shame as AWW 4.03. 70 P
you are well encount'red here, my cousin mowbray 2H4 4.02. 1
when ladies crave to be encount'red with. 1H6 2.02. 46
once i encount'red him, and thus i said: 4.07. 37
he shall be encount'red with a man as good as 2H6 4.02.116 P
but match to match i have encount'red him, | and 5.02. 10
whom i encount'red as the battles join'd. 3H6 1.01. 15
in blood of those that had encount'red him. 1.04. 13
face | blushing to be encount'red with a cloud. TIT 2.04. 32
that i am thus encount'red | with clamorous TIM 2.02. 36
were my thoughts tiring when we encount'red. 3.06. 5 P
middle of the night, | been thus encount'red. HAM 1.02.199
that was thus good | encount'red yet his better. TNK 5.03.123

ENCOUNT'RING 2 FR 0.0002 REL FR 2 V 0 P
like vassalage at /unawares encount'ring | the TRO 3.02. 38
our powers, with smiling fronts encount'ring, COR 1.06. 8

ENCOURAG'D 1 FR 0.0001 REL FR 1 V 0 P
come on refresh'd, new–added, and encourag'd; JC 4.03.209

ENCOURAGE 4 FR 0.0004 REL FR 3 V 1 P
let us go thank him, and encourage him. AYL 1.02.240
my dilemmas, encourage myself in my certainty, AWW 3.06. 75 P
with | reward did threaten and encourage him, WT 3.02.164
encourage him, and tell him all our reasons; R3 3.01.175

ENCOURAGEMENT 2 FR 0.0002 REL FR 1 V 1 P
as well for the encouragement of the like, which MM 1.02.187 P
lines of fair comfort and encouragement. R3 5.02. 6

ENCOURAGING 1 FR 0.0001 REL FR 1 V 0 P
as 'twere encouraging the greeks to fight, LUC 1402

ENCRIMSON'D 1 FR 0.0001 REL FR 1 V 0 P
in bloodless white and the encrimson'd mood, LC 201

ENCROACHING 1 FR 0.0001 REL FR 1 V 0 P
king | and lofty, proud, encroaching tyranny, 2H6 4.01. 96

ENCUMB'RED 1 FR 0.0001 REL FR 1 V 0 P
with arms encumb'red thus, or this headshake, HAM 1.05.174

/END* 3 FR 0.0003 REL FR 3 V 0 P
possession of the bride, | /end ere i do begin. AWW 2.05. 27
/end in one purpose, and be all well borne H5 1.02.212
/and /in /the /end /meet /the /old /course /of LR 3.07.101

END* 336 FR 0.0379 REL FR 255 V 81 P
at | which end o' th' beam should bow. TMP 2.01.132
the latter end of his commonwealth forgets the 2.01.158 P
and with each end of thy blue bow dost crown 4.01. 80
at the farthest | in the very end of harvest! 4.01.115
shortly shall all my labors end, and thou 4.01.264
to work mine end upon their senses that | this 5.01. 53
for what i will, i will, and there an end. TGV 1.03. 65
letter hath she deliver'd, and there an end. 2.01.162 P
you always end ere you begin. 2.04. 31 P
a slave, that still an end turns me to shame! 4.04. 62
go thou with her to the west end of the wood; 5.03. 9
i'll woo you like a soldier, at arms' end, | and 5.04. 57
if i were young again, the sword should end it. WIV 1.01. 41 P
is petter that friends is the sword, and end it; 1.01. 43 P
we three to hear it and end it between them. 1.01.142 P
i will make an end of my dinner; 1.02. 12 P
in faith, at the latter end of a sea–coal fire. 1.04. 9 P
hard by, at street end; he will be here anon. 4.02. 39 P
degrees, | but here they live, to end. MM 2.02. 99
my troth, i'll go with thee to the lane's end. 4.03.178 P
for 'tis a physic | that's bitter to sweet end. 4.06. 8
for truth is truth | to th' end of reck'ning. 5.01. 46
and by the doom of death end woes and all. ERR 1.01. 2
my woes end likewise with the evening sun. 1.01. 27
that the world may witness that my end | was 1.01. 33
fast'ned ourselves at either end the mast, | and 1.01. 85
but here must end the story of my life, | and 1.01.137
wend, | but to procrastinate his liveless end. 1.01.158
and therefore, to the world's end, will have 2.02.107 P
house, go thou | and buy a rope's end; 4.01. 16
and told thee to what purpose and what end. 4.01. 97
you sent me for a rope's end as soon: 4.01. 98
to what end did i bid thee hie thee home? 4.04. 15
to a rope's end, sir, and to that end am i 4.04. 16
rope's end, sir, and to that end am i return'd. 4.04. 16
and to that end, sir, i will welcome you. 4.04. 17
respice finem, respect your end, or rather, the 4.04. 41 P
like the parrot, "beware the rope's end." 4.04. 43 P
you always end with a jade's trick, i know you ADO 1.01.144 P
was't not to this end | that thou began'st to 1.01.310
graces will appear, and there's an end. 2.01.124 P
grace command me any service to the world's end? 2.01.264 P
to what end? 2.03.156 P
this is the end of the charge: 3.03. 74 P
what is the end of study, let me know. LLL 1.01. 55
but to jig off a tune at the tongue's end, 3.01. 12 P
you withal, to the end to crave your assistance. 5.01.116 P
thumb, he is not so big as the end of his club. 5.01.132 P
therefore i'll darkly end the argument. 5.02. 23
were, and to what end | their shallow shows and 5.02.304
speak for yourselves, my wit is at an end. 5.02.430
for the latter end of his name. 5.02.627 P
humors | even to the opposed end of our intents; 5.02.758
at the twelvemonth's end | i'll change my black 5.02.833
our wooing doth not end like an old play: 5.02.874
a twelvemonth an' a day, | and then 'twill end. 5.02.878
it should have followed in the end of our show. 5.02.888 P
thy love ne'er alter till thy sweet life end! MND 2.02. 61
say i — | and then end life when i end loyalty! 2.02. 63
say i — | and then end life when i end loyalty! 2.02. 63
league whose date till death shall never end. 3.02.373
and i will sing it in the latter end of a play, 4.01.217 P
skill, | that is the true beginning of our end. 5.01.111
a while, | i'll end my exhortation after dinner. MV 1.01.104
rank, | in end of autumn turned to the rams, 1.03. 81
a man's son may, but in the end truth will out. 2.02. 80 P
if thou keep promise, i shall end this strife, 2.03. 20
why, the end is, he hath lost a ship. 3.01. 16 P
i would it might prove the end of his losses. 3.01. 18 P
then, if he lose, he makes a swan–like end, 3.02. 44
wife, | tell her the process of antonio's end, 4.01.274
manage, and to that end riders dearly hir'd; AYL 1.01. 13 P
i hope i shall see an end of him; 1.01.164 P
it please your ladyships, you may see the end, 1.02.114 P
well, i'll end the song. 2.05. 31 P
hold death a while at the arm's end. 2.06. 10 P
the fairest boughs, | or at every sentence end, 3.02.136
and to that end i have been with sir oliver 3.03. 42 P
is said, "many a man knows no end of his goods." 3.03. 53 P
a man has good horns, and knows no end of them. 3.03. 54 P
as we do trust they'll end, in true delights. 5.04.198
hortensio, to what end are all these words? SHR 1.02.248
reign, | and 'tis my hope to end successfully. 4.01.189
him, | and bring our horses unto long–lane end; 4.03.185
stand aside and see the end of this controversy. 5.01. 62 P
let's follow, to see the end of this ado. 5.01.142
the fouler fortune mine, and there an end. 5.02. 98
/an end, sir, to your business! AWW 2.02. 63
is something at the latter end of a dinner, but 2.05. 28 P
come night, end day! 3.02.128
you may so in the end. 4.02. 68
what e'er the course, the end is the renown. 4.04. 36
all yet seems well, and if it end so meet, | the 5.03.333
journeys end in lovers meeting, | every wise TN 2.03. 43
if thou hast her not i' th' end, call me cut. 2.03.187 P
and the end — what should that alphabetical 2.05.118 P
and o shall end, i hope. 2.05.132 P
this shall end without the perdition of souls. 3.04.289 P
h'as hurt me, and there's th' end on't. 5.01.197 P
at the stave's end as well as a man in his case 5.01.285 P
was my negligence, | not weighing well the end; WT 1.02.258
some place | where chance may nurse or end it. 2.03.183
carriage of it | will clear or end the business. 3.01. 18
but to make an end of the ship, to see how the 3.03. 97 P
at upper end o' th' table, now i' th' middle; 4.04. 59
every lane's end, every shop, church, session, 4.04.685 P
this day all things begun come to ill end, | yea JN 3.01. 94
pains | will bring this labor to an happy end. 3.02. 10
there end thy brave, and turn thy face in peace; 5.02.159
good uncle, let this end where it begun; R2 1.01.158
with her companion, grief, must end her life. 1.02. 55
the daintiest last, to make the end most sweet: 1.03. 68
winters and four wanton springs | end in a word: 1.03.215
to foreign passages, and in the end, | having my 1.03.272
the bloody office of his timeless end. 4.01. 5
woman, do not so, | to make my end too sudden. 5.01. 17
my guilt be on my head, and there an end. 5.01. 69
my puny drawer to what end he gave me the sugar, 1H4 2.04. 30 P
if not, the end of life cancels all bands, | and 3.02.157
bid my lieutenant peto meet me at town's end. 4.02. 9 P
to the latter end of a fray and the beginning of 4.02. 79
content | to entertain the lag end of my life 5.01. 24
and they are for the town's end, to beg during 5.03. 38 P
honor comes unlook'd for, and there's an end. 5.03. 61 P
which would have been as speedy in your end | as 5.04. 55
for the hour is come | to end the one of us, and 5.04. 69
but in the end, to stop my ear indeed, | thou 2H4 1.01. 79
set | on bloody courses, the rude scene may end, 1.01.159
let the end try the man. 2.02. 47 P
a death's–head, do not bid me remember mine end. 2.04.235 P
till thy return — well, hearken a' th' end. 2.04.280 P
let time shape, and there an end. 3.02.332 P
briefly, to this end: 4.01. 54
/and either end in peace, which god so frame! 4.01.178
for he hath found to end one doubt by death 4.01.197
if god doth give successful end | to this debate 4.04. 1
this apoplexy will certain be his end. 4.04.130
conjoins with my disease, | and helps to end me. 4.05. 64
even there my life must end. 4.05.235
was lately here in the end of a displeasing play ep 8 P
and there's an end. H5 2.01. 10 P
'a made a finer end, and went away and it had 2.03. 11 P
and smile upon his finger's end, i knew there 2.03. 15 P
to that end, | as matching to his youth and 2.04.129
and there is an end. 3.02.141 P
our expectation hath this day an end. 3.03. 44
that we should dress us fairly for our end. 4.01. 10
but i think we shall never see the end of it. 4.01. 90 P
your cousin, in the latter end, and she must be 5.02.314 P
him, | by magic verses have contriv'd his end? 1H6 1.01. 27
age of care, | argue the end of edmund mortimer. 2.05. 7
must die, | for that's the end of human misery. 3.02.137
work | to bring this matter to the wished end. 3.03. 28
by water shall he die, and take his end. 2H6 1.04. 33
"by water shall he die, and take his end." 1.04. 65
here let them end it, and god defend the right! 2.03. 55
and, in the end being rescued, i have seen | him 3.01.364
mine hair be fix'd an end, as one distract; 3.02.318
but if thy arms be to no other end, | the king 5.01. 39
o, let the vile world end, | and the premised 5.02. 40
it will outrun you, father, in the end. 3H6 1.02. 14
here must i stay, and here my life must end. 1.04. 26
pass'd over to the end they were created, 2.05. 39
then no, my lord. my suit is at an end. 3.02. 81
and to that end i shortly mind to leave you. 4.01. 64
sprawl'st thou? take that, to end thy agony. 5.05. 39
false–boding woman, end thy frantic curse, R3 1.03.246
my hair doth stand an end to hear her curses. 1.03.303
and award | either of you to be the other's end. 2.01. 15
i see (as in a map) the end of all. 2.04. 54
and frantic outrage, end thy damned spleen, | or 2.04. 64
die | until your lordship came to see his end, 3.05. 53
and to that end we wish'd your lordship here, 3.05. 67
and when /mine oratory drew /to /an end, | i bid 3.07. 20
at lower end of the hall, hurl'd up their caps, 3.07. 35
he wonders to what end you have assembled | such 3.07. 84
at hand, | ensues his piteous and unpitied end. 4.04. 74
bloody thou art, bloody will be thy end; 4.04.195
sweetly in force unto her fair live's end. 4.04.351
awake, | and in a bloody battle end thy days! 5.03.155
to as much end | as give a crutch to th' dead. H8 1.01.171
the lag end of their lewdness and be laugh'd at. 1.03. 35
what warlike voice, | and to what end is this? 1.04. 51
certainly | the cardinal is the end of this. 2.01. 40
dying, | go with me like good angels to my end, 2.01. 75
and when old time shall lead him to his end, 2.01. 93
nicholas vaux, | who undertakes you to your end. 2.01. 97
heaven has an end in all; 2.01.124
look into these affairs see this main end, | the 2.02. 40
i was | from any private malice in his end, 3.02.268
and fear'd | she'll with the labor end. 5.01. 20
and the end | was ever to do well; 5.02. 71
i see your end, | 'tis my undoing. 5.02. 96
will leave all as i found it, and there an end. TRO 1.01. 88 P
the gods are above, time must friend or end. 1.02. 78 P
to end a tale of length, | troy in our weakness 1.03.136
be call'd to the world's end after my name; 3.02.201 P
the end crowns all, | and that old common 4.05.224
common arbitrator, time, | will one day end it. 4.05.226
i reak not though i end my life to–day. 5.06. 26
he hath done famously, he did it to that end. COR 1.01. 37 P
shall attend and shrug, | i' th' end admire; 1.09. 5
his honors | from where he should begin and end, 2.01.225
out | to him, or our authorities, for an end. 2.01.244
and is content | to spend the time to end it. 2.02.129
both divine and human, | seal what i end withal! 3.01.142
and suffer it | a brand to th' end a' th' world. 3.01.302
and the end of it | unknown to the beginning. 3.01.326
what then? | he'ld make an end of thy posterity. 4.02. 26
set at upper end o' th' table; 4.05.192 P
their talk at table, and their thanks at end; 4.07. 4
grace to both parts | than seek the end of one, 5.03.122
great son, | the end of war's uncertain; 5.03.141
an end, | this is the last. 5.03.171
and, to this end, | he bow'd his nature, never 5.06. 23
to reap the fame | which he did end all his, and 5.06. 36
but there to end | where he was to begin, and 5.06. 64
by my soul, were there worse end than death, TIT 2.03.302
death, | that end upon them should be executed. 2.03.303
then have i kept it to a worthy end. 3.01.173
when will this fearful slumber have an end? 3.01.252
then i have brought up a neck to a fair end. 4.04. 49 P
titus | hath ordain'd to an honorable end, | for 5.03. 22
which, but their children's end, nought could ROM pr 11
this but begins the woe others must end. 3.01.120
his fault concludes but what the law should end, 3.01.185
vile earth, to earth resign, end motion here, 3.02. 59
there is no end, no limit, measure, bound, | in 3.02.125
ah sir, ah sir, death's the end of all! 3.03. 92
some half a dozen friends, | and there an end. 3.04. 28
poison, i see, hath been his timeless end. 5.03.162
and i cannot think but, in the end, the TIM 3.03. 30 P
believe't, my lord and i have made an end: 3.04. 55
lips, let four words go by and language end! 5.01.220
whose end is purpos'd by the mighty gods? JC 2.02. 27
fear, | seeing that death, a necessary end, 2.02. 36
must end that work the ides of march begun. 5.01.113
the end of this day's business ere it come! 5.01.123
but it sufficeth that the day will end, | and 5.01.124
the day will end, | and then the end is known. 5.01.125
and where i did begin, there shall i end; 5.03. 24
were out, the man would die, | and there an end; MAC 3.04. 79
i'll spend | unto a dismal and a fatal end. 3.05. 21
by his worth, for then | it hath no end. 5.09. 12
and each particular hair to stand an end, | like HAM 1.05. 19
to shatter all his bulk | and end his being. 2.01. 93
to what end, my lord? 2.02.282 P
the humorous man shall end his part in peace, 2.02.322 P
a sea of troubles, | and by opposing, end them. 3.01. 59
and by a sleep to say we end | the heart–ache 3.01. 60
is from the purpose of playing, whose end, both 3.02. 21 P
but, orderly to end where i begun, | our wills 3.02.210
and my return shall be the end of /my business. 3.02.318 P
life in excrements, | start up and stand an end. 3.04.122
come, sir, to draw toward an end with you. 3.04.216
officers do the king best service in the end: 4.02. 17 P
two dishes, but to one table — that's the end. 4.03. 25 P
indeed without an oath i'll make an end on't. 4.05. 57 P
they say 'a made a good end — "for bonny sweet 4.05.186 P
as make your bouts more violent to that end — 4.07.158
'tis on such ground and to such wholesome end LR 2.04.144
depriv'd that benefit, | to end itself by death? 4.06. 62
your business of the world hath so an end, | and 5.01. 45
is this the promis'd end? 5.03.264
and duty, | but seeming so, for my peculiar end; OTH 1.01. 60
here is my journey's end, here is my butt | and 5.02.267
but soon that war had end, and the time's state ANT 1.02. 91
and to that end | assemble /we immediate council 1.04. 74
whose bosom was my crownet, my chief end, | like 4.12. 27
there is left us | ourselves to end ourselves. 4.14. 22
o, make an end | of what i have begun. 4.14.105

the miserable change now at my end | lament nor 4.15. 51
no friend | but resolution and the briefest end. 4.15. 91
not | for such an end thou seek'st — as base as CYM 1.06.144
to what end? 2.02. 42
son, let your mother end. 3.01. 39
and there's an end. 3.01. 82 P
i see into thy end and am almost | a man already 3.04.166
and my end | can make good use of either. 3.05. 63
dry and die, | but for the end it works to. 3.06. 32
'lack, to what end? 5.03. 59
again, | but end it by some means for imogen. 5.03. 83
then shall posthumus end his miseries, britain 5.04.143 P
and how you shall speed in your journey's end, i 5.04.183 P
but failing of her end by his strange absence, 5.05. 57
let me end the story: | i slew him there. 5.05.286
more it shap'd | unto my end of stealing them. 5.05.347
it was wise nature's end in the donation, | to 5.05.367
then shall posthumus end his miseries, britain 5.05.441 P
and yet the end of all is bought thus dear, PER 1.01. 98
sea she lies in, yet the end | must be as 'tis. 3.03. 11
it upon me and mine | to the end of generation! 3.03. 25
money enough in the end to buy him a wooden one? 4.06.173 P
be a troubler of your peace, | i will end here. 5.01.152
was my mother, who did end | the minute i began. 5.01.211
shall be returning | ere you can end this feast, TNK 1.01.224
like old importment's bastard) has this end, 1.03. 80
a thousand differing ways to one sure end. 1.05. 14
court hurry is over, we will have an end of it. 2.01. 18 P
shape shall make me, | or end my fortunes. 2.03. 22
the point is this — | an end, and that is all. 3.02. 38
and, if you can love, end this difference. 3.06.278
i'll choose, | and end their strife. 4.02. 3
to end the quarrel? 4.02. 57
would i might end first! 4.02. 57
how far is't now to th' end o' th' world, my 5.02. 72
i had no end in't else; 5.03. 75
burst of clamor | is sure th' end o' th' combat. 5.03. 78
or what fierce sulphur else, to this end made, 5.04. 64
power could give his will, bounds, comes on end, 5.04. 67
legs, on his hind hoofs | /... on end he stands, 5.04. 77
o miserable end of our alliance! 5.04. 86
in whose end | the visages of bridegrooms we'll 5.04.126
purpose it was meant ye), | we have our end; ep 15
upon his compass'd crest now stand on end, | his VEN 272
end without audience and are never done. 846
find sweet beginning, but unsavory end; 1138
the shame and fault finds no excuse nor end. LUC 238
a little harm done to a great good end | for 528
end thy ill aim before thy shoot be ended; 579
wilt thou sort an hour great strifes to end? 899
in vain | some happy mean to end a hapless life. 1045
foul deed, my life's fair end shall free it. 1208
thou wast not to this end from me derived. 1755
and kiss'd the fatal knife, to end his vow; 1843
of the fiend, | augur of the fever's end, | to PHT 7
but beauty's waste hath in the world an end, SON 9.11
against this coming end you should prepare, 13. 3
thy end is truth's and beauty's doom and date. 14.14
all losses are restor'd, and sorrows end. 30.14
way, | when what i seek (my weary travel's end) 50. 2
shore, | so do our minutes hasten to their end, 60. 2
when in the least of them my life hath end; 92. 6
now all is done, have what shall have no end, 110. 9
"i hate" she alter'd with an end | that follow'd 145. 9
is this thy body's end? 146. 8
END–ALL 1 FR 0.0001 REL FR 1 V 0 P
blow | might be the be–all and the end–all — MAC 1.07. 5
ENDAMAGE 2 FR 0.0002 REL FR 2 V 0 P
him, | your slander never can endamage him; TGV 3.02. 43
and lay new platforms to endamage them. 1H6 2.01. 77
ENDAMAGEMENT 1 FR 0.0001 REL FR 1 V 0 P
have hither march'd to your endamagement. JN 2.01.209
ENDANGER 2 FR 0.0002 REL FR 1 V 1 P
i hold him but a fool that will endanger | his TGV 5.04.133
think'st thou i'll endanger my soul gratis? WIV 2.02. 16 P
ENDART 1 FR 0.0001 REL FR 1 V 0 P
but no more deep will i endart mine eye | than ROM 1.03. 98
/ENDEAR'D 1 FR 0.0001 REL FR 1 V 0 P
when you were more /endear'd to it than now, 2H4 2.03. 11
ENDEAR'D 2 FR 0.0002 REL FR 1 V 1 P
so infinitely endear'd — TIM 1.02.227
i am so much endear'd to that lord; 3.02. 31 P
ENDEARED 2 FR 0.0002 REL FR 2 V 0 P
and thou, to be endeared to a king, | made it no JN 4.02.228
thy bosom is endeared with all hearts, | which i SON 31. 1
/ENDEAVOR 1 FR 0.0001 REL FR 0 V 1 P
/their /endeavor /keeps /in /the /wonted /pace; HAM 2.02.338 P
ENDEAVOR 16 FR 0.0018 REL FR 11 V 5 P
should produce | without sweat or endeavor: TMP 2.01.161
only to despite them, i will endeavor any thing. ADO 2.02. 31 P
th' endeavor of this present breath may buy LLL 1.01. 5
with all the fierce endeavor of your wit | to 5.02.853
and use thou all th' endeavor of a man | in MV 3.04. 48
endeavor thyself to sleep, and leave thy vain TN 4.02. 96 P
by so much | we must awake endeavor for defense,
JN 2.01. 81
with excellent endeavor of drinking good and 2H4 4.03.120 P
setting endeavor in continual motion; H5 1.02.185
you will endeavor for your french part of such a 5.02.213 P
and with your best endeavor have stirr'd up | my 2H6 3.01.163
but i'll endeavor deeds to match these words, TRO 4.05.259
why should our endeavor be so lov'd and the 5.10. 39 P
beget opinion | of my more fierce endeavor. LR 2.01. 34
may best discover, | and look on their endeavor. ANT 4.10. 9
us, | we with our travels will endeavor. PER 2.04. 56
ENDEAVOR'D 1 FR 0.0001 REL FR 1 V 0 P
endeavor'd my advancement to the throne. 1H6 2.05. 69
ENDEAVORS 9 FR 0.0010 REL FR 7 V 2 P
for all your fair endeavors, and entreat, | out LLL 5.02.730
my best endeavors shall be done herein. MV 2.02.173
be found in the calendar of my past endeavors, AWW 1.03. 5 P
dear sir, to my endeavors give consent, | of 2.01 153
and with my best endeavors, in your absence, WT 4.04.531
pains, and strong endeavors | to bring your most H5 5.02. 25
means to live well endeavors to trust to himself R3 1.04.143 P
which went | beyond all man's endeavors. H8 3.02.169
my endeavors | have ever come too short of my 3.02.169
ENDED 37 FR 0.0041 REL FR 30 V 7 P
our revels now are ended. TMP 4.01.148
when you went onward on this ended action, | i ADO 1.01.297
the music ended, | we'll fit the /hid–fox with a 2.03. 41
when after that the holy rites are ended, | i'll 5.04. 68
nay, my choler is ended. LLL 2.01.206
that you bought, | and he ended the market. 3.01.110 P
with vildest torture, let my life be ended. AWW 2.01.174
was the greatest, but that i have not ended yet. 4.03. 92 P
i mean the business is not ended, as fearing to 4.03. 96 P
all is well ended, if this suit be won, | that ep 2
heavens had been pleas'd, would we had so ended!
TN 2.01. 21 P
lady, | dear queen, that ended when i but began, WT 5.03. 45
thee, king harry, | this sword hath ended him. 1H4 5.03. 9
when every thing is ended, then you come. 2H4 4.03. 27
exceeding well, his cares are now all ended. 5.02. 3
our simple supper ended, give me leave | in this 2H6 2.02. 2
and, now the battle's ended, | if friend or foe, 3H6 2.06. 44
troy is ours, and our sharp wars are ended. TRO 5.09. 10
is it ended then? COR 4.03. 16 P
you have ended my business, and i will merrily 4.03. 38 P
my life were better ended by their hate, | than ROM 2.02. 77
death | was woe enough if it had ended there; 3.02.115
whereto i am going, | after my speech is ended. JC 3.01.251
tongue | hath almost ended his live's history. 5.05. 40
this business is well ended. HAM 2.02. 85
the griefs are ended | by seeing the worst, OTH 1.03.202
and 'twas i | that the mad brutus ended. ANT 3.11. 38
doctor, your service for this time is ended, CYM 1.05. 30
my speech of insultment ended on his dead body, 3.05.141 P
how ended she? 5.05. 30
the sports | once ended, we'll perform. TNK 2.03. 59
came home before the business | was fully ended. 4.01. 5
how was it ended? 4.01. 25
his day's hot task hath ended in the west; VEN 530
end thy ill aim before thy shoot be ended; LUC 579
lamenting philomele had ended | the well–tun'd 1079
got the lady gay, | for now my song is ended. PP 15.16
ENDER 1 FR 0.0001 REL FR 1 V 0 P
that is, to you, my origin and ender; LC 222
ENDING 15 FR 0.0017 REL FR 14 V 1 P
art to enchant, | and my ending is despair, TMP ep 15
ear, | as ending anthem of my endless dolor. TGV 3.01.242
and the rheum | for ending thee no sooner. MM 3.01. 32
a good l'envoy, ending in the goose; LLL 3.01. 99 P
it makes | foretell the ending of mortality. JN 5.07. 5
point, | still ending at the arrival of an hour. 1H4 5.02. 84
ending with "brother, son, and all are dead." 2H4 1.01. 81
yields his engrossments to the ending father. 4.05. 79
by, | from this day to the ending of the world, H5 4.03. 58
the passion ending, doth the purpose lose. HAM 3.02.195
here our play has ending. PER 5.03.102
what ending could be | of more content? TNK 5.04. 15
saith that the world hath ending with thy life. VEN 12
begins the sad dirge of her certain ending: LUC 1612
that wear this world out to the ending doom. SON 55.12
ENDINGS 2 FR 0.0002 REL FR 0 V 2 P
very ominous endings. ADO 5.02. 40 P
answer the particular endings of his soldiers, H5 4.01.156 P
ENDLESS 12 FR 0.0013 REL FR 10 V 2 P
ear, | as ending anthem of my endless dolor. TGV 3.01.242
notable coward, an infinite and endless liar, an AWW 3.06. 10 P
thou and endless night | have done me shame. JN 5.06. 12
to dwell in solemn shades of endless night. R2 1.03.177
shall be extinct with age and endless /night; 1.03.222
shall in procession sing her endless praise. 1H6 1.06. 20
from thy endless goodness send prosperous life, H8 5.04. 1 P
(between whose endless jar justice resides) TRO 1.03.117
for, to say truth, it were an endless thing, TNK pr 22
we are an endless mine to one another; 2.02. 79
me | to endless date of never–ending woes? LUC 935
and peace proclaims olives of endless age. SON 107. 8
ENDOW *(also due*)*
ENDOW 1 FR 0.0001 REL FR 1 V 0 P
all — | will i withal endow a child of thine; R3 4.04.250
ENDOW'D 4 FR 0.0004 REL FR 3 V 1 P
i endow'd thy purposes | with words that made TMP 1.02.357
though she were endow'd with all that adam had ADO 2.01.251 P
hast thou not forgot, | wherein i thee endow'd. LR 2.04.181
look whom she best endow'd she gave the more; SON 11.11
ENDOWED 1 FR 0.0001 REL FR 1 V 0 P
how shall she be endowed, | if she be mated with TIM 1.01.139
ENDOWMENTS 5 FR 0.0005 REL FR 4 V 1 P
base men by his endowments are made great. R2 2.03.139
catalogue of his endowments had been tabled by CYM 1.04. 5 P
virtue and cunning were endowments greater PER 3.02. 27
and how achiev'd you these endowments which 5.01.116
with all her best endowments, all those beauties TNK 4.02. 8
ENDOWS 1 FR 0.0001 REL FR 1 V 0 P
and such stuff within | endows a man but he. CYM 1.01. 24
ENDS 51 FR 0.0057 REL FR 42 V 9 P
thus neglecting worldly ends, all dedicated | to TMP 1.02. 89
with colors fairer painted their foul ends. 1.02.143
and most poor matters | point to rich ends. 3.01. 4
more grave and wrinkled than the aims and ends MM 1.03. 5
ere you flout old ends any further, examine your ADO 1.01.288 P
thou hast it ad dunghill, at the fingers' ends, LLL 5.01. 78 P
curtsy, sweet hearts — and so the measure ends. 5.02.221
here she comes, and her passion ends the play. MND 5.01.315 P
thus thisby ends; 5.01.346
all, | that ends this strange eventful history, AYL 2.07.164
in this forest let us do those ends | that here 5.04.170
till they attain to their abhorr'd ends; AWW 4.03. 23 P
all's well that ends well! 4.04. 35
all's well that ends well yet, | though time 5.01. 25
ay, sir, i have them at my fingers' ends. TN 1.03. 78 P
as it were, from the ends of oppos'd winds. WT 1.01. 31 P
but that which ends all counsel, true redress: JN 3.04. 24
wrath | out of the bloody fingers' ends of john. 3.04.168
for sorrow ends not when it seemeth done. R2 1.02. 61
more are men's ends mark'd than their lives 2.01. 11
though death be poor, it ends a mortal woe. 2.01.152
and so ends my catechism. 1H4 5.01.141 P
and drinks off candles' ends for flap–dragons, 2H4 2.04.246 P
with henry's death the english circle ends, 1H6 1.02.136
defer no time, delays have dangerous ends, 3.02. 33
that those which fly before the battle ends 2H6 4.02.178
'tis done by me, and ends in "margaret." R3 1.03.238
with odd old ends stol'n forth of holy writ, 1.03.336
in him stuff that puts him to these ends; H8 1.01. 58
but be brought to know our ends are honest, 3.01.154
mine own ends | have been mine so, that evermore 3.02.171
wealth i have drawn together | for mine own ends 3.02.212
let all the ends thou aim'st at be thy country's 3.02.447
as near as the extremest ends | of parallels, as TRO 1.03.167
the same you are not, which, for your best ends, COR 3.02. 47
only their ends | you have respected; 5.03. 4
these violent delights have violent ends, | and ROM 2.06. 9
never knewest, but the extremity of both ends. TIM 4.03.301 P
who can bring noblest minds to basest ends! 4.03.464
do) | loves for his own ends, not for you. MAC 3.05. 13
o my breast, | thy hope ends here! 4.03.114
thoughts are ours, their ends none of our own: HAM 3.02.213
us | there's a divinity that shapes our ends, 5.02. 10
harbor more craft and more corrupter ends | than LR 2.02.102
and make the hearts of romans serve your ends! ANT 3.02. 37
i was of late as petty to his ends | as is the 3.12. 8
to do that thing that ends all other deeds, 5.02. 5
to his bold ends honor and golden ingots, TNK 1.02. 17
me, | the law will have the honor of our ends. 3.06.130
chin, | and where she ends, she doth anew begin. VEN 60
he, | "leave me, and then the story aptly ends; 716
ENDU'D 1 FR 0.0001 REL FR 1 V 0 P
withal, | are men endu'd with worthy qualities. TGV 5.04.153
ENDUE *(also indue, etc.)*
ENDUE 1 FR 0.0001 REL FR 1 V 0 P
tribunes | endue you with the people's voice. COR 2.03.139
ENDUES 1 FR 0.0001 REL FR 1 V 0 P
and it endues | our other healthful members even OTH 3.04.146
ENDURANCE *(also indurance)*
ENDURANCE 2 FR 0.0002 REL FR 1 V 1 P
o, she misus'd me past the endurance of a block; ADO 2.01.239 P
prove the thousand part | of my endurance, thou PER 5.01.136
/ENDUR'D 1 FR 0.0001 REL FR 1 V 0 P
/finding | /who /'twas /that /so /endur'd, /with LR 5.03.212
ENDUR'D 17 FR 0.0019 REL FR 14 V 3 P
talk, is most tolerable, and not to be endur'd. ADO 3.03. 36 P
not to be endur'd! AYL 4.03. 69 P
that have endur'd shrewd days and nights with us 5.04.173
your betters have endur'd me say my mind, | and SHR 4.03. 75
o vild, | intolerable, not to be endur'd! 5.02. 94
whose honesty till now | endur'd all weathers. WT 5.01.195
back | of such as have before endur'd the like. R2 5.05. 30
what extremities he endur'd, and in the reproof 1H4 1.02.190 P
i grieve to hear what torments you endur'd, 1H6 1.04. 57
of those gross taunts that oft i have endur'd. R3 1.03.105
save for a night of groans | endur'd of her, for 4.04.304
as his bare head | in hell–black night endur'd, LR 3.07. 60
the wonder is, he hath endur'd so long, | he but 5.03.317
endur'd a sea | that almost burst the deck. PER 4.01. 55
be, hath endur'd a grief | might equal yours, if 5.01. 87
durst better have endur'd cold iron than done it TNK 2.06. 10
the mortal moon hath her eclipse endur'd, | and SON 107. 5
ENDURE 78 FR 0.0088 REL FR 59 V 19 P
and would no more endure | this wooden slavery TMP 3.01. 61
o valentine, this i endure for thee! TGV 5.03. 15
i could not endure a husband with a beard on his ADO 2.01. 29 P
dish i love not, i cannot endure my lady tongue. 2.01.275 P
she cannot endure to hear tell of a husband. 2.01.347 P
in his youth that he cannot endure in his age. 2.03.239 P
is but prolong'd, have patience and endure. 4.01.254
to be so moral when he shall endure | the like 5.01. 30
that could endure the toothache patiently, 5.01. 36
he shall endure such public shame as the rest of LLL 1.01.130 P
a world of torments though i should endure, | i 5.02.353
choice, | you can endure the livery of a nun, MND 1.01. 70
i will no longer endure it, though yet i know no AYL 1.01. 24 P
strong in me, and i will no longer endure it; 1.01. 71 P
which erst was irksome to me, | i will endure; 3.05. 96
patience and mine to endure her loud alarums, SHR 1.01.127 P
that mortal ears might hardly endure the din? 1.01.173
i could endure any thing before but a cat, and AWW 4.03.237 P
in grain, sir, 'twill endure wind and weather. TN 1.05.237 P
youth's a stuff will not endure." 2.03. 52
as hardly | will he endure your sight as yet, i WT 4.04.470
his face, | not able to endure the sight of day, R2 3.02. 52
and majesty might never yet endure | the moody 1H4 1.03. 18
man of good temper would endure this tempest of
2H4 2.01. 81 P
knowest sir john cannot endure an apple–john. 2.04. 2 P
i cannot endure such a fustian rascal. 2.04.189 P
and it will endure cold as another man's sword H5 2.01. 9 P
god of his mercy give | you patience to endure, 2.02.180
their eyes, and then they will endure handling, 5.02.310 P
but now the substance shall endure the like, 1H6 2.03. 38
how i am brav'd, and must perforce endure it! 2.04.115
have done, for more i hardly can endure. 2H6 1.04. 38
uneath may she endure the flinty streets, | to 2.04. 8
i am able to endure much. 4.02. 56 P
words as no christian ear can endure to hear. 4.07. 40 P
shall i endure the sight of somerset? 5.01. 90
and mortal eyes cannot endure the devil. R3 1.02. 45
these eyes could not endure that beauty's wrack; 1.02.127
they do me wrong, and i will not endure it! 1.03. 42
no, | i must have patience to endure the load; 3.07.230
lords, | can ye endure to hear this arrogance? H8 3.02.278
to endure more miseries and greater far | than 3.02.389
their dear brothers, are able to endure. 5.03. 63 P
by th' vows | we have made to endure friends, COR 1.06. 58
servant, or endure | your heaviest censure. 5.06.140
why, i have patience to endure all this. TIT 2.03. 88
did endure | to have his princely paws par'd all 2.03.151
shall i endure this monstrous villainy? 4.04. 51
i'll not endure him. ROM 1.05. 76
you'll not endure him! 1.05. 79
i did endure | not seldom, nor no slight checks, TIM 2.02.139
to battle, | and not endure all threats? 3.05. 43
both | endure the winter's cold as well as he; JC 1.02. 99
for we will shake him, or worse days endure. 1.02.322
but when they should endure the bloody spur, 4.02. 25
brutus, bait not me, | i'll not endure it. 4.03. 29
o ye gods, ye gods, must i endure all this? 4.03. 41
once, | i have the patience to endure it now. 4.03.192
even so great men great losses should endure. 4.03.193
and will endure | our setting down before't. MAC 5.04. 9
let me endure your wrath, if't be not so. 5.05. 35

the terms of our estate may not endure | hazard HAM 3.03. 5
i'll not endure it. LR 1.03. 5
open night's too rough | for nature to endure. 3.04. 3
pour on, i will endure. 3.04. 18
i never shall endure her. 5.01. 15
men must endure | their going hence even as 5.02. 9
the moor (howbeit that i endure him not) | is of OTH 2.01.288
or suffocating streams, | i'll not endure it. 3.03.390
i will indeed no longer endure it; 4.02.178 P
in the state | cannot endure my absence. ANT 1.02.172
the sight and could not | endure a further view. 3.10. 17
yet he that can endure | to follow with 3.13. 43
our subjects, sir, | will not endure his yoke; CYM 3.05. 5
thou art condemn'd, and must | endure our law. 5.05.299
and as they last, their verdour still endure, VEN 507
pure | doth in her poison'd closet yet endure." LUC 1659
love | a dateless lively heat, still to endure, SON 153. 6

ENDURED 4 FR 0.0004 REL FR 4 V 0 P
he shall be endured. ROM 1.05. 76
such a night as this | till now i ne'er endured. PER 3.02. 6
who endured | the beaks of ravens, talents of TNK 1.01. 40
to think their dolor others have endured. LUC 1582

ENDURES 1 FR 0.0001 REL FR 1 V 0 P
which easily endures not article | tying him to COR 2.03.196

ENDURING 1 FR 0.0001 REL FR 1 V 0 P
he so troubles me, | 'tis past enduring. WT 2.01. 2

ENDUR'ST 1 FR 0.0001 REL FR 1 V 0 P
thou divine imogen, what thou endur'st, CYM 2.01. 57

ENDYMION 1 FR 0.0001 REL FR 1 V 0 P
the moon sleeps with endymion | and would not be MV 5.01.109

ENEMIES' 9 FR 0.0010 REL FR 9 V 0 P
you came in arms to spill mine enemies' blood, JN 3.01.102
and fill up | her enemies' ranks — i must 5.02. 29
we will not fly but to our enemies' throats. 1H6 1.01. 98
for i have seen our enemies' overthrow. 3.02.111
of their observant toil the enemies' weight — TRO 1.03.203
can show /for rome | her enemies' marks upon me. COR 3.03.111
and chastised with arms | our enemies' pride; TIT 1.01. 33
to know our enemies' minds, we rip their hearts, LR 4.06.260
sands that will not bear your enemies' boats, CYM 3.01. 21

ENEMIES 107 FR 0.0121 REL FR 95 V 12 P
lady) hath mine enemies | brought to this shore; TMP 1.02.179
and these, mine enemies, are all knit up | in 3.03. 89
this hour | lies at my mercy all mine enemies. 4.01.263
that's not so, sir; we are your enemies. TGV 4.01. 8
how they might hurt their enemies — if they ADO 5.01. 98
i know you two are rival enemies. MND 4.01.142
cool'd my friends, heated mine enemies; MV 3.01. 58 P
well, and overthrown | more than your enemies. AYL 1.02.255
of men | their graces serve them but as enemies? 2.03. 11
such friends are thine enemies, knave. AWW 1.03. 41 P
i have many enemies in orsino's court, | else TN 2.01. 45
a vulgar proof | that very oft we pity enemies. 3.01.125
bloody and so dear, | hast made thine enemies? 5.01. 72
that the time's enemies may not have this | to JN 4.02. 61
o, let me have no subject enemies | when adverse 4.02.171
arm you against your other enemies, | i'll make 4.02.249
blood, | but bloody with the enemies of his kin. R2 2.01.183
yield stinging nettles to mine enemies; 3.02. 18
throw death upon thy sovereign's enemies. 3.02. 22
lies | the mightiest of thy greatest enemies, 5.06. 32
thee out three such enemies again as that fiend 1H4 2.04.368 P
and stiff | under the hoofs of vaunting enemies, 5.03. 42
forth | to know the numbers of our enemies. 2H4 4.01. 4
off | that might so much as think you enemies. 4.01.144
from enemies heavens keep your majesty, | and, 4.04. 94
thou wilt not, why then be enemies with me too. H5 2.01.103 P
those that were your father's enemies | have 2.02. 29
more dazzled and drove back his enemies | than 1H6 1.01. 13
enclosed were they with their enemies. 1.01.136
fled, | but that they left me midst my enemies. 1.02. 24
should strike such terror to his enemies. 2.03. 24
loyal friends, | as it disanimates his enemies. 3.01.182
and digest | your angry choler on your enemies. 4.01.168
voice, | by sight of these our baleful enemies. 5.04.122
have i overcome mine enemies in this presence? 2H6 2.03. 98 P
and ban thine enemies, both mine and thine! 2.04. 25
do him good, | so mighty are his vowed enemies. 3.01.220
weaves tedious snares to trap mine enemies. 3.01.340
he shall have the skins of our enemies, to make 4.02. 23 P
for our enemies shall /fall before us, inspir'd 4.02. 35 P
the frenchmen are our enemies. 4.02.170 P
priests pray for enemies, but princes kill. 5.02. 71
hath made us by-words to our enemies. 3H6 1.01. 42
ay, to be murther'd by his enemies. 1.01.260
so far'd our father with his enemies, | so fled 2.01. 18
so fled his enemies my warlike father; 2.01. 19
and who shines now but henry's enemies? 2.06. 10
nor how to shroud yourself from enemies? 4.03. 40
all these the enemies to our poor bark. 5.04. 28
throne, | repurchas'd with the blood of enemies. 5.07. 2
too, | for they that were your enemies are his, R3 1.01.130
days, | which here you urge to prove us enemies, 1.03.145
news, | that this same very day your enemies, 3.02. 49
this day those enemies are put to death, | and i 3.02.103
how mine enemies | to-day at pomfret bloodily 3.04. 89
look back, defend thee, here are enemies! 3.05. 19
please you; | but i had rather kill two enemies. 4.02. 71
two deep enemies, | foes to my rest and my sweet 4.02. 72
i lurk'd, | to watch the waning of mine enemies. 4.04. 4
and teach me how to curse mine enemies! 4.04.117
whisper the spirits of thine enemies | and 4.04.193
in arms, | if not to fight with foreign enemies, 4.04.529
not to be taught | that you have many enemies, H8 2.04.159
far | than my weak-hearted enemies dare offer. 3.02.390
mine age | have left me naked to mine enemies. 3.02.457
if they shall fail, i, with mine enemies, | will 5.01.123
your enemies are many, and not small; 5.01.128
like fathers, | when you curse them as enemies. COR 1.01. 78
thou mad'st thine enemies shake, as if the world 1.04. 60
you have been a scourge to her enemies, you have 2.03. 91 P
fast, | we have as many friends as enemies. 3.01.231
killing our enemies, the blood he hath lost 3.01.297
your enemies, with nodding of their plumes, 3.03.126
you, sir, he has as many friends as enemies; 4.05.206 P
your enemies and his find something in him. 4.06.106
his hate, | and therein show'd like enemies. 4.06.114
and brought to yoke, the enemies of rome. TIT 1.01. 69
thine, | that hath thrown down so many enemies, 3.01.163
with him, | and work confusion on his enemies. 5.02. 8
sent to me, | to be a torment to mine enemies? 5.02. 42
goths, | or at the least make them his enemies. 5.02. 79
out, | and sent her enemies unto the grave. 5.03.103
out | to beg relief among rome's enemies, | who 5.03.106
rebellious subjects, enemies to peace, ROM 1.01. 81
where be these enemies? 5.03.291
be at a breakfast of enemies than a dinner of TIM 1.02. 76 P
all those flatterers were thine enemies then, 1.02. 82 P
to feed | than such that do e'en enemies exceed. 1.02.204
and slain in fight many of your enemies. 3.05. 63
when man was wish'd to love his enemies! 4.03.466
those enemies of timon's and mine own | whom you 5.04. 56
in terms of friendship with thine enemies. JC 3.01.203
the enemies of caesar shall say this: 3.01.212
the stake, | and bay'd about with many enemies, 4.01. 49
wrong i mine enemies? 4.02. 38
rather have | such men my friends than enemies. 5.04. 29
our enemies have beat us to the pit. 5.05. 23
the poor advanc'd makes friends of enemies. HAM 3.02.205
none but his enemies. 4.05.145
but as /a pawn | to wage against thine enemies, LR 1.01.156
o'er our heads, | find out their enemies now. 3.02. 51
you valiant and strong-hearted enemies, | you TNK 5.01. 8
wish their office | to any of their enemies. 5.03. 36
light, | for light and lust are deadly enemies; LUC 674
eyes | of all the greeks that are thine enemies. 1470
and each (though enemies to /either's reign) SON 28. 5
knows | her pretty looks have been mine enemies, 139.10

/ENEMY 3 FR 0.0003 REL FR 3 V 0 P
here shall he see | /no /enemy | /but /winter AYL 2.05. 44
/nor /do /i /as /an /enemy /to /peace | /troop 2H4 4.01. 61
/in /disguise | /followed /his /enemy /king, LR 5.03.221

ENEMY 163 FR 0.0184 REL FR 136 V 27 P
of naples, being an enemy | to me inveterate, TMP 1.02.121
entertainment till | mine enemy has more pow'r. 1.02.467
and valentine i'll hold an enemy, | aiming at TGV 2.06. 29
ay, if his enemy deliver it; 3.02. 35
fenton, | i will not be your friend nor enemy. WIV 3.04. 89
o cunning enemy, that, to catch a saint, | with MM 2.02.179
be friends with me than fight with mine enemy. ADO 4.01.299 P
is claudio thine enemy? 4.01.300 P
but lend it rather to thine enemy, | who, if he MV 1.03.135
friend, | engag'd my friend to his mere enemy, 3.02.262
she would not hold out enemy for ever | for 4.01.447
but i did find him still mine enemy. AYL 1.02.226
this roof | the enemy of all your graces lives. 2.03. 18
here shall he see | no enemy | but winter and 2.05. 7
politic with my friend, smooth with mine enemy, 5.04. 46 P
dead, excessive grief the enemy to the living. AWW 1.01. 56 P
if the living be enemy to the grief, the excess 1.01. 57 P
be able for thine enemy | rather in power than 1.01. 65
man is enemy to virginity; 1.01.112 P
a friend, | a phoenix, captain, and an enemy, 1.01.168
whom i am sure he knows not from the enemy. 3.06. 24 P
i am sure care's an enemy to life. TN 1.03. 2 P
wherein the pregnant enemy does much. 2.02. 28
consider, he's an enemy to mankind. 3.04. 98 P
as thou usest him, and thy sworn enemy, andrew 3.04.170 P
on base and ground enough, | orsino's enemy. 5.01. 76
now my sworn friend and then mine enemy; WT 1.02.167
know't, | it will let in and out the enemy, 1.02.205
a cup, | to give mine enemy a lasting wink; 1.02.317
though fortune, visible an enemy, | should chase 5.01.216
town, | being no further enemy to you | than the JN 2.01.243
so mak'st thou faith an enemy to faith, | and 3.01.263
but are gone | to offer service to your enemy; 5.01. 34
on the casque | of thy adverse pernicious enemy. R2 1.03. 82
norfolk, so fare as to mine enemy: 1.03.193
proportionable to the enemy | is all unpossible. 2.02.125
that they have let the dangerous enemy | measure 3.02.124
and, though mine enemy, restor'd again | to all 4.01. 88
for though mine enemy thou hast ever been, 5.06. 28
devil alone | as owen glendower for an enemy. 1H4 1.03.117
foes, | which art my nearest and dearest enemy? 3.02.123
so are the horses of the enemy | in general 4.03. 25
quality, | but stand against us like an enemy. 4.03. 37
name were not so terrible to the enemy as it is. 2H4 1.02.218 P
he presents no mark to the enemy, the foeman may 3.02.266 P
off a mile, | in goodly form comes on the enemy, 4.01. 20
his friends | that, plucking to unfix an enemy, 4.01.206
dale, a most furious knight and valorous enemy. 4.03. 39 P
it, as with an enemy | that had before my face 4.05.166
join'd with an enemy proclaim'd, and from his H5 2.02.168
to weigh | the enemy more mighty than he seems, 2.04. 44
who disgrac'd, what terms the enemy stood on; 3.06. 74 P
so much | unto an enemy of craft and vantage, 3.06.144
why, the enemy is loud, you hear him all night. 4.01. 75 P
if the enemy is an ass and a fool, and a prating 4.01. 77 P
it may be his enemy is a gentleman of great sort 4.07.135 P
a friend to alanson, and an enemy to our person. 4.07.157 P
it possible dat i sould love de enemy of france? 5.02.169 P
possible you should love the enemy of france, 5.02.172 P
arm, arm! the enemy doth make assault! 1H6 2.01. 38
usurer, | froward by nature, enemy to peace, 3.01. 18
out of hand, | and set upon our boasting enemy. 3.02.103
but when they heard he was thine enemy, | they 3.03. 71
latest glory of thy praise | that i, thy enemy, 4.02. 34
he fables not, i hear the enemy. 4.02. 42
'tis known to you he is mine enemy; 2H6 1.01.148
nay more, an enemy unto you all, | and no great 1.01.149
stirr'd up | my liefest liege to be mine enemy. 3.01.164
a fox, | by nature prov'd an enemy to the flock, 3.01.258
crafty kern, | hath he conversed with the enemy, 3.01.368
although the duke was enemy to him, | yet he 3.02. 57
attracts the same for aidance 'gainst the enemy, 3.02.165
friend, | and 'tis well seen he found an enemy. 3.02.185
hast thou not spirit to curse thine enemy? 3.02.308
with the tongue of an enemy be a good counsellor 4.02.171 P
in love, | but that thou art so fast mine enemy. 5.02. 21
and defense | to give the enemy way, and to 5.02. 76
france | when as the enemy hath been ten to one; 3H6 1.02. 74
allegiance, | will apprehend you as his enemy. 3.01. 71
that king lewis | becomes your enemy, for 4.01. 30
i never sued to friend nor enemy; R3 1.02.167
courtesy, | i must be held a rancorous enemy. 1.03. 50
my soul, | and to myself become an enemy. 2.02. 37
one that hath ever been god's enemy. 5.03.252
then if you fight against god's enemy, | god 5.03.253
a thing devised by the enemy. 5.03.306
my lord, the enemy is past the marsh, | after 5.03.345
to love, although i knew | he were mine enemy? H8 2.04. 31
that | you are mine enemy, and make my challenge 2.04. 77
wherein he appears | as i would wish mine enemy. 3.02. 28
but what the repining enemy commends, | that TRO 1.03.243
you know an enemy intends you harm; 2.02. 39
when they charge on heaps | the enemy flying. 3.02. 29
as to one | that would be rid of such an enemy. 4.05.164
know caius martius is chief enemy to the people. COR 1.01. 8 P
cominius, martius your old enemy | (who is of 1.02. 12
say, has our general met the enemy? 1.04. 3
where is the enemy? 1.06. 47
he was your enemy, ever spake against | your 2.03.179
that he's your fixed enemy, and revoke | your 2.03.250
rather | follow thine enemy in a fiery gulf 3.02. 91
as enemy to the people and his country. 3.03.118
the people's enemy is gone, is gone! 3.03.136
our enemy is banish'd, he is gone! hoo! hoo! 3.03.137
say their great enemy is gone, and they | stand 4.02. 6
/hate i, and my love's upon | this enemy town. 4.04. 24
and more a friend than e'er an enemy; 4.05.146
popular ignorance, given your enemy your shield, 5.02. 41 P
the blot and enemy to our general name! TIT 2.03.183
besides, this sorrow is an enemy, | and would 3.01.267
she is thy enemy, and i thy friend. 5.02. 29
a montague, | the only son of your great enemy. ROM 1.05.137
it is to me | that i must love a loathed enemy. 1.05.141
'tis but thy name that is my enemy; 2.02. 38
to myself, | because it is an enemy to thee; 2.02. 56
i have been feasting with mine enemy, | where on 2.03. 49
in twain | to sunder his that was thine enemy? 5.03.100
free, and must my house | be my retentive enemy? TIM 3.04. 81
i'll believe him as an enemy, and give over my 4.03.454 P
caesar was ne'er so much your enemy | as that JC 2.02.112
as a friend or an enemy? 3.03. 21 P
'tis better that the enemy seek us; 4.03.199
the enemy, marching along by them, | by them 4.03.207
the enemy increaseth every day; 4.03.216
you said the enemy would not come down, | but 5.01. 2
the enemy comes on in gallant show; 5.01. 13
myself have to mine own turn'd enemy. 5.03. 2
whether yond troops are friend or enemy. 5.03. 18
i dare assure thee that no enemy | shall ever 5.04. 21
jewel | given to the common enemy of man, | to MAC 3.01. 68
bosoms, | whose execution takes your enemy off, 3.01.104
both of you | know banquo was your enemy. 3.01.114
all know, security | is mortals' chiefest enemy. 3.05. 33
i would not hear your enemy say so, | nor shall HAM 1.02.170
doth try, | directly seasons him his enemy. 3.02.209
wronged, | his madness is poor hamlet's enemy. 5.02.239
i profess | myself an enemy to all other joys LR 1.01. 73
moreover, to descry | the strength o' th' enemy. 4.05. 14
combine together 'gainst the enemy; 5.01. 29
employ you | against the general enemy ottoman. OTH 1.03. 49
men should put an enemy in their mouths to steal 2.03.290 P
that thrust had been mine enemy indeed, | but 5.01. 24
darts, | though enemy, lost aim and could not? ANT 4.14. 71
you have prevail'd, i am no further your enemy; CYM 1.04.160 P
he's for his master, | and enemy to my son. 1.05. 29
than | thyself domestic officers) thine enemy. 3.01. 64
say, "thus mine enemy fell, | and thus i set my 3.03. 91
sorry that i must report ye | my master's enemy. 3.05. 4
from this time forth | i wear it as your enemy. 3.05. 14
and if mine enemy | but fear the sword like me, 3.06. 25
and though he came our enemy, remember | he was 4.02.245
the enemy full-hearted, | lolling the tongue 5.03. 7
me, | this sword shall prove he's honor's enemy. PER 2.05. 64
what canst thou wish thine enemy to be? 4.06.158
carrier of that honor which | his enemy come in, TNK 1.02.109
because another | first sees the enemy, shall i 2.02.194
thus mistakes, the which, to you being enemy, 3.01. 49
thou art so brave an enemy | that no man but thy 3.06. 43
you charg'd | upon the left wing of the enemy, 3.06. 75
strove to show | mine enemy in this business, 5.01. 21
finding their enemy to be so curst, | they all VEN 887
her mansion batter'd by the enemy, | her sacred LUC 1171
"mine enemy was strong, my poor self weak | (and 1646

ENEMY'S 11 FR 0.0012 REL FR 7 V 4 P
i would i had any drum of the enemy's. AWW 4.01. 61 P
a drum now of the enemy's — 4.01. 64 P
and driven into despair an enemy's hope, | who R2 2.02. 47
as many holes in an enemy's battle as thou hast 2H4 3.02.154 P
every gash was an enemy's grave. COR 2.01.156 P
writing destruction on the enemy's castle? TIT 3.01.169
and from her bosom took the enemy's point, 5.03.111
the enemy's drum is heard, and fearful scouring TIM 5.02. 15
mine enemy's dog, | though he had bit me, should LR 4.07. 35
the enemy's in view, draw up your powers. 5.01. 51
false-play'd my glory | unto an enemy's triumph. ANT 4.14. 20

/ENEW 1 FR 0.0001 REL FR 1 V 0 P
and follies doth /enew | as falcon doth the fowl MM 3.01. 90

ENFEEBLED 3 FR 0.0003 REL FR 3 V 0 P
my people are with sickness much enfeebled, | my H5 3.06.145
famish'd, | or with light skirmishes enfeebled. 1H6 1.04. 69
then lack'd i matter, that enfeebled mine. SON 86.14

ENFEEBLES 1 FR 0.0001 REL FR 1 V 0 P
and the air on't | revengingly enfeebles me, or CYM 5.02. 4

ENFEOFF'D 1 FR 0.0001 REL FR 1 V 0 P
streets, | enfeoff'd himself to popularity, 1H4 3.02. 69

ENFETTER'D 1 FR 0.0001 REL FR 1 V 0 P
sin, | his soul is so enfetter'd to her love, OTH 2.03.345

ENFOLDINGS *(also infold)*

ENFOLDINGS 1 FR 0.0001 REL FR 0 V 1 P
not the air of the court in these enfoldings? WT 4.04.731 P

/ENFORC'D 1 FR 0.0001 REL FR 1 V 0 P
/and /are /enforc'd /from /our /most /quiet 2H4 4.01. 71

ENFORC'D 21 FR 0.0023 REL FR 17 V 4 P
when inward joy enforc'd my heart to smile! TGV 1.02. 63
and by an eminent body that enforc'd | the law MM 4.04. 22
i, being else by faith enforc'd | to call young ADO 5.04. 8
i was enforc'd to send it after him, | i was MV 5.01.216

what tranio did, myself enforc'd him to; SHR 5.01.129
we are enforc'd to farm our royal realm, | the R2 1.04. 45
but with nimble wing | we were enforc'd, for 1H4 5.01. 65
to the which course if i be enforc'd, if you do 2H4 4.03. 50 P
the earl of warwick and the duke enforc'd me. 3H6 1.01.229
enforc'd thee? 1.01.230
safety, | enforc'd us to this execution? R3 3.05. 46
hand, | because she was enforc'd, stain'd, and TIT 5.03. 38
nor his offenses enforc'd, for which he suffer'd JC 3.02. 40 P
adulterers by an enforc'd obedience of planetary LR 1.02.124 P
within this hour be off, thy mistress enforc'd, CYM 4.01. 17 P
master's garments | (which he enforc'd from me), 5.05.283
and enforc'd the god | snatch up the goodly boy TNK 4.02. 16
"as from this cold flint i enforc'd this fire, LUC 181
each one by him enforc'd retires his ward; 303
enforc'd by sympathy | of those fair suns set in 1229
and therefore art enforc'd to seek anew | some SON 82. 7

ENFORCE 36 FR 0.0040 REL FR 32 V 4 P
being awake, enforce them to this place; TMP 5.01.100
now i want | spirits to enforce, art to enchant, ep 14
nor how my father would enforce me marry | vain TGV 4.03. 16
so to enforce or qualify the laws | as to your MM 1.01. 65
here till he come and enforce them against him. 5.01.266 P
shall i enforce thy love? LLL 4.01. 81 P
wit | to enforce the pained impotent to smile. 5.02.854
work | than customary bounty can enforce you. MV 3.04. 9
or with a base and boist'rous sword enforce | a AYL 2.03. 32
shall in despite enforce a watery eye. SHR in.1. 128
i will no more enforce mine office on you, AWW 2.01.126
to enforce these rights so forcibly withheld. JN 1.01. 18
with swifter spleen than powder can enforce, 2.01.448
properly, | i will enforce it eas'ly to my love. 2.01.515
dying men | enforce attention like deep harmony. R2 2.01. 6
against aumerle we will enforce his trial. 4.01. 90
you not asham'd to enforce a poor widow to so 2H4 2.01. 82 P
that lack of means enforce you not to evils, 5.05. 67
and hunger will enforce them to be more eager. 1H6 1.02. 38
me, | and could it not enforce them to relent, 2H6 4.04. 17
will you enforce me to a world of cares? R3 3.07.223
enforce his pride, | and his old hate unto you; COR 2.03.219
enforce him with his envy to the people, | and 3.03. 3
a din confus'd | enforce the present execution 3.03. 21
earth, | thus i enforce thy rotten jaws to open, ROM 5.03. 47
if wrongs be evils and enforce us kill, | what TIM 3.05. 36
thou rather shalt enforce it with thy smile 5.04. 45
sometime with prayers, | enforce their charity. LR 2.03. 20
the law (with all his might to enforce it on) OTH 1.02. 16
the time, the place, the torture, o, enforce it! 5.02.369
you do not hold the method to enforce | the like ANT 1.03. 7
to enforce no further | the griefs between ye: 2.02. 99
know | we will extenuate rather than enforce. 5.02.125
we'll enforce it from thee | by a sharp torture. CYM 4.03. 11
a constant nobility enforce a freedom out of TNK 2.01. 34 P
me, but enjoy't till | i may enforce my remedy. 3.01.123

ENFORCED 12 FR 0.0013 REL FR 11 V 1 P
flower, | lamenting some enforced chastity. MND 3.01.200
rack, | where men enforced do speak any thing. MV 3.02. 33
portia, forgive me this enforced wrong, | and in 5.01.240
word, | though in some part enforced to digress, SHR 3.02.107
weep | upon the spot of this enforced cause — JN 5.02. 30
it so, | which finds it an enforced pilgrimage. R2 1.03.264
of the pridge, but he is enforced to retire, and H5 3.06. 94 P
stones | enforced from the old assyrian slings; 4.07. 62
looks | are at my service, like enforced smiles; R3 3.05. 9
and decay | it useth an enforced ceremony. JC 4.02. 21
who, much enforced, shows a hasty spark, | and 4.03.112
yield to my love, if not, enforced hate, | in LUC 668

ENFORCEDLY 1 FR 0.0001 REL FR 1 V 0 P
but thou | dost it enforcedly. TIM 4.03.241

ENFORCEMENT 7 FR 0.0008 REL FR 7 V 0 P
let gentleness my strong enforcement be, | in AYL 2.07.118
and by what rough enforcement | you got it from AWW 5.03.107
upon enforcement flies with greatest speed, | so 2H4 1.01.120
desire, | and his enforcement of the city wives, R3 3.07. 8
your mere enforcement shall acquittance me 3.07.233
the leisure and enforcement of the time 5.03.238
by foul enforcement might be done to me, | from LUC 1623

ENFORCES 2 FR 0.0002 REL FR 0 V 2 P
a monarch, and his countenance enforces homage. H5 3.07. 28 P
wink and yield, as love is blind and enforces. 5.02.301 P

ENFORCEST 1 FR 0.0001 REL FR 0 V 1 P
by virtue thou enforcest laughter — thy silly LLL 3.01. 75 P

ENFRANCHED 1 FR 0.0001 REL FR 1 V 0 P
him he has | hipparchus, my enfranched bondman, ANT 3.13.149

ENFRANCHIS'D 4 FR 0.0004 REL FR 3 V 1 P
belike that now she hath enfranchis'd them TGV 2.04. 90
with a muzzle and enfranchis'd with a clog, ADO 1.03. 33 P
of great nature thence | freed and enfranchis'd, WT 2.02. 59
and being enfranchis'd, bid him come to me; TIM 1.01.106

ENFRANCHISE *(also franchise, etc.)*

ENFRANCHISE 4 FR 0.0004 REL FR 3 V 1 P
"silvia, this night i will enfranchise thee." TGV 3.01.151
sirrah costard, i will enfranchise thee. LLL 3.01.120 P
sister, | i will perform it to enfranchise you. R3 1.01.110
take in that kingdom, and enfranchise that; ANT 1.01. 23

ENFRANCHISED 1 FR 0.0001 REL FR 1 V 0 P
were | he is enfranchised and come to light. TIT 4.02.125

ENFRANCHISEMENT 6 FR 0.0006 REL FR 6 V 0 P
request | th' enfranchisement of arthur, whose JN 4.02. 52
his golden uncontroll'd enfranchisement, | more R2 1.03. 90
to beg | enfranchisement immediate on his knees, 3.03.114
pawn their swords /for my enfranchisement. 2H6 5.01.113
to beg enfranchisement for publius cimber. JC 3.01. 57
out, | "liberty, freedom, and enfranchisement!" 3.01. 81

ENFRANCHISING 1 FR 0.0001 REL FR 1 V 0 P
enfranchising his mouth, his back, his breast. VEN 396

ENFREED 1 FR 0.0001 REL FR 1 V 0 P
for the enfreed antenor, the fair cressid. TRO 4.01. 39

ENFREEDOMING 1 FR 0.0001 REL FR 0 V 1 P
thee at liberty, enfreedoming thy person: LLL 3.01.124 P

ENGAG'D 15 FR 0.0017 REL FR 14 V 1 P
wars, | and i to thee engag'd a prince's word, ERR 5.01.162
enough, i am engag'd, i will challenge him. ADO 4.01.331 P
o spite! too old to be engag'd to young. MND 1.01.138
indeed | i have engag'd myself to a dear friend, MV 3.02.261
friend, | engag'd my friend to his mere enemy, 3.02.262
noble she was, and thought | i stood engag'd; AWW 5.03. 96
cross | we are impressed and engag'd to fight — 1H4 1.01. 21
indeed his king) to be engag'd in wales, | there 4.03. 95
and westmerland, that was engag'd, did bear it, 5.02. 43
which hath our several honors all engag'd | to TRO 2.02.124
and i do stand engag'd to many greeks, | even in 5.03. 68
'tis all engag'd, some forfeited and gone, | and TIM 2.02.146
than honesty to honesty engag'd | that this JC 2.01.127
that, struggling to be free, | art more engag'd; HAM 3.03. 69
retire, we have engag'd ourselves too far. ANT 4.07. 1

ENGAGE 5 FR 0.0005 REL FR 5 V 0 P
this to be true, | i do engage my life. AYL 5.04.166
pawn, | engage it to the trial, if thou darest. R2 4.01. 56
pawn, | engage it to the trial, if thou dar'st. 4.01. 71
i will engage my word to thee | that i will by 1H4 2.04.514
of a sacred vow | i here engage my words. OTH 3.03.462

ENGAGED 3 FR 0.0003 REL FR 3 V 0 P
hold it sin | to break the vow i am engaged in. LLL 4.03.176
who hither come engaged by my oath | (which god R2 1.03. 17
we all that are engaged to this loss | knew that 2H4 1.01.180

ENGAGEMENTS 1 FR 0.0001 REL FR 1 V 0 P
all my engagements i will construe to thee, JC 2.01.307

ENGAGING 1 FR 0.0001 REL FR 1 V 0 P
engaging and redeeming of himself | with such a TRO 5.05. 39

ENGENDER 1 FR 0.0001 REL FR 1 V 0 P
from my cold heart let heaven engender hail, ANT 3.13.159

ENGENDERS 6 FR 0.0006 REL FR 6 V 0 P
too young, | and abstinence engenders maladies. LLL 4.03.291
for it engenders choler, planteth anger, | and SHR 4.01.172
and that engenders thunder in his breast, | and 1H6 3.01. 39
the presence of a king engenders love | amongst 3.01.180
up, | for every cloud engenders not a storm. 3H6 5.03. 13
engenders the black toad and adder blue, | the TIM 4.03.181

ENGEND'RED 4 FR 0.0004 REL FR 4 V 0 P
it is engend'red in the /eyes, | with gazing fed MV 3.02. 67
of drops that sacred pity hath engend'red; AYL 2.07.123
but kill'st the mother that engend'red thee! JC 5.03. 71
it is engend'red. OTH 1.03.403

ENGEND'RING 1 FR 0.0001 REL FR 0 V 1 P
man, as i do hate the engend'ring of toads. TRO 2.03.158 P

ENGILDS 1 FR 0.0001 REL FR 1 V 0 P
who more engilds the night | than all yon fiery MND 3.02.187

ENGINE 10 FR 0.0011 REL FR 9 V 1 P
sword, pike, knife, gun, or need of any engine, TMP 2.01.162
and here an engine fit for my proceeding! TGV 3.01.138
they place before his hand that made the engine, TRO 1.03.208
but let him, like an engine | not portable, lie 2.03.134
when he walks, he moves like an engine, and the COR 5.04. 19 P
o, that delightful engine of her thoughts, TIT 3.01. 82
or who hath brought the fatal engine in | that 5.03. 86
which, like an engine, wrench'd my frame of LR 1.04.268
yet his eye | is like an engine bent, or a sharp TNK 5.03. 42
once more the engine of her thoughts began: VEN 367

ENGINER *(also ingener)*

ENGINER 2 FR 0.0002 REL FR 1 V 1 P
then there's achilles, a rare enginer! TRO 2.03. 8 P
for 'tis the sport to have the enginer | hoist HAM 3.04.206

ENGINES 4 FR 0.0004 REL FR 2 V 2 P
tokens, and all these engines of lust, are not AWW 3.05. 19 P
and she shall file our engines with advice, TIT 2.01.123
and, o you mortal engines, whose rude throats OTH 3.03.355
with treachery and devise engines for my life. 4.02.216 P

ENGIRT 4 FR 0.0004 REL FR 4 V 0 P
my body round engirt with misery — | for what's 2H6 3.01.200
that gold must round engirt these brows of mine, 5.01. 99
this siege that hath engirt his marriage, | this LUC 221
corrupted, | grossly engirt with daring infamy: 1173

ENGIRTS 1 FR 0.0001 REL FR 1 V 0 P
so white a friend engirts so white a foe: VEN 364

/ENGLAND 4 FR 0.0004 REL FR 4 V 0 P
/if /my /word /be /sterling /yet /in /england, R2 4.01.264
/in /england /the /most /valiant /gentleman. 2H4 4.01.130
so happy be the issue, brother /england, | of H5 5.02. 12
/be /shortly /known /to /him /from /england HAM 5.02. 71

ENGLAND 243 FR 0.0274 REL FR 193 V 50 P
were i in england now (as once i was) and had TMP 2.02. 28 P
as soon quarrel at it as any man in england. WIV 1.01.291 P
where england? ERR 3.02.125 P
to falconbridge, the young baron of england? MV 1.02. 67 P
he hath a third at mexico, a fourth for england, 1.03. 20 P
they have in england | a coin that bears the 2.07. 55
from tripolis, from mexico, and england, | from 3.02.268
they live like the old robin hood of england. AYL 1.01.116 P
were big enough for the bed of ware in england, TN 3.02. 48 P
the borrowed majesty, of england here. JN 1.01. 4
even till that england, hedg'd in with the main, 2.01. 26
my lord chatillion may from england bring | that 2.01. 46
what england says, say briefly, gentle lord, 2.01. 52
england, impatient of your just demands, | hath 2.01. 56
peace be to england, if that war return | from 2.01. 89
if that war return | from france to england, 2.01. 90
england we love, and for that england's sake 2.01. 91
but thou from loving england art so far | that 2.01. 94
england was geffrey's right, | and this is 2.01.105
england and ireland, /anjou, touraine, maine, 2.01.152
'tis france, for england. 2.01.202
england for itself. 2.01.202
doth not the crown of england prove the king? 2.01.273
england, thou hast not sav'd one drop of blood 2.01.341
speak, citizens, for england. who's your king? 2.01.362
the king of england, when we know the king. 2.01.363
by east and west let france and england mount 2.01.381
of spain, the lady blanch, | is near to england. 2.01.424
speak england first, that hath been forward 2.01.482
brother of england, how may we content | this 2.01.547
france friend with england, what becomes of me? 3.01. 35
and from the mouth of england | add thus much 3.01.152
brother of england, you blaspheme in this. 3.01.161
or the light loss of england for a friend. 3.01.206
england, i will fall from thee. 3.01.320
cousin, away for england! 3.03. 6
for england, cousin, go. 3.03. 71
and bloody england into england gone, 3.04. 8
and bloody england into england gone, 3.04. 8
well could i bear that england had this praise, 3.04. 15
to england, if you will. 3.04. 68
is now in england ransacking the church, 3.04.172
for england go; 3.04.181
from france to england. 4.02.110
heaven take my soul, and england keep my bones! 4.03. 10
how easy dost thou take all england up | from 4.03.142
and england now is left | to tug and scamble, 4.03.145
up the womb | of your dear mother england, blush 5.02.153
lead me to the revolts of england here. 5.04. 7
of the part of england. 5.06. 2
this england never did, nor never shall, | lie 5.07.112
us rue, | if england to itself do rest but true. 5.07.118
save back to england, all the world's my way. R2 1.03.207
as were our england in reversion his, | and he 1.04. 35
plot, this earth, this realm, this england, 2.01. 50
england, bound in with the triumphant sea, 2.01. 61
that england, that was wont to conquer others, 2.01. 65
for sleeping england long time have i watch'd, 2.01. 77
landlord of england art thou now, not king, 2.01.113
our uncle york lord governor of england; 2.01.220
and i am come to seek that name in england, 2.03. 71
if that my cousin king be king in england, | it 2.03.123
my lords of england, let me tell you this: 2.03.140
of death to me | than bullingbrook to england. 3.01. 32
crowns | than bullingbrook's return to england, 4.01. 17
gallows standing in england when thou art king? 1H4 1.02. 59 P
when i am king of england i shall command all 2.04. 14 P
i'll be sworn upon all the books in england, i 2.04. 50 P
lives not three good men unhang'd in england, 2.04.131 P
swear truth out of england but he would make you 2.04.306 P
shall the son of england prove a thief and take 2.04.409 P
with the sea | that chides the banks of england, 3.01. 44
england, from trent and severn hitherto, | by 3.01. 73
wars | that all in england did repute him dead; 5.01. 54
day, | england did never owe so sweet a hope, 5.02. 67
nor can one england brook a double reign | of 5.04. 66
humors, there's not a better wench in england. 2H4 2.01.149 P
did all the chevalry of england move | to do 2.03. 20
it is the foul–mouth'd'st rogue in england. 2.04. 72 P
up | whiles england shall have generation. 4.02. 49
england shall double gild his treble guilt, 4.05.128
england shall give him office, honor, might; 4.05.129
send to prison | th' immediate heir of england! 5.02. 71
the laws of england are at my commandement. 5.03.136 P
never king of england | had nobles richer and H5 1.02.126
hearts have left their bodies here in england, 1.02.128
that england, being empty of defense, | hath 1.02.153
for once the eagle (england) being in prey, | to 1.02.169
divide your happy england into four, | whereof 1.02.214
we never valu'd this poor seat of england, | and 1.02.269
now all the youth of england are on fire, | and 2.pr. 1
o england! 2.pr. 16
no king of england, if not king of france! 2.02.193
for england his approaches makes as fierce | as 2.04. 9
no, with no more than if we heard that england 2.04. 24
embassadors from harry king of england | do 2.04. 65
from our brother of england? 2.04. 75
full intent | back to our brother of england. 2.04.115
what to him from england? 2.04.116
for i desire | nothing but odds with england. 2.04.129
and leave your england as dead midnight, still, 3.pr. 19
whose limbs were made in england, show us here 3.01. 26
cry, "god for harry, england, and saint george!" 3.01. 34
let him greet england with our sharp defiance. 3.05. 37
bar harry england, that sweeps through our land 3.05. 48
and let him say to england that we send | to 3.05. 62
say thou to harry of england, though we seem'd 3.06.119 P
england shall repent his folly, see his weakness 3.06.124 P
alas, poor harry of england! 3.07.130 P
and peevish fellow is this king of england, to 3.07.133 P
that island of england breeds very valiant 3.07.140 P
go with my brothers to my lords of england. 4.01. 30
that england shall crouch down in fear, and 4.02. 37
but one ten thousand of those men in england 4.03. 17
no, faith, my coz, wish not a man from england. 4.03. 30
and gentlemen in england, now a–bed, | shall 4.03. 64
thou dost not wish more help from england, coz? 4.03. 73
valorous, and thrice–worthy seigneur of england. 4.04. 63 P
universal world, or in france, or in england! 4.08. 10 P
and then to callice, and to england then, 4.08.125
to england will i steal, and there i'll steal; 5.01. 87
face, | most worthy brother england, fairly met! 5.02. 10
great kings of france and england: 5.02. 24
shall mock at me, i cannot speak your england. 5.02.103 P
hand, and say, "harry of england, i am thine"; 5.02.237 P
but i will tell thee aloud, "england is thine, 5.02.239 P
sooner persuade harry of england than a general 5.02.278 P
is't so, my lords of england? 5.02.331 P
the contending kingdoms | of france and england, 5.02.350
bleeding sword 'twixt england and fair france. 5.02.355
small most greatly lived | this star of england. ep 6
bands crown'd king | of france and england, did ep 10
they lost france, and made his england bleed; ep 12
england ne'er lost a king of so much worth. 1H6 1.01. 7
england ne'er had a king until his time: 1.01. 8
records | england all olivers and rolands bred 1.02. 30
third son to the third edward, king of england. 2.04. 84
ay, we may march in england, or in france, | not 3.01.186
and was he not in england prisoner? 3.03. 70
crossing the sea from england into france, 4.01. 89
from thence to england, where i hope ere long 4.01.171
servant in arms to harry king of england, | and 4.02. 4
the fraud of england, not the force of france, 4.04. 36
never to england shall he bear his life, | but 4.04. 38
between the realms of england and of france. 5.01. 6
before that england give the french the foil. 5.03. 23
i'll over then to england with this news, | and 5.03.167
since, lords of england, it is thus agreed 5.04.116
nor be rebellious to the crown of england, 5.04.171
thou, nor thy nobles, to the crown of england. 5.04.172
to cross the seas to england and be crown'd 5.05. 90
in sight of england and her lordly peers, 2H6 1.01. 11
great king of england, and my gracious lord, 1.01. 24
ambassador for henry king of england, that the 1.01. 46 P
crown her queen of england ere the thirtieth of 1.01. 49 P
brave peers of england, pillars of the state, 1.01. 75
o peers of england, shameful is this league, 1.01. 98
methinks the realms of england, france, and 1.01.232
bookish rule hath pull'd fair england down. 1.01.259
is this the fashions in the court of england? 1.03. 43

as i was cause | your highness came to england, 1.03. 66
i | in england work your grace's full content. 1.03. 67
but can do more in england than the king. 1.03. 71
all | cannot do more in england than the nevils: 1.03. 73
why, suffolk, england knows thine insolence. 2.01. 31
the greatest man in england but the king. 2.02. 82
and humphrey is no little man in england. 3.01. 20
as firmly as i hope for fertile england. 3.01. 88
night by night, in studying good for england. 3.01.111
heard of, | that england was defam'd by tyranny. 3.01.123
i will stir up in england some black storm 3.01.349
troubles the silver spring where england drinks. 4.01. 72
was never merry world in england since gentlemen 4.02. 8 P
there shall be in england seven halfpenny loaves 4.02. 65 P
for thereby is england main'd, and fain to go 4.02.162 P
that the laws of england may come out of your 4.07. 6 P
my mouth shall be the parliament of england. 4.07. 15 P
spare england, for it is your native coast. 4.08. 50
for yet may england curse my wretched reign. 4.09. 49
it shall ne'er be said, while england stands, 4.10. 42
and now in england to our heart's great sorrow, 3H6 1.01.128
what good is this to england and himself! 1.01.177
the crown of england, father, which is yours. 1.02. 9
and when came george from burgundy to england? 2.01.143
for king of england shalt thou be proclaim'c 2.01.194
where did you dwell when i was king of england? 3.01. 74
fair queen of england, worthy margaret, | sit 3.03. 1
not montague that of itself | england is safe, 4.01. 40
by the grace of god, king of england and france, 4.07. 72 P
and once again proclaim us king of england. 4.08. 53
/thence we look'd toward england, | and cited up R3 1.04. 13
woe, woe for england, not a whit for me! 3.04. 80
miserable england! 3.04.103
the peace of england, and our persons' safety, 3.05. 45
happy were england, would this virtuous prince 3.07. 78
and do intend to make her queen of england. 4.04.264
he makes for england, here to claim the crown. 4.04.468
fight, gentlemen of england! 5.03.338
england hath long been mad and scarr'd herself: 5.05. 23
and make poor england weep in streams of blood! 5.05. 37
not a man in england | can advise me like you; H8 1.01.134
england and france might through their amity 1.01.181
the duke | shall govern england.'" 1.02.171
for little england | you'ld venture an emballing 2.03. 46
say, henry king of england, come into the court. 2.04. 6 P
henry king of england, etc. 2.04. 8 P
say, katherine queen of england, come into the 2.04. 10 P
katherine queen of england, etc. 2.04. 12 P
katherine queen of england, come into the court. 2.04.126 P
in england | but little for my profit; 3.01. 82
to the high and mighty princess of england, 5.04. 3 P
she shall be, to the happiness of england, | an 5.04. 56
i'll to england. MAC 2.03.137
are bestow'd | in england and in ireland, not 3.01. 30
some holy angel | fly to the court of england, 3.06. 46
bring you word | macduff is fled to england. 4.01.142
fled to england! 4.01.142
and here from gracious england have i offer | of 4.03. 43
which often, since my here-remain in england, 4.03.148
gracious england hath | lent us good siward, and 4.03.189
he shall with speed to england | for the demand HAM 3.01.169
to england send him, or confine him where | your 3.01.186
and he to england shall along with you. 3.03. 4
i must to england, you know that? 3.04.200
tend, and every thing is bent | for england. 4.03. 46
for england. 4.03. 46
but come, for england! 4.03. 49 P
come, for england! 4.03. 53 P
and, england, if my love thou hold'st at aught 4.03. 58
do it, england, | for like the hectic in my 4.03. 65
th' embassador that was bound for england — if 4.06. 11 P
and guildenstern hold their course for england, 4.06. 28 P
born — he that is mad, and sent into england. 5.01.148 P
ay, marry, why was he sent into england? 5.01.149 P
king, | as england was his faithful tributary, 5.02. 39
to th' embassadors of england gives | this 5.02.351
i cannot live to hear the news from england, 5.02.354
and our affairs from england come too late. 5.02.368
you from the polack wars, and you from england, 5.02.376
i learn'd it in england, where indeed they are OTH 2.03. 76 P
o sweet england! 2.03. 88 P
hath chid down all the majesty of england, STM II.C 73
nay, any where that not adheres to england, II.C 129

ENGLAND'S 64 FR 0.0072 REL FR 63 V 1 P
and for that england's sake | with burden of our JN 2.01. 91
in brief, we are the king of england's subjects: 2.01.267
fifteen thousand hearts of england's breed — 2.01.275
arthur of britain england's king and yours. 2.01.311
king john, your king and england's, doth 2.01.313
save what is opposite to england's love. 3.01.254
directly lead | thy foot to england's throne. 3.04.130
then england's ground, farewell, sweet soil, R2 1.03.306
gaunt's rebukes, nor england's private wrongs, 2.01.166
dar'd once to touch a dust of england's ground? 2.03. 91
shall ill become the flower of england's face, 3.03. 97
and quickly bring us word of england's fall. H5 3.05. 68
invites the king of england's stay at home; 5.pr. 37
arms, | of england's coat one half is cut away. 1H6 1.01. 81
or tear the lions out of england's coat; 1.05. 28
a little herd of england's timorous deer, 4.02. 46
and saint george, talbot and england's right, 4.02. 55
farewell talbot, france, and england's honor! 4.03. 23
his false hopes, the trust of england's honor, 4.04. 20
death's revenge, thy youth, and england's fame: 4.06. 39
whose life was england's glory, gallia's wonder. 4.07. 48
he doth intend she shall be england's queen. 5.01. 45
and let her head fall into england's lap. 5.03. 26
you, | if happy england's royal king be free. 5.03.115
that marg'ret may be england's royal queen. 5.05. 24
long live queen margaret, england's happiness! 2H6 1.01. 37
over of the king of england's own proper cost 1.01. 60 P
i never read but england's kings have had 1.01.128
even as i have of fertile england's soil. 1.01.238
his new bride and england's dear-bought queen, 1.01.252
not half so bad as thine to england's king, 1.04. 47
which is infallible, to england's crown. 2.02. 5
long live our sovereign richard, england's king! 2.02. 63
god and king henry govern england's realm. 2.03. 30
and twice by awkward wind from england's bank 3.02. 83
bid them blow towards england's blessed shore, 3.02. 90
and even with this i lost fair england's view, 3.02.110
death, | or banished fair england's territories, 3.02.245
beest death, i'll give thee england's treasure, 3.03. 2
to entertain great england's lawful king! 5.01. 4
outcast of naples, england's bloody scourge! 5.01.118
the rightful heir to england's royal seat. 5.01.178
what, was it you that would be england's king? 3H6 1.04. 70
the next degree is england's royal throne; 2.01.193
there to be crowned england's royal king; 2.06. 88
seat | of england's true-anointed lawful king. 3.03. 29
sister, | to england's king in lawful marriage. 3.03. 57
then, england's messenger, return in post, | and 3.03.222
should not become my wife and england's queen. 4.01. 26
then, for his mind, be edward england's king, 4.03. 48
come hither, england's hope. 4.06. 68
once more we sit in england's royal throne, 5.07. 1
small joy have i in being england's queen. R3 1.03.109
die neither mother, wife, nor england's queen! 1.03.208
shall lose the royalty of england's throne. 3.04. 40
cry, "god save richard, england's royal king!" 3.07. 22
long live richard, england's worthy king! 3.07.240
nor mother, wife, nor england's counted queen. 4.01. 46
rest thy unrest on england's lawful earth, 4.04. 29
infer fair england's peace by this alliance. 4.04.343
and who is england's king but great york's heir? 4.04.472
arm, fight, and conquer for fair england's sake! 5.03.158
made precious by the foil | of england's chair, 5.03.251
importing denmark's health and england's too, HAM 5.02. 21

ENGLISH *(also anglish)*

ENGLISH 143 FR 0.0161 REL FR 105 V 38 P
her will, out of honesty into english. WIV 1.03. 50 P
of god's patience and the king's english. 1.04. 6 P
here's a fellow frights english out of his wits. 2.01.139 P
mock-water, in our english tongue, is valor, 2.03. 60 P
keep their limbs whole and hack our english. 3.01. 78 P
they speak english? 4.03. 6 P
till thou art able to woo her in good english. 5.05.134 P
the taunt of one that makes fritters of english? 5.05.143 P
lief be a list of an english kersey as be pil'd, MM 1.02. 33 P
that i have a poor pennyworth in the english. MV 1.02. 72 P
narrow seas that part | the french and english, 2.08. 29
sure they are bastards to the english, the AWW 2.03. 94 P
h'as led the drum before the english tragedians. 4.03.266 P
sir, 'a has an english /name, but his fisnomy is 4.05. 39 P
of thy unnatural uncle, english john. JN 2.01. 10
than now the english bottoms have waft o'er 2.01. 73
though all these english and their discipline 2.01.261
much work for tears in many an english mother, 2.01.303
there stuck no plume in any english crest | that 2.01.317
troop of huntsmen come | our lusty english, all 2.01.322
full thirty thousand marks of english coin. 2.01.530
to train ten thousand english to their side, 3.04.175
now hear our english king, | for thus his 5.02.128
fly, noble english, you are bought and sold! 5.04. 10
when english measure backward their own ground 5.05. 3
the english lords | by his persuasion are again 5.05. 10
verge | that ever was surveyed by english eye, R2 1.01. 94
lo, as at english feasts, so i regreet | the 1.03. 67
my native english, now i must forgo, | and now 1.03.160
and sigh'd my english breath in foreign clouds, 3.01. 20
her pasters' grass with faithful english blood. 3.03.100
besides himself, are all the english peers, 3.04. 88
that reacheth from the restful english court 4.01. 12
the blood of english shall manure the ground, 4.01.137
forthwith a power of english shall we levy, 1H4 1.01. 22
that never spake other english in his life than 2.04. 24 P
i can speak english, lord, as well as you, | for 3.01.119
for i was train'd up in the english court, 3.01.120
to the harp | many an english ditty lovely well, 3.01.122
my wife can speak no english, i no welsh. 3.01.191
that douglas and the english rebels met | the 3.02.165
was alway yet the trick of our english nation, 2H4 1.02.215 P
with a great power of english and of scots, 4.04. 98
rigol hath divorc'd | so many english kings. 4.05. 37
and to the english court assemble now, | from 4.05.121
this is the english, not the turkish court, 5.02. 47
o noble english, that could entertain | with H5 1.02.111
with winged heels, as english mercuries. 2.pr. 7
policy | seek to divert the english purposes. 2.pr. 15
and my noble peers, | these english monsters! 2.02. 85
thus comes the english with full power upon us, 2.04. 1
left by the fatal and neglected english | upon 2.04. 13
take up the english short, and let them know 2.04. 72
or close the wall up with our english dead. 3.01. 2
on, on, you /noblest english, | whose blood is 3.01. 17
their bodies to the lust of english youth | to 3.05. 30
they bid us to the english dancing-schools, 3.05. 32
i thought upon one pair of english legs | did 3.06.149
and my way shall be pav'd with english faces. 3.07. 81 P
i would fain be about the ears of the english. 3.07. 84 P
he longs to eat the english. 3.07. 91 P
the english lie within fifteen hundred paces of 3.07.125 P
if the english had any apprehension, they would 3.07.135 P
ay, but these english are shrowdly out of beef. 3.07.152 P
french | do the low-rated english play at dice; 4.pr. 19
the poor condemned english, | like sacrifices, 4.pr. 22
be friends, you english fools, be friends, we 4.01.222 P
but it is no english treason to cut french 4.01.227 P
that their hot blood may spin in english eyes, 4.02. 10
the english are embattled, you french peers. 4.02. 14
mark then abounding valor in our english: 4.03.104
to smother up the english in our throngs, | if 4.05. 20
where is the number of our english dead? 4.08.102
the english beach | pales in the flood with men, 5.pr. 9
he could not speak english in the native garb, 5.01. 76 P
he could not therefore handle an english cudgel. 5.01. 77 P
correction teach you a good english condition. 5.01. 79 P
so are you, princes english, every one. 5.02. 11
you english princes all, i do salute you. 5.02. 22
confess it brokenly with your english tongue. 5.02.106 P
i am glad thou canst speak no better english, 5.02.123 P
kate, dost thou understand thus much english? 5.02.193 P
boy, half french, half english, that shall go to 5.02.208 P
and for my english moi'ty, take the word of a 5.02.215 P
by mine honor, in true english, i love thee, 5.02.221 P
for thy voice is music and thy english broken; 5.02.244 P
break thy mind to me in broken english — wilt 5.02.246 P
my royal cousin, teach you our princess english? 5.02.282 P
perfectly i love her, and that is good english. 5.02.284 P
that english may as french, french englishmen, 5.02.367
awake, awake, english nobility! 1H6 1.01. 78
france is revolted from the english quite, 1.01. 90
the english army is grown weak and faint; 1.01.158
late did he shine upon the english side; 1.02. 3
otherwhiles the famish'd english, like pale 1.02. 7
and drive the english forth the bounds of france 1.02. 54
assign'd am i to be the english scourge. 1.02.129
with henry's death the english circle ends, 1.02.136
and how the english have the suburbs won. 1.04. 2
espials have informed me | how the english, in 1.04. 9
our english troops retire, i cannot stay them; 1.05. 2
they call'd us for our fierceness english dogs, 1.05. 25
walls, | rescu'd is orleance from the english! 1.06. 2
and for the right | of english henry, shall this 2.01. 36
the special watchmen of our english weal, | i 3.01. 66
i, as sure as english henry lives | and as his 3.02. 80
and all the troops of english after him. 3.03. 32
ill, | who then but english henry will be lord, 3.03. 66
english john talbot, captains, /calls you forth, 4.02. 3
upon no christian soul but english talbot. 4.02. 30
if we be english deer, be then in blood, | not 4.02. 48
thou princely leader of our english strength, 4.03. 17
we english warriors wot not what it means. 4.07. 55
the english army, that divided was | into two 5.02. 11
blood, | and heir-apparent to the english crown. 2H6 1.01.152
was rightful heir unto the english crown | and 1.03.184
resolve thee, richard, claim the english crown. 3H6 1.01. 49
yet not so wealthy as an english yeoman. 1.04.123
iron of naples hid with english gilt, | whose 2.02.139
torment myself to catch the english crown; 3.02.179
that bona shall be wife to the english king. 3.03.139
to edward, but not to the english king. 3.03.140
my quarrel and this english queen's are one. 3.03.216
but henry now shall wear the english crown, 4.03. 49
edward's fruit, true heir to th' english crown. 4.04. 24
these english woes shall make me smile in france R3 4.04.115
like heathen gods, | shone down the english; H8 1.01. 20
there is no english soul | more stronger to 1.01.146
all the good our english | have got by the late 1.03. 5
to think an english courtier may be wise | and 1.03. 22
because they speak no english, thus they pray'd 1.04. 65
pray speak in english. 3.01. 46
ever yet committed | may be absolv'd in english. 3.01. 50
would i had never trod this english earth, | or 3.01.143
shall this lady, | when she has so much english. 5.04. 14
faith, here's an english tailor come hither for MAC 2.03. 13 P
lives in the english court, and is receiv'd | of 3.06. 26
the english pow'r is near, led on by malcolm, 5.02. 1
thanes, | and mingle with the english epicures! 5.03. 8
the english force, so please you. 5.03. 18
drug, | would scour these english hence? 5.03. 56
seek him out | upon the english party. LR 4.06.250
are nothing to your english. OTH 2.03. 79 P

ENGLISH'D 1 FR 0.0001 REL FR 0 V 1 P
voice of her behavior (to be english'd rightly) WIV 1.03. 48 P

/ENGLISHMAN 1 FR 0.0001 REL FR 0 V 1 P
is your /englishman so exquisite in his drinking OTH 2.03. 80 P

ENGLISHMAN 10 FR 0.0011 REL FR 7 V 3 P
then i have as much mock-vater as de englishman. WIV 2.03. 63 P
he borrow'd a box of the ear of the englishman, MV 1.02. 80 P
crow, | thinking this voice an armed englishman; JN 5.02.145
for that my grandsire was an englishman, 5.04. 42
where ever englishman durst set his foot. R2 1.01. 66
though banish'd, yet a true-born englishman. 1.03.309
an englishman? H5 4.07.124 P
i do not know that englishman alive | with whom R3 2.01. 70
that any englishman dare give me counsel? H8 3.01. 84
till looking on an englishman, the fairest that PP 15. 3

ENGLISHMAN'S 1 FR 0.0001 REL FR 1 V 0 P
win | a soul so easy as that englishman's." H5 2.02.125

ENGLISHMEN 5 FR 0.0005 REL FR 5 V 0 P
from the wounds of slaughtered englishmen, | the R2 3.03. 44
ten | we shall have each a hundred englishmen. H5 3.07.157
that english may as french, french englishmen, 5.02.367
are up | and put the englishmen unto the sword. 2H6 3.01.284
and temper clay with blood of englishmen. 3.01.311

ENGLISHWOMAN 1 FR 0.0001 REL FR 0 V 1 P
the princess is the better englishwoman. H5 5.02.121 P

ENGLUTS 1 FR 0.0001 REL FR 1 V 0 P
that it engluts and swallows other sorrows, OTH 1.03. 57

ENGLUTTED 2 FR 0.0002 REL FR 2 V 0 P
near the gulf, | thou needs must be englutted. H5 4.03. 83
have slaves and peasants | this night englutted! TIM 2.02.166

ENGRAFF'D 2 FR 0.0002 REL FR 0 V 2 P
been so lewd and so much engraff'd to falstaff. 2H4 2.02. 63 P
'tis not an engraff'd madness, but a most thick TNK 4.03. 49 P

ENGRAFTED *(see engraff'd, ingraft, ingrafted)*

ENGRAV'D 2 FR 0.0002 REL FR 2 V 0 P
thoughts | are visibly character'd and engrav'd, TGV 2.07. 4
read, | shall be engrav'd the sack of orleance, 1H6 2.02. 15

ENGRAVE 1 FR 0.0001 REL FR 1 V 0 P
thereon engrave | "edward" and "york"; R3 4.04.272

ENGRAVEN 1 FR 0.0001 REL FR 1 V 0 P
base, | that it will live engraven in my face. LUC 203

ENGROSS 2 FR 0.0002 REL FR 2 V 0 P
to engross up glorious deeds on my behalf; 1H4 3.02.148
not sleeping, to engross his idle body, | but R3 3.07. 76

ENGROSS'D *(also ingross'd)*

ENGROSS'D 2 FR 0.0002 REL FR 1 V 1 P
engross'd opportunities to meet her; WIV 2.02.196 P
which in a set hand fairly is engross'd | that R3 3.06. 2

ENGROSSED 2 FR 0.0002 REL FR 2 V 0 P
for this they have engrossed and pil'd up | the 2H4 4.05. 70
and my next self thou harder hast engrossed: SON 133. 6

ENGROSSEST 1 FR 0.0001 REL FR 1 V 0 P
if thou engrossest all the griefs are thine, AWW 3.02. 65

ENGROSSING 1 FR 0.0001 REL FR 1 V 0 P
kiss | a dateless bargain to engrossing death! ROM 5.03.115

ENGROSSMENTS 1 FR 0.0001 REL FR 1 V 0 P
yields his engrossments to the ending father. 2H4 4.05. 79

ENGUARD 1 FR 0.0001 REL FR 1 V 0 P
he may enguard his dotage with their pow'rs, LR 1.04.326

ENHEARSE *(see inhearse, etc.)*

ENIGMA 2 FR 0.0002 REL FR 1 V 1 P
some enigma, some riddle — come, thy l'envoy — LLL 3.01. 71
your enigma? COR 2.03. 90 P
ENIGMATICAL 1 FR 0.0001 REL FR 1 V 0 P
your answer, sir, is enigmatical, | but, for my ADO 5.04. 27
ENJAIL'D 1 FR 0.0001 REL FR 1 V 0 P
within my mouth you have enjail'd my tongue, R2 1.03.166
ENJOIN 2 FR 0.0002 REL FR 2 V 0 P
any heavy weight | that he'll enjoin me to. ADO 5.01.278
we enjoin thee, | as thou art liegeman to us, WT 2.03.173
ENJOIN'D 8 FR 0.0009 REL FR 6 V 2 P
up those logs that you are enjoin'd to pile! TMP 3.01. 17
last night she enjoin'd me to write some lines TGV 2.01. 87 P
as you enjoin'd me, i have writ your letter 2.01.104
and it was enjoin'd him in rome for want of LLL 5.02.712 P
i am enjoin'd by oath to observe three things: MV 2.09. 9
of enjoin'd penitents | there's four or five, to AWW 3.05. 94
accurs'd am i | to be by oath enjoin'd to this. WT 3.03. 53
and am enjoin'd | by holy lawrence to fall ROM 4.02. 19
ENJOINETH 1 FR 0.0001 REL FR 1 V 0 P
and since lord helicane enjoineth us, | we with PER 2.04. 55
ENJOY 54 FR 0.0061 REL FR 44 V 10 P
that i should win what you would enjoy? WIV 2.02.240 P
you shall, /and you will, enjoy ford's wife. 2.02.254 P
we prize not to the worth | whiles we enjoy it, ADO 4.01.219
being out of heart that you cannot enjoy her. LLL 3.01. 45 P
and will you persever to enjoy her? AYL 5.02. 4 P
consent with both that we may enjoy each other. 5.02. 9 P
so shall you quietly enjoy your hope, | and SHR 3.02.136
let me enjoy my private. TN 3.04. 89 P
where you may | enjoy your mistress — from the WT 4.04.528
as beauty, | that you might well enjoy her. 5.01.215
and like thy brother, to enjoy thy land; JN 1.01.135
leap, | the one in fear to lose what they enjoy, R2 2.04. 13
enjoy, | the other to enjoy by rage and war. 2.04. 14
you shall enjoy them, every thing set off | that 2H4 4.01.143
doubt not but your majesty | shall soon enjoy. 4.04. 12
rich, | that have abundance and enjoy it not. 4.04.108
must kings neglect, that private men enjoy! H5 4.01.237
upon condition i may quietly | enjoy mine own, 1H6 5.03.154
your grace shall well and quietly enjoy. 5.03.159
under him, | and still enjoy thy regal dignity. 5.04.132
court | and may enjoy such quiet walks as these? 2H6 4.10. 17
enjoy the kingdom after my decease. 3H6 1.01.175
now you are heir, therefore enjoy it now. 1.02. 12
a crown it is that seldom kings enjoy. 3.01. 65
and that is, to enjoy thee for my love. 3.02. 95
as you suppose | you should enjoy, were you this R3 1.03.151
little joy you may suppose in me | that i enjoy, 1.03.153
his bed | did i enjoy the golden dew of sleep, 4.01. 83
shall these enjoy our lands? 5.03.336
wear it, enjoy it, and make much of it. 5.05. 7
bade me enjoy it, with the place and honors, H8 3.02.248
i do enjoy | at ample point all that i did TRO 3.03. 88
which is a comfort | that all but we enjoy. COR 5.03.106
a valiant son–in–law thou shalt enjoy, | one fit TIT 1.01.311
now perforce we will enjoy | that nice–preserved 2.03.134
matter, | enjoy the honey–heavy dew of slumber. JC 2.01.230
him, you should enjoy half his revenue for ever, LR 1.02. 53 P
i wake him, you should enjoy half his revenue." 1.02. 56 P
mean you to enjoy him? 5.03. 78
and all the tribe of hell, thou shalt enjoy her; OTH 1.03.357 P
the next night following enjoy not desdemona, 4.02.215 P
enjoy thy plainness, | it nothing ill becomes ANT 2.06. 78
(i was about to say) enjoy your — but | it is CYM 1.06. 91
t' enjoy thy banish'd lord and this great land! 2.01. 65
as far, t' enjoy | a second night of such sweet 2.04. 43
i love her as a woman, to enjoy her. TNK 2.02.164
know i love him, | for i would fain enjoy him? 2.04. 30
though i think | i never shall enjoy her, yet 3.06.268
they cannot both enjoy you. 3.06.275
to touch the pillar, | he shall enjoy her; 3.06.296
"may you never more enjoy the light," etc. 4.01.104
that love best their loves shall not enjoy." VEN 1164
quoth he, "this night i must enjoy thee. LUC 512
scope, | with what i most enjoy contented least; SON 29. 8
ENJOY'D 11 FR 0.0012 REL FR 9 V 2 P
he hath enjoy'd nothing of ford's but his WIV 5.05.112 P
are, | are with more spirit chased than enjoy'd. MV 2.06. 13
of his, | it was alanson that enjoy'd my love. 1H6 5.04. 73
from that contented hap which i enjoy'd, | i R3 1.03. 83
it, and, though i am sold, | not yet enjoy'd. ROM 3.02. 28
neither can be enjoy'd | if both remain alive: LR 5.01. 58
that i have enjoy'd the dearest bodily part of CYM 1.04.149 P
no, he hath enjoy'd her. 2.04.126
once with a time when i enjoy'd a playfellow; TNK 1.03. 50
o happiness enjoy'd but of a few, | and, if LUC 22
enjoy'd no sooner but despised straight, | past SON 129. 5
ENJOYED 2 FR 0.0002 REL FR 2 V 0 P
joy is little less in joy | than hope enjoyed. R2 2.03. 16
the wand'ring prince and dido once enjoyed, TIT 2.03. 22
ENJOYER 1 FR 0.0001 REL FR 1 V 0 P
now proud as an enjoyer, and anon | doubting the SON 75. 5
ENJOYING 7 FR 0.0008 REL FR 5 V 2 P
shall be crown'd with your enjoying her. WIV 3.05.136 P
imposition, as for the enjoying of thy life, who MM 1.02.189 P
which makes me fear th' enjoying of my love; MV 3.02. 29
but for thy world enjoying but this land, | is R2 2.01.111
it is not worth th' enjoying. 2H6 3.01.334
and the enjoying of our griefs together. TNK 2.02. 60
the free enjoying of that face i die for — | o, 2.03. 3
ENJOYS 8 FR 0.0009 REL FR 7 V 1 P
man, | and king o'er him and all that he enjoys. JN 2.01.240
a member of the country's peace, | enjoys it; H5 4.01.282
or count them happy that enjoys the sun? 2H6 2.04. 39
shade, | all which secure and sweetly he enjoys, 3H6 2.05. 50
while he enjoys the honor and his ease. 4.06. 52
a little joy enjoys the queen thereof, | for i R3 1.03.154
more than the world enjoys. CYM 1.04. 79 P
but his place, for still the world enjoys it, SON 9.10
ENJOY'T 1 FR 0.0001 REL FR 1 V 0 P
me, but enjoy't till | i may enforce my remedy. TNK 3.01.122
ENKINDLE 2 FR 0.0002 REL FR 2 V 0 P
home, | might yet enkindle you unto the crown, MAC 1.03.121
edmund, enkindle all the sparks of nature, | to LR 3.07. 86
ENKINDLED 3 FR 0.0003 REL FR 3 V 0 P
with that same weak wind which enkindled it. JN 5.02. 87
will, | my will enkindled by mine eyes and ears, TRO 2.02. 63
impatience | which seem'd too much enkindled; JC 2.01.249
ENLARD 1 FR 0.0001 REL FR 1 V 0 P
that were to enlard his fat–already pride, | and TRO 2.03.195
ENLARG'D 3 FR 0.0003 REL FR 3 V 0 P
once, | enlarg'd him and made a friend of him, 1H4 3.02.115
her obsequies have been as far enlarg'd | as we HAM 5.01.226
thy praise | to tie up envy, evermore enlarg'd: SON 70.12
/ENLARGE 1 FR 0.0001 REL FR 1 V 0 P
/and /doth /enlarge /his /rising /with /the 2H4 1.01.204
ENLARGE 7 FR 0.0008 REL FR 6 V 1 P
he shall enlarge him; TN 5.01.278
exeter, | enlarge the man committed yesterday, H5 2.02. 40
we'll yet enlarge that man, | though cambridge, 2.02. 57
water, | which never ceaseth to enlarge itself, 1H6 1.02.134
lest your displeasure should enlarge itself | to TRO 5.02. 37
then in my tent, cassius, enlarge your griefs, JC 4.02. 46
third is up, till death enlarge his confine. ANT 3.05. 12 P
ENLARGEMENT 5 FR 0.0005 REL FR 4 V 1 P
take this key, give enlargement to the swain, LLL 3.01. 5 P
her womb, which, for enlargement striving, 1H4 3.01. 30
with sweet enlargement doth dismiss me hence. 1H6 2.05. 30
at our enlargement what are thy due fees? 3H6 4.06. 5
yet you are curb'd from that enlargement by CYM 2.03.120
ENLARGETH 1 FR 0.0001 REL FR 0 V 1 P
in other places she enlargeth her mirth so far WIV 2.02.222 P
ENLIGHTEN 1 FR 0.0001 REL FR 1 V 0 P
and, to enlighten thee, gave eyes to blindness, SON 152.11
ENLINK'D 1 FR 0.0001 REL FR 1 V 0 P
fell feats | enlink'd to waste and desolation? H5 3.03. 18
ENMESH 1 FR 0.0001 REL FR 1 V 0 P
make the net | that shall enmesh them all. OTH 2.03.362
ENMITIES 1 FR 0.0001 REL FR 1 V 0 P
how lesser enmities may give way to greater. ANT 2.01. 43
ENMITY 21 FR 0.0023 REL FR 21 V 0 P
whose enmity he flung aside, and breasted | the TMP 2.01.117
the enmity and discord which of late | sprung ERR 1.01. 5
jealousy | to sleep by hate and fear no enmity? MND 4.01.145
despair, and be at enmity | with cozening hope. R2 2.02. 68
while covert enmity | under the smile of safety 2H4 in 9
too, | hath been enacted through your enmity. 1H6 3.01.116
dens, | poor harmless lambs abide their enmity. 3H6 2.05. 75
brittany, | till storms be past of civil enmity. 4.06. 98
made peace of enmity, fair love of hate, R3 2.01. 51
'tis death to me to be at enmity; 2.01. 61
that long have frown'd upon their enmity! 5.05. 21
to stand the push and enmity of those | this TRO 2.02.137
of a doit, break out | to bitterest enmity; COR 4.04. 18
myself, | set deadly enmity between two friends, TIT 5.01.131
who drown'd their enmity in my true tears, | and 5.03.107
sweet, | and i am proof against their enmity. ROM 2.02. 73
his lady's lie, | poor sacrifices of our enmity! 5.03.304
effect | holds such an enmity with blood of man HAM 1.05. 65
choose | to wage against the enmity o' th' air, LR 2.04.209
deed, | reproach, disdain, and deadly enmity, LUC 503
'gainst death and all–oblivious enmity | shall SON 55. 9
ENMITY'S 1 FR 0.0001 REL FR 1 V 0 P
and to poor we | thine enmity's most capital; COR 5.03.104
ENNOBLE 1 FR 0.0001 REL FR 1 V 0 P
promotions | are daily given to ennoble those R3 1.03. 80
ENNOBLED 1 FR 0.0001 REL FR 1 V 0 P
now | the praised of the king, who, so ennobled, AWW 2.03.172
ENOBARB 1 FR 0.0001 REL FR 1 V 0 P
strong enobarb | is weaker than the wine, and ANT 2.07.122
ENOBARBUS 14 FR 0.0015 REL FR 13 V 1 P
enobarbus! ANT 1.02. 83
how now, enobarbus? 1.02.130
good enobarbus, 'tis a worthy deed, | and shall 2.02. 1
good enobarbus! 2.02.174 P
good enobarbus, make yourself my guest | whilst 2.02.243
enobarbus, welcome! 2.07. 86
why, enobarbus? 3.02. 53
what shall we do, enobarbus? 3.13. 1
call for enobarbus, | he shall not hear thee, or 4.05. 7
enobarbus! 4.05. 17
enobarbus, antony | hath after thee sent all thy 4.06. 19
mock not, enobarbus, | i tell you true. 4.06. 24
poor enobarbus did | before thy face repent! 4.09. 9
enobarbus? 4.09. 10
ENORMITY 1 FR 0.0001 REL FR 0 V 1 P
in what enormity is martius poor in, that you COR 2.01. 16 P
ENORMOUS 2 FR 0.0002 REL FR 2 V 0 P
shall find time | from this enormous state — LR 2.02.169
o great corrector of enormous times, | shaker of TNK 5.01. 62
/ENOUGH 3 FR 0.0003 REL FR 2 V 1 P
/i'll /read /enough, | /when /i /do /see /the R2 4.01.273
/they /are /apt /enough /to /dislocate /and LR 4.02. 65
/put /money /enough /in /your /purse. OTH 1.03.380 P
ENOUGH 331 FR 0.0374 REL FR 204 V 127 P
blow till thou burst thy wind, if room enough! TMP 1.01. 8 P
man) my library | was dukedom large enough: 1.02.110
there's wood enough within. 1.02.314
space enough | have i in such a prison. 1.02.493
i'll fish for thee, and get thee wood enough. 2.02.161
beat him enough. 3.02. 85
sir, i know that well enough. TGV 2.01. 50 P
enough; 2.04.143
but you, sir thurio, are not sharp enough: 3.02. 67
thanks is good enough for such a present. 4.04. 49 P
if we recover that, we are sure enough. 5.01. 12
now let me die, for i have liv'd long enough. WIV 3.03. 45 P
i have had ford enough. 3.05. 35 P
which they'll do fast enough of themselves, and 4.01. 67 P
there is no woman's gown big enough for him; 4.02. 70 P
we cannot misuse /him enough. 4.02.103 P
wind were but long enough /to /say /my /prayers, 4.05.102 P
the white will decipher her well enough. 5.02. 10 P
this is enough to be the decay of lust and 5.05.144 P
are not these large enough? MM 1.04. 2
having waste ground enough, | shall we desire to 2.02.169
is scarce truth enough alive to make societies 3.02.227 P
but security enough to make fellowships accurs'd 3.02.228 P
this news is old enough, yet it is every day's 3.02.230 P
your thief, your true man thinks it big enough; 4.02. 45 P
your thief, your thief thinks it little enough; 4.02. 46 P
if not true, none were enough. 4.03.168 P
enough, my lord. 5.01.215
is't not enough thou hast suborn'd these women 5.01.306
lay bolts enough upon him. 5.01.346 P
bear it with you, lest i come not time enough. ERR 4.01. 41
ay, but not rough enough. 5.01. 58
ay, but not enough. 5.01. 61
not show itself modest enough without a badge of ADO 1.01. 22 P
that if he have wit enough to keep himself warm, 1.01. 68 P
i have almost matter enough in me for such an 1.01.279 P
uncle, and money enough in his purse, such a man 2.01. 15 P
i know you well enough, you are signior antonio. 2.01.112 P
i am sure you know him well enough. 2.01.133 P
proof enough to misuse the prince, to vex 2.02. 28 P
no, faith, thou sing'st well enough for a shift. 2.03. 78 P
faith, like enough. 2.03.103 P
if you will follow me, i will show you enough, 3.02.121 P
if your husband have stables enough, you'll see 3.04. 48 P
it is not seen enough, you should wear it in 3.04. 71 P
there is not chastity enough in language 4.01. 97
enough, i am engag'd, i will challenge him. 4.01.331 P
the law, go to, and a rich fellow enough, go to, 4.02. 84 P
thou hast mettle enough in thee to kill care. 5.01.133 P
fire enough for a flint, pearl enough for a LLL 4.02. 88 P
enough for a flint, pearl enough for a swine: 4.02. 89 P
will you find men worthy enough to present them? 5.01.124 P
he is not quantity enough for that worthy's 5.01.131 P
and that were enough to hang us all. MND 1.02. 76 P
enough; hold, or cut bow–strings. 1.02.111 P
skin, | weed wide enough to wrap a fairy in; 2.01.256
is't not enough, is't not enough, young man, 2.02.125
is't not enough, is't not enough, young man, 2.02.125
but if i had wit enough to get out of this wood, 3.01.149 P
this wood, i have enough to serve mine owe turn. 3.01.150 P
enough, enough, my lord; 4.01.154
enough, enough, my lord; 4.01.154
you have enough. 4.01.154
it is not enough to speak, but to speak true. 5.01.121 P
have the grace of god, sir, and he hath enough. MV 2.02.151 P
parts that become thee happily enough | and in 2.02.182
the patch is kind enough, but a huge feeder, 2.05. 46
thou dost deserve enough, and yet enough | may 2.07. 27
and yet enough | may not extend so far as to the 2.07. 27
that i had a title good enough to keep his name 3.01. 13 P
no, none that thou hast wit enough to make. 4.01.127
the greatness whereof i cannot enough commend, 4.01.159 P
for if the jew do cut but deep enough, | i'll 4.01.280
in summer, where the ways are fair enough. 5.01.264
my father's love is enough to honor him enough. AYL 1.02. 83 P
my father's love is enough to honor him enough. 1.02. 84 P
thou art thy father's daughter, there's enough. 1.03. 58
in a holiday humor, and like enough to consent. 4.01. 69 P
how it be in tune, so it make noise enough. 4.02. 9 P
the priest was good enough, for all the old 5.01. 3 P
marry, i fare well, for here is cheer enough. SHR in.2. 101
take her with all faults, and money enough. 1.01.130 P
know | one rich enough to be petruchio's wife 1.02. 67
why, give him gold enough, and marry him to a 1.02. 78 P
help thee to a wife | with wealth enough, and 1.02. 86
her only fault, and that is faults enough, | is 1.02. 88
tell me her father's name, and 'tis enough; 1.02. 94
he was skillful enough to have liv'd still, if AWW 1.01. 30 P
and have ability enough to make such knaveries 1.03. 12 P
as 'tis receiv'd, | and is enough for both. 2.01. 5
my praises towards him, | knowing him is enough. 2.01.104
if there be breadth enough in the world, i will 3.02. 24 P
choughs' language, gabble enough, and good 4.01. 20 P
language, gabble enough, and good enough. 4.01. 20 P
three hours 'twill be time enough to go home. 4.01. 25 P
enough, no more! TN 1.01. 7
these clothes are good enough to drink in, and 1.03. 11 P
but it becomes /me well enough, does't not? 1.03.100 P
not yet old enough for a man, nor young enough 1.05.156 P
enough for a man, nor young enough for a boy; 1.05.157 P
ay, he does well enough if he be dispos'd, and 2.03. 81 P
not think i have wit enough to lie straight in 2.03.136 P
reason for't, but i have reason good enough. 2.03.146 P
this fellow is wise enough to play the fool, 3.01. 60
to one of your receiving | enough is shown; 3.01.121
the sheet were big enough for the bed of ware in 3.02. 47 P
let there be gall enough in thy ink, though thou 3.02. 49 P
i am not tall enough to become the function well 4.02. 6 P
nor lean enough to be thought a good studient; 4.02. 7 P
though i confess, on base and ground enough, 5.01. 75
upon, | the centre is not big enough to bear | a WT 2.01.102
that's enough. 2.03. 30
which is enough, i'll warrant, | as this world 2.03. 72
that's true enough, | though 'tis a saying, sir, 3.02. 57
oath, | places remote enough are in bohemia, 3.03. 31
which if i have not enough consider'd (as too 4.02. 17 P
purse is not hot enough to purchase your spice. 4.03.119 P
can dream of yet, | enough then for your wonder. 4.04.389
worthy enough a herdsman, yea, him too, | that 4.04.435
shores, most certain | to miseries enough; 4.04.568
i am a poor fellow, sir. i know ye well enough. 4.04.639 P
sir, you have done enough, and have perform'd 5.01. 1
there's time enough for that; 5.03.128
give with our niece a dowry large enough, | for JN 2.01.469
enough. 3.03. 66
the ocean, | enough to stifle such a villain up. 4.03.133
let hell want pains enough to torture me. 4.03.138
york | hath power enough to serve our turn. R2 3.02. 90
thou hast said enough. 3.02.203
though you are old enough to be my heir. 3.03.205
presence | were enough noble to be upright judge 4.01.118
what hole in hell were hot enough for him? 1H4 1.02.108 P
time enough to go to bed with a candle, i 2.01. 43 P
the stony–hearted villains know it well enough. 2.02. 27 P
there's enough to make us all. 2.02. 58 P
you are straight enough in the shoulders, you 2.04.149 P
and since your coming hither have done enough 3.01.176
thou that art like enough, through vassal fear, 3.02.124
as a gentleman need to be, virtuous enough: 3.03. 15 P
go to, i know you well enough. 3.03. 64 P
one, they'll find linen enough on every hedge. 4.02. 48 P
tut, tut, good enough to toss, food for powder, 4.02. 65 P
like enough you do. 4.04. 7
two paces of the vilest earth | is room enough. 5.04. 92
for this i shall have time enough to mourn; 2H4 1.01.136

to look with forehead bold and big enough | upon 1.03. 8
i think we are so /a body strong enough, | even 1.03. 66
and never shall have length of life enough | to 2.03. 58
i was prick'd well enough before, and you could 3.02.111 P
like enough, and thy father's shadow. 3.02.128 P
and the dungeon your place, a place deep enough; 4.03. 8 P
thou art not firm enough, since griefs are green 4.05.203
i will devise matter enough out of this shallow 5.01. 78 P
save that there was not time enough to hear, H5 1.01. 84
and — pauca, there's enough too! 2.01. 79
go down upon him, you have power enough, | and 3.05. 53
for we know enough, if we know we are the king's 4.01.131 P
there is not work enough for all our hands, 4.02. 19
scarce blood enough in all their sickly veins 4.02. 20
the fellow has mettle enough in his belly. 4.08. 63 P
enough, captain, you have astonish'd him. 5.01. 39 P
there is not enough leek to swear by. 5.01. 50 P
ave fausse french enough to deceive de most sage 5.02.218 P
how may i reverently worship thee enough? 1H6 1.02.145
enough; 2.05. 21
and strong enough to issue out and fight. 4.02. 20
it were enough to fright the realm of france! 4.07. 82
yes, there is remedy enough, my lord. 5.03.135
it is enough, i'll think upon the questions. 2H6 1.02. 82
the king is old enough himself | to give his 1.03.116
if he be old enough, what needs your grace | to 1.03.118
she'll gallop far enough to her destruction. 1.03.151
fear not, neighbor, you shall do well enough. 2.03. 61 P
that's bad enough, for i am but reproach; 2.04. 96
enough, sweet suffolk, thou torment'st thyself, 3.02.329
a wilderness is populous enough, | so suffolk 3.02.360
enough to purchase such another island, | so 3.03. 3
is't not enough to break into my garden, | and 4.10. 33
'tis not enough our foes are this time fled, 5.03. 21
you are old enough now, and yet methinks you 3H6 1.01.113
richard, enough; 1.02. 35
were shame enough to shame thee, wert thou not 1.04.120
methinks 'tis prize enough to be his son. 2.01. 20
why, so i am — in mind, and that's enough. 3.01. 60
of force enough to bid his brother battle; 5.01. 77
you shall have wine enough, my lord, anon. R3 1.04.162
ay, gentle cousin, were it light enough. 3.01.117
nay, like enough, for i stay dinner there. 3.02.121
being now seen possible enough, got credit, H8 1.01. 37
employment, | and far enough from court too. 2.01. 49
that's christian care enough. 2.02.130
sharp enough, | lord, for thy justice! 3.02. 92
well, i have told you enough of this. TRO 1.01. 13 P
why, paris hath color enough. 1.02. 99 P
he having color enough, and the other higher, is 1.02.103 P
wit, i can tell you, and he's man good enough. 1.02.191 P
cries, "o, enough, patroclus, | or give me ribs 1.03.176
'tis dry enough), will, with great speed of 1.03.329
to devise imposition enough than for us to 3.02. 80 P
princes, enough, so please you. 4.05.117
you may have every day enough of hector, | if 4.05.263
here's agamemnon, an honest fellow enough, and 5.01. 51 P
he's one honest enough; COR 1.01. 53 P
they say there's grain enough? 1.01.196
menenius, you are known well enough too. 2.01. 46 P
follows it that i am known well enough too? 2.01. 63 P
this character, if i be known well enough too? 2.01. 65 P
come, sir, come, we know you well enough. 2.01. 66 P
come, enough. 3.01.139
enough, with over-measure. 3.01.140
h'as said enough. 3.01.161
you might have been enough the man you are, 3.02. 19
general," but he was always good enough for him. 4.05.182 P
fear not thy sons, they shall do well enough. TIT 2.03.305
i know | there is enough written upon this earth 4.01. 84
'tis sure enough, and you knew how, | but if you 4.01. 95
look ye draw home enough, and 'tis there 4.03. 3
i am not mad, i know thee well enough. 5.02. 21
tut, i have work enough for you to do. 5.02.150
enough of this, i pray thee hold thy peace. ROM 1.03. 49
he dare, | it is enough i may but call her mine. 2.06. 8
you shall find me apt enough to that, sir, and 3.01. 41 P
ay, a scratch, a scratch, marry, 'tis enough. 3.01. 93
nor so wide as a church-door, but 'tis enough, 3.01. 97 P
death | was woe enough if it had ended there; 3.02.115
for it was bad enough before their spite. 4.01. 31
no, not till thursday, there is time enough. 4.02. 36
'tis not enough to help the feeble up, | but to TIM 1.01.107
so kind to heart, 'tis not enough to give; 1.02.219
and thou know'st well enough (although thou 3.01. 41 P
one may reach deep enough and yet | find little. 3.04. 15
certain as your waiting, | 'twere sure enough. 3.04. 48
what, he's poor, and that's revenge enough. 3.04. 63 P
no foes, that were enough | to overcome him. 3.05. 69
the gods keep you old enough that you may live 3.05.103
lend to each man enough, that one need not lend 3.06. 73 P
enough to make a whore forswear her trade, | and 4.03.134
would thou wert clean enough to spit upon! 4.03.359
not all the whips of heaven are large enough — 5.01. 61
and come to me, | i'll give you gold enough. 5.01.104
your plague, you his, | and last so long enough! 5.01.190
now is it rome indeed and room enough, | when JC 1.02.156
where wilt thou find a cavern dark enough | to 2.01. 80
not erebus itself were dim enough | to hide thee 2.01. 84
they do) bear fire enough | to kindle cowards, 2.01.120
that is enough to satisfy the senate. 2.02. 72
with courtesy and with respect enough, | but not 4.02. 15
have not you love enough to bear with me, | when 4.03.119
this hill is far enough. 5.03. 12
safe, antony, brutus is safe enough. 5.04. 20
till then, enough. come, friends. MAC 1.03.156
who committed treason enough for god's sake, yet 2.03. 10 P
enough. 4.01. 72
and yet, i' faith, | with wit enough for thee. 4.02. 43
we have willing dames enough; 4.03. 73
i have liv'd long enough: 5.03. 22
now near enough; 5.06. 1
damn'd be him that first cries, "hold, enough!" 5.08. 34
the chariest maid is prodigal enough | if she HAM 1.03. 36
your modesties have not craft enough to color. 2.02.280 P
wise men know well enough what monsters you make 3.01.138 P
i have heard of your paintings, well enough. 3.01.142 P
is there not rain enough in the sweet heavens 3.03. 45
which is not tomb enough and continent | to hide 4.04. 64
thither with modesty enough and likelihood to 5.01.208 P
as he's for a king, /th' art poor enough. LR 1.04. 22 P
should undo excess, | and each man have enough. 4.01. 71
affliction till it do cry out itself | "enough, 4.06. 77
till it do cry out itself | "enough, enough," 4.06. 77
i remember thine eyes well enough. 4.06.136 P
i know thee well enough, thy name is gloucester. 4.06.177
thy friendly hand | put strength enough to't. 4.06.231
nay, it is possible enough to judgment. OTH 1.03. 9
she oft bestows on me, | you would have enough. 2.01.102
i cannot speak enough of this content, | it 2.01.196
i can stand well enough, and i speak well enough 2.03.115 P
can stand well enough, and i speak well enough. 2.03.116 P
why, but you are now well enough. 2.03.294 P
poor and content is rich, and rich enough, | but 3.03.172
it were enough | to put him to ill thinking. 3.04. 28
ere it be demanded | (as like enough it will) i 3.04.190
she says enough; 4.02. 20
wine enough, | cleopatra's health to drink. ANT 1.02. 12
for they have entertained cause enough | to draw 2.01. 46
therefore | make space enough between you. 2.03. 24
o silius, silius, | i have done enough; 3.01. 12
all may be well enough. 3.03. 47
yes, like enough! 3.13. 29
mark antony but late, | enough to fetch him in. 4.01. 14
enough to purchase what you have made known. 5.02.148
you have land enough of your own, but he added CYM 1.02. 17 P
if there were wealth enough for the /purchase, 1.04. 83 P
gentlemen, enough of this. 1.04.120 P
i have enough; 2.02. 46
this foolish imogen, i should have gold enough. 2.03. 9 P
thou wert dignified enough, | even to the point 2.03.127
this is not strong enough to be believ'd | of 2.04.131
madam, 's enough for you — and too much too. 3.02. 69
now methinks | thy favor's good enough. 3.04. 49
she's far enough, and what he learns by this 3.05.102
though valor | becomes thee well enough. 4.02.156
'tis enough | that, britain, i have kill'd thy 5.01. 19
is't enough i am sorry? 5.04. 11
that i return'd with simular proof enough | to 5.05.200
it is enough you know, and it is fit, | what PER 1.01.105
enough. 1.01.158
my pistol's length, | i'll make him sure enough; 1.01.167
courage enough. 3.01. 39
not enough barbarous, had not o'erboard thrown 4.02. 66
your honor knows what 'tis to say well enough. 4.06. 32 P
and have not money enough in the end to buy him 4.06.172 P
not but i shall find them tractable enough. 4.06.199 P
that, | for truth can never be confirm'd enough, 5.01.201
you | have said enough to shake me from the arm TNK 1.03. 92
strong enough to laugh at misery | and bear the 2.02. 2
were there not maids enough? 2.02.121
and like enough the duke hath taken notice 2.02.227
'twill disturb us, | we shall have time enough. 3.03. 16
cousin, thrust the buckle | through far enough. 3.06. 62
a gammon of bacon that will never be enough. 4.03. 39 P
it is enough my hearing shall be punish'd | with 5.03. 7
o, what pity | enough for such a chance! 5.03. 60
sore eyes and 'tis enough to infect the city STM II.C 10 P
"within this limit is relief enough, | sweet VEN 235
but soft, enough — too much, i fear — | lest PP 18.49
'tis not enough that through the cloud thou SON 34. 5
and like enough thou know'st thy estimate; 87. 2
they had not still enough your worth to sing: 106.12
ye | even that your pity is enough to cure me. 111.14
is't not enough to torture me alone, | but slave 133. 3
more than enough am i that vex thee still, | to 135. 3

ENOW 10 FR 0.0011 REL FR 6 V 4 P
we were christians enow before, e'en as many as MV 3.05. 22 P
his back, | enow to press a royal merchant down, 4.01. 29
we have french quarrels enow, if you could tell H5 4.01.223 P
were enow | to purge this field of such a 4.02. 28
to die, we are enow | to do our country loss; 4.03. 20
we are enow yet living in the field | to smother 4.05. 19
maid, | spare for no faggots, let there be enow. 1H6 5.04. 56
have napkins enow about you, here you'll sweat MAC 2.03. 6 P
liars and swearers enow to beat the honest men 4.02. 57 P
are | evils enow to darken all his goodness: ANT 1.04. 11

ENPATRON 1 FR 0.0001 REL FR 1 V 0 P
be, | since i their altar, you enpatron me. LC 224

ENPIERCED 1 FR 0.0001 REL FR 1 V 0 P
i am too sore enpierced with his shaft | to soar ROM 1.04. 19

ENRAG'D 14 FR 0.0015 REL FR 11 V 3 P
who, all enrag'd, will banish valentine; TGV 2.06. 38
that she loves him with an enrag'd affection; ADO 2.03.100 P
don john had made, away went claudio enrag'd; 3.03.159 P
from the rude sea's enrag'd and foamy mouth TN 5.01. 78
eyes | that never saw the giant world enrag'd, JN 5.02. 57
with grief, being now enrag'd with grief, | are 2H4 1.01.144
to frown upon th' enrag'd northumberland! 1.01.152
that hath enrag'd him on to offer strokes, | as 4.01.209
here, there, and every where, enrag'd he slew. 1H6 1.01.124
or whether his fall enrag'd him, or how 'twas, COR 1.03. 63 P
why is my lord enrag'd against his love? ANT 4.12. 31
being so enrag'd, desire doth lend her force VEN 29
his love, perceiving how he was enrag'd, | grew 317
here all enrag'd, such passion her assails LUC 1562

ENRAGE 2 FR 0.0002 REL FR 2 V 0 P
but let the ruffian boreas once enrage | the TRO 1.03. 38
blunt not the heart, enrage it. MAC 4.03.229

ENRAGED 3 FR 0.0003 REL FR 3 V 0 P
match, | the sea enraged is not half so deaf, JN 2.01.451
upon th' enraged soldiers in their spoil, | as H5 3.03. 25
to his great master, who, /thereat enraged, LR 4.02. 75

ENRAGES 1 FR 0.0001 REL FR 1 V 0 P
grows worse and worse, | question enrages him. MAC 3.04.117

ENRANK 1 FR 0.0001 REL FR 1 V 0 P
no leisure had he to enrank his men; 1H6 1.01.115

ENRAPT 1 FR 0.0001 REL FR 1 V 0 P
am like a prophet suddenly enrapt | to tell thee TRO 5.03. 65

ENRICH 10 FR 0.0011 REL FR 9 V 1 P
but herein mean i to enrich my pain, | to have MND 1.01.250
whose lands and revenues enrich the new duke; AYL 1.01.102 P
henry is able to enrich his queen, | and not to 1H6 5.05. 51
with what his valor did enrich his wit, | his R3 3.01. 85
but praying, to enrich his watchful soul. 3.07. 77
enrich the time to come with smooth-fac'd peace, 5.05. 33
what lady's that which doth enrich the hand | of ROM 1.05. 41
would testify, t' enrich mine inventory. CYM 2.02. 30
down the rich, enrich the poor with treasures; VEN 1150
shall profit thee, and much enrich thy book. SON 77.14

ENRICH'D *(also rich'd)*

ENRICH'D 11 FR 0.0012 REL FR 9 V 2 P
the captive is enrich'd; LLL 4.01. 76 P
of beauty's tutors have enrich'd you with? 4.03.320
till twice five summers have enrich'd our fields R2 1.03.141
which more enrich'd | shall be your love and 2.03. 61
if thy pocket were enrich'd with any other 1H4 3.03.161 P
whose chin is but enrich'd | with one appearing H5 3.pr. 22
for then this land was famously enrich'd | with R3 2.03. 19
he likewise enrich'd poor straggling soldiers TIM 5.01. 6
did outsell her gift, | and yet enrich'd it too. CYM 2.04.103
you were at wars when she the grave enrich'd, TNK 1.03. 51
with th' annexions of fair gems enrich'd, | and LC 208

ENRICHED 1 FR 0.0001 REL FR 1 V 0 P
as art and practice hath enriched any | that we MM 1.01. 12

ENRICHES 1 FR 0.0001 REL FR 1 V 0 P
name | robs me of that which not enriches him, OTH 3.03.160

/ENRIDGED 1 FR 0.0001 REL FR 1 V 0 P
horns welk'd and waved like the /enridged sea. LR 4.06. 71

ENRINGS 1 FR 0.0001 REL FR 1 V 0 P
ivy so | enrings the barky fingers of the elm. MND 4.01. 44

ENROB'D 1 FR 0.0001 REL FR 1 V 0 P
that quaint in green she shall be loose enrob'd, WIV 4.06. 41

ENROBE 1 FR 0.0001 REL FR 1 V 0 P
enrobe the roaring waters with my silks, | and, MV 1.01. 34

ENROLL'D 3 FR 0.0003 REL FR 2 V 1 P
who was enroll'd 'mongst wonders, and when we, H8 1.02.119
towards her deserved children is enroll'd | in COR 3.01.290
of his death is enroll'd in the capitol: JC 3.02. 38 P

ENROLLED 5 FR 0.0005 REL FR 5 V 0 P
governor | awakes me all the enrolled penalties MM 1.02.166
term, | which i hope well is not enrolled there. LLL 1.01. 38
the which i hope is not enrolled there; 1.01. 41
which i hope well is not enrolled there. 1.01. 46
his oath enrolled in the parliament; 3H6 2.01.173

ENROOTED 1 FR 0.0001 REL FR 1 V 0 P
his foes are so enrooted with his friends | that 2H4 4.01.205

ENROUNDED 1 FR 0.0001 REL FR 1 V 0 P
no note | how dread an army hath enrounded him; H5 4.pr. 36

ENSCHEDUL'D 1 FR 0.0001 REL FR 1 V 0 P
you have enschedul'd briefly in your hands. H5 5.02. 73

ENSCONC'D 1 FR 0.0001 REL FR 1 V 0 P
and therein so ensconc'd his secret evil, | that LUC 1515

ENSCONCE *(also insconce)*

ENSCONCE 2 FR 0.0002 REL FR 0 V 2 P
yet you, rogue, will ensconce your rags, your WIV 2.02. 26 P
not see me, i will ensconce me behind the arras. 3.03. 89 P

ENSCONCING 1 FR 0.0001 REL FR 0 V 1 P
ensconcing ourselves into seeming knowledge, AWW 2.03. 4 P

ENSEAMED 1 FR 0.0001 REL FR 1 V 0 P
to live | in the rank sweat of an enseamed bed, HAM 3.04. 92

ENSEAR 1 FR 0.0001 REL FR 1 V 0 P
ensear thy fertile and conceptious womb, | let TIM 4.03.187

ENSEIGNE 1 FR 0.0001 REL FR 0 V 1 P
vous deja oublie ce que je vous ai enseigne? H5 3.04. 43 P

ENSEMBLE 1 FR 0.0001 REL FR 0 V 1 P
je reciterai une autre fois ma lecon ensemble: H5 3.04. 58 P

ENSHELTER'D 1 FR 0.0001 REL FR 1 V 0 P
turkish fleet | be not enshelter'd and embay'd, OTH 2.01. 18

ENSHIELD 1 FR 0.0001 REL FR 1 V 0 P
proclaim an enshield beauty ten times louder MM 2.04. 80

ENSHRINES 1 FR 0.0001 REL FR 1 V 0 P
burgundy | enshrines thee in his heart, and 1H6 3.02.119

ENSIGN *(also ancient*, aunchiant, aunchient)*

ENSIGN 6 FR 0.0006 REL FR 6 V 0 P
streaming the ensign of the christian cross R2 4.01. 94
beauty's ensign yet | is crimson in thy lips and ROM 5.03. 94
on our former ensign | two mighty eagles fell, JC 5.01. 79
this ensign here of mine was turning back; 5.03. 3
a roman and a british ensign wave | friendly CYM 5.05.480
scorning his churlish drum and ensign red, VEN 107

ENSIGNS 2 FR 0.0002 REL FR 2 V 0 P
hang up your ensigns, let your drums be still, 1H6 5.04.174
owe, | mine honor's ensigns humbled at thy feet. TIT 1.01.252

ENSINEWED 1 FR 0.0001 REL FR 1 V 0 P
that are ensinewed to this action | acquitted by 2H4 4.01.170

ENSKIED 1 FR 0.0001 REL FR 1 V 0 P
i hold you as a thing enskied, and sainted, | by MM 1.04. 34

ENSNAR'D 2 FR 0.0002 REL FR 2 V 0 P
why he hath thus ensnar'd my soul and body? OTH 5.02.302
thy beauty hath ensnar'd thee to this night, LUC 485

ENSNARE 2 FR 0.0002 REL FR 1 V 1 P
a web as this will i ensnare as great a fly as OTH 2.01.168 P
myself a weakling, do not then ensnare me; LUC 584

ENSNARETH 1 FR 0.0001 REL FR 1 V 0 P
spider | whose deadly web ensnareth thee about? R3 1.03.242

ENSTATE 1 FR 0.0001 REL FR 1 V 0 P
ours, | we do enstate and widow you with all, MM 5.01.424

ENSTEEP'D 1 FR 0.0001 REL FR 1 V 0 P
traitors ensteep'd to enclog the guiltless keel, OTH 2.01. 70

ENSU'D 1 FR 0.0001 REL FR 1 V 0 P
with demure confidence | this pausingly ensu'd: H8 1.02.168

ENSUE 15 FR 0.0017 REL FR 13 V 2 P
stomach, to bear up | against what should ensue. TMP 1.02.158
why then let kibes ensue. WIV 1.03. 32 P
if we obey them not, this will ensue: ERR 2.02.191
what doth ensue | but moody and dull melancholy, 5.01. 78
of thy misprision must perforce ensue | some MND 3.02. 90
doth it therefore ensue that you should love his AYL 1.03. 31 P
we had a kind of light what would ensue. JN 4.03. 61
let not to-morrow then ensue to-day; R2 2.01.197
what will ensue hereof, there's none can tell; 2.01.212
what perils past, what crosses to ensue, | would 2H4 3.01. 55
in france, | not seeing what is likely to ensue. 1H6 3.01.187
sir, i foretold you then what would ensue. TRO 4.05.217
the purchase made, the fruits are to ensue; OTH 2.03. 9
i know repentant tears ensue the deed, LUC 502
and shame that might ensue | by that her death, 1263

ENSUED 1 FR 0.0001 REL FR 1 V 0 P
before him, branded | his baseness that ensued? ANT 4.14. 77

ENSUES 7 FR 0.0008 REL FR 7 V 0 P
what of her ensues | i list not prophesy; WT 4.01. 25
be minist'red, | or overthrow incurable ensues. JN 5.01. 16

at hand, | ensues his piteous and unpitied end. R3 4.04. 74
nor what ensues, but have a fog in them | that i CYM 3.02. 79
what now ensues, to the judgment of your eye | i PER 1.ch. 41
and what ensues in this fell storm | shall for 3.ch. 53
and as one shifts, another straight ensues: LUC 1104
ENSUING 11 FR 0.0012 REL FR 9 V 2 P
but heart's sorrow, | and a clear life ensuing. TMP 3.03. 82
the next ensuing hour some foul mischance TGV 2.02. 11
hath holp to effect your ensuing marriage — ADO 3.02. 99 P
my life, | how happy then were my ensuing death! R2 2.01. 68
england ere the thirtieth of may next ensuing. 2H6 1.01. 49 P
instinct men's minds mistrust | ensuing danger; R3 2.03. 43
and th' ensuing night | made it a fool and H8 1.01. 27
yet i can give you inkling | of an ensuing evil, 2.01.141
his name remains | to th' ensuing age abhorr'd." COR 5.03.148
breath | nothing to think on but ensuing death. PER 2.01. 7
of things long since, or any thing ensuing? VEN 1078
ENSWATH'D 1 FR 0.0001 REL FR 1 V 0 P
sleided silk feat and affectedly | enswath'd, LC 49
ENTAIL 3 FR 0.0003 REL FR 2 V 1 P
of it, and cut th' entail from all remainders, AWW 4.03.279 P
i here entail | the crown to thee and to thine 3H6 1.01.194
to entail him and his heirs unto the crown, 1.01.235
ENTAME 1 FR 0.0001 REL FR 1 V 0 P
that can entame my spirits to your worship. AYL 3.05. 48
ENTANGLED 3 FR 0.0003 REL FR 2 V 1 P
bleeding, the more entangled by your hearing. COR 2.01. 77 P
to be entangled with those mouth–made vows, ANT 1.03. 30
of love | tied, weav'd, entangled, with so true, TNK 1.03. 42
ENTANGLES 1 FR 0.0001 REL FR 1 V 0 P
very force entangles | itself with strength. ANT 4.14. 48
ENTENDRE 1 FR 0.0001 REL FR 0 V 1 P
your majesty entendre bettre que moi. H5 5.02.264 P
/ENTER 1 FR 0.0001 REL FR 1 V 0 P
ulysses, /enter /you. TRO 2.03.141
ENTER 86 FR 0.0097 REL FR 74 V 12 P
and sorceries terrible | to enter human hearing, TMP 1.02.265
no noise, and enter. 4.01.216
what lets but one may enter at her window? TGV 3.01.113
this day my sister should the cloister enter, MM 1.02.177
that shall be up at heaven and enter there | ere 2.02.152
injunctions i am bound | to enter publicly. 4.03. 97
say he dines forth, and let no creature enter. ERR 2.02.210
ay, and let none enter, lest i break your pate. 2.02.218
that may with foul intrusion enter in, | and 3.01.103
were shut, | and i denied to enter in my house? 4.04. 64
good people, enter and lay hold on him. 5.01. 91
saw'st thou him enter at the abbey here? 5.01.279
he ought to enter into a quarrel with fear and ADO 2.03.194 P
forbid the sun to enter, like favorites | made 3.01. 9
course, | before we enter his forbidden gates, LLL 2.01. 26
oath, | to let you enter his /unpeopled house. 2.01. 88
his enter and exit shall be strangling a snake; 5.01.134 P
have spoken your speech, enter into that brake; MND 3.01. 75 P
pyramus, enter. 3.01.101 P
she is to enter now, and i am to spy her through 5.01.185 P
let not the sound of shallow fopp'ry enter | my MV 2.05. 35
of me, | let it not enter in your mind of love. 2.08. 42
abhor it, fear it, do not enter it. AYL 2.03. 28
which i take to be too little for pomp to enter. AWW 4.05. 52 P
not open my lips so wide as a bristle may enter, TN 1.05. 2 P
my niece is desirous you should enter, if your 3.01. 75 P
i mean, to go, sir, to enter. 3.01. 81 P
the competitors enter. 4.02. 10 P
you must not enter. WT 2.03. 26
to enter conquerors, and to proclaim | arthur of JN 2.01.310
that it may enter butcher mowbray's breast! R2 1.02. 48
yea, at all points, and longs to enter in. 1.03. 2
point, | that it may enter mowbray's waxen coat, 1.03. 75
unless you please to enter in the castle, | and 2.03.160
key, | that no man enter till my tale be done. 5.03. 37
deny the sheriff, so, if not, let him enter. 1H4 2.04.496 P
enter our gates, dispose of us and ours, | for H5 3.03. 49
come, uncle exeter, | go you and enter harflew; 3.03. 52
terms, | such as will enter at a lady's ear, 5.02.100
the gates, here's gloucester that would enter. 1H6 1.03. 17
must your bold verdict enter talk with lords?" 3.01. 63
enter, go in, the market bell is rung. 3.02. 16
dangerous ends, | enter and cry "the dolphin!" 3.02. 34
on us thou canst not enter but by death; 4.02. 18
the armorer and his man, to enter the lists, 2H6 2.03. 50
enter his chamber, view his breathless corpse, 3.02.132
the passage where thy words should enter. 3H6 1.03. 22
york, | but that we enter as into our dukedom? 4.07. 9
by fair or foul means we must enter in, | for 4.07. 14
the gates are open, let us enter too. 5.01. 60
can curses pierce the clouds and enter heaven? R3 1.03.194
kind sister, thanks, we'll enter all together. 4.01. 11
saw ye none enter since i slept? H8 4.02. 86
your grace may enter now. 5.02. 42
matter of the world | enter his thoughts, save TRO 2.03.187
come, come, enter my tent. 5.01. 87
as subtle | as ariachne's broken woof to enter. 5.02.152
confusion | may enter 'twixt the gap of both, COR 3.01.111
tarpeian, never more | to enter our rome gates. 3.03.104
i'll enter. 4.04. 24
come enter with us. 5.03.206
almost at point to enter. 5.04. 61
come knock and enter, and no sooner in, | but ROM 1.04. 33
to enter in the thoughts of desperate men! 5.01. 36
but they enter my master's house merrily, and go TIM 2.02.101 P
and enter in our ears like great triumphers | in 5.01.196
heart before, | to say thou't enter friendly. 5.04. 49
let 'em enter. JC 2.01. 76
enter, sir, the castle. MAC 5.07. 29
"i saw him enter such a house of sale," HAM 2.01. 58
ever | the soul of nero enter this firm bosom, 3.02.394
these words like daggers enter in my ears. 3.04. 95
good my lord, enter, | the tyranny of the open LR 3.04. 1
good my lord, enter here. 3.04. 4
good my lord, enter. 3.04. 5
good my lord, enter here. 3.04. 22
enter the city, clip your wives, your friends, ANT 4.08. 8
with this tidings, | shall enter me with him. 4.14.113
and let instructions enter | where folly now CYM 1.05. 47
then i'll enter. 3.06. 24
enter your /musit, lest this match between 's TNK 3.01. 97
now let 'em enter, and before the gods | tender 5.01. 1
sir, they enter. 5.01. 7
better proof than thy spear's point can enter; VEN 626
and will not let a false sound enter there, 780
to make the breach and enter this sweet city. LUC 469
ENTER'D 6 FR 0.0006 REL FR 6 V 0 P
i have not yet | enter'd my house. MV 5.01.273
shook | the bosom of my conscience, enter'd me, H8 2.04.183
i accuse | the city ports by this hath enter'd, COR 5.06. 6
your native town you enter'd like a post, | and 5.06. 49
before i enter'd here i call'd, and thought | to CYM 3.06. 46
closes, he is enter'd | his radiant roof. 5.04.120
ENTERED 1 FR 0.0001 REL FR 1 V 0 P
days, | since i have entered into these wars. 1H6 1.02.132
ENTERING 2 FR 0.0002 REL FR 0 V 2 P
death, perchance entering into some monastery, MM 4.02.201 P
for entering his fee–simple without leave. 2H6 4.10. 25 P
ENTERLUDE 4 FR 0.0004 REL FR 2 V 2 P
to play in our enterlude before the duke and the MND 1.02. 6 P
in this same enterlude it doth befall | that i, 5.01.155
one, sir, in this enterlude — one sir topas, TN 5.01.372 P
an enterlude! LR 5.03. 89
/ENTERPRISE 1 FR 0.0001 REL FR 1 V 0 P
/doth /this /bold /enterprise /bring /forth 2H4 1.01.178
ENTERPRISE 34 FR 0.0038 REL FR 32 V 2 P
she'll take the enterprise upon her, father, MM 4.01. 65
a trim exploit, a manly enterprise, | to conjure MND 3.02.157
and so far blameless proves my enterprise, 3.02.350
would counsel you to a more equal enterprise. AYL 1.02.178 P
both from his enterprise and from the world, 5.04.162
be magnanimious in the enterprise and go on; AWW 3.06. 67 P
yea, thrust this enterprise into my heart, | and JN 5.02. 90
and hath sent for you | to line his enterprise, 1H4 2.03. 83
infect | the very life–blood of our enterprise, 4.01. 29
a larger dare to our great enterprise, | than if 4.01. 78
troth | sworn to us in your younger enterprise. 5.01. 71
this present enterprise set off his head, | i do 5.01. 88
myself, | prevented from a damned enterprise. H5 2.02.164
the enterprise whereof | shall be to you as us, 2.02.182
ne'er heard i of a warlike enterprise | more 1H6 2.01. 44
north, | appear, and aid me in this enterprise. 5.03. 7
and whet on warwick to this enterprise. 3H6 1.02. 37
so thrive i in my enterprise | and dangerous R3 4.04.236
sacrifice, | he offers in another's enterprise, TRO 1.02.283
of all high designs, | the enterprise is sick! 1.03.103
in execution | of any bold or noble enterprise, JC 1.02.298
romans | to undergo with me an enterprise | of 1.03.123
not stain | the even virtue of our enterprise, 2.01.133
the heavens speed thee in thine enterprise! 2.04. 41
i wish your enterprise to–day may thrive. 3.01. 13
what enterprise, popilius? 3.01. 14
he wish'd to–day our enterprise might thrive. 3.01. 16
that made you break this enterprise to me? MAC 1.07. 48
to some enterprise | that hath a stomach in't, HAM 1.01. 99
through your dominions for this enterprise, | on 2.02. 78
think death no hazard in this enterprise. PER 1.01. 5
find | it greets me as an enterprise of kindness 4.03. 38
how to draw out, fit to this enterprise, | the TNK 1.01.160
the dangers of his loathsome enterprise; LUC 184
ENTERPRISES 3 FR 0.0003 REL FR 3 V 0 P
in his enterprises | discomfited great douglas, 1H4 3.02.113
ripe for exploits and mighty enterprises. H5 1.02.121
and enterprises of great pitch and moment | with HAM 3.01. 85
ENTERS 8 FR 0.0009 REL FR 7 V 1 P
no, not a creature enters in my house. ERR 5.01. 92
receiveth as the sea, nought enters there, | of TN 1.01. 11
stage, | are idly bent on him that enters next, R2 5.02. 25
fliers at the very heels, | with them he enters; COR 1.04. 50
that, when he enters the confines of a tavern, ROM 3.01. 6 P
of the grave | this viperous slander enters. CYM 3.04. 39
through which it enters to surprise her heart, VEN 890
soft pity enters at an iron gate. LUC 595
ENTERTAIN 44 FR 0.0049 REL FR 37 V 7 P
approach, rich ceres, her to entertain. TMP 4.01. 75
entertain him | to be my fellow–servant to your TGV 2.04.104
sweet lady, entertain him for your servant. 2.04.110
therefore know /thou, for this i entertain thee. 4.04. 70
i will entertain bardolph; WIV 1.03. 10 P
as many devils entertain; 1.03. 54 P
the best way were to entertain him with hope, 2.01. 67 P
i'll entertain myself like one that i am not 2.01. 86 P
lest thou a feverous life shouldst entertain, MM 3.01. 74
i'll entertain the /offer'd fallacy. ERR 2.02.186
since mine own doors refuse to entertain me, 3.01.120
pond, | and do a willful stillness entertain, MV 1.01. 90
then entertain him, then forswear him; AYL 3.02.416 P
and take a lodging fit to entertain | such SHR 1.01. 44
time, | to entertain it so merrily with a fool. AWW 2.02. 61
address yourself to entertain them sprightly, WT 4.04. 53
the misplac'd john should entertain an hour, JN 3.04.133
and entertain a cheerful disposition. R2 2.02. 4
content | to entertain the lag end of my life 1H4 5.01. 24
but entertain no more of it, good brothers, 2H4 5.02. 54
that could entertain | with half their forces H5 1.02.111
now entertain conjecture of a time | when 4.pr. 1
i did not entertain thee as thou art. 1H6 2.03. 72
still, | for here we entertain a solemn peace. 5.04.175
to entertain my vows of thanks and praise! 2H6 4.09. 14
to entertain great england's lawful king! 5.01. 4
to entertain these fair well–spoken days, | i am R3 1.01. 29
and entertain a score or two of tailors | to 1.02.256
therefore for god's sake entertain good comfort, 1.03. 4
there's few or none will entertain it. 1.04.132 P
to entertain your highness and your empress. TIT 5.03. 32
pray entertain them, give them guide to us. TIM 1.01.243
lasts | to entertain me as your steward still. 4.03.489
all that serv'd brutus, i will entertain them. JC 5.05. 60
you, sir, i entertain for one of my hundred; LR 3.06. 79 P
but entertain it, | and, though thou think me ANT 2.07. 63
follow you, | so please you entertain me. CYM 4.02.394
and until then your entertain shall be | as doth PER 1.01.119
to entertain | the labor of each knight in his 2.02. 14
"in tarquin's likeness i did entertain thee; LUC 596
wrack, | yet for thy honor did i entertain him; 842
the weary time she cannot entertain, | for now 1361
and entertain my love, else lasting shame | on 1629
to entertain the time with thoughts of love, SON 39.11
/ENTERTAIN'D 2 FR 0.0002 REL FR 2 V 0 P
you, brother mine, that /entertain'd ambition, TMP 5.01. 75
/which /entertain'd, /limbs /are /his TRO 1.03.354
ENTERTAIN'D 15 FR 0.0017 REL FR 10 V 5 P
when every grief is entertain'd that's offer'd, TMP 2.01. 16
thou hast entertain'd | a fox to be the shepherd TGV 4.04. 91
and entertain'd 'em deeply in her heart. 5.04.102
your brother is royally entertain'd by leonato, ADO 1.03. 43 P
being entertain'd for a perfumer, as i was 1.03. 58 P
mother i am returning, entertain'd my convoy, AWW 4.03. 89 P
yet tell'st thou not how thou wert entertain'd. 1H6 1.04. 38
romeo, | who had but newly entertain'd revenge, ROM 3.01.171
and entertain'd me with mine own device. TIM 1.02.150
let the presents | be worthily entertain'd. 1.02.185
do so, my friends. see them well entertain'd. 2.02. 44
your highness is not entertain'd with that LR 1.04. 58 P
let him be so entertain'd amongst you as suits CYM 1.04. 28 P
all entertain'd, each passion labors so, | that VEN 969
devil, | he entertain'd a show so seeming just, LUC 1514
ENTERTAINED 2 FR 0.0002 REL FR 2 V 0 P
sebastian, i have entertained thee, | partly TGV 4.04. 63
for they have entertained cause enough | to draw ANT 2.01. 46
ENTERTAINER 1 FR 0.0001 REL FR 1 V 0 P
that's offer'd, | comes to th' entertainer — TMP 2.01. 17
ENTERTAINING 1 FR 0.0001 REL FR 1 V 0 P
he burns | with entertaining great hyperion. TRO 2.03.197
ENTERTAINMENT 39 FR 0.0044 REL FR 22 V 17 P
i will resist such entertainment till | mine TMP 1.02.466
i spy entertainment in her. WIV 1.03. 44 P
the stealth of our most mutual entertainment MM 1.02.154
and advis'd him for th' entertainment of death. 3.02.213 P
some entertainment for them in their tents. LLL 4.03.370
as concerning some entertainment of time, some 5.01.119 P
can in this desert place buy entertainment, AYL 2.04. 72
who gave me fresh array and entertainment, 4.03.143
and, for an entrance to my entertainment, | i do SHR 2.01. 54
have you so soon forgot the entertainment | her 3.01. 2
quality worthy your lordship's entertainment. AWW 3.06. 12 P
if you give him not john drum's entertainment, 3.06. 38 P
of strangers i' th' adversary's entertainment. 4.01. 15 P
in me have i learn'd from my entertainment. TN 1.05.215 P
pardon me, sir, your bad entertainment. 2.01. 33 P
wherein our entertainment shall shame us: WT 1.01. 8 P
this entertainment | may a free face put on, 1.02.111
o, that is entertainment | my bosom likes not, 1.02.118
welcome | give entertainment to the might of it, 2H4 4.05.173
done | in entertainment to my princely queen. 2H6 1.01. 72
billeted, already in th' entertainment, and to COR 4.03. 44 P
i have deserv'd no better entertainment | in 4.05. 9
gues? but /by my entertainment with him if thou 5.02. 64 P
embrace and hug | with amplest entertainment. TIM 1.01. 45
set a fair fashion on our entertainment, | which 1.02.147
let's be provided to show them entertainment. 1.02.179
but do not dull thy palm with entertainment | of HAM 1.03. 64
man, what lenten entertainment the players shall 2.02.316 P
more appear like entertainment than yours. 2.02.375 P
use some gentle entertainment to laertes before 5.02.207 P
which shall be needful for your entertainment. LR 2.04.206
would invent some other custom of entertainment. OTH 2.03. 35 P
note if your lady strain his entertainment 3.03.250
back to caesar, | tell him thy entertainment. ANT 3.13.140
the rest | that fell away have entertainment, 4.06. 16
commendation for my more free entertainment. CYM 1.04.155 P
as if the entertainment in our court | had not a PER 2.03. 55
that she may not be raw in her entertainment. 4.02. 56 P
witness the entertainment that he gave. VEN 1108
ENTERTAINMENTS 1 FR 0.0001 REL FR 0 V 1 P
have a care of your entertainments. WIV 4.05. 75 P
ENTERTAIN'ST 3 FR 0.0003 REL FR 2 V 1 P
but thou with mildness entertain'st thy wooers, SHR 2.01.250
if thou entertain'st my love, let it appear in TN 2.05.175 P
or entertain'st a hope to blast my wishes, TNK 2.02.170
ENTHRALL'D 3 FR 0.0003 REL FR 2 V 1 P
o cross! too high to be enthrall'd to /low. MND 1.01.136
no money of me, but being enthrall'd as i am, it WT 4.04.232 P
what though i be enthrall'd, he seems a knight, 1H6 5.03.101
ENTHRALLED 2 FR 0.0002 REL FR 2 V 0 P
love hath chas'd sleep from my enthralled eyes, TGV 2.04.134
so is mine eye enthralled to thy shape; MND 3.01.139
ENTHRON'D *(also thron'd, etc.)*
ENTHRON'D 4 FR 0.0004 REL FR 4 V 0 P
sol | in noble eminence enthron'd and spher'd TRO 1.03. 90
and antony | enthron'd i' th' market–place, did ANT 2.02.215
in chairs of gold | were publicly enthron'd. 3.06. 5
pieces, keep enthron'd | in your dear heart! TNK 1.03. 10
ENTHRONED 2 FR 0.0002 REL FR 2 V 0 P
sway, | it is enthroned in the hearts of kings, MV 4.01.194
after | so many courses of the sun enthroned, H8 2.03. 6
ENTICE *(also 'ticed)*
ENTICE 6 FR 0.0006 REL FR 6 V 0 P
do i entice you? MND 2.01.199
we will entice the duke of burgundy | to leave 1H6 3.03. 19
to entice his own | to evil should be done by PER 1.ch. 27
he lisps in 's neighing able to entice | a TNK 5.02. 66
as if some mermaid did their ears entice, | some LUC 1411
addict to vice, | quickly him they will entice; PP 20.42
ENTICEMENTS 1 FR 0.0001 REL FR 0 V 1 P
their promises, enticements, oaths, tokens, and AWW 3.05. 18 P
ENTICETH 1 FR 0.0001 REL FR 1 V 0 P
enticeth thee to view | her countless glory, PER 1.01. 30
ENTICING 2 FR 0.0002 REL FR 2 V 0 P
them) | would make a volume of enticing lines, 1H6 5.05. 14
and plac'd a choir of such enticing birds | that 2H6 1.03. 89
ENTIRE 8 FR 0.0009 REL FR 7 V 1 P
being but the one half of an entire sum LLL 2.01.130
heard | of your entire affection to bianca, SHR 4.02. 23
divides one thing entire to many objects, | like R2 2.02. 17
pure fear and entire cowardice doth not make 2H4 2.04.325 P
a carbuncle entire, as big as thou art, | were COR 1.04. 55
and the man entire | upon the next encounter JC 1.03.155
that stands | aloof from th' entire point. LR 1.01.240
world | of one entire and perfect chrysolite, OTH 5.02.145
/ENTIRELY 1 FR 0.0001 REL FR 0 V 1 P
/that /so /tenderly /and /entirely /loves /him. LR 1.02. 96 P
ENTIRELY 8 FR 0.0009 REL FR 6 V 2 P
times a day, if not many days entirely drunk. MM 4.02.150 P
sure | that benedick loves beatrice so entirely? ADO 3.01. 37
other slow arts entirely keep the brain; LLL 4.03.321
so do i, my lord, | they are entirely welcome. MV 3.02.225

know, madam, you love your gentlewoman entirely. AWW 1.03.100 P
and subdue my father | entirely to her love; OTH 3.04. 60
all the office of my heart, | entirely honor. 3.04.114
and her fortunes mingled | with thine entirely. ANT 4.14. 25
ENTITLE 3 FR 0.0003 REL FR 3 V 0 P
with that which we lovers entitle "affected." LLL 2.01.232
age, | i may entitle thee my loving father. SHR 4.05. 61
that which in mean men we entitle patience | is R2 1.02. 33
ENTITLED *(also intitled)*
ENTITLED 1 FR 0.0001 REL FR 1 V 0 P
more, | entitled in /thy parts do crowned sit, SON 37. 7
ENTIT'LING *(also intituled)*
ENTIT'LING 1 FR 0.0001 REL FR 1 V 0 P
ignorant in that, as you | in so entit'ling me; WT 2.03. 71
ENTOMB 3 FR 0.0003 REL FR 3 V 0 P
if thou wouldst not entomb thyself alive | and TRO 3.03.186
that darkness does the face of earth entomb, MAC 2.04. 9
"your tunes entomb | within your hollow swelling LUC 1121
ENTOMB'D 2 FR 0.0002 REL FR 1 V 1 P
or to be entomb'd in an ass's pack–saddle. COR 2.01. 89 P
dead, | entomb'd upon the very hem o' th' sea, TIM 5.04. 66
ENTOMBED 2 FR 0.0002 REL FR 2 V 0 P
between whose hills her head entombed is; LUC 390
when you entombed in men's eyes shall lie; SON 81. 8
ENTOMBS 1 FR 0.0001 REL FR 1 V 0 P
entombs her outcry in her lips' sweet fold. LUC 679
ENTRAILS 11 FR 0.0012 REL FR 9 V 2 P
and peg thee in his knotty entrails till | thou TMP 1.02.295
cold, wither'd, and of intolerable entrails? WIV 5.05.153 P
from the earth, as if his entrails were hairs; H5 3.07. 13 P
hath thy fiery heart so parch'd thine entrails 3H6 1.04. 87
and throw them in the entrails of the wolf? R3 4.04. 23
heart | to revel in the entrails of my lambs. 4.04.229
and entrails feed the sacrificing fire, | whose TIT 1.01.144
and shows the ragged entrails of this pit: 2.03.230
plucking the entrails of an offering forth, JC 2.02. 39
turns our swords | in our own proper entrails. 5.03. 96
in the poison'd entrails throw; MAC 4.01. 5
ENTRANC'D 1 FR 0.0001 REL FR 1 V 0 P
she hath not been | entranc'd above five hours. PER 3.02. 94
/ENTRANCE 1 FR 0.0001 REL FR 1 V 0 P
/after /the /prompter, /for /our /entrance; ROM 1.04. 8
ENTRANCE 20 FR 0.0022 REL FR 18 V 2 P
his own doors being shut against his entrance. ERR 4.03. 89
and, for an entrance to my entertainment, | i do SHR 2.01. 54
i will answer you with gait and entrance — but TN 3.01. 82 P
thou | these rural latches to his entrance open, WT 4.04.438
our just and lineal entrance to our own; JN 2.01. 85
we fling wide ope, | and give you entrance; 2.01.450
is mann'd, my lord, | against thy entrance. R2 3.03. 22
no more the thirsty entrance of this soil 1H4 1.01. 5
that we do make our entrance several ways; 1H6 2.01. 30
if we have entrance, as i hope we shall, | and 3.02. 6
admit him entrance, griffith; H8 4.02.107
achilles stands i' th' entrance of his tent. TRO 3.03. 38
head, that he gives entrance to such companions? COR 4.05. 12 P
that was thy joy, | be barr'd his entrance here. TIT 1.01.383
stains | the stony entrance of this sepulchre? ROM 5.03.141
that croaks the fatal entrance of duncan | under MAC 1.05. 39
breach in nature | for ruin's wasteful entrance; 2.03.114
beware | of entrance to a quarrel, but being in, HAM 1.03. 66
therefore to make his entrance more sweet, PER 2.03. 64
no penetrable entrance to her plaining: LUC 559
ENTRANCES 1 FR 0.0001 REL FR 1 V 0 P
they have their exits and their entrances, | and AYL 2.07.141
ENTRAP 5 FR 0.0005 REL FR 4 V 1 P
cunning times put on | to entrap the wisest. MV 3.02.101
a golden mesh t' entrap the hearts of men 3.02.122
poison, entrap thee by some treacherous device, AYL 1.01.150 P
sought to entrap me by intelligence, | rated 1H4 4.03. 98
o, seek not to entrap me, gracious lord, | a PER 2.05. 45
ENTRAPP'D 1 FR 0.0001 REL FR 1 V 0 P
hath now entrapp'd the noble–minded talbot: 1H6 4.04. 37
ENTRE 1 FR 0.0001 REL FR 0 V 1 P
heureux que je tombe entre les mains d'un H5 4.04. 56 P
ENTREASUR'D *(also intreasured)*
ENTREASUR'D 1 FR 0.0001 REL FR 1 V 0 P
balm'd and entreasur'd | with full bags of PER 3.02. 65
ENTREAT 120 FR 0.0135 REL FR 106 V 14 P
and do entreat | thou pardon me my wrongs. TMP 5.01.118
i rather would entreat thy company | to see the TGV 1.01. 5
i do entreat your patience | to hear me speak 4.04.111
to him again, entreat him, | kneel down before MM 2.02. 43
let me entreat you speak the former language. 2.04.140
if for this night he entreat you to his bed, 3.01.262 P
we shall entreat you to abide here till he come 5.01.265 P
'tis my deserving, and i do entreat it. 5.01.477
they did entreat me to acquaint her of it, | but ADO 3.01. 40
friar, i must entreat your pains, i think. 5.04. 18
do one thing for me that i shall entreat. LLL 3.01.153
shall i entreat thy love? 4.01. 82 P
for all your fair endeavors, and entreat, | out 5.02.730
i do entreat your grace to pardon me. MND 1.01. 58
here are your parts, and i am to entreat you, 1.02. 99 P
"i would request you," or "i would entreat you, 3.01. 41 P
if she cannot entreat, i can compel. 3.02.248
thou canst compel no more than she entreat. 3.02.249
i would entreat you rather to put on | your MV 2.02.201
he did entreat me, past all saying nay, | to 3.02.229
entreat some power to change this currish jew. 4.01.292
sir, i entreat you home with me to dinner. 4.01.401
ring, and doth entreat | your company at dinner. 4.02. 7
grace, you shall not entreat him to a second, AYL 1.02.206 P
i did not then entreat to have her stay, | it 1.03. 69
will never have her unless thou entreat for her. 4.03. 72 P
let me entreat of you | to pardon me yet for a SHR in.2. 118
you would entreat me rather go than stay. 3.02.192
let us entreat you stay till after dinner. 3.02.198
let me entreat you. 3.02.199
let me entreat you. 3.02.200
i am content you shall entreat me stay, | but 3.02.202
but yet not stay, entreat me how you can. 3.02.203
to marry with her though she would entreat. 4.02. 33
but i, who never knew how to entreat, | nor 4.03. 7
nor never needed that i should entreat, | am 4.03. 8
go and entreat my wife | to come to me forthwith 5.02. 86
o ho, entreat her! 5.02. 87
this drives me to entreat you | that presently AWW 2.05. 63
and rather muse than ask why i entreat you, 2.05. 65
i will entreat you, when you see my son, | to 3.02. 92
more i'll entreat you | written to bear along. 3.02. 94
i could hardly entreat him back. TN 3.04. 58 P
i must entreat of you some of that money. 3.04.340
pursue him, and entreat him to a peace; 5.01.380
my last good deed was to entreat his stay; WT 1.02. 97
nor entreat the north | to make his bleak winds JN 5.07. 39
to entreat your majesty to visit him. R2 1.04. 56
and so let me entreat you leave the house. 1H4 2.04.518
but do not use it oft, let me entreat you. 3.01.174
gower, shall i entreat you with me to dinner? 2H4 2.01.182 P
if my tongue cannot entreat you to acquit me, ep 18 P
entreat you to your wonted furtherance? 1H6 5.03. 21
entreat her not the worse in that i pray | you 2H6 2.04. 81
by them, | yet did i purpose as they do entreat; 3.02.282
o, let me entreat thee cease. 3.02.339
my gracious lord, entreat him, speak him fair. 4.01.120
i'll send some holy bishop to entreat; 4.04. 9
i'll write unto them and entreat them fair; 3H6 1.01.271
let me entreat (for i command no more) | that 4.06. 59
came to you, | would not entreat for life? R3 1.04.260
come thou on my side, and entreat for me, | as 1.04.265
first, madam, i entreat true peace of you, 2.01. 63
to entreat of her | to meet you at the tower and 3.01.138
he doth entreat your grace, my noble lord, | to 3.07. 59
do, good my lord, your citizens entreat you. 3.07.201
/'zounds, /i'll entreat no more. 3.07.219
either be patient and entreat me fair, | or with 4.04.152
and entreat | an hour of revels with 'em. H8 1.04. 71
and did entreat your highness to this course 2.04.217
how that the cardinal did entreat his holiness 3.02. 32
i humbly do entreat your highness' pardon, | my 4.02.104
entreat her fair, and, by my soul, fair greek, TRO 4.04.113
can scarce entreat you to be odd with him. 4.05.265
dost thou entreat me, hector? 4.05.268
shall | concur together, severally entreat him. 4.05.274
and entreat them | for my wounds' sake to give COR 2.02.137
let us entreat by honor of his name, | whom TIT 1.01. 39
but entreat of thee | to pardon mutius and to 1.01.362
sweet lords, entreat her hear me but a word. 2.03.138
do thou entreat her show a woman's pity. 2.03.147
andronicus, i will entreat the king. 2.03.304
grave tribunes, once more i entreat of you — 3.01. 31
but he will not entreat his son for us. 4.04. 94
if tamora entreat him, then he will, | for i can 4.04. 95
/do entreat her eyes | to twinkle in their ROM 2.02. 16
my lord, we must entreat the time alone. 4.01. 40
i must entreat you honor me so much | as to TIM 1.02.169
behalf, i come to entreat your honor to supply; 3.01. 17 P
consent of love | entreat thee back to athens, 5.01.141
i would not (so with love i might entreat you) JC 1.02.166
shall i entreat a word? 2.01.100
i do entreat you, not a man depart, | save i 3.02. 60
yet when we can entreat an hour to serve, | we MAC 2.01. 22
i entreat you both | that, being of so young HAM 2.02. 10
and he beseech'd me to entreat your majesties 3.01. 22
let his queen–mother all alone entreat him | to 3.01.182
should win your displeasure to entreat me to't. LR 2.02.113 P
i'll entreat for thee. 2.02.154
i entreat you | to bring but five and twenty; 2.04.247
my lord, entreat him by no means to stay. 2.04.299
neither to speak of him, entreat for him, or any 3.03. 5 P
naked soul, | which i'll entreat to lead me. 4.01. 45
you and her husband entreat her to splinter; OTH 2.03.323 P
'tis as i should entreat you wear your gloves, 3.03. 77
i would i might entreat your honor | to scan 3.03.244
i do entreat that we may sup together. 4.01.262
to entreat your captain | to soft and gentle ANT 2.02. 2
i shall entreat him | to answer like himself. 2.02. 3
good queen, let us entreat you. 5.02.158
t' entreat your grace but in a small request, CYM 1.06.181
this one thing only | i will entreat: 5.05. 84
a twelvemonth longer let me entreat you | to PER 2.04. 45
more | let me entreat to know at large the cause 5.01. 62
i must needs entreat you | this afternoon to TNK 2.05. 45
and let me entreat you | by all the honesty and 3.03. 13
last let me entreat, sir. 3.06.210
if she entreat again, do any thing, | lie with 5.02. 17
entreat their mediation to the king, | give up STM II.C 145
"i have been wooed, as i entreat thee now, VEN 97
ENTREATED 12 FR 0.0013 REL FR 10 V 2 P
being entreated to it by your friend. TGV 3.02. 45
silvia | entreated me to call and know her mind. 4.03. 2
since the youth will not be entreated, his own AYL 1.02.150 P
fain dissuade him, but he will not be entreated. 1.02.161 P
do what you can, yours will not be entreated. SHR 5.02. 89
for god's sake fairly let her be entreated. R2 3.01. 37
the dolphin, whom of succors we entreated, H5 3.03. 45
and i entreated her come forth | and bear this ROM 5.03.260
am i entreated | to speak and strike? JC 2.01. 55
therefore i have entreated him along | with us HAM 1.01. 26
which she entreated. ANT 2.02.222
which do not be entreated to, but weigh | what 2.06. 32
ENTREATIES 11 FR 0.0012 REL FR 10 V 1 P
i should have given him tears unto entreaties, AYL 1.02.238
to satisfy your highness and the entreaties | of WT 1.02.232
th' entreaties of your mistress? 1.02.234
and will not temporize with my entreaties. JN 5.02.125
but if she be obdurate | to mild entreaties, god R3 3.01. 40
grace, | on our entreaties, to amend your fault! 3.07.115
but penetrable to your kind entreaties, | albeit 3.07.225
if entreaties | will render you no remedy, this H8 5.01.149
if i might in entreaties find success — | as TRO 4.05.149
a day of kings' entreaties a mother should not COR 1.03. 8 P
and with our fair entreaties haste them on. 5.01. 74
ENTREATING 2 FR 0.0002 REL FR 2 V 0 P
humbly entreating from your royal thoughts | a AWW 2.01.127
i am entreating of myself to do | that which you TNK 1.01.206
ENTREATMENTS 1 FR 0.0001 REL FR 1 V 0 P
set your entreatments at a higher rate | than a HAM 1.03.122
ENTREATS 14 FR 0.0015 REL FR 12 V 2 P
and my speech entreats | that i may know the let H5 5.02. 64
by me entreats, great lord, thou wouldst 1H6 2.02. 40
tell her the king, that may command, entreats. R3 4.04.345
and heartily entreats you take good comfort. H8 4.02.119
to be a heinous sin, | yield at entreats; TIT 1.01.449
here, | and at my lovely tamora's entreats, | i 1.01.483
entreats your company to–morrow to hunt with him TIM 1.02.187 P
steps in to cassio and entreats his pause; OTH 2.03.229
there's one cassio entreats her a little favor 3.01. 26 P
caesar entreats | not to consider in what case ANT 3.13. 53
dispatch, | the lamb entreats the butcher. CYM 3.04. 96
for them to play upon, entreats you pity him. PER 2.01. 61
still she entreats, and prettily entreats, | for VEN 73
still she entreats, and prettily entreats, | for 73
ENTREATY 12 FR 0.0013 REL FR 8 V 4 P
it is not my consent, | but my entreaty too. MM 4.01. 67
then she puts you to entreaty, and there begins AYL 4.01. 79 P
door | upon entreaty have a present alms, | if SHR 4.03. 5
at the good queen's entreaty. WT 1.02.220
use no entreaty, for it is in vain. 1H6 5.04. 85
my mild entreaty shall not make you guilty. 3H6 3.01. 91
has half by the entreaty and grant of the whole COR 4.05.199 P
to timon's cave | with letters of entreaty, TIM 5.02. 11
pleasures more into command | than to entreaty. HAM 2.02. 29
with an entreaty, herein further shown, | that 2.02. 76
and at my entreaty forbear his presence until LR 1.02.160 P
reconciles them to his entreaty, and himself to ANT 2.07. 8 P
ENT'RED 23 FR 0.0026 REL FR 17 V 6 P
and thorns, | which ent'red their frail shins. TMP 4.01.181
master, i am here ent'red in bond for you. ERR 4.04.125
you shall see her chamber–window ent'red, even ADO 3.02.113 P
forsook his scene, and ent'red in a brake; MND 3.02. 15
within this bosom never ent'red yet | the JN 4.02.254
nothing but some band that he is ent'red into R2 5.02. 65
master fang, have you ent'red the action? 2H4 2.01. 1 P
it is ent'red. 2.01. 2 P
good master snare, i have ent'red him and all. 2.01. 9 P
since my exion is ent'red and my case so openly 2.01. 30 P
with maiden walls that war hath /never ent'red. H5 5.02.323 P
pucelle is ent'red into orleance | in spite of 1H6 1.05. 36
here ent'red pucelle and her practisants. 3.02. 20
no way to that, for weakness, which she ent'red. 3.02. 25
against the greeks that would have ent'red troy. 3H6 2.01. 52
but being ent'red, | i doubt not, i, but we 4.07. 32
dreams | that ever ent'red in a drowsy head R3 5.03.228
like to an ent'red tide, they all rush by | and TRO 3.03.159
that they of rome are ent'red in our counsels, COR 1.02. 2
alone he ent'red | the mortal gate of th' city, 2.02.110
powers | are ent'red in the roman territories, 4.06. 40
but, sith i am ent'red in this cause so far OTH 3.03.411
into whose port | ne'er ent'red wanton sound) to TNK 5.01.148
ENTRENCH'D *(also intrench'd)*
ENTRENCH'D 1 FR 0.0001 REL FR 0 V 1 P
it was this very sword entrench'd it. AWW 2.01. 44 P
ENT'RING 5 FR 0.0005 REL FR 3 V 2 P
we proclaim it in an hour before his ent'ring, MM 4.04. 9 P
and very near upon | the duke is ent'ring; 4.06. 15
the revellers are ent'ring, brother, make good ADO 2.01. 84 P
where fame, late ent'ring at his heedful ears, 3H6 3.03. 63
his grace is ent'ring. H8 1.04. 21
ENTRY 1 FR 0.0001 REL FR 1 V 0 P
i hear a knocking | at the south entry. MAC 2.02. 63
ENTWIST 1 FR 0.0001 REL FR 1 V 0 P
woodbine the sweet honeysuckle | gently entwist; MND 4.01. 43
ENUR'D *(also inur'd)*
ENUR'D 1 FR 0.0001 REL FR 1 V 0 P
not to be tempted would she be enur'd, | and now LC 251
ENVELOP 2 FR 0.0002 REL FR 2 V 0 P
wholesom'st spirits of the night | envelop you, MM 4.02. 74
t' envelop and contain celestial spirits. H5 1.01. 31
ENVENOM 2 FR 0.0002 REL FR 2 V 0 P
envenom him with words, or get thee gone, | and JN 3.01. 63
of his | did hamlet so envenom with his envy HAM 4.07.103
ENVENOM'D 2 FR 0.0002 REL FR 2 V 0 P
is in /thy hand, | unbated and envenom'd. HAM 5.02.317
the point envenom'd too! 5.02.321
ENVENOMED 2 FR 0.0002 REL FR 2 V 0 P
with whose envenomed and fatal sting, | your 2H6 3.02.267
for piercing steel, and darts envenomed, | shall JC 5.03. 76
ENVENOMS 1 FR 0.0001 REL FR 1 V 0 P
what is comely | envenoms him that bears it! AYL 2.03. 15
ENVERNESS 1 FR 0.0001 REL FR 1 V 0 P
from hence to enverness, | and bind us further MAC 1.04. 42
/ENVIED 1 FR 0.0001 REL FR 1 V 0 P
our hearts nor outward eyes | /envied the great, PER 2.03. 26
ENVIED 4 FR 0.0004 REL FR 4 V 0 P
they will not stick to say you envied him, | and H8 2.02.126
the mutinous parts | that envied his receipt; COR 1.01.112
from time to time | envied against the people, 3.03. 95
thee fight, | when i have envied thy behavior. ANT 2.06. 75
ENVIES 2 FR 0.0002 REL FR 2 V 0 P
what low'ring star now envies thy estate, | that 2H6 3.01.206
and here, i hope, is none that envies it. PER 2.03. 14
ENVIOUS 38 FR 0.0043 REL FR 36 V 2 P
and he shall appear to the envious a scholar, a MM 3.02.145 P
berowne is like an envious sneaping frost | that LLL 1.01.100
but none can drive him from the envious plea MV 3.02.282
an envious emulator of every man's good parts, a AYL 1.01.143 P
my father's rough and envious disposition 1.02.241
more free from peril than the envious court? 2.01. 4
like envious floods o'errun her lovely face, SHR in.2. 65
whose rocky shore beats back the envious siege R2 2.01. 62
when he perceives the envious clouds are bent 3.03. 65
from envious malice of thy swelling heart. 1H6 3.01. 26
so will this base and envious discord breed. 3.01.193
the envious barking of your saucy tongue 3.04. 33
this fellow here, with envious carping tongue, 4.01. 90
with envious looks laughing at thy shame, | that 2H6 2.04. 12
and when i start, the envious people laugh, 2.04. 35
the envious load that lies upon his heart; 3.01.157
shrub, | to make an envious mountain on my back, 3H6 3.02.157
whose envious gulf did swallow up his life. 5.06. 25
the envious slanders of her false accusers; R3 1.03. 26
but still the envious flood | stopp'd in my soul 1.04. 37
that trick of state | was a deep envious one. H8 2.01. 45
follow your envious courses, men of malice! 3.02.243
carry gentle peace | to silence envious tongues. 3.02.446
grows to an envious fever | of pale and TRO 1.03.133
subjects all | to envious and calumniating time. 3.03.174
expecting ever when some envious surge | will in TIT 3.01. 96
as is the bud bit with an envious worm, | ere he ROM 1.01.151

arise, fair sun, and kill the envious moon, 2.02. 4
be not her maid, since she is envious; 2.02. 7
arm | an envious thrust from tybalt hit the life 3.01.168
can heaven be so envious? 3.02. 40
what envious streaks | do lace the severing 3.05. 7
make | our purpose necessary, and not envious; JC 2.01.178
see what a rent the envious casca made; 3.02.175
clamb'ring to hang, an envious sliver broke, HAM 4.07.173
devils take 'em | that are so envious to me! TNK 2.02.263
iron | came music's origin), what envious flint, 5.04. 61
each envious brier his weary legs do scratch, VEN 705
ENVIOUSLY 1 FR 0.0001 REL FR 1 V 0 P
spurns enviously at straws, speaks things in HAM 4.05. 6
ENVIRON 3 FR 0.0003 REL FR 2 V 1 P
in thy danger | (if ever danger do environ thee) TGV 1.01. 16
and dull and crudy vapors which environ it, 2H4 4.03. 99 P
and the gloomy shade of death | environ you, 1H6 5.04. 90
ENVIRON'D 3 FR 0.0003 REL FR 3 V 0 P
wert thou environ'd with a brazen wall. 3H6 2.04. 4
a legion of foul fiends | environ'd me, and R3 1.04. 59
a rock, | environ'd with a wilderness of sea, TIT 3.01. 94
ENVIRONED 4 FR 0.0004 REL FR 4 V 0 P
the trembling lamb environed with wolves. 3H6 1.01.242
environed he was with many foes, | and stood 2.01. 50
environed with all these hideous fears, | and ROM 4.03. 50
the fift, an hand environed with clouds, PER 2.02. 36
ENVY 59 FR 0.0066 REL FR 52 V 7 P
who with age and envy | was grown into a hoop? TMP 1.02.258
stands at a guard with envy; MM 1.03. 51
either this is envy in you, folly, or mistaking. 3.02.141 P
axe, bear half the keenness | of thy sharp envy. MV 4.01.126
owe no man hate, envy no man's happiness, glad AYL 3.02. 74 P
is it for him you do envy me so? SHR 2.01. 18
she bore a mind that envy could not but call TN 2.01. 29 P
that very envy and the tongue of loss | cried 5.01. 58
but now i envy at their liberty, | and will JN 3.04. 73
with rival–hating envy, set on you | to wake our R2 1.03.131
house, | against the envy of less happier lands; 2.01. 49
me sin | in envy that my lord northumberland 1H4 1.01. 79
either envy, therefore, or misprision | is 1.03. 27
some | envy your great deservings and good name, 4.03. 35
the world, | if he outlive the envy of this day, 5.02. 66
look pale | with envy of each other's happiness, H5 5.02.351
but more, when envy breeds unkind division: 1H6 4.01.193
as lean–fac'd envy in her loathsome cave. 2H6 3.02.315
or gather wealth, i care not with what envy. 4.10. 21
exempt from envy, but not from disdain, | unless 3H6 3.03.127
you envy my advancement and my friends'. R3 1.03. 74
go, go, poor soul, i envy not thy glory, | to 4.01. 63
whom envy hath immur'd within your walls — 4.01. 99
no black envy | shall make my grave. H8 2.01. 85
what envy reach you? 2.02. 88
'em, | envy and base opinion set against 'em, 3.01. 36
you turn the good we offer into envy. 3.01.113
of what coarse metal ye are moulded, envy, | how 3.02.239
that make | envy and crooked malice nourishment 5.02. 79
the devil | and his disciples only envy at, | ye 5.02.147
and thou art as full of envy at his greatness as TRO 2.01. 33 P
i have said my prayers, and devil envy say amen. 2.03. 21 P
to cressid as what envy can say worst shall be a 3.02. 96 P
have the gods envy? 4.04. 28
how now, thou /core of envy? 5.01. 4
why, thou damnable box of envy, thou, what means 5.01. 25 P
a serpent i abhor | more than thy fame and envy. COR 1.08. 4
enforce him with his envy to the people, | and 3.03. 3
such as become a soldier | rather than envy you. 3.03. 57
the cruelty and envy of the people, | permitted 4.05. 74
weeded from my heart | a root of ancient envy. 4.05.103
here lurks no treason, here no envy swells, TIT 1.01.153
it up again | with poisonous spite and envy. TIM 1.02.139
like wrath in death and envy afterwards; JC 2.01.164
he, | did that they did in envy of great caesar; 5.05. 70
did not together pluck such envy from him | as HAM 4.07. 74
did hamlet so envenom with his envy | that he 4.07.103
sum of my disgraces by | addition of his envy! ANT 5.02.164
even to the point of envy, if 'twere made CYM 2.03.128
but envy much | thou hast robb'd me of this deed 4.02.158
that monster envy, oft the wrack | of earned PER 4.ch. 12
marks, | that cleon's wife, with envy rare, | a 4.ch. 37
us, envy of ill men | crave our acquaintance; TNK 2.02. 90
do such a justice thou thyself wilt envy. 3.06.155
there is but envy in that light which shows 5.03. 21
perchance that envy of so rich a thing, LUC 39
wrath, envy, treason, rape, and murther's rages, 909
praise cannot be so thy praise | to tie up envy, SON 70.12
do i envy those jacks that nimble leap | to kiss 128. 5
ENVYING 2 FR 0.0002 REL FR 2 V 0 P
until the heavens, envying earth's good hap, R2 1.01. 23
i sin in envying his nobility; COR 1.01.230
ENVY'S 3 FR 0.0003 REL FR 3 V 0 P
means can carry me | out of his envy's reach, i MV 4.01. 10
faded, | by envy's hand and murder's bloody axe. R2 1.02. 21
advanc'd above pale envy's threat'ning reach. TIT 2.01. 4
ENWHEEL 1 FR 0.0001 REL FR 1 V 0 P
thee, and on every hand, | enwheel thee round! OTH 2.01. 87
ENWOMBED 1 FR 0.0001 REL FR 1 V 0 P
catalogue of those | that were enwombed mine. AWW 1.03.144
ENWRAPS 1 FR 0.0001 REL FR 1 V 0 P
and though 'tis wonder that enwraps me thus, TN 4.03. 3
EO 1 FR 0.0001 REL FR 1 V 0 P
glorious, | et bonum quo antiquius, eo melius. PER 1.ch. 10
EPHESIAN 1 FR 0.0001 REL FR 0 V 1 P
it is thine host, thine ephesian, calls. WIV 4.05. 18 P
EPHESIANS 1 FR 0.0001 REL FR 0 V 1 P
ephesians, my lord, of the old church. 2H4 2.02.150 P
EPHESUS 13 FR 0.0014 REL FR 13 V 0 P
more, if any born at ephesus be seen | at any ERR 1.01. 16
syracusian born | come to the bay of ephesus, he 1.01. 19
and for what cause thou cam'st to ephesus. 1.01. 30
asia, | and, coasting homeward, came to ephesus; 1.01.134
try all the friends thou hast in ephesus; 1.01.152
in ephesus i am but two hours old, | as strange 2.02.148
sir, sir, i shall have law in ephesus, | to your 4.01. 83
that i should be attach'd in ephesus; 4.04. 6
your honor has through ephesus pour'd forth PER 3.02. 43
his woeful queen we leave at ephesus, | unto 4.ch. 3
my temple stands in ephesus, hie thee thither, 5.01.240
toward ephesus | turn our blown sails; 5.01.254
at ephesus the temple see, | our king and all 5.02. 17
EPICURE 1 FR 0.0001 REL FR 0 V 1 P
pompey gives him, else he is a very epicure. ANT 2.07. 52 P
EPICUREAN 2 FR 0.0002 REL FR 1 V 1 P
what a damn'd epicurean rascal is this! WIV 2.02.287 P
epicurean cooks | sharpen with cloyless sauce ANT 2.01. 24
EPICURES 1 FR 0.0001 REL FR 1 V 0 P
thanes, | and mingle with the english epicures! MAC 5.03. 8
EPICURISM 1 FR 0.0001 REL FR 1 V 0 P
epicurism and lust | makes it more like a tavern LR 1.04.244
EPICURUS 1 FR 0.0001 REL FR 1 V 0 P
you know that i held epicurus strong, | and his JC 5.01. 76
EPIDAMIUM 7 FR 0.0008 REL FR 7 V 0 P
prosperous voyages i often made | to epidamium, ERR 1.01. 41
a league from epidamium had we sail'd | before 1.01. 62
therefore give out you are of epidamium, | lest 1.02. 1
there's a bark of epidamium | that stays but 4.01. 85
sheep, | what ship of epidamium stays for me? 4.01. 94
by men of epidamium he and i, | and the twin 5.01.350
and me they left with those of epidamium. 5.01.354
EPIDAURUS 1 FR 0.0001 REL FR 1 V 0 P
to us, | of corinth that, of epidaurus this. ERR 1.01. 93
EPIGRAM 1 FR 0.0001 REL FR 0 V 1 P
thou think i care for a satire or an epigram? ADO 5.04.102 P
EPILEPSY 1 FR 0.0001 REL FR 1 V 0 P
my lord is fall'n into an epilepsy. OTH 4.01. 50
EPILEPTIC 1 FR 0.0001 REL FR 1 V 0 P
a plague upon your epileptic visage! LR 2.02. 81
EPILOGUE 7 FR 0.0008 REL FR 1 V 6 P
page, it is an epilogue or discourse, to make LLL 3.01. 81
will it please you to see the epilogue, or to MND 5.01.353 P
no epilogue, i pray you; 5.01.355 P
let your epilogue alone. 5.01.362 P
is not the fashion to see the lady the epilogue; AYL ep 2 P
'tis true that a good play needs no epilogue. ep 5 P
that am neither a good epilogue, nor cannot ep 8 P
EPILOGUES 1 FR 0.0001 REL FR 0 V 1 P
prove the better by the help of good epilogues. AYL ep 7 P
EPISTLES 2 FR 0.0002 REL FR 0 V 2 P
drop in his way some obscure epistles of love, TN 2.03.155 P
but as a madman's epistles are no gospels, so it 5.01.287 P
EPISTROPHUS 1 FR 0.0001 REL FR 1 V 0 P
corses of the kings | epistrophus and cedius; TRO 5.05. 11
EPITAPH 14 FR 0.0015 REL FR 11 V 3 P
invention, | hang her an epitaph upon her tomb, ADO 5.01.284
hear an extemporal epitaph on the death of the LLL 4.02. 51 P
than to live still and write mine epitaph. MV 4.01.118
so in approof lives not his epitaph | as in your AWW 1.02. 50
the grave, | but not rememb'red in thy epitaph! 1H4 5.04.101
mouth, | not worshipp'd with a waxen epitaph. H5 1.02.233
make thine epitaph, | that death in me at TIM 4.03.379
why, i was writing of my epitaph; 5.01.185
better have a bad epitaph than their ill report HAM 2.02.526 P
with the hobby–horse, whose epitaph is, "for o, 3.02.135 P
and hath as oft a sland'rous epitaph | as record CYM 3.03. 52
please you wit | the epitaph is for marina writ PER 4.04. 32
will wed me, | and soldiers sing my epitaph. TNK 3.06.285
or i shall live your epitaph to make, | or you SON 81. 1
EPITAPHS 4 FR 0.0004 REL FR 4 V 0 P
family's old monument | hang mournful epitaphs, ADO 4.01.207
let's talk of graves, of worms, and epitaphs, R2 3.02.145
and her epitaphs | in glitt'ring golden PER 4.03. 43
and had their epitaphs, the people's curses. TNK 2.02.110
EPITHET *(also epithite, etc.)*
EPITHET 2 FR 0.0002 REL FR 1 V 1 P
a most singular and choice epithet. LLL 5.01. 15 P
they will not answer to that epithet; 5.02.171
EPITHETON 1 FR 0.0001 REL FR 0 V 1 P
as a congruent epitheton appertaining to thy LLL 1.02. 14 P
EPITHITE *(also epithet)*
EPITHITE 1 FR 0.0001 REL FR 0 V 1 P
a good epithite! ADO 5.02. 66 P
EPITHITES 2 FR 0.0002 REL FR 1 V 1 P
holofernes, the epithites are sweetly varied, LLL 4.02. 8 P
horribly stuff'd with epithites of war, | /and, OTH 1.01. 14
EPITOME 1 FR 0.0001 REL FR 1 V 0 P
this is a poor epitome of yours, | which by th' COR 5.03. 68
EQUAL *(also egall, etc.)*
/EQUAL 1 FR 0.0001 REL FR 1 V 0 P
/i /have /in /equal /balance /justly /weigh'd 2H4 4.01. 67
EQUAL 54 FR 0.0061 REL FR 50 V 4 P
bestow thy fawning smiles on equal mates, | and TGV 3.01.158
soul, | were equal poise of sin and charity. MM 2.04. 68
him from her, she is no equal for his birth. ADO 2.01.165 P
and justice always whirls in equal measure: LLL 4.03.381
the forfeit | be nominated for an equal pound MV 1.03.149
would counsel you to a more equal enterprise. AYL 1.02.178 P
have fought with equal fortune, and continue | a AWW 1.02. 2
his equal had awak'd them, and his honor, 1.02. 38
stars have fail'd | to equal my great fortune. 2.05. 76
mad as he, | if sad and merry madness equal be. TN 3.04. 15
now grown in grace | equal with wond'ring. WT 4.01. 25
to him, and will make | her portion equal his. 4.04.386
you equal potents, fiery kindled spirits! JN 2.01.358
her dowry shall weigh equal with a queen; 2.01.486
on equal terms to give /him chastisement? R2 4.01. 22
even as we are, to equal with the king. 2H4 1.03. 67
in equal rank with the best govern'd nation, 5.02.137
my duty to you both, on equal love. H5 5.02. 23
poor gentleman, his wrong doth equal mine. 1H6 2.05. 22
my vows are equal partners with thy vows. 3.02. 85
and poise the cause in justice' equal scales, 2H6 2.01.200
to equal him, i will make myself a knight 4.02.119 P
and let thy tongue be equal with thy heart. 5.01. 89
so is the equal poise of this fell war. 3H6 2.05. 13
wishing his foot were equal with his eye, | and 3.02.137
unless my hand and strength could equal them. 3.02.145
blame, | if this foul deed were by to equal it. 5.05. 55
equal in lustre, were now best, now worst, | as H8 1.01. 29
(for he is equal rav'nous | as he is subtile, 1.01.159
two equal men. 2.02.107
assurance | of equal friendship and proceeding. 2.04. 18
he has no equal. COR 1.01.253
i thought to crush him in an equal force, | true 1.10. 14
if she be mated with an equal husband? TIM 1.01.140
in equal scale weighing delight and dole, HAM 1.02. 13
and rewards | hast ta'en with equal thanks; 3.02. 68
faults | can never be so equal that your love ANT 3.04. 35
to tell them that this world did equal theirs 4.15. 77
his taints and honors | wag'd equal with him. 5.01. 31
i shall unfold equal discourtesy | to your best CYM 2.03. 96
less, and so more equal ballasting | to thee, 3.06. 77
were my fortunes equal to my desires, i could PER 2.01.111 P
to equal any single crown a' th' earth | i' th' 4.03. 8
be, hath endur'd a grief | might equal yours, if 5.01. 88
parentage — good parentage — | to equal mine! 5.01. 98
that thou thoughts' thy griefs might equal mine, 5.01.131
and earn'st a deity | equal with mars. TNK 1.01.228
his mind nurse equal | to these so diff'ring 1.03. 32
since that | your question's with your equal, 3.01. 55
that, having two fair gauds of equal sweetness, 4.02. 53
were i to lose one — they are equal precious — 5.01.155
in the passage | the gods have been most equal. 5.04.115
then son and father weep with equal strife | who LUC 1791
which should example where your equal grew? SON 84. 4
/EQUALITIES 1 FR 0.0001 REL FR 0 V 1 P
he values most, for /equalities are so weigh'd, LR 1.01. 5 P
EQUALITY 2 FR 0.0002 REL FR 2 V 0 P
whose equality | by our best eyes cannot be JN 2.01.327
equality of two domestic powers | breed ANT 1.03. 47
EQUALL'D 2 FR 0.0002 REL FR 2 V 0 P
nor was not to be equall'd" — thus your verse WT 5.01.101
was above mine, | else surely his had equall'd. TIM 3.04. 32
EQUALLY 11 FR 0.0012 REL FR 7 V 4 P
go to, sir, you weigh equally; MM 4.02. 30 P
his part, and equally rememb'red by don pedro. ADO 1.01. 12 P
her gifts may henceforth be bestow'd equally. AYL 1.02. 33 P
divided it | into three limits very equally: 1H4 3.01. 72
length, | consisting equally of horse and foot; R3 5.03.294
merits and our safety | may equally determine. LR 5.03. 45
that your love | can equally move with them. ANT 3.04. 36
to her dishonor and equally to me disloyal." CYM 3.04. 31 P
that equally canst poise sternness with pity, TNK 1.01. 86
it concerns your credit | and my oath equally. 3.06.224
ne'er settled equally, but high or low, | that VEN 1139
EQUALNESS 1 FR 0.0001 REL FR 1 V 0 P
should divide | our equalness to this. ANT 5.01. 48
EQUALS 4 FR 0.0004 REL FR 4 V 0 P
here, | in quantity equals not one of yours. 1H4 3.01. 96
on me, whose all not equals edward's moi'ty? R3 1.02.249
this and my food are equals, there's no odds; TIM 1.02. 60
"yet did i not, as some my equals did, | demand LC 148
EQUINOCTIAL 1 FR 0.0001 REL FR 0 V 1 P
the vapians passing the equinoctial of queubus. TN 2.03. 24 P
EQUINOX 1 FR 0.0001 REL FR 1 V 0 P
his vice, | 'tis to his virtue a just equinox, OTH 2.03.124
/EQUIPAGE 1 FR 0.0001 REL FR 1 V 0 P
/i /will /retort /the /sum /in /equipage. WIV 2.02. 1
EQUIPAGE 1 FR 0.0001 REL FR 1 V 0 P
brought | to march in ranks of better equipage; SON 32.12
/EQUITY 1 FR 0.0001 REL FR 1 V 0 P
/and /thou, /his //yoke–fellow /of /equity, LR 3.06. 37
EQUITY 3 FR 0.0003 REL FR 2 V 1 P
for this down–trodden equity, we tread | in JN 2.01.241
two arrant cowards, there's no equity stirring. 1H4 2.02.100 P
and equity exil'd your highness' land. 2H6 3.01.146
EQUIVALENT 1 FR 0.0001 REL FR 1 V 0 P
who stood equivalent with mighty kings, | but PER 5.01. 91
EQUIVOCAL 2 FR 0.0002 REL FR 1 V 1 P
what an equivocal companion is this! AWW 5.03.250 P
being strong on both sides, are equivocal. OTH 1.03.217
EQUIVOCATE 1 FR 0.0001 REL FR 0 V 1 P
god's sake, yet could not equivocate to heaven. MAC 2.03. 11 P
EQUIVOCATES 1 FR 0.0001 REL FR 0 V 1 P
in conclusion, equivocates him in a sleep, and, MAC 2.03. 35 P
EQUIVOCATION 2 FR 0.0002 REL FR 1 V 1 P
begin | to doubt th' equivocation of the fiend MAC 5.05. 42
speak by the card, or equivocation will undo us. HAM 5.01.138 P
EQUIVOCATOR 3 FR 0.0003 REL FR 0 V 3 P
faith, here's an equivocator, that could swear MAC 2.03. 8 P
o, come in, equivocator. 2.03. 11 P
may be said to be an equivocator with lechery: 2.03. 31 P
'ER *(also her*)*
'ER 1 FR 0.0001 REL FR 0 V 1 P
therefore briefly yield 'er, for she must PER 3.01. 53 P
ERCLES' *(also hercules', etc.)*
ERCLES' 1 FR 0.0001 REL FR 0 V 1 P
this is ercles' vein, a tyrant's vein; MND 1.02. 40 P
ERCLES 1 FR 0.0001 REL FR 0 V 1 P
i could play ercles rarely, or a part to tear a MND 1.02. 29 P
ERE *(also yer)*
/ERE 3 FR 0.0003 REL FR 3 V 0 P
/thou /torments /me /ere /i /come /to /hell! R2 4.01.270
/which /long /ere /this /we /offer'd /to /the 2H4 4.01. 75
/ere /they /have /done /their /mischief, LR 4.02. 55
ERE 386 FR 0.0436 REL FR 313 V 73 P
have sunk the sea within the earth or ere | it TMP 1.02. 11
if thou rememb'rest aught ere thou cam'st here, 1.02. 51
candied be they, | and melt ere they molest! 2.01.280
for yet ere supper–time must i perform | much 3.01. 95
i swam, ere i could recover the shore, five and 3.02. 14 P
quickly, spirit, | thou shalt ere long be free. 5.01. 87
me, and return | or ere your pulse twice beat. 5.01.103
have inly wept, | or should have spoke ere this. 5.01.201
bud | is eaten by the canker ere it blow, | even TGV 1.01. 46
'twill be this hour ere i have done weeping; 2.03. 1 P
you always end ere you begin. 2.04. 31 P
and, ere i part with thee, confer at large | of 3.01.255
unhappy were you, madam, ere i came; 5.04. 29
inconstancy falls off ere it begins. 5.04.113
twenty lascivious turtles ere one chaste man. WIV 2.01. 81 P
heed, ere summer comes or cuckoo–birds do sing. 2.01.123
been into thames, ere i will leave her thus. 3.05.127 P
may i not go out ere he come? 4.02. 50 P
otherwise you might slip away ere he came. 4.02. 53 P
and where you find a maid | that, ere she sleep, 5.05. 50
why, every fault's condemn'd ere it be done. MM 2.02. 38
be up at heaven and enter there | ere sun–rise, 2.02.153
sick for, ere i'ld yield | my body up to shame. 2.04.103
dear sir, ere long i'll visit you again. 3.01. 46
both work | ere this rude beast will profit. 3.02. 33
ere he would have hang'd a man for the getting a 3.02.117 P
as it is, | you shall hear more ere morning. 4.02. 95
ere twice the sun hath made his journal greeting 4.03. 88
persons with me, ere you make that my report. 5.01.336 P
but ere they came — o, let me say no more! ERR 1.01. 94

ere the ships could meet by twice five leagues, 1.01.100
town, | dies ere the weary sun set in the west. 1.02. 7
ere i learn love, i'll practice to obey. 2.01. 29
it was two ere i left him, and now the clock 4.02. 54
i'll give thee, ere i leave thee, so much money, 4.04. 2
i will discharge thee ere i go from thee: 4.04.119
will cost him a thousand pound ere 'a be cur'd. ADO 1.01. 90 P
i shall see thee, ere i die, look pale with love 1.01.247 P
ere you flout old ends any further, examine your 1.01.288 P
is, | saying i lik'd her ere i went to wars. 1.01.305
and she will die ere she make her love known, 2.03.175 P
his excellence did earn it, ere he had it. 3.01. 99
drink some wine ere you go; fare you well. 3.05. 53 P
orb, | as chaste as is the bud ere it be blown; 4.01. 58
and yet, ere i go, let me go with that i came, 5.02. 47 P
not erect in this age his own tomb ere he dies, 5.02. 78 P
let's have a dance ere we are married, that we 5.04.118 P
so, ere you find where light in darkness lies, LLL 1.01. 78
now here is three studied ere ye'll thrice wink; 1.02. 51 P
fast for thy offenses ere thou be pardoned. 1.02.146 P
sweet hearts, we shall be rich ere we depart, 5.02. 1
she might 'a' been /a grandam ere she died. 5.02. 17
that same berowne i'll torture ere i go. 5.02. 60
one word in private with you ere i die. 5.02.254
ere i will yield my virgin patent up | unto his MND 1.01. 80
and ere a man hath power to say "behold!" 1.01.147
/yours /would i catch, fair hermia, ere i go; 1.01.187
for ere demetrius look'd on hermia's eyne, | he 1.01.242
hath rotted ere his youth attain'd a beard. 2.01. 95
again | ere the leviathan can swim a league. 2.01.174
and ere i take this charm from off her sight 2.01.183
ere he do leave this grove, | thou shalt fly him 2.01.245
and look thou meet me ere the first cock crow. 2.01.267
your kindred hath made my eyes water ere now. 3.01.195 P
we may effect this business yet ere day. 3.02.395
my lord, | was i betrothed ere i /saw hermia; 4.01.172
tongue, | we will make amends ere long; 5.01.434
you shall seek all day ere you find them, and MV 1.01.117 P
nerissa, ere i will be married to a spunge. 1.02. 99 P
you shall look fairer ere i give or hazard. 2.09. 22
ere i ope his letter, | i pray you tell me how 3.02.232
ere thou shalt lose for me one drop of blood. 4.01.113
dew, | and saw the lion's shadow ere himself, 5.01. 8
my master will be here ere morning. 5.01. 48 P
what, are we cuckolds ere we have deserv'd it? 5.01.265
entreaties, | ere he should thus have ventur'd. AYL 1.02.239
and ere we have thy youthful wages spent, 2.03. 67
i partly guess; for i have lov'd ere now. 2.04. 24
for you'll be rotten ere you be half ripe, and 3.02.119 P
the horn, | it was a crest ere thou wast born; 4.02. 14
sir, a word ere you go. SHR 1.02.227
his lecture will be done ere you have tun'd. 3.01. 23
to put on better ere he go to church. 3.02.126
belly, ere i should come by a fire to thaw me. 4.01. 8 P
ere three days pass, which hath as long lov'd me 4.02. 38
and 'twill be supper-time ere you come there. 4.03.190
it shall be seven ere i go to horse. 4.03.191
alone, | i will not go to-day, and ere i do, 4.03.194
list, | or ere i journey to your father's house. 4.05. 8
ere they can hide their levity in honor. AWW 1.02. 35
a man may draw his heart out ere 'a pluck one. 1.03. 88 P
ere twice the horses of the sun shall bring 2.01.161
ere twice in murk and occidental damp | moist 2.01.163
possession of the bride, | /end ere i do begin. 2.05. 27
'twill be two days ere i shall see you, so | i 2.05. 70
you some sport with the fox ere we case him. 3.06.103 P
but that your daughter, ere she seems as won, 3.07. 31
ere i can perfect mine intents, to kneel. 4.04. 4
a thousand sallets ere we light on such another 4.05. 14 P
me, that i hope i shall see him ere i die. 4.05. 85 P
i have ere now, sir, been better known to you, 5.02. 2 P
foot of time | steals ere we can effect them. 5.03. 42
ere my heart | durst make too bold a herald of 5.03. 45
or, ere they meet, in me, o nature, cesse! 5.03. 72
have seen him damn'd ere i'd have challeng'd him TN 3.04.285 P
opinion of pythagoras ere i will allow of thy 4.02. 58 P
that went on crutches ere he was born desire yet WT 1.01. 40 P
's | with one soft kiss a thousand furlongs ere 1.02. 95
ere i could make thee open thy white hand | /and 1.02.103
been | (or i am much deceiv'd) cuckolds ere now, 1.02.191
come between | ere you can say she's honest: 2.01. 76
would have shed water out of fire ere done't; 3.02.193
pass | the same i am, ere ancient'st order was, 4.01. 10
if ever you have spent time worse ere now; 4.01. 30
ere they can behold | bright phoebus in his 4.04.123
why, how now, father? | speak ere thou diest. 4.04.451
for ere thou canst report, i will be there; JN 1.01. 25
and so, ere answer knows what question would, 1.01.200
but, ere sunset, | set armed discord 'twixt 3.01.110
to ashes, ere our blood shall quench that fire. 3.01.345
and ere our coming see thou shake the bags | of 3.03. 7
out | to all our sorrows, and ere long i doubt. 4.02.102
that, ere the next ascension-day at noon, | your 4.02.151
and grapple with him ere he come so nigh. 5.01. 61
and wish (so please my sovereign) ere i move, R2 1.01. 45
but ere i last receiv'd the sacrament | i did 1.01.139
ere my tongue | shall wound my honor with such 1.01.190
confess thy treasons ere thou fly the realm; 1.03.198
ere the six years that he hath to spend | can 1.03.219
ere further leisure yield them further means 1.04. 40
perhaps they had ere this, but that they stay 2.01.289
ere her native king | shall falter under foul 3.02. 25
but ere the crown he looks for live in peace, 3.03. 95
and ere thou bid good night, to quite their 5.01. 43
ere foul sin gathering head | shall break into 5.01. 58
and beg thy pardon ere he do accuse thee. 5.02.113
my mouth, | unless a pardon ere i rise or speak. 5.03. 32
it was, villain, ere thy hand did set it down. 5.03. 54
i'll starve ere i'll rob a foot further. 1H4 2.02. 21 P
ere i lead this life long, i'll sew 2.04.116 P
i'll see thee damn'd ere i call thee coward, but 2.04.146 P
ere break the smallest parcel of this vow. 3.02.159
have thirty miles to ride yet ere dinner-time. 3.03.198
he did, my lord, four days ere i set forth, 4.01. 22
whole | ere he by sickness had been visited, 4.01. 26
ere the king | dismiss his power he means to 4.04. 36
yet once ere night | i will embrace him with a 5.02. 72
i'll make it greater ere i part from thee, | and 5.04. 71
but priam found the fire ere he his tongue, 2H4 1.01. 74
and i my percy's death ere thou report'st it. 1.01. 75
saying that ere long they should call me madam? 2.01.101 P
wine, and it perfumes the blood ere one can say, 2.04. 28 P
sent away post, i will see you again ere i go. 2.04.378 P
but, ere they come, bid them o'er-read these 3.01. 2
and, ere they be dismiss'd, let them march by. 4.02. 96
ere you with grief had spoke and i had heard 4.05.141
i have been merry twice and once ere now. 5.03. 40 P
i hope to see london once ere i die. 5.03. 60 P
'twill be two a' clock ere they come from the 5.05. 3 P
i will lay odds that, ere this year expire, | we 5.05.105
their promises, | ere he take ship for france; H5 2.pr. 30
mess, ere theise eyes of mine take themselves to 3.02.114 P
first go yourself to hazard, ere you have them. 3.07. 87 P
and my poor soldiers tell me, yet ere night, 4.03.116
out of my mouth, ere it is made and finished. 4.07. 43 P
thy head, | for i intend to have it ere long. 1H6 1.03. 88
pray god she prove not masculine ere long, | if 2.01. 22
and death approach not ere my tale be done. 2.05. 62
and ere that we will suffer such a prince, | so 3.01. 97
or i would see his heart out ere the priest 3.01.120
his days may finish ere that hapless time. 3.01.200
i trust ere long to choke thee with thine own, 3.02. 46
and there will we be too, ere it be long, | or 3.02. 75
but ere we go, regard this dying prince, | the 3.02. 86
where i hope ere long | to be presented, by your 4.01.171
for ere the glass, that now begins to run, 4.02. 35
speak to thy father ere thou yield thy breath! 4.07. 24
tush, women have been captivate ere now. 5.03.107
her queen of england ere the thirtieth of may 2H6 1.01. 49 P
i prophesied france will be lost ere long. 1.01.146
ere thou go, | give up thy staff. 2.03. 22
resign | as ere thy father henry made it mine; 2.03. 34
but i will remedy this gear ere long, | or sell 3.01. 91
ere you can take due orders for a priest. 3.01.274
shall pay to me her maidenhead ere they have it. 4.07.122 P
my sword like a great pin, ere thou and i part. 4.10. 29 P
in chines of beef ere thou sleep in thy sheath, 4.10. 57 P
i know, ere they will have me go to ward, 5.01.112
set, | i would speak blasphemy ere bid you fly. 5.02. 85
let us pursue him ere the writs go forth. 5.03. 26
but 'twas ere i was born. 3H6 1.03. 39
frown hath made thee faint and fly ere this! 1.04. 48
but ere sunset i'll make thee curse the deed. 2.02.116
ere my knee rise from the earth's cold face, | i 2.03. 35
so many weeks ere the poor fools will ean, | so 2.05. 36
so many years ere i shall shear the fleece: 2.05. 37
may yet, ere night, yield both my life and them 2.05. 59
to take their rooms, ere i can place myself: 3.02.132
yet i confess that often ere this day, | when i 3.03.131
yet, ere thou go, but answer me one doubt: 3.03.238
but, ere i go, hastings and montague, | resolve 4.01.134
sun, | ere he attain his easeful western bed: 5.03. 6
must by the roots be hewn up yet ere night. 5.04. 69
ere ye come there, be sure to hear some news. 5.05. 48
ere you were queen, ay, or your husband king, R3 1.03.120
what you have been ere this, and what you are; 1.03.131
'twas full two years ere i could get a tooth. 2.04. 29
his nurse? why, she was dead ere thou wast born. 2.04. 33
would long ere this have met us on the way. 3.01. 21
shall we hear from you, catesby, ere we sleep? 3.01.188
well, catesby, ere a fortnight make me older, 3.02. 60
that he will lose his head ere give consent 3.04. 38
and die ere men can say, "god save the queen!" 4.01. 62
lo, ere i can repeat this curse again, | within 4.01. 77
ere from this war thou turn a conqueror, | or i 4.04.185
for that thou hast | misus'd ere us'd, by times 4.04.396
soul | ere i let fall the windows of mine eyes: 5.03.116
i died for hope ere i could lend thee aid, | but 5.03.173
i am sure the emperor | paid ere he promis'd, H8 1.01.186
his suit was granted | ere it was ask'd — but 1.01.187
the other moi'ty ere you ask is given; 1.02. 12
should find a running banket, ere they rested, 1.04. 12
ere a determinate resolution, he | (i mean the 2.04.177
was hector arm'd and gone ere ye came to ilium? TRO 1.02. 48 P
whose wit was mouldy ere /your grandsires had 2.01.105 P
you hang'd like clatpoles ere i come any more to 2.01.117 P
you must be watch'd ere you be made tame, must 3.02. 43 P
shall fight your hearts out ere i part you — 3.02. 52 P
kindred, though they be long ere they be woo'd, 3.02.110 P
howsoever, he shall pay for me ere he has me. 3.03.297 P
come, you'll do him wrong ere you are ware. 4.02. 55 P
ere the first sacrifice, within this hour, | we 4.02. 64
that give a coasting welcome ere it comes, | and 4.05. 59
shouldst have my office | ere that correction. 5.06. 5
this with our pikes, ere we become rakes; COR 1.01. 23 P
/unroof'd the city | ere so prevail'd with me; 1.01.219
with t' other, | ere stay behind this business. 1.01.243
that could be brought to bodily act ere rome 1.02. 5
which was | to take in many towns ere (almost) 1.02. 24
slaves, | ere yet the fight be done, pack up. 1.05. 8
where, ere we do repose us, we will write | to 1.09. 74
ere in our own house i do shade my head, | the 2.01.195
have you | ere now denied the asker; 2.03.206
dispos'd | ere they lack'd power to cross you. 3.02. 23
ere you go, hear this: 4.02. 38
in parts remote, | to fright them, ere destroy. 4.05.143
and to be executed ere they wipe their lips. 4.05.216 P
all places yields to him ere he sits down, | and 4.07. 28
i shall ere long have knowledge | of my success. 5.01. 61
ere he express himself or move the people | with 5.06. 54
and that you'll say ere half an hour pass. TIT 3.01.191
do me some service ere i come to thee. 5.02. 44
and yours, close fighting ere i did approach. ROM 1.01.107
ere he can spread his sweet leaves to the air 1.01.152
ere we may think her ripe to be a bride. 1.02. 11
five times in that ere once in our /five wits. 1.04. 47
but that thou overheardst, ere i was ware, | my 2.02.103
doth cease to be | ere one can say it lightens. 2.02.120
now, ere the sun advance his burning eye, | the 2.03. 5
i'll tell thee ere thou ask it me again. 2.03. 48
is something stale and hoar ere it be spent. 2.04.133 P
for a score, | when it hoars ere it be spent. 2.04.139
lest mine be about your ears ere it be out. 3.01. 82 P
for, ere i | could draw to part them, was stout 3.01.172
wife, go you to her ere you go to bed, 3.04. 15
go you to juliet ere you go to bed; 3.04. 31
be much in years | ere i again behold my romeo! 3.05. 47
ere he that should be husband comes to woo. 3.05.119
and ere this hand, by thee to romeo's seal'd, 4.01. 56
and there die strangled ere my romeo comes? 4.03. 35
i have watch'd ere now | all night for lesser 4.04. 9
some minute ere the time | of her awakening, 5.03.257
ere we depart, we'll share a bounteous time | in TIM 1.01.254
recanting goodness, sorry ere 'tis shown; 1.02. 17
you make me marvel wherefore ere this time | had 2.02.124
he did behoove his anger, ere 'twas spent, | as 3.05. 22
to let the meat cool ere we can agree upon the 3.06. 68 P
from the bone | ere thou relieve the beggar. 4.03.529
come hither, ere my tree hath felt the axe, 5.01.211
ere thou hadst power or we had cause of fear, 5.04. 15
but ere we could arrive the point propos'd, JC 1.02.110
come, casca, you and i will yet, ere day, | see 1.03.153
and ere day | we will awake him and be sure of 1.03.163
ere i can tell thee what thou shouldst do there. 2.04. 5
the end of this day's business ere it come! 5.01.123
yet ere night | we shall try fortune in a second 5.03.109
that will be ere the set of sun. MAC 1.01. 5
was it so late, friend, ere you went to bed, 2.03. 22
ere we will eat our meal in fear, and sleep | in 3.02. 17
ere the bat hath flown | his cloister'd flight, 3.02. 40
ere to black hecat's summons | the shard-borne 3.02. 41
blood hath been shed ere now, i' th' olden time, 3.04. 74
ere humane statute purg'd the gentle weal; 3.04. 75
which must be acted ere they may be scann'd. 3.04.139
great business must be wrought ere noon: 3.05. 22
profound, | i'll catch it ere it come to ground; 3.05. 25
and unfold | his message ere he come, that a 3.06. 47
rome, | a little ere the mightiest julius fell, HAM 1.01.114
or ere those shoes were old | with which she 1.02.147
ere yet the salt of most unrighteous tears | had 1.02.154
we'll teach you to drink /deep ere you depart. 1.02.175
or ere this | i should 'a' fatted all the region 2.02.578
make us again count o'er ere love be done! 3.02.162
speak with you in her closet ere you go to bed. 3.02.331 P
liege, | i'll call upon you ere you go to bed, 3.03. 34
force, | to be forestalled ere we come to fall, 3.03. 49
ere we were two days old at sea, a pirate of 4.06. 15 P
how long will a man lie i' th' earth ere he rot? 5.01.163 P
must be edified by the margent ere you had done. 5.02.156 P
a son for her cradle ere she had a husband for LR 1.01. 15 P
ere i was risen from the place that showed | my 2.04. 29
a hundred thousand flaws | or ere i'll weep. 2.04.286
i'll speak a prophecy ere i go: 3.02. 80 P
i will have my revenge ere i depart his house. 3.05. 1 P
ere long you are like to hear | (if you dare 4.02. 19
hairs in my beard ere the black ones were there. 4.06. 98 P
flesh and fell, | ere they shall make us weep! 5.03. 25
have been demanded | ere you had spoke so far. 5.03. 63
ere i taste bread, thou art in nothing less 5.03. 94
ere i would say i would drown myself for the OTH 1.03.314 P
your hollander a vomit ere the next pottle can 2.03. 84 P
ere it be demanded | (as like enough it will) i 3.04.189
i kiss'd thee ere i kill'd thee. 5.02.358
sir, | he fell upon me, ere admitted, then; ANT 2.02. 75
yet, ere we put ourselves in arms, dispatch we 2.02.165
ere the ninth hour, i drunk him to his bed; 2.05. 21
i have a mind to strike thee ere thou speak'st; 2.05. 42
we'll feast each other ere we part, and let's 2.06. 60
tell of her approach, | long ere she did appear; 3.06. 46
you were half blasted ere i knew you; 3.13.105
house of death | ere death dare come to us? 4.15. 82
as a crow, or less, ere left | to after-eye him. CYM 1.03. 15
ere i could tell him | how i would think on him 1.03. 26
or ere i could | give him that parting kiss 1.03. 33
did softly press the rushes ere he waken'd | the 2.02. 13
be many caesars, | ere such another julius. 3.01. 12
fear, ere wildness | vanquish my staider senses. 3.04. 9
ere clean it o'erthrow nature, makes it valiant. 3.06. 20
you shall have better cheer | ere you depart, 3.06. 67
citizen a wanton as | to seem to die ere sick. 4.02. 9
while nature will | than die ere i hear more. 5.05.152
ere i arise, i will prefer my sons; 5.05.326
ere the stroke | of yet this scarce-cold battle, 5.05.468
a war did cease | (ere bloody hands were wash'd) 5.05.485
our men be vanquish'd ere they do resist, | and PER 1.02. 27
how i might stop this tempest ere it came, | and 1.02. 98
yet, ere you shall depart, this we desire, | as 1.03. 38
that all those eyes ador'd them ere their fall 2.04. 11
your master will be dead ere you return, 3.02. 7
come | give me your flowers, ere the sea mar it. 4.01. 26
weep ere you fail; TNK 1.01. 95
shall be returning | ere you can end this feast, 1.01.224
garlands, | ere they have time to wish 'em ours. 2.02. 17
he'll eat a horn-book ere he fail. 2.03. 42
lest this match between 's | be cross'd ere met. 3.01. 98
maypole, and again, | ere another year run out, 3.05.146
for, ere the sun set, both shall sleep for ever. 3.06.184
ere i departed, a great likelihood | of both 4.01. 6
ever affected any man ere she beheld palamon? 4.03. 63 P
and ye shall have ere long, | i dare say, many a ep 15
his meaning struck her ere his words begun. VEN 462
and, ere he says "adieu," | the honey fee of 537
been gone," quoth she, "sweet boy, ere this, 613
lust's winter comes ere summer half be done; 802
an expir'd date, cancell'd ere well begun: LUC 26
the merchant fears, ere rich at home he lands." 336
thus treason works ere traitors be espied. 361
that twice she doth begin ere once she speaks. 567
receipt | ere he can see his own abomination. 704
climb | his wonted height, yet ere he go to bed, 776
fair, | ere he arrive his weary noontide prick, 781
of mine | as i ere this was pure to collatine. 826
"madam, ere i was up," replied the maid, | "the 1277
myself was stirring ere the break of day, | and 1280
of day, | and ere i rose was tarquin gone away. 1281
ere she with blood had stain'd her stain'd 1316
ere once she can discharge one word of woe; 1605
"but ere i name him, you fair lords," quoth she 1688
in thee thy summer ere thou be distill'd: SON 6. 2
with beauty's treasure ere it be self-kill'd. 6. 4
ere beauty's dead fleece made another gay: 68. 8
love that well, which thou must leave ere long. 73.14
ere you were born was beauty's summer dead. 104.14

to be diseas'd ere that there was true needing. 118. 8
tale, | ere long espied a fickle maid full pale, LC 5
consents bewitch'd, ere he desire, have granted, 131
/EREBUS 1 FR 0.0001 REL FR 1 V 0 P
as night, | and his affections dark as /erebus: MV 5.01. 87
EREBUS 2 FR 0.0002 REL FR 1 V 1 P
deep, with erebus and tortures vile also. 2H4 2.04.157 P
not erebus itself were dim enough | to hide thee JC 2.01. 84
ERECT 4 FR 0.0004 REL FR 3 V 1 P
if a man do not erect in this age his own tomb ADO 5.02. 78 P
within their chiefest temple i'll erect | a tomb 1H6 2.02. 12
erect his statue and worship it, | and make my 2H6 3.02. 80
him troilus, and on him erect | a second hope, TRO 4.05.108
ERECTED 2 FR 0.0002 REL FR 1 V 1 P
by mistaking the place where i erected it. WIV 2.02.217 P
ours | were not erected by their hands from whom
TIM 5.04. 23
ERECTING 1 FR 0.0001 REL FR 0 V 1 P
youth of the realm in erecting a grammar school; 2H6 4.07. 33 P
/ERECTION 1 FR 0.0001 REL FR 1 V 0 P
/must /we /rate /the /cost /of /the /erection, 2H4 1.03. 44
ERECTION 2 FR 0.0002 REL FR 1 V 1 P
they mistook their erection. WIV 3.05. 40 P
defeat and quell | the source of all erection. TIM 4.03.164
ERECTS 1 FR 0.0001 REL FR 1 V 0 P
and there erects | thy noble deeds as valor's 1H6 3.02.119
ERE'T 5 FR 0.0005 REL FR 4 V 1 P
they will then ere't be long. MM 4.02. 76
ere't be disburdened with a liberal tongue. R2 2.01.229
and therefore i'll uncrown him ere't be long. 3H6 3.03.232
and therefore i'll uncrown him ere't be long." 4.01.111
o, joy's e'en made away ere't can be born! TIM 1.02.106 P
EREWHILE *(also yerwhile)*
EREWHILE 3 FR 0.0003 REL FR 3 V 0 P
else your memory is bad, going o'er it erewhile. LLL 4.01. 97
i am as fair now as i was erewhile. MND 3.02.274
that young swain that you saw here but erewhile, AYL 2.04. 89
ERGA 1 FR 0.0001 REL FR 0 V 1 P
tanta est erga te mentis integritas, regina H8 3.01. 40 P
ERGO *(also argal, argo)*
ERGO 7 FR 0.0008 REL FR 1 V 6 P
ergo, light wenches will burn. ERR 4.03. 56 P
in minority, | ergo i come with this apology." LLL 5.02.593
but i pray you, ergo, old man, ergo, i beseech MV 2.02. 57 P
ergo, old man, ergo, i beseech you, talk you of 2.02. 57 P
ergo, master launcelot. 2.02. 60 P
ergo, thou liest. SHR 4.03.127 P
ergo, he that kisses my wife is my friend. AWW 1.03. 49 P
ERINGOES 1 FR 0.0001 REL FR 0 V 1 P
hail kissing-comfits, and snow eringoes; WIV 5.05. 20 P
ERMENGARE 1 FR 0.0001 REL FR 1 V 0 P
grandmother, | was lineal of the lady ermengare, H5 1.02. 82
ERMITES *(also hermits)*
ERMITES 1 FR 0.0001 REL FR 1 V 0 P
heap'd up to them, | we rest your ermites. MAC 1.06. 20
ERN *(also earns*, yearn, etc.)*
ERN 2 FR 0.0002 REL FR 2 V 0 P
for my manly heart doth ern. H5 2.03. 3
he is dead, | and we must ern therefore. 2.03. 6
ERN'D 1 FR 0.0001 REL FR 1 V 0 P
how it ern'd my heart when i beheld | in london R2 5.05. 76
EROS 27 FR 0.0030 REL FR 26 V 1 P
how now, friend eros? ANT 3.05. 1 P
eros, mine armor, eros! 4.04. 1
eros, mine armor, eros! 4.04. 1
eros, come, mine armor, eros! 4.04. 2
eros, come, mine armor, eros! 4.04. 2
thou fumblest, eros, and my queen's a squire 4.04. 14
go, eros, send his treasure after; 4.05. 12
what, eros, eros! 4.12. 30
what, eros, eros! 4.12. 30
eros, ho! 4.12. 42
eros, ho! 4.12. 49
eros, thou yet behold'st me? 4.14. 1
my good knave eros, now thy captain is | even 4.14. 12
she, eros, has | pack'd cards with caesar's, and 4.14. 18
nay, weep not, gentle eros, there is left us 4.14. 21
unarm, eros, the long day's task is done, | and 4.14. 35
apace, eros, apace. 4.14. 41
eros! 4.14. 50
eros! 4.14. 50
come, eros, eros! 4.14. 54
come, eros, eros! 4.14. 54
thou art sworn, eros, | that when the exigent 4.14. 62
eros, | wouldst thou be window'd in great rome, 4.14. 71
now, eros. 4.14. 93
thou teachest me, o valiant eros, what | i 4.14. 96
my queen and eros | have by their brave 4.14. 97
and, eros, | thy master dies thy scholar: 4.14.101
ERPINGHAM 3 FR 0.0003 REL FR 2 V 1 P
sir thomas erpingham, sir john ramston, | sir R2 2.01.283
good morrow, old sir thomas erpingham. H5 4.01. 13
under sir /thomas erpingham. 4.01. 94 P
ERR 16 FR 0.0018 REL FR 16 V 0 P
but, fearing lest my jealous aim might err, TGV 3.01. 28
because authority, though it err like others, MM 2.02.134
all these old witnesses — i cannot err — ERR 5.01.318
else, does err. AWW 2.03.183
i of you shall borrow, | err in bestowing it. 3.07. 12
for worthy wolsey | (who cannot err), he did it. H8 1.01.174
what error leads must err; TRO 5.02.111
host, and make discovery | err in report of us. MAC 5.04. 7
sense | is apoplex'd, for madness would not err, HAM 3.04. 73
for nature so prepost'rously to err | (being not OTH 1.03. 62
that will confess perfection so could err 1.03.100
of a sir so rare, | which you know cannot err. CYM 1.06.176
these her women | can trip me, if i err, who 5.05. 35
fits kings as they are men, for they may err. PER 1.02. 43
view us their mortal herd, behold who err, | and TNK 1.04. 5
to say they err i dare not be so bold, SON 131. 7
ERRAND *(also arrand, arrant*, errant*)*
ERRAND 11 FR 0.0012 REL FR 8 V 3 P
he came of an errand to me from parson hugh. WIV 1.04. 76 P
i must of another errand to sir john falstaff 3.04.109 P
him, he were as good go a mile on his errand. MM 3.02. 37 P
my errand is to you, fair youth, | my gentle AYL 4.03. 6
but hast thou done thy errand to baptista? SHR 4.04. 14
no lady living | so meet for this great errand. WT 2.02. 44
accord i'll off, | but first i'll do my errand. 2.03. 65
upon which errand | i now go toward him; 5.01.231
to thee, king john, my holy errand is: JN 3.01.137
i know thy errand, i will go with thee. H5 4.01.308
to know my errand, madam. JC 2.04. 3
ERRANDS 2 FR 0.0002 REL FR 1 V 1 P
she comes of errands, does she? WIV 4.02.174 P
unmeritable man, | meet to be sent on errands; JC 4.01. 13
ERRANT* *(also arrand, arrant*, errand)*
ERRANT* 3 FR 0.0003 REL FR 3 V 0 P
tortive and errant from his course of growth. TRO 1.03. 9
let me come in, and you shall know my errant. ROM 3.03. 79
each errant step beside is torment. TNK 3.02. 34
ERR'D 3 FR 0.0003 REL FR 3 V 0 P
err'd in this point which now you censure him, MM 2.01. 15
nor forward of revenge, though they much err'd. 3H6 4.08. 46
and doubting lest he had err'd or sinn'd, | to PER 1.03. 21
ERRED 1 FR 0.0001 REL FR 1 V 0 P
things right true my heart and eyes have erred, SON 137.13
ERREST 1 FR 0.0001 REL FR 0 V 1 P
madman, thou errest. TN 4.02. 42 P
ERRING 5 FR 0.0005 REL FR 4 V 1 P
if i can check my erring love, i will; TGV 2.04.213
the life of man | runs his erring pilgrimage, AYL 3.02.130
th' extravagant and erring spirit hies | to his HAM 1.01.154
a frail vow betwixt an erring barbarian and /a OTH 1.03.355 P
and yet how nature erring from itself — 3.03.227
ERRONEOUS 2 FR 0.0002 REL FR 2 V 0 P
erroneous, mutinous, and unnatural, | this 3H6 2.05. 90
erroneous vassals, the great king of kings R3 1.04.195
/ERROR 1 FR 0.0001 REL FR 0 V 1 P
body, she will find the /error of her choice. OTH 1.03.351 P
ERROR 34 FR 0.0038 REL FR 29 V 5 P
that one error | fills him with faults; TGV 5.04.111
but thou art full of error — i am sound. MM 1.02. 54 P
what error drives our eyes and ears amiss? ERR 2.02.184
that by this sympathized one day's error | have 5.01.398
not guiltless here | under some biting error. ADO 4.01.170
her | upon the error that you heard debated. 5.04. 3
pardon, sir, error: LLL 5.01.130 P
we are again forsworn, in will and error. 5.02.471
the error that love makes | is likewise yours. 5.02.771
to take from thence all error with his might, MND 3.02.368
this is the greatest error of all the rest. 5.01.246 P
what damned error but some sober brow | will MV 3.02. 78
and many an error by the same example | will 4.01.221
error i' th' bill, sir, error i' th' bill! SHR 4.03.145 P
error i' th' bill, sir, error i' th' bill! 4.03.145 P
religious in mine error, i adore | the sun, that AWW 1.03.205
that this may be some error, but no madness, TN 4.03. 10
of good and bad, that makes and unfolds error, WT 4.01. 2
smoke, | to make a faithless error in your ears; JN 2.01.230
or else was wrangling somerset in th' error? 1H6 2.04. 6
and yet thy tongue will not confess thy error. 2.04. 67
i find, | the error of our eye directs our mind. TRO 5.02.110
what error leads must err; 5.02.111
and mountainous error be too highly heap'd | for COR 2.03.120
o hateful error, melancholy's child, | why dost JC 5.03. 67
o error, soon conceiv'd, | thou never com'st 5.03. 69
i do not so secure me in the error | but the OTH 1.03. 10
it is the very error of the moon, | she comes 5.02.109
my boys, | there was our error. CYM 5.05.260
tells us life's but breath, to trust it error. PER 1.01. 46
and 'twere no error if i told you all you were STM II.C 95
what country by the nature of your error II.C 126
and childish error that they are afraid; VEN 898
if this be error and upon me proved, | i never SON 116.13
ERRORS 13 FR 0.0014 REL FR 13 V 0 P
smoth'red in errors, feeble, shallow, weak, ERR 3.02. 35
for me, | and thereupon these errors are arose. 5.01.389
to burn the errors that these princes hold ADO 4.01.163
my love with words and errors still she feeds, TRO 5.03.111
more mischance | on plots and errors happen. HAM 5.02.395
make us | adore our errors, laugh at 's while we ANT 3.13.114
yet these that we count errors may become him: TNK 4.02. 31
of foes, | to eat up errors by opinion bred, LUC 937
so are those errors that in thee are seen | to SON 96. 7
book both my willfulness and errors down, | and 117. 9
what wretched errors hath my heart committed, 119. 5
eyes, | for they in thee a thousand errors note, 141. 2
that abroad you see | are errors of the blood, LC 184
ERRS 3 FR 0.0003 REL FR 3 V 0 P
and as he errs, doting on hermia's eyes, | so i, MND 1.01.230
that errs in ignorance and not in cunning, | i OTH 3.03. 49
is't frailty that thus errs? 4.03. 99
ERST 7 FR 0.0008 REL FR 7 V 0 P
thy company, which erst was irksome to me, | i AYL 3.05. 95
that erst brought sweetly forth | the freckled H5 5.02. 48
that erst did follow thy proud chariot-wheels 2H6 2.04. 13
or slunk not saturnine, as tarquin erst, | that TIT 4.01. 63
speak, rome's dear friend, as erst our ancestor, 5.03. 80
gripe not at earthly joys as erst they did; PER 1.01. 49
which erst from heat did canopy the herd, | and SON 12. 6
ERUDITION 1 FR 0.0001 REL FR 1 V 0 P
thrice fam'd beyond, /beyond all erudition; TRO 2.03.243
ERUPTION 1 FR 0.0001 REL FR 1 V 0 P
this bodes some strange eruption to our state. HAM 1.01. 69
ERUPTIONS 3 FR 0.0003 REL FR 2 V 1 P
are good at such eruptions and sudden breaking LLL 5.01.114 P
oftentimes breaks forth | in strange eruptions; 1H4 3.01. 27
and fearful, as these strange eruptions are. JC 1.03. 78
ERYNGO *(see eringoes)*
ESCALUS 8 FR 0.0009 REL FR 8 V 0 P
escalus! MM 1.01. 1
old escalus, | though first in question, is thy 1.01. 45
'tis one thing to be tempted, escalus, | another 2.01. 17
he hath carried | notice to escalus and angelo, 4.03.130
come, escalus, | you must walk by us on our 5.01. 16
you, lord escalus, | sit with my cousin; 5.01.245
thanks, good friend escalus, for thy much 5.01.528
antonio, the duke's eldest son, | that, escalus. AWW 3.05. 77
ESCANES 2 FR 0.0002 REL FR 2 V 0 P
no, escanes, know this of me, | antiochus from PER 2.04. 1
old escanes, whom helicanus late | advanc'd in 4.04. 15
ESCAP'D 8 FR 0.0009 REL FR 6 V 2 P
i escap'd upon a butt of sack which the sailors TMP 2.02.121 P
with some of the sailors that escap'd the wrack. MV 3.01.104 P
myself, well mounted, hardly have escap'd. JN 5.06. 42
that hardly we escap'd the pride of france. 1H6 3.02. 40
i wonder how the king escap'd our hands. 3H6 1.01. 1
the happy hollow of a tree | escap'd the hunt. LR 2.03. 3
we'll spill the blood | that has to-day escap'd. ANT 4.08. 4
discover'd how | and by whose means he escap'd, TNK 4.01. 20
ESCAP'DST 1 FR 0.0001 REL FR 0 V 1 P
here; swear then how thou escap'dst. TMP 2.02.127 P
ESCAPE *(also scape, etc.)*
ESCAPE 21 FR 0.0023 REL FR 17 V 4 P
for our escape | is much beyond our loss. TMP 2.01. 2
a hat, a muffler, and a kerchief, and so escape. WIV 4.02. 72 P
give him leave to escape hence, he would not. MM 4.02.148 P
anon, i wot not by what strong escape, | he ERR 5.01.148
on, | and i for my escape have put on his; SHR 1.01.230
favor and for a week escape a great deal of AWW 3.06. 92 P
mine own escape unfoldeth to my hope, | whereto
TN 1.02. 19
ay, and privy | to this their late escape. WT 2.01. 95
of this escape and whither they are bound; 4.04.663
and i'll direct thee how thou shalt escape | by 1H6 4.05. 10
heard | the happy tidings of his good escape. 3H6 2.01. 7
no, 'tis impossible he should escape; 2.06. 38
unsavory news! but how made he escape? 4.06. 80
rome will despise her for this foul escape. TIT 4.02.113
as pure as snow, thou shalt not escape calumny. HAM 3.01.136 P
if he by chance escape your venom'd stuck, | our 4.07.161
the bloody proclamation to escape, | that LR 5.03.184
child, | for thy escape would teach me tyranny, OTH 1.03.197
thus i do escape the sorrow | of antony's death. ANT 4.14. 94
my father's to be hang'd for his escape; TNK 3.02. 22
said of me | concerning the escape of palamon? 4.01. 2
ESCAPED 1 FR 0.0001 REL FR 1 V 0 P
that edward is escaped from your brother, | and 3H6 4.06. 78
ESCAPEND 1 FR 0.0001 REL FR 1 V 0 P
man, of pelf, | ne aught escapend but himself; PER 2.ch. 36
ESCAPES 4 FR 0.0004 REL FR 2 V 2 P
thousand escapes of wit | make thee the father MM 4.01. 62
and he that escapes me without some broken limb
AYL 1.01.127 P
and in him that escapes, it were not sin to H5 4.01.182 P
even he escapes not | language unmannerly; H8 1.02. 26
ESCHEATOR *(see cheater)*
ESCHEW'D *(also 'schew)*
ESCHEW'D 1 FR 0.0001 REL FR 1 V 0 P
what cannot be eschew'd must be embrac'd. WIV 5.05.237
/ESCOTED 1 FR 0.0001 REL FR 0 V 1 P
/how /are /they /escoted? HAM 2.02.346 P
ESCRIMERS *(see scrimers)*
ESPECIAL 4 FR 0.0004 REL FR 3 V 1 P
"i have, upon especial cause, | mov'd with 1H6 4.01. 55
hamlet, this deed, for thine especial safety — HAM 4.03. 40
defense, | and for your rapier most especial, 4.07. 98
there is especial commission come from venice to OTH 4.02.220 P
ESPECIALLY 18 FR 0.0020 REL FR 3 V 15 P
gentleman, | especially against his very friend. TGV 3.02. 41
strifes, contended especially to know himself. MM 3.02.233 P
for the walk, and especially when i walk away. ADO 2.01. 89 P
it had, my lord, especially against benedick. 2.03.117 P
of the world, and especially of my own people, AYL 1.01.169 P
i especially think, under mars. AWW 1.01.193 P
especially he hath incurr'd the everlasting 4.03. 8 P
especially for those occasions | at eltam place 1H6 3.01.154
live, | especially since charles must father it. 5.04. 71
especially to you, fair queen, fair thoughts be TRO 3.01. 45 P
would you proceed especially against caius COR 1.01. 26 P
especially in pride. 2.01. 19 P
hope the ladies of rome, especially his mother, 5.04. 6 P
especially upon bare friendship without security TIM 3.01. 42 P
what three things does drink especially provoke? MAC 2.03. 26 P
thereabout of it especially when he speaks of HAM 2.02.447 P
be without you, especially that of cleopatra's, ANT 1.02.174 P
of the people, especially of the younger sort? PER 4.02. 97 P
ESPERANCE 4 FR 0.0004 REL FR 4 V 0 P
o esperance! 1H4 2.03. 71
now esperance! 5.02. 96
my heart, | an esperance so obstinately strong, TRO 5.02.121
stands still in esperance, lives not in fear. LR 4.01. 4
ESPIALS 2 FR 0.0002 REL FR 2 V 0 P
the prince's espials have informed me | how the 1H6 1.04. 8
by your espials were discovered | two mightier 4.03. 6
ESPIED 4 FR 0.0004 REL FR 4 V 0 P
now question me no more, we are espied. TIT 2.03. 48
pit | where i espied the panther fast asleep. 2.03.194
thus treason works ere traitors be espied. LUC 361
tale, | ere long espied a fickle maid full pale, LC 5
ESPIES 3 FR 0.0003 REL FR 2 V 1 P
but do it when the next thing he espies | may be MND 2.01.262
too curious dreg espies my sweet lady in the TRO 3.02. 65 P
from whence | lysimachus our tyrian ship espies, PER 5.ch. 18
ESPOUSAL *(see spousal)*
ESPOUS'D 3 FR 0.0003 REL FR 3 V 0 P
and so espous'd to death, with blood he seal'd H5 4.06. 26
i have perform'd my task, and was espous'd; 2H6 1.01. 9
place | i lead espous'd my bride along with me. TIT 1.01.328
ESPOUSE 4 FR 0.0004 REL FR 3 V 1 P
doll tearsheet she by name, and her espouse. H5 2.01. 77
the said henry shall espouse the lady margaret, 2H6 1.01. 46 P
he should espouse elizabeth her daughter. R3 4.05. 8
and in the sacred /pantheon her espouse. TIT 1.01.242
ESPOUSED 1 FR 0.0001 REL FR 1 V 0 P
that kings might be espoused to more fame, | but LUC 20
ESPY 4 FR 0.0004 REL FR 4 V 0 P
when his love he doth espy, | let her shine as MND 3.02.105
he doth espy | himself love's traitor. JN 2.01.506
securely i espy | virtue with valor couched in R2 1.03. 97
proud, | adonis' trampling courser doth espy; VEN 261
ESQUIRE 7 FR 0.0008 REL FR 3 V 4 P
he shall not abuse robert shallow, esquire. WIV 1.01. 4 P
robert shallow, esquire, saith he is wrong'd. 1.01.107 P
sir, a poor esquire of this county, and one of 2H4 3.02. 57 P
will i visit master robert shallow, esquire. 4.03.129 P
suffolk, | sir richard ketly, davy gam, esquire; H5 4.08.104
that alexander iden, an esquire of kent, | took 2H6 4.10. 43
a poor esquire of kent, that loves his king. 5.01. 75
ESQUIRES 2 FR 0.0002 REL FR 2 V 0 P
six thousand and two hundred good esquires; H5 1.01. 14
of knights, esquires, and gallant gentlemen, 4.08. 84
ESSAY 1 FR 0.0001 REL FR 0 V 1 P

wrote this but as an essay or taste of my virtue LR 1.02. 45 P
ESSAYS 1 FR 0.0001 REL FR 1 V 0 P
and worse essays prov'd thee my best of love. SON 110. 8
ESSENCE 4 FR 0.0004 REL FR 4 V 0 P
she is my essence, and i leave to be, | if i be TGV 3.01.182
of what he's most assur'd | (his glassy essence) MM 2.02.120
her honor is an essence that's not seen; OTH 4.01. 16
as love in twain | had the essence but in one, PHT 26
ESSENTIAL 1 FR 0.0001 REL FR 1 V 0 P
and in th' essential vesture of creation | does OTH 2.01. 64
ESSENTIALLY 3 FR 0.0003 REL FR 2 V 1 P
thou art essentially made, without seeming so. 1H4 2.04.492 P
hath not essentially but by circumstance | the 2H6 5.02. 39
out, | that i essentially am not in madness, HAM 3.04.187
ESSEX 1 FR 0.0001 REL FR 1 V 0 P
'tis not thy southern power | of essex, norfolk, 3H6 1.01.156
EST 17 FR 0.0019 REL FR 4 V 13 P
hic est /sigeia tellus; SHR 3.01. 28
i am lucentio, "hic est," son unto vincentio of 3.01. 32 P
i know you not, "hic est /sigeia tellus," i 3.01. 42 P
'tis "semper idem," for "obsque hoc nihil est." 2H4 5.05. 28 P
la main? elle est appelee de hand. H5 3.04. 7 P
c'est bien dit, madame, il est fort bon anglois. 3.04. 19 P
il est trop difficile, madame, comme je pense. 3.04. 27 P
"le chien est retourne a son propre vomissement, 3.07. 64 P
car ce soldat ici est dispose tout /a /cette 4.04. 35 P
encore qu'il est contre son jurement de 4.04. 50 P
il est content a vous donner la liberte, le 4.04. 52 P
o seigneur! le jour est perdu, tout est perdu! 4.05. 2
o seigneur! le jour est perdu, tout est perdu! 4.05. 2
donc votre est france et vous etes mienne. 5.02.183 P
il est /meilleur que l'anglois lequel je parle. 5.02.189 P
tanta est erga te mentis integritas, regina H8 3.01. 40 P
my lords, "ira furor brevis est," | but yond man TIM 1.02. 28
ESTABLISH *(also stablish, etc.)*
ESTABLISH 5 FR 0.0005 REL FR 5 V 0 P
establish him in his true sense again, | and i ERR 4.04. 48
of it, | but to establish here a peace indeed, 2H4 4.01. 86
consent, | and what we do establish he confirms. 2H6 3.01.317
to–morrow | mean to establish caesar as a king; JC 1.03. 86
know | we will establish our estate upon | our MAC 1.04. 37
ESTABLISH'D 3 FR 0.0003 REL FR 2 V 1 P
of their life, | establish'd then this law: H5 1.02. 50
any wholesome act establish'd against the rich, COR 1.01. 83 P
we were establish'd | the people's magistrates. 3.01.200
ESTABLISHED 4 FR 0.0004 REL FR 3 V 1 P
contrary to thy established proclaimed edict and LLL 1.01.259 P
in venice | can alter a decree established. MV 4.01.219
and peace established between these realms. 1H6 5.03. 92
rais'd in blood, and one in blood established; R3 5.03.247
/ESTATE 2 FR 0.0002 REL FR 2 V 0 P
/question /surveyors, /know /our /own /estate, 2H4 1.03. 53
/who, /having /seen /me /in /my /worst /estate, LR 5.03.210
ESTATE 50 FR 0.0056 REL FR 36 V 14 P
and some donation freely to estate | on the TMP 4.01. 85
my right of her | i do estate unto demetrius. MND 1.01. 98
nor is my whole estate | upon the fortune of MV 1.01. 43
antonio, | how much i have disabled mine estate, 1.01.123
his letter there | will show you his estate. 3.02.236
my creditors grow cruel, my estate is very low, 3.02.316 P
i will forget the condition of my estate, to AYL 1.02. 15 P
was old sir rowland's will i estate upon you, 5.02. 11 P
fie, doff this habit, shame to your estate, | an SHR 3.02.100
never ransom nature | from her inaidible estate; AWW 2.01.119
if not to thy estate, | a balance more replete. 2.03.175
though my estate be fall'n, i was well born, 3.07. 4
mine own occasion mellow | what my estate is! TN 1.02. 44
not match above her degree, neither in estate, 1.03.110 P
of great estate, of fresh and stainless youth; 1.05.259
but when i came to man's estate, | with hey ho, 5.01.393
neighbors, is grown into an unspeakable estate. WT 4.02. 40 P
dispute his own estate? 4.04.400
luck, being in so preposterous estate as we are. 5.02.148 P
how wildly then walks my estate in france! JN 4.02.128
showing as in a model our firm estate, | when R2 3.04. 42
i pray you, what thinks he of our estate? H5 4.01. 96 P
it pleas'd | to shine on my contemptible estate. 1H6 1.02. 75
what low'ring star now envies thy estate, | that 2H6 3.01.206
that your estate requires and mine can yield. 3H6 3.03.150
if warwick knew in what estate he stands, | 'tis 4.03. 18
by how much the estate is green and yet R3 2.02.127
breach of duty this way | is business of estate; H8 2.02. 69
pray'rs remember | th' estate of my poor queen. 5.01. 74
it gives me an estate of seven years' health, in COR 2.01.114 P
let me dispute with thee of thy estate. ROM 3.03. 63
and my estate deserves an heir more rais'd TIM 1.01.119
prompted you in the ebb of your estate | and 2.02.141
whose death he's stepp'd | into a great estate. 2.02.224
done and past, and his estate shrinks from him. 3.02. 7 P
supported his estate, nay, timon's money | has 3.02. 69
suspect still comes where an estate is least. 4.03.514
then do we sin against our own estate, | when we 5.01. 41
we will establish our estate upon | our eldest, MAC 1.04. 37
and wish th' estate o' th' world were now undone 5.05. 49
'a poisons him i' th' garden for his estate. HAM 3.02.261 P
the terms of our estate may not endure | hazard 3.03. 5
'twas of some estate. 5.01.221
pawn the moi'ty of my estate to your ring, which CYM 1.04.109 P
would i had put my estate and my neighbor's on 1.04.123 P
so think of your estate. 5.05. 74
our youths we could pick up some pretty estate, PER 4.02. 33 P
advanc'd in time to great and high estate. 4.04. 16
and i will estate your daughter in what i have TNK 2.01. 11 P
for that he color'd with his high estate, LUC 92
ESTATES 8 FR 0.0009 REL FR 7 V 1 P
which you on all estates will execute | that lie LLL 5.02.845
o, that estates, degrees, and offices | were not MV 2.09. 41
put such difference betwixt their two estates; AWW 1.03.112 P
kindred | and egally indeed to all estates — R3 3.07.213
that have | by this so sicken'd their estates, H8 1.01. 82
all these | owes their estates unto him. TIM 3.03. 5
and, should we shift estates, yours would be ANT 5.02.152
fit you | with dignities becoming your estates. CYM 5.05. 22
ESTEEM 28 FR 0.0031 REL FR 25 V 3 P
with other gentlemen of good esteem | are TGV 1.03. 40
yourself, held precious in the world's esteem, LLL 2.01. 4
and are you grown so high in his esteem, MND 3.02.294
sort, | as this their jangling i esteem a sport. 3.02.353
do i labor for a greater esteem than may in some AYL 5.02. 56 P
fleet, | i would esteem him worth a dozen such. SHR in.1. 27
of such possessions, and so high esteem, in.2. 15
she is of good esteem, | her dowry wealthy, and 4.05. 64
to esteem | a senseless help when help past AWW 2.01.123
and our esteem | was made much poorer by it; 5.03. 1
serv'd you, and beseech' | so to esteem of us; WT 2.03.149
steps | esteem as foil wherein thou art to set R2 1.03.266
beside five hundred prisoners of esteem, | lets 1H6 3.04. 8
esteem none friends but such as are his friends, 4.01. 5
is betroth'd | unto another lady of esteem. 5.05. 27
than from true evidence of good esteem | he be 2H6 3.02. 21
nor should thy prowess want praise and esteem, 5.02. 22
a man in much esteem with th' king, and truly H8 4.01.109
esteems her no more than i esteem an addle egg. TRO 1.02.132 P
and esteem no act | but that of hand. 1.03.199
what things again most dear in the esteem, | and 3.03.129
than you, | here in verona, ladies of esteem, ROM 1.03. 70
life, | and live a coward in thine own esteem, MAC 1.07. 43
and the poor state | esteem him as a lamb, being 4.03. 54
what do you esteem it at? CYM 1.04. 78 P
creatures vild, as cats and dogs | of no esteem. 5.05.253
sing to the ear that doth thy lays esteem, | and SON 100. 7
lack, | sland'ring creation with a false esteem: 127.12
ESTEEM'D 12 FR 0.0013 REL FR 9 V 3 P
how is the man esteem'd here in the city? ERR 5.01. 4
a man of sovereign /parts, /peerless esteem'd, LLL 2.01. 44
feast to–night | my best esteem'd acquaintance. MV 2.02.172
are not with me esteem'd above thy life. 4.01.285
the world esteem'd thy father honorable, | but i AYL 1.02.225
rather than i would be so pill'd esteem'd: 1H6 1.04. 33
my dear lord and most esteem'd friend, your TRO 3.01. 64 P
notwithstanding, thou shalt be no less esteem'd. TIM 2.02.106 P
so this side of our known world esteem'd him) HAM 1.01. 85
a great cause, they should be esteem'd nothing. ANT 1.02.140 P
her own price | proclaims how she esteem'd him; CYM 1.01. 52
queen | the basest jewel will be well esteem'd, SON 96. 6
ESTEEMED 4 FR 0.0004 REL FR 3 V 1 P
but, most esteemed greatness, will you hear the LLL 5.02.885 P
who for this seven years hath esteemed him | no SHR in.1. 122
he with the romans was esteemed so | as seely LUC 1811
'tis better to be vile than vile esteemed, SON 121. 1
ESTEEMETH 1 FR 0.0001 REL FR 1 V 0 P
by one whom she esteemeth as his friend. TGV 3.02. 37
ESTEEMING 1 FR 0.0001 REL FR 1 V 0 P
that love is merchandiz'd whose rich esteeming SON 102. 3
ESTEEMS 6 FR 0.0006 REL FR 4 V 2 P
for me and my possessions she esteems not. TGV 3.01. 79
and coy, | and nought esteems my aged eloquence. 3.01. 83
and he esteems himself happy that he hath fall'n H5 4.04. 60 P
he esteems her no more than i esteem an addle TRO 1.02.131 P
i hope my noble lord esteems me honest. OTH 4.02. 65
"alas, he nought esteems that face of thine, VEN 631
ESTEEM'ST 2 FR 0.0002 REL FR 1 V 1 P
how esteem'st thou me? i account of her beauty. TGV 2.01. 61 P
which thou esteem'st the ornament of life, | and MAC 1.07. 42
EST–IL 1 FR 0.0001 REL FR 0 V 1 P
est–il impossible d'echapper la force de ton H5 4.04. 16 P
ESTIMABLE 2 FR 0.0002 REL FR 1 V 1 P
flesh taken from a man | is not so estimable, MV 1.03.166
i could not with such estimable wonder overfar TN 2.01. 27 P
ESTIMATE 6 FR 0.0006 REL FR 6 V 0 P
rate | worth name of life in thee hath estimate: AWW 2.01.180
seymour, | none else of name and noble estimate. R2 2.03. 56
it holds his estimate and dignity | as well TRO 2.02. 54
my dear wive's estimate, her womb's increase COR 3.03.114
if he will touch the estimate. but for that — TIM 1.01. 14
and like enough thou know'st thy estimate; SON 87. 2
ESTIMATION 21 FR 0.0023 REL FR 10 V 11 P
to be of worth and worthy estimation, | and not TGV 2.04. 56
he cannot plead his estimation with you; MM 4.02. 26 P
rout | against your yet ungalled estimation, ERR 3.01.102
whose estimation do you mightily hold up — to a ADO 2.02. 24 P
good repute, carriage, bearing, and estimation." LLL 1.01.269 P
if thou beest rated by thy estimation, | thou MV 2.07. 26
to let him lack a reverend estimation, for i 4.01.163 P
scale do turn | but in the estimation of a hair, 4.01.331
lack'd the sense to know | her estimation home. AWW 5.03. 4
i speak not this in estimation, | as what i 1H4 1.03.272
dear men | of estimation and command in arms. 4.04. 32
the odds | of his great name and estimation, 5.01. 98
and he is a man of no estimation in the world, H5 3.06. 14 P
beggar the estimation which you priz'd | richer TRO 2.02. 91
who, in a cheap estimation, is worth all your COR 2.01. 91 P
them at all into their estimation and report. 2.02. 28 P
the people, to earn a dearer estimation of them; 2.03. 97 P
i were here, he would use me with estimation. 5.02. 52 P
you shall know now that i am in estimation; 5.02. 61 P
do they hold the same estimation they did when i HAM 2.02.334 P
adversities | make head against my estimation! OTH 1.03.274
ESTIMATIONS 1 FR 0.0001 REL FR 0 V 1 P
so your brace of unprizable estimations, the one CYM 1.04. 91 P
ESTRANGED 2 FR 0.0002 REL FR 2 V 0 P
it, | that thou art then estranged from thyself? ERR 2.02.120
will you not dance? how come you thus estranged? LLL 5.02.213

ESTRIDGE *(also ostridge)*
ESTRIDGE 1 FR 0.0001 REL FR 1 V 0 P
in that mood | the dove will peck the estridge; ANT 3.13.196
ESTRIDGES 1 FR 0.0001 REL FR 1 V 0 P
all plum'd like estridges, that with the wind 1H4 4.01. 98
/ET 1 FR 0.0001 REL FR 0 V 1 P
of the army, agamemnon, /et /cetera. TRO 3.03.278 P
ET 31 FR 0.0035 REL FR 7 V 24 P
video, et gaudeo. LLL 5.01. 31 P
et vous aussi; votre serviteur. TN 3.01. 72 P
ete en angleterre, et tu bien parles le langage. H5 3.04. 1 P
de hand. et les doigts? 3.04. 8 P
de hand, de fingres, et de nailes. 3.04. 18 P
et le coude? 3.04. 23 P
de nick. et le menton? 3.04. 34 P
par la grace de dieu, et en peu de temps. 3.04. 41 P
d' elbow, de nick, et de sin. 3.04. 49 P
comment appelez–vous le pied et la robe? 3.04. 50 P
le foot, madame, et le count. 3.04. 51 P
le foot et le count! 3.04. 52 P
gros, et impudique, et non pour les dames de 3.04. 53 P
et non pour les dames de honneur d'user. 3.04. 54 P
le foot et le count! 3.04. 56 P
vomissement, et la /truie lavee au bourbier." 3.07. 65 P
via! les eaux et terre. 4.02. 4
rien puis? l'air et feu? 4.02. 5
ma vie, et je vous donnerai deux cents ecus. 4.04. 42 P
et je m'estime heureux que je tombe entre les 4.04. 55 P
et tres /distingue seigneur d'angleterre. 4.04. 57 P
et quand vous avez le possession de moi — let 5.02.181 P
donc votre est france et vous etes mienne. 5.02.184 P
du monde, mon tres cher et devin deesse? 5.02.217 P
les dames et demoiselles pour etre baisees 5.02.258 P
noster henricus, rex angliae, et heres franciae. 5.02.341 P
"ego et rex meus" | was still inscrib'd; H8 3.02.314
et tu, brute? — then fall, caesar! JC 3.01. 77
hic et ubique? HAM 1.05.156
glorious, | et bonum quo antiquius, eo melius. PER 1.ch. 10
"et opus exegi, quod nec jovis ira, nec ignis" TNK 3.05. 88
ETCETERAS 1 FR 0.0001 REL FR 1 V 0 P
and are etceteras no things? 2H4 2.04.184
ETC. 28 FR 0.0031 REL FR 24 V 4 P
and down, down, adown–a, etc. WIV 1.04. 43
to shallow, etc." 3.01. 26
then sigh not so, etc. ADO 2.03. 74
philomele, with melody, etc. MND 2.02. 24
heigh–ho, sing, etc. AYL 2.07.190
country folks would lie, | in spring time, etc. 5.03. 25
a life was but a flower, | in spring time, etc. 5.03. 29
crowned with the prime, | in spring time, etc. 5.03. 33
get this ring | and /are by me with child, etc." AWW 5.03.313
when i came to man's estate, | with hey ho, etc. TN 5.01.394
men shut their gate, | for the rain, etc. 5.01.396
when i came, alas, to wive, | with hey ho, etc. 5.01.398
could i never thrive, | for the rain, etc. 5.01.400
when i came unto my beds, | with hey ho, etc. 5.01.402
still had drunken heads, | for the rain, etc. 5.01.404
while ago the world begun, | /with hey ho, etc. 5.01.406
england and france, and lord of ireland, etc." 3H6 4.07. 73 P
henry king of england, etc. H8 2.04. 8 P
katherine queen of england, etc. 2.04. 12 P
shall rome, etc. JC 2.01. 47
"shall rome, etc." 2.01. 51
"in her excellent white bosom, these, etc." HAM 2.02.113 P
we convent, etc. TNK 1.05. 10
to your health, etc. 3.03. 12
"may you never more enjoy the light," etc. 4.01.104
"o fair, o sweet," etc. 4.01.114
"when cynthia with her borrowed light," etc. 4.01.153
"i will be true, my stars, my fate," etc. 4.03. 57
ETE 1 FR 0.0001 REL FR 0 V 1 P
alice, tu as ete en angleterre, et tu bien H5 3.04. 1 P
/ETERNAL 1 FR 0.0001 REL FR 1 V 0 P
that this his love was an /eternal plant, 3H6 3.03.124
ETERNAL 39 FR 0.0044 REL FR 35 V 4 P
but go to hell for an eternal moment or so, i WIV 2.01. 49 P
it would give eternal food to his jealousy. 2.01.101 P
degree | stands in attainder of eternal shame. LLL 1.01.157
for thy sake, and my poor doing eternal; AWW 2.03.233 P
bedded her, and sworn to make the 'not' eternal. 3.02. 22 P
a contract of eternal bond of love, | confirm'd TN 5.01.156
to–morrow as to–day, | and to be boy eternal. WT 1.02. 65
holding th' eternal spirit, against her will, JN 3.04. 18
shame and eternal shame, nothing but shame! H5 4.05. 10
i kiss these fingers for eternal peace, | and 1H6 5.03. 48
by the eternal god, whose name and power | thou 2H6 1.04. 25
the mortal worm might make the sleep eternal. 3.02.263
o thou eternal mover of the heavens, | look with 3.03. 19
wrath | hath in eternal darkness folded up. R3 1.03.268
fall | into the blind cave of eternal night. 5.03. 62
they promis'd me eternal happiness, | and H8 4.02. 90
man fancy | with so eternal and so fix'd a soul. TRO 5.02.166
no noise, but silence and eternal sleep. TIT 1.01.155
and fame's eternal date, for virtue's praise! 1.01.168
me down, | that i may slumber an eternal sleep! 2.04. 15
and keep eternal spring–time /on /thy face, | so 3.01. 21
but heaven keeps his part in eternal life. ROM 4.05. 70
th' eternal devil to keep his state in rome | as JC 1.02.160
and mine eternal jewel | given to the common MAC 3.01. 67
me this, | and an eternal curse fall on you! 4.01.105
but this eternal blazon must not be | to ears of HAM 1.05. 21
what feast is toward in thine eternal cell, 5.02.365
proof, | or, by the worth of mine eternal soul, OTH 3.03.361
i will be hang'd if some eternal villain, | some 4.02.130
life in rome | would be eternal in our triumph. ANT 5.01. 66
why hast thou cast into eternal sleeping | those VEN 951
having solicited th' eternal power | that his LUC 345
day | and barren rage of death's eternal cold? SON 13.12
but thy eternal summer shall not fade, | nor 18. 9
when in eternal lines to time thou grow'st. 18.12
forth | eternal numbers to outlive long date. 38.12
rased, | and brass eternal slave to mortal rage; 64. 4
so that eternal love in love's fresh case 108. 9
remove | to spend her living in eternal love. LC 238
ETERNALLY 2 FR 0.0002 REL FR 2 V 0 P
with us | these couples shall eternally be knit. MND 4.01.181
shall be led | to those that love eternally. TNK 2.02.117
ETERNAL'S 1 FR 0.0001 REL FR 1 V 0 P
by penitence th' eternal's wrath's appeas'd: TGV 5.04. 81
ETERNE 2 FR 0.0002 REL FR 2 V 0 P
but in them nature's copy's not eterne. MAC 3.02. 38
on mars's armor forg'd for proof eterne | with HAM 2.02.490
ETERNITY 14 FR 0.0015 REL FR 12 V 2 P
keen edge, | and make us heirs of all eternity. LLL 1.01. 7
had he himself eternity and could put breath WT 5.02. 98 P
because i wish'd this world's eternity. 2H6 2.04. 90
to fight, | let mars divide eternity in twain, TRO 2.03.245
of a god but eternity and a heaven to throne in. COR 5.04. 24 P
must die, | passing through nature to eternity. HAM 1.02. 73
eternity was in our lips and eyes, | bliss in ANT 1.03. 35
there constant to eternity it lives. TNK pr 14
or sells eternity to get a toy? LUC 214
"thou ceaseless lackey to eternity, | with some 967
turtle's loyal breast | to eternity doth rest. PHT 58
know | time's thievish progress to eternity. SON 77. 8
rank remain | beyond all date, even to eternity; 122. 4
honoring, | or laid great bases for eternity, 125. 3
ETERNIZ'D 1 FR 0.0001 REL FR 1 V 0 P
york | shall be eterniz'd in all age to come. 2H6 5.03. 31
ETES 2 FR 0.0002 REL FR 0 V 2 P

je pense que vous etes le gentilhomme de bonne H5 4.04. 2 P
donc votre est france et vous etes mienne. 5.02.184 P
ETES–VOUS 1 FR 0.0001 REL FR 0 V 1 P
ecoutez: comment etes–vous appele? H5 4.04. 25 P
ETHIOP 3 FR 0.0003 REL FR 3 V 0 P
whom jove would swear | juno but an ethiop were, LLL 4.03.116
away, you ethiop! MND 3.02.257
such ethiop words, blacker in their effect AYL 4.03. 35
ETHIOPE 4 FR 0.0004 REL FR 4 V 0 P
her fair) | shows julia but a swarthy ethiope. TGV 2.06. 26
i'll hold my mind were she an ethiope. ADO 5.04. 38
shield | is a black ethiope reaching at the sun; PER 2.02. 20
jove would swear | juno but an ethiope were, PP 16.16
ETHIOPIAN 1 FR 0.0001 REL FR 0 V 1 P
is he dead, my ethiopian? WIV 2.03. 27 P
ETHIOPIAN'S 1 FR 0.0001 REL FR 1 V 0 P
or ethiopian's tooth, or the fann'd snow that's WT 4.04.364
ETHIOP'S 1 FR 0.0001 REL FR 1 V 0 P
of night | as a rich jewel in an ethiop's ear — ROM 1.05. 46
ETHIOPS 1 FR 0.0001 REL FR 1 V 0 P
and ethiops of their sweet complexion crack. LLL 4.03.264
ETNA 1 FR 0.0001 REL FR 0 V 1 P
i will be thrown into etna, as i have been into WIV 3.05.126 P
ETON 4 FR 0.0004 REL FR 2 V 2 P
steal my nan away, | and marry her at eton. WIV 4.04. 75
for so soon as i came beyond eton, they threw me 4.05. 67 P
and with him at eton | immediately to marry. 4.06. 24
i came yonder at eton to marry mistress anne 5.05.183 P
ETRE 1 FR 0.0001 REL FR 0 V 1 P
et demoiselles pour etre baisees devant leur H5 5.02.258 P
EUNUCH 13 FR 0.0014 REL FR 11 V 2 P
though argus were her eunuch and her guard. LLL 3.01.199
to be sung | by an athenian eunuch to the harp." MND 5.01. 45
thou shalt present me as an eunuch to him, | it TN 1.02. 56
be you his eunuch, and your mute i'll be; 1.02. 62
gelded the commonwealth, and made it an eunuch; 2H6 4.02.166 P
into a pipe | small as an eunuch, or the virgin COR 3.02.114
and if she do, i would i were an eunuch. TIT 2.03.128
thou, eunuch mardian! ANT 1.05. 8
i take no pleasure | in aught an eunuch has. 1.05. 10
as well a woman with an eunuch play'd | as with 2.05. 5
in rome | that photinus an eunuch and your maids 3.07. 14
hence, saucy eunuch, peace! 4.14. 25
nor the voice of unpav'd eunuch to boot, can CYM 2.03. 30 P
EUNUCHS 1 FR 0.0001 REL FR 0 V 1 P
would send them to th' turk, to make eunuchs of. AWW 2.03. 88 P
EUPHRATES 1 FR 0.0001 REL FR 1 V 0 P
from euphrates | his conquering banner shook, ANT 1.02.101
EURIPHILE 4 FR 0.0004 REL FR 4 V 0 P
euriphile, | thou wast their nurse; CYM 3.03.103
by good euriphile, our mother. 4.02.234
and words, | save that euriphile must be fidele. 4.02.238
their nurse, euriphile | (whom for the theft i 5.05.340
EUROPA 3 FR 0.0003 REL FR 2 V 1 P
thou wast a bull for thy europa, love set on thy WIV 5.05. 3 P
gold, | and all europa shall rejoice at thee, ADO 5.04. 45
at thee, | as once europa did at lusty jove, 5.04. 46
EUROPE 10 FR 0.0011 REL FR 6 V 4 P
would not bless our europe with your daughter, TMP 2.01.125
lady, | no court in europe is too good for thee, WT 2.02. 3
good cheap at the dearest chandler's in europe. 1H4 3.03. 46 P
and sisters, and sir john with all europe." 2H4 2.02.134 P
i were simply the most active fellow in europe. 4.03. 22 P
were it the mistress court of mighty europe; H5 2.04.133
it is the best horse of europe. 3.07. 5 P
whose bloody deeds shall make all europe quake. 1H6 1.01.156
slain | the flow'r of europe for his chevalry, 3H6 2.01. 71
lose it for a revenue | of any king's in europe! CYM 2.03.144
EVADE 1 FR 0.0001 REL FR 1 V 0 P
if he evade us there, | enforce him with his COR 3.03. 2
EVADES 1 FR 0.0001 REL FR 1 V 0 P
evades them with a bumbast circumstance OTH 1.01. 13
EVANS 1 FR 0.0001 REL FR 0 V 1 P
tell master parson evans i will do what i can WIV 1.04. 33 P
EVASION 4 FR 0.0004 REL FR 3 V 1 P
no more evasion. MM 1.01. 50
there can be no evasion | to blench from this TRO 2.02. 67
but his evasion, wing'd thus swift with scorn, 2.03.114
an admirable evasion of whoremaster man, to lay LR 1.02.127 P
EVASIONS 1 FR 0.0001 REL FR 0 V 1 P
his evasions have ears thus long. TRO 2.01. 69 P
EVE* 4 FR 0.0004 REL FR 2 V 2 P
all–hallond eve. MM 2.01.126 P
"with a child of our grandmother eve, a female; LLL 1.01.264 P
had he been adam, he had tempted eve. 5.02.322
what eve, what serpent, hath suggested thee | to R2 3.04. 75
EVEN* *(also e'en, ev'n*, and compounds)*
/EVEN* 6 FR 0.0006 REL FR 4 V 2 P
did you speak of me /even now before this honest 2H4 2.04.301 P
/even /by /those /men /that /most /have /done 4.01. 79
like niobe, all tears — why, she, /even /she — HAM 1.02.149
beggar that i am, i am /even poor in thanks — 2.02.272 P
/whose /reverence /even /the //head–lugg'd /bear LR 4.02. 42
/to /make /him /even /o'er /the /time /he /has 4.07. 79
EVEN* 623 FR 0.0704 REL FR 553 V 70 P
another way so high a hope that even | ambition TMP 2.01.241
even now, we heard a hollow burst of bellowing 2.01.311
these sweet thoughts do even refresh my labors, 3.01. 14
even here i will put off my hope, and keep it 3.03. 7
and even with such–like valor men hang and drown 3.03. 59
i will plague them all, | even to roaring. 4.01.193
some heavenly music (which even now i do) | to 5.01. 52
to call brother | would even infect my mouth, i 5.01.131
where, but even now, with strange and several 5.01.232
even in a dream, were we divided from them, 5.01.239
even as i would, when i to love begin. TGV 1.01. 10
even so by love the young and tender wit | is 1.01. 47
bud, | losing his verdure, even in the prime, 1.01. 49
even with the speediest expedition | i will 1.03. 37
hast thou observ'd that? even she, i mean. 2.01. 44 P
even she; and is she not a heavenly saint? 2.04.145
even as one heat another heat expels, | or as 2.04.192
even in the milk–white bosom of thy love. 3.01.252
even now about it! i will pardon you. 3.02. 97
my will is even this, | that presently you hie 4.02. 93
even for this time i spend in talking to thee. 4.02.104
even from a heart | as full of sorrows as the 4.03. 32
taught him, even as one would say precisely, 4.04. 5 P
intend confession | at patrick's cell this even, 5.02. 42
page's wife, who even now gave me good eyes too, WIV 1.03. 59 P
good even and twenty, good master page! 2.01.195 P
even as you came in to me, her assistant or 2.02.262 P
mine host, an old fat woman even now with me, 4.05. 25 P
herself might be her chooser) | even to my wish. 4.06. 12
(even strong against that match | and firm for 4.06. 27
worm, thou wast o'erlook'd even in thy birth. 5.05. 83
unhappily, even so. MM 1.02.156
slip, | even like an o'ergrown lion in a cave, 1.03. 22
even so her plenteous womb | expresseth his full 1.04. 43
even for our kitchens | we kill the fowl of 2.02. 84
from thee — even from thy virtue. 2.02.161
and even so | the general subject to a 2.04. 26
even so. heaven keep your honor! 2.04. 34
death we fear | that makes these odds all even. 3.01. 41
good even, good father. 3.02.214 P
the time is come even now. 4.01. 22 P
even with the stroke and line of his great 4.02. 80
good even. friar, where's the provost? 4.03.149 P
even so may angelo, | in all his dressings, 5.01. 55
out | most audible, even from his proper tongue, 5.01.408
your highness said even now i made you a duke; 5.01.515 P
even now, even here, not half an hour since. ERR 2.02. 14
even now, even here, not half an hour since. 2.02. 14
for even her very words | didst thou deliver to 2.02.163
even in the spring of love, thy love–springs rot 3.02. 3
husband, even my soul | doth for a wife abhor. 3.02.158
even just the sum that i do owe to you | is 4.01. 7
come, come, you know i gave it you even now. 4.01. 55
even now a tailor call'd me in his shop, | and 4.03. 7
even now we hous'd him in the abbey here, | and 5.01.188
even for the service that long since i did thee, 5.01.191
even for the blood | that then i lost for thee, 5.01.193
me, | even in the strength and height of injury: 5.01.200
him, even so much that joy could not show itself ADO 1.01. 21 P
even he. 1.03. 51 P
therefore i will even take sixpence in earnest 2.01. 40 P
even to the next willow, about your own business 2.01.187 P
who even now | is couched in the woodbine 3.01. 29
'tis even so. 3.02. 76 P
even she — leonato's hero, your hero, every 3.02.106 P
ent'red, even the night before her wedding–day. 3.02.113 P
a very even way, but no such friend. 4.01.264 P
what they weigh, even to the utmost scruple — 5.01. 93
i have deceiv'd even your very eyes. 5.01.232 P
yea, even i alone. 5.01.264
run smoothly in the even road of a blank verse, 5.02. 34 P
now the number is even. LLL 4.03.207
were not you here but even now, disguis'd? 5.02.433
even so: my tale is told. 5.02.720
humors | even to the opposed end of our intents; 5.02.758
and even that falsehood, in itself a sin, | thus 5.02.775
and even for that do i love you the more: MND 2.01.202
tell true, even for my sake! 3.02. 68
and me, put in two scales, | will even weigh; 3.02.133
(who even but now did spurn me with his foot), 3.02.225
groves may tread | even till the eastern gate, 3.02.391
and, in a word, but even now worth this, | and MV 1.01. 35
that shall be rack'd, even to the uttermost, 1.01.181
even there where merchants most do congregate, 1.03. 49
even for that i thank you; 2.01. 22
sweet, | even in the lovely garnish of a boy. 2.06. 45
and weigh thy value with an even hand. 2.07. 25
and even there, his eye being big with tears, 2.08. 46
wall, | even in the force and road of casualty. 2.09. 30
is | even as the flourish when true subjects bow 3.02. 49
or no, | so, thrice–fair lady, stand i, even so, 3.02.146
and even now, but now, | this house, these 3.02.169
you | even at that time i may be married too. 3.02.194
even such a husband | hast thou of me as she is 3.05. 83
even from the gallows did his fell soul fleet, 4.01.135
even so void is your false heart of truth. 5.01.189
even he that had held up the very life | of my 5.01.214
i swear to thee, even by thine own fair eyes, 5.01.242
as soon as you, | and even but now return'd; 5.01.272
is it even so? AYL 1.01. 85 P
even he, madam. 1.02.152 P
upon my body | even till i shrink with cold, i 2.01. 9
choke their service up | even with the having. 2.03. 62
peace, i say. good even to /you, friend. 2.04. 69
my lord, he is but even now gone hence; 2.07. 3
even by the squand'ring glances of the fool. 2.07. 57
bubble reputation | even in the cannon's mouth. 2.07.153
even so. 3.03. 56 P
good even, good master what–ye–call't; 3.03. 73 P
even a toy in hand here, sir. 3.03. 76 P
i have promis'd to make all this matter even: 5.04. 18
from hence i go | to make these doubts all even. 5.04. 25
when earthly things made even | atone together. 5.04.109
even daughter, welcome, in no less degree. 5.04.148
even as a flatt'ring dream or worthless fancy. SHR in.1. 44
even as the waving sedges play with wind. in.2. 53
even he, biondello. 1.02.222
good sooth, even thus; 3.02.116
even to the uttermost, as i please, in words. 4.03. 80
even in these honest mean habiliments; 4.03.170
and the moon changes even as your mind. 4.05. 20
what you will have it nam'd, even that it is, 4.05. 21
even such a woman oweth to her husband; 5.02.156
the care i have had to even your content, i wish AWW 1.03. 3 P
even so it was with me when i was young. 1.03.128
but will you make it even? 2.01.191
even to the world's pleasure and the increase of 2.04. 36 P
even to the utmost syllable of your worthiness. 3.06. 70 P
who had even tun'd his bounty to sing happiness 4.03. 9 P
her story true, even to the point of her death. 4.03. 56 P
know, | to make the even truth in pleasure flow. 5.03.326
into abatement and low price | even in a minute. TN 1.01. 14
to thee the book even of my secret soul. 1.04. 14
comptible, even to the least sinister usage. 1.05.176 P
and sing them loud even in the dead of night; 1.05.271
even so quickly may one catch the plague? 1.05.295
even now, sir — on a moderate pace i have since 2.02. 3 P
is't even so? 2.03.105 P
to die, even when they to perfection grow! 2.04. 41
even with the swiftness of putting on. 2.05.171 P
against you, even to a mortal arbitrement, but 3.04.261 P
even such and so | in favor was my brother, and 3.04.380
even what it please my lord, that shall become 5.01.116
even for the vows | we made each other but so 5.01.214
were you a woman, as the rest goes even, | i 5.01.239
my affairs | do even drag me homeward; WT 1.02. 24
and many a man there is (even at this present, 1.02.192
even for your son's sake, and thereby for 1.02.337
me | even so as i mine own course have set down. 1.02.340
even now i met him | with customary compliment, 1.02.370
i ey'd them | even to their ships. 2.01. 36
even as bad as those | that vulgars give bold'st 2.01. 93
even thou, that hast | a heart so tender o'er it 2.03.132
even thou, and none but thou. 2.03.135
rare | even then will rush to knowledge. 3.01. 21
even pushes 'gainst our heart — the party tried 3.02. 2
course, | even to the guilt or the purgation. 3.02. 7
with a love even such, | so and no other, as 3.02. 65
even since it could speak, from an infant, 3.02. 70
ay, my lord, even so | as it is here set down. 3.02.138
he hallow'd but even now. 3.03. 77 P
and children are even now to be afresh lamented. 4.02. 24 P
i will even take my leave of you, and pace 4.03.112 P
even now i tremble | to think your father, by 4.04. 18
i love a ballad but even too well, if it be 4.04.188 P
even here undone! 4.04.441
even he, my lord. 4.04.473
bless'd in this man, as i may say, even bless'd. 4.04.827 P
then, even now, | i might have look'd upon my 5.01. 52
that even your ears | should rift to hear me, 5.01. 65
i thought of her, | even in these looks i made. 5.01.228
expose the child were even then lost when it was 5.02. 72 P
even with such life of majesty (warm life, | as 5.03. 35
even till that england, hedg'd in with the main, JN 2.01. 26
even till that utmost corner of the west 2.01. 29
while they weigh so even, | we hold our town for 2.01.332
with course disturb'd even thy confining shores, 2.01.338
even till unfenced desolation | leave them as 2.01.386
and lay this angiers even with the ground, 2.01.399
well, | made to run even upon even ground, 2.01.576
well, | made to run even upon even ground, 2.01.576
and even before this truce, but new before, | no 3.01.233
even for that name, | which till this time my 3.01.306
even to that drop ten thousand wiry /friends 3.04. 64
even in the instant of repair and health, | the 3.04.113
for even the breath of what i mean to speak 3.04.127
not gone already, | even at that news he dies; 3.04.164
even in the matter of mine innocence; 4.01. 64
even with the fierce looks of these bloody men. 4.01. 73
even at my gates, with ranks of foreign pow'rs; 4.02.244
even so i have. 5.01. 27
and even there, methinks an angel spake. 5.02. 64
even in the jaws of danger and of death. 5.02.116
hand which had the strength, even at your door, 5.02.137
even at the crying of your nation's crow, 5.02.144
and even at hand a drum is ready brac'd | that 5.02.169
this news was brought to richard but even now. 5.03. 12
even on that altar where we swore to you | dear 5.04. 19
life, | which bleeds away even as a form of wax 5.04. 24
but even this night, whose black contagious 5.04. 33
even this ill night your breathing shall expire, 5.04. 36
even with a treacherous fine of all your lives, 5.04. 38
calmly run on in obedience | even to our ocean, 5.04. 57
even now he sung. 5.07. 12
even so must i run on, and even so stop. 5.07. 67
even so must i run on, and even so stop. 5.07. 67
afoot | even to the frozen ridges of the alps, R2 1.01. 64
even from the tongueless caverns of the earth, 1.01.105
even in the best blood chamber'd in his bosom, 1.01.149
where shame doth harbor, even in mowbray's face. 1.01.195
a' gaunt, | even in the lusty havior of his son. 1.03. 77
and make us wade even in our kinred's blood: 1.03.138
even in the glasses of thine eyes | i see thy 1.03.208
his face thou hast, for even so look'd he, 2.01.176
even through the hollow eyes of death | i spy 2.01.270
even in condition of the worst degree, | in 2.03.108
even at his feet to lay my arms and power, 3.03. 39
all must be even in our government. 3.04. 36
rue, even for ruth, here shortly shall be seen, 3.04.106
think i am dead, and that even here thou takest, 5.01. 38
even so, or with much more contempt, men's eyes 5.02. 27
even such, they say, as stand in narrow lanes 5.03. 8
death, | trembling even at the name of mortimer. 1H4 1.03.144
even with the bloody payment of your deaths. 1.03.186
a head, | for, bear ourselves as even as we can, 1.03.285
that's even as fair as — at hand, quoth the 2.01. 49 P
one horse, my lord, he brought even now. 2.03. 68
of sugar, clapp'd even now into my hand by an 2.04. 23 P
what, four? thou saidst but two even now. 2.04.197 P
seven? why, there were but four even now. 2.04.203 P
of land, | and then he runs straight and even. 3.01.113
and curbs himself even of his natural scope 3.01.169
even in the presence of the crowned king. 3.02. 54
and even as i was then is percy now. 3.02. 96
yea, even the slightest worship of his time, 3.02.151
'tis catching hither, even to our camp. 4.01. 30
and even those some | envy your great deservings 4.03. 34
him | even at the heels in golden multitudes. 4.03. 73
that even our love durst not come near your 5.01. 63
even those we love | that are misled upon your 5.01.104
and even in thy behalf i'll thank myself | for 5.04. 97
deeds | even in the bosom of our adversaries. 5.05. 31
of bold rebellion | even with the rebels' blood. 2H4 in 27
even such a man, so faint, so spiritless, | so 1.01. 70
fire | even to the dullest peasant in his camp, 1.01.113
out of his keeper's arms, even so my limbs, 1.01.143
even as we are, to equal with the king. 1.03. 67
even like those that are kin to the king, for 2.02.111 P
even such kin as the parish heckfers are to the 2.02.157 P
daughter, | give even way unto my rough affairs; 2.03. 2
even to the eyes of richard | gave him defiance. 3.01. 64
and that same word even now cries out on us. 3.01. 94
that even our corn shall seem as light as chaff, 4.01.193
with you, lord bishop, | it is even so. 4.02. 16

even there my life must end. 4.05.235
bad humors on the knight, that's the even of it. H5 2.01.122 P
how smooth and even they do bear themselves! 2.02. 3
for if you hide the crown | even in your hearts, 2.04. 98
now he weighs time | even to the utmost grain; 2.04.138
have in these parts from morn till even fought, 3.01. 20
even so. what are you? 4.01. 41 P
even as men wrack'd upon a sand, that look to be 4.01. 97 P
but in plain shock and even play of battle, 4.08.109
so swift a pace hath thought that even now | you 5.pr. 15
the even mead, that erst brought sweetly forth 5.02. 48
even so our houses, and ourselves, and children, 5.02. 56
mars his true moving, even as in the heavens, 1H6 1.02. 1
by my consent, we'll even let them alone. 1.02. 44
and even these three days have i watch'd | if i 1.04. 16
is it even so? 2.02. 44
even like a man new haled from the rack, | so 2.05. 3
and even since then hath richard been obscur'd, 2.05. 26
who in a moment even with the earth | shall lay 4.02. 12
even as i have of fertile england's soil. 2H6 1.01.238
did vow upon his knees he would be even with me. 1.03.200 P
and even as willingly at thy feet i leave it 2.03. 35
even so remorseless have they borne him hence; 3.01.213
even so myself bewails good gloucester's case 3.01.217
and even with this i lost fair england's view, 3.02.110
even so suspicious is this tragedy. 3.02.194
away even now, or i will drag thee hence. 3.02.229
and even now my burthen'd heart would break, 3.02.320
even now be gone. 3.02.352
even thus two friends condemn'd | embrace, and 3.02.353
majesty | that even now he cries aloud for him. 3.02.378
even as a splitted bark, so sunder we; 3.02.411
may, even in their wives' and children's sight, 4.02.179
presence, even the presence of lord mortimer, 4.07. 30 P
at us, as who should say, i'll be even with you. 4.07. 95 P
even to affright thee with the view thereof. 5.01.207
even of the bonny beast he lov'd so well. 5.02. 12
even at this sight | my heart is turn'd to stone 5.02. 49
shall be to me even as the dew to fire, | and 5.02. 53
sturdy rebel sits, | even in the chair of state. 3H6 1.01. 51
even in the lukewarm blood of henry's heart. 1.02. 34
yea, even my foes will shed fast–falling tears, 1.04.162
even with those wings | which sometime they have 2.02. 29
even then that sunshine brew'd a show'r for him, 2.02.156
even as thou wilt, sweet warwick, let it be; 2.06. 99
from scotland am i stol'n, even of pure love, 3.01. 13
even in the downfall of his mellow'd years, 3.03.104
now, warwick, tell me, even upon thy conscience, 3.03.113
'tis even so, yet you are warwick still. 5.01. 47
even with the dearest blood your bodies bear. 5.01. 69
my manors that i had, | even now forsake me; 5.02. 25
even now we heard the news. 5.02. 32
even so? R3 1.01. 88
it again, and even with the word | this hand, 1.02.188
even so thy breast encloseth my poor heart: 1.02.204
/'zounds, 'tis even now at my elbow, persuading 1.04.145 P
how he did lap me | even in his /own garments, 2.01.117
posterity, | even to the general all–ending day. 3.01. 78
even where his raging eye or savage heart, 3.05. 83
and even here brake off, and came away. 3.07. 41
even that (i hope) which pleaseth god above 3.07.109
away, | and that my path were even to the crown, 3.07.157
widow, | even in the afternoon of her best days, 3.07.186
even when you please, for you will have it so. 3.07.243
from which even here i slip my /weary head, 4.04.112
and all i have — ay, and myself and all — 4.04.249
even he that makes her queen. 4.04.266
even so. how think you of it? 4.04.267
below, | even of your metal, of your very blood; 4.04.302
hour, | even for revenge mock my destruction! 5.01. 9
swine | is now even in the centry of this isle, 5.02. 11
pitch our tent, even here in bosworth field. 5.03. 1
whose figure even this instant cloud puts on H8 1.01.225
even he escapes not | language unmannerly; 1.02. 26
even as the axe falls, if i be not faithful! 2.01. 61
even of her | that when the greatest stroke of 2.02. 34
spread then, | even of yourself, lord cardinal. 2.02.125
heard him play, | even the billows of the sea, 3.01. 10
set against 'em, | i know my life so even. 3.01. 37
noble temper, | a soul as even as a calm; 3.01.166
saw you not even now a blessed troop | invite me 4.02. 87
boat | whose weak untimber'd sides but even now TRO 1.03. 43
even so | doth valor's show and valor's worth 1.03. 45
even this. 1.03.217
even so much. 1.03.283
even such a passion doth embrace my bosom: 3.02. 35
even already | they clap the lubber ajax on the 3.03.138
even then when they sit idly in the sun. 3.03.233
to behold his visage, | even to my full of view. 3.03.241
true, | even in soul of sound good–fellowship — 4.01. 53
even in the birth of our own laboring breath. 4.04. 38
i charge thee use her well, even for my charge; 4.04.126
even she. 4.05. 17
you are an odd man, give even or give none. 4.05. 41
that you are odd, and he is even with you. 4.05. 44
one that knows the youth | even to his inches, 4.05.111
even in the fan and wind of your fair sword, 5.03. 41
even in the faith of valor, to appear | this 5.03. 69
even with the vail and dark'ning of the sun, 5.08. 7
which he is, even to the altitude of his virtue. COR 1.01. 40 P
ne'er came from the lungs, but even thus — 1.01.108
even so most fitly | as you malign our senators 1.01.112
even to the court, the heart, to th' seat o' th' 1.01.136
thou wast a soldier | even to /cato's wish, not 1.04. 57
even like a fawning greyhound in the leash, | to 1.06. 38
at home, upon my brother's guard, even there, 1.10. 25
even when the navel of the state was touch'd, 3.01.123
even as she speaks, why, their hearts were yours 3.02. 87
power must try him — even this | so criminal, 3.03. 80
even from this instant, banish him our city, 3.03.101
they charg'd him even | as those should do that 4.06.112
in this action, sir, | even by your own. 4.07. 6
even to my person, than i thought he would 4.07. 9
them, but he could not | carry his honors even. 4.07. 37
peace | even with the same austerity and garb 4.07. 44
part, and i am out, | even to a full disgrace. 5.03. 42
even he, your wife, this lady, and myself, | are 5.03. 77
i, | even in theirs and in the commons' ears, 5.06. 4
even so | as with a man by his own alms 5.06. 9
with bloody passage led your wars even to | the 5.06. 75
even thou hast strook upon my crest, | and with TIT 1.01.364
even as an adder when she doth unroll | to do 2.03. 35
even at thy teat thou hadst thy tyranny; 2.03.145
offended me, | even for his sake am i pitiless. 2.03.162
i, | even like a stony image, cold and numb. 3.01.258
even in their throats that hath committed them. 3.01.274
but even with law, against the willful sons | of 4.04. 8
even so mayest thou the giddy men of rome. 4.04. 87
the meeting | even at his father's house, the 4.04.103
even thus he rates the babe — | "for i must 5.01. 33
even by my god i swear to thee i will. 5.01. 86
even now i curse the day — and yet i think 5.01.125
even when their sorrows almost was forgot, | and 5.01.137
even from /hyperion's rising in the east, 5.02. 56
when he is here, even at thy solemn feast, | i 5.02.115
even in the time | when it should move ye to 5.03. 91
even such delight | among fresh fennel buds ROM 1.02. 28
even or odd, of all days in the year, | come 1.03. 16
for even the day before, she broke her brow, 1.03. 38
woos | even now the frozen bosom of the north, 1.04.101
a rhyme i learnt even now | of one i danc'd 1.05.142
good even to my ghostly confessor. 2.06. 21
lips, | who, even in pure and vestal modesty, 3.03. 38
o, he is even in my mistress' case, | just in 3.03. 84
even so lies she, | blubb'ring and weeping, 3.03. 86
but thankful even for hate that is meant love. 3.05.148
of your woes, | and lead you even to death. 5.03.220
even he drops down | the knee before him, and TIM 1.01. 60
make sacred even his stirrup, and through him 1.01. 82
mountain's top | even on their knees and /hands, 1.01. 87
figures are | even such as they give out. 1.01.160
my lord, you take us even at the best. 1.02.152
good even, varro. what, | you come for money? 2.02. 9
of whom, even to the state's best health, i have 2.02.197
nought | but even the mere necessities upon't. 4.03.376
that thou art even natural in thine art. 5.01. 85
even such heaps and sums of love and wealth | as 5.01.152
good even, casca; JC 1.03. 1
sit | even at noon–day upon the market–place, 1.03. 27
myself | even in the aim and very flash of it. 1.03. 52
not stain | the even virtue of our enterprise, 2.01.133
who did hide their faces | even from darkness. 2.01.278
he, | let me a little show it, even in this — 3.01. 71
then walk we forth, even to the market–place, 3.01.108
even at the base of pompey's statue | (which all 3.02.188
even so. 4.03.157
even so great men great losses should endure. 4.03.193
on | upon the left hand of the even field. 5.01. 17
even so, lucilius. 5.01. 92
even by the rule of that philosophy | by which i 5.01.100
i will be here again, even with a thought. 5.03. 19
even with the sword that kill'd thee. 5.03. 46
of grief, | that it runs over even at his eyes. 5.05. 14
even for that our love of old, i prithee | hold 5.05. 27
the sin of my ingratitude even now | was heavy MAC 1.04. 15
unnatural, | even like the deed that's done. 2.04. 11
both sides are even; 3.04. 10
me strange | even to the disposition that i owe, 3.04.112
all together, | even till destruction sicken; 4.01. 60
and even now, | to crown my thoughts with acts, 4.01.148
perchance even there where i did find my doubts. 4.03. 25
for even now | i put myself to thy direction, 4.03.121
even so? 5.01. 65 P
and many unrough youths that even now | protest 5.02. 10
your several loves, | and make us even with you. 5.09. 28
king, | whose image even but now appear'd to us, HAM 1.01. 81
and even the like precurse of /fear'd events, 1.01.121
good even, sir. 1.02.167
but even then the morning cock crew loud, | and 1.02.218
extinct in both | even in their promise, as it 1.03.119
that it went hand in hand even with the vow | i 1.05. 49
cut off even in the blossoms of my sin, 1.05. 76
charge you withal, be even and direct with me, 2.02.287 P
even those you were wont to take such delight in 2.02.327 P
even with the very comment of thy soul | observe 3.02. 79
that even our loves should with our fortunes 3.02.201
even to the teeth and forehead of our faults, 3.03. 63
i'll silence me even here; 3.04. 4
look where he goes, even now, out at the portal! 3.04.136
let it feed | even on the pith of life. 4.01. 23
to bear all smooth and even, | this sudden 4.03. 7
death, and danger dare, | even for an egg–shell. 4.04. 53
brands the harlot | even here, between the 4.05.120
but even his mother shall uncharge the practice, 4.07. 67
why, even in that was heaven ordinant. 5.02. 48
perform'd | even while men's minds are wild, 5.02.394
all these bounds, even from this line to this, LR 1.01. 63
she, whom even but now was your /best object, 1.01.214
but even for want of that for which i am richer 1.01.230
which even but now, demanding after you, 3.02. 65
he was met even now | as mad as the vex'd sea, 4.04. 1
methinks the ground is even. 4.06. 3
i am even | the natural fool of fortune. 4.06.190
no further, sir, a man may rot even here. 5.02. 8
their going hence even as their coming hither, 5.02. 10
it came even from the heart of — o, she's dead! 5.03.225
even so. cover their faces. 5.03.243
even now, now, very now, an old black ram | is OTH 1.01. 88
the cyprus wars | (which even now stands in act) 1.01.151
appearance, | even on the instant. 1.02. 38
but let your sentence | even fall upon my life. 1.03.120
even from my boyish days | to th' very moment 1.03.132
subdu'd | even to the very quality of my lord. 1.03.251
even till we make the main and th' aerial blue 2.01. 39
for even her folly help'd her to an heir. 2.01.137
should increase | even as our days do grow! 2.01.195
for even out of that will i cause these of 2.01.274 P
upon his peace and quiet | even to madness. 2.01.311
friends all, but now, even now; 2.03.179
even as again they were | when you yourself did 2.03.238
even so as one would beat his offenseless dog to 2.03.274 P
even as her appetite shall play the god | with 2.03.347
i heard thee say even now, thou lik'st not that, 3.03.109
even then this forked plague is fated to us 3.03.276
even so my bloody thoughts, with violent pace, 3.03.457
'tis even so; 3.04.145
our other healthful members even to a sense | of 3.04.147
and many worthy and chaste dames even thus, 4.01. 46
give me the addition | whose want even kills me. 4.01.105
she was here even now; 4.01.132 P
by that same handkerchief you gave me even now? 4.01.150 P
in her bed, even the bed she hath contaminated. 4.01.208 P
the shambles, | that quicken even with blowing. 4.02. 67
the world | even from the east to th' west! 4.02.144
and even from this instant do build on thee a 4.02.205 P
that even his stubbornness, his checks, his 4.03. 20
it is even so. 5.01. 29
even he, sir; did you know him? 5.01. 92
even like thy chastity. 5.02.276
and he himself confess'd it but even now, | that 5.02.321
and even but now he spake | (after long seeming 5.02.327
his honor | even till a lethe'd dullness — how ANT 2.01. 27
round, even to faultiness. 3.03. 30
i will be even with thee, doubt it not. 3.07. 1
even this repays me. 3.11. 71
i will contend | even with his pestilent scythe. 3.13.193
begins to rage, he's hunted | even to falling. 4.01. 8
antony part here, even here | do we shake hands. 4.12. 19
horse, even with a thought | the rack dislimns, 4.14. 9
eros, now thy captain is | even such a body. 4.14. 13
of this seleucus does | even make me wild. 5.02.154
i honor him | even out of your report. CYM 1.01. 55
rather shunn'd to go even with what i heard than 1.04. 44 P
make her go back, even to the yielding, had i 1.04.105 P
but even the very middle of my heart | is warm'd 1.06. 27
even to the point of envy, if 'twere made 2.03.128
for even to vice | they are not constant, but 2.05. 29
creatures, would even renew me with your eyes. 3.02. 42 P
even then | the princely blood flows in his 3.03. 92
which to read | would be even mortal to me. 3.04. 18
but we'll even | all that good time will give us 3.04.181
i will pursue her | even to augustus' throne. 3.05.101
even there, thou villain posthumus, will i kill 3.05.131 P
but even before, i was | at point to sink for 3.06. 16
i'll follow those that even now fled hence, 4.02. 98
he went hence even now. 4.02.189
even so | these herblets shall, which we upon 4.02.286
even when i wake, it is | without me, as within 4.02.306
even to the note o' th' king, or i'll fall in 4.03. 44
even for whom my life | is every breath a death; 5.01. 26
is this most constant wife, who, even now, 5.05.449
a bride | for embracements even of jove himself; PER 1.01. 7
o my distressed lord, even such our griefs are; 1.04. 7
for riches strew'd herself even in her streets; 1.04. 23
poor men that were cast away before us even now. 2.01. 19 P
this strict charge, even as he left his life, 2.01.125
even in your armors, as you are address'd, 2.03. 94
even in the height and pride of all his glory, 2.04. 6
shrivell'd up | those bodies, even to loathing; 2.04. 10
even in his throat — unless it be the king — 2.05. 56
even as my life my blood that fosters it. 2.05. 89
patience, good sir, | even for this charge. 3.01. 27
even at the first | thy loss is more than can 3.01. 34
your personal pain, but even | your purse, still 3.02. 46
even now | did the sea toss up upon our shore 3.02. 49
even on my /eaning time, but whether there 3.04. 6
wench, | even /ripe for marriage /rite; 4.ch. 17
which | even women have cast off, melt thee, but 4.01. 7
continual action are even as good as rotten. 4.02. 8 P
that even her art sisters the natural roses; 5.ch. 7
expect even here, where is a kingly patient, 5.01. 71
appetite, | that loathes even as it longs. TNK 1.03. 90
and even each thing | our haste does leave 1.04. 11
arcite, | even in the wagging of a wanton leg, 2.02. 15
even from the bottom of these miseries, | from 2.02. 56
and me too, | even when you please, of life. 2.02.225
even the very plum–broth | and marrow of my 3.05. 5
for, if my brother but even now had ask'd me 4.02. 47
sails that must these vessels port even where 5.01. 29
even with an eye–glance, to choke mars's drum 5.01. 80
of many mortal millions, may even now, | by 5.03. 24
victor's wreath | even then fell off his head; 5.04. 80
saw her, and | even then proclaim'd your fancy. 5.04.118
even by the rule you have among yourselves, STM II.C 46
why even your hurly | cannot proceed but by II.C 113
even as the sun with purple–color'd face | had VEN 1
and even now | to tie the rider she begins to 39
even as an empty eagle, sharp by fast, | tires 55
even so she kiss'd his brow, his cheek, his chin 59
now, | even by the stern and direful god of war, 98
morn till night, even where i list to sport me. 154
for men will kiss even by their own direction." 216
glow, | even as a dying coal revives with wind, 338
even as the wind is hush'd before it raineth, 458
or morn or weary even? 495
even so poor birds, deceiv'd with painted grapes 601
even so she languisheth in her mishaps, | as 603
wood, | even so confounded in the dark she lay, 827
even so the timorous yelping of the hounds 881
even at this word she hears a merry horn, 1025
auspicious to the hour, | even there he starts; LUC 348
even so, the curtain drawn, his eyes begun | to 374
that even for anger makes the lily pale | and 478
"i have debated, even in my soul, | what wrong, 498
a swallowing gulf that even in plenty wanteth. 557
even in the moment that we call them ours. 868
even so the maid with swelling drops gan wet 1228
even so this pattern of the worn–out age 1350
"for even as subtile sinon here is painted, | so 1541
even so his sighs, his sorrows, make a saw, | to 1672
even here she sheathed in her harmless breast 1723
"even thus," quoth she, "the warlike god PP 11. 5
"even thus," quoth she, "the warlike god unlac'd 11. 7
"even thus," quoth she, "he seized on my lips," 11. 9
cheered and check'd even by the self–same sky, SON 15. 6
stars twire not, thou /gild'st th' even: 28.12
even so my sun one early morn did shine | with 33. 9
all men make faults, and even i in this, 35. 5
even for this, let us divided live, | and our 39. 5
who lead thee in their riot even there | where 41.11
and for my sake even so doth she abuse me, 42. 7
who even but now come back again, assured | of 45.11
and even thence thou wilt be stol'n, i fear, 48.13
even in the eyes of all posterity | that wear 55.11

fill | thy hungry eyes even till they wink with 56. 6
even of five hundreth courses of the sun, | show 59. 6
utt'ring bare truth, even so as foes commend. 69. 4
but let your love even with my life decay; 71.12
breath most breathes, even in the mouths of men. 81.14
even such a beauty as you master now. 106. 8
even as when first i hallowed thy fair name. 108. 8
even to thy pure and most most loving breast. 110.14
ye | even that your pity is enough to cure me. 111.14
even those that said i could not love you dearer 115. 2
but bears it out even to the edge of doom. 116.12
even so, being full of your ne'er-cloying 118. 5
rank remain | beyond all date, even to eternity; 122. 4
nor that full star that ushers in the even 132. 7
even there resolv'd my reason into tears, LC 296
EVEN-CHRISTEN 1 FR 0.0001 REL FR 0 V 1 P
hang themselves, more than their even-christen. HAM 5.01. 28 P
EVEN'D 1 FR 0.0001 REL FR 1 V 0 P
content my soul | till i am even'd with him, OTH 2.01.299
EVEN-HANDED 1 FR 0.0001 REL FR 1 V 0 P
this even-handed justice | commends th' MAC 1.07. 10
EVENING 21 FR 0.0023 REL FR 17 V 4 P
and give some evening music to her ear. TGV 4.02. 17
this evening coming. 4.03. 42
lady, a happy evening! 5.01. 7
will not miss you morning nor evening prayer, as WIV 2.02. 99 P
my woes end likewise with the evening sun. ERR 1.01. 27
and about evening come yourself alone | to know 3.01. 96
at him upon my knees every morning and evening. ADO 2.01. 29 P
how still the evening is, | as hush'd on purpose 2.03. 38
say, what abridgment have you for this evening? MND 5.01. 39
i'll about it this evening, and i will presently AWW 3.06. 74 P
before the dew of evening fall, shall fleet | in JN 2.01.285
this evening must i leave you, gentle kate. 1H4 2.03.106
this evening, on the east side of the grove. 2H6 2.01. 42
and made an evening at the noontide prick. 3H6 1.04. 34
fall | like a bright exhalation in the evening, H8 3.02.226
now, | or shall i come to you at evening mass? ROM 4.01. 38
'twas on a summer's evening, in his tent, | that JC 3.02.172
any further delay than this very evening. LR 1.02. 93 P
i have this present evening from my sister 2.01.101
to hear him | sing in an evening, what a heaven TNK 2.04. 19
plains, | all our evening sport from us is fled, PP 17.31
EVENLY 3 FR 0.0003 REL FR 2 V 1 P
athwart his affection ranges evenly with mine. ADO 2.02. 7 P
shall run | in a new channel fair and evenly. 1H4 3.01.102
and when you find him evenly deriv'd | from his H5 2.04. 91
EVEN-PLEACH'D 1 FR 0.0001 REL FR 1 V 0 P
her hedges even-pleach'd, | like prisoners H5 5.02. 42
/EVENT 2 FR 0.0002 REL FR 1 V 1 P
as the /event stamps them, but they have a good ADO 1.02. 7 P
/you /cast /th' /event /of /war, /my /noble 2H4 1.01.166
EVENT 27 FR 0.0030 REL FR 24 V 3 P
mark his condition, and th' event, then tell me TMP 1.02.117
and crown what i profess with kind event | if i 3.01. 69
success | will fashion the event in better shape ADO 4.01.235
and most prepost'rous event that draweth from my LLL 1.01.242 P
i'll after him, and see the event of this. SHR 3.02.127
those tender limbs of thine to the event | of AWW 3.02.104
for this night, to bed, and dream on the event. TN 2.03.176 P
come, let's see the event. 3.04.395 P
if th' event o' th' journey | prove as WT 3.01. 11
day, | no common wind, no customed event, | but JN 3.04.155
merry, | but heaviness foreruns the good event. 2H4 4.02. 82
but that it doth presage some ill event. 1H6 4.01.191
with hope to find the like event in love, | but 5.05.105
lord suffolk, you and i must talk of that event. 2H6 3.01.326
in this the heaven figures some event. 3H6 2.01. 32
manner | daring th' event to th' teeth, are all H8 1.02. 36
act | such and no other than event doth form it, TRO 2.02.120
eyes for th' time, | but hearts for the event. COR 2.01.270
i'll show you how t' observe a strange event. TIM 3.04. 17
let our just censures | attend the true event, MAC 5.04. 15
of thinking too precisely on th' event — | a HAM 4.04. 41
puff'd | makes mouths at the invisible event, 4.04. 50
well, well, th' event. LR 1.04.348
sir, the event | is yet to name the winner. CYM 3.05. 14
the unborn event | i do commend to your content; PER 4.ch. 45
let th' event, | that never-erring arbitrator, TNK 1.02.113
"what uncouth ill event | hath thee befall'n, LUC 1598
EVENTFUL 1 FR 0.0001 REL FR 1 V 0 P
all, | that ends this strange eventful history, AYL 2.07.164
EVENTS 14 FR 0.0015 REL FR 12 V 2 P
these are not natural events, they strengthen TMP 5.01.227
but leave we him to his events, with a prayer MM 3.02.238 P
you are not satisfied | of these events at full. MV 5.01.297
make conclusion | of these most strange events. AYL 5.04.127
that their events can never fall out good. R2 2.01.214
but heaven hath a hand in these events, | to 5.02. 37
o heavy times, begetting such events! 3H6 2.05. 63
that hath been breeder of these dire events. TIT 5.03.178
of dire combustion and confus'd events | new MAC 2.03. 58
and even the like precurse of /fear'd events, HAM 1.01.121
there are many events in the womb of time which OTH 1.03.370 P
all strange and terrible events are welcome, ANT 4.15. 3
high events as these | strike those that make 5.02.360
"it shall be cause of war and dire events, | and VEN 1159
EVER *(also e'er, ev'r, and compounds)*
/EVER 4 FR 0.0004 REL FR 3 V 1 P
"that /ever turn'd their eyes to mortal views! LLL 5.02.163
/the /emptier /ever /dancing /in /the /air, R2 4.01.186
'a came /ever in the rearward of the fashion, 2H4 3.02.315 P
/lear /and /him | /that /ever /ear /received, LR 5.03.216
EVER 681 FR 0.0769 REL FR 523 V 158 P
would i might | but ever see that man! TMP 1.02.169
but omit, my fortunes | will ever after droop. 1.02.184
for nothing natural | i ever saw so noble. 1.02.420
we have lost your son, | i fear for ever. 2.01.133
three inches of it, | can lay to bed for ever; 2.01.284
said, "as proper a man as ever went on four legs 2.02. 61 P
for any emperor that ever trod on neat's-leather 2.02. 70 P
my mistress, dearest, | and i thus humble ever. 3.01. 87
was there ever man a coward that hath drunk so 3.02. 27 P
let me live here ever; 4.01.122
which may make this island | thine own for ever, 4.01.218
and deeper than did ever plummet sound | i'll 5.01. 56
business more than nature | was ever conduct of. 5.01.244
home-keeping youth have ever homely wits. TGV 1.01. 2
in thy danger | (if ever danger do environ thee) 1.01. 16
ever since you lov'd her. 2.01. 65 P
i have lov'd her ever since i saw her, and still 2.01. 66 P
excellent device, was there ever heard a better, 2.01.139
it is the unkindest tied that ever any man tied. 2.03. 38 P
man | (a rashness that i ever yet have shunn'd), 3.01. 30
tow'r, | the key whereof myself have ever kept; 3.01. 36
take no repulse, what ever she doth say; 3.01.100
far exceed the love | i ever bore my daughter, 3.01.167
the blackest news that ever thou heardst. 3.01.286 P
say | no grief did ever come so near thy heart 4.03. 19
didst thou ever see me do such a trick? 4.04. 39 P
bear witness, heaven, i have my wish for ever. 5.04.119
kind fellow as ever servant shall come in house WIV 1.04. 11 P
i detest, an honest maid as ever broke bread. 1.04.151 P
did you ever hear the like? 2.01. 69 P
his own gravity and patience that ever you saw. 3.01. 54 P
y' are overthrown, y' are undone for ever! 3.03. 96 P
or bid farewell to your good life for ever. 3.03.120 P
of villainous smell that ever offended nostril. 3.05. 92 P
that any madness i ever yet beheld seem'd but 4.02. 27 P
let me for ever be your table-sport. 4.02.162 P
discretions of a oman as ever i did look upon. 4.04. 2 P
me more wit than ever i learn'd before in my 4.05. 60 P
him, master /brook, that ever govern'd frenzy. 5.01. 19 P
that ever the devil could have made you our 5.05.149 P
and he was ever precise in promise-keeping. MM 1.02. 75 P
you | how i have ever lov'd the life removed, 1.03. 8
to come that she was ever respected with man, 2.01.168 P
if ever i was respected with her, or she with me 2.01.176 P
ever till now, | when men were fond, i smil'd 2.02.185
sister, by redeeming him, | should die for ever. 2.04.108
complexion, shall keep the body of it ever fair. 3.01.184 P
if ever he return, and i can speak to him, i 3.01.192 P
if peradventure he shall ever return to have 3.01.204 P
his love toward her ever most kind and natural; 3.01.220 P
ever your fresh whore and your powder'd bawd, an 3.02. 59 P
but if ever the duke return (as our prayers are 3.02.154 P
i have heard it was ever his manner to do so. 4.02.134 P
and hold you ever to our special drift, | though 4.05. 2
yet my husband | knows not that ever he knew me. 5.01.187
my knees, | or else for ever be confixed here, 5.01.232
was there ever any man thus beaten out of season ERR 2.02. 47
for ever hous'd where it gets possession. 3.01.106
and ever, as it blaz'd, they threw on him 5.01.172
nor ever didst thou draw thy sword on me; 5.01.267
he's return'd, and as pleasant as ever he was. ADO 1.01. 37 P
it ever changes with the next block. 1.01. 76 P
she is the sweetest lady that ever i look'd on. 1.01.188 P
thou wast ever an obstinate heretic in the 1.01.234 P
prove that ever i lose more blood with love than 1.01.250 P
well, if ever thou dost fall from this faith, 1.01.255 P
may, but if ever the sensible benedick bear it, 1.01.262 P
if this should ever happen, thou wouldst be 1.01.269 P
sad but when she sleeps, and not ever sad then; 2.01.344 P
ladies, sigh no more, | men were deceivers ever, 2.03. 63
the fraud of men was ever so, | since summer 2.03. 72
in all outward behaviors seem'd ever to abhor. 2.03. 97 P
to praise him more than ever man did merit. 3.01. 19
a bed | as ever beatrice shall couch upon? 3.01. 46
piece of lechery that ever was known in the 3.03.168 P
ever since you left it. 3.04. 69 P
sir, by my troth he is, as ever broke bread; 3.05. 39 P
and seem'd i ever otherwise to you? 4.01. 55
why ever wast thou lovely in my eyes? 4.01.130
mourn, | if ever love had interest in his liver, 4.01.231
flat burglary as ever was committed. 4.02. 50 P
small have continual plodders ever won, | save LLL 1.01. 86
as i look'd for, but the best that ever i heard. 1.01.280 P
if ever i do see the merry days of desolation 1.02.159 P
/clock, | still a-repairing, ever out of frame, 3.01.191
did you ever hear better? 4.01. 95
love, whose month is ever may, | spied a blossom 4.03.100
for all the wealth that ever i did see, | i 4.03.147
and ever and anon they made a doubt | presence 5.02.101
of the fairest dames | that ever turn'd their — 5.02.161
or ever but in vizards show their faces? 5.02.271
by being once false for ever to be true | to 5.02.773
or to abjure | for ever the society of men. MND 1.01. 66
for aught that i could ever read, | could ever 1.01.132
ever read, | could ever hear by tale or history, 1.01.133
if then true lovers have been ever cross'd, | it 1.01.150
by all the vows that ever men have broke | (in 1.01.175
broke | (in number more than ever women spoke), 1.01.176
did ever keep your counsels, never wrong'd you; 3.02.308
this dear, | if ever i thy face by daylight see. 3.02.427
more than cool reason ever comprehends. 5.01. 6
wittiest partition that ever i heard discourse, 5.01.167 P
o night, which ever art when day is not! 5.01.171
this is the silliest stuff that ever i heard. 5.01.210 P
issue, there create, | ever shall be fortunate. 5.01.406
all the couples three | ever true in loving be; 5.01.408
owner of it blest | ever shall in safety rest. 5.01.420
your father was ever virtuous, and holy men at MV 1.02. 27 P
and the worst fall that ever fell, i hope i 1.02. 90 P
of all the men that ever my foolish eyes look'd 1.02.117 P
hour, | for lovers ever run before the clock. 2.06. 4
that ever holds. 2.06. 8
you will to bed, | i will ever be your head. 2.09. 71
a gossip in that as ever knapp'd ginger or made 3.01. 9 P
unpleasant'st words | that ever blotted paper! 3.02.252
most impenetrable cur | that ever kept with men. 3.03. 19
as i have ever found thee honest-true, | so let 3.04. 46
she would not hold out enemy for ever | for 4.01.447
which i did make him swear to keep for ever. 4.02. 14
being ever from their cradles bred together, AYL 1.01.108 P
if ever he go alone again, i'll never wrastle 1.01.161 P
sworn it away before ever he saw those pancakes 1.02. 79 P
is the first time that ever i heard breaking of 1.02.138 P
and she believes, where ever they are gone, 2.02. 15
a lover | as ever sigh'd upon a midnight pillow. 2.04. 27
but if thy love were ever like to mine — | as 2.04. 28
folly | that ever love did make thee run into, 2.04. 35
well then, if ever i thank any man, i'll thank 2.05. 25 P
if ever you have look'd on better days, | if 2.07.113
if ever been where bells have knoll'd to church, 2.07.114
church, | if ever sat at any good man's feast, 2.07.115
feast, | if ever from your eyelids wip'd a tear, 2.07.116
wast ever in court, shepherd? 3.02. 33 P
did you ever cure any so? 3.02.406 P
your chestnut was ever the only color. 3.04. 11 P
if ever (as that ever may be near) | you meet in 3.05. 28
dear phebe, | if ever (as that ever may be near) 3.05. 28
"who ever lov'd that lov'd not at first sight?" 3.05. 82
where ever sorrow is, relief would be. 3.05. 86
for ever and a day. 4.01.145 P
say "a day," without the "ever." 4.01.146 P
did you ever hear such railing? 4.03. 46 P
but kindness, nobler ever than revenge, | and 4.03.128
i will marry you, if ever i marry woman, and 5.02.113 P
i will satisfy you, if ever i satisfied man, and 5.02.115 P
the first time that i ever saw him | methought 5.04. 28
these, | which never were, nor no man ever saw. SHR in.2. 96
rehears'd, | that ever katherina will be woo'd. 1.02.125
you, | did you yet ever see baptista's daughter? 1.02.250
was ever gentleman thus griev'd as i? 2.01. 37
did ever dian so become a grove | as kate this 2.01.258
was ever match clapp'd up so suddenly? 2.01.325
was ever man so beaten? 4.01. 2 P
was ever man so ray'd? 4.01. 3 P
was ever man so weary? 4.01. 3 P
peter, didst ever see the like? 4.01.179 P
forswear bianca and her love for ever. 4.02. 26
first, tell me, have you ever been at pisa? 4.02. 93
and will repute you ever | the patron of my life 4.02.113
master, if ever i said loose-bodied gown, sew me 4.03.135 P
but bid bianca farewell for ever and a day. 4.04. 97
i have brought him up ever since he was three 5.01. 82 P
by being ever kept, it is ever lost. AWW 1.01.131 P
by being ever kept, it is ever lost. 1.01.132 P
who ever strove | to show her merit, that did 1.01.226
wilt thou ever be a foul-mouth'd and calumnious 1.03. 56 P
if ever we are nature's, these are ours. 1.03.129
did ever in so true a flame of liking | wish 1.03.211
thus he his special nothing ever prologues. 2.01. 92
i see things may serve long, but not serve ever. 2.02. 59 P
let the white death sit on thy cheek for ever, 2.03. 71
your bed | find fairer fortune, if you ever wed! 2.03. 92
i give | me and my service, ever whilst i live, 2.03.103
disdain | rather corrupt me ever! 2.03.116
or i will throw thee from my care for ever 2.03.162
if ever thou be'st bound in thy scarf and beaten 2.03.225 P
undone, and forfeited to cares for ever! 2.03.267
and shall do so ever, though i took him at 's 2.05. 41 P
and ever shall | with true observance seek to 2.05. 73
madam, my lord is gone, for ever gone. 3.02. 46
when you find him out, you have him ever after. 3.06. 93 P
and will for ever | do thee all rights of 4.02. 16
say thou art mine, and ever | my love, as it 4.02. 36
ever a friend whose thoughts more truly labor 4.04. 17
gentlewoman that ever nature had praise for 4.05. 9 P
the master i speak of ever keeps a good fire. 4.05. 48 P
if her fortunes ever stood | necessitied to help 5.03. 84
if you shall prove | this ring was ever hers, 5.03.125
by jove, if ever i knew man, 'twas you. 5.03.287
i'll love her dearly, ever, ever dearly. 5.03.316
i'll love her dearly, ever, ever dearly. 5.03.316
decays the wise, doth ever make the better fool. TN 1.05. 76 P
if ever thou shalt love, | in the sweet pangs of 2.04. 15
and wish'd to see thee ever cross-garter'd: 2.05.154 P
servingman than ever she bestow'd upon me. 3.02. 6 P
sav'd by believing rightly can ever believe such 3.02. 72 P
answer make but thanks, | and thanks, and ever. 3.03. 15
so soon as ever thou seest him, draw, and, as 3.04.177 P
more approbation than ever proof itself would 3.04.181 P
will it be ever thus? 4.01. 47
i were the first that ever dissembled in such a 4.02. 5 P
fool, as ever thou wilt deserve well at my hand, 4.02. 80 P
thee more than ever the bearing of letter did. 4.02.111 P
and, having sworn truth, ever will be true. 4.03. 33
greatest promise that ever came into my note. WT 1.01. 36 P
then didst thou utter, | "i am yours for ever." 1.02.105
the one for ever earn'd a royal husband; 1.02.107
my lord, | if ever i were willful-negligent, 1.02.255
if ever fearful | to do a thing, where i the 1.02.258
he is dishonor'd by a man which ever | profess'd 1.02.455
(which was as gross as ever touch'd conjecture, 2.01.176
for ever | unvenerable be thy hands, if thou 2.03. 77
is rotten | as ever oak or stone was sound. 2.03. 91
for the babe | is counted lost for ever, perdita 3.03. 33
i am gone for ever. 3.03. 58
if ever you have spent time worse ere now; 4.01. 30
o that ever i was born! 4.03. 50 P
you speak, sweet, | i'ld have you do it ever; 4.04.137
sea, that you might ever do | nothing but that; 4.04.141
this is the prettiest low-born lass that ever 4.04.156
i the fairest youth | that ever made eye swerve, 4.04.374
force and knowledge | more than was ever man's, 4.04.375
if i may ever know thou dost but sigh | that 4.04.427
unworthy thee — if ever, henceforth, thou 4.04.437
as you have ever been my father's honor'd friend 4.04.493
o that ever i | had squar'd me to thy counsel! 5.01. 51
if ever truth were pregnant by circumstance. 5.02. 30 P
thrice a day, ever since the death of hermione, 5.02.106 P
first gentleman-like tears that ever we shed. 5.02.145 P
excels what ever yet you look'd upon | or hand 5.03. 16
to see the life as lively mock'd as ever | still 5.03. 19
scarce any joy | did ever so long live; 5.03. 52
what fine chisel | could ever yet cut breath? 5.03. 79
son, have i not ever said | how that ambitious JN 1.01. 31
my bed was ever to thy son as true | as thine 2.01.124
day | ever in france shall be kept festival. 3.01. 76
thou ever strong upon the stronger side! 3.01.117
i will pray | (if ever i remember to be holy) 3.03. 15
you, | what ever torment you do put me to. 4.01. 83
that ever wall-ey'd wrath or staring rage 4.03. 49
thread | that ever spider twisted from her womb 4.03.128
by all the blood that ever fury breath'd, | the 5.02.127
where ever englishman durst set his foot. R2 1.01. 66
verge | that ever was surveyed by english eye, 1.01. 94
no, bullingbrook, if ever i were traitor, | my 1.03.201
have ever made me sour my patient cheek, | or 2.01.169

we, | because we ever have been near the king. 2.02.134
farewell at once, for once, for all, and ever. 2.02.148
prove | that ever fell upon this cursed earth. 4.01.147
to effect | what ever i shall happen to devise. 4.01.330
for ever may my knees grow to the earth, | my 5.03. 30
for ever will i walk upon my knees, | and never 5.03. 93
for though mine enemy thou hast ever been, 5.06. 28
did i ever call for thee to pay thy part? 1H4 1.02. 51 P
most omnipotent villain that ever cried "stand!" 1.02.109 P
to be as true-bred cowards as ever turn'd back; 1.02.184 P
which ever and anon | he gave his nose and 1.03. 38
veriest varlet that ever chew'd with a tooth. 2.02. 24 P
o, we are undone, both we and ours for ever! 2.02. 87 P
laughter for a month, and a good jest for ever. 2.02. 96 P
our plot is a good plot as ever was laid, our 2.03. 17 P
that ever this fellow should have fewer words 2.04. 98 P
still run and roar'd, as ever i heard bull-calf. 2.04.260 P
and ever since thou hast blush'd extempore. 2.04.316 P
one of these harlotry players as ever i see! 2.04.396 P
hand, | as ever off'red foul play in a state. 3.02.169
making you ever better than his praise | by 5.02. 58
that ever said i heark'ned for your death. 5.04. 52
this is the strangest tale that ever i heard. 5.04.154
thus ever did rebellion find rebuke. 5.05. 1
his tongue | sounds ever after as a sullen bell, 2H4 1.01.102
as if he had writ man ever since his father was 1.02. 27 P
well, i cannot last ever, but it was alway yet 1.02.214 P
and whether i shall ever see thee again or no, 2.04. 67 P
prove that ever i dress myself handsome till thy 2.04.279 P
good phrases are surely, and ever were, very 3.02. 70 P
when ever yet was your appeal denied? 4.01. 88
against ill chances men are ever merry, | but 4.02. 81
which ever in the haunch of winter sings | the 4.04. 92
of it, | let god for ever keep it from my head, 4.05.174
very latest counsel | that ever i shall breathe. 4.05.183
so merrily, | and ever among so merrily." 5.03. 22
sum | than ever at one time the clergy yet | did H5 1.01. 80
as 'tis ever common | that men are merriest when 1.02.271
as ever you come of women, come in quickly to 2.01.117 P
treason and murther ever kept together, | as two 2.02.105
bosom, if ever man went to arthur's bosom. 2.03. 10 P
then, if ever thou dar'st acknowledge it, i will 4.01.209 P
if ever thou come to me and say, after to-morrow 4.01.213 P
if ever i live to see it, i will challenge it. 4.01.217 P
if alive and ever dare to challenge this glove, 4.07.126 P
as ever his black shoe trod upon god's ground 4.07.141 P
was ever known so great and little loss, | on 4.08.110
omit | all the occurrences, what ever chanc'd, 5.pr. 40
if ever thou beest mine, kate, as i have a 5.02.203 P
who ever saw the like? 1H6 1.02. 22
i'll rear | than rhodope's /of memphis ever was. 1.06. 22
hate, | will i for ever and my faction wear, 2.04.109
priest | should ever get that privilege of me. 3.01.121
hearts, | because i ever found them as myself. 3.02. 98
for ever should they be expuls'd from france, 3.03. 25
there is no hope that ever i will stay, | if the 4.05. 30
prayers | shall suffolk ever have of margaret. 5.03.174
the happiest gift that ever marquess gave, | the 2H6 1.01. 15
the fairest queen that ever king receiv'd. 1.01. 16
my lord, hang me if ever i spake the words. 1.03.197 P
pay, | nor ever had one penny bribe from france. 3.01.109
didst ever hear a man so penitent? 3.02. 4
if ever lady wrong'd her lord so much, | thy 3.02.211
cask | that ever did contain a thing of worth. 3.02.410
was ever feather so lightly blown to and fro as 4.08. 55 P
was ever king that joy'd an earthly throne | and 4.09. 1
by the best blood that ever was broach'd, and 4.10. 37 P
the most complete champion that ever i heard! 4.10. 56 P
the crown to thee and to thine heirs for ever, 3H6 1.01.195
hear | that things ill got had ever bad success? 2.02. 46
was ever son so ru'd a father's death? 2.05.109
was ever father so bemoan'd his son? 2.05.110
was ever king so griev'd for subjects' woe? 2.05.111
can oxford, that did ever fence the right, | now 3.03. 98
but if you ever chance to have a child, | look 5.05. 65
shall rue the hour that ever thou wast born. 5.06. 43
if ever he have child, abortive be it, R3 1.02. 21
if ever he have wife, let her be made | more 1.02. 26
thou dost confirm his happiness for ever. 1.02.208
was ever woman in this humor woo'd? 1.02.227
was ever woman in this humor won? 1.02.228
so do i ever — being well advis'd; 1.03.317
when ever buckingham doth turn his hate | upon 2.01. 32
if ever any grudge were lodg'd between us; 2.01. 66
thee | that ever wretched age hath look'd upon. 3.04.105
covert'st shelt'red traitor | that ever liv'd. 3.05. 34
still live they, and for ever let them last! 4.02. 7
that ever yet this land was guilty of. 4.03. 3
name | that ever grac'd me with thy company? 4.04.175
than ever you /or yours by me were harm'd! 4.04.239
but how long shall that title "ever" last? 4.04.350
dreams | that ever ent'red in a drowsy head 5.03.228
one that hath ever been god's enemy. 5.03.252
and ever since a fresh admirer | of what i saw H8 1.01. 3
fear | to cope malicious censurers, which ever, 1.02. 78
ten times more ugly | than ever they were fair. 1.02.118
the fairest hand i ever touch'd! 1.04. 75
if ever any malice in your heart | were hid 2.01. 80
ever belov'd and loving may his rule be; 2.01. 92
one stroke has taken | for ever from the world. 2.01.118
but to be commanded | for ever by your grace, 2.02.119
she | so good a lady that no tongue could ever 2.03. 3
heart, which ever yet | affected eminence, 2.03. 28
this burthen, 'tis too weak | ever to get a boy. 2.03. 44
ever in fear to kindle your dislike, | yea, 2.04. 25
was the hour | i ever contradicted your desire? 2.04. 28
yourself, who ever yet | have stood to charity, 2.04. 85
nor ever more | upon this business my appearance 2.04.132
whether ever i | did broach this business to 2.04.149
or ever | have to you, but with thanks to god 2.04.152
you ever | have wish'd the sleeping of this 2.04.163
to his music plants and flowers | ever sprung, 3.01. 7
the willing'st sin i ever yet committed | may be 3.01. 49
was put into you, ever casts | such doubts, as 3.01.170
matter against him that for ever mars | the 3.02. 21
ever god bless your highness! 3.02.136
and ever may your highness yoke together | (as i 3.02.150
have ever come too short of my desires, | yet 3.02.170
which ever has and ever shall be growing, | till 3.02.178
which ever has and ever shall be growing, | till 3.02.178
that for your highness' good i ever labor'd 3.02.191
truth | toward the king, my ever royal master, 3.02.273
of a rude stream that must for ever hide me. 3.02.364
in that one woman i have lost for ever. 3.02.409
no sun shall ever usher forth mine honors, | or 3.02.410
pray'rs | for ever and for ever shall be yours. 3.02.427
pray'rs | for ever and for ever shall be yours. 3.02.427
they are ever forward | in celebration of this 4.01. 9
thou hast the sweetest face i ever look'd on. 4.01. 43
is the goodliest woman | that ever lay by man — 4.01. 70
stomach, ever ranking | himself with princes; 4.02. 34
and be ever double | both in his words and 4.02. 38
ever witness for him | those twins of learning 4.02. 57
that christendom shall ever speak his virtue. 4.02. 63
so may he ever do, and ever flourish, | when i 4.02.125
so may he ever do, and ever flourish, | when i 4.02.125
and not ever | the justice and the truth o' th' 5.01.129
the god of heaven | both now and ever bless her! 5.01.165
and the end | was ever to do well; 5.02. 72
you were ever good at sudden commendations, 5.02.157
a shrewd turn, and he's your friend for ever." 5.02.211
long, and ever happy, to the high and mighty 5.04. 2 P
lady | heaven ever laid up to make parents happy 5.04. 7
where ever the bright sun of heaven shall shine, 5.04. 50
yesternight fairer than ever i saw her look, or TRO 1.01. 32 P
and shame whereof hath ever since kept hector 1.02. 35 P
ay, if i ever saw him before and knew him. 1.02. 65 P
that she was never yet that ever knew | love got 1.02.290
truer, | than ever greek did couple in his arms, 1.03.276
consent | that ever hector and achilles meet, 1.03.362
with the first glance that ever — pardon me — 3.02.118
if ever you prove false one to another, since i 3.02.199 P
writes me that man, how dearly ever parted, 3.03. 96
the welcome ever smiles, | and farewell goes out 3.03.168
the man's undone for ever, for if hector break 3.03.258 P
crown of falsehood, | if ever she leave troilus! 4.02.101
of more strong link asunder than can ever COR 1.01. 71
we have ever your good word. 1.01.166
was ever man so proud as is this martius? 1.01.252
what ever have been thought /on in this state 1.02. 4
'tis sworn between us we shall ever strike 1.02. 35
bear | th' addition nobly ever! 1.09. 66
ever right. 2.01.191
menenius, ever, ever. 2.01.192
menenius, ever, ever. 2.01.192
and their blaze | shall darken him for ever. 2.01.259
ever spake against | your liberties and the 2.03.179
such as cannot rule, | nor ever will be ruled. 3.01. 41
a graver bench | than ever frown'd in greece. 3.01.107
does forget that ever | he heard the name of 3.01.258
he hath been us'd | ever to conquer, and to have 3.03. 26
which doth ever cool | i' th' absence of the 4.01. 43
moe noble blows than ever thou wise words, | and 4.02. 21
and to pluck from them their tribunes for ever. 4.03. 24 P
a strange one as ever i look'd on. 4.05. 20 P
since i have ever followed thee with hate, 4.05. 98
thy love | as ever in ambitious strength i did 4.05.112
he was ever too hard for him; 4.05.184 P
i ever said we were i' th' wrong when we 4.06.154 P
which out of daily fortune ever taints | the 4.07. 38
for i have ever verified my friends | (of whom 5.02. 17
'tis the first time that ever | i was forc'd to 5.06.104
as the most noble corse that ever herald | did 5.06.143
if ever bassianus, caesar's son, | were gracious TIT 1.01. 10
and if thy sons were ever dear to thee, | o, 1.01.107
whose friend in justice thou hast ever been, 1.01.180
if ever tamora | were gracious in those princely 1.01.428
terms | that ever ear did hear to such effect, 2.03.111
that ever eye with sight made heart lament! 2.03.205
o tamora, was ever heard the like? 2.03.276
expecting ever when some envious surge | will in 3.01. 96
did ever raven sing so like a lark | that gives 3.01.158
that ever death should let life bear his name, 3.01.248
the woefull'st man that ever liv'd in rome. 3.01.289
your lordships, /that, when ever you have need, 4.02. 15
by this our mother is for ever sham'd. 4.02.112
was ever seen | an emperor in rome thus 4.04. 1
revenge, to do | as much as ever coriolanus did. 4.04. 68
too like the sire for ever being good. 5.01. 50
mother, | as sure a card as ever won the set; 5.01.100
of me, | as true a dog as ever fought at head. 5.01.102
ten thousand worse than ever yet i did | would i 5.03.187
the weaker vessels, are ever thrust to the wall; ROM 1.01. 16 P
if ever you disturb our streets again | your 1.01. 96
who ever would have thought it? 3.02. 42
that ever i should live to see thee dead! 3.02. 63
did ever dragon keep so fair a cave? 3.02. 74
was ever book containing such vile matter | so 3.02. 83
o, think'st thou we shall ever meet again? 3.05. 51
i cannot choose but ever weep the friend. 3.05. 77
henceforward i am ever rul'd by you. 4.02. 22
o, weraday, that ever i was born! 4.05. 15
day, most woeful day | that ever, ever, i did 4.05. 51
most woeful day | that ever, ever, i did yet 4.05. 51
your lordship ever binds him. TIM 1.01.104
mind he carries | that ever govern'd man. 1.01.281
i gave it freely ever, and there's none | can 1.02. 10
my heart is ever at your service, my lord. 1.02. 75 P
we should think ourselves for ever perfect. 1.02. 87 P
as good a trick as ever hangman serv'd thief. 2.02. 94 P
he's ever sending. 3.02. 32 P
have i been ever free, and must my house | be my 3.04. 80
we banish thee for ever. 3.05. 97
ever at the best, hearing well of your lordship. 3.06. 27 P
where ever we shall meet, for timon's sake 4.02. 24
i'll ever serve his mind with my best will; 4.02. 49
perfumes, and have forgot | that ever timon was. 4.03.208
what man didst thou ever know unthrift that was 4.03.311 P
thou talk'st of, didst thou ever know belov'd? 4.03.314 P
thou ever young, fresh, lov'd, and delicate 4.03.384
grant i may ever love, and rather woo | those 4.03.467
but tell me true | (for i must ever doubt, 4.03.507
performance is ever the duller for his act, 5.01. 24
of their love, | ever to read them thine. 5.01.155
as proper men as ever trod upon neat's-leather JC 1.01. 25 P
that noble minds keep ever with their likes; 1.02.311
who ever knew the heavens menace so? 1.03. 44
man | that ever lived in the tide of times. 3.01.257
remember | the first time ever caesar put it on; 3.02.171
and to your heirs for ever — common pleasures, 3.02.250
ever note, lucilius, | when love begins to 4.02. 19
him better | than ever thou lovedst cassius. 4.03.107
roman, | that ever brutus will go bound to rome; 5.01.111
for ever, and for ever, farewell, cassius! 5.01.116
for ever, and for ever, farewell, cassius! 5.01.116
for ever, and for ever, farewell, brutus! 5.01.119
for ever, and for ever, farewell, brutus! 5.01.119
my sight was ever thick; 5.03. 21
it is impossible that ever rome | should breed 5.03.100
enemy | shall ever take alive the noble brutus; 5.04. 22
to alter favor ever is to fear. MAC 1.05. 72
your servants ever | have theirs, themselves, 1.06. 25
with a most indissoluble tie | for ever knit. 3.01. 18
you to the grave, | and beggar'd yours for ever? 3.01. 90
much, shall banquo's issue ever | reign in this 4.01.102
may be rightly just, | what ever i shall think. 4.03. 31
more suffer, and more sundry ways than ever, 4.03. 48
my ever gentle cousin, welcome hither. 4.03.161
let not your ears despise my tongue for ever, 4.03.201
the heaviest sound | that ever yet they heard. 4.03.203
this push | will cheer me ever, or /disseat me 5.03. 21
the first that ever scotland | in such an honor 5.09. 29
some say that ever 'gainst that season comes HAM 1.01.158
do not for ever with thy vailed lids | seek for 1.02. 70
the same, my lord, and your poor servant ever. 1.02.162
foe in heaven | or ever i had seen that day, 1.02.183
if thou didst ever thy dear father love — 1.05. 23
spite, | that ever i was born to set it right! 1.05.189
having ever seen in the prenominate crimes | the 2.01. 43
if, once i be a widow, ever i be a wife! 3.02.223
let not ever | the soul of nero enter this firm 3.02.393
one part wisdom | and ever three parts coward — 4.04. 43
'a was the first that ever bore arms. 5.01. 33 P
i lov'd you ever. 5.01.290
if thou didst ever hold me in thy heart, 5.02.346
to thee and thine hereditary ever | remain this LR 1.01. 79
my heart and me | hold thee from this for ever. 1.01.116
lear, | whom i have ever honor'd as my king, 1.01.140
nor shall ever see | that face of hers again. 1.01.263
yet he hath ever but slenderly known himself. 1.01.293 P
you should enjoy half his revenue for ever, and 1.02. 53 P
thou dost think | i have cast off for ever. 1.04.310
and most poorest shape | that ever penury, in 2.03. 8
i have serv'd you ever since i was a child; 3.07. 73
if ever thou wilt thrive, bury my body, | and 4.06.247
if ever i return to you again, | i'll bring you 5.02. 3
instant way | where they shall rest for ever. 5.03.151
heart, if ever i | did hate thee or thy father. 5.03.178
she's gone for ever! 5.03.260
does redeem all sorrows | that ever i have felt. 5.03.268
i might have sav'd her, now she's gone for ever! 5.03.271
her voice was ever soft, | gentle, and low, an 5.03.273
if ever i did dream of such a matter, | abhor me OTH 1.01. 5
(how ever this may gall him with some check) 1.01.148
if it prove lawful prize, he's made for ever. 1.02. 51
would ever have, t' incur a general mock, | run 1.02. 69
which ever as she could with haste dispatch, 1.03.148
thus do i ever make my fool my purse; 1.03.383
she that was ever fair, and never proud, | had 2.01.148
she was a wight (if ever such /wight were) — 2.01.158
you'll be asham'd for ever. 2.03.163
what wound did ever heal but by degrees? 2.03.371
what ever shall become of michael cassio, | he's 3.03. 8
to him that ever fears he shall be poor. 3.03.174
i am bound to thee for ever. 3.03.213
(for he conjur'd her she should ever keep it) 3.03.294
shall ever medicine thee to that sweet sleep 3.03.332
o now, for ever | farewell the tranquil mind! 3.03.347
if ever mortal eyes do see them bolster | more 3.03.399
be in me remorse, | what bloody business ever. 3.03.469
i am your own for ever. 3.03.480
they are not ever jealious for the cause, | but 3.04.160
nor ever heard — nor ever did suspect. 4.02. 2
nor ever heard — nor ever did suspect. 4.02. 2
or that i do not yet, and ever did, | and ever 4.02.156
and ever will (though he do shake me off | to 4.02.157
build on thee a better opinion than ever before. 4.02.206 P
i have greater reason to believe now than ever 4.02.213 P
i am maim'd for ever. help ho! murther, murther! 5.01. 27
but did you ever tell him she was false? 5.02.178
did i, charmian, | ever love caesar so? ANT 1.05. 67
you, whom no brother | did ever love so dearly. 2.02.150
and his quails ever | beat mine, inhoop'd, at 2.03. 38
caesar and he are greater friends than ever. 2.05. 48
let him for ever go — let him not, charmian — 2.05.115
then is caesar and he for ever knit together. 2.06.115 P
i have ever held my cap off to thy fortunes. 2.07. 57
caesar and antony have ever won | more in their 3.01. 16
that ever i should call thee castaway! 3.06. 40
best of comfort, | and ever welcome to us. 3.06. 90
pray you | be ever known to patience. 3.06. 98
the world, that i | have lost my way for ever. 3.11. 4
you have been a boggler ever, | but when we in 3.13.110
one ever near thee. 4.05. 7
of the full-fortun'd caesar ever shall | be 4.15. 24
wishers were ever fools — o, come, come, come, 4.15. 37
but if there be, nor ever were one such, | it's 5.02. 96
which i will be ever to pay and yet pay still. CYM 1.04. 37 P
a lady to the worthiest sir that ever | country 1.06.160
was there ever man had such luck? 2.01. 1 P
a voucher, | stronger than ever law could make; 2.02. 40
loss, the most coldest that ever turn'd up ace. 2.03. 2 P
garment | that ever hath but clipt his body, is 2.03.134
to ears and tongues | be theme and hearing ever) 3.01. 4
and, to kill the marvel, | shall be so ever. 3.01. 11
with shame | (the first that ever touch'd him) 3.01. 25
hardness ever | of hardiness is mother. 3.06. 21
and shalt be ever. 4.02. 46
who ever yet could sound thy bottom? 4.02.204
did see man die, scarce ever look'd on blood, 4.04. 36
to pick that bolt, | then free for ever! 5.04. 11
than a band of clotens | had ever scar for. 5.05.305
thou art my brother, so we'll hold thee ever. 5.05.399
the truest princess | that ever swore her faith. 5.05.417

as from thence | sorrow were ever ras'd, and PER 1.01. 17
and if that ever my low fortunes better, | i'll 2.01.142
when peers thus knit, a kingdom ever stands. 2.04. 58
to this world | that ever was prince's child. 3.01. 31
i hold it ever | virtue and cunning were 3.02. 26
'tis known, i ever | have studied physic; 3.02. 31
as ever hit my nostril. 3.02. 62
thou hast a heart | that ever cracks for woe! 3.02. 77
our wonder, and sets up | your fame for ever. 3.02. 97
in our story, she | would ever with marina be: 4.ch. 20
the fates, | to foster it, not ever to preserve. 4.03. 15
proceeding | who ever but his approbation added, 4.03. 26
did you ever hear the like? 4.05. 1 P
did you ever dream of such a thing? 4.05. 5 P
but i am out of the road of rutting for ever. 4.05. 9 P
marry, hang her up for ever! 4.06.137 P
enough, | though doubts did ever sleep. 5.01.202
more power on him | than ever he had on thee, TNK 1.01. 88
thing, nor be so hardy | ever to take a husband. 1.01.205
spinsters, we | should hold you here for ever. 1.03. 24
both heaven and earth | friend thee for ever! 1.04. 2
we are prisoners | i fear for ever, cousin. 2.02. 4
wife, ever begetting | new births of love; 2.02. 80
possible our friendship | should ever leave us. 2.02.115
lady, | if ever thou hast felt what sorrow was, 2.02.276
place | where i may ever dwell in sight of her? 2.03. 82
it so) as ever | these eyes yet look'd on. 2.04. 10
that ever dream'd, or vow'd her maidenhead | to 2.04. 13
not, | let me find that my father ever hated — 2.05. 58
by him, like a shadow, | i'll ever dwell. 2.06. 35
thou most perfidious | that ever gently look'd! 3.01. 36
falsest cousin | that ever blood made kin! 3.01. 38
for, ere the sun set, both shall sleep for ever. 3.06.184
all the chaste nights i have ever pleas'd you — 3.06.200
and all the longing maids that ever lov'd, | if 3.06.246
where ever they shall travel, ever strangers 3.06.255
shall travel, ever strangers | to one another. 3.06.255
eyes, and as noble | as ever fame yet spoke of. 3.06.277
ye are a good man | and ever bring good news. 4.01. 25
and between | ever was "palamon, fair palamon," 4.01. 81
pray did you ever hear | of one young palamon? 4.01.116
as ever you heard, but say nothing. 4.01.135
as if she ever meant to /crown his valor. 4.02.109
too, as ever he may go upon 's legs, for in the 4.03. 14 P
cries, "o, that ever i did it behind the arras!" 4.03. 54 P
understand you she ever affected any man ere she 4.03. 62 P
darkness, which ever was | the dam of horror, 5.03. 22
'twas ever likely: 5.03. 68
he is a good one | as ever strook at head. 5.03.109
you'll see't done now for ever. 5.04. 25
the simplest things that ever stood in such a STM II.C 21
forgiven | is safer wars than ever you can make, II.C 112
would they not wish the feast might ever last, VEN 447
that ever yet betoken'd | wrack to the seaman, 453
of bristly pikes that ever threat his foes, 620
nor sun nor wind will ever strive to kiss you: 1082
yet ever to obtain his will resolving, | though LUC 129
if ever man were mov'd with woman's moans, | be 587
tears | that ever modest eyes with sorrow shed. 683
and ever let his unrecalling crime | have time 993
next, vouchsafe t' afford | (if ever, love, thy 1306
it easeth some, though none it ever cured, | to 1581
and ever since, as pitying lucrece' woes, 1747
so beauty blemish'd once, for ever lost, | in PP 13.11
love, whose month was ever may, | spied a 16. 2
my love shall in my verse ever live young. SON 19.14
fire, | are both with thee, where ever i abide; 45. 2
against that time (if ever that time come) 49. 1
to play the watchman ever for thy sake. 61.12
for slander's mark was ever yet the fair; 70. 2
why write i still all one, ever the same, | and 76. 5
then hate me when thou wilt, if ever, now, | now 90. 1
that in thy face sweet love should ever dwell; 93.10
be | to one, of one, still such, and ever so. 105. 4
proved, | i never writ, nor no man ever loved. 116.14
this i do vow and this shall ever be: 123.13
come, | chiding that tongue that, ever sweet, 145. 6
who ever shunn'd by precedent | the destin'd ill LC 155
knew vows were ever brokers to defiling, 173
that's to ye sworn to none was ever said, | for 180
teen, | or any of my leisures ever charmed. 193

EVER–ANGRY 1 FR 0.0001 REL FR 1 V 0 P
and penetrate the breasts | of ever–angry bears. TMP 1.02.289

EVER–BLINDED 1 FR 0.0001 REL FR 1 V 0 P
and in their songs curse ever–blinded fortune TNK 2.02. 38

EVER–BURNING 2 FR 0.0002 REL FR 2 V 0 P
sicily, | and be my heart an ever–burning hell! TIT 3.01.242
witness, you ever–burning lights above, | you OTH 3.03.463

EVER–DURING 1 FR 0.0001 REL FR 1 V 0 P
whose crime will bear an ever–during blame. LUC 224

EVER–ESTEEMED 1 FR 0.0001 REL FR 0 V 1 P
him i (as my ever–esteemed duty pricks me on) LLL 1.01.265 P

EVER–FIXED 2 FR 0.0002 REL FR 2 V 0 P
and quench the guards of th' ever–fixed pole; OTH 2.01. 15
o no, it is an ever–fixed mark | that looks on SON 116. 5

EVER–GENTLE 1 FR 0.0001 REL FR 1 V 0 P
you ever–gentle gods, take my breath from me, LR 4.06.217

EVER–HARMLESS 1 FR 0.0001 REL FR 1 V 0 P
with your sedg'd crowns and ever–harmless looks, TMP 4.01.129

EVERLASTING 22 FR 0.0024 REL FR 17 V 5 P
to put me into everlasting liberty if i tell you WIV 3.03. 31 P
where you shall be an everlasting leiger; MM 3.01. 58
a devil in an everlasting garment hath him; ERR 4.02. 33
be condemn'd into everlasting redemption for ADO 4.02. 56 P
and me | for everlasting bond of fellowship — MND 1.01. 85
hath incurr'd the everlasting displeasure of the AWW 4.03. 8 P
souls | that to their everlasting residence, JN 2.01.284
swore to you | dear amity and everlasting love. 5.04. 20
perpetual triumph, an everlasting bonfire light! 1H4 3.03. 41 P
reproach and everlasting shame | sits mocking in H5 4.05. 4
the treasury of everlasting joy. 2H6 2.01. 18
set ope thy everlasting gates | to entertain my 4.09. 13
by all the everlasting gods, i'll go! TRO 5.03. 5
pronounc'd | my everlasting doom of banishment. TIT 3.01. 51
a devil, | to live and burn in everlasting fire, 5.01.148
will ne'er wear out the everlasting flint; ROM 2.06. 17
o, here | will i set up my everlasting rest, 5.03.110
timon hath made his everlasting mansion | upon TIM 5.01.215
therefore our everlasting farewell take: JC 5.01.115
go the primrose way to th' everlasting bonfire. MAC 2.03. 19 P
or that the everlasting had not fix'd | his HAM 1.02.131
consent | to tarquin's everlasting banishment. LUC 1855

EVERLASTINGLY 4 FR 0.0004 REL FR 4 V 0 P
flow'r | and make rough winter everlastingly. TGV 2.04.163
services | and true subjection everlastingly. JN 5.07.105
i'll hate him everlastingly | that bids me be of R2 3.02.207
say i will love her everlastingly. R3 4.04.349

EVER–LIVING 1 FR 0.0001 REL FR 1 V 0 P
conqueror, | that ever–living man of memory, 1H6 4.03. 51

EVERMORE 26 FR 0.0029 REL FR 22 V 4 P
so shall i evermore be bound to thee; WIV 4.06. 54
crest, | with loyal blazon, evermore be blest! 5.05. 64
he hath evermore had the liberty of the prison; MM 4.02.147 P
like my lady's eldest son, evermore tattling. ADO 2.01. 9 P
so study evermore is overshot: LLL 1.01.142
i evermore did love you, hermia, | did ever keep MND 3.02.307
for it, | and will for evermore be true to it. 4.01.176
some that will evermore peep through their eyes, MV 1.01. 52
above, | in love and service to you evermore. 4.01.414
evermore cross'd and cross'd, nothing but SHR 4.05. 10
whom i am now in ward, evermore in subjection. AWW 1.01. 5 P
we make, | to rest without a spot for evermore. JN 5.07.107
evermore thank's the exchequer of the poor, R2 2.03. 65
and after summer evermore succeeds | barren 2H6 2.04. 2
that evermore they pointed | to th' good of your H8 3.02.172
paris and i kiss evermore for him. TRO 4.05. 34
now help, or woe betide thee evermore! TIT 4.02. 56
evermore weeping for your cousin's death? ROM 3.05. 69
evermore show'ring? 3.05.130
thine evermore, most dear lady, whilst this HAM 2.02.123 P
'tis evermore /the prologue to his sleep. OTH 2.03.129
that she reserves it evermore about her | to 3.03.295
so, on your patience evermore attending, | new PER 5.03.101
i may not evermore acknowledge thee, | lest my SON 36. 9
thy praise | to tie up envy, evermore enlarg'd: 70.12
care, | and frantic mad with evermore unrest; 147.10

EVER–PRESERV'D 1 FR 0.0001 REL FR 0 V 1 P
by the obligation of our ever–preserv'd love, HAM 2.02.285 P

EVER–RUNNING 1 FR 0.0001 REL FR 1 V 0 P
and follows so the ever–running year | with H5 4.01.276

EVER–VALIANT 1 FR 0.0001 REL FR 1 V 0 P
that ever–valiant and approved scot, | at 1H4 1.01. 54

/EVERY 2 FR 0.0002 REL FR 2 V 0 P
/that /every /day /under /his /household /roof R2 4.01.282
sith /every action that hath gone before, TRO 1.03. 13

EVERY 599 FR 0.0677 REL FR 467 V 132 P
though every drop of water swear against it, TMP 1.01. 59
to every article. 1.02.195
now in the waist, the deck, in every cabin, | i 1.02.197
and mine, invisible | to every eyeball else. 1.02.303
every day some sailor's wife, | the masters of 2.01. 4
when every grief is entertain'd that's offer'd, 2.01. 16
here is every thing advantageous to life. 2.01. 50 P
but | for every trifle are they set upon me, 2.02. 8
i'll show thee every fertile inch o' th' island; 2.02.148
are created | of every creature's best! 3.01. 48
and these fresh nymphs encounter every one | in 4.01.137
probable) of every | these happen'd accidents; 5.01.249
every man shift for all the rest, and let no man 5.01.256 P
where | every third thought shall be my grave. 5.01.312
that every day with parle encounter me, | in thy TGV 1.02. 5
and be in eye of every exercise | worthy his 1.03. 32
giving a gentle kiss to every sedge | he 2.07. 29
that longs for every thing that he can come by. 3.01.125
fee'd every slight occasion that could but WIV 2.02.197 P
the pittie–ward, the park–ward — every way; 3.01. 6 P
old windsor way, and every way but the town way. 3.01. 6 P
if he be amaz'd, he will every way be mock'd. 5.03. 19 P
strew good luck, ouphes, on every sacred room, 5.05. 57
with juice of balm and every precious flow'r; 5.05. 62
good husband, let us every one go home, | and 5.05.241
so every scope by the immoderate use | turns to MM 1.02.127
why, every fault's condemn'd ere it be done. 2.02. 38
for every pelting, petty officer | would use his 2.02.112
news is old enough, yet it is every day's news. 3.02.230 P
every true man's apparel fits your thief. 4.02. 43 P
so every true man's apparel fits your thief. 4.02. 46 P
find | by every syllable a faithful verity. 4.03.126
every letter he hath writ hath disvouch'd other. 4.04. 1 P
for they say, every why hath a wherefore. ERR 2.02. 43 P
who, every word by all my wit being scann'd, 2.02.150
that every churl affords. 3.01. 24
if every one knows us, and we know none, | 'tis 3.02.152
ill–fac'd, worse bodied, shapeless every where; 4.02. 20
friend, | and every one doth call me by my name: 4.03. 3
he hath every month a new sworn brother. ADO 1.01. 72 P
can cross him any way, i bless myself every way. 1.03. 68 P
at him upon my knees every morning and evening. 2.01. 28 P
tell him there is measure in every thing, and so 2.01. 71 P
in every good thing. 2.01.152 P
let every eye negotiate for itself, | and trust 2.01.178
she speaks poniards, and every word stabs. 2.01.248 P
thus goes every one to the world but i, and i am 2.01.318 P
your grace is too costly to wear every day. 2.01.329 P
in every thing but in loving benedick. 2.03.162 P
so turns she every man the wrong side out, | and 3.01. 68
why, every day to–morrow. 3.01.101
every one /can master a grief but he that has it 3.02. 28 P
leonato's hero, your hero, every man's hero. 3.02.107 P
i, but god send every one their heart's desire! 3.04. 60 P
doth not every earthly thing | cry shame upon 4.01.120
lamented, pitied, and excus'd | of every hearer; 4.01.217
and every lovely organ of her life | shall come 4.01.226
two gowns, and every thing handsome about him. 4.02. 85 P
and let it answer every strain for strain, | as 5.01. 12
in every lineament, branch, shape, and form; 5.01. 14
no food, | and but one meal on every day beside, LLL 1.01. 40
lights, | that give a name to every fixed star, 1.01. 89
and every godfather can give a name. 1.01. 93
for every man with his affects is born, | not by 1.01.151
— be to me, and every man that dares not fight! 1.01.227 P
for every object that the one doth catch | the 2.01. 70
that every one her own hath garnished | with 2.01. 78
thy own wish wish i thee in every place. 2.01.178
and every jest but a word. 2.01.216
the neck of the wax, and every one give ear. 4.01. 59
on thy picture, and my heart on thy every part. 4.01. 86 P
thou shin'st in every tear that i do weep, | no 4.03. 32
courses as swift as thought in every power, 4.03.327
and gives to every power a double power, | above 4.03.328
then homeward every man attach the hand | of his 4.03.372
and every one his love–feat will advance | unto 5.02.123
for, ladies, we will every one be mask'd, | and 5.02.127
this is the flow'r that smiles on every one, 5.02.331
it is vara fine, | for every one pursents three. 5.02.488
roll | to every varied object in his glance; 5.02.765
the cuckoo then on every tree | mocks married 5.02.898
the cuckoo then on every tree | mocks married 5.02.907
my fortunes every way as fairly rank'd | (if not MND 1.01.101
so the boy love is perjur'd every where; 1.01.241
here is the scroll of every man's name, which is 1.02. 4 P
that would hang us, every mother's son. 1.02. 78 P
flood, thorough fire, | i do wander every where, 2.01. 6
here, | and hang a pearl in every cowslip's ear. 2.01. 15
hath every pelting river made so proud | that 2.01. 91
sit down, every mother's son, and rehearse your 3.01. 73 P
and so every one according to his cue. 3.01. 75 P
horse, hound, hog, bear, fire, at every turn. 3.01.111
and when she weeps, weeps every little flower, 3.01.199
thou run'st before me, shifting every place, 3.02.423
known, | that every man should take his own, 3.02.459
every region near | seem all one mutual cry. 4.01.116
parted eye, | when every thing seems double. 4.01.190
i will tell you every thing, right as it fell 4.02. 31 P
every man look o'er his part; 4.02. 37 P
gaping wide, | every one lets forth his sprite, 5.01.381
every elf and fairy sprite | hop as light as 5.01.393
consecrate, | every fairy take his gait, | and 5.01.416
and every object that might make me fear MV 1.01. 20
a stage, where every man must play a part, | and 1.01. 78
for the four winds blow in from every coast 1.01.168
he is every man in no man. 1.02. 60 P
bonnet in germany, and his behavior every where. 1.02. 76 P
you may tell every finger i have with my ribs. 2.02.106 P
to these injunctions every one doth swear | that 2.09. 17
where every something, being blent together, 3.02.181
and every word in it a gaping wound | issuing 3.02.265
how every fool can play upon the word! 3.05. 43 P
every offense is not a hate at first. 4.01. 68
if every ducat in six thousand ducats | were in 4.01. 85
were in six parts, and every part a ducat, | i 4.01. 86
when every goose is cackling, would be thought 5.01.105
say many young gentlemen flock to him every day, AYL 1.01.117 P
an envious emulator of every man's good parts, a 1.01.144 P
thus men may grow wiser every day. 1.02.137 P
sermons in stones, and good in every thing. 2.01. 17
teeth, sans eyes, sans taste, sans every thing. 2.07.166
that every eye which in this forest looks 3.02. 7
shall see thy virtue witness'd every where. 3.02. 8
orlando, carve on every tree | the fair, the 3.02. 9
tongues i'll hang on every tree, | that shall 3.02.127
the fairest boughs, | or at every sentence end, 3.02.136
read to know | the quintessence of every sprite 3.02.139
else sighing every minute and groaning every 3.02.303 P
minute and groaning every hour would detect the 3.02.303 P
are, every one fault seeming monstrous till his 3.02.354 P
and every thing about you demonstrating a 3.02.380 P
and i set him every day to woo me. 3.02.409 P
for every passion something and for no passion 3.02.413 P
me rosalind and come every day to my cote and 3.02.427 P
betray themselves to every modern censure worse 4.01. 6 P
boy that abuses every one's eyes because his own 4.01.214 P
'tis hymen peoples every town, | high wedlock 5.04.143
honor, and renown | to hymen, god of every town! 5.04.146
hearing how that every day | men of great worth 5.04.154
and after, every of this happy number, | that 5.04.172
and give them friendly welcome every one. SHR in.1. 103
to be whipt at the high cross every morning. 1.01.133 P
haste, | and every day i cannot come to woo. 2.01.115
hearing thy mildness prais'd in every town, 2.01.191
to cast thy wand'ring eyes on every stale, 3.01. 90
curtis, in every office but thine, and therefore 4.01. 35 P
and every officer his wedding garment on? 4.01. 48 P
the carpets laid, and every thing in order? 4.01. 50 P
my father is here look'd for every day, | to 4.02.117
go hop me over every kennel home, | for you 4.03. 98
sun, | that every thing i look on seemeth green; 4.05. 47
to see him every hour, to sit and draw | his AWW 1.01. 93
of every line and trick of his sweet favor. 1.01. 96
woman born but /or every blazing star or at an 1.03. 87 P
mere word's a slave | debosh'd on every tomb, on 2.03.138
on every tomb, on every grave | a lying trophy, 2.03.138
general offense, and every man should beat thee. 2.03.254 P
in every thing i wait upon his will. 2.04. 54
let every word weigh heavy of her worth, | that 3.04. 31
every night he comes | with musics of all sorts, 3.07. 39
therefore we must every one be a man of his own 4.01. 17 P
nor believe he can have every thing in him by 4.03.145 P
he has every thing that an honest man should not 4.03.259 P
that every braggart shall be found an ass. 4.03.336
there's place and means for every man alive. 4.03.339
which bow the head, and nod at every man. 4.05.106 P
which warp'd the line of every other favor, 5.03. 49
you boggle shrewdly, every feather starts you. 5.03.232
and every particle and utensil labell'd to my TN 1.05.246 P
meeting, | every wise man's son doth know." 2.03. 44
business might be every thing and their intent 2.04. 77 P
be every thing and their intent every where, for 2.04. 77 P
for every one of these letters are in my name. 2.05.141 P
for every reason excites to this, that my lady 2.05.165 P
i will do every thing that thou wilt have me. 2.05.178 P
the orb like the sun, it shines every where. 3.01. 39 P
check at every feather | that comes before his 3.01. 64
by maidhood, honor, truth, and every thing, | i 3.01.150
he does obey every point of the letter that i 3.02. 77 P
why, every thing adheres together, that no dram 3.04. 78 P
deity in my nature | of here and every where. 5.01.228
but a toy, | for the rain it raineth every day. 5.01.392
and we'll strive to please you every day. 5.01.408
in every one of these no man is free | but that WT 1.02.251
for every inch of woman in the world, | ay, 2.01.137
ay, every dram of woman's flesh is false, | if 2.01.138

myself on every post | proclaim'd a strumpet; 3.02.101
whose every word deserves | to taste of thy most 3.02.178
every 'leven wether tods, every tod yields pound 4.03. 32 P
tods, every tod yields pound and odd shilling; 4.03. 32 P
but that our feasts | in every mess have folly, 4.04. 11
of chance, and flies | of every wind that blows. 4.04.541
the which shall point you forth at every sitting 4.04.561
every lane's end, every shop, church, session, 4.04.685 P
every lane's end, every shop, church, session, 4.04.685 P
i will tell the king all, every word, yea, and 4.04.699 P
as every present time doth boast itself | above 5.01. 96
every wink of an eye some new grace will be born 5.02.110 P
your exultation | partake to every one. 5.03.132
i would give it every foot to have this face; JN 1.01.146
is the young dolphin every way complete: 2.01.433
since all and every part of what we would | doth 4.02. 38
to seek out sorrow that dwells every where. R2 1.02. 72
every tedious stride i make | will but remember 1.03.268
and every thing is left at six and seven. 2.02.122
and darts his light through every guilty hole, 3.02. 43
for every man that bullingbrook hath press'd 3.02. 58
that every stride he makes upon my land | is 3.03. 92
state, for every one doth so | against a change; 3.04. 27
so, | i speak no more than every one doth know. 3.04. 91
and by every other appointment to be ourselves. 1H4 1.02.175 P
be his dole, say i, every man to his business. 2.02. 77 P
they were bound, every man of them, or i am a 2.04.178 P
and the soul of every man | prophetically do 3.02. 37
the push | of every beardless vain comparative, 3.02. 67
for every honor sitting on his helm | would they 3.02.142
account | that he shall render every glory up, 3.02.150
they are, | if promises be kept on every hand, 3.02.168
every loop from whence | the eye of reason may 4.01. 71
one, they'll find linen enough on every hedge. 4.02. 48 P
(who is, if every owner were well plac'd, 4.03. 94
yea, every man | shall be my friend again, and 5.01.107
hence therefore, every leader to his charge, 5.01.118
ride, | the which in every language i pronounce, 2H4 in 7
every minute now | should be the father of some 1.01. 7
me, and counsel every man | the aptest way for 1.01.212
and every part about you blasted with antiquity? 1.02.184 P
an ass and a beast, to bear every knave's wrong. 2.01. 38 P
it would be every man's thought, and thou art a 2.02. 56 P
a blessed fellow to think as every man thinks. 2.02. 57 P
every man would think me an hypocrite indeed. 2.02. 59 P
knight" — every man must know that, as oft as 2.02.110 P
for in every thing the purpose must weigh with 2.02.175 P
and asking every one for sir john falstaff. 2.04.360
turnbull street, and every third word a lie, 3.02.307 P
and the examples | of every minute's instance 4.01. 83
every thing set off | that might so much as 4.01.143
that every slight and false–derived cause, | yea 4.01.188
yea, every idle, nice, and wanton reason, 4.01.189
when every thing is ended, then you come. 4.03. 27
and every thing lies level to our wish. 4.04. 7
but peace puts forth her olive every where. 4.04. 87
read, | with every course in his particular. 4.04. 90
bee, tolling from every flower | /the /virtuous 4.05. 74
now, | from every region, apes of idleness! 4.05.122
dog | shall flesh his tooth on every innocent. 4.05.132
'tis /all in every part. 5.05. 29 P
whose guiltless drops | are every one a woe, a H5 1.02. 26
therefore let every man now task his thought, 1.02.309
reigns solely in the breast of every man. 2.pr. 4
not now | but every rub is smoothed on our way. 2.02.188
line, | in every branch truly demonstrative; 2.04. 89
and bend up every spirit | to his full height. 3.01. 16
that every wretch, pining and pale before, 4.pr. 41
sun, | his liberal eye doth give to every one, 4.pr. 44
every subject's duty is the king's, but every 4.01.176 P
the king's, but every subject's soul is his own. 4.01.177 P
therefore should every soldier in the wars do as 4.01.178 P
in the wars do as every sick man in his bed, 4.01.178 P
his bed, wash every mote out of his conscience; 4.01.179 P
'tis certain, every man that dies ill, the ill 4.01.186 P
of every fool whose sense no more can feel | but 4.01.235
that every one may pare his nails with a wooden 4.04. 71 P
then every soldier kill his prisoners, | give 4.06. 37
hath caus'd every soldier to cut his prisoner's 4.07. 9 P
so are you, princes english, every one. 5.02. 11
attire, | and every thing that seems unnatural. 5.02. 62
the king hath granted every article: 5.02.332
here, there, and every where, enrag'd he slew. 1H6 1.01.124
i had | that walk'd about me every minute while; 1.04. 54
for every drop of blood was drawn from him 2.02. 8
upon the which, that every one may read, | shall 2.02. 14
our windows are broke down in every street, 3.01. 84
and if your grace mark every circumstance, | you 3.01.152
fift | was in the mouth of every sucking babe, 3.01.196
sell every man his life as dear as mine, | and 4.02. 53
you fled for vantage, every one will swear; 4.05. 28
blood, | and stablish quietness on every side. 5.01. 10
so let them have their answers every one. 5.01. 25
have i sought every country far and near, | and, 5.04. 3
let them be whipt through every market town, 2H6 2.01.155
pointing–stock | to every idle rascal follower. 2.04. 47
when every one will give the time of day, | he 3.01. 14
for every word you speak in his behalf | is 3.02.208
ay, every joint should seem to curse and ban; 3.02.319
with every several pleasure in the world; 3.02.363
away, and throughout every town | proclaim them 4.02.176
the streets, and at every corner have them kiss. 4.07.136 P
you shall have pay and every thing you wish. 5.01. 47
thou art as opposite to every good | as the 3H6 1.04.134
and every drop cries vengeance for his death 1.04.148
proclaim'd | in every borough as we pass along, 2.01.195
there is no wrong, but every thing is right. 2.02.132
size, | to disproportion me in every part, 3.02.160
of storm, | as every loyal subject ought to do. 4.07. 44
up, | for every cloud engenders not a storm. 5.03. 13
be augmented | in every county as we go along. 5.03. 23
for every word i speak, | ye see i drink the 5.04. 74
with trembling wings misdoubteth every bush; 5.06. 14
since every jack became a gentleman, | there's R3 1.03. 71
and every man that means to live well endeavors 1.04.142 P
i every day expect an embassage | from my 2.01. 3
where every horse bears his commanding rein 2.02.128
ready with every nod to tumble down | into the 3.04.100
speak and look back, and pry on every side, 3.05. 6
flag | to be the aim of every dangerous shot; 4.04. 89
and every hour more competitors | flock to the 4.04.504
every man's conscience is a thousand men, | to 5.02. 17
and every tongue brings in a several tale, | and 5.03.194
and every tale condemns me for a villain. 5.03.195
and every one did threat | to–morrow's vengeance 5.03.205
go, gentlemen, every man unto his charge. 5.03.307
a man, | daring an opposite to every danger. 5.04. 3
every man that stood | show'd like a mine. H8 1.01. 21
every man, | after the hideous storm that 1.01. 89
why, we take | from every tree, lop, bark, and 1.02. 96
to every county | where this is question'd send 1.02. 98
let there be letters writ to every shire, | of 1.02.103
him — every day | it would infect his speech — 1.02.132
who fed him every minute | with words of 1.02.149
his dews fall every where. 1.03. 57
'tis most true | these news are every where; 2.02. 38
every tongue speaks 'em, | and every true heart 2.02. 38
speaks 'em, | and every true heart weeps for't. 2.02. 39
a wise council to them | of every realm, that 2.04. 52
every thing that heard him play, | even the 3.01. 9
to taint that honor every good tongue blesses, 3.01. 55
to hear such news as this | once every hour. 3.02. 25
your brain, and every function of your power, 3.02.187
ye appear in every thing may bring my ruin! 3.02.242
in her days every man shall eat in safety 5.04. 33
thou lay'st in every gash that love hath given TRO 1.01. 62
where every flower | did, as a prophet, weep 1.02. 9
he hath the joints of every thing, but every 1.02. 27 P
but every thing so out of joint that he is a 1.02. 28 P
then every thing include itself in power, 1.03.119
so every step, | exampled by the first pace that 1.03.131
and every greek of mettle, let him know, | what 1.03.258
grumblest and railest every hour on achilles, 2.01. 32 P
every tithe soul, 'mongst many thousand dismes, 2.02. 19
knows almost every /grain /of /pluto's /gold, 3.03.197
with every joint a wound, and that to–morrow! 4.01. 30
for every false drop in her bawdy veins, | a 4.01. 70
for every scruple | of her contaminated carrion 4.01. 71
an odd man, lady? every man is odd. 4.05. 42
out | at every joint and motive of her body. 4.05. 57
of their thoughts | to every ticklish reader! 4.05. 61
the fall of every phrygian stone will cost | a 4.05.223
i'll kill thee every where, yea, o'er and o'er. 4.05.256
you may have every day enough of hector, | if 4.05.263
my soul | of every syllable that here was spoke. 5.02.117
vow, | but vows to every purpose must not hold; 5.03. 24
life every man holds dear, but the dear man 5.03. 27
there, and every where, he leaves and takes, 5.05. 26
bastard in valor, in every thing illegitimate. 5.07. 18 P
with every minute you do change a mind, | and COR 1.01.182
madam, i will obey you in every thing hereafter. 1.03.103 P
of martius' tongue | from every meaner man. 1.06. 27
every gash was an enemy's grave. 2.01.155 P
but 'tis thought of every one coriolanus will 2.02. 3 P
reproof and rebuke from every ear that heard it. 2.02. 33 P
whose every motion | was tim'd with dying cries. 2.02.109
wherein every one of us has a single honor, in 2.03. 44 P
depopulate the city, and | be every man himself? 3.01.264
let every feeble rumor shake your hearts! 3.03.125
by the good gods | i'ld with thee every foot. 4.01. 57
like a great sea–mark, standing every flaw, 5.03. 74
with voices and applause of every sort, TIT 1.01.230
princely shall be thy usage every way. 1.01.266
and every thing | in readiness for hymenaeus 1.01.324
my foes i do repute you every one, | so trouble 1.01.366
when every thing doth make a gleeful boast? 2.03. 11
the birds chaunt melody on every bush, | the 2.03. 12
yet every mother breeds not sons alike — | do 2.03.146
sung | sweet varied notes, enchanting every ear! 3.01. 86
my aunt lavinia | follows me every where, i know 4.01. 2
and blazoning our unjustice every where? 4.04. 18
be every one officious | to make this banket, 5.02.201
examine every married lineament, | and see how ROM 1.03. 83
in the pantry, and every thing in extremity. 1.03.102 P
in, | but every man betake him to his legs. 1.04. 34
care keeps his watch in every old man's eye, 2.03. 35
by too and suffer every knave to use me at his 2.04.155 P
i am so vex'd that every part about me quivers. 2.04.161 P
and every tongue that speaks | but romeo's name 3.02. 32
lives, and every cat and dog | and little mouse, 3.03. 30
dog | and little mouse, every unworthy thing, 3.03. 31
time | every good hap to you that chances here. 3.03.171
i must hear from thee every day in the hour, 3.05. 44
every one prepare | to follow this fair corse 4.05. 92
when every feather sticks in his own wing, TIM 2.01. 30
when every room | hath blaz'd with lights and 2.02.160
every man has his fault, and honesty is his. 3.01. 27 P
of the same piece | is every flatterer's sport. 3.02. 65
every man here's so. 3.06. 19 P
for every grize of fortune | is smooth'd by that 4.03. 16
for every storm that blows — i to bear this, 4.03.266
that speak'st with every tongue | to every 4.03.388
speak'st with every tongue | to every purpose! 4.03.389
our captain hath in every figure skill, | an 5.03. 7
bid every noise be still; peace yet again! JC 1.02. 14
ordinary oaths my love | to every new protester; 1.02. 74
put it by thrice, every time gentler than other; 1.02.230 P
and at every putting–by mine honest neighbors 1.02.230 P
and land, | in every place, save here in italy. 1.03. 88
so every bondman in his own hand bears | the 1.03.101
yes, every man of them; 2.01. 90
and every one doth wish | you had but that 2.01. 91
yourself | which every noble roman bears of you. 2.01. 93
betimes, | and every man hence to his idle bed; 2.01.117
when every drop of blood | that every roman 2.01.136
every drop of blood | that every roman bears, 2.01.137
and so good morrow to you every one. 2.01.228
which sometime hath his hour with every man. 2.01.251
that every like is not the same, o caesar, | the 2.02.128
they are all fire, and every one doth shine; 3.01. 64
ay, every man away. 3.01.119
and put a tongue | in every wound of caesar, 3.02.229
to every roman citizen he gives, | to every 3.02.241
to every several man, seventy–five drachmaes. 3.02.242
answer every man directly. 3.03. 9 P
then to answer every man directly and briefly, 3.03. 15 P
that every nice offense should bear his comment. 4.03. 8
you wrong me every way; 4.03. 55
the enem; increaseth every day; 4.03.216
every thing is well. 4.03.236
farewell every one. 4.03.238
alas, thou hast misconstrued every thing! 5.03. 84
octavius' tent | how every thing is chanc'd. 5.04. 32
and every one did bear | thy praises in his MAC 1.03. 98
are regist'red where every day i turn | the leaf 1.03.151
by doing every thing | safe toward your love and 1.04. 26
all our service | in every point twice done, and 1.06. 15
air, | shall blow the horrid deed in every eye, 1.07. 24
how is't with me, when every noise appalls me? 2.02. 55
let every man be master of his time | till seven 3.01. 40
the house–keeper, the hunter, every one, 3.01. 96
that every minute of his being thrusts | against 3.01.116
provide, | your charms and every thing beside. 3.05. 19
pains, | and every one shall share i' th' gains. 4.01. 40
every one that does so is a traitor, and must be 4.02. 49 P
every one. 4.02. 53 P
smacking of every sin | that has a name; 4.03. 59
than on her feet, | died every day she liv'd. 4.03.111
let every soldier hew him down a bough, | and 5.04. 4
give every man thy ear, but few thy voice, HAM 1.03. 68
into every brain | that looks so many fadoms to 1.04. 76
you, | for every man hath business and desire, 1.05.130
use every man after his desert, and who shall 2.02.529 P
where every god did seem to set his seal | to 3.04. 61
to all, | to you yourself, to us, to every one. 4.01. 15
tend, and every thing is bent | for england. 4.03. 45
for every thing is seal'd and done | that else 4.03. 56
known, | the ratifiers and props of every word, 4.05.106
every fool can tell that. 5.01.146 P
every hour | he flashes into one gross crime or LR 1.03. 3
and himself upbraids us | on every trifle. 1.03. 7
father's curse | pierce every sense about thee! 1.04.301
yes, that, on every dream, | each buzz, each 1.04.324
smooth every passion | that in the natures of 2.02. 75
with every gale and vary of their masters, 2.02. 79
fit, | though the rain it raineth every day." 3.02. 77
when every case in law is right; 3.02. 87
search every acre in the high–grown field, | and 4.04. 7
to say "ay" and "no" to every thing that i said! 4.06. 99 P
they told me i was every thing. 4.06.105 P
ay, every inch a king! 4.06.107
every one hears that, | which can distinguish 4.06.210
will be too short, | and every measure fail me. 4.07. 3
and wheeling stranger | of here and every where. OTH 1.01.137
at every house i'll call | (i may command at 1.01.180
of years, of country, credit, every thing, | to 1.03. 97
good night to every one. 1.03.288
for every minute is expectancy | of more 2.01. 41
before, behind thee, and on every hand, 2.01. 86
if after every tempest come such calms, | may 2.01.185
fleet, every man put himself into triumph; 2.02. 3 P
every inordinate cup is unbless'd, and the 2.03.307 P
i'll intermingle every thing he does | with 3.03. 25
though i am bound to every act of duty, | i am 3.03.134
so help me every spirit sanctified, | as i have 3.04.126
think every bearded fellow that's but yok'd 4.01. 66
scorns | that dwell in every region of his face, 4.01. 83
she haunts me in every place. 4.01.133 P
and put in every honest hand a whip | to lash 4.02.142
every day thou daff'st me with some device, iago 4.02.175 P
do kill the other, | every way makes my gain. 5.01. 14
but every puny whipster gets my sword. 5.02.244
whom every thing becomes — to chide, to laugh, ANT 1.01. 49
/whose every passion fully strives | to make 1.01. 50
if every of your wishes had a womb, | and 1.02. 38
a womb, | and /fertile every wish, a million. 1.02. 39
thy biddings have been done, and every hour, 1.04. 34
they ear and wound | with keels of every kind. 1.04. 50
he shall have every day a several greeting, | or 1.05. 77
mark antony is every hour in rome | expected. 2.01. 29
every time | serves for the matter that is then 2.02. 9
them up, | i'll think them every one an antony, 2.05. 14
the holding every man shall /bear as loud | as 2.07.111
land, supplying every stage | with an augmented 3.06. 54
very action speaks | in every power that moves. 3.12. 36
for every ten that they make, the devils mar 5.02.276 P
o' th' haven, | and questionedst every sail. CYM 1.03. 2
i heard than in my every action to be guided by 1.04. 45 P
and every day that comes comes to decay | a 1.05. 56
whose touch | (whose every touch) would force 1.06.101
every jack slave hath his bellyful of fighting, 2.01. 20 P
should undertake every companion that you give 2.01. 27 P
but not every man patient after the noble temper 2.03. 4 P
with every thing that pretty is, my lady sweet, 2.03. 25
mother, | and every day do honor to her grave. 3.03.105
woman, from every one | the best she hath, and 3.05. 72
every good servant does not all commands; 5.01. 6
even for whom my life | is every breath a death; 5.01. 27
'tween man and man they weigh not every stamp; 5.04. 24
every villain | be call'd posthumus leonatus, 5.05.223
the king | of every virtue gives renown to men! PER 1.01. 14
and all good men, as every prince should do; 1.01. 51
since every worth in show commends itself. 2.03. 6
who freely give to every one that come | to 2.03. 60
round, | and every one with claps can sound, 3.ch. 36
we every day | expect him here: 4.01. 33
be not a conscience to be us'd in every trade, 4.02. 12 P
well, if we had of every nation a traveller, we 4.02.113 P
thou art the damned door–keeper to every 4.06.165
to the choleric fisting of every rogue | thy ear 4.06.167
god | for every graff would send a caterpillar, 5.01. 60
and the bear's, | and vault to every thing! TNK 1.01. 54
every hour in't will | take hostage of thee for 1.01.183
where every evil | hath a good color; 1.02. 38
misery | it is to live abroad, and every where! 2.02. 98
see the sports, then every man to 's tackle! 2.03. 55
i'll bring you every needful thing. 3.01. 99
every day | they'ld fight about you; 3.06.220
business withal, fits it to every question. 4.03. 8 P
bow, | who conquers where he comes in every jar, VEN 100
and yields at last to every light impression? 566
so to so, | for love can comment upon every woe. 714
and every tongue more moving than your own, 776

that lends embracements unto every stranger. 790
shrill–tongu'd tapsters answering every call, 849
so, | that every present sorrow seemeth chief, 970
and every beauty robb'd of his effect. 1132
for every little grief to wet his eyes; 1179
fight, | and every one to rest himself betakes, LUC 125
let, | till every minute pays the hour his debt. 329
whose grim aspect sets every joint a–shaking; 452
remain | the scornful mark of every open eye; 520
for kings like gods should govern every thing. 602
"they think not but that every eye can see | the 750
shape every bush a hideous shapeless devil. 973
mad, | himself himself seek every hour to kill! 998
fly, | but eagles gaz'd upon with every eye. 1015
revealing day through every cranny spies, | and 1086
thus cavils she with every thing she sees: 1093
when every part a part of woe doth bear. 1327
lie | imagine every eye beholds their blame, 1343
her blue blood chang'd to black in every vein, 1454
for every tear he falls a troyan bleeds; 1551
blood | circles her body in on every side, | who 1739
but smile and jest at every gentle offer. PP 4.12
young, | and truth in every shepherd's tongue, 19.18
every thing did banish moan, | save the 20. 7
every one that flatters thee | is no friend in 20.29
every man will be thy friend, | whilst thou hast 20.33
thus of every grief in heart | he with thee doth 20.53
session interdict | every fowl of tyrant wing, PHT 10
the lovely gaze where every eye doth dwell SON 5. 2
beauty o'ersnow'd and bareness every where: 5. 8
when every private widow well may keep, | by 9. 7
when i consider every thing that grows | holds 15. 1
and every fair from fair sometime declines, | by 18. 7
and every fair with his fair doth rehearse, 21. 4
and though they be outstripp'd by every pen, 32. 6
excellent | for every vulgar paper to rehearse? 38. 4
care, | art left the prey of every vulgar thief. 48. 8
since every one hath, every one, one shade, 53. 3
since every one hath, every one, one shade, 53. 3
and you, but one, can every shadow lend: 53. 4
and you in every blessed shape we know. 53.12
eye, | and all my soul, and all my every part; 62. 2
that every word doth almost /tell my name, 76. 7
my verse | as every alien pen hath got my use, 78. 3
of their fair subject, blessing every book. 82. 4
his wit, | making his style admired every where. 84.12
"amen" | to every hymn that able spirit affords 85. 7
and every humor hath his adjunct pleasure, 91. 5
where beauty's veil doth cover every blot, | and 95.11
what old december's bareness every where! 97. 4
hath put a spirit of youth in every thing, 98. 3
and make time's spoils despised every where. 100.12
the owner's tongue doth publish every where. 102. 4
but that wild music burthens every bough, | and 102.11
creating every bad a perfect best | as fast as 114. 7
it is the star to every wand'ring bark, | whose 116. 7
that every tongue says beauty should look so. 127.14
grace, | and suit thy pity like in every part. 132.12
anon their gazes lend | to every place at once, LC 27
and every light occasion of the wind | upon his 86
EVE'S 4 FR 0.0004 REL FR 1 V 3 P
it was eve's legacy, and cannot be ta'en from TGV 3.01.338 P
so curses all eve's daughters, of what WIV 4.02. 24 P
wert as witty a piece of eve's flesh as any in TN 1.05. 28 P
how like eve's apple doth thy beauty grow, | if SON 93.13
/EVIDENCE 1 FR 0.0001 REL FR 1 V 0 P
/trial /first, /bring /in /their /evidence. LR 3.06. 35
EVIDENCE 10 FR 0.0011 REL FR 9 V 1 P
comes not that blood as modest evidence | to ADO 4.01. 37
but thou art too fine in thy evidence, therefore AWW 5.03.269 P
than from true evidence of good esteem | he be 2H6 3.02. 21
(that now give evidence against my soul) | for R3 1.04. 67
where is the evidence that doth accuse me? 1.04.183
and so his peers upon this evidence | have found H8 2.01. 26
forehead of our faults, | to give in evidence. HAM 3.03. 64
and give true evidence to his love, which stands ANT 1.03. 74
end in the donation, | to be his evidence now. CYM 5.05.368
his scarlet lust came evidence to swear | that LUC 1650
EVIDENCES 1 FR 0.0001 REL FR 0 V 1 P
and many other evidences proclaim her, with all WT 5.02. 38 P
EVIDENT 7 FR 0.0008 REL FR 6 V 1 P
why, this is evident to any formal capacity, TN 2.05.117 P
your honor and your goodness is so evident WT 2.02. 41
so clear, so shining, and so evident, | that it 1H6 2.04. 23
hath not a tomb so evident as a chair | t' extol COR 4.07. 52
we must find | an evident calamity, though we 5.03.112
sign about her, | more evident than this; CYM 2.04.120
but that thou none lov'st is most evident; SON 10. 4
EVIL *(also ev'l)*
/EVIL 2 FR 0.0002 REL FR 2 V 0 P
corrects the /ill /aspects /of /planets /evil, TRO 1.03. 92
/of /our /nature /come | /in /further /evil? HAM 5.02. 70
EVIL 68 FR 0.0076 REL FR 59 V 9 P
in my false brother | awak'd an evil nature, and TMP 1.02. 93
to bring this woman to evil for your good. WIV 3.05. 96 P
no man means evil but the devil, and we shall 5.02. 13 P
i do it not in evil disposition, | but from lord MM 1.02.118
a thirsty evil, and when we drink we die. 1.02.130
when evil deeds have their permissive pass, 1.03. 38
those many had not dar'd to do that evil | if 2.02. 91
i do repent me as it is an evil, | and take the 2.03. 35
and in my heart the strong and swelling evil 2.04. 6
the evil that thou causest to be done, | that is 3.02. 20
time | unfold the evil which is here wrapp'd up 5.01.117
well, angelo, your evil quits you well. 5.01.496
ill deeds is doubled with an evil word. ERR 3.02. 20
no evil lost is wail'd when it is gone. 4.02. 24
sir, like an evil angel, and bid you forsake 4.03. 20 P
so politic a state of evil that they will not ADO 5.02. 63 P
there is no evil angel but love. LLL 1.02.173 P
ay marry, there — some flattery for this evil. 4.03.282
the boy replied, "an angel is not evil; 5.02.105
an evil soul producing holy witness | is like a MV 1.03. 99
a gracious voice, | obscures the show of evil? 3.02. 77
at my hand, but we must do good against evil. AWW 2.05. 48 P
in goodness, but greater a great deal in evil. 4.03.288 P
but the beauteous evil | are empty trunks TN 3.04.369
canst with thine eyes at once see good and evil, WT 1.02.303
do as the heavens have done, forget your evil, 5.01. 5
on their departure most of all show evil. JN 3.04.115
and broke out | to acquaint you with this evil, 5.06. 25
could out of thee extract one spark of evil H5 2.02.101
there is some soul of goodness in things evil, 4.01. 4
given | to dream on evil or to work my downfall. 2H6 3.01. 73
ah, what a sign it is of evil life, | where 3.03. 5
made impudent with use of evil deeds, | i would 3H6 1.04.117
how evil it beseems thee | to flatter henry and 4.07. 84
the owl shriek'd at thy birth, an evil sign; 5.06. 44
o, he hath kept an evil diet long, | and R3 1.01.139
tell them that god bids us do good for evil: 1.03.334
then be your eyes the witness of their evil. 3.04. 67
whose tenor | was, were he evil us'd, he would H8 1.02.207
yet i can give you inkling | of an ensuing evil, 2.01.141
men's evil manners live in brass, their virtues 4.02. 45
planets | in evil mixture to disorder wander, TRO 1.03. 95
or, shedding, breed a nursery of like evil, | to 1.03.319
most that | which would increase his evil. COR 1.01.179
the evil that men do lives after them, | the JC 3.02. 75
thy evil spirit, brutus. 4.03.282
'tis call'd the evil: MAC 4.03.146
let my disclaiming from a purpos'd evil | free HAM 5.02.241
from my throat, | i'll tell thee thou dost evil. LR 1.01.166
and all that we are evil in, by a divine 1.02.126 P
your brother's evil disposition made him seek 3.05. 6 P
thou worse than any name, read thine own evil. 5.03.157
it is too true an evil; OTH 1.01.160
and would do much | to cure him of this evil. 2.03.144
are you of good or evil? 5.01. 65
entice his own | to evil should be done by none. PER 1.ch. 28
where every evil | hath a good color; TNK 1.02. 38
where ev'ry seeming good's | a certain evil; 1.02. 40
for unstain'd thoughts do seldom dream on evil; LUC 87
o unlook'd–for evil, | when virtue is profan'd 846
and the dire thought of his committed evil 972
ill, | no more than wax shall be accounted evil, 1245
and therein so ensconc'd his secret evil, | that 1515
my female evil | tempteth my better angel from PP 2. 5
but not to tell of good or evil luck, | of SON 14. 3
true | that better is by evil still made better, 119.10
shown, | unless this general evil they maintain: 121.13
my female evil | tempteth my better angel from 144. 5
EVIL–EY'D 1 FR 0.0001 REL FR 1 V 0 P
of most stepmothers, | evil–ey'd unto you. CYM 1.01. 72
EVILLY 2 FR 0.0002 REL FR 2 V 0 P
this act so evilly borne shall cool the hearts JN 3.04.149
and wonder of good deeds evilly bestow'd! TIM 4.03.461
EVILS* 27 FR 0.0030 REL FR 25 V 2 P
looks in a glass that shows what future evils, MM 2.02. 95
raze the sanctuary | and pitch our evils there? 2.02.171
and this same progeny of evils comes | from our MND 2.01.115
and all th' embossed sores and headed evils, AYL 2.07. 67
oppress'd with two weak evils, age and hunger, 2.07.132
any of the principal evils that he laid to the 3.02.352 P
yet these fix'd evils sit so fit in him, | that AWW 1.01.102
you your leave, that i may bear my evils alone. TN 2.01. 6 P
less appear so, in comforting your evils, | than WT 2.03. 56
which has | my evils conjur'd to remembrance, 5.03. 40
evils that take leave, | on their departure most JN 3.04.114
of other, | turning past evils to advantages. 2H4 4.04. 78
that lack of means enforce you not to evils, 5.05. 67
of these known evils, but to give me leave | by R3 1.02. 79
nor build their evils on the graves of great men H8 2.01. 67
prayers | i should repent the evils i have done. TIT 5.03.186
if wrongs be evils and enforce us kill, | what TIM 3.05. 36
brow by night, | when evils are most free? JC 2.01. 79
for warnings and portents | and evils imminent, 2.02. 81
no use, | if you give place to accidental evils. 4.03.146
a devil more damn'd | in evils to top macbeth. MAC 4.03. 57
these evils thou repeat'st upon thyself | hath 4.03.112
appears in cassio, | and looks not on his evils. OTH 2.03.135
are | evils enow to darken all his goodness: ANT 1.04. 11
the evils she hatch'd were not effected; CYM 5.05. 60
the curse of heaven and men succeed their evils! PER 1.04.104
cave–keeping evils that obscurely sleep. LUC 1250
EVITATE 1 FR 0.0001 REL FR 1 V 0 P
since therein she doth evitate and shun | a WIV 5.05.228
EV'L *(also evil)*
/EV'L 1 FR 0.0001 REL FR 1 V 0 P
the dram of /ev'l | doth all the noble substance HAM 1.04. 36
EV'N* *(also e'en, even*, and compounds)*
EV'N* 28 FR 0.0031 REL FR 17 V 11 P
mine eyes, ev'n sociable to the show of thine, TMP 5.01. 63
o, give ye good ev'n! TGV 2.01. 98 P
and ev'n that pow'r which gave me first my oath 2.06. 4
and ev'n in kind love i do conjure thee, | who 2.07. 2
why, ev'n what fashion thou best likes, lucetta. 2.07. 52
madam, good ev'n to your ladyship. 4.02. 85
good ev'n, audrey. AYL 5.01. 13 P
god ye good ev'n, william. 5.01. 14 P
and good ev'n to you, sir. 5.01. 15 P
good ev'n, gentle friend. 5.01. 16 P
ev'n as soon as thou canst, for thou hast to AWW 2.03.224 P
were you not ev'n now with the countess olivia? TN 2.02. 1 P
which must be ev'n as swiftly followed as | i WT 1.02.409
'a parted ev'n just between twelve and one, ev'n H5 2.03. 12 P
twelve and one, ev'n at the turning o' th' tide; 2.03. 13 P
ev'n as your horse bears your praises, who would 3.07. 76 P
ev'n to the hall, to hear what shall become | of H8 2.01. 2
ev'n with all my heart | would i were dead, so TIT 5.03.172
i should ev'n die with pity | to see another LR 4.07. 52
where not to be ev'n jump | as they are, here TNK 1.02. 40
you must ev'n take it patiently. 4.01.115
good ev'n, good men. 4.01.116
ev'n thus all day long. 4.03. 18 P
ev'n when you will. 5.02. 87
i must ev'n leave you here. 5.02.102
ev'n he that led you to this banket shall 5.04. 22
ev'n very here | i sund'red you. 5.04. 99
ev'n in this thought through the dark night he LUC 729
EV'R *(also e'er, ever, and compounds)*
EV'R 3 FR 0.0003 REL FR 3 V 0 P
no figures of ourselves shall we ev'r see | to TNK 2.02. 33
/void'st of honor | that ev'r bore gentle token! 3.01. 37
lose the noblest sight | that ev'r was seen. 5.02.100
/EV'RY 1 FR 0.0001 REL FR 1 V 0 P
(which, /ev'ry innocent wots well, comes in TNK 1.03. 79
EV'RY 16 FR 0.0018 REL FR 13 V 3 P
a space whose ev'ry cubit | seems to cry out, TMP 2.01.257
good faith, ev'ry dram of it, and i will not AWW 2.03.221 P
and ev'ry hair that's on't, helen, that's dead, 5.03. 77
the tract of ev'ry thing | would by a good H8 1.01. 40
lead in your ladies, ev'ry one. 1.04.103
if my actions | were tried by ev'ry tongue, 3.01. 35
were tried by ev'ry tongue, ev'ry eye saw 'em, 3.01. 35
he owes | for ev'ry word. TIM 1.02.199
where ev'ry seeming good's | a certain evil; TNK 1.02. 39
would he would do so ev'ry day! 2.04. 27
and ev'ry day discourse you into health, | as i 3.06. 38
lards it, that she farces ev'ry business withal, 4.03. 7 P
and palamon is sweet, and ev'ry good thing. 4.03. 87 P
you should observe her ev'ry way. 5.02. 14
ev'ry blow that falls | threats a brave life, 5.03. 3
the which he will not ev'ry hour survey, | for SON 52. 3
EWE 4 FR 0.0004 REL FR 3 V 1 P
sour ringlets make, | whereof the ewe not bites; TMP 5.01. 38
for the ewe that will not hear her lamb when it ADO 3.03. 70 P
why he hath made the ewe bleak for the lamb; MV 4.01. 74
an old black ram | is tupping your white ewe. OTH 1.01. 89
EWER 1 FR 0.0001 REL FR 1 V 0 P
another bear the ewer, the third a diaper, | and SHR in.1. 57
EWERS 1 FR 0.0001 REL FR 1 V 0 P
basins and ewers to lave her dainty hands; SHR 2.01.348
EWES 11 FR 0.0012 REL FR 6 V 5 P
pied | should fall as jacob's hire, the ewes, MV 1.03. 80
he stuck them up before the fulsome ewes, | who 1.03. 86
or is your gold and silver ewes and rams? 1.03. 95
we are still handling our ewes, and their fells AYL 3.02. 53 P
of my pride is to see my ewes graze and my lambs 3.02. 76 P
in you, to bring the ewes and the rams together, 3.02. 79 P
no inch farther, | but milk my ewes, and weep. WT 4.04.450
how a score of ewes now? 2H4 3.02. 49 P
a score of good ewes may be worth ten pounds. 3.02. 50 P
so many days my ewes have been with young, | so 3H6 2.05. 35
my flocks feed not, my ewes breed not, | my rams PP 17. 1
EW'R 1 FR 0.0001 REL FR 0 V 1 P
i dreamt of a silver basin and ew'r to–night. TIM 3.01. 7 P
EXACT* 8 FR 0.0009 REL FR 7 V 1 P
but what my power might else exact — like one TMP 1.02. 99
thou mayst with better face | exact the penalty. MV 1.03.137
attributed to the true and exact performer, i AWW 3.06. 61 P
good | to set the exact wealth of all our states 1H4 4.01. 46
shapes, | severals and generals of grace exact, TRO 1.03.180
i have with exact view perus'd thee, hector, 4.05.232
an exact command, | larded with many several HAM 5.02. 19
and in the most exact regard support | the LR 1.04.265
EXACTED 1 FR 0.0001 REL FR 1 V 0 P
when have i aught exacted at your hands, | /but 2H6 4.07. 69
EXACTEST 1 FR 0.0001 REL FR 1 V 0 P
call me before th' exactest auditors, | and set TIM 2.02.156
EXACTING 1 FR 0.0001 REL FR 1 V 0 P
disguised | pay with falsehood false exacting, MM 3.02.281
EXACTION 3 FR 0.0003 REL FR 3 V 0 P
i gain | by the exaction of the forfeiture? MV 1.03.164
still exaction! H8 1.02. 52
in what kind, let's know, | is this exaction? 1.02. 54
EXACTIONS 3 FR 0.0003 REL FR 3 V 0 P
and daily new exactions are devis'd, | as blanks R2 2.01.249
on you as putter–on | of these exactions, yet H8 1.02. 25
these exactions | (whereof my sovereign would 1.02. 47
EXACTLY 6 FR 0.0006 REL FR 6 V 0 P
ariel, thy charge | exactly is perform'd; TMP 1.02.238
but then exactly do | all points of my command. 1.02.500
it, and exactly begg'd | your grace's pardon, R2 1.01.140
armed at point exactly, cap–a–pe, | appears HAM 1.02.200
'tis exactly valued, | not petty things admitted ANT 5.02.139
could be so rarely and exactly wrought, | since CYM 2.04. 75
EXACTS 1 FR 0.0001 REL FR 1 V 0 P
and where thou now exacts the penalty, | which MV 4.01. 22
EXALT 1 FR 0.0001 REL FR 1 V 0 P
in his own grace he doth exalt himself, | more LR 5.03. 67
EXALTED 3 FR 0.0003 REL FR 2 V 1 P
uses me with a more exalted respect than any one TN 2.05. 27 P
stream | do kiss the most exalted shores of all. JC 1.01. 60
to be exalted with the threat'ning clouds; 1.03. 8
EXAMINATION 5 FR 0.0005 REL FR 1 V 4 P
take their examination yourself, and bring it me ADO 3.05. 49 P
we are now to examination these men. 3.05. 59 P
i will go before and show him their examination. 4.02. 66 P
be but your lordship present at his examination, AWW 3.06. 28 P
where's his examination? H8 1.01.116
EXAMINATIONS 1 FR 0.0001 REL FR 1 V 0 P
on the contrary | urg'd on the examinations, H8 2.01. 16
EXAMIN'D 4 FR 0.0004 REL FR 1 V 3 P
examin'd my parts with most judicious iliads; WIV 1.03. 60 P
them this morning examin'd before your worship. ADO 3.05. 47 P
which are the offenders that are to be examin'd? 4.02. 8 P
honesty, and that | i have not heard examin'd. AWW 3.05. 63
EXAMINE 12 FR 0.0013 REL FR 4 V 8 P
old ends any further, examine your conscience, ADO 1.01.288 P
i could wish he would modestly examine himself, 2.03.208 P
certain, we have the exhibition to examine. 4.02. 6 P
master constable, you go not the way to examine; 4.02. 34 P
pray you examine him upon that point. 5.01.313 P
know of your youth, examine well your blood, MND 1.01. 68
thou stand for my father and examine me upon the 1H4 2.04.376 P
the pains but to examine the wars of pompey the H5 4.01. 69 P
come hither, sirrah, i must examine thee. 2H6 4.02. 97 P
for examine | their counsels and their cares; COR 1.01.149
examine other beauties. ROM 1.01.228
examine every married lineament, | and see how 1.03. 83
EXAMINED 1 FR 0.0001 REL FR 1 V 0 P
mine eye hath well examined his parts, | and JN 1.01. 89
EXAMINES 1 FR 0.0001 REL FR 0 V 1 P
old justice that examines all such offenders, AYL 4.01.199 P
EXAMPLE 34 FR 0.0038 REL FR 24 V 10 P
as, for example, thou thyself art a wicked MM 1.02. 25 P
rigor of the statute, | to make him an example. 1.04. 68
no such example have we. 4.02. 97
to correct yourself, for the example of others. ADO 5.01.323 P
that i may example my digression by some mighty LLL 1.02.116 P
i will example it: 3.01. 83 P

ill, to example ill, | would from my forehead 4.03.122
should his sufferance be by christian example? MV 3.01. 71 P
and many an error by the same example | will 4.01.221
and the misery is, example, that so terrible AWW 3.05. 21 P
there is example for't: TN 2.05. 39 P
if i could find example | of thousands that had WT 1.02.357
hang him, he'll be made an example. 4.04.817 P
order in so fierce a cause, | doth want example. JN 3.04. 13
grow great by your example and put on | the 5.01. 52
sovereign, lest example | breed, by his H5 2.02. 45
men to love their present pains | upon example; 4.01. 19
be hang'd up for example at their doors. 2H6 4.02.180
too, as myself, for example, that am a butcher. 4.07. 53 P
things done without example, in their issue H8 1.02. 90
he stepp'd before me happily | for my example. 4.02. 11
he was ill, and gave | the clergy ill example. 4.02. 44
and by his rare example made the coward | turn COR 2.02.104
there's much example for't: TIM 1.02. 46 P
like workmen, i'll example you with thievery: 4.03.435
i'll make thee an example. OTH 2.03.251
(save that they say the wars must make example 3.03. 65
o, /he has given example for our flight, | most ANT 3.10. 27
that some, turn'd coward | but by example (o, a CYM 5.03. 36
your advice | is cried up with example. TNK 1.02. 13
honor, would be loath | to take example by her. 2.02.146
by whose example thou reveng'd mayst be. LUC 1194
which should example where your equal grew? SON 84. 4
what are precepts worth | of stale example? LC 268

EXAMPLED 3 FR 0.0003 REL FR 3 V 0 P
a jest, | exampled by this heinous spectacle. JN 4.03. 56
for hear her but exampled by herself: H5 1.02.156
exampled by the first pace that is sick | of his TRO 1.03.132

EXAMPLES 7 FR 0.0008 REL FR 6 V 1 P
but that frailty hath examples for his falling, MM 3.01.186 P
and the examples | of every minute's instance 2H4 4.01. 82
as fear may teach us out of late examples | left H5 2.04. 12
most liberal, | they are set here for examples. H8 1.03. 62
can, | and three examples of the like hath been COR 4.06. 51
examples gross as earth exhort me: HAM 4.04. 46
or forc'd examples, 'gainst her own content, LC 157

EXASPERATE 3 FR 0.0003 REL FR 1 V 2 P
the youth in your sight only to exasperate you, TN 3.02. 19 P
why art thou then exasperate, thou idle TRO 5.01. 30 P
report | hath so exasperate /the king that he MAC 3.06. 38

EXASPERATES 1 FR 0.0001 REL FR 1 V 0 P
to take the widow | exasperates, makes mad her LR 5.01. 60

EXCEED 20 FR 0.0022 REL FR 19 V 1 P
my wrath shall far exceed the love | i ever bore TGV 3.01.166
beauties, livings, friends, | exceed account. MV 3.02.157
flood of fortune | so far exceed all instance, TN 4.03. 12
his deeds exceed all speech: 1H6 1.01. 15
and thou shalt find that i exceed my sex. 1.02. 90
let not her penance exceed the king's commission 2H6 2.04. 75
the lustre of the better shall exceed | by TRO 1.03.360
son | will or exceed the common or be caught COR 4.01. 32
as far as doth the capitol exceed | the meanest 4.02. 39
whom you have banish'd — does exceed you all. 4.02. 42
to feed | than such that do e'en enemies exceed. TIM 1.02.204
and him, he shall not exceed you three hits. HAM 5.02.166 P
the time, but let it not | exceed three days. OTH 3.03. 63
do not exceed | the prescript of this scroll. ANT 3.08. 4
to make some good, but others to exceed, | and PER 2.03. 16
(millions of rates) | exceed the wine of others. TNK 1.04. 30
wilt thou exceed in all, or dost thou do it | to 3.06. 46
as if the dead the living should exceed; VEN 292
guilt being great, the fear doth still exceed; LUC 229
you did exceed | the barren tender of a poet's SON 83. 3

EXCEEDED 4 FR 0.0004 REL FR 4 V 0 P
but justly, as you have exceeded all promise, AYL 1.02.244
in execution | upon offenders hath exceeded law, 2H6 1.03.133
that nature nev'r exceeded nor nev'r shall. TNK 2.03. 12
rhyme, | exceeded by the height of happier men. SON 32. 8

EXCEEDETH 1 FR 0.0001 REL FR 1 V 0 P
the number of the king exceedeth our. 1H4 4.03. 28

EXCEEDING 27 FR 0.0030 REL FR 15 V 12 P
o exceeding puppet! TGV 2.01. 94 P
those, for their parents were exceeding poor, ERR 1.01. 56
and she is exceeding wise. ADO 2.03.161 P
joy to wear it, for my heart is exceeding heavy. 3.04. 25 P
by my troth, i am exceeding ill. 3.04. 53 P
cousin do not look exceeding narrowly to thee. 5.04.116 P
the schoolmaster is exceeding fantastical, too LLL 5.02.528 P
you grow exceeding strange. MV 1.01. 67
i say't, is an honest exceeding poor man and, 2.02. 52 P
but this exceeding posting day and night | must AWW 5.01. 1
with strife to please you, day exceeding day. ep 4
very brief, and to exceeding good sense — less. TN 3.04.158 P
john, methinks they are exceeding poor and bare, 1H4 4.02. 68 P
before god, i am exceeding weary. 2H4 2.02. 1 P
word, and a word of exceeding good command, by 3.02. 76 P
very well, go to, very good, exceeding good. 3.02.274 P
exceeding ill. 4.05. 11
exceeding well, his cares are now all ended. 5.02. 3
hath, | exceeding the nine sibyls of old rome: 1H6 1.02. 56
grace, | to work exceeding miracles on earth. 5.04. 41
that living wrought me such exceeding trouble. 2H6 5.01. 70
exceeding those that i can wish upon thee, | o, R3 1.03.217
o, very mad, exceeding mad, in love too; H8 1.04. 28
exceeding wise, fair–spoken, and persuading; 4.02. 52
but breeds the giver a return exceeding | all TIM 1.01.279
this fellow's of exceeding honesty, | and knows OTH 3.03.258
exceeding pleasant; CYM 1.06. 59

EXCEEDINGLY 5 FR 0.0005 REL FR 2 V 3 P
o, my good knave costard, exceedingly well met! LLL 3.01.143 P
in faith, it is exceedingly well aim'd. 1H4 1.03.282
exceedingly well read, and profited | in strange 3.01.164
exceedingly, my lord, it is very sultry — as HAM 5.02.100 P
i have been to–night exceedingly well cudgell'd; OTH 2.03.365 P

EXCEEDS 12 FR 0.0013 REL FR 8 V 4 P
am put to know that your own science | exceeds, MM 1.01. 6
exceeds her as much in beauty as the first of ADO 1.01.191 P
o, that exceeds, they say. 3.04. 17 P
my mind exceeds the compass of her wheel. 3H6 4.03. 47
for to be wise and love | exceeds man's might; TRO 3.02.157
i, it exceeds peace as far as day does night; COR 4.05.221 P
and our oppression | exceeds what we expected. ANT 4.07. 3
my mistress exceeds in goodness the hugeness of CYM 1.04.144 P
go before | this lout as he exceeds our lords, 5.02. 9
chiefly in love, whose leave exceeds commission: VEN 568
which far exceeds his barren skill to show. LUC 81
that in my mind thy worst all best exceeds? SON 150. 8

EXCEL 7 FR 0.0008 REL FR 6 V 1 P
govern, sir, | t' excel the golden age. TMP 2.01.169
i do excel thee in my rapier as much as thou LLL 1.02. 74 P
how far dost thou excel | no thought can think, 4.03. 39
an earl, | although in glorious titles he excel. 1H6 5.05. 38
valor and pride excel themselves in hector, TRO 4.05. 79
so did this horse excel a common one, | in shape VEN 293
same, | and that unfair which fairly doth excel: SON 5. 4

EXCELLANT 1 FR 0.0001 REL FR 0 V 1 P
ay, dat is very good, excellant. WIV 3.01. 99 P

EXCELL'D 2 FR 0.0002 REL FR 1 V 1 P
i could not /but believe she excell'd many. CYM 1.04. 74 P
their virtue lost, wherein they late excell'd, VEN 1131

EXCELLENCE 20 FR 0.0022 REL FR 17 V 3 P
lends | the smallest scruple of her excellence, MM 1.01. 37
his excellence did earn it, ere he had it. ADO 3.01. 99
have found the ground of study's excellence LLL 4.03.296
what is thy excellence in a galliard, knight? TN 1.03.120 P
so much the more our carver's excellence, WT 5.03. 30
as she, | and she a fair divided excellence, JN 2.01.439
and breathing to his breathless excellence | the 4.03. 66
hath got the voice in hell for excellence; H5 2.02.113
they humbly sue unto your excellence | to have a 1H6 5.01. 4
i do greet your excellence | with letters of 5.04. 94
for france, | as procurator to your excellence, 2H6 1.01. 3
voice, | "jesu maintain your royal excellence!" 1.01.161
your grace | to be protector of his excellence? 1.03.119
of her that loves him with that excellence H8 2.02. 33
we'll put on those shall praise your excellence, HAM 4.07.131
not ignorant of what excellence laertes is — 5.02.136 P
lest i should compare with him in excellence, 5.02.139 P
sluttery, to such neat excellence oppos'd, CYM 1.06. 44
others but stewards of their excellence. SON 94. 8
kind, | still constant in a wondrous excellence, 105. 6

EXCELLENCIES 1 FR 0.0001 REL FR 0 V 1 P
(as he thinks) with excellencies, that it is his TN 2.03.151 P

EXCELLENCY 3 FR 0.0003 REL FR 1 V 2 P
so securely on the excellency of her honor, that WIV 2.02.243 P
is there not a double excellency in this? 3.03.176 P
it is the witness still of excellency | to put a ADO 2.03. 46

/EXCELLENT 1 FR 0.0001 REL FR 0 V 1 P
my /excellent good friends! HAM 2.02.224 P

EXCELLENT 127 FR 0.0143 REL FR 47 V 80 P
excellent. TMP 3.02.110 P
of tongue) a kind | of excellent dumb discourse. 3.03. 39
by line and level" is an excellent pass of pate; 4.01.243 P
o excellent motion! TGV 2.01. 94 P
o excellent device, was there ever heard a 2.01.139
you are a gentleman of excellent breeding, WIV 2.02.225 P
foot would give an excellent motion to thy gait 3.03. 63 P
that will be excellent. 4.04. 70
o, it is excellent | to have a giant's strength; MM 2.02.107
i know a wench of excellent discourse, | pretty ERR 3.01.109
trencherman, he hath an excellent stomach. ADO 1.01. 52 P
he were an excellent man that were made just in 2.01. 6 P
think i do not know you by your excellent wit? 2.01.122 P
your father got excellent husbands, if a maid 2.01.324 P
she were an excellent wife for benedick. 2.01.351 P
of good discourse, an excellent musician, and 2.03. 34 P
i pray thee get us some excellent music; 2.03. 85 P
she's an excellent sweet lady, and (out of all 2.03.159 P
having so swift and excellent a wit | as she is 3.01. 89
indeed he hath an excellent good name. 3.01. 98
graceful, and excellent fashion, yours is worth 3.04. 22 P
count sent me — they are an excellent perfume. 3.04. 63 P
so tempted, and he had an excellent strength; LLL 1.02.174 P
else none at all in aught proves excellent. 4.03.351
an excellent device! 5.01.137 P
o excellent! MND 3.02.247
of themselves, they may pass for excellent men. 5.01.216 P
o noble judge! o excellent young man! MV 4.01.246
young men, of excellent growth and presence. AYL 1.02.121 P
to deny so fair and excellent ladies any thing. 1.02.185 P
o excellent young man! 1.02.213 P
an excellent color. 3.04. 11 P
so" is good, very good, very excellent good; 5.01. 27 P
it will be pastime passing excellent, | if it be SHR in.1. 67
thou didst it excellent. in.1. 89
'tis a very excellent piece of work, madam lady; 1.01.253 P
o excellent motion! fellows, let's be gone. 1.02.278
he was excellent indeed, madam. AWW 1.01. 28 P
there was excellent command — to charge in with 3.06. 48 P
then hadst thou had an excellent head of hair. TN 1.03. 95 P
excellent! 1.03.102 P
think, by the excellent constitution of thy leg, 1.03.132 P
ha, ha, excellent! 1.03.141 P
perceive in you so excellent a touch of modesty, 2.01. 12 P
by my troth, the fool has an excellent breast. 2.03. 19 P
excellent! 2.03. 29 P
excellent good, i' faith. 2.03. 45 P
excellent! i smell a device. 2.03.162 P
excellent wench, say i. 2.05.109 P
the cur is excellent at faults. 2.05.128 P
of tartar, thou most excellent devil of wit! 2.05.205 P
most excellent accomplish'd lady, the heavens 3.01. 84 P
accosted her, and with some excellent jests, 3.02. 22 P
why, this is excellent. 5.01. 24 P
fresh piece | of excellent witchcraft, whom of WT 4.04.423
an excellent plot, very good friends. 1H4 2.03. 19 P
o jesu, this is excellent sport, i' faith! 2.04.390 P
faith, and let it be an excellent good thing. 2H4 2.02. 33 P
be old utis, it will be an excellent stratagem. 2.04. 20 P
now you are in an excellent good temperality. 2.04. 23 P
which was an excellent good word before it was 2.04.149 P
be accommodated — which is an excellent thing. 3.02. 80 P
most excellent, i' faith! 3.02.107 P
which is the birth, becomes excellent wit. 4.03.102 P
second property of your excellent sherris is the 4.03.103 P
and till'd with excellent endeavor of drinking 4.03.120 P
excellent, madame! H5 3.04. 60 P
there is very excellent services committed at 3.06. 3 P
most valiantly, with excellent discipline. 3.06. 11 P
poet makes a most excellent description of it. 3.06. 37 P
fortune is an excellent moral. 3.06. 38 P
you have an excellent armor; 3.07. 3 P
lord, it is a most absolute and excellent horse. 3.07. 26 P
excellent pucelle, if thy name be so, | let me 1H6 1.02.110
child | that for the beauty thinks it excellent. 2H6 3.01.230
o excellent device! and make a sop of him. R3 1.04.157 P
that excellent grand tyrant of the earth | that 4.04. 52
of an excellent | and unmatch'd wit and judgment H8 2.04. 46
so excellent in art, and still so rising, | that 4.02. 62
here, here's an excellent place, here we may see TRO 1.02.181 P
laughs out a loud applause, | cries, "excellent! 1.03.164
yet god achilles still cries, "excellent! 1.03.169
and i'll tell you excellent news of your husband COR 1.03. 90 P
the defense of a town, our general is excellent. 4.05.170 P
will beget | a very excellent piece of villainy. TIT 2.03. 7
your plantan leaf is excellent for that. ROM 1.02. 51
many for many virtues excellent, | none but for 2.03. 13
so 'tis. this comes off well and excellent. TIM 1.01. 29
excellent! 3.03. 27 P
most vicious strain, | and call it excellent. 4.03.214
only i will promise him an excellent piece. 5.01. 19
excellent workman! 5.01. 31
so excellent a king, that was, to this, HAM 1.02.139
"in her excellent white bosom, these, etc." 2.02.113 P
excellent well, you are a fishmonger. 2.02.174 P
this most excellent canopy, the air, look you, 2.02.299 P
cried in the top of mine — an excellent play, 2.02.439 P
excellent, i' faith — of the chameleon's dish, 3.02. 93 P
and there is much music, excellent voice, in 3.02.368 P
of infinite jest, of most excellent fancy. 5.01.185 P
/gentleman, full of most excellent differences, 5.02.107 P
this is the excellent foppery of the world, that LR 1.02.118 P
gentle, and low, an excellent thing in woman. 5.03.274
/an excellent /courtesy! OTH 2.01.175 P
'fore /god, an excellent song. 2.03. 75 P
excellent well. 2.03.117 P
excellent wretch! 3.03. 90
excellent good. what trumpet is that same? 4.01.213
excellent falsehood! ANT 1.01. 40
good now, some excellent fortune! 1.02. 26 P
o, excellent, i love long life better than figs. 1.02. 32 P
play one scene | of excellent dissembling, and 1.03. 79
he plied them both with excellent praises. 3.02. 14
excellent. 3.03. 25
first, a very excellent good conceited thing; CYM 2.03. 17 P
for my vantage, excellent; 5.05.198
of tyre | are excellent in making ladies trip, PER 2.03.102
and that their measures are as excellent. 2.03.103
reserve | that excellent complexion, which did 4.01. 40
speaks well, and has excellent good clothes; 4.02. 48 P
he's excellent i' th' woods, | bring him to th' TNK 2.03. 53
wrestled, | the best men call'd it excellent; 2.03. 76
'twas an excellent dance, and for a preface, | i 3.05.150
treason | in service of so excellent a beauty, 3.06.162
i cannot, sir, they are both too excellent: 3.06.286
bad in the best, though excellent in neither. PP 7.18
too excellent | for every vulgar paper to SON 38. 3

EXCELLENTLY 6 FR 0.0006 REL FR 1 V 5 P
i like the new tire within excellently, if the ADO 3.04. 13 P
excellently. AWW 4.03.210 P
for besides that it is excellently well penn'd, TN 1.05.173 P
excellently done, if god did all. 1.05.236 P
this letter, being so excellently ignorant, will 3.04.188 P
the thing he means to kill, more excellently. TRO 4.01. 25

EXCELLETH 1 FR 0.0001 REL FR 1 V 0 P
not | to darken her whose light excelleth thine; LUC 191

EXCELLING 3 FR 0.0003 REL FR 3 V 0 P
silvia let us sing, | that silvia is excelling; TGV 4.02. 50
thou cunning'st pattern of excelling nature, | i OTH 5.02. 11
for from the stillitory of thy face excelling VEN 443

EXCELS 7 FR 0.0008 REL FR 5 V 2 P
she excels each mortal thing | upon the dull TGV 4.02. 51
that you shall say my cunning drift excels. 4.02. 83
he excels his brother for a coward, yet his AWW 4.03.288 P
excels what ever yet you look'd upon | or hand WT 5.03. 16
than any man's, yet his leg excels all men's, ROM 2.05. 41 P
this second match, | for it excels your first; 3.05.223
one that excels the quirks of blazoning pens, OTH 2.01. 63

/EXCEPT 1 FR 0.0001 REL FR 0 V 1 P
/except they are busied about a counterfeit SHR 4.04. 91 P

EXCEPT 36 FR 0.0040 REL FR 30 V 6 P
letter in the letter, | except mine own name; TGV 1.02.117
she gave me none, except an angry word. 2.01.158 P
now no discourse, except it be of love; 2.04.140
except my mistress. 2.04.154
sweet, except not any, | except thou wilt except 2.04.154
any, | except thou wilt except against my love. 2.04.155
any, | except thou wilt except against my love. 2.04.155
except i be by silvia in the night, | there is 3.01.178
to none of these, except it be the last, ERR 5.01. 55
except to steal your thoughts, my gentle queen. MV 2.01. 12
except in that country he had the honor to be AWW 4.03.268 P
why, let her except before excepted. TN 1.03. 7 P
i know not why, except to get the land; JN 1.01. 73
the sea | (except this city now by us besieg'd) 2.01.489
which fear, not reverence, makes thee to except. R2 1.01. 72
except the marshal and such officers | appointed 1.03. 44
faith, none for me, except the northeast wind, 1.04. 6
us, | except like curs to tear us all to pieces. 2.02.139
of fox, | except, o signieur, thou do give to me H5 4.04. 10
go'st | except it be to pray against thy foes. 1H6 1.01. 43
quite, | except some petty towns of no import. 1.01. 91
mourn not, except thou sorrow for my good, 2.05.111
peace | more than i do, except i be provok'd? 3.01. 34
except you mean with obstinate repulse | to slay 3.01.113
then be at peace, except ye thirst for blood. 3.01.117
not resolute, except so much were done, | for 2H6 3.01.267
words, | except a sword or sceptre balance it. 5.01. 9
no, gracious lord, except i cannot do it. 3H6 3.02. 47
richard except, those whom we fight against R3 5.03.243
best respect in rome | (except immortal caesar), JC 1.02. 60
except they meant to bathe in reeking wounds, MAC 1.02. 39
more willingly part withal — except my life, HAM 2.02.216 P
except my life, except my life, except my life. 2.02.217 P
except my life, except my life, except my life. 2.02.217 P
except she bend her humor, shall be assur'd | to CYM 1.05. 81
desire is death, which physic did except. SON 147. 8

EXCEPTED 6 FR 0.0006 REL FR 3 V 3 P
excuse | hath he excepted most against my love. TGV 1.03. 83

i am lov'd of all ladies, only you excepted; ADO 1.01.125 P
man of italy, | always excepted my dear claudio. 3.01. 93
dinners and suppers and sleeping–hours excepted. AYL 3.02. 97 P
why, let her except before excepted. TN 1.03. 7 P
is it excepted i should know no secrets | that JC 2.01.281
EXCEPTING 4 FR 0.0004 REL FR 3 V 1 P
to–night, excepting your worship's presence, ha' ADO 3.05. 30 P
excepting one, i would he were the best | in all R2 4.01. 31
excepting none but good duke humphrey; 2H6 1.01.193
he that doth naught with her (excepting one) R3 1.01. 99
EXCEPTION 5 FR 0.0005 REL FR 4 V 1 P
the true minute when | exception bid him speak, AWW 1.02. 40
his prisoners, | but with proviso and exception, 1H4 1.03. 78
how modest in exception, and withal | how H5 2.04. 34
honor, and exception | roughly awake, i here HAM 5.02.231
hast taken against me a most just exception; OTH 4.02.207 P
EXCEPTIONS 6 FR 0.0006 REL FR 5 V 1 P
lest he should take exceptions to my love, | and TGV 1.03. 81
and yet she takes exceptions at your person. 5.02. 3
lady, takes great exceptions to your ill hours. TN 1.03. 6 P
'tis positive against all exceptions, lords, H5 4.02. 25
and he first took exceptions at this badge, 1H6 4.01.105
but you will take exceptions to my boon. 3H6 3.02. 46
EXCEPTLESS 1 FR 0.0001 REL FR 1 V 0 P
forgive my general and exceptless rashness, TIM 4.03.495
EXCESS 16 FR 0.0018 REL FR 15 V 1 P
and now excess of it will make me surfeit. TGV 3.01.222
the blood of youth burns not with such excess LLL 5.02. 73
nor borrow | by taking nor by giving of excess, MV 1.03. 62
in measure rain thy joy, scant this excess! 3.02.112
to the grief, the excess makes it soon mortal. AWW 1.01. 58 P
food of love, play on, | give me excess of it; TN 1.01. 2
to garnish, | is wasteful and ridiculous excess. JN 4.02. 16
it was excess of wine that set him on, | and on H5 2.02. 42
but my true love is grown to such excess | i ROM 2.06. 33
shame, that they wanted cunning in excess, TIM 5.04. 28
so distribution should undo excess, | and each LR 4.01. 70
cannot restrain | from the excess of laughter. OTH 4.01. 99
yet i wish him | excess and overflow of power, TNK 1.03. 4
more, the profit of excess | is but to surfeit, LUC 138
shall worms, inheritors of this excess, | eat up SON 146. 7
want cries some, but where excess begs all. LC 42
EXCESSIVE 1 FR 0.0001 REL FR 0 V 1 P
dead, excessive grief the enemy to the living. AWW 1.01. 56 P
EXCHANG'D 3 FR 0.0003 REL FR 3 V 0 P
that some night–tripping fairy had exchang'd 1H4 1.01. 87
for him was i exchang'd and ransomed. 1H6 1.04. 29
just to the time, not with the time exchang'd, SON 109. 7
EXCHANGE 31 FR 0.0035 REL FR 19 V 12 P
why then we'll make exchange: TGV 2.02. 6
to learn his wit t' exchange the bad for better. 2.06. 13
give me so much of your time in exchange of it, WIV 2.02.233 P
away myself for you, and dote upon the exchange. ADO 2.01.309 P
what shalt thou exchange for rags? LLL 4.01. 82 P
th' allusion holds in the exchange. 4.02. 41 P
indeed, the collusion holds in the exchange. 4.02. 43 P
i say, th' allusion holds in the exchange. 4.02. 45 P
the pollution holds in the exchange, for the 4.02. 46 P
on me, | for i am much asham'd of my exchange. MV 2.06. 35
for i have bills for money by exchange | from SHR 4.02. 89
love | made me exchange my state with tranio, 5.01.125
for she would not exchange flesh with one that WT 4.04.280 P
outside of thy poverty we must make an exchange; 4.04.633 P
what an exchange had this been, without boot! 4.04.674 P
what a boot is here, with this exchange! 4.04.676 P
that i shall make this northren youth exchange 1H4 3.02.145
in exchange of a hundred and fifty soldiers, 4.02. 13 P
desir'd my cressid in right great exchange, TRO 3.03. 21
th' exchange of thy love's faithful vow for mine ROM 2.02.127
we met, we woo'd, and made exchange of vow, 2.03. 62
it cannot countervail the exchange of joy | that 2.06. 4
or present, i'd exchange | for this one wish, TIM 4.03.520
hit, | or quit in answer of the third exchange, HAM 5.02.269
exchange forgiveness with me, noble hamlet. 5.02.329
husband's life, | and the exchange my brother! LR 4.06.273
there's my exchange. 5.03. 97
let's exchange charity. 5.03.167
exchange me for a goat, | when i shall turn the OTH 3.03.180
as i my poor self did exchange for you, | to CYM 1.01.119
being | is to exchange one misery with another, 1.05. 55
EXCHEQUER 7 FR 0.0008 REL FR 2 V 5 P
you have an exchequer of words and, i think, no TGV 2.04. 43 P
evermore thank's the exchequer of the poor, R2 2.03. 65
for all the coin in thy father's exchequer. 1H4 2.02. 36 P
the hill, 'tis going to the king's exchequer. 2.02. 55 P
rob me the exchequer the first thing thou doest, 3.03.183 P
for our losses, his exchequer is too poor; H5 3.06.130 P
veins, | for she hath no exchequer now but his, SON 67.11
EXCHEQUERS 1 FR 0.0001 REL FR 0 V 1 P
them both, and they shall be exchequers to me. WIV 1.03. 71 P
EXCITE 2 FR 0.0002 REL FR 2 V 0 P
and enmity of those | this quarrel would excite? TRO 2.02.138
and the grim alarm | excite the mortified man. MAC 5.02. 5
EXCITED 1 FR 0.0001 REL FR 1 V 0 P
beaten for loyalty | excited me to treason. CYM 5.05.345
EXCITEMENTS 2 FR 0.0002 REL FR 2 V 0 P
excitements to the field, or speech for truce, TRO 1.03.182
excitements of my reason and my blood, | and let HAM 4.04. 58
EXCITES 1 FR 0.0001 REL FR 0 V 1 P
for every reason excites to this, that my lady TN 2.05.165 P
/EXCLAIM 1 FR 0.0001 REL FR 0 V 1 P
/to /make /them /exclaim /against /their /own HAM 2.02.351 P
EXCLAIM 10 FR 0.0011 REL FR 8 V 2 P
love, | and be my vantage to exclaim on you. MV 3.02.174
of sorrow that e'er i heard virgin exclaim in, AWW 1.03.118 P
say, gentlemen, what makes you thus exclaim? 1H6 4.01. 83
to weep | or to exclaim on fortune's fickleness. 5.03.134
that thus you do exclaim you'll go with him? 2H6 4.08. 35
come, come, dispatch, 'tis bootless to exclaim. R3 3.04.102
you are amaz'd, my liege, at her exclaim. TRO 5.03. 91
exclaim no more against it. OTH 2.03.310 P
place, | where fearfully the dogs exclaim aloud: VEN 886
against the thing he sought he would exclaim: LC 313
EXCLAIM'D 3 FR 0.0003 REL FR 3 V 0 P
the french exclaim'd, the devil was in arms; 1H6 1.01.125
when she exclaim'd on hastings, you, and i, R3 3.03. 16
he broke his whipstock and exclaim'd against TNK 1.02. 86
EXCLAIMING 1 FR 0.0001 REL FR 1 V 0 P
she stays, exclaiming on the direful night, | he LUC 741
EXCLAIMS 8 FR 0.0009 REL FR 8 V 0 P
doth more solicit me than your exclaims | to R2 1.02. 2
besides, all french and france exclaims on thee, 1H6 3.03. 60
and york as fast upon your grace exclaims, 4.04. 30
fill'd it with cursing cries and deep exclaims. R3 1.02. 52
the trumpet sounds, be copious in exclaims. 4.04.135
and arm the vinds of infants to exclaims. TIT 4.01. 86
and sighing it again, exclaims on death. VEN 930
here she exclaims against repose and rest, | and LUC 757
EXCLAMATION 5 FR 0.0005 REL FR 3 V 2 P
for i hear as good exclamation on your worship ADO 3.05. 25 P
her so | that we shall stop her exclamation. JN 2.01.558
temper would endure this tempest of exclamation? 2H4 2.01. 81 P
or else you suffer | too hard an exclamation. H8 1.02. 52
his pride, no exclamation | can curb his heat, LUC 705
EXCLAMATIONS 1 FR 0.0001 REL FR 1 V 0 P
of war | thus will i drown your exclamations. R3 4.04.154
EXCLUDES 1 FR 0.0001 REL FR 1 V 0 P
excludes all pity from our threat'ning looks: ERR 1.01. 10
EXCOMMUNICATE 2 FR 0.0002 REL FR 2 V 0 P
thou shalt stand curs'd and excommunicate, | and JN 3.01.173
more, | if thou stand excommunicate and curs'd? 3.01.223
EXCOMMUNICATION 1 FR 0.0001 REL FR 0 V 1 P
learned writer to set down our excommunication, ADO 3.05. 63 P
EXCREMENT* 5 FR 0.0005 REL FR 2 V 3 P
being, as it is, so plentiful an excrement? ERR 2.02. 78 P
thus, dally with my excrement, with my mustachio LLL 5.01.104 P
and these assume but valor's excrement | to MV 3.02. 87
let me pocket up my pedlar's excrement. WT 4.04.714 P
by a composture stol'n | from gen'ral excrement; TIM 4.03.442
EXCREMENTS 1 FR 0.0001 REL FR 1 V 0 P
your bedded hair, like life in excrements, HAM 3.04.121
EXCUSABLE 1 FR 0.0001 REL FR 1 V 0 P
that were excusable, that, and thousands more ANT 3.04. 2
EXCUS'D 11 FR 0.0012 REL FR 6 V 5 P
that they may hold excus'd our lawless lives; TGV 4.01. 52
lamented, pitied, and excus'd | of every hearer; ADO 4.01.216
well excus'd. AWW 5.03. 55
all murthers past do stand excus'd in this; JN 4.03. 51
i will not excuse you, you shall not be excus'd, 2H4 5.01. 5 P
no excuse shall serve, you shall not be excus'd. 5.01. 6 P
sir john, you shall not be excus'd. 5.01. 12 P
sir john, you shall not be excus'd. 5.01. 21 P
they are then excus'd, my lord, when they see H5 5.02.302 P
y' are excus'd; H8 2.04.162
and purge | myself condemned and myself excus'd. ROM 5.03.227

EXCUSE *(also 'scuse, etc.)*
EXCUSE 88 FR 0.0099 REL FR 70 V 18 P
to go — | excuse it not, for i am peremptory. TGV 1.03. 71
and with the vantage of mine own excuse | hath 1.03. 82
teach me, thy tempted subject, to excuse it! 2.06. 8
i will not hear thy vain excuse, | but, as thou 3.01.168
i must excuse myself, master ford. WIV 3.02. 53 P
to him, and excuse his throwing into the water, 3.03.194 P
i something do excuse the thing i hate, | for MM 2.04.119
let me excuse me, and believe me so, | my mirth 4.01. 12
good signior angelo, you must excuse us all, ERR 3.01. 1
but she will well excuse | why at this time the 3.01. 92
you use this dalliance to excuse | your breach 4.01. 48
why seek'st thou then to cover with excuse ADO 4.01.174
your own good thoughts excuse me, and farewell. LLL 2.01.175
for our rude transgression | some fair excuse. 5.02.432
in your rich wisdom to excuse or hide | the 5.02.732
excuse me so, coming too short of thanks | for 5.02.738
hear my excuse, | my love, my life, my soul, MND 3.02.245
for your play needs no excuse. 5.01.356 P
never excuse; 5.01.356 P
her foot, | unless she do it under this excuse, MV 2.04. 36
man, | to excuse the current of thy cruelty. 4.01. 64
it will be a good excuse for me hereafter to AYL 3.03. 93 P
and what wit could wit have to excuse that? 4.01.170 P
that you might excuse | his broken promise, and 4.03.153
bear answer back | how you excuse my brother, 4.03.180
i hope this reason stands for my excuse. SHR in.2. 124
which at more leisure i will so excuse | as you 3.02.108
as a bristle may enter, in way of thy excuse. TN 1.05. 3 P
make your excuse wisely, you were best. 1.05. 30 P
if there were no other excuse why they should WT 1.01. 43 P
excuse it is to beat usurping down. JN 2.01.119
doth make the fault the worse by th' excuse: 4.02. 31
and thy abundant goodness shall excuse | this R2 5.03. 65
quit all offenses with as clear excuse | as well 1H4 3.02. 19
it hath the excuse of youth and heat of blood, 5.02. 17
love, | pleading so wisely in excuse of it! 2H4 4.05.180
you must excuse me, master robert shallow. 5.01. 3 P
i will not excuse you, you shall not be excus'd, 5.01. 4 P
not be admitted, there is no excuse shall serve, 5.01. 6 P
i humbly pray them to admit th' excuse | of time H5 5.pr. 3
i know it will excuse | this sudden execution of 1H6 5.05. 98
pray god the duke of york excuse himself! 2H6 1.03.178
clarence, excuse me to the king my brother; 3H6 5.05. 46
me have | some patient leisure to excuse myself. R3 1.02. 82
make | no excuse current but to hang thyself. 1.02. 84
excuse me, | the king has sent me otherwhere. H8 2.02. 58
my lord cardinal, | i do excuse you; 2.04.157
like your grace | to let my tongue excuse all. 5.02.184
excuse me. TRO 1.02. 81 P
what's his excuse? 2.03.163
for him at supper, you will make his excuse. 3.01. 77 P
well, i'll make 's excuse. 3.01. 90 P
you'll remember your brother's excuse? 3.01.143 P
give me excuse, good madam, i will obey you in COR 1.03.102 P
and i must excuse | what cannot be amended. 4.07. 11
there was a yielding — this admits no excuse. 5.06. 68
age | to keep mine own, excuse it how she can. TIT 4.02.105
what, shall this speech be spoke for our excuse? ROM 1.04. 1
the excuse that thou dost make in this delay 2.05. 33
is longer than the tale thou dost excuse. 2.05. 34
thee | doth much excuse the appertaining rage 3.01. 63
this shall not excuse the injuries | that thou 3.01. 66
made your minister | thus to excuse yourself. TIM 2.02.132
business, but he would not hear my excuse. 3.06. 14 P
majesty and skill | both countenance and excuse. HAM 4.01. 32
these bloody accidents must excuse my manners OTH 5.01. 94
yet must antony | no way excuse his foils, when ANT 1.04. 24
the gods give men | to excuse their after wrath. 5.02.287
our hence–going | and our return, to excuse. CYM 3.02. 64
why should excuse be born or e'er begot? 3.02. 65
she pray'd me to excuse her keeping close, 3.05. 46
i will not have excuse with saying this | loud PER 2.03. 96
"let me excuse thy courser, gentle boy, | and VEN 403
o strange excuse! 791
what excuse can my invention make | when thou LUC 225
might have excuse to work upon his wife, | as in 235
the shame and fault finds no excuse nor end. 238
she with blood had stain'd her stain'd excuse. 1316
where no excuse can give the fault amending. 1614
"o, teach me how to make mine own excuse, | or 1653
by my excuse shall claim excuse's giving." 1715
shall sum my count, and make my old excuse," SON 2.11
loving offenders, thus i will excuse ye: 42. 5
thus can my love excuse the slow offense | of my 51. 1
o, what excuse will my poor beast then find, 51. 5
but love, for love, thus shall excuse my jade: 51.12
excuse not silence so, for't lies in thee | to 101.10
let me excuse thee: 139. 9
EXCUSED 1 FR 0.0001 REL FR 1 V 0 P
and by despairing shalt thou stand excused | for R3 1.02. 86
EXCUSE'S 1 FR 0.0001 REL FR 1 V 0 P
by my excuse shall claim excuse's giving." LUC 1715
EXCUSES 8 FR 0.0009 REL FR 7 V 1 P
not be excus'd, excuses shall not be admitted, 2H4 5.01. 5 P
clifford, devise excuses for thy faults. 3H6 2.06. 71
/i will be deaf to pleading and excuses, | nor ROM 3.01.192
but | you patch'd up your excuses. ANT 2.02. 56
what bare excuses mak'st thou to be gone! VEN 188
thither, | he makes excuses for his being there. LUC 114
"why hunt i then for color or excuses? 267
nor fold my fault in cleanly coin'd excuses; 1073
EXCUSEZ–MOI 2 FR 0.0002 REL FR 0 V 2 P
excusez–moi, alice; H5 3.04. 28 P
excusez–moi, je vous supplie, mon tres puissant 5.02.256 P
EXCUSING 2 FR 0.0002 REL FR 2 V 0 P
and oftentimes excusing of a fault | doth make JN 4.02. 30
excusing /thy sins more than /thy sins are; SON 35. 8
EXECRABLE 1 FR 0.0001 REL FR 1 V 0 P
give sentence on this execrable wretch | that TIT 5.03.177
EXECRATIONS 2 FR 0.0002 REL FR 1 V 1 P
cease, gentle queen, these execrations, | and 2H6 3.02.305
i'll see some issue of my spiteful execrations. TRO 2.03. 7 P
EXECUTE 23 FR 0.0026 REL FR 16 V 7 P
i would, by contraries, | execute all things; TMP 2.01.149
whom here you have warrant to execute, is no MM 4.02.157 P
which you on all estates will execute | that lie LLL 5.02.845
the villainy you teach me, i will execute, and MV 3.01. 72 P
one thing more rests, that thyself execute — SHR 1.01.246
must either stay to execute them thyself, or WT 4.02. 15 P
to execute the charge my father gave me | for 5.01.162
thy men | to execute the noble duke at callice. R2 4.01. 82
i have a jest to execute that i cannot manage 1H4 1.02.161 P
(a business that this night may execute), 3.01. 81
whom with my bare fists i would execute, | if i 1H6 1.04. 36
more can i bear than you dare execute. 2H6 4.01.130
brother | to execute the like upon thyself — 3H6 2.04. 10
work thou the way — and that /shall execute. 5.07. 25
misdeeds, | yet execute thy wrath in me alone! R3 1.04. 71
your office, sergeant; execute it. H8 1.01.198
we'll execute your purpose, and put on | a form TRO 3.03. 50
as heart can think or courage execute. 4.01. 14
about, | in fellest manner execute your arms. 5.07. 6
him with determin'd sword | to execute upon him. OTH 2.03.228
to vex her i will execute in the clothes that CYM 3.05.142 P
off, or the common hangman shall execute it. PER 4.06.128 P
and settle again to execute their preordain'd TNK 4.03. 72 P
EXECUTED 19 FR 0.0021 REL FR 9 V 10 P
he hath stol'n, otherwise he had been executed; TGV 4.04. 32 P
claudio | be executed by nine to–morrow morning. MM 2.01. 34
let claudio be executed by four of the clock, 4.02.121 P
who is to be executed in th' afternoon? 4.02.128 P
deliver'd him to his liberty or executed him? 4.02.133 P
let this barnardine be this morning executed, 4.02.171 P
awake till you are executed, and sleep 4.03. 33 P
prison, | and see our pleasure herein executed. 5.01.521
to his hands, and commands shall be executed. TN 3.04. 28 P
that is like to be executed for robbing a church H5 3.06.101 P
and sometimes red, but his nose is executed, and 3.06.105 P
for treason executed in our late king's days? 1H6 2.04. 91
over, | because his purpose is not executed. 2H6 3.01.256
george, | be executed in his father's sight. R3 5.03. 96
and to be executed ere they wipe their lips. COR 4.05.216 P
come, | this vengeance on me had they executed: TIT 2.03.113
death, | that end upon them should be executed. 2.03.303
and what is written shall be executed. 5.02. 15
our spirit, | he shall be executed presently. TIM 3.05.102
EXECUTING 2 FR 0.0002 REL FR 2 V 0 P
and executing th' outward face of royalty | with TMP 1.02.104
if murthering innocents be executing, | why then 3H6 5.06. 32
EXECUTION 48 FR 0.0054 REL FR 41 V 7 P
like it, | the execution of it shall make known: TGV 1.03. 36
o'ernight | that wait for execution in the morn. 4.02.133
to th' hopeful execution do i leave you | of MM 1.01. 59
the provost hath | a warrant for 's execution. 1.04. 74
i have seen | when, after execution, judgment 2.02. 11
will help you to–morrow in your execution. 4.02. 23 P
as if to carry him to execution, and show'd him 4.02.151 P
vale, | the place of /death and sorry execution, ERR 5.01.121
whereof the execution did cry out | against the WT 1.02.260
own mouth — thereon | his execution sworn. 1.02.446
be swift like lightning in the execution, | and R2 1.03. 79
over | to execution and the hand of death. 3.01. 30
form | and present execution of our wills — 2H4 4.01.172
in the arm | that was uprear'd to execution. 4.01.212
retrait is made and execution stay'd. 4.03. 72
confederates | to york, to present execution. 4.03. 74
doing the execution and the act | for which we H5 2.02. 17
use his good pleasure, and put him to execution; 3.06. 56 P
my father's execution | was nothing less than 1H6 2.05. 99
presently, | and then do execution on the watch. 3.02. 35

ay, ay; away with her to execution! 5.04. 54
will excuse | this sudden execution of my will. 5.05. 99
thy cruelty in execution | upon offenders hath 2H6 1.03.132
from thence, unto the place of execution. 2.03. 6
refrain | the execution of my big–swoll'n heart 3H6 2.02.111
but, sirs, be sudden in the execution, | withal R3 1.03.345
safety, | enforc'd us to this execution? 3.05. 46
too late, | 'tis like a pardon after execution. H8 4.02.121
of their souls | by reason guide his execution. TRO 1.03.210
the will is infinite and the execution confin'd, 3.02. 82 P
hath done to–day | mad and fantastic execution, 5.05. 38
hold that purpose and to put it | in execution. COR 2.01.241
enforce the present execution | of what we 3.03. 21
back to rome, and prepare for your execution. 5.02. 48 P
throats are sentenc'd, and stay upon execution. 5.04. 8 P
she doth unroll | to do some fatal execution? TIT 2.03. 36
man but i | do execution on my flesh and blood. 4.02. 84
castaway, | do shameful execution on herself, 5.03. 76
which craves as desperate an execution | as that ROM 4.01. 69
so is he now in execution | of any bold or noble JC 1.02.297
steel, | which smok'd with bloody execution, MAC 1.02. 18
is execution done on cawdor? 1.04. 1
bosoms, | whose execution takes your enemy off, 3.01.104
the sway, revenue, execution of the rest, LR 1.01.137
iago doth give up | the execution of his wit, OTH 3.03.466
why, one that rode to 's execution, man, | could CYM 3.02. 70
pass'd slightly | his careless execution, where TNK 1.03. 29
let us put it in execution; 4.03.100 P
EXECUTIONER 12 FR 0.0013 REL FR 10 V 2 P
here is in our prison a common executioner, who MM 4.02. 9 P
call your executioner, and off with barnardine's 4.02.206 P
the common executioner, | whose heart th' AYL 3.05. 3
i would not be thy executioner; 3.05. 8
and like an executioner | cut off the heads of R2 3.04. 33
the deed, |-and i'll provide his executioner, 2H6 3.01.276
then, executioner, unsheathe thy sword. 3H6 2.02.123
think'st thou i am an executioner? 5.06. 30
executing, | why then thou art an executioner. 5.06. 33
and edward, | as blameful as the executioner? R3 1.02.119
wish thy death, | i will not be thy executioner. 1.02.185
us, | play judge and executioner all himself, CYM 4.02.128
EXECUTIONERS 2 FR 0.0002 REL FR 2 V 0 P
but soft, here come my executioners. R3 1.03.338
and they themselves become | the executioners. TNK 5.04.122
EXECUTOR 2 FR 0.0002 REL FR 2 V 0 P
says such baseness | had never like executor. TMP 3.01. 13
thee, | which used lives th' executor to be. SON 4.14
EXECUTORS 3 FR 0.0003 REL FR 3 V 0 P
let's choose executors and talk of wills; R2 3.02.148
delivering o'er to executors pale | the lazy H5 1.02.203
and their executors, the knavish crows, | fly 4.02. 51
EXECUT'ST 1 FR 0.0001 REL FR 1 V 0 P
'tis thou that execut'st the traitor's treason; LUC 877
EXEGI 1 FR 0.0001 REL FR 1 V 0 P
"et opus exegi, quod nec jovis ira, nec ignis" TNK 3.05. 88
EXEMPT 9 FR 0.0010 REL FR 9 V 0 P
be it my wrong you are from me exempt, | but ERR 2.02.171
and this our life, exempt from public haunt, AYL 2.01. 15
corrupted, and exempt from ancient gentry? 1H6 2.04. 93
is not quite exempt | from envious malice of thy 3.01. 25
true nobility is exempt from fear: 2H6 4.01.129
exempt from envy, but not from disdain, | unless 3H6 3.03.127
madam, yourself is not exempt from this; R3 2.01. 18
and with a care exempt themselves from fear; H8 1.02. 89
who would not wish to be from wealth exempt, TIM 4.02. 31
EXEMPTED 1 FR 0.0001 REL FR 1 V 0 P
exempted be from me the arrogance | to choose AWW 2.01.195
EXEQUIES 1 FR 0.0001 REL FR 1 V 0 P
but see his exequies fulfill'd in roan. 1H6 3.02.133
EXERCISE 20 FR 0.0022 REL FR 19 V 1 P
that they may work, | all exercise on thee; TMP 1.02.328
and be in eye of every exercise | worthy his TGV 1.03. 32
he's all my exercise, my mirth, my matter; WT 1.02.166
as nature | will bear up with this exercise, so 3.02.241
his youth | the rich advantage of good exercise. JN 4.02. 60
dare | to gentle exercise and proof of arms. 1H4 5.02. 54
for hunting was his daily exercise. 3H6 4.06. 85
i am in your debt for your last exercise; R3 3.02.110
be mov'd, | to draw him from his holy exercise. 3.07. 64
and swelling o'er with arts and exercise. TRO 4.04. 78
thy exercise hath been too violent for | a COR 1.05. 15
whose meal and exercise | are still together, 4.04. 14
that show of such an exercise may color | your HAM 3.01. 44
report | for art and exercise in your defense, 4.07. 97
hard at hand comes the master and main exercise, OTH 2.01.262 P
and prayer, | much castigation, exercise devout, 3.04. 41
i' th' common show–place, where they exercise. ANT 3.06. 12
no longer exercise | upon a valiant race thy CYM 5.04. 82
they are now starv'd for want of exercise; PER 1.04. 38
o, never | shall we two exercise, like twins of TNK 2.02. 18
EXERCISES 5 FR 0.0005 REL FR 2 V 3 P
for any or for all these exercises | he said TGV 1.03. 11
allow me such exercises as may become a AYL 1.01. 72 P
to his princely exercises than formerly he hath WT 4.02. 33 P
their sons with arts and martial exercises; 2H4 4.05. 73
all my mirth, forgone all custom of exercises; HAM 2.02.297 P
/EXETER 1 FR 0.0001 REL FR 1 V 0 P
/when /last /i /was /at /exeter, | /the /mayor R3 4.02.103
EXETER 25 FR 0.0028 REL FR 21 V 4 P
that late broke from the duke of exeter, | his R2 2.01.281
uncle of exeter, | enlarge the man committed H5 2.02. 39
my lord of westmerland, and uncle exeter, | we 2.02. 70
come, uncle exeter, | go you and enter harflew; 3.03. 51
is the duke of exeter safe? 3.06. 5 P
the duke of exeter is as magnanimous as 3.06. 6 P
the duke of exeter doth love thee well. 3.06. 22
but exeter hath given the doom of death | for 3.06. 44
the duke of exeter has very gallantly maintain'd 3.06. 91 P
and the duke of exeter is master of the pridge. 3.06. 95 P
dear lord gloucester, and my good lord exeter, 4.03. 9
words, | harry the king, bedford and exeter, 4.03. 53
go you with me, uncle of exeter. 4.07.183
here, uncle exeter, fill this glove with crowns, 4.08. 57
go, uncle exeter, | and brother clarence, and 5.02. 83
which is so plain that exeter doth wish | his 1H6 3.01.199
cousin of exeter, frowns, words, and threats 3H6 1.01. 72
exeter, thou art a traitor to the crown, | in 1.01. 80
art thou against us, duke of exeter? 1.01.147
ah, exeter! 1.01.191
exeter, so will i. 1.01.212
nay, take me with thee, good sweet exeter; 2.05.137
cousin of exeter, what thinks your lordship? 4.08. 34
no, exeter, these graces challenge grace; 4.08. 48
bishop of exeter, his elder brother, | with many R3 4.04.501
EXHALATION 2 FR 0.0002 REL FR 2 V 0 P
no natural exhalation in the sky, | no scope of JN 3.04.153
fall | like a bright exhalation in the evening, H8 3.02.226
EXHALATIONS 2 FR 0.0002 REL FR 1 V 1 P
do you behold these exhalations? 1H4 2.04.320 P
the exhalations whizzing in the air | give so JC 2.01. 44
/EXHAL'D 1 FR 0.0001 REL FR 1 V 0 P
it is some meteor that the sun /exhal'd | to be ROM 3.05. 13
EXHAL'D 2 FR 0.0002 REL FR 2 V 0 P
light, | and be no more an exhal'd meteor, | a 1H4 5.01. 19
let their exhal'd unwholesome breaths make sick LUC 779
EXHALE 2 FR 0.0002 REL FR 2 V 0 P
and doting death is near, | therefore exhale. H5 2.01. 62
and what these sorrows could not thence exhale, R3 1.02.165
EXHALES 1 FR 0.0001 REL FR 1 V 0 P
for 'tis thy presence that exhales this blood R3 1.02. 58
/EXHAL'ST 1 FR 0.0001 REL FR 1 V 0 P
/exhal'st this vapor vow, in thee it is: PP 3.11
EXHAL'ST 1 FR 0.0001 REL FR 1 V 0 P
my earth dost shine, | exhal'st this vapor–vow; LLL 4.03. 68
EXHAUST 1 FR 0.0001 REL FR 1 V 0 P
dimpled smiles from fools exhaust their mercy; TIM 4.03.120
EXHIBIT 4 FR 0.0004 REL FR 1 V 3 P
i'll exhibit a bill in the parliament for the WIV 2.01. 28 P
they should exhibit their petitions in the MM 4.04. 10 P
tears exhibit my tongue. MV 2.03. 10 P
plantagenet | we do exhibit to your majesty. 1H6 3.01.150
EXHIBITERS 1 FR 0.0001 REL FR 1 V 0 P
than cherishing th' exhibiters against us; H5 1.01. 74
EXHIBITION 6 FR 0.0006 REL FR 4 V 2 P
like exhibition thou shalt have from me. TGV 1.03. 69
certain, we have the exhibition to examine. ADO 4.02. 5 P
prescrib'd his pow'r, | confin'd to exhibition? LR 1.02. 25
wife, | due reference of place and exhibition, OTH 1.03.237
petticoats, nor caps, nor any petty exhibition; 4.03. 74 P
with tomboys hir'd with that self exhibition CYM 1.06.122
EXHORT 2 FR 0.0002 REL FR 1 V 1 P
man, and exhort all the world to be cowards; 2H6 4.10. 74 P
examples gross as earth exhort me: HAM 4.04. 46
EXHORTATION 1 FR 0.0001 REL FR 1 V 0 P
a while, | i'll end my exhortation after dinner. MV 1.01.104
EXIGENT 3 FR 0.0003 REL FR 3 V 0 P
spent, | wax dim, as drawing to their exigent; 1H6 2.05. 9
why do you cross me in this exigent? JC 5.01. 19
that when the exigent should come, which now ANT 4.14. 63
EXIL'D 7 FR 0.0008 REL FR 7 V 0 P
to /them again | that were with him exil'd. AYL 5.04.165
purchase honor, | and not the king exil'd thee; R2 1.03.283
and equity exil'd your highness' land. 2H6 3.01.146
beguil'd, | both you and i, for romeo is exil'd. ROM 3.02.133
as calling home our exil'd friends abroad | that MAC 5.09. 32
to be exil'd, and thrown | from leonati seat, CYM 5.04. 59
i sue for exil'd majesty's repeal, | let him LUC 640
EXILE 26 FR 0.0029 REL FR 24 V 2 P
since his exile she hath despis'd me most, TGV 3.02. 3
and let them be recall'd from their exile; 5.04.155
they willfully themselves exile from light, MND 3.02.386
put themselves into voluntary exile with him, AYL 1.01.102 P
that /she would have follow'd her exile, or have 1.01.109 P
now, my co–mates and brothers in exile, | hath 2.01. 1
the dateless limit of thy dear exile; R2 1.03.151
me | he shortens four years of my son's exile, 1.03.217
omitting suffolk's exile, my soul's treasure? 2H6 3.02.382
condemning some to death, and some to exile; COR 1.06. 35
vagabond exile, fleaing, pent to linger | but 3.03. 89
greasy caps in hooting at | coriolanus' exile. 4.06.132
a kiss | long as my exile, | sweet as my revenge! 5.03. 45
bewray what life | we have led since thy exile. 5.03. 96
thou art an exile, and thou must not stay. TIT 3.01.284
offense | immediately we do exile him hence. ROM 3.01.187
for exile hath more terror in his look, | much 3.03. 13
from the world, | and world's exile is death; 3.03. 20
and sayest thou yet that exile is not death? 3.03. 43
becomes thy friend, | and turns it to exile: 3.03.140
grief of my son's exile hath stopp'd her breath. 5.03.211
he takes his part | to draw upon an exile. CYM 1.01.166
the exile of her minion is too new, | she hath 2.03. 41
since the exile of posthumus, most retir'd 3.05. 36
who find in my exile the want of breeding, | the 4.04. 26
't may be she joy'd to jest at my exile, | 't PP 14. 9
EXION 1 FR 0.0001 REL FR 0 V 1 P
since my exion is ent'red and my case so openly 2H4 2.01. 30 P
EXIST 2 FR 0.0002 REL FR 2 V 0 P
orbs, | from whom we do exist and cease to be; LR 1.01.112
that by your virtuous means i may again | exist, OTH 3.04.112
EXISTS 1 FR 0.0001 REL FR 1 V 0 P
for thou exists on many a thousand grains | that MM 3.01. 20
EXIT 2 FR 0.0002 REL FR 0 V 2 P
his enter and exit shall be strangling a snake; LLL 5.01.134 P
keep some state in thy exit, and vanish. 5.02.594 P
EXITS 1 FR 0.0001 REL FR 1 V 0 P
they have their exits and their entrances, | and AYL 2.07.141
EXORCISER 1 FR 0.0001 REL FR 1 V 0 P
no exorciser harm thee! CYM 4.02.276
EXORCISMS 1 FR 0.0001 REL FR 0 V 1 P
will her ladyship behold and hear our exorcisms? 2H6 1.04. 4 P
EXORCIST 2 FR 0.0002 REL FR 2 V 0 P
is there no exorcist | beguiles the truer office AWW 5.03.304
thou, like an exorcist, hast conjur'd up | my JC 2.01.323
/EXPECT 1 FR 0.0001 REL FR 1 V 0 P
/and /be't /of /less /expect | /that /matter TRO 1.03. 70
EXPECT 35 FR 0.0039 REL FR 30 V 5 P
it is my promise, | and they expect it from me. TMP 4.01. 42
if /you do, expect spoon–meat, or bespeak a long ERR 4.03. 60 P
than you must expect of me to tell you how. ADO 1.01. 16 P
to–morrow then i will expect your coming, 5.01.296
i do expect return | of thrice three times the MV 1.03.158
my young master doth expect your reproach. 2.05. 20 P
we all expect a gentle answer, jew! 4.01. 34
soul, let's in, and there expect their coming. 5.01. 49
better news in store for you | than you expect. 5.01.275
and | my people did expect my hence departure WT 1.02.450
do all expect that you should rouse yourself, H5 1.02.123
expect saint martin's summer, halcyons' days, 1H6 1.02.131
renowned talbot doth expect my aid, | and i am 4.03. 12
and here i will expect thy coming. 5.03.145
fourteen days | at bristow i expect my soldiers, 2H6 3.01.328
expect your highness' doom, of life or death. 4.09. 12
and do expect him here some two hours hence. 3H6 5.01. 10
i every day expect an embassage | from my R3 2.01. 3
with hate in those where i expect most love! 2.01. 35
untimely storms makes men expect a dearth. 2.03. 35
it so, | 'tis more than we deserve or i expect. 2.03. 37
win the duke of york, | anon expect him here; 3.01. 39
what other | would you expect? H8 5.02.129
no talk of timon, nothing of him expect. TIM 5.02. 14
good, i will expect you. JC 1.02.293 P
you | where rather i'll expect victorious life ANT 4.02. 43
riveted trim, | and at the port expect you. 4.04. 23
what shalt thou expect | to be depender on a CYM 1.05. 57
my grief and as certain as i expect my revenge. 3.04. 25 P
when expect you them? 4.02.341
for comfort is too far for us to expect. PER 1.04. 59
were more than you expect, or more than's fit, 2.03. 5
we every day | expect him here: 4.01. 34
expect even here, where is a kingly patient, 5.01. 71
the things we are, for that which we expect; LUC 149
EXPECTANCE 1 FR 0.0001 REL FR 1 V 0 P
there is expectance here from both the sides, TRO 4.05.146
EXPECTANCY 1 FR 0.0001 REL FR 1 V 0 P
for every minute is expectancy | of more OTH 2.01. 41
/EXPECTATION 2 FR 0.0002 REL FR 2 V 0 P
/conjecture, /expectation, /and /surmise | /of 2H4 1.03. 23
/now /expectation, /tickling /skittish /spirits, TRO pr 20
EXPECTATION 25 FR 0.0028 REL FR 20 V 5 P
better bett'red expectation than you must expect ADO 1.01. 16 P
upon this, i will never trust my expectation. 2.03.212 P
oft expectation fails, and most oft there AWW 2.01.142
fresh expectation troubled not the land | with JN 4.02. 7
plot, good friends, and full of expectation; 1H4 2.03. 19 P
the hope and expectation of thy time | is ruin'd 3.02. 36
now possess'd | the utmost man of expectation, 2H4 1.03. 65
my death | thou hast seal'd up my expectation. 4.05.103
to find, | you stand in coldest expectation. 5.02. 31
survive, | to mock the expectation of the world, 5.02.126
for now sits expectation in the air, | and hides H5 2.pr. 8
and collected, | as were a war in expectation. 2.04. 20
our expectation hath this day an end. 3.03. 44
expectation whirls me round; TRO 3.02. 18
it opens the eyes of expectation. TIM 5.01. 23
the livelong day, with patient expectation, | to JC 1.01. 41
hang'd himself on th' expectation of plenty. MAC 2.03. 5 P
rest | that are within the note of expectation 3.03. 10
th' expectation and rose of the fair state, HAM 3.01.152
our preparation stands | in expectation of them. LR 4.04. 23
there were no expectation of our prosperity. OTH 2.01.280 P
should have borne men, and expectation fainted, ANT 3.06. 47
our expectation that it would be thus | hath CYM 3.05. 28
a mistress, expectation | most guiltless on't. TNK 3.01. 14
lo where our sister is in expectation, | yet 5.03.105
EXPECTATIONS 1 FR 0.0001 REL FR 0 V 1 P
and return'd me expectations and comforts of OTH 4.02.189 P
EXPECTED 11 FR 0.0012 REL FR 10 V 1 P
of despair, | when it is least expected. MM 4.03.111
supply, | that was expected by the dolphin here, JN 5.03. 10
all the expected good w' are like to hear | for H8 ep 8
shall all repair, | what honey is expected? TRO 1.03. 83
much more a fresher man, | had i expected thee. 5.06. 21
'twas to pardon | when it was less expected. COR 5.01. 19
mark antony is every hour in rome | expected. ANT 2.01. 30
and our oppression | exceeds what we expected. 4.07. 3
expected to prove so worthy as since he hath CYM 1.04. 2 P
he was expected then, | but not approach'd. 2.04. 38
"i am," quoth he, "expected of my friends, | and VEN 718
EXPECTERS 1 FR 0.0001 REL FR 1 V 0 P
interview | to the expecters of our troyan part; TRO 4.05.156
EXPECTING 7 FR 0.0008 REL FR 6 V 1 P
thus expecting thy reply, i profane my lips on LLL 4.01. 84 P
the coming space, | expecting absent friends. AWW 2.03.182
expecting but the aid | of buckingham to welcome R3 4.04.438
expecting ever when some envious surge | will in TIT 3.01. 96
gifts, | expecting in return twenty for one? TIM 4.03.510
within | with bloody veins, expecting overthrow, PER 1.04. 94
swell in their pride, the onset still expecting. LUC 432
EXPECTS 4 FR 0.0004 REL FR 3 V 1 P
my father at the road | expects my coming, there TGV 1.01. 54
tell you, expects performance of your promises. 2H6 1.04. 2 P
please you, save the thanks this prince expects. TRO 4.04.117
that thou expects not, nor i look'd not for. ROM 3.05.110
EXPEDIENCE 4 FR 0.0004 REL FR 4 V 0 P
are making hither with all due expedience, | and R2 2.01.287
did decree | in forwarding this dear expedience. 1H4 1.01. 33
and will with all expedience charge on us. H5 4.03. 70
the cause of our expedience to the queen, | and ANT 1.02.178
EXPEDIENT 8 FR 0.0009 REL FR 7 V 1 P
therefore is it most expedient for the wise, if ADO 5.02. 83 P
shall seem expedient on the now–born brief, AWW 2.03.179
his marches are expedient to this town, | his JN 2.01. 60
who painfully with much expedient march | have 2.01.223
the angry lords with all expedient haste. 4.02.268
expedient manage must be made, my liege, | ere R2 1.04. 39
a breach that craves a quick expedient stop! 2H6 3.01.288
tears) | i will with all expedient duty see you. R3 1.02.216
EXPEDIENTLY 1 FR 0.0001 REL FR 1 V 0 P
do this expediently, and turn him going. AYL 3.01. 18
EXPEDITION 24 FR 0.0027 REL FR 17 V 7 P
even with the speediest expedition | i will TGV 1.03. 37
shall be employ'd | to hasten on his expedition. 1.03. 77
longer than swiftest expedition | will give thee 3.01.164
time, | so much they spur their expedition. 5.01. 6
that the bark expedition put forth to–night, and ERR 4.03. 38 P
good expedition be my friend, and comfort | the WT 1.02.458
how much unlook'd for is this expedition! JN 2.01. 79
did set forth | upon his irish expedition; 1H4 1.03.150
not what impediments | drag back our expedition. 4.03. 19
for you before your expedition to shrewsbury. 2H4 1.02.102 P
be honest, and god bless your expedition! 1.02.222 P
poor and old motion, the expedition of thought? 4.03. 34 P
that may give furth'rance to our expedition; H5 1.02.301

of god, | putting it straight in expedition. 2.02.191
and of great expedition and knowledge in th' 3.02. 77 P
this expedition was by york and talbot | too 1H6 4.04. 2
levied host, | collected for this expedition. 4.04. 32
then fiery expedition be my wing, | jove's R3 4.03. 54
who intercepts me in my expedition? 4.04.136
he had, before this last expedition, twenty–five COR 2.01.153 P
his expedition promises | present approach. TIM 5.02. 3
bending their expedition toward philippi. JC 4.03.170
th' expedition of my violent love | outrun the MAC 2.03.110
this more stubborn and boist'rous expedition. OTH 1.03.228 P
/EXPEDITION'S 1 FR 0.0001 REL FR 1 V 0 P
priories shall pay | this /expedition's charge. JN 1.01. 49
EXPEDITIOUS 1 FR 0.0001 REL FR 1 V 0 P
and sail so expeditious, that shall catch | your TMP 5.01.316
EXPEL 6 FR 0.0006 REL FR 6 V 0 P
peace | should not expel these inconveniences, H5 5.02. 66
in the repeal, as hasty | to expel him thence. COR 4.07. 33
be of any power | to expel sickness, but prolong TIM 3.01. 63
with variable objects shall expel | this HAM 3.01.172
should patch a wall t' expel the /winter's flaw! 5.01.216
follow | this sound of hope doth labor to expel, VEN 976
EXPELL'D 1 FR 0.0001 REL FR 1 V 0 P
expell'd remorse and nature, whom, with TMP 5.01. 76
EXPELS 2 FR 0.0002 REL FR 2 V 0 P
even as one heat another heat expels, | or as TGV 2.04.192
expels the seeds of fear and th' apprehension TNK 5.01. 36
EXPEND 4 FR 0.0004 REL FR 4 V 0 P
i would expend it with all willingness. 2H6 3.01.150
will | as to expend your time with us a while HAM 2.02. 23
if i would time expend with such /a snipe | but OTH 1.03.385
heirs | may the two latter darken and expend; PER 3.02. 29
EXPENSE 19 FR 0.0021 REL FR 17 V 2 P
wilt thou, after the expense of so much money, WIV 2.02.141 P
and that, my state being gall'd with my expense, 3.04. 5
do so. this jest shall cost me some expense. ERR 3.01.123
i implore so much expense of thy royal sweet LLL 5.02.522 P
if i have thanks, it is a dear expense. MND 1.01.249
a third thinks, without expense at all, | by 1H6 1.01. 76
and what expense by th' hour | seems to flow H8 3.02.108
as honor, loss of time, travail, expense, TRO 2.02. 4
no care, no stop, so senseless of expense, TIM 2.02. 1
that i might so have rated my expense | as i had 2.02.126
we shall not spend a large expense of time MAC 5.09. 26
they keep, | what company, at what expense; HAM 2.01. 9
to have th' expense and waste of his revenues. LR 2.01.100
that horse and sail and high expense | can stead PER 3.ch. 20
and care in us | at whose expense 'tis done. 4.03. 46
his banners sable, trimm'd with rich expense, 5.ch. 19
and moan th' expense of many a vanish'd sight; SON 30. 8
and husband nature's riches from expense; 94. 6
th' expense of spirit in a waste of shame | is 129. 1
EXPENSES 2 FR 0.0002 REL FR 1 V 1 P
hold, there's expenses for thee. TN 3.01. 43 P
for your expenses and sufficient charge, | among 1H6 5.05. 92
EXPERIENC'D 3 FR 0.0003 REL FR 3 V 0 P
thereto | clerk–like experienc'd, which no less WT 1.02.392
the greekish ears | to his experienc'd tongue, TRO 1.03. 68
as best thou art experienc'd, since thou know'st COR 4.05.139
EXPERIENCE 21 FR 0.0023 REL FR 14 V 7 P
experience is by industry achiev'd, | and TGV 1.03. 22
his years but young, but his experience old; 2.04. 69
receiv'd none, unless experience be a jewel — WIV 2.02.204 P
this — your long experience of /her wisdom, ERR 3.01. 89
how hast thou purchased this experience? LLL 3.01. 26 P
yes, i have gain'd my experience. AYL 4.01. 26 P
and your experience makes you sad. 4.01. 27 P
make me merry than experience to make me sad — 4.01. 28 P
than at home, | where small experience grows. SHR 1.02. 52
reading | and manifest experience had collected AWW 1.03.223
and of his old experience th' only darling, | he 2.01.107
sinn'd against his experience and transgress'd 2.05. 10 P
why art thou old, and want'st experience? 2H6 5.01.171
bold her bashful years with your experience; R3 4.04.326
of age, | grave witnesses of true experience, TIT 5.03. 78
i shall have so much experience for my pains; OTH 2.03.367 P
pawn their experience to their present pleasure, ANT 1.04. 32
experience, manhood, honor, ne'er before | did 3.10. 22
experience, o, thou disprov'st report! CYM 4.02. 34
peace, peace, and give experience tongue. PER 1.02. 37
experience for me many bulwarks builded | of LC 152
EXPERIENCES 1 FR 0.0001 REL FR 0 V 1 P
action to be guided by others' experiences: CYM 1.04. 46 P
EXPERIMENT 2 FR 0.0002 REL FR 1 V 1 P
to make another experiment of his suspicion. WIV 4.02. 35 P
of heaven, not me, make an experiment. AWW 2.01.154
EXPERIMENTAL 1 FR 0.0001 REL FR 1 V 0 P
which with experimental seal doth warrant | the ADO 4.01.166
EXPERIMENTS 2 FR 0.0002 REL FR 2 V 0 P
of art, | and hold me pace in deep experiments. 1H4 3.01. 48
you | are singled forth to try thy experiments. TIT 2.03. 69
EXPERT 3 FR 0.0003 REL FR 2 V 1 P
a valiant and most expert gentleman. H5 3.07.129 P
town, | placing therein some expert officers, 1H6 3.02.127
pilot | of very expert and approv'd allowance; OTH 2.01. 49
EXPERTNESS 2 FR 0.0002 REL FR 0 V 2 P
what his valor, honesty, and expertness in wars; AWW 4.03.178 P
what say you to his expertness in war? 4.03.265 P
EXPIATE 2 FR 0.0002 REL FR 2 V 0 P
make haste, the hour of death is expiate. R3 3.03. 24
then look i death my days should expiate. SON 22. 4
EXPIRATION 3 FR 0.0003 REL FR 3 V 0 P
then, at the expiration of the year, | come LLL 5.02.804
art come | before the expiration of thy time, R2 2.03.111
if, till the expiration of your month, | you LR 2.04.202
EXPIR'D 6 FR 0.0006 REL FR 6 V 0 P
i would his troubles likewise were expir'd, 1H6 2.05. 31
till term of eighteen months | be full expir'd. 2H6 1.01. 68
your time's expir'd, | either expound now, or PER 1.01. 89
if in which time expir'd he not return, | i 2.04. 47
my twelve months are expir'd, and tyrus stands 3.03. 2
an expir'd date, cancell'd ere well begun: LUC 26
EXPIRE 9 FR 0.0010 REL FR 9 V 0 P
constancies | expire before their fashions." AWW 1.02. 63
even this ill night your breathing shall expire, JN 5.04. 36
i will lay odds that, ere this year expire, | we 2H4 5.05.105
and expire the term | of a despised life clos'd ROM 1.04.109
lives | expire before the flowers in their caps, MAC 4.03.172
where you may abide till your date expire. PER 3.04. 14
now that cannot finish | till one of us expire. TNK 5.01. 19
we expire, | and not without men's pity; 5.04. 4
lie, | as the death–bed whereon it must expire, SON 73.11
EXPIRED 1 FR 0.0001 REL FR 1 V 0 P
to work my mind, when body's work's expired; SON 27. 4
EXPIRES 1 FR 0.0001 REL FR 1 V 0 P
that's a month before | this bond expires, i do MV 1.03.158
EXPIRING 1 FR 0.0001 REL FR 1 V 0 P
and thus expiring do foretell of him: R2 2.01. 32
EXPLAIN *(see plain*)*
EXPLICATION 1 FR 0.0001 REL FR 0 V 1 P
as it were in via, in way, of explication; LLL 4.02. 14 P
EXPLOIT 16 FR 0.0018 REL FR 12 V 4 P
a trim exploit, a manly enterprise, | to conjure MND 3.02.157
come forth to view | the issue of th' exploit. MV 3.02. 60
who are sick | for breathing and exploit. AWW 1.02. 17
i will grace the attempt for a worthy exploit. 3.06. 68 P
some hurts, and say i got them in exploit. 4.01. 38 P
will they adventure upon the exploit themselves, 1H4 1.02.172 P
imagination of some great exploit | drives him 1.03.199
gilded over your night's exploit on gadshill. 2H4 1.02.149 P
i shall as famous be by this exploit | as 1H6 2.03. 5
but mine it will, that no exploit have done. 4.05. 27
gold | will tempt unto a close exploit of death? R3 4.02. 35
who (but for dreaming on this fond exploit) 5.03.330
in hand | any exploit worthy the name of honor. JC 2.01.317
such an exploit have i in hand, ligarius, | had 2.01.318
i will work him | to an exploit, now ripe in my HAM 4.07. 64
and, in the fleshment of this /dread exploit, LR 2.02.123
EXPLOIT'S 1 FR 0.0001 REL FR 0 V 1 P
what exploit's in hand? where sups he to–night? TRO 3.01. 81 P
EXPLOITS 7 FR 0.0008 REL FR 6 V 1 P
his rest to do more exploits with his mace than ERR 4.03. 28 P
ripe for exploits and mighty enterprises. H5 1.02.121
of all exploits since first i follow'd arms, 1H6 2.01. 43
thy late exploits done in the heart of france 2H6 1.01.196
whose high exploits and honorable deeds TIT 5.01. 11
time, thou anticipat'st my dread exploits: MAC 4.01.144
obdurate vassals fell exploits effecting, | in LUC 429
EXPOS'D 6 FR 0.0006 REL FR 6 V 0 P
expos'd unto the sea (which hath requit it) TMP 3.03. 71
that for thy mother's fault art thus expos'd WT 3.03. 50
too | expos'd this paragon to th' fearful usage 5.01.153
expos'd myself | from certain and possess'd TRO 3.03. 6
o, you shall be expos'd, my lord, to dangers 4.04. 68
trunks, | to the conflicting elements expos'd, TIM 4.03.230
EXPOSE 5 FR 0.0005 REL FR 4 V 1 P
and expose | those tender limbs of thine to the AWW 3.02.103
for his sake | did i expose myself (pure for his TN 5.01. 83
which aided to expose the child were even then WT 5.02. 71 P
why do fond men expose themselves to battle, TIM 3.05. 42
expose thyself to feel what wretches feel, LR 3.04. 34
EXPOSING 2 FR 0.0002 REL FR 2 V 0 P
exposing what is mortal and unsure | to all that HAM 4.04. 51
cheek, | exposing it (but o, the harder heart! CYM 3.04.161
EXPOSITION 5 FR 0.0005 REL FR 3 V 2 P
i have an exposition of sleep come upon me. MND 4.01. 39 P
the law, your exposition | hath been most sound. MV 4.01.237
reverence | your exposition on the holy text 2H4 4.02. 7
a most courteous exposition. ROM 2.04. 56 P
strict edict, | your exposition misinterpreting, PER 1.01.112
EXPOSITOR 1 FR 0.0001 REL FR 1 V 0 P
which his fair tongue, conceit's expositor, LLL 2.01. 72
EXPOSTULATE 5 FR 0.0005 REL FR 4 V 1 P
the time now serves not to expostulate: TGV 3.01.253
nay, stay not to expostulate, make speed, | or 3H6 2.05.135
more bitterly could i expostulate, | save that, R3 3.07.192
madam, to expostulate | what majesty should be, HAM 2.02. 86
i'll not expostulate with her, lest her body and OTH 4.01.205 P
EXPOSTULATION 1 FR 0.0001 REL FR 1 V 0 P
nay, we must use expostulation kindly, | for it TRO 4.04. 60
EXPOSTURE 1 FR 0.0001 REL FR 1 V 0 P
more than a wild exposture to each chance | that COR 4.01. 36
EXPOSURE 2 FR 0.0002 REL FR 2 V 0 P
dirt, | to weaken /or discredit our exposure, TRO 1.03.195
that suffer in exposure, let us meet | and MAC 2.03.127
EXPOUND 5 FR 0.0005 REL FR 3 V 2 P
an ass, if he go about /t' expound this dream. MND 4.01.207 P
me here behind to expound the meaning or moral SHR 4.04. 79 P
expound unto me, boy. H5 4.04. 58
stew, and to expound | his beastly mind to us, CYM 1.06.152
either expound now, or receive your sentence. PER 1.01. 90
EXPOUNDED 2 FR 0.0002 REL FR 2 V 0 P
and this way have you well expounded it. JC 2.02. 91
which read and not expounded, 'tis decreed, | as PER 1.01. 57
/EXPRESS 1 FR 0.0001 REL FR 1 V 0 P
/strove | /who /should /express /her /goodliest. LR 4.03. 17
EXPRESS 40 FR 0.0045 REL FR 31 V 9 P
on mine honor, | my words express my purpose. MM 2.04.148
having the hour limited, and an express command, 4.02.166 P
that shall express my true love's fasting pain. LLL 4.03.120
neither rhyme nor reason can express how much. AYL 3.02.398 P
to express the like kindness, myself, that have SHR 2.01. 77 P
groan, | yet i express to you a mother's care. AWW 1.03.148
less, | resolvedly more leisure shall express. 5.03.332
if this suit be won, | that you express content; ep 3
me in manners the rather to express myself. TN 2.01. 15 P
to the contrary i have express commandment. WT 2.02. 8
being counted falsehood, shall (as i express it) 3.02. 27
that ballad–makers cannot be able to express it. 5.02. 25 P
the sums i have collected shall express. JN 4.02.142
face, | as bid me tell my tale in express words, 4.02.234
and we give express charge that, in our marches H5 3.06.108 P
from him i have express commandement | that thou 1H6 1.03. 20
glansdale, | let me have your express opinions, 1.04. 64
i can express no kinder sign of love | than this 2H6 1.01. 18
as i in justice and true right express it. 5.02. 25
with that which here his passion doth express? TRO 5.02.162
or express yourself in a more comfortable sort. COR 1.03. 1 P
minded, | wave thus to express his disposition, 1.06. 74
let deeds express | what's like to be their 3.01.132
ere he express himself or move the people | with 5.06. 54
whereby we might express some part of our zeals, TIM 1.02. 86 P
these well express in thee thy latter spirits: 5.04. 74
do, t' express his love and friending to you, HAM 1.05.185
how express and admirable in action! 2.02.305 P
with us, | we shall express our duty in his eye, 4.04. 6
mean time we shall express our darker purpose. LR 1.01. 36
could best express how slow his soul sail'd on, CYM 1.03. 13
no farther with your din | express impatience, 5.04.112
father, to express | my commendations great, PER 2.02. 8
in glitt'ring golden characters express | a 4.03. 44
if such vows | stand for express will, all the TNK 3.06.229
"my tongue cannot express my grief for one, VEN 1069
her joy with heav'd–up hand she doth express, LUC 111
for more it is than i can well express, | and 1286
that may express my love, or thy dear merit? SON 108. 4
me words, and words express | the manner of my 140. 3
EXPRESS'D 15 FR 0.0017 REL FR 15 V 0 P
one (as you are well express'd | by all external MM 2.04.136
henceforth my wooing mind shall be express'd LLL 5.02.412
sum or sums as are | express'd in the condition, MV 1.03.148
save of joy | express'd and not express'd. 3.02.183
save of joy | express'd and not express'd. 3.02.183
it is not so express'd, but what of that? 4.01.260
scorn'd a fair color, or express'd it stol'n, AWW 5.03. 50
that hath express'd himself in all his deeds | a TIT 1.01.422
would be well express'd | in our condition. TIM 1.01. 76
but not express'd in fancy, rich, not gaudy, HAM 1.03. 71
old thing 'twas, but it express'd her fortune, OTH 4.03. 29
whose inward ill no outward harm express'd. LUC 91
than that tongue that more hath more express'd. SON 23.12
i see their antique pen would have express'd 106. 7
at randon from the truth vainly express'd; 147.12
EXPRESSED 1 FR 0.0001 REL FR 1 V 0 P
proud with his form, in his eye pride expressed; LLL 2.01.237
EXPRESSETH 1 FR 0.0001 REL FR 1 V 0 P
womb | expresseth his full tilth and husbandry. MM 1.04. 44
EXPRESSING 3 FR 0.0003 REL FR 3 V 0 P
shapes, such gesture, and such sound expressing TMP 3.03. 37
past all expressing. MV 3.05. 73
one thing expressing, leaves out difference. SON 105. 8
EXPRESSION *(see expressure)*
EXPRESSIVE 1 FR 0.0001 REL FR 0 V 1 P
be more expressive to them, for they wear AWW 2.01. 52 P
EXPRESSLY 11 FR 0.0012 REL FR 10 V 1 P
dine, | when i to /feast expressly am forbid; LLL 1.01. 62
the words expressly are "a pound of flesh." MV 4.01.307
for your physicians have expressly charg'd, | in SHR in.2. 121
away, | and i expressly am forbid to touch it; 4.01.171
here, | to whom expressly i bring greeting too. H5 2.04.112
'tis expressly against the law of arms. 4.07. 1 P
the king's will from his mouth expressly? H8 3.02.235
expressly proves | that no man is the lord of TRO 3.03.114
the prince expressly hath | forbid this bandying ROM 3.01. 88
and i am sent expressly to your lordship. TIM 2.02. 32
their face their manners most expressly told: LUC 1397
EXPRESSURE 3 FR 0.0003 REL FR 2 V 1 P
th' expressure that it bears, green let it be, WIV 5.05. 67
manner of his gait, the expressure of his eye, TN 2.03.157 P
than breath or pen can give expressure to. TRO 3.03.204
EXPULS'D 1 FR 0.0001 REL FR 1 V 0 P
for ever should they be expuls'd from france, 1H6 3.03. 25
EXPULSION 2 FR 0.0002 REL FR 2 V 0 P
rome, | no, not th' expulsion of the tarquins. COR 5.04. 43
more hateful than the foul expulsion is | of thy CYM 2.01. 60
EXQUISITE 13 FR 0.0014 REL FR 3 V 10 P
i mean that her beauty is exquisite, but her TGV 2.01. 54 P
who, the most exquisite claudio? ADO 1.03. 50 P
most radiant, exquisite, and unmatchable beauty TN 1.05.170 P
thy exquisite reason, dear knight? 2.03.143 P
i have no exquisite reason for't, but i have 2.03.145 P
my most exquisite sir topas! 4.02. 62 P
'tis the way | to call hers, exquisite, in ROM 1.01.229
virtuous lord, my very exquisite friend. TIM 3.02. 29 P
she's a most exquisite lady. OTH 2.03. 18 P
your /englishman so exquisite in his drinking? 2.03. 80 P
this is a more exquisite song than the other. 2.03. 98 P
and jewels | of rich and exquisite form, their CYM 1.06.190
that she hath all courtly parts more exquisite 3.05. 71
EXSUFFLICATE 1 FR 0.0001 REL FR 1 V 0 P
soul | to such exsufflicate and /blown surmises, OTH 3.03.182
/EXTANT 1 FR 0.0001 REL FR 1 V 0 P
/but /in /this /extant /moment, /faith /and TRO 4.05.168
EXTANT 5 FR 0.0005 REL FR 2 V 3 P
ay, and an ox too; both the proofs are extant. WIV 5.05.120 P
is there no virtue extant? 1H4 2.04.119 P
his name's gonzago, the story is extant, and HAM 3.02.262 P
she is all the beauty extant! TNK 2.02.147
that you yourself, being extant, well might show SON 83. 6
EXTEMPORAL 3 FR 0.0003 REL FR 1 V 2 P
assist me, some extemporal god of rhyme, for i LLL 1.02.183 P
will you hear an extemporal epitaph on the death 4.02. 50 P
as i with sudden and extemporal speech | purpose 1H6 3.01. 6
EXTEMPORALLY 2 FR 0.0002 REL FR 2 V 0 P
quick comedians | extemporally will stage us, ANT 5.02.217
note, | and sings extemporally a woeful ditty, VEN 836
EXTEMPORE 5 FR 0.0005 REL FR 1 V 4 P
you may do it extempore, for it is nothing but MND 1.02. 68 P
it is extempore, from my mother–wit. SHR 2.01.263
at us, and we may do any thing extempore. WT 4.04.677 P
we be merry, shall we have a play extempore? 1H4 2.04.280 P
and ever since thou hast blush'd extempore. 2.04.316 P
EXTEND 17 FR 0.0019 REL FR 13 V 4 P
the sole drift of my purpose doth extend | not a TMP 5.01. 29
to buy his favor, i extend this friendship. MV 1.03.168
enough | may not extend so far as to the lady; 2.07. 28
god, that would not extend his might only where AWW 1.03.113 P
it, and extend to you what further becomes his 3.06. 69 P
i extend my hand to him thus, quenching my TN 2.05. 65 P
it reaches far, and where 'twill not extend, H8 1.01.111
to lacedaemon did my land extend. TIM 2.02.151
you shall offend him and extend his passion. MAC 3.04. 56
that we our largest bounty may extend | where LR 1.01. 52
patience, good iago, | that i extend my manners; OTH 2.01. 98
you do extend | these thoughts of horror further ANT 5.02. 62
i do extend him, sir, within himself, | crush CYM 1.01. 25
under her colors are wonderfully to extend him, 1.04. 21 P
forespent on us, | we must extend our notice. 2.03. 60
sometimes they do extend | their view right on; LC 25
and supplicant their sighs to you extend | to 276
EXTENDED 6 FR 0.0006 REL FR 5 V 1 P

when vice makes mercy, mercy's so extended, MM 4.02.112
of worst — extended | with vildest torture, let AWW 2.01.173
extended or contracted all proportions | to a 5.03. 51
the report of her is extended more than can be WT 4.02. 43 P
formed in th' applause | where th' are extended; TRO 3.03.120
hath with his parthian force | extended asia; ANT 1.02.101
EXTENDS 1 FR 0.0001 REL FR 1 V 0 P
that mercy which fierce fire and iron extends, JN 4.01.119
EXTENT 5 FR 0.0005 REL FR 4 V 1 P
make an extent upon his house and lands. AYL 3.01. 17
in this uncivil and unjust extent | against thy TN 4.01. 53
and, for the extent | of egall justice, us'd in TIT 4.04. 3
in this garb, /lest /my extent to the players, HAM 2.02.373 P
and front of my offending | hath this extent, no OTH 1.03. 81
EXTENUATE 6 FR 0.0006 REL FR 6 V 0 P
you may not so extenuate his offense | for i MM 2.01. 27
a husband, | and so extenuate the 'forehand sin. ADO 4.01. 50
you up | (which by no means we may extenuate) MND 1.01.120
nothing extenuate, | nor set down aught in OTH 5.02.342
know | we will extenuate rather than enforce. ANT 5.02.125
is alive, | her rash suspect she doth extenuate, VEN 1010
EXTENUATED 1 FR 0.0001 REL FR 0 V 1 P
his glory not extenuated, wherein he was worthy; JC 3.02. 39 P
EXTENUATES 1 FR 0.0001 REL FR 1 V 0 P
persist | in doing wrong extenuates not wrong, TRO 2.02.187
EXTENUATION 1 FR 0.0001 REL FR 1 V 0 P
yet such extenuation let me beg | as, in reproof 1H4 3.02. 22
EXTERIOR 4 FR 0.0004 REL FR 4 V 0 P
that she were a maid, | by these exterior shows? ADO 4.01. 40
exterior form, outward accoutrement, | but from JN 1.01.211
teacheth this prostrate and exterior bending. 2H4 4.05.148
it, | sith nor th' exterior nor the inward man HAM 2.02. 6
EXTERIORLY 1 FR 0.0001 REL FR 1 V 0 P
in my form, | which, howsoever rude exteriorly, JN 4.02.257
EXTERIORS 1 FR 0.0001 REL FR 0 V 1 P
so course o'er my exteriors with such a greedy WIV 1.03. 65 P
EXTERMIN'D 1 FR 0.0001 REL FR 1 V 0 P
your sorrow and my grief | were both extermin'd. AYL 3.05. 89
EXTERN 2 FR 0.0002 REL FR 2 V 0 P
and figure of my heart | in complement extern, OTH 1.01. 63
canopy, | with my extern the outward honoring, SON 125. 2
/EXTERNAL 1 FR 0.0001 REL FR 1 V 0 P
/and /these /external /manners /of /laments R2 4.01.296
EXTERNAL 6 FR 0.0006 REL FR 6 V 0 P
are well express'd | by all external warrants), MM 2.04.137
should well agree with our external parts? SHR 5.02.168
having no external thing to lose | but the word JN 2.01.571
her virtues, graced with external gifts, | do 1H6 5.05. 3
poison, 'twould appear | by external swelling; ANT 5.02.346
in all external grace you have some part, | but SON 53.13
EXTINCT 4 FR 0.0004 REL FR 4 V 0 P
shall be extinct with age and endless /night; R2 1.03.222
heat, extinct in both | even in their promise, HAM 1.03.118
glister with new fire, or be | to-day extinct. TNK 5.01. 70
i am extinct, | there is but envy in that light 5.03. 20
EXTINCTED 1 FR 0.0001 REL FR 1 V 0 P
give renew'd fire to our extincted spirits, OTH 2.01. 81
EXTINCTURE 1 FR 0.0001 REL FR 1 V 0 P
both fire from hence and chill extincture hath. LC 294
EXTINGUISH 1 FR 0.0001 REL FR 1 V 0 P
/and natural graces that extinguish art; 1H6 5.03.192
EXTINGUISHING 1 FR 0.0001 REL FR 1 V 0 P
face, | extinguishing his conduct in this case; LUC 313
EXTINGUIT 1 FR 0.0001 REL FR 1 V 0 P
"qui me alit, me extinguit." PER 2.02. 33
EXTIRP 1 FR 0.0001 REL FR 0 V 1 P
but it is impossible to extirp it quite, friar, MM 3.02.102 P
EXTIRPATE 1 FR 0.0001 REL FR 1 V 0 P
should presently extirpate me and mine | out of TMP 1.02.125
EXTIRPED 1 FR 0.0001 REL FR 1 V 0 P
with us, | but be extirped from our provinces. 1H6 3.03. 24
EXTOL 4 FR 0.0004 REL FR 4 V 0 P
flatter and praise, commend, extol their graces; TGV 3.01.102
i so deserv'd of you, | that you extol me thus? MM 5.01.503
mother, | who has a charter to extol her blood, COR 1.09. 14
evident as a chair | t' extol what it hath done. 4.07. 53
EXTOLL'D 1 FR 0.0001 REL FR 1 V 0 P
if i should pay you for't as 'tis extoll'd, | it TIM 1.01.167
EXTOLMENT 1 FR 0.0001 REL FR 0 V 1 P
but, in the verity of extolment, i take him to HAM 5.02.116 P
EXTON 3 FR 0.0003 REL FR 3 V 0 P
sir pierce of exton, who | lately came from the R2 5.05.100
exton, thy fierce hand | hath with the king's 5.05.109
exton, i thank thee not, for thou hast wrought 5.06. 34
EXTORT 5 FR 0.0005 REL FR 4 V 1 P
would so offend a virgin and extort | a poor MND 3.02.160
that you will not extort from me what i am TN 2.01. 13 P
do not extort thy reasons from this clause, 3.01.153
till the injurious romans did extort | this CYM 3.01. 47
and so extort from 's that | which we have done, 4.04. 12
EXTORTED 2 FR 0.0002 REL FR 2 V 0 P
are my chests fill'd up with extorted gold? 2H6 4.07. 99
life | extorted treasure in the womb of earth, HAM 1.01.137
EXTORTION 1 FR 0.0001 REL FR 1 V 0 P
into your own hands, card'nal, by extortion; H8 3.02.285
EXTORTIONS 1 FR 0.0001 REL FR 1 V 0 P
bags | are lank and lean with thy extortions. 2H6 1.03.129
EXTRACT 1 FR 0.0001 REL FR 1 V 0 P
could out of thee extract one spark of evil H5 2.02.101
EXTRACTED *(also extraught)*
EXTRACTED 1 FR 0.0001 REL FR 0 V 1 P
of many simples, extracted from many objects, AYL 4.01. 17 P
EXTRACTING 2 FR 0.0002 REL FR 1 V 1 P
hand in the pocket and extracting /it clutch'd? MM 3.02. 47 P
a most extracting frenzy of mine own | from my TN 5.01.281
EXTRAORDINARILY 2 FR 0.0002 REL FR 0 V 2 P
me, and i mean not to sweat extraordinarily. 2H4 1.02.210 P
beats as extraordinarily as heart would desire, 2.04. 24 P
EXTRAORDINARY 5 FR 0.0005 REL FR 3 V 2 P
thee there's something extraordinary in thee. WIV 3.03. 69 P
me how to remember any extraordinary pleasure. AYL 1.02. 7 P
by some severals | of head-piece extraordinary? WT 1.02.227
these signs have mark'd me extraordinary, | and 1H4 3.01. 40
with community, | afford no extraordinary gaze, 3.02. 78
EXTRAUGHT *(also extracted)*
EXTRAUGHT 1 FR 0.0001 REL FR 1 V 0 P
thou not, knowing whence thou art extraught, 3H6 2.02.142
EXTRAVAGANCY 1 FR 0.0001 REL FR 0 V 1 P
my determinate voyage is mere extravagancy. TN 2.01. 12 P
EXTRAVAGANT 4 FR 0.0004 REL FR 2 V 2 P
simple, a foolish extravagant spirit, full of LLL 4.02. 66 P
th' extravagant and erring spirit hies | to his HAM 1.01.154
in an extravagant and wheeling stranger | of OTH 1.01.136
but they are now in a most extravagant vagary. TNK 4.03. 73 P
EXTREME 17 FR 0.0019 REL FR 16 V 1 P
hot fire, | but qualify the fire's extreme rage, TGV 2.07. 22
be not as extreme in submission as in offense; WIV 4.04. 11
the extreme parts of time extremely forms | all LLL 5.02.740
yet extreme gusts will blow out fire and all; SHR 2.01.135
therefore fire, for i have caught extreme cold. 4.01. 45 P
worthy sake | to th' extreme edge of hazard. AWW 3.03. 6
when i was dry with rage and extreme toil, 1H4 1.03. 31
death, | but that the extreme peril of the case, R3 3.05. 44
or i with grief and extreme age shall perish 4.04.186
the extreme dangers, and the drops of blood COR 4.05. 69
and almost broke my heart with extreme laughter. TIT 5.01.113
temp'ring extremities with extreme sweet. ROM 2.pr. 14
are now within a foot | of th' extreme verge. LR 4.06. 26
but, being wrought, | perplexed in the extreme; OTH 5.02.346
and extreme fear can neither fight nor fly, LUC 230
savage, extreme, rude, cruel, not to trust, SON 129. 4
had, having, and in quest to have, extreme, | a 129.10
EXTREMELY 8 FR 0.0009 REL FR 7 V 1 P
the extreme parts of time extremely forms | all LLL 5.02.740
extremely stretch'd and conn'd with cruel pain, MND 5.01. 80
stirr'd | with such an agony he sweat extremely, H8 2.01. 33
to hear the city | abus'd extremely, and to cry, ep 6
nay, urg'd extremely for't, and show'd what TIM 3.02. 12 P
you play the child extremely. TNK 2.02.204
extremely lov'd him, infinitely lov'd him; 2.04. 15
if you do, | your teeth will bleed extremely. 3.05. 81
EXTREMES 18 FR 0.0020 REL FR 17 V 1 P
which otherwise would grow into extremes. SHR in.1. 138
to chide at your extremes it not becomes me. WT 4.04. 6
comfort, to be us'd | in undeserv'd extremes. JN 4.01.107
fierce extremes | in their continuance will not 5.07. 13
course from the inwards to the parts' extremes. 2H4 4.03.107 P
but always resolute in most extremes. 1H6 4.01. 38
who can be patient in such extremes? 3H6 1.01.215
by so much is the wonder in extremes. 3.02.115
death, | do to this body what extremes you can; TRO 4.02.102
and do not break into these deep extremes. TIT 3.01.215
'twixt my extremes and me this bloody knife ROM 4.01. 62
'twixt two extremes of passion, joy and grief, LR 5.03.199
to the time o' th' year between the extremes ANT 1.05. 51
no midway | 'twixt these extremes at all. 3.04. 20
a settled valor | (not tainted with extremes) TNK 4.02.101
thy weal and woe are both of them extremes; VEN 987
devise extremes beyond extremity, | to make him LUC 969
extremity still urgeth such extremes. 1337
EXTREMEST 10 FR 0.0011 REL FR 8 V 2 P
gentleman to the extremest shore of my modesty, MM 3.02.251 P
my purse, my person, my extremest means, | lie MV 1.01.138
stood on th' extremest verge of the swift brook, AYL 2.01. 42
to prove it on thee to the extremest point | of R2 4.01. 47
with the very extremest inch of possibility; 2H4 4.03. 35 P
to take her in her heart's extremest hate, R3 1.02.231
as near as the extremest ends | of parallels, as TRO 1.03.167
capital kind, | deserves th' extremest death. COR 3.03. 82
to kill, i grant, is sin's extremest gust, | but TIM 3.05. 54
and from th' extremest upward of thy head | to LR 5.03.137
EXTREMITIES 5 FR 0.0005 REL FR 4 V 1 P
what blows, what extremities he endur'd, and in 1H4 1.02.189 P
be too noble, | but when extremities speak. COR 3.02. 41
to say extremities was the trier of spirits, 4.01. 4
temp'ring extremities with extreme sweet. ROM 2.pr. 14
would run to these and these extremities; JC 2.01. 31
/EXTREMITY 1 FR 0.0001 REL FR 1 V 0 P
/make /much /more, | /and /top /extremity. LR 5.03.208
EXTREMITY 30 FR 0.0034 REL FR 21 V 9 P
any extremity rather than a mischief. WIV 4.02. 73 P
not what i seek, show no color for my extremity; 4.02.161 P
mark'd | to bear the extremity of dire mishap! ERR 1.01.141
passion | ne'er brake into extremity of rage. 5.01. 48
o time's extremity, | hast thou so crack'd and 5.01.308
her eye, | which she must dote on in extremity. MND 3.02. 3
those that are in extremity of either are AYL 4.01. 5 P
a fool, | and turn'd into the extremity of love. 4.03. 23
to save your life in this extremity, | this SHR 4.02.103
but in the extremity of the one, it must needs WT 5.02. 19 P
little better, extremity of weather continuing, 5.02.119 P
life, | which false hope lingers in extremity. R2 2.02. 72
'tis she | that /tempers him to this extremity. R3 1.01. 65
they say in great extremity, and fear'd | she'll H8 5.01. 19
shall to the edge of all extremity | pursue each TRO 4.05. 68
in the extremity of great and little, | valor 4.05. 78
now this extremity | hath brought me to thy COR 4.05. 78
oft, | extremity of griefs would make men mad; TIT 4.01. 19
in the pantry, and every thing in extremity. ROM 1.03.102 P
never knewest, but the extremity of both ends. TIM 4.03.301 P
my youth i suff'red much extremity for love — HAM 2.02.190 P
quantity, | in neither aught, or in extremity. 3.02.168
thy uncover'd body this extremity of the skies. LR 3.04.102 P
proceed upon just grounds | to this extremity. OTH 5.02.139
thy tongue | may take off some extremity, which CYM 3.04. 17
graves, and smiling | extremity out of act. PER 5.01.139
extremity, that sharpens sundry wits, | makes me TNK 1.01.118
devise extremes beyond extremity, | to make him LUC 969
extremity still urgeth such extremes. 1337
find, | when swift extremity can seem but slow? SON 51. 6
EXULT 2 FR 0.0002 REL FR 1 V 1 P
that you insult, exult, and all at once, | over AYL 3.05. 36
i would exult, man. TN 2.05. 7 P
EXULTATION 1 FR 0.0001 REL FR 1 V 0 P
your exultation | partake to every one. WT 5.03.131
EXULTING 1 FR 0.0001 REL FR 1 V 0 P
more exulting? TNK 5.03. 89
EYASES *(also niesse)*
/EYASES 1 FR 0.0001 REL FR 0 V 1 P
/an /aery /of /children, /little /eyases, /that HAM 2.02.339 P
EYAS-MUSKET 1 FR 0.0001 REL FR 0 V 1 P
how now, my eyas-musket, what news with you? WIV 3.03. 22 P
EY'D 5 FR 0.0005 REL FR 5 V 0 P
full many a lady | i have ey'd with best regard, TMP 3.01. 40
that, when he wak'd, of force she must be ey'd. MND 3.02. 40
i ey'd them | even to their ships. WT 2.01. 35
ey'd awry | distinguish form; R2 2.02. 19
for as you were when first your eye i ey'd, SON 104. 2
EYE *(also e'e)*
/EYE 1 FR 0.0001 REL FR 1 V 0 P
/is /it mine /eye, or valentinus' praise, | her TGV 2.04.196
EYE 495 FR 0.0559 REL FR 443 V 52 P
the fringed curtains of thine eye advance | and TMP 1.02.409
with an eye of green in't. 2.01. 56 P
where she, at least, is banish'd from your eye, 2.01.127
the setting of thine eye and cheek proclaim | a 2.01.229
our master | cap'ring to eye her. 5.01.238
and be in eye of every exercise | worthy his TGV 1.03. 32
that not an eye that sees you but is a physician 2.01. 40 P
they say that love hath not an eye at all. 2.04. 96
i read your fortune in your eye. 2.04.143
myself | to be regarded in her sun-bright eye. 3.01. 88
nought but mine eye | could have persuaded me; 5.04. 64
spy | more fresh in julia's with a constant eye? 5.04.115
the appetite of her eye did seem to scorch me up WIV 1.03. 67 P
have not your worship a wart above your eye? 1.04.147 P
as long as i have an eye to make difference of 2.01. 56 P
take heed, have open eye, for thieves do foot by 2.01.122
sir john, as you have one eye upon my follies, 2.02.186 P
lead mine eyes, or eye your master's heels? 3.02. 4 P
i see how thine eye would emulate the diamond. 3.03. 55 P
no man their works must eye. 5.05. 48
dishonor not your eye | by throwing it on any MM 5.01. 22
methinks i see a quick'ning in his eye. 5.01.495
as, nimble jugglers that deceive the eye, ERR 1.02. 98
there's nothing situate under heaven's eye | but 2.01. 16
i know his eye doth homage otherwhere, | or else 2.01.104
since that my beauty cannot please his eye, 2.01.114
ear, | that never object pleasing in thine eye, 2.02.115
a fool, | to put the finger in the eye and weep, 2.02.204
let not my sister read it in your eye; 3.02. 9
it is a fault that springeth from your eye. 3.02. 55
mine eye's clear eye, my dear heart's dearer 3.02. 62
mightst thou perceive austerely in his eye 4.02. 2
hath not else his eye | stray'd his affection in 5.01. 50
in mine eye she is the sweetest lady that ever i ADO 1.01.187 P
i look'd upon her with a soldier's eye, | that 1.01.298
i have a good eye, uncle, i can see a church by 2.01. 82 P
let every eye negotiate for itself, | and trust 2.01.178
and in her eye there hath appear'd a fire | to 4.01.162
life, | into the eye and prospect of his soul, 4.01.229
your niece regards me with an eye of favor. 5.04. 22
that eye my daughter lent her, 'tis most true. 5.04. 23
and i do with an eye of love requite her. 5.04. 24
study me how to please the eye indeed | by LLL 1.01. 80
the eye indeed | by fixing it upon a fairer eye, 1.01. 81
who dazzling so, that eye shall be his heed, 1.01. 82
beauty is bought by judgment of the eye, | not 2.01. 15
his eye begets occasion for his wit, | for every 2.01. 69
will you prick't with your eye? 2.01.189
did make their retire | to the court of his eye, 2.01.235
proud with his form, in his eye pride expressed; 2.01.237
methought all his senses were lock'd in his eye, 2.01.242
that in words which his eye hath disclos'd. 2.01.251
i only have made a mouth of his eye, | by adding 2.01.252
king cophetua set eye upon the pernicious and 4.01. 65 P
thy eye jove's lightning bears, thy voice his 4.02.115
o, but her eye — by this light, but for her eye 4.03. 9 P
by this light, but for her eye, i would not love 4.03. 9 P
"did not the heavenly rhetoric of thine eye, 4.03. 58
by heaven, the wonder in a mortal eye! 4.03. 83
i | will praise a hand, a foot, a face, an eye, 4.03.182
what peremptory eagle-sighted eye | dares look 4.03.222
might shake off fifty, looking in her eye: 4.03.239
if that she learn not of her eye to look: 4.03.248
world | teaches such beauty as a woman's eye? 4.03.309
it adds a precious seeing to the eye: 4.03.330
his tongue filed, his eye ambitious, his gait 5.01. 11 P
the virtue of your eye must break my oath. 5.02.348
with eyes best seeing, heaven's fiery eye, | by 5.02.375
this proves you wise and rich, for in my eye — 5.02.379
squier, | and laugh upon the apple of her eye? 5.02.475
there's an eye | wounds like a leaden sword. 5.02.480
form'd by the eye and therefore, like the eye, 5.02.762
form'd by the eye and therefore, like the eye, 5.02.762
varying in subjects as the eye doth roll | to 5.02.764
the sudden hand of death close up mine eye! 5.02.815
me, | behold the window of my heart, mine eye, 5.02.838
my ear should catch your voice, my eye your eye, MND 1.01.188
my ear should catch your voice, my eye your eye, 1.01.188
in thy eye that shall appear | when thou wak'st, 2.02. 32
can, | deserve a sweet look from demetrius' eye, 2.02.127
so is mine eye enthralled to thy shape; 3.01.139
the moon methinks looks with a wat'ry eye; 3.01.198
then, what it was that next came in her eye, 3.02. 2
as wild geese that the creeping fowler eye, | or 3.02. 20
cupid's archery, | sink in apple of his eye. 3.02.104
night, that from the eye his function takes, 3.02.177
thou art not by mine eye, lysander, found; 3.02.181
then crush this herb into lysander's eye; 3.02.366
and then i will her charmed eye release | from 3.02.376
and sleep, that sometimes shuts up sorrow's eye, 3.02.435
i'll apply | /to your eye, | gentle lover, 3.02.451
in the sight | of thy former lady's eye; 3.02.457
the object and the pleasure of mine eye, | is 4.01.170
methinks i see these things with parted eye, 4.01.189
the eye of man hath not heard, the ear of man 4.01.211 P
the poet's eye, in a fine frenzy rolling, | doth 5.01. 12
within the eye of honor, be assur'd | my purse, MV 1.01.137
a christian by, | will be worth a jewess' eye. 2.05. 43
within whose empty eye | there is a written 2.07. 63
and even there, his eye being big with tears, 2.08. 46
not learning more than the fond eye doth teach, 2.09. 27
proper, my eye shall be the stream | and wat'ry 3.02. 46
glancing an eye of pity on his losses, | that 4.01. 27
to view with hollow eye and wrinkled brow | an 4.01.270
eyes he doubly sees himself, | in each eye, one. 5.01.245
if i had a thunderbolt in mine eye, i can tell AYL 1.02.214 P
poke, | and, looking on it with lack-lustre eye, 2.07. 21
and as mine eye doth his effigies witness | most 2.07.193
survey | with thy chaste eye, from thy pale 3.02. 3
that every eye which in this forest looks 3.02. 7
a blue eye and sunken, which you have not; 3.02.374 P

thou tell'st me there is murder in mine eye: 3.05. 10
now show the wound mine eye hath made in thee. 3.05. 20
did make offense, his eye did heal it up. 3.05.117
"whiles the eye of man did woo me, | that could 4.03. 47
if that an eye may profit by a tongue, | then 4.03. 83
he threw his eye aside, | and mark what object 4.03.102
shall in despite enforce a watery eye. SHR in.1. 128
it is best | put finger in the eye, and she knew 1.01. 79
whose sudden sight hath thrall'd my wounded eye. 1.01.220
to make mine eye the witness | of that report 2.01. 52
because his painted skin contents the eye? 4.03.178
and draw | his arched brows, his hawking eye, AWW 1.01. 94
that makes me see, and cannot feed mine eye? 1.01.221
her eye is sick on't; 1.03.136
wet, | the many–color'd iris, rounds thine eye? 1.03.152
darling, | he bade me store up, as a triple eye, 2.01.108
fair maid, send forth thine eye. 2.03. 52
where the impression of mine eye infixing, 5.03. 47
was in mine eye | the dust that did offend it. 5.03. 54
for mine eye, | while i was speaking, oft was 5.03. 81
mine eye too great a flatterer for my mind. TN 1.05.309
worth stooping for, there it lies in your eye; 2.02. 15 P
his gait, the expressure of his eye, forehead, 2.03.158 P
thine eye | hath stay'd upon some favor that it 2.04. 23
o, for a stone–bow, to hit him in the eye! 2.05. 46 P
ay, and you had any eye behind you, you might 2.05.136 P
at every feather | that comes before his eye. 3.01. 65
haply your eye shall light upon some toy | you 3.03. 44
if it please the eye of one, it is with me as 3.04. 22 P
dearly, | him will i tear out of that cruel eye, 5.01.127
sir page, | look on me with your welkin eye. WT 1.02.136
present | th' abhorr'd ingredient to his eye, 2.01. 43
whole matter | and copy of the father — eye, 2.03.100
bring | tincture or lustre in her lip, her eye, 3.02.205
i the fairest youth | that ever made eye swerve, 4.04.374
to have an open ear, a quick eye, and a nimble 4.04.671 P
the sun looking with a southward eye upon him, 4.04.790 P
i'ld bid you mark | her eye, and tell me for 5.01. 64
hermione as is her picture, | affront his eye. 5.01. 75
the other, when she has obtain'd your eye, 5.01.105
my liege, | your eye hath too much youth in't. 5.01.225
she had one eye declin'd for the loss of her 5.02. 74 P
every wink of an eye some new grace will be born 5.02.110 P
the fixure of her eye has motion in't, | as we 5.03. 67
mine eye hath well examined his parts, | and JN 1.01. 89
here | before the eye and prospect of your town, 2.01.208
my lord, and in her eye i find | a wonder, or a 2.01.496
the shadow of myself form'd in her eye, | which, 2.01.498
drawn in the flattering table of her eye. 2.01.503
drawn in the flattering table of her eye! 2.01.504
clapp'd on the outward eye of fickle france, 2.01.583
why holds thine eye that lamentable rheum, 3.01. 22
turning with splendor of his precious eye | the 3.01. 79
hubert, throw thine eye | on yon young boy. 3.03. 59
she looks upon them with a threat'ning eye. 3.04.120
but for containing fire to harm mine eye. 4.01. 66
i will not touch thine eye | for all the 4.01.121
to seek the beauteous eye of heaven to garnish, 4.02. 15
of a wicked heinous fault | lives in his eye; 4.02. 72
a fearful eye thou hast. 4.02.106
or turn'd an eye of doubt upon my face, | as bid 4.02.233
distrust | govern the motion of a kingly eye. 5.01. 47
unthread the rude eye of rebellion, | and 5.04. 11
the cruel pangs of death | right in thine eye. 5.04. 60
o cousin, thou art come to set mine eye. 5.07. 51
verge | that ever was surveyed by english eye, R2 1.01. 94
the last leave of thee takes my weeping eye. 1.02. 74
o, let no noble eye profane a tear | for me, if 1.03. 59
i espy | virtue with valor couched in thine eye. 1.03. 98
all places that the eye of heaven visits | are 1.03.275
o, had thy grandsire with a prophet's eye | seen 2.01.104
or if it be, 'tis with false sorrow's eye, 2.02. 26
look on my wrongs with an indifferent eye. 2.03.116
that when the searching eye of heaven is hid 3.02. 37
so may you by my dull and heavy eye: 3.02.196
behold, his eye, | as bright as is the eagle's, 3.03. 68
love | than my unpleased eye see your courtesy. 3.03.193
thine eye begins to speak, set thy tongue there; 5.03.125
to thread the postern of a small needle's eye." 5.05. 17
i do see | danger and disobedience in thine eye. 1H4 1.03. 16
and on my face he turn'd an eye of death, 1.03.143
hast thou never an eye in thy head? 2.01. 28 P
but chiefly a villainous trick of thine eye, and 2.04.404 P
of a cheerful look, a pleasing eye, and a most 2.04.423 P
not an eye | but is a–weary of thy common sight, 3.02. 87
whence | the eye of reason may pry in upon us. 4.01. 72
no eye hath seen such scarecrows. 4.02. 38 P
with some fine color that may please the eye 5.01. 75
i see a strange confession in thine eye. 2H4 1.01. 94
have you not a moist eye, a dry hand, a yellow 1.02.180 P
when richard, with his eye brimful of tears, 3.01. 67
his eye is hollow, and he changes much. 4.05. 6
at, how shall we stretch our eye | when capital H5 2.02. 55
as black and white, my eye will scarcely see it. 2.02.104
not working with the eye without the ear, | and 2.02.135
then lend the eye a terrible aspect; 3.01. 9
have at the very eye of that proverb with "a pox 3.07.119 P
sun, | his liberal eye doth give to every one, 4.pr. 44
sweats in the eye of phoebus, and all night 4.01.273
that face to face, and royal eye to eye, | you 5.02. 30
that face to face, and royal eye to eye, | you 5.02. 30
i have but with a /cursitory eye | o'erglanc'd 5.02. 77
thing he sees there, let thine eye be thy cook. 5.02.149 P
face will wither, a full eye will wax hollow; 5.02.161 P
one eye thou hast to look to heaven for grace; 1H6 1.04. 83
the sun with one eye vieweth all the world. 1.04. 84
two girls, which hath the merriest eye — | i 2.04. 15
my side | that any purblind eye may find it out. 2.04. 21
that it will glimmer through a blindman's eye. 2.04. 24
no shape but his can please your dainty eye. 5.03. 38
day, | he knits his brow and shows an angry eye, 2H6 3.01. 15
look with a gentle eye upon this wretch! 3.03. 20
i lost mine eye in laying the prize aboard, 4.01. 25
any life be left in thee, | throw up thine eye! 3H6 2.05. 85
upon thy wounds, that kills mine eye and heart! 2.05. 87
wishing his foot were equal with his eye, | and 3.02.137
but is he gracious in the people's eye? 3.03.117
i speak, | ye see i drink the water of my eye. 5.04. 75
have now the fatal object in my eye | where my 5.06. 16
and many an orphan's water–standing eye — | men 5.06. 40
a cherry lip, a bonny eye, a passing pleasing R3 1.01. 94
no sleep close up that deadly eye of thine, 1.03.224
o, if thine eye be not a flatterer, | come thou 1.04.264
even where his raging eye or savage heart, 3.05. 83
that seems disgracious in the city's eye, | and 3.07.112
made prize and purchase of his wanton eye, 3.07.187
the world, | whose unavoided eye is murtherous. 4.01. 55
tear–falling pity dwells not in this eye. 4.02. 65
if i be so disgracious in your eye, | let me 4.04.178
myself, | look on my forces with a gracious eye; 5.03.109
such noble scenes as draw the eye to flow, | we H8 pr 4
him in eye | still him in praise, and being 1.01. 30
him — let some graver eye | pierce into that — 1.01. 67
and his eye revil'd | me as his abject object; 1.01.126
were tried by ev'ry tongue, ev'ry eye saw 'em, 3.01. 35
and came to th' eye o' th' king, wherein was 3.02. 31
and anon he casts | his eye against the moon. 3.02.118
paper in the packet, | to bless your eye withal. 3.02.130
helen, to change, would give an eye to boot. TRO 1.02.239 P
whose med'cinable eye | corrects the /ill 1.03. 91
as will stop the eye of helen's needle, for whom 2.01. 80 P
at /unawares encount'ring | the eye of majesty. 3.02. 39
nor doth the eye itself, | that most pure spirit 3.03.105
but eye to eye opposed | salutes each other with 3.03.107
but eye to eye opposed | salutes each other with 3.03.107
the present eye praises the present object. 3.03.180
since things in motion sooner catch the eye 3.03.183
the lustre in your eye, heaven in your cheek, 4.04.118
there's language in her eye, her cheek, her lip, 4.05. 55
why dost thou so oppress me with thine eye? 4.05.241
thou green sarcenet flap for a sore eye, thou 5.01. 32 P
one eye yet looks on thee, | but with my heart 5.02.107
but with my heart the other eye doth see. 5.02.108
i find, | the error of our eye directs our mind. 5.02.110
look how thy eye turns pale! 5.03. 81
follow me, sirs, and my proceedings eye, | it is 5.07. 7
the kingly–crowned head, the vigilant eye, | the COR 1.01.115
reechy neck, | clamb'ring the walls to eye him; 2.01.210
turns up the white o' th' eye to his discourse. 4.05.196 P
and is no less apparent | to th' vulgar eye, 4.07. 21
sit in gold, his eye | red as 'twould burn rome; 5.01. 63
every flaw, | and saving those that eye thee! 5.03. 75
he is able to pierce a corslet with his eye, 5.04. 21 P
serve your lust, shadowed from heaven's eye, TIT 2.01.130
what signifies my deadly–standing eye, | my 2.03. 32
pit, | where never man's eye may behold my body: 2.03.177
that ever eye with sight made heart lament! 2.03.205
my heart suspects more than mine eye can see. 2.03.213
for such a sight will blind a father's eye. 2.04. 53
o, that which i would hide from heaven's eye, 4.02. 59
and, as i earnestly did fix mine eye | upon the 5.01. 22
is the pearl that pleas'd your empress' eye, 5.01. 42
can the son's eye behold his father bleed? 5.03. 65
take thou some new infection to thy eye, | and ROM 1.02. 49
and with unattainted eye | compare her face with 1.02. 85
when the devout religion of mine eye | maintains 1.02. 88
by, | herself pois'd with herself in either eye; 1.02. 95
but no more deep will i endart mine eye | than 1.03. 98
care i | what curious eye doth cote deformities? 1.04. 31
her eye discourses, i will answer it. 2.02. 13
there lies more peril in thine eye | than twenty 2.02. 71
now, ere the sun advance his burning eye, | the 2.03. 5
care keeps his watch in every old man's eye, 2.03. 35
stabb'd with a white wench's black eye, run 2.04. 14 P
hildings and harlots, thisby a grey eye or so, 2.04. 43 P
what eye but such an eye would spy out such a 3.01. 21 P
what eye but such an eye would spy out such a 3.01. 21 P
than the death/–darting eye of cockatrice. 3.02. 47
i'll say yon grey is not the morning's eye, 3.05. 19
and trust me, love, in my eye so do you; 3.05. 58
green, so quick, so fair an eye | as paris hath. 3.05.220
what a mental power | this eye shoots forth! TIM 1.01. 32
h'as caught me in his eye, i will present | my 4.03.469
for the eye sees not itself | but by reflection, JC 1.02. 52
turn | your hidden worthiness into your eye, 1.02. 57
set honor in one eye and death i' th' other, 1.02. 86
and that same eye whose bend doth awe the world 1.02.123
have an eye to cinna; 2.03. 2 P
a friendly eye could never see such faults. 4.03. 90
the eye wink at the hand; MAC 1.04. 52
yet let that be | which the eye fears, when it 1.04. 53
bear welcome in your eye, | your hand, your 1.05. 64
air, | shall blow the horrid deed in every eye, 1.07. 24
'tis the eye of childhood | that fears a painted 2.02. 51
masking the business from the common eye | for 3.01.124
present him eminence both with eye and tongue: 3.02. 31
night, | scarf up the tender eye of pitiful day, 3.02. 47
eye of newt and toe of frog, | wool of bat and 4.01. 14
all swoll'n and ulcerous, pitiful to the eye, 4.03.151
your eye in scotland | would create soldiers, 4.03.186
a mote it is to trouble the mind's eye. HAM 1.01.112
joy, | with an auspicious, and a dropping eye, 1.02. 11
and let thine eye look like a friend on denmark. 1.02. 69
breath, | no, nor the fruitful river in the eye, 1.02. 80
here in the cheer and comfort of our eye, | our 1.02.116
in my mind's eye, horatio. 1.02.185
nay then i have an eye of you! 2.02.290 P
soldier's, scholar's, eye, tongue, sword, | th' 3.01.151
an eye like mars, to threaten and command, | a 3.04. 57
you, | that you do bend your eye on vacancy, 3.04.117
with us, | we shall express our duty in his eye, 4.04. 6
your judgment 'pear | as day does to your eye. 4.05.153
burn out the sense and virtue of mine eye! 4.05.156
he swore had neither motion, guard, nor eye, 4.07.101
and you, the judges, bear a wary eye. 5.02.279
me still remain | the true blank of thine eye. LR 1.01.159
a still–soliciting eye, and such a tongue | that 1.01.231
he gives the web and the pin, /squinies the eye, 3.04.117 P
you have one eye left | to see some mischief on 3.07. 81
who hast not in thy brows an eye discerning 4.02. 52
going to put out | the other eye of gloucester. 4.02. 72
but, o poor gloucester, | lost he his other eye? 4.02. 81
high–grown field, | and bring him to our eye. 4.04. 8
whose power | will close the eye of anguish. 4.04. 15
that eye that told you so look'd but a–squint. 5.03. 72
in impatient thoughts | by being in his eye. OTH 1.03.243
her eye must be fed; 2.01.225 P
that /has an eye can stamp and counterfeit 2.01.243 P
with my personal eye | will i look to't. 2.03. 5
what an eye she has! 2.03. 22 P
an inviting eye; and yet methinks right modest. 2.03. 24 P
it, my father's eye | should hold her loathed, 3.04. 61
make it a darling like your precious eye. 3.04. 66
do you perceive the gastness of her eye? 5.01.106
sweetest innocent | that e'er did lift up eye. 5.02.200
i know by that same eye there's some good news. ANT 1.03. 19
kill me when they do not | eye well to you. 1.03. 97
this in the public eye? 3.06. 11
in eye of caesar's battle, from which place | we 3.09. 2
whose eye beck'd forth my wars and call'd them 4.12. 26
nor once be chastis'd with the sober eye | of 5.02. 54
long | as he could make me with /this eye or ear CYM 1.03. 9
air, and then | have turn'd mine eye and wept. 1.03. 22
it cannot be i' th' eye: 1.06. 39
takes prisoner the wild motion of mine eye, 1.06.103
then by–peeping in an eye | base and illustrious 1.06.108
night, that dawning | may bare the raven's eye! 2.02. 49
take this too, | it is a basilisk unto mine eye, 2.04.107
no single soul | can we set eye on; 4.02.131
as small a drop of pity | as a wren's eye, 4.02.305
or fruitful object be | in eye of imogen, that 5.04. 56
of wiving, | fairness which strikes the eye — 5.05.168
harmless lightning) throws her eye | on him, her 5.05.394
to the judgment of your eye | i give my cause, PER 1.ch. 41
desert, because thine eye | presumes to reach, 1.01. 32
archer hits the mark | his eye doth level at, so 1.01.163
her face was to mine eye beyond all wonder; 1.02. 75
this by the eye of cynthia hath she vowed, | and 2.05. 11
of mortal loathsomeness from the blest eye | of TNK 1.01. 45
first with mine eye of all those beauties in her 2.02.168
that | i ear'd her language, liv'd in her eye, o 3.01. 29
what an eye, | of what a fiery sparkle and quick 4.02. 12
of an eye as heavy | as if he had lost his 4.02. 27
surfeit of her eye hath distemper'd the other 4.03. 70 P
'tween her mind and eye become the pranks and 4.03. 80 P
this business, were't one eye | against another, 5.01. 21
not that thy rare green eye — which never yet 5.01.144
not taint mine eye | with dread sights it may 5.03. 9
the belief | both seal'd with eye and ear. 5.03. 15
knights must kindle | their valor at your eye. 5.03. 30
yet his eye | is like an engine bent, or a sharp 5.03. 41
long time his eye | will dwell upon his object; 5.03. 48
i see one eye of yours conceives a tear, | the 5.03.137
with burning eye did hotly overlook them, VEN 178
sprite, | and with a heavy, dark, disliking eye, 182
thine eye darts forth the fire that burneth me, 196
and dead, | statue contenting but the eye alone, 213
his eye, which scornfully glisters like fire, 275
and this i do to captivate the eye | of the fair 281
broad breast, full eye, small head, and nostril 296
nigh, | for all askance he holds her in his eye. 342
but, when his glutton eye so full hath fed, 399
sky, | so is her face illumin'd with her eye, 486
do surfeit by the eye and pine the maw; 602
sawest thou not signs of fear lurk in mine eye? 644
presenteth to mine eye | the picture of an angry 661
so glides he in the night from venus' eye, 816
her eye seen in the tears, tears in her eye, 962
her eye seen in the tears, tears in her eye, 962
being prison'd in her eye like pearls in glass, 980
trifles, unwitnessed with eye or ear, | thy 1023
and then she reprehends her mangling eye, | that 1065
for oft the eye mistakes, the brain being 1068
whose downward eye still looketh for a grave, 1106
in their pure ranks his traitor eye encloses, LUC 73
save sometime too much wonder of his eye, 95
which must be lodestar to his lustful eye; 179
my heart shall never countermand mine eye. 276
that eye which looks on her confounds his wits; 290
that eye which him beholds, as more divine, 291
the eye of heaven is out, and misty night 356
and in his will his willful eye he tired. 417
his eye, which late this mutiny restrains, 426
his drumming heart cheers up his burning eye, 435
eye, | his eye commends the leading to his hand; 436
only he hath an eye to gaze on beauty, | and 496
remain | the scornful mark of every open eye; 520
here with a cockatrice' dead–killing eye | he 540
with heavy eye, knit brow, and strengthless pace 709
"they think not but that every eye can see | the 750
face, | and tarquin's eye may read the mot afar, 830
fly, | but eagles gaz'd upon with every eye. 1015
"o eye of eyes, | why pry'st thou through my 1088
will fix a sharp knife to affright mine eye, 1138
day, | as shaming any eye should thee behold, 1143
set, | each flow'r moist'ned like a melting eye, 1227
for then the eye interprets to the ear | the 1325
her, with a steadfast eye | receives the scroll 1339
lie | imagine every eye beholds their blame, 1343
her earnest eye did make him more amazed. 1356
was left unseen, save to the eye of mind: 1426
thy eye kindled the fire that burneth here, 1475
and here in troy, for trespass of thine eye, 1476
his eye drops fire, no water thence proceeds; 1552
and round about her tear–distained eye | blue 1586
outruns the eye that doth behold his haste, 1668
did not the heavenly rhetoric of thine eye, PP 3. 1
she show'd for favors to allure his eye; 4. 6
thine eye jove's lightning seems, thy voice his 5.11
the sun look'd on the world with glorious eye, 6.11
an englishman, the fairest that eye could see, 15. 3
when as thine eye hath chose the dame, | and 18. 1
the lovely gaze where every eye doth dwell SON 5. 2
head, each under eye | doth homage to his 7. 2
is it for fear to wet a widow's eye | that thou 9. 1
sometime too hot the eye of heaven shines, | and 18. 5
an eye more bright than theirs, less false in 20. 5
mine eye hath play'd the painter and hath 24. 1
spread | but as the marigold at the sun's eye, 25. 6
then can i drown an eye (unus'd to flow) | for 30. 5
hath dear religious love stol'n from mine eye 31. 6
flatter the mountain tops with sovereign eye, 33. 2
mine eye and heart are at a mortal war, | how to 46. 1
mine eye my heart /thy picture's sight would bar 46. 3

my heart mine eye the freedom of that right. 46. 4
betwixt mine eye and heart a league is took, 47. 1
when that mine eye is famish'd for a look, | or 47. 3
with my love's picture then my eye doth feast, 47. 5
another time mine eye is my heart's guest, | and 47. 7
and scarcely greet me with that sun, thine eye, 49. 6
it is my love that keeps mine eye awake, | mine 61.10
sin of self–love possesseth all mine eye, | and 62. 1
parts of thee that the world's eye doth view 69. 1
by seeing farther than the eye hath shown. 69. 8
light, | and place my merit in the eye of scorn, 88. 2
for there can live no hatred in thine eye, 93. 5
for as you were when first your eye i ey'd, 104. 2
hath motion, and mine eye may be deceiv'd; 104.12
of hand, of foot, of lip, of eye, of brow, | i 106. 6
since i left you, mine eye is in my mind, | and 113. 1
or whether shall i say mine eye saith true, 114. 3
mine eye well knows what with his gust is 114.11
that mine eye loves it and doth first begin. 114.14
me from myself thy cruel eye hath taken, | and 133. 5
wound me not with thine eye but with thy tongue, 139. 3
dear heart, forbear to glance thine eye aside; 139. 6
denote | love's eye is not so true as all men's: 148. 8
o, how can love's eye be true, | that is so 148. 9
more perjur'd eye, | to swear against the truth 152.13
but at my mistress' eye love's brand new fired, 153. 9
each eye that saw him did enchant the mind, LC 89
the accident which brought me to her eye | upon 247
religious love put out religion's eye. 250
"o, that infected moisture of his eye, | o, that 323

EYEBALL 1 FR 0.0001 REL FR 1 V 0 P
and mine, invisible | to every eyeball els§. TMP 1.02.303

EYEBALLS 10 FR 0.0011 REL FR 10 V 0 P
and make his eyeballs roll with wonted sight. MND 3.02.369
your bugle eyeballs, nor your cheek of cream AYL 3.05. 47
and put my eyeballs in thy vaulty brows, | and JN 3.04. 30
o, were mine eyeballs into bullets turn'd, 1H6 4.07. 79
upon thy eyeballs murderous tyranny | sits in 2H6 3.02. 49
his eyeballs further out than when he lived, 3.02.169
thy crown does sear mine eyeballs. MAC 4.01.113
i'll wake mine eyeballs /out first. CYM 3.04.101
look in mine eyeballs, there thy beauty lies; VEN 119
rolling his greedy eyeballs in his head. LUC 368

EYE–BEAMS 1 FR 0.0001 REL FR 1 V 0 P
as thy eye–beams, when their fresh rays have LLL 4.03. 27

EYEBROW 1 FR 0.0001 REL FR 1 V 0 P
a woeful ballad | made to his mistress' eyebrow. AYL 2.07.149

EYEBROWS 2 FR 0.0002 REL FR 2 V 0 P
pray now | what color are your eyebrows? WT 2.01. 13
nose | that has been blue, but not her eyebrows. 2.01. 15

EYE–DROPS 1 FR 0.0001 REL FR 1 V 0 P
have wash'd his knife | with gentle eye–drops. 2H4 4.05. 87

EYE–GLANCE 1 FR 0.0001 REL FR 1 V 0 P
even with an eye–glance, to choke mars's drum TNK 5.01. 80

EYE–GLASS 1 FR 0.0001 REL FR 1 V 0 P
or your eye–glass | is thicker than a cuckold's WT 1.02.268

/EYELESS 1 FR 0.0001 REL FR 1 V 0 P
/the /impetuous /blasts /with /eyeless /rage LR 3.01. 8

EYELESS 4 FR 0.0004 REL FR 4 V 0 P
lends his light | to grubs and eyeless skulls? ROM 5.03.126
the gilded newt and eyeless venom'd worm, | with TIM 4.03.182
turn out that eyeless villain; LR 3.07. 96
that eyeless head of thine was first fram'd 4.06.227

EYELID 1 FR 0.0001 REL FR 1 V 0 P
let love forbid | sleep his seat on thy eyelid. MND 2.02. 81

EYELIDS 14 FR 0.0015 REL FR 13 V 1 P
why | doth it not then our eyelids sink? TMP 2.01.201
advanc'd their eyelids, lifted up their noses 4.01.177
love, | and on my eyelids shall conjecture hang, ADO 4.01.106
humor it with turning up your eyelids, sigh a LLL 3.01. 13 P
the juice of it on sleeping eyelids laid | will MND 2.01.170
feast, | if ever from your eyelids wip'd a tear, AYL 2.07.116
and on your eyelids crown the god of sleep, 1H4 3.01.214
but rather drows'd and hung their eyelids down, 3.02. 81
that thou no more wilt weigh my eyelids down, 2H4 3.01. 7
theme | until my eyelids will no longer wag. HAM 5.01.267
her eyelids, cases to those heavenly jewels PER 3.02. 98
she vail'd her eyelids, who like sluices stopp'd VEN 956
thee, | and keep my drooping eyelids open wide, SON 27. 7
keep open | my heavy eyelids to the weary night? 61. 2

EYE–OFFENDING 2 FR 0.0002 REL FR 2 V 0 P
her chamber round | with eye–offending brine; TN 1.01. 29
patch'd with foul moles and eye–offending marks, JN 3.01. 47

EYE'S 5 FR 0.0005 REL FR 5 V 0 P
mine eye's clear eye, my dear heart's dearer ERR 3.02. 62
my eye's too quick, my heart o'erweens too much, 3H6 3.02.144
the clear eye's moiety and the dear heart's part SON 46.12
mine eye's due is /thy outward part, | and my 46.13
awakes my heart to heart's and eye's delight. 47.14

EYES' 5 FR 0.0005 REL FR 5 V 0 P
fade | to /wanny ashes, thy eyes' windows fall, ROM 4.01.100
senses grow imperfect | by your eyes' anguish. LR 4.06. 6
thy eyes' shrowd tutor, that hard heart of thine VEN 500
heavy heart's lead, melt at mine eyes' red fire! 1073
why of eyes' falsehood hast thou forged hooks, SON 137. 7

/EYES 12 FR 0.0013 REL FR 11 V 1 P
it is engend'red in the /eyes, | with gazing fed MV 3.02. 67
/mine /eyes /are /full /of /tears, /i /cannot R2 4.01.244
/nay, /if /i /turn /mine /eyes /upon /myself, 4.01.247
/their /eyes /of /fire /sparkling /through 2H4 4.01.119
/the /tears /that /thy /poor /eyes /let /fall TIT 3.02. 18
/mine /eyes /are /cloy'd /with /view /of 3.02. 55
her /eyes in heaven | would through the airy ROM 2.02. 20
thou turn'st my /eyes into my /very soul, | and HAM 3.04. 89
/want'st /thou /eyes /at /trial, /madam? LR 3.06. 24 P
/to /know | /what /guests /were /in /her /eyes, 4.03. 21
/the /holy /water /from /her /heavenly /eyes, 4.03. 30
where cupid got new fire — my mistress' /eyes. SON 153.14

EYES 793 FR 0.0896 REL FR 709 V 84 P
wipe thou thine eyes, have comfort. TMP 1.02. 25
it is a hint | that wrings mine eyes to't. 1.02.135
those are pearls that were his eyes: 1.02.399
who with mine eyes (never since at ebb) beheld 1.02.436
at the first sight | they have chang'd eyes. 1.02.442
i wish mine eyes | would, with themselves, shut 2.01.191
to be asleep | with eyes wide open — standing, 2.01.214
as mine eyes open'd, | i saw their weapons drawn 2.01.319
thy eyes are almost set in thy head. 3.02. 9 P
must | bestow upon the eyes of this young couple 4.01. 40
all eyes! 4.01. 59
mine eyes, ev'n sociable to the show of thine, 5.01. 63
scarce think | their eyes do offices of truth, 5.01.156
o, that you had mine eyes, or your own eyes had TGV 2.01. 71 P
or your own eyes had the lights they were wont 2.01. 71 P
why, my grandam, having no eyes, look you, wept 2.03. 13 P
did hold his eyes lock'd in her crystal looks. 2.04. 89
why, lady, love hath twenty pair of eyes. 2.04. 95
love hath chas'd sleep from my enthralled eyes, 2.04.134
love doth to her eyes repair, | to help him of 4.02. 46
her eyes are grey as glass, and so are mine; 4.04.192
i should have scratch'd out your unseeing eyes, 4.04.204
black men are pearls in beauteous ladies' eyes. 5.02. 12
such pearls as put out ladies' eyes, | for i had 5.02. 13
who even now gave me good eyes too, examin'd my WIV 1.03. 60 P
whether had you rather lead mine eyes, or eye 3.02. 3 P
hath he any eyes? 3.02. 30 P
he capers, he dances, he has eyes of youth; 3.02. 67 P
but do not like to stage me to their eyes; MM 1.01. 68
you that have worn your eyes almost out in the 1.02.110 P
and feast upon her eyes? 2.02.178
and those eyes, the break of day, | lights that 4.01. 3
millions of false eyes | are stuck upon thee. 4.01. 59
o, i will to him and pluck out his eyes! 4.03.119
comes home to–morrow — nay, dry your eyes — 4.03.127
command these fretting waters from your eyes 4.03.146
am pale at mine heart to see thine eyes so red; 4.03.152 P
her shall you hear disproved to her eyes, | till 5.01.161
i, | fixing our eyes on whom our care was fix'd, ERR 1.01. 84
what error drives our eyes and ears amiss? 2.02.184
and yet would herein others' eyes were worse: 4.02. 26
with these nails i'll pluck out these false eyes 4.04.104
who give their eyes the liberty of gazing? 5.01. 53
and, gazing in mine eyes, feeling my pulse, 5.01.244
i see two husbands, or mine eyes deceive me. 5.01.332
pick out mine eyes with a ballad–maker's pen and ADO 1.01.252 P
may i be so converted and see with these eyes? 2.03. 22 P
disdain and scorn ride sparkling in her eyes, 3.01. 51
you look with your eyes as other women do. 3.04. 91 P
are our eyes our own? 4.01. 71
do not live, hero, do not ope thine eyes; 4.01.123
why ever wast thou lovely in my eyes? 4.01.130
out of all eyes, tongues, minds, and injuries. 4.01.243
i have deceiv'd even your very eyes. 5.01.232 P
let me see his eyes, | that when i note another 5.01.259
die in thy lap, and be buried in thy eyes; 5.02.103 P
your light grows dark by losing of your eyes. LLL 1.01. 79
the heart's still rhetoric disclosed with eyes, 2.01.229
that all eyes saw his eyes enchanted with gazes. 2.01.247
that all eyes saw his eyes enchanted with gazes. 2.01.247
hat penthouse–like o'er the shop of your eyes; 3.01. 18 P
with two pitch–balls stuck in her face for eyes; 3.01.197
my lips on thy foot, my eyes on thy picture, and 4.01. 85 P
his bias leaves, and makes his book thine eyes, 4.02.109
yes, for her two eyes. 4.03. 10 P
her hairs were gold, crystal the other's eyes. 4.03.140
your eyes do make no /coaches; 4.03.153
my eyes are then no eyes, nor i berowne. 4.03.228
my eyes are then no eyes, nor i berowne. 4.03.228
o, if the streets were paved with thine eyes, 4.03.274
from women's eyes this doctrine i derive: 4.03.298
you have in that forsworn the use of eyes, | and 4.03.306
then when ourselves we see in ladies' eyes, 4.03.312
such fiery numbers as the prompting eyes | of 4.03.319
but love, first learned in a lady's eyes, 4.03.324
a lover's eyes will gaze an eagle blind. 4.03.331
from women's eyes this doctrine i derive: 4.03.347
i thought to close mine eyes some half an hour; 5.02. 90
their "eyes," villain, their "eyes." 5.02.162 P
their "eyes," villain, their "eyes." 5.02.162 P
"that /ever turn'd their eyes to mortal views! 5.02.163
"once to behold with your sun–beamed eyes, | — 5.02.169
eyes, | — with your sun–beamed eyes" — 5.02.170
you were best call it "daughter–beamed eyes." 5.02.172
with eyes best seeing, heaven's fiery eye, | by 5.02.375
have the plague, and caught it of your eyes. 5.02.421
love | put on by us, if, in your heavenly eyes, 5.02.767
those heavenly eyes, that look into these faults 5.02.769
i would my father look'd but with my eyes. MND 1.01. 56
rather your eyes must with his judgment look. 1.01. 57
well | beteem them from the tempest of my eyes. 1.01.131
o hell! to choose love by another's eyes. 1.01.140
your eyes are lodestars, and your tongue's sweet 1.01.183
and thence from athens turn away our eyes, | to 1.01.218
and as he errs, doting on hermia's eyes, | so i, 1.01.230
love looks not with the eyes, but with the mind, 1.01.234
wings, and no eyes, figure unheedy haste; 1.01.237
if i do it, let the audience look to their eyes. 1.02. 26 P
asleep, | and drop the liquor of it in her eyes; 2.01.178
and with the juice of this i'll streak her eyes, 2.01.257
anoint his eyes, | but do it when the next thing 2.01.261
half that wish the wisher's eyes be press'd! 2.02. 65
on whose eyes i might approve | this flower's 2.02. 68
upon thy eyes i throw | all the power this charm 2.02. 78
for she hath blessed and attractive eyes. 2.02. 91
how came her eyes so bright? 2.02. 92
if so, my eyes are oft'ner wash'd than hers. 2.02. 93
and leads me to your eyes, where i o'erlook 2.02.121
hop in his walks and gambol in his eyes; 3.01.165
and light them at the fiery glow–worm's eyes, 3.01.170
to fan the moonbeams from his sleeping eyes. 3.01.173
your kindred hath made my eyes water ere now. 3.01.194 P
but hast thou yet latch'd the athenian's eyes 3.02. 36
i'll charm his eyes against she do appear. 3.02. 99
to conjure tears up in a poor maid's eyes | with 3.02.158
than all yon fiery oes and eyes of light. 3.02.188
to follow me and praise my eyes and face? 3.02.223
but that my nails can reach unto thine eyes. 3.02.298
that i have 'nointed an athenian's eyes; 3.02.351
stood now within the pretty flouriets' eyes 4.01. 55
undo | this hateful imperfection of her eyes. 4.01. 63
o, how mine eyes do loathe his visage now! 4.01. 79
thou wak'st, with thine own fool's eyes peep. 4.01. 84
i must confess, | made mine eyes water; 5.01. 69
eyes, do you see? 5.01.279
hath spied him already with those sweet eyes. 5.01.322 P
a tomb | must cover thy sweet eyes. 5.01.329
his eyes were green as leeks. 5.01.335
some that will evermore peep through their eyes, MV 1.01. 52
sometimes from her eyes | i did receive fair 1.01.163
the men that ever my foolish eyes look'd upon, 1.02.118 P
soly led | by nice direction of a maiden's eyes; 2.01. 14
i would o'erstare the sternest eyes that look, 2.01. 27
indeed, if you had your eyes, you might fail of 2.02. 75 P
and in such eyes as ours appear not faults, 2.02.183
is saying, hood mine eyes | thus with my hat, 2.02.193
thou shalt see, thy eyes shall be thy judge, 2.05. 1
and fair she is, if that mine eyes be true, 2.06. 54
hath not a jew eyes? 3.01. 59 P
beshrow your eyes, | they have o'erlook'd me and 3.02. 14
move these eyes? 3.02.116
but her eyes — | how could he see to do them? 3.02.123
that thinks he hath done well in people's eyes, 3.02.142
my eyes, my lord, can look as swift as yours: 3.02.197
their savage eyes turn'd to a modest gaze, | by 5.01. 78
i swear to thee, even by thine own fair eyes, 5.01.242
in both my eyes he doubly sees himself, | in 5.01.244
if you saw yourself with your eyes, or knew AYL 1.02.175 P
but let your fair eyes and gentle wishes go with 1.02.186 P
with his eyes full of anger. 1.03. 40 P
and wip'd our eyes | of drops that sacred pity 2.07.122
with eyes severe and beard of formal cut, | full 2.07.155
sans teeth, sans eyes, sans taste, sans every 2.07.166
of many faces, eyes, and hearts, | to have the 3.02.151
thao eyes, that are the frail'st and softest 3.05. 12
and if mine eyes can wound, now let them kill 3.05. 16
lie not, to say mine eyes are murtherers! 3.05. 19
but now mine eyes, | which i have darted at thee 3.05. 24
nor i am sure there is no force in eyes | that 3.05. 26
life, | i think she means to tangle my eyes too! 3.05. 44
he said mine eyes were black and my hair black, 3.05.130
nothing, is to have rich eyes and poor hands. 4.01. 24 P
abuses every one's eyes because his own are out, 4.01.214 P
wounded it is, but with the eyes of a lady. 5.02. 24 P
look into happiness through another man's eyes! 5.02. 45 P
to set her before your eyes to–morrow, human as 5.02. 67 P
shall have no more eyes to see withal than a cat SHR 1.02.115 P
but youth in ladies' eyes that flourisheth. 2.01.340
to cast thy wand'ring eyes on every stale, 3.01. 90
and since mine eyes are witness of her lightness 4.02. 24
as those two eyes become that heavenly face? 4.05. 32
pardon, old father, my mistaking eyes, | that 4.05. 45
and dart not scornful glances from those eyes, 5.02.137
and thine eyes | see it so grossly shown in thy AWW 1.03.177
the honor, sir, that flames in your fair eyes, 2.03. 80
me leave to use | the help of mine own eyes. 2.03.108
for i submit | my fancy to your eyes. 2.03.168
where thou | wast shot at with fair eyes, to be 3.02.107
o, ransom, ransom! do not hide mine eyes. 4.01. 67
did astonish the survey | of richest eyes, whose 5.03. 17
close | her eyes myself could win me to believe, 5.03.119
beguiles the truer office of mine eyes? 5.03.305
mine eyes smell onions, i shall weep anon. 5.03.320
o, when mine eyes did see olivia first, TN 1.01. 18
my tongue blabs, then let mine eyes not see. 1.02. 63
item, two grey eyes, with lids to them; 1.05.248 P
and subtle stealth | to creep in at mine eyes. 1.05.298
occasion more mine eyes will tell tales of me. 2.01. 41 P
that methought her eyes had lost her tongue, 2.02. 20
"his eyes do show his days are almost done." 2.03.104
i pray you let us satisfy our eyes | with the 3.03. 22
that i am ready to distrust mine eyes | and 4.03. 13
after him i love | more than i love these eyes, 5.01.135
his eyes were set at eight i' th' morning. 5.01.199 P
your precious self had then not cross'd the eyes WT 1.02. 79
to have nor eyes nor ears nor thought, then say 1.02.275
and all eyes | blind with the pin and web but 1.02.290
canst with thine eyes at once see good and evil, 1.02.303
me, that bare eyes | to see alike mine honor as 1.02.309
wafting his eyes to th' contrary and falling | a 1.02.372
spotless | i' th' eyes of heaven and to you — i 2.01.132
let him that makes but trifles of his eyes 2.03. 63
flatness of my misery, yet with eyes | of pity, 3.02.122
begin some speech, her eyes | became two spouts; 3.03. 25
so far that i have eyes under my service which 4.02. 35 P
but sweeter than the lids of juno's eyes | or 4.04.121
stand and read | as 'twere my daughter's eyes; 4.04.174
that you may | (for i do fear eyes over) to 4.04.654
i might have look'd upon my queen's full eyes, 5.01. 53
stars, stars, | and all eyes else dead coals! 5.01. 68
on one another, to tear the cases of their eyes. 5.02. 13 P
there was casting up of eyes, holding up of 5.02. 47 P
and that which angled for mine eyes (caught the 5.02. 83 P
be thou as lightning in the eyes of france; JN 1.01. 24
these eyes, these brows, were moulded out of his 2.01.100
those heaven–moving pearls from his poor eyes, 2.01.169
by these french | /confronts /your city's eyes, 2.01.215
equality | by our best eyes cannot be censured. 2.01.328
keep men's eyes | and strain their cheeks to 3.03. 45
or if that thou couldst see me without eyes, 3.03. 48
without eyes, ears, and harmful sound of words 3.03. 51
out at mine eyes in tender womanish tears. 4.01. 36
must you with hot irons burn out both mine eyes? 4.01. 39
will you put out mine eyes, | these eyes that 4.01. 56
these eyes that never did nor never shall | so 4.01. 57
approaching near these eyes, would drink my 4.01. 62
and told me hubert should put out mine eyes, | i 4.01. 69
my eyes are out | even with the fierce looks of 4.01. 72
none, but to lose your eyes. 4.01. 90
must needs want pleading for a pair of eyes. 4.01. 98
cut out my tongue, | so i may keep mine eyes. 4.01.101
o, spare mine eyes, | though to no use but still 4.01.101
nay, it perchance will sparkle in your eyes; 4.01.114
and look'd upon, i hope, with cheerful eyes. 4.02. 2
with eyes as red as new–enkindled fire, | and 4.02.163
wrinkled brows, with nods, with rolling eyes. 4.02.192
and foul imaginary eyes of blood | presented 4.02.265
trust not those cunning waters of his eyes, 4.03.107
and snarleth in the gentle eyes of peace; 4.03.150
so shall inferior eyes, | that borrow their 5.01. 50
startles mine eyes, and makes me more amaz'd 5.02. 51

commend these waters to those baby eyes | that 5.02. 56
he is forsworn if e'er those eyes of yours 5.04. 31
mowbray, impartial are our eyes and ears. R2 1.01.115
and for our eyes do hate the dire aspect | of 1.03.127
even in the glasses of thine eyes | i see thy 1.03.208
even through the hollow eyes of death | i spy 2.01.270
for sorrow's eyes, glazed with blinding tears, 2.02. 16
with the eyes of heavy mind | i see thy glory 2.04. 18
tears drawn from her eyes by your foul wrongs; 3.01. 15
and with rainy eyes | write sorrow on the bosom 3.02.146
kinsmen digg'd their graves with weeping eyes. 3.03.169
nay, dry your eyes — | tears show their love, 3.03.202
your hearts of sorrow, and your eyes of tears. 4.01.332
through casements darted their desiring eyes 5.02. 14
as in a theatre the eyes of men, | after a 5.02. 23
men's eyes | did scowl on gentle richard. 5.02. 27
his eyes do drop no tears, his prayers are in 5.03.101
they jar | their watches on unto mine eyes, the 5.05. 52
those opposed eyes, | which, like the meteors of 1H4 1.01. 9
shall show more goodly and attract more eyes 1.02.214
why dost thou bend thine eyes upon the earth, 2.03. 42
give me a cup of sack to make my eyes look red, 2.04.385 P
for tears do stop the flood–gates of her eyes. 2.04.394
been, | so common–hackney'd in the eyes of men, 3.02. 40
that, being daily swallowed by men's eyes, 3.02. 70
seen, but with such eyes | as, sick and blunted 3.02. 76
when it shines seldom in admiring eyes; 3.02. 80
all our lives shall be stuck full of eyes, | for 5.02. 8
nothing confutes me but eyes, and nobody sees me 5.04.127 P
we will not trust our eyes | without our ears: 5.04.136
hath by instinct knowledge from others' eyes 2H4 1.01. 86
but these mine eyes saw him in bloody state, 1.01.107
at last i spied his eyes, and methought he had 2.02. 81 P
to rain upon remembrance with mine eyes, | that 2.03. 59
and giddy /mast | seal up the ship–boy's eyes, 3.01. 19
even to the eyes of richard | gave him defiance. 3.01. 64
whose dangerous eyes may well be charm'd asleep 4.02. 39
that all their eyes may bear those tokens home 4.02. 64
that i will dazzle all the eyes of france, | yea H5 1.02.279
base | that hath not noble lustre in your eyes. 3.01. 30
mess, ere theise eyes of mine take themselves to 3.02.114 P
with a muffler afore his eyes, to signify to you 3.06. 31 P
that their hot blood may spin in english eyes, 4.02. 10
the gum down–roping from their pale–dead eyes, 4.02. 48
and all my mother came into mine eyes | and gave 4.06. 31
i must perforce compound | with /mistful eyes, 4.06. 34
his eyes are humbler than they us'd to be. 4.07. 67
and your eyes advance | after your thoughts, 5.pr. 44
as we are now glad to behold your eyes — | your 5.02. 14
your eyes, which hitherto have borne in them 5.02. 15
though they have their eyes, and then they will 5.02.309 P
his sparkling eyes, replete with wrathful fire, 1H6 1.01. 12
their mothers' moist'ned eyes babes shall suck, 1.01. 49
wounds will i lend the french in stead of eyes, 1.01. 87
one of thy eyes and thy cheek's side struck off! 1.04. 75
fain would mine eyes be witness with mine ears 2.03. 9
these eyes, like lamps whose wasting oil is 2.05. 8
when death doth close his tender–dying eyes, 3.03. 48
these eyes, that see thee now well colored, 4.02. 37
so seems this gorgeous beauty to mine eyes. 5.03. 64
and dimm'd mine eyes, that i can read no further 2H6 1.01. 55
sword should shed hot blood, mine eyes no tears. 1.01.118
why are thine eyes fix'd to the sullen earth, 1.02. 5
thine eyes and thoughts | beat on a crown, the 2.01. 19
let me see thine eyes. 2.01.103
mine eyes are full of tears, my heart of grief. 2.03. 17
my tear–stain'd eyes to see her miseries. 2.04. 16
nod their heads, and throw their eyes on thee! 2.04. 22
red sparkling eyes blab his heart's malice, 3.01.154
whose flood begins to flow within mine eyes; 3.01.199
tears, and with dimm'd eyes | look after him, 3.01.218
run, go, help, help! o henry, ope thine eyes! 3.02. 35
look not upon me, for thine eyes are wounding. 3.02. 51
and bid mine eyes be packing with my heart, 3.02.111
mine eyes should sparkle like the beaten flint, 3.02.317
and cry out for thee to close up mine eyes, | to 3.02.395
he hath no eyes, the dust hath blinded them. 3.03. 14
close up his eyes, and draw the curtain close, 3.03. 32
the sight of me is odious in their eyes; 4.04. 46
oppose thy steadfast–gazing eyes to mine, | see 4.10. 45
i vow by heaven these eyes shall never close. 3H6 1.01. 24
or is it fear | that makes him close his eyes? 1.03. 11
and in that hope i throw mine eyes to heaven, 1.04. 37
and if thine eyes can water for his death, | i 1.04. 82
child, | to bid the father wipe his eyes withal, 1.04.139
so | that hardly can i check my eyes from tears. 1.04.151
dazzle mine eyes, or do i see three suns? 2.01. 25
and though man's face be fearful to their eyes, 2.02. 27
till either death hath clos'd these eyes of mine 2.03. 31
i throw my hands, mine eyes, my heart to thee, 2.03. 36
and let our hearts and eyes, like civil war, 2.05. 77
with fiery eyes sparkling for very wrath, | and 2.05.131
from such a cause as fills mine eyes with tears 3.03. 13
these eyes, that now are dimm'd with death'i 5.02. 16
lad, | with tearful eyes add water to the sea, 5.04. 8
life | i pour the helpless balm of my poor eyes. R3 1.02. 13
and mortal eyes cannot endure the devil. 1.02. 45
these eyes could not endure that beauty's wrack; 1.02.127
out of my sight, thou dost infect mine eyes! 1.02.148
thine eyes, sweet lady, have infected mine. 1.02.149
those eyes of thine from mine have drawn salt 1.02.153
these eyes, which never shed remorseful tear — 1.02.155
time | my manly eyes did scorn an humble tear; 1.02.164
with curses in her mouth, tears in her eyes, 1.02.232
and will she yet abase her eyes on me, | that 1.02.246
and cheer his grace with quick and merry eyes. 1.03. 5
with thy scorns drew'st rivers from his eyes, 1.03.175
your eyes drop millstones, when fools' eyes fall 1.03.352
drop millstones, when fools' eyes fall tears. 1.03.352
what sights of ugly death within /my eyes! 1.04. 23
and, in the holes | where eyes did once inhabit, 1.04. 30
(as 'twere in scorn of eyes) reflecting gems, 1.04. 31
your eyes do menace me. 1.04.170
all springs reduce their currents to mine eyes, 2.02. 68
days, | how many of you have mine eyes beheld! 2.04. 56
then be your eyes the witness of their evil. 3.04. 67
which hitherto hath held /my eyes from rest; 4.01. 81
me | that look into me with considerate eyes. 4.02. 30

that had his teeth before his eyes | to worry 4.04. 49
that reigns in galled eyes of weeping souls, 4.04. 53
till that my nails were anchor'd in thine eyes; 4.04.232
and bid her wipe her weeping eyes withal. 4.04.278
soul | ere i let fall the windows of mine eyes: 5.03.116
another spread on 's breast, mounting his eyes, H8 1.02.205
heaven will one day open | the king's eyes, that 2.02. 42
from me, as if ruin | leap'd from his eyes. 3.02.206
let's dry our eyes; 3.02.431
and saint–like | cast her fair eyes to heaven, 4.01. 84
mark her eyes! 4.02. 98
mine eyes grow dim. 4.02.164
along, | how earnestly he cast his eyes upon me! 5.02. 12
in the open ulcer of my heart | her eyes, her TRO 1.01. 54
use, or purblind argus, all eyes and no sight. 1.02. 30 P
queen hecuba laugh'd that her eyes ran o'er. 1.02.143 P
a more temperate fire under the pot of her eyes. 1.02.147 P
did her eyes run o'er too? 1.02.147 P
i could live and die in the eyes of troilus. 1.02.243 P
have you any eyes? 1.02.252 P
nothing of that shall from mine eyes appear. 1.02.295
a prince | do a fair message to his kingly eyes? 1.03.219
looks | know them from eyes of other mortals? 1.03.225
modest as morning when she coldly eyes | the 1.03.229
i see them not with my old eyes, what are they? 1.03.365
than in the pride and salt scorn of his eyes, 1.03.370
will, | my will enkindled by mine eyes and ears, 2.02. 63
lend me ten thousand eyes, | and i will fill 2.02.101
practice your eyes with tears! 2.02.108
do in our eyes begin to lose their gloss, | yea, 2.03.119
more dregs than water, if my /fears have eyes. 3.02. 68 P
question me | why such unplausive eyes are bent, 3.03. 43
he shall as soon read in the eyes of others | as 3.03. 77
not, but commends itself | to others' eyes; 3.03.105
whiles others play the idiots in her eyes! 3.03.135
sleep kill those pretty eyes, | and give as soft 4.02. 4
stretch thy chest, and let thy eyes spout blood; 4.05. 10
my own searching eyes | shall find him by his 4.05.161
now, hector, i have fed mine eyes on thee; 4.05.231
cold palsies, raw eyes, dirt–rotten livers, 5.01. 20 P
minds sway'd by eyes are full of turpitude. 5.02.112
that doth invert th' attest of eyes and ears, 5.02.122
will 'a swagger himself out on 's own eyes? 5.02.136 P
their eyes o'ergalled with recourse of tears, 5.03. 55
and i have a rheum in mine eyes too, and such an 5.03.104 P
your eyes, half out, weep out at pandar's fall; 5.10. 48
mark'd you his lip and eyes? COR 1.01.255
you could turn your eyes toward the napes of 2.01. 39 P
whither do you follow your eyes so fast? 2.01. 99 P
dear, | such eyes the widows in corioles wear, 2.01.178
and carry with us ears and eyes for th' time, 2.01.269
his honors in their eyes and his actions in 2.02. 29 P
and the eyes of th' ignorant | more learned than 3.02. 76
within thine eyes sate twenty thousand deaths, 3.03. 70
a younger man's, | and venomous to thine eyes. 4.01. 23
has the porter his eyes in his head, that he 4.05. 12 P
go whip him 'fore the people's eyes — his 4.06. 61
or those doves' eyes, | which can make gods 5.03. 27
these eyes are not the same i wore in rome. 5.03. 38
which should | make our eyes flow with joy, 5.03. 99
thing to make | mine eyes to sweat compassion. 5.03.196
unholy braggart, | 'fore your own eyes and ears? 5.06.119
son, | were gracious in the eyes of royal rome, TIT 1.01. 11
gracious triumpher in the eyes of rome! 1.01.170
were gracious in those princely eyes of thine, 1.01.429
and faster bound to aaron's charming eyes | than 2.01. 16
the palace full of tongues, of eyes, and ears; 2.01.127
will not permit mine eyes once to behold | the 2.03.218
will whole months of tears thy father's eyes? 2.04. 55
titus, prepare thy aged eyes to weep, | or, if 3.01. 59
good titus, dry thine eyes. 3.01.138
the closing up of our most wretched eyes. 3.01.262
an enemy, | and would usurp upon my wat'ry eyes, 3.01.268
that both mine eyes were rainy like to his; 5.01.117
men | have miserable, mad, mistaking eyes. 5.02. 66
should, without eyes, see pathways to his will! ROM 1.01.172
being purg'd, a fire sparkling in lovers' eyes, 1.01.191
nor bide th' encounter of assailing eyes, | nor 1.01.213
by giving liberty unto thine eyes: 1.01.227
lies | find written in the margent of his eyes. 1.03. 86
that book in many's eyes doth share the glory, 1.03. 91
i conjure thee by rosaline's bright eyes, | by 2.01. 17
/do entreat her eyes | to twinkle in their 2.02. 16
what if her eyes were there, they in her head? 2.02. 18
unto the white–upturned wond'ring eyes | of 2.02. 29
i have night's cloak to hide me from their eyes, 2.02. 75
he lent me counsel, and i lent him eyes. 2.02. 81
sleep dwell upon thine eyes, peace in thy breast 2.02.186
not truly in their hearts, but in their eyes. 2.03. 68
other reason but because thou hast hazel eyes. 3.01. 20 P
here all eyes gaze on us. 3.01. 53
men's eyes were made to look, and let them gaze; 3.01. 54
that /th' runaway's eyes may wink, and romeo 3.02. 6
or those eyes /shut, that makes thee answer ay, 3.02. 49
i saw the wound, i saw it with mine eyes — 3.02. 52
to prison, eyes, ne'er look on liberty! 3.02. 58
how should they when that wise men have no eyes? 3.03. 62
mist–like infold me from the search of eyes. 3.03. 73
some say the lark and loathed toad change eyes; 3.05. 31
for still thy eyes, which i may call the sea, 3.05.132
need and oppression starveth in thy eyes, 5.01. 70
eyes, look your last! 5.03.112
whose eyes are on this sovereign lady fix'd, TIM 1.01. 68
to show lord timon that mean eyes have seen 1.01. 93
mine eyes cannot hold out water, methinks. 1.02.106 P
joy had the like conception in our eyes, | and 1.02.110
they only now come but to feast thine eyes. 1.02.127
'tis pity bounty had not eyes behind, | that man 1.02.163
to a wasteful cock | and set mine eyes at flow. 2.02.163
do't in your parents' eyes! 4.01. 8
heart, | for showing me again the eyes of man! 4.03. 51
through the window/–bars bore at men's eyes, 4.03.117
put armor on thine ears and on thine eyes, 4.03.124
the tongues, the eyes, and hearts of men | at 4.03.261
for his undone lord than mine eyes for you. 4.03.481
whose eyes do never give | but thorough lust and 4.03.484
it opens the eyes of expectation. 5.01. 23
lend me a fool's heart and a woman's eyes, | and 5.01.157

i have not from your eyes that gentleness | and JC 1.02. 33
have wish'd that noble brutus had his eyes. 1.02. 62
looks with such ferret and such fiery eyes | as 1.02.186
themselves | betwixt your eyes and night? 2.01. 99
which so appearing to the common eyes, | we 2.01.179
had i as many eyes as thou hast wounds, 3.01.200
passion, i see, is catching, /for mine eyes, 3.01.283
soul, his eyes are red as fire with weeping. 3.02.115
before the eyes of both our armies here | (which 4.02. 43
o, i could weep | my spirit from mine eyes! 4.03.100
canst thou hold up thy heavy eyes awhile, | and 4.03.256
i think it is the weakness of mine eyes | that 4.03.276
of grief, | that it runs over even at his eyes. 5.05. 14
night hangs upon mine eyes, my bones would rest, 5.05. 41
what a haste looks through his eyes! MAC 1.02. 46
mine eyes are made the fools o' th' other senses 2.01. 44
business which informs | thus to mine eyes. 2.01. 49
they pluck out mine eyes. 2.02. 56
to th' amazement of mine eyes | that look'd 2.04. 19
thou hast no speculation in those eyes | which 3.04. 94
show his eyes, and grieve his heart; 4.01.110
start, eyes! 4.01.116
o, i could play the woman with mine eyes, | and 4.03.230
you see her eyes are open. 5.01. 24 P
all annoyance, | and still keep eyes upon her. 5.01. 77
come, | he may approve our eyes and speak to it. HAM 1.01. 29
the sensible and true avouch | of mine own eyes. 1.01. 58
had left the flushing in her galled eyes, | she 1.02.155
by their oppress'd and fear–surprised eyes, 1.02.203
and fix'd his eyes upon you? 1.02.233
all the earth o'erwhelm them, to men's eyes. 1.02.257
make thy two eyes, like stars, start from their 1.05. 17
he seem'd to find his way without his eyes, 2.01. 95
their eyes purging thick amber and plum–tree gum 2.02.198 P
with eyes like carbuncles, the hellish pyrrhus 2.02.463
have made milch the burning eyes of heaven, 2.02.517
not turn'd his color and has tears in 's eyes. 2.02.520 P
tears in his eyes, distraction in his aspect, 2.02.555
indeed | the very faculties of eyes and ears. 2.02.566
note, | for i mine eyes will rivet to his face, 3.02. 85
have you eyes? 3.04. 65
ha, have you eyes? 3.04. 67
eyes without feeling, feeling without sight, 3.04. 78
ears without hands or eyes, smelling sans all, 3.04. 79
forth at your eyes your spirits wildly peep, 3.04.119
who like not in their judgment, but their eyes, 4.03. 5
shall i beg leave to see your kingly eyes, when 4.07. 45 P
father, with wash'd eyes | cordelia leaves you. LR 1.01.268
where are his eyes? 1.04.227
old fond eyes, | beweep this cause again, i'll 1.04.301
how far your eyes may pierce i cannot tell: 1.04.345
why, to keep one's eyes of either side 's nose, 1.05. 22 P
take vantage, heavy eyes, not to behold | this 2.02.171
their noses are led by their eyes but blind men, 2.04. 69 P
your blinding flames | into her scornful eyes! 2.04.166
her eyes are fierce, but thine | do comfort, and 2.04.172
pluck out his eyes. 3.07. 5 P
thy cruel nails | pluck out his poor old eyes, 3.07. 57
upon these eyes of thine i'll set my foot. 3.07. 68
i have no way, and therefore want no eyes; 4.01. 18
thee in my touch, | i'ld say i had eyes again. 4.01. 24
bless thy sweet eyes, they bleed. 4.01. 54
gloucester's eyes? 4.02. 72
where was his son when they did take his eyes? 4.02. 88
show'dst the king, | and to revenge thine eyes. 4.02. 96
great ignorance, gloucester's eyes being out, 4.05. 9
and dizzy 'tis, to cast one's eyes so low! 4.06. 12
alack, i have no eyes. 4.06. 60
below, methought his eyes | were two full moons; 4.06. 69
i remember thine eyes well enough. 4.06.136 P
what, with the case of eyes? 4.06.144
no eyes in your head, nor no money in your purse 4.06.145 P
your eyes are in a heavy case, your purse in a 4.06.146 P
a man may see how this world goes with no eyes. 4.06.151 P
get thee glass eyes, | and, like a scurvy 4.06.170
if thou wilt weep my fortunes, take my eyes. 4.06.176
salt, | to use his eyes for garden water–pots, 4.06.196
wipe thine eyes; 5.03. 23
and turn our impress'd lances in our eyes 5.03. 50
place where thee he got | cost him his eyes. 5.03.174
had i your tongues and eyes, i'ld use them so 5.03.259
mine eyes are not o' th' best; 5.03.280
of whom his eyes had seen the proof | at rhodes, OTH 1.01. 28
look to her, moor, if thou hast eyes to see; 1.03.292
in | as to throw out our eyes for brave othello, 2.01. 38
of her revolt, | for she had eyes, and chose me. 3.03.189
wear your eyes thus, not jealious nor secure. 3.03.198
such a seeming | to seel her father's eyes up, 3.03.210
if ever mortal eyes do see them bolster | more 3.03.399
let me see your eyes; | look in my face. 4.02. 25
or that mine eyes, mine ears, or any sense 4.02.154
mine eyes do itch; 4.03. 58
/forth of my heart those charms, thine eyes, are 5.01. 35
for you're fatal then | when your eyes roll so. 5.02. 38
of one whose subdu'd eyes, | albeit unused to 5.02.348
those his goodly eyes, | that o'er the files and ANT 1.01. 2
eternity was in our lips and eyes, | bliss in 1.03. 35
would stand and make his eyes grow in my brow; 1.05. 32
could not with graceful eyes attend those wars 2.02. 60
so many mermaids, tended her i' th' eyes, | and 2.02.207
pays his heart | for what his eyes eat only. 2.02.226
or i'll spurn thine eyes | like balls before me; 2.05. 63
if our eyes had authority, here they might take 2.06. 95 P
move in't, are the holes where eyes should be, 2.07. 15 P
the april's in her eyes, it is love's spring, 3.02. 43
i have eyes upon him, | and his affairs come to 3.06. 62
to see't mine eyes are blasted. 3.10. 4
mine eyes did sicken at the sight and could not 3.10. 16
how i convey my shame out of thine eyes | by 3.11. 52
the wise gods seel our eyes, | in our own filth 3.13.112
would you mingle eyes | with one that ties his 3.13.156
nod unto the world | and mock our eyes with air. 4.14. 7
with her modest eyes | and still conclusion, 4.15. 27
but it is tidings | to wash the eyes of kings. 5.01. 28
but i'll catch thine eyes | though they had 5.02.156
sure mine nails | are stronger than mine eyes. 5.02.224
never be beheld | of eyes again so royal! 5.02.318
here abide the hourly shot | of angry eyes, not CYM 1.01. 90

and with mine eyes i'll drink the words you send 1.01.100
could behold the sun with as firm eyes as he. 1.04. 12 P
hath nature given them eyes | to see this 1.06. 32
ay, madam, with his eyes in flood with laughter. 1.06. 74
mine eyes are weak. 2.02. 3
mary–buds begin to ope their golden eyes; 2.03. 24
(whose remembrance yet | lives in men's eyes, 3.01. 3
creatures, would even renew me with your eyes. 3.02. 43 P
first kill him, and in her eyes; 3.05.138 P
our very eyes | are sometimes like our judgments 4.02.301
wipe thine eyes: 4.02.402
fires, have both their eyes | and ears so cloy'd 4.04. 18
your death has eyes in 's head then; 5.04.178 P
there are none want eyes to direct them the way 5.04.185 P
have the best use of eyes to see the way of 5.04.189 P
mine eyes | were not in fault, for she was 5.05. 62
he eyes us not, forbear. 5.05.124
to glad your ear and please your eyes. PER 1.ch. 4
gives heaven countless eyes to view men's acts, 1.01. 73
blows dust in others' eyes, to spread itself; 1.01. 97
and the sore eyes see clear | to stop the air 1.01. 99
here pleasures court mine eyes, and mine eyes 1.02. 6
court mine eyes, and mine eyes shun them, | and 1.02. 6
drew sleep out of mine eyes, blood from my 1.02. 96
are but felt, and seen with mischief's eyes, 1.04. 8
deep our woes | into the air, our eyes to weep, 1.04. 14
our cheeks and hollow eyes do witness it. 1.04. 51
men | be like a beacon fir'd t' amaze your eyes. 1.04. 87
tidings to the contrary | are brought your eyes; 2.ch. 16
have neither in our hearts nor outward eyes 2.03. 25
that all those eyes ador'd them ere their fall 2.04. 11
the good gods | throw their best eyes upon't! 3.01. 37
her hither | to have blest mine eyes with her! 3.03. 9
which did steal | the eyes of young and old. 4.01. 41
your ears unto your eyes i'll reconcile. 4.04. 22
maid, | my lord, that ne'er before invited eyes, 5.01. 85
pray you turn your eyes upon me. 5.01.101
her eyes as jewel–like | and cas'd as richly, 5.01.110
and thick slumber | hangs upon mine eyes. 5.01.235
(then weaker than your eyes) laid by his club; TNK 1.01. 67
wrinching our holy begging in our eyes | to make 1.01.156
so adieu, | and heaven's good eyes look on you! 1.04. 13
without your noble hand to close mine eyes, | or 2.02. 93
i have, | beshrew mine eyes for't! 2.02.157
still blossom | as her bright eyes shine on ye, 2.02.234
her bright eyes break each morning 'gainst thy 2.03. 9
it so) as ever | these eyes yet look'd on. 2.04. 11
i have not clos'd mine eyes | save when my lids 3.02. 27
with thy twinkling eyes look right and straight 3.05.117
and why her eyes command me | stay here to love 3.06.169
the misadventure of their own eyes kill 'em; 3.06.190
by your own eyes, by strength, | in which you 3.06.205
they are princes | as goodly as your own eyes, 3.06.276
alone | and only beautiful, and these the eyes, 4.02. 38
the circles of his eyes show /fire within him, 4.02. 81
and in his rolling eyes sits victory, | as if 4.02.108
torturing convulsions from his globy eyes | had 5.01.113
of mine eyes | were i to lose one — they are 5.01.154
for they would glance their eyes | toward my 5.03. 61
that four such eyes should be so fix'd on one 5.03.145
i'll close thine eyes, prince; 5.04. 96
they breed sore eyes and 'tis enough to infect STM II.C 10 P
which bred more beauty in his angry eyes: VEN 70
then why not lips on lips, since eyes in eyes? 120
then why not lips on lips, since eyes in eyes? 120
mine eyes are grey, and bright, and quick in 140
red cheeks and fiery eyes blaze forth her wrong; 219
her eyes petitioners to his eyes suing, | his 356
her eyes petitioners to his eyes suing, | his 356
his eyes saw her eyes as they had not seen them, 357
his eyes saw her eyes as they had not seen them, 357
her eyes wooed still, his eyes disdain'd the 358
eyes wooed still, his eyes disdain'd the wooing: 358
with tears which chorus–like her eyes did rain. 360
"had i no eyes but ears, my ears would love 433
though neither eyes nor ears to hear nor see, 437
and these mine eyes, true leaders to their queen 503
for my sick heart commands mine eyes to watch. 584
his eyes like glow–worms shine when he doth fret 621
to which love's eyes pays tributary gazes, | nor 632
whereon with fearful eyes they long have gazed, 927
o yes, it may, thou hast no eyes to see, | but 939
those eyes that taught all other eyes to see? 952
those eyes that taught all other eyes to see? 952
o, how her eyes and tears did lend and borrow! 961
which seen, her eyes /as murd'red with the view, 1031
so at his bloody view her eyes are fled | into 1037
from their dark beds once more leap her eyes, 1050
her eyes are mad that they have wept till now. 1062
mine eyes are turn'd to fire, my heart to lead: 1072
she lifts the coffer–lids that close his eyes, 1127
for every little grief to wet his eyes; 1179
persuade | the eyes of men without an orator; LUC 30
in silent wonder of still–gazing eyes. 84
but she, that never cop'd with stranger eyes, 99
more than his eyes were open'd to the light. 105
when heavy sleep had clos'd up mortal eyes. 163
mine eyes forgo their light, my false heart 228
hand, | and gaz'd for tidings in my eager eyes, 254
so, the curtain drawn, his eyes begun | to wink, 374
lies, | to be admir'd of lewd unhallowed eyes. 392
her eyes like marigolds had sheath'd their light 397
she much amaz'd breaks ope her lock'd–up eyes, 446
quick–shifting antics, ugly in her eyes. 459
who, angry that the eyes fly from their lights, 461
for those thine eyes betray thee unto mine. 483
her pity–pleading eyes are sadly fixed | in the 561
where subjects' eyes do learn, do read, do look. 616
from their own misdeeds askaunce their eyes! 637
tears | that ever modest eyes with sorrow shed. 683
and my true eyes have never practic'd how | to 748
and bids her eyes hereafter still be blind; 758
and scarce hath eyes his treasure to behold, 857
let ghastly shadows his lewd eyes affright, 971
tongue shall utter all, mine eyes like sluices, 1076
light to all fair eyes that light will borrow; 1083
"o eye of eyes, | why pry'st thou through my 1088
with thy tickling beams eyes that are sleeping; 1090
wip'd the brinish pearl from her bright eyes, 1213
then they drown their eyes or break their hearts 1239
and dying eyes gleam'd forth their ashy lights, 1378
the very eyes of men through loop–holes thrust, 1383
that one might see those far–off eyes look sad. 1386
in ajax' eyes blunt rage and rigor roll'd, | but 1398
staring on priam's wounds with her old eyes, 1448
on this sad shadow lucrece spends her eyes, 1457
and with my knife scratch out the angry eyes 1469
she throws her eyes about the painting round, 1499
an humble gait, calm looks, eyes wailing still, 1508
"look, look how list'ning priam wets his eyes, 1548
her eyes, though sod in tears, look'd red and 1592
that my poor beauty had purloin'd his eyes, 1651
with sad set eyes, and wretched arms across, 1662
to drown /one woe, one pair of weeping eyes. 1680
to check the tears in collatinus' eyes. 1817
his bias leaves, and makes his book thine eyes, PP 5. 5
lord, how mine eyes throw gazes to the east! 14.13
not daring trust the office of mine eyes. 14.16
hath his hope, and eyes their wished sight: 14.22
but thou, contracted to thine own bright eyes, SON 1. 5
to say within thine own deep–sunken eyes | were 2. 7
the eyes ('fore duteous) now converted are 7.11
by children's eyes, her husband's shape in mind. 9. 8
but from thine eyes my knowledge i derive, | and 14. 9
can make you live yourself in eyes of men: 16.12
if i could write the beauty of your eyes, | and 17. 5
so long as men can breathe or eyes can see, | so 18.13
which steals men's eyes and women's souls 20. 8
to hear with eyes belongs to love's fine wit. 23.14
that hath his windows glazed with thine eyes. 24. 8
now see what good turns eyes for eyes have done: 24. 9
now see what good turns eyes for eyes have done: 24. 9
mine eyes have drawn thy shape, and thine for me 24.10
yet eyes this cunning want to grace their art, 24.13
when in disgrace with fortune and men's eyes, 29. 1
when most i wink, then do mine eyes best see, 43. 1
when to unseeing eyes thy shade shines so! 43. 8
mine eyes be blessed made | by looking on thee 43. 9
through heavy sleep on sightless eyes doth stay! 43.12
(a closet never pierc'd with crystal eyes), 46. 6
even in the eyes of all posterity | that wear 55.11
you live in this, and dwell in lovers' eyes. 55.14
fill | thy hungry eyes even till they wink with 56. 6
their thoughts (although their eyes were kind) 69.11
thine eyes, that taught the dumb on high to sing 78. 5
when you entombed in men's eyes shall lie; 81. 8
which eyes not yet created shall o'er–read, 81.10
there lives more life in one of your fair eyes 83.13
and all things turns to fair that eyes can see! 95.12
and, for they look'd but with divining eyes, 106.11
have eyes to wonder, but lack tongues to praise. 106.14
how have mine eyes out of their spheres been 119. 7
for why should others' false adulterate eyes 121. 5
therefore my mistress' eyes are raven black, 127. 9
her eyes so suited, and they mourners seem | at 127.10
my mistress' eyes are nothing like the sun; 130. 1
thine eyes i love, and they, as pitying me, 132. 1
as those two /mourning eyes become thy face. 132. 9
what dost thou to mine eyes | that they behold 137. 1
if eyes, corrupt by over–partial looks, | be 137. 5
or mine eyes seeing this, say this is not, | to 137.11
things right true my heart and eyes have erred, 137.13
bear thine eyes straight, though thy proud heart 140.14
in faith, i do not love thee with mine eyes, 141. 1
whom thine eyes woo as mine importune thee. 142.10
what eyes hath love put in my head, | which have 148. 1
if that be fair whereon my false eyes dote, 148. 5
lest eyes well seeing thy foul faults should 148.14
defect, | commanded by the motion of thine eyes? 149.12
and, to enlighten thee, gave eyes to blindness, 152.11
sometimes her levell'd eyes their carriage ride, LC 22
these often bath'd she in her fluxive eyes, 50
that maidens' eyes stuck over all his face. 81
that did his picture get | to serve their eyes, 135
"'among the many that mine eyes have seen, | not 190
believ'd her eyes when they t' assail begun, 262
"this said, his wat'ry eyes he did dismount, 281
but with the inundation of the eyes | what rocky 290

EYESIGHT 7 FR 0.0008 REL FR 7 V 0 P
doth falsely blind the eyesight of his look. LLL 1.01. 76
did stumble with haste in his eyesight to be; 2.01.239
that he did hold me dear | as precious eyesight, 5.02.445
or is it fantasy that plays upon our eyesight? 1H4 5.04.135
the precious treasure of his eyesight lost. ROM 1.01.233
either my eyesight fails, or thou lookest pale. 3.05. 57
dearer than eyesight, space, and liberty, LR 1.01. 56

EYE–SORE 2 FR 0.0002 REL FR 2 V 0 P
estate, | an eye–sore to our solemn festival! SHR 3.02.101
survive, | and be an eye–sore in my golden coat; LUC 205

EYE–STRINGS 1 FR 0.0001 REL FR 1 V 0 P
i would have broke mine eye–strings, crack'd CYM 1.03. 17

EYE–WINK 1 FR 0.0001 REL FR 0 V 1 P
you, they could never get an eye–wink of her. WIV 2.02. 71 P

EYNE 13 FR 0.0014 REL FR 13 V 0 P
(those clouds removed) upon our watery eyne. LLL 5.02.206
for ere demetrius look'd on hermia's eyne, | he MND 1.01.242
made me compare with hermia's sphery eyne! 2.02. 99
to what, my love, shall i compare thine eyne? 3.02.138
me thy chink, to blink through with mine eyne! 5.01.177
"if the scorn of your bright eyne | have power AYL 4.03. 50
while counterfeit supposes blear'd thine eyne. SHR 5.01.117
of the vine, | plumpy bacchus with pink eyne! ANT 2.07.114
the cat, with eyne of burning coal, | now PER 3.ch. 5
thy soft hands, sweet lips, and crystal eyne, VEN 633
and wipe the dim mist from thy doting eyne, LUC 643
with swelling drops gan wet | her circled eyne, 1229
oft did she heave her napkin to her eyne, LC 15

EY'ST 1 FR 0.0001 REL FR 1 V 0 P
wherefore ey'st him so? CYM 5.05.114

FA 6 FR 0.0006 REL FR 2 V 4 P
ut, re, sol, la, mi, fa. LLL 4.02.100 P
i'll try how you can sol, fa, and sing it. SHR 1.02. 17
lord, | c fa ut, that loves with all affection. 3.01. 76
carry no crotchets, i'll re you, i'll fa you. ROM 4.05.119 P
and you re us and fa us, you note us. 4.05.120 P
fa, sol, la, mi. LR 1.02.137 P

FABIAN 7 FR 0.0008 REL FR 1 V 6 P
come thy ways, signior fabian. TN 2.05. 1 P
signior fabian, stay you by this gentleman till 3.04.257 P
fabian can scarce hold him yonder. 3.04.282 P
come hither, fabian; 3.04.377 P
and for his cowardship, ask fabian. 3.04.388 P
good master fabian, grant me another request. 5.01. 2 P
see him deliver'd, fabian, bring him hither. 5.01.315

FABLE 5 FR 0.0005 REL FR 4 V 1 P
sans fable, she herself revil'd you there. ERR 4.04. 73
by the world, i recount no fable: LLL 5.01.106 P
let aesop fable in a winter's night, | his 3H6 5.05. 25
but that's a fable. OTH 5.02.286
and, to say verity, and not to fable, | we are a TNK 3.05.105

FABLES 2 FR 0.0002 REL FR 2 V 0 P
i never may believe | these antic fables, nor MND 5.01. 3
he fables not, i hear the enemy. 1H6 4.02. 42

FABRIC 4 FR 0.0004 REL FR 4 V 0 P
and, like the baseless fabric of this vision, TMP 4.01.151
or counsel shake | the fabric of his folly, WT 1.02.429
muniments and petty helps | in this our fabric, COR 1.01.119
when it stands | against a falling fabric. 3.01.246

FABULOUS 2 FR 0.0002 REL FR 2 V 0 P
i see report is fabulous and false. 1H6 2.03. 18
thought's compass, that former fabulous story, H8 1.01. 36

/FAC'D 1 FR 0.0001 REL FR 1 V 0 P
/the /face /which /fac'd /so /many /follies, R2 4.01.285

FAC'D 7 FR 0.0008 REL FR 3 V 4 P
yet i have fac'd it with a card of ten. SHR 2.01.405
thou hast fac'd many things. 4.03.122 P
i will neither be fac'd nor brav'd. 4.03.125 P
that fac'd and braved me in this matter so? 5.01.121
so, for fear i should be fac'd out of my way. H5 3.07. 82 P
malice and malice fac'd with wit turn him to? TRO 5.01. 58 P
out his passage | till he fac'd the slave; MAC 1.02. 20

/FACE 11 FR 0.0012 REL FR 11 V 0 P
/that /it /may /show /me /what /a /face /i /have R2 4.01.266
/so /many /blows /upon /this /face /of /mine, 4.01.278
/was /this /face /the /face | /that /every /day 4.01.281
/was /this /face /the /face | /that /every /day 4.01.281
/was /this /the /face | /that, /like /the /sun, 4.01.283
/is /this /the /face /which /fac'd /so /many 4.01.285
/a /brittle /glory /shineth /in /this /face, 4.01.287
/as /brittle /as /the /glory /is /the /face, 4.01.288
/soon /my /sorrow /hath /destroy'd /my /face. 4.01.291
/hath /destroy'd | /the /shadow /of /your /face. 4.01.293
/of /eggs | /to /apply /to /his /bleeding /face. LR 3.07.107

FACE 469 FR 0.0530 REL FR 381 V 88 P
and executing th' outward face of royalty | with TMP 1.02.104
more — | and yet methinks i see it in thy face, 2.01.206
no woman's face remember, | save, from my glass, 3.01. 49
as a nose on a man's face, or a weathercock on a TGV 2.01.136
but chiefly for thy face and thy behavior, 4.04. 67
and pinch'd the lily–tincture of her face, 4.04.155
this face of mine | were full as lovely as is 4.04.185
what says she to my face? 5.02. 8
nay then the wanton lies; my face is black. 5.02. 10
what is in silvia's face, but i may spy | more 5.04.114
by this hat, then he in the red face had it; WIV 1.01.170 P
he is not show his face. 2.03. 32 P
then, if you speak, you must not show your face, MM 1.04. 12
or, if you show your face, you must not speak. 1.04. 13
but as she spit in his face, so she defied him. 2.01. 84 P
beseech you, sir, look in this gentleman's face. 2.01.148 P
doth your honor mark his face? 2.01.149 P
doth your honor see any harm in his face? 2.01.153 P
a book, his face is the worst thing about him. 2.01.155 P
if his face be the worst thing about him, how 2.01.156 P
first, let her show /her face, and after speak. 5.01.168
i will not show my face | until my husband bid 5.01.169
this is a strange abuse. let's see thy face. 5.01.205
this is that face, thou cruel angelo, | which 5.01.207
show your sheep–biting face, and be hang'd an 5.01.354 P
what, wilt thou flout me thus unto my face, ERR 1.02. 91
fie, how impatience low'reth in your face! 2.01. 86
me, | and hurl the name of husband in my face, 2.02.135
but here's a villain that would face me down 3.01. 6
thou wouldst have chang'd thy face for a name, 3.01. 47
and break it in your face, so he break it not 3.01. 76
shoe, but her face nothing like so clean kept: 3.02.102 P
/of his heart's meteors tilting in his face? 4.02. 6
did this companion with the saffron face | revel 4.04. 61
to scorch your face, and to disfigure you. 5.01.183
and with no face, as 'twere, outfacing me, 5.01.245
have written strange defeatures in my face: 5.01.300
though now this grained face of mine be hid | in 5.01.312
other shall scape a predestinate scratch'd face. ADO 1.01.135 P
it worse, and 'twere such a face as yours were. 1.01.137 P
john's melancholy in signior benedick's face — 2.01. 13 P
not endure a husband with a beard on his face, i 2.01. 30 P
to put a strange face on his own perfection. 2.03. 47
and when was he wont to wash his face? 3.02. 56 P
she shall be buried with her face upwards. 3.02. 68 P
is this face hero's? 4.01. 71
blushing apparitions | to start into her face, a 4.01.160
man | shall face to face be brought to margaret, 5.01.298
man | shall face to face be brought to margaret, 5.01.298
matter, | that you have such a february face, 5.04. 41
sweet, let me see your face. 5.04. 55
with that face? LLL 1.02.140 P
fair fall the face it covers! 2.01.124
favor, sweet welkin, i must sigh in thy face: 3.01. 67
with two pitch–balls stuck in her face for eyes; 3.01.197
anon falleth like a crab on the face of terra, 4.02. 6 P
as doth thy face through tears of mine give 4.03. 31
i | will praise a hand, a foot, a face, an eye, 4.03.182
the sea will ebb and flow, heaven show his face; 4.03.212
no face is fair that is not full so black. 4.03.249
i'll find a fairer face not wash'd to–day. 4.03.269
look, here's thy love; my foot and her face see. 4.03.273
without the beauty of a woman's face? 4.03.297
now, for not looking on a woman's face, | you 4.03.305
and if my face were but as fair as yours, | my 5.02. 32
o that your face were not so full of o's! 5.02. 45
here comes boyet, and mirth is in his face. 5.02. 79
grace, | despite of suit, to see a lady's face. 5.02.129
but while 'tis spoke each turn away /her face. 5.02.148
vouchsafe to show the sunshine of your face, 5.02.201

my face is but a moon, and clouded too. 5.02.203
that hid the worse and show'd the better face. 5.02.388
can any face of brass hold longer out? 5.02.395
because thou hast no face. 5.02.608 P
a death's face in a ring. 5.02.612 P
the face of an old roman coin, scarce seen. 5.02.613 P
the carv'd–bone face on a flask. 5.02.615 P
he no more shall see my face; MND 1.01.202
and i may hide my face, let me play thisby too. 1.02. 51 P
that | it is not night when i do see your face, 2.01.221
name, and half his face must be seen through the 3.01. 37 P
to follow me and praise my eyes and face? 3.02.223
and dar'st not stand, nor look me in the face. 3.02.424
this dear, | if ever i thy face by daylight see. 3.02.427
methinks i am marvail's hairy about the face; 4.01. 25 P
chink, | to spy and i can hear my thisby's face. 5.01.193
thou mayst with better face | exact the penalty. MV 1.03.136
than i have of my face when i /last saw him. 2.02. 98 P
ambitious head | spets in the face of heaven, is 2.07. 45
turning his face, he put his hand behind him, 2.08. 47
make room, and let him stand before our face. 4.01. 16
will ne'er wear hair on 's face that had it. 5.01.158
and with a kind of umber smirch my face; AYL 1.03.112
with his satchel | and shining morning face, 2.07.146
most truly limn'd and living in your face, | be 2.07.194
let no face be kept in mind | but the fair of 3.02. 94
like envious floods o'errun her lovely face, SHR in.2. 65
and paint your face, and use you like a fool. 1.01. 65
o yes, i saw sweet beauty in her face, | such as 1.01.167
he will throw a figure in her face, and so 1.02.114 P
i never yet beheld that special face | which i 2.01. 11
what, you mean my face? 2.01.234
that thinks with oaths to face the matter out. 2.01.289
and threw the sops all in the sexton's face, 3.02.173
why, she hath a face of her own. 4.01.100 P
face not me; 4.03.124 P
as those two eyes become that heavenly face? 4.05. 32
youth, thou bear'st thy father's face; AWW 1.02. 19
"was this fair face the cause," quoth she, 1.03. 70
that the first face of neither on the start 3.02. 50
his face i know not. 3.05. 51
is taken, and it shall be read to his face. 4.03.114 P
lord your son with a patch of velvet on 's face. 4.05. 95 P
but it is your carbinado'd face. 4.05.101 P
heat, | shall not behold her face at ample view; TN 1.01. 26
come, throw it o'er my face. 1.05.165
good madam, let me see your face. 1.05.230 P
from your lord to negotiate with my face? 1.05.232 P
thy tongue, thy face, thy limbs, actions, and 1.05.292
he does smile his face into more lines than is 3.02. 78 P
as, a sad face, a reverend carriage, a slow 3.04. 72 P
and do all they can to face me out of my wits. 4.02. 93 P
that face of his i do remember well, | yet, when 5.01. 51
taught him to face me out of his acquaintance, 5.01. 88
one face, one voice, one habit, and two persons, 5.01.216
this entertainment | may a free face put on, WT 1.02.112
looking on the lines | of my boy's face, 1.02.154
i saw his heart in 's face. 1.02.447
there's not a grain of it the face to sweeten 2.01.156
her face o' fire | with labor, and the thing she 4.04. 60
and pluck it o'er your brows, muffle your face, 4.04.651
he hath a trick of cordelion's face, | the JN 1.01. 85
with half that face would he have all my land — 1.01. 93
my face so thin | that in mine ear i durst not 1.01.141
i would give it every foot to have this face; 1.01.146
your face hath got five hundred pound a year, 1.01.152
yet sell your face for five pence and 'tis dear. 1.01.153
look here upon thy brother geffrey's face: 2.01. 99
stand in his face to contradict his claim. 2.01.280
turn face to face and bloody point to point; 2.01.390
turn face to face and bloody point to point; 2.01.390
what say'st thou, boy? look in the lady's face. 2.01.495
in this the antique and well–noted face | of 4.02. 21
or turn'd an eye of doubt upon my face, | as bid 4.02.233
you taught me how to know the face of right, 5.02. 88
there end thy brave, and turn thy face in peace; 5.02.159
face to face, | and frowning brow to brow, R2 1.01. 15
face to face, | and frowning brow to brow, 1.01. 15
o, let my sovereign turn away his face, | and 1.01.111
where shame doth harbor, even in mowbray's face. 1.01.195
nor never look upon each other's face, | nor 1.03.185
or bend one wrinkle on my sovereign's face. 2.01.170
his face thou hast, for even so look'd he, 2.01.176
his treasons will sit blushing in his face, 3.02. 51
of twenty thousand men | did triumph in my face, 3.02. 77
shall ill become the flower of england's face, 3.03. 97
then set before my face the lord aumerle. 4.01. 6
his face still combating with tears and smiles, 5.02. 32
shall i for love speak treason to thy face? 5.03. 44
look upon his face: 5.03.100
to look upon my sometimes royal master's face. 5.05. 75
and on my face he turn'd an eye of death, 1H4 1.03.143
and only stays but to behold the face | of that 1.03.275
and in thy face strange motions have appear'd, 2.03. 60
be not forgot upon the face of the earth, then 2.04.129 P
geese, i'll never wear hair on my face more. 2.04.139 P
give me them that will face me. 2.04.151 P
if i tell thee a lie, spit in my face, call me 2.04.194 P
my masters, for a true face and good conscience. 2.04.501 P
slept in his face and rend'red such aspect | as 3.02. 82
do thou amend thy face, and i'll amend my life. 3.03. 24 P
why, sir john, my face does you no harm. 3.03. 28 P
i never see thy face but i think upon hell–fire 3.03. 31 P
way given to virtue, i would swear by thy face; 3.03. 34 P
but for the light in thy face, the son of utter 3.03. 37 P
'sblood, i would my face were in your belly! 3.03. 49 P
look upon his face; 3.03. 77 P
over his /country's wrongs, and by this face, 4.03. 82
to face the garment of rebellion | with some 5.01. 74
no, i know this face full well. 5.03. 19
but let my favors hide thy mangled face, | and 5.04. 96
will not stick to say his face is a face royal. 2H4 1.02. 23 P
will not stick to say his face is a face royal. 1.02. 23 P
he may keep it still at a face royal, for a 1.02. 24 P
a white hair in your face but should have his 1.02.160 P
go wash thy face, and draw the action. 2.01.149 P
thy name, or to know thy face to–morrow, or to 2.02. 14 P
discern no part of his face from the window. 2.02. 80 P
come let me wipe thy face. 2.04.217 P
now, the lord bless that sweet face of thine! 2.04.293 P
and his face is lucifer's privy–kitchen, where 2.04.333 P
let us sway on and face them in the field. 4.01. 24
it illumineth the face, which as a beacon gives 4.03.108 P
that had before my face murdered my father, 4.05.167
him laugh till his face be like a wet cloak ill 5.01. 84 P
and i dare swear you borrow not that face | of 5.02. 28
the "solus" in thy most mervailous face, | the H5 2.01. 47
good bardolph, put thy face between his sheets, 2.01. 83 P
his face is all bubukles, and whelks, and knobs, 3.06.102 P
each battle sees the other's umber'd face. 4.pr. 9
upon his royal face there is no note | how dread 4.pr. 35
to ice with fanning in his face with a peacock's 4.01.200 P
gashes | that bloodily did yawn upon his face. 4.06. 14
he smil'd me in the face, raught me his hand, 4.06. 21
right joyous are we to behold your face, | most 5.02. 9
that face to face, and royal eye to eye, | you 5.02. 30
that face to face, and royal eye to eye, | you 5.02. 30
kate, whose face is not worth sunburning, that 5.02.147 P
pate will grow bald, a fair face will wither, a 5.02.161 P
of beauty, can do no more spoil upon my face. 5.02.231 P
though i speak it before his face, if he be not 5.02.241 P
durst not presume to look once in the face. 1H6 1.01.140
do what thou dar'st, i beard thee to thy face. 1.03. 44
am i dar'd and bearded to my face? 1.03. 45
because till now we never saw your face. 3.04. 24
and pale destruction meets thee in the face. 4.02. 27
knows | that suffolk doth not flatter, face, or 5.03.142
for thou hast given me in this beauteous face 2H6 1.01. 21
proud prelate, in thy face | i see thy fury. 1.01.142
if so, gaze on, and grovel on thy face, | until 1.02. 9
i could set my ten commandements in your face. 1.03.142
abrook | the abject people gazing on thy face, 2.04. 11
humphrey, in thy face i see | the map of honor, 3.01.202
in face, in gait, in speech, he doth resemble. 3.01.373
what, dost thou turn away and hide thy face? 3.02. 74
to drain | upon his face an ocean of salt tears, 3.02.143
see how the blood is settled in his face. 3.02.160
but see, his face is black and full of blood, 3.02.168
hath this lovely face | rul'd like a wandering 4.04. 15
it will be prov'd to thy face that thou hast men 4.07. 38 P
but boldly stand and front him to his face. 5.01. 86
and, if thou canst for blushing, view this face, 3H6 1.04. 46
but that thy face is vizard–like, unchanging, 1.04.116
and yet be seen to wear a woman's face? 1.04.140
that face of his the hungry cannibals | would 1.04.152
duke in high despite, | laugh'd in his face; 2.01. 60
not his that spoils her young before her face. 2.02. 14
and though man's face be fearful to their eyes, 2.02. 27
boy, | and let his manly face, which promiseth 2.02. 40
ere my knee rise from the earth's cold face, | i 2.03. 35
it is my father's face, | whom in this conflict 2.05. 61
is this our foeman's face? 2.05. 82
the red rose and the white are on his face, 2.05. 97
for (though before his face i speak the words) 2.06. 39
look, as i blow this feather from my face, | and 3.01. 84
tears, | and frame my face to all occasions. 3.02.185
blow, | and with the other fling it at thy face, 5.01. 51
but 'twas thy heavenly face that set me on. R3 1.02.182
for by his face straight shall you know his 3.04. 53
what of his heart perceive you in his face | by 3.04. 54
/her face defac'd with scars of infamy, | /her 3.07.126
o, when, i say, i look'd on richard's face, 4.01. 70
perish | and never more behold thy face again. 4.04.187
what good is cover'd with the face of heaven, 4.04.240
be this cold corpse on the earth's cold face; 5.03.266
is but merely | a fit or two o' th' face — but H8 1.03. 7
desir'd | to him brought viva voce to his face; 2.01. 18
thou hast the sweetest face i ever look'd on. 4.01. 43
how long her face is drawn! 4.02. 97
be what they will, may stand forth face to face, 5.02. 82
be what they will, may stand forth face to face, 5.02. 82
door, he should be a brazier by his face, for, 5.03. 41 P
my armed fist | i'll /pash him o'er the face. TRO 2.03.203
here is a man — but 'tis before his face, | i 2.03.229
the beauty that is borne here in the face | the 3.03.103
a lion that will fly | with his face backward. 4.01. 21
come, come, thou boy–queller, show thy face, 5.05. 45
turn thy false face, thou traitor, | and pay thy 5.06. 6
shalt see me once more strike at tullus' face. COR 1.01.240
and when my face is fair, you shall perceive 1.09. 69
palate adversely, i make a crooked face at it. 2.01. 57 P
from face to foot | he was a thing of blood, 2.02.108
appearance, and thy face | bears a command in't; 4.05. 60
i knew by his face that there was something in 4.05.154 P
he had, sir, a kind of face, methought — i 4.05.155 P
should consume it, i have not the face | to say, 4.06.116
requires nor child nor woman's face to see. 5.03.130
the tartness of his face sours ripe grapes. 5.04. 18 P
o tamora, thou bearest a woman's face — TIT 2.03.136
and wonder greatly that man's face can fold | in 2.03.266
ah, now thou turn'st away thy face for shame! 2.04. 28
yet do thy cheeks look red as titan's face 2.04. 31
and keep eternal spring–time /on /thy face, | so 3.01. 21
aaron will have his soul black like his face. 3.01.205
the welkin with his big–swoll'n face? 3.01.223
side, | although my seal be stamped in his face. 4.02.127
this growing image of thy fiend–like face? 5.01. 45
till he be brought unto the empress' face | for 5.03. 7
sorrowful drops upon thy blood/–stain'd face, 5.03.154
compare her face with some that i shall show, ROM 1.02. 86
"yea," quoth he, "dost thou fall upon thy face? 1.03. 41
"yea," quoth my husband, "fall'st upon thy face? 1.03. 55
read o'er the volume of young paris' face, | and 1.03. 81
slave | come hither, cover'd with an antic face, 1.05. 56
foot, | nor arm nor face, /nor /any /other /part 2.02. 41
thou knowest the mask of night is on my face, 2.02. 85
good peter, to hide her face, for her fan's the 2.04.107 P
to hide her face, for her fan's the fairer face. 2.04.108 P
news | by playing it to me with so sour a face. 2.05. 24
though his face be better than any man's, yet 2.05. 40 P
and he will make the face of heaven so fine 3.02. 23
o serpent heart, hid with a flow'ring face! 3.02. 73
thursday, | or never after look me in the face. 3.05.162
being spoke behind your back, than to your face. 4.01. 28
poor soul, thy face is much abus'd with tears. 4.01. 29
and what i spake, i spake it to my face. 4.01. 34
thy face is mine, and thou hast sland'red it. 4.01. 35
have i thought /long to see this morning's face, 4.05. 41
of death | is partly to behold my lady's face, 5.03. 29
let me peruse this face. 5.03. 74
paint till a horse may mire upon your face: TIM 4.03.148
whom thy upward face | hath to the marbled 4.03.190
let me behold thy face. 4.03.493
set him before me, let me see his face. JC 1.02. 20
tell me, good brutus, can you see your face? 1.02. 51
you that, i'll ne'er look you i' th' face again. 1.02.282 P
whereto the climber–upward turns his face; 2.01. 23
if not the face of men, | the sufferance of our 2.01.114
when they shall see | the face of caesar, they 2.02. 12
and, in his mantle muffling up his face, | even 3.02.187
him off | if at philippi we do face him there, 4.03.211
thinking by this face | to fasten in our 5.01. 10
to see my best friend ta'en before my face! 5.03. 35
and when my face is cover'd, as 'tis now, 5.03. 44
titinius' face is upward. 5.03. 93
hold then my sword, and turn away thy face, 5.05. 47
to find the mind's construction in the face: MAC 1.04. 12
your face, my thane, is as a book, where men 1.05. 62
i would, while it was smiling in my face, | have 1.07. 56
false face must hide what the false heart doth 1.07. 82
that darkness does the face of earth entomb, 2.04. 9
there's blood upon thy face. 3.04. 13
new sorrows | strike heaven on the face, that it 4.03. 6
go prick thy face, and over–red thy fear, | thou 5.03. 14
take thy face hence. 5.03. 19
tyrant, show thy face! 5.07. 14
winds of heaven | visit her face too roughly. HAM 1.02.142
then saw you not his face? 1.02.229
he falls to such perusal of my face | as 'a 2.01. 87
why, thy face is valanc'd since i saw thee last; 2.02.423 P
plucks off my beard and blows it in my face, 2.02.573
god hath given you one face, and you make 3.01.143 P
note, | for i mine eyes will rivet to his face, 3.02. 85
each opposite that blanks the face of joy | meet 3.02.220
heaven's face does glow | o'er this solidity and 3.04. 48
painting of a sorrow, | a face without a heart? 4.07.109
come, let me wipe thy face. 5.02.294
nor shall ever see | that face of hers again. LR 1.01.264
so your face bids me, though you say nothing. 1.04.195 P
why one's nose stands i' th' middle on 's face? 1.05. 20 P
my face i'll grime with filth, | blanket my 2.03. 9
(although as yet the face of it is cover'd 3.01. 20
and broke them in the sweet face of heaven: 3.04. 89 P
dust which the rude wind | blows in your face. 4.02. 31
whose face between her forks presages snow; 4.06.119
was this a face | to be oppos'd against the 4.07. 30
knavery's plain face is never seen till us'd. OTH 2.01.312
cunning, | i have no judgment in an honest face. 3.03. 50
is now begrim'd and black | as mine own face. 3.03.388
scorns | that dwell in every region of his face, 4.01. 83
let me see your eyes; | look in my face. 4.02. 26
know we this face or no? 5.01. 88
out, strumpet! weep'st thou for him to my face? 5.02. 77
but there's no goodness in thy face, if antony ANT 2.05. 37
hadst thou narcissus in thy face, to me | thou 2.05. 96
what counts harsh fortune casts upon my face, 2.06. 54
but there is never a fair woman has a true face. 2.06.100 P
he has a cloud in 's face. 3.02. 51
i look'd her in the face, and saw her led 3.03. 9
bear'st thou her face in mind? 3.03. 29
though you fled | from that great face of war, 3.13. 5
till like a boy you see him cringe his face, 3.13.100
poor enobarbus did | before thy face repent! 4.09. 10
neck, his face subdu'd | to penetrative shame, 4.14. 74
and would gladly | look him i' th' face. 5.02. 32
his face was as the heav'ns, and therein stuck 5.02. 79
no, but he fled forward still, toward your face. CYM 1.02. 16 P
thy garments cut to pieces before /her face: 4.01. 18 P
not lack | the flower that's like thy face, pale 4.02.221
but his jovial face — | murther in heaven? 4.02.311
let's see the boy's face. 4.02.359
to the face of peril | myself i'll dedicate. 5.01. 28
done aught but well, | whose face i never saw? 5.04. 36
and full of face | as heaven ha- lent her all PER 1.ch. 23
her face the book of praises, where is read 1.01. 15
her face, like heaven, enticeth thee to view 1.01. 30
how durst thy tongue move anger to our face? 1.02. 54
against the face of death | i sought the 1.02. 71
her face was to mine eye beyond all wonder; 1.02. 75
she has a good face, speaks well, and has 4.02. 47 P
on her, | but cast their gazes on marina's face; 4.03. 33
which, to betray, dost, with thine angel's face, 4.03. 47
he swears | never to wash his face, nor cut his 4.04. 28
as it were to stink afore the face of the gods. 4.06.136 P
the free enjoying of that face i die for — | o, TNK 2.03. 3
woman, | his face, methinks, goes that way. 2.05. 21
or i'll proclaim him, | and to his face, no man. 2.06. 31
content and anger | in me have but one face. 3.01.108
that face of yours | will bear the curses else 3.06.186
in my face, dear sister, | i find no anger to 3.06.188
good heaven, | what a sweet face has arcite! 4.02. 7
and yet inviting, | has this brown manly face! 4.02. 42
should be a stout man, by his face a prince 4.02. 77
knight he spoke of, | but of a face far sweeter; 4.02. 95
in 's face appears | all the fair hopes of what 4.02. 98
in his face | the livery of the warlike maid 4.02.105
a young handsome wench then, show his face — ep 6
even as the sun with purple–color'd face | had VEN 1
panting he lies, and breatheth in her face. 62
"is thine own heart to thine own face affected? 157
the sun doth burn my face, i must remove." 186
for from the stillitgry of thy face excelling 443
sky, | so is her face illumin'd with her eye, 486
whose beams upon his hairless face are fix'd, 487
incorporate then they seem, face grows to face. 540
incorporate then they seem, face grows to face. 540
her face doth reek and smoke, her blood doth 555
"alas, he nought esteems that face of thine, 631
"didst thou not mark my face? 643
my face is full of shame, my heart of teen, 808
some catch her by the neck, some kiss her face, 872
to wash the foul face of the sluttish ground, 983
his face seems twain, each several limb is 1067
what face remains alive that's worth the viewing 1076

"to see his face the lion walk'd along | behind 1093
if he did see his face, why then i know | he 1109
and stains her face with his congealed blood. 1122
within whose face beauty and virtue strived LUC 52
this heraldry in lucrece' face was seen, 64
base, | that it will live engraven in my face. 203
stay, | and blows the smoke of it into his face, 312
"the color in thy face, | that even for anger 477
fixed | in the remorseless wrinkles of his face; 562
cooling his hot face in the chastest tears 682
let not the jealous day behold that face, 800
reproach is stamp'd in collatinus' face, | and 829
sorrow | (for why her face wore sorrow's livery) 1222
the face of either cipher'd either's heart, 1396
their face their manners most expressly told: 1397
a hand, a foot, a face, a leg, a head | stood 1427
to find a face where all distress is stell'd. 1444
his face, though full of cares, yet show'd 1503
such signs of truth in his plain face she spied, 1532
but such a face should bear a wicked mind. 1540
saw, | amazedly in her sad face he stares: 1591
with a joyless smile she turns away | the face, 1712
about the mourning and congealed face | of that 1744
he falls, and bathes the pale fear in his face, 1775
in thy glass and tell the face thou viewest, SON 3. 1
now is the time that face should form another, 3. 2
a woman's face with nature's own hand painted 20. 1
black night beauteous and her old face new. 27.12
kissing with golden face the meadows green, 33. 3
to ride | with ugly rack on his celestial face, 33. 6
to dry the rain on my storm–beaten face, | for 34. 6
methinks no face so gracious is as mine, | no 62. 5
so love's face | may still seem love to me, 93. 2
that in thy face sweet love should ever dwell; 93.10
rise, resty muse, my love's sweet face survey, 100. 9
and there appears a face | that overgoes my 103. 6
fairing the foul with art's false borrow'd face, 127. 6
thy face hath not the power to make love groan; 131. 6
a thousand groans, but thinking on thy face, 131.10
as those two /mourning eyes become thy face. 132. 9
is not, | to put fair truth upon so foul a face? 137.12
and therefore from my face she turns my foes, 139.11
to follow that which flies before her face, 143. 7
that maidens' eyes stuck over all his face. LC 81
whose sights till then were levell'd on my face, 282
FACERE 1 FR 0.0001 REL FR 0 V 1 P
facere, as it were, replication, or rather LLL 4.02. 15 P
FACE'S 2 FR 0.0002 REL FR 2 V 0 P
his face's own margent did cote such amazes LLL 2.01.246
which tarquin view'd in her fair face's field, LUC 72
FACES 56 FR 0.0063 REL FR 43 V 13 P
smote the air | for breathing in their faces; TMP 4.01.173
ne'er so black, say they have angels' faces. TGV 3.01.103
there are no faces truer than those that are so ADO 1.01. 27 P
or ever but in vizards show their faces? LLL 5.02.271
false, we have given thee faces. 5.02.622 P
he's a god or a painter, for he makes faces. 5.02.643 P
to gaze on christian fools with varnish'd faces; MV 2.05. 33
of many faces, eyes, and hearts, | to have the AYL 3.02.151
as many as have good beards, or good faces, or ep 21 P
nor can we be distinguish'd by our faces | for SHR 1.01.200
i learn'd it out of women's faces. WT 2.01. 12
damask roses, | masks for faces and for noses; 4.04.221
plackets where they should bear their faces? 4.04.244 P
compare our faces, and be judge yourself. JN 1.01. 79
with ladies' faces and fierce dragons' spleens, 2.01. 68
which then blew bitterly against our faces, R2 1.04. 7
by the means whereof 'a faces it out, but fights H5 3.02. 33 P
and my way shall be pav'd with english faces. 3.07. 81 P
than midday sun fierce bent against their faces. 1H6 1.01. 14
that i in rage might shoot them at your faces! 4.07. 80
your wives and daughters before your faces. 2H6 4.08. 31 P
smile in men's faces, smooth, deceive, and cog, R3 1.03. 48
we know each other's faces; 3.04. 10
high–rear'd bulwarks, stand before our faces. 5.03.242
ye have angels' faces, but heaven knows your H8 3.01.145
flew up, and had their faces | been loose, this 4.01. 74
whose bright faces | cast thousand beams upon me 4.02. 88
and faces pale | with flight and agued fear! COR 1.04. 37
they lie deadly that tell you have good faces. 2.01. 62 P
with the colic, you make faces like mummers, set 2.01. 74 P
bid them wash their faces, | and keep their 2.03. 60
off, and sprinkles in your faces | your reeking TIM 3.06. 92
wear timon's livery, | that see i by our faces; 4.02. 18
and half their faces buried in their cloaks, JC 2.01. 74
who did hide their faces | even from darkness. 2.01.277
i'll gild the faces of the grooms withal, | for MAC 2.02. 53
their hands and faces were all badg'd with blood 2.03.102
and make our faces vizards to our hearts, 3.02. 34
shame itself, | why do you make such faces? 3.04. 66
what are these faces? 4.02. 79
have grey beards, that their faces are wrinkled, HAM 2.02.197 P
murtherer, leave thy damnable faces and begin. 3.02.253 P
i have seen better faces in my time | than LR 2.02. 93
even so. cover their faces. 5.03.243
all men's faces are true, whatsome'er their ANT 2.06. 97 P
although they wear their faces to the bent | of CYM 1.01. 13
upon their faces. 4.02.285
with faces fit for masks, or rather fairer 5.03. 21
there's business in these faces. 5.05. 23
poor women's faces are their own faults' books. LUC 1253
that two red fires in both their faces blazed; 1353
you might behold triumphing in their faces; 1388
about him were a press of gaping faces, | which 1408
glass fell wherein they view'd their faces. 1526
heavenly touches ne'er touch'd earthly faces." SON 17. 8
they are the lords and owners of their faces, 94. 7
FACIANT 1 FR 0.0001 REL FR 1 V 0 P
dii faciant laudis summa sit ista tuae! 3H6 1.03. 48
FACILE 2 FR 0.0002 REL FR 1 V 1 P
facile, precor gelida quando /pecus /omne sub LLL 4.02. 93 P
so may he with more facile question bear it, OTH 1.03. 23
FACILITY 3 FR 0.0003 REL FR 1 V 2 P
affect the letter, for it argues facility. LLL 4.02. 55
for the elegancy, facility, and golden cadence 4.02.122 P
he drinks you, with facility, your dane dead OTH 2.03. 82 P
FACINERIOUS 1 FR 0.0001 REL FR 0 V 1 P
and he's of a most facinerious spirit that will AWW 2.03. 29 P
FACING 1 FR 0.0001 REL FR 0 V 1 P
richer than innocency, stands for the facing. MM 3.02. 10 P
FACIT 2 FR 0.0002 REL FR 0 V 2 P
cucullus non facit monachum: MM 5.01.262 P
lady, "cucullus non facit monachum": TN 1.05. 56 P
/FACT 1 FR 0.0001 REL FR 1 V 0 P
'ad been a kindness | becoming well thy /fact. PER 4.03. 12
FACT 13 FR 0.0014 REL FR 12 V 1 P
and indeed his fact, till now in the government MM 4.02.136 P
should she kneel down in mercy of this fact, 5.01.434
where both not sin, and yet a sinful fact. AWW 3.07. 47
past all shame | (those of your fact are so), so WT 3.02. 85
this fact was infamous | and ill beseeming any 1H6 4.01. 30
and a fouler fact | did never traitor in the 2H6 1.03.173
whom we have apprehended in the fact, | raising 2.01.169
were more than one | confederate in the fact; TIT 4.01. 39
nor did he soil the fact with cowardice | (/an TIM 3.05. 16
damned fact! MAC 3.06. 10
lack humanity | so much as this fact comes to? CYM 3.02. 17
ay, if the fact be known; LUC 239
the powers to whom i pray abhor this fact, | how 349
FACTION 19 FR 0.0021 REL FR 16 V 3 P
this fellow were a king for our wild faction! TGV 4.01. 37
i will bandy with thee in faction; AYL 5.01. 55 P
and all the rest revolted faction traitors? R2 2.02. 57
may turn the tide of fearful faction, | and 1H4 4.01. 67
hate, | will i for ever and my faction wear, 1H6 2.04.109
grown to this faction in the temple garden, 2.04.125
forsaken your pernicious faction | and join'd 4.01. 59
her faction will be full as strong as ours. 3H6 5.03. 17
or any of your faction? R3 1.03. 57
which they upon the adverse faction want. 5.03. 13
is wit stirring, and leave the faction of fools. TRO 2.01.119 P
fraction is more our wish than their faction. 2.03. 99 P
themselves, | and drave great mars to faction. 3.03.190
my faction if thou strengthen with thy friends, TIT 1.01.214
thou and thy faction shall repent this rape. 1.01.404
all, | and rase their faction and their family, 1.01.451
they are the faction. JC 2.01. 77
so, | hamlet is of the faction that is wronged, HAM 5.02.238
two domestic powers | breed scrupulous faction; ANT 1.03. 48
FACTIONARY 1 FR 0.0001 REL FR 0 V 1 P
always factionary on the party of your general. COR 5.02. 29 P
FACTIONS 7 FR 0.0008 REL FR 6 V 1 P
that here you maintain several factions; 1H6 1.01. 71
hollow upon this plain, so many hollow factions. TRO 1.03. 80
to draw emulous factions and bleed to death upon 2.03. 73 P
side factions, and give out | conjectural COR 1.01.193
princes, that strive by factions and by friends TIT 1.01. 18
world | when sects and factions were newly born. TIM 3.05. 30
known to commit outrages | and cherish factions. 3.05. 72
FACTIOUS 10 FR 0.0011 REL FR 10 V 0 P
a cause | such factious emulations shall arise! 1H6 4.01.113
this factious bandying of their favorites, | but 4.01.190
make up no factious numbers for the matter, | in 2H6 2.01. 39
and chop away that factious pate of his. 5.01.135
thou factious duke of york, descend my throne, 3H6 1.01. 74
grey | were factious for the house of lancaster; R3 1.03.127
you have been factious one against the other. 2.01. 20
makes factious feasts, rails on our state of war TRO 1.03.191
the dull and factious nobles of the greeks 2.02.209
be factious for redress of all these griefs, JC 1.03.118
FACTO 1 FR 0.0001 REL FR 1 V 0 P
it cures her ipso facto | the melancholy humor TNK 5.02. 37
FACTOR 4 FR 0.0004 REL FR 4 V 0 P
percy is but my factor, good my lord, | to 1H4 3.02.147
or lowly factor for another's gain; R3 3.07.134
only reserv'd their factor to buy souls | and 4.04. 72
which i (the factor for the rest) have done | in CYM 1.06.188
FACTOR'S 1 FR 0.0001 REL FR 1 V 0 P
made | to epidamium, till my factor's death, ERR 1.01. 41
FACTORS 1 FR 0.0001 REL FR 1 V 0 P
this great world, | chief factors for the gods: ANT 2.06. 10
FACULTIES 9 FR 0.0010 REL FR 6 V 3 P
as notes whose faculties inclusive were | more AWW 1.03.226
and such other gambol faculties 'a has, that 2H4 2.04.251 P
which neither know | my faculties nor person, H8 1.02. 73
their natures, and preformed faculties, | to JC 1.03. 67
this duncan | hath borne his faculties so meek, MAC 1.07. 17
how infinite in faculties, in form and moving! HAM 2.02.304 P
indeed | the very faculties of eyes and ears. 2.02.566
attributes | the faculties of other instruments TNK 1.02. 68
again to execute their preordain'd faculties, 4.03. 72 P
FACULTY 2 FR 0.0002 REL FR 2 V 0 P
by night, | unseen, yet crescive in his faculty. H5 1.01. 66
and heart | have faculty by nature to subsist, SON 122. 6
FADE *(also vade, etc.)*
FADE 6 FR 0.0006 REL FR 6 V 0 P
nothing of him that doth fade, | but doth suffer TMP 1.02.400
how chance the roses there do fade so fast? MND 1.01.129
the roses in thy lips and cheeks shall fade | to ROM 4.01. 99
rise, and fade. CYM 5.04.106
but thy eternal summer shall not fade, | nor SON 18. 9
show, | they live unwoo'd, and unrespected fade, 54.10
FADED 4 FR 0.0004 REL FR 4 V 0 P
and, like this insubstantial pageant faded, TMP 4.01.155
this is a man, old, wrinkled, faded, withered, SHR 4.05. 43
is hack'd down, and his summer leaves all faded, R2 1.02. 20
it faded on the crowing of the cock. HAM 1.01.157
FADETH 1 FR 0.0001 REL FR 1 V 0 P
such day | as after sunset fadeth in the west, SON 73. 6
FADGE 2 FR 0.0002 REL FR 1 V 1 P
we will have, if this fadge not, an antic. LLL 5.01.147 P
how will this fadge? TN 2.02. 33
FADING 6 FR 0.0006 REL FR 6 V 0 P
one fading moxent's mirth | with twenty watchful TGV 1.01. 30
my wasting lamps some fading glimmer left, | my ERR 5.01.316
he makes a swan–like end, | fading in music. MV 3.02. 45
if that my fading breath permit | and death 1H6 2.05. 61
to the wide world and all her fading sweets: SON 19. 7
dost thou upon thy fading mansion spend? 146. 6
FADINGS 1 FR 0.0001 REL FR 0 V 1 P
such delicate burthens of dildos and fadings, WT 4.04.195 P
FADOM *(also fathom)*
FADOM 6 FR 0.0006 REL FR 4 V 2 P
full fadom five thy father lies, | of his bones TMP 1.02.397
thirty fadom. AWW 4.01. 58 P
of april, forty thousand fadom above water, and WT 4.04.277 P
o' my conscience, | wish him ten fadom deep. H8 2.01. 51
spanish blades, | of healths five fadom deep; ROM 1.04. 85
another of his fadom they have none | to lead OTH 1.01.152
FADOM–LINE 1 FR 0.0001 REL FR 1 V 0 P
where fadom–line could never touch the ground, 1H4 1.03.204
FADOMS 4 FR 0.0004 REL FR 4 V 0 P
my staff, | bury it certain fadoms in the earth, TMP 5.01. 55
or the profound seas hides | in unknown fadoms, WT 4.04.491
reply not in how many fadoms deep | they lie TRO 1.01. 50
brain | that looks so many fadoms to the sea HAM 1.04. 77
FAGGOT 1 FR 0.0001 REL FR 1 V 0 P
or brought a faggot to bright–burning troy? TIT 3.01. 69
FAGGOTS 1 FR 0.0001 REL FR 1 V 0 P
maid, | spare for no faggots, let there be enow. 1H6 5.04. 56
FAIL 70 FR 0.0079 REL FR 61 V 9 P
i will not fail your ladyship. TGV 4.03. 45
she will not fail, for lovers break not hours, 5.01. 4
woman, commend me to her, i will not fail her. WIV 2.02. 93 P
wherein if he chance to fail, he hath sentenc'd MM 3.02.257 P
thus fail not to do your office, as you will 4.02.125 P
and tell him i will not fail him at supper, for ADO 1.01.277 P
we will not fail. 5.01.330
i pray you fail me not. MND 1.02.106 P
a million fail, confounding oath on oath. 3.02. 93
i will not fail you. MV 1.01. 72
had your eyes, you might fail of the knowing me; 2.02. 76 P
tell gentle jessica | i will not fail her; 2.04. 20
but if you fail, without more speech, my lord, 2.09. 7
next, if i fail | of the right casket, never in 2.09. 11
lastly, | if i do fail in fortune of my choice, 2.09. 15
if he fail of that, | he will have other means AYL 2.03. 24
i'll not fail, if i live. 5.02.122
shall get a sire, if i fail not of my cunning. SHR 2.01.411
myself in my incertain grounds to fail | as AWW 3.01. 15
and trusty business in a main danger fail you. 3.06. 15 P
adieu till then, then fail not. 4.02. 64
for the fail | of any point in't shall not only WT 2.03.170
it cannot fail, but by | the violation of my 4.04.476
what dangers, by his highness' fail of issue, 5.01. 27
meeting, wherein it is at our pleasure to fail; 1H4 1.02.171 P
if truth and upright innocency fail me, | i'll 2H4 5.02. 39
a jove, | that if requiring fail he will compel; H5 2.04.101
with me, | my purpose should not fail with me, 3.02. 16
though thy speech doth fail, | one eye thou hast 1H6 1.04. 82
that, if it chance the one of us do fail, | the 2.01. 31
crown for this, | or all my fence shall fail. 2H6 2.01. 51
and if thou fail us, all our hope is done. 3H6 3.03. 33
and, if i fail not in my deep intent, | clarence R3 1.01.149
he his title to the crown | upon our fail? H8 1.02.145
i shall not fail t' approve the fair conceit 2.03. 74
my realms stood in | by this my issue's fail, 2.04.199
if my sight fail not, | you should be lord 4.02.108
if they shall fail, i, with mine enemies, | will 5.01.123
persuasions to the contrary | fail not to use, 5.01.148
if he fail, | yet go we under our opinion still TRO 1.03.381
fall greeks, fail fame, honor or go or stay, 5.01. 43
sweet honey and sweet notes together fail. 5.10. 44
to fail in the disposing of those chances COR 4.07. 40
rights fouler, strengths by strengths do fail. 4.07. 55
that, if you fail in our request, the blame 5.03. 90
i will not fail, 'tis twenty year till then. ROM 2.02.169
if all else fail, myself have power to die. 3.05.242
obedience, fail in children! TIM 4.01. 4
be that the uttermost, and fail not then. JC 2.01.214
if we should fail? MAC 1.07. 59
we fail? 1.07. 59
to the sticking place, | and we'll not fail. 1.07. 61
fail not our feast. 3.01. 27
if this should fail, | and that our drift look HAM 4.07.150
sister in the least | would fail her obligation. LR 2.04.142
will be too short, | and every measure fail me. 4.07. 3
"this fail you not to do, as you will —" OTH 4.01.228 P
but if we fail, | we then can do't at land. ANT 3.07. 52
the queen | of audience nor desire shall fail, 3.12. 21
be false and perjur'd | from thy great fail. CYM 3.04. 64
and i will never fail | beginning nor supplyment 3.04.178
weep ere you fail; TNK 1.01. 95
or it shall be, | on fail of some condition? 1.02.105
he'll eat a horn–book ere he fail. 2.03. 42
o state of nature, fail together in me, | since 3.02. 31
all offices are done | save what i fail in. 3.02. 37
nay, and she fail me once — you can tell, arcas 3.05. 46
and with thy teeth thou hold, will either fail. 3.05. 50
if he fail, | he's neither man nor soldier. 3.06. 3
we dare not fail thee, theseus. 3.06.305
FAIL'D 7 FR 0.0008 REL FR 6 V 1 P
hath all his ventures fail'd? MV 3.02.267
wherein toward me my homely stars have fail'd AWW 2.05. 75
that in such intelligence hath seldom fail'd. 4.05. 83 P
that, had the king in his last sickness fail'd, H8 1.02.184
and 'cause he fail'd | his presence at the MAC 3.06. 21
he hath not fail'd to pester us with message HAM 1.02. 22
freckled nell — that never fail'd her master. TNK 3.05. 27
FAILING 6 FR 0.0006 REL FR 6 V 0 P
to those have shut him up, which failing, TIM 1.01. 98
full of decay and failing? 4.03.460
or failing so, yet that i put the moor | at OTH 2.01.300
there would be something failing | in him that CYM 1.01. 21
they failing, | i must die much your debtor. 2.04. 7
but failing of her end by his strange absence, 5.05. 57
FAILS 9 FR 0.0010 REL FR 9 V 0 P
my sails | must fill, or else my project fails, TMP ep 12
oft expectation fails, and most oft there AWW 2.01.142
pure innocence | persuades when speaking fails. WT 2.02. 40
and now my sight fails, and my brain is giddy. 2H4 4.04.110
till lionel's issue fails, his should not reign. 2H6 2.02. 56
it fails not yet, but flourishes in thee, | and 2.02. 57
earth below | fails in the promis'd largeness. TRO 1.03. 5
their obedience fails | to th' greater bench. COR 3.01.165
either my eyesight fails, or thou lookest pale. ROM 3.05. 57
FAIL'ST 1 FR 0.0001 REL FR 1 V 0 P
and when thou fail'st (as god forbid the hour!) 3H6 2.01.190
FAIN 70 FR 0.0079 REL FR 38 V 32 P
but i would fain die a dry death. TMP 1.01. 67 P
i perceive i must be fain to bear with you. TGV 1.01.120 P
by my victuals, and would fain have meat. 2.01.174 P
mine honor in my necessity, am fain to shuffle, WIV 2.02. 25 P
master /brook below would fain speak with you, 2.02.145 P

i am fain to dine and sup with water and bran; MM 4.03.152 P
but i was fain to forswear it. 4.03.172 P
that outward courtesies would fain proclaim 5.01. 15
upon a wrong'd — i would fain have said a maid! 5.01. 21
i know you'ld fain be gone. 5.01.120
we would fain have either. ERR 3.01. 66
i would fain have it a match, and i doubt not ADO 2.01.368 P
i would fain know what you have to say. 3.05. 29 P
melancholy and would fain have it beaten away. 5.01.123 P
all, | that he was fain to seal on cupid's name. LLL 5.02. 9
they are thirsty, fools would fain have drink. 5.02.372
the holy suit which fain it would convince, 5.02.746
challenger's youth i would fain dissuade him, AYL 1.02.160 P
i would fain see this meeting. 3.03. 46 P
which such as you are fain to be beholding to 4.01. 59 P
me, signior gremio, i would fain be doing. SHR 2.01. 74
most fain would steal | what law does vouch mine AWW 2.05. 81
general's looks, we shall be fain to hang you. 4.03.240 P
to come into me, | which i would fain shut out. 5.03.115
i would fain say, bleed tears; WT 5.02. 88 P
on, i must be fain to pawn both my plate and the 2H4 2.01.141 P
fain would i go to meet the archbishop, | but 2.03. 65
mistress tearsheet would fain hear some music. 2.04. 12 P
as i perceiv'd his grace would fain have done, H5 1.01. 85
i wad full fain heard some question 'tween you 3.02.118 P
for i would fain be about the ears of the 3.07. 84 P
i would fain see the man, that hath but two legs 4.07.161 P
but i would fain see it once, and please god of 4.07.163 P
fain would mine eyes be witness with mine ears 1H6 2.03. 9
are glad and fain by flight to save themselves. 3.02.114
fain would i woo her, yet i dare not speak: 5.03. 65
yea, man and birds are fain of climbing high. 2H6 2.01. 8
ah, york, no man alive so fain as i! 3.01.244
fain would i go to chafe his paly lips | with 3.02.141
is england main'd, and fain to go with a staff, 4.02.163 P
the good old man would fain that all were well, 3H6 4.07. 31
my soul is heavy, and i fain would sleep. R3 1.04. 74
how fain, like pilate, would i wash my hands 1.04.272
would fain have come with me to meet your grace, 3.01. 29
which he fain | would have flung from him; H8 2.01. 24
pibbles, that i was fain to draw mine honor in, 5.03. 57 P
i would fain have arm'd to-day, but my nell TRO 3.01.136 P
i would fain see them meet, that that same young 5.04. 5 P
fain would i dwell on form, fain, fain deny ROM 2.02. 88
fain would i dwell on form, fain, fain deny 2.02. 88
form, fain, fain deny | what i have spoke, but 2.02. 88
one paris, that would fain lay knife aboard; 2.04.202 P
i would forget it fain, | but o, it presses to 3.02.109
how fain would i have hated all mankind, | and TIM 4.03.499
that, to my thinking, he would fain have had it. JC 1.02.240 P
which the poor heart would fain deny, and dare MAC 5.03. 28
i would fain prove so. HAM 2.02.131
been such a time — i would fain know that — 2.02.153
and fain i would beguile | the tedious day with 3.02.226
i have a speech a' fire that fain would blaze, 4.07.190
respect of that, i would fain think it were not. LR 1.02. 64 P
your countenance which i would fain call master. 1.04. 28 P
thy fool to lie — i would fain learn to lie. 1.04.180 P
night | against my fire, and wast thou fain, 4.07. 37
gallants that would fain have a measure to the OTH 2.03. 31 P
for i would very fain speak with you. 4.01.167 P
know i love him, | for i would fain enjoy him? TNK 2.04. 30
i perceive | you would fain be at that fight. 3.06. 60
o, sir, you would fain be nibbling. 5.02. 87
and now she weeps, and now she fain would speak, VEN 221

FAINING 2 FR 0.0002 REL FR 2 V 0 P
with faining voice verses of faining love, | and MND 1.01. 31
with faining voice verses of faining love, | and 1.01. 31

FAINT 52 FR 0.0058 REL FR 49 V 3 P
i have's mine own, | which is most faint. TMP ep 3
chaunting faint hymns to the cold fruitless moon MND 1.01. 73
i | upon faint primrose beds were wont to lie, 1.01.215
fair love, you faint with wand'ring in the wood; 2.02. 35
than my faint means would grant continuance. MV 1.01.125
i faint almost to death. AYL 2.04. 66
weakness possesseth me, and i am faint. JN 5.03. 17
backward their own ground | in faint retire. 5.05. 4
i am the /cygnet to this pale faint swan | who 5.07. 21
but if you faint, as fearing to do so, | stay, R2 2.01.297
makes me with heavy nothing faint and shrink. 2.02. 32
breathless and faint, leaning upon my sword, 1H4 1.03. 32
in thy faint slumbers i by thee have watch'd, 2.03. 47
even such a man, so faint, so spiritless, | so 2H4 1.01. 70
state, | rend'ring faint quittance, wearied and 1.01.108
of indigent faint souls past corporal toil, | a H5 1.01. 16
the muster of his kingdom too faint a number; 3.06.131 P
the english army is grown weak and faint; 1H6 1.01.158
why faint you, lords? 3H6 1.01.129
and i am faint, and cannot fly their fury; 1.04. 23
frown hath made thee faint and fly ere this! 1.04. 48
can pluck the diadem from faint henry's head, 2.01.153
this soft courage makes your followers faint. 2.02. 57
and much effuse of blood doth make me faint. 2.06. 28
of so high a courage, | and warriors faint! 5.04. 51
the faint defects of age | must be the scene of TRO 1.03.172
what he hath done, | nor faint in the pursuit. 2.02.142
leave this faint puling, and lament as i do, COR 4.02. 52
if fear hath made thee faint, as me it hath — TIT 2.03.234
into some house, benvolio, | or i shall faint. ROM 3.01.106
i have a faint cold fear thrills through my 4.03. 15
at first | to set a gloss on faint deeds, hollow TIM 1.02. 16
has friendship such a faint and milky heart, 3.01. 54
and with their faint reply this answer join: 3.03. 25
o, i grow faint. JC 2.04. 43
but i am faint, my gashes cry for help. MAC 1.02. 42
i have perceiv'd a most faint neglect of late, LR 1.04. 68 P
i faint, o iras, charmian! ANT 2.05.110
i am faint. CYM 4.02. 63
you come in faint for want of meat, depart 5.04.161 P
quail to remember — give me leave, i faint. 5.05.149
maiden pinks, of odor faint, | daisies TNK 1.01. 4
i know you are faint — then i'll talk further 3.03. 7
who is so faint that dares not be so bold | to VEN 401
with her plenty press'd, she faint with dearth, 545
hot, faint, and weary, with her hard embracing, 559
grew i not faint? 645
thought of it doth make my faint heart bleed, 669
"as burning fevers, agues pale and faint, 739
faint not, faint heart, but stoutly say, 'so be LUC 1209
faint not, faint heart, but stoutly say, 'so be 1209
o, how i faint when i of you do write, | knowing SON 80. 1

FAINTED 3 FR 0.0003 REL FR 3 V 0 P
and now he fainted, | and cried, in fainting, AYL 4.03.148
should have borne men, and expectation fainted, ANT 3.06. 47
(as if with grief or travail he had fainted), LUC 1543

FAINTER 1 FR 0.0001 REL FR 1 V 0 P
but in a fainter kind — o, not like me, | for CYM 3.02. 55

FAINT-HEARTED 3 FR 0.0003 REL FR 3 V 0 P
faint-hearted woodvile, prizest him 'fore me? 1H6 1.03. 22
farewell, faint-hearted and degenerate king, 3H6 1.01.183
faint-hearted boy, arise and look upon her. TIT 3.01. 65

FAINTING 8 FR 0.0009 REL FR 8 V 0 P
herself (almost at fainting under | the pleasing ERR 1.01. 45
and cried, in fainting, upon rosalind. AYL 4.03.149
out of the weak door of our fainting land. JN 5.07. 78
that i may kindly give one fainting kiss. 1H6 2.05. 40
and that my fainting words do warrant death. 2.05. 95
fainting, despair; R3 5.03.172
o brother, help me with thy fainting hand — TIT 2.03.233
never fainting | under the weight of arms; TNK 4.02.129

/FAINTLY 1 FR 0.0001 REL FR 1 V 0 P
/faintly /spoke | /after /the /prompter, /for ROM 1.04. 7

FAINTLY 11 FR 0.0012 REL FR 10 V 1 P
i faintly broke with thee of arthur's death; JN 4.02.227
where it perceives it is but faintly borne. R2 1.03.281
he prays but faintly, and would be denied, | we 5.03.103
and faintly through a rusty beaver peeps. H5 4.02. 44
faintly besiege us one hour in a month. 1H6 1.02. 8
'twas very faintly he said, "rise"; COR 5.01. 66
but faintly, nothing like the image and horror LR 1.02.174 P
why do you speak so faintly? | are you not well? OTH 3.03.282
now he denies it faintly, and laughs it out. 4.01.112
her two blue windows faintly she upheaveth, VEN 482
he faintly flies, sweating with guilty fear; LUC 740

FAINTNESS 2 FR 0.0002 REL FR 2 V 0 P
faintness constraineth me | to measure out my MND 3.02.428
bewray'd the faintness of my master's heart. 1H6 4.01.107

FAINTS 9 FR 0.0010 REL FR 8 V 1 P
travel much oppressed, | and faints for succor. AYL 2.04. 75
it faints me | to think what follows. H8 2.03.103
come between us, good benvolio, my wits faints. ROM 2.04. 68 P
he faints. my lord, my lord! LR 5.03.312
alas, he faints! o cassio, cassio, cassio! OTH 5.01. 84
and in our sports my better cunning faints ANT 2.03. 35
he that faints now, shame take him! TNK 3.06.121
affection faints not like a pale-fac'd coward, VEN 569
here manly hector faints, here troilus sounds, LUC 1486

/FAIR* 6 FR 0.0006 REL FR 6 V 0 P
/it /not /shame /thee /in /so /fair /a /troop R2 4.01.231
/name /it, /fair /cousin. 4.01.304
"/fair /cousin"? 4.01.305
/with /the /blood | /of /fair /king /richard, 2H4 1.01.205
/to /tell /you, /fair /beholders, /that /our TRO pr 26
/on /his /fair /worth /and /single /chivalry. 4.04.148

FAIR* 879 FR 0.0993 REL FR 768 V 111 P
and confer fair milan | with all the honors on TMP 1.02.126
if the ill spirit have so fair a house, | good 1.02.459
of the king's fair daughter claribel to the king 2.01. 71 P
us, and the fair soul herself | weigh'd between 2.01.130
fair encounter | of two most rare affections! 3.01. 74
as i hope | for quiet days, fair issue, and long 4.01. 24
should wrangle, | and i would call it fair play. 5.01.175
and all the fair effects of future hopes. TGV 1.01. 50
of all the fair resort of gentlemen | that every 1.02. 4
what think'st thou of the fair sir eglamour? 1.02. 9
not so fair, boy, as well-favor'd. 2.01. 49 P
that she is not so fair as (of you) well favor'd 2.01. 52 P
so painted to make her fair, that no man counts 2.01. 59 P
name) | made use and fair advantage of his days; 2.04. 68
she is fair; 2.04.199
to love fair silvia, shall i be forsworn; 2.06. 2
and silvia (witness heaven, that made her fair) 2.06. 25
but when his fair course is not hindered, | he 2.07. 27
beseeming such a wife as your fair daughter. 3.01. 66
if i be not by her fair influence | foster'd, 3.01.183
but silvia is too fair, too true, too holy, | to 4.02. 5
holy, fair, and wise is she; 4.02. 41
is she kind as she is fair? 4.02. 44
is she not passing fair? 4.04.148
well, | she, in my judgment, was as fair as you; 4.04.151
she says it is a fair one. 5.02. 9
but pearls are fair; 5.02. 11
vouchsafe me, for my meed, but one fair look: 5.04. 23
he's a good dog, and a fair dog — can there be WIV 1.01. 96 P
he is good, and fair. 1.01. 97 P
here comes fair mistress anne. 1.01.259 P
i will wait on him, fair mistress anne. 1.01.263 P
two thousand, fair woman, and i'll vouchsafe 2.02. 42 P
like a fair house built on another man's ground, 2.02.215 P
peace your tattlings! what is "fair," william? 4.01. 25 P
with the dear love i bear to fair anne page, 4.06. 9
each fair installment, coat, and sev'ral crest, 5.05. 63
buckled below fair knighthood's bending knee: 5.05. 72
do not these fair yokes | become the forest 5.05.107
and the fair sister | to her unhappy brother MM 1.04. 19
gentle and fair, your brother kindly greets you. 1.04. 24
unless you have the grace by your fair prayer 1.04. 69
be you content, fair maid, | it is the law, not 2.02. 79
repent you, fair one, of the sin you carry? 2.03. 19
how now, fair maid? 2.04. 30
heaven shield my mother play'd my father fair! 3.01.140
hand that hath made you fair hath made you good; 3.01.181 P
complexion, shall keep the body of it ever fair. 3.01.184 P
good morning to you, fair and gracious daughter. 4.03.112
my decayed fair | a sunny look of his would soon ERR 2.01. 98
so he would keep fair quarter with his bed! 2.01.108
keep then fair league and truce with thy true 2.02.145
plead you to me, fair dame? 2.02.147
look sweet, speak fair, become disloyalty; 3.02. 11
bear a fair presence, though your heart be 3.02. 13
for gazing on your beams, fair sun, being by. 3.02. 56
but her fair sister, | possess'd with such a 3.02.159
that would refuse so fair an offer'd chain. 3.02.181
her trim, the merry wind | blows fair from land: 4.01. 91
didst speak him fair? 4.02. 16
you saw they speak us fair, give us gold: 4.04.152 P
that bore thee at a burthen two fair sons. 5.01.344
and this fair gentlewoman, her sister here, 5.01.374
for a high praise, too brown for a fair praise, ADO 1.01.172 P
all prompting me how fair young hero is, 1.01.304
if thou dost love fair hero, cherish it, | and i 1.01.308
disguise, | and tell fair hero i am claudio, 1.01.322
true root but by the fair weather that you make 1.03. 24 P
i have woo'd in thy name, and fair hero is won. 2.01.299 P
one woman is fair, yet i am well; 2.03. 27 P
fair, or i'll never look on her; 2.03. 32 P
they say the lady is fair; 2.03.231 P
she's a fair lady. 2.03.245 P
fair beatrice, i thank you for your pains. 2.03.249 P
but fare thee well, most foul, most fair! 4.01.103
surely i do believe your fair cousin is wrong'd. 4.01.259 P
good morrow to this fair assembly. 5.04. 34
i'll tell you largely of fair hero's death. 5.04. 69
soft and fair, friar. which is beatrice? 5.04. 72
fair weather after you! LLL 1.02.144 P
single you | as our best-moving fair solicitor. 2.01. 29
the only soil of his fair virtue's gloss, | if 2.01. 47
which his fair tongue, conceit's expositor, 2.01. 72
navarre had notice of your fair approach, | and 2.01. 81
fair princess, welcome to the court of navarre. 2.01. 90
"fair" i give you back again, and "welcome" i 2.01. 91 P
not for the world, fair madam, by my will. 2.01. 99
now fair befall your mask! 2.01.123
fair fall the face it covers! 2.01.124
and hold fair friendship with his majesty. 2.01.140
your fair self should make | a yielding 'gainst 2.01.150
you may not come, fair princess, within my gates 2.01.171
though so denied fair harbor in my house. 2.01.174
sweet health and fair desires consort your grace 2.01.177
to feel only looking on fairest of fair: 2.01.241
i thank my beauty, i am fair that shoot, | and 4.01. 11
not fair? 4.01. 15
yes, madam, fair. 4.01. 16
where fair is not, praise cannot mend the brow. 4.01. 17
fair payment for foul words is more than due. 4.01. 19
nothing but fair is that which you inherit. 4.01. 20
o heresy in fair, fit for these days! 4.01. 22
hand, though foul, shall have fair praise. 4.01. 23
"by heaven, that thou art fair, is most 4.01. 60 P
more fairer than fair, beautiful than beauteous, 4.01. 62 P
then thou, fair sun, which on my earth dost 4.03. 67
as fair as day. 4.03. 88
spied a blossom passing fair | playing in the 4.03.101
the cull'd sovereignty | do meet, as at a fair, 4.03.231
do meet, as at a fair, in her fair cheek, 4.03.231
no face is fair that is not full so black. 4.03.249
and therefore is she born to make black fair. 4.03.257
i'll prove her fair, or talk till doomsday here. 4.03.270
man attach the hand | of his fair mistress. 4.03.373
and merry hours | forerun fair love, strewing 4.03.377
and if my face were but as fair as yours, | my 5.02. 32
fair as a text b in a copy-book. 5.02. 42
what was sent to you from fair dumaine? 5.02. 47
fair lady — 5.02.239
fair lord — | take that for your fair lady. 5.02.239
fair lord — | take that for your fair lady. 5.02.240
a calf, fair lady! 5.02.248
no, a fair lord calf. 5.02.248
fair ladies mask'd are roses in their bud; 5.02.295
fair sir, god save you! where's the princess? 5.02.310
all hail, sweet madam, and fair time of day! 5.02.339
"fair" in "all hail" is foul, as i conceive. 5.02.340
for our rude transgression | some fair excuse. 5.02.432
i was, fair madam. 5.02.435
thou part'st a fair fray. 5.02.484
that is all one, my fair, sweet, honey monarch, 5.02.527 P
for all your fair endeavors, and entreat, | out 5.02.730
for your fair sakes have we neglected time, 5.02.755
to those that make us both — fair ladies, you; 5.02.774
a beard, fair health, and honesty; 5.02.824
now, fair hippolyta, our nuptial hour | draws on MND 1.01. 1
be advis'd, fair maid. 1.01. 46
therefore, fair hermia, question your desires, 1.01. 67
for you, fair hermia, look you arm yourself | to 1.01.117
god speed fair helena! whither away? 1.01.180
call you me fair? 1.01.181
that fair again unsay. 1.01.181
demetrius loves your fair, o happy fair! 1.01.182
demetrius loves your fair, o happy fair! 1.01.182
/yours /would i catch, fair hermia, ere i go; 1.01.187
through athens i am thought as fair as she. 1.01.227
i will go tell him of fair hermia's flight; 1.01.246
and make him with fair /aegles break his faith, 2.01. 79
he took | at a fair vestal throned by /the west, 2.01.158
where is lysander and fair hermia? 2.01.189
do i speak you fair? 2.01.199
fair love, you faint with wand'ring in the wood; 2.02. 35
amen, amen, to that fair prayer, say i — | and 2.02. 62
"ladies," or "fair ladies, i would wish you," or 3.01. 39 P
"if i were fair, thisby, i were only thine." 3.01.103
and thy fair virtue's force (perforce) doth move 3.01.140
that would not let him bide — | fair helena! 3.02.187
my love, my life, my soul, fair helena! 3.02.246
i am as fair now as i was erewhile. 3.02.274
opening on neptune with fair blessed beams, 3.02.392
and kiss thy fair large ears, my gentle joy. 4.01. 4
and bless it to all fair prosperity. 4.01. 90
we will, fair queen, up to the mountain's top, 4.01.109
my lord, fair helen told me of their stealth, 4.01.160
them, | fair helena in fancy following me. 4.01.163
fair lovers, you are fortunately met; 4.01.177
my next is, "most fair pyramus." 4.01.201 P
my moans, | for parting my fair pyramus and me! 5.01.189
and she is fair and, fairer than that word, | of MV 1.01.162
eyes | i did receive fair speechless messages. 1.01.164
to furnish thee to belmont, to fair portia. 1.01.182
and i pray god grant them a fair departure. 1.02.111 P
look'd upon, was the best deserving a fair lady. 1.02.119 P
rest you fair, good signior, | your worship was 1.03. 59
"fair sir, you spet on me on wednesday last, 1.03.126
for an equal pound | of your fair flesh, to be 1.03.150
i like not fair terms and a villain's mind. 1.03.179
then stood as fair | as any comer i have look'd 2.01. 20

in faith, 'tis a fair hand, | and whiter than 2.04. 12
paper it writ on | is the fair hand that writ. 2.04. 14
was not that letter from fair jessica? 2.04. 28
fair jessica shall be my torch–bearer. 2.04. 39
and fair she is, if that mine eyes be true, 2.06. 54
therefore, like herself, wise, fair, and true, 2.06. 56
hazard all | do it in hope of fair advantages; 2.07. 19
now | for princes to come view fair portia. 2.07. 43
they come | as o'er a brook to see fair portia. 2.07. 47
and such fair ostents of love | as shall 2.08. 44
text, | hiding the grossness with fair ornament? 3.02. 80
fair portia's counterfeit! 3.02.115
the view, | chance as fair, and choose as true: 3.02.132
fair lady, by your leave, | i come by note, to 3.02.139
a thousand times more fair, ten thousand times 3.02.154
but now i was the lord | of this fair mansion, 3.02.168
i got a promise of this fair one here | to have 3.02.206
heart, | i shall obey you in all fair commands. 3.04. 36
fair thoughts and happy hours attend on you! 3.04. 41
say how i lov'd you, speak me fair in death; 4.01.275
fair sir, you are well o'erta'en. 4.02. 5
i swear to thee, even by thine own fair eyes, 5.01.242
in summer, where the ways are fair enough. 5.01.264
fair ladies, you drop manna in the way | of 5.01.294
besides that they are fair with their feeding, AYL 1.01. 12 P
for those that she makes fair she scarce makes 1.02. 37 P
when nature hath made a fair creature, may she 1.02. 43 P
fair princess, you have lost much good sport. 1.02. 99 P
no, fair princess; 1.02.170 P
guilty to deny so fair and excellent ladies any 1.02.185 P
but let your fair eyes and gentle wishes go with 1.02.186 P
ay. fare you well, fair gentleman. 1.02.248
fair sir, i pity her, | and wish, for her sake 2.04. 75
and says, if ladies be but young and fair, 2.07. 37
in fair round belly with good capon lin'd, 2.07.154
carve on every tree | the fair, the chaste, and 3.02. 10
be kept in mind | but the fair of rosalind." 3.02. 95
fair youth, i would i could make thee believe i 3.02.385 P
well, i am not fair, and therefore i pray the 3.03. 33 P
my fair rosalind, i come within an hour of my 4.01. 42 P
have liv'd many a fair year though hero had 4.01.101 P
my errand is to you, fair youth, | my gentle 4.03. 6
she says i am not fair, that i lack manners; 4.03. 15
good morrow, fair ones. 4.03. 75
"the boy is fair, | of female favor, and bestows 4.03. 85
a fair name. wast born i' the forest here? 5.01. 22 P
and you, fair sister. 5.02. 18 P
that bring these tidings to this fair assembly. 5.04.153
for the great desire i had | to see fair padua, SHR 1.01. 2
have access to our fair mistress and be happy 1.01.117 P
about a schoolmaster for the fair bianca, | and 1.02.166
i no whit be behind in duty | to fair bianca, so 1.02.175
listen to me, and if you speak me fair, | i'll 1.02.179
he that has the two fair daughters? 1.02.221
fair leda's daughter had a thousand wooers, 1.02.242
then well one more may fair bianca have; 1.02.243
you will have gremio to keep you fair. 2.01. 17
daughter | call'd katherina, fair and virtuous? 2.01. 43
your daughter, | unto bianca, fair and virtuous. 2.01. 91
be the jacks fair within, the gills fair without 4.01. 49 P
the jacks fair within, the gills fair without, 4.01. 50 P
i tell you, sir, she bears me fair in hand. 4.02. 3
fair lovely maid, once more good day to thee. 4.05. 33
young budding virgin, fair, and fresh, and sweet 4.05. 37
happy the parents of so fair a child! 4.05. 39
fair sir, and you my merry mistress, | that with 4.05. 53
my fair bianca, bid my father welcome, | while i 5.02. 4
now fair befall thee, good petruchio! 5.02.111
the wisdom of your duty, fair bianca, | hath 5.02.127
thy fame, as whirlwinds shake fair buds, | and 5.02.140
tribute at thy hands | but love, fair looks, and 5.02.153
she inherits, which makes fair gifts fairer; AWW 1.01. 41 P
'save you, fair queen! 1.01.106 P
"was this fair face the cause," quoth she, 1.03. 70
now, fair one, does your business follow us? 2.01. 99
fair maid, send forth thine eye. 2.03. 52
to each of you one fair and virtuous mistress 2.03. 57
the honor, sir, that flames in your fair eyes, 2.03. 80
fair one, i think not so. 2.03. 98
she is young, wise, fair, | in these to nature 2.03.131
where thou | wast shot at with fair eyes, to be 3.02.107
he is too good and fair for death and me, | whom 3.04. 16
she's a fair creature; 3.06.116
but, fair soul, | in your fine frame hath love 4.02. 3
the time is fair again. 5.03. 36
scorn'd a fair color, or express'd it stol'n, 5.03. 50
send forth your amorous token for fair maudlin. 5.03. 68
vanquish'd thereto by the fair grace and speech 5.03.133
i will buy me a son–in–law in a fair, and toll 5.03.148 P
of) | that he did seek the love of fair olivia. TN 1.02. 34
there is a fair behavior in thee, captain, | and 1.02. 47
with this thy fair and outward character. 1.02. 51
bless you, fair shrew. 1.03. 47 P
fair lady, do you think you have fools in hand? 1.03. 64 P
'tis a fair young man, and well attended. 1.05.102 P
but, if you were the devil, you are fair. 1.05.251
farewell, fair cruelty. 1.05.288
bore a mind that envy could not but call fair. 2.01. 29 P
roses, whose fair flow'r | being once display'd, 2.04. 38
away, breath, | i am slain by a fair cruel maid. 2.04. 54
cesario is your servant's name, fair princess. 3.01. 97
for the fair kindness you have show'd me here, 3.04.342
let thy fair wisdom, not thy passion, sway | in 4.01. 52
but i bespake you fair, and hurt you not. 5.01.189
we were, fair queen, | two lads that thought WT 1.02. 62
than they | should not produce fair issue. 2.01.150
that i now may be | in fair bohemia, and 4.01. 21
or i'll be thine, my fair, | or not my father's; 4.04. 42
shepherdess | (a fair one are you!), 4.04. 78
what fair swain is this | which dances with your 4.04.166
how now, fair shepherd? 4.04.345
swain seems to wash | the hand was fair before! 4.04.367
whose joy is nothing else | but fair posterity) 4.04.409
will i break my oath | to this my fair belov'd. 4.04.492
there present yourself and your fair princess 4.04.544
happy be you! | all that you speak shows fair. 4.04.623
and your fair princess — goddess! 5.01.131
of this fair couple), meets he on the way | the 5.01.190

please you to interpose, fair madam, kneel, 5.03.119
claim | to this fair island and the territories, JN 1.01. 10
at least from fair five hundred pound a year. 1.01. 69
(fair fall the bones that took the pains for me! 1.01. 78
till then, fair boy, | will i not think of home, 2.01. 30
as she, | and she a fair divided excellence, 2.01.439
for /anjou and fair touraine, maine, poictiers, 2.01.487
and this rich fair town | we make him lord of. 2.01.552
when his fair angels would salute my palm, | but 2.01.590
but thou art fair, and at thy birth, dear boy, 3.01. 51
to tread down fair respect of sovereignty, | and 3.01. 58
'tis true, fair daughter, and this blessed day 3.01. 75
to curse the fair proceedings of this day. 3.01. 97
i pandulph, of fair milan cardinal, | and from 3.01.138
o fair return of banish'd majesty! 3.01.321
fair day, adieu! 3.01.326
i remember to be holy) | for your fair safety; 3.03. 16
o fair affliction, peace! 3.04. 36
note | in the fair multitude of those her hairs! 3.04. 62
o lord, my boy, my arthur, my fair son! 3.04.103
is it not fair writ? 4.01. 37
knew you of this fair work? 4.03.116
and make fair weather in your blust'ring land. 5.01. 21
that, having our fair order written down, | both 5.02. 4
according to the fair play of the world, | let 5.02.118
favor and the form | of this most fair occasion, 5.04. 51
as i, | to try the fair adventure of to–morrow. 5.05. 22
since the more fair and crystal is the sky, R2 1.01. 41
the fair reverence of your highness curbs me 1.01. 54
i'll answer thee in any fair degree | or 1.01. 80
the one my duty owes,' but my fair name, 1.01.167
or seven fair branches springing from one root. 1.02. 13
appointed to direct these fair designs. 1.03. 45
might from our quiet confines fright fair peace, 1.03.137
fields | shall not regreet our fair dominions, 1.03.142
the flowers fair ladies, and thy steps no more 1.03.290
whom fair befall in heaven 'mongst happy souls, 2.01.129
a king | but by fair sequence and succession? 2.01.199
the wind sits fair for news to go for ireland, 2.02.123
and yet your fair discourse hath been as sugar, 2.03. 6
and stain'd the beauty of a fair queen's cheeks 3.01. 14
from richard's night to bullingbrook's fair day. 3.02.218
the news is very fair and good, my lord: 3.03. 5
the fresh green lap of fair king richard's land, 3.03. 47
our fair appointments may be well perus'd. 3.03. 53
that any harm should stain so fair a show! 3.03. 71
and all the number of his fair demands | shall 3.03.123
not, | to look so poorly and to speak so fair? 3.03.128
all apart, | and show fair duty to his majesty. 3.03.188
fair cousin, you debase your princely knee | to 3.03.190
shall i so much dishonor my fair stars | on 4.01. 21
by that fair sun which shows me where thou 4.01. 35
or rather do not see, | my fair rose wither; 5.01. 8
join not with grief, fair woman, do not so, | to 5.01. 16
and wilt thou pluck my fair son from mine age, 5.02. 92
and the blessed sun himself a fair hot wench in 1H4 1.02. 9 P
by phoebus, he, "that wand'ring knight so fair." 1.02. 16 P
that's even as fair as — at hand, quoth the 2.01. 49 P
doubt not but to die a fair death for all this, 2.02. 14 P
and show it a fair pair of heels and run from it 2.04. 48 P
sirs, by'r lady, you fought fair, so did you, 2.04.298 P
these promises are fair, the parties sure, | and 3.01. 1
shall run | in a new channel fair and evenly. 3.01.102
the moon shines fair, you may away by night. 3.01.140
sung by a fair queen in a summer's bow'r, | with 3.01.207
where you did give a fair and natural light, 5.01. 18
and from this swarm of fair advantages | you 5.01. 55
we offer fair, take it advisedly. 5.01.114
the arms are fair | when the intent of bearing 5.02. 87
in this fair rescue thou hast brought to me. 5.04. 50
for doing these fair rites of tenderness. 5.04. 98
day, | and since this business so fair is done, 5.05. 43
grant that our hopes (yet likely of fair birth) 2H4 1.03. 63
grace, my lord, tap for tap, and so part fair. 2.01.193 P
fair daughter, you do draw my spirits from me 2.03. 46
then feed and be fat, my fair calipolis. 2.04.179
how a good yoke of bullocks at /stamford fair? 3.02. 38 P
health and fair greeting from our general, | the 4.01. 27
and bloody insurrection | with your fair honors. 4.01. 41
but /write her fair words still in foulest terms 4.04.104
wages, about the sack he lost at /hinckley fair? 5.01. 25 P
well, you must now speak sir john falstaff fair, 5.02. 33
i like this fair proceeding of the king's. 5.05. 97
make you merry with fair katherine of france, ep 29 P
the king is full of grace and fair regard. H5 1.01. 22
till satisfied | that fair queen isabel, his 1.02. 81
know the pleasure | of our fair cousin dolphin; 1.02.235
that this fair action may on foot be brought. 1.02.310
you with my rapier, as i may, in fair terms. 2.01. 57 P
cut thy throat one time or other in fair terms, 2.01. 70 P
now sits the wind fair, and we will aboard. 2.02. 12
that grows not in a fair consent with ours; 2.02. 22
we doubt not of a fair and lucky war, | since 2.02.184
if my father render fair return, | it is against 2.04.127
shall be soon dispatch'd, with fair conditions. 2.04.144
disguise fair nature with hard–favor'd rage; 3.01. 8
your fresh fair virgins and your flow'ring 3.03. 14
and your fair show shall suck away their souls, 4.02. 17
no, my fair cousin. 4.03. 19
to our sister, | health and fair time of day; 5.02. 3
to our most fair and princely cousin katherine; 5.02. 4
will you, fair sister, | go with the princes, or 5.02. 90
fair katherine, and most fair, | will you 5.02. 98
fair katherine, and most fair, | will you 5.02. 98
o fair katherine, if you will love me soundly 5.02.104 P
what says she, fair one? 5.02.117 P
pate will grow bald, a fair face will wither, a 5.02.161 P
speak, my fair, and fairly, i pray thee. 5.02.167 P
what say'st thou, my fair flower–de–luce? 5.02.210 P
and therefore tell me, most fair katherine, will 5.02.234 P
i would have her learn, my fair cousin, how 5.02.283 P
who cannot see many a fair french city for one 5.02.317 P
french city for one fair french maid that stands 5.02.318 P
take her, fair son,(and from her blood raise up 5.02.348
bleeding sword 'twixt england and fair france. 5.02.355
in your fair minds let this acceptance take. ep 14
by guileful fair words peace may be obtain'd. 1H6 1.01. 77
fair maid, is't thou wilt do these wondrous 1.02. 64

be not dismay'd, fair lady, nor misconster | the 2.03. 73
that cause, fair nephew, that imprison'd me 2.05. 55
and so farewell, and fair be all thy hopes, 2.05.113
by fair persuasions, mix'd with sug'red words, 3.03. 18
then here i take my leave of thee, fair son, 4.05. 52
am | to woo so fair a dame to be his wife | and 5.03.124
fair margaret knows | that suffolk doth not 5.03.141
lady of so high resolve | (as is fair margaret) 5.05. 76
change two dukedoms for a duke's fair daughter. 2H6 1.01.219
bookish rule hath pull'd fair england down. 1.01.259
and in thy sons, fair slips of such a stock. 2.02. 58
have you laid fair the bed? 3.02. 11
and even with this i lost fair england's view, 3.02.110
death, | or banished fair england's territories, 3.02.245
my gracious lord, entreat him, speak him fair. 4.01.120
i think he hath a very fair warning. 4.06. 10 P
but i must make fair weather yet a while, | till 5.01. 30
i'll write unto them and entreat them fair; 3H6 1.01.271
i bear | upon my target three fair shining suns. 2.01. 40
how now, fair lords? 2.01. 95
fair queen of england, worthy margaret, | sit 3.03. 1
why, say, fair queen, whence springs this deep 3.03. 12
that virtuous lady bona, thy fair sister, | to 3.03. 56
i like it well that our fair queen and mistress 3.03.167
and yours, fair queen? 3.03.171
and mine, fair lady bona, joins with yours. 3.03.217
son edward, she is fair and virtuous, 3.03.245
till then fair hope must hinder live's decay; 4.04. 16
by fair or foul means we must enter in, | for 4.07. 14
fair lords, take leave and stand not to reply. 4.08. 23
as good to chide the waves as speak them fair. 5.04. 24
i, that am curtail'd of this fair proportion, R3 1.01. 18
to entertain these fair well–spoken days, | i am 1.01. 29
his noble queen | well strook in years, fair, 1.01. 92
curse not thyself, fair creature — thou art 1.02.132
shine out, fair sun, till i have bought a glass, 1.02.262
because i cannot flatter and look fair, | smile 1.03. 47
she may help you to many fair preferments, | and 1.03. 94
now fair befall thee and thy noble house! 1.03.281
made peace of enmity, fair love of hate, 2.01. 51
o my fair cousin, i must not say so. 3.01.106
now fair befall you! 3.05. 47
in peace, | your bounty, virtue, fair humility; 3.07. 17
and reverend looker–on of two fair queens. 4.01. 30
a mother only mock'd with two fair babes; 4.04. 87
either be patient and entreat me fair, | or with 4.04.152
virtuous and fair, royal and gracious. 4.04.205
this fair alliance quickly shall call home | to 4.04.313
infer fair england's peace by this alliance. 4.04.343
sweetly in force unto her fair live's end. 4.04.351
holy king henry and thy fair son edward, 5.01. 4
lines of fair comfort and encouragement. 5.02. 6
arm, fight, and conquer for fair england's sake! 5.03.158
jocund | in the remembrance of so fair a dream. 5.03.233
our ancient word of courage, fair saint george, 5.03.349
rescue, fair lord, or else the day is lost! 5.04. 6
smile heaven upon this fair conjunction, | that 5.05. 20
by god's fair ordinance conjoin together! 5.05. 31
with smiling plenty, and fair prosperous days! 5.05. 34
would with treason wound this fair land's peace! 5.05. 39
ten times more ugly | than ever they were fair. H8 1.02.118
night he dedicates | to fair content and you. 1.04. 3
the very thought of this fair company | clapp'd 1.04. 8
life, | they are a sweet society of fair ones. 1.04. 14
you, if these fair ladies | pass away frowning. 1.04. 32
y' are welcome, my fair guests. 1.04. 35
red wine first must rise | in their fair cheeks, 1.04. 44
of this so noble and so fair assembly | this 1.04. 67
and under your fair conduct | crave leave to 1.04. 70
you hold a fair assembly; 1.04. 87
what fair lady's that? 1.04. 91
a dozen healths | to drink to these fair ladies, 1.04.106
you, that have so fair parts of woman on you, 2.03. 27
that you may, fair lady, | perceive i speak 2.03. 58
i shall not fail t' approve the fair conceit 2.03. 74
the king already | hath married the fair lady. 3.02. 42
for him, | there's more in't than fair visage. 3.02. 88
and saint–like | cast her fair eyes to heaven, 4.01. 84
simony was fair play; 4.02. 36
and fair purgation to the world than malice, 5.02.187
is, a fair young maid that yet wants baptism, 5.02.196
they are come already, | as if we kept a fair here! 5.03. 69
more covetous of wisdom and fair virtue | than 5.04. 24
and when fair cressid comes into my thoughts — TRO 1.01. 30
thou answer'st she is fair, | pourest in the 1.01. 52
if she be fair, 'tis better for her; 1.01. 67 P
kin to me, therefore she's not so fair as helen. 1.01. 75 P
she would be as fair a' friday as helen is on 1.01. 76 P
say i she is not fair? 1.01. 79
fools on both sides, helen must needs be fair, 1.01. 90
a prince | do a fair message to his kingly eyes? 1.03.219
fair leave and large security. 1.03.223
fair lord aeneas, let me touch your hand; 1.03.304
of his eyes, | should he scape hector fair. 1.03.371
it, | but i would have the soil of her fair rape 2.02.148
that lays thee out says thou art a fair corse, 2.03. 32 P
yea, like fair fruit in an unwholesome dish, 2.03.120
why will he not upon our fair request | untent 2.03.167
fair be to you, my lord, and to all this fair 3.01. 43 P
to you, my lord, and to all this fair company! 3.01. 43 P
fair desires, in all fair measure, fairly guide 3.01. 44 P
fair desires, in all fair measure, fairly guide 3.01. 44 P
especially to you, fair queen, fair thoughts be 3.01. 45 P
fair queen, fair thoughts be your fair pillow! 3.01. 45 P
fair queen, fair thoughts be your fair pillow! 3.01. 46 P
dear lord, you are full of fair words. 3.01. 47 P
you speak your fair pleasure, sweet queen. 3.01. 48 P
fair prince, here is good broken music. 3.01. 49 P
few words to fair faith. 3.02. 95 P
if to–morrow be a fair day, by aleven of the 3.03.295 P
for the enfreed antenor, the fair cressid. 4.01. 39
who, in your thoughts, deserves fair helen best, 4.01. 54
fair diomed, you do as chapmen do, | dispraise 4.01. 76
nor play at subtile games — fair virtues all, 4.04. 87
entreat her fair, and, by my soul, fair greek, 4.04.113
entreat her fair, and, by my soul, fair greek, 4.04.113
fair lady cressid, | so please you, save the 4.04.116
pleads your fair usage, and to diomed | you 4.04.119

here art thou in appointment fresh and fair, 4.05. 1
i'll take that winter from your lips, fair lady; 4.05. 24
stand fair, i pray thee, let me look on thee. 4.05.235
and bent of amorous view | on the fair cressid. 4.05.283
a token from her daughter, my fair love, | both 5.01. 40
so now, fair prince of troy, i bid good night. 5.01. 71
farewell, revolted fair! 5.02.186
even in the fan and wind of your fair sword, 5.03. 41
o, 'tis fair play. 5.03. 43
present the fair steed to my lady cressid. 5.05. 2
most putrefied core, so fair without, | thy 5.08. 1
now the fair goddess fortune | fall deep in love COR 1.05. 20
and when my face is fair, you shall perceive 1.09. 69
how now, my as fair as noble ladies — and the 2.01. 97 P
on fair ground | i could beat forty of them. 3.01.241
the vengeance, | could he not speak 'em fair? 3.01.262
come, go with us, speak fair. 3.02. 70
only fair speech. 3.02. 96
buy | their mercy at the price of one fair word, 3.03. 91
an heir | of these fair edifices 'fore my wars 4.04. 3
if he slay me, | he does fair justice; 4.04. 25
you have made fair work, i fear me. 4.06. 88
you have made fair work! 4.06.100
you have made fair hands, | you and your crafts! 4.06.117
you have crafted fair! 4.06.118
and with our fair entreaties haste them on. 5.01. 74
how fair the tribune speaks to calm my thoughts! TIT 1.01. 46
fair lords, your fortunes are alike in all, 1.01.174
clear up, fair queen, that cloudy countenance; 1.01.263
ascend, fair queen, pantheon. 1.01.333
it, | with words, fair looks, and liberality? 2.01. 92
listen, fair madam, let it be your glory | to 2.03.139
fair philomela, why, she but lost her tongue, 2.04. 38
let fools do good, and fair men call for grace, 3.01.204
his child is like to her, fair as you are. 4.02.154
then i have brought up a neck to a fair end. 4.04. 49 P
yield to his humor, smooth and speak him fair, 5.02.140
in fair verona, where we lay our scene, | from ROM pr 2
shuts up his windows, locks fair daylight out, 1.01.139
a right good mark–man! and she's fair i love. 1.01.206
a right fair mark, fair coz, is soonest hit. 1.01.207
a right fair mark, fair coz, is soonest hit. 1.01.207
she is too fair, too wise, wisely too fair, | to 1.01.221
she is too fair, too wise, wisely too fair, | to 1.01.221
these happy masks that kiss fair ladies' brows, 1.01.230
being black, puts us in mind they hide the fair. 1.01.231
show me a mistress that is passing fair, | what 1.01.234
where i may read who pass'd that passing fair? 1.01.236
lies my consent and fair according voice. 1.02. 19
trudge about | through fair verona, find those 1.02. 35
my fair niece rosaline, /and livia; 1.02. 69 P
a fair assembly. 1.02. 71
sups the fair rosaline whom thou so loves, 1.02. 83
tut, you saw her fair, none else being by, 1.02. 94
and what obscur'd in this fair volume lies 1.03. 85
for fair without the fair within to hide. 1.03. 90
for fair without the fair within to hide. 1.03. 90
the game was ne'er so fair, and i am /done. 1.04. 39
tell | a whispering tale in a fair lady's ear, 1.05. 23
show a fair presence and put off these frowns, 1.05. 73
that fair for which love groan'd for and would 2.pr. 3
with tender juliet /match'd is now not fair. 2.pr. 4
speak to my gossip venus one fair word, | one 2.01. 11
my invocation | is fair and honest; 2.01. 28
arise, fair sun, and kill the envious moon, 2.02. 4
that thou, her maid, art far more fair than she. 2.02. 6
neither, fair maid, if either thee dislike. 2.02. 61
in truth, fair montague, i am too fond, | and 2.02. 98
aught so good but, strain'd from that fair use, 2.03. 19
is set | on the fair daughter of rich capulet. 2.03. 58
god ye good den, fair gentlewoman. 2.04.110 P
romeo that spoke him fair, bid him bethink | how 3.01.153
did ever dragon keep so fair a cave? 3.02. 74
of fair demesnes, youthful and nobly /lien'd, 3.05.180
green, so quick, so fair an eye | as paris hath. 3.05.220
and yourself | had part in this fair maid, now 4.05. 67
and stick your rosemary | on this fair corse, 4.05. 80
to follow this fair corse unto her grave. 4.05. 93
within this three hours will fair juliet wake. 5.02. 25
grief | it is supposed the fair creature died, 5.03. 51
ah, dear juliet, | why art thou yet so fair? 5.03.102
the maid is fair, a' th' youngest for a bride, TIM 1.01.123
faults that are rich are fair. 1.02. 13
have done our pleasures much grace, fair ladies, 1.02.146
set a fair fashion on our entertainment, | which 1.02.147
let them be receiv'd, | not without fair reward. 1.02.191
fault), | but with a noble fury and fair spirit, 3.05. 18
striving to make an ugly deed look fair. 3.05. 25
why, /i say, my lords, h'as done fair service, 3.05. 62
much of this will make | black white, foul fair, 4.03. 29
but if he sack fair athens, | and take our 5.01.171
write them together, yours is as fair a name; JC 1.02.144
it was a vision fair and fortunate. 2.02. 84
fair is foul, and foul is fair, | hover through MAC 1.01. 11
fair is foul, and foul is fair, | hover through 1.01. 11
so foul and fair a day i have not seen. 1.03. 38
and seem to fear | things that do sound so fair? 1.03. 52
fair and noble hostess, | we are your guest 1.06. 24
bless you, fair dame! 4.02. 65
together with that fair and warlike form | in HAM 1.01. 47
take thy fair hour, laertes, time be thine, 1.02. 62
why, 'tis a loving and a fair reply. 1.02.121
most fair return of greetings and desires. 2.02. 60
why — "one fair daughter, and no more, | the 2.02.407
soft you now, | the fair ophelia. 3.01. 88
are you fair? 3.01.104 P
that if you be honest and fair, /your /honesty 3.01.106 P
th' expectation and rose of the fair state, 3.01.152
that's a fair thought to lie between maids' legs 3.02.118 P
and thou shalt live in this fair world behind, 3.02.175
from the fair forehead of an innocent love | and 3.04. 43
could you on this fair mountain leave to feed, 3.04. 66
that to the use of actions fair and good | he 3.04.163
for who, that's but a queen, fair, sober, wise, 3.04.189
go seek him out, speak fair, and bring the body 4.01. 36
divided from herself and her fair judgment, 4.05. 85
and from her fair and unpolluted flesh | may 5.01.239
what, the fair ophelia! 5.01.242

down, | devis'd a new commission, wrote it fair. 5.02. 32
a baseness to write fair, and labor'd much | how 5.02. 34
before he was sent for, yet was his mother fair, LR 1.01. 23 P
remain this ample third of our fair kingdom, 1.01. 80
is queen of us, of ours, and our fair france. 1.01.257
come, my fair cordelia. 1.01.282
your name, fair gentlewoman? 1.04.236
for there was never yet fair woman but she made 3.02. 35 P
this seems a fair deserving, and must draw me 3.03. 23
fair daylight? 4.07. 51
for your claim, fair /sister, | i bar it in the 5.03. 84
since thy outside looks so fair and warlike, 5.03.143
(a fellow almost damn'd in a fair wife), | that OTH 1.01. 21
partly i find it is) that your fair daughter, 1.01.122
whether a maid so tender, fair, and happy, | so 1.02. 66
and such fair question | as soul to soul 1.03.113
how i did thrive in this fair lady's love, | and 1.03.125
your son–in–law is far more fair than black. 1.03.290
if she be fair and wise, fairness and wit, | the 2.01.129
how if fair and foolish? 2.01.135
she never yet was foolish that was fair, | for 2.01.136
does foul pranks which fair and wise ones do. 2.01.142
she that was ever fair, and never proud, | had 2.01.148
o my fair warrior! 2.01.182
not i, for this fair island. 2.03.142
though other things grow fair against the sun, 2.03.376
to make me jealious | to say my wife is fair, 3.03.184
some swift means of death | for the fair devil. 3.03.479
how is't with you, my most fair bianca? 3.04.170
a fair woman! 4.01.179 P
who art so lovely fair and smell'st so sweet 4.02. 68
was this fair paper, this most goodly book, 4.02. 71
what name, fair lady? 4.02.118
and taketh away with him the fair desdemona, 4.02.225 P
to make itself, in thee, fair and admir'd! ANT 1.01. 51
i have fair /meanings, sir. 2.06. 66
and fair words to them. 2.06. 66
but there is never a fair woman has a true face. 2.06. 99 P
of the stars give light | to thy fair way! 3.02. 66
the morn is fair. good morrow, general. 4.04. 24
and our advantage serves | for a fair victory. 4.07. 12
and bids thee study on what fair demands | thou 5.02. 10
think | so fair an outward and such stuff within CYM 1.01. 23
of bloody affirmation) his to be more fair, 1.04. 59 P
as fair and as good — a kind of hand–in–hand 1.04. 70 P
had been something too fair and too good for any 1.04. 71 P
i should get ground of your fair mistress; 1.04.104 P
spectacles so precious | 'twixt fair and foul? 1.06. 38
a lady | so fair, and fasten'd to an empery 1.06.120
keep unshak'd | that temple, thy fair mind, that 2.01. 64
hail, thou fair heaven! 3.03. 7
a sland'rous epitaph | as record of fair act; 3.03. 53
for she's fair and royal, | and that she hath 3.05. 70
prithee, fair youth, | think us no churls; 3.06. 63
fair youth, come in. 3.06. 89
this forwardness | makes our hopes fair. 4.02.343
like his ancestry, | moulded the stuff so fair, 5.04. 49
before thee stands this fair hesperides, | with PER 1.01. 27
fair glass of light, i lov'd you, and could 1.01. 76
you are a fair viol, and your sense the strings; 1.01. 81
succeeding from so fair a tree | as your fair 1.01.114
from so fair a tree | as your fair self, doth 1.01.115
and i'll tell you, he hath a fair daughter, and 2.01.108 P
as you would be denied | of your fair courtesy. 2.03.106
and she is fair too, is she not? 2.05. 35
as a fair day in summer; wondrous fair. 2.05. 36
as a fair day in summer; wondrous fair. 2.05. 36
then, as you are as virtuous as fair, | resolve 2.05. 67
make | us weep to hear your fate, fair creature, 3.02.103
is she not a fair creature? 4.06. 43 P
welcome, fair one! 5.01. 65
fair /one, all goodness that consists in beauty, 5.01. 70
he is promis'd to be wived | to fair marina, but 5.02. 11
did wed | at pentapolis the fair thaisa. 5.03. 4
of the air, | bird melodious, or bird fair, | is TNK 1.01. 17
as you wish your womb may thrive with fair ones, 1.01. 27
you were that time fair; 1.01. 62
that was a fair boy certain, but a fool | to 2.02.120
they could not be to one so fair. 2.02.123
she is wondrous fair! 2.02.147
bereave you | of your fair cousin's company. 2.02.224
if that | get him a wife so noble and so fair, 2.02.230
once more | i would but see this fair one. 2.02.232
her, | and, if she be as gentle as she's fair, 2.03. 15
and yet he had a cousin, fair as he too; 2.04. 16
"fair gentle maid, good morrow. 2.04. 24
pirithous, | dispose of this fair gentleman. 2.05. 32
you have honor'd her fair birthday with your 2.05. 36
kiss her fair hand, sir. 2.05. 37
you skip them in me, and with them, fair coz, 3.01. 52
but the whole week's not fair | if any day it 3.01. 65
i thank thee, arcite, | thou art yet a fair foe; 3.06. 8
that too much, fair cousin, | is but a debt to 3.06. 18
defy me in these fair terms, and you show | more 3.06. 25
that fortunate bright star, the fair emilia, 3.06.146
ask that lady | why she is fair, and why her 3.06.169
that fair hand, and that honest heart you gave 3.06.197
accompanied | with three fair knights, appear 3.06.292
by fair and knightly strength to touch the 3.06.295
and between | ever was "palamon, fair palamon," 4.01. 81
that methought she appear'd like the fair nymph 4.01. 86
"o fair, o sweet," etc. 4.01.114
the wind's fair. 4.01.147
a fair wood. 4.01.151
that, having two fair gauds of equal sweetness, 4.02. 53
return'd, | and with them their fair knights. 4.02. 67
now, my fair sister, | you must love one of them 4.02. 67
all the fair hopes of what he undertakes, | and 4.02. 99
this anatomy | had by his young fair fere a boy, 5.01.116
i give thee thanks | for this fair token, which 5.01.133
he's a very fair one. 5.02. 46
a very fair hand, and casts himself th' accounts 5.02. 58
yes, by this fair hand, will i. 5.02. 86
my cousin palamon | has made so fair a choice. 5.02. 92
on others, on /him | live in fair dwelling. 5.03. 55
one kiss from fair emilia. 5.04. 94
and by her fair immortal hand she swears | from VEN 80
but my lips with those fair lips of thine — 115

though mine be not so fair, yet are they red — 116
fair flowers that are not gath'red in their 131
his low'ring brows o'erwhelming his fair sight, 183
speak, fair, but speak fair words, or else be 208
fair, but speak fair words, or else be mute. 208
eye | of the fair breeder that is standing by." 282
with one fair hand she heaveth up his hat, | her 351
her other tender hand his fair cheek feels: 352
but when he saw his love, his youth's fair fee, 393
fair fall the wit that can so well defend her! 472
like the fair sun, when in his fresh array | he 483
"fair queen," quoth he, "if any love you owe me, 523
swear nature's death for framing thee so fair. 744
sith in thy pride so fair a hope is slain. 762
of those fair arms which bound him to her breast 812
having lost the fair discovery of her way. 828
venus salutes him with this fair good morrow: 859
the crystal tide that from her two cheeks fair 957
the foul boar's conquest on her fair delight, 1030
having no fair to lose, you need not fear, | the 1083
lurk'd like two thieves, to rob him of his fair. 1086
flames the waist | of collatine's fair love, LUC 7
venus' doves, doth challenge that fair field; 58
which tarquin view'd in her fair face's field, 72
doth yet in his fair welkin once appear, | till 116
"fair torch, burn out thy light, and lend it not 190
let fair humanity abhor the deed | that spots 195
his foul thoughts might compass his fair fair, 346
his foul thoughts might compass his fair fair, 346
look as the fair and fiery–pointed sun, 372
without the bed her other fair hand was, | on 393
from this fair throne to heave the owner out. 413
laud, | and mak'st fair reputation but a bawd. 623
thou their fair life, and they thy fouler grave; 661
besides, his soul's fair temple is defaced, | to 719
sick | the life of purity, the supreme fair, 780
or toads infect fair founts with venom mud? 850
lends light to all fair eyes that light will 1083
foul deed, my life's fair end shall free it. 1208
nor why her fair cheek? over–wash'd with woe. 1225
of those fair suns set in her mistress' sky, 1230
mild patience bid fair lucrece speak | to the 1268
so fair a form lodg'd not a mind so ill. 1530
love, what spite hath thy fair color spent? 1600
"but ere i name him, you fair lords," quoth she 1688
for 'tis a meritorious fair design | to chase 1692
she utters this, "he, he, fair lords, 'tis he, 1721
but now that fair fresh mirror, dim and old, 1760
for his foul act by whom thy fair wife bleeds? 1824
strong arms from forth her fair streets chased. 1834
by heaven's fair sun that breeds the fat earth's 1837
my better angel is a man (right fair), | my PP 2. 3
devil, | wooing his purity with her fair pride. 2. 8
then thou, fair sun, that on this earth doth 3.10
then fell she on her back, fair queen, and 4.13
fair is my love, but not so fair as fickle, 7. 1
fair is my love, but not so fair as fickle, 7. 1
fair was the morn when the fair queen of love, 9. 1
fair was the morn when the fair queen of love, 9. 1
"did i see a fair sweet youth | here in these 9. 9
sweet rose, fair flower, untimely pluck'd, soon 10. 1
fair creature, kill'd too soon by death's sharp 10. 4
was ever may, | spied a blossom passing fair, 16. 3
let those repair | that are either true or fair; PHT 66
"this fair child of mine | shall sum my count, SON 2.10
for where is she so fair whose unear'd womb 3. 5
for thou art much too fair | to be death's 6.13
who lets so fair a house fall to decay, | which 13. 9
neither in inward worth nor outward fair | can 16.11
and every fair from fair sometime declines, | by 18. 7
and every fair from fair sometime declines, | by 18. 7
nor lose possession of that fair thou ow'st, 18.10
o, carve not with thy hours my love's fair brow, 19. 9
and every fair with his fair doth rehearse, 21. 4
and every fair with his fair doth rehearse, 21. 4
me, my love is as fair | as any mother's child, 21.10
princes' favorites their fair leaves spread 25. 5
points on me graciously with fair aspect, | and 26.10
when in dead night /thy fair imperfect shade 43.11
assured | of /thy fair health, recounting it to 45.12
and says in him /thy fair appearance lies. 46. 8
the rose looks fair, but fairer we it deem | for 54. 3
before these bastard signs of fair were born, 68. 3
to thy fair flower add the rank smell of weeds: 69.12
for slander's mark was ever yet the fair; 70. 2
and found such fair assistance in my verse | as 78. 2
words which writers use | of their fair subject, 82. 4
thou art as fair in knowledge as in hue, 82. 5
thou, truly fair, wert truly sympathiz'd | in 82.11
and therefore to your fair no painting set; 83. 2
there lives more life in one of your fair eyes 83.13
the cause of this fair gift in me is wanting, 87. 7
and all things turns to fair that eyes can see! 95.12
to me, fair friend, you never can be old, | for 104. 1
"fair," "kind," and "true" is all my argument, 105. 9
"fair," "kind," and "true" varying to other 105.10
"fair," "kind," and "true" have often liv'd 105.13
even as when first i hallowed thy fair name. 108. 8
in the old age black was not counted fair, | or 127. 1
they mourners seem | at such who, not born fair, 127.11
and in my will no fair acceptance shine? 135. 8
let no unkind, no fair beseechers kill; 135.13
is not, | to put fair truth upon so foul a face? 137.12
the better angel is a man right fair, | the 144. 3
for i have sworn thee fair, and thought thee 147.13
if that be fair whereon my false eyes dote, 148. 5
for i have sworn thee fair; 152.13
and when in his fair parts she did abide, | she LC 83
i have receiv'd from many a several fair, 206
with th' annexions of fair gems enrich'd, | and 208
showing fair nature is both kind and tame; 311

FAIR–BETROTHED 1 FR 0.0001 REL FR 1 V 0 P

prince, the fair–betrothed of your daughter, PER 5.03. 71

FAIRER 43 FR 0.0048 REL FR 34 V 9 P

with colors fairer painted their foul ends. TMP 1.02.143
she hath been fairer, madam, than she is: TGV 4.04.149
there are fairer things than poulcats sure. WIV 4.01. 28 P
sir, your company is fairer than honest. MM 4.03.175 P

the eye indeed | by fixing it upon a fairer eye, LLL 1.01. 81
why, it is a fairer name than french crown! 3.01.141 P
more fairer than fair, beautiful than beauteous, 4.01. 62 P
i'll find a fairer face not wash'd to–day. 4.03.269
and she is fair and, fairer than that word, | of MV 1.01.162
if any man in italy have a fairer table, which 2.02.158 P
you shall look fairer ere i give or hazard. 2.09. 22
and were his daughter fairer than she is, | she SHR 1.02.240
she inherits, which makes fair gifts fairer; AWW 1.01. 41 P
and in your bed | find fairer fortune, if you 2.03. 92
fairer prove your honor | than in my thought it 5.03.183
where should he find it fairer than in blanch? JN 2.01.427
is yet the cover of a fairer mind | than to be 4.02.258
falls upon thee in a more fairer sort; 2H4 4.05.200
helen of greece was fairer far than thou, 3H6 2.02.146
fairer than tongue can name thee, let me have R3 1.02. 81
my babes were destin'd to a fairer death, | if 4.04.220
if grace had blest thee with a fairer life. 4.04.221
so much fairer | and spotless shall mine H8 3.02.300
look'd yesternight fairer than ever i saw her TRO 1.01. 32 P
he hath a lady, wiser, fairer, truer, | than 1.03.275
him that my lady | was fairer than his grandam, 1.03.299
the clearer, /ajax, and your virtues the fairer. 2.03.154 P
one fairer than my love! ROM 1.02. 92
to hide her face, for her fan's the fairer face. 2.04.108 P
time, with his fairer hand, | offering the TIM 5.01.123
i would not wish them to a fairer death. MAC 5.09. 15
you shall be yet far fairer than you are. ANT 1.02. 17
you have seen and prov'd a fairer former fortune 1.02. 33
or rather fairer | than those for preservation CYM 5.03. 21
not juno's mantle fairer than your tresses, TNK 1.01. 63
fairer spoken | was never gentleman. 2.04. 20
fairer promises | in such a body yet i never 4.02.118
"thrice fairer than myself," thus she began, VEN 7
none fairer, nor none falser to deface her. PP 7. 6
shall hate be fairer lodg'd than gentle love? SON 10.10
but fairer we it deem | for that sweet odor 54. 3
grows fairer than at first, more strong, far 119.12
all aids, themselves made fairer by their place, LC 117

FAIREST 49 FR 0.0055 REL FR 45 V 4 P
wine and sugar of the best, and the fairest, WIV 2.02. 69 P
year, i'll rent the fairest house in it after MM 2.01.241 P
the fairest grant is the necessity. ADO 1.01.317
death is the fairest cover for her shame | that 4.01.116
to feel only looking on fairest of fair: LLL 2.01.241
a stand where you may make the fairest shoot. 4.01. 10
and thereupon thou speak'st the fairest shoot. 4.01. 12
too, | i were the fairest goddess on the ground. 5.02. 36
"a holy parcel of the fairest dames | that ever 5.02.160
the fairest is confession. 5.02.432
no — which was the fairest dame | that liv'd, MND 5.01.293
bring me the fairest creature northward born, MV 2.01. 4
all the pictures fairest lin'd | are but black AYL 3.02. 92
but upon the fairest boughs, | or at every 3.02.135
carry him gently to my fairest chamber, | and SHR in.1. 46
she was the fairest creature in the world, | and in.2. 66
the fairest flow'rs o' th' season | are our WT 4.04. 81
were i the fairest youth | that ever made eye 4.04.373
princess (she | the fairest i have yet beheld), 5.01. 87
is full of weeds, her fairest flowers chok'd up, R2 3.04. 44
and your fairest daughter and mine, my 2H4 3.02. 6 P
my dog, | his fairest daughter is contaminated. H5 4.05. 16
o fairest beauty, do not fear nor fly, | for i 1H6 5.03. 46
the fairest queen that ever king receiv'd. 2H6 1.01. 16
the fairest hand i ever touch'd! H8 1.04. 75
two of the fairest stars in all the heaven, ROM 2.02. 15
hope his honor will conceive the fairest of me. TIM 3.02. 54 P
away, and mock the time with fairest show: MAC 1.07. 81
fairest cordelia, that art most rich being poor, LR 1.01.250
and, sweetest, fairest, | as i my poor self did CYM 1.01.118
i'll place it | upon this fairest prisoner. 1.01.123
thanks, fairest lady. 1.06. 31
good morrow, fairest: sister, your sweet hand. 2.03. 86
is one of the fairest that i have look'd upon. 2.04. 32
o sweetest, fairest lily! 4.02.201
with fairest flowers | whilst summer lasts and i 4.02.218
his chiefest seat, | the fairest in all syria — PER 1.ch. 19
who makes the fairest show means most deceit. 1.04. 75
"the fairest, sweetest, and best lies here, 4.04. 34
she is all happy as the fairest of all, | and, 5.01. 49
fairest emily, | the gods by their divine TNK 5.03.106
"o fairest mover on this mortal round, | would VEN 368
a lording's daughter, the fairest one of three, PP 15. 1
an englishman, the fairest that eye could see, 15. 3
from fairest creatures we desire increase, SON 1. 1
time | i see descriptions of the fairest wights, 106. 2
thou art the fairest and most precious jewel. 131. 4
thy black is fairest in my judgment's place. 131.12
hand | the fairest votary took up that fire, 154. 5

FAIREST–BODING 1 FR 0.0001 REL FR 1 V 0 P
the sweetest sleep and fairest–boding dreams R3 5.03.227

FAIR–EY'D 3 FR 0.0003 REL FR 3 V 0 P
the fair–ey'd maids shall weep our banishments, TNK 2.02. 37
of all the world, | dwells fair–ey'd honor. 2.05. 29
and fair–ey'd emily, upon their knees | begg'd 4.01. 8

FAIR–FAC'D 3 FR 0.0003 REL FR 3 V 0 P
if fair–fac'd, | she would swear the gentleman ADO 3.01. 61
i shall show you peace and fair–fac'd league; JN 2.01.417
amongst the fair–fac'd breeders of our clime. TIT 4.02. 68

FAIRIES' 2 FR 0.0002 REL FR 2 V 0 P
she is the fairies' midwife, and she comes | in ROM 1.04. 54
time out a' mind the fairies' coachmakers. 1.04. 61

/FAIRIES 1 FR 0.0001 REL FR 1 V 0 P
/fairies, skip hence — | i have forsworn his MND 2.01. 61

FAIRIES 26 FR 0.0029 REL FR 18 V 8 P
urchins, ouphes, and fairies, green and white, WIV 4.04. 50
let the supposed fairies pinch him sound, | and 4.04. 62
my nan shall be the queen of all the fairies, 4.04. 71
us properties | and tricking for our fairies. 4.04. 79
till we see the light of our fairies. 5.02. 2 P
where is nan now, and her troop of fairies, and 5.03. 12 P
trib, trib, fairies; 5.04. 1 P
fairies, black, grey, green, and white, | you 5.05. 37
they are fairies, he that speaks to them shall 5.05. 47
fairies use flow'rs for their charactery. 5.05. 73
about him, fairies, sing a scornful rhyme, | and 5.05. 91
pinch him, fairies, mutually! 5.05. 99
and these are not fairies? 5.05.121 P
four times in the thought they were not fairies, 5.05.122 P
of all rhyme and reason, that they were fairies. 5.05.126 P
your desires, and fairies will not pinse you. 5.05.130 P
fairies, away! MND 2.01.144
i'll give thee fairies to attend on thee; 3.01.157
fairies, be gone, and be /all /ways away. 4.01. 41
and we fairies, that do run | by the triple 5.01.383
it was told me i should be rich by the fairies. WT 3.03.118 P
sing, | like elves and fairies in a ring, MAC 4.01. 42
fairies and gods | prosper it with thee! LR 4.06. 29
from fairies and the tempters of the night CYM 2.02. 9
with female fairies will his tomb be haunted, 4.02.217
what fairies haunt this ground? 5.04.133

FAIRING 1 FR 0.0001 REL FR 1 V 0 P
fairing the foul with art's false borrow'd face, SON 127. 6

FAIRINGS 1 FR 0.0001 REL FR 1 V 0 P
depart, | if fairings come thus plentifully in. LLL 5.02. 2

FAIRLY 49 FR 0.0055 REL FR 39 V 10 P
fairly spoke. TMP 4.01. 31
in earnest, they parted very fairly in jest. TGV 2.05. 13 P
say 'tis grossly done, so it be fairly done, no WIV 2.02.143 P
my very worthy cousin, fairly met! MM 5.01. 1
then fairly i bespoke the officer | to go in ERR 5.01.233
my fortunes every way as fairly rank'd | (if not MND 1.01.101
is to come fairly off from the great debts MV 1.01.128
after some oration fairly spoke | by a beloved 3.02.178
thou offer'st fairly to thy brothers' wedding: AYL 5.04.167
blow our nails together, and fast it fairly out. SHR 1.01.108 P
you, sir, i'll have them very fairly bound — 1.02.145
and there it is in writing, fairly drawn. 3.01. 70
letters for her name fairly set down in studs, 3.02. 61 P
house–keeper goes as fairly as to say a careful TN 4.02. 9 P
that they may fairly note this act of mine! 4.03. 35
and the true blood which peeps fairly through't, WT 4.04.148
fairly offer'd. 4.04.378
too fairly, hubert, for so foul effect. JN 4.01. 38
for god's sake fairly let her be entreated. R2 3.01. 37
our soldiers stand full fairly for the day. 1H4 5.03. 29
so fought, so followed, and so fairly won, 2H4 1.01. 21
thou dost thy office fairly. H5 3.06.139
that we should dress us fairly for our end. 4.01. 10
face, | most worthy brother england, fairly met! 5.02. 10
the venom of such looks we fairly hope | have 5.02. 18
speak, my fair, and fairly, i pray thee. 5.02.168 P
which in a set hand fairly is engross'd | that R3 3.06. 2
but how long fairly shall her sweet life last? 4.04.352
so now y' are fairly seated. H8 1.04. 31
fairly answer'd. 3.02.179
would i were fairly out on't! 5.02.144
find a way out | to let the troop pass fairly; 5.03. 85
th' unworthiest shows as fairly in the mask. TRO 1.03. 84
what troy means fairly shall be spoke aloud. 1.03.259
desires, in all fair measure, fairly guide them! 3.01. 44 P
furnish you fairly for this interchange; 3.03. 33
a second hope, as fairly built as hector. 4.05.109
th' vulgar eye, that he bears all things fairly, COR 4.07. 21
you gave us the counterfeit fairly last night. ROM 2.04. 45 P
containing such vile matter | so fairly bound? 3.02. 84
they are fairly welcome. TIM 1.02.176
i shall accept them fairly; 1.02.184
how fairly this lord strives to appear foul! 3.03. 31 P
i tell you, must show fairly outwards, should HAM 2.02.374 P
(to this good purpose, that so fairly shows) ANT 2.02.144
i pray greet him fairly. PER 5.01. 10
so we may fairly carry | our swords and cause TNK 3.06.259
they prevail'd, had their suits fairly granted: 4.01. 27
same, | and that unfair which fairly doth excel: SON 5. 4

FAIRNESS 4 FR 0.0004 REL FR 4 V 0 P
gambols with the wind | upon supposed fairness, MV 3.02. 94
good addition | to th' fairness of my power. COR 1.09. 73
if she be fair and wise, fairness and wit, | the OTH 2.01.129
of wiving, | fairness which strikes the eye — CYM 5.05.168

FAIR–PLAY 1 FR 0.0001 REL FR 1 V 0 P
send fair–play orders and make compremise, JN 5.01. 67

FAIRS* 5 FR 0.0005 REL FR 3 V 2 P
be seen | at any syracusian marts and fairs; ERR 1.01. 17
i am compar'd to twenty thousand fairs. LLL 5.02. 37
at wakes and wassails, meetings, markets, fairs: 5.02.318
he haunts wakes, fairs, and bear–baitings. WT 4.03.102 P
come, march to wakes and fairs and market towns. LR 3.06. 74 P

FAIR–SPOKEN 1 FR 0.0001 REL FR 1 V 0 P
exceeding wise, fair–spoken, and persuading; H8 4.02. 52

FAIR'ST 2 FR 0.0002 REL FR 2 V 0 P
now, my fair'st friend, | i would i had some WT 4.04.112
if there be one among the fair'st of greece TRO 1.03.265

FAIRY 40 FR 0.0045 REL FR 34 V 6 P
monster, your fairy, which you say is a harmless TMP 4.01.196 P
which you say is a harmless fairy, has done 4.01.197 P
yet this is your harmless fairy, monster! 4.01.212 P
and ask him why, that hour of fairy revel, | in WIV 4.04. 59
must my sweet nan present the fairy queen; 4.06. 20
crier hobgoblin, make the fairy oyes. 5.05. 41
heavens defend me from that welsh fairy, lest he 5.05. 81 P
well said, fairy hugh. 5.05.131 P
this is the fairy land. ERR 2.02.189
a fiend, a fairy, pitiless and rough; 4.02. 35
and i serve the fairy queen, | to dew her orbs MND 2.01. 8
those be rubies, fairy favors, | in those 2.01. 12
but room, fairy! 2.01. 58
when thou hast stolen away from fairy land, 2.01. 65
the fairy land buys not the child of me. 2.01.122
not for thy fairy kingdom. 2.01.144
skin, | weed wide enough to wrap a fairy in; 2.01.256
come, now a roundel and a fairy song; 2.02. 1
do no wrong, | come not near our fairy queen. 2.02. 12
here, | so near the cradle of the fairy queen? 3.01. 78
captain of our fairy band, | helena is here at 3.02.110
my fairy lord, this must be done with haste, 3.02.378
i have a venturous fairy that shall seek | the 4.01. 35
and her fairy sent | to bear him to my bower in 4.01. 60
sent | to bear him to my bower in fairy land. 4.01. 61
but first i will release the fairy queen. 4.01. 70
fairy king, attend and mark; 4.01. 93
these antic fables, nor these fairy toys. 5.01. 3
lovers, to bed, 'tis almost fairy time. 5.01.364
every elf and fairy sprite | hop as light as 5.01.393
hand in hand, with fairy grace, | will we sing, 5.01.399
of day, | through this house each fairy stray. 5.01.402
consecrate, | every fairy take his gait, | and 5.01.416
this is fairy gold, boy, and 'twill prove so. WT 3.03.123 P
that some night–tripping fairy had exchang'd 1H4 1.01. 87
no fairy takes, nor witch hath power to charm, HAM 1.01.163
to this great fairy i'll commend thy acts, ANT 4.08. 12
victuals, i should think | here were a fairy. CYM 3.06. 41
have you a working pulse, and are no fairy? PER 5.01.153
or like a fairy, trip upon the green, | or like VEN 146

FAIRY–LIKE 1 FR 0.0001 REL FR 1 V 0 P
and, fairy–like, to pinch the unclean knight; WIV 4.04. 58

FAIS 1 FR 0.0001 REL FR 0 V 1 P
je m'en fais la repetition de tous les mots que H5 3.04. 25 P

FAIT 1 FR 0.0001 REL FR 0 V 1 P
ma foi, il fait fort /chaud. WIV 1.04. 51 P

FAITES 1 FR 0.0001 REL FR 0 V 1 P
commande a vous dire que vous faites vous pret; H5 4.04. 34 P

FAITH *(also fay, feith)*

/FAITH 22 FR 0.0024 REL FR 15 V 7 P
now, by my /faith, lords, 'twas a glorious day. 2H6 5.03. 29
/faith, some certain dregs of conscience are yet R3 1.04.121 P
/in /this /extant /moment, /faith /and /troth, TRO 4.05.168
good /faith, 'tis day. ROM 4.04. 21
/faith, /there /has /been /much /to /do /on HAM 2.02.352 P
/no, /faith, /lords /and /great /men /will /not LR 1.04.152 P
/faith, /once /or /twice /she /heav'd /the /name 4.03. 25
/yes, /faith; OTH 3.03. 52
/i' /faith, i fear it has. 3.03.215
/faith, that's with watching, 'twill away again. 3.03.285
no, /faith; 3.03.311
no, /faith, my lord. 3.04. 54
/i' /faith! is't true? 3.04. 75
/i' /faith, you are to blame. 3.04. 97
no, /by /my /faith, bianca. 3.04.187
/faith, that he did — i know not what he did. 4.01. 32
poor rogue, i think, /i' /faith, she loves me. 4.01.111
/faith, the cry goes that you marry her. 4.01.123 P
/faith, i must, she'll rail in the streets else. 4.01.163 P
/faith, i intend so. 4.01.165 P
/faith, i have heard too much; 4.02.182 P
good /faith, how foolish are our minds! 4.03. 23

FAITH 421 FR 0.0475 REL FR 238 V 183 P
yes, faith, and all his lords, the duke of milan TMP 1.02.438
faith, sir, you need not fear. 3.03. 43
in breaking faith with julia whom i lov'd; TGV 4.02. 11
company, | upon whose faith and honor i repose. 4.03. 26
to praise his faith which i would have 4.04.102
whose dear sake thou didst then rend thy faith 5.04. 47
thou hast no faith left now, unless thou'dst two 5.04. 50
better have none | than plural faith, which is 5.04. 52
common friend, that's without faith or love, 5.04. 62
i' faith, i'll eat nothing. WIV 1.01.279 P
if he do, i' faith, and find any body in the 1.04. 4 P
have a posset for't soon at night, in faith, at 1.04. 9 P
good faith, it is such another nan; 1.04.149 P
i' faith, that we will; 1.04.158 P
i' faith, but you do, in my mind. 2.01. 39 P
faith, thou hast some crotchets in thy head now. 2.01.154 P
that was of late an heretic, | as firm as faith. 4.04. 10
faith, sir, few of any wit in such matters. MM 2.01.268 P
yes, faith, sir. 3.02. 62 P
nor heard from her, | upon my faith and honor. 5.01.224
faith, my lord, i spoke it but according to the 5.01.504 P
faith, no, he comes too late, | and so tell your ERR 3.01. 49
faith, i saw it not; 3.02.131 P
if my breast had not been made of faith, and my 3.02.145
faith, stay here this night, they will surely do 4.04.151 P
faith, niece, you tax signior benedick too much, ADO 1.01. 46 P
he wears his faith but as the fashion of his hat 1.01. 75 P
why, i' faith, methinks she's too low for a high 1.01.171 P
in faith, hath not the world one man but he will 1.01.197 P
go to, i' faith, and thou wilt needs thrust thy 1.01.200 P
and in faith, my lord, i spoke mine. 1.01.225 P
if ever thou dost fall from this faith, thou 1.01.256 P
in faith, she's too curst. 2.01. 20 P
yes, faith, it is my cousin's duty to make 2.01. 52 P
against whose charms faith melteth into blood. 2.01.180
your saying, by my faith you say honestly. 2.01.235 P
i' faith, lady, i think your blazon to be true, 2.01.296 P
in faith, lady, you have a merry heart. 2.01.312 P
no, faith, thou sing'st well enough for a shift. 2.03. 77 P
faith, like enough. 2.03.103 P
and your gown's a most rare fashion, i' faith. 3.04. 15 P
but, in faith, honest as the skin between his 3.05. 11 P
well said, i' faith, neighbor verges. 3.05. 35 P
an honest soul, i' faith, sir, by my troth he is 3.05. 38 P
in faith, i will go. 4.01.296 P
in faith, my hand meant nothing to my sword. 5.01. 57
i' faith, i thank him, he hath bid me to a 5.01.154 P
i, being else by faith enforc'd | to call young 5.04. 8
if i break faith, this word shall speak for me: LLL 1.01.153
i' faith, your hand is out. 4.01.133
ah, never faith could hold, if not to beauty 4.02.106
i' faith, i will not. 4.03. 8 P
in faith, secrets! 4.03. 24 P
you would for paradise break faith and troth, 4.03.141
say when that he shall hear | faith infringed, 4.03.144
our loving lawful, and our faith not torn. 4.03.281
yes, in good faith. 5.02.280
and quick berowne hath plighted faith to me. 5.02.283
my faith and this the princess i did give; 5.02.454
he is a marvellous good neighbor, faith, and a 5.02.582 P
faith, unless you play the honest troyan, the 5.02.675 P
nay, faith; MND 1.02. 47 P
and make him with fair /aegles break his faith, 2.01. 79
bearing the badge of faith to prove them true? 3.02.127
disparage not the faith thou dost not know, 3.02.174
fine, i' faith! 3.02.284
and all the faith, the virtue of my heart, | the 4.01.169
thanks, i' faith, for silence is only MV 1.01.111
content, in faith, i'll seal to such a bond, 1.03.152
in faith, 'tis a fair hand, | and whiter than 2.04. 12
love–news, in faith. 2.04. 14
are wont | to keep obliged faith unforfeited! 2.06. 7
mean to solemnize | the bargain of your faith, i 3.02.193
and do you, gratiano, mean good faith? 3.02.210
yes, faith, my lord. 3.02.211
thou almost mak'st me waver in my faith | to 4.01.130

stealing her soul with many vows of faith, | and 5.01. 19
in faith, i gave it to the judge's clerk. 5.01.143
and so riveted with faith unto your flesh. 5.01.169
now, in faith, gratiano, | you give your wife 5.01.174
lord | will never more break faith advisedly. 5.01.253
no, faith, hate him not, for my sake. AYL 1.03. 35 P
i' faith, coz, 'tis he. 3.02.216 P
but, good faith, i had as lief have been myself 3.02.254 P
now, by the faith of my love, i will. 3.02.428 P
i' faith, his hair is of a good color. 3.04. 10 P
as, by my faith, i see no more in you | than 3.05. 38
no, faith, proud mistress, hope not after it. 3.05. 45
by my faith, you have great reason to be sad. 4.01. 21 P
no, faith, die by attorney. 4.01. 94 P
yes, faith, will i, fridays and saturdays and 4.01.116 P
but, i' faith, i should have been a woman by 4.03.175 P
faith, the priest was good enough, for all the 5.01. 3 P
faith, sir, so, so. 5.01. 26 P
it is to be all made of faith and service, | and 5.02. 89
i' faith, i' faith, and both in a tune, like two 5.03. 14 P
i' faith, i' faith, and both in a tune, like two 5.03. 14 P
faith, we met, and found the quarrel was upon 5.04. 49 P
by my faith, he is very swift and sententious. 5.04. 62 P
mine, | thy faith my fancy to thee doth combine. 5.04.150
you to a love, that your true faith doth merit; 5.04.188
i'll pheeze you, in faith. SHR in.1. 1 P
i' faith, sir, you shall never need to fear. 1.01. 61
faith, as you say, there's small choice in 1.01.134 P
so could i, faith, boy, to have the next wish 1.01.239
faith, sirrah, and you'll not knock, i'll ring 1.02. 16
you lie, in faith, for you are call'd plain kate 2.01.185
come, you wasp, i' faith you are too angry. 2.01.209
faith, gentlemen, now i play a merchant's part, 2.01.326
faith, mistress, then i have no cause to stay. 3.01. 86
i' faith, he'll have a lusty widow now, | that 4.02. 50
faith, he is gone unto the taming-school. 4.02. 54
faith, as cold as can be. 4.03. 37
faith, nothing; 4.04. 78 P
nay, faith, i'll see the church a' your back, 5.01. 4 P
his faith, his sweet disaster; AWW 1.01.173
what one, i' faith? 1.01.178 P
faith, madam, i have other holy reasons, such as 1.03. 32 P
faith, i do. 1.03.101 P
good faith, across! 2.01. 67
now, by my faith and honor, | if seriously i may 2.01. 80
but a trifle neither, in good faith, if the 2.02. 34 P
yes, good faith, ev'ry dram of it, and i will 2.03.221 P
a good knave, i' faith, and well fed. 2.04. 38
faith, yes: 2.05. 85
sir, betake thee to thy faith, for seventeen 4.01. 76 P
faith, sir, h'as led the drum before the english 4.03.266 P
faith, sir, 'a has an english /name, but his 4.05. 39 P
faith, there's a dozen of 'em, with delicate 4.05.104 P
faith, sir, he did love her, but how? 5.03.243 P
faith, i know more than i'll speak. 5.03.256 P
faith, i'll home to-morrow, sir toby. TN 1.03.105 P
faith, i can cut a caper. 1.03.121 P
surprise her with discourse of my dear faith; 1.04. 25
apt, in good faith, very apt. 1.05. 26 P
give me faith, say i. 1.05.129 P
faith, so they say, but i think it rather 2.03. 11 P
here comes the fool, i' faith. 2.03. 15 P
'twas very good, i' faith. 2.03. 25 P
excellent good, i' faith. 2.03. 45 P
very sweet and contagious, i' faith. 2.03. 55 P
good, i' faith. come, begin. 2.03. 71 P
it is his grounds of faith that all that look on 2.03.152 P
what years, i' faith? 2.04. 27
in faith, they are as true of heart as we. 2.04.106
i' faith, or i either? 2.05.192 P
no, faith, i'll not stay a jot longer. 3.02. 1 P
well held out, i' faith! 4.01. 5 P
plight me the full assurance of your faith, 4.03. 26
since you to non-regardance cast my faith, | and 5.01.121
hold little faith, though thou hast too much 5.01.171
whose foundation | is pil'd upon his faith, and WT 1.02.430
form | (which on my faith deserves high speech) 2.01. 70
contrary to the faith and allegiance of a true 3.02. 19 P
honor, nor my lusts | burn hotter than my faith. 4.04. 35
wouldst adventure | to mingle faith with him! 4.04.460
but by | the violation of my faith, and then 4.04.477
(as, in faith, i mean not | to see him any more) 4.04.494
it is requir'd | you do awake your faith. 5.03. 95
sirrah, look to't, i' faith i will, i' faith. JN 2.01.140
sirrah, look to't, i' faith i will, i' faith. 2.01.140
and, by my faith, this league that we have made 2.01.545
that broker that still breaks the pate of faith, 2.01.568
since kings break faith upon commodity, | gain, 2.01.597
yea, faith itself to hollow falsehood change! 3.01. 95
the lady constance speaks not from her faith, 3.01.210
which only lives but by the death of faith, 3.01.212
that faith would live again by death of need. 3.01.214
o then tread down my need, and faith mounts up; 3.01.215
keep my need up, and faith is trodden down! 3.01.216
gave the sound of words | was deep-sworn faith, 3.01.231
play fast and loose with faith? 3.01.242
unswear faith sworn, and on the marriage-bed 3.01.245
i may disjoin my hand, but not my faith. 3.01.262
so mak'st thou faith an enemy to faith, | and 3.01.263
so mak'st thou faith an enemy to faith, | and 3.01.263
a voluntary zeal and an unurg'd faith | to your 5.02. 10
and welcome home again discarded faith. 5.04. 12
faith, none for me, except the northeast wind, R2 1.04. 6
they break their faith to god as well as us. 3.02.101
and sends allegiance and true faith of heart 3.03. 37
there is /my bond of faith, | to tie thee to my 4.01. 76
in faith, | it is a conquest for a prince to 1H4 1.01. 76
who, i rob? i a thief? not i, by my faith. 1.02.138 P
i have done, i' faith. 1.03.258
in faith, it is exceedingly well aim'd. 1.03.282
hast no faith in thee? 2.01. 31 P
i know a trick worth two of that, i' faith. 2.01. 37 P
nay, by my faith, i think you are more beholding 2.01. 88 P
we'll jure ye, faith. 2.02. 92 P
in faith, | i'll know your business, harry, that 2.03. 79
in faith, i'll break thy little finger, harry, 2.03. 87
faith, and i'll send him packing. 2.04.297 P
faith, i ran when i saw others run. 2.04.302 P
faith, tell me now in earnest, how came 2.04.303 P
not a whit, i' faith, i lack some of thy 2.04.371 P
o jesu, this is excellent sport, i' faith! 2.04.390 P
a goodly portly man, i' faith, and a corpulent, 2.04.422 P
i'll tickle ye for a young prince, i' faith. 2.04.444 P
stuff | as puts me from my faith. 3.01.153
in faith, he is a worthy gentleman, 3.01.163
scope | when you come 'cross his humor, faith, 3.01.170
in faith, my lord, you are too willful-blame, 3.01.175
is the wind in that door, i' faith? 3.03. 88 P
there's neither faith, truth, nor womanhood in 3.03.110 P
there's no more faith in thee than in a stew'd 3.03.112 P
but, sirrah, there's no room for faith, truth, 3.03.153 P
lopp'd off — | and yet, in faith, it is not; 4.01. 44
faith, and so we should, | where now remains a 4.01. 52
ay, by my faith, that bears a frosty sound. 4.01.128
faith, sir john, 'tis more than time that i were 4.02. 54 P
faith, for their poverty, i know not where they 4.02. 70 P
and violation of all faith and troth | sworn to 5.01. 70
and yet, in faith, thou bearest thee like a king 5.04. 36
by my faith, i am afraid he would prove the 5.04.123 P
in mine own house, most beastly, in good faith. 2H4 2.01. 14 P
faith, you said so before. 2.01.137 P
i' faith, i am loath to pawn my plate, so god 2.01.154 P
faith, it does me, though it discolors the 2.02. 4 P
yes, faith, and let it be an excellent good 2.02. 33 P
i' faith, sweet heart, methinks now you are in 2.04. 22 P
but, i' faith, you have drunk too much canaries, 2.04. 26 P
sick of a calm, yea, good faith. 2.04. 36 P
no, by my faith, i must live among my neighbors; 2.04. 74 P
longer ago than wed'sday last, i' good faith — 2.04. 87 P
a tame cheater, i' faith, you may stroke him as 2.04. 98 P
peesel, be quiet, 'tis very late, i' faith. 2.04.162 P
i' faith, i love thee. 2.04.218 P
i' faith, and thou follow'dst him like a church. 2.04.230 P
no, faith, boys, none. 2.04.324 P
it is well said, in faith, sir, and it is well 3.02. 68 P
most excellent, i' faith! 3.02.107 P
very singular good, in faith, well said, sir 3.02.109 P
that we have, that we have, in faith, sir john, 3.02.217 P
faith, i'll bear no base mind. 3.02.240 P
well said, i' faith, wart, th' art a good scab. 3.02.276 P
will you thus break your faith? 4.02.112
good faith, this same young sober-blooded boy 4.03. 87 P
for, by my faith, it very well becomes you. 5.02. 50
faith, i will live so long as i may, that's the H5 2.01. 14 P
faith, he's very ill. 2.01. 84 P
sate | crowned with faith and constant loyalty. 2.02. 5
an irishman, a very valiant gentleman, i' faith. 3.02. 67 P
by faith and honor, | our madams mock at us, and 3.05. 27
by my faith, sir, but it is; 3.07.110 P
no, faith, my coz, wish not a man from england. 4.03. 30
i' faith, kate, my wooing is fit for thy 5.02.122 P
urge me farther than to say "do you in faith?" 5.02.128 P
give me your answer, i' faith, do, and so clap 5.02.129 P
no, faith, is't not, kate; 5.02.190 P
as i have a saving faith within me tells me thou 5.02.204 P
but, in faith, kate, the elder i wax, the better 5.02.228 P
faith, i have been a truant in the law, | and 1H6 2.04. 7
the law, | good faith, i am no wiser than a daw. 2.04. 18
should reign among professors of one faith. 5.01. 14
give thee her hand, for sign of plighted faith. 5.03.162
faith, holy uncle, would't were come to that! 2H6 2.01. 37
let it come, i' faith, and i'll pledge you all, 2.03. 66 P
e'er i prov'd thee false or fear'd thy faith. 3.01.205
ay, by my faith, the field is honorable, and 4.02. 50 P
false king, why hast thou broken faith with me, 5.01. 91
o, where is faith? 5.01.166
fight closer or, good faith, you'll catch a blow 3H6 3.02. 23
thy faith irrevocable | that only warwick's 3.03.247
(for trust not him that hath once broken faith), 4.04. 30
ay, by my faith, for a poor earl to give. 5.01. 32
good faith, good faith, the saying did not hold R3 2.04. 16
good faith, good faith, the saying did not hold 2.04. 16
good faith, and when i met this holy man | the 3.02.116
for which your honor and your faith is pawn'd, 4.02. 89
faith, none, but humphrey hour, that call'd your 4.04.176
thy broken faith hath made the prey for worms. 4.04.386
by the false faith of him whom most i trusted; 5.01. 17
faith, and so it did. H8 1.01.167
faith, my lord, | i hear of none but the new 1.03. 16
the faith they have in tennis and tall stockings 1.03. 30
faith, how easy? 1.04. 17
by my faith, | and thank your lordship. 1.04. 24
you do not doubt my faith, sir? 2.01.143
'twill require | a strong faith to conceal it. 2.01.145
in faith, for little england | you'ld venture an 2.03. 46
so deep suspicion, where all faith was meant. 3.01. 53
was rather | (if there be faith in men) meant 5.02.186
faith, i'll not meddle in it, let her be as she TRO 1.01. 66 P
faith, to say truth, brown and not brown. 1.02. 96 P
faith, sir, superficially. 3.01. 10 P
sweet queen, that's a sweet queen — i' faith — 3.01. 71 P
love? ay, that it shall, i' faith. 3.01.112 P
in love, i' faith, to the very tip of the nose. 3.01.127 P
few words to fair faith. 3.02. 95 P
your uncle's word and my firm faith. 3.02.108 P
in faith, i lie, | my thoughts were like 3.02.121
and yet, good faith, i wish'd myself a man, | or 3.02.127
pretty, i' faith. 3.02.135 P
tell me, noble diomed — faith, tell me true, 4.01. 52
in this i do not call your faith in question 4.04. 84
in faith, i cannot. what would you have me do? 5.02. 23
in faith, i do not. come hither once again. 5.02. 49
in faith i will lo, never trust me else. 5.02. 59
o beauty, where is thy faith? 5.02. 67
shall not have it, diomed, faith, you shall not. 5.02. 85
the fractions of her faith, orts of her love, 5.02.158
and greasy relics | of her o'er-eaten faith, are 5.02.160
no, faith, young troilus, doff thy harness, 5.03. 31
even in the faith of valor, to appear | this 5.03. 69
i must not break my faith. 5.03. 71
a fine spot, in good faith. COR 1.03. 53 P
yet, by the faith of men, | we have some old 2.01.187
faith, there hath been many great men that have 2.02. 7 P
faith, look you, one cannot tell how to say that 4.05.169 P
faith, we hear fearful news. 4.06.139
good faith, i'll prove him, | speed how it will. 5.01. 60
faith, sir, if you had told as many lies in his 5.02. 24 P
faith, not me. TIT 2.01.102
faith, i can tell her age unto an hour. ROM 1.03. 11
nay, he's a flower, in faith, a very flower. 1.03. 78
pray — grant thou, lest faith turn to despair. 1.05.104
very well took, i' faith, wisely, wisely. 2.04.126 P
heart, and, i' faith, i will tell her as much. 2.04.173 P
i' faith, i am sorry that thou art not well. 2.05. 53
no faith, no honesty in men, all perjur'd, | all 3.02. 86
dost thou with him | that is renowm'd for faith? 3.05. 62
my husband is on earth, my faith in heaven; 3.05.205
how shall that faith return again to earth, 3.05.206
faith, here it is. 3.05.212
faith, you'll be sick to-morrow | for this 4.04. 7
in your bed, | he'll fright you up, i' faith. 4.05. 11
faith, we may put up our pipes and be gone. 4.05. 96 P
no money, on my faith, but the gleek; 4.05.114 P
faith, i know not what to say. 4.05.138 P
in faith, i will. 5.03. 74
faith, for the worst is filthy, and would not TIM 1.02.153 P
else i should tell him well (i' faith, i should) 1.02.161
faith, nothing but an empty box, sir, which, in 3.01. 16 P
faith, i perceive our masters may throw their 3.04.100 P
of this untrod state | with all true faith. JC 3.01.137
there are no tricks in plain and simple faith; 4.02. 22
faith, here's an equivocator, that could swear MAC 2.03. 8 P
faith, here's an english tailor come hither for 2.03. 12 P
faith, sir, we were carousing till the second 2.03. 24 P
speak'st with all thy wit, and yet, i' faith, 4.02. 42
at no time broke my faith, would not betray 4.03.128
but what, in faith, make you from wittenberg? HAM 1.02.168
offend you, heartily, | yes, faith, heartily. 1.05.135
in faith, | my lord, not i. 1.05.145
nor i, my lord, in faith. 1.05.146
faith, as you may season it in the charge: 2.01. 28
faith, her privates we. 2.02.234 P
excellent, i' faith — of the chameleon's dish, 3.02. 93 P
faith, i must leave thee, love, and shortly too; 3.02.173
i like thy wit well, in good faith. 5.01. 45 P
faith, e'en with losing his wits. 5.01.159 P
faith, if 'a be not rotten before 'a die — as 5.01.165 P
no, faith, not a jot, but to follow him thither 5.01.207 P
nay, good my lord, for my ease, in good faith. 5.02.105 P
sir, yet, in faith, if you did, it would not 5.02.134 P
three of the carriages, in faith, are very dear 5.02.151 P
must be a faith that reason without miracle LR 1.01.222
sir, in good faith, in sincere verity, | under 2.02.105
faith, he is posted hence on serious matter. 4.05. 8
yes, faith. 4.07. 70
and, by the faith of man, | i know my price, i OTH 1.01. 10
faith, he to-night hath boarded a land carract. 1.02. 50
she swore, in faith 'twas strange, 'twas passing 1.03.160
my life upon her faith! 1.03.294
in faith, too much; 2.01.103
good faith, a little one; 2.03. 66 P
in faith, he's penitent; 3.03. 63
faith, that was not so well; 4.01.273
faith, half asleep. 4.02. 97
for, in good faith, | i am a child to chiding. 4.02.113
thou hast serv'd me with much faith; ANT 2.07. 58
held to fools does make | our faith mere folly; 3.13. 43
no, faith; not so much as his patience. CYM 1.02. 7 P
faith, yes, to be put to the arbiterment of 1.04. 49 P
faith, | i shall unfold equal discourtesy | to 2.03. 95
if thy faith be not tainted with the breach of 3.04. 26 P
away, away, | corrupters of my faith! 3.04. 83
faith, i'll lie down and sleep. 4.02.294
good faith, | i tremble still with fear; 4.02.302
thy name well fits thy faith; 4.02.381
thy faith thy name. 4.02.381
the truest princess | that ever swore her faith. 5.05.417
i do not doubt thy faith; PER 1.02.111
i'll take thy word for faith, not ask thine oath 1.02.120
faith, master, i am thinking of the poor men 2.01. 18 P
faith, by no means, she hath so strictly tied 2.05. 8
faith, they listen'd to me as they would have 4.02. 98 P
thou sayest true, i' faith, so they must: 4.02.126 P
faith, some do, and some do not. 4.02.129 P
ay, by my faith, they shall not be chang'd yet. 4.02.135 P
faith, i must ravish her, or she'll disfurnish 4.06. 11 P
faith, there's no way to be rid on't but by the 4.06. 15 P
faith, she would serve after a long voyage at 4.06. 44 P
faith, my acquaintance lies little amongst them. 4.06.195 P
no, good faith; 5.01.177
you well descry | a figure of truth, of faith, 5.03. 92
which is not catching | where there is faith? TNK 1.02. 46
almost puts | faith in a fever, and deifies 1.02. 66
i am not | against your faith, yet i continue 1.03. 97
beauty, | thus let me seal my vow'd faith. 2.05. 39
out with't, faith! 3.03. 33
about this hour my cousin gave his faith | to 3.06. 1
faith, so am i. 3.06. 61
faith, very little. love has us'd you kindly. 3.06. 67
as i love most, and in that faith will perish, 3.06.163
by that faith, | that fair hand, and that honest 3.06.196
ye make my faith reel. 3.06.212
my virgin's faith has fled me; 4.02. 46
faith, i'll tell you; 4.03. 30 P
in faith, i will not. 5.03. 29
faith, 'a says true. STM II.C 141 P
o, never faith could hold, if not to beauty PP 5. 2
her faith, her oaths, her tears, and all were 7.12
where her faith was firmly fix'd in love, 17. 7
as men, | in faith, you had not had it then." 18.36
jollity, | and purest faith unhappily forsworn, SON 66. 4
yet in good faith some say that thee behold, 131. 5
in faith, i do not love thee with mine eyes, 141. 1
and new faith torn | in vowing new hate after 152. 3
thee, | and all my honest faith in thee is lost; 152. 8

FAITH-BREACH 1 FR 0.0001 REL FR 1 V 0 P
now minutely revolts upbraid his faith-breach; MAC 5.02. 18

FAITH'D 1 FR 0.0001 REL FR 1 V 0 P
or worth in thee | make thy words faith'd? LR 2.01. 70

FAITHFUL 36 FR 0.0040 REL FR 36 V 0 P
find | by every syllable a faithful verity. MM 4.03.126
our old and faithful friend, we are glad to see 5.01. 2
to myself forsworn, to thee i'll faithful prove; LLL 4.02.107
some thousand verses of a faithful lover. 5.02. 50

i'll change my black gown for a faithful friend. 5.02.834
there shall the pairs of faithful lovers be MND 4.01. 91
of life, | i will your very faithful feeder be, AYL 2.04. 99
youth and kind | will the faithful offer take 4.03. 60
you are there followed by a faithful shepherd — 5.02. 81
give yourself to this most faithful shepherd? 5.04. 14
your faithful subject i, a gentleman, | born in JN 1.01. 50
grief, | like true, inseparable, faithful loves, 3.04. 66
i do bequeath my faithful services | and true 5.07.104
her pasters' grass with faithful english blood. R2 3.03.100
his heart | to faithful service of your majesty. 3.03.118
and god forbid, my dear and faithful lord, H5 1.02. 13
never did faithful subject more rejoice | at the 2.02.161
your faithful service, and your toil in war; 1H6 3.04. 21
king henry's faithful and anointed queen. 5.05. 91
that, as i am a christian faithful man, | i R3 1.04. 4
so season'd with your faithful love to me, 3.07.149
even as the axe falls, if i be not faithful! H8 2.01. 61
these | your faithful friends o' th' suburbs? 5.03. 72
approved warriors, and my faithful friends, | i TIT 5.01. 1
exchange of thy love's faithful vow for mine. ROM 2.02.127
she, there dead, /that romeo's faithful wife. 5.03.232
be set | as that of true and faithful juliet. 5.03.302
he was my friend, faithful and just to me; JC 3.02. 85
do faithful homage and receive free honors; MAC 3.06. 36
i will be faithful. HAM 2.02.115
as of a man faithful and honorable. 2.02.130
king, | as england was his faithful tributary, 5.02. 39
this hath been | your faithful servant. CYM 1.01.174
day serves not light more faithful than i'll be. PER 1.02.110
the wind, | faithful friends are hard to find: PP 20.32
to know | faithful friend from flatt'ring foe. 20.56

FAITHFULL'ST 1 FR 0.0001 REL FR 1 V 0 P
my soul the faithfull'st off'rings have breath'd TN 5.01.114

FAITHFULLY 13 FR 0.0014 REL FR 12 V 1 P
of that which hath so faithfully been paid. LLL 2.01.156
i'll serve thee true and faithfully till then. 5.02.831
and we will answer all things faithfully. MV 5.01.299
as you have whisper'd faithfully you were, | and AYL 2.07.192
but wilt thou faithfully? AWW 4.01. 86
was faithfully confirm'd by the rector of the 4.03. 58 P
as faithfully as i deny the devil. JN 1.01.252
yet their own authors faithfully affirm | that H5 1.02. 43
have follow'd both my fortunes faithfully, | of H8 4.02.141
if thou dost love, pronounce it faithfully; ROM 2.02. 94
i should not urge it half so faithfully. TIM 3.02. 41
if you serve faithfully, i dare assure you TNK 2.05. 56
that gave her promise faithfully she would | be 3.05. 43

FAITHFULNESS 2 FR 0.0002 REL FR 2 V 0 P
other thought | but faithfulness and courage. PER 1.01. 63
and for your faithfulness | we will advance you, 1.01.153

FAITHLESS 4 FR 0.0004 REL FR 4 V 0 P
o faithless coward! MM 3.01.136
excuse, | that she is issue to a faithless jew. MV 2.04. 37
smoke, | to make a faithless error in your ears; JN 2.01.230
a most unnatural and faithless service. H8 2.01.123

FAITH'S 1 FR 0.0001 REL FR 1 V 0 P
love is dying, faith's defying, | heart's PP 17. 3

FAITHS 7 FR 0.0008 REL FR 6 V 1 P
and by my two faiths and troths, my lord, i ADO 1.01.226 P
the faiths of men ne'er stained with revolt; JN 4.02. 6
and keep our faiths firm and inviolable. 5.02. 7
show now your mended faiths, | and instantly 5.07. 75
that, were our royal faiths martyrs in love, 2H4 4.01.191
oaths are straws, men's faiths are wafer–cakes, H5 2.03. 51
"shall plight your honorable faiths to me | with LUC 1690

FAITORS 1 FR 0.0001 REL FR 0 V 1 P
down, faitors! 2H4 2.04.159 P

FALCHION 8 FR 0.0009 REL FR 7 V 1 P
the pommel of caesar's falchion. LLL 5.02.614 P
came edward to my side | with purple falchion, 3H6 1.04. 12
thy murd'rous falchion smoking in his blood; R3 1.02. 94
with my good biting falchion | i would have made LR 5.03.277
his falchion on a flint he softly smiteth, LUC 176
so under his insulting falchion lies | harmless 509
i fear'd by tarquin's falchion to be slain, 1046
with shining falchion in my chamber came | a 1626

FALC'NER'S 1 FR 0.0001 REL FR 1 V 0 P
o, for a falc'ner's voice, | to lure this ROM 2.02.158

FALC'NERS 1 FR 0.0001 REL FR 0 V 1 P
we'll e'en to't like /french falc'ners — fly at HAM 2.02.430 P

FALCON 8 FR 0.0009 REL FR 6 V 2 P
follies doth /enew | as falcon doth the fowl, is MM 3.01. 91
the horse his curb, and the falcon her bells, so AYL 3.03. 80 P
my falcon now is sharp and passing empty, | and SHR 4.01.190
when my good falcon made her flight across | thy WT 4.04. 15
but what a point, my lord, your falcon made, 2H6 2.01. 5
out ere i part you — the falcon as the tercel, TRO 3.02. 52 P
a falcon, tow'ring in her pride of place, | was MAC 2.04. 12
which, like a falcon tow'ring in the skies, LUC 506

FALCONBRIDGE *(also faulconbridge)*

FALCONBRIDGE 5 FR 0.0005 REL FR 4 V 1 P
and the beauteous heir | of jaques falconbridge, LLL 2.01. 42
not offended, | she is an heir of falconbridge. 2.01.205
what say you then to falconbridge, the young MV 1.02. 66 P
the thrice–victorious lord of falconbridge, 1H6 4.07. 67
stern falconbridge commands the narrow seas, 3H6 1.01.239

FALCON'S 3 FR 0.0003 REL FR 3 V 0 P
as confident as is the falcon's flight | against R2 1.03. 61
and bears his thoughts above his falcon's pitch. 2H6 2.01. 12
so doves do peck the falcon's piercing talons, 3H6 1.04. 41

FALCONS' 1 FR 0.0001 REL FR 1 V 0 P
trembling fear, as fowl hear falcons' bells. LUC 511

FALCONS 1 FR 0.0001 REL FR 1 V 0 P
as falcons to the lure, away she flies, | the VEN 1027

FALL* *(also fault)*

/FALL* 5 FR 0.0005 REL FR 4 V 1 P
/rise /thus /nimbly /by /a /true /king's /fall. R2 4.01.318
/more /likely /to /fall /in /than /to /get /o'er 2H4 1.01.171
for our enemies shall /fall before us, inspir'd 2H6 4.02. 35 P
/the /tears /that /thy /poor /eyes /let /fall TIT 3.02. 18
/come, /let's /fall /to, /and, /gentle /girl, 3.02. 34

FALL* 327 FR 0.0369 REL FR 279 V 48 P
fall to't, yarely, or we run ourselves aground. TMP 1.01. 3 P
hand, do you the like, | to fall it on gonzalo. 2.01.296
on prosper fall and make him | by inch–meal a 2.02. 2
i'll fall flat, | perchance he will not mind me. 2.02. 16
same cloud cannot choose but fall by pailfuls. 2.02. 24 P
no sweet aspersion shall the heavens let fall 4.01. 18
that the blind mole may not | hear a foot fall; 4.01.195
to the show of thine, | fall fellowly drops. 5.01. 64
wouldst thou then counsel me to fall in love? TGV 1.02. 2
to take a paper up that i let fall. 1.02. 71
the building fall | and leave no memory of what 5.04. 9
save the fall is in the ord "dissolutely." WIV 1.01.254 P
why then all the dukes fall upon the king. MM 1.02. 3 P
cut a little, | than fall, and bruise to death. 2.01. 6
to be tempted, escalus, | another thing to fall. 2.01. 18
some rise by sin, and some by virtue fall; 2.01. 38
if any thing fall to you upon this, more than 4.02.178 P
a blasting and a scandalous breath to fall | on 5.01.122
proceed, solinus, to procure my fall, | and by ERR 1.01. 1
as easy mayst thou fall | a drop of water in the 2.02.125
i will fall prostrate at his feet, | and never 5.01.114
well, if ever thou dost fall from this faith, ADO 1.01.255 P
that she shall fall in love with benedick, and i 2.01.381 P
stomach, he shall fall in love with beatrice. 2.01.384 P
lady, and her death shall fall heavy on you. 5.01.149 P
bad parts didst thou first fall in love with me? 5.02. 60 P
fair fall the face it covers! LLL 2.01.124
submissive fall his princely feet before, | and 4.01. 90
the people fall a–hooting. 4.02. 59
fall in the fresh lap of the crimson rose, | and MND 2.01.108
fool, | i did upbraid her and fall out with her. 4.01. 50
and, as she fled, her mantle she did fall, 5.01.142
you shall see it will fall pat as i told you. 5.01.187 P
and the worst fall that ever fell, i hope i MV 1.02. 90 P
streak'd and pied | should fall as jacob's hire, 1.03. 80
did in eaning time | fall parti–color'd lambs, 1.03. 88
your father, i fall into charybdis, your mother. 3.05. 17 P
good youth, or it will fall | to cureless ruin. 4.01.141
to come in disguis'd against me to try a fall. AYL 1.01.126 P
may she not by fortune fall into the fire? 1.02. 44 P
you shall try but one fall. 1.02.204 P
you will try in time, in despite of a fall. 1.03. 25 P
you should fall into so strong a liking with old 1.03. 27 P
welcome, fall to. 2.07.171
for though he go as softly as foot can fall, he 3.02.328 P
why, now fall down, | or if thou canst not, o, 3.05. 17
foulness, and she'll fall in love with my anger. 3.05. 67 P
i pray you do not fall in love with me, | for i 3.05. 72
would have gone near | to fall in love with him; 3.05.126
dignity, | and fall into our rustic revelry. 5.04.177
measure heap'd in joy, to th' measures fall. 5.04.179
i would be loath to fall into my dreams again. SHR in.2. 126 P
fall to them as you find your stomach serves you 1.01. 38
that, all amaz'd, the priest let fall the book, 3.02.161
will you let it fall? 4.01.155
and my prayers pluck down, | fall on thy head! AWW 1.01. 70
(those bated that inherit but the fall | of the 2.01. 13
of you one fair and virtuous mistress | fall, 2.03. 58
when better fall, for your avails they fell. 3.01. 22
emboss'd him, you shall see his fall to–night; 3.06.100 P
before, because i would not fall out with thee. 4.05. 57 P
my fore–past proofs, howe'er the matter fall, 5.03.121
that strain again, it had a dying fall; TN 1.01. 4
or, if both break, your gaskins fall. 1.05. 25 P
being once display'd, doth fall that very hour. 2.04. 39
"if this fall into thy hand, revolve. 2.05.143 P
better | to fall before the lion than the wolf! 3.01.129
i should my tears let fall upon your cheek, 5.01.240
frighted, thou let'st fall | from dis's waggon! WT 4.04.117
(fair fall the bones that took the pains for me! JN 1.01. 78
before the dew of evening fall, shall fleet | in 2.01.285
men, | which in the very meeting fall, and die. 3.01. 33
pray that their burthens may not fall this day, 3.01. 90
and dost thou now fall over to my foes? 3.01.127
england, i will fall from thee. 3.01.320
john may stand, then arthur needs must fall: 3.04.139
but what shall i gain by young arthur's fall? 3.04.141
then let the worst unheard fall on your head. 4.02.136
foreknowing that the truth will fall out so. 4.02.154
seek out king john and fall before his feet; 5.04. 13
fall like amazing thunder on the casque | of thy R2 1.03. 81
that their events can never fall out good. 2.01.214
these signs forerun the death or fall of kings. 2.04. 15
fall to the base earth from the firmament. 2.04. 20
weak men must fall, for heaven still guards the 3.02. 62
hath now himself met with the fall of leaf. 3.04. 49
thee | to make a second fall of cursed man? 3.04. 76
here did she fall a tear, here in this place 3.04.104
would he not fall down, | since pride must have 5.05. 87
since pride must have a fall, and break the neck 5.05. 88
my lord, will't please you to fall to? 5.05. 98
he never did fall off, my sovereign liege, | but 1H4 1.03. 94
if he fall in, good night, or sink or swim. 1.03.194
every man | prophetically do forethink thy fall. 3.02. 38
should, how would thy guts fall about thy knees! 3.03.152 P
you two never meet but you fall to some discord. 2H4 2.04. 56 P
shall we fall foul for toys? 2.04.169
the wicked might not fall in love with thee; 2.04.320 P
and though we here fall down, | we have supplies 4.02. 44
fish–meals, that they fall into a kind of male 4.03. 92 P
may they fall | as those that i am come to tell 4.04. 95
i know thee not, old man, fall to thy prayers. 5.05. 47
did contend | without much fall of blood, whose H5 1.02. 25
and thus thy fall hath left a kind of blot | to 2.02.138
thine, methinks, is like | another fall of man. 2.02.142
if your pure maidens fall into the hand | of hot 3.03. 20
and quickly bring us word of england's fall. 3.05. 68
so, and ride not warily, fall into foul bogs. 3.07. 57 P
some of them will fall to–morrow, i hope. 3.07. 72 P
i pray you fall to; 5.01. 37 P
a good leg will fall, a straight back will stoop 5.02.159 P
if all things fall out right, | i shall as 1H6 2.03. 4
red, | and fall on my side so against your will. 2.04. 51
stones, we'll fall to it with our teeth. 3.01. 89 P
and so thrive richard as thy foes may fall! 3.01.173
till bones and flesh and sinews fall away, | so 3.01.192
a prophet to the fall of all our foes! 3.02. 32
lets fall his sword before your highness' feet, 3.04. 9
not rascal–like, to fall down with a pinch, 4.02. 49
the coward horse that bears me fall and die! 4.06. 47
and let her head fall into england's lap. 5.03. 26
makes me from wond'ring fall to weeping joys, 2H6 1.01. 34
and her attainture will be humphrey's fall. 1.02.106
a fall off of a tree. 2.01. 94
come, leave your drinking, and fall to blows. 2.03. 79 P
and should you fall, he is the next will mount. 3.01. 22
by wicked means to frame our sovereign's fall. 3.01. 52
this way fall i to death. 3.02.412
come, come, let's fall in with them. 4.02. 30 P
that not a tear can fall for rutland's death? 3H6 1.04. 88
must edward fall, which peril heaven forefend! 2.01.191
and, now i fall, thy tough commixtures melts, 2.06. 6
i fear her not, unless she chance to fall. 3.02. 24
me, | he's very likely now to fall from him, 3.03.209
i long till edward fall by war's mischance, 3.03.254
and, by my fall, the conquest to my foe. 5.02. 10
th' untimely fall of virtuous lancaster. R3 1.02. 4
wits | and fall something into a slower method: 1.02.116
that fall out | in sharing that which you have 1.03.157
and if they fall, they dash themselves to pieces 1.03.259
drop millstones, when fools' eyes fall tears. 1.03.352
come, shall we fall to work? 1.04.153 P
when great leaves fall, then winter is at hand; 2.03. 33
prince, | to stay him from the fall of vanity; 3.07. 97
is that by sudden floods and fall of waters 4.04.510
i wish'd might fall on me when i was found 5.01. 14
this is the day wherein i wish'd to fall | by 5.01. 16
lest his son george fall | into the blind cave 5.03. 61
that they may crush down with a heavy fall | the 5.03.111
soul | ere i let fall the windows of mine eyes: 5.03.116
think on me, | and fall thy edgeless sword. 5.03.135
and with guilty fear | let fall thy lance. 5.03.143
think on me, | and fall thy edgeless sword. 5.03.163
may (if they think it well) let fall a tear; H8 pr 6
his dews fall every where. 1.03. 57
your fortunes, fall away | like water from ye, 2.01.129
you inkling | of an ensuing evil, if it fall, 2.01.141
will have his will, and she must fall. 2.01.167
killing care and grief of heart | fall asleep, 3.01. 14
once | the burthen of my sorrows fall upon ye. 3.01.111
from her | will fall some blessing to this land, 3.02. 51
fit for a fool to fall by. 3.02.214
i shall fall | like a bright exhalation in the 3.02.225
fall into th' compass of a praemunire — | that 3.02.340
mark but my fall, and that that ruin'd me: 3.02.439
the dews of heaven fall thick in blessings on 4.02.133
or i fall into | the trap is laid for me! 5.01.141
stone a–rolling, | 'twould fall upon ourselves. 5.02.140
to make parents happy | may hourly fall upon ye! 5.04. 8
and make him fall | his crest that prouder than TRO 1.03.378
walls will stand till they fall of themselves. 2.03. 9 P
my cousin will fall out with you. 3.01. 85 P
out with fortune, | must fall out with men too. 3.03. 76
in the eyes of others | as feel in his own fall; 3.03. 78
which when they fall, as being slippery standers 3.03. 84
down another, and together | die in the fall. 3.03. 87
hector would have them fall upon him thus. 4.05.137
the fall of every phrygian stone will cost | a 4.05.223
fall greeks, fail fame, honor or go or stay, 5.01. 43
and all troy on thee, | fall all together. 5.03. 62
fall down before him like a mower's swath. 5.05. 25
so, ilion, fall thou next! 5.08. 11
your eyes, half out, weep out at pandar's fall; 5.10. 48
or whether his fall enrag'd him, or how 'twas, COR 1.03. 63 P
goddess fortune | fall deep in love with thee, 1.05. 21
so it must fall out | to him, or our authorities 2.01.243
nature is, he fall in rage | with their refusal, 2.03.258
stop, | or all will fall in broil. 3.01. 33
him | a mile before his tent, fall down, and 5.01. 5
but the fall of either | makes the survivor heir 5.06. 17
shall he die, | and i'll renew me in his fall. 5.06. 48
body hearing it | should straight fall mad, or TIT 2.03.104
confusion fall — 2.03.184
brother, hast thou hurt thee with the fall? 2.03.203
doth rise and fall between thy rosed lips, 2.04. 24
shall, | lo hand in hand lucius and i will fall. 5.03.136
to see it techy and fall out wi' th' dug! ROM 1.03. 32
"yea," quoth he, "dost thou fall upon thy face? 1.03. 41
thou wilt fall backward when thou hast more wit, 1.03. 42
thou wilt fall backward when thou comest to age, 1.03. 56
eyes | of mortals that fall back to gaze on him, 2.02. 30
women may fall, when there's no strength in men. 2.03. 80
it beats as it would fall in twenty pieces. 2.05. 49
in the wanton summer air, | and yet not fall; 2.06. 20
didst thou not fall out with a tailor for 3.01. 27 P
and fall upon the ground, as i do now, | taking 3.03. 69
why should you fall into so deep an o? 3.03. 90
fade | to /wanny ashes, thy eyes' windows fall, 4.01.100
by holy lawrence to fall prostrate here | and 4.02. 20
veins | that the life–weary taker may fall dead, 5.01. 62
that state of fortune fall into my keeping, TIM 1.01.150
so fall to't: 1.02. 70
that now they are at fall, want treasure, cannot 2.02.205
tear me, take me, and the gods fall upon you! 3.04. 99
thou have thyself fall in the confusion of men, 4.03.324 P
hath /sense withal | of it own fall, restraining 5.01.148
ours is the fall, i fear, our foes the snare. 5.02. 17
this, | whose fall the mark of his ambition is. 5.03. 10
and schools should fall | for private faults in 5.04. 25
which in the bluster of thy wrath must fall 5.04. 41
you yourselves shall set out for reproof | fall, 5.04. 58
our droplets which | from niggard nature fall, 5.04. 77
run to your houses, fall upon your knees, | pray JC 1.01. 53
that this shall be, or we will fall for it? 2.01.128
prevent, | let antony and caesar fall together. 2.01.161
as low as to thy foot doth cassius fall, | to 3.01. 56
et tu, brute? — then fall, caesar! 3.01. 77
thus did mark antony bid me fall down; 3.01.124
here didst thou fall, and here thy hunters stand 3.01.205
i know not what may fall, i like it not. 3.01.243
o, what a fall was there, my countrymen! 3.02.190
they fall their crests, and like deceitful jades 4.02. 26
for fear of what might fall, so to prevent | the 5.01.104
that is a step | on which i must fall down, or MAC 1.04. 49
like | the sovereignty will fall upon macbeth. 2.04. 30
but wail his fall | who i myself struck down. 3.01.121
me this, | and an eternal curse fall on you! 4.01.105
of the happy throne, | and fall of many kings. 4.03. 69
let fall thy blade on vulnerable crests, | i 5.08. 11
and never did the cyclops' hammers fall | on HAM 2.02.489
and fall a–cursing, like a very drab, | a 2.02.586

tree, | but fall unshaken when they mellow be. 3.02.191
force, | to be forestalled ere we come to fall, 3.03. 49
where th' offense is, let the great axe fall. 4.05.219
under the which he shall not choose but fall; 4.07. 65
woe | fall ten times /treble on that cursed head 5.01.247
to laertes before you fall to play. 5.02.207 P
is special providence in the fall of a sparrow. 5.02.220 P
let it fall rather, though the fork invade | the LR 1.01.144
your fore–vouch'd affection | fall into taint; 1.01.221
all the stor'd vengeances of heaven fall | on 2.04.162
by the pow'rful sun, | to fall and blister! 2.04.168
then let fall | your horrible pleasure. 3.02. 18
the younger rises when the old doth fall. 3.03. 25
and not fall | to quarrel with your great 4.06. 37
fall, and cease! 5.03.265
to fall in love with what she fear'd to look on! OTH 1.03. 98
but let your sentence | even fall upon my life. 1.03.120
it so fell out) | the town might fall in fright. 2.03.232
for that i heard the clink and fall of swords, 2.03.234
my speech should fall into such vild success 3.03.222
may fall to match you with her country forms, 3.03.237
i will fashion to fall out between twelve and 4.02.236 P
your attempt, and he shall fall between us. 4.02.238 P
it is their husbands' faults | if wives do fall. 4.03. 87
angel from his side, | and fall to reprobance. 5.02.209
and the wide arch | of the rang'd empire fall! ANT 1.01. 34
help me away, dear charmian, i shall fall. 1.03. 15
and, when we are put off, fall to their throats: 2.07. 72
take heed you fall not. 2.07.129
shall fall you for refusing him at sea, | being 3.07. 39
fall not a tear, i say, one of them rates | all 3.11. 69
and it portends alone | the fall of antony! 3.13.155
grace grow where those drops fall, my hearty 4.02. 38
she hath sold me, and i fall | under this plot. 4.12. 48
it smites me | beneath the fall i have. 5.02.172
and, when we fall, | we answer others' merits in 5.02.177
dost fall? 5.02.293
unless it had been the fall of an ass, which is CYM 1.02. 37 P
if you fall in the adventure, our crows shall 3.01. 81 P
be sprightly, for you fall 'mongst friends. 3.06. 74
to the note o' th' king, or i'll fall in them. 4.03. 44
the hazard therefore due fall on me by | the 4.04. 46
that's love, | to have them fall no more: 5.01. 13
with mars fall out, with juno chide, | that thy 5.04. 32
my tears that fall | prove holy water on thee! 5.05.268
covering heavens | fall on their heads like dew! 5.05.351
die, | for by his fall my honor must keep high. PER 1.01.149
yet those which see them fall | have scarce 1.04. 48
that all those eyes ador'd them ere their fall 2.04. 11
left without a roof | soon fall to ruin — your 2.04. 37
does fall in travail with her fear; 3.ch. 52
which the people's prayers still fall upon you, 3.03. 19
fill'd, | and wishes fall out as they're will'd. 5.02. 16
if we let fall the nobleness of this, | and the TNK pr 15
our losses fall so thick we must needs leave. pr 32
her twinning cherries shall their sweetness fall 1.01.178
let them break and fall | off me with that 1.02. 73
what will | the fall o' th' stroke do damage? 1.02.113
when he bids 'em charge, | fall on like fire. 2.02.250
that let fall | the birch upon the breeches of 3.05.110
if i fall, curse me, and say i was a coward, 3.06.104
only a little let him fall before me, | that i 3.06.178
better they fall by th' law than one another. 3.06.225
if ye fall in't, | think how you maim your honor 3.06.236
let it not fall again, sir. 3.06.272
if i fall from that mouth, i fall with favor, 3.06.282
if i fall from that mouth, i fall with favor, 3.06.282
for me, a hair shall never fall of these men. 3.06.287
nor shall he grudge to fall, | nor think he dies 3.06.297
young handsome men | shall never fall for me; 4.02. 4
so neither for my sake should fall untimely. 4.02. 69
fair fall the wit that can so well defend her! VEN 472
the mellow plum doth fall, the green sticks fast 527
their lips together glued, fall to the earth. 546
and now 'tis dark, and going i shall fall." 719
"but if thou fall, o, then imagine this, | the 721
adon, "you will fall again | into your idle 769
wounding itself to death, rise up and fall, LUC 466
hind'ring their present fall by this dividing; 551
who, if it wink, shall thereon fall and die. 1139
for one's offense why should so many fall, | to 1483
falls, through wind, before the fall should be. PP 10. 6
who lets so fair a house fall to decay, | which SON 13. 9
be, | to stand in thy affairs, fall by thy side. 151.12
her "love" for whose dear love i rise and fall. 151.14
or monarch's hands that lets not bounty fall LC 41

FALLACY 1 FR 0.0001 REL FR 1 V 0 P
i'll entertain the /offer'd fallacy. ERR 2.02.186

FALLEN 4 FR 0.0004 REL FR 4 V 0 P
did fly, | that fallen am i in dark uneven way, MND 3.02.417
what, art thou fallen? TIT 2.03.198
did hold her so, | but now her price is fallen. LR 1.01.197
and am fallen out with my more headier will, 2.04.110

FALLETH 3 FR 0.0003 REL FR 2 V 1 P
and anon falleth like a crab on the face of LLL 4.02. 6 P
and at his look she flatly falleth down, | for VEN 463
with this she falleth in the place she stood, 1121

FALLIABLE 1 FR 0.0001 REL FR 0 V 1 P
but this is most falliable, the worm's an odd ANT 5.02.257 P

FALLIBLE 1 FR 0.0001 REL FR 0 V 1 P
your resolution with hopes that are fallible, MM 3.01.169 P

FALLING 26 FR 0.0029 REL FR 20 V 6 P
who, falling in the flaws of her own youth, MM 2.03. 11
but that frailty hath examples for his falling, 3.01.186 P
who, falling there to find his fellow forth ERR 1.02. 37
argument of his own scorn by falling in love — ADO 2.03. 11 P
which, falling in the land, | hath every pelting MND 2.01. 90
falling out that year on ash we'nsday was four MV 2.05. 26 P
let me see — what think you of falling in love? AYL 1.02. 25 P
wafting his eyes to th' contrary and falling | a WT 1.02.372
and falling from a hill, he was so bruis'd 1H4 5.05. 21
is held from falling with so weak a wind | that 2H4 4.05. 99
gloucester stumbled, and in falling | strook me R3 1.04. 18
o my lord, | press not a falling man too far! H8 3.02.333
and sometimes falling ones. 4.01. 55
'tis a cruelty | to load a falling man. 5.02.112
falling in, after falling out, may make them TRO 3.01.103 P
falling in, after falling out, may make them 3.01.103 P
shall my prompted sword | falling on diomed. 5.02.176
when it stands | against a falling fabric. COR 3.01.246
'tis very like, he hath the falling sickness. JC 1.02.254
and honest casca, we have the falling sickness. 1.02.256
in 's rouse, | there falling out at tennis"; HAM 2.01. 57
begins to rage, he's hunted | even to falling. ANT 4.01. 8
whose top to climb | is certain falling, or so CYM 3.03. 48
so slipp'ry that | the fear's as bad as falling; 3.03. 49
touch'd, some falling | merely through fear, 5.03. 10
he vails his tail that, like a falling plume, VEN 314

FALLING–FROM 1 FR 0.0001 REL FR 0 V 1 P
of gold, and the falling–from of his friends, TIM 4.03.400 P

FALLING–OFF 1 FR 0.0001 REL FR 1 V 0 P
hamlet, what /a falling–off was there | from me, HAM 1.05. 47

/FALL'N 1 FR 0.0001 REL FR 1 V 0 P
/a /gallant /horse /fall'n /in /first /rank, TRO 3.03.161

FALL'N 45 FR 0.0050 REL FR 35 V 10 P
and it had not fall'n flat–long. TMP 2.01.181 P
though he hath fall'n by prompture of the blood, MM 2.04.178
o, she is fall'n | into a pit of ink, that the ADO 4.01.139
grieve not that i am fall'n to this for you; MV 4.01.266
he's fall'n in love with your foulness, and AYL 3.05. 66 P
is tir'd, my master and mistress fall'n out. SHR 4.01. 55 P
though my estate be fall'n, i was well born, AWW 3.07. 4
that you are not fall'n | from the report that 5.01. 12
that has fall'n into the unclean fishpond of her 5.02. 20 P
where but by chance a silver drop hath fall'n, JN 3.04. 63
lords | by his persuasion are again fall'n off, 5.05. 11
am i not fall'n away vilely since this last 1H4 3.03. 1 P
his highness is fall'n into this same whoreson 2H4 1.02.107 P
i think you are fall'n into the disease, for you 1.02.118 P
happy that he hath fall'n into the hands of one H5 4.04. 61 P
bright star of venus, fall'n down on the earth, 1H6 1.02.144
this sudden mischief never could have fall'n. 2.01. 59
and humphrey with the peers be fall'n at jars: 2H6 1.01.253
against thee, are all fall'n upon thee; R3 1.03.179
now margaret's curse is fall'n upon our heads, 3.03. 15
lo you, my lord, | the net has fall'n upon me! H8 1.01.203
with me, a poor weak woman, fall'n from favor? 3.01. 20
nay, and you weep | i am fall'n indeed. 3.02.376
i am a poor fall'n man, unworthy now | to be thy 3.02.413
greatness, once fall'n out with fortune, | must TRO 3.03. 75
wife is when she's fall'n out with her husband. COR 4.03. 33 P
things have fall'n out, sir, so unluckily | that ROM 3.04. 1
so noble a master fall'n, all gone, and not TIM 4.02. 6
you were retir'd, your friends fall'n off, 5.01. 59
my way of life | is fall'n into the sear, the MAC 5.03. 23
and be not from his reason fall'n thereon, | let HAM 2.02.165
mistook | fall'n on th' inventors' heads: 5.02.385
but have i fall'n, or no? LR 4.06. 56
my lord is fall'n into an epilepsy. OTH 4.01. 50
there's fall'n between him and my lord | an 4.01.224
fall'n in the practice of a /damned slave, 5.02.292
to follow with allegiance a fall'n lord | does ANT 3.13. 44
the star is fall'n. 4.14.106
of the war, | the soldier's pole is fall'n! 4.15. 65
y' are fall'n into a princely hand, fear nothing 5.02. 22
confounded one the other, or have fall'n both. CYM 1.04. 51 P
a strange infection | is fall'n into thy ear! 3.02. 4
with hunger, | i am fall'n in this offense. 3.06. 63
am i fall'n much away? TNK 3.06. 66
the flow'r is fall'n, the tree descends. 5.01.169

FALL'N–OFF 1 FR 0.0001 REL FR 1 V 0 P
our wars against | the fall'n–off britains, that CYM 3.07. 6

FALLOW* 3 FR 0.0003 REL FR 2 V 1 P
how does your fallow greyhound, sir? WIV 1.01. 89 P
that from the seedness the bare fallow brings MM 1.04. 42
her fallow leas | the darnel, hemlock, and rank H5 5.02. 44

FALLOWS 1 FR 0.0001 REL FR 1 V 0 P
and all our vineyards, fallows, meads, and H5 5.02. 54

FALLS' 1 FR 0.0001 REL FR 1 V 0 P
with their fresh falls' haste | add to his flow, LUC 650

FALLS 66 FR 0.0074 REL FR 59 V 7 P
desolate isle, else falls | upon your heads — TMP 3.03. 80
inconstancy falls off ere it begins. TGV 5.04.113
to whose falls | melodious birds sings madrigals WIV 3.01. 17
"to shallow rivers, to whose falls —" | heaven 3.01. 29
sense your brother's life | falls into forfeit; MM 1.04. 66
o, pardon me, my lord, it oft falls out, | to 2.04.117
the capon burns, the pig falls from the spit; ERR 1.02. 44
and with his legs falls into the cinquepace ADO 2.01. 78 P
then down upon her knees she falls, weeps, sobs, 2.03.146 P
for it so falls out | that what we have we prize 4.01.217
which falls into mine ears as profitless | as 5.01. 4
and "tailor" cries, and falls into a cough; MND 2.01. 54
and, at our stamp, here o'er and o'er one falls; 3.02. 25
this falls out better than i could devise. 3.02. 35
a throstle sing, he falls straight a–cap'ring. MV 1.02. 61 P
since this fortune falls to you, | be content, 3.02.133
and so did mine too, as the matter falls; 3.02.202
falls not the axe upon the humbled neck | but AYL 3.05. 5
brains are forfeit to the next tile that falls. AWW 4.03.191 P
to be well thank'd, | what e'er falls more. 5.01. 37
but falls into abatement and low price | even in TN 1.01. 13
grief boundeth where /it falls, | not with the R2 1.02. 58
the ripest fruit first falls, and so doth he; 2.01.153
since not to be avoided it falls on me. 1H4 5.05. 13
how quickly nature falls into revolt | when gold 2H4 4.05. 65
falls upon thee in a more fairer sort; 4.05.200
and so falls it out | with rivers, vaughan, grey R3 3.02. 64
thus margaret's curse falls heavy on my neck: 5.01. 25
and richard falls in height of all his pride! 5.03.176
even as the axe falls, if i be not faithful! H8 2.01. 61
and, as the long divorce of steel falls on me, 2.01. 76
that when the greatest stroke of fortune falls 2.02. 35
nips his root, | and then he falls as i do. 3.02.358
and when he falls, he falls like lucifer, 3.02.371
and when he falls, he falls like lucifer, 3.02.371
when many times the captive grecian falls, TRO 5.03. 40
and now falls on her bed, and then starts up, ROM 3.03.100
on romeo cries, | and then down falls again. 3.03.102
misgiving still | falls shrewdly to the purpose. JC 3.01.146
itself, | and falls on th' other — how now? MAC 1.07. 28
he falls to such perusal of my face | as 'a HAM 2.01. 87
rebellious to his arm, lies where it falls, 2.02.470
of his fell sword | th' unnerved father falls. 2.02.474
pyrrhus' bleeding sword | now falls on priam. 2.02.492
are mortis'd and adjoin'd, which, when it falls, 3.03. 20
it falls right. 4.07. 70
honor's bound, | when majesty falls to folly. LR 1.01.149
love cools, friendship falls off, brothers 1.02.107 P
the king falls from bias of nature; 1.02.111 P
preferment falls on him that cuts him off. 4.05. 38
/by /this /hand, falls me thus about my neck — OTH 4.01.135 P
each drop she falls would prove a crocodile. 4.01.246
the woman falls; sure he hath kill'd his wife. 5.02.236
some falls are means the happier to arise. CYM 4.02.403
her modesty will blow so far she falls for't. TNK 2.02.144
i wish his weary soul that falls may win it. 3.06.100
ev'ry blow that falls | threats a brave life, 5.03. 3
stroke laments | the place whereon it falls, and 5.03. 5
neck, | he on her belly falls, she on her back. VEN 594
yet sometimes falls an orient drop beside, 981
and lo there falls into thy boundless flood LUC 653
for every tear he falls a troyan bleeds; 1551
in key–cold lucrece' bleeding stream | he falls, 1775
and falls, through wind, before the fall should PP 10. 6
by whose falls | melodious birds sing madrigals. 19. 7
pomp, nor falls | under the blow of thralled SON 124. 6

FALL'ST 4 FR 0.0004 REL FR 4 V 0 P
but, seeing thou fall'st on me so luckily, | i 1H4 5.04. 33
then if thou fall'st, o cromwell, | thou fall'st H8 3.02.448
o cromwell, | thou fall'st a blessed martyr! 3.02.449
"yea," quoth my husband, "fall'st upon thy face? ROM 1.03. 55

FALOROUS *(also valorous)*

FALOROUS 1 FR 0.0001 REL FR 0 V 1 P
captain jamy is a marvellous falorous gentleman, H5 3.02. 76 P

/FALSE 5 FR 0.0005 REL FR 4 V 1 P
/him, | /he /takes /false /shadows /for /true TIT 3.02. 80
/what, /frighted /with /false /fire? HAM 3.02.266 P
/i /should /be /false /persuaded | /i /had LR 1.04.233
/false /justicer, /why /hast /thou /let /her 3.06. 56
/and /thyself /bewray | /when /false /opinion, 3.06.112

FALSE 313 FR 0.0353 REL FR 275 V 38 P
thy false uncle — | dost thou attend me? TMP 1.02. 77
in my false brother | awak'd an evil nature, and 1.02. 92
sweet lord, you play me false. 5.01.172
concerns | unless it have a false interpreter. TGV 1.02. 75
her true perfection, or my false transgression, 2.04.197
without false vantage, or base treachery. 4.01. 29
already have i been false to valentine, | and 4.02. 1
he plays false, father. 4.02. 59 P
but yet so false that he grieves my very 4.02. 61 P
thou subtile, perjur'd, false, disloyal man, 4.02. 95
'twere false, if i should speak it; 4.02.106
to worship shadows and adore false shapes, 4.02.130
unless i prove false traitor to myself. 4.04.105
though his false finger have profan'd the ring, 4.04.136
rather than have false proteus rescue me. 5.04. 35
cannot be) | i do detest false perjur'd proteus. 5.04. 39
a liar as i do despise one that is false, or as WIV 1.01. 69 P
no, it is false, if it is a pick–purse. 1.01.160 P
see the hell of having a false woman! 2.02.292 P
and tie the wiser souls | to thy false seeming! MM 2.04. 15
metal in restrained means | to make a false one. 2.04. 49
are, | and credulous to false prints. 2.04.130
my false o'erweighs your true. 2.04.170
disguised | pay with falsehood false exacting, 3.02.281
millions of false eyes | are stuck upon thee. 4.01. 59
run with these false and most contrarious 4.01. 61
it seems hid, | and hide the false seems true. 5.01. 67
mouth, what he doth know | is true and false; 5.01.156
'tis false. 5.01.290
and from my false hand cut the wedding–ring, ERR 2.02.137
for if we two be one, and thou play false, | i 2.02.142
muffle your false love with some show of 3.02. 8
villain, thou speak'st false in both. 4.04.100
dissembling harlot, thou art false in all, | and 4.04.101
with these nails i'll pluck out these false eyes 4.04.104
and that is false thou dost report to us. 5.01.179
soul | as this is false he burthens me withal! 5.01.209
and this is false you burthen me withal. 5.01.269
once before he won it of me with false dice, ADO 2.01.280 P
be sworn, if he be so, his conceit is false. 2.01.298 P
of the false sweet bait that we lay for it. 3.01. 33
not a false gallop. 3.04. 94 P
but if all aim but this be levell'd false, | the 4.01.237
that you are little better than false knaves, 4.02. 21 P
say to you, it is thought you are false knaves. 4.02. 28 P
in a false quarrel there is no true valor. 5.01.120 P
marry, sir, they have committed false report; 5.01.215 P
dead upon mine and my master's false accusation; 5.01.242 P
persuade my heart to this false perjury? LLL 4.03. 60
hair | should ravish doters with a false aspect: 4.03.256
o, i smell false latin, "dunghill" for unguem. 5.01. 79 P
false, we have given thee faces. 5.02.622 P
we to ourselves prove false, | by being once 5.02.772
by being once false for ever to be true | to 5.02.773
when the false troyan under sail was seen, | by MND 1.01.174
true love turn'd, and not a false turn'd true. 3.02. 91
all three | to fashion this false sport, in 3.02.194
to prove him false that says i love thee not. 3.02.253
my lady his mother play'd false with a smith. MV 1.02. 44 P
whose hearts are all as false | as stairs of 3.02. 83
even so void is your false heart of truth. 5.01.189
this is the very false gallop of verses; AYL 3.02.113 P
they are both the confirmer of false reckonings. 3.04. 32 P
an instrument, and play false strains upon thee? 4.03. 68 P
go get thee gone, thou false deluding slave, SHR 4.03. 31
fly with false aim, move the still–peering air AWW 3.02.110
the story then goes false, you threw it him 5.03.229
a false conclusion. TN 2.03. 6 P
and words are grown so false, i am loath to 3.01. 24 P
where being apprehended, his false cunning 5.01. 86
but were they false | as o'er–dy'd blacks, as WT 1.02.131
false | as dice are to be wish'd by one that 1.02.132
that false villain | whom i employ'd was 2.01. 48
ay, every dram of woman's flesh is false, | if 2.01.138
they shall not see | to bring false generations. 2.01.148
innocence shall make | false accusation blush, 3.02. 31
i am false of heart that way, and that he knew, 4.03.108 P
fear, my doricles, | you woo'd me the false way. 4.04.151
how if it be false, son? 5.02.161 P
if it be ne'er so false, a true gentleman may 5.02.162 P
and if she did play false, the fault was hers, JN 1.01.118
false blood to false blood join'd! 3.01. 2

false blood to false blood join'd! 3.01. 2
as true as i believe you think them false | that 3.01. 27
i'll fill these dogged spies with false reports; 4.01.128
i idly heard — if true or false i know not. 4.02.124
whose tongue soe'er speaks false, | not truly 4.03. 91
why should i then be false, since it is true 5.04. 28
like a false traitor and injurious villain; R2 1.01. 91
fetch from false mowbray their first head and 1.01. 97
through the false passage of thy throat thou 1.01.125
on pain to be found false and recreant, | to 1.03.106
on pain to be found false and recreant, | both 1.03.111
or if it be, 'tis with false sorrow's eye, 2.02. 26
life, | which false hope lingers in extremity. 2.02. 72
thy knee, | whose duty is deceivable and false. 2.03. 84
and will maintain what thou hast said is false 4.01. 27
as false, by heaven, as heaven itself is true. 4.01. 64
his prayers are full of false hypocrisy, | ours 5.03.107
thou judgest false already. 1H4 1.02. 66 P
(for recreation sake) prove a false thief, for 1.02.155 P
rather let me have it as you are a false thief. 2.01. 93 P
'sblood, my lord, they are false. 2.04.443 P
stuffing the ears of men with false reports. 2H4 in 8
tongues | they bring smooth comforts false, in 40
of wrenching the true cause the false way. 2.01.111 P
that great northumberland, then false to him, 3.01. 89
as a false favorite doth his prince's name, | in 4.02. 25
now fie upon my false french! H5 5.02.220 P
no prophet will i trust, if she prove false. 1H6 1.02.150
of /aire, | nor any of his false confederates. 2.02. 21
i see report is fabulous and false. 2.03. 18
unless my study and my books be false, | the 2.04. 56
where false plantagenet dare not be seen. 2.04. 74
should be found such false dissembling guile? 4.01. 63
you, his false hopes, the trust of england's 4.04. 20
as for your spiteful false objections, | prove 2H6 1.03.155
false fiend, avoid! 1.04. 40
york and impious beauford, that false priest, 2.04. 53
back, | by false accuse doth level at my life. 3.01.160
i shall not want false witness to condemn me, 3.01.168
false allegations to o'erthrow his state? 3.01.181
beshrew the winners, for they play'd me false! 3.01.184
ah, that my fear were false, ah, that it were! 3.01.193
e'er i prov'd thee false or fear'd thy faith. 3.01.205
but now return we to the false duke humphrey. 3.01.322
or thou not false like him? 3.02.119
if my suspect be false, forgive me, god, | for 3.02.139
dares not warwick, if false suffolk dare him? 3.02.203
i would, false murd'rous coward, on thy knee 3.02.220
from such fell serpents as false suffolk is; 3.02.266
the false revolting normans thorough thee 4.01. 87
that's false. 4.02.140
they call false caterpillars, and intend their 4.04. 37
false king, why hast thou broken faith with me, 5.01. 91
back'd by the power of warwick, that false peer, 3H6 1.01. 52
fell clifford, and thee, false frenchwoman. 1.04.149
by that false woman as this king by thee. 2.02.149
thy sly conveyance and thy lord's false love, 3.03.160
and tell false edward, thy supposed king, | that 3.03.223
cross the seas and bid false edward battle; 3.03.235
"go tell false edward, the supposed king, | that 4.01. 93
be as true and just | as i am subtle, false, and R3 1.01. 37
i fear me both are false. 1.02.194
the envious slanders of her false accusers; 1.03. 26
can this dark monarchy afford false clarence?" 1.04. 51
"clarence is come — false, fleeting, perjur'd 1.04. 55
for false forswearing and for murther too. 1.04.202
here | by false intelligence or wrong surmise 2.01. 55
and i for comfort have but one false glass, 2.02. 53
keep you from them, and from such false friends! 3.01. 15
god keep me from false friends! 3.01. 16
to warn false traitors from the like attempts. 3.05. 49
slander myself as false to edward's bed, | throw 4.04.208
i never was nor never will be false. 4.04.493
false to his children and his wive's allies; 5.01. 15
by the false faith of him whom most i trusted; 5.01. 17
my surveyor is false; H8 1.01.222
nought be trusted | for speaking false in that. 2.04.137
woe upon ye | and all such false professors! 3.01.115
ever casts | such doubts, as false coin, from it 3.01.171
lay upon my credit, | i answer is most false. 3.02.266
if i be false, or swerve a hair from truth, TRO 3.02.184
from false to false, among false maids in love, 3.02.190
from false to false, among false maids in love, 3.02.190
from false to false, among false maids in love, 3.02.190
when th' have said as false | as air, as water, 3.02.191
the heart of falsehood, | "as false as cressid." 3.02.196
if ever you prove false one to another, since i 3.02.199 P
men be troiluses, all false women cressids, and 3.02.203 P
for every false drop in her bawdy veins, | a 4.01. 70
you'll be so true to him, to be false to him. 4.02. 56 P
he lov'd me — o false wench! 5.02. 70
o false cressid! 5.02.178
false, false, false! 5.02.178
false, false, false! 5.02.178
false, false, false! 5.02.178
turn thy false face, thou traitor, | and pay thy 5.06. 6
would you have me | false to my nature? COR 3.02. 15
gave me his clothes made a false report of him. 4.05.151 P
"boy," false hound! 5.06.112
if thou swear'st, | thou mayest prove false. ROM 2.02. 92
affection makes him false, he speaks not true. 3.01.177
methinks false hearts should never have sound TIM 1.02.234
when your false masters eat of my lord's meat? 3.04. 50
slink all away, leave their false vows with him, 4.02. 11
that he may never more false title plead, | nor 4.03.154
i am sick of this false world, and will love 4.03.375
you should have fear'd false times when you did 4.03.513
and may diseases lick up their false bloods! 4.03.532
and each false | be as a cantherizing to the 5.01.132
cannot, is false; JC 2.02. 63
the strings, my lord, are false. 4.03.291
wouldst not play false, | and yet wouldst MAC 1.05. 21
false face must hide what the false heart doth 1.07. 82
face must hide what the false heart doth know. 1.07. 82
but | a dagger of the mind, a false creation, 2.01. 38
is an office | which the false man does easy. 2.03.137
luxurious, avaricious, false, deceitful, 4.03. 58
my first false speaking | was this upon myself. 4.03.130
then fly, false thanes, | and mingle with the 5.03. 7
if thou speak'st false, | upon the next tree 5.05. 37
day, | thou canst not then be false to any man. HAM 1.03. 80
makes marriage vows | as false as dicers' oaths, 3.04. 45
how cheerfully on the false trail they cry! 4.05.110
o, this is counter, you false danish dogs! 4.05.111
it is the false steward, that stole his master's 4.05.173 P
false of heart, light of ear, bloody of hand; LR 3.04. 92 P
true or false, it hath made thee earl of 3.05. 17 P
and false. 3.07. 49
could else out-frown false fortune's frown. 5.03. 6
false to thy gods, thy brother, and thy father, 5.03.135
'tis a pageant | to keep us in false gaze. OTH 1.03. 19
to be suspected — fram'd to make women false. 1.03.398
reputation is an idle and most false imposition; 2.03.268 P
for such things in a false disloyal knave | are 3.03.121
why, say they are vild and false, | as where's 3.03.136
if she be false, /o, /then heaven /mocks itself! 3.03.278
ha, ha, false to me? 3.03.333
heaven truly knows that thou art false as hell. 4.02. 39
to whom, my lord? with whom? how am i false? 4.02. 40
"i call'd my love false love; 4.03. 55
she was false as water. 5.02.134
art rash as fire to say | that she was false. 5.02.135
that she was false to wedlock? 5.02.142
my husband say she was false? 5.02.152
he says thou toldst him that his wife was false. 5.02.173
but did you ever tell him she was false? 5.02.178
she false with cassio? 5.02.182
throned gods), | who have been false to fulvia? ANT 1.03. 29
o most false love! 1.03. 62
where have you this? 'tis false. 2.01. 18
false, false; 4.04. 7
false, false; 4.04. 7
o this false soul of egypt! 4.12. 25
that the false huswife fortune break her wheel, 4.15. 44
she is fool'd | with a most false effect; CYM 1.05. 43
and i the truer, | so to be false with her. 1.05. 44
a father cruel, and a step-dame false, | a 1.06. 1
to try your taking of a false report, which hath 1.06.173
and makes | diana's rangers false themselves, 2.03. 69
look thorough a casement to allure false hearts, 2.04. 34
allure false hearts, | and be false with them. 2.04. 35
o, above measure false! 2.04.113
what false italian | (as poisonous tongu'd as 3.02. 4
whose false oaths prevail'd | before my perfect 3.03. 66
false to his bed? 3.04. 40
what is it to be false? 3.04. 40
that's false to 's bed? 3.04. 44
i false? 3.04. 46
true honest men being heard, like false aeneas, 3.04. 58
false aeneas, | were in his time thought false; 3.04. 59
goodly and gallant shall be false and perjur'd 3.04. 63
thus may poor fools | believe false teachers. 3.04. 85
therein false strook, can take no greater wound, 3.04.114
grant, heavens, that which i fear | prove false! 3.05. 53
for true to thee | were to prove false, which i 3.05.158
my dear lord, | thou art one o' th' false ones. 3.06. 15
be companion with them, | since leonatus' false. 3.06. 88
dream often so, | and never false. 4.02.353
wherein i am false, i am honest; 4.03. 42
and my false spirits | quail to remember — give 5.05.148
if it be true that i interpret false, | then PER 1.01.124
and a fellow | false as thy title to her. TNK 2.02.172
in manners this was false position. 3.05. 51
can that be, when | venus i have said is false? 5.04. 45
i was false, | yet never treacherous. 5.04. 92
gives false alarms, suggesteth mutiny, | and in VEN 651
sometime true news, sometime false doth bring, 658
and will not let a false sound enter there, 780
age, but thy false dart | mistakes that aim and 941
thy coward heart with false bethinking grieves." 1024
"it shall be fickle, false, and full of fraud, 1141
borne by the trustless wings of false desire, LUC 2
o rash false heat, wrapp'd in repentant cold, 48
when at collatium this false lord arrived, 50
him go, | rather than triumph in so false a foe. 77
devil, | little suspecteth the false worshipper: 86
eyes forgo their light, my false heart bleed? 228
divine, | unto a view so false will not incline, 292
his true respect will prison false desire, | and 642
thou ravisher, thou traitor, thou false thief, 888
eater of youth, false slave to false delight, 927
eater of youth, false slave to false delight, 927
to hide the truth of this false night's abuses. 1075
and for my sake serve thou false tarquin so. 1197
nor ashy pale the fear that false hearts have. 1512
false creeping craft and perjury should thrust 1517
so priam's trust false sinon's tears doth 1560
look'd black, and that false tarquin stain'd. 1743
unskillful in the world's false forgeries. PP 1. 4
persuade my heart to this false perjury? 3. 3
shifting change, as is false women's fashion; SON 20. 4
more bright than theirs, less false in rolling, 20. 5
thee, | thine, by thy beauty being false to me. 41.14
why should false painting imitate his cheek, 67. 5
to show false art what beauty was of yore. 68.14
o, lest your true love may seem false in this, 72. 9
thou mayst be false, and yet i know it not. 92.14
in many's looks the false heart's history | is 93. 7
o, never say that i was of false heart, | though 109. 1
for why should others' false adulterate eyes 121. 5
fairing the foul with art's false borrow'd face, 127. 6
lack, | sland'ring creation with a false esteem: 127.12
as rare | as any she belied with false compare. 130.14
and to be sure that is not false i swear, | a 131. 9
erred, | and to this false plague are they now 137.14
unlearned in the world's false subtilties. 138. 4
and seal'd false bonds of love as oft as mine, 142. 7
if that be fair whereon my false eyes dote, 148. 5
cried, "o false blood, thou register of lies, LC 52
which remain'd the foil | of this false jewel, 154
o, that false fire which in his cheek so glowed, 324

FALSE-BODING 1 FR 0.0001 REL FR 1 V 0 P
false-boding woman, end thy frantic curse, R3 1.03.246

FALSE-DERIVED 1 FR 0.0001 REL FR 1 V 0 P
that every slight and false-derived cause, | yea 2H4 4.01.188

FALSE-FAC'D 1 FR 0.0001 REL FR 1 V 0 P
cities be | made all of false-fac'd soothing! COR 1.09. 44

FALSE-HEART 1 FR 0.0001 REL FR 1 V 0 P
i am thy king, and thou a false-heart traitor. 2H6 5.01.143

FALSE-HEARTED 1 FR 0.0001 REL FR 0 V 1 P
that same diomed's a false-hearted rogue, a most TRO 5.01. 88 P

FALSEHOOD 38 FR 0.0043 REL FR 35 V 3 P
did beget of him | a falsehood in its contrary, TMP 1.02. 95
way is to slander valentine | with falsehood, TGV 3.02. 32
she twits me with my falsehood to my friend; 4.02. 8
but since your falsehood shall become you well 4.02.129
disguised | pay with falsehood false exacting, MM 3.02.281
by falsehood and corruption doth it shame. ERR 2.01.113
(which is a great argument of falsehood) if i LLL 1.02.170 P
and even that falsehood, in itself a sin, | thus 5.02.775
o, what a goodly outside falsehood hath! MV 1.03.102
being counted falsehood, shall (as i express it) WT 3.02. 27
this is mere falsehood. 3.02.141
yea, faith itself to hollow falsehood change! JN 3.01. 95
and falsehood falsehood cures, as fire cools 3.01.277
and falsehood falsehood cures, as fire cools 3.01.277
and i will turn thy falsehood to thy heart, R2 4.01. 39
nicholas as truly as a man of falsehood may. 1H4 2.01. 65 P
whiles thy consuming canker eats his falsehood. 1H6 2.04. 71
by treason, falsehood, and by treachery, | our 5.04.109
right, | now buckler falsehood with a pedigree? 3H6 3.03. 99
either betray'd by falsehood of his guard | or 4.04. 8
kings | confound your hidden falsehood and award R3 2.01. 14
how may he wound, | and worthily, my falsehood! H8 2.04. 97
false maids in love, | upbraid my falsehood! TRO 3.02.191
let them say, to stick the heart of falsehood, 3.02.195
make cressid's name the very crown of falsehood, 4.02.100
religion of mine eye | maintains such falsehood, ROM 1.02. 89
if you suspect my husbandry or falsehood, | call TIM 2.02.155
your bait of falsehood take this carp of truth, HAM 2.01. 60
excellent falsehood! ANT 1.01. 40
with hands | made hard with hourly falsehood CYM 1.06.107
made hard with hourly falsehood (falsehood, as 1.06.107
and falsehood | is worse in kings than beggars. 3.06. 13
torture shall | winnow the truth from falsehood. 5.05.134
but his falsehood! TNK 2.02.228
it is a falsehood she is in, which is with 4.03. 93 P
to unmask falsehood and bring truth to light, LUC 940
it might unused stay | from hands of falsehood, SON 48. 4
why of eyes' falsehood hast thou forged hooks, 137. 7

FALSEHOODS 1 FR 0.0001 REL FR 0 V 1 P
is in, which is with falsehoods to be combated. TNK 4.03. 94 P

FALSELY 18 FR 0.0020 REL FR 13 V 5 P
ay, or very falsely pocket up his report. TMP 2.01. 68 P
as easy | falsely to take away a life true made MM 2.04. 47
prov'd my lady hero hath been falsely accus'd, ADO 5.02. 97 P
doth falsely blind the eyesight of his look. LLL 1.01. 76
that be true love, which is falsely attempted? 1.02.171 P
thou speak'st it falsely, as i love mine honor, AWW 5.03.113
haste | had falsely thrust upon contrary feet, JN 4.02.198
by all my hopes, most falsely doth he lie. R2 1.01. 68
and i thine, most truly falsely, must needs be H5 5.02.191 P
my witness, i am falsely accus'd by the villain. 2H6 1.03.189 P
falsely to draw me in these vile suspects. R3 1.03. 88
of england's chair, where he is falsely set; 5.03.251
laid falsely | i' th' plain way of his merit. COR 3.01. 60
and impotence | was falsely borne in hand, sends HAM 2.02. 67
the witness, | and he's indicted falsely. OTH 3.04.154
o, falsely, falsely murder'd! 5.02.117
o, falsely, falsely murder'd! 5.02.117
that censures falsely what they see aright? SON 148. 4

FALSENESS 3 FR 0.0003 REL FR 3 V 0 P
would of that seed grow to a greater falseness, 2H4 3.01. 90
falseness cannot come from thee, for thou PER 5.01.120
did livery falseness in a pride of truth. LC 105

FALSE-PLAY'D 1 FR 0.0001 REL FR 1 V 0 P
and false-play'd my glory | unto an enemy's ANT 4.14. 19

FALSER 4 FR 0.0004 REL FR 4 V 0 P
me, | for i am falser than vows made in wine. AYL 3.05. 73
and that i dare not, falser: JC 2.02. 63
trod thy ground, | a falser nev'r seem'd friend. TNK 3.06.142
none fairer, nor none falser to deface her. PP 7. 6

FALSE-SELF 1 FR 0.0001 REL FR 1 V 0 P
now | thy false-self and thy friend had but this TNK 2.02.207

FALSE-SPEAKING 2 FR 0.0002 REL FR 2 V 0 P
i smiling credit her false-speaking tongue, PP 1. 7
simply i credit her false-speaking tongue; SON 138. 7

FALSEST 1 FR 0.0001 REL FR 1 V 0 P
falsest cousin | that ever blood made kin! TNK 3.01. 37

FALSIFY 1 FR 0.0001 REL FR 1 V 0 P
i am, | by so much shall i falsify men's hopes, 1H4 1.02.211

FALSING 1 FR 0.0001 REL FR 0 V 1 P
nay, not sure, in a thing falsing. ERR 2.02. 94 P

FALSTAFF 71 FR 0.0080 REL FR 17 V 54 P
if sir john falstaff have committed WIV 1.01. 31 P
is falstaff there? 1.01. 67 P
is sir john falstaff here? 1.01. 98 P
falstaff will learn the /humor of the age, 1.03. 83
and i to /ford shall eke unfold | how falstaff, 1.03. 97
his might | for thee to fight, | john falstaff." 2.01. 19 P
my name is nym, and falstaff loves your wife. 2.01.134 P
i will seek out falstaff. 2.01.140 P
into't, and i have a disguise to sound falstaff. 2.01.238 P
detect my wife, be reveng'd on falstaff, and 2.02.311 P
sir john falstaff. 3.02. 22 P
sir john falstaff! 3.02. 23 P
bids me search — there i shall find falstaff. 3.02. 46 P
as the earth is firm that falstaff is there. 3.02. 48 P
i will to my honest knight falstaff, and drink 3.02. 88 P
what, sir john falstaff! 3.03.139 P
and we will yet have more tricks with falstaff. 3.03.191 P
another errand to sir john falstaff from my two 3.04.110 P
that falstaff at that oak shall meet with us, 4.04. 42
as falstaff, she, and i are newly met, | let 4.04. 53
go, send to falstaff straight. 4.04. 75
speak with sir john falstaff from master slender 4.05. 5 P
fat falstaff | hath a great scene; 4.06. 16
at the abuse of falstaff as he will chafe at the 5.03. 8 P
sir john falstaff, serve got, and leave your 5.05.129 P
falstaff, /bardolph, /peto, and gadshill shall 1H4 1.02.162 P
falstaff sweats to death, | and lards the lean 2.02.108
tell me flatly i am no proud jack like falstaff, 2.04. 12 P

to drive away the time till falstaff come, i 2.04. 29 P
falstaff and the rest of the thieves are at the 2.04. 87 P
i prithee call in falstaff. 2.04.109 P
and, falstaff, you carried your guts away as 2.04.258 P
and now i remember me, his name is falstaff. 2.04.426 P
i speak it, there is virtue in that falstaff; 2.04.430 P
abominable misleader of youth, falstaff, that 2.04.463 P
but for sweet jack falstaff, kind jack falstaff, 2.04.475 P
but for sweet jack falstaff, kind jack falstaff, 2.04.476 P
kind jack falstaff, true jack falstaff, valiant 2.04.476 P
true jack falstaff, valiant jack falstaff, and 2.04.476 P
as he is, old jack falstaff, banish not him thy 2.04.478 P
have much to say in the behalf of that falstaff. 2.04.485 P
falstaff! 2.04.528 P
what should poor jack falstaff do in the days of 3.03.166 P
but if i be not jack falstaff, then am i a jack. 5.04.139 P
falstaff, and't please your lordship. 2H4 1.02. 59 P
sir john falstaff! 1.02. 65 P
sir john falstaff, a word with you. 1.02. 92 P
snare, we must arrest sir john falstaff. 2.01. 8 P
as far in the devil's book as thou and falstaff, 2.02. 46 P
been so lewd and so much engraff'd to falstaff. 2.02. 63 P
and the boy that i gave falstaff. 2.02. 70 P
"john falstaff, knight" — every man must know 2.02.109 P
"sir john falstaff, knight, to the son of the 2.02.119 P
usest him, jack falstaff with my /familiars, 2.02.132 P
how might we see falstaff bestow himself 2.02.169 P
and asking every one for sir john falstaff. 2.04.360
falstaff, good night. 2.04.366
then was jack falstaff, now sir john, a boy, and 3.02. 25 P
my captain, sir john falstaff, a tall gentleman, 3.02. 61 P
are not you sir john falstaff? 4.03. 10 P
i think you are sir john falstaff, and in that 4.03. 16 P
now, falstaff, where have you been all this 4.03. 26
fare you well, falstaff. 4.03. 84
well, you must now speak sir john falstaff fair, 5.02. 33
go carry sir john falstaff to the fleet. 5.05. 91
any thing i know) falstaff shall die of a sweat, ep 30 P
for falstaff he is dead, | and we must ern H5 2.03. 5
sir john falstaff. 4.07. 51 P
if sir john falstaff had not play'd the coward. 1H6 1.01.131
but o, the treacherous falstaff wounds my heart, 1.04. 35
whither away, sir john falstaff, in such haste? 3.02.104

FALSTAFF'S 9 FR 0.0010 REL FR 0 V 9 P
rightly) is, "i am sir john falstaff's." WIV 1.03. 48 P
going to my wife, and falstaff's boy with her. 3.02. 36 P
and falstaff's boy with her! 3.02. 38 P
some special suspicion of falstaff's being here, 3.03.188 P
the very instant of falstaff's and our meeting, 5.03. 15 P
master /brook, falstaff's a knave, a cuckoldly 5.05.110 P
i have remov'd falstaff's horse, and he frets 1H4 2.02. 2 P
in earnest, how came falstaff's sword so hack'd? 2.04.304 P
here come two of sir john falstaff's men, as i 2H4 3.02. 53 P

FALSTAFFS 1 FR 0.0001 REL FR 0 V 1 P
if he were twenty sir john falstaffs, he shall WIV 1.01. 3 P

FALTER 1 FR 0.0001 REL FR 1 V 0 P
king | shall falter under foul rebellion's arms. R2 3.02. 26

FALT'RING 1 FR 0.0001 REL FR 1 V 0 P
and leave the falt'ring feeble souls alive? LUC 1768

FAM'D 11 FR 0.0012 REL FR 10 V 1 P
he was much fam'd. AWW 1.02. 71
from his most fam'd of famous ancestors, H5 2.04. 92
buried in your dunghills, | they shall be fam'd; 4.03.100
as bold in war | as he is fam'd for mildness, 3H6 2.01.156
your grace hath still been fam'd for virtuous, 4.06. 26
fam'd be thy tutor, and thy parts of nature TRO 2.03.242
and thy parts of nature | thrice fam'd beyond, 2.03.243
but it was fam'd with more than with one man? JC 1.02.153
for joy whereof | the fam'd cassibelan, who was CYM 3.01. 30
blasts my bays and my fam'd works makes lighter TNK pr 20
they are fam'd to be a pair of absolute men. 2.01. 26 P

/FAME 1 FR 0.0001 REL FR 1 V 0 P
that's their /fame in peace. TRO 1.03.236

FAME 85 FR 0.0096 REL FR 79 V 6 P
shame hath a bastard fame, well managed; ERR 3.02. 19
my lord, i have play'd the part of lady fame. ADO 2.01.214 P
her wrongs, | gives her fame which never dies. 5.03. 6
with shame | lives in death with glorious fame." 5.03. 8
let fame, that all hunt after in their lives, LLL 1.01. 1
too much to know is to know nought but fame; 1.01. 92
ignorant, all–telling fame | doth noise abroad, 2.01. 21
confounds thy fame, as whirlwinds shake fair SHR 5.02.140
that you seek, | that fame may cry you loud. AWW 2.01. 17
letters sent me | that sets him high in fame. 5.03. 31
with the memorials and the things of fame | that TN 3.03. 23
tongue of loss | cried fame and honor on him. 5.01. 59
i am in good name and fame with the very best. 2H4 2.04. 75 P
i in the clear sky of fame o'ershine you as much 4.03. 51 P
thee guard and keep, most royal imp of fame! 5.05. 42
to fill king edward's fame with prisoner kings, H5 1.02.162
in bloody field, | doth win immortal fame." 3.02. 11
i would give all my fame for a pot of ale and 3.02. 13 P
heart of gold, | a lad of life, an imp of fame, 4.01. 45
coward of france, how much he wrongs his fame, 1H6 2.01. 16
i find thou art no less than fame hath bruited, 2.03. 68
or else reproach be talbot's greatest fame! 3.02. 76
his fame lives in the world, his shame in you. 4.04. 46
death's revenge, thy youth, and england's fame: 4.06. 39
to save a paltry life and slay bright fame, 4.06. 45
fatal this marriage, cancelling your fame, 2H6 1.01. 99
in cruelty will i seek out my fame. 5.02. 60
where fame, late ent'ring at his heedful ears, 3H6 3.03. 63
that's not my fear, my meed hath got me fame: 4.08. 38
there's nothing differs but the outward fame. R3 1.04. 83
i say, without characters fame lives long. 3.01. 81
for now he lives in fame though not in life. 3.01. 88
having heard by fame | of this so noble and so H8 1.04. 66
star–like rise as great in fame as she was, 5.04. 46
host, | having his ear full of his airy fame, TRO 1.03.144
that breath fame blows, that praise, sole pure, 1.03.244
foes, | and fame in time to come canonize us, 2.02.202
when fame shall in our islands sound her trump, 3.03.210
is at stake, | my fame is shrowdly gor'd. 3.03.228
on whose bright crest fame with her loud'st oyes 4.05.143
fall greeks, fail fame, honor or go or stay, 5.01. 43
fame, at the which he aims, | in whom already COR 1.01.263
him seek danger where he was like to find fame. 1.03. 13 P
a serpent i abhor | more than thy fame and envy. 1.08. 4
hath won, | with fame, a name to martius caius; 2.01.164
whence men have read | his fame unparallel'd, 5.02. 16
holp to reap the fame | which he did end all his 5.06. 35
the man is noble and his fame folds in | this 5.06.124
my noble lord and father, live in fame! TIT 1.01.158
you that survive, and you that sleep in fame! 1.01.173
soldiers and rome's servitors | repose in fame; 1.01.353
he lives in fame, that died in virtue's cause. 1.01.390
the emperor's court is like the house of fame, 2.01.126
that for a fantasy and trick of fame | go to HAM 4.04. 61
and set a double varnish on the fame | the 4.07.132
maid | that paragons description and wild fame; OTH 2.01. 62
that he you hurt is of great fame in cyprus, 3.01. 45
so is the fame. ANT 2.02.163
fine egyptian cookery | shall have the fame. 2.06. 64
acquire too high a fame when him we serve's away 3.01. 15
hours, | unregist'red in vulgar fame, you have 3.13.119
i' th' name of fame and honor which dies i' th' CYM 3.03. 51
tyre, | fame answering the most strange inquire, PER 3.ch. 22
our wonder, and sets up | your fame for ever. 3.02. 97
wife, when fame | had spread his cursed deed, 5.03. 95
remember that your fame | knolls in the ear o' TNK 1.01.133
by my troth, i think fame but stammers 'em, they 2.01. 27 P
whose doughty dismal fame | from dis to daedalus 3.05.114
eyes, and as noble | as ever fame yet spoke of. 3.06.277
fame and honor, | methinks, from hence, as from 4.02. 21
their fame has fir'd me so — till they appear. 4.02.153
that kings might be espoused to more fame, | but LUC 20
which of them both should underprop her fame. 53
he stories to her ears her husband's fame, | won 106
i give | a badge of fame to slander's livery, 1054
so of shame's ashes shall my fame be bred, | for 1188
my shame be his that did my fame confound; 1202
and all my fame that lives disbursed be | to 1203
troy had been bright with fame, and not with 1491
act will be | my fame and thy perpetual infamy.' 1638
to make me tongue–tied, speaking of your fame. SON 80. 4
and such a counterpart shall fame his wit, 84.11
give my love fame faster than time wastes life, 100.13
she that her fame so to herself contrives, | the LC 243
of wealth, of filial fear, law, kindred, fame! 270

FAME'S 2 FR 0.0002 REL FR 2 V 0 P
when, for fame's sake, for praise, an outward LLL 4.01. 32
and fame's eternal date, for virtue's praise! TIT 1.01.168

FAMILIAR 38 FR 0.0043 REL FR 24 V 14 P
it is a familiar beast to man, and signifies WIV 1.01. 20 P
i can construe the action of her familiar style, 1.03. 46 P
though 'tis my familiar sin | with maids to seem MM 1.04. 31
mean time let wonder seem familiar, | and to the ADO 5.04. 70
by a familiar demonstration of the working, my LLL 1.02. 9 P
love is a familiar; 1.02.172 P
the king is a noble gentleman, and my familiar, 5.01. 96 P
to make modern and familiar things supernatural AWW 2.03. 2 P
quenching my familiar smile with an austere TN 2.05. 66 P
hearts | with humble and familiar courtesy, R2 1.04. 26
this wen to be as familiar with me as my dog, 2H4 2.02.106 P
be not too familiar with poins, for he misuses 2.02.127 P
be | as things acquainted and familiar to us, 5.02.139
of it he will unloose, | familiar as his garter; H5 1.01. 47
strain | that haunted us in our familiar paths. 2.04. 52
would have me as familiar with men's pockets as 3.02. 47 P
and for the world, familiar to us and unknown, 3.07. 37 P
familiar in his mouth as household words, 4.03. 52
i think her old familiar is asleep. 1H6 3.02.122
now, ye familiar spirits, that are cull'd | out 5.03. 10
with him, he has a familiar under his tongue, he 2H6 4.07.108 P
made tame and most familiar to my nature; TRO 3.03. 10
it is familiar — but at the author's drift, 3.03.113
yea, so familiar? 5.02. 8
that we have been familiar, | ingrate COR 5.02. 85
too familiar | is my dear son with such sour ROM 3.03. 6
so in use, | and dreadful objects so familiar, JC 3.01.266
enough, | but not with such familiar instances, 4.02. 16
direness, familiar to my slaughterous thoughts, MAC 5.05. 14
be thou familiar, but by no means vulgar: HAM 1.03. 61
dear my lord, | be not familiar with her. LR 5.01. 16
/ear | that he is too familiar with his wife. OTH 1.03.396
good wine is a good familiar creature, if it be 2.03.309 P
be familiar with | my playfellow, your hand, ANT 3.13.124
we are familiar at first. CYM 1.04.101 P
his favor is familiar to me. 5.05. 93
made familiar | to me and to my aid the blest PER 3.02. 34
nor that affable familiar ghost | which nightly SON 86. 9

FAMILIARITY 4 FR 0.0004 REL FR 1 V 3 P
i hope, upon familiarity will grow more content. WIV 1.01.249 P
you, when i have held familiarity with fresher AWW 5.02. 3 P
added to their familiarity | (which was as gross WT 2.01.175
me to be no more so familiarity with such poor 2H4 2.01.100 P

FAMILIARLY 4 FR 0.0004 REL FR 3 V 1 P
because that i familiarly sometimes | do use you ERR 2.02. 26
talks as familiarly of roaring lions | as maids JN 2.01.459
and talks as familiarly of john a' gaunt as if 2H4 3.02.320 P
familiarly shall call thy dorset brother; R3 4.04.316

/FAMILIARS 1 FR 0.0001 REL FR 0 V 1 P
jack falstaff with my /familiars, john with my 2H4 2.02.133 P

FAMILIARS 1 FR 0.0001 REL FR 1 V 0 P
so his familiars to his buried fortunes | slink TIM 4.02. 10

FAMILIES 1 FR 0.0001 REL FR 1 V 0 P
we are, in one another, families: TNK 2.02. 82

FAMILY 6 FR 0.0006 REL FR 6 V 0 P
come they of noble family? H5 2.02.129
parliament | let us assail the family of york. 3H6 1.01. 65
to advance | thy name and honorable family, TIT 1.01.239
the deed | that hath dishonored all our family: 1.01.345
all, | and rase their faction and their family, 1.01.451
signior, is all your family within? OTH 1.01. 84

FAMILY'S 1 FR 0.0001 REL FR 1 V 0 P
and on your family's old monument | hang ADO 4.01.206

FAMINE 12 FR 0.0013 REL FR 8 V 4 P
'a was the very genius of famine, yet lecherous 2H4 3.02.314 P
(leash'd in, like hounds) should famine, sword, H5 pr 7
lean famine, quartering steel, and climbing fire 1H6 4.02. 11
famine and no other hath slain me. 2H6 4.10. 60 P
that never fear'd any, am vanquish'd by famine, 4.10. 75 P
famine is in thy cheeks, | need and oppression ROM 5.01. 69
them lie | till famine and the ague eat them up. MAC 5.05. 4
shall thou hang alive, | till famine cling thee; 5.05. 39
e'en as the o'erflowing nilus presageth famine. ANT 1.02. 50 P
at thy heel | did famine follow, whom thou 1.04. 59
yet famine, | ere clean it o'erthrow nature, CYM 3.06. 19
fuel, | making a famine where abundance lies, SON 1. 7

FAMISH 10 FR 0.0011 REL FR 6 V 4 P
what, did he marry me to famish me? SHR 4.03. 3
that have a sword, and yet am ready to famish! 2H6 4.10. 2 P
or else you famish — that's a threefold death. 3H6 5.04. 32
are all resolv'd rather to die than to famish? COR 1.01. 5 P
suffer us to famish, and their store–houses 1.01. 80 P
whilst their own birds famish in their nests; TIT 2.03.154
set him breast–deep in earth and famish him, 5.03.179
a dog, and thou shalt famish a dog's death. TIM 2.02. 87 P
it, | or can conceal his hunger till he famish? PER 1.04. 12
but rather famish them amid their plenty, VEN 20

FAMISH'D 11 FR 0.0012 REL FR 9 V 2 P
i am famish'd in his service; MV 2.02.106 P
rogue, you filthy famish'd correctioner, if you 2H4 5.04. 20 P
his soldiers sick and famish'd in their march; H5 3.05. 57
otherwhiles the famish'd english, like pale 1H6 1.02. 7
for aught i see, this city must be famish'd, 1.04. 68
on his will | till paris was besieg'd, famish'd, 2H6 1.03.172
kent, | took odds to combat a poor famish'd man. 4.10. 44
these famish'd beggars weary of their lives, R3 5.03.329
and scants us with a single famish'd kiss, TRO 4.04. 47
but let the famish'd flesh slide from the bone TIM 4.03.528
when that mine eye is famish'd for a look, | or SON 47. 3

FAMISHING 1 FR 0.0001 REL FR 1 V 0 P
delay | commends us to a famishing hope. TNK 1.01.167

FAMOUS 32 FR 0.0036 REL FR 29 V 3 P
she | is daughter to this famous duke of milan, TMP 5.01.192
to this town by that most famous warrior, | duke ERR 5.01.368
the one as famous for a scolding tongue, | as is SHR 1.02.252
he was famous, sir, in his profession, and it AWW 1.01. 26 P
this place is famous for the creatures | of prey WT 3.03. 12
by their breed, and famous by their birth, R2 2.01. 52
hand | upon my head and all this famous land. 5.06. 36
a famous rebel art thou, colevile. 2H4 4.03. 63
and a famous true subject took him. 4.03. 64 P
from his most fam'd of famous ancestors, H5 2.04. 92
your grandfather of famous memory, an't please 4.07. 92 P
king henry the fift, too famous to live long! 1H6 1.01. 6
i shall as famous be by this exploit | as 2.03. 5
deriv'd | from famous edmund langley, duke of 2.05. 85
and we will make thee famous through the world. 3.03. 13
so, in the famous ancient city tours, | in 2H6 1.01. 5
hath made the wizard famous in his death. 5.02. 69
saint albons battle won by famous york | shall 5.03. 30
were he as famous and as bold in war | as he is 3H6 2.01.155
thy famous grandfather | doth live again in thee 5.04. 52
that julius caesar was a famous man; R3 3.01. 84
duke | in the seat royal of this famous isle? 3.01.164
famous plantagenet, most gracious prince, | lend 3.07.100
together with all famous colleges | almost in H8 3.02. 66
the other, though unfinish'd, yet so famous, 4.02. 61
desire | my famous cousin to our grecian tents. TRO 4.05.151
let the birds fly, and like the famous ape, | to HAM 3.04.194
word | menecrates and menas, famous pirates, ANT 1.04. 48
the earth shall clip in it | a pair so famous. 5.02.360
thine uncle | (famous in caesar's praises, no CYM 3.01. 6
yon sometimes famous princes, like thyself, PER 1.01. 34
more famous yet 'twixt po and silver trent. TNK pr 12

FAMOUSED 1 FR 0.0001 REL FR 1 V 0 P
the painful warrior famoused for /fight, | after SON 25. 9

FAMOUSLY 2 FR 0.0002 REL FR 1 V 1 P
for then this land was famously enrich'd | with R3 2.03. 19
i say unto you, what he hath done famously, he COR 1.01. 36 P

FAN 16 FR 0.0018 REL FR 13 V 3 P
mistress bridget lost the handle of her fan, i WIV 2.02. 13 P
see him walk before a lady and to bear her fan! LLL 4.01.145
to fan the moonbeams from his sleeping eyes. MND 3.01.173
the air of paradise did fan the house | and AWW 3.02.125
rascal, i could brain him with his lady's fan. 1H4 2.03. 23 P
give me my fan. 2H6 1.03.138
distinction, with a broad and powerful fan, TRO 1.03. 27
even in the fan and wind of your fair sword, 5.03. 41
nodding of their plumes, | fan you into despair! COR 3.03.127
my fan, peter. ROM 2.04.106 P
banners flout the sky | and fan our people cold. MAC 1.02. 50
to fetch her fan, her gloves, her mask, nor OTH 4.02. 9
and is become the bellows and the fan | to cool ANT 1.01. 9
the love i bear him | made me to fan you thus, CYM 1.06.177
fan | from me the witless chaff of such a writer TNK pr 18
to fan and blow them dry again she seeks. VEN 52

FANATICAL 1 FR 0.0001 REL FR 0 V 1 P
i abhor such fanatical phantasimes, such LLL 5.01. 18 P

FANCIES' 1 FR 0.0001 REL FR 1 V 0 P
so soon | is by your fancies' thankful doom. PER 5.02. 20

FANCIES 16 FR 0.0018 REL FR 14 V 2 P
confines call'd to enact | my present fancies. TMP 4.01.122
idle dream | and rack thee in their fancies. MM 4.01. 64
to fit your fancies to your father's will; MND 1.01.118
the humor of forty fancies prick'd in't for a SHR 3.02. 69 P
our fancies are more giddy and unfirm, | more TN 2.04. 33
thy jealousies | (fancies too weak for boys, too WT 3.02.181
sware they were his fancies or his good–nights. 2H4 3.02.318 P
play with your fancies: H5 3.pr. 7
of sorriest fancies your companions making, MAC 3.02. 9
as she is troubled with thick–coming fancies, 5.03. 38
be as your fancies teach you; OTH 3.03. 88
and his spirits should hunt | after new fancies. 3.04. 63
spent | with your fine fancies quaintly /eche: PER 3.ch. 13
are not prophets | when oft our fancies are. TNK 5.03.103
for other ruffians, as their fancies wrought, STM II.C 84
here what tributes wounded fancies sent me, | of LC 197

FANCY 55 FR 0.0062 REL FR 45 V 10 P
and the best comforter | to an unsettled fancy, TMP 5.01. 59
cannot your grace win her to fancy him? TGV 3.01. 67
are either rich or poor | as fancy values them; MM 2.02.151
not angry with me, madam, | speaking my fancy: ADO 3.01. 95
there is no appearance of fancy in him, unless 3.02. 31 P
unless it be a fancy that he hath to strange 3.02. 32 P
unless he have a fancy to this foolery, as it 3.02. 37 P
as it appears he hath, he is no fool for fancy, 3.02. 38 P
this child of fancy, that armado hight, | for LLL 1.01.170
smelling out the odoriferous flowers of fancy, 4.02.125 P
them, | fair helena in fancy following me. MND 4.01.163
tell me where is fancy bred, | or in the heart MV 3.02. 63
and fancy dies | in the cradle where it lies. 3.02. 68

you meet in some fresh cheek the power of fancy, AYL 3.05. 29
chewing the food of sweet and bitter fancy, | lo 4.03.101
mine, | thy faith my fancy to thee doth combine. 5.04.150
even as a flatt'ring dream or worthless fancy. SHR in.1. 44
face | which i could fancy more than any other. 2.01. 12
o then belike you fancy riches more: 2.01. 16
bianca | doth fancy any other but lucentio? 4.02. 2
and my idolatrous fancy | must sanctify his AWW 1.01. 97
for i submit | my fancy to your eyes. 2.03.168
we must every one be a man of his own fancy, not 4.01. 17 P
in fancy's course | are motives of more fancy, 5.03.215
so full of shapes is fancy | that it alone is TN 1.01. 14
that, should she fancy, it should be one of my 2.05. 25 P
let fancy still my sense in lethe steep; 4.01. 62
accusation | than your own weak–hing'd fancy) WT 2.03.119
i am — and by my fancy. 4.04.482
on't, lest your fancy | may think anon it moves. 5.03. 60
tush, that was but his fancy, blame him not. 1H6 4.01.178
yet so my fancy may be satisfied, | and peace 5.03. 91
although we fancy not the cardinal, | yet must 2H6 1.03. 94
make yourself mirth with your particular fancy, H8 2.03.101
madam, such good dreams | possess your fancy. 4.02. 94
that the blest gods, as angry with my fancy, TRO 4.04. 25
never did young man fancy | with so eternal and 5.02.165
my very wishes | and the buildings of my fancy; COR 2.01.200
but not express'd in fancy, rich, not gaudy, HAM 1.03. 71
of infinite jest, of most excellent fancy. 5.01.185 P
in faith, are very dear to fancy, very 5.02.151 P
each buzz, each fancy, each complaint, dislike, LR 1.04.325
may all the building in my fancy pluck | upon my 4.02. 85
venus where we see | the fancy outwork nature. ANT 2.02.201
wants stuff | to vie strange forms with fancy; 5.02. 98
an antony were nature's piece 'gainst fancy, 5.02. 99
the /brake i meant, is gone | after his fancy. TNK 3.02. 2
o, who can find the bent of woman's fancy? 4.02. 33
what a mere child is fancy, | that, having two 4.02. 52
how she continues this fancy! 4.03. 48 P
saw her, and | even then proclaim'd your fancy. 5.04.118
from forth dull sleep by dreadful fancy waking, LUC 450
that eye could see, | her fancy fell a–turning. PP 15. 4
worthy blame, | as well as fancy, partial might. 18. 4
towards this afflicted fancy fastly drew, | and, LC 61
FANCY–FREE 1 FR 0.0001 REL FR 1 V 0 P
passed on, | in maiden meditation, fancy–free. MND 2.01.164
FANCY–MONGER 1 FR 0.0001 REL FR 0 V 1 P
if i could meet that fancy–monger, i would give AYL 3.02.364 P
FANCY'S 8 FR 0.0009 REL FR 8 V 0 P
wishes and tears, poor fancy's followers. MND 1.01.155
together, | more witnesseth than fancy's images, 5.01. 25
let us all ring fancy's knell. MV 3.02. 70
as all impediments in fancy's course | are AWW 5.03.214
seen, | orsino's mistress and his fancy's queen. TN 5.01.388
nor shall not, when my fancy's on my play. H8 5.01. 60
what horrible fancy's this? OTH 4.02. 26
a martial man to be soft fancy's slave! LUC 200
FANCY–SICK 1 FR 0.0001 REL FR 1 V 0 P
all fancy–sick she is and pale of cheer | with MND 3.02. 96
FANE 1 FR 0.0001 REL FR 1 V 0 P
being naked, sick, nor fane nor capitol, | the COR 1.10. 20
FANES 1 FR 0.0001 REL FR 1 V 0 P
are worse | than priests and fanes that lie. CYM 4.02.242
FANG 5 FR 0.0005 REL FR 2 V 3 P
as the icy fang | and churlish chiding of the AYL 2.01. 6
master fang, have you ent'red the action? 2H4 2.01. 1 P
good master fang, hold him sure. 2.01. 25 P
do your offices, master fang and master snare, 2.01. 41 P
destruction fang mankind! TIM 4.03. 23
FANG'D 1 FR 0.0001 REL FR 1 V 0 P
whom i will trust as i will adders fang'd, HAM 3.04.203
FANGLED 1 FR 0.0001 REL FR 1 V 0 P
be not, as is our fangled world, a garment CYM 5.04.134
FANGLESS 1 FR 0.0001 REL FR 1 V 0 P
so that his power, like to a fangless lion, 2H4 4.01.216
FANGS 5 FR 0.0005 REL FR 4 V 1 P
cause, | but, since i am a dog, beware my fangs. MV 3.03. 7
and yet (by the very fangs of malice i swear) i TN 1.05.184 P
the swords of soldiers are his teeth, his fangs, JN 2.01.353
in his anointed flesh /rash boarish fangs. LR 3.07. 58
under whose sharp fangs on his back doth lie VEN 663
FANN'D 2 FR 0.0002 REL FR 2 V 0 P
fann'd with the eastern wind, turns to a crow MND 3.02.142
tooth, or the fann'd snow that's bolted | by th' WT 4.04.364
/FANNING 1 FR 0.0001 REL FR 1 V 0 P
silken streamers the young phoebus /fanning. H5 3.pr. 6
FANNING 2 FR 0.0002 REL FR 1 V 1 P
the sun to ice with fanning in his face with a H5 4.01.200 P
fanning the hairs, who wave like feath'red wings VEN 306
FAN'S 1 FR 0.0001 REL FR 0 V 1 P
to hide her face, for her fan's the fairer face. ROM 2.04.107 P
FANS 2 FR 0.0002 REL FR 2 V 0 P
with scarfs and fans, and double change of SHR 4.03. 57
with divers–color'd fans, whose wind did seem ANT 2.02.203
FANTASIED 1 FR 0.0001 REL FR 1 V 0 P
land, | i find the people strangely fantasied, JN 4.02.144
FANTASIES 4 FR 0.0004 REL FR 4 V 0 P
eyes, | and make her full of hateful fantasies. MND 2.01.258
such shaping fantasies, that apprehend | more 5.01. 5
wounds | with many legions of strange fantasies, JN 5.07. 18
thou hast no figures nor no fantasies, | which JC 2.01.231
FANTASTIC 6 FR 0.0006 REL FR 6 V 0 P
to be fantastic may become a youth | of greater TGV 2.07. 47
plays such fantastic tricks before high heaven MM 2.02.121
snow | by thinking on fantastic summer's heat? R2 1.03.299
hath done to–day | mad and fantastic execution, TRO 5.05. 38
therewith fantastic garlands did she make | of HAM 4.07.168
call, | soothing the humor of fantastic wits? VEN 850
FANTASTICAL 15 FR 0.0017 REL FR 3 V 12 P
this is fery fantastical humors and jealousies. WIV 3.03.170 P
it was a mad fantastical trick of him to steal MM 3.02. 92 P
if the old fantastical duke of dark corners had 4.03.157 P
like a scotch jig, and full as fantastical; ADO 2.01. 76 P
his words are a very fantastical banquet, just 2.03. 21 P
the schoolmaster is exceeding fantastical, too LLL 5.02.529 P
longing and liking, proud, fantastical, apish, AYL 3.02.411 P
ne'er a fantastical knave of them all shall 3.03.106 P
nor the musician's, which is fantastical; 4.01. 12 P
is fancy | that it alone is high fantastical. TN 1.01. 15
seems to be the more noble in being fantastical. WT 4.04.752 P
are ye fantastical, or that indeed | which MAC 1.03. 53
thought, whose murther yet is but fantastical, 1.03.139
for bragging and telling her fantastical lies. OTH 2.01.223 P
he's as fantastical, too, as ever he may go upon TNK 4.03. 13 P
FANTASTICALLY 2 FR 0.0002 REL FR 1 V 1 P
with a head fantastically carv'd upon it with a 2H4 3.02.311 P
king'd, | her sceptre so fantastically borne, H5 2.04. 27
FANTASY 15 FR 0.0017 REL FR 15 V 0 P
said, | raise up the organs of her fantasy, WIV 5.05. 51
fie on sinful fantasy! 5.05. 93
and stol'n the impression of her fantasy | with MND 1.01. 32
hast thou been drawn to by thy fantasy? AYL 2.04. 31
it is to be all made of fantasy, | all made of 5.02. 94
or is it fantasy that plays upon our eyesight? 1H4 5.04.135
upon me | than i have drawn it in my fantasy. 2H4 5.02. 13
idle brain, | begot of nothing but vain fantasy, ROM 1.04. 98
from the main opinion he held once | of fantasy, JC 2.01.197
and things unluckily charge my fantasy. 3.03. 2
horatio says 'tis but our fantasy, | and will HAM 1.01. 23
is not this something more than fantasy? 1.01. 54
that for a fantasy and trick of fame | go to 4.04. 61
i nothing but to please his fantasy. OTH 3.03.299
she tells them 'tis a causeless fantasy | and VEN 897
FAP 1 FR 0.0001 REL FR 0 V 1 P
and being fap, sir, was, as they say, cashier'd; WIV 1.01.178 P
/FAR* 4 FR 0.0004 REL FR 3 V 1 P
/if /on /my /credit /you /dare /build /so /far LR 3.01. 35
/the /marshal /of /france, /monsieur /la /far. 4.03. 8 P
/with /her — /as /far /as /we /call /hers. 5.01. 13
distemper'd | /far worse than now she shows. TNK 4.01.120
FAR* 301 FR 0.0340 REL FR 268 V 33 P
'tis far off — | and rather like a dream than TMP 1.02. 44
know thus far forth: 1.02.177
who is so far from italy removed | i ne'er again 2.01.111
but she as far surpasseth sycorax | as great'st 3.02.102
that shall catch | your royal fleet far off. 5.01.317
some to discover islands far away; TGV 1.03. 9
a word (for far behind his worth | comes all the 2.04. 71
his heart as far from fraud as heaven from earth 2.07. 78
her chamber is aloft, far from the ground, | and 3.01.114
my wrath shall far exceed the love | i ever bore 3.01.166
swear), | i am so far from granting thy request, 4.02.101
thou'dst two, | and that's far worse than none: 5.04. 51
he's as far from jealousy as i am from giving WIV 2.01.103 P
enlargeth her mirth so far that there is shrewd 2.02.223 P
(so far forth as herself might be her chooser) 4.06. 11
tongue far from heart — play with all virgins MM 1.04. 33
life, | nature dispenses with the deed so far, 3.01.134
and we discovered | two ships from far, making ERR 1.01. 92
far more, far more, to you do i decline. 3.02. 44
far more, far more, to you do i decline. 3.02. 44
far from her nest the lapwing cries away; 4.02. 27
my lord, in truth, thus far i witness with him: 5.01.255
thus far can i praise him: ADO 2.01.378 P
were not his requests so far | from reason's LLL 2.01.149
how far dost thou excel | no thought can think, 4.03. 39
dumaine, thy love is far from charity, | that in 4.03.125
"this hector far surmounted hannibal. 5.02.670
and phibbus' car | shall shine from far, | and MND 1.02. 36
bachelor and a maid, | so far be distant; 2.02. 60
and so far blameless proves my enterprise, 3.02.350
and so far am i glad it so did sort, | as this 3.02.352
that hatred is so far from jealousy | to sleep 4.01.144
him, i will run as far as god has any ground. MV 2.02.110 P
enough | may not extend so far as to the lady; 2.07. 28
yet look how far | the substance of my praise 3.02.126
it, so far this shadow | doth limp behind the 3.02.128
you press me far, and therefore i will yield. 4.01.425
love did run from venice, | as far as belmont. 5.01. 17
how far that little candle throws his beams! 5.01. 90
us, | maids as we are, to travel forth so far! AYL 1.03.109
thou hast a lady far more beautiful | than any SHR in.2. 62
it shall be so far forth friendly maintain'd 1.01.136 P
petruchio, since we are stepp'd thus far in, | i 1.02. 83
that were my state far worser than it is, | i 1.02. 91
that never read so far | to know the cause why 3.01. 9
travel you far on, or are you at the farthest? 4.02. 73
two, | but then up farther, and as far as rome, 4.02. 75
forward, i pray, since we have come so far, 4.05. 12
had it stretch'd so far, would have made nature AWW 1.01. 20 P
he did look far | into the service of the time, 1.02. 26
do not plunge thyself too far in anger, lest 2.03.211 P
whilst i from far | his name with zealous fervor 3.04. 10
do you think i am so far deceiv'd in him? 3.06. 6 P
lest, reposing too far in his virtue, which he 3.06. 14 P
and let me buy your friendly help thus far, 3.07. 15
he hath out–villain'd villainy so far, that the 4.03.273 P
and therefore know how far i may be pitied. 5.03.161
that, yet thus far i will boldly publish her: TN 2.01. 28 P
for i am now so far in offense with my niece 4.02. 69 P
flood of fortune | so far exceed all instance, 4.03. 12
so far beneath your soft and tender breeding, 5.01.323
to mingle friendship far is mingling bloods. WT 1.02.109
'tis far gone, | when i shall gust it last. 1.02.218
how far off, how near, | which way to be 1.02.404
best haste, and go not | too far i' th' land; 3.03. 11
so far that i have eyes under my service which 4.02. 35 P
is it not too far gone? 4.04.344
him call me rogue for being so far officious, 4.04.839 P
my lord's almost so far transported that | he'll 5.03. 69
i am sorry, sir, i have thus far stirr'd you; 5.03. 74
i'll not seek far | (for him, i partly know his 5.03.141
near or far off, well won is still well shot, JN 1.01.174
but thou from loving england art so far | that 2.01. 94
and now 'tis far too huge to be blown out | with 5.02. 86
a nurse, | too far in years to be a pupil now. R2 1.03.171
since thou hast far to go, bear not along | the 1.03.199
as far as land will let me, by your side. 1.03.252
how far brought you high herford on his way? 1.04. 2
renowned for their deeds as far from home, | for 2.01. 53
york is too far gone with grief, | or else he 2.01.184
your husband, he is gone to save far off, 2.02. 80
how far is it, my lord, to berkeley now? 2.03. 1
how far is it to berkeley? 2.03. 51
and far surmounts our labor to attain it. 2.03. 64
how far off lies your power? 3.02. 63
richard not far from hence hath hid his head. 3.03. 6
how far off from the mind of bullingbrook | it 3.03. 45
so far be mine, my most redoubted lord, | as my 3.03.198
the restful english court | as far as callice, 4.01. 13
better far off than, near, be ne'er the near. 5.01. 88
as far as to the sepulchre of christ — | whose 1H4 1.01. 19
and elsewhere, so far as my coin would stretch, 1.02. 54 P
ginger, to be deliver'd as far as charing–cross. 2.01. 25 P
bear my own flesh so far afoot again for all the 2.02. 36 P
so far afoot, i shall be weary, love. 2.03. 84
and so far will i trust thee, gentle kate. 2.03.112
how! so far? 2.03.113
with cheese and garlic in a windmill, far, 3.01.160
you strain too far. 4.01. 75
my judgment is we should not step too far 2H4 1.03. 20
thou thinkest me as far in the devil's book as 2.02. 45 P
how far forth you do like their articles. 4.02. 53
spoke and i had heard | the course of it so far. 4.05.142
civil swords and native fire | as far as france. 5.05.107
or shall we sparingly show you far off | the H5 1.02.239
they seem to threaten | runs far before them. 2.04. 71
so far my king and master; 3.06.136 P
followers so far out of his knowledge! 3.07.134 P
since then my office hath so far prevail'd, 5.02. 29
thus far, with rough and all–unable pen, | our ep 1
a far more glorious star thy soul will make 1H6 1.01. 55
but with a baser man of arms by far | once in 1.04. 30
better far, i guess, | that we do make our 2.01. 29
as far as i could well discern | for smoke and 2.02. 26
have i sought every country far and near, | and, 5.04. 3
she'll gallop far enough to her destruction. 2H6 1.03.151
far truer spoke than meant. 3.01.183
might happily have prov'd far worse than his. 3.01.306
as far as i could ken thy chalky cliffs, | when 3.02.101
far be it we should honor such as these | with 4.01.123
set limb to limb, and thou art far the lesser; 4.10. 47
i am far better born than is the king; 5.01. 28
far be the thought of this from henry's heart, 3H6 1.01. 70
my title's good, and better far than his. 1.01.130
and creep into it far before thy time? 1.01.237
helen of greece was fairer far than thou, 2.02.146
like to a dismal clangor heard from far, 2.03. 18
enjoys, | is far beyond a prince's delicates — 2.05. 51
jest withal, | but far unfit to be a sovereign. 3.02. 92
so do i wish the crown, being so far off, | and 3.02.140
alas, you know, 'tis far from hence to france; 4.01. 4
rest, | yet thus far fortune maketh us amends, 4.07. 2
how far hence is thy lord, mine honest fellow? 5.01. 2
how far off is our brother montague? 5.01. 4
thus far our fortune keeps an upward course, 5.03. 1
shall for thy love kill a far truer love; R3 1.02.190
far be it from my heart, the thought thereof! 1.03.149
the prince my brother hath outgrown me far. 3.01.104
and, as it were far off, sound thou lord 3.01.170
nay, for a need, thus far come near my person: 3.05. 85
yet touch this sparingly, as 'twere far off, 3.05. 93
see, | how far i am from the desire of this. 3.07.236
in | so far in blood that sin will pluck on sin. 4.02. 64
though far more cause, yet much less spirit to 4.04.197
thus far into the bowels of the land | have we 5.02. 3
how far into the morning is it, lords? 5.03.234
o, you go far. H8 1.01. 38
and't may be said | it reaches far, and where 1.01.111
dangerous for /him | to ruminate on this so far, 1.02.180
as far as i see, all the good our english | have 1.03. 5
employment, | and far enough from court too. 2.01. 49
you that thus far have come to pity me, | hear 2.01. 56
yet thus far we are one in fortunes: 2.01.121
how far i have proceeded, | or how far further 2.04. 90
or how far further shall, is warranted | by a 2.04. 91
to this point, | and thus far clear him. 2.04.168
yourself to say | how far you satisfied me. 2.04.212
both of his truth and him (which was too far), 3.01. 65
other comforts) far hence | in mine own country, 3.01. 90
far from his succor, from the king, from all 3.02.261
o my lord, | press not a falling man too far! 3.02.333
in a sea of glory, | but far beyond my depth. 3.02.361
to endure more miseries and greater far | than 3.02.389
and thus far hear me, cromwell, | and when i am 3.02.431
yet thus far, griffith, give me leave to speak 4.02. 32
who hath so far | given ear to our complaint, of 5.01. 47
my commission | bid ye so far forget yourselves? 5.02.177
thus far, | my most dread sovereign, may it like 5.02.182
when i might see from far some forty 5.03. 51 P
there's troilus will not come far behind him. TRO 1.02. 57 P
that we come short of our suppose so far | that 1.03. 11
than i | as far as toucheth my particular, | yet 2.02. 9
she is as far high–soaring o'er thy praises | as 4.04.124
holds honor far more precious–dear than life. 5.03. 28
how far off lie these armies? COR 1.04. 8
hark you, far off! 1.04. 19
and thus far having stretch'd it (here be with 3.02. 74
theirs, so far | as thou hast power and person. 3.02. 85
as far as doth the capitol exceed | the meanest 4.02. 39
the meanest house in rome, so far my son, | this 4.02. 40
i, it exceeds peace as far as day does night; 4.05.222 P
for i dare so far free him — made him fear'd, 4.07. 47
that brought her for this high good turn so far? TIT 1.01.397
this, | as far from help as limbo is from bliss! 3.01.149
not far, one muliteus my countryman | his wife 4.02.152
so close, | so far from sounding and discovery, ROM 1.01.150
that thou, her maid, art far more fair than she. 2.02. 6
wert thou as far | as that vast shore /wash'd 2.02. 82
goose, proves thee far and wide a broad goose. 2.04. 86 P
more fierce and more inexorable far | than empty 5.03. 38
and thus far i confirm you. TIM 1.02. 94 P
i am so far already in your gifts — 1.02.172
you befriend me so far as to use mine own words 3.02. 58 P
and, if it be so far beyond his health, 3.04. 74
the place, it cannot be far | where he abides. 5.01. 1
and i will set this foot of mine as far | as who JC 1.03.119
may well stretch so far | as to annoy us all; 2.01.159
have i in conquest stretch'd mine arm so far, 2.02. 66
nay, press not so upon me, stand far off. 3.02.167
fly therefore, noble cassius, fly far off. 5.03. 11
this hill is far enough. 5.03. 12
far from this country pindarus shall run, 5.03. 49
how far is't call'd to /forres? MAC 1.03. 39
thou art so far before, | that swiftest wing of 1.04. 16

is't far you ride? 3.01. 23
as far, my lord, as will fill up the time 3.01. 24
i am in blood | stepp'd in so far that, should i 3.04.136
yet so far hath discretion fought with nature HAM 1.02. 5
it fits your wisdom so far to believe it | as he 1.03. 25
quarrelling, | drabbing — you may go so far. 2.01. 26
'a is far gone. 2.02.189 P
so far from cheer and from /your former state, 3.02.164
them so well, | they shall go far with little. 4.05.140
so far he topp'd /my thought, | that i, in 4.07. 88
her obsequies have been as far enlarg'd | as we 5.01.226
free me so far in your most generous thoughts, 5.02.242
whose nature is so far from doing harms | that LR 1.02.180
well, you may fear too far. 1.04.328
safer than trust too far. 1.04.328
how far your eyes may pierce i cannot tell: 1.04.345
let him fly far. 2.01. 56
his picture | i will send far and near, that all 2.01. 82
the shrill–gorg'd lark so far | cannot be seen 4.06. 58
far off methinks i hear the beaten drum. 4.06.285
still, still, far wide! 4.07. 49
have been demanded | ere you had spoke so far. 5.03. 63
your son–in–law is far more fair than black. OTH 1.03.290
i'll not be far from you. 2.01.266 P
but, sith i am ent'red in this cause so far 3.03.411
i'll set a bourn how far to be belov'd. ANT 1.01. 16
you shall be yet far fairer than you are. 1.02. 17
her die twenty times upon far poorer moment. 1.02.142 P
tempt him not so too far; 1.03. 11
do | so far ask pardon as befits mine honor | to 2.02. 97
there, | my music playing far off, i will betray 2.05. 11
follow the noise so far as we have quarter; 4.03. 21
retire, we have engag'd ourselves too far. 4.07. 1
you speak him far. CYM 1.01. 24
you must not so far prefer her 'fore ours of 1.04. 65 P
being so far provok'd as i was in france, i 1.04. 67 P
only, thus far you shall answer: 1.04.157 P
having thus far proceeded | (unless thou 1.05. 15
so far i read aloud — | but even the very 1.06. 26
who is as far | from thy report as thou from 1.06.145
i'll make a journey twice as far, t' enjoy | a 2.04. 43
read, and tell me | how far 'tis thither. 3.02. 50
how far it is | to this same blessed milford. 3.02. 58
was the theme, my name | was not far off. 3.03. 60
why hast thou gone so far, | to be unbent when 3.04.107
thus far, and so farewell. 3.05. 1
she's far enough, and what he learns by this 3.05.102
of thy story, | so far as thou wilt speak it. 3.06. 92
absolute madness could so far have rav'd | to 4.02.135
pray how far thither? 4.02.292
in that he spake too far. 5.05.309
whose arm seems far too short to hit me here. PER 1.02. 8
for comfort is too far for us to expect. 1.04. 59
we have heard your miseries as far as tyre, 1.04. 88
how far is his court distant from this shore? 2.01.106 P
ye speak, | diana's temple is not distant far, 3.04. 13
your kindness | we have stretch'd thus far, let 5.01. 55
her modesty will blow so far she falls for't. TNK 2.02.144
the matter's too far driven between him | and 2.03. 43
not far, sir. | are there such games to–day? 2.03. 63
this; but far off, prince. 2.05. 5
emily my sovereign), how far | i may be proud. 3.01. 16
cousin, thrust the buckle | through far enough. 3.06. 62
and she answered me | so far from what she was, 4.01. 39
from the far shore, thick set with reeds and 4.01. 54
that, believe me, | she left me far behind her. 4.01. 99
three or four | i saw from far off cross her — 4.01.100
like the great–ey'd juno's, but far sweeter, 4.02. 20
knight he spoke of, | but of a face far sweeter; 4.02. 95
twenty times had been far better, | for there 5.02. 7
how far is't now to th' end o' th' world, my 5.02. 72
sometime he scuds far off, and there he stares, VEN 301
"by this, poor wat, far off upon a hill, 697
by this, far off, she hears some huntsman hallow 973
which far exceeds his barren skill to show. LUC 81
far from the purpose of his coming thither, | he 113
and doth so far proceed | that what is vile 251
and lust, the thief, far poorer than before. 693
yet with the fault i thus far can dispense: 1279
met far from home, wond'ring each other's chance 1596
(and far the weaker with so strong a fear), | my 1647
for then my thoughts (from far where i abide) SON 27. 5
the other to complain | how far i toil, still 28. 8
from limits far remote, where thou dost stay. 44. 4
"thus far the miles are measur'd from thy friend 50. 4
thee | so far from home into my deeds to pry, 61. 6
from me far off, with others all too near. 61.14
so far from variation or quick change? 76. 2
doth bear, | my saucy bark (inferior far to his) 80. 7
how far a modern quill doth come too short, 83. 7
lilies that fester smell far worse than weeds. 94.14
fairer than at first, more strong, far greater. 119.12
no, it was builded far from accident; 124. 5
coral is far more red than her lips' red; 130. 2
that music hath a far more pleasing sound; 130.10
thus far for love my love–suit, sweet, fulfill. 136. 4
only my plague thus far i count my gain, | that 141.13

FARBOROUGH 1 FR 0.0001 REL FR 0 V 1 P
his own person, for i am his grace's farborough; LLL 1.01.184 P

FARCED *(also force*)*

FARCED 1 FR 0.0001 REL FR 1 V 0 P
the farced title running 'fore the king, | the H5 4.01.263

FARCES 1 FR 0.0001 REL FR 0 V 1 P
lards it, that she farces ev'ry business withal, TNK 4.03. 7 P

FARCY *(see fashions*)*

FAR'D 2 FR 0.0002 REL FR 2 V 0 P
so far'd our father with his enemies, | so fled 3H6 2.01. 18
so it far'd | good space between these kinsmen; TNK 5.03.128

FARDELS *(also farthel)*

FARDELS 1 FR 0.0001 REL FR 1 V 0 P
who would fardels bear, | to grunt and sweat HAM 3.01. 75

FARDINGALES *(also farthingale)*

FARDINGALES 1 FR 0.0001 REL FR 1 V 0 P
with ruffs and cuffs, and fardingales, and SHR 4.03. 56

/FARE 1 FR 0.0001 REL FR 0 V 1 P
/fare /you /well, /sir. LR 4.07. 93 P

FARE 142 FR 0.0160 REL FR 92 V 50 P
to the elements | be free, and fare thou well! TMP 5.01.319
fare thee well, commend me to them both. WIV 2.02.131 P
well, fare you well. 3.02. 84 P
fare you well. 4.05. 82 P
fare you well, sir. 5.03. 6 P
so fare you well. MM 1.01. 58
once more fare you well. 1.01. 72
i thank you. fare you well. 1.01. 75
so for this time, pompey, fare you well. 2.01.250 P
fare you well. 2.01.275 P
fare you well. 2.02.142
fare you well, good father. 3.01.268 P
i am going to visit the prisoner. fare you well. 3.02.258 P
well; you'll answer this one day. fare ye well. 4.03.163 P
i shall, sir. fare you well. 4.04. 18 P
you are a merry man, sir, fare you well. ERR 3.02.178
you have no stomach, signior, fare you well. ADO 2.03.256 P
drink some wine ere you go; fare you well. 3.05. 53 P
but fare thee well, most foul, most fair! 4.01.103
so will it fare with claudio: 4.01.222
well, fare you well, my lord. 5.01. 48
fare you well, boy, you know my mind. 5.01.185 P
fare you well now. 5.02. 46 P
fare you well. 5.03. 28
fare you well. LLL 1.02.131 P
a gallant lady. monsieur, fare you well. 2.01.196
well, i will do it, sir; fare you well. 3.01.156 P
fare thee well, nymph. MND 2.01.245
but fare you well; 2.02.131
but fare ye well; 3.02.243
fare ye well, | we leave you now with better MV 1.01. 58
fare ye well a while, | i'll end my exhortation 1.01.103
fare you well! i'll grow a talker for this gear. 1.01.110
but fare you well, | i have some business. 2.02.203
but fare thee well, there is a ducat for thee, 2.03. 4
fare you well, your suit is cold." 2.07. 73
so fare you well till we shall meet again. 3.04. 40
fare you well, jessica. 3.04. 44
give me your hand, bassanio, fare you well! 4.01.265
fare you well! pray heaven i be deceiv'd in you! AYL 1.02.197 P
but fare thee well, thou art a gallant youth. 1.02.229
ay. fare you well, fair gentleman. 1.02.248
have with you. fare you well. 1.02.256
sir, fare you well. 1.02.283
fare you well. 1.02.286
fare you well. 3.05. 63
so fare you well; 5.02.120 P
marry, i fare well, for here is cheer enough. SHR in.2. 101
that dare leave two together, fare you well. AWW 2.01. 98
i must not hear thee, fare thee well, kind maid! 2.01.145
so, my good window of lettice, fare thee well! 2.03.213 P
fare you well, my lord, and believe this of me: 2.05. 42 P
coward, i'd compel it of you, but fare you well. 4.03.322 P
fare ye well, sir, i am for france too. 4.03.328 P
fare you well, gentlemen. TN 1.03. 60 P
fare you well! 1.05.282
fare ye well at once; 2.01. 39 P
"fare thee well, and god have mercy upon one of 3.04.166 P
fare thee well! 3.04.216
fare thee well. 4.02. 57 P
fare thee well. 4.02. 60 P
then fare thee well, i must go buy spices for WT 4.03.116 P
madam, fare you well, | i'll send those powers JN 3.03. 69
fare you well! 3.04. 99
fare thee well! 5.02.160
poison'd — ill fare! 5.07. 35
norfolk, so fare as to mine enemy: R2 1.03.193
so fare you well, | unless you please to enter 2.03.159
fare thee well, great heart! 1H4 5.04. 87
fare you well! 2H4 1.02.226 P
fare you well; 2.02.165 P
well, fare thee well. 2.04.382 P
and truer–hearted man — well, fare thee well. 2.04.384 P
fare you well, gentlemen both, i thank you. 3.02.289 P
fare you well, gentle gentlemen. 3.02.299 P
fare you well, falstaff. 4.03. 84
fare you well. H5 1.02.297
and so, montjoy, fare you well. 3.06.162
keep thy word; fare thee well. 4.01.221 P
and so fare thee well; 4.03.126
fare ye well. 5.01. 79 P
rack, | so fare my limbs with long imprisonment; 1H6 2.05. 4
how dost thou fare? 4.06. 27
sheriff, farewell, and better than i fare, 2H6 2.04.100
how would it fare with your departed souls? 4.07.116
what fare? 3H6 2.01. 95
then fare you well, for i will hence again, | i 4.07. 48
fare you well. R3 1.04. 99 P
o my lord aburga'ny, fare you well! H8 1.01.211
so fare you well, my little good lord cardinal. 3.02.349
fare ye well, good niece. TRO 1.02.276 P
fare ye well, with all my heart. 3.03.299 P
fare thee well. 5.06. 19
fare you well then. COR 1.03.106 P
fare you well. 1.05. 17
fare you well. 2.03.150
fare ye well! 4.01. 44
fare you well. TIM 1.01.108
well fare you, gentleman; 1.01.163
fare thee well, fare thee well. 1.01.262
fare thee well, fare thee well. 1.01.262
fare thee well. 3.01. 44 P
fare thee well, commend me to thy honorable 3.02. 27 P
and how fare you? 3.06. 26 P
if they will fare so harshly o' th' trumpet's 3.06. 34 P
why, fare thee well; 4.03.100
fare you well. JC 1.02.286 P
fare you well. 3.01. 14
fare thee well! 3.01.150
the last of all the romans, fare thee well! 5.03. 99
so fare you well at once, for brutus' tongue 5.05. 39
give me your hand first. fare you well, my lord. 5.05. 49
fare thee well, lord, | i would not be the MAC 4.03. 34
fare thee well, | these evils thou repeat'st 4.03.111
fare you well. 5.06. 6
so fare you well. HAM 1.02.250
fare thee well at once! 1.05. 88
god buy ye, fare ye well. 2.01. 66
fare you well, my lord. 2.02.218 P
fare you well, my liege, | i'll call upon you 3.03. 33
rain'd many a tear" — | fare you well, my dove! 4.05.168 P
fare thee well, king; LR 1.01.180
you may do then in time. fare you well, sir. 2.01. 13 P
conceive, and fare thee well. 4.02. 24
so fare you well. 4.05. 36
fare thee well. 4.05. 40
now fare ye well, good sir. 4.06. 32
now, fellow, fare thee well. 4.06. 41
why, fare thee well, i will o'erlook thy paper. 5.01. 50
fare thee well awhile. ANT 1.02.111
farewell, my dearest sister, fare thee well! 3.02. 39
fare thee well! 3.02. 41
fare you well. 4.03. 2
fare thee well, dame, what e'er becomes of me. 4.04. 29
so fare thee well! 5.02.314
fare thee well, pisanio; CYM 1.05. 84
our crows shall fare the better for you; 3.01. 81 P
fare you well. 3.05. 15
you shall fare well, you shall have the PER 4.02. 79 P
fare thee well, thou art a piece of virtue, and 4.06.111
how do things fare? TNK 5.04. 45
fare well i could not, for i supp'd with sorrow. PP 14. 6

/FARES 1 FR 0.0001 REL FR 1 V 0 P
/how /fares /your /grace? 2H4 4.05. 49

FARES 31 FR 0.0035 REL FR 29 V 2 P
spirit, | how fares the king and 's followers? TMP 5.01. 7
how fares my gracious sir? 5.01.253
how fares your majesty? LLL 5.02.726
how fares my noble lord? SHR in.2. 100
how fares my kate? what, sweeting, all amort? 4.03. 36
dear gentlewoman, | how fares our gracious lady? WT 2.02. 19
go, | see how he fares. 2.03. 18
badly, i fear. how fares your majesty? JN 5.03. 2
how fares your majesty? 5.07. 34
how fares our noble uncle lancaster? R2 2.01. 71
harry, how fares your uncle? 2.03. 23
cheerly, my lord, how fares your grace? 1H4 5.04. 44
how fares my lord? 2H6 3.02. 33
how fares my gracious lord? 3.02. 37
how fares my lord? 3.03. 1
how fares my brother? 3H6 2.01. 8
this battle fares like to the morning's war, 2.05. 1
and see our gentle queen how well she fares. 5.05. 89
richard of york, how fares our loving brother? R3 3.01. 96
how fares our cousin, noble lord of york? 3.01.101
be of good cheer. mother, how fares your grace? 4.01. 37
tell me, how fares our loving mother? 5.03. 82
how fares our cousin hamlet? HAM 3.02. 92 P
how fares my lord? 3.02.267 P
how fares your grace? LR 3.04.125
how does my royal lord? how fares your majesty? 4.07. 43
how fares my mistress? CYM 5.05.235
so surfeit–taking tarquin fares this night: LUC 698
so fares it with this fault–full lord of rome, 715
to ask the spotted princess how she fares. 721
he hath no power to ask her how she fares. 1594

/FAREWELL 1 FR 0.0001 REL FR 0 V 1 P
/go /to, /farewell. OTH 1.03.380 P

FAREWELL 378 FR 0.0427 REL FR 308 V 70 P
"farewell, my wife and children!" TMP 1.01. 61
"farewell, brother!" 1.01. 62
farewell, master; farewell, farewell! 2.02.178
farewell, master; farewell, farewell! 2.02.178
farewell, master; farewell, farewell! 2.02.178
and now farewell | till half an hour hence. 3.01. 90
as much to you at home; and so farewell. TGV 1.01. 62
julia, farewell! 2.02. 16
farewell. 4.02. 84
farewell. 4.04.178
well, farewell, i am in great haste now. WIV 1.04.161 P
farewell to your worship. 1.04.162 P
farewell. 2.01.121
farewell, my hearts. 3.02. 87 P
or bid farewell to your good life for ever. 3.03.119 P
till then farewell, sir; 3.04. 92
farewell, gentle mistress; farewell, nan. 3.04. 94
farewell, gentle mistress; farewell, nan. 3.04. 94
farewell, mistress page. 4.01. 82 P
farewell. MM 2.01.211 P
farewell. 3.01.173 P
farewell. 3.02. 63 P
farewell, good pompey. 3.02. 68 P
farewell, good friar, i prithee pray for me. 3.02.180 P
farewell. 3.02.184 P
farewell till then. ERR 1.02. 30
farewell therefore hero! ADO 2.01.182
do so, farewell. 2.03. 89 P
contempt, farewell, and maiden pride, adieu! 3.01.109
farewell, | thou pure impiety and impious purity 4.01.103
you kill me to deny it. farewell. 4.01.291 P
and so farewell. 4.01.335 P
until to–morrow morning, lords, farewell. 5.01.328
farewell, my lords, we look for you to–morrow. 5.01.329
and so farewell. LLL 1.02.143 P
your own good thoughts excuse me, and farewell. 2.01.175
farewell to me, sir, and welcome to you. 2.01.214
farewell, mad wenches, you have simple wits. 5.02.264
farewell, worthy lord! 5.02.736
farewell, sweet playfellow, pray thou for us; MND 1.01.220
farewell, thou lob of spirits; 2.01. 16
and farewell, friends; 5.01.345
good heart as i can bid the other four farewell. MV 1.02.128 P
this letter, do it secretly, | and so farewell. 2.03. 8
farewell, good launcelot. 2.03. 15
his words were "farewell, mistress!" 2.05. 45
farewell, and if my fortune be not cross'd, | i 2.05. 56
then farewell heat, and welcome frost! 2.07. 75
farewell, good charles. AYL 1.01.163 P
farewell, kind master. 2.06. 3 P
farewell, good signior love. 3.02.291 P
farewell, good master oliver: 3.03. 98 P
farewell, monsieur traveller: 4.01. 33 P
kind offer, when i make curtsy, bid me farewell. ep 23 P
children in good bringing–up, | and so farewell. SHR 1.01.100
farewell; 1.01.109 P
yours, if you talk of tales, and so farewell. 2.01.217
farewell, sweet masters both, i must be gone. 3.01. 85

me, | for i must hence, and farewell to you all. 3.02.197
and so farewell, signior lucentio. 4.02. 40
but bid bianca farewell for ever and a day. 4.04. 97
farewell! AWW 1.01. 70
heaven bless him! | farewell, bertram. 1.01. 74
farewell, pretty lady, | you must howd the 1.01. 77
little helen, farewell. 1.01.188 P
farewell! 1.01.212 P
so farewell. 1.01.215 P
farewell, young lords! 2.01. 1
and you, my lords, farewell! 2.01. 2
farewell, young lords! 2.01. 10
i say farewell. 2.01. 17
farewell. — come hither to me. 2.01. 23
i am your accessary, and so farewell. 2.01. 35
farewell, captain. 2.01. 38 P
after them, and take a more dilated farewell. 2.01. 57 P
farewell, monsieur! 2.05. 46 P
farewell; 2.05. 77
farewell. 2.05. 89
farewell. 3.06. 83 P
farewell, fair cruelty. TN 1.05.288
farewell. 2.01. 43 P
of her, she is very willing to bid you farewell. 2.03.101 P
"farewell, dear heart, since i must needs be 2.03.102
farewell. 2.03.176 P
farewell. 2.04. 78 P
farewell. 2.05.158 P
farewell, and take her, but direct thy feet 5.01.168
to save both, | farewell, our brother. WT 1.02. 27
farewell, we are gone. 2.03.130
farewell! 3.03. 53
farewell, my friend. 4.04.659
farewell, chatillion. JN 1.01. 30
farewell, gentle cousin. 3.03. 17
coz, farewell. 3.03. 17
and so farewell. 4.02. 95
farewell, old gaunt! R2 1.02. 44
farewell, old gaunt! 1.02. 54
sister, farewell, i must to coventry. 1.02. 56
and loving farewell of our several friends. 1.03. 51
farewell, my blood, which if to–day thou shed, 1.03. 57
farewell, my lord, securely i espy | virtue with 1.03. 97
farewell, my liege, now no way can i stray; 1.03.206
cousin, farewell; 1.03.247
cousin, farewell! 1.03.249
then england's ground, farewell, sweet soil, 1.03.306
"farewell!" 1.04. 11
would the word "farewell" have length'ned hours 1.04. 16
my liege, farewell! 2.01.211
save bidding farewell to so sweet a guest | as 2.02. 8
farewell! 2.02.142
farewell at once, for once, for all, and ever. 2.02.148
farewell! 2.04. 4
farewell! 2.04. 16
lords, farewell! 3.01. 32
thorough his castle wall, and farewell king! 3.02.170
uncle, farewell, and, cousin, adieu! 5.03.144
farewell, you shall find me in eastcheap. 1H4 1.02.157 P
farewell, the latter spring! 1.02.158 P
farewell, all–hallown summer! 1.02.158 P
farewell. 1.02.193 P
farewell, my lord. 1.02.194 P
farewell, kinsman! 1.03.234
cousin, farewell! 1.03.292
farewell, good brother, we shall thrive, i trust 1.03.300
farewell, you muddy knave. 2.01. 96 P
farewell, and stand fast. 2.02. 72 P
men, | he shall be answerable, and so farewell. 2.04.522
i will, captain, farewell. 4.02. 10 P
and so farewell. 4.03.111
write again | to other friends, and so farewell, 4.04. 41
say thy prayers, and farewell. 5.01.124 P
poor jack, farewell! 5.04.103
at idle times as thou mayst and so farewell. 2H4 2.02.130 P
farewell, hostess, farewell, doll. 2.04.374 P
farewell, hostess, farewell, doll. 2.04.374 P
farewell, good wenches, if i be not sent away 2.04.377 P
farewell, farewell. 2.04.381 P
farewell, farewell. 2.04.381 P
farewell, hostess. H5 2.03. 59 P
farewell; adieu. 2.03. 63 P
farewell, good salisbury, and good luck go with 4.03. 11
farewell, kind lord; 4.03. 12
farewell, my masters, to my task will i. 1H6 1.01.152
mayor, farewell; thou dost but what thou mayst. 1.03. 86
talbot, farewell, thy hour is not yet come. 1.05. 13
and so farewell until i meet thee next. 2.04.113
farewell, ambitious richard. 2.04.114
and so farewell, and fair be all thy hopes, 2.05.113
so farewell, talbot, i'll no longer trust thee. 3.03. 84
if he miscarry, farewell wars in france! 4.03. 16
else farewell talbot, france, and england's 4.03. 23
lucy, farewell, no more my fortune can, | but 4.03. 43
so farewell, reignier! 5.03.169
farewell, my lord! 5.03.173
farewell, sweet madam! 5.03.175
lordings, farewell, and say, when i am gone, | i 2H6 1.01.145
farewell, good king; 2.03. 37
and so, sir john, farewell! 2.04. 84
what, gone, my lord, and bid me not farewell? 2.04. 85
sheriff, farewell, and better than i fare, 2.04.100
ay, ay, farewell, thy office is discharg'd. 2.04.103
yet now farewell, and farewell life with thee! 3.02.356
yet now farewell, and farewell life with thee! 3.02.356
farewell, my lord, trust not the kentish rebels. 4.04. 57
and so farewell, for i must hence again. 4.05. 12
iden, farewell, and be proud of thy victory. 4.10. 72 P
farewell, faint–hearted and degenerate king, 3H6 1.01.183
farewell, my gracious lord, i'll to my castle. 1.01.206
and takes her farewell of the glorious sun! 2.01. 22
away, away! once more, sweet lords, farewell. 2.03. 48
now, brother king, farewell, and sit you fast, 4.01.119
now for awhile farewell, good duke of york. 4.03. 57
bishop, farewell! 4.05. 28
farewell, my sovereign. 4.08. 24
farewell, my hector, and my troy's true hope. 4.08. 25
and all at once, once more a happy farewell. 4.08. 31
farewell, sweet lords, let's meet at coventry. 4.08. 32
with a groan, | "o, farewell, warwick!" 5.02. 47
for warwick bids you all farewell, to meet in 5.02. 49
farewell sour annoy! 5.07. 45
brother, farewell, i will unto the king, | and R3 1.01.107
i must perforce. farewell. 1.01.116
bid me farewell. 1.02.222
you, | imagine i have said farewell already. 1.02.224
madam, farewell. 2.04. 67
farewell, until we meet again in heaven. 3.03. 26
and so, my good lord mayor, we bid farewell. 3.05. 71
farewell, my /cousin, farewell, gentle friends. 3.07.247
farewell, my /cousin, farewell, gentle friends. 3.07.247
farewell, thou woeful welcomer of glory! 4.01. 89
so foolish sorrows bids your stones farewell. 4.01.103
farewell till then. 4.03. 35
farewell, york's wife, and queen of sad 4.04.114
and so farewell. 4.04.430
farewell. 4.05. 21
farewell! 5.03. 97
my /lord, farewell. H8 1.01.226
farewell! 2.01.134
nay then, farewell! 3.02.222
by a piece of scarlet, | farewell nobility! 3.02.281
so farewell — to the little good you bear me. 3.02.350
farewell? 3.02.351
a long farewell to all my greatness! 3.02.351
farewell | the hopes of court! 3.02.458
farewell, | my lord. 4.02.164
griffith, farewell. 4.02.165
this contagious sickness, | farewell all physic! 5.02. 62
farewell. TRO 2.01.126
farewell. who shall answer him? 2.01.127
farewell, sweet queen. 3.01.145 P
ever smiles, | and farewell goes out sighing. 3.03.169
farewell, my lord; 3.03.214
ajax, farewell. 4.05.148
why then farewell, | thou never shalt mock 5.02. 98
farewell till then. 5.02.106
troilus, farewell! 5.02.107
farewell, revolted fair! 5.02.186
o, farewell, dear hector! 5.03. 80
farewell; 5.03. 89
farewell, the gods with safety stand about thee! 5.03. 94
farewell, bastard. 5.07. 22 P
farewell. COR 1.02. 37
farewell. 1.02. 37
farewell. 1.02. 38
well, then farewell. 1.03.111 P
so farewell. 1.05. 24
a brief farewell. 4.01. 1
farewell, my wife, my mother, | i'll do well yet 4.01. 20
when i am forth, | bid me farewell, and smile. 4.01. 50
thank you, sir, farewell. 4.04. 11
farewell, kind neighbors! 4.06. 24
farewell, farewell. 4.06. 26
farewell, farewell. 4.06. 26
make this his latest farewell to their souls. TIT 1.01.149
farewell, my sons, see that you make her sure. 2.03.187
now farewell, flatt'ry; 3.01.253
farewell, andronicus, my noble father, | the 3.01.288
farewell, proud rome, till lucius come again; 3.01.290
farewell, lavinia, my noble sister, | o, would 3.01.292
farewell, andronicus, revenge now goes | to lay 5.02.146
i know thou dost, and, sweet revenge, farewell. 5.02.148
bid him farewell, commit him to the grave, | do 5.03.170
farewell, my coz. ROM 1.01.195
farewell, thou canst not teach me to forget. 1.01.237
what i have spoke, but farewell compliment! 2.02. 89
farewell, ancient lady, farewell, "lady, lady, 2.04.143 P
farewell, ancient lady, farewell, "lady, lady, 2.04.143 P
farewell, be trusty, and i'll quit thy pains. 2.04.192
farewell, commend me to thy mistress. 2.04.193
hie to high fortune! honest nurse, farewell. 2.05. 78
therefore farewell, i see thou knowest me not. 3.01. 65
and bid him come to take his last farewell. 3.02.143
farewell, good night. 3.03.172
farewell. 3.03.175
farewell, my lord. 3.04. 33
farewell, farewell! one kiss, and i'll descend. 3.05. 42
farewell, farewell! one kiss, and i'll descend. 3.05. 42
farewell! 3.05. 48
farewell, dear father! 4.01.126
farewell! 4.03. 14
farewell! 5.01. 84
live and be prosperous, and farewell, good 5.03. 42
thou art a fool to bid me farewell twice. TIM 1.01.263
farewell, and come with better music. 1.02.245 P
farewell, timon! 4.03.169
and so farewell and thrive. 4.03.533
do so. farewell both. JC 1.02.294 P
farewell, cicero. 1.03. 40
why, farewell, portia. 4.03.190
farewell, good messala. 4.03.231
farewell every one. 4.03.238
therefore our everlasting farewell take: 5.01.115
for ever, and for ever, farewell, cassius! 5.01.116
for ever, and for ever, farewell, brutus! 5.01.119
farewell to you, and you, and you, volumnius. 5.05. 31
farewell to thee too, strato. 5.05. 33
farewell, good strato. 5.05. 50
nev'r shook hands, nor bade farewell to him, MAC 1.02. 21
lay it to thy heart, and farewell." 1.05. 14 P
farewell, father. 2.04. 39
farewell. 3.01. 39
o, farewell, honest /soldier. HAM 1.01. 16
farewell, and let your haste commend your duty. 1.02. 39
we doubt it nothing, heartily farewell. 1.02. 41
your loves, as mine to you, farewell. 1.02.253
farewell. 1.03. 1
farewell, my blessing season this in thee! 1.03. 81
farewell, ophelia, and remember well | what i 1.03. 84
farewell. 1.03. 87
farewell! how now, ophelia, what's the matter? 2.01. 71
but farewell it, for i will use no art. 2.02. 99
farewell! 3.01.132 P
get thee to a nunn'ry, farewell! 3.01.137 P
farewell! 3.01.140 P
thou wretched, rash, intruding fool, farewell! 3.04. 31
farewell, dear mother. 4.03. 49 P
farewell. 4.06. 29 P
sweets to the sweet, farewell! 5.01.243
bid them farewell, cordelia, though unkind, LR 1.01.260
bid farewell to your sisters. 1.01.267
so farewell to you both. 1.01.275
so farewell. 2.01. 32
farewell: 2.04.219
farewell, dear sister, farewell, my lord of 3.07. 12 P
dear sister, farewell, my lord of gloucester. 3.07. 12 P
farewell, sweet lord, and sister. 3.07. 21
edmund, farewell. 3.07. 22
bid me farewell, and let me hear thee going. 4.06. 31
farewell! 4.06. 41
farewell; OTH 1.01.144
so farewell. 1.01.159
go to, farewell. do you hear, roderigo? 1.03.376 P
farewell. 2.01.284 P
shall i deny you? no. farewell, my lord. 3.03. 86
farewell, my desdemona, i'll come to thee 3.03. 87
farewell, farewell! 3.03.238
farewell, farewell! 3.03.238
o now, for ever | farewell the tranquil mind! 3.03.348
farewell content! 3.03.348
farewell the plumed troops and the big wars 3.03.349
o, farewell, | farewell the neighing steed and 3.03.350
farewell the neighing steed and the shrill trump 3.03.351
jove's dread clamors counterfeit, | farewell! 3.03.357
farewell! 5.02.124
o, farewell! 5.02.125
for your going, | but bid farewell, and go. ANT 1.03. 33
farewell. 1.04. 80
farewell, my lord. 1.04. 81
dress, | which will become you both, farewell. 2.04. 5
farewell. 2.04. 10
let neptune hear we bid a loud farewell | to 2.07.132
good fortune, worthy soldier, and farewell. 3.02. 22
farewell, my dearest sister, fare thee well! 3.02. 39
farewell, farewell! 3.02. 66
farewell, farewell! 3.02. 66
farewell! 3.02. 66
before i strike this bloody stroke, farewell. 4.14. 91
'tis said, man, and farewell. 4.14. 92
farewell, great chief. shall i strike now? 4.14. 93
farewell, and thanks! 5.02.207
get thee hence, farewell. 5.02.259
farewell. 5.02.261
ay, ay, farewell. 5.02.264
well, get thee gone, farewell. 5.02.278
farewell, kind charmian, iras, long farewell. 5.02.292
farewell, kind charmian, iras, long farewell. 5.02.292
well, madam, we must take a short farewell, CYM 3.04.185
thus far, and so farewell. 3.05. 1
so farewell, noble lucius. 3.05. 12
brother, farewell. 4.02. 30
farewell, you're angry. 5.03. 63
antioch, farewell, for wisdom sees those men PER 1.01.134
so farewell to your highness. 1.01.167
loath to bid farewell, we take our leaves. 2.05. 13
thee, whiles i say | a priestly farewell to her. 3.01. 69
farewell! TNK 1.01.167
farewell, my beauteous sister. 1.01.219
once more, farewell all. 1.01.225
sir, farewell. 1.03. 1
if that will lose ye, farewell, palamon! 2.02.177
farewell, kind window. 2.02.274
farewell, father! 2.06. 37
give me your hand, farewell. 3.01. 98
farewell. 3.01.123
farewell. 3.03. 51
once more farewell, my cousin. 3.06.106
farewell, arcite. 3.06.106
one farewell! 5.01. 32
why, let it be so; farewell, coz! 5.01. 33
farewell, sir! 5.01. 33
farewell, sister, | i am like to know your 5.03. 36
let us bid farewell; 5.04. 19
farewell. 5.04. 92
bids him farewell, and look well to her heart, VEN 580
"farewell," quoth she, "and come again to–morrow PP 14. 5
farewell, sweet /lass, thy like ne'er was | for 17.33
once do frown, | then farewell his great renown; 20.46
farewell, thou art too dear for my possessing, SON 87. 1

FAREWELLS 2 FR 0.0002 REL FR 2 V 0 P
he should have had a volume of farewells; R2 1.04. 18
as many farewells as be stars in heaven, | with TRO 4.04. 44

FAR–FET 1 FR 0.0001 REL FR 1 V 0 P
if york, with all his far–fet policy, | had been 2H6 3.01.293

FARING 1 FR 0.0001 REL FR 1 V 0 P
as tender nurse her babe from faring ill. SON 22.12

FARM 8 FR 0.0009 REL FR 7 V 1 P
then at my farm | i have a hundred milch–kine to SHR 2.01.356
we are enforc'd to farm our royal realm, | the R2 1.04. 45
it — | like to a tenement or pelting farm. 2.01. 60
the earl of wiltshire hath the realm in farm. 2.01.256
to buy a slobb'ry and a dirty farm | in that H5 3.05. 13
think i had sold my farm to buy my crown. 5.02.125 P
for a state, | but keep a farm and carters. HAM 2.02.167
to pay five ducats, five, i would not farm it; 4.04. 20

FARMER 1 FR 0.0001 REL FR 0 V 1 P
here's a farmer, that hang'd himself on th' MAC 2.03. 4 P

FARMER'S 3 FR 0.0003 REL FR 2 V 1 P
since once he play'd a farmer's eldest son. SHR in.1. 84
to hear | as will a chestnut in a farmer's fire? 1.02.209
thou hast seen a farmer's dog bark at a beggar? LR 4.06.155 P

FARM–HOUSE 1 FR 0.0001 REL FR 0 V 1 P
anne page is, at a farm–house a–feasting; WIV 2.03. 87 P

FARMS 1 FR 0.0001 REL FR 1 V 0 P
and with this horrible object, from low farms, LR 2.03. 17

FAR–OFF 4 FR 0.0004 REL FR 4 V 0 P
like far–off mountains turned into clouds. MND 4.01.188
and if we did but glance a far–off look, 2H6 3.01. 10
and spies a far–off shore where he would tread, 3H6 3.02.136
that one might see those far–off eyes look sad. LUC 1386

FARRE *(also farther)*

FARRE 1 FR 0.0001 REL FR 1 V 0 P

no, not our kin, | farre than deucalion off. WT 4.04.431
FARROW 1 FR 0.0001 REL FR 1 V 0 P
sow's blood, that hath eaten | her nine farrow; MAC 4.01. 65
FAR'ST 2 FR 0.0002 REL FR 2 V 0 P
how far'st thou, mirror of all martial men? 1H6 1.04. 74
i know thee now: how far'st thou, soldier? ANT 2.06. 71
FARTHEL *(also fardels)*
FARTHEL 7 FR 0.0008 REL FR 0 V 7 P
is that in this farthel will make him scratch WT 4.04.708 P
the condition of that farthel? 4.04.718 P
the farthel there? 4.04.754 P
what's i' th' farthel? 4.04.754 P
there lies such secrets in this farthel and box, 4.04.756 P
i was by at the opening of the farthel, heard 5.02. 3 P
heard them talk of a farthel and i know not what 5.02.116 P
FARTHER *(also farre)*
FARTHER 47 FR 0.0053 REL FR 39 V 8 P
'tis time | i should inform thee farther. TMP 1.02. 23
sit down, | for thou must now know farther. 1.02. 33
please you, farther. 1.02. 65
i'll go farther off. 3.02. 73 P
stand farther. — come, proceed. 3.02. 86
and have you nuns no farther privileges? MM 1.04. 1
let me hear you speak farther. 3.01.205 P
i will disparage her no farther till you are my ADO 3.02.128 P
prince, let me go no farther to mine answer: 5.01.230 P
what if i stray'd no farther, but chose here? MV 2.07. 35
you | make no moe offers, use no farther means, 4.01. 81
gentlemen, importune me no farther, | for how i SHR 1.01. 48
to seek their fortunes farther than at home, 1.02. 51
but then up farther, and as far as rome, | and 4.02. 75
when i feel and see her no farther trust her; WT 2.01.136
being now awake, i'll queen it no inch farther, 4.04.449
but | i could afflict you farther. 5.03. 75
to meet displeasure farther from the doors, JN 5.01. 60
nor near nor farther off, my gracious lord, R2 3.02. 64
but yet no farther wise | than harry percy's 1H4 2.03.107
time | did push it out of farther question. H5 1.01. 5
then if you urge me farther than to say "do you 5.02.128 P
tut, were it farther off, i'll pluck it down. 3H6 3.02.195
no farther than the tower, and, as i guess, R3 4.01. 8
my part, i'll not meddle nor make no farther. TRO 1.01. 14 P
that you may be abhorr'd | farther than seen, COR 1.04. 33
of your voices, and so trouble you no farther. 2.03.110 P
to know our farther pleasure in this case, | to ROM 1.01.101
and yet no farther than a wanton's bird, | that 2.02.177
to pry | in what i farther shall intend to do, 5.03. 34
tempt me no farther. JC 4.03. 36
your thoughts, | which can interpret farther; MAC 3.06. 2
he shall in strangeness stand no farther off OTH 3.03. 12
your honor | to scan this thing no farther; 3.03.245
pray you stand farther from me. ANT 1.03. 18
from egypt, 'tis | a space for farther travel. 2.01. 31
torch is out, | lie down and stray no farther. 4.14. 47
it is an earnest of a farther good | that i mean CYM 1.05. 65
home, i grant | we were to question farther; 2.04. 52
no farther halting. 3.05. 92
no farther with your din | express impatience, 5.04.111
there's no farther necessity of qualities can PER 4.02. 48 P
apprehension | which still is farther off it, go TNK 5.01. 37
how far i toil, still farther off from thee. SON 28. 8
for thou /not farther than my thoughts canst 47.11
by seeing farther than the eye hath shown. 69. 8
flesh stays no farther reason, | but, rising at 151. 8
FARTHEST 14 FR 0.0015 REL FR 12 V 2 P
spring come to you at the farthest | in the very TMP 4.01.114
five summers have i spent in farthest greece, ERR 1.01.132
here | come from the farthest steep of india? MND 2.01. 69
be ready at the farthest by five of the clock. MV 2.02.115 P
travel you far on, or are you at the farthest? SHR 4.02. 73
sir, at the farthest for a week or two, | but 4.02. 74
was the farthest off you could have been to him, WT 4.04.703 P
my mouth, | the farthest limit of my embassy. JN 1.01. 22
sun | should in the farthest east begin to draw ROM 1.01.135
that vast shore /wash'd with the farthest sea, 2.02. 83
this foot of mine as far | as who goes farthest. JC 1.03.120
and as my farthest band | shall pass on thy ANT 3.02. 26
upon the farthest earth remov'd from thee, | for SON 44. 6
should transport me farthest from your sight. 117. 8
FARTHING 1 FR 0.0001 REL FR 0 V 1 P
marry, sir, halfpenny farthing. LLL 3.01.148 P
FARTHINGALE *(also fardingales)*
FARTHINGALE 3 FR 0.0003 REL FR 1 V 2 P
what compass will you wear your farthingale?" TGV 2.07. 51
make water against a gentlewoman's farthingale? 4.04. 38 P
motion to thy gait in a semicircled farthingale. WIV 3.03. 64 P
FARTHINGS 2 FR 0.0002 REL FR 0 V 2 P
o, that's the latin word for three farthings: LLL 3.01.137 P
three farthings — remuneration. 3.01.138 P
FARTUOUS 1 FR 0.0001 REL FR 0 V 1 P
your ear, she's as fartuous a civil modest wife, WIV 2.02. 97 P
FAR–UNWORTHY 1 FR 0.0001 REL FR 1 V 0 P
i swear, | whose far–unworthy deputy i am, | he 2H6 3.02.286
FAS 1 FR 0.0001 REL FR 1 V 0 P
sit fas aut nefas, till i find the stream | to TIT 2.01.133
FASHION *(also fashon)*
/FASHION 1 FR 0.0001 REL FR 0 V 1 P
/these /are /now /the /fashion, /and /so HAM 2.02.342 P
FASHION 98 FR 0.0110 REL FR 58 V 40 P
in the same fashion as you gave in charge, TMP 5.01. 8
what fashion, madam, shall i make your breeches?
TGV 2.07. 49
why, ev'n what fashion thou best likes, lucetta. 2.07. 52
besides, the fashion of the time is chang'd) 3.01. 86
how shall i fashion me to wear a cloak? 3.01.135
uncivil touch, | thou friend of an ill fashion! 5.04. 61
by gar, 'tis no the fashion of france; WIV 3.03.172 P
daughter | in such a righteous fashion as i do, 3.04. 79
that mourn'd for fashion, ignorant what to fear, ERR 1.01. 73
aspect, | and fashion your demeanor to my looks, 2.02. 33
the fineness of the gold, and chargeful fashion, 4.01. 29
wears his faith but as the fashion of his hat: ADO 1.01. 76 P
the fashion of the world is to avoid cost, and 1.01. 97 P
of all than to fashion a carriage to rob love 1.03. 29 P
what fashion will you wear the garland of? 2.01.188 P
and i doubt not but to fashion it, if you three 2.01.369 P
mean time i will so fashion the matter that hero 2.02. 46 P
awake carving the fashion of a new doublet; 2.03. 17 P
thou knowest that the fashion of a doublet, or a 3.03.118 P
i mean the fashion. 3.03.121 P
yes, the fashion is the fashion. 3.03.122 P
yes, the fashion is the fashion. 3.03.122 P
thou not what a deformed thief this fashion is? 3.03.124 P
say, what a deformed thief this fashion is, how 3.03.131 P
i see, and i see that the fashion wears out more 3.03.139 P
art not thou thyself giddy with the fashion too, 3.03.141 P
out of thy tale into telling me of the fashion? 3.03.143 P
and your gown's a most rare fashion, i' faith. 3.04. 15 P
graceful, and excellent fashion, yours is worth 3.04. 23 P
success | will fashion the event in better shape 4.01.235
a man in all the world's new fashion planted, LLL 1.01.164
or ratherest unconfirmed fashion, to insert 4.02. 18 P
heard your guilty rhymes, observ'd your fashion, 4.03.137
her favor turns the fashion of the days, | for 4.03.258
therefore met your loves | in their own fashion, 5.02.784
all three | to fashion this false sport, in MND 3.02.194
is not in the fashion to choose me a husband. MV 1.02. 22 P
that thou but leadest this fashion of thy malice 4.01. 18
it was upon this fashion bequeath'd me by will AYL 1.01. 2 P
and greasy citizens, | 'tis just the fashion. 2.01. 56
thou art not for the fashion of these times, 2.03. 59
shepherd's passion | is much upon my fashion. 2.04. 61
but yet, for fashion sake, i thank you too for 3.02.255 P
it is not the fashion to see the lady the ep 1 P
it is my fashion when i see a crab. SHR 2.01.229
'tis some odd humor pricks him to this fashion; 3.02. 72
well, | according to the fashion and the time. 4.03. 95
why, here is the note of the fashion to testify. 4.03.129 P
wears her cap out of fashion, richly suited, but AWW 1.01.157 P
dost thou garter up thy arms a' this fashion? 2.03.250 P
and cross–garter'd, a fashion she detests; TN 2.05.200 P
and he went | still in this fashion, color, 3.04.382
denied, which 'longs | to women of all fashion; WT 3.02.104
as i will fashion it, shall happily meet | to 1H4 1.03.297
yea, two and two, newgate fashion. 3.03. 90 P
by my troth, this is the old fashion, you two 2H4 2.04. 55 P
'a came /ever in the rearward of the fashion, 3.02.316 P
that i will deeply put the fashion on | and wear 5.02. 52
that you should fashion, wrest, or bow your H5 1.02. 14
though it appear a little out of fashion, 4.01. 83
it is not a fashion for the maids in france to 5.02.265 P
within the weak list of a country's fashion. 5.02.270 P
upholding the nice fashion of your country in 5.02.273 P
i scorn thee and thy fashion, peevish boy. 1H6 2.04. 76
i will, | or let me lose the fashion of a man! H8 4.02.159
and in this fashion, | all our abilities, gifts, TRO 1.03.178
wit would be out of fashion. 2.03.216 P
to have done is to hang | quite out of fashion, 3.03.152
say i, to fashion in | my sequent protestation: 4.04. 65
wars and lechery, nothing else holds fashion. 5.02.195 P
how the dispatch is made, and in what fashion, COR 1.01.277
he did fashion | after the inveterate hate he 2.03.225
set a fair fashion on our entertainment, | which TIM 1.02.147
and he will (after his sour fashion) tell you JC 1.02.180
but men may construe things after their fashion, 1.03. 34
no color for the thing he is, | fashion it thus: 2.01. 30
send him but hither, and i'll fashion him. 2.01.220
and stal'd by other men, | begin his fashion. 4.01. 39
bear with him, brutus, 'tis his fashion. 4.03.135
slaying is the word, | it is a deed in fashion. 5.05. 5
favor, | hold it a fashion and a toy in blood, HAM 1.03. 6
importun'd me with love | in honorable fashion. 1.03.111
ay, fashion you may call it. go to, go to. 1.03.112
appurtenance of welcome is fashion and ceremony. 2.02.372 P
the glass of fashion and the mould of form, 3.01.153
beating puts him thus | from fashion of himself. 3.01.175
alexander look'd a' this fashion i' th' earth? 5.01.198 P
all with me's meet that i can fashion fit. LR 1.02.184
is it the fashion, that discarded fathers 3.04. 72
only i do not like the fashion of your garments. 3.06. 80 P
i prattle out of fashion, and i dote | in mine OTH 2.01.206
(which i will fashion to fall out between twelve 4.02.236 P
let's do't after the high roman fashion, | and ANT 4.15. 87
poor i am stale, a garment out of fashion, | and CYM 3.04. 51
guise o' th' world, i will begin | the fashion: 5.01. 33
sighs and groans and tears may grace the fashion LUC 1319
shifting change, as is false women's fashion; SON 20. 4
whereto th' inviting time our fashion calls; 124. 8
FASHIONABLE 2 FR 0.0002 REL FR 2 V 0 P
for time is like a fashionable host | that TRO 3.03.165
to promise is most courtly and fashionable; TIM 5.01. 27
/FASHION'D 1 FR 0.0001 REL FR 1 V 0 P
/copy /and /book, | /that /fashion'd /others. 2H4 2.03. 32
FASHION'D 8 FR 0.0009 REL FR 8 V 0 P
of his own pure brain, | fashion'd to beatrice. ADO 5.04. 88
but sway'd and fashion'd by the hand of heaven. MV 1.03. 93
i never saw a better fashion'd gown, | more SHR 4.03.101
for putting on so new a fashion'd robe. JN 4.02. 27
and fashion'd thee that instrument of ill, | who 1H6 3.03. 65
to be fashion'd | into what pitch he please. H8 2.02. 48
undoubtedly | was fashion'd to much honor. 4.02. 50
is fashion'd for the journey, dull and heavy. TIM 2.02.219
FASHIONED 1 FR 0.0001 REL FR 1 V 0 P
mould, that fashioned thee | made him a man; R2 1.02. 23
FASHIONING 2 FR 0.0002 REL FR 1 V 1 P
sometimes fashioning them like pharaoh's ADO 3.03.133 P
fashioning our humors | even to the opposed end LLL 5.02.757
FASHION–MONGERS 1 FR 0.0001 REL FR 0 V 1 P
with these strange flies, these fashion–mongers, ROM 2.04. 33 P
FASHION–MONGING 1 FR 0.0001 REL FR 1 V 0 P
scambling, outfacing, fashion–monging boys, ADO 5.01. 94
FASHION'S 1 FR 0.0001 REL FR 1 V 0 P
a man of fire–new words, fashion's own knight. LLL 1.01.178
FASHIONS* 9 FR 0.0010 REL FR 6 V 3 P
no, not to be so odd and from all fashions | as ADO 3.01. 72
old fashions please me best; SHR 3.01. 80
with the lampass, infected with the fashions, 3.02. 52 P
constancies | expire before their fashions." AWW 1.02. 63
report of fashions in proud italy, | whose R2 2.01. 21
laughter the wearing out of six fashions, which 2H4 5.01. 80 P
is this the fashions in the court of england? 2H6 1.03. 43
of tailors | to study fashions to adorn my body: R3 1.02.257
shall you, and taste gentlemen of all fashions. PER 4.02. 79 P
FASHON *(also fashion)*
FASHON 1 FR 0.0001 REL FR 0 V 1 P
dat it is not be de fashon pour les ladies of H5 5.02.261 P
FAST* 137 FR 0.0154 REL FR 116 V 21 P
stand fast, good fate, to his hanging, make the TMP 1.01. 30 P
vent thy groans | as fast as mill–wheels strike. 1.02.281
speaking, moving — | and yet so fast asleep. 2.01.215
to fast, like one that takes diet; TGV 2.01. 24 P
now can i break my fast, dine, sup, and sleep, 2.04.141
haply when they have judg'd me fast asleep, 3.01. 25
sir valentine, whither away so fast? 3.01. 51
fellows, stand fast; i see a passenger. 4.01. 1
by my halidom, i was fast asleep. 4.02.135 P
which they'll do fast enough of themselves, and WIV 4.01. 67 P
as surfeit is the father of much fast, | so MM 1.02.126
she is fast my wife, | save that we do the 1.02.147
with profits of the mind — study and fast. 1.04. 61
as fast lock'd up in sleep as guiltless labor 4.02. 66
a vow'd contract, | was fast belock'd in thine; 5.01.210
you have no stomach, having broke your fast: ERR 1.02. 50
but we that know what 'tis to fast and pray, 1.02. 51
she that doth fast till you come home to dinner; 1.02. 89
why, how now, dromio, where run'st thou so fast? 3.02. 72 P
by running fast. 4.02. 30
let us come in, that we may bind him fast, | and 5.01. 40
i am resolved, 'tis but a three years' fast: LLL 1.01. 24
not to see ladies, study, fast, not sleep. 1.01. 48
you shall fast a week with bran and water. 1.01.301 P
no penance, but 'a must fast three days a week. 1.02.129 P
thou shalt fast for thy offenses ere thou be 1.02.146 P
i will fast, being loose. 1.02.155 P
no, sir, that were fast and loose; 1.02.157 P
your wit's too hot, it speeds too fast, 'twill 2.01.119
a bargain well is as cunning as fast and loose: 3.01.103
soft, whither away so fast? 4.03.184
to fast, to study, and to see no woman — | flat 4.03.288
say, can you fast? 4.03.290
how chance the roses there do fade so fast? MND 1.01.129
night's swift dragons cut the clouds full fast, 3.02.379
i followed fast, but faster he did fly, | that 3.02.416
i cannot tell, i make it breed as fast. MV 1.03. 96
fast bind, fast find — | a proverb never stale 2.05. 54
fast bind, fast find — | a proverb never stale 2.05. 54
i will make fast the doors, and gild myself 2.06. 49
who comes so fast in silence of the night? 5.01. 25
as fast as she answers thee with frowning looks, AYL 3.05. 68 P
why now, as fast as she can marry us. 4.01.134 P
that as fast as you pour affection in, /it runs 4.01.209 P
blow our nails together, and fast it fairly out. SHR 1.01.108 P
and kiss on kiss | she vied so fast, protesting 2.01.309
and better 'twere that both of us did fast, 4.01.173
and for this night we'll fast for company. 4.01.177
not too fast! TN 1.05.293
to her need i have | a vessel rides fast by, but WT 4.04.501
me | upon good friday and ne'er broke his fast. JN 1.01.235
o lewis, stand fast! 3.01.208
play fast and loose with faith? 3.01.242
you shall find with me | fast to the chair. 4.01. 5
run more fast. 4.02.269
he tires betimes that spurs too fast betimes; R2 2.01. 36
within me grief hath kept a tedious fast; 2.01. 75
some fathers feed upon | is my strict fast — i 2.01. 80
cut off the heads of /too fast growing sprays, 3.04. 34
old, | i doubt not but to ride as fast as york. 5.02.115
farewell, and stand fast. 1H4 2.02. 72 P
pound i could run as fast as thou canst. 2.04.148 P
fast asleep behind the arras, and snorting like 2.04.528 P
do pelt so fast at one another's pate | that 1H6 3.01. 82
i think the duke of burgundy will fast | before 3.02. 42
and york as fast upon your grace exclaims, 4.04. 30
damsel of france, i think i have you fast: 5.03. 30
we will make fast within a hallow'd verge. 2H6 1.04. 22
these news, as fast as horse can carry them — 1.04. 74
fresh, | and sees fast by a butcher with an axe, 3.02.189
whither goes vaux so fast? what news, i prithee? 3.02.367
in love, | but that thou art so fast mine enemy. 5.02. 21
now, brother king, farewell, and sit you fast, 3H6 4.01.119
the gates made fast? 4.07. 10
this hand, fast wound about thy coal–black hair, 5.01. 54
now, montague, sit fast, i seek for thee, | that 5.02. 3
it is his policy | to haste thus fast, to find 5.04. 63
good morrow, neighbor, whither away so fast? R3 2.03. 1
and since, methinks i would not grow so fast, 2.04. 14
my uncle grew so fast | that he could gnaw a 2.04. 27
you said that idle weeds are fast in growth: 3.01.103
to sleep the /nights, and fast the /days; 4.04.118
whither away so fast? H8 2.01. 1
straight | springs out into fast gait, then 3.02.116
all fast? 5.02. 3
we must with all our main of power stand fast; TRO 2.03.262
which are devour'd | as fast as they are made, 3.03.149
to this valiant greek | comes fast upon. 4.03. 3
stand fast, and wear a castle on thy head! 5.02.187
lay hold upon him, priam, hold him fast, | he is 5.03. 59
if you'll stand fast, we'll beat them to their COR 1.04. 41
whither do you follow your eyes so fast? 2.01. 99 P
malignantly remain | fast foe to th' plebeii, 2.03.184
stand fast, | we have as many friends as enemies 3.01.230
friends now fast sworn, | whose double bosoms 4.04. 12
pit | where i espied the panther fast asleep. TIT 2.03.194
my niece, that flies away so fast? 2.04. 11
look that you bind them fast. 5.02.165
was that my father that went hence so fast? ROM 1.01.162
wisely and slow, they stumble that run fast. 2.03. 94
fast, i warrant her, she. 4.05. 1
bankrupts, hold fast; TIM 4.01. 8
fast asleep? JC 2.01.229
stand fast together, lest some friend of 3.01. 87
weeping as fast as they stream forth thy blood, 3.01.201
stand fast, titinius; we must out and talk. 5.01. 22
let us rather | hold fast the mortal sword, and MAC 4.03. 3
yet all this while in a most fast sleep. 5.01. 8 P
her very guise, and, upon my life, fast asleep. 5.01. 20 P
and for the day confin'd to fast in fires, HAM 1.05. 11
said, old mole, canst work i' th' earth so fast? 1.05.162
make, | fell into a sadness, then into a fast, 2.02.147
upon another's heel, | so fast they follow. 4.07.164
woo't fight, woo't fast, woo't tear thyself? 5.01.275
and 'tis our fast intent | to shake all cares LR 1.01. 38
bind fast his corky arms. 3.07. 29
but i pray you, sir, | are you fast married? OTH 1.02. 11

wilt thou be fast to my hopes, if i depend on 1.03.362 P
drops tears as fast as the arabian trees | their 5.02.350
but i had rather fast from all, four days, ANT 2.07.102
hath at fast and loose | beguil'd me to the very 4.12. 28
took, | as we do air, fast as 'twas minist'red, CYM 1.01. 45
bed, | and will continue fast to your affection, 1.06.138
(i fast and pray'd for their intelligence) thus: 4.02.347
spreads like a plane | fast by a brook, and TNK 2.06. 6
even as an empty eagle, sharp by fast, | tires VEN 55
mellow plum doth fall, the green sticks fast, 527
were beauty under twenty locks kept fast, | yet 575
the dove sleeps fast that this night–owl will LUC 360
shame, | thy private feasting to a public fast, 891
charging the sour–fac'd groom to hie as fast 1334
back to the strait that forc'd him on so fast 1670
as fast as thou shalt wane, so fast thou grow'st SON 11. 1
fast as thou shalt wane, so fast thou grow'st, 11. 1
and die as fast as they see others grow, | and 12.12
best | as fast as objects to his beams assemble? 114. 8
me | under that bond that him as fast doth bind. 134. 8

FAST–CLOSED 1 FR 0.0001 REL FR 1 V 0 P
than battery can | to our fast–closed gates; JN 2.01.447

FASTED 1 FR 0.0001 REL FR 0 V 1 P
when you fasted, it was presently after dinner; TGV 2.01. 28 P

FASTEN 4 FR 0.0004 REL FR 3 V 1 P
therefore fasten your ear on my advisings: MM 3.01.197 P
come, i will fasten on this sleeve of thine: ERR 2.02.173
to fasten in our thoughts that they have courage JC 5.01. 11
if i can fasten but one cup upon him, | with OTH 2.03. 48

FASTEN'D 3 FR 0.0003 REL FR 3 V 0 P
while i was speaking, oft was fasten'd to't. AWW 5.03. 82
fasten'd and fix'd the shame on't in himself, WT 2.03. 15
fair, and fasten'd to an empery | would make the CYM 1.06.120

/FASTENED 1 FR 0.0001 REL FR 1 V 0 P
/he /fastened /on /my /neck /and /bellowed /out LR 5.03.213

FASTENS 1 FR 0.0001 REL FR 1 V 0 P
bridle on a ragged bough | nimbly she fastens (o VEN 38

FASTER 18 FR 0.0020 REL FR 12 V 6 P
i'll bring my wood home faster. TMP 2.02. 72 P
falls into the cinquepace faster and faster, ADO 2.01. 79 P
falls into the cinquepace faster and faster, 2.01. 79 P
i followed fast, but faster he did fly, | that MND 3.02.416
o, ten times faster venus' pigeons fly | to seal MV 2.06. 5
hearts of men | faster than gnats in cobwebs. 3.02.123
and faster than his tongue | did make offense, AYL 3.05.116
he sings several tunes faster than you'll tell WT 4.04.184 P
the other grow | faster than thought or time. 4.04.554
the more it is trodden on, the faster it grows, 1H4 2.04.401 P
faster than spring–time show'rs comes thought on 2H6 3.01.337
and faster bound to aaron's charming eyes | than TIT 2.01. 16
which ten times faster glides than the sun's ROM 2.05. 5
upon thee, and then thou wouldst sin the faster. TIM 1.02.240 P
the water which they beat to follow faster, | as ANT 2.02.196
decrease not, but grow faster than the years; PER 1.02. 85
which strook her sad, and then it faster rock'd, LUC 262
give my love fame faster than time wastes life, SON 100.13

FASTEST 2 FR 0.0002 REL FR 1 V 1 P
he that runs fastest gets the ring. SHR 1.01.140 P
grew like the summer grass, fastest by night, H5 1.01. 65

FAST–FALLING 1 FR 0.0001 REL FR 1 V 0 P
yea, even my foes will shed fast–falling tears, 3H6 1.04.162

FAST–GROWING 1 FR 0.0001 REL FR 1 V 0 P
whom our fast–growing scene must find | at PER 4.ch. 6

FASTING 13 FR 0.0014 REL FR 10 V 3 P
she is not to be /kiss'd fasting, in respect of TGV 3.01.323 P
from fasting maids whose minds are dedicate | to MM 2.02.154
that shall express my true love's fasting pain. LLL 4.03.120
and thank heaven, fasting, for a good man's love AYL 3.05. 58
ten thousand years together, naked, fasting, WT 3.02.211
horn–ring, to keep my pack from fasting. 4.04.600 P
paw, | a fasting tiger safer by the tooth, JN 3.01.260
and therein fasting, hast thou made me gaunt. R2 2.01. 81
and give their fasting horses provender, | and H5 4.02. 58
hath ever since kept hector fasting and waking. TRO 1.02. 35 P
while pride is fasting in his wantonness! 3.03.137
fasting and prayer, | much castigation, exercise OTH 3.04. 40
discourse is heavy, fasting; CYM 3.06. 90

FASTING–DAYS 1 FR 0.0001 REL FR 0 V 1 P
have flesh for /holidays, fish for fasting–days, PER 2.01. 82 P

FAST–LOST 1 FR 0.0001 REL FR 1 V 0 P
feast–won, fast–lost; TIM 2.02.171

FASTLY 1 FR 0.0001 REL FR 1 V 0 P
towards this afflicted fancy fastly drew, | and, LC 61

FAST'NED 5 FR 0.0005 REL FR 5 V 0 P
had fast'ned him unto a small spare mast, | such ERR 1.01. 79
fast'ned ourselves at either end the mast, | and 1.01. 85
some stay to see him fast'ned in the earth. TIT 5.03.183
o strange and fast'ned villain! LR 2.01. 77
in a net, | so fast'ned in her arms adonis lies; VEN 68

FASTOLFE *(see falstaff)*

FASTS 4 FR 0.0004 REL FR 4 V 0 P
thoughts have punish'd me | with bitter fasts, TGV 2.04.131
if frosts and fasts, hard lodging and thin weeds LLL 5.02.801
a thousand men have broke their fasts to–day 3H6 2.02.127
suppler souls | than in our priest–like fasts: COR 5.01. 56

FAT* 71 FR 0.0080 REL FR 35 V 36 P
by the bare scalp of robin hood's fat friar, TGV 4.01. 36
i shall think the worse of fat men, as long as i WIV 2.01. 56 P
i am glad the fat knight is not here. 4.02. 29 P
my maid's aunt, the fat woman of brainford, has 4.02. 75 P
the poor unvirtuous fat knight shall be any 4.02.217 P
appoint a meeting with this old fat fellow, 4.04. 14
there's an old woman, a fat woman, gone up into 4.05. 11 P
a fat woman? 4.05. 15 P
tarries the coming down of thy fat woman. 4.05. 21 P
mine host, an old fat woman even now with me, 4.05. 24 P
they would melt me out of my fat drop by drop, 4.05. 98 P
fat falstaff | hath a great scene; 4.06. 16
match, and yet is she a wondrous fat marriage. ERR 3.02. 93 P
how dost thou mean a fat marriage? 3.02. 94 P
there is a fat friend at your master's house, 5.01.415
fat paunches have lean pates; LLL 1.01. 26
your pennyworth is good, and your goose be fat. 3.01.102
a fat l'envoy — ay, that's a fat goose. 3.01.104
a fat l'envoy — ay, that's a fat goose. 3.01.104
then the boy's fat l'envoy, the goose that you 3.01.109
wits they have — gross gross, fat fat. 5.02.268
wits they have — gross gross, fat fat. 5.02.268
smile | when i a fat and bean–fed horse beguile, MND 2.01. 45
i will feed fat the ancient grudge i bear him. MV 1.03. 47
"sweep on, you fat and greasy citizens, | 'tis AYL 2.01. 55
that good pasture makes fat sheep; 3.02. 27 P
ask marian hacket, the fat ale–wife of wincot, SHR in.2. 21 P
six score fat oxen standing in my stalls, | and 2.01.358
how say you to a fat tripe finely broil'd? 4.03. 20
it is as fat and fulsome to mine ear | as TN 5.01.109
praise, and make 's | as fat as tame things. WT 1.02. 92
the fat ribs of peace | must by the hungry now JN 3.03. 9
and traders riding to london with fat purses. 1H4 1.02.127 P
lies that this same fat rogue will tell us when 1.02.187 P
if i hang, i'll make a fat pair of gallows; 2.01. 67 P
no, ye fat chuffs, i would your store were here! 2.02. 89 P
how the fat rogue roar'd! 2.02.111 P
prithee come out of that fat room, and lend me 2.04. 1 P
england, and one of them is fat and grows old, 2.04.131 P
'zounds, ye fat paunch, and ye call me coward, 2.04.144 P
haunts thee in the likeness of an old fat man, a 2.04.448 P
if to be fat be to be hated, then pharaoh's 2.04.472 P
well known, my gracious lord, | a gross fat man. 2.04.511
as fat as butter. 2.04.511
i'll procure this fat rogue a charge of foot, 2.04.545 P
away, | advantage feeds him fat while men delay. 3.02.180
why, you are so fat, sir john, that you must 3.03. 21 P
death hath not strook so fat a deer to–day, 5.04.107
did you not tell me this fat man was dead? 5.04.132
put all my substance into that fat belly of his, 2H4 2.01. 75 P
and look if the fat villain have not transform'd 2.02. 71 P
you make fat rascals, mistress doll. 2.04. 41 P
then feed and be fat, my fair calipolis. 2.04.179
how? you fat fool, i scorn you. 2.04.296 P
if you be not too much cloy'd with fat meat, our ep 27 P
turn'd away the fat knight with the great belly H5 4.07. 48 P
want their porridge and their fat bull–beeves: 1H6 1.02. 9
your country's fat shall pay your pains the hire R3 5.03.258
would they but fat their thoughts | with this TRO 2.02. 48
luxury, with his fat rump and potato finger, 5.02. 55 P
doth fat me with the very thoughts of it! TIT 3.01.203
let me have men about me that are fat, JC 1.02.192
and duller shouldst thou be than the fat weed HAM 1.05. 32
we fat all creatures else to fat us, and we fat 4.03. 22 P
we fat all creatures else to fat us, and we fat 4.03. 22 P
to fat us, and we fat ourselves for maggots; 4.03. 22 P
your fat king and your lean beggar is but 4.03. 23 P
he's fat, and scant of breath. 5.02.287
julius caesar | grew fat with feasting there. ANT 2.06. 65
then mine host | and his fat spouse, that TNK 3.05.128
fair sun that breeds the fat earth's store, | by LUC 1837

FATAL 44 FR 0.0049 REL FR 41 V 3 P
son | that floated with thee on the fatal raft? ERR 5.01.349
a very dangerous flat, and fatal, where the MV 3.01. 5 P
and fatal opposite that you could possibly have TN 3.04.267 P
of that fatal country sicilia, prithee speak no WT 4.02. 20 P
a deed of slander with thy fatal hand | upon my R2 5.06. 35
fatal to all those | that wear those colors on 1H4 5.04. 26
left by the fatal and neglected english | upon H5 2.04. 13
with fatal mouths gaping on girded harflew. 3.pr. 27
troyan, | to have me fold up parca's fatal web? 5.01. 20
bent | the fatal balls of murthering basilisks. 5.02. 17
accursed fatal hand | that hath contriv'd this 1H6 1.04. 76
and now i fear that fatal prophecy | which in 3.01.194
but burning fatal to the talbonites! 3.02. 28
place barrels of pitch upon the fatal stake, 5.04. 57
fatal this marriage, cancelling your fame, 2H6 1.01. 99
and blood | as did the fatal brand althaea burnt 1.01.234
with whose envenomed and fatal sting, | your 3.02.267
ah, hark, the fatal followers do pursue, | and i 3H6 1.04. 22
face, | the fatal colors of our striving houses; 2.05. 98
bring forth that fatal screech–owl to our house 2.06. 56
brought from thence the thracian fatal steeds, 4.02. 21
to bend the fatal instruments of war | against 5.01. 87
and richard but a /ragged fatal rock? 5.04. 27
have now the fatal object in my eye | where my 5.06. 16
fatal and ominous to noble peers! R3 3.03. 10
tumble down | into the fatal bowels of the deep. 3.04.101
she doth unroll | to do some fatal execution? TIT 2.03. 36
breeds, | unless the nightly owl or fatal raven; 2.03. 97
a very fatal place it seems to me. 2.03.202
then all too late i bring this fatal writ, | the 2.03.264
or who hath brought the fatal engine in | that 5.03. 86
from forth the fatal loins of these two foes | a ROM pr 5
all | the unlucky manage of this fatal brawl: 3.01.143
his /agile arm beats down their fatal points, 3.01.166
fir'd | doth hurry from the fatal cannon's womb. 5.01. 65
their shadows seem | a canopy most fatal, under JC 5.01. 87
that croaks the fatal entrance of duncan | under MAC 1.05. 39
art thou not, fatal vision, sensible | to 2.01. 36
it was the owl that shriek'd, the fatal bellman, 2.02. 3
i'll spend | unto a dismal and a fatal end. 3.05. 21
so sweet was ne'er so fatal. OTH 5.02. 20
for you're fatal then | when your eyes roll so. 5.02. 37
wreath'd up in fatal folds just in his way, VEN 879
and kiss'd the fatal knife, to end his vow; LUC 1843

FATALLY 1 FR 0.0001 REL FR 1 V 0 P
shame | when cressy battle fatally was struck, H5 2.04. 54

FATAL–PLOTTED 1 FR 0.0001 REL FR 1 V 0 P
and give the king this fatal–plotted scroll. TIT 2.03. 47

FAT–ALREADY 1 FR 0.0001 REL FR 1 V 0 P
that were to enlard his fat–already pride, | and TRO 2.03.195

FAT–BRAIN'D 1 FR 0.0001 REL FR 0 V 1 P
to mope with his fat–brain'd followers so far H5 3.07.133 P

/FATE 1 FR 0.0001 REL FR 1 V 0 P
"/tell /me what /fate /awaits the duke of 2H6 1.04. 32

FATE 50 FR 0.0056 REL FR 47 V 3 P
stand fast, good fate, to his hanging, make the TMP 1.01. 30 P
i and my fellows | are ministers of fate. 3.03. 61
but fate (ordaining he should be a cuckold) held WIV 3.05.104 P
money buys lands, and wives are sold by fate. 5.05.233
my bending down | reprieve thee from thy fate, MM 3.01.144
o fate! ADO 4.01.115
that he should be my fool and i his fate. LLL 5.02. 68
then fate o'errules, that, one man holding troth MND 3.02. 92
fate, show thy force: TN 1.05.310
the malignancy of my fate might perhaps 2.01. 4 P
since fate (against thy better disposition) WT 3.03. 28
o god, that one might read the book of fate, 2H4 3.01. 45
us fear | the native mightiness and fate of him. H5 2.04. 64
and of buxom valor, hath, by cruel fate, | and 3.06. 26
till with thy warlike sword, despite of fate, 1H6 4.06. 8
"tell me what fate awaits the duke of suffolk?" 2H6 1.04. 64
let me say | 'tis but the fate of place, and the H8 1.02. 75
and you, o fate! 2.03. 85
is like that mirth fate turns to sudden sadness. TRO 1.01. 40
if to my sword his fate be not the glory, | a 4.01. 27
mine honor keeps the weather of my fate. 5.03. 26
not fate, obedience, nor the hand of mars 5.03. 52
fate, hear me what i say! 5.06. 25
this day's black fate on moe days doth depend, ROM 3.01.119
he is a man (setting his fate aside) | of comely TIM 3.05. 14
hard fate! 3.05. 74
which fate and metaphysical aid doth seem | to MAC 1.05. 29
what should be spoken here, where our fate, 2.03.121
rather than so, come fate into the list, | and 3.01. 70
must embrace the fate | of that dark hour. 3.01.136
he shall spurn fate, scorn death, and bear | his 3.05. 30
double sure, | and take a bond of fate: 4.01. 84
if thou art privy to thy country's fate, | which HAM 1.01.133
my fate cries out, | and makes each petty artere 1.04. 81
comfort like to this | succeeds in unknown fate. OTH 2.01.193
lives in bliss | who, certain of his fate, loves 3.03.168
"cursed fate that gave thee to the moor!" 3.03.426
and bid me, when my fate would have me wiv'd, 3.04. 64
dear lies dead, | and your unblest fate hies. 5.01. 34
who can control his fate? 5.02.265
in alexandria, where | i will oppose his fate. ANT 3.13.169
and drink carouses to the next day's fate, 4.08. 34
do not please sharp fate | to grace it with your 4.14.135
live, and make | us weep to hear your fate, fair PER 3.02.103
our life, this daring deed | of fate in wedlock. TNK 1.01.165
must | with him stand to the mercy of our fate, 1.02.102
yet fate hath brought them off. 1.03. 41
"i will be true, my stars, my fate," etc. 4.03. 57
for me, i am the mistress of my fate, | and with LUC 1069
cries, | and look upon myself and curse my fate, SON 29. 4

FATED 5 FR 0.0005 REL FR 5 V 0 P
one midnight | fated to th' purpose, did antonio TMP 1.02.129
the fated sky | gives us free scope, only doth AWW 1.01.217
as it hath fated her to be my motive | and 4.04. 20
air | hang fated o'er men's faults light on thy LR 3.04. 68
even then this forked plague is fated to us OTH 3.03.276

FATES 15 FR 0.0017 REL FR 13 V 2 P
egeon, whom the fates have mark'd | to bear the ERR 1.01.140
far, | and make and mar | the foolish fates." MND 1.02. 38
and i, like helen, till the fates me kill. 5.01.197
o fates, come, come, | cut thread and thrum, 5.01.285
gentleman, according to fates and destinies, and MV 2.02. 62 P
thy fates open their hands, let thy blood and TN 2.05.146 P
o, the fates! WT 4.04. 20
what fates impose, that men must needs abide; 3H6 4.03. 58
men at some time are masters of their fates; JC 1.02.139
if not, the fates with traitors do contrive. 2.03. 16
fates, we will know your pleasures. 3.01. 98
as harbingers preceding still the fates | and HAM 1.01.122
our wills and fates do so contrary run | that 3.02.211
that the strict fates had pleas'd you had PER 3.03. 8
nurses are not the fates, | to foster it, not 4.03. 14

FAT–GUTS 1 FR 0.0001 REL FR 0 V 1 P
peace, ye fat–guts, lie down. 1H4 2.02. 31 P

/FATHER 15 FR 0.0017 REL FR 12 V 3 P
sir proteus, your /father calls for you: TGV 1.03. 88
/thing, /in /honor, /had /my /father /lost, 2H4 4.01.111
/my /father /from /the /breast /of /bullingbrook 4.01.122
/but /if /your /father /had /been /victor /there 4.01.132
/if /that /fly /had /a /father /and /mother? TIT 3.02. 60
that i, the son of a dear /father murthered, HAM 2.02.583
like my sisters, | /to /love /my /father /all. LR 1.01.104
/to /his /father, /that /so /tenderly /and 1.02. 96 P
/which /they /will /make /an /obedient /father. 1.04.235 P
/she /kick'd /the /poor /king /her /father. 3.06. 48 P
/a /father, /and /a /gracious /aged /man, 4.02. 41
/or /twice /she /heav'd /the /name /of "/father" 4.03. 25
/father! 4.03. 28
/the /question /of /cordelia /and /her /father 5.03. 58
/burst /heaven, /threw /him /on /my /father, 5.03.214

FATHER 844 FR 0.0954 REL FR 663 V 181 P
if by your art, my dearest father, you have TMP 1.02. 1
a full poor cell, | and thy no greater father. 1.02. 21
thy father was the duke of milan and | a prince 1.02. 54
sir, are not you my father? 1.02. 55
and thy father | was duke of milan, and his only 1.02. 57
full fadom five thy father lies, | of his bones 1.02.397
the ditty does remember my drown'd father. 1.02.406
at ebb) beheld | the king my father wrack'd. 1.02.437
why speaks my father so ungently? 1.02.445
pity move my father | to be inclin'd my way! 1.02.447
o dear father, | make not too rash a trial of 1.02.467
beseech you, father. 1.02.474
my father | is hard at study; 3.01. 19
o my father, | i have broke your hest to say so! 3.01. 36
men than you, good friend, | and my dear father. 3.01. 52
so rare a wond'red father and a wise | makes 4.01.123
blessings | of a glad father compass thee about! 5.01.180
i chose her when i could not ask my father | for 5.01.190
and second father | this lady makes him to me. 5.01.195
my father at the road | expects my coming, there TGV 1.01. 53
madam, | dinner is ready, and your father stays. 1.02.128
i fear'd to show my father julia's letter, 1.03. 80
my father stays my coming; 2.02. 13
my mother weeping, my father wailing, my sister 2.03. 7 P
this shoe is my father; 2.03. 15 P
no, this left shoe is my father; 2.03. 15 P
is my mother, and this my father — a vengeance 2.03. 18 P
now come i to my father: 2.03. 24 P
"father, your blessing." 2.03. 24 P
now should i kiss my father; 2.03. 26 P
here comes my father. 2.04. 48 P
sir valentine, your father is in good health: 2.04. 50
the honor and regard of such a father. 2.04. 60
madam, my lord your father would speak with you. 2.04.116
my foolish rival, that her father likes | (only 2.04.174
now presently i'll give her father notice | of 2.06. 36
child, | nor fearing me as if i were her father; 3.01. 71
he plays false, father. 4.02. 59 P
nor how my father would enforce me marry | vain 4.03. 16

ay, and her father is make her a petter penny. WIV 1.01. 60 P
my father desires your worships' company. 1.01.261 P
i hope i have your good will, father page. 3.02. 60 P
o boy, thou hadst a father! 3.04. 37 P
i had a father, mistress anne; 3.04. 38 P
anne the jest how my father stole two geese out 3.04. 40 P
your father and my uncle hath made motions. 3.04. 63 P
you may ask your father, here he comes. 3.04. 66 P
must needs go in, | her father will be angry. 3.04. 93
her father hath commanded her to slip | away 4.06. 23
her father means she shall be all in white; 4.06. 35
which means she to deceive, father or mother? 4.06. 46
whoa ho, ho! father page! 5.05.177 P
pardon, good father! good my mother, pardon! 5.05.216
as surfeit is the father of much fast, | so MM 1.02.126
holy father, throw away that thought; 1.03. 1
therefore indeed, my father, | i have on angelo 1.03. 39
whom i would save, had a most noble father! 2.01. 7
whose father died at hallowmas. 2.01.124 P
i do confess it, and repent it, father. 2.03. 29
heaven shield my mother play'd my father fair! 3.01.140
what's your will, father? 3.01.175 P
show me how, good father. 3.01.238 P
fare you well, good father. 3.01.269 P
bless you, good father friar. 3.02. 11 P
and you, good brother father. 3.02. 13 P
good even, good father. 3.02.214 P
wit | make thee the father of their idle dream 4.01. 63
she'll take the enterprise upon her, father, 4.01. 65
welcome, father. 4.02. 72
pardon me, good father, it is against my oath. 4.02.181 P
look you, sir, here comes your ghostly father. 4.03. 49 P
here in the prison, father, | there died this 4.03. 69
this shall be done, good father, presently. 4.03. 82
a ghostly father, belike. 5.01.126
as the plain bald pate of father time himself. ERR 2.02. 70 P
i never saw my father in my life. 5.01.320
these ducats pawn i for my father here. 5.01.390
it shall not need, thy father hath his life. 5.01.391
lady, for you are like an honorable father. ADO 1.01.112 P
if signior leonato be her father, she would not 1.01.113 P
and i will break with her, and with her father, 1.01.309
then after to her father will i break, | and the 1.01.326
niece, i trust you will be rul'd by your father. 2.01. 51 P
cousin's duty to make cur'sy and say, "father, 2.01. 53 P
or else make another cur'sy and say, "father, as 2.01. 55 P
and hath withdrawn her father to break with him 2.01.156 P
i have broke with her father, and his good will 2.01.299 P
your father got excellent husbands, if a maid 2.01.324 P
father, by your leave, | will you with free and 4.01. 23
o my father, | prove you that any man with me 4.01.180
bring me a father that so lov'd his child, 5.01. 8
you must be father to your brother's daughter, 5.04. 15
to her decrepit, sick, and bedred father; LLL 1.01.138
consider who the king your father sends, | to 2.01. 2
your father here doth intimate | the payment of 2.01.128
entire sum | disbursed by my father in his wars. 2.01.131
if then the king your father will restore | but 2.01.137
withal, | and have the money by our father lent, 2.01.147
you do the king my father too much wrong, | and 2.01.153
from special officers | of charles his father. 2.01.162
like her mother, for her father is but grim. 2.01.256
and, as a certain father saith — 4.02.148 P
sir, tell not me of the father, i do fear 4.02.149 P
what a joyful father wouldest thou make me! 5.01. 76 P
the king, your father — 5.02.719
to you your father should be as a god; MND 1.01. 47
i would my father look'd but with my eyes. 1.01. 56
you, pyramus' father; 1.02. 63 P
myself, thisby's father; 1.02. 64 P
your mother, and to master peascod, your father. 3.01.187 P
yea, and my father. 4.01.196
daughter curb'd by the will of a dead father. MV 1.02. 25 P
your father was ever virtuous, and holy men at 1.02. 27 P
o father abram, what these christians are, 1.03.160
but if my father had not scanted me, | and 2.01. 17
son, for indeed my father did something smack, 2.02. 17 P
o heavens, this is my true–begotten father, who, 2.02. 36 P
his father, though i say't, is an honest 2.02. 52 P
well, let his father be what 'a will, we talk of 2.02. 54 P
talk not of master launcelot, father, for the 2.02. 61 P
do you know me, father? 2.02. 69 P
do you not know me, father? 2.02. 73 P
it is a wise father that knows his own child. 2.02. 76 P
father, i am glad you are come; 2.02.107 P
to him, father, for i am a jew if i serve the 2.02.112 P
to him, father. 2.02.119 P
that would, sir, as my father shall specify — 2.02.124 P
and have a desire, as my father shall specify — 2.02.128 P
me wrong, doth cause me, as my father, being, i 2.02.133 P
say it, though old man, yet poor man, my father. 2.02.140 P
go, father, with thy son. 2.02.152
father, in. 2.02.156 P
father, come, i'll take my leave of the jew in 2.02.167 P
i am sorry thou wilt leave my father so. 2.03. 1
i would not have my father | see me in talk with 2.03. 8
if e'er the jew her father come to heaven, | it 2.04. 33
i have a father, you a daughter, lost. 2.05. 57
approach, | here dwells my father jew. 2.06. 25
the sins of the father are to be laid upon the 3.05. 2 P
may partly hope that your father got you not, 3.05. 11 P
i fear you are damn'd both by father and mother; 3.05. 16 P
thus when i shun scylla, your father, i fall 3.05. 17 P
and the spirit of my father, which i think is AYL 1.01. 22 P
i have as much of my father in me as you, albeit 1.01. 49 P
he was my father, and he is thrice a villain 1.01. 57 P
villain that says such a father begot villains. 1.01. 58 P
my father charg'd you in his will to give me 1.01. 67 P
the spirit of my father grows strong in me, and 1.01. 70 P
poor allottery my father left me by testament, 1.01. 73 P
duke's daughter, be banish'd with her father? 1.01.106 P
you could teach me to forget a banish'd father, 1.02. 6 P
if my uncle, thy banish'd father, had banish'd 1.02. 10 P
had banish'd thy uncle, the duke my father, so 1.02. 11 P
have taught my love to take thy father for mine; 1.02. 12 P
you know my father hath no child but i, nor none 1.02. 17 P
he hath taken away from thy father perforce, i 1.02. 20 P
mistress, you must come away to your father. 1.02. 58 P
one that old frederick, your father, loves. 1.02. 82 P
lie, the poor old man, their father, making such 1.02.130 P
the world esteem'd thy father honorable, | but i 1.02.225
i would thou hadst told me of another father. 1.02.230
were i my father, coz, would i do this? 1.02.231
my father lov'd sir rowland as his soul, | and 1.02.235
but is all this for your father? 1.03. 10 P
no, some of it is for my child's father. 1.03. 11 P
the duke my father lov'd his father dearly. 1.03. 29 P
the duke my father lov'd his father dearly. 1.03. 29 P
hate him, for my father hated his father dearly; 1.03. 33 P
hate him, for my father hated his father dearly; 1.03. 33 P
my father was no traitor. 1.03. 63
else had she with her father rang'd along. 1.03. 68
no, let my father seek another heir. 1.03. 99
son) | of him i was about to call his father — 2.03. 21
the thrifty hire i sav'd under your father, 2.03. 39
i am the duke | that lov'd your father. 2.07.196
here in the forest on the duke your father. 3.04. 34 P
thy father's father wore it, | and thy father 4.02. 15
father wore it, | and thy father bore it. 4.02. 16
i'll have no father, if you be not he; 5.04.122
gave me my being and my father first, | a SHR 1.01. 11
she delights, i will wish him to her father. 1.01.112 P
hortensio, though her father be very rich, any 1.01.124 P
that till the father rid his hands of her, 1.01.181
for so your father charg'd me at our parting; 1.01.213
antonio, my father, is deceas'd, | and i have 1.02. 54
her father is baptista minola, | an affable and 1.02. 97
i know her father, though i know not her, | and 1.02.101
not her, | and he knew my deceased father well. 1.02.102
my father dead, my fortune lives for me, | and i 1.02.191
to whom my father is not all unknown, | and were 1.02.239
her father keeps from all access of suitors, 1.02.259
you knew my father well, and in him me, | left 2.01.116
for i tell you, father, | i am as peremptory as 2.01.130
your father hath consented | that you shall be 2.01.269
here comes your father. 2.01.279
father, 'tis thus: 2.01.290
provide the feast, father, and bid the guests, 2.01.316
father, and wife, and gentlemen, adieu. 2.01.321
'tis known my father hath no less | than three 2.01.377
and let your father make her the assurance, 2.01.387
your father were a fool | to give thee all, and 2.01.400
but suppos'd lucentio | must get a father, 2.01.408
your father prays you leave your books, | and 3.01. 82
how does my father? 3.02. 93
the narrow–prying father, minola, | the quaint 3.02.146
dine with my father, drink a health to me, | for 3.02.196
father, be quiet, he shall stay my leisure. 3.02.217
in gait and countenance surely like a father. 4.02. 65
he is my father, sir, and, sooth to say, | in 4.02. 99
my father is here look'd for every day, | to 4.02.117
with such austerity as 'longeth to a father. 4.04. 7
i told him that your father was at venice, | and 4.04. 15
i pray you stand good father to me now, | give 4.04. 21
that like a father you will deal with him, | and 4.04. 44
there doth my father lie; 4.04. 56
lucentio's father is arriv'd in padua, | and how 4.04. 65
with the deceiving father of a deceitful son. 4.04. 83 P
pardon, old father, my mistaking eyes, | that 4.05. 45
now i perceive thou art a reverent father. 4.05. 48
age, | i may entitle thee my loving father. 4.05. 61
i do assure thee, father, so it is. 4.05. 74
lucentio that his father is come from pisa, and 5.01. 28 P
his father is come from padua and here looking 5.01. 30 P
art thou his father? 5.01. 32 P
didst thou never see thy /master's father, 5.01. 53 P
i thank my good father, i am able to maintain it 5.01. 76 P
thy father! 5.01. 77 P
father baptista, i charge you see that he be 5.01. 92 P
pardon, sweet father. 5.01.112
pardon, dear father. 5.01.113
then pardon him, sweet father, for my sake. 5.01.130
not pale, bianca, thy father will not frown. 5.01.138 P
my fair bianca, bid my father welcome, | while i 5.02. 4
you, sir, a father. AWW 1.01. 7 P
this young gentlewoman had a father — o, that 1.01. 17 P
remembrance of her father never approaches her 1.01. 49 P
bertram, and succeed thy father | in manners, as 1.01. 61
lady, | you must hold the credit of your father. 1.01. 78
i think not on my father, | and these great 1.01. 79
as when thy father and myself in friendship 1.02. 25
much repairs me | to talk of your good father. 1.02. 31
her father bequeath'd her to me, and she herself 1.03.101 P
you know my father left me some prescriptions 1.03.221
gerard de narbon was my father, | in what he did 2.01.101
not one of those but had a noble father. 2.03. 62
i am sure thy father drunk wine — but if thou 2.03. 99 P
child begotten of thy body that i am father to, 3.02. 59 P
five descents | since the first father wore it. 3.07. 25
i have heard my father name him. TN 1.02. 28
my father was that sebastian of messaline, whom 2.01. 17 P
the lady olivia's father took much delight in. 2.04. 12 P
my father had a daughter lov'd a man, | as it 2.04.107
then lead the way, good father, and heavens so 4.03. 34
call forth the holy father. 5.01.142
o, welcome, father! 5.01.150
father, i charge thee by thy reverence | here to 5.01.151
sebastian was my father — | such a sebastian 5.01.232
my father had a mole upon his brow. 5.01.242
i will respect thee as a father, if | thou WT 1.02.461
the whole matter | and copy of the father — eye 2.03.100
to see this bastard kneel | and call me father? 2.03.156
no father owning it (which is indeed | more 3.02. 88
the emperor of russia was my father. 3.02.119
or death, upon the earth | of its right father. 3.03. 46
my father nam'd me autolycus, who being, as i am 4.03. 24 P
but my father hath made her mistress of the 4.03. 39 P
even now i tremble | to think your father, by 4.04. 19
my father and the gentlemen are in sad talk, and 4.04.310 P
o, father, you'll know more of that hereafter. 4.04.343
have you a father? 4.04.392
methinks a father | is at the nuptial of his son 4.04.394
more, | is not your father grown incapable | of 4.04.397
but as good reason | the father (all whose joy 4.04.408
i not acquaint | my father of this business. 4.04.413
why, how now, father? | speak ere thou diest. 4.04.450
yea, | to die upon the bed my father died, | to 4.04.455
from my succession wipe me, father, i | am heir 4.04.480
i' th' love | that i have borne your father? 4.04.517
your discontenting father strive to qualify, 4.04.532
sent by the king your father | to greet him and 4.04.556
him, with | what you (as from your father) shall 4.04.559
preserver of my father, now of me, | the 4.04.586
shall satisfy your father. 4.04.622
should i now meet my father, | he would not call 4.04.657
away from his father with his clog at his heels. 4.04.679 P
no honest man, neither to his father nor to me, 4.04.701 P
for she did print your royal father off, 5.01.125
amity too, of your brave father, whom | (though 5.01.136
to execute the charge my father gave me | for 5.01.162
you have a holy father, | a graceful gentleman, 5.01.170
fled from his father, from his hopes, and with 5.01.184
on the way | the father of this seeming lady and 5.01.191
he's with the king your father. 5.01.196
o my poor father! 5.01.202
should chase us with my father, pow'r no jot 5.01.217
my father will grant precious things as trifles. 5.01.222
i will to your father. 5.01.229
but i was a gentleman born before my father; 5.02.140 P
and then the two kings call'd my father brother; 5.02.142 P
princess, my sister, call'd my father father; 5.02.143 P
princess, my sister, call'd my father father; 5.02.144 P
is well known — and, as i think, one father; JN 1.01. 60
and were our father, and this son like him, | o 1.01. 81
o old sir robert, father, on my knee | i give 1.01. 82
because he hath a half–face like my father! 1.01. 92
my gracious liege, when that my father liv'd, 1.01. 95
your brother did employ my father much — 1.01. 96
shores | between my father and my mother lay, 1.01.106
lay, | as i have heard my father speak himself, 1.01.107
had of your father claim'd this son for his? 1.01.122
friend, your father might have kept | this calf, 1.01.123
my brother might not claim him, nor your father, 1.01.126
my father gave me honor, yours gave land. 1.01.164
then, good my mother, let me know my father; 1.01.249
king richard cordelion was thy father. 1.01.253
madam, i would not wish a better father. 1.01.260
with all my heart i thank thee for my father! 1.01.270
liker in feature to his father geffrey | than 2.01.126
i think | his father never was so true begot — 2.01.130
a good mother, boy, that blots thy father. 2.01.132
since i first call'd my brother's father dad. 2.01.467
good father cardinal, cry thou amen | to my keen 3.01.181
bethink you, father, for the difference | is 3.01.204
good reverend father, make my person yours, 3.01.224
sir, | my reverend father, let it not be so! 3.01.249
father, to arms! 3.01.300
father, i may not wish the fortune thine; 3.01.333
will | as dear be to thee as thy father was. 3.03. 4
and, father cardinal, i have heard you say 3.04. 76
of lancaster, | the honorable father to my foe, R2 1.01.136
you would have bid me argue like a father. 1.03.238
son, | for that i was his father edward's son, 2.01.125
of whom thy father, prince of wales, was first. 2.01.172
hot youth | as when brave gaunt, thy father, and 2.03.100
you are my father, for methinks in you | i see 2.03.117
o then my father, | will you permit that i shall 2.03.118
he should have found his uncle gaunt a father 2.03.127
where is the duke my father with his power? 3.02.143
my father hath a power, inquire of him, | and 3.02.186
cousin, i am too young to be your father, 3.03.204
o loyal father of a treacherous son! 5.03. 60
my soul the father, and these two beget | a 5.05. 7
should be the father to so blest a son — | a 1H4 1.01. 80
with the rusty curb of old father antic the law? 1.02. 61 P
but that i think his father loves him not | and 1.03.231
is there not my father, my uncle, and myself? 2.03. 24 P
lies are like their father that begets them, 2.04.225 P
he says he comes from your father. 2.04.289 P
here was sir john bracy from your father; 2.04.334 P
chid to–morrow when thou comest to thy father. 2.04.374 P
do thou stand for my father and examine me upon 2.04.376 P
o, the father, how he holds his countenance! 2.04.392 P
do thou stand for me, and i'll play my father. 2.04.434 P
that grey iniquity, that father ruffian, that 2.04.454 P
to meet your father and the scottish power, | as 3.01. 84
my father glendower is not ready yet, | nor 3.01. 86
fie, cousin percy, how you cross my father! 3.01.145
good father, tell her that she and my aunt percy 3.01.194
thou think i'll fear thee as i fear thy father? 3.03.150 P
good friends with my father and may do any thing 3.03.181 P
these letters come from your father. 4.01. 14
but yet i would your father had been here. 4.01. 60
my father and glendower being both away, | the 4.01.131
my father and my uncle and myself | did give him 4.03. 54
home, | my father gave him welcome to the shore; 4.03. 59
my father, in kind heart and pity mov'd, | swore 4.03. 64
little higher than his vow | made to my father, 4.03. 76
in rage dismiss'd my father from the court, 4.03.100
if your father will do me any honor, so; 5.04.140 P
/where hotspur's father, old northumberland, 2H4 in 36
now | should be the father of some stratagem. 1.01. 8
writ man ever since his father was a bachelor. 1.02. 27 P
head for liking his father to a singing–man of 2.01. 90 P
that i should be sad, now my father is sick, 2.02. 40 P
heart bleeds inwardly that my father is so sick, 2.02. 48 P
to the son of the king nearest his father, harry 2.02.120 P
the time was, father, that you broke your word 2.03. 10
threw many a northward look to see his father 2.03. 13
and thy father is to give me thanks for it. 2.04.322 P
the king your father is at westminster, | and 2.04.355
you, reverend father, and these noble lords 4.01. 38
in very ample virtue of his father, | to hear 4.01.161
the subjects of his substitute, my father, | and 4.02. 28
lords, | i hear the king my father is sore sick. 4.03. 77
blood he did naturally inherit of his father, he 4.03.118 P
what would my lord and father? 4.04. 18
o my royal father! 4.04.112
the king your father is dispos'd to sleep. 4.05. 17
my father! 4.05. 34
and filial tenderness | shall, o dear father, 4.05. 40
yields his engrossments to the ending father. 4.05. 79
thy wish was father, harry, to that thought: 4.05. 92
depending | hath fed upon the body of my father; 4.05.159

that had before my face murdered my father, 4.05.167
health, peace, and happiness to my royal father! 4.05.226
i'll be your father and your brother too. 5.02. 57
i then did use the person of your father, | the 5.02. 73
whereon (as an offender to your father) | i gave 5.02. 81
be now the father and propose a son, | hear your 5.02. 92
you shall be as a father to my youth, | my voice 5.02.118
you, | my father is gone wild into his grave; 5.02.123
in which you, father, shall have foremost hand. 5.02.140
whiles his most mighty father on a hill | stood H5 1.02.108
my most redoubted father, | it is most meet we 2.04. 14
if my father render fair return, | it is against 2.04.127
so, if a son that is by his father sent about 4.01.147 P
should be impos'd upon his father that sent him; 4.01.150 P
endings of his soldiers, the father of his son, 4.01.156 P
fault | my father made in compassing the crown! 4.01.294
his father was called philip of macedon, as i 4.07. 20 P
here comes your father. 5.02.280 P
father, i know, and oft have shot at them, 1H6 1.04. 3
father, i warrant you, take you no care, | i'll 1.04. 21
was not thy father, richard earl of cambridge, 2.04. 90
my father was attached, not attainted, 2.04. 96
declare the cause | my father, earl of cambridge 2.05. 54
the fift | (succeeding his father bullingbrook) 2.05. 83
thy father, earl of cambridge then, deriv'd 2.05. 84
a prince, | so kind a father of the commonweal, 3.01. 98
lives | and as his father here was conqueror, 3.02. 81
i do remember how my father said | a stouter 3.04. 18
o, think upon the conquest of my father, | my 4.01.148
i met in travel toward his warlike father! 4.03. 36
should bring thy father to his drooping chair. 4.05. 5
then let me stay, and, father, do you fly. 4.05. 21
part of thy father may be sav'd in thee. 4.05. 38
for live i will not if my father die. 4.05. 51
o, twice my father, twice am i thy son! 4.06. 6
speak to thy father ere thou yield thy breath! 4.07. 24
for though her father be the king of naples, 5.03. 94
and if my father please, i am content. 5.03.127
thou art no father nor no friend of mine. 5.04. 9
dost thou deny thy father, cursed drab? 5.04. 32
live, | especially since charles must father it. 5.04. 71
her father is no better than an earl, | although 5.05. 37
yes, my lord, her father is a king, | the king 5.05. 39
and deliver'd /over to the king her father" — 2H6 1.01. 52 P
and deliver'd over to the king her father, and 1.01. 60 P
o father, maine is lost! 1.01.209
main chance, father, you meant, but i meant 1.01.212
edward the black prince died before his father, 2.02. 18
father, the duke hath told the truth; 2.02. 28
then, father salisbury, kneel we together, | and 2.02. 59
resign | as ere thy father henry made it mine; 2.03. 34
john cade, so term'd of our suppos'd father — 4.02. 32 P
my father was a mortimer — 4.02. 39 P
for his father had never a house but the cage. 4.02. 52 P
villain, thy father was a plasterer, | and thou 4.02.132
who hateth him and honors not his father, 4.08. 16
this small inheritance my father left me 4.10. 18
shall be the surety for their traitor father. 5.01.116
ay, noble father, if our words will serve. 5.01.139
and so to arms, victorious father, | to quell 5.01.211
wast thou ordain'd, dear father, | to lose thy 5.02. 45
my noble father, | three times to–day i holp him 5.03. 7
lord stafford's father, duke of buckingham, | is 3H6 1.01. 10
that this is true, father, behold his blood. 1.01. 13
earl of northumberland, he slew thy father, 1.01. 54
he durst not sit there, had your father liv'd. 1.01. 63
thy father was a traitor to the crown. 1.01. 79
/thy father was, as thou art, duke of york, 1.01.105
father, tear the crown from the usurper's head. 1.01.114
sweet father, do so, set it on your head. 1.01.115
wherein my grandsire and my father sat? 1.01.125
whose heir my father was, and i am his. 1.01.140
where i shall kneel to him that slew my father! 1.01.162
seeing thou hast prov'd so unnatural a father! 1.01.218
father, you cannot disinherit me. 1.01.226
the crown of england, father, which is yours. 1.02. 9
it will outrun you, father, in the end. 1.02. 14
and, father, do but think | how sweet a thing it 1.02. 28
ay, with five hundred, father, for a need. 1.02. 67
whose father slew my father, he shall die. 1.03. 5
whose father slew my father, he shall die. 1.03. 5
thy father hath. 1.03. 39
thy father slew my father; 1.03. 47
thy father slew my father; 1.03. 47
to me, | and thrice cried, "courage, father! 1.04. 10
with downright payment show'd unto my father. 1.04. 32
thy father bears the type of king of naples, 1.04.121
child, | to bid the father wipe his eyes withal, 1.04.139
i wonder how our princely father scap'd; 2.01. 1
where our right valiant father is become. 2.01. 10
so far'd our father with his enemies, | so fled 2.01. 18
so fled his enemies my warlike father; 2.01. 19
your princely father and my loving lord! 2.01. 47
by many hands your father was subdu'd, | but 2.01. 56
where your brave father breath'd his latest gasp 2.01.108
him, | which argued thee a most unloving father. 2.02. 25
got, | my careless father fondly gave away"? 2.02. 38
whose father for his hoarding went to hell? 2.02. 48
and would my father had left me no more! 2.02. 50
my gracious father, by your kingly leave, | i'll 2.02. 63
my royal father, cheer these noble lords, | and 2.02. 78
unsheathe your sword, good father; 2.02. 80
who should succeed the father but the son? 2.02. 94
i slew thy father, call'st thou him a child? 2.02.113
whose father bears the title of a king | (as if 2.02.140
his father revell'd in the heart of france, 2.02.150
this is the hand that stabb'd thy father york, 2.04. 6
my father, being the earl of warwick's man, 2.05. 65
and pardon, father, for i knew not thee! 2.05. 70
thy father gave thee life too soon, | and hath 2.05. 92
was ever father so bemoan'd his son? 2.05.110
and so obsequious will thy father be, | /e'en 2.05.118
fly, father, fly! 2.05.125
do, | or as thy father and his father did, 2.06. 15
do, | or as thy father and his father did, 2.06. 15
i mean our princely father, duke of york. 2.06. 51
which in the time of death he gave our father. 2.06. 67
old, | my father and my grandfather were kings; 3.01. 77
your grace my sons should call you father. 3.02.100
a happy thing | to be the father unto many sons. 3.02.105
the ghostly father now hath done his shrift. 3.02.107
because thy father henry did usurp, | and thou 3.03. 79
and more than so, my father, | even in the 3.03.103
queen, | you have a father able to maintain you, 3.03.154
of york | my father came untimely to his death? 3.03.187
father of warwick, know you what this means? 5.01. 81
ah, that thy father had been so resolv'd! 5.05. 22
thy father, minos, that denied our course; 5.06. 22
two cliffords, as the father and the son, | and 5.07. 7
/reignier, her father, to the king of france 5.07. 38
what though i kill'd her husband and her father? R3 1.01.154
is to become her husband and her father: 1.01.156
when my father york and edward wept | to hear 1.02.156
nor when thy warlike father, like a child, 1.02.159
i, that kill'd her husband and his father, | to 1.02.230
poor clarence did forsake his father, warwick, 1.03.134
the curse my noble father laid on thee | when 1.03.173
when that our princely father york | blest his 1.04.235
good grandam, tell us, is our father dead? 2.02. 1
if that our noble father were alive? 2.02. 7
bade me rely on him as on my father, | and he 2.02. 25
ah for our father, for our dear lord clarence! 2.02. 72
so hath this, both by his father and mother. 2.03. 22
better it were they all came by his father, | or 2.03. 23
or by his father there were none at all; 2.03. 24
my princely father, then had wars in france, 3.05. 88
being nothing like the noble duke my father. 3.05. 92
as being got, your father then in france, | and 3.07. 10
being the right idea of your father, | both in 3.07. 13
besides, he hates me for my father warwick, 4.01. 85
ay, i thank god, my father, and yourself. 4.04.156
as sometimes margaret | did to thy father, 4.04.275
and here receive we from our father stanley 5.02. 5
the father rashly slaughter'd his own son, | the 5.05. 25
play'd | the part my father meant to act upon H8 1.02.195
after "the duke his father," with the "knife," 1.02.203
outgo | his father by as much as a performance 1.02.208
i had it from my father. 1.04. 27
in haste too, | lest he should help his father. 2.01. 44
my noble father, henry of buckingham, | who 2.01.107
me | a little happier than my wretched father. 2.01.120
the king, your father, was reputed for | a 2.04. 45
my father, king of spain, was reckon'd one | the 2.04. 48
my father lov'd you, | he said he did, and with 3.02.154
"o father abbot, | an old man, broken with the 4.02. 20
will beget a thousand, here will be father, 5.03. 38 P
lest hector or my father should perceive me, | i TRO 1.01. 36
she's a fool to stay behind her father, let her 1.01. 81 P
that white hair is my father, and all the rest 1.02.162 P
and the rude son should strike his father dead; 1.03.115
a prince call'd hector — priam is his father — 1.03.261
should not our father | bear the great sway of 2.02. 34
but pardon, father nestor, were your days | as 2.03.253
shall i call you father? 2.03.256
thou must to thy father, and be gone from 4.02. 92 P
i have forgot my father, | i know no touch of 4.02. 96
lady, a word. i'll bring you to your father. 4.05. 53
cassandra, call my father to persuade. 5.03. 30
do not, dear father. 5.03. 76
was not a man my father? COR 4.02. 18
he call'd me father; 5.01. 3
thee no worse than thy old father menenius does! 5.02. 70 P
rome, | lov'd me above the measure of a father, 5.03. 10
and the father tearing | his country's bowels 5.03.102
he kill'd my father! 5.06.122 P
see, lord and father, how we have perform'd TIT 1.01.142
my noble lord and father, live in fame! 1.01.158
thanks, noble titus, father of my life! 1.01.253
father, and in that name doth nature speak — 1.01.371
dear father, soul and substance of us all — 1.01.374
deeds | a father and a friend to thee and rome. 1.01.423
the cruel father and his traitorous sons, | to 1.01.452
come let us go, and make thy father blind, | for 2.04. 52
o noble father, you lament in vain: 3.01. 27
sweet father, cease your tears, for at your 3.01.136
stay, father, for that noble hand of thine, 3.01.162
sweet father, if i shall be thought thy son, 3.01.179
farewell, andronicus, my noble father, | the 3.01.288
ay, when my father was in rome she did. 4.01. 7
and father of that chaste dishonored dame, 4.01. 90
thy father hath full oft | for his ungrateful 4.01.110
look how the black slave smiles upon the father, 4.02.120
i wrote the letter that thy father found, | and 5.01.106
pledges | unto my father and my uncle marcus, 5.01.164
can the son's eye behold his father bleed? 5.03. 65
my father and lavinia shall forthwith | be 5.03.193
was that my father that went hence so fast? ROM 1.01.162
deny thy father and refuse thy name; 2.02. 34
good morrow, father. 2.03. 31
my ghostly father, no; 2.03. 45
dead," | thy father or thy mother, nay, or both, 3.02.119
is father, mother, tybalt, romeo, juliet, | all 3.02.123
where is my father and my mother, nurse? 3.02.127
father, what news? 3.03. 4
well, well, thou hast a careful father, child, 3.05.107
i pray you tell my lord and father, madam, | i 3.05.120
here comes your father, tell him so yourself; 3.05.124
good father, i beseech you on my knees, | hear 3.05.158
having displeas'd my father, to lawrence' cell, 3.05.232
my father capulet will have it so, | and i am 4.01. 2
her father counts it dangerous | that she do 4.01. 9
come you to make confession to this father? 4.01. 22
are you at leisure, holy father, now, | or shall 4.01. 37
farewell, dear father! 4.01.126
is my father well? 5.01. 14
see thou deliver it to my lord and father. 5.03. 24
this, | to press before thy father to a grave? 5.03.215
this letter he early bid me give his father, 5.03.275
freely, good father. TIM 1.01.110
ventidius lately | buried his father, by whose 2.02.223
my knowing, timon has been this lord's father, 3.02. 67
if thou wilt curse, thy father (that poor rag) 4.03.271
had he not resembled | my father as he slept, i MAC 2.02. 13
ha, good father, | thou seest the heavens, as 2.04. 4
farewell, father. 2.04. 39
but that myself should be the root and father 3.01. 5
they hail'd him father to a line of kings. 3.01. 59
for donalbain | to kill their gracious father? 3.06. 10
they should find | what 'twere to kill a father; 3.06. 20
my father is not dead, for all your saying. 4.02. 37
yes, he is dead. how wilt thou do for a father? 4.02. 38
was my father a traitor, mother? 4.02. 44 P
but how wilt thou do for a father? 4.02. 60 P
sign that i should quickly have a new father. 4.02. 63 P
thy royal father | was a most sainted king; 4.03.108
those foresaid lands | so by his father lost; HAM 1.01.104
surrender of those lands | lost by his father, 1.02. 24
than is the throne of denmark to thy father. 1.02. 49
lids | seek for thy noble father in the dust. 1.02. 71
to give these mourning duties to your father. 1.02. 88
but you must know your father lost a father, 1.02. 89
but you must know your father lost a father, 1.02. 89
that father lost, lost his, and the survivor 1.02. 90
woe, and think of us | as of a father, for, let 1.02.108
than that which dearest father bears his son 1.02.111
but no more like my father | than i to hercules. 1.02.152
my father — methinks i see my father. 1.02.184
my father — methinks i see my father. 1.02.184
my lord, the king your father. 1.02.191
the king my father? 1.02.191
a figure like your father, | armed at point 1.02.199
i knew your father, | these hands are not more 1.02.211
i stay too long — but here my father comes. 1.03. 52
call thee hamlet, | king, father, royal dane. 1.04. 45
if thou didst ever thy dear father love — 1.05. 23
as thus, "i know his father and his friends, 2.01. 14
thou still hast been the father of good news. 2.02. 42
would make mouths at him while my father liv'd, 2.02.365 P
of his fell sword | th' unnerved father falls. 2.02.474
play something like the murther of my father 2.02.595
her father and myself, | we'll so bestow 3.01. 31
where's your father? 3.01.129 P
looks, and my father died within 's two hours. 3.02.127 P
a villain kills my father, and for that | i, his 3.03. 76
'a took my father grossly, full of bread, | with 3.03. 80
hamlet, thou hast thy father much offended. 3.04. 9
mother, you have my father much offended. 3.04. 10
my father, in his habit as he lived! 3.04.135
thy loving father, hamlet. 4.03. 50
father and mother is man and wife, man and wife 4.03. 51 P
that have a father kill'd, a mother stain'd, 4.04. 57
she speaks much of her father, says she hears 4.05. 4
conceit upon her father. 4.05. 45
first, her father slain; 4.05. 79
o thou vile king, | give me my father! 4.05.117
cries cuckold to my father, brands the harlot 4.05.119
where is my father? 4.05.129
i'll be reveng'd | most throughly for my father. 4.05.137
to know the certainty | of your dear father, 4.05.142
but they wither'd all when my father died. 4.05.185 P
that he which hath your noble father slain 4.07. 4
and so have i a noble father lost, | a sister 4.07. 25
i lov'd your father, and we love ourself, | and 4.07. 34
laertes, was your father dear to you? 4.07.107
not that i think you did not love your father, 4.07.110
/pass of practice | requite him for your father. 4.07.139
as much as child e'er lov'd, or father found; LR 1.01. 59
lov'd as my father, as my master follow'd, | as 1.01.141
i am sorry then you have so lost a father | that 1.01.246
the jewels of our father, with wash'd eyes 1.01.268
love well our father; 1.01.271
i think our father will hence to–night. 1.01.284 P
if our father carry authority with such 1.01.304 P
if our father would sleep till i wak'd him, you 1.02. 52 P
the father should be as ward to the son, and the 1.02. 73 P
and the bond crack'd 'twixt son and father. 1.02.109 P
there's son against father: 1.02.110 P
there's father against child. 1.02.111 P
my father compounded with my mother under the 1.02.128 P
/come, /come, when saw you my father last? 1.02.152 P
a credulous father and a brother noble, | whose 1.02.179
did my father strike my gentleman for chiding of 1.03. 1
my lady's father. 1.04. 79 P
"my lady's father"? 1.04. 80 P
so kind a father! 1.05. 32 P
i have been with your father, and given him 2.01. 2 P
my father hath set guard to take my brother, 2.01. 16
my father watches: 2.01. 20
i hear my father coming. 2.01. 28
come before my father. 2.01. 31
father, father! 2.01. 35
father, father! 2.01. 35
a bond | the child was bound to th' father; 2.01. 48
he whom my father nam'd, your edgar? 2.01. 92
riotous knights | that tended upon my father? 2.01. 95
i hear that you have shown your father | a 2.01.105
our father he hath writ, so hath our sister, 2.01.122
puppet's part against the royalty of her father. 2.02. 37 P
the dear father | would with his daughter speak, 2.04.101
i pray you, father, being weak, seem so. 2.04.201
these daughters' hearts | against their father, 2.04.275
and must draw me | that which my father loses: 3.03. 24
your old kind father, whose frank heart gave all 3.04. 20
i lov'd him, friend, | no father his son dearer; 3.04.169
seek out where thy father is, that he may be 3.05. 18 P
and thou shalt find a /dearer father in my love. 3.05. 25 P
upon your traitorous father are not fit for your 3.07. 8 P
my father, //parti–ey'd? 4.01. 10
o dear father, | it is thy business that i go 4.04. 23
therefore, thou happy father, | think that the 4.06. 72
son | was kinder to his father than my daughters 4.06.115
well pray you, father. 4.06.219
sit you down, father; 4.06.255
come, father, i'll bestow you with a friend. 4.06.286
o, wind up | of this child–changed father! 4.07. 16
o my dear father, restoration hang | thy 4.07. 25
had you not been their father, these white 4.07. 29
my fire, and wast thou fain, poor father, | to 4.07. 37
here, father, take the shadow of this tree | for 5.02. 1
false to thy gods, thy brother, and thy father, 5.03.135
heart, if ever i | did hate thee or thy father. 5.03.179
how have you known the miseries of your father? 5.03.181
habit | met i my father with his bleeding rings, 5.03.190
call up her father. OTH 1.01. 67

who would be a father! 1.01.164
those are the raised father and his friends. 1.02. 29
and let her speak of me before her father. 1.03.116
her father lov'd me, oft invited me; 1.03.128
my noble father, | i do perceive here a divided 1.03.180
to you, preferring you before her father, | so 1.03.187
to put my father in impatient thoughts | by 1.03.242
she has deceiv'd her father, and may thee. 1.03.293
she did deceive her father, marrying you, | and 3.03.206
and subdue my father | entirely to her love; 3.04. 59
if happily you my father do suspect | an 4.02. 44
her father? 4.02.126
an antique token | my father gave my mother. 5.02.217
wherefore my father should revengers want, ANT 2.06. 11
that despiteful rome | cast on my noble father. 2.06. 23
thy father, pompey, would ne'er have made this 2.06. 82 P
your caesar's father oft | (when he hath mus'd 3.13. 82
if that thy father live, let him repent | thou 3.13.134
his father | was call'd sicilius, who did join CYM 1.01. 28
for which their father, | then old and fond of 1.01. 36
who to my father was a friend, to me | known but 1.01. 98
betwixt two charming words, comes in my father, 1.03. 35
his father and i were soldiers together, to whom 1.04. 26 P
a father cruel, and a step–dame false, | a 1.06. 1
the king my father shall be made acquainted | of 1.06.149
betwixt a father by thy step–dame govern'd, | a 2.01. 58
against | obedience, which you owe your father. 2.03.112
i will inform your father. 2.03.152
and do't, i' th' court, before | her father. 2.04.149
most venerable man which i | did call my father, 2.05. 4
a sickness, say | she'll home to her father; 3.02. 75
who | the king his father call'd guiderius — 3.03. 88
morgan call'd, | they take for natural father. 3.03.107
up my disobedience 'gainst the king | my father, 3.04. 89
no court, no father, nor no more ado | with that 3.04.131
this done, spurn her home to her father, who may 4.01. 19 P
the weight as much, | as i do love my father. 4.02. 18
die, i'ld say | "my father, not this youth." 4.02. 24
cowards father cowards and base things sire base 4.02. 26
i'm not their father, yet who this should be 4.02. 28
why, worthy father, what have we to lose, | but 4.02.124
to th' east, | my father hath a reason for't. 4.02.256
and rather father thee than master thee. 4.02.395
whose father then (as men report | thou orphans' 5.04. 39
then (as men report | thou orphans' father art) 5.04. 40
been a grandsire and begot | a father to me; 5.04.124
then spare not the old father. 5.05.327
that call me father | and think they are my sons 5.05.328
you are my father too, and did relieve me | to 5.05.400
with whom the father liking took, | and her to PER 1.ch. 25
bad child, worse father, to entice his own | to 1.ch. 27
which labor | i found that kindness in a father. 1.01. 67
he's father, son, and husband mild; 1.01. 68
where now /you're both a father and a son | by 1.01.127
(which pleasures fits a husband, not a father), 1.01.129
found, the sinful father | seem'd not to strike, 1.02. 77
which my dead father did bequeath to me, | with 2.01.124
since i have here my father gave in his will. 2.01.134
it pleaseth you, my royal father, to express 2.02. 8
a knight of sparta, my renowned father, | and 2.02. 18
a prince of macedon, my royal father, | and the 2.02. 24
what is't | to me, my father? 2.03. 58
alas, my father, it befits not me | unto a 2.03. 66
the king my father, sir, has drunk to you — 2.03. 75
resolve your angry father if my tongue | did 2.05. 68
i love the king your father, and yourself, 4.01. 32
my father, as nurse says, did never fear, | but 4.01. 52
and to her father turn our thoughts again, 5.ch. 12
that had some power, | my father, and a king. 5.01.149
the king my father did in tharsus leave me, 5.01.170
and another /life | to pericles thy father. 5.01.208
the king my father gave you such a ring. 5.03. 39
we are father, friends, acquaintance; TNK 2.02. 81
base, | my father the mean keeper of his prison, 2.04. 3
my father said so; 2.05. 6
your father | sure is a happy sire then. 2.05. 8
body | and fiery mind illustrate a brave father. 2.05. 22
not, | let me find that my father ever hated — 2.05. 58
my father | durst better have endur'd cold iron 2.06. 9
of the wrong he did | to me and to my father. 2.06. 26
farewell, father! 2.06. 37
now my father, | twenty to one, is truss'd up in 3.04. 16
what e'er her father says, if you perceive | her 5.02. 33
besides, my father must be hang'd to–morrow, 5.02. 80
state | stands many a father with his child. 5.04. 3
sin | to wish that i their father had not been. LUC 210
their father was too weak, and they too strong, 865
that thou art doting father of his fruit. 1064
till lucrece' father, that beholds her bleed, 1732
live again and see | thy father die, and not thy 1771
see | thy father die, and not thy father thee!" 1771
then son and father weep with equal strife | who 1791
the father says, "she's mine." 1795
you know | you had a father, let your son say so SON 13.14
as a decrepit father takes delight | to see his 37. 1
"father," she says, "though in me you behold LC 71
"o father, what a hell of witchcraft lies | in 288

FATHER'D 2 FR 0.0002 REL FR 2 V 0 P
my sex, | being so father'd and so husbanded? JC 2.01.297
father'd he is, and yet he's fatherless. MAC 4.02. 27

/FATHERED 1 FR 0.0001 REL FR 1 V 0 P
/he /childed /as /i /fathered! LR 3.06.110

FATHER–IN–LAW 4 FR 0.0004 REL FR 4 V 0 P
my stranger soul | was my great father–in–law, R3 1.04. 49
afford | be to thy person, noble father–in–law! 5.03. 81
may give me | remembrance of my father–in–law, H8 3.02. 8
land | of noble buckingham, my father–in–law; 3.02.256

FATHERLESS 2 FR 0.0002 REL FR 2 V 0 P
our fatherless distress was left unmoan'd, R3 2.02. 64
father'd he is, and yet he's fatherless. MAC 4.02. 27

FATHERLY 3 FR 0.0003 REL FR 2 V 1 P
by that fatherly and kindly power | that you ADO 4.01. 74
you | you have show'd a tender fatherly regard, SHR 2.01.286
but take this service i have done fatherly. CYM 2.03. 35 P

/FATHER'S 2 FR 0.0002 REL FR 2 V 0 P
/noble /and /right //well–rememb'red /father's? 2H4 4.01.110
you have my /father's house — but what, we are ANT 2.07.128

FATHER'S 235 FR 0.0265 REL FR 211 V 24 P
weeping again the king my father's wrack, | this TMP 1.02.391
my father's loss, the weakness which i feel, 1.02.488
my father's of a better nature, sir, | than he 1.02.497
ten times more gentle than her father's crabbed; 3.01. 8
and my father's precepts | i therein do forget. 3.01. 58
your father's in some passion | that works him 4.01.143
those at her father's churlish feet she tender'd TGV 3.01.227
urge not my father's anger, eglamour, | but 4.03. 27
i see i cannot get thy father's love, WIV 3.04. 1
albeit i will confess thy father's wealth | was 3.04. 13
yet seek my father's love, still seek it, sir. 3.04. 19
this is my father's choice. 3.04. 31
there my father's grave | did utter forth a MM 3.01. 85
would rather have one of your father's getting. ADO 2.01.322 P
some such strange bull leapt your father's cow, 5.04. 49
my father's wit and my mother's tongue assist me LLL 1.02. 95 P
omne bene, say i, being of an old father's mind: 4.02. 32
dine to–day at the father's of a certain pupil 4.02.153 P
for the remembrance of my father's death. 5.02.810
but in this kind, wanting your father's voice, MND 1.01. 54
if you yield not to your father's choice, | you 1.01. 69
to die | for disobedience to your father's will, 1.01. 87
you have her father's love, demetrius, | let me 1.01. 93
to fit your fancies to your father's will; 1.01.118
steal forth thy father's house to–morrow night; 1.01.164
stand'st between her father's ground and mine! 5.01.175
you should refuse to perform your father's will, MV 1.02. 94 P
sort than your father's imposition depending on 1.02.104 P
i be obtain'd by the manner of my father's will. 1.02.108 P
lady, in your father's time, a venetian, a 1.02.112 P
in me | to be ashamed to be my father's child! 2.03. 17
how i shall take her from her father's house, 2.04. 30
be patient, for your father's remembrance, be at AYL 1.01. 64 P
my father's love is enough to honor him enough. 1.02. 83 P
and all the world was of my father's mind. 1.02.236
my father's rough and envious disposition 1.02.241
and pity her for her good father's sake; 1.02.281
thou art thy father's daughter, there's enough. 1.03. 58
the clownish fool out of your father's court? 1.03.130
thy father's father wore it, | and thy father 4.02. 15
for my father's house and all the revenue that 5.02. 10 P
and by my father's love and leave am arm'd SHR 1.01. 5
ah, tranio, what a cruel father's he! 1.01.185
tell me her father's name, and 'tis enough; 1.02. 94
i am my father's heir and only son. 2.01.364
love concerneth us to add | her father's liking, 3.02.129
beggars that come unto my father's door | upon 4.03. 4
love, | will we return unto thy father's house, 4.03. 53
kate, we will unto your father's | even in these 4.03.169
to feast and sport us at thy father's house. 4.03.183
long, | i am content, in a good father's care, 4.04. 31
once more toward our father's. 4.05. 1
list, | or ere i journey to your father's house. 4.05. 8
my father's bears more toward the market–place; 5.01. 9
going, madam, weep o'er my father's death anew; AWW 1.01. 3 P
youth, thou bear'st thy father's face; 1.02. 19
thy father's moral parts | mayst thou inherit 1.02. 21
since the physician at your father's died? 1.02. 70
something in't | more than my father's skill, 1.03.243
of my dear father's gift stands chief in power, 2.01.112
whom both sovereign power and father's voice | i 2.03. 54
she had her breeding at my father's charge — 2.03.114
i am all the daughters of my father's house, TN 2.04.120
made her flight across | thy father's ground. WT 4.04. 16
or i'll be thine, my fair, | or not my father's; 4.04. 43
it is my father's will i should take on me | the 4.04. 71
my lord, | you know /your father's temper. 4.04.467
you have ever been my father's honor'd friend, 4.04.493
it is my father's music | to speak your deeds; 4.04.518
forgiveness, | as 'twere i' th' father's person; 4.04.550
but that you have your father's bosom there, 4.04.563
shall not at your father's house these seven 4.04.578
he comes not | like to his father's greatness. 5.01. 89
your father's image is so hit in you | (his very 5.01.127
and your father's bless'd | (as he from heaven 5.01.174
that "once," i see, by your good father's speed, 5.01.210
how found | thy father's court? 5.03.125
and in the mean time sojourn'd at my father's; JN 1.01.103
my father's land, as was my father's will. 1.01.115
my father's land, as was my father's will. 1.01.115
your father's wife did after wedlock bear him; 1.01.117
my mother's son did get your father's heir; 1.01.128
your father's heir must have your father's land. 1.01.129
your father's heir must have your father's land. 1.01.129
shall then my father's will be of no force | to 1.01.130
this, in our foresaid holy father's name, | pope 3.01.145
spar'd, | shall wait upon your father's funeral. 5.07. 98
heir, | as he is but my father's brother's son, R2 1.01.117
shall i seem crestfallen in my father's sight? 1.01.188
in some large measure to thy father's death, 1.02. 26
die, | who was the model of thy father's life. 1.02. 28
which his triumphant father's hand had won. 2.01.181
my father's goods are all distrain'd and sold, 2.03.131
lie | in earth as quiet as thy father's skull; 4.01. 69
for all the coin in thy father's exchequer. 1H4 2.02. 36 P
thy father's beard is turn'd white with the news 2.04.358 P
your father's sickness is a maim to us. 4.01. 42
this absence of your father's draws a curtain 4.01. 73
yet this before my father's majesty: 5.01. 96
live upon my head | and on his father's. 5.02. 21
like enough, and thy father's shadow. 2H4 3.02.129 P
so indeed, but much of the father's substance! 3.02.131 P
i am not here against your father's peace, | but 4.02. 31
blood, | my father's purposes have been mistook, 4.02. 56
thou mightst win the more thy father's love, 4.05.179
so shall i live to speak my father's words: 5.02.107
the breath no sooner left his father's body, H5 1.01. 25
shall strike his father's crown into the hazard. 1.02.263
we'll chide this dolphin at his father's door. 1.02.308
those that were your father's enemies | have 2.02. 29
and if your father's highness | do not, in grant 2.04.120
by my hand i swear, and my father's soul, the 3.02. 90 P
now beshrew my father's ambition! 5.02.225 P
and did upbraid me with my father's death; 1H6 2.05. 48
therefore, good uncle, for my father's sake, 2.05. 51
my father's execution | was nothing less than 2.05. 99
so shall his father's wrongs be recompens'd. 3.01.160
thy father's charge shall clear thee from that 4.05. 42
it warm'd thy father's heart with proud desire 4.06. 11
speak, thy father's care: 4.06. 26
if thou wilt fight, fight by thy father's side, 4.06. 56
come, come, and lay him in his father's arms, 4.07. 29
at your father's castle walls | we'll crave a 5.03.129
joan, this kills thy father's heart outright! 5.04. 2
was better worth than all my father's lands, 2H6 1.03. 86
his father's acts commenc'd in burning troy! 3.02.118
to free us from his father's wrathful curse, | i 3.02.155
he made a chimney in my father's house, and the 4.02.148 P
me, that, for his father's sake, henry the fift 4.02.157 P
shall be their father's bail, and bane to those 5.01.120
now, by my father's badge, old nevil's crest, 5.01.202
than drops of blood were in my father's veins. 3H6 1.01. 97
my father's blood | hath stopp'd the passage 1.03. 21
then let my father's blood open it again, | he 1.03. 23
that is my office, for my father's sake. 1.04.109
see, ruthless queen, a hapless father's tears! 1.04.156
for my oath, here's for my father's death. 1.04.175
lose his birthright by his father's fault, | and 2.02. 35
that wash'd his father's fortunes forth of 2.02.157
it is my father's face, | whom in this conflict 2.05. 61
how will my mother for a father's death | take 2.05.103
was ever son so ru'd a father's death? 2.05.109
your father's head, which clifford placed there; 2.06. 53
and rear it in the place your father's stands. 2.06. 86
pity they should lose their father's lands. 3.02. 31
i will not ruinate my father's house, | who gave 5.01. 83
suppose that i am now my father's mouth: 5.05. 18
and thou usurp'st my father's right and mine. 5.05. 37
told the sad story of my father's death, | and R3 1.02.160
thou loathed issue of thy father's loins! 1.03.231
as loath to lose him, not your father's death; 2.02. 10
you cannot guess who caus'd your father's death. 2.02. 19
you wept not for our father's death; 2.02. 62
he for his father's sake so loves the prince 3.01.165
i am their father's mother, i will see them. 4.01. 22
her father's brother | would be her lord? 4.04.337
my father's death — 4.04.376
george, | be executed in his father's sight. 5.03. 96
truly pitying | my father's loss, like a most H8 2.01.113
of a king | so great as our dread father's, in a TRO 2.02. 27
thou art, great lord, my father's sister's son, 4.05.120
and this sinister | bounds in my father's"; 4.05.129
a' my word, the father's son. COR 1.03. 57 P
one on 's father's moods. 1.03. 66 P
rome, | then let my father's honors live in me, TIT 1.01. 7
lavinia, live, outlive thy father's days, | and 1.01.167
for my father's sake, | that gave thee life when 2.03.158
for such a sight will blind a father's eye. 2.04. 53
will whole months of tears thy father's eyes? 2.04. 55
hath made thee handless in thy father's sight? 3.01. 67
and for our father's sake, and mother's care, 3.01.181
more than remembrance of my father's death. 3.01.240
shall seize this prey out of his father's hands. 4.02. 96
the meeting | even at his father's house, the 4.04.103
a sight to vex the father's soul withal. 5.01. 52
i play'd the cheater for thy father's hand, 5.01.111
he craves a parley at your father's house, 5.01.159
let him, | as he regards his aged father's life. 5.02.130
since 'tis my father's mind | that i repair to 5.03. 1
and with thy shame thy father's sorrow die! 5.03. 47
our father's tears despis'd, and basely cozen'd 5.03.101
not to his father's, i spoke with his man. ROM 2.04. 3
hath sent a letter to his father's house. 2.04. 7
romeo, will you come to your father's? 2.04.140 P
pleas'd the gods to remember my father's age, TIM 1.02. 2
your royal father's murther'd. MAC 2.03.100
no less material to me | than is his father's, 3.01.136
sirrah, your father's dead, | and what will you 4.02. 30
have you your father's leave? HAM 1.02. 57
with which she followed my poor father's body, 1.02.148
my father's brother, but no more like my father 1.02.152
my lord, i came to see your father's funeral. 1.02.176
if it assume my noble father's person, | i'll 1.02.243
my father's spirit — in arms! 1.02.254
i am thy father's spirit, | doom'd for a certain 1.05. 9
the serpent that did sting thy father's life 1.05. 39
more than his father's death, that thus hath put 2.02. 8
his father's death and our /o'erhasty marriage. 2.02. 57
which i have told thee of my father's death. 3.02. 77
it springs | all from her father's death — and 4.05. 76
with pestilent speeches of his father's death, 4.05. 91
that i am guiltless of your father's death, 4.05.150
to show yourself indeed your father's son | more 4.07.125
i had my father's signet in my purse, | which 5.02. 49
mine and my father's death come not upon thee, 5.02.330
as here i give | her father's heart from her. LR 1.01.126
our father's love is to the bastard edmund | as 1.02. 17
th' untented woundings of a father's curse 1.04.300
what, did my father's godson seek your life? 2.01. 91
why, madam, if i were your father's dog, | you 2.02.136
have been your tenant, and your father's tenant, 4.01. 13
edgar, | the food of thy abused father's wrath! 4.01. 22
love, dear love, and our ag'd father's right. 4.04. 28
my name is edgar, and thy father's son. 5.03.170
here is her father's house, i'll call aloud. OTH 1.01. 74
/if /you /please, | /be't at her father's. 1.03.240
such a seeming | to seel her father's eyes up, 3.03.210
it, my father's eye | should hold her loathed, 3.04. 61
i am glad thy father's dead. 5.02.204
rich in his father's honor, creeps apace | into ANT 1.03. 50
thou dost o'er–count me of my father's house; 2.06. 27
sat | caesarion, whom they call my father's son, 3.06. 6
i something fear my father's wrath, but nothing CYM 1.01. 86
your son's my father's friend, he takes his part 1.01.165
"justice, and your father's wrath, should he 3.02. 40 P
that they | had been my father's sons, then had 3.06. 76
so sure as you your father's. 5.05.332
/yon king's to me like to my father's picture, PER 2.03. 37
have hearken'd to their father's testament. 4.02. 99 P
letters of good credit, sir, | my father's dead. 5.03. 78
my father's to be hang'd for his escape; TNK 3.02. 22
i in my father's life | to take prerogative and STM III 8
quoth she, "this was thy father's guise — VEN 1177
"here was thy father's bed, here in my breast; 1183
if in the child the father's image lies, | where LUC 1753

FATHERS' 6 FR 0.0006 REL FR 6 V 0 P
as thriftless sons their scraping fathers' gold. R2 5.03. 69
of us, | the emptying of our fathers' luxury, H5 3.05. 6
i stabb'd your fathers' bosoms, split my breast. 3H6 2.06. 30
for by my fathers' reverent tomb i vow | they TIT 2.03.296
and give him burial in his fathers' grave. 5.03.192
but, woe the while, our fathers' minds are dead, JC 1.03. 82
FATHERS 41 FR 0.0046 REL FR 35 V 6 P
o, that our fathers would applaud our loves, TGV 1.03. 48
that indeed know not their fathers, and 3.01.319 P
now, as fond fathers, | having bound up the MM 1.03. 23
truly the lady fathers herself. ADO 1.01.111 P
you, the wall is down that parted their fathers. MND 5.01.352 P
wilt thou change fathers? AYL 1.03. 91
but what talk we of fathers, when there is such 3.04. 38 P
fathers commonly | do get their children; SHR 2.01.409
judgments are | mere fathers of their garments; AWW 1.02. 62
the pleasure that some fathers feed upon | is my R2 2.01. 79
so, their fathers being so sick as yours at this 2H4 2.02. 30 P
for this the foolish over-careful fathers | have 4.05. 67
the patterns that by god and by french fathers H5 2.04. 61
for husbands, fathers, and betrothed lovers, 2.04.108
whose blood is fet from fathers of war-proof! 3.01. 18
fathers that, like so many alexanders, | have in 3.01. 19
those whom you call'd fathers did beget you. 3.01. 23
your fathers taken by the silver beards, | and 3.03. 36
and slew your fathers, and with colors spread 3H6 1.01. 91
with reverend fathers and well-learned bishops. R3 3.05.100
he is within, with two right reverend fathers, 3.07. 61
the children live whose fathers thou hast 4.04.391
whom our fathers | have in their own land beaten 5.03.333
these reverend fathers, men | of singular H8 2.04. 58
by all the reverend fathers of the land | and 2.04.206
come, reverend fathers, | bestow your counsels 3.01.181
learned and reverend fathers of his order, 4.01. 26
o' th' state, who care for you like fathers, COR 1.01. 77
hear me, grave fathers! TIT 3.01. 1
you and i have heard our fathers say | there was JC 1.02.158
whose common theme | is death of fathers, and HAM 1.02.104
gules, horridly trick'd | with blood of fathers, 2.02.458
sons at perfect age and fathers declin'd, the LR 1.02. 72 P
fathers that wear rags | do make their children 2.04. 48
but fathers that bear bags | shall see their 2.04. 50
that discarded fathers | should have thus little 3.04. 72
fathers, from hence trust not your daughters' OTH 1.01.170
those rich-left heirs that let their fathers lie CYM 4.02.226
so children temporal fathers do appease; 5.04. 12
"remember what your fathers were, and conquer!" TNK 2.02. 36
you fathers are fine fools. 5.02. 28
FATHOM *(also fadom, etc.)*
FATHOM 4 FR 0.0004 REL FR 1 V 3 P
didst know how many fathom deep i am in love! AYL 4.01.206 P
fathom and half, fathom and half! poor tom! LR 3.04. 37 P
fathom and half, fathom and half! poor tom! 3.04. 37 P
air | (so many fathom down precipitating), 4.06. 50
FATHOMLESS 1 FR 0.0001 REL FR 1 V 0 P
and buckle in a waist most fathomless | with TRO 2.02. 30
FATIGATE 1 FR 0.0001 REL FR 1 V 0 P
spirit | requick'ned what in flesh was fatigate, COR 2.02.117
FAT-KIDNEY'D 1 FR 0.0001 REL FR 0 V 1 P
peace, ye fat-kidney'd rascal! 1H4 2.02. 5 P
FATNESS 1 FR 0.0001 REL FR 1 V 0 P
for in the fatness of these pursy times | virtue HAM 3.04.153
FAT'S 1 FR 0.0001 REL FR 1 V 0 P
we may go whistle; all the fat's i' th' fire. TNK 3.05. 39
FATS 1 FR 0.0001 REL FR 1 V 0 P
in thy fats our cares be drown'd, | with thy ANT 2.07.115
FATTED 2 FR 0.0002 REL FR 2 V 0 P
and crows are fatted with the murrion flock; MND 2.01. 97
this | i should 'a' fatted all the region kites HAM 2.02.579
FATTER 1 FR 0.0001 REL FR 1 V 0 P
would he were fatter! JC 1.02.198
FATTEST 2 FR 0.0002 REL FR 1 V 1 P
me, i am here a windsor stag, and the fattest, i WIV 5.05. 13 P
most subject is the fattest soil to weeds, | and 2H4 4.04. 54
FATTING 2 FR 0.0002 REL FR 2 V 0 P
he is frank'd up to fatting for his pains — R3 1.03.313
that i lay fatting like a swine, to fight, | and TNK 3.06. 12
FATUUS 2 FR 0.0002 REL FR 1 V 1 P
hadst been an ignis fatuus or a ball of wildfire 1H4 3.03. 39 P
tile, | we have been fatuus, and labored vainly. TNK 3.05. 41
FAT-WITTED 1 FR 0.0001 REL FR 0 V 1 P
thou art so fat-witted with drinking of old sack 1H4 1.02. 2 P
FAUCET-SELLER *(see forset-seller)*
FAUGH *(see foh, fough)*
FAULCONBRIDGE *(also falconbridge)*
FAULCONBRIDGE 12 FR 0.0013 REL FR 12 V 0 P
son, | as i suppose, to robert faulconbridge. JN 1.01. 52
the son and heir to that same faulconbridge. 1.01. 56
whether hadst thou rather be a faulconbridge, 1.01.134
go, faulconbridge, now hast thou thy desire, | a 1.01.176
hast thou denied thyself a faulconbridge? 1.01.251
the bastard faulconbridge | is now in england 3.04.171
stand by, or i shall gall you, faulconbridge. 4.03. 94
what wilt thou do, renowned faulconbridge? 4.03.101
my lord, your valiant kinsman, faulconbridge, 5.03. 5
that misbegotten devil faulconbridge, | in spite 5.04. 4
beaumont, grandpre, roussi, and faulconbridge, H5 3.05. 44
grandpre and roussi, faulconbridge and foix, 4.08. 99
FAULT *(also fall*)*
/FAULT 3 FR 0.0003 REL FR 3 V 0 P
/like /or /find /fault, /do /as /your /pleasures TRO pr 30
accursed, if the /fault be prov'd in them — TIT 2.03.291
/his /fault /is /much, /and /the /good /king LR 2.02.141
FAULT 174 FR 0.0196 REL FR 139 V 35 P
i do forgive | thy rankest fault — all of them; TMP 5.01.132
pardon the fault, i pray. TGV 1.02. 40
and pray her to a fault for which i chid her. 1.02. 52
the kind of the launces have this very fault. 2.03. 3 P
well, that fault may be mended with a breakfast. 3.01.325 P
but were you banish'd for so small a fault? 4.01. 31
than he, to take a fault upon me that he did, i 4.04. 14 P
'tis your fault, 'tis your fault; WIV 1.01. 93 P
'tis your fault, 'tis your fault; 1.01. 94 P
his worst fault is, that he is given to prayer; 1.04. 13 P
but nobody but has his fault — but let that 1.04. 15 P
ay, for fault of a better. 1.04. 17 P
'tis my fault, master page. i suffer for it. 3.03.218 P
good heart, that was not her fault. 3.05. 39 P
a fault done first in the form of a beast (o 5.05. 8 P
the form of a beast (o jove, a beastly fault!) 5.05. 9 P
and then another fault in the semblance of a 5.05. 10 P
of a fowl — think on't, jove, a foul fault! 5.05. 11 P
whether it be the fault and glimpse of newness, MM 1.02.158
sith 'twas my fault to give the people scope, 1.03. 35
none, | and some condemned for a fault alone. 2.01. 40
i do beseech you let it be his fault, | and not 2.02. 35
condemn the fault, and not the actor of it? 2.02. 37
it doth know | that's like my brother's fault. 2.02.138
is this her fault, or mine? 2.02.162
i have bethought me of another fault. 5.01.456
i thought it was a fault, but knew it not, | yet 5.01.463
for she will /score your fault upon my pate: ERR 1.02. 65
that's not my fault, he's master of my state. 2.01. 95
it is a fault that springeth from your eye. 3.02. 55
that's a fault that water will mend. 3.02.105 P
a grievous fault! say, woman, didst thou so? 5.01.206
the fault will be in the music, cousin, if you ADO 2.01. 69 P
to be whipt? what's his fault? 2.01.221 P
but margaret was in some fault for this, 5.04. 4
if broken then, it is no fault of mine: LLL 4.03. 69
it were a fault to snatch words from my tongue. 5.02.382
i made a little fault in "great." 5.02.559 P
and i will have you and that fault withal; 5.02.866
and i shall find you empty of that fault, 5.02.868
his folly, helena, is no fault of mine. MND 1.01.200
would that fault were mine! 1.01.201
'tis partly my own fault, | which death, or 3.02.243
shall lose a hair through bassanio's fault. MV 3.02.302
if i could add a lie unto a fault, | i would 5.01.186
pardon this fault, and by my soul i swear | i 5.01.247
let me the knowledge of my fault bear with me: AYL 1.03. 46
the worst fault you have is to be in love. 3.02.282 P
'tis a fault i will not change for your best 3.02.283 P
are, every one fault seeming monstrous till his 3.02.354 P
woman that cannot make her fault her husband's 4.01.174 P
at the hedge-corner, in the coldest fault? SHR in.1. 20
her only fault, and that is faults enough, | is 1.02. 88
patience, i pray you, 'twas a fault unwilling. 4.01.156
some undeserved fault | i'll find about the 4.01.199
we'd find no fault with the tithe-woman if i AWW 1.03. 84 P
'tis not his fault, the spark. 2.01. 25
that's all the fault. 3.06.112
there's something in me that reproves my fault; TN 3.04.203
but such a headstrong potent fault it is | that 3.04.204
have done offense, i take the fault on me; 3.04.313
and that with us | you did continue fault, and WT 1.02. 85
of | which comes to me in name of fault, i must 3.02. 60
you have made fault | i' th' boldness of your 3.02.217
that for thy mother's fault art thus expos'd 3.03. 50
no fault could you make | which you have not 5.01. 2
and if she did play false, the fault was hers, JN 1.01.118
which fault lies on the hazards of all husbands 1.01.119
your fault was not your folly; 1.01.262
is it my fault that i was geffrey's son? 4.01. 22
and oftentimes excusing of a fault | doth make 4.02. 30
doth make the fault the worse by th' excuse: 4.02. 31
discredit more in hiding of the fault | than did 4.02. 33
than did the fault before it was so patch'd. 4.02. 34
the image of a wicked heinous fault | lives in 4.02. 71
this is my fault. R2 1.01.142
which made the fault that we cannot correct, 1.02. 5
to smooth his fault i should have been more mild 1.03.240
thee, | and minister correction to thy fault! 2.03.105
my gracious uncle, let me know my fault, | on 2.03.106
intended, or committed, was this fault? 5.03. 33
my reformation, glitt'ring o'er my fault, 1H4 1.02.213
or misprision | is guilty of this fault, and not 1.03. 28
if sack and sugar be a fault, god help the 2.04.470 P
you must needs learn, lord, to amend this fault; 3.01.178
neither, 'tis a woman's fault. 3.01.240 P
midwives say the children are not in the fault, 2H4 2.02. 25 P
as to one it pleases me, for fault of a better, 2.02. 41 P
see, thy fault france hath in thee found out, H5 2.pr. 20
i do confess my fault, | and do submit me to 2.02. 76
and i repent my fault more than my death, 2.02.152
my fault, but not my body, pardon, sovereign. 2.02.165
a! that's a foul fault. 3.02.136 P
think not upon the fault | my father made in 4.01.293
you take it for your own fault and not mine; 4.08. 54 P
or will you blame and lay the fault on me? 1H6 2.01. 57
i did correct him for his fault the other day, 2H6 1.03.199 P
pity was all the fault that was in me; 3.01.125
and lowly words were ransom for their fault. 3.01.127
o, 'tis a fault too too unpardonable! 3H6 1.04.106
shall for the fault make forfeit of his head. 2.01.197
'tis not my fault, | nor wittingly have i 2.02. 7
lose his birthright by his father's fault, | and 2.02. 35
o monstrous fault, to harbor such a thought! 3.02.164
ah, what a shame, ah, what a fault were this! 5.04. 12
alack, my lord, that fault is none of yours; R3 1.01. 47
my brother kill'd no man, his fault was thought, 2.01.105
grace, | on our entreaties, to amend your fault! 3.07.115
it is your fault that you resign | the supreme 3.07.117
gentlemen, | whose fault is this? H8 1.04. 43
might have mercy on the fault thou gav'st him; 3.02.262
alas, it is my vice, my fault: TRO 4.04.102
'tis troilus' fault. 4.04.143
this fault in us i find, | the error of our eye 5.02.109
what miscarries | shall be the general's fault, COR 1.01.267
he's poor in no one fault, but stor'd with all. 2.01. 18 P
lay | a fault on us, your tribunes, that we 2.03.227
lay the fault on us. 2.03.234
that this fell fault of my accursed sons — TIT 2.03.290
and that shall be the ransom for their fault. 3.01.156
and for that vild fault | two of her brothers 5.02.172
the youngest of that name, for fault of a worse. ROM 2.04.122 P
his fault concludes but what the law should end, 3.01.185
thy fault our law calls death, but the kind 3.03. 25
and if aught in this | miscarried by my fault, 5.03.267
every man has his fault, and honesty is his. TIM 3.01. 27 P
(/an honor in him which buys out his fault), 3.05. 17
i must needs say you have a little fault; 5.01. 87
and for this fault | assemble all the poor men JC 1.01. 56
the fault, dear brutus, is not in our stars, 1.02.140
i would it were my fault to sleep so soundly. 2.01. 4
if it were so, it was a grievous fault, | and 3.02. 79
fie, 'tis a fault to heaven, | a fault against HAM 1.02.101
a fault against the dead, a fault to nature, 1.02.102
a fault against the dead, a fault to nature, 1.02.102
take corruption | from that particular fault: 1.04. 36
my fault is past, but, o, what form of prayer 3.03. 51
do you smell a fault? LR 1.01. 16 P
i cannot wish the fault undone, the issue of it 1.01. 17 P
the fault of it i'll answer. 1.03. 10
you should, the fault | would not scape censure, 1.04.209
o most small fault, | how ugly didst thou in 1.04.266
why dost thou call him knave? what is his fault? 2.02. 89
never (o fault!) 5.03.193
is not almost a fault | t' incur a private check OTH 3.03. 66
that's a fault. 3.04. 55
upon his blood | and new-create /this fault? 4.01.276
till that the nature of your fault be known | to 5.02.336
i have made no fault. ANT 2.05. 74
o, that his fault should make a knave of thee, 2.05.102
is antony or we in fault for this? 3.13. 2
against the flint and hardness of my fault, 4.09. 16
it is your fault that i have lov'd posthumus: CYM 1.01.144
but that's no fault of his. 2.03. 57
my fault being nothing (as i have told you oft) 3.03. 65
if you kill me for my fault, i should | have 3.06. 56
so, sir, i yoke me | in my good brother's fault. 4.02. 20
mine eyes | were not in fault, for she was 5.05. 63
the more my fault | to scape his hands where i PER 4.02. 74
gone, | and 'tis your fault i am bereft him so. VEN 381
with much ado the cold fault cleanly out; 694
"'tis not my fault, the boar provok'd my tongue, 1003
the shame and fault finds no excuse nor end. LUC 238
the fault is thine, | for those thine eyes 482
the fault unknown is as a thought unacted. 527
when pattern'd by thy fault foul sin may say 629
and by their mortal fault brought in subjection 724
nor fold my fault in cleanly coin'd excuses; 1073
yet with the fault i thus far can dispense: 1279
where no excuse can give the fault amending. 1614
if broken, then it is no fault of mine. PP 3.12
for to thy sensual fault i bring in sense — SON 35. 9
say that thou didst forsake me for some fault, 89. 1
some say thy fault is youth, some wantonness, 96. 1
FAULT-FULL 1 FR 0.0001 REL FR 1 V 0 P
so fares it with this fault-full lord of rome, LUC 715
FAULTINESS 1 FR 0.0001 REL FR 1 V 0 P
round, even to faultiness. ANT 3.03. 30
FAULTLESS 3 FR 0.0003 REL FR 3 V 0 P
and look thyself be faultless, thou wert best. 2H6 2.01.185
that faultless may condemn a nobleman! 3.02. 24
steep'd in the faultless blood of pretty rutland R3 1.03.177
FAULT'S 5 FR 0.0005 REL FR 5 V 0 P
the fault's your own. TMP 2.01.136
why, every fault's condemn'd ere it be done. MM 2.02. 38
that for the fault's love is th' offender 4.02.113
then, angelo, thy fault's thus manifested; 5.01.412
the fault's | bloody; TIM 3.05. 1
FAULTS' 1 FR 0.0001 REL FR 1 V 0 P
poor women's faces are their own faults' books. LUC 1253
FAULTS 106 FR 0.0119 REL FR 93 V 13 P
assaults | mercy itself, and frees all faults. TMP ep 18
more hair than wit, and more faults than hairs, TGV 3.01.354 P
faults than hairs, and more wealth than faults." 3.01.354 P
"and more faults than hairs" — 3.01.364 P
"and more wealth than faults." 3.01.367 P
why, that word makes the faults gracious. 3.01.368 P
for we cite our faults | that they may hold 4.01. 51
that one error | fills him with faults; 5.04.112
what a world of vild ill-favor'd faults | looks WIV 3.04. 32
his offense | for i have had such faults; MM 2.01. 28
to fine the faults whose fine stands in record, 2.02. 40
to have it added to the faults of mine, | and 2.04. 72
no stronger | than faults may shake our frames), 2.04.133
from our faults, as faults from seeming, free! 3.02. 39
from our faults, as faults from seeming, free! 3.02. 39
striking | kills for faults of his own liking! 3.02.268
he should pursue | faults proper to himself. 5.01.110
laws for all faults, | but faults so 5.01.319
but faults so countenanc'd, that the strong 5.01.320
they say best men are moulded out of faults, 5.01.439
but, for those earthly faults, i quit them all, 5.01.483
white and red, | her faults will ne'er be known, LLL 1.02.100
for blush in cheeks by faults are bred | and 1.02.101
heavenly eyes, that look into these faults, 5.02.769
you are attaint with faults and perjury: 5.02.819
and in such eyes as ours appear not faults, MV 2.02.183
but myself, against whom i know most faults. AYL 3.02.281 P
would take her with all faults, and money enough SHR 1.01.129 P
her only fault, and that is faults enough, | is 1.02. 88
hortensio, have you told him all her faults? 1.02.186
such were our faults, or then we thought them AWW 1.03.135
with sainted vow my faults to have amended. 3.04. 7
would be proud, if our faults whipt them not, 4.03. 73 P
our rash faults | make trivial price of serious 5.03. 60
two faults, madonna, that drink and good counsel TN 1.05. 43 P
the cur is excellent at faults. 2.05.128 P
so forcing faults upon hermione, | i little like WT 3.01. 16
all faults i make, when i shall come to know 3.02.219
to pardon me all the faults i have committed to 5.02.150 P
a time | to punish this offense in other faults. 1H4 5.02. 7
chide him for faults, and do it reverently, 2H4 4.04. 37
with such a heady currance, scouring faults; H5 1.01. 34
if little faults, proceeding on distemper, 2.02. 54
their faults are open, | arrest them to the 2.02.142
or, if he were not privy to those faults, | yet, 2H6 3.01. 47
tut, these are petty faults to faults unknown, 3.01. 64
tut, these are petty faults to faults unknown, 3.01. 64
my lord, these faults are easy, quickly answer'd 3.01.133
clifford, devise excuses for thy faults. 3H6 2.06. 71
while we devise fell tortures for thy faults. 2.06. 72
and i forgive and quite forget old faults, | and 3.03.200
and, richard, do not frown upon my faults, | for 5.01.101
duty, and thy faults | provoke us hither now to R3 1.04.224
have mercies | more than i dare make faults. H8 2.01. 71
his faults lie open to the laws, let them, | not 3.02.334
so may he rest, his faults lie gently on him! 4.02. 31
he hath faults (with surplus) to tire in COR 1.01. 45 P

and all his faults | to martius shall be honors, 1.01.274
a nettle, and | the faults of fools but folly. 2.01.191
consul's worthiness, | so can i name his faults. 3.01.277
to suffer lawful censure for such faults | as 3.03. 46
what faults he made before the last, i think 5.06. 63
i do remit these young men's heinous faults. TIT 1.01.484
calm thee, and bear the faults of titus' age, 4.04. 29
for their fell faults our brothers were beheaded 5.03.100
faults that are rich are fair. TIM 1.02. 13
to forget their faults, i drink to you. 1.02.107 P
wilt thou whip thine own faults in other men? 5.01. 39
should fall | for private faults in them. 5.04. 26
for aye | on thy low grave, on faults forgiven. 5.04. 79
that have known the earth so full of faults. JC 1.03. 45
i do not like your faults. 4.03. 89
a friendly eye could never see such faults. 4.03. 90
check'd like a bondman, all his faults observ'd, 4.03. 97
but breathe his faults so quaintly | that they HAM 2.01. 31
even to the teeth and forehead of our faults, 3.03. 63
who, dipping all his faults in their affection, 4.07. 19
loath to call | your faults as they are named. LR 1.01.271
who covers faults, at last with shame derides. 1.01.281
fated o'er men's faults light on thy daughters! 3.04. 68
/oft my jealousy | shapes faults that are not), OTH 3.03.148
but i do think it is their husbands' faults | if 4.03. 86
and taunt my faults | with such full license as ANT 1.02.107
a man who is th' /abstract of all faults | that 1.04. 9
his faults, in him, seem as the spots of heaven, 1.04. 12
for our faults | can never be so equal that your 3.04. 34
gods will give us | some faults to make us men. 5.01. 33
all faults that name, nay, that hell knows, CYM 2.05. 27
you | should have ta'en vengeance on my faults, 5.01. 8
you snatch some hence for little faults; 5.01. 12
should let their ears hear their faults hid! PER 1.02. 62
of all the faults beneath the heavens, the gods 4.03. 20
in men's nativity | are nature's faults, not LUC 539
men's faults do seldom to themselves appear, 633
that all the faults which in thy reign are made 804
poor women's faults that they are so fulfill'd 1258
outfacing faults in love with love's ill rest. PP 1. 8
since that our faults in love thus smother'd be. 1.14
all men make faults, and even i in this, SON 35. 5
i can set down a story | of faults conceal'd, 88. 7
both grace and faults are lov'd of more and less 96. 3
thou mak'st faults graces that to thee resort. 96. 4
the ills that were not, grew to faults assured, 118.10
me, | and in our faults by lies we flattered be. 138.14
eyes well seeing thy foul faults should find. 148.14
lest guilty of my faults thy sweet self prove: 151. 4

FAULTY 3 FR 0.0003 REL FR 3 V 0 P
my youth | hath faulty wand'red and irregular, 1H4 3.02. 27
that i am faulty in duke humphrey's death. 2H6 3.02.202
however faulty, yet should find respect | for H8 5.02.110

FAUSSE 1 FR 0.0001 REL FR 0 V 1 P
your majestee ave fausse french enough to H5 5.02.218 P

FAUSTUSES 1 FR 0.0001 REL FR 0 V 1 P
three german devils, three doctor faustuses. WIV 4.05. 70 P

FAUT 1 FR 0.0001 REL FR 0 V 1 P
il faut que j'apprenne a parler. H5 3.04. 4 P

/FAVOR 1 FR 0.0001 REL FR 1 V 0 P
may help these lovers | /into /your /favor. OTH 1.03.201

FAVOR 136 FR 0.0153 REL FR 111 V 25 P
good my lord, give me thy favor still. TMP 4.01.204
her beauty is exquisite, but her favor infinite. TGV 2.01. 55 P
confirm his welcome with some special favor. 2.04.101
kiss, | and, of so great a favor growing proud, 2.04.161
pray, sir, by your good favor — for surely, sir MM 4.02. 32 P
sir, a good favor you have, but that you have a 4.02. 33 P
seen them both, and will discover the favor. 4.02.173 P
do me the favor to dilate at full | what have ERR 1.01.122
yet will i favor thee in what i can; 1.01.149
when i like your favor, for god defend the lute ADO 2.01. 94 P
how much i am in the favor of margaret, the 2.02. 13 P
well, for your favor, sir, why, give god thanks, 3.03. 19 P
your niece regards me with an eye of favor. 5.04. 22
by thy favor, sweet welkin, i must sigh in thy LLL 3.01. 67
as thou wilt win my favor, good my knave, | do 3.01.152
her favor turns the fashion of the days, | for 4.03.258
but, rosaline, you have a favor too? 5.02. 30
but as fair as yours, | my favor were as great: 5.02. 33
hold, rosaline, this favor thou shalt wear, 5.02.130
and that 'a wears next his heart for a favor. 5.02.715 P
therefore if you my favor mean to get, | a 5.02.820
o, were favor so, | /yours /would i catch, fair MND 1.01.186
to buy his favor, i extend this friendship. MV 1.03.168
that for this favor | he presently become a 4.01.386
of female favor, and bestows himself | like a AYL 4.03. 86
some lively touches of my daughter's favor. 5.04. 27
woo, | and free access and favor as the rest; SHR 2.01. 97
this favor will i do you for his sake; 4.02.104
carries no favor in't but bertram's. AWW 1.01. 83
of every line and trick of his sweet favor. 1.01. 96
good fortune and the favor of the king | smile 2.03.177
himself into a man's favor and for a week escape 3.06. 92 P
nay, i'll read it first, by your favor. 4.03.217 P
which warp'd the line of every other favor, 5.03. 49
give a favor from you | to sparkle in the 5.03. 74
if you priz'd my lady's favor at any thing more TN 2.03.122 P
eye | hath stay'd upon some favor that it loves. 2.04. 24
a little, by your favor. 2.04. 25
he brought me out o' favor with my lady about a 2.05. 8 P
she did show favor to the youth in your sight 3.02. 18 P
do, he'll smile, and take't for a great favor. 3.02. 83 P
i know your favor well, | though now you have no 3.04.329
even such and so | in favor was my brother, and 3.04.381
that screws me from my true place in your favor, 5.01.123
you have given me such clear lights of favor, 5.01.336
methinks | my favor here begins to warp. WT 1.02.365
to it own protection | and favor of the climate. 2.03.179
the crown and comfort of my life, your favor, 3.02. 94
they were to be known by garment, not by favor. 5.02. 49 P
to whom in favor she shall give the day, | and JN 2.01.393
speak on with favor, we are bent to hear. 2.01.422
my soul | but i do love the favor and the form 5.04. 50
creature pluck a glove | and wear it as a favor, R2 5.03. 18
but neither my good word nor princely favor. 5.06. 42
looks | of favor from myself and all our house, 1H4 5.01. 31
heart | and ripens in the sunshine of his favor, 2H4 4.02. 12
wear thou this favor for me and stick it in thy H5 4.07.153 P
the glove which i have given him for a favor 4.07.172
which to reduce into our former favor | you are 5.02. 63
if not of hell, the heavens sure favor him. 1H6 2.01. 47
fortune in favor makes him lag behind. 3.03. 34
and this is mine, sweet henry, favor him. 4.01. 81
henceforth i charge you, as you love our favor, 4.01.135
we thank you all for this great favor done | in 2H6 1.01. 71
what though the common people favor him, 1.01.158
hath won the greatest favor of the commons, 1.01.192
hence, | i care not whither, for i beg no favor; 2.04. 92
us'd to command, untaught to plead for favor. 4.01.122
justice with favor have i always done; 4.07. 67
i am commanded, with your leave and favor, 3H6 3.03. 60
way, | if we will keep in favor with the king, R3 1.01. 79
may | but beg one favor at thy gracious hand, 1.02.207
since i am crept in favor with myself, | i will 1.02.258
and i myself secure, in grace and favor. 3.04. 91
pray give me favor, sir: H8 1.01.168
and then let's dream | who's best in favor. 1.04.108
the spaniard, tied by blood and favor to her, 2.02. 89
and my favor | to him that does best, god forbid 2.02.113
much joy and favor to you; 2.02.117
with me, a poor weak woman, fall'n from favor? 3.01. 20
one | hath crawl'd into the favor of the king, 3.02.103
may he continue | long in his highness' favor, 3.02.396
a man of his place, and so near our favor, | to 5.02. 30
are a little, | by your good favor, too sharp; 5.02.109
th' other day that troilus, for a brown favor TRO 1.02. 93 P
call it melancholy, if you will favor the man; 2.03. 87 P
are without him, as place, riches, and favor — 3.03. 82
i know your favor, lord ulysses, well. 4.05.213
but your favor is well appear'd by your tongue. COR 4.03. 9 P
and to my fortunes and the people's favor TIT 1.01. 54
and to the love and favor of my country | commit 1.01. 58
thracian tyrant in his tent | may favor tamora, 1.01.139
receive him then to favor, saturnine, | that 1.01.421
ay, but the citizens favor lucius, | and will 4.04. 79
out of her favor where i am in love. ROM 1.01.168
o, what more favor can i do to thee, | than with 5.03. 98
then, under favor, pardon me | if i speak like a TIM 3.05. 40
fortune's tender arm | with favor never clasp'd, 4.03.251
as well as i do know your outward favor. JC 1.02. 91
i may discover them | by any mark of favor. 2.01. 76
give me your favor; MAC 1.03.149
to alter favor ever is to fear. 1.05. 72
your leave and favor to return to france, | from HAM 1.02. 51
for hamlet, and the trifling of his favor, 1.03. 5
itself, | she turns to favor and to prettiness. 4.05.189
an inch thick, to this favor she must come. 5.01.194 P
to dismantle | so many folds of favor. LR 1.01.218
that hath depriv'd me of your grace and favor, 1.01.229
for taking one's part that's out of favor. 1.04.100 P
but, by your favor, | how near's the other army? 4.06.211
defeat thy favor with an usurp'd beard. OTH 1.03.340 P
satiety a fresh appetite, loveliness in favor, 2.01.229 P
cassio entreats her a little favor of speech. 3.01. 26 P
know him | were he in favor as in humor alter'd. 3.04.125
unpin me — have grace and favor /in /them. 4.03. 21
so tart a favor | to trumpet such good tidings! ANT 2.05. 38
which he achiev'd by th' minute, lost his favor. 3.01. 20
he did ask favor. 3.13.133
for idiots in this case of favor would | be CYM 1.06. 42
uncertain favor! 3.03. 64
time hath nothing blurr'd those lines of favor 4.02.104
on greatness' favor dream as i have done, | wake 5.04.128
his favor is familiar to me. 5.05. 93
unite | his favor with the radiant cymbeline, 5.05.475
voice and favor! PER 5.03. 13
and now and then a favor and a frisk. TNK 3.05. 30
if you but favor, our country pastime made is. 3.05.102
if i fall from that mouth, i fall with favor, 3.06.282
oak, | and in it stuck the favor of his lady. 4.02.138
petition of grace and acceptance into her favor. 4.03. 89 P
if thou wilt deign this favor, for thy meed | a VEN 15
"pity," she cries, "some favor, some remorse!" 257
both favor, savor, hue, and qualities, | whereat 747
let those who are in favor with their stars | of SON 25. 1
the most sweet favor or deformed'st creature, 113.10
have i not seen dwellers on form and favor 125. 5

FAVORABLE 5 FR 0.0005 REL FR 5 V 0 P
happier the man whom favorable stars | allots SHR 4.05. 40
heavens look | with an aspect more favorable. WT 2.01.107
unless some dull and favorable hand | will 2H4 4.05. 2
prince, | lend favorable ear to our requests, R3 3.07.101
h'as had most favorable and happy speed: OTH 2.01. 67

FAVORABLY 1 FR 0.0001 REL FR 0 V 1 P
which the time shall more favorably minister. OTH 2.01.270 P

FAVOR'D 2 FR 0.0002 REL FR 1 V 1 P
she is not so fair as (of you) well favor'd. TGV 2.01. 53 P
and those senators | that always favor'd him. COR 3.03. 8

FAVORER 2 FR 0.0002 REL FR 2 V 0 P
do not i know you for a favorer | of this new H8 5.02.115
for being now a favorer to the britain, | no CYM 5.03. 74

FAVORERS 2 FR 0.0002 REL FR 2 V 0 P
friends, followers, favorers of my right, | if TIT 1.01. 9
and come to us as favorers, not as foes. PER 1.04. 73

/FAVORING 1 FR 0.0001 REL FR 1 V 0 P
man, | commend unto his lips thy /favoring hand. ANT 4.08. 23

FAVORING 1 FR 0.0001 REL FR 0 V 1 P
imperfect in favoring the first complaint, hasty COR 2.01. 50 P

FAVORITE 2 FR 0.0002 REL FR 2 V 0 P
as a false favorite doth his prince's name, | in 2H4 4.02. 25
the great man down, you mark his favorite flies, HAM 3.02.204

FAVORITE'S 1 FR 0.0001 REL FR 1 V 0 P
not scissor'd just | to such a favorite's glass? TNK 1.02. 55

FAVORITES 6 FR 0.0006 REL FR 6 V 0 P
enter, like favorites | made proud by princes, ADO 3.01. 9
ye favorites of a king, are we not high? R2 3.02. 88
of all the favorites that the absent king | in 1H4 4.03. 86
this factious bandying of their favorites, | but 1H6 4.01.190
him, his sons, his favorites, and his friends. 3H6 1.01. 56
great princes' favorites their fair leaves SON 25. 5

FAVOR'S 3 FR 0.0003 REL FR 3 V 0 P
/in favor's like the work we have in hand, JC 1.03.129
now methinks | thy favor's good enough. CYM 3.04. 49
lord, how your favor's chang'd | with this PER 4.01. 24

/FAVORS 2 FR 0.0002 REL FR 2 V 0 P
/well /remember | /the /favors /of /these /men. R2 4.01.168
/i'll /court /his /favors. HAM 5.02. 78

FAVORS 42 FR 0.0047 REL FR 35 V 7 P
but when i call to mind your gracious favors TGV 3.01. 6
thank me for this more than for all the favors 3.01.161
would fain proclaim | favors that keep within. MM 5.01. 16
know | by favors several which they did bestow. LLL 5.02.125
and change you favors too, so shall your loves 5.02.134
come on then, wear the favors most in sight. 5.02.136
"out of your favors, heavenly spirits, vouchsafe 5.02.166
therefore change favors, and, when they repair, 5.02.292
once disclos'd, | the ladies did change favors; 5.02.468
your favors, embassadors of love; 5.02.778
those be rubies, fairy favors, | in those MND 2.01. 12
seeking sweet favors for this hateful fool, | i 4.01. 49
as one unworthy all the former favors | that i SHR 4.02. 30
boy, | to fly the favors of so good a king, | to AWW 3.02. 29
if the duke continue these favors towards you, TN 1.04. 1 P
is he inconstant, sir, in his favors? 1.04. 7 P
i saw your niece do more favors to the count's 3.02. 6 P
earth, | and do thee favors with my royal hands. R2 3.02. 11
blood, | and stain my favors in a bloody mask, 1H4 3.02.136
but let my favors hide thy mangled face, | and 5.04. 96
for he misuses thy favors so much that he swears 2H4 2.02.128 P
hath dull'd and cloy'd with gracious favors — H5 2.02. 9
captain, i thee beseech to do me favors. 3.06. 21
or bound my horse for her favors, i could lay on 5.02.141 P
that can rhyme themselves into ladies' favors, 5.02.157 P
brows, | as frowning at the favors of the world? 2H6 1.02. 4
ah, know you not the city favors them, | and 3H6 1.01. 67
and hastings as he favors edward's cause! 4.01.144
noted, | and generally, whoever the king favors, H8 2.01. 47
you have, by fortune and his highness' favors, 2.04.111
is that poor man that hangs on princes' favors! 3.02.367
upon your favors swims with fins of lead, | and COR 1.01.180
for thy favors done | to us in our election this TIT 1.01.234
beg nor fear | your favors nor your hate. MAC 1.03. 61
about her waist, or in the middle of her favors? HAM 2.02.233 P
with robber's hands my hospitable favors | you LR 3.07. 40
favors? ANT 3.13. 85
disdaining me and throwing favors on | the low CYM 3.05. 75
deserve, | and yet are steep'd in favors; 5.04.131
hung with the painted favors of their ladies, TNK 2.02. 11
she show'd him favors to allure his eye; PP 4. 6
a thousand favors from a maund she drew, | of LC 36

FAWN* 14 FR 0.0015 REL FR 14 V 0 P
how i would make him fawn, and beg, and seek, LLL 5.02. 62
the more you beat me, i will fawn on you. MND 2.01.204
a doe, i go to find my fawn | and give it food. AYL 2.07.128
i am too old to fawn upon a nurse, | too far in R2 1.03.170
dogs, easily won to fawn on any man! 3.02.130
the rod, | and fawn on rage with base humility, 5.01. 33
and take foul scorn to fawn on him by sending. 1H6 4.04. 35
my love, forbear to fawn upon their frowns. 3H6 4.01. 75
than spend a fawn upon 'em | for the inheritance COR 3.02. 67
then they could smile, and fawn upon his debts, TIM 3.04. 51
know | that i do fawn on men and hug them hard, JC 1.02. 75
if thou dost bend, and pray, and fawn for him, 3.01. 45
hasting to feed her fawn hid in some brake. VEN 876
on whom frown'st thou that i do fawn upon? SON 149. 6

FAWN'D 2 FR 0.0002 REL FR 2 V 0 P
your /teeth like apes, and fawn'd like hounds, JC 5.01. 41
they that fawn'd on him before | use his company PP 20.47

FAWNETH 2 FR 0.0002 REL FR 2 V 0 P
the more it grows, and fawneth on her still. TGV 4.02. 15
as the grim lion fawneth o'er his prey, | sharp LUC 421

FAWNING 6 FR 0.0006 REL FR 6 V 0 P
bestow thy fawning smiles on equal mates, | and TGV 3.01.158
how like a fawning publican he looks! MV 1.03. 41
this fawning greyhound then did proffer me! 1H4 1.03.252
even like a fawning greyhound in the leash, | to COR 1.06. 38
low-crooked curtsies, and base spaniel fawning. JC 3.01. 43
of the knee | where thrift may follow fawning. HAM 3.02. 62

FAWNS 2 FR 0.0002 REL FR 2 V 0 P
and when the lion fawns upon the lamb, | the 3H6 4.08. 49
look when he fawns he bites; R3 1.03.289

FAY *(also faith, feith)*

/FAY 1 FR 0.0001 REL FR 0 V 1 P
/for, /by /my /fay, /i /cannot /reason. HAM 2.02.265 P

FAY 2 FR 0.0002 REL FR 2 V 0 P
by my fay, a goodly nap, | but did i never speak SHR in.2. 81
ah, sirrah, by my fay, it waxes late, | i'll to ROM 1.05.126

FE 4 FR 0.0004 REL FR 0 V 4 P
fe, fe, fe, fe! WIV 1.04. 51 P
fe, fe, fe, fe! 1.04. 51 P
fe, fe, fe, fe! 1.04. 51 P
fe, fe, fe, fe! 1.04. 51 P

FEALTY 5 FR 0.0005 REL FR 5 V 0 P
them | upon some other pawn for fealty. TGV 2.04. 91
truth | and lasting fealty to the new-made king. R2 5.02. 45
all my sons, | as pledges of my fealty and love; 2H6 5.01. 50
deserts, | romans, forget your fealty to me. TIT 1.01.257
our fealty and tenantius' right | with honor to CYM 5.04. 73

/FEAR 4 FR 0.0004 REL FR 3 V 1 P
/i /fear /your /disposition; LR 4.02. 31
/kingdom /so /much /fear /and /danger /that /his 4.03. 5 P
/the /king, /with /others /whom, /i /fear, 5.01. 26
will and what they can, | what need we /fear? PER 1.04. 77

FEAR 691 FR 0.0781 REL FR 593 V 98 P
sir, | i fear you have done yourself some wrong; TMP 1.02.444
we have lost your son, | i fear for ever. 2.01.133
the bottom run | by their own fear or sloth. 2.01.228
moon-calf's gaberdine for fear of the storm. 2.02.111 P
faith, sir, you need not fear. 3.03. 43
amends, with which | i fear a madness held me. 5.01.116
i saw you last that i fear me will never out of 5.01.283 P
i shall not fear fly-blowing. 5.01.284 P
so, by your circumstance, i fear you'll prove. TGV 1.01. 37
i fear she'll prove as hard to you in telling 1.01.139 P
i fear my julia would not deign my lines, 1.01.152
have i shunn'd the fire for fear of burning, 1.03. 78
for fear thou shouldst lose thy tongue. 2.03. 46 P
i fear me, it will make me scandaliz'd. 2.07. 61
i fear me, he will scarce be pleas'd withal. 2.07. 67
that is the least, lucetta, of my fear: 2.07. 68
and, that thou must perceive my fear of this, 3.01. 33
fear not but that she will love you | now 3.02. 1
that all the travellers do fear so much. 4.01. 6

sir thurio, fear not you, i will so plead, 4.02. 82
i fear i am attended by some spies. 5.01. 10
fear not: 5.01. 11
fear not; 5.03. 13
there is no fear of got in a riot. WIV 1.01. 37 P
shall desire to hear the fear of got, and not to 1.01. 38 P
be drunk with those that have the fear of god, 1.01.184 P
leaving the fear of /god on the left hand, and 2.02. 23 P
i fear you love mistress page. 3.03. 75 P
and i fear not mine own shame so much as his 3.03.122 P
i quak'd for fear, lest the lunatic knave would 3.05.103 P
why yet there want not many that do fear | in 4.04. 39
fear not you that. 4.04. 78
/brook, i fear not goliah with a weaver's beam, 5.01. 22 P
fear not you; MM 1.02.106 P
i do fear — too dreadful; 1.03. 34
he (to give fear to use and liberty, | which 1.04. 62
law, | setting it up to fear the birds of prey, 2.01. 2
and the knaves, you need not to fear the bawds. 2.01.235 P
as we love it, | but as we stand in fear — 2.03. 34
for thou dost fear the soft and tender fork | of 3.01. 16
yet death we fear | that makes these odds all 3.01. 40
o, i do fear thee, claudio, and i quake, | lest 3.01. 73
nature is a paradise | to what we fear of death. 3.01.131
i fear you not. 3.02.163 P
fear me not. 4.01. 69
nor, gentle daughter, fear you not at all. 4.01. 70
my lord, her wits, i fear me, are not firm. 5.01. 33
fearing death, | than that which lives to fear. 5.01.398
that mourn'd for fashion, ignorant what to fear, ERR 1.01. 73
i greatly fear my money is not safe. 1.02.105
for fear you ne'er see chain nor money more. 3.02.177
meet a sergeant, 'a turns back for very fear. 4.02. 56
fear me not, man, i will not break away; 4.04. 1
come, stand by me, fear nothing. 5.01.185
unless the fear of death doth make me dote, | i 5.01.195
undertakes them with a most christian–like fear. ADO 2.03.192 P
if he do fear god, 'a must necessarily keep 2.03.193 P
to enter into a quarrel with fear and trembling. 2.03.195 P
and so will he do, for the man doth fear god, 2.03.197 P
fear you not my part of the dialogue. 3.01. 31
lay thy hand upon thy sword, | i fear thee not. 5.01. 55
if it should give your age such cause of fear. 5.01. 56
tush, fear not, man, we'll tip thy horns with 5.04. 44
then if she fear, or be to blame, | by this you LLL 1.02.103
i fear too much rubbing. 4.01.139
sir, you have done this in the fear of god, very 4.02.147 P
me of the father, i do fear colorable colors. 4.02.149 P
i fear these stubborn lines lack power to move. 4.03. 53
your grace needs not fear it. 4.03.197
for fear their colors should be wash'd away. 4.03.267
yet fear not thou, but speak audaciously." 5.02.104
cuckoo, cuckoo" — o word of fear, | unpleasing 5.02.901
cuckoo, cuckoo" — o word of fear, | unpleasing 5.02.910
that all their elves for fear | creep into MND 2.01. 30
fear not, my lord! your servant shall do so. 2.01.268
for beasts that meet me run away for fear. 2.02. 95
lysander, look how i do quake with fear. 2.02.148
i swoon almost with fear. 2.02.154
by'r lakin, a parlous fear. 3.01. 13 P
this will put them out of fear. 3.01. 22 P
i fear it, i promise you. 3.01. 28 P
or "i would entreat you, not to fear, not to 3.01. 41 P
i led them on in this distracted fear, | and 3.02. 31
for thou, i fear, hast given me cause to curse. 3.02. 46
for fear lest day should look their shames upon, 3.02.385
jealousy | to sleep by hate and fear no enmity? 4.01.145
or in the night, imagining some fear, | how easy 5.01. 21
alack, | i fear my thisby's promise is forgot! 5.01.173
you, whose gentle hearts do fear | the smallest 5.01.219
i fear we shall outsleep the coming morn | as 5.01.365
and every object that might make me fear MV 1.01. 20
i fear he will prove the weeping philosopher 1.02. 48 P
therefore for fear of the worst, i pray thee set 1.02. 95 P
you need not fear, lady, the having any of these 1.02.100 P
why, fear not, man, i will not forfeit it. 1.03.156
which makes me fear th' enjoying of my love; 3.02. 29
ay, but i fear you speak upon the rack, | where 3.02. 32
and shudd'ring fear, and green–eyed jealousy! 3.02.110
make it less, | for fear i surfeit. 3.02.114
therefore, i promise you, i fear you. 3.05. 3 P
truly then i fear you are damn'd both by father 3.05. 15 P
nay, you need not fear us, lorenzo, launcelot 3.05. 31 P
wherein doth sit the dread and fear of kings; 4.01.192
we are no tell–tales, madam, fear you not. 5.01.123
while i live i'll fear no other thing | so sore, 5.01.306
the fear of your adventure would counsel you to AYL 1.02.177 P
lie there what hidden woman's fear there will — 1.03.119
abhor it, fear it, do not enter it. 2.03. 28
i fear you have sold your own lands to see other 4.01. 22 P
as those that fear they hope, and know they fear 5.04. 4
those that fear they hope, and know they fear. 5.04. 4
fear not, my lord, we can contain ourselves, SHR in.1. 100
i' faith, sir, you shall never need to fear. 1.01. 61
ashore | i kill'd a man and fear i was descried. 1.01.232
tush, tush, fear boys with bugs. 1.02.210
for fear, i promise you, if i look pale. 2.01.143
now i fear thee not. 2.01.399
fear not, sweet wench, they shall not touch thee 3.02.238
i fear it is too choleric a meat. 4.03. 19
i cannot tell, i fear 'tis choleric. 4.03. 22
fear you not him. 4.04. 10
tut, fear not me. 4.04. 13
fear not, baptista, we will content you, go to; 5.01.135 P
is running away, when fear proposes the safety. AWW 1.01.202 P
that your valor and fear makes in you is a 1.01.203 P
what they are, there were no fear in marriage, 1.03. 51 P
my fear hath catch'd your fondness! 1.03.170
we should submit ourselves to an unknown fear. 2.03. 6 P
you shall not need to fear me. 3.05. 29 P
life and in the highest compulsion of base fear, 3.06. 30 P
but my heart hath the fear of mars before it, 4.01. 29 P
knows himself a braggart, | let him fear this; 4.03.335
you either fear his humor or my negligence, that TN 1.04. 5 P
hang'd in this world needs to fear no colors. 1.05. 6 P
he shall see none to fear. 1.05. 8 P
that saying was born, of "i fear no colors." 1.05. 10 P
what, and fear to find | mine eye too great a 1.05.308

abuse | myself, my servant, and, i fear me, you. 3.01.114
love, | the rather by these arguments of fear, 3.03. 12
and fear to kill a woodcock lest thou dispossess 4.02. 59 P
it is the baseness of thy fear | that makes thee 5.01.146
fear not, cesario, take thy fortunes up, | be 5.01.148
little faith, though thou hast too much fear. 5.01.171
free | but that his negligence, his folly, fear, WT 1.02.252
'twas a fear | which oft infects the wisest: 1.02.261
fear o'ershades me. 1.02.457
you need not fear it, sir. 2.02. 56
do not you fear. 2.02. 63
fear you his tyrannous passion more, alas, 2.03. 28
i have here alive, | that i should fear to die? 3.02.108
son, with mere conceit and fear | of the queen's 3.02.144
my lord, and fear | we have landed in ill time: 3.03. 2
which i fear the wolf will sooner find than the 3.03. 66 P
but, i fear, the angle that plucks our son 4.02. 46 P
i fear, sir, my shoulder–blade is out. 4.03. 72 P
your greatness | hath not been us'd to fear. 4.04. 18
with wisdom i might fear, my doricles, | you 4.04.150
have | as little skill to fear as i have purpose 4.04.152
fear not thou, man, thou shalt lose nothing here 4.04.255 P
will he endure your sight as yet, i fear. 4.04.470
my lord, | fear none of this. 4.04.590
fear not, man, here's no harm intended to thee. 4.04.629 P
that you may | (for i do fear eyes over) to 4.04.654
fear thou no wife; 5.01. 68
kings of our fear, until our fears, resolv'd, JN 2.01.371
but on this day let seamen fear no wrack; 3.01. 92
is assailed in our tent, | and ta'en, i fear. 3.02. 7
her highness is in safety, fear you not. 3.02. 8
i fear some outrage, and i'll follow her. 3.04.106
fear not you. 4.01. 7
and more, more strong than lesser is my fear, 4.02. 42
i fear will issue thence | the foul corruption 4.02. 80
not knowing what they fear, but full of fear. 4.02.146
not knowing what they fear, but full of fear. 4.02.146
let not the world see fear and sad distrust 5.01. 46
badly, i fear. how fares your majesty? 5.03. 2
the king, i fear, is poison'd by a monk. 5.06. 23
which fear, not reverence, makes thee to except. R2 1.01. 72
tear | the slavish motive of recanting fear, 1.01.193
and all too soon, i fear, the king shall rue. 1.03.205
urge doubts to them that fear. 2.01.299
and will, i fear, revolt on herford's side. 2.02. 89
i fear me, never. 2.02.149
leap, | the one in fear to lose what they enjoy, 2.04. 13
fear not, my lord, that power that made you king 3.02. 27
one day too late, i fear me, noble lord, | hath 3.02. 67
to fear the foe, since fear oppresseth strength, 3.02.180
to fear the foe, since fear oppresseth strength, 3.02.180
fear, and be slain — no worse can come to fight 3.02.183
this ague fit of fear is overblown, | an easy 3.02.190
horror, fear, and mutiny | shall here inhabit, 4.01.142
the love of wicked men converts to fear, | that 5.01. 66
that fear to hate, and hate turns one or both 5.01. 67
i fear, i fear — 5.02. 64
i fear, i fear — 5.02. 64
what should you fear? 5.02. 64
thy revengeful hand, thou hast no cause to fear. 5.03. 42
fear, and not love, begets his penitence. 5.03. 56
yet am i sick for fear, speak it again, | twice 5.03.133
i no friend will rid me of this living fear?" 5.04. 2
within this coffin i present | thy buried fear. 5.06. 31
are all scattered and possess'd with fear | so 1H4 2.02.105
in very sincerity of fear and cold heart will he 2.03. 30 P
i fear my brother mortimer doth stir | about his 2.03. 81
on fire, | and not in fear of your nativity. 3.01. 25
thou that art like enough, through vassal fear, 3.02.124
i fear thee as i fear the roaring of the lion's 3.03.146 P
i fear thee as i fear the roaring of the lion's 3.03.146 P
dost thou think i'll fear thee as i fear thy 3.03.150 P
thou think i'll fear thee as i fear thy father? 3.03.150 P
that shows the ignorant a kind of fear | before 4.01. 74
spoke of in scotland as this term of fear. 4.01. 85
i am out of fear | of death or death's hand for 4.01.135
such as fear the report of a caliver worse than 4.02. 19 P
tut, never fear me, i am as vigilant as a cat to 4.02. 58 P
he is, sir john. i fear we shall stay too long. 4.02. 77 P
well, | you speak it out of fear and cold heart. 4.03. 7
i hold as little counsel with weak fear | as you 4.03. 11
and i fear, sir michael, | what with the 4.04. 13
i fear the power of percy is too weak | to wage 4.04. 19
why, my good lord, you need not fear, | there is 4.04. 21
i hope no less, yet needful 'tis to fear, | and, 4.04. 34
a prodigy of fear, and a portent | of broached 5.01. 20
come near your sight | for fear of swallowing; 5.01. 64
scape shot–free at london, i fear the shot here, 5.03. 31 P
i fear thou art another counterfeit, | and yet, 5.04. 35
and all his men | upon the foot of fear, fled 5.05. 20
and hold'st it fear or sin | to speak a truth. 2H4 1.01. 95
to this weight such lightness with their fear 1.01.122
in his flight, | stumbling in fear, was took. 1.01.131
never fear that. 1.03. 80
fear we broadsides? 2.04.182
see now whether pure fear and entire cowardice 2.04.325 P
this offer comes from mercy, not from fear. 4.01.148
to give admittance to a thought of fear. 4.01.151
fear you not that; 4.01.183
therefore rouse up fear and trembling, and do 4.03. 14 P
the people fear me, for they do observe 4.04.121
and by whose power i well might lodge a fear 4.05.207
o god, i fear all will be overturn'd! 5.02. 19
brothers, you /mix your sadness with some fear: 5.02. 46
fear not your advancements, i will be the man 5.05. 78 P
a color that i fear you will die in, sir john. 5.05. 87 P
fear no colors, go with me to dinner. 5.05. 88 P
first my fear, then my cur'sy, last my speech. ep 1 P
my fear, is your displeasure, my cur'sy, my duty ep 2 P
but fear the main intendment of the scot, | who H5 1.02.144
shake in their fear, and with pale policy | seek 2.pr. 14
as fear may teach us out of late examples | left 2.04. 12
and let us do it with no show of fear, | no, 2.04. 23
humorous youth, | that fear attends her not. 2.04. 29
and let us fear | the native mightiness and fate 2.04. 63
he'll drop his heart into the sink of fear, 3.05. 59
so, for fear i should be fac'd out of my way. 3.07. 82 P
thawing cold fear, that mean and gentle all 4.pr. 45

should possess him with any appearance of fear, 4.01.111 P
and form, | creating awe and fear in other men? 4.01.247
soldiers' hearts, | possess them not with fear! 4.01.290
that england shall crouch down in fear, and 4.02. 37
i fear thou wilt once more come again for a 4.03.128 P
talbot is taken, whom we wont to fear; 1H6 1.02. 14
then come a' god's name, i fear no woman. 1.02.102
since henry's death, i fear, there is conveyance 1.03. 2
none durst come near for fear of sudden death. 1.04. 48
so great fear of my name 'mongst them were 1.04. 50
a witch by fear, not force, like hannibal, 1.05. 21
for pale they look with fear, as witnessing 2.04. 63
'tis not for fear, but anger, that thy cheeks 2.04. 65
beside, i fear me, if thy thoughts were sifted, 3.01. 24
and we, for fear, compell'd to shut our shops. 3.01. 85
ay, but, i fear me, with a hollow heart. 3.01.136
and now i fear that fatal prophecy | which in 3.01.194
i fear we should have seen decipher'd there 4.01.184
but, if i bow, they'll say it was for fear. 4.05. 29
now he is gone, my lord, you need not fear. 5.02. 17
of all base passions, fear is most accurs'd. 5.02. 18
o fairest beauty, do not fear nor fly, | for i 5.03. 46
such fierce alarums both of hope and fear, | as 5.05. 85
ay, grief, i fear me, both at first and last. 5.05.102
and no great friend, i fear me, to the king. 2H6 1.01.150
i fear me, lords, for all this flattering gloss, 1.01.163
nay, fear not, man, | we are alone, here's none 1.02. 68
and thus, i fear, at last | hume's knavery will 1.02.104
ay, what else? fear you not her courage. 1.04. 5 P
madam, sit you and fear not. 1.04. 21
and fear not, neighbor, you shall do well enough 2.03. 60 P
drink, and fear not your man. 2.03. 65 P
be merry, peter, and fear not thy master. 2.03. 70 P
but fear not thou, until thy foot be snar'd, 2.04. 56
if it be fond, call it a woman's fear; 3.01. 36
which fear, if better reasons can supplant, | i 3.01. 37
ah, that my fear were false, ah, that it were! 3.01.193
for, good king henry, thy decay i fear. 3.01.194
world, | to rid us from the fear we have of him. 3.01.234
let pale–fac'd fear keep with the mean–born man, 3.01.335
i fear me you but warm the starved snake, | who, 3.01.343
they say, in him they fear your highness' death; 3.02.249
it is thee i fear. 4.01.117
shalt have cause to fear before i leave thee. 4.01.118
true nobility is exempt from fear: 4.01.129
i fear neither sword nor fire. 4.02. 59 P
he need not fear the sword, for his coat is of 4.02. 60 P
but methinks he should stand in fear of fire, 4.02. 62 P
fear not that, i warrant thee. 4.03. 17 P
i fear me, love, if that i had been dead, | thou 4.04. 23
trust nobody, for fear you /be betray'd. 4.04. 58
the palsy, and not fear, provokes me. 4.07. 93
fear frames disorder, and disorder wounds 5.02. 32
think'st thou that we fear them? 3H6 1.02. 53
i'll win them, fear it not. 1.02. 60
what should we fear? 1.02. 68
or is it fear | that makes him close his eyes? 1.03. 10
what, multitudes, and fear? 1.04. 39
or more than common fear of clifford's rigor, 2.01.126
as the rocks cheer them that fear their wrack: 2.02. 5
to kings that fear their subjects' treachery? 2.05. 45
not that i fear to stay, but love to go 2.05.138
i fear thy overthrow | more than my body's 2.06. 3
my love and fear glu'd many friends to thee, 2.06. 5
i fear her not, unless she chance to fall. 3.02. 24
ay, but, i fear me, in another sense. 3.02. 60
seest what's pass'd, go fear thy king withal. 3.03.226
fear not that, my lord. 4.02. 5
my fear to hope, my sorrows unto joys, | at our 4.06. 4
by doubtful fear | my joy of liberty is half 4.06. 62
what, fear not, man, but yield me up the keys, 4.07. 37
that's not my fear, my meed hath got me fame: 4.08. 38
die thou, and die our fear, | for warwick was a 5.02. 1
'twere childish weakness to lament or fear. 5.04. 38
the thief doth fear each bush an officer. 5.06. 12
which now mistrust no parcel of my fear, | and 5.06. 38
i, that have neither pity, love, nor fear. 5.06. 68
and then, to purge his fear, i'll be thy death. 5.06. 88
and his physicians fear him mightily. R3 1.01.137
i fear me both are false. 1.02.194
i fear our happiness is at the height. 1.03. 41
i fear thy justice will take hold | on me and 2.01.132
as well the fear of harm, as harm apparent, | in 2.02.130
i fear, i fear 'twill prove a giddy world. 2.03. 5
i fear, i fear 'twill prove a giddy world. 2.03. 5
come, come, we fear the worst; all will be well. 2.03. 31
truly, the hearts of men are full of fear. 2.03. 38
why, what should you fear? 3.01.143
i fear no uncles dead. 3.01.146
and if they live, i hope i need not fear. 3.01.148
lord, | bid him not fear the separated council: 3.02. 20
fear you the boar, and go so unprovided? 3.02. 73
intend some fear, | be not you spoke with but by 3.07. 45
but sure i fear we shall not win him to it. 3.07. 80
i fear he will. 3.07. 82
the boy is foolish, and i fear not him. 4.02. 55
and soon i'll rid you from the fear of them. 4.02. 77
if thou didst fear to break an oath with him, 4.04.378
thou wilt revolt and fly to him, i fear. 4.04.477
the fear of that holds off my present aid. 4.05. 5
hath no friends but what are friends for fear, 5.02. 20
and with guilty fear | let fall thy lance. 5.03.142
what do i fear? 5.03.182
o ratcliffe, i fear, i fear! 5.03.214
o ratcliffe, i fear, i fear! 5.03.214
our necessary actions in the fear | to cope H8 1.02. 77
in fear our motion will be mock'd or carp'd at, 1.02. 86
and with a care exempt themselves from fear; 1.02. 89
men fear the french would prove perfidious, | to 1.02.156
the duke | said, 'twas the fear indeed, and that 1.02.158
nay, ladies, fear not; 1.04. 51
i fear, with dancing is a little heated. 1.04.100
i fear, too much. 1.04.101
i fear, too many curses on their heads | that 2.01.138
i fear he will indeed. 2.02. 10
me, my lords, | i love him not, nor fear him; 2.02. 50
ever in fear to kindle your dislike, | yea, 2.04. 25
near mine honor | (more near my life, i fear), 3.01. 72

but cardinal sins and hollow hearts i fear ye. 3.01.104
now the time | gives way to us) i much fear. 3.02. 16
o, fear him not, | his spell in that is out. 3.02. 19
i fear, the story of his anger. 3.02.209
be just, and fear not; 3.02.446
let's sit down quiet | for fear we wake her; 4.02. 82
i fear nothing | what can be said against me. 5.01.125
more than, i fear, you are provided for. 5.02. 92
but those, we fear, | w' have frighted with our ep 3
that, i fear, | all the expected good w' are ep 7
that knows his valor, and knows not his fear, TRO 1.03.268
more spungy to suck in the sense of fear, | more 2.02. 12
that we have stol'n what we do fear to keep! 2.02. 93
we fear to warrant in our native place! 2.02. 96
nor fear of bad success in a bad cause, | can 2.02.117
death, i fear me, | sounding destruction, or 3.02. 22
i fear it much, and i do fear besides | that i 3.02. 26
much, and i do fear besides | that i shall lose 3.02. 26
blind fear, that seeing reason leads, finds 3.02. 71 P
than blind reason stumbling without fear. 3.02. 72 P
to fear the worst oft cures the worse. 3.02. 73 P
o, let my lady apprehend no fear. 3.02. 74 P
i fear | we shall be much unwelcome. 4.01. 45
fear not my truth: 4.04.107
the general state, i fear, | can scarce entreat 4.05.264
fear me not, my lord. 5.02. 62
i do not speak of flight, of fear, of death, 5.10. 12
it should be now, but that my fear is this, 5.10. 53
"come on, you cowards, you were got in fear, COR 1.03. 33
they fear us not, but issue forth their city. 1.04. 23
and faces pale | with flight and agued fear! 1.04. 38
if any fear | /lesser his person than an ill 1.06. 69
fear not our care, sir. 1.07. 5
and in true fear | they gave us our demands." 3.01.134
thy mother rather feel thy pride than fear | thy 3.02.126
we hear not of him, neither need we fear him; 4.06. 1
you have made fair work, i fear me. 4.06. 88
but i fear | they'll roar him in again. 4.06.123
to have | this true which they so seem to fear. 4.06.151
go home, | and show no sign of fear. 4.06.152
them weep and shake with fear and sorrow, 5.03.100
and fear not, lords, and you, lavinia; TIT 1.01.471
i am surprised with an uncouth fear, | a 2.03.211
now | was i a child to fear i know not what. 2.03.221
if fear hath made thee faint, as me it hath — 2.03.234
fear not thy sons, they shall do well enough. 2.03.305
for fear they die before their pardon come. 3.01.175
stand by me, lucius, do not fear thine aunt. 4.01. 5
fear her not, lucius, somewhat doth she mean. 4.01. 9
that made me to fear, | although, my lord, i 4.01. 21
and rape, i fear, was root of thy annoy. 4.01. 49
why should you fear? is not your city strong? 4.04. 78
again, | and bury all thy fear in my devices. 4.04.112
murther or detested rape | can couch for fear, 5.02. 38
i fear the emperor means no good to us. 5.03. 10
fear me not. ROM 1.01. 36 P
no, marry, i fear thee! 1.01. 37 P
i fear, too early, for my mind misgives | some 1.04.106
ay, so i fear, the more is my unrest. 1.05.120
we will have vengeance for it, fear thou not. 3.05. 87
and i will do it without fear or doubt, | to 4.01. 87
if no inconstant toy, nor womanish fear, | abate 4.01.119
give me, give me! o, tell not me of fear! 4.01.121
i have a faint cold fear thrills through my 4.03. 15
i fear it is, and yet methinks it should not, 4.03. 28
his looks i fear, and his intents i doubt. 5.03. 44
for fear of that, i still will stay with thee, 5.03.106
fear comes upon me. 5.03.135
o, much i fear some ill unthrifty thing. 5.03.136
what fear is this which startles in your ears? 5.03.194
a huge man, i should fear to drink at meals, TIM 1.02. 50 P
i should fear those that dance before me now 1.02.143
thou giv'st so long, timon (i fear me), thou 1.02.241 P
for i do fear, | when every feather sticks in 2.01. 29
i fear it. 2.02. 12
sun's, but not, like his, recoverable, | i fear. 3.04. 14
i am of your fear for that. 3.04. 16
piety, and fear, | religion to the gods, peace, 4.01. 15
i will fear to catch it, and give way. 4.03.352 P
ours is the fall, i fear, our foes the snare. 5.02. 17
break his wind | with fear and horrid flight. 5.04. 13
ere thou hadst power or we had cause of fear, 5.04. 15
i do fear the people | choose caesar for their JC 1.02. 79
ay, do you fear it? 1.02. 80
love | the name of honor more than i fear death. 1.02. 89
fear him not, caesar, he's not dangerous, | he 1.02.196
but i fear him not. 1.02.198
yet if my name were liable to fear, | i do not 1.02.199
thee what is to be fear'd | than what i fear; 1.02.212
for fear of opening my lips and receiving the 1.02.249 P
transformed with their fear, who swore they saw 1.03. 24
it is the part of men to fear and tremble | when 1.03. 54
and put on fear, and cast yourself in wonder, 1.03. 60
to make them instruments of fear and warning 1.03. 70
yet i fear him, | for in the ingrafted love he 2.01.183
there is no fear in him; 2.01.190
never fear that. 2.01.202
things are beyond all use, | and i do fear them. 2.02. 26
seems to me most strange that men should fear, 2.02. 35
if he should stay at home to-day for fear. 2.02. 43
call it my fear | that keeps you in the house, 2.02. 50
i know will be, much that i fear may chance. 2.04. 32
i fear our purpose is discovered. 3.01. 17
casca, be sudden, for we fear prevention. 3.01. 19
the multitude, beside themselves with fear, 3.01.180
i fear there will a worse come in his place. 3.02.111
i fear i wrong the honorable men | whose daggers 3.02.151
i do fear it. 3.02.152
you'll bear me a bang for that, i fear. 3.03. 18 P
some that smile have in their hearts, i fear, 4.01. 50
for fear of what might fall, so to prevent | the 5.01.104
and seem to fear | things that do sound so fair? MAC 1.03. 51
who neither beg nor fear | your favors nor your 1.03. 60
yet do i fear thy nature, | it is too full o' 1.05. 16
and that which rather thou dost fear to do 1.05. 24
to alter favor ever is to fear. 1.05. 72
walk, for fear | the very stones prate of my 2.01. 57
list'ning their fear, i could not say "amen," 2.02. 26
and i fear | thou play'dst most foully for't; 3.01. 2
there is none but he | whose being i do fear; 3.01. 54
ere we will eat our meal in fear, and sleep | in 3.02. 17
this is the very painting of your fear; 3.04. 60
flaws and starts | (imposters to true fear) 3.04. 63
your cheeks, | when mine is blanch'd with fear. 3.04.115
is the initiate fear that wants hard use: 3.04.142
bear | his hopes 'bove wisdom, grace, and fear; 3.05. 31
thou hast harp'd my fear aright. 4.01. 74
what need i fear of thee? 4.01. 82
that i may tell pale-hearted fear it lies, | and 4.01. 85
not | whether it was his wisdom or his fear. 4.02. 5
all is the fear, and nothing is the love; 4.02. 12
when we hold rumor | from what we fear, yet know 4.02. 20
from what we fear, yet know not what we fear, 4.02. 20
poor bird, thou'dst never fear the net nor lime, 4.02. 34
i speak not as in absolute fear of you. 4.03. 38
but fear not yet | to take upon you what is 4.03. 69
yet do not fear, | scotland hath foisons to fill 4.03. 87
what need we fear who knows it, when none can 5.01. 37 P
remove to dunsinane | i cannot taint with fear. 5.03. 3
"fear not, macbeth, no man that's born of woman 5.03. 6
shall never sag with doubt, nor shake with fear. 5.03. 10
go prick thy face, and over-red thy fear, | thou 5.03. 14
linen cheeks of thine | are counsellors to fear. 5.03. 17
country round, | hang those that talk of fear. 5.03. 36
"fear not, till birnan wood | do come to 5.05. 43
such a one | am i to fear, or none. 5.07. 4
most like; it /harrows me with fear and wonder. HAM 1.01. 44
almost to jelly with the act of fear, | stand 1.02.205
the virtue of his will, but you must fear, | his 1.03. 16
fear it, ophelia, fear it, my dear sister, | and 1.03. 33
fear it, ophelia, fear it, my dear sister, | and 1.03. 33
be wary then, best safety lies in fear: 1.03. 43
o, fear me not. 1.03. 51
why, what should be the fear? 1.04. 64
lord, i do not know, | but truly i do fear it. 2.01. 83
a blanket, in the alarm of fear caught up — 2.02.509
/for women's fear and love hold quantity, | in 3.02.167
know, | and as my love is siz'd, my fear is so. 3.02.170
love is great, the littlest doubts are fear; 3.02.171
most holy and religious fear it is | to keep 3.03. 8
for we will fetters put about this fear, | which 3.03. 25
i'll /warr'nt you, fear me not. 3.04. 6
let him go, gertrude, do not fear our person: 4.05.123
now fear i this will give it start again, 4.07.193
dangerous, | which let thy wisdom fear. 5.01.263
i do not fear it, i have seen you both; 5.02.262
that's my fear. LR 1.02.166 P
that is wise and says little, to fear judgment, 1.04. 16 P
well, you may fear too far. 1.04.328
let me still take away the harms i fear, | not 1.04.329
the harms i fear, | not fear still to be taken. 1.04.330
inform her full of my particular fear, | and 1.04.337
apt | to have his ear abus'd, wisdom bids fear. 2.04.307
shall see cordelia | (as fear not but you shall) 3.01. 47
cannot carry | th' affliction nor the fear. 3.02. 49
stands still in esperance, lives not in fear. 4.01. 4
plainly, | i fear i am not in my perfect mind. 4.07. 62
fear /me not. | she and the duke her husband! 5.01. 16
bosom | of such a thing as thou — to fear, not OTH 1.02. 71
o, but i fear — how lost you company? 2.01. 91
for i fear | my soul hath her content so 2.01.190
garb | (for i fear cassio with my night-cap too) 2.01.307
i fear the trust othello puts him in, | on some 2.03.126
yet wild, the people's hearts brimful of fear, 2.03.214
draw | the smallest fear or doubt of her revolt, 3.03.188
when she seem'd to shake and fear your looks, 3.03.207
/i' /faith, i fear it has. 3.03.215
speak of her, though i may fear | her will, 3.03.235
my fears | (as worthy cause i have to fear i am) 3.03.254
fear not my government. 3.03.256
devils themselves | should fear to seize thee; 4.02. 37
quick, quick, fear nothing; 5.01. 3
and yet i fear you; 5.02. 37
why i should fear i know not, | since guiltiness 5.02. 38
but yet i feel i fear. 5.02. 39
o, my fear interprets. what, is he dead? 5.02. 73
'tis a lost fear; 5.02.269
this did i fear, but thought he had no weapon; 5.02.360
in time we hate that which we often fear. ANT 1.03. 12
but how the fear of us | may cement their 2.01. 47
thy angel | becomes a fear, as being o'erpow'r'd 2.03. 23
thou canst not fear us, pompey, with thy sails; 2.06. 24
i fear me you'll be in till then. 2.07. 32 P
the least cause | for what you seem to fear. 3.02. 36
rashness, and they them | for fear and doting. 3.11. 15
to be furious | is to be frighted out of fear, 3.13.195
his fretted fortunes give him hope and fear | of 4.12. 8
she had a prophesying fear | of what hath come 4.14.120
are fall'n into a princely hand, fear nothing. 5.02. 22
that you did fear is done. 5.02.335
i something fear my father's wrath, but nothing CYM 1.01. 86
notwithstanding, i fear not my ring. 1.04. 98 P
you have some religion in you, that you fear. 1.04.137 P
my lord, i fear, | has forgot britain. 1.06.112
i lodge in fear; 2.02. 49
fear it not, sir. 2.04. 1
and we will fear no poison, which attends | in 3.03. 77
put thyself | into a havior of less fear, ere 3.04. 9
if thou fear to strike and to make me certain it 3.04. 29 P
fear not, 'tis empty of all things but grief. 3.04. 69
fear and niceness | (the handmaids of all women, 3.04.155
grant, heavens, that which i fear | prove false! 3.05. 52
and if mine enemy | but fear the sword like me, 3.06. 26
i fear some ambush. 4.02. 65
to thy further fear, | nay, to thy mere 4.02. 91
those that i reverence, those i fear — the wise 4.02. 95
at fools i laugh, not fear them. 4.02. 96
defect of judgment | is oft the cause of fear. 4.02.112
all himself, | for we do fear the law? 4.02.129
then on good ground we fear, | if we do fear 4.02.143
if we do fear this body hath a tail | more 4.02.144
i fear 'twill be reveng'd. 4.02.154
fear no more the heat o' th' sun, | nor the 4.02.258
fear no more the frown o' th' great, | thou art 4.02.264
fear no more the lightning flash. 4.02.270
fear not slander, censure rash. 4.02.272
good faith, | i tremble still with fear; 4.02.303
we fear not | what can from italy annoy us, but 4.03. 33
some falling | merely through fear, that the 5.03. 11
to no more payments, fear no more tavern-bills, 5.04.159 P
lord, | now fear is from me, i'll speak troth. 5.05.274
by flight i'll shun the danger which i fear. PER 1.01.142
and what was first but fear what might be done, 1.02. 14
'tis time to fear when tyrants seems to kiss. 1.02. 79
which fear so grew in me, i hither fled, | under 1.02. 80
antiochus you fear, | and justly too, i think, 1.02.102
and justly too, i think, you fear the tyrant, 1.02.103
that's the least fear; 1.04. 71
does fall in travail with her fear; 3.ch. 52
i do not fear the flaw, | it hath done to me the 3.01. 39
pure surprise and fear | made me to quit the 3.02. 17
fear not, my lord, but think | your grace, that 3.03. 17
my father, as nurse says, did never fear, | but 4.01. 52
this is the fear we bring; TNK pr 21
power | (unless we fear that apes can tutor 's) 1.02. 43
but that we fear the gods in him, he brings not 1.02. 94
we are prisoners | i fear for ever, cousin. 2.02. 4
near the gods in nature, they should fear her; 2.02.242
me use my sword | against th' advice of fear. 3.01. 60
in me hath grief slain fear, and, but for one 3.02. 5
come forth and fear not, here's no theseus. 3.03. 3
but i must fear you first. 3.03. 9
fear me not. 3.03. 51
shall threaten me | i fear less than my fortune. 3.06.125
or fear of my miscarrying on his scape, | or 4.01. 50
fear he cannot, | he shows no such soft temper. 4.02.102
expels the seeds of fear and th' apprehension 5.01. 36
to my petition, | season'd with holy fear. 5.01.149
fear their gay skins with thought of their sharp STM III 18
when lo the unback'd breeder, full of fear, VEN 320
which purchase if thou make, for fear of slips, 515
sawest thou not signs of fear lurk in mine eye? 644
that if i love thee, i thy death should fear. 660
bleed, | and fear doth teach it divination: 670
danger deviseth shifts, wit waits on fear. 690
the fear whereof doth make him shake and shudder 880
who, overcome by doubt and bloodless fear, 891
them leave quaking, bids them fear no more — 899
a second fear through all her sinews spread, 903
i felt a kind of fear | when as i met the boar, 998
thou art as full of fear | as one with treasure 1021
having no fair to lose, you need not fear, | the 1083
some hedge, because he would not fear him; 1094
"it shall suspect where is no cause of fear, 1153
it shall not fear where it should most mistrust, 1154
put fear to valor, courage to the coward. 1158
birds never lim'd no secret bushes fear: LUC 88
till sable night, mother of dread and fear, 117
but honest fear, bewitch'd with lust's foul 173
here pale with fear he doth premeditate | the 183
guilt being great, the fear doth still exceed; 229
and extreme fear can neither fight nor fly, 230
o, how her fear did make her color rise! 257
forc'd it to tremble with her loyal fear! 261
"then childish fear, avaunt, debating, die! 274
so heedful fear | is almost chok'd by unresisted 281
they fright him, yet he still pursues his fear. 308
marking what he tells | with trembling fear, as 511
"this deed will make thee only lov'd for fear, 610
if but for fear of this, thy will remove: 614
he faintly flies, sweating with guilty fear; 740
and therefore now i need not fear to die. 1052
that dying fear through all her body spread, 1266
bright things stain'd) a kind of heavy fear. 1435
nor ashy pale the fear that false hearts have. 1512
(and far the weaker with so strong a fear), | my 1647
he falls, and bathes the pale fear in his face, 1775
but soft, enough — too much, i fear — | lest PP 18.49
is it for fear to wet a widow's eye | that thou SON 9. 1
who with his fear is put besides his part, | or 23. 2
so i, for fear of trust, forget to say | the 23. 5
and even thence thou wilt be stol'n, i fear, 48.13
i was not sick of any fear from thence: 86.12
then need i not to fear the worst of wrongs, 92. 5
for fear of which, hear this, thou age unbred: 104.13
yet fear her, o thou minion of her pleasure, 126. 9
for fear of harms that preach in our behoof. LC 165
stand forth | of wealth, of filial fear, law, 270

/FEAR'D 2 FR 0.0002 REL FR 2 V 0 P

and even the like precurse of /fear'd events, HAM 1.01.121
against thine enemies, ne'er /fear'd to lose it, LR 1.01.156

FEAR'D 52 FR 0.0058 REL FR 49 V 3 P

of it, but i fear'd | lest i might anger thee. TMP 4.01.168
i fear'd to show my father julia's letter, TGV 1.03. 80
time the rod | /becomes more mock'd than fear'd; MM 1.03. 27
i should have fear'd her had she been a devil." LLL 5.02.106
i am fear'd in field and town. MND 3.02.398
this aspect of mine | hath fear'd the valiant; MV 2.01. 9
vanity, | having vainly fear'd too little. AWW 5.03.123
that noble honor'd lord, is fear'd and lov'd? WT 5.01.158
done, | what we so fear'd he had a charge to do. JN 4.02. 75
indeed we fear'd his sickness was past cure. 4.02. 86
fear'd by their breed, and famous by their birth R2 2.01. 52
to monarchize, be fear'd, and kill with looks, 3.02.165
mighty and to be fear'd, than my condition, 1H4 1.03. 6
the king himself is to be fear'd as the lion. 3.03.149 P
thence | he was much fear'd by his physicians. 4.01. 24
others' eyes | that what he fear'd is chanced. 2H4 1.01. 87
chok'd the respect of likely peril fear'd, | and 1.01.184
she hath been then more fear'd than harm'd, my H5 1.02.155
never was monarch better fear'd and lov'd | than 2.02. 25
where they fear'd the death, they have borne 4.01.172 P
wherein thou art less happy, being fear'd, 4.01.248
so much fear'd abroad | that with his name the 1H6 2.03. 16
have made thee fear'd and honor'd of the people; 2H6 1.01.198
'tis to be fear'd they all will follow him. 3.01. 30
e'er i prov'd thee false or fear'd thy faith. 3.01.205
for i, that never fear'd any, am vanquish'd by 4.10. 75 P
for warwick was a bug that fear'd us all. 3H6 5.02. 2
if thou hadst fear'd to break an oath by him, R3 4.04.381
example, in their issue | are to be fear'd. H8 1.02. 91
and fear'd | she'll with the labor end. 5.01. 19

she shall be lov'd and fear'd: 5.04. 30
makes fear'd and talk'd of more than seen — COR 4.01. 31
for if | i had fear'd death, of all the men i' 4.05. 81
for i dare so far free him — made him fear'd, 4.07. 47
you should have fear'd false times when you did TIM 4.03.513
i rather tell thee what is to be fear'd | than JC 1.02.211
say, i fear'd caesar, honor'd him, and lov'd him 3.01.129
of nature | reigns that which would be fear'd. MAC 3.01. 50
i fear'd he did but trifle | and meant to wrack HAM 2.01.109
he shall never more | be fear'd of doing harm. LR 2.01.111
to fall in love with what she fear'd to look on! OTH 1.03. 98
belov'd of those | that only have fear'd caesar; ANT 1.04. 38
antony | as you did love, but as you fear'd him. 3.13. 57
in these fear'd /hopes | i barely gratify your CYM 2.04. 6
a drop of pity | as a wren's eye, fear'd gods, a 4.02.305
and danger, which i fear'd, is at antioch, PER 1.02. 7
draw thy fear'd sword | that does good turns to TNK 1.01. 48
i fear'd thy fortune, and my joints did tremble. VEN 642
touch'd no unknown baits, nor fear'd no hooks, LUC 103
but happy monarchs still are fear'd for love; 611
i fear'd by tarquin's falchion to be slain, 1046
but when i fear'd, i was a loyal wife: 1048

FEARED 2 FR 0.0002 REL FR 2 V 0 P
the voice and echo, | the numbers of the feared. 2H4 3.01. 98
for she being feared of all, now fearing one; R3 4.04.103

FEAREST 1 FR 0.0001 REL FR 1 V 0 P
and full of wretchedness, | and fearest to die? ROM 5.01. 69

FEARETH 1 FR 0.0001 REL FR 1 V 0 P
one sweetly flatters, th' other feareth harm, LUC 172

/FEARFUL 1 FR 0.0001 REL FR 1 V 0 P
/but /rather /show /a /while /like /fearful /war 2H4 4.01. 63

FEARFUL 97 FR 0.0109 REL FR 92 V 5 P
of him, for | he's gentle, and not fearful. TMP 1.02.469
power guide us | out of this fearful country! 5.01.106
some whirlwind bear | unto a ragged, fearful, TGV 1.02.118
death is a fearful thing. MM 3.01.115
virtue is bold, and goodness never fearful. 3.01.208 P
yet since i see you fearful, that neither my 4.02.189 P
did but convey unto our fearful minds | a ERR 1.01. 67
there is not a more fearful wild-fowl than your MND 3.01. 32 P
and in the modesty of fearful duty | i read as 5.01.101
through which the fearful lovers are to whisper. 5.01.164
left in the fearful guard | of an unthrifty MV 1.03.175
a man may, if he were of a fearful heart, AYL 3.03. 48 P
black and fearful | on the opposer. AWW 3.01. 5
deliver, when the courtesy of it is so fearful. TN 1.05.207 P
i may be negligent, foolish, and fearful: WT 1.02.250
if ever fearful | to do a thing, where i the 1.02.258
too | expos'd this paragon to th' fearful usage 5.01.153
must | with fearful bloody issue arbitrate. JN 1.01. 38
the fearful difference of incensed kings — 3.01.238
a fearful eye thou hast. 4.02.106
whilst he that hears makes fearful action | with 4.02.191
black, fearful, comfortless, and horrible. 5.06. 20
but, lords, we hear this fearful tempest sing, R2 2.01.263
and lean-look'd prophets whisper fearful change, 2.04. 11
covering your fearful land | with hard bright 3.02.110
to watch the fearful bending of thy knee, 3.03. 73
a mighty and a fearful head they are, | if 1H4 3.02.167
may turn the tide of fearful faction, | and 4.01. 67
i, | make fearful musters and prepar'd defense, 2H4 in 12
hazard | and fearful meeting of their opposite. 4.01. 16
hear | a fearful battle rend'red you in music; H5 1.01. 44
confirm'd conspiracy with fearful france, | and 2.pr. 27
'tis a fearful odds. 4.03. 5
thou ominous and fearful owl of death, | our 1H6 4.02. 15
now, york, or never, steel thy fearful thoughts, 2H6 3.01.331
and after all this fearful homage done, | give 3.02.224
the mind, | and makes it fearful and degenerate; 4.04. 2
the fearful french, whom you late vanquished, 4.08. 42
this is the palace of the fearful king, | and 3H6 1.01. 25
base, fearful, and despairing henry! 1.01.178
and though man's face be fearful to their eyes, 2.02. 27
sometime they have us'd with fearful flight, 2.02. 30
having the fearful flying hare in sight, | with 2.05.130
should leave the helm and, like a fearful lad, 5.04. 7
for did i but suspect a fearful man, | he should 5.04. 44
that edward shall be fearful of his life, | and 5.06. 87
to fright the souls of fearful adversaries, | he R3 1.01. 11
so full of fearful dreams, of ugly sights, 1.04. 3
methoughts i saw a thousand fearful wracks; 1.04. 24
gone | to brecknock while my fearful head is on! 4.02.122
i have learn'd that fearful commenting | is 4.03. 51
that with a fearful soul | leads discontented 4.04.311
this, this all-souls' day to my fearful soul, 5.01. 18
the leisure and the fearful time | cuts off the 5.03. 97
cold fearful drops stand on my trembling flesh. 5.03.181
o ratcliffe, i have dream'd a fearful dream! 5.03.212
i am fearful; H8 5.01. 87
you that will be less fearful than discreet; COR 3.01.150
and more, | more fearful, is deliver'd. 4.06. 64
what more fearful? 4.06. 64
a fearful army, led by caius martius 4.06. 75
faith, we hear fearful news. 4.06.139
would make such fearful and confused cries, | as TIT 2.03.102
and see a fearful sight of blood and death. 2.03.216
when will this fearful slumber have an end? 3.01.252
but let them hear what fearful words i utter. 5.02.168
the fearful passage of their death-mark'd love, ROM pr 9
shall bitterly begin his fearful date | with 1.04.108
she steal love's sweet bait from fearful hooks. 2.pr. 8
romeo, come forth, come forth, thou fearful man: 3.03. 1
that pierc'd the fearful hollow of thine ear; 3.05. 3
there's a fearful point! 4.03. 32
it thee, | so fearful were they of infection. 5.02. 16
and fearful scouring | doth choke the air with TIM 5.02. 15
and fearful, as these strange eruptions are. JC 1.03. 78
for now, this fearful night, | there is no stir 1.03.126
what a fearful night is this! 1.03.137
and come down | with fearful bravery, thinking 5.01. 10
no; nor more fearful. MAC 5.07. 9
like a guilty thing | upon a fearful summons. HAM 1.01.149
end, | like quills upon the fearful porpentine. 1.05. 20
have found a safe redress, but now grow fearful, LR 1.04.206
how fearful | and dizzy 'tis, to cast one's eyes 4.06. 11
main article i do approve | in fearful sense. OTH 1.03. 12
difficult weight, | and fearful to be granted. 3.03. 83
o my lord, my lord, | forgive my fearful sails! ANT 3.11. 55
to break it with a fearful dream of him, | and CYM 3.04. 43
hath been to me | as fearful as a siege. 3.04.134
and in a time | when fearful wars point at me; 4.03. 7
and by those fearful objects to prepare | this PER 1.01. 43
time, | fearful consumers, you will all devour! TNK 1.01. 70
i am cruel fearful. ep 3
as fearful of him, part, through whom he rushes. VEN 630
pursue these fearful creatures o'er the downs, 677
whereon with fearful eyes they long have gazed, 927
bare and unpeopled in this fearful flood. LUC 1741
o fearful meditation! SON 65. 9

FEARFULL'ST 1 FR 0.0001 REL FR 1 V 0 P
i prophesy the fearfull'st time to thee | that R3 3.04.104

FEARFULLY 10 FR 0.0011 REL FR 9 V 1 P
a night | did thisby fearfully o'ertrip the dew, MV 5.01. 7
breast, | and i do fearfully believe 'tis done, JN 4.02. 74
ran fearfully among the trembling reeds, | and 1H4 1.03.105
it | as fearfully as doth a galled rock H5 3.01. 12
and fearfully did menace me with death | if i ROM 5.03.133
head | looks fearfully in the confined deep. LR 4.01. 74
must seem to do that fearfully which you commit PER 4.02.117 P
place, | where fearfully the dogs exclaim aloud: VEN 886
all sleeping, | nymphs /back peeping fearfully. PP 17.28
the roses fearfully on thorns did stand, | /one SON 99. 8

FEARFULNESS 1 FR 0.0001 REL FR 1 V 0 P
men, | and keep us all in servile fearfulness. JC 1.01. 75

FEARING 30 FR 0.0034 REL FR 29 V 1 P
or fearing else some messenger, that might her TGV 2.01.167
but, fearing lest my jealous aim might err, 3.01. 28
child, | nor fearing me as if i were her father; 3.01. 71
good we oft might win, | by fearing to attempt. MM 1.04. 79
that life is better life, past fearing death, 5.01.397
first were we sad, fearing you would not come, SHR 3.02. 98
not ended, as fearing to hear of it hereafter. AWW 4.03. 96 P
not fearing the displeasure of your master, 5.03.235
but if you faint, as fearing to do so, | stay, R2 2.01.297
where fearing dying pays death servile breath. 3.02.185
mind, | if you suppose as fearing you it shook. 1H4 3.01. 22
happy, being fear'd, | than they in fearing. H5 4.01.249
not fearing death, nor shrinking for distress, 1H6 4.01. 37
for she being feared of all, now fearing one; R3 4.04.103
and fearing he would rise (he was so virtuous), H8 2.02.127
than man could give him, he died fearing god. 4.02. 68
i speak not "be thou true" as fearing thee, TRO 4.04. 62
not fearing outward force, so shall my lungs COR 3.01. 77
fearing to strengthen that impatience | which JC 2.01.248
life | cuts off so many years of fearing death. 3.01.102
that have abridg'd | his time of fearing death. 3.01.105
it spills itself in fearing to be spilt. HAM 4.05. 20
but, fearing since how it might work, hath sent ANT 4.14.125
therefore the earth, fearing to be o'erflowed, PER 4.04. 40
i rail'd on thee, fearing my love's decesse. VEN 1002
sit, | long after fearing to creep forth again; 1036
fearing some hard news from the warlike band LUC 255
but she, sound sleeping, fearing no such thing, 363
my love, the loss whereof still fearing! PP 7.10
alas, why, fearing of time's tyranny, | might i SON 115. 9

FEARLESS 4 FR 0.0004 REL FR 3 V 1 P
reakless, and fearless of what's past, present, MM 4.02.144 P
free speech and fearless i to thee allow. R2 1.01.123
and fearless minds climb soonest unto crowns. 3H6 4.07. 62
which shows him hardy, fearless, proud of TNK 4.02. 80

FEAR'S 2 FR 0.0002 REL FR 2 V 0 P
so slipp'ry that | the fear's as bad as falling; CYM 3.03. 49
against love's fire fear's frost hath LUC 355

/FEARS 2 FR 0.0002 REL FR 1 V 1 P
more dregs than water, if my /fears have eyes. TRO 3.02. 67 P
tyrannous, and tyrants' /fears | decrease not, PER 1.02. 84

FEARS 83 FR 0.0093 REL FR 76 V 7 P
to watch, like one that fears robbing; TGV 2.01. 25 P
than i meant, to pluck all fears out of you. MM 4.02.191 P
faults are bred | and fears by pale white shown: LLL 1.02.102
thus weak, lost with their fears thus strong, MND 3.02. 27
throttle their practic'd accent in their fears, 5.01. 97
for he fears none. SHR 1.02.210
now, for my life, hortensio fears his widow. 5.02. 16
but such traitors | his majesty seldom fears. AWW 2.01. 97
and mak'st /conjectural fears to come into me, 5.03.114
fall, | shall /tax my fears of little vanity, 5.03.122
i am question'd by my fears of what may chance WT 1.02. 11
kings of our fear, until our fears, resolv'd, JN 2.01.371
me, | for i am sick and capable of fears, 3.01. 12
with wrongs, and therefore full of fears, | a 3.01. 13
fears, | a widow, husbandless, subject to fears, 3.01. 14
to fears, | a woman, naturally born to fears; 3.01. 15
why then your fears, which (as they say) attend 4.02. 56
why seek'st thou to possess me with these fears? 4.02.203
and those thy fears might have wrought fears in 4.02.236
those thy fears might have wrought fears in me. 4.02.236
and indent with fears, | when they have lost and 1H4 1.03. 87
to-morrow in the battle | which of us fears. 4.03. 14
he that but fears the thing he would not know 2H4 1.01. 85
your spirit is too true, your fears too certain. 1.01. 92
all these bold fears | thou seest with peril i 4.05.195
when he sees reason of fears, as we do, his H5 4.01.108 P
of fears, as we do, his fears, out of doubt, be 4.01.109 P
that fears his fellowship to die with us. 4.03. 39
tell him his fears are shallow, without instance R3 3.02. 25
he fears, my lord, you mean no good to him. 3.07. 87
his fears were that the interview betwixt H8 1.01.180
i do not think he fears death. 2.01. 37
fears, and despairs, and all these for his 2.02. 28
you wrong the king's love with these fears, 3.01. 81
your fears are worse. 3.01.124
your virtues | with these weak women's fears. 3.01.169
more pangs and fears than wars or women have; 3.02.370
prayers then would seek you, not their fears. 5.02.118
/seeks his praise more than he fears his peril, TRO 1.03.267
though no man lesser fears the greeks than i 2.02. 8
and inches so diminutive | as fears and reasons? 2.02. 32
off | all fears attending on so dire a project. 2.02.134
fears make devils of cherubins, they never see 3.02. 69 P
no, nor a man that fears you less than he, COR 1.04. 14
and make the rabble | call our cares fears; 3.01.137
to die by himself fears it not from another. 5.02.105 P
environed with all these hideous fears, | and ROM 4.03. 50
their fears of hostile strokes, their aches, TIM 5.01.199
to atone your fears | with my more noble meaning 5.04. 58
how foolish do your fears seem now, calphurnia! JC 2.02.105
but yet have i a mind | that fears him much; 3.01.145
present fears | are less than horrible MAC 1.03.137
yet let that be | which the eye fears, when it 1.04. 53
eye of childhood | that fears a painted devil. 2.02. 52
fears and scruples shake us. 2.03.129
our fears in banquo | stick deep, and in his 3.01. 48
confin'd, bound in | to saucy doubts and fears. 3.04. 24
actions do not, | our fears do make us traitors. 4.02. 4
i have almost forgot the taste of fears. 5.05. 9
where little fears grow great, great love grows HAM 3.02.172
my fears forgetting manners, to /unseal | their 5.02. 17
way to loyalty, something fears me to think of. LR 3.05. 3 P
to him that ever fears he shall be poor. OTH 3.03.174
let me be thought too busy in my fears | (as 3.03.253
and all great fears, which now import their ANT 2.02.132
touch more rare | subdues all pangs, all fears. CYM 1.01.136
routs us but | the villainy of our fears. 5.02. 13
/one | that fears not to do harm; TNK 1.02. 71
griefs, angers, fears, my friend shall suffer? 2.02.188
only this fears me, | the law will have the 3.06.129
who fears a sentence or an old man's saw | shall LUC 244
then who fears sinking where such treasure lies? 280
the merchant fears, ere rich at home he lands." 336
wrapp'd and confounded in a thousand fears, 456
in black mourn i, all fears scorn i, | love hath PP 17.13
but weep to have that which it fears to lose. SON 64.14
but what's so blessed-fair that fears no blot? 92.13
not mine own fears, nor the prophetic soul | of 107. 1
applying fears to hopes, and hopes to fears, 119. 3
applying fears to hopes, and hopes to fears, 119. 3
it fears not policy, that heretic, | which works 124. 9
the aloes of all forces, shocks, and fears. LC 273
shook off my sober guards and civil fears; 298

FEAR'ST 3 FR 0.0003 REL FR 3 V 0 P
oft provok'st, yet grossly fear'st | thy death, MM 3.01. 18
then thou art | as great as that thou fear'st. TN 5.01.150
fear'st thou that, antonio? 5.01.221

FEAR-SURPRISED 1 FR 0.0001 REL FR 1 V 0 P
by their oppress'd and fear-surprised eyes, HAM 1.02.203

/FEAST 1 FR 0.0001 REL FR 1 V 0 P
dine, | when i to /feast expressly am forbid; LLL 1.01. 62

FEAST 107 FR 0.0121 REL FR 94 V 13 P
one feast, one house, one mutual happiness. TGV 5.04.173
impiety has made a feast of thee. MM 1.02. 57 P
and feast upon her eyes? 2.02.178
cheer and great welcome makes a merry feast. ERR 3.01. 26
face | revel and feast it at my house to-day, 4.04. 62
go to a gossips' feast, and go with me — 5.01.406
with all my heart, i'll gossip at this feast. 5.01.408
what, a feast, a feast? ADO 5.01.153 P
what, a feast, a feast? 5.01.153 P
they have been at a great feast of languages, LLL 5.01. 37 P
three, | we'll hold a feast in great solemnity. MND 4.01.185
for i do feast to-night | my best esteem'd MV 2.02.171
who riseth from a feast | with that keen 2.06. 8
and we are stay'd for at bassanio's feast. 2.06. 48
our feast shall be much honored in your marriage 3.02.212
church, | if ever sat at any good man's feast, AYL 2.07.115
provide the feast, father, and bid the guests, SHR 2.01.316
go to the feast, revel and domineer, | carouse 3.02.224
you know there wants no junkets at the feast. 3.02.248
to feast and sport us at thy father's house. 4.03.183
out of hope of all but my share of the feast. 5.01.141
feast with the best, and welcome to my house. 5.02. 8
the solemn feast | shall more attend upon the AWW 2.03.180
how shall i feast him? TN 3.04. 2
what am i to buy for our sheep-shearing feast? WT 4.03. 37 P
my father hath made her mistress of the feast, 4.03. 40 P
i prithee darken not | the mirth o' th' feast. 4.04. 42
that which you are, mistress o' th' feast. 4.04. 68
i was promis'd them against the feast, but they 4.04.235 P
shall our feast be kept with slaughtered men? JN 3.01.302
to feast upon whole thousands of the french. 5.02.178
this feast of battle with mine adversary. R2 1.03. 92
of appetite | by bare imagination of a feast? 1.03.297
seldom but sumptuous, show'd like a feast, | and 1H4 3.02. 58
end of a fray and the beginning of a feast 4.02. 79
did feast together, and in two year after | were 2H4 3.01. 59
or else a feast | and takes away the stomach — 4.04.106
this day is call'd the feast of crispian: H5 4.03. 40
will yearly on the vigil feast his neighbors, 4.03. 45
to keep our great saint george's feast withal. 1H6 1.01.154
and feast and banquet in the open streets, | to 1.06. 13
to feast so great a warrior in my house. 2.03. 82
now thou art come unto a feast of death, | a 4.05. 7
'tis like you would not feast him like a friend, 2H6 3.02.184
again | to york-place, where the feast is held. H8 4.01. 94
yourself shall feast with us before you go, TRO 1.03.308
next | to feast with me and see me at my tent. 4.05.229
there diomed doth feast with him to-night, | who 4.05.280
patroclus, let us feast him to the height. 5.01. 3
yet cam'st thou to a morsel of this feast, COR 1.09. 10
the feast smells well, but i | appear not like a 4.05. 5
as it were, a parcel of their feast, and to be 4.05.216 P
if the emperor's court can feast two brides, TIT 1.01.489
when he is here, even at thy solemn feast, | i 5.02.115
emperor and the empress too | feast at my house, 5.02.128
feast at my house, and he shall feast with them. 5.02.128
you know your mother means to feast with me, 5.02.184
this is the feast that i have bid her to, | and 5.02.192
more stern and bloody than the centaurs' feast. 5.02.203
the feast is ready which the careful titus 5.03. 21
this night i hold an old accustom'd feast, ROM 1.02. 20
at this same ancient feast of capulet's | sups 1.02. 82
that i will show you shining at this feast, 1.02. 98
this night you shall behold him at our feast; 1.03. 80
an ill-beseeming semblance for a feast. 1.05. 74
our wedding cheer to a sad burial feast; 4.05. 87
thou art going to lord timon's feast? TIM 1.01.260
i could wish my best friend at such a feast. 1.02. 80 P
they only now come but to feast thine eyes. 1.02.127
i'll once more feast the rascals. 3.04.112
feast your ears with the music awhile, if they 3.06. 33 P
here's a noble feast toward. 3.06. 60 P
make not a city feast of it, to let the meat 3.06. 67 P
may you a better feast never behold, | you knot 3.06. 88
henceforth be no feast | whereat a villain's not 3.06.102

here, i will mend thy feast. 4.03.282
have fear'd false times when you did feast: 4.03.513
you know it is the feast of lupercal. JC 1.01. 67
i dreamt to–night that i did feast with caesar, 3.03. 1
course, | chief nourisher in life's feast. MAC 2.02. 37
it had been as a gap in our great feast, | and 3.01. 12
fail not our feast. 3.01. 27
the feast is sold | that is not often vouch'd, 3.04. 32
he fail'd | his presence at the tyrant's feast, 3.06. 22
my news shall be the fruit to that great feast. HAM 2.02. 52
go to your rest, at night we'll feast together. 2.02. 84
what feast is toward in thine eternal cell, 5.02.365
we had much more monstrous matter of feast, ANT 2.02.182 P
barber'd ten times o'er, goes to the feast; 2.02.224
we'll feast each other ere we part, and let's 2.06. 60
this is not yet an alexandrian feast. 2.07. 96
since pompey's feast, as menas says, is troubled 3.02. 5
see it done, | and feast the army; 4.01. 15
venison first shall be the lord o' th' feast, CYM 3.03. 75
best woodman and | are master of the feast. 3.06. 29
'twas at a feast — o, would | our viands had 5.05.155
as friends to antioch, we may feast in tyre. PER 1.03. 39
feast here awhile, | until our stars that frown 1.04.107
prepare for mirth, for mirth becomes a feast. 2.03. 7
come, queen a' th' feast — | for, daughter, so 2.03. 17
striv'd | god neptune's annual feast to keep, 5.ch. 17
keep the feast full, bate not an hour on't. TNK 1.01.220
shall be returning | ere you can end this feast, 1.01.224
would they not wish the feast might ever last, VEN 447
should by his stealing in disturb the feast?" 450
with my love's picture then my eye doth feast, SON 47. 5
invited | to any sensual feast with thee alone; 141. 8
FEASTED 5 FR 0.0005 REL FR 5 V 0 P
while she with harlots feasted in my house. ERR 5.01.205
as if you were a feasted one and not | the WT 4.04. 63
when i have feasted with queen margaret? 2H6 4.01. 58
the place which i have feasted, does it now TIM 3.04. 82
three kings i had newly feasted, and did want ANT 2.02. 76
FEAST–FINDING 1 FR 0.0001 REL FR 1 V 0 P
feast–finding minstrels, tuning my defame, LUC 817
FEASTING 10 FR 0.0011 REL FR 8 V 2 P
i have no mind of feasting forth to–night; MV 2.05. 37
that does take | your mind from feasting. WT 4.04.347
i have been feasting with mine enemy, | where on ROM 2.03. 49
this vault a feasting presence full of light. 5.03. 86
not be, by the persuasion of his new feasting. TIM 3.06. 8 P
is full liberty of feasting from this present OTH 2.02. 9 P
julius caesar | grew fat with feasting there. ANT 2.06. 65
shame, | thy private feasting to a public fast, LUC 891
justice is feasting while the widow weeps, 906
sometime all full with feasting on your sight, SON 75. 9
FEAST'S 1 FR 0.0001 REL FR 1 V 0 P
the feast's solemnity | shall want till your TNK 1.01.221
FEASTS 18 FR 0.0020 REL FR 17 V 1 P
and sat at good men's feasts, and wip'd our eyes AYL 2.07.122
as clear | as friendship wears at feasts, keep WT 1.02.344
but that our feasts | in every mess have folly, 4.04. 10
and now he feasts, mousing the flesh of men, JN 2.01.354
nor met with fortune other than at feasts, 5.02. 58
lo, as at english feasts, so i regreet | the R2 1.03. 67
makes factious feasts, rails on our state of war TRO 1.03.191
is, and feasts the nobles of the state | at his COR 4.04. 9
feasts are too proud to give thanks to the gods. TIM 1.02. 61
what needs these feasts, pomps, and vainglories? 1.02.242 P
therefore be abhorr'd | all feasts, societies, 4.03. 21
free from our feasts and banquets bloody knives; MAC 3.06. 35
tie up the libertine in a field of feasts, ANT 2.01. 23
to do, for i perceive | four feasts are toward. 2.06. 73
seal it with feasts. CYM 5.05.483
i never at great feasts | sought to betray a TNK 5.01.102
therefore are feasts so solemn and so rare, SON 52. 5
for feasts of love i have been call'd unto, LC 181
FEAST–WON 1 FR 0.0001 REL FR 1 V 0 P
feast–won, fast–lost; TIM 2.02.171
/FEAT 2 FR 0.0002 REL FR 2 V 0 P
and if you break the ice and do this /feat, SHR 1.02.265
if that thy prosperous and artificial /feat PER 5.01. 72
FEAT 8 FR 0.0009 REL FR 8 V 0 P
and got a calf in that same noble feat | much ADO 5.04. 50
all the husbands | that cannot do that feat, WT 2.03.111
up | each corporal agent to this terrible feat. MAC 1.07. 80
his occasions, true, | so feat, so nurse–like. CYM 5.05. 88
i dare not praise | my feat in horsemanship, yet TNK 2.05. 13
me language such | as thou hast show'd me feat! 3.01. 45
force and great feat | must put my garland on, 5.01. 43
blood, | with sleided silk feat and affectedly LC 48
FEATED 1 FR 0.0001 REL FR 1 V 0 P
to th' more mature | a glass that feated them, CYM 1.01. 49
FEATER 1 FR 0.0001 REL FR 1 V 0 P
garments sit upon me, | much feater than before. TMP 2.01.273
FEATHER 24 FR 0.0027 REL FR 19 V 5 P
with raven's feather from unwholesome fen | drop TMP 1.02.322
a feather will turn the scale. MM 4.02. 30 P
a crow without feather? ERR 3.01. 81
without a fin, there's a fowl without a feather: 3.01. 82
of forty fancies prick'd in't for a feather: SHR 3.02. 69 P
you boggle shrewdly, every feather starts you. AWW 5.03.232
check at every feather | that comes before his TN 3.01. 64
i am a feather for each wind that blows. WT 2.03.154
there lies a downy feather which stirs not. 2H4 4.05. 32
fanning in his face with a peacock's feather. H5 4.01.201 P
there's not a piece of feather in our host — 4.03.112
was ever feather so lightly blown to and fro as 2H6 4.08. 55 P
and of their feather many moe proud birds, 3H6 2.01.170
look, as i blow this feather from my face, | and 3.01. 84
for both of you are birds of self–same feather. 3.03.161
of fool and feather that they got in france, H8 1.03. 25
feather of lead, bright smoke, cold fire, sick ROM 1.01.180
i am not of that feather to shake off | my TIM 1.01.100
when every feather sticks in his own wing, 2.01. 30
secrecy to the king and queen moult no feather. HAM 2.02.295 P
this feather stirs, she lives! LR 5.03.266
inform her tongue — the swan's down feather, ANT 3.02. 48
and your lord | (the best feather of our wing) CYM 1.06.186
anon he starts at stirring of a feather; VEN 302
FEATHER–BED 1 FR 0.0001 REL FR 0 V 1 P
peril of my life with the edge of a feather–bed, MV 2.02.165 P
FEATHER'D 2 FR 0.0002 REL FR 2 V 0 P
of feather'd cupid seel with wanton dullness OTH 1.03.269
in feather'd briefness sails are fill'd, | and PER 5.02. 15
FEATHERED 3 FR 0.0003 REL FR 3 V 0 P
rise from the ground like feathered mercury, 1H4 4.01.106
within your hollow swelling feathered breasts, LUC 1122
one of her feathered creatures broke away, SON 143. 2
FEATHERS 16 FR 0.0018 REL FR 13 V 3 P
when fowls have no feathers, and fish have no ERR 3.01. 79
what plume of feathers is he that indited this LLL 4.01. 94
lark, | because his feathers are more beautiful? SHR 4.03.176
and most courteous feathers, which bow the head, AWW 4.05.105 P
be mercury, set feathers to thy heels, | and fly JN 4.02.174
hen, if her feathers turn back in any show of 2H4 2.04.100 P
swiftness add | more feathers to our wings; H5 1.02.307
his feathers are but borrow'd, | for he's 2H6 3.01. 75
his shaft | to soar with his light feathers, and ROM 1.04. 20
these growing feathers pluck'd from caesar's JC 1.01. 72
sir, and a forest of feathers — if the rest of HAM 3.02.275 P
hadst thou been aught but goss'mer, feathers, LR 4.06. 49
paphos might with the crow | vie feathers white. PER 4.ch. 33
tires with her beak on feathers, flesh, and bone VEN 56
fleet–wing'd duty with thought's feathers flies. LUC 1216
have added feathers to the learned's wing, | and SON 78. 7
FEATH'RED 2 FR 0.0002 REL FR 2 V 0 P
the hairs, who wave like feath'red wings. VEN 306
tyrant wing, | save the eagle, feath'red king; PHT 11
FEATLY 2 FR 0.0002 REL FR 2 V 0 P
foot it featly here and there, | and, sweet TMP 1.02.379
she dances featly. WT 4.04.176
FEATS 14 FR 0.0015 REL FR 12 V 2 P
in the figure of a lamb, the feats of a lion. ADO 1.01. 15 P
and the feats he hath done about turnbull street 2H4 3.02.306 P
and with your puissant arm renew their feats. H5 1.02.116
do with his smirch'd complexion all fell feats 3.03. 17
with advantages | what feats he did that day. 4.03. 51
maid, is't thou wilt do these wondrous feats? 1H6 1.02. 64
call'd upon | for high feats done to th' crown, H8 1.01. 61
in that day's feats, | when he might act the COR 2.02. 95
me | why you /proceeded not against these feats, HAM 4.07. 6
more than pertains to feats of broils and battle OTH 1.03. 87
tell them your feats, whilst they with joyful ANT 4.08. 9
no whit less | than in his feats deserving it), CYM 3.01. 7
i sit and tell | the warlike feats i have done, 3.03. 90
aptly will suppose | what pageantry, what feats, PER 5.02. 6
FEATUR'D 2 FR 0.0002 REL FR 2 V 0 P
how wise, how noble, young, how rarely featur'd, ADO 3.01. 60
hope, | featur'd like him, like him with friends SON 29. 6
/FEATURE 1 FR 0.0001 REL FR 1 V 0 P
/for /shame | /bemonster /not /thy /feature. LR 4.02. 63
FEATURE 13 FR 0.0014 REL FR 11 V 2 P
he is complete in feature and in mind | with all TGV 2.04. 73
doth my simple feature content you? AYL 3.03. 3 P
none, | nor know i you by voice or any feature. TN 3.04.353
thou hast, sebastian, done good feature shame. 3.04.366
boy | liker in feature to his father geffrey JN 2.01.126
comment that my passion made | upon thy feature, 4.02.264
her peerless feature, joined with her birth, 1H6 5.05. 68
cheated of feature by dissembling nature, R3 1.01. 19
creature, and complete | in mind and feature. H8 3.02. 50
to show virtue her feature, scorn her own image, HAM 3.02. 23 P
bid him | report the feature of octavia, her ANT 2.05.112
for feature, laming | the shrine of venus or CYM 5.05.163
crow or dove, it shapes them to your feature. SON 113.12
FEATURELESS 1 FR 0.0001 REL FR 1 V 0 P
harsh, featureless, and rude, barrenly perish: SON 11.10
FEATURES 3 FR 0.0003 REL FR 1 V 2 P
how features are abroad | i am skilless of; TMP 3.01. 52
your features, lord warrant us! what features? AYL 3.03. 5 P
your features, lord warrant us! what features? 3.03. 5 P
FEAZ'D 1 FR 0.0001 REL FR 0 V 1 P
dishonorable ragged than an old feaz'd ancient: 1H4 4.02. 31 P
FEBRUARY 1 FR 0.0001 REL FR 1 V 0 P
matter, | that you have such a february face, ADO 5.04. 41
FECKS 1 FR 0.0001 REL FR 1 V 0 P
i' fecks! WT 1.02.120
/FED 1 FR 0.0001 REL FR 1 V 0 P
many together, | and then they /fed on him. TNK 3.02. 19
FED 38 FR 0.0043 REL FR 34 V 4 P
o, i have fed upon this woe already, | and now TGV 3.01.221
fed in heart, whose flames aspire, | as thoughts WIV 5.05. 97
at board he fed not for my urging it; ERR 5.01. 64
he hath never fed of the dainties that are bred LLL 4.02. 24
fed with the same food, hurt with the same MV 3.01. 60 P
with gazing fed, and fancy dies | in the cradle 3.02. 68
with oaths kept waking, and with brawling fed; SHR 4.03. 10
i will show myself highly fed and lowly taught. AWW 2.02. 3 P
a good knave, i' faith, and well fed. 2.04. 38
of peace | must by the hungry now be fed upon. JN 3.03. 10
whilst you have fed upon my signories, R2 3.01. 22
and being fed by us you us'd us so | as that 1H4 5.01. 59
depending | hath fed upon the body of my father; 2H4 4.05.159
fed from my trencher, kneel'd down at the board, 2H6 4.01. 57
who fed him every minute | with words of H8 1.02.149
that was he | that fed him with his prophecies? 2.01. 23
ye follow my disgraces | as if it fed ye, and 3.02.241
now, hector, i have fed mine eyes on thee; TRO 4.05.231
half–supp'd sword, that frankly would have fed, 5.08. 19
disobedience, fed | the ruin of the state. COR 3.01.117
sensibly fed | of that self blood that first TIT 4.02.122
whereof their mother daintily hath fed, | eating 5.03. 61
we both have fed as well, and we can both JC 1.02. 98
so valiant, | and in his commendations i am fed; MAC 1.04. 55
of appetite had grown | by what it fed on, and HAM 1.02.145
and eat of the fish that hath fed of that worm. 4.03. 28 P
"the hedge–sparrow fed the cuckoo so long, LR 1.04.215
her eye must be fed; OTH 2.01.225 P
i slept the next night well, fed well, was free 3.03.340
smoky light | that's fed with stinking tallow: CYM 1.06.110
protest my ears were never better fed | with PER 2.05. 27
your grace, that fed my country with your corn, 3.03. 18
unless the earth with thy increase be fed? VEN 170
but, when his glutton eye so full hath fed, 399
under whose simple semblance he hath fed | upon 795
he fed them with his sight, they him with 1104
the spring that those shrunk pipes had fed, LUC 1455
within be fed, without be rich no more: SON 146.12
FEDARY *(also federary, feodary)*
FEDARY 1 FR 0.0001 REL FR 1 V 0 P
if not a fedary, but only he, | owe and succeed MM 2.04.122
FEDERARY *(also fedary, feodary)*
FEDERARY 1 FR 0.0001 REL FR 1 V 0 P
and camillo is | a federary with her, and one WT 2.01. 90
FEE 28 FR 0.0031 REL FR 26 V 2 P
to plead for love deserves more fee than hate. TGV 1.02. 48
here is thy fee, arrest him, officer. ERR 4.01. 76
working this, and thy fee is a thousand ducats. ADO 2.02. 53 P
mistook by me, | pleading for a lover's fee. MND 3.02.113
go, tubal, fee me an officer; MV 3.01.126 P
remembrance of us, as a tribute, | not as fee. 4.01.423
clerk, | a prating boy, that begg'd it as a fee. 5.01.164
ay, and i'll give them him without a fee. 5.01.290
not helping, death's my fee, | but, if i help, AWW 2.01.189
which heaven shall take in nature of a fee; JN 2.01.170
and i should rob the deathsman of his fee, 2H6 3.02.217
ay, here's a deer whose skin's a keeper's fee: 3H6 3.01. 22
but, now thy beauty is propos'd my fee, | my R3 1.02.169
take thou the fee and tell him what i say, | for 1.04.277
orator | as if the golden fee for which i plead 3.05. 96
gain the popedom | and fee my friends in rome). H8 3.02.213
so should i rob my sweet sons of their fee. TIT 2.03.179
i do not set my life at a pin's fee, | and for HAM 1.04. 65
him threescore thousand crowns in annual fee, 2.02. 73
pole | a ranker rate, should it be sold in fee. 4.04. 22
and /the fee bestow | upon the foul disease. LR 1.01.163
besides this treasure for a fee, | the gods PER 3.02. 74
about that neck | which is my fee, and which i TNK 1.01.198
but when he saw his love, his youth's fair fee, VEN 393
"adieu," | the honey fee of parting tend'red is: 538
her pleading hath deserv'd a greater fee; 609
they buy thy help, but sin ne'er gives a fee, LUC 913
but that your trespass now becomes a fee, | mine SON 120.13
FEEBLE 33 FR 0.0037 REL FR 26 V 7 P
to measure kingdoms with his feeble steps; TGV 2.07. 10
smoth'red in errors, feeble, shallow, weak, ERR 3.02. 35
son | knows not my feeble key of untun'd cares? 5.01.311
which cannot hear a lady's feeble voice, | which JN 3.04. 41
about the burning crest | of the old, feeble, 5.04. 35
shall wound my honor with such feeble wrong, R2 1.01.191
but if without him we be thought too feeble, 2H4 1.03. 19
francis feeble! 3.02.147 P
what trade art thou, feeble? 3.02.149 P
well said, courageous feeble! 3.02.159 P
let that suffice, most forcible feeble. 3.02.168 P
i am bound to thee, reverend feeble. 3.02.170 P
then, mouldy, bullcalf, feeble, and shadow. 3.02.248 P
swiftly will this feeble the woman's tailor run 3.02.268 P
to view the sick and feeble parts of france; H5 2.04. 22
and, with a feeble gripe, says, "dear my lord, 4.06. 22
and pluck the crown from feeble henry's head. 2H6 5.01. 2
house, | so was his will in his old feeble body. 5.03. 13
and pluck'd two crutches from my feeble hands, R3 2.02. 58
let every feeble rumor shake your hearts! COR 3.03.125
emperor, upon my feeble knee | i beg this boon, TIT 2.03.288
heaven, | and bow this feeble ruin to the earth; 3.01.207
'tis not enough to help the feeble up, | but to TIM 1.01.107
amaze me | a man of such a feeble temper should JC 1.02.129
old feeble carrions, and such suffering souls 2.01.130
vouchsafe good morrow from a feeble tongue. 2.01.313
will crowd a feeble man almost to death. 2.04. 36
not, fool, thou canst not, thou art feeble. TNK 2.02.214
thy mark is feeble age, but thy false dart VEN 941
feeble desire, all recreant, poor, and meek, LUC 710
and leave the falt'ring feeble souls alive? 1768
her feeble force will yield at length, | when PP 18.33
car, | like feeble age he reeleth from the day, SON 7.10
FEEBLED 1 FR 0.0001 REL FR 1 V 0 P
shall that victorious hand be feebled here, JN 5.02.146
FEEBLENESS 1 FR 0.0001 REL FR 1 V 0 P
than his that shakes for age and feebleness. TIT 1.01.188
FEEBLING 1 FR 0.0001 REL FR 1 V 0 P
and feebling such as stand not in their liking COR 1.01.195
FEEBLY 1 FR 0.0001 REL FR 1 V 0 P
of coriolanus | should not be utter'd feebly. COR 2.02. 83
FEE'D 4 FR 0.0004 REL FR 3 V 1 P
fee'd every slight occasion that could but WIV 2.02.197 P
i am no fee'd post, lady; TN 1.05.284
thou wouldst be fee'd, i see, to make me sport: 3H6 1.04. 92
them but in his house | i keep a servant fee'd. MAC 3.04.131
/FEED 1 FR 0.0001 REL FR 1 V 0 P
bait, | the other rotted with delicious /feed. TIT 4.04. 93
FEED 92 FR 0.0104 REL FR 80 V 12 P
all abundance, | to feed my innocent people. TMP 2.01.165
i will stand to, and feed, | although my last, 3.03. 49
to feed on such sweet honey | and kill the bees TGV 1.02.103
though the chameleon love can feed on the air, i 2.01.173 P
hath more mind to feed on your blood than live 2.04. 27 P
is by, | and feed upon the shadow of perfection. 3.01.177
as those that feed grow full, as blossoming time MM 1.04. 41
such meet food to feed it as signior benedick? ADO 1.01.121 P
sheep, sweet lamb, unless we feed on your lips. LLL 2.01.220
feed him with apricocks and dewberries, | with MND 3.01.166
i will feed fat the ancient grudge i bear him. MV 1.03. 47
in hate, to feed upon | the prodigal christian. 2.05. 14
fish withal — if it will feed nothing else, it 3.01. 53 P
will feed nothing else, it will feed my revenge. 3.01. 54 P
my friend to his mere enemy, | to feed my means. 3.02.263
he lets me feed with his hinds, bars me the AYL 1.01. 19 P
he will put on us, as pigeons feed their young. 1.02. 93 P
take that, and he that doth the ravens feed, 2.03. 43
bring us where we may rest ourselves and feed. 2.04. 73
flocks, and bounds of feed | are now on sale, 2.04. 83
there is nothing | that you will feed on; 2.04. 86
sit down and feed, and welcome to our table. 2.07.105
down your venerable burthen, | and let him feed. 2.07.168
we sing, | feed yourselves with questioning; 5.04.138
than feed it with such overroasted flesh. SHR 4.01.175
a dish that i do love to feed upon. 4.03. 24
that makes me see, and cannot feed mine eye? AWW 1.01.221
a worm i' th' bud, | feed on her damask cheek. TN 2.04.112
you beguile the time and feed your knowledge 3.03. 41
brought in matter that should feed this fire; JN 5.02. 85
the pleasure that some fathers feed upon | is my R2 2.01. 79
feed not thy sovereign's foe, my gentle earth, 3.02. 12
than feed on cates and have him talk to me | in 1H4 3.01.161

looks, | and we shall feed like oxen at a stall, 5.02. 14
a stage | to feed contention in a ling'ring act; 2H4 1.01.156
doth the old boar feed in the old frank? 2.02.146 P
then feed and be fat, my fair calipolis. 2.04.179
gold, | nor care i who doth feed upon my cost; H5 4.03. 25
where i was wont to feed you with my blood, 1H6 5.03. 14
if wind and fuel be brought to feed it with. 2H6 3.01.303
now the word "sallet" must serve me to feed on. 4.10. 15 P
leaving thy trunk for crows to feed upon. 4.10. 84
unreasonable creatures feed their young, | and 3H6 2.02. 26
glory, | to feed my humor wish thyself no harm. R3 4.01. 64
my lord, you feed too much on this dislike. TRO 2.03.225
to feed for /aye her lamp and flames of love, 3.02.160
feed arrogance and are the proud man's fees. 3.03. 49
in awe, which else | would feed on one another? COR 1.01.188
and entrails feed the sacrificing fire, | whose TIT 1.01.144
i'll make you feed on berries and on roots, 4.02.177
and feed on curds and whey, and suck the goat, 4.02.178
and feed his humor kindly as we may, | till time 4.03. 29
he doth me wrong to feed me with delays. 4.03. 43
what e'er i forge to feed his brain-sick humors, 5.02. 71
will't please your highness feed? 5.03. 54
and i feed | most hungerly on your sight. TIM 1.01.252
happier is he that has no friend to feed | than 1.02.203
on what i hate i feed not. 4.03.306 P
in a baser temple | than where swine feed! 5.01. 49
know his gross patchery, love him, feed him, 5.01. 96
meat doth this our caesar feed | that JC 1.02.149
to feed were best at home; MAC 3.04. 34
feed, and regard him not. 3.04. 57
but thy good spirits | to feed and clothe thee? HAM 3.02. 59
promise-cramm'd — you cannot feed capons so. 3.02. 94 P
safe | that live and feed upon your majesty. 3.03. 10
could you on this fair mountain leave to feed, 3.04. 66
let it feed | even on the pith of life. 4.01. 22
market of his time | be but to sleep and feed? 4.04. 35
or feed upon such nice and waterish diet, | or OTH 3.03. 15
or feed on nourishing dishes, or keep you warm, 3.03. 78
now i feed myself | with most delicious poison. ANT 1.05. 26
other women cloy | the appetites they feed, but 2.02.236
feed, and sleep. 5.02.187
vomit emptiness, | not so allur'd to feed. CYM 1.06. 46
and it gave me present hunger | to feed again, 2.04.138
should by the minute feed on life, and ling'ring 5.05. 51
yet i feed | on mother's flesh which did me PER 1.01. 64
are, who though they feed | on sweetest flowers, 1.01.132
sight, | and not so much to feed on as delight; 1.04. 29
then men must comfort you, men must feed you, 4.02. 91 P
bring her fruit | fit for the gods to feed on; TNK 2.02.239
thou shalt feed | upon the sweetness of a noble 2.03. 10
ravenous fishes | would feed on /one another. STM II.C 87
the earth's increase why shouldst thou feed, VEN 169
feed where thou wilt, on mountain or in dale; 232
fold in the object that did feed her sight. 822
hasting to feed her fawn hid in some brake. 876
to feed oblivion with decay of things, | to blot LUC 947
my flocks feed not, my ewes breed not, | my rams PP 17. 1
and see the shepherds feed their flocks, | by 19. 6
so shalt thou feed on death, that feeds on men, SON 146.13

/FEEDER 1 FR 0.0001 REL FR 1 V 0 P
/thou, /beastly /feeder, /art /so /full /of /him 2H4 1.03. 95

FEEDER 5 FR 0.0005 REL FR 5 V 0 P
the patch is kind enough, but a huge feeder, MV 2.05. 46
of life, | i will your very faithful feeder be, AYL 2.04. 99
with eager feeding food doth choke the feeder; R2 2.01. 37
wast, | the tutor and the feeder of my riots. 2H4 5.05. 62
being nurse and feeder of the other four! VEN 446

FEEDERS 3 FR 0.0003 REL FR 3 V 0 P
and the feeders | digest/'t with a custom, i WT 4.04. 11
have been oppress'd | with riotous feeders, when TIM 2.02.159
to be abus'd | by one that looks on feeders? ANT 3.13.109

FEEDETH 2 FR 0.0002 REL FR 2 V 0 P
the sight of lovers feedeth those in love. AYL 3.04. 57
she feedeth on the steam as on a prey, | and VEN 63

FEEDING 17 FR 0.0019 REL FR 14 V 3 P
besides that they are fair with their feeding, AYL 1.01. 12 P
and so dies with feeding his own stomach. AWW 1.01.143 P
and boasts himself | to have a worthy feeding; WT 4.04.169
with eager feeding food doth choke the feeder; R2 2.01. 37
grew by our feeding to so great a bulk | that 1H4 5.01. 62
like a horse | full of high feeding, madly hath 2H4 1.01. 10
upon myself, | and so shall starve with feeding. COR 4.02. 51
of our blood | with wine and feeding, we have 5.01. 55
and they have nurs'd this woe, in feeding life; TIT 3.01. 74
gorging and feeding from our soldiers' hands, JC 5.01. 81
that sleep and feeding may prorogue his honor ANT 2.01. 26
in feeding them with those my former fortunes 4.15. 53
i pray you, for it is not worth the feeding. 5.02.270 P
you talk of feeding me to breed me strength; TNK 3.01.119
which but to-day by feeding is allay'd, SON 56. 3
to bitter sauces did i frame my feeding, | and, 118. 6
feeding on that which doth preserve the ill, 147. 3

FEEDS 23 FR 0.0026 REL FR 23 V 0 P
deer, he breaks the pale, | and feeds from home; ERR 2.01.101
they do consume the thing that feeds their fury. SHR 2.01.133
away, | advantage feeds him fat while men delay. 1H4 3.02.180
of such as your oppression feeds upon, 1H6 4.01. 58
feeds in the bosom of such great commanders, 4.03. 48
a hand as fruitful as the land that feeds us; H8 1.03. 56
my love with words and errors still she feeds, TRO 5.03.111
and infinite breast | teems and feeds all; TIM 4.03.179
that feeds and breeds by a composture stol'n 4.03.441
one that feeds | on objects, arts, and JC 4.01. 36
feeds on this wonder, keeps himself in clouds, HAM 4.05. 89
monster which doth mock | the meat it feeds on. OTH 3.03.167
jealious | to say my wife is fair, feeds well, 3.03.184
our dungy earth alike | feeds beast as man; ANT 1.01. 36
who starves the ears she feeds, and makes them PER 5.01.112
fair nymph | that feeds the lake with waters, or TNK 4.01. 87
and glutton-like she feeds, yet never filleth; VEN 548
her sad behavior feeds his vulture folly, | a LUC 556
the orphan pines while the oppressor feeds, 905
as from a mountain spring that feeds a dale, 1077
die, | for sparing justice feeds iniquity. 1687
brow, | feeds on the rarities of nature's truth, SON 60.11
so shalt thou feed on death, that feeds on men, 146.13

FEED'ST 3 FR 0.0003 REL FR 2 V 1 P
that feed'st me with the very name of meat. SHR 4.03. 32
where feed'st thou a' days, apemantus? TIM 4.03.293 P
feed'st thy light's flame with self-substantial SON 1. 6

FEE-FARM 1 FR 0.0001 REL FR 0 V 1 P
a kiss in fee-farm! TRO 3.02. 50 P

FEE-GRIEF 1 FR 0.0001 REL FR 1 V 0 P
or is it a fee-grief | due to some single breast MAC 4.03.196

/FEEL 1 FR 0.0001 REL FR 1 V 0 P
/by /those /that /feel /their /sharpness. LR 5.03. 57

FEEL 114 FR 0.0128 REL FR 96 V 18 P
my father's loss, the weakness which i feel, TMP 1.02.488
but i feel not | this deity in my bosom. 2.01.277
no matter, since i feel | the best is past. 3.03. 50
i pray thee let me feel thy cloak upon me. TGV 3.01.136
he can command, lets it straight feel the spur; MM 1.02.162
doubtfully, thou couldst not feel his meaning? ERR 2.01. 51 P
so plainly, i could too well feel his blows; 2.01. 53 P
sir, that i might not feel your blows. 4.04. 26 P
give me your hand, and let me feel your pulse. 4.04. 52
there is my hand, and let it feel your ear. 4.04. 53
that i love her, i feel. ADO 1.01.228 P
that i neither feel how she should be lov'd nor 1.01.230 P
to that grief | which they themselves not feel, 5.01. 22
to feel only looking on fairest of fair: LLL 2.01.241
you for it, | though i alone do feel the injury. MND 3.02.219
i feel too much thy blessing; MV 3.02.113
here feel we not the penalty of adam, | the AYL 2.01. 5
your lips will feel them the sooner. 3.02. 60 P
i smell sweet savors, and i feel soft things. SHR in.2. 71
(she being now at hand) thou shalt soon feel, to 4.01. 31 P
this 'tis to feel a tale, not to hear a tale. 4.01. 63 P
though little he do feel it, set down sharply. AWW 3.04. 33
methinks i feel this youth's perfections | with TN 1.05.296
than when i feel and see her no farther trust WT 2.01.136
as you feel doing thus — and see withal | the 2.01.153
and see withal | the instruments that feel. 2.01.154
thee than it), so thou | shalt feel our justice; 3.02. 90
favor, | i do give lost, for i do feel it gone, 3.02. 95
the tortures he shall feel, will break the back 4.04.769 P
too well i feel | the different plague of each JN 3.04. 59
in their continuance will not feel themselves. 5.07. 14
i live with bread like you, feel want, | taste R2 3.02.175
me rather had my heart might feel your love 3.03.192
shall feel this day as sharp to them as thorn. 4.01.323
doth he feel it? 1H4 5.01.137 P
feel, masters, how i shake, look you, i warrant 2H4 2.04.105 P
i feel me much to blame | so idly to profane the 2.04.361
all | that feel the bruises of the days before, 4.01. 98
you speak this to feel other men's minds. H5 4.01.126 P
of every fool whose sense no more can feel | but 4.01.235
i feel such sharp dissension in my breast, 1H6 5.05. 84
and with my fingers feel his hand unfeeling. 2H6 3.02.145
so thou wilt let me live, and feel no pain. 3.03. 4
i feel remorse in myself with his words; 4.07.105 P
and they shall feel the vengeance of my wrath. 3H6 4.01. 82
they often feel a world of restless cares; R3 1.04. 81
how dost thou feel thyself now? 1.04.120 P
whereof | we cannot feel too little, hear too H8 1.02.128
cruel | that she should feel the smart of this? 2.01.166
which | i then did feel full sick, and yet not 2.04.205
for i feel | the last fit of my greatness — 3.01. 77
our ends are honest, | you'ld feel more comfort. 3.01.155
now i feel | of what coarse metal ye are moulded 3.02.238
thou shouldst feel | my sword i' th' life-blood 3.02.276
i feel my heart new open'd. 3.02.366
and i feel within me | a peace above all earthly 3.02.378
methinks | (out of a fortitude of soul i feel), 3.02.388
now, methinks, i feel a little ease. 4.02. 4
which i feel | i am not worthy yet to wear. 4.02. 91
feel then. TRO 2.01. 11 P
in the eyes of others | as feel in his own fall; 3.03. 78
be myself, nor have cognition | of what i feel; 5.02. 64
did see and hear, devise, instruct, walk, feel, COR 1.01.102
him for a volsce, | and he shall feel mine edge. 1.04. 29
let | thy mother rather feel thy pride than fear 3.02.126
with what he would say, let him feel your sword, 5.06. 55
they must take it /in sense that feel it. ROM 1.01. 27 P
me they shall feel while i am able to stand, and 1.01. 28 P
this love feel i, that feel no love in this. 1.01.182
this love feel i, that feel no love in this. 1.01.182
such comfort as do lusty young men feel | when 1.02. 26
thou canst not speak of that thou dost not feel. 3.03. 64
so shall you feel the loss, but not the friend 3.05. 75
what shall be done, he will not hear, till feel. TIM 2.02. 7
i feel my master's passion. 3.01. 56
and i perceive you feel | the dint of pity. JC 3.02.193
and i feel now | the future in the instant. MAC 1.05. 57
but i must also feel it as a man: 4.03.221
now does he feel | his secret murthers sticking 5.02. 16
now does he feel his title | hang loose about 5.02. 20
seeming to feel this blow, with flaming top HAM 2.02.475
he hath writ this to feel my affection to your LR 1.02. 86 P
that she may feel | how sharper than a serpent's 1.04.287
expose thyself to feel what wretches feel, 3.04. 34
expose thyself to feel what wretches feel, 3.04. 34
that will not see | because he does not feel, 4.01. 69
he does not feel, feel your pow'r quickly; 4.01. 69
he'll not feel wrongs | which tie him to an 4.02. 13
feel you your legs? 4.06. 65
let's see, | i feel this pin prick. 4.07. 55
speak what we feel, not what we ought to say: 5.03.325
cannot but feel this wrong as 'twere their own; OTH 1.02. 97
to the felt absence now i feel a cause. 3.04.182
but yet i feel i fear. 5.02. 39
villain of the earth, | and feel i am so most. ANT 4.06. 30
thought, but thought will do't, i feel. 4.06. 35
never | o'ertake pursu'd success, but i do feel, 5.02.103
i partly feel thee. 5.02.322
that are betray'd | do feel the treason sharply, CYM 3.04. 86
hear him groan, | nor feel him where he strook. 5.03. 70
must feel war's blow, who spares not innocence: PER 1.02. 93
who cannot feel nor see the rain, being in't, TNK 1.01.120
and feel our fiery horses | like proud seas 2.02. 19
now i feel my shackles. 2.02.157
do not you feel it thaw you? 3.03. 18
and i feel myself, | with this refreshing, able 3.06. 8
or, if you feel yourself not fitting yet | and 3.06. 36
what may be done? for now i feel compassion. 3.06.271
art thou a woman's son and canst not feel | what VEN 201
me my hand," saith he, "why dost thou feel it?" 373
may feel her heart (poor citizen!) LUC 465
upon my cheeks what helpless shame i feel." 756
save where thou art not, though i feel thou art, SON 48.10
now, | and for that sorrow which i then did feel 120. 2

FEELER'S 1 FR 0.0001 REL FR 1 V 0 P
would force the feeler's soul | to th' oath of CYM 1.06.101

FEELING 37 FR 0.0041 REL FR 31 V 6 P
a touch, a feeling | of their afflictions, and TMP 5.01. 21
and frame some feeling line | that may discover TGV 3.02. 75
indeed with most painful feeling of thy speech. MM 1.02. 37 P
he had some feeling of the sport; 3.02.119 P
and, gazing in mine eyes, feeling my pulse, ERR 5.01.244
thou hast no feeling of it, moth. LLL 3.01.114 P
which we /of taste and feeling are — for those 4.02. 29
love's feeling is more soft and sensible | than 4.03.334
to whose feeling sorrows i might be some allay WT 4.02. 7 P
no hearing, no feeling, but my sir's song, and 4.04.612 P
then feeling what small things are boisterous JN 4.01. 94
gives but the greater feeling to the worse. R2 1.03.301
i have had feeling of my cousin's wrongs, | and 2.03.141
this earth shall have a feeling, and these 3.02. 24
thou mine, | and that's a feeling disputation, 1H4 3.01.203
have you that holy feeling in your souls | to R3 1.04.250
that wound beyond their feeling to the quick. TIT 4.02. 28
yet let me weep for such a feeling loss. ROM 3.05. 74
feeling so the loss, | i cannot choose but ever 3.05. 76
feeling in itself | a lack of timon's aid, hath TIM 5.01.146
fatal vision, sensible | to feeling as to sight? MAC 2.01. 37
eyes without feeling, feeling without sight, HAM 3.04. 78
eyes without feeling, feeling without sight, 3.04. 78
has this fellow no feeling of his business? 5.01. 65 P
doth from my senses take all feeling else, LR 3.04. 13
who, by the art of known and feeling sorrows, 4.06.222
and have ingenious feeling | of my huge sorrows! 4.06.280
thou mayst say, | and prove it in thy feeling. CYM 5.05. 68
know the world, see heaven, but, feeling woe, PER 1.01. 48
"say that the sense of feeling were bereft me, VEN 439
with cold-pale weakness numbs each feeling part: 892
the life and feeling of her passion | she hoards LUC 1317
being from the feeling of her own grief brought 1578
which is so deemed | not by our feeling, but by SON 121. 4
nor tender feeling to base touches prone, | nor 141. 6
have of my suffering youth some feeling pity LC 178
feeling it break, with bleeding groans they pine 275

FEELINGLY 6 FR 0.0006 REL FR 4 V 2 P
do i speak feelingly now? MM 1.02. 34 P
that feelingly persuade me what i am." AYL 2.01. 11
he shall find himself most feelingly personated. TN 2.03.159 P
i see it feelingly. LR 4.06.149
true sorrow then is feelingly suffic'd | when LUC 1112
here feelingly she weeps troy's painted woes, 1492

FEELING-PAINFUL 1 FR 0.0001 REL FR 1 V 0 P
thy passion maketh | more feeling-painful: LUC 1679

/FEELS 1 FR 0.0001 REL FR 1 V 0 P
compulsive course | nev'r /feels retiring ebb, OTH 3.03.455

FEELS 9 FR 0.0010 REL FR 7 V 2 P
one who never feels | the wanton stings and MM 1.04. 58
other lives merrily because he feels no pain; AYL 3.02.322 P
though she be, she feels her young one kick. AWW 5.03.302
nor feals not what he owes, but by reflection; TRO 3.03. 99
your ignorance (which finds not till it feels, COR 3.03.129
he does confess he feels himself distracted, HAM 3.01. 5
sir, he that sleeps feels not the toothache; CYM 5.04.172 P
at his love, and scorns the heat he feels, VEN 311
her other tender hand his fair cheek feels: 352

FEEL'ST 3 FR 0.0003 REL FR 3 V 0 P
what care | for what thou feel'st not? TNK 1.01.181
what thou feel'st being able | to make mars 1.01.181
see thy blood warm when thou feel'st it cold. SON 2.14

FEEL'T 4 FR 0.0004 REL FR 4 V 0 P
this pearl she gave me, i do feel't and see't, TN 4.03. 2
on 's | have the disease, and feel't not. WT 1.02.207
but i do see't, and feel't, | as you feel doing 2.01.152
i feel't upon my bones. TIM 3.06.119

FEES 5 FR 0.0005 REL FR 4 V 1 P
so you shall pay your fees | when you depart, WT 1.02. 53
at our enlargement what are thy due fees? 3H6 4.06. 5
feed arrogance and are the proud man's fees. TRO 3.03. 49
lawyers' fingers, who straight dream on fees; ROM 1.04. 73
the rest of your fees, o gods — the senators of TIM 3.06. 79 P

FEE-SIMPLE 7 FR 0.0008 REL FR 1 V 6 P
if the devil have him not in fee-simple, with WIV 4.02.210 P
he will sell the fee-simple of his salvation, AWW 4.03.278 P
for entering his fee-simple without leave. 2H6 4.10. 25 P
and the rivell'd fee-simple of the tetter, take TRO 5.01. 22 P
man should buy the fee-simple of my life for an ROM 3.01. 32 P
the fee-simple! o simple! 3.01. 34 P
did in freedom stand | and was my own fee-simple LC 144

/FEET 1 FR 0.0001 REL FR 1 V 0 P
/have /secret /feet | /in /some /of /our /best LR 3.01. 32

FEET 57 FR 0.0064 REL FR 48 V 9 P
come, | i'll manacle thy neck and feet together. TMP 1.02.462
beat the ground | for kissing of their feet; 4.01.174
that the foul lake | o'erstunk their feet. 4.01.184
at her father's churlish feet she tender'd, TGV 3.01.227
whence he came, lest he catch cold on 's feet. ERR 3.01. 37
i will fall prostrate at his feet, | and never 5.01.114
end, canary to it with your feet, humor it with LLL 3.01. 13 P
submissive fall his princely feet before, | and 4.01. 90
her feet were much too dainty for such tread! 4.03.275
the stairs, as he treads on them, kiss his feet. 5.02.330
them had in them more feet than the verses would AYL 3.02.165 P
the feet might bear the verses. 3.02.167 P
ay, but the feet were lame and could not bear 3.02.169 P
than legs, nor no more shoes than feet — nay, SHR in.2. 10 P
nay, sometime more feet than shoes, or such in.2. 11 P
you as surely as your feet hits the ground they TN 3.04.277 P
her, but direct thy feet | where thou and i, 5.01.168
haste | had falsely thrust upon contrary feet, JN 4.02.198
seek out king john and fall before his feet; 5.04. 13
way, | doing annoyance to the treacherous feet, R2 3.02. 16
even at his feet to lay my arms and power, 3.03. 39
where subjects' feet | may hourly trample on 3.03.156
over whose acres walk'd those blessed feet 1H4 1.01. 25
so 'a bade me lay more clothes on his feet. H5 2.03. 23 P

kneeling at our feet but a weak and worthless 3.06.132 P
under my feet i stamp thy cardinal's hat; 1H6 1.03. 49
yet are these feet, whose strengthless stay is 2.05. 13
lets fall his sword before your highness' feet, 3.04. 9
stinking and fly–blown lies here at our feet. 4.07. 76
that, when thou com'st to kneel at henry's feet, 5.03.194
thyself | from top of honor to disgrace's feet? 2H6 1.02. 49
my stay, my guide, and lanthorn to my feet; 2.03. 25
and even as willingly at thy feet i leave it 2.03. 35
to tread them with her tender–feeling feet. 2.04. 9
the ruthless flint doth cut my tender feet, 2.04. 34
and kneel for grace and mercy at my feet: 3H6 1.01. 75
kneel'd /at my feet and bid me be advis'd? R3 2.01.108
do buss the clouds, | must kiss their own feet. TRO 4.05.221
and at thy feet i kneel, with tears of joy TIT 1.01.161
owe, | mine honor's ensigns humbled at thy feet. 1.01.252
as cerberus at the thracian poet's feet, 2.04. 51
weep, they humbly at my feet | receive my tears, 3.01. 41
to–night | have my old feet stumbled at graves! ROM 5.03.122
and bow'd like bondmen, kissing caesar's feet; JC 5.01. 42
thee, | oft'ner upon her knees than on her feet, MAC 4.03.110
to kiss the ground before young malcolm's feet, 5.08. 28
bent, | to lay our service freely at your feet, HAM 2.02. 31
to see't, | that going shall be us'd with feet. LR 3.02. 94
i look down towards his feet; OTH 5.02.286
smooth success | be strew'd before your feet! ANT 1.03.101
at the feet sat | caesarion, whom they call my 3.06. 5
i am prompt | to lay my crown at 's feet, and 3.13. 76
and put | my clouted brogues from off my feet, CYM 4.02.214
time | post /on the lame feet of my rhyme, PER 4.ch. 48
sweet, | lie 'fore bride and bridegroom's feet, TNK 1.01. 14
at whose great feet i offer up my penner. 3.05.124
your unreverent knees, | make them your feet: STM II.C 111

FEEZE *(see feaz'd, pheese, pheeze)*

FEHEMENTLY 1 FR 0.0001 REL FR 0 V 1 P
i most fehemently desire you you will also look WIV 3.01. 8 P

FEIGN 10 FR 0.0011 REL FR 8 V 2 P
the poet | did feign that orpheus drew trees, MV 5.01. 80
in poetry may be said as lovers they do feign. AYL 3.03. 22 P
a poet, i might have some hope thou didst feign. 3.03. 27 P
if i do feign, you witnesses above | punish my TN 5.01.137
if i do feign, | o, let me in my present 2H4 4.05.151
that suffolk doth not flatter, face, or feign. 1H6 5.03.142
and all that poets feign of bliss and joy. 3H6 1.02. 31
but old folks — many feign as they were dead, ROM 2.05. 16
go, bid my woman feign a sickness, say | she'll CYM 3.02. 74
one god is god of both (as poets feign), | one PP 8.13

FEIGN'D 4 FR 0.0004 REL FR 1 V 3 P
it is the more like to be feign'd. TN 1.05.196 P
pleasant hill | feign'd fortune to be thron'd. TIM 1.01. 64
where thou hast feign'd him a worthy fellow. 1.01.223 P
that's not feign'd, he is so. 1.01.224 P

FEIGNED 6 FR 0.0006 REL FR 6 V 0 P
burns under feigned ashes of forg'd love, | and 1H6 3.01.189
were but a feigned friend to our proceedings. 3H6 4.02. 11
hath turn'd my feigned prayer on my head, | and R3 5.01. 21
his feigned ecstasies | shall be no shelter to TIT 4.04. 21
accident | i had a feigned letter of my master's CYM 5.05.279
dismiss your vows, your feigned tears, your VEN 425

FEIGNING 3 FR 0.0003 REL FR 2 V 1 P
most friendship is feigning, most loving mere AYL 2.07.181
for the truest poetry is the most feigning, and 3.03. 20 P
since lowly feigning was call'd compliment. TN 3.01. 99

FEITH *(also faith, fay)*

FEITH 1 FR 0.0001 REL FR 0 V 1 P
it sall be vary gud, gud feith, gud captens bath H5 3.02.102 P

FELICITATE 1 FR 0.0001 REL FR 1 V 0 P
and find i am alone felicitate | in your dear LR 1.01. 75

FELICITY 2 FR 0.0002 REL FR 2 V 0 P
a wife of such wood were felicity. LLL 4.03.245
thy heart, | absent thee from felicity a while, HAM 5.02.347

FELL* 148 FR 0.0167 REL FR 126 V 22 P
they fell together all, as by consent; TMP 2.01.203
then all together | they fell upon me, bound me, ERR 5.01.247
fell over the threshold, and broke my shin. LLL 3.01.117
the fourth turn'd on the toe, and down he fell. 5.02.114
for oberon is passing fell and wrath, | because MND 2.01. 20
yet mark'd i where the bolt of cupid fell. 2.01.165
it fell upon a little western flower, | before 2.01.166
will tell you every thing, right as it fell out. 4.02. 32 P
know that i as snug the joiner am | a lion fell, 5.01.224
approach, ye furies fell! 5.01.284
and the worst fall that ever fell, i hope i MV 1.02. 90 P
nothing that my nose fell a–bleeding on black 2.05. 24 P
the curse never fell upon our nation till now, i 3.01. 85 P
which i denying, they fell sick and died. 3.04. 71
even from the gallows did his fell soul fleet, 4.01.135
my pride fell with my fortunes, | i'll ask him AYL 1.02.252
courtship too well, for there he fell in love. 3.02.346 P
who quickly fell before him, in which hurtling 4.03.131
such a cuff | that down fell priest and book, SHR 3.02.164
heard how her horse fell and she under her horse 4.01. 74 P
when better fall, for your avails they fell. AWW 3.01. 22
and my desires, like fell and cruel hounds, TN 1.01. 21
alas, sir, how fell you besides your five wits? 4.02. 86 P
and rouse from sleep that fell anatomy | which JN 3.04. 40
of that fell poison which assaileth him. 5.07. 9
our cousin herford and fell mowbray fight. R2 1.02. 46
fell sorrow's tooth doth never rankle more 1.03.302
prove | that ever fell upon this cursed earth. 4.01.147
down fell their hose. 1H4 2.04.215 P
the other night i fell asleep here behind the 3.03. 97 P
knowest in the state of innocency adam fell, and 3.03.165 P
and such a flood of greatness fell on you, 5.01. 48
to noise abroad that harry monmouth fell | under 2H4 in 29
by whose fell working i was first advanc'd, 4.05.206
revenge from ebon den with fell alecto's snake, 5.05. 37
do with his smirch'd complexion all fell feats H5 3.03. 17
that never may ill office, or fell jealousy, 5.02.363
so fell that noble earl | and was beheaded. 1H6 2.05. 90
fell banning hag, enchantress, hold thy tongue! 5.03. 42
and this fell tempest shall not cease to rage 2H6 3.01.351
from such fell serpents as false suffolk is; 3.02.266
stand, villain, stand, or i'll fell thee down. 4.02.115 P
they fell before thee like sheep and oxen, and 4.03. 3 P
with the bear's fell paw | hath clapp'd his tail 5.01.153
for his death | 'gainst thee, fell clifford, and 3H6 1.04.149
fell gently down, as if they struck their 2.01.132
so is the equal poise of this fell war. 2.05. 13
how fell? 2.05. 89
while we devise fell tortures for thy faults. 2.06. 72
fell warwick's brother, and by that our foe. 4.04. 12
after he once fell in with mistress shore. R3 3.05. 51
but he fell to himself again, and sweetly | in H8 2.01. 35
that wretch betray'd, | and without trial fell; 2.01.111
both | fell by our servants, by those men we 2.01.122
say something that is sad, | speak how i fell. 2.01.136
by that sin fell the angels; 3.02.441
in the choir, fell off | a distance from her; 4.01. 64
for since the cardinal fell that title's lost. 4.01. 96
he fell sick suddenly and grew so ill | he could 4.02. 15
one of which fell with him, | unwilling to 4.02. 59
princely care foreseeing those fell mischiefs 5.01. 49
me till her pink'd porringer fell off her head, 5.03. 48 P
they fell on, i made good my place; 5.03. 53 P
and fell so roundly to a large confession, | to TRO 3.02.154
to–morrow do i meet thee, fell as death; 4.05.269
heavens bless my lord from fell aufidius! COR 1.03. 45
sail, so men obey'd | and fell below his stem. 2.02.107
hath — | out of this fell devouring receptacle, TIT 2.03.235
two of thy whelps, fell curs of bloody kind, 2.03.281
that this fell fault of my accursed sons — 2.03.290
would have dropp'd his knife, and fell asleep, 2.04. 50
that down fell both the ram's horns in the court 4.03. 73
for their fell faults our brothers were beheaded 5.03.100
and, as he fell, did romeo turn and fly. ROM 3.01.174
this fell whore of thine | hath in her more TIM 4.03. 62
one winter's brush | fell from their boughs, and 4.03.265
but all, save thee, | i fell with curses. 4.03.501
me to cut down, | and shortly must i fell it. 5.01.207
hand thus, and then the people fell a–shouting. JC 1.02.223 P
caesar, for he swounded, and fell down at it; 1.02.248 P
he fell down in the market–place, and foam'd at 1.02.252 P
mean by that, but i am sure caesar fell down. 1.02.258 P
marry, before he fell down, when he perceiv'd 1.02.263 P
and so he fell. 1.02.268 P
all pity chok'd with custom of fell deeds; 3.01.269
all the while ran blood) great caesar fell. 3.02.189
then i, and you, and all of us fell down, 3.02.191
with this she fell distract, | and, her 4.03.155
on our former ensign | two mighty eagles fell, 5.01. 80
his soldiers fell to spoil, | whilst we by 5.03. 7
and, to conclude, | the victory fell on us. MAC 1.02. 58
visitings of nature | shake my fell purpose, nor 1.05. 46
in a woman's ear | would murther as it fell. 2.03. 86
to do worse to you were fell cruelty, | which is 4.02. 71
are bright still, though the brightest fell. 4.03. 22
chickens, and their dam, | at one fell swoop? 4.03.219
but for mine, | fell slaughter on their souls. 4.03.227
and my fell of hair | would at a dismal treatise 5.05. 11
of the article /design'd, | his fell to hamlet. HAM 1.01. 95
rome, | a little ere the mightiest julius fell, 1.01.114
as they fell out by time, by means, and place, 2.02.127
fell into a sadness, then into a fast, | thence 2.02.147
but with the whiff and wind of his fell sword 2.02.473
madam, it so fell out that certain players | we 3.01. 16
and herself | fell in the weeping brook. 4.07.175
between the pass and fell incensed points | of 5.02. 61
had i but time — as this fell sergeant, death, 5.02.336
to his unnatural purpose, in fell motion, | with LR 2.01. 50
how fell you out? say that. 2.02. 86
altitude | which thou hast perpendicularly fell. 4.06. 54
good–years shall devour them, flesh and fell, 5.03. 24
pursue, | lest by his clamor (as it so fell out) OTH 2.03.231
her salt tears fell from her, and soft'ned the 4.03. 46
more fell than anguish, hunger, or the sea! 5.02.362
sir, | he fell upon me, ere admitted, then; ANT 2.02. 75
the rest | that fell away have entertainment, 4.06. 16
much like an argument that fell out last night, CYM 1.04. 56 P
where each of us fell in praise of our country 1.04. 57 P
say, "thus mine enemy fell, | and thus i set my 3.03. 91
good time with him, | you say he is so fell. 4.02.109
country's cause | fell bravely and were slain, 5.04. 72
and what ensues in this fell storm | shall for PER 3.ch. 53
virtue /preserv'd from fell destruction's blast, 5.03. 89
whose sovereigns fell before | the wrath of TNK 1.01. 39
of his gyves | might call fell things to listen, 3.02. 15
"there was three fools fell out about an howlet: 3.05. 67
thou wor'st that day the three kings fell, but 3.06. 71
she stay'd, | and fell, scarce to be got away. 4.01.102
and fell to what disorder | his power could give 5.04. 66
victor's wreath | even then fell off his head; 5.04. 80
and fell i not downright? VEN 645
as life for honor in fell battle's rage, | honor LUC 145
obdurate vassals fell exploits effecting, | in 429
black stage for tragedies and murthers fell! 766
when their glass fell wherein they view'd their 1526
then fell she on her back, fair queen, and PP 4.13
she bade love last, and yet she fell a–turning. 7.16
her, | and as he fell to her, she fell to him. 11. 4
her, | and as he fell to her, she fell to him. 11. 4
that eye could see, | her fancy fell a–turning. 15. 4
as it fell upon a day, | in the merry month of 20. 1
till nature, as she wrought thee, fell a–doting, SON 20.10
when i have seen by time's fell hand defaced 64. 1
when that fell arrest | without all bail shall 74. 1
drugs poison him that so fell sick of you. 118.14
cupid laid by his brand and fell asleep: 153. 1
all quit, but, spite of heaven's fell rage, LC 13
ay me, i fell, and yet do question make | what i 321

FELL'D 2 FR 0.0002 REL FR 2 V 0 P
dispark'd my parks and fell'd my forest woods, R2 3.01. 23
flew on him, and amongst them fell'd him dead, LR 4.02. 76

FELLEST 2 FR 0.0002 REL FR 2 V 0 P
about, | in fellest manner execute your arms. TRO 5.07. 6
so, fellest foes, | whose passions and whose COR 4.04. 18

/FELLIES 1 FR 0.0001 REL FR 1 V 0 P
all the spokes and /fellies from her wheel, HAM 2.02.495

FELL–LURKING 1 FR 0.0001 REL FR 1 V 0 P
they may astonish these fell–lurking curs. 2H6 5.01.146

FELLOW 317 FR 0.0358 REL FR 163 V 154 P
i have great comfort from this fellow. TMP 1.01. 28 P
fellow trinculo, we'll fill him by and by again. 2.02.176 P
to be your fellow | you may deny me, but i'll be 3.01. 84
my fellow ministers | are like invulnerable. 3.03. 65
were on land, | this fellow could not drown. 5.01.218
this fellow were a king for our wild faction! TGV 4.01. 37
and goes me to the fellow that whips the dogs: 4.04. 24 P
kind fellow as ever servant shall come in house WIV 1.04. 10 P
here's a fellow frights english out of his wits. 2.01.139 P
'twas a good sensible fellow — well. 2.01.147 P
appoint a meeting with this old fat fellow, 4.04. 14
my shoulders for the fellow of this walk — and 5.05. 26 P
fellow, why dost thou show me thus to th' world? MM 1.02.116
next, this is a respected fellow; 2.01.163 P
truly, sir, i am a poor fellow that would live. 2.01.223 P
a shy fellow was the duke, and i believe i know 3.02.130 P
a very superficial, ignorant, unweighing fellow. 3.02.140 P
that fellow is a fellow of much license; 3.02.204 P
that fellow is a fellow of much license; 3.02.204 P
receive some instruction from my fellow partner. 4.02. 18 P
here's a fellow will help you to–morrow in your 4.02. 22 P
a saucy friar, | a very scurvy fellow. 5.01.136
silence that fellow. 5.01.181
we shall find this friar a notable fellow. 5.01.267 P
o thou damnable fellow! 5.01.339 P
such a fellow is not to be talk'd withal. 5.01.344 P
if any woman wrong'd by this lewd fellow | (as i 5.01.509
who, falling there to find his fellow forth ERR 1.02. 37
arrest me, foolish fellow, if thou dar'st. 4.01. 75
a wolf, nay worse, a fellow all in buff; 4.02. 36
the fellow is distract, and so am i, | and here 4.03. 42
the fellow finds his vein, | and, yielding to 4.04. 80
hath the fellow any wit that told you this? ADO 1.02. 17 P
a good sharp fellow. 1.02. 18 P
let him be a handsome fellow, or else make 2.01. 54 P
but that the white–bearded fellow speaks it. 2.03.119 P
a marvellous witty fellow, i assure you, but i 4.02. 25 P
pray thee, fellow, peace. 4.02. 44 P
what else, fellow? 4.02. 52 P
i am a wise fellow, and, which is more, an 4.02. 80 P
the law, go to, and a rich fellow enough, go to, 4.02. 83 P
go to, and a fellow that hath had losses, and 4.02. 84 P
how her acquaintance grew with this lewd fellow. 5.01.332
my fellow scholars, and to keep those statutes LLL 1.01. 17
this, fellow. what wouldst? 1.01.182 P
thou shalt know her, fellow, by the rest that 4.01. 44 P
thou fellow, a word. 4.01.100
this fellow pecks up wit as pigeons pease, | and 5.02.315
fellow hector, she is gone; 5.02.672 P
good hay, sweet hay, hath no fellow. MND 4.01. 34 P
this fellow doth not stand upon points. 5.01.118 P
i shot his fellow of the self–same flight | the MV 1.01.141
i'll prove the prettier fellow of the two, | and 3.04. 64
for the poor rude world | hath not her fellow. 3.05. 83
it is the stubbornest young fellow of france, AYL 1.01.142 P
to catch the strong fellow by the leg. 1.02.212 P
this fellow will but join you together as they 3.03. 86 P
they say you are a melancholy fellow. 4.01. 3 P
good my lord, like this fellow. 5.04. 52 P
is not this a rare fellow, my lord? 5.04.104 P
this fellow i remember | since once he play'd a SHR in.1. 83
has my fellow tranio stol'n your clothes? 1.01.223 P
your fellow tranio here, to save my life, | puts 1.01.228
were it not that my fellow schoolmaster | doth 3.02.138
and my new mistress and myself, fellow curtis. 4.01. 25 P
fellow grumio! 4.01.109 P
fellow, you — and thus much for greeting. 4.01.112 P
th' art a tall fellow; 4.04. 17
not unknown to you, madam, i am a poor fellow. AWW 1.03. 14 P
and indeed such a fellow, to say precisely, were 2.02. 12 P
for two ordinaries, to be a pretty wise fellow. 2.03.202 P
a very tainted fellow, and full of wickedness. 3.02. 87
lady, | the fellow has a deal of that too much, 3.02. 90
'tis a most gallant fellow. 3.05. 78
is not this a strange fellow, my lord, that so 3.06. 86 P
was misled with a snipt–taffata fellow there, 4.05. 2 P
i am a woodland fellow, sir, that always lov'd a 4.05. 47 P
i am a fellow o' th' strangest mind i' th' world TN 1.03.112 P
yond young fellow swears he will speak with you. 1.05.139 P
o fellow, come, the song we had last night. 2.04. 42
shall this fellow live? 2.05. 62 P
thee a steward still, the fellow of servants, 2.05.156 P
thou art a merry fellow and car'st for nothing. 3.01. 26 P
this fellow is wise enough to play the fool, 3.01. 60
good maria, let this fellow be look'd to. 3.04. 61 P
went away now, "let this fellow be look'd to"; 3.04. 76 P
"fellow"! 3.04. 77 P
"malvolio," nor after my degree, but "fellow." 3.04. 78 P
thou art, thou art but a scurvy fellow." 3.04.148 P
go to, go to, thou art a foolish fellow, | let 4.01. 3
maintain no words with him, good fellow. 4.02. 99 P
i know thee well; how dost thou, my good fellow? 5.01. 11 P
but for thee, fellow — fellow, thy words are 5.01. 98
thee, fellow — fellow, thy words are madness. 5.01. 98
a fellow of the royal bed, which owe | a moi'ty WT 3.02. 38
what manner of fellow was he that robb'd you? 4.03. 84 P
a fellow, sir, that i have known to go about 4.03. 86 P
this is a brave fellow. 4.04.201 P
thou talkest of an admirable conceited fellow. 4.04.203 P
how now, good fellow? 4.04.628 P
i am a poor fellow, sir. 4.04.630 P
i am a poor fellow, sir. i know ye well enough. 4.04.638 P
bed of majesty again | with a sweet fellow to't? 5.01. 34
art as honest a true fellow as any is in bohemia 5.02.157 P
thou art a tall fellow of thy hands and that 5.02.164 P
thou art no tall fellow of thy hands and that 5.02.166 P
thou wouldst be a tall fellow of thy hands. 5.02.167 P
ay, by any means prove a tall fellow. 5.02.170 P
venture to be drunk, not being a tall fellow, 5.02.172 P
a good blunt fellow. JN 1.01. 71
"god–a–mercy, fellow!" 1.01.185
fellow, be gone! 3.01. 36
tell me, thou fellow, is not france forsworn? 3.01. 62
by, | a fellow by the hand of nature mark'd, 4.02.221
go, fellow, get thee home, provide some carts, R2 2.02.106
we'll serve him too, and be his fellow so. 3.02. 99
fellow, give place, here is no longer stay. 5.05. 95
which many a good tall fellow had destroyed | so 1H4 1.03. 62
poor fellow never joy'd since the price of oats 2.01. 12 P
each takes his fellow for an officer. 2.02.107
that ever this fellow should have fewer words 2.04. 98 P
that same mad fellow of the north, percy, and he 2.04.335 P
a fellow of no mark nor likelihood. 3.02. 45

a mad fellow met me on the way and told me i had 4.02. 36 P
this is the strangest fellow, brother john. 5.04.155
he was some hilding fellow that had stol'n | the 2H4 1.01. 57
i am the fellow with the great belly, and he my 1.02.146 P
stand from him, fellow, wherefore hang'st thou 2.01. 68
thou art a blessed fellow to think as every man 2.02. 57 P
and that i am a proper fellow of my hands, and 2.02. 68 P
a good shallow young fellow. 2.04.237 P
a good–limb'd fellow, young, strong, and of good 3.02.103 P
peace, fellow, peace, stand aside, know you 3.02.119 P
'fore god, a likely fellow! 3.02.175 P
well said, th' art a good fellow. 3.02.239 P
and this same half–fac'd fellow, shadow, give me 3.02.265 P
there was a little quiver fellow, and 'a would 3.02.281 P
i shall ne'er see such a fellow. 3.02.286 P
i were simply the most active fellow in europe. 4.03. 21 P
say, with the hook–nos'd fellow of rome, "there, 4.03. 41 P
but thou, like a kind fellow, gavest thyself 4.03. 69 P
master bardolph, and welcome, my tall fellow. 5.01. 58 P
brow will do with a fellow that never had the 5.01. 83 P
a wretched and peevish fellow is this king of H5 3.07.132 P
call yonder fellow hither. 4.07.118
thy vow, sirrah, when thou meet'st the fellow. 4.07.145 P
this was my glove, here is the fellow of it; 4.08. 29 P
look, here is the fellow of it. 4.08. 40 P
glove with crowns, | and give it to this fellow. 4.08. 58
keep it, fellow, | and wear it for an honor in 4.08. 58
the fellow has mettle enough in his belly. 4.08. 62 P
know to be no petter than a fellow, look you now 5.01. 7 P
if thou canst love a fellow of this temper, kate 5.02.146 P
take a fellow of plain and uncoin'd constancy, 5.02.153 P
face, if he be not fellow with the best king, 5.02.242 P
this fellow here, with envious carping tongue, 1H6 4.01. 90
how now, fellow? wouldst any thing with me? 2H6 1.03. 10 P
take this fellow in, and send for his master 1.03. 33 P
fellow, what miracle dost thou proclaim? 2.01. 58
good fellow, tell us here the circumstance, 2.01. 72
tell me, good fellow, cam'st thou here by chance 2.01. 85
i never saw a fellow worse bestead, | or more 2.03. 56
fellow, thank god, and the good wine in thy 2.03. 95 P
the truth and innocence of this poor fellow, 2.03.103
come, fellow, follow us for thy reward. 2.03.105
here i am, thou particular fellow. 4.02.112 P
fellow kings, i tell you that that lord say hath 4.02.164 P
if this fellow be wise, he'll never call ye jack 4.06. 9 P
come, fellow soldier, make thou proclamation. 3H6 4.07. 70
how far hence is thy lord, mine honest fellow? 5.01. 2
i tell thee, fellow, | he that doth naught with R3 1.01. 98
but first i'll turn yon fellow in his grave, 1.02.260
what wouldst thou, fellow? 1.04. 85
go, fellow, go, return unto thy lord, | bid him 3.02. 19
go on before, i'll talk with this good fellow. 3.02. 95
gramercy, fellow. there, drink that for me. 3.02.106
this is all–souls' day, fellow, is it not? 5.01. 10
and who doth lead them but a paltry fellow, 5.03.323
or to see a fellow | in a long motley coat H8 pr 15
but this top–proud fellow, | whom from the flow 1.01.151
a french song and a fiddle has no fellow. 1.03. 41
i find him a fit fellow. 2.02.116
that good fellow, | if i command him, follows my 2.02.132
this same cranmer's | a worthy fellow, and hath 3.02. 72
and from this fellow? 3.02.279
you are a saucy fellow, | deserve we no more 4.02.100
but this fellow | let me ne'er see again. 4.02.107
me | wait else at door, a fellow councillor, 5.02. 17
there is a fellow somewhat near the door, he 5.03. 40 P
you great fellow, | stand close up, or i'll make 5.03. 87
there's a fellow! TRO 1.02.200 P
what sneaking fellow comes yonder? 1.02.226 P
a paltry, insolent fellow! 2.03.208 P
it should seem, fellow, thou hast not seen the 3.01. 37 P
a strange fellow here | writes me that man, how 3.03. 95
here's agamemnon, an honest fellow enough, and 5.01. 51 P
fellow, commend my service to her beauty; 5.05. 3
'fore me, this fellow speaks! COR 1.01.120
o noble fellow! 1.04. 52
that's a brave fellow; 2.02. 5 P
ill as you, and make me | your fellow tribune. 3.01. 52
what have you to do here, fellow? 4.05. 22 P
where is this fellow? 4.05. 50
but reason with the fellow, | before you punish 4.06. 52
wife, his child, | and this brave fellow too: 5.01. 30
i tell thee, fellow, | thy general is my lover. 5.02. 13
therefore, fellow, | i must have leave to pass. 5.02. 22
prithee, fellow, remember my name is menenius, 5.02. 28 P
nay, but, fellow, fellow — 5.02. 58 P
nay, but, fellow, fellow — 5.02. 58 P
a noble fellow, i warrant him. 5.02.109 P
the worthy fellow is our general. 5.02.110 P
this fellow had a volscian to his mother; 5.03.178
the plebeians have got your fellow tribune. 5.04. 36
how now, good fellow, wouldst thou speak with us
TIT 4.04. 39
whipt and tormented and — god–den, good fellow.
ROM 1.02. 56
stay, fellow, i can read. 1.02. 63 P
am i like such a fellow? 3.01. 10 P
now, fellow, what is there? 4.04. 14
and be prosperous, and farewell, good fellow. 5.03. 42
this fellow here, lord timon, this thy creature, TIM 1.01.116
where thou hast feign'd him a worthy fellow. 1.01.223 P
the fellow that sits next him, now parts bread 1.02. 46 P
a brave fellow! 1.02. 55 P
the fellow | loaden with irons wiser than the 3.05. 49
mend me, thou saucy fellow? JC 1.01. 18
fellow, come from the throng, look upon caesar. 1.02. 21
what a blunt fellow is this grown to be! 1.02.295
come hither, fellow; which way hast thou been? 2.04. 21
what, is the fellow mad? 3.01. 10
quality | there is no fellow in the firmament. 3.01. 62
how now, fellow? 3.02.261
a barren–spirited fellow; 4.01. 36
get you hence, sirrah; saucy fellow, hence! 4.03.134
fellow thou, awake! 4.03.300
that ever rome | should breed thy fellow. 5.03.101
thou art a fellow of a good respect; 5.05. 45
fellow, wilt thou bestow thy time with me? 5.05. 61
remembrance cannot parallel | a fellow to it. MAC 2.03. 63
would not betray | the devil to his fellow, and 4.03.129
i prithee do not mock me, fellow student, | i HAM 1.02.177
come on, you hear this fellow in the cellarage, 1.05.151
periwig–pated fellow tear a passion to totters, 3.02. 9 P
i would have such a fellow whipt for o'erdoing 3.02. 13 P
we shall know by this fellow. 3.02.141 P
has this fellow no feeling of his business? 5.01. 65 P
this fellow might be in 's time a great buyer of 5.01.103 P
i will speak to this fellow. 5.01.117 P
him, horatio, a fellow of infinite jest, of most 5.01.185 P
a very honest–hearted fellow, and as poor as the LR 1.04. 19 P
dost thou know me, fellow? 1.04. 26 P
what says the fellow there? 1.04. 46 P
i thank thee, fellow. 1.04. 87 P
this fellow has banish'd two on 's daughters, 1.04.102 P
thou wast a pretty fellow when thou hadst no 1.04.191 P
fellow, i know thee. 2.02. 13 P
why, what a monstrous fellow art thou, thus to 2.02. 25 P
thou art a strange fellow. a tailor make a man? 2.02. 56 P
what, art thou mad, old fellow? 2.02. 85
this is some fellow | who, having been prais'd 2.02. 95
this is a fellow of the self–same color | our 2.02.138
being the very fellow which of late | display'd 2.04. 40
and she will tell you who that fellow is | that 3.01. 48
where is this straw, my fellow? 3.02. 69
in, fellow, there, into th' hovel; 3.04.174
let him take the fellow. 3.04.177
fellow, where goest? 4.01. 29
i' th' last night's storm i such a fellow saw, 4.01. 32
is that the naked fellow? 4.01. 40
sirrah, naked fellow — 4.01. 51
come hither, fellow. 4.01. 53
now, fellow, fare thee well. 4.06. 41
that fellow handles his bow like a crow–keeper; 4.06. 87 P
half–blooded fellow, yes. 5.03. 80
did i not, fellow? 5.03.276
he's a good fellow, i can tell you that; 5.03.285
(a fellow almost damn'd in a fair wife), | that OTH 1.01. 21
you see this fellow that is gone before: 2.03.121
there comes a fellow crying out for help, | and 2.03.226
myself the crying fellow did pursue, | lest by 2.03.230
o, that's an honest fellow. 3.03. 5
think every bearded fellow that's but yok'd 4.01. 66
some base notorious knave, some scurvy fellow. 4.02.140
the same indeed, a very valiant fellow. 5.01. 52
let this fellow | be nothing of our strife; ANT 2.02. 79
go to the fellow, good alexas, bid him | report 2.05.111
there's a strong fellow, menas. 2.07. 88
where is the fellow? 3.03. 1
the fellow has good judgment. 3.03. 25
what art thou, fellow? 3.13. 86
to let a fellow that will take rewards | and say 3.13.123
of me | as when mine empire was your fellow too, 4.02. 22
come, good fellow, put thine iron on. 4.04. 3
seest thou, my good fellow? 4.04. 9
here is a rural fellow | that will not be denied 5.02.233
and that she should love this fellow, and refuse CYM 1.02. 25 P
he's a strange fellow himself, and knows it not. 2.01. 35 P
a worthy fellow, | albeit he comes on angry 2.03. 55
profane fellow! 2.03.124
come, fellow, be thou honest, | do thou thy 3.04. 64
why, good fellow, | what shall i do the while? 3.04.127
and the fellow dares not deceive me. 4.01. 25 P
but for thee, fellow, | who needs must know of 4.03. 9
yes indeed do i, fellow. 5.04.177 P
i tell thee, fellow, there are none want eyes to 5.04.185 P
dangerous fellow, hence! 5.05.237
he was a wise fellow and had good discretion PER 1.03. 4 P
you shall not need, my fellow peers of tyre, 1.03. 10
good fellow, what's that? 2.01. 53 P
now, afore me, a handsome fellow! 2.01. 80 P
and, /with her fellow maids, /is now upon | the 5.01. 50
and a fellow | false as thy title to her. TNK 2.02.171
wrastling and running. — 'tis a pretty fellow. 2.03. 67
this fellow has a vengeance trick o' th' hip. 2.03. 70
other curses a suing fellow and her garden–house 4.03. 56 P
nay, this' a sound fellow i tell you, let's mark STM II.C 89 P
all thy fellow birds do sing, | careless of thy PP 20.25

FELLOW–FAULT 1 FR 0.0001 REL FR 0 V 1 P
till his fellow–fault came to match it. AYL 3.02.355 P

FELLOWLY 1 FR 0.0001 REL FR 1 V 0 P
to the show of thine, | fall fellowly drops. TMP 5.01. 64

FELLOW'S 6 FR 0.0006 REL FR 3 V 3 P
what muffled fellow's that? MM 5.01.486
cry down | this ipswich fellow's insolence; H8 1.01.138
what fellow's this? COR 4.05. 19 P
a whoreson mad fellow's it was. HAM 5.01.176 P
sir, this young fellow's mother could; LR 1.01. 13 P
this fellow's of exceeding honesty, | and knows OTH 3.03.258

FELLOWS' 2 FR 0.0002 REL FR 1 V 1 P
keep your fellows' counsels and your own, and ADO 3.03. 86 P
him a livery | more guarded than his fellows'; MV 2.02.155

FELLOWS 71 FR 0.0080 REL FR 50 V 21 P
he hath lost his fellows, | and strays about to TMP 1.02.417
my brother's servants | were then my fellows, 2.01.274
i and my fellows | are ministers of fate. 3.03. 60
thou and thy meaner fellows your last service 4.01. 35
two of these fellows you | must know and own, 5.01.274
fellows, stand fast; i see a passenger. TGV 4.01. 1
have made you four tall fellows skip like rats. WIV 2.01.229 P
you were good soldiers and tall fellows; 2.02. 11 P
after him, fellows, bring him to the block. MM 4.03. 65
bring you these fellows on. ADO 5.01.331
i am more bound to you than your fellows, for LLL 1.02.151 P
sky, | so, at his sight, away his fellows fly; MND 3.02. 24
nature hath fram'd strange fellows in her time: MV 1.01. 51
go to thy fellows, bid them cover the table, 3.05. 58 P
in extremity of either are abominable fellows, AYL 4.01. 6 P
now, fellows, you are welcome. SHR in.1. 79
man, there be good fellows in the world, and a 1.01.128 P
o excellent motion! fellows, let's be gone. 1.02.278
worthy fellows, and like to prove most sinewy AWW 2.01. 59 P
of all the learned and authentic fellows — 2.03. 12 P
italian fields | where noble fellows strike. 2.03.291
do you not hear, fellows? take away the lady. TN 1.05. 39 P
these lords, my noble fellows, if they please, WT 2.03.143
we are but plain fellows, sir. 4.04.721 P
jack, whose fellows are these that come after? 1H4 4.02. 62 P
and, fellows, soldiers, friends, | better 5.02. 75
these fellows woll do well, master shallow. 2H4 3.02.287 P
and such fellows are perfit in the great H5 3.06. 70 P
god, why should they mock poor fellows thus? 4.03. 92
for these fellows of infinite tongue, that can 5.02.156 P
thou shalt find the best king of good fellows. 5.02.243 P
i have fought with pembroke and his fellows, 3H6 4.03. 54
fellows in arms, and my most loving friends, R3 5.02. 1
his noble friends and fellows, whom to leave H8 2.01. 73
to village curs, | bark when their fellows do: 2.04.161
y' have made a fine hand, fellows! 5.03. 70
what mean these fellows? know they not achilles?
TRO 3.03. 70
strike, fellows, strike, this is the man i seek. 5.08. 10
come on, my fellows! COR 1.04. 27
march on, my fellows! 1.06. 85
i think our fellows are asleep. 4.05. 2 P
come, we are fellows and friends: 4.05.183 P
than when these fellows ran about the streets, 4.06. 28
crows, | as yonder lady o'er her fellows shows. ROM 1.05. 49
thou art like one of these fellows that, when he 3.01. 5 P
honest good fellows, ah, put up, put up, | for 4.05. 98
all those which were his fellows but of late — TIM 1.01. 78
these old fellows | have their ingratitude in 2.02.214
give't these fellows | to whom 'tis instant due. 2.02.229
alack, my fellows, what should i say to you? 4.02. 3
more of our fellows. 4.02. 15
we are fellows still, | serving alike in sorrow. 4.02. 18
good fellows all, | the latest of my wealth i'll 4.02. 22
meet, for timon's sake | let's yet be fellows. 4.02. 25
one of my fellows had the speed of him, | who, MAC 1.05. 35
a rumor | of many worthy fellows that were out, 4.03.183
what should such fellows as i do crawling HAM 3.01.127 P
this, give these fellows some means to the king, 4.06. 14 P
these good fellows will bring thee where i am. 4.06. 27 P
negligence you please, | you and your fellows; LR 1.03. 13
advise your fellows so. 1.03. 23
fellows, hold the chair, | upon these eyes of 3.07. 67
these fellows have some soul, | and such a one OTH 1.01. 54
dark | by roderigo and fellows that are scap'd. 5.01.113
we bid a loud farewell | to these great fellows. ANT 2.07.133
whip him, fellows, | till like a boy you see him 3.13. 99
me well, | and kings have been your fellows. 4.02. 13
well, my good fellows, wait on me to–night. 4.02. 20
nay, good my fellows, do not please sharp fate 4.14.135
into contempt the suits | of princely fellows, CYM 3.04. 90
had there such fellows liv'd when you were babes STM II.C 63

FELLOW–SERVANT 1 FR 0.0001 REL FR 1 V 0 P
him | to be my fellow–servant to your ladyship. TGV 2.04.105

/FELLOWSHIP 1 FR 0.0001 REL FR 1 V 0 P
/grief /hath /mates, /and /bearing /fellowship. LR 3.06.107

FELLOWSHIP 17 FR 0.0019 REL FR 12 V 5 P
in love, i hope — sweet fellowship in shame. LLL 4.03. 47
and me | for everlasting bond of fellowship — MND 1.01. 85
is scattered and disjoin'd from fellowship. JN 3.04. 3
manhood, nor good fellowship in thee, nor thou 1H4 1.02.140 P
but out upon this half–fac'd fellowship! 1.03.208
all the titles of good fellowship come to you! 2.04.278 P
that fears his fellowship to die with us. H5 4.03. 39
here was a royal fellowship of death! 4.08.101
and all the fellowship i hold now with him | is H8 3.01.121
but kneels and holds up hands for fellowship, COR 5.03.175
if sour woe delights in fellowship | and needly ROM 3.02.116
his fellowship i' th' cause against your city, TIM 5.02. 12
you, by the rights of our fellowship, by the HAM 2.02.284 P
shoes, get me a fellowship in a cry of players? 3.02.277 P
of /the sea and skies | parted our fellowship. OTH 2.01. 93
it is to have a name in great men's fellowship. ANT 2.07. 12 P
pain, | and fellowship in woe doth woe assuage, LUC 790

FELLOWSHIPS 1 FR 0.0001 REL FR 0 V 1 P
security enough to make fellowships accurs'd. MM 3.02.228 P

FELLOW'ST 1 FR 0.0001 REL FR 1 V 0 P
thou co–active art, | and fellow'st nothing. WT 1.02.142

FELLS* 2 FR 0.0002 REL FR 1 V 1 P
our ewes, and their fells you know are greasy. AYL 3.02. 54 P
hews down and fells the hardest–timber'd oak. 3H6 2.01. 55

FELL'ST 1 FR 0.0001 REL FR 1 V 0 P
but better 'twere | thou fell'st into my fury, ANT 4.12. 41

FELON 2 FR 0.0002 REL FR 2 V 0 P
above the felon or what trespass else. 2H6 3.01.132
and apprehend thee for a felon here. ROM 5.03. 69

FELONIOUS 1 FR 0.0001 REL FR 1 V 0 P
or foul felonious thief that fleec'd poor 2H6 3.01.129

FELONY 2 FR 0.0002 REL FR 1 V 1 P
treason, felony, | sword, pike, knife, gun, or TMP 2.01.161
and i will make it felony to drink small beer. 2H6 4.02. 67 P

FELT* 44 FR 0.0049 REL FR 39 V 5 P
not a soul | but felt a fever of the mad, and TMP 1.02.209
dead | if i in thought felt not her very sorrow. TGV 4.04.172
but i felt it hot in her breath. ERR 3.02.131 P
that since have felt the vigor of his rage. 4.04. 78
and when this hail some heat from hermia felt, MND 1.01.244
our nation till now, i never felt it till now. MV 3.01. 86 P
which might be felt, that we, the poorer born, AWW 1.01.182
i have felt so many quirks of joy and grief 3.02. 49
was | before the child himself felt he was sick. JN 4.02. 88
have felt the worst of death's destroying wound, R2 3.02.139
i put my hand into the bed and felt them, and H5 2.03. 23 P
then i felt to his knees, and so up'ard and 2.03. 24 P
i, | or felt that pain which i did for him once, 3H6 1.01.221
thy mother felt more than a mother's pain, | and 5.06. 49
the last was i that felt thy tyranny. R3 5.03.168
life | felt so much cold as over shoes in snow? 5.03.326
or felt the flatteries that grow upon it! H8 3.01.144
for then, and not till then, he felt himself, 4.02. 65
on the nipple | of my dug and felt it bitter, ROM 1.03. 31
he jests at scars that never felt a wound. 2.02. 1
show'r of your gifts, | and sweetly felt it. TIM 5.01. 71
come hither, ere my tree hath felt the axe, 5.01.211
that it resounds | as if it felt with scotland, MAC 4.03. 7
malady is fix'd, | the lesser is scarce felt. LR 3.04. 9
stratagem, to shoe | a troop of horse with felt. 4.06.185
does redeem all sorrows | that ever i have felt. 5.03.268
it /yet hath felt no age nor known no sorrow. OTH 3.04. 37
to the felt absence now i feel a cause. 3.04.182
ill tidings tell | themselves when they be felt. ANT 2.05. 88
died of the biting of it, what pain she felt. 5.02.254 P
i had rather | you felt than make't my boast. CYM 2.03.111

the city's usuries, | and felt them knowingly; 3.03. 46
not imagin'd, felt. 4.02.307
the more of you 'twas felt, the more it shap'd 5.05.346
here they are but felt, and seen with mischief's PER 1.04. 8
then discourse our woes, felt several years, 1.04. 18
lady, | if ever thou hast felt what sorrow was, TNK 2.02.276
say i felt | compassion to 'em both, how would 3.06.212
he has felt | without doubt what he fights for, 4.02. 96
smooth moist hand, were it with thy hand felt, VEN 143
and having felt the sweetness of the spoil, 553
i felt a kind of fear | when as i met the boar, 998
when more is felt than one hath power to tell. LUC 1288
what freezings have i felt, what dark days seen! SON 97. 3
FELT'ST 1 FR 0.0001 REL FR 1 V 0 P
which, i hope, thou felt'st i was displeas'd. ERR 2.02. 19
FEMALE 19 FR 0.0021 REL FR 15 V 4 P
"with a child of our grandmother eve, a female; LLL 1.01.264 P
the female ivy so | enrings the barky fingers of MND 4.01. 43
of female favor, and bestows himself | like a AYL 4.03. 86
in the boorish is company — of this female — 5.01. 49 P
is, abandon the society of this female, or, 5.01. 51 P
that thou carry | this female bastard hence, and WT 2.03.175
and clap their female joints | in stiff unwieldy R2 3.02.114
my brain i'll prove the female to my soul, | my 5.05. 6
so the son of the female is the shadow of the 2H4 3.02.129 P
the founder of this law and female bar. H5 1.02. 42
no female | should be inheritrix in salique land 1.02. 50
to hold in right and title of the female; 1.02. 89
to bar your highness claiming from the female, 1.02. 92
anon, as patient as the female dove, | when that HAM 5.01.286
with female fairies will his tomb be haunted, CYM 4.02.217
took a peer, | who died and left a female heir, PER 1.ch. 22
who to thy female knights | allow'st no more TNK 5.01.140
my female evil | tempteth my better angel from PP 2. 5
my female evil | tempteth my better angel from SON 144. 5
FEMALES 4 FR 0.0004 REL FR 4 V 0 P
are masters to their females, and their lords: ERR 2.01. 24
a knavish lad, | thus to make poor females mad. MND 3.02.441
year, | when flesh is cheap and females dear, 2H4 5.03. 19
being proud, as females are, to see him woo her, VEN 309
FEMETARY *(also femiter)*
FEMETARY 1 FR 0.0001 REL FR 1 V 0 P
hemlock, and rank femetary | doth root upon, H5 5.02. 45
FEMININE 1 FR 0.0001 REL FR 0 V 1 P
a soul feminine saluteth us. LLL 4.02. 81 P
FEMITER *(also femetary)*
/FEMITER 1 FR 0.0001 REL FR 1 V 0 P
crown'd with rank /femiter and furrow–weeds, LR 4.04. 3
FEN 3 FR 0.0003 REL FR 2 V 1 P
with raven's feather from unwholesome fen | drop TMP 1.02.322
or, as 'twere perfum'd by a fen. 2.01. 49 P
that his fen | makes fear'd and talk'd of more COR 4.01. 30
FENC'D 1 FR 0.0001 REL FR 1 V 0 P
a sheep–cote fenc'd about with olive–trees? AYL 4.03. 77
FENCE 15 FR 0.0017 REL FR 10 V 5 P
at sword and dagger with a master of fence WIV 1.01.284 P
alas, sir, i cannot fence. 2.03. 15 P
despite his nice fence and his active practice, ADO 5.01. 75
sir boy, i'll whip you from your foining fence, 5.01. 84
he will fence with his own shadow. MV 1.02. 61 P
he had been valiant, and so cunning in fence, TN 3.04.284 P
at mine hostess' door, | teach us some fence! JN 2.01.290
crown for this, | or all my fence shall fail. 2H6 2.01. 51
my master, he hath learnt so much fence already. 2.03. 78 P
where's captain margaret, to fence you now? 3H6 2.06. 75
can oxford, that did ever fence the right, | now 3.03. 98
which he hath giv'n for fence impregnable, | and 4.01. 44
dive in the earth, | and fence not athens! TIM 4.01. 3
which fence the roots they grow by and defend PER 1.02. 31
shame assail'd, the red should fence the white. LUC 63
FENCER 1 FR 0.0001 REL FR 0 V 1 P
they say he has been fencer to the sophy. TN 3.04.279 P
FENCER'S 1 FR 0.0001 REL FR 0 V 1 P
and yours as blunt as the fencer's foils, which ADO 5.02. 13 P
FENCING 4 FR 0.0004 REL FR 1 V 3 P
that time in the tongues that i have in fencing, TN 1.03. 93 P
this is the right fencing grace, my lord, tap 2H4 2.01.193 P
ay, or drinking, fencing, swearing, quarrelling, HAM 2.01. 25
without any more virginal fencing, will you use PER 4.06. 57 P
FENNEL 3 FR 0.0003 REL FR 1 V 2 P
well, and eats cunger and fennel, and drinks off 2H4 2.04.245 P
among fresh fennel buds shall you this night ROM 1.02. 29
there's fennel for you, and columbines. HAM 4.05.180 P
FENNY 1 FR 0.0001 REL FR 1 V 0 P
fillet of a fenny snake, | in the cauldron boil MAC 4.01. 12
FENS 2 FR 0.0002 REL FR 2 V 0 P
that the sun sucks up | from bogs, fens, flats, TMP 2.02. 2
breath i hate | as reek a' th' rotten fens, COR 3.03.121
FEN–SUCK'D 1 FR 0.0001 REL FR 1 V 0 P
you fen–suck'd fogs, drawn by the pow'rful sun, LR 2.04.167
FENTON 18 FR 0.0020 REL FR 8 V 10 P
but notwithstanding, master fenton, i'll be WIV 1.04.145 P
what say you to young master fenton? 3.02. 66 P
gentle master fenton, | yet seek my father's 3.04. 18
and how does good master fenton? 3.04. 34 P
what does master fenton here? 3.04. 68
good master fenton, come not to my child. 3.04. 72
no, good master fenton. 3.04. 74
knowing my mind, you wrong me, master fenton. 3.04. 76
good master fenton, | i will not be your friend 3.04. 88
look on master fenton." 3.04. 97 P
or, in sooth, i would master fenton had her. 3.04.106 P
as my word, but speciously for master fenton. 3.04.109 P
master fenton, talk not to me, my mind is heavy; 4.06. 1 P
i will hear you, master fenton, and i will (at 4.06. 6 P
here comes master fenton. 5.05.214 P
how now, master fenton? 5.05.215 P
fenton, heaven give thee joy! 5.05.236
master fenton, | heaven give you many, many 5.05.239
FEODARY *(also fedary, federary)*
FEODARY 1 FR 0.0001 REL FR 1 V 0 P
art thou a feodary for this act, and look'st CYM 3.02. 21
FER 5 FR 0.0005 REL FR 0 V 5 P
monsieur le fer. H5 4.04. 26 P
he says his name is master fer. 4.04. 27 P
master fer! 4.04. 28 P
i'll fer him, and firk him, and ferret him. 4.04. 28 P
i do not know the french for fer, and ferret, 4.04. 30 P
FERDINAND 8 FR 0.0009 REL FR 8 V 0 P
all afire with me, the king's son, ferdinand, TMP 1.02.212
you grant with me | that ferdinand is drown'd? 2.01.244
them, while i visit | young ferdinand, whom they 3.03. 92
o ferdinand, | do not smile at me that i boast 4.01. 8
my dear son ferdinand. 5.01.139
and ferdinand, her brother, found a wife | where 5.01.210
and bid my cousin ferdinand come hither; SHR 4.01.151
ferdinand, | my father, king of spain, was H8 2.04. 47
FERE 2 FR 0.0002 REL FR 2 V 0 P
me, as with the woeful fere | and father of that TIT 4.01. 89
this anatomy | had by his young fair fere a boy, TNK 5.01.116
FERN–SEED 2 FR 0.0002 REL FR 0 V 2 P
we have the receipt of fern–seed, we walk 1H4 2.01. 87 P
to the night than to fern–seed for your walking 2.01. 89 P
FERRARA 1 FR 0.0001 REL FR 1 V 0 P
a league between his highness and ferrara. H8 3.02.323
/FERRERS 1 FR 0.0001 REL FR 1 V 0 P
john duke of norfolk, walter lord /ferrers, R3 5.05. 13
FERRET 3 FR 0.0003 REL FR 1 V 2 P
i'll fer him, and firk him, and ferret him. H5 4.04. 29 P
i do not know the french for fer, and ferret, 4.04. 30 P
looks with such ferret and such fiery eyes | as JC 1.02.186
FERRY 2 FR 0.0002 REL FR 1 V 1 P
to the common ferry | which trades to venice. MV 3.04. 53
silver on the tip of your tongue, or no ferry. TNK 4.03. 21 P
FERRYMAN 1 FR 0.0001 REL FR 1 V 0 P
with that sour ferryman which poets write of, R3 1.04. 46
/FERTILE 1 FR 0.0001 REL FR 1 V 0 P
a womb, | and /fertile every wish, a million. ANT 1.02. 39
FERTILE 14 FR 0.0015 REL FR 12 V 2 P
springs, brine–pits, barren place and fertile. TMP 1.02.338
i'll show thee every fertile inch o' th' island; 2.02.148
with adorations, fertile tears, | with groans TN 1.05.255
from heartiness, from bounty, fertile bosom, WT 1.02.113
fertile the isle, the temple much surpassing 3.01. 2
and all the fertile land within that bound, | to 1H4 3.01. 76
drinking good and good store of fertile sherris, 2H4 4.03.121 P
our fertile france, put up her lovely visage? H5 5.02. 37
look on thy country, look on fertile france, 1H6 3.03. 44
even as i have of fertile england's soil. 2H6 1.01.238
as firmly as i hope for fertile england. 3.01. 88
ensear thy fertile and conceptious womb, | let TIM 4.03.187
he hath much land, and fertile; HAM 5.02. 85 P
and, though he in a fertile climate dwell, OTH 1.01. 70
FERTILE–FRESH 1 FR 0.0001 REL FR 1 V 0 P
more fertile–fresh than all the field to see; WIV 5.05. 68
FERTILITY 2 FR 0.0002 REL FR 2 V 0 P
the soil's fertility from wholesome flowers. R2 3.04. 39
lie on heaps, | corrupting in it own fertility. H5 5.02. 40
FERULA 1 FR 0.0001 REL FR 1 V 0 P
ones, | and humble with a ferula the tall ones, TNK 3.05.112
FERVENCY 1 FR 0.0001 REL FR 1 V 0 P
on his hook, which he | with fervency drew up. ANT 2.05. 18
FERVOR 4 FR 0.0004 REL FR 4 V 0 P
far | his name with zealous fervor sanctify. AWW 3.04. 11
and let your fervor, like my master's, be TN 1.05.287
or, wing'd with fervor of her love, she's flown CYM 3.05. 61
and to him in his barge with fervor hies. PER 5.ch. 20
FERY *(also vara, vary*, very)*
FERY 6 FR 0.0006 REL FR 0 V 6 P
it is that fery person for all the orld, as just WIV 1.01. 49 P
fery goot. 1.01.144 P
it is a fery discretion answer, save the fall is 1.01.253 P
fery well; what is it? 3.01. 51 P
this is fery fantastical humors and jealousies. 3.03.170 P
admirable pleasures and fery honest knaveries. 4.04. 81 P
FESCUE 1 FR 0.0001 REL FR 1 V 0 P
do but put | a fescue in her fist, and you shall TNK 2.03. 34
FESTE 1 FR 0.0001 REL FR 0 V 1 P
feste, the jester, my lord, a fool that the lady TN 2.04. 11 P
FESTER 3 FR 0.0003 REL FR 3 V 0 P
their poor bodies | must lie and fester. H5 4.03. 88
well might they fester 'gainst ingratitude, COR 1.09. 30
lilies that fester smell far worse than weeds. SON 94.14
/FESTINATE 1 FR 0.0001 REL FR 0 V 1 P
you are going, to a most /festinate preparation; LR 3.07. 10 P
FESTINATELY 1 FR 0.0001 REL FR 0 V 1 P
to the swain, bring him festinately hither. LLL 3.01. 6 P
FESTIVAL 6 FR 0.0006 REL FR 4 V 2 P
planet, nor i cannot woo in festival terms. ADO 5.02. 41 P
estate, | an eye–sore to our solemn festival! SHR 3.02.101
i pick'd and cut most of their festival purses; WT 4.04.614 P
day | ever in france shall be kept festival. JN 3.01. 76
as is the night before some festival | to an ROM 3.02. 29
all things that we ordained festival, | turn 4.05. 84
FESTIVALS 2 FR 0.0002 REL FR 2 V 0 P
transported shall be at high festivals | before 1H6 1.06. 26
it hath been sung at festivals, | on ember–eves PER 1.ch. 5
FEST'RED 2 FR 0.0002 REL FR 2 V 0 P
this fest'red joint cut off, the rest rest sound R2 5.03. 85
as fest'red members rot but by degree, | till 1H6 3.01.191
FEST'RING 1 FR 0.0001 REL FR 1 V 0 P
lies fest'ring in his shroud, where, as they say ROM 4.03. 43
FET 2 FR 0.0002 REL FR 2 V 0 P
whose blood is fet from fathers of war–proof! H5 3.01. 18
forthwith from ludlow the young prince be fet R3 2.02.121
FETCH *(also vetch)*
/FETCH 3 FR 0.0003 REL FR 3 V 0 P
/fetch /hither /richard, /that /in /common /view R2 4.01.155
/some /of /you, /and /fetch /a //looking–glass. 4.01.268
/i'll /fetch /some /flax /and /whites /of /eggs LR 3.07.106
FETCH 123 FR 0.0139 REL FR 89 V 34 P
thou call'dst me up at midnight to fetch dew TMP 1.02.228
fetch in our wood, and serves in offices | that 1.02.312
fetch us in fuel, and be quick, thou'rt best, 1.02.366
nor fetch in firing | at requiring, | nor scrape 2.02.181
i will fetch off my bottle, though i be o'er 4.01.213 P
i'll fetch them, sir. 5.01. 32
ariel, | fetch me the hat and rapier in my cell. 5.01. 84
and with a corded ladder fetch her down; TGV 3.01. 40
"inprimis, she can fetch and carry." 3.01.275 P
nay, a horse cannot fetch, but only carry, 3.01.276 P
ay, forsooth, i'll fetch it you. WIV 1.04. 48 P
doctor caius, i am come to fetch you home. 2.03. 52 P
go fetch me a quart of sack — put a toast in't. 3.05. 3 P
could fetch your brother from the manacles | of MM 2.04. 93
think you i can a resolution fetch | from 3.01. 81
go in to him, and fetch him out. 4.03. 34 P
place where he abides, | and he may fetch him. 5.01.253
go fetch him hither, let me look upon him. 5.01.469
my charge was but to fetch you from the mart ERR 1.02. 74
go back again, thou slave, and fetch him home. 2.01. 75
hence, prating peasant! fetch thy master home. 2.01. 81
go fetch me something: i'll break ope the gate. 3.01. 73
go, get thee gone, fetch me an iron crow. 3.01. 84
get you home | and fetch the chain; 3.01.115
i'll fetch my sister to get her good will. 3.02. 70
why, give it to my wife, and fetch your money. 4.01. 54
go fetch it, sister. 4.02. 47
to the centaur, fetch our stuff from thence; 4.04.149
to fetch my poor distracted husband hence. 5.01. 39
us, | and will not suffer us to fetch him out, 5.01.157
then, | who parted with me to go fetch a chain, 5.01.221
master, shall i fetch your stuff from shipboard? 5.01.409
you speak this to fetch me in, my lord. ADO 1.01.223 P
i will fetch you a toothpicker now from the 2.01.266 P
fetch you a hair off the great cham's beard, do 2.01.268 P
of the town are come to fetch you to church. 3.04. 97 P
fetch hither the swain, he must carry me a LLL 3.01. 49 P
and sail upon the land | to fetch me trifles, MND 2.01.133
fetch me that flow'r; 2.01.169
fetch me this herb, and be thou here again | ere 2.01.173
and they shall fetch thee jewels from the deep, 3.01.158
the squirrel's hoard, and fetch thee new nuts. 4.01. 36
fetch that gallant hither. AYL 2.02. 17
i will fetch up your goats, audrey. 3.03. 1 P
i must go fetch the /thirdborough. SHR in.1. 11 P
and fetch shrill echoes from the hollow earth. in.2. 46
we will fetch thee straight | adonis painted by in.2. 49
go, rascals, go, and fetch my supper in. 4.01.139
i like it well, good grumio, fetch it me. 4.03. 21
my boy shall fetch the scrivener presently. 4.04. 59
go on, and fetch our horses back again. 4.05. 9
go fetch them hither. 5.02.103
none better than to let him fetch off his drum, AWW 3.06. 19 P
the love of laughter, let him fetch his drum; 3.06. 34 P
let him fetch off his drum in any hand. 3.06. 42 P
good mother, fetch my bail. 5.03.295
fetch him off, i pray you, he speaks nothing but TN 1.05.106 P
i will fetch you light and paper and ink. 4.02.117 P
fetch malvolio hither. 5.01.278
i do, and will fetch off bohemia for't; WT 1.02.334
of him what he is, fetch me to th' sight of him. 3.03.134 P
it makes the course of thoughts to fetch about, JN 4.02. 24
fetch from false mowbray their first head and R2 1.01. 97
since last i went to france to fetch his queen. 1.01.131
kiss me, and bid me fetch thee thirty shillings? 2H4 2.01.102 P
be kin to us, or they will fetch it from japhet. 2.02.118 P
as i return, i will fetch off these justices. 3.02.301 P
fetch forth the lazar kite of cressid's kind, H5 2.01. 76
/or i will fetch thy rim out at thy throat | in 4.04. 14
i will fetch him. 4.07.169 P
go forth and fetch their conqu'ring caesar in; 5.pr. 28
sirrah, go fetch the beadle hither straight. 2H6 2.01.137
now fetch me a stool hither by and by. 2.01.138 P
from off the gates of york fetch down the head, 3H6 2.06. 52
that it is meet so few should fetch the prince. R3 2.02.139
of council out, | must fetch him in he papers. H8 1.01. 80
fetch me a dozen crab–tree staves, and strong 5.03. 7 P
i'll fetch her. TRO 3.02. 33 P
you know of him, but yet go fetch him hither, go 4.02. 57 P
i'll fetch you one. 5.02. 61
let's fetch him off, or make remain alike. COR 1.04. 62
him, and i'll go fetch thy sons | to back thy TIT 2.03. 53
now will i fetch the king to find them here, 2.03.206
then i'll go fetch an axe. 3.01.184
go fetch them hither to us presently. 5.03. 59
fetch me my rapier, boy. ROM 1.05. 55
to fetch a ladder, by the which your love | must 2.05. 73
go, villain, fetch a surgeon. 3.01. 94
the cords | that romeo bid thee fetch? 3.02. 35
ay, marry, go, i say, and fetch him hither. 4.02. 30
hold, take these keys and fetch more spices, 4.04. 1
sirrah, fetch drier logs. 4.04. 16
nay, we will all of us be there to fetch him. JC 2.01.212
i come to fetch you to the senate–house. 2.02. 59
and look where publius is come to fetch me. 2.02.108
i'll fetch him presently. 3.01.142
go fetch fire. 3.02.257 P
fetch the will hither, and we shall determine 4.01. 8
my drift, | and i believe it is a fetch of wit: HAM 2.01. 38
go get thee in, and fetch me a sup of liquor. 5.01. 60 P
fetch forth the stocks! LR 2.02.125
fetch forth the stocks! 2.02.133
fetch me a better answer. 2.04. 91
i fetch my life and being | from men of royal OTH 1.02. 21
fetch desdemona hither. 1.03.120
i must fetch his necessaries ashore. 2.01.284 P
fetch me the handkerchief, my mind misgives. 3.04. 89
to fetch her fan, her gloves, her mask, nor 4.02. 9
shall i go fetch your night–gown? 4.03. 34
from hence, | i'll fetch the general's surgeon. 5.01.100
mark antony but late, | enough to fetch him in. ANT 4.01. 14
the strong–wing'd mercury should fetch thee up, 4.15. 35
go fetch | my best attires. 5.02.227
i'll fetch a turn about the garden, pitying CYM 1.01. 81
i will fetch my gold and have our two wagers 1.04.167 P
service thou dost me, fetch that suit hither. 3.05.127 P
might break out and swear | he'd fetch us in; 4.02.141
pray you fetch him hither. 4.02.251
if you'll go fetch him, | we'll say our song 4.02.253
fetch breath that may proclaim them louder, that PER 1.04. 15
come away, or i'll fetch th' with a wanton. 2.01. 17 P
fetch hither all my boxes in my closet. 3.02. 81
to fetch his daughter home, who first is gone. 4.04. 20
FETCH'D 1 FR 0.0001 REL FR 1 V 0 P
and with forms being fetch'd | from glist'ring H5 2.02.116
FETCHED 1 FR 0.0001 REL FR 1 V 0 P
and as she fetched breath, away he skips, | and PP 11.11
FETCHES* 5 FR 0.0005 REL FR 2 V 3 P
of wheat, rye, barley, fetches, oats, and pease; TMP 4.01. 61
hark how hard he fetches breath. 1H4 2.04.530 P
does so blush, and fetches her wind so short, as TRO 3.02. 31 P
she fetches her breath as short as a new–ta'en 3.02. 33 P

mere fetches, | the images of revolt and flying LR 2.04. 89
FETCHING 1 FR 0.0001 REL FR 1 V 0 P
fetching mad bounds, bellowing and neighing loud MV 5.01. 73
FETCH'T 1 FR 0.0001 REL FR 1 V 0 P
fetch't, let me see't. OTH 3.04. 85
FETLOCK 1 FR 0.0001 REL FR 1 V 0 P
wounded steeds | fret fetlock deep in gore, and H5 4.07. 79
FETLOCKS 2 FR 0.0002 REL FR 2 V 0 P
that stain'd their fetlocks in his smoking blood 3H6 2.03. 21
short–jointed, fetlocks shag and long, | broad VEN 295
FETTER 4 FR 0.0004 REL FR 4 V 0 P
free your life, | but fetter you till death. MM 3.01. 66
fetter strong madness in a silken thread, ADO 5.01. 25
but rather reason thus with reason fetter: TN 3.01.155
fetter him, | till he be brought unto the TIT 5.03. 6
FETTER'D 2 FR 0.0002 REL FR 2 V 0 P
that in their chains fetter'd the kingly lion, 3H6 5.07. 11
thou art fetter'd | more than my shanks and CYM 5.04. 8
FETTERING 1 FR 0.0001 REL FR 0 V 1 P
be patient, there is no fettering of authority. AWW 2.03.237 P
FETTERS 2 FR 0.0002 REL FR 2 V 0 P
for we will fetters put about this fear, | which HAM 3.03. 25
these strong egyptian fetters i must break, | or ANT 1.02.116
FETTLE 1 FR 0.0001 REL FR 1 V 0 P
but fettle your fine joints 'gainst thursday ROM 3.05.153
FETT'RED 2 FR 0.0002 REL FR 2 V 0 P
as is our wretches fett'red in our prisons; H5 1.02.243
hast prisoner held, fett'red in amorous chains, TIT 2.01. 15
FEU 2 FR 0.0002 REL FR 1 V 1 P
volant, the pegasus, chez les narines de feu! H5 3.07. 15 P
rien puis? l'air et feu? 4.02. 5
/FEUD 1 FR 0.0001 REL FR 1 V 0 P
had not impressure made | /of /our /rank /feud; TRO 4.05.132
FEUDARY *(see fedary, federary, feodary)*
/FEVER 1 FR 0.0001 REL FR 1 V 0 P
/brought /ourselves /into /a /burning /fever, 2H4 4.01. 56
FEVER 24 FR 0.0027 REL FR 23 V 1 P
not a soul | but felt a fever of the mad, and TMP 1.02.209
but that there is so great a fever on goodness, MM 3.02.222 P
there died this morning of a cruel fever | one 4.03. 70
he is sick, my lord, | of a strange fever. 5.01.152
thereof the raging fire of fever bred, | and ERR 5.01. 75
bred, | and what's a fever but a fit of madness? 5.01. 76
but, a fever, she | reigns in my blood and will LLL 4.03. 93
a fever in your blood! 4.03. 95
fire, | to make a shaking fever in your walls, JN 2.01.228
this fever, that hath troubled me so long, 5.03. 3
ay me, this tyrant fever burns me up, | and will 5.03. 14
thinks thou the fiery fever will go out | with H5 4.01.253
grows to an envious fever | of pale and TRO 1.03.133
and 'tis this fever that keeps troy on foot, 1.03.135
the fever whereof all our power is sick. 1.03.139
till the high fever seethe your blood to froth, TIM 4.03.430
he had a fever when he was in spain, | and when JC 1.02.119
after life's fitful fever he sleeps well. MAC 3.02. 23
the white hand of a lady fever thee, | shake ANT 3.13.138
a fever with the absence of her son; CYM 4.03. 2
almost puts | faith in a fever, and deifies TNK 1.02. 66
desire of liberty, a fever, madness, | 'hath set 1.04. 42
in the distraction of this madding fever? SON 119. 8
my love is as a fever, longing still | for that 147. 1
FEVEROUS 4 FR 0.0004 REL FR 4 V 0 P
lest thou a feverous life shouldst entertain, MM 3.01. 74
my heart beats thicker than a feverous pulse, TRO 3.02. 36
as if the world | were feverous and did tremble. COR 1.04. 61
say, the earth | was feverous, and did shake. MAC 2.03. 61
FEVER'S 1 FR 0.0001 REL FR 1 V 0 P
of the fiend, | augur of the fever's end, | to PHT 7
FEVERS 2 FR 0.0002 REL FR 2 V 0 P
your potent and infectious fevers heap | on TIM 4.01. 22
"as burning fevers, agues pale and faint, VEN 739
FEVER–WEAK'NED 1 FR 0.0001 REL FR 1 V 0 P
and as the wretch whose fever–weak'ned joints, 2H4 1.01.140
FEW 71 FR 0.0080 REL FR 57 V 14 P
in few, they hurried us aboard a bark, | bore us TMP 1.02.144
few in millions | can speak like us. 2.01. 7
here have i few attendants, | and subjects none 5.01.166
company | some few odd lads you remember not. 5.01.255
faith, sir, few of any wit in such matters. MM 2.01.268 P
in few, bestow'd her on her own lamentation, 3.01.227 P
is it sad, and few words? 3.02. 51 P
but few of any sort, and none of name. ADO 1.01. 7 P
hath drops too few to wash her clean again, 4.01.141
gracious, though few have the grace to do it. LLL 5.01.140 P
the liker you; few taller are so young. 5.02.836
here are a few of the unpleasant'st words | that MV 3.02.251
but in a few, | signior hortensio, thus it SHR 1.02. 52
'twixt such friends as we | few words suffice; 1.02. 66
love all, trust a few, | do wrong to none. AWW 1.01. 64
all deaths are too few, the sharpest too easy. WT 4.04.780 P
but few, | and those but mean. 5.01. 92
there's few or none do know me; JN 4.03. 3
i have too few to take my leave of you, | when R2 1.03.255
with some few private friends upon this coast. 3.03. 4
and some few vanities that make him light; 3.04. 86
cut's saddle, put a few flocks in the point. 1H4 2.01. 5 P
in few, his death, whose spirit lent a fire 2H4 1.01.112
never so few, and never yet more need. 1.01.215
thou hast stol'n that which after some few hours 4.05.101
thus then in few: H5 1.02.245
and this man | hath, for a few light crowns, 2.02. 89
he hath heard that men of few words are the best 3.02. 37 P
but his few bad words are match'd with as few 3.02. 39 P
bad words are match'd with as few good deeds; 3.02. 39 P
look you, a few disputations with you, as partly 3.02. 95 P
shall a few sprays of us, | the emptying of our 3.05. 5
sorry am i his numbers are so few, | his 3.05. 56
and those few i have | almost no better than so 3.06.146
i am afeard there are few die well that die in a 4.01.141 P
we few, we happy few, we band of brothers; 4.03. 60
we few, we happy few, we band of brothers; 4.03. 60
since they, so few, watch such a multitude. 1H6 1.01.161
these few days' wonder will be quickly worn. 2H6 2.04. 69
who having pinch'd a few and made them cry, 3H6 2.01. 16
us | with some few bands of chosen soldiers, 3.03.204
my sovereign liege, no letters, and few words, 4.01. 86
for few men rightly temper with the stars; 4.06. 29
in few words, | if you'll not here proclaim 4.07. 53
there's few or none will entertain it. R3 1.04.131 P
that it is meet so few should fetch the prince. 2.02.139
and thus i took the vantage of those few: 3.07. 37
i am solicited, not by a few, | and those of H8 1.02. 18
but few now give so great ones. 1.03. 63
you few that lov'd me | and dare be bold to weep 2.01. 71
few are angels; 5.02. 47
this good man (few of you deserve that title), 5.02.173
(but few now living can behold that goodness) 5.04. 21
few words to fair faith. TRO 3.02. 95 P
at a few drops of women's rheum, which are | as COR 5.06. 45
few come within the compass of my curse — TIT 5.01.126
that few things loves better | than to abhor TIM 1.01. 59
'tis in few words, but spacious in effect: 3.05. 96
i would attend his leisure | for a few words. MAC 3.02. 4
and these few precepts in thy memory | look thou HAM 1.03. 58
give every man thy ear, but few thy voice, 1.03. 68
in few, ophelia, | do not believe his vows, for 1.03.126
few words, but, to effect, more than all yet: LR 3.01. 52
here's a few flow'rs, but 'bout midnight, more: CYM 4.02.283
few love to hear the sins they love to act; PER 1.01. 92
we are a few of those collected here | that TNK 3.05.103
i'll warrant ye he had not so few last night 4.01.137
being so few and well dispos'd, they show 4.02.122
o happiness enjoy'd but of a few, | and, if LUC 22
"few words," quoth she, "shall fit the trespass 1613
or none, or few, do hang | upon those boughs SON 73. 2
/FEWER 1 FR 0.0001 REL FR 1 V 0 P
/draw /anew /the /model | /in /fewer /offices, 2H4 1.03. 47
FEWER 3 FR 0.0003 REL FR 1 V 2 P
fellow should have fewer words than a parrot, 1H4 2.04. 98 P
in the name of jesu christ, speak fewer. H5 4.01. 65 P
the fewer men, the greater share of honor. 4.03. 22
FEWEST 2 FR 0.0002 REL FR 2 V 0 P
the fewest roses are cropp'd from the tree 1H6 2.04. 41
if i have fewest, i subscribe in silence. 2.04. 44
FEWNESS 1 FR 0.0001 REL FR 1 V 0 P
fewness and truth, 'tis thus: MM 1.04. 39
FIA *(also via)*
FIA 1 FR 0.0001 REL FR 0 V 1 P
"fia!" MV 2.02. 11 P
/FICKLE 1 FR 0.0001 REL FR 1 V 0 P
dwells in the /fickle grace of her he follows. LR 2.04.186
FICKLE 13 FR 0.0014 REL FR 13 V 0 P
clapp'd on the outward eye of fickle france, JN 2.01.583
of fickle changelings and poor discontents, 1H4 5.01. 76
and giddy fortune's furious fickle wheel, | that H5 3.06. 27
in france, amongst a fickle, wavering nation. 1H6 4.01.138
o fortune, fortune, all men call thee fickle; ROM 3.05. 60
if thou art fickle, what dost thou with him 3.05. 61
be fickle, fortune: 3.05. 62
"it shall be fickle, false, and full of fraud, VEN 1141
fair is my love, but not so fair as fickle, PP 7. 1
loss, | o frowning fortune, cursed, fickle dame! 17.10
whilst as fickle fortune smil'd, | thou and i 20.27
in thy power | dost hold time's fickle glass, SON 126. 2
tale, | ere long espied a fickle maid full pale, LC 5
FICKLENESS 1 FR 0.0001 REL FR 1 V 0 P
to weep | or to exclaim on fortune's fickleness. 1H6 5.03.134
FICO *(also figo)*
FICO 1 FR 0.0001 REL FR 0 V 1 P
a fico for the phrase! WIV 1.03. 30 P
FICTION 3 FR 0.0003 REL FR 2 V 1 P
i could condemn it as an improbable fiction. TN 3.04.128 P
and, for thy fiction, | why, thy verse swells TIM 5.01. 83
but in a fiction, in a dream of passion, | could HAM 2.02.552
FIDDLE 2 FR 0.0002 REL FR 2 V 0 P
a french song and a fiddle has no fellow. H8 1.03. 41
the devil fiddle 'em! 1.03. 42
FIDDLER 3 FR 0.0003 REL FR 2 V 1 P
while she did call me rascal fiddler | and SHR 2.01.157
fiddler, forbear, you grow too forward, sir. 3.01. 1
unless the fiddler apollo get his sinews to make TRO 3.03.303 P
FIDDLESTICK 2 FR 0.0002 REL FR 0 V 2 P
the devil rides upon a fiddlestick. 1H4 2.04.487 P
here's my fiddlestick, here's that shall make ROM 3.01. 48 P
FIDELE 9 FR 0.0010 REL FR 9 V 0 P
fidele, sir. CYM 3.06. 60
to our rock, | you and fidele play the cooks. 4.02.164
poor sick fidele! 4.02.166
whilst summer lasts and i live here, fidele, 4.02.219
and words, | save that euriphile must be fidele. 4.02.238
fidele, sir. 4.02.379
fidele, sir. 5.05.118
that sweet rosy lad | who died, and was fidele. 5.05.122
this is sure fidele. 5.05.260
FIDELE'S 1 FR 0.0001 REL FR 1 V 0 P
the boy fidele's sickness | did make my way long CYM 4.02.148
FIDELICET 2 FR 0.0002 REL FR 0 V 2 P
master page (fidelicet master page) and there is WIV 1.01.138 P
and there is myself (fidelicet myself) and the 1.01.139 P
FIDELITY 1 FR 0.0001 REL FR 0 V 1 P
by my fidelity, this is not well, master ford; WIV 4.02.153 P
FIDES 1 FR 0.0001 REL FR 1 V 0 P
"sic spectanda fides." PER 2.02. 38
FIDIUS 1 FR 0.0001 REL FR 1 V 0 P
proh deum, medius fidius, ye are all dunces! TNK 3.05. 11
FIDIUS'D 1 FR 0.0001 REL FR 0 V 1 P
not have been so fidius'd for all the chests in COR 2.01.131 P
/FIE 4 FR 0.0004 REL FR 4 V 0 P
/fie, /brother, /fie, /teach /her /not /thus /to TIT 3.02. 21
/brother, /fie, /teach /her /not /thus /to /lay 3.02. 21
/fie, /fie, /how /franticly /i /square /my /talk 3.02. 31
/fie, /fie, /how /franticly /i /square /my /talk 3.02. 31
FIE 163 FR 0.0184 REL FR 127 V 36 P
fie, what a spendthrift is he of his tongue! TMP 2.01. 24
fie, fie, how wayward is this foolish love, TGV 1.02. 57
fie, fie, how wayward is this foolish love, 1.02. 57
fie, fie, unreverend tongue, to call her bad, 2.06. 14
fie, fie, unreverend tongue, to call her bad, 2.06. 14
fie on thee, jolthead, thou canst not read. 3.01.290 P
fie, what the ignorance is! WIV 1.01.176 P
fie, fie, fie! 2.02.313 P
fie, fie, fie! 2.02.313 P
fie, fie, fie! 2.02.313 P
fie, fie, master ford, are you not asham'd? 3.03.214 P
fie, fie, master ford, are you not asham'd? 3.03.214 P
fie on her! 4.01. 62 P
and to call "horum," — fie upon you! 4.01. 68 P
fie, fie, he'll never come. 4.04. 18 P
fie, fie, he'll never come. 4.04. 18 P
fie, privacy? 4.05. 22 P
fie! 4.05. 23 P
fie on sinful fantasy! 5.05. 93
fie on lust and luxury! 5.05. 94
o, fie, fie, fie! MM 2.02.171
o, fie, fie, fie! 2.02.171
o, fie, fie, fie! 2.02.171
fie, these filthy vices! 2.04. 42
o, fie, fie, fie! 3.01.147
o, fie, fie, fie! 3.01.147
o, fie, fie, fie! 3.01.147
fie, sirrah, a bawd, a wicked bawd! 3.02. 19
fie upon him, he will discredit our mystery. 4.02. 28 P
fie, how impatience low'reth in your face! ERR 2.01. 86
self–harming jealousy — fie, beat it hence! 2.01.102
fie, brother, how the world is chang'd with you: 2.02.152
fie, now you run this humor out of breath. 4.01. 57
fie on thee, wretch! 5.01. 27
fie upon thee, art not asham'd? ADO 3.04. 28 P
fie, fie, they are not to be named, my lord, 4.01. 95
fie, fie, they are not to be named, my lord, 4.01. 95
all gentle tongues — | fie, painted rhetoric! LLL 4.03.235
fie, demetrius! MND 2.01.239
fie, fie, you counterfeit, you puppet, you! 3.02.288
fie, fie, you counterfeit, you puppet, you! 3.02.288
fie, fie! MV 1.01. 46
fie, fie! 1.01. 46
fie, fie, gratiano, where are all the rest? 2.06. 62
fie, fie, gratiano, where are all the rest? 2.06. 62
fie, what a question's that, | if thou wert near 3.04. 79
if you deny me, fie upon your law! 4.01.101
fie on thee! i can tell what thou wouldst do. AYL 2.07. 62
let's hear. o fie, the treble jars. SHR 3.01. 39
fie, doff this habit, shame to your estate, | an 3.02.100
fie, fie on all tir'd jades, on all mad masters, 4.01. 1 P
fie, fie on all tir'd jades, on all mad masters, 4.01. 1 P
fie on her! 4.02. 34
signior petruchio, fie, you are to blame. 4.03. 48
fie, fie, 'tis lewd and filthy. 4.03. 65
fie, fie, 'tis lewd and filthy. 4.03. 65
o, fie, fie, fie! 4.03.163
o, fie, fie, fie! 4.03.163
o, fie, fie, fie! 4.03.163
fie, what a foolish duty call you this? 5.02.125
fie, fie, unknit that threat'ning unkind brow, 5.02.136
fie, fie, unknit that threat'ning unkind brow, 5.02.136
fie, that you'll say so! TN 1.03. 25 P
fie on him! 1.05.107 P
fie on him, jezebel! 2.05. 41 P
fie, thou dishonest sathan! 4.02. 31 P
fie, fie, no thought of him; WT 2.03. 18
fie, fie, no thought of him; 2.03. 18
and my near'st of kin | cry fie upon my grave! 3.02. 54
fie, daughter, when my old wife liv'd, upon 4.04. 55
and says to his wife, "fie upon this quiet life! 1H4 2.04.104 P
you will not touch the true prince, no, fie! 2.04.301 P
fie, cousin percy, how you cross my father! 3.01.145
fie, fie, fie, sir john! 2H4 1.02.185 P
fie, fie, fie, sir john! 1.02.185 P
fie, fie, fie, sir john! 1.02.185 P
fie, this is hot weather, gentlemen. 3.02. 92 P
now fie upon my false french! H5 5.02.220 P
fie, lords, that you, being supreme magistrates, 1H6 1.03. 57
fie, uncle beauford, i have heard you preach 3.01.127
fie, de la pole, disable not thyself. 5.03. 67
fie, joan, that thou wilt be so obstacle! 5.04. 17
fie, coward woman and soft–hearted wretch! 2H6 3.02.307
fie on ambitions! 4.10. 1 P
fie on myself, that have a sword, and yet am 4.10. 1 P
fie! 5.01.213
fie, what a slug is hastings, that he comes not R3 3.01. 22
fie, what an indirect and peevish course | is 3.01. 31
a very fresh fish here — fie, fie, fie upon H8 2.03. 86
fie, fie, fie upon | this compell'd fortune! 2.03. 86
fie, fie, fie upon | this compell'd fortune! 2.03. 86
fie, fie, my brother! TRO 2.02. 25
fie, fie, my brother! 2.02. 25
fie, for godly shame! 2.02. 32
fie, fie upon her! 4.05. 54
fie, fie upon her! 4.05. 54
fie, savage, fie! 5.03. 49
fie, savage, fie! 5.03. 49
fie, you confine yourself most unreasonably. COR 1.03. 76 P
fie, fie, fie! 3.01.195
fie, fie, fie! 3.01.195
fie, fie, fie! 3.01.195
fie, fie, fie! 4.02. 54
fie, fie, fie! 4.02. 54
fie, fie, fie! 4.02. 54
fie, treacherous hue, that will betray with TIT 4.02.117
fie, publius, fie, thou art too much deceiv'd. 5.02.155
fie, publius, fie, thou art too much deceiv'd. 5.02.155
fie, how my bones ache! ROM 2.05. 26
fie, fie, thou shamest thy shape, thy love, thy 3.03.122
fie, fie, thou shamest thy shape, thy love, thy 3.03.122
fie, fie, what, are you mad? 3.05.157
fie, fie, what, are you mad? 3.05.157
fie, you slug–a–bed! 4.05. 2
fie, th' art a churl. TIM 1.02. 26
fie, fie, fie, fie! 2.02. 9
fie, fie, fie, fie! 2.02. 9
fie, fie, fie, fie! 2.02. 9
fie, fie, fie, fie! 2.02. 9
fie, no, do not believe it; 3.02. 8 P
fie, for shame! MAC 3.04. 73
fie, my lord, fie, a soldier, and afeard? 5.01. 36 P
fie, my lord, fie, a soldier, and afeard? 5.01. 37 P
fie, 'tis a fault to heaven, | a fault against HAM 1.02.101
fie on't, ah fie! 1.02.135
fie on't, ah fie! 1.02.135
o, fie, hold, hold, my heart, | and you, my 1.05. 93
fie upon't, foh! 2.02.587
by saint charity, | alack, and fie for shame! 4.05. 59
fie, sir, fie! LR 2.04.164

fie, sir, fie! 2.04.164
fie on this storm! 3.01. 49
his word was still, 'fie, foh, and fum, | i 3.04.183
fie, fie, fie! 4.06.129
fie, fie, fie! 4.06.129
fie, fie, fie! 4.06.129
o, fie upon thee, slanderer! OTH 2.01.113
fie, there is no such man; it is impossible. 4.02.134
o fie upon them! 4.02.145
o, fie upon thee, strumpet! 5.01.121
as i? /fough, fie upon thee! 5.01.123
fie, | your sword upon a woman? 5.02.223
fie, wrangling queen! ANT 1.01. 48
fie upon "but yet"! 2.05. 51
o fie, fie, fie! 3.11. 31
o fie, fie, fie! 3.11. 31
o fie, fie, fie! 3.11. 31
fie, you must give way. CYM 1.01.158
fie! 1.06. 9
fie, fie upon her, she's able to freeze the god PER 4.06. 3 P
fie, fie upon her, she's able to freeze the god 4.06. 3 P
fie, sir! TNK 2.02.203
fie, fie, | what tediosity and disensanity | is 3.05. 1
fie, fie, | what tediosity and disensanity | is 3.05. 1
his cheeks, cries, "fie, no more of love! VEN 185
"fie, liveless picture, cold and senseless stone 211
"fie, fie," he says, "you crush me, let me go, 611
"fie, fie," he says, "you crush me, let me go, 611
"fie, fie, fond love, thou art as full of fear 1021
"fie, fie, fond love, thou art as full of fear 1021
"fie, fie, fie," now would she cry, | "tereu, PP 20.13
"fie, fie, fie," now would she cry, | "tereu, 20.13
"fie, fie, fie," now would she cry, | "tereu, 20.13

/FIELD 1 FR 0.0001 REL FR 1 V 0 P
/to /abide /a /field | /where /nothing /but /the 2H4 2.03. 36

FIELD 166 FR 0.0187 REL FR 156 V 10 P
more fertile–fresh than all the field to see; WIV 5.05. 68
you, | to make it wander in an unknown field? ERR 3.02. 38
he rather means to lodge you in the field, LLL 2.01. 85
and i to be a corporal of his field, | and wear 3.01.187
saint cupid, then! and, soldiers, to the field! 4.03.363
this field shall hold me, and so hold your vow: 5.02.345
that oft in field with targe and shield did make 5.02.553
the fold stands empty in the drowned field, MND 2.01. 96
ay, in the temple, in the town, the field, | you 2.01.238
i am fear'd in field and town. 3.02.398
have i not heard great ord'nance in the field, SHR 1.02.203
my household stuff, my field, my barn, | my 3.02.231
petruchio, go thy ways, the field is won. 4.05. 23
to–morrow to th' field. AWW 3.01. 23
to challenge him the field, and then to break TN 2.03.127 P
hand | of cordelion knighted in the field. JN 1.01. 54
speed then to take advantage of the field. 2.01.297
back to the stained field, | you equal potents, 2.01.357
beds, | that here come sacrifices for the field. 2.01.420
whom zeal and charity brought to the field | as 2.01.565
of war | when he intendeth to become the field. 5.01. 55
desires your majesty to leave the field, | and 5.03. 6
say king john, sore sick, hath left the field. 5.04. 6
from forth the noise and rumor of the field, 5.04. 45
up, | last in the field, and almost lords of it! 5.05. 8
for jesu christ in glorious christian field, R2 4.01. 93
the field of golgotha and dead men's skulls. 4.01.144
to the field!" 1H4 2.03. 50
make haste, percy is already in the field. 4.02. 75 P
the prince of wales from such a field as this, 5.04. 12
boys | seek percy and thyself about the field, 5.04. 32
brother, let us to the highest of the field, 5.04.160
how goes the field? 5.05. 16
who in a bloody field by shrewsbury | hath 2H4 in 24
towns | between that royal field of shrewsbury in 34
and westmerland and stafford fled the field; 1.01. 18
saw you the field? 1.01. 24
aiming at their safety, | fly from the field. 1.01.125
night in the windmill in saint george's field? 3.02.195 P
let us sway on and face them in the field. 4.01. 24
and sword and shield, | in bloody field, | doth H5 3.02. 10
more sharper than your swords, hie to the field! 3.05. 39
to purge this field of such a hilding foe; 4.02. 29
for our approach shall so much dare the field, 4.02. 36
bones, | ill–favoredly become the morning field. 4.02. 40
to the field! 4.02. 60
with rainy marching in the painful field; 4.03.111
we are enow yet living in the field | to smother 4.05. 19
all's not done — yet keep the french the field. 4.06. 2
as in this glorious and well–foughten field | we 4.06. 18
us, bid them come down, | or void the field; 4.07. 59
that we may wander o'er this bloody field | to 4.07. 72
to view the field in safety, and dispose | of 4.07. 82
your horsemen peer | and gallop o'er the field. 4.07. 86
then call we this the field of agincourt, 4.07. 90
thousand french | that in the field lie slain; 4.08. 81
and whilst a field should be dispatch'd and 1H6 1.01. 72
his sword did ne'er leave striking in the field. 1.04. 81
leap o'er the walls for refuge in the field. 2.02. 25
nails | shall pitch a field when we are dead. 3.01.103
dare ye come forth and meet us in the field? 3.02. 61
came to the field and vanquished his foes. 3.02. 96
but where's the great alcides of the field, 4.07. 60
me this once, that france may get the field. 5.03. 12
did he so often lodge in open field, | in 2H6 1.01. 80
the cardinal's not my better in the field. 1.03.110
by my faith, the field is honorable, and there 4.02. 50 P
tut, when struck'st thou one blow in the field? 4.07. 80 P
meet me to–morrow in saint george's field, | you 5.01. 46
to keep thee from the tempest of the field. 5.01.197
we are those which chas'd you from the field, 3H6 1.01. 90
if not, our swords shall plead it in the field. 1.01.103
when i return with victory /from the field 1.01.261
she shall not need, we'll meet her in the field. 1.02. 65
the army of the queen hath got the field. 1.04. 1
i think it cites us, brother, to the field, 2.01. 34
i would your highness would depart the field, 2.02. 73
head, | or bide the mortal fortune of the field? 2.02. 83
at saint albons field | this lady's husband, sir 3.02. 1
him, | while he himself keeps in the cold field? 4.03. 14
methinks the power that edward hath in field 4.08. 35
lords, to the field! 5.01.113
we, having now the best at barnet field, | will 5.03. 20
that stabb'd me in the field by tewksbury: R3 1.04. 56
who told me, in the field at tewksbury, | when 2.01.112
told me, when we both lay in the field | frozen 2.01.115
is in the field, and still his power increaseth. 4.03. 48
we must be brief when traitors brave the field. 4.03. 57
pitch our tent, even here in bosworth field. 5.03. 1
saddle white surrey for the field to–morrow. 5.03. 64
arm, arm, my lord, the foe vaunts in the field. 5.03.288
i think there be six richmonds in the field; 5.04. 11
lily, | that once was mistress of the field, and H8 3.01.152
her foes shake like a field of beaten corn, 5.04. 31
let him to field, troilus, alas, hath none. TRO 1.01. 5
what news, aeneas, from the field to–day? 1.01.108
was harness'd light, | and to the field goes he; 1.02. 9
hark, they are coming from the field. 1.02.177 P
excitements to the field, or speech for truce, 1.03.182
achilles will not to the field to–morrow. 2.03.162
they're come from the field. 3.01.148
ajax goes up and down the field, asking for 3.03.244 P
week by days, | did haunt you in the field. 4.01. 11
that swore to ride before him to the field. 4.04.142
come, come, to field with him. 4.04.143
be divided | by any voice or order of the field? 4.05. 70
i pray you let us see you in the field; 4.05.266
in what place of the field doth calchas keep? 4.05.278
there is a thousand hectors in the field: 5.05. 19
tail, | along the field i will the troyan trail. 5.08. 22
stand ho! yet are we masters of the field. 5.10. 1
sort, dragg'd through the shameful field. 5.10. 5
our army's in the field. COR 1.02. 17
are you lords a' th' field? 1.06. 47
if we lose the field, | we cannot keep the town. 1.07. 4
the treasure in this field achiev'd and city, 1.09. 33
trumpets shall | i' th' field prove flatterers, 1.09. 43
he prov'd best man i' th' field, and for his 2.02. 97
and till we call'd | both field and city ours, 2.02.121
his valiant sons | in coffins from the field, TIT 1.01. 35
knighted in field, slain manfully in arms, | in 1.01.196
marry, go before to field, he'll be your ROM 3.01. 58
upon the sweetest flower of all the field. 4.05. 29
alcibiades, your heart's in the field now. TIM 1.02. 73 P
the lands thou hast | lie in a pitch'd field. 1.02.225
on | upon the left hand of the even field. JC 5.01. 17
if you dare fight to–day, come to the field; 5.01. 65
and tell me what thou not'st about the field. 5.03. 22
and come, young cato, let us to the field. 5.03.107
i will proclaim my name about the field. 5.04. 3
so call the field to rest, and let's away, | to 5.05. 80
since his majesty went into the field, i have MAC 5.01. 4 P
ay, and brought off the field. 5.09. 10
such a sight as this | becomes the field, but HAM 5.02.402
when usurers tell their gold i' th' field, | and LR 3.02. 91
a little fire in a wild field were like an old 3.04.111 P
search every acre in the high–grown field, | and 4.04. 7
wife), | that never set a squadron in the field, OTH 1.01. 22
us'd | their dearest action in the tented field; 1.03. 85
of moving accidents by flood and field, | of 1.03.135
fulvia thy wife first came into the field. ANT 1.02. 88
time we twain | did show ourselves i' th' field, 1.04. 74
caesar and lepidus | are in the field, a mighty 2.01. 17
tie up the libertine in a field of feasts, 2.01. 23
of parthia | we have jaded out o' th' field. 3.01. 34
if from the field i shall return once more | to 3.13.173
antony | is come into the field. 4.06. 7
to th' field, to th' field! CYM 4.02. 42
to th' field, to th' field! 4.02. 42
resist are grown | the mortal bugs o' th' field. 5.03. 51
to be i' th' field, and ask "what news?" 5.03. 65
that without covering, save yon field of stars, PER 1.01. 37
him, if he i' th' blood–siz'd field lay swoll'n, TNK 1.01. 99
yet in the field to strike a battle for her; 2.02.252
run | swifter than wind upon a field of corn, 2.03. 77
in a field | that their crowns' titles tried. 3.01. 21
honor'd friend, | to you i give the field; 4.02.150
whose havoc in vast field | unearthed skulls 5.01. 51
are they i' th' field? 5.02.100
making my arms his field, his tent my bed. VEN 108
wrack to the seaman, tempest to the field, 454
they basely fly, and dare not stay the field. 894
venus' doves, doth challenge that fair field; LUC 58
which tarquin view'd in her fair face's field, 72
their brave hope, bold hector, march'd to field, 1430
and dig deep trenches in thy beauty's field, SON 2. 2

FIELD–BED 1 FR 0.0001 REL FR 1 V 0 P
this field–bed is too cold for me to sleep. ROM 2.01. 40

FIELD–DEW 1 FR 0.0001 REL FR 1 V 0 P
with this field–dew consecrate, | every fairy MND 5.01.415

FIELDED 1 FR 0.0001 REL FR 1 V 0 P
march from hence | to help our fielded friends! COR 1.04. 12

FIELD'S 1 FR 0.0001 REL FR 1 V 0 P
"the field's chief flower, sweet above compare, VEN 8

FIELDS 31 FR 0.0035 REL FR 26 V 5 P
and i will bring the doctor about by the fields. WIV 2.03. 78 P
go about the fields with me through frogmore, i 2.03. 86 P
welcome to the wide fields too base to be mine. LLL 2.01. 93 P
that won three fields of sultan solyman, | i MV 2.01. 26
in respect it is in the fields, it pleaseth me AYL 3.02. 17 P
shall furnish me to those italian fields | where AWW 2.03.290
a cock'red silken wanton, brave our fields, JN 5.01. 70
till twice five summers have enrich'd our fields R2 1.03.141
no more shall trenching war channel her fields, 1H4 1.01. 7
to chase these pagans in those holy fields, 1.01. 24
till fields, and blows, and groans applaud our 1.03.302
were strangely clamorous to the frighted fields. 3.01. 39
he doth fill fields with harness in the realm, 3.02.101
we will our youth lead on to higher fields, 2H4 4.04. 3
this cockpit hold | the vasty fields of france? H5 pr 12
and lie pavilion'd in the fields of france. 1.02.129
sharp as a pen, and 'a /babbl'd of green fields. 2.03. 17 P
fatal and neglected english | upon our fields. 2.04. 14
sweat drops of gallant youth in our rich fields! 3.05. 25
and a sweet retire | from off these fields, 4.03. 87
spoil'd your summer fields and fruitful vines, R3 5.02. 8
and give me swift transportance to these fields TRO 3.02. 11
glorious deeds, but in these fields of late, 3.03.188
the fields are fragrant and the woods are green. TIT 2.02. 2
the fields are near, and you are gallant grooms. 4.02.164
led by their master to the flow'red fields, 5.01. 15
and, this last night, here in philippi fields. JC 5.05. 19
ascension is | more sweet than our blest fields. CYM 5.04.117
and pecks of crows in the foul fields of thebes. TNK 1.01. 42
fame, | won in the fields of fruitful italy; LUC 107
that hills and valleys, dales and fields, | and PP 19. 3

/FIEND 5 FR 0.0005 REL FR 2 V 3 P
/fiend, /thou /torments /me /ere /i /come /to R2 4.01.270
this is the foul /fiend flibbertigibbet; LR 3.04.115 P
/the /foul /fiend /bites /my /back. 3.06. 17 P
/the /foul /fiend /haunts /poor /tom /in /the 3.06. 29 P
/howe'er /thou /art /a /fiend, | /a /woman's 4.02. 66

FIEND 61 FR 0.0069 REL FR 36 V 25 P
but one fiend at a time, | i'll fight their TMP 3.03.102
a fiend, a fairy, pitiless and rough; ERR 4.02. 35
avoid then, fiend! 4.03. 65
more company! the fiend is strong within him. 4.04.107
the fiend is at mine elbow and tempts me, saying MV 2.02. 2 P
well, the most courageous fiend bids me pack. 2.02. 10 P
says the fiend; 2.02. 11 P
says the fiend; 2.02. 11 P
rouse up a brave mind," says the fiend, "and run 2.02. 13 P
"bouge," says the fiend. 2.02. 20 P
"fiend," say i, "you counsel well." 2.02. 21 P
the jew, i should be rul'd by the fiend, who, 2.02. 26 P
the fiend gives the more friendly counsel: 2.02. 30 P
i will run, fiend; 2.02. 31 P
up, | signior baptista, for this fiend of hell, SHR 1.01. 88
why, he's a devil, a devil, a very fiend. 3.02.155
lo, how hollow the fiend speaks within him! TN 3.04. 91 P
the fiend is rough, and will not be roughly us'd 3.04.111 P
a fiend like thee might bear my soul to hell. 3.04.217
out, hyperbolical fiend! 4.02. 25 P
there is not yet so ugly a fiend of hell | as JN 4.03.123
the poison | is as a fiend confin'd to tyrannize 5.07. 47
three such enemies again as that fiend douglas, 1H4 2.04.368 P
no, let the fiend give fire. 2H4 2.04.182
the fiend hath prick'd down bardolph 2.04.332 P
and whatsoever cunning fiend it was | that H5 2.02.111
i think this talbot be a fiend of hell. 1H6 2.01. 46
scoff on, vile fiend and shameless courtezan! 3.02. 45
foul fiend of france, and hag of all despite, 3.02. 52
false fiend, avoid! 2H6 1.04. 40
o, beat away the busy meddling fiend | that lays 3.03. 21
what black magician conjures up this fiend | to R3 1.02. 34
accurs'd the offspring of so foul a fiend! TIT 4.02. 79
fiend angelical! ROM 3.02. 75
when thou didst bower the spirit of a fiend | in 3.02. 81
o most wicked fiend! 3.05.235
bring thou this fiend of scotland and myself; MAC 4.03.233
to doubt th' equivocation of the fiend | that 5.05. 42
thou marble–hearted fiend, | more hideous when LR 1.04.259
away, the foul fiend follows me! 3.04. 46 P
whom the foul fiend hath led through fire and 3.04. 52 P
tom some charity, whom the foul fiend vexes. 3.04. 61 P
take heed o' th' foul fiend. 3.04. 80 P
from lenders' books, and defy the foul fiend. 3.04. 98 P
fury of his heart, when the foul fiend rages, 3.04.131 P
peace, smulkin, peace, thou fiend! 3.04.141 P
how to prevent the fiend, and to kill vermin. 3.04.159 P
pray, innocent, and beware the foul fiend. 3.06. 8 P
bless thee, good man's son, from the foul fiend! 4.01. 58 P
proper deformity /shows not in the fiend | so 4.02. 60
it was some fiend; 4.06. 72
often 'twould say, | "the fiend, the fiend!" 4.06. 79
often 'twould say, | "the fiend, the fiend!" 4.06. 79
o most delicate fiend! CYM 5.05. 47
ay, so thou dost, | italian fiend! 5.05.210
hold'st a place for which the pained'st fiend PER 4.06.163
and whether that my angel be turn'd fiend, PP 2. 9
harbinger, | foul precurrer of the fiend, PHT 6
and whether that my angel be turn'd fiend SON 144. 9
who like a fiend | from heaven to hell is flown 145.11
the naked and concealed fiend he cover'd, | that LC 317

FIEND–LIKE 2 FR 0.0002 REL FR 2 V 0 P
this growing image of thy fiend–like face? TIT 5.01. 45
of this dead butcher and his fiend–like queen, MAC 5.09. 35

FIEND'S 1 FR 0.0001 REL FR 1 V 0 P
'tis the spite of hell, the fiend's arch–mock, OTH 4.01. 70

FIENDS' 1 FR 0.0001 REL FR 1 V 0 P
the gods inherit, | beneath is all the fiends': LR 4.06.127

/FIENDS 1 FR 0.0001 REL FR 0 V 1 P
/five /fiends /have /been /in /poor /tom /at LR 4.01. 58 P

FIENDS 13 FR 0.0014 REL FR 12 V 1 P
they are devils' additions, the names of fiends; WIV 2.02.299 P
floods o'erswell, and fiends for food howl on! H5 2.01. 93
arrayed in flames like to the prince of fiends, 3.03. 16
a legion of foul fiends | environ'd me, and R3 1.04. 58
gapes, hell burns, fiends roar, saints pray, 4.04. 75
with the spleen | of all the under fiends. COR 4.05. 92
a thousand fiends, a thousand hissing snakes, TIT 2.03.100
and be these juggling fiends no more believ'd, MAC 5.08. 19
the hill of heaven | as low as to the fiends!" HAM 2.02.497
from heaven, | and fiends will snatch at it. OTH 5.02.275
and all the fiends of hell | divide themselves CYM 2.04.129
or else | thou art straightway with the fiends. 3.05. 83
beauty hath nought to do with such foul fiends. VEN 638

FIERCE 41 FR 0.0046 REL FR 41 V 0 P
with all the fierce endeavor of your wit | to LLL 5.02.853
there is no following her in this fierce vein. MND 3.02. 82
and though she be but little, she is fierce. 3.02.325
but as the fierce vexation of a dream. 4.01. 69
the proud control of fierce and bloody war, | to JN 1.01. 17
with ladies' faces and fierce dragons' spleens, 2.01. 68
such temperate order in so fierce a cause, 3.04. 12
even with the fierce looks of these bloody men. 4.01. 73
that mercy which fierce fire and iron extends, 4.01.119
hearts | to fierce and bloody inclination. 5.02.158
fierce extremes | in their continuance will not 5.07. 13
his rash fierce blaze of riot cannot last, | for R2 2.01. 33
in war was never lion rag'd more fierce, | in 2.01.173
thy fierce hand | hath with the king's blood 5.05.109
for england his approaches makes as fierce | as H5 2.04. 9
therefore in fierce tempest is he coming, | in 2.04. 99
when down the hill he holds his fierce career? 3.03. 23
than midday sun fierce bent against their faces. 1H6 1.01. 14
such fierce alarums both of hope and fear, | as 5.05. 85
for he is fierce and cannot brook hard language. 2H6 4.09. 45

no beast so fierce but knows some touch of pity. R3 1.02. 71
what had he | to do in these fierce vanities? H8 1.01. 54
fierce to their skill, and to their fierceness TRO 1.01. 8
the fierce polydamas | hath beat down menon; 5.05. 6
wish, not fierce and terrible | only in strokes, COR 1.04. 57
would i | wash my fierce hand in 's heart. 1.10. 27
but fierce andronicus would not relent. TIT 2.03.165
more fierce and more inexorable far | than empty ROM 5.03. 38
o, the fierce wretchedness that glory brings us! TIM 4.02. 30
fierce fiery warriors fight upon the clouds | in JC 2.02. 19
domestic fury and fierce civil strife | shall 3.01.263
more composition and fierce quality | than doth, LR 1.02. 12
beget opinion | of my more fierce endeavor. 2.01. 34
her eyes are fierce, but thine | do comfort, and 2.04.172
nor thy fierce sister | in his anointed flesh 3.07. 57
yet have i fierce affections, and think | what ANT 1.05. 17
this fierce abridgment | hath to it CYM 5.05.382
although assail'd with fortune fierce and keen, PER 5.03. 88
or what fierce sulphur else, to this end made, TNK 5.04. 64
the keen teeth from the fierce tiger's /jaws, SON 19. 3
or some fierce thing replete with too much rage, 23. 3
FIERCELY 1 FR 0.0001 REL FR 1 V 0 P
battles join'd, and both sides fiercely fought; 3H6 2.01.121
FIERCENESS 4 FR 0.0004 REL FR 3 V 1 P
it sorts well with your fierceness. H5 4.01. 63 P
they call'd us for our fierceness english dogs, 1H6 1.05. 25
to their skill, and to their fierceness valiant, TRO 1.01. 8
the breath of tigers, yea, the fierceness too, TNK 5.01. 40
FIERCEST 1 FR 0.0001 REL FR 1 V 0 P
to call the fiercest tyrant from his rage, | and TNK 5.01. 78
/FIERY 2 FR 0.0002 REL FR 2 V 0 P
from forth day's path and titan's /fiery wheels. ROM 2.03. 4
must send thee hence | /with /fiery /quickness; HAM 4.03. 43
FIERY 49 FR 0.0055 REL FR 47 V 2 P
the delighted spirit | to bathe in fiery floods, MM 3.01.121
alas, how fiery, and how sharp, he looks! ERR 4.04. 50
out | such fiery numbers as the prompting eyes LLL 4.03.319
with eyes best seeing, heaven's fiery eye, | by 5.02.375
but i might see young cupid's fiery shaft MND 2.01.161
and light them at the fiery glow-worm's eyes, 3.01.170
than all yon fiery oes and eyes of light. 3.02.188
even till the eastern gate, all fiery red, 3.02.391
how fiery and forward our pedant is! SHR 3.01. 48
bring | their fiery torcher his diurnal ring, AWW 2.01.162
bound and high curvet | of mars's fiery steed. 2.03.283
land, | rash, inconsiderate, fiery voluntaries, JN 2.01. 67
you equal potents, fiery kindled spirits! 2.01.358
and quench /his fiery indignation | even in the 4.01. 63
and cull'd these fiery spirits from the world, 5.02.114
sun | from out the fiery portal of the east, R2 3.03. 64
mounted upon a hot and fiery steed, | which his 5.02. 8
the front of heaven was full of fiery shapes 1H4 3.01. 14
the front of heaven was full of fiery shapes, 3.01. 37
the clouds | to turn and wind a fiery pegasus, 4.01.109
and look whether the fiery trigon, his man, be 2H4 2.04.265 P
full of nimble, fiery, and delectable shapes, 4.03.100 P
thinks thou the fiery fever will go out | with H5 4.01.253
hath thy fiery heart so parch'd thine entrails 3H6 1.04. 87
with fiery eyes sparkling for very wrath, | and 2.05.131
that phaeton should check thy fiery steeds, 2.06. 12
then fiery expedition be my wing, | jove's R3 4.03. 54
and by the bright tract of his fiery car | gives 5.03. 20
inspire us with the spleen of fiery dragons! 5.03.350
mars | beck'ning with fiery truncheon my retire, TRO 5.03. 53
follow thine enemy in a fiery gulf | than COR 3.02. 91
strike the proud cedars 'gainst the fiery sun, 5.03. 60
in the instant came | the fiery tybalt, with his ROM 1.01.109
looks with such ferret and such fiery eyes | as JC 1.02.186
hand, | most bloody, fiery, and most terrible. 1.03.130
fierce fiery warriors fight upon the clouds | in 2.02. 19
the flash and outbreak of a fiery mind, | a HAM 2.01. 33
i' th' darkest night, | stick fiery off indeed. 5.02.257
lord, | you know the fiery quality of the duke, LR 2.04. 92
"fiery"? 2.04. 96
"fiery"? 2.04.104
the fiery duke? 2.04.104
of heaven, | more fiery by night's blackness; ANT 1.04. 13
the fiery orbs above and the twinn'd stones CYM 1.06. 35
and feel our fiery horses | like proud seas TNK 2.02. 19
body | and fiery mind illustrate a brave father. 2.05. 22
of what a fiery sparkle and quick sweetness, 4.02. 13
red cheeks and fiery eyes blaze forth her wrong; VEN 219
shall neigh (no dull flesh) in his fiery race, SON 51.11
FIERY-FOOTED 1 FR 0.0001 REL FR 1 V 0 P
gallop apace, you fiery-footed steeds, | towards ROM 3.02. 1
FIERY-POINTED 1 FR 0.0001 REL FR 1 V 0 P
look as the fair and fiery-pointed sun, LUC 372
FIERY-RED 1 FR 0.0001 REL FR 1 V 0 P
bloody with spurring, fiery-red with haste. R2 2.03. 58
FIFE* 10 FR 0.0011 REL FR 8 V 2 P
was no music with him but the drum and the fife, ADO 2.03. 14 P
and the vile squealing of the wry-neck'd fife, MV 2.05. 30
took | mordake earl of fife and eldest son | to 1H4 1.01. 71
i shall have none but mordake earl of fife. 1.01. 95
from fife, great king, | where the norweyan MAC 1.02. 48
no, cousin, i'll to fife. 2.04. 36
beware macduff, | beware the thane of fife. 4.01. 72
seize upon fife, give to th' edge o' th' sword 4.01.151
the thane of fife had a wife; 5.01. 42 P
the spirit-stirring drum, th' ear-piercing fife, OTH 3.03.352
FIFES 1 FR 0.0001 REL FR 1 V 0 P
the trumpets, sackbuts, psalteries, and fifes, COR 5.04. 49
/FIFT 1 FR 0.0001 REL FR 1 V 0 P
that hector, by the /fift hour of the sun, TRO 2.01.122
FIFT 26 FR 0.0029 REL FR 19 V 7 P
or the fift, if i. LLL 5.01. 54 P
and there is a forerunner come from a fift, the MV 1.02.125 P
if i could bid the fift welcome with so good 1.02.127 P
the fift, the countercheck quarrelsome; AYL 5.04. 95 P
or fourth, or fift borough, i'll answer him by SHR in.1. 13 P
and the fift did whirl about | the other four in JN 4.02.183
harry the fift is crown'd! 2H4 4.05.119
for the fift harry from curb'd license plucks 4.05.130
harry the fourth, or fift? 5.03.114
king henry the fift, too famous to live long! 1H6 1.01. 6
henry the fift, thy ghost i invocate: 1.01. 52
henry the fift he first train'd to the wars; 1.04. 79
long after this, when henry the fift 2.05. 82
which in the time of henry nam'd the fift | was 3.01.195
ever-living man of memory, | henry the fift. 4.03. 52
verified | henry the fift did sometime prophesy: 5.01. 31
the fift was edmund langley, duke of york; 2H6 2.02. 15
to edmund langley, edward the third's fift /son, 2.02. 46
for his father's sake, henry the fift (in whose 4.02.157 P
henry the fift, that made all france to quake, 4.08. 17
is cade the son of henry the fift, | that thus 4.08. 34
the name of henry the fift hales them to an 4.08. 57 P
i am the son of henry the fift, | who made the 3H6 1.01.107
and after that wise prince, henry the fift, 3.03. 85
lost | all that which henry the fift had gotten? 3.03. 90
the fift, an hand environed with clouds, PER 2.02. 36
FIFTEEN 17 FR 0.0019 REL FR 11 V 6 P
hadst thou not fifteen pence? WIV 2.02. 14
a blind bitch's puppies, fifteen i' th' litter; 3.05. 11 P
alas, fifteen wives is nothing! MV 2.02.161 P
these fifteen years you have been in a dream, SHR in.2. 79
these fifteen years! in.2. 81
and slept above some fifteen year or more. in.2. 113
my life, amounts not to fifteen thousand pole, AWW 4.03.167 P
it is fifteen years since i saw my country; WT 4.02. 4 P
fifteen hundred shorn, what comes the wool to? 4.03. 33 P
twice fifteen thousand hearts of england's breed JN 2.01.275
no, fifteen hundred foot, five hundred horse, 2H4 2.01.173
full fifteen earls and fifteen hundred knights, H5 1.01. 13
full fifteen earls and fifteen hundred knights, 1.01. 13
english lie within fifteen hundred paces of your 3.07.126 P
full fifteen hundred, besides common men. 4.08. 79
sir, march is wasted fifteen days. JC 2.01. 59
driven to | when fifteen once has found us! TNK 2.04. 7
FIFTEENS 1 FR 0.0001 REL FR 0 V 1 P
he that made us pay one and twenty fifteens, and 2H6 4.07. 22 P
FIFTEENTH 1 FR 0.0001 REL FR 1 V 0 P
that suffolk should demand a whole fifteenth 2H6 1.01.133
FIFTH *(see fift, etc.)*
FIFT'S 1 FR 0.0001 REL FR 1 V 0 P
harry the fift's the man. 2H4 5.03.117
FIFTY 31 FR 0.0035 REL FR 10 V 21 P
make you a hundred and fifty pounds jointure. WIV 3.04. 48 P
yes, your beggar of fifty; MM 3.02.126 P
sore, then l to sore makes fifty sores o' sorel: LLL 4.02. 60
might shake off fifty, looking in her eye: 4.03.239
i will kill thee a hundred and fifty ways: AYL 5.01. 57 P
have as many diseases as two and fifty horses. SHR 1.02. 81 P
spurio, a hundred and fifty; AWW 4.03.162 P
lodowick, and gratii, two hundred fifty each; 4.03.164 P
vaumond, bentii, two hundred fifty each; 4.03.165 P
are germane to him (though remov'd fifty times) WT 4.04.774 P
but if i fought not with fifty of them, i am a 1H4 2.04.186 P
not two or three and fifty upon poor old jack, 2.04.187 P
and, as i think, his age some fifty, or, by'r 2.04.424 P
in exchange of a hundred and fifty soldiers, 4.02. 14 P
i had a hundred and fifty totter'd prodigals 4.02. 34 P
not three of my hundred and fifty left alive, 5.03. 37 P
and northumberland | are fifty thousand strong. 2H4 3.01. 96
reclaim'd | to your obedience fifty fortresses, 1H6 3.04. 6
the turk, that two and fifty kingdoms hath, 4.07. 73
"here's but two and fifty hairs on your chin — TRO 1.02.157 P
"two and fifty hairs," quoth he, "and one white. 1.02.161 P
let the request be fifty talents. TIM 2.02.193 P
great and instant occasion to use fifty talents, 3.01. 19 P
he cannot want fifty — five hundred talents. 3.02. 38
mine, fifty talents. 3.04. 93 P
forty, fifty, a hundred ducats a-piece for his HAM 2.02.365 P
what, fifty of my followers at a clap? LR 1.04.294
and fifty men dismiss'd? 2.04.207
what, fifty followers? 2.04.237
thy fifty yet doth double five and twenty, | and 2.04.259
let me have a child at fifty, to whom herod of ANT 1.02. 28 P
FIFTY-FIVE 1 FR 0.0001 REL FR 0 V 1 P
that's fifty-five year ago. 2H4 3.02.210 P
FIFTYFOLD 1 FR 0.0001 REL FR 0 V 1 P
him laughing to his grave, fiftyfold a cuckold! ANT 1.02. 67 P
FIG* *(see fico, figo)*
FIG* 6 FR 0.0006 REL FR 4 V 2 P
will | give it a plum, a cherry, and a fig. JN 2.01.162
this, and fig me like | the bragging spaniard. 2H4 5.03.118
the fig of spain. H5 3.06. 59
and i'll pledge you all, and a fig for peter! 2H6 2.03. 67 P
a fig! OTH 1.03.319 P
and these fig leaves | have slime upon them, ANT 5.02.351
/FIGHT 3 FR 0.0003 REL FR 3 V 0 P
/shadows /and /the /shows /of /men, /to /fight; 2H4 1.01.193
/and /they /did /fight /with /queasiness, 1.01.196
the painful warrior famoused for /fight, | after SON 25. 9
FIGHT 261 FR 0.0295 REL FR 224 V 37 P
at a time, | i'll fight their legions o'er. TMP 3.03.103
repent, | but yet i slew him manfully in fight, TGV 4.01. 28
light, | with all his might | for thee to fight, WIV 2.01. 18
i had rather hear them scold than fight. 2.01.232 P
to see thee fight, to see thee foin, to see thee 2.03. 24 P
if you should fight, you go against the hair of 2.03. 40 P
warrant you, he's the man should fight with him. 3.01. 68 P
and yet my nature never in the fight | to do in MM 1.03. 42
and counsel him to fight against his passion, ADO 3.01. 83
be friends with me than fight with mine enemy. 4.01.298 P
— be to me, and every man that dares not fight! LLL 1.01.228 P
so breathed, that certain he would fight, yea, 5.02.653
i will not fight with a pole like a northren man 5.02.694 P
we cannot fight for love, as men may do. MND 2.01.241
thou seest these lovers seek a place to fight; 3.02.354
i view the fight than thou that mak'st the fray. MV 3.02. 62
any thing so sudden but the fight of two rams, AYL 5.02. 30 P
you go so much backward when you fight. AWW 1.01.200 P
me the count's youth to fight with him, hurt him TN 3.02. 35 P
sir, he will fight with you for 's oath sake. 3.04.297 P
no, my lord, i'll fight. WT 1.02.162
against this cruelty fight on thy side, | poor 2.03.191
you denied to fight with me this other day, 5.02.128 P
the aweless lion could not wage the fight, | nor JN 1.01.266
to parley or to fight, therefore prepare. 2.01. 78
then after fight who shall be king of it? 2.01.400
thou fortune's champion that dost never fight 3.01.118
and, like a dog that is compell'd to fight, 4.01.115
the french fight coldly, and retire themselves. 5.03. 13
not light, | if i be traitor or unjustly fight! R2 1.01. 83
our cousin herford and fell mowbray fight. 1.02. 46
me — | and as i truly fight, defend me heaven! 1.03. 25
me — | and as i truly fight, defend me heaven! 1.03. 41
right, | so be thy fortune in this royal fight! 1.03. 56
against a bird, do i with mowbray fight. 1.03. 62
gentle and as jocund as to jest | go i to fight: 1.03. 96
and dares him to set forward to the fight. 1.03.109
to fight with glendower and his complices. 3.01. 43
then if angels fight, | weak men must fall, for 3.02. 61
and so your follies fight against yourself. 3.02.182
and be slain — no worse can come to fight, 3.02.183
and fight and die is death destroying death, 3.02.184
no, good my lord, let's fight with gentle words, 3.03.131
cross | we are impressed and engag'd to fight — 1H4 1.01. 21
leading the men of /herfordshire to fight 1.01. 39
third, if he fight longer than he sees reason, 1.02.185 P
but i remember, when the fight was done, | when 1.03. 30
the lives of those that he did lead to fight 1.03. 82
slain, | and all the currents of a heady fight; 2.03. 55
as thou hast done, and then say it was in fight! 2.04.262 P
he would make you believe it was done in fight, 2.04.307 P
spleen, | to fight against me under percy's pay, 3.02.126
we'll fight with him to-night. 4.03. 1
side, | try fortune with him in a single fight. 5.01.100
and, nephew, challeng'd you to single fight. 5.02. 46
to fight with glendower and the earl of march. 5.05. 40
the very same day did i fight with one samson 2H4 3.02. 32 P
the manner and true order of the fight | this 4.04.100
while that the armed hand doth fight abroad, H5 1.02.178
i dare not fight, but i will wink and hold out 2.01. 7 P
they will eat like wolves and fight like devils. 3.07.151 P
have only stomachs to eat and none to fight. 3.07.154 P
and yet i determine to fight lustily for him. 4.01.189 P
ay, he said so, to make us fight cheerfully; 4.01.192 P
horses provender, | and after fight with them? 4.02. 59
fight valiantly to-day! 4.03. 12
that he which hath no stomach to this fight, 4.03. 35
more help, could fight this royal battle! 4.03. 75
if they will fight with us, bid them come down, 4.07. 58
'tis the gage of one that i should fight withal, 4.07.123 P
give me my steeled coat, i'll fight for france. 1H6 1.01. 85
bedford, if thou be slack, i'll fight it out. 1.01. 99
i must inform you of a dismal fight | betwixt 1.01.105
more than three hours the fight continued, 1.01.120
recreants, | fight till the last gasp; 1.02.127
what she says i'll confirm. we'll fight it out. 1.02.128
i myself fight not once in forty year. 1.03. 91
hark, countrymen, either renew the fight, | or 1.05. 27
'tis thought, lord talbot, when the fight began, 2.02. 22
broil, | and set this unaccustom'd fight aside. 3.01. 93
we and our wives and children all will fight, 3.01.100
will ye, like soldiers, come and fight it out? 3.02. 66
let this dissension first be tried by fight, 4.01.116
and strong enough to issue out and fight. 4.02. 20
prosper our colors in this dangerous fight! 4.02. 56
burdeaux with his power | to fight with talbot. 4.03. 5
york set him on to fight and die in shame, 4.04. 8
to fight i will, but not to fly the foe. 4.05. 37
and leave my followers here to fight and die? 4.05. 45
fight, soldiers, fight! 4.06. 1
fight, soldiers, fight! 4.06. 1
and had the maidenhood | of thy first fight, i 4.06. 18
if thou wilt fight, fight by thy father's side, 4.06. 56
if thou wilt fight, fight by thy father's side, 4.06. 56
french, | he left me proudly, as unworthy fight. 4.07. 43
alas, my lord, i cannot fight; 2H6 1.03.213 P
i shall never be able to fight a blow. 1.03.216 P
sirrah, or you must fight, or else be hang'd. 1.03.217
so please your highness to behold the fight. 2.03. 51
or more afraid to fight, than is the appellant, 2.03. 57
fight for credit of the prentices. 2.03. 71 P
the lives of those which we have lost in fight 4.01. 21
fight for your king, your country, and your 4.05. 11
come, then, let's go fight with them. 4.06. 13 P
my foot shall fight with all the strength thou 4.10. 50
o, i could hew up rocks and fight with flint, 5.01. 24
and fight against that monstrous rebel cade, 5.01. 62
clifford, i say, come forth and fight with me. 5.02. 5
you'll nor fight nor fly. 5.02. 74
let's fight it out, and not stand cavilling thus 3H6 1.01.117
lord clifford vows to fight in thy defense. 1.01.160
fight it out!" 1.04. 10
so cowards fight when they can fly no further, 1.04. 40
but all in vain, they had no heart to fight, 2.01.135
you were, | making another head to fight again. 2.01.141
be it with resolution then to fight. 2.02. 77
and hearten those that fight in your defense. 2.02. 79
for god's sake, lords, give signal to the fight. 2.02.100
this man whom hand to hand i slew in fight | may 2.05. 56
bear thee hence, and let them fight that will, 2.05.121
fight closer or, good faith, you'll catch a blow 3.02. 23
why shall we fight if you pretend no title? 4.07. 57
by this i challenge him to single fight. 4.07. 75
warwick, wilt thou leave the town, and fight? 5.01.107
and, as we hear, march on to fight with us. 5.03. 9
and he that will not fight for such a hope | go 5.04. 55
lords, for edward is at hand, | ready to fight; 5.04. 61
give signal to the fight, and to it, lords! 5.04. 72
you fight in justice; 5.04. 81
be valiant, and give signal to the fight. 5.04. 82
to fight on edward's party for the crown, | and R3 1.03.137
thou didst receive the sacrament to fight | in 1.04.203
the mighty warwick and did fight for me? 2.01.111
my prayers on the adverse party fight, | and 4.04.191
in arms, | if not to fight with foreign enemies, 4.04.529
men, | to fight against this guilty homicide. 5.02. 18
of butchered princes fight in thy behalf. 5.03.122
arm, fight, and conquer for fair england's sake! 5.03.158
god and good angels fight on richmond's side, 5.03.175
god and our good cause fight upon our side; 5.03.240
those whom we fight against | had rather have us 5.03.243
then if you fight against god's enemy, | god 5.03.253
if you do fight against your country's foes, 5.03.257
if you do fight in safeguard of your wives, 5.03.259
fight, gentlemen of england! 5.03.338
fight, bold yeomen! 5.03.338
truth with such a show | as fool and fight is, H8 pr 19
at a playhouse and fight for bitten apples, that 5.03. 61 P
i cannot fight upon this argument; TRO 1.01. 92

can helenus fight, uncle? 1.02.222 P
yes, he'll fight indifferent well. 1.02.223 P
ajax draw | the sort to fight with hector; 1.03.375
of helen's needle, for whom he comes to fight. 2.01. 81 P
the weakest spleen | to fight for and maintain! 2.02.129
well may we fight for her whom, we know well, 2.02.161
you must prepare to fight without achilles. 2.03.227
but he that disciplin'd thine arms to fight, 2.03.244
you shall fight your hearts out ere i part you 3.02. 51 P
o virtuous fight, | when right with right wars 3.02.171
know my mind, i'll fight no more 'gainst troy. 3.03. 56
shall ajax fight with hector? 3.03.225
he must fight singly to–morrow with hector, and 3.03.247 P
aeneas | consent upon the order of their fight, 4.05. 90
i am not warm yet, let us fight again. 4.05.118
this white beard, i'd fight with thee to–morrow. 4.05.209
within my soul there doth conduce a fight | of 5.02.147
unarm, unarm, and do not fight to–day. 5.03. 3
now, young man, meanest thou to fight to–day? 5.03. 29
troilus, i would not have you fight to–day. 5.03. 50
we'll forth and fight, | do deeds worth praise, 5.03. 92
i'll fight with him alone. stand, diomed. 5.06. 9
turn, slave, and fight. 5.07. 13 P
if the son of a whore fight for a whore, he 5.07. 21 P
lean upon one crutch, and fight with t' other, COR 1.01.242
and fight | with hearts more proof than shields. 1.04. 24
slaves, | ere yet the fight be done, pack up. 1.05. 8
been too violent for | a second course of fight. 1.05. 16
to aufidius thus | i will appear, and fight. 1.05. 20
shall bear the business in some other fight, 1.06. 82
i'll fight with none but thee, for i do hate 1.08. 1
rome, that all alone martius did fight | within 2.01.162
whom with all praise i point at, saw him fight, 2.02. 90
for i will fight | against my cank'red country 4.05. 90
run away till i am bigger, but then i'll fight. 5.03.128
and, romans, fight for freedom in your choice. TIT 1.01. 17
if to fight for king and commonweal | were piety 1.01.114
o lord, they fight! i will go call the watch. ROM 5.03. 71
and slain in fight many of your enemies. TIM 3.05. 63
fierce fiery warriors fight upon the clouds | in JC 2.02. 19
it is a creature that i teach to fight, | to 4.01. 31
if you dare fight to–day, come to the field; 5.01. 65
night | we shall try fortune in a second fight. 5.03.110
thy personal venture in the rebels' fight, | his MAC 1.03. 91
against the undivulg'd pretense i fight | of 2.03.131
and let them fight | against the churches; 4.01. 52
the most diminutive of birds, will fight, | her 4.02. 10
would create soldiers, make our women fight, 4.03.187
i'll fight, till from my bones my flesh be 5.03. 32
let us be beaten, if we cannot fight. 5.06. 8
fly, | but bear–like i must fight the course. 5.07. 2
the tyrant's people on both sides do fight, 5.07. 25
i'll not fight with thee. 5.08. 22
fight for a plot | whereon the numbers cannot HAM 4.04. 62
i will fight with him upon this theme | until my 5.01.266
woo't weep, woo't fight, woo't fast, woo't tear 5.01.275
to fear judgment, to fight when i cannot choose, LR 1.04. 16 P
before you fight the battle, ope this letter. 5.01. 40
were it my cue to fight, i should have known it OTH 1.02. 83
were we before our armies, and to fight, | i ANT 2.02. 26
and we shall talk before we fight. 2.06. 2
i have seen thee fight, | when i have envied thy 2.06. 74
we came hither to fight with you. 2.06.102 P
canidius, we | will fight with him by sea. 3.07. 28
so hath my lord dar'd him to single fight. 3.07. 30
i'll fight at sea. 3.07. 48
o noble emperor, do not fight by sea, | trust 3.07. 61
how appears the fight? 3.10. 8
i' th' midst o' th' fight, | when vantage like a 3.10. 11
leaving the fight in heighth, flies after her. 3.10. 20
hearted, breath'd, | and fight maliciously; 3.13.178
the next time i do fight, | i'll make death love 3.13.191
the last of many battles | we mean to fight. 4.01. 12
he will not fight with me, domitius? 4.02. 1
soldier, | by sea and land i'll fight; 4.02. 5
woo't thou fight well? 4.02. 7
you that will fight, | follow me close, i'll 4.04. 33
determine this great war in single fight! 4.04. 37
had once prevail'd | to make me fight at land! 4.05. 3
go forth, agrippa, and begin the fight. 4.06. 1
i fight against thee? 4.06. 36
i would they'ld fight i' th' fire or i' th' air; 4.10. 3
we'ld fight there too. 4.10. 4
or, like the parthian, i shall flying fight — CYM 1.06. 20
they dare not fight with me because of the queen 2.01. 19 P
and to fight | against my lady's kingdom. 5.01. 18
so i'll fight | against the part i come with; 5.01. 24
stand, stand, and fight! 5.02. 13
fight i will no more, | but yield me to the 5.03. 76
and then they fight like compell'd bears, would TNK 3.01. 68
that i lay fatting like a swine, to fight, | and 3.06. 12
i perceive | you would fain be at that fight. 3.06. 60
will you fight bare–arm'd? 3.06. 63
fight bravely, cousin. 3.06.101
decider of all injuries, | say, "fight again!" 3.06.154
every day | they'ld fight about you; 3.06.221
lady, you shall see men fight now. 4.02.143
and, as the gods regard ye, fight with justice. 5.01. 15
we'll go with you, | i will not lose the fight. 5.02.103
for mast'ring her that foil'd the god of fight! VEN 114
but in one minute's fight brings beauty under; 746
teaching them thus to use it in the fight, LUC 62
yet their ambition makes them still to fight, 68
leaden slumber with live's strength doth fight, 124
and extreme fear can neither fight nor fly, 230
flesh being proud, desire doth fight with grace, 712
conceit and grief an eager combat fight, | what 1298
as 'twere encouraging the greeks to fight, 1402
combat doubtful, that love with love did fight, PP 15. 5
like a thousand vanquish'd men in bloody fight! 17.24
crooked eclipses 'gainst his glory fight, | and SON 60. 7
upon thy side against myself i'll fight, | and 88. 3
FIGHTER 4 FR 0.0004 REL FR 1 V 3 P
you have yourself been a great fighter, though WIV 2.03. 43 P
i am no fighter. TN 3.04.242 P
i must confess to you, sir, i am no fighter. WT 4.03.107 P
a feast | fits a dull fighter and a keen guest. 1H4 4.02. 80
FIGHTEST 1 FR 0.0001 REL FR 1 V 0 P
and fightest with the sword of deborah. 1H6 1.02.105
FIGHTETH 1 FR 0.0001 REL FR 1 V 0 P
he fighteth as one weary of his life. 1H6 1.02. 26
FIGHTING 14 FR 0.0015 REL FR 11 V 3 P
ancientry, stealing, fighting — hark you now! WT 3.03. 63 P
thou shalt have twelve thousand fighting men! R2 3.02. 70
wilt thou leave fighting a' days and foining a' 2H4 2.04.232 P
of fighting men they have full threescore H5 4.03. 3
thrice up again, and fighting; 4.06. 5
there's some among you have beheld me fighting; COR 3.01.223
and yours, close fighting ere i did approach. ROM 1.01.107
o, step between her and her fighting soul. HAM 3.04.113
in my heart there was a kind of fighting | that 5.02. 4
on the earth, | and fighting foot to foot. ANT 3.07. 66
every jack slave hath his bellyful of fighting, CYM 2.01. 20 P
to note the fighting conflict of her hue, | how VEN 345
like straggling slaves for pillage fighting, LUC 428
encamp'd in hearts, but fighting outwardly. LC 203
FIGHTS 16 FR 0.0018 REL FR 13 V 3 P
up with your fights; WIV 2.02.136
where one on his side fights, thousands will fly R2 2.02.147
means whereof 'a faces it out, but fights not. H5 3.02. 33 P
his horse is slain, and all on foot he fights, R3 5.04. 4
pertaining thereunto, as fights and fireworks, H8 1.03. 27
now here he fights on galathe his horse | and TRO 5.05. 20
fights dragon–like, and does achieve as soon COR 4.07. 23
successful in the battles that he fights, | with TIT 1.01. 66
he fights as you sing prick–song, keeps time, ROM 2.04. 20 P
villain, that fights by the book of arithmetic! 3.01.102 P
which in the scuffles of great fights hath burst ANT 1.01. 7
/on reason, | it eats the sword it fights with. 3.13.199
to all the under world the loves and fights | of TNK 4.02. 24
he has felt | without doubt what he fights for, 4.02. 97
his red lips, after fights, are fit for ladies. 4.02.111
the coward fights, and will not be dismay'd. LUC 273
FIGHT'ST 2 FR 0.0002 REL FR 2 V 0 P
then, thou fight'st against thy countrymen | and 1H6 3.03. 74
nobly, york, 'tis for a crown thou fight'st. 2H6 5.02. 16
FIGO *(also fico)*
FIGO 2 FR 0.0002 REL FR 2 V 0 P
die and be damn'd! and figo for thy friendship! H5 3.06. 57
the figo for thee then! 4.01. 60
FIGS 4 FR 0.0004 REL FR 3 V 1 P
with purple grapes, green figs, and mulberries; MND 3.01.167
o, excellent, i love long life better than figs. ANT 1.02. 32 P
he brings you figs. 5.02.235
a simple countryman, that brought her figs. 5.02.339
FIG'S–END 1 FR 0.0001 REL FR 0 V 1 P
bless'd fig's–end! OTH 2.01.251 P
FIGUR'D 4 FR 0.0004 REL FR 4 V 0 P
figur'd quite o'er with burning meteors. JN 5.02. 53
gown, | my figur'd goblets for a dish of wood, R2 3.03.150
'tis figur'd in my tongue. R3 1.02.193
which hath not figur'd to thee my true spirit? SON 108. 2
/FIGURE 1 FR 0.0001 REL FR 1 V 0 P
/when /we /see /the /figure /of /the /house, 2H4 1.03. 43
FIGURE 45 FR 0.0050 REL FR 34 V 11 P
bravely the figure of this harpy hast thou TMP 3.03. 83
to yourself; why, she woos you by a figure. TGV 2.01.148 P
what figure? 2.01.149 P
this weak impress of love is as a figure 3.02. 6
by spells, by th' figure, and such daub'ry as WIV 4.02.177 P
what figure of us think you he will bear? MM 1.01. 16
before so noble and so great a figure | be 1.01. 49
doing, in the figure of a lamb, the feats of a ADO 1.01. 14 P
a most fine figure! LLL 1.02. 55 P
what is the figure? what is the figure? 5.01. 64 P
what is the figure? what is the figure? 5.01. 64 P
his power | to leave the figure or disfigure it. MND 1.01. 51
wings, and no eyes, figure unheedy haste; 1.01.237
a coin that bears the figure of an angel MV 2.07. 56
there i shall see mine own figure. AYL 3.02.289 P
for it is a figure in rhetoric that drink, being 5.01. 41 P
a little, he will throw a figure in her face, SHR 1.02.114 P
man | that the great figure of a council frames AWW 3.01. 12
resolveth from his figure 'gainst the fire? JN 5.04. 25
them, | and shall the figure of god's majesty, R2 4.01.125
whose white investments figure innocence, | the 2H4 4.01. 45
since a crooked figure may | attest in little H5 pr 15
poor key–cold figure of a holy king, | pale R3 1.02. 5
whose figure even this instant cloud puts on H8 1.01.225
aim | and that unbodied figure of the thought TRO 1.03. 16
is seen | the baby figure of the giant mass | of 1.03.345
and renders back | his figure and his heat. 3.03.123
there shall no figure at such rate be set | as ROM 5.03.301
our captain hath in every figure skill, | an TIM 5.03. 7
in the same figure, like the king that's dead. HAM 1.01. 41
well may it sort that this portentous figure 1.01.109
a figure like your father, | armed at point 1.02.199
a foolish figure! 2.02. 98
what would your gracious figure? 3.04.104
frowning, now thou art an o without a figure. LR 1.04.193 P
the native act and figure of my heart | in OTH 1.01. 62
make me | the fixed figure for the time of scorn 4.02. 54
cadwal, | once arviragus, in as like a figure, CYM 3.03. 96
may you well descry | a figure of truth, of PER 5.03. 92
and, by a figure, even the very plum–broth | and TNK 3.05. 5
and sweetly, by a figure, trace and turn, boys. 3.05. 21
or company, or by a figure, choris, | that 'fore 3.05.107
wound arcite to | the spoiling of his figure. 5.03. 59
he hath not only lent the king his figure, | his STM II.C 102
steal from his figure, and no pace perceiv'd, SON 104.10
FIGURED 1 FR 0.0001 REL FR 1 V 0 P
or he refus'd to take /her figured proffer, PP 4.10
FIGURE'S 1 FR 0.0001 REL FR 1 V 0 P
though light, take pieces for the figure's sake; CYM 5.04. 25
/FIGURES 1 FR 0.0001 REL FR 1 V 0 P
hoo, hearts, tongues, /figures, scribes, bards, ANT 3.02. 16
FIGURES 17 FR 0.0019 REL FR 13 V 4 P
if it be but to scrape the figures out of your WIV 4.02.216 P
spirit, full of forms, figures, shapes, objects, LLL 4.02. 66 P
figures pedantical — these summer flies | have 5.02.408
he apprehends a world of figures here, | but not 1H4 1.03.209
/or /else | we fortify in paper and in figures, 2H4 1.03. 56
well, for there is figures in all things. H5 4.07. 33 P
i speak but in the figures and comparisons of it 4.07. 44 P
in this the heaven figures some event. 3H6 2.01. 32
these pencill'd figures are | even such as they TIM 1.01.159
and write in thee the figures of their love, 5.01.154
thou hast no figures nor no fantasies, | which JC 2.01.231
the arras, figures, | why, such and such; CYM 2.02. 26
never saw i figures | so likely to report 2.04. 82
no figures of ourselves shall we ev'r see | to TNK 2.02. 33
him i utter learned things | and many figures; 3.05. 15
they were but sweet, but figures of delight, SON 98.11
laund'ring the silken figures in the brine LC 17
FIGURING 3 FR 0.0003 REL FR 2 V 1 P
thou art always figuring diseases in me; MM 1.02. 53 P
figuring the natures /of the times deceas'd, 2H4 3.01. 81
figuring that they their passions likewise lent LC 199
FILBERTS 1 FR 0.0001 REL FR 1 V 0 P
i'll bring thee | to clust'ring filberts, and TMP 2.02.171
FILCH 2 FR 0.0002 REL FR 2 V 0 P
you have been so earnest | to have me filch it? OTH 3.03.315
what 'twere to filch affection from another! TNK 2.02.210
FILCH'D 1 FR 0.0001 REL FR 1 V 0 P
cunning hast thou filch'd my daughter's heart, MND 1.01. 36
FILCHES 1 FR 0.0001 REL FR 1 V 0 P
but he that filches from me my good name | robs OTH 3.03.159
FILCHING 3 FR 0.0003 REL FR 1 V 2 P
his filching was like an unskillful singer, he WIV 1.03. 25 P
nym and bardolph are sworn brothers in filching, H5 3.02. 45 P
anon | doubting the filching age will steal his SON 75. 6
FIL'D* 3 FR 0.0003 REL FR 2 V 1 P
i would have fil'd keys off that hung in chains. WT 4.04.611 P
so, | for banquo's issue have i fil'd my mind, MAC 3.01. 64
and precious phrase by all the muses fil'd. SON 85. 4
FILE* 17 FR 0.0019 REL FR 13 V 4 P
the greater file of the subject held the duke to MM 3.02.136 P
day, | great mars, i put myself into thy file; AWW 3.03. 9
or it is upon a file with the duke's other 4.03.204 P
our present musters grow upon the file | to five 2H4 1.03. 10
he makes up the file | of all the gentry; H8 1.01. 75
and front but in that file | where others tell 1.02. 42
still, when suddenly a file of boys behind 'em, 5.03. 55 P
for our gentlemen, | the common file (a plague! COR 1.06. 43
the city, i mean of us a' th' right–hand file? 2.01. 23 P
and she shall file our engines with advice, TIT 2.01.123
the valued file | distinguishes the swift, the MAC 3.01. 94
now, if you have a station in the file, | not i' 3.01.101
i have a file | of all the gentry. 5.02. 8
for three performers are the file when all | the CYM 5.03. 30
these impediments | will i file off; TNK 3.01. 85
the wolves would jaw me, so | he had this file. 3.02. 8
else grant | the file and quality i hold i may 5.01.161
FILED 3 FR 0.0003 REL FR 2 V 1 P
his discourse peremptory, his tongue filed, his LLL 5.01. 10 P
more sharp than filed steel, did spur me forth, TN 3.03. 5
tell, | smooth not thy tongue with filed talk, PP 18. 8
FILES* 8 FR 0.0009 REL FR 7 V 1 P
mile–end, to instruct for the doubling of files. AWW 4.03.270 P
let him choose | out of my files, his projects COR 5.06. 33
are his files | as full as thy report? TIM 5.02. 1
that o'er the files and musters of the war ANT 1.01. 3
within our files there are, | of those that 4.01. 12
keep close | till i provide him files and food, TNK 2.06. 7
i have brought you food and files. 3.03. 2
things needful — files and shirts and perfumes. 3.03. 48
FILIAL 4 FR 0.0004 REL FR 4 V 0 P
love, and filial tenderness | shall, o dear 2H4 4.05. 39
bound | in filial obligation for some term | to HAM 1.02. 91
save what beats there — filial ingratitude! LR 3.04. 14
stand forth | of wealth, of filial fear, law, LC 270
FILII 1 FR 0.0001 REL FR 1 V 0 P
intrate, filii; TNK 3.05.137
FILIUS 1 FR 0.0001 REL FR 0 V 1 P
latin, praeclarissimus filius noster henricus, H5 5.02.341 P
FILL 74 FR 0.0083 REL FR 62 V 12 P
fill all thy bones with aches, make thee roar TMP 1.02.370
fellow trinculo, we'll fill him by and by again. 2.02.176 P
toe to crown he'll fill our skins with pinches, 4.01.233
tide | will shortly fill the reasonable /shores 5.01. 81
gentle breath of yours my sails | must fill, or ep 12
there wanteth but a mean to fill your song. TGV 1.02. 92
were dry, i am able to fill it with my tears; 2.03. 52 P
i dare not for my head fill my belly; MM 4.03.154 P
tell | how many inches doth fill up one mile. LLL 5.02.193
to fill up your grace's request in my stead. MV 4.01.160 P
only in the world i fill up a place, which may AYL 1.02.191 P
well said, master, mum, and gaze your fill. SHR 1.01. 73
i fill a place, i know't. AWW 1.02. 69
in fine, delivers me to fill the time, | herself 3.07. 33
that thought to fill his grave in quiet; WT 4.04.454
i'll fill your grave up. 5.03.101
shall, | if not fill up the measure of her will, JN 2.01.556
i'll fill these dogged spies with false reports; 4.01.128
bosom, and fill up | her enemies' ranks — i 5.02. 28
go thou and fill another room in hell. R2 5.05.107
days, | or fill up chronicles in time to come, 1H4 1.03.171
he doth fill fields with harness in the realm, 3.02.101
of him, | to fill the mouth of deep defiance up, 3.02.116
fill me a bottle of sack. 4.02. 1 P
to fill up the rooms of them as have bought out 4.02. 32 P
they'll fill a pit as well as better. 4.02. 66 P
mocks | and changes fill the cup of alteration 2H4 3.01. 52
a number of shadows fill up the muster–book. 3.02.134 P
"fill the cup, and let it come, | i'll pledge 5.03. 53
to fill king edward's fame with prisoner kings, H5 1.02.162
here, uncle exeter, fill this glove with crowns, 4.08. 57
to fill the world with vicious qualities. 1H6 5.04. 35
and dead men's cries do fill the empty air, 2H6 5.02. 4
york, | or i will fill the house with armed men, 3H6 1.01.167
no more words till they have flow'd their fill. 2.05. 72
i'll bear thee hence, where i may weep my fill. 2.05.113
mine such as fill my heart with unhop'd joys. 3.03.172
should she live, to fill the world with words? 5.05. 44
that fill his ears with such dissentious rumors. R3 1.03. 46
a queen in jest, only to fill the scene. 4.04. 91
fill me a bowl of wine. 5.03. 63
that fill the court with quarrels, talk, and H8 1.03. 20
his end, | goodness and he fill up one monument! 2.01. 94
and i will fill them with prophetic tears. TRO 2.02.102
behold thy fill. 4.05.236
sword, thou hast thy fill of blood and death. 5.08. 4
absence did but fill /ithaca full of months. COR 1.03. 84 P

for i can smooth and fill his aged ears | with TIT 4.04. 96
'twill fill your stomachs, please you eat of it. 5.03. 29
his strides, his lobbies fill with tendance, TIM 1.01. 80
ay, to see meat fill knaves, and wine heat fools 1.01.261
fill me some wine. 3.01. 8 P
pass by and curse thy fill, but pass and stay 5.04. 73
whose ransoms did the general coffers fill; JC 3.02. 89
fill, lucius, till the wine o'erswell the cup; 4.03.161
and fill me from the crown to the toe topful MAC 1.05. 42
lord, as will fill up the time | 'twixt this and 3.01. 24
give me some wine, fill full. 3.04. 87
and your maids could not fill up | the cestern 4.03. 62
scotland hath foisons to fill up your will | of 4.03. 88
let him demand his fill. HAM 4.05.130
in their wills — fill thy purse with money. OTH 1.03.347 P
where be the sacred vials thou shouldst fill ANT 1.03. 63
fill till the cup be hid. 2.07. 87
and he will fill thy wishes to the brim | with 3.13. 18
all my sad captains, fill our bowls once more; 3.13.183
counsellor should fill the bores of hearing, CYM 3.02. 57
lop that doubt, he'll fill this land with arms, PER 1.02. 90
as do you love, fill to your mistress' lips — 2.03. 51
stuff up his lust, as minutes fill up hours; LUC 297
"to fill with worm–holes stately monuments, | to 946
although to–day thou fill | thy hungry eyes even SON 56. 5
your love and pity doth th' impression fill 112. 1
ay, fill it full with wills, and my will one. 136. 6

FILL'D 31 FR 0.0035 REL FR 29 V 2 P
the nine men's morris is fill'd up with mud, MND 2.01. 98
that one body should be fill'd | with all graces AYL 3.02.142
and fill'd | her sweet perfections with one self TN 1.01. 37
they were blanks, rather than fill'd with me! 3.01.104
time as long again | would be fill'd up, my WT 1.02. 4
he (most humane | and fill'd with honor) to my 3.02.166
of like sorrow, | so fill'd, and so becoming; 3.03. 22
it is all fill'd up with guts and midriff. 1H4 3.03.155 P
his hours fill'd up with riots, banquets, sports H5 1.01. 56
so the proportions of defense are fill'd; 2.04. 45
who, with a body fill'd and vacant mind, | gets 4.01.269
have fill'd their pockets full of pebble stones; 1H6 3.01. 80
and princes' courts be fill'd with my reproach. 2H6 3.02. 69
are my chests fill'd up with extorted gold? 4.07. 99
as doth a sail, fill'd with a fretting gust, 3H6 2.06. 35
thy place is fill'd, thy sceptre wrung from thee 3.01. 16
the wrinkles in my brows, now fill'd with blood, 5.02. 19
fill'd it with cursing cries and deep exclaims. R3 1.02. 52
have your mouth fill'd up | before you open it. H8 2.03. 87
of my desires, | yet fill'd with my abilities. 3.02.171
are smother'd up, leads fill'd, and ridges COR 2.01.211
till now you have gone on and fill'd the time TIM 5.04. 3
a vomit ere the next pottle can be fill'd. OTH 2.03. 85 P
if he fill'd | his vacancy with his ANT 1.04. 25
that tub | both fill'd and running — ravening CYM 1.06. 49
in feather'd briefness sails are fill'd, | and PER 5.02. 15
heavy cheers, | sacred vials fill'd with tears, TNK 1.05. 5
with clamors fill'd | the dispers'd air, who, LUC 1804
if it were fill'd with your most high deserts? SON 17. 2
hours have drain'd his blood and fill'd his brow 63. 3
but when your countenance fill'd up his line, 86.13

FILLET 2 FR 0.0002 REL FR 2 V 0 P
fillet of a fenny snake, | in the cauldron boil MAC 4.01. 12
some in her threaden fillet still did bide, LC 33

FILLETH 1 FR 0.0001 REL FR 1 V 0 P
and glutton–like she feeds, yet never filleth; VEN 548

FILL–HORSE 1 FR 0.0001 REL FR 0 V 1 P
chin than dobbin my fill–horse has on his tail. MV 2.02. 95 P

/FILLING 1 FR 0.0001 REL FR 1 V 0 P
/owes /two /buckets, /filling /one /another, R2 4.01.185

FILLING 8 FR 0.0009 REL FR 6 V 2 P
for filling a bottle with a tun–dish. MM 3.02.172 P
glass, by filling the one doth empty the other. AYL 5.01. 42 P
in filling | the whole realm by your teaching H8 5.02. 50
filling the air with swords advanc'd and darts, COR 1.06. 61
see | filling the aged wrinkles in my cheeks, TIT 3.01. 7
the one is filling still, never complete; TIM 4.03.244
filling their hearers | with strange invention. MAC 3.01. 31
like ivory conduits coral cesterns filling: LUC 1234

FILLIP 2 FR 0.0002 REL FR 1 V 1 P
if i do, fillip me with a three–man beetle. 2H4 1.02.228 P
you fillip me a' th' head. TRO 4.05. 45

FILLOP 1 FR 0.0001 REL FR 1 V 0 P
pibbles on the hungry beach | fillop the stars; COR 5.03. 59

FILLS* 13 FR 0.0014 REL FR 10 V 3 P
that one error | fills him with faults; TGV 5.04.112
place, | or in his eminence that fills it up, MM 1.02.164
grief fills the room up of my absent child, JN 3.04. 93
by so much fills their hearts with deadly hate. R2 2.02.131
which he fills | with treacherous crowns; H5 2.pr. 21
dark | fills the wide vessel of the universe. 4.pr. 3
whose glory fills the world with loud report. 1H6 2.02. 43
from such a cause as fills mine eyes with tears 3H6 3.03. 13
it fills a man full of obstacles. R3 1.04.139 P
thee, | now fills thy sleep with perturbations. 5.03.161
you draw backward, we'll put you i' th' fills. TRO 3.02. 46 P
hound that hunts, but one that fills up the cry. OTH 2.03.364 P
for sure he fills it up with great ability — 3.03.247

FILLY 1 FR 0.0001 REL FR 1 V 0 P
beguile, | neighing in likeness of a filly foal; MND 2.01. 46

FILM 2 FR 0.0002 REL FR 2 V 0 P
her whip of cricket's bone, the lash of film, ROM 1.04. 66
it will but skin and film the ulcerous place, HAM 3.04.147

FILS 1 FR 0.0001 REL FR 0 V 1 P
in french, notre tres cher fils henri, roi H5 5.02.339 P

FILTH 10 FR 0.0011 REL FR 9 V 1 P
i have us'd thee | (filth as thou art) with TMP 1.02.346
his filth within being cast, he would appear | a MM 3.01. 92
sink, whose filth and dirt | troubles the silver 2H6 4.01. 71
rebellious hinds, the filth and scum of kent, 4.02.122
sweep the court clean of such filth as thou art. 4.07. 32 P
my face i'll grime with filth, | blanket my LR 2.03. 9
filth, thou liest! OTH 5.02.231
in our own filth drop our clear judgments, make ANT 3.13.113
old receptacles, or common shores, of filth, PER 4.06.175
mire | and unperceiv'd fly with the filth away, LUC 1010

/FILTHS 1 FR 0.0001 REL FR 1 V 0 P
/seem /vild, | /filths /savor /but /themselves. LR 4.02. 39

FILTHS 1 FR 0.0001 REL FR 1 V 0 P
to general filths | convert o' th' instant, TIM 4.01. 6

FILTHY 20 FR 0.0022 REL FR 10 V 10 P
fie, these filthy vices! MM 2.04. 42
maw or clothe a back | from such a filthy vice; 3.02. 23
fie, fie, 'tis lewd and filthy. SHR 4.03. 65
off me, scurvy, old, filthy, scurvy lord! AWW 2.03.236 P
a filthy officer he is in those suggestions for 3.05. 17 P
made on you all and sung to filthy tunes, let a 1H4 2.02. 45 P
dowlas, filthy dowlas. 3.03. 69 P
you filthy bung, away! 2H4 2.04.128 P
rogue, you filthy famish'd correctioner, if you 5.04. 20 P
o'erblows the filthy and contagious clouds | of H5 3.03. 31
a scurvy railing knave, a very filthy rogue. TRO 5.04. 29 P
and yet he's but a filthy piece of work. TIM 1.01.199 P
faith, for the worst is filthy, and would not 1.02.153 P
is fair, | hover through the fog and filthy air. MAC 1.01. 12
and wash this filthy witness from your hand. 2.02. 44
filthy hags, | why do you show me this? 4.01.115
hundred–pound, filthy worsted–stocking knave; LR 2.02. 17 P
hard, hard. o filthy traitor! 3.07. 32
hates the slime | that sticks on filthy deeds. OTH 5.02.149
she was too fond of her most filthy bargain. 5.02.157

FILTHY–MANTLED 1 FR 0.0001 REL FR 1 V 0 P
i' th' filthy–mantled pool beyond your cell, TMP 4.01.182

FIN* 3 FR 0.0003 REL FR 3 V 0 P
fowls have no feathers, and fish have no fin. ERR 3.01. 79
for a fish without a fin, there's a fowl without 3.01. 82
la fin couronne les /oeuvres. 2H6 5.02. 28

FINALLY 1 FR 0.0001 REL FR 0 V 1 P
and the three party is (lastly and finally) mine WIV 1.01.140 P

FINCH 1 FR 0.0001 REL FR 1 V 0 P
the finch, the sparrow, and the lark, | the MND 3.01.130

FINCH–EGG 1 FR 0.0001 REL FR 0 V 1 P
finch–egg! TRO 5.01. 36 P

FIN'D 3 FR 0.0003 REL FR 3 V 0 P
for the momentary trick | be perdurably fin'd? MM 3.01.114
the nobles hath he fin'd | for ancient quarrels, R2 2.01.247
that i have fin'd these bones of mine for ransom H5 4.07. 69

/FIND 8 FR 0.0009 REL FR 8 V 0 P
/shouldst /thou /find /one /heinous /article, R2 4.01.233
/i /find /myself /a /traitor /with /the /rest; 4.01.248
/which /if /we /find /outweighs /ability, 2H4 1.03. 45
/dead /vomit /up, | /and /howl'st /to /find /it. 1.03.100
/and /find /our /griefs /heavier /than /our 4.01. 69
/like /or /find /fault, /do /as /your /pleasures TRO pr 30
/you /shall /find | /some /that /will /thank LR 3.01. 36
sir, /find /we in life, to lock it | from action CYM 4.04. 2

FIND 556 FR 0.0628 REL FR 423 V 133 P
prescience | i find my zenith doth depend upon TMP 1.02.181
best know'st | what torment i did find thee in; 1.02.287
his fellows, | and strays about to find 'em. 1.02.418
i find | they are inclin'd to do so. 2.01.192
i find not | myself dispos'd to sleep. 2.01.201
i could find in my heart to beat him — 2.02.155 P
he is drown'd | whom thus we stray to find, and 3.03. 9
of | our human generation you shall find | many, 3.03. 33
which now we find | each putter–out of five for 3.03. 47
for thou shalt find she will outstrip all praise 4.01. 10
there shalt thou find the mariners asleep 5.01. 98
voyage | did claribel her husband find at tunis, 5.01.209
find this grand liquor that hath gilded 'em? 5.01.280
if i lose them, thus find i by their loss — TGV 2.06. 21
thereby to find | that which thyself hast now 3.01. 31
him we go to find. 3.01.191 P
go, sirrah, find him out. come, valentine. 3.01.261
go, get thee hence, and find my dog again, | or 4.04. 59
where thou shalt find me sad and solitary. 4.04. 89
o, sir, i find her milder than she was, | and 5.02. 2
ay, sir, you shall find me reasonable. WIV 1.01.210 P
i' faith, and find any body in the house, here 1.04. 4 P
ay me, he'll find the young man there, and be 1.04. 65 P
you shall find it a great charge; 1.04.101 P
i will find you twenty lascivious turtles ere 2.01. 80 P
i will be patient; i will find out this. 2.01.126 P
if i do find it — well. 2.01.143 P
if i find her honest, i lose not my labor; 2.01.238 P
bids me search — there i shall find falstaff. 3.02. 46 P
how i love you, and you shall one day find it. 3.03. 81 P
ascend my chambers, search, seek, find out. 3.03.163 P
i cannot find him. 3.03.199 P
you, | and as i find her, so am i affected. 3.04. 91
did he search for you, and could not find you? 3.05. 82 P
i shall find you anon. 4.02.140 P
if you find a man there, he shall die a flea's 4.02.150 P
if i find not what i seek, show no color for my 4.02.161 P
if they can find in their hearts the poor 4.02.217 P
go you, and where you find a maid | that, ere 5.05. 49
the jewel that we find, we stoop and take't, MM 2.01. 24
hoping you'll find good cause to whip them all. 2.01.137
i advise you let me not find you before me again 2.01.246 P
to sue to live, i find i seek to die, | and, 3.01. 42
i seek to die, | and, seeking death, find life. 3.01. 43
me desire to know how you find claudio prepar'd. 3.02.239 P
but shall you on your knowledge find this way? 4.01. 36
for i do find your hangman is a more penitent 4.02. 49 P
me for your own turn, you shall find me yare; 4.02. 58 P
where you shall find, within these two days he 4.02.198 P
now, sir, how do you find the prisoner? 4.03. 66
you shall find | your safety manifested. 4.03. 89
say, which you shall find | by every syllable a 4.03.125
have way, my lord, | to find this practice out. 5.01.239
him your kind pains | to find out this abuse, 5.01.247
you shall find this friar a notable fellow. 5.01.266 P
i find an apt remission in myself; 5.01.498
hopeless to find, yet loath to leave unsought ERR 1.01.135
who, falling there to find his fellow forth 1.02. 37
so i, to find a mother and a brother, | in quest 1.02. 39
i could find out countries in her. 3.02.114 P
cliffs, but i could find no whiteness in them. 3.02.127 P
me, i could find in my heart to stay here still, 4.04.155 P
discover how, and thou shalt find me just. 5.01.203
i find here that don /pedro hath bestow'd much ADO 1.01. 9 P
and i would i could find in my heart that i had 1.01.126 P
you shall find her the infernal ate in good 2.01.255 P
find me a meet hour to draw don pedro and the 2.02. 33 P
there shalt thou find my cousin beatrice 3.01. 2
i could find in my heart to bestow it all of 3.05. 21 P
but they shall find, awak'd in such a kind, 4.01.197
then we find | the virtue that possession would 4.01.220
shall i not find a woodcock too? 5.01.157 P
i can find out no rhyme to "lady" but "baby," an 5.02. 37 P
conscience) find no impediment to the contrary, 5.02. 84 P
so, ere you find where light in darkness lies, LLL 1.01. 78
you find not the apostraphas, and so miss the 4.02.119 P
leaves the wind, | all unseen, can passage find; 4.03.104
but i a beam do find in each of three. 4.03.160
i'll find a fairer face not wash'd to–day. 4.03.269
/let us once lose our oaths to find ourselves, 4.03.358
where will you find men worthy enough to present 5.01.124 P
we need more light to find your meaning out. 5.02. 21
and i shall find you empty of that fault, 5.02.868
find you out a bed; MND 2.02. 39
either death, or you, i'll find immediately. 2.02.156
find out moonshine, find out moonshine. 3.01. 54 P
find out moonshine, find out moonshine. 3.01. 54 P
the wind, | and helena of athens look thou find. 3.02. 95
i'll find demetrius and revenge this spite. 3.02.420
go, one of you, find out the forester, | for now 4.01.103
dispatch, i say, and find the forester. 4.01.108
how shall we find the concord of this discord? 5.01. 60
unless you can find sport in their intents, 5.01. 79
she will find him by starlight. 5.01.314 P
you shall seek all day ere you find them, and MV 1.01.117 P
more advised watch | to find the other forth, 1.01.143
or to find both | or bring your latter hazard 1.01.150
fast bind, fast find — | a proverb never stale 2.05. 54
find the girl, | she hath the stones upon her, 2.08. 21
i pray thee let us go and find him out | and 2.08. 51
too long a pause for that which you find there. 2.09. 53
where i did hear of her, but cannot find her. 3.01. 82 P
with so much, and so much to find the thief, and 3.01. 93 P
if you do love me, you will find me out. 3.02. 41
what find i here? 3.02.114
thee honest–true, | so let me find thee still. 3.04. 47
i cannot find it, 'tis not in the bond. 4.01.262
i give you, | and find it out by proclamation; 4.01.436
there you shall find that portia was the doctor, 5.01.269
there you shall find three of your argosies 5.01.276
which thou shalt find i will most kindly requite AYL 1.01.138 P
but i did find him still mine enemy. 1.02.226
i'll make him find him. 2.02. 19
i could find in my heart to disgrace my man's 2.04. 4 P
and little reaks to find the way to heaven | by 2.04. 81
beast, | for i can no where find him like a man. 2.07. 2
a doe, i go to find my fawn | and give it food. 2.07.128
go find him out, | and we will nothing waste 2.07.133
find out thy brother, wheresoe'er he is; 3.01. 5
he that sweetest rose will find, | must find 3.02.111
find, | must find love's prick and rosalind. 3.02.112
dead shepherd, now i find thy saw of might, 3.05. 81
i'll go find a shadow, and sigh till he come. 4.01.216 P
we shall find a time, audrey, patience, gentle 5.01. 1 P
how did you find the quarrel on the seventh 5.04. 66 P
fall to them as you find your stomach serves you SHR 1.01. 38
and weep, | till i can find occasion of revenge. 2.01. 36
mistake me not, i speak but as i find. 2.01. 66
ay, if the fool could find it where it lies. 2.01.212
no, not a whit, i find you passing gentle: 2.01.242
and sullen, | and now i find report a very liar; 2.01.244
if once i find thee ranging, | hortensio will be 3.01. 91
a grumbling groom, and that the girl shall find. 3.02.153
of you all shall find when he comes home. 4.01. 88 P
fault | i'll find about the making of the bed, 4.01.200
agreement | me shall you find ready and willing 4.04. 34
you shall find of the king a husband, madam; AWW 1.01. 6 P
will repeat, | which men full true shall find: 1.03. 61
we'd find no fault with the tithe–woman if i 1.03. 84 P
/loneliness, and find | your salt tears' head. 1.03.171
that seeks not to find that her search implies, 1.03.216
to return | and find your grace in health. 2.01. 7
find what you seek, | that fame may cry you loud 2.01. 16
you shall find in the regiment of the spinii one 2.01. 42 P
and in your bed | find fairer fortune, if you 2.03. 92
honor | flies where you bid it, i find that she, 2.03.170
thou shall find what it is to be proud of thy 2.03.226 P
did you find me in yourself, sir, or were you 2.04. 33 P
in yourself, sir, or were you taught to find me? 2.04. 34 P
and much fool may you find in you, even to the 2.04. 36 P
since i cannot yet find in my heart to repent. 2.05. 12 P
find you that there? 3.02. 76
if your lordship find him not a hilding, hold me 3.06. 3 P
deal of discoveries, but when you find him out, 3.06. 93 P
tell me what a sprat you shall find him, which 3.06.105 P
i find my tongue is too foolhardy, but my heart 4.01. 28 P
if you could find out a country where but women 4.03.326 P
and you shall find yourself to be well thank'd, 5.01. 36
find him, and bring him hither. 5.03.204
where did you find it then? 5.03.274
life, | in your denial i would find no sense. TN 1.05.266
what, and fear to find | mine eye too great a 1.05.308
him will my revenge find notable cause to work. 2.03.153 P
he shall find himself most feelingly personated. 2.03.158 P
make a third, where he shall find the letter; 2.03.174 P
o, where | sad true lover never find my grave, 2.04. 65
where shall i find you? 3.02. 51 P
he were open'd and you find so much blood in his 3.02. 61 P
firm, | you should find better dealing. 3.03. 18
he will find it comes from a clodpole. 3.04.189 P
you'll find it otherwise, i assure you; 3.04.229 P
as you are like to find him in the proof of his 3.04.265 P
i could not find him at the elephant, | yet 4.03. 5
and i find it | and that to the infection of my WT 1.02.144
if i could find example | of thousands that had 1.02.357
fear the wolf will sooner find than the master. 3.03. 67 P
not for issue, | the crown will find an heir. 5.01. 47
his mind) to find thee | an honorable husband. 5.03.142
where should he find it fairer than in blanch? JN 2.01.427
where should he find it purer than in blanch? 2.01.429
find liable to our crown and dignity, | shall 2.01.490
my lord, and in her eye i find | a wonder, or a 2.01.496
judge, | that i can find should merit any hate. 2.01.520
so we could find some pattern of our shame. 3.04. 16
in true blood | shall find but bloody safety, 3.04.148
and bind the boy which you shall find with me 4.01. 4
and find th' inheritance of this poor child, 4.02. 97
land, | i find the people strangely fantasied, 4.02.144
i'll find a thousand shifts to get away. 4.03. 7

with colors idlely spread, | and find no check? 5.01. 73
strike up our drums, to find this danger out. 5.02.179
and thou shalt find it, dolphin, do not doubt. 5.02.180
i in the black brow of night, | to find you out. 5.06. 18
find shapes of grief, more than himself, to wail R2 2.02. 22
and i must find that title in your tongue, 2.03. 72
to find out right with wrong — it may not be; 2.03.145
post you to london and you will find it so, | i 3.04. 90
and in this thought they find a kind of ease, 5.05. 28
find we a time for frighted peace to pant | and 1H4 1.01. 2
farewell, you shall find me in eastcheap. 1.02.157 P
but i will find him when he lies asleep, | and 1.03.221
thou need'st him, there thou shalt find him. 2.02. 71 P
books in england, i could find in my heart — 2.04. 50 P
canst thou now find out to hide thee from this 2.04.264 P
irregular, | find pardon on my true submission. 3.02. 28
do not think so, you shall not find it so, | and 3.02.129
thou shalt find me tractable to any honest 3.03.172 P
where shall i find one that can steal well? 3.03.188 P
present want | seems more than we shall find it. 4.01. 45
one, they'll find linen enough on every hedge. 4.02. 47 P
title, the which we find | too indirect for long 4.03.104
and find a time | to punish this offense in 5.02. 6
and thou shalt find a king that will revenge 5.03. 12
nay, you shall find no boy's play here, i can 5.04. 75 P
thus ever did rebellion find rebuke. 5.05. 1
about it, you know where to find me. 2H4 1.02.243 P
in another place, | and find me worse provided. 2.03. 50
and see if thou canst find out sneak's noise. 2.04. 11 P
i'll see if i can find out sneak. 2.04. 21 P
which should not find a ground to root upon 3.01. 91
as chaff, | and good from bad find no partition. 4.01.194
find him, my lord of warwick, chide him hither. 4.05. 62
though no man be assur'd what grace to find, 5.02. 30
and you shall find his vanities forespent | were H5 2.04. 36
and when you find him evenly deriv'd | from his 2.04. 91
and, be assur'd, you'll find a difference, | as 2.04.134
if i find a hole in his coat, i will tell him my 3.06. 84 P
then shall we find to-morrow they have only 3.07.153 P
the wars of pompey the great, you shall find, i 4.01. 70 P
you, you shall find the ceremonies of the wars, 4.01. 72 P
i am a king that find thee; 4.01.259
absence, | seek through your camp to find you. 4.01.286
our bodies shall no doubt | find native graves; 4.03. 96
the maps of the orld, i warrant you sall find, 4.07. 24 P
that shall find himself aggrief'd at this glove; 4.07.162 P
you find it otherwise, and henceforth let a 5.01. 77 P
thou wouldst find me such a plain king that thou 5.02.124 P
thou shalt find the best king of good fellows. 5.02.242 P
and thou shalt find that i exceed my sex. 1H6 1.02. 90
and thou shalt find me at the governor's. 1.04. 20
i find thou art no less than fame hath bruited, 2.03. 68
my side | that any purblind eye may find it out. 2.04. 21
i'll find friends to wear my bleeding roses, 2.04. 72
ah, thou shalt find us ready for thee still; 2.04.104
or thou shouldst find thou hast dishonor'd me. 3.01. 9
and that we find the slothful watch but weak, 3.02. 7
and they shall find dear deer of us, my friends. 4.02. 54
and, now it is my chance to find thee out, 5.04. 4
ten to one | we shall not find like opportunity. 5.04.158
with hope to find the like event in love, | but 5.05.105
yet i do find it so; 2H6 1.02. 96
well, sir, we must have you find your legs. 2.01.144 P
they in seeking that | shall find their deaths, 2.02. 76
man, | and find no harbor in a royal heart. 3.01.336
for in the shade of death i shall find joy; 3.02. 54
i'll have an iris that shall find thee out. 3.02.407
unless i find him guilty, he shall not die. 4.02. 96 P
where shall it find a harbor in the earth? 5.01.168
wilt thou go dig a grave to find out war, | and 5.01.169
not knowing how to find the open air | but 3H6 3.02.177
air | but toiling desperately to find it out — 3.02.178
he shall here find his friends with horse and 4.05. 12
he'll soon find means to make the body follow. 4.07. 26
shalt find | men well inclin'd to hear what thou 4.08. 15
to haste thus fast, to find us unprovided. 5.04. 63
but i do find more pain in banishment | than R3 1.03.167
and would not let it forth | to find the empty, 1.04. 39
if thou dost find him tractable to us, 3.01.174
at crosby house, there shall you find us both. 3.01.190
and hopes to find you forward | upon his party 3.02. 46
where you shall find me well accompanied | with 3.05. 99
i myself | find in myself no pity to myself? 5.03.203
they may believe, | may here find truth too. H8 pr 9
bosom up my counsel, | you'll find it wholesome. 1.01.113
could not find | his hour of speech a minute — 1.02.120
if he may | find mercy in the law, 'tis his; 1.02.212
some of these | should find a running banket, 1.04. 12
i would i were, | they should find easy penance. 1.04. 17
which they would have your grace | find out, and 1.04. 84
the card'nal instantly will find employment, 2.01. 48
you'll find a most unfit time to disturb him. 2.02. 60
i find him a fit fellow. 2.02.116
your graces find me here part of a huswife | (i 3.01. 24
madam, you'll find it so. 3.01.168
which | i find at such proud rate, that it 3.02.127
till i find more than will or words to do it 3.02.236
no doubt | in time will find their fit rewards. 3.02.245
cranmer will find a friend will not shrink from 4.01.107
pray for heartily, that it may find | good time, 5.01. 21
pray heaven the king may never find a heart 5.02. 77
i shall both find your lordship judge and juror, 5.02. 95
yet should find respect | for what they have 5.02.110
but i find none. 5.02.171
and find a way out | to let the troop pass 5.03. 84
or i'll find | a marshalsea shall hold ye play 5.03. 85
none think flattery, for they'll find 'em truth. 5.04. 16
your presence, | and ye shall find me thankful. 5.04. 72
troy, | that find such cruel battle here within? TRO 1.01. 3
jove | to find persistive constancy in men? 1.03. 21
you go, | and find the welcome of a noble foe. 1.03.309
find hector's purpose | pointing on him. 1.03.330
could not you find out that by her attributes? 3.01. 35 P
who do methinks find out | some thing not worth 3.03. 90
we met by chance, you did not find me here. 4.02. 71
if i might in entreaties find success — | as 4.05.149
shall find him by his large and portly size. 4.05.162
this fault in us i find, | the error of our eye 5.02.109
you shall find | no public benefit which you COR 1.01.151
where he should find you lions, finds you hares; 1.01.171
you'll find | th' have not prepar'd for us. 1.02. 29
him seek danger where he was like to find fame. 1.03. 13 P
what good condition can a treaty find | i' th' 1.10. 6
where i find him, were it | at home, upon my 1.10. 24
when i find the ass in compound with the major 2.01. 58 P
we hope to find you our friend; 2.03.104 P
rage, when it shall find | the harm of unscann'd 3.01.310
like a citizen, | you find him like a soldier; 3.03. 54
from the volscian state to find you out there. 4.03. 11 P
and you'll look pale | before you find it other. 4.06.102
your enemies and his find something in him. 4.06.106
we must find | an evident calamity, though we 5.03.111
in a male tiger, that shall our poor city find. 5.04. 29 P
we must proceed as we do find the people. 5.06. 15
alone, | i'll find a day to massacre them all, TIT 1.01.450
till i find the stream | to cool this heat, a 2.01.133
yet have i heard — o, could i find it now! 2.03.150
now will i fetch the king to find them here, 2.03.206
hour, | to find thy brother bassianus dead. 2.03.252
look, sirs, if you can find the huntsman out, 2.03.278
then which way shall i find revenge's cave? 3.01.270
what would she find? 4.01. 46
inspire me, that i may this treason find! 4.01. 67
and who should find them but the empress' 4.03. 74
can couch for fear, but i will find them out, 5.02. 38
and find out /murderers in their guilty /caves; 5.02. 52
i'll find some cunning practice out of hand, 5.02. 77
thy hap | to find another that is like to thee, 5.02.102
and now i find it, therefore bind them sure, 5.02.160
find those persons out | whose names are written ROM 1.02. 35
find them out whose names are written here! 1.02. 38 P
but i am sent to find those persons whose names 1.02. 42 P
and can never find what names the writing person 1.02. 43 P
and find delight writ there with beauty's pen; 1.03. 82
lies | find written in the margent of his eyes. 1.03. 86
turn back, dull earth, and find thy centre out. 2.01. 2
thou art, | if any of my kinsmen find thee here. 2.02. 65
and but thou love me, let them find me here; 2.02. 76
kind | we sucking on her natural bosom find: 2.03. 12
of you tell me where i may find the young romeo? 2.04.119 P
and if i cannot, i'll find those that shall. 2.04.152 P
you shall find me apt enough to that, sir, and 3.01. 41 P
me to-morrow, and you shall find me a grave man. 3.01. 98 P
i'll find romeo | to comfort you, i wot well 3.02.138
o, find him! 3.02.142
where thou shalt live till we can find a time 3.03.150
i'll find out your man, | and he shall signify 3.03.169
if you could find out but a man | to bear a 3.05. 96
find thou the means, and i'll find such a man. 3.05.103
find thou the means, and i'll find such a man. 3.05.103
i have a head, sir, that will find out logs, 4.04. 18
going to find a barefoot brother out, | one of 5.02. 5
go, some of you, whoe'er you find attach. 5.03.173
like your work, | and you shall find i like it. TIM 1.01.161
to me in words, | but find supply immediate. 2.01. 27
one may reach deep enough and yet | find little. 3.04. 16
where he shall find | th' unkindest beast more 4.01. 35
men daily find it. 4.03.174
o, thou shalt find — 4.03.232
find what thou want'st by free and offer'd light 5.01. 45
him no further, thus you still shall find him. 5.01.213
if you do find them deck'd with ceremonies. JC 1.01. 65
about | to find ourselves dishonorable graves. 1.02.138
and find a time | both meet to hear and answer 1.02.169
you shall find | that heaven hath infus'd them 1.03. 68
to find out you. who's that? metellus cimber? 1.03.134
praetor's chair, | where brutus may but find it; 1.03.144
to pompey's porch, where you shall find us. 1.03.147
day | where wilt thou find a cavern dark enough 2.01. 80
we shall find of him | a shrewd contriver; 2.01.157
they could not find a heart within the beast. 2.02. 40
years, | i shall not find myself so apt to die; 3.01.160
what? shall i find you here? 4.01. 10
not how, | but i do find it cowardly and vile, 5.01.103
come, cassius' sword, and find titinius' heart. 5.03. 90
i shall find time, cassius; 5.03.103
i shall find time. 5.03.103
when you do find him, or alive or dead, | he 5.04. 24
to find the mind's construction in the face: MAC 1.04. 12
do you find | your patience so predominant in 3.01. 85
if it find heaven, must find it out to-night. 3.01.141
if it find heaven, must find it out to-night. 3.01.141
they should find | what 'twere to kill a father; 3.06. 19
where such as thou mayst find him. 4.02. 82
as i shall find the time to friend, i will. 4.03. 10
perchance even there where i did find my doubts. 4.03. 25
cast | the water of my land, find her disease, 5.03. 51
do we but find the tyrant's power to-night, 5.06. 7
let me find him, fortune! 5.07. 22
know | where we shall find him most convenient. HAM 1.01.175
i find thee apt, | and duller shouldst thou be 1.05. 31
of bias, | by indirections find directions out. 2.01. 63
he seem'd to find his way without his eyes, 2.01. 95
that we find out the cause of this effect, | or 2.02.101
lead me, i will find | where truth is hid, 2.02.157
than natural, if philosophy could find it out. 2.02.368 P
nor do we find him forward to be sounded, | but 3.01. 7
if she find him not, | to england send him, or 3.01.185
i have sent to seek him, and to kind the body. 4.03. 1
if your messenger find him not there, seek him 4.03. 34 P
but if indeed you find him not within this month 4.03. 35 P
but greatly to find quarrel in a straw | when 4.04. 55
or by collateral hand | they find us touch'd, we 4.05.208
alexander, till 'a find it stopping a bunghole? 5.01.204 P
in the dark | grop'd i to find out them, had my 5.02. 14
for you shall find in him the continent of what 5.02.110 P
heart | i find she names my very deed of love; LR 1.01. 71
and find i am alone felicitate | in your dear 1.01. 75
thou losest here, a better where to find. 1.01.261
perus'd, i find it not fit for your o'erlooking. 1.02. 38 P
i begin to find an idle and fond bondage in the 1.02. 49 P
convey the business as i shall find means, and 1.02.102 P
find out this villain, edmund, it shall lose 1.02.114 P
thou lov'st, | shall find thee full of labors. 1.04. 7
thou shalt find | that i'll resume the shape 1.04.308
and shall find time | from this enormous state 2.02.168
o'er our heads, | find out their enemies now. 3.02. 51
if i find him comforting the king, it will stuff 3.05. 20 P
and thou shalt find a /dearer father in my love. 3.05. 24 P
villain, thou shalt find — 3.07. 34
if you do find him, pray you give him this; 4.05. 33
as we shall find their merits and our safety 5.03. 44
and most wise consent | (as partly i find it is) OTH 1.01.122
that you shall surely find him, | lead to the 1.01.157
driven | to find out practices of cunning hell 1.03.102
if you do find me foul in her report, | the 1.03.117
and prompt alacrity | i find in hardness; 1.03.233
and let me find a charter in your voice | t' 1.03.245
body, she will find the /error of her choice. 1.03.351 P
i find it still, when i have /list to sleep. 2.01.104
she'll find a white that shall her blackness 2.01.133
her delicate tenderness will find itself abus'd, 2.01.232 P
do you find some occasion to anger cassio, 2.01.266 P
and bring him jump when he may cassio find 2.03.386
lodging lose this napkin, | and let him find it. 3.03.322
but now i find i had suborn'd the witness, | and 3.04.153
if i do find him fit, i'll move your suit | and 3.04.166
work, that you should find it in your chamber, 4.01.152 P
i do not find that thou deal'st justly with me. 4.02.173 P
respect and acquaintance, but i find none. 4.02.190 P
scurvy, and begin to find myself fopp'd in it. 4.02.194 P
i am sorry to find you thus; 5.01. 81
then must thou needs find out new heaven, new ANT 1.01. 17
find me to marry me with octavius caesar, and 1.02. 29 P
if you find him sad, | say i am dancing; 1.03. 3
you shall find there | a man who is th' 1.04. 8
so find we profit | by losing of our prayers. 2.01. 7
your mother came to sicily and did find | her 2.06. 45
but you shall find the band that seems to tie 2.06.120 P
once 'tis offer'd, | shall never find it more. 2.07. 84
you shall not find, | though you be therein 3.02. 34
i find thee | most fit for business. 3.03. 36
should i find them | so saucy with the hand of 3.13. 97
say that i wish he never find more cause | to 4.05. 15
us what she says, | and how you find of her. 5.01. 68
and you shall find | a conqueror that will pray 5.02. 26
further than you shall | find cause in caesar. 5.02. 64
you shall find | a benefit in this change; 5.02.127
no, be assur'd you shall not find me, daughter, CYM 1.01. 70
and shall find it so | in all that i can do. 1.06. 30
masterless leave both | to who shall find them. 2.04. 61
give me leave to spare when you shall find | you 2.04. 65
could i find out | the woman's part in me — for 2.05. 19
so caesar shall not find them. 3.01. 76
you shall find us in our salt-water girdle. 3.01. 79 P
shall we find | the sharded beetle in a safer 3.03. 19
and you shall find me, wretched man, a thing 3.04. 19
shalt hereafter find | it is no act of common 3.04. 90
from thy heart, or rip | thy heart to find it. 3.05. 87
go, | and find not her whom thou pursuest. 3.05.160
i cannot find those runagates, that villain 4.02. 62
find | the ooze, to show what coast thy sluggish 4.02.204
may seem to those | which chance to find us. 4.02.332
never | find such another master. 4.02.374
us | find out the prettiest daisied plot we can, 4.02.398
these present wars shall find i love my country, 4.03. 43
who find in my exile the want of breeding, | the 4.04. 26
could not find death where i did hear him groan, 5.03. 69
well, i will find him; 5.03. 73
so graze, as you find pasture. 5.04. 2
dream as i have done, | wake, and find nothing. 5.04.129
many dream not to find, neither deserve, | and 5.04.130
to himself unknown, without seeking find, and be 5.04.139 P
he shall be happy that can find him, if | our 5.05. 6
her honor confident | than i did truly find her, 5.05.188
to himself unknown, without seeking find, and be 5.05.436 P
if in his grave he rest, we'll find him there; PER 2.04. 30
whom if you find, and win unto return, | you 2.04. 52
portage quit | with all thou canst find here. 3.01. 36
whom our fast-growing scene must find | at 4.ch. 6
when he shall come and find | our paragon to all 4.01. 34
how dost thou find the inclination of the people 4.02. 96 P
yet i find | it greets me as an enterprise of 4.03. 37
i desire to find him so, that i may worthily 4.06. 51 P
doubt not but i shall find them tractable enough 4.06.199 P
where we shall find | the moi'ty of a number, TNK 1.01.213
i pity | decays where e'er i find them, but such 1.02. 32
go and find out | the bones of your dead lords, 1.04. 6
here age must find us, | and which is heaviest, 2.02. 28
i find the court here, | i am sure, a more 2.02. 99
dare assure you | you'll find a loving mistress. 2.05. 57
not, | let me find that my father ever hated — 2.05. 58
if the law | find me, and then condemn me for't, 2.06. 14
would i could find a fine frog! 3.04. 12
ye | as kind a kinsman as you force me find | a 3.06. 21
you'll find it. 3.06. 49
we shall find | too many hours to die in, gentle 3.06.111
sister, | i find no anger to 'em, nor no ruin: 3.06.189
believe you'll find it so. 4.01. 47
i'll find him out to-morrow." 4.01. 69
o, who can find the bent of woman's fancy? 4.02. 33
we should give her physic till we find that — 5.02. 29
you'll find it so. she comes. pray /humor her. 5.02. 40
you, we shall find | some blind priest for the 5.02. 77
that neither could find other, get herself 5.03. 26
to find a nation of such barbarous temper | that STM II.C 131
find sweet beginning, but unsavory end; VEN 1138
when shall he think to find a stranger just LUC 159
where it may find | some purer chest to close so 760
to find some desp'rate instrument of death, 1038
heat nor freezing cold, | will we find out; 1146
to find a face where all distress is stell'd. 1444
and turn'd it thus, "it cannot be, i find, | but 1539
or (at the least) this refuge let me find: 1654
leaves the wind | all unseen gan passage find, PP 16. 6
smell — | a cripple soon can find a halt — 18.10
the wind, | faithful friends are hard to find: 20.32
which you hold in lease | find no determination; SON 13. 6
go well, | by oft predict that i in heaven find: 14. 8
to find where your true image pictur'd lies, 24. 6
mind, | for thee, and for myself, no quiet find. 27.14
both find each other, and i lose both twain, 42.11
was | shall reasons find of settled gravity — 49. 8
o, what excuse will my poor beast then find, 51. 5

your praise shall still find room, | even in the 55.10
pry, | to find out shames and idle hours in me, 61. 7
and thou shalt find | those children nurs'd, 77.10
o, what a happy title do i find, | happy to have 92.11
and thou in this shalt find thy monument, | when 107.13
but thence i learn, and find the lesson true, 118.13
now i find true | that better is by evil still 119. 9
and thou shalt find it merits not reproving, 142. 4
eyes well seeing thy foul faults should find. 148.14
bidding them find their sepulchres in mud, LC 46
what's sweet to do, to do will aptly find: 88
the goodly objects which abroad they find | of 137
sought their shame that so their shame did find, 187
FINDER 1 FR 0.0001 REL FR 0 V 1 P
the bar and crown thee for a finder of madmen. TN 3.04.140 P
FINDER/–OUT 1 FR 0.0001 REL FR 0 V 1 P
and subtle knave, a finder/–out of occasion; OTH 2.01.242 P
FINDER–OUT 1 FR 0.0001 REL FR 0 V 1 P
for had i been the finder–out of this secret, it WT 5.02.121 P
FIND–FAULTS 1 FR 0.0001 REL FR 0 V 1 P
our places stops the mouth of all find–faults, H5 5.02.272 P
/FINDING 1 FR 0.0001 REL FR 1 V 0 P
/finding | /who /'twas /that /so /endur'd, /with LR 5.03.211
FINDING 17 FR 0.0019 REL FR 14 V 3 P
finding yourself desir'd of such a person, MM 2.04. 91
who, being overjoy'd with finding a bird's nest, ADO 2.01.223 P
and therefore, finding barren practicers, LLL 4.03.322
but take a taste of my finding him, and relish AYL 3.02.233 P
finding | myself thus alter'd with't. WT 1.02.383
aspect, | finding thee fit for bloody villainy, JN 4.02.225
the north, | finding his usurpation most unjust, 1H6 2.05. 68
and finding him, the searchers of the town, ROM 5.02. 8
dedicate themselves, | finding it so inclin'd. MAC 4.03. 76
and finding | by this encompassment and drift of HAM 2.01. 9
finding ourselves too slow of sail, we put on a 4.06. 17 P
and finding little comfort to relieve them, | i PER 1.02. 99
not finding in | the circuit of my breast any TNK 3.01. 45
finding their enemy to be so curst, | they all VEN 887
hue, | finding thy worth a limit past my praise, SON 82. 6
finding the first conceit of love there bred, 108.13
finding myself in honor so forbid, | with safest LC 150
FINDINGS 1 FR 0.0001 REL FR 0 V 1 P
go you the next way with your findings; WT 3.03.128 P
FINDS 50 FR 0.0056 REL FR 39 V 11 P
it is the lesser blot, modesty finds, | women to TGV 5.04.108
in corporal sufferance finds a pang as great MM 3.01. 79
the fellow finds his vein, | and, yielding to ERR 4.04. 80
and finds his trusty thisby's mantle slain; MND 5.01.145
before thisby comes back and finds her lover? 5.01.313 P
he finds the joys of heaven here on earth; MV 3.05. 76
finds tongues in trees, books in the running AYL 2.01. 16
and finds no other advantage in the process but AWW 1.01. 15 P
make title to as much love as she finds. 1.03.103 P
virginity and devours up all the fry it finds. 4.03.221 P
if not, be it his that finds it. TN 2.02. 16 P
and he finds that now scarce to be worth talking 3.04.298 P
his parts, | and finds them perfect richard. JN 1.01. 90
finds brotherhood in thee no sharper spur? R2 1.02. 9
it so, | which finds it an enforced pilgrimage. 1.03.264
who finds the heifer dead and bleeding fresh, 2H6 3.02.188
who finds the partridge in the puttock's nest 3.02.191
such safety finds | the trembling lamb environed 3H6 1.01.241
that who finds edward | shall have a high reward 5.05. 9
upon my life, she finds (although i cannot) R3 1.02.253
and finds the testy gentleman so hot | that he 3.04. 37
since virtue finds no friends) a wife, a true H8 3.01.126
finds safer footing than blind reason stumbling TRO 3.02. 71 P
finds bottom in th' uncomprehensive depth, 3.03.198
where he should find you lions, finds you hares; COR 1.01.171
your ignorance (which finds not till it feels, 3.03.129
riddling confession finds but riddling shrift. ROM 2.03. 56
that heaven finds means to kill your joys with 5.03.293
where my stomach finds meat, or, rather, where i TIM 4.03.294 P
sake | he finds himself beholding to us all. JC 3.02. 67
he finds thee in the stout norweyan ranks, MAC 1.03. 95
the night is long that never finds the day. 4.03.240
"anon he finds him | striking too short at HAM 2.02.468
hath sate on her, and finds it christian burial. 5.01. 4 P
yet nature finds itself scourg'd by the sequent LR 1.02.105 P
this, let him be whipt that first finds it so. 1.04.165 P
that he which finds him shall deserve our thanks 2.01. 61
all's not offense that indiscretion finds | and 2.04.196
when resty sloth | finds the down pillow hard. CYM 3.06. 35
who finds her, give her burying, | she was the PER 3.02. 72
to spy advantages, and where he finds 'em, TNK 4.02.133
which superstition | here finds allowance — on 5.04. 54
the warm effects which she in him finds missing VEN 605
here kennell'd in a brake she finds a hound, 913
the shame and fault finds no excuse nor end. LUC 238
and who she finds forlorn she doth lament. 1500
that he finds means to burn his troy with water. 1561
who finds his lucrece clad in mourning black, 1585
wherein it finds a joy above the rest, | but SON 91. 6
love | which alters when it alteration finds, 116. 3
FIND'ST 5 FR 0.0005 REL FR 4 V 1 P
where fires thou find'st unrak'd and hearths WIV 5.05. 44
voice, and bring me word how thou find'st him. TN 4.02. 67 P
and when thou find'st a man that's like thyself, TIT 5.02. 99
thou find'st to be too busy is some danger. HAM 3.04. 33
and give the letters which thou find'st about me LR 4.06.248
/FINE* 5 FR 0.0005 REL FR 4 V 1 P
to /fine his title with some shows of truth, H5 1.02. 72
thou hast affected the /fine strains of honor, COR 5.03.149
/nature /is /fine /in /love, /and /where /'tis HAM 4.05.162
/is /fine /in /love, /and /where /'tis /fine, 4.05.162
/is /this /the /fine /of /his /fines, /and /the 5.01.106 P
FINE* 100 FR 0.0113 REL FR 71 V 29 P
fine apparition! TMP 1.02.317
spirit, fine spirit, i'll free thee | within two 1.02.421
thou hast done well, fine ariel! 1.02.495
these be fine things, and if they be not sprites 2.02.116
how fine my master is! 5.01.262
as of a knight well–spoken, neat, and fine; TGV 1.02. 10
a fine volley of words, gentlemen, and quickly 2.04. 33 P
hark, what fine change is in the music. 4.02. 68 P
i have a fine hawk for the bush. WIV 3.03.231 P
him not in fee–simple, with fine and recovery, 4.02.211 P
whip me with their fine wits till i were as 4.05.100 P
are not finely touch'd | but to fine issues; MM 1.01. 36
to fine the faults whose fine stands in record, 2.02. 40
to fine the faults whose fine stands in record, 2.02. 40
may he not do it by fine and recovery? ERR 2.02. 74 P
yes, to pay a fine for a periwig, and recover 2.02. 75 P
and the fine is (for the which i may go the ADO 1.01.245 P
that thou began'st to twist so fine a story? 1.01.311
but for a fine, quaint, graceful, and excellent 3.04. 22 P
i said thou hadst a fine wit. 5.01.160 P
"true," said she, "a fine little one." 5.01.161 P
or study where to meet some mistress fine, LLL 1.01. 63
a most fine figure! 1.02. 55 P
as to speak "dout," fine, when he should say 5.01. 20 P
no, sir, but it is vara fine, | for every one 5.02.487
fine, i' faith! MND 3.02.284
the poet's eye, in a fine frenzy rolling, | doth 5.01. 12
garter, it would have been a fine tragedy; 5.01.359 P
and speak of frays | like a fine bragging youth, MV 3.04. 69
state, | which humbleness may drive unto a fine. 4.01.372
to quit the fine for one half of his goods, | i 4.01.381
a fine musician to instruct our mistress; SHR 1.02.173
i will be sure my katherine shall be fine. 2.01.317
we will have rings and things, and fine array; 2.01.323
fine linen, turkey cushions boss'd with pearl, 2.01.353
deceiv'd, | our fine musician groweth amorous. 3.01. 63
there were none fine but adam, rafe, and gregory 4.01.136
o fine villain! 5.01. 66 P
let her in fine consent, | as we'll direct her AWW 3.07. 19
in fine, delivers me to fill the time, | herself 3.07. 33
soul, | in your fine frame hath love no quality? 4.02. 4
in fine, made a groan of her last breath, and 4.03. 52 P
there's a dozen of 'em, with delicate fine hats, 4.05.105 P
are motives of more fancy, and, in fine, | her 5.03.215
but thou art too fine in thy evidence, therefore 5.03.268 P
o, she that hath a heart of that fine frame | to TN 1.01. 32
present our services to a fine new prince | one WT 2.01. 17
what fine chisel | could ever yet cut breath? 5.03. 78
paying the fine of rated treachery | even with a JN 5.04. 37
even with a treacherous fine of all your lives, 5.04. 38
o for a fine thief, of the age of two and twenty 1H4 3.03.188 P
in this fine age were not thought flattery, 4.01. 2
with some fine color that may please the eye 5.01. 75
'a shot a fine shoot. 2H4 3.02. 44 P
other, less fine in carat, /is more precious, 4.05.161
but thou, most fine, most honor'd, most renown'd 4.05.163
"a cup of wine that's brisk and fine, | and 5.03. 46
in fine, redeem'd i was as i desir'd. 1H6 1.04. 34
y' have made a fine hand, fellows! H8 5.03. 70
troth, sweet /lord, thou hast a fine forehead. TRO 3.01.108 P
sounding destruction, or some joy too fine, 3.02. 23
the grief is fine, full, perfect, that i taste, 4.04. 3
a fine spot, in good faith. COR 1.03. 52 P
commons," be it either | for death, for fine, or 3.03. 15
then let them, | if i say fine, cry "fine!" 3.03. 16
then let them, | if i say fine, cry "fine!" 3.03. 16
by her fine foot, straight leg, and quivering ROM 2.01. 19
but i'll amerce you with so strong a fine | that 3.01.190
and he will make the face of heaven so fine 3.02. 23
but fettle your fine joints 'gainst thursday 3.05.153
thy verse swells with stuff so fine and smooth TIM 5.01. 84
sir, in respect of a fine workman, i am but, as JC 1.01. 10 P
receives rebuke from norway, and, in fine, HAM 2.02. 69
sweet, and by very much more handsome than fine. 2.02.445 P
frenchman gave you, bring you in fine together, 4.07.133
here's fine revolution, and we had the trick to 5.01. 90 P
to have his fine pate full of fine dirt? 5.01.107 P
to have his fine pate full of fine dirt? 5.01.108 P
and in fine withdrew | to mine own room again, 5.02. 15
fine word, "legitimate"! LR 1.02. 18
sir, in fine, | seeing how loathly opposite i 2.01. 48
i was a fine fool to take it. OTH 4.01.150 P
a fine woman! 4.01.178 P
your fine egyptian cookery | shall have the fame ANT 2.06. 63
a very fine one. o, how he loves caesar! 3.02. 7
how fine this tyrant | can tickle where she CYM 1.01. 84
such gain the cap of him that makes him fine, 3.03. 25
spent | with your fine fancies quaintly /eche: PER 3.ch. 13
would i could find a fine frog! TNK 3.04. 12
is not this a fine song? 4.01.105
o, a very fine one! 4.01.105
is't not a fine young gentleman? 4.01.118
yes, he's a fine man. 4.01.120
they show | great and fine art in nature. 4.02.123
you fathers are fine fools. 5.02. 28
that's fine indeed. 5.02. 50
that's a fine maid! 5.02. 70
time's office is to fine the hate of foes, | to LUC 936
to hear with eyes belongs to love's fine wit. SON 23.14
for blunting the fine point of seldom pleasure. 52. 4
FINE–BAITED 1 FR 0.0001 REL FR 0 V 1 P
and lead him on with a fine–baited delay, till WIV 2.01. 95 P
FINELESS 1 FR 0.0001 REL FR 1 V 0 P
but riches fineless is as poor as winter | to OTH 3.03.173
FINELY 13 FR 0.0014 REL FR 11 V 2 P
go, brew me a pottle of sack finely. WIV 3.05. 29 P
fairies, | finely attired in a robe of white. 4.04. 72
we'll betray him finely. 5.03. 20 P
spirits are not finely touch'd | but to fine MM 1.01. 35
why, she that bears the bow. | finely put off! LLL 4.01.110
finely put on! 4.01.113
finely put on indeed! 4.01.116
we will turn it finely off, sir; 5.02.510
how say you to a fat tripe finely broil'd? SHR 4.03. 20
such and so finely bolted didst thou seem. H5 2.02.137
he dances very finely, very comely, | and, for a TNK 5.02. 48
and will perfume me finely against the wedding. 5.02. 89
my palamon i hope will grow too, finely, | now 5.02. 95
FINEM 1 FR 0.0001 REL FR 0 V 1 P
mistress, respice finem, respect your end, or ERR 4.04. 41 P
FINENESS 3 FR 0.0003 REL FR 3 V 0 P
the fineness of the gold, and chargeful fashion, ERR 4.01. 29
the fineness of which metal is not found | in TRO 1.03. 22
or those that with the fineness of their souls 1.03.209
FINER 6 FR 0.0006 REL FR 1 V 5 P
the fine is (for the which i may go the finer), ADO 1.01.245 P
of his verbosity finer than the staple of his LLL 5.01. 17 P
your accent is something finer than you could AYL 3.02.341 P
i'll confine myself no finer than i am. TN 1.03. 10 P
not noted, is't, | but of the finer natures? WT 1.02.226
'a made a finer end, and went away and it had H5 2.03. 11 P
FINE'S 1 FR 0.0001 REL FR 1 V 0 P
still the fine's the crown; AWW 4.04. 35
/FINES 1 FR 0.0001 REL FR 0 V 1 P
/is /this /the /fine /of /his /fines, /and /the HAM 5.01.106 P
FINES 4 FR 0.0004 REL FR 3 V 1 P
o'ercharging your free purses with large fines; 1H6 1.03. 64
on your heads | clap round fines for neglect. H8 5.03. 80
the last, i think | might have found easy fines; COR 5.06. 64
his recognizances, his fines, his double HAM 5.01.105 P
FINEST 3 FR 0.0003 REL FR 1 V 2 P
love | inhabits in the finest wits of all. TGV 1.01. 44
hath the finest mad devil of jealousy in him, WIV 5.01. 18 P
of nothing but the finest part of pure love. ANT 1.02.147 P
FINGER 63 FR 0.0071 REL FR 45 V 18 P
though his false finger have profan'd the ring, TGV 4.04.136
but i'll ne'er put my finger in the fire, and WIV 1.04. 86 P
i see a sword out, my finger itches to make one. 2.03. 45 P
in his fortunes with the finger of my substance. 3.02. 75 P
dare no more stretch this finger of mine than he MM 5.01.314
a fool, | to put the finger in the eye and weep, ERR 2.02.204
ring — | the ring i saw upon his finger now — 4.04.139
he did, and from my finger snatch'd that ring. 5.01.277
my poor shoulder, and with his royal finger, LLL 5.01.103 P
another, with his finger and his thumb, | cried, 5.02.111
i will kiss thy royal finger, and take leave. 5.02.882 P
if i cut my finger, i shall make bold with you. MND 3.01.183 P
you may tell every finger i have with my ribs. MV 2.02.107 P
but when this ring | parts from this finger, 3.02.184
a thing stuck on with oaths upon your finger, 5.01.168
nor pluck it from his finger, for the wealth 5.01.173
but you see my finger | hath not the ring upon 5.01.187
as lief thou didst break his neck as his finger. AYL 1.01.147 P
it is best | put finger in the eye, and she knew SHR 1.01. 79
though thy little finger be arm'd in a thimble. 4.03.148 P
"when thou canst get the ring upon my finger, AWW 3.02. 58 P
and on your finger in the night i'll put 4.02. 61
her leave at court, | i saw upon her finger. 5.03. 80
that she would never put it from her finger, 5.03.109
sir, much like | the same upon your finger. 5.03.226
"when from my finger you can get this ring | and 5.03.312
the very mould and frame of hand, nail, finger. WT 2.03.103
whereto my finger, like a dial's point, | is R2 5.05. 53
and 'twixt his finger and his thumb he held | a 1H4 1.03. 37
in faith, i'll break thy little finger, harry, 2.03. 87
for they never prick their finger but they say, 2H4 2.02.112 P
temp'ring between my finger and my thumb, and 4.03.130 P
one spark of evil | that might annoy my finger? H5 2.02.102
prick not your finger as you pluck it off, 1H6 2.04. 49
thy hand is but a finger to my fist, | thy leg a 2H6 4.10. 48
do not honor him so much | to prick thy finger, 3H6 1.04. 55
look how my ring encompasseth thy finger, | even R3 1.02.203
man's pie is freed | from his ambitious finger. H8 1.01. 53
ground, | then lays his finger on his temple; 3.02.115
where a finger | could not be wedg'd in more. 4.01. 57
the king will suffer but the little finger | of 5.02.141
he, that dares most, but wag his finger at thee. 5.02.166
peace, troyan, lay thy finger on thy lips! TRO 1.03.240
with his fat rump and potato finger, tickles 5.02. 56 P
would your cambric were sensible as your finger, COR 1.03. 85 P
me about with his finger and his thumb as one 4.05.153 P
for you to displace it with your little finger, 5.04. 5 P
upon his bloody finger he doth wear | a precious TIT 2.03.226
worm | prick'd from the lazy finger of a /maid. ROM 1.04. 69
but chiefly to take thence from her dead finger 5.03. 30
but must not break my back to heal his finger. TIM 2.01. 24
by each at once her choppy finger laying | upon MAC 1.03. 44
finger of birth–strangled babe | ditch–deliver'd 4.01. 30
that they are not a pipe for fortune's finger HAM 3.02. 70
lay thy finger thus; OTH 2.01.221 P
for let our finger ache, and it endues | our 3.04.146
scorn | to point his slow /unmoving finger at! 4.02. 55
my ring i hold dear as my finger, 'tis part of CYM 1.04.133 P
that diamond upon your finger, say | how came it 5.05.137
which then he wore | upon his honor'd finger, to 5.05.184
long, | and with a finger of so deep a cunning, TNK 1.03. 43
and griping it, the needle his finger pricks, LUC 319
as on the finger of a throned queen | the basest SON 96. 5
FINGER'D 3 FR 0.0003 REL FR 3 V 0 P
the king was slily finger'd from the deck! 3H6 5.01. 44
finger'd their packet, and in fine withdrew | to HAM 5.02. 15
who, finger'd to make man his lawful music, PER 1.01. 82
FINGER–END 1 FR 0.0001 REL FR 1 V 0 P
with trial–fire touch me his finger–end. WIV 5.05. 84
FINGERING 3 FR 0.0003 REL FR 2 V 1 P
and bow'd her hand to teach her fingering; SHR 2.01.150
to learn the order of my fingering, | i must 3.01. 65
if you can penetrate her with your fingering, so CYM 2.03. 15 P
FINGER'S 2 FR 0.0002 REL FR 1 V 1 P
and smile upon his finger's end, i knew there H5 2.03. 15 P
why, this hath not a finger's dignity. TRO 1.03.204
FINGERS' 3 FR 0.0003 REL FR 1 V 2 P
thou hast it ad dunghill, at the fingers' ends, LLL 5.01. 78 P
ay, sir, i have them at my fingers' ends. TN 1.03. 78 P
wrath | out of the bloody fingers' ends of john. JN 3.04.168
FINGERS 41 FR 0.0046 REL FR 25 V 16 P
your monster, and the devil take your fingers! TMP 3.02. 81 P
come put some lime upon your fingers, and away 4.01.246 P
monster, lay–to your fingers. 4.01.250 P
or let him hold his fingers thus, and through MND 3.01. 70 P
ivy so | enrings the barky fingers of the elm. 4.01. 44
in sweet clothes, rings put upon his fingers, SHR in.1. 38
and not worthy to touch fortune's fingers. TN 2.05.157 P
but to be paddling palms and pinching fingers, WT 1.02.115
and ring these fingers with thy household worms, JN 3.04. 31
come | to thrust his icy fingers in my maw, 5.07. 37
unless you call three fingers in the ribs bare. 1H4 4.02. 74 P
one, 'tis alike as my fingers is to my fingers, H5 4.07. 30 P
'tis alike as my fingers is to my fingers, and 4.07. 30 P
i kiss these fingers for eternal peace, | and 1H6 5.03. 48
and with my fingers feel his hand unfeeling. 2H6 3.02.145
do not, porpentine, do not, my fingers itch. TRO 2.01. 26 P
/these your white enchanting fingers touch'd, 3.01.151
and he hath cut those pretty fingers off | that TIT 2.04. 42
o'er lawyers' fingers, who straight dream on ROM 1.04. 73
my fingers itch. 3.05.164
for i'll try if they can lick their fingers. 4.02. 4 P

an ill cook that cannot lick his own fingers; 4.02. 7 P
that cannot lick his fingers goes not with me. 4.02. 8 P
he was very loath to lay his fingers off it. JC 1.02.242 P
peace, | shaking the bloody fingers of thy foes, 3.01.198
now | contaminate our fingers with base bribes? 4.03. 24
and still your fingers on your lips, i pray. HAM 1.05.187
these ventages with your fingers and /thumbs, 3.02.358 P
paddling in your neck with his damn'd fingers, 3.04.185
cull–cold maids do dead men's fingers call them. 4.07.171
i prithee take thy fingers from my throat. 5.01.260
you had not kiss'd your three fingers so oft, OTH 2.01.173 P
yet again, your fingers to your lips? 2.01.176 P
the fingers of the pow'rs above do tune | the CYM 5.05.466
weav'd the sleided silk | with fingers long, PER 4.ch. 22
the gout had knit his fingers into knots, TNK 5.01.112
gone, | she locks her lily fingers one in one. VEN 228
he bends her fingers, holds her pulses hard, 476
with thy sweet fingers when thou gently sway'st SON 128. 3
o'er whom /thy fingers walk with gentle gait, 128.11
give them /thy fingers, me thy lips to kiss. 128.14

FINGRE 3 FR 0.0003 REL FR 0 V 3 P
d' hand, de fingre, de nailes, d' arma, de H5 3.04. 29 P
d' hand, de fingre, de nailes — 3.04. 45 P
d' hand, de fingre, de nailes, d' arma, d' elbow 3.04. 58 P

FINGRES 4 FR 0.0004 REL FR 0 V 4 P
je pense qu'ils sont appeles de fingres, oui, de H5 3.04. 11 P
qu'ils sont appeles de fingres, oui, de fingres. 3.04. 11 P
les doigts, de fingres. 3.04. 12 P
de hand, de fingres, et de nailes. 3.04. 18 P

FING'RING 1 FR 0.0001 REL FR 1 V 0 P
you would be fing'ring them, to anger me. TGV 1.02. 98

FINICAL 1 FR 0.0001 REL FR 0 V 1 P
glass–gazing, superserviceable, finical rogue; LR 2.02. 19 P

FINISH 10 FR 0.0011 REL FR 9 V 1 P
shall that finish the jest? LLL 2.01.221
how thus we met, and these things finish. AYL 5.04.140
god may finish it when he will, 'tis not a hair 2H4 1.02. 23 P
his days may finish ere that hapless time. 1H6 3.01.200
to run, | finish the process of his sandy hour, 4.02. 36
day, | how many days will finish up the year, 3H6 2.05. 28
break to powder, | and finish all foul thoughts. ANT 4.09. 18
finish, good lady, the bright day is done, | and 5.02.193
i had you down and might | have made you finish. CYM 5.05.412
the glass is running now that cannot finish TNK 5.01. 18

FINISH'D 5 FR 0.0005 REL FR 4 V 1 P
the nuptial finish'd, | let him be whipt and MM 5.01.512
i took him sleeping — that is finish'd too — MND 3.02. 38
he bids be done is finish'd with his bidding. COR 5.04. 23 P
thou hast finish'd joy and moan. CYM 4.02.273
wet cheeks | were present when she finish'd. 5.05. 36

FINISHED 4 FR 0.0004 REL FR 3 V 1 P
he finished indeed his mortal act | that day TN 5.01.247
man, | left to be finished by such as she, | and JN 2.01.438
out of my mouth, ere it is made and finished. H5 4.07. 43 P
her monument | is almost finished, and her PER 4.03. 43

FINISHER 1 FR 0.0001 REL FR 1 V 0 P
he that of greatest works is finisher | oft does AWW 2.01.136

FINLESS 1 FR 0.0001 REL FR 1 V 0 P
and of a dragon and a finless fish, | a 1H4 3.01.149

/FINNY 1 FR 0.0001 REL FR 1 V 0 P
how from the /finny subject of the sea | these PER 2.01. 48

FINS 2 FR 0.0002 REL FR 1 V 1 P
and his fins like arms! TMP 2.02. 34 P
upon your favors swims with fins of lead, | and COR 1.01.180

FINSBURY 1 FR 0.0001 REL FR 1 V 0 P
as if thou never walk'st further than finsbury. 1H4 3.01.252

FIN'ST 3 FR 0.0003 REL FR 3 V 0 P
toys for your head | of the new'st and fin'st, WT 4.04.320
head | of the new'st and fin'st, fin'st wear–a? 4.04.320
our dear'st repute | with their fin'st palate; TRO 1.03.338

FIRAGO 1 FR 0.0001 REL FR 0 V 1 P
a very devil, i have not seen such a firago. TN 3.04.274 P

FIR'D 4 FR 0.0004 REL FR 4 V 0 P
is that lead slow which is fir'd from a gun? LLL 3.01. 62
as violently as hasty powder fir'd | doth hurry ROM 5.01. 64
men | be like a beacon fir'd t' amaze your eyes. PER 1.04. 87
their fame has fir'd me so — till they appear. TNK 4.02.153

/FIRE 4 FR 0.0004 REL FR 3 V 1 P
/their /eyes /of /fire /sparkling /through 2H4 4.01.119
/what, /frighted /with /false /fire? HAM 3.02.266 P
/arms, /arms, /sword, /fire! LR 3.06. 55
the circles of his eyes show /fire within him, TNK 4.02. 81

FIRE 300 FR 0.0339 REL FR 243 V 57 P
to th' welkin's cheek, | dashes the fire out. TMP 1.02. 5
to swim, to dive into the fire, to ride | on the 1.02.191
the fire and cracks | of sulphurous roaring the 1.02.203
he does make our fire, | fetch in our wood, and 1.02.311
oaths are straw | to th' fire i' th' blood. 4.01. 53
the dread rattling thunder | have i given fire, 5.01. 45
fire that's closest kept burns most of all. TGV 1.02. 30
have i shunn'd the fire for fear of burning, 1.03. 78
yourself, sweet lady, for you gave the fire. 2.04. 37 P
which, like a waxen image 'gainst a fire, 2.04.201
thou wouldst as soon go kindle fire with snow 2.07. 19
as seek to quench the fire of love with words. 2.07. 20
i do not seek to quench your love's hot fire, 2.07. 21
in faith, at the latter end of a sea–coal fire. WIV 1.04. 9 P
but i'll ne'er put my finger in the fire, and 1.04. 86 P
till the wicked fire of lust have melted him in 2.01. 68 P
give fire! 2.02.137
would run through fire and water for such a kind 3.04.103 P
the oil that's in me should set hell on fire; 5.05. 35 P
come, will this wood take fire? 5.05. 88
lust is but a bloody fire, | kindled with 5.05. 95
and laugh this sport o'er by a country fire — 5.05.242
light is an effect of fire, and fire will burn: ERR 4.03. 56 P
light is an effect of fire, and fire will burn: 4.03. 56 P
thereof the raging fire of fever bred, | and 5.01. 75
beard they have sing'd off with brands of fire, 5.01.171
is the opinion that fire cannot melt out of me; ADO 1.01.232 P
and have cleft his club to make the fire too. 2.01.254 P
therefore let benedick, like cover'd fire, 3.01. 77
what fire is in mine ears? 3.01.107
and in her eye there hath appear'd a fire | to 4.01.162
'tis won as towns with fire — so won, so lost. LLL 1.01.146
fire enough for a flint, pearl enough for a 4.02. 88 P
not to anger bent, is music and sweet fire. 4.02.116
whence doth spring the true promethean fire. 4.03.300
they sparkle still the right promethean fire; 4.03.348
and stand between her back, sir, and the fire, 5.02.476
and by that fire which burn'd the carthage queen MND 1.01.173
over pale, | thorough flood, thorough fire, | i 2.01. 5
and run through fire i will for thy sweet sake. 2.02.103
a hog, a headless bear, sometime a fire, | and 3.01.109
horse, hound, hog, bear, fire, at every turn. 3.01.111
glimmering light | by the dead and drowsy fire, 5.01.392
where phoebus' fire scarce thaws the icicles, MV 2.01. 5
his tedious measures with the unbated fire 2.06. 11
"the fire seven times tried this: 2.09. 63
well be amity and life | 'tween snow and fire, 3.02. 31
may she not by fortune fall into the fire? AYL 1.02. 44 P
the property of rain is to wet and fire to burn; 3.02. 27 P
to hear | as will a chestnut in a farmer's fire? SHR 1.02.209
though little fire grows great with little wind, 2.01.134
yet extreme gusts will blow out fire and all; 2.01.135
i am sent before to make a fire, and they are 4.01. 4 P
belly, ere i should come by a fire to thaw me. 4.01. 8 P
but i with blowing the fire shall warm myself; 4.01. 9 P
a fire, good curtis. 4.01. 16 P
o, ay, curtis, ay, and therefore fire, fire; 4.01. 19 P
o, ay, curtis, ay, and therefore fire, fire; 4.01. 19 P
but wilt thou make a fire, or shall i complain 4.01. 29 P
in every office but thine, and therefore fire. 4.01. 36 P
there's fire ready, and therefore, good grumio, 4.01. 39 P
why, therefore fire, for i have caught extreme 4.01. 44 P
they sit conferring by the parlor fire. 5.02.102
dance canary | with spritely fire and motion, AWW 2.01. 75
that ride upon the violent speed of fire, | fly 3.02.109
yet in his idle fire, | to buy his will, it 3.07. 26
if the quick fire of youth light not your mind, 4.02. 5
that always lov'd a great fire, and the master i 4.05. 48 P
the master i speak of ever keeps a good fire. 4.05. 49 P
that leads to the broad gate and the great fire. 4.05. 55 P
when oil and fire, too strong for reason's force 5.03. 7
groans that thunder love, with sighs of fire. TN 1.05.256
fire and brimstone! 2.05. 50 P
your dormouse valor, to put fire in your heart, 3.02. 20 P
as doth that orbed continent the fire | that 5.01.271
given to the fire, a moi'ty of my rest | might WT 2.03. 8
together with the dam | commit them to the fire! 2.03. 96
it is an heretic that makes the fire, | not she 2.03.115
and see it instantly consum'd with fire. 2.03.134
go, take it to the fire, | for thou set'st on 2.03.141
would have shed water out of fire ere done't; 3.02.193
her face o' fire | with labor, and the thing she 4.04. 60
and now, instead of bullets wrapp'd in fire, JN 2.01.227
when the rich blood of kings is set on fire! 2.01.351
as fire cools fire | within the scorched veins 3.01.277
as fire cools fire | within the scorched veins 3.01.277
to ashes, ere our blood shall quench that fire. 3.01.345
but for containing fire to harm mine eye. 4.01. 66
the fire is dead with grief, | being create for 4.01.105
that mercy which fierce fire and iron extends, 4.01.119
with eyes as red as new–enkindled fire, | and 4.02.163
be stirring as the time, be fire with fire, 5.01. 48
be stirring as the time, be fire with fire, 5.01. 48
brought in matter that should feed this fire; 5.02. 85
resolveth from his figure 'gainst the fire? 5.04. 25
and against this fire | do i shrink up. 5.07. 33
ire, | in rage, deaf as the sea, hasty as fire. R2 1.01. 19
hath love in thy old blood no living fire? 1.02. 10
who can hold a fire in his hand | by thinking on 1.03.294
terror than the elements | of fire and water, 3.03. 56
be he the fire, i'll be the yielding water; 3.03. 58
in winter's tedious nights sit by the fire 5.01. 40
tongue, | and in compassion weep the fire out, 5.01. 48
that hand shall burn in never–quenching fire 5.05.108
is that the rebels have consum'd with fire | our 5.06. 2
thou hadst fire and sword on thy side, and yet 1H4 2.04.317 P
and the fire of grace be not quite out of thee, 2.04.383 P
the heavens were all on fire, the earth did 3.01. 23
then the earth shook to see the heavens on fire, 3.01. 24
as slow | as hot lord percy is on fire to go. 3.01.264
my oath should be "by this fire, that/'s god's 3.03. 35 P
of yours with fire any time this two and thirty 3.03. 47 P
i am on fire | to hear this rich reprisal is so 4.01.117
but priam found the fire ere he his tongue, 2H4 1.01. 74
whose spirit lent a fire | even to the dullest 1.01.112
took fire and heat away | from the best–temper'd 1.01.114
breaks like a fire | out of his keeper's arms, 1.01.142
bosom burns | with an incensed fire of injuries. 1.03. 14
at the round table by a sea–coal fire, upon 2.01. 88 P
no, let the fiend give fire. 2.04.182
we bear our civil swords and native fire | as 5.05.106
o for a muse of fire, that would ascend | the H5 pr 1
famine, sword, and fire | crouch for employment. pr 7
with /blood and sword and fire, to win your 1.02.131
now all the youth of england are on fire, | and 2.pr. 1
cock is up, | and flashing fire will follow. 2.01. 53
the fuel is gone that maintain'd that fire. 2.03. 44 P
and knobs, and flames a' fire, and his lips 3.06.103 P
and it is like a coal of fire, sometimes plue 3.06.104 P
he is pure air and fire; 3.07. 21 P
fire answers fire, and through their paly flames 4.pr. 8
fire answers fire, and through their paly flames 4.pr. 8
his sparkling eyes, replete with wrathful fire, 1H6 1.01. 12
famine, quartering steel, and climbing fire, 4.02. 11
from the dolphin's crest thy sword struck fire, 4.06. 10
the time of night when troy was set on fire, 2H6 1.04. 17
nay then, this spark will prove a raging fire, 3.01.302
burns with revenging fire, whose hopeful colors 4.01. 97
i fear neither sword nor fire. 4.02. 59 P
but methinks he should stand in fear of fire, 4.02. 63 P
but first go and set london bridge on fire, and, 4.06. 14 P
shall be to me even as the dew to fire, | and 5.02. 53
as red as fire? nay then, her wax must melt. 3H6 3.02. 51
a little fire is quickly trodden out, | which, 4.08. 7
i need not add more fuel to your fire, | for 5.04. 70
the fire that mounts the liquor till't run o'er H8 1.01.144
quench, | or but allay, the fire of passion. 1.01.149
my drops of tears | i'll turn to sparks of fire. 2.04. 73
only envy at, | ye blew the fire that burns ye. 5.02.148
was a more temperate fire under the pot of her TRO 1.02.146 P
a noble man that hath no spark of fire | to 1.03.294
come in, come in, i'll go get a fire. 3.02. 59 P
when we vow to weep seas, live in fire, eat 3.02. 78 P
but it lies as coldly in him as fire in a flint, 3.03.257 P
no, | than is the coal of fire upon the ice, COR 1.01.173
they'll sit by th' fire, and presume to know 1.01.191
will be his fire | to kindle their dry stubble; 2.01.257
o'erborne their way, consum'd with fire, and 4.06. 78
one fire drives out one fire; 4.07. 54
one fire drives out one fire; 4.07. 54
till he had forg'd himself a name a' th' fire 5.01. 14
you'll see your rome embrac'd with fire before 5.02. 7
blow out the intended fire your city is ready to 5.02. 46 P
thou art preparing fire for us; 5.02. 71 P
as certain as i know the sun is fire. 5.04. 45
away with him, and make a fire straight, | and TIT 1.01.127
and entrails feed the sacrificing fire, | whose 1.01.144
set fire on barns and haystalks in the night, 5.01.133
a devil, | to live and burn in everlasting fire, 5.01.148
that quench the fire of your pernicious rage ROM 1.01. 84
of lead, bright smoke, cold fire, sick health, 1.01.180
being purg'd, a fire sparkling in lovers' eyes, 1.01.191
tut, man, one fire burns out another's burning, 1.02. 45
and quench the fire, the room is grown too hot. 1.05. 28
and in their triumph die, like fire and powder, 2.06. 10
the fire i' th' flint | shows not till it be TIM 1.01. 22
hot ardent zeal would set whole realms on fire; 3.03. 33 P
up, | let your close fire predominate his smoke, 4.03.143
whereon hyperion's quick'ning fire doth shine: 4.03.184
and her pale fire she snatches from the sun; 4.03.438
struck but thus much show of fire from brutus. JC 1.02.177
now, | did i go through a tempest dropping fire. 1.03. 10
not sensible of fire, remain'd unscorch'd. 1.03. 18
who swore they saw | men, all in fire, walk up 1.03. 25
those that with haste will make a mighty fire 1.03.107
toward the north | he first presents his fire, 2.01.110
they do) bear fire enough | to kindle cowards, 2.01.120
might fire the blood of ordinary men, | and turn 3.01. 37
they are all fire, and every one doth shine; 3.01. 64
as fire drives out fire, so pity pity — | hath 3.01.171
as fire drives out fire, so pity pity — | hath 3.01.171
soul, his eyes are red as fire with weeping. 3.02.115
fire! 3.02.204 P
and with the brands fire the traitors' houses. 3.02.255
go fetch fire. 3.02.257 P
that carries anger as the flint bears fire, 4.03.111
and, her attendants absent, swallow'd fire. 4.03.156
are those my tents where i perceive the fire? 5.03. 13
the conquerors can but make a fire of him; 5.05. 55
what hath quench'd them hath given me fire. MAC 2.02. 2
become | a woman's story at a winter's fire, 3.04. 64
fire burn, and cauldron bubble. 4.01. 11
fire burn, and cauldron bubble. 4.01. 21
fire burn, and cauldron bubble. 4.01. 36
as stars with trains of fire and dews of blood, HAM 1.01.117
whether in sea or fire, in earth or air, | th' 1.01.153
as it is a–making, | you must not take for fire. 1.03.120
near, | and gins to pale his uneffectual fire. 1.05. 90
"doubt thou the stars are fire, | doubt that the 2.02.116
this majestical roof fretted with golden fire, 2.02.301 P
roasted in wrath and fire, | and thus o'er–sized 2.02.461
let virtue be as wax | and melt in her own fire. 3.04. 85
time qualifies the spark and fire of it. 4.07.113
i have a speech a' fire that fain would blaze, 4.07.190
let all the battlements their ord'nance fire. 5.02.270
the lady brach may stand by th' fire and stink. LR 1.04.112 P
being oil to fire, snow to the colder moods; 2.02. 77
like the wreath of radiant fire | on /flick'ring 2.02.107
spit, fire! 3.02. 14
nor rain, wind, thunder, fire are my daughters. 3.02. 15
such sheets of fire, such bursts of horrid 3.02. 46
fiend hath led through fire and through flame, 3.04. 52 P
now a little fire in a wild field were like an 3.04.111 P
look, here comes a walking fire. 3.04.114 P
and bring you where both fire and food is ready. 3.04.153
should have stood that night | against my fire, 4.07. 37
but i am bound | upon a wheel of fire, that mine 4.07. 46
from heaven, | and fire us hence like foxes. 5.03. 23
the fire | is spied in populous cities. OTH 1.01. 76
give renew'd fire to our extincted spirits, 2.01. 81
poison, or fire, or suffocating streams, | i'll 3.03.389
fire and brimstone! 4.01.234
thou art rash as fire to say | that she was 5.02.134
wash me in steep–down gulfs of liquid fire! 5.02.280
by the fire | that quickens nilus' slime, i go ANT 1.03. 68
the sighs of octavia blow the fire up in caesar, 2.06.127 P
i would they'ld fight i' th' fire or i' th' air; 4.10. 3
i am fire and air; 5.02.289
yet | the fire of rage is in him, and 'twere CYM 1.01. 77
i stand on fire: | come to the matter. 5.05.168
but my unspotted fire of love to you. PER 1.01. 53
that were to blow at fire in hope to quench it, 1.04. 4
the which hath fire in darkness, none in light: 2.03. 44
him, | a fire from heaven came and shrivell'd up 2.04. 9
thou hast as chiding a nativity | as fire, air, 3.01. 33
hast thou had, my dear, | no light, no fire. 3.01. 57
get fire and meat for these poor men. 3.02. 3
make a fire within. 3.02. 80
and yet the fire of life kindle again | the 3.02. 83
the fire and cloths. 3.02. 87
when he bids 'em charge, | fall on like fire. TNK 2.02.250
we may go whistle; all the fat's i' th' fire. 3.05. 39
a fire ill take her! does she flinch now? 3.05. 52
they shall stand in fire up to the nav'l, and in 4.03. 43 P
/th' other, "this fire!" 4.03. 54 P
our stars must glister with new fire, or be 5.01. 69
could | no more be hid in him than fire in flax, 5.03. 98
and like him possess'd | with fire malevolent, 5.04. 63
i comment not — the hot horse, hot as fire, 5.04. 65
she red and hot as coals of glowing fire, | he VEN 35
she bathes in water, yet her fire must burn. 94
love is a spirit all compact of fire, | not 149
thine eye darts forth the fire that burneth me, 196
his eye, which scornfully glisters like fire, 275
free vent of words love's fire doth assuage, 334
pale, and by and by | it flash'd forth fire, as 348
else, suffer'd, it will set the heart on fire: 388
that dares not be so bold | to touch the fire, 402
or in the ocean drench'd, or in the fire? 494
desire, | as air and water do abate the fire. 654
mine eyes are turn'd to fire, my heart to lead: 1072

heavy heart's lead, melt at mine eyes' red fire! 1073
as dry combustious matter is to fire. 1162
and to collatium bears the lightless fire, LUC 4
that from the cold stone sparks of fire do fly, 177
"as from this cold flint i enforc'd this fire, 181
against love's fire fear's frost hath 355
thou blowest the fire when temperance is thaw'd, 884
thy eye kindled the fire that burneth here, 1475
had been bright with fame, and not with fire." 1491
his eye drops fire, no water thence proceeds; 1552
are balls of quenchless fire to burn thy city. 1554
for sinon in his fire doth quake with cold, 1556
and in that cold, hot burning fire doth dwell; 1557
times with sighs she gives her sorrow fire, 1604
doubt, | till my bad angel fire my good one out. PP 2.14
not to anger bent, is music and sweet fire. 5.12
she burnt with love, as straw with fire flameth, 7.13
the other two, slight air and purging fire, SON 45. 1
mars his sword nor war's quick fire shall burn 55. 7
in me thou seest the glowing of such fire | that 73. 9
doubt, | till my bad angel fire my good one out. 144.14
and his love–kindling fire did quickly steep 153. 3
which borrow'd from this holy fire of love | a 153. 5
for my help lies | where cupid got new fire — 153.14
hand | the fairest votary took up that fire, 154. 5
which from love's fire took heat perpetual, 154.10
love's fire heats water, water cools not love. 154.14
both fire from hence and chill extincture hath. LC 294
o, that false fire which in his cheek so glowed, 324

FIRE–BRAND 3 FR 0.0003 REL FR 2 V 1 P
nor lead me, like a fire–brand, in the dark TMP 2.02. 6
dreamt she was deliver'd of a fire–brand, and 2H4 2.02. 90 P
our fire–brand brother, paris, burns us all. TRO 2.02.110

FIRE–BRANDS 1 FR 0.0001 REL FR 0 V 1 P
come, brands ho, fire–brands! JC 3.03. 36 P

FIRED 1 FR 0.0001 REL FR 1 V 0 P
but at my mistress' eye love's brand new fired, SON 153. 9

FIRE–DRAKE 1 FR 0.0001 REL FR 0 V 1 P
that fire–drake did i hit three times on the H8 5.03. 44 P

FIRE/–EY'D 1 FR 0.0001 REL FR 1 V 0 P
lenity, | and fire/–ey'd fury be my conduct now! ROM 3.01.124

FIRE–EY'D 1 FR 0.0001 REL FR 1 V 0 P
and to the fire–ey'd maid of smoky war | all hot 1H4 4.01.114

FIRE–NEW 4 FR 0.0004 REL FR 3 V 1 P
a man of fire–new words, fashion's own knight. LLL 1.01.178
some excellent jests, fire–new from the mint, TN 3.02. 22 P
your fire–new stamp of honor is scarce current. R3 1.03.255
/despite thy victor–sword and fire–new fortune, LR 5.03.133

FIRE–ROB'D 1 FR 0.0001 REL FR 1 V 0 P
and the fire–rob'd god, | golden apollo, a poor WT 4.04. 29

FIRE'S 2 FR 0.0002 REL FR 1 V 1 P
hot fire, | but qualify the fire's extreme rage, TGV 2.07. 22
but his nose is executed, and his fire's out. H5 3.06.106 P

/FIRES 1 FR 0.0001 REL FR 1 V 0 P
such falsehood, then turn tears to /fires; ROM 1.02. 89

FIRES 25 FR 0.0028 REL FR 24 V 1 P
where fires thou find'st unrak'd and hearths WIV 5.05. 44
and where two raging fires meet together, | they SHR 2.01.132
fires? WT 3.02.176
for violent fires soon burn out themselves; R2 2.01. 34
he fires the proud tops of the eastern pines 3.02. 42
by their watchful fires | sit patiently and inly H5 4.pr. 23
is kindling coals that fires all my breast, 3H6 2.01. 83
sprites and fires! TRO 5.01. 66 P
or, by the fires of heaven, i'll leave the foe COR 1.04. 39
the fires i' th' lowest hell fold in the people! 3.03. 68
praise the gods, | and make triumphant fires! 5.05. 3
consider the true cause | why all these fires, JC 1.03. 63
stars, hide your fires, | let not light see my MAC 1.04. 50
and for the day confin'd to fast in fires, HAM 1.05. 11
you sulph'rous and thought–executing fires, LR 3.02. 4
have buoy'd up | and quench'd the stelled fires; 3.07. 61
and shot their fires | into th' abysm of hell. ANT 3.13.146
made lud's–town with rejoicing fires bright, CYM 3.01. 32
behold their quarter'd fires, have both their 4.04. 18
if fires be hot, knives sharp, or waters deep, PER 4.02.146
let the temples | burn bright with sacred fires, TNK 5.01. 3
the heavenly fires | did scorch his mortal son, 5.01. 91
puffs forth another wind that fires the torch. LUC 315
lights are soon blown out, huge fires abide, 647
that two red fires in both their faces blazed; 1353

FIRE–SHOVEL 1 FR 0.0001 REL FR 0 V 1 P
and in callice they stole a fire–shovel. H5 3.02. 45 P

FIREWORK 1 FR 0.0001 REL FR 0 V 1 P
or show, or pageant, or antic, or firework. LLL 5.01.112 P

FIREWORKS 1 FR 0.0001 REL FR 1 V 0 P
pertaining thereunto, as fights and fireworks, H8 1.03. 27

FIRING 2 FR 0.0002 REL FR 2 V 0 P
nor fetch in firing | at requiring, | nor scrape TMP 2.02.181
wild motion of mine eye, | firing it only here; CYM 1.06.104

FIRK 2 FR 0.0002 REL FR 0 V 2 P
i'll fer him, and firk him, and ferret him. H5 4.04. 28 P
know the french for fer, and ferret, and firk. 4.04. 31 P

FIRM 41 FR 0.0046 REL FR 37 V 4 P
who was so firm, so constant, that this coil TMP 1.02.207
you are already love's firm votary | and cannot TGV 3.02. 58
as the earth is firm that falstaff is there. WIV 3.02. 48 P
and the firm fixture of thy foot would give an 3.03. 62 P
that was of late an heretic, | as firm as faith. 4.04. 10
against that match | and firm for doctor caius) 4.06. 28
(a man of stricture and firm abstinence) | my MM 1.03. 12
my lord, her wits, i fear me, are not firm. 5.01. 33
as there is no firm reason to be rend'red | why MV 4.01. 53
firm and irrevocable is my doom | which i have AYL 1.03. 83
nor is your firm resolve unknown to me, | in the SHR 2.01. 92
mine from all the world, | by your firm promise; 2.01.385
but, were my worth as is my conscience firm, TN 3.03. 17
that no supporter but the huge firm earth | can JN 3.01. 72
and keep our faiths firm and inviolable. 5.02. 7
showing as in a model our firm estate, | when R2 3.04. 42
peace shall stand as firm as rocky mountains. 2H4 4.01.186
thou art not firm enough, since griefs are green 4.05.203
bardolph, a soldier firm and sound of heart, H5 3.06. 25
for thou art fram'd of the firm truth of valor. 4.03. 14
all, | according to their firm proposed natures. 5.02.334
before his legs be firm to bear his body. 2H6 3.01.190
now, sister, let us hear your firm resolve. 3H6 3.03.129
what pledge have we of thy firm loyalty? 3.03.239
of us, | and the compact is firm and true in me. R3 2.02.133
look your heart be firm, | or else his head's 4.04.495
though my heart's content firm love doth bear, TRO 1.02.294
to blench from this and to stand firm by honor. 2.02. 68
your uncle's word and my firm faith. 3.02.108 P
not yet mature, yet matchless, firm of word, 4.05. 97
for who so firm that cannot be seduc'd? JC 1.02.312
that, and my firm nerves | shall never tremble. MAC 3.04.101
blood, | then the charm is firm and good. 4.01. 38
ever | the soul of nero enter this firm bosom, HAM 3.02.394
nothing. i have sworn, i am firm. LR 1.01.245
on that, | and fix most firm thy resolution. OTH 5.01. 5
"say the firm roman to great egypt sends | this ANT 1.05. 43
to chance and hazard, | from firm security. 3.07. 48
could behold the sun with as firm eyes as he. CYM 1.04. 12 P
the heavens hold firm | the walls of thy dear 2.01. 62
and the firm soil win of the wat'ry main, SON 64. 7

FIRMAMENT 6 FR 0.0006 REL FR 3 V 3 P
betwixt the firmament and it you cannot thrust a WT 3.03. 85 P
fall to the base earth from the firmament. R2 2.04. 20
what, hath the firmament moe suns than one? TIT 5.03. 17
quality | there is no fellow in the firmament. JC 3.01. 62
look you, this brave o'erhanging firmament, this HAM 2.02.301 P
maidenl'est star in the firmament twinkled on my LR 1.02.132 P

FIRMLY 10 FR 0.0011 REL FR 9 V 1 P
and stands so firmly on his wive's frailty, yet WIV 2.01.234 P
for how i firmly am resolv'd you know: SHR 1.01. 49
as firmly as yourself were still in place, | yea 1.02.156
and here i firmly vow | never to woo her more, 4.02. 28
as firmly as i hope for fertile england. 2H6 3.01. 88
last, i firmly am resolv'd | you shall have aid. 3H6 3.03.219
for now he firmly takes me for revenge, | and, TIT 5.02. 73
i will maintain | my truth and honor firmly. LR 5.03.101
what he beheld, on that he firmly doted, | and LUC 416
where her faith was firmly fix'd in love, PP 17. 7

FIRMNESS 2 FR 0.0002 REL FR 2 V 0 P
the unstooping firmness of my upright soul. R2 1.01.121
weary of solid firmness, melt itself | into the 2H4 3.01. 48

FIRM–SET 1 FR 0.0001 REL FR 1 V 0 P
thou /sure and firm–set earth, | hear not my MAC 2.01. 56

/FIRST 6 FR 0.0006 REL FR 4 V 2 P
/but /first sheathe thy impatience, throw cold WIV 2.03. 84 P
/we /first /survey /the /plot, /then /draw /the 2H4 1.03. 42
/a /gallant /horse /fall'n /in /first /rank, TRO 3.03.161
/i'll /see /their /trial /first, /bring /in LR 3.06. 35
/arraign /her /first, /'tis /goneril. 3.06. 46 P
that stands | in the /first place with arcite, TNK 4.02. 76

FIRST 575 FR 0.0650 REL FR 457 V 118 P
through all the signories it was the first, TMP 1.02. 71
not hair), | was the first man that leapt; 1.02.214
when thou cam'st first, | thou strok'st me and 1.02.332
that you have, | which first was mine own king; 1.02.342
at the first sight | they have chang'd eyes. 1.02.441
the first | that e'er i sigh'd for. 1.02.446
adrian, for a good wager, first begins to crow? 2.01. 29 P
as fresh as when we put them on first in afric, 2.01. 70 P
my doublet as fresh as the first day i wore it? 2.01.103 P
brain him, | having first seiz'd his books; 3.02. 89
remember | first to possess his books; 3.02. 92
let/'t alone | and do the murther first. 4.01.232
i did say so, | when first i rais'd the tempest. 5.01. 6
first, noble friend, | let me embrace thine age, 5.01.120
a breakfast, nor | befitting this first meeting. 5.01.165
rigg'd as when | we first put out to sea. 5.01.225
first, you have learn'd, like sir proteus, to TGV 2.01. 18 P
and ev'n that pow'r which gave me first my oath 2.06. 4
at first i did adore a twinkling star, | but now 2.06. 9
for scorn at first makes after–love the more. 3.01. 95
read over julia's heart (thy first best love), 5.04. 46
mistress anne, yourself shall go first. WIV 1.01.307 P
truly i will not go first; 1.01.309 P
but let thine inherit first, for i protest mine 2.01. 73 P
as my mother was, the first hour i was born. 2.02. 38
/brook, i will first make bold with your money; 2.02.252 P
and moreover, bully — but first, master guest, 2.03. 73 P
think i shall drink in pipe–wine first with him; 3.02. 90 P
let me stop this way first. 3.03.164 P
wealth | was the first motive that i woo'd thee, 3.04. 14
first, an intolerable fright, to be detected 3.05.108 P
i'll first direct my men what they shall do with 4.02. 99 P
a fault done first in the form of a beast (o 5.05. 8 P
though first in question, is thy secondary. MM 1.01. 46
first, and it like you, the house is a respected 2.01.162 P
evil | if the first that did th' edict infringe 2.02. 92
so you must be the first that gives this 2.02.106
in her the continuance of her first affection; 3.01.240 P
first, that your stay with him may not be long; 3.01.246 P
i'll be hang'd first; 3.02.168 P
first, here's young master rash, he's in for a 4.03. 4 P
but send me flavius first. 4.05. 10
first, his integrity | stands without blemish; 5.01.107
first, hath this woman | most wrongfully accus'd 5.01.139
first, for this woman, | to justify this worthy 5.01.158
first, let her show /her face, and after speak. 5.01.168
thou art the first knave that e'er mad'st a duke 5.01.356
first, provost, let me bail these gentle three. 5.01.357
whipt first, sir, and hang'd after. 5.01.507
i could not speak with dromio since at first | i ERR 2.02. 5
why, first — for flouting me, and then 2.02. 45
but, like a shrew, you first begin to brawl. 4.01. 51
first he denied you had in him no right. 4.02. 7
first he did praise my beauty, then my speech. 4.02. 15
him, | after you first forswore it on the mart, 5.01.262
antipholus, thou cam'st from corinth first? 5.01.363
cuts for the senior, till then, lead thou first. 5.01.423
much in beauty as the first of may doth the last ADO 1.01.192 P
the first suit is hot and hasty, like a scotch 2.01. 74 P
men was ever so, | since summer first was leavy. 2.03. 73
impossible, she may wear her heart out first. 2.03.204 P
you must hang it first, and draw it afterwards. 3.02. 24 P
first, who think you the most desartless man to 3.03. 9 P
vildly, i should first tell thee how the prince, 3.03.148 P
partly by his oaths, which first possess'd them, 3.03.156 P
we'll be friends first. 4.01.297 P
and write god first, for god defend but god 4.02. 19 P
but that's no matter, let him kill one first. 5.01. 81
first, i ask thee what they have done; 5.01.220 P
in the rare semblance that i lov'd it first. 5.01.252
swimmer, troilus the first employer of pandars, 5.02. 31 P
bad parts didst thou first fall in love with me? 5.02. 60 P
my good parts did you first suffer love for me? 5.02. 65 P
first, of my word; 5.04.121 P
the first and second cause will not serve my LLL 1.02.177 P
why, villain, thou must know first. 3.01.159 P
first praise me, and again say no? 4.01. 14
i assure ye it was a buck of the first head. 4.02. 10 P
am i the first that have been perjur'd so? 4.03. 49
at the first op'ning of the gorgeous east, 4.03.219
consider what you first did swear unto: 4.03.287
but love, first learned in a lady's eyes, 4.03.324
but be first advis'd, | in conflict that you get 4.03.365
first, from the park let us conduct them thither 4.03.371
these four worthies in their first show thrive, 5.02.538
there is five in the first show. 5.02.540
yet, since love's argument was first on foot, 5.02.747
first, good peter quince, say what the play MND 1.02. 8 P
and look thou meet me ere the first cock crow. 2.01.267
first, pyramus must draw a sword to kill himself 3.01. 10 P
doth move me | on the first view to say, to 3.01.141
two of the first, /like coats in heraldry, | due 3.02.213
but first i will release the fairy queen. 4.01. 70
choice of which your highness will see first. 5.01. 43
the trusty thisby, comin‹ first by night, | did 5.01.140
first, rehearse your song by rote, | to each 5.01.397
that self way | which you did shoot the first, i MV 1.01.149
and thankfully rest debtor for the first. 1.01.152
first, there is the neapolitan prince. 1.02. 39 P
first, forward to the temple; 2.01. 44
the unbated fire | that he did pace them first? 2.06. 12
this first, of gold, who this inscription bears, 2.07. 4
first, never to unfold to any one | which casket 2.09. 10
play with them the first boy for a thousand 3.02.213 P
lady, | when i did first impart my love to you, 3.02.253
first go with me to church and call me wife, 3.02.303
i will anon, first let us go to dinner. 3.05. 86
every offense is not a hate at first. 4.01. 68
you taught me first to beg, and now methinks 4.01.439
to part so slightly with your wive's first gift, 5.01.167
the first inter'gatory | that my nerissa shall 5.01.300
you my better, in that you are the first born, AYL 1.01. 47 P
it is the first time that ever i heard breaking 1.02.138 P
have so mightily persuaded him from a first. 1.02.207 P
first, for his weeping into the needless stream: 2.01. 46
you touch'd my vein at first. 2.07. 94
till he be first suffic'd, | oppress'd with two 2.07.131
at first the infant, | mewling and puking in the 2.07.143
you must borrow me gargantua's mouth first; 3.02.226 P
upon the hundred neck | but first begs pardon. 3.05. 6
"who ever lov'd that lov'd not at first sight?" 3.05. 82
you were better speak first, and when you were 4.01. 73 P
when from the first to last betwixt us two 4.03.139
the first time that i ever saw him | methought 5.04. 28
the first, the retort courteous; 5.04. 92 P
first, in this forest let us do those ends 5.04.170
gave me my being and my father first, | a SHR 1.01. 11
tell me thine first. 1.01.191
but i will charm him first to keep his tongue. 1.01.209
i should knock you first, | and then i know 1.02. 13
whom would to god i had well knock'd at first, 1.02. 34
you | to give you over at this first encounter, 1.02.105
any man, | until the elder sister first be wed. 1.02.261
i knew you at the first | you were a moveable. 2.01.196
i'll see thee hang'd on sunday first. 2.01.299
she says she'll see thee hang'd first. 2.01.300
i am your neighbor, and was suitor first. 2.01.334
first, as you know, my house within the city 2.01.346
first were we sad, fearing you would not come, 3.02. 98
that take it on you at the first so roundly. 3.02.214
first, know my horse is tir'd, my master and 4.01. 54 P
what, master, read you? first resolve me that. 4.02. 7
first, tell me, have you ever been at pisa? 4.02. 93
for our first merriment hath made thee jealous. 4.05. 76
first kiss me, kate, and we will. 5.01.143
to come at first when he doth send for her, 5.02. 68
come on, i say, and first begin with her. 5.02.133
i say she shall, and first begin with her. 5.02.135
never virgin /got till virginity was first lost. AWW 1.01.129 P
in friendship | first tried our soldiership! 1.02. 26
that least lend it you shall lack you first. 1.02. 68
without rescue in the first assault or ransom 1.03.116 P
greater than shows itself at the first view | to 2.05. 68
that the first face of neither on the start 3.02. 50
he was first smok'd by the old lord lafew. 3.06.103 P
first, give me trust, the count he is my husband 3.07. 8
five descents | since the first father wore it. 3.07. 25
this is the first truth that e'er thine own 4.01. 32 P
"first demand of him, how many horse the duke is 4.03.129 P
nay, i'll read it first, by your favor. 4.03.217 P
altogether so great as the first in goodness, 4.03.287 P
a self–gracious remembrance, did first propose. 4.05. 74 P
my good lord, you were the first that found me! 5.02. 42 P
and i was the first that lost thee. 5.02. 44 P
but first i beg my pardon — the young lord 5.03. 12
and the first view shall kill | all repetition. 5.03. 21
at first | i stuck my choice upon her, ere my 5.03. 44
which better than the first, o dear heaven, 5.03. 71
you, that have turn'd off a first so noble wife, 5.03.220
this ring was mine, i gave it his first wife. 5.03.279
o, when mine eyes did see olivia first, TN 1.01. 18
answer by the method, in the first of his heart. 1.05.226 P
'tis not the first time i have constrain'd one 2.03. 67 P
nay, but first, let me see, let me see, let me 2.05.111 P
sport, mark his first approach before my lady. 2.05.198 P
to–morrow, sir. best first go see your lodging. 3.03. 20
though i strook him first, yet it's no matter 4.01. 36 P
i would i were the first that ever dissembled in 4.02. 5 P
the captain that did bring me first on shore 5.01.274
me, it was she | first told me thou wast mad. 5.01.349
if you first sinn'd with us, and that with us WT 1.02. 84
what was my first? 1.02. 98
will take again your queen as yours at first, 1.02.336
makes but trifles of his eyes | first hand me. 2.03. 64
accord i'll off, | but first i'll do my errand. 2.03. 65
what they did | than to perform it first. 3.02. 57
but, first, how the poor souls roar'd, and the 3.03. 98 P
and let's first see moe ballads. 4.04.273 P

pedlar, let's have the first choice. 4.04.313 P
they throng who should buy first, as if my 4.04.601 P
be such | as, walk'd your first queen's ghost, 5.01. 80
shall be when your first queen's again in breath 5.01. 83
the stars, i see, will kiss the valleys first; 5.01.206
and there was the first gentleman–like tears 5.02.144 P
first, you, my liege; 5.03. 22
now it coldly stands), when first i woo'd her! 5.03. 36
perform'd in this wide gap of time since first 5.03.154
for our advantage — therefore hear us first: JN 2.01.206
did display them when we first march'd forth; 2.01.320
from first to last, the onset and retire | of 2.01.326
since i first call'd my brother's father dad. 2.01.467
speak england first, that hath been forward 2.01.482
that hath been forward first | to speak unto 2.01.482
that i did so when i was first assur'd. 2.01.535
let thy vow | first made to heaven, first be to 3.01.266
made to heaven, first be to heaven perform'd, 3.01.266
therefore thy later vows, against thy first, 3.01.288
since the birth of cain, the first male child, 3.04. 79
the first of april died | your noble mother; 4.02.120
your breath first kindled the dead coal of wars 5.02. 83
but when it first did help to wound itself. 5.07.114
first, heaven be the record to my speech, | in R2 1.01. 30
first, the fair reverence of your highness curbs 1.01. 54
from false mowbray their first head and spring. 1.01. 97
or, if misfortune miss the first career, | be 1.02. 49
of those physicians that first wounded thee. 2.01. 99
the ripest fruit first falls, and so doth he; 2.01.153
of whom thy father, prince of wales, was first. 2.01.172
the first departing of the king for ireland. 2.01.290
hold out my horse, and i will first be there. 2.01.300
had you first died, and he been thus trod down, 2.03.126
if on the first, how heinous e'er it be, | to 5.03. 34
say "pardon" first, and afterwards "stand up." 5.03.112
"pardon" should be the first word of thy speech. 5.03.114
that they are not the first of fortune's slaves, 5.05. 24
taste of it first, as thou art wont to do. 5.05. 99
first, to thy sacred state wish i all happiness. 5.06. 6
where i first bow'd my knee | unto this king of 1H4 1.03.245
bit than i have been since the first cock. 2.01. 18 P
marry, i'll see thee hang'd first. 2.01. 40 P
first, pardon me, my lord. 2.04.507
rob me the exchequer the first thing thou doest, 3.03.183 P
i would the state of time had first been whole 4.01. 25
whose power was in the first proportion, | and 4.04. 15
we were the first and dearest of your friends. 5.01. 33
but what mean i | to speak so true at first? 2H4 in 28
yet the first bringer of unwelcome news | hath 1.01.100
since i perceiv'd the first white hair of my 1.02.242 P
and first, lord marshal, what say you to it? 1.03. 4
all our loves, | first let them try themselves. 2.03. 56
"when arthur first in court" — empty the jordan 2.04. 33 P
i'll see her damn'd first, to pluto's damned 2.04.156 P
the first humane principle i would teach them 4.03.123 P
by whose fell working i was first advanc'd, 4.05.206
unto the lodging where i first did swound? 4.05.233
first my fear, then my cur'sy, last my speech. ep 1 P
france win, | then with scotland first begin." H5 1.02.168
he that strikes the first stroke, i'll run him 2.01. 64 P
by this sword, he that makes the first thrust, 2.01. 99 P
that shall first spring and be most delicate. 2.04. 40
you must first go yourself to hazard, ere you 3.07. 87 P
'tis not the first time you were overshot. 3.07.124 P
suffolk first died, and york, all haggled over, 4.06. 11
his daughter first; 5.02.333
but first, to try her skill, | reignier, stand 1H6 1.02. 60
she takes upon her bravely at first dash. 1.02. 71
henry the fift he first train'd to the wars; 1.04. 79
of all exploits since first i follow'd arms, 2.01. 43
didst thou at first, to flatter us withal, 2.01. 51
how, or which way, should they first break in? 2.01. 71
since henry monmouth first began to reign, 2.05. 23
first, lean thine aged back against mine arm, 2.05. 43
got | first to my god and next unto your grace. 3.04. 12
when first this order was ordain'd, my lords, 4.01. 33
first let me know, and then i'll answer you. 4.01. 88
and he first took exceptions at this badge, 4.01.105
let this dissension first be tried by fight, 4.01.116
nay, let it rest where it began at first. 4.01.121
stay, | if the first hour i shrink and run away. 4.05. 31
the life thou gav'st me first was lost and done, 4.06. 7
and had the maidenhood | of thy first fight, i 4.06. 18
you shall first receive | the sum of money which 5.01. 51
she was the first fruit of my bach'lorship. 5.04. 13
first let me tell you whom you have condemn'd: 5.04. 36
ay, grief, i fear me, both at first and last. 5.05.102
we here create thee the first duke of suffolk, 2H6 1.01. 64
and william de la pole, first duke of suffolk. 1.02. 30
i'll be the first, sure. 1.03. 7 P
first, for i cannot flatter thee in pride; 1.03.166
"first of the king: what shall of him become?" 1.04. 29
the first, edward the black prince, prince of 2.02. 11
for richard, the first son's heir, being dead, 2.02. 31
and in this private plot be we the first | that 2.02. 60
holden at bury the first of this next month. 2.04. 71
first note that he is near you in descent, | and 3.01. 21
and, had i first been put to speak my mind, | i 3.01. 43
wolves are gnarling who shall gnaw thee first. 3.01.192
which mates him first that first intends deceit. 3.01.265
which mates him first that first intends deceit. 3.01.265
first let my words stab him, as he hath me. 4.01. 66
the first thing we do, let's kill all the 4.02. 76 P
but claret wine this first year of our reign. 4.06. 4 P
but first go and set london bridge on fire, and, 4.06. 14 P
first let me ask of /these | if they can brook i 5.01.109
the first i warrant thee, if dreams prove true. 5.01.195
plantagenet shall speak first. 3H6 1.01.121
first shall war unpeople this my realm; 1.01.126
how began it first? 1.02. 5
first will i see the coronation, | and then to 2.06. 96
first, to do greetings to thy royal person, 3.03. 52
ay, that's the first thing that we have to do, 4.03. 62
but, with the first of all your chief affairs, 4.06. 58
so first the harmless sheep doth yield his 5.06. 8
thou been kill'd when first thou didst presume, 5.06. 35
but first i'll turn yon fellow in his grave, R3 1.02.260
i do the wrong, and first begin to brawl. 1.03.323

the first that there did greet my stranger soul 1.04. 48
first, madam, i entreat true peace of you, 2.01. 63
but he, poor man, by your first order died, 2.01. 88
first, he commends him to your noble self. 3.02. 8
therefore — to speak, and to avoid the first, 3.07.151
first, if all obstacles were cut away, | and 3.07.156
for first was he contract to lady lucy — | your 3.07.179
first, mighty liege, tell me your highness' 4.04.447
the first was i that help'd thee to the crown; 5.03.167
devis'd at first to keep the strong in awe: 5.03.310
the first and happiest hearers of the town, | be H8 pr 24
climb steep hills | requires slow pace at first. 1.01.132
first, it was usual with him — every day | it 1.02.132
he would have all as merry | as, first, good 1.04. 6
the red wine first must rise | in their fair 1.04. 43
first, kildare's attendure, | then deputy of 2.01. 41
who first rais'd head against usurping richard, 2.01.108
bitter than | 'tis sweet at first t' acquire — 2.03. 9
my conscience first receiv'd a tenderness, 2.04.171
first, methought | i stood not in the smile of 2.04.187
first i began in private | with you, my lord of 2.04.207
oppression i did reek | when i first mov'd you. 2.04.210
the question did at first so stagger me, 2.04.213
he did unseal them, and the first he view'd, 3.02. 79
first, that, without the king's assent or 3.02.310
the duke of suffolk is the first, and claims 4.01. 17
strangely | with me since first you knew me. 4.02.113
first, mine own service to your grace, the next, 4.02.115
toward the king first, then his laws, in filling 5.02. 50
when we first put this dangerous stone a–rolling 5.02.139
exampled by the first pace that is sick | of his TRO 1.03.132
let us, like merchants, first show foul wares, 1.03.358
shall exceed | by showing the worse first. 1.03.361
since the first sword was drawn about this 2.02. 18
not bear it so, 'a should eat swords first. 2.03.218 P
with the first glance that ever — pardon me — 3.02.118
women had men's privilege | of speaking first. 3.02.129
retort that heat again | to the first /giver. 3.03.102
ere the first sacrifice, within this hour, | we 4.02. 64
the first was menelaus' kiss, this, mine; 4.05. 32
dead | since first i saw yourself and diomed 4.05.215
first, all you peers of greece, go to my tent; 4.05.271
she will sing any man at first sight. 5.02. 9
first, you know caius martius is chief enemy to COR 1.01. 7 P
against him first; 1.01. 28 P
he, | "that i receive the general food at first 1.01.131
to run, | lead'st first to win some vantage. 1.01.160
the rabble should have first /unroof'd the city 1.01.218
more attain'd than by | a place below the first; 1.01.266
sprang not more in joy at first hearing he was a 1.03. 16 P
man–child than now in first seeing he had prov'd 1.03. 17 P
let the first budger die the other's slave, 1.08. 5
imperfect in favoring the first complaint, hasty 2.01. 50 P
than crave the hire which first we do deserve. 2.03.114
so then the volsces stand but as at first, 3.01. 4
not martius, we'll proceed | in our first way. 3.01.332
said | my praises made thee first a soldier, so, 3.02.108
first hear me speak. 3.03. 41
my first son, | whither /wilt thou go? 4.01. 33
know thou first, | i lov'd the maid i married; 4.05.113
heart | than when i first my wedded mistress saw 4.05.117
let me commend thee first to those that shall 4.05.144
thought he would | when first i did embrace him; 4.07. 10
first he was | a noble servant to them, but he 4.07. 35
once more offer'd | the first conditions, which 5.03. 14
first, the gods bless you for your tidings; 5.04. 58
'tis the first time that ever | i was forc'd to 5.06.104
ten years are spent since first he undertook TIT 1.01. 31
from whence at first she weigh'd her anchorage, 1.01. 73
first thrash the corn, then after burn the straw 2.03.123
of that self blood that first gave life to you, 4.02.123
to him, at the first approach you must kneel, 4.03.110 P
first hang the child, that he may see it sprawl 5.01. 51
first know thou, i begot him on the empress. 5.01. 87
o any thing, of nothing first /create! ROM 1.01.177
ne'er saw her match since first the world begun. 1.02. 93
that presses them and learns them first to bear, 1.04. 93
by love, that first did prompt me to inquire; 2.02. 80
a gentleman of the very first house, of the 2.04. 24 P
very first house, of the first and second cause. 2.04. 25 P
but first let me tell ye, if ye should lead her 2.04.165 P
this second match, | for it excels your first; 3.05.223
your first is dead, or 'twere as good he were 3.05.224
that from my first have been inclin'd to thrift, TIM 1.01.118
ceremony was but devis'd at first | to set a 1.02. 15
but his occasions might have wooed me first; 3.03. 15
i was the first man | that e'er received gift 3.03. 16
worth of thrice the sum | h'ad sent to me first, 3.03. 23
meat cool ere we can agree upon the first place; 3.06. 68 P
soft, take thy physic first — thou too — and 3.06.100
more whore, more mischief first; 4.03.168
thou like us from our first swath proceeded 4.03.252
first mend /my company, take away thyself. 4.03.283
let us first see peace in athens. 4.03.456 P
second masters, | upon their first lord's neck. 4.03.506
when thy first griefs were but a mere conceit, 5.04. 14
who were the motives that you first went out; 5.04. 27
since cassius first did whet me against caesar, JC 2.01. 61
of a dreadful thing | and the first motion, all 2.01. 64
toward the north | he first presents his fire, 2.01.110
o caesar, read mine first; 3.01. 6
casca, you are the first that rears your hand. 3.01. 30
and turn preordinance and first decree | into 3.01. 38
first, marcus brutus, will i shake with you; 3.01.185
pardon — | i will myself into the pulpit first, 3.01.236
remember | the first time ever caesar put it on; 3.02.171
this day i breathed first: 5.03. 23
give me your hand first. fare you well, my lord. 5.05. 49
first, as i am his kinsman and his subject, MAC 1.07. 13
when first they put the name of king upon me, 3.01. 57
at first | and last, the hearty welcome. 3.04. 1
got, | boil thou first i' th' charmed pot. 4.01. 9
here's another, | more potent than the first. 4.01. 76
thou other gold–bound brow, is like the first. 4.01.114
my first false speaking | was this upon myself. 4.03.130
that even now | protest their first of manhood. 5.02. 11
your right noble son, | lead our first battle. 5.06. 4
and damn'd be him that first cries, "hold, 5.08. 34

the first that ever scotland | in such an honor 5.09. 29
from the first corse till he that died to–day, HAM 1.02.105
inquire me first what danskers are in paris, 2.01. 7
give first admittance to th' embassadors; 2.02. 51
upon our first, he sent out to suppress | his 2.02. 61
yet he knew me not at first, 'a said i was a 2.02.188 P
the first row of the pious chanson will show you 2.02.419 P
whose end, both at the first and now, was and is 3.02. 21 P
none wed the second but who kill'd the first. 3.02.180
die thy thoughts when thy first lord is dead. 3.02.215
i stand in pause where i shall first begin, 3.03. 42
in the corner of his jaw, first mouth'd, to be 4.02. 18 P
first, her father slain; 4.05. 79
when i shall, first asking you pardon thereunto, 4.07. 45 P
'a was the first that ever bore arms. 5.01. 33 P
cain's jaw–bone, that did the first murder! 5.01. 77 P
if hamlet give the first or second hit, | or 5.02.268
i'll play this bout first, set it by a while. 5.02.284
goneril, | our eldest–born, speak first. LR 1.01. 54
we first address toward you, who with this king 1.01.190
this, let him be whipt that first finds it so. 1.04.164 P
you we first seize on. 2.01.116
he that first lights on him | holla the other. 3.01. 54
in, boy, go first. 3.04. 26
at curfew, and walks /till /the first cock; 3.04.116 P
first let me talk with this philosopher. 3.04.154
let me wipe it first, it smells of mortality. 4.06.133
the first time that we smell the air | we wawl 4.06.179
eyeless head of thine was first fram'd flesh 4.06.227
until their greater pleasures first be known 5.03. 2
we are not the first | who with best meaning 5.03. 3
we'll see 'em starv'd first. 5.03. 25
and from first to last | told him our pilgrimage 5.03.196
that, from your first of difference and decay, 5.03.289
where each second | stood heir to th' first. OTH 1.01. 38
to leave that latest which concerns him first, 1.03. 28
first, i must tell thee this: 2.01.218 P
me with what violence she first lov'd the moor, 2.01.222 P
they do suggest at first with heavenly shows, 2.03.352
fruits that blossom first will first be ripe. 2.03.377
fruits that blossom first will first be ripe. 2.03.377
he did, from first to last. why dost thou ask? 3.03. 96
this was her first remembrance from the moor. 3.03.291
why, that the moor first gave to desdemona, 3.03.308
which at the first are scarce found to distaste, 3.03.327
i gave her such a one; 'twas my first gift. 3.03.436
be hang'd for his labor — first to be hang'd, 4.01. 38 P
ay, 'twas he that told me on her first. 5.02.147
and pledge of love | which i first gave her. 5.02.215
fulvia thy wife first came into the field. ANT 1.02. 88
italy, | upon the first encounter, drave them. 1.02. 94
yet at the first | i saw the treasons planted. 1.03. 25
not if the small come first. 2.02. 12
when she first met mark antony, she purs'd up 2.02.186 P
first, madam, he is well. 2.05. 31
most meet | that first we come to words, and 2.06. 3
but, first | or last, your fine egyptian cookery 2.06. 62
source, and the first stone | drop in my neck; 3.13.160
had we done so at first, we had droven them home 4.07. 5
if she first meet the curled antony, | he'll 5.02.301
would hazard the winning both of first and last. CYM 1.04. 93 P
we are familiar at first. 1.04.102 P
flattering rascal, upon him | will i first work. 1.05. 28
which first, perchance, she'll prove on cats and 1.05. 38
fill'd and running — ravening first the lamb, 1.06. 49
first, a very excellent good conceited thing; 2.03. 16 P
make them, | must first induce you to believe; 2.04. 63
first, her bedchamber | (where i confess i slept 2.04. 66
or less — at first? 2.05. 15
with shame | (the first that ever touch'd him) 3.01. 25
who was the first of britain which did put | his 3.01. 59
but first of all, | how we may steal from hence; 3.02. 61
but first, how get hence. 3.02. 64
report was once | first with the best of note. 3.03. 58
the venison first shall be the lord o' th' feast 3.03. 75
ne'er long'd my mother so | to see me first, as 3.04. 3
i'll wake mine eyeballs /out first. 3.04.101
first, make yourself but like one. 3.04.167
the first service thou dost me, fetch that suit 3.05.127 P
let it be thy first service, go. 3.05.128 P
first kill him, and in her eyes; 3.05.138 P
the ground that gave them first has them again: 4.02.289
but first, and't please the gods, | i'll hide my 4.02.387
a sin in war, | damn'd in the first beginners!), 5.03. 37
first, she confess'd she never lov'd you; 5.05. 37
first pay me for the nursing of thy sons, | and 5.05.322
and at first meeting lov'd, | continu'd so, 5.05.379
how first met them? 5.05.386
but your ring first, | and here the bracelet of 5.05.415
all love the womb that their first being bred, PER 1.01.107
that have their first conception by misdread, 1.02. 12
and what was first but fear what might be done, 1.02. 14
draw lots who first shall die to lengthen life. 1.04. 46
who is the first that doth prefer himself? 2.02. 17
even at the first | thy loss is more than can 3.01. 34
"he that will give most shall have her first." 4.02. 60 P
to fetch his daughter home, who first is gone. 4.04. 20
first, i would have you note, this is an 4.06. 49 P
prithee tell me one thing first. 4.06.156 P
first, what is your place? 5.01. 20
first, sir, i pray, | what is your title? 5.01.202
cleon, but i am | for other service first. 5.01.254
that can | from first to last resolve you. 5.03. 61
beseech you first, go with me to my house, 5.03. 65
that, after holy tie and first night's stir, TNK pr 6
and the first sound this child hear be a hiss, pr 16
in that honor | first nature styl'd it in — 1.01. 83
your first thought is more | than others' 1.01.135
since first we went to school, may we perceive 1.02. 14
i saw her first. 2.02.160
i, that first saw her; 2.02.167
first with mine eye of all those beauties in her 2.02.168
because another | first sees the enemy, shall i 2.02.194
first, i saw him: 2.04. 7
in a morning, first | he bows his noble body, 2.04. 22
but i must fear you first. 3.03. 9
base cousin, | dar'st thou break first? 3.03. 45
i first appear, though rude, and raw, and muddy, 3.05.122

that's mine then. | i'll arm you first. 3.06. 53
when i saw you charge first, | methought i heard 3.06. 82
seeing | and first bequeathing of the soul to) 3.06.148
which cannot want due mercy, i beg first. 3.06.209
would i might end first! 4.02. 57
methinks, of him that's first with palamon. 4.02. 90
but first, by your leave, | i' th' way of 5.02. 19
cure her first this way; 5.02. 22
higher, | anon the other, then again the first, 5.03.126
a steed that emily | did first bestow on him — 5.04. 50
in this place first you fought; 5.04. 99
lady | did lie in you, for you first saw her, 5.04.117
first, 'tis a sin | which oft th' apostle did STM II.C 93
struck dead at first, what needs a second VEN 250
all strain court'sy who shall cope him first. 888
both would strive who first should dry his tears 1092
with kissing him i should have kill'd him first, 1118
first red as roses that on lawn we lay, | then LUC 258
first like a trumpet doth his tongue begin | to 470
first hovering o'er the paper with her quill. 1297
a flower that dies when first it gins to bud, PP 13. 3
and for a woman wert thou first created, | till SON 20. 9
the first my thought, the other my desire, 45. 3
that god forbid, that made me first your slave, 58. 1
since mind at first in character was done! 59. 8
at first the very worst of fortune's might; 90.12
for as you were when first your eye i ey'd, 104. 2
since first i saw you fresh, which yet are green 104. 8
even as when first i hallowed thy fair name. 108. 8
finding the first conceit of love there bred, 108.13
o, 'tis the first, 'tis flatt'ry in my seeing, 114. 9
that mine eye loves it and doth first begin. 114.14
grows fairer than at first, more strong, far 119.12
FIRST-BEGOTTEN 1 FR 0.0001 REL FR 1 V 0 P
the first-begotten and the lawful heir | of 1H6 2.05. 65
FIRST-BORN 8 FR 0.0009 REL FR 7 V 1 P
that bites the first-born infants of the spring. LLL 1.01.101
i'll rail against all the first-born of egypt. AYL 2.05. 61 P
but let one spirit of the first-born cain 2H4 1.01.157
i am his first-born son, that was the last TIT 1.01. 5
thrice-noble titus, spare my first-born son! 1.01.120
that touches this my first-born son and heir! 4.02. 92
primrose, first-born child of ver, | merry TNK 1.01. 7
with april's first-born flowers, and all things SON 21. 7
FIRST-CONCEIVED 1 FR 0.0001 REL FR 1 V 0 P
can chase away the first-conceived sound? 2H6 3.02. 44
FIRST-FRUITS 1 FR 0.0001 REL FR 1 V 0 P
my second joy | and first-fruits of my body, WT 3.02. 97
/FIRSTLINGS 1 FR 0.0001 REL FR 1 V 0 P
/the /vaunt /and /firstlings /of /those /broils, TRO pr 27
FIRSTLINGS 2 FR 0.0002 REL FR 2 V 0 P
the very firstlings of my heart shall be | the MAC 4.01.147
my heart shall be | the firstlings of my hand. 4.01.148
FIRST'S 1 FR 0.0001 REL FR 1 V 0 P
sir, sir, the first's for me! let her go by. SHR 1.02.254
/FISH 1 FR 0.0001 REL FR 1 V 0 P
/froze /them /up, | /as /fish /are /in /a /pond. 2H4 1.01.200
FISH 47 FR 0.0053 REL FR 19 V 28 P
what strange fish | hath made his meal on thee? TMP 2.01.113
a man or a fish? 2.02. 25 P
a fish, he smells like a fish; 2.02. 25 P
a fish, he smells like a fish; 2.02. 26 P
a strange fish! 2.02. 27 P
(as once i was) and had but this fish painted, 2.02. 28 P
this is no fish, but an islander, that hath 2.02. 35 P
i'll fish for thee, and get thee wood enough. 2.02.161
no more dams i'll make for fish, | nor fetch in 2.02.180
why, thou debosh'd fish thou, was there ever man 3.02. 26 P
lie, being but half a fish and half a monster? 3.02. 29 P
one of them | is a plain fish, and no doubt 5.01.266
no, they are both as whole as a fish. TGV 2.05. 19 P
the luce is the fresh fish, the salt fish is an WIV 1.01. 22 P
is the fresh fish, the salt fish is an old coat. 1.01. 22 P
of more pre-eminence than fish and fowls, | are ERR 2.01. 23
o, signior balthazar, either at flesh or fish, 3.01. 22
fowls have no feathers, and fish have no fin. 3.01. 79
for a fish without a fin, there's a fowl without 3.01. 82
bait the hook well, this fish will bite. ADO 2.03.108 P
the pleasant'st angling is to see the fish | cut 3.01. 26
but fish not with this melancholy bait | for MV 1.01.101
to bait fish withal — if it will feed nothing 3.01. 53 P
no more than a fish loves water. AWW 3.06. 85 P
henceforth eat no fish of fortune's butt'ring. 5.02. 8 P
of a fish that appear'd upon the coast on WT 4.04.275 P
was turn'd into a cold fish for she would not 4.04.279 P
eyes (caught the water though not the fish), was 5.02. 84 P
and of a dragon and a finless fish, | a 1H4 3.01.149
she's neither fish nor flesh, a man knows not 3.03.127 P
up fish street! 2H6 4.08. 1 P
a very fresh fish here — fie, fie, fie upon H8 2.03. 86
whiles others fish with craft for great opinion, TRO 4.04.103
he'll be to rome | as is the aspray to the fish, COR 4.07. 34
than baits to fish, or honey-stalks to sheep, TIT 4.04. 91
'tis well thou art not fish; ROM 1.01. 30 P
the fish lives in the sea, and 'tis much pride 1.03. 89
a man may fish with the worm that hath eat of a HAM 4.03. 27 P
and eat of the fish that hath fed of that worm. 4.03. 28 P
fight when i cannot choose, and to eat no fish. LR 1.04. 17 P
the dish, | poor tributary rivers as sweet fish. CYM 4.02. 36
they say they're half fish, half flesh. PER 2.01. 25 P
be got now-a-days unless thou canst fish for't. 2.01. 69 P
have flesh for /holidays, fish for fasting-days, 2.01. 81 P
here's a fish hangs in the net, like a poor 2.01.116 P
he that will fish | for my least minnow, let him TNK 1.01.115
soon as they /move, as aspray do the fish, 1.01.138
FISH'D 2 FR 0.0002 REL FR 1 V 1 P
that "sort" was well fish'd for. TMP 2.01.105 P
and his pond fish'd by his next neighbor — by WT 1.02.195
FISHER 2 FR 0.0002 REL FR 1 V 1 P
the fisher with his pencil and the painter with ROM 1.02. 40 P
me, | no fisher but the ungrown fry forbears; VEN 526
FISHERMEN 5 FR 0.0005 REL FR 5 V 0 P
three were taken up | by fishermen of corinth, ERR 1.01.111
but by and by rude fishermen of corinth | by 5.01.352
the fishermen, that /walk upon the beach, LR 4.06. 17
peace be at your labor, honest fishermen. PER 2.01. 52
through a small glade cut by the fishermen, | i TNK 4.01. 64
FISHERMEN'S 1 FR 0.0001 REL FR 0 V 1 P
by drop, and liquor fishermen's boots with me. WIV 4.05. 98 P
FISHERS 2 FR 0.0002 REL FR 2 V 0 P
and would have reft the fishers of their prey, ERR 1.01.115
sea | these fishers tell the infirmities of men, PER 2.01. 49
FISHES 13 FR 0.0014 REL FR 11 V 2 P
the beasts, the fishes, and the winged fowls ERR 2.01. 18
a thousand men that fishes gnaw'd upon; R3 1.04. 25
as rav'nous fishes, do a vessel follow | that is H8 1.02. 79
and other skins | of ill-shap'd fishes, and ROM 5.01. 44
water, | as beasts and birds and fishes. TIM 4.03.423
on the beasts themselves, the birds and fishes; 4.03.424
he fishes, drinks, and wastes | the lamps of ANT 1.04. 4
far off, i will betray | tawny/-finn'd fishes; 2.05. 12
and tell the fishes he's the queen's son, cloten CYM 4.02.153
master, i marvel how the fishes live in the sea. PER 2.01. 27 P
canst thou catch any fishes then? 2.01. 66 P
and men like ravenous fishes | would feed on STM II.C 86
the fishes spread on it their golden gills; VEN 1100
FISHIFIED 1 FR 0.0001 REL FR 0 V 1 P
o flesh, flesh, how art thou fishified! ROM 2.04. 38 P
FISH-LIKE 1 FR 0.0001 REL FR 0 V 1 P
a very ancient and fish-like smell; TMP 2.02. 26 P
FISH-MEALS 1 FR 0.0001 REL FR 0 V 1 P
their blood, and making many fish-meals, that 2H4 4.03. 92 P
FISHMONGER 2 FR 0.0002 REL FR 0 V 2 P
excellent well, you are a fishmonger. HAM 2.02.174 P
me not at first, 'a said i was a fishmonger. 2.02.189 P
FISHPOND 1 FR 0.0001 REL FR 0 V 1 P
into the unclean fishpond of her displeasure, AWW 5.02. 21 P
FISNOMY *(also physiognomy)*
FISNOMY 1 FR 0.0001 REL FR 0 V 1 P
but his fisnomy is more hotter in france than AWW 4.05. 40 P
FIST 10 FR 0.0011 REL FR 8 V 2 P
his | but buffets better than a fist of france. JN 2.01.465
and i but fist him once, and 'a come but within 2H4 2.01. 21 P
give me thy fist, thy fore-foot to me give. H5 2.01. 67
fame, | of parents good, of fist most valiant. 4.01. 46
nor hold the sceptre in his childish fist, | nor 2H6 1.01.245
thy hand is but a finger to my fist, | thy leg a 4.10. 48
and wring the aweful sceptre from his fist, 3H6 2.01.154
he would pun thee into shivers with his fist, as TRO 2.01. 40 P
with my armed fist | i'll /pash him o'er the 2.03.202
do but put | a fescue in her fist, and you shall TNK 2.03. 34
FISTING 2 FR 0.0002 REL FR 2 V 0 P
unbuckling helms, fisting each other's throat, COR 4.05.125
to the choleric fisting of every rogue | thy ear PER 4.06.167
FISTS 1 FR 0.0001 REL FR 1 V 0 P
whom with my bare fists i would execute, | if i 1H6 1.04. 36
FISTULA 1 FR 0.0001 REL FR 0 V 1 P
a fistula, my lord. AWW 1.01. 34 P
FIT* 179 FR 0.0202 REL FR 144 V 35 P
could control thee, | if now 'twere fit to do't. TMP 1.02.441
he's in his fit now, and does not talk after the 2.02. 73 P
wine afore, it will go near to remove his fit. 2.02. 75 P
worth, | and you an officer fit for the place. TGV 1.02. 45
fit me with such weeds | as may beseem some 2.07. 42
and here an engine fit for my proceeding! 3.01.138
would better fit his chamber than this shadow. 4.04.120
which served me as fit, by all men's judgments, 4.04.162
and fit for great employment, worthy lord. 5.04.157
trust me, i thought on her. she'll fit it. WIV 2.01.161 P
in state as wholesome as in state 'tis fit, 5.05. 59
young man | more fit to do another such offense MM 2.03. 14
fit thy consent to my sharp appetite, | lay by 2.04.161
and fit his mind to death, for his soul's rest. 2.04.187
maid will i frame and make fit for his attempt. 3.01.256 P
these letters at fit time deliver me. 4.05. 1
come, i have found you out a stand most fit, 4.06. 10
of your honor, | i thought your marriage fit; 5.01.420
bred, | and what's a fever but a fit of madness? ERR 5.01. 76
day | a most outrageous fit of madness took him, 5.01.139
look what will serve is fit: ADO 1.01.318
lovest, | and i will fit thee with the remedy. 1.01.319
we'll fit the /hid-fox with a pennyworth. 2.03. 42
you of a worse title, and i will fit her to it. 3.02.111 P
but it would better fit your honor to change 3.02.115 P
the most senseless and fit man for the constable 3.03. 23 P
fit in his place and time. LLL 1.01. 98
o heresy in fair, fit for these days! 4.01. 22
maids' girdles for your waist should be fit. 4.01. 50
by my troth, most pleasant. how both did fit it! 4.01.129
smoothly off, so obscenely as it were, so fit. 4.01.143
i say none so fit as to present the nine 5.01.123 P
to fit your fancies to your father's will; MND 1.01.118
of every man's name, which is thought fit, 1.02. 5 P
how fit a word | is that vile name to perish on 2.02.106
is fit for treasons, stratagems, and spoils; MV 5.01. 85
and take a lodging fit to entertain | such SHR 1.01. 44
within my house, | fit to instruct her youth. 1.01. 95
any means light on a fit man to teach her that 1.01.111 P
was it fit for a servant to use his master so, 1.02. 31 P
for learning and behavior | fit for her turn, 1.02.169
it skills not much, we'll fit him to our turn — 3.02.132
i'll have no bigger, this doth fit the time, 4.03. 69
yet these fix'd evils sit so fit in him, | that AWW 1.01.102
nay, i'll fit you, | and not be all day neither. 2.01. 90
will your answer serve fit to all questions? 2.02. 20 P
as fit as ten groats is for the hand of an 2.02. 21 P
your constable, it will fit any question. 2.02. 31 P
most monstrous size that must fit all demands. 2.02. 33 P
it were fit you knew him, lest, reposing too far 3.06. 13 P
for folly that he wisely shows is fit, | but TN 3.01. 67
it doth not fit me. 3.03. 38
you may have very fit occasion for't; 3.04.173 P
fit for the mountains and the barbarous caves, 4.01. 48
what fit is this, good lady? WT 3.02.174
well you fit our ages | with flow'rs of winter. 4.04. 78
no milliner can so fit his customers with gloves 4.04.192 P
which 'tis not fit you know, i not acquaint | my 4.04.412
if he think it fit to shore them again, and that 4.04.837 P
say, | but i will fit it with some better /time. JN 3.03. 26
a ghost, | as dim and meagre as an ague's fit, 3.04. 85
of repair and health, | the fit is strongest; 3.04.114
aspect, | finding thee fit for bloody villainy, 4.02.225
this ague fit of fear is overblown, | an easy R2 3.02.190
impatient of his fit, breaks like a fire | out 2H4 1.01.142
thou mightst mend him and make him fit to go. 3.02.165 P
is it fit this soldier keep his oath? H5 4.07.132 P
kate, my wooing is fit for thy understanding. 5.02.122 P
a goodly prize, fit for the devil's grace! 1H6 5.03. 33
a child, | fit to be made companion with a king. 5.03.149
approves her fit for none but for a king. 5.05. 69
that were a state fit for his holiness. 2H6 1.03. 64
a' god's name see the lists and all things fit; 2.03. 54
not fit to govern and rule multitudes, | which 5.01. 94
i am a subject fit to jest withal, | but far 3H6 3.02. 91
and shall be thought most fit | for your best R3 3.01. 66
is but merely | a fit or two o' th' face — but H8 1.03. 7
and fit it with such furniture as suits | the 2.01. 99
conscience, | thou art a cure fit for a king. 2.02. 75
i find him a fit fellow. 2.02.116
madam, | it's fit this royal session do proceed, 2.04. 66
for i feel | the last fit of my greatness — 3.01. 78
fit for a fool to fall by. 3.02.214
no doubt | in time will find their fit rewards. 3.02.245
and better would fit achilles much | to throw TRO 3.03.207
and fit it is, | because i am the store-house COR 1.01.132
tell valeria | we are fit to bid her welcome. 1.03. 44
he cannot but with measure fit the honors 2.02.123
pray you go fit you to the custom, and | take to 2.02.142
the violent fit a' th' time craves it as physic 3.02. 33
were fit for thee to use as they to claim, | in 3.02. 83
sir, 'tis fit | you make strong party, or defend 3.02. 93
enjoy, | one fit to bandy with thy lawless sons, TIT 1.01.312
aaron, arm thy heart, and fit thy thoughts, | to 2.01. 12
i am as able and as fit as thou | to serve, and 2.01. 33
unless some fit or frenzy do possess her; 4.01. 17
lucius, i'll fit thee, and withal my boy | shall 4.01.114
sir, that is as fit as can be to serve for your 4.03. 95 P
as you think fit to furnish me to-morrow? ROM 4.02. 35
upon them, fit to open | these dead men's tombs. 5.03.200
affect company, | nor is he fit for't indeed. TIM 1.02. 32
i see thou art a fool, and fit for thy master. 3.01. 49 P
fit i meet them. 5.01. 54
and when the fit was on him, i did mark | how he JC 1.02.120
indeed he is not fit. 2.01.153
let's carve him as a dish fit for the gods, 2.01.173
gods, | not hew him as a carcass fit for hounds; 2.01.174
there is no hour so fit | as caesar's death's 3.01.153
is it fit, | the threefold world divided, he 4.01. 13
then comes my fit again. MAC 3.04. 20
the fit is momentary, upon a thought | he will 3.04. 54
if such a one be fit to govern, speak. 4.03.101
fit to govern? 4.03.102
let's follow. 'tis not fit thus to obey him. HAM 1.04. 88
i hold it fit that we shake hands and part, 1.05.128
but, if you hold it fit, after the play | let 3.01.181
black, hands apt, drugs fit, and time agreeing, 3.02.255
when he is fit and season'd for his passage? 3.03. 86
you must translate, 'tis fit we understand them. 4.01. 2
in his lawless fit, | behind the arras hearing 4.01. 8
we would not understand what was most fit, | but 4.01. 20
and botch the words up fit to their own thoughts 4.05. 10
of time and means | may fit us to our shape. 4.07.150
and /thus a while the fit will work on him; 5.01.285
their repair hither, and say you are not fit. 5.02.218 P
i | return those duties back as are right fit, LR 1.01. 97
perus'd, i find it not fit for your o'erlooking. 1.02. 38 P
i have heard him oft maintain it to be fit that, 1.02. 72 P
all with me's meet that i can fashion fit. 1.02.184
that which ordinary men are fit for, i am 1.04. 34 P
which i best /thought it fit | to answer from 2.01.123
to take the indispos'd and sickly fit | for the 2.04.111
you yet, nor am provided | for your fit welcome. 2.04.233
must make content with his fortunes fit, 3.02. 76
father are not fit for your beholding. 3.07. 8 P
i thought it fit | to send the old and miserable 5.03. 45
till fit time | of law and course of direct OTH 1.02. 85
state, | i crave fit disposition for my wife, 1.03.236
he's a soldier fit to stand by caesar | and give 2.03.122
if you think fit, or that it may be done, | give 3.01. 51
although 'tis fit that cassio have his place — 3.03.246
if i do find him fit, i'll move your suit | and 3.04.166
this is his second fit; 4.01. 51
i find thee | most fit for business. ANT 3.03. 37
being in these wars, | and say'st it is not fit. 3.07. 4
it were fit | that all the plagues of hell CYM 1.06.110
if he shall think it fit | a saucy stranger in 1.06.150
his mistress, only | for the most worthiest fit. 1.06.162
it is not fit /your lordship should undertake 2.01. 26 P
but it is fit i should commit offense to my 2.01. 28 P
ay, it is fit for your lordship only. 2.01. 30 P
is it fit i went to look upon him? 2.01. 42 P
no costlier than would fit | a franklin's 3.02. 76
forethinking this, i have already fit | ('tis in 3.04.168
to some shade, | and fit you to your manhood. 3.04.192
how fit his garments serve me! 4.01. 2 P
by him that made the tailor, not be fit too? 4.01. 4 P
with faces fit for masks, or rather fairer 5.03. 21
and will fit you | with dignities becoming your 5.05. 21
the fit and apt construction of thy name, 5.05.444
it is enough you know, and it is fit, | what PER 1.01.105
fit counsellor and servant for a prince, | who 1.02. 63
it's fit it should be so, for princes are | a 2.02. 10
were more than you expect, or more than's fit, 2.03. 5
some other is more fit. 2.03. 23
none fit for th' dead! TNK 1.01.141
how to draw out, fit to this enterprise, | the 1.01.160
juno would | resume her ancient fit of jealousy 1.02. 22
bring her fruit | fit for the gods to feed on; 2.02.239
all dues | fit for the honor you have won; 2.05. 61
go thy ways, i'll remember thee, i'll fit thee! 3.05. 58
that no man but thy cousin's fit to kill thee. 3.06. 44
"traitor," | i am a villain fit to lie unburied. 3.06.171
fit for my modest suit and your free granting. 3.06.235
his red lips, after fights, are fit for ladies. 4.02.111
well she knew | what hour my fit would take me. 5.02. 10
so, | and when your fit comes, fit her home, and 5.02. 11
so, | and when your fit comes, fit her home, and 5.02. 11
words," quoth she, "shall fit the trespass best, LUC 1613
FITCHEW 2 FR 0.0002 REL FR 1 V 1 P
the fitchew nor the soiled horse goes to't LR 4.06.122
'tis such another fitchew! OTH 4.01.146 P
FITCHOOK 1 FR 0.0001 REL FR 0 V 1 P
a moile, a cat, a fitchook, a toad, a lezard, an TRO 5.01. 61 P
FITFUL 1 FR 0.0001 REL FR 1 V 0 P

after life's fitful fever he sleeps well. MAC 3.02. 23
FITLY 6 FR 0.0006 REL FR 4 V 2 P
even so most fitly | as you malign our senators COR 1.01.112
that can judge as fitly of his worth | as i can 4.02. 34
so fitly? TIM 3.04.110
and nothing more, may fitly like your grace, LR 1.01.200
from whence i will fitly bring you to hear my 1.02.169 P
rich misers to nothing so fitly as to a whale: PER 2.01. 30 P
FITMENT 2 FR 0.0002 REL FR 1 V 1 P
'twas a fitment for | the purpose i then CYM 5.05.409
when she should do for clients her fitment, and PER 4.06. 6 P
/FITNESS 1 FR 0.0001 REL FR 1 V 0 P
/were't /my /fitness | /to /let /these /hands LR 4.02. 63
FITNESS 8 FR 0.0009 REL FR 5 V 3 P
all my others parts | of necessary fitness? MM 2.04. 23
an answer of such fitness for all questions? AWW 2.02. 28 P
'tis a needful fitness | that we adjourn this H8 2.04.232
hands shall strike | when fitness calls them on, TRO 1.03.202
of no more soul nor fitness for the world | than COR 2.01.250
and that their fitness now | does unmake you. MAC 1.07. 53
if his fitness speaks, mine is ready; HAM 5.02.201 P
for 'tis said a woman's fitness comes by fits. CYM 4.01. 6 P
/FITS* 1 FR 0.0001 REL FR 1 V 0 P
where hope is coldest and despair most /fits. AWW 2.01.144
FITS* 48 FR 0.0054 REL FR 38 V 10 P
and in these fits i leave them, while i visit TMP 3.03. 91
that fits as well as "tell me, good my lord, TGV 2.07. 50
every true man's apparel fits your thief. MM 4.02. 43 P
so every true man's apparel fits your thief. 4.02. 47 P
belike his wife, acquainted with his fits, | on ERR 4.03. 90
thy jealous fits | hath scar'd thy husband from 5.01. 85
and it better fits my blood to be disdain'd of ADO 1.03. 28 P
i love to cope him in these sullen fits, | for AYL 2.01. 67
a spare life, look you, it fits my humor well; 3.02. 19 P
a bountiful answer that fits all questions. AWW 2.02. 15 P
is like a barber's chair that fits all buttocks: 2.02. 17 P
for i must go | where it fits not you to know. WT 4.04.298
and fits the mounting spirit like myself; JN 1.01.206
a feast | fits a dull fighter and a keen guest. 1H4 4.02. 80
you do know these fits | are with his highness 2H4 4.04.114
it fits us then to be as provident | as fear may H5 2.04. 11
whose church-like humors fits not for a crown. 2H6 1.01.247
that time best fits the work we have in hand. 1.04. 20
where it best fits to be, in henry's hand. 2.03. 44
it fits we thus proceed, or else no witness H8 5.01.107
well said, my lord! well, you say so in fits. TRO 3.01. 57 P
in you, | which better fits a lion than a man. 5.03. 38
a better head her glorious body fits | than his TIT 1.01.187
to cool this heat, a charm to calm these fits, 2.01.134
this valley fits the purpose passing well. 2.03. 84
for no name fits thy nature but thy own! 2.03.119
why dost thou laugh? it fits not with this hour. 3.01.265
his fits, his frenzy, and his bitterness? 4.04. 12
this closing with him fits his lunacy. 5.02. 70
it fits when such a villain is a guest. ROM 1.05. 75
and best knows | the fits o' th' season. MAC 4.02. 17
it fits your wisdom so far to believe it | as he HAM 1.03. 25
such thanks | as fits a king's remembrance. 2.02. 26
look for such observancy | as fits the bridal. OTH 3.04.150
the foul'st best fits | my latter part of life. ANT 4.06. 37
as the fits and stirs of 's mind | could best CYM 1.03. 12
it fits us therefore ripely | our chariots and 3.05. 22
for 'tis said a woman's fitness comes by fits. 4.01. 6 P
thy name well fits thy faith; 4.02.381
your child | (which pleasures fits a husband, PER 1.01.129
it fits thee not | to ask the reason why, 1.01.156
fits kings as they are men, for they may err. 1.02. 43
and i (as fits my nature) do obey you. 2.01. 4
if it be a day fits you, search out of the 2.01. 54 P
business withal, fits it to every question. TNK 4.03. 8 P
and now the happy season once more fits | that VEN 327
plagu'd with cramps and gouts and painful fits, LUC 856
the humble salve which wounded bosoms fits! SON 120.12
FITTED* 15 FR 0.0017 REL FR 11 V 4 P
he may be so fitted | that his soul sicken not. MM 2.04. 40
been drinking all night, i am not fitted for't. 4.03. 44 P
i hope to see you one day fitted with a husband. ADO 2.01. 57 P
well fitted in arts, glorious in arms; LLL 2.01. 45
that will be time, and may by us be fitted. 4.03.379
and i hope here is a play fitted. MND 1.02. 65 P
there is not one word apt, one player fitted. 5.01. 65
part | was aptly fitted and naturally perform'd. SHR in.1. 87
she better would have fitted me or clarence; 3H6 4.01. 54
are, | fitted by kind for rape and villainy. TIT 2.01.116
well are you fitted, had you but a moor. 5.02. 85
in madness, thoughts and remembrance fitted. HAM 4.05.179 P
time | (when she had fitted you with her craft), CYM 5.05. 55
fitted and shap'd just to that strength of STM III 4
have mine eyes out of their spheres been fitted SON 119. 7
/FITTER 1 FR 0.0001 REL FR 1 V 0 P
/and /her /father | /requires /a /fitter /place. LR 5.03. 59
FITTER 10 FR 0.0011 REL FR 7 V 3 P
dispose of her | to some more fitter place; MM 2.02. 17
but fitter time for that. 5.01.493
against your son, there is no fitter matter. AWW 4.05. 76 P
thou art fitter to be worn in my cap than to 2H4 1.02. 15 P
me, there are other men fitter to go out than i. 3.02.115 P
place, | fitter for sickness and for crazy age. 1H6 3.02. 89
and fitter is my study and my books | than 5.01. 22
for he was fitter for that place than earth. R3 1.02.108
the fitter then the gods should have her. PER 4.01. 10
fitter for girls and schoolboys) will be seen, TNK 3.06. 34
FITTEST 4 FR 0.0004 REL FR 3 V 1 P
this course i fittest choose, | for forty ducats ERR 4.03. 95
devise the fittest time and safest way | to hide AYL 1.03.135
the fittest time to corrupt a man's wife is when COR 4.03. 32 P
madam, do you, 'tis fittest. LR 4.07. 42
FITTETH 3 FR 0.0003 REL FR 2 V 1 P
reck'ning, it fitteth the spirit of a tapster. LLL 1.02. 40 P
humbler, | it fitteth not a prelate so to plead. 1H6 3.01. 57
best fitteth my degree or your condition. R3 3.07.143
FITTING 10 FR 0.0011 REL FR 8 V 2 P
a silly answer, and fitting well a sheep. TGV 1.01. 81 P
and any thing that is fitting to be known — WT 4.04.720 P
o my sweet sir, news fitting to the night, JN 5.06. 19
as fitting best to quittance their deceit 1H6 2.01. 14
indeed, left nothing fitting for your purpose R3 3.07. 18
it, | as needful in our loves, fitting our duty? HAM 1.01.173
and fitting for a princess | descended of so ANT 5.02.326
fitting my bounty and thy state, i'll give it; CYM 5.05. 98
or, if you feel yourself not fitting yet | and TNK 3.06. 36
order it | fitting the persons that must use it. 4.02.151
FITT'ST 2 FR 0.0002 REL FR 2 V 0 P
o' th' night | are strewings fitt'st for graves. CYM 4.02.285
can, fitt'st time | for best solicitation? TNK 1.01.169
FITZWATER 3 FR 0.0003 REL FR 3 V 0 P
fitzwater, thou art damn'd to hell for this. R2 4.01. 43
my lord fitzwater, i do remember well | the very 4.01. 60
thy pains, fitzwater, shall not be forgot, 5.06. 17
/FIVE 4 FR 0.0004 REL FR 3 V 1 P
than common sleep of all these /five the sense. MND 4.01. 82
deck'd with /five flower-de-luces on each side, 1H6 1.02. 99
five times in that ere once in our /five wits. ROM 1.04. 47
/five /fiends /have /been /in /poor /tom /at LR 4.01. 58 P
FIVE 127 FR 0.0143 REL FR 87 V 40 P
had i not | four, or five, women once that TMP 1.02. 47
full fadom five thy father lies, | of his bones 1.02.397
would continue in it five weeks without changing 2.01.184 P
they say there's but five upon this isle: 3.02. 5 P
the shore, five and thirty leagues off and on. 3.02. 14 P
each putter-out of five for one will bring us 3.03. 48
where, for one shot of five pence, thou shalt TGV 2.05. 9 P
pence, thou shalt have five thousand welcomes. 2.05. 10 P
had drunk himself out of his five sentences. WIV 1.01.175 P
it is his five senses. 1.01.176 P
a omans as i will desires among five thousand, 3.03.220 P
among five thousand, and five hundred too. 3.03.221 P
to prison was worth five thousand of you all. MM 1.02. 61 P
let me have claudio's head sent me by five. 4.02.123 P
pounds, of which he made five marks ready money. 4.03. 7 P
and five years since there was some speech of 5.01.217
since which time of five years | i never spake 5.01.222
ere the ships could meet by twice five leagues, ERR 1.01.100
five summers have i spent in farthest greece, 1.01.132
soon at five a' clock, | please you, i'll meet 1.02. 26
at five a' clock | i shall receive the money for 4.01. 10
five hundred ducats, villain, for a rope? 4.04. 13
i'll serve you, sir, five hundred at the rate. 4.04. 14
by this i think the dial points at five. 5.01.118
conflict four of his five wits went halting off, ADO 1.01. 66 P
five shillings to one on't, with any man that 3.03. 78 P
'tis almost five a' clock, cousin, 'tis time you 3.04. 52 P
cain's birth, that's not five weeks old as yet? LLL 4.02. 35
and raught not to five weeks when he came to 4.02. 40
the last of the five vowels, if "you" repeat 5.01. 53 P
for he hath been five thousand year a boy. 5.02. 11
will change habits, and present the other five. 5.02.539
there is five in the first show. 5.02.540
whole world again | i cannot pick out five such, 5.02.545
be ready at the farthest by five of the clock. MV 2.02.115 P
i have five hundred crowns, | the thrifty hire i AYL 2.03. 38
five and twenty, sir. 5.01. 19 P
of enjoin'd penitents | there's four or five, to AWW 3.05. 95
some four or five descents | since the first 3.07. 24
five or six thousand, but very weak and 4.03.131 P
"five or six thousand horse," i said — i will 4.03.148 P
who hath for four or five removes come short 5.03.131
some four or five attend him — | all, if you TN 1.04. 36
alas, sir, how fell you besides your five wits? 4.02. 86 P
the second and the third, nine, and some five; WT 2.01.145
three pound of sugar, five pound of currants, 4.03. 38 P
and five or six honest wives that were present. 4.04.270 P
five justices' hands at it, and witnesses more 4.04.283 P
at least from fair five hundred pound a year. JN 1.01. 69
a half-fac'd groat five hundred pound a year! 1.01. 94
your face hath got five hundred pound a year, 1.01.152
yet sell your face for five pence and 'tis dear. 1.01.153
poictiers, and anjou, these five provinces, 2.01.528
my lord, they say five moons were seen to-night; 4.02.182
five moons? 4.02.185
till twice five summers have enrich'd our fields R2 1.03.141
forsooth, five years, and as much as to — 1H4 2.04. 42 P
five year! 2.04. 45 P
for this advertisement is five days old. 3.02.172
to five and twenty thousand men of choice, | and 2H4 1.03. 11
whether our present five and twenty thousand 1.03. 16
what, is the king but five and twenty thousand? 1.03. 68
no, fifteen hundred foot, five hundred horse, 2.01.173
and told him there were five more sir johns, and 2.04. 6 P
as hector of troy, worth five of agamemnon, and 2.04.220 P
john, let me have five hundred of my thousand. 5.05. 83 P
river sala, in the year | eight hundred five. H5 1.02. 64
with four or five most vile and ragged foils 4.pr. 50
five hundred poor i have in yearly pay, | who 4.01.298
there's five to one; 4.03. 4
why, now thou hast unwish'd five thousand men; 4.03. 76
five hundred were but yesterday dubb'd knights. 4.08. 86
and of all other men | but five and twenty. 4.08.106
there hath at least five frenchmen died to-night 1H6 2.02. 9
beside five hundred prisoners of esteem, | lets 3.04. 8
these five days have i hid me in these woods and 2H6 4.10. 2 P
i have eat no meat these five days, yet, come 4.10. 39 P
yet, come thou and thy five men, and if i do not 4.10. 40 P
what, with five thousand men? 3H6 1.02. 66
ay, with five hundred, father, for a need. 1.02. 67
five men to twenty! 1.02. 71
will but amount to five and twenty thousand, 2.01.181
thou and oxford, with five thousand men, | shall 3.03.234
and yet within these five hours hastings liv'd, R3 3.06. 8
five have i slain to-day in stead of him. 5.04. 12
five tribunes to defend their vulgar wisdoms, COR 1.01.215
five times, martius, | i have fought with thee; 1.10. 7
i'll have five hundred voices of that sound. 2.03.211
i twice five hundred, and their friends to piece 2.03.212
five times he hath return'd | bleeding to rome, TIT 1.01. 33
romans, of five and twenty valiant sons, | half 1.01. 79
this monument five hundreth years hath stood, 1.01.350
five times in that ere once in our /five wits. ROM 1.04. 47
spanish blades, | of healths five fadom deep; 1.04. 85
some five and twenty years, and then we mask'd. 1.05. 37
wits than, i am sure, i have in my whole five. 2.04. 73 P
ay, my good lord, five talents is his debt, TIM 1.01. 95
the five best senses | acknowledge thee their 1.02.123
and late, five thousand; 2.01. 1
my former sum, | which makes it five and twenty. 2.01. 3
of friends, | i clear'd him with five talents. 2.02.226
to be rememb'red | with those five talents. 2.02.229
he cannot want fifty — five hundred talents. 3.02. 38
five thousand mine. 3.04. 29
five thousand crowns, my lord. 3.04. 95 P
five thousand drops pays that. 3.04. 96
to pay five ducats, five, i would not farm it; HAM 4.04. 20
to pay five ducats, five, i would not farm it; 4.04. 20
five days we do allot thee, for provision | to LR 1.01.173
i entreat you | to bring but five and twenty; 2.04.248
what, must i come to you | with five and twenty? 2.04.254
thy fifty yet doth double five and twenty, | and 2.04.259
what need you five and twenty? 2.04.261
or five? 2.04.261
bless thy five wits! 3.04. 58 P
bless thy five wits! 3.06. 57 P
some five or six and thirty of his knights, 3.07. 16
this present hour of five till the bell have OTH 2.02. 10 P
every ten that they make, the devils mar five. ANT 5.02.277 P
with five times so much conversation, i should CYM 1.04.103 P
hath the king | five times redeem'd from death. 1.05. 63
she hath not been | entranc'd above five hours. PER 3.02. 94
were you a gamester at five, or at seven? 4.06. 75 P
his age some five and twenty. TNK 4.02.116
even of five hundreth courses of the sun, | show SON 59. 6
but my five wits nor my five senses can 141. 9
but my five wits nor my five senses can 141. 9
FIVE-AND-THIRTY 1 FR 0.0001 REL FR 0 V 1 P
hot-bloods between fourteen and five-and-thirty, ADO 3.03.132 P
/FIVE-FINGER-TIED 1 FR 0.0001 REL FR 1 V 0 P
and with another knot, /five-finger-tied, | the TRO 5.02.157
FIVEFOLD 1 FR 0.0001 REL FR 1 V 0 P
and spirit | do give thee fivefold blazon. TN 1.05.293
FIVES 1 FR 0.0001 REL FR 0 V 1 P
ray'd with the yellows, past cure of the fives, SHR 3.02. 54 P
FIVESCORE 2 FR 0.0002 REL FR 2 V 0 P
not to five weeks when he came to fivescore. LLL 4.02. 40
a wither'd hermit, fivescore winters worn, 4.03.238
FIX 4 FR 0.0004 REL FR 4 V 0 P
fix thy foot. COR 1.08. 4
and, as i earnestly did fix mine eye | upon the TIT 5.01. 22
on that, | and fix most firm thy resolution. OTH 5.01. 5
will fix a sharp knife to affright mine eye, LUC 1138
FIX'D 32 FR 0.0036 REL FR 30 V 2 P
my wife hath sent to him, the hour is fix'd, the WIV 2.02.290 P
i, | fixing our eyes on whom our care was fix'd, ERR 1.01. 84
yet these fix'd evils sit so fit in him, | that AWW 1.01.102
but my intents are fix'd and will not leave me. 1.01.229
fasten'd and fix'd the shame on't in himself, WT 2.03. 15
the statue is but newly fix'd, 5.03. 47
that the fix'd sentinels almost receive | the H5 4.pr. 6
why are thine eyes fix'd to the sullen earth, 2H6 1.02. 5
mine hair be fix'd an end, as one distract; 3.02.318
whereof the root was fix'd in virtue's ground, 3H6 3.03.125
in the air | and be not fix'd in doom perpetual, R3 4.04. 12
and fix'd on spiritual object, he should still H8 3.02.132
great in fame as she was, | and so stand fix'd. 5.04. 47
whose patience | is as a virtue fix'd, to-day TRO 1.02. 5
man fancy | with so eternal and so fix'd a soul. 5.02.166
nay, that's most fix'd. TIM 1.01. 9
whose eyes are on this sovereign lady fix'd, 1.01. 68
and fix'd his head upon our battlements. MAC 1.02. 23
or that the everlasting had not fix'd | his HAM 1.02.131
and fix'd his eyes upon you? 1.02.233
fix'd on the summit of the highest mount, | to 3.03. 18
my frame of nature | from the fix'd place; LR 1.04.269
how unremovable and fix'd he is | in his own 2.04. 93
but where the greater malady is fix'd, | the 3.04. 8
i fix'd my note | constantly on them; TNK 1.04. 19
in great hope she had fix'd her liking on this 4.03. 64 P
that four such eyes should be so fix'd on one 5.03.145
whose beams upon his hairless face are fix'd, VEN 487
where her faith was firmly fix'd in love, PP 17. 7
as those gold candles fix'd in heaven's air: SON 21.12
"truth needs no color with his color fix'd, 101. 6
to every place at once, and no where fix'd, LC 27
FIXED 16 FR 0.0018 REL FR 15 V 1 P
of night, | you orphan heirs of fixed destiny, WIV 5.05. 39
lights, | that give a name to every fixed star, LLL 1.01. 89
take, | an ass's nole i fixed on his head. MND 3.02. 17
there thy fixed foot shall grow | till thou have TN 1.04. 17
by this time from their fixed beds of lime | had JN 2.01.219
four fixed, and the fift did whirl about | the 4.02.183
and meteors fright the fixed stars of heaven, R2 2.04. 9
to which is fixed, as an aim or butt, H5 1.02.186
look you, is fixed upon a spherical stone, which 3.06. 35 P
the horsemen sit like fixed candlesticks, | with 4.02. 45
strong fixed is the house of lancaster, | and 1H6 2.05.102
deliver'd strongly through my fixed teeth, 2H6 3.02.313
that he's your fixed enemy, and revoke | your COR 2.03.250
make me | the fixed figure for the time of scorn OTH 4.02. 54
her pity-pleading eyes are sadly fixed | in the LUC 561
and little stars shot from their fixed places, 1525
FIXES 1 FR 0.0001 REL FR 1 V 0 P
as dice are to be wish'd by one that fixes | no WT 1.02.133
FIXING 2 FR 0.0002 REL FR 2 V 0 P
i, | fixing our eyes on whom our care was fix'd, ERR 1.01. 84
the eye indeed | by fixing it upon a fairer eye, LLL 1.01. 81
FIXTURE 1 FR 0.0001 REL FR 0 V 1 P
and the firm fixture of thy foot would give an WIV 3.03. 63 P
FIXURE 2 FR 0.0002 REL FR 2 V 0 P
the fixure of her eye has motion in't, | as we WT 5.03. 67
calm of states | quite from their fixure! TRO 1.03.101
FLAG* 7 FR 0.0008 REL FR 6 V 1 P
stand for your own, unwind your bloody flag, H5 1.02.101
this token serveth for a flag of truce | betwixt 1H6 3.01.138
a garish flag | to be the aim of every dangerous R3 4.04. 88
set up the bloody flag against all patience, and COR 2.01. 75 P
and death's pale flag is not advanced there. ROM 5.03. 96
life, | i must show out a flag and sign of love, OTH 1.01.156
body, | like to a vagabond flag upon the stream, ANT 1.04. 45
FLAGGING 1 FR 0.0001 REL FR 1 V 0 P
and flagging wings | cleep dead men's graves, 2H6 4.01. 5
FLAGON 1 FR 0.0001 REL FR 0 V 1 P
'a pour'd a flagon of rhenish on my head once. HAM 5.01.180 P
FLAGS 3 FR 0.0003 REL FR 3 V 0 P
these flags of france, that are advanced here JN 2.01.207
than was his loss, to course your flying flags, ANT 3.13. 11

the semblance | of their white flags display'd, PER 1.04. 72
FLAIL 1 FR 0.0001 REL FR 1 V 0 P
or like /an /idle thresher with a flail, | fell 3H6 2.01.131
FLAKES 1 FR 0.0001 REL FR 1 V 0 P
these white flakes | did challenge pity of them. LR 4.07. 29
FLAKY 1 FR 0.0001 REL FR 1 V 0 P
on, | and flaky darkness breaks within the east. R3 5.03. 86
FLAM'D 1 FR 0.0001 REL FR 1 V 0 P
the deck, in every cabin, | i flam'd amazement. TMP 1.02.198
FLAME 27 FR 0.0030 REL FR 24 V 3 P
yards and boresprit, would i flame distinctly, TMP 1.02.200
the flame will back descend | and turn him to no WIV 5.05. 85
"after my flame lacks oil, to be the snuff | of AWW 1.02. 59
did ever in so true a flame of liking | wish 1.03.211
if i did love you in my master's flame, | with TN 1.05.264
quenching the flame of bold rebellion | even 2H4 in 26
love, | and will at last break out into a flame: 1H6 3.01.190
put in her tender heart th' aspiring flame | of R3 4.04.328
no, by the flame of yonder glorious heaven, | he TRO 5.06. 23
but a small thing would make it flame again; COR 4.03. 21 P
intended fire your city is ready to flame in, 5.02. 46 P
our gentle flame | provokes itself and like the TIM 1.01. 23
which did flame and burn | like twenty torches JC 1.03. 16
the murderer's gibbet throw | into the flame. MAC 4.01. 67
son, | upon the heat and flame of thy distemper HAM 3.04.123
there lives within the very flame of love | a 4.07.114
fiend hath led through fire and through flame, LR 3.04. 52 P
the flame o' th' taper | bows toward her, and CYM 2.02. 19
murther's as near to lust as flame to smoke; PER 1.01.138
have skipp'd thy flame — at seventy thou canst TNK 5.01. 87
and to the flame thus speaks advisedly: LUC 180
the turtle fled | in a mutual flame from hence. PHT 24
feed'st thy light's flame with self-substantial SON 1. 6
though absence seem'd my flame to qualify! 109. 2
why | my most full flame should afterwards burn 115. 4
not one whose flame my heart so much as warmed,
LC 191
roses | that flame through water which their hue 287
FLAME-COLOR'D 1 FR 0.0001 REL FR 0 V 1 P
a fair hot wench in flame-color'd taffata; 1H4 1.02. 10 P
FLAMEN 1 FR 0.0001 REL FR 1 V 0 P
hoar the flamen, | that /scolds against the TIM 4.03.155
FLAMENS 1 FR 0.0001 REL FR 1 V 0 P
seld-shown flamens | do press among the popular COR 2.01.213
FLAMES 15 FR 0.0017 REL FR 14 V 1 P
desire, | fed in heart, whose flames aspire, WIV 5.05. 97
the honor, sir, that flames in your fair eyes, AWW 2.03. 80
arrayed in flames like to the prince of fiends, H5 3.03. 16
and knobs, and flames a' fire, and his lips 3.06.103 P
and through their paly flames | each battle sees 4.pr. 8
and the premised flames of the last day | knit 2H6 5.02. 41
and burns me up with flames that tears would 3H6 2.01. 84
to feed for /aye her lamp and flames of love, TRO 3.02.160
did from the flames of troy upon his shoulder JC 1.02.113
when i to sulph'rous and tormenting flames HAM 1.05. 3
threat'ning the flames | with bisson rheum, a 2.02.505
dart your blinding flames | into her scornful LR 2.04.165
blow that nearness out that flames between ye, TNK 5.01. 10
to phoebus thou | add'st flames, hotter than his 5.01. 91
and girdle with embracing flames the waist | of LUC 6
FLAMETH 1 FR 0.0001 REL FR 1 V 0 P
she burnt with love, as straw with fire flameth, PP 7.13
FLAMING 10 FR 0.0011 REL FR 9 V 1 P
shall to my flaming wrath be oil and flax. 2H6 5.02. 55
is too flaming a praise for a good complexion. TRO 1.02.104 P
blow, with flaming top | stoops to his base, and HAM 2.02.475
to flaming youth let virtue be as wax | and melt 3.04. 84
if i quench thee, thou flaming minister, | i can OTH 5.02. 8
which is but cold in flaming, thy /lone bosom PER 4.01. 5
bid him that we, whom flaming war doth scorch, TNK 1.01. 91
are by his flaming torch dimm'd and controll'd. LUC 448
a creeping creature, with a flaming light, | and 1627
saw his right | flaming in the phoenix' sight; PHT 35
/FLAMINIUS 1 FR 0.0001 REL FR 1 V 0 P
/flaminius! TIM 2.02.185
FLAMINIUS 6 FR 0.0006 REL FR 0 V 6 P
flaminius, honest flaminius, you are very TIM 3.01. 7 P
flaminius, honest flaminius, you are very 3.01. 7 P
thou there under thy cloak, pretty flaminius? 3.01. 15 P
flaminius, i have noted thee always wise. 3.01. 31 P
draw nearer, honest flaminius. 3.01. 39 P
flaminius? 3.04. 34 P
FLANDERS 3 FR 0.0003 REL FR 3 V 0 P
lord — | and shipp'd from thence to flanders? 3H6 4.05. 21
bold | to carry into flanders the great seal. H8 3.02.319
go you to france or flanders, | to any german STM II.C 127
FLANK 2 FR 0.0002 REL FR 2 V 0 P
that the boar had trench'd | in his soft flank, VEN 1053
and nousling in his flank, the loving swine 1115
FLANNEL 1 FR 0.0001 REL FR 0 V 1 P
i am not able to answer the welsh flannel; WIV 5.05.163 P
FLAP 1 FR 0.0001 REL FR 0 V 1 P
thou green sarcenet flap for a sore eye, thou TRO 5.01. 32 P
FLAP-DRAGON 1 FR 0.0001 REL FR 0 V 1 P
thou art easier swallow'd than a flap-dragon. LLL 5.01. 42 P
FLAP-DRAGON'D 1 FR 0.0001 REL FR 0 V 1 P
the ship, to see how the sea flap-dragon'd it; WT 3.03. 98 P
FLAP-DRAGONS 1 FR 0.0001 REL FR 0 V 1 P
and drinks off candles' ends for flap-dragons, 2H4 2.04.246 P
FLAP-EAR'D 1 FR 0.0001 REL FR 1 V 0 P
a whoreson, beetle-headed, flap-ear'd knave! SHR 4.01.157
FLAP-JACKS 1 FR 0.0001 REL FR 0 V 1 P
and, moreo'er, puddings and flap-jacks, and thou
PER 2.01. 82 P
FLAP-MOUTH'D 1 FR 0.0001 REL FR 1 V 0 P
another flap-mouth'd mourner, black and grim, VEN 920
FLARING 1 FR 0.0001 REL FR 1 V 0 P
with ribands pendant, flaring 'bout her head; WIV 4.06. 42
FLASH 4 FR 0.0004 REL FR 4 V 0 P
secure of thunder's crack or lightning flash, TIT 2.01. 3
myself | even in the aim and very flash of it. JC 1.03. 52
the flash and outbreak of a fiery mind, | a HAM 2.01. 33
fear no more the lightning flash. CYM 4.02.270
FLASH'D 1 FR 0.0001 REL FR 1 V 0 P
pale, and by and by | it flash'd forth fire, as VEN 348
FLASHES 4 FR 0.0004 REL FR 3 V 1 P
a naked gull, | which flashes now a phoenix. TIM 2.01. 32
your songs, your flashes of merriment, that were HAM 5.01.190 P
hour | he flashes into one gross crime or other LR 1.03. 4
gently quench | thy nimble, sulphurous flashes! PER 3.01. 6
FLASHING 1 FR 0.0001 REL FR 1 V 0 P
cock is up, | and flashing fire will follow. H5 2.01. 53
FLASK 2 FR 0.0002 REL FR 1 V 1 P
the carv'd-bone face on a flask. LLL 5.02.615 P
like powder in a skilless soldier's flask, | is ROM 3.03.132
FLAT 24 FR 0.0027 REL FR 17 V 7 P
i'll fall flat, | perchance he will not mind me. TMP 2.02. 16
and flat meads thatch'd with stover, them to 4.01. 63
nay, now you are too flat, | and mar the concord TGV 1.02. 90
word, | which in the soldier is flat blasphemy. MM 2.02.131
the flat transgression of a schoolboy, who, ADO 2.01.222 P
why, this is flat perjury, to call a prince's 4.02. 42 P
flat burglary as ever was committed. 4.02. 50 P
hath sold him a bargain, a goose, that's flat. LLL 3.01.101
flat treason 'gainst the kingly state of youth. 4.03.289
they call the place, a very dangerous flat, and MV 3.01. 5 P
why, this is flat knavery, to take upon you SHR 5.01. 36 P
rebellion, flat rebellion! JN 3.01.298
that's flat. 1H4 1.03.218
march through coventry with them, that's flat. 4.02. 39 P
the flat unraised spirits that hath dar'd | on H5 pr 9
up | the lees and dregs of a flat tamed piece; TRO 4.01. 63
to unbuild the city, and to lay all flat. COR 3.01.197
that is the way to lay the city flat, | to bring 3.01.203
down with the nose, | down with it flat; TIM 4.03.158
stale, flat, and unprofitable | seem to me all HAM 1.02.133
that we are made of stuff so flat and dull 4.07. 31
till of this flat a mountain you have made | t' 5.01.252
strike flat the thick rotundity o' th' world! LR 3.02. 7
which else an easy battery might lay flat, for CYM 1.04. 22 P
FLAT-LONG 1 FR 0.0001 REL FR 0 V 1 P
and it had not fall'n flat-long. TMP 2.01.181 P
FLATLY 5 FR 0.0005 REL FR 2 V 3 P
he tells me flatly there's no mercy for me in MV 3.05. 32 P
you, sir, he tells you flatly what his mind is. SHR 1.02. 77 P
he flatly says he'll not lay down his arms. JN 5.02.126
and tell me flatly i am no proud jack like 1H4 2.04. 11 P
and at his look she flatly falleth down, | for VEN 463
FLATNESS 1 FR 0.0001 REL FR 1 V 0 P
that he did but see | the flatness of my misery, WT 3.02.122
FLATS 5 FR 0.0005 REL FR 5 V 0 P
fens, flats, on prosper fall and make him | by TMP 2.02. 2
but i should think of shallows and of flats, MV 1.01. 26
passing these flats, are taken by the tide — JN 5.06. 40
eats not the flats with more impiteous haste HAM 4.05.101
i'll tread these flats. CYM 3.03. 11
/FLATTER 1 FR 0.0001 REL FR 1 V 0 P
/yet /have /learn'd | /to /insinuate, /flatter, R2 4.01.165
FLATTER 47 FR 0.0053 REL FR 43 V 4 P
i will not flatter her. TGV 2.04.147
o, flatter me; for love delights in praises. 2.04.148
flatter and praise, commend, extol their graces; 3.01.102
think not i flatter, for i swear i do not — 4.03. 12
little, | unless i flatter with myself too much. 4.04.188
to flatter up these powers of mine with rest, LLL 5.02.814
i am not bid for love, they flatter me, | but MV 2.05. 13
desire him not to flatter with his lord, | nor TN 1.05.303
further i will not flatter you, my lord, | that JN 2.01.516
i mock my name, great king, to flatter thee. R2 2.01. 87
should dying men flatter with those that live? 2.01. 88
no, no, men living flatter those that die. 2.01. 89
thoughts tending to content flatter themselves 5.05. 23
by god, i cannot flatter, i do defy | the 1H4 4.01. 6
my blood begins to flatter me that thou dost — H5 5.02.223 P
didst thou at first, to flatter us withal, 1H6 2.01. 51
margaret knows | that suffolk doth not flatter, 5.03.142
so should i give consent to flatter sin. 5.05. 25
first, for i cannot flatter thee in pride; 2H6 1.03.166
thee | to flatter henry and forsake thy brother! 3H6 4.07. 85
'tis sin to flatter, "good" was little better: 5.06. 3
but since you teach me how to flatter you, R3 1.02.223
because i cannot flatter and look fair, | smile 1.03. 47
flatter my sorrow with report of it; 4.04.246
fool, do not flatter: 5.03.192
that will give good words to thee will flatter COR 1.01.167
he dislikes, to flatter them for their love. 2.02. 23 P
your multiplying spawn how can he flatter — 2.02. 78
will, sir, flatter my sworn brother, the people, 2.03. 96 P
let them | regard me as i do not flatter, and 3.01. 67
he would not flatter neptune for his trident, 3.01.255
in a fiery gulf | than flatter him in a bower. 3.02. 92
andronicus, i do not flatter thee, | but honor TIT 1.01.212
for i should ne'er flatter thee. TIM 1.02. 39 P
bid them flatter thee. 4.03.231
i flatter not, but say thou art a caitiff. 4.03.235
nay, do not think i flatter, | for what HAM 3.02. 56
he cannot flatter, he, | an honest mind and LR 2.02. 98
to flatter caesar, would you mingle eyes | with ANT 3.13.156
they do abuse the king that flatter him, | for PER 1.02. 38
the one doth flatter thee in thoughts unlikely, VEN 989
so, | to flatter thee with an infringed oath; LUC 1061
hold | only to flatter fools and make them bold: 1559
priam's trust false sinon's tears doth flatter, 1560
so flatter i the swart-complexion'd night, SON 28.11
flatter the mountain tops with sovereign eye, 33. 2
thus have i had thee as a dream doth flatter: 87.13
FLATTER'D 11 FR 0.0012 REL FR 8 V 3 P
and yet the painter flatter'd her a little, TGV 4.04.187
that i have fondly flatter'd /her withal. SHR 4.02. 31
now shall he try his friends that flatter'd him. R2 2.02. 85
many great men that have flatter'd the people, COR 2.02. 8 P
he that loves to be flatter'd is worthy o' th' TIM 1.01.226 P
they never flatter'd thee. 4.03.270
why should the poor be flatter'd? HAM 3.02. 59
contemn'd, | than still contemn'd and flatter'd. LR 4.01. 2
they flatter'd me like a dog, and told me i had 4.06. 97 P
tale lie death, | i hear him as he flatter'd. ANT 1.02. 99
lepidus flatters both, | of both is flatter'd; 2.01. 15
FLATTERED 4 FR 0.0004 REL FR 4 V 0 P
where be the bending peers that flattered thee? R3 4.04. 95
he says he does, being then most flattered. JC 2.01.208
the thing the which is flattered, but a spark PER 1.02. 40
me, | and in our faults by lies we flattered be. SON 138.14
/FLATTERER 1 FR 0.0001 REL FR 1 V 0 P
/i /have /a /king /here /to /my /flatterer. R2 4.01.308
FLATTERER 14 FR 0.0015 REL FR 12 V 2 P
hope, and keep it | no longer for my flatterer. TMP 3.03. 8
mine eye too great a flatterer for my mind. TN 1.05.309
he is a flatterer, | a parasite, a keeper-back R2 2.02. 69
let him that is no coward nor no flatterer, 1H6 2.04. 31
o, if thine eye be not a flatterer, | come thou R3 1.04.264
from the glass-fac'd flatterer | to apemantus, TIM 1.01. 58
to be flatter'd is worthy o' th' flatterer. 1.01.227 P
upright | and say, "this man's a flatterer"? 4.03. 15
be thou a flatterer now, and seek to thrive | by 4.03.210
of men, | thou hadst been a knave and flatterer. 4.03.276
conceit me, | either a coward or a flatterer. JC 3.01.193
i know, sir, i am no flatterer. LR 2.02.110 P
thou art | no flatterer. PER 1.02. 61
sense | to critic and to flatterer stopped are. SON 112.11
FLATTERER'S 2 FR 0.0002 REL FR 2 V 0 P
of the same piece | is every flatterer's sport. TIM 3.02. 65
a flatterer's would not, though they do appear JC 4.03. 91
/FLATTERERS 1 FR 0.0001 REL FR 1 V 0 P
/for /when /i /was /a /king /my /flatterers R2 4.01.306
FLATTERERS 11 FR 0.0012 REL FR 9 V 2 P
a thousand flatterers sit within thy crown, R2 2.01.100
but basely led | by flatterers, and what they 2.01.242
trumpets shall | i' th' field prove flatterers, COR 1.09. 43
call'd them | time-pleasers, flatterers, foes to 3.01. 45
would all those flatterers were thine enemies TIM 1.02. 81 P
thy flatterers yet wear silk, drink wine, lie 4.03.206
canst thou nearest compare to thy flatterers? 4.03.319 P
lions with toils, and men with flatterers; JC 2.01.206
but when i tell him he hates flatterers | he 2.01.207
o you flatterers! 5.01. 44
flatterers? 5.01. 45
FLATTEREST 1 FR 0.0001 REL FR 1 V 0 P
thou, now a-dying, sayest thou flatterest me. R2 2.01. 90
/FLATTERIES 1 FR 0.0001 REL FR 1 V 0 P
/must /be /us'd | /with /checks /as /flatteries, LR 1.03. 20
FLATTERIES 5 FR 0.0005 REL FR 5 V 0 P
wounds me with the flatteries of his tongue. R2 3.02.216
or felt the flatteries that grow upon it! H8 3.01.144
and spend our flatteries to drink those men TIM 1.02.137
who, stuck and spangled /with /your flatteries, 3.06. 91
with a discovery of the infinite flatteries 5.01. 36
/FLATTERING 1 FR 0.0001 REL FR 1 V 0 P
/flattering /myself /as /if /it /were /the /moor TIT 3.02. 72
FLATTERING 18 FR 0.0020 REL FR 14 V 4 P
o, you are a flattering boy, now i see you'll be WIV 3.02. 7 P
i cannot be said to be a flattering honest man) ADO 1.03. 31 P
that flattering tongue of yours won me. AYL 4.01.184 P
drawn in the flattering table of her eye. JN 2.01.503
drawn in the flattering table of her eye! 2.01.504
no, it is stopp'd with other flattering sounds, R2 2.01. 17
thou dost give me flattering busses. 2H4 2.04.268 P
i fear me, lords, for all this flattering gloss, 2H6 1.01.163
off, | flattering me with impossibilities. 3H6 3.02.143
the flattering index of a direful pageant; R3 4.04. 85
if i may trust the flattering truth of sleep, ROM 5.01. 1
lave our honors in these flattering streams, MAC 3.02. 33
lay not that flattering unction to your soul, HAM 3.04.145
he, compact, and flattering his displeasure, LR 2.02.118
here comes a flattering rascal, upon him | will CYM 1.05. 27
flattering, hers; 2.05. 23
his flattering "holla," or his "stand, i say"? VEN 284
and with such-like flattering, | "pity but he PP 20.39
FLATTERING-SWEET 1 FR 0.0001 REL FR 1 V 0 P
dream, | too flattering-sweet to be substantial. ROM 2.02.141
FLATTERS 7 FR 0.0008 REL FR 7 V 0 P
'tis not her glass, but you, that flatters her, AYL 3.05. 54
we thank you both, yet one but flatters us, | as R2 1.01. 25
lepidus flatters both, | of both is flatter'd; ANT 2.01. 14
he flatters you, makes war upon your life. PER 1.02. 45
rejoice, | and flatters her it is adonis' voice. VEN 978
th' one sweetly flatters, th' other feareth harm LUC 172
every one that flatters thee | is no friend in PP 20.29
FLATTER'ST 1 FR 0.0001 REL FR 1 V 0 P
thou flatter'st misery. TIM 4.03.234
FLATTERY 23 FR 0.0026 REL FR 20 V 3 P
so conceitless, | to be seduced by thy flattery, TGV 4.02. 97
the sweet breath of flattery conquers strife. ERR 3.02. 28
ay marry, there — some flattery for this evil. LLL 4.03.282
cold, i smile and say, | "this is no flattery: AYL 2.01. 10
in this fine age were not thought flattery, 1H4 4.01. 2
proverb with "there is flattery in friendship." H5 3.07.114 P
stead of homage sweet, | but poison'd flattery? 4.01.251
the voice nor the heart of flattery about me, i 5.02.288 P
all color | of base insinuating flattery, | i 1H6 2.04. 35
by flattery hath he won the commons' hearts; 2H6 3.01. 28
but know i come not | to hear such flattery now, H8 5.02.159
and the words i utter | let none think flattery, 5.04. 16
tongue can do | i' th' way of flattery further. COR 3.02.137
he watered his new plants with dews of flattery, 5.06. 22
be | to counsel deaf, but not to flattery! TIM 1.02.250
i kiss thy hand, but not in flattery, caesar; JC 3.01. 52
dread to speak | when power to flattery bows? LR 1.01.148
out of her own love and flattery, not out of my OTH 4.01.129 P
mine ears, that /heard her flattery, nor my CYM 5.05. 64
him, | for flattery is the bellows blows up sin, PER 1.02. 39
villainy | so well as soft and tender flattery. 4.04. 45
sweet flattery! SON 42.14
drink up the monarch's plague, this flattery? 114. 2
FLATT'RED 2 FR 0.0002 REL FR 1 V 1 P
i have trod a measure, i have flatt'red a lady, AYL 5.04. 44 P
who, flatt'red by their leader's jocund show, LUC 296
/FLATT'RING 1 FR 0.0001 REL FR 1 V 0 P
/o /flatt'ring /glass, | /like /to /my R2 4.01.279
FLATT'RING 4 FR 0.0004 REL FR 4 V 0 P
even as a flatt'ring dream or worthless fancy. SHR in.1. 44
flatt'ring himself in project of a power | much 2H4 1.03. 29
let him return, and flatt'ring thoughts retire; LUC 641
to know | faithful friend from flatt'ring foe. PP 20.56
FLATT'RY 3 FR 0.0003 REL FR 3 V 0 P
now farewell, flatt'ry; TIT 3.01.253
your vows, your feigned tears, your flatt'ry, VEN 425
o, 'tis the first, 'tis flatt'ry in my seeing, SON 114. 9
FLAUNTS 1 FR 0.0001 REL FR 1 V 0 P
i, in these my borrowed flaunts, behold | the WT 4.04. 23
/FLAVINA 1 FR 0.0001 REL FR 1 V 0 P
'twas /flavina. TNK 1.03. 54
FLAVINA 1 FR 0.0001 REL FR 1 V 0 P
that you shall never (like the maid flavina) TNK 1.03. 84

FLAVIO 1 FR 0.0001 REL FR 1 V 0 P
labio and flavio, set our battles on. JC 5.03.108
FLAVIO'S 1 FR 0.0001 REL FR 1 V 0 P
go call at flavio's house, | and tell him where MM 4.05. 6
FLAVIUS 3 FR 0.0003 REL FR 2 V 1 P
but send me flavius first. MM 4.05. 10
flavius! TIM 1.02.157
murellus and flavius, for pulling scarfs off JC 1.02.285 P
FLAW* 6 FR 0.0006 REL FR 6 V 0 P
my love to thee is sound, sans crack or flaw. LLL 5.02.415
beams, | do calm the fury of this mad–bred flaw. 2H6 3.01.354
like a great sea–mark, standing every flaw, COR 5.03. 74
should patch a wall t' expel the /winter's flaw! HAM 5.01.216
observe how antony becomes his flaw, | and what ANT 3.12. 34
i do not fear the flaw, | it hath done to me the PER 3.01. 39
FLAW'D 3 FR 0.0003 REL FR 3 V 0 P
for france hath flaw'd the league, and hath H8 1.01. 95
'em, which hath flaw'd the heart | of all their 1.02. 21
but his flaw'd heart | (alack, too weak the LR 5.03.197
FLAWS* 5 FR 0.0005 REL FR 5 V 0 P
who, falling in the flaws of her own youth, MM 2.03. 11
as flaws congealed in the spring of day. 2H4 4.04. 35
o, these flaws and starts | (imposters to true MAC 3.04. 62
shall break into a hundred thousand flaws | or LR 2.04.285
gusts and foul flaws to herdmen and to herds. VEN 456
/FLAX 1 FR 0.0001 REL FR 1 V 0 P
/i'll /fetch /some /flax /and /whites /of /eggs LR 3.07.106
FLAX 4 FR 0.0004 REL FR 2 V 2 P
what, a hodge–pudding? a bag of flax? WIV 5.05.151 P
it hangs like flax on a distaff; TN 1.03.102 P
shall to my flaming wrath be oil and flax. 2H6 5.02. 55
could | no more be hid in him than fire in flax, TNK 5.03. 98
FLAXEN 1 FR 0.0001 REL FR 1 V 0 P
as white as snow, | /all flaxen was his pole, HAM 4.05.196
FLAX–WENCH 1 FR 0.0001 REL FR 1 V 0 P
a name | as rank as any flax–wench that puts to WT 1.02.277
FLAY'D *(also flea*, etc.)*
FLAY'D 3 FR 0.0003 REL FR 0 V 3 P
he has a son, who shall be flay'd alive; WT 4.04.783 P
remember "ston'd," and "flay'd alive." 4.04.805 P
one, i hope i shall not be flay'd out of it. 4.04.815 P
FLAYING 1 FR 0.0001 REL FR 1 V 0 P
what flaying? WT 3.02.176
FLEA* *(also flay'd, etc.)*
FLEA* 6 FR 0.0006 REL FR 2 V 4 P
man's blood in his belly than will sup a flea. LLL 5.02.692 P
thou flea, thou nit, thou winter–cricket thou! SHR 4.03.109
in his liver as will clog the foot of a flea, TN 3.02. 62 P
'a saw a flea stick upon bardolph's nose, and 'a H5 2.03. 40 P
say, that's a valiant flea that dare eat his 3.07.145 P
with her nails | she'll flea thy wolvish visage. LR 1.04.308
/FLEA'D 1 FR 0.0001 REL FR 0 V 1 P
the gentleman is half /flea'd already. WT 4.04.641 P
FLEA'D 1 FR 0.0001 REL FR 1 V 0 P
yonder, | that does appear as he were flea'd? COR 1.06. 22
FLEAING 1 FR 0.0001 REL FR 1 V 0 P
vagabond exile, fleaing, pent to linger | but COR 3.03. 89
FLEANCE 9 FR 0.0010 REL FR 9 V 0 P
goes fleance with you? MAC 3.01. 35
fleance his son, that keeps him company, | whose 3.01.134
thou know'st that banquo and his fleance lives. 3.02. 37
fly, good fleance, fly, fly, fly! 3.03. 17
yet he's good that did the like for fleance. 3.04. 17
most royal sir, fleance is scap'd. 3.04. 19
you may say (if't please you) fleance kill'd, 3.06. 6
please you) fleance kill'd, | for fleance fled. 3.06. 7
so should fleance. 3.06. 20
FLEA'S 1 FR 0.0001 REL FR 0 V 1 P
find a man there, he shall die a flea's death. WIV 4.02.151 P
FLEAS 2 FR 0.0002 REL FR 0 V 2 P
villainous house in all london road for fleas. 1H4 2.01. 15 P
and your chamber–lye breeds fleas like a loach. 2.01. 21 P
FLECKLED 1 FR 0.0001 REL FR 1 V 0 P
and fleckled darkness like a drunkard reels ROM 2.03. 3
FLED* 98 FR 0.0110 REL FR 90 V 8 P
then | she's fled unto that peasant valentine; TGV 5.02. 35
that leads toward mantua, whither they are fled. 5.02. 47
we'll follow him that's fled — | the thicket is 5.03. 10
meet the duke, villain, do not say they be fled. WIV 4.05. 72 P
then they fled | into this abbey, whither we ERR 5.01.154
and then you fled into this abbey here, | from 5.01.264
your brother the bastard is fled from messina. ADO 5.01.190 P
did he not say my brother was fled? 5.01.205 P
treachery, | and fled he is upon this villainy. 5.01.250
men, | a third is fled, that had a hand in it. 5.01.267
john is the author of all, who is fled and gone. 5.02. 99 P
thou runaway, thou coward, art thou fled? MND 3.02.405
and, as she fled, her mantle she did fall, 5.01.142
now am i dead, | now am i fled; 5.01.302
fled with a christian! MV 2.08. 16
with my hate to her, | and wherefore i am fled; AWW 2.03.288
wife some two months since fled from his house. 4.03. 47 P
lest that the treachery of the two fled hence WT 2.01.195
fled from his father, from his hopes, and with 5.01.184
and truth of all this realm | is fled to heaven; JN 4.03.145
all their powerful friends, are fled to him. R2 2.02. 55
and all the household servants fled with him 2.02. 60
the nobles they are fled, the commons they are 2.02. 88
our countrymen are gone and fled, | as well 2.04. 16
thy friends are fled to wait upon thy foes, 2.04. 23
are gone to bullingbrook, dispers'd and fled. 3.02. 74
men | did triumph in my face, and they are fled; 3.02. 77
men | upon the foot of fear, fled with the rest, 1H4 5.05. 20
and westmerland and stafford fled the field; 2H4 1.01. 18
that arrows fled not swifter toward their aim 1.01.123
the rogue fled from me like quicksilver. 2.04.228 P
cowardly fled, not having struck one stroke. 1H6 1.01.134
i would ne'er have fled, | but that they left me 1.02. 23
the day begins to break, and night is fled, 2.02. 1
grief | that such a valiant company are fled. 3.02.125
for fly he could not, if he would have fled; 4.04. 43
that basely fled when noble talbot stood. 4.05. 17
you fled for vantage, every one will swear; 4.05. 28
for that which we have fled | during the life, 4.07. 49
for with his soul fled all my worldly solace; 2H6 3.02.151
what, is he fled? 4.08. 65
he is fled, my lord, and all his powers do yield 4.09. 10
because the unconquer'd soul of cade is fled. 4.10. 65 P
'tis not enough our foes are this time fled, 5.03. 21
for, as i hear, the king is fled to london, | to 5.03. 24
so fled his enemies my warlike father; 3H6 2.01. 19
them, no hope to win the day, | so that we fled: 2.01.137
'twas odds, belike, when valiant warwick fled: 2.01.148
you said so much before, and yet you fled. 2.02.106
for all your friends are fled, | and warwick 2.05.125
think you, lords, that clifford fled with them? 2.06. 37
and fled (as he hears since) to burgundy. 4.06. 79
and somerset, with oxford, fled to her; 5.03. 15
as i hear, is fled | to richmond, in the parts R3 4.02. 48
well, let that rest. dorset is fled to richmond. 4.02. 85
morton is fled to richmond, | and buckingham, 4.03. 46
proclaim a pardon to the soldiers fled | that in 5.05. 16
either to harbor fled, | or made a toast for TRO 1.03. 44
and flies fled under shade, why then the thing 1.03. 51
when blows have made me stay, i fled from words. COR 2.02. 72
you rememb'red, marcus, she's gone, she's fled. TIT 4.03. 5
and gladly shunn'd who gladly fled from me. ROM 1.01.130
life | of stout mercutio, and then tybalt fled; 3.01.169
this was my lord's best hope, now all are fled, TIM 3.03. 35
fled to his house amaz'd. JC 3.01. 96
thou /art fled to brutish beasts, | and men have 3.02.104
this morning are they fled away and gone, | and 5.01. 83
are stol'n away and fled, which puts upon them MAC 2.04. 26
there's but one down; the son is fled. 3.03. 20
the worm that's fled | hath nature that in time 3.04. 28
please you) fleance kill'd, | for fleance fled. 3.06. 7
bring you word | macduff is fled to england. 4.01.142
fled to england! 4.01.142
that fled the snares of watchful tyranny, 5.09. 33
fled this way, sir, when by no means he could — LR 2.01. 42
by the noise i made, | full suddenly he fled. 2.01. 56
head, | dogs leapt the hatch, and all are fled. 3.06. 73
fled from her wish, and yet said, "now i may"; OTH 2.01.151
from him that fled some strange indignity 2.03.245
toward peloponnesus are they fled. ANT 3.10. 30
i have fled myself, and have instructed cowards 3.11. 7
what though you fled | from that great face of 3.13. 4
no, but he fled forward still, toward your face. CYM 1.02. 15 P
'tis certain she is fled. 3.05. 66
i'll follow those that even now fled hence, 4.02. 98
made good the passage, cried to those that fled, 5.03. 23
why fled you from the court? 5.05.387
my lord, prince pericles is fled. PER 1.01.160
which fear so grew in me, i hither fled, | under 1.02. 80
my virgin's faith has fled me; TNK 4.02. 46
"call it not love, for love to heaven is fled, VEN 793
love's golden arrow at him should have fled, 947
so at his bloody view her eyes are fled | into 1037
and blushing fled, and left her all alone. PP 9.14
plains, | all our evening sport from us is fled, 17.31
phoenix and the turtle fled | in a mutual flame PHT 23
give warning to the world that i am fled | from SON 71. 3
or if they have, where is my judgment fled, 148. 3
FLEDGE *(also flidge)*
FLEDGE 1 FR 0.0001 REL FR 0 V 1 P
your master, whose chin is not yet fledge. 2H4 1.02. 20 P
FLEE 1 FR 0.0001 REL FR 1 V 0 P
thump then, and i flee. LLL 3.01. 65
FLEEC'D 1 FR 0.0001 REL FR 1 V 0 P
felonious thief that fleec'd poor passengers, 2H6 3.01.129
FLEECE 10 FR 0.0011 REL FR 9 V 1 P
hang on her temples like a golden fleece, MV 1.01.170
we are the jasons, we have won the fleece. 3.02.241
would you had won the fleece that he hath lost. 3.02.242
fleece them! 1H4 2.02. 85 P
worthy saint michael, and the golden fleece, 1H6 4.07. 69
so many years ere i shall shear the fleece: 3H6 2.05. 37
first the harmless sheep doth yield his fleece, 5.06. 8
my fleece of woolly hair that now uncurls, TIT 2.03. 34
with her own white fleece her voice controll'd LUC 678
ere beauty's dead fleece made another gay: SON 68. 8
FLEECES 1 FR 0.0001 REL FR 1 V 0 P
and do not shear the fleeces that i graze. AYL 2.04. 79
FLEER 2 FR 0.0002 REL FR 2 V 0 P
tush, tush, man, never fleer and jest at me; ADO 5.01. 58
face, | to fleer and scorn at our solemnity? ROM 1.05. 57
FLEER'D 1 FR 0.0001 REL FR 1 V 0 P
one rubb'd his elbow thus, and fleer'd, and LLL 5.02.109
FLEERING 1 FR 0.0001 REL FR 1 V 0 P
to such a man | that is no fleering tell–tale. JC 1.03.117
FLEERS 1 FR 0.0001 REL FR 1 V 0 P
and mark the fleers, the gibes, and notable OTH 4.01. 82
FLEET* 25 FR 0.0028 REL FR 22 V 3 P
hast dispos'd, | and all the rest o' th' fleet. TMP 1.02.226
and for the rest o' th' fleet | (which i 1.02.232
that shall catch | your royal fleet far off. 5.01.317
i am sure he is in the fleet; ADO 2.01.143 P
how all the other passions fleet to air, | as MV 3.02.108
even from the gallows did his fell soul fleet, 4.01.135
to him every day, and fleet the time carelessly, AYL 1.01.118 P
if echo were as fleet, | i would esteem him SHR in.1. 26
make | with the most noble bottom of our fleet, TN 5.01. 57
shall fleet | in dreadful trial of our kingdom's JN 2.01.285
go carry sir john falstaff to the fleet. 2H4 5.05. 91
and his brave fleet | with silken streamers the H5 3.pr. 5
for so appears this fleet majestical, | holding 3.pr. 16
so cares and joys abound, as seasons fleet. 2H6 2.04. 4
shall waft them over with our royal fleet. 3H6 3.03.253
yet do they all confirm | a turkish fleet, and OTH 1.03. 8
have there injointed them with an after fleet. 1.03. 35
a segregation of the turkish fleet: 2.01. 10
if that the turkish fleet | be not enshelter'd 2.01. 17
and sufferance | on most part of their fleet. 2.01. 24
the mere perdition of the turkish fleet, every 2.02. 3 P
in caesar's fleet | are those that often have ANT 3.07. 36
sever'd navy too | have knit again, and fleet, 3.13.171
my fleet hath yielded to the foe, and yonder 4.12. 11
to darkness fleet souls that fly backwards. CYM 5.03. 25
FLEETER 2 FR 0.0002 REL FR 2 V 0 P
their conceits have wings | fleeter than arrows, LLL 5.02.261
ay, fleeter than the roe. SHR in.2. 48
FLEET–FOOT 1 FR 0.0001 REL FR 1 V 0 P
or as the fleet–foot roe that's tir'd with VEN 561
FLEETING 5 FR 0.0005 REL FR 5 V 0 P
is come — false, fleeting, perjur'd clarence, R3 1.04. 55
and i, hence fleeting, here remain with thee. ANT 1.03.104
now the fleeting moon | no planet is of mine. 5.02.240
a dream, a breath, a froth of fleeting joy. LUC 212
from thee, the pleasure of the fleeting year! SON 97. 2
FLEET'ST 1 FR 0.0001 REL FR 1 V 0 P
make glad and sorry seasons as thou fleet'st, SON 19. 5
FLEET–WING'D 1 FR 0.0001 REL FR 1 V 0 P
for fleet–wing'd duty with thought's feathers LUC 1216
FLEMING 1 FR 0.0001 REL FR 0 V 1 P
i will rather trust a fleming with my butter, WIV 2.02.302 P
FLEMISH 1 FR 0.0001 REL FR 0 V 1 P
behavior hath this flemish drunkard pick'd (with WIV 2.01. 23 P
/FLESH 3 FR 0.0003 REL FR 3 V 0 P
/you /were /advis'd /his /flesh /was /capable 2H4 1.01.172
/beats /in /this /hollow /prison /of /my /flesh, TIT 3.02. 10
/dislocate /and /tear | /thy /flesh /and /bones. LR 4.02. 66
FLESH 141 FR 0.0159 REL FR 96 V 45 P
throats had hanging at 'em | wallets of flesh? TMP 3.03. 46
flesh and blood, | you, brother mine, that 5.01. 74
thy pulse | beats as of flesh and blood; 5.01.114
methinks his flesh is punish'd, he shall have no WIV 4.04. 23 P
start, | it is the flesh of a corrupted heart. 5.05. 87
follow it as the flesh and fortune shall better MM 2.01.253 P
false, | i do digest the poison of thy flesh, ERR 2.02.143
o, signior balthazar, either at flesh or fish, 3.01. 22
the mountain of mad flesh that claims marriage 4.04.154 P
may season give | to her foul tainted flesh! ADO 4.01.143
as pretty a piece of flesh as any is in messina, 4.02. 82 P
i will be flesh and blood, | for there was never 5.01. 34
i would see his own person in flesh and blood. LLL 1.01.185 P
simplicity of man to hearken after the flesh. 1.01.218 P
my sweet ounce of man's flesh, my incony jew! 3.01.135
is the liver–vein, which makes flesh a deity, 4.03. 72
as true we are as flesh and blood can be. 4.03.211
for an equal pound | of your fair flesh, to be MV 1.03.150
a pound of man's flesh taken from a man | is not 1.03.165
neither, | as flesh of muttons, beefs, or goats. 1.03.167
be launcelot, thou art mine own flesh and blood. 2.02. 92 P
my own flesh and blood to rebel! 3.01. 34 P
i say, my daughter is my flesh and my blood. 3.01. 37 P
between thy flesh and hers than between jet and 3.01. 39 P
if he forfeit, thou wilt not take his flesh. 3.01. 52 P
that he would rather have antonio's flesh | than 3.02.286
me | that i shall hardly spare a pound of flesh 3.03. 33
which is a pound of this poor merchant's flesh, 4.01. 23
have | a weight of carrion flesh than to receive 4.01. 41
the pound of flesh which i demand of him | is 4.01. 99
the jew shall have my flesh, blood, bones, and 4.01.112
by this the jew may claim | a pound of flesh, to 4.01.232
are there balance here to weigh | the flesh? 4.01.256
a pound of that same merchant's flesh is thine, 4.01.299
and you must cut this flesh from off his breast, 4.01.302
the words expressly are "a pound of flesh." 4.01.307
then thy bond, take thou thy pound of flesh, 4.01.308
therefore prepare thee to cut off the flesh. 4.01.324
thou less nor more | but just a pound of flesh. 4.01.326
and so riveted with faith unto your flesh. 5.01.169
in respect of a good piece of flesh indeed! AYL 3.02. 66 P
his arm | the lioness had torn some flesh away, 4.03.147
tarry in despite of the flesh and the blood. SHR in.2. 127 P
than feed it with such overroasted flesh. 4.01.175
i am driven on by the flesh, and he must needs AWW 1.03. 29 P
creature, as you and all flesh and blood are, 1.03. 36 P
my wife is the cherisher of my flesh and blood; 1.03. 47 P
he that cherishes my flesh and blood loves my 1.03. 47 P
my flesh and blood loves my flesh and blood; 1.03. 48 P
he that loves my flesh and blood is my friend; 1.03. 48 P
if she had partaken of my flesh, and cost me the 4.05. 11 P
witty a piece of eve's flesh as any in illyria. TN 1.05. 28 P
this once, and let your flesh and blood obey it. 5.01. 33 P
ay, every dram of woman's flesh is false, | if WT 2.01.138
would not exchange flesh with one that lov'd her 4.04.280 P
a changeling, and none of your flesh and blood. 4.04.689 P
she being none of your flesh and blood, your 4.04.693 P
your flesh and blood has not offended the king, 4.04.694 P
king, and so your flesh and blood is not to be 4.04.695 P
and now he feasts, mousing the flesh of men, JN 2.01.354
within this wall of flesh | there is a soul 3.03. 20
and flesh his spirit in a warlike soil, 5.01. 71
banish'd this frail sepulchre of our flesh | as R2 1.03.196
as now our flesh is banish'd from this land; 1.03.197
as if this flesh which walls about our life 3.02.167
and mock not flesh and blood | with solemn 3.02.171
whilst my gross flesh sinks downward, here to 5.05.112
i'll not bear my own flesh so far afoot again 1H4 2.02. 35 P
horse–back–breaker, this huge hill of flesh — 2.04.243 P
she's neither fish nor flesh, a man knows not 3.03.127 P
thou seest i have more flesh than another man, 3.03.167 P
wound my thoughts worse than thy sword my flesh. 5.04. 80
could not all this flesh | keep in a little life 5.04.102
majesty, by this light flesh and corrupt blood, 2H4 2.04.295 P
for suffering flesh to be eaten in thy house, 2.04.344 P
grace says that which his flesh rebels against. 2.04.350 P
dog | shall flesh his tooth on every innocent. 4.05.132
year, | when flesh is cheap and females dear, 5.03. 19
name not religion, for thou lov'st the flesh, 1H6 1.01. 41
till bones and flesh and sinews fall away, | so 3.01.192
did flesh his puny sword in frenchmen's blood! 4.07. 36
god knows thou art a collop of my flesh, | and 5.04. 18
bear that proportion to my flesh and blood | as 2H6 1.01.233
men's flesh preserv'd so whole do seldom win. 3.01.301
eagle | tire on the flesh of me and of my son! 3H6 1.01.269
stab poniards in our flesh till all were told, 2.01. 98
cold fearful drops stand on my trembling flesh. R3 5.03.181
own natures frail, and capable | of our flesh; H8 5.02. 47
good traders in the flesh, set this in your TRO 5.10. 45 P
spirit | requick'ned what in flesh was fatigate, COR 2.02.117
best of my flesh, | forgive my tyranny; 5.03. 42
ad /manes fratrum sacrifice his flesh | before TIT 1.01. 98
man but i | do execution on my flesh and blood. 4.02. 84
eating the flesh that she herself hath bred. 5.03. 62
and 'tis known i am a pretty piece of flesh. ROM 1.01. 29 P
makes my flesh tremble in their different 1.05. 90
o flesh, flesh, how art thou fishified! 2.04. 37 P
o flesh, flesh, how art thou fishified! 2.04. 38 P
fiend | in mortal paradise of such sweet flesh? 3.02. 82
buy food, and get thyself in flesh. 5.01. 84
stars | from this world–wearied flesh. 5.03.112

that /scolds against the quality of flesh | and TIM 4.03.156
but let the famish'd flesh slide from the bone 4.03.528
and men are flesh and blood, and apprehensive; JC 3.01. 67
fight, till from my bones my flesh be hack'd. MAC 5.03. 32
o, that this too too sallied flesh would melt, HAM 1.02.129
blazon must not be | to ears of flesh and blood. 1.05. 22
thousand natural shocks | that flesh is heir to; 3.01. 62
is man and wife, man and wife is one flesh — so 4.03. 52 P
and from her fair and unpolluted flesh | may 5.01.239
come, i'll flesh ye, come on, young master. LR 2.02. 46 P
but yet thou art my flesh, my blood, my daughter 2.04.221
or rather a disease that's in my flesh, | which 2.04.222
should have thus little mercy on their flesh? 3.04. 73
'twas this flesh begot | those pelican daughters 3.04. 74
our flesh and blood, my lord, is grown so vild 3.04.145
in his anointed flesh /rash boarish fangs. 3.07. 58
eyeless head of thine was first fram'd flesh 4.06.227
good–years shall devour them, flesh and fell, 5.03. 24
he means in flesh. ANT 1.02. 18 P
it is reported thou didst eat strange flesh, 1.04. 67
though written in our flesh, we shall remember 5.02.119
if you buy ladies' flesh at a million a dram, CYM 1.04.135 P
to let an arrogant piece of flesh threat us, 4.02.127
how now, my flesh? 5.05.264
i feed | on mother's flesh which did me breed. PER 1.01. 65
and she an eater of her mother's flesh | by the 1.01.130
they say they're half fish, half flesh. 2.01. 25 P
go home, and we'll have flesh for /holidays, 2.01. 81 P
for flesh and blood, sir, white and red, you 4.06. 34 P
but are you flesh and blood? 5.01.152
flesh of thy flesh, thaisa, | thy burden at the 5.03. 46
flesh of thy flesh, thaisa, | thy burden at the 5.03. 46
videlicet, the way of flesh — you have me? TNK 5.02. 35
tires with her beak on feathers, flesh, and bone VEN 56
my flesh is soft and plump, my marrow burning, 142
the flesh being proud, desire doth fight with LUC 712
desperate, with her nails her flesh doth tear; 739
if the dull substance of my flesh were thought, SON 44. 1
shall neigh (no dull flesh) in his fiery race, 51.11
flesh stays no farther reason, | but, rising at 151. 8

FLESH'D 6 FR 0.0006 REL FR 5 V 1 P
you are well flesh'd. TN 4.01. 39 P
full bravely hast thou flesh'd | thy maiden 1H4 5.04.130
the head | which princes, flesh'd with conquest, 2H4 1.01.149
the kindred of him hath been flesh'd upon us; H5 2.04. 50
and the flesh'd soldier, rough and hard of heart 3.03. 11
albeit they were flesh'd villains, bloody dogs, R3 4.03. 6

FLESHES 1 FR 0.0001 REL FR 0 V 1 P
and this night he fleshes his will in the spoil AWW 4.03. 16 P

FLESH–FLY 1 FR 0.0001 REL FR 1 V 0 P
than to suffer | the flesh–fly blow my mouth. TMP 3.01. 63

FLESHLY 1 FR 0.0001 REL FR 1 V 0 P
nay, in the body of this fleshly land, | this JN 4.02.245

FLESHMENT 1 FR 0.0001 REL FR 1 V 0 P
and, in the fleshment of this /dread exploit, LR 2.02.123

FLESHMONGER 1 FR 0.0001 REL FR 0 V 1 P
and was the duke a fleshmonger, a fool, and a MM 5.01.333 P

FLEUR–DE–LYS *(see flower–de–luce, etc.)*

FLEW 8 FR 0.0009 REL FR 7 V 1 P
the tailor that made the wings she flew withal. MV 3.01. 27 P
and what a pitch she flew above the rest! 2H6 2.01. 6
i think) flew up, and had their faces | been H8 4.01. 74
breach whereout | hector's great spirit flew. TRO 4.05.246
flew on him, and amongst them fell'd him dead, LR 4.02. 76
of corn, | curling the wealthy ears, never flew. TNK 2.03. 78
but still before that flew | the lightning of 3.06. 84
by | the swiftest hours, observed as they flew, LC 60

FLEW'D 1 FR 0.0001 REL FR 1 V 0 P
so flew'd, so sanded; MND 4.01.120

FLEXIBLE 2 FR 0.0002 REL FR 2 V 0 P
women are soft, mild, pitiful, and flexible; 3H6 1.04.141
wind | makes flexible the knees of knotted oaks, TRO 1.03. 50

FLEXURE 2 FR 0.0002 REL FR 1 V 1 P
will it give place to flexure and low bending? H5 4.01.255
legs are legs for necessity, not for flexure. TRO 2.03.106 P

/FLIBBERTIGIBBET 1 FR 0.0001 REL FR 0 V 1 P
/flibbertigibbet, /of /mopping /and /mowing, LR 4.01. 61 P

FLIBBERTIGIBBET 1 FR 0.0001 REL FR 0 V 1 P
this is the foul /fiend flibbertigibbet; LR 3.04.115 P

/FLICK'RING 1 FR 0.0001 REL FR 1 V 0 P
radiant fire | on /flick'ring phoebus' front — LR 2.02.108

FLIDGE *(also fledge)*

FLIDGE 1 FR 0.0001 REL FR 0 V 1 P
for his own part, knew the bird was flidge, and MV 3.01. 29 P

FLIERS 4 FR 0.0004 REL FR 4 V 0 P
fortune widens them, | not for the fliers. COR 1.04. 45
following the fliers at the very heels, | with 1.04. 49
he stopp'd the fliers, | and by his rare example 2.02.103
though you, it seems, come from the fliers? CYM 5.03. 2

/FLIES* 1 FR 0.0001 REL FR 1 V 0 P
/common /people /swarm /like /summer /flies, 3H6 2.06. 8

FLIES* 57 FR 0.0064 REL FR 53 V 4 P
that flies her fortune when it follows her. TGV 5.02. 50
"love like a shadow flies when substance love WIV 2.02.207
pursuing that that flies, and flying what 2.02.208
these summer flies | have blown me full of LLL 5.02.408
apollo flies, and daphne holds the chase; MND 2.01.231
speed, | when cowardice pursues and valor flies. 2.01.234
why then my taxing like a wild goose flies, AYL 2.07. 86
and what dole of honor | flies where you bid it, AWW 2.03.170
of chance, and flies | of every wind that blows. WT 4.04.540
he is to behold him with flies blown to death. 4.04.790 P
upon enforcement flies with greatest speed, | so 2H4 1.01.120
thus with imagin'd wing our swift scene flies H5 3.pr. 1
warm kept, are like flies at bartholomew–tide, 5.02.308 P
between two hawks, which flies the higher pitch, 1H6 2.04. 11
he that flies so will ne'er return again. 4.05. 19
yet have i gold flies from another coast — | i 2H6 1.02. 93
we'll all assist you; he that flies shall die. 3H6 1.01. 30
my soul flies through these wounds to seek out 1.04.178
they never then had sprung like summer flies; 2.06. 17
so flies the reakless shepherd from the wolf; 5.06. 7
to give us our reward, thy conscience flies out. R3 1.04.130 P
hope is swift and flies with swallow's wings, 5.02. 23
and flies fled under shade, why then the thing TRO 1.03. 51
and reason flies the object of all harm. 2.02. 41
but flies the grasps of love | with wings more 4.02. 13
summer butterflies, | or butchers killing flies. COR 4.06. 95
my niece, that flies away so fast? TIT 2.04. 11
now to the goths, as swift as swallow flies, 4.02.172
be thus afflicted with these strange flies, ROM 2.04. 33 P
courtship lives | in carrion flies than romeo; 3.03. 35
flies may do this, but i from this must fly; 3.03. 41
provokes itself and like the current flies TIM 1.01. 24
but flies an eagle flight, bold, and forth on, 1.01. 49
of winter show'rs, | these flies are couch'd. 2.02.172
of fortune, trencher–friends, time's flies, 3.06. 96
what, with worms and flies? MAC 4.02. 32
the great man down, you mark his favorite flies, HAM 3.02.204
as flies to wanton boys are we to th' gods, LR 4.01. 36
fertile climate dwell, | plague him with flies. OTH 1.01. 71
o, ay, as summer flies are in the shambles, 4.02. 66
our separation so abides and flies, | that thou, ANT 1.03.102
like a cow in /june — | hoists sails and flies. 3.10. 15
leaving the fight in heighth, flies after her. 3.10. 20
till the flies and gnats of nile | have buried 3.13.166
our valor is to chase what flies. CYM 3.03. 42
i'll hide my master from the flies, as deep | as 4.02.388
show | thy spite on mortal flies: 5.04. 31
swear to th' gods that winter kills the flies, PER 4.03. 50
the meanest bird | that flies i' th' purer air! 4.06.102
flies like a parthian quiver from our rages, TNK 2.02. 50
he stamps, and bites the poor flies in his fume. VEN 316
as falcons to the lure, away she flies, | the 1027
he faintly flies, sweating with guilty fear; LUC 740
fleet–wing'd duty with thought's feathers flies. 1216
a crow that flies in heaven's sweetest air. SON 70. 4
to follow that which flies before her face, 143. 7
so run'st thou after that which flies from thee, 143. 9

FLIETH 1 FR 0.0001 REL FR 1 V 0 P
the duke of alanson flieth to his side. 1H6 1.01. 95

FLIGHT* 56 FR 0.0063 REL FR 53 V 3 P
with all the cunning manner of our flight, TGV 2.04.180
of their disguising and pretended flight, | who, 2.06. 37
and when the flight is made to one so dear, | of 2.07. 12
for theseus' perjury and unjust flight; 4.04.168
these likelihoods confirm her flight from hence: 5.02. 43
for him thou labor'st by thy flight to shun, MM 3.01. 12
and challeng'd cupid at the flight, and my ADO 1.01. 40 P
my lord, your brother john is ta'en in flight, 5.04.125
i will go tell him of fair hermia's flight; MND 1.01.246
and in our flight | tell me how it came this 4.01. 99
tongue, lose thy light, | moon, take thy flight, 5.01.305
i shot his fellow of the self–same flight | the MV 1.01.141
none so well as you, of my daughter's flight. 3.01. 25 P
pursuit that will be made | after my flight. AYL 1.03.137
away, and for our flight. AWW 2.05. 92
that pitiful rumor may report my flight | to 3.02.127
camillo's flight, | added to their familiarity WT 2.01.174
when my good falcon made her flight across | thy 4.04. 15
he's irremovable, | resolv'd for flight. 4.04.508
change your purpose | but undergo this flight: 4.04.543
complaint may be to the flight of my master. 4.04.710 P
we will untread the steps of damned flight, JN 5.04. 52
new flight, | and happy newness, that intends 5.04. 60
as confident as is the falcon's flight | against R2 1.03. 61
quite from the flight of all thy ancestors. 1H4 3.02. 31
that turn'd their backs, and in his flight, 2H4 1.01.130
to save myself by flight. 1H6 3.02.105
are glad and fain by flight to save themselves. 3.02.114
to wall thee from the liberty of flight; 4.02. 24
thee how thou shalt escape | by sudden flight. 4.05. 11
flight cannot stain the honor you have won, 4.05. 26
yes, your renowned name. shall flight abuse it? 4.05. 41
then talk no more of flight, it is no boot; 4.06. 52
our soldiers', like the night–owl's lazy flight, 3H6 2.01.130
sometime they have us'd with fearful flight, 2.02. 30
bootless is flight, they follow us with wings, 2.03. 12
no way to fly, nor strength to hold out flight. 2.06. 24
our treasure seiz'd, our soldiers put to flight, 3.03. 36
my lord, i like not of this flight of edward's; 4.06. 89
i do not speak of flight, of fear, of death, TRO 5.10. 12
and faces pale | with flight and agued fear! COR 1.04. 38
as a flight of fowl | scatter'd by winds and TIT 5.03. 68
but flies an eagle flight, bold, and forth on, TIM 1.01. 49
break his wind | with fear and horrid flight. 5.04. 13
banquo, thy soul's flight, | if it find heaven, MAC 3.01.140
ere the bat hath flown | his cloister'd flight, 3.02. 41
his flight was madness. 4.02. 3
where the flight | so runs against all reason. 4.02. 13
but if /thy flight lay toward the roaring sea, LR 3.04. 10
o, /he has given example for our flight, | most ANT 3.10. 27
history of my know!edge | touching her flight. CYM 3.05.100
but that her flight prevented it, she had 5.05. 46
by flight i'll shun the danger which i fear. PER 1.01.142
unapt for tender smell, or speedy flight, | make LUC 695
with some mischance cross tarquin in his flight. 968
the scars of battle scapeth by the flight, | and LC 244

FLIGHTS* 2 FR 0.0002 REL FR 2 V 0 P
(a time that lovers' flights doth still conceal) MND 1.01.212
and flights of angels sing thee to thy rest! HAM 5.02.360

FLIGHTY 1 FR 0.0001 REL FR 1 V 0 P
the flighty purpose never is o'ertook | unless MAC 4.01.145

FLINCH 3 FR 0.0003 REL FR 2 V 1 P
time, or flinch in property | of what i spoke, AWW 2.01.187
if he flinch, chide me for it. TRO 3.02.106 P
a fire ill take her! does she flinch now? TNK 3.05. 52

FLING 8 FR 0.0009 REL FR 8 V 0 P
bed, | and here i'll fling the pillow, there the SHR 4.01.201
the mouth of passage shall we fling wide ope, JN 2.01.449
else would i have a fling at winchester. 1H6 3.01. 64
fling up his cap, and say, "god save his majesty 2H6 4.08. 15
blow, | and with the other fling it at thy face, 3H6 5.01. 51
cromwell, i charge thee, fling away ambition! H8 3.02.440
and fling my wanton arms | in at her window! TNK 2.02.237
at length | i fling my cap up; 3.05. 17

FLINT 24 FR 0.0027 REL FR 22 V 2 P
fire enough for a flint, pearl enough for a LLL 4.02. 88 P
make his heart of flint that you shall love, TN 1.05.286
go to flint castle, there i'll pine away — | a R2 3.02.209
to whose flint bosom my condemned lord | is 5.01. 3
notwithstanding, being incens'd, he is flint, 2H4 4.04. 33
the ruthless flint doth cut my tender feet, 2H6 2.04. 34
mine eyes should sparkle like the beaten flint, 3.02.317
o, i could hew up rocks and fight with flint, 5.01. 24
i would to god my heart were flint, like R3 1.03.139
but it lies as coldly in him as fire in a flint, TRO 3.03.257 P
whilst with no softer cushion than the flint | i COR 5.03. 53
to them | as unrelenting flint to drops of rain. TIT 2.03.141
my heart is not compact of flint nor steel, 5.03. 88
will ne'er wear out the everlasting flint; ROM 2.06. 17
the fire i' th' flint | shows not till it be TIM 1.01. 22
searching the window for a flint, i found | this JC 2.01. 36
that carries anger as the flint bears fire, 4.03.111
against the flint and hardness of my fault, ANT 4.09. 16
weariness | can snore upon the flint, when resty CYM 3.06. 34
make raging battery upon shores of flint." PER 4.04. 43
iron | came music's origin), what envious flint, TNK 5.04. 61
nay, more than flint, for stone at rain VEN 200
his falchion on a flint he softly smiteth, LUC 176
"as from this cold flint i enforc'd this fire, 181

FLINT–HEARTED 1 FR 0.0001 REL FR 1 V 0 P
"o, pity," gan she cry, "flint–hearted boy, VEN 95

FLINTS 2 FR 0.0002 REL FR 2 V 0 P
from brassy bosoms and rough hearts of flints, MV 4.01. 31
/shards, flints, and pebbles should be thrown on HAM 5.01.231

FLINTY 12 FR 0.0013 REL FR 12 V 0 P
through flinty tartar's bosom would peep forth AWW 4.04. 7
the flinty ribs of this contemptuous city. JN 2.01.384
may tear a passage thorough the flinty ribs | of R2 5.05. 20
let us resolve to scale their flinty bulwarks. 1H6 2.01. 27
uneath may she endure the flinty streets, | to 2H6 2.04. 8
because thy flinty heart, more hard than they, 3.02. 99
thou stern, obdurate, flinty, rough, remorseless 3H6 1.04.142
as thou hast shown it flinty by thy deeds, | i 2.01.202
and disclaim'st | flinty mankind, whose eyes do TIM 4.03.484
hath made the flinty and steel /couch of war OTH 1.03.230
as he thus went counting | the flinty pavement, TNK 5.04. 59
"art thou obdurate, flinty, hard as steel? VEN 199

FLIRTED *(see flurted)*

FLIRT–GILLS 1 FR 0.0001 REL FR 0 V 1 P
scurvy knave, i am none of his flirt–gills, i am ROM 2.04.153 P

FLOAT 3 FR 0.0003 REL FR 3 V 0 P
and are upon the mediterranean float | bound TMP 1.02.234
o'er | did never float upon the swelling tide JN 2.01. 74
but float upon a wild and violent sea | each way MAC 4.02. 21

FLOATED 1 FR 0.0001 REL FR 1 V 0 P
son | that floated with thee on the fatal raft? ERR 5.01.349

FLOATING 2 FR 0.0002 REL FR 2 V 0 P
and floating straight, obedient to the stream, ERR 1.01. 86
all boats alike | show'd mastership in floating; COR 4.01. 7

FLOATS 1 FR 0.0001 REL FR 1 V 0 P
but such a vessel 'tis that floats but for | the TNK 5.04. 83

/FLOCK 1 FR 0.0001 REL FR 1 V 0 P
/more /and /less /do /flock /to /follow /him. 2H4 1.01.209

FLOCK 19 FR 0.0021 REL FR 16 V 3 P
and crows are fatted with the murrion flock; MND 2.01. 97
i am a tainted wether of the flock, | meetest MV 4.01.114
say many young gentlemen flock to him every day, AYL 1.01.117 P
what is he that shall buy his flock and pasture? 2.04. 88
buy thou the cottage, pasture, and the flock, 2.04. 92
come, to our flock. 3.05. 80
hath kill'd the flock of all affections else TN 1.01. 35
as your good flock shall prosper. WT 4.04. 70
i should leave grazing, were i of your flock, 4.04.109
subjects afore thee like a flock of wild geese, 1H4 2.04.138 P
better show'd with you | when that your flock, 2H4 4.02. 5
of society that they flock together in consent, 5.01. 70 P
till they have snar'd the shepherd of the flock, 2H6 2.02. 73
a fox, | by nature prov'd an enemy to the flock, 3.01.258
so many hours must i tend my flock, | so many 3H6 2.05. 31
to london, | and many giddy people flock to him. 4.08. 5
hour more competitors | flock to the rebels, and R3 4.04.505
now 'mongst this flock of drunkards | am i to OTH 2.03. 59
"sometime he runs among a flock of sheep, | to VEN 685

FLOCKS* 7 FR 0.0008 REL FR 6 V 1 P
his cote, his flocks, and bounds of feed | are AYL 2.04. 83
cut's saddle, put a few flocks in the point. 1H4 2.01. 6 P
my soldiers, gathered flocks of friends, | /and 3H6 2.01.112
but leave their flocks, and under your fair H8 1.04. 70
my flocks feed not, my ewes breed not, | my rams PP 17. 1
herds stands weeping, flocks all sleeping, 17.27
and see the shepherds feed their flocks, | by 19. 6

FLOOD 55 FR 0.0062 REL FR 51 V 4 P
tut, man, i mean thou'lt lose the flood, and, in TGV 2.03. 41 P
and, in losing the flood, lose thy voyage, and, 2.03. 42 P
to drown me in thy /sister's flood of tears. ERR 3.02. 46
'tis in grain, noah's flood could not do it. 3.02.106 P
need the bridge much broader than the flood? ADO 1.01.316
thorough flood, thorough fire, | i do wander MND 2.01. 5
marking th' embarked traders on the flood; 2.01.127
like signiors and rich burghers on the flood, MV 1.01. 10
and bid the main flood bate his usual height; 4.01. 72
there is sure another flood toward, and these AYL 5.04. 35 P
yet doth this accident and flood of fortune | so TN 4.03. 11
so, by a roaring tempest on the flood, | a whole JN 3.04. 1
but now i breathe again | aloft the flood, and 4.02.139
flight, | and like a bated and retired flood, 5.04. 53
all unwarily | devoured by the unexpected flood. 5.07. 64
upon agreement, of swift severn's flood, | who 1H4 1.03.103
and such a flood of greatness fell on you, 5.01. 48
so looks the strond whereon the imperious flood 2H4 1.01. 62
nature's hand | keep the wild flood confin'd! 1.01.154
never came reformation in a flood | with such a H5 1.01. 33
the english beach | pales in the flood with men, 5.pr. 10
return thee therefore with a flood of tears, 1H6 3.03. 56
whose flood begins to flow within mine eyes; 2H6 3.01.199
sometime the flood prevails, and then the wind; 3H6 2.05. 9
and half our sailors swallow'd in the flood? 5.04. 5
but still the envious flood | stopp'd in my soul R3 1.04. 37
i pass'd, methought, the melancholy flood, 1.04. 45
as doth a rock against the chiding flood, H8 3.02.197
let it be call'd the wild and wand'ring flood, TRO 1.01.102
his youth in flood, | i'll prove this troth with 1.03.300
ungrateful rome, | like a bold flood o'er–beat. COR 4.05.131
dry, | with miry slime left on them by a flood? TIT 3.01.126
although she lave them hourly in the flood. 4.02.103
bark thy body is, | sailing in this salt flood; ROM 3.05.134
this confluence, this great flood of visitors. TIM 1.01. 42
upon the beached verge of the salt flood, | who 5.01.216
now | leap in with me into this angry flood, JC 1.02.103
when went there by an age since the great flood 1.02.152
stir you up | to such a sudden flood of mutiny. 3.02.211

the affairs of men | which, taken at the flood, 4.03.219
what if it tempt you toward the flood, my lord, HAM 1.04. 69
of moving accidents by flood and field, | of OTH 1.03.135
nothing at all, it is a high-wrought flood. 2.01. 2
like molestation view | on the enchafed flood. 2.01. 17
ay, madam, with his eyes in flood with laughter. CYM 1.06. 74
half the flood | hath their keel cut. PER 3.ch. 45
she saw me, and straight sought the flood. TNK 4.01. 95
hath dropp'd a precious jewel in the flood, | or VEN 824
self-love had never drown'd him in the flood. LUC 266
and lo there falls into thy boundless flood 653
deep woes roll forward like a gentle flood, 1118
no flood by raining slaketh. 1677
bare and unpeopled in this fearful flood. 1741
"o jove," quoth she, "why was not i a flood?" PP 6.14
she perus'd, sigh'd, tore, and gave the flood, LC 44

FLOOD-GATE 1 FR 0.0001 REL FR 1 V 0 P
is of so flood-gate and o'erbearing nature OTH 1.03. 56

FLOOD-GATES 2 FR 0.0002 REL FR 2 V 0 P
for tears do stop the flood-gates of her eyes. 1H4 2.04.394
but through the flood-gates breaks the silver VEN 959

FLOODS 11 FR 0.0012 REL FR 11 V 0 P
the delighted spirit | to bathe in fiery floods, MM 3.01.121
therefore the moon, the governess of floods, MND 2.01.103
all, | that in crossways and floods have burial, 3.02.383
that orpheus drew trees, stones, and floods; MV 5.01. 80
like envious floods o'errun her lovely face, SHR in.2. 65
great floods have flown | from simple sources; AWW 2.01.139
where it shall mingle with the state of floods, 2H4 5.02.132
between the floods of sala and of /elbe; H5 1.02. 45
let floods o'erswell, and fiends for food howl 2.01. 93
is that by sudden floods and fall of waters R3 4.04.510
but floods of tears will drown my oratory, | and TIT 5.03. 90

FLOOR 4 FR 0.0004 REL FR 4 V 0 P
smallest monstrous mouse that creeps on floor, MND 5.01.220
look how the floor of heaven | is thick inlaid MV 5.01. 58
though i had found | gold strew'd i' th' floor. CYM 3.06. 49
o' th' floor; 4.02.212

FLORA 1 FR 0.0001 REL FR 1 V 0 P
no shepherdess, but flora, | peering in april's WT 4.04. 2

FLORENCE 11 FR 0.0012 REL FR 8 V 3 P
vincentio's son, brought up in florence, | it SHR 1.01. 14
bills for money by exchange | from florence, and 4.02. 90
and florence is denied before he comes. AWW 1.02. 12
madam, he's gone to serve the duke of florence. 3.02. 52
towards florence is he? 3.02. 68
perverted a young gentlewoman here in florence, 4.03. 15 P
an advertisement to a proper maid in florence, 4.03.213 P
in florence was it from a casement thrown me, 5.03. 93
prove that i husbanded her bed in florence, 5.03.126
he stole from florence, taking no leave, and i 5.03.143 P
he's now in florence. OTH 1.03. 45

FLORENCE'S 1 FR 0.0001 REL FR 0 V 1 P
is this captain in the duke of florence's camp? AWW 4.03.193 P

FLORENTINE 9 FR 0.0010 REL FR 7 V 2 P
much honor on a young florentine call'd claudio. ADO 1.01. 11 P
i will some other be, some florentine, | some SHR 1.01.204
that the florentine will move us | for speedy AWW 1.02. 6
discover that which shall undo the florentine. 4.01. 73
will you undertake to betray the florentine? 4.03.293 P
here's a petition from a florentine, | who hath 5.03.130
i am, my lord, a wretched florentine, | derived 5.03.158
one michael cassio, a florentine | (a fellow OTH 1.01. 20
i never knew a florentine more kind and honest. 3.01. 40

FLORENTINES 2 FR 0.0002 REL FR 1 V 1 P
the florentines and senoys are by th' ears, AWW 1.02. 1
i, with a troop of florentines, will suddenly 3.06. 22 P

FLORENTIUS' 1 FR 0.0001 REL FR 1 V 0 P
be she as foul as was florentius' love, | as old SHR 1.02. 69

FLORIZEL 4 FR 0.0004 REL FR 2 V 2 P
th' king's, which florizel | i now name to you; WT 4.01. 22
when saw'st thou the prince florizel, my son? 4.02. 26 P
i have serv'd prince florizel, and in my time 4.03. 13 P
one that gives out himself prince florizel, 5.01. 85

FLOUR 1 FR 0.0001 REL FR 1 V 0 P
all | from me do back receive the flour of all, COR 1.01.145

FLOURIETS' *(also flow'rets)*

FLOURIETS' 1 FR 0.0001 REL FR 1 V 0 P
stood now within the pretty flouriets' eyes MND 4.01. 55

FLOURISH 23 FR 0.0026 REL FR 20 V 3 P
of your title to him | doth flourish the deceit. MM 4.01. 74
needs not the painted flourish of your praise: LLL 2.01. 14
lend me the flourish of all gentle tongues — 4.03.234
is | even as the flourish when true subjects bow MV 3.02. 49
grave, | or flourish to the height of my degree. 1H6 2.04.111
wither one rose, and let the other flourish; 3H6 2.05.101
poor painted queen, vain flourish of my fortune! R3 1.03.240
i call'd thee then vain flourish of my fortune; 4.04. 82
a flourish, trumpets! 4.04.149
live and flourish! 5.03.130
live and flourish! 5.03.138
edward's unhappy sons do bid thee flourish. 5.03.153
so may he ever do, and ever flourish, | when i H8 4.02.125
he shall flourish, | and like a mountain cedar 5.04. 52
why do the emperor's trumpets flourish thus? TIT 4.02. 49
athens again, and flourish | with the highest. TIM 5.01. 10
love between them like the palm might flourish, HAM 5.02. 40
sir — after what flourish your nature will. 5.02.180 P
be fortunate and flourish in peace and plenty." CYM 5.04.144 P
be fortunate and flourish in peace and plenty." 5.05.441 P
he hopes by you his fortunes yet may flourish. PER 2.02. 47
canst make | a cripple flourish with his crutch, TNK 5.01. 82
time doth transfix the flourish set on youth, SON 60. 9

FLOURISH'D 4 FR 0.0004 REL FR 4 V 0 P
struck anointed kings | and flourish'd after, WT 1.02.359
once was mistress of the field, and flourish'd, H8 3.01.152
to him that flourish'd for her with his sword. TIT 1.01.310
whilst bloody treason flourish'd over us. JC 3.02.192

FLOURISHES 4 FR 0.0004 REL FR 3 V 1 P
otherwise a seducer flourishes, and a poor maid AWW 5.03.146 P
it fails not yet, but flourishes in thee, | and 2H6 2.02. 57
come, | and flourishes his blade in spite of me. ROM 1.01. 78
tediousness the limbs and outward flourishes, HAM 2.02. 91

FLOURISHETH 1 FR 0.0001 REL FR 1 V 0 P
but youth in ladies' eyes that flourisheth. SHR 2.01.340

FLOURISHING 3 FR 0.0003 REL FR 3 V 0 P
i better brook than flourishing peopled towns: TGV 5.04. 3
one flourishing branch of his most royal root, R2 1.02. 18
to rome, | renowned titus, flourishing in arms. TIT 1.01. 38

FLOUT 21 FR 0.0023 REL FR 14 V 7 P
"flout 'em and /scout 'em, | and scout 'em and TMP 3.02.121
and /scout 'em, | and scout 'em and flout 'em! 3.02.122
what, wilt thou flout me thus unto my face, ERR 1.02. 91
yea, dost thou jeer and flout me in the teeth? 2.02. 22
ere you flout old ends any further, examine your ADO 1.01.288 P
to write to one that she knew would flout her. 2.03.142 P
"by my own spirit, for i should flout him, if he 2.03.144 P
that lie and cog and flout, deprave and slander, 5.01. 95
of wit-crackers cannot flout me out of my humor. 5.04.101 P
and therefore never flout at me for what i have 5.04.107 P
o poverty in wit, kingly-poor flout! LLL 5.02.269
bruise me with scorn, confound me with a flout, 5.02.397
eye, | but you must flout my insufficiency? MND 2.02.128
why will you suffer her to flout me thus? 3.02.327
nature hath given us wit to flout at fortune, AYL 1.02. 45 P
of them all shall flout me out of my calling. 3.03.107 P
these scroyles of angiers flout you, kings, JN 2.01.373
and what offense it is to flout his friends. 1H6 4.01. 75
i could have given my uncle's grace a flout, R3 2.04. 24
you bring me to do — and then you flout me too. TRO 4.02. 26
where the norweyan banners flout the sky | and MAC 1.02. 49

FLOUTED 4 FR 0.0004 REL FR 4 V 0 P
shall i be flouted thus by dunghill grooms? 1H6 1.03. 14
this, | to be so flouted in this royal presence? R3 2.01. 79
certainly, | he flouted us downright. COR 2.03.160
deal, | but sorrow flouted at is double death. TIT 3.01.245

FLOUTING 3 FR 0.0003 REL FR 1 V 2 P
first — for flouting me, and then wherefore — ERR 2.02. 45
or do you play the flouting jack, to tell us ADO 1.01.183 P
we shall be flouting; AYL 5.01. 12 P

FLOUTING-STOCK *(see vlouting-stocks, vlouting-stog)*

FLOUTS 2 FR 0.0002 REL FR 2 V 0 P
full of comparisons and wounding flouts, | which LLL 5.02.844
her silence flouts me, and i'll be reveng'd. SHR 2.01. 29

FLOW 30 FR 0.0034 REL FR 27 V 3 P
i'll teach you how to flow. TMP 2.01.222
being that i flow in grief, | the smallest twine ADO 4.01.249
the sea will ebb and flow, heaven show his face; LLL 4.03.212
doth it not flow as hugely as the sea, | till AYL 2.07. 72
know, | to make the even truth in pleasure flow. AWW 5.03.326
if wit flow from't | as boldness from my bosom, WT 2.02. 50
the moon's men doth ebb and flow like the sea, 1H4 1.02. 32 P
by and by in as high a flow as the ridge of the 1.02. 38 P
floods, | and flow henceforth in formal majesty. 2H4 5.02.133
whose flood begins to flow within mine eyes; 2H6 3.01.199
are the fount that makes small brooks to flow; 3H6 4.08. 54
such noble scenes as draw the eye to flow, | we H8 pr 4
whom from the flow of gall i name not, but 1.01.152
expense by th' hour | seems to flow from him! 3.02.109
you flow to great /distraction. TRO 5.02. 41
which should | make our eyes flow with joy, COR 5.03. 99
may call the sea, | do ebb and flow with tears; ROM 3.05.133
let it flow this way, my good lord. TIM 1.02. 54
flow this way? 1.02. 55 P
to maintain it, | nor cease his flow of riot. 2.02. 3
of your estate | and your great flow of debts. 2.02.142
to a wasteful cock | and set mine eyes at flow. 2.02.163
scorn'dst our brains' flow, and those our 5.04. 76
of great ones, | that ebb and flow by th' moon. LR 5.03. 19
they take the flow o' th' nile | by certain ANT 2.07. 17
flow, flow, | you heavenly blessings, on her! CYM 3.05.160
flow, flow, | you heavenly blessings, on her! 3.05.160
he did not flow | from honorable courses. PER 4.03. 27
with their fresh falls' haste | add to his flow, LUC 651
then can i drown an eye (unus'd to flow) | for SON 30. 5

FLOW'D 5 FR 0.0005 REL FR 4 V 1 P
thus your verse | flow'd with her beauty once. WT 5.01.102
in me | hath proudly flow'd in vanity till now; 2H4 5.02.130
no more words till they have flow'd their fill. 3H6 2.05. 72
is he for the numbers that petrarch flow'd in. ROM 2.04. 39 P
with brinish current downward flow'd apace: LC 284

FLOWED *(also flown*)*

FLOWED 1 FR 0.0001 REL FR 1 V 0 P
the river hath thrice flowed, no ebb between, 2H4 4.04.125

FLOWER 44 FR 0.0049 REL FR 40 V 4 P
i am that flower" — LLL 5.02.655
it fell upon a little western flower, | before MND 2.01.166
hast thou the flower there? 2.01.247
and when she weeps, weeps every little flower, 3.01.199
flower of this purple dye, | hit with cupid's 3.02.102
have with our needles created both one flower, 3.02.204
dian's bud o'er cupid's flower | hath such force 4.01. 73
hey nonino, | how that a life was but a flower, AYL 5.03. 28
if thou beest yet a fresh uncropped flower, AWW 5.03.327
true cuckold but calamity, so beauty's a flower. TN 1.05. 52 P
not a flower, not a flower sweet, | on my black 2.04. 59
not a flower, not a flower sweet, | on my black 2.04. 59
to crop at once a too long withered flower. R2 2.01.134
and when they from thy bosom pluck a flower, 3.02. 19
shall ill become the flower of england's face, 3.03. 97
nettle, danger, we pluck this flower, safety. 1H4 2.03. 10 P
bee, tolling from every flower | /the /virtuous 2H4 4.05. 74
that you on my behalf would pluck a flower. 1H6 2.04.129
pronouncing that the paleness of this flower 4.01.106
where every flower | did, as a prophet, weep TRO 1.02. 9
and /cull their flower, ajax shall cope the best 2.03.264
flower of warriors, | how is't with titus COR 1.06. 32
verona's summer hath not such a flower. ROM 1.03. 77
nay, he's a flower, in faith, a very flower. 1.03. 78
nay, he's a flower, in faith, a very flower. 1.03. 78
within the infant rind of this weak flower 2.03. 23
pink for flower. 2.04. 58 P
he is not the flower of courtesy, but, i'll 2.05. 43 P
upon the sweetest flower of all the field. 4.05. 29
lies, | flower as she was, deflowered by him. 4.05. 37
sweet flower, with flowers thy bridal bed i 5.03. 12
look like th' innocent flower, | but be the MAC 1.05. 65
to dew the sovereign flower and drown the weeds. 5.02. 30
not lack | the flower that's like thy face, pale CYM 4.02.221
how she gins | to blow into life's flower again! PER 3.02. 95
"the field's chief flower, sweet above compare, VEN 8
bid thee crop a weed, thou pluck'st a flower. 946
sweet rose, fair flower, untimely pluck'd, soon PP 10. 1
a flower that dies when first it gins to bud, 13. 3
a doubtful good, a gloss, a glass, a flower, 13. 5
whose action is no stronger than a flower? SON 65. 4
to thy fair flower add the rank smell of weeds: 69.12
i might as yet have been a spreading flower, LC 75
reserv'd the stalk and gave him all my flower. 147

FLOWER'D 1 FR 0.0001 REL FR 0 V 1 P
why then is my pump well flower'd. ROM 2.04. 60 P

FLOWER-DE-LUCE 1 FR 0.0001 REL FR 0 V 1 P
what say'st thou, my fair flower-de-luce? H5 5.02.210 P

FLOWER-DE-LUCES 2 FR 0.0002 REL FR 2 V 0 P
cropp'd are the flower-de-luces in your arms, 1H6 1.01. 80
deck'd with /five flower-de-luces on each side, 1.02. 99

FLOWERET *(see flouriets', flow'rets)*

FLOWER'S 1 FR 0.0001 REL FR 1 V 0 P
approve | this flower's force in stirring love. MND 2.02. 69

FLOWERS 57 FR 0.0064 REL FR 52 V 5 P
smelling out the odoriferous flowers of fancy, LLL 4.02.124 P
fair love, strewing her way with flowers. 4.03.377
crowns him with flowers, and makes him all her MND 2.01. 27
lull'd in these flowers with dances and delight; 2.01.254
"thisby, the flowers of odious savors sweet" — 3.01. 82
sing while thou on pressed flowers dost sleep. 3.01.159
with coronet of fresh and fragrant flowers; 4.01. 52
full of rose-water and bestrew'd with flowers, SHR in.1. 56
in speech, yet sweet as spring-time flowers. 2.01.246
the flowers fair ladies, and thy steps no more R2 1.03.290
the soil's fertility from wholesome flowers. 3.04. 39
is full of weeds, her fairest flowers chok'd up, 3.04. 44
fumble with the sheets, and play with flowers, H5 2.03. 14 P
to his music plants and flowers | ever sprung, H8 3.01. 6
strew me over | with maiden flowers, that all 4.02.169
he's one of the flowers of troy, i can tell you. TRO 1.02.187 P
strew flowers before them! COR 5.05. 3
as fresh as morning dew distill'd on flowers? TIT 2.03.201
and i hang the head | as flowers with frost, or 4.04. 71
with baleful weeds and precious-juiced flowers. ROM 2.03. 8
our bridal flowers serve for a buried corse; 4.05. 89
give me those flowers. 5.03. 9
flower, with flowers thy bridal bed i strew — 5.03. 12
he came with flowers to strew his lady's grave, 5.03.281
and do you now strew flowers in his way, | that JC 1.01. 50
lives | expire before the flowers in their caps, MAC 4.03.172
"larded all with sweet flowers, | which bewept HAM 4.05. 38
where souls do couch on flowers, we'll hand in ANT 4.14. 51
yet the dew's on ground, gather those flowers; CYM 1.05. 1
with fairest flowers | whilst summer lasts and i 4.02.218
who though they feed | on sweetest flowers, yet PER 1.01.133
of her weed | to strow thy green with flowers. 4.01. 14
come | give me your flowers, ere the sea mar it. 4.01. 26
canst not thou work such flowers in silk, wench? TNK 2.02.127
keep these flowers, | we'll see how near art can 2.02.148
and fruit and flowers more blessed, that still 2.02.233
any nymph, | that makes the stream seem flowers! 3.01. 9
and she must gather flowers to bury you, | and 4.01. 78
all day long but pick flowers with proserpine. 4.03. 25 P
her, stuck in as sweet flowers as the season is 4.03. 83 P
on, where she sticks | the queen of flowers. 5.01. 45
wishing her cheeks were gardens full of flowers, VEN 65
fair flowers that are not gath'red in their 131
lie, | these forceless flowers like sturdy trees 152
whose blood upon the fresh flowers being shed 665
the flowers are sweet, their colors fresh and 1079
as flowers dead lie withered on the ground, | as PP 13. 9
yet not for me, shine sun to succor flowers! 14.28
a cap of flowers, and a kirtle | embroidered all 19.11
but flowers distill'd, though they with winter SON 5.13
virtuous wish would bear your living flowers, 16. 7
with april's first-born flowers, and all things 21. 7
when beauty liv'd and died as flowers do now, 68. 2
smell | of different flowers in odor and in hue, 98. 6
more flowers i noted, yet i none could see | but 99.14
among weeds, or flowers with flowers gather'd. 124. 4
among weeds, or flowers with flowers gather'd. 124. 4

FLOWER-SOFT 1 FR 0.0001 REL FR 1 V 0 P
with the touches of those flower-soft hands, ANT 2.02.210

/FLOWING 1 FR 0.0001 REL FR 1 V 0 P
/flowing and swelling o'er with arts and TRO 4.04. 78

FLOWING 4 FR 0.0004 REL FR 4 V 0 P
be in their flowing cups freshly rememb'red. H5 4.03. 55
tidings would call forth her flowing tides. 1H6 1.01. 83
does purpose honor to you no less flowing | than H8 2.03. 62
have i to-night fluster'd with flowing cups, OTH 2.03. 58

FLOWN* *(also flowed)*

FLOWN* 7 FR 0.0008 REL FR 5 V 2 P
great floods have flown | from simple sources; AWW 2.01.139
and, having flown over many knavish professions, WT 4.03. 99 P
with youthful wings is flown | from this bare 2H4 4.05.228
ere the bat hath flown | his cloister'd flight, MAC 3.02. 40
o, well flown, bird! LR 4.06. 91 P
love, she's flown | to her desir'd posthumus. CYM 3.05. 61
a fiend | from heaven to hell is flown away: SON 145.12

FLOW'R 23 FR 0.0026 REL FR 23 V 0 P
disdain to root the summer-swelling flow'r | and TGV 2.04.162
with juice of balm and every precious flow'r; WIV 5.05. 62
do as the carrion does, not as the flow'r, MM 2.02.166
this is the flow'r that smiles on every one, LLL 5.02.331
fetch me that flow'r; MND 2.01.169
roses, whose fair flow'r | being once display'd, TN 2.04. 38
slain | the flow'r of europe for his chevalry, 3H6 2.01. 71
may prove a beauteous flow'r when next we meet. ROM 2.02.122
the flow'r that i would pluck | and put between TNK 1.03. 66
what flow'r is this? 2.02.119
these brave knights, and i, a virgin flow'r, 5.01.167
the flow'r is fall'n, the tree descends. 5.01.169
no flow'r was nigh, no grass, herb, leaf, or VEN 1055
a purple flow'r sprung up, check'red with white, 1168
bows her head, the new-sprung flow'r to smell, 1171
"poor flow'r," quoth she, "this was thy father's 1177
wherein i will not kiss my sweet love's flow'r." 1188
set, | each flow'r moist'ned like a melting eye, LUC 1227
no man inveigh against the withered flow'r, 1254
chide rough winter that the flow'r hath kill'd; 1255
the summer's flow'r is to the summer sweet, SON 94. 9
but if that flow'r with base infection meet, 94.11
form delivers to the heart | of bird, of flow'r, 113. 6

FLOW'R-DE-LUCE 2 FR 0.0002 REL FR 2 V 0 P
of all kinds, | the flow'r-de-luce being one! WT 4.04.127
on which i'll toss the flow'r-de-luce of france. 2H6 5.01. 11

FLOW'RED 1 FR 0.0001 REL FR 1 V 0 P
led by their master to the flow'red fields, TIT 5.01. 15
FLOW'RETS *(also flouriets')*
FLOW'RETS 1 FR 0.0001 REL FR 1 V 0 P
nor bruise her flow'rets with the armed hoofs 1H4 1.01. 8
FLOW'RING 4 FR 0.0004 REL FR 4 V 0 P
fresh fair virgins and your flow'ring infants. H5 3.03. 14
me | and hath detain'd me all my flow'ring youth 1H6 2.05. 56
or as the snake roll'd in a flow'ring bank, 2H6 3.01.228
o serpent heart, hid with a flow'ring face! ROM 3.02. 73
FLOW'RS 22 FR 0.0024 REL FR 22 V 0 P
who with thy saffron wings upon my flow'rs TMP 4.01. 78
pense" write | in em'rald tuffs, flow'rs purple, WIV 5.05. 70
fairies use flow'rs for their charactery. 5.05. 73
away before me to sweet beds of flow'rs, TN 1.01. 39
give me those flow'rs there, dorcas. WT 4.04. 73
well you fit our ages | with flow'rs of winter. 4.04. 79
the fairest flow'rs o' th' season | are our 4.04. 81
here's flow'rs for you: 4.04.103
these are flow'rs | of middle summer, and i 4.04.106
i would i had some flow'rs o' th' spring that 4.04.113
for the flow'rs now, that, frighted, thou let'st 4.04.117
come, take your flow'rs. 4.04.132
because sweet flow'rs are slow and weeds make R3 2.04. 15
my /unblown flow'rs, new–appearing sweets! 4.04. 10
those springs | on chalic'd flow'rs that lies; CYM 2.03. 23
when flow'rs are none, | to winter–ground thy 4.02.228
here's a few flow'rs, but 'bout midnight, more: 4.02.283
you were as flow'rs, now wither'd; 4.02.286
these flow'rs are like the pleasures of the 4.02.296
upon your never–withering banks of flow'rs. 5.04. 98
of all flow'rs | methinks a rose is best. TNK 2.02.135
weeds take root with precious flow'rs, | the LUC 870
FLOW'RY 5 FR 0.0005 REL FR 4 V 1 P
a resolution fetch | from flow'ry tenderness? MM 3.01. 82
what angel wakes me from my flow'ry bed? MND 3.01.129
come sit thee down upon this flow'ry bed, 4.01. 1
they'll be for the flow'ry way that leads to the AWW 4.05. 54 P
to do observance | to flow'ry may, in dian's TNK 2.05. 51
FLOWS 9 FR 0.0010 REL FR 9 V 0 P
could control the moon, make flows and ebbs, TMP 5.01.270
scarce confesses | that his blood flows; MM 1.03. 52
the night of dew that on my cheeks down flows; LLL 4.03. 28
his ebbs, /his flows, /as if | the passage and TRO 2.03.130
blood is cak'd, 'tis cold, it seldom flows; TIM 2.02.216
who is so full of grace that it flows over | on ANT 5.02. 24
then | the princely blood flows in his cheek, he CYM 3.03. 93
see what our general of ebbs and flows | out TNK 5.01.163
thus ebbs and flows the current of her sorrow, LUC 1569
FLUELLEN 12 FR 0.0013 REL FR 4 V 8 P
captain fluellen, you must come presently to the H5 3.02. 54 P
i say gud day, captain fluellen. 3.02. 83 P
how now, captain fluellen, come you from the 3.06. 1 P
how now, fluellen, cam'st thou from the bridge? 3.06. 88 P
what men have you lost, fluellen? 3.06. 97 P
know'st thou fluellen? 4.01. 52
captain fluellen! 4.01. 64 P
they did, fluellen. 4.07. 96
what think you, captain fluellen? 4.07.131 P
here, fluellen, wear thou this favor for me and 4.07.153 P
follow fluellen closely at the heels. 4.07.171
for i do know fluellen valiant | and, touch'd 4.07.179
FLUENT 1 FR 0.0001 REL FR 0 V 1 P
it is a theme as fluent as the sea; H5 3.07. 33 P
FLUENTLY 1 FR 0.0001 REL FR 1 V 0 P
her, | and fluently persuade her to a peace. TNK 3.05. 87
FLUNG 5 FR 0.0005 REL FR 5 V 0 P
whose enmity he flung aside, and breasted | the TMP 2.01.117
which he fain | would have flung from him; H8 2.01. 25
matrons flung gloves, | ladies and maids their COR 2.01.263
he's flung in rage from this ingrateful seat TIM 4.02. 45
wild in nature, broke their stalls, flung out, MAC 2.04. 16
FLURTED 1 FR 0.0001 REL FR 1 V 0 P
and now flurted | by peace, for whom he fought, TNK 1.02. 18
FLUSH 3 FR 0.0003 REL FR 3 V 0 P
now the time is flush, | when crouching marrow TIM 5.04. 8
all his crimes broad blown, as flush as may, HAM 3.03. 81
blood to think on't, and flush youth revolt. ANT 1.04. 52
FLUSHING 1 FR 0.0001 REL FR 1 V 0 P
had left the flushing in her galled eyes, | she HAM 1.02.155
FLUSTER'D 1 FR 0.0001 REL FR 1 V 0 P
have i to–night fluster'd with flowing cups, OTH 2.03. 58
FLUTE 4 FR 0.0004 REL FR 0 V 4 P
francis flute, the bellows–mender. MND 1.02. 42 P
flute, you must take thisby on you. 1.02. 44 P
and, flute, you thisby. 1.02. 56 P
flute, the bellows–mender! 4.01.202 P
FLUTES 2 FR 0.0002 REL FR 2 V 0 P
which to the tune of flutes kept stroke, and ANT 2.02.195
these drums, these trumpets, flutes! 2.07.131
/FLUTTER'D 1 FR 0.0001 REL FR 1 V 0 P
i | /flutter'd your volscians in corioles. COR 5.06.115
FLUX 2 FR 0.0002 REL FR 1 V 1 P
"thus misery doth part | the flux of company." AYL 2.01. 52
than tar, the very uncleanly flux of a cat. 3.02. 68 P
FLUXIVE 1 FR 0.0001 REL FR 1 V 0 P
these often bath'd she in her fluxive eyes, LC 50
/FLY* 8 FR 0.0009 REL FR 8 V 0 P
/fly away, /fly away, breath, | i am slain by a TN 2.04. 53
/fly away, /fly away, breath, | i am slain by a 2.04. 53
/that /i /have /kill'd, /my /lord — /a /fly. TIT 3.02. 53
/alas, /my /lord, /i /have /but /kill'd /a /fly. 3.02. 59
/how /if /that /fly /had /a /father /and /mother 3.02. 60
/poor /harmless /fly, | /that, /with /his 3.02. 63
/sir, /it /was /a /black //ill–favor'd /fly, 3.02. 66
/but /that /between /us /we /can /kill /a /fly 3.02. 77
FLY* 244 FR 0.0275 REL FR 223 V 21 P
be't to fly, | to swim, to dive into the fire, TMP 1.02.190
you, did | my heart fly to your service, there 3.01. 65
/her peacocks fly amain. 4.01. 74
neptune, and do fly him | when he comes back; 5.01. 35
on the bat's back i do fly | after summer 5.01. 91
less shall she that hath love's wings to fly, TGV 2.07. 11
i fly not death, to fly his deadly doom: 3.01.185
i fly not death, to fly his deadly doom: 3.01.185
death, | but, fly i hence, i fly away from life. 3.01.187
death, | but, fly i hence, i fly away from life. 3.01.187
sight, | we two in great amazedness will fly; WIV 4.04. 56
fly, run, hue and cry, villain! 4.05. 91 P
nay, do not fly, i think we have watch'd you now 5.05.103
life, | so fly i from her that would be my wife. ERR 3.02.155
"fly pride," says the peacock: 4.03. 80
fly, be gone! 5.01.184
or hide your heads like cowards, and fly hence. LLL 5.02. 86
lysander and myself will fly this place. MND 1.01.203
thou shalt fly him and he shall seek thy love. 2.01.246
do, as a monster, fly my presence thus. 2.02. 97
pray, masters, fly, masters! 3.01.105 P
sky, | so, at his sight, away his fellows fly; 3.02. 24
i followed fast, but faster he did fly, | that 3.02.416
as they fly by them with their woven wings. MV 1.01. 14
o, ten times faster venus' pigeons fly | to seal 2.06. 5
morning early will we both | fly toward belmont. 4.01.457
therefore devise with me how we may fly, AYL 1.03.100
i fly thee, for i would not injure thee. 3.05. 9
by this hand, it will not kill a fly. 4.01.111 P
'twill fly with the smoke out at the chimney. 4.01.164 P
i fly, biondello; SHR 5.01. 2 P
what is infirm from your sound parts shall fly, AWW 2.01.167
now, dian, from thy altar do i fly, | and to 2.03. 74
and all the honors that can fly from us | shall 3.01. 20
boy, | to fly the favors of so good a king, | to 3.02. 29
fly with false aim, move the still–peering air 3.02.110
and that you fly them as you swear them lordship 5.03.156
methinks his words do from such passion fly TN 3.04.373
for their better safety, to fly away by night." WT 3.02. 21 P
that shepherd be not in hand–fast, let him fly. 4.04.769 P
and fly, like thought, from them to me again. JN 4.02.175
fly, noble english, you are bought and sold! 5.04. 10
said | king john did fly an hour or two before 5.05. 17
the uglier seem the clouds that in it fly. R2 1.01. 42
confess thy treasons ere thou fly the realm; 1.03.198
one on his side fights, thousands will fly. 2.02.147
all souls that will be safe, fly from my side, 3.02. 80
a rendezvous, a home to fly unto, | if that the 1H4 4.01. 57
sake, to fly | out of your sight and raise this 5.01. 65
aiming at their safety, | fly from the field. 2H4 1.01.125
o, fly to scotland, | till that the nobles and 2.03. 50
o, with what wings shall his affections fly 4.04. 65
wasteful vengeance | that shall fly with them; H5 1.02.284
and so our scene must to the battle fly; 4.pr. 48
men, they have no wings to fly from god. 4.01.168 P
fly o'er them all, impatient for their hour. 4.02. 52
good argument, i hope, we will not fly — | and 4.03.113
tarry, sweet soul, for mine, then fly abreast, 4.06. 17
and so i shall catch the fly, your cousin, in 5.02.313 P
another would fly swift, but wanteth wings; 1H6 1.01. 75
all fly to him? 1.01. 96
o, whither shall we fly from this reproach? 1.01. 97
we will not fly but to our enemies' throats. 1.01. 98
me, | when he sees me go back one foot or fly. 1.02. 21
and while i live, i'll ne'er fly from a man. 1.02.103
my grisly countenance made others fly, | none 1.04. 47
as you fly from your oft–subdued slaves. 1.05. 32
what? will you fly, and leave lord talbot? 3.02.107
for fly he could not, if he would have fled; 4.04. 43
and fly would talbot never, though he might. 4.04. 44
and shall i fly? 4.05. 13
fly, to revenge my death, if i be slain. 4.05. 18
then let me stay, and, father, do you fly. 4.05. 21
to fight i will, but not to fly the foe. 4.05. 37
if death be so apparent, then both fly. 4.05. 44
and soul with soul from france to heaven fly. 4.05. 55
wilt thou yet leave the battle, boy, and fly, 4.06. 28
fly, to revenge my death when i am dead; 4.06. 30
all these are sav'd if thou wilt fly away. 4.06. 41
before young talbot from old talbot fly | the 4.06. 46
have won, | and if i fly, i am not talbot's son. 4.06. 51
the regent conquers, and the frenchmen fly. 5.03. 1
o fairest beauty, do not fear nor fly, | for i 5.03. 46
were it not good your grace could fly to heaven? 2H6 2.01. 17
true; made the lame to leap and fly away. 2.01.158
you made in a day, my lord, whole towns to fly. 2.01.160
and, fly thou how thou canst, they'll tangle 2.04. 55
fly, fly, fly! 4.02.113 P
fly, fly, fly! 4.02.113 P
fly, fly, fly! 4.02.113 P
that those which fly before the battle ends 4.02.178
fly, my lord! 4.04. 27
the citizens fly and forsake their houses; 4.04. 50
knowledge the wing wherewith we fly to heaven, 4.07. 74
alas, he hath no home, no place to fly to; 4.08. 38
let no soldier fly. 5.02. 36
you'll not fight nor fly. 5.02. 74
us | by what we can, which can no more but fly. 5.02. 77
set, | i would speak blasphemy ere bid you fly. 5.02. 85
but fly you must. 5.02. 86
but when the duke is slain, they'll quickly fly. 3H6 1.01. 69
sound drums and trumpets, and the king will fly. 1.01.118
ah, whither shall i fly to scape their hands? 1.03. 1
followers to the eager foe | turn back and fly, 1.04. 4
and i am faint, and cannot fly their fury; 1.04. 23
so cowards fight when they can fly no further, 1.04. 40
frown hath made thee faint and fly ere this! 1.04. 48
foes, | but never once again turn back and fly. 2.01.185
proclaims him king, and many fly to him. 2.02. 71
then 'twas my turn to fly, and now 'tis thine. 2.02.105
whither shall we fly? 2.03. 11
i'll kill my horse, because i will not fly. 2.03. 24
and give them leave to fly that will not stay; 2.03. 50
fly, father, fly! 2.05.125
fly, father, fly! 2.05.125
and whither fly the gnats but to the sun? 2.06. 9
no way to fly, nor strength to hold out flight. 2.06. 24
what are they that fly there? 4.03. 28
come therefore let us fly while we may fly, | if 4.04. 34
come therefore let us fly while we may fly, | if 4.04. 34
ah, couldst thou fly! 5.02. 32
why then i would not fly. 5.02. 33
fly, lords, and save yourselves, | for warwick 5.02. 48
if case some one of you would fly from us, 5.04. 34
to fly the boar before the boar pursues | were R3 3.02. 28
helms, | and i did scorn it and disdain to fly. 3.04. 83
if yet your gentle souls fly in the air | and be 4.04. 11
wilt thou, o god, fly from such gentle lambs, 4.04. 22
catesby, fly to the duke. 4.04.442
thou wilt revolt and fly to him, i fear. 4.04.477
which in his dearest need will fly from him. 5.02. 21
then fly. 5.03.185
where my chaff | and corn shall fly asunder; H8 5.01.111
now good angels | fly o'er thy royal head, and 5.01.160
heels | and fly like chidden mercury from jove, TRO 2.02. 45
in circumvention deliver a fly from a spider, 2.03. 16 P
his painted wings, | and fly with me to cressid! 3.02. 15
and with his arms outstretch'd as he would fly 3.03.167
and thou shalt hunt a lion that will fly | with 4.01. 20
fly not, for shouldst thou take the river styx, 5.04. 19
i do not fly, but advantageous care | withdrew 5.04. 21
and there they fly or die, like scaling sculls 5.05. 22
why then fly on, i'll hunt thee for thy hide. 5.06. 31
if i fly, martius, | hollow me like a hare. COR 1.08. 6
for him | shall fly out of itself. 1.10. 19
to issue out of one skull, they would fly east, 2.03. 22 P
which way do you judge my wit would fly? 2.03. 26 P
do they still fly to th' roman? 4.07. 1
if you'ld save your life, fly to your house. 5.04. 35
which made me down to throw my books, and fly — TIT 4.01. 25
sweet scrolls to fly about the streets of rome! 4.04. 16
is the sun dimm'd, that gnats do fly in it? 4.04. 82
things | as willingly as one would kill a fly, 5.01.142
the door | that so my sad decrees may fly away, 5.02. 11
your consent gives strength to make /it fly. ROM 1.03. 99
and, as he fell, did romeo turn and fly. 3.01.174
flies may do this, but i from this must fly; 3.03. 41
fly hence and leave me, think upon these gone, 5.03. 60
i will fly, like a dog, the heels a' th' ass. TIM 1.01.272 P
his promises fly so beyond his state | that what 1.02.197
fly, damned baseness, | to him that worships 3.01. 47
fly, whilst thou art blest and free. 4.03.535
wing | will make him fly an ordinary pitch, JC 1.01. 73
his coward lips did from their color fly, | and 1.02.122
fly not, stand still; 3.01. 83
and kites | fly o'er our heads, and downward 5.01. 85
o, look, titinius, look, the villains fly! 5.03. 1
fly further off, my lord, fly further off; 5.03. 9
fly further off, my lord, fly further off; 5.03. 9
fly therefore, noble cassius, fly far off. 5.03. 11
fly therefore, noble cassius, fly far off. 5.03. 11
fly, fly, my lord, there is no tarrying here. 5.05. 30
fly, fly, my lord, there is no tarrying here. 5.05. 30
fly, my lord, fly. 5.05. 43
fly, my lord, fly. 5.05. 43
fly, good fleance, fly, fly, fly! MAC 3.03. 17
fly, good fleance, fly, fly, fly! 3.03. 17
fly, good fleance, fly, fly, fly! 3.03. 17
fly, good fleance, fly, fly, fly! 3.03. 17
some holy angel | fly to the court of england, 3.06. 46
what had he done, to make him fly the land? 4.02. 1
in a place | from whence himself does fly? 4.02. 8
whither should i fly? 4.02. 73
bring me no more reports, let them fly all. 5.03. 1
then fly, false thanes, | and mingle with the 5.03. 7
doctor, the thanes fly from me. 5.03. 49
i cannot fly, | but bear–like i must fight the 5.07. 1
/french falc'ners — fly at any thing we see; HAM 2.02.430 P
have, | than fly to others that we know not of? 3.01. 81
my words fly up, my thoughts remain below: 3.03. 97
let the birds fly, and like the famous ape, | to 3.04.194
with as much speed as thou wouldest fly death. 4.06. 24 P
o sir, fly this place, | intelligence is given LR 2.01. 20
fly, brother. 2.01. 32
let him fly far. 2.01. 56
not gone yet, if the wild geese fly that way. 2.04. 46 P
the fool will stay, | and let the wise man fly. 2.04. 83
and the small gilded fly | does lecher in my 4.06.112
bade her wrong stay, and her displeasure fly; OTH 2.01.153
as this will i ensnare as great a fly as cassio. 2.01.169 P
thy freer thoughts | may not fly forth of egypt. ANT 1.05. 12
our hearts, and never | fly off our loves again! 2.02.152
this was but as a fly by an eagle; 2.02.181 P
and the shelters whither | the routed fly; 3.01. 9
with all their sixty, fly and turn the rudder. 3.10. 3
fly, | and make your peace with caesar. 3.11. 5
fly? not we. 3.11. 6
bid them all fly; 4.12. 15
bid them all fly, be gone. 4.12. 17
thy death and fortunes bid thy followers fly. 4.14.111
i shall flying fight — | rather, directly fly. CYM 1.06. 21
have done, his spirits fly out | into my story; 3.03. 90
o jove, i think | foundations fly the wretched: 3.06. 7
that it would fly | from so divine a temple to 4.02. 54
soft, what are you | that fly me thus? 4.02. 71
thus smiling, as some fly had tickled slumber, 4.02.210
till it fly out and show them princes born. 4.04. 54
or betimes | let's reinforce, or fly. 5.02. 18
to darkness fleet souls that fly backwards. 5.03. 25
forthwith they fly | chickens, the way which 5.03. 41
i know he'll quickly fly my friendship too. 5.03. 62
or we appeal, | and from thy justice fly. 5.04. 92
as thou | wilt live, fly after, and like an PER 1.01.161
law, | i never kill'd a mouse, nor hurt a fly; 4.01. 77
the petty wrens of tharsus will fly hence | and 4.03. 22
you have heard me say, when i did fly from tyre, 5.03. 50
with them any discord bring, | but from it fly! TNK 1.01. 24
compell'd bears, would fly | were they not tied. 3.01. 68
like meeting of two tides, fly strongly from us, 3.06. 30
and justifying my love, i must not fly from't. 3.06. 42
i had rather see a wren hawk at a fly | than 5.03. 2
and whe'er he run or fly they know not whether; VEN 304
they basely fly, and dare not stay the field. 894
that from the cold stone sparks of fire do fly, LUC 177
and extreme fear can neither fight nor fly, 230
who, angry that the eyes fly from their lights, 461
mire | and unperceiv'd fly with the filth away, 1010
gnats are unnoted wheresoe'er they fly, | but 1014
at gaze, | wildly determining which way to fly, 1150
and from his lips did fly | thin winding breath, 1406
and through her wounds doth fly | live's lasting 1728
to sing, | and heavy ignorance aloft to fly, SON 78. 6
and now she would the caged cloister fly: LC 249
o, that forc'd thunder from his heart did fly, 325
FLY–BITTEN 1 FR 0.0001 REL FR 0 V 1 P
bed–hangers and these fly–bitten /tapestries. 2H4 2.01.146 P

FLY–BLOWING 1 FR 0.0001 REL FR 0 V 1 P
i shall not fear fly–blowing. TMP 5.01.284 P
FLY–BLOWN 1 FR 0.0001 REL FR 1 V 0 P
stinking and fly–blown lies here at our feet. 1H6 4.07. 76
FLYING* 19 FR 0.0021 REL FR 18 V 1 P
and slaves they are to me that send them flying: TGV 3.01.141
grief, | and on the justice of my flying hence, 4.03. 29
that that flies, and flying what pursues." WIV 2.02.208
flying between the cold moon and the earth, MND 2.01.156
air, | and thou art flying to a fresher clime. R2 1.03.285
and with his pistol kills a sparrow flying. 1H4 2.04.346 P
believe me, lords, for flying at the brook, | i 2H6 2.01. 1
so shouldst thou either turn my flying soul, 3.02.397
having the fearful flying hare in sight, | with 3H6 2.05.130
flying for succor to his servant banister, H8 2.01.109
when they charge on heaps | the enemy flying. TRO 3.02. 29
there is nor flying hence, nor tarrying here. MAC 5.05. 47
fetches, | the images of revolt and flying off. LR 2.04. 90
than was his loss, to course your flying flags, ANT 3.13. 11
or, like the parthian, i shall flying fight — CYM 1.06. 20
seen, all flying | through a strait lane; 5.03. 6
"our britain's harts die flying, not our men. 5.03. 24
and clamors through the wild air flyinğ! TNK 1.05. 6
by me, | uncouple at the timorous flying hare, VEN 674
FO 4 FR 0.0004 REL FR 4 V 0 P
fo, fo, come, tell a pin. you are forsworn. TRO 5.02. 22
fo, fo, come, tell a pin. you are forsworn. 5.02. 22
fo, fo, /adieu, you palter. 5.02. 48
fo, fo, /adieu, you palter. 5.02. 48
FOAL 1 FR 0.0001 REL FR 1 V 0 P
beguile, | neighing in likeness of a filly foal; MND 2.01. 46
FOALS 1 FR 0.0001 REL FR 1 V 0 P
it him, it foals me straight | and able horses. TIM 2.01. 9
FOAM 4 FR 0.0004 REL FR 4 V 0 P
lie where the light foam of the sea may beat TIM 4.03.378
that rig'st the bark and plough'st the foam, 5.01. 50
th' ambitious ocean swell, and rage, and foam, JC 1.03. 7
join, and shoot their foam at simois' banks. LUC 1442
FOAM'D 2 FR 0.0002 REL FR 1 V 1 P
down in the market–place, and foam'd at mouth, JC 1.02.253 P
me | with his sword drawn, foam'd at the mouth, CYM 5.05.276
FOAMING 5 FR 0.0005 REL FR 4 V 1 P
all but mariners | plung'd in the foaming brine, TMP 1.02.211
that they may break his foaming courser's back, R2 1.02. 51
of the camp will do among foaming bottles and H5 3.06. 78 P
and once again bestride our foaming steeds, 3H6 2.01.183
for do but stand upon the foaming shore, | the OTH 2.01. 11
FOAMS 3 FR 0.0003 REL FR 3 V 0 P
and foams at mouth, and he is arm'd and at it, TRO 5.05. 36
if not, he foams at mouth, and by and by OTH 4.01. 54
at whose burthen | the anger'd ocean foams, with ANT 2.06. 21
FOAMY 1 FR 0.0001 REL FR 1 V 0 P
from the rude sea's enrag'd and foamy mouth TN 5.01. 78
FOB *(also fubb'd)*
FOB 1 FR 0.0001 REL FR 0 V 1 P
you must not think to fob off our disgrace with COR 1.01. 94 P
FOCATIVE 2 FR 0.0002 REL FR 0 V 2 P
what is the focative case, william? WIV 4.01. 51 P
remember, william, focative is caret. 4.01. 53 P
FODDER 1 FR 0.0001 REL FR 0 V 1 P
the sheep for fodder follow the shepherd, the TGV 1.01. 89 P
FOE 74 FR 0.0083 REL FR 73 V 1 P
see what thou wert, if fortune thy foe were not, WIV 3.03. 65 P
with targe and shield did make my foe to sweat, LLL 5.02.553
lay breath so bitter on your bitter foe. MND 3.02. 44
i know | our party may well meet a prouder foe. JN 5.01. 79
of lancaster, | the honorable father to my foe, R2 1.01.136
feed not thy sovereign's foe, my gentle earth, 3.02. 12
to fear the foe, since fear oppresseth strength, 3.02.180
gives in your weakness strength unto your foe, 3.02.181
steel | over the glittering helmet of my foe! 4.01. 51
i am the king's friend, and will rid his foe. 5.04. 11
it is most meet we arm us 'gainst the foe; H5 2.04. 15
fortune is bardolph's foe, and frowns on him; 3.06. 39
to purge this field of such a hilding foe; 4.02. 29
here's gloucester, a foe to citizens, | one that 1H6 1.03. 62
defac'd | by wasting ruin of the cruel foe. 3.03. 46
was not the duke of orleance thy foe? 3.03. 69
powers, | and seek how we may prejudice the foe. 3.03. 91
he doth, my lord, and is become your foe. 4.01. 65
to fight i will, but not to fly the foe. 4.05. 37
imagine him a frenchman, and thy foe. 4.07. 26
and to preserve my sovereign from his foe, | say 2H6 3.01.271
and for myself, foe as he was to me, | might 3.02. 59
and all my followers to the eager foe | turn 3H6 1.04. 3
wailing our losses, whiles the foe doth rage, 2.03. 26
the foe is merciless, and will not pity; 2.06. 25
if friend or foe, let him be gently used. 2.06. 45
the scatt'red foe that hopes to rise again; 2.06. 93
my gracious lord, henry your foe is taken, | and 3.02.118
the more we stay, the stronger grows our foe. 3.03. 40
but i return his sworn and mortal foe. 3.03.257
his guard | or by his foe surpris'd at unawares; 4.04. 9
fell warwick's brother, and by that our foe. 4.04. 12
hands, | i here proclaim myself thy mortal foe; 5.01. 94
come to me, friend or foe, | and tell me who is 5.02. 5
and, by my fall, the conquest to my foe. 5.02. 10
is prisoner to the foe, his state usurp'd, | his 5.04. 77
intelligence or wrong surmise | hold me a foe — R3 2.01. 56
arm, arm, my lord, the foe vaunts in the field. 5.03.288
heat not a furnace for your foe so hot | that it H8 1.01.140
i hold my most malicious foe, and think not | at 2.04. 83
you go, | and find the welcome of a noble foe. TRO 1.03.309
i'll leave the foe | and make my wars on you. COR 1.04. 39
malignantly remain | fast foe to th' plebeii, 2.03.184
innovator, | a foe to th' public weal. 3.01.175
thou shalt not stir one foot to seek a foe. ROM 1.01. 80
uncle, this is a montague, our foe; 1.05. 61
but to his foe suppos'd he must complain, | and 2.pr. 7
being held a foe, he may not have access | to 2.pr. 9
for lo | my intercession likewise steads my foe. 2.03. 54
that thought is bounty's foe; TIM 2.02.232
touch'd to death, | he did oppose his foe; 3.05. 20
a foe to tyrants, and my country's friend. JC 5.04. 5
so they | doubly redoubled strokes upon the foe. MAC 1.02. 38
would i had met my dearest foe in heaven | or HAM 1.02.182
swoopstake, you will draw both friend and foe, 4.05.143
of being taken by the insolent foe | and sold to OTH 1.03.137
my fleet hath yielded to the foe, and yonder ANT 4.12. 11
such a foe, good heavens! CYM 3.06. 27
our foe was princely, | and though you took his 4.02.249
and though you took his life, as being our foe, 4.02.250
who dares not stand his foe, i'll be his friend; 5.03. 60
i thank thee, arcite, | thou art yet a fair foe; TNK 3.06. 8
kinsman as you force me find | a beneficial foe, 3.06. 22
so white a friend engirts so white a foe: VEN 364
him go, | rather than triumph in so false a foe. LUC 77
begin | to sound a parley to his heartless foe, 471
and wast afeard to scratch her wicked foe, 1035
myself thy friend will kill myself thy foe, 1196
know | her honor is ta'en prisoner by the foe, 1608
be suddenly revenged on my foe, | thine, mine, 1683
longing to hear the hateful foe bewray'd. 1698
to slay herself, that should have slain her foe. 1827
to know | faithful friend from flatt'ring foe. PP 20.56
thyself thy foe, to thy sweet self too cruel. SON 1. 8
FOEMAN 1 FR 0.0001 REL FR 0 V 1 P
the foeman may with as great aim level at the 2H4 3.02.266 P
FOEMAN'S 1 FR 0.0001 REL FR 1 V 0 P
is this our foeman's face? 3H6 2.05. 82
FOEMEN 2 FR 0.0002 REL FR 2 V 0 P
aid, | unto his dastard foemen is betray'd. 1H6 1.01.144
what valiant foemen, like to autumn's corn, 3H6 5.07. 3
FOEMEN'S 1 FR 0.0001 REL FR 1 V 0 P
than foemen's marks upon his batt'red shield, TIT 4.01.127
FOE'S 1 FR 0.0001 REL FR 1 V 0 P
my life is my foe's debt. ROM 1.05.118
/FOES 1 FR 0.0001 REL FR 1 V 0 P
/we /scarcely /think /our /miseries /our /foes. LR 3.06.103
FOES 78 FR 0.0088 REL FR 74 V 4 P
'mongst all foes that a friend should be the TGV 5.04. 72
pity two such friends should be long foes. 5.04.118
of pale distemperatures and foes to life? ERR 5.01. 82
strangers and foes do sunder, and not kiss. AWW 2.05. 86
from courtly friends, with camping foes to live, 3.04. 14
sir, the better for my foes and the worse for my TN 5.01. 12 P
now my foes tell me plainly i am an ass; 5.01. 18 P
so that by my foes, sir, i profit in the 5.01. 19 P
worse for my friends and the better for my foes. 5.01. 23 P
dy'd in the dying slaughter of their foes. JN 2.01.323
and dost thou now fall over to my foes? 3.01.127
against the pope, and count his friends my foes. 3.01.171
nor friends, nor foes, to me welcome you are: R2 2.03.170
thy friends are fled to wait upon thy foes, 2.04. 23
since foes have scope to beat both thee and me. 3.03.141
why, harry, do i tell thee of my foes, | which 1H4 3.02.122
his foes are so enrooted with his friends | that 2H4 4.01.205
go'st | except it be to pray against thy foes. 1H6 1.01. 43
when i have chased all thy foes from hence, 1.02.115
and know us by these colors for thy foes, | for 2.04.105
and have our bodies slaught'red by thy foes. 3.01.101
and so thrive richard as thy foes may fall! 3.01.173
goes, | for friendly counsel cuts off many foes. 3.01.184
a prophet to the fall of all our foes! 3.02. 32
came to the field and vanquished his foes. 3.02. 96
and none your foes but such as shall pretend 4.01. 6
still | you may behold confusion of your foes. 4.01. 77
infancy | crowned in paris in despite of foes? 2H6 1.01. 94
snar'd, | nor never seek prevention of thy foes. 2.04. 57
and had i twenty times so many foes, | and each 2.04. 60
but both of you were vowed duke humphrey's foes, 3.02.182
'tis not enough our foes are this time fled, 5.03. 21
accurs'd be he that seeks to make them foes! 3H6 1.01.205
yea, even my foes will shed fast–falling tears, 1.04.162
environed he was with many foes, | and stood 2.01. 50
or shall we on the helmets of our foes | tell 2.01.163
upon our foes, | but never once again turn back 2.01.184
lord, cheer up your spirits, our foes are nigh, 2.02. 56
that to my foes this body must be prey, | yet 2.03. 39
i rather wish you foes than hollow friends. 4.01.139
so other foes may set upon our backs. 5.01. 61
foes to my rest and my sweet sleep's disturbers, R3 4.02. 73
if you do fight against your country's foes, 5.03.257
advance our standards, set upon our foes. 5.03.348
her foes shake like a field of beaten corn, H8 5.04. 31
whose present courage may beat down our foes, TRO 2.02.201
time–pleasers, flatterers, foes to nobleness. COR 3.01. 45
still your own foes) deliver you as most 3.03.131
so, fellest foes, | whose passions and whose 4.04. 18
that with his sons, a terror to our foes, | hath TIT 1.01. 29
to quit the bloody wrongs upon her foes. 1.01.141
my foes i do repute you every one, | so trouble 1.01.366
by working wreakful vengeance on thy foes. 5.02. 32
sons, | the emperor himself and all thy foes, 5.02.117
now goes | to lay a complot to betray thy foes. 5.02.147
come, come, lavinia, look, thy foes are bound. 5.02.166
from forth the fatal loins of these two foes | a ROM pr 5
and let the foes quietly cut their throats TIM 3.05. 44
if there were no foes, that were enough | to 3.05. 69
i have kept back their foes, | while they have 3.05.105
ours is the fall, i fear, our foes the snare. 5.02. 17
peace, | shaking the bloody fingers of thy foes, JC 3.01.198
would make good of bad, and friends of foes! MAC 2.04. 41
we have met with foes | that strike beside us. 5.07. 28
and all foes | the cup of their deservings. LR 5.03.304
ripp'd, | came crying 'mongst his foes, | a CYM 5.04. 46
and come to us as favorers, not as foes. PER 1.04. 73
shows, | that are quick–ey'd pleasure's foes! TNK 1.05. 8
you royal germane foes, that this day come | to 5.01. 9
of bristly pikes that ever threat his foes, VEN 620
goes | are like a labyrinth to amaze his foes. 684
ear, | to hearken if his foes pursue him still. 699
time's office is to fine the hate of foes, | to LUC 936
"let him have time to see his friends his foes, 988
cries, | and bitter words to ban her cruel foes; 1460
kill me with spites, yet we must not be foes. SON 40.14
utt'ring bare truth, even so as foes commend. 69. 4
and therefore from my face she turns my foes, 139.11
FOG 6 FR 0.0006 REL FR 4 V 2 P
anon | with drooping fog as black as acheron, MND 3.02.357
more puzzled than the egyptians in their fog. TN 4.02. 44 P
to lose itself in a fog, where being three parts COR 2.03. 31 P
and stain the sun with fog, as sometime clouds TIT 3.01.212
is fair, | hover through the fog and filthy air. MAC 1.01. 12
but have a fog in them | that i cannot look CYM 3.02. 79
FOGGY 4 FR 0.0004 REL FR 4 V 0 P
like foggy south, puffing with wind and rain? AYL 3.05. 50
is not their climate foggy, raw, and dull, | on H5 3.05. 16
see, | sits in a foggy cloud, and stays for me. MAC 3.05. 35
"o hateful, vaporous, and foggy night! LUC 771
FOGS 3 FR 0.0003 REL FR 3 V 0 P
have suck'd up from the sea | contagious fogs; MND 2.01. 90
blasts and fogs upon thee! LR 1.04.299
you fen–suck'd fogs, drawn by the pow'rful sun, 2.04.167
FOH *(also fough)*
FOH 7 FR 0.0008 REL FR 3 V 4 P
foh! WIV 1.03. 29 P
foh, sir, why, you bald–pated, lying rascal, you MM 5.01.351 P
foh, prithee stand away. AWW 5.02. 16 P
foh! H5 3.04. 56 P
fie upon't, foh! HAM 2.02.587
came, | his word was still, 'fie, foh, and fum, LR 3.04.183
foh, one may smell in such, a will most rank, OTH 3.03.232
FOI 3 FR 0.0003 REL FR 0 V 3 P
ma foi, il fait fort /chaud. WIV 1.04. 51 P
ma foi, j'oublie les doigts, mais je me H5 3.04. 9 P
ma foi, je ne veux point que vous abaissez votre 5.02.253 P
FOIL* 14 FR 0.0015 REL FR 12 V 2 P
grace she ow'd, | and put it to the foil. TMP 3.01. 46
and for your love i would be loath to foil him, AYL 1.01.130 P
that did but lately foil the sinowy charles, 2.02. 14
steps | esteem as foil wherein thou art to set R2 1.03.266
than that which hath no foil to set it off. 1H4 1.02.215
one sudden foil shall never breed distrust. 1H6 3.03. 11
before that england give the french the foil. 5.03. 23
and make him, naked, foil a man at arms. 3H6 5.04. 42
made precious by the foil | of england's chair, R3 5.03.250
knight shall use his foil and target, the lover HAM 2.02.321 P
i'll be your foil, laertes; 5.02.255
and must not foil | the precious note of it with CYM 2.03.121
palamon | is but his foil, to him, a mere dull TNK 4.02. 26
which remain'd the foil | of this false jewel, LC 153
FOIL'D 6 FR 0.0006 REL FR 5 V 1 P
wherein if i be foil'd, there is but one sham'd AYL 1.02.187 P
if he were foil'd, | why then we do our main TRO 1.03.371
nose that bled, or foil'd some debile wretch — COR 1.09. 48
for mast'ring her that foil'd the god of fight! VEN 114
fram'd the love, and yet she foil'd the framing, PP 7.15
after a thousand victories once foil'd, | is SON 25.10
FOILS 8 FR 0.0009 REL FR 6 V 2 P
and yours as blunt as the fencer's foils, which ADO 5.02. 13 P
with four or five most vile and ragged foils H5 4.pr. 50
will not peruse the foils, so that, with ease, HAM 4.07.136
let the foils be brought, the gentleman willing, 5.02.175 P
give us the foils. 5.02.254
give them the foils, young osric. 5.02.259
these foils have all a length? 5.02.265
yet must antony | no way excuse his foils, when ANT 1.04. 24
FOIN 2 FR 0.0002 REL FR 0 V 2 P
to see thee fight, to see thee foin, to see thee WIV 2.03. 24 P
he will foin like any devil, he will spare 2H4 2.01. 16 P
FOINING 2 FR 0.0002 REL FR 1 V 1 P
sir boy, i'll whip you from your foining fence, ADO 5.01. 84
leave fighting a' days and foining a' nights, 2H4 2.04.232 P
FOINS 1 FR 0.0001 REL FR 0 V 1 P
come, no matter vor your foins. LR 4.06.245 P
FOIS 2 FR 0.0002 REL FR 0 V 2 P
je reciterai une autre fois ma lecon ensemble: H5 3.04. 57 P
c'est assez pour une fois: allons–nous a diner. 3.04. 61 P
FOISON 6 FR 0.0006 REL FR 6 V 0 P
of it own kind, all foison, all abundance, | to TMP 2.01.164
earth's increase, foison plenty, | barns and 4.01.110
the bare fallow brings | to teeming foison, even MM 1.04. 43
or the mean, if dearth | or foison follow. ANT 2.07. 20
breath blows down | the teeming ceres' foison, TNK 5.01. 53
speak of the spring and foison of the year, SON 53. 9
FOISONS 1 FR 0.0001 REL FR 1 V 0 P
scotland hath foisons to fill up your will | of MAC 4.03. 88
FOIST 1 FR 0.0001 REL FR 1 V 0 P
what thou dost foist upon us that is old, | and SON 123. 6
/FOIX 1 FR 0.0001 REL FR 1 V 0 P
/foix, lestrake, bouciqualt, and charolois; H5 3.05. 45
FOIX 1 FR 0.0001 REL FR 1 V 0 P
grandpre and roussi, faulconbridge and foix, H5 4.08. 99
FOLD* 18 FR 0.0020 REL FR 17 V 1 P
fold it over and over, | 'tis threefold too TGV 1.01.108
thus will i fold them one upon another; 1.02.125
the fold stands empty in the drowned field, MND 2.01. 96
we will descend and fold him in our arms. R2 1.03. 54
troyan, | to have me fold up parca's fatal web? H5 5.01. 20
then, | to make the fox surveyor of the fold? 2H6 3.01.253
shall from your neck unloose his amorous fold, TRO 3.03.223
the fires i' th' lowest hell fold in the people! COR 3.03. 68
and wonder greatly that man's face can fold | in TIT 2.03.266
here, marcus, fold it in the oration, | for 4.03.116
approach the fold and cull th' infected forth, TIM 5.04. 43
closet, take forth paper, fold it, write upon't, MAC 5.01. 6 P
fold down the leaf where i have left. CYM 2.02. 4
but forty thousand fold we had rather have 'em TNK 1.04. 36
the sheep are gone to fold, birds to their nest, VEN 532
fold in the object that did feed her sight. 822
entombs her outcry in her lips' sweet fold. LUC 679
nor fold my fault in cleanly coin'd excuses; 1073
/FOLDED 1 FR 0.0001 REL FR 1 V 0 P
/our /tenfold /grief | /with /folded /arms. TIT 3.02. 7
FOLDED 7 FR 0.0008 REL FR 7 V 0 P
the folded meaning of your words' deceit. ERR 3.02. 36
regent of love–rhymes, lord of folded arms, LLL 3.01.181
they shoot but calm words folded up in smoke, JN 2.01.229
wrath | hath in eternal darkness folded up. R3 1.03.268
folded the writ up in the form of th' other, HAM 5.02. 51
shame folded up in blind concealing night, LUC 675
of folded schedules had she many a one, | which LC 43
FOLDS 4 FR 0.0004 REL FR 4 V 0 P
the man is noble and his fame folds in | this COR 5.06.124
to dismantle | so many folds of favor. LR 1.01.218
wreath'd up in fatal folds just in his way, VEN 879
here folds she up the tenure of her woe, | her LUC 1310
FOLIO 1 FR 0.0001 REL FR 0 V 1 P
write, pen, for i am for whole volumes in folio. LLL 1.02.185 P
FOLK *(also voke)*
FOLK 3 FR 0.0003 REL FR 2 V 1 P
walk aside the true folk, and let the traitors LLL 4.03.209
and the old folk (time's doting chronicles) 2H4 4.04.126

and the more pity that great folk should have HAM 5.01. 27 P
FOLKS 12 FR 0.0013 REL FR 7 V 5 P
we must give folks leave to prate; WIV 1.04.121 P
old folks, you know, have discretion, as they 2.02.129 P
nonino, | these pretty country folks would lie, AYL 5.03. 24
see, to beguile the old folks, how the young SHR 1.02.139 P
how the young folks lay their heads together! 1.02.139 P
how likes gremio these quick–witted folks? 5.02. 38
with good old folks and let them tell /thee R2 5.01. 41
poor market folks that come to sell their corn. 1H6 3.02. 15
o monstrous coward! what, to come behind folks?
2H6 4.07. 84 P
but old folks — many feign as they were dead, ROM 2.05. 16
fools are not mad folks. CYM 2.03.101
will poor folks lie, | that have afflictions on 3.06. 9
/FOLLIES 2 FR 0.0002 REL FR 2 V 0 P
/must /i /ravel /out | /my //weav'd–up /follies? R2 4.01.229
/the /face /which /fac'd /so /many /follies, 4.01.285
FOLLIES 11 FR 0.0012 REL FR 7 V 4 P
but you are so without these follies, that these TGV 2.01. 38 P
follies, that these follies are within you, and 2.01. 38 P
as you have one eye upon my follies, as you hear WIV 2.02.186 P
and follies doth /enew | as falcon doth the fowl MM 3.01. 90
hath laugh'd at such shallow follies in others, ADO 2.03. 10 P
see | the pretty follies that themselves commit, MV 2.06. 37
you, that are thus so tender o'er his follies, WT 2.03.128
and so your follies fight against yourself. R2 3.02.182
i think thou art enamored | on his follies. 1H4 5.02. 70
surrey can be, | and all that love his follies. H8 3.02.275
o my follies! LR 3.07. 91
/FOLLOW 2 FR 0.0002 REL FR 2 V 0 P
/more /and /less /do /flock /to /follow /him. 2H4 1.01.209
/let's /follow /the /old /earl, /and /get /the LR 3.07.103
FOLLOW 314 FR 0.0355 REL FR 225 V 89 P
follow me. TMP 1.02.460
follow. 1.02.465
follow me. 1.02.495
come, follow. speak not for him. 1.02.502
i'll bear him no more sticks, but follow thee, 2.02.163
let's follow it, and after do our work. 3.02.148 P
lead, monster, we'll follow. 3.02.150 P
wilt come? i'll follow stephano. 3.02.152 P
are of suppler joints) follow them swiftly, 3.03.107
follow, i pray you. 3.03.109
for a little | follow, and do me service. 4.01.266
the sheep for fodder follow the shepherd, the TGV 1.01. 89 P
here follow her vices. 3.01.321 P
dispatch, sweet gentlemen, and follow me. 5.02. 48
and i will follow, more for silvia's love | than 5.02. 53
and i will follow, more to cross that love 5.02. 55
outrun us, | but moyses and valerius follow him. 5.03. 8
we'll follow him that's fled — | the thicket is 5.03. 10
let him follow. WIV 1.03. 13 P
follow. 1.03. 15 P
bardolph, follow him. 1.03. 16 P
follow my heels, rugby. 1.04.125 P
i follow, mine host, i follow. 2.01.195 P
i follow, mine host, i follow. 2.01.195 P
follow me, /lads of peace; 3.01.110 P
follow, follow, follow. 3.01.111 P
follow, follow, follow. 3.01.111 P
follow, follow, follow. 3.01.111 P
follow, gentlemen, follow. 3.01.112 P
follow, gentlemen, follow. 3.01.113 P
well, i will smite his noddles. pray you follow. 3.01.126 P
you like a man than follow him like a dwarf. 3.02. 6 P
follow your friend's counsel. 3.03.137 P
follow me, gentlemen. 3.03.169 P
nay, follow him, gentlemen, see the issue of his 3.03.174 P
and not follow the imaginations of your own 4.02.156 P
will you follow, gentlemen? 4.02.195 P
i beseech you follow; 4.02.196 P
follow me, i'll tell you strange things of this 5.01. 26 P
follow. 5.01. 29 P
follow. 5.01. 30 P
follow me. 5.02. 14 P
follow me into the pit, and when i give the 5.04. 2 P
but i shall follow it as the flesh and fortune MM 2.01.253 P
wrong to th' appetite, | to follow as it draws! 2.04.177
follow. 4.02. 55 P
we must follow the leaders. ADO 2.01.151 P
the ladies follow her, and but one visor remains 2.01.157 P
if you will follow me, i will show you enough, 3.02.120 P
i thought there would a scab follow. 3.03.100 P
come follow me, boy; 5.01. 83
come, sir boy, come follow me. 5.01. 83
as it shall follow in my correction, and god LLL 1.01.213 P
your moral, and do you follow with my l'envoy: 3.01. 93 P
moth, follow. 3.01.133 P
i beseech you follow. 5.01.148 P
with duty and desire we follow you. MND 1.01.127
hence, get thee gone, and follow me no more. 2.01.194
draw, | and i shall have no power to follow you. 2.01.198
me leave, | unworthy as i am, to follow you. 2.01.207
or, if thou follow me, do not believe | but i 2.01.236
i'll follow thee and make a heaven of hell, | to 2.01.243
i'll follow you, i'll lead you about a round, 3.01.106
to follow me and praise my eyes and face? 3.02.223
to break loose — take on as you would follow, 3.02.258
bear my folly back, | and follow you no further. 3.02.316
now follow, if thou dar'st, to try whose right, 3.02.336
follow? nay; i'll go with thee, cheek by jowl. 3.02.338
follow me then | to plainer ground. 3.02.403
follow my voice; we'll try no manhood here. 3.02.412
the duke was here, and bid us follow him? 4.01.195
and he did bid us follow to the temple. 4.01.197
let's follow him, | and by the way let's recount 4.01.198
one of the twenty to follow mine own teaching. MV 1.02. 17 P
why, all the boys in venice follow him, | crying 2.08. 23
follow not, | i'll have no speaking, i will have 3.03. 16
i'll follow him no more with bootless prayers. 3.03. 20
that i follow thus | a losing suit against him. 4.01. 61
of a strange nature is the suit you follow, 4.01.177
which if thou follow, this strict court of 4.01.204
on, and i will follow thee | to the last gasp, AYL 2.03. 69
foolish shepherd, wherefore do you follow her, 3.05. 49
i follow you. SHR 4.04. 72
husband, let's follow, to see the end of this 5.01.142
might with effects of them follow our friends, AWW 1.01.184
i follow him not | by any token of presumptuous 1.03.197
now, fair one, does your business follow us? 2.01. 99
go to, follow. 5.02. 54 P
and i follow him to his country for justice. 5.03.144 P
a should follow, but o does. TN 2.05.130 P
if you will see it, follow me. 2.05.204 P
will laugh yourselves into stitches, follow me. 3.02. 69 P
i'll follow this good man, and go with you, 4.03. 32
but rather follow | our forceful instigation? WT 2.01.162
come follow us, | we are to speak in public; 2.01.196
go thou away, | i'll follow instantly. 3.03. 14
art thus expos'd | to loss, and what may follow! 3.03. 51
follow me, girls. 4.04.313 P
follow us to the court. 4.04.432
i will but look upon the hedge and follow you. 4.04.826 P
make proselytes | of who she but bid follow. 5.01.109
therefore follow me | and mark what way i make. 5.01.232
lames report to follow it and undoes description 5.02. 57 P
come, follow us; 5.02.174 P
bequeath thy land to him, and follow me? JN 1.01.149
madam, i'll follow you unto the death. 1.01.154
will i not think of home, but follow arms. 2.01. 31
i fear some outrage, and i'll follow her. 3.04.106
away that child, | and follow me with speed. 4.03.157
remote, | and follow unacquainted colors here? 5.02. 32
percy | shall follow in your conduct speedily. 1H4 3.01.195
i'll follow, as they say, for reward. 5.04.162 P
be your patient to follow your prescriptions, 2H4 1.02.129 P
you follow the young prince up and down, like 1.02.163 P
i am your shadow, my lord, i'll follow you. 2.02.159 P
follow me, ned. 2.02.176 P
"the time shall come," thus did he follow it, 3.01. 75
we shall all follow, cousin. 3.02. 35 P
the heat is past, follow no further now; 4.03. 24
him, | and we with sober speed will follow you. 4.03. 80
i'll follow you, good master robert shallow. 5.01. 60 P
o, let their bodies follow, my dear liege, H5 1.02.130
cock is up, | and flashing fire will follow. 2.01. 53
follow, follow! 3.pr. 17
follow, follow! 3.pr. 17
hair, that will not follow | these cull'd and 3.pr. 23
follow your spirit; 3.01. 33
follow me! 4.04. 65
and he that will not follow bourbon now, | let 4.05. 12
follow fluellen closely at the heels. 4.07.171
follow, good cousin warwick. 4.07.175
follow, and see there be no harm between them. 4.07.182
with purpose to relieve and follow them, 1H6 1.01.133
ascend, brave talbot, we will follow thee. 2.01. 28
we'll follow them with all the power we have. 2.02. 33
if talbot do but thunder, rain will follow. 3.02. 59
cowardly knight, ill fortune follow thee! 3.02.109
burgundy | to leave the talbot and to follow us. 3.03. 20
then follow thou thy desp'rate sire of crete, 4.06. 54
yes, my good lord, i'll follow presently. 2H6 1.02. 60
follow i must, i cannot go before | while 1.02. 61
lord cardinal, i will follow eleanor, | and 1.03.148
follow the knave, and take this drab away. 2.01.153
come, fellow, follow us for thy reward. 2.03.105
that erst did follow thy proud chariot–wheels 2.04. 13
'tis to be fear'd they all will follow him. 3.01. 30
and you that be the king's friends, follow me. 4.02.181
and you that love the commons, follow me. 4.02.182
we'll follow cade, we'll follow cade! 4.08. 33 P
we'll follow cade, we'll follow cade! 4.08. 33 P
we'll follow the king and clifford. 4.08. 53 P
go some, and follow him, | and he that brings 4.08. 65
follow me, soldiers, we'll devise a mean | to 4.08. 68
i know our safety is to follow them, | for, as i 5.03. 23
whom should he follow but his natural king? 3H6 1.01. 82
nay, go not from me, i will follow thee. 1.01.213
have forsworn thy colors | will follow mine, if 1.01.252
till then, i'll follow her. 1.01.262
bootless is flight, they follow us with wings, 2.03. 12
and prince shall follow with a fresh supply. 3.03.237
you that love me and warwick, follow me. 4.01.123
myself in person will straight follow you. 4.01.133
you that will follow me to this attempt, 4.02. 26
but follow me, and edward shall be ours. 4.03. 25
i'll follow you, and tell what answer | lewis 4.03. 55
he'll soon find means to make the body follow. 4.07. 26
and all those friends that deign to follow me. 4.07. 39
lamb, | the lamb will never cease to follow him. 4.08. 50
go you before, and i will follow you. R3 1.01.144
or like obedient subjects follow him | to his 2.02. 45
pursues | were to incense the boar to follow us, 3.02. 29
the rest that love me, rise, and follow me. 3.04. 79
had rather have us win than him they follow: 5.03.244
for what is he they follow? 5.03.245
directed, we will follow | in the main battle, 5.03.298
i'll follow and outstare him. H8 1.01.129
do a vessel follow | that is new trimm'd, but 1.02. 79
and heav'nly blessings | follow such creatures. 2.03. 58
how eagerly ye follow my disgraces | as if it 3.02.240
follow your envious courses, men of malice! 3.02.243
do you not follow the young lord paris? TRO 3.01. 2 P
on, lord, we'll follow you. 4.01. 50
follow his torch, he goes to calchas' tent. 5.01. 85
follow me, sirs, and my proceedings eye, | it is 5.07. 7
follow cominius; COR 1.01.246
we must follow you, | right worthy you priority. 1.01.246
nay, let them follow. 1.01.248
pray follow. 1.01.251
follow 's. 1.04. 42
express his disposition, | and follow martius. 1.06. 75
whither do you follow your eyes so fast? 2.01. 98 P
therefore follow me, and i'll direct you how you 2.03. 46 P
i charge thee, | and follow to thine answer. 3.01.176
he must come, | or what is worst will follow. 3.01.334
rather | follow thine enemy in a fiery gulf 3.02. 91
go see him out at gates, and follow him, | as he 3.03.138
i'll follow thee a month, devise with thee 4.01. 38
follow your function, go, and batten on cold 4.05. 32 P
and they follow him | against us brats with no 4.06. 92
corse that ever herald | did follow to his urn. 5.06.144
follow, my lord, and i'll soon bring her back. TIT 1.01.289
and i have horse will follow where the game 2.02. 23
thou shalt not bail them, see thou follow me. 2.03.299
come, marcus, let us go. publius, follow me. 4.03.121
be bold in us, we'll follow where thou lead'st, 5.01. 13
i beseech you follow straight. ROM 1.03.103 P
we follow thee. juliet, the county stays. 1.03.104
and follow thee my lord throughout the world. 2.02.148
follow me this jest now, till thou hast worn out 2.04. 61 P
i will follow you. 2.04.142 P
follow me close, for i will speak to them. 3.01. 37
to follow this fair corse unto her grave. 4.05. 93
on the moment | follow his strides, his lobbies TIM 1.01. 80
i do not always follow lover, elder brother, and 2.02.121 P
i'll follow and inquire him out. 4.02. 48
follow thy drum, | with man's blood paint the 4.03. 59
flatteries | that follow youth and opulency. 5.01. 37
what tributaries follow him to rome, | to grace JC 1.01. 33
as i was, i plunged in | and bade him follow; 1.02.106
if the redress will follow, thou receivest | thy 2.01. 57
for he will never follow any thing | that other 2.01.151
foot, | and with a heart new–fir'd i follow you, 2.01.332
follow me then. 2.01.334
but will follow | the fortunes and affairs of 3.01.134
prepare the body then, and follow us. 3.01.253
then follow me, and give me audience, friends. 3.02. 2
those that will follow cassius, go with him; 3.02. 6
we'll hear him, we'll follow him, we'll die with 3.02.208 P
his pow'rs betimes before, | and we will follow. 4.03.308
i will follow. 5.05. 43
octavius, then take him to follow thee, | that 5.05. 66
and it must follow, as the night the day, | thou HAM 1.03. 79
it will not speak, then i will follow it. 1.04. 63
it waves me forth again, i'll follow it. 1.04. 68
it waves me still. — | go on, i'll follow thee. 1.04. 79
go on, i'll follow thee. 1.04. 86
let's follow. 'tis not fit thus to obey him. 1.04. 88
nay, let's follow him. 1.04. 91
follow him, friends, we'll hear a play to–morrow 2.02.535 P
follow that lord, and look you mock him not. 2.02.545 P
of the knee | where thrift may follow fawning. 3.02. 62
follow him at foot, tempt him with speed aboard. 4.03. 54
follow her close, give her good watch, i pray 4.05. 74
upon another's heel, | so fast they follow. 4.07.164
let's follow, gertrude. 4.07.191
give it start again, | therefore let's follow. 4.07.194
but to follow him thither with modesty enough 5.01.207 P
who is this they follow? 5.01.218
the corse they follow did with desp'rate hand 5.01.220
to my purposes, they follow the king's pleasure. 5.02.200 P
follow my mother! 5.02.327
i follow thee. 5.02.332
ruinous disorders follow us disquietly to our LR 1.02.114 P
other day, what should follow these eclipses. 1.02.141 P
follow me, thou shalt serve me. 1.04. 40 P
if thou follow him, thou must needs wear my 1.04.103 P
commanded me to follow, and attend | the leisure 2.04. 36
follow me not, | stay here. 2.04. 59
all that follow their noses are led by their 2.04. 69 P
i would have none but knaves follow it, since a 2.04. 76 P
to follow in a house where twice so many | have 2.04.262
up, | and follow me, that will to some provision 3.06. 96
follow me, lady. 3.07. 95
i should show | what party i do follow. 4.05. 40
go follow them to prison. 5.03. 27
i would not follow him then. OTH 1.01. 40
i follow him to serve my turn upon him. 1.01. 42
in following him, i follow but myself; 1.01. 58
follow thou the wars; 1.03.340 P
i do follow here in the chase, not like a hound 2.03.363 P
to follow still the changes of the moon | with 3.03.178
and let worse follow worse, till the worst of ANT 1.02. 66 P
till the worst of all follow him laughing to his 1.02. 66 P
/abstract of all faults | that all men follow. 1.04. 10
at thy heel | did famine follow, whom thou 1.04. 59
the water which they beat to follow faster, | as 2.02.196
follow me, and receive't. 2.03. 43
will e'en but kiss octavia, and we'll follow. 2.04. 3
and what may follow, | to try a larger fortune. 2.06. 33
or the mean, if dearth | or foison follow. 2.07. 20
i'll never follow thy pall'd fortunes more. 2.07. 82
sword is warm, | the fugitive parthians follow. 3.01. 7
i'll yet follow | the wounded chance of antony, 3.10. 34
why should he follow? 3.13. 6
follow me. 3.13. 28
endure | to follow with allegiance a fall'n lord 3.13. 44
be thou sorry | to follow caesar in his triumph, 3.13.136
follow the noise so far as we have quarter; 4.03. 21
fight, | follow me close, i'll bring you to't. 4.04. 34
follow his chariot, like the greatest spot | of 4.12. 35
pray let us follow 'em. CYM 1.04.172 P
let's follow him and pervert the present wrath 2.04.151
own love will out of this advise you, follow. 3.02. 45 P
son, i say, follow the king. 3.05. 53
would i had wings to follow it! 3.05.156 P
i'll follow those that even now fled hence, 4.02. 98
physic, must | all follow this and come to dust. 4.02.269
i'll follow, sir. 4.02.387
sigh, | and leaving so his service, follow you, 4.02.393
let thy effects | so follow, to be most unlike 5.04.136
follow me then. lord helicane, a word. PER 2.04. 21
well, follow me, my masters, you shall have your 4.02. 53 P
performance shall follow. 4.02. 63 P
come your ways, follow me. 4.02.145 P
queens, | follow your soldier. TNK 1.01.211
sir, | i'll follow you at heels; 1.01.221
striving, and to follow | the common stream, 1.02. 9
by any generous bond to follow him | follows his 1.02. 50
and let us follow | the becking of our chance. 1.02.115
stood staggering whether he should follow | his 4.01. 10
we'll follow cheerfully. 5.04. 39
the dire imagination she did follow | this sound VEN 975
to follow that which flies before her face, SON 143. 7
follow'd it as gentle day | doth follow night, 145.11
/FOLLOW'D 1 FR 0.0001 REL FR 1 V 0 P
/he's /follow'd /both /with /body /and /with 2H4 1.01.203
FOLLOW'D 34 FR 0.0038 REL FR 24 V 10 P
thence i have follow'd it, | or it hath drawn me TMP 1.02.394
that calf–like they my lowing follow'd through 4.01.179
follow'd her with a doting observance; WIV 2.02.195 P

you here, that you follow'd not to leonato's? ADO 1.01.205 P
well follow'd: judas was hang'd on an elder. LLL 5.02.606 P
they would be better if well follow'd. MV 1.02. 11 P
that /she would have follow'd her exile, or have AYL 1.01.109 P
devil lead the measure, such are to be follow'd. AWW 2.01. 56 P
o, had i but follow'd the arts! TN 1.03. 94 P
how with a sportful malice it was follow'd | may 5.01.365
hear me, and the words that follow'd | should be WT 5.01. 66
but i follow'd me close, came in, foot and hand, 1H4 2.04.216 P
of all exploits since first i follow'd arms, 1H6 2.01. 43
and follow'd with a rabble that rejoice | to see 2H6 2.04. 32
we follow'd then our lord, our sovereign king. R3 1.03.146
now | came to me as i follow'd henry's corse, 4.01. 66
that dear saint which then i weeping follow'd — 4.01. 69
and follow'd with the general throng and sweat H8 pr 28
after the hideous storm that follow'd, was | a 1.01. 90
(nay, let 'em be unmanly), yet are follow'd. 1.03. 4
but what follow'd? 4.01. 81
have follow'd both my fortunes faithfully, | of 4.02.141
as he hath follow'd you, with all despite; COR 3.03.139
are they so follow'd? HAM 2.02.335 P
lov'd as my father, as my master follow'd, | as LR 1.01.141
that follow'd me so near (o, our lives' 5.03.185
and decay, | have follow'd your sad steps — 5.03.290
nor all masters | cannot be truly follow'd. OTH 1.01. 44
what was he that you follow'd with your sword? 2.03.284 P
o, | i follow'd that i blush to look upon. ANT 3.11. 12
a fitment for | the purpose i then follow'd. CYM 5.05.410
much follow'd both, for both much money gi'n, TNK pr 2
haply so long until | the follow'd make pursuit? 1.02. 52
with an end | that follow'd it as gentle day SON 145.10

FOLLOW'DST 1 FR 0.0001 REL FR 0 V 1 P
i' faith, and thou follow'dst him like a church. 2H4 2.04.230 P

/FOLLOWED 1 FR 0.0001 REL FR 1 V 0 P
/in /disguise | /followed /his /enemy /king, LR 5.03.221

FOLLOWED 29 FR 0.0032 REL FR 28 V 1 P
it should have followed in the end of our show. LLL 5.02.887 P
he followed you; MND 3.02.311
for love i followed him. 3.02.311
i followed fast, but faster he did fly, | that 3.02.416
this wood, | and i in fury hither followed them, 4.01.162
you are there followed by a faithful shepherd — AYL 5.02. 81
which, followed well, would demonstrate them now AWW 1.02. 47
which must be ev'n as swiftly followed as | i WT 1.02.409
cry | hath followed certain men unto this house. 1H4 2.04.508
followed him | even at the heels in golden 4.03. 72
so fought, so followed, and so fairly won, 2H4 1.01. 21
you see this chase is hotly followed, friends. H5 2.04. 68
be the thronging troops that followed thee? R3 4.04. 96
since i have ever followed thee with hate, COR 4.05. 98
why followed not, when she said, "tybalt's dead, ROM 3.02.118
how this lord is followed! TIM 1.01. 39
but followed | the sug'red game before thee. 4.03.258
mark how the blood of caesar followed it, | as JC 3.02.178
with which she followed my poor father's body, HAM 1.02.148
indeed, my lord, it followed hard upon. 1.02.179
but kept a reservation to be followed | with LR 2.04.252
followed the old man forth. he is return'd. 2.04.295
i little thought | you would have followed. ANT 3.11. 56
thee, would have still | followed thy heels. 4.05. 6
o antony, | i have followed thee to this; 5.01. 36
o, behold, | how pomp is followed! 5.02.151
nay, followed him till he had melted from | the CYM 1.03. 20
so | followed my banishment, and this twenty 3.03. 69
/wear) i followed | for my most serious decking. TNK 1.03. 73

FOLLOWER 10 FR 0.0011 REL FR 7 V 3 P
you were wont to be a follower, but now you are WIV 3.02. 2 P
to become | the follower of so poor a gentleman. MV 2.02.148
suit, | a gentleman, and follower of my lady's. TN 5.01.277
pointing–stock | to every idle rascal follower. 2H6 2.04. 47
till at the last | i seem'd his follower, not COR 5.06. 38
go before to field, he'll be your follower; ROM 3.01. 58
i'll receive him gladly, | but not one follower. LR 2.04.293
beware my follower. 3.04.140 P
gratitude, but be a diligent follower of mine. CYM 3.05.120 P
youngest follower of thy drum, instruct this day TNK 5.01. 57

FOLLOWERS' 1 FR 0.0001 REL FR 0 V 1 P
me, but only my followers' base and ignominious 2H6 4.08. 63 P

/FOLLOWERS 3 FR 0.0003 REL FR 3 V 0 P
/by /your /person /and /your /followers R2 4.01.224
/like /to /my /followers /in /prosperity, 4.01.280
/with /a /double /surety /binds /his /followers. 2H4 1.01.191

FOLLOWERS 39 FR 0.0044 REL FR 32 V 7 P
spirit, | how fares the king and 's followers? TMP 5.01. 7
think, no other treasure to give your followers; TGV 2.04. 45 P
host, i must turn away some of my followers. WIV 1.03. 5 P
to the world's end, will have bald followers. ERR 2.02.107 P
wishes and tears, poor fancy's followers. MND 1.01.155
invite the duke and all 's contented followers. AYL 5.02. 15 P
could not sway her house, command her followers, TN 4.03. 17
your followers i will whisper to the business, WT 1.02.437
what became of his bark and his followers? 5.02. 67 P
discharge my followers, let them hence away, R2 3.02.217
with poins, and other his continual followers. 2H4 4.04. 53
perfectness of time | cast off his followers, 4.04. 75
he hath intent his wonted followers | shall all 5.05. 98
coronets, | promis'd to harry and his followers. H5 2.pr. 11
he hath betray'd his followers, whose 3.06.135 P
with his fat–brain'd followers so far out of his 3.07.133 P
thou wilt mind | thy followers of repentance; 4.03. 85
truce | betwixt ourselves and all our followers. 1H6 3.01.139
and leave my followers here to fight and die? 4.05. 45
and i to norfolk with my followers. 3H6 1.01.208
and all my followers to the eager foe | turn 1.04. 3
ah, hark, the fatal followers do pursue, | and i 1.04. 22
this soft courage makes your followers faint. 2.02. 57
that his chief followers lodge in towns about 4.03. 13
brave followers, yonder stands the thorny wood, 5.04. 67
when he had done, some followers of mine own, R3 3.07. 34
where be thy tenants and thy followers? 4.04.480
in this | are dogg'd with two strange followers. TRO 1.03.364
'tis for the followers fortune widens them, COR 1.04. 44
and, countrymen, my loving followers, | plead my TIT 1.01. 3
friends, followers, favorers of my right, | if 1.01. 9
dismiss your followers, and, as suitors should, 1.01. 44
state, | will use you nobly and your followers. 1.01.260
what, fifty of my followers at a clap? LR 1.04.294
she have restrain'd the riots of your followers, 2.04.143
what, fifty followers? 2.04.237
to make his followers weep. ANT 4.02. 24
thy death and fortunes bid thy followers fly. 4.14.111
not live to wear | all your true followers out. 4.14.134

FOLLOWEST 1 FR 0.0001 REL FR 0 V 1 P
thou for wages followest thy master, thy master TGV 1.01. 91 P

/FOLLOWING 1 FR 0.0001 REL FR 1 V 0 P
assaulted, | /for /following /her /affairs. LR 2.02.150

FOLLOWING 31 FR 0.0035 REL FR 24 V 7 P
bear) | had made provision for her following me, ERR 1.01. 47
in manner and form following, sir, all those LLL 1.01.205 P
the form, and taken following her into the park, 1.01.207 P
put together, is in manner and form following. 1.01.209 P
for the following, sir? 1.01.212 P
following the signs, woo'd but the sign of she. 5.02.469
with pretty and with swimming gait | following MND 2.01.131
there is no following her in this fierce vein. 3.02. 82
them, | fair helena in fancy following me. 4.01.163
of the sun, | following darkness like a dream, 5.01.386
talk with you, walk with you, and so following; MV 1.03. 36 P
now on the sunday following shall bianca | be SHR 2.01.395
back, not following | my leash unwillingly. WT 4.04.465
following the mirror of all christian kings, H5 2.pr. 6
and his advantage following your decease, | that 2H6 3.01. 25
the crown, | in following this usurping henry. 3H6 1.01. 81
each following day | became the next day's H8 1.01. 16
following the fliers at the very heels, | with COR 1.04. 49
but with a rearward following tybalt's death, ROM 3.02.121
if, on the tenth day following, | thy banish'd LR 1.01.176
knowing nought (like dogs) but following. 2.02. 80
a hill, lest it break thy neck with following; 2.04. 73 P
in following him, i follow but myself; OTH 1.01. 58
see suitors following, and not look behind: 2.01.157
and cassio following him with determin'd sword 2.03.227
if thou the next night following enjoy not 4.02.215 P
since | thou hast been whipt for following him. ANT 3.13.137
will in that kingdom spend our following days. PER 5.03. 81
following the dead–cold ashes of their sons, TNK 4.02. 5
what following sorrow may on this arise. LUC 186
in personal duty, following where he haunted. LC 130

FOLLOWS 66 FR 0.0074 REL FR 49 V 17 P
the shepherd for food follows not the sheep; TGV 1.01. 90 P
master, thy master for wages follows not thee: 1.01. 92 P
it follows not that she will love sir thurio. 3.02. 50
that flies her fortune when it follows her. 5.02. 50
and follows close the rigor of the statute, | to MM 1.04. 67
granted in course — and now follows all — we 3.01.249 P
disquiet, horror, and perturbation follows her. ADO 2.01.261 P
how follows that? LLL 1.01. 98
the more i hate, the more he follows me. MND 1.01.198
proof, | because what follows is pure innocence. MV 1.01.145
a good divine that follows his own instructions; 1.02. 15 P
then it follows thus: SHR 1.01.201
but follows it, my lord, to bring me down | must AWW 2.03.112
respect than any one else that follows her. TN 2.05. 27 P
what follows? 2.05.100 P
soft, here follows prose. 2.05.142 P
to do this deed, | promotion follows. WT 1.02.357
and what to her adheres, which follows after, 4.01. 28
what follows this? 4.04.365
this follows, if you will not change your 4.04.542
what follows if we disallow of this? JN 1.01. 16
how ill it follows, after you have labor'd so 2H4 2.02. 28 P
it follows then the cat must stay at home, | yet H5 1.02.174
or else what follows? 2.04. 96
and follows so the ever–running year | with 4.01.276
and the liberty that follows our places stops 5.02.271 P
pride went before, ambition follows him. 2H6 1.01.180
our ranks are broke, and ruin follows us. 3H6 2.03. 10
g, | it follows in his thought that i am he. R3 1.01. 59
without her, follows to myself and thee, 4.04.407
now this follows | (which, as i take it, is a H8 1.01.174
if i command him, follows my appointment; 2.02.133
it faints me | to think what follows. 2.03.104
then follows, that | i weigh'd the danger which 2.04.197
charles, good night. | well, sir, what follows? 5.01. 79
and am right sorry to repeat what follows. 5.01. 96
and what follows then? 5.02. 62
that string, | and hark what discord follows. TRO 1.03.110
when degree is suffocate, | follows the choking, 1.03.126
more ready to cry out, "who knows what follows?" 2.02. 13
i had your heart before, this follows it. 5.02. 83
follows it that i am known well enough too? COR 2.01. 63 P
these | in honor follows coriolanus. 2.01.165
barr'd, it follows | nothing is done to purpose. 3.01.148
my aunt lavinia | follows me every where, i know TIT 4.01. 2
what's he that follows here, that would not ROM 1.05.132
the swallow follows not summer more willing than TIM 3.06. 29 P
the throng that follows caesar at the heels, JC 2.04. 34
the love that follows us sometime is our trouble MAC 1.06. 11
now follows that you know young fortinbras, HAM 1.02. 17
nay, that follows not. 2.02.413 P
what follows then, my lord? 2.02.414 P
look you now what follows: 3.04. 63
was under ursa major, so that it follows, i am LR 1.02.130 P
would buy a halter, | so the fool follows after. 1.04.321
and seeks for gain, | and follows but for form, 2.04. 79
dwells in the /fickle grace of her he follows. 2.04.186
away, the foul fiend follows me! 3.04. 46 P
so the acquittance follows. CYM 5.04.170 P
happy what follows! PER 3.01. 31
bond to follow him | follows his tailor, haply TNK 1.02. 51
how his longing | follows his friend: 1.03. 27
against /thy own edict, follows thy sister, 3.06.145
what follows more, she murthers with a kiss. VEN 54
covers the shame that follows sweet delight." LUC 357
for still temptation follows where thou art. SON 41. 4

FOLLOW'ST 1 FR 0.0001 REL FR 1 V 0 P
and a loyal sir | to him thou follow'st! TMP 5.01. 70

FOLLY 85 FR 0.0096 REL FR 59 V 26 P
the folly of this island! TMP 3.02. 4 P
however — but a folly bought with wit, | or TGV 1.01. 34
with wit, | or else a wit by folly vanquished. 1.01. 35
the young and tender wit | is turn'd to folly, 1.01. 48
lord, lord! to see what folly reigns in us! 1.02. 15
back | and ask remission for my folly past. 1.02. 65
your own present folly, and her passing 2.01. 75 P
your folly. 2.04. 17 P
and how quote you my folly? 2.04. 18 P
well then i'll double your folly. 2.04. 21 P
car, | and with thy daring folly burn the world? 3.01.155
that the folly of my soul dares not present WIV 2.02.244 P
he gives her folly motion and advantage; 3.02. 35 P
why, this is your own folly. 5.05.194 P
either this is envy in you, folly, or mistaking. MM 3.02.141 P
nor no great argument of her folly, for i will ADO 2.03.234 P
sweet leaves, shade folly. LLL 4.03. 42
folly, in wisdom hatch'd, | hath wisdom's 5.02. 70
folly in fools bears not so strong a note | as 5.02. 75
to check their folly, passion's solemn tears. 5.02.118
his folly, helena, is no fault of mine. MND 1.01.200
quiet go, | to athens will i bear my folly back, 3.02.315
if thou remembr'est not the slightest folly AYL 2.04. 34
so is all nature in love mortal in folly. 2.04. 56 P
and they that are most galled with my folly, 2.07. 50
the wise man's folly is anatomiz'd | even by the 2.07. 56
suits | his folly to the mettle of my speech? 2.07. 82
friendship is feigning, most loving mere folly. 2.07.181
all's brave that youth mounts and folly guides. 3.04. 46 P
he uses his folly like a stalking–horse, and 5.04.106 P
see | cold wisdom waiting on superfluous folly. AWW 1.01.105
for i know you lack not folly to commit them, 1.03. 11 P
as mad in folly, lack'd the sense to know | her 5.03. 3
infirmity, for the better increasing your folly! TN 1.05. 79 P
no, indeed, sir, the lady olivia has no folly. 3.01. 32 P
for folly that he wisely shows is fit, | but 3.01. 67
i prithee vent thy folly somewhere else, | thou 4.01. 10
vent my folly! 4.01. 12 P
vent my folly! 4.01. 14 P
how sometimes nature will betray its folly! WT 1.02.151
is free | but that his negligence, his folly, 1.02.252
i were willful–negligent, | it was my folly; 1.02.256
or counsel shake | the fabric of his folly, 1.02.429
but that our feasts | in every mess have folly, 4.04. 11
and then i lost | (all mine own folly) the 5.01.135
your fault was not your folly; JN 1.01.262
thing the purpose must weigh with the folly. 2H4 2.02.176 P
covering discretion with a coat of folly, | as H5 2.04. 38
england shall repent his folly, see his weakness 3.06.124 P
o, too much folly is it, well i wot, | to hazard 1H6 4.06. 32
humors that his valor is crush'd into folly, his TRO 1.02. 23 P
into folly, his folly sauc'd with discretion. 1.02. 23 P
common curse of mankind, folly and ignorance, be 2.03. 28 P
that wisdom knits not, folly may easily untie. 2.03.101 P
uncle, what folly i commit, i dedicate to you. 3.02.102 P
his insolence draws folly from my lips, | but 4.05.258
sweet honey greek, tempt me no more to folly. 5.02. 18
wondrous malicious, | or be accus'd of folly. COR 1.01. 89
nor did you think it folly | to keep your great 1.02. 19
a nettle, and | the faults of fools but folly. 2.01.191
he said 'twas folly, | for one poor grain or two 5.01. 26
kill, | what folly 'tis to hazard life for ill! TIM 3.05. 37
what? quite unmann'd in folly? MAC 3.04. 72
to do good sometime | accounted dangerous folly. 4.02. 77
would blaze, | but that this folly drowns it. HAM 4.07.191
honor's bound, | when majesty falls to folly. LR 1.01.149
that let thy folly in | and thy dear judgment 1.04.271
from rest, | and must needs taste his folly. 2.04.291
for even her folly help'd her to an heir. OTH 2.01.137
in him that folly and green minds look after; 2.01.246 P
she turn'd to folly, and she was a whore. 5.02.132
though age from folly could not give me freedom, ANT 1.03. 57
hence, | therefore be deaf to my unpitied folly, 1.03. 98
held to fools does make | our faith mere folly; 3.13. 43
a day, and, being aged, | die of this folly! CYM 1.01.158
instructions enter | where folly now possesses? 1.05. 48
that it was folly in me, thou mayst say, | and 5.05. 67
the sun has seen my folly. TNK 3.04. 3
lo, cousin, lo, our folly has undone us. 3.06.107
how love is wise in folly, foolish witty. VEN 838
her sad behavior feeds his vulture folly, | a LUC 556
or tyrant folly lurk in gentle breasts? 851
short | his time of folly and his time of sport; 992
without this, folly, age, and cold decay. SON 11. 6
and folly (doctor–like) controlling skill, | and 66.10

FOLLY–FALL'N 1 FR 0.0001 REL FR 1 V 0 P
but wise /men, folly–fall'n, quite taint their TN 3.01. 68

FOLLY'S 1 FR 0.0001 REL FR 1 V 0 P
burying in lucrece' wound his folly's show. LUC 1810

/FOND 3 FR 0.0003 REL FR 3 V 0 P
as praises, of whose taste the wise are /fond, R2 2.01. 18
/o /thou /fond /many, /with /what /loud 2H4 1.03. 91
for though /fond nature bids us all lament, ROM 4.05. 82

FOND 61 FR 0.0069 REL FR 57 V 4 P
counsel thee | that art a votary to fond desire? TGV 1.01. 52
if this fond love were not a blinded god? 4.04.196
now, as fond fathers, | having bound up the MM 1.03. 23
not with fond sicles of the tested gold, | or 2.02.149
when men were fond, i smil'd and wond'red how. 2.02.186
by heaven, fond wretch, thou know'st not what 5.01.105
how many fond fools serve mad jealousy? ERR 2.01.116
prove | more fond on her than she upon her love; MND 2.01.266
o, i am out of breath in this fond chase! 2.02. 88
shall we their fond pageant see? 3.02.114
you see how simple and how fond i am. 3.02.317
not learning more than the fond eye doth teach, MV 2.09. 27
that thou art so fond | to come abroad with him 3.03. 9
why would you be so fond to overcome | the bonny AYL 2.03. 7
with a world | of pretty, fond, adoptious AWW 1.01.174
fond done, done fond, | was this king priam's 1.03. 72
fond done, done fond, | was this king priam's 1.03. 72
my lord, this is a fond and desp'rate creature, 5.03.178
and i (poor monster) fond as much on him; TN 2.02. 34
are you so fond of your young prince as we | do WT 1.02.164
th' effects of his fond jealousies so grieving 4.01. 18
for thee, fond boy, | if i may ever know thou 4.04.426
you are as fond of grief as of your child. JN 3.04. 92
then, have i reason to be fond of grief? 3.04. 98
we make woe wanton with this fond delay, | once R2 5.01.101
thou fond mad woman, | wilt thou conceal this 5.02. 95
away, fond woman, were he twenty times my son, 5.02.101

i laugh to see your ladyship so fond | to think 1H6 2.03. 45
fond man, remember that thou hast a wife, | then 5.03. 81
if it be fond, call it a woman's fear; 2H6 3.01. 36
what's more dangerous than this fond affiance! 3.01. 74
for i, too fond, might have prevented this. R3 3.04. 81
who (but for dreaming on this fond exploit) 5.03.330
women | 'tis fond to wail inevitable strokes, COR 4.01. 26
when she, poor hen, fond of no second brood, 5.03.162
what beg'st thou then? fond woman, let me go. TIT 2.03.172
in truth, fair montague, i am too fond, | and ROM 2.02. 98
/thou fond mad man, hear me a little speak. 3.03. 52
grant i may never prove so fond, | to trust man TIM 1.02. 64
why do fond men expose themselves to battle, 3.05. 42
be not fond | to think that caesar bears such JC 3.01. 39
i'll wipe away all trivial fond records, | all HAM 1.05. 99
i begin to find an idle and fond bondage in the LR 1.02. 49 P
old fond eyes, | beweep this cause again, i'll 1.04.301
i am a very foolish fond old man, | fourscore 4.07. 59
i confess it is my shame to be so fond, but it OTH 1.03.318 P
these are old fond paradoxes to make fools laugh 2.01.138 P
all my fond love thus do i blow to heaven. 3.03.445
if you are so fond over her iniquity, give her 4.01.197 P
she was too fond of her most filthy bargain. 5.02.157
then old and fond of issue, took such sorrow CYM 1.01. 37
or to be fond upon | another's way of speech, TNK 1.02. 46
fie, fond love, thou art as full of fear | as VEN 1021
those that much covet are with gain so fond, LUC 134
or what fond beggar, but to touch the crown, 216
full of foul hope and full of fond mistrust; 284
his hot heart, which fond desire doth scorch, 314
true grief is fond and testy as a child, | who 1094
thy heat of lust, fond paris, did incur | this 1473
or who is he so fond will be the tomb, | of his SON 3. 7
being fond on praise, which makes your praises 84.14

FONDER 1 FR 0.0001 REL FR 1 V 0 P
tear, | tamer than sleep, fonder than ignorance, TRO 1.01. 10

FONDLING 1 FR 0.0001 REL FR 1 V 0 P
"fondling," she saith, "since i have hemm'd thee VEN 229

FONDLY 10 FR 0.0011 REL FR 10 V 0 P
how fondly dost thou reason! ERR 4.02. 57
that i have fondly flatter'd /her withal. SHR 4.02. 31
but if you fondly pass our proffer'd offer, JN 2.01.258
plays fondly with her tears and smiles in R2 3.02. 9
makes him speak fondly like a frantic man, | yet 3.03.185
how fondly dost thou spur a forward horse! 4.01. 72
fondly brought here and foolishly sent hence. 2H4 4.02.119
got, | my careless father fondly gave away"? 3H6 2.02. 38
which fondly you would here impose on me. R3 3.07.147
contrive, | to cipher me how fondly i did dote; LUC 207

FONDNESS 3 FR 0.0003 REL FR 3 V 0 P
part, and in obsequious fondness | crowd to his MM 2.04. 28
my fear hath catch'd your fondness! AWW 1.03.170
been, out of fondness, superstitious to him? H8 3.01.131

/FONT 1 FR 0.0001 REL FR 1 V 0 P
/not /that /name /was /given /me /at /the /font, R2 4.01.256

FONT 1 FR 0.0001 REL FR 1 V 0 P
to bring thee to the gallows, not to the font. MV 4.01.400

FONTIBELL 1 FR 0.0001 REL FR 1 V 0 P
they told me that your name was fontibell. AWW 4.02. 1

/FOOD 1 FR 0.0001 REL FR 0 V 1 P
/black /angel, /i /have /no /food /for /thee. LR 3.06. 32 P

FOOD 70 FR 0.0079 REL FR 57 V 13 P
some food we had, and some fresh water, that | a TMP 1.02.160
thy food shall be | the fresh–brook mussels, 1.02.463
the shepherd for food follows not the sheep; TGV 1.01. 90 P
know'st thou not his looks are my soul's food? 2.07. 15
in, | by longing for that food so long a time. 2.07. 17
young ravens must have food. WIV 1.03. 35 P
it would give eternal food to his jealousy. 2.01.101 P
my food, my fortune, and my sweet hope's aim, ERR 3.02. 63
in food, in sport, and life–preserving rest | to 5.01. 83
she hath such meet food to feed it as signior ADO 1.01.121 P
thither, this may prove food to my displeasure. 1.03. 66 P
and one day in a week to touch no food, | and LLL 1.01. 39
food for his rage, repasture for his den." 4.01. 93
from lovers' food till morrow deep midnight. MND 1.01.223
but like a sickness did i loathe this food; 4.01.173
fed with the same food, hurt with the same MV 3.01. 61 P
hard food for midas, i will none of thee; 3.02.102
what, wouldst thou have me go and beg my food?
AYL 2.03. 31
yond man | if he for gold will give us any food; 2.04. 65
to live i' th' sun, | seeking the food he eats, 2.05. 40
o, i die for food! 2.06. 2 P
i will either be food for it or bring it for 2.06. 7 P
be food for it or bring it for food to thee. 2.06. 8 P
as i do live by food, i met a fool, | who laid 2.07. 14
i almost die for food, and let me have it. 2.07.104
then forbear your food a little while, | whiles, 2.07.127
a doe, i go to find my fawn | and give it food. 2.07.129
chewing the food of sweet and bitter fancy, | lo 4.03.101
there, | food to the suck'd and hungry lioness? 4.03.126
i care not what, so it be wholesome food. SHR 4.03. 16
if music be the food of love, play on, | give me TN 1.01. 1
my life, my joy, my food, my all the world! JN 3.04.104
with eager feeding food doth choke the feeder; R2 2.01. 37
that brings me food to make misfortune live? 5.05. 71
good enough to toss, food for powder, food for 1H4 4.02. 65 P
to toss, food for powder, food for powder; 4.02. 66 P
no, percy, thou art dust, | and food for — 5.04. 86
she either gives a stomach and no food — | such 2H4 4.04.105
floods o'erswell, and fiends for food howl on! H5 2.01. 93
and that's but unwholesome food, they say. 2.03. 57 P
the other lords, like lions wanting food, | do 1H6 1.02. 27
still sweet love is food for fortune's tooth. TRO 4.05.293
he, | "that i receive the general food at first COR 1.01.131
there let him stand and rave and cry for food. TIT 5.03.180
shut up in prison, kept without my food, | whipt ROM 1.02. 55
buy food, and get thyself in flesh. 5.01. 84
and in despite i'll cram thee with more food. 5.03. 48
this and my food are equals, there's no odds; TIM 1.02. 60
unmatched mind, | care of your food and living; 4.03.517
if thy revenges hunger for that food | which 5.04. 32
for food and diet, to some enterprise | that HAM 1.01. 99
nor earth to me give food, nor heaven light, 3.02.216
you'll vouchsafe me raiment, bed, and food." LR 2.04.156
should tear this hand | for lifting food to't? 3.04. 16
have been tom's food for seven long year. 3.04.139
and bring you where both fire and food is ready. 3.04.153
edgar, | the food of thy abused father's wrath! 4.01. 22
the food that to him now is as luscious as OTH 1.03.347 P
they are all but stomachs, and we all but food; 3.04.104
music, moody food | of us that trade in love. ANT 2.05. 1
and throw between them all the food thou hast, 3.05. 14
even before, i was | at point to sink for food. CYM 3.06. 17
who wanteth food and will not say he wants it, PER 1.04. 11
thy food is such | as hath been belch'd on by 4.06.168
uses | (the food and nourishment of noble minds) TNK 2.02. 52
keep close | till i provide him files and food, 2.06. 7
food took i none these two days — | sipp'd some 3.02. 26
i have brought you food and files. 3.03. 2
he ten times pines that pines beholding food, LUC 1115
so are you to my thoughts as food to life, | or SON 75. 1

'FOOL 1 FR 0.0001 REL FR 1 V 0 P
what 'fool is she, that knows i am a maid, | and TGV 1.02. 53

/FOOL* 12 FR 0.0013 REL FR 3 V 9 P
/peace, /fool, /i /have /not /done. TRO 2.03. 56 P
/agamemnon /is /a /fool, /achilles /is /a /fool, 2.03. 58 P
/agamemnon /is /a /fool, /achilles /is /a /fool, 2.03. 58 P
/achilles /is /a /fool, /thersites /is /a /fool, 2.03. 59 P
/and, /as /aforesaid, /patroclus /is /a /fool. 2.03. 60 P
/the /lamenting /fool /in //sea–salt /tears. TIT 3.02. 20
why, /fool? LR 1.04. 98 P
/the /sweet /and /bitter /fool | /will 1.04.144
/dost /thou /call /me /fool, /boy? 1.04.148 P
/this /is /not /altogether /fool, /my /lord. 1.04.151 P
/not /let /me /have /all /the /fool /to /myself, 1.04.155 P
/whilst /thou, /a /moral /fool, /sits /still 4.02. 58

FOOL* 380 FR 0.0429 REL FR 194 V 186 P
not a holiday fool there but would give a piece TMP 2.02. 29 P
i am a fool | to weep at what i am glad of. 3.01. 73
let it alone, thou fool, it is but trash. 4.01.224
the dropsy drown this fool! 4.01.230
for a god, | and worship this dull fool! 5.01.298
so, by your circumstance, you call me fool. TGV 1.01. 36
and he that is so yoked by a fool, | methinks 1.01. 40
why, fool, i meant not thee, i meant thy master. 2.05. 49 P
i am but a fool, look you, and yet i have the 3.01.263 P
come, fool, come; try me in thy paper. 3.01.299 P
alas, poor fool, why do i pity him | that with 4.04. 93
true — from a gentleman to a fool. 5.02. 24
i hold him but a fool that will endanger | his 5.04.133
though page be a secure fool, and stands so WIV 2.01.233 P
good mother, do not marry me to yond fool. 3.04. 83
"will you cast away your child on a fool, and a 3.04. 96 P
that hath the jealious fool to her husband! 4.02.131 P
you are a tedious fool. MM 2.01.115 P
merely, thou art death's fool, | for him thou 3.01. 11
and was the duke a fleshmonger, a fool, and a 5.01.334 P
you, sirrah, that knew me for a fool, a coward, 5.01.500
i familiarly sometimes | do use you for my fool, ERR 2.02. 27
come, come, no longer will i be a fool, | to put 2.02.203
his man with scissors nicks him like a fool; 5.01.175
peace, fool, thy master and his man are here, 5.01.178
cupid at the flight, and my uncle's fool, ADO 1.01. 41 P
what is he for a fool that betroths himself to 1.03. 47 P
he is the prince's jester, a very dull fool; 2.01.138 P
for the fool will eat no supper that night. 2.01.149 P
the prince's fool! 2.01.204 P
i thank it — poor fool, it keeps on the windy 2.01.314 P
much another man is a fool when he dedicates his 2.03. 8 P
of me, he shall never make me such a fool. 2.03. 26 P
as it appears he hath, he is no fool for fancy, 3.02. 38 P
tush, i may as well say the fool's the fool. 3.03.123 P
my cousin's a fool, and thou art another. 3.04. 11 P
what means the fool, trow? 3.04. 59 P
lady, i am not such a fool to think what i list, 3.04. 82 P
call me a fool, | trust not my reading, nor my 4.01.164
i speak not like a dotard nor a fool, | as under 5.01. 59
for "school," "fool," a babbling rhyme: 5.02. 39 P
is the fool sick? LLL 2.01.184
become me to be vain, /indiscreet, or a fool, 4.02. 30
for so they say the fool said, and so say i, and 4.03. 4 P
say the fool said, and so say i, and i the fool: 4.03. 5 P
the clown bore it, the fool sent it, and the 4.03. 16 P
sweet clown, sweeter fool, sweetest lady! 4.03. 17 P
now, in thy likeness, one more fool appear! 4.03. 44
what fool is not so wise | to lose an oath to 4.03. 70
three fools lack'd me fool to make up the mess. 4.03.203
that he should be my fool and i his fate. 5.02. 68
when they are catch'd, | as wit turn'd fool; 5.02. 70
and wit's own grace to grace a learned fool. 5.02. 72
i am a fool, and full of poverty. 5.02.380
all the fool mine? 5.02.384
the hedge–priest, the fool, and the boy: 5.02.543 P
seeking sweet favors for this hateful fool, | i MND 4.01. 49
but man is but /a /patch'd fool, if he will 4.01.210 P
let me play the fool: MV 1.01. 79
this melancholy bait | for this fool gudgeon, 1.01.102
what says that fool of hagar's offspring, ha? 2.05. 44
that many may be meant | by the fool multitude, 2.09. 26
still more fool i shall appear | by the time i 2.09. 73
this is the fool that lent out money gratis! 3.03. 2
i'll not be made a soft and dull–ey'd fool | to 3.03. 14
how every fool can play upon the word! 3.05. 43 P
the fool hath planted in his memory | an army of 3.05. 66
not fortune sent in this fool to cut off the AYL 1.02. 46 P
the dullness of the fool is the whetstone of the 1.02. 55 P
where learn'd you that oath, fool? 1.02. 62 P
thou art a fool; 1.03. 80
you are a fool. 1.03. 87
the clownish fool out of your father's court? 1.03.130
and thus the hairy fool, | much marked of the 2.01. 40
ay, now am i in arden, the more fool i. 2.04. 16 P
peace, fool, he's not thy kinsman. 2.04. 67
a fool, a fool! 2.07. 12
a fool, a fool! 2.07. 12
i met a fool i' th' forest, | a motley fool. 2.07. 12
i met a fool i' th' forest, | a motley fool. 2.07. 13
as i do live by food, i met a fool, | who laid 2.07. 14
in good set terms, and yet a motley fool. 2.07. 17
"good morrow, fool," quoth i. 2.07. 18
he, | "call me not fool till heaven hath sent me 2.07. 19
hear | the motley fool thus moral on the time, 2.07. 29
o noble fool! 2.07. 33
a worthy fool! 2.07. 34
what fool is this? 2.07. 35
o worthy fool! 2.07. 36
o that i were a fool! 2.07. 42
he that a fool doth very wisely hit | doth very 2.07. 53
even by the squand'ring glances of the fool. 2.07. 57
out, fool! 3.02. 99 P
peace, you dull fool, i found them on a tree. 3.02.115 P
i was seeking for a fool when i found you. 3.02.285 P
which i take to be either a fool or a cipher. 3.02.290 P
a material fool! 3.03. 32 P
i had rather have a fool to make me merry than 4.01. 28 P
herself, for she will breed it like a fool! 4.01.176 P
come, come, you are a fool, | and turn'd into 4.03. 22
a saying, "the fool doth think he is wise, but 5.01. 31 P
but the wise man knows himself to be a fool." 5.01. 32 P
he's as good at any thing, and yet a fool. 5.04.105 P
thou art a fool; SHR in.1. 26
and paint your face, and use you like a fool. 1.01. 65
any man is so very a fool to be married to hell? 1.01.125 P
ay, if the fool could find it where it lies. 2.01.212
go, fool, and whom thou keep'st command. 2.01.257
your father were a fool | to give thee all, and 2.01.400
i told you, i, he was a frantic fool, | hiding 3.02. 12
but what a fool am i to chat with you, | when i 3.02.121
tut, she's a lamb, a dove, a fool to him! 3.02.157
i see a woman may be made a fool, | if she had 3.02.220
away, you three–inch fool! i am no beast. 4.01. 26 P
the more fool you for laying on my duty. 5.02.129
think him a great way fool, soly a coward; AWW 1.01.101
if we could, i will be a fool in question, 2.02. 39 P
time, | to entertain it so merrily with a fool. 2.02. 61
go to, thou art a witty fool, i have found thee. 2.04. 32 P
profitable, and much fool may you find in you, 2.04. 35 P
this dialogue between the fool and the soldier? 4.03. 98 P
whipt for getting the shrieve's fool with child, 4.03.187 P
"dian, the count's a fool, and full of gold" — 4.03.211
for count of this, the count's a fool, i know it 4.03.229
that you would think truth were a fool. 4.03.254 P
dost thou profess thyself — a knave or a fool? 4.05. 23 P
a fool, sir, at a woman's service, and a knave 4.05. 24 P
for thee, thou art both knave and fool. 4.05. 33 P
though you are a fool and a knave, you shall eat 5.02. 53 P
he's a very fool and a prodigal. TN 1.03. 24 P
for besides that he's a fool, he's a great 1.03. 30 P
"better a witty fool than a foolish wit." 1.05. 36 P
take the fool away. 1.05. 38 P
go to, y' are a dry fool; 1.05. 41 P
for give the dry fool drink, then is the fool 1.05. 44 P
the dry fool drink, then is the fool not dry; 1.05. 45 P
the lady bade take away the fool, therefore i 1.05. 53 P
good madonna, give me leave to prove you a fool. 1.05. 58 P
good fool, for my brother's death. 1.05. 67 P
i know his soul is in heaven, fool. 1.05. 69 P
the more fool, madonna, to mourn for your 1.05. 70 P
take away the fool, gentlemen. 1.05. 71 P
what think you of this fool, malvolio? 1.05. 73 P
decays the wise, doth ever make the better fool. 1.05. 77 P
pass his word for twopence that you are no fool. 1.05. 81 P
day with an ordinary fool that has no more brain 1.05. 85 P
there is no slander in an allow'd fool, though 1.05. 94 P
madonna, as if thy eldest son should be a fool; 1.05.113 P
what's a drunken man like, fool? 1.05.130 P
like a drown'd man, a fool, and a madman. 1.05.131 P
one draught above heat makes him a fool, the 1.05.132 P
madonna, and the fool shall look to the madman. 1.05.137 P
here comes the fool, i' faith. 2.03. 15 P
by my troth, the fool has an excellent breast. 2.03. 19 P
and so sweet a breath to sing, as the fool has. 2.03. 21 P
begin, fool. 2.03. 68 P
break promise with him and make a fool of him. 2.03.128 P
plant you two, and let the fool make a third, 2.03.174 P
a fool that the lady olivia's father took much 2.04. 11 P
bear again, and we will fool him black and blue, 2.05. 10 P
i knew 'twas i, for many do call me fool. 2.05. 81 P
i do not now fool myself, to let imagination 2.05.164 P
art not thou the lady olivia's fool? 3.01. 31 P
she will keep no fool, sir, till she be married, 3.01. 33 P
i am indeed not her fool, but her corrupter of 3.01. 35 P
but the fool should be as oft with your master 3.01. 40 P
this fellow is wise enough to play the fool, 3.01. 60
i wish it might, for now i am your fool. 3.01.144
of some great man and now applies it to a fool. 4.01. 13 P
fool! 4.02. 74 P
fool! 4.02. 76 P
fool, i say! 4.02. 78 P
good fool, as ever thou wilt deserve well at my 4.02. 80 P
ay, good fool. 4.02. 85 P
fool, there was never man so notoriously abus'd; 4.02. 87 P
i am as well in my wits, fool, as thou art. 4.02. 88 P
if you be no better in your wits than a fool. 4.02. 90 P
fool, fool, fool, i say! 4.02.102 P
fool, fool, fool, i say! 4.02.102 P
fool, fool, fool, i say! 4.02.102 P
good fool, help me to some light and some paper. 4.02.105 P
good fool, some ink, paper, and light; 4.02.109 P
fool, i'll requite it in the highest degree. 4.02.118 P
you can fool no more money out of me at this 5.01. 41 P
well edified when the fool delivers the madman. 5.01.290 P
alas, poor fool, how have they baffled thee! 5.01.369
"by the lord, fool, i am not mad." 5.01.373 P
or else a fool | that seest a game play'd home, WT 1.02.247
if industriously | i play'd the fool, it was my 1.02.257
ignorant by age, | or thou wert born a fool. 2.01.174
that did but show thee, of a fool, inconstant 3.02.186
the love i bore your queen — lo, fool again! 3.02.228
must know | the royal fool thou cop'st with — 4.04.424
ha, ha, what a fool honesty is! 4.04.595 P
what a fool art thou, | a ramping fool, to brag JN 3.01.121
a ramping fool, to brag and stamp and swear 3.01.122
a lunatic lean–witted fool, | presuming on an R2 2.01.115
wife, thou art a fool. 5.02. 68
what a wasp–stung and impatient fool | art thou 1H4 1.03.236
but i tell you, my lord fool, out of this nettle 2.03. 9 P
thou clay–brain'd guts, thou knotty–pated fool, 2.04.227 P
/a fool go with thy soul, whither it goes! 5.03. 22
the slaves of life, and life, time's fool, | and 5.04. 81
you'll be a fool still. 2H4 2.01.157 P
me not, he was a fool that taught them me. 2.01.192 P

thou art a great fool. 2.01.195 P
you virtuous ass, you bashful fool, must you be 2.02. 75 P
how? you fat fool, i scorn you. 2.04.296 P
how ill white hairs becomes a fool and jester! 5.05. 48
why, 'tis a gull, a fool, a rogue, that now and H5 3.06. 67 P
if the enemy is an ass and a fool, and a prating 4.01. 77 P
look you, be an ass and a fool, and a prating 4.01. 79 P
of every fool whose sense no more can feel | but 4.01.235
come back, fool. 2H6 1.03. 8 P
what a peevish fool was that of crete | that 3H6 5.06. 18
yet, for all his wings, the fool was drown'd. 5.06. 20
fool, fool, thou whet'st a knife to kill thyself R3 1.03.243
fool, fool, thou whet'st a knife to kill thyself 1.03.243
relenting fool, and shallow, changing woman! 4.04.431
fool, of thyself speak well; 5.03.192
fool, do not flatter: 5.03.192
truth with such a show | as fool and fight is, H8 pr 19
th' ensuing night | made it a fool and beggar. 1.01. 28
of fool and feather that they got in france, 1.03. 25
he was a fool — | for he would needs be 2.02.131
fit for a fool to fall by. 3.02.214
she's a fool to stay behind her father, let her TRO 1.01. 81 P
the wise and fool, the artist and unread, | the 1.03. 24
thou art proclaim'd fool, i think. 2.01. 25 P
i know that, fool. 2.01. 65 P
ay, but that fool knows not himself. 2.01. 66 P
peace, fool! 2.01. 82 P
peace and quietness, but the fool will not — he 2.01. 84 P
i am patroclus' knower, and patroclus is a fool. 2.03. 54 P
agamemnon is a fool to offer to command achilles 2.03. 62 P
achilles, achilles is a fool to be commanded /of 2.03. 63 P
thersites is a fool to serve such a fool, and 2.03. 64 P
thersites is a fool to serve such a fool, and 2.03. 64 P
a fool, and this patroclus is a fool positive. 2.03. 65 P
why am i a fool? 2.03. 66 P
achilles hath inveigled his fool from him. 2.03. 91 P
it was a strong composure a fool could disunite. 2.03. 99 P
that itself will leave | to be another's fool. 3.02.150
the fool slides o'er the ice that you should 3.03.215
i'll send the fool to ajax and desire him | t' 3.03.235
why, thou full dish of fool, from troy. 5.01. 9 P
no, no, good night, i'll be your fool no more. 5.02. 32
away, you fool! COR 1.03. 39
rather than fool it so, | let the high office 2.03.121
ay, fool, is that a shame? 4.02. 17
note but this fool. 4.02. 17
which not to cut would show thee but a fool, 4.05. 97
what fool hath added water to the sea? TIT 3.01. 68
of my dug and felt it bitter, pretty fool, | to ROM 1.03. 31
and, pretty fool, it stinted and said, "ay." 1.03. 48
o, i am fortune's fool! 3.01.136
i would the fool were married to her grave! 3.05.140
peace, you mumbling fool! 3.05.173
man, | and then to have a wretched puling fool, 3.05.183
thou art a fool to bid me farewell twice. TIM 1.01.263
stay, here comes the fool with apemantus, let's 2.02. 46 P
how dost, fool? 2.02. 50 P
there's the fool hangs on your back already. 2.02. 55 P
where's the fool now? 2.02. 58 P
speak to 'em, fool. 2.02. 65 P
gramercies, good fool; how does your mistress? 2.02. 67 P
fool, i will go with you to lord timon's. 2.02. 88 P
ay, fool. 2.02. 97 P
i think no usurer but has a fool to his servant; 2.02. 98 P
my mistress is one, and i am her fool. 2.02. 99 P
what is a whoremaster, fool? 2.02.107 P
a fool in good clothes, and something like thee. 2.02.108 P
thou art not altogether a fool. 2.02.115 P
come with me, fool, come. 2.02.120 P
now i see thou art a fool, and fit for thy 3.01. 49 P
rest, and 'mongst lords /i be thought a fool. 3.03. 21
the learned pate | ducks to the golden fool. 4.03. 18
like thyself, | a madman so long, now a fool. 4.03.221
a fool of thee. depart. 4.03.232
he was but a fool that brought | my answer back. JC 4.03. 84
no boasting like a fool; MAC 4.01.153
i am so much a fool, should i stay longer, | it 4.02. 28
why should i play the roman fool, and die | on 5.08. 1
/wringing it thus) you'll tender me a fool. HAM 1.03.109
that he may play the fool no where but in 's own 3.01.132 P
if thou wilt needs marry, marry a fool, for wise 3.01.138 P
most pitiful ambition in the fool that uses it. 3.02. 45 P
they fool me to the top of my bent. 3.02.384 P
thou wretched, rash, intruding fool, farewell! 3.04. 31
every fool can tell that. 5.01.146 P
strike my gentleman for chiding of his fool? LR 1.03. 1
my fool? 1.04. 42 P
go you and call my fool hither. 1.04. 43 P
where's my fool? 1.04. 47 P
but where's my fool? 1.04. 72 P
into france, sir, the fool hath much pin'd away. 1.04. 74 P
go you call hither my fool. 1.04. 77 P
this is nothing, fool. 1.04.128 P
he will not believe a fool. 1.04.135 P
a bitter fool! 1.04.136 P
my boy, between a bitter fool and a sweet one? 1.04.138 P
a schoolmaster that can teach thy fool to lie — 1.04.180 P
i had rather be any kind o' thing than a fool, 1.04.186 P
i am better than thou art now, i am a fool, thou 1.04.194 P
not only, sir, this your all–licens'd fool, 1.04.201
sir, more knave than fool, after your master. 1.04.314
nuncle lear, tarry, take the fool with thee. 1.04.316 P
would buy a halter, | so the fool follows after. 1.04.321
yes indeed, thou wouldst make a good fool. 1.05. 38 P
if thou wert my fool, nuncle, i'ld have thee 1.05. 41 P
smile you my speeches, as i were a fool? 2.02. 82
rogues and cowards | but ajax is their fool. 2.02.125
why, fool? 2.04. 66 P
but knaves follow it, since a fool gives it. 2.04. 77 P
but i will tarry, the fool will stay, | and let 2.04. 82
the knave turns fool that runs away, | the fool 2.04. 84
that runs away, | the fool no knave, perdie. 2.04. 85
where learn'd you this, fool? 2.04. 86 P
not i' th' stocks, fool. 2.04. 87 P
father, fool me not so much | to bear it tamely; 2.04.275
o fool, i shall go mad! 2.04.286
none but the fool, who labors to outjest | his 3.01. 16
and a codpiece — that's a wise man and a fool. 3.02. 41 P
poor fool and knave, i have one part in my heart 3.02. 72
bad is the trade that must play fool to sorrow, 4.01. 38
services are due, | /a fool usurps my /bed. 4.02. 28
o vain fool! 4.02. 61
i am even | the natural fool of fortune. 4.06.191
and my poor fool is hang'd! 5.03.306
thus do i ever make my fool my purse; OTH 1.03.383
now, my sick fool roderigo, | whom love hath 2.03. 51
to be now a sensible man, by and by a fool, and 2.03.306 P
for whiles this honest fool | plies desdemona to 2.03.353
o wretched fool, | that lov'st to make thine 3.03.375
for honesty's a fool | and loses that it works 3.03.382
i was a fine fool to take it. 4.01.150 P
you are a fool; go to. 4.02.148
what should such a fool | do with so good a wife 5.02.233
o fool, fool, fool! 5.02.323
o fool, fool, fool! 5.02.323
o fool, fool, fool! 5.02.323
the world transform'd | into a strumpet's fool. ANT 1.01. 13
i'll seem the fool i am not. 1.01. 42
out, fool, i forgive thee for a witch. 1.02. 40 P
when it concerns the fool or coward. 1.02. 96
thou teachest like a fool: the way to lose him. 1.03. 10
cries, "fool lepidus!" 3.05. 17
that's the way | to fool their preparation, and 5.02.225
poor venomous fool, | be angry, and dispatch. 5.02.305
had measur'd how long a fool you were upon the CYM 1.02. 24 P
to have smell'd like a fool. 2.01. 16 P
you are a fool granted, therefore your issues, 2.01. 46 P
do you call me fool? 2.03.101
i am sprited with a fool, | frighted, and 2.03.139
thou art some fool, | i am loath to beat thee. 4.02. 85
this cloten was a fool, an empty purse, | there 4.02.113
this, the fool had borne | my head as i do his. 4.02.116
ay me, most credulous fool, | egregious 5.05.210
opinion's but a fool, that makes us scan | the PER 2.02. 56
to wisdom he's a fool that will not yield; 2.04. 54
in silken bags, | to please the fool and death. 3.02. 42
that sharpens sundry wits, | makes me a fool. TNK 1.01.119
fair boy certain, but a fool | to love himself. 2.02.120
thou dar'st not, fool, thou canst not, thou art 2.02.214
fool, | away with this strain'd mirth! 3.03. 42
you are a fool. 3.05. 79
then the beast–eating clown, and next the fool, 3.05.131
childishly, | so sillily, as if she were a fool, 4.01. 40
i am a fool, my reason is lost in me; 4.02. 34
the poor fool prays her that he may depart. VEN 578
"how much a fool was i | to be of such a weak 1015
the wise dumb, and teach the fool to speak. 1146
"fool, fool," quoth she, "his wounds will not be LUC 1568
"fool, fool," quoth she, "his wounds will not be 1568
let my unsounded self, suppos'd a fool, | now 1819
what fool is not so wise | to break an oath, to PP 3.13
he rose and ran away, ah, fool too froward! 4.14
so true a fool is love that in your will SON 57.13
love's not time's fool, though rosy lips and 116. 9
thou blind fool, love, what dost thou to mine 137. 1

FOOL–BEGG'D 1 FR 0.0001 REL FR 1 V 0 P
this fool–begg'd patience in thee will be left. ERR 2.01. 41

FOOL–BORN 1 FR 0.0001 REL FR 1 V 0 P
reply not to me with a fool–born jest, | presume 2H4 5.05. 55

FOOL'D 3 FR 0.0003 REL FR 3 V 0 P
being fool'd, by fool'ry thrive! AWW 4.03.338
that you are fool'd, discarded, and shook off 1H4 1.03.178
she is fool'd | with a most false effect; CYM 1.05. 42

FOOLERIES 1 FR 0.0001 REL FR 1 V 0 P
thy by–gone fooleries were but spices of it. WT 3.02.184

FOOLERY 13 FR 0.0014 REL FR 1 V 12 P
now he shall see his own foolery. WIV 4.02. 37 P
well, sir, there rest in your foolery. ERR 4.03. 34 P
unless he have a fancy to this foolery, as it ADO 3.02. 37 P
the little foolery that wise men have makes a AYL 1.02. 90 P
cousin, thrown upon thee in holiday foolery; 1.03. 14 P
and that may you be bold to say in your foolery. TN 1.05. 13 P
foolery, sir, does walk about the orb like the 3.01. 38 P
here has been too much homely foolery already. WT 4.04.333 P
and manhood is call'd foolery when it stands COR 3.01.245
as much foolery as i have, so much wit thou TIM 2.02.117 P
it was mere foolery, i did not mark it. JC 1.02.236 P
there was more foolery yet, if i could remember 1.02.287 P
it is but foolery, but it is such a kind of HAM 5.02.215 P

FOOLHARDINESS 1 FR 0.0001 REL FR 1 V 0 P
foolhardiness, not i. COR 1.04. 46

FOOLHARDY 2 FR 0.0002 REL FR 1 V 1 P
i find my tongue is too foolhardy, but my heart AWW 4.01. 29 P
open the door, secure, foolhardy king! R2 5.03. 43

FOOLING 10 FR 0.0011 REL FR 2 V 8 P
in this kind of merry fooling, am nothing to you TMP 2.01.177 P
but, after all this fooling, i would not have it MM 1.02. 70 P
pray you let's have no more fooling about it, MV 2.02. 83 P
and't be thy will, put me into good fooling! TN 1.05. 32 P
see, sir, how your fooling grows old, and people 1.05.110 P
thou wast in very gracious fooling last night, 2.03. 22 P
why, this is the best fooling, when all is done. 2.03. 29 P
beshrew me, the knight's in admirable fooling. 2.03. 80 P
while i stand fooling here, his jack of the R2 5.05. 60
i do not like this fooling. TRO 5.02.101

/FOOLISH 1 FR 0.0001 REL FR 1 V 0 P
/no /more, /the /text /is /foolish. LR 4.02. 37

FOOLISH 97 FR 0.0109 REL FR 67 V 30 P
foolish wench, | to th' most of men this is a TMP 1.02.480
fie, fie, how wayward is this foolish love, TGV 1.02. 57
my foolish rival, that her father likes | (only 2.04.174
for 'tis no trusting to yond foolish lout — 4.04. 66
shall we send that foolish carrion, mistress WIV 3.03.193 P
i mine, to build upon a foolish woman's promise. 3.05. 41 P
thou art as foolish christian creatures as i 4.01. 71 P
so play the foolish throngs with one that MM 2.04. 24
thou foolish friar, and thou pernicious woman, 5.01.241
the sun shines, let foolish gnats make sport, ERR 2.02. 30
arrest me, foolish fellow, if thou dar'st. 4.01. 75
vicious, ungentle, foolish, blunt, unkind, 4.02. 21
simple, a foolish extravagant spirit, full of LLL 4.02. 66 P
sweet, | your wits makes wise things foolish. 5.02.374
wise things seem foolish and rich things but 5.02.378
an't shall please you, a foolish mild man, an 5.02.581 P
far, | and make and mar | the foolish fates." MND 1.02. 38
who would set his wit to so foolish a bird? 3.01.134 P
a foolish heart, that i leave here behind. 3.02.319
the men that ever my foolish eyes look'd upon, MV 1.02.118 P
these foolish drops do something drown my manly 2.03. 13 P
quail | to bring again these foolish runaways. AYL 2.02. 21
you foolish shepherd, wherefore do you follow 3.05. 49
and the foolish chroniclers of that age found it 4.01.105 P
it but time lost to hear such a foolish song. 5.03. 40 P
where is the foolish knave i sent before? SHR 4.01.127
here, sir — as foolish as i was before. 4.01.128
fie, what a foolish duty call you this? 5.02.125
i would your duty were as foolish too. 5.02.126
of one count rossillion, a foolish idle boy, but AWW 4.03.215 P
decay'd, ingenious, foolish, rascally knave. 5.02. 24 P
and of a foolish knight that you brought in one TN 1.03. 15 P
"better a witty fool tyan a foolish wit." 1.05. 36 P
treasure of your time with a foolish knight" — 2.05. 78 P
go to, go to, thou art a foolish fellow, | let 4.01. 3
i prithee, foolish greek, depart from me. 4.01. 18
what foolish boldness brought thee to their 5.01. 70
and the rain, | a foolish thing was but a toy, 5.01.391
i may be negligent, foolish, and fearful: WT 1.02.250
that could conceive a gross and foolish sire 3.02.197
sir, royal sir, forgive a foolish woman. 3.02.227
lame, foolish, crooked, swart, prodigious, JN 3.01. 46
how now, foolish rheum? 4.01. 33
why, foolish boy, the king is left behind, | and R2 2.03. 97
peace, foolish woman. 5.02. 80
his brother–in–law, the foolish mortimer, | who, 1H4 1.03. 80
eye, and a foolish hanging of thy nether lip, 2.04.404 P
do, | make blind itself with foolish tenderness. 3.02. 91
but for these foolish officers, i beseech you i 2H4 2.01.107 P
what foolish master taught you these manners, 2.01.189 P
me there all the foolish and dull and crudy 4.03. 98 P
for this the foolish over–careful fathers | have 4.05. 67
o foolish youth, | thou seek'st the greatness 4.05. 96
him, do bear themselves like foolish justices; 5.01. 67 P
foolish curs, that run winking into the mouth of H5 3.07.143 P
come, 'tis a foolish saying. 4.01.202 P
what is the trust or strength of foolish man? 1H6 3.02.112
in great affairs, | too full of foolish pity; 2H6 3.01.225
tut, that's a foolish observation. 3H6 2.06.108
so foolish sorrows bids your stones farewell. R3 4.01.103
the boy is foolish, and i fear not him. 4.02. 55
o foolish cressid! TRO 4.02. 17
this foolish, dreaming, superstitious girl 5.03. 79
me, and the foolish fortune of this girl, and 5.03.102 P
same scurvy doting foolish /young knave's sleeve 5.04. 3 P
neither foolish in our stands | nor cowardly in COR 1.06. 2
no, foolish tribune, no; TIT 1.01.343
why, foolish lucius, dost thou not perceive 3.01. 53
we have a trifling foolish banquet towards. ROM 1.05.122
back, foolish tears, back to your native spring, 3.02.102
how foolish do your fears seem now, calphurnia! JC 2.02.105
a foolish thought, to say a sorry sight. MAC 2.02. 19
a foolish figure! HAM 2.02. 98
who was in life a foolish prating knave. 3.04.215
of it, a knavish speech sleeps in a foolish ear. 4.02. 24 P
on whose foolish honesty | my practices ride LR 1.02.181
i am a very foolish fond old man, | fourscore 4.07. 59
i am old and foolish. 4.07. 83
how if fair and foolish? OTH 2.01.135
she never yet was foolish that was fair, | for 2.01.136
hast thou for her that's foul and foolish? 2.01.140 P
there's none so foul and foolish thereunto, 2.01.141
to have a foolish wife. 3.03.304
far | (prick'd to't by foolish honesty and love) 3.03.412
see how he prizes the foolish woman your wife! 4.01.176 P
good /faith, how foolish are our minds! 4.03. 23
most part, too, they are foolish that are so. ANT 3.03. 31
thou foolish thing! CYM 1.01.150
a foolish suitor to a wedded lady | that hath 1.06. 2
therefore your issues, being foolish, do not 2.01. 47 P
if i could get this foolish imogen, i should 2.03. 8 P
come, you're a young foolish sapling, and must PER 4.02. 88 P
why /are you foolish? can it be undone? 4.03. 1
to marry us, for here they are nice and foolish. TNK 5.02. 79
how love is wise in folly, foolish witty. VEN 838
for sportive words and utt'ring foolish things. LUC 1813
dissuade one foolish heart from serving thee, SON 141.10

FOOLISH–COMPOUNDED 1 FR 0.0001 REL FR 0 V 1 P
the brain of this foolish–compounded clay, man, 2H4 1.02. 7 P

FOOLISHLY 5 FR 0.0005 REL FR 2 V 3 P
sorry should be thus foolishly lost at a game of MM 1.02.190 P
may not speak wisely what wise men do foolishly. AYL 1.02. 87 P
fool doth very wisely hit | doth very foolishly, 2.07. 54
fondly brought here and foolishly sent hence. 2H4 4.02.119
in peace what already i have foolishly suff'red. OTH 4.02.180 P

FOOLISHNESS 1 FR 0.0001 REL FR 1 V 0 P
come on, sir knave, have done your foolishness, ERR 1.02. 72

FOOL'RY 4 FR 0.0004 REL FR 4 V 0 P
o, what a scene of fool'ry have i seen, | of LLL 4.03.161
not so strong a note | as fool'ry in the wise, 5.02. 76
being fool'd, by fool'ry thrive! AWW 4.03.338
but this is fool'ry. CYM 3.02. 73

FOOL'S 13 FR 0.0014 REL FR 7 V 6 P
tush, i may as well say the fool's the fool. ADO 3.03.123 P
thou wak'st, with thine own fool's eyes peep. MND 4.01. 84
did i deserve no more than a fool's head? MV 2.09. 59
with one fool's head i came to woo, | but i go 2.09. 75
according to the fool's bolt, sir, and such AYL 5.04. 64 P
by how much "a fool's bolt is soon shot." H5 3.07.122 P
will you set your wit to a fool's? TRO 2.01. 86 P
no, i warrant you, the fool's will shame it. 2.01. 87 P
fool's play, by heaven, hector. 5.03. 43
if ye should lead her in a fool's paradise, as ROM 2.04.166 P
always a villain's office, or a fool's. TIM 4.03.237
lend me a fool's heart and a woman's eyes, | and 5.01.157
this fool's speed | be cross'd with slowness; CYM 3.05.161

FOOLS' 3 FR 0.0003 REL FR 2 V 1 P
and wretched fools' secrets heedfully o'er–eye. LLL 4.03. 78
kind of fools no better than the fools' zanies. TN 1.05. 89 P
drop millstones, when fools' eyes fall tears. R3 1.03.352

/FOOLS 3 FR 0.0003 REL FR 3 V 0 P
/old /fools /are /babes /again, /and /must /be LR 1.03. 19
should play bo–peep, | and go the /fools among." 1.04.178
/fools /do /those /villains /pity /who /are 4.02. 54

FOOLS 105 FR 0.0118 REL FR 78 V 27 P

did lie, | though fools at home condemn 'em. TMP 3.03. 27
you fools! 3.03. 60
for why, the fools are mad, if left alone. TGV 3.01. 99
wrench awe from fools and tie the wiser souls MM 2.04. 14
lose a thing | that none but fools would keep. 3.01. 8
o heaven, the vanity of wretched fools! 5.01.164
unfeeling fools can with such wrongs dispense: ERR 2.01.103
how many fond fools serve mad jealousy? 2.01.116
lord, lest i should prove the mother of fools. ADO 2.01.286 P
these shallow fools have brought to light, who 5.01.233 P
the hour that fools should ask. LLL 2.01.122
that you three fools lack'd me fool to make up 4.03.203
then fools you were these women to forswear, 4.03.352
or keeping what is sworn, you will prove fools. 4.03.353
they are worse fools to purchase mocking so. 5.02. 59
folly in fools bears not so strong a note | as 5.02. 75
let us complain to them what fools were here, 5.02.302
i dare not call them fools; 5.02.371
they are thirsty, fools would fain have drink. 5.02.372
which shallow laughing hearers give to fools. 5.02.860
lord, what fools these mortals be! MND 3.02.115
hearing them, would call their brothers fools. MV 1.01. 99
to gaze on christian fools with varnish'd faces; 2.05. 33
there be fools alive, iwis, | silver'd o'er, and 2.09. 68
o, these deliberate fools! 2.09. 80
and i do know | a many fools, that stand in 3.05. 68
that fools may not speak wisely what wise men do AYL 1.02. 86 P
the little wit that fools have was silenc'd, the 1.02. 89 P
and yet it irks me the poor dappled fools, 2.01. 22
here shall he see | gross fools as he, | and if 2.05. 56
a greek invocation, to call fools into a circle. 2.05. 59 P
that fools should be so deep contemplative; 2.07. 31
to blow on whom i please, for so fools have; 2.07. 49
'tis such fools as you | that makes the world 3.05. 52
beasts, which in all tongues are call'd fools. 5.04. 38 P
fair lady, do you think you have fools in hand? TN 1.03. 65 P
and those that are fools, let them use their 1.05. 15 P
think they have thee do very oft prove fools; 1.05. 34 P
so at these set kind of fools no better than the 1.05. 89 P
with leasing, for thou speak'st well of fools! 1.05. 98 P
and fools are as like husbands as pilchers are 3.01. 34 P
wise men that give fools money get themselves a 4.01. 22 P
do not weep, good fools, | there is no cause. WT 2.01.118
women and fools, break off your conference. JN 2.01.150
mingled his royalty with cap'ring fools, | had 1H4 3.02. 63
well, thus we play the fools with the time, and 2H4 2.02.142 P
they are generally fools and cowards, which some 4.03. 94 P
be friends, you english fools, be friends, we H5 4.01.222 P
belike your lordship takes us then for fools, 1H6 3.02. 62
so many weeks ere the poor fools will ean, | so 3H6 2.05. 36
i will converse with iron–witted fools | and R3 4.02. 28
fools on both sides, helen must needs be fair, TRO 1.01. 90
asses, fools, dolts! 1.02.241 P
is wit stirring, and leave the faction of fools. 2.01.119 P
see, we fools! 3.02.123
testy magistrates (alias fools) as any in rome. COR 2.01. 45 P
a nettle, and | the faults of fools but folly. 2.01.191
if you are learn'd, | be not as common fools; 3.01.100
valiant ignorance, | and perish constant fools. 4.06.105
and patient fools, | whose children he hath 5.06. 51
ye, and are you such fools | to square for this? TIT 2.01. 99
let fools do good, and fair men call for grace, 3.01.204
part, fools! ROM 1.01. 64
sick and green, | and none but fools do wear it; 2.02. 9
to see meat fill knaves, and wine heat fools. TIM 1.01.261
we make ourselves fools to disport ourselves, 1.02.136
thus honest fools lay out their wealth on 1.02.235
you fools of fortune, trencher–friends, time's 3.06. 96
slaves and fools, | pluck the grave wrinkled 4.01. 4
dimpled smiles from fools exhaust their mercy; 4.03.120
thou art the cap of all the fools alive. 4.03.358
why old men, fools, and children calculate, JC 1.03. 65
true quality | with that which melteth fools — 3.01. 42
as much as to say, they are fools that marry. 3.03. 17 P
should the wars do with these jigging fools? 4.03.137
eyes are made the fools o' th' other senses, MAC 2.01. 44
then the liars and swearers are fools; 4.02. 56 P
and all our yesterdays have lighted fools | the 5.05. 22
and we fools of nature | so horridly to shake HAM 1.04. 54
these tedious old fools! 2.02.219 P
on necessity, fools by heavenly compulsion, LR 1.02.122 P
"fools had ne'er less grace in a year, | for 1.04.166
a night pities neither wise men nor fools. 3.02. 13 P
cold night will turn us all to fools and madmen. 3.04. 78 P
that we are come | to this great stage of fools. 4.06.183
paradoxes to make fools laugh i' th' alehouse. OTH 2.01.138 P
to suckle fools and chronicle small beer. 2.01.160
and fools as gross | as ignorance made drunk. 3.03.404
thus credulous fools are caught, | and many 4.01. 45
the loyalty well held to fools does make | our ANT 3.13. 42
wishers were ever fools — o, come, come, come, 4.15. 37
she shines not upon fools, lest the reflection CYM 1.02. 32 P
fools are not mad folks. 2.03.101
thus may poor fools | believe false teachers. 3.04. 84
for when fools shall — | who is here? 3.05. 79
at fools i laugh, not fear them. 4.02. 96
e'er dull'd sleep | did mock sad fools withal. PER 5.01.162
with us, | make talk for fools and cowards. TNK 3.03. 12
"there was three fools fell out about an howlet: 3.05. 67
you fathers are fine fools. 5.02. 28
foes, | and merry fools to mock at him resort; LUC 989
"out, idle words, servants to shallow fools! 1016
hold | only to flatter fools and make them bold: 1559
to this i witness call the fools of time, SON 124.13
like fools that in th' imagination set | the LC 136

FOOL'S–HEAD 1 FR 0.0001 REL FR 0 V 1 P
you shall have anne — fool's–head of your own. WIV 1.04.126 P

/FOOT 1 FR 0.0001 REL FR 1 V 0 P
/the /instant /action, /a /cause /on /foot — 2H4 1.03. 37

FOOT 177 FR 0.0200 REL FR 136 V 41 P
foot it featly here and there, | and, sweet TMP 1.02.379
what, i say, | my foot my tutor? 1.02.470
and i will kiss thy foot. 2.02.149
i'll kiss thy foot. 2.02.152
that the blind mole may not | hear a foot fall; 4.01.195
and ye that on the sands with printless foot 5.01. 34
me | upon the rising of the mountain foot | that TGV 5.02. 46
sometimes the beam of her view gilded my foot, WIV 1.03. 61 P
have open eye, for thieves do foot by night. 2.01.122
firm fixture of thy foot would give an excellent 3.03. 63 P
while other jests are something rank on foot, 4.06. 22
which i did think with slower foot came on, MM 5.01.395
longer from head to foot than from hip to hip: ERR 3.02.113 P
with a good leg and a good foot, uncle, and ADO 2.01. 14 P
bring you the length of prester john's foot, 2.01.268 P
ever, | one foot in sea and one on shore, | to 2.03. 64
the crown of his head to the sole of his foot, 3.02. 9 P
(which is baser) guided by her foot (which is LLL 1.02.168 P
i profane my lips on thy foot, my eyes on thy 4.01. 85 P
you hear that i | will praise a hand, a foot, a 4.03.182
look, here's thy love; my foot and her face see. 4.03.273
no, to the death we will not move a foot, | nor 5.02.146
do not you know my lady's foot by th' squier, 5.02.474
loves her by the foot. 5.02.668 P
yet, since love's argument was first on foot, 5.02.747
(who even but now did spurn me with his foot), MND 3.02.225
beard | and foot me as you spurn a stranger cur MV 1.03.118
and never dare misfortune cross her foot, 2.04. 35
i would my daughter were dead at my foot, and 3.01. 88 P
would she were hears'd at my foot, and the 3.01. 90 P
that thou with license of free foot hast caught, AYL 2.07. 68
would detect the lazy foot of time as well as a 3.02.304 P
and why not the swift foot of time? 3.02.306 P
for though he go as softly as foot can fall, he 3.02.328 P
power, which were on foot | in his own conduct, 5.04.156
in his waning age | set foot under thy table. SHR 2.01.402
why, thy horn is a foot, and so long am i at the 4.01. 28 P
you pluck my foot awry. 4.01.147
what say you to a neat's foot? 4.03. 17
there will we mount, and thither walk on foot. 4.03.186
and place your hands below your husband's foot; 5.02.177
it no more merits | the tread of a man's foot. AWW 2.03.275
hearing so much, will speed her foot again, 3.04. 37
th' inaudible and noiseless foot of time 5.03. 41
there thy fixed foot shall grow | till thou have TN 1.04. 17
wilt thou set thy foot o' my neck? 2.05.188 P
in his liver as will clog the foot of a flea, 3.02. 62 P
occasion whereon my services are now on foot, WT 1.01. 3 P
horsing foot on foot? 1.02.288
horsing foot on foot? 1.02.288
but jumps twelve foot and a half by th' squier. 4.04.339 P
proceed; | no foot shall stir. 5.03. 98
i would give it every foot to have this face; JN 1.01.146
a foot of honor better than i was, | but many a 1.01.182
i was, | but many a many foot of land the worse. 1.01.183
whose foot spurns back the ocean's roaring tides 2.01. 24
and wheresoe'er this foot of mine doth tread, 3.03. 62
directly lead | thy foot to england's throne. 3.04.130
methinks i see this hurly all on foot; 3.04.169
when i strike my foot | upon the bosom of the 4.01. 2
of all this isle, | three foot of it doth hold; 4.02.100
the better foot before. 4.02.170
nor attend the foot | that leaves the print of 4.03. 25
if thou but frown on me, or stir thy foot, | or 4.03. 96
hand, | it may lie gently at the foot of peace, 5.02. 76
shall, | lie at the proud foot of a conqueror, 5.07.113
where ever englishman durst set his foot. R2 1.01. 66
my gage | upon this overweening traitor's foot, 1.01.147
myself i throw, dread sovereign, at thy foot, 1.01.165
nimble mischance, that art so light of foot, 3.04. 92
now in as low an ebb as the foot of the ladder, 1H4 1.02. 37 P
i am join'd with no foot land–rakers, no 2.01. 73 P
if i travel but four foot by the squier further 2.02. 12 P
i'll starve ere i'll rob a foot further. 2.02. 21 P
nether–stocks, and mend them and foot them too. 2.04.117 P
came in, foot and hand, and with a thought seven 2.04.217 P
ye cuckoo, but afoot he will not budge a foot. 2.04.354 P
i'll procure this fat rogue a charge of foot, 2.04.546 P
when i from france set foot at ravenspurgh, 3.02. 95
i have procur'd thee, jack, a charge of foot. 3.03.186 P
and all his men | upon the foot of fear, fled 5.05. 20
no, fifteen hundred foot, five hundred horse, 2H4 2.01.173
and laid his love and life under my foot, | yea, 3.01. 63
cured, | stoop tamely to the foot of majesty. 4.02. 42
on the top on't (colevile kissing my foot), to 4.03. 49 P
that this fair action may on foot be brought. H5 1.02.310
le foot, madame, et le count. 3.04. 51 P
le foot et le count! 3.04. 52 P
le foot et le count! 3.04. 56 P
d' elbow, de nick, de sin, de foot, le count. 3.04. 59 P
and her foot, look you, is fixed upon a 3.06. 35 P
swear by her foot, that she may tread out the 3.07. 95 P
me, | when he sees me go back one foot or fly. 1H6 1.02. 21
nay, stand thou back, i will not budge a foot: 1.03. 38
stoop then and set your knee against my foot, 3.01.168
your troops of horsemen with his bands of foot, 4.01.165
if son to talbot, die at talbot's foot. 4.06. 53
but fear not thou, until thy foot be snar'd, 2H6 2.04. 56
to mow down thorns that would annoy our foot 3.01. 67
my foot shall fight with all the strength thou 4.10. 50
and tread it under foot with all contempt, 5.01.209
day | is not itself, nor have we won one foot, 5.03. 6
and give no foot of ground!" 3H6 1.04. 15
when he might spurn him with his foot away? 1.04. 58
not he that sets his foot upon her back. 2.02. 16
wishing his foot were equal with his eye, | and 3.02.137
we say that shore's wife hath a pretty foot, | a R3 1.01. 93
or, by saint paul, i'll strike thee to my foot, 1.02. 41
length, | consisting equally of horse and foot; 5.03.294
shall have the leading of this foot and horse. 5.03.297
his horse is slain, and all on foot he fights, 5.04. 4
as much as one sound cudgel of four foot | (you H8 5.03. 19
and 'tis this fever that keeps troy on foot, TRO 1.03.135
i would thou didst itch from head to foot; 2.01. 27 P
as if his foot were on brave hector's breast 3.03.140
eye, her cheek, her lip, | nay, her foot speaks; 4.05. 56
fix thy foot. COR 1.08. 4
from face to foot | he was a thing of blood, 2.02.108
the service of the foot | being once gangren'd, 3.01.304
by the good gods | i'ld with thee every foot. 4.01. 57
and to be on foot at an hour's warning. 4.03. 45 P
mars, i tell thee, | we have a power on foot; 4.05.119
unless by using means i lame the foot | of our 4.07. 7
come on, my lords, the better foot before. TIT 2.03.192
approach you must kneel, then kiss his foot, 4.03.111 P
thou shalt not stir one foot to seek a foe. ROM 1.01. 80
and foot it, girls. 1.05. 26
by her fine foot, straight leg, and quivering 2.01. 19
it is nor hand nor foot, | nor arm nor face, 2.02. 40
and all my fortunes at thy foot i'll lay, | and 2.02.147
and for a hand and a foot and a body, though 2.05. 41 P
o, so light a foot | will ne'er wear out the 2.06. 16
so shall no foot upon the churchyard tread, 5.03. 5
what cursed foot wanders this way to–night, | to 5.03. 19
down, | not one accompanying his declining foot. TIM 1.01. 88
mean eyes have seen | the foot above the head. 1.01. 94
it requires swift foot. 5.01.228
set but thy foot | against our rampir'd gates 5.04. 46
and i will set this foot of mine as far | as who JC 1.03.119
and too impatiently stamp'd with your foot. 2.01.244
set on your foot, | and with a heart new–fir'd i 2.01.331
as low as to thy foot doth cassius fall, | to 3.01. 56
nor our strong sorrow | upon the foot of motion. MAC 2.03.125
i wish your horses swift and sure of foot; 3.01. 37
my lord, from head to foot. HAM 1.02.228
head to foot | now is he total gules, horridly 2.02.456
follow him at foot, tempt him with speed aboard. 4.03. 54
keep thy foot out of brothels, thy hand out of LR 3.04. 96 P
upon these eyes of thine i'll set my foot. 3.07. 68
you are now within a foot | of th' extreme verge 4.06. 25
near and on speedy foot; 4.06.213
head | to the descent and dust below thy foot, 5.03.138
he, swift of foot, | outran my purpose; OTH 2.03.232
at whose foot, | to mend the petty present, i ANT 1.05. 44
on the earth, | and fighting foot to foot. 3.07. 66
on the earth, | and fighting foot to foot. 3.07. 66
our foot | upon the hills adjoining to the city 4.10. 4
now from head to foot | i am marble–constant; 5.02.239
arm me, audacity, from head to foot, | or, like CYM 1.06. 19
cupids | of silver, each on one foot standing, 2.04. 90
and thus i set my foot on 's neck," even then 3.03. 92
court i'll knock her back, foot her home again. 3.05.144 P
his foot mercurial, his martial thigh, | the 4.02.310
the holy eagle | stoop'd, as to foot us. 5.04.116
and life, must he set foot | upon this kingdom. TNK 2.02.246
i'll cut my green coat a foot above my knee, 3.04. 19
come forth, and foot it. 3.05.137
aged cramp | had screw'd his square foot round, 5.01.111
"and when thou hast on foot the purblind hare, VEN 679
in his hold–fast foot the weak mouse panteth. LUC 555
the cedar stoops not to the base shrub's foot, 664
this said, he sets his foot upon the light, 673
a hand, a foot, a face, a leg, a head | stood 1427
which bleeding under pyrrhus' proud foot lies. 1449
no matter then although my foot did stand | upon SON 44. 5
what strong hand can hold his swift foot back? 65.11
of hand, of foot, of lip, of eye, of brow, | i 106. 6

FOOTBALL 2 FR 0.0002 REL FR 1 V 1 P
me, | that like a football you do spurn me thus? ERR 2.01. 83
nor tripp'd neither, you base football player. LR 1.04. 86 P

FOOTBOY 2 FR 0.0002 REL FR 1 V 1 P
not like a christian footboy or a gentleman's SHR 3.02. 71 P
wait like a lousy footboy | at chamber–door? H8 5.02.174

FOOTBOYS 2 FR 0.0002 REL FR 2 V 0 P
like peasant footboys do they keep the walls, 1H6 3.02. 69
door 'mongst pursuivants, | pages, and footboys. H8 5.02. 25

FOOT–CLOTH 3 FR 0.0003 REL FR 2 V 1 P
bare–headed plodded by my foot–cloth mule | and 2H6 4.01. 54
thou dost ride in a foot–cloth, dost thou not? 4.07. 46 P
times to–day my foot–cloth horse did stumble, R3 3.04. 84

FOOTED 4 FR 0.0004 REL FR 3 V 1 P
for he is footed in this land already. H5 2.04.143
there is part of a power already footed: LR 3.03. 13 P
"swithold footed thrice the 'old, | he met the 3.04.120
with the traitors | late footed in the kingdom? 3.07. 45

FOOTFALL 1 FR 0.0001 REL FR 1 V 0 P
way, and mount | their pricks at my footfall; TMP 2.02. 12

FOOTING 16 FR 0.0018 REL FR 14 V 2 P
nymphs encounter every one | in country footing. TMP 4.01.138
but hark, i hear the footing of a man. MV 5.01. 24
there your charity would have lack'd footing. WT 3.03.111 P
shall we, upon the footing of our land, | send JN 5.01. 66
who strongly hath set footing in this land: R2 2.02. 48
loud | on the unsteadfast footing of a spear. 1H4 1.03.193
when talbot hath set footing once in france 1H6 3.03. 64
nor set no footing on this unkind shore"? 2H6 3.02. 87
along | upon the giddy footing of the hatches, R3 1.04. 17
that little thought, when she set footing here, H8 3.01.183
'twixt his stretch'd footing and the scaffolage, TRO 1.03.156
should once set footing in your generous bosoms? 2.02.155
finds safer footing than blind reason stumbling 3.02. 72 P
whose footing here anticipates our thoughts | a OTH 2.01. 76
dance on the sands, and yet no footing seen. VEN 148
the earth, in love with thee, thy footing trips, 722

FOOT–LICKER 1 FR 0.0001 REL FR 1 V 0 P
and i, thy caliban, | for aye thy foot–licker. TMP 4.01.219

FOOTMAN 5 FR 0.0005 REL FR 1 V 4 P
what, by a horseman, or a footman? WT 4.03. 64 P
a footman, sweet sir, a footman. 4.03. 65 P
a footman, sweet sir, a footman. 4.03. 65 P
he should be a footman by the garments he has 4.03. 66 P
trot like a servile footman all day long, | even TIT 5.02. 55

FOOTMEN 1 FR 0.0001 REL FR 1 V 0 P
which doth most consist | of war–mark'd footmen, ANT 3.07. 44

FOOT–PATH 2 FR 0.0002 REL FR 1 V 1 P
jog on, jog on, the foot–path way, | and merrily WT 4.03.123
both stile and gate, horse–way and foot–path. LR 4.01. 56 P

FOOTSTEPS 1 FR 0.0001 REL FR 1 V 0 P
for it shall strew the footsteps of my rising. JN 1.01.216

FOOTSTOOL 1 FR 0.0001 REL FR 1 V 0 P
our seat, | and made our footstool of security. 3H6 5.07. 14

FOPP'D 1 FR 0.0001 REL FR 0 V 1 P
scurvy, and begin to find myself fopp'd in it. OTH 4.02.194 P

FOPPERY 3 FR 0.0003 REL FR 0 V 3 P
the grossness of the foppery into a receiv'd WIV 5.05.124 P
i had as lief have the foppery of freedom as the MM 1.02.133 P
this is the excellent foppery of the world, that LR 1.02.118 P

FOPPISH 1 FR 0.0001 REL FR 1 V 0 P
in a year, | for wise men are grown foppish, LR 1.04.167

FOPP'RY 1 FR 0.0001 REL FR 1 V 0 P
let not the sound of shallow fopp'ry enter | my MV 2.05. 35

FOPS 1 FR 0.0001 REL FR 1 V 0 P
bed, | go to th' creating a whole tribe of fops, LR 1.02. 14
FOR *(also ver*, vor)*
/FOR 64 FR 0.0072 REL FR 50 V 14 P
FOR 8100 FR 0.9156 REL FR 6055 V 2045 P
FORAGE 4 FR 0.0004 REL FR 4 V 0 P
and he from forage will incline to play. LLL 4.01. 91
forage, and run | to meet displeasure farther JN 5.01. 59
whelp | forage in blood of french nobility. H5 1.02.110
with blindfold fury she begins to forage; VEN 554
FORAGERS 1 FR 0.0001 REL FR 1 V 0 P
hive | to whom the foragers shall all repair, TRO 1.03. 82
FORBADE *(also forbod)*
FORBADE 4 FR 0.0004 REL FR 3 V 1 P
he swears she's a witch, forbade her my house, WIV 4.02. 86 P
forbade my tongue to speak of mortimer, | but i 1H4 1.03.220
forbade all names; COR 5.01. 12
forbade the boy he should not pass those grounds PP 9. 8
/FORBEAR 1 FR 0.0001 REL FR 1 V 0 P
/no, /forbear, | the lethargy must have his OTH 4.01. 52
FORBEAR 59 FR 0.0066 REL FR 51 V 8 P
better forbear till proteus make return. TGV 2.07. 14
villain, forbear. 3.01.202 P
sirrah, i say, forbear. 3.01.205
love, lend me patience to forbear a while. 5.04. 27
forbear, forbear, i say; 5.04.122
forbear, forbear, i say; 5.04.122
forbear; here's company. WIV 2.03. 17 P
oman, forbear. 4.01. 55 P
forbear it therefore, give your cause to heaven. MM 4.03.124
till he come home again, i would forbear. ERR 2.01. 31
to hear, or forbear hearing? LLL 1.01.196 P
or to forbear both. 1.01.198 P
forbear till this company be past. 1.02.126 P
peace, peace, forbear: 5.02.439
therefore forbear a while. MV 3.02. 3
forbear, and eat no more. AYL 2.07. 88
forbear, i say, | he dies that touches any 2.07. 97
then forbear your food a little while, | whiles, 2.07.127
fiddler, forbear, you grow too forward, sir. SHR 3.01. 1
i can hardly forbear hurling things at him. TN 3.02. 81 P
good my lord, forbear. WT 5.03. 80
either forbear, | quit presently the chapel, or 5.03. 85
bagot, forbear, thou shalt not take it up. R2 4.01. 30
what, canst thou not forbear me half an hour? 2H4 4.05.109
my lord, it were your duty to forbear. 1H6 3.01. 52
do, | let me persuade you to forbear a while. 3.01.105
o no, forbear! 4.07. 49
ah, nell, forbear! 2H6 2.04. 58
forbear, i say! 3.02. 46
forbear to judge, for we are sinners all. 3.03. 31
spirits | you cannot but forbear to murther me. 4.07. 76
forbear awhile, we'll hear a little more. 3H6 3.01. 27
my lords, forbear this talk; 4.01. 6
my love, forbear to fawn upon their frowns. 4.01. 75
forbear your conference with the noble duke. R3 1.01.104
forbear to sleep the /nights, and fast the /days 4.04.118
this is too much. | forbear for shame, my lords. H8 5.02.121
villains, forbear, we are the empress' sons. TIT 5.02.162
gentlemen, for shame, forbear this outrage! ROM 3.01. 87
mean time forbear, | and let mischance be slave 5.03.220
for love of god, forbear him. HAM 5.01.273
dear sir, forbear. LR 1.01.162
and at my entreaty forbear his presence until 1.02.160 P
i'll forbear, | and am fallen out with my more 2.04.109
godliness i have, | i did full hard forbear him. OTH 1.02. 10
forbear me. ANT 1.02.121
i wish, forbear. 1.03. 11
my precious queen, forbear, | and give true 1.03. 73
forbear me till anon. 2.07. 39
forbear, seleucus. 5.02.175
we must forbear. CYM 1.01. 68
your majesty, | forbear sharp speeches to her. 3.05. 39
ghost unlaid forbear thee! 4.02.278
he eyes us not, forbear. 5.05.124
forbear your suffrages. PER 2.04. 41
if that you love prince pericles, forbear. 2.04. 42
you | to forbear the absence of your king; 2.04. 46
ay me, but yet thou mightst my seat forbear, SON 41. 9
dear heart, forbear to glance thine eye aside; 139. 6
FORBEARANCE 6 FR 0.0006 REL FR 4 V 2 P
i shall crave your forbearance a little. MM 4.01. 22 P
learn him forbearance from so foul a wrong. R2 4.01.120
tut, tut, here is a mannerly forbearance. 1H6 2.04. 19
have a continent forbearance till the speed of LR 1.02.167 P
should learn, being taught, forbearance. CYM 2.03. 98
she restrain'd, | and pray'd me oft forbearance; 2.05. 10
FORBEARS 2 FR 0.0002 REL FR 2 V 0 P
let this my sword report what speech forbears. 2H6 4.10. 54
me, | no fisher but the ungrown fry forbears; VEN 526
FORBEAR'T 1 FR 0.0001 REL FR 1 V 0 P
i could well forbear't. ANT 2.07. 98
FORBID 76 FR 0.0086 REL FR 65 V 11 P
and oftentimes have purpos'd to forbid | sir TGV 3.01. 26
have i not forbid her my house? WIV 4.02.173 P
coin heaven's image | in stamps that are forbid. MM 2.04. 46
thou flout me thus unto my face, | being forbid? ERR 1.02. 92
not so, but indeed, god forbid it should be so." ADO 1.01.217 P
not shortly, god forbid it should be otherwise. 1.01.220 P
forbid the sun to enter, like favorites | made 3.01. 9
a child his new coat and forbid him to wear it. 3.02. 7 P
so, | to know the thing i am forbid to know: LLL 1.01. 60
dine, | when i to /feast expressly am forbid; 1.01. 62
of progeny | forbid the smiling courtesy of love 5.02.745
let love forbid | sleep his seat on thy eyelid. MND 2.02. 80
why then you left me (o, the gods forbid!) 3.02.276
marry, god forbid, the boy was the very staff of MV 2.02. 66 P
you may as well forbid the mountain pines | to 4.01. 75
away, | and i expressly am forbid to touch it; SHR 4.01.171
marry, god forbid! 4.02. 78
no, sir, god forbid, but asham'd to kiss. 5.01.146
the gods forbid else! AWW 3.05. 74
let it be forbid, sir, so should i be a great 4.03. 45 P
fortune forbid my outside have not charm'd her! TN 2.02. 18
be it forbid, my lord! WT 1.02.241
as well | forbid the sea for to obey the moon 1.02.427
the higher pow'rs forbid! 3.02.202
how can the law forbid my tongue to curse? JN 3.01.190
from whose obedience i forbid my soul, 4.03. 64
now, afore god — god forbid i say true! R2 2.01.200
now god in heaven forbid! 2.02. 51
the king of heaven forbid our lord the king 3.03.101
marry, god forbid! 4.01.114
did you beg any? god forbid! 1H4 5.02. 35
and god forbid a shallow scratch should drive 5.04. 11
but yet, god forbid, sir, but a knave should 2H4 5.01. 44 P
and god forbid, my dear and faithful lord, H5 1.02. 13
god forbid any malice should prevail, | that 2H6 3.02. 23
and therefore do they cry, though you forbid, 3.02.264
for god forbid so many simple souls | should 4.04. 10
no; god forbid your grace should be forsworn. 3H6 1.02. 18
and when thou fail'st (as god forbid the hour!) 2.01.190
god forbid that, for he'll take vantages. 3.02. 25
god forbid that i should wish them sever'd 4.01. 21
if any such be here — as god forbid! 5.04. 48
god in heaven forbid | we should infringe the R3 3.01. 40
favor | to him that does best, god forbid else. H8 2.02.114
the lord forbid! 3.02. 54
and jove forbid there should be done amongst us TRO 2.02.127
jupiter forbid, | and say in thunder, "achilles 2.03.198
which you do here forbid me, royal priam. 5.03. 75
hector! the gods forbid! 5.10. 3
the gods forbid! COR 3.01.232
now the good gods forbid | that our renowned 3.01.288
god forbid i should be so bold to press to TIT 4.03. 91 P
god forbid! ROM 1.03. 4
hath | forbid this bandying in verona streets. 3.01. 89
no, no, this shall forbid it. 4.03. 23
lord, | join with me to forbid him her resort, TIM 1.01.127
he shall live a man forbid; MAC 1.03. 21
and yet your beards forbid me to interpret 1.03. 46
but that i am forbid | to tell the secrets of my HAM 1.05. 13
poor ophelia, | and therefore i forbid my tears. 4.07.186
this courtesy, forbid thee, shall the duke LR 3.03. 21
i was forbid it. 5.01. 47
the heavens forbid | but that our loves and OTH 2.01.193
that | which heaven hath forbid the ottomites? 2.03.171
marry, /god forbid! 2.03.261 P
marry, heaven forbid! 5.01. 72
wrinkles forbid! ANT 1.02. 20 P
the gods forbid! 4.02. 19
the gods forbid! 5.02.213
and heaven forbid | that kings should let their PER 1.02. 61
heaven forbid, man! TNK 4.01.140
marry, god forbid that! STM II.C 96 P
but i forbid thee one most heinous crime, | o, SON 19. 8
that god forbid, that made me first your slave, 58. 1
or who his spoil /of beauty can forbid? 65.12
finding myself in honor so forbid, | with safest LC 150
FORBIDDEN *(also forbod)*
FORBIDDEN 5 FR 0.0005 REL FR 4 V 1 P
course, | before we enter his forbidden gates, LLL 2.01. 26
why have those banish'd and forbidden legs R2 2.03. 90
men, | forbidden late to carry any weapon, 1H6 3.01. 79
nay, if we be forbidden stones, we'll fall to it 3.01. 89 P
that use is not forbidden usury, | which happies SON 6. 5
FORBIDDENLY 1 FR 0.0001 REL FR 1 V 0 P
that you have touch'd his queen | forbiddenly. WT 1.02.417
FORBIDDINGS 1 FR 0.0001 REL FR 1 V 0 P
but all these poor forbiddings could not stay LUC 323
FORBIDS 6 FR 0.0006 REL FR 6 V 0 P
the treason that my haste forbids me show. R2 5.03. 50
he forbids it, | being free from vainness and H5 5.pr. 19
not open, | the cardinal of winchester forbids. 1H6 1.03. 19
that at her hands which the king's king forbids. R3 4.04.346
enforcement of the time | forbids to dwell upon, 5.03.239
the obligation of our blood forbids | a gory TRO 4.05.122
FORBID'T 1 FR 0.0001 REL FR 0 V 1 P
now gods forbid't, and i have a gown here! PER 2.01. 78 P
FORBOD *(also forbade, forbidden)*
FORBOD 2 FR 0.0002 REL FR 2 V 0 P
my bloody judge forbod my tongue to speak, | no LUC 1648
to be forbod the sweets that seems so good | for LC 164
FORBORNE 1 FR 0.0001 REL FR 1 V 0 P
rome, | forborne the getting of a lawful race, ANT 3.13.107
FORCA 1 FR 0.0001 REL FR 1 V 0 P
"piu per dolcera que per forca." PER 2.02. 27
/FORC'D 1 FR 0.0001 REL FR 1 V 0 P
of deaths put on by cunning and /forc'd cause, HAM 5.02.383
FORC'D 37 FR 0.0041 REL FR 36 V 1 P
that would have forc'd your honor and your love. TGV 5.04. 22
that he hath forc'd me to tell him he is indeed MM 3.02.253 P
forc'd me to seek delays for them and me. ERR 1.01. 74
me | that i am forc'd to lay my reverence by, ADO 5.01. 64
be forc'd | to give my hand oppos'd against my SHR 3.02. 8
with these forc'd thoughts, i prithee darken not WT 4.04. 41
fram'd, but forc'd | by need and accident. 5.01. 91
'tis like the forc'd gait of a shuffling nag. 1H4 3.01.133
but he hath forc'd us to compel this offer, 2H4 4.01.145
the pretty and sweet manner of it forc'd | those H5 4.06. 28
art thou king, and wilt be forc'd? 3H6 1.01.230
forc'd by the tide to combat with the wind; 2.05. 6
sea | forc'd to retire by fury of the wind. 2.05. 8
man, | and forc'd to live in scotland a forlorn; 3.03. 26
the region of my breast, which forc'd such way, H8 2.04.185
but thou hast forc'd me | (out of thy honest 3.02.429
that i was forc'd to wheel | three or four miles COR 1.06. 19
first time that ever | i was forc'd to scold. 5.06.105
forc'd in the ruthless, vast, and gloomy woods? TIT 4.01. 53
be that heart that forc'd us to this shift! 4.01. 72
inhuman traitors, you constrain'd and forc'd. 5.02.177
put out of office | before i were forc'd out! TIM 1.02.202
ground | do stand but in a forc'd affection, JC 4.03.205
were they not forc'd with those that should be MAC 5.05. 5
black, | nor windy suspiration of forc'd breath, HAM 1.02. 79
whom the rigor of our state | forc'd to cry out. LR 5.01. 23
so shall i clothe me in a forc'd content, | and OTH 3.04.120
may frame herself | to th' way she's forc'd to. ANT 5.01. 56
be enclouded, | and forc'd to drink their vapor. 5.02.213
forc'd to content, but never to obey, | panting VEN 61
forc'd it to tremble with her loyal fear! LUC 261
till life to death acquit my forc'd offense. 1071
that was not forc'd, that never was inclin'd 1657
back to the strait that forc'd him on so fast 1670
where thou art forc'd to break a twofold truth: SON 41.12
or forc'd examples, 'gainst her own content, LC 157
o, that forc'd thunder from his heart did fly, 325
FORCE* *(also farced, etc.)*
/FORCE* 1 FR 0.0001 REL FR 1 V 0 P
/was /force /perforce /compell'd /to /banish 2H4 4.01.114
FORCE* 123 FR 0.0139 REL FR 119 V 4 P
and would not force the letter to my view! TGV 1.02. 54
(which, unrevers'd, stands in effectual force) 3.01.225
ay, much is the force of heaven-bred poesy. 3.02. 71
love you 'gainst the nature of love — force ye. 5.04. 58
i'll force thee yield to my desire. 5.04. 59
the law by th' nose, | when he would force it? MM 3.01.109
by force took dromio and my son from them, | and ERR 5.01.353
maintain his part but in the force of his will. ADO 1.01.237 P
and take her hearing prisoner with the force 1.01.324
our late edict shall strongly stand in force: LLL 1.01. 11
we must of force dispense with this decree, 1.01.147
your oath once broke, you force not to forswear. 5.02.440
approve | this flower's force in stirring love. MND 2.02. 69
and thy fair virtue's force (perforce) doth move 3.01.140
that, when he wak'd, of force she must be ey'd. 3.02. 40
flower | hath such force and blessed power. 4.01. 74
wall, | even in the force and road of casualty. MV 2.09. 30
but of force | must yield to such inevitable 4.01. 56
there is no force in the decrees of venice. 4.01.102
his sceptre shows the force of temporal power, 4.01.190
dear sir, of force i must attempt you further. 4.01.421
your gentleness shall force, | more than your AYL 2.07.102
more than your force move us to gentleness. 2.07.103
nor i am sure there is no force in eyes | that 3.05. 26
camp i'll show, | their force, their purposes; AWW 4.01. 85
oil and fire, too strong for reason's force, 5.03. 7
fate, show thy force: TN 1.05.310
to force that on you in a shameful cunning 3.01.116
force me to keep you as a prisoner, | not like a WT 1.02. 52
force her hence. 2.03. 62
had force and knowledge | more than was ever 4.04.374
whom of force must know | the royal fool thou 4.04.423
hope is i shall so prevail | to force him after; 4.04.665
shall then my father's will be of no force | to JN 1.01.130
of no more force to dispossess me, sir, | than 1.01.132
against whose fury and unmatched force | the 1.01.265
and force perforce | keep stephen langton, 3.01.142
use our commission in his utmost force. 3.03. 11
for do we must what force will have us do. R2 3.03.207
it must of force. 1H4 2.03.117
i am sorry i should force you to believe | that 2H4 1.01.105
(as, force perforce, the age will pour it in), 4.04. 46
it shall not force | this lineal honor from me. 4.05. 45
with ample and brim fullness of his force, H5 1.02.150
force a play: 2.pr. 32
cut their passage through the force of france, 2.02. 16
impossible d'echapper la force de ton bras? 4.04. 16 P
where is my strength, my valor, and my force? 1H6 1.05. 1
a witch by fear, not force, like hannibal, 1.05. 21
the other yet may rise against their force. 2.01. 32
and those occasions, uncle, were of force: 3.01.156
all our general force | might with a sally of 4.04. 3
the fraud of england, not the force of france, 4.04. 36
of mine | which thou didst force from talbot, my 4.06. 24
whether it be through force of your report, | my 5.05. 79
that maine which by main force warwick did win, 2H6 1.01.210
and force perforce i'll make him yield the crown 1.01.258
leave | to show some reason, of no little force, 1.03.163
which now they hold by force and not by right; 2.02. 30
and turns the force of them upon thyself. 3.02.332
or dare to bring thy force so near the court. 5.01. 22
a man, | to force a spotless virgin's chastity, 5.01.186
i will, | for hither we have broken in by force. 3H6 1.01. 29
orator, | inferring arguments of mighty force. 2.02. 44
and force the tyrant from his seat by war. 3.03.206
there shall i rest secure from force and fraud. 4.04. 33
of force enough to bid his brother battle; 5.01. 77
sweetly in force unto her fair live's end. R3 4.04.351
thus doth he force the swords of wicked men | to 5.01. 23
the force of his own merit makes his way — | a H8 1.01. 64
that has denied | the force of this commission. 1.02.101
and force them with a constancy, the cardinal 3.02. 2
force should be right, or rather, right and TRO 1.03.116
force him with /praises — pour in, pour /in, 2.03.223 P
the edge of steel | or force of greekish sinews. 3.01.153
the hunter for thy life | with all my force, 4.01. 19
time, force, and death, | do to this body what 4.02.101
with such a careless force and forceless care 5.05. 40
i thought to crush him in an equal force, | true COR 1.10. 14
not fearing outward force, so shall my lungs 3.01. 77
why force you this? 3.02. 51
are stronger than | your gates against my force. 5.02. 89
and strike her home by force, if not by words; TIT 2.01.118
me most, | and force you to commiseration. 5.03. 93
being the time the potion's force should cease. ROM 5.03.249
head, sword, force, means, but is lord timon's? TIM 2.02.167
yet our old love made a particular force, | and 5.02. 8
good reasons must of force give place to better: JC 4.03.203
the english force, so please you. MAC 5.03. 18
could force his soul so to his own conceit HAM 2.02.553
it is to a bawd than the force of honesty can 3.01.112 P
and what's in prayer but this twofold force, 3.03. 48
in) return, and force | their scanted courtesy. LR 3.02. 66
of them, jointing their force 'gainst caesar, ANT 1.02. 92
hath with his parthian force | extended asia; 1.02.100
our force by land | hath nobly held; 3.13.169
and to-night i'll force | the wine peep through 3.13.189
for his best force | is forth to man his galleys 4.11. 2
very force entangles | itself with strength. 4.14. 48
would force the feeler's soul | to th' oath of CYM 1.06.101
will force him think i have pick'd the lock and 2.02. 41
sinks my knee, | as then your force did. 5.05.414
by you reliev'd, would force me to my duty; PER 3.03. 22
at once subduing | thy force and thy affection; TNK 1.01. 85
either presuming them to have some force, | or 1.01.194
not | my sister her petition, in that force, 1.01.201
ye | as kind a kinsman as you force me find | a 3.06. 21
can force his cousin | by fair and knightly 3.06.294
force and great feat | must put my garland on, 5.01. 43
that mayst force the king | to be his subject's 5.01. 83
with waters | that drift-winds force to raging. 5.03.100
desire doth lend her force | courageously to VEN 29

rank | perforce will force it overflow the bank. 72
fire, | so lucrece must i force to my desire." LUC 182
if thou deny, then force must work my way, | for 513
this forced league doth force a further strife, 689
for me, i force not argument a straw, | since 1021
of strange kinds | is form'd in them by force, 1243
her feeble force will yield at length, | when PP 18.33
sweet love, renew thy force, be it not said SON 56. 1
in their wealth, some in their body's force, 91. 2
for these, of force, must your oblations be, LC 223
her eye | upon the moment did her force subdue, 248
FORCED 8 FR 0.0009 REL FR 8 V 0 P
which forced marriage would have brought upon WIV 5.05.230
tak'st up the princess by that forced baseness WT 2.03. 79
child, | his little kingdom of a forced grave. JN 4.02. 98
than from it issued forced drops of blood. H5 4.01.297
for what is wedlock forced, but a hell, | an age 1H6 5.05. 62
did you by indirect and forced courses | subdue OTH 1.03.111
this forced league doth force a further strife, LUC 689
"how may this forced stain be wip'd from me? 1701
FORCEFUL 1 FR 0.0001 REL FR 1 V 0 P
but rather follow | our forceful instigation? WT 2.01.163
FORCELESS 2 FR 0.0002 REL FR 2 V 0 P
with such a careless force and forceless care TRO 5.05. 40
lie, | these forceless flowers like sturdy trees VEN 152
FORCES 23 FR 0.0026 REL FR 22 V 1 P
then turn your forces from this paltry siege, JN 2.01. 54
his forces strong, his soldiers confident. 2.01. 61
our general forces at bridgenorth shall meet. 1H4 3.02.178
who is it like should lead his forces hither? 2H4 1.03. 81
come all his forces back? 2.01.172
great accompt, | on your imaginary forces work. H5 pr 18
with half their forces the full pride of france, 1.02.112
never went with his forces into france | but 1.02.147
but gather we our forces out of hand, | and set 1H6 3.02.102
my forces and my power of men are yours. 3.03. 83
set from our o'ermatch'd forces forth for aid. 4.04. 11
his brother are hard by, with the king's forces. 2H6 4.02.114 P
then what intends these forces thou dost bring? 5.01. 60
away betimes, before his forces join, | and take 3H6 4.08. 62
at southam i did leave him with his forces, 5.01. 9
nay rather, wilt thou draw thy forces hence, 5.01. 25
myself, | look on my forces with a gracious eye; R3 5.03.109
is the guess of their true strength and forces, LR 5.01. 52
i will try the forces | of these thy compounds CYM 1.05. 18
is lucius general of the forces? 3.07. 11
with hostile forces he'll o'erspread the land, PER 1.02. 24
/aulis meet us with | the forces you can raise, TNK 1.01.213
the aloes of all forces, shocks, and fears. LC 273
FORCIBLE 3 FR 0.0003 REL FR 1 V 2 P
out of his right sense, so forcible is thy wit. ADO 5.02. 56 P
let that suffice, most forcible feeble. 2H4 3.02.167 P
but i have reasons strong and forcible. 3H6 1.02. 3
FORCIBLY 2 FR 0.0002 REL FR 2 V 0 P
to enforce these rights so forcibly withheld. JN 1.01. 18
forcibly prevents | our lock'd embrasures, TRO 4.04. 36
FORCING 3 FR 0.0003 REL FR 3 V 0 P
so forcing faults upon hermione, | i little like WT 3.01. 16
into the hand | of hot and forcing violation? H5 3.03. 21
but with much forcing of his disposition. HAM 3.01. 12
/FORD 2 FR 0.0002 REL FR 1 V 1 P
and i to /ford shall eke unfold | how falstaff, WIV 1.03. 96
and through flame, through /ford and whirlpool, LR 3.04. 53 P
FORD 59 FR 0.0066 REL FR 4 V 55 P
how now, mistress ford? WIV 1.01.191 P
mistress ford, by my troth, you are very well 1.01.192 P
which of you know ford of this town? 1.03. 36 P
and thou this to mistress ford. 1.03. 74 P
sir alice ford! 2.01. 51 P
but that the name of page and ford differs! 2.01. 71 P
both young and old, one with another, ford. 2.01.114
he loves the gallimaufry, ford. 2.01.115
how now, master ford! 2.01.168 P
there is one mistress ford, sir — i pray come a 2.02. 44 P
well, on. mistress ford, you say — 2.02. 47 P
well; mistress ford, what of her? 2.02. 54 P
mistress ford; come, mistress ford — 2.02. 58 P
mistress ford; come, mistress ford — 2.02. 58 P
master ford her husband will be from home. 2.02. 88 P
mistress ford and mistress page, have i 2.02.152 P
in this town, her husband's name is ford. 2.02.192 P
want no mistress ford, master /brook, you shall 2.02.260 P
do you know ford, sir? 2.02.269 P
i would you knew ford, sir, that you might avoid 2.02.276 P
well met, master ford. 3.02. 50 P
i must excuse myself, master ford. 3.02. 53 P
is come in at your back door, mistress ford, and 3.03. 25 P
mistress ford, i cannot cog, i cannot prate, 3.03. 48 P
i cannot cog, i cannot prate, mistress ford. 3.03. 49 P
mistress ford, mistress ford! 3.03. 85 P
mistress ford, mistress ford! 3.03. 85 P
o mistress ford, what have you done? 3.03. 94 P
o well–a–day, mistress ford, having an honest 3.03. 99 P
call your men, mistress ford. 3.03.144 P
good master ford, be contented. 3.03.166 P
you use me well, master ford, do you? 3.03.202 P
you do yourself mighty wrong, master ford. 3.03.208 P
fie, fie, master ford, are you not asham'd? 3.03.214 P
sir, i come to your worship from mistress ford. 3.05. 34 P
mistress ford? 3.05. 35 P
i have had ford enough. 3.05. 35 P
i was thrown into the ford; 3.05. 36 P
i have my belly full of ford. 3.05. 37 P
master /brook, you shall cuckold ford. 3.05.138 P
master ford, awake! 3.05.140 P
awake, master ford! 3.05.141 P
a hole made in your best coat, master ford. 3.05.142 P
mistress ford desires you to come suddenly. 4.01. 5 P
mistress ford, your sorrow hath eaten up my 4.02. 1 P
not only, mistress ford, in the simple office of 4.02. 4 P
what ho, gossip ford! what ho! 4.02. 9 P
why, this passes, master ford. 4.02.122 P
indeed, master ford, this is not well indeed. 4.02.126 P
come hither, mistress ford, mistress ford, the 4.02.129 P
mistress ford, mistress ford, the honest woman, 4.02.129 P
by my fidelity, this is not well, master ford; 4.02.154 P
master ford, you must pray, and not follow the 4.02.155 P
let them say of me, "as jealous as ford, that 4.02.163 P

go, mistress ford, | send quickly to sir john, 4.04. 82
mistress ford, good heart, is beaten black and 4.05.111 P
that same knave ford, her husband, hath the 5.01. 18 P
i'll tell you strange things of this knave ford, 5.01. 27 P
for he to–night shall lie with mistress ford. 5.05.245
FORDID *(also foredo, etc.)*
FORDID 1 FR 0.0001 REL FR 1 V 0 P
upon her own despair, | that she fordid herself. LR 5.03.256
FORDOES 1 FR 0.0001 REL FR 1 V 0 P
love, | whose violent property fordoes itself, HAM 2.01.100
FORD'S 12 FR 0.0013 REL FR 0 V 12 P
i do mean to make love to ford's wife. WIV 1.03. 44 P
has ford's wife and page's wife acquainted each 2.02.108 P
siege to the honesty of this ford's wife. 2.02.235 P
you shall, /and you will, enjoy ford's wife. 2.02.254 P
ford's a knave, and i will aggravate his style; 2.02.283 P
what hath pass'd between me and ford's wife? 3.05. 62 P
gives intelligence of ford's approach; 3.05. 85 P
in her invention and ford's wive's distraction, 3.05. 85 P
in the basket, a couple of ford's knaves, his 3.05. 98 P
is he at master ford's already, think'st thou? 4.01. 1 P
three of master ford's brothers watch the door 4.02. 51 P
enjoy'd nothing of ford's but his buck–basket, 5.05.112 P
FORDS 1 FR 0.0001 REL FR 1 V 0 P
sounds make lesser noise than shallow fords, LUC 1329
'FORE *(also afore, before, tofore)*
/'FORE 1 FR 0.0001 REL FR 1 V 0 P
we will post | to athens /'fore our army. TNK 1.04. 49
'FORE 38 FR 0.0043 REL FR 27 V 11 P
at any time 'fore noon. MM 2.02.160
'fore god, they are both in a tale. ADO 4.02. 30 P
'fore me, i speak in respect — AWW 2.03. 26 P
'fore god, i think so. 2.03. 45 P
'fore whose throne 'tis needful, | ere i can 4.04. 3
to prate and talk for life and honor 'fore | who WT 3.02. 41
come on, | contract us 'fore these witnesses. 4.04.390
(for so i see she must be) 'fore leontes. 4.04.545
not a month | 'fore your queen died, she was 5.01.226
to stop their marches 'fore we are inflam'd. JN 5.01. 7
'fore god, a likely fellow! 2H4 3.02.175 P
'fore god, would you would. 3.02.296 P
'fore god, you have here goodly dwelling and 5.03. 5 P
'fore god, his grace is bold to trust these H5 2.02. 1
the farced title running 'fore the king, | the 4.01.263
which like a mighty whiffler 'fore the king 5.pr. 12
faint–hearted woodvile, prizest him 'fore me? 1H6 1.03. 22
to bring my whole cause 'fore his holiness, H8 2.04.120
what would you 'fore our tent? TRO 1.03.215
'fore all the greekish heads, which with one 1.03.221
'fore me, this fellow speaks! COR 1.01.120
of these fair edifices 'fore my wars | have i 4.04. 3
go whip him 'fore the people's eyes — his 4.06. 61
your soldiers use him as the grace 'fore meat, 4.07. 3
unholy braggart, | 'fore your own eyes and ears? 5.06.119
'fore god, my lord, well spoken, with good HAM 2.02.466 P
'fore /god, they have given me a rouse already. OTH 2.03. 64 P
'fore /god, an excellent song. 2.03. 75 P
'fore /god, this is a more exquisite song than 2.03. 98 P
must not so far prefer her 'fore ours of italy. CYM 1.04. 65 P
a season) 'fore noble lucius | present yourself, 3.04.172
sweet, | lie 'fore bride and bridegroom's feet, TNK 1.01. 14
lords | lie blist'ring 'fore the visitating sun, 1.01.146
that 'fore thy dignity will dance a morris. 3.05.108
and all we'll dance an antic 'fore the duke, 4.01. 75
thy priest, | am humbled 'fore thine altar. 5.01.143
i am like to know your husband 'fore yourself 5.03. 37
the eyes ('fore duteous) now converted are SON 7.11
FORE–ADVIS'D 1 FR 0.0001 REL FR 1 V 0 P
as you were fore–advis'd, had touch'd his spirit COR 2.03.191
FORE–BEMOANED 1 FR 0.0001 REL FR 1 V 0 P
o'er | the sad account of fore–bemoaned moan, SON 30.11
FORE–BETRAY'D 1 FR 0.0001 REL FR 1 V 0 P
would yet again betray the fore–betray'd, | and LC 328
FORECAST 1 FR 0.0001 REL FR 1 V 0 P
alas, that warwick had no more forecast, | but, 3H6 5.01. 42
FOREDO *(also fordid, etc.)*
FOREDO 1 FR 0.0001 REL FR 1 V 0 P
did with desp'rate hand | foredo it own life. HAM 5.01.221
FOREDOES 1 FR 0.0001 REL FR 1 V 0 P
that either makes me, or foredoes me quite. OTH 5.01.129
FOREDONE 2 FR 0.0002 REL FR 2 V 0 P
snores, | all with weary task foredone. MND 5.01.374
your eldest daughters have foredone themselves, LR 5.03.292
FORE–END 1 FR 0.0001 REL FR 1 V 0 P
to heaven than in all | the fore–end of my time. CYM 3.03. 73
FOREFATHER 1 FR 0.0001 REL FR 1 V 0 P
is still deriv'd | from some forefather grief; R2 2.02. 35
FOREFATHERS' 2 FR 0.0002 REL FR 2 V 0 P
no, if i digg'd up thy forefathers' graves | and 3H6 1.03. 27
and madly play with my forefathers' joints, ROM 4.03. 51
FOREFATHERS 1 FR 0.0001 REL FR 0 V 1 P
our forefathers had no other books but the score 2H6 4.07. 34 P
FOREFEND *(also forfend, etc.)*
FOREFEND 5 FR 0.0005 REL FR 5 V 0 P
to be made, but by | (as heavens forefend!) WT 4.04.530
must edward fall, which peril heaven forefend! 3H6 2.01.191
thy unprepared spirit, | no, /heaven forefend! OTH 5.02. 32
o heavens forefend! 5.02.186
marry, the gods forefend! CYM 5.05.287
FOREFINGER 2 FR 0.0002 REL FR 1 V 1 P
as tib's rush for tom's forefinger, as a pancake AWW 2.02. 23 P
agot–stone | on the forefinger of an alderman, ROM 1.04. 56
FORE–FOOT 1 FR 0.0001 REL FR 1 V 0 P
give me thy fist, thy fore–foot to me give. H5 2.01. 67
FOREGOERS 1 FR 0.0001 REL FR 1 V 0 P
our acts we them derive | than our foregoers. AWW 2.03.137
FOREGONE 4 FR 0.0004 REL FR 4 V 0 P
by our remembrances of days foregone, | such AWW 1.03.134
but this denoted a foregone conclusion. OTH 3.03.428
than all the actions that i have foregone | or TNK 1.01.173
then can i grieve at grievances foregone, | and SON 30. 9
'FOREHAND *(also aforehand, beforehand)*
'FOREHAND 1 FR 0.0001 REL FR 1 V 0 P
a husband, | and so extenuate the 'forehand sin. ADO 4.01. 50
FOREHAND 3 FR 0.0003 REL FR 2 V 1 P
and carried you a forehand shaft a fourteen and 2H4 3.02. 47 P
sleep, | had the forehand and vantage of a king. H5 4.01.280
crowns | the sinow and the forehand of our host, TRO 1.03.143

FOREHEAD 23 FR 0.0026 REL FR 14 V 9 P
and so buffets himself on the forehead, crying, WIV 4.02. 25 P
in her forehead, arm'd and reverted, making war ERR 3.02.123 P
i will have a rechate winded in my forehead, or ADO 1.01.241 P
the bull's horns and set them in my forehead, 1.01.264 P
would from my forehead wipe a perjur'd note: LLL 4.03.123
nor did not with unbashful forehead woo | the AYL 2.03. 50
so is the forehead of a married man more 3.03. 60 P
through the army with this rhyme in 's forehead. AWW 4.03.234 P
gait, the expressure of his eye, forehead, and TN 2.03.158 P
the trick of 's frown, his forehead, nay, the WT 2.03.101
and in his forehead sits | a bare–ribb'd death, JN 5.02.176
to look with forehead bold and big enough | upon 2H4 1.03. 8
hid'st thou that forehead with a golden crown R3 4.04.140
as smiles upon the forehead of this action | for TRO 2.02.205
troth, sweet /lord, thou hast a fine forehead. 3.01.108 P
than hector's forehead when it spit forth blood COR 1.03. 42
the night than with the forehead of the morning. 2.01. 52 P
by her high forehead and her scarlet lip, | by ROM 2.01. 18
even to the teeth and forehead of our faults, HAM 3.03. 63
from the fair forehead of an innocent love | and 3.04. 43
i have a pain upon my forehead, here. OTH 3.03.284
and her forehead | as low as she would wish it. ANT 3.03. 33
brand not my forehead with thy piercing light, LUC 1091
FOREHEAD'S 1 FR 0.0001 REL FR 1 V 0 P
ay, but her forehead's low, and mine's as high. TGV 4.04.193
FOREHEADS 1 FR 0.0001 REL FR 1 V 0 P
or to apes | with foreheads villainous low. TMP 4.01.249
FOREHORSE 2 FR 0.0002 REL FR 2 V 0 P
i shall stay here the forehorse to a smock, AWW 2.01. 30
either i am | the forehorse in the team, or i am TNK 1.02. 59
/FOREIGN 1 FR 0.0001 REL FR 1 V 0 P
/turn'd /her | /to /foreign /casualties, /gave LR 4.03. 44
FOREIGN 28 FR 0.0031 REL FR 28 V 0 P
is no bar | to stop the foreign spirits, but MV 2.07. 46
breeds | a native slip to us from foreign seeds. AWW 1.03.146
secure | and confident from foreign purposes, JN 2.01. 28
never such a pow'r | for any foreign preparation 4.02.111
even at my gates, with ranks of foreign pow'rs; 4.02.244
of soul | to stranger blood, to foreign royalty. 5.01. 11
a long apprenticehood | to foreign passages, and R2 1.03.272
and sigh'd my english breath in foreign clouds, 3.01. 20
to busy giddy minds | with foreign quarrels, 2H4 4.05.214
that he should, for a foreign purse, so sell H5 2.02. 10
may it be possible that foreign hire | could out 2.02.100
grieve thee more than streams of foreign gore. 1H6 3.03. 55
when foreign princes shall be certified | that 4.01.144
this tongue hath parley'd unto foreign kings 2H6 4.07. 77
'gainst foreign storms than any home–bred 3H6 4.01. 38
till we meet warwick with his foreign pow'r. 4.01.149
soul | leads discontented steps in foreign soil, R3 4.04.312
in arms, | if not to fight with foreign enemies, 4.04.529
men than they can be | out of a foreign wisdom, H8 1.03. 29
as great embassadors | from foreign princes. 1.04. 56
kept him a foreign man still, which so griev'd 2.02.128
or else | to foreign princes, "ego et rex meus" 3.02.314
either thou | must as a foreign recreant be led COR 5.03.114
and then dreams he of cutting foreign throats, ROM 1.04. 83
malice domestic, foreign levy, nothing, | can MAC 3.02. 25
and foreign mart for implements of war, | why HAM 1.01. 74
and pour our treasures into foreign laps; OTH 4.03. 88
and yourself, | with more than foreign heart. PER 4.01. 33
FOREIGNERS 1 FR 0.0001 REL FR 1 V 0 P
when adverse foreigners affright my towns | with JN 4.02.172
FOREKNOWING 3 FR 0.0003 REL FR 3 V 0 P
foreknowing that the truth will fall out so. JN 4.02.154
fate, | which, happily, foreknowing may avoid, HAM 1.01.134
foreknowing well, if there he came to lie, | why VEN 245
FOREKNOWLEDGE 1 FR 0.0001 REL FR 0 V 1 P
he seems to have a foreknowledge of that too, TN 1.05.143 P
FOREMOST 5 FR 0.0005 REL FR 5 V 0 P
valor, | goes foremost in report through italy. ADO 3.01. 97
in which you, father, shall have foremost hand. 2H4 5.02.140
this most wise rebellion, thou goest foremost; COR 1.01.158
my wife comes foremost; 5.03. 22
that struck the foremost man of all this world JC 4.03. 22
FORENAM'D 1 FR 0.0001 REL FR 0 V 1 P
this forenam'd maid hath yet in her the MM 3.01.239 P
FORENOON 2 FR 0.0002 REL FR 0 V 2 P
out a good wholesome forenoon in hearing a cause COR 2.01. 69 P
let me be married to three kings in a forenoon, ANT 1.02. 27 P
FORE–PAST 1 FR 0.0001 REL FR 1 V 0 P
my fore–past proofs, howe'er the matter fall, AWW 5.03.121
FORE–RANK 1 FR 0.0001 REL FR 1 V 0 P
within the fore–rank of our articles. H5 5.02. 97
FORE–RECITED 1 FR 0.0001 REL FR 1 V 0 P
bid him recount | the fore–recited practices, H8 1.02.127
FORERUN 4 FR 0.0004 REL FR 4 V 0 P
and merry hours | forerun fair love, strewing LLL 4.03.377
these signs forerun the death or fall of kings. R2 2.04. 15
woe is forerun with woe. 3.04. 28
o, this same thought did but forerun my need, ROM 5.01. 53
FORERUNNER 3 FR 0.0003 REL FR 1 V 2 P
and there is a forerunner come from a fift, the MV 1.02.124 P
arthur, that great forerunner of thy blood, JN 2.01. 2
there comes with them a forerunner, my lord, TIM 1.02.119 P
FORERUNNING 1 FR 0.0001 REL FR 1 V 0 P
to public thanks, | forerunning more requital. MM 5.01. 8
FORERUNS 1 FR 0.0001 REL FR 1 V 0 P
merry, | but heaviness foreruns the good event. 2H4 4.02. 82
FORESAID *(also aforesaid)*
FORESAID 6 FR 0.0006 REL FR 4 V 2 P
cracking the stones of the foresaid pruins — MM 2.01.107 P
with the parents of the foresaid child or pupil, LLL 4.02.156 P
this, in our foresaid holy father's name, | pope JN 3.01.145
to charles, the foresaid duke of lorraine; H5 1.02. 83
king's course, | and break the foresaid peace. H8 1.01.190
those foresaid lands | so by his father lost; HAM 1.01.103
FORESAW 1 FR 0.0001 REL FR 1 V 0 P
weep what it foresaw | in hector's wrath. TRO 1.02. 10
FORESAY 1 FR 0.0001 REL FR 1 V 0 P
let ord'nance | come as the gods foresay it; CYM 4.02.146
FORESEE 6 FR 0.0006 REL FR 5 V 1 P
that you foresee not what impediments | drag 1H4 4.03. 18
i foresee with grief | the utter loss of all the 1H6 5.04.111
cassandra doth foresee, and i myself | am like a TRO 5.03. 64
away | of him that, his particular to foresee, TIM 4.03.159

i make not, but foresee. ANT 1.02. 15
pray then, foresee me one. 1.02. 16 P
FORESEEING 1 FR 0.0001 REL FR 1 V 0 P
grace | and princely care foreseeing those fell H8 5.01. 49
FORESEES 1 FR 0.0001 REL FR 1 V 0 P
my master through his art foresees the danger TMP 2.01.297
FORESHOW 1 FR 0.0001 REL FR 1 V 0 P
and your looks foreshow | you have a gentle PER 4.01. 85
FORESHOW'D 1 FR 0.0001 REL FR 1 V 0 P
which foreshow'd our princely eagle, | th' CYM 5.05.473
FORESIGHT 1 FR 0.0001 REL FR 1 V 0 P
but her foresight could not forestall their will LUC 728
FORESKIRT 1 FR 0.0001 REL FR 1 V 0 P
honor's train | is longer than his foreskirt. H8 2.03. 98
FORESLOW 1 FR 0.0001 REL FR 1 V 0 P
foreslow no longer, make we hence amain. 3H6 2.03. 56
FORESPENT 4 FR 0.0004 REL FR 4 V 0 P
hard | a gentleman, almost forespent with speed, 2H4 1.01. 37
and you shall find his vanities forespent | were H5 2.04. 36
forespent with toil, as runners with a race, | i 3H6 2.03. 1
towards himself, his goodness forespent on us, CYM 2.03. 59
FORESPOKE 1 FR 0.0001 REL FR 1 V 0 P
thou hast forespoke my being in these wars, ANT 3.07. 3
FORE–SPURRER 1 FR 0.0001 REL FR 1 V 0 P
as this fore–spurrer comes before his lord. MV 2.09. 95
FOREST 45 FR 0.0050 REL FR 27 V 18 P
the forest is not three leagues off; TGV 5.01. 11
as he in penance wander'd through the forest; 5.02. 38
(sometime a keeper here in windsor forest) WIV 4.04. 29
stag, and the fattest, i think, i' th' forest. 5.05. 13 P
yokes | become the forest better than the town? 5.05.108
met we on hill, in dale, forest, or mead, | by MND 2.01. 83
through the forest have i gone, | but athenian 2.02. 66
they say he is already in the forest of arden, AYL 1.01.114 P
to seek my uncle in the forest of arden. 1.03.107
well, this is the forest of arden. 2.04. 15 P
if this uncouth forest yield any thing savage, i 2.06. 6 P
i met a fool i' th' forest, | a motley fool. 2.07. 12
that every eye which in this forest looks 3.02. 7
but whether wisely or no, let the forest judge. 3.02.122 P
that i am in this forest and in man's apparel? 3.02.229 P
there's no clock in the forest. 3.02.301 P
then there is no true lover in the forest, else 3.02.302 P
here in the skirts of the forest, like fringe 3.02.336 P
there is a man haunts the forest, that abuses 3.02.360 P
you shall tell me where in the forest you live. 3.02.431 P
me in this place of the forest and to couple us. 3.03. 45 P
he attends here in the forest on the duke your 3.04. 33 P
where in the purlieus of this forest stands | a 4.03. 76
within an hour, and pacing through the forest, 4.03.100
is a youth here in the forest lays claim to you. 5.01. 7 P
a fair name. wast born i' the forest here? 5.01. 22 P
obscured in the circle of this forest. 5.04. 34
that i have so often met in the forest. 5.04. 42 P
men of great worth resorted to this forest, 5.04.155
in this forest let us do those ends | that here 5.04.170
dispark'd my parks and fell'd my forest woods, R2 3.01. 23
what is this forest call'd? 2H4 4.01. 1
'tis gaultree forest, and't shall please your 4.01. 2
west of this forest, scarcely off a mile, | in 4.01. 19
whose hand is that the forest bear doth lick? 3H6 2.02. 13
him | in secret ambush on the forest side, | and 4.06. 83
and made the forest tremble when they roar'd. 5.07. 12
the forest walks are wide and spacious, | and TIT 2.01.114
to see the general hunting in this forest? 2.03. 59
of athens is become a forest of beasts. TIM 4.03.348 P
thou wast the forest to this hart, | and this JC 3.01.207
who can impress the forest, bid the tree | unfix MAC 4.01. 95
bane, | till birnan forest come to dunsinane. 5.03. 60
sir, and a forest of feathers — if the rest of HAM 3.02.275 P
that shook the aged forest with their echoes, TNK 2.02. 47
FORESTALL 7 FR 0.0008 REL FR 6 V 1 P
and might not you | forestall our sport, to make LLL 5.02.473
forestall prescience, and esteem no act | but TRO 1.03.199
i shall forestall thee, lord ulysses, thou! 4.05.230
i will forestall their repair hither, and say HAM 5.02.218 P
this night forestall him of the coming day! CYM 3.05. 69
"thus i forestall thee, if thou mean to chide, LUC 484
her foresight could not forestall their will. 728
FORESTALL'D 2 FR 0.0002 REL FR 2 V 0 P
i had forestall'd this dear and deep rebuke 2H4 4.05.140
i will beg | a ragged and forestall'd remission. 5.02. 38
FORESTALLED 1 FR 0.0001 REL FR 1 V 0 P
force, | to be forestalled ere we come to fall, HAM 3.03. 49
FOREST–BORN 1 FR 0.0001 REL FR 1 V 0 P
but, my good lord, this boy is forest–born, AYL 5.04. 30
FORESTER 6 FR 0.0006 REL FR 4 V 2 P
then, forester, my friend, where is the bush LLL 4.01. 7
and, like a forester, the groves may tread MND 3.02.390
go, one of you, find out the forester, | for now 4.01.103
dispatch, i say, and find the forester. 4.01.108
do you hear, forester? AYL 3.02.297 P
have you no song, forester, for this purpose? 4.02. 6 P
FORESTERS 1 FR 0.0001 REL FR 0 V 1 P
let us be diana's foresters, gentlemen of the 1H4 1.02. 26 P
FORESTS 3 FR 0.0003 REL FR 3 V 0 P
knight of his train, to trace the forests wild; MND 2.01. 25
with shadowy forests and with champains rich'd, LR 1.01. 64
have from the forests shook three summers' pride SON 104. 4
FORETELL 5 FR 0.0005 REL FR 4 V 1 P
it makes | foretell the ending of mortality. JN 5.07. 5
and thus expiring do foretell of him: R2 2.01. 32
whose heavy looks foretell | some dreadful story 3H6 2.01. 43
but when he performs, astronomers foretell it: TRO 5.01. 92 P
foretell new storms to those already spent; LUC 1589
FORETELLING 1 FR 0.0001 REL FR 1 V 0 P
foretelling this same time's condition | and the 2H4 3.01. 78
FORETELLS 3 FR 0.0003 REL FR 3 V 0 P
foretells | the great apollo suddenly will have WT 2.03.199
foretells a tempest and a blust'ring day. 1H4 5.01. 6
foretells the nature of a tragic volume. 2H4 1.01. 61
FORETHINK 1 FR 0.0001 REL FR 1 V 0 P
every man | prophetically do forethink thy fall. 1H4 3.02. 38
FORETHINKING 1 FR 0.0001 REL FR 1 V 0 P
forethinking this, i have already fit | ('tis in CYM 3.04.168
FORETHOUGHT 1 FR 0.0001 REL FR 1 V 0 P
alter not the doom | forethought by heaven! JN 3.01.312
FORETOLD 4 FR 0.0004 REL FR 4 V 0 P
these our actors | (as i foretold you) were all TMP 4.01.149
are well foretold that danger lurks within. 3H6 4.07. 12
which he himself | foretold should be his last, H8 4.02. 27
sir, i foretold you then what would ensue. TRO 4.05.217
FORE–VOUCH'D 1 FR 0.0001 REL FR 1 V 0 P
or your fore–vouch'd affection | fall into taint LR 1.01.220
FOREWARD 1 FR 0.0001 REL FR 1 V 0 P
my foreward shall be drawn out all in length, R3 5.03.293
FOREWARN 2 FR 0.0002 REL FR 1 V 1 P
forewarn him that he use no scurrilous words in WT 4.04.213 P
sin | which oft th' apostle did forewarn us of, STM II.C 94
FOREWARN'D 1 FR 0.0001 REL FR 1 V 0 P
well, i will arm me, being thus forewarn'd. 3H6 4.01.113
FOREWARNED 1 FR 0.0001 REL FR 1 V 0 P
my lords, we were forewarned of your coming, 3H6 4.07. 17
FOREWARNING 1 FR 0.0001 REL FR 1 V 0 P
but well forewarning wind | did seem to say, 2H6 3.02. 85
FOREWEARIED 1 FR 0.0001 REL FR 1 V 0 P
forewearied in this action of swift speed, JN 2.01.233
FORFEIT 30 FR 0.0034 REL FR 23 V 7 P
sense your brother's life | falls into forfeit; MM 1.04. 66
your brother is a forfeit of the law, | and you 2.02. 71
why, all the souls that were were forfeit once, 2.02. 73
admonition, and still forfeit in the same kind! 3.02.193 P
is no greater forfeit to the law than angelo who 4.02.158 P
our states are forfeit, seek not to undo us. LLL 5.02.425
that you stand forfeit, being those that sue? 5.02.427
let the forfeit | be nominated for an equal MV 1.03.148
why, fear not, man, i will not forfeit it. 1.03.156
i am sure, if he forfeit, thou wilt not take his 3.01. 51 P
i will have the heart of him if he forfeit, for, 3.01.127 P
is very low, my bond to the jew is forfeit; 3.02.317 P
sworn | to have the due and forfeit of my bond. 4.01. 37
the law, | the penalty and forfeit of my bond. 4.01.207
on forfeit of my hands, my head, my heart. 4.01.212
why, this bond is forfeit, | and lawfully by 4.01.230
and yet, thy wealth being forfeit to the state, 4.01.365
my soul upon the forfeit, that your lord | will 5.01.252
that with the divine forfeit of his soul upon AWW 3.06. 32 P
i know his brains are forfeit to the next tile 4.03.190 P
shall for the fault make forfeit of his head. 3H6 2.01.197
the forfeit, sovereign, of my servant's life, R3 2.01.100
to forfeit all your goods, lands, tenements, H8 3.02.342
your lives shall pay the forfeit of the peace. ROM 1.01. 97
breast | by some vile forfeit of untimely death. 1.04.111
did forfeit (with his life) all /those his lands HAM 1.01. 88
quite crack'd, | i having ta'en the forfeit. CYM 5.05.208
might | omit a ward, or forfeit an offense, TNK 5.03. 63
suppos'd as forfeit to a confin'd doom. SON 107. 4
myself i'll forfeit, so that other mine | thou 134. 3
FORFEITED 5 FR 0.0005 REL FR 4 V 1 P
undone, and forfeited to cares for ever! AWW 2.03.267
a widower, his vows are forfeited to me, and my 5.03.142 P
when they have lost and forfeited themselves? 1H4 1.03. 88
wales, | there without ransom to lie forfeited; 4.03. 96
'tis all engag'd, some forfeited and gone, | and TIM 2.02.146
FORFEITERS 1 FR 0.0001 REL FR 1 V 0 P
though forfeiters you cast in prison, yet | you CYM 3.02. 38
FORFEITING 2 FR 0.0002 REL FR 2 V 0 P
by forfeiting a traitor and a coward. 1H6 4.03. 27
is, beside forfeiting | our own brains and the H8 pr 19
FORFEITS 4 FR 0.0004 REL FR 4 V 0 P
stand like the forfeits in a barber's shop, | as MM 5.01.321
and therewithal | remit thy other forfeits. 5.01.520
despising many forfeits and subduements, | when TRO 4.05.187
he forfeits his own blood that spills another. TIM 3.05. 87
FORFEITURE 8 FR 0.0009 REL FR 8 V 0 P
i gain | by the exaction of the forfeiture? MV 1.03.164
drive him from the envious plea | of forfeiture, 3.02.283
duke | will never grant this forfeiture to hold. 3.03. 25
thou wilt not only loose the forfeiture, | but, 4.01. 24
to cut the forfeiture from that bankrout there. 4.01.122
why doth the jew pause? take thy forfeiture. 4.01.335
thou shalt have nothing but the forfeiture, | to 4.01.343
'twas due on forfeiture, my lord, six weeks TIM 2.02. 30
FORFEITURES 1 FR 0.0001 REL FR 1 V 0 P
i oft deliver'd from his forfeitures | many that MV 3.03. 22
FORFEND *(also forefend)*
FORFEND 5 FR 0.0005 REL FR 5 V 0 P
o, forfend it, god, | that in a christian R2 4.01.129
now heaven forfend, the holy maid with child? 1H6 5.04. 65
marry, god forfend! 2H6 3.02. 30
now heavens forfend such scarcity of /youth! TRO 1.03.302
the gods of rome forfend | i should be author to TIT 1.01.434
FORFENDED 1 FR 0.0001 REL FR 1 V 0 P
found my brother's way | to the forfended place? LR 5.01. 11
FORGAVE 2 FR 0.0002 REL FR 1 V 1 P
slander her love, and he forgave it her. MV 5.01. 22
and forgave him with all their hearts. JC 1.02.272 P
FORG'D 8 FR 0.0009 REL FR 8 V 0 P
be forg'd in your thoughts be servants to you! AWW 1.01. 75
as you yourself have forg'd against yourself 1H4 5.01. 68
book | of forg'd rebellion with a seal divine. 2H4 4.01. 92
that therefore i have forg'd, or am not able 1H6 3.01. 12
burns under feigned ashes of forg'd love, | and 3.01.189
far, until | it forg'd him some design, which, H8 1.02.181
till he had forg'd himself a name a' th' fire COR 5.01. 14
fall | on mars's armor forg'd for proof eterne HAM 2.02.490
FORGE 5 FR 0.0005 REL FR 4 V 1 P
come, to the forge with it, then shape it. WIV 4.02.223 P
in the quick forge and working–house of thought, H5 5.pr. 23
but, by the forge that /stithied mars his helm, TRO 4.05.255
what e'er i forge to feed his brain–sick humors, TIT 5.02. 71
that i should forge | quarrels unjust against MAC 4.03. 82
FORGED 6 FR 0.0006 REL FR 6 V 0 P
where it was forged, with my rapier's point. R2 4.01. 40
for though he seem with forged quaint conceit 1H6 4.01.102
of denmark | is by a forged process of my death HAM 1.05. 37
damn'd pisanio | hath with his forged letters CYM 4.02.318
love is all truth, lust full of forged lies. VEN 804
why of eyes' falsehood hast thou forged hooks, SON 137. 7
FORGERIES 4 FR 0.0004 REL FR 4 V 0 P
these are the forgeries of jealousy; MND 2.01. 81
there put on him | what forgeries you please: HAM 2.01. 20
such shadows are the weak brain's forgeries, LUC 460
unskillful in the world's false forgeries. PP 1. 4
FORGERY 3 FR 0.0003 REL FR 3 V 0 P
and now, to soothe your forgery and his, | sends 3H6 3.03.175
that i, in forgery of shapes and tricks, | come HAM 4.07. 89
guilty of treason, forgery, and shift, | guilty LUC 920
FORGES 4 FR 0.0004 REL FR 3 V 1 P
and then to return and swear the lies he forges. AWW 4.01. 23 P
to me the difference forges dread; WT 4.04. 17
what his breast forges, that his tongue must COR 3.01.257
i should make very forges of my cheeks, | that OTH 4.02. 74
/FORGET 1 FR 0.0001 REL FR 1 V 0 P
/as /if /we /should /forget /we /had /no /hands, TIT 3.02. 32
FORGET 95 FR 0.0107 REL FR 83 V 12 P
dost thou forget | from what a torment i did TMP 1.02.250
i forget; 3.01. 13
and my father's precepts | i therein do forget. 3.01. 59
i will forget that julia is alive, | rememb'ring TGV 2.06. 27
what might we do to make the girl forget | the 3.02. 29
one julia, that his changing thoughts forget, 4.04.119
know then, i here forget all former griefs, 5.04.142
if you forget your qui's, your /quae's, and your WIV 4.01. 77 P
oak | of herne the hunter, let us not forget. 5.05. 76
but, whilst i live, forget to drink after thee. MM 1.02. 39 P
written down, yet forget not that i am an ass. ADO 4.02. 77 P
masters, do not forget to specify, when time and 5.01.255 P
it doth forget to do the thing it should; LLL 1.01.144
i would forget her, but, a fever, she | reigns 4.03. 93
forget the shames that you have stain'd me with, MV 1.03.139
you could teach me to forget a banish'd father, AYL 1.02. 5 P
well, i will forget the condition of my estate, 1.02. 15 P
mean time, forget this new–fall'n dignity, | and 5.04.176
would not the beggar then forget himself? SHR in.1. 41
i could not forget you, for i never saw you 5.01. 50 P
be this sweet helen's knell, and now forget her. AWW 5.03. 67
have minded you | of what you should forget. WT 3.02.226
do as the heavens have done, forget your evil, 5.01. 5
virtues, i cannot forget | my blemishes in them, 5.01. 7
for new–made honor doth forget men's names; JN 1.01.187
we like not this, thou dost forget thyself. 3.01.134
for then 'tis like i should forget myself. 3.04. 49
o, if i could, what grief should i forget! 3.04. 50
if i were mad, i should forget my son, | or 3.04. 57
i would not have you, lord, forget yourself, 4.03. 83
i, by marking of your rage, forget | your worth, 4.03. 85
forget, forgive, conclude and be agreed, | our R2 1.01.156
how dare thy joints forget | to pay their aweful 3.03. 75
or that i could forget what i have been! 3.03.138
forget to pity him, lest thy pity prove | a 5.03. 57
thou't forget me when i am gone. 2H4 2.04.277 P
how might a prince of my great hopes forget | so 5.02. 68
your highness pleased to forget my place, | the 5.02. 77
and shall forget the office of our hand | sooner H5 2.02. 33
old men forget; 4.03. 49
go, let's not forget | the noble duke of bedford 1H6 3.02.131
quite to forget this quarrel, and the cause. 4.01.136
be patient, gentle nell, forget this grief. 2H6 2.04. 26
ah, gloucester, teach me to forget myself! 2.04. 27
you forget | that we are those which chas'd you 3H6 1.01. 89
did i forget that by the house of york | my 3.03.186
and i forgive and quite forget old faults, | and 3.03.200
they quite forget their loss of liberty. 4.06. 15
but we now forget | our title to the crown and 4.07. 45
let me put in your minds, if you forget, | what R3 1.03.130
shall i forget myself to be myself? 4.04.420
my commission | bid ye so far forget yourselves? H8 5.02.177
of olympus, forget that thou art jove, the king TRO 2.03. 10 P
upon their ancient malice will forget | with the COR 2.01.228
i would they would forget me, like the virtues 2.03. 57
forget not | with what contempt he wore the 2.03.220
does forget that ever | he heard the name of 3.01.258
and when i do forget | the least of these TIT 1.01.255
deserts, | romans, forget your fealty to me. 1.01.257
be rul'd by me, forget to think of her. ROM 1.01.225
o, teach me how i should forget to think. 1.01.226
he that is strooken blind cannot forget | the 1.01.232
farewell, thou canst not teach me to forget. 1.01.237
and she was wean'd — i never shall forget it — 1.03. 24
a thousand years, | i never should forget it: 1.03. 47
i shall forget, to have thee still stand there, 2.02.172
and i'll still stay, to have thee still forget, 2.02.174
i would forget it fain, | but o, it presses to 3.02.109
to forget their faults, i drink to you. TIM 1.02.107 P
forget | what we are sorry for ourselves in thee 5.01.138
forget not, in your speed, antonio, | to touch JC 1.02. 6
you forget yourself | to hedge me in. 4.03. 29
urge me no more, i shall forget myself; 4.03. 35
i do forget. MAC 3.04. 83
horatio — or i do forget myself. HAM 1.02.161
most necessary 'tis that we forget | to pay 3.02.192
do not forget! 3.04.110
and labor'd much | how to forget that learning, 5.02. 35
i will forget my nature. LR 1.05. 32 P
pray you now forget, and forgive; 4.07. 83
the best sometimes forget. OTH 2.03.241
my general will forget my love and service. 3.03. 18
nay, you must forget that. 4.01.180 P
born that day | when i forget to send to antony, ANT 1.05. 64
to forget them quite | were to remember that the 2.02.100
you put me to forget a lady's manners | by being CYM 2.03.105
you must forget to be a woman; 3.04.154
forget that rarest treasure of your cheek, 3.04.160
and forget | your laborsome and dainty trims, 3.04.163
see if 'twill teach us to forget our own? PER 1.04. 3
be wise then | and here forget 'em; TNK 3.06.223
forget i love her? 3.06.257
her voice is stopp'd, her joints forget to bow, VEN 1061
forget to say | the perfect ceremony of love's SON 23. 5
after my death, dear love, forget me quite, 72. 3
FORGETFUL 5 FR 0.0005 REL FR 5 V 0 P
the crown | upon the head of this forgetful man, 1H4 1.03.161
and we forgetful | in our long absence. H8 2.03.105
which my mother gave me | makes me forgetful? JC 4.03.121
bear with me, good boy, i am much forgetful. 4.03.255
return, forgetful muse, and straight redeem | in SON 100. 5
FORGETFULNESS 6 FR 0.0006 REL FR 6 V 0 P
torment me for my love's forgetfulness! TGV 2.02. 12
down, | and steep my senses in forgetfulness? 2H4 3.01. 8
gulf | of dark forgetfulness and deep oblivion. R3 3.07.129
ingrate forgetfulness shall poison rather | than COR 5.02. 86
toward thee forgetfulness too general gross; TIM 5.01.144

thee | were to import forgetfulness in me. SON 122.14
FORGETIVE 1 FR 0.0001 REL FR 0 V 1 P
apprehensive, quick, forgetive, full of nimble, 2H4 4.03. 99 P
FORGETS 4 FR 0.0004 REL FR 3 V 1 P
end of his commonwealth forgets the beginning. TMP 2.01.158 P
who in rage forgets | aged contusions and all 2H6 5.03. 2
war, | forgets the shows of love to other men. JC 1.02. 47
forgets school–doing, being therein train'd TNK 5.04. 68
FORGET'ST 3 FR 0.0003 REL FR 3 V 0 P
what thou hast been, | which thou forget'st. TMP 1.02.263
to get, | and what thou hast, forget'st. MM 3.01. 23
that thou forget'st so long | to speak of that SON 100. 1
FORGETTING 6 FR 0.0006 REL FR 6 V 0 P
deed | the pow'rs, delaying (not forgetting), TMP 3.03. 73
forgetting (like a good man) your late censure H8 3.01. 64
forget, | forgetting any other home but this. ROM 2.02.175
forgetting thy great deeds when neighbor states, TIM 4.03. 95
my fears forgetting manners, to /unseal | their HAM 5.02. 17
forgetting shame's pure blush and honor's wrack. VEN 558
FORGING 1 FR 0.0001 REL FR 1 V 0 P
till forging nature be condemn'd of treason, VEN 729
FORGIVE 79 FR 0.0089 REL FR 65 V 14 P
o, forgive me my sins! TMP 3.02.130 P
here have kill'd your king, i do forgive thee, 5.01. 78
my mouth, i do forgive | thy rankest fault — 5.01.131
forgive me, that i do not dream on thee, TGV 2.04.172
forgive me, valentine; 5.04. 74
forgive them what they have committed here | and 5.04.154
heaven forgive me! WIV 2.01. 28 P
well — heaven forgive you, and all of us, i 2.02. 56 P
heaven forgive my sins at the day of judgment! 3.03.212 P
heaven forgive our sins! 5.05. 31 P
heaven forgive him! MM 2.01. 37
and forgive us all! 2.01. 37
thy slanders i forgive, and therewithal | remit 5.01.519
forgive him, angelo, that brought you home | the 5.01.532
why then god forgive me! ADO 4.01.281 P
i forgive thy duty. LLL 4.02.143 P
if he would despise me, i would forgive him, for MV 1.02. 64 P
cursed be my tribe | if i forgive him! 1.03. 52
and love, | forgive a moi'ty of the principal, 4.01. 26
portia, forgive me this enforced wrong, | and in 5.01.240
his taken labors bid him me forgive; AWW 3.04. 12
i forgive you the praise. TN 1.05.192 P
o good antonio, forgive me your trouble. 2.01. 34 P
sir, royal sir, forgive a foolish woman. WT 3.02.227
forget your evil, | with them, forgive yourself. 5.01. 6
god shall forgive you cordelion's death | the JN 2.01. 12
then god forgive the sin of all those souls 2.01.283
thrust but these men away, and i'll forgive you, 4.01. 82
forgive the comment that my passion made | upon 4.02.263
forget, forgive, conclude and be agreed, | our R2 1.01.156
much harm upon me, hal, god forgive thee for it! 1H4 1.02. 92 P
god forgive me! 1.03.255
and god forgive them that so much have sway'd 3.02.130
hostess, i forgive thee. 3.03.170 P
how i came by the crown, o god forgive, | and 2H4 4.05.218
which i beseech your highness to forgive, H5 2.02.153
yet, forgive me, god, | that i do brag thus! 3.06.150
him i forgive my death that killeth me, | when 1H6 1.02. 20
forgive me, country, and sweet countrymen, | and 3.03. 81
if my suspect be false, forgive me, god, | for 2H6 3.02.139
o god, forgive him! 3.03. 29
and i forgive and quite forget old faults, | and 3H6 3.03.200
o, god forgive my sins, and pardon thee! 5.06. 60
if thy revengeful heart cannot forgive, | lo R3 1.02.173
if i chance to talk a little wild, forgive me; H8 1.04. 26
be what they will, i heartily forgive 'em; 2.01. 65
were hid against me, now to forgive me frankly. 2.01. 81
i as free forgive you | as i would be forgiven. 2.01. 82
i forgive all. 2.01. 83
and god forgive me! 2.01.136
and pray forgive me; 3.01.175
heaven forgive me! 3.02.135
i forgive him. 3.02.336
the morning, are unapt | to give or to forgive; COR 5.01. 53
best of my flesh, | forgive my tyranny; 5.03. 43
but do not say | for that, "forgive our romans." 5.03. 44
god forgive me! ROM 4.05. 7
forgive me, cousin! 5.03.101
forgive my general and exceptless rashness, TIM 4.03.495
if he scape, | heaven forgive him too! MAC 4.03.235
god, god, forgive us all! 5.01. 75
"forgive me my foul murther"? HAM 3.03. 52
forgive me this my virtue, | for in the fatness 3.04.152
kind gods, forgive me that, and prosper him! LR 3.07. 92
pray you now forget, and forgive; 4.07. 83
if thou'rt noble, | i do forgive thee. 5.03.167
/god forgive us our sins! OTH 2.03.111 P
o heaven forgive me! 3.03.373
o, heaven forgive us! 4.02. 88
out, fool, i forgive thee for a witch. ANT 1.02. 40 P
but, sir, forgive me, | since my becomings kill 1.03. 95
o my lord, my lord, | forgive my fearful sails! 3.11. 55
infamous, | forgive me in thine own particular, 4.09. 20
the malice towards you to forgive you, live, CYM 5.05.419
heavens forgive it! PER 4.03. 39
i will forgive | the trespass thou hast done me, TNK 3.01. 76
thou kill'st me, | the gods and i forgive thee. 3.06. 98
forgive me, cousin. 5.04. 93
i do forgive thy robb'ry, gentle thief, SON 40. 9
FORGIVEN 7 FR 0.0008 REL FR 5 V 2 P
lady, | i have forgiven and forgotten all, AWW 5.03. 9
if the sins of your youth are forgiven you, WT 3.03.121 P
all the gentlewomen here have forgiven me; 2H4 ep 22 P
i as free forgive you | as i would be forgiven. H8 2.01. 83
for aye | on thy low grave, on faults forgiven. TIM 5.04. 79
your spirit | to send him hence forgiven. TNK 5.04.120
to kneel to be forgiven | is safer wars than STM II.C 111
FORGIVENESS 9 FR 0.0010 REL FR 7 V 2 P
it sound that i | must ask my child forgiveness! TMP 5.01.198
your bawd — he doth oft'ner ask forgiveness. MM 4.02. 51 P
asks thee there, son, forgiveness, | as 'twere WT 4.04.549
then asks bohemia forgiveness; 5.02. 52 P
more sins for this forgiveness prosper may. R2 5.03. 84
forgiveness, horse! 5.05. 90
exchange forgiveness with me, noble hamlet. HAM 5.02.329
ask her forgiveness? LR 2.04.152
i'll kneel down | and ask of thee forgiveness. 5.03. 11
/FORGO 1 FR 0.0001 REL FR 1 V 0 P
/my /manors, /rents, /revenues /i /forgo; R2 4.01.212
FORGO 8 FR 0.0009 REL FR 8 V 0 P
forgo the purpose | that you resolv'd t' effect. TMP 3.03. 12
forgo the easier. JN 3.01.207
years, | my native english, now i must forgo, R2 1.03.160
and let us not forgo | that for a trifle that 1H6 4.01.149
must i needs forgo | so good, so noble, and so H8 3.02.422
i am unarm'd, forgo this vantage, greek. TRO 5.08. 9
quite forgo | the way which promises assurance, ANT 3.07. 45
mine eyes forgo their light, my false heart LUC 228
FORGOING 1 FR 0.0001 REL FR 1 V 0 P
for compound sweet forgoing simple savor, SON 125. 7
FORGONE 1 FR 0.0001 REL FR 0 V 1 P
all my mirth, forgone all custom of exercises; HAM 2.02.296 P
/FORGOT 1 FR 0.0001 REL FR 1 V 0 P
/that /to /laertes /i /forgot /myself, | /for HAM 5.02. 76
FORGOT 95 FR 0.0107 REL FR 80 V 15 P
hast thou forgot | the foul witch sycorax, who TMP 1.02.257
hast thou forgot her? 1.02.259
i had forgot that foul conspiracy | of the beast 4.01.139
tutor | (for long agone i have forgot to court; TGV 3.01. 85
and worthless valentine shall be forgot. 3.02. 10
she dreams on him that has forgot her love; 4.04. 81
what have i forgot? WIV 1.04.165 P
forsooth, i have forgot. 4.01. 76 P
alack, when once our grace we have forgot, MM 4.04. 33
and may it be that you have quite forgot | a ERR 3.02. 1
what say you, lords? why, this was quite forgot. LLL 1.01.141
"the hobby–horse is forgot." 3.01. 29 P
but have you forgot your love? 3.01. 33 P
and to speak troth, i have forgot our way. MND 2.02. 36
time | for parting us — o, is all forgot? 3.02.201
alack, | i fear my thisby's promise is forgot! 5.01.173
i had forgot — three months — you told me so. MV 1.03. 67
that dost not bite so nigh | as benefits forgot; AYL 2.07.186
i have forgot your name; SHR in.1. 86
have you so soon forgot the entertainment | her 3.01. 2
what, have you forgot me? 5.01. 49 P
forgot you? 5.01. 50 P
i have forgot him. AWW 1.01. 82
hast thou forgot thyself? TN 5.01.141
what have we twain forgot? WT 4.04.660
the one i have almost forgot — your pardon — 5.01.104
my lord, i had forgot to tell your lordship: R2 2.02. 93
have you forgot the duke of /herford, boy? 2.03. 36
lord, for that is not forgot | which ne'er i did 2.03. 37
i had forgot myself, am i not king? 3.02. 83
thy pains, fitzwater, shall not be forgot, 5.06. 17
be not forgot upon the face of the earth, then 1H4 2.04.129 P
i have forgot the map. 3.01. 6
king | have any way your good deserts forgot, 4.03. 46
hand, | forgot your oath to us at doncaster, 5.01. 58
my nephew's trespass may be well forgot, | it 5.02. 16
him to the heart, but he hath forgot that. 2H4 2.04. 9 P
we meet like men that had forgot to speak. 5.02. 22
yet all shall be forgot, | but he'll remember H5 4.03. 49
knaveries, and mocks — i have forgot his name. 4.07. 50 P
hath he forgot he is his sovereign? 1H6 4.01. 52
was broke in twain (by whom i have forgot, | but 2H6 1.02. 26
but if she have forgot | honor and virtue, and 2.01.190
can, | that this my death may never be forgot! 4.01.133
why, warwick, hath thy knee forgot to bow? 5.01.161
hath she forgot already that brave prince, R3 1.02.239
'tis time to speak, my pains are quite forgot. 1.03.116
/'zounds, he dies! i had forgot the reward. 1.04.125 P
almost forgot my pray'rs to content him? H8 3.01.132
when time is old /and hath forgot itself, | when TRO 3.02.185
as if he were forgot, and, princes all, | lay 3.03. 40
what, are my deeds forgot? 3.03.144
fast as they are made, forgot as soon | as done. 3.03.149
i have forgot my father, | i know no touch of 4.02. 96
by jupiter, forgot! COR 1.09. 90
it is so, sir. truly, i have forgot you. 4.03. 3 P
like a dull actor now | i have forgot my part, 5.03. 41
even when their sorrows almost was forgot, | and TIT 5.01.137
i have forgot why i did call thee back. ROM 2.02.170
i have forgot that name, and that name's woe. 2.03. 46
i cannot think but your age has forgot me, | it TIM 3.05. 92
perfumes, and have forgot | that ever timon was. 4.03.207
have you forgot me, sir? 4.03.472
i have forgot all men. 4.03.473
/grant'st th' art a man, i have forgot thee. 4.03.474
you have forgot the will i told you of. JC 3.02.238
i have almost forgot the taste of fears. MAC 5.05. 9
is, "for o, for o, the hobby–horse is forgot." HAM 3.02.135 P
have you forgot me? 3.04. 14
alack, | i had forgot. 'tis so concluded on. 3.04.201
antiquity forgot, custom not known, | the 4.05.105
thy half o' th' kingdom hast thou not forgot, LR 2.04.180
great thing of us forgot! 5.03.237
have you forgot all place of sense and duty? OTH 2.03.167
how comes it, michael, you are thus forgot? 2.03.188
by heaven, i would most gladly have forgot it. 4.01. 19
i had forgot thee. 5.02.103
that truth should be silent i had almost forgot. ANT 2.02.108 P
my lord, i fear, | has forgot britain. CYM 1.06.113
i had almost forgot | t' entreat your grace but 1.06.180
is too new, | she hath not yet forgot him. 2.03. 42
her andirons | (i had forgot them) were two 2.04. 89
(i forgot to ask him one thing, i'll remember't 3.05.130 P
for cloten | is quite forgot. 4.02.244
while, | till that his rage and anger be forgot, PER 1.02.107
what i have been i have forgot to know, | but 2.01. 71
th' unfriendly elements | forgot thee utterly, 3.01. 58
i have forgot it quite; TNK 4.03. 11 P
take, | the blemish that will never be forgot, LUC 536
and never be forgot in mighty rome | th' 1644
all my merry jigs are quite forgot, | all my PP 17. 5
and all the rest forgot for which he toil'd. SON 25.12
that i in your sweet thoughts would be forgot, 71. 7
repay, | forgot upon your dearest love to call, 117. 3
do i not think on thee when i forgot | am of 149. 3
FORGOTTEN 15 FR 0.0017 REL FR 11 V 4 P
love | is by a newer object quite forgotten. TGV 2.04.195
into a thousand that i have forgotten. AYL 2.04. 32
lady, | i have forgiven and forgotten all, AWW 5.03. 9
on a forgotten matter we can hardly make TN 2.03.160 P
that thou hast forgotten to demand that truly 1H4 1.02. 4 P
and i have not forgotten what the inside of a 3.03. 7 P
only compound me with forgotten dust; 2H4 4.05.115
may this be wash'd in lethe and forgotten? 5.02. 72
but all | was either pitied in him or forgotten. H8 2.01. 29
and when i am forgotten, as i shall be, | and 3.02.432
dull brain was wrought | with things forgotten. MAC 1.03.150
if he had been forgotten, | it had been as a gap 3.01. 11
die two months ago, and not forgotten yet? HAM 3.02.131 P
is a very antony, | and i am all forgotten. ANT 1.03. 91
although in me each part will be forgotten. SON 81. 4
FORK 3 FR 0.0003 REL FR 3 V 0 P
for thou dost fear the soft and tender fork | of MM 3.01. 16
of dog, | adder's fork and blind–worm's sting, MAC 4.01. 16
though the fork invade | the region of my heart; LR 1.01.144
FORK'D 4 FR 0.0004 REL FR 1 V 3 P
knee–deep, o'er head and ears a fork'd one! WT 1.02.186
he was for all the world like a fork'd redish, 2H4 3.02.311 P
"the fork'd one," quoth he, "pluck't out, and TRO 1.02.164 P
such a poor, bare, fork'd animal as thou art. LR 3.04.107 P
FORKED 4 FR 0.0004 REL FR 4 V 0 P
should in their own confines with forked heads AYL 2.01. 24
were there a serpent seen, with forked tongue, 2H6 3.02.259
even then this forked plague is fated to us OTH 3.03.276
a forked mountain, or blue promontory | with ANT 4.14. 5
FORKS 1 FR 0.0001 REL FR 1 V 0 P
whose face between her forks presages snow; LR 4.06.119
FORLORN 25 FR 0.0028 REL FR 24 V 1 P
"poor forlorn proteus, passionate proteus: TGV 1.02.121
thou gentle nymph, cherish thy forlorn swain. 5.04. 12
speed | to some forlorn and naked hermitage, LLL 5.02.795
as well as one so great and so forlorn | may WT 2.02. 20
'a was so forlorn, that his dimensions to any 2H4 3.02.312 P
now for the honor of the forlorn french! 1H6 1.02. 19
as he stood by, whilest i, his forlorn duchess, 2H6 2.04. 45
be poisonous too, and kill thy forlorn queen. 3.02. 77
speak, captain, shall i stab the forlorn swain? 4.01. 65
art then forsaken, as thou went'st forlorn! 3H6 3.01. 54
man, | and forc'd to live in scotland a forlorn; 3.03. 26
the trees, though summer, yet forlorn and lean, TIT 2.03. 94
some say that ravens foster forlorn children 2.03.153
long have i been forlorn, and all for thee. 5.02. 81
to, | like a forlorn and desperate castaway, 5.03. 75
to hovel thee with swine and rogues forlorn | in LR 4.07. 38
the forlorn soldier, that /so nobly fought, | he CYM 5.05.405
poor queen of love, in thine own law forlorn, VEN 251
thy lips | make modest dian cloudy and forlorn, 725
whereat she leaps, that was but late forlorn. 1026
and who she finds forlorn she doth lament. LUC 1500
for shade, | when cytherea (all in love forlorn) PP 6. 3
i, | love hath forlorn me, living in thrall; 17.14
she, poor bird, as all forlorn, | lean'd her 20. 9
and from the forlorn world his visage hide, SON 33. 7
FORM 114 FR 0.0128 REL FR 99 V 15 P
believe me, sir, | it carries a brave form. TMP 1.02.412
nor can imagination form a shape, | besides 3.01. 56
dissolves to water, and doth lose his form. TGV 3.02. 8
o thou senseless form, | thou shalt be 4.04.198
words | can no way change you to a milder form, 5.04. 56
a fault done first in the form of a beast (o WIV 5.05. 9 P
o place, o form, | how often dost thou with thy MM 2.04. 12
by cold gradation and weal–balanc'd form, | we 4.03.100
thou hast thine own form. ERR 2.02.198
be brief — only to the plain form of marriage, ADO 4.01. 2 P
in every lineament, branch, shape, and form; 5.01. 14
in manner and form following, sir, all those LLL 1.01.205 P
sitting with her upon the form, and taken 1.01.207 P
put together, is in manner and form following. 1.01.209 P
for the form — in some form. 1.01.211 P
for the form — in some form. 1.01.211 P
proud with his form, in his eye pride expressed; 2.01.237
this is the ape of form, monsieur the nice, 5.02.325
their form confounded makes most form in mirth, 5.02.519
their form confounded makes most form in mirth, 5.02.519
to whom you are but as a form in wax | by him MND 1.01. 49
love can transpose to form and dignity. 1.01.233
take it, prince, and if my form lie there, MV 2.07. 61
as haply shall become | the form of my intent. TN 1.02. 55
that wonderful promise, to read him by his form, 3.04.265 P
if spirits can assume both form and suit, | you 5.01.235
whom i from meaner form | have bench'd and WT 1.02.313
praise her but for this her without–door form 2.01. 69
bear his name whose form thou bearest: JN 1.01.160
exterior form, outward accoutrement, | but from 1.01.211
all form is formless, order orderless, | save 3.01.253
stuffs out his vacant garments with his form; 3.04. 97
i will not keep this form upon my head | when 3.04.101
face | of plain old form is much disfigured, 4.02. 22
and you have slander'd nature in my form, 4.02.256
without this object, | form such another? 4.03. 45
life, | which bleeds away even as a form of wax 5.04. 24
but i do love the favor and the form | of this 5.04. 50
you are born | to set a form upon that indigest 5.07. 26
i am a scribbled form, drawn with a pen | upon a 5.07. 32
ey'd awry | distinguish form; R2 2.02. 20
tradition, form, and ceremonious duty, | for you 3.02.173
a pale | keep law and form and due proportion, 3.04. 41
but not the form of what he should attend. 1H4 1.03.210
and by the necessary form of this | king richard 2H4 3.01. 87
off a mile, | in goodly form comes on the enemy, 4.01. 20
had not been here to dress the ugly form | of 4.01. 39
acquitted by a true substantial form | and 4.01.171
crowd us and crush us to this monstrous form 4.02. 34
for now a time is come to mock at form. 4.05.118
return into london under the form of a soldier. H5 3.06. 69 P
art thou aught else but place, degree, and form, 4.01.246
shall name your highness in this form, and with 5.02.338 P
did he not, contrary to form of law, | devise 2H6 3.01. 58
we may digest our complots in some form. R3 3.01.200
or that we would, against the form of law, 3.05. 42
both in your form and nobleness of mind; 3.07. 14
i'll draw the form and model of our battle, 5.03. 24
insisture, course, proportion, season, form, TRO 1.03. 87
act | such and no other than event doth form it, 2.02.120
put on | a form of strangeness as we pass along. 3.03. 51
salutes each other with each other's form; 3.03.108
/brother's leg — to what form but that he is, 5.01. 57 P

predecessors have, | your honor with your form. COR 2.02.144
him | where he shall answer, by a lawful form 3.01.323
fain would i dwell on form, fain, fain deny ROM 2.02. 88
who stand so much on the new form, that they 2.04. 34 P
thy form cries out thou art; 3.03.109
thy noble shape is but a form of wax, 3.03.126
for it wrought on her | the form of death. 5.03.246
'tis a good form. TIM 1.01. 17
they labor'd | to bring manslaughter into form, 3.05. 27
however he puts on this tardy form. JC 1.02.299
in ranks and squadrons and right form of war, 2.02. 20
brutus, this sober form of yours hides wrongs, 4.02. 40
in form as palpable | as this which now i draw. MAC 2.01. 40
together with that fair and warlike form | in HAM 1.01. 47
form of the thing, each word made true and good, 1.02.210
o'er-leavens | the form of plausive manners — 1.04. 30
and there assume some other horrible form, 1.04. 72
how infinite in faculties, in form and moving! 2.02.305 P
the glass of fashion and the mould of form, 3.01.153
that unmatch'd form and stature of blown youth 3.01.159
what he spake, though it lack'd form a little, 3.01.163
age and body of the time his form and pressure. 3.02. 24 P
but, o, what form of prayer | can serve my turn? 3.03. 51
hill, | a combination and a form indeed, | where 3.04. 60
his form and cause conjoin'd, preaching to 3.04.126
folded the writ up in the form of th' other, 5.02. 51
and seeks for gain, | and follows but for form, LR 2.04. 79
upon his life | without the form of justice, yet 3.07. 25
in putting on the mere form of civil and humane OTH 2.01.239 P
what form? 4.02.138
any sense | delighted them /in any other form; 4.02.155
and jewels | of rich and exquisite form, their CYM 1.06.190
makes me look dismal will i clip to form, | and PER 5.03. 74
so sorrow, wanting form, | is press'd with TNK 1.01.108
now 'twill take form, the heats are gone 1.01.152
any gross stuff | to form me like your blazon, 3.01. 47
give up yourself to form, obey the magistrate, STM II.C 146
so fair a form lodg'd not a mind so ill. LUC 1530
now is the time that face should form another, SON 3. 2
that thou no form of thee hast left behind, 9. 6
your sweet issue your sweet form should bear. 13. 8
thy beauty's form in table of my heart; 24. 2
how would thy shadow's form form happy show | to 43. 6
how would thy shadow's form form happy show | to 43. 6
affords | in polish'd form of well-refined pen. 85. 8
so ill, | to set a form upon desired change, 89. 6
where time and outward form would show it dead. 108.14
for it no form delivers to the heart | of bird, 113. 5
have i not seen dwellers on form and favor 125. 5
"his qualities were beauteous as his form, | for LC 99
playing the place which did no form receive, 241

FORMAL 11 FR 0.0012 REL FR 10 V 1 P
prayers, | to make of him a formal man again: ERR 5.01.105
with eyes severe and beard of formal cut, | full AYL 2.07.155
are you so formal, sir? SHR 3.01. 61
i know not what, but formal in apparel, | in 4.02. 40
this is evident to any formal capacity, there is TN 2.05.117 P
floods, | and flow henceforth in formal majesty. 2H4 5.02.133
thus, like the formal vice, iniquity, | i R3 3.01. 82
do, | with untir'd spirits and formal constancy. JC 2.01.227
bones, | no noble rite nor formal ostentation — HAM 4.05.216
crown'd with snakes, | not like a formal man. ANT 2.05. 41
her hair, nor loose nor tied in formal plat, LC 29

FORMALLY 2 FR 0.0002 REL FR 2 V 0 P
instruct me | how i may formally in person bear MM 1.03. 47
and formally, according to our law, | depose him R2 1.03. 29

FORM'D 6 FR 0.0006 REL FR 5 V 1 P
i say, or chang'd 'em, | or else new form'd 'em; TMP 1.02. 83
form'd by the eye and therefore, like the eye, LLL 5.02.762
leg, it was form'd under the star of a galliard. TN 1.03.133 P
the shadow of myself form'd in her eye, | which, JN 2.01.498
and therefore are they form'd as marble will; LUC 1241
of strange kinds | is form'd in them by force, 1243

FORMED 1 FR 0.0001 REL FR 1 V 0 P
till he behold them formed in th' applause TRO 3.03.119

FORMER 62 FR 0.0070 REL FR 58 V 4 P
so the remembrance of my former love | is by a TGV 2.04.194
know then, i here forget all former griefs, 5.04.142
let me entreat you speak the former language. MM 2.04.140
the former hero! hero that is dead! ADO 5.04. 65
in the sight | of thy former lady's eye; MND 3.02.457
you to your former honor i bequeath, | your AYL 5.04.186
charg'd, | in peril to incur your former malady, SHR in.2. 122
as one unworthy all the former favors | that i 4.02. 30
m.o.a.i. this simulation is not as the former; TN 2.05.140 P
holy | than to rejoice the former queen is well? WT 5.01. 30
she shall not be so young | as was your former, 5.01. 79
now, had i not the dash of my former life in me, 5.02.113 P
our former scruple in our strong-barr'd gates, JN 2.01.370
then speak again, not all thy former tale, | but 3.01. 25
soul, | to think our former state a happy dream, R2 5.01. 18
which to his former strength may be restored 2H4 3.01. 42
out, | may waste the memory of the former days. 4.05.215
that i have turn'd away my former self; 5.05. 58
as did the former lions of your blood. H5 1.02.124
i pray thee bear my former answer back: 4.03. 90
which to reduce into our former favor | you are 5.02. 63
and bless us with her former qualities. 5.02. 67
thou maintain the former words thou spak'st? 1H6 3.04. 31
hath sullied all his gloss of former honor | by 4.04. 6
and in thy thought o'errun my former time; 3H6 1.04. 45
great albion's queen in former golden days; 3.03. 7
my noble queen, let former grudges pass, | and 3.03.195
bona, | and replant henry in his former state. 3.03.198
i will never more remember | our former hatred, R3 2.01. 24
master, till the last | made former wonders its. H8 1.01. 18
thought's compass, that former fabulous story, 1.01. 36
the former agents, if they did complain, | what COR 1.01.123
it is your former promise. 1.01.238
in this action outdone his former deeds doubly. 2.01.136 P
out of that i'll work | myself a former fortune. 5.03.202
he owes nine thousand, besides my former sum, TIM 2.01. 2
offering the fortunes of his former days, | the 5.01.124
his former days, | the former man may make him. 5.01.125
on our former ensign | two mighty eagles fell, JC 5.01. 79
and with his former title greet macbeth. MAC 1.02. 65
this sore night | hath trifled former knowings. 2.04. 4
malice | remains in danger of her former tooth. 3.02. 15
my former speeches have but hit your thoughts, 3.06. 1
a third is like the former. 4.01.115
so by my former lecture and advice, | shall you HAM 2.01. 64
so far from cheer and from /your former state, 3.02.164
if you come slack of former services, | you LR 1.03. 9
madam, my former suit. OTH 3.04.110
us, | or scant our former having in despite: 4.03. 91
i can again thy former light restore, | should i 5.02. 9
you have seen and prov'd a fairer former fortune ANT 1.02. 33
thou must not take my former sharpness ill. 3.03. 35
if that the former dare but what it can, | no 3.13. 80
when my good stars, that were my former guides, 3.13.145
in feeding them with those my former fortunes 4.15. 53
their friends | o'erborne i' th' former wave. CYM 5.03. 48
but immortality attends the former, | making a PER 3.02. 30
in her into their former law and regiment. TNK 4.03. 96 P
to-morrow sharp'ned in his former might. SON 56. 4
amiss | the second burthen of a former child! 59. 4
sure i am the wits of former days | to subjects 59.13
they are but dressings of a former sight. 123. 4

FORMERLY 6 FR 0.0006 REL FR 3 V 3 P
incurr'd | the danger formerly by me rehears'd. MV 4.01.362
it was formerly better, marry, yet 'tis a AWW 1.01.163 P
exercises than formerly he hath appear'd. WT 4.02. 33 P
that never | they shall abound as formerly. H8 1.01. 83
of me aught | but what is like me formerly. COR 4.01. 53
him of letters he had formerly wrote to pompey; ANT 3.05. 10 P

/FORMLESS 1 FR 0.0001 REL FR 1 V 0 P
/husks | /and /formless /ruin /of /oblivion; TRO 4.05.167

FORMLESS 1 FR 0.0001 REL FR 1 V 0 P
all form is formless, order orderless, | save JN 3.01.253

FORMS 26 FR 0.0029 REL FR 23 V 3 P
which are as easy broke as they make forms. MM 2.04.126
in all his dressings, caracts, titles, forms, 5.01. 56
a foolish extravagant spirit, full of forms, LLL 4.02. 66 P
the extreme parts of time extremely forms | all 5.02.740
of straying shapes, of habits, and of forms, 5.02.763
bodies forth | the forms of things unknown, the MND 5.01. 15
the which he vents | in mangled forms. AYL 2.07. 42
in women's waxen hearts to set their forms! TN 2.02. 30
and in such forms which here were presuppos'd 5.01.350
to lay down likelihoods and forms of hope. 2H4 1.03. 35
in forms imaginary, th' unguided days | and 4.04. 59
and with forms being fetch'd | from glist'ring H5 2.02.116
and the cares of it, and the forms of it, and 4.01. 73 P
they turn to vicious forms, ten times more ugly H8 1.02.117
make 'em, and | appear in forms more horrid), 3.02.196
nothing been but shapes and forms of slaughter. TRO 5.03. 12
misshapen chaos of well/-seeming forms, ROM 1.01.179
pluck down forms, windows, any thing. JC 3.02.259 P
together with all forms, moods, /shapes of grief HAM 1.02. 82
all saws of books, all forms, all pressures past 1.05.100
function suiting | with forms to his conceit? 2.02.557
are | who, trimm'd in forms and visages of duty, OTH 1.01. 50
may fall to match you with her country forms, 3.03.237
wants stuff | to vie strange forms with fancy; ANT 5.02. 98
blot with hell-born sin such saint-like forms. LUC 1519
applied to cautels, all strange forms receives, LC 303

FORNICATION 4 FR 0.0004 REL FR 2 V 2 P
might have been accus'd in fornication, adultery MM 2.01. 81 P
condemn'd upon the act of fornication | to lose 5.01. 70
she that accuses him of fornication, | in 5.01.195
bless me, what a fry of fornication is at door! H8 5.03. 36 P

FORNICATIONS 1 FR 0.0001 REL FR 0 V 1 P
and given to fornications, and to taverns, and WIV 5.05.158 P

FORNICATRESS 1 FR 0.0001 REL FR 1 V 0 P
see you the fornicatress be remov'd. MM 2.02. 23

/FORRES 1 FR 0.0001 REL FR 1 V 0 P
how far is't call'd to /forres? MAC 1.03. 39

FORREST 3 FR 0.0003 REL FR 3 V 0 P
dighton and forrest, who i did suborn | to do R3 4.03. 4
thus," quoth forrest, "girdling one another 4.03. 10
which /once," quoth forrest, "almost chang'd my 4.03. 15

FORSAKE 27 FR 0.0030 REL FR 25 V 2 P
forsake unsounded deeps to dance on sands. TGV 3.02. 80
an evil angel, and bid you forsake your liberty. ERR 4.03. 21 P
hast power to choose, and they none to forsake. AWW 2.03. 56
in such a scarre | that we'll forsake ourselves. 4.02. 39
i must | forsake the court. WT 1.02.362
wilt thou forsake thy fortune, | bequeath thy JN 1.01.148
walls they'll tear down than forsake the siege. 1H6 1.02. 40
if you forsake the offer of their love. 4.02. 14
see, they forsake me! 5.03. 24
home to your cottages, forsake this groom: 2H6 4.02.124
the citizens fly and forsake their houses; 4.04. 50
that will forsake thee and go home in peace. 4.08. 10
thee | to flatter henry and forsake thy brother! 3H6 4.07. 85
my manors that i had, | even now forsake me; 5.02. 25
poor clarence did forsake his father, warwick, R3 1.03.134
who told me how the poor soul did forsake | the 2.01.110
sweet partner, | i must not yet forsake you. H8 1.04.104
and, till my soul forsake, | shall cry for 2.01. 89
i must now forsake ye. 2.01.132
to borrow of men, men would forsake the gods. TIM 3.06. 75 P
he she lov'd prov'd mad, | and did forsake her. OTH 4.03. 28
you must forsake this room and go with us. 5.02.330
forsake thy seat, i do beseech thee, captain, ANT 2.07. 38
jealous of catching, swiftly doth forsake him, VEN 321
lust, | and for himself himself he must forsake: LUC 157
since sweets and beauties do themselves forsake, SON 12.11
say that thou didst forsake me for some fault, 89. 1

FORSAKEN 6 FR 0.0006 REL FR 5 V 1 P
either to make him a garland, as being forsaken, ADO 2.01.219 P
forsaken your pernicious faction | and join'd 1H6 4.01. 59
art then forsaken, as thou went'st forlorn! 3H6 3.01. 54
thou didst love so dear, | so soon forsaken? ROM 2.03. 67
most choice forsaken, and most lov'd despis'd, LR 1.01.251
of him, myself, and thee i am forsaken, | a SON 133. 7

FORSAKETH 1 FR 0.0001 REL FR 1 V 0 P
forsaketh yet the lists | by reason of his 1H6 5.05. 32

FORSET-SELLER 1 FR 0.0001 REL FR 0 V 1 P
between an orange-wife and a forset-seller, and COR 2.01. 71 P

FORSOOK 11 FR 0.0012 REL FR 10 V 1 P
belike she thinks that proteus hath forsook her? TGV 4.04.146
forsook his scene, and ent'red in a brake; MND 3.02. 15
dead, forsook, cast off, | and none of you will JN 5.07. 35
no, my good lord, he hath forsook the court, R2 2.03. 26
but his red color hath forsook his cheeks. R3 2.01. 86
who | have all forsook me, hath devour'd the COR 4.05. 76
his comfortable temper has forsook him, he's TIM 3.04. 71 P
hath she forsook so many noble matches? OTH 4.02.125
narcissus so himself himself forsook, | and died VEN 161
for where they lay the shadow had forsook them, 176
"it cannot be" she in that sense forsook, | and LUC 1538

FORSOOTH 47 FR 0.0053 REL FR 24 V 23 P
no, i thank you, forsooth, heartily; WIV 1.01.267 P
i am not a-hungry, i thank you, forsooth. 1.01.270 P
ay, forsooth. 1.04. 19 P
no, forsooth; 1.04. 22 P
ay, forsooth; 1.04. 25 P
ay, forsooth, i'll fetch it you. 1.04. 48 P
ay, forsooth; to desire her to — 1.04. 79 P
ay, forsooth; 2.01.164 P
ay, forsooth; 2.02. 86 P
i had rather, forsooth, go before you like a man 3.02. 5 P
to the laundress, forsooth. 3.03.153 P
and, forsooth, to search his house for his 3.05. 77 P
forsooth, i have forgot. 4.01. 76 P
from the two parties, forsooth. 4.05.105 P
ay, forsooth, i have spoke with her, and we have 5.02. 4 P
forsooth, took on him as a conjurer, | and, ERR 5.01.243
speaks — | note notes, forsooth, and nothing. ADO 2.03. 57
o, and i, forsooth, in love! LLL 3.01.174
but that, forsooth, the bouncing amazon, | your MND 2.01. 70
and tender me (forsooth) affection, | but by 3.02.230
her height, forsooth, she hath prevail'd with 3.02.293
all, forsooth, /deifying the name of rosalind. AYL 3.02.362 P
i must, forsooth, be forc'd | to give my hand SHR 3.02. 8
no, no, forsooth, i dare not for my life. 4.03. 1
i am going, forsooth. AWW 1.03. 96 P
he will, forsooth, have all my prisoners, | and 1H4 1.03.140
forsooth, five years, and as much as to — 2.04. 42 P
and now, forsooth, takes on him to reform | some 4.03. 78
because, forsooth, the king of scots is crown'd. 1H6 4.01.157
and yet, forsooth, she is a virgin pure. 5.04. 83
no, forsooth; 2H6 1.03. 30 P
because the king, forsooth, will have it so. 1.03.115
forsooth, a blind man at saint albon's shrine, 2.01. 61
most true, forsooth; 2.01. 91
black, forsooth, coal-black as jet. 2.01.110
peter, forsooth. 2.03. 81 P
and you, forsooth, had the good duke to keep. 3.02.183
that complains unto the king | that i, forsooth, R3 1.03. 44
nay forsooth, my friends, | they that must weigh H8 3.01. 87
forsooth, an inventory, thus importing | the 3.02.124
and then, forsooth, the faint defects of age TRO 1.03.172
loves, but thou wilt frame | thyself, forsooth, COR 3.02. 85
yea forsooth, and your mistriship be emperial. TIT 4.04. 40 P
ay forsooth ROM 4.02. 12
yes, forsooth, i will hold my tongue; LR 1.04.194 P
forsooth, a great arithmetician, | one michael OTH 1.01. 19
yes, forsooth; i wish you joy o' th' worm. ANT 5.02.279 P

/FORSWEAR 1 FR 0.0001 REL FR 1 V 0 P
/all /pomp /and /majesty /i /do /forswear; R2 4.01.211

FORSWEAR 27 FR 0.0030 REL FR 14 V 13 P
forswear not thyself, sweet youth, for i am not TGV 2.05. 3 P
love bade me swear, and love bids me forswear. 2.06. 6
you'll forswear this again. MM 3.02.166 P
but i was fain to forswear it. 4.03.172 P
who heard me to deny it or forswear it? ERR 5.01. 25
then fools you were these women to forswear, LLL 4.03.352
i do forswear them, and i here protest, | by 5.02.410
your oath once broke, you force not to forswear. 5.02.440
as waggish boys in game themselves forswear, MND 1.01.240
then entertain him, then forswear him; AYL 3.02.416 P
to forswear the full stream of the world and to 3.02.419 P
country copulatives, to swear and to forswear, 5.04. 56 P
forswear bianca and her love for ever. SHR 4.02. 26
but do forswear her | as one unworthy all the 4.02. 29
deny him, forswear him, or else we are all 5.01.111 P
and i thought that, i'd forswear it. TN 1.03. 88 P
certain, or forswear to wear iron about you. 3.04.252 P
forswear themselves as often as they speak. WT 5.01.200
longer than he sees reason, i'll forswear arms. 1H4 1.02.185 P
i'll forswear keeping house afore i'll be in 2H4 2.04.204 P
be, to forswear thin potations and to addict 4.03.124 P
you be not swing'd, i'll forswear half-kirtles. 5.04. 21 P
ay, but thou usest to forswear thyself. 3H6 5.05. 75
it, | accuse some innocent, and forswear myself, TIT 5.01.130
forswear it, sight! ROM 1.05. 52
enough to make a whore forswear her trade, | and TIM 4.03.134
love him dearly, | comfort forswear me! OTH 4.02.159

FORSWEARING 2 FR 0.0002 REL FR 2 V 0 P
thus, | by now forswearing that he is forsworn. 1H4 5.02. 38
for false forswearing and for murther too. R3 1.04.202

FORSWEAR'T 2 FR 0.0002 REL FR 2 V 0 P
if it be not, forswear't. AWW 1.03.183
bears not one, | let villainy itself forswear't. WT 1.02.361

FORSWORE 11 FR 0.0012 REL FR 9 V 2 P
prosper'd since i forswore myself at primero. WIV 4.05.101 P
which he forswore most monstrously to have. ERR 5.01. 11
yes, that you did, sir, and forswore it too. 5.01. 24
him, | after you first forswore it on the mart, 5.01.262
night, which he forswore on tuesday morning. ADO 5.01.168 P
a woman i forswore, but i will prove, | thou LLL 4.03. 62
thou being a goddess, i forswore not thee. 4.03. 63
why, love forswore me in my mother's womb; 3H6 3.02.153
ay, and forswore himself — which jesu pardon! R3 1.03.135
a woman i forswore; PP 3. 5
thou being a goddess, i forswore not thee: 3. 6

FORSWORN 66 FR 0.0074 REL FR 60 V 6 P
boy's scandall'd company | i have forsworn. TMP 4.01. 91
to leave my julia, shall i be forsworn; TGV 2.06. 1
to love fair silvia, shall i be forsworn; 2.06. 2
to wrong my friend, i shall be much forsworn. 2.06. 3
hath she forsworn me? 3.01.213
no valentine, if silvia have forsworn me. 3.01.215
forsworn my company, and rail'd at me, | that i 3.02. 4
she bids me think how i have been forsworn | in 4.02. 10
lips away, | that so sweetly were forsworn, MM 4.01. 2
that angelo's forsworn, is it not strange? 5.01. 38
and true he swore, though yet forsworn he were. ERR 4.02. 10
they are both forsworn: 5.07.212
you swear, my lord, you shall not be forsworn. ADO 1.01.154 P
necessity will make us all forsworn | three LLL 1.01.149

i am forsworn "on mere necessity." 1.01.154
i shall be forsworn (which is a great argument 1.02.169 P
our lady help my lord! he'll be forsworn. 2.01. 98
"if love make me forsworn, how shall i swear to 4.02.105
though to myself forsworn, to thee i'll faithful 4.02.107
ay me, i am forsworn! 4.03. 45
it sin in me, | that i am forsworn for thee; 4.03.114
therefore of all hands must we be forsworn. 4.03.215
o, nothing so sure, and thereby all forsworn. 4.03.279
in that each of you have forsworn his book, 4.03.293
you have in that forsworn the use of eyes, | and 4.03.306
and in that vow we have forsworn our books. 4.03.316
it is religion to be thus forsworn: 4.03.360
light wenches may prove plagues to men forsworn; 4.03.382
we are again forsworn, in will and error. 5.02.471
yet swear not, lest ye be forsworn again. 5.02.832
hence — | i have forsworn his bed and company. MND 2.01. 62
how to choose right, but then i am forsworn. MV 3.02. 11
make me wish a sin, | that i had been forsworn. 3.02. 14
was good, and yet was not the knight forsworn. AYL 1.02. 67 P
swear by that that is not, you are not forsworn. 1.02. 77 P
would all the world but he had quite forsworn! SHR 4.02. 35
love, | and have forsworn you with hortensio. 4.02. 47
tranio, you jest, but have you both forsworn me? 4.02. 48
tell me, thou fellow, is not france forsworn? JN 3.01. 62
you are forsworn, forsworn! 3.01.101
you are forsworn, forsworn! 3.01.101
to swear, swears only not to be forsworn, | else 3.01.284
but thou dost swear only to be forsworn, | and 3.01.286
and most forsworn, to keep what thou dost swear; 3.01.287
he is forsworn if e'er those eyes of yours 5.04. 31
i task the earth to the like, forsworn aumerle, R2 4.01. 52
i have forsworn his company hourly any time this 1H4 2.02. 15 P
thus, | by now forswearing that he is forsworn. 5.02. 38
do you think i'll be forsworn? H5 4.08. 12 P
the northern lords that have forsworn thy colors 3H6 1.01.251
no; god forbid your grace should be forsworn. 1.02. 18
fo, fo, come, tell a pin. you are forsworn. TRO 5.02. 22
doves' eyes, | which can make gods forsworn? COR 5.03. 28
the thing i have forsworn to grant may never 5.03. 80
she hath forsworn to love, and in that vow | do ROM 1.01.223
all forsworn, all naught, all dissemblers. 3.02. 87
trust to't, bethink you, i'll not be forsworn. 3.05.195
is it more sin to wish me thus forsworn, | or to 3.05.236
i am yet | unknown to woman, never was forsworn, MAC 4.03.126
lest she should steal a kiss and die forsworn. VEN 726
if love make me forsworn, how shall i swear to PP 5. 1
though to myself forsworn, to thee i'll constant 5. 3
jollity, | and purest faith unhappily forsworn, SON 66. 4
prove thee virtuous, though thou art forsworn. 88. 4
in loving thee thou know'st i am forsworn, | but 152. 1
but thou art twice forsworn, to me love swearing 152. 2

/FOR'T 2 FR 0.0002 REL FR 1 V 1 P
/and /are /most /tyrannically /clapp'd /for't. HAM 2.02.341 P
/king /his /master | /will /check /him /for't. LR 2.02.142

FOR/'T 1 FR 0.0001 REL FR 0 V 1 P
if i die for/'t (as no less is threat'ned me), LR 3.03. 17 P

FOR'T 95 FR 0.0107 REL FR 65 V 30 P
heavens thank you for't! TMP 1.02.175
here's a garment for't. 4.01.242 P
there's another garment for't. 4.01.244 P
thou art pinch'd for't now, sebastian. 5.01. 74
i am woe for't, sir. 5.01.139
he did, i think verily he had been hang'd for't; TGV 4.04. 15 P
sure as i live, he had suffer'd for't. 4.04. 16 P
he hath kill'd, otherwise he had suffer'd for't. 4.04. 33 P
and she shall thank you for't, if e'er you know 4.04.179
and we'll have a posset for't soon at night, in WIV 1.04. 8 P
blessing on your heart for't! 2.02.107 P
ages smack of this vice, and he | to die for't! MM 2.02. 6
there shall be order for't. 2.02. 25
and you tell me that he shall die for't. 2.04.143
i will proclaim thee, angelo, look for't! 2.04.151
been drinking all night, i am not fitted for't. 4.03. 44 P
what reason have you for't? LLL 5.02.709 P
i'll die for't but some woman had the ring! MV 5.01.208
i will stand for't a little, though therefore i AWW 1.01.133 P
broke thy pate, | and ask'd thee mercy for't. 2.01. 67
he says he has a stratagem for't. 3.06. 35 P
but i con him no thanks for't, in the nature he 4.03.152 P
way to-morrow, | i'll give him reasons for't. TN 1.05.306
i have no exquisite reason for't, but i have 2.03.145 P
there is example for't: 2.05. 39 P
thee so, for i will show thee no reason for't." 3.04.152 P
you may have very fit occasion for't; 3.04.173 P
i shall be much bound to you for't. 3.04.270 P
i will live to be thankful to thee for't. 4.02. 83 P
physic for't there's none. WT 1.02.200
i do, and will fetch off bohemia for't; 1.02.334
by some putter-on | that will be damn'd for't. 2.01.142
if this prove true, they'll pay for't. 2.01.146
your suspicion, | be blam'd for't how you might. 2.01.161
and vengeance for't | not dropp'd down yet. 3.02.201
i am sorry for't. 3.02.218
i am sorry for't. 2H6 4.02. 95 P
i am sorry for't. H8 2.01. 9
that blood will make 'em one day groan for't. 2.01.106
speaks 'em, | and every true heart weeps for't. 2.02. 39
and venture maidenhead for't, and so would you 2.03. 25
if the king blame me for't, i'll lay ye all | by 5.03. 78
could be content to give him good report for't, COR 1.01. 33 P
o, he is wounded, i thank the gods for't. 2.01.121 P
well assur'd | they ne'er did service for't; 3.01.122
target from thy brawn, | or lose mine arm for't. 4.05.121
being banish'd for't, he came unto my hearth, 5.06. 29
let him die for't. 5.06.119
if i should pay you for't as 'tis extoll'd, | it TIM 1.01.167
affect company, | nor is he fit for't indeed. 1.02. 32
there's much example for't: 1.02. 46 P
i am to thank you for't. 1.02.151
he is so kind that he now | pays interest for't; 1.02.200
nay, urg'd extremely for't, and show'd what 3.02. 12 P
i see no sense for't, | but his occasions might 3.03. 14
if he care not for't, he will supply us easily; 4.03.404 P
napkins enow about you, here you'll sweat for't. MAC 2.03. 6 P
and i fear | thou play'dst most foully for't; 3.01. 3
the moment on't, for't must be done to-night, 3.01.130
freely, or the /blank verse shall halt for't. HAM 2.02.325 P
of an unfee'd lawyer, you gave me nothing for't. LR 1.04.130 P
who can arraign me for't? 5.03.160
we are very sorry for't. OTH 1.03. 73
i humbly thank you for't. 3.01. 39
beshrew him for't! 4.02.128
i should venture purgatory for't. 4.03. 77 P
honest iago hath ta'en order for't. 5.02. 72
the dryness of his bones | call on him for't. ANT 1.04. 28
for't cannot be | we shall remain in friendship, 2.02.112
i am paid for't now. 2.05.108
i ask no more, | and the gods yield you for't! 4.02. 33
she dies for't. 4.12. 49
i am sorry for't; CYM 4.02. 93
to th' east, | my father hath a reason for't. 4.02.256
youth, i blame ye not, | you had a motive for't. 5.05.268
i am sorry for't, my lord. 5.05.270
and thou shalt die for't. 5.05.310
oppression, and the poor worm doth die for't. PER 1.01.102
i thank thee for't, and heaven forbid | that 1.02. 61
art one, | who now reprov'dst me for't — 1.02. 95
now do i see he had some reason for't; 1.03. 7 P
be got now-a-days unless thou canst fish for't. 2.01. 70 P
i thank thee for't. 2.01.133
upon a worm against my will, | but i wept for't. 4.01. 79
sail seas in cockles, have and wish but for't, 4.04. 2
and i did love him for't. TNK 1.03. 35
her modesty will blow so far she falls for't. 2.02.144
i have, | beshrew mine eyes for't! 2.02.157
and hang for't afterward! 2.02.264
mark how his body's made for't. 2.03. 71
if the law | find me, and then condemn me for't, 2.06. 14
made her groan a month for't; 3.03. 35
if he keep touch, he dies for't. 3.03. 53
on one | that two must needs be blind for't! 5.03.146
for't lies in thee | to make him much outlive a SON 101.10

FORT* 4 FR 0.0004 REL FR 2 V 2 P
ma foi, il fait fort /chaud. WIV 1.04. 51 P
c'est bien dit, madame, il est fort bon anglois. H5 3.04. 19 P
am i come to scale | thy never-conquered fort; LUC 482
if in this blemish'd fort i make some hole 1175

FORTED 1 FR 0.0001 REL FR 1 V 0 P
a forted residence 'gainst the tooth of time MM 5.01. 12

/FORTH 7 FR 0.0008 REL FR 6 V 1 P
/yet /did /you /say, "/go /forth!" 2H4 1.01.175
/doth /this /bold /enterprise /bring /forth 1.01.178
/come, /bring /forth /the /prisoners. R3 3.03. 1
/athenian /bay | /put /forth /toward /phrygia, TRO pr 7
/since /his /coming /forth /is /thought /of, LR 4.03. 4 P
/the /name /of "/father" | /pantingly /forth, 4.03. 26
/forth of my heart those charms, thine eyes, are OTH 5.01. 35

FORTH 395 FR 0.0446 REL FR 347 V 48 P
know thus far forth: TMP 1.02.177
come forth, i say, there's other business for 1.02.315
devil himself | upon thy wicked dam, come forth! 1.02.320
and your affection not gone forth, i'll make you 1.02.449
of it in the sea, bring forth more islands. 2.01. 94 P
but nature should bring forth, | of it own kind, 2.01.163
are in, and sends me forth | (for else his 2.01.298
if thou beest trinculo, come forth. 2.02.103 P
i warrant, | and bring thee forth brave brood. 3.02.105
noontide sun, call'd forth the mutinous winds, 5.01. 42
op'd, and let 'em forth | by my so potent art. 5.01. 49
very duke | which was thrust forth of milan, who 5.01.160
at least bring forth a wonder, to content ye 5.01.170
for it is you that have chalk'd forth the way 5.01.203
put forth their sons to seek preferment out: TGV 1.03. 7
i shall inquire you forth. 2.04.186
rascally knave her husband will be forth. WIV 2.02.266 P
and when i suddenly call you, come forth, and 3.03. 11 P
were call'd forth by their mistress to carry me 3.05. 98 P
come, come forth! 4.02.120 P
what honest clothes you send forth to bleaching! 4.02.121 P
come forth, sirrah! 4.02.136 P
let them from forth a sawpit rush at once | with 4.04. 54
(so far forth as herself might be her chooser) 4.06. 11
for if our virtues | did not go forth of us, MM 1.01. 34
lead forth and bring you back in happiness! 1.01. 74
they put forth to steal. 1.02. 14 P
my father's grave | did utter forth a voice. 3.01. 86
come forth! 4.01. 49
cannot but yield you forth to public thanks, 5.01. 7
whom it concerns to hear this matter forth, | do 5.01.255
who, falling there to find his fellow forth ERR 1.02. 37
and the heedful slave | is wand'red forth, in 2.02. 3
say he dines forth, and let no creature enter. 2.02.210
if any bark put forth, come to the mart, | where 3.02.150
is there any ships puts forth to-night? 4.03. 35 P
that the bark expedition put forth to-night, and 4.03. 38 P
say, wherefore didst thou lock me forth to-day? 4.04. 95
i did not, gentle husband, lock thee forth. 4.04. 97
then let your servants bring my husband forth. 5.01. 93
nor send him forth, that we may bear him hence. 5.01.158
with thy command | let him be brought forth, and 5.01.160
you'll be made bring deformed forth, i warrant ADO 3.03.172 P
you must call forth the watch that are their 4.02. 34 P
let the watch come forth. 4.02. 37 P
call her forth, brother, here's the friar ready. 5.04. 39
/pecus /omne sub umbra ruminat — and so forth. LLL 4.02. 94 P
now step i forth to whip hypocrisy. 4.03.149
call them forth quickly, we will do so. 5.02.889 P
of mirth, | turn melancholy forth to funerals: MND 1.01. 14
stand forth, demetrius. 1.01. 24
stand forth, lysander. 1.01. 26
steal forth thy father's house to-morrow night; 1.01.164
quince, call forth your actors by the scroll. 1.02. 14 P
speak, pyramus. thisby, stand forth. 3.01. 81 P
must be answered, | and forth my mimic comes. 3.02. 19
and as imagination bodies forth | the forms of 5.01. 14
gaping wide, | every one lets forth his sprite, 5.01.381
believe me, sir, had i such venture forth, | the MV 1.01. 15
more advised watch | to find the other forth, 1.01.143
therefore go forth, | try what my credit can in 1.01.179
i am bid forth to supper, jessica. 2.05. 11
i have no mind of feasting forth to-night; 2.05. 37
come forth to view | the issue of th' exploit. 3.02. 59
well, i'll set you forth. 3.05. 90
antonio and old shylock, both stand forth. 4.01.175
padua, | and it is meet i presently set forth. 4.01.404
hand, | and bring your music forth into the air. 5.01. 53
here | shall witness i set forth as soon as you, 5.01.271
stand you both forth now. AYL 1.02. 71 P
'gainst the lady | will suddenly break forth. 1.02.283
us, | maids as we are, to travel forth so far! 1.03.109
the wretched animal heav'd forth such groans 2.01. 36
he went but forth to wash him in the hellespont 4.01.103 P
ta'en his bow and arrows and is gone forth — to 4.03. 5 P
could not drop forth such giant-rude invention, 4.03. 34
it shall be so far forth friendly maintain'd SHR 1.01.136 P
draw forth thy weapon, we are beset with thieves 3.02.236
call forth nathaniel, joseph, nicholas, philip, 4.01. 89 P
call them forth. 4.01. 97 P
i call them forth to credit her. 4.01.104 P
orders grey, | as he forth walked on his way" — 4.01.146
lay forth the gown. 4.03. 62
call forth an officer. 5.01. 91 P
me them soundly forth unto their husbands. 5.02.104
to choose from forth the royal blood of france, AWW 2.01.196
fair maid, send forth thine eye. 2.03. 52
whose great decision hath much blood let forth 3.01. 3
then go thou forth, | and fortune play upon thy 3.03. 6
juno, sent him forth | from courtly friends, 3.04. 13
come, bring forth this counterfeit module, h'as 4.03. 98 P
bring him forth, h'as sat i' th' stocks all 4.03.101 P
through flinty tartar's bosom would peep forth 4.04. 7
distracted clouds give way, so stand thou forth; 5.03. 35
send forth your amorous token for fair maudlin. 5.03. 68
on thee, lafew, | to bring forth this discov'ry. 5.03.151
item, one neck, one chin, and so forth. TN 1.05.249 P
more sharp than filed steel, did spur me forth, 3.03. 5
arguments of fear, | set forth in your pursuit. 3.03. 13
in the habit of some sir of note, and so forth. 3.04. 74 P
call forth the holy father. 5.01.142
to make us say, | "this is put forth too truly." WT 1.02. 14
doings of the world, | sometime puts forth. 1.02.254
your attendants, i | shall bring emilia forth. 2.02. 14
is good) hath brought you forth a daughter — 2.03. 66
therefore bring forth, | and in apollo's name, 3.02.117
the casting forth to crows thy baby-daughter 3.02.191
time's news | be known when 'tis brought forth. 4.01. 27
his free arms and weeping | his welcomes forth; 4.04.549
the which shall point you forth at every sitting 4.04.561
of such affections, | step forth mine advocate. 5.01.221
and ready mounted are they to spit forth | their JN 2.01.211
where we'll set forth | in best appointment all 2.01.295
did display them when we first march'd forth; 2.01.320
fortune shall cull forth | out of one side her 2.01.391
that spits forth death and mountains, rocks and 2.01.458
arise forth from the couch of lasting night, 3.04. 27
that none so small advantage shall step forth 3.04.151
rush forth | and bind the boy which you shall 4.01. 3
young lad, come forth; 4.01. 8
come forth. do as i bid you do. 4.01. 71
with me | from forth the streets of pomfret, 4.02.148
up | from forth this morsel of dead royalty! 4.03.143
from forth the noise and rumor of the field, 5.04. 45
a maim | as to be cast forth in the common air, R2 1.03.157
go, say i sent thee forth to purchase honor, 1.03.282
where doth the world thrust forth a vanity — 2.01. 24
from forth thy reach he would have laid thy 2.01.106
now hath my soul brought forth her prodigy, 2.02. 64
from forth the ranks of many thousand french, 2.03.102
bring forth these men. 3.01. 1
which didst lead me forth | of that sweet way i 3.02.204
eagle's, lightens forth | controlling majesty. 3.03. 69
call forth bagot. 4.01. 1
cousin, stand forth, and look upon that man. 4.01. 7
the lion dying thrusteth forth his paw, | and 5.01. 29
from whence set forth in pomp | she came adorned 5.01. 78
which elder years | may happily bring forth. 5.03. 22
how shall we part with them in setting forth? 1H4 1.02.168 P
why, we will set forth before or after them and 1.02.169 P
did set forth | upon his irish expedition; 1.03.149
bid butler lead him forth into the park. 2.03. 72
to-day will i set forth, to-morrow you. 2.03.116
go call him forth. 2.04.527 P
diseased nature oftentimes breaks forth | in 3.01. 26
i | and my good lord of worcester will set forth 3.01. 83
the earl of westmerland set forth to-day, | with 3.02.170
he did, my lord, four days ere i set forth, 4.01. 22
the king himself in person is set forth, | or 4.01. 91
prince of wales stepp'd forth before the king, 5.02. 45
his lordship is walk'd forth into the orchard. 2H4 1.01. 4
come, we will all put forth, body and goods. 1.01.186
lend me a thousand pound to furnish me forth? 1.02.224 P
the powers that you already have sent forth 3.01.100
and send discoverers forth | to know the numbers 4.01. 3
we have sent forth already. 4.01. 5
how far forth you do like their articles. 4.02. 53
but peace puts forth her olive every where. 4.04. 87
graffing, with a dish of caraways, and so forth. 5.03. 3 P
on this unworthy scaffold to bring forth | so H5 pr 10
i may, and to put forth | my rightful hand in a 1.02.292
but till the king come forth, and not till then, 2.pr. 41
fetch forth the lazar kite of cressid's kind, 2.01. 76
then forth, dear countrymen! 2.02.189
of brabant and of orleance, shall make forth, 2.04. 5
'tis meet we all go forth | to view the sick and 2.04. 21
now forth, lord constable and princes all, | and 3.05. 67
for forth he goes, and visits all his host, 4.pr. 32
go forth and fetch their conqu'ring caesar in; 5.pr. 28
with hair, | put forth disorder'd twigs; 5.02. 44
that erst brought sweetly forth | the freckled 5.02. 48
tidings would call forth her flowing tides. 1H6 1.01. 83
and goliases | it sendeth forth to skirmish. 1.02. 34
and drive the english forth the bounds of france 1.02. 54
out of a great deal of old iron i chose forth. 1.02.101
bring forth the body of old salisbury, | and 2.02. 4
and makes him roar these accusations forth. 3.01. 40
dare ye come forth and meet us in the field? 3.02. 61
english john talbot, captains, /calls you forth, 4.02. 3
set from our o'ermatch'd forces forth for aid. 4.04. 11
then call our captains and our colors forth, 5.03.128
bring forth that sorceress condemn'd to burn. 5.04. 1
put forth thy hand, reach at the glorious gold. 2H6 1.02. 11

stand forth, dame eleanor cobham, gloucester's 2.03. 1
he that loos'd them forth their brazen caves, 3.02. 89
therefore bring forth the soldiers of our prize, 4.01. 8
stood | and duly waited for my coming forth? 4.01. 62
god, to shoot forth thunder | upon these paltry, 4.01.104
clifford, i say, come forth and fight with me. 5.02. 5
let us pursue him ere the writs go forth. 5.03. 26
and issue forth and bid them battle straight. 3H6 1.02. 70
may bring forth | a bird that will revenge upon 1.04. 35
and watch'd him how he singled clifford forth. 2.01. 12
wash'd his father's fortunes forth of france, 2.02.157
from london by the king was i press'd forth; 2.05. 64
in hewing rutland when his leaves put forth, 2.06. 48
bring forth that fatal screech–owl to our house 2.06. 56
bring forth the gallant, let us hear him speak. 5.05. 12
and yet brought forth less than a mother's hope, 5.06. 50
lo, in these windows that let forth thy life | i R3 1.02. 12
and let the soul forth that adoreth thee, | i 1.02.176
with odd old ends stol'n forth of holy writ, 1.03.336
and would not let it forth | to find the empty, 1.04. 38
are you drawn forth among a world of men | to 1.04.181
i am not barren to bring forth complaints. 2.02. 67
may send forth plenteous tears to drown the 2.02. 70
yet to draw forth your noble ancestry | from the 3.07.198
from forth the kennel of thy womb hath crept | a 4.04. 47
grace | to breakfast once, forth of my company. 4.04.177
i will lead forth my soldiers to the plain, 5.03.291
whom their o'ercloyed country vomits forth | to 5.03.318
stand forth, and with bold spirit relate what H8 1.02.129
to–day he puts forth | the tender leaves of 3.02.352
no sun shall ever usher forth mine honors, | or 3.02.410
embalm me, | then lay me forth. 4.02.171
be what they will, may stand forth face to face, 5.02. 82
i think he went not forth to–day. TRO 1.02.220 P
that the prais'd himself bring the praise forth; 1.03.242
and doth boil | (as 'twere from forth us all) a 1.03.350
when thou art forth in the incursions, thou 2.01. 29 P
cressid comes forth to him. 5.02. 6
how poor andromache shrills her dolors forth! 5.03. 84
we'll forth and fight, | do deeds worth praise, 5.03. 92
sigh'd forth proverbs — | that hunger broke COR 1.01.205
upon power, and throw forth greater themes | for 1.01.220
mutiners, | your valor puts well forth; 1.01.251
some parcels of their power are forth already, 1.02. 32
with his mail'd hand then wiping, forth he goes, 1.03. 35
than hector's forehead when it spit forth blood 1.03. 42
good madam, pardon me, indeed i will not forth. 1.03. 88 P
the volsces have an army forth; 1.03. 96 P
hark, our drums | are bringing forth our youth. 1.04. 16
they fear us not, but issue forth their city. 1.04. 23
we render you the tenth, to be ta'en forth, 1.09. 34
done — | you /shout me forth | in acclamations 1.09. 50
to give forth | the corn a' th' store–house 3.01.113
so if the time thrust forth | a cause for thy 4.01. 40
when i am forth, | bid me farewell, and smile. 4.01. 49
if he had gone forth consul, found it so. 4.06. 35
thrusts forth his horns again into the world, 4.06. 44
lest i let forth your half–pint of blood. 5.02. 56 P
that brought you forth this boy, to keep your 5.03.126
till from forth this place | i lead espous'd my TIT 1.01.327
you | are singled forth to try thy experiments. 2.03. 69
i pour'd forth tears in vain | to save your 2.03.163
is torn from forth that pretty hollow cage, 3.01. 84
and prompt me that my tongue may utter forth 5.03. 12
i am the turned forth, be it known to you, 5.03.109
and on the ragged stones beat forth our souls, 5.03.133
but throw her forth to beasts and birds to prey: 5.03.198
from forth the fatal loins of these two foes | a ROM pr 5
peer'd forth the golden window of the east, | a 1.01.119
call her forth to me. 1.03. 1
from forth day's path and titan's /fiery wheels. 2.03. 4
romeo, come forth, come forth, thou fearful man: 3.03. 1
romeo, come forth, come forth, thou fearful man: 3.03. 1
joy | than thou went'st forth in lamentation. 3.03.154
they are all forth. 4.02. 44
for shame, bring juliet forth, her lord is come. 4.05. 22
seal'd up the doors and would not let us forth, 5.02. 11
bring forth the parties of suspicion. 5.03.222
and i entreated her come forth | and bear this 5.03.260
a picture, sir. when comes your book forth? TIM 1.01. 26
what a mental power | this eye shoots forth! 1.01. 32
but flies an eagle flight, bold, and forth on, 1.01. 49
mine heir from forth the beggars of the world, 1.01.138
so soon as dinner's done, we'll forth again, 2.02. 14
pray is my lord ready to come forth? 3.04. 35 P
from forth thy plenteous bosom, one poor root! 4.03.186
within this mile break forth a hundred springs; 4.03.418
and send forth us to make their sorrowed render, 5.01.149
approach the fold and cull th' infected forth, 5.04. 43
no, i am promis'd forth. JC 1.02.289 P
is the bright day that brings forth the adder, 2.01. 14
whether caesar will come forth to–day or no; 2.01.194
think you to walk forth? 2.02. 8
caesar shall forth; 2.02. 10
yet caesar shall go forth; 2.02. 28
themselves blaze forth the death of princes. 2.02. 31
they would not have you to stir forth to–day. 2.02. 38
plucking the entrails of an offering forth, 2.02. 39
and caesar shall go forth. 2.02. 48
do not go forth to–day; 2.02. 50
thy lord look well, | for he went sickly forth; 2.04. 14
then walk we forth, even to the market–place, 3.01.108
what, shall we forth? 3.01.119
weeping as fast as they stream forth thy blood, 3.01.201
i have no will to wander forth of doors, | yet 3.03. 3
forth of doors, | yet something leads me forth. 3.03. 4
must be taught, and train'd, and bid go forth; 4.01. 35
for, from this day forth, | i'll use you for my 4.03. 48
if that thou be'st a roman, take it forth. 4.03.103
make forth, the generals would have some words. 5.01. 25
why didst thou send me forth, brave cassius? 5.03. 80
pardon, and set forth | a deep repentance. MAC 1.04. 6
bring forth men–children only! 1.07. 72
and | sent forth great largess to your offices. 2.01. 14
maggot–pies and choughs and rooks brought forth 3.04.124
men | already at a point, was setting forth. 4.03.135
comes the king forth, i pray you? 4.03.140
unlock her closet, take forth paper, fold it, 5.01. 6 P
producing forth the cruel ministers | of this 5.09. 34
did coldly furnish forth the marriage tables. HAM 1.02.181
would not, in plain terms, from this time forth, 1.03.132
it waves me forth again, i'll follow it. 1.04. 68
of sale," | videlicet, a brothel, or so forth. 2.01. 59
forth at your eyes your spirits wildly peep, 3.04.119
o, from this time forth, | my thoughts be bloody 4.04. 65
breaking forth | in rank and not–to–be–endur'd LR 1.04.203
fetch forth the stocks! 2.02.125
fetch forth the stocks! 2.02.133
/panting forth | from goneril his mistress 2.04. 31
give me my servant forth. 2.04.115
bid them come forth and hear me, | or at their 2.04.117
followed the old man forth. he is return'd. 2.04.295
come forth. 3.04. 45 P
a /century send forth; 4.04. 6
but are my brother's pow'rs set forth? 4.05. 1
our troops set forth to–morrow, stay with us; 4.05. 16
i pray you, sir, go forth, | and give us truth OTH 2.01. 57
forth my sword; 5.01. 10
uncle, i must come forth. 5.02.254
where is that viper? bring the villain forth. 5.02.285
from this time forth i never will speak word. 5.02.304
then we bring forth weeds | when our quick winds ANT 1.02.109
your old smock brings forth a new petticoat, and 1.02.168 P
no vessel can peep forth, but 'tis as soon 1.04. 53
thy freer thoughts | may not fly forth of egypt. 1.05. 12
and, breathless, pow'r breathe forth. 2.02.232
"but yet" is as a jailer to bring forth | some 2.05. 52
your letters did withhold our breaking forth, 3.06. 79
with labor, and throes forth | each minute some. 3.07. 80
unto a muss, kings would start forth | and cry, 3.13. 91
call forth my household servants, let's to–night 4.02. 9
he goes forth gallantly. 4.04. 36
go forth, agrippa, and begin the fight. 4.06. 1
sea is given, | they have put forth the haven — 4.10. 7
his best force | is forth to man his galleys. 4.11. 3
whose eye beck'd forth my wars and call'd them 4.12. 26
which your death | will never let come forth. 5.02. 46
antony | shall be brought drunken forth, and i 5.02.219
were you but riding forth to air yourself, CYM 1.01.110
will she not forth? 2.03. 38
but from this time forth | i wear it as your 3.05. 13
fidele's sickness | did make my way long forth. 4.02.149
sir, step you forth; 5.05.130
my lord of rome, | call forth your soothsayer. 5.05.426
thy lopp'd branches point | thy two sons forth; 5.05.455
he must not live to trumpet forth my infamy, PER 1.01.145
he, doing so, put forth to seas, | where when 2.ch. 27
grisled north | disgorges such a tempest forth, 3.ch. 48
your honor has through ephesus pour'd forth 3.02. 43
well, call forth, call forth. 4.06. 33 P
well, call forth, call forth. 4.06. 33 P
yet i was mortally brought forth, and am | no 5.01.104
but brought forth | a maid–child call'd marina, 5.03. 5
whereto he'll infuse pow'r and press you forth TNK 1.01. 73
forth and levy | our worthiest instruments, 1.01.162
but when could grief | cull forth, as unpang'd 1.01.169
come forth and fear not, here's no theseus. 3.03. 3
"he s' buy me a white cut, forth for to ride, 3.04. 22
come forth, and foot it. 3.05.137
which doubt not will bring forth comfort. 4.03.101 P
with hand armipotent from forth blue clouds 5.01. 54
thine eye darts forth the fire that burneth me, VEN 196
she had not brought forth thee, but died unkind. 204
red cheeks and fiery eyes blaze forth her wrong; 219
but lo from forth a copse that neighbors by, | a 259
and forth she rushes, snorts, and neighs aloud. 262
the air, and forth again | as from a furnace, 273
pale, and by and by | it flash'd forth fire, as 348
who plucks the bud before one leaf put forth? 416
sit, | long after fearing to creep forth again; 1036
made | to set forth that which is so singular? LUC 32
puffs forth another wind that fires the torch. 315
rushing from forth a cloud, bereaves our sight, 373
who, peeping forth this tumult to behold, | are 447
from forth dull sleep by dreadful fancy waking, 450
with grief thus breathes she forth her spite 762
me good | is to let forth my foul defiled blood. 1029
with gold, but stol'n from forth thy gate. 1068
no, | and forth with bashful innocence doth hie. 1341
and dying eyes gleam'd forth their ashy lights, 1378
would break, | she throws forth tarquin's name: 1717
by our strong arms from forth her fair streets 1834
not, | green plants bring not forth their dye; PP 17.26
her well, | and set her person forth to sale. 18.12
and make me travel forth without my cloak, | to SON 34. 2
let him bring forth | eternal numbers to outlive 38.11
and all–oblivious enmity | shall you pace forth; 55.10
for i am sham'd by that which i bring forth, 72.13
alack, what poverty my muse brings forth, | that 103. 1
thou usurer, that put'st forth all to use, | and 134.10
breath'd forth the sound that said "i hate" | to 145. 2
how coldly those impediments stand forth | of LC 269

FORTHCOMING 3 FR 0.0003 REL FR 2 V 1 P
i charge you see that he be forthcoming. SHR 5.01. 93 P
we'll see your trinkets here all forthcoming. 2H6 1.04. 53
means | your lady is forthcoming yet at london. 2.01.175

FORTHLIGHT 1 FR 0.0001 REL FR 0 V 1 P
lusty pudding, and master forthlight the tilter, MM 4.03. 16 P

FORTHRIGHT 1 FR 0.0001 REL FR 1 V 0 P
or /hedge aside from the direct forthright, TRO 3.03.158

FORTH–RIGHTS 1 FR 0.0001 REL FR 1 V 0 P
trod indeed | through forth–rights and meanders! TMP 3.03. 3

FORTHWITH 24 FR 0.0027 REL FR 23 V 1 P
bear me forthwith unto his creditor, | and, ERR 4.04.120
then meet me forthwith at the notary's; MV 1.03.172
and therefore frolic, we will hence forthwith, SHR 4.03.182
and entreat my wife | to come to me forthwith. 5.02. 87
leave and part, for you must part forthwith. R2 5.01. 70
forthwith a power of english shall we levy, 1H4 1.01. 22
bonfires in france forthwith i am to make, | to 1H6 1.01.153
i must go victual orleance forthwith. 1.05. 14
and now forthwith shall articles be drawn 3H6 3.03.135
joy, | to him forthwith in holy wedlock bands. 3.03.243
see that forthwith duke edward be convey'd 4.03. 52
i'll hence forthwith unto the sanctuary, | to 4.04. 31
forthwith that edward be pronounc'd a traitor, 4.06. 54
forthwith we'll send him hence to brittany, 4.06. 97
forthwith from ludlow the young prince be fet R3 2.02.121
be acquainted | forthwith for what you come. H8 2.02.108
that forthwith | you be convey'd to th' tower a 5.02.123
and i will give a taste thereof forthwith | to TRO 1.03.387
and /for /him forthwith, | ere the first 4.02. 63
my father and lavinia shall forthwith | be TIT 5.03.193
i your commission will forthwith dispatch, | and HAM 3.03. 3
on th' instant, i will be return'd forthwith. OTH 4.03. 8 P
forthwith they fly | chickens, the way which CYM 5.03. 41
whereat a waxen torch forthwith he lighteth, LUC 178

FORTIFICATION 1 FR 0.0001 REL FR 1 V 0 P
this fortification, gentlemen, shall we see't? OTH 3.02. 5

FORTIFIED 5 FR 0.0005 REL FR 4 V 1 P
he's fortified against any denial. TN 1.05.145 P
what he hath won, that hath he fortified. JN 3.04. 10
for i protest we are well fortified, | and 1H6 4.02. 19
ears, | that are so fortified against our story, HAM 1.01. 32
which fortified her visage from the sun, LC 9

FORTIFIES 1 FR 0.0001 REL FR 1 V 0 P
great dunsinane he strongly fortifies. MAC 5.02. 12

FORTIFY 7 FR 0.0008 REL FR 6 V 1 P
/or /else | we fortify in paper and in figures, 2H4 1.03. 56
and fortify it strongly 'gainst the french. H5 3.03. 53
one, | and view the frenchmen how they fortify. 1H6 1.04. 61
and therefore fortify your hold, my lord. 3H6 1.02. 52
extend him, be it but to fortify her judgment, CYM 1.04. 21 P
and fortify yourself in your decay | with means SON 16. 3
for such a time do i now fortify | against 63. 9

FORTINBRAS 12 FR 0.0013 REL FR 11 V 1 P
us, | was, as you know, by fortinbras of norway, HAM 1.01. 82
did slay this fortinbras, who, by a seal'd 1.01. 86
/return'd | to the inheritance of fortinbras, 1.01. 92
now, sir, young fortinbras, | of unimproved 1.01. 95
now follows that you know young fortinbras, 1.02. 17
writ | to norway, uncle of young fortinbras — 1.02. 28
sends out arrests | on fortinbras, which he, in 2.02. 68
tell him that by his license fortinbras | craves 4.04. 2
the nephew to old norway, fortinbras. 4.04. 14
that our last king hamlet overcame fortinbras. 5.01.144 P
young fortinbras, with conquest come from poland 5.02.350
do prophesy th' election lights | on fortinbras, 5.02.356

FORTITUDE 5 FR 0.0005 REL FR 4 V 1 P
smile, | infused with a fortitude from heaven, TMP 1.02.154
fame, | despairing of his own arm's fortitude, 1H6 2.01. 17
methinks | (out of a fortitude of soul i feel), H8 3.02.388
devotion, patience, courage, fortitude, | i have MAC 4.03. 94
the fortitude of the place is best known to you; OTH 1.03.222 P

FORTNIGHT *(also vortnight)*

FORTNIGHT 9 FR 0.0010 REL FR 6 V 3 P
last, a fortnight afore michaelmas? WIV 1.01.205 P
a fortnight hold we this solemnity, | in nightly MND 5.01.369
bespeak him a fortnight before. MV 3.01.126 P
for what offense have i this fortnight been | a 1H4 2.03. 38
your majesty hath been this fortnight ill, | and 2H4 3.01.104
well, catesby, ere a fortnight make me older, R3 3.02. 60
had inkling this fortnight what we intend to do, COR 1.01. 58 P
a fortnight and odd days. ROM 1.03. 15
within a fortnight? LR 1.04.295

FORTRESS 3 FR 0.0003 REL FR 3 V 0 P
this fortress built by nature for herself R2 2.01. 43
god is our fortress, in whose conquering name 1H6 2.01. 26
be the ram to batter | the fortress of it; ANT 3.02. 31

FORTRESS'D 1 FR 0.0001 REL FR 1 V 0 P
are weakly fortress'd from a world of harms. LUC 28

FORTRESSES 1 FR 0.0001 REL FR 1 V 0 P
reclaim'd | to your obedience fifty fortresses, 1H6 3.04. 6

FORTS 2 FR 0.0002 REL FR 2 V 0 P
hath slain their governors, surpris'd our forts, 2H6 4.01. 89
oft breaking down the pales and forts of reason, HAM 1.04. 28

FORTUNA 2 FR 0.0002 REL FR 1 V 1 P
put it, as they say, to fortuna de la /guerra. LLL 5.02.530 P
si fortuna me tormenta, spero contenta. 2H4 5.05. 96

FORTUNATE 19 FR 0.0021 REL FR 14 V 5 P
deserve as full as fortunate a bed | as ever ADO 3.01. 45
so hung upon with love, so fortunate | (but MND 3.02.233
issue, there create, | ever shall be fortunate. 5.01.406
that i should questionless be fortunate! MV 1.01.176
bless you, my fortunate lady! AWW 2.04. 14 P
fortunate mistress (let my prophecy | come home WT 4.04.648
account | nothing so strong and fortunate as i. 1H4 5.01. 38
thou shalt be fortunate | if thou receive me for 1H6 1.02. 91
then on, my lords, and france be fortunate! 5.02. 21
thee, | for thou art fortunate in all thy deeds. 3H6 4.06. 25
well–minded clarence, be thou fortunate! 4.08. 27
i am most fortunate thus accidentally to COR 4.03. 37 P
makes me less gracious, or thee more fortunate; TIT 2.01. 32
it was a vision fair and fortunate. JC 2.02. 84
as he was fortunate, i rejoice at it; 3.02. 25 P
whilst the wheel'd seat | of fortunate caesar, ANT 4.14. 76
britain be fortunate and flourish in peace and CYM 5.04.144 P
britain be fortunate and flourish in peace and 5.05.441 P
that fortunate bright star, the fair emilia, TNK 3.06.146

FORTUNATELY 3 FR 0.0003 REL FR 3 V 0 P
fair lovers, you are fortunately met; MND 4.01.177
who hath most fortunately been inform'd | of my LR 2.02.167
most fortunately. OTH 2.01. 61

FORTUNATE–UNHAPPY 1 FR 0.0001 REL FR 0 V 1 P
services with thee, the fortunate–unhappy." TN 2.05.159 P

/FORTUNE 3 FR 0.0003 REL FR 2 V 1 P
/knows /on /whom /fortune /would /then /have 2H4 4.01.131
/deserv'd /at /the /hands /of /fortune, /that HAM 2.02.241 P
since that /respects /of /fortune are his love, LR 1.01.248

FORTUNE 343 FR 0.0387 REL FR 287 V 56 P
by accident most strange, bountiful fortune TMP 1.02.178
thou let'st thy fortune sleep — die, rather; 2.01.216
your content | tender your own good fortune? 2.01.270
for all is but fortune. 5.01.257 P
some to the wars, to try their fortune there; TGV 1.03. 8
wishing me with him, partner of his fortune, 1.03. 59
i read your fortune in your eye. 2.04.143
because myself do want my servants' fortune. 3.01.147
if crooked fortune had not thwarted me. 4.01. 22
nothing but my fortune. 4.01. 41
which heaven and fortune still rewards with 4.03. 31
witness good bringing up, fortune, and truth: 4.04. 69
that flies her fortune when it follows her. 5.02. 50

well, heaven send anne page no worse fortune! WIV 1.04. 33 P
see what thou wert, if fortune thy foe were not, 3.03. 65 P
now heaven send thee good fortune! 3.04.101 P
it were my master's fortune to have her or no. 4.05. 48 P
'tis, 'tis his fortune. 4.05. 49 P
follow it as the flesh and fortune shall better MM 2.01.253 P
you, fortune hath convey'd to my understanding; 3.01.185 P
him, the portion and sinew of her fortune, her 3.01.221 P
more than thanks and good fortune, by the saint 4.02.179 P
to try her gracious fortune with lord angelo, 5.01. 76
fortune had left to both of us alike | what to ERR 1.01.105
my food, my fortune, and my sweet hope's aim, 3.02. 63
i to this fortune that you see me in. 5.01.356
to be a well–favor'd man is the gift of fortune, ADO 3.03. 15 P
and given way unto this course of fortune, | by 4.01.157
nor fortune made such havoc of my means, | nor 4.01.195
i thank my fortune for it, | my ventures are not MV 1.01. 41
estate | upon the fortune of this present year: 1.01. 44
you lead me to the caskets | to try my fortune. 2.01. 24
may turn by fortune from the weaker hand: 2.01. 34
/page, | and so may i, blind fortune leading me, 2.01. 36
good fortune then! 2.01. 45
o rare fortune! 2.02.111 P
to swear upon a book, i shall have good fortune. 2.02.160 P
well, if fortune be a woman, she's a good wench 2.02.166 P
farewell, and if my fortune be not cross'd, | i 2.05. 56
lastly, | if i do fail in fortune of my choice, 2.09. 15
fortune now | to my heart's hope! 2.09. 19
for who shall go about | to cozen fortune, and 2.09. 38
it so, | let fortune go to hell for it, not i. 3.02. 21
but let me to my fortune and the caskets. 3.02. 39
the continent and summary of my fortune. 3.02.130
since this fortune falls to you, | be content, 3.02.133
this, | and hold your fortune for your bliss, 3.02.136
your fortune stood upon the caskets there, | and 3.02.201
provided that your fortune | achiev'd her 3.02.207
for herein fortune shows herself more kind 4.01.267
mock the good huswife fortune from her wheel, AYL 1.02. 32 P
fortune reigns in gifts of the world, not in the 1.02. 41 P
may she not by fortune fall into the fire? 1.02. 44 P
nature hath given us wit to flout at fortune, 1.02. 46 P
hath not fortune sent in this fool to cut off 1.02. 46 P
indeed there is fortune too hard for nature, 1.02. 48 P
nature, when fortune makes nature's natural the 1.02. 49 P
as wit and fortune will. 1.02.104 P
one out of suits with fortune, | that could give 1.02.246
that can translate the stubbornness of fortune 2.01. 19
yet fortune cannot recompense me better | than 2.03. 75
sun, | and rail'd on lady fortune in good terms, 2.07. 16
me not fool till heaven hath sent me fortune." 2.07. 19
the residue of your fortune, | go to my cave and 2.07.196
but he comes arm'd in his fortune, and prevents 4.01. 61 P
know into what straits of fortune she is driven, 5.02. 64 P
shall share the good of our returned fortune, 5.04.174
to deck his fortune with his virtuous deeds. SHR 1.01. 16
and by good fortune i have lighted well | on 1.02.167
my father dead, my fortune lives for me, | and i 1.02.191
whatever fortune stays him from his word. 3.02. 23
the fouler fortune mine, and there an end. 5.02. 98
the mightiest space in fortune nature brings AWW 1.01.222
have fought with equal fortune, and continue | a 1.02. 2
fortune, she said, was no goddess, that had put 1.03.111 P
and in your bed | find fairer fortune, if you 2.03. 92
good fortune and the favor of the king | smile 2.03.177
stars have fail'd | to equal my great fortune. 2.05. 76
love and credence | upon thy promising fortune. 3.03. 3
and fortune play upon thy prosperous helm | as 3.03. 7
which well approves | y' are great in fortune. 3.07. 14
i am a man whom fortune hath cruelly scratch'd. 5.02. 26 P
the knave with fortune that she should scratch 5.02. 30 P
let the justices make you and fortune friends; 5.02. 34 P
but when i had subscrib'd | to mine own fortune, 5.03. 97
fortune forbid my outside have not charm'd her! TN 2.02. 18
the parts that fortune hath bestow'd upon her, 2.04. 83
her, | tell her, i hold as giddily as fortune; 2.04. 84
'tis but fortune, all is fortune. 2.05. 23 P
'tis but fortune, all is fortune. 2.05. 23 P
yet doth this accident and flood of fortune | so 4.03. 11
time, fortune, do cohere and jump | that i am 5.01.252
all the occurrence of my fortune since | hath 5.01.257
as by strange fortune | it came to us, i do in WT 2.03.179
which may, if fortune please, both breed thee, 3.03. 48
o lady fortune, | stand you auspicious! 4.04. 51
let myself and fortune | tug for the time to 4.04.496
fortune speed us! 4.04.667
to be honest, i see fortune would not suffer me: 4.04.831 P
though fortune, visible an enemy, | should chase 5.01.216
in the blossoms of their fortune. 5.02.125 P
wilt thou forsake thy fortune, | bequeath thy JN 1.01.148
brother, adieu, good fortune come to thee! 1.01.180
fortune shall cull forth | out of one side her 2.01.391
nature and fortune join'd to make thee great. 3.01. 52
but fortune, o, | she is corrupted, chang'd, and 3.01. 54
france is a bawd to fortune and king john, 3.01. 60
that strumpet fortune, that usurping john! 3.01. 61
bidding me depend | upon thy stars, thy fortune, 3.01.126
father, i may not wish the fortune thine; 3.01.333
lady, with me, with me thy fortune lies. 3.01.337
there where my fortune lives, there my life dies 3.01.338
when fortune means to men most good, | she looks 3.04.119
nor met with fortune other than at feasts, 5.02. 58
right, | so be thy fortune in this royal fight! R2 1.03. 56
however god or fortune cast my lot, | there 1.03. 85
and patient underbearing of his fortune, | as 1.04. 29
and, as my fortune ripens with thy love, | it 2.03. 48
which, till my infant fortune comes to years, 2.03. 66
and crossly to thy good all fortune goes. 2.04. 24
myself, a prince by fortune of my birth, | near 3.01. 16
thy joys, friends, fortune, and thy state, | for 3.02. 72
and that my fortune runs against the bias. 3.04. 5
for the fortune of us that are the moon's men 1H4 1.02. 31 P
"look when his infant fortune came to age" | and 1.03.253
on, | to see how fortune is dispos'd to us, 4.01. 38
a day | wherein the fortune of ten thousand men 4.04. 9
it rain'd down fortune show'ring on your head, 5.01. 47
side, | try fortune with him in a single fight. 5.01.100
and i embrace this fortune patiently, | since 5.05. 12
the fortune of the day quite turn'd from him, 5.05. 18
and, in the fortune of my lord your son, 2H4 1.01. 15
god send the wench no worse fortune! 2.02.140 P
"si fortune me tormente, sperato me contento." 2.04.181
will fortune never come with both hands full, 4.04.103
i would not take a /knighthood for my fortune. 5.03.127 P
fortune is painted blind, with a muffler afore H5 3.06. 30 P
eyes, to signify to you that fortune is blind; 3.06. 32 P
fortune is an excellent moral. 3.06. 38 P
fortune is bardolph's foe, and frowns on him; 3.06. 39
o mechante fortune! 4.05. 5
doth fortune play the huswife with me now? 5.01. 80
fortune made his sword; ep 6
which caesar and his fortune bare at once. 1H6 1.02.139
cowardly knight, ill fortune follow thee! 3.02.109
fortune in favor makes him lag behind. 3.03. 34
lucy, farewell, no more my fortune can, | but 4.03. 43
but dies, betray'd to fortune by your strife. 4.04. 39
commit them to the fortune of the sea. 5.01. 50
witness the fortune he hath had in france. 2H6 3.01.292
thy fortune, york, hadst thou been regent there, 3.01.305
my lord of york, try what your fortune is. 3.01.309
to see their day, and them our fortune give. 5.02. 89
trull | upon their woes whom fortune captivates! 3H6 1.04.115
which promiseth | successful fortune, steel thy 2.02. 41
ay, good my lord, and leave us to our fortune. 2.02. 75
why, that's my fortune too, therefore i'll stay. 2.02. 76
head, | or bide the mortal fortune of the field? 2.02. 83
mine | or fortune given me measure of revenge. 2.03. 32
breathe we, lords, good fortune bids us pause, 2.06. 31
where i must take like seat unto my fortune, 3.03. 10
and meaner than myself have had like fortune. 4.01. 71
by living low, where fortune cannot hurt me, 4.06. 20
consent, | for on thy fortune i repose myself. 4.06. 47
rest, | yet thus far fortune maketh us amends, 4.07. 2
i'll leave you to your fortune and be gone | to 4.07. 55
if fortune serve me, i'll requite this kindness. 4.07. 78
thus far our fortune keeps an upward course, 5.03. 1
nor i, but stoop with patience to my fortune. 5.05. 6
poor painted queen, vain flourish of my fortune! R3 1.03.240
it cannot be, for he bewept my fortune, | and 1.04.244
weep, | to chide my fortune, and torment myself? 2.02. 35
your state of fortune, and your due of birth, 3.07.120
me, | the right and fortune of his happy stars, 3.07.172
men, | since you will buckle fortune on my back, 3.07.228
thou to richmond, and good fortune guide thee! 4.01. 91
i call'd thee then vain flourish of my fortune; 4.04. 82
unto the dignity and height of fortune, | the 4.04.244
heaven and fortune bar me happy hours! 4.04.400
fortune and victory sit on thy helm! 5.03. 79
and put thy fortune to the arbitrement | of 5.03. 89
blind priest, like the eldest son of fortune, H8 2.02. 20
that when the greatest stroke of fortune falls 2.02. 35
if that quarrel, fortune, do divorce | it from 2.03. 14
fie, fie, fie upon | this compell'd fortune! 2.03. 87
you have, by fortune and his highness' favors, 2.04.111
in spite of fortune | will bring me off again. 3.02.219
and valor's worth divide | in storms of fortune; TRO 1.03. 47
in self–same key | retires to chiding fortune. 1.03. 54
rate, | and do a deed that never fortune did, 2.02. 90
greatness, once fall'n out with fortune, | must 3.03. 75
not so with me, | fortune and i are friends. 3.03. 88
me, and the foolish fortune of this girl, and 5.03.102 P
till when, go seek thy fortune. 5.06. 19
'tis for the followers fortune widens them, COR 1.04. 44
now the fair goddess fortune | fall deep in love 1.05. 20
this man has marr'd his fortune. 3.01.253
which else would put you to your fortune and 3.02. 60
which out of daily fortune ever taints | the 4.07. 38
i purpose not to wait on fortune till | these 5.03.119
out of that i'll work | myself a former fortune. 5.03.202
will you be put in mind of his blind fortune, 5.06.117
with honor and with fortune is return'd, | from TIT 1.01. 67
whose wisdom hath her fortune conquered. 1.01.336
and had you not by wondrous fortune come, | this 2.03.112
and ours with thine, befall what fortune will. 5.03. 3
ay, mine own fortune in my misery. ROM 1.02. 58
hie to high fortune! honest nurse, farewell. 2.05. 78
thou /pouts /upon thy fortune and thy love. 3.03.144
o fortune, fortune, all men call thee fickle; 3.05. 60
o fortune, fortune, all men call thee fickle; 3.05. 60
be fickle, fortune: 3.05. 62
unhappy fortune! 5.02. 17
his large fortune, | upon his good and gracious TIM 1.01. 55
pleasant hill | feign'd fortune to be thron'd. 1.01. 64
whom fortune with her ivory hand wafts to her, 1.01. 70
this throne, this fortune, and this hill, 1.01. 73
when fortune in her shift and change of mood 1.01. 84
to build his fortune i will strain a little, 1.01.143
that state of fortune fall into my keeping, 1.01.150
it pleases time and fortune to lie heavy | upon 3.05. 10
you fools of fortune, trencher–friends, time's 3.06. 96
not | one friend to take his fortune by the arm, 4.02. 7
can bear great fortune | but by contempt of 4.03. 7
for every grize of fortune | is smooth'd by that 4.03. 16
but for thy sword and fortune, trod upon them — 4.03. 96
joy for his fortune; JC 3.02. 28 P
fortune is merry, | and in this mood will give 3.02.266
which, taken at the flood, leads on to fortune; 4.03.219
night | we shall try fortune in a second fight. 5.03.110
and fortune, on his damned /quarrel smiling, MAC 1.02. 14
disdaining fortune, with his brandish'd steel, 1.02. 17
our separated fortune | shall keep us both the 2.03.138
times past which held you | so under fortune, 3.01. 77
so weary with disasters, tugg'd with fortune, 3.01.111
that the malevolence of fortune nothing | takes 3.06. 28
let me find him, fortune! 5.07. 22
in the secret parts of fortune? HAM 2.02.235 P
out, out, thou strumpet fortune! 2.02.493
the slings and arrows of outrageous fortune, 3.01. 57
whether love lead fortune, or else fortune love. 3.02.203
whether love lead fortune, or else fortune love. 3.02.203
and hitherto doth love on fortune tend, | for 3.02.206
take thy fortune; 3.04. 32
what is mortal and unsure | to all that fortune, 4.04. 52
the queen carouses to thy fortune, hamlet. 5.02.289
for me, with sorrow i embrace my fortune. 5.02.388
that when we are sick in fortune — often the LR 1.02.119 P
briefness and fortune, work! 2.01. 18
a good man's fortune may grow out at heels. 2.02.157
fortune, good night! 2.02.173
fortune, that arrant whore, | ne'er turns the 2.04. 52
how malicious is my fortune, that i must repent 3.05. 9 P
the lowest and most dejected thing of fortune, 4.01. 3
i am even | the natural fool of fortune. 4.06.191
lest that th' infection of his fortune take 4.06.233
fortune /love you! 5.01. 46
your valiant strain, | and fortune led you well. 5.03. 41
/despite thy victor–sword and fire–new fortune, 5.03.133
what art thou | that hast this fortune on me? 5.03.166
if fortune brag of two she lov'd and hated, 5.03.281
what a /full fortune does the thick–lips owe OTH 1.01. 66
to as proud a fortune | as this that i have 1.02. 23
what cannot be preserv'd when fortune takes, 1.03.206
in the degree of this fortune as cassio does? 2.01.237 P
fool | plies desdemona to repair his fortune, 2.03.354
and let her down the wind | to prey at fortune. 3.03.263
would you would bear your fortune like a man! 4.01. 61
it is my wretched fortune. 4.02.128
he knows not yet of his honorable fortune. 4.02.235 P
old thing 'twas, but it express'd her fortune, 4.03. 29
thou speak'st of | i found by fortune, and did 5.02.226
good sir, give me good fortune. ANT 1.02. 14 P
good now, some excellent fortune! 1.02. 26 P
you have seen and prov'd a fairer former fortune 1.02. 33
prithee tell her but a worky–day fortune. 1.02. 54 P
am i not an inch of fortune better than she? 1.02. 58 P
you were but an inch of fortune better than i, 1.02. 59 P
alexas — come, his fortune, his fortune! 1.02. 63 P
alexas — come, his fortune, his fortune! 1.02. 63 P
isis, keep decorum, and fortune him accordingly! 1.02. 74 P
make thee a fortune from me. 2.05. 49
and what may follow, | to try a larger fortune. 2.06. 34
what counts harsh fortune casts upon my face, 2.06. 54
pompey doth this day laugh away his fortune. 2.06.105 P
pleas'd fortune does of marcus crassus' death 3.01. 2
good fortune, worthy soldier, and farewell. 3.02. 22
our fortune lies | upon this jump. 3.08. 5
our fortune on the sea is out of breath, | and 3.10. 24
fortune knows | we scorn her most when most she 3.11. 73
fortune pursue thee! 3.12. 25
wisdom and fortune combating together, | if that 3.13. 79
he thinks, being twenty times of better fortune, 4.02. 3
if fortune be not ours to–day, it is | because 4.04. 4
fortune and antony part here, even here | do we 4.12. 19
that the false huswife fortune break her wheel, 4.15. 44
not being fortune, he's but fortune's knave, | a 5.02. 3
who was once at point | (o giglet fortune!) CYM 3.01. 31
man, a thing | the most disdain'd of fortune. 3.04. 20
you could wear a mind | dark as your fortune is, 3.04.144
hast stuck to the bare fortune of that beggar 3.05.118 P
fortune put them into my hand! 4.01. 23 P
fortune brings in some boats that are not 4.03. 46
our pleasure his full fortune doth confine, 5.04.110
till fortune, tir'd with doing bad, | threw him PER 2.ch. 37
thanks, fortune, yet, that, after all /thy 2.01.121
'tis more by fortune, lady, than my merit. 2.03. 12
all fortune to the good simonides! 2.05. 24
but fortune, mov'd, | varies again; 3.ch. 46
a good constraint of fortune it belches upon us. 3.02. 55
your shakes of fortune, though they haunt you 3.03. 6
his courses to be ordered | by lady fortune, 4.04. 48
though most ungentle fortune | have plac'd me in 4.06. 96
though wayward fortune did malign my state, | my 5.01. 89
although assail'd with fortune fierce and keen, 5.03. 88
fortune at you | dimpled her cheek with smiles. TNK 1.01. 65
and't might be, | to dure ill–dealing fortune. 1.03. 5
and in their songs curse ever–blinded fortune 2.02. 38
from all that fortune can inflict upon us, | i 2.02. 57
false–self and thy friend had but this fortune 2.02.207
for all the fortune of my life hereafter, | yon 2.02.235
arcite shall have a fortune, | if he dare make 2.02.250
tell me, o lady fortune | (next after emily my 3.01. 15
so little dream'st upon my fortune that | thou 3.01. 24
i can tell your fortune. 3.05. 78
so, love and fortune for me! 3.06. 16
shall threaten me | i fear less than my fortune. 3.06.125
o'er us the victors have | fortune, whose title 5.04. 17
and with our patience anger tott'ring fortune, 5.04. 20
never fortune | did play a subtler game. 5.04.112
i fear'd thy fortune, and my joints did tremble. VEN 642
reck'ning his fortune at such high proud rate LUC 19
"then love and fortune be my gods, my guide! 351
to hold their cursed–blessed fortune long. 866
loss, | o frowning fortune, cursed, fickle dame! PP 17.10
whilst as fickle fortune smil'd, | thou and i 20.27
but if fortune once do frown, | then farewell 20.45
nor can i fortune to brief minutes tell, SON 14. 5
whilst i, whom fortune of such triumph bars, 25. 3
when in disgrace with fortune and men's eyes, 29. 1
and shalt by fortune once more re–survey | these 32. 3
join with the spite of fortune, make me bow, 90. 3
o, for my sake do you /with fortune chide, | the 111. 1

FORTUNED 1 FR 0.0001 REL FR 1 V 0 P
that you will wonder what hath fortuned. TGV 5.04.169

FORTUNE'S 45 FR 0.0050 REL FR 34 V 11 P
now thou goest from fortune's office to nature's AYL 1.02. 40 P
peradventure this is not fortune's work neither, 1.02. 51 P
now, sir, muddied in fortune's mood, and smell AWW 5.02. 4 P
fortune's displeasure is but sluttish if it 5.02. 6 P
henceforth eat no fish of fortune's butt'ring. 5.02. 8 P
a paper from fortune's close–stool to give to a 5.02. 17 P
here is a purr of fortune's, sir, or of 5.02. 19 P
sir, or of fortune's cat — but not a musk–cat 5.02. 19 P
and not worthy to touch fortune's fingers. TN 2.05.157 P
thou fortune's champion that dost never fight JN 3.01.118
some unborn sorrow, ripe in fortune's womb, | is R2 2.02. 10
that they are not the first of fortune's slaves, 5.05. 24
who is sweet fortune's minion and her pride, 1H4 1.01. 83
be what thou wilt, i am fortune's steward — get 2H4 5.03.130 P
and giddy fortune's furious fickle wheel, | that H5 3.06. 27
to weep | or to exclaim on fortune's fickleness. 1H6 5.03.134
be slack | to play my part in fortune's pageant. 2H6 1.02. 67
yield not thy neck | to fortune's yoke, but let 3H6 3.03. 17
though fortune's malice overthrow my state, | my 4.03. 46
that i may conquer fortune's spite | by living 4.06. 19
by spying and avoiding fortune's malice, | for 4.06. 28

of which metal is not found | in fortune's love; TRO 1.03. 23
how some men creep in skittish fortune's hall, 3.03.134
still sweet love is food for fortune's tooth. 4.05.293
fortune's blows, | when most strook home, being COR 4.01. 7
safe out of fortune's shot, and sits aloft, TIT 2.01. 2
o, i am fortune's fool! ROM 3.01.136
a whining mammet, in her fortune's tender, | to 3.05.184
shall demonstrate these quick blows of fortune's TIM 1.01. 91
whom fortune's tender arm | with favor never 4.03.250
being nature's livery, or fortune's star, | his HAM 1.04. 32
on fortune's /cap we are not the very button. 2.02.229 P
'gainst fortune's state would treason have 2.02.511
a man that fortune's buffets and rewards | hast 3.02. 67
that they are not a pipe for fortune's finger 3.02. 70
lord, who hath receiv'd you | at fortune's alms. LR 1.01.278
a most poor man, made tame to fortune's blows, 4.06.221
could else out-frown false fortune's frown. 5.03. 6
up in some other course, | to fortune's alms. OTH 3.04.122
not being fortune, he's but fortune's knave, | a ANT 5.02. 3
pray you tell him | i am his fortune's vassal, 5.02. 29
and turn the giddy round of fortune's wheel; LUC 952
so i, made lame by fortune's dearest spite, SON 37. 3
at first the very worst of fortune's might; 90.12
it might for fortune's bastard be unfather'd, 124. 2

/FORTUNES 2 FR 0.0002 REL FR 1 V 1 P
your good will to have mine own good /fortunes. AWW 2.04. 16 P
year to year — the /battles, sieges, /fortunes, OTH 1.03.130

FORTUNES 123 FR 0.0139 REL FR 105 V 18 P
but omit, my fortunes | will ever after droop. TMP 1.02.183
knit a knot in his fortunes with the finger of WIV 3.02. 75 P
and hear at large discoursed all our fortunes; ERR 5.01.396
of me my daughter, and with her my fortunes. ADO 2.01.303 P
to my fortunes and me. LLL 2.01.224
my fortunes every way as fairly rank'd | (if not MND 1.01.101
thou know'st that all my fortunes are at sea, MV 1.01.177
in the same abundance as your good fortunes are; 1.02. 4 P
i do in birth deserve her, and in fortunes, | in 2.07. 32
this, | and instantly unlock my fortunes here. 2.09. 52
testament, with that i will go buy my fortunes. AYL 1.01. 74 P
my pride fell with my fortunes, | i'll ask him 1.02.252
at seventeen years many their fortunes seek, 2.03. 73
my fortunes were more able to relieve her; 2.04. 77
as yet to question you about your fortunes. 2.07.172
hand, | and let me all your fortunes understand. 2.07.200
to seek their fortunes farther than at home, SHR 1.02. 51
and think it not the worst of all your fortunes 4.02.105
love make your fortunes twenty times above | her AWW 2.03. 82
do thine own fortunes that obedient right 2.03.160
if her fortunes ever stood | necessitied to help 5.03. 84
as thy lord, | to call his fortunes thine. TN 1.04. 40
above my fortunes, yet my state is well: 1.05.278
"above my fortunes, yet my state is well: 1.05.290
"cousin toby, my fortunes, having cast me on 2.05. 69 P
at your heels than fortunes before you. 2.05.137 P
why then build me thy fortunes upon the basis of 3.02. 33 P
and suits well for a servant with my fortunes. 3.04. 6
fear not, cesario, take thy fortunes up, | be 5.01.148
i'll put | my fortunes to your service, which WT 1.02.440
unclasp'd my practice, quit his fortunes here 3.02.167
i think you know my fortunes | do all lie there. 4.04.590
have sold their fortunes at their native homes, JN 2.01. 69
backs, | to make a hazard of new fortunes here. 2.01. 71
their fortunes both are weigh'd. R2 3.04. 84
to bear our fortunes in our own strong arms, 1H4 1.03.298
the very utmost bound | of all our fortunes. 4.01. 52
to dignify the times, | since caesar's fortunes. 2H4 1.01. 23
he is retir'd, to ripe his growing fortunes, 4.01. 13
we ready are to try our fortunes | to the last 4.02. 43
his fortunes i will weep, and 'twixt each groan 2H6 3.01.221
should see the bottom | of all our fortunes; 5.02. 79
and where this breach now in our fortunes made 5.02. 82
wash'd his father's fortunes forth of france, 3H6 2.02.157
yet thus far we are one in fortunes: H8 2.01.121
once perceive | the least rub in your fortunes, 2.01.129
alas, poor wenches, where are now your fortunes? 3.01.148
have follow'd both my fortunes faithfully, | of 4.02.141
possess'd conveniences | to doubtful fortunes, TRO 3.03. 8
that he would pawn his fortunes | to hopeless COR 3.01. 15
my fortunes and my friends at stake requir'd | i 3.02. 63
and that to prove more fortunes | th' art tir'd, 4.05. 93
and to my fortunes and the people's favor TIT 1.01. 54
whose fortunes rome's best citizens applaud! 1.01.164
fair lords, your fortunes are alike in all, 1.01.174
and all my fortunes at thy foot i'll lay, | and ROM 2.02.147
long may he live in fortunes! shall we in? TIM 1.01.282
more welcome are ye to my fortunes | than my 1.02. 19
are ye to my fortunes | than my fortunes to me. 1.02. 20
like brothers commanding one another's fortunes! 1.02.105 P
honor, and fortunes, keep with you, lord timon! 1.02.229
men and men's fortunes could i frankly use | as 2.02.179
shall perceive how you | mistake my fortunes; 2.02.184
that timon's fortunes 'mong his friends can sink 2.02.231
so his familiars to his buried fortunes | slink 4.02. 10
as 'twere a knell unto our master's fortunes, 4.02. 26
thy great fortunes | are made thy chief 4.02. 43
is divident, touch them with several fortunes, 4.03. 5
but in thy fortunes am unlearn'd and strange. 4.03. 57
offering the fortunes of his former days, | the 5.01.124
the fortunes and affairs of noble brutus JC 3.01.135
even our loves should with our fortunes change: HAM 3.02.201
if the rest of my fortunes turn turk with me — 3.02.276 P
a little, | lest you may mar your fortunes. LR 1.01. 95
keeps our fortunes from us till our oldness 1.02. 48 P
must make content with his fortunes fit, 3.02. 76
if thou wilt weep my fortunes, take my eyes. 4.06.176
was first fram'd flesh | to raise my fortunes. 4.06.228
thou dost make thy way | to noble fortunes. 5.03. 30
and fortunes | in an extravagant and wheeling OTH 1.01.135
the gloss of your new fortunes with this more 1.03.227 P
my downright violence and storm of fortunes 1.03.249
parts | did i my soul and fortunes consecrate. 1.03.254
and, my fortunes against any lay worth naming, 2.03.323 P
i am desperate of my fortunes if they check me 2.03.331 P
hath founded his good fortunes on your love, 3.04. 94
and seize upon the fortunes of the moor, | for 5.02.366
we'll know all our fortunes. ANT 1.02. 44 P
mine, and most of our fortunes to-night, shall 1.02. 45 P
your fortunes are alike. 1.02. 55
say to me, whose fortunes shall rise higher, 2.03. 16
i will give thee, | and make thy fortunes proud; 2.05. 69
i have ever held my cap off to thy fortunes. 2.07. 57
i'll never follow thy pall'd fortunes more. 2.07. 82
as i pleas'd, | making and marring fortunes. 3.11. 65
lord of his fortunes he salutes thee, and 3.12. 11
women are not | in their best fortunes strong, 3.12. 30
judgments are | a parcel of their fortunes, and 3.13. 32
that of his fortunes you should make a staff 3.13. 68
o, my fortunes have | corrupted honest men! 4.05. 16
his fretted fortunes give him hope and fear | of 4.12. 8
and her fortunes mingled | with thine entirely. 4.14. 24
thy death and fortunes bid thy followers fly. 4.14.111
in feeding them with those my former fortunes 4.15. 53
for | his fortunes all lie speechless, and his CYM 1.05. 52
to her is now as low as were | thy fortunes. 3.02. 11
not beneath him in fortunes, beyond him in the 4.01. 11 P
inform us of thy fortunes, for it seems | they 4.02.361
to have bereft a prince of all his fortunes; PER 2.01. 9
were my fortunes equal to my desires, i could 2.01.111 P
and if that ever my low fortunes better, | i'll 2.01.142
he hopes by you his fortunes yet may flourish. 2.02. 47
you have fortunes coming upon you. 4.02.116 P
child, and stood between | her and her fortunes. 4.03. 32
my fortunes — parentage — good parentage — 5.01. 97
riding, her fortunes brought the maid aboard us, 5.03. 11
i have heard the fortunes | of your dead lords, TNK 1.01. 56
for whose fortunes | i will now in and kneel, 1.03. 93
that our fortunes | were twin'd together. 2.02. 63
shape shall make me, | or end my fortunes. 2.03. 22
king of pigmies, | for he tells fortunes rarely. 3.04. 16
and that which we profanely term our fortunes STM III 2
cancell'd my fortunes, and enchained me | to LUC 934

FORTUNE-TELL 1 FR 0.0001 REL FR 0 V 1 P
i'll conjure you, i'll fortune-tell you! WIV 4.02.186 P

FORTUNE-TELLER 1 FR 0.0001 REL FR 1 V 0 P
a threadbare juggler and a fortune-teller, | a ERR 5.01.240

FORTUNE-TELLING 1 FR 0.0001 REL FR 0 V 1 P
to pass under the profession of fortune-telling. WIV 4.02.176 P

FORTY 31 FR 0.0035 REL FR 20 V 11 P
i had rather than forty shillings i had my book WIV 1.01.198 P
that stabb'd pots, and i think forty more — all MM 4.03. 18 P
a ring he hath of mine worth forty ducats, | and ERR 4.03. 83
choose, | for forty ducats is too much to lose. 4.03. 96
girdle round about the earth | in forty minutes. MND 2.01.176
and the humor of forty fancies prick'd in't for SHR 3.02. 69 P
i had rather than forty shillings i had such a TN 2.03. 20 P
i had rather than forty pound i were at home. 5.01.177 P
of april, forty thousand fadom above water, and WT 4.04.277 P
the language i have learnt these forty years, R2 1.03.159
seal-ring of my grandfather's worth forty mark. 1H4 3.03. 82 P
three or four bonds of forty pound a-piece, and 3.03.102 P
forty let it be! 4.01.130
you shall have forty, sir. 2H4 3.02.232 P
moy shall not serve, i will have forty moys, H5 4.04. 13
i myself fight not once in forty year. 1H6 1.03. 91
forty pence, no. H8 2.03. 89
within these forty hours surrey durst better 3.02.253
see from far some forty truncheoners draw to her 5.03. 51 P
on fair ground | i could beat forty of them. COR 3.01.242
rome, i have been thy soldier forty years, | and TIT 1.01.193
death | thou shalt continue two and forty hours, ROM 4.01.105
hold, there is forty ducats; 5.01. 59
my father liv'd, give twenty, forty, fifty, a HAM 2.02.365 P
forty thousand brothers | could not with all 5.01.269
and mine, a hundred forty. OTH 1.03. 4
o, that the slave had forty thousand lives! 3.03.442
hop forty paces through the public street; ANT 2.02.229
forty days longer we do respite you; PER 1.01.116
but forty thousand fold we had rather have 'em TNK 1.04. 36
when forty winters shall besiege thy brow, | and SON 2. 1

FORTY-EIGHT 1 FR 0.0001 REL FR 0 V 1 P
i have years on my back forty-eight. LR 1.04. 39 P

/FORWARD 1 FR 0.0001 REL FR 1 V 0 P
/and /that /his /forward /spirit | /would /lift 2H4 1.01.173

FORWARD 78 FR 0.0088 REL FR 60 V 18 P
his forward voice now is to speak well of his TMP 2.02. 90 P
now forward with your tale. 3.02. 83 P
as the most forward bud | is eate, by the canker TGV 1.01. 45
well — you'll still be too forward. 2.01. 11 P
but let our plot go forward. WIV 4.04. 12
you | look forward on the journey you shall go. MM 4.03. 58
nay, forward, old man, do not break off so, ERR 1.01. 96
a very forward march-chick! ADO 1.03. 56 P
answer for that, and now forward with thy tale. 3.03.102 P
and now forward, for we have put thee in LLL 5.02.619 P
but i will forward with my device. 5.02.662 P
it goes not forward, doth it? MND 4.02. 6 P
if our sport had gone forward, we had all been 4.02. 17 P
first, forward to the temple; MV 2.01. 44
duke that the wrastling might not go forward. AYL 1.02.182 P
man's good wit seconded with the forward child, 3.03. 13 P
go forward, this contents; SHR 1.01.163
am bold to show myself a forward guest | within 2.01. 51
you are marvellous forward. 2.01. 73
fiddler, forbear, you grow too forward, sir. 3.01. 1
how fiery and forward our pedant is! 3.01. 48
gentlemen, forward to the bridal dinner. 3.02.219
they shall go forward, kate, at thy command. 3.02.222
forward, i pray, since we have come so far, 4.05. 12
well, forward, forward! 4.05. 24
well, forward, forward! 4.05. 24
whoever charges on his forward breast, | i am AWW 3.02.113
let's take the instant by the forward top; 5.03. 39
she's as forward of her breeding as | she is i' WT 4.04.580
that hath been forward first | to speak unto JN 2.01.482
or rather then set forward, for 'twill be | two 4.03. 19
and dares him to set forward to the fight. R2 1.03.109
sound, trumpets, and set forward, combatants. 1.03.117
how fondly dost thou spur a forward horse! 4.01. 72
when a jest is so forward, and afoot too! 1H4 2.02. 47 P
are they not some of them set forward already? 2.03. 28 P
i will set forward to-night. 2.03. 35 P
on wednesday next, harry, you shall set forward, 3.02.173
what need i be so forward with him that calls 5.01.128 P
and bending forward strook his armed heels 2H4 1.01. 44
grace of york, in god's name then set forward. 4.01.225
go forward, and be chok'd with thy ambition! 1H6 2.04.112
makes them thus forward in his banishment. 2H6 3.02.253
and inclin'd to blood, | if you go forward; 4.02.127
come, march forward. 4.02.190 P
and long live thou, and these thy forward sons! 3H6 1.01.203
you promis'd knighthood to our forward son, 2.02. 58
forward, away! 2.05.139
if that go forward, henry's hope is done. 3.03. 58
we'll forward towards warwick and his mates; 4.07. 82
nor forward of revenge, though they much err'd. 4.08. 46
i came into the world with my legs forward. 5.06. 71
short summers lightly have a forward spring. R3 3.01. 94
boy, | bold, quick, ingenious, forward, capable: 3.01.155
and hopes to find you forward | upon his party 3.02. 46
makes me most forward in this princely presence 3.04. 64
but on thy side i may not be too forward, | lest 5.03. 94
let him on. | go forward. H8 1.02.177
of my alleged reasons, drives this forward. 2.04.226
let his grace go forward, | and dare us with his 3.02.281
they are ever forward | in celebration of this 4.01. 9
arrested him at york, and brought him forward, 4.02. 13
but when goes this forward? COR 4.05.213 P
that have been thus forward in my right, | i TIT 1.01. 56
can i go forward when my heart is here? ROM 2.01. 1
forward, not permanent, sweet, not lasting, HAM 1.03. 8
nor do we find him forward to be sounded, | but 3.01. 7
no, but he fled forward still, toward your face. CYM 1.02. 15 P
that it would be thus | hath made us forward. 3.05. 29
set we forward. 5.05.479
forward to th' temple! TNK 1.01.130
set you forward, | for i will see you gone. 1.01.217
pray, forward. 2.02.122
will ye go forward, cousin? 2.02.126
and i go forward. 3.05. 16
well, sir, go forward, we will edify. 3.05. 98
deep woes roll forward like a gentle flood, LUC 1118
the forward violet thus did i chide: SON 99. 1

FORWARDING 1 FR 0.0001 REL FR 1 V 0 P
did decree | in forwarding this dear expedience. 1H4 1.01. 33

FORWARDNESS 5 FR 0.0005 REL FR 4 V 1 P
be entreated, his own peril on his forwardness. AYL 1.02.150 P
gloucester, why doubt'st thou of my forwardness?
1H6 1.01.100
stanley, i will requite thy forwardness. 3H6 4.05. 23
this cheers my heart, to see your forwardness. 5.04. 65
this forwardness | makes our hopes fair. CYM 4.02.342

FORWARDS 1 FR 0.0001 REL FR 1 V 0 P
in sequent toil all forwards do contend. SON 60. 4

FOSTER 2 FR 0.0002 REL FR 2 V 0 P
some say that ravens foster forlorn children TIT 2.03.153
the fates, | to foster it, not ever to preserve. PER 4.03. 15

FOSTER'D 2 FR 0.0002 REL FR 2 V 0 P
if i be not by her fair influence | foster'd, TGV 3.01.184
one bred of alms and foster'd with cold dishes, CYM 2.03.114

FOSTERED 2 FR 0.0002 REL FR 2 V 0 P
war, | that, like a lion fostered up at hand, JN 5.02. 75
with that dear blood which it hath fostered; R2 1.03.126

FOSTER-NURSE 2 FR 0.0002 REL FR 2 V 0 P
which i did store to be my foster-nurse | when AYL 2.03. 40
our foster-nurse of nature is repose, | the LR 4.04. 12

FOSTERS 1 FR 0.0001 REL FR 1 V 0 P
even as my life my blood that fosters it. PER 2.05. 89

FOST'RING 1 FR 0.0001 REL FR 0 V 1 P
earth's god, and body's fost'ring patron" — LLL 1.01.221 P

FOUGH *(also foh)*

/FOUGH 1 FR 0.0001 REL FR 1 V 0 P
as i? /fough, fie upon thee! OTH 5.01.123

/FOUGHT 1 FR 0.0001 REL FR 1 V 0 P
/or /ill, /as /this /day's /battle's /fought. LR 4.07. 96

FOUGHT 69 FR 0.0078 REL FR 56 V 13 P
he hath fought with a warrener. WIV 1.04. 27 P
is a fray to be fought between sir hugh the 2.01.200 P
had we fought, i doubt we should have been too ADO 5.01.118 P
had four quarrels, and like to have fought one. AYL 5.04. 47 P
have fought with equal fortune, and continue | a AWW 1.02. 2
'twixt joy and sorrow was fought in paulina! WT 5.02. 73 P
heart, | and fought the holy wars in palestine, JN 2.01. 4
what a noble combat hast /thou fought | between 5.02. 43
many a time hath banish'd norfolk fought | for R2 4.01. 92
under whose colors he had fought so long. 4.01.100
how thirty at least he fought with, what wards, 1H4 1.02.189 P
what, fought you with them all? 2.04.184 P
all, but if i fought not with fifty of them, i 2.04.186 P
sirs, by'r lady, you fought fair, so did you, 2.04.298 P
o douglas, hadst thou fought at holmedon thus, 5.03. 14
both at an instant and fought a long hour by 5.04.148 P
so fought, so followed, and so fairly won, 2H4 1.01. 21
so fought the noble douglas" — | stopping my 1.01. 77
god, and not we, hath safely fought to-day. 4.02.121
have in these parts from morn till even fought, H5 3.01. 20
and if he be not fought withal, my lord, | let 3.05. 2
that fought with us upon saint crispin's day. 4.03. 67
fought on the day of crispin crispianus. 4.07. 91
fought a most prave pattle here in france. 4.07. 95 P
this acknowledgment, | that god fought for us. 4.08.120
the battles of the lord of hosts he fought; 1H6 1.01. 31
whilst a field should be dispatch'd and fought, 1.01. 72
and fought so long, till that his thighs with 2H6 3.01.362
now, by my sword, well hast thou fought to-day; 5.03. 15
after the bloody fray at wakefield fought, 3H6 2.01.107
battles join'd, and both sides fiercely fought; 2.01.121
when i have fought with pembroke and his fellows 4.03. 54
if by the way they be not fought withal. R3 4.05. 18
knew thy grandsire, | and once fought with him. TRO 4.05.197
o, well fought, my youngest brother! 5.06. 12
you have fought together? COR 1.01.232
well fought; 1.06. 1
we have at disadvantage fought, and did | retire 1.06. 49
by all the battles wherein we have fought, | by 1.06. 56
tullus, | alone i fought in your corioles walls, 1.08. 8
five times, martius, | i have fought with thee; 1.10. 8
titus lartius writes they fought together, but 2.01.127 P
for rome, he fought | beyond the mark of others. 2.02. 88
for your voices i have fought; 2.03.126
for they have fought for rome, and all in vain; TIT 3.01. 73
of me, | as true a dog as ever fought at head. 5.01.102
that true hand that fought rome's quarrel out, 5.03.102
when i have fought with the men, i will be civil ROM 1.01. 22 P
came more and more, and fought on part and part, 1.01.114

some twenty of them fought in this black strife, 3.01.178
here, | i dreamt my master and another fought, 5.03.138
who like a good and hardy soldier fought MAC 1.02. 4
in the unshrinking station where he fought, 5.09. 8
yet so far hath discretion fought with nature HAM 1.02. 5
partner in the cause 'gainst which he fought, ANT 2.02. 59
at pharsalia, | where caesar fought with pompey. 3.07. 32
are those that often have 'gainst pompey fought; 3.07. 37
o my brave emperor, this is fought indeed! 4.07. 4
and have fought | not as you serv'd the cause, 4.08. 5
he hath fought to-day | as if a god, in hate of 4.08. 24
but that my master rather play'd than fought CYM 1.01.162
for all was lost | but that the heavens fought; 5.03. 4
that the poor soldier that so richly fought, 5.05. 3
the forlorn soldier, that /so nobly fought, | he 5.05.405
when you caught hurt in parting two that fought; PER 4.01. 87
and now flurted | by peace, for whom he fought, TNK 1.02. 19
fought out together where death's self was 1.03. 40
in this place first you fought; 5.04. 99
from the strond of dardan, where they fought, LUC 1436
FOUGHT'ST 1 FR 0.0001 REL FR 1 V 0 P
did famine follow, whom thou fought'st against ANT 1.04. 59
/FOUL 4 FR 0.0004 REL FR 2 V 2 P
when blood is nipp'd and ways be /foul, | then LLL 5.02.916
/foul deeds will rise, | though all the earth HAM 1.02.256
/the /foul /fiend /bites /my /back. LR 3.06. 17 P
/the /foul /fiend /haunts /poor /tom /in /the 3.06. 29 P
FOUL 257 FR 0.0290 REL FR 210 V 47 P
what foul play had we, that we came from thence? TMP 1.02. 60
by foul play (as thou say'st) were we heav'd 1.02. 62
with colors fairer painted their foul ends. 1.02.143
hast thou forgot | the foul witch sycorax, who 1.02.258
it is foul weather in us all, good sir, | when 2.01.142
very foul. 2.01.143
looks like a foul bumbard that would shed his 2.02. 21 P
voice is to utter foul speeches and to detract. 2.02. 91 P
for which foul deed | the pow'rs, delaying (not 3.03. 72
i had forgot that foul conspiracy | of the beast 4.01.139
that the foul lake | o'erstunk their feet. 4.01.183
/shores | that now lie foul and muddy. 5.01. 82
the next ensuing hour some foul mischance TGV 2.02. 11
'tis a foul thing when a cur cannot keep himself 4.04. 10 P
creep in here, and throw foul linen upon him, as WIV 3.03.131 P
ramm'd me in with foul shirts and smocks, socks, 3.05. 90 P
smocks, socks, foul stockings, greasy napkins, 3.05. 90 P
me in the name of foul clothes to datchet-lane. 3.05. 99 P
for a search, and away went i for foul clothes. 3.05.106 P
of a fowl — think on't, jove, a foul fault! 5.05. 11 P
and do him right that, answering one foul wrong, MM 2.02.103
wit in them, | but in the less foul profanation. 2.02.128
mercy | is nothing kin to foul redemption. 2.04.113
that appears not foul in the truth of my spirit. 3.01.206 P
to accuse this worthy man, but, in foul mouth, 5.01.307
that may with foul intrusion enter in, | and ERR 3.01.103
nature, drawing of an antic, | made a foul blot; ADO 3.01. 64
but fare thee well, most foul, most fair! 4.01.103
may season give | to her foul tainted flesh! 4.01.143
only foul words — and thereupon i will kiss 5.02. 50 P
foul words is but foul wind, and foul wind is 5.02. 52 P
foul words is but foul wind, and foul wind is 5.02. 52 P
but foul wind, and foul wind is but foul breath, 5.02. 52 P
wind, and foul wind is but foul breath, and foul 5.02. 53 P
is but foul breath, and foul breath is noisome; 5.02. 53 P
fair payment for foul words is more than due. LLL 4.01. 19
a giving hand, though foul, shall have fair 4.01. 23
come, you talk greasily, your lips grow foul. 4.01.137
a foul word. 4.03. 3 P
her amber hairs for foul hath amber coted. 4.03. 85
"fair" in "all hail" is foul, as i conceive. 5.02.340
time, | play'd foul play with our oaths. 5.02.756
contriv'd | to bait me with this foul derision? MND 3.02.197
cleanse the foul body of th' infected world, AYL 2.07. 60
most mischievous foul sin, in chiding sin: 2.07. 64
away honesty upon a foul slut were to put good 3.03. 36 P
not a slut, though i thank the gods i am foul. 3.03. 39 P
foul is most foul, being foul to be a scoffer. 3.05. 62
foul is most foul, being foul to be a scoffer. 3.05. 62
foul is most foul, being foul to be a scoffer. 3.05. 62
a poor house, as your pearl in your foul oyster. 5.04. 61 P
sure together, | as the winter to foul weather. 5.04.136
death, how foul and loathsome is thine image! SHR in.1. 35
balm his foul head in warm distilled waters, in.1. 48
should be infused with so foul a spirit! in.2. 16
be she as foul as was florentius' love, | as old 1.02. 69
jades, on all mad masters, and all foul ways! 4.01. 2 P
inprimis, we came down a foul hill, my master 4.01. 67 P
will, | what is she but a foul contending rebel, 5.02.159
our modesty and make foul the clearness of our AWW 1.03. 6 P
cannot recover your niece, i am a foul way out. TN 2.03.185 P
hang him, foul collier! 3.04.117 P
so bloody, must | lead on to some foul issue. WT 2.03.153
mischief and break a foul gap into the matter, 4.04.197 P
patch'd with foul moles and eye-offending marks, JN 3.01. 47
o foul revolt of french inconstancy! 3.01.322
too fairly, hubert, for so foul effect. 4.01. 38
the foul corruption of a sweet child's death. 4.02. 81
it is apparent foul play and 'tis shame | that 4.02. 93
so foul a sky clears not without a storm, | pour 4.02.108
and foul imaginary eyes of blood | presented 4.02.265
ah, foul shrewd news! 5.05. 14
with a foul traitor's name stuff i thy throat, R2 1.01. 44
how god and good men hate so foul a liar. 1.01.114
that he is a traitor, foul and dangerous, | to 1.03. 39
tears drawn from her eyes by your foul wrongs; 3.01. 15
king | shall falter under foul rebellion's arms. 3.02. 26
we'll make foul weather with despised tears; 3.03.161
learn him forbearance from so foul a wrong. 4.01.120
is a foul traitor to proud herford's king, | and 4.01.135
and future ages groan for this foul act. 4.01.138
ere foul sin gathering head | shall break into 5.01. 58
treason, foul treason! 5.02. 72
i know she is come to pray for your foul sin. 5.03. 82
by breaking through the foul and ugly mists | of 1H4 1.02.202
will she hold out water in foul way? 2.01. 84 P
home without boots, and in foul weather too! 3.01. 67
hand, | as ever off'red foul play in a state. 3.02.169
for nothing can seem foul to those that win. 5.01. 8
shall we fall foul for toys? 2H4 2.04.169
the body of our kingdom | how foul it is, what 3.01. 39
"the time will come, that foul sin, gathering 3.01. 76
sir, for they have marvail's foul linen. 5.01. 35 P
if you grow foul with me, pistol, i will scour H5 2.01. 56 P
a! that's a foul fault. 3.02.136 P
the blind and blood soldier with foul hand 3.03. 34
so, and ride not warily, fall into foul bogs. 3.07. 57 P
camp to camp, through the foul womb of night, 4.pr. 4
who like a foul and ugly witch doth limp | so 4.pr. 21
the /gimmal'd bit | lies foul with chaw'd-grass, 4.02. 50
foul fiend of france, and hag of all despite, 1H6 3.02. 52
and take foul scorn to fawn on him by sending. 4.04. 35
to ashes, | thou foul accursed minister of hell! 5.04. 93
and call these foul offenders to their answers, 2H6 2.01.199
or foul felonious thief that fleec'd poor 3.01.129
virtue is chok'd with foul ambition, | and 3.01.143
foul subornation is predominant, | and equity 3.01.145
tongue | (the agent of thy foul inconstancy) 3.02.115
all the foul terrors in dark-seated hell — 3.02.328
breathe foul contagious darkness in the air. 4.01. 7
breast from harboring foul deceitful thoughts. 4.07.103
hence, heap of wrath, foul indigested lump, | as 5.01.157
foul stigmatic, that's more than thou canst tell 5.01.215
and spread they shall be, to thy foul disgrace, 3H6 1.01.253
and after many scorns, many foul taunts, | they 2.01. 64
nor dam, | but like a foul misshapen stigmatic, 2.02.136
unless thou rescue him from foul despair? 3.03.215
by fair or foul means we must enter in, | for 4.07. 14
to plague thee for thy foul misleading me. 5.01. 97
blame, | if this foul deed were by to equal it. 5.05. 55
foul devil, for god's sake hence, and trouble us R3 1.02. 50
blush, blush, thou lump of foul deformity; 1.02. 57
in thy foul throat thou li'st! 1.02. 93
foul wrinkled witch, what mak'st thou in my 1.03.163
foul shame upon you, you have all mov'd mine. 1.03.248
a legion of foul fiends | environ'd me, and 1.04. 58
before i'll see the crown so foul misplac'd. 3.02. 44
blood, | that foul defacer of god's handiwork, 4.04. 51
bottled spider, that foul bunch-back'd toad! 4.04. 81
'tis full of thy foul wrongs. 4.04.375
by underhand corrupted foul injustice, | if that 5.01. 6
this foul swine | is now even in the centry of 5.02. 10
a base foul stone, made precious by the foil 5.03.250
his noble jury and foul cause can witness. H8 3.02.269
but, thus much, they are foul ones. 3.02.300
let us, like merchants, first show foul wares, TRO 1.03.358
moor, | if foul desire had not conducted you? TIT 2.03. 79
and then they call'd me foul adulteress, 2.03.109
no, no, they would not do so foul a deed; 3.01.118
o, why should nature build so foul a den, 4.01. 59
accurs'd the offspring of so foul a fiend! 4.02. 79
rome will despise her for this foul escape. 4.02.113
ingrateful rome requites with foul contempt, 5.01. 12
revenge, which makes the foul offender quake. 5.02. 40
face | for testimony of her foul proceedings. 5.03. 8
and bakes the /elf-locks in foul sluttish hairs, ROM 1.04. 90
hands, and they unwash'd too, 'tis a foul thing. 1.05. 4 P
to whose foul mouth no healthsome air breathes 4.03. 34
seek, and know how this foul murder comes. 5.03.198
how fairly this lord strives to appear foul! TIM 3.03. 31 P
us, | his days are foul and his drink dangerous. 3.05. 73
much of this will make | black white, foul fair, 4.03. 29
that this foul deed shall smell above the earth JC 3.01.274
fair is foul, and foul is fair, | hover through MAC 1.01. 11
fair is foul, and foul is fair, | hover through 1.01. 11
so foul and fair a day i have not seen. 1.03. 38
though all things foul would wear the brows of 4.03. 23
foul whisp'rings are abroad. 5.01. 71
all is not well, | i doubt some foul play. HAM 1.02.255
till the foul crimes done in my days of nature 1.05. 12
revenge his foul and most unnatural murther. 1.05. 25
murther most foul, as in the best it is, | but 1.05. 27
but this most foul, strange, and unnatural. 1.05. 28
appeareth nothing to me but a foul and pestilent 2.02.302 P
and my imaginations are as foul | as vulcan's 3.02. 83
"forgive me my foul murther"? 3.03. 52
fit, | but, like the owner of a foul disease, 4.01. 21
the foul practice | hath turn'd itself on me. 5.02.317
and /the fee bestow | upon the foul disease. LR 1.01.164
who's there, besides foul weather? 3.01. 1
'tis foul. 3.02. 24
away, the foul fiend follows me! 3.04. 46 P
whom the foul fiend hath led through fire and 3.04. 52 P
tom some charity, whom the foul fiend vexes. 3.04. 61 P
take heed o' th' foul fiend. 3.04. 80 P
from lenders' books, and defy the foul fiend. 3.04. 98 P
this is the foul /fiend flibbertigibbet; 3.04.115 P
fury of his heart, when the foul fiend rages, 3.04.131 P
pray, innocent, and beware the foul fiend. 3.06. 8 P
do me no foul play, friends. 3.07. 31
bless thee, good man's son, from the foul fiend! 4.01. 58 P
o thou foul thief, where hast thou stow'd my OTH 1.02. 62
thou hast practic'd on her with foul charms, 1.02. 73
who e'er he be that in this foul proceeding 1.03. 65
if you do find me foul in her report, | the 1.03.117
were parted | with foul and violent tempest. 2.01. 34
hast thou for her that's foul and foolish? 2.01.140 P
there's none so foul and foolish thereunto, 2.01.141
but does foul pranks which fair and wise ones do 2.01.142
to the history of lust and foul thoughts. 2.01.258 P
give me to know | how this foul rout began; 2.03.210
as where's that palace whereinto foul things 3.03.137
rank, | foul disproportions, thoughts unnatural. 3.03.233
o, 'tis foul in her. 4.01.201 P
the purest of their wives | is foul as slander. 4.02. 19
or keep it as a cestern for foul toads | to knot 4.02. 61
for my lord | from any other foul unlawful touch 4.02. 84
o, my good lord, yonder's foul murthers done! 5.02.106
o, she was foul! 5.02.200
sorrow to behold a foul knave uncuckolded; ANT 1.02. 73 P
break to powder, | and finish all foul thoughts. 4.09. 18
this foul egyptian hath betrayed me. 4.12. 10
spectacles so precious | 'twixt fair and foul? CYM 1.06. 38
more hateful than the foul expulsion is | of thy 2.01. 60
the foul opinion | you had of her pure honor 2.04. 58
so bad | as with foul incest to abuse your soul; PER 1.01.126
attribute cry out, | "she died by foul play." 4.03. 19
see how belief may suffer by foul show! 4.04. 23
on whom foul death hath made this slaughter. 4.04. 37
and pecks of crows in the foul fields of thebes. TNK 1.01. 42
or to go tiptoe | before the street be foul? 1.02. 58
you are now too foul; 3.03. 51
seeks all foul means | of boist'rous and rough 5.04. 71
wash your foul minds with tears, and those same STM II.C 108
"were i hard-favor'd, foul, or wrinkled old, VEN 133
gusts and foul flaws to herdmen and to herds. 456
foul words and frowns must not repel a lover; 573
beauty hath nought to do with such foul fiends. 638
foul cank'ring rust the hidden treasure frets, 767
by this black-fac'd night, desire's foul nurse, 773
like many clouds consulting for foul weather. 972
to wash the foul face of the sluttish ground, 983
'tis he, foul creature, that hath done thee 1005
the foul boar's conquest on her fair delight, 1030
"but this foul, grim, and urchin-snouted boar, 1105
and this ambitious foul infirmity, | in having LUC 150
honest fear, bewitch'd with lust's foul charm, 173
o foul dishonor to my household's grave! 198
o impious act, including all foul harms! 199
full of foul hope and full of fond mistrust; 284
that his foul thoughts might compass his fair 346
who like a foul usurper went about | from this 412
right, | nor aught obeys but his foul appetite. 546
yet, foul night-waking cat, he doth but dally, 554
and stoop to honor, not to foul desire. 574
with foul offenders thou perforce must bear, 612
when pattern'd by thy fault foul sin may say 629
devours his will, that liv'd by foul devouring. 700
says, her subjects with foul insurrection | have 722
"o night, thou furnace of foul reeking smoke! 799
troth, | thou foul abettor, thou notorious bawd! 886
me good | is to let forth my foul defiled blood. 1029
my live's foul deed, my life's fair end shall 1208
by foul enforcement might be done to me, | from 1623
may my pure mind with the foul act dispense, 1704
for his foul act by whom thy fair wife bleeds? 1824
and so to publish tarquin's foul offense; 1852
harbinger, | foul precurrer of the fiend, PHT 6
distill'd from limbecks foul as hell within, SON 119. 2
fairing the foul with art's false borrow'd face, 127. 6
and all they foul that thy complexion lack. 132.14
is not, | to put fair truth upon so foul a face? 137.12
devil, | wooing his purity with her foul pride. 144. 8
eyes well seeing thy foul faults should find. 148.14
eye, | to swear against the truth so foul a lie! 152.14
and knew the patterns of his foul beguiling, LC 170
and bastards of his foul adulterate heart. 175
FOULED 1 FR 0.0001 REL FR 1 V 0 P
no hat upon his head, his stockins fouled, HAM 2.01. 76
FOULER 10 FR 0.0011 REL FR 9 V 1 P
in't, | which seems a little fouler than it is, MM 2.04.146
the fouler fortune mine, and there an end. SHR 5.02. 98
and a fouler fact | did never traitor in the 2H6 1.03.173
fouler than heart can think thee, thou canst R3 1.02. 83
never hung poison on a fouler toad. 1.02.147
were, | and he that slew them fouler than he is. 4.04.121
rights by rights fouler, strengths by strengths COR 4.07. 55
that's fouler. OTH 4.01.203 P
labor when i wash my brain | and it grow fouler. ANT 2.07.100
thou their fair life, and they thy fouler grave; LUC 661
FOULEST 3 FR 0.0003 REL FR 3 V 0 P
/write her fair words still in foulest terms? 2H4 4.04.104
o, 'twas the foulest deed to slay that babe, R3 1.03.182
love that tells close offices | the foulest way, TNK 5.01.123
FOUL-FAC'D 1 FR 0.0001 REL FR 1 V 0 P
but if black scandal or foul-fac'd reproach R3 3.07.231
FOULLY 4 FR 0.0004 REL FR 4 V 0 P
dost thou desire her foully for those things MM 2.02.173
the life of helen, lady, | was foully snatch'd. AWW 5.03.154
mouth | live scandaliz'd and foully spoken of. 1H4 1.03.154
and i fear | thou play'dst most foully for't; MAC 3.01. 3
FOUL-MOUTH'D 3 FR 0.0003 REL FR 1 V 2 P
thou ever be a foul-mouth'd and calumnious knave AWW 1.03. 56 P
vilely of you, like a foul-mouth'd man as he is, 1H4 3.03.107 P
have never been foul-mouth'd against thy law, TNK 5.01. 98
FOUL-MOUTH'D'ST 1 FR 0.0001 REL FR 0 V 1 P
it is the foul-mouth'd'st rogue in england. 2H4 2.04. 72 P
FOULNESS 5 FR 0.0005 REL FR 3 V 2 P
lov'd her so, that, speaking of her foulness, ADO 4.01.153
well, prais'd be the gods for thy foulness! AYL 3.03. 40 P
he's fall'n in love with your foulness, and 3.05. 66 P
th' contrary | the foulness is the punishment. H8 3.02.183
it is no vicious blot, murther, or foulness, LR 1.01.227
FOUL-SPOKEN 1 FR 0.0001 REL FR 1 V 0 P
foul-spoken coward, that thund'rest with thy TIT 2.01. 58
FOUL'ST 2 FR 0.0002 REL FR 2 V 0 P
and let the foul'st contempt | shut door upon me H8 2.04. 42
the foul'st best fits | my latter part of life. ANT 4.06. 37
/FOUND 3 FR 0.0003 REL FR 3 V 0 P
/in /twelve, | /found /truth /in /all /but /one; R2 4.01.171
off, | and say you /found them in mine honesty. TIM 2.02.135
/motley /here, | /the /other /found /out /there. LR 1.04.147
FOUND 237 FR 0.0268 REL FR 189 V 48 P
found a wife | where he himself was lost; TMP 5.01.210
that we have safely found | our king and company 5.01.221
and bestow your luggage where you found it. 5.01.299
till i have found each letter in the letter, TGV 1.02.116
this i speak in print, for in print i found it. 2.01.169 P
if he had found the young man, he would have WIV 1.04. 49 P
it will be found so, master page. 2.03. 51 P
i found thee of more value | than stamps in gold 3.04. 15
i have done so, but he's not to be found. MM 1.02.175
vantage best have took | found out the remedy. 2.02. 75
thief too, sir, for we have found upon him, sir, 3.02. 16 P
but my brother-justice have i found so severe, 3.02.253 P
wish | you had not found me here so musical. 4.01. 11
good friar, i know you do, and have found it. 4.01. 53
come, i have found you out a stand most fit, 4.06. 10
let this friar be found. 5.01.133
what ruins are in me that can be found, | by him ERR 2.01. 96
in her buttocks, i found it out by the bogs. 3.02.117 P
i found it by the barrenness, hard in the palm 3.02.120 P
i see, sir, you have found the goldsmith now. 4.03. 46

and if he found her accordant, he meant to take ADO 1.02. 14 P
i found him here as melancholy as a lodge in a 2.01.214 P
she found "benedick" and "beatrice" between the 2.03.137 P
since, but i think now 'tis not to be found; LLL 1.02.113 P
you found his mote, the king your mote did see; 4.03.159
have found the ground of study's excellence 4.03.296
in leaden contemplation have found out | such 4.03.318
as to rejoice at friends but newly found. 5.02.751
forest have i gone, | but athenian found i none, MND 2.02. 67
thou art not by mine eye, lysander, found; 3.02.181
that i sleeping here was found | with these 4.01.101
and i have found demetrius like a jewel, | mine 4.01.191
but how i caught it, found it, or came by it, MV 1.01. 3
my lord bassanio, since you have found antonio, 1.01. 69
and by adventuring both | i oft found both. 1.01.144
hast thou found my daughter? 3.01. 80 P
as i have ever found thee honest–true, | so let 3.04. 46
within these ten days if that thou beest found AYL 1.03. 43
they found the bed untreasur'd of their mistress 2.02. 7
i have by hard adventure found mine own. 2.04. 45
peace, you dull fool, i found them on a tree. 3.02.115 P
for look here what i found on a palm tree. 3.02.175 P
i found him under a tree, like a dropp'd acorn. 3.02.234 P
i was seeking for a fool when i found you. 3.02.286 P
foolish chroniclers of that age found it was — 4.01.105 P
approach the man | and found it was his brother, 4.03.120
and found the quarrel was upon the seventh cause 5.04. 49 P
o tranio, till i found it to be true, | i never SHR 1.01.148
on, | i found the effect of love in idleness, 1.01.151
by being once lost, may be ten times found; AWW 1.01.131 P
i wish might be found in the calendar of my past 1.03. 4 P
my father, | in what he did profess, well found. 2.01.102
i have now found thee. 2.03.206 P
go to, thou art a witty fool, i have found thee. 2.04. 32 P
therefore am i found | so much unsettled. 2.05. 62
it, since i have found | myself in my incertain 3.01. 14
with her but once | and found her wondrous cold, 3.06.113
over–pay and pay again | when i have found it. 3.07. 17
that every braggart shall be found an ass. 4.03.336
my good lord, you were the first that found me! 5.02. 42 P
i found it not. 5.03.274
was like this maid, | i found you wondrous kind. 5.03.310
could possibly have found in any part of illyria TN 3.04.268 P
yet there he was, and there i found this credit, 4.03. 6
you'll be found, | be you beneath the sky. WT 1.02.179
an heir, if that which is lost be not found." 3.02.136 P
show those things you found about her, those 4.04.696 P
not have an heir | till his lost child be found? 5.01. 40
old shepherd deliver the manner how he found it; 5.02. 5 P
i heard the shepherd say, he found the child. 5.02. 7 P
the king's daughter is found. 5.02. 23 P
has the king found his heir? 5.02. 29 P
the letters of antigonus found with it, which 5.02. 34 P
out of himself for joy of his found daughter, as 5.02. 50 P
the child were even then lost when it was found. 5.02. 72 P
turn, good lady, | our perdita is found. 5.03.121
how found | thy father's court? 5.03.124
there | my mate, that's never to be found again, 5.03.134
thou hast found mine, | but how, is to be 5.03.138
whom i found | with many hundreds treading on JN 4.02.148
found it too precious–princely for a grave. 4.03. 40
they found him dead and cast into the streets, 5.01. 39
on pain to be found false and recreant, | to R2 1.03.106
on pain to be found false and recreant, | both 1.03.111
from ravenspurgh to cotshall will be found | in 2.03. 9
he should have found his uncle gaunt a father 2.03.127
i would to god, my lords, he might be found. 5.03. 4
and you have found me, for accordingly | you 1H4 1.03. 3
till he hath found a time to pay us home. 1.03.288
but roguery to be found in villainous man, yet a 2.04.125 P
what hast thou found? 2.04.532 P
rebellion lay in his way, and he found it. 5.01. 28 P
but priam found the fire ere he his tongue, 2H4 1.01. 74
for he hath found to end one doubt by death 4.01.197
had found some months asleep and leapt them over 4.04.124
my lord, i found the prince in the next room, 4.05. 82
in, | and found no course of breath within your 4.05.150
see, thy fault france hath in thee found out, H5 2.pr. 20
as we his subjects have in wonder found, 2.04.135
'tis sure they found some place | but weakly 1H6 2.01. 73
hearts, | because i ever found them as myself. 3.02. 98
there should be found such false dissembling 4.01. 63
in, | we should have found a bloody day of this. 4.07. 34
gloss, | he will be found a dangerous protector. 2H6 1.01.164
"a staff is quickly found to beat a dog." 3.01.171
friend, | and 'tis well seen he found an enemy. 3.02.185
if after three days' space thou here be'st found 3.02.295
if thou be found by me, thou art but dead. 3.02.387
our scouts have found the adventure very easy; 3H6 4.02. 18
a purse of gold that (by chance) i found. R3 1.04.140 P
time, | found that the issue was not his begot; 3.05. 90
i wish'd might fall on me when i was found 5.01. 14
this found i on my tent this morning. 5.03.303
ye have found him, cardinal. H8 1.04. 86
is he found guilty? 2.01. 7
have found him guilty of high treason. 2.01. 27
never found again | but where they mean to sink 2.01.130
but that slander, sir, | is found a truth now; 2.01.154
lord, have great care | i be not found a talker. 2.02. 78
the king hath found | matter against him that 3.02. 20
and wot you what i found | there (on my 3.02.122
if what i now pronounce you have found true; 3.02.163
the duke by law | found his deserts. 3.02.267
found thee a way, out of his wrack, to rise in; 3.02.437
and found the blessedness of being little; 4.02. 66
i will leave all as i found it, and there an end TRO 1.01. 88 P
the fineness of which metal is not found | in 1.03. 22
the nature of the sickness found, ulysses, 1.03.140
and when i have the bloody hector found, 5.07. 4
i therein would have found issue. COR 1.03. 21 P
but you have found, | scaling his present 2.03.248
if he had gone forth consul, found it so. 4.06. 35
the last, i think | might have found easy fines; 5.06. 64
i found a friend, and sure as death i swore | i TIT 1.01.487
must we pursue, and i have found the path: 2.01.111
but out alas, here have we found him dead. 2.03.258
who found this letter? 2.03.293
o, thus i found her straying in the park, 3.01. 88
the old man hath found their guilt, | and sends 4.02. 26
i wrote the letter that thy father found, | and 5.01.106
then most sought where most might not be found, ROM 1.01.127
to seek him here that means not to be found. 2.01. 42
older when you have found him than he was when 2.04.121 P
what hast thou found? 2.04.131 P
else, when he is found, that hour is his last. 3.01.195
i dreamt my lady came and found me dead — 5.01. 6
romeo's man, we found him in the churchyard. 5.03.182
my occasions have found time to use 'em toward a TIM 2.02.191 P
they have all been touch'd and found base metal, 3.03. 6
the window for a flint, i found | this paper, JC 2.01. 36
if it be found so, some will dear abide it. 3.02.114
i found it in his closet, 'tis his will. 3.02.129
he will be found like brutus, like himself. 5.04. 25
my life | i found no man but he was true to me. 5.05. 35
so brutus should be found. 5.05. 58
which unwip'd we found | upon their pillows. MAC 2.03.103
take a homely man's advice, | be not found here; 4.02. 69
children, servants, all | that could be found. 4.03.212
that i have found | the very cause of hamlet's HAM 2.02. 48
he hath found | the head and source of all your 2.02. 54
he truly found | it was against your highness. 2.02. 64
why, 'tis found so. 5.01. 8 P
where i found, horatio — | ah, royal knavery! 5.02. 18
as much as child e'er lov'd, or father found; LR 1.01. 59
thy banish'd trunk be found in our dominions, 1.01.177
i found it thrown in at the casement of my 1.02. 60 P
found you no displeasure in him by word nor 1.02.156 P
to have found a safe redress, but now grow 1.04.206
and found — dispatch. 2.01. 58
and found him pight to do it, with curst speech 2.01. 65
your son and daughter found this trespass worth 2.04. 44
that when we have found the king — in which 3.01. 53
not peace at my bidding, there i found 'em, 4.06.103 P
but have you never found my brother's way | to 5.01. 10
i must be found. OTH 1.02. 30
when, being not at your lodging to be found, 1.02. 45
'tis well i am found by you. 1.02. 47
and found good means | to draw from her a prayer 1.03.151
i never found man that knew how to love himself. 1.03.313 P
cyprus, | i have found great love amongst them. 2.01.205
knave, and the woman hath found him already. 2.01.248 P
i found them close together | at blow and thrust 2.03.237
i am glad i have found this napkin; 3.03.290
which at the first are scarce found to distaste, 3.03.327
i found not cassio's kisses on her lips. 3.03.341
i found it in my chamber. 3.04.188
i will be found most cunning in my patience; 4.01. 90
i should have found in some place of my soul | a 4.02. 52
he found it then; 5.02. 66
than what he found himself was apt and true. 5.02.177
thou speak'st of | i found by fortune, and did 5.02.226
no, alas, i found it, | and i did give't my 5.02.230
found in the pocket of the slain roderigo, | and 5.02.309
discontented paper, | found in his pocket too; 5.02.315
i found it in my chamber: 5.02.320
i should have found it afterwards well done, ANT 2.07. 79
when antony found julius caesar dead, | he cried 3.02. 54
wept | when at philippi he found brutus slain. 3.02. 56
i found you as a morsel, cold upon | dead 3.13.116
for when she saw | (which never shall be found) 4.14.122
i found her trimming up the diadem | on her dead 5.02.342
but found their courage | worthy his frowning at CYM 2.04. 22
found no opposition | but what he look'd for 2.05. 17
though i had found | gold strew'd i' th' floor. 3.06. 48
how found you him? 4.02.209
have i not found it | murd'rous to th' senses? 4.02.327
in seeking him, | and will, no doubt, be found. 4.03. 21
having found the back door open | of the 5.03. 45
but none of 'em can be found. 5.03. 88
stepp'd before targes of proof, cannot be found. 5.05. 5
when i wak'd, i found | this label on my bosom, 5.05.429
which labor | i found that kindness in a father. PER 1.01. 67
he has found the meaning. 1.01.109
he hath found the meaning, | for which we mean 1.01.143
which by my knowledge found, the sinful father 1.02. 77
buried at tharsus, | and found at sea again! 5.01.197
found there rich jewels, recovered her, and 5.03. 24
now do i long to hear how you were found, | how 5.03. 56
where shall be shown you all was found with her; 5.03. 66
had not the loving gods found this place for us, TNK 2.02.108
yes, and have found me so. 2.02.183
driven to | when fifteen once has found us! 2.04. 7
if we be found, we are wretched. 3.06.109
for i gave him | more mercy than you found, sir, 3.06.182
doubt, but mercy may be found if you so seek it. STM II.C 147
and swear i found you where you did fulfill LUC 1635
and as goods lost are seld or never found, | as PP 13. 7
and losing her, my friend hath found that loss; SON 42.10
as 'twixt a miser and his wealth is found: 75. 4
and found such fair assistance in my verse | as 78. 2
doth he give, | and found it in thy cheek; 79.11
i found (or thought i found) you did exceed 83. 3
i found (or thought i found) you did exceed 83. 3
found a kind of meetness | to be diseas'd ere 118. 7
a maid of dian's this advantage found, | and his 153. 2
but found no cure: 153.13
found yet moe letters sadly penn'd in blood, LC 47

/FOUNDATION 1 FR 0.0001 REL FR 1 V 0 P
/model, | /consent /upon /a /sure /foundation, 2H4 1.03. 52

FOUNDATION 6 FR 0.0006 REL FR 5 V 1 P
god save the foundation! ADO 5.01.318 P
whose foundation | is pil'd upon his faith, and WT 1.02.429
there is no sure foundation set on blood; JN 4.02.104
the frame and huge foundation of the earth 1H4 3.01. 16
flat, | to bring the roof to the foundation, COR 3.01.204
for passage, earth's foundation shakes, | which VEN 1047

FOUNDATIONS 3 FR 0.0003 REL FR 3 V 0 P
in those foundations which i build upon, | the WT 2.01.101
do slope | their heads to their foundations; MAC 4.01. 58
o jove, i think | foundations fly the wretched: CYM 3.06. 7

FOUNDED 2 FR 0.0002 REL FR 2 V 0 P
whole as the marble, founded as the rock, | as MAC 3.04. 21
hath founded his good fortunes on your love, OTH 3.04. 94

FOUNDER* 4 FR 0.0004 REL FR 4 V 0 P
the founder of this law and female bar. H5 1.02. 42
idly suppos'd the founder of this law, | who 1.02. 59
but in this point | all his tricks founder, and H8 3.02. 40
and that will founder the best hobby–horse | (if TNK 5.02. 52

FOUNDER'D 1 FR 0.0001 REL FR 1 V 0 P
i shall think or phoebus' steeds are founder'd TMP 4.01. 30

FOUND'RED 1 FR 0.0001 REL FR 0 V 1 P
i have found'red ninescore and odd posts, and 2H4 4.03. 36 P

FOUNDST 1 FR 0.0001 REL FR 1 V 0 P
by whose direction foundst thou out this place? ROM 2.02. 79

FOUNT 3 FR 0.0003 REL FR 3 V 0 P
desire | to meet me at the consecrated fount, MM 4.03. 98
you are the fount that makes small brooks to 3H6 4.08. 54
each cheek a river running from a fount | with LC 283

FOUNTAIN 17 FR 0.0019 REL FR 14 V 3 P
by fountain clear, or spangled starlight sheen, MND 2.01. 29
or mead, | by paved fountain or by rushy brook, 2.01. 84
weep for nothing, like diana in the fountain, AYL 4.01.154 P
a woman mov'd is like a fountain troubled, SHR 5.02.142
thou sheer, immaculate, and silver fountain, R2 5.03. 61
my sweet lady in the fountain of our love? TRO 3.02. 66 P
my mind is troubled, like a fountain stirr'd, 3.03.308
would the fountain of your mind were clear again 3.03.310 P
like to a bubbling fountain stirr'd with wind, TIT 2.04. 23
and thou, and i, sit round about some fountain, 3.01.123
and in the fountain shall we gaze so long | till 3.01.127
which, like a fountain with an hundred spouts, JC 2.02. 77
head, the fountain of your blood | is stopp'd, MAC 2.03. 98
the fountain from the which my current runs | or OTH 4.02. 59
mud not the fountain that gave drink to thee, LUC 577
the poisoned fountain clears itself again, | and 1707
and from the purple fountain brutus drew | the 1734

FOUNTAINS 5 FR 0.0005 REL FR 5 V 0 P
the skies, the fountains, every region near MND 4.01.116
with purple fountains issuing from your veins — ROM 1.01. 85
stray lower, where the pleasant fountains lie. VEN 234
roses have thorns, and silver fountains mud, SON 35. 2
have emptied all their fountains in my well, LC 255

FOUNTS 2 FR 0.0002 REL FR 2 V 0 P
and proofs as clear as founts in july when | we H8 1.01.154
or toads infect fair founts with venom mud? LUC 850

FOUR 140 FR 0.0158 REL FR 70 V 70 P
had i not | four, or five, women once that TMP 1.02. 47
drowning to be afeard now of your four legs; 2.02. 60 P
a man as ever went on four legs cannot make him 2.02. 61 P
this is some monster of the isle with four legs, 2.02. 65 P
four legs and two voices; 2.02. 89 P
when three or four of his blind brothers and TGV 4.04. 4 P
company of three or four gentleman–like dogs, 4.04. 17 P
i would have made you four tall fellows skip WIV 2.01.229 P
vat be all you, one, two, tree, four, come for? 2.03. 22 P
and three or four more of their growth, we'll 4.04. 49
i was three or four times in the thought they 5.05.121 P
block and your axe to–morrow, four a' clock. MM 4.02. 53 P
let claudio be executed by four of the clock, 4.02.121 P
effect, i crave but four days' respite; 4.02.160 P
for some four suits of peach–color'd satin, 4.03. 10 P
in our last conflict four of his five wits went ADO 1.01. 66 P
four days ago. LLL 1.01.122
of all the four, or the three, or the two, or 1.02. 79 P
or the three, or the two, or one of the four. 1.02. 80 P
is that one of the four complexions? 1.02. 83 P
of door, | and stayed the odds by adding four. 3.01. 92
out of door, | staying the odds by adding four. 3.01. 98
four woodcocks in a dish! 4.03. 80
true, true, we are four. 4.03.207
we four indeed confronted were with four | in 5.02.367
we four indeed confronted were with four | in 5.02.367
and if these four worthies in their first show 5.02.538
these four will change habits, and present the 5.02.539
four happy days bring in | another moon; MND 1.01. 2
four days will quickly steep themselves in night 1.01. 7
four nights will quickly dream away the time; 1.01. 8
two of both kinds makes up four. 3.02.438
for the four winds blow in from every coast MV 1.01.168
the four strangers seek for you, madam, to take 1.02.123 P
good heart as i can bid the other four farewell, 1.02.128 P
'tis now but four of clock, we have two hours 2.04. 8
on ash we'nsday was four year in th' afternoon. 2.05. 26 P
from the four corners of the earth they come 2.07. 39
some three or four of you | go give him 4.01.147
duke, and three or four loving lords have put AYL 1.01.101 P
undone three tailors, i have had four quarrels, 5.04. 47 P
i'll leave her houses three or four as good, SHR 2.01.366
or four and twenty times the pilot's glass AWW 2.01.165
of enjoin'd penitents | there's four or five, to 3.05. 95
some four or five descents | since the first 3.07. 24
who hath for four or five removes come short 5.03.131
and speaks three or four languages word for word TN 1.03. 26 P
if she be, it's four to one she'll none of me. 1.03.106 P
some four or five attend him — | all, if you 1.04. 36
does not our lives consist of the four elements? 2.03. 10 P
as kisses, if your four negatives make your two 5.01. 21 P
she hath made me four and twenty nosegays for WT 4.03. 41 P
four pounds of pruins, and as many of raisins o' 4.03. 48 P
pray let's see these four threes of herdsmen. 4.04.336 P
ay, and have been so any time these four hours. 5.02.136 P
four fixed, and the fift did whirl about | the JN 4.02.183
whirl about | the other four in wondrous motion. 4.02.184
of his banish'd years | pluck'd four away. R2 1.03.211
four lagging winters and four wanton springs 1.03.214
four lagging winters and four wanton springs 1.03.214
me | he shortens four years of my son's exile, 1.03.217
to–morrow morning by four a' clock early, at 1H4 1.02.125 P
an' it be not four by the day, i'll be hang'd. 2.01. 1 P
if i travel but four foot by the squier further 2.02. 12 P
you four shall front them in the narrow lane; 2.02. 60 P
with three or four loggerheads amongst three or 2.04. 4 P
amongst three or four score hogsheads. 2.04. 5 P
there be four of us here have ta'en a thousand 2.04.158 P
a hundred upon poor four of us. 2.04.162 P
through the doublet, four through the hose, my 2.04.167 P
we four set upon some dozen — 2.04.174 P
four rogues in buckrom let drive at me — 2.04.196 P
what, four? thou saidst but two even now. 2.04.197 P
four, hal, i told thee four. 2.04.198 P
four, hal, i told thee four. 2.04.198 P

ay, ay, he said four. 2.04.199 P
these four came all afront, and mainly thrust at 2.04.200 P
seven? why, there were but four even now. 2.04.203 P
ay, four, in buckrom suits. 2.04.205 P
we two saw you four set on four and bound them, 2.04.253 P
we two saw you four set on four and bound them, 2.04.253 P
then did we two set on you four, and, with a 2.04.256 P
money that i borrow'd — three or four times, 3.03. 18 P
and money lent you, four and twenty pound. 3.03. 74 P
hal, three or four bonds of forty pound a–piece, 3.03.101 P
he did, my lord, four days ere i set forth, 4.01. 22
you had not four such swingebucklers in all the 2H4 3.02. 21 P
than your number, you must have but four here, 3.02.189 P
and here's four harry ten shillings in french 3.02.221 P
four of which you please. 3.02.242 P
come, sir john, which four will you have? 3.02.246 P
i should make four dozen of such bearded 5.01. 63 P
out of six fashions, which is four terms, or two 5.01. 80 P
is it four a' clock? H5 1.01. 93
land | until four hundred one and twenty years 1.02. 57
of our redemption | four hundred twenty–six; 1.02. 61
divide your happy england into four, | whereof 1.02.214
three or four times. 2.03. 19 P
is digt himself four yard under the countermines 3.02. 62 P
with any that treads but on four /pasterns. 3.07. 12 P
with four or five most vile and ragged foils 4.pr. 50
gentlemen, | eight thousand and four hundred; 4.08. 85
of my leek, or i will peat his pate four days. 5.01. 41 P
four of their lords i'll change for one of ours. 1H6 1.01.151
come, let us four to dinner. 2.04.132
you four, from hence to prison back again; 2H6 2.03. 5
you shall have four /and you'll be rul'd by him. 3H6 3.02. 30
upon the stroke of four. R3 3.02. 5
and towards three or four a' clock | look for 3.05.101
their lips were four red roses on a stalk, 4.03. 12
upon the stroke of four. 5.03.235
what four thron'd ones could have weigh'd | such H8 1.01. 11
over her, are four barons | of the cinque–ports. 4.01. 48
as much as one sound cudgel of four foot | (you 5.03. 19
has not past three or four hairs on his chin — TRO 1.02.112 P
'tis not four days gone | since i heard thence; COR 1.02. 6
was forc'd to wheel | three or four miles about, 1.06. 20
not outward, which of you | but is four volsces? 1.06. 78
and four shall quickly draw out my command, 1.06. 84
yet, to my teen be it spoken, i have but four — ROM 1.03. 13
hath presented to you | four milk–white horses, TIM 1.02.183
lips, let four words go by and language end! 5.01.220
three or four wenches, where i stood, cried, JC 1.02.271 P
you know sometimes he walks four hours together HAM 2.02.160
richer than that which four successive kings 5.02.273
let four captains | bear hamlet, like a soldier, 5.02.395
upon the world for four times seven years, and OTH 1.03.312 P
to do, for i perceive | four feasts are toward. ANT 2.06. 73
but i had rather fast from all, four days, 2.07.102
and if thou canst awake by four o' th' clock, CYM 2.02. 6
by the four opposing /coigns | which the world PER 3.ch. 17
three or four thousand chequins were as pretty a 4.02. 26 P
three or four | i saw from far off cross her — TNK 4.01. 99
now with child by him — | there must be four. 4.01.130
i'll warrant you within these three or four days 5.02.104
that four such eyes should be so fix'd on one 5.03.145
a bushel, and beef at four nobles a stone, list STM II.C 3 P
being nurse and feeder of the other four! VEN 446
were never four such lamps together mix'd, | had 489
my life, being made of four, with two alone SON 45. 7

FOUR–INCH'D 1 FR 0.0001 REL FR 0 V 1 P
a bay trotting–horse over four–inch'd bridges, LR 3.04. 57 P

FOURSCORE 13 FR 0.0014 REL FR 5 V 8 P
i have liv'd fourscore years and upward; WIV 3.01. 56 P
a man of fourscore pound a year; MM 2.01.123 P
are you of fourscore pounds a year? 2.01.195 P
genoa, as i heard, one night fourscore ducats. MV 3.01.109 P
fourscore ducats at a sitting! 3.01.111 P
fourscore ducats! 3.01.112 P
from /seventeen years till now almost fourscore AYL 2.03. 71
seek, | but at fourscore it is too late a week; 2.03. 74
the coast on we'nsday the fourscore of april, WT 4.04.276 P
sir, | you have undone a man of fourscore three, 4.04.453
goes up and down in from fourscore to thirteen, TIM 2.02.113 P
your father's tenant, | these fourscore years. LR 4.01. 14
fourscore and upward, not an hour more nor less; 4.07. 60

FOURTEEN 25 FR 0.0028 REL FR 17 V 8 P
which for this fourteen years we have let slip, MM 1.03. 21
hot–bloods between fourteen and five–and–thirty, ADO 3.03.132 P
if she say i am not fourteen pence on the score SHR in.2. 23 P
thou be'st not an ass, i am a youth of fourteen. AWW 2.03.101 P
a good report — after fourteen years' purchase. TN 4.01. 23 P
fourteen they shall not see | to bring false WT 2.01.147
full fourteen weeks before the course of time. JN 1.01.113
which fourteen hundred years ago were nail'd 1H4 1.01. 26
he, and answers, "some fourteen," an hour after; 2.04.108 P
nor shall we need his help these fourteen days. 3.01. 87
he /cannot draw his power this fourteen days. 4.01.126
a forehand shaft a fourteen and fourteen and a 2H4 3.02. 47 P
shaft a fourteen and fourteen and a half, that 3.02. 47 P
board a dozen or fourteen gentlewomen that live H5 2.01. 33 P
within fourteen days | at bristow i expect my 2H6 3.01.327
she hath not seen the change of fourteen years; ROM 1.02. 9
she's not fourteen. 1.03. 12
i'll lay fourteen of my teeth — | and yet, to 1.03. 12
spoken, i have but four — | she's not fourteen. 1.03. 14
come lammas–eve at night shall she be fourteen. 1.03. 17
on lammas–eve at night shall she be fourteen, 1.03. 21
for that i am some twelve or fourteen moonshines LR 1.02. 5
who at fourteen years | he sought to murder, but PER 5.03. 8
and what this fourteen years no razor touch'd, 5.03. 75
i told them — who | a lass of fourteen brided. TNK 5.01.109

FOURTH 20 FR 0.0022 REL FR 15 V 5 P
the fourth turn'd on the toe, and down he fell. LLL 5.02.114
he hath a third at mexico, a fourth for england, MV 1.03. 20 P
the fourth, the reproof valiant; AYL 5.04. 94 P
third, or fourth, or fift borough, i'll answer SHR in.1. 13 P
him, | and long live henry, fourth of that name! R2 4.01.112
harry the fourth, or fift? 2H4 5.03.114
harry the fourth. 5.03.115
henry the fourth, grandfather to this king, 1H6 2.05. 63
being but fourth of that heroic line. 2.05. 78
crown'd by the name of henry the fourth, 2H6 2.02. 23
the fourth son, york claims it from the third; 2.02. 55
henry the fourth by conquest got the crown. 3H6 1.01.132
lords, | resign'd the crown to henry the fourth, 1.01.139
and after john of gaunt, henry the fourth, 3.03. 83
"edward the fourth, by the grace of god, king of 4.07. 71 P
long live edward the fourth! 4.07. 76
the fourth would return for conscience' sake to COR 2.03. 32 P
a fourth? MAC 4.01.116
there was a fourth man, in a silly habit, | that CYM 5.03. 86
what is the fourth? PER 2.02. 31

FOUTRE 2 FR 0.0002 REL FR 2 V 0 P
a foutre for the world and worldlings base! 2H4 5.03. 99
a foutre for thine office! 5.03.115

FOWL 15 FR 0.0017 REL FR 10 V 5 P
fowl weather? TMP 2.01.143
then another fault in the semblance of a fowl — WIV 5.05. 10 P
for our kitchens | we kill the fowl of season. MM 2.02. 85
follies doth /enew | as falcon doth the fowl, is 3.01. 91
without a fin, there's a fowl without a feather: ERR 3.01. 82
alas, poor hurt fowl! ADO 2.01.202 P
o, ay, stalk on, stalk on, the fowl sits. 2.03. 93 P
worse than a struck fowl or a hurt wild duck. 1H4 4.02. 19 P
had not your man put up the fowl so suddenly, 2H6 2.01. 44
that taught his son the office of a fowl! 3H6 5.06. 19
as a flight of fowl | scatter'd by winds and TIT 5.03. 68
but you know strange fowl light upon neighboring CYM 1.04. 89 P
coucheth the fowl below with his wings' shade, LUC 507
trembling fear, as fowl hear falcons' bells. 511
session interdict | every fowl of tyrant wing, PHT 10

FOWLER 1 FR 0.0001 REL FR 1 V 0 P
as wild geese that the creeping fowler eye, | or MND 3.02. 20

FOWLS 4 FR 0.0004 REL FR 4 V 0 P
and the winged fowls | are their males' subjects ERR 2.01. 18
of more pre–eminence than fish and fowls, | are 2.01. 23
ay, when fowls have no feathers, and fish have 3.01. 79
as lagging fowls before the northern blast. LUC 1335

/FOX 1 FR 0.0001 REL FR 0 V 1 P
/hide /fox, /and /all /after. HAM 4.02. 30 P

FOX 34 FR 0.0038 REL FR 20 V 14 P
a fox to be the shepherd of thy lambs. TGV 4.04. 92
i'll warrant we'll unkennel the fox. WIV 3.03.164 P
and furr'd with fox and lambskins too, to MM 3.02. 8 P
come you to seek the lamb here of the fox, 5.01.298
the fox, the ape, and the humble–bee, | were LLL 3.01. 84
the fox, the ape, and the humble–bee, | were 3.01. 89
the fox, the ape, and the humble–bee, | were 3.01. 95
this lion is a very fox for his valor. MND 5.01.231 P
his discretion, and the fox carries the goose. 5.01.234 P
for the goose carries not the fox. 5.01.236 P
an old italian fox is not so kind, my boy. SHR 2.01.403
o, will you eat | no grapes, my royal fox? AWW 2.01. 70
grapes, and if my royal fox | could reach them. 2.01. 71
you some sport with the fox ere we case him. 3.06.102 P
sir toby will be sworn that i am no fox, but he TN 1.05. 80 P
for all this, though it be as rank as a fox. 2.05.124 P
nor no more truth in thee than in a drawn fox, 1H4 3.03.113 P
eyes, | for treason is but trusted like the fox, 5.02. 9
to wake a wolf is as bad as smell a fox. 2H4 1.02.155 P
o signieur dew, thou diest on point of fox, H5 4.04. 9
the fox barks not when he would steal the lamb. 2H6 3.01. 55
then, | to make the fox surveyor of the fold? 3.01.253
let him die, in that he is a fox, | by nature 3.01.257
but when the fox hath once got in his nose, 3H6 4.07. 25
this holy fox, | or wolf, or both (for he is H8 1.01.158
as fox to lamb, or wolf to heifer's calf, | pard TRO 3.02.193
thou wert the lion, the fox would beguile thee; TIM 4.03.328 P
if thou wert the lamb, the fox would eat thee; 4.03.329 P
if thou wert the fox, the lion would suspect 4.03.330 P
a fox, when one has caught her, | and such a LR 1.04.317
hog in sloth, fox in stealth, wolf in greediness 3.04. 93 P
ingrateful fox, 'tis he. 3.07. 28
subtle as the fox for prey, | like warlike as CYM 3.03. 40
hare, | or at the fox which lives by subtilty, VEN 675

FOXES 2 FR 0.0002 REL FR 2 V 0 P
where foxes, geese. COR 1.01.172
from heaven, | and fire us hence like foxes. LR 5.03. 23

FOXSHIP 1 FR 0.0001 REL FR 1 V 0 P
hadst thou foxship | to banish him that strook COR 4.02. 18

FRACTED 2 FR 0.0002 REL FR 2 V 0 P
his heart is fracted and corroborate. H5 2.01.124
and my reliances on his fracted dates | have TIM 2.01. 22

FRACTION 1 FR 0.0001 REL FR 0 V 1 P
their fraction is more our wish than their TRO 2.03. 98 P

FRACTIONS 2 FR 0.0002 REL FR 2 V 0 P
the fractions of her faith, orts of her love, TRO 5.02.158
distasteful looks, and these hard fractions, TIM 2.02.211

FRAGILE 1 FR 0.0001 REL FR 1 V 0 P
that nature's fragile vessel doth sustain | in TIM 5.01.201

FRAGMENT 3 FR 0.0003 REL FR 1 V 2 P
from whence, fragment? TRO 5.01. 8 P
it is some poor fragment, some slender ort of TIM 4.03.399 P
nay, you were a fragment | of cneius pompey's — ANT 3.13.117

FRAGMENTS 4 FR 0.0004 REL FR 3 V 1 P
discourse is sometime guarded with fragments, ADO 1.01.286 P
the fragments, scraps, the bits and greasy TRO 5.02.159
go get you home, you fragments! COR 1.01.222
like fragments in hard voyages, became | the CYM 5.03. 44

FRAGRANT *(also vagram)*

FRAGRANT 6 FR 0.0006 REL FR 6 V 0 P
beds of roses, | and a thousand fragrant posies. WIV 3.01. 20
with coronet of fresh and fragrant flowers; MND 4.01. 52
the fields are fragrant and the woods are green. TIT 2.02. 2
one hour's storm will drown the fragrant meads, 2.04. 54
bed of roses, | with a thousand fragrant posies, PP 19.10
which, like a canker in the fragrant rose, SON 95. 2

FRAIL 19 FR 0.0021 REL FR 16 V 3 P
and thorns, | which ent'red their frail shins. TMP 4.01.181
we are all frail. MM 2.04.121
nay, women are frail too. 2.04.124
nay, call us ten times frail, | for we are soft 2.04.128
strong corruption | inhabits our frail blood. TN 3.04.357
some suppose the soul's frail dwelling–house) JN 5.07. 3
banish'd this frail sepulchre of our flesh | as R2 1.03.196
my ransom is this frail and worthless trunk; H5 3.06.154
she did corrupt frail nature with some bribe, 3H6 3.02.155
or else his head's assurance is but frail. R3 4.04.496
which perforce | i, her frail son, amongst my H8 3.02.148
in our own natures frail, and capable | of our 5.02. 46
if sanctimony and a frail vow betwixt an erring OTH 1.03.355 P
she that in wisdom never was so frail | to 2.01.154
than thy continent, | crack thy frail case! ANT 4.14. 41
the one is but frail and the other casual. CYM 1.04. 91 P
the holding or loss of that you term her frail. 1.04. 96 P
hath taught | my frail mortality to know itself, PER 1.01. 42
not my tongue be mute, my frail joints shake? LUC 227

FRAILER 1 FR 0.0001 REL FR 1 V 0 P
or on my frailties why are frailer spies, SON 121. 7

FRAIL'ST 1 FR 0.0001 REL FR 1 V 0 P
eyes, that are the frail'st and softest things, AYL 3.05. 12

FRAILTIES 4 FR 0.0004 REL FR 4 V 0 P
and when we have our naked frailties hid, | that MAC 2.03.126
been laden with like frailties which before ANT 5.02.123
all frailties that besiege all kinds of blood, SON 109.10
or on my frailties why are frailer spies, 121. 7

FRAILTY 12 FR 0.0013 REL FR 7 V 5 P
and stands so firmly on his wive's frailty, yet WIV 2.01.234 P
let her consider his frailty, and then judge of 3.05. 50 P
but that frailty hath examples for his falling, MM 3.01.186 P
himself (by the instruction of his frailty) many 3.02.246 P
alas, /our frailty is the cause, not we! TN 2.02. 31
and from the organ–pipe of frailty sings | his JN 5.07. 23
than another man, and therefore more frailty. 1H4 3.03.168 P
out of which frailty | and want of wisdom, you, H8 5.02. 47
when we will tempt the frailty of our powers, TRO 4.04. 96
frailty, thy name is woman! HAM 1.02.146
is't frailty that thus errs? OTH 4.03. 99
desires for sport, and frailty, as men have? 4.03.101

FRAM'D 19 FR 0.0021 REL FR 17 V 2 P
yet had he fram'd to himself (by the instruction MM 3.02.245 P
but nature never fram'd a woman's heart | of ADO 3.01. 49
save this of hers, fram'd by thy villainy! 5.01. 71
he is compos'd and fram'd of treachery, | and 5.01.249
nature hath fram'd strange fellows in her time: MV 1.01. 51
tells us | 'tis not a visitation fram'd, but WT 5.01. 91
for thou art fram'd of the firm truth of valor. H5 4.03. 14
his head by nature fram'd to wear a crown, | his 3H6 4.06. 72
fram'd in the prodigality of nature — | young, R3 1.02.243
honor'd mould | wherein this trunk was fram'd, COR 5.03. 23
here's a young lad fram'd of another leer: TIT 4.02.119
no big–bon'd men fram'd of the cyclops' size, 4.03. 47
'twas time and griefs | that fram'd him thus. TIM 5.01.123
eyeless head of thine was first fram'd flesh LR 4.06.227
to be suspected — fram'd to make women false. OTH 1.03.398
she's fram'd as fruitful | as the free elements. 2.03.341
when nature fram'd this piece, she meant thee a PER 4.02.139 P
wherein she fram'd thee in high heaven's despite VEN 731
she fram'd the love, and yet she foil'd the PP 7.15

FRAME 49 FR 0.0055 REL FR 43 V 6 P
and frame some feeling line | that may discover TGV 3.02. 75
the maid will i frame and make fit for his MM 3.01.255 P
her madness hath the oddest frame of sense, 5.01. 61
it is needful that you frame the season for your ADO 1.03. 25 P
chid i for that at frugal nature's frame? 4.01.128
whose spirits toil in frame of villainies. 4.01.189
/clock, | still a–repairing, ever out of frame, LLL 3.01.191
like to lysander sometime frame thy tongue; MND 3.02.360
o, wherefore, nature, didst thou lions frame? 5.01.291
and frame your mind to mirth and merriment, SHR in.2. 135
and therefore frame your manners to the time. 1.01.227
soul, | in your fine frame hath love no quality? AWW 4.02. 4
o, she that hath a heart of that fine frame | to TN 1.01. 32
the very mould and frame of hand, nail, finger. WT 2.03.103
if | his going i could frame to serve my turn, 4.04.509
the frame and huge foundation of the earth 1H4 3.01. 16
his back, and the whole frame stands upon pins. 2H4 3.02.144 P
/and either end in peace, which god so frame! 4.01.178
i tell you, madam, were the whole frame here, 1H6 2.03. 54
law, | and never yet could frame my will to it, 2.04. 8
it, | and therefore frame the law unto my will. 2.04. 9
by wicked means to frame our sovereign's fall. 2H6 3.01. 52
tears, | and frame my face to all occasions. 3H6 3.02.185
but you frame | things that are known alike, H8 1.02. 44
their good loves, but thou wilt frame | thyself, COR 3.02. 84
serve, if he | can thereto frame his spirit. 3.02. 97
thou art my warrior, | i /holp to frame thee. 5.03. 63
make true wars, | i'll frame convenient peace. 5.03.191
one do i personate of lord timon's frame, | whom TIM 1.01. 69
at duty, more than i could frame employment; 4.03.262
but let the frame of things disjoint, both the MAC 3.02. 16
our state to be disjoint and out of frame, HAM 1.02. 20
with my disposition, that this goodly frame, the 2.02.298 P
put your discourse into some frame, and /start 3.02.309 P
frame the business after your own wisdom. LR 1.02. 98 P
wrench'd my frame of nature | from the fix'd 1.04.268
some bloody passion shakes your very frame. OTH 5.02. 44
hands, | that yarely frame the office. ANT 2.02.211
that she preparedly may frame herself | to th' 5.01. 55
frame yourself | to orderly /solicits, and be CYM 2.03. 46
that an invisible instinct should frame them 4.02.177
made many princes thither frame | to seek her as PER 1.ch. 32
mistress, either frame | your will to mine — 2.05. 81
do here present this machine, or this frame. TNK 3.05.113
and to her will frame all thy ways, | spare not PP 18.13
those hours that with gentle work did frame SON 5. 1
my body is the frame wherein 'tis held, | and 24. 3
say | to this composed wonder of your frame, 59.10
to bitter sauces did i frame my feeding, | and, 118. 6

FRAMED 3 FR 0.0003 REL FR 2 V 1 P
and here he hath framed a letter to a sequent of LLL 4.02.138 P
i framed to the harp | many an english ditty 1H4 3.01.121
that from the prime creation e'er she framed." R3 4.03. 19

FRAMES 3 FR 0.0003 REL FR 3 V 0 P
no stronger | than faults may shake our frames), MM 2.04.133
that the great figure of a council frames | by AWW 3.01. 12
fear frames disorder, and disorder wounds 2H6 5.02. 32

FRAMING 3 FR 0.0003 REL FR 3 V 0 P
in framing an artist, art hath thus decreed, PER 2.03. 15
swear nature's death for framing thee so fair. VEN 744
fram'd the love, and yet she foil'd the framing, PP 7.15

FRAMPAL 1 FR 0.0001 REL FR 1 V 0 P
now to be frampal, now to piss o' th' nettle! TNK 3.05. 57

FRAMPOLD 1 FR 0.0001 REL FR 0 V 1 P

she leads a very frampold life with him, good WIV 2.02. 90 P
FRANCAIS *(see francois)*
/FRANCE 5 FR 0.0005 REL FR 3 V 2 P
/from /france /there /comes /a /power | /into LR 3.01. 30
/france /spreads /his /banners /in /our 4.02. 56
/why /the /king /of /france /is /so /suddenly 4.03. 1 P
/the /marshal /of /france, /monsieur /la /far. 4.03. 8 P
/touches /us, /as /france /invades /our /land, 5.01. 25
FRANCE 369 FR 0.0417 REL FR 320 V 49 P
let the court of france show me such another. WIV 3.03. 54 P
by gar, 'tis no the fashion of france; 3.03.172 P
it is not jealous in france. 3.03.173 P
where france? ERR 3.02.122 P
the salt rheum that ran between france and it. 3.02.128 P
tell him, the daughter of the king of france, LLL 2.01. 30
breast, | and go well satisfied to france again. 2.01.152
/on saturday we will return to france. 4.01. 6
to a lady of france that he call'd rosaline. 4.01.105
man when king pippen of france was a little boy, 4.01.120 P
shall we resolve to woo these girls of france? 4.03.368
before the legs of this sweet lass of france." 5.02.555
his doublet in italy, his round hose in france, MV 1.02. 75 P
it is the stubbornest young fellow of france, AYL 1.01.143 P
to choose from forth the royal blood of france, AWW 2.01.196
france is a dog-hole, and it no more merits 2.03.274
france is a stable, we that dwell in't jades, 2.03.284
therefore we marvel much our cousin france 3.01. 7
"till i have no wife, i have nothing in france." 3.02. 75 P
nothing in france, until he have no wife! 3.02. 79
"till i have no wife, i have nothing in france." 3.02. 99 P
nothing in france, until he has no wife! 3.02.100
shalt have none, rossillion, none in france; 3.02.101
you came, i think, from france? 3.05. 46
he stole from france, | as 'tis reported, for 3.05. 52
he travel higher, or return again into france? 4.03. 42 P
his lordship will next morning for france. 4.03. 78 P
i am for france. 4.03.318 P
fare ye well, sir, i am for france too. 4.03.329 P
his fisnomy is more hotter in france than there. 4.05. 40 P
sir, i have seen you in the court of france. 5.01. 10
now say, chatillion, what would france with us? JN 1.01. 1
speaks the king of france | in my behavior to 1.01. 2
philip of france, in right and true behalf | of 1.01. 7
so answer france. 1.01. 20
be thou as lightning in the eyes of france; 1.01. 24
would not cease | till she had kindled france, 1.01. 33
i am a soldier, and now bound to france. 1.01.150
richard, we must speed | for france, for france, 1.01.179
we must speed | for france, for france, for it 1.01.179
till angiers, and the right thou hast in france, 2.01. 22
peace be to france — if france in peace permit 2.01. 84
if france in peace permit | our just and lineal 2.01. 84
if not, bleed france, and peace ascend to heaven 2.01. 86
if that war return | from france to england, 2.01. 90
whom hast thou this great commission, france, 2.01.110
who is it thou dost call usurper, france? 2.01.120
i do defy thee, france. 2.01.155
than e'er the coward hand of france can win. 2.01.158
'tis france, for england. 2.01.202
these flags of france, that are advanced here 2.01.207
who by the hand of france this day hath made 2.01.302
crest | that is removed by a staff of france; 2.01.318
france, hast thou yet more blood to cast away? 2.01.334
in this hot trial more than we of france, 2.01.342
by east and west let france and england mount 2.01.381
france, shall we knit our pow'rs, | and lay this 2.01.398
austria and france shoot in each other's mouth. 2.01.414
his | but buffets better than a fist of france. 2.01.465
i see a yielding in the looks of france; 2.01.474
philip of france, if thou be pleas'd withal, 2.01.531
and france, whose armor conscience buckled on, 2.01.564
clapp'd on the outward eye of fickle france, 2.01.583
france friend with england, what becomes of me? 3.01. 35
and with her golden hand hath pluck'd on france 3.01. 57
france is a bawd to fortune and king john, 3.01. 60
tell me, thou fellow, is not france forsworn? 3.01. 62
day | ever in france shall be kept festival. 3.01. 76
philip of france, on peril of a curse, | let go 3.01.191
and raise the power of france upon his head, 3.01.193
look'st thou pale, france? 3.01.195
look to that, devil, lest that france repent, 3.01.196
france, thou mayst hold a serpent by the tongue, 3.01.258
france, thou shalt rue this hour within this 3.01.323
well then, france shall rue. 3.01.325
france, i am burn'd up with inflaming wrath, | a 3.01.340
the blood and dearest-valued blood of france. 3.01.343
o'erbearing interruption, spite of france? 3.04. 9
yet i remember, when i was in france, | young 4.01. 14
how goes all in france? 4.02.109
from france to england. 4.02.110
that such an army could be drawn in france, 4.02.118
how wildly then walks my estate in france! 4.02.128
under whose conduct came those pow'rs of france 4.02.129
the count melune, a noble lord of france, 4.03. 15
hail, noble prince of france! 5.02. 68
since last i went to france to fetch his queen. R2 1.01.131
hie thee to france, | and cloister thee in some 5.01. 22
sometimes queen, prepare thee hence for france. 5.01. 37
with all swift speed you must away to france. 5.01. 54
my wife to france, from whence set forth in pomp 5.01. 78
weep thou for me in france, i for thee here; 5.01. 87
when i from france set foot at ravenspurgh, 1H4 3.02. 95
civil swords and native fire | as far as france. 2H4 5.05.107
make you merry with fair katherine of france, ep 29 P
this cockpit hold | the vasty fields of france? H5 pr 12
as touching france, to give a greater sum | than 1.01. 79
and generally to the crown and seat of france, 1.01. 88
task our thoughts, concerning us and france. 1.02. 6
why the law salique, that they have in france, 1.02. 11
to make against your highness' claim to france 1.02. 36
unjustly gloze | to be the realm of france, and 1.02. 41
law | was not devised for the realm of france; 1.02. 55
make claim and title to the crown of france. 1.02. 68
wearing the crown of france, till satisfied 1.02. 80
great | was re-united to the crown of france. 1.02. 85
so do the kings of france unto this day. 1.02. 90
making defeat on the full power of france, 1.02.107
with half their forces the full pride of france, 1.02.112
and lie pavilion'd in the fields of france. 1.02.129
never went with his forces into france | but 1.02.147
when all her chevalry hath been in france, | and 1.02.157
whom she did send to france | to fill king 1.02.161
old and true, | "if that you will france win, 1.02.167
therefore to france, my liege! 1.02.213
whereof take you one quarter into france, | and 1.02.215
france being ours, we'll bend it to our awe, 1.02.224
o'er france and all her almost kingly dukedoms, 1.02.227
your highness, lately sending into france, | did 1.02.246
there's nought in france | that can be with a 1.02.251
we will in france, by god's grace, play a set 1.02.262
that all the courts of france will be disturb'd 1.02.265
when i do rouse me in my throne of france. 1.02.275
that i will dazzle all the eyes of france, | yea 1.02.279
for we have now no thought in us but france, 1.02.302
see, thy fault france hath in thee found out, 2.pr. 20
have for the gilt of france (o guilt indeed!) 2.pr. 26
confirm'd conspiracy with fearful france, | and 2.pr. 27
their promises, | ere he take ship for france; 2.pr. 30
and thence to france shall we convey you safe, 2.pr. 37
and we'll be all three sworn brothers to france. 2.01. 13 P
we must to france together; 2.01. 91 P
cut their passage through the force of france, 2.02. 16
and sworn unto the practices of france | to kill 2.02. 90
for me, the gold of france did not seduce, 2.02.155
now, lords, for france; 2.02.182
no king of england, if not king of france! 2.02.193
let us to france, like horse-leeches, my boys, 2.03. 55
to view the sick and feeble parts of france; 2.04. 22
ordinance of times, | unto the crown of france. 2.04. 84
that caves and womby vaultages of france | shall 2.04.124
read | in your own losses, if he stay in france. 2.04.139
cull'd and choice-drawn cavaliers to france? 3.pr. 24
les seigneurs de france pour tout le monde. 3.04. 56 P
withal, my lord, | let us not live in france; 3.05. 3
to new-store france with bastard warriors. 3.05. 31
charles delabreth, high constable of france, 3.05. 40
this your air of france | hath blown that vice 3.06.151
though france himself and such another neighbor 3.06.157
is simply the most active gentleman of france. 3.07. 98 P
were better than a churlish turf of france. 4.01. 15
why do you stay so long, my lords of france? 4.02. 38
the constable of france. 4.03. 89
those that leave their valiant bones in france, 4.03. 98
smell whereof shall breed a plague in france. 4.03.103
i was not angry since i came to france | until 4.07. 55
fought a most prave pattle here in france. 4.07. 95 P
as any's in the universal world, or in france, 4.08. 10 P
charles delabreth, high constable of france, 4.08. 92
jacques of chatillion, admiral of france, | the 4.08. 93
great master of france, the brave sir guichard 4.08. 95
where ne'er from france arriv'd more happy men. 4.08.126
the emperor's coming in behalf of france, | to 5.pr. 38
till harry's back-return again to france. 5.pr. 41
your thoughts, straight back again to france. 5.pr. 45
is dead i' th' spittle | of a malady of france, 5.01. 82
unto our brother france, and to our sister, 5.02. 2
great kings of france and england: 5.02. 24
our fertile france, put up her lovely visage? 5.02. 37
alas, she hath from france too long been chas'd, 5.02. 38
it possible dat i sould love de enemy of france? 5.02.170 P
possible you should love the enemy of france, 5.02.172 P
loving me, you should love the friend of france; 5.02.173 P
for i love france so well that i will not part 5.02.173 P
kate, when france is mine and i am yours, then 5.02.175 P
am yours, then yours is france and you are mine. 5.02.176 P
je quand sur le possession de france, et quand 5.02.181 P
donc votre est france et vous etes mienne. 5.02.183 P
de most sage demoiselle dat is en france. 5.02.219 P
ireland is thine, france is thine, and henry 5.02.240 P
leur noces, il n'est pas la coutume de france. 5.02.259 P
is not be de fashon pour les ladies of france — 5.02.262 P
for the maids in france to kiss before they are 5.02.265 P
your majesty demands, that the king of france, 5.02.337 P
henri, roi d'angleterre, heritier de france; 5.02.340 P
the contending kingdoms | of france and england, 5.02.350
bleeding sword 'twixt england and fair france. 5.02.355
bands crown'd king | of france and england, did ep 10
that they lost france, and made his england ep 12
sad tidings bring i to you out of france, | of 1H6 1.01. 58
me they concern, regent i am of france. 1.01. 84
give me my steeled coat, i'll fight for france. 1.01. 85
france is revolted from the english quite, 1.01. 90
thoughts, | wherewith already france is overrun. 1.01.102
whom all france with their chief assembled 1.01.139
bonfires in france forthwith i am to make, | to 1.01.153
drive the english forth the bounds of france. 1.02. 54
wretched shall france be only in my name. 1.04. 97
france, triumph in thy glorious prophetess! 1.06. 8
all france will be replete with mirth and joy, 1.06. 15
before the kings and queens of france. 1.06. 27
coward of france, how much he wrongs his fame, 2.01. 16
and what a terror he had been to france. 2.02. 17
so much applauded through the realm of france? 2.02. 36
is this the scourge of france? 2.03. 15
to cross the seas and to be crown'd in france. 3.01.179
ay, we may march in england, or in france, | not 3.01.186
paysans, la pauvre gens de france, | poor market 3.02. 14
france, thou shalt rue this treason with thy 3.02. 36
that hardly we escap'd the pride of france. 3.02. 40
foul fiend of france, and hag of all despite, 3.02. 52
base muleters of france! 3.02. 68
prick'd on by public wrongs sustain'd in france, 3.02. 78
france were no place for henry's warriors, | nor 3.03. 22
for ever should they be expuls'd from france, 3.03. 25
the princely charles of france, thy countryman. 3.03. 38
brave burgundy, undoubted hope of france, | stay 3.03. 41
look on thy country, look on fertile france, 3.03. 44
eyes, | see, see the pining malady of france! 3.03. 49
besides, all french and france exclaims on thee, 3.03. 60
when talbot hath set footing once in france 3.03. 64
that hath so long been resident in france? 3.04. 14
with charles, the rightful king of france." 4.01. 60
crossing the sea from england into france, 4.01. 89
in france, amongst a fickle, wavering nation. 4.01.138
themselves, and lost the realm of france! 4.01.147
to be our regent in these parts of france; 4.01.163
if he miscarry, farewell wars in france! 4.03. 16
never so needful on the earth of france, | spur 4.03. 18
else farewell talbot, france, and england's 4.03. 23
we mourn, france smiles; 4.03. 32
the fraud of england, not the force of france, 4.04. 36
and soul with soul from france to heaven fly. 4.05. 55
and left us to the rage of france his sword. 4.06. 3
and like me to the peasant boys of france, | to 4.06. 48
of all his wars within the realm of france? 4.07. 71
it were enough to fright the realm of france! 4.07. 82
a phoenix that shall make all france afeard. 4.07. 93
between the realms of england and of france. 5.01. 6
charles, | a man of great authority in france, 5.01. 18
mean | shall be transported presently to france. 5.01. 40
then march to paris, royal charles of france, 5.02. 4
then on, my lords, and france be fortunate! 5.02. 21
me this once, that france may get the field. 5.03. 12
that france must vail her lofty-plumed crest 5.03. 25
now, france, thy glory droopeth to the dust. 5.03. 29
damsel of france, i think i have you fast: 5.03. 30
reignier of france, i give thee kingly thanks, 5.03.163
the utter loss of all the realm of france. 5.04.112
peaceful truce shall be proclaim'd in france, 5.04.117
and of such great authority in france | as his 5.05. 41
therefore shipping, post, my lord, to france, 5.05. 87
i had in charge at my depart for france, | as 2H6 1.01. 2
in presence of the kings of france and sicil, 1.01. 6
from being regent | i' th' parts of france, till 1.01. 67
heat, | to conquer france, his true inheritance? 1.01. 82
receiv'd deep scars in france and normandy? 1.01. 87
how france and frenchmen might be kept in awe, 1.01. 92
defacing monuments of conquer'd france, 1.01.102
for france, 'tis ours; 1.01.106
france should have torn and rent my very heart 1.01.126
she should have stay'd in france, and starv'd in 1.01.135
have stay'd in france, and starv'd in france, 1.01.135
i prophesied france will be lost ere long. 1.01.146
thy late exploits done in the heart of france 1.01.196
which i will win from france, or else be slain. 1.01.213
methinks the realms of england, france, and 1.01.232
for i had hope of france, | even as i have of 1.01.237
and stol'st away the ladies' hearts of france, 1.03. 52
if york have ill demean'd himself in france, 1.03.103
thy sale of offices and towns in france, | if 1.03.135
man | to be your regent in the realm of france. 1.03.161
till france be won into the dolphin's hands. 1.03.170
sent his poor queen to france, from whence she 2.02. 25
through the realm | for soldiers' pay in france, 3.01. 62
welcome, lord somerset. what news from france? 3.01. 83
for i had hope of france | as firmly as i hope 3.01. 87
my lord, that you took bribes of france, | and, 3.01.104
by means whereof his highness hath lost france. 3.01.106
pay, | nor ever had one penny bribe from france. 3.01.109
witness the fortune he hath had in france. 3.01.292
he never would have stay'd in france so long. 3.01.295
to france, sweet suffolk! 3.02.405
by thee anjou and maine were sold to france. 4.01. 86
i go of message from the queen to france; 4.01.114
the lord say, which sold the towns in france; 4.07. 21 P
unto mounsieur basimecu, the dolphin of france? 4.07. 29 P
the giving up of some more towns in france. 4.07.133 P
henry the fift, that made all france to quake, 4.08. 17
will he conduct you through the heart of france, 4.08. 36
to france, to france, and get what you have lost 4.08. 49
to france, to france, and get what you have lost 4.08. 49
on which i'll toss the flow'r-de-luce of france. 5.01. 11
talk not of france, sith thou hast lost it all. 3H6 1.01.110
ay, and their colors, often borne in france, 1.01.127
many a battle have i won in france | when as the 1.02. 73
she-wolf of france, but worse than wolves of 1.04.111
of france, but worse than wolves of france, 1.04.111
his father revell'd in the heart of france, 2.02.150
wash'd his father's fortunes forth of france, 2.02.157
from whence shall warwick cut the sea to france, 2.06. 89
and, having france thy friend, thou shalt not 2.06. 92
my queen and son are gone to france for aid; 3.01. 28
no, mighty king of france; 3.03. 4
it shall be eas'd if france can yield relief. 3.03. 20
what brings thee to france? 3.03. 46
fift, | who by his prowess conquered all france: 3.03. 86
these peers of france should smile at that. 3.03. 91
and better 'twere you troubled him than france. 3.03.155
is this th' alliance that he seeks with france? 3.03.177
that lewis of france is sending over masquers 3.03.224
for mocking marriage with a dame of france. 3.03.255
alas, you know, 'tis far from hence to france; 4.01. 4
as well as lewis of france or the earl of 4.01. 11
yet, to have join'd with france in such alliance 4.01. 36
but the safer when 'tis back'd with france. 4.01. 41
'tis better using france than trusting france. 4.01. 42
'tis better using france than trusting france. 4.01. 42
what letters or what news | from france? 4.01. 85
that lewis of france is sending over masquers 4.01. 94
be sent for, to return from france with speed; 4.06. 61
king of england and france, and lord of ireland, 4.07. 72 P
the queen from france hath brought a puissant 5.02. 31
the friends of france our shrouds and tacklings? 5.04. 18
to the king of france | hath pawn'd the sicils 5.07. 38
away with her, and waft her hence to france. 5.07. 41
i'll win our ancient right in france again, | or R3 3.01. 92
my princely father, then had wars in france, 3.05. 88
lucy, | and his contract by deputy in france, 3.07. 6
as being got, your father then in france, | and 3.07. 10
to bona, sister to the king of france. 3.07.182
to, | and will to france, hoping the consequence 4.04. 6
english woes shall make me smile in france. 4.04.115
lash hence these overweening rags of france, 5.03.328
how have ye done | since last we saw in france? H8 1.01. 2
for france hath flaw'd the league, and hath 1.01. 95
only to show his pomp as well in france | as 1.01.163
england and france might through their amity 1.01.181
for this | is nam'd, your wars in france. 1.02. 60
not long before your highness sped to france, 1.02.151
is't possible the spells of france should juggle 1.03. 1
of fool and feather that they got in france, 1.03. 25
your leave and favor to return to france, | from HAM 1.02. 51
my thoughts and wishes bend again toward france, 1.02. 55
and they in france of the best rank and station 1.03. 73

her brother is in secret come from france, 4.05. 88
since he went into france i have been in 5.02.210 P
attend the lords of france and burgundy, LR 1.01. 34
the princes, france and burgundy, | great rivals 1.01. 45
love | the vines of france and milk of burgundy 1.01. 84
call france. 1.01.126
here's france and burgundy, my noble lord. 1.01.188
is queen of us, of ours, and our fair france. 1.01.257
thou hast her, france, let her be thine, for we 1.01.262
of leave–taking between france and him. 1.01.303 P
and france in choler parted? 1.02. 23
since my young lady's going into france, sir, 1.04. 73 P
why, the hot–bloodied france, that dowerless 2.04.212
which are to france the spies and speculations 3.01. 24
intelligent party to the advantages of france. 3.05. 12 P
the army of france is landed. 3.07. 2 P
sir, what letters had you late from france? 3.07. 42
therefore great france | my mourning and 4.04. 25
am i in france? 4.07. 75
i have seen him in france. CYM 1.04. 11 P
than any the rarest of our ladies in france. 1.04. 61 P
being so far provok'd as i was in france, i 1.04. 67 P
(the factor for the rest) have done | in france. 1.06.189
go you to france or flanders, | to any german STM II.C 127
FRANCE'S 1 FR 0.0001 REL FR 1 V 0 P
but joan de pucelle shall be france's saint. 1H6 1.06. 29
FRANCES 1 FR 0.0001 REL FR 0 V 1 P
o, marry me to one frances! LLL 3.01.121 P
FRANCHIS'D 1 FR 0.0001 REL FR 1 V 0 P
keep | my bosom franchis'd and allegiance clear, MAC 2.01. 28
FRANCHISE *(also enfranchise, etc.)*
FRANCHISE 1 FR 0.0001 REL FR 1 V 0 P
mangled, whose repair and franchise | shall, by CYM 3.01. 56
FRANCHISEMENT 1 FR 0.0001 REL FR 0 V 1 P
a vous donner la liberte, le franchisement. H5 4.04. 53 P
FRANCHISES 1 FR 0.0001 REL FR 1 V 0 P
and | your franchises, whereon you stood, COR 4.06. 86
FRANCIAE 1 FR 0.0001 REL FR 0 V 1 P
noster henricus, rex angliae, et heres franciae. H5 5.02.342 P
FRANCIS 33 FR 0.0037 REL FR 4 V 29 P
go, get you to francis seacole, bid him bring ADO 3.05. 57 P
come, friar francis, be brief — only to the 4.01. 1 P
francis flute, the bellows–mender. MND 1.02. 42 P
at the saint francis here beside the port. AWW 3.05. 36
sir robert waterton, and francis /coint — | all R2 2.01.284
their christen names, as tom, dick, and francis. 1H4 2.04. 8 P
and do thou never leave calling "francis," that 2.04. 32 P
francis! 2.04. 34 P
francis! 2.04. 36 P
come hither, francis. 2.04. 39 P
how long hast thou to serve, francis? 2.04. 41 P
francis! 2.04. 43 P
but, francis, darest thou be so valiant as to 2.04. 46 P
francis! 2.04. 51 P
how old art thou, francis? 2.04. 53 P
francis! 2.04. 56 P
nay, but hark you, francis: 2.04. 58 P
francis! 2.04. 63 P
anon, francis? 2.04. 65 P
no, francis; 2.04. 65 P
but to–morrow, francis; 2.04. 66 P
or, francis, a' thursday; 2.04. 66 P
or indeed, francis, when thou wilt. 2.04. 67 P
but, francis! 2.04. 67 P
for look you, francis, your white canvas doublet 2.04. 74 P
francis! 2.04. 77 P
what's a' clock, francis? 2.04. 96 P
some sack, francis. 2H4 2.04.281 P
look to th' door there, francis. 2.04.353 P
and black george barnes, and francis pickbone, 3.02. 20 P
francis feeble! 3.02.147 P
holy saint francis, what a change is here! ROM 2.03. 65
saint francis be my speed! 5.03.121
FRANCISCAN 1 FR 0.0001 REL FR 1 V 0 P
holy franciscan friar! brother, ho! ROM 5.02. 1
FRANCISCO 2 FR 0.0002 REL FR 1 V 1 P
is he dead, my francisco? WIV 2.03. 28 P
get thee to bed, francisco. HAM 1.01. 7
FRANCOIS 1 FR 0.0001 REL FR 0 V 1 P
sauf votre honneur, le francois que vous parlez, H5 5.02.188 P
FRANK* 11 FR 0.0012 REL FR 9 V 2 P
how now, sweet frank, why art thou melancholy? WIV 2.01.150 P
frank nature, rather curious than in haste, AWW 1.02. 20
thy frank election make; 2.03. 55
doth the old boar feed in the old frank? 2H4 2.02.147 P
therefore with frank and with uncurbed plainness H5 1.02.244
never be the native | of our so frank donation. COR 3.01.130
but to be frank and give it thee again, ROM 2.02.131
old kind father, whose frank heart gave all — LR 3.04. 20
bearing with frank appearance | their purposes OTH 1.03. 38
'tis a good hand, | a frank one. 3.04. 44
and being frank she lends to those are free: SON 4. 4
FRANK'D 2 FR 0.0002 REL FR 2 V 0 P
he is frank'd up to fatting for his pains — R3 1.03.313
my son george stanley is frank'd up in hold; 4.05. 3
FRANKER 1 FR 0.0001 REL FR 1 V 0 P
and duty that i bear you | with franker spirit; OTH 3.03.195
FRANKFORD 1 FR 0.0001 REL FR 0 V 1 P
gone, cost me two thousand ducats in frankford! MV 3.01. 84 P
FRANKLIN 1 FR 0.0001 REL FR 0 V 1 P
there's a franklin in the wild of kent hath 1H4 2.01. 55 P
FRANKLIN'S 1 FR 0.0001 REL FR 1 V 0 P
costlier than would fit | a franklin's huswife. CYM 3.02. 77
FRANKLINS 1 FR 0.0001 REL FR 0 V 1 P
let boors and franklins say it, i'll swear it. WT 5.02.160 P
FRANKLY 10 FR 0.0011 REL FR 9 V 1 P
down for your deliverance | as frankly as a pin. MM 3.01.105
were hid against me, now to forgive me frankly. H8 2.01. 81
speak frankly as the wind, | it is not TRO 1.03.253
half–supp'd sword, that frankly would have fed, 5.08. 19
to be controll'd in that he frankly gave. TIT 1.01.420
men and men's fortunes could i frankly use | as TIM 2.02.179
that very frankly he confess'd his treasons, MAC 1.04. 5
we may of their encounter frankly judge, | and HAM 3.01. 33
and will this brother's wager frankly play. 5.02.253
me another, to make me frankly despise myself. OTH 2.03.298 P
FRANKNESS 1 FR 0.0001 REL FR 0 V 1 P
pardon the frankness of my mirth, if i answer H5 5.02.291 P
FRANTIC 15 FR 0.0017 REL FR 14 V 1 P
go bind this man, for he is frantic too. ERR 4.04.113
to make frantic, lunatic. LLL 5.01. 26 P
the lover, all as frantic, | sees helen's beauty MND 5.01. 10
if that i do not dream, or be not frantic | (as AYL 1.03. 49
i told you, i, he was a frantic fool, | hiding SHR 3.02. 12
makes him speak fondly like a frantic man, | yet R2 3.03.185
thou frantic woman, what dost thou make here? 5.03. 89
let frantic talbot triumph for a while, | and 1H6 3.03. 5
false–boding woman, end thy frantic curse, R3 1.03.246
o, preposterous | and frantic outrage, end thy 2.04. 64
and the beholders of this frantic play, | th' 4.04. 68
sly frantic wretch, that holp'st to make me TIT 4.04. 59
die, frantic wretch, for this accursed deed! 5.03. 64
frantic with grief thus breathes she forth her LUC 762
care, | and frantic mad with evermore unrest; SON 147.10
/FRANTICLY 1 FR 0.0001 REL FR 1 V 0 P
/fie, /how /franticly /i /square /my /talk, TIT 3.02. 31
FRANTICLY 1 FR 0.0001 REL FR 1 V 0 P
dumbly she passions, franticly she doteth, | she VEN 1059
FRATERETTO 1 FR 0.0001 REL FR 0 V 1 P
frateretto calls me, and tells me nero is an LR 3.06. 6 P
FRATRUM 1 FR 0.0001 REL FR 1 V 0 P
a pile | ad /manes fratrum sacrifice his flesh TIT 1.01. 98
FRAUD 6 FR 0.0006 REL FR 6 V 0 P
his heart as far from fraud as heaven from earth TGV 2.07. 78
the fraud of men was ever so, | since summer ADO 2.03. 72
the fraud of england, not the force of france, 1H6 4.04. 36
there shall i rest secure from force and fraud. 3H6 4.04. 33
"it shall be fickle, false, and full of fraud, VEN 1141
kinds | is form'd in them by force, by fraud, or LUC 1243
FRAUDFUL 1 FR 0.0001 REL FR 1 V 0 P
hangs on the cutting short that fraudful man. 2H6 3.01. 81
/FRAUGHT 1 FR 0.0001 REL FR 1 V 0 P
/fraught /with /the /ministers /and /instruments TRO pr 4
FRAUGHT 7 FR 0.0008 REL FR 7 V 0 P
a vessel of our country richly fraught. MV 2.08. 30
took the phoenix and her fraught from candy, TN 5.01. 61
i am so fraught with curious business that | i WT 4.04.514
lo, as the bark that hath discharg'd his fraught TIT 1.01. 71
(whereof i know you are fraught) and put away LR 1.04.220
swell, bosom, with thy fraught, | for 'tis of OTH 3.03.449
if after this command thou fraught the court CYM 1.01.126
/FRAUGHTAGE 1 FR 0.0001 REL FR 1 V 0 P
/there /disgorge | /their /warlike /fraughtage. TRO pr 13
FRAUGHTAGE 1 FR 0.0001 REL FR 1 V 0 P
our fraughtage, sir, | i have convey'd aboard, ERR 4.01. 87
FRAUGHTED 1 FR 0.0001 REL FR 1 V 0 P
o cruel speeding, fraughted with gall. PP 17.16
FRAUGHTING 1 FR 0.0001 REL FR 1 V 0 P
swallow'd and | the fraughting souls within her. TMP 1.02. 13
FRAY 16 FR 0.0018 REL FR 14 V 2 P
there is a fray to be fought between sir hugh WIV 2.01.200 P
you are almost come to part almost a fray. ADO 5.01.114 P
thou part'st a fair fray. LLL 5.02.484
when truth kills truth, o devilish–holy fray! MND 3.02.129
your hands than mine are quicker for a fray; 3.02.342
heavens shield lysander, if they mean a fray! 3.02.447
i view the fight than thou that mak'st the fray. MV 3.02. 62
signior hortensio, come you to part the fray? SHR 1.02. 23
the latter end of a fray and the beginning of a 1H4 4.02. 79
though many dearer, in this bloody fray. 5.04.108
after the bloody fray at wakefield fought, 3H6 2.01.107
right glad i am he was not at this fray. ROM 1.01.117
what fray was here? 1.01.173
where are the vile beginners of this fray? 3.01.141
benvolio, who began this bloody fray? 3.01.151
i heard a bustling rumor, like a fray, | and the JC 2.04. 18
FRAY'D 1 FR 0.0001 REL FR 0 V 1 P
so short, as if she were fray'd with a spirit. TRO 3.02. 32 P
FRAYS 1 FR 0.0001 REL FR 1 V 0 P
and speak of frays | like a fine bragging youth, MV 3.04. 68
FRECKLED 3 FR 0.0003 REL FR 3 V 0 P
a freckled whelp, hag–born) not honor'd with | a TMP 1.02.283
brought sweetly forth | the freckled cowslip, H5 5.02. 49
and freckled nell — that never fail'd her TNK 3.05. 27
FRECKLE–FAC'D 1 FR 0.0001 REL FR 1 V 0 P
o, he that's freckle–fac'd? TNK 4.02.120
FRECKLES 1 FR 0.0001 REL FR 1 V 0 P
favors, | in those freckles live their savors. MND 2.01. 13
FREDERICK 5 FR 0.0005 REL FR 2 V 3 P
heard speak of mariana, the sister of frederick, MM 3.01.210 P
her brother frederick was wrack'd at sea, having 3.01.216 P
one that old frederick, your father, loves. AYL 1.02. 82 P
that calling | to be adopted heir to frederick. 1.02.234
duke frederick, hearing how that every day | men 5.04.154
/FREE 1 FR 0.0001 REL FR 1 V 0 P
/leaving /free /things /and /happy /shows LR 3.06.105
FREE 197 FR 0.0222 REL FR 183 V 14 P
forget | from what a torment i did free thee? TMP 1.02.251
i'll free thee | within two days for this. 1.02.421
delicate ariel, | i'll set thee free for this. 1.02.443
thou shalt be as free | as mountain winds; 1.02.499
shall free thee from the tribute which thou 2.01.293
thought is free." 3.02.123
quickly, spirit, | thou shalt ere long be free. 5.01. 87
bravely, my diligence. thou shalt be free. 5.01.241
set caliban and his companions free; 5.01.252
then to the elements | be free, and fare thou 5.01.319
pardon'd be, | let your indulgence set me free. ep 20
and, that my love may appear plain and free, TGV 5.04. 82
to give me leave | to have free speech with you; MM 1.01. 77
whether thou art tainted or free. 1.02. 43 P
ignomy in ransom and free pardon | are of two 2.04.111
if you'll implore it, that will free your life, 3.01. 65
from our faults, as faults from seeming, free! 3.02. 39
i am your free dependant. 4.03. 91
who is as free from touch or soil with her | as 5.01.141
and now, dear maid, be you as free to us. 5.01.388
free from these slanders and this open shame! ERR 4.04. 67
will you with free and unconstrained soul | give ADO 4.01. 24
a most acute juvenal, volable and free of grace! LLL 3.01. 66
you are not free, | for the lord's tokens on you 5.02.422
no, they are free that gave these tokens to us. 5.02.424
for mine own part, i breathe free breath. 5.02.722 P
shall i say to you, | "let them be free! MV 4.01. 94
more free from peril than the envious court? AYL 2.01. 4
that thou with license of free foot hast caught, 2.07. 68
if he be free, | why then my taxing like a wild 2.07. 85
husband we set his youngest free for a husband, SHR 1.01.138 P
are not the streets as free | for me as for you? 1.02.231
the younger then i? free, and not before. 1.02.262
elder, set the younger free | for our access — 1.02.266
woo, | and free access and favor as the rest; 2.01. 97
and rather than it shall, i will be free, | even 4.03. 79
the fated sky | gives us free scope, only doth AWW 1.01.218
health shall live free, and sickness freely die. 2.01.168
whom i know | is free for me to ask, thee to 2.01.200
me, | whom i myself embrace to set him free." 3.04. 17
now, sir, thought is free. TN 1.03. 69 P
guiltless, and of free disposition, is to take 1.05. 92 P
in voices well divulg'd, free, learn'd, and 1.05.260
and the free maids that weave their thread with 2.04. 45
my remembrance is very free and clear from any 3.04.227 P
i will be free from thee. 4.01. 41
this entertainment | may a free face put on, WT 1.02.112
in every one of these no man is free | but that 1.02.251
infirmities that honesty | is never free of. 1.02.264
from our free person she should be confin'd, 2.01.194
evident | that your free undertaking cannot miss 2.02. 42
innocent soul, | more free than he is jealous. 2.03. 30
which i would free — if i shall be condemn'd 3.02.111
yet we free thee | from the dead blow of it. 4.04.433
see | leontes opening his free arms and weeping 4.04.548
you swear | never to marry but by my free leave? 5.01. 70
mountains and rocks | more free from motion, no, JN 2.01.453
can taste the free breath of a sacred king? 3.01.148
prince, | and free from other misbegotten hate, R2 1.01. 33
from giving reins and spurs to my free speech, 1.01. 55
free speech and fearless i to thee allow. 1.01.123
courageously, and with a free desire, 1.03.115
my claim | to my inheritance of free descent. 2.03.136
as thou liv'st in peace, die free from strife, 5.06. 27
him | up to his pleasure, ransomless and free. 1H4 5.05. 28
i have three pound to free mouldy and bullcalf. 2H4 3.02.244 P
free from gross passion, or of mirth or anger, H5 2.02.132
let gallows gape for dog, let man go free, | and 3.06. 42
sin to think that, making god so free an offer, 4.01.183 P
being free from vainness and self–glorious pride 5.pr. 20
king, | and take with you free power to ratify, 5.02. 86
vocation | and free my country from calamity. 1H6 1.02. 81
o'ercharging your free purses with large fines; 1.03. 64
they set him free without his ransom paid, | in 3.03. 72
go, and be free again, as suffolk's friend. 5.03. 59
my hand would free her, but my heart says no. 5.03. 61
for princes should be free. 5.03.114
you, | if happy england's royal king be free. 5.03.115
free from oppression or the stroke of war, | my 5.03.155
it's sign she hath been liberal and free. 5.04. 82
the purest spring is not so free from mud | as i 2H6 3.01.101
free lords, cold snow melts with the sun's hot 3.01.223
to free us from his father's wrathful curse, | i 3.02.155
loyalty, | free from a stubborn opposite intent, 3.02.251
these hands are free from guiltless 4.07.102
that their wives be as free as heart can wish or 4.07.124 P
and here pronounce free pardon to them all 4.08. 9
and from that torment i will free myself, | or 3H6 3.02.180
to do, | to free king henry from imprisonment, 4.03. 63
and men | to set him free from his captivity. 4.05. 13
but, warwick, after god, thou set'st me free, 4.06. 16
and therefore i yield thee my free consent. 4.06. 36
untainted, unexamin'd, free, at liberty. R3 3.06. 9
if you do free your children from the sword, 5.03.261
with | free pardon to each man that has denied H8 1.02.100
i as free forgive you | as i would be forgiven. 2.01. 82
and free us from his slavery. 2.02. 43
in christian kingdoms) | have their free voices. 2.02. 93
if he know | that i am free of your report, he 2.04. 99
yea, upon mine honor, | i free you from't. 2.04.158
could speak this with as free a soul as i do! 3.01. 32
and to deliver | (like free and honest men) our 3.01. 60
courtiers as free, as debonair, unarm'd, | as TRO 1.03.235
blood | than to make up a free determination 2.02.170
by my place and message, | to be a speaker free. 4.04.131
his heart and hand both open and both free, 4.05.100
thou art too gentle and too free a man. 4.05.139
strike a free march. 5.10. 30
of my son, he should | be free as is the wind. COR 1.09. 89
he did solicit you in free contempt | when he 2.03.200
ask'd, as free | as words to little purpose. 3.02. 88
"thou liest" unto thee with a voice as free | as 3.03. 73
for i dare so far free him — made him fear'd, 4.07. 47
before | but to be rough, unswayable, and free. 5.06. 25
ransomless here we set our prisoners free. TIT 1.01.274
they are free men, but i am banished: ROM 3.03. 42
and this shall free thee from this present shame 4.01.118
my free drift | halts not particularly, but TIM 1.01. 45
stirrup, and through him | drink the free air. 1.01. 83
i'll pay the debt and free him. 1.01.103
grateful virtue i am bound | to your free heart, 1.02. 6
honor, lord lucius | (out of his free love) hath 1.02.182
being free itself, it thinks all others so. 2.02.233
have i been ever free, and must my house | be my 3.04. 80
fly, whilst thou art blest and free. 4.03.535
what thou want'st by free and offer'd light. 5.01. 45
i was born free as caesar, so were you; JC 1.02. 97
brow by night, | when evils are most free? 2.01. 79
nor with such free and friendly conference, | as 4.02. 17
so, i am free; 5.03. 47
free from the bondage you are in, messala; 5.05. 54
let us speak | our free hearts each to other. MAC 1.03.155
defect, | which else should free have wrought. 2.01. 19
free from our feasts and banquets bloody knives; 3.06. 35
do faithful homage and receive free honors; 3.06. 36
the time is free. 5.09. 21
of your audience been most free and bounteous. HAM 1.03. 93
is it a free visitation? 2.02.275 P
make mad the guilty, and appall the free, 2.02.564
but of our demands | most free in his reply. 3.01. 14
your majesty and we that have free souls, it 3.02.242 P
o limed soul, that, struggling to be free, | art 3.03. 68
sword, and thy free awe | pays homage to us — 4.03. 61
most generous, and free from all contriving, 4.07.135
free me so far in your most generous thoughts, 5.02.242
heaven make thee free of it! 5.02.332

no port is free, no place | that guard and most LR 2.03. 3
o, are you free? 2.04.132
when the mind's free, | the body's delicate; 3.04. 11
bear free and patient thoughts. 4.06. 80
i would not my unhoused free condition | put OTH 1.02. 26
for if such actions may have passage free, 1.02. 98
with his free duty recommends you thus, | and 1.03. 41
but the free comfort which from thence he hears; 1.03.213
but to be free and bounteous to her mind. 1.03.265
the moor is of a free and open nature, | that 1.03.399
she is of so free, so kind, so apt, so bless'd a 2.03.320 P
when this advice is free i give, and honest, 2.03.337
she's fram'd as fruitful | as the free elements. 2.03.342
your converse and business | may be more free. 3.01. 39
i am not bound to that all slaves are free /to. 3.03.135
is free of speech, sings, plays, and dances 3.03.185
i would not have your free and noble nature, 3.03.199
and hold her free, i do beseech your honor. 3.03.255
next night well, fed well, was free and merry; 3.03.340
blank of his displeasure | for my free speech! 3.04.129
but well and free, | if thou so yield him, there ANT 2.05. 27
if antony | be free and healthful — so tart a 2.05. 38
of health thou say'st, and thou say'st free. 2.05. 56
free, madam, no; 2.05. 57
i not constrain'd, but did it | on my free will. 3.06. 57
when i did make thee free, swor'st thou not then 4.14. 81
commendation for my more free entertainment. CYM 1.04.155 P
(your lord, i mean) laughs from 's free lungs; 1.06. 68
be, will 's free hours languish for | assured 1.06. 72
did extort | this tribute from us, we were free. 3.01. 48
to pick that bolt, | then free for ever! 5.04. 11
bring'st good news, i am call'd to be made free. 5.04.194 P
of me, | antiochus from incest lived not free; PER 2.04. 2
funeral, | and leave us to our free election. 2.04. 33
would set me free from this unhallowed place, 4.06.100
maintain | i am as worthy and as free a lover, TNK 2.02.179
the free enjoying of that face i die for — | o, 2.03. 3
say i ventur'd | to set him free? 2.04. 31
thebes, | and therein wretched, although free. 3.01. 27
fit for my modest suit and your free granting. 3.06.235
you whose free nobleness do make my cause | your 5.01. 73
free vent of words love's fire doth assuage, VEN 334
or free that soul which wretchedness hath LUC 900
foul deed, my life's fair end shall free it. 1208
me, | from that, alas, thy lucrece is not free. 1624
and being frank she lends to those are free: SON 4. 4
and take thou my oblation, poor but free, 125.10
but thou wilt not, nor he will not be free, 134. 5
me, | he pays the whole, and yet am i not free. 134.14
for maiden–tongu'd he was, and thereof free; LC 100
kept hearts in liveries, but mine own was free, 195

FREED 5 FR 0.0005 REL FR 5 V 0 P
yield him my virginity, | thou mightst be freed! MM 3.01. 98
of great nature thence | freed and enfranchis'd, WT 2.02. 59
no man's pie is freed | from his ambitious H8 1.01. 52
rather than have 'em | freed of this plight, and TNK 1.04. 34
let guiltless souls be freed from guilty woe: LUC 1482

FREEDOM 37 FR 0.0041 REL FR 28 V 9 P
freedom, high–day! TMP 2.02.186 P
high–day, freedom! 2.02.186 P
freedom, high–day, freedom! 2.02.186 P
freedom, high–day, freedom! 2.02.187 P
a heart as willing | as bondage e'er of freedom. 3.01. 89
end, and thou | shalt have the air at freedom. 4.01.265
miss thee, | but yet thou shalt have freedom. 5.01. 96
have the foppery of freedom as the mortality of MM 1.02.133 P
teeth my bonds in sunder, | i gain'd my freedom; ERR 5.01.251
and doth impeach the freedom of the state, | if MV 3.02.278
upon your charter and your city's freedom! 4.01. 39
shall i play my freedom at tray–trip, and become TN 2.05.190 P
i speak it in the freedom of my knowledge: WT 1.01. 11 P
having my freedom, boast of nothing else | but R2 1.03.273
why, what concerns his freedom unto me? 1H6 5.03.116
till you had recover'd your ancient freedom. 2H6 4.08. 27 P
of comfort, kingdom, kindred, freedom, life. R3 4.04.224
now, madam, may his highness live in freedom, H8 1.02.200
you cannot with such freedom purge yourself 5.01.102
i request you | to give my poor host freedom. COR 1.09. 87
and, romans, fight for freedom in your choice. TIT 1.01. 17
seems a–sleeping, | or a keeper with my freedom, TIM 1.02. 68
may | have an immediate freedom of repeal. JC 3.01. 54
freedom! 3.01. 78
out, | "liberty, freedom, and enfranchisement!" 3.01. 81
let's all cry, "peace, freedom, and liberty!" 3.01.110
freedom lives hence, and banishment is here. LR 1.01.181
though age from folly could not give me freedom,
ANT 1.03. 57
the arm'd rest, courtiers of beauteous freedom, 2.06. 17
where i have liv'd at honest freedom, paid CYM 3.03. 71
if of my freedom 'tis the main part, take | no 5.04. 16
nobility enforce a freedom out of bondage, TNK 2.01. 34 P
let that one say so, | and use thy freedom; 2.02.198
your gentle daughter gave me freedom once; 5.04. 24
steal thine own freedom, and complain on theft. VEN 160
my heart mine eye the freedom of that right. SON 46. 4
self, that did in freedom stand | and was my own LC 143

FREEDOMS 1 FR 0.0001 REL FR 1 V 0 P
and | dispropertied their freedoms, holding them COR 2.01.248

FREE–FOOTED 1 FR 0.0001 REL FR 1 V 0 P
this fear, | which now goes too free–footed. HAM 3.03. 26

FREE–HEARTED 1 FR 0.0001 REL FR 0 V 1 P
complete, free–hearted gentleman of athens, thy TIM 3.01. 10 P

FREELIER 1 FR 0.0001 REL FR 0 V 1 P
i should freelier rejoice in that absence COR 1.03. 3 P

FREELY 58 FR 0.0065 REL FR 50 V 8 P
and some donation freely to estate | on the TMP 4.01. 85
that i am freely dissolv'd, and dissolutely. WIV 1.01.251 P
all their petitions are as freely theirs | as MM 1.04. 82
speak freely, syracusian, what thou wilt. ERR 5.01.286
as freely, son, as god did give her me. ADO 4.01. 26
you have no reason, i do it freely. 4.01.258 P
and i must freely have the half of any thing MV 3.02.249
i freely told you all the wealth i had | ran in 3.02.254
we freely cope your courteous pains withal. 4.01.412
any, freely give unto /you this young scholar, SHR 2.01. 78 P
freely have they leave | to stand on either part AWW 1.02. 14
health shall live free, and sickness freely die. 2.01.168
see what may be done, so you confess freely; 4.03.247 P
and thou shalt live as freely as thy lord, | to TN 1.04. 39
most freely i confess, myself and toby | set 5.01.359
a great deal too dear for what's given freely. WT 1.01. 18 P
since it could speak, from an infant, freely, 3.02. 70
hear | the accuser and the accused freely speak. R2 1.01. 17
and lands restor'd again be freely granted. 3.03. 41
now, bagot, freely speak thy mind, | what thou 4.01. 2
my lord, | before i freely speak my mind herein, 4.01.327
that freely rend'red me these news for true. 2H4 1.01. 27
this present peace, | you would drink freely. 4.02. 75
with full mouth | speak freely of our acts, or H5 1.02.231
leave | freely to render what we have in charge? 1.02.238
master, this prisoner freely give i thee, | and 2H6 4.01. 12
then, thy husband's lands i freely give thee. 3H6 3.02. 55
and montague, | speak freely what you think. 4.01. 28
speak freely. H8 1.02.131
or gentleman that is not freely merry | is not 1.04. 36
in committing freely | your scruple to the voice 2.02. 86
scholars allow'd freely to argue for her. 2.02.112
opposing freely | the beauty of her person to 4.01. 67
face to face, | and freely urge against me. 5.02. 83
it is spoke freely out of many mouths — | how COR 4.06. 65
freely, good father. TIM 1.01.110
i gave it freely ever, and there's none | can 1.02. 10
and come freely | to gratulate thy plenteous 1.02.124
may the passive drugs of it | freely /command, 4.03.255
so green and pale | at what it did so freely? MAC 1.07. 38
which have freely gone | with this affair along. HAM 1.02. 15
bent, | to lay our service freely at your feet, 2.02. 31
and the lady shall say her mind freely, or the 2.02.325 P
i embrace it freely, | and will this brother's 5.02.252
my boat sails freely, both with wind and stream. OTH 2.03. 63
confess yourself freely to her; 2.03.318 P
i think it freely; 2.03.329 P
shall have time | to speak your bosom freely. 3.01. 55
therefore confess thee freely of thy sin; 5.02. 53
world | shall bear the olive freely. ANT 4.06. 6
make your full reference freely to my lord, 5.02. 23
prison'd bird, | and sing our bondage freely. CYM 3.03. 44
speak freely. 5.05.119
give answer to this boy, and do it freely, | or, 5.05.131
given me leave to speak, | freely will i speak. PER 1.02.102
who freely give to every one that come | to 2.03. 60
i thank both him and you, and pledge him freely. 2.03. 78
fee, and which i freely lend | to do these poor TNK 1.01.198

FREEMAN 2 FR 0.0002 REL FR 2 V 0 P
now be a freeman, and with this good sword, JC 5.03. 41
could i persuade him to become a freeman, | he TNK 2.06. 24

FREEMEN 1 FR 0.0001 REL FR 0 V 1 P
than that caesar were dead, to live all freemen? JC 3.02. 24 P

FREENESS 1 FR 0.0001 REL FR 1 V 0 P
we'll learn our freeness of a son–in–law: CYM 5.05.421

FREER 5 FR 0.0005 REL FR 3 V 2 P
we shall have the freer wooing at master page's. WIV 3.02. 85 P
never did captive with a freer heart | cast off R2 1.03. 88
their punishment | might have the freer course. LR 4.02. 94
thy freer thoughts | may not fly forth of egypt. ANT 1.05. 11
thou shalt be then freer than a jailer; CYM 5.04.196 P

FREES 1 FR 0.0001 REL FR 1 V 0 P
assaults | mercy itself, and frees all faults. TMP ep 18

FREESTONE–COLORED
1 FR 0.0001 REL FR 1 V 0 P
has a leathern hand, | a freestone–colored hand. AYL 4.03. 25

FREE'T 1 FR 0.0001 REL FR 1 V 0 P
would i could free't! CYM 3.06. 79

FREE–TOWN 1 FR 0.0001 REL FR 1 V 0 P
to old free–town, our common judgment–place. ROM 1.01.102

FREEZE 11 FR 0.0012 REL FR 9 V 2 P
freeze, freeze, thou bitter sky, | that dost not AYL 2.07.184
freeze, freeze, thou bitter sky, | that dost not 2.07.184
greybeard, thy love doth freeze. SHR 2.01.338
soon hot, my very lips might freeze to my teeth, 4.01. 6 P
of all his people, and freeze up their zeal, JN 3.04.150
and cold hearts freeze | allegiance in them; H8 1.02. 61
nay, you must not freeze, | two women plac'd 1.04. 21
made trees, | and the mountain tops that freeze, 3.01. 4
harrow up thy soul, freeze thy young blood, HAM 1.05. 16
upon her, she's able to freeze the god priapus, PER 4.06. 3 P
prince, i shall not then | freeze in my saddle. TNK 2.05. 48

FREEZES 3 FR 0.0003 REL FR 2 V 1 P
tut, thou art all ice, thy kindness freezes. R3 4.02. 22
that almost freezes up the heat of life. ROM 4.03. 16
part burns, and the deceiving part freezes: TNK 4.03. 44 P

FREEZING 2 FR 0.0002 REL FR 2 V 0 P
shall we discourse | the freezing hours away? CYM 3.03. 39
that knows not parching heat nor freezing cold, LUC 1145

FREEZINGS 1 FR 0.0001 REL FR 1 V 0 P
what freezings have i felt, what dark days seen! SON 97. 3

FREIGHT *(see fraught, etc.)*

/FRENCH 1 FR 0.0001 REL FR 0 V 1 P
we'll e'en to't like /french falc'ners — fly at HAM 2.02.430 P

FRENCH 150 FR 0.0169 REL FR 99 V 51 P
french thrift, you rogues — myself and skirted WIV 1.03. 84
the very yea and the no is, the french doctor, 1.04. 94 P
the welsh priest and caius the french doctor. 2.01.201 P
doctor caius, the renown'd french physician. 3.01. 61 P
gallia and gaul, french and welsh, soul–curer 3.01. 97 P
pil'd, as thou art pil'd, for a french velvet. MM 1.02. 34 P
a french crown more. 1.02. 52 P
the french king's daughter with yourself to LLL 1.01.135
and ransom him to any french courtier for a new 1.02. 62 P
will you win your love with a french brawl? 3.01. 9 P
how meanest thou? brawling in french? 3.01. 10 P
why, it is a fairer name than french crown! 3.01.141 P
some of your french crowns have no hair at all; MND 1.02. 97 P
how say you by the french lord, monsieur le /bon MV 1.02. 54 P
he hath neither latin, french, nor italian, and 1.02. 70 P
narrow seas that part | the french and english, 2.08. 29
is like one of our french wither'd pears, it AWW 1.01.161 P
they say our french lack language to deny | if 2.01. 20
as your french crown for your taffety punk, as 2.02. 22 P
to the english, the french ne'er got 'em. 2.03. 95 P
they say the french count has done most 3.05. 3 P
well, diana, take heed of this french earl. 3.05. 12 P
italian, or french, let him speak to me, | i'll 4.01. 72
siege | and merciless proceeding by these french JN 2.01.214
behold, the french amaz'd vouchsafe a parle, 2.01.226
play | upon the dancing banners of the french, 2.01.308
o foul revolt of french inconstancy! 3.01.322
if but a dozen french | were there in arms, they 3.04.173
the french, my lord; 4.02.161
told of a many thousand warlike french | that 4.02.199
now keep your holy word, go meet the french, 5.01. 5
go i to make the french lay down their arms. 5.01. 24
to feast upon whole thousands of the french. 5.02.178
the french fight coldly, and retire themselves. 5.03. 13
put spirit in the french; 5.04. 2
for if the french be lords of this loud day, 5.04. 14
but when he frowned it was against the french, R2 2.01.178
from forth the ranks of many thousand french, 2.03.102
speak it in french, king, say "pardonne moy." 5.03.119
the chopping french we do not understand. 5.03.124
one power against the french, | and one against 2H4 1.03. 71
/to french and welsh he leaves his back unarm'd, 1.03. 79
but who is substituted against the french, | i 1.03. 84
harry ten shillings in french crowns for you. 3.02.221 P
the french embassador upon that instant | crav'd H5 1.01. 91
which salique land the french unjustly gloze 1.02. 40
there left behind and settled certain french; 1.02. 47
nor did the french possess the salique land 1.02. 56
and did seat the french | beyond the river sala, 1.02. 62
who on the french ground play'd a tragedy, 1.02.106
whelp | forage in blood of french nobility. 1.02.110
we must not only arm t' invade the french, | but 1.02.136
the french, advis'd by good intelligence | of 2.pr. 12
and now to our french causes. 2.02. 60
the patterns that by god and by french fathers 2.04. 61
th' embassador from the french comes back, 3.pr. 28
and fortify it strongly 'gainst the french. 3.03. 53
the french is gone off, look you, and there is 3.06. 92 P
none of the french upbraided or abus'd in 3.06.111 P
i have | almost no better than so many french; 3.06.147
like a kern of ireland, your french hose off, 3.07. 53 P
the confident and overlusty french | do the 4.pr. 18
be friends, we have french quarrels enow, if you 4.01.223 P
indeed the french may lay twenty french crowns 4.01.225 P
may lay twenty french crowns to one they will 4.01.226 P
it is no english treason to cut french crowns, 4.01.228 P
the english are embattled, you french peers. 4.02. 14
that our french gallants shall to–day draw out, 4.02. 22
the french are bravely in their battles set, 4.03. 69
gay new coats o'er the french soldiers' heads 4.03.118
ask me this slave in french | what is his name. 4.04. 23
discuss the same in french unto him. 4.04. 29 P
i do not know the french for fer, and ferret, 4.04. 30 P
the french might have a good prey of us, if he 4.04. 75 P
all's not done — yet keep the french the field. 4.06. 2
the french have reinforc'd their scatter'd men. 4.06. 36
here comes the herald of the french, my liege. 4.07. 66
here is the number of the slaught'red french. 4.08. 74
this note doth tell me of ten thousand french 4.08. 80
as yet the lamentation of the french | invites 5.pr. 36
and, princes french, and peers, health to you 5.02. 8
against the french that met them in their bent 5.02. 16
you will love me soundly with your french heart, 5.02.105 P
i will tell thee in french, which i am sure will 5.02.178 P
the kingdom as to speak so much more french. 5.02.186 P
i shall never move thee in french, unless it be 5.02.186 P
compound a boy, half french, half english, that 5.02.208 P
endeavor for your french part of such a boy; 5.02.214 P
majestee ave fausse french enough to deceive de 5.02.218 P
now fie upon my false french! 5.02.220 P
them than in the tongues of the french council; 5.02.277 P
see many a fair french city for one fair french 5.02.318 P
city for one fair french maid that stands in my 5.02.318 P
and with this addition, in french, notre tres 5.02.339 P
that english may as french, french englishmen, 5.02.367
that english may as french, french englishmen, 5.02.367
or shall we think the subtile–witted french 1H6 1.01. 25
unto the french the dreadful judgment day | so 1.01. 29
wounds will i lend the french in stead of eyes, 1.01. 87
betwixt the stout lord talbot and the french. 1.01.106
by three and twenty thousand of the french | was 1.01.113
the french exclaim'd, the devil was in arms; 1.01.125
now for the honor of the forlorn french! 1.02. 19
'tis the french dolphin sueth to thee thus. 1.02.112
here, said they, is the terror of the french, 1.04. 42
gone, | remember to avenge me on the french." 1.04. 94
my lord, my lord, the french have gather'd head. 1.04.100
if underneath the standard of the french | she 2.01. 23
besides, all french and france exclaims on thee, 3.03. 60
and that the french were almost ten to one, 4.01. 21
ten thousand french have ta'en the sacrament 4.02. 28
maz'd with a yelping kennel of french curs! 4.02. 47
upon my death the french can little boast; 4.05. 24
into the clust'ring battle of the french; 4.07. 13
had death been french, then death had died 4.07. 28
so, rushing in the bowels of the french, | he 4.07. 42
'tis a mere french word; 4.07. 54
and turn again unto the warlike french. 5.02. 3
before that england give the french the foil. 5.03. 23
perhaps i shall be rescu'd by the french, | and 5.03.104
betwixt our nation and the aspiring french; 5.04. 99
our sovereign and the french king charles, | for 2H6 1.01. 41
it is agreed between the french king charles, 1.01. 44 P
anjou and maine are given to the french, | paris 1.01.214
anjou and maine both given unto the french! 1.01.236
let somerset be regent o'er the french, 1.03.205
boys went to span–counter for french crowns), i 4.02.158 P
and more than that, he can speak french, and 4.02.167 P
the fearful french, whom you late vanquished, 4.08. 42
who made the dolphin and the french to stoop, 3H6 1.01.108
thither gone to crave the french king's sister 3.01. 30
cog, | duck with french nods and apish courtesy, R3 1.03. 49
to–day the french, | all clinquant, all in gold, H8 1.01. 18
upon this french going out, took he upon him 1.01. 73
the peace between the french and us not values 1.01. 88
the londoners | concerning the french journey. 1.02.155
men fear the french would prove perfidious, | to 1.02.156
a french song and a fiddle has no fellow. 1.03. 41
you can speak the french tongue; 1.04. 57
see this main end, | the french king's sister. 2.02. 41
th' bishop of bayonne, then french embassador, 2.04.173
duchess of alanson, | the french king's sister; 3.02. 86
there's a french salutation to your french slop. ROM 2.04. 44 P
there's a french salutation to your french slop. 2.04. 44 P

come hither for stealing out of a french hose. MAC 2.03. 14 P
seen myself, and serv'd against, the french, HAM 4.07. 83
as i take it, six french rapiers and poniards, 5.02.149 P
six barb'ry horses against six french swords, 5.02.161 P
that's the french bet against the danish. 5.02.163 P
do you know the french knight that cow'rs i' the PER 4.02.105 P

FRENCH–CROWN–COLOR 1 FR 0.0001 REL FR 0 V 1 P
beard, or your french–crown–color beard, your MND 1.02. 95 P

FRENCHMAN 13 FR 0.0014 REL FR 8 V 5 P
i have heard the frenchman hath good skill in WIV 2.01.222 P
to be a dutchman to–day, a frenchman to–morrow, ADO 3.02. 33 P
i think the frenchman became his surety and MV 1.02. 82 P
i reason'd with a frenchman yesterday, | who 2.08. 27
which is the frenchman? AWW 3.05. 77
one captain dumaine be i' th' camp, a frenchman; 4.03.176 P
who's that? a frenchman? 4.05. 38 P
before the frenchman speak a word of it. H5 1.01. 97
done like a frenchman — turn and turn again! 1H6 3.03. 85
imagine him a frenchman, and thy foe. 4.07. 26
varnish on the fame | the frenchman gave you, HAM 4.07.133
there is a frenchman his companion, one | an CYM 1.06. 64
to be by | and hear him mock the frenchman. 1.06. 76

FRENCHMAN'S 1 FR 0.0001 REL FR 1 V 0 P
than you should stoop unto a frenchman's mercy. 2H6 4.08. 48

FRENCHMEN 13 FR 0.0014 REL FR 12 V 1 P
or die, be you the sons | of worthy frenchmen. AWW 2.01. 12
since frenchmen are so braid, | marry that will, 4.02. 73
of english legs | did march three frenchmen. H5 3.06.150
one, | and view the frenchmen how they fortify. 1H6 1.04. 61
frenchmen, i'll be a salisbury to you. 1.04.106
we'll try what these dastard frenchmen dare. 1.04.111
us, | this happy night the frenchmen are secure, 2.01. 11
hath at least five frenchmen died to–night. 2.02. 9
the regent conquers, and the frenchmen fly. 5.03. 1
as little shall the frenchmen gain thereby. 5.04.115
peace, | and keep the frenchmen in allegiance. 5.05. 43
how france and frenchmen might be kept in awe, 2H6 1.01. 92
the frenchmen are our enemies. 4.02.169 P

FRENCHMEN'S 5 FR 0.0005 REL FR 5 V 0 P
wade to the market–place in frenchmen's blood, JN 2.01. 42
hither return all gilt with frenchmen's blood. 2.01.316
if i to–day die not with frenchmen's rage, 1H6 4.06. 34
did flesh his puny sword in frenchmen's blood! 4.07. 36
is talbot slain, the frenchmen's only scourge, 4.07. 77

FRENCHWOMAN 2 FR 0.0002 REL FR 2 V 0 P
yea, i it was, proud frenchwoman. 2H6 1.03.140
fell clifford, and thee, false frenchwoman. 3H6 1.04.149

FRENZIES 1 FR 0.0001 REL FR 1 V 0 P
life–poisoning pestilence, and frenzies wood, VEN 740

FRENZY 12 FR 0.0013 REL FR 11 V 1 P
him, master /brook, that ever govern'd frenzy. WIV 5.01. 19 P
and, yielding to him, humors well his frenzy. ERR 4.04. 81
the poet's eye, in a fine frenzy rolling, | doth MND 5.01. 12
blood, | and melancholy is the nurse of frenzy. SHR in.2. 133
a most extracting frenzy of mine own | from my TN 5.01.281
the lady constance in a frenzy died | three days JN 4.02.122
behold, /distraction, frenzy, and amazement, TRO 5.03. 85
unless some fit or frenzy do possess her; TIT 4.01. 17
his fits, his frenzy, and his bitterness? 4.04. 12
that | from one bad thing to worse, not frenzy, CYM 4.02.134
where, in a frenzy, in my master's garments 5.05.282
and his untimely frenzy thus awaketh: LUC 1675

FRENZY'S 1 FR 0.0001 REL FR 1 V 0 P
mouldeth goblins swift as frenzy's thoughts. TRO 5.10. 29

FREQUENT 4 FR 0.0004 REL FR 3 V 1 P
from court and is less frequent to his princely WT 4.02. 32 P
for there, they say, he daily doth frequent, R2 5.03. 6
basest groom | that doth frequent your house. PER 4.06.191
that i have frequent been with unknown minds, SON 117. 5

FREQUENTS 1 FR 0.0001 REL FR 1 V 0 P
thy creature, | by night frequents my house. TIM 1.01.117

/FRESH 2 FR 0.0002 REL FR 2 V 0 P
/the /fresh /and /yet /unbruised /greeks /do TRO pr 14
/with /a /bridegroom's /fresh /alacrity | /let 4.04.145

FRESH 101 FR 0.0114 REL FR 88 V 13 P
some food we had, and some fresh water, that | a TMP 1.02.160
the fresh springs, brine–pits, barren place and 1.02.338
garments are now as fresh as when we put them on 2.01. 69 P
garments seem now as fresh as when we were at 2.01. 98 P
my doublet as fresh as the first day i wore it? 2.01.103 P
'tis fresh morning with me | when you are by at 3.01. 33
use such vigilance | as when they are fresh. 3.03. 17
and these fresh nymphs encounter every one | in 4.01.137
spy | more fresh in julia's with a constant eye? TGV 5.04.115
the luce is the fresh fish, the salt fish is an WIV 1.01. 22 P
a wither'd servingman a fresh tapster. 1.03. 18 P
with the story of the prodigal, fresh and new. 4.05. 8 P
ever your fresh whore and your powder'd bawd, an MM 3.02. 59 P
to those fresh morning drops upon the rose, | as LLL 4.03. 26
when their fresh rays have smote | the night of 4.03. 27
fall in the fresh lap of the crimson rose, | and MND 2.01.108
sighs of love, that costs the fresh blood dear. 3.02. 97
with coronet of fresh and fragrant flowers; 4.01. 52
joy and fresh days of love | accompany your 5.01. 29
you meet in some fresh cheek the power of fancy, AYL 3.05. 29
who gave me fresh array and entertainment, 4.03.143
budding virgin, fair, and fresh, and sweet, SHR 4.05. 37
if thou beest yet a fresh uncropped flower, AWW 5.03.327
o spirit of love, how quick and fresh art thou, TN 1.01. 9
which she would keep fresh | and lasting in her 1.01. 30
and then 'twas fresh in murmur (as, you know, 1.02. 32
of great estate, of fresh and stainless youth; 1.05.259
to be, cast thy humble slough and appear fresh. 2.05.149 P
tempests are kind and salt waves fresh in love. 3.04.384
physics the subject, makes old hearts fresh. WT 1.01. 39 P
fresh horses! 3.01. 21
and thou, fresh piece | of excellent witchcraft, 4.04.422
kisses the hands | of your fresh princess; 4.04.551
whose fresh complexion and whose heart together 4.04.574
how green you are and fresh in this old world! JN 3.04.145
fresh expectation troubled not the land | with 4.02. 7
the fresh green lap of fair king richard's land, R2 3.03. 47
and wash him fresh again with true–love tears. 5.01. 10
fresh as a bridegroom, and his chin new reap'd 1H4 1.03. 34
hast thou lost the fresh blood in thy cheeks, 2.03. 44
some six or seven fresh men set upon us — 2.04.181 P
thus did i keep my person fresh and new, | my 3.02. 55
as many fresh streams meet in one salt sea; H5 1.02.209
your fresh fair virgins and your flow'ring 3.03. 14
move | with casted slough and fresh legerity. 4.01. 23
shall we go send them dinners and fresh suits, 4.02. 57
besides, they all are fresh. 4.03. 4
brave duke, thy friendship makes us fresh. 1H6 3.03. 86
who finds the heifer dead and bleeding fresh, 2H6 3.02.188
his wonted sleep under a fresh tree's shade, 3H6 2.05. 49
and prince shall follow with a fresh supply. 3.03.237
and ever since a fresh admirer | of what i saw H8 1.01. 3
a very fresh fish here — fie, fie, fie upon 2.03. 86
alter'd that the old name | is fresh about me. 4.01. 99
fresh kings are come to troy; TRO 2.03.261
here art thou in appointment fresh and fair, 4.05. 1
fresh embassies and suits, | nor from the state COR 5.03. 17
as fresh as morning dew distill'd on flowers? TIT 2.03.201
then fresh tears | stood on her cheeks, as doth 3.01.111
long | till the fresh taste be taken from that 3.01.128
with tears augmenting the fresh morning's dew, ROM 1.01.132
among fresh fennel buds shall you this night 1.02. 29
thou ever young, fresh, lov'd, and delicate TIM 4.03.384
good gentlemen, look fresh and merrily; JC 2.01.224
for i am fresh of spirit, and resolv'd | to meet 5.01. 90
new supplies of men, | began a fresh assault. MAC 1.02. 33
of sleep | we put fresh garments on him. LR 4.07. 21
inflame it and to give satiety a fresh appetite, OTH 2.01.228 P
indeed she's a most fresh and delicate creature. 2.03. 20 P
the changes of the moon | with fresh suspicions? 3.03.179
/her name, that was as fresh | as dian's visage, 3.03.386
the fresh streams ran by her, and murmur'd her 4.03. 44
spirits a time, | to be more fresh, reviving. CYM 1.05. 42
fresh lily, | and whiter than the sheets! 2.02. 15
whose remembrance | is yet fresh in their grief. 2.04. 15
'tis their fresh supplies. 5.02. 16
'tis strange he hides him in fresh cups, soft 5.03. 71
of this poor infant, this fresh new sea–farer, PER 3.01. 41
to–night, | for look how fresh she looks! 3.02. 79
therefore let's have fresh ones, what e'er we 4.02. 10 P
give me fresh garments. 5.01.214
thousand fresh water–flowers of several colors, TNK 4.01. 85
making them red and pale with fresh variety — VEN 21
dainties to taste, fresh beauty for the use, 164
when in his fresh array | he cheers the morn, 483
whose blood upon the fresh flowers being shed 665
semblance he hath fed | upon fresh beauty, 796
love's gentle spring doth always fresh remain, 801
flowers are sweet, their colors fresh and trim, 1079
with their fresh falls' haste | add to his flow, LUC 650
but now that fair fresh mirror, dim and old, 1760
with young adonis, lovely, fresh, and green, PP 4. 2
thou that art now the world's fresh ornament, SON 1. 9
whose fresh repair if now thou not renewest, 3. 3
and that fresh blood which youngly thou 11. 3
and in fresh numbers number all your graces, 17. 6
since first i saw you fresh, which yet are green 104. 8
of this most balmy time | my love looks fresh, 107.10
so that eternal love in love's fresh case 108. 9
fresh to myself, if i had self–applied | love to LC 76
in whose fresh regard | weak sights their sickly 213

FRESH–BROOK 1 FR 0.0001 REL FR 1 V 0 P
thy food shall be | the fresh–brook mussels, TMP 1.02.464

FRESHER 10 FR 0.0011 REL FR 9 V 1 P
not a blemish, | but fresher than before; TMP 1.02.219
too, | hast thou beheld a fresher gentlewoman? SHR 4.05. 29
i have held familiarity with fresher clothes; AWW 5.02. 3 P
air, | and thou art flying to a fresher clime. R2 1.03.285
they'll be in fresher robes, or they will pluck H5 4.03.117
there's fresher air, my lord, | in the next H8 1.04.101
for it grows again | fresher than e'er it was, 2.01.155
i would have been much more a fresher man, | had TRO 5.06. 20
fresher than may, sweeter | than her gold TNK 3.01. 5
some fresher stamp of the time–bettering days. SON 82. 8

FRESHES 1 FR 0.0001 REL FR 1 V 0 P
i'll not show him | where the quick freshes are. TMP 3.02. 67

FRESHEST 3 FR 0.0003 REL FR 3 V 0 P
turn then my freshest reputation to | a savor WT 1.02.420
i do | to th' freshest things now reigning, and 4.01. 13
to accomplish, | my best and freshest men; COR 5.06. 34

FRESHLY 8 FR 0.0009 REL FR 5 V 3 P
we, in all our trim, freshly beheld | our royal, TMP 5.01.236
the drowsy and neglected act | freshly on me — MM 1.02.171
looks he as freshly as he did the day he AYL 3.02.230 P
but freshly looks, and overbears attaint | with H5 4.pr. 39
be in their flowing cups freshly rememb'red. 4.03. 55
witness, | yet freshly pitied in our memories. H8 5.02. 66
be jointed to the old stock, and freshly grow; CYM 5.04.143 P
be jointed to the old stock, and freshly grow; 5.05.440 P

FRESHNESS 2 FR 0.0002 REL FR 1 V 1 P
notwithstanding their freshness and glosses, TMP 2.01. 63 P
whose youth and freshness | wrinkles apollo's, TRO 2.02. 78

FRET* 15 FR 0.0017 REL FR 13 V 2 P
good sister, let us dine, and never fret; ERR 2.01. 6
do not fret yourself too much in the action, MND 4.01. 13 P
look not big, nor stamp, nor stare, nor fret, SHR 3.02.228
wounded steeds | fret fetlock deep in gore, and H5 4.07. 79
let henry fret, and all the world repine. 1H6 5.02. 20
so york must sit, and fret, and bite his tongue, 2H6 1.01.230
rave, and fret, that i may sing and dance. 3H6 1.04. 91
'twere something that would fret the string, H8 3.02.105
that fret the clouds are messengers of day. JC 2.01.104
fret till your proud heart break; 4.03. 42
me what instrument you will, though you fret me, HAM 3.02.371 P
with cadent tears fret channels in her cheeks, LR 1.04.285
pure shame and aw'd resistance made him fret, VEN 69
eyes like glow–worms shine when he doth fret, 621
abide, | and with the wind in greater fury fret. LUC 648

FRETFUL 3 FR 0.0003 REL FR 2 V 1 P
john, you are so fretful you cannot live long. 1H4 3.03. 11 P
though parting be a fretful corrosive, | it is 2H6 3.02.403
contending with the fretful elements; LR 3.01. 4

FRETS* 10 FR 0.0011 REL FR 9 V 1 P
i did but tell her she mistook her frets, | and SHR 2.01.149
devilish spirit, | "frets, call you these?" 2.01.152
horse, and he frets like a gumm'd velvet. 1H4 2.02. 2 P
and take no care | who chafes, who frets, or MAC 4.01. 91
that struts and frets his hour upon the stage, 5.05. 25
he frets | that lepidus of the triumpherate ANT 3.06. 27
which he frets at rather | than any jot obeys; TNK 5.04. 70
still is he sullen, still he low'rs and frets, VEN 75
foul cank'ring rust the hidden treasure frets, 767
these means, as frets upon an instrument, LUC 1140

FRETTED* 5 FR 0.0005 REL FR 3 V 2 P
clothes that fretted in their own grease. WIV 3.05.113 P
till they have fretted us a pair of graves R2 3.03.167
this majestical roof fretted with golden fire, HAM 2.02.301 P
his fretted fortunes give him hope and fear | of ANT 4.12. 8
th' chamber | with golden cherubins is fretted. CYM 2.04. 88

FRETTEN 1 FR 0.0001 REL FR 1 V 0 P
when they are fretten with the gusts of heaven; MV 4.01. 77

FRETTING 4 FR 0.0004 REL FR 4 V 0 P
command these fretting waters from your eyes MM 4.03.146
'twas a commodity lay fretting by you; SHR 2.01.328
and he may well in fretting spend his gall — 1H6 1.02. 16
as doth a sail, fill'd with a fretting gust, 3H6 2.06. 35

FRIAR 80 FR 0.0090 REL FR 62 V 18 P
by the bare scalp of robin hood's fat friar, TGV 4.01. 36
at friar patrick's cell, | where i intend holy 4.03. 43
that silvia at friar patrick's cell should meet 5.01. 3
for friar laurence met them both, | as he in 5.02. 37
may formally in person bear | like a true friar. MM 1.03. 48
i am the provost. what's your will, good friar? 2.03. 2
bless you, good father friar. 3.02. 12 P
bless you, friar. 3.02. 77 P
what news abroad, friar? 3.02. 83 P
what news, friar, of the duke? 3.02. 86 P
something too crabbed that way, friar. 3.02. 98 P
but it is impossible to extirp it quite, friar, 3.02.103 P
thou art deceiv'd in me, friar. 3.02.169 P
farewell, good friar, i prithee pray for me. 3.02.180 P
so please you, this friar hath been with him, 3.02.212 P
good friar, i know you do, and have found it. 4.01. 53
friar, not i; 4.03. 53 P
this letter then to friar peter give; 4.03.137
good even. friar, where's the provost? 4.03.149 P
friar, thou knowest not the duke so well as i do 4.03.161 P
nay, friar, i am a kind of bur, i shall stick. 4.03.179 P
i would friar peter — 4.06. 9
o, peace, the friar is come. 4.06. 9
one that i would were here, friar lodowick. 5.01.125
my lord, i know him, 'tis a meddling friar. 5.01.127
this' a good friar, belike! 5.01.131
let this friar be found. 5.01.133
but yesternight, my lord, she and that friar, 5.01.134
a saucy friar, | a very scurvy fellow. 5.01.135
know you that friar lodowick that she speaks of? 5.01.143
good friar, let's hear it. 5.01.162
is this the witness, friar? 5.01.167
thou foolish friar, and thou pernicious woman, 5.01.241
there is another friar that set them on, | let 5.01.248
not you say you knew that friar lodowick to be a 5.01.260 P
we shall find this friar a notable fellow. 5.01.267 P
why, thou unreverend and unhallowed friar, 5.01.305
for the friar and you | must have a word anon. 5.01.358
do you the office, friar, which consummate, 5.01.378
hither, isabel, | your friar is now your prince. 5.01.382
there was a friar told me of this man. 5.01.479
friar, advise him, | i leave him to your hand. 5.01.485
come, friar francis, be brief — only to the ADO 4.01. 1 P
friar, you come to marry her. 4.01. 7 P
stand thee by, friar. 4.01. 23
friar! 4.01.114
friar, it cannot be. 4.01.170
signior leonato, let the friar advise you, | and 4.01.244
friar, i must entreat your pains, i think. 5.04. 18
in which, good friar, i shall desire your help. 5.04. 31
call her forth, brother, here's the friar ready. 5.04. 39
before this friar, and swear to marry her. 5.04. 57
give me your hand before this holy friar — | i 5.04. 58
soft and fair, friar. which is beatrice? 5.04. 72
"it was the friar of orders grey, | as he forth SHR 4.01.145
whom he supposes to be a friar, from the time of AWW 4.03.109 P
go thou to friar /penker; R3 3.05.104
sir, a chartreux friar, | his confessor, who fed H8 1.02.148
and there she shall at friar lawrence' cell | be ROM 2.04.181
then hie you hence to friar lawrence' cell, 2.05. 68
o friar, the damned use that word in hell; 3.03. 47
o holy friar, o tell me, holy friar, | where's 3.03. 81
o holy friar, o tell me, holy friar, | where's 3.03. 81
o, tell me, friar, tell me, | in what vile part 3.03.105
i'll to the friar to know his remedy; 3.05.241
tell me not, friar, that thou hearest of this, 4.01. 50
i'll send a friar with speed | to mantua, with 4.01.123
what, is my daughter gone to friar lawrence? 4.02. 11
now, afore god, this reverend holy friar, | all 4.02. 31
what if it be a poison which the friar 4.03. 24
dost thou not bring me letters from the friar? 5.01. 13
hast thou no letters to me from the friar? 5.01. 31
holy franciscan friar! brother, ho! 5.02. 1
this same should be the voice of friar john. 5.02. 2
friar john, go hence, | get me an iron crow, and 5.02. 20
o comfortable friar! 5.03.148
here is a friar, that trembles, sighs, and weeps 5.03.184
a great suspicion. stay the friar too. 5.03.187
here is a friar, and /slaughter'd romeo's man, 5.03.199
but he which bore my letter, friar john, | was 5.03.250

FRIAR'S 2 FR 0.0002 REL FR 1 V 1 P
as the nun's lip to the friar's mouth, nay, as AWW 2.02. 27 P
this letter doth make good the friar's words, ROM 5.03.286

FRIARS 1 FR 0.0001 REL FR 1 V 0 P
and all the priests and friars in my realm 1H6 1.06. 19

FRIDAY 3 FR 0.0003 REL FR 1 V 2 P
me | upon good friday and ne'er broke his fast. JN 1.01.235
soul that thou soldest him on good friday last, 1H4 1.02.115 P
would be as fair a' friday as helen is on sunday TRO 1.01. 76 P

FRIDAYS 2 FR 0.0002 REL FR 0 V 2 P
say to thee again) would eat mutton on fridays. MM 3.02.182 P
faith, will i, fridays and saturdays and all. AYL 4.01.116 P

/FRIEND 4 FR 0.0004 REL FR 3 V 1 P
command, i mean, /friend. TRO 3.01. 25 P
/the /friend /hath /lost /his /friend, | /and LR 5.03. 55
/the /friend /hath /lost /his /friend, | /and 5.03. 55
/do, /good /my /friend. in happy time, iago. OTH 3.01. 30

FRIEND 452 FR 0.0511 REL FR 352 V 100 P
thy case, dear friend, | shall be my president: TMP 2.01.290
art foresees the danger | that you, his friend, 2.01.298
you cannot tell who's your friend. 2.02. 85 P
voice now is to speak well of his friend; 2.02. 91 P
be not afeard — thy good friend trinculo. 2.02.102 P
more that i may call men than you, good friend, 3.01. 51
first, noble friend, | let me embrace thine age, 5.01.120
else | betideth here in absence of thy friend; TGV 1.01. 59
deliver'd by a friend that came from him. 1.03. 54
unto the secret, nameless friend of yours; 2.01.105
that's the letter i writ to her friend. 2.01.160 P
to wrong my friend, i shall be much forsworn. 2.06. 3
i to myself am dearer than a friend, | for love 2.06. 23
enemy, | aiming at silvia as a sweeter friend. 2.06. 30
know, worthy prince, sir valentine, my friend, 3.01. 10
to cross my friend in his intended drift, | than 3.01. 18
for love of you, not hate unto my friend, | hath 3.01. 46
to match my friend sir thurio to my daughter. 3.01. 62
friend valentine, a word. 3.01.205
from hence, from silvia, and from me thy friend. 3.01.220
by one whom she esteemeth as his friend. 3.02. 37
gentleman, | especially against his very friend. 3.02. 41
being entreated to it by your friend. 3.02. 45
to hate young valentine and love my friend. 3.02. 65
she twits me with my falsehood to my friend; 4.02. 8
yet valentine thy friend | survives, to whom, 4.02.108
your servant and your friend; 4.03. 4
"friend," quoth i, "you mean to whip the dog?" 4.04. 25 P
thou counterfeit to thy true friend! 5.04. 53
in love | who respects friend? 5.04. 54
uncivil touch, | thou friend of an ill fashion! 5.04. 61
thou common friend, that's without faith or love 5.04. 62
faith or love, | for such is a friend now! 5.04. 63
now i dare not say | i have one friend alive; 5.04. 66
all foes that a friend should be the worst! 5.04. 72
here is got's plessing, and your friend, and WIV 1.01. 75 P
may be beholding to his friend for a man. 1.01.273 P
alas! he speaks but for his friend. 1.04.114 P
honest, and gentle, and one that is your friend; 1.04.140 P
servingman, and friend simple by your name, 3.01. 2 P
if fortune thy foe were not, nature thy friend. 3.03. 65 P
but if you have a friend here, convey, convey 3.03.117 P
there is a gentleman, my dear friend; 3.03.122 P
fenton, | i will not be your friend nor enemy. 3.04. 89
there is a friend of mine come to town, tells me 4.05. 76 P
one word, good friend. lucio, a word with you. MM 1.02.142
i thank you, good friend lucio. 1.02.192
he hath got his friend with child. 1.04. 29
where were you born, friend? 2.01.193 P
friend hast thou none, | for thine own bowels, 3.01. 28
here's a gentleman, and a friend of mine. 3.02. 42 P
when | the steeled jailer is the friend of men. 4.02. 87
our old and faithful friend, we are glad to see 5.01. 2
thanks, good friend escalus, for thy much 5.01.528
me | as if i were their well-acquainted friend, ERR 4.03. 2
you have done wrong to this my honest friend, 5.01. 19
buried some dear friend? 5.01. 50
if any friend will pay the sum for him, | he 5.01.131
haply i see a friend will save my life, | and 5.01.284
there is a fat friend at your master's house, 5.01.415
do, good friend. ADO 1.01. 92 P
my dear friend leonato hath invited you all. 1.01.148 P
the sixt of july. your loving friend, benedick. 1.01.283 P
o, i cry you mercy, friend, go you with me, and 1.02. 26 P
lady, will you walk about with your friend? 2.01. 87 P
give not this rotten orange to your friend, 4.01. 32
to link my dear friend to a common stale. 4.01. 65
a very even way, but no such friend. 4.01.264 P
or that i had any friend would be a man for my 4.01.318 P
what is your name, friend? 4.02. 10 P
i will never love that which my friend hates. 5.02. 70 P
forester, my friend, where is the bush | that we LLL 4.01. 7
he's a good friend of mine. 4.01. 54
my familiar, i do assure ye, very good friend; 5.01. 96 P
tongue, | nor never come in vizard to my friend, 5.02.404
i'll change my black gown for a faithful friend. 5.02.834
but, gentle friend, for love and courtesy | lie MND 2.02. 56
and good night, sweet friend. 2.02. 60
to join with men in scorning your poor friend? 3.02.216
and the death of a dear friend, would go near to 5.01.288 P
yet, to supply the ripe wants of my friend, MV 1.03. 63
take | a breed for barren metal of his friend? 1.03.134
very wisely to me, "my honest friend launcelot, 2.02. 15 P
your worship's friend and launcelot, sir. 2.02. 56 P
friend launcelot, what's the news? 2.04. 9
what, and my old venetian friend salerio? 3.02.219
i pray you tell me how my good friend doth. 3.02.233
some dear friend dead, else nothing in the world 3.02.245
indeed | i have engag'd myself to a dear friend, 3.02.261
friend, | engag'd my friend to his mere enemy, 3.02.262
lady, | the paper as the body of my friend, 3.02.264
is it your dear friend that is thus in trouble? 3.02.291
the dearest friend to me, the kindest man, | the 3.02.292
before a friend of this description | shall lose 3.02.301
wife, | and then away to venice to your friend; 3.02.304
when it is paid, bring your true friend along. 3.02.308
but let me hear the letter of your friend. 3.02.314
repent but you that you shall lose your friend, 4.01.278
i and my friend | have by your wisdom been this 4.01.408
a friend. 5.01. 26
a friend! 5.01. 27
what friend? 5.01. 27
your name, i pray you, friend? 5.01. 27
my friend /stephano, signify, i pray you, 5.01. 51
give welcome to my friend; 5.01.133
had held up the very life | of my dear friend. 5.01.215
peace, i say. good even to /you, friend. AYL 2.04. 69
is not so sharp | as friend rememb'red not. 2.07.189
vows | 'twixt the souls of friend and friend; 3.02.134
vows | 'twixt the souls of friend and friend; 3.02.134
good ev'n, gentle friend. 5.01. 16 P
how old are you, friend? 5.01. 18 P
i have been politic with my friend, smooth with 5.04. 45 P
of all | my best beloved and approved friend, SHR 1.02. 3
my old friend grumio! 1.02. 21 P
and my good friend petruchio! 1.02. 21 P
and tell me now, sweet friend, what happy gale 1.02. 48
but th' art too much my friend, | and i'll not 1.02. 63
now shall my friend petruchio do me grace, | and 1.02.131
no, say'st me so, friend? what countryman? 1.02.189
how now, my friend, why dost thou look so pale? 2.01.142
is't possible, friend litio, that mistress 4.02. 1
and keep thy friend | under thy own life's key. AWW 1.01. 66
loves, | a mother, and a mistress, and a friend, 1.01.167
wherein our dearest friend | prejudicates the 1.02. 7
he that loves my flesh and blood is my friend; 1.03. 49 P
ergo, he that kisses my wife is my friend. 1.03. 50 P
sir, i am a poor friend of yours that loves you. 2.02. 43 P
this is your devoted friend, sir, the manifold 4.03.235 P
ever a friend whose thoughts more truly labor 4.04. 17
you have them ill to friend | till your deeds 5.03.182
not a friend, not a friend greet | my poor TN 2.04. 61
a friend, not a friend greet | my poor corpse, 2.04. 61
'save thee, friend, and thy music! 3.01. 1 P
thy friend, as thou usest him, and thy sworn 3.04.169 P
in leaving his friend here in necessity and 3.04.387 P
i prithee, gentle friend, | let thy fair wisdom, 4.01. 51
th' other for some while a friend. WT 1.02.108
mine honest friend, | will you take eggs for 1.02.160
now my sworn friend and then mine enemy; 1.02.167
good expedition be my friend, and comfort | the 1.02.458
and ingratitude | to you and toward your friend, 3.02. 69
the minister to poison | my friend polixenes; 3.02.161
now, my fair'st friend, | i would i had some 4.04.112
to make you garlands of, and my sweet friend, 4.04.128
you have ever been my father's honor'd friend, 4.04.493
farewell, my friend. 4.04.659
give you all greetings that a king, at friend, 5.01.140
by your desires, | i am friend to them and you. 5.01.231
may swear it in the behalf of his friend; 5.02.163 P
in sooth, good friend, your father might have JN 1.01.123
france friend with england, what becomes of me? 3.01. 35
or the light loss of england for a friend. 3.01.206
and, my good friend, thy voluntary oath | lives 3.03. 23
good friend, thou hast no cause to say so yet, 3.03. 30
i'll tell thee what, my friend, | he is a very 3.03. 60
alas, i then have chid away my friend! 4.01. 86
he show'd his warrant to a friend of mine. 4.02. 70
a friend. what art thou? 5.06. 2
thou art my friend that know'st my tongue so 5.06. 8
to a dear friend of the good duke of york's R2 3.04. 70
but that is lost for being richard's friend; 5.02. 42
"have i no friend will rid me of this living 5.04. 2
"have i no friend?" 5.04. 4
i am the king's friend, and will rid his foe. 5.04. 11
tell me, gentle friend, | how went he under him? 5.05. 81
here is /a dear, a true industrious friend, 1H4 1.01. 62
for i shall never hold that man my friend 1.03. 90
so much land | to any well-deserving friend; 3.01.136
once, | enlarg'd him and made a friend of him, 3.02.115
every man | shall be my friend again, and i'll 5.01.108
bell, | rememb'red tolling a departing friend. 2H4 1.01.103
for fault of a better, to call my friend — i 2.02. 42 P
the part of a careful friend and a true subject, 2.04.322 P
good master corporate bardolph, stand my friend, 3.02.221 P
for my old dame's sake, stand my friend. 3.02.230 P
enemy, | he doth unfasten so and shake a friend, 4.01.207
till his friend sickness /have determin'd me? 4.05. 81
a friend i' th' court is better than a penny in 5.01. 30 P
the knave is mine honest friend, sir, therefore 5.01. 50 P
o, good my lord, you have lost a friend indeed, 5.02. 27
sir john, i am thy pistol and thy friend, | and 5.03. 93
there stands your friend for the devil; H5 3.07.118 P
a friend. 4.01. 36 P
art thou his friend? 4.01. 58
a friend. 4.01. 92 P
disorder, that hath spoil'd us, friend us now! 4.05. 17
angers, look you, kill his best friend, clytus. 4.07. 38 P
as alexander kill'd his friend clytus, being in 4.07. 45 P
man challenge this, he is a friend to alanson, 4.07.156 P
he is my dear friend, and please you. 4.07.166 P
him, he's a friend of the duke alanson's. 4.08. 17 P
i will tell you asse my friend, captain gower: 5.01. 4 P
loving me, you should love the friend of france; 5.02.173 P
his crown shall be the ransom of my friend; 1H6 1.01.150
thou art no friend to god or to the king. 1.03. 25
wherefore is charles impatient with his friend? 2.01. 54
richard plantagenet, my friend, is he come? 2.05. 34
see, noble charles, the beacon of our friend, 3.02. 29
go, and be free again, as suffolk's friend. 5.03. 59
thou art no father nor no friend of mine. 5.04. 9
and no great friend, i fear me, to the king. 2H6 1.01.150
'tis like you would not feast him like a friend, 3.02.184
tell me, my friend, art thou the man that slew 5.01. 71
if friend or foe, let him be gently used. 3H6 2.06. 45
and, having france thy friend, thou shalt not 2.06. 92
our earl of warwick, edward's greatest friend. 3.03. 45
my lord and sovereign and thy vowed friend, | i 3.03. 50
before thy coming, lewis was henry's friend. 3.03.143
and still is friend to him and margaret. 3.03.144
and joy that thou becom'st king henry's friend. 3.03.201
so much his friend, ay, his unfeigned friend, 3.03.202
so much his friend, ay, his unfeigned friend, 3.03.202
so long as edward is thy constant friend | and 4.01. 77
were but a feigned friend to our proceedings. 4.02. 11
the lord hastings, the king's chiefest friend. 4.03. 11
what news, my friend? 4.06. 77
our trusty friend, unless i be deceiv'd. 4.07. 41
how thou canst, have wind and tide thy friend, 5.01. 53
come to me, friend or foe, | and tell me who is 5.02. 5
i never sued to friend nor enemy; R3 1.02.167
my friend, i spy some pity in thy looks. 1.04.263
when i have most need to employ a friend, | and 2.01. 36
friend, | and most assured that he is a friend, 2.01. 37
and at the other is my good friend catesby; 3.02. 22
dar'st thou resolve to kill a friend of mine? 4.02. 69
some light-foot friend post to the duke of 4.04.440
hath any well-advised friend proclaim'd | reward 4.04.515
will leave us never an understanding friend. H8 pr 22
be to yourself | as you would to your friend. 1.01.136
that is not freely merry | is not my friend. 1.04. 37
what friend of mine | that had to him deriv'd 2.04. 31
foe, and think not | at all a friend to truth. 2.04. 84
or be a known friend, 'gainst his highness' 3.01. 85
be more | to me, your friend, than any. 3.02.190
cranmer will find a friend will not shrink from 4.01.107
with th' king, and truly | a worthy friend. 4.01.110
stand these poor people's friend, and urge the 4.02.157
to't, give your friend | some touch of your late 5.01. 12
and thy integrity is rooted | in us, thy friend. 5.01.115
i thank you, | you are always my good friend; 5.02. 94
a shrewd turn, and he's your friend for ever." 5.02.211
the gods are above, time must friend or end. TRO 1.02. 78 P
friend, you! 3.01. 1 P
friend, know me better, i am the lord pandarus. 3.01. 11 P
not so, friend. 3.01. 16 P
at whose pleasure, friend? 3.01. 23 P
friend, we understand not one another; 3.01. 27 P
my dear lord and most esteem'd friend, your 3.01. 64 P
and i'll grow friend with danger. 4.04. 70
ajax hath lost a friend, | and foams at mouth, 5.05. 35
note me this, good friend: COR 1.01.127
thy friend no less | than those she placeth 1.05. 23
we hope to find you our friend; 2.03.104 P
him joy, and make him good friend to the people! 2.03.135 P
be that you seem, truly your country's friend, 3.01.217
i prithee, noble friend, home to thy house; 3.01.233
what would you have, friend? 4.05. 7 P
and more a friend than e'er an enemy; 4.05.146
but as a discontented friend, grief-shot | with 5.01. 44
friend, | art thou certain this is true? 5.04. 43
whose friend in justice thou hast ever been, TIT 1.01.180
deeds | a father and a friend to thee and rome. 1.01.423
lose not so noble a friend on vain suppose, 1.01.440
i found a friend, and sure as death i swore | i 1.01.487
she is thy enemy, and i thy friend. 5.02. 29
speak, rome's dear friend, as erst our ancestor, 5.03. 80
and op'd their arms to embrace me as a friend. 5.03.108
my very friend, hath got this mortal hurt | in ROM 3.01.110
not romeo, prince, he was mercutio's friend; 3.01.184
o tybalt, tybalt, the best friend i had! 3.02. 61
a sin-absolver, and my friend profess'd, | to 3.03. 50
law that threat'ned death becomes thy friend, 3.03.139
we'll keep no great ado — a friend or two, 3.04. 23
thou gone so, love — lord, ay, husband, friend! 3.05. 43
loss, but not the friend | which you weep for. 3.05. 75
i cannot choose but ever weep the friend. 3.05. 77
and you be mine, i'll give you to my friend; 3.05.191
the world is not thy friend, nor the world's law 5.01. 72
here's one, a friend, and one that knows you 5.03.123
tell me, good my friend, | what torch is yond, 5.03.124
to shake off | my friend when he must need me. TIM 1.01.101
what have you there, my friend? 1.01.154
make thy requests to thy friend. 1.01.269 P
i could wish my best friend at such a feast. 1.02. 79 P
happier is he that has no friend to feed | than 1.02.203
mine honest friend, | i prithee but repair to me 2.02. 24
contain thyself, good friend. 2.02. 26
some good necessity | touches his friend, which 2.02.228
thou disease of a friend, and not himself! 3.01. 53
he is my very good friend, and an honorable 3.02. 2 P
virtuous lord, my very exquisite friend. 3.02. 29 P
him | his friend that dips in the same dish? 3.02. 66
bounties over me | to mark me for his friend; 3.02. 79
what do ye ask of me, my friend? 3.04. 45
fortune to lie heavy | upon a friend of mine, 3.05. 11
friend, or brother, | he forfeits his own blood 3.05. 86
ah, my good friend, what cheer? 3.06. 40 P
not | one friend to take his fortune by the arm, 4.02. 7
i am thy friend, and pity thee, dear timon. 4.03. 98
lord, but therefore | came not my friend nor i. 5.01. 79
i met a courier, one mine ancient friend, | whom 5.02. 6
a hand | over your friend that loves you. JC 1.02. 36
till then, my noble friend, chew upon this: 1.02.171
i do know him by his gait, | he is a friend. 1.03.133
lest some friend of caesar's | should chance — 3.01. 87
soft, who comes here? a friend of antony's. 3.01.122
i know that we shall have him well to friend. 3.01.143
then, in a friend, it is cold modesty. 3.01.213
and in the pulpit, as becomes a friend, | speak 3.01.229
in this assembly, any dear friend of caesar's, 3.02. 18 P
if then that friend demand why brutus rose 3.02. 20 P
he was my friend, faithful and just to me; 3.02. 85
a plain blunt man | that love my friend, and 3.02.219
as a friend or an enemy? 3.03. 21 P
as a friend. 3.03. 22 P
thou hast describ'd | a hot friend cooling. 4.02. 19
a friend should bear his friend's infirmities; 4.03. 86
whether yond troops are friend or enemy. 5.03. 18
to see my best friend ta'en before my face! 5.03. 35
a foe to tyrants, and my country's friend. 5.04. 5
marcus brutus, i, | brutus, my country's friend; 5.04. 8
this is not brutus, friend, but, i assure you, 5.04. 26
that's not an office for a friend, my lord. 5.05. 29
hail, brave friend! MAC 1.02. 5
a friend. 2.01. 11
was it so late, friend, ere you went to bed, 2.03. 22
and to our dear friend banquo, whom we miss; 3.04. 89
as i shall find the time to friend, i will. 4.03. 10
and let thine eye look like a friend on denmark. HAM 1.02. 69
sir, my good friend — i'll change that name 1.02.163
for /loan oft loses both itself and friend, 1.03. 76
"good sir," or so, or "friend," or "gentleman," 2.01. 46
but as your daughter may conceive, friend, look 2.02.185 P
o, old friend! 2.02.422 P
dost thou hear me, old friend? 2.02.537 P
for who not needs shall never lack a friend, 3.02.207
and who in want a hollow friend doth try, 3.02.208
liberty if you deny your griefs to your friend. 3.02.339 P
swoopstake, you will draw both friend and foe, 4.05.143
and you must put me in your heart for friend, 4.07. 2
remember him hereafter as my honorable friend. LR 1.01. 28 P
how now, my noble friend? 2.01. 86
our good old friend, | lay comforts to your 2.01.125
good dawning to thee, friend. art of this house? 2.02. 1 P
i am sorry for thee, friend, 'tis the /duke's 2.02.152
the king grows mad, i'll tell thee, friend, | i 3.04.165
i lov'd him, friend, | no father his son dearer; 3.04.168
come hither, friend; 3.06. 86
good friend, i prithee take him in thy arms; 3.06. 88
and drive toward dover, friend, where thou shalt 3.06. 91
good friend, be gone, | thy comforts can do me 4.01. 15
come hither, friend, | tell me what more thou 4.02. 96

here, friend, 's another purse; 4.06. 28
friend! 4.06. 46
take that of me, my friend, who have the power 4.06.169
come, father, i'll bestow you with a friend. 4.06.286
'tis noble kent, your friend. 5.03.269
and bade me, if i had a friend that lov'd her, OTH 1.03.164
i have profess'd me thy friend, and i confess me 1.03.337 P
this likewise is a friend. 2.01. 95
dost thou hear, mine honest friend? 3.01. 21 P
no, i hear not your honest friend; i hear you. 3.01. 22 P
thou dost conspire against thy friend, iago, 3.03.142
cassio's my worthy friend — | my lord, i see y' 3.03.223
and from hence | i'll love no friend, sith love 3.03.380
my friend is dead; 3.03.474
'save you, friend cassio! 3.04.169
this is some token from a newer friend; 3.04.181
or to be naked with her friend in bed | an hour, 4.01. 3
good friend, go to him; 4.02.150
my friend and my dear countryman | roderigo! 5.01. 89
lies slain here, cassio, | was my dear friend. 5.01.102
my friend, thy husband, honest, honest iago. 5.02.154
"good friend," quoth he, | "say the firm roman ANT 1.05. 42
my honorable friend, agrippa! 2.02.173 P
prithee, friend, | pour out the pack of matter 2.05. 53
how now, friend eros? 3.05. 1 P
she | from egypt drive her all–disgraced friend, 3.12. 22
please, our master | will leap to be his friend; 3.13. 51
i'll give thee, friend, | an armor all of gold; 4.08. 26
come, we have no friend | but resolution and the 4.15. 90
friend and companion in the front of war, | the 5.01. 44
you, | that we remain your friend, and so adieu. 5.02.189
who to my father was a friend, to me | known but CYM 1.01. 98
your son's my father's friend, he takes his part 1.01.165
whom i commend to you as a noble friend of mine. 1.04. 32 P
i profess myself her adorer, not her friend. 1.04. 69 P
had i admittance, and opportunity to friend. 1.04.106 P
you are a friend, and therein the wiser. 1.04.134 P
boldness be my friend! 1.06. 18
say his name, good friend. 4.02.376
who dares not stand his foe, i'll be his friend; 5.03. 60
thy friend? 5.05.111
no, friend, cannot you beg? PER 2.01. 63 P
hark you, my friend. you said you could not beg? 2.01. 85 P
o, not all, my friend, not all; 2.01. 91 P
but hark you, my friend, 'twas we that made up 2.01.148 P
only, my friend, i yet am unprovided | of a pair 2.01.160
how his longing | follows his friend: TNK 1.03. 27
both heaven and earth | friend thee for ever! 1.04. 2
your friend and i have chanc'd to name you here, 2.01. 16 P
have i call'd thee friend? 2.02.182
griefs, angers, fears, my friend shall suffer? 2.02.188
false–self and thy friend had but this fortune 2.02.207
why should a friend be treacherous? 2.02.229
to the games, my friend. 2.03. 62
and you, emilia — and you, friend — and all — 2.05. 49
my friend, carry your tail without offense | or 3.05. 34
friend, you must eat no white bread; 3.05. 80
trod thy ground, | a falser nev'r seem'd friend. 3.06.142
o' my conscience, | was never soldier's friend. 4.02. 88
pray speak him, friend. 4.02. 91
honor'd friend, | to you i give the field; 4.02.149
good friend, be royal. 4.02.154
fix'd her liking on this gentleman, my friend. 4.03. 65 P
take upon you, young sir her friend, the name of 4.03. 76 P
ah ha, my friend, my friend! 5.04. 23
ah ha, my friend, my friend! 5.04. 23
if you'll stand our friend to procure our pardon STM II.C 143 P
so white a friend engirts so white a foe: VEN 364
on shore | gazing upon a late embarked friend, 818
or were he not my dear friend, this desire LUC 234
but as he is my kinsman, my dear friend, | the 237
"but if thou yield, i rest thy secret friend: 526
"my husband is thy friend, for his sake spare me 582
wilt thou be the humble suppliant's friend, 897
myself thy friend will kill myself thy foe, 1196
here friend by friend in bloody channel lies, 1487
here friend by friend in bloody channel lies, 1487
and friend to friend gives unadvised wounds, 1488
and friend to friend gives unadvised wounds, 1488
for being both to me, both to each friend, | i PP 2.11
o yes, dear friend, i pardon crave of thee, 10.11
one that flatters thee | is no friend in misery. 20.30
every man will be thy friend, | whilst thou hast 20.33
he that is thy friend indeed, | he will help 20.49
to know | faithful friend from flatt'ring foe. 20.56
but if the while i think on thee, dear friend, SON 30.13
suff'ring my friend for my sake to approve her. 42. 8
and losing her, my friend hath found that loss; 42.10
my friend and i are one; 42.13
far the miles are measur'd from thy friend." 50. 4
in true plain words by thy true–telling friend; 82.12
to me, fair friend, you never can be old, | for 104. 1
grind | on newer proof, to try an older friend, 110.11
pity me then, dear friend, and i assure ye 111.13
for that deep wound it gives my friend and me! 133. 2
but slave to slavery my sweet'st friend must be? 133. 4
use, | and sue a friend came debtor for my sake, 134.11
but being both from me, both to each friend, | i 144.11
who hateth thee that i do call my friend? 149. 5

FRIENDED 3 FR 0.0003 REL FR 3 V 0 P

for the fault's love is th' offender friended. MM 4.02.113
not friended by his wish, to your high person; H8 1.02.140
and be friended | with aptness of the season; CYM 2.03. 47

FRIENDING 1 FR 0.0001 REL FR 1 V 0 P

do, t' express his love and friending to you, HAM 1.05.185

FRIENDLESS 1 FR 0.0001 REL FR 1 V 0 P

alas, i am a woman, friendless, hopeless! H8 3.01. 80

FRIENDLINESS 1 FR 0.0001 REL FR 1 V 0 P

of such childish friendliness | to yield your COR 2.03.175

FRIENDLY 38 FR 0.0043 REL FR 33 V 5 P

will, | and not depending on his friendly wish. TGV 1.03. 62
no, truly, but in friendly recompense. ADO 5.04. 83
it is not friendly, 'tis not maidenly. MND 3.02.217
the fiend gives the more friendly counsel: MV 2.02. 31 P
for i must tell you friendly in your ear, | sell AYL 3.05. 59
and give them friendly welcome every one. SHR in.1. 103
be so far forth friendly maintain'd till by 1.01.136 P
and in my house you shall be friendly lodg'd. 4.02.108
and let me buy your friendly help thus far, AWW 3.07. 15
i will seem friendly, as thou hast advis'd me. WT 1.02.350
(a prosperous south–wind friendly) we have 5.01.161
this friendly treaty of our threat'ned town? JN 2.01.481
let's drink together friendly and embrace, 2H4 4.02. 63
argument, look you, and friendly communication; H5 3.02. 98 P
goes, | for friendly counsel cuts off many foes. 1H6 3.01.184
to draw conditions of a friendly peace, | which 5.01. 38
give me assurance with some friendly vow, | that 3H6 4.01.141
desire | to reconcile me to his friendly peace. R3 2.01. 60
that which company | would not be friendly to. H8 5.01. 76
you into love, | standing your friendly lord. COR 2.03.190
and take our friendly senators by th' hands, 4.05.132
and going | about their functions friendly. 4.06. 9
will ye bestow them friendly on andronicus? TIT 1.01.219
did you not use his daughter very friendly? 4.02. 40
and left no friendly drop | to help me after? ROM 5.03.163
which looks like man | is friendly with him. TIM 5.01.119
heart before, | to say thou't enter friendly. 5.04. 49
nor with such free and friendly conference, | as JC 4.02. 17
a friendly eye could never see such faults. 4.03. 90
the gods to–day stand friendly, that we may, 5.01. 93
now, my friendly knave, i thank thee, there's LR 1.04. 93 P
now let thy friendly hand | put strength enough 4.06.230
my lord and you again | as friendly as you were. OTH 3.03. 7
to sicily and did find | her welcome friendly. ANT 2.06. 46
receive it friendly; CYM 3.05. 13
and a british ensign wave | friendly together. 5.05.481
not see thee, or else look friendly upon thee. PER 4.06. 89 P
sorrow that friendly sighs sought still to dry; VEN 964

FRIEND'S 9 FR 0.0010 REL FR 6 V 3 P

and, for your friend's sake, will be glad of you TGV 3.02. 63
follow your friend's counsel. WIV 3.03.138 P
made this match, and his friend's reputation, ADO 2.02. 38 P
have some countenance at his friend's request. 2H4 5.01. 45 P
i weigh my friend's affection with mine own. TIM 1.02.216
a friend should bear his friend's infirmities; JC 4.03. 86
hast such noble sense of thy friend's wrong! OTH 5.01. 32
"had my friend's muse grown with this growing SON 32.10
but then my friend's heart let my poor heart 133.10

FRIENDS' 4 FR 0.0004 REL FR 4 V 0 P

you envy my advancement and my friends'. R3 1.03. 74
set them upright at their dear friends' door, TIT 5.01.136
spurn to their graves | of their friends' gift? TIM 1.02.142
i have known frights, fury, friends' behests, TNK 1.04. 40

/FRIENDS 5 FR 0.0005 REL FR 3 V 2 P

left and abandoned of his velvet /friends: AYL 2.01. 50
even to that drop ten thousand wiry /friends JN 3.04. 64
the day, my /friends, and all things stay for me H5 4.01.309
/what /have /you, /my /good /friends, /deserv'd HAM 2.02.240 P
/diffidences, /banishment /of /friends, LR 1.02.148 P

FRIENDS 489 FR 0.0552 REL FR 413 V 76 P

the wrack of all my friends, nor this man's TMP 1.02.489
what harmony is this? my good friends, hark! 3.03. 18
welcome, my friends all! 5.01.125
he leaves his friends to dignify them more; TGV 1.01. 64
i /leave myself, my friends, and all, for love. 1.01. 65
what maintenance he from his friends receives, 1.03. 68
what say you to a letter from your friends | of 2.04. 51
your friends are well and have them much 2.04.123
that stays to bear my letters to my friends, 3.01. 53
but she i mean is promis'd by her friends | unto 3.01.106
my friends — 4.01. 7
'twere pity two such friends should be long foes 5.04.118
it is petter that friends is the sword, and end WIV 1.01. 42 P
grated upon my good friends for three reprieves 2.02. 7 P
in hell for swearing to gentlemen my friends, 2.02. 11 P
i desire you that we may be friends; 3.01.118 P
well money'd, and his friends | potent at court. 4.04. 88
dow'r | remaining in the coffer of her friends, MM 1.02.151
that she made friends | to the strict deputy; 1.02.180
his friends still wrought reprieves for him; 4.02.135 P
your friends, sir — the hangman. 4.03. 26 P
there's other of our friends | will greet us 4.05. 12
try all the friends thou hast in ephesus; ERR 1.01.152
i will hold friends with you, lady. ADO 1.01. 91 P
what is it, my good friends? 3.05. 8 P
nor my bad life reft me so much of friends, 4.01.196
mind, | ability in means, and choice of friends, 4.01.199
we'll be friends first. 4.01.297 P
you dare easier be friends with me than fight 4.01.298 P
come, come, we are friends. 5.04.117 P
you'll ne'er be friends with him, 'a kill'd your LLL 5.02. 13
only to part friends. 5.02.220
i must needs be friends with thee. 5.02.549
since to wail friends lost | is not by much so 5.02.749
as to rejoice at friends but newly found. 5.02.751
or else it stood upon the choice of friends — MND 1.01.139
to seek new friends and /stranger /companies. 1.01.219
i grant you, friends, if you should fright the 1.02. 79 P
honest neighbors will not make them friends. 3.01.146 P
good morrow, friends. 4.01.139
joy, gentle friends, joy and fresh days of love 5.01. 29
and farewell, friends; 5.01.345
sweet friends, to bed. 5.01.368
give me your hands, if we be friends, | and 5.01.437
if worthier friends had not prevented me. MV 1.01. 61
lend it not | as to thy friends, for when did 1.03.133
i would be friends with you, and have your love, 1.03.138
for we have friends | that purpose merriment. 2.02.202
sweet friends, your patience for my long abode; 2.06. 21
nine a' clock — our friends all stay for you. 2.06. 63
thwarted my bargains, cool'd my friends, heated 3.01. 57 P
sweet a bar | should sunder such sweet friends. 3.02.120
i might in virtues, beauties, livings, friends, 3.02.156
leave, | i bid my very friends and countrymen, 3.02.223
bid your friends welcome, show a merry cheer — 3.02.312
and in the hearing of these many friends | i 5.01.241
i shall do my friends no wrong, for i have none AYL 1.02.189 P
or, if we did derive it from our friends, 1.03. 62
that your poor friends must woo your company? 2.07. 10
and content is without three good friends; 3.02. 26 P
back, friends! 3.02.158 P
lord, it is a hard matter for friends to meet; 3.02.184 P
my friends told me as much, and i thought no 4.01.183 P
put you in your best array, bid your friends; 5.02. 72 P
such friends as time in padua shall beget. SHR 1.01. 45
since this bar in law makes us friends, it shall 1.01.136 P
house and ply his book, welcome his friends, 1.01.196
i take my leave | to see my friends in padua, 1.02. 2
'twixt such friends as we | few words suffice; 1.02. 65
strive mightily, but eat and drink as friends. 1.02.277
make friends, invite, and proclaim the banes, 3.02. 16
gentlemen and friends, i thank you for your 3.02.184
neighbors and friends, though bride and 3.02.246
might with effects of them follow our friends, AWW 1.01.184
when thou hast none, remember thy friends. 1.01.214 P
i am out a' friends, madam, and i hope to have 1.03. 39 P
and i hope to have friends for my wive's sake. 1.03. 40 P
such friends are thine enemies, knave. 1.03. 41 P
madam — in great friends, for the knaves come 1.03. 42 P
my friends were poor, but honest, so's my love. 1.03.195
the coming space, | expecting absent friends. 2.03.182
i pray you make us friends, i will pursue the 2.05. 13 P
sent him forth | from courtly friends, with 3.04. 14
you, and take your leave of all your friends. 4.03.312 P
let the justices make you and fortune friends; 5.02. 34 P
destroy our friends and after weep their dust; 5.03. 64
what country, friends, is this? TN 1.02. 1
now good morrow, friends. 2.04. 1
belong you to the lady olivia, friends? 5.01. 8 P
better for my foes and the worse for my friends. 5.01. 13 P
just the contrary: the better for thy friends. 5.01. 14 P
of myself, and by my friends i am abus'd; 5.01. 20 P
the worse for my friends and the better for my 5.01. 23 P
though it please you to be one of my friends. 5.01. 26 P
you bid | these unknown friends to 's welcome, WT 4.04. 65
for it is | a way to make us better friends, 4.04. 66
and, friends unknown, you shall bear witness 4.04.384
yourself, assisted with your honor'd friends, 5.01.113
be friends awhile, and both conjointly bend JN 2.01.379
gone to be friends? 3.01. 2
against the pope, and count his friends my foes. 3.01.171
to do your pleasure and continue friends. 3.01.252
divers dear friends slain? 3.04. 7
we shall see and know our friends in heaven. 3.04. 77
the little number of your doubtful friends. 5.01. 36
and is't not pity, o my grieved friends, | that 5.02. 24
i did not think the king so stor'd with friends. 5.04. 1
away, my friends! 5.04. 60
which since we cannot do to make you friends, R2 1.01.197
and loving farewell of our several friends. 1.03. 51
that thou returnest no greeting to thy friends? 1.03.254
whether our kinsman come to see his friends. 1.04. 22
my countrymen, my loving friends," | as were our 1.04. 34
the french, | and not against his friends. 2.01.179
with all their powerful friends, are fled to him 2.02. 55
now shall he try his friends that flatter'd him. 2.02. 85
as in a soul rememb'ring my good friends, | and, 2.03. 47
nor friends, nor foes, to me welcome you are: 2.03.170
thy friends are fled to wait upon thy foes, 2.04. 23
overthrows thy joys, friends, fortune, and thy 3.02. 72
you, feel want, | taste grief, need friends: 3.02.176
with some few private friends upon this coast. 3.03. 4
us, | and we are barren and bereft of friends, 3.03. 84
till time lend friends, and friends their 3.03.132
lend friends, and friends their helpful swords. 3.03.132
therefore, friends, | as far as to the sepulchre 1H4 1.01. 18
dangerous, the friends you have nam'd uncertain, 2.03. 11 P
as ever was laid, our friends true and constant: 2.03. 17 P
a good plot, good friends, and full of 2.03. 18 P
an excellent plot, very good friends. 2.03. 19 P
call you that backing of your friends? 2.04.150 P
may have drawn together | your tenants, friends, 3.01. 89
i am good friends with my father and may do any 3.03.181 P
and that his friends by deputation could not 4.01. 32
i must go write again | to other friends, and so 4.04. 41
we were the first and dearest of your friends. 5.01. 33
and, fellows, soldiers, friends, | better 5.02. 75
lest your retirement do amaze your friends. 5.04. 6
to see what friends are living, who are dead. 5.04.161
and letters, and make friends with speed — 2H4 1.01.214
and, my most noble friends, i pray you all 1.03. 2
come, i'll be friends with thee, jack. 2.04. 65 P
since richard and northumberland, great friends, 3.01. 58
fellow, young, strong, and of good friends. 3.02.103 P
such order that thy friends shall ring for thee. 3.02.186 P
have a desire to stay with my friends, else, sir 3.02.226 P
my friends and brethren in these great affairs, 4.01. 6
his foes are so enrooted with his friends | that 4.01.205
and thou shalt prove a shelter to thy friends, 4.04. 42
let there be no noise made, my gentle friends, 4.05. 1
and all /my friends, which thou must make thy 4.05.204
/my friends, which thou must make thy friends, 4.05.204
blessed are they that have been my friends, and 5.03.138 P
what, are ancient pistol and you friends yet? H5 2.01. 3 P
i will bestow a breakfast to make you friends, 2.01. 12 P
come, shall i make you two friends? 2.01. 90 P
corporal nym, and thou wilt be friends, be 2.01.102 P
nym, and thou wilt be friends, be friends; 2.01.103 P
you see this chase is hotly followed, friends. 2.04. 68
once more unto the breach, dear friends, once 3.01. 1
and calls them brothers, friends, and countrymen 4.pr. 34
be friends, you english fools, be friends, we 4.01.222 P
you english fools, be friends, we have french 4.01.222 P
he never kill'd any of his friends. 4.07. 41 P
captain, you must needs be friends with him. 4.08. 61
artois, | wallon, and picardy are friends to us, 1H6 2.01. 10
i'll find friends to wear my bleeding roses, 2.04. 72
for these my friends in spite of thee shall wear 2.04.106
see here, my friends and loving countrymen, 3.01.137
amongst his subjects and his loyal friends, | as 3.01.181
i'll by a sign give notice to our friends, 3.02. 8
in spite of burgundy and all his friends. 3.03. 73
esteem none friends but such as are his friends, 4.01. 5
esteem none friends but such as are his friends, 4.01. 5
and what offense it is to flout his friends. 4.01. 75
good my lords, be friends. 4.01.133
and they shall find dear deer of us, my friends. 4.02. 54
that sund'red friends greet in the hour of death 4.03. 42
and purchase friends and give to courtezans, 2H6 1.01.223
for it is known we were but hollow friends? 3.02. 66
even thus two friends condemn'd | embrace, and 3.02.353
if he revenge it not, yet will his friends; 4.01.146
and you that be the king's friends, follow me. 4.02.181

unless by robbing of your friends and us. 4.08. 40
call buckingham, and all the friends thou hast, 5.01.193
him, his sons, his favorites, and his friends. 3H6 1.01. 56
thy kinsmen and thy friends, i'll have more 1.01. 96
my soldiers, gathered flocks of friends, | /and 2.01.112
gently down, as if they struck their friends. 2.01.132
with all the friends that thou, brave earl of 2.01.179
would thy best friends did know | how it doth 2.02. 54
for all your friends are fled, | and warwick 2.05.125
my love and fear glu'd many friends to thee, 2.06. 5
when clifford cannot spare his friends an oath. 2.06. 78
but say, is warwick friends with margaret? 4.01.115
i rather wish you foes than hollow friends. 4.01.139
speak suddenly, my lords, are we all friends? 4.02. 4
for warwick and his friends, god and saint 4.02. 29
king edward's friends must down. 4.04. 28
shall here find his friends with horse and men 4.05. 12
now that god and friends | have shaken edward 4.06. 1
in, | for hither will our friends repair to us. 4.07. 15
open the gates, we are king henry's friends. 4.07. 28
and all those friends that deign to follow me. 4.07. 39
the bruit thereof will bring you many friends. 4.07. 64
in warwickshire i have true–hearted friends, 4.08. 9
in oxfordshire shalt muster up thy friends. 4.08. 18
who should that be? belike unlook'd–for friends. 5.01. 14
we are advertis'd by our loving friends | that 5.03. 18
our slaught'red friends the tackles; 5.04. 15
the friends of france our shrouds and tacklings? 5.04. 18
and i no friends to back my suit /at /all | but R3 1.02.235
a liberal rewarder of his friends; 1.03.123
thy friends suspect for traitors while thou 1.03.222
and take deep traitors for thy dearest friends! 1.03.223
wherein, my friends, have i offended you? 1.04.177
since i have made my friends at peace on earth. 2.01. 6
no, no, good friends, god wot, | for then this 2.03. 18
keep you from them, and from such false friends! 3.01. 15
god keep me from false friends! 3.01. 16
your friends at pomfret, they do need the priest 3.02.114
be patient, they are friends — ratcliffe and 3.05. 21
which now the loving haste of these our friends, 3.05. 54
"thanks, gentle citizens and friends," quoth i, 3.07. 38
my god, | deferr'd the visitation of my friends. 3.07.107
your very worshipful and loving friends, | and 3.07.138
then, on the other side, i check'd my friends. 3.07.150
farewell, my /cousin, farewell, gentle friends. 3.07.247
no, to their lives ill friends were contrary. 4.04.217
throng many doubtful hollow–hearted friends, 4.04.435
no, my good lord, my friends are in the north. 4.04.483
cold friends to me! 4.04.484
i'll muster up my friends and meet your grace 4.04.488
as i by friends am well advertised, | sir edward 4.04.499
fellows in arms, and my most loving friends, 5.02. 1
in god's name cheerly on, courageous friends, 5.02. 14
i doubt not but his friends will turn to us. 5.02. 19
he hath no friends but what are friends for fear 5.02. 20
hath no friends but what are friends for fear, 5.02. 20
so long sund'red friends should dwell upon. 5.03.100
your friends are up and buckle on their armor. 5.03.211
thou — will our friends prove all true? 5.03.213
and your arms be prais'd, victorious friends; 5.05. 1
general throng and sweat | of thousand friends; H8 pr 29
and it stretches | beyond you to your friends. 1.02.142
his noble friends and fellows, whom to leave 2.01. 73
for those you make friends | and give your 2.01.127
or which of your friends | have i not strove to 2.04. 29
till i may | be by my friends in spain advis'd, 2.04. 55
fears, | your hopes and friends are infinite. 3.01. 82
nay forsooth, my friends, | they that must weigh 3.01. 87
since virtue finds no friends) a wife, a true 3.01.126
no friends, no hope, no kindred weep for me, 3.01.150
we profess, peacemakers, friends, and servants. 3.01.167
gain the popedom | and fee my friends in rome). 3.02.213
be friends, for shame, my lords! 5.02.194
these | your faithful friends o' th' suburbs? 5.03. 72
wounds, friends, and what else dear that is TRO 2.02. 5
not so with me, | fortune and i are friends. 3.03. 88
with such a costly loss of wealth and friends. 4.01. 61
to–night all friends. 4.05.270
masters, my good friends, mine honest neighbors, COR 1.01. 62
i tell you, friends, most charitable care | have 1.01. 65
"true is it, my incorporate friends," quoth he, 1.01.130
you, my good friends, this says the belly, mark 1.01.141
where i know | our greatest friends attend us. 1.01.245
march from hence | to help our fielded friends! 1.04. 12
breathe you, my friends. 1.06. 1
we have heard | the charges of our friends. 1.06. 6
by th' vows | we have made to endure friends, 1.06. 58
nature teaches beasts to know their friends. 2.01. 6 P
her enemies, you have been a rod to her friends; 2.03. 92 P
five hundred, and their friends to piece 'em. 2.03.212
and tell those friends | they have chose a 2.03.213
my nobler friends, i crave their pardons. 3.01. 65
fast, | we have as many friends as enemies. 3.01.231
say | honor and policy, like unsever'd friends, 3.02. 42
my fortunes and my friends at stake requir'd | i 3.02. 63
hear me, my masters, and my common friends — 3.03.108
dearest mother, and | my friends of noble touch; 4.01. 49
friends now fast sworn, | whose double bosoms 4.04. 12
shall grow dear friends | and interjoin their 4.04. 21
come, we are fellows and friends: 4.05.183 P
you, sir, he has as many friends as enemies; 4.05.206 P
which friends, sir, as it were, durst not (look 4.05.206 P
it) his friends whilest he's in directitude. 4.05.208 P
here do we make his friends | blush that the 4.06. 4
is not much miss'd but with his friends; 4.06. 13
for his best friends, if they | should say, "be 4.06.111
to awaken his regard | for 's private friends. 5.01. 24
good my friends, | if you have heard your 5.02. 8
general talk of rome | and of his friends there, 5.02. 10
for i have ever verified my friends | (of whom 5.02. 17
not with such friends | that thought them sure 5.03. 7
suits, | nor from the state nor private friends, 5.03. 18
with dews of flattery, | seducing so my friends; 5.06. 23
romans, friends, followers, favorers of my right TIT 1.01. 9
princes, that strive by factions and by friends 1.01. 18
that i will here dismiss my loving friends; 1.01. 53
friends, that have been thus forward in my right 1.01. 56
my faction if thou strengthen with thy friends, 1.01.214
lie thy bones, sweet mutius, with thy friends, 1.01.387
that i have reconcil'd your friends and you. 1.01.467
nay, nay, sweet emperor, we must all be friends. 1.01.479
you are my guest, lavinia, and your friends. 1.01.490
you so desperate grown to threat your friends? 2.01. 40
for shame, be friends, and join for that you jar 2.01.103
do this and purchase us thy lasting friends." 2.03.275
sweet girl, for here are none but friends, 4.01. 61
and secretly to greet the empress' friends. 4.02.174
approved warriors, and my faithful friends, | i 5.01. 1
myself, | set deadly enmity between two friends, 5.01.131
and see the ambush of our friends be strong, | i 5.03. 9
me, | for when no friends are by, men praise 5.03.118
some loving friends convey the emperor hence, 5.03.191
both by myself and many other friends, | but he, ROM 1.01.146
romeo he cries aloud, | "hold, friends! 3.01.165
friends, part!" 3.01.165
to blaze your marriage, reconcile your friends, 3.03.151
therefore we'll have some half a dozen friends, 3.04. 27
freedom, | or my friends, if i should need 'em. TIM 1.02. 69
a breakfast of enemies than a dinner of friends. 1.02. 77 P
o, no doubt, my good friends, but the gods 1.02. 88 P
how had you been my friends else? 1.02. 90 P
i, what need we have any friends, if we should 1.02. 96 P
we call our own than the riches of our friends? 1.02.103 P
o my friends! 1.02.167
methinks, i could deal kingdoms to my friends, 1.02.220
ready for his friends. 1.02.230
do so, my friends. see them well entertain'd. 2.02. 44
conscience lack | to think i shall lack friends? 2.02.176
for by these | shall i try friends. 2.02.183
i am wealthy in my friends. 2.02.184
poor, | imprison'd, and in scarcity of friends, 2.02.225
timon's fortunes 'mong his friends can sink. 2.02.231
his friends, like physicians, | thrive, give him 3.03. 11
now his friends are dead, | doors, that were 3.03. 36
go, bid all my friends again, | lucius, lucullus 3.04.110
it seem in the trial of his several friends. 3.06. 6 P
my worthy friends, will you draw near? 3.06. 58 P
for these my present friends, as they are to me 3.06. 82 P
but only painted, like his varnish'd friends? 4.02. 36
this ingrateful seat | of monstrous friends; 4.02. 46
and the falling–from of his friends, drove him 4.03.400 P
what vilder thing upon the earth than friends, 4.03.463
of his | has been but a try for his friends? 5.01. 9
you were retir'd, your friends fall'n off, 5.01. 59
but for all this, my honest–natur'd friends, | i 5.01. 86
timon, | look out and speak to friends. 5.01.128
tell my friends, | tell athens, in the sequence 5.01.207
force, | and made us speak like friends. 5.02. 9
but let not therefore my good friends be griev'd JC 1.02. 43
and, gentle friends, | let's kill him boldly, 2.01.171
brutus, | and, friends, disperse yourselves; 2.01.222
that your best friends shall wish i had been 2.02.125
good friends, go in, and taste some wine with me 2.02.126
me, | and we, like friends, will straightway go 2.02.127
so are we caesar's friends, that have abridg'd 3.01.104
will you be prick'd in number of our friends, 3.01.216
friends am i with you all, and love you all, 3.01.220
then follow me, and give me audience, friends. 3.02. 2
friends, romans, countrymen, lend me your ears! 3.02. 73
have patience, gentle friends, i must not read 3.02.140
good friends, sweet friends, let me not stir you 3.02.210
good friends, sweet friends, let me not stir you 3.02.210
i come not, friends, to steal away your hearts. 3.02.216
why, friends, you go to do you know not what. 3.02.235
our best friends made, our means stretch'd, 4.01. 44
to lock such rascal counters from his friends, 4.03. 80
love, and be friends, as two such men should be, 4.03.131
that we have tried the utmost of our friends, 4.03.214
did i not meet thy friends? 5.03. 81
friends, i owe moe tears | to this dead man than 5.03.101
rather have | such men my friends than enemies. 5.04. 29
come, poor remains of friends, rest on this rock 5.05. 1
till then, enough. come, friends. MAC 1.03.156
would make good of bad, and friends of foes! 2.04. 41
for certain friends that are both his and mine, 3.01.120
pronounce it for me, sir, to all our friends, 3.04. 7
sit, worthy friends; 3.04. 52
worthy lord, | your noble friends do lack you. 3.04. 83
do not muse at me, my most worthy friends, | i 3.04. 84
as honor, love, obedience, troops of friends, 5.03. 25
i would the friends we miss were safe arriv'd. 5.09. 1
as calling home our exil'd friends abroad | that 5.09. 32
friends to this ground. HAM 1.01. 15
those friends thou hast, and their adoption 1.03. 62
and now, good friends, | as you are friends, 1.05.140
as you are friends, scholars, and soldiers, 1.05.141
once more remove, good friends. 1.05.163
as thus, "i know his father and his friends, 2.01. 14
welcome, my good friends! 2.02. 58
my /excellent good friends! 2.02.224 P
and sure, dear friends, my thanks are too dear a 2.02.273 P
welcome, good friends. 2.02.422 P
follow him, friends, we'll hear a play to–morrow 2.02.535 P
my good friends, i'll leave you /till night. 2.02.546 P
the poor advanc'd makes friends of enemies. 3.02.205
leave me, friends. 3.02.387
friends both, go join you with some further aid: 4.01. 33
we'll call up our wisest friends | and let them 4.01. 38
to his good friends thus wide i'll ope my arms, 4.05.146
choice of whom your wisest friends you will, 4.05.205
o, yet defend me, friends, i am but hurt. 5.02.324
where they boast | to have well–armed friends. LR 3.07. 20
good my friends, consider | you are my guests. 3.07. 30
do me no foul play, friends. 3.07. 31
yet my mind | was then scarce friends with him. 4.01. 35
letters that he speaks of | may be my friends. 4.06.257
you lords and noble friends, know our intent. 5.03.297
all friends shall taste | the wages of their 5.03.303
friends of my soul, you twain | rule in this 5.03.320
those are the raised father and his friends. OTH 1.02. 29
the goodness of the night upon you, friends! 1.02. 35
our friends at least. 2.01. 57
news, friends: 2.01.202
o, they are our friends — but one cup, i'll 2.03. 37 P
friends all, but now, even now; 2.03.179
and her friends? 4.02.126
and the time's state | made friends of them, ANT 1.02. 92
too | of many our contriving friends in rome 1.02.182
noble friends, | that which combin'd us was most 2.02. 17
or friends with caesar, or not captive to him, 2.05. 44
and friends with caesar. 2.05. 47
caesar and he are greater friends than ever. 2.05. 48
he's friends with caesar, | in state of health 2.05. 55
having a son and friends, since julius caesar, 2.06. 12
my /father's house — but what, we are friends? 2.07.128
that have my heart parted betwixt two friends 3.06. 77
friends, come hither: 3.11. 2
friends, be gone, | i have myself resolv'd upon 3.11. 8
friends, be gone, you shall | have letters from 3.11. 15
have letters from me to some friends that will 3.11. 16
none but friends: say boldly. 3.13. 47
so haply are they friends to antony. 3.13. 48
mine honest friends, | i turn you not away, but, 4.02. 29
grow where those drops fall, my hearty friends! 4.02. 38
enter the city, clip your wives, your friends, 4.08. 8
and carouse together | like friends long lost. 4.12. 13
i have done my work ill, friends. 4.14.105
bear me, good friends, where cleopatra bides, 4.14.131
i have led you oft, carry me now, good friends, 4.14.139
help, friends below, let's draw him hither. 4.15. 13
assist, good friends. 4.15. 31
look you sad, friends? 5.01. 26
hear me, good friends — | but i will tell you 5.01. 48
as all the tuned spheres, and that to friends; 5.02. 84
dignity | as we greet modern friends withal, and 5.02.167
but he does buy my injuries, to be friends; CYM 1.01.105
nor has no friends | so much as but to prop him? 1.05. 59
and other noble friends | are partners in the 1.06.183
and, 'tis thought, one of leonatus' friends. 2.01. 38 P
you know that we | must not continue friends. 2.04. 49
be sprightly, for you fall 'mongst friends. 3.06. 74
'mongst friends? 3.06. 74
my friends, | the boy hath taught us manly 4.02.396
for friends kill friends, and the disorder's 5.02. 15
for friends kill friends, and the disorder's 5.02. 15
some their friends | o'erborne i' th' former 5.03. 47
as friends to antioch, we may feast in tyre. PER 1.03. 39
an armor, friends? 2.01.120
to beg of you, kind friends, this coat of worth, 2.01.136
a lasting storm, | whirring me from my friends. 4.01. 20
what were thy friends? 5.01.125
what were thy friends? 5.01.139
well, my companion friends, | if this but answer 5.01.237
cannot weep | when our friends don their helms, TNK 1.03. 19
where are our friends and kindreds? 2.02. 8
we are father, friends, acquaintance; 2.02. 81
by your leaves, honest friends: 2.03. 60
your person i am friends with, | and i could 3.06. 39
the other lose his head, | and all his friends; 3.06.297
arcite, | i am friends again till that hour. 3.06.300
ye | now usage like to princes and to friends. 3.06.306
the stage of death, | whom i adopt my friends. 5.04.124
friends, masters, countrymen — STM II.C 27
me set up before your thoughts, good friends, II.C 90
to hunt the boar with certain of his friends. VEN 588
that thrive well take counsel of their friends. 640
"i am," quoth he, "expected of my friends, | and 718
his honor, his affairs, his friends, his state, LUC 45
but will is deaf and hears no heedful friends; 495
would purchase thee a thousand thousand friends, 963
"let him have time to see his friends his foes, 988
all thy friends are lapp'd in lead; PP 20.24
the wind, | faithful friends are hard to find: 20.32
like him, like him with friends possess'd, SON 29. 6
for precious friends hid in death's dateless 30. 6
and all those friends which i thought buried. 31. 4

FRIENDSHIP 47 FR 0.0053 REL FR 37 V 10 P

the law of friendship bids me to conceal, | but TGV 3.01. 5
i desire you in friendship, and i will one way WIV 3.01. 87 P
friendship is constant in all other things ADO 2.01.175
is there any way to show such friendship? 4.01.263 P
and hold fair friendship with his majesty. LLL 2.01.140
all school–days friendship, childhood innocence? MND 3.02.202
for when did friendship take | a breed for MV 1.03.133
to buy his favor, i extend this friendship. 1.03.168
i do in friendship counsel you | to leave this AYL 1.02.261
most friendship is feigning, most loving mere 2.07.181
as when thy father and myself in friendship AWW 1.02. 25
to mingle friendship far is mingling bloods. WT 1.02.109
as clear | as friendship wears at feasts, keep 1.02.344
'tis a point of friendship. 1H4 5.01.122 P
but a colossus can do thee that friendship. 5.01.124 P
and friendship shall combine, and brotherhood. H5 2.01.109
die and be damn'd! and figo for thy friendship! 3.06. 57
proverb with "there is flattery in friendship." 3.07.115 P
but join in friendship, as your lords have done. 1H6 3.01.145
brave duke, thy friendship makes us fresh. 3.03. 86
they are so link'd in friendship | that young 3H6 4.01.116
he little thought of this divided friendship. R3 1.04.238
have no cause to hold my friendship doubtful. 4.04.492
assurance | of equal friendship and proceeding. H8 2.04. 18
love, friendship, charity, are subjects all | to TRO 3.03.173
ease thy smart | by friendship nor by speaking." 4.04. 20
so shalt thou show me friendship. ROM 5.03. 41
but where there is true friendship, there needs TIM 1.02. 18
upon bare friendship without security. 3.01. 42 P
has friendship such a faint and milky heart, 3.01. 54
that their society (as their friendship) may 4.01. 31
or to live | but in a dream of friendship, | to 4.02. 34
noble timon, | what friendship may i do thee? 4.03. 71
promise me friendship, but perform none. 4.03. 73 P
in terms of friendship with thine enemies. JC 3.01.203
but in the beaten way of friendship, what make HAM 2.02.270 P
love cools, friendship falls off, brothers LR 1.02.106 P
some friendship will it lend you 'gainst the 3.02. 62
if i do vow a friendship, i'll perform it | to OTH 3.03. 21
for't cannot be | we shall remain in friendship, ANT 2.02.113
seems to tie their friendship together will be 2.06.121 P
i know he'll quickly fly my friendship too. CYM 5.03. 62
i do not think it possible our friendship TNK 2.02.114
friendship, blood, | and all the ties between us 2.02.172
more | come near thee with such friendship. 3.06.103
by all our friendship, sir, by all our dangers, 3.06.202
in scorn or friendship, nill i conster whether. PP 14. 8

FRIENDSHIP'S 2 FR 0.0002 REL FR 2 V 0 P
friendship's full of dregs; TIM 1.02.233
knighthood, gentry, and sweet friendship's oath, LUC 569
FRIENDSHIPS 1 FR 0.0001 REL FR 0 V 1 P
and my profit therein the heaping friendships. WT 4.02. 20 P
FRIEZE* 4 FR 0.0004 REL FR 3 V 1 P
shall i have a coxcomb of frieze? WIV 5.05.138 P
no jutty, frieze, | buttress, nor coign of MAC 1.06. 6
comes from my pate as birdlime does from frieze, OTH 2.01.126
you most coarse frieze capacities, ye /jane TNK 3.05. 8
FRIGHT 36 FR 0.0040 REL FR 30 V 6 P
o, 'twas a din to fright a monster's ear, | to TMP 2.01.314
fright me with urchin–shows, pitch me i' th' 2.02. 5
first, an intolerable fright, to be detected WIV 3.05.109 P
will shake her chain, and fright us with it. ERR 4.03. 76
to fright them hence with that dread penalty. LLL 1.01.127
no devil will fright thee then so much as she. 4.03.271
you would fright the duchess and the ladies, MND 1.02. 75 P
if you should fright the ladies out of their 1.02. 79 P
this is to make an ass of me, to fright me, if 3.01.121 P
to fright the animals and to kill them up | in AYL 2.01. 62
this will so fright them both that they will TN 3.04.195 P
both form and suit, | you come to fright us. 5.01.236
do your best | to fright me with your sprites; WT 2.01. 28
the bug which you would fright me with, i seek. 3.02. 92
the lion in his den, | and fright him there? JN 5.01. 58
might from our quiet confines fright fair peace, R2 1.03.137
and fright our native peace with self–borne arms 2.03. 80
and meteors fright the fixed stars of heaven, 2.04. 9
put on his ugliest mask | to fright our party. 2H4 1.01. 67
that, when i come to woo ladies, i fright them. H5 5.02.228 P
it were enough to fright the realm of france! 1H6 4.07. 82
sits in grim majesty, to fright the world. 2H6 3.02. 50
nay, do not fright us with an angry look. 5.01.126
to fright the souls of fearful adversaries, | he R3 1.01. 11
may fright the hopeful mother at the view, | and 1.02. 24
in parts remote, | to fright them, ere destroy. COR 4.05.143
and would not, but in fury, fright my youth, TIT 4.01. 24
in your bed, | he'll fright you up, i' faith. ROM 4.05. 11
stood on ceremonies, | yet now they fright me. JC 2.02. 14
to fright you thus methinks i am too savage; MAC 4.02. 70
it so fell out) | the town might fall in fright. OTH 2.03.232
these stops of thine fright me the more; 3.03.120
and never fright the silly lamb that day. VEN 1098
they fright him, yet he still pursues his fear. LUC 308
and fright her with confusion of their cries. 445
and fright her crying babe with tarquin's name; 814
/FRIGHTED 1 FR 0.0001 REL FR 0 V 1 P
/what, /frighted /with /false /fire? HAM 3.02.266 P
FRIGHTED 15 FR 0.0017 REL FR 14 V 1 P
thou hast frighted the word out of his right ADO 5.02. 55 P
ay, but not frighted me, therefore i'll sleep SHR 5.02. 43
that, frighted, thou let'st fall | from dis's WT 4.04.117
find we a time for frighted peace to pant | and 1H4 1.01. 2
were strangely clamorous to the frighted fields. 3.01. 39
nature's soft nurse, how have i frighted thee, 2H4 3.01. 6
we fear, | w' have frighted with our trumpets; H8 ep 4
where ladies shall be frighted | and, gladly COR 1.09. 5
and, being thus frighted, swears a prayer or two ROM 1.04. 87
shall i be frighted when a madman stares? JC 4.03. 40
war, whose several ranges | frighted each other? ANT 3.13. 6
to be furious | is to be frighted out of fear, 3.13.195
with a fool, | frighted, and ang'red worse. CYM 2.03.140
who, frighted from my country, did wed | at PER 5.03. 3
as the poor frighted deer that stands at gaze, LUC 1149
FRIGHTFUL 2 FR 0.0002 REL FR 2 V 0 P
their music frightful as the serpent's hiss, 2H6 3.02.326
thy school–days frightful, desp'rate, wild, and R3 4.04.170
FRIGHTING 3 FR 0.0003 REL FR 2 V 1 P
thou shalt be punish'd for thus frighting me, JN 3.01. 11
frighting her pale–fac'd villages with war | and R2 2.03. 94
but a plague break thy neck — for frighting me! TRO 5.04. 32 P
FRIGHTS 8 FR 0.0009 REL FR 6 V 2 P
here's a fellow frights english out of his wits. WIV 2.01.139 P
he | that frights the maidens of the villagery, MND 2.01. 35
on her frights and griefs | (which never tender WT 2.02. 21
about, | startles and frights consideration, JN 4.02. 25
afore i'll be in these tirrits and frights. 2H4 2.04.205 P
frights, changes, horrors, | divert and crack, TRO 1.03. 98
bell, it frights the isle | from her propriety. OTH 2.03.175
since i have known frights, fury, friends' TNK 1.04. 40
FRINGE 1 FR 0.0001 REL FR 0 V 1 P
of the forest, like fringe upon a petticoat. AYL 3.02.336 P
FRINGED 1 FR 0.0001 REL FR 1 V 0 P
the fringed curtains of thine eye advance | and TMP 1.02.409
FRINGES 1 FR 0.0001 REL FR 1 V 0 P
begin to part | their fringes of bright gold. PER 3.02.100
FRIPPERY 1 FR 0.0001 REL FR 0 V 1 P
we know what belongs to a frippery. TMP 4.01.226 P
FRISK 2 FR 0.0002 REL FR 2 V 0 P
were as twinn'd lambs that did frisk i' th' sun, WT 1.02. 67
and now and then a favor and a frisk. TNK 3.05. 30
FRISKINS 1 FR 0.0001 REL FR 0 V 1 P
become the pranks and friskins of her madness. TNK 4.03. 80 P
FRITTERS 1 FR 0.0001 REL FR 0 V 1 P
the taunt of one that makes fritters of english? WIV 5.05.143 P
FRIVOLOUS 3 FR 0.0003 REL FR 2 V 1 P
to leave frivolous circumstances, i pray you SHR 5.01. 26 P
when for so slight and frivolous a cause | such 1H6 4.01.112
your oath, my lord, is vain and frivolous. 3H6 1.02. 27
FRIZ 1 FR 0.0001 REL FR 1 V 0 P
here's friz and maudline. TNK 3.05. 25
FRO 3 FR 0.0003 REL FR 2 V 1 P
precinct | i was employ'd in passing to and fro, 1H6 2.01. 69
debating to and fro | how france and frenchmen 2H6 1.01. 91
so lightly blown to and fro as this multitude? 4.08. 56 P
FROCK 1 FR 0.0001 REL FR 1 V 0 P
and good | he likewise gives a frock or livery, HAM 3.04.164
FROG 3 FR 0.0003 REL FR 2 V 1 P
eye of newt and toe of frog, | wool of bat and MAC 4.01. 14
poor tom, that eats the swimming frog, the toad, LR 3.04.129 P
would i could find a fine frog! TNK 3.04. 12
FROGMORE 3 FR 0.0003 REL FR 0 V 3 P
slender, go you through the town to frogmore. WIV 2.03. 75 P
go about the fields with me through frogmore, i 2.03. 86 P
and another gentleman — from frogmore, over the 3.01. 33 P
FROISSARD 1 FR 0.0001 REL FR 1 V 0 P
froissard, a countryman of ours, records 1H6 1.02. 29

FROLIC 2 FR 0.0002 REL FR 2 V 0 P
darkness like a dream, | now are frolic. MND 5.01.387
and therefore frolic, we will hence forthwith, SHR 4.03.182
/FROM 28 FR 0.0031 REL FR 27 V 1 P
/give /this /heavy /weight /from /off /my /head, R2 4.01.204
/and /this /unwieldy /sceptre /from /my /hand, 4.01.205
/pride /of /kingly /sway /from /out /my /heart; 4.01.206
/you /will, /so /i /were /from /your /sights. 4.01.315
/action /of /their /bodies /from /their /souls, 2H4 1.01.195
/king /richard, /scrap'd /from /pomfret /stones; 1.01.205
/derives /from /heaven /his /quarrel /and /his 1.01.206
/and /are /enforc'd /from /our /most /quiet 4.01. 71
/either /from /the /king /or /in /the /present 4.01.106
/my /father /from /the /breast /of /bullingbrook 4.01.122
/shillings /i /won /from /you /at /betting? H5 2.01.105 P
when i return with victory /from the field 3H6 1.01.261
/and /charg'd /us /from /his /soul /to /love R3 1.04.237
/from /isles /of /greece | /the /princes TRO pr 1
/from /th' /athenian /bay | /put /forth /toward pr 6
/troth, | /strain'd /purely /from /all /hollow 4.05.169
/letters, /my /lord, /from /hamlet: HAM 4.07. 36
/be /shortly /known /to /him /from /england 5.02. 71
/i /would /breed /from /hence /occasions, /and LR 1.03. 24
/from /france /there /comes /a /power | /into 3.01. 30
/and, /from /some /knowledge /and /assurance, 3.01. 41
/and /disbranch | /from /her /material /sap, 4.02. 35
/thence, | /as /pearls /from /diamonds /dropp'd. 4.03. 22
/the /holy /water /from /her /heavenly /eyes, 4.03. 30
/that /stripp'd /her /from /his /benediction, 4.03. 43
/burning /shame | /detains /him /from /cordelia. 4.03. 47
why did you throw your wedded lady /from you? CYM 5.05.261
the which the gods protect thee /from! PER 2.01.129
FROM 2807 FR 0.3173 REL FR 2467 V 340 P
i have great comfort from this fellow. TMP 1.01. 28 P
thy hand, | and pluck my magic garment from me. 1.02. 24
what foul play had we, that we came from thence? 1.02. 60
turn'd you to, | which is from my remembrance! 1.02. 65
smile, | infused with a fortitude from heaven, 1.02.154
me | from mine own library with volumes that | i 1.02.167
to fetch dew | from the still–vex'd bermoothes, 1.02.229
forget | from what a torment i did free thee? 1.02.251
terrible | to enter human hearing, from argier, 1.02.265
with raven's feather from unwholesome fen | drop 1.02.322
sycorax my mother, | which thou tak'st from me. 1.02.332
whiles you do keep from me | the rest o' th' 1.02.343
as a spy, to win it | from me, the lord on't. 1.02.457
come, from thy ward, | for i can here disarm 1.02.472
this is unwonted | which now came from him. 1.02.499
who is so far from italy removed | i ne'er again 2.01.111
where she, at least, is banish'd from your eye, 2.01.127
eye and cheek proclaim | a matter from thee; 2.01.230
she that from naples | can have no note, unless 2.01.247
she that from whom | we all were sea–swallow'd, 2.01.250
shall free thee from the tribute which thou 2.01.293
heavens keep him from these beasts! 2.01.324
infections that the sun sucks up | from bogs, 2.02. 2
hast thou not dropp'd from heaven? 2.02.137 P
i'll get thee | young scamels from the rock. 2.02.172
face remember, | save, from my glass, mine own; 3.01. 50
from me he got it. 3.02. 53
give him blows, | and take his bottle from him. 3.02. 65
three | from milan did supplant good prospero, 3.03. 70
and your ways, whose wraths to guard you from — 3.03. 79
and hinder them from what this ecstasy | may now 3.03.108
it is my promise, | and they expect it from me. 4.01. 42
art | i have from their confines call'd to enact 4.01.121
come hither from the furrow and be merry. 4.01.135
from toe to crown he'll fill our skins with 4.01.233
beard like winter's drops | from eaves of reeds. 5.01. 17
you have | been justled from your senses, know 5.01.158
was milan thrust from milan, that his issue 5.01.205
they strengthen | from strange to stranger. 5.01.228
even in a dream, were we divided from them, 5.01.239
but release me from my bands | with the help of ep 9
as you from crimes would pardon'd be, | let your ep 19
to milan let me hear from thee by letters | of TGV 1.01. 57
from a pound to a pin? 1.01.108
why? couldst thou perceive so much from her? 1.01.134 P
sir, i could perceive nothing at all from her; 1.01.136 P
go, go, be gone, to save your ship from wrack, 1.01.148
receiving them from such a worthless post. 1.01.153
"to julia" — say, from whom? 1.02. 35
and sent, i think, from proteus. 1.02. 38
or two | of commendations sent from valentine, 1.03. 53
deliver'd by a friend that came from him. 1.03. 54
what maintenance he from his friends receives, 1.03. 68
like exhibition thou shalt have from me. 1.03. 69
to be a spokesman from madam silvia. 2.01.146 P
borrows his wit from your ladyship's looks, and 2.04. 38 P
what say you to a letter from your friends | of 2.04. 51
thankful | to any happy messenger from thence. 2.04. 53
for from our infancy | we have convers'd and 2.04. 62
to me | with commendation from great potentates, 2.04. 79
if this be he you oft have wish'd to hear from. 2.04.103
when you have done, we look to hear from you. 2.04.120
now tell me: how do all from whence you came? 2.04.122
love hath chas'd sleep from my enthralled eyes, 2.04.134
should from her vesture chance to steal a kiss, 2.04.160
get such a secret from me but by a parable. 2.05. 39 P
his tears pure messengers sent from his heart, 2.07. 77
his heart as far from fraud as heaven from earth 2.07. 78
heart as far from fraud as heaven from earth. 2.07. 78
else, no worldly good should draw from me. 3.01. 9
and should she thus be stol'n away from you, 3.01. 15
know | that i had any light from thee of this. 3.01. 49
upon advice, hath drawn my love from her, | and, 3.01. 73
worth, | and kept severely from resort of men, 3.01.108
her chamber is aloft, far from the ground, | and 3.01.114
as thou lov'st thy life, make speed from hence. 3.01.169
to die is to be banish'd from myself, | and 3.01.171
banish'd from her | is self from self, a deadly 3.01.172
banish'd from her | is self from self, a deadly 3.01.173
death, | but, fly i hence, i fly away from life. 3.01.187
from hence, from silvia, and from me thy friend. 3.01.220
from hence, from silvia, and from me thy friend. 3.01.220
from hence, from silvia, and from me thy friend. 3.01.220
a team of horse shall not pluck that from me; 3.01.267 P
was eve's legacy, and cannot be ta'en from her. 3.01.339 P

you | now valentine is banish'd from her sight. 3.02. 2
but say this weed her love from valentine, | it 3.02. 49
therefore, as you unwind her love from him, 3.02. 51
from milan. 4.01. 19
youth | thrust from the company of aweful men. 4.01. 44
myself was from verona banished | for practicing 4.01. 45
and i from mantua, for a gentleman, | who, in my 4.01. 48
swear), | i am so far from granting thy request, 4.02.101
sweet lady, let me rake it from the earth. 4.02.115
hence, | to keep me from a most unholy match, 4.03. 30
even from a heart | as full of sorrows as the 4.03. 32
one that i sav'd from drowning, when three or 4.04. 3 P
as a present to mistress silvia from my master; 4.04. 7 P
what, didst thou offer her this from me? 4.04. 54 P
squirrel was stol'n from me by the hangman's 4.04. 56 P
this ring i gave him when he parted from me, 4.04. 97
from whom? 4.04.113
from my master, sir proteus, madam. 4.04.114
tell him from me, | one julia, that his changing 4.04.118
true — from a gentleman to a fool. 5.02. 24
these likelihoods confirm her flight from hence: 5.02. 43
much to do | to keep them from uncivil outrages. 5.04. 17
and rescue you from him | that would have forc'd 5.04. 21
come, come, a hand from either. 5.04.116
and let them be recall'd from their exile; 5.04.155
he came of an errand to me from parson hugh. WIV 1.04. 76 P
he's as far from jealousy as i am from giving 2.01.103 P
far from jealousy as i am from giving him cause, 2.01.103 P
will be absence from his house between ten and 2.02. 84 P
master ford her husband will be from home. 2.02. 88 P
worship that her husband is seldom from home, 2.02.101 P
could drive her then from the ward of her purity 2.02.248 P
me, her assistant or go–between parted from me. 2.02.263 P
and another gentleman — from frogmore, over the 3.01. 32 P
keep a gamester from the dice, and a good 3.01. 37 P
the dice, and a good studient from his book, and 3.01. 38 P
/god pless you from his mercy sake, all of you! 3.01. 42 P
veil of modesty from the so–seeming mistress 3.02. 41 P
we'll teach him to know turtles from jays. 3.03. 42 P
to sir john falstaff from my two mistresses. 3.04.110 P
sir, i come to your worship from mistress ford. 3.05. 33 P
i have receiv'd from her another ambassy of 3.05.129 P
and the rest of their company from their sport, 4.02. 34 P
let them from forth a sawpit rush at once | with 4.04. 54
with sir john falstaff from master slender. 4.05. 5 P
speak from thy lungs military. 4.05. 17 P
things to have spoken with her too from him. 4.05. 41 P
eton, they threw me off from behind one of them, 4.05. 67 P
from the two parties, forsooth. 4.05.105 P
from time to time i have acquainted you | with 4.06. 8
i have a letter from her | of such contents as 4.06. 12
like a poor old man, but i came from her, master 5.01. 16 P
heavens defend me from that welsh fairy, lest he 5.05. 81 P
from which we would not have you warp. MM 1.01. 14
our haste from hence is of so quick condition 1.01. 53
captain and all the rest from their functions; 1.02. 13 P
but from lord angelo by special charge. 1.02.119
from too much liberty, my lucio, liberty: 1.02.125
from whom we thought it meet to hide our love 1.02.152
tongue far from heart — play with all virgins 1.04. 33
that from the seedness the bare fallow brings 1.04. 42
the duke is very strangely gone from hence; 1.04. 50
infinite distance | from his true–meant design. 1.04. 55
some run from brakes of ice and answer none, 2.01. 39
ere sun–rise, prayers from preserved souls, 2.02.153
from fasting maids whose minds are dedicate | to 2.02.154
from thee — even from thy virtue. 2.02.161
from thee — even from thy virtue. 2.02.161
wrench awe from fools and tie the wiser souls 2.04. 14
to pardon him that hath from nature stol'n | a 2.04. 43
could fetch your brother from the manacles | of 2.04. 93
and from this testimony of your own sex | (since 2.04.131
so then you hope of pardon from lord angelo? 3.01. 1
would bark your honor from that trunk you bear, 3.01. 71
a resolution fetch | from flow'ry tenderness? 3.01. 82
he would give't thee, from this rank offense, 3.01. 99
to take life | from thine own sister's shame? 3.01.139
of wilderness | ne'er issu'd from his blood. 3.01.142
my bending down | reprieve thee from thy fate, 3.01.144
redeem your brother from the angry law; 3.01.201 P
in death to take this poor maid from the world! 3.01.232 P
but keeps you from dishonor in doing it. 3.01.237 P
of the benefit defends the deceit from reproof. 3.01.258 P
maw or clothe a back | from such a filthy vice; 3.02. 23
from their abominable and beastly touches | i 3.02. 24
from our faults, as faults from seeming, free! 3.02. 39
from our faults, as faults from seeming, free! 3.02. 39
trick of him to steal from the state, and usurp 3.02. 93 P
of gracious order, late come from the /see, | in 3.02.219
/see, | in special business from his holiness. 3.02.220
receiv'd no sinister measure from his judge, but 3.02.243 P
what is the news from this good deputy? 4.01. 27
which from the vineyard to the garden leads; 4.01. 33
have you to say | when you depart from him, but, 4.01. 68
assist him, it shall redeem you from your gyves; 4.02. 11 P
receive some instruction from my fellow partner. 4.02. 17 P
that you swerve not from the smallest article of 4.02.103 P
to save me from the danger that might come | if 4.03. 85
and from thence, | by cold gradation and 4.03. 99
he hath releas'd him, isabel, from the world, 4.03.115
command these fretting waters from your eyes 4.03.146
and to deliver us from devices hereafter, which 4.04. 12 P
sometimes you do blench from this to that, | as 4.05. 5
not being believ'd, | or wring redress from you. 5.01. 32
i came to her from claudio, and desir'd her | to 5.01. 75
heaven shield your grace from woe, | as i, thus 5.01.118
who is as free from touch or soil with her | as 5.01.141
touch or soil with her | as she from one ungot. 5.01.142
to speak, as from his mouth, what he doth know 5.01.155
the body | that took away the match from isabel, 5.01.211
spake with her, saw her, nor heard from her, 5.01.223
as there comes light from heaven, and words from 5.01.225
comes light from heaven, and words from breath, 5.01.225
true, | let me in safety raise me from my knees, 5.01.231
and then to glance from him | to th' duke 5.01.309
out | most audible, even from his proper tongue, 5.01.408
sprung from the rancorous outrage of your duke ERR 1.01. 6
excludes all pity from our threat'ning looks: 1.01. 10

why thou departedst from thy native home, | and 1.01. 29
drew me from kind embracements of my spouse; 1.01. 43
from whom my absence was not six months old 1.01. 44
a league from epidamium had we sail'd | before 1.01. 62
and we discovered | two ships from far, making 1.01. 92
thus have you heard me sever'd from my bliss, 1.01.118
my present business calls me from you now. 1.02. 29
the capon burns, the pig falls from the spit; 1.02. 44
so great a charge from thine own custody? 1.02. 61
i from my mistress come to you in post: 1.02. 63
my charge was but to fetch you from the mart 1.02. 74
and from the mart he's somewhere gone to dinner. 2.01. 5
th' alluring beauty took | from my poor cheek? 2.01. 90
deer, he breaks the pale, | and feeds from home; 2.01.101
since at first | i sent him from the mart! 2.02. 6
it, | that thou art then estranged from thyself? 2.02.120
ah, do not tear away thyself from me; 2.02.124
as take from me thyself and not me too. 2.02.129
and from my false hand cut the wedding-ring, 2.02.137
by thee, and this thou didst return from him: 2.02.157
be it my wrong you are from me exempt, | but 2.02.171
if aught possess thee from me, it is dross, 2.02.177
you would keep from my heels, and beware of an 3.01. 18
either get thee from the door, or sit down at 3.01. 33
go get thee from the door. 3.01. 35
let him walk from whence he came, lest he catch 3.01. 37
thou that keep'st me out from the house i owe? 3.01. 42
your wife, sir knave! go get you from the door. 3.01. 64
it is a fault that springeth from your eye. 3.02. 55
a lamp of her and run from her by her own light. 3.02. 97 P
quarters, will not measure her from hip to hip. 3.02.111 P
no longer from head to foot than from hip to hip 3.02.113 P
longer from head to foot than from hip to hip: 3.02.113 P
arm, that i, amaz'd, ran from her as a witch. 3.02.144 P
road, | and if the wind blow any way from shore, 3.02.148
as from a bear a man would run for life, | so 3.02.154
life, | so fly i from her that would be my wife. 3.02.155
her trim, the merry wind | blows fair from land: 4.01. 91
far from her nest the lapwing cries away; 4.02. 27
some blessed power deliver us from hence! 4.03. 44
i have serv'd him from the hour of my nativity 4.04. 30 P
driven out of doors with it when i go from home, 4.04. 36 P
lam'd me, i shall beg with it from door to door. 4.04. 39 P
free from these slanders and this open shame! 4.04. 67
and did not i in rage depart from thence? 4.04. 76
i will discharge thee ere i go from thee: 4.04.119
she that would be your wife now ran from you. 4.04.148
to the centaur, fetch our stuff from thence; 4.04.149
sad, | and much different from the man he was; 5.01. 46
namely, some love that drew him off from home. 5.01. 56
hath scar'd thy husband from the use of wits. 5.01. 86
and it shall privilege him from your hands 5.01. 95
and take perforce my husband from the abbess. 5.01.117
he broke from those that had the guard of him, 5.01.149
this woman lock'd me out this day from dinner; 5.01.218
from whence, i think, you are come by miracle. 5.01.265
he did, and from my finger snatch'd that ring. 5.01.277
by force took dromio and my son from them, | and 5.01.353
antipholus, thou cam'st from corinth first? 5.01.363
no, sir, not i, i came from syracuse. 5.01.364
i came from corinth, my most gracious lord — 5.01.366
this purse of ducats i receiv'd from you, | and 5.01.385
sir, i must have that diamond from you. 5.01.392
master, shall i fetch your stuff from shipboard? 5.01.409
signior mountanto return'd from the wars or no? ADO 1.01. 31 P
but when you depart from me, sorrow abides and 1.01.101 P
he is no hypocrite, but prays from his heart. 1.01.151 P
if ever thou dost fall from this faith, thou 1.01.255 P
from my house — if i had it — 1.01.281 P
than to fashion a carriage to rob love from any. 1.03. 30 P
i came yonder from a great supper. 1.03. 42 P
i pray you dissuade him from her, she is no 2.01.165 P
you a toothpicker now from the furthest inch of 2.01.266 P
they have the truth of this from hero; 2.03.222 P
proudly, if i perceive the love come from her; 2.03.226 P
the brain awe a man from the career of his humor 2.03.241 P
no, not to be so odd and from all fashions | as 3.01. 72
from the crown of his head to the sole of his 3.02. 8 P
at once, as a german from the waist downward, 3.02. 35 P
all slops, and a spaniard from the hip upward, 3.02. 36 P
this shame derives itself from unknown loins"? 4.01.135
hence from her, let her die. 4.01.154
therein do men from children nothing differ. 5.01. 33
sir boy, i'll whip you from your foining fence, 5.01. 84
god bless me from a challenge! 5.01.144 P
let me hear from you. 5.01.150 P
your brother the bastard is fled from messina. 5.01.190 P
your overkindness doth wring tears from me. 5.01.293
and either i must shortly hear from him, or i 5.02. 58 P
the sight whereof i think you had from me, 5.04. 25
you had from me, | from claudio, and the prince. 5.04. 26
in my cousin's hand, stol'n from her pocket, 5.04. 89
your oath is pass'd to pass away from these. LLL 1.01. 49
hid and barr'd, you mean, from common sense. 1.01. 57
when mistresses from common sense are hid; 1.01. 64
won, | save base authority from others' books. 1.01. 87
how well this yielding rescues thee from shame! 1.01.118
the worth of many a knight | from tawny spain, 1.01.173
a letter from the magnificent armado. 1.01.191 P
event that draweth from my snow-white pen the 1.01.242 P
and by east from the west corner of thy 1.01.246 P
would deliver me from the reprobate thought of 1.02. 60 P
his requests so far | from reason's yielding, 2.01.150
for such a sum from special officers | of 2.01.161
and yours from long living! 2.01.192
their own worth from where they were glass'd, 2.01.244
is that lead slow which is fir'd from a gun? 3.01. 62
i give thee thy liberty, set thee from durance, 3.01.128 P
i have a letter from monsieur berowne to one 4.01. 53
and he from forage will incline to play. 4.01. 91
from my lord to my lady. 4.01.102
from which lord to which lady? 4.01.103
from my lord berowne, a good master of mine, 4.01.104
put l to sore, then sorel jumps from thicket, 4.02. 58
me by costard, and sent me from don armado. 4.02. 92 P
ay, sir, from one monsieur berowne, one of the 4.02.129 P
is sworn | ne'er to pluck thee from thy /thorn; 4.03.110
would from my forehead wipe a perjur'd note: 4.03.123
dumaine, thy love is far from charity, | that in 4.03.125
saw sighs reek from you, noted well your passion 4.03.138
i post from love; good lover, let me go. 4.03.186
from women's eyes this doctrine i derive: 4.03.298
from whence doth spring the true promethean fire 4.03.300
from women's eyes this doctrine i derive: 4.03.347
the law, | and who can sever love from charity? 4.03.362
from the park let us conduct them thither; 4.03.371
we will be singuled from the barbarous. 5.01. 82 P
look you what i have from the loving king. 5.02. 4
what was sent to you from fair dumaine? 5.02. 47
and quite divorce his memory from his part. 5.02.150
it were a fault to snatch words from my tongue. 5.02.382
sea-sick, i think, coming from muscovy. 5.02.393
from morn till night, out of his pavilion. 5.02.654
of sorrow justle it | from what it purpos'd; 5.02.749
remote from all the pleasures of the world; 5.02.796
to weed this wormwood from your fructful brain, 5.02.847
you shall this twelvemonth term from day to day 5.02.850
well | beteem them from the tempest of my eyes. MND 1.01.131
from athens is her house remote seven leagues; 1.01.159
and thence from athens turn away our eyes, | to 1.01.218
from lovers' food till morrow deep midnight. 1.01.223
and when this hail some heat from hermia felt, 1.01.244
and phibbus' car | shall shine from far, | and 1.02. 36
hath | a lovely boy stolen from an indian king; 2.01. 22
then slip i from her bum, down topples she, 2.01. 53
when thou hast stolen away from fairy land, 2.01. 65
here | come from the farthest steep of india? 2.01. 69
through the glimmering night | from perigenia, 2.01. 78
have suck'd up from the sea | contagious fogs; 2.01. 89
same progeny of evils comes | from our debate, 2.01.116
comes | from our debate, from our dissension; 2.01.116
as from a voyage, rich with merchandise. 2.01.134
thou shalt not from this grove | till i torment 2.01.146
and certain stars shot madly from their spheres, 2.01.153
and loos'd his love-shaft smartly from his bow, 2.01.159
and ere i take this charm from off her sight 2.01.183
i'll run from thee and hide me in the brakes, 2.01.227
can, | deserve a sweet look from demetrius' eye, 2.02.127
to pluck this crawling serpent from my breast! 2.02.146
but i will not stir from this place, do what 3.01.122 P
what angel wakes me from my flow'ry bed? 3.01.129
and they shall fetch thee jewels from the deep, 3.01.158
the honey-bags steal from the humble-bees, | and 3.01.168
and pluck the wings from painted butterflies, 3.01.172
to fan the moonbeams from his sleeping eyes. 3.01.173
he murther cries, and help from athens calls. 3.02. 26
some hats, from yielders all things catch. 3.02. 30
he have stolen away | from sleeping hermia? 3.02. 52
and from thy hated presence part i /so: 3.02. 80
go, | swifter than arrow from the tartar's bow. 3.02.101
night, that from the eye his function takes, 3.02.177
what love could press lysander from my side? 3.02.185
or i will shake thee from me like a serpent! 3.02.261
by night | and stol'n my love's heart from him? 3.02.284
tear | impatient answers from my gentle tongue? 3.02.287
and from each other look thou lead them thus, 3.02.363
to take from thence all error with his might, 3.02.368
her charmed eye release | from monster's view, 3.02.377
they willfully themselves exile from light, 3.02.386
shine, comforts, from the east, | that i may 3.02.432
from these that my poor company detest. 3.02.434
eye, | steal me a while from mine own company. 3.02.436
from off the head of this athenian swain, | that 4.01. 65
that hatred is so far from jealousy | to sleep 4.01.144
our intent | was to be gone from athens, where 4.01.152
masters, the duke is coming from the temple, and 4.02. 15 P
doth glance from heaven to earth, from earth to 5.01. 13
from heaven to earth, from earth to heaven; 5.01. 13
when i from thebes came last a conqueror. 5.01. 51
i read as much as from the rattling tongue | of 5.01.102
hecat's team | from the presence of the sun, 5.01.385
fairy sprite | hop as light as bird from brier, 5.01.394
moan to be abridg'd | from such a noble rate, MV 1.01.127
is to come fairly off from the great debts 1.01.128
and from your love i have a warranty | to 1.01.132
sometimes from her eyes | i did receive fair 1.01.163
for the four winds blow in from every coast 1.01.168
god defend me from these two! 1.02. 52 P
and there is a forerunner come from a fift, the 1.02.125 P
this jacob from our holy abram was | (as his 1.03. 72
three months from twelve; 1.03.104
a pound of man's flesh taken from a man | is not 1.03.165
pluck the young sucking cubs from the she-bear, 2.01. 29
may turn by fortune from the weaker hand: 2.01. 34
will serve me to run from this jew my master. 2.02. 2 P
and, to run away from the jew, i should be rul'd 2.02. 25 P
was not that letter from fair jessica? 2.04. 28
how i shall take her from her father's house, 2.04. 30
who riseth from a feast | with that keen 2.06. 8
the scarfed bark puts from her native bay, 2.06. 15
from the four corners of the earth they come 2.07. 39
of double ducats, stol'n from me by my daughter! 2.08. 19
lord, | you must be gone from hence immediately. 2.09. 8
then be gleaned | from the true seed of honor? 2.09. 47
pick'd from the chaff and ruin of the times | to 2.09. 48
lord, | from whom he bringeth sensible regreets: 2.09. 89
what news from genoa? 3.01. 79 P
hath an argosy cast away, coming from tripolis. 3.01.100 P
it out in length, | to stay you from election. 3.02. 24
as from her lord, her governor, her king. 3.02.165
which when you part from, lose, or give away, 3.02.172
but when this ring | parts from this finger, 3.02.184
from this finger, then parts life from hence; 3.02.184
for i am sure you can wish none from me; 3.02.191
what's the news from venice? 3.02.238
that steals the color from bassanio's cheek — 3.02.244
from tripolis, from mexico, and england, | from 3.02.268
from tripolis, from mexico, and england, | from 3.02.268
from lisbon, barbary, and india, | and not one 3.02.269
but none can drive him from the envious plea 3.02.282
i oft deliver'd from his forfeitures | many that 3.03. 22
soul, | from out the state of hellish cruelty! 3.04. 21
pity, void and empty | from any dram of mercy. 4.01. 6
from brassy bosoms and rough hearts of flints, 4.01. 31
from stubborn turks, and tartars never train'd 4.01. 32
a messenger with letters from the doctor, | new 4.01.108
letters from the doctor, | new come from padua. 4.01.109
came you from padua, from bellario? 4.01.119
came you from padua, from bellario? 4.01.119
from both, my lord. bellario greets your grace. 4.01.120
to cut the forfeiture from that bankrout there. 4.01.122
even from the gallows did his fell soul fleet, 4.01.135
till thou canst rail the seal from off my bond, 4.01.139
this letter from bellario doth commend | a young 4.01.143
come you from old bellario? 4.01.169
it droppeth as the gentle rain from heaven 4.01.185
from which ling'ring penance | of such misery 4.01.271
and you must cut this flesh from off his breast, 4.01.302
i pray you give me leave to go from hence, | i 4.01.395
and for your love i'll take this ring from you. 4.01.427
night | did jessica steal from the wealthy jew, 5.01. 15
and with an unthrift love did run from venice, 5.01. 16
he is not, nor we have not heard from him. 5.01. 35
tell him there's a post come from my master, 5.01. 46 P
nor pluck it from his finger, for the wealth 5.01.173
lie not a night from home. 5.01.230
it comes from padua, from bellario. 5.01.268
it comes from padua, from bellario. 5.01.268
from the rich jew, a special deed of gift, 5.01.292
that differs not from the stalling of an ox? AYL 1.01. 10 P
gave me his countenance seems to take from me. 1.01. 18 P
not take this hand from thy throat till this 1.01. 60 P
obscuring and hiding from me all gentleman-like 1.01. 69 P
being ever from their cradles bred together, 1.01.108 P
either you might stay him from his intendment, 1.01.133 P
underhand means labor'd to dissuade him from it; 1.01.141 P
he hath taken away from thy father perforce, i 1.02. 20 P
from henceforth i will, coz, and devise sports. 1.02. 24 P
mock the good huswife fortune from her wheel, 1.02. 32 P
now thou goest from fortune's office to nature's 1.02. 40 P
have so mightily persuaded him from a first. 1.02.207 P
deed | hadst thou descended from another house. 1.02.228
thus must i from the smoke into the smother, 1.02.287
from tyrant duke unto a tyrant brother. 1.02.288
your safest haste, | and get you from our court. 1.03. 42
or, if we did derive it from our friends, 1.03. 62
way | to hide us from pursuit that will be made 1.03.136
more free from peril than the envious court? 2.01. 4
and this our life, exempt from public haunt, 2.01. 15
that from the hunter's aim had ta'en a hurt, 2.01. 34
from /seventeen years till now almost fourscore 2.03. 71
or if thou hast not broke from company 2.04. 40
instead of her, from whom i took two cods and, 2.04. 52 P
and then he drew a dial from his poke, | and, 2.07. 20
and so, from hour to hour, we ripe and ripe, 2.07. 26
and then, from hour to hour, we rot and rot; 2.07. 27
of bare distress hath ta'en from me the show 2.07. 95
feast, | if ever from your eyelids wip'd a tear, 2.07.116
with thy chaste eye, from thy pale sphere above, 3.02. 3
"from the east to western inde, | no jewel is 3.02. 88
from whence you have studied your questions. 3.02.274 P
i drave my suitor from his mad humor of love to 3.02.418 P
of many simples, extracted from many objects, 4.01. 17 P
men have died from time to time and worms have 4.01.107 P
when last the young orlando parted from you | he 4.03. 98
hurtling | from miserable slumber i awaked. 4.03.132
when from the first to last betwixt us two 4.03.139
in some little measure draw a belief from you, 5.02. 57 P
and from hence i go | to make these doubts all 5.04. 24
thy daughter, | hymen from heaven brought her, 5.04.112
both from his enterprise and from the world, 5.04.162
both from his enterprise and from the world, 5.04.162
tell him from me, as he will win my love, | he SHR in.1. 109
how my men will stay themselves from laughter in.1. 134
call home thy ancient thoughts from banishment, in.2. 31
and fetch shrill echoes from the hollow earth. in.2. 46
being all this time abandon'd from your bed. in.2. 115
that i should yet absent me from your bed. in.2. 123
from all such devils, good lord deliver us! 1.01. 66
now, | affection is not rated from the heart. 1.01.160
nay, then 'tis time to stir him from his trance. 1.01.177
while i make way from hence to save my life. 1.01.234
gale | blows you to padua here from old verona? 1.02. 49
and her withholds from me /and other more, 1.02.121
i met, | upon agreement from us to his liking, 1.02.182
her father keeps from all access of suitors, 1.02.259
it is extempore, from my mother-wit. 2.01.263
kate, | and bring you from a wild kate to a kate 2.01.277
why then the maid is mine from all the world, 2.01.384
was ajax, call'd so from his grandfather. 3.01. 53
whatever fortune stays him from his word. 3.02. 23
being restrain'd to keep him from stumbling, 3.02. 58 P
hath all so long detain'd you from your wife, 3.02.103
i stay too long from her. 3.02.110
signior gremio, came you from the church? 3.02.149
as willingly as e'er i came from school. 3.02.150
it, thou mayst slide from my shoulder to my heel 4.01. 15 P
and walter's dagger was not come from sheathing; 4.01.135
bring it from the dresser | and serve it thus to 4.01.163
speak, | and sits as one new risen from a dream. 4.01.186
bills for money by exchange | from florence, and 4.02. 90
lucentio that his father is come from pisa, and 5.01. 28 P
his father is come from padua and here looking 5.01. 30 P
and, as the jest did glance away from me, | 'tis 5.02. 61
and dart not scornful glances from those eyes, 5.02.137
in delivering my son from me, i bury a second AWW 1.01. 1 P
your commendations, madam, get from her tears. 1.01. 46 P
her sorrows takes all livelihood from her cheek. 1.01. 51 P
bless our poor virginity from underminers and 1.01.120 P
a certainty, vouch'd from our cousin austria, 1.02. 5
home, | i quickly were dissolved from my hive, 1.02. 66
breeds | a native slip to us from foreign seeds. 1.03.146
i am from humble, he from honored name; 1.03.156
i am from humble, he from honored name; 1.03.156
king, | had from the conversation of my thoughts 1.03.234
warlike principles | do not throw from you; 2.01. 2
never ransom nature | from her inaidible estate; 2.01.119
humbly entreating from your royal thoughts | a 2.01.127
great floods have flown | from simple sources; 2.01.140
what is infirm from your sound parts shall fly, 2.01.167
exempted be from me the arrogance | to choose 2.01.195
to choose from forth the royal blood of france, 2.01.196
from whence thou cam'st, how tended on, but rest 2.01.207
from below your duke to beneath your constable, 2.02. 30 P

now, dian, from thy altar do i fly, | and to 2.03. 74
know'st she has rais'd me from my sickly bed. 2.03.111
from lowest place /when virtuous things proceed, 2.03.125
when rather from our acts we them derive | than 2.03.136
honor and wealth from me. 2.03.144
or i will throw thee from my care for ever 2.03.162
dissuade me from believing thee a vessel of too 2.03.204 P
there's letters from my mother; 2.03.276
in earth, from whence god send her quickly! 2.04. 12 P
you have it from his own deliverance. 2.05. 4 P
i have, sir, as i was commanded from you, 2.05. 54
so that from point to point now have you heard 3.01. 1
and all the honors that can fly from us | shall 3.01. 20
is't i | that chase thee from thy country, and 3.02.103
it i | that drive thee from the sportive court, 3.02.106
that from the bloody course of war | my dearest 3.04. 8
whilst i from far | his name with zealous fervor 3.04. 10
sent him forth | from courtly friends, with 3.04. 14
grant, reprieve him from the wrath | of greatest 3.04. 28
you came, i think, from france? 3.05. 46
he stole from france, | as 'tis reported, for 3.05. 52
whom i am sure he knows not from the enemy. 3.06. 24 P
and by midnight look to hear further from me. 3.06. 77 P
counsel i have spoken | is so from word to word; 3.07. 10
hath succeeded in his house | from son to son, 3.07. 24
nothing steads us | to chide him from our eaves, 3.07. 42
i swore i leapt from the window of the citadel 4.01. 55 P
art, will lead thee on | to gather from thee. 4.01. 82
keep him muffled | till we do hear from them. 4.01. 91
but have no power | to give it from me. 4.02. 41
house, | bequeathed down from many ancestors, 4.02. 43
house, | bequeathed down from many ancestors, 4.02. 47
wife some two months since fled from his house. 4.03. 48 P
the particular confirmations, point from point, 4.03. 62 P
from the time of his remembrance to this very 4.03.109 P
dare not shake the snow from off their cassocks, 4.03.168 P
paris, from whence he was whipt for getting the 4.03.186 P
of it, and cut th' entail from all remainders, 4.03.280 P
not this to suggest thee from thy master thou 4.05. 45 P
his highness comes post from marsellis, of as 4.05. 80 P
from the report that goes upon your goodness, 5.01. 13
a paper from fortune's close-stool to give to a 5.02. 16 P
strikes some scores away | from the great compt; 5.03. 57
give a favor from you | to sparkle in the 5.03. 74
in florence was it from a casement thrown me, 5.03. 93
by what rough enforcement | you got it from her. 5.03.108
that she would never put it from her finger, 5.03.109
here's a petition from a florentine, | who hath 5.03.130
he stole from florence, taking no leave, and i 5.03.143 P
florentine, | derived from the ancient capilet. 5.03.159
"when from my finger you can get this ring | and 5.03.312
let us from point to point this story know, | to 5.03.325
how now, what news from her? TN 1.01. 22
but from her handmaid do return this answer: 1.01. 24
not three hours' travel from this very place. 1.02. 23
for but a month ago i went from hence, | and 1.02. 31
from the count orsino, is it? 1.05.101 P
if it be a suit from the count, i am sick, or 1.05.108 P
but this is from my commission; 1.05.189 P
in me have i learn'd from my entertainment. 1.05.215 P
you any commission from your lord to negotiate 1.05.231 P
you will not extort from me what i am willing to 2.01. 13 P
before you took me from the breach of the sea 2.01. 22 P
thou wilt drop, that they come from my niece, 2.03.165 P
having come from a day-bed, where i have left 2.05. 48 P
though our silence be drawn from us with cars, 2.05. 63 P
pension of thousands to be paid from the sophy. 2.05.181 P
to solicit that | than music from the spheres. 3.01.110
do not extort thy reasons from this clause, 3.01.153
some excellent jests, fire-new from the mint, 3.02. 22 P
we shall have a rare letter from him; 3.02. 56 P
answer'd in repaying | what we took from them, 3.03. 34
note, that keeps you from the blow of the law. 3.04.153 P
he will find it comes from a clodpole. 3.04.190 P
is very free and clear from any image of offense 3.04.228 P
methinks his words do from such passion fly 3.04.373
i prithee, foolish greek, depart from me. 4.01. 18
i will be free from thee. 4.01. 41
an ounce or two of this malapert blood from you. 4.01. 44 P
took the phoenix and her fraught from candy, 5.01. 61
from the rude sea's enrag'd and foamy mouth 5.01. 78
that screws me from my true place in your favor, 5.01.123
clad | which from the womb i did participate. 5.01.238
and died that day when viola from her birth 5.01.244
continent the fire | that severs day from night. 5.01.272
own | from my remembrance clearly banish'd his. 5.01.282
you shall from this time be | your master's 5.01.325
write from it, if you can, in hand or phrase, 5.01.332
sweet sister, | we will not part from hence. 5.01.385
as it were, from the ends of oppos'd winds. WT 1.01. 31 P
you had drawn oaths from him not to stay. 1.02. 29
say this to him, | he's beat from his best ward. 1.02. 33
derive a liberty | from heartiness, from bounty, 1.02.113
derive a liberty | from heartiness, from bounty, 1.02.113
think it — | from east, west, north, and south. 1.02.203
i from thee departed | thy penitent reform'd. 1.02.238
behind, restraining | from course requir'd; 1.02.245
whom i from meaner form | have bench'd and 1.02.313
if from me he have wholesome beverage, | account 1.02.346
a lip of much contempt, speeds from me, and | so 1.02.373
(from him that has most cause to grieve it 2.01. 77
now, from the oracle | they will bring all, 2.01.185
from our free person she should be confin'd, 2.01.194
and honor from th' access of gentle visitors. 2.02. 10
if wit flow from't | as boldness from my bosom, 2.02. 51
him of that humor | that presses him from sleep. 2.03. 39
from all dishonesty he can. 2.03. 47
i say, i come | from your good queen. 2.03. 58
from those you sent to th' oracle are come | an 2.03.194
being well arriv'd from delphos, are both landed 2.03.196
my part no other | but what comes from myself, 3.02. 25
for honor, | 'tis a derivative from me to mine, 3.02. 44
even since it could speak, from an infant, 3.02. 70
of my body, from his presence | i am barr'd, 3.02. 97
(starr'd most unluckily) is from my breast 3.02. 99
and from thence have brought | this seal'd-up 3.02.126
the fury spent, anon | did this break from her: 3.03. 27
if the bear be gone from the gentleman and how 3.03.129 P
is of late much retir'd from court and is less 4.02. 32 P
from whom i have this intelligence, that he is 4.02. 36 P
that he is seldom from the house of a most 4.02. 37 P
they say, that from very nothing, and beyond the 4.02. 38 P
can be thought to begin from such a cottage. 4.02. 43 P
from whose simplicity i think it not uneasy to 4.02. 49 P
my money and apparel ta'en from me, and these 4.03. 62 P
frighted, thou let'st fall | from dis's waggon! 4.04.118
what maids lack from head to heel. 4.04.227
bless me from marrying a usurer! 4.04.268 P
that does take | your mind from feasting. 4.04.347
the gifts she looks from me are pack'd and 4.04.358
know man from man? 4.04.400
thou shalt), we'll bar thee from succession, 4.04.429
yet we free thee | from the dead blow of it. 4.04.434
court | hides not his visage from our cottage, 4.04.445
from my succession wipe me, father, i | am heir 4.04.480
save him from danger, do him love and honor, 4.04.510
you may | enjoy your mistress — from the whom, 4.04.528
him, with | what you (as from your father) shall 4.04.559
horn-ring, to keep my pack from fasting. 4.04.600 P
and scar'd my choughs from the chaff, i had not 4.04.617 P
and those that you'll procure from king leontes? 4.04.621
here's nobody will steal that from thee. 4.04.632 P
stealing away from his father with his clog at 4.04.679 P
receives not thy nose court-odor from me? 4.04.733 P
i insinuate, /that toze from thee thy business, 4.04.735 P
or, from the all that are, took something good 5.01. 14
eyes, | have taken treasure from her lips — 5.01. 54
and from him | give you all greetings that a 5.01.139
good my lord, | she came from libya. 5.01.157
most royal sir, from thence; 5.01.159
from him, whose daughter | his tears proclaim'd 5.01.159
i have from your sicilian shores dismiss'd; 5.01.164
purge all infection from our air whilest you 5.01.169
father's bless'd | (as he from heaven merits it) 5.01.175
sir, | bohemia greets you from himself by me; 5.01.181
fled from his father, from his hopes, and with 5.01.184
fled from his father, from his hopes, and with 5.01.184
i now came from him. 5.01.186
most sorry, you have broken from his liking, 5.01.212
she lifted the princess from the earth, and so 5.02. 76 P
till, from one sign of dolor to another, she did 5.02. 87 P
from thy admiring daughter took the spirits, 5.03. 41
to take off so much grief from you as he | will 5.03. 55
still methinks | there is an air comes from her. 5.03. 78
for from him | dear life redeems you. 5.03.102
she has liv'd, | or how stol'n from the dead. 5.03.115
and from your sacred vials pour your graces 5.03.122
let's from this place. 5.03.146
lead us from hence, where we may leisurely 5.03.152
then take my king's defiance from my mouth, JN 1.01. 21
come from the country to be judg'd by you | that 1.01. 45
at least from fair five hundred pound a year. 1.01. 69
might have kept | this calf, bred from his cow, 1.01.124
calf, bred from his cow, from all the world; 1.01.124
would i might never stir from off this place, 1.01.145
from henceforth bear his name whose form thou 1.01.160
something about, a little from the right, | in 1.01.170
but from the inward motion to deliver | sweet, 1.01.212
nor keep his princely heart from richard's hand. 1.01.267
and coops from other lands her islanders, | even 2.01. 25
secure | and confident from foreign purposes, 2.01. 28
my lord chatillion may from england bring | that 2.01. 46
then turn your forces from this paltry siege, 2.01. 54
if that war return | from france to england, 2.01. 90
but thou from loving england art so far | that 2.01. 94
from whom hast thou this great commission, 2.01.110
france, | to draw my answer from thy articles? 2.01.111
from that supernal judge that stirs good 2.01.112
but, ass, i'll take that burthen from your back, 2.01.145
those heaven-moving pearls from his poor eyes, 2.01.169
removed from thy sin-conceiving womb. 2.01.182
by this time from their fixed beds of lime | had 2.01.219
walls | can hide you from our messengers of war, 2.01.260
we for the worthiest hold the right from both. 2.01.282
heralds, from off our tow'rs we might behold, 2.01.325
from first to last, the onset and retire | of 2.01.326
we from the west will send destruction | into 2.01.409
i from the north. 2.01.411
our thunder from the south | shall rain their 2.01.411
from north to south — | austria and france 2.01.413
mountains and rocks | more free from motion, no, 2.01.453
nay, ask me if i can refrain from love, | for i 2.01.525
makes it take head from all indifferency, | from 2.01.579
from all direction, purpose, course, intent — 2.01.580
hath drawn him from his own determin'd aid, 2.01.584
from a resolv'd and honorable war | to a most 2.01.585
she is corrupted, chang'd, and won from thee; 3.01. 55
and from pope innocent the legate here, | do in 3.01.139
archbishop | of canterbury, from that holy see? 3.01.144
and from the mouth of england | add thus much 3.01.152
who in that sale sells pardon from himself; 3.01.167
doth revolt | from his allegiance to an heretic, 3.01.175
is purchase of a heavy curse from rome, | or the 3.01.205
the lady constance speaks not from her faith, 3.01.210
speaks not from her faith, | but from her need. 3.01.211
o, be remov'd from him, and answer well! 3.01.218
as now again to snatch our palm from palm, 3.01.244
england, i will fall from thee. 3.01.320
is scattered and disjoin'd from fellowship. 3.04. 3
arise forth from the couch of lasting night, 3.04. 27
and rouse from sleep that fell anatomy | which 3.04. 40
i tore them from their bonds, and cried aloud, 3.04. 70
and chase the native beauty from his cheek, 3.04. 83
of all his people shall revolt from him, | and 3.04.165
i am best pleas'd to be from such a deed. 4.01. 85
from france to england. 4.02.110
but this from rumor's tongue | i idly heard — 4.02.123
with me | from forth the streets of pomfret, 4.02.148
and fly, like thought, from them to me again. 4.02.175
who brought that letter from the cardinal? 4.03. 14
from whose obedience i forbid my soul, 4.03. 64
you shall think the devil is come from hell. 4.03.100
that ever spider twisted from her womb | will 4.03.128
up | from forth this morsel of dead royalty! 4.03.143
now powers from home and discontents at home 4.03.151
take again | from this my hand, as holding of 5.01. 3
and from his holiness use all your power | to 5.01. 6
that borrow their behaviors from the great, 5.01. 51
to meet displeasure farther from the doors, 5.01. 60
that i must draw this metal from my side | to be 5.02. 16
would bear thee from the knowledge of thyself, 5.02. 35
to give us warrant from the hand of heaven, 5.02. 66
and cull'd these fiery spirits from the world, 5.02.114
from the king | i come to learn how you have 5.02.120
arms, | from out the circle of his territories. 5.02.136
resolveth from his figure 'gainst the fire? 5.04. 25
from forth the noise and rumor of the field, 5.04. 45
me | that any accent breaking from thy tongue 5.06. 14
and from the organ-pipe of frailty sings | his 5.07. 23
who half an hour since came from the dolphin, 5.07. 83
and brings from him such offers of our peace 5.07. 84
prince, | and free from other misbegotten hate, R2 1.01. 33
from giving reins and spurs to my free speech, 1.01. 55
fetch from false mowbray their first head and 1.01. 97
even from the tongueless caverns of the earth, 1.01.105
it issues from the rancor of a villain, | a 1.01.143
one, | take honor from me, and my life is done. 1.01.183
o, god defend my soul from such deep sin! 1.01.187
or seven fair branches springing from one root. 1.02. 13
take from my mouth the wish of happy years. 1.03. 94
might from our quiet confines fright fair peace, 1.03.137
and all unlook'd for from your highness' mouth. 1.03.155
which robs my tongue from breathing native 1.03.173
then thus i turn me from my country's light, 1.03.176
as now our flesh is banish'd from this land; 1.03.197
my name be blotted from the book of life, | and 1.03.202
and i from heaven banish'd as from hence! 1.03.203
and i from heaven banish'd as from hence! 1.03.203
hath from the number of his banish'd years 1.03.210
return with welcome home from banishment. 1.03.212
and pluck nights from me, but not lend a morrow; 1.03.228
know, | from where you do remain let paper show. 1.03.250
of world | i wander from the jewels that i love. 1.03.270
when time shall call him home from banishment, 1.04. 21
renowned for their deeds as far from home, | for 2.01. 53
and who abstains from meat that is not gaunt? 2.01. 76
from forth thy reach he would have laid thy 2.01.106
blood | with fury from his native residence. 2.01.119
head | should run thy head from thy unreverent 2.01.123
away, and take from time | his charters and his 2.01.195
i have from le port blanc, | a bay in britain, 2.01.277
that late broke from the duke of exeter, | his 2.01.281
redeem from broking pawn the blemish'd crown, 2.01.293
more than with parting from my lord the king. 2.02. 13
is still deriv'd | from some forefather grief; 2.02. 35
way | from ravenspurgh to cotshall will be found 2.03. 9
sent from my brother worcester, whencesoever. 2.03. 22
from the most gracious regent of this land, 2.03. 77
from forth the ranks of many thousand french, 2.03.102
and royalties | pluck'd from my arms perforce — 2.03.121
and yet we hear no tidings from the king, 2.04. 3
fall to the base earth from the firmament. 2.04. 20
to wash your blood | from off my hands, here in 3.01. 6
with tears drawn from her eyes by your foul 3.01. 15
from my own windows torn my household coat, 3.01. 24
and when they from thy bosom pluck a flower, 3.02. 19
but when from under this terrestrial ball | he 3.02. 41
of night being pluck'd from off their backs, 3.02. 45
can wash the balm off from an anointed king; 3.02. 55
all souls that will be safe, fly from my side, 3.02. 80
from richard's night to bullingbrook's fair day. 3.02.218
richard not far from hence hath hid his head. 3.03. 6
rain'd from the wounds of slaughtered englishmen 3.03. 44
how far off from the mind of bullingbrook | it 3.03. 45
that from this castle's tottered battlements 3.03. 52
sun | from out the fiery portal of the east, 3.03. 64
that hath dismiss'd us from our stewardship, 3.03. 78
have torn their souls by turning them from us, 3.03. 83
currents that spring from one most gracious head 3.03.108
northumberland comes back from bullingbrook. 3.03.142
the soil's fertility from wholesome flowers. 3.04. 39
that reacheth from the restful english court 4.01. 12
in thy treacherous ear | from /sun to /sun. 4.01. 55
i come to thee | from plume-pluck'd richard, who 4.01.108
ascend his throne, descending now from him, 4.01.111
learn him forbearance from so foul a wrong. 4.01.120
from which awak'd, the truth of what we are 5.01. 19
as from my death-bed, thy last living leave. 5.01. 39
to pluck him headlong from the usurped throne. 5.01. 65
from whence set forth in pomp | she came adorned 5.01. 78
ay, hand from hand, my love, and heart from 5.01. 82
hand from hand, my love, and heart from heart. 5.01. 82
where rude misgoverned hands from windows' tops 5.02. 5
he, from the one side to the other turning, 5.02. 18
what news from oxford? 5.02. 52
and wilt thou pluck my fair son from mine age, 5.02. 92
an' never will i rise up from the ground | till 5.02.116
and from the common'st creature pluck a glove 5.03. 17
i tore it from the traitor's bosom, king; 5.03. 55
from whence this stream through muddy passages 5.03. 62
our scene is alt'red from a serious thing, | and 5.03. 79
his words come from his mouth, ours from our 5.03.102
words come from his mouth, ours from our breast; 5.03.102
that would divorce this terror from my heart" — 5.04. 9
is pointing still, in cleansing them from tears. 5.05. 54
that jade hath eat bread from my royal hand, 5.05. 85
who | lately came from the king, commands the 5.05.101
i have from oxford sent to london | the heads of 5.06. 13
as thou liv'st in peace, die free from strife, 5.06. 27
from your own mouth, my lord, did i this deed. 5.06. 37
to wash this blood off from my guilty hand. 5.06. 50
came | a post from wales loaden with heavy news, 1H4 1.01. 37
uneven and unwelcome news | came from the north, 1.01. 51
sir walter blunt, new lighted from his horse, 1.01. 63
but let him from my thoughts. 1.01. 91
of life in thee, from praying to purse-taking. 1.02.103 P
rob them, cut this head off from my shoulders. 1.02.166 P
to smother up his beauty from the world, | that, 1.02.199
sure | i will from henceforth rather be myself, 1.03. 5
or you shall hear in such a kind from me | as 1.03.121
from whence he intercepted did return | to be 1.03.151
send danger from the east unto the west, | so 1.03.195
so honor cross it from the north to south, | and 1.03.196
to pluck bright honor from the pale-fac'd moon, 1.03.202

when you and he came back from ravenspurgh — 1.03.248
thou variest no more from picking of purses than 2.01. 50 P
purses than giving direction doth from laboring; 2.01. 51 P
if they scape from your encounter, then they 2.02. 62 P
been | a banish'd woman from my harry's bed? 2.03. 39
what is't that takes from thee | thy stomach, 2.03. 40
butler brought those horses from the sheriff? 2.03. 67
show it a fair pair of heels and run from it? 2.04. 48 P
taken from us it is: 2.04.161 P
with a word, outfac'd you from your prize, and 2.04.256 P
now find out to hide thee from this open and 2.04.264 P
he says he comes from your father. 2.04.289 P
here was sir john bracy from your father; 2.04.334 P
my noble lord, from eastcheap. 2.04.441 P
thou art violently carried away from grace, 2.04.446 P
the goats ran from the mountains, and the herds 3.01. 38
i can call spirits from the vasty deep. 3.01. 52
thrice from the banks of wye | and 3.01. 64
england, from trent and severn hitherto, | by 3.01. 73
the remnant northward lying off from trent. 3.01. 78
from whom you now must steal and take no leave, 3.01. 92
methinks my moi'ty, north from burton here, | in 3.01. 95
and cuts me from the best of all my land | a 3.01. 98
much | as on the other side it takes from you. 3.01.110
stuff | as puts me from my faith. 3.01.153
thou pourest down from these swelling heavens 3.01.199
hang in the air a thousand leagues from hence, 3.01.224
quite from the flight of all thy ancestors. 3.02. 31
and then i stole all courtesy from heaven, | and 3.02. 50
that i did pluck allegiance from men's hearts, 3.02. 52
loud shouts and salutations from their mouths, 3.02. 53
when i from france set foot at ravenspurgh, 3.02. 95
holds from all soldiers chief majority | and 3.02.109
your majesty's good thoughts away from me! 3.02.131
or i will tear the reckoning from his heart. 3.02.152
these letters come from your father. 4.01. 14
letters from him! why comes he not himself? 4.01. 15
of our proceedings kept the earl from hence, 4.01. 65
side | must keep aloof from strict arbitrement, 4.01. 70
every loop from whence | the eye of reason may 4.01. 71
rise from the ground like feathered mercury, 4.01.106
as if an angel /dropp'd down from the clouds 4.01.108
prodigals lately come from swine–keeping, from 4.02. 35 P
from swine–keeping, from eating draff and husks. 4.02. 35 P
the truth, stol'n from my host at saint albons, 4.02. 46 P
i come with gracious offers from the king, | if 4.03. 30
you conjure from the breast of civil peace 4.03. 43
rated mine uncle from the council–board, | in 4.03. 99
in rage dismiss'd my father from the court, 4.03.100
looks | of favor from myself and all our house, 5.01. 31
and from this swarm of fair advantages | you 5.01. 55
on, | and, his corruption being ta'en from us, 5.02. 22
i thank him that he cuts me from my tale, | for 5.02. 90
the prince of wales from such a field as this, 5.04. 12
i'll make it greater ere i part from thee, | and 5.04. 71
the fortune of the day quite turn'd from him, 5.05. 18
and falling from a hill, he was so bruis'd 5.05. 21
i, from the orient to the drooping west 2H4 in 3
from rumor's tongues | they bring smooth in 39
i bring you certain news from shrewsbury. 1.01. 12
came you from shrewsbury? 1.01. 24
spake with one, my lord, that came from thence, 1.01. 25
more than he haply may retail from me. 1.01. 32
of him | i did demand what news from shrewsbury. 1.01. 40
say, morton, didst thou come from shrewsbury? 1.01. 64
i ran from shrewsbury, my noble lord, | where 1.01. 65
hath by instinct knowledge from others' eyes 1.01. 86
from whence with life he never more sprung up. 1.01.111
from the best–temper'd courage in his troops, 1.01.115
for from his metal was his party steeled, 1.01.116
aiming at their safety, | fly from the field. 1.01.125
sweet earl, divorce not wisdom from your honor, 1.01.162
this present grief had wip'd it from my mind. 1.01.211
is return'd with some discomfort from wales. 1.02.104 P
it hath it original from much grief, from study, 1.02.115 P
it hath it original from much grief, from study, 1.02.115 P
and fubb'd off, from this day to that day, that 2.01. 35 P
stand from him, fellow, wherefore hang'st thou 2.01. 68
with such more than impudent sauciness from you, 2.01.113 P
you, can thrust me from a level consideration. 2.01.113 P
i do desire deliverance from these officers, 2.01.127 P
comes the king back from wales, my noble lord? 2.01.176 P
hath in reason taken from me all ostentation of 2.02. 50 P
'a had him from me christian, and look if the 2.02. 71 P
discern no part of his face from the window. 2.02. 80 P
o that this blossom could be kept from cankers! 2.02. 94 P
be kin to us, or they will fetch it from japhet. 2.02.118 P
from a god to a bull? 2.02.173 P
from a prince to a prentice? 2.02.174 P
you do draw my spirits from me | with new 2.03. 46
the rogue fled from me like quicksilver. 2.04.228 P
o jesu, are you come from wales? 2.04.293 P
weak and wearied posts | come from the north, 2.04.357
new–dated letters from northumberland, | their 4.01. 8
health and fair greeting from our general, | the 4.01. 27
but this is mere digression from my purpose. 4.01.138
here come i from our princely general | to know 4.01.139
to tell you from his grace | that he will give 4.01.140
offer, | and it proceeds from policy, not love. 4.01.146
this offer comes from mercy, not from fear. 4.01.148
this offer comes from mercy, not from fear. 4.01.148
as chaff, | and good from bad find no partition. 4.01.194
hath been with scorn shov'd from the court, 4.02. 37
and heir from heir shall hold his quarrel up 4.02. 48
the leaders, having charge from you to stand, 4.02. 99
it, and makes it course from the inwards to the 4.03.106 P
the blood weeps from my heart when i do shape, 4.04. 58
from enemies heavens keep your majesty, | and, 4.04. 94
stand from him, give him air, he'll straight be 4.04.116
that from this golden rigol hath divorc'd | so 4.05. 36
thy due from me | is tears and heavy sorrows of 4.05. 37
my due from thee is this imperial crown, | which 4.05. 41
which, as immediate from thy place and blood, 4.05. 42
it shall not force | this lineal honor from me. 4.05. 46
this from thee | will i to mine leave, as 'tis 4.05. 46
where is the crown? who took it from my pillow? 4.05. 57
bee, tolling from every flower | /the /virtuous 4.05. 74
is held from falling with so weak a wind | that 4.05. 99
now, | from every region, apes of idleness! 4.05.122
for the fift harry from curb'd license plucks 4.05.130
let me no more from this obedience rise, | which 4.05.146
of it, | let god for ever keep it from my head, 4.05.174
wings is flown | from this bare wither'd trunk. 4.05.229
we hope no otherwise from your majesty. 5.02. 62
to pluck down justice from your aweful bench? 5.02. 86
one pistol come from the court with news. 5.03. 81 P
from the court? 5.03. 82 P
sir, you come with news from the court, i take 5.03.110 P
two a' clock ere they come from the coronation. 5.05. 4 P
rouse up revenge from ebon den with fell 5.05. 37
given to the church, | would they strip from us; H5 1.01. 11
sequestration | from open haunts and popularity. 1.01. 59
deriv'd from edward, his great–grandfather. 1.01. 89
but this, which they produce from pharamond: 1.02. 37
to bar your highness claiming from the female, 1.02. 92
titles | usurp'd from you and your progenitors. 1.02. 95
great–grandsire's tomb, | from whom you claim; 1.02.104
our inland from the pilfering borderers. 1.02.142
cannot defend our own doors from the dog, | let 1.02.218
call in the messengers sent from the dolphin. 1.02.221
for we hear | your greeting is from him, not 1.02.236
your greeting is from him, not from the king. 1.02.236
that men are merriest when they are from home. 1.02.272
mock mothers from their sons, mock castles down; 1.02.286
and hides a sword, from hilts unto the point, 2.pr. 9
the king is set from london, and the scene | is 2.pr. 34
and from the powd'ring–tub of infamy | fetch 2.01. 75
we carry not a heart with us from hence | that 2.02. 21
fetch'd | from glist'ring semblances of piety; 2.02.117
free from gross passion, or of mirth or anger, 2.02.132
myself, | prevented from a damned enterprise. 2.02.164
and from his coffers | receiv'd the golden 2.02.168
the king will be gone from southampton. 2.03. 45 P
embassadors from harry king of england | do 2.04. 65
from our brother of england? 2.04. 75
from him, and thus he greets your majesty: 2.04. 76
pick'd from the worm–holes of long–vanish'd days 2.04. 86
days, | nor from the dust of old oblivion rak'd, 2.04. 87
from his most fam'd of famous ancestors, 2.04. 92
indirectly held | from him, the native and true 2.04. 95
what to him from england? 2.04.116
th' embassador from the french comes back, 3.pr. 28
whose blood is fet from fathers of war–proof! 3.01. 18
have in these parts from morn till even fought, 3.01. 20
if i should take from another's pocket to put 3.02. 49 P
now, captain fluellen, come you from the bridge? 3.06. 1 P
and i must speak with him from the pridge. 3.06. 86 P
how now, fluellen, cam'st thou from the bridge? 3.06. 88 P
there be nothing compell'd from the villages; 3.06.109 P
he bounds from the earth, as if his entrails 3.07. 13 P
from the rising of the lark to the lodging of 3.07. 31 P
from camp to camp, through the foul womb of 4.pr. 4
and from the tents | the armorers, accomplishing 4.pr. 11
this ruin'd band | walking from watch to watch, 4.pr. 30
walking from watch to watch, from tent to tent, 4.pr. 30
beholding him, plucks comfort from his looks. 4.pr. 42
thus may we gather honey from the weed, | and 4.01. 11
and from heart–string | i love the lovely bully. 4.01. 47
men, they have no wings to fly from god. 4.01.168 P
will go out | with titles blown from adulation? 4.01.254
but like a lackey, from the rise to set, 4.01.272
take from them now | the sense of reck'ning, /if 4.01.290
opposed numbers | pluck their hearts from them. 4.01.292
than from it issued forced drops of blood. 4.01.297
the gum down–roping from their pale–dead eyes, 4.02. 48
i will the banner from a trumpet take, | and use 4.02. 61
no, faith, my coz, wish not a man from england. 4.03. 30
as one man more methinks would share from me, 4.03. 32
by, | from this day to the ending of the world, 4.03. 58
thou dost not wish more help from england, coz? 4.03. 73
and a sweet retire | from off these fields, 4.03. 87
so full a voice issue from so empty a heart; 4.04. 68 P
from helmet to the spur all blood he was. 4.06. 6
those waters from me which i would have stopp'd, 4.06. 29
rascals that ran from the battle ha' done this 4.07. 6 P
stones | enforced from the old assyrian slings; 4.07. 62
to sort our nobles from our common men. 4.07. 74
great sort, quite from the answer of his degree. 4.07.136 P
together, i pluck'd this glove from his helm. 4.07.155 P
all offenses, my lord, come from the heart. 4.08. 46 P
never came any from mine that might offend your 4.08. 47 P
or take that praise from god | which is his only 4.08.115
where ne'er from france arriv'd more happy men. 4.08.126
being free from vainness and self–glorious pride 5.pr. 20
signal, and ostent | quite from himself to god. 5.pr. 22
as in good time he may, from ireland coming, 5.pr. 31
and from my weary limbs | honor is cudgell'd. 5.01. 84
alas, she hath from france too long been chas'd, 5.02. 38
son, and from her blood raise up | issue to me, 5.02.348
prosper this realm, keep it from civil broils, 1H6 1.01. 53
make him burst his lead and rise from death. 1.01. 64
france is revolted from the english quite, 1.01. 90
o, whither shall we fly from this reproach? 1.01. 97
lord, | retiring from the siege of orleance, 1.01.111
to keep the horsemen off from breaking in. 1.01.119
i'll hale the dolphin headlong from his throne, 1.01.149
supply, | and hardly keeps his men from mutiny, 1.01.160
the king from eltam i intend to send, | and sit 1.01.176
which by a vision sent to her from heaven 1.02. 52
come, come from behind, | i know thee well, 1.02. 66
be not amaz'd, there's nothing hid from me; 1.02. 68
vocation | and free my country from calamity. 1.02. 81
and while i live, i'll ne'er fly from a man. 1.02.103
love, | for my profession's sacred from above. 1.02.114
when i have chased all thy foes from hence, 1.02.115
drive them from orleance and be immortaliz'd. 1.02.148
from him i have express commandement | that thou 1.03. 20
then broke i from the officers that led me, 1.04. 44
and from my shoulders crack my arms asunder, 1.05. 11
are from their hives and houses driven away. 1.05. 24
sheep run not half so treacherous from the wolf, 1.05. 30
the wolf, | or horse or oxen from the leopard, 1.05. 31
as you fly from your oft–subdued slaves. 1.05. 32
walls, | rescu'd is orleance from the english! 1.06. 2
for every drop of blood was drawn from him 2.02. 8
rous'd on the sudden from their drowsy beds, 2.02. 23
from off this brier pluck a white rose with me. 2.04. 30
pluck a red rose from off this thorn with me. 2.04. 33
the fewest roses are cropp'd from the tree 2.04. 41
spring crestless yeomen from so deep a root? 2.04. 85
corrupted, and exempt from ancient gentry? 2.04. 93
even like a man new haled from the rack, | so 2.05. 3
now declare, sweet stem from york's great stock, 2.05. 41
i derived am | from lionel duke of clarence, 2.05. 75
he | from john of gaunt doth bring his pedigree, 2.05. 77
deriv'd | from famous edmund langley, duke of 2.05. 85
from envious malice of thy swelling heart. 3.01. 26
from whence you spring by lineal descent. 3.01.165
by thrusting out a torch from yonder tower, 3.02. 23
away, captains, let's get us from the walls, 3.02. 71
not to be gone from hence; 3.02. 94
with us, | but be extirped from our provinces. 3.03. 24
for ever should they be expuls'd from france, 3.03. 25
one drop of blood drawn from thy country's bosom 3.03. 54
my gracious sovereign, as i rode from callice, 4.01. 9
writ to your grace from th' duke of burgundy. 4.01. 12
to tear the garter from thy craven's leg, 4.01. 15
letter | sent from our uncle duke of burgundy. 4.01. 49
crossing the sea from england into france, 4.01. 89
much less to take occasion from their mouths 4.01.130
from thence to england, where i hope ere long 4.01.171
to wall thee from the liberty of flight; 4.02. 24
set from our o'ermatch'd forces forth for aid. 4.04. 11
from bought and sold lord talbot, | who, ring'd 4.04. 13
to beat assailing death from his weak /legions; 4.04. 16
drops bloody sweat from his war–wearied limbs, 4.04. 18
charge shall clear thee from that stain. 4.05. 42
no more can i be severed from your side | than 4.05. 48
and soul with soul from france to heaven fly. 4.05. 55
i gave thee life, and rescu'd thee from death. 4.06. 5
when from the dolphin's crest thy sword struck 4.06. 10
and from the pride of gallia rescued thee. 4.06. 15
orleance, that drew blood | from thee, my boy, 4.06. 17
of mine | which thou didst force from talbot, my 4.06. 24
words of yours draw life–blood from my heart. 4.06. 43
before young talbot from old talbot fly | the 4.06. 46
heart | suddenly made him from my side to start 4.07. 12
to scorn, | anon, from thy insulting tyranny, 4.07. 19
but from their ashes shall be rear'd | a phoenix 4.07. 92
have you perus'd the letters from the pope, 5.01. 1
free from oppression or the stroke of war, | my 5.03.155
swain, | but issued from the progeny of kings; 5.04. 38
virtuous and holy, chosen from above, | by 5.04. 39
hath been | a virgin from her tender infancy, 5.04. 50
with letters of commission from the king. 5.04. 95
detract so much from that prerogative | as to be 5.04.142
for more, | be cast from possibility of all. 5.04.146
usurp'st, | of benefit proceeding from our king, 5.04.152
to save your subjects from such massacre | and 5.04.160
and so conduct me where, from company, | i may 5.05.100
makes me from wond'ring fall to weeping joys, 2H6 1.01. 34
we here discharge your grace from being regent 1.01. 66
blotting your names from books of memory, 1.01.100
we'll quickly hoise duke humphrey from his seat. 1.01.169
which i will win from france, or else be slain. 1.01.213
thyself | from top of honor to disgrace's feet? 1.02. 49
away from me, and let me hear no more! 1.02. 50
a spirit rais'd from depth of under ground, 1.02. 79
when from saint albons we do make return, 1.02. 83
yet have i gold flies from another coast — | i 1.02. 93
i dare not say from the rich cardinal | and from 1.02. 94
and from the great and new–made duke of suffolk; 1.02. 95
my house, and lands, and wife and all, from me. 1.03. 18 P
till thou speak, thou shalt not pass from hence. 1.04. 27
if you mean to save yourself from whipping, leap 2.01.140 P
they come to berwick, from whence they came. 2.01.156
raising up wicked spirits from under ground, 2.01.170
his poor queen to france, from whence she came, 2.02. 25
clarence, from whose line | i claim the crown, 2.02. 34
henry doth claim the crown from john of gaunt, 2.02. 54
the fourth son, york claims it from the third; 2.02. 55
you four, from hence to prison back again; 2.03. 5
from thence, unto the place of execution. 2.03. 6
go, take hence that traitor from our sight, 2.03.100
your grace, we'll take her from the sheriff. 2.04. 17
gloucester, hide thee from their hateful looks, 2.04. 23
wouldst have me rescue thee from this reproach? 2.04. 64
man, | what e'er occasion keeps him from us now. 3.01. 3
from meaning treason to our royal person | as is 3.01. 70
welcome, lord somerset. what news from france? 3.01. 83
the purest spring is not so free from mud | as i 3.01.101
as i am clear from treason to my sovereign. 3.01.102
pay, | nor ever had one penny bribe from france. 3.01.109
that doit that e'er i wrested from the king, 3.01.112
that you will clear yourself from all suspense. 3.01.140
from treason's secret knife and traitors' rage 3.01.174
thus is the shepherd beaten from thy side, | and 3.01.191
world, | to rid us from the fear we have of him. 3.01.234
say as you think, and speak it from your souls: 3.01.247
set | to guard the chicken from a hungry kite, 3.01.249
and to preserve my sovereign from his foe, | say 3.01.271
great lords, from ireland am i come amain, | to 3.01.282
collected choicely, from each county some, | and 3.01.313
why, then from ireland come i with my strength, 3.01.380
than from true evidence of good esteem | he be 3.02. 21
wren, | by crying comfort from a hollow breast, 3.02. 43
and twice by awkward wind from england's bank 3.02. 83
when from thy shore the tempest beat us back, 3.02.102
view, | i took a costly jewel from my neck, | a 3.02.106
to free us from his father's wrathful curse, | i 3.02.155
if from this presence thou dar'st go with me. 3.02.228
they will by violence tear him from your palace, 3.02.246
loyalty, | free from a stubborn opposite intent, 3.02.251
from such fell serpents as false suffolk is; 3.02.266
an answer from the king, my lord of salisbury! 3.02.270
sent from a sort of tinkers to the king. 3.02.277
an answer from the king, or we will all break in 3.02.278
go, salisbury, and tell them all from me, | i 3.02.279
now, by the ground that i am banish'd from, 3.02.334
and banished i am, if but from thee. 3.02.351
if i depart from thee, i cannot live, | and in 3.02.388
where, from thy sight, i should be raging mad, 3.02.394
from thee to die were torture more than death. 3.02.401
let me hear from thee; 3.02.405

and from his bosom purge this black despair! 3.03. 23
graves, and from their misty jaws | breathe foul 4.01. 6
fed from my trencher, kneel'd down at the board, 4.01. 57
thrust from the crown | by shameful murther of a 4.01. 94
i go of message from the queen to france; 4.01.114
true nobility is exempt from fear: 4.01.129
go to, sirrah, tell the king from me, that, for 4.02.156 P
descended from the duke of clarence' house, 4.04. 29
aid of your honor from the tower to defend the 4.05. 4 P
the tower to defend the city from the rebels. 4.05. 5 P
these hands are free from guiltless 4.07.102
this breast from harboring foul deceitful 4.07.103
we come ambassadors from the king | unto the 4.08. 7
the duke of york is newly come from ireland, 4.09. 24
his arms are only to remove from thee | the duke 4.09. 29
thither, | until his army be dismiss'd from him. 4.09. 40
and sends the poor well pleased from my gate. 4.10. 23
ne'er shall this blood be wiped from thy point, 4.10. 69
tell kent from me, she hath lost her best man, 4.10. 73 P
from ireland thus comes york to claim his right, 5.01. 1
and pluck the crown from feeble henry's head. 5.01. 2
a messenger from henry, our dread liege, | to 5.01. 17
is to remove proud somerset from the king, 5.01. 36
to heave the traitor somerset from hence, | and 5.01. 61
go bid her hide him quickly from the duke. 5.01. 84
if it be banish'd from the frosty head, | where 5.01.167
to wring the widow from her custom'd right, 5.01.188
to keep thee from the tempest of the field. 5.01.197
and from thy burgonet i'll rend thy bear, | and 5.01.208
and if thou dost not hide thee from the bear, 5.02. 2
him off, | persuaded him from any further act: 5.03. 10
you have defended me from imminent death. 5.03. 19
far be the thought of this from henry's heart, 3H6 1.01. 70
we are those which chas'd you from the field, 1.01. 90
father, tear the crown from the usurper's head. 1.01.114
all will revolt from me and turn to him. 1.01.151
and i unto the sea, from whence i came. 1.01.209
nay, go not from me, i will follow thee. 1.01.213
i here divorce myself | both from thy table, 1.01.248
now phaeton hath tumbled from his car, | and 1.04. 33
point | made issue from the bosom of the boy; 1.04. 81
so | that hardly can i check my eyes from tears. 1.04.151
hard-hearted clifford, take me from the world, 1.04.167
from clifford's and northumberland's pursuit. 2.01. 3
ah, would she break from hence, that this my 2.01. 75
and when came george from burgundy to england? 2.01.143
he was lately sent | from your kind aunt, 2.01.146
can pluck the diadem from faint henry's head, 2.01.153
and wring the aweful sceptre from his fist, 2.01.154
like to a dismal clangor heard from far, 2.03. 18
ere my knee rise from the earth's cold face, | i 2.03. 35
clifford too, | have chid me from the battle; 2.05. 17
and i, that, haply, take them from him now, 2.05. 58
from london by the king was i press'd forth; 2.05. 64
for from my heart thine image ne'er shall go; 2.05.116
from whence that tender spray did sweetly spring 2.06. 50
from off the gates of york fetch down the head, 2.06. 52
from whence shall warwick cut the sea to france, 2.06. 89
from scotland am i stol'n, even of pure love, 3.01. 13
place is fill'd, thy sceptre wrung from thee, 3.01. 16
and in conclusion wins the king from her | with 3.01. 50
look, as i blow this feather from my face; | and 3.01. 84
that from his loins no hopeful branch may spring 3.02.126
to cross me from the golden time i look for! 3.02.127
and chides the sea that sunders him from thence, 3.02.138
and so i chide the means that keeps me from it, 3.02.141
seeking a way, and straying from the way, | not 3.02.176
and from that torment i will free myself, | or 3.02.180
from such a cause as fills mine eyes with tears 3.03. 13
from worthy edward, king of albion, | my lord 3.03. 49
springs not from edward's well-meant honest love 3.03. 67
love, | but from deceit bred by necessity; 3.03. 68
from these our henry lineally descends. 3.03. 87
exempt from envy, but not from disdain, | unless 3.03.127
sun, | exempt from envy, but not from disdain, 3.03.127
from giving aid which late i promised. 3.03.148
sent from your brother, marquess montague. 3.03.164
these from our king unto your majesty. 3.03.165
from whom i know not. 3.03.166
that i am clear from this misdeed of edward's; 3.03.183
did i put henry from his native right? 3.03.190
and force the tyrant from his seat by war. 3.03.206
me, | he's very likely now to fall from him, 3.03.209
unless thou rescue him from foul despair? 3.03.215
tell him from me that he hath done me wrong, 3.03.231
i came from edward as ambassador, | but i return 3.03.256
alas, you know, 'tis far from hence to france; 4.01. 4
what letters or what news | from france? 4.01. 85
"tell him from me that he hath done me wrong, 4.01.110
and brought from thence the thracian fatal 4.02. 21
tent | but to defend his person from night-foes? 4.03. 22
embassade | then i degraded you from being king, 4.03. 33
nor how to shroud yourself from enemies? 4.03. 40
to do, | to free king henry from imprisonment, 4.03. 63
and i the rather wain me from despair | for love 4.04. 17
there shall i rest secure from force and fraud. 4.04. 33
and men | to set him free from his captivity. 4.05. 13
lord — | and shipp'd from thence to flanders? 4.05. 21
shield thee from warwick's frown, | and pray 4.05. 28
have shaken edward from the regal seat, | and 4.06. 2
be sent for, to return from france with speed; 4.06. 61
that edward is escaped from your brother, | and 4.06. 78
and from the bishop's huntsmen rescu'd him; 4.06. 84
seas, | and brought desired help from burgundy. 4.07. 6
from ravenspurgh haven before the gates of york, 4.07. 8
edward from belgia, | with hasty germans and 4.08. 1
where is the post that came from valiant oxford? 5.01. 1
where is the post that came from montague? 5.01. 5
the drum your honor hears marcheth from warwick. 5.01. 13
the king was slily finger'd from the deck! 5.01. 44
and kept low shrubs from winter's pow'rful wind. 5.02. 15
the queen from france hath brought a puissant 5.02. 31
and blow it to the source from whence it came; 5.03. 11
we will not from the helm to sit and weep, | but 5.04. 21
from shelves and rocks that threaten us with 5.04. 23
if case some one of you would fly from us, 5.04. 34
and ne'er have stol'n the breech from lancaster. 5.05. 24
so flies the reakless shepherd from the wolf; 5.06. 7
from those that wish the downfall of our house! 5.06. 65
thou /keep'st me from the light, | but i will 5.06. 84
thus have we swept suspicion from our seat, 5.07. 13
that i love the tree from whence thou sprang'st, 5.07. 31
and from the cross-row plucks the letter g, R3 1.01. 55
from whence this present day he is delivered? 1.01. 69
cursed the blood that let this blood from hence! 1.02. 16
load, | taken from paul's to be interred there; 1.02. 30
from cold and empty veins where no blood dwells. 1.02. 59
nails should rent that beauty from my cheeks. 1.02.126
never came poison from so sweet a place. 1.02.146
those eyes of thine from mine have drawn salt 1.02.153
from wayward sickness and no grounded malice. 1.03. 29
and i | are come from visiting his majesty. 1.03. 32
from that contented hap which i enjoy'd, | i 1.03. 83
far be it from my heart, the thought thereof! 1.03.149
in sharing that which you have pill'd from me! 1.03.158
with thy scorns drew'st rivers from his eyes, 1.03.175
from bitterness of soul | denounc'd against thee 1.03.178
and soothe the devil that i warn thee from? 1.03.297
methoughts that i had broken from the tower 1.04. 9
who from my cabin tempted me to walk | upon the 1.04. 12
because i will be guiltless from the meaning. 1.04. 94
him, from the which no warrant can defend me. 1.04.111 P
take not the quarrel from his pow'rful arm; 1.04.217
go you to him from me. 1.04.234
you | from this earth's thralldom to the joys of 1.04.248
being pent from liberty, as i am now, | if two 1.04.258
embassage | from my redeemer to redeem me hence; 2.01. 4
by heaven, my soul is purg'd from grudging hate, 2.01. 9
madam, yourself is not exempt from this; 2.01. 18
did, | and yet go current from suspicion! 2.01. 95
all this from my remembrance brutish wrath 2.01.119
yet from my dugs he drew not this deceit. 2.02. 30
but death hath snatch'd my husband from my arms, 2.02. 57
and pluck'd two crutches from my feeble hands, 2.02. 58
forthwith from ludlow the young prince be fet 2.02.121
part the queen's proud kindred from the prince. 2.02.150
god keep you from them, and from such false 3.01. 15
keep you from them, and from such false friends! 3.01. 15
god keep me from false friends! 3.01. 16
and from her jealous arms pluck him perforce. 3.01. 36
can from his mother win the duke of york, | anon 3.01. 38
then, taking him from thence that is not there, 3.01. 53
or else reported | successively from age to age, 3.01. 73
methinks the truth should live from age to age, 3.01. 76
he is all the mother's, from the top to toe. 3.01.156
shall we hear from you, catesby, ere we sleep? 3.01.188
one from the lord stanley. 3.02. 3
have this crown of mine cut from my shoulders 3.02. 43
lords at pomfret, when they rode from london, 3.02. 83
god bless the prince from all the pack of you! 3.03. 5
he liv'd from all attainder of suspects. 3.05. 32
to warn false traitors from the like attempts. 3.05. 49
but nothing /spake in warrant from himself. 3.07. 33
be mov'd, | to draw him from his holy exercise. 3.07. 64
prince, | to stay him from the fall of vanity; 3.07. 97
but as successively, from blood to blood, | your 3.07.135
that i would rather hide me from my greatness — 3.07.161
which god defend that i should wring from him! 3.07.173
ancestry | from the corruption of abusing times 3.07.199
from all the impure blots and stains thereof; 3.07.234
see, | how far i am from the desire of this. 3.07.236
the lord protect him from that kingly title! 4.01. 19
i am their mother, who shall bar me from them? 4.01. 21
and take thy office from thee on my peril. 4.01. 25
and live with richmond, from the reach of hell. 4.01. 42
go hie thee, hie thee from this slaughter-house, 4.01. 43
you shall have letters from me to my son | in 4.01. 49
scarce the blood was well wash'd from his hands 4.01. 67
which issued from my other angel husband, | and 4.01. 68
which hitherto hath held /my eyes from rest; 4.01. 81
and soon i'll rid you from the fear of them. 4.02. 77
that from the prime creation e'er she framed." 4.03. 19
wilt thou, o god, fly from such gentle lambs, 4.04. 22
from forth the kennel of thy womb hath crept | a 4.04. 47
to have him suddenly convey'd from hence. 4.04. 76
from which even here i slip my /weary head, 4.04.112
from all the slaughters, wretch, that thou hast 4.04.139
ere from this war thou turn a conqueror, | or i 4.04.185
then know that from my soul i love thy daughter. 4.04.256
that thou dost love my daughter from thy soul; 4.04.259
so from thy soul's love didst thou love her 4.04.260
and from my heart's love i do thank thee for it. 4.04.261
the purple sap from her sweet brother's body, 4.04.277
if i did take the kingdom from your sons, | to 4.04.294
and you shall understand from me her mind. 4.04.429
what from your grace i shall deliver to him. 4.04.448
safe-conducting the rebels from their ships? 4.04.482
him, they came from buckingham | upon his party. 4.04.525
sir christopher, tell richmond this from me: 4.05. 1
and here receive we from our father stanley 5.02. 5
from tamworth thither is but one day's march. 5.02. 13
which in his dearest need will fly from him. 5.02. 21
least | south from the mighty power of the king. 5.03. 38
and give him from me this most needful note. 5.03. 41
from troop to troop | went through the army, 5.03. 70
i, by attorney, bless thee from thy mother, 5.03. 83
good angels guard thee from the boar's annoy! 5.03.151
what, from myself? 5.03.185
to see if any mean to shrink from me. 5.03.222
if you do free your children from the sword, 5.03.261
i would these dewy tears were from the ground. 5.03.284
from the dead temples of this bloody wretch 5.05. 5
man's pie is freed | from his ambitious finger. H8 1.01. 53
beneficial sun, | and keep it from the earth. 1.01. 57
if not from hell, the devil is a niggard, | or 1.01. 70
(and take it from a heart that wishes towards 1.01.103
and from a mouth of honor quite cry down | this 1.01.137
whom from the flow of gall i name not, but 1.01.152
but | from sincere motions, by intelligence, 1.01.153
for from this league | peep'd harms that menac'd 1.01.182
to see you ta'en from liberty, to look on | the 1.01.205
here is a warrant from | the king t' attach lord 1.01.216
master — | whose honor heaven shield from soil! 1.02. 26
which compels from each | the sixt part of his 1.02. 57
and with a care exempt themselves from fear; 1.02. 89
we must not rend our subjects from our laws, 1.02. 93
why, we take | from every tree, lop, bark, and 1.02. 96
hour | to hear from him a matter of some moment; 1.02.163
a general welcome from his grace | salutes ye 1.04. 1
i had it from my father. 1.04. 27
as great embassadors | from foreign princes. 1.04. 56
pray tell 'em thus much from me: 1.04. 77
which he fain | would have flung from him; 2.01. 25
employment, | and far enough from court too. 2.01. 49
one stroke has taken | for ever from the world. 2.01.118
me, | this from a dying man receive as certain: 2.01.125
fall away | like water from ye, never found 2.01.130
good angels keep it from us! 2.01.142
by commission and main power, took 'em from me, 2.02. 6 P
heaven keep me from such counsel! 2.02. 37
and free us from his slavery. 2.02. 43
man will work us all | from princes into pages. 2.02. 47
from these sad thoughts that work too much upon 2.02. 57
fortune, do divorce | it from the bearer, 'tis a 2.03. 15
as from a blushing handmaid, to his highness; 2.03. 72
knows yet | but from this lady may proceed a gem 2.03. 78
whilst our commission from rome is read, | let 2.04. 1
put me off, | and take your good grace from me? 2.04. 22
gave notice | he was from thence discharg'd? 2.04. 34
yea, from my soul | refuse you for my judge, 2.04. 81
warranted | by a commission from the consistory, 2.04. 92
the cure is to | remove these thoughts from you; 2.04.102
with me, a poor weak woman, fall'n from favor? 3.01. 20
madam, you wander from the good we aim at. 3.01.138
utterly | grow from the king's acquaintance, by 3.01.161
casts | such doubts, as false coin, from it. 3.01.171
from her | will fall some blessing to this land, 3.02. 50
speedily i wish | to hear from rome. 3.02. 90
expense by th' hour | seems to flow from him! 3.02.109
to steal from spiritual leisure a brief span 3.02.140
duty to you | and throw it from their soul, 3.02.194
he parted frowning from me, as if ruin | leap'd 3.02.205
from me, as if ruin | leap'd from his eyes. 3.02.206
no new device to beat this from his brains? 3.02.217
and, from that full meridian of my glory, | i 3.02.224
till you hear further from his highness. 3.02.232
the king's will from his mouth expressly? 3.02.235
far from his succor, from the king, from all 3.02.261
far from his succor, from the king, from all 3.02.261
from all | that might have mercy on the fault 3.02.261
i was | from any private malice in his end, 3.02.268
and from this fellow? 3.02.279
sins, the articles | collected from his life. 3.02.294
and from these shoulders, | these ruin'd pillars 3.02.381
go get thee from me, cromwell! 3.02.412
behold | the lady anne pass from her coronation? 4.01. 3
the duke of buckingham came from his trial. 4.01. 5
six miles off | from ampthill, where the 4.01. 28
in the choir, fell off | a distance from her; 4.01. 65
newly preferr'd from the king's secretary, | the 4.01.102
will find a friend will not shrink from him. 4.01.107
though from an humble stock, undoubtedly | was 4.02. 49
from his cradle | he was a scholar, and a ripe 4.02. 50
actions | to keep mine honor from corruption, 4.02. 71
is staying | a gentleman, sent from the king, to 4.02.106
you should be lord ambassador from the emperor, 4.02.109
but poverty could never draw 'em from me), 4.02.149
came you from the king, my lord? 5.01. 6
from your affairs | i hinder you too long. 5.01. 53
now, lovell, from the queen what is the news? 5.01. 61
that was sent to me from the council pray'd me 5.02. 2
you, | from hence you be committed to the tower, 5.02. 89
unless we sweep 'em from the door with cannons 5.03. 13
when i might see from far some forty 5.03. 51 P
from all parts they are coming, | as if we kept 5.03. 68
when they pass back from the christening. 5.03. 74
th' are come already from the christening. 5.03. 83
from thy endless goodness send prosperous life, 5.04. 1 P
from her shall read the perfect /ways of honor, 5.04. 37
(when heaven shall call her from this cloud of 5.04. 44
who from the sacred ashes of her honor | shall 5.04. 45
sorts, | for womanish it is to be from thence. TRO 1.01.107
what news, aeneas, from the field to-day? 1.01.108
hark, they are coming from the field. 1.02.177 P
ay, a token from troilus. 1.02.280 P
nothing of that shall from mine eyes appear. 1.02.295
tortive and errant from his course of growth. 1.03. 9
calm of states | quite from their fixure! 1.03.101
peaceful commerce from dividable shores, | the 1.03.105
from the tongue of roaring typhon dropp'd, 1.03.160
from his deep chest laughs out a loud applause, 1.03.163
from troy. 1.03.214
looks | know them from eyes of other mortals? 1.03.225
he hears nought privately that comes from troy. 1.03.249
nor i from troy come not to whisper with him. 1.03.250
tell him from me | i'll hide my silver beard in 1.03.295
so shall each lord of greece, from tent to tent. 1.03.307
that can from hector bring those honors off, 1.03.334
he that meets hector issues from our choice, 1.03.347
and doth boil | (as 'twere from forth us all) a 1.03.350
what heart receives from hence a conquering part 1.03.352
what glory our achilles shares from hector, 1.03.366
then would come some matter from him; 2.01. 8 P
i would thou didst itch from head to foot; 2.01. 27 P
thus once again says nestor from the greeks: 2.02. 2
heels | and fly like chidden mercury from jove, 2.02. 45
to blench from this and to stand firm by honor. 2.02. 68
less than little wit from them that they have, 2.03. 13 P
in circumvention deliver a fly from a spider, 2.03. 16 P
heaven bless thee from a tutor, and discipline 2.03. 29 P
achilles hath inveigled his fool from him. 2.03. 91 P
be led | at your request a little from himself. 2.03.181
that ajax makes | when they go from achilles. 2.03.184
here's a lord — come knights from east to west, 2.03.263
to speak with paris from the prince troilus. 3.01. 38 P
they're come from the field. 3.01.148
from cupid's shoulder pluck his painted wings, 3.02. 14
from my weakness draws | my very soul of counsel 3.02.132
if i be false, or swerve a hair from truth, 3.02.184
from false to false, among false maids in love, 3.02.190
myself | from certain and possess'd conveniences 3.03. 7
fortunes, sequest'ring from me all | that time, 3.03. 8
sense, behold itself, | not going from itself; 3.03.107
or /hedge aside from the direct forthright, 3.03.158

shall from your neck unloose his amorous fold, 3.03.223
and, like /a dewdrop from the lion's mane, | be 3.03.224
i come from the worthy achilles — 3.03.282 P
and to procure safe–conduct from agamemnon. 3.03.287 P
borne to greece | than cressid borne from troy. 4.01. 48
our joys no longer, | i would not from thee. 4.02. 11
must to thy father, and be gone from troilus. 4.02. 92 P
i will not go from troy. 4.02.109
lips blow to their deities, take thee from me. 4.04. 27
and is it true that i must go from troy? 4.04. 30
what, and from troilus too? 4.04. 31
from troy and troilus. 4.04. 32
kindly, | for it is parting from us. 4.04. 61
of his | in aspiration lifts him from the earth. 4.05. 16
i'll take that winter from your lips, fair lady; 4.05. 24
thou shouldst not bear from me a greekish member 4.05.130
that any /drop thou borrow'dst from thy mother, 4.05.133
a thought of added honor torn from hector. 4.05.145
there is expectance here from both the sides, 4.05.146
from heart of very heart, great hector, welcome. 4.05.171
his insolence draws folly from my lips, | but 4.05.258
so much, | after we part from agamemnon's tent, 4.05.285
from whence, fragment? 5.01. 8 P
why, thou full dish of fool, from troy. 5.01. 9 P
from my great purpose in to–morrow's battle. 5.01. 38
here is a letter from queen hecuba, | a token 5.01. 39
a token from her daughter, my fair love, | both 5.01. 40
nay, do not snatch it from me. 5.02. 81
spur them to ruthful work, rein them from ruth. 5.03. 48
here's a letter come from yond poor girl. 5.03. 99 P
words, mere words, no matter from the heart; 5.03.108
care | withdrew me from the odds of multitude. 5.04. 22
which ne'er came from the lungs, but even thus COR 1.01.108
veins | from me receive that natural competency 1.01.139
all | from me do back receive the flour of all, 1.01.145
but it proceeds or comes from them to you, | and 1.01.153
from them to you, | and no way from yourselves. 1.01.154
o, doubt not that, | i speak from certainties. 1.02. 31
should not sell him an hour from her beholding; 1.03. 9 P
a cruel war i sent him, from whence he return'd, 1.03. 14 P
as children from a bear, the volsces shunning 1.03. 31
heavens bless my lord from fell aufidius! 1.03. 45
the threshold till my lord return from the wars. 1.03. 75 P
there came news from him last night. 1.03. 93 P
that we with smoking swords may march from hence 1.04. 11
have you run | from slaves that apes would beat! 1.04. 36
the shepherd knows not thunder from a tabor 1.06. 25
of martius' tongue | from every meaner man. 1.06. 27
they did budge | from rascals worse than they. 1.06. 45
(though thanks to all) must i select from all; 1.06. 81
and from this time, | for what he did before 1.09. 62
look, here's a letter from him; 2.01.108 P
the senate has letters from the general, wherein 2.01.134 P
from whom i have receiv'd not only greetings, 2.01.197
his honors | from where he should begin and end, 2.01.225
reproof and rebuke from every ear that heard it. 2.02. 33 P
when blows have made me stay, i fled from words. 2.02. 72
from face to foot | he was a thing of blood, 2.02.108
and might well | be taken from the people. 2.02.146
and ran | from th' noise of our own drums." 2.03. 54
from him pluck'd | either his gracious promise, 2.03.192
have chose a consul that will from them take 2.03.214
took from you | th' apprehension of his present 2.03.223
from whence came | that ancus martius, numa's 2.03.238
'twas from the canon. 3.01. 90
he that would take from you all your power. 3.01.181
martius would have all from you; 3.01.194
and from thence | into destruction cast him. 3.01.212
valiantness was mine, thou suck'st it from me; 3.02.129
cog their hearts from them, and come home 3.02.133
to take | from rome all season'd office, and to 3.03. 64
from time to time | envied against the people, 3.03. 94
even from this instant, banish him our city, 3.03.101
of precipitation | from off the rock tarpeian, 3.03.103
you shall | hear from me still, and never of me 4.01. 52
one seven years | from these old arms and legs, 4.01. 56
i have a note from the volscian state to find 4.03. 10 P
ripe aptness to take all power from the people, 4.03. 23 P
and to pluck from them their tribunes for ever. 4.03. 24 P
tell you most strange things from rome, all 4.03. 41 P
you take my part from me, sir, i have the most 4.03. 50 P
word thou hast spoke hath weeded from my heart 4.05.102
should from yond cloud speak divine things, 4.05.104
once more to hew thy target from thy brawn, | or 4.05.120
we would muster all | from twelve to seventy, 4.05.129
his mother and his wife | hear nothing from him. 4.06. 19
not moving | from th' casque to th' cushion, but 4.07. 43
good will | must have that thanks from rome, 5.01. 46
from whence? 5.02. 4
from rome. 5.02. 4
our general | will no more hear from thence. 5.02. 6
cannot office me from my son coriolanus. 5.02. 63 P
to die by himself fears it not from another. 5.02.105 P
suits, | nor from the state nor private friends, 5.03. 18
heaven, that kiss | i carried from thee, dear; 5.03. 47
that's curdied by the frost from purest snow 5.03. 66
for we'll | hear nought from rome in private. 5.03. 93
nay, go not from us thus. 5.03.131
that thou restrain'st from me the duty which 5.03.167
this martius is grown from man to dragon: 5.04. 13 P
mark what mercy his mother shall bring from him. 5.04. 27 P
bear from hence his body, | and mourn you for 5.06.141
takes from aufidius a great part of blame. 5.06.145
from weary wars against the barbarous goths, TIT 1.01. 28
his valiant sons | in coffins from the field, 1.01. 35
from where he circumscribed with his sword, 1.01. 68
from whence at first she weigh'd her anchorage, 1.01. 73
rest, | secure from worldly chances and mishaps! 1.01.152
and welcome, nephews, from successful wars, 1.01.172
people's hearts, and wean them from themselves. 1.01.211
bear his betroth'd from all the world away. 1.01.286
till from forth this place | i lead espous'd my 1.01.327
i would not part a bachelor from the priest. 1.01.488
serve your lust, shadowed from heaven's eye, 2.01.130
jove shield your husband from his hounds to–day! 2.03. 70
why are you sequest'red from all your train, 2.03. 75
dismounted from your snow–white goodly steed, 2.03. 76
the milk thou suck'st from her did turn to 2.03.144
vain | to save your brother from the sacrifice, 2.03.164
o, keep me from their worse than killing lust, 2.03.175
from this /unhallow'd and blood–stained hole? 2.03.210
sirs, drag them from the pit unto the prison, 2.03.283
as from a conduit with /three issuing spouts, 2.04. 30
but, lovely niece, that mean is cut from thee. 2.04. 40
that shall distill from these two ancient /urns, 3.01. 17
to rescue my two brothers from their death, 3.01. 49
then, | from these devourers to be banished! 3.01. 57
is torn from forth that pretty hollow cage, 3.01. 84
the fresh taste be taken from that clearness, 3.01.128
this, | as far from help as limbo is from bliss! 3.01.149
this, | as far from help as limbo is from bliss! 3.01.149
to ransom my two nephews from their death; 3.01.172
let me redeem my brothers both from death. 3.01.180
a hand that warded him | from thousand dangers, 3.01.195
as for thee, boy, go get thee from my sight; 3.01.283
perhaps, she cull'd it from among the rest. 4.01. 44
boy | shall carry from me to the empress' sons 4.01.115
ay, some mad message from his mad grandfather. 4.02. 3
i may, | i greet your honors from andronicus — 4.02. 5
o, that which i would hide from heaven's eye, 4.02. 59
tell the empress from me, i am of age | to keep 4.02.104
and from your womb where you imprisoned were 4.02.124
aid, | and that it comes from old andronicus, 4.03. 16
if you will have revenge from hell, you shall. 4.03. 39
news, news from heaven! 4.03. 78
why, didst thou not come from heaven? 4.03. 89
from heaven! 4.03. 90 P
him deliver the pigeons to the emperor from you. 4.03. 97 P
i know from whence this same device proceeds. 4.04. 52
lucius, | and will revolt from me to succor him. 4.04. 80
to pluck proud lucius from the warlike goths. 4.04.110
i have received letters from great rome | which 5.01. 2
brave slip, sprung from the great andronicus, 5.01. 9
from our troops i stray'd | to gaze upon a 5.01. 20
the child | and bear it from me to the emperess. 5.01. 54
that codding spirit had they from their mother, 5.01. 99
oft have i digg'd up dead men from their graves, 5.01.135
there is a messenger from rome | desires to be 5.01.152
welcome, aemilius, what's the news from rome? 5.01.155
sent from below | to join with him and right his 5.02. 3
sent from th' infernal kingdom | to ease the 5.02. 30
even from /hyperion's rising in the east, 5.02. 56
and from her bosom took the enemy's point, 5.03.111
from the place where you behold us pleading, 5.03.130
life i did, | i do repent it from my very soul. 5.03.190
from ancient grudge break to new mutiny, | where ROM pr 3
from forth the fatal loins of these two foes | a pr 5
i will push montague's men from the wall, and 1.01. 17 P
with purple fountains issuing from your veins — 1.01. 85
from those bloody hands | throw your mistempered 1.01. 86
that westward rooteth from this city side, | so 1.01.122
and gladly shunn'd who gladly fled from me. 1.01.130
to draw | the shady curtains from aurora's bed, 1.01.136
bed, | away from light steals home my heavy son, 1.01.137
so close, | so far from sounding and discovery, 1.01.150
could we but learn from whence his sorrows grow, 1.01.154
arm'd, | from love's weak childish bow she lives 1.01.211
severity | cuts beauty off from all posterity. 1.01.220
say thou hadst suck'd wisdom from thy teat. 1.03. 68
dun, we'll draw thee from the mire | /of /this 1.04. 41
worm | prick'd from the lazy finger of a /maid. 1.04. 69
and, being anger'd, puffs away from thence, 1.04.102
this wind you talk of blows us from ourselves: 1.04.104
thus from my lips, by thine, my sin is purg'd. 1.05.107
sin from my lips? 1.05.109
my only love sprung from my only hate! 1.05.138
she steal love's sweet bait from fearful hooks. 2.pr. 8
i have night's cloak to hide me from their eyes, 2.02. 75
goes toward love as schoolboys from their books, 2.02.156
but love from love, toward school with heavy 2.02.157
bird, | that lets it hop a little from his hand, 2.02.178
from forth day's path and titan's /fiery wheels. 2.03. 4
and from her womb children of divers kind | we 2.03. 11
aught so good but, strain'd from that fair use, 2.03. 19
revolts from true birth, stumbling on abuse. 2.03. 20
the sun not yet thy sighs from heaven clears, 2.03. 73
that stretches from an inch narrow to an ell 2.04. 84 P
and from nine till twelve | is /three long hours 2.05. 10
and yet thou wilt tutor me from quarrelling! 3.01. 29 P
arm | an envious thrust from tybalt hit the life 3.01.168
a gentler judgment vanish'd from his lips — 3.03. 10
here from verona art thou banished. 3.03. 15
hence "banished" is banish'd from the world, 3.03. 19
and steal immortal blessing from her lips, | who 3.03. 37
flies may do this, but i from this must fly; 3.03. 41
mist–like infold me from the search of eyes. 3.03. 73
i come from lady juliet. 3.03. 80
with blood removed but little from her own? 3.03. 96
name, | shot from the deadly level of a gun, 3.03.103
of wax, | digressing from the valor of a man; 3.03.127
or by the break of day /disguis'd from hence. 3.03.168
and he shall signify from time to time | every 3.03.170
since arm from arm that voice doth us affray, 3.05. 33
i must hear from thee every day in the hour, 3.05. 44
wilt thou wash him from his grave with tears? 3.05. 70
ay, madam, from the reach of these my hands. 3.05. 85
one who, to put thee from thy heaviness, | hath 3.05.108
unless that husband send it me from heaven | by 3.05.207
speak'st thou from thy heart? 3.05.226
and from my soul too, else beshrew them both. 3.05.227
herself alone, | may be put from her by society. 4.01. 14
that cop'st with death himself to scape from it; 4.01. 75
paris, | from off the battlements of any tower, 4.01. 78
and then awake as from a pleasant sleep. 4.01.106
the morning comes | to rouse thee from thy bed, 4.01.108
this shall free thee from this present shame, 4.01.118
see where she comes from shrift with merry look. 4.02. 15
and pluck the mangled tybalt from his shroud, 4.03. 52
but i will watch you from such watching now. 4.04. 12
and cruel death hath catch'd it from my sight! 4.05. 48
your part in her you could not keep from death, 4.05. 69
turn from their office to black funeral: 4.05. 85
news from verona! 5.01. 12
dost thou not bring me letters from the friar? 5.01. 13
hast thou no letters to me from the friar? 5.01. 31
fir'd | doth hurry from the fatal cannon's womb. 5.01. 65
welcome from mantua! 5.02. 3
but chiefly to take thence from her dead finger 5.03. 30
thee, | and never from this /palace of dim night 5.03.107
stars | from this world–wearied flesh. 5.03.112
come from that nest | of death, contagion, and 5.03.151
we took this mattock and this spade from him, 5.03.185
as he was coming from this churchyard's side. 5.03.186
that calls our person from our morning rest? 5.03.189
banish'd the new–made bridegroom from this city, 5.03.235
you, to remove that siege of grief from her, 5.03.237
mean | to rid her from this second marriage, 5.03.241
to help to take her from her borrowed grave, 5.03.248
came i to take her from her kindred's vault, 5.03.254
but then a noise did scare me from the tomb, 5.03.262
and then in post he came from mantua | to this 5.03.273
a thing slipp'd idlely from me. TIM 1.01. 20
/gum, which /oozes | from whence 'tis nourish'd. 1.01. 22
from the glass–fac'd flatterer | to apemantus, 1.01. 58
with one man beckon'd from the rest below, 1.01. 74
that from my first have been inclin'd to thrift, 1.01.118
mine heir from forth the beggars of the world, 1.01.138
i thank you, you shall hear from me anon. 1.01.153
wait attendance | till you hear further from me. 1.01.162
service, from whose help | i deriv'd liberty. 1.02. 7
provided that i shall have much help from you: 1.02. 90 P
have you that charitable title from thousands, 1.02. 91 P
taste, touch, all, pleas'd from thy table rise; 1.02.126
i'll lock thy heaven from thee. 1.02.248 P
takes no accompt | how things go from him, nor 2.02. 4
be round with him, now he comes from hunting. 2.02. 8
from isidore; 2.02. 27
goes up and down in from fourscore to thirteen, 2.02.113 P
greet him from me, | bid him suppose some good 2.02.226
my lord, and which i hear from common rumors, 3.02. 5 P
done and past, and his estate shrinks from him. 3.02. 7 P
i have receiv'd some small kindnesses from him, 3.02. 21 P
and tell him this from me, i count it one of my 3.02. 55 P
is wealthy too, | whom he redeem'd from prison. 3.03. 4
first man | that e'er received gift from him; 3.03. 17
they have e'en put my breath from me, the slaves 3.04.103
you only speak from your distracted soul; 3.04.113
pluck the grave wrinkled senate from the bench, 4.01. 5
the lin'd crutch from thy old limping sire, 4.01. 14
nothing i'll bear from thee | but nakedness, 4.01. 32
from our companion thrown into his grave, | so 4.02. 9
who would not wish to be from wealth exempt, 4.02. 31
he's flung in rage from this ingrateful seat 4.02. 45
sun, draw from the earth | rotten humidity; 4.03. 1
lug your priests and servants from your sides, 4.03. 32
stout men's pillows from below their heads. 4.03. 33
whose dimpled smiles from fools exhaust their 4.03.120
to foresee, | smells from the general weal. 4.03.160
of the war | derive some pain from you. 4.03.162
from forth thy plenteous bosom, one poor root! 4.03.186
mind, | that from it all consideration slips — 4.03.196
melancholy sprung | from change of future. 4.03.204
hadst thou like us from our first swath 4.03.252
one winter's brush | fell from their boughs, and 4.03.265
and her pale fire she snatches from the sun; 4.03.438
by a composture stol'n | from gen'ral excrement; 4.03.442
h'as almost charm'd me from my profession, by 4.03.450 P
thou shalt build from men; 4.03.526
but let the famish'd flesh slide from the bone 4.03.528
rid me these villains from your companies; 5.01.101
from high to low throughout, that whoso please 5.01.209
man was riding | from alcibiades to timon's cave 5.02. 10
were not erected by their hands from whom | you 5.04. 23
our droplets which | from niggard nature fall, 5.04. 77
and drive away the vulgar from the streets; JC 1.01. 70
growing feathers pluck'd from caesar's wing 1.01. 72
fellow, come from the throng, look upon caesar. 1.02. 21
i have not from your eyes that gentleness | and 1.02. 33
did from the flames of troy upon his shoulder 1.02.113
so from the waves of tiber | did i the tired 1.02.114
his coward lips did from their color fly, | and 1.02.122
struck but thus much show of fire from brutus. 1.02.177
may be wrought | from that it is dispos'd; 1.02.310
throw, | as if they came from several citizens, 1.02.317
clean from the purpose of the things themselves. 1.03. 35
why birds and beasts from quality and kind, 1.03. 64
all these things change from their ordinance, 1.03. 66
cassius from bondage will deliver cassius. 1.03. 90
is when it disjoins | remorse from power; 2.01. 19
my ancestors did from the streets of rome | the 2.01. 53
were dim enough | to hide thee from prevention. 2.01. 85
of any promise that hath pass'd from him. 2.01.140
quite from the main opinion he held once | of 2.01.196
augurers | may hold him from the capitol to–day. 2.01.201
y' have ungently, brutus, | stole from my bed; 2.01.238
who did hide their faces | even from darkness. 2.01.278
vouchsafe good morrow from a feeble tongue. 2.01.313
brave son, deriv'd from honorable loins! 2.01.322
signifies that from you great rome shall suck 2.02. 87
fray, | and the wind brings it from the capitol. 2.04. 19
that will be thaw'd from the true quality | with 3.01. 41
but was indeed | sway'd from the point, by 3.01.219
with ate by his side come hot from hell, | shall 3.01.271
stand from the hearse, stand from the body. 3.02.165 P
stand from the hearse, stand from the body. 3.02.165 P
is come | to do you salutation from his master. 4.02. 5
(which should perceive nothing but love from us) 4.02. 44
their charges off | a little from this ground. 4.02. 49
for, from this day forth, | i'll use you for my 4.03. 48
from the hard hands of peasants their vile trash 4.03. 74
to lock such rascal counters from his friends, 4.03. 80
o, i could weep | my spirit from mine eyes! 4.03.100
yes, cassius, and, from henceforth, | when you 4.03.121
had you your letters from your wife, my lord? 4.03.181
from which advantage shall we cut him off | if 4.03.210
thy instrument, | i'll take it from thee; 4.03.272
coming from sardis, on our former ensign | two 5.01. 79
gorging and feeding from our soldiers' hands, 5.01. 81
i slew the coward, and did take it from him. 5.03. 4
far from this country pindarus shall run, 5.03. 49
the gods defend him from so great a shame! 5.04. 23
free from the bondage you are in, messala; 5.05. 54
upon him) from the western isles | of kerns and MAC 1.02. 12

till he unseam'd him from the nave to th' chops, 1.02. 22
so from that spring whence comfort seem'd to 1.02. 27
from fife, great king, | where the norweyan 1.02. 48
say from whence | you owe this strange 1.03. 75
to give thee from our royal master thanks, 1.03.101
he bade me, from him, call thee thane of cawdor; 1.03.105
from hence to enverness, | and bind us further 1.04. 42
the wonder of it, came missives from the king, 1.05. 6 P
all that impedes thee from the golden round, 1.05. 28
and fill me from the crown to the toe topful 1.05. 42
golden opinions from all sorts of people, 1.07. 33
from this time | such i account thy love. 1.07. 38
have pluck'd my nipple from his boneless gums, 1.07. 57
proceeding from the heat-oppressed brain? 2.01. 39
and take the present horror from the time, 2.01. 59
and wash this filthy witness from your hand. 2.02. 44
why did you bring these daggers from the place? 2.02. 45
ocean wash this blood | clean from my hand? 2.02. 58
as from your graves rise up, and walk like 2.03. 79
for, from this instant, | there's nothing 2.03. 92
if there come truth from them — | as upon thee, 3.01. 6
from the bill | that writes them all alike: 3.01. 99
with barefac'd power sweep him from my sight, 3.01.118
masking the business from the common eye | for 3.01.124
done to-night, | and something from the palace; 3.01.131
is banquo gone from court? 3.02. 1
from hence to th' palace gate | make it their 3.03. 13
from thence, the sauce to meat is ceremony, 3.04. 35
is often thus, | and hath been from his youth. 3.04. 53
on their crowns, | and push us from our stools. 3.04. 81
for from broad words, and 'cause he fail'd | his 3.06. 21
(from whom this tyrant holds the due of birth) 3.06. 25
fortune nothing | takes from his high respect. 3.06. 29
free from our feasts and banquets bloody knives; 3.06. 35
if th' hadst rather hear it from our mouths, 4.01. 62
hear it from our mouths, | or from our masters'? 4.01. 63
sweaten | from the murderer's gibbet throw 4.01. 66
from this moment | the very firstlings of my 4.01.146
in a place | from whence himself does fly? 4.02. 8
when we hold rumor | from what we fear, yet know 4.02. 20
and here from gracious england have i offer | of 4.03. 43
upon thyself | hath banish'd me from scotland. 4.03.113
hath from my soul | wip'd the black scruples, 4.03.115
wisdom plucks me | from over-credulous haste. 4.03.120
keep it not from me, quickly let me have it. 4.03.200
and i must be from thence! | my wife kill'd too? 4.03.212
i have seen her rise from her bed, throw her 5.01. 5 P
i will set down what comes from her, to satisfy 5.01. 33 P
remove from her the means of all annoyance, 5.01. 76
fight, till from my bones my flesh be hack'd. 5.03. 32
fancies, | that keep her from her rest. 5.03. 39
pluck from the memory a rooted sorrow, | raze 5.03. 41
doctor, the thanes fly from me. 5.03. 49
were i from dunsinane away and clear, | profit 5.03. 61
creeps in this petty pace from day to day, | to 5.05. 20
macduff was from his mother's womb | untimely 5.08. 15
yond same star that's westward from the pole HAM 1.01. 36
task | does not divide the sunday from the week, 1.01. 76
from whence though willingly i came to denmark 1.02. 52
lord, wrung from me my slow leave | by laborsome 1.02. 58
from the first corse till he that died to-day, 1.02.105
and what make you from wittenberg, horatio? 1.02.164
but what, in faith, make you from wittenberg? 1.02.168
in haste away | and vanish'd from our sight. 1.02.220
from top to toe? 1.02.228
my lord, from head to foot. 1.02.228
do not sleep, | but let me hear from you. 1.03. 4
from this time | be something scanter of your 1.03.120
would not, in plain terms, from this time forth, 1.03.132
and indeed it takes | from our achievements, 1.04. 21
take corruption | from that particular fault: 1.04. 36
bring with thee airs from heaven, or blasts from 1.04. 41
with thee airs from heaven, or blasts from hell, 1.04. 41
two eyes, like stars, start from their spheres, 1.05. 17
what /a falling-off was there | from me, whose 1.05. 48
from the table of my memory | i'll wipe away all 1.05. 98
my lord, come from the grave | to tell us this. 1.05.125
him | so much from th' understanding of himself, 2.02. 9
gather | so much as from occasion you may glean, 2.02. 16
th' embassadors from norway, my good lord, | are 2.02. 40
say, voltemand, what from our brother norway? 2.02. 59
receives rebuke from norway, and, in fine, 2.02. 69
came this from hamlet to her? 2.02.114
that she should lock herself from /his resort, 2.02.143
take this from this, if this be otherwise. 2.02.156
and be not from his reason fall'n thereon, | let 2.02.165
you cannot take from me any thing that i will 2.02.215 P
the players shall receive from you. 2.02.317 P
wind is southerly i know a hawk from a hand-saw. 2.02.379 P
all the spokes and /fellies from her wheel, 2.02.495
that from her working all the visage wann'd, 2.02.554
get from him why he puts on this confusion, 3.01. 2
but from what cause 'a will by no means speak. 3.01. 6
from whose bourn | no traveller returns, puzzles 3.01. 78
transform honesty from what it is to a bawd than 3.01.111 P
beating puts him thus | from fashion of himself. 3.01.175
of his grief | sprung from neglected love. 3.01.178
thing so o'erdone is from the purpose of playing 3.02. 20 P
for what advancement may i hope from thee | that 3.02. 57
so far from cheer and from /your former state, 3.02.164
so far from cheer and from /your former state, 3.02.164
sport and repose lock from me day and night, 3.02.217
frame, and /start not so wildly from my affair. 3.02.309 P
you would sound me from my lowest note to /the 3.02.366 P
armor of the mind | to keep itself from noyance, 3.03. 13
from the fair forehead of an innocent love | and 3.04. 43
a deed | as from the body of contraction plucks 3.04. 46
what judgment | would step from this to this? 3.04. 71
that from a shelf the precious diadem stole, 3.04.100
will reword, which madness | would gambol from. 3.04.144
would from a paddock, from a bat, a gib, | such 3.04.190
would from a paddock, from a bat, a gib, | such 3.04.190
to keep it from divulging, let it feed | even on 4.01. 22
and from his mother's closet hath he dragg'd him 4.01. 35
is bestow'd, my lord, | we cannot get from him. 4.03. 13
go, captain, from me greet the danish king. 4.04. 1
o, from this time forth, | my thoughts be bloody 4.04. 65
should i your true-love know | from another one? 4.05. 24
it springs | all from her father's death — and 4.05. 76
divided from herself and her fair judgment, 4.05. 85
her brother is in secret come from france, 4.05. 88
cry to be heard, as 'twere from heaven to earth, 4.05.217
i do not know from what part of the world | i 4.06. 5
i should be greeted, if not from lord hamlet. 4.06. 6
it came from th' embassador that was bound for 4.06. 10 P
direct me | to him from whom you brought them. 4.06. 34
from hamlet? who brought them? 4.07. 38
did not together pluck such envy from him | as 4.07. 74
most generous, and free from all contriving, 4.07.135
collected from all simples that have virtue 4.07.144
can save the thing from death | that is but 4.07.145
pull'd the poor wretch from her melodious lay 4.07.182
lie, sir, 'twill away again from me to you. 5.01.128 P
and from her fair and unpolluted flesh | may 5.01.239
i prithee take thy fingers from my throat. 5.01.260
up from my cabin, | my sea-gown scarf'd about me 5.02. 12
an earnest conjuration from the king, | as 5.02. 38
i should impart a thing to you from his majesty. 5.02. 90 P
come, hamlet, come, and take this hand from me. 5.02.225
if hamlet from himself be ta'en away, | and when 5.02.234
let my disclaiming from a purpos'd evil | free 5.02.241
thy heart, | absent thee from felicity a while, 5.02.347
fortinbras, with conquest come from poland, | to 5.02.350
i cannot live to hear the news from england, 5.02.354
and our affairs from england come too late. 5.02.368
not from his mouth, | had it th' ability of life 5.02.372
you from the polack wars, and you from england, 5.02.376
you from the polack wars, and you from england, 5.02.376
and from his mouth whose voice will draw /on 5.02.392
to shake all cares and business from our age, LR 1.01. 39
all these bounds, even from this line to this, 1.01. 63
orbs, | from whom we do exist and cease to be; 1.01.112
my heart and me | hold thee from this for ever. 1.01.116
as here i give | her father's heart from her. 1.01.126
the bow is bent and drawn, make from the shaft. 1.01.143
or, whilst i can vent clamor from my throat, 1.01.165
to shield thee from disasters of the world, 1.01.174
that good effects may spring from words of love. 1.01.185
i would not from your love make such a stray 1.01.209
that stands | aloof from th' entire point. 1.01.240
'tis strange that from their cold'st neglect 1.01.254
then must we look from his age to receive not 1.01.296 P
are we like to have from him as this of kent's 1.01.301 P
it is a letter from my brother that i have not 1.02. 37 P
keeps our fortunes from us till our oldness 1.02. 48 P
till you can derive from him better testimony of 1.02. 81 P
the king falls from bias of nature; 1.02.111 P
from whence i will fitly bring you to hear my 1.02.168 P
shall i hear from you anon? 1.02.177 P
whose nature is so far from doing harms | that 1.02.180
when he returns from hunting, | i will not speak 1.03. 7
after dinner, i will not part from thee yet. 1.04. 41 P
late transport you | from what you rightly are. 1.04.222
my frame of nature | from the fix'd place; 1.04.269
drew from my heart all love, | and added to the 1.04.269
and from her derogate body never spring | a babe 1.04.280
these hot tears, which break from me perforce, 1.04.298
you know than comes from her demand out of the 1.05. 3 P
when i dissuaded him from his intent, | and 2.01. 64
i have this present evening from my sister 2.01.101
best /thought it fit | to answer from our home; 2.01.124
several messengers | from hence attend dispatch. 2.01.125
the messengers from our sister and the king. 2.02. 50 P
and constrains the garb | quite from his nature. 2.02. 98
i know 'tis from cordelia, | who hath most 2.02.166
shall find time | from this enormous state — 2.02.169
and with this horrible object, from low farms, 2.03. 17
strange that they should so depart from home, 2.04. 1
or they impose, this usage, | coming from us. 2.04. 27
ere i was risen from the place that showed | my 2.04. 29
forth | from goneril his mistress salutations; 2.04. 32
i would divorce me from thy /mother's tomb, 2.04.131
wholesome end | as clears her from all blame. 2.04.145
out, varlet, from my sight! 2.04.187
i am now from home, and out of that provision 2.04.205
from those that she calls servants or from mine? 2.04.244
from those that she calls servants or from mine? 2.04.244
'tis his own blame hath put himself from rest, 2.04.290
they took from me the use of mine own house, 3.03. 3 P
doth from my senses take all feeling else, 3.04. 13
defend you | from seasons such as these? 3.04. 32
bless thee from whirlwinds, star-blasting, and 3.04. 59 P
out of plackets, thy pen from lenders' books, 3.04. 97 P
who is whipt from tithing to tithing, and 3.04.134 P
i had a son, | now outlaw'd from my blood; 3.04.167
i will not be long from you. 3.06. 3 P
these hairs which thou dost ravish from my chin 3.07. 38
sir, what letters had you late from france? 3.07. 42
which came from one that's of a neutral heart, 3.07. 48
of a neutral heart, | and not from one oppos'd. 3.07. 49
the lamentable change is from the best, | the 4.01. 5
bless thee, good man's son, from the foul fiend! 4.01. 58 P
from that place | i shall no leading need. 4.01. 77
eye discerning | thine honor from thy suffering, 4.02. 53
'tis from your sister. 4.02. 83
and when your mistress hears thus much from you, 4.05. 34
from the dread summit of this chalky bourn. 4.06. 57
what thing was that | which parted from you? 4.06. 68
down from the waist they are centaurs, | though 4.06.124
i would not take this from report; 4.06.141
and the creature run from the cur? 4.06.157 P
who redeems nature from the general curse 4.06.206
you ever-gentle gods, take my breath from me, 4.06.217
from the loath'd warmth whereof deliver me, and 4.06.267 P
so should my thoughts be sever'd from my griefs, 4.06.282
that parts us shall bring a brand from heaven, 5.03. 22
i should answer | from a full-flowing stomach. 5.03. 74
and from th' extremest upward of thy head | to 5.03.137
led him, begg'd for him, sav'd him from despair; 5.03.192
and from first to last | told him our pilgrimage 5.03.196
it came even from the heart of — o, she's dead! 5.03.225
he hath commission from thy wife and me | to 5.03.253
that, from your first of difference and decay, 5.03.289
bear them from hence. 5.03.319
believe | that, from the sense of all civility, OTH 1.01.131
from hence trust not your daughters' minds | by 1.01.170
my life and being | from men of royal siege, and 1.02. 22
something from cyprus, as i may divine; 1.02. 39
run from her guardage to the sooty bosom | of 1.02. 70
a messenger from the galleys. 1.03. 13
write from us to him, post-post-haste. dispatch! 1.03. 46
hath rais'd me from my bed, nor doth the general 1.03. 54
she is abus'd, stol'n from me, and corrupted 1.03. 60
me the story of my life | from year to year — 1.03.130
even from my boyish days | to th' very moment 1.03.132
to draw from her a prayer of earnest heart 1.03.152
with all my heart | i would keep from thee. 1.03.195
that smiles steals something from the thief; 1.03.208
but the free comfort which from thence he hears; 1.03.213
what from the cape can you discern at sea? 2.01. 1
comes from my pate as birdlime does from frieze, 2.01.126
comes from my pate as birdlime does from frieze, 2.01.126
fled from her wish, and yet said, "now i may"; 2.01.151
and duck again as low | as hell's from heaven! 2.01.189
i have brought you from venice. 2.01.264 P
i'll not be far from you. 2.01.266 P
or from what other course you please, which the 2.01.268 P
liberty of feasting from this present hour of 2.02. 9 P
from whence ariseth this? 2.03.169
bell, it frights the isle | from her propriety. 2.03.176
i had rather have this tongue cut from my mouth 2.03.221
from him that fled some strange indignity 2.03.245
was not that cassio parted from my wife? 3.03. 37
he did, from first to last. why dost thou ask? 3.03. 96
they're close dilations, working from the heart, 3.03.123
/then, | from one that so imperfectly /conjects, 3.03.149
but he that filches from me my good name | robs 3.03.159
souls of all my tribe defend | from jealousy! 3.03.176
nor from mine own weak merits will i draw | the 3.03.187
therefore, as i am bound, | receive it from me. 3.03.196
consider what is spoke | comes from /my love. 3.03.217
and yet how nature erring from itself — 3.03.227
this was her first remembrance from the moor. 3.03.291
hast stol'n it from her? 3.03.310
profit, and from hence | i'll love no friend, 3.03.379
arise, black vengeance, from the hollow hell! 3.03.447
he was born | drew all such humors from him. 3.04. 31
of yours requires | a sequester from liberty: 3.04. 40
this is a trick to put me from my suit. 3.04. 87
from his very arm | puff'd his own brother — 3.04.136
either from venice, or some unhatch'd practice 3.04.141
heaven keep the monster from othello's mind! 3.04.163
what make you from home? 3.04.169
this is some token from a newer friend; 3.04.181
the devil's teeth, | from whence you have them. 3.04.185
jealious now | that this is from some mistress, 3.04.186
cannot restrain | from the excess of laughter. 4.01. 99
i warrant, something from venice. 4.01.214
'tis lodovico — | this comes from the duke. 4.01.215
the fountain from the which my current runs | or 4.02. 59
for my lord | from any other foul unlawful touch 4.02. 84
the world | even from the east to th' west! 4.02.144
keep'st from me all conveniency than suppliest 4.02.176 P
jewels you have had from me to deliver desdemona 4.02.186 P
and even from this instant do build on thee a 4.02.205 P
take me from this world with treachery and 4.02.216 P
commission come from venice to depute cassio in 4.02.220 P
that song to-night | will not go from my mind; 4.03. 31
her salt tears fell from her, and soft'ned the 4.03. 46
not to pick bad from bad, but by bad mend. 4.03.105
of gold and jewels that i bobb'd from him | as 5.01. 16
some good man bear him carefully from hence, 5.01. 99
yea, curse his better angel from his side, | and 5.02.208
which i have /here recover'd from the moor. 5.02.240
look of thine will hurl my soul from heaven, 5.02.274
from the possession of this heavenly sight! 5.02.278
wrench his sword from him. 5.02.288
from this time forth i never will speak word. 5.02.304
news, my good lord, from rome. ANT 1.01. 18
your dismission | is come from caesar, therefore 1.01. 27
whose better issue in the war from italy, | upon 1.02. 93
from euphrates | his conquering banner shook, 1.02.101
shook, from syria | to lydia and to ionia, 1.02.102
from sicyon how the news? speak there! 1.02.113
the man from sicyon — is there such an one? 1.02.114
what our contempts doth often hurl from us, | we 1.02.123
i must from this enchanting queen break off; 1.02.128
i must with haste from hence. 1.02.132
deities to take the wife of a man from him, it 1.02.163 P
under us require, | our quick remove from hence. 1.02.196
hold the method to enforce | the like from him. 1.03. 8
pray you stand farther from me. 1.03. 18
though age from folly could not give me freedom, 1.03. 57
give me freedom, | it does from childishness. 1.03. 58
nilus' slime, i go from hence | thy soldier, 1.03. 69
from alexandria | this is the news: 1.04. 3
that drums him from his sport and speaks as loud 1.04. 29
it hath been taught us from the primal state 1.04. 41
when thou once | was beaten from modena, where 1.04. 57
yet, coming from him, that great med'cine hath 1.05. 36
from silvius, sir. 2.01. 18
since he went from egypt, 'tis | a space for 2.01. 30
can from the lap of egypt's widow pluck | the 2.01. 37
and have my learning from some true reports 2.02. 47
hours had bound me up | from mine own knowledge. 2.02. 91
hoop should hold us staunch from edge to edge 2.02.115
and from this hour | the heart of brothers 2.02.146
welcome from egypt, sir. 2.02.171 P
from the barge | a strange invisible perfume 2.02.211
will sometimes | divide me from your bosom. 2.03. 2
would i had never come from thence, nor you 2.03. 11 P
o, from italy! 2.05. 23
make thee a fortune from me. 2.05. 49
merchandise which thou hast brought from rome 2.05.104
lead me from hence; 2.05.109
to tell us | (for this is from the present) how 2.06. 30
merit thou wilt hear me, | rise from thy stool. 2.07. 56
no, pompey, i have kept me from the cup. 2.07. 66
but i had rather fast from all, four days, 2.07.102
octavia weeps | to part from rome; 3.02. 4
you take from me a great part of myself; 3.02. 24
sweet octavia, | you shall hear from me still; 3.02. 60
him, he not /took't, | or did it from his teeth. 3.04. 10
already, will their good thoughts call from him. 3.06. 21

take from his heart, take from his brain, from 3.07. 11
take from his heart, take from his brain, from 3.07. 11
his heart, take from his brain, from 's time, 3.07. 11
that from tarentum and brundusium | he could so 3.07. 21
to chance and hazard, | from firm security. 3.07. 48
from th' head of /actium | beat th' approaching 3.07. 51
from which place | we may the number of the 3.09. 2
have letters from me to some friends that will 3.11. 16
thy beck might from the bidding of the gods 3.11. 60
let him appear that's come from antony. 3.12. 1
such as i am, i come from antony. 3.12. 7
she | from egypt drive her all–disgraced friend, 3.12. 22
from antony win cleopatra, promise, | and in our 3.12. 27
add more, | from thine invention, offers. 3.12. 29
though you fled | from that great face of war, 3.13. 5
from which the world should note | something 3.13. 21
a messenger from caesar. 3.13. 37
spirits | to hear from me you had left antony, 3.13. 70
from his all–obeying breath i hear | the doom of 3.13. 77
authority melts from me. 3.13. 90
from my cold heart let heaven engender hail, 3.13.159
if from the field i shall return once more | to 3.13.173
or from caesar's camp | say "i am none of thine. 4.05. 8
tears | wash the congealment from your wounds, 4.08. 10
com'st thou smiling from | the world's great 4.08. 17
of ajax cannot keep | the battery from my heart. 4.14. 39
from me awhile. 4.14. 43
turn from me then that noble countenance, 4.14. 85
o charmian, i will never go from hence. 4.15. 1
were | as plates dropp'd from his pocket. 5.02. 92
to that destruction which i'll guard them from 5.02.132
now from head to foot | i am marble–constant; 5.02.239
there's dolabella sent from caesar; call him. 5.02.324
her bed, | and bear her women from the monument. 5.02.357
the other, from their nursery | were stol'n, and CYM 1.01. 59
your highness, | i will from hence to–day. 1.01. 80
and cere up my embracements from a next | with 1.01.116
thou basest thing, avoid hence, from my sight! 1.01.125
why came you from your master? 1.01.169
/this eye or ear | distinguish him from others, 1.03. 10
nay, followed him till he had melted from | the 1.03. 20
good pisanio, | when shall we hear from him? 1.03. 23
of the north | shakes all our buds from growing. 1.03. 37
him, i doubt not, a great deal from the matter. 1.04. 16 P
and i will bring from thence that honor of hers 1.04.130 P
a dram, you cannot preserve it from tainting. 1.04.136 P
signior jachimo will not from it. 1.04.171 P
shall from this practice but make hard your 1.05. 24
hath the king | five times redeem'd from death. 1.05. 63
do't as from thyself. 1.05. 67
of rome, | comes from my lord with letters. 1.06. 11
arm me, audacity, from head to foot, | or, like 1.06. 19
he furnaces | the thick sighs from him, whiles 1.06. 67
(your lord, i mean) laughs from 's free lungs; 1.06. 68
to hide me from the radiant sun, and solace | i' 1.06. 86
that from my mutest conscience to my tongue 1.06.116
queen, and you | recoil from your great stock. 1.06.128
is as far | from thy report as thou from honor, 1.06.146
is as far | from thy report as thou from honor, 1.06.146
from gallia | i cross'd the seas on purpose and 1.06.201
and this her son | cannot take two from twenty, 2.01. 55
from fairies and the tempters of the night 2.02. 9
so like you, sir, ambassadors from rome; 2.03. 54
yet you are curb'd from that enlargement by 2.03.120
which you might from relation likewise reap, 2.04. 86
she stripp'd it from her arm. 2.04.101
being corrupted, | hath stol'n it from her? 2.04.117
by jupiter, i had it from her arm. 2.04.121
oppose and she | should from encounter guard. 2.05. 19
which then they had to take from 's, to resume 3.01. 15
him) he was carried | from off our coast, twice 3.01. 26
caesar can hide the sun from us with a blanket, 3.01. 43 P
romans did extort | this tribute from us, we 3.01. 48
receive it from me then: 3.01. 65
madam, here is a letter from my lord. 3.02. 25
but first of all, | how we may steal from hence; 3.02. 62
in time, from our hence–going | and our return, 3.02. 63
thus | draws us a profit from all things we see; 3.03. 18
have never wing'd from view o' th' nest, nor 3.03. 28
th' nest, nor /know not | what air's from home. 3.03. 29
thou toldst me, when we came from horse, the 3.04. 1
breaks that sigh | from th' inward of thee? 3.04. 6
but from proof as strong as my grief and as 3.04. 24 P
tear, took pity | from most true wretchedness. 3.04. 61
be false and perjur'd | from thy great fail. 3.04. 64
you can borrow | from youth of such a season) 3.04.172
be suspected of | your carriage from the court. 3.04.187
here is a box, i had it from the queen, | what's 3.04.188
my emperor hath wrote i must from hence, | and 3.05. 2
but from this time forth | i wear it as your 3.05. 13
from whence he moves | his war for britain. 3.05. 25
woman, from every one | the best she hath, and 3.05. 72
i'll have this secret from thy heart, or rip 3.05. 86
from whose so many weights of baseness cannot 3.05. 88
(the bitterness of it i now belch from my heart) 3.05.134 P
when from the mountain top pisanio show'd thee, 3.06. 5
it would fly | from so divine a temple to commix 4.02. 55
ay, and that | from one bad thing to worse, not 4.02.134
my throat, i have ta'en | his head from him. 4.02.151
honor untaught, | civility not seen from other; 4.02.179
have skipp'd from sixteen years of age to sixty, 4.02.199
and put | my clouted brogues from off my feet, 4.02.214
from this most bravest vessel of the world 4.02.319
but what from rome? 4.02.336
from the spungy south to this part of the west, 4.02.349
i may wander | from east to occident, cry out 4.02.372
i'll hide my master from the flies, as deep | as 4.02.388
we'll enforce it from thee | by a sharp torture. 4.03. 11
the roman legions, all from gallia drawn, | are 4.03. 24
we fear not | what can from italy annoy us, but 4.03. 34
i heard no letter from my master since | i wrote 4.03. 36
nor hear i from my mistress, who did promise 4.03. 38
let us from it. 4.04. 1
in life, to lock it | from action and adventure? 4.04. 3
and so extort from 's that | which we have done, 4.04. 12
upon our note, | to know from whence we are. 4.04. 21
you see, not wore him | from my remembrance. 4.04. 24
away, boy, from the troops, and save thyself; 5.02. 14
cam'st thou from where they made the stand? 5.03. 1
though you, it seems, come from the fliers? 5.03. 2
and shielded him | from this earth–vexing smart. 5.04. 42
my throes, | that from me was posthumus ripp'd, 5.04. 45
and thrown | from leonati seat, and cast | from 5.04. 60
seat, and cast | from her his dearest one, 5.04. 61
for this from stiller seats we came, | our 5.04. 69
or we appeal, | and from thy justice fly. 5.04. 92
and when from a stately cedar shall be lopp'd 5.04.140 P
is not this boy reviv'd from death? 5.05.120
torture shall | winnow the truth from falsehood. 5.05.134
o, get thee from my sight, | thou gav'st me 5.05.236
i had it from the queen. 5.05.242
lord, | now fear is from me, i'll speak troth. 5.05.274
master's garments | (which he enforc'd from me), 5.05.283
i would not thy good deeds should from my lips 5.05.288
the offender, | and take him from our presence. 5.05.301
after this strange starting from your orbs, 5.05.371
why fled you from the court? 5.05.387
other by–dependances, | from chance to chance; 5.05.391
whose containing | is so from sense in hardness, 5.05.431
and when from a stately cedar shall be lopp'd 5.05.437 P
from the which | we were dissuaded by our wicked 5.05.462
from south to west on wing soaring aloft, 5.05.471
climb to their nostrils | from our blest altars. 5.05.478
was sung, | from ashes ancient gower is come, PER 1.ch. 2
as from thence | sorrow were ever ras'd, and 1.01. 16
my riches to the earth from whence they came; 1.01. 52
succeeding from so fair a tree | as your fair 1.01.114
/'schew no course to keep them from the light. 1.01.136
from a well–experienc'd archer hits the mark 1.01.162
amazement shall drive courage from the state, 1.02. 26
from whence | they have their nourishment? 1.02. 55
i have power | to take thy life from thee. 1.02. 57
from whence an issue i might propagate, | are 1.02. 73
sleep out of mine eyes, blood from my cheeks, 1.02. 96
from whence we had our being and our birth. 1.02.114
tyre, i now look from thee then, and to tharsus 1.02.115
intend my travel, where i'll hear from thee, 1.02.116
what from antioch? 1.03. 18
lord thaliard from antiochus is welcome. 1.03. 30
from him i come | with message unto princely 1.03. 31
now message must return from whence it came. 1.03. 35
to eat honey like a drone | from others' labors; 2.ch. 19
lost, | by waves from coast to coast is toss'd. 2.ch. 34
wash'd me from shore to shore, and left /me 2.01. 6
and having thrown him from your wat'ry grave, 2.01. 10
how from the /finny subject of the sea | these 2.01. 48
and from their wat'ry empire recollect | all 2.01. 50
since he gains from his subjects the name of 2.01.104 P
how far is his court distant from this shore? 2.01.106 P
and knights come from all parts of the world to 2.01.109 P
you'll remember from whence you had them. 2.01.152 P
from the dejected state wherein he is, | he 2.02. 46
and will awake him from his melancholy. 2.03. 91
of me, | antiochus from incest lived not free; 2.04. 2
him, | a fire from heaven came and shrivell'd up 2.04. 9
knights, from my daughter this i let you know, 2.05. 2
known, | which from her by no means can i get. 2.05. 6
coal, | now couches from the mouse's hole; 3.ch. 6
at last from tyre, | fame answering the most 3.ch. 21
in brass, | having call'd them from the deep! 3.01. 4
heaven can make | to herald thee from the womb. 3.01. 34
your lady | take from my heart all thankfulness! 3.03. 4
a lasting storm, | whirring me from my friends. 4.01. 20
and from the ladder–tackle washes off | a 4.01. 60
industry they skip | from /stem to stern. 4.01. 63
he did not flow | from honorable courses. 4.03. 28
from bourn to bourn, region to region. 4.04. 4
would set me free from this unhallowed place, 4.06.100
if thou dost | hear from me, it shall be for thy 4.06.116
to take from you the jewel you hold so dear. 4.06.154 P
gods | would safely deliver me from this place! 4.06.180
with other virtues, which i'll keep from boast, 4.06.184
from whence | lysimachus our tyrian ship espies, 5.ch. 17
sir, there is a barge put off from meteline, 5.01. 3
but the main grief springs from the loss | of a 5.01. 29
my derivation was from ancestors | who stood 5.01. 90
from the deck | you may discern the place. 5.01.114
falseness cannot come from thee, for thou 5.01.120
thee — that thou cam'st | from good descending? 5.01.128
thou hadst been toss'd from wrong to injury, 5.01.130
who, frighted from my country, did wed | at 5.03. 3
you have heard me say, when i did fly from tyre, 5.03. 50
that can | from first to last resolve you. 5.03. 61
virtue /preserv'd from fell destruction's blast, 5.03. 89
and make him cry from under ground, "o, fan TNK pr 18
fan | from me the witless chaff of such a writer pr 19
play do not keep | a little dull time from us, pr 31
with them any discord bring, | but from it fly! 1.01. 24
of mortal loathsomeness from the blest eye | of 1.01. 45
able to lock jove from a synod, shall | by 1.01.176
from henceforth i'll not dare | to ask you any 1.01.203
cousin, i charge you | boudge not from athens. 1.01.223
there | that does command my rapier from my hip, 1.02. 56
sib to him be suck'd | from me with leeches! 1.02. 73
at adventure humm'd /one | from musical coinage, 1.03. 76
have said enough to shake me from the arm | of 1.03. 92
who from the mounted heavens | view us their 1.04. 4
bear 'em speedily | from our kind air, to them 1.04. 38
i' th' deliverance, will break from one of them; 2.01. 42 P
flies like a parthian quiver from our rages, 2.02. 50
even from the bottom of these miseries, | from 2.02. 56
from all that fortune can inflict upon us, | i 2.02. 57
to keep us from corruption of worse men. 2.02. 72
might, like women, | woo us to wander from. 2.02. 76
no hard oppressor | dare take this from us; 2.02. 85
chances, | were we from hence, would sever us. 2.02. 95
what 'twere to filch affection from another! 2.02.210
no, but from this place to remove your lordship; 2.02.261
which will seek of me | some news from earth, 3.01. 80
tell me | news from all parts o' th' world. 3.04. 13
"the george alow came from the south, | from the 3.05. 59
from the south, | from the coast of barbary–a; 3.05. 60
doughty dismal fame | from dis to daedalus, from 3.05.115
from dis to daedalus, from post to pillar, | is 3.05.115
like meeting of two tides, fly strongly from us, 3.06. 30
dreadful clap of thunder | break from the troop. 3.06. 84
if i fall from that mouth, i fall with favor, 3.06.282
and she answered me | so far from what she was, 4.01. 39
from the far shore, thick set with reeds and 4.01. 54
or as iris | newly dropp'd down from heaven. 4.01. 88
three or four | i saw from far off cross her — 4.01.100
they come from all parts of the dukedom to him. 4.01.136
methinks, from hence, as from a promontory 4.02. 22
hence, as from a promontory | pointed in heaven, 4.02. 22
love, this only | from this hour is complexion. 4.02. 43
from the noble duke your brother, | madam, i 4.02. 55
from whence come you, sir? 4.02. 71
from the knights. 4.02. 71
then from this gather | how i should tender you. 5.01. 24
with hand armipotent from forth blue clouds 5.01. 54
to call the fiercest tyrant from his rage, | and 5.01. 78
torturing convulsions from his globy eyes | had 5.01.113
o thou that from eleven to ninety reign'st | in 5.01.130
flows | out from the bowels of her holy altar 5.01.164
you must not from her, | but still preserve her 5.02.105
a life more worthy from him than all women, | i 5.03.143
what | hath wak'd us from our dream? 5.04. 48
as they say, from iron | came music's origin), 5.04. 60
one kiss from fair emilia. 5.04. 94
the gods my justice | take from my hand, and 5.04.121
and call your lovers from the stage of death, 5.04.123
till now grown up | had been ta'en from you, and STM II.C 66
god, | that i from such an humble bench of birth III 6
and tithe of knees | from elder kinsmen, and him III 10
courageously to pluck him from his horse. VEN 30
she swears | from his soft bosom never to remove 81
from morn till night, even where i list to sport 154
seeds spring from seeds and beauty breedeth 167
"the sun that shines from heaven shines but warm 193
the heat i have from thence doth little harm, 195
and when from thence he struggles to be gone, 227
to shelter thee from tempest and from rain: 238
to shelter thee from tempest and from rain: 238
and from her twining arms doth urge releasing. 256
but lo from forth a copse that neighbors by, | a 259
and forth again | as from a furnace, vapors doth 274
flash'd forth fire, as lightning from the sky. 348
care, | is how to get my palfrey from the mare." 384
throwing the base thong from his bending crest, 395
remove your siege from my unyielding heart, | to 423
for from the stillitory of thy face excelling 443
as if from thence they borrowed all their shine. 488
to drive infection from the dangerous year! 508
"a thousand kisses buys my heart from me, | and 517
such nectar from his lips she had not suck'd. 572
for stealing moulds from heaven that were divine 730
yet from mine ear the tempting tune is blown; 778
with this he breaketh from the sweet embrace 811
look how a bright star shooteth from the sky, 815
so glides he in the night from venus' eye, 816
from his moist cabinet mounts up on high, | and 854
from whose silver breast | the sun ariseth in 855
from whom each lamp and shining star doth borrow 861
she wildly breaketh from their strict embrace, 874
the crystal tide that from her two cheeks fair 957
that from their dark beds once more leap her 1050
kill'd | was melted like a vapor from her sight, 1166
since he himself is reft from her by death. 1174
from the besieged ardea all in post, | borne by LUC 1
are weakly fortress'd from a world of harms. 28
he should keep unknown | from thievish ears, 35
in that white intituled | from venus' doves, 58
then virtue claims from beauty beauty's red, 59
proving from world's minority their right: 67
could pick no meaning from their parling looks, 100
far from the purpose of his coming thither, | he 113
they scatter and unloose it from their bond, 136
and now this lustful lord leapt from his bed, 169
that from the cold stone sparks of fire do fly, 177
"as from this cold flint i enforc'd this fire, 181
fearing some hard news from the warlike band 255
part is youth, and beats these from the stage. 278
he takes it from the rushes where it lies, | and 318
that shuts him from the heaven of his thought, 338
hath barr'd him from the blessed thing he sought 340
so from himself impiety hath wrought, | that for 341
rushing from forth a cloud, bereaves our sight, 373
from this fair throne to heave the owner out. 413
from forth dull sleep by dreadful fancy waking, 450
from sleep disturbed, heedfully doth view | the 454
who, angry that the eyes fly from their lights, 461
the shame that from them no device can take, 535
from earth's dark womb some gentle gust doth get 549
blow these pitchy vapors from their biding, 550
she puts the period often from his place, | and 565
thing | from vassal actors can be wip'd away; 608
from a pure heart command thy rebel will; 625
that from their own misdeeds askaunce their eyes 637
and wipe the dim mist from thy doting eyne, 643
and bids it leap from thence, where it may find 760
that is as clear from this attaint of mine | as 825
in me, | from me by strong assault it is bereft: 835
coming from thee, i could not put him back, 843
a thousand crosses keep them from thy aid: 912
come, | from the creation to the general doom. 924
to pluck the quills from ancient ravens' wings, 949
"the baser is he, coming from a king, | to shame 1002
said, from her betumbled couch she starteth, 1037
so vanisheth | as smoke from aetna, that in air 1042
or that which from discharged cannon fumes. 1043
with gold, but stol'n from forth thy gate. 1068
as from a mountain spring that feeds a dale, 1077
some dark deep desert, seated from the way, 1144
ay me, the bark pill'd from the lofty pine, 1167
wip'd the brinish pearl from her bright eyes, 1213
"on what occasion break | those tears from thee, 1271
till after a deep groan) "tarquin from hence?" 1276
so i commend me from our house in grief, | my 1308
from that suspicion which the world might bear 1321
and from the tow'rs of troy there would appear 1382
and from his lips did fly | thin winding breath, 1406
and from the walls of strong–besieged troy, 1429
and from the strond of dardan, where they fought 1436
let guiltless souls be freed from guilty woe: 1482

and little stars shot from their fixed places, 1525
and from her tongue "can lurk" from "cannot" 1537
from her tongue "can lurk" from "cannot" took: 1537
"such devils steal effects from lightless hell, 1555
that patience is quite beaten from her breast; 1563
being from the feeling of her own grief brought 1578
met far from home, wond'ring each other's chance 1596
me, | from that, alas, thy lucrece is not free. 1624
from lips new waxen pale begins to blow | the 1663
suppose thou dost defend me | from what is past: 1685
"how may this forced stain be wip'd from me? 1701
may any terms acquit me from this chance? 1706
and why not i from this compelled stain?" 1708
that blow did bail it from the deep unrest | of 1725
live's lasting date from cancell'd destiny. 1729
and from the purple fountain brutus drew | the 1734
and bubbling from her breast, it doth divide 1737
thou wast not to this end from me derived. 1755
o, from thy cheeks my image thou hast torn, 1762
by this starts collatine as from a dream, | and 1772
or keep him from heart–easing words so long, 1782
who pluck'd the knife from lucrece' side, 1807
such childish humor from weak minds proceeds; 1825
by our strong arms from forth her fair streets 1834
evil | tempteth my better angel from my side; PP 2. 6
doth cite each moving sense from idle rest, 14.15
sworn | ne'er to pluck thee from thy /thorn, 16.12
plains, | all our evening sport from us is fled, 17.31
complain, | scarce i could from tears refrain; 20.16
to know | faithful friend from flatt'ring foe. 20.56
from this session interdict | every fowl of PHT 9
the turtle fled | in a mutual flame from hence. 24
from fairest creatures we desire increase, SON 1. 1
but when from highmost pitch, with weary car, 7. 9
car, | like feeble age he reeleth from the day, 7.10
are | from his low tract and look another way: 7.12
in one of thine, from that which thou departest, 11. 2
call thine, when thou from youth convertest. 11. 4
which erst from heat did canopy the herd, | and 12. 6
not from the stars do i my judgment pluck, | and 14. 1
but from thine eyes my knowledge i derive, | and 14. 9
if from thyself to store thou wouldst convert; 14.12
you, | as he takes from you, i ingraft you new. 15.14
and every fair from fair sometime declines, | by 18. 7
pluck the keen teeth from the fierce tiger's 19. 3
as tender nurse her babe from faring ill. 22.12
foil'd, | is from the book of honor rased quite, 25.11
for then my thoughts (from far where i abide) 27. 5
how far i toil, still farther off from thee. 28. 8
at break of day arising | from sullen earth) 29.12
and heavily from woe to woe tell o'er | the sad 30.10
hath dear religious love stol'n from mine eye 31. 6
and from the forlorn world his visage hide, 33. 7
the region cloud hath mask'd him from me now. 33.12
to that sweet thief which sourly robs from me. 35.14
doth it steal sweet hours from love's delight. 36. 8
me, | unless thou take that honor from thy name. 36.12
when i am sometime absent from thy heart, | thy 41. 2
from limits far remote, where thou dost stay. 44. 4
upon the farthest earth remov'd from thee, | for 44. 6
by those swift messengers return'd from thee, 45.10
it might unused stay | from hands of falsehood, 48. 4
from whence at pleasure thou mayst come and part 48.12
eye, | when love converted from the thing it was 49. 7
far the miles are measur'd from thy friend." 50. 4
his rider lov'd not speed, being made from thee. 50. 8
of my dull bearer, when from thee i speed: 51. 2
from where thou art, why should i haste me 51. 3
since from thee going he went willful–slow, 51.13
is it thy spirit that thou send'st from thee 61. 5
thee | so far from home into my deeds to pry, 61. 6
from me far off, with others all too near. 61.14
that he shall never cut from memory | my sweet 63.11
time's best jewel from time's chest lie hid? 65.10
with all these, from these would i be gone, 66.13
the world that i am fled | from this vile world, 71. 4
save what is had or must from you be took. 75.12
so far from variation or quick change? 76. 2
those children nurs'd, deliver'd from thy brain, 77.11
and he stole that word | from thy behavior; 79.10
from hence your memory death cannot take, 81. 3
your name from hence immortal life shall have, 81. 5
i was not sick of any fear from thence: 86.12
be absent from thy walks, and in my tongue | thy 89. 9
and husband nature's riches from expense; 94. 6
like a winter hath my absence been | from thee, 97. 2
from you have i been absent in the spring, 98. 1
or from their proud lap pluck them where they 98. 8
that smells, | if not from my love's breath? 99. 3
but sweet or color it had stol'n from thee. 99.15
have from the forests shook three summers' pride 104. 4
steal from his figure, and no pace perceiv'd, 104.10
as easy might i from myself depart | as from my 109. 3
might i from myself depart | as from my soul, 109. 4
to know my shames and praises from your tongue; 112. 6
should transport me farthest from your sight. 117. 8
distill'd from limbecks foul as hell within, 119. 2
therefore to give them from me was i bold, | to 122.11
no, it was builded far from accident; 124. 5
than in the breath that from my mistress reeks. 130. 8
me from myself thy cruel eye hath taken, | and 133. 5
and therefore from my face she turns my foes, 139.11
no news but health from their physicians know; 140. 8
dissuade one foolish heart from serving thee, 141.10
or, if it do, not from those lips of thine, 142. 5
so run'st thou after that which flies from thee, 143. 9
evil | tempteth my better angel from my /side, 144. 6
but being both from me, both to each friend, | i 144.11
a fiend | from heaven to hell is flown away: 145.12
"i hate" from hate away she threw, | and sav'd 145.13
at randon from the truth vainly express'd; 147.12
o, from what pow'r hast thou this pow'rful might 150. 1
which borrow'd from this holy fire of love | a 153. 5
which from love's fire took heat perpetual, 154.10
from off a hill whose concave womb reworded | a LC 1
a plaintful story from a sist'ring vale, | my 2
which fortified her visage from the sun, 9
true to bondage, would not break from thence, 34
a thousand favors from a maund she drew, | of 36
if that from him there may be aught applied 68
'that horse his mettle from his rider takes; 107
o appetite, from judgment stand aloof! 166
i have receiv'd from many a several fair, 206
"'lo this device was sent me from a nun, | or 232
each cheek a river running from a fount | with 283
both fire from hence and chill extincture hath. 294
o, that forc'd thunder from his heart did fly, 325

FROM'T 5 FR 0.0005 REL FR 3 V 2 P
if wit flow from't | as boldness from my bosom, WT 2.02. 50
yea, upon mine honor, | i free you from't. H8 2.04.158
told him on't, but i could ne'er get him from't. TIM 3.01. 29 P
some other hour, i should derive much from't; 3.04. 69 P
and justifying my love, i must not fly from't. TNK 3.06. 42

/FRONT 1 FR 0.0001 REL FR 1 V 0 P
/to /take /the /safest /occasion /by /the /front OTH 3.01. 49

FRONT 22 FR 0.0024 REL FR 19 V 3 P
"accost" is front her, board her, woo her, TN 1.03. 56 P
but flora, | peering in april's front. WT 4.04. 3
you four shall front them in the narrow lane; 1H4 2.02. 60 P
the front of heaven was full of fiery shapes 3.01. 14
the front of heaven was full of fiery shapes, 3.01. 37
but death doth front thee with apparent spoil, 1H6 4.02. 26
but boldly stand and front him to his face. 2H6 5.01. 86
charg'd our main battle's front and, breaking in 3H6 1.01. 8
war hath smooth'd his wrinkled front; R3 1.01. 9
and front but in that file | where others tell H8 1.02. 42
for yonder walls, that pertly front your town, TRO 4.05.219
think to front his revenges with the easy groans COR 5.02. 42 P
front to front | bring thou this fiend of MAC 4.03.232
front to front | bring thou this fiend of 4.03.232
ay, on the front. 5.09. 13
hyperion's curls, the front of jove himself, HAM 3.04. 56
radiant fire | on /flick'ring phoebus' front — LR 2.02.108
the very head and front of my offending | hath OTH 1.03. 80
and devotion of their view | upon a tawny front; ANT 1.01. 6
land i can be able | to front this present time. 1.04. 79
friend and companion in the front of war, | the 5.01. 44
lays, | as philomel in summer's front doth sing, SON 102. 7

FRONTED 1 FR 0.0001 REL FR 1 V 0 P
those wars | which fronted mine own peace. ANT 2.02. 61

FRONTIER 2 FR 0.0002 REL FR 2 V 0 P
endure | the moody frontier of a servant brow. 1H4 1.03. 19
the main of poland, sir, | or for some frontier? HAM 4.04. 16

FRONTIERS 1 FR 0.0001 REL FR 1 V 0 P
of palisadoes, frontiers, parapets, | of 1H4 2.03. 52

FRONTING 2 FR 0.0002 REL FR 2 V 0 P
fly | towards fronting peril and oppos'd decay! 2H4 4.04. 66
or, like a gate of steel | fronting the sun, TRO 3.03.122

FRONTLET 1 FR 0.0001 REL FR 0 V 1 P
what makes that frontlet on? LR 1.04.189 P

FRONTS 4 FR 0.0004 REL FR 4 V 0 P
why stand these royal fronts amazed thus? JN 2.01.356
what well–appointed leader fronts us here? 2H4 4.01. 25
and abutting fronts | the perilous narrow ocean H5 pr 21
our powers, with smiling fronts encount'ring, COR 1.06. 8

FROST 13 FR 0.0014 REL FR 12 V 1 P
o' th' earth | when it is bak'd with frost. TMP 1.02.256
so full of frost, of storm, and cloudiness? ADO 5.04. 42
berowne is like an envious sneaping frost | that LLL 1.01.100
then farewell heat, and welcome frost! MV 2.07. 75
she was, good curtis, before this frost; SHR 4.01. 22 P
the third day comes a frost, a killing frost, H8 3.02.355
the third day comes a frost, a killing frost, 3.02.355
that's curdied by the frost from purest snow COR 5.03. 66
and i hang the head | as flowers with frost, or TIT 4.04. 71
death lies on her like an untimely frost | upon ROM 4.05. 28
since frost itself as actively doth burn, | and HAM 3.04. 87
love's fire fear's frost hath dissolution. LUC 355
sap check'd with frost and lusty leaves quite SON 5. 7

/FROSTS 1 FR 0.0001 REL FR 1 V 0 P
/as /despair | /that /frosts /will /bite /them. 2H4 1.03. 41

FROSTS 4 FR 0.0004 REL FR 4 V 0 P
if frosts and fasts, hard lodging and thin weeds LLL 5.02.801
hoary–headed frosts | fall in the fresh lap of MND 2.01.107
blots thy beauty, as frosts do bite the meads, SHR 5.02.139
like little frosts that sometime threat the LUC 331

FROSTY 9 FR 0.0010 REL FR 9 V 0 P
age is as a lusty winter, | frosty, but kindly. AYL 2.03. 53
his hand | by thinking on the frosty caucasus? R2 1.03.295
ay, by my faith, that bears a frosty sound. 1H4 4.01.128
quick blood, spirited with wine, | seem frosty? H5 3.05. 22
whiles a more frosty people | sweat drops of 3.05. 24
if it be banish'd from the frosty head, | where 2H6 5.01.167
for all the frosty nights that i have watch'd, TIT 3.01. 5
but if my frosty signs and chaps of age, | grave 5.03. 77
fire, | he red for shame, but frosty in desire. VEN 36

FROSTY–SPIRITED 1 FR 0.0001 REL FR 0 V 1 P
what a frosty–spirited rogue is this! 1H4 2.03. 20 P

FROTH 16 FR 0.0018 REL FR 4 V 12 P
froth and scum, thou liest! WIV 1.01.164
let me see thee froth and /lime. 1.03. 14 P
(as i said), master froth here, this very man, MM 2.01.100 P
as you know, master froth, i could not give you 2.01.103 P
and i beseech you, look into master froth here, 2.01.122 P
was't not at hallowmas, master froth? 2.01.125 P
good master froth, look upon his honor; 2.01.148 P
how could master froth do the constable's wife 2.01.157 P
come hither to me, master froth. 2.01.203 P
master froth, i would not have you acquainted 2.01.204 P
they will draw you, master froth, and you will 2.01.205 P
no more of it, master froth. 2.01.211 P
and anon swallow'd with yest and froth, as WT 3.03. 93 P
till the high fever seethe your blood to froth, TIM 4.03.430
who once a day with his embossed froth | the 5.01.217
a dream, a breath, a froth of fleeting joy. LUC 212

FROTHY 1 FR 0.0001 REL FR 1 V 0 P
whose frothy mouth bepainted all with red, VEN 901

FROWARD 14 FR 0.0015 REL FR 14 V 0 P
no, trust me, she is peevish, sullen, froward, TGV 3.01. 68
that wench is stark mad or wonderful froward. SHR 1.01. 69
is intolerable curst | and shrowd and froward, 1.02. 90
for she's not froward, but modest as the dove; 2.01.293
and if she /be froward, | then hast thou taught 4.05. 78
and brings your froward wives | as prisoners to 5.02.119
and when she is froward, peevish, sullen, sour, 5.02.157
come, come, you froward and unable worms! 5.02.169
but a harsh hearing when women are froward. 5.02.183
froward by nature, enemy to peace, | lascivious, 1H6 3.01. 18
ah, froward clarence, how evil it beseems thee 3H6 4.07. 84
or like the froward infant still'd with dandling VEN 562
then woos best when most his choice is froward. 570
he rose and ran away, ah, fool too froward! PP 4.14

FROWN 51 FR 0.0057 REL FR 45 V 6 P
of my purpose doth extend | not a frown further. TMP 5.01. 30
i here could pluck his highness' frown upon you 5.01.127
how angerly i taught my brow to frown, | when TGV 1.02. 62
if she do frown, 'tis not in hate of you, | but 3.01. 96
ay, ay, antipholus, look strange and frown, ERR 2.02.110
i frown upon him; yet he loves me still. MND 1.01.194
he doth nothing but frown, as who should say, MV 1.02. 46 P
now i do frown on thee with all my heart, | and AYL 3.05. 15
mind, for i protest her frown might kill me. 4.01.110 P
say that she frown, i'll say she looks as clear SHR 2.01.172
thou canst not frown, thou canst not look 2.01.247
gentles, methinks you frown, | and wherefore 3.02. 93
not pale, bianca, thy father will not frown. 5.01.139 P
to bandy word for word and frown for frown; 5.02.172
to bandy word for word and frown for frown; 5.02.172
i frown the while, and perchance wind up my TN 2.05. 59 P
to put on yellow stockings and to frown | upon 5.01.338
the trick of 's frown, his forehead, nay, the WT 2.03.101
we have in hand are angry, | and frown upon 's. 3.03. 6
the grappling vigor and rough frown of war | is JN 3.01.104
did nor never shall | so much as frown on you? 4.01. 58
if thou but frown on me, or stir thy foot, | or 4.03. 96
and heaven itself doth frown upon the land. 4.03.159
to frown upon th' enrag'd northumberland! 2H4 1.01.152
but if you frown upon this proffer'd peace, 1H6 4.02. 9
whose smile and frown, like to achilles' spear, 2H6 5.01.100
whose frown hath made thee faint and fly ere 3H6 1.04. 48
shield thee from warwick's frown, | and pray 4.05. 28
and, richard, do not frown upon my faults, | for 5.01.101
and let my griefs frown on the upper hand. R3 4.04. 37
the sky doth frown and low'r upon our army. 5.03.283
but, in the wind and tempest of her frown, TRO 1.03. 26
frown on, you heavens, effect your rage with 5.10. 6
show our general louts | how you can frown, than COR 3.02. 67
prepare thy brow to frown. know'st thou me yet? 4.05. 63
heart | that dies in tempest of thy angry frown. TIT 1.01.458
and virtue stoops and trembles at her frown; 2.01. 11
i will frown as i pass by, and let them take it ROM 1.01. 40 P
i'll frown and be perverse, and say thee nay, 2.02. 96
you are too much of late i' th' frown. LR 1.04.190 P
could else out–frown false fortune's frown. 5.03. 6
fear no more the frown o' th' great, | thou art CYM 4.02.264
and may save | but to look back in frown. 5.03. 28
until our stars that frown lend us a smile. PER 1.04.108
doth she stroke his cheek, now doth he frown, VEN 45
a smile recures the wounding of a frown. 465
when he did frown, o, had she then gave over, 571
but if fortune once do frown, | then farewell PP 20.45
for at a frown they in their glory die. SON 25. 8
when i shall see thee frown on my defects, 49. 2
bring me within the level of your frown, | but 117.11

FROWN'D 4 FR 0.0004 REL FR 4 V 0 P
that all without desert have frown'd on me; R3 2.01. 68
that long have frown'd upon their enmity! 5.05. 21
a graver bench | than ever frown'd in greece. COR 3.01.107
so frown'd he once, when, in an angry parle, HAM 1.01. 62

FROWNED 1 FR 0.0001 REL FR 1 V 0 P
but when he frowned it was against the french, R2 2.01.178

FROWNING 15 FR 0.0017 REL FR 12 V 3 P
a better bad habit of frowning than the count MV 1.02. 59 P
the beards of hercules and frowning mars, | who, 3.02. 85
as fast as she answers thee with frowning looks, AYL 3.05. 68 P
hang'd in the frowning wrinkle of her brow! JN 2.01.505
and frowning brow to brow, ourselves will hear R2 1.01. 16
brows, | as frowning at the favors of the world? 2H6 1.02. 4
their verdict up | unto the frowning judge? R3 1.04.185
you, if these fair ladies | pass away frowning. H8 1.04. 33
he parted frowning from me, as if ruin | leap'd 3.02.205
the grey–ey'd morn smiles on the frowning night, ROM 2.03. 1
thou hadst no need to care for her frowning, now LR 1.04.192 P
found their courage | worthy his frowning at. CYM 2.04. 23
he goes hence frowning; 3.05. 18
loss, | o frowning fortune, cursed, fickle dame! PP 17.10
what though her frowning brows be bent, | her 18.25

FROWNINGLY 1 FR 0.0001 REL FR 1 V 0 P
what, look'd he frowningly? HAM 1.02.231

FROWNS 24 FR 0.0027 REL FR 23 V 1 P
master, sir thurio frowns on you. TGV 2.04. 3 P
o that your frowns would teach my smiles such MND 1.01.195
the day frowns more and more; WT 3.03. 54
when perchance it frowns | more upon humor than JN 4.02.213
to dog his heels and curtsy at his frowns, | to 1H4 3.02.127
looks pale, | killing their fruit with frowns? H5 3.05. 18
fortune is bardolph's foe, and frowns on him; 3.06. 39
cousin of exeter, frowns, words, and threats 3H6 1.01. 72
for this world frowns, and edward's sun is 2.03. 7
and smooth the frowns of war with peaceful looks 2.06. 32
smiles at her news, while warwick frowns at his. 3.03.168
my love, forbear to fawn upon their frowns. 4.01. 75
heaven | that frowns on me looks sadly upon him. R3 5.03.287
wherefore frowns he thus? H8 5.01. 87
show a fair presence and put off these frowns, ROM 1.05. 73
even his stubbornness, his checks, his frowns — OTH 4.03. 20
our graver business | frowns at this levity. ANT 2.07.121
you do not meet a man but frowns. CYM 1.01. 1
if there be such a dart in princes' frowns, PER 1.02. 53
when he frowns | to seal his will with. TNK 4.02. 86
he smiles | he shows a lover, when he frowns, a 4.02.136
is grav'd, and seems to bury what it frowns on,. 5.03. 46
foul words and frowns must not repel a lover; VEN 573
is writ in moods and frowns and wrinkles strange SON 93. 8

FROWN'ST 1 FR 0.0001 REL FR 1 V 0 P
on whom frown'st thou that i do fawn upon? SON 149. 6

/FROZE 1 FR 0.0001 REL FR 1 V 0 P
/word, /rebellion, /it /had /froze /them /up, 2H4 1.01.199

FROZE 2 FR 0.0002 REL FR 2 V 0 P
and all the conduits of my blood froze up, | yet ERR 5.01.314
cold–moving nods, | they froze me into silence. TIM 2.02.213

FROZEN 13 FR 0.0014 REL FR 12 V 1 P
a little time will melt her frozen thoughts, TGV 3.02. 9

twenty adieus, my frozen muscovits. LLL 5.02.265
the hall | and milk comes frozen home in pail; 5.02.915
master and mistress are almost frozen to death. SHR 4.01. 37 P
afoot | even to the frozen ridges of the alps, R2 1.01. 64
six frozen winters spent, | return with welcome 1.03.211
darest with thy frozen admonition | make pale 2.01.117
throw in the frozen bosoms of our part | hot 2H6 5.02. 35
when we both lay in the field | frozen (almost) R3 2.01.116
as frozen water to a starved snake. TIT 3.01.251
woos | even now the frozen bosom of the north, ROM 1.04.101
what wax so frozen but dissolves with temp'ring, VEN 565
'tween frozen conscience and hot burning will, LUC 247
FRUCTFUL *(also fruitful)*
FRUCTFUL 1 FR 0.0001 REL FR 1 V 0 P
to weed this wormwood from your fructful brain, LLL 5.02.847
FRUCTIFY 1 FR 0.0001 REL FR 1 V 0 P
those parts that do fructify in us more than he. LLL 4.02. 29
FRUGAL 2 FR 0.0002 REL FR 1 V 1 P
i was then frugal of my mirth. WIV 2.01. 27 P
chid i for that at frugal nature's frame? ADO 4.01.128
/FRUIT 1 FR 0.0001 REL FR 1 V 0 P
/which /to /prove /fruit | /hope /gives /not /so 2H4 1.03. 39
FRUIT 36 FR 0.0040 REL FR 30 V 6 P
the weakest kind of fruit | drops earliest to MV 4.01.115
he dies that touches any of this fruit | till i AYL 2.07. 98
truly, the tree yields bad fruit. 3.02.116 P
it will be the earliest fruit i' th' country; 3.02.119 P
call'd jove's tree, when it drops /such fruit. 3.02.237 P
ripe | the bloom that promiseth a mighty fruit. JN 2.01.473
the ripest fruit first falls, and so doth he; R2 2.01.153
if then the tree may be known by the fruit, as 1H4 2.04.429 P
be known by the fruit, as the fruit by the tree, 2.04.429 P
but i pray god the fruit of her womb miscarry. 2H4 5.04. 13 P
best | neighbor'd by fruit of baser quality; H5 1.01. 62
looks pale, | killing their fruit with frowns? 3.05. 18
she was the first fruit of my bach'lorship. 1H6 5.04. 13
murther not then the fruit within my womb, 5.04. 63
whose fruit thou art | and never of the nevils' 2H6 3.02.214
the leaves and fruit maintain'd with beauty's 3H6 3.03.126
or tears i blast or drown | king edward's fruit, 4.04. 24
not like the fruit of such a goodly tree. 5.06. 52
witness the loving kiss i give the fruit. 5.07. 32
the royal tree hath left us royal fruit, | which R3 3.07.167
the fruit she goes with | i pray for heartily, H8 5.01. 20
yea, like fair fruit in an unwholesome dish, TRO 2.03.120
as hercules | did shake down mellow fruit. COR 4.06.100
and here's the base fruit of her burning lust. TIT 5.01. 43
tree, | and by his side his fruit of bastardy. 5.01. 48
and wish his mistress were that kind of fruit ROM 2.01. 35
my news shall be the fruit to that great feast. HAM 2.02. 52
which now, the fruit unripe, sticks on the tree, 3.02.190
i as a tree | whose boughs did bend with fruit; CYM 3.03. 61
hang there like fruit, my soul, | till the tree 5.05.263
to taste the fruit of yon celestial tree | (or PER 1.01. 21
with golden fruit, but dangerous to be touch'd; 1.01. 28
and fruit and flowers more blessed, that still TNK 2.02.233
i would bring her fruit | fit for the gods to 2.02.238
that thou art doting father of his fruit. LUC 1064
me | but hope of orphans and unfathered fruit, SON 97.10
FRUIT–DISH 1 FR 0.0001 REL FR 0 V 1 P
as it were, in a fruit–dish, a dish of some MM 2.01. 92 P
FRUITERER 1 FR 0.0001 REL FR 0 V 1 P
i fight with one samson stockfish, a fruiterer, 2H4 3.02. 32 P
FRUITFUL *(also fructful)*
FRUITFUL 15 FR 0.0017 REL FR 13 V 2 P
one fruitful meal would set me to't. MM 4.03.154 P
of arts, | i am arriv'd for fruitful lombardy, SHR 1.01. 3
thousand ducats by the year | of fruitful land, 2.01.370
that one day bloom'd and fruitful were the next. 1H6 1.06. 7
and suffer you to breathe in fruitful peace, 5.04.127
spoil'd your summer fields and fruitful vines, R3 5.02. 8
a hand as fruitful as the land that feeds us; H8 1.03. 56
together with a recompense more fruitful | than TIM 5.01.150
breath, | no, nor the fruitful river in the eye, HAM 1.02. 80
didst intend | to make this creature fruitful. LR 1.04.277
she's fram'd as fruitful | as the free elements. OTH 2.03.341
an oily palm be not a fruitful prognostication, ANT 1.02. 52 P
ram thou thy fruitful tidings in mine ears, 2.05. 24
or fruitful object be | in eye of imogen, that CYM 5.04. 55
fame, | won in the fields of fruitful italy; LUC 107
FRUITFULLY 2 FR 0.0002 REL FR 0 V 2 P
most fruitfully, i am there before my legs. AWW 2.02. 70 P
not, time and place will be fruitfully offer'd. LR 4.06.265 P
FRUITFULNESS 1 FR 0.0001 REL FR 1 V 0 P
this argues fruitfulness and liberal heart; OTH 3.04. 38
FRUITION 1 FR 0.0001 REL FR 1 V 0 P
arrive | where i may have fruition of her love. 1H6 5.05. 9
FRUITLESS 5 FR 0.0005 REL FR 5 V 0 P
faint hymns to the cold fruitless moon. MND 1.01. 73
shall seem a dream and fruitless vision, | and 3.02.371
and hear thou there how many fruitless pranks TN 4.01. 55
upon my head they plac'd a fruitless crown, MAC 3.01. 60
"therefore, despite of fruitless chastity, VEN 751
FRUITS 9 FR 0.0010 REL FR 8 V 1 P
if you will then see the fruits of the sport, TN 2.05.197 P
to bear and he to taste | their fruits of duty. R2 3.04. 63
but stay thee, 'tis the fruits of love i mean. 3H6 3.02. 58
the fruits of love i mean, my loving liege. 3.02. 59
this is the fruits of rashness! R3 2.01.135
which done, she took the fruits of my advice; HAM 2.02.145
the purchase made, the fruits are to ensue; OTH 2.03. 9
yet fruits that blossom first will first be ripe 2.03.377
this is the fruits of whoring. 5.01.116
FRUIT–TREE 1 FR 0.0001 REL FR 1 V 0 P
tips with silver all these fruit–tree tops — ROM 2.02.108
FRUIT–TREES 2 FR 0.0002 REL FR 2 V 0 P
her fruit–trees all unprun'd, her hedges ruin'd, R2 3.04. 45
do wound the bark, the skin of our fruit–trees, 3.04. 58
FRUSH 1 FR 0.0001 REL FR 1 V 0 P
i'll frush it and unlock the rivets all, | but TRO 5.06. 29
FRUSTRATE 6 FR 0.0006 REL FR 6 V 0 P
the sea mocks | our frustrate search on land. TMP 3.03. 10
to frustrate prophecies, and to rase out 2H4 5.02.127
to frustrate both his oath and what beside | may 3H6 2.01.175
tyrant's rage, | and frustrate his proud will. LR 4.06. 64
being so frustrate, tell him he mocks | the ANT 5.01. 2
at least to frustrate striving, and to follow TNK 1.02. 9
FRUTIFY 1 FR 0.0001 REL FR 0 V 1 P
i hope, an old man, shall frutify unto you — MV 2.02.134 P
FRY* 8 FR 0.0009 REL FR 3 V 5 P
but thine doth fry. SHR 2.01.338
virginity and devours up all the fry it finds. AWW 4.03.221 P
bless me, what a fry of fornication is at door! H8 5.03. 36 P
fry, lechery, fry! TRO 5.02. 56 P
fry, lechery, fry! 5.02. 57 P
what, you egg! | young fry of treachery! MAC 4.02. 84
and tumbles, driving the poor fry before him, PER 2.01. 31 P
me, | no fisher but the ungrown fry forbears; VEN 526
FRYING 1 FR 0.0001 REL FR 0 V 1 P
th' tother place, such burning, frying, boiling, TNK 4.03. 32 P
FUBB'D *(also fob)*
FUBB'D 4 FR 0.0004 REL FR 0 V 4 P
and resolution thus fubb'd as it is with the 1H4 1.02. 60 P
and borne, and have been fubb'd off, and fubb'd 2H4 2.01. 34 P
and have been fubb'd off, and fubb'd off, and 2.01. 34 P
and fubb'd off, and fubb'd off, from this day to 2.01. 35 P
FUEL 5 FR 0.0005 REL FR 4 V 1 P
fetch us in fuel, and be quick, thou'rt best, TMP 1.02.366
the fuel is gone that maintain'd that fire. H5 2.03. 43 P
if wind and fuel be brought to feed it with. 2H6 3.01.303
i need not add more fuel to your fire, | for 3H6 5.04. 70
thy light's flame with self–substantial fuel, SON 1. 6
FUGITIVE 3 FR 0.0003 REL FR 3 V 0 P
lord, | and thou be thrust out like a fugitive? 1H6 3.03. 67
sword is warm, | the fugitive parthians follow. ANT 3.01. 7
me in register | a master–leaver and a fugitive. 4.09. 22
FULFILL 9 FR 0.0010 REL FR 9 V 0 P
for servants must their masters' minds fulfill. ERR 4.01.113
but it does fulfill my vow; WT 4.04.486
then | spurn at his edict, and fulfill a man's? R3 1.04.198
do reek and smoke, | fulfill your pleasure. JC 3.01.159
good alive, | and to fulfill his prince' desire, PER 2.ch. 21
thy princely office how canst thou fulfill, LUC 628
and swear i found you where you did fulfill 1635
thus far for love my love–suit, sweet, fulfill. SON 136. 4
will will fulfill the treasure of thy love, | ay 136. 5
FULFILL'D 8 FR 0.0009 REL FR 6 V 2 P
will have fulfill'd their secret purposes; WT 5.01. 36
the oracle is fulfill'd; 5.02. 23 P
another elevated that the oracle was fulfill'd. 5.02. 75 P
but see his exequies fulfill'd in roan. 1H6 3.02.133
th' name of god, | your pleasure be fulfill'd! H8 2.04. 57
but their pleasures | must be fulfill'd, and i 5.02. 19
to tell him his commandment is fulfill'd, | that HAM 5.02.370
poor women's faults that they are so fulfill'd LUC 1258
/FULFILLING 1 FR 0.0001 REL FR 1 V 0 P
/and /corresponsive /and /fulfilling /bolts TRO pr 18
FULFILLS 1 FR 0.0001 REL FR 1 V 0 P
for charity itself fulfills the law, | and who LLL 4.03.361
FULHAM *(see fullam)*
/FULL 5 FR 0.0005 REL FR 5 V 0 P
/other /down, /unseen, /and /full /of /water: R2 4.01.187
/bucket /down /and /full /of /tears /am /i, 4.01.188
/mine /eyes /are /full /of /tears, /i /cannot 4.01.244
/beastly /feeder, /art /so /full /of /him, 2H4 1.03. 95
what a /full fortune does the thick–lips owe OTH 1.01. 66
FULL 448 FR 0.0506 REL FR 374 V 74 P
than prospero, master of a full poor cell, | and TMP 1.02. 20
when i have deck'd the sea with drops full salt, 1.02.155
thou did promise | to bate me a full year. 1.02.250
full fadom five thy father lies, | of his bones 1.02.397
full many a lady | i have ey'd with best regard, 3.01. 39
any | with so full soul but some defect in her 3.01. 44
i am full of pleasure, | let us be jocund. 3.02.116
the isle is full of noises, | sounds, and sweet 3.02.135
may | with full and holy rite be minist'red, 4.01. 17
so full cf valor that they smote the air | for 4.01.172
for love, thou know'st, is full of jealousy. TGV 2.04.177
the gentleman | is full of virtue, bounty, worth 3.01. 65
i now am full resolv'd to take a wife | and turn 3.01. 76
heart | as full of sorrows as the sea of sands, 4.03. 33
and full of new–found oaths, which he will break 4.04.130
mine | were full as lovely as is this of hers; 4.04.186
and full as much (for more there cannot be) | i 5.04. 38
they are reformed, civil, full of good, | and 5.04.156
how full of chollors i am and trempling of mind! WIV 3.01. 11 P
i have my belly full of ford. 3.05. 36 P
pray heaven it be not full of knight again. 4.02.112 P
you are wise and full of gibes and 4.05. 80 P
in our remove be thou at full ourself. MM 1.01. 43
but thou art full of error — i am sound. 1.02. 54 P
as those that feed grow full, as blossoming time 1.04. 41
womb | expresseth his full tilth and husbandry. 1.04. 44
place, | and with full line of his authority, 1.04. 56
you shall have your full time of imprisonment, 4.02. 12 P
to do it, | he says, to veil full purpose. 4.06. 4
and all probation will make up full clear, 5.01.157
do me the favor to dilate at full | what have ERR 1.01.122
they say this town is full of cozenage: 1.02. 97
a table full of welcome makes scarce one dainty 3.01. 23
company, | and we shall make full satisfaction. 5.01.400
when the achiever brings home full numbers. ADO 1.01. 9 P
you have it full, benedick. 1.01.109 P
you must not make the full show of this till you 1.03. 19 P
like a scotch jig, and full as fantastical; 2.01. 75 P
as a measure, full of state and ancientry; 2.01. 77 P
it seems her affections have their full bent. 2.03.223 P
gentleman | deserve as full as fortunate a bed 3.01. 45
more moving, delicate, and full of life, | into 4.01.228
thou villain, thou art full of piety, as shall 4.02. 78 P
but what was true, and very full of proof. 5.01.105
so full of frost, of storm, and cloudiness? 5.04. 42
when i do it i shall do it on a full stomach. LLL 1.02.149 P
a foolish extravagant spirit, full of forms, 4.02. 66 P
no face is fair that is not full so black. 4.03.249
o that your face were not so full of o's! 5.02. 45
you took the moon at full, but now she's changed 5.02.214
trim gallants, full of courtship and of state. 5.02.363
i am a fool, and full of poverty. 5.02.380
have blown me full of maggot ostentation. 5.02.409
full merrily | hath this brave /manage, this 5.02.481
as love is full of unbefitting strains, | all 5.02.760
full of straying shapes, of habits, and of forms 5.02.763
we have receiv'd your letters full of love; 5.02.777
full of dear guiltiness, and therefore this: 5.02.791
full of comparisons and wounding flouts, | which 5.02.844
full of vexation come i, with complaint MND 1.01. 22
full often hath she gossip'd by my side, | and 2.01.125
eyes, | and make her full of hateful fantasies. 2.01.258
grey, | whose note full many a man doth mark, 3.01.132
night's swift dragons cut the clouds full fast, 3.02.379
here come the lovers, full of joy and mirth. 5.01. 28
o wall, full often hast thou heard my moans, 5.01.188
being so full of unmannerly sadness in his youth MV 1.02. 50 P
up the gross | of full three thousand ducats. 1.03. 56
come, the full stop. 3.01. 15 P
but the full sum of me | is sum of something; 3.02.157
of the law | hath full relation to the penalty, 4.01.248
from my master, with his horn full of good news. 5.01. 47 P
nought so stockish, hard, and full of rage, 5.01. 81
you are not satisfied | of these events at full. 5.01.297
young fellow of france, full of ambition, an AYL 1.01.143 P
school'd and yet learned, full of noble device, 1.01.167 P
me not with the full weight that i love thee. 1.02. 8 P
with his mouth full of news. 1.02. 92 P
o, how full of briers is this working–day world! 1.03. 12 P
with his eyes full of anger. 1.03. 40 P
full of the pasture, jumps along by him | and 2.01. 53
sullen fits, | for then he's full of matter. 2.01. 68
full of strange oaths, and bearded like the pard 2.07.150
cut, | full of wise saws and modern instances; 2.07.156
thy huntress' name that my full life doth sway. 3.02. 4
you are full of pretty answers; 3.02.270 P
inconstant, full of tears, full of smiles; 3.02.412 P
inconstant, full of tears, full of smiles; 3.02.412 P
to forswear the full stream of the world and to 3.02.420 P
and his kissing is as full of sanctity as the 3.04. 13 P
you | that makes the world full of ill–favor'd 3.05. 53
full of rose–water and bestrew'd with flowers, SHR in.1. 56
for i have it full. 1.01.198
heart | unto a mad–brain rudesby full of spleen, 3.02. 10
infected with the fashions, full of windgalls, 3.02. 52 P
carouse full measure to her maidenhead, | be mad 3.02.225
come, you are so full of cony–catching! 4.01. 43 P
son, | who will of thy arrival be full joyous. 4.05. 70
withal, full oft we see | cold wisdom waiting on AWW 1.01.104
i am so full of businesses, i cannot answer thee 1.01.206 P
will repeat, | which men full true shall find: 1.03. 61
for your passions | have to the full appeach'd. 1.03.191
but what at full i know, thou know'st no part, 2.01.132
a very tainted fellow, and full of wickedness. 3.02. 87
from point, to the full arming of the verity. 4.03. 62 P
"dian, the count's a fool, and full of gold" — 4.03.211
so full of shapes is fancy | that it alone is TN 1.01. 14
are you full of them? 1.03. 77 P
my words are as full of peace as matter. 1.05.210 P
my bosom is full of kindness, and i am yet so 2.01. 39 P
practice | as full of labor as a wise man's art; 3.01. 66
witty, so it be eloquent and full of invention. 3.02. 44 P
between me and the full prospect of my hopes. 3.04. 82 P
but thy intercepter, full of despite, bloody as 3.04.222 P
plight me the full assurance of your faith, 4.03. 26
the shoots that i have, | to be full like me; WT 1.02.129
it becomes thy oath full well, | thou to me thy 4.04.300
your heart is full of something that does take 4.04.346
though full of our displeasure, yet we free thee 4.04.433
thou must know the king is full of grief. 4.04.765 P
i might have look'd upon my queen's full eyes, 5.01. 53
there was not full a month | between their 5.01.117
full fourteen weeks before the course of time. JN 1.01.113
hand, | but with a heart full of unstained love. 2.01. 16
the cannons have their bowels full of wrath, 2.01.210
full thirty thousand marks of english coin. 2.01.530
with wrongs, and therefore full of fears, | a 3.01. 13
full of unpleasing blots and sightless stains, 3.01. 45
is all too wanton and too full of gawds | to 3.03. 36
my head with more ill news, for it is full. 4.02.134
possess'd with rumors, full of idle dreams, 4.02.145
not knowing what they fear, but full of fear. 4.02.146
men's mouths are full of it. 4.02.161
full warm of blood, of mirth, of gossiping. 5.02. 59
high–stomach'd are they both and full of ire, R2 1.01. 18
one vial full of edward's sacred blood, | one 1.02. 17
o, full of careful business are his looks! 2.02. 75
and lie full low, grav'd in the hollow ground. 3.02.140
'twill make me think the world is full of rubs, 3.04. 4
is full of weeds, her fairest flowers chok'd up, 3.04. 44
and spur thee on with full as many lies | as may 4.01. 53
i see your brows are full of discontent, | your 4.01.331
'tis full three months since i did see him last. 5.03. 2
his prayers are full of false hypocrisy, | ours 5.03.107
as full of valure as of royal blood! 5.05.113
i protest my soul is full of woe | that blood 5.06. 45
go, i will stuff your purses full of crowns; 1H4 1.02.132 P
as full of peril and adventerous spirit | as to 1.03.191
plot, good friends, and full of expectation; 2.03. 18 P
and our induction full of prosperous hope. 3.01. 2
the front of heaven was full of fiery shapes 3.01. 14
the front of heaven was full of fiery shapes, 3.01. 37
with his presence glutted, gorg'd, and full. 3.02. 84
thy looks are full of speed. 3.02.162
our hands are full of business, let's away, 3.02.179
images, | as full of spirit as the month of may, 4.01.101
the better part of ours are full of rest. 4.03. 27
soul | shall pay full dearly for this encounter, 5.01. 84
all our lives shall be stuck full of eyes, | for 5.02. 8
no, i know this face full well. 5.03. 19
our soldiers stand full fairly for the day. 5.03. 29
full bravely hast thou flesh'd | thy maiden 5.04.130
like a horse | full of high feeding, madly hath 2H4 1.01. 10
this is the news at full. 1.01.135
and come against us in full puissance, | need 1.03. 77
empty vessel bear such a huge full hogshead? 2.04. 62 P
come we to full points here? 2.04.184
our battle is more full of names than yours, 4.01.152
hath the prince john a full commission, | in 4.01.160
for full well he knows | he cannot so precisely 4.01.202
you as much as the full moon doth the cinders of 4.03. 52 P
quick, forgetive, full of nimble, fiery, and 4.03. 99 P
will fortune never come with both hands full, 4.04.103
i am here, brother, full of heaviness. 4.05. 8
full fifteen earls and fifteen hundred knights, H5 1.01. 13
the king is full of grace and fair regard. 1.01. 22
making defeat on the full power of france, 1.02.107

with half their forces the full pride of france, 1.02.112
congreeing in a full and natural close, | like 1.02.182
things, having full reference | to one consent, 1.02.205
either our history shall with full mouth | speak 1.02.230
but i will rise there with so full a glory 1.02.278
thus comes the english with full power upon us, 2.04. 1
to-morrow shall you bear our full intent | back 2.04.114
to-morrow shall you know our mind at full. 2.04.140
and bend up every spirit | to his full height. 3.01. 17
i wad full fain heard some question 'tween you 3.02.118 P
good to bruise an injury till it were full ripe. 3.06.122 P
fighting men they have full threescore thousand. 4.03. 3
he is as full of valor as of kindness, 4.03. 15
i did never know so full a voice issue from so 4.04. 67 P
he was full of jests, and gipes, and knaveries, 4.07. 48 P
full fifteen hundred, besides common men. 4.08. 79
giving full trophy, signal, and ostent | quite 5.pr. 21
with full accord to all our just demands, 5.02. 71
that the tongues of men are full of deceits? 5.02.118 P
dat de tongeus of de mans is be full of deceits: 5.02.119 P
face will wither, a full eye will wax hollow; 5.02.161 P
by starts the full course of their glory. ep 4
lords, view these letters full of bad mischance. 1H6 1.01. 89
having full scarce six thousand in his troop, 1.01.112
and in a vision full of majesty | will'd me to 1.02. 79
have fill'd their pockets full of pebble stones; 3.01. 80
'twas full of darnel; 3.02. 44
valiant and virtuous, full of haughty courage, 4.01. 35
so full replete with choice of all delights, 5.05. 17
till term of eighteen months | be full expir'd. 2H6 1.01. 68
we'll see these things effected to the full. 1.02. 84
i | in england work your grace's full content. 1.03. 67
my lord, i long to hear it at full. 2.02. 6
we know your mind at full. 2.02. 77
mine eyes are full of tears, my heart of grief. 2.03. 17
a man | unsounded yet and full of deep deceit. 3.01. 57
in great affairs, | too full of foolish pity; 3.01.225
to make commotion, as full well he can, | under 3.01.358
full often, like a shag-hair'd crafty kern, 3.01.367
but see, his face is black and full of blood, 3.02.168
staring full ghastly, like a strangled man; 3.02.170
teeth, | with full as many signs of deadly hate, 3.02.314
and boding screech-owls make the consort full! 3.02.327
sweet is the country, because full of riches, 4.07. 62
hath made me full of sickness and diseases. 4.07. 89
witty, courteous, liberal, full of spirit. 3H6 1.02. 43
and full as oft came edward to my side | with 1.04. 11
that she was coming with a full intent | to dash 2.01.117
who look'd full gently on his warlike queen, 2.01.123
full well hath clifford play'd the orator, 2.02. 43
how many makes the hour full complete, | how 2.05. 26
ay, full as dearly as i love myself. 3.02. 37
with my talk and tears | (both full of truth) i 3.03.159
mine full of sorrow and heart's discontent. 3.03.173
these news i must confess are full of grief, 4.04. 13
his looks are full of peaceful majesty, | his 4.06. 71
her faction will be full as strong as ours. 5.03. 17
so full of fearful dreams, of ugly sights, R3 1.04. 3
days — | so full of dismal terror was the time. 1.04. 7
it fills a man full of obstacles. 1.04.139 P
treacherous, and full of guile | be he unto me! 2.01. 38
i prithee peace, my soul is full of sorrow. 2.01. 97
and, in his full and ripened years, himself, 2.03. 14
o, full of danger is the duke of gloucester, 2.03. 27
truly, the hearts of men are full of fear. 2.03. 38
man | that looks not heavily and full of dread. 2.03. 40
'twas full two years ere i could get a tooth. 2.04. 29
the precedent was full as long a-doing, | and 3.06. 7
full of wise care is this your counsel, madam; 4.01. 47
why should calamity be full of words? 4.04.126
'tis full of thy foul wrongs. 4.04.375
body | by thee was punched full of deadly holes. 5.03.125
sad, high, and working, full of state and woe: H8 pr 3
the office did | distinctly his full function. 1.01. 45
anger is like | a full hot horse, who being 1.01.133
of beauty | shall shine at full upon them. 1.04. 60
o, this is full of pity! 2.01.137
if the duke be guiltless, | 'tis full of woe; 2.01.140
private, | full of sad thoughts and troubles. 2.02. 15
sign your place and calling, in full seeming, 2.04.108
which | i then did feel full sick, and yet not 2.04.205
shall give you | the full cause of our coming. 3.01. 29
i was set at work | among my maids, full little, 3.01. 75
have i with all my full affections | still met 3.01.129
you are full of heavenly stuff, and bear the 3.02.137
and, from that full meridian of my glory, | i 3.02.224
man, full surely | his greatness is a-ripening, 3.02.356
am sure have shown at full their royal minds — 4.01. 8
which when the people | had the full view of, 4.01. 71
and with the same full state pac'd back again 4.01. 93
foretold should be his last, full of repentance, 4.02. 27
vows, gifts, tears, and love's full sacrifice, TRO 1.02.282
host, | having his ear full of his airy fame, 1.03.144
in full as proud a place | as broad achilles; 1.03.189
great jove's accord, | nothing so full of heart. 1.03.239
how if he had biles — full, all over, generally 2.01. 2 P
and thou art as full of envy at his greatness as 2.01. 33 P
unrespective sieve, | because we now are full. 2.02. 72
your breath with full consent bellied his sails; 2.02. 74
your full consent | gave wings to my propension, 2.02.132
dear lord, you are full of fair words. 3.01. 47 P
nell, he is full of harmony. 3.01. 52 P
full of protest, of oath and big compare, 3.02.175
to behold his visage, | even to my full of view. 3.03.241
the grief is fine, full, perfect, that i taste, 4.04. 3
the grecian youths are full of quality; 4.04. 76
there in the full convive we. 4.05.272
why, thou full dish of fool, from troy. 5.01. 9 P
whissing lungs, bladders full of imposthume, 5.01. 21 P
minds sway'd by eyes are full of turpitude. 5.02.112
full merrily the humble-bee doth sing, | till he 5.10. 41
absence did but fill /ithaca full of months. COR 1.03. 84 P
that being pass'd for consul with full voice, 3.03. 59
and thou art too full | of the wars' surfeits to 4.01. 45
spite, | to be full quit of those my banishers, 4.05. 83
sprightly, /waking, audible, and full of vent. 4.05.223 P
part, and i am out, | even to a full disgrace. 5.03. 42
which by th' interpretation of full time | may 5.03. 69
of consuls, senators, patricians, | a city full; 5.04. 54
of tribunes, such as you, | a sea and land full. 5.04. 55
doth more than counterpoise a full third part 5.06. 77
full well, andronicus, | agree these deeds with TIT 1.01.305
full well shalt thou perceive how much i dare. 2.01. 44
full well i wot the ground of all this grudge. 2.01. 48
for that i am prepar'd and full resolv'd, 2.01. 57
what, hast not thou full often strook a doe, 2.01. 93
the palace full of tongues, of eyes, and ears; 2.01.127
for i have heard my grandsire say full oft, 4.01. 18
thy father hath full oft | for his ungrateful 4.01.110
a charitable wish, and full of love. 4.02. 43
and now be it known to you my full intent. 4.02.151
are, | that my report is just and full of truth. 5.03.115
full soon the canker death eats up that plant. ROM 2.03. 30
was this, that was so full of his ropery? 2.04.146 P
thy head is as full of quarrels as an egg is 3.01. 22 P
as full of quarrels as an egg is full of meat, 3.01. 23 P
well thou knowest, is cross and full of sin. 4.03. 5
for i am sure you have your hands full all, | in 4.03. 11
my heart itself plays "my heart is full." 4.05.107 P
art thou so bare and full of wretchedness, | and 5.01. 68
the letter was not nice but full of charge, | of 5.02. 18
this vault a feasting presence full of light. 5.03. 86
full half an hour. 5.03.130
friendship's full of dregs; TIM 1.02.233
how full of valor did he bear himself | in the 3.05. 64
on each bush | lays her full mess before you. 4.03.421
full of decay and failing? 4.03.460
rumor hold for true that he's | so full of gold? 5.01. 4
are his files | as full as thy report? 5.02. 2
our town till we | have seal'd thy full desire. 5.04. 54
that have known the earth so full of faults. JC 1.03. 45
thy full petition at the hand of brutus! 2.01. 58
danger knows full well | that caesar is more 2.02. 44
our reasons are so full of good regard | that 3.01.224
and that they know full well | that gave me 3.02.219
such as he is, full of regard and honor. 4.02. 12
are full of rest, defense, and nimbleness. 4.03.202
on such a full sea are we now afloat, | and we 4.03.222
now is that noble vessel full of grief, | that 5.05. 13
and will labor | to make thee full of growing. MAC 1.04. 29
he is full so valiant, | and in his 1.04. 54
it is too full o' th' milk of human kindness 1.05. 17
o, full of scorpions is my mind, dear wife! 3.02. 36
the table's full. 3.04. 45
give me some wine, fill full. 3.04. 87
about his throne | that speak him full of grace. 4.03.159
i have supp'd full with horrors; 5.05. 13
tale | told by an idiot, full of sound and fury, 5.05. 27
fortinbras, | of unimproved mettle hot and full, HAM 1.01. 96
and full proportions are all made | out of his 1.02. 32
and here give up ourselves, in the full bent, 2.02. 30
full thirty times hath phoebus' cart gone round 3.02.155
'a took my father grossly, full of bread, | with 3.03. 80
his liberty is full of threats to all, | to you 4.01. 14
my soul is full of discord and dismay. 4.01. 45
our sovereign process, which imports at full, 4.03. 63
amiss, | so full of artless jealousy is guilt, 4.05. 19
to have his fine pate full of fine dirt? 5.01.107 P
/gentleman, full of most excellent differences, 5.02.107 P
you see how full of changes his age is; LR 1.01.288 P
may carry through itself to that full issue 1.04. 3
thou lov'st, | shall find thee full of labors. 1.04. 7
when were you wont to be so full of songs, 1.04.170 P
inform her full of my particular fear, | and 1.04.337
by the noise i made, | full suddenly he fled. 2.01. 56
as full of grief as age, wretched in both. 2.04.273
i have full cause of weeping, but this heart 2.04.284
full oft 'tis seen, | our means secure us, and 4.01. 19
below, methought his eyes | were two full moons; 4.06. 70
he's full of alteration | and self-reproving — 5.01. 3
the wheel is come full circle, i am here. 5.03.175
(being full of supper and distemp'ring draughts) OTH 1.01. 99
godliness i have, | i did full hard forbear him. 1.02. 10
and is in full commission here for cyprus. 2.01. 29
him, and the man commands | like a full soldier. 2.01. 36
in her, she's full of most bless'd condition. 2.01.249 P
and there is full liberty of feasting from this 2.02. 9 P
and, i'll warrant her, full of game. 2.03. 19 P
he'll be as full of quarrel and offense | as my 2.03. 50
it shall be full of poise and difficult weight, 3.03. 82
for i know thou'rt full of love and honesty, 3.03.118
rather have lost my purse | full of crusadoes; 3.04. 26
and when they are full | they belch us. 3.04.105
is this the noble moor whom our full senate 4.01.264
speak, for my heart is full. 5.02.175
i am full sorry | that he approves the common ANT 1.01. 59
with such full license as both truth and malice 1.02.108
but my full heart | remains in use with you. 1.03. 43
full surfeits and the dryness of his bones 1.04. 27
auguring hope | says it will come to th' full. 2.01. 11
that stands upon the swell at the full of tide, 3.02. 49
my spirit | /thy full supremacy thou knew'st, 3.11. 59
love, i am full of lead. 3.11. 72
the full caesar will | answer his emptiness! 3.13. 35
'tis a brave army, | and full of purpose. 4.03. 12
make your full reference freely to my lord, 5.02. 23
who is so full of grace that it flows over | on 5.02. 24
me present hunger | to feed again, though full. CYM 2.04.138
should tread a course | pretty and full of view; 3.04.147
are | full weak to undertake our wars against 3.07. 5
gods are more full of mercy. 5.04. 13
our pleasure his full fortune doth confine, 5.04.110
battle, at this instant | is full accomplish'd: 5.05.470
and full of face | as heaven had lent her all PER 1.ch. 23
a city on whom plenty held full hand, | for 1.04. 22
their tables were stor'd full, to glad the sight 1.04. 28
how thaliard came full bent with sin | and hid 2.ch. 23
and entreasur'd | with full bags of spices! 3.02. 66
mortally, | yet glance full wond'ringly on us. 3.03. 7
market narrowly, meteline is full of gallants. 4.02. 3 P
and his army full | of bread and sloth. TNK 1.01.158
keep the feast full, bate not an hour on't. 1.01.220
this world's a city full of straying streets, 1.05. 15
but have you a full promise of her? 2.01. 13 P
i'll have a gown full of 'em — and of these: 2.02.128
and his full poise | becomes the rider's load. 5.04. 81
wishing her cheeks were gardens full of flowers, VEN 65
broad breast, full eye, small head, and nostril 296
when lo the unback'd breeder, full of fear, 320
full gently now she takes him by the hand, | a 361
but, when his glutton eye so full hath fed, 399
whose full perfection all the world amazes, 634
love is all truth, lust full of forged lies. 804
my face is full of shame, my heart of teen, 808
full of respects, yet nought at all respecting, 911
here overcome, as one full of despair, | she 955
thou art as full of fear | as one with treasure 1021
"it shall be fickle, false, and full of fraud, 1141
"it shall be sparing, and too full of riot, 1147
full of foul hope and full of fond mistrust; LUC 284
full of foul hope and full of fond mistrust; 284
which gives the watch-word to his hand full soon 370
his face, though full of cares, yet show'd 1503
youth is full of pleasance, age is full of care, PP 12. 2
youth is full of pleasance, age is full of care, 12. 2
youth is full of sport, age's breath is short, 12. 5
have you not heard it said full oft, | a woman's 18.41
full many a glorious morning have i seen SON 33. 1
thy beauty and thy years full well befits, | for 41. 3
the canker-blooms have full as deep a dye | as 54. 5
as call it winter, which, being full of care, 56.13
sometime all full with feasting on your sight, 75. 9
was it the proud full sail of his great verse, 86. 1
why | my most full flame should afterwards burn 115. 4
to give full growth to that which still doth 115.14
so, being full of your ne'er-cloying sweetness, 118. 5
my brain | full character'd with lasting memory, 122. 2
is perjur'd, murd'rous, bloody, full of blame, 129. 3
nor that full star that ushers in the even 132. 7
ay, fill it full with wills, and my will one. 136. 6
tale, | ere long espied a fickle maid full pale, LC 5

FULL-ACORN'D 1 FR 0.0001 REL FR 1 V 0 P
like a full-acorn'd boar, a german /one, | cried CYM 2.05. 16

FULLAM 1 FR 0.0001 REL FR 1 V 0 P
for gourd and fullam holds, | and high and low WIV 1.03. 85

FULL-CHARG'D 1 FR 0.0001 REL FR 1 V 0 P
i' th' level | of a full-charg'd confederacy, H8 1.02. 3

FULLER 2 FR 0.0002 REL FR 2 V 0 P
them, | by them shall make a fuller number up, JC 4.03.208
a fuller blast ne'er shook our battlements. OTH 2.01. 6

FULLERS 1 FR 0.0001 REL FR 1 V 0 P
off | the spinsters, carders, fullers, weavers, H8 1.02. 33

FULLEST 1 FR 0.0001 REL FR 1 V 0 P
but performs | the bidding of the fullest man, ANT 3.13. 87

FULL-FED 1 FR 0.0001 REL FR 1 V 0 P
look as the full-fed hound or gorged hawk, LUC 694

FULL-FLOWING 1 FR 0.0001 REL FR 1 V 0 P
i should answer | from a full-flowing stomach. LR 5.03. 74

FULL-FORTUN'D 1 FR 0.0001 REL FR 1 V 0 P
show | of the full-fortun'd caesar ever shall ANT 4.15. 24

FULL-FRAUGHT 2 FR 0.0002 REL FR 2 V 0 P
should be full-fraught with serviceable vows. TGV 3.02. 70
to /mark /the full-fraught man and best indued H5 2.02.139

FULL-GORG'D 1 FR 0.0001 REL FR 1 V 0 P
and till she stoop, she must not be full-gorg'd, SHR 4.01.191

FULL-GROWN 1 FR 0.0001 REL FR 1 V 0 P
hath | one daughter, and a full-grown wench, PER 4.ch. 16

FULL-HEARTED 1 FR 0.0001 REL FR 1 V 0 P
the enemy full-hearted, | lolling the tongue CYM 5.03. 7

FULL-MANN'D 1 FR 0.0001 REL FR 1 V 0 P
and, with the rest full-mann'd, from th' head of ANT 3.07. 51

FULLNESS 6 FR 0.0006 REL FR 6 V 0 P
whose fullness of perfection lies in him. JN 2.01.440
with ample and brim fullness of his force, H5 1.02.150
such is the fullness of my heart's content. 2H6 1.01. 35
wanton in fullness, seek to hide themselves | in MAC 1.04. 34
to lapse in fullness | is sorer than to lie for CYM 3.06. 12
hungry eyes even till they wink with fullness, SON 56. 6

FULL-WING'D 1 FR 0.0001 REL FR 1 V 0 P
in a safer hold | than is the full-wing'd eagle. CYM 3.03. 21

FULLY 14 FR 0.0015 REL FR 12 V 2 P
to th' observer doth thy history | fully unfold. MM 1.01. 29
to instruct her fully in those sciences, SHR 2.01. 57
nathaniel's coat, sir, was not fully made, | and 4.01.132
and inform'd her fully | i could not answer in AWW 5.03. 97
here had the conquest fully been seal'd up, | if 1H6 1.01.130
not there | at once and fully satisfied), H8 2.04.149
of this feast, | having fully din'd before. COR 1.09. 11
nothing undone that may fully discover him their 2.02. 20 P
to seek him there, | to oppose his hatred fully. 3.01. 20
had you not fully laid my state before me, TIM 2.02.125
king, it will stuff his suspicion more fully. LR 3.05. 21 P
/whose every passion fully strives | to make ANT 1.01. 50
our hour | is fully out. 4.09. 32
came home before the business | was fully ended. TNK 4.01. 5

FULSOME 5 FR 0.0005 REL FR 4 V 1 P
he stuck them up before the fulsome ewes, | who MV 1.03. 86
it is as fat and fulsome to mine ear | as TN 5.01.109
and stop this gap of breath with fulsome dust, JN 3.04. 32
i that was wash'd to death with fulsome wine, R3 5.03.132
/'zounds, that's fulsome! OTH 4.01. 37 P

FULVIA 14 FR 0.0015 REL FR 12 V 2 P
fulvia perchance is angry; ANT 1.01. 20
pays shame | when shrill-tongu'd fulvia scolds. 1.01. 32
why did he marry fulvia, and not love her? 1.01. 41
fulvia thy wife first came into the field. 1.02. 88
fulvia thy wife is dead. 1.02.118
fulvia is dead. 1.02.156
fulvia is dead. 1.02.158
fulvia? 1.02.159 P
if there were no more women but fulvia, then had 1.02.166 P
for not alone | the death of fulvia, with more 1.02.180
throned gods), | who have been false to fulvia? 1.03. 29
can fulvia die? 1.03. 58
so fulvia told me. 1.03. 75
truth is, that fulvia, | to have me out of egypt 2.02. 94

FULVIA'S 4 FR 0.0004 REL FR 4 V 0 P
where's fulvia's process? ANT 1.01. 28
rail thou in fulvia's phrase, and taunt my 1.02.107
you should safe my going, | is fulvia's death. 1.03. 56
in fulvia's death, how mine receiv'd shall be. 1.03. 65

FUM 1 FR 0.0001 REL FR 1 V 0 P
came, | his word was still, 'fie, foh, and fum, LR 3.04.183

FUMBLE 2 FR 0.0002 REL FR 1 V 1 P

for after i saw him fumble with the sheets, and H5 2.03. 14 P
what dost thou wrap and fumble in thy arms? TIT 4.02. 58
FUMBLES 1 FR 0.0001 REL FR 1 V 0 P
to them, | he fumbles up into a loose adieu; TRO 4.04. 46
FUMBLEST 1 FR 0.0001 REL FR 1 V 0 P
thou fumblest, eros, and my queen's a squire ANT 4.04. 14
FUMBLING 1 FR 0.0001 REL FR 1 V 0 P
and, with a palsy fumbling on his gorget, TRO 1.03.174
FUME 5 FR 0.0005 REL FR 5 V 0 P
quoth she, "i'll fume with them." SHR 2.01.152
her fume needs no spurs, | she'll gallop far 2H6 1.03.150
love is a smoke made with the fume of sighs, ROM 1.01.190
shall be a fume, and the receipt of reason | a MAC 1.07. 66
he stamps, and bites the poor flies in his fume. VEN 316
FUMES 3 FR 0.0003 REL FR 3 V 0 P
begin to chase the ignorant fumes that mantle TMP 5.01. 67
at nothing, | which the brain makes of fumes. CYM 4.02.301
or that which from discharged cannon fumes. LUC 1043
FUMING 1 FR 0.0001 REL FR 1 V 0 P
in a field of feasts, | keep his brain fuming; ANT 2.01. 24
FUMITORY *(see femetary, femiter)*
FUNCTION 17 FR 0.0019 REL FR 14 V 3 P
mine were the very cipher of a function, | to MM 2.02. 39
you have paid the heavens your function, and the 3.02.249 P
night, that from the eye his function takes, MND 3.02.177
or what is he of basest function, | that says AYL 2.07. 79
am not tall enough to become the function well, TN 4.02. 7 P
of this compact | seal'd in my function, by my 5.01.161
still, still so, | and own no other function. WT 4.04.143
each hath his place and function to attend: 1H6 1.01.173
art reverent | touching thy spiritual function, 3.01. 50
the office did | distinctly his full function. H8 1.01. 45
your brain, and every function of your power, 3.02.187
follow your function, go, and batten on cold COR 4.05. 32 P
shakes so my single state of man that function MAC 1.03.140
an' his whole function suiting | with forms to HAM 2.02.556
shall play the god | with his weak function. OTH 2.03.348
some of your function, mistress; 4.02. 27
governs me to go about | doth part his function, SON 113. 3
FUNCTIONS 8 FR 0.0009 REL FR 6 V 2 P
captain and all the rest from their functions; MM 1.02. 13 P
above their functions and their offices. LLL 4.03.329
divide | the state of man in divers functions, H5 1.02.184
their particular functions and wonder at him. 3.07. 38 P
as if those organs /had /deceptious functions, TRO 5.02.123
and going | about their functions friendly. COR 4.06. 9
my operant powers their functions leave to do, HAM 3.02.174
of nature should again | do their due functions. CYM 5.05.258
FUNDAMENTAL 2 FR 0.0002 REL FR 2 V 0 P
you heard | the fundamental reasons of this war, AWW 3.01. 2
that leave the fundamental part of state | more COR 3.01.151
FUNERAL 24 FR 0.0027 REL FR 22 V 2 P
a very scurvy tune to sing at a man's funeral. TMP 2.02. 44 P
spar'd, | shall wait upon your father's funeral. JN 5.07. 98
were our tears wanting to this funeral, | these 1H6 1.01. 82
for my good, | only give order for my funeral. 2.05.112
my sighing breast shall be thy funeral bell; 3H6 2.05.117
but safer triumph is this funeral pomp, | that TIT 1.01.176
physic, | and you must needs bestow her funeral; 4.02.163
no funeral rite, nor man in mourning weed, | no 5.03.196
turn from their office to black funeral: ROM 4.05. 85
a friend, | speak in the order of his funeral. JC 3.01.230
not consent | that antony speak in his funeral. 3.01.233
you shall not in your funeral speech blame us, 3.01.245
not have any hand at all | about his funeral. 3.01.249
men), | come i to speak in caesar's funeral. 3.02. 84
directly, i am going to caesar's funeral. 3.03. 20 P
eye, | with mirth in funeral, and with dirge in HAM 1.02. 12
my lord, i came to see your father's funeral. 1.02.176
the funeral bak'd-meats | did coldly furnish 1.02.180
his means of death, his obscure funeral — | no 4.05.214
army shall | in solemn show attend this funeral, ANT 5.02.364
or, dead, give 's cause to mourn his funeral, PER 2.04. 32
this funeral path brings to your household's TNK 1.05. 11
and in their funeral songs for these two cousins 3.06.248
and give grace unto | the funeral of arcite, in 5.04.126
FUNERALS 3 FR 0.0003 REL FR 3 V 0 P
of mirth, | turn melancholy forth to funerals: MND 1.01. 14
son | did graciously plead for his funerals; TIT 1.01.381
his funerals shall not be in our camp, | lest it JC 5.03.105
/FUR 1 FR 0.0001 REL FR 1 V 0 P
//belly-pinched /wolf | /keep /their /fur /dry, LR 3.01. 14
FUR 1 FR 0.0001 REL FR 1 V 0 P
priest, | you fur your gloves with reason. TRO 2.02. 38
FURBISH 1 FR 0.0001 REL FR 1 V 0 P
and furbish new the name of john a' gaunt, R2 1.03. 76
FURBISH'D 1 FR 0.0001 REL FR 1 V 0 P
with furbish'd arms and new supplies of men, MAC 1.02. 32
FURIES' 1 FR 0.0001 REL FR 1 V 0 P
then, pistol, lay thy head in furies' lap. 2H4 5.03.106
FURIES 4 FR 0.0004 REL FR 2 V 2 P
approach, ye furies fell! MND 5.01.284
and of limbo and of furies and i know not what. AWW 5.03.261 P
in his rages, and his furies, and his wraths, H5 4.07. 35 P
seize on him, furies, take him unto torment!" R3 1.04. 57
FURIOUS 15 FR 0.0017 REL FR 12 V 3 P
give ground if you see him furious. TN 3.04.304 P
shock | and furious close of civil butchery, 1H4 1.01. 13
so soon ta'en prisoner, and that furious scot, 2H4 1.01.126
dale, a most furious knight and valorous enemy. 4.03. 39 P
o braggard vile and damned furious wight! H5 2.01. 60
and giddy fortune's furious fickle wheel, | that 3.06. 27
rancorous spite, more furious raging broils, 1H6 4.01.185
good queen, and whet not on these furious peers, 2H6 2.01. 33
frightful, desp'rate, wild, and furious, | thy R3 4.04.170
in rome | how furious and impatient they be, TIT 2.01. 76
here comes the furious tybalt back again. ROM 3.01.121
who can be wise, amaz'd, temp'rate, and furious, MAC 2.03.108
to be furious | is to be frighted out of fear, ANT 3.13.194
you are most hot and furious when you win. CYM 2.03. 5 P
o' th' sun, | nor the furious winter's rages, 4.02.259
FURLONGS 2 FR 0.0002 REL FR 1 V 1 P
i give a thousand furlongs of sea for an acre of TMP 1.01. 65 P
's | with one soft kiss a thousand furlongs ere WT 1.02. 95
FURNACE 4 FR 0.0004 REL FR 4 V 0 P
sighing like furnace, with a woeful ballad AYL 2.07.148
heat not a furnace for your foe so hot | that it H8 1.01.140
and forth again | as from a furnace, vapors doth VEN 274
"o night, thou furnace of foul reeking smoke! LUC 799
FURNACE-BURNING 1 FR 0.0001 REL FR 1 V 0 P
serves to quench my furnace-burning heart; 3H6 2.01. 80
FURNACES 1 FR 0.0001 REL FR 1 V 0 P
he furnaces | the thick sighs from him, whiles CYM 1.06. 66
FURNISH 21 FR 0.0023 REL FR 17 V 4 P
i will furnish it anon with new contents. TMP 2.02.143 P
of, | to furnish me upon my longing journey. TGV 2.07. 85
which is the best to furnish me to-morrow. ADO 3.01.103
to furnish thee to belmont, to fair portia. MV 1.01.182
a wealthy hebrew of my tribe, | will furnish me. 1.03. 58
of clock, we have two hours | to furnish us. 2.04. 9
that thee may furnish, and my prayers pluck down AWW 1.01. 69
gift | shall furnish me to those italian fields 2.03.290
skill, and wrath can furnish man withal. TN 3.04.232 P
the revenue whereof shall furnish us | for our R2 1.04. 46
lend me a thousand pound to furnish me forth? 2H4 1.02.224 P
accord | to furnish /him with all appertinents H5 2.02. 87
if king lewis vouchsafe to furnish us | with 3H6 3.03.203
that he may furnish and instruct great teachers H8 1.02.113
to furnish rome, and to prepare the ways | you 3.02.328
furnish you fairly for this interchange; TRO 3.03. 33
as you think fit to furnish me to-morrow? ROM 4.02. 35
hath sent to your lordship to furnish him, TIM 3.01. 19 P
there's not so much left to furnish out | a 3.04.114
did coldly furnish forth the marriage tables. HAM 1.02.181
to furnish me with some swift means of death OTH 3.03.478
FURNISH'D 20 FR 0.0022 REL FR 14 V 6 P
he furnish'd me | from mine own library with TMP 1.02.166
let him be furnish'd with divines, and have all MM 3.02.209 P
i am not furnish'd with the present money: ERR 4.01. 34
what gold and jewels she is furnish'd with, MV 2.04. 31
he is furnish'd with my opinion, which, better'd 4.01.157 P
he was furnish'd like a hunter. AYL 3.02.245 P
i am not furnish'd like a beggar, therefore to ep 10 P
we are not furnish'd like bohemia's son, | nor WT 4.04.588
all furnish'd, all in arms; 1H4 4.01. 97
semblably furnish'd like the king himself. 5.03. 21
and he is furnish'd with no certainties | more 2H4 1.01. 31
he then, that is not furnish'd in this sort, 1H6 4.01. 39
i had, i saw well chosen, ridden, and furnish'd. H8 2.02. 3 P
my wolsey, see it furnish'd. 2.02.140
'tis furnish'd well with men, | and men are JC 3.01. 66
i shall be furnish'd to inform you rightly ANT 1.04. 77
when he was less furnish'd than now he is with CYM 1.04. 8 P
if she be furnish'd with a mind so rare, | she 1.06. 16
i'll see you furnish'd, and because you say TNK 2.05. 44
yet | and furnish'd with your old strength, i'll 3.06. 37
FURNISHED 3 FR 0.0003 REL FR 3 V 0 P
city | is richly furnished with plate and gold, SHR 2.01.347
well furnished by the duke of britain | with R2 2.01.285
to an honor'd triumph strangely furnished. PER 2.02. 53
FURNISHINGS 1 FR 0.0001 REL FR 1 V 0 P
whereof, perchance, these are but furnishings — LR 3.01. 29
FURNITURE 5 FR 0.0005 REL FR 5 V 0 P
worse | for this poor furniture and mean array. SHR 4.03.180
i'd give bay curtal and his furniture, | my AWW 2.03. 59
receive | money and order for their furniture. 1H4 3.03.202
here | without discharge, money, or furniture, 2H6 1.03.169
and fit it with such furniture as suits | the H8 2.01. 99
FURNIVAL 1 FR 0.0001 REL FR 1 V 0 P
of wingfield, lord furnival of sheffield, | the 1H6 4.07. 66
FUROR 1 FR 0.0001 REL FR 1 V 0 P
my lords, "ira furor brevis est," | but yond man TIM 1.02. 28
FURR'D 5 FR 0.0005 REL FR 2 V 3 P
by order of law a furr'd gown to keep him warm; MM 3.02. 7 P
and furr'd with fox and lambskins too, to 3.02. 8 P
not able to travel with her furr'd pack, she 2H6 4.02. 48 P
robes and furr'd gowns hide all. LR 4.06.165
thee all this, | yea, and furr'd moss besides. CYM 4.02.228
FURROW 2 FR 0.0002 REL FR 2 V 0 P
come hither from the furrow and be merry. TMP 4.01.135
thou canst help time to furrow me with age, R2 1.03.229
FURROWED 1 FR 0.0001 REL FR 1 V 0 P
draw the huge bottoms through the furrowed sea, H5 3.pr. 12
FURROWS 1 FR 0.0001 REL FR 1 V 0 P
but when in thee time's furrows i behold, | then SON 22. 3
FURROW-WEEDS 1 FR 0.0001 REL FR 1 V 0 P
crown'd with rank /femiter and furrow-weeds, LR 4.04. 3
FURTHER *(also vurther)*
/FURTHER 2 FR 0.0002 REL FR 1 V 1 P
item, /it /is /further /agreed /between /them, 2H6 1.01. 50 P
/of /our /nature /come | /in /further /evil? HAM 5.02. 70
FURTHER 199 FR 0.0225 REL FR 155 V 44 P
hear a little further, | and then i'll bring TMP 1.02.135
and let's make further search | for my poor son. 2.01.323
trinculo, run into no further danger. 3.02. 68 P
interrupt the monster one word further, and, by 3.02. 69 P
prithee stand further off. 3.02. 84 P
by'r lakin, i can go no further, sir, | my old 3.03. 1
of my purpose doth extend | not a frown further. 5.01. 30
well, i will look further into't, and i have a WIV 2.01.237 P
let's obey his humor a little further. 4.02.199 P
conscience, pursue him with any further revenge? 4.02.208 P
fat knight shall be any further afflicted, we 4.02.218 P
well, i will muse no further. 5.05.239
you this note, and by me this further charge: MM 4.02.103 P
attempt you, i will go further than i meant, to 4.02.190 P
that apprehends no further than this world, 5.01.481
ere you flout old ends any further, examine your ADO 1.01.288 P
we will hear further of it by your daughter, let 2.03.205 P
wonder not till further warrant. 3.02.112 P
for my sake, my dear, | lie further off yet; MND 2.02. 44
for love and courtesy | lie further off, in 2.02. 57
bear my folly back, | and follow you no further. 3.02.316
briers, | i can no further crawl, no further go; 3.02.444
briers, | i can no further crawl, no further go; 3.02.444
dear sir, of force i must attempt you further. MV 4.01.421
i will no further offend you than becomes me for AYL 1.01. 79 P
no man in good earnest, nor no further in sport, 1.02. 27 P
i pray you bear with me, i cannot go no further. 2.04. 10 P
dear master, i can go no further. 2.06. 1 P
but do not look for further recompense | than 3.05. 97
i durst go no further than the lie 5.04. 85 P
i will speak with you further anon. AWW 1.03.127 P
indeed give us a further use to be made than 2.03. 35 P
you presently | attend his further pleasure. 2.04. 53
i hope i need not to advise you further, but i 3.05. 25 P
though there were no further danger known but 3.05. 27 P
shall be for me, and, to requite you further, 3.05. 99
extend to you what further becomes his greatness 3.06. 70 P
and by midnight look to hear further from me. 3.06. 77 P
i know not how i shall assure you further | but 3.07. 2
prithee get thee further. 5.02. 14 P
sirrah, inquire further after me. 5.02. 52 P
we'll sift this matter further. 5.03.124
do they charge me further? 5.03.167
trip no further, pretty sweeting; TN 2.03. 42
of your pains, | i will no further chide you. 3.03. 3
if thou dar'st tempt me further, draw thy sword. 4.01. 42
along with you, it may awake my bounty further. 5.01. 44 P
so please you, these things further thought on, 5.01.316
town, | being no further enemy to you | than the JN 2.01.243
further i will not flatter you, my lord, | that 2.01.516
which for our goods we do no further ask | than 4.02. 64
peace, | and be no further harmful than in show. 5.02. 77
further i say, and further will maintain | upon R2 1.01. 98
and further will maintain | upon his bad life to 1.01. 98
ere further leisure yield them further means 1.04. 40
ere further leisure yield them further means 1.04. 40
mistake not, uncle, further than you should. 3.03. 15
take not, good cousin, further than you should, 3.03. 16
his coming hither hath no further scope | than 3.03.112
and shall it in more shame be further spoken, 1H4 1.03.177
no further go in this | than i by letters shall 1.03.292
but four foot by the squier further afoot, i 2.02. 13 P
i'll starve ere i'll rob a foot further. 2.02. 22 P
not an inch further. 2.03.114
as if thou never walk'st further than finsbury. 3.01.252
and further, i have learn'd, | the king himself 4.01. 90
proceeded further — cut me off the heads | of 4.03. 85
nor claim no further than your new-fall'n right, 5.01. 44
to approve my youth further, i will not. 2H4 1.02.191 P
the heat is past, follow no further now; 4.03. 24
comes to no further use | but to be known and 4.04. 72
for us, we will consider of this further. H5 2.04.113
question, my lords, no further of the case, 1H6 2.01. 72
give it you | in earnest of a further benefit, 5.03. 16
dimm'd mine eyes, that i can read no further. 2H6 1.01. 55
"item, it is further agreed between them, that 1.01. 57 P
to keep, until your further time of trial. 3.01.138
his eyeballs further out than when he lived, 3.02.169
him off, | persuaded him from any further act: 5.03. 10
so cowards fight when they can fly no further, 3H6 1.04. 40
while i use further conference with warwick. 3.03.111
then further: 3.03.119
my thoughts aim at a further matter: 4.01.125
and, as i further have to understand, | is new 4.04. 10
to consider further, that | what his high hatred H8 1.01.106
till you know | how he determines further. 1.01.214
me, | i have no further gone in this than by | a 1.02. 69
but benefit no further | than vainly longing. 1.02. 80
anon advise you | further in the proceeding. 1.02.108
adding further | that, had the king in his last 1.02.183
canst thou say further? 1.02.187
for further life in this world i ne'er hope, 2.01. 69
or how far further shall, is warranted | by a 2.04. 91
that we adjourn this court till further day. 2.04.233
till you hear further from his highness. 3.02.232
lord cardinal, the king's further pleasure is — 3.02.337
further, sir, | stands in the gap and trade of 5.01. 35
till further trial in those charges | which will 5.01.103
to have heard you | without indurance further. 5.01.121
there to remain till the king's further pleasure 5.02.125
from both the sides, | what further you will do. TRO 4.05.147
before we proceed any further, hear me speak. COR 1.01. 1 P
without any further deed to have them at all 2.02. 27 P
left your voices, | i have no further with you." 2.03.173
pass no further. 3.01. 24
it will be dangerous to go on — no further. 3.01. 26
not poison any further. 3.01. 88
and therefore law shall scorn him further trial 3.01.267
the which shall turn you to no further harm 3.01.282
being of catching nature, | spread further. 3.01.309
i muse my mother | does not approve me further, 3.02. 8
tongue can do | i' th' way of flattery further. 3.02.137
shall i be charg'd no further than this present? 3.03. 42
consider further: 3.03. 52
i'll know no further. 3.03. 87
and we'll no further. 4.02. 1
tongues | plot some device of further misery, TIT 3.01.134
can vengeance be pursued further than death? ROM 5.03. 55
what further woe conspires against mine age? 5.03.212
well; what further? TIM 1.01.120
wait attendance | till you hear further from me. 1.01.162
come, sermon me no further. 2.02.172
trouble him no further, thus you still shall 5.01.213
you one), | nor construe any further my neglect, JC 1.02. 45
i might entreat you) | be any further mov'd. 1.02.167
i urg'd you further; 2.01.243
your best friends shall wish i had been further. 2.02.125
fly further off, my lord, fly further off; 5.03. 9
fly further off, my lord, fly further off; 5.03. 9
to enverness, | and bind us further to you. MAC 1.04. 43
when i burnt in desire to question them further, 1.05. 4 P
we will speak further. 1.05. 71
we will proceed no further in this business: 1.07. 31
i'll devil-porter it no further. 2.03. 17 P
most bloody piece of work, | to know it further. 2.03.129
and went further, which is now | our point of 3.01. 84
foreign levy, nothing, | can touch him further. 3.02. 26
i dare not speak much further, | but cruel are 4.02. 17
to suppress | his further gait herein, in that HAM 1.02. 31
giving to you no further personal power | to 1.02. 36
which is no further | than the main voice of 1.03. 27
speak, i'll go no further. 1.05. 1
with an entreaty, herein further shown, | that 2.02. 76
how may we try it further? 2.02.159
good gentlemen, give him a further edge, | and 3.01. 26
have you any further trade with us? 3.02.334 P
friends both, go join you with some further aid: 4.01. 33
let's further think of this, | weigh what 4.07.148
without debatement further, more or less, | he 5.02. 45
there is further compliment of leave-taking LR 1.01.302 P
we shall further think of it. 1.01.307 P

and that without any further delay than this 1.02. 93 P
i will look further into't. 1.04. 71 P
my daughter no further with any thing you know 1.05. 2 P
i will talk further with you. 3.01. 43
poor tom's a–cold. i cannot daub it further. 4.01. 52
then shall you go no further. 4.02. 11
go thou further off: 4.06. 30
in, trouble him no more | till further settling. 4.07. 81
no further, sir, a man may rot even here. 5.02. 8
they are ready | to–morrow, or at further space, 5.03. 53
no further conscionable than in putting on the OTH 2.01.238 P
a satisfaction of my thought, | no further harm. 3.03. 98
i will hear further reason for this. 4.02.244 P
beseech you, sir, trouble yourself no further. 4.03. 1
to enforce no further | the griefs between ye: ANT 2.02. 99
let me hear agrippa further speak. 2.02.123
me have thy hand | further this act of grace; 2.02.146
trouble yourselves no further; 2.04. 1
you praise caesar, say "caesar," go no further. 3.02. 13
no further, sir. 3.02. 23
the sight and could not | endure a further view. 3.10. 17
and there i will attend | what further comes. 3.10. 32
case thou stand'st | further than he is /caesar. 3.13. 55
peace! | hark further. 4.09. 11
these thoughts of horror further than you shall 5.02. 63
you have prevail'd, i am no further your enemy; CYM 1.04.159 P
no further service, doctor, | until i send for 1.05. 44
if you seek | for further satisfying, under her 2.04.134
to thy further fear, | nay, to thy mere 4.02. 91
further to boast were neither true nor modest, 5.05. 18
peace, peace, see further. 5.05.124
be silent; let's see further. 5.05.127
what became of him | i further know not. 5.05.286
further to question me of your king's departure. PER 1.03. 11
if further yet you will be satisfied | why (as 1.03. 15
and further, he desires to know of you | of 2.03. 79
and for further grief — god give you joy! 2.05. 87
but i'll see further: 4.01. 99
thebes and the temptings in't before we further TNK 1.02. 4
no further! 1.03. 1
which shall be then | beyond further requiring. 1.03. 26
are faint — then i'll talk further with you. 3.03. 7
note her a little further. 4.03. 29 P
i'll no step further. 5.03. 1
my good lord, | your sister will no further. 5.03. 11
this way she runs, and now she will no further, VEN 905
this forced league doth force a further strife, LUC 689
"for further i could say, 'this man's untrue,' LC 169

FURTHERANCE 2 FR 0.0002 REL FR 2 V 0 P
entreat you to your wonted furtherance? 1H6 5.03. 21
by your furtherance i am cloth'd in steel, | and PER 2.01.154

FURTHERER 1 FR 0.0001 REL FR 1 V 0 P
thy brother was a furtherer in the act. TMP 5.01. 73

FURTHERMORE 3 FR 0.0003 REL FR 2 V 1 P
furthermore, | i pray you show my youth old MV 4.02. 10
and furthermore, we'll have the lord say's head 2H6 4.02.160 P
and furthermore tell him, we desire to know of PER 2.03. 73

FURTHEST 2 FR 0.0002 REL FR 1 V 1 P
toothpicker now from the furthest inch of asia, ADO 2.01.267 P
or here or elsewhere to the furthest verge R2 1.01. 93

FURTH'RANCE 1 FR 0.0001 REL FR 1 V 0 P
that may give furth'rance to our expedition; H5 1.02.301

/FURY 2 FR 0.0002 REL FR 2 V 0 P
/but /my /deeds /shall /stay /thy /fury /soon. 2H6 4.01.113
/with /eyeless /rage | /catch /in /their /fury, LR 3.01. 9

FURY 72 FR 0.0081 REL FR 64 V 8 P
allaying both their fury and my passion | with TMP 1.02.393
fury, fury! 4.01.257
fury, fury! 4.01.257
nobler reason, 'gainst my fury | do i take part. 5.01. 26
such as the fury of ungovern'd youth | thrust TGV 4.01. 43
he would never have boarded me in this fury. WIV 2.01. 89 P
that here and there his fury had committed. ERR 5.01.147
and she were not possess'd with a fury, exceeds ADO 1.01.191 P
i keep her as a vessel of thy law's fury, and LLL 1.01.274 P
what zeal, what fury, hath inspir'd thee now? 4.03.225
this wood, | and i in fury hither followed them, MND 4.01.162
i do oppose | my patience to his fury, and am MV 4.01. 11
they do consume the thing that feeds their fury. SHR 2.01.133
of his rage, skill, fury, and impetuosity. TN 3.04.194 P
the fury spent, anon | did this break from her: WT 3.03. 26
then, till the fury of his highness settle, 4.04.471
against whose fury and unmatched force | the JN 1.01.265
himself | in mortal fury half so peremptory, 2.01.454
so | as doth the fury of two desperate men, 3.01. 32
by all the blood that ever fury breath'd, | the 5.02.127
blood | with fury from his native residence. R2 2.01.119
an oath of mickle might, and fury shall abate. H5 2.01. 66
tell him my fury shall abate, and i | the crowns 4.04. 47
duke | hath banish'd moody discontented fury, 1H6 3.01.123
you tempt the fury of my three attendants, 4.02. 10
mad ire and wrathful fury makes me weep, | that 4.03. 28
none, | dizzy–ey'd fury and great rage of heart 4.07. 11
proud prelate, in thy face | i see thy fury. 2H6 1.01.143
beams, | do calm the fury of this mad–bred flaw. 3.01.354
on sheep or oxen could i spend my fury. 5.01. 27
house of york | is as a fury to torment my soul; 3H6 1.03. 31
and i am faint, and cannot fly their fury; 1.04. 23
and were i strong, i would not shun their fury. 1.04. 24
i dare your quenchless fury to more rage. 1.04. 28
sea | forc'd to retire by fury of the wind. 2.05. 8
and men ne'er spend their fury on a child. 5.05. 57
what, lost in the labyrinth of thy fury? TRO 2.03. 2 P
embarquements all of fury, shall lift up | their COR 1.10. 22
whose fury not dissembled speaks his griefs. TIT 1.01.438
and would not, but in fury, fright my youth, 4.01. 24
he'll so awake as he in fury shall | cut off the 4.04. 25
welcome, dread fury, to my woeful house; 5.02. 82
ah, why should wrath be mute and fury dumb? 5.03.184
lenity, | and fire/–ey'd fury be my conduct now! ROM 3.01.124
acts /denote | the unreasonable fury of a beast. 3.03.111
sin upon my head, | by urging me to fury: 5.03. 63
fault), | but with a noble fury and fair spirit, TIM 3.05. 18
in that beastly fury | he has been known to 3.05. 70
it is a cause worthy my spleen and fury, | that 3.05.112
know you the quality of lord timon's fury? 3.06.108 P
and, thy fury spent, | confounded be thyself! 4.03.128
make thine own self the conquest of thy fury; 4.03.337 P
domestic fury and fierce civil strife | shall JC 3.01.263
o, yet i do repent me of my fury, | that i did MAC 2.03.106
that lesser hate him | do call it valiant fury; 5.02. 14
tale | told by an idiot, full of sound and fury, 5.05. 27
that in the fury of his heart, when the foul LR 3.04.131 P
in her prophetic fury sew'd the work; OTH 3.04. 72
i understand a fury in your words, | /but /not 4.02. 32
shouldst come like a fury crown'd with snakes, ANT 2.05. 40
that antony may seem to spend his fury | upon 4.06. 9
but better 'twere | thou fell'st into my fury, 4.12. 41
look | for fury not to be resisted. CYM 3.01. 67
never saw | such noble fury in so poor a thing; 5.05. 8
but whisper'd, to | the loudness of his fury. TNK 1.02. 88
since i have known frights, fury, friends' 1.04. 40
and both upon our guards, then let our fury, 3.06. 29
grew kinder, and his fury was assuag'd. VEN 318
with blindfold fury she begins to forage; 554
or stop the headlong fury of his speed. LUC 501
abide, | and with the wind in greater fury fret. 648
spend'st thou thy fury on some worthless song, SON 100. 3

/FURZE 1 FR 0.0001 REL FR 0 V 1 P
ground, long heath, brown /furze, any thing. TMP 1.01. 66 P

FURZES 1 FR 0.0001 REL FR 1 V 0 P
follow'd through | tooth'd briers, sharp furzes, TMP 4.01.180

FUST 1 FR 0.0001 REL FR 1 V 0 P
and godlike reason | to fust in us unus'd. HAM 4.04. 39

FUSTIAN 4 FR 0.0004 REL FR 0 V 4 P
the servingmen in their new fustian, /their SHR 4.01. 47 P
a fustian riddle! TN 2.05.108 P
i cannot endure such a fustian rascal. 2H4 2.04.189 P
and discourse fustian with one's own shadow? OTH 2.03.280 P

FUSTILARIAN 1 FR 0.0001 REL FR 0 V 1 P
you fustilarian! 2H4 2.01. 60 P

FUSTY 3 FR 0.0003 REL FR 2 V 1 P
at this fusty stuff | the large achilles, on his TRO 1.03.161
were as good crack a fusty nut with no kernel. 2.01.101 P
that with the fusty plebeians hate thine honors, COR 1.09. 7

/FUT 1 FR 0.0001 REL FR 0 V 1 P
/fut, i should have been that i am, had the LR 1.02.131 P

FUTURE 14 FR 0.0015 REL FR 14 V 0 P
and all the fair effects of future hopes. TGV 1.01. 50
looks in a glass that shows what future evils, MM 2.02. 95
may token to the future our past deeds. AWW 4.02. 63
for present comfort, and for future good, | to WT 5.01. 32
and future ages groan for this foul act. R2 4.01.138
me | and give me signs of future accidents. 1H6 5.03. 4
but that my heart's on future mischief set, | i 2H6 5.02. 84
now, and provide | for thine own future safety. H8 3.02.421
three talents on the present; in future, all. TIM 1.01.141
the future comes apace; 2.02.148
melancholy sprung | from change of future. 4.03.204
and i feel now | the future in the instant. MAC 1.05. 58
that future strife | may be prevented now. LR 1.01. 44
he'ld lay the future open. CYM 3.02. 29

FUTURELY 1 FR 0.0001 REL FR 1 V 0 P
that i have foregone | or futurely can cope. TNK 1.01.174

FUTURITY 1 FR 0.0001 REL FR 1 V 0 P
sorrows, | nor purpos'd merit in futurity, | can OTH 3.04.117

G 4 FR 0.0004 REL FR 4 V 0 P
which says that g | of edward's heirs the R3 1.01. 39
and from the cross–row plucks the letter g, 1.01. 55
and says a wizard told him that by g | his issue 1.01. 56
and, for my name of george begins with g, | it 1.01. 58

GABBLE 3 FR 0.0003 REL FR 1 V 2 P
but wouldst gabble like | a thing most brutish, TMP 1.02.356
choughs' language, gabble enough, and good AWW 4.01. 20 P
but to gabble like tinkers at this time of night TN 2.03. 87 P

GABERDINE 3 FR 0.0003 REL FR 1 V 2 P
my best way is to creep under his gaberdine; TMP 2.02. 38 P
dead moon–calf's gaberdine for fear of the storm 2.02.111 P
dog, | and spet upon my jewish gaberdine, | and MV 1.03.112

GABR'EL'S 1 FR 0.0001 REL FR 1 V 0 P
and gabr'el's pumps were all unpink'd i' th' SHR 4.01.133

GAD 2 FR 0.0002 REL FR 2 V 0 P
and with a gad of steel will write these words, TIT 4.01.103
all this done | upon the gad? LR 1.02. 26

GADDING 1 FR 0.0001 REL FR 1 V 0 P
now, my headstrong, where have you been gadding? ROM 4.02. 16

GADSHILL 8 FR 0.0009 REL FR 0 V 8 P
now shall we know if gadshill have set a match. 1H4 1.02.106 P
morning by four a' clock early, at gadshill, 1.02.125 P
gadshill lies to–night in rochester. 1.02.129 P
and gadshill shall rob those men that we have 1.02.163 P
good morrow, master gadshill. 2.01. 53 P
when thou ran'st up gadshill in the night to 3.03. 38 P
gilded over your night's exploit on gadshill. 2H4 1.02.149 P
me, as you did when you ran away by gadshill. 2.04.307 P

/GADSLUGS 1 FR 0.0001 REL FR 1 V 0 P
now by /gadslugs i swear i scorn the term; H5 2.01. 30

GAG'D 1 FR 0.0001 REL FR 1 V 0 P
something too prodigal | hath left me gag'd. MV 1.01.130

GAGE 18 FR 0.0020 REL FR 16 V 2 P
pale trembling coward, there i throw my gage, R2 1.01. 69
and interchangeably hurl down my gage | upon 1.01.146
throw down, my son, the duke of norfolk's gage. 1.01.161
rage must be withstood, | give me his gage. 1.01.174
take but my shame, | and i resign my gage. 1.01.176
cousin, throw up your gage, do you begin. 1.01.186
there is my gage, the manual seal of death, 4.01. 25
there is my gage, aumerle, in gage to thine. 4.01. 34
there is my gage, aumerle, in gage to thine. 4.01. 34
and that thou art so, there i throw my gage, 4.01. 46
some honest christian trust me with a gage — 4.01. 83
these differences shall all rest under gage 4.01. 86
your differences shall all rest under gage 4.01.105
power | did gage them both in an unjust behalf 1H4 1.03.173
give me any gage of thine, and i will wear it in H5 4.01.208 P
'tis the gage of one that i should fight withal, 4.07.122 P
that one for all, or all for one, we gage: LUC 144
pawn'd honest looks, but laid no words to gage. 1351

GAGED 1 FR 0.0001 REL FR 1 V 0 P
a moi'ty competent | was gaged by our king, HAM 1.01. 91

GAGG'D 2 FR 0.0002 REL FR 0 V 2 P
and minister occasion to him, he is gagg'd. TN 1.05. 88 P
and you smile not, he's gagg'd." 5.01.376 P

GAGING 1 FR 0.0001 REL FR 1 V 0 P
both taxing me and gaging me to keep | an oath TRO 5.01. 41

GAGNE 1 FR 0.0001 REL FR 0 V 1 P
j'ai gagne deux mots d'anglois vitement. H5 3.04. 13 P

/GAIN 2 FR 0.0002 REL FR 2 V 0 P
/your /care /is /gain /of /care, /by /new /care R2 4.01.197
/and /might /by /no /suit /gain /our /audience. 2H4 4.01. 76

GAIN 69 FR 0.0078 REL FR 63 V 6 P
if happ'ly won, perhaps a hapless gain; TGV 1.01. 32
his bonds, | and gain a husband by his liberty. ERR 5.01.341
if study's gain be thus, and this be so, | study LLL 1.01. 67
day, what should i gain | by the exaction of the MV 1.03.163
chooseth me shall gain what many men desire"; 2.07. 5
chooseth me shall gain what many men desire." 2.07. 37
chooseth me shall gain what many men desire." 2.09. 24
his brother, gain nothing under him but growth, AYL 1.01. 14 P
'twill bring you gain, or perish on the seas. SHR 2.01.329
the gain i seek is, quiet /in the match. 2.01.330
if both gain, all | the gift doth stretch itself AWW 2.01. 3
some other times we drown our gain in tears! 4.03. 68 P
them ill to friend | till your deeds gain them; 5.03.183
the loss, the gain, the ord'ring on't, is all WT 2.01.169
that for thine own gain shouldst defend mine JN 1.01.242
gain, be my lord, for i will worship thee. 2.01.598
but what shall i gain by young arthur's fall? 3.04.141
one, | and yet we ventur'd for the gain propos'd 2H4 1.01.183
a strange tongue, wherein, to gain the language, 4.04. 69
to upbraid | my gain of it by their assistances, 4.05.193
us withal, | make us partakers of a little gain, 1H6 2.01. 52
by me they nothing gain and if i stay, | 'tis 4.06. 36
charms, | and try if they can gain your liberty. 5.03. 32
as little shall the frenchmen gain thereby. 5.04.115
my mind presageth happy gain and conquest. 3H6 5.01. 71
and of our labors thou shalt reap the gain. 5.07. 20
for me to joy and weep their gain and loss; R3 2.04. 59
forward | upon his party for the gain thereof; 3.02. 47
or lowly factor for another's gain; 3.07.134
and then marry her — | uncertain way of gain! 4.02. 63
of ten times double gain of happiness. 4.04.324
the gain of my attempt | the least of you shall 5.03.267
(indeed to gain the popedom | and fee my friends H8 3.02.212
so i grow stronger, you more honor gain. 5.02.215
our sufferance is a gain to them. COR 1.01. 22 P
we give you any thing, we hope to gain by you. 2.03. 72 P
and might not gain so great a happiness | as TIT 2.04. 20
only be men's works, and death their gain! TIM 5.01.222
whom we, to gain our peace, have sent to peace, MAC 3.02. 20
lated traveller apace | to gain the timely inn, 3.03. 7
we go to gain a little patch of ground | that HAM 4.04. 18
i will gain nothing but my shame and the odd 5.02.177 P
that sir which serves and seeks for gain, | and LR 2.04. 78
neglecting an attempt of ease and gain | to wake OTH 1.03. 29
do kill the other, | every way makes my gain. 5.01. 14
choice of loss | than gain which darkens him. ANT 3.01. 24
to gain the cap of him that makes him fine, CYM 3.03. 25
to gain his color | i'ld let a parish of such 4.02.167
her countless glory, which desert must gain; PER 1.01. 31
reign, | losing a mite, a mountain gain. 2.ch. 8
a deed might gain her love or your displeasure. 2.05. 54
despise profit where you have most gain. 4.02.118 P
if that thy master would gain by me, | proclaim 4.06.182
and her gain | she gives the cursed bawd. 5.ch. 10
labor through, | our gain but life and weakness. TNK 1.02. 12
and bare weeds | the gain o' th' martialist, who 1.02. 16
execution, where nor gain | made him regard, or 1.03. 29
despair to gain doth traffic oft for gaining, LUC 131
those that much covet are with gain so fond, 134
that they prove bankrout in this poor rich gain. 140
"what win i if i gain the thing i seek? 211
a captive victor that hath lost in gain, 730
having no other pleasure of his gain | but 860
nothing could be used to turn them both to gain, PP 15.10
if i lose thee, my loss is my love's gain, | and SON 42. 9
when i have seen the hungry ocean gain 64. 5
and gain by ills thrice more than i have spent. 119.14
only my plague thus far i count my gain, | that 141.13
a youthful suit — it was to gain my grace — LC 79

GAIN'D 11 FR 0.0012 REL FR 9 V 2 P
teeth my bonds in sunder, | i gain'd my freedom; ERR 5.01.251
thy grace being gain'd cures all disgrace in me. LLL 4.03. 65
yes, i have gain'd my experience. AYL 4.01. 26 P
must be as boisterously maintain'd as gain'd; JN 3.04.136
lost wherein such preparation was gain'd; H5 4.01.182 P
hath gain'd thy daughter princely liberty. 1H6 5.03.140
for i mine own gain'd knowledge should profane OTH 1.03.384
for i have gain'd by't. ANT 2.06. 52
so gain'd the sur–addition leonatus; CYM 1.01. 33
who hath gain'd | of education all the grace, PER 4.ch. 8
thy grace being gain'd cures all disgrace in me. PP 3. 8

GAINER 2 FR 0.0002 REL FR 1 V 1 P
the expense of so much money, be now a gainer? WIV 2.02.141 P
and i by this will be a gainer too, | for, SON 88. 9

/GAIN–GIVING 1 FR 0.0001 REL FR 0 V 1 P
but it is such a kind of /gain–giving, as would HAM 5.02.216 P

GAINING 2 FR 0.0002 REL FR 2 V 0 P
despair to gain doth traffic oft for gaining, LUC 131
or, gaining more, the profit of excess | is but 138

GAINS 8 FR 0.0009 REL FR 6 V 2 P
he gains by death that hath such means to die: ERR 3.02. 51
laugh'd at my losses, mock'd at my gains, MV 3.01. 56 P
and to thy worth will add right worthy gains. R2 5.06. 12
when they are gone, then must i count my gains. R3 1.01.162
pains, | and every one shall share i' th' gains. MAC 4.01. 40
you had of her pure honor gains or loses | your CYM 2.04. 59
since he gains from his subjects the name of PER 2.01.104 P
his, | and, proud of many, lives upon his gains? SON 67.12

GAINSAID 1 FR 0.0001 REL FR 1 V 0 P
you are too great to be by me gainsaid, | your 2H4 1.01. 91

GAINSAY 4 FR 0.0004 REL FR 4 V 0 P
wanted | less impudence to gainsay what they did WT 3.02. 56
gentlemen, what i should say | my tears gainsay; 3H6 5.04. 74
if it be known to him | that i gainsay my deed, H8 2.04. 96
but the just gods gainsay | that any /drop thou TRO 4.05.132

GAINSAYING 1 FR 0.0001 REL FR 1 V 0 P
and in that | i'll no gainsaying. WT 1.02. 19

GAINSAYS 1 FR 0.0001 REL FR 1 V 0 P
and whosoe'er gainsays king edward's right, | by 3H6 4.07. 74

'GAINST *(also against)*

'GAINST 114 FR 0.0128 REL FR 113 V 1 P
nobler reason, 'gainst my fury | do i take part. TMP 5.01. 26

which, like a waxen image 'gainst a fire, TGV 2.04.201
and love you 'gainst the nature of love — force 5.04. 58
a forted residence 'gainst the tooth of time MM 5.01. 12
was complaint | intended 'gainst lord angelo, 5.01.154
a yielding 'gainst some reason in my breast, LLL 2.01.151
thou hear the nemean lion roar | 'gainst thee, 4.01. 89
'gainst whom the world cannot hold argument, 4.03. 59
flat treason 'gainst the kingly state of youth. 4.03.289
needs give sentence 'gainst the merchant there. MV 4.01.205
the party 'gainst the which he doth contrive 4.01.352
of the duke only, 'gainst all other voice: 4.01.356
be valued 'gainst your wive's commandement. 4.01.451
hath ta'en displeasure 'gainst his gentle niece, AYL 1.02.278
his malice 'gainst the lady | will suddenly 1.02.282
venice | to buy apparel 'gainst the wedding–day. SHR 2.01.315
since you set up your rest 'gainst remedy. AWW 2.01.135
once in a sea–fight 'gainst the count his TN 3.03. 26
'gainst knaves and thieves men shut their gate, 5.01.395
even pushes 'gainst our heart — the party tried WT 3.02. 2
my great profaneness 'gainst thine oracle! 3.02.154
their iron indignation 'gainst your walls; JN 2.01.212
put thee down, 'gainst whom these arms we bear, 2.01.346
resolveth from his figure 'gainst the fire? 5.04. 25
or complot any ill | 'gainst us, our state, our R2 1.03.190
inform, | merely in hate, 'gainst any of us all, 2.01.243
will the king severely prosecute | 'gainst us, 2.01.245
into | for gay apparel 'gainst the triumph day. 5.02. 66
that you did nothing purpose 'gainst the state, 1H4 5.01. 43
'gainst all the world will rightfully maintain. 2H4 4.05.224
impartial spirit | as you have done 'gainst me. 5.02.117
'gainst him whose wrongs gives edge unto the H5 1.02. 27
me | are heavy orisons 'gainst this poor wretch! 2.02. 53
but thou ('gainst all proportion) didst bring in 2.02.109
it is most meet we arm us 'gainst the foe; 2.04. 15
and fortify it strongly 'gainst the french. 3.03. 53
a piece of ord'nance 'gainst it i have plac'd, 1H6 1.04. 15
proceed no straiter 'gainst our uncle gloucester 2H6 3.02. 20
attracts the same for aidance 'gainst the enemy, 3.02.165
these dread curses, like the sun 'gainst glass, 3.02.330
of capital treason 'gainst the king and crown. 5.01.107
breathe out invectives 'gainst the officers. 3H6 1.04. 43
cries vengeance for his death | 'gainst thee, 1.04.149
show thy descent by gazing 'gainst the sun; 2.01. 92
'gainst foreign storms than any home–bred 4.01. 38
be those numberless offenses | 'gainst me, that H8 2.01. 85
a known friend, 'gainst his highness' pleasure 3.01. 85
know my mind, i'll fight no more 'gainst troy. TRO 3.03. 56
but 'gainst your privacy | the reasons are more 3.03.191
well might they fester 'gainst ingratitude, COR 1.09. 30
if 'gainst yourself you be incens'd, we'll put 1.09. 56
their rotten privilege and custom 'gainst | my 1.10. 23
in soothing them we nourish 'gainst our senate 3.01. 69
with aufidius, leads a power 'gainst rome, | and 4.06. 67
strike the proud cedars 'gainst the fiery sun, 5.03. 60
fettle your fine joints 'gainst thursday next, ROM 3.05.153
yea, 'gainst th' authority of manners, pray'd TIM 2.02.138
that 'gainst the stream of virtue they may 4.01. 27
warr'st thou 'gainst athens? 4.03.103
and hardy soldier fought | 'gainst my captivity. MAC 1.02. 5
point against point, rebellious arm 'gainst arm, 1.02. 56
contending 'gainst obedience, as they would make 2.04. 17
'gainst nature still! 2.04. 27
some say that ever 'gainst that season comes HAM 1.01.158
not fix'd | his canon 'gainst /self–slaughter! 1.02.132
to be a preparation 'gainst the polack; 2.02. 63
'gainst fortune's state would treason have 2.02.511
have you not spoken 'gainst the duke of cornwall LR 2.01. 23
upon his party 'gainst the duke of albany? 2.01. 26
'gainst parricides did all the thunder bend, 2.01. 46
and danger | speak 'gainst so great a number? 2.04.240
your high–engender'd battles 'gainst a head | so 3.02. 23
friendship will it lend you 'gainst the tempest. 3.02. 62
combine together 'gainst the enemy; 5.01. 29
conspirant 'gainst this high illustrious prince, 5.03.136
if e'er my will did trespass 'gainst his love, OTH 4.02.152
of them, jointing their force 'gainst caesar, ANT 1.02. 92
partner in the cause 'gainst which he fought, 2.02. 59
i did not think to draw my sword 'gainst pompey, 2.02.153
natural luck, | he beats thee 'gainst the odds. 2.03. 28
but he hath wag'd | new wars 'gainst pompey; 3.04. 4
made use of him in the wars 'gainst pompey, 3.05. 8 P
are those that often have 'gainst pompey fought; 3.07. 37
an antony were nature's piece 'gainst fancy, 5.02. 99
surges, crack'd | as easily 'gainst our rocks. CYM 3.01. 29
in caesar's name pronounce i 'gainst thee; 3.01. 66
didst set up my disobedience 'gainst the king 3.04. 88
action | 'gainst the pannonians and dalmatians, 3.07. 3
pieces of gold 'gainst this which then he wore 5.05.183
'gainst whom i am too little to contend, | since PER 1.02. 17
her to meteline, 'gainst whose shore | riding, 5.03. 10
t' instruct me 'gainst a capital grief indeed — TNK 1.01.123
that it shall make a counter–reflect 'gainst 1.01.127
eyes break each morning 'gainst thy window, 2.03. 9
are you, that, 'gainst the tenor of my laws, 3.06.133
beside, i have another oath 'gainst yours, | of 3.06.230
'gainst the which there is | no deafing — but 5.03. 8
if i told you all you were in arms 'gainst god. STM II.C 95
rising 'gainst him that god himself installs, II.C 105
god himself installs, | but rise 'gainst god? II.C 106
'gainst venom'd sores the only sovereign plaster VEN 916
and dotes on what he looks, 'gainst law or duty. LUC 497
'gainst whom the world could not hold argument, PP 3. 2
that 'gainst thyself thou stick'st not to SON 10. 6
and nothing 'gainst time's scythe can make 12.13
and 'gainst myself a lawful plea commence. 35.11
'gainst death and all–oblivious enmity | shall 55. 9
crooked eclipses 'gainst his glory fight, | and 60. 7
potions of eisel 'gainst my strong infection, 111.10
or forc'd examples, 'gainst her own content, LC 157
love's arms are peace, 'gainst rule, 'gainst 271
'gainst rule, 'gainst sense, 'gainst shame, 271
'gainst rule, 'gainst sense, 'gainst shame, 271
to leave the batt'ry that you make 'gainst mine, 277

/GAIT 2 FR 0.0002 REL FR 2 V 0 P
/had /no /legs /that /practic'd /not /his /gait; 2H4 2.03. 23
/so /that /in /speech, /in /gait, | /in /diet, 2.03. 28

GAIT 35 FR 0.0039 REL FR 26 V 9 P
great juno, comes, i know her by her gait. TMP 4.01.102
up his head, as it were, and strut in his gait? WIV 1.04. 30 P
motion to thy gait in a semicircled farthingale. 3.03. 64 P
a gait, a state, a brow, a breast, a waist, | a LLL 4.03.183
his eye ambitious, his gait majestical, and his 5.01. 11 P
which she with pretty and with swimming gait MND 2.01.130
hath well beguil'd | the heavy gait of night. 5.01.368
consecrate, | every fairy take his gait, | and 5.01.416
voice, gait, and action of a gentlewoman. SHR in.1. 132
as kate this chamber with her princely gait? 2.01.259
in gait and countenance surely like a father. 4.02. 65
there do muster true gait, eat, speak, and move AWW 2.01. 54 P
good youth, address thy gait unto her, | be not TN 1.04. 15
the shape of his leg, the manner of his gait, 2.03.157 P
i will answer you with gait and entrance — but 3.01. 82 P
hath not my gait in it the measure of the court? WT 4.04.732 P
'tis like the forc'd gait of a shuffling nag. 1H4 3.01.133
should with his lion gait walk the whole world, H5 2.02.122
in face, in gait, in speech, he doth resemble. 2H6 3.01.373
straight | springs out into fast gait, then H8 3.02.116
eyes, her hair, her cheek, her gait, her voice, TRO 1.01. 54
'tis he, i ken the manner of his gait, | he 4.05. 14
thy fill, but pass and stay not here thy gait." TIM 5.04. 73
'tis cinna, i do know him by his gait, | he is a JC 1.03.132
to suppress | his further gait herein, in that HAM 1.02. 31
accent of christians nor the gait of christian, 3.02. 31 P
good gentleman, go your gait, and let poor voke LR 4.06.237 P
methought thy very gait did prophesy | a royal 5.03.176
i know his gait, 'tis he. OTH 5.01. 23
what majesty is in her gait? ANT 3.03. 17
what need i | affect another's gait, which is TNK 1.02. 45
"look, the world's comforter, with weary gait, VEN 529
and solemn night with slow sad gait descended LUC 1081
and give the harmless show | an humble gait, 1508
o'er whom /thy fingers walk with gentle gait, SON 128.11

GALATHE 1 FR 0.0001 REL FR 1 V 0 P
now here he fights on galathe his horse | and TRO 5.05. 20

GALE 3 FR 0.0003 REL FR 3 V 0 P
what happy gale | blows you to padua here from SHR 1.02. 48
a little gale will soon disperse that cloud, 3H6 5.03. 10
with every gale and vary of their masters, LR 2.02. 79

GALEN 4 FR 0.0004 REL FR 0 V 4 P
has no more knowledge in hibocrates and galen —
WIV 3.01. 66 P
so i say, both of galen and paracelsus. AWW 2.03. 11 P
i have read the cause of his effects in galen, 2H4 1.02.117 P
prescription in galen is but empiricutic, and, COR 2.01.117 P

GALES 1 FR 0.0001 REL FR 1 V 0 P
and promise you calm seas, auspicious gales, TMP 5.01.315

GALIEN 1 FR 0.0001 REL FR 0 V 1 P
my galien? WIV 2.03. 29 P

GALL* 33 FR 0.0037 REL FR 29 V 4 P
'twould be my tyranny to strike and gall them MM 1.03. 36
which a dismiss'd offense would after gall, 2.02.102
can tie the gall up in the slanderous tongue? 3.02.188
thou grievest my gall. LLL 5.02.237
gall! bitter. 5.02.237
let there be gall enough in thy ink, though thou TN 3.02. 49 P
stand by, or i shall gall you, faulconbridge. JN 4.03. 94
thou wert better gall the devil, salisbury. 4.03. 95
save how to gall and pinch this bullingbrook, 1H4 1.03.229
well, i am loath to gall a new–heal'd wound. 2H4 1.02.147 P
and he may well in fretting spend his gall — 1H6 1.02. 16
gall, worse than gall, the daintiest that they 2H6 3.02.322
gall, worse than gall, the daintiest that they 3.02.322
whom from the flow of gall i name not, but H8 1.01.152
a slave whose gall coins slanders like a mint, TRO 1.03.193
you have the honey still, but these the gall; 2.02.144
o deadly gall, and theme of all our scorns, 4.05. 30
out, gall! 5.01. 35 P
a choking gall, and a preserving sweet. ROM 1.01.194
now seeming sweet, convert to bitt'rest gall. 1.05. 92
and take my milk for gall, you murth'ring MAC 1.05. 48
gall of goat, and slips of yew | sliver'd in the 4.01. 27
and lack gall | to make oppression bitter, or HAM 2.02.577
this contagion, that, if i gall him slightly, 4.07.147
a pestilent gall to me! LR 1.04.114 P
from my heart all love, | and added to the gall. 1.04.270
(how ever this may gall him with some check) OTH 1.01.148
these sentences, to sugar or to gall, | being 1.03.216
let it not gall your patience, good iago, | that 2.01. 97
words you send, | though ink be made of gall. CYM 1.01.101
let 'em suffer | the gall of hazard, so they TNK 2.02. 66
thy honey turns to gall, thy joy to grief! LUC 889
o cruel speeding, fraughted with gall. PP 17.16

/GALLANT 1 FR 0.0001 REL FR 1 V 0 P
/or, /like /a /gallant /horse /fall'n /in /first TRO 3.03.161

GALLANT 55 FR 0.0062 REL FR 38 V 17 P
this gallant which thou seest | was in the wrack TMP 1.02.414
beheld | our royal, good, and gallant ship; 5.01.237
pieces with age to show himself a young gallant! WIV 2.01. 22 P
nay, keep your way, little gallant; 3.02. 1 P
count, count comfect, a sweet gallant surely! ADO 4.01.317 P
a gallant lady. monsieur, fare you well. LLL 2.01.196
the king's command, and this most gallant, 5.01.121 P
and this gallant gentleman, judas machabeus; 5.01.126 P
this gallant pins the wenches on his sleeve; 5.02.321
lover, that kills himself most gallant for love. MND 1.02. 23 P
never did i hear | such gallant chiding; 4.01.115
where is this young gallant that is so desirous AYL 1.02.200 P
but fare thee well, thou art a gallant youth. 1.02.229
a gallant curtle–axe upon my thigh, | a 1.03.117
fetch that gallant hither. 2.02. 17
why so: this gallant will command the sun. SHR 4.03.196
'tis a most gallant fellow. AWW 3.05. 78
sat i' th' stocks all night, poor gallant knave. 4.03.102 P
is monsieur parolles, the gallant militarist — 4.03.141 P
it is a gallant child; WT 1.01. 38 P
before i drew this gallant head of war, | and JN 5.02.113
know the gallant monarch is in arms, | and like 5.02.148
and what said the gallant? R2 5.03. 15
on holy–rood day, the gallant hotspur there, 1H4 1.01. 52
a gallant prize? 1.01. 75
this gallant hotspur, this all–praised knight, 3.02.140
and a head | of gallant warriors, noble 4.04. 26
a gallant knight he was, his name was blunt, 5.03. 20
gentleman, by heaven, and a most gallant leader. 2H4 3.02. 62 P
sweat drops of gallant youth in our rich fields! H5 3.05. 25
world, but i did see him do as gallant service. 3.06. 15 P
and there is gallant and most prave passages. 3.06. 92 P
white hand of my lady, he's a gallant prince. 3.07. 93 P
to horse, you gallant princes! 4.02. 15
o, 'tis a gallant king! 4.07. 10 P
of knights, esquires, and gallant gentlemen, 4.08. 84
and, like a gallant in the brow of youth, 2H6 5.03. 4
and, gallant warwick, do but answer this: 3H6 5.01. 40
bring forth the gallant, let us hear him speak. 5.05. 12
she is a gallant creature, and complete | in H8 3.02. 49
hector's a gallant man. TRO 1.02. 39 P
is't not a gallant man too, is't not? 1.02.213 P
this challenge that the gallant hector sends, 1.03.321
i have, thou gallant troyan, seen thee oft, 4.05.183
god give you joy, sir, of your gallant bride! TIT 1.01.400
the fields are near, and you are gallant grooms. 4.02.164
that gallant spirit hath aspir'd the clouds, ROM 3.01.117
make gallant, young, and noble gentleman, | the 3.05.113
make gallant show and promise of their mettle; JC 4.02. 24
the enemy comes on in gallant show; 5.01. 13
but this gallant | had witchcraft in't, he grew HAM 4.07. 84
goodly and gallant shall be false and perjur'd CYM 3.04. 63
sure he's a gallant gentleman. PER 2.03. 32
she's a gallant lady. 5.01. 66
the master loveless, or kill the gallant knight: PP 15. 6

GALLANTLY 3 FR 0.0003 REL FR 2 V 1 P
on, | his cushes on his thighs, gallantly arm'd, 1H4 4.01.105
duke of exeter has very gallantly maintain'd the H5 3.06. 91 P
he goes forth gallantly. ANT 4.04. 36

GALLANTRY 1 FR 0.0001 REL FR 0 V 1 P
helenus, antenor, and all the gallantry of troy. TRO 3.01.136 P

GALLANTS 15 FR 0.0017 REL FR 9 V 6 P
gallants, i am not as i have been. ADO 3.02. 15 P
and all the gallants of the town are come to 3.04. 96 P
the gallants shall be task'd: LLL 5.02.126
ladies, withdraw; the gallants are at hand. 5.02.308
trim gallants, full of courtship and of state. 5.02.363
come, where be these gallants? who's at home? SHR 3.02. 87
gallants, lads, boys, hearts of gold, all the 1H4 2.04.277 P
that our french gallants shall to–day draw out, H5 4.02. 22
good morrow, gallants, want ye corn for bread? 1H6 3.02. 41
the reformation of our travell'd gallants, H8 1.03. 19
a brace of cyprus gallants that would fain have OTH 2.03. 31 P
'tis a night of revels, the gallants desire it. 2.03. 44 P
market narrowly, meteline is full of gallants. PER 4.02. 4 P
and there he met with brave gallants of war, TNK 3.05. 61
"well hail'd, well hail'd, you jolly gallants! 3.05. 63

GALLANT–SPRINGING
1 FR 0.0001 REL FR 1 V 0 P
when gallant–springing brave plantagenet, | that R3 1.04.221

GALLANT'ST 1 FR 0.0001 REL FR 1 V 0 P
dost overshine the gallant'st dames of rome, TIT 1.01.317

GALL'D 8 FR 0.0009 REL FR 7 V 1 P
and that, my state being gall'd with my expense, WIV 3.04. 5
'a has a little gall'd me, i confess; SHR 5.02. 60
how i am gall'd — mightst bespice a cup, | to WT 1.02.316
an ass, | spurr'd, gall'd, and tir'd by jauncing R2 5.05. 94
upon the daring huntsman that has gall'd him; H8 3.02.207
or else it would have gall'd his surly nature, COR 2.03.195
the bull, being gall'd, gave aries such a knock TIT 4.03. 72
let the gall'd jade winch, our withers are HAM 3.02.242 P

GALLED 8 FR 0.0009 REL FR 8 V 0 P
and they that are most galled with my folly, AYL 2.07. 50
wherein have you been galled by the king? 2H4 4.01. 89
as fearfully as doth a galled rock | o'erhang H5 3.01. 12
that reigns in galled eyes of weeping souls, R3 4.04. 53
some galled goose of winchester would hiss. TRO 5.10. 54
had left the flushing in her galled eyes, | she HAM 1.02.155
welcomes to their cost | the galled traveller, TNK 3.05.129
ranks began | to break upon the galled shore, LUC 1440

GALLERY 4 FR 0.0004 REL FR 4 V 0 P
your gallery | have we pass'd through, not WT 5.03. 10
to me, | for in my gallery thy picture hangs; 1H6 2.03. 37
avoid the gallery. H8 5.01. 86
are coming, we will withdraw | into the gallery. PER 2.02. 59

GALLEY 1 FR 0.0001 REL FR 1 V 0 P
aboard my galley i invite you all. ANT 2.06. 80

GALLEYS 6 FR 0.0006 REL FR 6 V 0 P
two galliasses | and twelve tight galleys. SHR 2.01.379
in a sea–fight 'gainst the count his galleys | i TN 3.03. 26
the galleys | have sent a dozen sequent OTH 1.02. 40
my letters say a hundred and seven galleys. 1.03. 3
a messenger from the galleys. 1.03. 13
his best force | is forth to xan his galleys. ANT 4.11. 3

GALLIA 12 FR 0.0013 REL FR 11 V 1 P
peace, i say, gallia and gaul, french and welsh, WIV 3.01. 97 P
and you withal shall make all gallia shake. H5 1.02.216
and /swear i got them in the gallia wars. 5.01. 89
and from the pride of gallia rescued thee. 1H6 4.06. 15
hath rais'd in gallia have arriv'd our coast, 3H6 5.03. 8
from gallia | i cross'd the seas on purpose and CYM 1.06.201
hear | the legion now in gallia sooner landed 2.04. 18
the pow'rs that he already hath in gallia | will 3.05. 24
and that the legions now in gallia are | full 3.07. 4
remaining now in gallia? 3.07. 12
to them the legions garrison'd in gallia, 4.02.333
the roman legions, all from gallia drawn, | are 4.03. 24

GALLIAN 2 FR 0.0002 REL FR 2 V 0 P
with more than half the gallian territories, 1H6 5.04.139
it seems, much loves | a gallian girl at home. CYM 1.06. 66

GALLIARD 4 FR 0.0004 REL FR 1 V 3 P
what is thy excellence in a galliard, knight? TN 1.03.120 P
go to church in a galliard and come home in a 1.03.128 P
leg, it was form'd under the star of a galliard. 1.03.133 P
france | that can be with a nimble galliard won; H5 1.02.252

GALLIA'S 1 FR 0.0001 REL FR 1 V 0 P
whose life was england's glory, gallia's wonder. 1H6 4.07. 48

GALLIASSES 1 FR 0.0001 REL FR 1 V 0 P
besides two galliasses | and twelve tight SHR 2.01.378

GALLIMAUFRY 2 FR 0.0002 REL FR 1 V 1 P
he loves the gallimaufry, ford. WIV 2.01.115
the wenches say is a gallimaufry of gambols, WT 4.04.328 P

GALLING 3 FR 0.0003 REL FR 2 V 1 P
galling the gleaned land with hot assays, H5 1.02.151
you gleeking and galling at this gentleman twice 5.01. 74 P
galling | his kingly hands haling ropes, | and, PER 4.01. 53

GALLONS 1 FR 0.0001 REL FR 0 V 1 P
item, sack, two gallons ... 5s.8d.. 1H4 2.04.537 P

GALLOP 6 FR 0.0006 REL FR 3 V 3 P

not a false gallop. ADO 3.04. 94 P
this is the very false gallop of verses; AYL 3.02.113 P
who doth he gallop withal? 3.02.326 P
your horsemen peer | and gallop o'er the field. H5 4.07. 86
she'll gallop far enough to her destruction. 2H6 1.03.151
gallop apace, you fiery-footed steeds, | towards ROM 3.02. 1
GALLOPING 1 FR 0.0001 REL FR 1 V 0 P
i did hear | the galloping of horse. MAC 4.01.140
GALLOPS 6 FR 0.0006 REL FR 5 V 1 P
a true man, or a thief, that gallops so? LLL 4.03.185
who time trots withal, who time gallops withal, AYL 3.02.311 P
gallops the zodiac in his glistering coach, TIT 2.01. 7
and in this state she gallops night by night ROM 1.04. 70
sometime she gallops o'er a courtier's nose, 1.04. 77
and gallops to the /tune of "light a' love." TNK 5.02. 54
GALLOW 1 FR 0.0001 REL FR 1 V 0 P
skies | gallow the very wanderers of the dark, LR 3.02. 44
GALLOWAY 1 FR 0.0001 REL FR 0 V 1 P
know we not galloway nags? 2H4 2.04.191 P
/GALLOWGLASSES 1 FR 0.0001 REL FR 1 V 0 P
isles | of kerns and /gallowglasses is supplied, MAC 1.02. 13
GALLOWGLASSES 1 FR 0.0001 REL FR 1 V 0 P
mighty power | of gallowglasses and stout kerns 2H6 4.09. 26
GALLOWS' 1 FR 0.0001 REL FR 1 V 0 P
one time or other break some gallows' back. 2H4 4.03. 29
GALLOWS 20 FR 0.0022 REL FR 7 V 13 P
upon him, his complexion is perfect gallows. TMP 1.01. 30 P
i prophesied, if a gallows were on land, | this 5.01.217
what with the sweat, what with the gallows, and MM 1.02. 83 P
ay, and a shrowd unhappy gallows too. LLL 5.02. 12
even from the gallows did his fell soul fleet, MV 4.01.135
to bring thee to the gallows, not to the font. 4.01.400
with a thief to the gallows; AYL 3.02.327 P
gallows and knock are too powerful on the WT 4.03. 28 P
in as high a flow as the ridge of the gallows. 1H4 1.02. 38 P
shall there be gallows standing in england when 1.02. 59 P
if i hang, i'll make a fat pair of gallows; 2.01. 67 P
hang'd among you, the gallows shall have wrong. 2H4 2.02. 97 P
let gallows gape for dog, let man go free, | and H5 3.06. 42
and you three shall be strangled on the gallows. 2H6 2.03. 8
mark'd for the gallows, lay your weapons down, 4.02.123
belong to th' gallows, and be hang'd, ye rogue! H8 5.03. 6 P
the gallows does well; HAM 5.01. 45 P
dost ill to say the gallows is built stronger 5.01. 47 P
argal, the gallows may do well to thee. 5.01. 48 P
a man would marry a gallows and beget young CYM 5.04.198 P
GALLOWSES 1 FR 0.0001 REL FR 0 V 1 P
there were desolation of jailers and gallowses! CYM 5.04.205 P
GALLOWS-MAKER 1 FR 0.0001 REL FR 0 V 1 P
the gallows-maker, for that outlives a thousand HAM 5.01. 43 P
GALLS* 7 FR 0.0008 REL FR 4 V 3 P
of our livers with the bitterness of your galls; 2H4 1.02.176 P
but the gout galls the one, and the pox pinches 1.02.230 P
enemies | have steep'd their galls in honey, and H5 2.02. 30
when they would seem soldiers, they have galls, TRO 1.03.237
the canker galls the infants of the spring | too HAM 1.03. 39
the heel of the courtier, he galls his kibe. 5.01.141 P
why, we have galls; OTH 4.03. 92
GALLUS 1 FR 0.0001 REL FR 1 V 0 P
gallus, go you along. ANT 5.01. 69
GAM 1 FR 0.0001 REL FR 1 V 0 P
suffolk, | sir richard ketly, davy gam, esquire; H5 4.08.104
GAMBOL 3 FR 0.0003 REL FR 2 V 1 P
hop in his walks and gambol in his eyes; MND 3.01.165
and such other gambol faculties 'a has, that 2H4 2.04.251 P
will reword, which madness | would gambol from. HAM 3.04.144
GAMBOLD 1 FR 0.0001 REL FR 0 V 1 P
is not a comonty a christmas gambold, or a SHR in.2. 138 P
GAMBOLS 4 FR 0.0004 REL FR 2 V 2 P
which /make such wanton gambols with the wind MV 3.02. 93
the wenches say is a gallimaufry of gambols, WT 4.04.328 P
where be your gibes now, your gambols, your HAM 5.01.189 P
i warrant her, she'll do the rarest gambols. TNK 3.05. 75
GAME 27 FR 0.0030 REL FR 22 V 5 P
cried game? WIV 2.03. 88 P
be thus foolishly lost at a game of tick-tack. MM 1.02.190 P
the gentles are at their game, and we will to LLL 4.02.166 P
so shall we stay, mocking intended game, | and 5.02.155
we have had pastimes here and pleasant game. 5.02.360
as waggish boys in game themselves forswear, MND 1.01.240
ay, that way goes the game. 3.02.289
or else a fool | that seest a game play'd home, WT 1.02.248
so thrive it in your game! JN 4.02. 95
have i not here the best cards for the game, 5.02.105
before the game is afoot thou still let'st slip. 1H4 1.03.278
he knows the game; how true he keeps the wind! 3H6 3.02. 14
this way, | under the color of his usual game, 4.05. 11
this way, my lord, for this way lies the game. 4.05. 14
of opportunity, | and daughters of the game. TRO 4.05. 63
the bull has the game, ware horns ho! 5.07. 12 P
and i have horse will follow where the game TIT 2.02. 23
the game was ne'er so fair, and i am /done. ROM 1.04. 39
if our betters play at that game, we must not TIM 1.02. 12
but followed | the sug'red game before thee. 4.03.259
at game, a-swearing, or about some act | that HAM 3.03. 91
and, i'll warrant her, full of game. OTH 2.03. 19 P
if thou dost play with him at any game, | thou ANT 2.03. 26
hark, the game is rous'd! CYM 3.03. 98
the game is up. 3.03.107
and we in herds thy game, i give thee thanks TNK 5.01.132
never fortune | did play a subtler game. 5.04.113
GAME'S 1 FR 0.0001 REL FR 1 V 0 P
the game's afoot! H5 3.01. 32
GAMES 6 FR 0.0006 REL FR 6 V 0 P
rewards | as victors wear at the olympian games. 3H6 2.03. 53
nor play at subtile games — fair virtues all, TRO 4.04. 87
the games are done, and caesar is returning. JC 1.02.178
the hardy youths strive for the games of honor, TNK 2.02. 10
to the games, my friend. 2.03. 62
not far, sir. | are there such games to-day? 2.03. 64
GAMESOME 3 FR 0.0003 REL FR 3 V 0 P
for thou art pleasant, gamesome, passing SHR 2.01.245
i am not gamesome; JC 1.02. 28
a stranger there | so merry and so gamesome. CYM 1.06. 60
GAMESTER 8 FR 0.0009 REL FR 3 V 5 P
keep a gamester from the dice, and a good WIV 3.01. 37 P
you are a gentleman and a gamester, sir. LLL 1.02. 42 P
now will i stir this gamester. AYL 1.01.164 P
sirrah, young gamester, your father were a fool SHR 2.01.400
lord, | and was a common gamester to the camp. AWW 5.03.188
the gentler gamester is the soonest winner. H5 3.06.113 P
you are a merry gamester, | my lord sands. H8 1.04. 45
were you a gamester at five, or at seven? PER 4.06. 75 P
GAMING 2 FR 0.0002 REL FR 2 V 0 P
as gaming, my lord. HAM 2.01. 24
there was 'a gaming, there o'ertook in 's rouse, 2.01. 56
GAMMON 2 FR 0.0002 REL FR 0 V 2 P
i have a gammon of bacon and two razes of ginger 1H4 2.01. 24 P
and there boil like a gammon of bacon that will TNK 4.03. 38 P
GAMOUTH 5 FR 0.0005 REL FR 5 V 0 P
art, | to teach you gamouth in a briefer sort, SHR 3.01. 67
why, i am past my gamouth long ago. 3.01. 71
yet read the gamouth of hortensio. 3.01. 72
"gamouth i am, the ground of all accord: 3.01. 73
call you this gamouth? 3.01. 79
GAN *(also began, can*)*
/GAN 1 FR 0.0001 REL FR 1 V 0 P
and often kiss'd, and often /gan to tear; LC 51
GAN 8 FR 0.0009 REL FR 8 V 0 P
gan vail his stomach and did grace the shame 2H4 1.01.129
when by and by the din of war gan pierce | his COR 2.02.115
gan to look | the way that they did, and to grin CYM 5.03. 37
brain | gan in your duller britain operate 5.05.197
"o, pity," gan she cry, "flint-hearted boy, VEN 95
even so the maid with swelling drops gan wet LUC 1228
leaves the wind | all unseen gan passage find, PP 16. 6
i held my city, | till thus he gan besiege me: LC 177
GANGREN'D 1 FR 0.0001 REL FR 1 V 0 P
the service of the foot | being once gangren'd, COR 3.01.305
GANYMED 8 FR 0.0009 REL FR 7 V 1 P
page, | and therefore look you call me ganymed. AYL 1.03.125
here comes young master ganymed, my new 3.02. 86 P
why, how now, ganymed, sweet ganymed? 4.03.157
why, how now, ganymed, sweet ganymed? 4.03.157
there is more in it. cousin ganymed! 4.03.159
and i for ganymed. 5.02. 86
and i for ganymed. 5.02. 91
and so am i for ganymed. 5.02.100
GANYMEDE 1 FR 0.0001 REL FR 1 V 0 P
just such another wanton ganymede | set /jove TNK 4.02. 15
GAP 12 FR 0.0013 REL FR 10 V 2 P
and leave the growth untried | of that wide gap, WT 4.01. 7
mischief and break a foul gap into the matter, 4.04.197 P
perform'd in this wide gap of time since first 5.03.154
and stop this gap of breath with fulsome dust, JN 3.04. 32
stands in the gap and trade of moe preferments, H8 5.01. 36
confusion | may enter 'twixt the gap of both, COR 3.01.111
it had been as a gap in our great feast, | and MAC 3.01. 12
it would make a great gap in your own honor and LR 1.02. 84 P
that i might sleep out this great gap of time ANT 1.05. 5
on cleopatra too, | and made a gap in nature. 2.02.218
and for the gap | that we shall make in time, CYM 3.02. 62
rather than a gap | should be in their dear TNK 1.04. 8
GAPE 11 FR 0.0012 REL FR 11 V 0 P
against it, | and gape at wid'st to glut him. TMP 1.01. 60
and heard thee, that made gape | the pine, and 1.02.292
whence they gape and point | at your industrious JN 2.01.375
which gape and rub the elbow at the news | of 1H4 5.01. 77
know the grave doth gape | for thee thrice wider 2H4 5.05. 53
the grave doth gape, and doting death is near, H5 2.01. 61
let gallows gape for dog, let man go free, | and 3.06. 42
may that ground gape, and swallow me alive, 3H6 1.01.161
or earth gape open wide and eat him quick, | as R3 1.02. 65
though hell itself should gape | and bid me hold HAM 1.02.244
would you, the /supervisor, grossly gape on? OTH 3.03.395
GAPES 2 FR 0.0002 REL FR 2 V 0 P
earth gapes, hell burns, fiends roar, saints R3 4.04. 75
lie, | and young affection gapes to be his heir; ROM 2.pr. 2
GAPING 10 FR 0.0011 REL FR 8 V 2 P
of night | that the graves, all gaping wide, MND 5.01.380
and every word in it a gaping wound | issuing MV 3.02.265
some men there are love not a gaping pig; 4.01. 47
be rend'red | why he cannot abide a gaping pig; 4.01. 54
gaping wounds | untwind the sisters three! 2H4 2.04.198
with fatal mouths gaping on girded harflew. H5 3.pr. 27
ye rude slaves, leave your gaping. H8 5.03. 3 P
descend | into this gaping hollow of the earth? TIT 2.03.249
who never leave gaping till they swallow'd the PER 2.01. 33 P
about him were a press of gaping faces, | which LUC 1408
GAPS 1 FR 0.0001 REL FR 1 V 0 P
of me, who stand /i' /th' gaps to teach you, PER 4.04. 8
GAR *(also god, got*)*
GAR 27 FR 0.0030 REL FR 0 V 27 P
by gar, it is a shallenge. WIV 1.04.108 P
by gar, i will cut all his two stones; 1.04.111 P
by gar, he shall not have a stone to throw at 1.04.112 P
by gar, i vill kill de jack priest; 1.04.117 P
by gar, i will myself have anne page. 1.04.119 P
by gar, if i have not anne page, i shall turn 1.04.124 P
by gar, he has save his soul, dat he is no come; 2.03. 6 P
by gar, jack rugby, he is dead already, if he be 2.03. 8 P
by gar, de herring is no dead so as i vill kill 2.03. 12 P
by gar, he is de coward jack priest of de vorld; 2.03. 31 P
by gar, then i have as much mock-vater as de 2.03. 62 P
by gar, me vill cut his ears. 2.03. 63 P
by gar, me do look he shall clapper-de-claw me, 2.03. 68 P
me, for, by gar, me vill have it. 2.03. 69 P
by gar, me vill kill de priest, for he speak for 2.03. 82 P
by gar, me dank you vor dat. 2.03. 90 P
by gar, i love you; 2.03. 90 P
by gar, 'tis good; vell said. 2.03. 96 P
by gar, you are de coward, de jack dog, john ape 3.01. 83 P
by gar, with all my heart. 3.01.122 P
by gar, he deceive me too. 3.01.123 P
by gar, 'tis no the fashion of france; 3.03.172 P
by gar, i see 'tis an honest woman. 3.03.222 P
dat is good, by gar; with all my heart! 3.03.241 P
by gar, i am cozen'd. 5.05.204 P
oon pesant, by gar. 5.05.206 P
by gar, i am cozen'd. 5.05.206 P
GARB 5 FR 0.0005 REL FR 3 V 2 P
he could not speak english in the native garb, H5 5.01. 76 P
even with the same austerity and garb | as he COR 4.07. 44
let me comply with you in this garb, /lest /my HAM 2.02.373 P
and constrains the garb | quite from his nature. LR 2.02. 97
abuse him to the moor in the /rank garb | (for i OTH 2.01.306
GARBAGE 2 FR 0.0002 REL FR 2 V 0 P
itself in a celestial bed | and prey on garbage. HAM 1.05. 57
first the lamb, | longs after for the garbage. CYM 1.06. 50
GARBOILS 2 FR 0.0002 REL FR 2 V 0 P
leisure read | the garboils she awak'd: ANT 1.03. 61
so much uncurbable her garboils, caesar, | made 2.02. 67
GARCON *(see garsoon)*
GARDE 1 FR 0.0001 REL FR 0 V 1 P
dieu vous garde, monsieur. TN 3.01. 71 P
GARDEN 35 FR 0.0039 REL FR 26 V 9 P
he hath a garden circummur'd with brick, | whose MM 4.01. 28
which from the vineyard to the garden leads; 4.01. 33
god saw him when he was hid in the garden. ADO 5.01.180 P
the west corner of thy curious-knotted garden. LLL 1.01.246 P
lombardy, | the pleasant garden of great italy, SHR 1.01. 4
as she went to the garden for parsley to stuff a 4.04.100 P
let the garden door be shut, and leave me to my TN 3.01. 92 P
you would seek us, | we are yours i' th' garden. WT 1.02.178
then make /your garden rich in gillyvors, | and 4.04. 98
what sport shall we devise here in this garden R2 3.04. 1
when our sea-walled garden, the whole land, | is 3.04. 43
and dress'd his land | as we this garden! 3.04. 57
old adam's likeness, set to dress this garden, 3.04. 73
good service in a garden where leeks did grow, H5 4.07. 99 P
should not in this best garden of the world, 5.02. 36
by which the world's best garden he achieved, ep 7
thy promises are like adonis' garden, | that one 1H6 1.06. 6
too loud, | the garden here is more convenient. 2.04. 4
grown to this faction in the temple garden, 2.04.125
them now, and they'll o'ergrow the garden, | and 2H6 3.01. 32
on a brick wall have i climb'd into this garden, 4.10. 7 P
is't not enough to break into my garden, | and 4.10. 33
wither, garden, and be henceforth a 4.10. 63 P
i saw good strawberries in your garden there. R3 3.04. 32
do you take the court for parish garden? H8 5.03. 2 P
'tis an unweeded garden | that grows to seed, HAM 1.02.135
'a poisons him i' th' garden for his estate. 3.02.261 P
salt, | to use his eyes for garden water-pots, LR 4.06.196
he's walking in the garden — thus, and spurns ANT 3.05. 16
i'll fetch a turn about the garden, pitying CYM 1.01. 81
this garden has a world of pleasures in't. TNK 2.02.118
and leap the garden, when i see her next, | and 2.02.216
blessed garden, | and fruit and flowers more 2.02.232
may i see the garden? 2.02.268
th' enamell'd knacks o' th' mead or garden! 3.01. 7
GARDENER 1 FR 0.0001 REL FR 1 V 0 P
and adam was a gardener. 2H6 4.02.134
GARDENERS 3 FR 0.0003 REL FR 2 V 1 P
but stay, here come the gardeners. R2 3.04. 24
as gardeners do with ordure hide those roots H5 2.04. 39
gardens, to the which our wills are gardeners; OTH 1.03.321 P
GARDEN-HOUSE 3 FR 0.0003 REL FR 2 V 1 P
and did supply thee at thy garden-house | in her MM 5.01.212
but tuesday night last gone, in 's garden-house, 5.01.229
curses a suing fellow and her garden-house. TNK 4.03. 56 P
GARDEN'S 1 FR 0.0001 REL FR 1 V 0 P
of that kind | our rustic garden's barren, and i WT 4.04. 84
GARDENS 3 FR 0.0003 REL FR 2 V 1 P
our bodies are our gardens, to the which our OTH 1.03.320 P
wishing her cheeks were gardens full of flowers, VEN 65
and many maiden gardens, yet unset, | with SON 16. 6
GARDEZ 1 FR 0.0001 REL FR 0 V 1 P
gardez ma vie, et je vous donnerai deux cents H5 4.04. 42 P
GARDINER 4 FR 0.0004 REL FR 4 V 0 P
where's gardiner? H8 2.02.108
prithee call gardiner to me, my new secretary. 2.02.115
come hither, gardiner. 2.02.120
/stokesly and gardiner, the one of winchester, 4.01.101
GARD'NER 1 FR 0.0001 REL FR 1 V 0 P
gard'ner, for telling me these news of woe, R2 3.04.100
GARD'NERS 1 FR 0.0001 REL FR 0 V 1 P
there is no ancient gentlemen but gard'ners, HAM 5.01. 30 P
GARDON *(also guerdon)*
GARDON 4 FR 0.0004 REL FR 0 V 4 P
gardon, o sweet gardon! LLL 3.01.170 P
gardon, o sweet gardon! 3.01.170 P
most sweet gardon! 3.01.172 P
gardon! 3.01.172 P
GARGANTUA'S 1 FR 0.0001 REL FR 0 V 1 P
you must borrow me gargantua's mouth first; AYL 3.02.225 P
GARGRAVE 2 FR 0.0002 REL FR 2 V 0 P
sir thomas gargrave, and sir william glansdale, 1H6 1.04. 63
sir thomas gargrave, hast thou any life? 1.04. 88
GARISH 2 FR 0.0002 REL FR 2 V 0 P
a garish flag | to be the aim of every dangerous R3 4.04. 88
night, | and pay no worship to the garish sun. ROM 3.02. 25
GARLAND *(also girlond)*
GARLAND 22 FR 0.0024 REL FR 17 V 5 P
what fashion will you wear the garland of? ADO 2.01.189 P
either to make him a garland, as being forsaken, 2.01.218 P
the rod had been made, and the garland too, for 2.01.228 P
too, for the garland he might have worn himself, 2.01.228 P
i'll crop, to make a garland for my head. 1H4 5.04. 73
so thou the garland wear'st successively. 2H4 4.05.201
be you contented, wearing now the garland, | to 5.02. 84
i wear the willow garland for his sake. 3H6 3.03.228
i'll wear the willow garland for his sake." 4.01.100
till richard wear the garland of the realm. R3 3.02. 40
how? wear the garland? dost thou mean the crown? 3.02. 41
him vild, that was your garland. COR 1.01.184
that caius martius | wears this war's garland; 1.09. 60
the third time home with the oaken garland. 2.01.125 P
since | he lurch'd all swords of the garland. 2.02.101
but hold thee, take this garland on thy brow; JC 5.03. 85
as peace should still her wheaten garland wear HAM 5.02. 41
"sing all a green willow must be my garland. OTH 4.03. 51
o, wither'd is the garland of the war, | the ANT 4.15. 64
force and great feat | must put my garland on, TNK 5.01. 44
let him | take off my wheaten garland, or else 5.01.160
the price and garland | to crown the question's 5.03. 16
GARLANDS 9 FR 0.0010 REL FR 8 V 1 P
to her let us garlands bring. TGV 4.02. 53
to make you garlands of, and my sweet friend, WT 4.04.128
bound with triumphant garlands will i come | and R3 4.04.333
and brought me garlands, griffith, which i feel H8 4.02. 91
therewith fantastic garlands did she make | of HAM 4.07.168
you say, must change his horns with garlands! ANT 1.02. 5 P

chariots, and | put garlands on thy head. 3.01. 11
the people's praises, won the garlands, | ere TNK 2.02. 16
whether my brows may not be girt with garlands, 2.03. 80
GARLIC 4 FR 0.0004 REL FR 2 V 2 P
beggar, though she smelt brown bread and garlic. MM 3.02.184 P
most dear actors, eat no onions nor garlic, for MND 4.02. 43 P
marry, garlic, | to mend her kissing with! WT 4.04.162
live | with cheese and garlic in a windmill, far 1H4 3.01.160
GARLIC-EATERS 1 FR 0.0001 REL FR 1 V 0 P
of occupation and | the breath of garlic-eaters! COR 4.06. 98
GARMENT 21 FR 0.0023 REL FR 15 V 6 P
thy hand, | and pluck my magic garment from me.
TMP 1.02. 24
here's a garment for't. 4.01.241 P
there's another garment for't. 4.01.244 P
as if the garment had been made for me; TGV 4.04.163
a devil in an everlasting garment hath him; ERR 4.02. 33
and every officer his wedding garment on? SHR 4.01. 49 P
that they were to be known by garment, not by WT 5.02. 48 P
son, | when i will wear a garment all of blood, 1H4 3.02.135
to face the garment of rebellion | with some 5.01. 74
this new and gorgeous garment, majesty, | sits 2H4 5.02. 44
dashing the garment of this peace, aboded | the H8 1.01. 93
his mean'st garment | that ever hath but clipt CYM 2.03.133
"his garment"! 2.03.139
you have abus'd me. | "his meanest garment"! 2.03.150
i'll be reveng'd. | "his mean'st garment"! well. 2.03.156
poor i am stale, a garment out of fashion, | and 3.04. 51
she held the very garment of posthumus in more 3.05.135 P
world, a garment | nobler than that it covers! 5.04.134
we that made up this garment through the rough PER 2.01.149 P
"who wears a garment shapeless and unfinish'd? VEN 415
"thus merely with the garment of a grace, | the LC 316
GARMENTS' 1 FR 0.0001 REL FR 1 V 0 P
richer than wealth, prouder than garments' cost, SON 91.10
GARMENTS 50 FR 0.0056 REL FR 31 V 19 P
did give us, with | rich garments, linens, TMP 1.02.164
on their sustaining garments not a blemish, 1.02.218
hence! hang not on my garments. 1.02.475
that our garments, being, as they were, drench'd 2.01. 62 P
methinks our garments are now as fresh as when 2.01. 69 P
talking that our garments seem now as fresh as 2.01. 97 P
and look how well my garments sit upon me, 2.01.272
how you should know my daughter by her garments?
WIV 5.05.196 P
say so, master, if your garments were thin. ERR 3.01. 70
and saw me court margaret in hero's garments, ADO 5.01.238 P
the man | by the athenian garments he hath on. MND 2.01.264
the man | by the athenian garments he had on? 3.02.349
look what notes and garments he doth give thee, MV 3.04. 51
wint'red garments must be lin'd, | so must AYL 3.02.105
description — | such garments and such years. 4.03. 85
our purses shall be proud, our garments poor, SHR 4.03.171
judgments are | mere fathers of their garments; AWW 1.02. 62
the cutting of my garments would serve the turn, 4.01. 46 P
me first on shore | hath my maid's garments. TN 5.01.275
be a footman by the garments he has left with WT 4.03. 66 P
in't) and change garments with this gentleman. 4.04.635 P
his garments are rich, but he wears them not 4.04.749 P
stuffs out his vacant garments with his form; JN 3.04. 97
the nonce, to immask our noted outward garments.
1H4 1.02.180 P
to beslubber our garments with it and swear it 2.04.310 P
it yearns me not if men my garments wear; H5 4.03. 26
witness the night, your garments, your lowliness 4.08. 52 P
thy garments are not spotted with our blood; R3 1.03.282
how he did lap me | even in his /own garments, 2.01.117
may i change these garments? COR 2.03.146
i shall shake thy bones | out of thy garments. 3.01.179
like our strange garments, cleave not to their MAC 1.03.145
long it could not be | till that her garments, HAM 4.07.181
only i do not like the fashion of your garments. LR 3.06. 80 P
in nothing am i chang'd | but in my garments. 4.06. 10
of sleep | we put fresh garments on him. 4.07. 21
the skill i have | remembers not these garments; 4.07. 66
"his garments"! now the devil — CYM 2.03.137
of thy late master's garments in thy possession? 3.05.124 P
i would these garments were come. 3.05.132 P
be those the garments? 3.05.146 P
how fit his garments serve me! 4.01. 2 P
thy garments cut to pieces before /her face: 4.01. 17 P
the garments of posthumus? 4.02.308
in a frenzy, in my master's garments | (which he 5.05.282
one, i like the manner of your garments well. PER 4.02.134 P
give me fresh garments. 5.01.214
hidden sun, | breaks through his baser garments. TNK 2.05. 24
you shall have garments, and | perfumes to kill 3.01. 85
some in their garments, though new-fangled ill, SON 91. 3
GARNER'D 1 FR 0.0001 REL FR 1 V 0 P
but there, where i have garner'd up my heart, OTH 4.02. 57
GARNERS 2 FR 0.0002 REL FR 2 V 0 P
foison plenty, | barns and garners never empty; TMP 4.01.111
take these rats thither | to gnaw their garners. COR 1.01.250
GARNISH 2 FR 0.0002 REL FR 2 V 0 P
sweet, | even in the lovely garnish of a boy. MV 2.06. 45
to seek the beauteous eye of heaven to garnish, JN 4.02. 15
GARNISH'D 2 FR 0.0002 REL FR 2 V 0 P
garnish'd like him, that for a tricksy word MV 3.05. 69
garnish'd and deck'd in modest complement, | not
H5 2.02.134
GARNISHED 1 FR 0.0001 REL FR 1 V 0 P
that every one her own hath garnished | with LLL 2.01. 78
GARRET 1 FR 0.0001 REL FR 0 V 1 P
he did speak them to me in the garret one night, 2H6 1.03.191 P
GARRISON 1 FR 0.0001 REL FR 1 V 0 P
no interest | in any of our towns of garrison. 1H6 5.04.168
GARRISON'D 2 FR 0.0002 REL FR 2 V 0 P
yes, it is already garrison'd. HAM 4.04. 24
to them the legions garrison'd in gallia, CYM 4.02.333
GARRISONS 1 FR 0.0001 REL FR 1 V 0 P
commons, | have i dispursed to the garrisons, 2H6 3.01.117
GARSOON 1 FR 0.0001 REL FR 0 V 1 P
i ha' married oon garsoon, a boy; WIV 5.05.205 P
GARTER *(also jarteer)*
GARTER 18 FR 0.0020 REL FR 6 V 12 P
being in love, could not see to garter his hose; TGV 2.01. 76 P
is (lastly and finally) mine host of the garter. WIV 1.01.141 P
mine host of the garter! 1.03. 1 P
pawn'd his horses to mine host of the garter. 2.01. 97 P
does he lie at the garter? 2.01.180 P
look where my ranting host of the garter comes. 2.01.189 P
good mine host o' th' garter, a word with you. 2.01.203 P
i'll be judgment by mine host of the garter. 3.01. 96 P
hear mine host of the garter. 3.01.100 P
cogging companion, the host of the garter. 3.01.121 P
pyramus and hang'd himself in thisby's garter, MND 5.01.359 P
why dost thou garter up thy arms a' this fashion AWW 2.03.250 P
of it he will unloose, | familiar as his garter; H5 1.01. 47
to tear the garter from thy craven's leg, 1H6 4.01. 15
knights of the garter were of noble birth, 4.01. 34
now, by my george, my garter, and my crown — R3 4.04.366
thy garter, blemish'd, pawn'd his knightly 4.04.370
lend me a garter. OTH 5.01. 82
GARTER'S 1 FR 0.0001 REL FR 1 V 0 P
sing, | like to the garter's compass, in a ring. WIV 5.05. 66
GARTERS 3 FR 0.0003 REL FR 0 V 3 P
and their garters of an indifferent knit; SHR 4.01. 92 P
hang thyself in thine own heir-apparent garters! 1H4 2.02. 44 P
hah, ha, he wears cruel garters. LR 2.04. 7 P
GART'RED 1 FR 0.0001 REL FR 0 V 1 P
on the other, gart'red with a red and blue list; SHR 3.02. 67 P
GASH 5 FR 0.0005 REL FR 4 V 1 P
a perilous gash, a very limb lopp'd off — | and 1H4 4.01. 43
thou lay'st in every gash that love hath given TRO 1.01. 62
every gash was an enemy's grave. COR 2.01.155 P
and each new day a gash | is added to her wounds MAC 4.03. 40
give me a gash, put me to present pain, | lest PER 5.01.191
GASH'D 1 FR 0.0001 REL FR 1 V 0 P
and his gash'd stabs look'd like a breach in MAC 2.03.113
GASHES 6 FR 0.0006 REL FR 6 V 0 P
kisses the gashes | that bloodily did yawn upon H5 4.06. 13
but i am faint, my gashes cry for help. MAC 1.02. 42
with twenty trenched gashes on his head, | the 3.04. 26
i see lives, the gashes | do better upon them. 5.08. 2
wounds, and kiss | the honor'd gashes whole. ANT 4.08. 11
that makes more gashes where no breach should be
VEN 1066
GASKINS 1 FR 0.0001 REL FR 0 V 1 P
or, if both break, your gaskins fall. TN 1.05. 25 P
GASP 8 FR 0.0009 REL FR 7 V 1 P
and i will follow thee | to the last gasp, with AYL 2.03. 70
cannot look greenly, nor gasp out my eloquence, H5 5.02.143 P
recreants, | fight till the last gasp; 1H6 1.02.127
neck, | and in his bosom spend my latter gasp. 2.05. 38
that makes him gasp, and stare, and catch the 2H6 3.02.371
your brave father breath'd his latest gasp, 3H6 2.01.108
and to the latest gasp cried out for warwick, 5.02. 41
lie speechless, and his name | is at last gasp. CYM 1.05. 53
/GASPING 1 FR 0.0001 REL FR 1 V 0 P
/gasping /for /life /under /great /bullingbrook, 2H4 1.01.208
GASPING 2 FR 0.0002 REL FR 2 V 0 P
and, gasping to begin some speech, her eyes WT 3.03. 25
and i, a gasping new-deliver'd mother, | have R2 2.02. 65
GASTED 1 FR 0.0001 REL FR 1 V 0 P
or whether gasted by the noise i made, | full LR 2.01. 55
GASTNESS 1 FR 0.0001 REL FR 1 V 0 P
do you perceive the gastness of her eye? OTH 5.01.106
GAT *(also got*)*
GAT 2 FR 0.0002 REL FR 2 V 0 P
praise him that gat thee, she that gave thee TRO 2.03.241
child, whom nature gat | for men to see, and PER 2.02. 6
GATE 55 FR 0.0062 REL FR 42 V 13 P
and to that vineyard is a planched gate, | that MM 4.01. 30
and bid them bring the trumpets to the gate. 4.05. 9
dromio, keep the gate. ERR 2.02.206
master, shall i be porter at the gate? 2.02.217
who are those at the gate? 3.01. 48
go fetch me something: i'll break ope the gate. 3.01. 73
no, but to the gate, and there will the devil ADO 2.01. 43 P
climb o'er the house to unlock the little gate. LLL 1.01.109
groves may tread | even till the eastern gate, MND 3.02.391
whiles we shut the gate upon one wooer, another MV 1.02.133
madam, there is alighted at your gate | a young 2.09. 86
villain, i say, knock me at this gate, | and rap SHR 1.02. 11
i bade the rascal knock upon your gate, | and 1.02. 37
knock at the gate? 1.02. 39 P
and come you now with "knocking at the gate"? 1.02. 43 P
he that knocks as he would beat down the gate? 5.01. 17 P
i am for the house with the narrow gate, which i AWW 4.05. 51 P
that leads to the broad gate and the great fire. 4.05. 54 P
there is at the gate a young gentleman much TN 1.05. 99 P
what is he at the gate, cousin? 1.05.117 P
there's one at the gate. 1.05.126 P
make me a willow cabin at your gate, | and call 1.05.268
'gainst knaves and thieves men shut their gate, 5.01.395
who keeps the gate here ho? where is the earl? 2H4 1.01. 1
please it your honor knock but at the gate, 1.01. 5
in | their heavy burthens at his narrow gate, H5 1.02.201
i think at the north gate, for there stands 1H6 1.04. 66
and sends the poor well pleased from my gate. 2H6 4.10. 23
open thy gate of mercy, gracious god! 3H6 1.04.177
and brought your prisoner to your palace gate. 3.02.119
that's clapp'd upon the court gate. H8 1.03. 18
or, like a gate of steel | fronting the sun, TRO 3.03.121
alone he ent'red | the mortal gate of th' city, COR 2.02.111
bring me but out at gate. 4.01. 47
before the palace gate | to brave the tribune in TIT 4.02. 35
peter, stay at the gate. ROM 2.05. 20 P
no porter at his gate, | but rather one that TIM 2.01. 10
go to the gate, somebody knocks. JC 2.01. 60
if a man were porter of hell gate, he should MAC 2.03. 2 P
they are, my lord, without the palace gate. 3.01. 46
from hence to th' palace gate | make it their 3.03. 13
there's knocking at the gate. 5.01. 67 P
beat at this gate, that let thy folly in | and LR 1.04.271
hot questrists after him, met him at gate, | who 3.07. 17
if wolves had at thy gate howl'd that /dearn 3.07. 63
both stile and gate, horse-way and foot-path. 4.01. 56 P
to saint peter, | and keeps the gate of hell! OTH 4.02. 92
hark, hark, the lark at heaven's gate sings, CYM 2.03. 20
boys, this gate | instructs you how t' adore the 3.03. 2
that, knowing sin within, will touch the gate. PER 1.01. 80
to love's alarms it will not ope the gate; VEN 424
soft pity enters at an iron gate. LUC 595
with gold, but stol'n from forth thy gate. 1068
from sullen earth) sings hymns at heaven's gate, SON 29.12
who glaz'd with crystal gate the glowing roses LC 286
GATES 86 FR 0.0097 REL FR 77 V 9 P
did antonio open | the gates of milan, and, i' TMP 1.02.130
who do prepare to meet him at the gates, | there MM 4.03.131
and why meet him at the gates, and /redeliver 4.04. 6 P
and gravest citizens | have hent the gates, and 4.06. 14
and here the abbess shuts the gates on us, | and ERR 5.01.156
for thee i'll lock up all the gates of love, ADO 4.01.105
hand | took up a beggar's issue at my gates, 4.01.132
for he carried the town gates on his back like a LLL 1.02. 72 P
as much as thou didst me in carrying gates. 1.02. 75 P
course, | before we enter his forbidden gates, 2.01. 26
may not come, fair princess, within my gates, 2.01.171
through athens gates have we devis'd to steal. MND 1.01.213
shall break the locks | of prison gates; 1.02. 34
who shut their coward gates on atomies, | should AYL 3.05. 13
i heard you were saucy at my gates, and allow'd TN 1.05.197 P
to the gates of tartar, thou most excellent 2.05.205 P
whiles other men have gates, and those gates WT 1.02.197
other men have gates, and those gates open'd, 1.02.197
welcome before the gates of angiers, duke. JN 2.01. 17
/your city's eyes, your winking gates; 2.01.215
have brought a countercheck before your gates, 2.01.224
have we ramm'd up our gates against the world. 2.01.272
you men of angiers, open wide your gates, | and 2.01.300
open your gates and give the victors way. 2.01.324
our former scruple in our strong-barr'd gates, 2.01.370
than battery can | to our fast-closed gates; 2.01.447
now, citizens of angiers, ope your gates, | let 2.01.536
even at my gates, with ranks of foreign pow'rs; 4.02.244
by his gates of breath | there lies a downy 2H4 4.05. 31
the gates of mercy shall be all shut up, | and H5 3.03. 10
enter our gates, dispose of us and ours, | for 3.03. 49
open your gates. 3.03. 51
open the gates, 'tis gloucester that calls. 1H6 1.03. 4
break up the gates, i'll be your warrantize. 1.03. 13
open the gates, here's gloucester that would 1.03. 17
open the gates, or i'll shut thee out shortly. 1.03. 26
open the gates unto the lord protector, | or 1.03. 27
these are the city-gates, the gates of roan, 3.02. 1
go to the gates of burdeaux, trumpeter, | summon 4.02. 1
will cry for vengeance at the gates of heaven. 5.04. 53
my sword therefore broke through london gates, 2H6 4.08. 24 P
set ope thy everlasting gates | to entertain my 4.09. 13
march'd through the city to the palace gates. 3H6 1.01. 92
off with his head, and set it on york gates, 1.04.179
see how the morning opes her golden gates, | and 2.01. 21
and on the gates of york | they set the same, 2.01. 65
yet that thy brazen gates of heaven may ope 2.03. 40
from off the gates of york fetch down the head, 2.06. 52
from ravenspurgh haven before the gates of york, 4.07. 8
the gates made fast? 4.07. 10
and shut the gates for safety of ourselves; 4.07. 18
open the gates, we are king henry's friends. 4.07. 28
ay, say you so? the gates shall then be opened. 4.07. 29
these gates must not be shut | but in the night 4.07. 35
the gates are open, let us enter too. 5.01. 60
of reason, | /let's shut our gates and sleep. TRO 2.02. 47
mine uncle down, | he shall unbolt the gates. 4.02. 3
strong as pluto's gates: 5.02.153
i'll bring you to the gates. 5.02.188
our gates, | which yet seem shut, we have but COR 1.04. 17
so, now the gates are ope; 1.04. 43
who upon the sudden | clapp'd to their gates. 1.04. 51
and shut your gates upon 's. 1.07. 6
alone martius did fight | within corioles gates; 2.01.163
was touch'd, | they would not thread the gates. 3.01.124
tarpeian, never more | to enter our rome gates. 3.03.104
go see him out at gates, and follow him, | as he 3.03.138
come, come, let's see him out at gates, come. 3.03.142
whether to knock against the gates of rome, | or 4.05.141
and sowl the porter of rome gates by th' ears. 4.05.201 P
have push'd out your gates the very defender of 5.02. 39 P
i have been blown out of your gates with sighs, 5.02. 75 P
are stronger than | your gates against my force. 5.02. 89
tide, | as the recomforted through th' gates. 5.04. 48
led your wars even to | the gates of rome. 5.06. 76
open the gates and let me in. TIT 1.01. 62
saturnine and his empress | beg at the gates, 3.01.298
the gates shut on me, and turn'd weeping out 5.03.105
great triumphers | in their applauding gates. TIM 5.01.197
against our rampir'd gates and they shall ope, 5.04. 47
are rid like madmen through the gates of rome. JC 3.02.269
the natural gates and alleys of the body, | and HAM 1.05. 67
go thrust him out at gates, and let him smell LR 3.07. 93
the gates of monarchs | are arch'd so high that CYM 3.03. 4
and on the gates of lud's-town set your heads. 4.02. 99
nor gates of steel so strong, but time decays? SON 65. 8
GATHER 25 FR 0.0028 REL FR 25 V 0 P
now does my project gather to a head: TMP 5.01. 1
gather the sequel by that went before. ERR 1.01. 95
the reason that i gather he is mad, | besides 4.03. 86
yet to me, | and i of him will gather patience. ADO 5.01. 19
having come to padua | to gather in some debts, SHR 4.04. 25
art, will lead thee on | to gather from thee. AWW 4.01. 82
by this we gather | you have tripp'd since. WT 1.02. 75
thus may we gather honey from the weed, | and H5 4.01. 11
to gather our soldiers, scatter'd and dispers'd, 1H6 2.01. 76
the rest i wish thee gather; 2.05. 96
men | that come to gather money for their corn. 3.02. 5
but gather we our forces out of hand, | and set 3.02.102
then gather strength and march unto him straight 4.01. 73
charge, | among the people gather up a tenth. 5.05. 93
but get you to smithfield and gather head, | and 2H6 4.05. 9
or gather wealth, i care not with what envy. 4.10. 21
and to gather | so much as from occasion you may
HAM 2.02. 15
now gather, and surmise. 2.02.108
and gather by him, as he is behav'd, | if't be 3.01. 34
you may gather more. LR 4.05. 32
yet the dew's on ground, gather those flowers; CYM 1.05. 1
and by them gather | their several virtues and 1.05. 22
is gone to th' wood to gather mulberries. TNK 4.01. 68
and she must gather flowers to bury you, | and 4.01. 78
then from this gather | how i should tender you. 5.01. 24
GATHER'D 6 FR 0.0006 REL FR 5 V 1 P
my lord, my lord, the french have gather'd head. 1H6 1.04.100
there's an army gather'd together in smithfield. 2H6 4.06. 11 P

that they had gather'd a wise council to them H8 2.04. 51
of him i gather'd honor, | which he to seek of CYM 3.01. 70
i shall be gather'd, | i think so, but i know TNK 5.01.170
among weeds, or flowers with flowers gather'd. SON 124. 4
GATHERED 4 FR 0.0004 REL FR 4 V 0 P
a night | medea gathered the enchanted herbs MV 5.01. 13
and more than may be gathered by thy shape. 1H6 2.03. 69
my soldiers, gathered flocks of friends, | /and 3H6 2.01.112
the goths have gathered head, and with a power TIT 4.04. 63
GATHERING 2 FR 0.0002 REL FR 2 V 0 P
ere foul sin gathering head | shall break into R2 5.01. 58
time will come, that foul sin, gathering head, 2H4 3.01. 76
GATHERS 1 FR 0.0001 REL FR 1 V 0 P
half way down | hangs one that gathers sampire, LR 4.06. 15
GATH'RED 2 FR 0.0002 REL FR 2 V 0 P
upon a gath'red lily almost withered. TIT 3.01.113
flowers that are not gath'red in their prime VEN 131
GAUD 1 FR 0.0001 REL FR 1 V 0 P
as the remembrance of an idle gaud | which in my MND 4.01.167
GAUDEO 1 FR 0.0001 REL FR 0 V 1 P
video, et gaudeo. LLL 5.01. 31 P
GAUDS *(also gawds)*
GAUDS 1 FR 0.0001 REL FR 1 V 0 P
that, having two fair gauds of equal sweetness, TNK 4.02. 53
GAUDY 9 FR 0.0010 REL FR 9 V 0 P
weeds | nip not the gaudy blossoms of your love LLL 5.02.802
therefore then, thou gaudy gold, | hard food for MV 3.02.101
the gaudy, blabbing, and remorseful day | is 2H6 4.01. 1
but not express'd in fancy, rich, not gaudy, HAM 1.03. 71
come, | let's have one other gaudy night. ANT 3.13.182
to tell the world 'tis but a gaudy shadow | that TNK 2.02.103
on, | under whose brim the gaudy sun would peep; VEN 1088
and when his gaudy banner is display'd, | the LUC 272
ornament, | and only herald to the gaudy spring, SON 1.10
GAUGE 1 FR 0.0001 REL FR 1 V 0 P
you shall not gauge me | by what we do to–night. MV 2.02.199
GAUL 1 FR 0.0001 REL FR 0 V 1 P
peace, i say, gallia and gaul, french and welsh, WIV 3.01. 97 P
GAULTIER *(see gualtier)*
GAULTREE 1 FR 0.0001 REL FR 1 V 0 P
'tis gaultree forest, and't shall please your 2H4 4.01. 2
GAUNT* 35 FR 0.0039 REL FR 31 V 4 P
old john of gaunt, time–honored lancaster, R2 1.01. 1
ah, gaunt, his blood was thine! 1.02. 22
call it not patience, gaunt, it is despair. 1.02. 29
farewell, old gaunt! 1.02. 44
farewell, old gaunt! 1.02. 54
and furbish new the name of john a' gaunt, 1.03. 76
old john of gaunt is grievous sick, my lord, 1.04. 54
what comfort, man? how is't with aged gaunt? 2.01. 72
old gaunt indeed, and gaunt in being old. 2.01. 74
old gaunt indeed, and gaunt in being old. 2.01. 74
and who abstains from meat that is not gaunt? 2.01. 76
watching breeds leanness, leanness is all gaunt. 2.01. 78
and therein fasting, hast thou made me gaunt. 2.01. 81
gaunt am i for the grave, gaunt as a grave, 2.01. 82
gaunt am i for the grave, gaunt as a grave, 2.01. 82
liege, old gaunt commends him to your majesty. 2.01.147
whereof our uncle gaunt did stand possess'd. 2.01.162
is not gaunt dead? 2.01.191
was not gaunt just? 2.01.192
lord of such hot youth | as when brave gaunt, 2.03.100
for methinks in you | i see old gaunt alive. 2.03.118
he should have found his uncle gaunt a father 2.03.127
head, | and by the buried hand of warlike gaunt, 3.03.109
indeed i am not john of gaunt, your grandfather, 1H4 2.02. 67 P
the seat of gaunt, dukedom of lancaster. 5.01. 45
john a' gaunt lov'd him well, and betted much 2H4 3.02. 44 P
as familiarly of john a' gaunt as if he had been 3.02.320 P
it, and told john a' gaunt he beat his own name, 3.02.324 P
he | from john of gaunt doth bring his pedigree, 1H6 2.05. 77
next to whom | was john of gaunt, the duke of 2H6 2.02. 14
the eldest son and heir of john of gaunt, 2.02. 22
henry doth claim the crown from john of gaunt, 2.02. 54
such hope have all the line of john of gaunt! 3H6 1.01. 19
then warwick disannuls great john of gaunt, 3.03. 81
and after john of gaunt, henry the fourth, 3.03. 83
GAUNTLET 3 FR 0.0003 REL FR 2 V 1 P
a scaly gauntlet now with joints of steel | must 2H4 1.01.146
by mars his gauntlet, thanks! TRO 4.05.177
there's my gauntlet, i'll prove it on a giant. LR 4.06. 90 P
GAUNTLETS 2 FR 0.0002 REL FR 2 V 0 P
their thimbles into armed gauntlets change, JN 5.02.156
but use your gauntlets though. TNK 3.06. 64
GAUNT'S 1 FR 0.0001 REL FR 1 V 0 P
not gaunt's rebukes, nor england's private R2 2.01.166
/GAVE 1 FR 0.0001 REL FR 1 V 0 P
/casualties, /gave /her /dear /rights | /to /his LR 4.03. 44
GAVE 252 FR 0.0284 REL FR 224 V 28 P
in the same fashion as you gave in charge, TMP 5.01. 8
but three glasses since, we gave out split — 5.01.223
(a lost mutton) gave your letter to her (a lac'd TGV 1.01. 96 P
and she (a lac'd mutton) gave me (a lost mutton) 1.01. 97 P
say, say; who gave it thee? 1.02. 37
she gave me none, except an angry word. 2.01.158 P
yourself, sweet lady, for you gave the fire. 2.04. 37 P
when i was sick, you gave me bitter pills, | and 2.04.149
and ev'n that pow'r which gave me first my oath 2.06. 4
i gave him gentle looks, thereby to find | that 3.01. 31
this ring i gave him when he parted from me, 4.04. 97
times | his julia gave it him at his departure: 4.04.135
why, this is the ring i gave to julia. 5.04. 93
at my depart | i gave this unto julia. 5.04. 97
behold her that gave aim to all thy oaths, | and 5.04.101
page's wife, who even now gave me good eyes too, WIV 1.03. 59 P
and gave such orderly and well–behav'd reproof 2.01. 58 P
deep | gave any tragic instance of our harm: ERR 1.01. 64
gave healthful welcome to their shipwrack'd 1.01.114
where have you left the money that i gave you? 1.02. 54
where is the gold i gave in charge to thee? 1.02. 70
to me, sir? why, you gave no gold to me. 1.02. 71
"where is the thousand marks i gave thee, 2.01. 65
the gold i gave to dromio is laid up | safe at 2.02. 1
home to the centaur with the gold you gave me. 2.02. 16
for this something that you gave me for nothing. 2.02. 52 P
were parchment, and the blows you gave were ink, 3.01. 13
come, come, you know i gave it you even now. 4.01. 55
you know i gave it you half an hour since. 4.01. 65
you gave me none, you wrong me much to say so. 4.01. 66
why, sir, i gave the money for the rope. 4.04. 12
he lent it me awhile, and i gave him use for it, ADO 2.01.279 P
beside | and prodigally gave them all to you. LLL 2.01. 12
who gave thee this letter? 4.01.101
no, they are free that gave these tokens to us. 5.02.424
and to confirm it plain, | you gave me this: 5.02.453
of lances the almighty, | gave hector a gift" — 5.02.645
gave hector a gift, the heir of ilion; 5.02.652
which straight she gave me, and her fairy sent MND 4.01. 60
in faith, i gave it to the judge's clerk. MV 5.01.143
gave it a judge's clerk! 5.01.157
now, by this hand, i gave it to a youth, | a 5.01.161
i gave my love a ring, and made him swear 5.01.170
my lord bassanio gave his ring away | unto the 5.01.179
what ring gave you, my lord? 5.01.184
if you did know to whom i gave the ring, | if 5.01.193
if you did know for whom i gave the ring, | and 5.01.194
and would conceive for what i gave the ring, 5.01.195
or half her worthiness that gave the ring, | or 5.01.200
by heaven, it is the same i gave the doctor! 5.01.257
something that nature gave me his countenance AYL 1.01. 18 P
who gave me fresh array and entertainment, 4.03.143
gave me my being and my father first, | a SHR 1.01. 11
grumio gave order how it should be done. 4.03.117
i gave him no order, i gave him the stuff. 4.03.118
i gave him no order, i gave him the stuff. 4.03.118
as she stood, | and gave this sentence then: AWW 1.03. 76
on 's bed of death | many receipts he gave me; 2.01.105
that gave him out incurable — 2.03. 14 P
this ring was mine, and, when i gave it helen, 5.03. 83
mine, 'twas helen's, | whoever gave it you. 5.03.105
finger, | unless she gave it to yourself in bed, 5.03.110
all that | he gave it to a commoner a' th' camp, 5.03.194
and this was it i gave him, being a–bed. 5.03.228
where did you buy it? or who gave it you? 5.03.271
i never gave it him. 5.03.276
this ring was mine, i gave it his first wife. 5.03.279
this pearl she gave me, i do feel't and see't, TN 4.03. 2
his life i gave him, and did thereto add | my 5.01. 80
to execute the charge my father gave me | for WT 5.01.162
that the oracle | gave hope thou wast in being, 5.03.127
my father gave me honor, yours gave land. JN 1.01.164
my father gave me honor, yours gave land. 1.01.164
the latest breath that gave the sound of words 3.01.230
that in your chambers gave you chastisement? 5.02.147
whereto thy tongue a party–verdict gave. R2 1.03.234
but you gave leave to my unwilling tongue 1.03.245
but if i could, by him that gave me life, | i 2.03.155
and there at venice gave | his body to that 4.01. 97
no joyful tongue gave him his welcome home, 5.02. 29
anon | he gave his nose and took't away again, 1H4 1.03. 39
my puny drawer to what end he gave me the sugar, 2.04. 31 P
and he of wales that gave amamon the bastinado 2.04.336 P
well, | and gave the tongue a helpful ornament, 3.01.123
and gave his countenance, against his name, | to 3.02. 65
home, | my father gave him welcome to the shore; 4.03. 59
gave him their heirs as pages, followed him 4.03. 72
he gave you all the duties of a man, | trimm'd 5.02. 55
my death, i gave him this wound in the thigh. 5.04.151 P
with that he gave his able horse the head, | and 2H4 1.01. 43
the box of the year that the prince gave you, he 1.02.195 P
prince gave you, he gave it like a rude prince, 1.02.195 P
and the boy that i gave falstaff. 2.02. 70 P
even to the eyes of richard | gave him defiance. 3.01. 65
the just proportion that we gave them out. 4.01. 23
give that which gave thee life unto the worms, 4.05.116
you won it, wore it, kept it, gave it me; 4.05.221
your father) | i gave bold way to my authority, 5.02. 82
up, | gave thee no instance why thou shouldst do H5 2.02.119
came into mine eyes | and gave me up to tears. 4.06. 32
and he that i gave it to in change promis'd to 4.08. 29 P
porter, remember what i gave in charge, | and 1H6 2.03. 1
i gave thee life, and rescu'd thee from death. 4.06. 5
i gave a noble to the priest | the morn that i 5.04. 23
i would the milk | thy mother gave thee, when 5.04. 28
the happiest gift that ever marquess gave, | the 2H6 1.01. 15
till suffolk gave two dukedoms for his daughter. 1.03. 87
i never gave them condign punishment. 3.01.130
things well, | according as i gave directions? 3.02. 12
the ruthless queen gave him to dry his cheeks 3H6 2.01. 61
got, | my careless father fondly gave away"? 2.02. 38
blood, | the noble gentleman gave up the ghost. 2.03. 22
thy father gave thee life too soon, | and hath 2.05. 92
which, whiles it lasted, gave king henry light. 2.06. 2
which in the time of death he gave our father. 2.06. 67
matter of marriage was the charge he gave me, 3.03.258
and warwick, doing what you gave in charge, | is 4.01. 32
'twas i that gave the kingdom to thy brother. 5.01. 34
who gave his blood to lime the stones together, 5.01. 84
whose arms gave shelter to the princely eagle, 5.02. 12
if to have done the thing you gave in charge R3 4.03. 25
thy head (all indirectly) gave direction. 4.04.226
nought rebell'd, | order gave each thing view; H8 1.01. 44
gave notice | he was from thence discharg'd? 2.04. 33
and that gave to me | many a groaning throe. 2.04.199
and your master) with his own hand gave me; 3.02.247
the king, that gave it. 3.02.251
out of the pain you suffer'd, gave no ear to't. 4.02. 8
to whom he gave these words: 4.02. 20
he gave his honors to the world again, | his 4.02. 29
he was ill, and gave | the clergy ill example. 4.02. 43
my mind gave me, | in seeking tales and 5.02.144
in daily thanks, that gave us such a prince, 5.02.150
i gave ye | power as he was a councillor to try 5.02.177
your full consent | gave wings to my propension, TRO 2.02.133
him that gat thee, she that gave thee suck; 2.03.241
neither gave to me | good word nor look. 3.03.143
human powers, | and gave him graceful posture. COR 2.01.221
whoever gave that counsel, to give forth | the 3.01.113
and in true fear | they gave us our demands." 3.01.135
and yet my mind gave me his clothes made a false 4.05.150 P
and cowardly nobles gave way unto your clusters, 4.06.122
gave him way | in all his own desires; 5.06. 31
to be controll'd in that he frankly gave. TIT 1.01.420
gave you a dancing–rapier by your side, | are 2.01. 39
that gave thee life when well he might have 2.03.159
ovid's metamorphosis, | my mother gave it me. 4.01. 43
of that self blood that first gave life to you, 4.02.123
gave aries such a knock | that down fell both 4.03. 72
and for my tidings gave me twenty kisses. 5.01.120
i gave thee mine before thou didst request it; ROM 2.02.128
you gave us the counterfeit fairly last night. 2.04. 45 P
cell, | and gave him what becomed love i might, 4.02. 26
then gave i her (so tutor'd by my art) | a 5.03.243
i gave it freely ever, and there's none | can TIM 1.02. 10
you gave | good words the other day of a bay 1.02.210
he gave me a jewel th' other day, and now he has 3.06.112 P
'tis said he gave unto | his steward a mighty 5.01. 7
star–like nobleness gave life and influence | to 5.01. 63
of your hand | gave sign for me to leave you. JC 2.01.247
the men that gave their country liberty. 3.01.118
that gave me public leave to speak of him. 3.02.220
when that rash humor which my mother gave me 4.03.120
o cassius, brutus gave the word too early, | who 5.03. 5
when those that gave the thane of cawdor to me MAC 1.03.119
i believe drink gave thee the lie last night. 2.03. 37 P
and then i prescripts gave her, | that she HAM 2.02.142
no, not i, | i never gave you aught. 3.01. 95
and will answer well | the death i gave him. 3.04.177
gave us not | that capability and godlike reason 4.04. 37
of very warlike appointment gave us chase. 4.06. 17 P
and gave you such a masterly report | for art 4.07. 96
varnish on the fame | the frenchman gave you, 4.07.133
he never gave commandement for their death. 5.02.374
if i gave them all my living, i'ld keep my LR 1.04.107 P
of an unfee'd lawyer, you gave me nothing for't. 1.04.130 P
what was th' offense you gave him? 2.02.114
i never gave him any. 2.02.115
the leisure of their answer, gave me cold looks: 2.04. 37
i gave you all — 2.04.250
and in good time you gave it. 2.04.250
i never gave you kingdom, call'd you children; 3.02. 17
old kind father, whose frank heart gave all — 3.04. 20
she gave strange eliads and most speaking looks 4.05. 25
she gave me for my pains a world of /sighs; OTH 1.03.159
why, that the moor first gave to desdemona, 3.03.308
"cursed fate that gave thee to the moor!" 3.03.426
i gave her such a one; 'twas my first gift. 3.03.436
for 'twas that hand that gave away my heart. 3.04. 45
the hearts of old gave hands; 3.04. 46
that which i gave you. 3.04. 53
she, dying, gave it me, | and bid me, when my 3.04. 63
alas the day, i never gave him cause. 3.04.158
by that same handkerchief you gave me even now? 4.01.149 P
she gave it him, and he hath giv'n it his whore. 4.01.176 P
handkerchief which i so lov'd, and gave thee, 5.02. 48
i never gave him token. 5.02. 61
i never gave it him. 5.02. 67
and pledge of love | which i first gave her. 5.02.215
an antique token | my father gave my mother. 5.02.217
dear general, i never gave you cause. 5.02.299
hardly gave audience, or | /vouchsaf'd to think ANT 1.04. 7
unto her | he gave the stablishment of egypt, 3.06. 9
parthia, and armenia | he gave to alexander; 3.06. 15
that day appear'd, and oft before gave audience, 3.06. 18
me at heels, to whom i gave | their wishes, do 4.12. 21
he added to your having, gave you some ground. CYM 1.02. 18 P
i gave him satisfaction! 2.01. 14 P
leaf's turn'd down | where philomele gave up. 2.02. 46
she gave it me, and said | she priz'd it once. 2.04.103
and it gave me present hunger | to feed again, 2.04.137
then, and thank | the man that gave them thee. 4.02. 85
the ground that gave them first has them again: 4.02.289
all curses madded hecuba gave the greeks, | and 4.02.313
the drug he gave me, which he said was precious 4.02.326
which gave advantage to an ancient soldier | (an 5.03. 15
silly habit, | that gave th' affront with them. 5.03. 87
if | that box i gave you was not thought by me 5.05.241
that confection | which i gave him for cordial, 5.05.247
till lucina reigned, | nature this dowry gave: PER 1.01. 9
although they gave their creatures in abundance, 1.04. 36
since i have here my father gave in his will. 2.01.134
the king my father gave you such a ring. 5.03. 39
and to those gentle uses gave me life. TNK 2.05. 7
that gave her promise faithfully she would | be 3.05. 43
about this hour my cousin gave his faith | to 3.06. 1
for i gave him | more mercy than you found, sir, 3.06.181
fair hand, and that honest heart you gave me — 3.06.197
and attentive | i gave my ear, when i might well 4.01. 57
did you nev'r see the horse he gave me? 5.02. 45
your gentle daughter gave me freedom once; 5.04. 24
her kind of ill | gave me some sorrow. 5.04. 27
and to arcite gave | the grace of the contention 5.04.107
which through the crystal tears gave light, VEN 491
when he did frown, o, had she then gave over, 571
the kiss i gave you is bestow'd in vain, | and 771
witness the entertainment that he gave. 1108
which virtue gave the golden age to gild | their LUC 60
mud not the fountain that gave drink to thee, 577
by him that gave it thee, | from a pure heart 624
in scorn of nature, art gave liveless life: 1374
so | that blushing red no guilty instance gave, 1511
look whom she best endow'd she gave the more; SON 11.11
were it not thy sour leisure gave sweet leave 39.10
and time that gave doth now his gift confound. 60. 8
these blenches gave my heart another youth, 110. 7
and, to enlighten thee, gave eyes to blindness, 152.11
she perus'd, sigh'd, tore, and gave the flood, LC 44
his real habitude gave life and grace | to 114
reserv'd the stalk and gave him all my flower. 147
o, how the channel to the stream gave grace! 285
that th' unexperient gave the tempter place, 318
GAVEST 3 FR 0.0003 REL FR 1 V 2 P
for the sugar thou gavest me, 'twas a pennyworth 1H4 2.04. 59 P
like a kind fellow, gavest thyself away gratis, 2H4 4.03. 69 P
"villain" back again | that late thou gavest me, ROM 3.01.126
GAVE'T 3 FR 0.0003 REL FR 3 V 0 P
the packet, cromwell, gave't you the king? H8 3.02. 76
of the thought | that gave't surmised shape. TRO 1.03. 17
/subscrib'd it, gave't th' impression, plac'd it HAM 5.02. 52
GAV'ST 16 FR 0.0018 REL FR 12 V 4 P
gav'st thou my letter to julia? TGV 1.01. 94 P
she whom thou gav'st to me to be my wife; ERR 5.01.198

the life thou gav'st me first was lost and done, 1H6 4.06. 7
to my determin'd time thou gav'st new date. 4.06. 9
them, gav'st the duke a clout | steep'd in the R3 1.03.176
might have mercy on the fault thou gav'st him; H8 3.02.262
thou gav'st thine ears (like tapsters that bade TIM 4.03.215
/crown i' th' middle and gav'st away both parts, LR 1.04.161 P
bald crown when thou gav'st thy golden one away. 1.04.163 P
thy mothers, for when thou gav'st them the rod, 1.04.173 P
lov'd, and gave thee, | thou gav'st to cassio. OTH 5.02. 49
get thee from my sight, | thou gav'st me poison. CYM 5.05.237
betray'd the hours thou gav'st me to repose? LUC 933
thou gav'st me thine not to give back again. SON 22.14
thyself thou gav'st, thy own worth then not 87. 9
or me, to whom thou gav'st it, else mistaking, 87.10

GAWDED 1 FR 0.0001 REL FR 1 V 0 P
their nicely gawded cheeks to th' wanton spoil COR 2.01.217

GAWDS *(also gauds)*

/GAWDS 1 FR 0.0001 REL FR 1 V 0 P
but for these other /gawds, | unbind my hands, SHR 2.01. 3

GAWDS 3 FR 0.0003 REL FR 3 V 0 P
bracelets of thy hair, rings, gawds, conceits, MND 1.01. 33
is all too wanton and too full of gawds | to JN 3.03. 36
all, with one consent, praise new-born gawds, TRO 3.03.176

GAWSEY 2 FR 0.0002 REL FR 2 V 0 P
sir nicholas gawsey hath for succor sent, | and 1H4 5.04. 45
make up to clifton, i'll to sir nicholas gawsey. 5.04. 58

GAY 12 FR 0.0013 REL FR 12 V 0 P
do their gay vestments his affections bait? ERR 2.01. 94
my gay apparel for an almsman's gown, | my R2 3.03.149
into | for gay apparel 'gainst the triumph day. 5.02. 66
the gay new coats o'er the french soldiers' H5 4.03.118
lady's lap, | and deck my body in gay ornaments, 3H6 3.02.149
never lack'd gold, and yet went never gay, OTH 2.01.150
therefore | to lay his gay comparisons apart, ANT 3.13. 26
fear their gay skins with thought of their sharp STM III 18
spur, | for rich caparisons or trappings gay? VEN 286
lullaby, the learned man hath got the lady gay, PP 15.15
ere beauty's dead fleece made another gay: SON 68. 8
painting thy outward walls so costly gay? 146. 4

GAYNESS 1 FR 0.0001 REL FR 1 V 0 P
our gayness and our gilt are all besmirch'd H5 4.03.110

GAZ'D 7 FR 0.0008 REL FR 7 V 0 P
for never gaz'd the moon | upon the water as WT 4.04.172
which rightly gaz'd upon | show nothing but R2 2.02. 18
eyes, | but have been gaz'd on like a comet. PER 5.01. 86
hand, | and gaz'd for tidings in my eager eyes, LUC 254
fly, | but eagles gaz'd upon with every eye. 1015
and still on him she gaz'd, and gazing still, 1531
thy youth's proud livery, so gaz'd on now, SON 2. 3

GAZE 31 FR 0.0035 REL FR 29 V 2 P
she that you gaze on so as she sits at supper? TGV 2.01. 43 P
peruse the traders, gaze upon the buildings, ERR 1.02. 13
gaze when you should, and that will clear your 3.02. 57
a lover's eyes will gaze an eagle blind. LLL 4.03.331
to gaze on christian fools with varnish'd faces; MV 2.05. 33
their savage eyes turn'd to a modest gaze, | by 5.01. 78
well said, master, mum, and gaze your fill. SHR 1.01. 73
frown, | and wherefore gaze this goodly company, 3.02. 94
no longer shall you gaze on't, lest your fancy WT 5.03. 60
with community, | afford no extraordinary gaze, 1H4 3.02. 78
if so, gaze on, and grovel on thy face, | until 2H6 1.02. 9
look how they gaze! 2.04. 20
death | to gaze upon these secrets of the deep? R3 1.04. 35
but gives all gaze and bent of amorous view | on TRO 4.05.282
youth with comeliness pluck'd all gaze his way; COR 1.03. 7 P
and in the fountain shall we gaze so long | till TIT 3.01.127
i stray'd | to gaze upon a ruinous monastery, 5.01. 21
eyes | of mortals that fall back to gaze on him, ROM 2.02. 30
here all eyes gaze on us. 3.01. 53
men's eyes were made to look, and let them gaze; 3.01. 54
you look pale, and gaze, | and put on fear, and JC 1.03. 59
and live to be the show and gaze o' th' time! MAC 5.08. 24
'tis a pageant | to keep us in false gaze. OTH 1.03. 19
vacancy, | had gone to gaze on cleopatra too, ANT 2.02.217
with our sprightly port make the ghosts gaze. 4.14. 52
teach 'em | boldly to gaze against bright arms, TNK 2.02. 35
you are going now to gaze upon my mistress, 3.01.117
only he hath an eye to gaze on beauty, | and LUC 496
as the poor frighted deer that stands at gaze, 1149
the lovely gaze where every eye doth dwell SON 5. 2
sun | delights to peep, to gaze therein on thee. 24.12

GAZED 2 FR 0.0002 REL FR 2 V 0 P
whereon with fearful eyes they long have gazed, VEN 927
and, blushing with him, wistly on him gazed; LUC 1355

GAZER 3 FR 0.0003 REL FR 3 V 0 P
and kill the innocent gazer with thy sight; 2H6 3.02. 53
shall make the gazer joy to see him tread. PER 2.01.159
whereat th' impartial gazer late did wonder, VEN 748

GAZERS 2 FR 0.0002 REL FR 2 V 0 P
i'll slay more gazers than the basilisk, | i'll 3H6 3.02.187
how many gazers mightst thou lead away, | if SON 96.11

GAZES 6 FR 0.0006 REL FR 6 V 0 P
that all eyes saw his eyes enchanted with gazes. LLL 2.01.247
she was more worth such gazes | than what you WT 5.01.226
on her, | but cast their gazes on marina's face; PER 4.03. 33
to which love's eyes pays tributary gazes, | nor VEN 632
lord, how mine eyes throw gazes to the east! PP 14.13
anon their gazes lend | to every place at once, LC 26

GAZETH 3 FR 0.0003 REL FR 3 V 0 P
now gazeth she on him, now on the ground; VEN 224
stalks, | and gazeth on her yet unstained bed. LUC 366
gilding the object whereupon it gazeth; SON 20. 6

GAZING 19 FR 0.0021 REL FR 18 V 1 P
dost thou know her by my gazing on her, and yet TGV 2.01. 46 P
at length the sun, gazing upon the earth, ERR 1.01. 88
for gazing on your beams, fair sun, being by. 3.02. 56
who give their eyes the liberty of gazing? 5.01. 53
and, gazing in mine eyes, feeling my pulse, 5.01.244
with gazing fed, and fancy dies | in the cradle MV 3.02. 68
still gazing in a doubt | whether those peals of 3.02.144
were i of your flock, | and only live by gazing. WT 4.04.110
presented them unto the gazing moon | so many H5 4.pr. 27
gazing on that which seems to dim thy sight? 2H6 1.02. 6
abrook | the abject people gazing on thy face, 2.04. 11
show thy descent by gazing 'gainst the sun; 3H6 2.01. 92
your flying flags, | and leave his navy gazing. ANT 3.13. 12
look | like patience gazing on kings' graves, PER 5.01.138
on shore | gazing upon a late embarked friend, VEN 818
stay, | his rage of lust by gazing qualified; LUC 424
gazing upon the greeks with little lust. 1384
and still on him she gaz'd, and gazing still, 1531
pitiful thrivers, in their gazing spent? SON 125. 8

GEAR 10 FR 0.0011 REL FR 6 V 4 P
disguis'd like muscovites, in shapeless gear; LLL 5.02.303
fare you well! i'll grow a talker for this gear. MV 1.01.110
be a woman, she's a good wench for this gear. 2.02.167 P
to this gear, the sooner the better. 2H6 1.04. 14 P
but i will remedy this gear ere long, | or sell 3.01. 91
will this gear ne'er be mended? TRO 1.01. 6 P
bed, chamber, pandar to provide this gear! 3.02.211
come, to this gear. TIT 4.03. 53
here's goodly gear! a sail, a sail! ROM 2.04.101 P
such soon-speeding gear | as will disperse 5.01. 60

GECK 2 FR 0.0002 REL FR 2 V 0 P
and made the most notorious geck and gull | that TN 5.01.343
and to become the geck and scorn | o' th' CYM 5.04. 67

GEESE 11 FR 0.0012 REL FR 5 V 6 P
stood on the pillory for geese he hath kill'd, TGV 4.04. 32 P
jest how my father stole two geese out of a pen, WIV 3.04. 40 P
since i pluck'd geese, play'd truant, and whipt 5.01. 25 P
spring is near when green geese are a-breeding. LLL 1.01. 97
as wild geese that the creeping fowler eye, | or MND 3.02. 20
subjects afore thee like a flock of wild geese, 1H4 2.04.138 P
together in consent, like so many wild geese. 2H4 5.01. 71 P
where foxes, geese. COR 1.01.172
you souls of geese, | that bear the shapes of 1.04. 34
geese, villain? MAC 5.03. 13
not gone yet, if the wild geese fly that way. LR 2.04. 46 P

GEFFREY 3 FR 0.0003 REL FR 3 V 0 P
doth contain that large | which died in geffrey; JN 2.01.102
that geffrey was thy elder brother born, | and 2.01.104
liker in feature to his father geffrey | than 2.01.126

GEFFREY'S 6 FR 0.0006 REL FR 6 V 0 P
behalf | of thy deceased brother geffrey's son, JN 1.01. 8
look here upon thy brother geffrey's face: 2.01. 99
england was geffrey's right, | and this is 2.01.105
and this is geffrey's in the name of god. 2.01.106
my name is constance, i was geffrey's wife, 3.04. 46
is it my fault that i was geffrey's son? 4.01. 22

GELD 3 FR 0.0003 REL FR 1 V 2 P
does your worship mean to geld and splay all the MM 2.01.230 P
by mine honor, | i'll geld 'em all; WT 2.01.147
'twas nothing to geld a codpiece of a purse; 4.04.610 P

GELDED 4 FR 0.0004 REL FR 2 V 2 P
lent, | than aquitaine, so gelded as it is. LLL 2.01.148
pity him, | bereft and gelded of his patrimony. R2 2.01.237
that that lord say hath gelded the commonwealth, 2H6 4.02.165 P
household, let me be gelded like a spaniel. PER 4.06.124 P

GELDING 4 FR 0.0004 REL FR 1 V 3 P
or a thief to walk my ambling gelding, than my WIV 2.02.305 P
me thy lantern, to see my gelding in the stable. 1H4 2.01. 35 P
the ostler bring my gelding out of the stable. 2.01. 96 P
gelding the opposed continent as much | as on 3.01.109

GELIDA 1 FR 0.0001 REL FR 0 V 1 P
precor gelida quando /pecus /omne sub umbra LLL 4.02. 93 P

GELIDUS 1 FR 0.0001 REL FR 1 V 0 P
/pene gelidus timor occupat artus: 2H6 4.01.117

GELT 2 FR 0.0002 REL FR 2 V 0 P
would he were gelt that had it, for my part, MV 5.01.144
years old | they must be all gelt for musicians, TNK 4.01.133

GEM 5 FR 0.0005 REL FR 5 V 0 P
never so rich a gem | was set in worse than gold MV 2.07. 54
of six preceding ancestors, that gem, AWW 5.03.196
yet | but from this lady may proceed a gem | to H8 2.03. 78
the brooch indeed | and gem of all the nation. HAM 4.07. 94
and by a gem of women, to be abus'd | by one ANT 3.13.108

GEMINY 1 FR 0.0001 REL FR 0 V 1 P
through the grate, like a geminy of baboons. WIV 2.02. 9 P

GEMS 4 FR 0.0004 REL FR 4 V 0 P
but 'tis that miracle and queen of gems | that TN 2.04. 85
(as 'twere in scorn of eyes) reflecting gems, R3 1.04. 31
sun and moon, with earth and sea's rich gems, SON 21. 6
with th' annexions of fair gems enrich'd, | and LC 208

GENDER 4 FR 0.0004 REL FR 3 V 1 P
is the great love the general gender bear him, HAM 4.07. 18
supply it with one gender of herbs or distract OTH 1.03.323 P
cestern for foul toads | to knot and gender in! 4.02. 62
that thy sable gender mak'st | with the breath PHT 18

GENDERS 1 FR 0.0001 REL FR 0 V 1 P
for thy cases and the numbers of the genders? WIV 4.01. 71 P

/GENERAL 2 FR 0.0002 REL FR 1 V 1 P
/for /all /the /country /in /a /general /voice 2H4 4.01.134
/who /hath /he /left /behind /him /general? LR 4.03. 7 P

GENERAL 195 FR 0.0220 REL FR 153 V 42 P
are you content to be our general? TGV 4.01. 59
so | the general subject to a well-wish'd king MM 2.04. 27
it is too general a vice, and severity must cure 3.02. 99 P
revenges to your heart, | and general honor. 4.03.136
when she did starve the general world beside LLL 2.01. 11
sole imperator and great general | of trotting 3.01.185
gait majestical, and his general behavior vain, 5.01. 11 P
the other half comes to the general state, MV 4.01.371
he is the general challenger. AYL 1.02.170 P
wouldst thou disgorge into the general world. 2.07. 69
had collected | for general sovereignty; AWW 1.03.224
methink'st thou art a general offense, and every 2.03.254 P
the general of our horse thou art, and we, 3.03. 1
the general is content to spare thee yet, | and, 4.01. 80
you are a merciful general. 4.03.126 P
our general bids you answer to what i shall ask 4.03.126 P
i'll whisper with the general, and know his 4.03.296 P
the general says, you that have so traitorously 4.03.304 P
is much more general than these lines import. JN 4.03. 17
the plot and the general course of the action. 1H4 2.03. 21 P
our general forces at bridgenorth shall meet. 3.02.178
should go so general current through the world. 4.01. 5
in general journey-bated and brought low. 4.03. 26
to gripe the general sway into your hand, 5.01. 57
health and fair greeting from our general, | the 2H4 4.01. 27
my brother general, the commonwealth, | i make 4.01. 93
here come i from our princely general | to know 4.01.139
for this contains our general grievances: 4.01.167
this will i show the general. 4.01.176
here comes our general. 4.03. 23 P
did, as heir general, being descended | of H5 1.02. 66
not too, | save ceremony, save general ceremony? 4.01.239
were now the general of our gracious empress, 5.pr. 30
of england than a general petition of monarchs. 5.02.279 P
hence grew the general wrack and massacre; 1H6 1.01.135
trumpeter, | summon their general unto the wall. 4.02. 2
all our general force | might with a sally of 4.04. 3
success unto our valiant general, | and 5.02. 8
have earnestly implor'd a general peace 5.04. 98
where's our general? 2H6 4.02.111 P
will parley with jack cade their general. 4.04. 13
now let the general trumpet blow his blast, 5.02. 43
a woman's general: 3H6 1.02. 68
their woes are parcell'd, mine is general. R3 2.02. 81
posterity, | even to the general all-ending day. 3.01. 78
i, | "this general applause and cheerful shout 3.07. 39
no less importing than our general good, | are 3.07. 68
and follow'd with the general throng and sweat H8 pr 28
not consulting, broke | into a general prophecy: 1.01. 92
a general welcome from his grace | salutes ye 1.04. 1
self, hath sent | one general tongue unto us: 2.02. 95
that time offer'd sorrow, | this, general joy. 4.01. 7
with a general taint | of the whole state; 5.02. 63
when that the general is not like the hive | to TRO 1.03. 81
one voice | call agamemnon head and general. 1.03.222
sends, | however it is spread in general name, 1.03.322
a scantling | of good or bad unto the general, 1.03.342
run — say so — did not the general run then? 2.01. 6 P
i was advertis'd their great general slept, 2.02.211
our noble general, do not do so. 2.03.226
please it our great general | to call together 2.03.259
please it our general pass strangely by him, 3.03. 39
what comes the general to speak with me? 3.03. 55
would you, my lord, aught with the general? 3.03. 58
you of this man that takes me for the general? 3.03.262 P
by priam and the general state of troy. 4.02. 67
our general doth salute you with a kiss. 4.05. 19
'twere better she were kiss'd in general. 4.05. 21
after the general, i beseech you next | to feast 4.05.228
the general state, i fear, | can scarce entreat 4.05.264
thanks and good night to the greeks' general. 5.01. 73
to square the general sex | by cressid's rule. 5.02.132
were i the general, thou shouldst have my office 5.06. 4
he, | "that i receive the general food at first COR 1.01.131
against whom cominius the general is gone, with 1.03. 97 P
say, has our general met the enemy? 1.04. 3
and hark, what noise the general makes! 1.05. 9
o general! 1.09. 11
i thank you, general; 1.09. 36
gifts, am bound to beg | of my lord general. 1.09. 81
the senate has letters from the general, wherein 2.01.134 P
and welcome, general, and y' are welcome all. 2.01.182
the present consul and last general | in our 2.02. 43
but by the yea and no | of general ignorance — 3.01.146
and you will rather show our general louts | how 3.02. 66
my sometime general, | i have seen thee stern, 4.01. 23
the defense of a town, our general is excellent. 4.05.170 P
here's he that was wont to thwack our general, 4.05.179 P
why do you say, "thwack our general"? 4.05.180 P
i do not say, "thwack our general," but he was 4.05.181 P
our general himself makes a mistress of him, 4.05.194 P
the news is, our general is cut i' th' middle, 4.05.197 P
he hath said | which was sometime his general, 5.01. 2
our general | will no more hear from thence. 5.02. 5
if you have heard your general talk of rome 5.02. 9
i tell thee, fellow, | thy general is my lover. 5.02. 14
always factionary on the party of your general. 5.02. 30 P
i am, as thy general is. 5.02. 37 P
our general has sworn you out of reprieve and 5.02. 49 P
i mean, thy general. 5.02. 54 P
my general cares not for you. 5.02. 55 P
i neither care for th' world nor your general; 5.02.102 P
let your general do his worst. 5.02.105 P
the worthy fellow is our general. 5.02.110 P
your ears against | the general suit of rome; 5.03. 6
how is it with our general? 5.06. 9
to see the general hunting in this forest? TIT 2.03. 59
the blot and enemy to our general name! 2.03.183
is warlike lucius general of the goths? 4.04. 69
what says our general? 5.01.162
then, dreadful trumpet, sound the general doom, ROM 3.02. 67
and then will i be general of your woes, | and 5.03.219
bold | (for that i knew it the most general way) TIM 2.02.200
to general filths | convert o' th' instant, 4.01. 6
bosoms, and their crop | be general leprosy! 4.01. 30
to foresee, | smells from the general weal. 4.03.160
wouldst have plung'd thyself | in general riot, 4.03.256
forgive my general and exceptless rashness, 4.03.495
toward thee forgetfulness too general gross; 5.01.144
whom, though in general part we were oppos'd, 5.02. 7
my noble general, timon is dead, | entomb'd upon 5.04. 65
if it be aught toward the general good, | set JC 1.02. 85
another general shout! 1.02.132
cause to spurn at him, | but for the general. 2.01. 12
are to the world in general as to caesar. 2.02. 29
and pity to the general wrong of rome — | as 3.01.170
whose ransoms did the general coffers fill; 3.02. 89
the greater part, the horse in general, | are 4.02. 29
what says my general? 5.01. 70
here comes the general. 5.04. 17
only in a general honest thought | and common 5.05. 71
inch | ten thousand dollars to our general use. MAC 1.02. 62
rock, | as broad and general as the casing air; 3.04. 22
i drink to th' general joy o' th' whole table, 3.04. 88
the general cause? 4.03.196
shall in the general censure take corruption HAM 1.04. 35
in unreclaimed blood, | of general assault. 2.01. 35
'twas caviary to the general, but it was — as i 2.02.437 P
gods, | in general synod take away her power! 2.02.494
and cleave the general ear with horrid speech, 2.02.563
did the king sigh, but /with a general groan. 3.03. 23
is the great love the general gender bear him, 4.07. 18
as well in the general dependants as in the duke LR 1.04. 61 P
who redeems nature from the general curse 4.06.206
general, | take thou my soldiers, prisoners, 5.03. 74
our present business | is general woe. 5.03.320
the duke does greet you, general, | and he OTH 1.02. 36
general, be advis'd, | he comes to bad intent. 1.02. 55
would ever have, t' incur a general mock, | run 1.02. 69

employ you | against the general enemy ottoman. 1.03. 49
nor doth the general care | take hold on me; 1.03. 54
but, good lieutenant, is your general wiv'd? 2.01. 60
'tis one iago, ancient to the general. 2.01. 66
our noble and valiant general, that upon certain 2.02. 2 P
isle of cyprus and our noble general othello! 2.02. 11 P
our general cast us thus early for the love of 2.03. 14 P
to the health of our general! 2.03. 86 P
for mine own part — no offense to the general, 2.03.106 P
were well | the general were put in mind of it. 2.03.132
the general speaks to you; 2.03.168
/thus it is, general: 2.03.224
are more ways to recover the general again. 2.03.272 P
our general's wife is now the general — i may 2.03.315 P
and bid "good morrow, general." 3.01. 2
and the general so likes your music, that he 3.01. 12 P
to hear music the general does not greatly care. 3.01. 16 P
the general and his wife are talking of it, 3.01. 43
my general will forget my love and service. 3.03. 18
why, how now, general? no more of that. 3.03.334
i had been happy, if the general camp, | pioners 3.03.345
i do attend here on the general, | and think it 3.04.193
how is it, general? 4.01. 59
/god save /thee, worthy general! 4.01.216
but with such general warranty of heaven | as i 5.02. 60
what is the matter? how now, general? 5.02.168
dear general, i never gave you cause. 5.02.299
speak to me home, mince not the general tongue; ANT 1.02.105
whose virtue and whose general graces speak 2.02.129
had our general | been what he knew himself, it 3.10. 25
the morn is fair. good morrow, general. 4.04. 24
good morrow, general. 4.04. 25
is lucius general of the forces? CYM 3.07. 11
alike conversant in general services, and more 4.01. 13 P
go tell their general we attend him here, | to PER 1.04. 79
both th' /heart and place | of general wonder. 4.ch. 11
characters express | a general praise to her, 4.03. 45
most wise in general, tell me, if thou canst, 5.01.183
see what our general of ebbs and flows | out TNK 5.01.163
that the cry | was general "a palamon!"; 5.03. 81
come, | from the creation to the general doom. LUC 924
many fall, | to plague a private sin in general? 1484
all these i better in one general best. SON 91. 8
shown, | unless this general evil they maintain: 121.13
and so the general of hot desire | was sleeping 154. 7
"that he did in the general bosom reign | of LC 127

GENERALLY 12 FR 0.0013 REL FR 4 V 8 P
generally allow'd for your many war–like, WIV 2.02.227 P
you were best to call them generally, man by man MND 1.02. 2 P
offenses as he hath generally tax'd their whole AYL 3.02.349 P
to whom we all rest generally beholding. SHR 1.02.272
he that so generally is at all times good must AWW 1.01. 7 P
generally thankful. 2.03. 38 P
wherein the king stands generally condemn'd. R2 2.02.132
they are generally fools and cowards, which some 2H4 4.03. 94 P
and generally to the crown and seat of france, H5 1.01. 88
and generally, whoever the king favors, | the H8 2.01. 47
if he had biles — full, all over, generally? TRO 2.01. 3 P
and, generally, in all shapes that man goes up TIM 2.02.112 P

/GENERAL'S 1 FR 0.0001 REL FR 0 V 1 P
that attends the /general's /wife be stirring, OTH 3.01. 25 P

GENERAL'S 8 FR 0.0009 REL FR 5 V 3 P
sir, by /the general's looks, we shall be fain AWW 4.03.239 P
that is intended in the general's name. 2H4 4.01.164
what a beard of the general's cut and a horrid H5 3.06. 77 P
the general's disdain'd | by him one step below, TRO 1.03.129
what miscarries | shall be the general's fault, COR 1.01.267
our general's wife is now the general — i may OTH 2.03.315 P
from hence, | i'll fetch the general's surgeon. 5.01.100
but this dotage of our general's | o'erflows the ANT 1.01. 1

GENERALS 7 FR 0.0008 REL FR 7 V 0 P
fought, | you are disputing of your generals. 1H6 1.01. 73
shapes, | severals and generals of grace exact, TRO 1.03.180
let me go in to see the generals. JC 4.03.124
for shame, you generals! 4.03.130
prepare you, generals. 5.01. 12
make forth, the generals would have some words. 5.01. 25
pray you hasten | your generals after. ANT 2.04. 2

GENERATION 12 FR 0.0013 REL FR 8 V 4 P
than of | our human generation you shall find TMP 3.03. 33
made his journal greeting | to yond generation, MM 4.03. 89
when the work of generation was | between these MV 1.03. 82
being but the second generation | removed from JN 2.01.181
beget | a generation of still–breeding thoughts; R2 5.05. 8
up | whiles england shall have generation. 2H4 4.02. 49
is this the generation of love — hot blood, hot TRO 3.01.131 P
is love a generation of vipers? 3.01.133 P
thy mother's of my generation; TIM 1.01.201 P
or he that makes his generation messes | to LR 1.01.117
it upon me and mine | to the end of generation! PER 3.03. 25
the god priapus, and undo a whole generation. 4.06. 4 P

GENERATIONS 1 FR 0.0001 REL FR 1 V 0 P
they shall not see | to bring false generations. WT 2.01.148

GENERATIVE 1 FR 0.0001 REL FR 0 V 1 P
and he is a motion generative, that's infallible MM 3.02.112 P

GENEROSITY 1 FR 0.0001 REL FR 1 V 0 P
to break the heart of generosity | and make bold COR 1.01.211

GENEROUS 12 FR 0.0013 REL FR 10 V 2 P
the generous and gravest citizens | have hent MM 4.06. 13
the posterior of the day, most generous sir, is LLL 5.01. 91 P
this is not generous, not gentle, not humble. 5.02.629
to be generous, guiltless, and of free TN 1.05. 91 P
should once set footing in your generous bosoms? TRO 2.02.155
of a most select and generous chief in that. HAM 1.03. 74
most generous, and free from all contriving, 4.07.135
free me so far in your most generous thoughts, 5.02.242
my mind as generous, and my shape as true, | as LR 1.02. 8
and the generous islanders | by you invited, do OTH 3.03.280
am i bound | by any generous bond to follow him TNK 1.02. 50
pleas'd | to show in generous terms your griefs, 3.01. 54

GENITIVE 2 FR 0.0002 REL FR 0 V 2 P
what is your genitive case plural, william? WIV 4.01. 57 P
genitive case? 4.01. 59 P

/GENITIVO 1 FR 0.0001 REL FR 0 V 1 P
/genitivo, horum, harum, horum. WIV 4.01. 61 P

GENITIVO 1 FR 0.0001 REL FR 0 V 1 P
genitivo, hujus. WIV 4.01. 43 P

GENIUS 7 FR 0.0008 REL FR 5 V 2 P
strong'st suggestion | our worser genius can, TMP 4.01. 27
one of these men is genius to the other: ERR 5.01.333
his very genius hath taken the infection of the TN 3.04.129 P
'a was the very genius of famine, yet lecherous 2H4 3.02.314 P
some say the genius /so | cries "/come" to him TRO 4.04. 50
the genius and the mortal instruments | are then JC 2.01. 66
and under him | my genius is rebuk'd, as it is MAC 3.01. 55

GENNETS *(also jennet)*

GENNETS 1 FR 0.0001 REL FR 0 V 1 P
coursers for cousins, and gennets for germans. OTH 1.01.113 P

GENOA 5 FR 0.0005 REL FR 1 V 4 P
what news from genoa? MV 3.01. 79 P
antonio, as i heard in genoa — 3.01. 98 P
/heard in genoa? 3.01.107 P
your daughter spent in genoa, as i heard, one 3.01.108 P
remember me | near twenty years ago in genoa, SHR 4.04. 4

GENOUX 1 FR 0.0001 REL FR 0 V 1 P
sur mes genoux /je vous donne mille H5 4.04. 54 P

GEN'RAL 1 FR 0.0001 REL FR 1 V 0 P
by a composture stol'n | from gen'ral excrement; TIM 4.03.442

GENS 2 FR 0.0002 REL FR 2 V 0 P
paysans, la pauvre gens de france, | poor market 1H6 3.02. 14
nothing but this; 'tis "bona terra, mala gens." 2H6 4.07. 56

GENTILHOMME 2 FR 0.0002 REL FR 0 V 2 P
que vous etes le gentilhomme de bonne qualite. H5 4.04. 2 P
je suis le gentilhomme de bonne maison; 4.04. 41 P

GENTILITY 2 FR 0.0002 REL FR 1 V 1 P
a dangerous law against gentility. LLL 1.01.128
him lies, mines my gentility with my education. AYL 1.01. 21 P

GENTILITY'S 1 FR 0.0001 REL FR 1 V 0 P
for pity's sake and true gentility's, | hear and TNK 1.01. 25

/GENTLE 3 FR 0.0003 REL FR 3 V 0 P
/gentle /northumberland, | /if /thy /offenses R2 4.01.229
/the /gentle /archbishop /of /york /is /up 2H4 1.01.189
/fall /to, /and, /gentle /girl, /eat /this. TIT 3.02. 34

GENTLE 394 FR 0.0445 REL FR 368 V 26 P
of him, for | he's gentle, and not fearful. TMP 1.02.469
ten times more gentle than her father's crabbed; 3.01. 8
their manners are more gentle, kind, than of 3.03. 32
gentle breath of yours my sails | must fill, or ep 11
what think'st thou of the gentle proteus? TGV 1.02. 14
i thank you, gentle servant — 'tis very clerkly 2.01.108
have patience, gentle julia. 2.02. 1
o gentle proteus, love's a mighty lord, | and 2.04.136
gentle girl, assist me; 2.07. 1
the current that with gentle murmur glides, 2.07. 25
giving a gentle kiss to every sedge | he 2.07. 29
i'll be as patient as a gentle stream, | and 2.07. 34
gentle lucetta, fit me with such weeds | as may 2.07. 42
on thurio, whom your gentle daughter hates, 3.01. 14
i gave him gentle looks, thereby to find | that 3.01. 31
ay, gentle thurio, for you know that love | will 4.02. 19
sir proteus, gentle lady, and your servant. 4.02. 91
good morrow, gentle lady. 4.03. 45
she is beholding to thee, gentle youth. 4.04.173
thou gentle nymph, cherish thy forlorn swain. 5.04. 12
if the gentle spirit of moving words | can no 5.04. 55
come, gentle master slender, come; WIV 1.01.300 P
and honest, and gentle, and one that is your 1.04.140 P
gentle master fenton, | yet seek my father's 3.04. 18
farewell, gentle mistress; farewell, nan. 3.04. 94
gentle isabella, | turn you the key, and know MM 1.04. 7
gentle and fair, your brother kindly greets you. 1.04. 24
gentle my lord, turn back. 2.02.143
gentle my lord, | let me entreat you speak the 2.04.139
nor, gentle daughter, fear you not at all. 4.01. 70
or reprieve | for the most gentle claudio. 4.02. 72
this is a gentle provost: 4.02. 86
my gentle varrius! 4.05. 13
first, provost, let me bail these gentle three. 5.01.357
gentle my liege — 5.01.428
wild, and yet, too, gentle; ERR 3.01.110
then, gentle brother, get you in again; 3.02. 25
possess'd with such a gentle sovereign grace, 3.02.160
i did not, gentle husband, lock thee forth. 4.04. 97
and, gentle master, i receiv'd no gold; 4.04. 98
methinks they are such a gentle nation that, but 4.04.153 P
i, gentle mistress. 5.01.371
and you too, gentle hero? ADO 2.01.374 P
wolves have preyed, and look, the gentle day, 5.03. 25
were all address'd to meet you, gentle lady, LLL 2.01. 83
not so, gentle beast. 2.01.222
park, | and in her train there is a gentle lady: 3.01.165
and, gentle longaville, where lies thy pain? 4.03.170
lend me the flourish of all gentle tongues — 4.03.234
nothing but peace and gentle visitation. 5.02.179
nothing but peace and gentle visitation. 5.02.181
gentle sweet, | your wits makes wise things 5.02.373
this is not generous, not gentle, not humble. 5.02.629
o, shall i say, i thank you, gentle wife? 5.02.826
there, gentle hermia, may i marry thee; MND 1.01.161
my gentle puck, come hither. 2.01.148
but, gentle friend, for love and courtesy | lie 2.02. 56
i pray thee, gentle mortal, sing again. 3.01.137
in show, | you would not use a gentle lady so; 3.02.152
stay, gentle helena; 3.02.245
tear | impatient answers from my gentle tongue? 3.02.287
come, thou gentle day! 3.02.418
apply | /to your eye, | gentle lover, remedy. 3.02.452
and kiss thy fair large ears, my gentle joy. 4.01. 4
and, gentle puck, take this transformed scalp 4.01. 64
how comes this gentle concord in the world, 4.01.143
joy, gentle friends, joy and fresh days of love 5.01. 29
why, gentle sweet, you shall see no such thing. 5.01. 87
you, whose gentle hearts do fear | the smallest 5.01.219
a very gentle beast, and of a good conscience. 5.01.227 P
which, touching but my gentle vessel's side, MV 1.01. 32
hie thee, gentle jew. 1.03.177
except to steal your thoughts, my gentle queen. 2.01. 12
tell gentle jessica | i will not fail her; 2.04. 19
it will be for his gentle daughter's sake, | and 2.04. 34
now, by my hood, a gentle, and no jew. 2.06. 51
a gentle riddance. 2.07. 78
a gentle scroll. 3.02.139
is that her gentle spirit | commits itself to 3.02.163
my lord bassanio and my gentle lady, | i wish 3.02.189
gentle lady, | when i did first impart my love 3.02.252
we all expect a gentle answer, jew! 4.01. 34
it droppeth as the gentle rain from heaven 4.01.185
and pardon me, my gentle gratiano, | for that 5.01.260
and in the gentle condition of blood you should AYL 1.01. 44 P
yet he's gentle, never school'd and yet learned, 1.01.166 P
your fair eyes and gentle wishes go with me to 1.02.186 P
gentle cousin, | let us go thank him, and 1.02.239
hath ta'en displeasure 'gainst his gentle niece, 1.02.278
o my gentle master! 2.03. 2
and wherefore are you gentle, strong, and 2.03. 6
your virtues, gentle master, | are sanctified 2.03. 12
and to you, gentle sir, and to you all. 2.04. 70
o most gentle jupiter, what tedious homily of 3.02.155 P
why, i am sorry for thee, gentle silvius. 3.05. 85
my gentle phebe did bid me give you this. 4.03. 7
women's gentle brain | could not drop forth such 4.03. 33
/in brief, he led me to the gentle duke, | who 4.03.142
find a time, audrey, patience, gentle audrey. 5.01. 2 P
good ev'n, gentle friend. 5.01. 16 P
this do, and do it kindly, gentle sirs; SHR in.1. 66
mi perdonato, gentle master mine; 1.01. 25
but, gentle sir, methinks you walk like a 2.01. 85 P
no, not a whit, i find you passing gentle: 2.01.242
with gentle conference, soft, and affable. 2.01.251
nay, i have ta'en you napping, gentle love, 4.02. 46
much good do it unto thy gentle heart! 4.03. 51
when you are gentle, you shall have one too, 4.03. 71
good morrow, gentle mistress, where away? 4.05. 27
lucentio, gentle sir. 4.05. 58
please it this matron and this gentle maid | to AWW 3.05. 97
gentle madam, | you never had a servant to whose 4.04. 14
one, | to wear your gentle limbs in my affairs, 5.01. 4
your gentle hands lend us, and take our hearts. ep 6
good gentle one, give me modest assurance if you TN 1.05.179 P
i come to whet your gentle thoughts | on his 3.01.105
i prithee, gentle friend, | let thy fair wisdom, 4.01. 51
i am one of those gentle ones that will use the 4.02. 32 P
by whose gentle help | i was preserv'd to serve 5.01.255
in whose success we are gentle — i beseech you, WT 1.02.394
gentle my lord, | you scarce can right me 2.01. 98
and honor from th' access of gentle visitors. 2.02. 10
gentle spectators, that i now may be | in fair 4.01. 20
be merry, gentle! 4.04. 46
wherefore, gentle maiden, | do you neglect them? 4.04. 85
for we must be gentle, now we are gentlemen. 5.02.152 P
what england says, say briefly, gentle lord, JN 2.01. 52
our trumpet call'd you to this gentle parle — 2.01.205
and make a riot on the gentle brow | of true 3.01.247
impose | some gentle order, and then we shall be 3.01.251
farewell, gentle cousin. 3.03. 17
o my gentle hubert, | we owe thee much! 3.03. 19
patience, good lady, comfort, gentle constance! 3.04. 22
he hath a stern look, but a gentle heart. 4.01. 87
o my gentle cousin, | hear'st thou the news 4.02.159
gentle kinsman, go | and thrust thyself into 4.02.166
this gentle offer of the perilous time. 4.03. 13
and snarleth in the gentle eyes of peace; 4.03.150
but since you are a gentle convertite, | my 5.01. 19
march | upon her gentle bosom, and fill up | her 5.02. 28
and their gentle hearts | to fierce and bloody 5.02.157
as gentle and as jocund as to jest | go i to R2 1.03. 95
draws the sweet infant breath of gentle sleep; 1.03.133
in peace was never gentle lamb more mild, | than 2.01.174
i thank thee, gentle percy, and be sure | i 2.03. 45
thanks, gentle uncle. 3.01. 42
feed not thy sovereign's foe, my gentle earth, 3.02. 12
speak to his gentle hearing kind commends. 3.03.126
no, good my lord, let's fight with gentle words, 3.03.131
men's eyes | did scowl on gentle richard. 5.02. 28
which with such gentle sorrow he shook off, 5.02. 31
sweet york, be patient. hear me, gentle liege. 5.03. 91
tell me, gentle friend, | how went he under him? 5.05. 81
we thank thee, gentle percy, for thy pains, 5.06. 11
me hear | of you, my gentle cousin westmerland, 1H4 1.01. 31
took, | when on the gentle severn's sedgy bank, 1.03. 98
and "gentle harry percy" and "kind cousin" — 1.03.254
this evening must i leave you, gentle kate. 2.03.106
and so far will i trust thee, gentle kate. 2.03.112
down, | and rest your gentle head upon her lap, 3.01.212
dare | to gentle exercise and proof of arms. 5.02. 54
i pray thee, loving wife, and gentle daughter, 2H4 2.03. 1
o gentle sleep! 3.01. 5
fare you well, gentle gentlemen. 3.02.299 P
good day to you, gentle lord archbishop, | and 4.02. 2
health to my lord, and gentle cousin, mowbray. 4.02. 78
let there be no noise made, my gentle friends, 4.05. 1
washing with kindly tears his gentle cheeks, 4.05. 83
have wash'd his knife | with gentle eye–drops. 4.05. 87
i break, and you, my gentle creditors, lose. ep 12 P
the narrow seas | to give you gentle pass; H5 2.pr. 39
and you, my gentle knight, give me your thoughts 2.02. 14
o then belike she was old and gentle, and you 3.07. 52 P
cold fear, that mean and gentle all | behold, as 4.pr. 45
have before gor'd the gentle bosom of peace with 4.01.165 P
so vile, | this day shall gentle his condition; 4.03. 63
come thou no more for ransom, gentle herald, 4.03.122
that i may know the let why gentle peace 5.02. 65
and plead his love–suit to her gentle heart? 5.02.101
the rather, gentle princess, because i love thee 5.02.202 P
you may not, my lord, despise her gentle suit. 1H6 2.02. 47
thanks, gentle duke. 3.02.121
that doth presume to boast of gentle blood. 4.01. 44
say, gentle princess, would you not suppose 5.03.110
no, gentle madam, i unworthy am | to woo so fair 5.03.123
deny me not, i prithee, gentle joan. 5.04. 20
be patient, gentle nell, forget this grief. 2H6 2.04. 26
thy greatest help is quiet, gentle nell. 2.04. 67
what did i then, but curs'd the gentle gusts, 3.02. 88
o henry, let me plead for gentle suffolk! 3.02.289
ungentle queen, to call him gentle suffolk! 3.02.290
cease, gentle queen, these execrations, | and 3.02.305
as mild and gentle as the cradle–babe | dying 3.02.392
look with a gentle eye upon this wretch! 3.03. 20
well, seeing gentle words will not prevail, 4.02.174
thanks, gentle norfolk. 3H6 1.01. 31
be patient, gentle earl of westmerland. 1.01. 61
be patient, gentle queen, and i will stay. 1.01.214

stay, gentle margaret, and hear me speak. 1.01.257
gentle son edward, thou wilt stay /with me? 1.01.259
ah, gentle clifford, kill me with thy sword 1.03. 16
where is the duke of norfolk, gentle warwick? 2.01.142
to whom do lions cast their gentle looks? 2.02. 11
had slept, | and we, in pity of the gentle king, 2.02.161
since thou deniedst the gentle king to speak. 2.02.172
smile, gentle heaven! 2.03. 6
brother, give me thy hand, and gentle warwick, 2.03. 44
o, pity, pity, gentle heaven, pity! 2.05. 96
for what doth cherish weeds but gentle air? 2.06. 21
then, gentle clarence, welcome unto warwick, 4.02. 6
speak gentle words and humbly bend thy knee, 5.01. 22
thanks, gentle somerset, sweet oxford, thanks. 5.04. 58
and see our gentle queen how well she fares. 5.05. 89
o, he was gentle, mild, and virtuous! R3 1.02.104
but, gentle lady anne, | to leave this keen 1.02.114
there's many a gentle person made a jack. 1.03. 72
ah, gentle villain, do not turn away! 1.03.162
what, dost thou scorn me for my gentle counsel? 1.03.296
who knows not that the gentle duke is dead? 2.01. 80
that deceit should steal such gentle shape, 2.02. 27
the tiger now hath seiz'd the gentle hind; 2.04. 50
i thank you, gentle uncle. 3.01.102
ay, gentle cousin, were it light enough. 3.01.117
go, gentle catesby, | and, as it were far off, 3.01.169
give mistress shore one gentle kiss the more. 3.01.185
which i presume he'll take in gentle part. 3.04. 20
"thanks, gentle citizens and friends," quoth i, 3.07. 38
we know your tenderness of heart | and gentle, 3.07.211
farewell, my /cousin, farewell, gentle friends. 3.07.247
to gratulate the gentle princes there. 4.01. 10
thus," quoth dighton, "lay the gentle babes." 4.03. 9
and buried, gentle tyrrel? 4.03. 28
if yet your gentle souls fly in the air | and be 4.04. 11
wilt thou, o god, fly from such gentle lambs, 4.04. 22
to worry lambs and lap their gentle blood, 4.04. 50
where is the gentle rivers, vaughan, grey? 4.04.147
i will be mild and gentle in my words. 4.04.161
th' advancement of your children, gentle lady. 4.04.242
stir with the lark to-morrow, gentle norfolk. 5.03. 56
for, gentle hearers, know, | to rank our chosen H8 pr 17
it was a gentle business, and becoming | the 2.03. 54
you bear a gentle mind, and heav'nly blessings 2.03. 57
display'd th' effects | of disposition gentle, 2.04. 87
i know you have a gentle, noble temper, | a soul 3.01.165
still in thy right hand carry gentle peace | to 3.02.445
softly, gentle patience. 4.02. 82
that gentle physic given in time had cur'd me; 4.02.122
and | with gentle travail, to the gladding of 5.01. 71
pace 'em not in their hands to make 'em gentle, 5.02. 57
ruffian boreas once enrage | the gentle thetis, TRO 1.03. 39
no less noble, much more gentle, and altogether 2.03.149 P
o gentle pandar, | from cupid's shoulder pluck 3.02. 13
sir, | during all question of the gentle truce; 4.01. 12
this is the most despiteful gentle greeting, 4.01. 33
go, gentle knight, | stand by our ajax. 4.05. 88
thou art too gentle and too free a man. 4.05.139
most gentle and most valiant hector, welcome! 4.05.227
but gentle tell me, of what honor was | this 4.05.287
you were conducted to a gentle bath | and balms COR 1.06. 63
my gentle martius, worthy caius, and | by 2.01.172
'tis a condition they account gentle. 2.03. 97 P
all | than to take in a town with gentle words, 3.02. 59
when most strook home, being gentle wounded, 4.01. 8
thanks, gentle tribune, noble brother marcus. TIT 1.01.171
nor with sour looks afflict his gentle heart. 1.01.441
under your patience, gentle empress, | 'tis 2.03. 66
o tamora, be call'd a gentle queen, | and with 2.03.168
speak, gentle niece: 2.04. 16
o gentle, aged men! 3.01. 23
speak, gentle sister, who hath mart'red thee? 3.01. 81
gentle lavinia, let me kiss thy lips, | or make 3.01.120
o gentle aaron! 3.01.157
calm thee, gentle lord, although i know | there 4.01. 83
o gentle aaron, we are all undone! 4.02. 55
go, gentle marcus, to thy nephew lucius; 5.02.122
name, | and therefore bind them, gentle publius. 5.02.157
thanks, gentle romans, may i govern so, | to 5.03.147
but, gentle people, give me aim a while, | for 5.03.149
alas that love, so gentle in his view, | should ROM 1.01.169
but woo her, gentle paris, get her heart, | my 1.02. 16
nay, gentle romeo, we must have you dance. 1.04. 13
content thee, gentle coz, let him alone, | 'a 1.05. 65
hand | this holy shrine, the gentle sin is this: 1.05. 94
o gentle romeo, | if thou dost love, pronounce 2.02. 93
but, i'll warrant him, as gentle as a lamb. 2.05. 44 P
gentle mercutio, put thy rapier up. 3.01. 84
this, uttered | with gentle breath, calm look, 3.01.156
come, gentle night, come, loving, black-brow'd 3.02. 20
ay, those attires are best, but, gentle nurse, 4.03. 1
good gentle youth, tempt not a desp'rate man. 5.03. 59
our gentle flame | provokes itself and like the TIM 1.01. 23
good morrow to thee, gentle apemantus! 1.01.178
till i be gentle, stay thou for thy good morrow 1.01.179
so thou wilt send thy gentle heart before, | to 5.04. 48
and be not jealous on me, gentle brutus: JC 1.02. 71
tell us the manner of it, gentle casca. 1.02.234
and, gentle friends, | let's kill him boldly, 2.01.171
kneel not, gentle portia. 2.01.278
i should not need, if you were gentle brutus. 2.01.279
that i am meek and gentle with these butchers! 3.01.255
you gentle romans — 3.02. 72
have patience, gentle friends, i must not read 3.02.140
gentle knave, good night; 4.03.269
his life was gentle, and the elements | so mix'd 5.05. 73
recommends itself | unto our gentle senses. MAC 1.06. 3
o gentle lady, | 'tis not for you to hear what i 2.03. 83
gentle my lord, sleek o'er your rugged looks, 3.02. 27
ere humane statute purg'd the gentle weal; 3.04. 75
my ever gentle cousin, welcome hither. 4.03.161
but, gentle heavens, | cut short all 4.03.231
this gentle and unforc'd accord of hamlet | sits HAM 1.02.123
thanks, rosencrantz and gentle guildenstern. 2.02. 33
thanks, guildenstern and gentle rosencrantz. 2.02. 34
o gentle son, | upon the heat and flame of thy 3.04.122
you to use some gentle entertainment to laertes 5.02.206 P
hail, gentle sir. LR 4.06.208
leave, gentle wax, and, manners, blame us not: 4.06.259
gentle, and low, an excellent thing in woman. 5.03.274
iago, | but that i love the gentle desdemona, OTH 1.02. 25
welcome, gentle signior, | we lack'd your 1.03. 50
come hither, gentle mistress. 1.03.178
o gentle lady, do not put me to't, | for i am 2.01.118
look if my gentle love be not rais'd up! 2.03.250
and then, of so gentle a condition! 4.01.193 P
ay, too gentle. 4.01.194 P
babes | do it with gentle means and easy tasks. 4.02.112
i cry your gentle pardon; 5.01. 93
your captain | to soft and gentle speech. ANT 2.02. 3
gentle lords, let's part, | you see we have 2.07.121
gentle octavia, | let your best love draw to 3.04. 20
nay, gentle madam, to him, comfort him. 3.11. 25
(i will subscribe) gentle adieus and greetings; 4.05. 14
nay, weep not, gentle eros, there is left us 4.14. 21
gentle, hear me: 4.15. 47
how calm and gentle i proceeded still | in all 5.01. 75
a ditch in egypt | be gentle grave unto me! 5.02. 58
be gentle to her. 5.02. 68
gentle madam, no. 5.02. 94
which towards you are most gentle, you shall 5.02.127
as sweet as balm, as soft as air, as gentle — 5.02.311
that he quit being, and his gentle lady, | big CYM 1.01. 38
you gentle gods, give me but this i have, | and 1.01.115
but, my gentle queen, | where is our daughter? 3.05. 29
he said he was gentle, but unfortunate; 4.02. 39
they are as gentle | as zephyrs blowing below 4.02.171
these gentle princes | (for such and so they are 5.05.336
o my gentle brothers, | have we thus met? 5.05.374
and /midwife gentle | to those that cry by night PER 3.01. 11
quiet and gentle thy conditions! 3.01. 29
thither, gentle mariner, | alter thy course for 3.01. 74
hush, my gentle neighbors! 3.02.106
my gentle babe marina, whom, | for she was born 3.03. 12
your looks foreshow | you have a gentle heart. 4.01. 86
assur'd | came of a gentle kind and noble stock, 5.01. 68
how, gentle cousin? TNK 2.02. 70
why, gentle madam? 2.02.136
her, | and, if she be as gentle as she's fair, 2.03. 15
"fair gentle maid, good morrow. 2.04. 24
and to those gentle uses gave me life. 2.05. 7
/void'st of honor | that ev'r bore gentle token! 3.01. 37
find | too many hours to die in, gentle cousin. 3.06.112
i thank him for his gentle patience, | he's a 5.02. 43
your gentle daughter gave me freedom once; 5.04. 24
whose gentle wind | shall cool the heat of this VEN 189
steps, | with gentle majesty and modest pride; 278
"let me excuse thy courser, gentle boy, | and 403
distemp'ring gentle love in his desire, | as air 653
love's gentle spring doth always fresh remain, 801
lo here the gentle lark, weary of rest, | from 853
for now she knows it is no gentle chase, | but 883
then, gentle shadow (truth i must confess), | i 1001
to the rough beast that knows no gentle right, LUC 545
earth's dark womb some gentle gust doth get, 549
or tyrant folly lurk in gentle breasts? 851
deep woes roll forward like a gentle flood, 1118
men prove beasts, let beasts bear gentle minds." 1148
their gentle sex to weep are often willing, 1237
know, gentle wench, it small avails my mood; 1273
but smile and jest at every gentle offer. PP 4.12
those hours that with gentle work did frame SON 5. 1
shall hate be fairer lodg'd than gentle love? 10.10
a woman's gentle heart, but not acquainted 20. 3
i do forgive thy robb'ry, gentle thief, 40. 9
gentle thou art, and therefore to be won, 41. 5
art, | within the gentle closure of my breast, 48.11
aid, | my verse alone had all thy gentle grace, 79. 2
your monument shall be my gentle verse, | which 81. 9
some say thy grace is youth and gentle sport; 96. 2
redeem | in gentle numbers time so idly spent; 100. 6
o'er whom /thy fingers walk with gentle gait, 128.11
ever sweet, | was us'd in giving gentle doom, 145. 7
that follow'd it as gentle day | doth follow 145.10
then, gentle cheater, urge not my amiss, | lest 151. 3
'gentle maid, | have of my suffering youth some LC 177

GENTLEFOLKS 1 FR 0.0001 REL FR 1 V 0 P
that the queen's kindred are made gentlefolks. R3 1.01. 95

GENTLE-HEARTED 1 FR 0.0001 REL FR 1 V 0 P
and here's to right our gentle-hearted king. 3H6 1.04.176

/GENTLEMAN 4 FR 0.0004 REL FR 3 V 1 P
/in /england /the /most /valiant /gentleman. 2H4 4.01.130
believe me, an absolute /gentleman, full of most HAM 5.02.107 P
/i /am /a /gentleman /of /blood /and /breeding, LR 3.01. 40
/alack, /poor /gentleman! 4.03. 47

GENTLEMAN 291 FR 0.0329 REL FR 163 V 128 P
i know the gentleman | to be of worth and worthy TGV 2.04. 55
mind | with all good grace to grace a gentleman. 2.04. 74
this gentleman is come to me | with commendation 2.04. 78
this is the gentleman i told your ladyship | had 2.04. 87
have done, have done; here comes the gentleman. 2.04. 99
besides, the gentleman | is full of virtue, 3.01. 64
friends | unto a youthful gentleman of worth, 3.01.107
now, as thou art a gentleman of blood, | advise 3.01.121
'tis an ill office for a gentleman, | especially 3.02. 40
and i from mantua, for a gentleman, | who, in my 4.01. 48
music and see the gentleman that you ask'd for. 4.02. 31 P
o eglamour, thou art a gentleman — | think not 4.03. 11
true — from a gentleman to a fool. 5.02. 24
where is the gentleman that was with her? 5.03. 6
thou art a gentleman and well deriv'd, | take 5.04.146
and a gentleman born, master parson, who writes WIV 1.01. 8 P
i say the gentleman had drunk himself out of his 1.01.174 P
yet i live like a poor gentleman born. 1.01.276 P
truly, an honest gentleman; 1.04.163 P
thou'rt a gentleman. 2.01.193 P
sir, i am a gentleman that have spent much. 2.02.160 P
you are a gentleman of excellent breeding, 2.02.225 P
and last, as i am a gentleman, you shall, /and 2.02.254 P
master shallow, and another gentleman — from 3.01. 32 P
yonder is a most reverend gentleman, who, belike 3.01. 52 P
the gentleman is of no having. 3.02. 72 P
to search for a gentleman that he says is here 3.03.108 P
there is a gentleman, my dear friend; 3.03.121 P
and, as i am a gentleman, i'll give thee | a 4.06. 4
alas, this gentleman, | whom i would save, had a MM 2.01. 6
well, sir, what did this gentleman to her? 2.01.146 P
here's a gentleman, and a friend of mine. 3.02. 41 P
a gentleman of all temperance. 3.02.237 P
for the poor gentleman to the extremest shore of 3.02.251 P
this gentleman told somewhat of my tale — 5.01. 84
meddler, | as he's reported by this gentleman; 5.01.146
more | than i stand debted to this gentleman. ERR 4.01. 31
both wind and tide stays for this gentleman, 4.01. 46
i met him, | and in his company that gentleman. 5.01.226
i see, lady, the gentleman is not in your books. ADO 1.01. 78 P
so some gentleman or other shall scape a 1.01.134 P
how tartly that gentleman looks! 2.01. 3 P
when i know the gentleman, i'll tell him what 2.01.144 P
the gentleman that danc'd with her told her she 2.01.237 P
doth not the gentleman | deserve as full as 3.01. 44
she would swear the gentleman should be her 3.01. 62
so rare a gentleman as signior benedick. 3.01. 91
'a goes up and down like a gentleman. 3.03.127 P
i am a gentleman, sir, and my name is conrade. 4.02. 13 P
write down master gentleman conrade. 4.02. 15 P
fence, | nay, as i am a gentleman, i will. 5.01. 85
"nay," said i, "the gentleman is wise." 5.01.164 P
"certain," said she, "a wise gentleman." 5.01.166 P
come, cousin, i am sure you love the gentleman. 5.04. 84
and, as i am a gentleman, betook myself to walk: LLL 1.01.234 P
you are a gentleman and a gamester, sir. 1.02. 42 P
the king is a noble gentleman, and my familiar, 5.01. 95 P
illustrate, and learned gentleman, before the 5.01.122 P
and this gallant gentleman, judas machabeus; 5.01.127 P
thrice-worthy gentleman! 5.01.144 P
which shall be either to this gentleman, | or to MND 1.01. 43
demetrius is a worthy gentleman. 1.01. 52
be kind and courteous to this gentleman. 3.01.164
your name, honest gentleman? 3.01.184 P
hath devour'd many a gentleman of your house. 3.01.193 P
master young gentleman, i pray you, which is the MV 2.02. 39 P
father, for the young gentleman, according to 2.02. 61 P
i know you not, young gentleman, but i pray you 2.02. 70 P
to become | the follower of so poor a gentleman. 2.02.148
a kinder gentleman treads not the earth. 2.08. 35
i was a gentleman; 3.02.255
honor, | how true a gentleman you send relief, 3.04. 6
upon his death unto the gentleman | that lately 4.01.384
antonio, gratify this gentleman, | for in my 4.01.406
most worthy gentleman, i and my friend | have by 4.01.408
you that keeping for a gentleman of my birth, AYL 1.01. 9 P
me such exercises as may become a gentleman, or 1.01. 72 P
young gentleman, your spirits are too bold for 1.02.173 P
gentleman, | wear this for me; 1.02.245
ay. fare you well, fair gentleman. 1.02.248
that i know you are a gentleman of good conceit. 5.02. 53 P
well met, honest gentleman. 5.03. 7 P
the motley-minded gentleman that i have so often 5.04. 41 P
belike some noble gentleman that means SHR in.1. 75
minola, | an affable and courteous gentleman. 1.02. 98
and i have met a gentleman | hath promis'd me to 1.02.171
here is a gentleman whom by chance i met, | upon 1.02.181
this gentleman is happily arriv'd, | my mind 1.02.212
baptista is a noble gentleman, | to whom my 1.02.238
what, this gentleman will out-talk us all. 1.02.246
you must, as we do, gratify this gentleman, | to 1.02.271
was ever gentleman thus griev'd as i? 2.01. 37
i am a gentleman of verona, sir, | that, hearing 2.01. 47
i am a gentleman — 2.01.219
if you strike me, you are no gentleman, | and if 2.01.222
and if no gentleman, why then no arms. 2.01.223
for such a one as leaves a gentleman | and makes 4.02. 19
sir, this is the gentleman i told you of. 4.04. 20
may beseem | the spouse of any noble gentleman. 4.05. 67
why, how now, gentleman? 5.01. 35 P
seem a sober ancient gentleman by your habit; 5.01. 73 P
and a gentleman | which i have sometime known. AWW 3.02. 84
been solicited by a gentleman his companion. 3.05. 15 P
there is a gentleman that serves the count 3.05. 56
is't not a handsome gentleman? 3.05. 80
my master hath been an honorable gentleman. 5.03.239 P
did love her, sir, as a gentleman loves a woman. 5.03.245 P
is at the gate a young gentleman much desires to TN 1.05. 99 P
a gentleman. 1.05.118 P
a gentleman? what gentleman? 1.05.119 P
a gentleman? what gentleman? 1.05.119 P
'tis a gentleman here — a plague o' these 1.05.120 P
i am a gentleman. 1.05.279
i am a gentleman." 1.05.291
'save you, gentleman. 3.01. 69 P
the young gentleman of the count orsino's is 3.04. 57 P
of the young gentleman gives him out to be of 3.04.185 P
notable report of valor, and drive the gentleman 3.04.192 P
gentleman, god save thee! 3.04.218 P
stay you by this gentleman till my return. 3.04.258 P
there's no remedy, the gentleman will, for his 3.04.306 P
promis'd me, as he is a gentleman and a soldier, 3.04.308 P
if this young gentleman | have done offense, i 3.04.312
as i am a gentleman, i will live to be thankful 4.02. 82 P
the count's gentleman, one cesario. 5.01.180 P
my gentleman, cesario? 5.01.183 P
how now, gentleman? how is't with you? 5.01.195 P
suit, | a gentleman, and follower of my lady's. 5.01.277
they say, poor gentleman, he's much distract. 5.01.280
it is a gentleman of the greatest promise that WT 1.01. 35 P
to this kernel, | this squash, this gentleman. 1.02.160
as you are certainly a gentleman, thereto 1.02.391
and how the poor gentleman roar'd, and the bear 3.03.100 P
water, nor the bear half din'd on the gentleman. 3.03.106 P
be gone from the gentleman and how much he hath 3.03.129 P
his sworn brother, a very simple gentleman! 4.04.596 P
in't) and change garments with this gentleman. 4.04.635 P
the gentleman is half /flea'd already. 4.04.640 P
sure | when i shall see this gentleman, thy 5.01.121
o my brother, | good gentleman! 5.01.148
a graceful gentleman, against whose person | (so 5.01.171
here comes a gentleman that happily knows more. 5.02. 20 P
this other day, because i was no gentleman born. 5.02.129 P
them not and think me still no gentleman born. 5.02.131 P
and try whether i am not now a gentleman born. 5.02.133 P
i know you are now, sir, a gentleman born. 5.02.135 P
but i was a gentleman born before my father; 5.02.139 P
not swear it, now i am a gentleman? 5.02.159 P

a true gentleman may swear it in the behalf of 5.02.162 P
your faithful subject i, a gentleman, | born in JN 1.01. 50
when this same lusty gentleman was got. 1.01.108
that smooth–fac'd gentleman, tickling commodity, 2.01.573
spoke like a sprightful noble gentleman. 4.02.177
to prove myself a loyal gentleman | even in the R2 1.01.148
throne, | a loyal, just, and upright gentleman. 1.03. 87
than was that young and princely gentleman. 2.01.175
a happy gentleman in blood and lineaments, | by 3.01. 9
blood, | to show the world i am a gentleman. 3.01. 27
a gentleman of mine i have dispatch'd | with 3.01. 40
just, | and, as i am a gentleman, i credit him. 3.03.120
in faith, he is a worthy gentleman, 1H4 3.01.163
as virtuously given as a gentleman need to be, 3.03. 15 P
his head, | i do not think a braver gentleman, 5.01. 89
dead | bears not alive so stout a gentleman. 5.04. 93
a gentleman well bred and of good name, | that 2H4 1.01. 26
after him came spurring hard | a gentleman, 1.01. 37
why should that gentleman that rode by travers 1.01. 55
yea–forsooth knave, to bear a gentleman in hand, 1.02. 36 P
as i am a gentleman! 2.01.136 P
as i am a gentleman! come, no more words of it. 2.01.138 P
i am a gentleman, thou art a drawer. 2.04.287 P
sir john falstaff, a tall gentleman, by heaven, 3.02. 61 P
honest gentleman, i know not your breeding. 5.03.107 P
by an irishman, a very valiant gentleman, i' H5 3.02. 67 P
captain jamy is a marvellous falorous gentleman, 3.02. 76 P
is simply the most active gentleman of france. 3.07. 97 P
a valiant and most expert gentleman. 3.07.129 P
i am a gentleman of a company. 4.01. 39 P
as good a gentleman as the emperor. 4.01. 42
a good old commander and a most kind gentleman. 4.01. 95 P
art thou a gentleman? 4.04. 5 P
o signieur dew should be a gentleman. 4.04. 7
he is a gentleman of a good house, and for his 4.04. 44 P
may be his enemy is a gentleman of great sort, 4.07.135 P
he be as good a gentleman as the devil is, as 4.07.137 P
and galling at this gentleman twice or thrice. 5.01. 74 P
let him that is a true–born gentleman | and 1H6 2.04. 27
poor gentleman, his wrong doth equal mine. 2.05. 22
so should we save a valiant gentleman | by 4.03. 26
him aid, | while he, renowned noble gentleman, 4.04. 24
did bear him like a noble gentleman. 2H6 1.01.184
look on my george, i am a gentleman: 4.01. 29
we will not leave one lord, one gentleman; 4.02.184
blood, | the noble gentleman gave up the ghost. 3H6 2.03. 22
york | the worthy gentleman did lose his life. 3.02. 7
a sweeter and a lovelier gentleman, | fram'd in R3 1.02.242
since every jack became a gentleman, | there's 1.03. 71
who slew to–day a riotous gentleman | lately 2.01.101
and finds the testy gentleman so hot | that he 3.04. 37
i know a discontented gentleman | whose humble 4.02. 36
inquire me out some mean poor gentleman, | whom 4.02. 53
before us | that gentleman of buckingham's; H8 1.02. 5
the gentleman is learn'd, and a most rare 1.02.111
shall hear | (this was his gentleman in trust) 1.02.125
lady | or gentleman that is not freely merry 1.04. 36
a bold brave gentleman. 4.01. 40
there is staying | a gentleman, sent from the 4.02.106
thomas, y' are a gentleman | of mine own way; 5.01. 27
and yet the gentleman | that was sent to me from 5.02. 1
you depend upon a notable gentleman; TRO 3.01. 6 P
o poor gentleman! 4.02. 87 P
bold gentleman! COR 1.05. 22
a gentleman. 4.05. 26 P
pray you, poor gentleman, take up some other 4.05. 29 P
this noble gentleman, lord titus here, | is in TIT 1.01.415
can you love the gentleman? ROM 1.03. 79
alone, | 'a bears him like a portly gentleman; 1.05. 66
come hither, nurse. what is yond gentleman? 1.05.128
but trust me, gentleman, i'll prove more true 2.02.100
a gentleman of the very first house, of the 2.04. 24 P
a gentleman, nurse, that loves to hear himself 2.04.147 P
your love says, like an honest gentleman, | an' 2.05. 55
"your love says, like an honest gentleman, 2.05. 60
this gentleman, the prince's near ally, | my 3.01.109
o courteous tybalt, honest gentleman, | that 3.02. 62
morn, | the gallant, young, and noble gentleman, 3.05.113
wrought | so worthy a gentleman to be her bride? 3.05.145
now provided | a gentleman of noble parentage, 3.05.179
o, he's a lovely gentleman! 3.05.218
him | a gentleman that well deserves a help, TIM 1.01.102
this gentleman of mine hath serv'd me long; 1.01.142
well fare you, gentleman; 1.01.163
my lord, that honorable gentleman, lord lucullus 1.02.187 P
complete, free–hearted gentleman of athens, thy 3.01. 10 P
a noble gentleman 'tis, if he would not keep so 3.01. 22 P
thy lord's a bountiful gentleman, but thou art 3.01. 40 P
my very good friend, and an honorable gentleman. 3.02. 2 P
i cannot pleasure such an honorable gentleman. 3.02. 57 P
o valiant cousin, worthy gentleman! MAC 1.02. 24
thane of cawdor lives | a prosperous gentleman; 1.03. 73
he was a gentleman on whom i built | an absolute 1.04. 13
or "friend," or "gentleman," | according to the HAM 2.01. 46
"i know the gentleman. 2.01. 53
most like a gentleman. 3.01. 11
speak | like a good child and a true gentleman. 4.05.149
months since | here was a gentleman of normandy: 4.07. 82
was he a gentleman? 5.01. 32 P
continent of what part a gentleman would see. 5.02.111 P
why do we wrap the gentleman in our more rawer 5.02.123 P
what imports the nomination of this gentleman? 5.02.127 P
let the foils be brought, the gentleman willing, 5.02.175 P
wrong, | but pardon't, as you are a gentleman. 5.02.227
do you know this noble gentleman, edmund? LR 1.01. 25 P
my father strike my gentleman for chiding of his 1.03. 1
much more worse | to have her gentleman abus'd, 2.02.149
the prince of darkness is a gentleman. 3.04.143 P
me whether a madman be a gentleman or a yeoman? 3.06. 10 P
he's a yeoman that has a gentleman to his son; 3.06. 12 P
yeoman that sees his son a gentleman before him. 3.06. 14 P
good gentleman, go your gait, and let poor voke 4.06.237 P
why, thou silly gentleman? OTH 1.03.307 P
this gentleman | steps in to cassio and entreats 2.03.228
alas, what does this gentleman conceive? 4.02. 95
alas, good gentleman! alas, good cassio! 5.01.115
herself | unto a poor but worthy gentleman. CYM 1.01. 7
and had (besides this gentleman in question) 1.01. 34
big of this gentleman, our theme, deceas'd | as 1.01. 39
here comes the gentleman, | the queen, and 1.01. 68
you all be better known to this gentleman, whom 1.04. 31 P
this gentleman at that time vouching (and upon 1.04. 58 P
madam, a noble gentleman of rome, | comes from 1.06. 10
thou wrong'st a gentleman, who is as far | from 1.06.145
when a gentleman is dispos'd to swear, it is not 2.01. 10 P
a gentleman. 2.03. 77
that this gentleman may render | of whom he had 5.05.135
this gentleman, whom i call polydore, | most 5.05.357
this gentleman, my cadwal, arviragus, | your 5.05.359
court, | where with it i may appear a gentleman; PER 2.01.141
sure he's a gallant gentleman. 2.03. 32
he's but a country gentleman: 2.03. 33
a gentleman of tyre, my name, pericles, | my 2.03. 81
names himself pericles, | a gentleman of tyre, 2.03. 87
lord, | a stranger and distressed gentleman, 2.05. 46
why should i love this gentleman? TNK 2.04. 1
fairer spoken | was never gentleman. 2.04. 21
are you a gentleman? 2.05. 6
pirithous, | dispose of this fair gentleman. 2.05. 32
with the mind and sword | of a true gentleman. 3.01. 57
is't not a fine young gentleman? 4.01.118
hope she had fix'd her liking on this gentleman, 4.03. 65 P
he's a kind gentleman, and i am much bound to 5.02. 44

GENTLEMAN–LIKE 5 FR 0.0005 REL FR 0 V 5 P
company of three or four gentleman–like dogs, TGV 4.04. 17 P
a most lovely gentleman–like man: MND 1.02. 87 P
and hiding from me all gentleman–like qualities. AYL 1.01. 69 P
was the first gentleman–like tears that ever we WT 5.02.144 P
which, as i take it, is a gentleman–like offer. ROM 2.04.178 P

GENTLEMAN'S 4 FR 0.0004 REL FR 0 V 4 P
beseech you, sir, look in this gentleman's face. MM 2.01.147 P
good enough, for all the old gentleman's saying. AYL 5.01. 4 P
a christian footboy or a gentleman's lackey. SHR 3.02. 71 P
or this gentleman's opinion by this worn out. CYM 1.04. 62 P

/GENTLEMEN 4 FR 0.0004 REL FR 4 V 0 P
i pray you, though you mock me, /gentlemen, MND 3.02.299
on, /gentlemen, away! MV 2.06. 58
wrath–kindled /gentlemen, be rul'd by me, R2 1.01.152
thanks, /gentlemen. 1H6 2.04.131

GENTLEMEN 190 FR 0.0214 REL FR 128 V 62 P
did it to minister occasion to these gentlemen, TMP 2.01.173 P
you are gentlemen of brave mettle; 2.01.182 P
of all the fair resort of gentlemen | that every TGV 1.02. 4
i am) | should censure thus on lovely gentlemen. 1.02. 19
alphonso | with other gentlemen of good esteem 1.03. 40
a fine volley of words, gentlemen, and quickly 2.04. 33 P
no more, gentlemen, no more; 2.04. 47 P
to sort some gentlemen well skill'd in music. 3.02. 91
about it, gentlemen! 3.02. 94
know, then, that some of us are gentlemen, 4.01. 42
now, gentlemen, | let's tune, and to it lustily 4.02. 24
i thank you for your music, gentlemen. 4.02. 86
dispatch, sweet gentlemen, and follow me. 5.02. 48
you hear all these matters denied, gentlemen; WIV 1.01.186 P
wife, bid these gentlemen welcome. 1.01.194 P
come, gentlemen, i hope we shall drink down all 1.01.196 P
in hell for swearing to gentlemen my friends, 2.02. 10 P
and lords, and gentlemen, with their coaches; 2.02. 64 P
de knight, de lords, de gentlemen, my patients. 2.03. 92 P
follow, gentlemen, follow. 3.01.112 P
gentlemen, i have dream'd to–night; 3.03.160 P
up, gentlemen, you shall see sport anon. 3.03.168 P
follow me, gentlemen. 3.03.169 P
nay, follow him, gentlemen, see the issue of his 3.03.174 P
let's go in, gentlemen, but, trust me, we'll 3.03.228 P
good gentlemen, let him /not strike the old 4.02.181 P
will you follow, gentlemen? 4.02.195 P
come, gentlemen. 4.02.200 P
let me speak with the gentlemen; 4.03. 6 P
bore many gentlemen (myself being one) | in hand MM 1.04. 51
that, when gentlemen are tir'd, gives them a sob ERR 4.03. 25 P
how many gentlemen have you lost in this action? ADO 1.01. 5 P
gentlemen both, we will not wake your patience. 5.01.102
gentlemen and soldiers, pardon me, i will not LLL 5.02.704 P
go, gentlemen, | will you prepare you for this MV 2.04. 21
gentlemen, my master antonio is at his house and 3.01. 74 P
they say many young gentlemen flock to him every AYL 1.01.117 P
truly, young gentlemen, though there was no 5.03. 34 P
gentlemen, importune me no farther, | for how i SHR 1.01. 48
gentlemen, that i may soon make good | what i 1.01. 74
gentlemen, content ye; 1.01. 90
gentlemen, god save you. 1.02.218
if you be gentlemen, | do me this right: 1.02.236
god save you, gentlemen! 2.01. 41 P
sirrah, lead these gentlemen | to my daughters, 2.01.108
be patient, gentlemen, i choose her for myself. 2.01.302
father, and wife, and gentlemen, adieu. 2.01.321
faith, gentlemen, now i play a merchant's part, 2.01.326
content you, gentlemen, i will compound this 2.01.341
well, gentlemen, | i am thus resolv'd: 2.01.392
why, gentlemen, you do me double wrong | to 3.01. 16
gentlemen and friends, i thank you for your 3.02.184
gentlemen, forward to the bridal dinner. 3.02.219
she shall, lucentio. come, gentlemen, let's go. 3.02.252
for our gentlemen that mean to see | the tuscan AWW 1.02. 13
gentlemen, | heaven hath through me restor'd the 2.03. 63
pray you, gentlemen, | i have felt so many 3.02. 48
brought you this letter, gentlemen? 3.02. 62
y' are welcome, gentlemen. 3.02. 91
tricks he hath had in him, which gentlemen have. 5.03.240 P
fare you well, gentlemen. TN 1.03. 60 P
take away the fool, gentlemen. 1.05. 72 P
my father and the gentlemen are in sad talk, and WT 4.04.310 P
sons and daughters will be all gentlemen born. 5.02.127 P
best say these robes are not gentlemen born. 5.02.132 P
for we must be gentle, now we are gentlemen. 5.02.153 P
young gentlemen would be as sad as night, | only JN 4.01. 15
come, gentlemen, let's all go visit him. R2 1.04. 63
and well met, gentlemen. 2.02. 41
gentlemen, will you go muster men? 2.02.108
gentlemen, go muster up your men, | and meet me 2.02.118
and all your southern gentlemen in arms | upon 3.02.202
us be diana's foresters, gentlemen of the shade, 1H4 1.02. 26 P
neighbor mugs, we'll call up the gentlemen. 2.01. 45 P
there are two gentlemen | have in this robbery 2.04.519
tenants, friends, and neighboring gentlemen. 3.01. 89
lieutenants, gentlemen of companies — slaves as 4.02. 24 P
a head | of gallant warriors, noble gentlemen. 4.04. 26
arm, gentlemen, to arms! 5.02. 41
o gentlemen, the time of life is short! 5.02. 81
good morrow, honest gentlemen. 2H4 3.02. 55 P
fie, this is hot weather, gentlemen. 3.02. 92 P
fare you well, gentlemen both, i thank you. 3.02.289 P
fare you well, gentle gentlemen. 3.02.299 P
of he, the worst of these three gentlemen! 5.02. 16
if the gentlemen will not, then the gentlemen do ep 23 P
not, then the gentlemen do not agree with the ep 23 P
why, how now, gentlemen? H5 2.02. 71
gentlemen both, you will mistake each other. 3.02.134 P
and gentlemen in england, now a–bed, | shall 4.03. 64
of knights, esquires, and gallant gentlemen, 4.08. 84
squires, | and gentlemen of blood and quality. 4.08. 90
great lords and gentlemen, what means this 1H6 2.04. 1
stay, lords and gentlemen, and pluck no more, 2.04. 39
and dare not take up arms like gentlemen. 3.02. 70
myself and divers gentlemen beside | were there 4.01. 25
say, gentlemen, what makes you thus exclaim? 4.01. 83
so many captains, gentlemen, and soldiers, 5.04.104
and bear the name and port of gentlemen? 2H6 4.01. 19
merry world in england since gentlemen came up. 4.02. 8 P
all scholars, lawyers, courtiers, gentlemen, 4.04. 36
the knights and gentlemen to come with thee. 3H6 4.08. 13
knights, and gentlemen, what i should say | my 5.04. 73
o gentlemen, see, see dead henry's wounds | open R3 1.02. 55
dukes, earls, lords, gentlemen — indeed of all. 2.01. 69
come, noble gentlemen, | let us survey the 5.03. 14
come, gentlemen, | let us consult upon 5.03. 44
once more, good night, kind lords and gentlemen. 5.03.107
cry mercy, lords and watchful gentlemen, | that 5.03.224
truly, gentlemen, | a bloody tyrant and a 5.03.245
go, gentlemen, every man unto his charge. 5.03.307
fight, gentlemen of england! 5.03.338
gentlemen, | the penance lies on you, if these H8 1.04. 31
gentlemen, | whose fault is this? 1.04. 42
see then, | by all your good leaves, gentlemen; 1.04. 85
a health, gentlemen! 1.04. 96
(whom, if he live, will scarce be gentlemen), 3.02.292
come, gentlemen, ye shall go my way, which | is 4.01.114
but for our gentlemen, | the common file (a COR 1.06. 42
on, lusty gentlemen! ROM 1.04.113
welcome, gentlemen! 1.05. 16
welcome, gentlemen! 1.05. 21
you are welcome, gentlemen! 1.05. 25
nay, gentlemen, prepare not to be gone, | we 1.05.121
i thank you, honest gentlemen, good night. 1.05.124
god ye good morrow, gentlemen. 2.04.109 P
gentlemen, can any of you tell me where i may 2.04.118 P
gentlemen, good den, a word with one of you. 3.01. 38
gentlemen, for shame, forbear this outrage! 3.01. 87
please you, gentlemen, | the time is unagreeable TIM 2.02. 39
how do you, gentlemen? 2.02. 66 P
lord timon myself, these gentlemen can witness; 3.02. 51 P
if i might beseech you, gentlemen, to repair 3.04. 68 P
with all my heart, gentlemen both; 3.06. 25 P
gentlemen, our dinner will not recompense this 3.06. 32 P
good gentlemen, look fresh and merrily; JC 2.01.224
i know not, gentlemen, what you intend, | who 3.01.151
gentlemen all — alas, what shall i say? 3.01.190
i thank you, gentlemen. MAC 1.03.129
kind gentlemen, your pains | are regist'red 1.03.150
gentlemen, rise, his highness is not well. 3.04. 51
where are these gentlemen? 4.01.155
deliver, | upon the witness of these gentlemen, HAM 1.02.194
two nights together had these gentlemen, 1.02.196
unhand me, gentlemen. 1.04. 84
come hither, gentlemen, | and lay your hands 1.05.157
so, gentlemen, | with all my love i do commend 1.05.182
good gentlemen, he hath much talk'd of you, 2.02. 19
and bring these gentlemen where hamlet is. 2.02. 37
gentlemen, you are welcome to elsinore. 2.02.370 P
well be with you, gentlemen! 2.02.380 P
good gentlemen, give him a further edge, | and 3.01. 26
there is no ancient gentlemen but gard'ners, 5.01. 30 P
gentlemen! 5.01.264
gentlemen, let's look to our business. OTH 2.03.112 P
do not think, gentlemen, i am drunk: 2.03.113 P
good lieutenant — /god's /will, gentlemen — 2.03.158
lieutenant — sir — montano — gentlemen — 2.03.166
this fortification, gentlemen, shall we see't? 3.02. 5
light, gentlemen! 5.01. 73
gentlemen all, i do suspect this trash | to be a 5.01. 85
stay you, good gentlemen. 5.01.105
do you see, gentlemen? 5.01.109
kind gentlemen, let's go see poor cassio dress'd 5.01.124
good gentlemen, let me have leave to speak. 5.02.195
by heaven, i do not, i do not, gentlemen. 5.02.232
they were parted | by gentlemen at hand. CYM 1.01.164
you as suits with gentlemen of your knowing to a 1.04. 29 P
let us leave here, gentlemen. 1.04. 99 P
gentlemen, enough of this. 1.04.120 P
up the confiners | and gentlemen of italy, most 4.02.338
with a supply | of roman gentlemen, by the 4.03. 26
sir, | in cambria are we born, and gentlemen. 5.05. 17
o gentlemen, help | mine and your mistress! 5.05.229
these two young gentlemen, that call me father 5.05.328
sir, for we are gentlemen | have neither in our PER 2.03. 24
come, gentlemen, we sit too long on trifles, 2.03. 92
thanks, gentlemen, to all, all have done well; 2.03.107
gentlemen, | why do you stir so early? 3.02. 11
gentlemen, this queen will live. 3.02. 92
shall you, and taste gentlemen of all fashions. 4.02. 78 P
we'll have no more gentlemen driven away. 4.06.129 P
that he have his. call up some gentlemen. 5.01. 6
ho, gentlemen! my lord calls. 5.01. 7
gentlemen, there is some of worth would come 5.01. 9
what means the /nun? she dies, help, gentlemen! 5.03. 15
by your leave, gentlemen. TNK 2.02.220
and take heed, as you are gentlemen, this 3.06.303
gentlemen, good night. ep 18
submit you to these noble gentlemen, | entreat STM II.C 144

GENTLENESS 18 FR 0.0020 REL FR 16 V 2 P

so, of his gentleness, | knowing i lov'd my TMP 1.02.165
the truth you speak doth lack some gentleness, 2.01.138
of breath — your gentleness | was guilty of it. LLL 5.02.735
i thought you lord of more true gentleness. MND 2.02.132
but, touch'd with humane gentleness and love, MV 4.01. 25
your gentleness shall force, | more than your AYL 2.07.102
more than your force move us to gentleness. 2.07.103
let gentleness my strong enforcement be, | in 2.07.118
and therefore sit you down in gentleness | and 2.07.124
the gentleness of all the gods go with thee! TN 2.01. 44
no way but gentleness — gently, gently. 3.04.110 P
(if thy rare qualities, sweet gentleness, | thy H8 2.04.138
manhood, learning, gentleness, virtue, youth, TRO 1.02.254 P
in humane gentleness, | welcome to troy! 4.01. 21
and will with deeds requite thy gentleness; TIT 1.01.237
i have not from your eyes that gentleness | and JC 1.02. 33
this milky gentleness and course of yours LR 1.04.341
blazon, holds me to | this gentleness of answer: TNK 3.01. 48
GENTLER 10 FR 0.0011 REL FR 8 V 2 P
you, | unless you were of gentler, milder mould. SHR 1.01. 60
we marry | a gentler scion to the wildest stock, WT 4.04. 93
the gentler gamester is the soonest winner. H5 3.06.113 P
whilst /by /a slave, no gentler than my dog, 4.05. 15
a gentler heart did never sway in court; 1H6 3.02.135
i am descended of a gentler blood. 5.04. 8
which you are out of, with a gentler spirit, COR 3.01. 55
a gentler judgment vanish'd from his lips — ROM 3.03. 10
put it by thrice, every time gentler than other; JC 1.02.230 P
how goes it now? he looks gentler than he did. OTH 4.03. 11
GENTLES 8 FR 0.0009 REL FR 6 V 2 P
will you go, gentles? WIV 3.02. 91 P
good wits will be jangling, but, gentles, agree: LLL 2.01.225
away, the gentles are at their game, and we will 4.02.166 P
gentles, perchance you wonder at this show; MND 5.01.127
but a dream, | gentles, do not reprehend. 5.01.429
gentles, methinks you frown, | and wherefore SHR 3.02. 93
but pardon, gentles all, | the flat unraised H5 pr 8
and the scene | is now transported, gentles, to 2.pr. 35
GENTLE–SLEEPING 1 FR 0.0001 REL FR 1 V 0 P
and there awake god's gentle–sleeping peace. R3 1.03.287
GENTLEST 2 FR 0.0002 REL FR 2 V 0 P
neptune and | the gentlest winds of heaven. PER 3.03. 37
for if it see the rud'st or gentlest sight, SON 113. 9
GENTLEWOMAN 43 FR 0.0048 REL FR 16 V 27 P
we talk on | often resort unto this gentlewoman? TGV 4.02. 74
gentlewoman, good day; 4.04.108
poor gentlewoman, my master wrongs her much. 4.04.141
a virtuous gentlewoman, mild and beautiful! 4.04.180
i know the young gentlewoman, she has good gifts WIV 1.01. 62 P
to desire this honest gentlewoman, your maid, to 1.04. 82 P
there is a gentlewoman in this town, her 2.02.191 P
he will maintain you like a gentlewoman. 3.04. 45 P
a gentlewoman of mine, | who, falling in the MM 2.03. 10
how heavily this befell to the poor gentlewoman. 3.01.219 P
here's a gentlewoman denies all that you have 5.01.281 P
did you converse, sir, with this gentlewoman? ERR 2.02.160
and this fair gentlewoman, her sister here, 5.01.374
woo'd margaret, the lady hero's gentlewoman, by ADO 3.03.145 P
hisperia, the princess' gentlewoman, | confesses AYL 2.02. 10
'twas where you woo'd the gentlewoman so well. SHR in.1. 85
voice, gait, and action of a gentlewoman. in.1. 132
brought up as best becomes a gentlewoman. 1.02. 87
too, | hast thou beheld a fresher gentlewoman? 4.05. 29
the sister to my wife, this gentlewoman, | thy 4.05. 62
this young gentlewoman had a father — o, that AWW 1.01. 17 P
was this gentlewoman the daughter of gerard de 1.01. 37 P
what say you of this gentlewoman? 1.03. 2 P
tell my gentlewoman i would speak with her — 1.03. 68 P
know, madam, you love your gentlewoman entirely. 1.03. 99 P
perverted a young gentlewoman here in florence, 4.03. 14 P
the most virtuous gentlewoman that ever nature 4.05. 9 P
let him approach. call in my gentlewoman. TN 1.05.163 P
gentlewoman, my lady calls. 1.05.164 P
dear gentlewoman, | how fares our gracious lady? WT 2.02. 18
a proper gentlewoman, sir, and a kinswoman of my 2H4 2.02.155 P
before this honest, virtuous, civil gentlewoman! 2.04.302 P
this virtuous gentlewoman to close with us. 2.04.327 P
you, gentlewoman — 2.04.348 P
you'll question this gentlewoman about me; H5 5.02.199 P
the late queen's gentlewoman? H8 3.02. 94
god ye good den, fair gentlewoman. ROM 2.04.110 P
one, gentlewoman, that god hath made, himself to 2.04.115 P
for the gentlewoman is young; 2.04.167 P
an ill thing to be off'red to any gentlewoman, 2.04.169 P
if this had not been a gentlewoman, she should HAM 5.01. 24 P
your name, fair gentlewoman? LR 1.04.236
if the gentlewoman that attends the /general's OTH 3.01. 24 P
GENTLEWOMAN'S 2 FR 0.0002 REL FR 1 V 1 P
make water against a gentlewoman's farthingale? TGV 4.04. 38 P
yes, and a gentlewoman's son. CYM 2.03. 78
/GENTLEWOMEN 1 FR 0.0001 REL FR 1 V 0 P
her /gentlewomen, like the nereides, | so many ANT 2.02.206
GENTLEWOMEN 7 FR 0.0008 REL FR 3 V 4 P
must your daughter and her gentlewomen carry. ADO 2.03.215 P
well, daughter, and you gentlewomen all, 5.04. 10
time, | and gentlewomen wear such caps as these. SHR 4.03. 70
all the gentlewomen here have forgiven me; 2H4 ep 22 P
the gentlemen do not agree with the gentlewomen, ep 24 P
dozen or fourteen gentlewomen that live honestly H5 2.01. 33 P
since that our brother dubb'd them gentlewomen, R3 1.01. 82
GENTLY 38 FR 0.0043 REL FR 31 V 7 P
to command | and do my spriting gently. TMP 1.02.298
i will roar you as gently as any sucking dove; MND 1.02. 82 P
woodbine the sweet honeysuckle | gently entwist; 4.01. 43
when the sweet wind did gently kiss the trees MV 5.01. 2
speak you so gently? AYL 2.07.106
carry him gently to my fairest chamber, | and SHR in.1. 46
take him up gently and to bed with him, | and in.1. 72
peace, peace, we must deal gently with him. TN 3.04. 96 P
no way but gentleness — gently, gently. 3.04.110 P
no way but gentleness — gently, gently. 3.04.110 P
being something gently consider'd, i'll bring WT 4.04.795 P
hand, | it may lie gently at the foot of peace, JN 5.02. 76
which gently laid my knighthood on my shoulder, R2 1.01. 79
who gently would dissolve the bands of life, 2.02. 71
i told him gently of our grievances, | of his 1H4 5.02. 36
may stroke him as gently as a puppy greyhound. 2H4 2.04. 98 P
gently to hear, kindly to judge, our play. H5 pr 34
peace, | and lay them gently on thy tender side. 1H6 5.03. 49
who look'd full gently on his warlike queen, 3H6 2.01.123
fell gently down, as if they struck their 2.01.132
if friend or foe, let him be gently used. 2.06. 45
must gently be preserv'd, cherish'd, and kept. R3 2.02.119
so may he rest, his faults lie gently on him! H8 4.02. 31
and bring our emperor gently in thy hand, TIT 5.03.138
would i were gently put out of office | before i TIM 1.02.201
march gently on to meet him. JC 4.02. 31
this way, my lord, the castle's gently rend'red: MAC 5.07. 24
hand, thus, but use all gently, for in the very HAM 3.02. 5 P
what's amiss, | may it be gently heard. ANT 2.02. 20
if thou and nature can so gently part, | the 5.02.294
dreadful thunders, gently quench | thy nimble, PER 3.01. 5
for when the west wind courts her gently, | how TNK 2.02.138
thou most perfidious | that ever gently look'd! 3.01. 36
to the shoulder–piece | gently they swell, like 4.02.128
arcite is gently visag'd; 5.03. 41
full gently now she takes him by the hand, | a VEN 361
the tiger would be tame and gently hear him; 1096
with thy sweet fingers when thou gently sway'st SON 128. 3
GENTRY 15 FR 0.0017 REL FR 13 V 2 P
shouldst not alter the article of thy gentry. WIV 2.01. 53 P
it well may serve | a nursery to our gentry, who AWW 1.02. 16
our gentry than our parents' noble names, | in WT 1.02.393
cause — | to grace the gentry of a land remote, JN 5.02. 31
corrupted, and exempt from ancient gentry? 1H6 2.04. 93
he makes up the file | of all the gentry; H8 1.01. 76
carry it but by the suit of the gentry to him COR 2.01.238
where gentry, title, wisdom, | cannot conclude 3.01.144
i have a file | of all the gentry. MAC 5.02. 9
you | to show us so much gentry and good will HAM 2.02. 22
of him, he is the card or calendar of gentry; 5.02.110 P
that we do incite | the gentry to this business. CYM 3.07. 7
i am brought hither | among th' italian gentry, 5.01. 18
if that thy gentry, britain, go before | this 5.02. 8
by knighthood, gentry, and sweet friendship'i LUC 569
GEOFFREY *(see geffrey, etc.)*
/GEORGE 1 FR 0.0001 REL FR 0 V 1 P
which is daughter to master /george page, which WIV 1.01. 46 P
GEORGE 41 FR 0.0046 REL FR 35 V 6 P
whither go you, george, hark you? WIV 2.01.149 P
you'll come to dinner, george. 2.01.157 P
good george, be not angry. 5.05.200 P
sir, or george seacole, for they can write and ADO 3.03. 11 P
now, by saint george, i am too young for you. SHR 2.01.236
and if his name be george, i'll call him peter; JN 1.01.186
saint george, that swing'd the dragon, and e'er 2.01.288
mine innocence and saint george to thrive! R2 1.03. 84
doit of staffordshire, and black george barnes, 2H4 3.02. 20 P
cry, "god for harry, england, and saint george!" H5 3.01. 34
between saint denis and saint george, compound a 5.02.207 P
god and saint george, talbot and england's right 1H6 4.02. 55
saint george and victory! 4.06. 1
knight of the noble order of saint george, 4.07. 68
look on my george, i am a gentleman: 2H6 4.01. 29
now, | the wanton edward, and the lusty george? 3H6 1.04. 74
lord george your brother, norfolk, and myself, 2.01.138
and when came george from burgundy to england? 2.01.143
god and saint george for us! 2.01.204
cry "saint george!" 2.02. 80
duke of gloucester, | and george, of clarence. 2.06.104
me be duke of clarence, george of gloucester, 2.06.106
warwick and his friends, god and saint george! 4.02. 29
and lo, where george of clarence sweeps along, 5.01. 76
saint george and victory! 5.01.113
lascivious edward, and thou perjur'd george, 5.05. 34
because my name is george. R3 1.01. 46
and, for my name of george begins with g, | it 1.01. 58
till george be pack'd with post–horse up to 1.01.146
now, by my george, my garter, and my crown — 4.04.366
thy george, profan'd, hath lost his lordly honor 4.04.369
but leave behind | your son, george stanley. 4.04.495
my son george stanley is frank'd up in hold; 4.05. 3
lest his son george fall | into the blind cave 5.03. 61
lest, being seen, thy brother, tender george, 5.03. 95
god and saint george! 5.03.270
this, and saint george to /boot! 5.03.301
after the battle let george stanley die. 5.03.346
our ancient word of courage, fair saint george, 5.03.349
but tell me, is young george stanley living? 5.05. 9
"the george alow came from the south, | from the TNK 3.05. 59
GEORGE'S 6 FR 0.0006 REL FR 4 V 2 P
saint george's half–cheek in a brooch. LLL 5.02.616 P
night in the windmill in saint george's field? 2H4 3.02.195 P
to keep our great saint george's feast withal. 1H6 1.01.154
meet me to–morrow in saint george's field, | you 2H6 5.01. 46
if i revolt, off goes young george's head; R3 4.05. 4
off with his son george's head! 5.03.344
GERARD 3 FR 0.0003 REL FR 1 V 2 P
his great right to be so — gerard de narbon. AWW 1.01. 27 P
gentlewoman the daughter of gerard de narbon? 1.01. 37 P
gerard de narbon was my father, | in what he did 2.01.101
/GERMAINS 1 FR 0.0001 REL FR 1 V 0 P
of nature's /germains tumble all together, MAC 4.01. 59
GERMAINS 1 FR 0.0001 REL FR 1 V 0 P
moulds, all germains spill at once | that makes LR 3.02. 8
GERMAN 10 FR 0.0011 REL FR 5 V 5 P
set spurs and away, like three german devils, WIV 4.05. 69 P
at once, as a german from the waist downward, ADO 3.02. 35 P
wife — | a woman, that is like a german /clock, LLL 3.01.190
how like you the young german, the duke of MV 1.02. 84 P
if there be here german, or dane, low dutch, AWW 4.01. 71
prodigal, or the german hunting in waterwork, is 2H4 2.01.145 P
holding in disdain the german women | for some H5 1.02. 48
your dane, your german, and your swag–bellied OTH 2.03. 77 P
but, | like a full–acorn'd boar, a german /one, CYM 2.05. 16
to any german province, spain or portigal, | nay STM II.C 128
GERMANE 4 FR 0.0004 REL FR 1 V 3 P
but those that are germane to him (though WT 4.04.773 P
thou a leopard, thou wert germane to the lion, TIM 4.03.340 P
the phrase would be more germane to the matter, HAM 5.02.158 P
you royal germane foes, that this day come | to TNK 5.01. 9
/GERMANS* 1 FR 0.0001 REL FR 0 V 1 P
sir, the /germans /desire to have three of your WIV 4.03. 1 P
GERMANS* 3 FR 0.0003 REL FR 1 V 2 P
germans are honest men. WIV 4.05. 72 P
with hasty germans and blunt hollanders, | hath 3H6 4.08. 2
coursers for cousins, and gennets for germans. OTH 1.01.113 P
GERMANY *(also jamany)*
/GERMANY 1 FR 0.0001 REL FR 0 V 1 P
/is /with /the /earl /of /kent /in /germany. LR 4.07. 90 P
GERMANY 5 FR 0.0005 REL FR 4 V 1 P
his round hose in france, his bonnet in germany, MV 1.02. 75 P
once dispatch'd him in an embassy | to germany, JN 1.01.100
affirm | that the land salique is in germany, H5 1.02. 44
sala, | is at this day in germany call'd meisen. 1.02. 53
the upper germany, can dearly witness, | yet H8 5.02. 65
GERMENS *(see germains)*
GERROLD *(also giraldo)*
GERROLD 1 FR 0.0001 REL FR 1 V 0 P
and sweetly we will do it, master gerrold. TNK 3.05. 22
GERTRUDE 13 FR 0.0014 REL FR 13 V 0 P
he tells me, my dear gertrude, he hath found HAM 2.02. 54
sweet gertrude, leave us two, | for we have 3.01. 28
what, gertrude? how does hamlet? 4.01. 6
o gertrude, come away! 4.01. 28
come, gertrude, we'll call up our wisest friends 4.01. 38
o gertrude, gertrude, | when sorrows come, they 4.05. 77
o gertrude, gertrude, | when sorrows come, they 4.05. 77
o my dear gertrude, this, | like to a 4.05. 94
let him go, gertrude, do not fear our person: 4.05.123
let him go, gertrude. 4.05.127
let's follow, gertrude. 4.07.191
good gertrude, set some watch over your son. 5.01.296
gertrude, do not drink. 5.02.290
GEST 1 FR 0.0001 REL FR 1 V 0 P
to let him there a month behind the gest WT 1.02. 41
/GESTS 1 FR 0.0001 REL FR 1 V 0 P
before, | and let the queen know of our /gests. ANT 4.08. 2
GESTURE 7 FR 0.0008 REL FR 4 V 3 P
too much muse | such shapes, such gesture, and TMP 3.03. 37
so near the heart as your gesture cries it out, AYL 5.02. 62 P
their dumbness, language in their very gesture; WT 5.02. 14 P
and their gesture sad, | investing lank–lean H5 4.pr. 25
to th' dumbness of the gesture | one might TIM 1.01. 33
i say, but mark his gesture. OTH 4.01. 87
his gesture imports it. 4.01.138 P
GESTURES 2 FR 0.0002 REL FR 2 V 0 P
as her winks and nods and gestures yield them, HAM 4.05. 11
must /conster | poor cassio's smiles, gestures, OTH 4.01.102
/GET 4 FR 0.0004 REL FR 4 V 0 P
/likely /to /fall /in /than /to /get /o'er; 2H4 1.01.171
/or /get /some /little /knife /between /thy TIT 3.02. 16
/get /thee /gone, | /i /see /thou /art /not /for 3.02. 57
/and /get /the /bedlam | /to /lead /him /where LR 3.07.103
GET 329 FR 0.0371 REL FR 234 V 95 P
and keep him tame, and get to naples with him, TMP 2.02. 69 P
i'll fish for thee, and get thee wood enough. 2.02.161
and sometimes i'll get thee | young scamels from 2.02.171
ca–caliban | has a new master, get a new man. 2.02.185
go, get you gone; TGV 1.02. 97
thou shalt never get such a secret from me but 2.05. 39 P
'tis well that i get it so. 2.05. 41 P
for "get you gone," she doth not mean "away!" 3.01.101
by seven a' clock i'll get you such a ladder. 3.01.126
i'll get me one of such another length. 3.01.133
go, get thee hence, and find my dog again, | or 4.04. 59
his love, | i'll get me such a color'd periwig. 4.04.191
get you home; WIV 2.01.152 P
you, they could never get an eye–wink of her. 2.02. 71 P
they could never get her so much as sip on a cup 2.02. 75 P
i see i cannot get thy father's love, 3.04. 1
get you home, boy. 4.01. 85 P
go get us properties | and tricking for our 4.04. 78
i'll do what i can to get you a pair of horns. 5.01. 6 P
get you gone, and let me hear no more of you. MM 2.01.206 P
what thou hast not, still thou striv'st to get, 3.01. 22
get thee away. ERR 1.02. 16
commends me to the thing i cannot get: 1.02. 34
blows long, i must get a sconce for my head, and 2.02. 37 P
either get thee from the door, or sit down at 3.01. 33
go get thee from the door. 3.01. 35
your wife, sir knave! go get you from the door. 3.01. 64
is something in the wind, that we cannot get in. 3.01. 69
go, get thee gone, fetch me an iron crow. 3.01. 84
get you home | and fetch the chain; 3.01.114
then, gentle brother, get you in again; 3.02. 25
i'll fetch my sister to get her good will. 3.02. 70
get thee gone, | buy thou a rope, and bring it 4.01. 19
therefore away, to get our stuff aboard. 4.04.158
some get within him, take his sword away: 5.01. 34
once did i get him bound, and sent him home, 5.01.145
with love than i will get again with drinking, ADO 1.01.251 P
in the world, if 'a could get her good will. 2.01. 16 P
niece, thou wilt never get thee a husband, if 2.01. 18 P
his head, and say, "get you to heaven, beatrice, 2.01. 45 P
beatrice, get you to heaven, here's no place for 2.01. 46 P
lady beatrice, i will get you one. 2.01.321 P
i pray thee get us some excellent music; 2.03. 85 P
i will go get her picture. 2.03.264 P
and bid those that are drunk get them to bed. 3.03. 43 P
get you some of this distill'd carduus 3.04. 73 P
go, get you to francis seacole, bid him bring 3.05. 57 P
only get the learned writer to set down our 3.05. 63 P
thou art sad, get thee a wife, get thee a wife. 5.04.122 P
thou art sad, get thee a wife, get thee a wife. 5.04.122 P
then will she get the upshoot by cleaving the LLL 4.01.136
in conflict that you get the sun of them. 4.03.366
sir, it were pity you should get your living by 5.02.496 P
therefore if you my favor mean to get, | a 5.02.820
hence, get thee gone, and follow me no more. MND 2.01.194
but if i had wit enough to get out of this wood, 3.01.150 P
and if i could, what should i get therefore? 3.02. 78
why, get you gone. who is't that hinders you? 3.02.318
get you gone, you dwarf; 3.02.328
mounsieur, get you your weapons in your hand, 4.01. 10 P
i will get peter quince to write a ballet of 4.01.214 P
get your apparel together, good strings to your 4.02. 35 P
how to get clear of all the debts i owe. MV 1.01.134
i cannot get a service, no; 2.02.156 P

a christian do not play the knave and get thee, 2.03. 12 P
"who chooseth me shall get as much as he 2.07. 7
"who chooseth me shall get as much as he 2.07. 23
"who chooseth me shall get as much as he 2.09. 36
"who chooseth me shall get as much as he 2.09. 50
with all my heart, so thou canst get a wife. 3.02.195
waste no time in words, | but get thee gone. 3.04. 55
launcelot, if you thus get my wife into corners! 3.05. 30 P
get thee gone, but do it. 4.01.397
i'll see if i can get my husband's ring, | which 4.02. 13
well, sir, get you in. AYL 1.01. 76 P
get you with him, you old dog. 1.01. 81 P
your safest haste, | and get you from our court. 1.03. 42
and get our jewels and our wealth together, 1.03.134
i earn that i eat, get that i wear, owe no man 3.02. 74 P
together, and to offer to get your living by the 3.02. 79 P
get you to church, and have a good priest that 3.03. 84 P
good | what i have said, bianca, get you in, SHR 1.01. 75
marry, sir, to get a husband for her sister. 1.01.120 P
to get her cunning schoolmasters to instruct her 1.01.187
and could not get him for my heart to do it. 1.02. 38
if without more words you will get you hence. 1.02.230
what, in my sight? bianca, get thee in. 2.01. 30
then tell me, if i get your daughter's love, 2.01.119
but suppos'd lucentio | must get a father, 2.01.408
fathers commonly | do get their children; 2.01.410
a child shall get a sire, if i fail not of my 2.01.411
tellus," disguis'd thus to get your love, "hic 3.01. 33 P
i am to get a man — what e'er he be, | it 3.02.131
sirrah, get you hence, | and bid my cousin 4.01.150
i prithee go, and get me some repast; 4.03. 15
mustard, | or else you get no beef of grumio. 4.03. 28
go get thee gone, thou false deluding slave, 4.03. 31
go get thee gone, i say. 4.03. 35
dally not with the gods, but get thee gone. 4.04. 68
your commendations, madam, get from her tears. AWW 1.01. 46 P
get thee a good husband, and use him as he uses 1.01.214 P
get you gone, sirrah. 1.03. 8 P
get you gone, sir, i'll talk with you more anon. 1.03. 64 P
"when thou canst get the ring upon my finger, 3.02. 57 P
prithee get thee further. 5.02. 13 P
"when from my finger you can get this ring | and 5.03.312
get you to your lord. TN 1.05.279
get thee to yond same sovereign cruelty. 2.04. 80
get ye all three into the box–tree; 2.05. 15 P
i'll get 'em all three all ready. 3.01. 91 P
get him to say his prayers, good sir toby, get 3.04.118 P
say his prayers, good sir toby, get him to pray. 3.04.119 P
therefore get you on, and give him his desire. 3.04.247 P
men that give fools money get themselves a good 4.01. 22 P
get him to bed, and let his hurt be look'd to. 5.01.208 P
go get aboard; WT 3.03. 7
well may i get aboard! 3.03. 57
think it not uneasy to get the cause of my son's 4.02. 50 P
barren, and i care not | to get slips of them. 4.04. 85
get you hence, for i must go | where it fits not 4.04.297
fear eyes over) to shipboard | get undescried. 4.04.655
i know not why, except to get the land; JN 1.01. 73
well, sir, by this you cannot get my land; 1.01. 97
who, as you say, took pains to get this son, 1.01.121
my mother's son did get your father's heir; 1.01.128
sir, | than was his will to get me, as i think. 1.01.133
well — marry, to confess — | could /he get me. 1.01.237
now, by this light, were i to get again, | madam 1.01.259
envenom him with words, or get thee gone, | and 3.01. 63
if i get down, and do not break my limbs, | i'll 4.03. 6
i'll find a thousand shifts to get away. 4.03. 7
avaunt, thou hateful villain, get thee gone! 4.03. 77
sirrah, get thee to plashy, to my sister R2 2.02. 90
go, fellow, get thee home, provide some carts, 2.02.106
that know the strong'st and surest way to get. 3.03.201
spur post, and get before him to the king, | and 5.02.112
worcester, get thee gone, for i do see | danger 1H4 1.03. 15
bardolph, get thee before to coventry; 4.02. 1 P
get posts and letters, and make friends with 2H4 1.01.214
of my hand than he shall get one /of his cheek, 1.02. 22 P
and i could get me but a wife in the stews, i 1.02. 53 P
i can get no remedy against this consumption of 1.02.236 P
mare, if i have any vantage of ground to get up. 2.01. 79 P
is't such a matter to get a pottle–pot's 2.02. 78 P
if they get ground and vantage of the king, 2.03. 53
come, get you down stairs. 2.04.195 P
get you down stairs. 2.04.203 P
and then, when they marry, they get wenches. 4.03. 94 P
then get thee gone, and dig my grave thyself, 4.05.110
i am fortune's steward — get on thy boots. 5.03.131 P
so get you hence in peace; H5 1.02.294
hound of crete, think'st thou my spouse to get? 2.01. 73
get you therefore hence, | poor miserable 2.02.177
and patches will i get unto these cudgell'd 5.01. 88
tells me thou shalt, i get thee with scambling, 5.02.204 P
swift–winged with desire to get a grave, | as 1H6 2.05. 15
priest | should ever get that privilege of me. 3.01.121
away, captains, let's get us from the walls, 3.02. 71
france, | either to get the town again, or die: 3.02. 79
so sure i swear to get the town, or die. 3.02. 84
we lose, they daily get; 4.03. 32
me this once, that france may get the field. 5.03. 12
go, get you to my house, | i will reward you for 2H6 3.02. 8
this get i by his death. 3.02. 70
so get thee gone, that i may know my grief, 3.02.346
now get thee hence, the king, thou know'st, is 3.02.386
come and get thee a sword, though made of a lath 4.02. 1 P
ay, marry, will we; therefore get ye gone. 4.02.153
but get you to smithfield and gather head, | and 4.05. 9
france, to france, and get what you have lost! 4.08. 49
me, and get a thousand crowns of the king by 4.10. 27 P
we shall to london get, where you are lov'd, 5.02. 81
thou hast spoke too much already; get thee gone. 3H6 1.01.258
then get your husband's lands, to do them good. 3.02. 40
what love, think'st thou, i sue so much to get? 3.02. 61
and yet i know not how to get the crown, | for 3.02.172
can i do this, and cannot get a crown? 3.02.194
'twas full two years ere i could get a tooth. R3 2.04. 29
my husband lost his life to get the crown, | and 2.04. 57
and look you get a prayer–book in your hand, 3.07. 47
o dorset, speak not to me, get thee gone! 4.01. 38
so get thee gone; 4.05. 6
this burthen, 'tis too weak | ever to get a boy. H8 2.03. 44
go get thee from me, cromwell! 3.02.412
get you gone, | and do as i have bid you. 5.01.155
you i' th' chamblet, get up o' th' rail, | i'll 5.03. 89
before | this happy child, did i get any thing. 5.04. 65
come in, come in, i'll go get a fire. TRO 3.02. 59 P
if my lord get a boy of you, you'll give him me. 3.02.104 P
unless the fiddler apollo get his sinews to make 3.03.304 P
pray thee get thee in. 4.02. 85 P
you train me to offend you, get you in. 5.03. 4
you, | upon the love you bear me, get you in. 5.03. 78
go get you home, you fragments! COR 1.01.222
him some way, | or wrath or craft may get him. 1.10. 16
for conscience' sake to help to get thee a wife. 2.03. 33 P
get you hence instantly, and tell those friends 2.03.213
go, get you to /your house; 3.01.229
get you gone. 3.01.230
now, pray, sir, get you gone; 4.02. 37
pray get you out. 4.05. 13 P
away? get you away. 4.05. 15 P
i cannot get him out o' th' house. 4.05. 21 P
go, masters, get you home, be not dismay'd. 4.06.149
one, | so trouble me no more, but get you gone. TIT 1.01.367
as for thee, boy, go get thee from my sight; 3.01.283
and come, i will go get a leaf of brass, | and 4.01.102
go get you gone, and pray be careful all, | and 4.03. 21
get me a ladder. 5.01. 53
but woo her, gentle paris, get her heart, | my ROM 1.02. 16
go get thee to thy love as was decreed, | ascend 3.03.146
well, get you gone, a' thursday be it then. 3.04. 30
get thee to church a' thursday, | or never after 3.05.161
hold, get you gone. 4.01.122
get thee to bed and rest, for thou hast need. 4.03. 13
go, you cot–quean, go, | get you to bed. 4.04. 7
thou knowest my lodging, get me ink and paper, 5.01. 25
no matter, get thee gone, | and hire those 5.01. 32
buy food, and get thyself in flesh. 5.01. 84
again — | nor get a messenger to bring it thee, 5.02. 15
get me an iron crow, and bring it straight 5.02. 21
go get thee hence, for i will not away. 5.03.160
get on your cloak and haste you to lord timon; TIM 2.01. 15
get you gone, | put on a most importunate aspect 2.01. 27
get you gone. 2.01. 32
told him on't, but i could ne'er get him from't. 3.01. 28 P
get you gone, sirrah. 3.01. 38 P
i prithee beat thy drum and get thee gone. 4.03. 97
get thee away, and take | thy beagles with thee. 4.03.174
get thee gone. 4.03.280
he covetously reserve it, how shall 's get it? 4.03.405 P
home, you idle creatures, get you home! JC 1.01. 1
out their shoes, to get myself into more work. 1.01. 29 P
should | so get the start of the majestic world 1.02.130
get me a taper in my study, lucius. 2.01. 7
get you to bed again, it is not day. 2.01. 39
impossible, | yea, get the better of them. 2.01.326
stay not to answer me, but get thee gone. 2.04. 2
i'll get me to a place more void, and there 2.04. 37
get thee apart and weep. 3.01.282
get you hence, sirrah; saucy fellow, hence! 4.03.134
go, pindarus, get higher on that hill; 5.03. 20
go get him surgeons. MAC 1.02. 44
thou shalt get kings, though thou be none. 1.03. 67
get thee to bed. 2.01. 32
go get some water, | and wash this filthy 2.02. 43
get on your night–gown, lest occasion call us 2.02. 67
get thee gone; 3.04. 30
get you gone, | and at the pit of acheron | meet 3.05. 14
with what i get, i mean, and so do they. 4.02. 33
but get thee back, my soul is too much charg'd 5.08. 5
get thee to bed, francisco. HAM 1.01. 7
get from him why he puts on this confusion, 3.01. 2
get thee /to a nunn'ry, why wouldst thou be a 3.01.120 P
get thee to a nunn'ry, farewell! 3.01.136 P
get you a place. 3.02. 91
shoes, get me a fellowship in a cry of players? 3.02.277 P
is bestow'd, my lord, | we cannot get from him. 4.03. 13
go get thee in, and fetch me a sup of liquor. 5.01. 60 P
now get you to my lady's /chamber, and tell her, 5.01.192 P
me not stay a jot for dinner, go get it ready. LR 1.04. 8 P
get you gone, | and hasten your return. 1.04.339
you houseless poverty, | nay, get thee in. 3.04. 27
get horses for your mistress. 3.07. 20
away, get thee away! 4.01. 15
/then, /prithee, get thee away. 4.01. 41
get thee glass eyes, | and, like a scurvy 4.06.170
come, and you get it, you shall get it by 4.06.202 P
and you get it, you shall get it by running. 4.06.203 P
get moe tapers; OTH 1.01.166
please | to get good guard and go along with me. 1.01.179
get weapons, ho! 1.01.181
i had rather to adopt a child than get it. 1.03.191
to get his place and to plume up my will | in 1.03.393
nay, get thee gone. 2.03.382
get me some poison, iago, this night. 4.01.204 P
get you away; 4.01.258
cogging, cozening slave, to get some office, 4.02.132
get you to bed on th' instant, i will be 4.03. 7 P
so get thee gone, good night. 4.03. 58
what, are you mad? i charge you, get you home. 5.02.194
be wise, and get you home. 5.02.223
to the queen, | and get her /leave to part. ANT 1.02.179
but come, away, | get me ink and paper. 1.05. 76
get thee gone. 2.03. 31
go get thee hence! 2.05. 95
get thee hence; 2.05.103
get thee back to caesar, | tell him thy 3.13.139
nerves, and can | get goal for goal of youth. 4.08. 22
get thee hence, farewell. 5.02.259
well, get thee gone, farewell. 5.02.278
those things i bid you do, get them dispatch'd, CYM 1.03. 39
i should get ground of your fair mistress; 1.04.104 P
if i could get this foolish imogen, i should 2.03. 8 P
so, get you gone. 2.03. 27 P
but first, how get hence. 3.02. 64
o, get thee from my sight, | thou gav'st me 5.05.236
if i can get him within my pistol's length, PER 1.01.166
and what a man cannot get, he may lawfully deal 2.01.114 P
known, | which from her by no means can i get. 2.05. 6
may we not get access to her, my lord? 2.05. 7
then with what haste you can, get you to bed. 2.05. 93
get fire and meat for these poor men. 3.02. 3
get linen. 3.02.108
is it a shame to get when we are old? 4.02. 29 P
get this done as i command you. 4.02. 61 P
we must either get her ravish'd or be rid of her 4.06. 5 P
get you and pray the gods | for success and TNK 1.01.208
fit of jealousy | to get the soldier work, that 1.02. 23
if that | get him a wife so noble and so fair, 2.02.230
may thy goodness | get thee a happy husband!" 2.04. 25
get many more such prisoners and such daughters, 2.06. 38
news from earth, they shall get none but this — 3.01. 80
get off your trinkets, you shall want nought. 3.03. 52
if we can get her dance, we are made again. 3.05. 74
shall grow to th' ground but i'll get mercy. 3.06.192
let's get her in. 4.01.149
let's get her in. 5.02.107
other, get herself | some part of a good name, 5.03. 26
although we grant you get the thing you seek? STM II.C 69
her help she sees, but help she cannot get, VEN 93
thou wast begot, to get it is thy duty. 168
care, | is how to get my palfrey from the mare." 384
or sells eternity to get a toy? LUC 214
earth's dark womb some gentle gust doth get, 549
thou sets the wolf where he the lamb may get; 878
"go get me hither paper, ink, and pen, | yet 1289
noon, | unlook'd on diest unless thou get a son. SON 7.14
"many there were that did his picture get | to LC 134

GETS 14 FR 0.0015 REL FR 8 V 6 P
and what he gets more of her than sharp words, WIV 2.01.183 P
for ever hous'd where it gets possession. ERR 3.01.106
alas, he gets nothing by that. ADO 1.01. 65 P
food he eats, | and pleas'd with what he gets, AYL 2.05. 41
he that runs fastest gets the ring. SHR 1.01.140 P
if percy be alive, thou gets not my sword, but 1H4 5.03. 51 P
gets him to rest, cramm'd with distressful bread H5 4.01.270
alas, i know not, how gets the tide in? H8 5.03. 18
how the murtherer gets the love of gonzago's HAM 3.02.264 P
grown so vild | that it doth hate what gets it. LR 3.04.146
but every puny whipster gets my sword. OTH 5.02.244
caesar gets money where | he loses hearts. ANT 2.01. 13
in our country of greece gets more with begging PER 2.01. 64 P
marina gets | all praises, which are paid as 4.ch. 33

GET'ST 1 FR 0.0001 REL FR 0 V 1 P
if thou get'st any leave of me, hang me; 2H4 1.02. 88 P

GETTER 1 FR 0.0001 REL FR 0 V 1 P
a getter of more bastard children than war's a COR 4.05.224 P

GETTING 11 FR 0.0012 REL FR 2 V 9 P
and it is for getting madam julietta with child. MM 1.02. 72 P
hang'd a man for the getting a hundred bastards, 3.02.117 P
once before him for getting a wench with child. 4.03.169 P
would rather have one of your father's getting. ADO 2.01.323 P
than you can the getting up of the negro's belly MV 3.05. 38 P
dowry of his wife, 'tis none of his own getting. AYL 3.03. 56 P
of men, though it be the getting of children. AWW 3.02. 42 P
he was whipt for getting the shrieve's fool with 4.03.186 P
in the between but getting wenches with child, WT 3.03. 61 P
and though he were unsatisfied in getting H8 4.02. 55
rome, | forborne the getting of a lawful race, ANT 3.13.107

GHASTLY 8 FR 0.0009 REL FR 8 V 0 P
wherefore this ghastly looking? TMP 2.01.309
why then let grievous, ghastly, gaping wounds 2H4 2.04.198
staring full ghastly, like a strangled man; 2H6 3.02.170
suspicion, ghastly looks | are at my service, R3 3.05. 8
drawn | upon a heap a hundred ghastly women, JC 1.03. 23
that thinks she hath beheld some ghastly sprite, LUC 451
let ghastly shadows his lewd eyes affright, 971
which, like a jewel hung in ghastly night, SON 27.11

/GHOST 1 FR 0.0001 REL FR 1 V 0 P
/do /his /ghost /the /wrong | /to /hold /your 2H4 2.03. 39

GHOST 31 FR 0.0035 REL FR 31 V 0 P
her brother's ghost his paved bed would break, MM 5.01.435
egeon art thou not? or else his ghost? ERR 5.01.338
were i the ghost that walk'd, i'ld bid you mark WT 5.01. 63
walk'd your first queen's ghost, it should take 5.01. 80
cheek, | and he will look as hollow as a ghost, JN 3.04. 84
henry the fift, thy ghost i invocate: 1H6 1.01. 52
news would cause him once more yield the ghost. 1.01. 67
i think this upstart is old talbot's ghost, | he 4.07. 87
i trust the ghost of talbot is not there. 5.02. 16
oft have i seen a timely–parted ghost, | of ashy 2H6 3.02.161
and do some service to duke humphrey's ghost. 3.02.231
sometime he talks as if duke humphrey's ghost 3.02.373
blood, | the noble gentleman gave up the ghost. 3H6 2.03. 22
be it lawful that i invocate thy ghost | to hear R3 1.02. 8
and often did i strive | to yield the ghost; 1.04. 37
marry, my uncle clarence angry ghost. 3.01.144
life, blind sight, poor mortal–living ghost, 4.04. 26
methinks i see my cousin's ghost | seeking out ROM 4.03. 55
our army lies, ready to give up the ghost. JC 5.01. 88
the ghost of caesar hath appear'd to me | two 5.05. 17
towards his design | moves like a ghost. MAC 2.01. 56
heaven, i'll make a ghost of him that lets me! HAM 1.04. 85
alas, poor ghost! 1.05. 4
ay, thou poor ghost, whiles memory holds a seat 1.05. 96
there needs no ghost, my lord, come from the 1.05.125
it is an honest ghost, that let me tell you. 1.05.138
it is a damned ghost that we have seen, | and my 3.02. 82
vex not his ghost. LR 5.03.314
ghost unlaid forbear thee! CYM 4.02.278
"grim–grinning ghost, earth's worm, what dost VEN 933
nor that affable familiar ghost | which nightly SON 86. 9

GHOSTED 1 FR 0.0001 REL FR 1 V 0 P
who at philippi the good brutus ghosted, | there ANT 2.06. 13

GHOSTLY 7 FR 0.0008 REL FR 6 V 1 P
look you, sir, here comes your ghostly father. MM 4.03. 48 P
a ghostly father, belike. 5.01.126
the ghostly father now hath done his shrift. 3H6 3.02.107
hence will i to my ghostly /sire's close cell, ROM 2.02.188
my ghostly father, no; 2.03. 45
good even to my ghostly confessor. 2.06. 21
heart, | being a divine, a ghostly confessor, 3.03. 49

GHOST'S 1 FR 0.0001 REL FR 0 V 1 P
i'll take the ghost's word for a thousand pound. HAM 3.02.286 P

GHOSTS 11 FR 0.0012 REL FR 11 V 0 P
at whose approach, ghosts, wand'ring here and MND 3.02.381
some haunted by the ghosts they have deposed, R2 3.02.158

unto the gazing moon | so many horrid ghosts. H5 4.pr. 28
the famish'd english, like pale ghosts, 1H6 1.02. 7
spirits walk, and ghosts break up their graves, 2H6 1.04. 19
all these fires, why all these gliding ghosts, JC 1.03. 63
and ghosts did shriek and squeal about the 2.02. 24
wife and children's ghosts will haunt me still. MAC 5.07. 16
with our sprightly port make the ghosts gaze. ANT 4.14. 52
or we poor ghosts will cry | to th' shining CYM 5.04. 88
how dare you ghosts | accuse the thunderer, 5.04. 94
GI' *(also give)*
GI' 1 FR 0.0001 REL FR 0 V 1 P
god gi' god–den. i pray, sir, can you read? ROM 1.02. 57 P
GIANT 12 FR 0.0013 REL FR 8 V 4 P
but it is tyrannous | to use it like a giant. MM 2.02.109
finds a pang as great | as when a giant dies. 3.01. 80
he is then a giant to an ape, but then is an ape ADO 5.01.201 P
some mollification for your giant, sweet lady. TN 1.05.204 P
colbrand the giant, that same mighty man? JN 1.01.225
eyes | that never saw the giant world enrag'd, 5.02. 57
sirrah, you giant, what says the doctor to my 2H4 1.02. 1 P
the world's whole strength | into one giant arm, 4.05. 45
a giant traitor! H8 1.02.199
the baby figure of the giant mass | of things to TRO 1.03.345
we do allowance give | before a sleeping giant. 2.03.138
there's my gauntlet, i'll prove it on a giant. LR 4.06. 90 P
GIANT–DWARF 1 FR 0.0001 REL FR 1 V 0 P
this senior/–junior, giant–dwarf, dan cupid, LLL 3.01.180
GIANTESS 1 FR 0.0001 REL FR 0 V 1 P
i had rather be a giantess, and lie under mount WIV 2.01. 79 P
GIANT–LIKE 2 FR 0.0002 REL FR 1 V 1 P
giant–like ox–beef hath devour'd many a MND 3.01.192 P
that thy rebellion looks so giant–like? HAM 4.05.122
GIANT–RUDE 1 FR 0.0001 REL FR 1 V 0 P
could not drop forth such giant–rude invention, AYL 4.03. 34
GIANT'S 2 FR 0.0002 REL FR 2 V 0 P
o, it is excellent | to have a giant's strength; MM 2.02.108
like a giant's robe | upon a dwarfish thief. MAC 5.02. 21
GIANTS 1 FR 0.0001 REL FR 1 V 0 P
are arch'd so high that giants may jet through CYM 3.03. 5
GIB 2 FR 0.0002 REL FR 1 V 1 P
am as melancholy as a gib cat or a lugg'd bear. 1H4 1.02. 74 P
wise, | would from a paddock, from a bat, a gib, HAM 3.04.190
GIBBER 1 FR 0.0001 REL FR 1 V 0 P
did squeak and gibber in the roman streets. HAM 1.01.116
GIBBET 3 FR 0.0003 REL FR 2 V 1 P
hang no more about me, i am no gibbet for you. WIV 2.02. 17 P
from the murderer's gibbet throw | into the MAC 4.01. 66
make | my country's high pyramides my gibbet, ANT 5.02. 61
GIBBET–MAKER 1 FR 0.0001 REL FR 0 V 1 P
ho, the gibbet–maker? TIT 4.03. 81 P
GIBBETS 3 FR 0.0003 REL FR 0 V 3 P
i had unloaded all the gibbets and press'd the 1H4 4.02. 37 P
on swifter than he that gibbets on the brewer's 2H4 3.02.264 P
would marry a gallows and beget young gibbets, i CYM 5.04.199 P
GIBE 1 FR 0.0001 REL FR 1 V 0 P
taunts | did gibe my missive out of audience. ANT 2.02. 74
GIBER 1 FR 0.0001 REL FR 0 V 1 P
to be a perfecter giber for the table than a COR 2.01. 82 P
GIBES *(also gipes)*
GIBES 5 FR 0.0005 REL FR 2 V 3 P
knave, to have his gibes and his mockeries! WIV 3.03.242 P
are wise and full of gibes and vlouting–stocks, 4.05. 80 P
where be your gibes now, your gambols, your HAM 5.01.189 P
and mark the fleers, the gibes, and notable OTH 4.01. 82
ready in gibes, quick–answer'd, saucy, and | as CYM 3.04.158
GIBING 2 FR 0.0002 REL FR 2 V 0 P
why, that's the way to choke a gibing spirit, LLL 5.02.858
to laugh at gibing boys, and stand the push | of 1H4 3.02. 66
GIBINGLY 1 FR 0.0001 REL FR 1 V 0 P
which most gibingly, ungravely, he did fashion COR 2.03.225
GIDDILY 2 FR 0.0002 REL FR 1 V 1 P
how giddily 'a turns about all the hot–bloods ADO 3.03.131 P
her, | tell her, i hold as giddily as fortune; TN 2.04. 84
GIDDINESS 1 FR 0.0001 REL FR 0 V 1 P
neither call the giddiness of it in question, AYL 5.02. 5 P
/GIDDY 1 FR 0.0001 REL FR 1 V 0 P
/an /habitation /giddy /and /unsure | /hath /he 2H4 1.03. 89
GIDDY 29 FR 0.0032 REL FR 24 V 5 P
art not thou thyself giddy with the fashion too, ADO 3.03.141 P
for man is a giddy thing, and this is my 5.04.108 P
giddy in spirit, still gazing in a doubt MV 3.02.144
touch'd with so many giddy offenses as he hath AYL 3.02.349 P
an ape, more giddy in my desires than a monkey. 4.01.153 P
am starv'd for meat, giddy for lack of sleep, SHR 4.03. 9
he that is giddy thinks the world turns round. 5.02. 20
"he that is giddy thinks the world turns round": 5.02. 26
our fancies are more giddy and unfirm, | more TN 2.04. 33
parts | against these giddy loose suggestions; JN 3.01.292
thou hast made me giddy | with these ill tidings 4.02.131
go, ye giddy goose. 1H4 3.01.228 P
wilt thou upon the high and giddy /mast | seal 2H4 3.01. 18
and now my sight fails, and my brain is giddy. 4.04.110
be it thy course to busy giddy minds | with 4.05.213
who hath been still a giddy neighbor to us; H5 1.02.145
by a vain, giddy, shallow, humorous youth, 2.04. 28
and giddy fortune's furious fickle wheel, | that 3.06. 27
that many have their giddy brains knock'd out; 1H6 3.01. 83
see how the giddy multitude do point | and nod 2H6 2.04. 21
to london, | and many giddy people flock to him. 3H6 4.08. 5
along | upon the giddy footing of the hatches, R3 1.04. 17
i fear, i fear 'twill prove a giddy world. 2.03. 5
i am giddy; TRO 3.02. 18
and giddy censure | will then cry out of martius COR 1.01.268
even so mayest thou the giddy men of rome. TIT 4.04. 87
hand, | to scatter and disperse the giddy goths, 5.02. 78
turn giddy, and be holp by backward turning; ROM 1.02. 47
and turn the giddy round of fortune's wheel; LUC 952
GIDDY–PACED 1 FR 0.0001 REL FR 1 V 0 P
of these most brisk and giddy–paced times. TN 2.04. 6
/GIFT 2 FR 0.0002 REL FR 2 V 0 P
then, as my /gift, and thine own acquisition TMP 4.01. 13
/loving /well /compos'd /with /gift /of /nature, TRO 4.04. 77
GIFT 66 FR 0.0074 REL FR 50 V 16 P
afore heaven, | i ratify this my rich gift. TMP 4.01. 8
of yours, and therefore the gift the greater. TGV 4.04. 58 P
the gift hath made me happy. 5.04.148
coach, letter after letter, gift after gift; WIV 2.02. 66 P
coach, letter after letter, gift after gift; 2.02. 66 P
and give them to a dog for a new–year's gift. 3.05. 9 P
not, but by gift of my chaste body | to his MM 5.01. 97
only his gift is in devising impossible slanders ADO 2.01.138 P
to be a well–favor'd man is the gift of fortune, 3.03. 15 P
may counterpoise this rich and precious gift? 4.01. 28
this is a gift that i have, simple; LLL 4.02. 65 P
but the gift is good in those /in whom it is 4.02. 70 P
of lances the almighty, | gave hector a gift" — 5.02.645
gave hector a gift, the heir of ilion; 5.02.652
i have no gift at all in shrewishness; MND 3.02.301
the other, that he do record a gift, | here in MV 4.01.388
clerk, draw a deed of gift. 4.01.394
to part so slightly with your wive's first gift, 5.01.167
from the rich jew, a special deed of gift, 5.01.292
young and fair, | they have the gift to know it; AYL 2.07. 38
i will not take her on gift of any man. 3.03. 68 P
and if the boy have not a woman's gift | to rain SHR in.1. 124
/neighbor, this is a gift very grateful, i am 2.01. 76 P
the gift doth stretch itself as 'tis receiv'd, AWW 2.01. 4
of my dear father's gift stands chief in power, 2.01.112
receive | the confirmation of my promis'd gift, 2.03. 50
proud scornful boy, unworthy this good gift, 2.03.151
his present gift | shall furnish me to those 2.03.289
but that he hath the gift of a coward to allay TN 1.03. 31 P
he would quickly have the gift of a grave. 1.03. 33 P
than i, that have not well the gift of tongue, 1H4 5.02. 77
the borrowed glories that by gift of heaven, H5 2.04. 79
he hath not the gift to woo in other places; 5.02.155 P
the happiest gift that ever marquess gave, | the 2H6 1.01. 15
is not a dukedom, sir, a goodly gift? 3H6 5.01. 31
i'll do thee service for so good a gift. 5.01. 33
why then 'tis mine, if but by warwick's gift. 5.01. 35
and, weakling, warwick takes his gift again, 5.01. 37
a greater gift than that i'll give my cousin. R3 3.01.115
a greater gift? o, that's the sword to it. 3.01.116
my lord, i claim the gift, my due by promise, 4.02. 88
a gift that heaven gives for him, which buys | a H8 1.01. 65
pandar | have not more gift in taciturnity. TRO 4.02. 73
'tis thought you have a goodly gift in horning, TIT 2.03. 67
no gift to him | but breeds the giver a return TIM 1.01.278
spurn to their graves | of their friends' gift? 1.02.142
a gift, i warrant. 3.01. 5 P
first man | that e'er received gift from him; 3.03. 17
and he wears jewels now of timon's gift, | for 3.04. 19
according to the gift which bounteous nature MAC 3.01. 97
virtue, | he hath a heavenly gift of prophecy, 4.03.157
revoke thy gift, | or, whilst i can vent clamor LR 1.01.164
i gave her such a one; 'twas my first gift. OTH 3.03.436
or made a gift of it, my father's eye | should 3.04. 61
and i will boot thee with what gift beside | thy ANT 2.05. 71
enough for the /purchase, or merit for the gift; CYM 1.04. 84 P
a thing for sale, and only the gift of the gods. 1.04. 85 P
her pretty action did outsell her gift, | and 2.04.102
to make my gift, | the more delay'd, delighted. 5.04.101
my good will is great, though the gift small. PER 3.04. 18
which by a gift of learning did bear the maid PP 15.14
which bounteous gift thou shouldst in bounty SON 11.12
and time that gave doth now his gift confound. 60. 8
the cause of this fair gift in me is wanting, 87. 7
so thy great gift, upon misprision growing, 87.11
thy gift, thy tables, are within my brain | full 122. 1
GIFTS 48 FR 0.0054 REL FR 35 V 13 P
win her with gifts, if she respect not words: TGV 3.01. 89
holy, | to be corrupted with my worthless gifts. 4.02. 6
know the young gentlewoman, she has good gifts. WIV 1.01. 63 P
pounds, and possibilities, is goot gifts. 1.01. 65 P
with such gifts that heaven shall share with you MM 2.02.147
when in the streets he meets such golden gifts. ERR 3.02.183
gifts that god gives. ADO 3.05. 43 P
and courteous breath), | gifts of rich value. MV 2.09. 91
that 'scuse serves many men to save their gifts, 4.01.444
wheel, that her gifts may henceforth be bestow'd AYL 1.02. 32 P
woman doth most mistake in her gifts to women. 1.02. 36 P
fortune reigns in gifts of the world, not in the 1.02. 41 P
heaven would that she these gifts should have, 3.02.153
your gifts are so good, here's none will hold SHR 1.01.105 P
she inherits, which makes fair gifts fairer; AWW 1.01. 41 P
book, and hath all the good gifts of nature. TN 1.03. 28 P
wherefore have these gifts a curtain before 'em? 1.03.126 P
royally attorney'd with interchange of gifts, WT 1.01. 28 P
the gifts she looks from me are pack'd and 4.04.358
of nature's gifts thou mayst with lilies boast, JN 3.01. 53
laid gifts before him, proffer'd him their oaths 1H4 4.03. 71
all the other gifts appertinent to man, as the 2H4 1.02.171 P
as, liking of the lady's virtuous gifts, | her 1H6 5.01. 43
her virtues, graced with external gifts, | do 5.05. 3
and tears have mov'd me, gifts could never. 2H6 4.07. 68
large gifts have i bestow'd on learned clerks, 4.07. 71
then i see you will part but with light gifts! R3 3.01.118
and which gifts | (saving your mincing) the H8 2.03. 30
words, vows, gifts, tears, and love's full TRO 1.02.282
all our abilities, gifts, natures, shapes, 1.03.179
that now | refus'd most princely gifts, am bound COR 1.09. 80
how proud i am of thee and of thy gifts | rome TIT 1.01.254
do, and with his gifts present | your lordships, 4.02. 14
a lord | basely insinuate and send us gifts. 4.02. 38
i am so far already in your gifts — TIM 1.02.172
he commands us to provide, and give great gifts, 1.02.192
for your own gifts, make yourselves prais'd; 3.06. 71 P
a usuring kindness, and, as rich men deal gifts, 4.03.509
travail'd in the great show'r of your gifts, 5.01. 70
witchcraft of his wits, with traitorous gifts — HAM 1.05. 43
o wicked wit and gifts that have the power | so 1.05. 44
upon a wretch whose natural gifts were poor | to 1.05. 51
rich gifts wax poor when givers prove unkind. 3.01.100
that i bobb'd from him | as gifts to desdemona; OTH 5.01. 17
since men take women's gifts for impudence. PER 2.03. 69
why do you make us love your goodly gifts | and 3.01. 23
petitions are not | without gifts understood, TNK 1.03. 15
than of your graces and your gifts to tell; SON 103.12
GIG 3 FR 0.0003 REL FR 1 V 2 P
to see great hercules whipping a gig, | and LLL 4.03.165
thou disputes like an infant; go whip thy gig. 5.01. 67 P
infamy, /manu cita — a gig of a cuckold's horn. 5.01. 69 P
GIGLET 1 FR 0.0001 REL FR 1 V 0 P
who was once at point | (o giglet fortune!) CYM 3.01. 31
GIGLETS 1 FR 0.0001 REL FR 0 V 1 P
away with those giglets too, and with the other MM 5.01.347 P
GIGLOT 1 FR 0.0001 REL FR 1 V 0 P
not born | to be the pillage of a giglot wench." 1H6 4.07. 41
GILBERT 3 FR 0.0003 REL FR 3 V 0 P
sir gilbert talbot, sir william stanley, R3 4.05. 13
la car, | one gilbert /perk, his /chancellor — H8 1.01.219
sir gilbert /perk his chancellor, and john car, 2.01. 20
GILD 13 FR 0.0014 REL FR 13 V 0 P
the sun begins to gild the western sky, | and TGV 5.01. 1
doors, and gild myself | with some moe ducats, MV 2.06. 49
shall gild her bridal bed and make her rich | in JN 2.01.491
to gild refined gold, to paint the lily, | to 4.02. 11
lent | shall point on me and gild my banishment. R2 1.03.147
i'll gild it with the happiest terms i have. 1H4 5.04.158
england shall double gild his treble guilt, 2H4 4.05.128
the sun doth gild our armor, up, my lords! H5 4.02. 1
or gild again the noble troops that waited H8 3.02.411
some with cunning gild their copper crowns, TRO 4.04.105
for which we lose our heads to gild his horns! 4.05. 31
i'll gild the faces of the grooms withal, | for MAC 2.02. 53
which virtue gave the golden age to gild | their LUC 60
/GILDED 1 FR 0.0001 REL FR 1 V 0 P
/would /he /hang /his /slender /gilded /wings TIT 3.02. 61
GILDED 20 FR 0.0022 REL FR 17 V 3 P
find this grand liquor that hath gilded 'em? TMP 5.01.280
sometimes the beam of her view gilded my foot, WIV 1.03. 61 P
gilded /tombs do worms infold. MV 2.07. 69
a green and gilded snake had wreath'd itself, AYL 4.03.108
away, | men are but gilded loam or painted clay. R2 1.01.179
hath a little gilded over your night's exploit 2H4 1.02.149 P
i saw him run after a gilded butterfly, and when COR 1.03. 60 P
the gilded newt and eyeless venom'd worm, | with TIM 4.03.182
offense's gilded hand may /shove by justice, HAM 3.03. 58
and the small gilded fly | does lecher in my LR 4.06.112
and laugh | at gilded butterflies, and hear poor 5.03. 13
and, in thy /attaint, | this gilded serpent. 5.03. 84
the stale of horses and the gilded puddle ANT 1.04. 62
med'cine hath | with his tinct gilded thee. 1.05. 37
a distaff to a lance, gilded pale looks; CYM 5.03. 34
whose rags sham'd gilded arms, whose naked 5.05. 4
not marble nor the gilded /monuments | of SON 55. 1
and gilded honor shamefully misplac'd, | and 66. 5
thee | to make him much outlive a gilded tomb, 101.11
saw how deceits were gilded in his smiling, LC 172
GILDING 2 FR 0.0002 REL FR 2 V 0 P
gilding the object whereupon it gazeth; SON 20. 6
gilding pale streams with heavenly alcumy; 33. 4
/GILD'ST 1 FR 0.0001 REL FR 1 V 0 P
stars twire not, thou /gild'st th' even: SON 28.12
GILL *(also jill)*
GILL 1 FR 0.0001 REL FR 1 V 0 P
jack hath not gill. LLL 5.02.875
GILLIAMS 1 FR 0.0001 REL FR 1 V 0 P
what ho! is gilliams with the packet gone? 1H4 2.03. 65
GILLIAN 1 FR 0.0001 REL FR 1 V 0 P
maud, bridget, marian, cic'ly, gillian, ginn! ERR 3.01. 31
GILLS* 2 FR 0.0002 REL FR 1 V 1 P
the jacks fair within, the gills fair without, SHR 4.01. 50 P
the fishes spread on it their golden gills; VEN 1100
GILLYVORS 2 FR 0.0002 REL FR 2 V 0 P
are our carnations and streak'd gillyvors, WT 4.04. 82
then make /your garden rich in gillyvors, | and 4.04. 98
/GILT 1 FR 0.0001 REL FR 0 V 1 P
a /gilt nutmeg. LLL 5.02.646 P
GILT 14 FR 0.0015 REL FR 10 V 4 P
the double gilt of this opportunity you let time TN 3.02. 25 P
hither return all gilt with frenchmen's blood. JN 2.01.316
wipe off the dust that hides our sceptre's gilt, R2 2.01.294
you do not all show like gilt twopences to me, 2H4 4.03. 51 P
have for the gilt of france (o guilt indeed!) H5 2.pr. 26
our gayness and our gilt are all besmirch'd 4.03.110
iron of naples hid with english gilt, | whose 3H6 2.02.139
dwarfish pages were | as cherubins, all gilt; H8 1.01. 23
if i could 'a' rememb'red a gilt counterfeit, TRO 2.03. 25 P
and /give to dust, that is a little gilt, | more 3.03.178
a little gilt, | more laud than gilt o'erdusted. 3.03.179
it more becomes a man | than gilt his trophy. COR 1.03. 40
and, having gilt the ocean with his beams, TIT 2.01. 6
when thou wast in thy gilt and thy perfume, they TIM 4.03.302 P
/GIMMAL'D 1 FR 0.0001 REL FR 1 V 0 P
and in their pale dull mouths the /gimmal'd bit H5 4.02. 49
GIMMORS 1 FR 0.0001 REL FR 1 V 0 P
i think by some odd gimmors or device | their 1H6 1.02. 41
GI'N *(also given, giv'n)*
GI'N 1 FR 0.0001 REL FR 1 V 0 P
much follow'd both, for both much money gi'n, TNK pr 2
GIN* *(also begin, etc.)*
GIN* 4 FR 0.0004 REL FR 3 V 1 P
now is the woodcock near the gin. TN 2.05. 83 P
ay, ay, so strives the woodcock with the gin. 3H6 1.04. 61
the net nor lime, | the pitfall nor the gin. MAC 4.02. 35
i gin to be a–weary of the sun, | and wish th' 5.05. 48
/GING 1 FR 0.0001 REL FR 0 V 1 P
rascals, there's a knot, a /ging, a pack, a WIV 4.02.118 P
GINGER 7 FR 0.0008 REL FR 0 V 7 P
for a commodity of brown paper and old ginger, MM 4.03. 5 P
marry, then ginger was not much in request, for 4.03. 7 P
in that as ever knapp'd ginger or made her MV 3.01. 9 P
anne, and ginger shall be hot i' th' mouth too. TN 2.03.117 P
a race or two of ginger, but that i may beg; WT 4.03. 47 P
have a gammon of bacon and two razes of ginger, 1H4 2.01. 25 P
and of the heat of the ginger. H5 3.07. 20 P
GINGERBREAD 1 FR 0.0001 REL FR 0 V 1 P
world, thou shouldst have it to buy gingerbread. LLL 5.01. 72 P
GINGERLY 1 FR 0.0001 REL FR 1 V 0 P
what is't that you | took up so gingerly? TGV 1.02. 70
GINN *(also jinny's)*
GINN 1 FR 0.0001 REL FR 1 V 0 P
maud, bridget, marian, cic'ly, gillian, ginn! ERR 3.01. 31
GINS* 9 FR 0.0010 REL FR 9 V 0 P
time after) | now gins to bite the spirits. TMP 3.03.106
be it by gins, by snares, by subtlety, 2H6 3.01.262
as whence the sun gins his reflection MAC 1.02. 25
near, | and gins to pale his uneffectual fire. HAM 1.05. 90
heaven's gate sings, | and phoebus gins arise, CYM 2.03. 21
see how she gins | to blow into life's flower PER 3.02. 94
and like a bold–fac'd suitor gins to woo him. VEN 6
and gins to chide, but soon she stops his lips, 46
a flower that dies when first it gins to bud, PP 13. 3

GIPES *(also gibes)*
GIPES 1 FR 0.0001 REL FR 0 V 1 P
he was full of jests, and gipes, and knaveries, H5 4.07. 49 P
GIPSIES 1 FR 0.0001 REL FR 0 V 1 P
and both in a tune, like two gipsies on a horse. AYL 5.03. 15 P
GIPSY 3 FR 0.0003 REL FR 2 V 1 P
dido a dowdy, cleopatra a gipsy, helen and hero ROM 2.04. 41 P
like a right gipsy, hath at fast and loose ANT 4.12. 28
thou art a changeling to him, a mere gipsy, TNK 4.02. 44
GIPSY'S 1 FR 0.0001 REL FR 1 V 0 P
bellows and the fan | to cool a gipsy's lust. ANT 1.01. 10
GIRALDO *(also gerrold)*
GIRALDO 1 FR 0.0001 REL FR 0 V 1 P
and penn'd by no worse man than giraldo, TNK 4.03. 13 P
GIRD 4 FR 0.0004 REL FR 3 V 1 P
i thank thee for that gird, good tranio. SHR 5.02. 58
men of all sorts take a pride to gird at me. 2H4 1.02. 6 P
the bishop hath a kindly gird. 1H6 3.01.131
being mov'd, he will not spare to gird the gods. COR 1.01.256
GIRDED 2 FR 0.0002 REL FR 2 V 0 P
with fatal mouths gaping on girded harflew. H5 3.pr. 27
and summer's green all girded up in sheaves SON 12. 7
GIRDING 1 FR 0.0001 REL FR 1 V 0 P
girding with grievous siege castles and towns; H5 1.02.152
GIRDLE 11 FR 0.0012 REL FR 7 V 4 P
if he be, he knows how to turn his girdle. ADO 5.01.142 P
i'll put a girdle round about the earth | in MND 2.01.175
stones, | that as a waist doth girdle you about, JN 2.01.217
nay, and i do, i pray god my girdle break. 1H4 3.03.151 P
times to see | the beachy girdle of the ocean 2H4 3.01. 50
suppose within the girdle of these walls | are H5 pr 19
knock me down with 'em, cleave me to the girdle!
TIM 3.04. 90
with their assigns, as girdle, /hangers, and so. HAM 5.02.150 P
but to the girdle do the gods inherit, | beneath LR 4.06.126
you shall find us in our salt-water girdle. CYM 3.01. 80 P
and girdle with embracing flames the waist | of LUC 6
GIRDLED 2 FR 0.0002 REL FR 1 V 1 P
for they are all girdled with maiden walls that H5 5.02.322 P
who now is girdled with a waist of iron | and 1H6 4.03. 20
GIRDLES 3 FR 0.0003 REL FR 2 V 1 P
one a' these maids' girdles for your waist LLL 4.01. 50
and bunches of keys at their girdles, and if a 2H4 1.02. 39 P
o thou wall | that girdles in those wolves, dive TIM 4.01. 2
GIRDLING 1 FR 0.0001 REL FR 1 V 0 P
"girdling one another | within their alablaster R3 4.03. 10
/GIRL 2 FR 0.0002 REL FR 2 V 0 P
/wound /it /with /sighing, /girl, /kill /it TIT 3.02. 15
/fall /to, /and, /gentle /girl, /eat /this. 3.02. 34
GIRL 54 FR 0.0061 REL FR 46 V 8 P
both, both, my girl. TMP 1.02. 61
gentle girl, assist me; TGV 2.07. 1
no, girl, i'll knit it up in silken strings, 2.07. 45
what might we do to make the girl forget | the 3.02. 29
why, this it is to be a peevish girl, | that 5.02. 49
his body for a girl that loves him not. 5.04.134
anne is a good girl, and i wish — WIV 1.04. 34 P
i think so, when i took a boy for a girl. 5.05.191 P
thou'rt i' th' right, girl, more o' that. MM 2.02.129
and jaquenetta is a true girl, and therefore LLL 1.01.312 P
i do love that country girl that i took in the 1.02.117 P
have with thee, my girl. 4.02.146 P
jessica, my girl, | look to my house. MV 2.05. 15
find the girl, | she hath the stones upon her, 2.08. 21
is an unlesson'd girl, unschool'd, unpractic'd, 3.02.159
shall we part, sweet girl? AYL 1.03. 98
there's a girl goes before the priest, and 4.01.140 P
for i will love thee ne'er the less, my girl. SHR 1.01. 77
if i achieve not this young modest girl. 1.01.156
poor girl, she weeps. 2.01. 24
go, girl, i cannot blame thee now to weep, | for 3.02. 27
a grumbling groom, and that the girl shall find. 3.02.153
in those unfledg'd days was my wife a girl; WT 1.02. 78
therefore no dancing, girl, some other sport. R2 3.04. 9
of neither, girl; 3.04. 12
kneel down and take my blessing, good my girl. 1H6 5.04. 25
why, here's a girl! 5.04. 80
'tis a girl | promises boys hereafter. H8 5.01.165
said i for this, the girl was like to him? 5.01.174
superstitious girl | makes all these bodements. TRO 5.03. 79
here's a letter come from yond poor girl. 5.03. 99 P
and the foolish fortune of this girl, and what 5.03.102 P
which is it, girl, of these? TIT 4.01. 32
lavinia, wert thou thus surpris'd, sweet girl? 4.01. 51
give signs, sweet girl, for here are none but 4.01. 61
because the girl should not survive her shame, 5.03. 41
where's this girl? ROM 1.03. 4
go, girl, seek happy nights to happy days. 1.03.105
well, girl, thou weep'st not so much for his 3.05. 78
but now i'll tell thee joyful tidings, girl. 3.05.104
how now, a conduit, girl? 3.05.129
since this same wayward girl is so reclaim'd. 4.02. 47
me some drink, titinius," | as a sick girl. JC 1.02.128
i inhabit then, protest me | the baby of a girl. MAC 3.04.105
you speak like a green girl, | unsifted in such HAM 1.03.101
o unhappy girl! OTH 1.01.163
cold, cold, my girl? 5.02.275
what, girl, though grey | do something mingle ANT 4.08. 19
it seems, much loves | a gallian girl at home. CYM 1.06. 66
art a man, and i | have suffered like a girl. PER 5.01.137
o heavens bless my girl! 5.01.223
tyrant from his rage, | and weep unto a girl; TNK 5.01. 79
"my girl," quoth she, "on what occasion break LUC 1270
"but tell me, girl, when went" (and there she 1275
GIRLOND *(also garland)*
GIRLOND 1 FR 0.0001 REL FR 1 V 0 P
wear the girlond | with joy that you have won. TNK 5.03.130
GIRLS 14 FR 0.0015 REL FR 13 V 1 P
shall we resolve to woo these girls of france? LLL 4.03.368
we are wise girls to mock our lovers so. 5.02. 58
those girls of italy, take heed of them. AWW 2.01. 19
boys, too green and idle | for girls of nine), o WT 3.02.182
follow me, girls. 4.04.313 P
between two girls, which hath the merriest eye 1H6 2.04. 15
and all the greekish girls shall tripping sing, TRO 3.03.211
and foot it, girls. ROM 1.05. 26
young boys and girls | are level now with men; ANT 4.15. 65
my noble girls! 4.15. 84
he words me, girls, he words me, that i should 5.02.191
golden lads and girls all must, | as CYM 4.02.262
that place them on the truth of girls and boys. 5.05.107
fitter for girls and schoolboys) will be seen, TNK 3.06. 34
GIRT 4 FR 0.0004 REL FR 4 V 0 P
i girt thee with the valiant sword of york: 1H6 3.01.170
duke of suffolk, | and girt thee with the sword. 2H6 1.01. 65
like to his island, girt in with the ocean, | or 3H6 4.08. 20
whether my brows may not be girt with garlands, TNK 2.03. 80
GIRTH 2 FR 0.0002 REL FR 1 V 1 P
one girth six times piec'd, and a woman's SHR 3.02. 60 P
when neither curb would crack, girth break, nor TNK 5.04. 74
GIRTHS 2 FR 0.0002 REL FR 2 V 0 P
and break'st | the stony girths of cities: TNK 5.01. 56
and now his woven girths he breaks asunder; VEN 266
GIS *(also jesus)*
GIS 1 FR 0.0001 REL FR 1 V 0 P
"by gis, and by saint charity, | alack, and fie HAM 4.05. 58
GIVE *(also gi')*
/GIVE 15 FR 0.0017 REL FR 14 V 1 P
/give /me /thy /hand, /terrestrial; WIV 3.01.105 P
/give /sorrow /leave /a /while /to /tutor /me R2 4.01.166
/give /me /the /crown. 4.01.181
/of /your /cares /you /give /me /with /your 4.01.194
/the /cares /i /give /i /have, /though /given 4.01.198
/i /give /this /heavy /weight /from /off /my 4.01.204
/mine /own /hands /i /give /away /my /crown, 4.01.208
/give /me /that /glass, /and /therein /will /i 4.01.276
/then /give /me /leave /to /go. 4.01.313
/to /take /is /not /to /give. R3 1.02.202
and /give /to dust, that is a little gilt, | more TRO 3.03.178
/for /we /would /give /much /to /use /violent 5.03. 21
/give /me /thy /knife, /i /will /insult /on /him TIT 3.02. 71
i will /give you way for these your letters, HAM 4.06. 32
/counsell'd /thee | /to /give /away /thy /land, LR 1.04.141
GIVE 1410 FR 0.1593 REL FR 1094 V 316 P
you cannot, give thanks you have liv'd so long, TMP 1.01. 24 P
shall we give o'er and drown? 1.01. 38 P
now would i give a thousand furlongs of sea for 1.01. 65 P
th' king of naples | to give him annual tribute, 1.02.113
appointed | master of this design, did give us, 1.02.163
'tis a good dullness, | and give it way. 1.02.186
since thou dost give me pains, | let me remember 1.02.242
me, wouldst give me | water with berries in't, 1.02.333
and that you will some good instruction give 1.02.425
the visitor will not give him o'er so. 2.01. 11 P
in his pocket, and give it his son for an apple. 2.01. 92 P
fool there but would give a piece of silver. 2.02. 29 P
when they will not give a doit to relieve a lame 2.02. 32 P
went on four legs cannot make him give ground"; 2.02. 61 P
i will give him some relief, if it be but for 2.02. 67 P
here is that which will give language to you, 2.02. 83 P
pray give me that, | i'll carry it to the pile. 3.01. 24
that dare not offer | what i desire to give; 3.01. 78
i do beseech thy greatness, give him blows, 3.02. 64
as you like this, give me the lie another time. 3.02. 77 P
i did not give the lie. 3.02. 78 P
give me thy hand. 3.02.111 P
and sweet airs, that give delight and hurt not. 3.02.136
give us kind keepers, heavens! what were these? 3.03. 20
bring the rabble | (o'er whom i give thee pow'r) 4.01. 38
do not give dalliance | too much the rein. 4.01. 51
good my lord, give me thy favor still. 4.01.204
give me thy hand. 4.01.220 P
give us particulars of thy preservation, | how 5.01.135
give me your hands. 5.01.213
over the boots? nay, give me not the boots. TGV 1.01. 27
give her no token but stones, for she's as hard 1.01.140 P
give me a note, your ladyship can set. 1.02. 78
ay, give it me, it's mine: 2.01. 3
o, give ye good ev'n! 2.01. 98 P
he should give her interest, and she gives it 2.01.102 P
give him leave, madam, he is a kind of chameleon 2.04. 25 P
think, no other treasure to give your followers; 2.04. 44 P
now presently i'll give her father notice | of 2.06. 36
sir thurio, give us leave, i pray, a while, | we 3.01. 1
never give her o'er, | for scorn at first makes 3.01. 94
will give thee time to leave our royal court, 3.01.165
the turn | to give the onset to thy good advice. 3.02. 93
and give some evening music to her ear. 4.02. 17
plac'd, | i give consent to go along with you, 4.03. 39
give her that ring and therewithal | this letter 4.04. 85
go give your master this. 4.04.118
i give thee this | for thy sweet mistress' sake, 4.04.176
and less than this, i am sure you cannot give. 5.04. 25
free, | all that was mine in silvia i give thee. 5.04. 83
and julia herself did give it me — | and julia 5.04. 98
thurio, give back, or else embrace thy death; 5.04.126
they may give the dozen white luces in their WIV 1.01. 16 P
give, when she is able to overtake seventeen 1.01. 53 P
give ear to his motions: 1.01.214 P
give her this letter; 1.02. 7 P
we must give folks leave to prate; 1.04.121 P
o mistress page, give me some counsel! 2.01. 41 P
meeting, give him a show of comfort in his suit, 2.01. 94 P
it would give eternal food to his jealousy. 2.01.101 P
but i'll give you a pottle of burnt sack to give 2.01.214 P
of burnt sack to give me recourse to him and 2.01.215 P
give your worship good morrow. 2.02. 33 P
give fire! 2.02.137
give us leave, drawer. 2.02.158 P
tell you, sir, if you will give me the hearing. 2.02.176 P
that could but niggardly give me sight of her; 2.02.198 P
not only bought many presents to give her, but 2.02.199 P
only give me so much of your time in exchange of 2.02.233 P
next, give me your hand; 2.02.253 P
give you good morrow, sir. 2.03. 21 P
pray you give me my gown, or else keep it in 3.01. 34 P
give me thy hand, celestial; 3.01.106 P
give your men the charge, we must be brief. 3.03. 7 P
of thy foot would give an excellent motion to 3.03. 63 P
husband, to give him such cause of suspicion! 3.03.100 P
into the water, and give him another hope, to 3.03.195 P
such a sickly creature, i give heaven praise. 3.04. 59 P
once to-night | give my sweet nan this ring. 3.04.100
and give them to a dog for a new-year's gift. 3.05. 8 P
give your worship good morrow. 3.05. 26 P
come, mother prat, come give me your hand. 4.02.182 P
i will give over all. 4.06. 2 P
i'll give thee | a hundred pound in gold more 4.06. 4
marrying, | to give our hearts united ceremony. 4.06. 51
me into the pit, and when i give the watch-ords, 5.04. 3 P
seese is not good to give putter; 5.05.140 P
fenton, heaven give thee joy! 5.05.236
fenton, | heaven give you many, many merry days! 5.05.240
lists of all advice | my strength can give you. MM 1.01. 7
yet give leave, my lord, | that we may bring you 1.01. 60
give me your hand, | i'll privily away. 1.01. 66
the heavens give safety to your purposes! 1.01. 73
to give me leave | to have free speech with you; 1.01. 76
why i desire thee | to give me secret harbor, 1.03. 4
sith 'twas my fault to give the people scope, 1.03. 35
he (to give fear to use and liberty, | which 1.04. 62
to know, when maidens sue, | men give like gods; 1.04. 81
no longer staying but to give the mother 1.04. 86
froth, i could not give you threepence again. 2.01.103 P
you'll be glad to give out a commission for more 2.01.239 P
do you your office, or give up your place, | and 2.02. 13
heaven give thee moving graces! 2.02. 36
give up your body to such sweet uncleanness | as 2.04. 54
this, | i had rather give my body than my soul. 2.04. 56
he shall not, isabel, if you give me love. 2.04.144
and now i give my sensual race the rein. 2.04.160
why give you me this shame? 3.01. 80
to his bed, give him promise of satisfaction. 3.01.263 P
warranted need, give him a better proclamation. 3.02.143 P
heaven give your spirits comfort! 4.02. 70
give him leave to escape hence, he would not. 4.02.148 P
i will give him a present shrift and advise him 4.02.207 P
forbear it therefore, give your cause to heaven. 4.03.124
at the gates, | there to give up their pow'r. 4.03.132
this letter then to friar peter give; 4.03.137
give notice to such men of sort and suit as are 4.04. 16 P
give the like notice | to valentius, rowland, 4.05. 7
give /me your hand, | and let the subject see, 5.01. 13
here is lord angelo shall give you justice; 5.01. 27
give us some seats. 5.01.165
now, good my lord, give me the scope of justice, 5.01.234
my lord, give me leave to question, you shall 5.01.271 P
o, give me pardon, | that i, your vassal, have 5.01.385
give up your keys. 5.01.462
give me your hand and say you will be mine, | he 5.01.492
therefore give out you are of epidamium, | lest ERR 1.02. 1
earnest, | upon what bargain do you give it me? 2.02. 25
amends next, to give you nothing for something. 2.02. 53 P
give me thy hand. 3.02. 69
nay, come, i pray you, sir, give me the chain: 4.01. 45
why, give it to my wife, and fetch your money. 4.01. 54
i do obey thee, till i give thee bail. 4.01. 80
give her this key, and tell her, in the desk 4.01.103
some other give me thanks for kindnesses; 4.03. 5
going to bed and says, "god give you good rest!" 4.03. 33 P
give me the ring of mine you had at dinner, | or 4.03. 68
master, be wise, and if you give it her, | the 4.03. 75
i'll give thee, ere i leave thee, so much money, 4.04. 2
give me your hand, and let me feel your pulse. 4.04. 52
you saw they speak us fair, give us gold: 4.04.152 P
who give their eyes the liberty of gazing? 5.01. 53
whom i beseech | to give me ample satisfaction 5.01.253
me up, i likewise give her most humble thanks; ADO 1.01.239 P
and i can give you intelligence of an intended 1.03. 44 P
having obtain'd her, give her to count claudio. 1.03. 63 P
name the day of marriage, and god give thee joy! 2.01.301 P
i give away myself for you, and dote upon the 2.01.308 P
cousins, god give you joy! 2.01.336 P
such assistance as i shall give you direction. 2.01.370 P
god give me patience!" 2.03.148 P
will rather die than give any sign of affection. 2.03.227 P
well, give them their charge, neighbor dogberry. 3.03. 7 P
why, give god thanks, and make no boast of it, 3.03. 19 P
god give me joy to wear it, for my heart is 3.04. 24 P
they stay for you to give your daughter to her 3.05. 54 P
free and unconstrained soul | give me this maid, 4.01. 25
as freely, son, as god did give her me. 4.01. 26
and what have i to give you back whose worth 4.01. 27
give not this rotten orange to your friend, 4.01. 32
and salt too little which may season give | to 4.01.142
give not me counsel, | nor let no comforter 5.01. 5
before | would give preceptial med'cine to rage, 5.01. 24
therefore give me no counsel, | my griefs cry 5.01. 31
if it should give your age such cause of fear. 5.01. 56
nay then give him another staff, this last was 5.01.138 P
give her the right you should have giv'n her 5.01.291
i humbly give you leave to depart, and if a 5.01.325 P
i give thee the bucklers. 5.02. 17 P
give us the swords, we have bucklers of our own. 5.02. 18 P
daughter, | and give her to young claudio. 5.04. 16
this same is she, and i do give you her. 5.04. 54
give me your hand before this holy friar — | i 5.04. 58
and give him light that it was blinded by. LLL 1.01. 83
lights, | that give a name to every fixed star, 1.01. 89
and every godfather can give a name. 1.01. 93
give me the paper, let me read the same, | and 1.01.116
it as the style shall give us cause to climb in 1.01.199 P
"fair" i give you back again, and "welcome" i 2.01. 91 P
we will give up our right in aquitaine, | and 2.01.139
i'll give you aquitaine and all that is his, 2.01.248
and you give him for my sake but one loving kiss 2.01.249
take this key, give enlargement to the swain, 3.01. 5 P
i give thee thy liberty, set thee from durance, 3.01.128 P
"no, i'll give you a remuneration": 3.01.139 P
the neck of the wax, and every one give ear. 4.01. 59
to whom shouldst thou give it? 4.01.102
god give you good morrow, master person. 4.02. 82 P
one with a paper, god give him grace to groan! 4.03. 19 P
doth thy face through tears of mine give light. 4.03. 31
o, who can give an oath? 4.03.246
take thou this, my sweet, and give me thine, 5.02.132
will you give horns, chaste lady? 5.02.252
madam, and pretty mistresses, give ear: 5.02.286
then wish me better, i will give you leave. 5.02.342
i cannot give you less. 5.02.384
god give thee joy of him! 5.02.448
my faith and this the princess i did give; 5.02.454
give it him. 5.02.628
i must rather give it the rein, for it runs 5.02.657 P

then, if i have much love, i'll give you some. 5.02.830
which shallow laughing hearers give to fools. 5.02.860
yoke | my soul consents not to give sovereignty. MND 1.01. 82
the rest i'll give to be to you translated. 1.01.191
i give him curses; yet he gives me love. 1.01.196
if it be, give it me, for i am slow of study. 1.02. 67 P
you come | to give their bed joy and prosperity. 2.01. 73
give me that boy, and i will go with thee. 2.01.143
only give me leave, | unworthy as i am, to 2.01.206
i pray thee give it me. 2.01.248
sleep give thee all his rest! 2.02. 64
who would give a bird the lie, though he cry 3.01.135 P
i'll give thee fairies to attend on thee; 3.01.157
ah, good demetrius, wilt thou give him me? 3.02. 63
i had rather give his carcass to my hounds. 3.02. 64
will you give her o'er? 3.02.130
nor none, in my mind, now you give her o'er. 3.02.135
give me your neaf, mounsieur mustardseed. 4.01. 19 P
that hermia should give answer of her choice? 4.01.136
the kinder we, to give them thanks for nothing. 5.01. 89
through the house give glimmering light | by the 5.01.391
give me your hands, if we be friends, | and 5.01.437
give him direction for this merry bond, | and i MV 1.03.173
give me your blessing; 2.02. 78 P
fooling about it, but give me your blessing. 2.02. 84 P
give him a present! 2.02.105 P
give him a halter. 2.02.105 P
give me your present to one master bassanio, who 2.02.108 P
give him a livery | more guarded than his 2.02.154
give him this letter, do it secretly, | and so 2.03. 7
"who chooseth me must give and hazard all he 2.07. 9
"who chooseth me must give and hazard all he 2.07. 16
must give — for what? 2.07. 17
i'll then nor give nor hazard aught for lead. 2.07. 21
"who chooseth me must give and hazard all he 2.09. 21
you shall look fairer ere i give or hazard. 2.09. 22
give me a key for this, | and instantly unlock 2.09. 51
leave, | i come by note, to give and to receive. 3.02.140
i give them with this ring, | which when you 3.02.171
which when you part from, lose, or give away, 3.02.172
look what notes and garments he doth give thee, 3.04. 51
and i be pleas'd to give ten thousand ducats 4.01. 45
so can i give no reason, nor i will not, | more 4.01. 59
go give him courteous conduct to this place. 4.01.148
give me your hand. 4.01.169
must needs give sentence 'gainst the merchant 4.01.205
i do beseech the court | to give the judgment. 4.01.244
give me your hand, bassanio, fare you well! 4.01.265
your wife would give you little thanks for that 4.01.288
the court awards it, and the law doth give it. 4.01.300
this bond doth give thee here no jot of blood; 4.01.306
give me my principal, and let me go. 4.01.336
why then the devil give him good of it! 4.01.345
i pray you give me leave to go from hence, | i 4.01.395
give me your gloves, i'll wear them for your 4.01.426
i will not shame myself to give you this. 4.01.431
the dearest ring in venice will i give you, 4.01.435
me vow | that i should neither sell, nor give, 4.01.443
give him the ring, and bring him, if thou canst, 4.01.453
inquire the jew's house out, give him this deed, 4.02. 1
that they did give the rings away to men; 4.02. 16
give order to my servants that they take | no 5.01.119
let me give light, but let me not be light, 5.01.129
give welcome to my friend; 5.01.133
a paltry ring | that she did give me, whose posy 5.01.148
you swore to me, when i did give /it you, | that 5.01.152
you give your wife too unkind a cause of grief; 5.01.175
the ring of me to give the worthy doctor. 5.01.222
give him this, | and bid him keep it better than 5.01.254
ay, and i'll give them him without a fee. 5.01.290
there do i give to you and jessica, | from the 5.01.291
you in his will to give me good education. AYL 1.01. 67 P
or give me the poor allottery my father left me 1.01. 73 P
and yet give no thousand crowns neither. 1.01. 86 P
if he come to–morrow, i'll give him his payment. 1.01.160 P
ay, my liege, so please you give us leave. 1.02.157 P
your own safety, and give over this attempt. 1.02.179 P
that could give more, but that her hand lacks 1.02.247
i will give thee mine. 1.03. 91
all this i give you, let me be your servant. 2.03. 46
yond man | if he for gold will give us any food; 2.04. 65
as many matters as he, but i give heaven thanks, 2.05. 36 P
i'll give you a verse to this note, that i made 2.05. 46 P
something to eat, i will give thee leave to die; 2.06. 12 P
give me leave | to speak my mind, and i will 2.07. 58
a doe, i go to find my fawn | and give it food. 2.07.129
give us some music, and, good cousin, sing. 2.07.173
give me your hand, | and let me all your 2.07.199
give me audience, good madam. 3.02.238 P
i would give him some good counsel, for he seems 3.02.364 P
in the which women still give the lie to their 3.02.390 P
well, the gods give us joy! 3.03. 47 P
is there none here to give the woman? 3.03. 67 P
proceed, proceed. i'll give her. 3.03. 72 P
give me your hand, orlando. 4.01.125 P
my gentle phebe did bid me give you this. 4.03. 7
occasion, | made him give battle to the lioness, 4.03.130
his broken promise, and to give this napkin, 4.03.154
give me your hand. art thou learned? 5.01. 38 P
that would i, had i kingdoms to give with her. 5.04. 8
me, | you'll give yourself to this most faithful 5.04. 14
you your word, o duke, to give your daughter; 5.04. 19
nor he durst not give me the lie direct; 5.04. 86 P
to you i give myself, for i am yours. 5.04.116
to you i give myself, for i am yours. 5.04.117
and give them friendly welcome every one. SHR in.1. 103
anon i'll give thee more instructions. in.1. 130
and if you give me any conserves, give me in.2. 7 P
me any conserves, give me conserves of beef. in.2. 7 P
why, give him gold enough, and marry him to a 1.02. 78 P
you | to give you over at this first encounter, 1.02.105
sir, give him head, i know he'll prove a jade. 1.02.247
you wrong me, signior gremio, give me leave. 2.01. 46
any, freely give unto /you this young scholar, 2.01. 79 P
if she do bid me pack, i'll give her thanks, 2.01.177
give me thy hand, kate, i will unto venice | to 2.01.314
i know not what to say, but give me your hands. 2.01.318
your father were a fool | to give thee all, and 2.01.401

then give me leave to have prerogative, | and 3.01. 6
then give me leave to read philosophy, | and 3.01. 13
you may go walk, and give me leave a while; 3.01. 59
to give my hand oppos'd against my heart | unto 3.02. 9
you all | that have beheld me give away myself 3.02.194
will you give thanks, sweet kate, or else shall 4.01.159
god give him joy! 4.02. 52
and give assurance to baptista minola, | as if 4.02. 69
take thou the bill, give me thy mete–yard, and 4.03.152 P
to me now, | give me bianca for my patrimony. 4.04. 22
nay, i will give thee a kiss; 5.01.148
and, being a winner, god give you good night! 5.02.187
from my hive, | to give some laborers room. AWW 1.02. 67
then give me pity | to her whose state is such that 1.03.213
but lend and give where she is sure to lose; 1.03.215
your honor | but give me leave to try success, 1.03.247
to give great charlemain a pen in 's hand | and 2.01. 77
i cannot give thee less, to be call'd grateful. 2.01.129
and such thanks i give | as one near death to 2.01.130
dear sir, to my endeavors give consent, | of 2.01.153
then shalt thou give me with thy kingly hand 2.01.193
give me some help here ho! 2.01.209
give helen this, | and urge her to a present 2.02. 63
which should indeed give us a further use to be 2.03. 35 P
i'd give bay curtal and his furniture, | my 2.03. 59
say i take you, but i give | me and my service, 2.03.102
give me leave to use | the help of mine own eyes 2.03.107
give me thy hand. 2.03.215 P
my lord, you give me most egregious indignity. 2.03.216 P
by thee, in what motion age will give me leave. 2.03.234 P
if you give him not john drum's entertainment, 3.06. 38 P
first, give me trust, the count he is my husband 3.07. 8
i must give myself some hurts, and say i got 4.01. 37 P
and great ones i dare not give; 4.01. 40 P
off, | but give thyself unto my sick desires, 4.02. 35
give me that ring. 4.02. 39
but have no power | to give it from me. 4.02. 41
will you give me a copy of the sonnet you writ 4.03.319 P
and i would give his wife my bauble, sir, to do 4.05. 30 P
i give thee not this to suggest thee from thy 4.05. 44 P
you | to give this poor petition to the king, 5.01. 19
master lavatch, give my lord lafew this letter. 5.02. 1 P
fortune's close–stool to give to a nobleman! 5.02. 17 P
give me your hand. 5.02. 41 P
brightest beams | distracted clouds give way, so 5.03. 35
give a favor from you | to sparkle in the 5.03. 74
you give away this hand, and that is mine; 5.03.170
you give away heaven's vows, and those are mine; 5.03.171
you give away myself, which is known mine; 5.03.172
i will return it home, | and give me mine again. 5.03.224
of all these ways, | how could you give it him? 5.03.276
food of love, play on, | give me excess of it; TN 1.01. 2
well, god give them wisdom that have it; 1.05. 14 P
for give the dry fool drink, then is the fool 1.05. 44 P
good madonna, give me leave to prove you a fool. 1.05. 58 P
give me faith, say i. 1.05.129 P
give me my veil. 1.05.165
give me modest assurance if you be the lady of 1.05.179 P
give us the place alone, we will hear this 1.05.218 P
i will give out divers schedules of my beauty. 1.05.245 P
and spirit | do give thee fivefold blazon. 1.05.293
way to–morrow, | i'll give him reasons for't. 1.05.306
if one knight give a — 2.03. 34 P
you would not give means for this uncivil rule. 2.03.123 P
give me some music. 2.04. 1
give me now leave to leave thee. 2.04. 72
let all the rest give place. 2.04. 79
strong a passion | as love doth give my heart; 2.04. 95
give her this jewel. 2.04.123
say | my love can give no place, bide no denay. 2.04.124
niece, give me this prerogative of speech" — 2.05. 70 P
i will not give my part of this sport for a 2.05.180 P
give me your hand, sir. 3.01. 93 P
give me leave, beseech you. 3.01.111
thy reason, dear venom, give thy reason. 3.02. 2 P
give me. 3.04.147 P
give them way till he take leave, and presently 3.04.197 P
deny, | that honor, sav'd, may upon asking give? 3.04.212
how with mine honor may i give him that | which 3.04.214
therefore get you on, and give him his desire. 3.04.248 P
let the matter slip, and i'll give him my horse, 3.04.286 P
give ground if you see him furious. 3.04.304 P
you tarry longer, | i shall give worse payment. 4.01. 20
these wise men that give fools money get 4.01. 22 P
take and give back affairs and their dispatch 4.03. 18
this is to give a dog and in recompense desire 5.01. 6 P
o, you give me ill counsel. 5.01. 31 P
that i shake off these names you give me. 5.01. 73
give me thy hand, | and let me see thee in thy 5.01.272
therefore perpend, my princess, and give ear. 5.01.299 P
what to say — we will give you sleepy drinks, WT 1.01. 13 P
i'll give him my commission | to let him there a 1.02. 40
though you perceive me not how i give line. 1.02.181
a cup, | to give mine enemy a lasting wink; 1.02.317
give scandal to the blood o' th' prince my son 1.02.330
i'll give no blemish to her honor, none. 1.02.341
give me thy hand, | be pilot to me, and thy 1.02.447
give me the boy. 2.01. 56
bad as those | that vulgars give bold'st titles; 2.01. 94
the oracle | give rest to th' minds of others — 2.01.191
give her the bastard, | thou dotard, thou art 2.03. 74
beseech your highness, give us better credit. 2.03.147
i do give lost, for i do feel it gone, | but 3.02. 95
and give my scene such growing | as you had 4.01. 16
bouget, | then my account i well may give, | and 4.03. 21
weeds to each part of you | does give a life; 4.04. 2
give me those flow'rs there, dorcas. 4.04. 73
so give alms; 4.04.138
do plainly give you out an unstain'd shepherd, 4.04.149
stomachers | for my lads to give their dears; 4.04.225
more, which will shame you to give him again. 4.04.240 P
i give my daughter to him, and will make | her 4.04.385
father | to greet him and to give him comforts. 4.04.557
omit | nothing may give us aid. 4.04.625
and they often give us soldiers the lie, but we 4.04.724 P
steel, therefore they do not give us the lie. 4.04.726 P
close with him, give him gold; 4.04.801 P
well, give me the moi'ty. 4.04.812 P

i will give you as much as this old man does 4.04.821 P
give me the office | to choose you a queen. 5.01. 77
so must thy grave | give way to what's seen now! 5.01. 98
from him | give you all greetings that a king, 5.01.140
give me the lie, do; 5.02.132 P
and to give me your good report to the prince my 5.02.151 P
give me thy hand: 5.02.156 P
and give me leave, | and do not say 'tis 5.03. 42
but began, | give me that hand of yours to kiss. 5.03. 46
i give heaven thanks i was not like to thee! JN 1.01. 83
i would give it every foot to have this face; 1.01.146
our country manners give our betters way. 1.01.156
brother by th' mother's side, give me your hand; 1.01.163
james gurney, wilt thou give us leave a while? 1.01.230
embrace him, love him, give him welcome hither. 2.01. 11
the rather that you give his offspring life, 2.01. 13
i give you welcome with a powerless hand, | but 2.01. 15
your strong hand shall help to give him strength 2.01. 33
and out of my dear love i'll give thee more 2.01.157
give grandame kingdom, and it grandame will 2.01.161
and it grandame will | give it a plum, a cherry, 2.01.162
or shall we give the signal to our rage, | and 2.01.265
open your gates and give the victors way. 2.01.324
to whom in favor she shall give the day, | and 2.01.393
we fling wide ope, | and give you entrance; 2.01.450
give with our niece a dowry large enough, | for 2.01.469
then do i give volquessen, touraine, maine, 2.01.527
made | will give her sadness very little cure. 2.01.546
that give you cause to prove my saying true. 3.01. 28
law cannot give my child his kingdom here, | for 3.01.187
give me thy hand. 3.03. 25
and too full of gawds | to give me audience. 3.03. 37
as i, | i could give better comfort than you do. 3.04.100
give me the iron, i say, and bind him here. 4.01. 74
that his compassion may | give life to yours. 4.01. 89
good lords, although my will to give is living, 4.02. 83
flood, and can give audience | to any tongue, 4.02.139
shall give a holiness, a purity, | to the yet 4.03. 53
at noon | my crown i should give off? 5.01. 27
to give us warrant from the hand of heaven, 5.02. 66
and shall i now give o'er the yielded set? 5.02.107
give me leave to speak. 5.02.162
my arm shall give thee help to bear thee hence, 5.04. 58
i have a kind soul that would give thanks, | and 5.07.108
rage must be withstood, | give me his gage. R2 1.01.174
but not a minute, king, that thou canst give. 1.03.226
and yet my letters–patents give me leave. 2.03.130
we all have strongly sworn to give him aid; 2.03.150
i'll give thee scope to beat, | since foes have 3.03.140
i'll give my jewels for a set of beads, | my 3.03.147
give richard leave to live till richard die? 3.03.174
uncle, give me your hands; 3.03.202
what you will have, i'll give, and willing too, 3.03.206
give some supportance to the bending twigs. 3.04. 32
on equal terms to give /him chastisement? 4.01. 22
what subject can give sentence on his king? 4.01.121
though he divide the realm and give thee half, 5.01. 60
thus give i mine, and thus take i thy heart. 5.01. 96
give me mine own again, 'twere no good part | to 5.01. 97
give me my boots, i say, saddle my horse. 5.02. 77
give me my boots, i say. 5.02. 87
then give me leave that /i may turn the key, 5.03. 36
till thou give joy, until thou bid me joy | by 5.03. 95
fellow, give place, here is no longer stay. 5.05. 95
take hence the rest, and give them burial here. 5.05.118
no, i'll give thee thy due, thou hast paid all 1H4 1.02. 52 P
i must give over this life, and i will give it 1.02. 95 P
give over this life, and i will give it over. 1.02. 95 P
he will give the devil his due. 1.02.119 P
god give thee the spirit of persuasion and him 1.02.152 P
good cousin, give me audience for a while. 1.03.211
and give it him | to keep his anger still in 1.03.225
is the next way to give poor jades the bots. 2.01. 9 P
nicholas' clerks, i'll give thee this neck. 2.01. 62 P
give me thy hand. 2.01. 91 P
give me my horse, you rogues, give me my horse, 2.02. 29 P
you rogues, give me my horse, and be hang'd! 2.02. 29 P
of ned, i give thee this pennyworth of sugar, 2.04. 22 P
i will give thee for it a thousand pound. 2.04. 61 P
"give my roan horse a drench," says he, and 2.04.106 P
give me a cup of sack, boy. 2.04.115 P
give me a cup of sack, rogue. 2.04.118 P
but i would give a thousand pound i could run as 2.04.147 P
give me them that will face me. 2.04.151 P
give me a cup of sack. 2.04.152 P
began to give me ground; 2.04.216 P
give you a reason on compulsion? 2.04.238 P
i would give no man a reason upon compulsion, i. 2.04.240 P
give him as much as will make him a royal man, 2.04.290 P
shall i give him his answer? 2.04.295 P
give me a cup of sack to make my eyes look red, 2.04.384 P
give me leave | to tell you once again that at 3.01. 35
i'll give thrice so much land | to any 3.01.135
lords, give us leave, the prince of wales and i 3.02. 1
yet doth he give us bold advertisement | that 4.01. 36
will you give me money, captain? 4.02. 4 P
you give him then advantage. 4.03. 2
did give him that same royalty he wears, | and 4.03. 55
where you did give a fair and natural light, 5.01. 18
hal, i prithee give me leave to breathe a while. 5.03. 44 P
give it me. what? is it in the case? 5.03. 52 P
give me life, which if i can save, so; 5.03. 59 P
i'll give you leave to powder me and eat me too 5.04.112 P
courtesy, | which i shall give away immediately. 5.05. 33
honor, for a silken point | i'll give my barony. 2H4 1.01. 54
by travers | give then such instances of loss? 1.01. 56
the which, if you give o'er | to stormy passion, 1.01.164
and give me leave to tell you you lie in your 1.02. 84 P
i give thee leave to tell me so? 1.02. 87 P
god give your lordship good time of day. 1.02. 93 P
say i am an old man, you should give me rest. 1.02.217 P
daughter, | give even way unto my rough affairs; 2.03. 2
rascal, is that all the comfort you give me? 2.04. 40 P
give crowns like pins! 2.04.174 P
come give 's some sack. 2.04.180 P
no, let the fiend give fire. 2.04.182
give me some sack, and, sweet heart, lie thou 2.04.183
give me my rapier, boy. 2.04.201 P

thou dost give me flattering busses. 2.04.268 P
and thy father is to give me thanks for it. 2.04.323 P
give me my sword and cloak. 2.04.366
give /then repose | to the wet //sea–boy in an 3.01. 26
come on, come on, give me your hand, sir, give 3.02. 1 P
give me your hand, sir, give me your hand, sir. 3.02. 2 P
give me your good hand, give me your worship's 3.02. 82 P
good hand, give me your worship's good hand. 3.02. 82 P
give me the spirit, master shallow. 3.02.259 P
half–fac'd fellow, shadow, give me this man. 3.02.265 P
o, give me the spare men, and spare me the great 3.02.269 P
o, give me always a little, lean, old, chopp'd, 3.02.274 P
bardolph, give the soldiers coats. 3.02.291 P
from his grace | that he will give you audience, 4.01.141
to give admittance to a thought of fear. 4.01.151
i give it you, and will maintain my word, | and 4.02. 67
lord, i beseech you give me leave to go through 4.03. 81 P
if god doth give successful end | to this debate 4.04. 1
but, being moody, give him time and scope, 4.04. 39
stand from him, give him air, he'll straight be 4.04.116
give that which gave thee life unto the worms, 4.05.116
england shall give him office, honor, might; 4.05.129
welcome | give entertainment to the might of it, 4.05.173
give me your hand, master bardolph. 5.01. 54 P
silence, i'll give you a health for that anon. 5.03. 24 P
give master bardolph some wine, davy. 5.03. 25 P
give me pardon, sir. 5.03.109 P
but mark the countenance that he will give me. 5.05. 8 P
strengths and qualities, | give you advancement. 5.05. 70
unless you give me your doublet and stuff me out 5.05. 81 P
to give a greater sum | than ever at one time H5 1.01. 79
hour, i think, is come | to give him hearing. 1.01. 93
may't please your majesty to give us leave 1.02.237
hence, did give ourself | to barbarous license; 1.02.270
that may give furth'rance to our expedition; 1.02.301
the narrow seas | to give you gentle pass; 2.pr. 39
give me thy fist, thy fore–foot to me give. 2.01. 67
give me thy fist, thy fore–foot to me give. 2.01. 67
pay, | and liquor likewise will i give to thee, 2.01.108
give me thy hand. 2.01.113
you, my gentle knight, give me your thoughts. 2.02. 14
sir, | you show great mercy if you give him life 2.02. 50
the taste whereof god of his mercy give | you 2.02.179
my love, give me thy lips. 2.03. 47
we'll give them present audience. 2.04. 67
hear the shrill whistle which doth order give 3.pr. 9
i would give all my fame for a pot of ale and 3.02. 13 P
the work ish give over, the trompet sound the 3.02. 89 P
it ish give over. 3.02. 91 P
therefore to our best mercy give yourselves, 3.03. 3
and give our vineyards to a barbarous people. 3.05. 4
and they will give | their bodies to the lust of 3.05. 29
send | to know what willing ransom he will give. 3.05. 63
and we give express charge that, in our marches 3.06.108 P
will take up that with "give the devil his due." 3.07.116 P
give them great meals of beef and iron and steel 3.07.149 P
rivets up, | give dreadful note of preparation. 4.pr. 14
sun, | his liberal eye doth give to every one, 4.pr. 44
give me any gage of thine, and i will wear it in 4.01.208 P
here's my glove; give me another of thine. 4.01.211 P
and bid thy ceremony give thee cure! 4.01.252
will it give place to flexure and low bending? 4.01.255
veins | to give each naked curtle–axe a stain, 4.02. 21
and give their fasting horses provender, | and 4.02. 58
signieur, thou do give to me | egregious ransom. 4.04. 10
peasant, unless thou give me crowns, brave 4.04. 38
his ransom he will give you two hundred crowns. 4.04. 45 P
kill his prisoners, | give the word through. 4.06. 38
o, give us leave, great king, | to view the 4.07. 81
i will give treason his payment into plows, i 4.08. 13 P
glove of alanson that your majesty is give me, 4.08. 37 P
give me thy glove, soldier. 4.08. 39 P
glove with crowns, | and give it to this fellow. 4.08. 58
give him the crowns; 4.08. 60
give me your answer, i' faith, do, and so clap 5.02.129 P
the rest, | and thereupon give me your daughter. 5.02.347
give me my steeled coat, i'll fight for france. 1H6 1.01. 85
back, you lords, and give us leave a while. 1.02. 70
shall we give o'er orleance, or no? 1.02.125
and straightway give thy soul to him thou 1.05. 7
renounce your soil, give sheep in lions' stead: 1.05. 29
to give their censure of these rare reports. 2.03. 10
that i may kindly give one fainting kiss. 2.05. 40
for my good, | only give order for my funeral. 2.05.112
to give me hearing what i shall reply. 3.01. 28
love for thy love and hand for hand i give. 3.01.135
but all the whole inheritance i give | that doth 3.01.163
i'll by a sign give notice to our friends, 3.02. 8
him, | and give him chastisement for this abuse. 4.01. 69
be patient, lords, and give them leave to speak. 4.01. 82
and give it out | that he is march'd to burdeaux 4.03. 3
give me their bodies, that i may bear them hence 4.07. 85
and give them burial as beseems their worth. 4.07. 86
one, | and means to give you battle presently. 5.02. 13
me | and give me signs of future accidents. 5.03. 4
i'll lop a member off and give it you | in 5.03. 15
before that england give the french the foil. 5.03. 23
i prithee give me leave to curse a while. 5.03. 43
sweet madam, give me hearing in a cause. 5.03.106
consent, and for thy honor give consent, | thy 5.03.136
to give thee answer of thy just demand. 5.03.144
give thee her hand, for sign of plighted faith. 5.03.162
reignier of france, i give thee kingly thanks, 5.03.163
o, give me leave, i have deluded you, | 'twas 5.04. 76
give consent | that marg'ret may be england's 5.05. 23
so should i give consent to flatter sin. 5.05. 25
where reignier sooner will receive than give. 5.05. 47
'tis thine they give away, and not their own. 2H6 1.01.221
and purchase friends and give to courtezans, 1.01.223
seal up your lips, and give no words but mum; 1.02. 89
is old enough himself | to give his censure. 1.03.117
give me my fan. 1.03.138
election, give me leave | to show some reason, 1.03.162
your grace shall give me leave, my lord of york, 1.04. 76
and give her as a prey to law and shame, | that 2.01.194
give me leave | in this close walk to satisfy 2.02. 2
i beseech your majesty give me leave to go; 2.03. 20
ere thou go, | give up thy staff. 2.03. 23
give up your staff, sir, and the king his realm. 2.03. 31
here, robin, and if i die, i give thee my aporn; 2.03. 74 P
when every one will give the time of day, | he 3.01. 14
but i can give the loser leave to chide. 3.01.182
what counsel give you in this weighty cause? 3.01.289
'twas men i lack'd, and you will give them me; 3.01.345
give thee thy hire and send thy soul to hell, 3.02.225
give me thy hand, | that i may dew it with my 3.02.339
beest death, i'll give thee england's treasure, 3.03. 2
i'll give a thousand pound to look upon him. 3.03. 13
give me some drink, and bid the apothecary 3.03. 17
master, this prisoner freely give i thee, | and 4.01. 12
and so much shall you give, or off goes yours. 4.01. 17
i'll give it, sir, and therefore spare my life. 4.01. 23
give him a box o' th' ear, and that will make 4.07. 86 P
me, and give me but the ten meals i have lost, 4.10. 61 P
i cannot give due action to my words, | except a 5.01. 8
we give thee for reward a thousand marks, | and 5.01. 79
give place! 5.01.104
sons, he says, shall give their words for him. 5.01.137
and defense | to give the enemy way, and to 5.02. 76
to see their day, and them our fortune give. 5.02. 89
peace thou! and give king henry leave to speak. 3H6 1.01.120
brother, though i be youngest, give me leave. 1.02. 1
my days, | and when i give occasion of offense, 1.03. 44
and give no foot of ground!" 1.04. 15
i give thee this to dry thy cheeks withal. 1.04. 83
i come to pierce it, or to give thee mine. 2.01.203
for god's sake, lords, give signal to the fight. 2.02.100
i prithee give no limits to my tongue, | i am a 2.02.119
what counsel give you? 2.03. 11
ope | and give sweet passage to my sinful soul! 2.03. 41
brother, give me thy hand, and gentle warwick, 2.03. 44
and give them leave to fly that will not stay; 2.03. 50
give me thy gold — if thou hast any gold — 2.05. 80
warwick, to give: 3.01. 42
nay then whip me; he'll rather give her two. 3.02. 28
lords, give us leave. i'll try this widow's wit. 3.02. 33
what service wilt thou do me if i give them? 3.02. 44
then, thy husband's lands i freely give thee. 3.02. 55
and give my tongue–tied sorrows leave to speak. 3.03. 22
let me give humble thanks for all at once. 3.03.221
therefore delay not, give thy hand to warwick, 3.03.246
and here, to pledge my vow, i give my hand. 3.03.250
to give the heir and daughter of lord scales 4.01. 52
you shall give me leave | to play the broker in 4.01. 62
give me assurance with some friendly vow, | that 4.01.141
ay, but give me worship and quietness, | i like 4.03. 16
warwick and clarence, give me both your hands. 4.06. 38
ay, by my faith, for a poor earl to give. 5.01. 32
and give more strength to that which hath too 5.04. 9
give signal to the fight, and to it, lords! 5.04. 72
be valiant, and give signal to the fight. 5.04. 82
witness the loving kiss i give the fruit. 5.07. 32
to give them thanks | that were the cause of my R3 1.01.127
to give me leave | by circumstance but to acquit 1.02. 76
but to give me leave | by circumstance /t' 1.02. 79
why then give way, dull clouds, to my quick 1.03.195
(that now give evidence against my soul) | for 1.04. 67
i will, my lord. god give your grace good rest! 1.04. 75
when he opens his purse to give us our reward, 1.04.129 P
where art thou, keeper? give me a cup of wine. 1.04.161
till that the duke give order for his burial; 1.04.281
and shall that tongue give pardon to a slave? 2.01.104
even in his /own garments, and did give himself 2.01.117
give me no help in lamentation, | i am not 2.02. 66
you go | to give your censures in this business? 2.02.144
give you good morrow, sir. 2.03. 6
i pray you, uncle, give me this dagger. 3.01.110
of my kind uncle, that i know will give, | and 3.01.113
and being but a toy, which is no grief to give. 3.01.114
a greater gift than that i'll give my cousin. 3.01.115
talk, | and give us notice of his inclination; 3.01.178
give mistress shore one gentle kiss the more. 3.01.185
but that i'll give my voice on richard's side 3.02. 53
we give to thee our guiltless blood to drink. 3.03. 14
and in the duke's behalf i'll give my voice, 3.04. 19
that he will lose his head ere give consent 3.04. 38
and to give order that no manner person | have 3.05.108
alive, | i give a sparing limit to my tongue. 3.07.194
god give your graces both | a happy and a joyful 4.01. 5
give me thy hand. 4.02. 3
give me some little breath, some pause, dear 4.02. 24
i say again, give out | that anne, my queen, is 4.02. 56
reverent, | give mine the benefit of seniory, 4.04. 36
to make amends i'll give it to your daughter; 4.04.295
pleaseth your majesty to give me leave, | i'll 4.04.487
we must both give and take, my loving lord. 5.03. 6
give me some ink and paper in my tent; 5.03. 23
and give him from me this most needful note. 5.03. 41
it, | and so god give you quiet rest to–night! 5.03. 43
give me some ink and paper. 5.03. 49
give me a watch. 5.03. 63
give me a bowl of wine. 5.03. 72
god give us leisure for these rites of love! 5.03.101
give me another horse! 5.03.177
why, then 'tis time to arm and give direction. 5.03.236
give me a calendar. 5.03.276
such as give | their money out of hope they may H8 pr 7
pray give me favor, sir: 1.01.168
to as much end | as give a crutch to th' dead. 1.01.172
and give thanks | to you that chok'd it. 1.02. 3
highness | would give it quick consideration, 1.02. 66
'tis time to give 'em physic, their diseases 1.03. 36
but few now give so great ones. 1.03. 63
good lord chamberlain, | go, give 'em welcome: 1.04. 57
then give my charge up to sir nicholas vaux, 2.01. 96
you make friends | and give your hearts to, when 2.01.128
yet i can give you inkling | of an ensuing evil, 2.01.140
i would your grace would give us but an hour 2.02. 79
give me your hand. 2.02.117
to give her the avaunt, it is a pity | would 2.03. 10
me, and so give me up | to the sharp'st kind of 2.04. 43
give heed to't: 2.04.170
we shall give you | the full cause of our coming 3.01. 28
that any englishman dare give me counsel? 3.01. 84
guilty | to give up willingly that noble title 3.01.140
to meet the least occasion that may give me 3.02. 7
my brethren mortal, | must give my tendance to. 3.02.149
give him a little earth for charity!" 4.02. 23
thus far, griffith, give me leave to speak him, 4.02. 32
honors to his age | than man could give him, he 4.02. 68
beseeching him to give her virtuous breeding — 4.02.134
to't, give your friend | some touch of your late 5.01. 12
come, come, give me your hand. 5.01. 94
give me thy hand, stand up; 5.01.115
they shall no more prevail than we give way to. 5.01.143
give her an hundred marks. i'll to the queen. 5.01.170
cruel men, and give it | to a most noble judge, 5.02.135
into whose hand i give thy life. 5.04. 11
one," quoth he, "pluck't out, and give it him." TRO 1.02.165 P
will he give you the nod? 1.02.196 P
helen, to change, would give an eye to boot. 1.02.239 P
i give to both your speeches, which were such 1.03. 62
enough, patroclus, | or give me ribs of steel! 1.03.177
shall give a scantling | of good or bad unto the 1.03.341
give pardon to my speech: 1.03.356
give him allowance for the better man, | for 1.03.376
and i will give a taste thereof forthwith | to 1.03.387
a stirring dwarf we do allowance give | before a 2.03.137
divide eternity in twain, | and give him half; 2.03.246
come, give me an instrument. 3.01. 94 P
and give me swift transportance to these fields 3.02. 11
words pay no debts, give her deeds; 3.02. 55 P
if my lord get a boy of you, you'll give him me. 3.02.105 P
nay, i'll give my word for her too. 3.02.109 P
to give me now a little benefit | out of those 3.03. 14
they will almost | give us a prince of blood, a 3.03. 26
if you give way, | or /hedge aside from the 3.03.157
than breath or pen can give expressure to. 3.03.204
wounds heal ill that men do give themselves. 3.03.229
rouse him and give him note of our approach, 4.01. 44
and give as soft attachment to thy senses | as 4.02. 5
we must give up to diomedes' hand | the lady 4.02. 65
the like allayment could i give my grief: 4.04. 8
sentinels, | to give thee nightly visitation. 4.04. 73
at the port, lord, i'll give her to thy hand, 4.04.111
lady, give me your hand, and, as we walk, | to 4.04.138
give with thy trumpet a loud note to troy, 4.05. 3
both take and give. 4.05. 37
the kiss you take is better than you give; 4.05. 38
i'll give you boot, i'll give you three for one. 4.05. 40
i'll give you boot, i'll give you three for one. 4.05. 40
you are an odd man, give even or give none. 4.05. 41
you are an odd man, give even or give none. 4.05. 41
give me a kiss | when helen is a maid again and 4.05. 49
that give a coasting welcome ere it comes, | and 4.05. 59
give me thy hand, my cousin. 4.05.157
that i may give the local wound a name, | and 4.05.244
give me your hand. 5.01. 84
give me some token for the surety of it. 5.02. 60
i'll give you something else. 5.02. 86
do not give advantage | to stubborn critics, apt 5.02.130
patroclus will give me any thing for the 5.02.192 P
but give me leave | to take that course by your 5.03. 73
or if you cannot weep, yet give some groans, 5.10. 49
could be content to give him good report for't, COR 1.01. 32 P
he that will give good words to thee will 1.01.167
factions, and give out | conjectural marriages, 1.01.193
beseech you give me leave to retire myself. 1.03. 27
give me excuse, good madam, i will obey you in 1.03.102 P
no, i'll nor sell nor give him; 1.04. 6
encount'ring, | may give you thankful sacrifice. 1.06. 9
than grateful | to us that give you truly. 1.09. 55
my noble steed, known to the camp, i give him, 1.09. 61
i request you | to give my poor host freedom. 1.09. 87
give your dispositions the reins and be angry at 2.01. 30 P
if the drink you give me touch my palate 2.01. 56 P
give way there, and go on! 2.01.193
that he will give them make i as little question 2.01.230
more pertinent | than the rebuke you give it. 2.02. 64
he covets less | than misery itself would give, 2.02.127
for my wounds' sake to give their suffrage. 2.02.138
what he requested | should be in them to give. 2.02.158
are you all resolv'd to give your voices? 2.03. 36 P
you must think, if we give you any thing, we 2.03. 71 P
and 'twere to give again — but 'tis no matter. 2.03. 83 P
man, and give it bountiful to the desirers. 2.03.102 P
and therefore give you our voices heartily. 2.03.105 P
the gods give you joy, sir, heartily! 2.03.111 P
the gods give him joy, and make him good friend 2.03.135 P
tribunes, give way, he shall to th' market–place 3.01. 31
to give forth | the corn a' th' store–house 3.01.113
why shall the people give | one that speaks thus 3.01.118
i'll give my reasons, | more worthier than their 3.01.119
and give way the while | to unstable slightness. 3.01.147
give me leave, | i'll go to him, and undertake 3.01.321
i | with my base tongue give to my noble heart 3.02.100
nor check my courage for what they can give, 3.03. 92
give him deserv'd vexation. 3.03.140
give me thy hand. | come. 4.01. 57
if he give me way, | i'll do his country service 4.04. 25
the morning, are unapt | to give or to forgive; 5.01. 53
each in either side | give the all–hail to thee, 5.03.139
yet give us our dispatch. 5.03.180
home, | they'll give him death by inches. 5.04. 39
we have all | great cause to give great thanks. 5.04. 60
and give away | the benefit of our levies, 5.06. 65
my grave lords, | must give this cur the lie; 5.06.106
give us the proudest prisoner of the goths, TIT 1.01. 96
i give him you, the noblest that survives, | the 1.01.102
give me a staff of honor for mine age, | but not 1.01.198
i give thee thanks in part of thy deserts, | and 1.01.236
ways, go give that changing piece | to him that 1.01.309
but let us give him burial as becomes, | give 1.01.347
give mutius burial with our bretheren. 1.01.348
god give you joy, sir, of your gallant bride! 1.01.400
only thus much i give your grace to know: 1.01.413
horn and hound we'll give your grace bon jour. 1.01.494
and give the king this fatal–plotted scroll. 2.03. 47
give me the poniard; 2.03.120
give me a sword, i'll chop off my hands too, 3.01. 72
lend me thy hand, and i will give thee mine. 3.01.187
good aaron, give his majesty my hand. 3.01.193
then give me leave, for losers will have leave 3.01.232
give signs, sweet girl, for here are none but 4.01. 61

well, god give her good rest! 4.02. 63
nurse, give it me, my sword shall soon dispatch 4.02. 86
go pack with him, and give the mother gold, 4.02.155
give it pallas. 4.03. 65
but give them to his master for a present. 4.03. 76
why, there it goes, god give his lordship joy! 4.03. 77
ado, | but give your pigeons to the emperor. 4.03.103
give me pen and ink. 4.03.106 P
god and saint steven give you god–den. 4.04. 42 P
let the emperor give his pledges | unto my 5.01.163
now give some surance that thou art revenge — 5.02. 46
but, gentle people, give me aim a while, | for 5.03.149
o now, sweet boy, give them their latest kiss! 5.03.169
give sentence on this execrable wretch | that 5.03.177
and give him burial in his fathers' grave. 5.03.192
what noise is this? give me my long sword ho! ROM 1.01. 75
grow, | we would as willingly give cure as know. 1.01.155
nurse, give leave a while, | we must talk in 1.03. 7
give me a torch, i am not for this ambling; 1.04. 11
give me a case to put my visage in, | a visor 1.04. 29
give room! 1.05. 26
give me my sin again. 1.05.110
and yet i would it were to give again. 2.02.129
but to be frank and give it thee again, | and 2.02.131
the more i give to thee, | the more i have, for 2.02.134
but to the earth some special good doth give; 2.03. 18
what counterfeit did i give you? 2.04. 47 P
i am a–weary, give me leave a while. 2.05. 25
to that, sir, and you will give me occasion. 3.01. 42 P
beg for justice, which thou, prince, must give: 3.01.180
give me my romeo, and, when i shall die, | take 3.02. 21
give me some aqua–vitae; 3.02. 88
give this ring to my true knight, | and bid him 3.02.142
i'll give thee armor to keep off that word: 3.03. 54
here, sir, a ring she bid me give you, sir. 3.03.163
give me thy hand. 3.03.172
shall give him such an unaccustom'd dram | that 3.05. 90
doth she not give us thanks? 3.05.142
and you be mine, i'll give you to my friend; 3.05.191
that she do give her sorrow so much sway; 4.01. 10
if in thy wisdom thou canst give no help, | do 4.01. 52
give me some present counsel, or, behold, 4.01. 61
and if thou darest, i'll give thee remedy. 4.01. 76
home, be merry, give consent | to marry paris. 4.01. 89
give me, give me! o, tell not me of fear! 4.01.121
give me, give me! o, tell not me of fear! 4.01.121
love give me strength! 4.01.125
and doth it give me such a sight as this? 4.05. 42
i will then give it you soundly. 4.05.112 P
what will you give us? 4.05.113 P
i will give you the minstrel. 4.05.115 P
then will i give you the serving–creature. 4.05.116 P
or, if his mind be writ, give me his letter. 5.02. 4
give me thy torch, boy. 5.03. 1
give me those flowers. 5.03. 9
give me that mattock and the wrenching iron. 5.03. 22
give me the light. 5.03. 25
o, give me thy hand, | one writ with me in sour 5.03. 81
this letter he early bid me give his father, 5.03.275
give me the letter, i will look on it. 5.03.278
o brother montague, give me thy hand. 5.03.296
but i can give thee more, | for i will /raise 5.03.298
give him thy daughter; TIM 1.01.144
figures are | even such as they give out. 1.01.160
give me your hand. 1.01.163
'tis rated | as those which sell would give; 1.01.169
pray entertain them, give them guide to us. 1.01.243
one to thyself, for i mean to give thee none. 1.01.266 P
i come to observe, i give thee warning on't. 1.02. 34
feasts are too proud to give thanks to the gods. 1.02. 61
he commands us to provide, and give great gifts, 1.02.192
so kind to heart, 'tis not enough to give; 1.02.219
thou wilt give away thyself in paper shortly. 1.02.241 P
once, i am sworn not to give regard to you. 1.02.245 P
steal but a beggar's dog | and give it timon, 2.01. 6
better than he, why, give my horse to timon, 2.01. 8
ask nothing, give it him, it foals me straight 2.01. 9
give me breath. 2.02. 33
were it all yours to give it in a breath, | how 2.02.153
a towardly prompt spirit — give thee thy due — 3.01. 35 P
like physicians, | thrive, give him over; 3.03. 12
but reserve still to give, lest your deities be 3.06. 72 P
and give them title, knee, and approbation 4.03. 37
as the moon does, by wanting light to give: 4.03. 68
give them diseases, leaving with thee their lust 4.03. 85
give us some gold, good timon; hast thou more? 4.03.133
up in thee, | i'ld give thee leave to hang it. 4.03.280
give it the beasts, to be rid of the men. 4.03.323 P
i will fear to catch it, and give way. 4.03.353 P
steal less for this i give you, | and gold 4.03.448
believe him as an enemy, and give over my trade. 4.03.454 P
whose eyes do never give | but thorough lust and 4.03.484
give to dogs | what thou deniest to men. 4.03.529
look you, i love you well, i'll give you gold, 5.01.100
and come to me, | i'll give you gold enough. 5.01.104
fear, | we sent to thee to give thy rages balm, 5.04. 16
which give some soil, perhaps, to my behaviors; JC 1.02. 42
alas, it cried, "give me some drink, titinius," 1.02.127
of the stars | give guess how near to day. 2.01. 3
give so much light that i may read by them. 2.01. 45
give me your hands all over, one by one. 2.01.112
for i can give his humor the true bent, | and i 2.01.210
to give this day a crown to mighty caesar. 2.02. 94
give me my robe, for i will go. 2.02.107
along, | and as a suitor will i give him this. 2.03. 12
sirrah, give place. 3.01. 10
this hope, that you shall give me reasons | why, 3.01.221
then follow me, and give me audience, friends. 3.02. 2
give him a statue with his ancestors. 3.02. 50
and will you give me leave? 3.02.160
and in this mood will give us any thing. 3.02.267
give the word ho! and stand. 4.02. 2
your griefs, | and i will give you audience. 4.02. 47
must i give way and room to your rash choler? 4.03. 39
i, that denied thee gold, will give my heart: 4.03.104
do you confess so much? give me your hand. 4.03.117
no use, | if you give place to accidental evils. 4.03.146
give me a bowl of wine. 4.03.158
good reasons must of force give place to better: 4.03.203
give me the gown. 4.03.239
i was sure your lordship did not give it me. 4.03.254
mark antony, shall we give sign of battle? 5.01. 23
your bad strokes, brutus, you give good words; 5.01. 30
give me thy hand, messala. 5.01. 72
our army lies, ready to give up the ghost. 5.01. 88
for the death | which he did give himself — i 5.01.102
and give these bills | unto the legions on the 5.02. 1
wreath of victory, | and bid me give it thee? 5.03. 83
thy brutus bid me give it thee, and i | will do 5.03. 86
keep this man safe, | give him all kindness; 5.04. 28
give me your hand first. fare you well, my lord. 5.05. 49
"give me!" MAC 1.03. 5
i'll give thee a wind. 1.03. 11
to give thee from our royal master thanks, 1.03.101
give me your favor; 1.03.149
give him tending, | he brings great news. 1.05. 37
come | give solely sovereign sway and masterdom. 1.05. 70
give me your hand. 1.06. 28
give me my sword. 2.01. 9
give me the daggers. 2.02. 50
give us a light there, ho! 3.03. 9
my royal lord, | you do not give the cheer. 3.04. 32
give me some wine, fill full. 3.04. 87
for mine own good | all causes shall give way. 3.04.135
we may again | give to our tables meat, sleep to 3.06. 34
i'll charm the air to give a sound, | while you 4.01.129
fife, give to th' edge o' th' sword | his wife, 4.01.151
give sorrow words. 4.03.209
come, come, come, come, give me your hand. 5.01. 67 P
we on | to give obedience where 'tis truly ow'd. 5.02. 26
give me my armor. 5.03. 33
give me mine armor. 5.03. 36
give me my staff. 5.03. 48
all our trumpets speak, give them all breath, 5.06. 9
bloodier villain | than terms can give thee out! 5.08. 8
give you good night. HAM 1.01. 16
barnardo hath my place. | give you good night. 1.01. 18
i do beseech you give him leave to go. 1.02. 61
to give these mourning duties to your father. 1.02. 88
give it an understanding, but no tongue. 1.02.249
as the winds give benefit | and convey /is 1.03. 2
act and place | may give his saying deed, which 1.03. 27
give thy thoughts no tongue, | nor any 1.03. 59
give every man thy ear, but few thy voice, 1.03. 68
give me up the truth. 1.03. 98
as to give words or talk with the lord hamlet. 1.03.134
and soldiers, | give me one poor request. 1.05.142
and therefore as a stranger give it welcome. 1.05.165
give him this money and these notes, reynaldo. 2.01. 1
and here give up ourselves, in the full bent, 2.02. 30
give first admittance to th' embassadors; 2.02. 51
to give th' assay of arms against your majesty. 2.02. 71
that it might please you to give quiet pass 2.02. 77
o, give me leave, | how does my good lord hamlet 2.02.170
at him while my father liv'd, give twenty, forty 2.02.365 P
come give us a taste of your quality, come, a 2.02.431 P
good gentlemen, give him a further edge, | and 3.01. 26
a lash that speech doth give my conscience! 3.01. 49
off this mortal coil, | must give us pause. 3.01. 67
to put them in, imagination to give them shape, 3.01.126 P
marry, i'll give thee this plague for thy dowry: 3.01.134 P
beget a temperance that may give it smoothness. 3.02. 8 P
give me that man | that is not passion's slave, 3.02. 71
give him heedful note, | for i mine eyes will 3.02. 84
nor earth to me give food, nor heaven light, 3.02.216
give o'er the play. 3.02.268 P
give me some light. away! 3.02.269 P
and /thumbs, give it breath with your mouth, and 3.02.358 P
to give them seals never my soul consent! 3.02.399
forehead of our faults, | to give in evidence. 3.03. 64
his seal | to give the world assurance of a man. 3.04. 62
as my great power thereof may give thee sense, 4.03. 59
follow her close, give her good watch, i pray 4.05. 74
i pray you give me leave. 4.05.114
o thou vile king, | give me my father! 4.05.117
that both the worlds i give to negligence, | let 4.05.135
i would give you some violets, but they wither'd 4.05.184 P
they find us touch'd, we will our kingdom give, 4.05.208
labor with your soul | to give it due content. 4.05.213
this, give these fellows some means to the king, 4.06. 14 P
that liberal shepherds give a grosser name, 4.07.170
now fear i this will give it start again, 4.07.193
give me leave. 5.01. 15 P
give me your pardon, sir. 5.02.226
give us the foils. 5.02.254
give them the foils, young osric. 5.02.259
if hamlet give the first or second hit, | or 5.02.268
give me the cups, | and let the kettle to the 5.02.274
stay, give me drink. 5.02.282
give him the cup. 5.02.283
as th' art a man, | give me the cup. 5.02.343
ears are senseless that should give us hearing, 5.02.369
give order that these bodies | high on a stage 5.02.377
give me the map there. LR 1.01. 37
as here i give | her father's heart from her. 1.01.125
give but that portion which yourself propos'd, 1.01.242
give me the letter, sir. 1.02. 40 P
i shall offend either to detain or give it: 1.02. 41 P
nuncle, give me an egg, and i'll give thee two 1.04.155 P
give me an egg, and i'll give thee two crowns. 1.04.156 P
head in, not to give it away to his daughters, 1.05. 30 P
my lord, if you/'ll give me leave, i will tread 2.02. 65 P
give you good morrow! 2.02.158
seeking to give | losses their remedies." 2.02.169
gives thee better counsel, give me mine again, i 2.04. 75 P
give me my servant forth. 2.04.115
thy tender–hefted nature shall not give | thee 2.04.171
give ear, sir, to my sister, | for those that 2.04.233
to no more | will i give place or notice. 2.04.249
you heavens, give me that patience, patience i 2.04.271
'tis best to give him way, he leads himself. 2.04.298
give me your hand. have you no more to say? 3.01. 51
this tempest will not give me leave to ponder 3.04. 24
give me thy hand. who's there? 3.04. 41 P
didst thou give all to thy daughters? 3.04. 49 P
wouldst thou give 'em all? 3.04. 64
to some provision | give thee quick conduct. 3.06. 97
to live till he be old, | give me some help! 3.07. 70
give me thy sword. a peasant stand up thus? 3.07. 80
give me your arm. 3.07. 98
give me thy arm; | poor tom shall lead thee. 4.01. 78
and give the distaff | into my husband's hands. 4.02. 17
if you do find him, pray you give him this; 4.05. 33
give me your hand. 4.06. 25
give me your arm. 4.06. 64
give the word. 4.06. 92 P
give me an ounce of civet; 4.06.130
give me your hand, | i'll lead you to some 4.06.223
and give the letters which thou find'st about me 4.06.248
give me your hand; 4.06.284
away, old man, give me thy hand, away! 5.02. 5
give me thy hand; 5.02. 7
this sword of mine shall give them instant way 5.03.150
/the /captain — | give it the captain. 5.03.252
give me a taper! OTH 1.01.141
might to enforce it on) | will give him cable. 1.02. 17
i here do give thee that with all my heart 1.03.193
heavens | give him defense against the elements, 2.01. 45
and give us truth who 'tis that is arriv'd. 2.01. 58
give renew'd fire to our extincted spirits, 2.01. 81
they give /their greeting to the citadel. 2.01. 94
would she give you so much of her lips | as of 2.01.100
/again to inflame it and to give satiety a fresh 2.01.228 P
fit to stand by caesar | and give direction; 2.03.123
give me answer to it. 2.03.196
give me to know | how this foul rout began; 2.03.209
the devil drunkenness to give place to the devil 2.03.296 P
when this advice is free i give, and honest, 2.03.337
give me advantage of some brief discourse | with 3.01. 52
these letters give, iago, to the pilot, | and by 3.02. 1
emilia here, | i give thee warrant of thy place. 3.03. 20
shall rather die | than give thy cause away. 3.03. 28
and give thy worst of thoughts | the worst of 3.03.132
she that so young could give out such a seeming 3.03.209
what will you give me now | for that same 3.03.305
a good wench, give it me. 3.03.313
give me the ocular proof, | or, by the worth of 3.03.360
the door of truth | will give you satisfaction, 3.03.408
give me a living reason she's disloyal. 3.03.409
witness that here iago doth give up | the 3.03.465
give me your hand. this hand is moist, my lady. 3.04. 36
did an egyptian to my mother give; 3.04. 56
my fate would have me wiv'd, | to give it her. 3.04. 65
but if i give my wife a handkerchief — 4.01. 10
may she give that? 4.01. 15
the worser that you give me the addition | whose 4.01.104
there, give it your hobby–horse. 4.01.154 P
over her iniquity, give her patent to offend, 4.01.197 P
i will give over my suit and repent my unlawful 4.02.198 P
give me thy hand, roderigo. 4.02.206 P
emilia, | give me my nightly wearing, and adieu. 4.03. 16
give me some help. 5.01. 55
come in, and give some help. 5.01. 59
thy rose, | i cannot give it vital growth again, 5.02. 14
i found by fortune, and did give my husband; 5.02.226
she give it cassio? 5.02.230
good sir, give me good fortune. ANT 1.02. 14 P
but how, but how? give me particulars. 1.02. 56 P
and let her die too, and give him a worse! 1.02. 65 P
why, sir, give the gods a thankful sacrifice. 1.02.161 P
in each thing give him way, cross him in nothing 1.03. 9
i am sorry to give breathing to my purpose — 1.03. 14
though age from folly could not give me freedom, 1.03. 57
are, or cease, | as you shall give th' advice. 1.03. 68
and give true evidence to his love, which stands 1.03. 74
to give a kingdom for a mirth, to sit | and keep 1.04. 18
and men's reports | give him much wrong'd. 1.04. 40
ha, ha! | give me to drink mandragora. 1.05. 4
by isis, i will give thee bloody teeth, | if 1.05. 70
how lesser enmities may give way to greater. 2.01. 43
but small to greater matters must give way. 2.02. 11
give me leave, caesar — 2.02.116
give me some music; 2.05. 1
give me mine angle, we'll to th' river; 2.05. 10
the gold i give thee will i melt and pour | down 2.05. 34
say 'tis not so, a province i will give thee, 2.05. 68
give to a gracious message | an host of tongues, 2.05. 86
but give me your hand, menas; 2.06. 94 P
i am the man | will give thee all the world. 2.07. 65
and shall, sir, give 's your hand. 2.07.127
thus i let you go, | and give you to the gods. 3.02. 64
let all the number of the stars give light | to 3.02. 65
give up yourself merely to chance and hazard, 3.07. 47
give me a kiss. 3.11. 70
for he partly begs | to be desir'd to give. 3.13. 67
give me grace to lay | my duty on your hand. 3.13. 81
give him no breath, but now | make boot of his 4.01. 8
give me thy hand, | thou hast been rightly 4.02. 10
mean you, sir, | to give them this discomfort? 4.02. 34
let's see how it will give off. 4.03. 22
come give me that: 4.04. 28
i give it you. 4.06. 23
give me thy hand; 4.08. 11
i'll give thee, friend, | an armor all of gold; 4.08. 26
give me thy hand. 4.08. 29
his fretted fortunes give him hope and fear | of 4.12. 8
vanish, or i shall give thee thy deserving, 4.12. 32
and give me | sufficing strokes for death. 4.14.116
give me some wine, and let me speak a little. 4.15. 42
but you gods will give us | some faults to make 5.01. 32
give her what comforts | the quality of her 5.01. 62
please | to give me conquer'd egypt for my son, 5.02. 19
dispose you as | yourself shall give us counsel. 5.02.187
i'll give thee leave | to play till doomsday. 5.02.231
give it nothing, i pray you, for it is not worth 5.02.269 P
give me my robe, put on my crown, i have 5.02.280
which the gods give men | to excuse their after 5.02.286
my other elements | i give to baser life. 5.02.290
lest i give cause | to be suspected of more CYM 1.01. 93
you gentle gods, give me but this i have, | and 1.01.115
fie, you must give way. 1.01.158
give him that parting kiss which i had set 1.03. 34
your voyage upon her and give me directly to 1.04.158 P
i was going, sir, | to give him welcome. 1.06. 55

give me your pardon. 1.06.162
every companion that you give offense to. 2.01. 27 P
i am advis'd to give her music a' mornings; 2.03. 12 P
but i'll never give o'er. 2.03. 16 P
the thanks i give | is telling you that i am 2.03. 88
you'll give me leave to spare when you shall 2.04. 65
her own command | shall give thee opportunity." 3.02. 19
i shall give thee opportunity at milford–haven. 3.04. 28 P
i'll give but notice you are dead, and send him 3.04.124
we'll even | all that good time will give us. 3.04.182
give me thy hand, here's my purse. 3.05.123 P
and such a welcome as i'ld give to him | (after 3.06. 72
occasion | hath cadwal now to give it motion? 4.02.188
give color to my pale cheek with thy blood, 4.02.330
if you will bless me, sir, and give me leave, 4.04. 44
peace, | i'll give no wound to thee. 5.01. 21
or we are romans and will give you that | like 5.03. 26
give me | the penitent instrument to pick that 5.04. 9
fitting my bounty and thy state, i'll give it; 5.05. 98
in private, if you please | to give me hearing. 5.05.116
give answer to this boy, and do it freely, | or, 5.05.131
spirits | quail to remember — give me leave, i 5.05.149
o, give me cord, or knife, or poison, | some 5.05.213
to the judgment of your eye | i give my cause, PER 1.ch. 42
then give my tongue like leave to love my head. 1.01.108
peace, peace, and give experience tongue. 1.02. 37
he would depart, i'll give some light unto you. 1.03. 17
have scarce strength left to give them burial. 1.04. 49
and give them life whom hunger starv'd half dead 1.04. 96
in conversation, | to whom i give my benison, 2.ch. 10
doing bad, | threw him ashore, to give him glad. 2.ch. 38
to give my tongue that heat to ask your help; 2.01. 75
d' ye take it, and the gods give thee good an't! 2.01.146 P
guest, | to whom this wreath of victory i give, 2.03. 10
who freely give to every one that come | to 2.03. 60
scorn now their hand should give them burial. 2.04. 12
or, dead, give 's cause to mourn his funeral, 2.04. 32
and for further grief — god give you joy! 2.05. 87
we here below | recall not what we give, and 3.01. 25
i time | to give thee hallow'd to thy grave, but 3.01. 59
give this to the pothecary, | and tell me how it 3.02. 9
which doth give me | a more content in course of 3.02. 38
"here i give to understand, | if e'er this 3.02. 68
who finds her, give her burying, | she was the 3.02. 72
i pray you give her air. 3.02. 91
beseeching you | to give her princely training, 3.03. 16
then give you up to the mask'd neptune and | the 3.03. 36
come | give me your flowers, ere the sea mar it. 4.01. 26
a proportion to live quietly, and so give over. 4.02. 27 P
why to give over, i pray you? 4.02. 28 P
"he that will give most shall have her first." 4.02. 59 P
spacious world, | i'd give it to undo the deed. 4.03. 6
peevish baggage would but give way to customers. 4.06. 19 P
i beseech your honor give me leave a word, and 4.06. 46 P
believe me, 'twere best i did give o'er. 5.01.166
yet give me leave: 5.01.168
give me a gash, put me to present pain, | lest 5.01.191
give me fresh garments. 5.01.214
give me my robes. 5.01.222
it is not good to cross him, give him way. 5.01.230
call | and give them repetition to the /life. 5.01.246
and give you gold for such provision | as our 5.01.257
this, my last boon, give me, | for such kindness 5.02. 3
give us the bones | of our dead kings, that we TNK 1.01. 49
and i will give you comfort | to give your dead 1.01.148
you comfort | to give your dead lords graves; 1.01.149
and i shall give you | to a most noble service 2.05. 33
give me language such | as thou hast show'd me 3.01. 44
quit me of these cold gyves, give me a sword, 3.01. 72
give me your hand, farewell. 3.01. 98
i could for each word give a cuff, my stomach 3.01.104
give me more wine. 3.03. 28
next gloves that i give her shall be dogskin; 3.05. 45
i would be sorry else. | give me your hand. 3.05. 78
give me some meditation, | and mark your cue. 3.05. 93
give us but a tree or twain | for a maypole, and 3.05.144
i'll give you cause, sweet cousin. 3.06. 69
give me thy noble hand. 3.06.101
i give consent. 3.06.279
i'll give ye | now usage like to princes and to 3.06.305
honor'd friend, | to you i give the field; 4.02.150
penn'worth on't to give half my state that both 4.03. 67 P
give me your aid | and bend your spirits towards 5.01. 47
give me, great mars, | some token of thy 5.01. 60
give me the victory of this question, which | is 5.01.127
game, i give thee thanks | for this fair token, 5.01.132
and we should give her physic till we find that 5.02. 29
and must needs be by | to give the service pay. 5.03. 32
give me your hands. 5.03.109
give them our present justice, since i know 5.03.132
sooner than such, to give us nectar with 'em, 5.04. 12
and give the tidings ear | that are most /dearly 5.04. 46
what disorder | his power could give his will, 5.04. 67
be yet unbroken, | give me thy last words; 5.04. 89
and while i live, | this day i give to tears. 5.04. 98
and give grace unto | the funeral of arcite, in 5.04.125
nature of your error | should give you harbor? STM II.C 127
give up yourself to form, obey the magistrate, II.C 146
my country's head | and give the law out there. III 8
place | to give the smooth and secter way to me III 11
so offers he to give what she did crave, | but VEN 88
give me one kiss, i'll give it thee again, | and 209
give me one kiss, i'll give it thee again, | and 209
"give me my hand," saith he, "why dost thou feel 373
"give me my heart," saith she, "and thou shalt 374
o, give it me, lest thy hard heart do steel it, 375
and give the sneaped birds more cause to sing. LUC 333
give physic to the sick, ease to the pained? 901
live | disdain to him disdained scraps to give. 987
i give | a badge of fame to slander's livery, 1053
her mistress she doth give demure good morrow, 1219
to give her so much grief, and not a tongue. 1463
and give the harmless show | an humble gait, 1507
and tell thy grief, that we may give redress. 1603
where no excuse can give the fault amending. 1614
that guides this hand to give this wound to me." 1722
and bids lucretius give his sorrow place, | and 1773
at last it rains, and busy winds give o'er: 1790
"i did give that life | which she too early and 1800
is it revenge to give thyself a blow | for his 1823
the romans plausibly did give consent | to 1854
the bounteous largess given thee to give? SON 4. 6
and your sweet semblance to some other give. 13. 4
to give away yourself keeps yourself still, 16.13
thou gav'st me thine not to give back again. 22.14
who all their parts of me to thee did give: 31.11
nor can thy shame give physic to my grief, 34. 9
that this shadow doth such substance give, 37.10
give thyself the thanks if aught in me | worthy 38. 5
when thou thyself dost give invention light? 38. 8
that by this separation i may give | that due to 39. 7
towards thee i'll run, and give him leave to go. 51.14
by that sweet ornament which truth doth give! 54. 2
(the voice of souls) give thee that /due, 69. 3
those same tongues that give thee so thine own, 69. 6
bell | give warning to the world that i am fled 71. 3
show, | of mouthed graves will give thee memory; 77. 6
and my sick muse doth give another place. 79. 4
beauty doth he give, | and found it in thy cheek 79.10
when others would give life and bring a tomb. 83.12
give not a windy night a rainy morrow, | to 90. 7
give my love fame faster than time wastes life, 100.13
then give me welcome, next my heaven the best, 110.13
to give full growth to that which still doth 115.14
eyes | give salutation to my sportive blood? 121. 6
therefore to give them from me was i bold, | to 122.11
give them /thy fingers, me thy lips to kiss. 128.14
to make me give the lie to my true sight, | and 150. 3

GIVE–A 1 FR 0.0001 REL FR 0 V 1 P
you jack'nape, give–a this letter to sir hugh. WIV 1.04.107 P

GIVEN *(also gi'n, giv'n)*
/GIVEN 5 FR 0.0005 REL FR 4 V 1 P
/cares /i /give /i /have, /though /given /away, R2 4.01.198
/for /i /have /given /here /my /soul's /consent 4.01.249
/not /that /name /was /given /me /at /the /font, 4.01.256
/authorities | /that /he /hath /given /away! LR 1.03. 18
/thy /other /titles /thou /hast /given /away, 1.04.149 P

GIVEN 194 FR 0.0219 REL FR 142 V 52 P
what a blow was there given! TMP 2.01.180 P
(like poison given to work a great time after) 3.03.105
have given you here a third of mine own life, 4.01. 3
the dread rattling thunder | have i given fire, 5.01. 45
my dukedom since you have given me again, | i 5.01.168
he would have given it you, but i, being in the TGV 1.02. 39
why, she hath given you a letter. 2.01.159 P
his worst fault is, that he is given to prayer; WIV 1.04. 13 P
she is given too much to allicholy and musing; 1.04.153 P
had myself twenty angels given me this morning, 2.02. 72 P
but have given largely to many to know what she 2.02.199 P
to many to know what she would have given; 2.02.200 P
the maid hath given consent to go with him. 4.06. 45
and have given ourselves without scruple to hell 5.05.148 P
and given to fornications, and to taverns, and 5.05.158 P
and given his deputation all the organs | of our MM 1.01. 20
if she had been a woman cardinally given, might 2.01. 80 P
if the devil have given thee proofs for sin, 3.02. 30
the deputy, sir, he has given him warning. 3.02. 34 P
what pleasure was he given to? 3.02.234 P
the better, given me by so holy a man. 4.03.113
me in my true complaint | and given me justice, 5.01. 25
scanted /men in hair he hath given them in wit. ERR 2.02. 81 P
and given way unto this course of fortune, | by ADO 4.01.157
it was given me by costard, and sent me from don LLL 4.02. 91 P
sitting on a close–stool, will be given to ajax; 5.02.577 P
false, we have given thee faces. 5.02.622 P
thou, lysander, thou hast given her rhymes, MND 1.01. 28
for thou, i fear, hast given me cause to curse. 3.02. 46
and the duke had not given him sixpence a day 4.02. 22 P
but there the duke was given to understand MV 2.08. 7
i would not have given it for a wilderness of 3.01.122 P
good sir, this ring was given me by my wife, 4.01.441
sweet lady, you have given me life and living, 5.01.286
i am given, sir, secretly to understand that AYL 1.01.123 P
though nature hath given us wit to flout at 1.02. 45 P
i should have given him tears unto entreaties, 1.02.238
methinks i have given him a penny and he renders 2.05. 28 P
most feigning, and lovers are given to poetry; 3.03. 20 P
truly, she must be given, or the marriage is not 3.03. 69 P
and would i had given him the best horse in SHR 1.01.142 P
but thanks be given, she's very well, and wants AWW 2.04. 4 P
given order for our horses, and to–night, | when 2.05. 25
madam, | if i had given you this at overnight, 3.04. 23
you have not given him his mother's letter? 4.03. 1 P
he hath given her his monumental ring, and 4.03. 17 P
it was not given me, nor i did not buy it. 5.03.272
sought is good, but given unsought is better. TN 3.01.156
might well have given us bloody argument. 3.03. 32
may i give him that | which i have given to you? 3.04.215
my head across and has given sir toby a bloody 5.01.175 P
and given your drunken cousin rule over me, yet 5.01.304 P
why you have given me such clear lights of favor 5.01.336
a great deal too dear for what's given freely. WT 1.01. 18 P
given to the fire, a moi'ty of my rest | might 2.03. 8
and i think they are given | to men of middle 4.04.107
up in my heart, which i have given already, 4.04.359
your worship had like to have given us one, if 4.04.727 P
have given him time | to land his legions all as JN 2.01. 58
as they have given these hairs their liberty!" 3.04. 72
and given away | to upstart unthrifts? R2 2.03.121
the rascal have not given me medicines to make 1H4 2.02. 18 P
and given my treasures and my rights of thee 2.03. 45
if that man should be lewdly given, he deceiveth 2.04.427 P
i was as virtuously given as a gentleman need to 3.03. 14 P
if thou wert any way given to virtue, i would 3.03. 33 P
but thou art altogether given over, and wert 3.03. 36 P
i have given them away to bakers' wives, they 3.03. 69 P
shrewsbury, | as i am truly given to understand, 4.04. 11
lord, lord, how this world is given to lying! 5.04.146 P
i have given over, i will speak no more; 2H4 2.03. 5
devout | by testament have given to the church, H5 1.01. 10
to whom the order of the siege is given, is 3.02. 66 P
have the pioners given o'er? 3.02. 87 P
but exeter hath given the doom of death | for 3.06. 44
the glove which i have given him for a favor 4.07.172
and thou hast given me most bitter terms. 4.08. 42
to celebrate the joy that god hath given us. 1H6 1.06. 14
which thou thyself hast given her woeful breast. 3.03. 51
i have a while given truce unto my wars, | to do 3.04. 3
before we met, or that a stroke was given, 4.01. 22
for thou hast given me in this beauteous face 2H6 1.01. 21
hath given the duchy of anjou, and maine, | unto 1.01.110
anjou and maine are given to the french, | paris 1.01.214
anjou and maine both given unto the french! 1.01.236
so am i given in charge, may't please your grace 2.04. 80
and too well given | to dream on evil or to work 3.01. 72
and given me notice of their villainies. 3.01.370
hath given them heart and courage to proceed. 4.04. 35
ye would never have given out these arms till 4.08. 26 P
that i have given no answer all this while; 5.01. 33
thus war hath given thee peace, for thou art 5.02. 29
mine | or fortune given me measure of revenge. 3H6 2.03. 32
hadst thou never given consent | that phaeton 2.06. 11
his majesty hath straitly given in charge | that R3 1.01. 85
promotions | are daily given to ennoble those 1.03. 80
what lawful quest have given their verdict up 1.04.184
i could have given my uncle's grace a flout, 2.04. 24
and given in earnest what i begg'd in jest. 5.01. 22
i cannot tell | what heaven hath given him — H8 1.01. 67
or has given all before, and he begins | a new 1.01. 71
the other moi'ty ere you ask is given; 1.02. 12
your grace has given a president of wisdom 2.02. 85
hath my behavior given to your displeasure, 2.04. 20
there's order given for her coronation. 3.02. 46
that gentle physic given in time had cur'd me; 4.02.122
heaven had pleas'd to have given me longer life 4.02.152
who hath so far | given ear to our complaint, of 5.01. 48
look'd | you would have given me your petition, 5.01.118
lay'st in every gash that love hath given me TRO 1.01. 62
such rich beholding | as they have often given. 3.03. 92
she hath not given so many good words breath 4.01. 74
of her o'er–eaten faith, are given to diomed. 5.02.160
and given to lartius and to martius battle. COR 1.06. 11
when corn was given them gratis, you repin'd, 3.01. 43
but that | which they have given to beggars. 3.01. 74
thus | given hydra here to choose an officer, 3.01. 93
as now at last | given hostile strokes, and that 3.03. 97
and he had been cannibally given, he might have 4.05.188 P
popular ignorance, given your enemy your shield, 5.02. 41 P
of your throats | i'd not have given a doit. 5.04. 57
he has betray'd your business, and given up, 5.06. 91
here goths have given me leave to sheathe my TIT 1.01. 85
pray to the devils, the gods have given us over. 4.02. 48
hark ye, lords, you see i have given her physic, 4.02.162
and when thou hast given it the emperor, | knock 4.03.118
legs be worth the sums | that are given for 'em. TIM 1.02.233
unwisely, not ignobly, have i given. 2.02.174
i have given you earnest. 4.03.168
what hast thou given? 4.03.270
he is a noble roman, and well given. JC 1.02.197
much he should, for he is given | to sports, to 2.01.188
he loves me well, and i have given him reasons; 2.01.219
hath given me some worthy cause to wish | things 4.02. 8
ill, | why hath it given me earnest of success, MAC 1.03.132
i have given suck, and know | how tender 'tis to 1.07. 54
what hath quench'd them hath given me fire. 2.02. 2
jewel | given to the common enemy of man, | to 3.01. 68
while 'tis a–making, | 'tis given with welcome. 3.04. 34
such sanctity hath heaven given his hand, | they 4.03.144
for where there is advantage to be given, | both 5.04. 11
both more and less have given him the revolt, 5.04. 12
very oft of late | given private time to you, HAM 1.03. 92
and hath given countenance to his speech, my 1.03.113
teder may he walk | than may be given you. 1.03.126
'tis given out that, sleeping in my orchard, | a 1.05. 35
what, have you given him any hard words of late? 2.01.104
duty and obedience, mark, | hath given me this. 2.02.108
by means, and place, | all given to mine ear. 2.02.128
or given my heart a /winking, mute and dumb, 2.02.137
god hath given you one face, and you make 3.01.143 P
they were given me by claudio. 4.07. 40
and given him notice that the duke of cornwall LR 2.01. 3 P
intelligence is given where you are hid; 2.01. 21
of his wits have given way to his impatience. 3.06. 4 P
your daughter (if you have not given her leave), OTH 1.01.133
'fore /god, they have given me a rouse already. 2.03. 64 P
that he hath devoted and given up himself to the 2.03.316 P
given to captivity me and my utmost hopes, |.i 4.02. 51
and yet he hath given me satisfying reasons. 5.01. 9
pompeius | /hath given the dare to caesar, and ANT 1.02.184
would she had never given you leave to come! 1.03. 21
i could have given less matter | a better ear. 2.01. 31
since i myself | have given myself the cause. 2.05. 84
when the best hint was given him, he not /took't 3.04. 9
he hath given his empire | up to a whore, who 3.06. 66
o, /he has given example for our flight, | most 3.10. 27
shall stay with us — order for sea is given, 4.10. 6
very honest woman — but something given to lie, 5.02.252 P
the one may be sold or given, or if there were CYM 1.04. 83 P
which the gods have given you? 1.04. 86 P
i have given him that | which, if he take, shall 1.05. 78
hath nature given them eyes | to see this 1.06. 32
son, | when you have given good morning to your 2.03. 61
(and praise | be given to your remembrance), the 2.04. 93
but it honors us | that we have given him cause. 3.05. 19
that will be given to th' loud of noise we make. 3.05. 44
to–day how many would have given their honors 5.03. 66
"given his mistress that confection | which i 5.05.246
two on 's are as good | as i have given out him. 5.05.312
my lord, since you have given me leave to speak, PER 1.02.101
sir, | we have given order be next our own. 2.03.110
which are paid as debts, | and not as given. 4.ch. 35
name | was given me by one that had some power, 5.01.148
been taken | when their last hurts were given, TNK 1.04. 26
i am given out to be better lin'd than it can 2.01. 5 P
has given a sum of money to her marriage, | a 4.01. 23
divine arbitrement | have given you this knight: 5.03.108
grac'd her altar, | and given you your love. 5.04.106
throne and sword, but given him his own name, STM II.C 103
the bounteous largess given thee to give? SON 4. 6
to subjects worse have given admiring praise. 59.14
wing, | and given grace a double majesty. 78. 8
and given to time your own dear–purchas'd right; 117. 6

GIVEN'T 2 FR 0.0002 REL FR 1 V 1 P
i should have given't you to–day morning. TN 5.01.286 P

it in rage, though calm'd have given't again. PER 2.01.132
/GIVER 1 FR 0.0001 REL FR 1 V 0 P
retort that heat again | to the first /giver. TRO 3.03.102
GIVER 3 FR 0.0003 REL FR 2 V 1 P
'tis indeed, madam, we thank the giver. TGV 2.04. 35 P
to him | but breeds the giver a return exceeding TIM 1.01.279
sir, y' are a noble giver. TNK 2.05. 38
GIVERS 1 FR 0.0001 REL FR 1 V 0 P
rich gifts wax poor when givers prove unkind. HAM 3.01.100
/GIVES 2 FR 0.0002 REL FR 2 V 0 P
/fruit | /hope /gives /not /so /much /warrant, 2H4 1.03. 40
sir, but she will none, she /gives you thanks. ROM 3.05.139
GIVES 141 FR 0.0159 REL FR 102 V 39 P
should give her interest, and she gives it him. TGV 2.01.103 P
she carves, she gives the leer of invitation. WIV 1.03. 45 P
and she gives you to notify that her husband 2.02. 83 P
no, he gives me the potions and the motions. 3.01.102 P
no, he gives me the proverbs and the no–verbs. 3.01.104 P
he gives her folly motion and advantage; 3.02. 35 P
the clock gives me my cue, and my assurance bids 3.02. 45 P
gives intelligence of ford's approach; 3.05. 84 P
you must be the first that gives this sentence, MM 2.02.106
the image of it gives me content already, and i 3.01.259 P
and his confessor, | gives me this instance. 4.03.129
i'll utter what my sorrow gives me leave. ERR 1.01. 35
are tir'd, gives them a sob and 'rests them; 4.03. 25 P
on decay'd men and gives them suits of durance; 4.03. 27 P
the world into her person, and so gives me out. ADO 2.01.209 P
and never gives to truth and virtue that | which 3.01. 69
gifts that god gives. 3.05. 43 P
her wrongs, | gives her fame which never dies. 5.03. 6
most rude melancholy, valor gives thee place. LLL 3.01. 68
"so sweet a kiss the golden sun gives not | to 4.03. 25
and gives the crutch the cradle's infancy. 4.03.241
and gives to every power a double power, | above 4.03.328
days) | in courtesy gives undeserving praise. 5.02.366
i give him curses; yet he gives me love. MND 1.01.196
turns them to shapes and gives to aery nothing 5.01. 16
the fiend gives the more friendly counsel: MV 2.02. 30 P
bassanio, who indeed gives rare new liveries. 2.02.109 P
it blesseth him that gives and him that takes. 4.01.187
this nothing that he so plentifully gives me, AYL 1.01. 17 P
therefore he gives them good leave to wander. 1.01.103 P
that gives not half so great a blow to hear | as SHR 1.02.208
the fated sky | gives us free scope, only doth AWW 1.01.218
spares my team and gives me leave to inn the 1.03. 44 P
of your birth and virtue gives you heraldry. 2.03.262 P
and common speech | gives him a worthy pass. 2.05. 53
it gives a very echo to the seat | where love is TN 2.04. 21
gives manhood more approbation than ever proof 3.04.180 P
the young gentleman gives him out to be of good 3.04.185 P
and he gives me the stuck in with such a mortal 3.04.275 P
one that gives out himself prince florizel, WT 5.01. 85
he gives the bastinado with his tongue; JN 2.01.463
gives but the greater feeling to the worse. R2 1.03.301
gives in your weakness strength unto your foe, 3.02.181
yet blessing on his heart that gives it me! 5.05. 64
gives o'er, and leaves his part–created cost | a 2H4 1.03. 60
which as a beacon gives warning to all the rest 4.03.108 P
she either gives a stomach and no food — | such 4.04.105
him whose wrongs gives edge unto the swords H5 1.02. 27
he gives you, upon his knees, a thousand thanks, 4.04. 59 P
whose want gives growth to th' imperfections 5.02. 69
that, in regard king henry gives consent, | of 1H6 5.04.124
wives, | and our king henry gives away his own, 2H6 1.01.130
dame eleanor gives gold to bring the witch; 1.02. 91
to believing souls | gives light in darkness, 2.01. 65
what instance gives lord warwick for his vow? 3.02.159
gives not the hawthorn bush a sweeter shade | to 3H6 2.05. 42
to mitigate the scorn he gives his uncle, | he R3 3.01.133
which after–hours gives leisure to repent. 4.04.293
car | gives token of a goodly day to–morrow. 5.03. 21
/'a gives us note | the force of his own merit H8 1.01. 63
a gift that heaven gives for him, which buys | a 1.01. 65
(though now the time | gives way to us) i much 3.02. 16
gives us more palm in beauty than we have, | yea TRO 3.01.157
for what he has he gives, what thinks he shows, 4.05.101
yet gives he not till judgment guide his bounty, 4.05.102
but gives all gaze and bent of amorous view | on 4.05.282
glove, | and gives memorial dainty kisses to it, 5.02. 80
it gives me an estate of seven years' health, in COR 2.01.114 P
wherein he gives my son the whole name of the 2.01.135 P
head, that he gives entrance to such companions? 4.05. 12 P
but that which gives my soul the greatest spurn TIT 3.01.101
that gives sweet tidings of the sun's uprise? 3.01.159
the fatal engine in | that gives our troy, our 5.03. 87
than your consent gives strength to make /it fly ROM 1.03. 99
that one short minute gives me in her sight. 2.06. 5
dream, that gives a dead man leave to think! 5.01. 7
the boy gives warning, something doth approach. 5.03. 18
none | can truly say he gives if he receives. TIM 1.02. 11
meat be belov'd more than the man that gives it. 3.06. 76 P
one day he gives us diamonds, next day stones. 3.06.120
which gives men stomach to disgest his words JC 1.02.301
security gives way to conspiracy. 2.03. 7 P
to every roman citizen he gives, | to every 3.02.241
and sudden push gives them the overthrow. 5.02. 5
thoughts that nature | gives way to in repose! MAC 2.01. 9
to the heat of deeds too cold breath gives. 2.01. 61
bellman, | which gives the stern'st good–night. 2.02. 4
soldier none | that christendom gives out. 4.03.192
gives him threescore thousand crowns in annual HAM 2.02. 73
gives me the lie i' th' throat | as deep as to 2.02.574
a paradox, but now the time gives it proof. 3.01.114 P
when the compulsive ardure gives the charge, 3.04. 86
and good | he likewise gives a frock or livery, 3.04.164
in many places | gives me superfluous death. 4.05. 96
to th' embassadors of england gives | this 5.02.351
have that scope | as dotage gives it. LR 1.04.293
the country gives me proof and president | of 2.03. 13
when a wise man gives thee better counsel, give 2.04. 75 P
but knaves follow it, since a fool gives it. 2.04. 77 P
who gives any thing to poor tom? 3.04. 51 P
he gives the web and the pin, /squinies the eye, 3.04.117 P
censur'd, that nature thus gives way to loyalty, 3.05. 3 P
in /these news | that gives them credit. OTH 1.03. 2
that gives me this bold show of courtesy. 2.01. 99
it gives me wonder great as my content | to see 2.01.183
he gives your hollander a vomit ere the next 2.03. 84 P
she gives it out that you shall marry her. 4.01.115
with the health that pompey gives him, else he ANT 2.07. 51 P
and gives his potent regiment to a trull | that 3.06. 95
he gives me so much of mine own as i | will 5.02. 20
the king | of every virtue gives renown to men! PER 1.01. 14
that gives heaven countless eyes to view men's 1.01. 73
to which that /blast gives heat and stronger 1.02. 41
and gives them what he will, not what they crave 2.03. 47
no less than it gives a good report to a number 4.06. 40 P
and her gain | she gives the cursed bawd. 5.ch. 11
them hungry, | the more she gives them speech. 5.01.113
chaucer (of all admir'd) the story gives; TNK pr 13
which gives me such lamenting | as wakes my 1.01. 57
the other presently gives it so sweet a rebuke 2.01. 43 P
goddess of it grant, she gives | victory too. 5.01. 71
to them, gives | the prejudice of disparity, 5.03. 87
gives false alarms, suggesteth mutiny, | and in VEN 651
by their suggestion gives a deadly groan. 1044
so guiltless she securely gives good cheer | and LUC 89
which gives the watch–word to his hand full soon 370
gives the hot charge, and bids them do their 434
not themselves but he that gives them knows! 833
they buy thy help, but sin ne'er gives a fee, 913
and friend to friend gives unadvised wounds, 1488
at last she smilingly with this gives o'er; 1567
times with sighs she gives her sorrow fire, 1604
nature's bequest gives nothing, but doth lend, SON 4. 3
so long lives this, and this gives life to thee. 18.14
blessed are you, whose worthiness gives scope, 52.13
the charter of thy worth gives thee releasing; 87. 3
to speak of that which gives thee all thy might? 100. 2
and gives thy pen both skill and argument. 100. 8
of age, | nor gives to necessary wrinkles place, 108.11
for that deep wound it gives my friend and me! 133. 2
"nor gives it satisfaction to our blood | that LC 162
GIVEST 3 FR 0.0003 REL FR 3 V 0 P
and givest such sarcenet surety for thy oaths 1H4 3.01.251
i'll take the gold thou givest me, | not all thy TIM 4.03.130
thou givest me somewhat to repair myself; PER 2.01.122
GIVE/'T 1 FR 0.0001 REL FR 1 V 0 P
talk, | wanting a hand to give/'t that accord? TIT 5.02. 18
GIVE'T 13 FR 0.0014 REL FR 11 V 2 P
give't not o'er so. MM 2.02. 43
yes, he would give't thee, from this rank 3.01. 99
i'll give't him. TN 3.04.171 P
give't or take't. 3.04.240 P
come on then, | and give't me in mine ear. WT 2.01. 32
give't to thy crone. 2.03. 77
give't me again. TRO 5.02. 70
this hint | when we shall hap to give't them. COR 3.03. 24
give't these fellows | to whom 'tis instant due. TIM 2.02.229
i'll have the work ta'en out, | and give't iago. OTH 3.03.297
for some purpose of import, | give't me again. 3.03.317
to lose't or give't away were such perdition 3.04. 67
alas, i found it, | and i did give't my husband. 5.02.231
GIVETH 1 FR 0.0001 REL FR 1 V 0 P
which giveth many wounds when one will kill. 1H6 2.05.110
/GIVING 1 FR 0.0001 REL FR 1 V 0 P
/i /am /not /in /the /giving /vein //to–day. R3 4.02.116
GIVING 40 FR 0.0045 REL FR 27 V 13 P
giving a gentle kiss to every sedge | he TGV 2.07. 29
far from jealousy as i am from giving him cause, WIV 2.01.104 P
a giving hand, though foul, shall have fair LLL 4.01. 23
nor borrow | by taking nor by giving of excess, MV 1.03. 62
hold out enemy for ever | for giving it to me. 4.01.448
giving thy sum of more | to that which had too AYL 2.01. 48
whom i took two cods and, giving her them again, 2.04. 52 P
by giving love, your sorrow and my grief | were 3.05. 88
a bank of violets, | stealing and giving odor. TN 1.01. 7
hand, | by giving it the worship of revenge. JN 4.03. 72
from giving reins and spurs to my free speech, R2 1.01. 55
giving him breath, | the traitor lives, the true 5.03. 72
of purses than giving direction doth from 1H4 2.01. 51 P
and his quick wit wasted in giving reckonings; 2H4 1.02.171 P
giving full trophy, signal, and ostent | quite H5 5.pr. 21
giving my verdict on the white rose side. 1H6 2.04. 48
to my majesty for giving up of normandy unto 2H6 4.07. 28 P
consult about the giving up of some more towns 4.07.132 P
by giving the house of lancaster leave to 3H6 1.02. 13
did, | giving no ground unto the house of york, 2.06. 16
from giving aid which late i promised. 3.03.148
were a malice that, giving itself the lie, would COR 2.02. 32 P
honor, in giving him our own voices with our own 2.03. 44 P
their base throats tear | with giving him glory. 5.06. 53
by giving liberty unto thine eyes: ROM 1.01.227
could you not take some occasion without giving? 3.01. 44 P
parts you'll suit | in giving him his right. TIM 2.02. 24
giving our holy virgins to the stain | of 5.01.173
giving myself a voluntary wound | here, in the JC 2.01.300
in a sleep, and, giving him the lie, leaves him. MAC 2.03. 35 P
giving to you no further personal power | to HAM 1.02. 36
giving more light than heat, extinct in both 1.03.118
or such ambiguous giving out, to note | that you 1.05.178
this is the monkey's own giving out. OTH 4.01.127 P
the gods will be strong with us for giving o'er. PER 4.02. 35 P
beds of eels as my giving out her beauty stirs 4.02.143 P
by my excuse shall claim excuse's giving." LUC 1715
nor his compeers by night | giving him aid, my SON 86. 8
ever sweet, | was us'd in giving gentle doom, 145. 7
all vows and consecrations giving place. LC 263
GIVING–BACK 1 FR 0.0001 REL FR 1 V 0 P
about the giving–back the great seal to us, H8 3.02.347
/GIVINGS–OUT 1 FR 0.0001 REL FR 1 V 0 P
his /givings–out were of an infinite distance MM 1.04. 54
GIV'N *(also gi'n, given)*
GIV'N 4 FR 0.0004 REL FR 3 V 1 P
her the right you should have giv'n her cousin, ADO 5.01.291
and giv'n unto the house of york such head | as 3H6 1.01.233
which he hath giv'n for fence impregnable, | and 4.01. 44
she gave it him, and he hath giv'n it his whore. OTH 4.01.177 P
/GIV'ST 1 FR 0.0001 REL FR 1 V 0 P
/that /not /only /giv'st | /me /cause /to /wail, R2 4.01.300
GIV'ST 5 FR 0.0005 REL FR 4 V 1 P
that thou for truth giv'st out are landed here? JN 4.02.130
thou that giv'st whores indulgences to sin. 1H6 1.03. 35
thou giv'st so long, timon (i fear me), thou TIM 1.02.240 P
thy words before thou giv'st them breath, OTH 3.03.119
mak'st | with the breath thou giv'st and tak'st, PHT 19
/GLAD 1 FR 0.0001 REL FR 1 V 0 P
and am /glad | to have you therein my companion. H8 3.02.142
GLAD 139 FR 0.0157 REL FR 87 V 52 P
i am a fool | to weep at what i am glad of. TMP 3.01. 74
so glad of this as they i cannot be, | who are 3.01. 92
i am right glad that he's so out of hope. 3.03. 11
blessings | of a glad father compass thee about! 5.01.180
for your friend's sake, will be glad of you — TGV 3.02. 63
i was, and held me glad of such a doom. 4.01. 32
and will be glad to do my benevolence to make WIV 1.01. 32 P
i am glad to see your worships well. 1.01. 79 P
master page, i am glad to see you. 1.01. 81 P
i am glad to see you, good master slender. 1.01. 88 P
i am glad i am so acquit of this tinderbox; 1.03. 24 P
i am glad he went not in himself; 1.04. 49 P
i am glad he is so quiet. 1.04. 89 P
/brook, i shall be glad to be your servant. 2.02.178 P
i shall be glad if he have deceiv'd me. 3.01. 12 P
you know yourself clear, why, i am glad of it; 3.03.116 P
truly, i am so glad you have nobody here. 4.02. 18 P
i am glad the fat knight is not here. 4.02. 29 P
but i am glad the knight is not here. 4.02. 36 P
i shall make my master glad with these tidings. 4.05. 56 P
i am glad, though you have ta'en a special stand 5.05.234 P
you'll be glad to give out a commission for more MM 2.01.239 P
are chosen, they are glad to choose me for them. 2.01.269 P
denial which he is most glad to receive. 3.01.166 P
i would be glad to receive some instruction from 4.02. 17 P
old and faithful friend, we are glad to see you. 5.01. 2
i am glad to see you in this merry vein. ERR 2.02. 20
here in messina will be very much glad of it. ADO 1.01. 19 P
i be but a poor man, i am glad to hear it. 3.05. 27 P
well, i am glad that all things sorts so well. 5.04. 7
my commendations — i would be glad to see it. LLL 2.01.182 P
and so far am i glad it so did sort, | as this MND 3.02.352
i am glad this parcel of wooers are so MV 1.02.108 P
four farewell, i should be glad of his approach. 1.02.129 P
father, i am glad you are come; 2.02.107 P
i am glad 'tis night, you do not look on me, 2.06. 34
i am glad on't. 2.06. 67
i am very glad of it. 3.01.116 P
i am glad of it. 3.01.117 P
i know he will be glad of our success; 3.02.240
i am heartily glad i came hither to you. AYL 1.01.159 P
no man's happiness, glad of other men's good, 3.02. 75 P
i am glad of your departure. 3.02.293 P
i am very glad to see you. 3.03. 75 P
glad that you thus continue your resolve | to SHR 1.01. 27
i am glad he's come, howsoe'er he comes. 3.02. 74 P
my tale, | i'll make him glad to seem vincentio, 4.02. 68
that you are well restor'd, my lord, i'm glad. AWW 2.03.147
i am heartily sorry that he'll be glad of this. 4.03. 63 P
wouldst thou not be glad to have the niggardly TN 2.05. 4 P
i am glad you did not nurse him. WT 2.01. 56
i am glad at heart | to be so rid o' th' 3.03. 14
as heartily as he is glad he hath him. JN 3.04.124
i am not glad that such a sore of time | should 5.02. 12
glad am i that your highness is so arm'd | to R2 3.02.104
and would be glad he met with some mischance, 1H4 1.03.232
by the lord, lads, i am glad you have the money. 2.04.276 P
marry, | and i am glad of it with all my heart. 3.01.126
i am glad to see your lordship abroad. 2H4 1.02. 94 P
i am glad to see you well, good master robert 3.02. 85 P
i am glad to see you, by my troth, master 3.02.192 P
i am glad of it. 4.02. 77
i am glad to see your worship. 5.01. 56 P
we are glad the dolphin is so pleasant with us, H5 1.02.259
as we are now glad to behold your eyes — | your 5.02. 14
i will be glad to hear you confess it brokenly 5.02.105 P
i am glad thou canst speak no better english, 5.02.123 P
unready? ay, and glad we scap'd so well. 1H6 2.01. 40
are glad and fain by flight to save themselves. 3.02.114
but you, my lord, were glad to be employ'd, | to 2H6 3.02.273
health and glad tidings to your majesty! 4.09. 7
did glad my heart with hope of this young 3H6 4.06. 93
well met, my lord, i am glad to see your honor. R3 3.02.108
i'm glad 'tis there. H8 1.03. 21
i am glad they are going, | for sure there's no 1.03. 42
i am glad | your grace is grown so pleasant. 1.04. 89
subject to your countenance — glad, or sorry 2.04. 26
i should be glad to hear such news as this 3.02. 24
i am glad your grace has made that right use of 3.02.386
and am right glad to catch this good occasion 5.01.109
i am glad | i came this way so happily; 5.02. 8
most reverend nestor, i am glad to clasp thee. TRO 4.05.204
i am glad on't, then we shall ha' means to vent COR 1.01.225
i am glad to see your ladyship. 1.03. 50 P
on 's heart, | that is not glad to see thee! 2.01.186
well met, and most glad of your company. 4.03. 48 P
sir, i have the most cause to be glad of yours. 4.03. 51 P
these are a side that would be glad to have 4.06.150
i am glad thou hast set thy mercy and thy honor 5.03.200
the cordial of mine age to glad my heart! TIT 1.01.166
right glad i am he was not at this fray. ROM 1.01.117
why, i am glad on't, this is well, stand up. 4.02. 28
i am glad y' are well. TIM 1.01. 1
i am right glad that his health is well, sir; 3.01. 13 P
i am glad that my weak words | have struck but JC 1.02.176
the common herd was glad he refus'd the crown, 1.02.264 P
i am glad on't. 1.03.137
part, | i shall be glad to learn of noble men. 4.03. 54
i am glad to see you well. HAM 1.02.160
i am very glad to see you. 1.02.167
i am glad to see thee well. 2.02.421 P
i am glad of it, a knavish speech sleeps in a 4.02. 23 P
and such a tongue | that i am glad i have not, LR 1.01.232
i am glad to see your highness. 2.04.128
if thou shouldst not be glad, | i would divorce 2.04.130
i am glad at soul i have no other child, | for OTH 1.03.196
i am glad on't; 'tis a worthy governor. 2.01. 30
i am glad of this, for now i shall have reason 3.03.193
i am glad i have found this napkin; 3.03.290
i am very glad to see you, signior; 4.01.220
/by /my /troth, i am glad on't. 4.01.238
i am glad to see you mad. 4.01.239
i am glad to see you. 5.01. 95

i am glad thy father's dead. 5.02.204
we have cause to be glad that matters are so ANT 2.02.175 P
that is not | glad at the thing they scowl at. CYM 1.01. 15
i am very glad on't. 1.01.164
i was glad i did atone my countryman and you. 1.04. 39 P
i am glad i was up so late, for that's the 2.03. 33 P
i am most glad | you think of other place. 3.04.140
i am glad to be constrain'd to utter that 5.05.141
and am right glad he is not standing here | to 5.05.296
to glad your ear and please your eyes. PER 1.ch. 4
to glad her presence, | the senate–house of 1.01. 9
tables were stor'd full, to glad the sight, 1.04. 28
would now be glad of bread and beg for it; 1.04. 41
doing bad, | threw him ashore, to give him glad. 2.ch. 38
who takes offense | at that would make me glad? 2.05. 72
i am glad on't with all my heart. 2.05. 74
i am glad to see your honor in good health. 4.06. 22 P
ourselves shall we ev'r see | to glad our age, TNK 2.02. 34
i am glad | you have so good a stomach. 3.03. 20
and i am glad my cousin palamon | has made so 5.02. 91
by my short life, | i am most glad on't. 5.04. 29
'tis the latest thing | i shall be glad of, 5.04. 30
i was as dearly sorry | as glad of arcite; 5.04.130
and am now as glad | as for him sorry. 5.04.130
make glad and sorry seasons as thou fleet'st, SON 19. 5
this told, i joy, but then no longer glad, | i 45.13
GLADDED 1 FR 0.0001 REL FR 1 V 0 P
th' world) should not | be gladded in't by me. H8 2.04.197
GLADDER 1 FR 0.0001 REL FR 1 V 0 P
i am gladder | i have so good meat to't. TNK 3.03. 21
GLADDING 1 FR 0.0001 REL FR 1 V 0 P
to the gladding of | your highness with an heir! H8 5.01. 71
GLADE 1 FR 0.0001 REL FR 1 V 0 P
through a small glade cut by the fishermen, | i TNK 4.01. 64
GLADLY 16 FR 0.0018 REL FR 13 V 3 P
gladly, my lord. MM 1.03. 18
i'll gladly learn. 2.03. 23
which though myself would gladly have embrac'd,
ERR 1.01. 69
i would gladly have him see his company AWW 4.03. 31 P
i would most gladly know the issue of it. WT 5.02. 8 P
his weary joints would gladly rise, i know, R2 5.03.105
but gladly would be better satisfied | how in 2H4 1.03. 6
man that he would gladly make show to the world
H5 3.06. 83 P
ladies shall be frighted | and, gladly quak'd, COR 1.09. 6
and gladly shunn'd who gladly fled from me. ROM 1.01.130
and gladly shunn'd who gladly fled from me. 1.01.130
very gladly. MAC 1.03.155
for his particular, i'll receive him gladly, LR 2.04.292
by heaven, i would most gladly have forgot it. OTH 4.01. 19
and would gladly | look him i' th' face. ANT 5.02. 31
thou that which thou receiv'st not gladly, | or SON 8. 3
GLADNESS 3 FR 0.0003 REL FR 3 V 0 P
than thine own gladness that thou art employ'd. AYL 3.05. 98
but sorrow that is couch'd in seeming gladness TRO 1.01. 39
with most gladness, | and do invite you to my ANT 2.02.166
GLADS 1 FR 0.0001 REL FR 1 V 0 P
your presence glads our days. PER 2.03. 21
GLAMIS 8 FR 0.0009 REL FR 8 V 0 P
hail, macbeth, hail to thee, thane of glamis! MAC 1.03. 48
by sinel's death i know i am thane of glamis, 1.03. 71
glamis, and thane of cawdor! 1.03.116
glamis thou art, and cawdor, and shalt be | what 1.05. 15
thou'ldst have, great glamis, | that which cries 1.05. 22
great glamis! 1.05. 54
"glamis hath murther'd sleep, and therefore 2.02. 39
king, cawdor, glamis, all, | as the weird women 3.01. 1
GLANC'D 1 FR 0.0001 REL FR 0 V 1 P
to strike at me, that your arrow hath glanc'd. WIV 5.05.235 P
GLANCE 14 FR 0.0015 REL FR 14 V 0 P
and then to glance from him | to th' duke MM 5.01.309
roll | to every varied object in his glance; LLL 5.02.765
titania, | glance at my credit with hippolyta, MND 2.01. 75
doth glance from heaven to earth, from earth to 5.01. 13
and, as the jest did glance away from me, | 'tis SHR 5.02. 61
as to vouchsafe one glance unto the ground. 2H6 1.02. 16
and if we did but glance a far–off look, 3.01. 10
with the first glance that ever — pardon me — TRO 3.02.118
for they yet glance by and scarcely bruise, LR 5.03.149
mortally, | yet glance full wond'ringly on us. PER 3.03. 7
for they would glance their eyes | toward my TNK 5.03. 61
but the mild glance that sly ulysses lent LUC 1399
why with the time do i not glance aside | to SON 76. 3
dear heart, forbear to glance thine eye aside; 139. 6
GLANCED 2 FR 0.0002 REL FR 2 V 0 P
in company i often glanced it; ERR 5.01. 66
caesar's ambition shall be glanced at. JC 1.02.320
GLANCES 3 FR 0.0003 REL FR 3 V 0 P
days | to the sweet glances of thy honor'd love, TGV 1.01. 4
even by the squand'ring glances of the fool. AYL 2.07. 57
and dart not scornful glances from those eyes, SHR 5.02.137
GLANCING 1 FR 0.0001 REL FR 1 V 0 P
glancing an eye of pity on his losses, | that MV 4.01. 27
GLANDERS 1 FR 0.0001 REL FR 0 V 1 P
possess'd with the glanders and like to mose in SHR 3.02. 50 P
GLANSDALE 1 FR 0.0001 REL FR 1 V 0 P
sir thomas gargrave, and sir william glansdale, 1H6 1.04. 63
GLARE *(also glaz'd*)*
GLARE 1 FR 0.0001 REL FR 1 V 0 P
in those eyes | which thou dost glare with! MAC 3.04. 95
/GLARES 1 FR 0.0001 REL FR 0 V 1 P
/look /where /he /stands /and /glares! LR 3.06. 23 P
GLARES 1 FR 0.0001 REL FR 1 V 0 P
look you how pale he glares! HAM 3.04.125
/GLASS 4 FR 0.0004 REL FR 4 V 0 P
/this /paper /while /the /glass /doth /come. R2 4.01.269
/give /me /that /glass, /and /therein /will /i 4.01.276
/o /flatt'ring /glass, | /like /to /my 4.01.279
/he /was /the /mark /and /glass, /copy /and 2H4 2.03. 31
GLASS 67 FR 0.0075 REL FR 59 V 8 P
face remember, | save, from my glass, mine own; TMP 3.01. 50
her eyes are grey as glass, and so are mine; TGV 4.04.192
looks in a glass that shows what future evils, MM 2.02. 95
methinks you are my glass, and not my brother: ERR 5.01.418
here (good my glass), take this for telling true LLL 4.01. 18
behold | her silver visage in the wat'ry glass, MND 1.01.210
what wicked and dissembling glass of mine | made 2.02. 98
i pray thee set a deep glass of rhenish wine on MV 1.02. 96 P
'tis not her glass, but you, that flatters her, AYL 3.05. 54
being pour'd out of a cup into a glass, by 5.01. 42 P
had i a glass, i would. SHR 2.01.233
or four and twenty times the pilot's glass AWW 2.01.165
i my brother know | yet living in my glass; TN 3.04.380
if this be so, as yet the glass seems true, | i 5.01.265
she would not live | the running of one glass. WT 1.02.306
i turn my glass, and give my scene such growing 4.01. 16
sworn, i think, | to show myself a glass. 4.04. 14
stone, not a ribbon, glass, pomander, brooch, 4.04.598 P
he was indeed the glass | wherein the noble 2H4 2.03. 21
never looks in his glass for love of any thing H5 5.02.148 P
for ere the glass, that now begins to run, 1H6 4.02. 35
these dread curses, like the sun 'gainst glass, 2H6 3.02.330
look in a glass, and call thy image so. 5.01.142
shine out, fair sun, till i have bought a glass, R3 1.02.262
and i for comfort have but one false glass, 2.02. 53
or else my kingdom stands on brittle glass. 4.02. 61
and like a glass | did break i' th' wrenching. H8 1.01.166
than in the glass of pandar's praise may be; TRO 1.02.285
pride is his own glass, his own trumpet, his own 2.03.155 P
pride hath no other glass | to show itself but 3.03. 47
so well as by reflection, i, your glass, | will JC 1.02. 68
who bears a glass | which shows me many more; MAC 4.01.119
the glass of fashion and the mould of form, HAM 3.01.153
you go not till i set you up a glass | where you 3.04. 19
yet fair woman but she made mouths in a glass. LR 3.02. 36 P
get thee glass eyes, | and, like a scurvy 4.06.170
to th' more mature | a glass that feated them, CYM 1.01. 49
for a man and his glass to confer in his own 4.01. 8 P
fair glass of light, i lov'd you, and could PER 1.01. 76
like one another's glass to trim them by; 1.04. 27
to me he seems like diamond to glass. 2.03. 36
crack the glass of her virginity, and make the 4.06.142 P
dear glass of ladies, | bid him that we, whom TNK 1.01. 90
not scissor'd just | to such a favorite's glass? 1.02. 55
as well | speak this, and act it in your glass, 3.01. 70
the glass is running now that cannot finish 5.01. 18
being prison'd in her eye like pearls in glass, VEN 980
for princes are the glass, the school, the book, LUC 615
wilt thou be glass wherein it shall discern 619
when their glass fell wherein they view'd their 1526
"poor broken glass, i often did behold | in thy 1758
torn, | and shiver'd all the beauty of my glass, 1763
brighter than glass, and yet as glass is, PP 7. 3
brighter than glass, and yet as glass is, 7. 3
bud, | a brittle glass that's broken presently: 13. 4
a doubtful good, a gloss, a glass, a flower, 13. 5
ground, | as broken glass no cement can redress: 13.10
look in thy glass and tell the face thou viewest SON 3. 1
thou art thy mother's glass, and she in thee 3. 9
left | a liquid prisoner pent in walls of glass, 5.10
my glass shall not persuade me i am old, | so 22. 1
but when my glass shows me myself indeed, 62. 9
thy glass will show thee how thy beauties /wear, 77. 1
the wrinkles which thy glass will truly show, 77. 5
look in your glass, and there appears a face 103. 6
your own glass shows you when you look in it. 103.14
in thy power | dost hold time's fickle glass, 126. 2
GLASS'D 1 FR 0.0001 REL FR 1 V 0 P
their own worth from where they were glass'd, LLL 2.01.244
GLASSES 11 FR 0.0012 REL FR 8 V 3 P
at least two glasses. TMP 1.02.240
which, but three glasses since, we gave out 5.01.223
ay, as the glasses where they view themselves, MM 2.04.125
then thou /wilt keep | my tears for glasses, and LLL 4.03. 38
you will not pay for the glasses you have burst? SHR in.1. 7 P
even in the glasses of thine eyes | i see thy R2 1.03.208
glasses, glasses, is the only drinking, and for 2H4 2.01.143 P
glasses, glasses, is the only drinking, and for 2.01.143 P
tears take up | the glasses of my sight! COR 3.02.117
and bears with glasses, elephants with holes, JC 2.01.205
two glasses, where herself herself beheld | a VEN 1129
GLASS–FAC'D 1 FR 0.0001 REL FR 1 V 0 P
from the glass–fac'd flatterer | to apemantus, TIM 1.01. 58
GLASS–GAZING 1 FR 0.0001 REL FR 0 V 1 P
whoreson, glass–gazing, superserviceable, LR 2.02. 18 P
/GLASSY 1 FR 0.0001 REL FR 1 V 0 P
like wrinkled pebbles in a /glassy stream, | you TNK 1.01.112
GLASSY 4 FR 0.0004 REL FR 4 V 0 P
of what he's most assur'd | (his glassy essence) MM 2.02.120
as plays the sun upon the glassy streams, 1H6 5.03. 62
shows his hoary leaves in the glassy stream, HAM 4.07.167
writ in the glassy margents of such books. LUC 102
GLAZ'D* *(also glare)*
GLAZ'D* 2 FR 0.0002 REL FR 2 V 0 P
who glaz'd upon me, and went surly by, | without JC 1.03. 21
who glaz'd with crystal gate the glowing roses LC 286
GLAZED 2 FR 0.0002 REL FR 2 V 0 P
for sorrow's eyes, glazed with blinding tears, R2 2.02. 16
that hath his windows glazed with thine eyes. SON 24. 8
GLEAM'D 1 FR 0.0001 REL FR 1 V 0 P
and dying eyes gleam'd forth their ashy lights, LUC 1378
/GLEAMS 1 FR 0.0001 REL FR 1 V 0 P
by thy gracious, golden, glittering /gleams, | i MND 5.01.274
GLEAN 4 FR 0.0004 REL FR 3 V 1 P
crop | to glean the broken ears after the man AYL 3.05.102
which is a wonder how his grace should glean it, H5 1.01. 53
can your beesom conspectuities glean out of this COR 2.01. 64 P
gather | so much as from occasion you may glean, HAM 2.02. 16
GLEAN'D 1 FR 0.0001 REL FR 0 V 1 P
when he needs what you have glean'd, it is but HAM 4.02. 20 P
GLEANED 3 FR 0.0003 REL FR 3 V 0 P
how much low peasantry would then be gleaned MV 2.09. 46
nor the pomp that may | be thereat gleaned, for WT 4.04.489
galling the gleaned land with hot assays, H5 1.02.151
GLEANING 1 FR 0.0001 REL FR 1 V 0 P
of gleaning all the land's wealth into one, H8 3.02.284
GLEEFUL 1 FR 0.0001 REL FR 1 V 0 P
when every thing doth make a gleeful boast? TIT 2.03. 11
GLEEK *(also glikes)*
GLEEK 2 FR 0.0002 REL FR 0 V 2 P
nay, i can gleek upon occasion. MND 3.01.146 P
no money, on my faith, but the gleek; ROM 4.05.114 P
GLEEKING 1 FR 0.0001 REL FR 0 V 1 P
i have seen you gleeking and galling at this H5 5.01. 74 P
GLENDOWER 20 FR 0.0022 REL FR 17 V 3 P
to fight with glendower and his complices. R2 3.01. 43
against the irregular and wild glendower, | was 1H4 1.01. 40
against that great magician, damn'd glendower, 1.03. 83
in changing hardiment with great glendower. 1.03.101
he never did encounter with glendower. 1.03.114
devil alone | as owen glendower for an enemy. 1.03.117
i'll steal to glendower and lord mortimer, 1.03.295
mortimer, my lord of york, and owen glendower? 2.03. 25 P
o, glendower. 2.04.340 P
that spirit percy, and that devil glendower? 2.04.369 P
lord mortimer, and cousin glendower, | will you 3.01. 3
as oft as he hears | owen glendower spoke of. 3.01. 12
land within that bound, | to owen glendower; 3.01. 77
my father glendower is not ready yet, | nor 3.01. 86
o that glendower were come! 4.01.124
my father and glendower being both away, | the 4.01.131
to fight with glendower and the earl of march. 5.05. 40
against the french, | and one against glendower; 2H4 1.03. 72
a certain instance that glendower is dead. 3.01.103
and, but for owen glendower, had been king, 2H6 2.02. 41
GLENDOWER'S 1 FR 0.0001 REL FR 1 V 0 P
and what with owen glendower's absence thence, 1H4 4.04. 16
GLIB* 4 FR 0.0004 REL FR 4 V 0 P
and i had rather glib myself than they | should WT 2.01.149
o, these encounterers, so glib of tongue, | that TRO 4.05. 58
as well of glib and slipp'ry creatures as | of TIM 1.01. 53
if for i want that glib and oily art | to speak LR 1.01.224
GLIDE 2 FR 0.0002 REL FR 2 V 0 P
his sprite, | in the church–way paths to glide. MND 5.01.382
a week, why may not i | glide thither in a day? CYM 3.02. 52
GLIDED 1 FR 0.0001 REL FR 1 V 0 P
that slily glided towards your majesty, | it 2H6 3.02.260
GLIDES 4 FR 0.0004 REL FR 4 V 0 P
the current that with gentle murmur glides, TGV 2.07. 25
and with indented glides did slip away | into a AYL 4.03.112
ten times faster glides than the sun's beams, ROM 2.05. 5
so glides he in the night from venus' eye, VEN 816
GLIDETH 1 FR 0.0001 REL FR 1 V 0 P
more water glideth by the mill | than wots the TIT 2.01. 85
GLIDING 1 FR 0.0001 REL FR 1 V 0 P
all these fires, why all these gliding ghosts, JC 1.03. 63
GLIKES *(also gleek)*
GLIKES 1 FR 0.0001 REL FR 1 V 0 P
the bastard's braves, and charles his glikes? 1H6 3.02.123
GLIMMER 2 FR 0.0002 REL FR 2 V 0 P
my wasting lamps some fading glimmer left, | my ERR 5.01.316
that it will glimmer through a blindman's eye. 1H6 2.04. 24
GLIMMERING 3 FR 0.0003 REL FR 3 V 0 P
not thou lead him through the glimmering night MND 2.01. 77
as yonder venus in her glimmering sphere. 3.02. 61
through the house give glimmering light | by the 5.01.391
GLIMMERS 1 FR 0.0001 REL FR 1 V 0 P
the west yet glimmers with some streaks of day; MAC 3.03. 5
GLIMPSE 2 FR 0.0002 REL FR 1 V 1 P
whether it be the fault and glimpse of newness, MM 1.02.158
man hath a virtue that he hath not a glimpse of, TRO 1.02. 25 P
GLIMPSES 1 FR 0.0001 REL FR 1 V 0 P
steel | revisits thus the glimpses of the moon, HAM 1.04. 53
GLISTER 2 FR 0.0002 REL FR 2 V 0 P
away, and glister like the god of war | when he JN 5.01. 54
our stars must glister with new fire, or be TNK 5.01. 69
GLISTERING 2 FR 0.0002 REL FR 2 V 0 P
and make stale | the glistering of this present, WT 4.01. 14
gallops the zodiac in his glistering coach, TIT 2.01. 7
GLISTERS 3 FR 0.0003 REL FR 3 V 0 P
"all that glisters is not gold, | often have you MV 2.07. 65
how he glisters | through my rust! WT 3.02.170
his eye, which scornfully glisters like fire, VEN 275
GLIST'RING 3 FR 0.0003 REL FR 3 V 0 P
down, down i come, like glist'ring phaeton, R2 3.03.178
fetch'd | from glist'ring semblances of piety; H5 2.02.117
than to be perk'd up in a glist'ring grief | and H8 2.03. 21
GLITTERING 6 FR 0.0006 REL FR 6 V 0 P
by thy gracious, golden, glittering /gleams, | i MND 5.01.274
the meagre cloddy earth to glittering gold. JN 3.01. 80
his glittering arms he will commend to rust, R2 3.03.116
steel | over the glittering helmet of my foe! 4.01. 51
glittering in golden coats like images, | as 1H4 4.01.100
yellow, glittering, precious gold? TIM 4.03. 26
GLITT'RING 3 FR 0.0003 REL FR 3 V 0 P
my reformation, glitt'ring o'er my fault, 1H4 1.02.213
in glitt'ring golden characters express | a PER 4.03. 44
smear with dust their glitt'ring golden tow'rs; LUC 945
GLOBE 10 FR 0.0011 REL FR 8 V 2 P
the solemn temples, the great globe itself, TMP 4.01.153
she is spherical, like a globe; ERR 3.02.114 P
we the globe can compass soon, | swifter than MND 4.01. 97
eye of heaven is hid | behind the globe, that R2 3.02. 38
why, thou globe of sinful continents, what a 2H4 2.04.285 P
for wheresoe'er thou art in this world's globe, 2H6 3.02.406
and make a sop of all this solid globe; TRO 1.03.113
memory holds a seat | in this distracted globe. HAM 1.05. 97
approach, thou beacon to this under globe, LR 2.02.163
and that th' affrighted globe | did yawn at OTH 5.02.100
GLOBES 2 FR 0.0002 REL FR 2 V 0 P
and whirl along with thee about the globes. TIT 5.02. 49
her breasts like ivory globes circled with blue, LUC 407
GLOBY 1 FR 0.0001 REL FR 1 V 0 P
torturing convulsions from his globy eyes | had TNK 5.01.113
GLOOMING 1 FR 0.0001 REL FR 1 V 0 P
a glooming peace this morning with it brings, ROM 5.03.305
GLOOMY 3 FR 0.0003 REL FR 3 V 0 P
but darkness and the gloomy shade of death 1H6 5.04. 89
forc'd in the ruthless, vast, and gloomy woods? TIT 4.01. 53
keep still possession of thy gloomy place, LUC 803
/GLORIES 1 FR 0.0001 REL FR 1 V 0 P
/you /may /my /glories /and /my /state /depose, R2 4.01.192
GLORIES 11 FR 0.0012 REL FR 11 V 0 P
the borrowed glories that by gift of heaven, H5 2.04. 79
ends, | dispersed are the glories it included. 1H6 1.02.137
'tis love i bear thy glories make me speak. 3H6 2.01.158
live | to bear his image and renew his glories! 5.04. 54
princes have but their titles for their glories, R3 1.04. 78
but shall we wear these glories for a day? 4.02. 5
all my glories | in that one woman i have lost H8 3.02.408
are all thy conquests, glories, triumphs, spoils JC 3.01.149
grace his speech | tending to caesar's glories, 3.02. 58
away, | to part the glories of this happy day. 5.05. 81

his victories, his triumphs, and his glories. VEN 1014
GLORIFIED 1 FR 0.0001 REL FR 1 V 0 P
till my attempt so much be glorified | as to my JN 5.02.111
GLORIFIES 1 FR 0.0001 REL FR 1 V 0 P
and as the bright sun glorifies the sky, | so is VEN 485
GLORIFY 3 FR 0.0003 REL FR 3 V 0 P
join | do glorify the banks that bound them in; JN 2.01.442
victory | we with our stately presence glorify, 1H6 1.01. 21
that we for thee may glorify the lord. 2H6 2.01. 73
GLORIOUS 48 FR 0.0054 REL FR 47 V 1 P
and in that glorious supposition think | he ERR 3.02. 50
with shame | lives in death with glorious fame." ADO 5.03. 8
study is like the heaven's glorious sun, | that LLL 1.01. 84
well fitted in arts, glorious in arms; 2.01. 45
this is the air, that is the glorious sun, TN 4.03. 1
the day, | and kiss him with a glorious victory. JN 2.01.394
to solemnize this day the glorious sun | stays 3.01. 77
and, by the glorious worth of my descent, | this R2 1.01.107
richard hath in heavenly pay | a glorious angel; 3.02. 61
for jesu christ in glorious christian field, 4.01. 93
and in the closing of some glorious day | be 1H4 3.02.133
his glorious deeds for my indignities. 3.02.146
to engross up glorious deeds on my behalf; 3.02.148
whereof | shall be to you as us, like glorious. H5 2.02.183
as in this glorious and well-foughten field | we 4.06. 18
a far more glorious star thy soul will make 1H6 1.01. 55
france, triumph in thy glorious prophetess! 1.06. 8
may never glorious sun reflex his beams | upon 5.04. 87
an earl, | although in glorious titles he excel. 5.05. 38
put forth thy hand, reach at the glorious gold. 2H6 1.02. 11
long, | or sell my title for a glorious grave. 3.01. 92
like to the glorious sun's transparent beams, 3.01.353
now, by my /faith, lords, 'twas a glorious day. 5.03. 29
and cried, "a crown, or else a glorious tomb! 3H6 1.04. 16
and takes her farewell of the glorious sun! 2.01. 22
three glorious suns, each one a perfect sun, 2.01. 26
head | be round impaled with a glorious crown. 3.02.171
that will encounter with our glorious sun, | ere 5.03. 5
made glorious summer by this son of york; R3 1.01. 2
and therefore is the glorious planet sol | in TRO 1.03. 89
whose glorious deeds, but in these fields of 3.03.188
thy stained name, | and they'll seem glorious. 5.02.180
no, by the flame of yonder glorious heaven, | he 5.06. 23
the glorious gods sit in hourly synod about thy COR 5.02. 68 P
a better head her glorious body fits | than his TIT 1.01.187
for thou art | as glorious to this night, being ROM 2.02. 27
and would in action glorious i had lost | those OTH 2.03.186
pride, pomp, and circumstance of glorious war! 3.03.354
most miserable | is the /desire that's glorious. CYM 1.06. 7
the purchase is to make men glorious, | et bonum PER 1.ch. 9
were not this glorious casket stor'd with ill. 1.01. 77
in the day's glorious walk or peaceful night, 1.02. 4
i sought the purchase of a glorious beauty, 1.02. 72
does, | build his statue to make him glorious. 2.ch. 14
name, | made glorious by his manly chivalry, LUC 109
grooms are sightless night, kings glorious day; 1013
the sun look'd on the world with glorious eye, PP 6.11
full many a glorious morning have i seen SON 33. 1
GLORIOUSLY 2 FR 0.0002 REL FR 2 V 0 P
let her shine as gloriously | as the venus of MND 3.02.106
who doth the world so gloriously behold | that VEN 857
/GLORY 4 FR 0.0004 REL FR 4 V 0 P
/made /glory /base, /and /sovereignty /a /slave; R2 4.01.251
/a /brittle /glory /shineth /in /this /face, 4.01.287
/as /brittle /as /the /glory /is /the /face, 4.01.288
/the /glory /of /our /troy /doth /this /day /lie TRO 4.04.147
GLORY 90 FR 0.0101 REL FR 85 V 5 P
the uncertain glory of an april day, | which now TGV 1.03. 85
determines | herself the glory of a creditor, MM 1.01. 39
start-up hath all the glory of my overthrow. ADO 1.03. 67 P
his glory shall be ours, for we are the only 2.01.385 P
no glory lives behind the back of such. 3.01.110
be called boy, but his glory is to subdue men. LLL 1.02.180 P
glory grows guilty of detested crimes, | when, 4.01. 31
and they thy glory through my grief will show. 4.03. 36
told my love, | in glory of my kinsman hercules. MND 5.01. 47
so doth the greater glory dim the less: MV 5.01. 93
how high thy glory tow'rs | when the rich blood JN 2.01.350
all days of glory, joy, and happiness. 3.04.117
till i have set a glory to this hand, | by 4.03. 71
up into your hand | the circle of my glory. 5.01. 2
put on | the lineal state and glory of the land! 5.07.102
mind | i see thy glory like a shooting star R2 2.04. 19
a puny subject strikes | at thy great glory. 3.02. 87
bent | to dim his glory and to stain the track 3.03. 66
and threat the glory of my precious crown. 3.03. 90
account | that he shall render every glory up, 1H4 3.02.150
percy, | to share with me in glory any more. 5.04. 64
but i will rise there with so full a glory H5 1.02.278
let him cry, "praise and glory on his head!" 4.pr. 31
by starts the full course of their glory. ep 4
in complete glory she reveal'd herself; 1H6 1.02. 83
glory is like a circle in the water, | which 1.02.133
whose glory fills the world with loud report. 2.02. 43
reign, | before whose glory i was great in arms, 2.05. 24
yet heavens have glory for this victory! 3.02.117
heart | ascribes the glory of his conquest got 3.04. 11
this is the latest glory of thy praise | that i, 4.02. 33
surely, by all the glory you have won, | and if 4.06. 50
whose life was england's glory, gallia's wonder. 4.07. 48
to know who hath obtain'd the glory of the day. 4.07. 52
tends to god's glory and my country's weal. 5.01. 27
now, france, thy glory droopeth to the dust. 5.03. 29
and will you pale your head in henry's glory, 3H6 1.04.103
he might have kept that glory to this day. 2.02.153
lo, now my glory smear'd in dust and blood! 5.02. 23
outlive thy glory like my wretched self! R3 1.03.202
birth, | the lineal glory of your royal house, 3.07.121
be hid | and in the vapor of my glory smother'd. 3.07.164
go, go, poor soul, i envy not thy glory, | to 4.01. 63
farewell, thou woeful welcomer of glory! 4.01. 89
the high imperial type of this earth's glory. 4.04.245
thy crown, usurp'd, disgrac'd his kingly glory. 4.04.371
in my chamber when | those suns of glory, those H8 1.01. 6
then you lost | the view of earthly glory. 1.01. 14
yet let 'em look they glory not in mischief, 2.01. 66
and, from that full meridian of my glory, | i 3.02.224
bladders, | this many summers in a sea of glory, 3.02.360
vain pomp and glory of this world, i hate ye! 3.02.365
say wolsey, that once trod the ways of glory, 3.02.435
the greatest monarch now alive may glory | in 5.02.198
what glory our achilles shares from hector, TRO 1.03.366
were it not glory that we more affected | than 2.02.195
so rich advantage of a promis'd glory | as 2.02.204
if to my sword his fate be not the glory, | a 4.01. 27
that we look'd | for no less spoil than glory — COR 5.06. 43
their base throats tear | with giving him glory. 5.06. 53
madam, let it be your glory | to see her tears, TIT 2.03.139
that book in many's eyes doth share the glory, ROM 1.03. 91
it stains the glory in that happy verse | which TIM 1.01. 16
like madness is the glory of this life, | as 1.02.134
o, the fierce wretchedness that glory brings us! 4.02. 30
who would be so mock'd with glory, or to live 4.02. 33
his glory not extenuated, wherein he was worthy; JC 3.02. 38 P
i shall have glory by this losing day | more 5.05. 36
to bear my part, | or show the glory of our art? MAC 3.05. 9
not let him partake in the glory of the action, ANT 3.05. 9 P
and false-play'd my glory | unto an enemy's 4.14. 19
no less in pity than his glory which | brought 5.02.362
whom | he serv'd with glory and admir'd success: CYM 1.01. 32
soul | embold'ned with the glory of her praise, PER 1.01. 4
enticeth thee to view | her countless glory, 1.01. 31
as jewels lose their glory if neglected, | so 2.02. 12
which tells /me in that glory once he was; 2.03. 38
even in the height and pride of all his glory, 2.04. 6
and what they win in't, boot and glory; TNK 1.02. 70
the gods will show their glory in a life | that 5.04. 43
"time's glory is to calm contending kings, | to LUC 939
words like wildfire burnt the shining glory | of 1523
for at a frown they in their glory die. SON 25. 8
suffic'd, | and by a part of all thy glory live. 37.12
crooked eclipses 'gainst his glory fight, | and 60. 7
which shall be most my glory, being dumb, | for 83.10
that to his subject lends not some small glory, 84. 6
that thou in losing me shall win much glory. 88. 8
some glory in their birth, some in their skill, 91. 1
even | doth half that glory to the sober west, 132. 8
GLORY'S 2 FR 0.0002 REL FR 2 V 0 P
that plotted thus our glory's overthrow? 1H6 1.01. 24
me, | whereas no glory's got to overcome. PER 1.04. 70
GLOSE *(also gloze)*
GLOSE 1 FR 0.0001 REL FR 1 V 0 P
they whom youth and ease have taught to glose. R2 2.01. 10
GLOSS 17 FR 0.0019 REL FR 14 V 3 P
a soil in the new gloss of your marriage as to ADO 3.02. 6 P
the only soil of his fair virtue's gloss, | if LLL 2.01. 47
if virtue's gloss will stain with any soil, | is 2.01. 48
'tis a commodity will lose the gloss with lying: AWW 1.01.153 P
conceit | to set a gloss upon his bold intent, 1H6 4.01.103
hath sullied all his gloss of former honor | by 4.04. 6
i fear me, lords, for all this flattering gloss, 2H6 1.01.163
your painted gloss discovers, | to men that H8 5.02.106
do in our eyes begin to lose their gloss, | yea, TRO 2.03.119
at first | to set a gloss on faint deeds, hollow TIM 1.02. 16
which would be worn now in their newest gloss, MAC 1.07. 34
to slubber the gloss of your new fortunes with OTH 1.03.227 P
before we further | sully our gloss of youth: TNK 1.02. 5
his breath and beauty set | gloss on the rose, VEN 936
good, | a shining gloss that vadeth suddenly, PP 13. 2
a doubtful good, a gloss, a glass, a flower, 13. 5
found, | as vaded gloss no rubbing will refresh, 13. 8
GLOSSES 1 FR 0.0001 REL FR 0 V 1 P
notwithstanding their freshness and glosses, TMP 2.01. 64 P
/GLOUCESTER 1 FR 0.0001 REL FR 0 V 1 P
/'tis /said, /the /bastard /son /of /gloucester. LR 4.07. 88 P
GLOUCESTER 110 FR 0.0124 REL FR 101 V 9 P
in the county of gloucester, justice of peace WIV 1.01. 5 P
thomas, my dear lord, my life, my gloucester, R2 1.02. 16
my brother gloucester, plain well-meaning soul, 2.01.128
get thee to plashy, to my sister gloucester, 2.02. 90
humphrey, my son of gloucester, | where is the 2H4 4.04. 12
warwick! gloucester! clarence! 4.05. 48
the duke of gloucester would speak with you. H5 3.02. 55 P
the duke of gloucester, to whom the order of the 3.02. 65 P
gloucester, 'tis true that we are in great 4.01. 1
my dear lord gloucester, and my good lord exeter 4.03. 9
warwick and talbot, salisbury and gloucester, 4.03. 54
my lord of warwick, and my brother gloucester, 4.07.170
brother clarence, and you, brother gloucester, 5.02. 84
gloucester, what e'er we like, thou art 1H6 1.01. 37
gloucester, why doubt'st thou of my forwardness? 1.01.100
open the gates, 'tis gloucester that calls. 1.03. 4
it is the noble duke of gloucester. 1.03. 6
the gates, here's gloucester that would enter. 1.03. 17
gloucester, thou wilt answer this before the 1.03. 52
here's gloucester, a foe to citizens, | one that 1.03. 62
gloucester, we'll meet to thy cost, be sure: 1.03. 82
abominable gloucester, guard thy head, | for i 1.03. 87
for the truce of winchester and gloucester; 2.04.118
humphrey of gloucester, if thou canst accuse, 3.01. 3
gloucester, i do defy thee. 3.01. 27
unreverent gloucester! 3.01. 49
uncles of gloucester and of winchester, | the 3.01. 65
pray, uncle gloucester, mitigate this strife. 3.01. 88
well, duke of gloucester, i will yield to thee; 3.01.134
o loving uncle, kind duke of gloucester, | how 3.01.142
when gloucester says the word, king henry goes, 3.01.183
is this the lord talbot, uncle gloucester, 3.04. 13
humphrey of gloucester, thou shalt well perceive 5.01. 58
gloucester, york, buckingham, somerset, 2H6 1.01. 69
my lord of gloucester, now ye grow too hot: 1.01.137
him "humphrey, the good duke of gloucester," 1.01.159
if gloucester be displac'd, he'll be protector. 1.01.177
i never saw but humphrey duke of gloucester 1.01.183
while gloucester bears this base and humble mind 1.02. 62
and thy ambition, gloucester. 2.01. 32
believe me, cousin gloucester, | had not your 2.01. 43
why, how now, uncle gloucester? 2.01. 48
gloucester, see here the tainture of thy nest, 2.01.184
was thomas of woodstock, duke of gloucester; 2.02. 16
stay, humphrey duke of gloucester! 2.03. 22
and humphrey duke of gloucester scarce himself, 2.03. 40
ah, gloucester, hide thee from their hateful 2.04. 23
ah, gloucester, teach me to forget myself! 2.04. 27
i muse my lord of gloucester is not come; 3.01. 1
gloucester is a man | unsounded yet and full of 3.01. 56
our kinsman gloucester is as innocent | from 3.01. 69
nay, gloucester, know that thou art come too 3.01. 95
my lord of gloucester, 'tis my special hope 3.01.139
say, "who's a traitor, gloucester he is none." 3.01.222
this gloucester should be quickly rid the world, 3.01.233
proceed no straiter 'gainst our uncle gloucester 3.02. 20
dead in his bed, my lord; gloucester is dead. 3.02. 29
ah, woe is me for gloucester, wretched man! 3.02. 72
richard, i will create thee duke of gloucester, 3H6 2.06.103
me be duke of clarence, george of gloucester, 2.06.106
richard, be duke of gloucester. 2.06.109
brother of gloucester, at saint albons field 3.02. 1
now, brother of gloucester, lord hastings, and 4.05. 16
he was convey'd by richard, duke of gloucester, 4.06. 81
"good gloucester" and "good devil" were alike, 5.06. 4
clarence and gloucester, love my lovely queen, 5.07. 26
is put unto the trust of richard gloucester, | a R3 1.03. 12
the duke of gloucester and your brothers, | and 1.03. 37
brother of gloucester, you mistake the matter: 1.03. 62
come, we know your meaning, brother gloucester; 1.03. 73
my lord of gloucester, i have too long borne 1.03.102
my lord of gloucester, in those busy days, 1.03.144
and in my company my brother gloucester, | who 1.04. 11
methought that gloucester stumbled, and in 1.04. 18
back to the duke of gloucester and tell him so. 1.04.115 P
and i will send you to my brother gloucester, 1.04.229
are deceiv'd, your brother gloucester hates you. 1.04.232
bid gloucester think /of this, and he will weep. 1.04.239
there wanteth now our brother gloucester here 2.01. 43
gloucester, we have done deeds of charity, 2.01. 50
for my good uncle gloucester | told me the king, 2.02. 20
o, full of danger is the duke of gloucester, 2.03. 27
"ay," quoth my uncle gloucester, | "small herbs 2.04. 12
the mighty dukes, | gloucester and buckingham. 2.04. 45
say, uncle gloucester, if our brother come, 3.01. 61
where is my lord, the duke of gloucester? 3.04. 46
to murther me and my good lord of gloucester? 3.05. 39
led in the hand of her kind aunt of gloucester? 4.01. 2
the lords of france and burgundy, gloucester. LR 1.01. 34
go you before to gloucester with these letters. 1.05. 1 P
occasions, noble gloucester, of some prize, 2.01.120
why, gloucester, gloucester, | i'ld speak with 2.04. 96
why, gloucester, gloucester, | i'ld speak with 2.04. 96
where is my lord of gloucester? 2.04.294
or false, it hath made thee earl of gloucester. 3.05. 18 P
seek out the traitor gloucester. 3.07. 3 P
dear sister, farewell, my lord of gloucester. 3.07. 13 P
my lord of gloucester hath convey'd him hence. 3.07. 15
go seek the traitor gloucester, | pinion him 3.07. 22
my most dear gloucester! 4.02. 25
going to put out | the other eye of gloucester. 4.02. 72
but, o poor gloucester, | lost he his other eye? 4.02. 80
but being widow, and my gloucester with her, 4.02. 84
gloucester, i live | to thank thee for the love 4.02. 94
i know thee well enough, thy name is gloucester. 4.06.177
find'st about me | to edmund earl of gloucester; 4.06.249
thou art armed, gloucester, let the trumpet 5.03. 90
upon edmund, supposed earl of gloucester, that 5.03.112 P
he that speaks for edmund earl of gloucester? 5.03.125
this is practice, gloucester. 5.03.152
GLOUCESTER'S 23 FR 0.0026 REL FR 22 V 1 P
that he did plot the duke of gloucester's death, R2 1.01.100
for gloucester's death, | i slew him not, but to 1.01.132
the best way is to venge my gloucester's death. 1.02. 36
not gloucester's death, nor herford's banishment 2.01.165
what thou dost know of noble gloucester's death, 4.01. 3
dead time when gloucester's death was plotted, 4.01. 10
thou wert cause of noble gloucester's death. 4.01. 37
my brother gloucester's voice? H5 4.01.307
the bishop and the duke of gloucester's men, 1H6 3.01. 78
he that breaks a stick of gloucester's grove 2H6 1.02. 33
still | under the surly gloucester's governance? 1.03. 47
that hath dishonored gloucester's honest name. 2.01.195
forth, dame eleanor cobham, gloucester's wife: 2.03. 1
even so myself bewails good gloucester's case 3.01.217
and gloucester's show | beguiles him as the 3.01.225
in life but double death, now gloucester's dead. 3.02. 55
is all thy comfort shut in gloucester's tomb? 3.02. 78
for gloucester's dukedom is too ominous. 3H6 2.06.107
o, in the duke of gloucester's purse. R3 1.04.128 P
of gloucester's treachery, | and of the loyal LR 4.02. 6
gloucester's eyes? 4.02. 72
great ignorance, gloucester's eyes being out, 4.05. 9
for gloucester's bastard son | was kinder to his 4.06.114
GLOUCESTERSHIRE 8 FR 0.0009 REL FR 4 V 4 P
as well as i love any woman in gloucestershire. WIV 3.04. 44 P
i'll make the best in gloucestershire know on't. 5.05.180 P
lord, | i am a stranger here in gloucestershire. R2 2.03. 3
fire | our town of ciceter in gloucestershire, 5.06. 3
a plague upon it, it is in gloucestershire — 1H4 1.03.243
you shall march | through gloucestershire; 3.02.176
you give me leave to go through gloucestershire, 2H4 4.03. 82 P
i'll through gloucestershire, and there will i 4.03.128 P
GLOVE 37 FR 0.0041 REL FR 18 V 19 P
sir, your glove. TGV 2.01. 1
madam, this glove. LLL 5.02. 48
by this white glove (how white the hand, god 5.02.411
this woman's an easy glove, my lord, she goes AWW 5.03.277 P
sentence is but a chev'ril glove to a good wit. TN 3.01. 12 P
ballad, knife, tape, glove, shoe-tie, bracelet, WT 4.04.599 P
and from the common'st creature pluck a glove R2 5.03. 17
now with joints of steel | must glove this hand; 2H4 1.01.147
here's my glove; give me another of thine. H5 4.01.211 P
after to-morrow, "this is my glove," by this 4.01.215 P
soldier, why wear'st thou that glove in thy cap? 4.07.120 P
if alive and ever dare to challenge this glove, 4.07.127 P
or if i can see my glove in his cap, which he 4.07.128 P
together, i pluck'd this glove from his helm. 4.07.155 P
that shall find himself aggrief'd at this glove; 4.07.163 P
the glove which i have given him for a favor 4.07.172
sir, know you this glove? 4.08. 6 P
know the glove? i know the glove is a glove. 4.08. 7 P
know the glove? i know the glove is a glove. 4.08. 7 P
know the glove? i know the glove is a glove. 4.08. 7 P
has strook the glove which your majesty is take 4.08. 26 P
my liege, this was my glove, here is the fellow 4.08. 28 P
i met this man with my glove in his cap, and i 4.08. 31 P
that this is the glove of alanson that your 4.08. 37 P

give me thy glove, soldier. 4.08. 39 P
here, uncle exeter, fill this glove with crowns, 4.08. 57
for i will throw my glove to death himself TRO 4.04. 63
and you this glove. when shall i see you? 4.04. 71
your quondam wife swears still by venus' glove. 4.05.179
of thee and me, and sighs, and takes my glove, 5.02. 79
o that i were a glove upon that hand, | that i ROM 2.02. 24
throw thy glove, | or any token of thine honor TIM 5.04. 49
then there's my glove; 5.04. 54
with glove or hat or handkerchief | still waving CYM 1.03. 11
by the light he spies | lucretia's glove, LUC 317
"this glove to wanton tricks | is not inur'd; 320
doors, the wind, the glove that did delay him, 325
GLOVER'S 1 FR 0.0001 REL FR 0 V 1 P
great round beard, like a glover's paring–knife? WIV 1.04. 21 P
GLOVES 18 FR 0.0020 REL FR 9 V 9 P
not mine: my gloves are on. TGV 2.01. 1
ay, by these gloves, did he, or i would i might WIV 1.01.153 P
pence a–piece of yead miller — by these gloves. 1.01.158 P
by these gloves, then 'twas he. 1.01.165 P
these gloves the count sent me — they are an ADO 3.04. 62 P
give me your gloves, i'll wear them for your MV 4.01.426
verily did think | that her old gloves were on, AYL 4.03. 26
milliner can so fit his customers with gloves. WT 4.04.192 P
was crow, | gloves as sweet as damask roses, 4.04.220
be the bondage of certain ribbons and gloves. 4.04.234 P
me a tawdry–lace and a pair of sweet gloves. 4.04.250 P
pockets as their gloves or their handkerchers; H5 3.02. 48 P
priest, | you fur your gloves with reason. TRO 2.02. 38
matrons flung gloves, | ladies and maids their COR 2.01.263
wore gloves in my cap; LR 3.04. 86 P
'tis as i should entreat you wear your gloves, OTH 3.03. 77
to fetch her fan, her gloves, her mask, nor 4.02. 9
the next gloves that i give her shall be dogskin TNK 3.05. 45
/GLOW 1 FR 0.0001 REL FR 1 V 0 P
to /glow the delicate cheeks which they did cool ANT 2.02.204
GLOW 6 FR 0.0006 REL FR 6 V 0 P
now the wasted brands do glow, | whilst the MND 5.01.375
and the red glow of scorn and proud disdain, AYL 3.04. 54
blush | and glow with shame of your proceedings, JN 4.01.113
the angry spot doth glow on caesar's brow, | and JC 1.02.183
heaven's face does glow | o'er this solidity and HAM 3.04. 48
he sees her coming, and begins to glow, | even VEN 337
GLOW'D 1 FR 0.0001 REL FR 1 V 0 P
of the war | have glow'd like plated mars, now ANT 1.01. 4
GLOWED 1 FR 0.0001 REL FR 1 V 0 P
o, that false fire which in his cheek so glowed, LC 324
GLOWING 5 FR 0.0005 REL FR 4 V 1 P
this lies glowing, i can tell you, and is almost COR 4.03. 25 P
that /blast gives heat and stronger glowing; PER 1.02. 41
she red and hot as coals of glowing fire, | he VEN 35
in me thou seest the glowing of such fire | that SON 73. 9
who glaz'd with crystal gate the glowing roses LC 286
GLOWING–HOT 1 FR 0.0001 REL FR 0 V 1 P
thames, and cool'd, glowing–hot, in that surge, WIV 3.05.120 P
GLOWS 2 FR 0.0002 REL FR 2 V 0 P
but there is something glows upon my cheek, PER 5.01. 95
to quench the coal which in his liver glows. LUC 47
GLOW–WORM 2 FR 0.0002 REL FR 2 V 0 P
the glow–worm shows the matin to be near, | and HAM 1.05. 89
now his /son's like a glow–worm in the night, PER 2.03. 43
GLOW–WORM'S 1 FR 0.0001 REL FR 1 V 0 P
and light them at the fiery glow–worm's eyes, MND 3.01.170
GLOW–WORMS 2 FR 0.0002 REL FR 2 V 0 P
and twenty glow–worms shall our lanthorns be, WIV 5.05. 78
his eyes like glow–worms shine when he doth fret VEN 621
GLOZ'D 1 FR 0.0001 REL FR 1 V 0 P
cause and question now in hand | have gloz'd, TRO 2.02.165
GLOZE *(also glose)*
GLOZE 3 FR 0.0003 REL FR 3 V 0 P
which salique land the french unjustly gloze H5 1.02. 40
become | high–witted tamora to gloze with all; TIT 4.04. 35
but i will gloze with him. PER 1.01.110
GLOZES 1 FR 0.0001 REL FR 1 V 0 P
now to plain–dealing, lay these glozes by: LLL 4.03.367
GLU'D 2 FR 0.0002 REL FR 2 V 0 P
my love and fear glu'd many friends to thee, 3H6 2.06. 5
in, which being glu'd together | makes morris, TNK 3.05.119
GLUE 1 FR 0.0001 REL FR 1 V 0 P
/friends | do glue themselves in sociable grief, JN 3.04. 65
GLUED 2 FR 0.0002 REL FR 2 V 0 P
have your lath glued within your sheath, | till TIT 2.01. 41
their lips together glued, fall to the earth. VEN 546
GLUES 1 FR 0.0001 REL FR 1 V 0 P
that glues my lips and will not let me speak. 3H6 5.02. 38
GLUT 1 FR 0.0001 REL FR 1 V 0 P
against it, | and gape at wid'st to glut him. TMP 1.01. 60
GLUTTED 1 FR 0.0001 REL FR 1 V 0 P
being with his presence glutted, gorg'd, and 1H4 3.02. 84
GLUTT'NOUS 1 FR 0.0001 REL FR 1 V 0 P
down th' int'rest into their glutt'nous maws. TIM 3.04. 52
/GLUTTON 1 FR 0.0001 REL FR 1 V 0 P
/thy /glutton /bosom /of /the /royal /richard, 2H4 1.03. 98
GLUTTON 4 FR 0.0004 REL FR 3 V 1 P
let him be damn'd like the glutton! 2H4 1.02. 34 P
but, when his glutton eye so full hath fed, VEN 399
love surfeits not, lust like a glutton dies; 803
pity the world, or else this glutton be, | to SON 1.13
GLUTTONING 1 FR 0.0001 REL FR 1 V 0 P
day by day, | or gluttoning on all, or all away. SON 75.14
GLUTTON–LIKE 1 FR 0.0001 REL FR 1 V 0 P
and glutton–like she feeds, yet never filleth; VEN 548
GLUTTON'S 1 FR 0.0001 REL FR 0 V 1 P
where the glutton's dogs lick'd his sores, and 1H4 4.02. 26 P
GLUTTONY 2 FR 0.0002 REL FR 0 V 2 P
gluttony and diseases make, i make them not. 2H4 2.04. 42 P
if the cook help to make the gluttony, you help 2.04. 44 P
GNARLED 1 FR 0.0001 REL FR 1 V 0 P
splits the unwedgeable and gnarled oak | than MM 2.02.116
GNARLING 2 FR 0.0002 REL FR 2 V 0 P
for gnarling sorrow hath less power to bite R2 1.03.292
and wolves are gnarling who shall gnaw thee 2H6 3.01.192
GNAT 4 FR 0.0004 REL FR 4 V 0 P
i sat, | to see a king transformed to a gnat! LLL 4.03.164
a grain, a dust, a gnat, a wandering hair, | any JN 4.01. 92
film, | her waggoner a small grey–coated gnat, ROM 1.04. 67
melted from | the smallness of a gnat to air, CYM 1.03. 21
GNATS 7 FR 0.0008 REL FR 7 V 0 P
the sun shines, let foolish gnats make sport, ERR 2.02. 30
hearts of men | faster than gnats in cobwebs. MV 3.02.123
and whither fly the gnats but to the sun? 3H6 2.06. 9
is the sun dimm'd, that gnats do fly in it? TIT 4.04. 82
till the flies and gnats of nile | have buried ANT 3.13.166
and princes not doing so are like to gnats, PER 2.03. 62
gnats are unnoted wheresoe'er they fly, | but LUC 1014
GNAW 7 FR 0.0008 REL FR 7 V 0 P
wolves are gnarling who shall gnaw thee first. 2H6 3.01.192
that he could gnaw a crust at two hours old; R3 2.04. 28
take these rats thither | to gnaw their garners. COR 1.01.250
the canker gnaw thy heart, | for showing me TIM 4.03. 50
doth, like a poisonous mineral, gnaw my inwards; OTH 2.01.297
and hell gnaw his bones! 4.02.136
alas, why gnaw you so your nether lip? 5.02. 43
GNAW'D 2 FR 0.0002 REL FR 2 V 0 P
but he, i thank him, gnaw'd in two my cords: ERR 5.01.290
a thousand men that fishes gnaw'd upon; R3 1.04. 25
GNAWING 3 FR 0.0003 REL FR 3 V 0 P
till, gnawing with my teeth my bonds in sunder, ERR 5.01.250
thy other hand | gnawing with thy teeth, and be TIT 3.01.261
to ease the gnawing vulture of thy mind, | by 5.02. 31
GNAWN 1 FR 0.0001 REL FR 0 V 1 P
my coffers ransack'd, my reputation gnawn at, WIV 2.02.293 P
GNAWS 2 FR 0.0002 REL FR 2 V 0 P
that gnaws the bowels of the commonwealth. 1H6 3.01. 73
the king is angry, see, he gnaws his lip. R3 4.02. 27
/GO 10 FR 0.0011 REL FR 9 V 1 P
/go /some /of /you, /and /fetch /a R2 4.01.268
/then /give /me /leave /to /go. 4.01.313
/go /some /of /you, /convey /him /to /the /tower 4.01.316
/yet /did /you /say, "/go /forth!" 2H4 1.01.175
/lavinia, /go /with /me. TIT 3.02. 81
/and /go /read /with /thee | /sad /stories 3.02. 82
/boy, /and /go /with /me, /thy /sight /is /young 3.02. 84
/go /thou. LR 3.07.106
/i /pray /you /go | /along /with /me. 4.03. 54
/go /to, /farewell. OTH 1.03.380 P
GO 1786 FR 0.2018 REL FR 1293 V 493 P
go make thyself like a nymph o' th' sea; TMP 1.02.301
go take this shape | and hither come in't. 1.02.303
go. 1.02.304
we would so, and then go a–batfowling. 2.01.185 P
go sleep, and hear us. 2.01.190 P
so, king, go safely on to seek thy son. 2.01.327
with a tang, | would cry to a sailor, 'go hang!' 2.02. 51
then to sea, boys, and let her go hang!" 2.02. 54
wine afore, it will go near to remove his fit. 2.02. 75 P
wilt thou go with me? 2.02.172
nor go neither; 3.02. 19 P
i'll go farther off. 3.02. 72 P
by'r lakin, i can go no further, sir, | my old. 3.03. 1
well, let him go. 3.03. 10
go bring the rabble | (o'er whom i give thee 4.01. 37
before you can say "come" and "go," | and 4.01. 44
go with me | to bless this twain, that they may 4.01.103
the trumpery in my house, go bring it hither, 4.01.186
i go, i go. 4.01.187
i go, i go. 4.01.187
wit shall not go unrewarded while i am king of 4.01.242 P
go to, carry this. 4.01.252 P
go, charge my goblins that they grind their 4.01.258
go, release them, ariel. 5.01. 30
go, sirrah, to my cell; 5.01.292
go to, away! 5.01.298
shall make it | go quick away — the story of my 5.01.305
it shall go hard but i'll prove it by another. TGV 1.01. 85 P
go, go, be gone, to save your ship from wrack, 1.01.148
go, go, be gone, to save your ship from wrack, 1.01.148
i must go send some better messenger: 1.01.151
go, get you gone; 1.02. 97
well, let us go. 1.02.129
come, come, will't please you go? 1.02.137
with them shall proteus go — | and in good time 1.03. 43
to–morrow be in readiness to go — | excuse it 1.03. 70
to–morrow thou must go. 1.03. 75
therefore i pray you go. 1.03. 89
go to, sir; tell me, do you know madam silvia? 2.01. 14 P
go; 2.02. 19
wilt thou go? 2.03. 58 P
well, i will go. 2.03. 59 P
come, sir thurio, | go with me. 2.04.118
good proteus, go with me to my chamber, | in 2.04.184
go on before; 2.04.186
if thou wilt, go with me to the alehouse; 2.05. 53 P
much charity in thee as to go to the ale with a 2.05. 58 P
wilt thou go? 2.05. 58 P
thou wouldst as soon go kindle fire with snow 2.07. 19
then let me go, and hinder not my course: 2.07. 33
but in what habit will you go along? 2.07. 39
if you think so, then stay at home and go not. 2.07. 62
then never dream on infamy, but go. 2.07. 64
him, | and presently go with me to my chamber, 2.07. 83
i will go to her alone. 3.01.127
o, could their master come and go as lightly, 3.01.142
go, base intruder! 3.01.157
him we go to find. 3.01.190 P
go, sirrah, find him out. come, valentine. 3.01.261
and must i go to him? 3.01.377 P
come, go with us, we'll bring thee to our crews, 4.01. 72
love | will creep in service where it cannot go. 4.02. 20
go to thy lady's grave and call hers thence, 4.02.116
host, will you go? 4.02.134 P
of sands, | to bear me company, and go with me; 4.03. 34
plac'd, | i give consent to go along with you, 4.03. 39
when will you go? 4.03. 42
go, get thee hence, and find my dog again, | or 4.04. 59
go presently, and take this ring with thee, 4.04. 71
go give your master this. 4.04.118
go on, good eglamour, | out at the postern by 5.01. 8
go thou with her to the west end of the wood; 5.03. 9
let go that rude uncivil touch, | thou friend of 5.04. 60
come, let us go, we will include all jars | with 5.04.160
go, sirrah, for all you are my man, go wait upon WIV 1.01.271 P
you are my man, go wait upon my cousin shallow. 1.01.271 P
i may not go in without your worship; 1.01.277 P
mistress anne, yourself shall go first. 1.01.307 P
truly i will not go first; 1.01.309 P
go your ways, and ask of doctor caius' house 1.02. 1 P
go, adieu. 1.03. 18 P
go, bear thou this letter to mistress page; 1.03. 72 P
go! 1.03. 81
i pray thee go to the casement, and see if you 1.04. 2 P
i'll go watch. 1.04. 7 P
go, and we'll have a posset for't soon at night, 1.04. 8 P
go into this closet. 1.04. 38 P
go, john, go inquire for my master; 1.04. 40 P
go, john, go inquire for my master; 1.04. 40 P
pray you go and vetch me in my closet /une 1.04. 45 P
but for you — well — go to. 1.04.154 P
go to then, there's sympathy. 2.01. 7 P
if i would but go to hell for an eternal moment 2.01. 49 P
or go thou | like sir actaeon he, with ringwood 2.01.117
whither go you, george, hark you? 2.01.149 P
go. 2.01.153 P
will you go, mistress page? 2.01.155 P
go in with us and see. 2.01.166 P
master page, will you go with us? 2.01.197 P
will you go with us to behold it? 2.01.206 P
will you go, an–heires? 2.01.219 P
go — a short knife and a throng! 2.02. 17 P
go. 2.02. 19 P
pay all, go to bed when she list, rise when she 2.02.119 P
look you, he may come and go between you both; 2.02.125 P
boy, go along with this woman. 2.02.132 P
go thy ways. 2.02.138 P
go to, via! 2.02.153 P
for they say, if money go before, all ways do 2.02.168 P
you go against the hair of your professions. 2.03. 40 P
you must go with me, master doctor. 2.03. 55 P
slender, go you through the town to frogmore. 2.03. 75 P
go about the fields with me through frogmore, i 2.03. 85 P
go before you like a man than follow him like a 3.02. 5 P
well met, mistress page. whither go you? 3.02. 9 P
i will go. 3.02. 49 P
cheer at home, and i pray you all go with me. 3.02. 52 P
heartily, some of you go home with me to dinner. 3.02. 79 P
master doctor, you shall go, so shall you, 3.02. 82 P
go home, john rugby, i come anon. 3.02. 86 P
will you go, gentles? 3.02. 90 P
i'll go hide me. 3.03. 35 P
go tell thy master i am alone. 3.03. 36 P
go to then. 3.03. 40 P
he's too big to go in there. what shall i do? 3.03.134 P
go take up these clothes here quickly. 3.03.146 P
let's go in, gentlemen, but, trust me, we'll 3.03.228 P
pray you go, master page. 3.03.238 P
can tell you how things go better than i can. 3.04. 65 P
she must needs go in, | her father will be angry 3.04. 92
go fetch me a quart of sack — put a toast in't. 3.05. 3 P
go, brew me a pottle of sack finely. 3.05. 28 P
to make one mad, let the proverb go with me: 3.05.151 P
go your ways and play, go. 4.01. 79 P
go your ways and play, go. 4.01. 79 P
which way should he go? 4.02. 46 P
may i not go out ere he come? 4.02. 50 P
i'll go out then. 4.02. 65 P
if you go out in your own semblance, you die, 4.02. 66 P
die, sir john — unless you go out disguis'd. 4.02. 67 P
go, go, sweet sir john. 4.02. 80 P
go, go, sweet sir john. 4.02. 80 P
let's go dress him like the witch of brainford. 4.02. 98 P
go up, i'll bring linen for him straight. 4.02.100 P
go, sirs, take the basket again on your 4.02.108 P
you are not to go loose any longer, you must be 4.02.123 P
but let our plot go forward. 4.04. 12
i'll go buy them vizards. 4.04. 70
that silk will i go buy. 4.04. 73
go, send to falstaff straight. 4.04. 75
go get us properties | and tricking for our 4.04. 78
go, mistress ford, | send quickly to sir john, 4.04. 82
go, knock and call; 4.05. 8 P
sent to her, seeing her go thorough the streets, 4.05. 31 P
go; 4.05. 51 P
hue and cry, villain, go! 4.05. 90 P
you shall hear how things go, and, i warrant, to 4.05.122 P
time | to take her by the hand and bid her go, 4.06. 37
hand and bid her go, | she shall go with him. 4.06. 38
the maid hath given consent to go with him. 4.06. 45
both, my good host, to go along with me. 4.06. 47
go, i'll hold. 5.01. 1 P
away, go. 5.01. 3 P
i am in haste, go along with me, i'll tell you 5.01. 23 P
go before into the park; 5.03. 4 P
we two must go together. 5.03. 4 P
go you, and where you find a maid | that, ere 5.05. 49
good husband, let us every one go home, | and 5.05.241
for if our virtues | did not go forth of us, MM 1.01. 34
away! let's go learn the truth of it. 1.02. 81 P
away, sir, you must go. 1.02.141
go to lord angelo, | and let him learn to know, 1.04. 79
go to; 2.01. 58 P
go to, go to; no matter for the dish, sir. 2.01. 95 P
go to, go to; no matter for the dish, sir. 2.01. 95 P
some piece of money, and go through with all. 2.01.270 P
go to; 2.02. 12
stands in record, | and let go by the actor. 2.02. 41
go to your bosom, | knock there, and ask your 2.02.136
go to; 'tis well. away! 2.02.156
grace go with you, benedicite! 2.03. 39
ay, but to die, and go we know not where; 3.01.117
go to your knees, and make ready. 3.01.169 P
go you to angelo, answer his requiring with a 3.01.243 P
to stead up your appointment, go in your place. 3.01.251 P
go mend, go mend. 3.02. 27
go mend, go mend. 3.02. 27
him, he were as good go a mile on his errand. 3.02. 37 P
go say i sent thee thither. 3.02. 63 P
go to kennel, pompey, go. 3.02. 85 P
go to kennel, pompey, go. 3.02. 85 P
go, away with her to prison. 3.02.190 P
go to, no more words. 3.02.206 P
to know, | grace to stand, and virtue go; 3.02.264
come, let us go, | our corn's to reap, for yet 4.01. 74
go to, sir, you weigh equally; 4.02. 30 P
well, go, prepare yourself. 4.02. 69

attempt you, i will go further than i meant, to 4.02.190 P
go in to him, and fetch him out. 4.03. 34 P
you | look forward on the journey you shall go. 4.03. 58
in that good path that i would wish it go, | and 4.03.133
nay, tarry, i'll go along with thee. 4.03.165 P
my troth, i'll go with thee to the lane's end. 4.03.177 P
go call at flavio's house, | and tell him where 4.05. 6
woe, | as i, thus wrong'd, hence unbelieved go! 5.01.119
go, do it instantly. 5.01.253
i will go darkly to work with her. 5.01.278 P
go take her hence, and marry her instantly. 5.01.377
go with him, provost. 5.01.379
go fetch him hither, let me look upon him. 5.01.469
go bear it to the centaur, where we host, | and ERR 1.02. 9
word, | and go indeed, having so good a mean. 1.02. 18
town, | and then go to my inn and dine with me? 1.02. 23
i will go lose myself, | and wander up and down 1.02. 30
i'll to the centaur to go seek this slave; 1.02.104
and when they see time, | they'll go or come; 2.01. 9
go back again, thou slave, and fetch him home. 2.01. 75
go back again, and be new beaten home? 2.01. 76
dromio, go bid the servants spread for dinner. 2.02.187
so, | and in this mist at all adventures go. 2.02.216
go bid them let us in. 3.01. 30
go get thee from the door. 3.01. 35
your wife, sir knave! go get you from the door. 3.01. 64
went in pain, master, this knave would go sore. 3.01. 65
go fetch me something: i'll break ope the gate. 3.01. 73
well, i'll break in: go borrow me a crow. 3.01. 80
go, get thee gone, fetch me an iron crow. 3.01. 84
a man may go over shoes in the grime of it. 3.02.104 P
go hie thee presently, post to the road, | and 3.02.147
go home with it, and please your wife withal, 3.02.173
while i go to the goldsmith's house, go thou 4.01. 15
house, go thou | and buy a rope's end; 4.01. 15
here, go: 4.02. 29
go fetch it, sister. 4.02. 47
go, dromio, there's the money, bear it straight, 4.02. 63
will you go with me? 4.03. 59
avaunt, thou witch! come, dromio, let us go. 4.03. 79
driven out of doors with it when i go from home, 4.04. 36 P
come go along, my wife is coming yonder. 4.04. 40
masters, let him go: 4.04.111
go bind this man, for he is frantic too. 4.04.113
if i let him go, | the debt he owes will be 4.04.117
i will discharge thee ere i go from thee: 4.04.119
go bear him hence. 4.04.130
sister, go you with me. 4.04.130
come go: 5.01.114
go, some of you, knock at the abbey–gate, | and 5.01.165
then, | who parted with me to go fetch a chain, 5.01.221
officer | to go in person with me to my house. 5.01.234
go call the abbess hither. 5.01.281
the pains | to go with us into the abbey here, 5.01.395
error | have suffer'd wrong, go keep us company, 5.01.399
go to a gossips' feast, and go with me — 5.01.406
go to a gossips' feast, and go with me — 5.01.406
come go with us, we'll look to that anon. 5.01.413
and now let's go hand in hand, not one before 5.01.426
your hand, leonato, we will go together. ADO 1.01.160 P
what key shall a man take you to go in the song? 1.01.186 P
go to, i' faith, and thou wilt needs thrust thy 1.01.200 P
the fine is (for the which i may go the finer), 1.01.245 P
go you and tell her of it. 1.02. 23 P
friend, go you with me, and i will use your 1.02. 26 P
shall we go prove what's to be done? 1.03. 73 P
well then, go you into hell. 2.01. 42 P
go to, mum, you are he. 2.01.123 P
come, will you go with me? 2.01.185 P
it may be i go under that title because i am 2.01.205 P
sin upon purpose, because they would go thither; 2.01.259 P
i will go on the slightest arrand now to the 2.01.264 P
county claudio, when mean you to go to church? 2.01.355 P
claudio, the time shall not go dully by us. 2.01.364 P
go in with me, and i will tell you my drift. 2.01.386 P
go you to the prince your brother; 2.02. 22 P
go then, find me a meet hour to draw don pedro 2.02. 33 P
i will presently go learn their day of marriage. 2.02. 56 P
then sigh not so, but let them go, | and be you 2.03. 66
shall we go seek benedick, and tell him of her 2.03.199 P
i will go get her picture. 2.03.263 P
then go we near her, that her ear lose nothing 3.01. 32
rather i will go to benedick | and counsel him 3.01. 82
come go in, | i'll show thee some attires, and 3.01.101
be consummate, and then go i toward arragon. 3.02. 2 P
go but with me to–night, you shall see her 3.02.112 P
why then take no note of him, but let him go, 3.03. 29 P
let us go sit here upon the church–bench till 3.03. 89 P
let us obey you to go with us. 3.03.176 P
drink some wine ere you go; fare you well. 3.05. 53 P
go, good partner, go, get you to francis seacole 3.05. 57 P
good partner, go, get you to francis seacole, 3.05. 57 P
come, let us go. 4.01.111
nay, i pray you let me go. 4.01.294 P
in faith, i will go. 4.01.296 P
go comfort your cousin. 4.01.334 P
defend but god should go before such villains! 4.02. 20 P
and it will go near to be thought so shortly. 4.02. 22 P
i assure you, but i will go about with him. 4.02. 26 P
master constable, you go not the way to examine; 4.02. 33 P
i will go before and show him their examination. 4.02. 65 P
and one that knows the law, go to, and a rich 4.02. 83 P
and a rich fellow enough, go to, and a fellow 4.02. 84 P
if you go on thus, you will kill yourself, | and 5.01. 1
go anticly, and show outward hideousness, | and 5.01. 96
prince, let me go no farther to mine answer: 5.01.230 P
go, i discharge thee of thy prisoner, and i 5.01.319 P
and yet, ere i go, let me go with that i came, 5.02. 47 P
ere i go, let me go with that i came, which is, 5.02. 47 P
will you go hear this news, signior? 5.02.101 P
and moreover i will go with thee to thy uncle's. 5.02.103 P
songs of woe, | round about her tomb they go. 5.03. 15
other weeds, | and then to leonato's we will go. 5.03. 31
well, sit you out; go home, berowne; adieu. LLL 1.01.110
and go we, lords, to put in practice that 1.01.306
proud of employment, willingly i go. 2.01. 35
breast, | and go well satisfied to france again. 2.01.152
go, tenderness of years, take this key, give 3.01. 4 P
but i go. 3.01. 55 P
go. 3.01.169
but being watch'd that it may still go right! 3.01.193
her, to watch for her, | to pray for her, go to! 3.01.201
trip and go, my sweet, deliver this paper into 4.02.140 P
good costard, go with me. 4.02.144 P
this same shall go. 4.03. 57
i post from love; good lover, let me go. 4.03.186
the treason and you go in peace away together. 4.03.190
thou disputes like an infant; go whip thy gig. 5.01. 66 P
go to, thou hast it ad dunghill, at the fingers' 5.01. 77 P
that same berowne i'll torture ere i go. 5.02. 60
go, sickness as thou art! 5.02.280
go, you are allow'd; 5.02.478
go bid them prepare. 5.02.509 P
therefore as he is, an ass, let him go. 5.02.625
i go woolward for penance. 5.02.711 P
but go with speed | to some forlorn and naked 5.02.794
go, philostrate, | stir up the athenian youth to MND 1.01. 11
come, | and come, egeus, you shall go with me; 1.01.115
demetrius and egeus, go along; 1.01.123
/yours /would i catch, fair hermia, ere i go; 1.01.187
i will go tell him of fair hermia's flight; 1.01.246
i must go seek some dewdrops here, | and hang a 2.01. 14
and see our moonlight revels, go with us; 2.01.141
give me that boy, and i will go with thee. 2.01.143
well — go thy way. 2.01.146
let me go; 2.01.235
stay, on thy peril; i alone will go. 2.02. 87
out of this wood do not desire to go; 3.01.152
therefore go with me. 3.01.156
so, | that thou shalt like an aery spirit go. 3.01.161
where shall we go? 3.01.163
about the wood go swifter than the wind, | and 3.02. 94
i go, i go, look how i go, | swifter than arrow 3.02.100
i go, i go, look how i go, | swifter than arrow 3.02.100
i go, i go, look how i go, | swifter than arrow 3.02.100
why should he stay, whom love doth press to go? 3.02.184
you are a tame man, go! 3.02.259
and now, so you will let me quiet go, | to 3.02.314
let me go. 3.02.316
follow? nay; i'll go with thee, cheek by jowl. 3.02.338
nay, go not back. 3.02.340
now, go thy way. 3.02.428
briers, | i can no further crawl, no further go; 3.02.444
nought shall go ill; 3.02.462
go, one of you, find out the forester, | for now 4.01.103
uncouple in the western valley, let them go. 4.01.107
go, bid the huntsmen wake them with their horns. 4.01.138
an ass, if he go about /t' expound this dream. 4.01.207 P
away, go, away! 4.02. 45 P
go bring them in; 5.01. 84
and, being done, thus wall away doth go. 5.01.205
friend, would go near to make a man look sad. 5.01.289 P
should i go to church | and see the holy edifice MV 1.01. 29
therefore go forth, | try what my credit can in 1.01.179
go presently inquire, and so will i, | where 1.01.183
i hope i shall make shift to go without him. 1.02. 91 P
sirrah, go before. 1.02.132
go to then, you come to me, and you say, 1.03.115
go with me to a notary, seal me there | your 1.03.144
and i will go and purse the ducats straight, 1.03.174
go, father, with thy son. 2.02.152
go to, here's a simple line of life! 2.02.160 P
hie thee, go. 2.02.172
i must go with you to belmont. 2.02.178 P
i be misconst'red in the place i go to, | and 2.02.188
go, gentlemen, | will you prepare you for this 2.04. 21
come go with me, peruse this as thou goest. 2.04. 38
but wherefore should i go? 2.05. 12
but yet i'll go in hate, to feed upon | the 2.05. 14
i am right loath to go; 2.05. 16
i beseech you, sir, go. 2.05. 19 P
but i will go. 2.05. 38
go you before me, sirrah, | say i will come. 2.05. 38
i will go before, sir. 2.05. 40 P
well, jessica, go in. 2.05. 51
come about, | bassanio presently will go aboard. 2.06. 65
go, draw aside the curtains and discover | the 2.07. 1
draw the curtains, go. 2.07. 78
i pray thee let us go and find him out | and 2.08. 51
for who shall go about | to cozen fortune, and 2.09. 37
head i came to woo, | but i go away with two. 2.09. 76
and it shall go hard but i will better the 3.01. 72 P
go, tubal, fee me an officer; 3.01.125 P
go, tubal, and meet me at our synagogue; 3.01.129 P
go, good tubal, at our synagogue, tubal. 3.01.130 P
it so, | let fortune go to hell for it, not i. 3.02. 21
go, hercules! 3.02. 60
deny not, | it will go hard with poor antonio. 3.02.290
first go with me to church and call me wife, 3.02.303
since i have your good leave to go away, | i 3.02.324
therefore go. 3.03. 31
madam, i go with all convenient speed. 3.04. 56
go in, sirrah, bid them prepare for dinner. 3.05. 46 P
go to thy fellows, bid them cover the table, 3.05. 58 P
i will anon, first let us go to dinner. 3.05. 86
go one, and call the jew into the court. 4.01. 14
you may as well go stand upon the beach | and 4.01. 71
go give him courteous conduct to this place. 4.01.148
pay the bond thrice | and let the christian go. 4.01.319
give me my principal, and let me go. 4.01.336
i pray you give me leave to go from hence, | i 4.01.395
go, gratiano, run and overtake him; 4.01.452
but go we in, i pray thee, jessica, | and 5.01. 36
why should we go in? 5.01. 50
go in, nerissa. 5.01.118
him, | and suffer'd him to go displeas'd away — 5.01.213
let us go in, | and charge us there upon 5.01.297
or go to bed now, being two hours to day. 5.01.303
go apart, adam, and thou shalt hear how he will AYL 1.01. 27 P
let me go, i say. 1.01. 65 P
testament, with that i will go buy my fortunes. 1.01. 74 P
if ever he go alone again, i'll never wrastle 1.01.161 P
kindle the boy thither, which now i'll go about. 1.01.173 P
duke that the wrastling might not go forward. 1.02.182 P
eyes and gentle wishes go with me to my trial; 1.02.186 P
let us go thank him, and encourage him. 1.02.240
shall we go, coz? 1.02.248
will you go, coz? 1.02.255
o my poor rosalind, whither wilt thou go? 1.03. 90
whither to go, and what to bear with us, | and 1.03.101
say what thou canst, i'll go along with thee. 1.03.105
why, whither shall we go? 1.03.106
he'll go along o'er the wide world with me; 1.03.132
now go /we /in content | to liberty, and not to 1.03.137
come, shall we go and kill us venison? 2.01. 21
why, whither, adam, wouldst thou have me go? 2.03. 29
what, wouldst thou have me go and beg my food? 2.03. 31
let me go with you, | i'll do the service of a 2.03. 53
but come thy ways, we'll go along together. 2.03. 66
master, go on, and i will follow thee | to the 2.03. 69
i pray you bear with me, i cannot go no further. 2.04. 9 P
go with me; 2.04. 97
i'll go sleep, if i can; 2.05. 60 P
and i'll go seek the duke, his banket is 2.05. 62 P
dear master, i can go no further. 2.06. 1 P
go seek him, tell him i would speak with him. 2.07. 7
a doe, i go to find my fawn | and give it food. 2.07.128
go find him out, | and we will nothing waste 2.07.133
of your fortune, | go to my cave and tell me. 2.07.197
shepherd, go off a little. 3.02.158 P
go with him, sirrah. 3.02.159 P
for though he go as softly as foot can fall, he 3.02.328 P
go with me to it and i'll show it you; 3.02.430 P
will you go? 3.02.432 P
come, sister, will you go? 3.02.435 P
tree, or shall we go with you to your chapel? 3.03. 66 P
go thou with me, and let me counsel thee. 3.03. 95 P
of as good as he, so he laugh'd and let me go. 3.04. 38 P
go hence a little, and i shall conduct you, | if 3.04. 55
you | than without candle may go dark to bed — 3.05. 39
will you go, sister? 3.05. 76
go with me, silvius. 3.05.139
go to! 4.01.130 P
ay, go your ways, go your ways; 4.01.182 P
ay, go your ways, go your ways; 4.01.182 P
i'll go find a shadow, and sigh till he come. 4.01.216 P
well, go your way to her (for i see love hath 4.03. 69 P
good sir, go with us. 4.03.178 P
will you go? 4.03.182 P
go you and prepare aliena; 5.02. 15 P
and from hence i go | to make these doubts all 5.04. 24
i durst go no further than the lie 5.04. 85 P
go by, saint jeronimy! SHR in.1. 9 P
go to thy cold bed, and warm thee. in.1. 9 P
i must go fetch the /thirdborough. in.1. 11 P
sirrah, go see what trumpet 'tis that sounds. in.1. 74
go, sirrah, take them to the buttery, | and give in.1. 102
sirrah, go you to barthol'mew my page, | and see in.1. 105
go in, bianca. 1.01. 91
why, and i trust i may go too, may i not? 1.01.102
you may go to the devil's dam; 1.01.105 P
go forward, this contents; 1.01.163
tranio, let's go. 1.01.245
pray you, sir, let him go while the humor lasts. 1.02.107 P
tarry, petruchio, i must go with thee, | for in 1.02.117
than perfume itself | to whom they go to. 1.02.153
sir, a word ere you go. 1.02.227
sir, sir, the first's for me! let her go by. 1.02.254
go ply thy needle, meddle not with her. 2.01. 25
talk not to me, i will go sit and weep, | till i 2.01. 35
you are too blunt, go to it orderly. 2.01. 45
you shall go see your pupils presently. 2.01.107
we will go walk a little in the orchard, | and 2.01.111
well, go with me and be not so discomfited. 2.01.163
signior petruchio, will you go with us, | or 2.01.166
i chafe you if i tarry. let me go. 2.01.241
go, fool, and whom thou keep'st command. 2.01.257
you may go walk, and give me leave a while; 3.01. 59
go, girl, i cannot blame thee now to weep, | for 3.02. 27
go to my chamber, put on clothes of mine. 3.02.113
to put on better ere he go to church. 3.02.126
you would entreat me rather go than stay. 3.02.192
do what thou canst, i will not go to–day, | no, 3.02.208
they shall go forward, kate, at thy command. 3.02.222
go to the feast, revel and domineer, | carouse 3.02.224
be mad and merry, or go hang yourselves; 3.02.226
nay, let them go, a couple of quiet ones. 3.02.240
she shall, lucentio. come, gentlemen, let's go. 3.02.252
go, rascals, go, and fetch my supper in. 4.01.139
go, rascals, go, and fetch my supper in. 4.01.139
then go with me to make the matter good. 4.02.115
go with me to clothe you as becomes you. 4.02.121
i prithee go, and get me some repast; 4.03. 15
go get thee gone, thou false deluding slave, 4.03. 31
go get thee gone, i say. 4.03. 35
go hop me over every kennel home, | for you 4.03. 98
go take it up unto thy master's use. 4.03.157
go take it hence, be gone, and say no more. 4.03.165
go call my men, and let us straight to him, 4.03.184
it shall be seven ere i go to horse. 4.03.191
i will not go to–day, and ere i do, | it shall 4.03.194
hath appointed me to go to saint luke's to bid 4.04.102 P
hap what hap may, i'll roundly go about her; 4.04.107
it shall go hard if cambio go without her. 4.04.108
it shall go hard if cambio go without her. 4.04.108
go on, and fetch our horses back again. 4.05. 9
say as he says, or we shall never go. 4.05. 11
petruchio, go thy ways, the field is won. 4.05. 23
come go along and see the truth hereof, | for 4.05. 75
you shall not choose but drink before you go. 5.01. 11
stay, officer, he shall not go to prison. 5.01. 95 P
i say he shall go to prison. 5.01. 96 P
fear not, baptista, we will content you, go to; 5.01.135 P
go, biondello, bid your mistress come to me. 5.02. 76
i go. 5.02. 77
go and entreat my wife | to come to me forthwith 5.02. 86
sirrah grumio, go to your mistress, | say i 5.02. 95
go fetch them hither. 5.02.103
well, go thy ways, old lad, for thou shalt ha't. 5.02.181
now go thy ways, thou hast tam'd a curst shrow. 5.02.188
qualities, there commendations go with pity: AWW 1.01. 43 P
go to, no more, lest it be rather thought you 1.01. 52 P
you go so much backward when you fight. 1.01.200 P
your ladyship's good will to go to the world, 1.03. 18 P

and he must needs go that the devil drives.		1.03. 29 P
go not about;		1.03.188
an intent — speak truly — | to go to paris?		1.03.219
go call before me all the lords in court.		2.03. 46
the property by what /it is should go, | not by		2.03.130
let the rest go.		2.03.148
go to, sir, you were beaten in italy for picking		2.03.258 P
go with me to my chamber, and advise me.		2.03.294
go.		2.03.299
go to, thou art a witty fool, i have found thee.		2.04. 32 P
madam, my lord will go away to–night, | a very		2.04. 39
let that go.		2.05. 76
go thou toward home, where i will never come		2.05. 90
then go thou forth, | and fortune play upon thy		3.03. 6
of lust, are not the things they go under.		3.05. 20 P
a pox on't, let it go, 'tis but a drum.		3.06. 46 P
be magnanimious in the enterprise and go on;		3.06. 67 P
i must go look my twigs. he shall be caught.		3.06.107
your brother he shall go along with me.		3.06.108
will you go see her?		3.06.117
three hours 'twill be time enough to go home.		4.01. 25 P
go tell the count rossillion, and my brother,		4.01. 89
death and honesty | go with your impositions, i		4.04. 29
go thy ways, i begin to be a–weary of thee, and		4.05. 56 P
go thy ways, let my horses be well look'd to,		4.05. 58 P
let us go see your son, i pray you.		4.05.102 P
go, go, provide.		5.01. 38
go, go, provide.		5.01. 38
go to, follow.		5.02. 54 P
go speedily and bring again the count.		5.03.152
i did go between them, as i said, but more than		5.03.258 P
will you go hunt, my lord?	TN	1.01. 16
marry, now i let go your hand, i am barren.		1.03. 79 P
why dost thou not go to church in a galliard and		1.03.128 P
well, go thy way, if sir toby would leave		1.05. 26 P
go to, y' are a dry fool;		1.05. 41 P
go you, malvolio;		1.05.107 P
go thou and seek the crowner, and let him sit o'		1.05.134 P
go look after him.		1.05.136 P
nor will you not that i go with you?		2.01. 2 P
the gentleness of all the gods go with thee!		2.01. 44
that danger shall seem sport, and i will go.		2.01. 48
to be up after midnight and to go to bed then,		2.03. 7 P
so that to go to bed after midnight is to go to		2.03. 8 P
to bed after midnight is to go to bed betimes.		2.03. 9 P
"shall i bid him go?"		2.03.109
"shall i bid him go, and spare not?"		2.03.111
go, sir, rub your chain with crumbs.		2.03.119 P
go shake your ears.		2.03.125 P
come, i'll go burn some sack, 'tis too late to		2.03.190 P
burn some sack, 'tis too late to go to bed now.		2.03.191 P
go to, thou art made if thou desir'st to be so;		2.05.155 P
i mean, to go, sir, to enter.		3.01. 81 P
go, write it in a martial hand, be curst and		3.02. 42 P
go about it.		3.02. 48 P
we'll call thee at the cubiculo. go.		3.02. 52 P
shall we go see the reliques of this town?		3.03. 19
to–morrow, sir. best first go see your lodging.		3.03. 20
go call him hither.		3.04. 14
wilt thou go to bed, malvolio?		3.04. 29 P
"go to, thou art made, if thou desir'st to be		3.04. 52 P
go off, i discard you.		3.04. 89 P
go off.		3.04. 90 P
go to, go to;		3.04. 95 P
go to, go to;		3.04. 95 P
go hang yourselves all!		3.04.123 P
go, sir andrew, scout me for him at the corner		3.04.176 P
i am one that had rather go with sir priest than		3.04.271 P
come, sir, i pray you go.		3.04.358
go to, go to, thou art a foolish fellow, | let		4.01. 3
go to, go to, thou art a foolish fellow, | let		4.01. 3
i'll go another way to work with him;		4.01. 33 P
let go thy hand.		4.01. 37
come, sir, i will not let you go.		4.01. 38 P
go with me to my house, | and hear thou there		4.01. 54
thou shalt not choose but go;		4.01. 57
topas, sir topas, good sir topas, go to my lady.		4.02. 23 P
now go with me and with this holy man | into the		4.03. 23
i'll follow this good man, and go with you,		4.03. 32
i go, sir, but i would not have you to think		5.01. 46 P
we should, for perpetuity, | go hence in debt.	WT	1.02. 6
you" many thousands moe | that go before it.		1.02. 9
but let him say so then, and let him go;		1.02. 35
verily, | you shall not go;		1.02. 50
will you go yet?		1.02. 51
yet go on, | th' offenses we have made you do		1.02. 82
go to, go to!		1.02.182
go to, go to!		1.02.182
go play, boy, play.		1.02.187
go play, boy, play.		1.02.190
go play, mamillius, thou'rt an honest man.		1.02.211
make that thy question, and go rot!		1.02.324
my lord, | go then;		1.02.343
this action i now go on | is for my better grace		2.01.121
go, do our bidding; hence!		2.01.125
i'll go in couples with her;		2.01.135
go, | see how he fares.		2.03. 17
go, take it to the fire, | for thou set'st on		2.03.141
go;		3.01. 21
if word nor oath | prevail not, go and see.		3.02.204
go on, go on;		3.02.214
go on, go on;		3.02.214
go get aboard;		3.03. 7
best haste, and go not | too far i' th' land;		3.03. 10
go thou away, | i'll follow instantly.		3.03. 13
let my sheep go.		3.03.126 P
go you the next way with your findings;		3.03.128 P
i'll go see if the bear be gone from the		3.03.129 P
but shall i go mourn for that, my dear?		4.03. 15
here and there, | i then do most go right.		4.03. 18
fellow, sir, that i have known to go about with		4.03. 86 P
i must go buy spices for our sheep–shearing.		4.03.116 P
ay, good brother, or go about to think.		4.04.217 P
for i must go | where it fits not you to know.		4.04.297
me too; let me go thither.		4.04.302
you have let him go, | and nothing marted with		4.04.351
have you thought on | a place whereto you'll go?		4.04.537
go to then.		4.04.692 P
this being done, let the law go whistle;		4.04.698 P
to go about to make me the king's brother–in–law		4.04.701 P
toward the sea–side, go on the right hand, i		4.04.825 P
go, cleomines;		5.01.112
upon which errand | i now go toward him;		5.01.232
which lets go by some sixteen years, and makes		5.03. 31
go together, | you precious winners all;		5.03.130
or else it must go wrong with you and me;	JN	1.01. 41
nay, i would have you go before me thither.		1.01.155
go, faulconbridge, now hast thou thy desire, | a		1.01.176
do, child, go to it grandame, child, | give		2.01.160
if lusty love should go in quest of beauty,		2.01.426
if zealous love should go in search of virtue,		2.01.428
go we, as well as haste will suffer us, | to		2.01.559
madam, | i may not go without you to the kings.		3.01. 66
thou mayst, thou shalt, i will not go with thee.		3.01. 67
a curse, | let go the hand of that arch–heretic,		3.01.192
do not let go thy hand.		3.01.195
knee i beg, go not to arms | against mine uncle.		3.01.308
which is the side that i must go withal?		3.01.327
cousin, go draw our puissance together.		3.01.339
i had a thing to say, but let it go.		3.03. 33
my blessing go with thee!		3.03. 71
for england, cousin, go.		3.03. 71
courage and comfort! all shall yet go well.		3.04. 4
what can go well, when we have run so ill?		3.04. 5
i prithee, lady, go away with me.		3.04. 20
o noble dolphin, | go with me to the king.		3.04.178
for england go;		3.04.181
let us go;		3.04.182
go stand within; let me alone with him.		4.01. 84
is this your promise? go to, hold your tongue.		4.01. 96
go closely in with me;		4.01.132
the color of the king doth come and go | between		4.02. 76
stay yet, lord salisbury, i'll go with thee,		4.02. 96
go | and thrust thyself into their companies;		4.02.166
go after him;		4.02.178
as good to die and go, as die and stay.		4.03. 8
go, bear him in thine arms.		4.03.139
now keep your holy word, go meet the french,		5.01. 5
go i to make the french lay down their arms.		5.01. 24
and send him word by me which way you go.		5.03. 7
whither dost thou go?		5.06. 3
as much good stay with thee as go with me!	R2	1.02. 57
though this be all, do not so quickly go;		1.02. 64
gentle and as jocund as to jest | go i to fight:		1.03. 96
go bear this lance to thomas duke of norfolk.		1.03.103
since thou hast far to go, bear not along | the		1.03.199
six years we banish him, and he shall go.		1.03.248
go, say i sent thee forth to purchase honor,		1.03.282
he is gone, and with him go these thoughts.		1.04. 37
come, gentlemen, let's all go visit him.		1.04. 63
go, bushy, to the earl of wiltshire straight,		2.01.215
so, | stay, and be secret, and myself will go.		2.01.298
he was — why, so go all which way it will!		2.02. 87
go, fellow, get thee home, provide some carts,		2.02.106
gentlemen, will you go muster men?		2.02.108
gentlemen, go muster up your men, | and meet me		2.02.118
the wind sits fair for news to go for ireland,		2.02.123
will you go along with us?		2.02.140
but we must win your grace to go with us | to		2.03.163
it may be i will go with you, but yet i'll pause		2.03.168
go to flint castle, there i'll pine away — | a		3.02.209
and let them go | to ear the land that hath some		3.02.211
go to the rude ribs of that ancient castle;		3.03. 32
go signify as much, while here we march | upon		3.03. 49
a' god's name let it go.		3.03.146
go bind thou up young dangling apricocks,		3.04. 29
go thou, and like an executioner | cut off the		3.04. 33
i will go root away | the noisome weeds which		3.04. 37
come, ladies, go | to;		3.04. 96
peace shall go sleep with turks and infidels,		4.01.139
then whither he goes, thither let me go.		5.01. 85
go count thy way with sighs, i mine with groans.		5.01. 89
come, let's go.		5.04. 10
go thou and fill another room in hell.		5.05.107
with cain go wander thorough shades of night,		5.06. 43
old, | and bootless 'tis to tell you we will go;	1H4	1.01. 29
we that take purses go by the moon and the seven		1.02. 14 P
if you will go, i will stuff your purses full of		1.02.131 P
if i tarry at home and go not, i'll hang you for		1.02.134 P
reasons for this adventure that he shall go.		1.02.151 P
well, i'll go with thee.		1.02.191 P
no further go in this | than i by letters shall		1.03.292
time enough to go to bed with a candle, i		2.01. 43 P
go to, homo is a common name to all men.		2.01. 95 P
up to the top of the hill, i'll go seek him.		2.02. 9 P
and i rob the thieves and go merrily to london,		2.02. 94 P
o, i could divide myself and go to buffets, for		2.03. 32 P
you | to line his enterprise, but if you go —		2.03. 83
have you henceforth question me | whither i go,		2.03.104
kate, | whither i go, thither shall you go too;		2.03.115
kate, | whither i go, thither shall you go too;		2.03.115
go thy ways, old jack, die when thou wilt;		2.04.127 P
go hide thee behind the arras, the rest walk up		2.04.500 P
go call him forth.		2.04.527 P
and "well, go to," | but mark'd him not a word.		3.01.156
go, ye giddy goose.		3.01.228 P
as slow | as hot lord percy is on fire to go.		3.01.264
go to, you are a woman, go.		3.03. 61 P
go to, you are a woman, go.		3.03. 61 P
go to, i know you well enough.		3.03. 64 P
go, you thing, go.		3.03.115 P
go, you thing, go.		3.03.115 P
go make ready breakfast;		3.03.170 P
go bear this letter to lord john of lancaster,		3.03.195
go, peto, to horse, to horse, for thou and i		3.03.197
should go so general current through the world.		4.01. 5
go to the king, and let there be impawn'd | some		4.03.108
i must go write again | to other friends, and so		4.04. 40
lord douglas, go you and tell him so.		5.02. 32
/a fool go with thy soul, whither it goes!		5.03. 22
lord john of lancaster, go you with him.		5.04. 3
go to the douglas, and deliver him | up to his		5.05. 27
go in with me, and counsel every man | the	2H4	1.01.212
go pluck him by the elbow, i must speak with him		1.02. 69 P
and yet in some respects i grant i cannot go.		1.02.168 P
go bear this letter to my lord of lancaster,		1.02.238 P
shall we go draw our numbers and set on?		1.03.109
go wash thy face, and draw the action.		2.01.149 P
go with her, with her, hook on, hook on.		2.01.161 P
come, go along with me, good master gower.		2.01.179
are to take soldiers up in counties as you go.		2.01.187 P
go to, i stand the push of your one thing that		2.02. 37 P
go.		2.02.165 P
o yet, for god's sake, go not to these wars!		2.03. 9
but i must go and meet with danger there, | or		2.03. 48
come, come, go in with me.		2.03. 62
fain would i go to meet the archbishop, | but		2.03. 65
more, pistol, i would not have you go off here.		2.04.136 P
pray thee go down, good ancient.		2.04.151 P
pray thee go down.		2.04.155 P
asia, | which cannot go but thirty mile a day,		2.04.165
sent away post, i will see you again ere i go.		2.04.378 P
go call the earls of surrey and of warwick;		3.01. 1
please it your grace | to go to bed.		3.01. 99
me, there are other men fitter to go out than i.		3.02.115 P
go to, peace, mouldy, you shall go.		3.02.116 P
go to, peace, mouldy, you shall go.		3.02.116 P
thou mightst mend him and make him fit to go.		3.02.165 P
come, thou shalt go to the wars in a gown.		3.02.184 P
and so i pray you go in with me to dinner.		3.02.190 P
come, i will go drink with you, but i cannot		3.02.191 P
i had as live be hang'd, sir, as go, and yet,		3.02.223 P
go to, stand aside.		3.02.228 P
go to, stand aside.		3.02.233 P
's prince, and let it go which way it will, he		3.02.237 P
go to, well.		3.02.245 P
so — very well, go to, very good, exceeding		3.02.274 P
and away again would 'a go, and again would 'a		3.02.285 P
go to, i have spoke at a word. god keep you!		3.02.297 P
return, and't shall go hard but i'll make him a		3.02.329 P
go, captain, and deliver to the army | this news		4.02. 69
go, my lord, | and let our army be discharged		4.02. 91
go, good lord hastings, | and, ere they be		4.02. 95
will not go off until they hear you speak.		4.02.100
our news shall go before us to his majesty,		4.03. 78
you give me leave to go through gloucestershire,		4.03. 81 P
let them go.		4.03.128 P
will't please your grace to go along with us?		4.05. 19
go seek him out.		4.05. 59
go to, i say, he shall have no wrong.		5.01. 52 P
that the great body of our state may go | in		5.02.136
rascal, and the child i go with do miscarry,		5.04. 9 P
come, i charge you both go with me, for the man		5.04. 16 P
fear no colors, go with me to dinner.		5.05. 88 P
go carry sir john falstaff to the fleet.		5.05. 91
then go we in, to know his embassy;	H5	1.01. 95
go, my dread lord, to your great–grandsire's		1.02.103
no, to the spittle go, | and from the		2.01. 74
go to.		2.01. 80
go, clear thy crystals.		2.03. 54
'tis meet we all go forth | to view the sick and		2.04. 21
go, and bring them.		2.04. 67
"knocks go and come;		3.02. 8
ay, or go to death;		3.02.116 P
come, uncle exeter, | go you and enter harflew;		3.03. 52
go down upon him, you have power enough, | and		3.05. 53
let gallows gape for dog, let man go free, | and		3.06. 42
therefore go speak, the duke will hear thy voice		3.06. 46
go therefore tell thy master here i am;		3.06.153
go bid thy master well advise himself.		3.06.159
who will go to hazard with me for twenty		3.07. 85 P
you must first go yourself to hazard, ere you		3.07. 87 P
'tis midnight, i'll go arm myself.		3.07. 89 P
go with my brothers to my lords of england.		4.01. 30
you may as well go about to turn the sun to ice		4.01.199 P
thinks thou the fiery fever will go out | with		4.01.253
i know thy errand, i will go with thee.		4.01.308
shall we go send them dinners and fresh suits,		4.02. 57
good salisbury, and good luck go with thee!		4.03. 11
and crispin crispian shall ne'er go by, | from		4.03. 57
let him go hence, and with his cap in hand		4.05. 13
let us on heaps go offer up our lives.		4.05. 18
go and tell them so.		4.07. 65
our heralds go with him;		4.07.116
pray thee go seek him, and bring him to my tent.		4.07.167 P
go you with me, uncle of exeter.		4.07.183
come, go /we in procession to the village;		4.08.113
go forth and fetch their conqu'ring caesar in;		5.pr. 28
go, go, you are a counterfeit cowardly knave.		5.01. 69 P
go, go, you are a counterfeit cowardly knave.		5.01. 69 P
go, uncle exeter, | and brother clarence, and		5.02. 83
warwick, and huntington, go with the king, | and		5.02. 85
go with the princes, or stay here with us?		5.02. 91
our gracious brother, i will go with them.		5.02. 92
that shall go to constantinople and take the		5.02.208 P
take my leave, | to go about my preparation.	1H6	1.01.166
me, | when he sees me go back one foot or fly.		1.02. 21
go call her in.		1.02. 60
i must go victual orleance forthwith.		1.05. 14
go, go, cheer up thy hungry–starved men;		1.05. 16
go, go, cheer up thy hungry–starved men;		1.05. 16
what means he now? go ask him whither he goes.		2.03. 28
belief, | i go to certify her talbot's here.		2.03. 32
go forward, and be chok'd with thy ambition!		2.04.112
enter, go in, the market bell is rung.		3.02. 16
but ere we go, regard this dying prince, | the		3.02. 86
but yet before we go, let's not forget | the		3.02.131
i go, my lord, in heart desiring still | you may		4.01. 76
go cheerfully together and digest | your angry		4.01.167
go to the gates of burdeaux, trumpeter, | summon		4.02. 1
come go, i will dispatch the horsemen straight;		4.04. 40
upon my blessing i command thee go.		4.05. 36
stay, go, do what you will, the like do i;		4.05. 50
go take their bodies hence.		4.07. 91
go, and be free again, as suffolk's friend.		5.03. 59
well, go to, we'll have no bastards live,		5.04. 70
i go. come, nell, thou wilt ride with us?	2H6	1.02. 59
i cannot go before | while gloucester bears this		1.02. 61
you shall go near | to call them both a pair of		1.02.102
suffolk, let them go.		1.03. 40
and so i pray you go in god's name, and leave us		1.04. 9 P
sirrah, go fetch the beadle hither straight.		2.01.137
you go about to torture me in vain.		2.01.143
i beseech your majesty give me leave to go;		2.03. 20

ere thou go, | give up thy staff. 2.03. 22
and go in peace, humphrey, no less belov'd 2.03. 26
lords, let him go. 2.03. 47
go, take hence that traitor from our sight, 2.03.100
all comfort go with thee, | for none abides with 2.04. 87
stanley, i prithee go, and take me hence, | i 2.04. 91
come, stanley, shall we go? 2.04.104
and go we to attire you for our journey. 2.04.106
go, lead the way, i long to see my prison. 2.04.110
go, get you to my house, | i will reward you for 3.02. 8
go call our uncle to our presence straight. 3.02. 15
run, go, help, help! o henry, ope thine eyes! 3.02. 35
yet do not go away. 3.02. 52
fain would i go to chafe his paly lips | with 3.02.141
if from this presence thou dar'st go with me. 3.02.228
go, salisbury, and tell them all from me, | i 3.02.279
come, warwick, come, good warwick, go with me, 3.02.298
mischance and sorrow go along with you! 3.02.300
go, speak not to me; 3.02.352
o, go not yet! 3.02.353
go tell this heavy message to the king. 3.02.379
i go. 3.02.408
i go of message from the queen to france; 4.01.114
therefore come you with us and let him go. 4.01.141
nobility think scorn to go in leather aprons. 4.02. 12 P
and in cheapside shall my palfrey go to grass; 4.02. 69 P
'twill go hard with you. 4.02.101 P
and inclin'd to blood, | if you go forward; 4.02.127
go to, sirrah, tell the king from me, that, for 4.02.156 P
is england main'd, and fain to go with a staff, 4.02.163 P
go to then, i ask but this: 4.02.170 P
spare none but such as go in clouted shoon, 4.02.185
come, then, let's go fight with them. 4.06. 13 P
but first go and set london bridge on fire, and, 4.06. 14 P
now go some and pull down the savoy; 4.07. 1 P
when honester men than thou go in their hose and 4.07. 50 P
go, take him away, i say, and strike off his 4.07.109 P
lord, when shall we go to cheapside and take up 4.07.126 P
that will forsake thee and go home in peace. 4.08. 10
that thus you do exclaim you'll go with him? 4.08. 35
go some, and follow him, | and he that brings 4.08. 65
i pray thee, buckingham, go and meet him, | and 4.09. 36
we twain will go into his highness' tent. 5.01. 55
go bid her hide him quickly from the duke. 5.01. 84
i know, ere they will have me go to ward, 5.01.112
wilt thou go dig a grave to find out war, | and 5.01.169
you were best to go to bed and dream again, | to 5.01.196
let us pursue him ere the writs go forth. 5.03. 26
nay, go not from me, i will follow thee. 3H6 1.01.213
brother, i go; 1.02. 60
keep thou the napkin and go boast of this, | and 1.04.159
shall we go throw away our coats of steel, | and 2.01.160
go rate thy minions, proud insulting boy! 2.02. 84
for from my heart thine image ne'er shall go; 2.05.116
but love to go | whither the queen intends. 2.05.138
and you must be contented | to go along with us; 3.01. 68
go where you will, the king shall be commanded; 3.01. 92
the king's, | to go with us unto the officers. 3.01. 98
and go we, brothers, to the man that took him, 3.02.121
widow, go you along. 3.02.123
if that go forward, henry's hope is done. 3.03. 58
seest what's pass'd, go fear thy king withal. 3.03.226
yet, ere thou go, but answer me one doubt: 3.03.238
and leave your brothers to go speed elsewhere. 4.01. 58
go to, we pardon thee; 4.01. 89
"go tell false edward, the supposed king, | that 4.01. 93
you in our behalf | go levy men, and make 4.01.131
but, ere i go, hastings and montague, | resolve 4.01.134
let them go, here is | the duke. 4.03. 29
huntsman, what say'st thou? wilt thou go along? 4.05. 25
go, trumpet, to the walls, and sound a parle. 5.01. 16
be augmented | in every county as we go along. 5.03. 23
man, | he should have leave to go away betimes, 5.04. 45
will not fight for such a hope | go home to bed, 5.04. 56
go bear them hence, i will not hear them speak. 5.05. 4
away with her, go bear her hence perforce. 5.05. 68
go tread the path that thou shalt ne'er return: R3 1.01.117
go you before, and i will follow you. 1.01.144
tressel and berkeley, go along with me. 1.02.221
marr'd, | that will i make before i let thee go. 1.03.165
catesby, i come. lords, will you go with me? 1.03.321
we go to use our hands, and not our tongues. 1.03.351
go, go, dispatch. 1.03.354
go, go, dispatch. 1.03.354
'tis no matter, let it go. 1.04.131 P
if you are hir'd for meed, go back again, | and 1.04.228
go you to him from me. 1.04.234
go, coward as thou art. 1.04.279
i'll go hide the body in some hole | till that 1.04.280
did, | and yet go current from suspicion! 2.01. 95
will you go | to comfort edward with our company 2.01.139
and go we to determine | who they shall be that 2.02.141
will you go | to give your censures in this 2.02.143
i, as a child, will go by thy direction. 2.02.153
a parlous boy! go to, you are too shrewd. 2.04. 35
stay, i will go with you. 2.04. 67
my gracious lady, go, | and thither bear your 2.04. 68
go, i'll conduct you to the sanctuary. 2.04. 73
if she deny, lord hastings, go with him, | and 3.01. 35
come on, lord hastings, will you go with me? 3.01. 58
i go, my lord. 3.01. 59
what, will you go unto the tower, my lord? 3.01.140
heart, | thinking on them, go i unto the tower. 3.01.150
go, gentle catesby, | and, as it were far off, 3.01.169
good catesby, go effect this business soundly. 3.01.186
go, fellow, go, return unto thy lord, | bid him 3.02. 19
go, fellow, go, return unto thy lord, | bid him 3.02. 19
go, bid thy master rise and come to me, | and we 3.02. 31
i'll go, my lord, and tell him what you say. 3.02. 34
fear you the boar, and go so unprovided? 3.02. 73
go on before, i'll talk with this good fellow. 3.02. 95
what, go you toward the tower? 3.02.118
come, will you go? 3.02.123
withdraw yourself a while, i'll go with you. 3.04. 41
go after, after, cousin buckingham. 3.05. 72
i go, and towards three or four a' clock | look 3.05.101
go, lovel, with all speed to doctor shaw; 3.05.103
go thou to friar /penker; 3.05.104
now will i go to take some privy order | to draw 3.05.106
i go; 3.07. 52
go, go up to the leads, the lord mayor knocks. 3.07. 55
go, go up to the leads, the lord mayor knocks. 3.07. 55
if thou wilt outstrip death, go cross the seas, 4.01. 41
go hie thee, hie thee from this slaughter–house, 4.01. 43
and i with all unwillingness will go. 4.01. 57
go, go, poor soul, i envy not thy glory, | to 4.01. 63
go, go, poor soul, i envy not thy glory, | to 4.01. 63
go thou to richmond, and good fortune guide thee 4.01. 91
go thou to richard, and good angels tend thee! 4.01. 92
go thou to sanctuary, and good thoughts possess 4.01. 93
go call him hither, boy. 4.02. 41
go, by this token. 4.02. 79
crown, | to her go i, a jolly thriving wooer. 4.03. 43
go muster men. 4.03. 56
go with me, | and in the breath of bitter words 4.04.132
go then, my mother, to thy daughter go, | make 4.04.325
go then, my mother, to thy daughter go, | make 4.04.325
shall i go win my daughter to thy will? 4.04.426
i go. 4.04.428
i go. 4.04.452
why, what wouldst thou do there before i go? 4.04.454
go then, and muster men; 4.04.494
i go, my lord. 5.03. 55
come, go with me, | under our tents i'll play 5.03.220
go, gentlemen, every man unto his charge. 5.03.307
o, you go far. H8 1.01. 38
your choler question | what 'tis you go about: 1.01.131
you, and i'll go along | by your prescription; 1.01.150
the rough brake | that virtue must go through. 1.02. 76
let him on. | go forward. 1.02.177
good lord chamberlain, | go, give 'em welcome: 1.04. 57
let it go round. 1.04. 97
hear what i say, and then go home and lose me. 2.01. 57
dying, | go with me like good angels to my end, 2.01. 75
go to; 2.02. 71
we are busy; go. 2.02. 80
go thy ways, kate. 2.04.134
therefore go on, | for no dislike i' th' world 2.04.223
let his grace go forward, | and dare us with his 3.02.281
go get thee from me, cromwell! 3.02.412
that had not half a week to go, like rams | in 4.01. 77
gentlemen, ye shall go my way, which | is to th' 4.01.114
meditating | on that celestial harmony i go to. 4.02. 80
go to, kneel. 4.02.103
i must to him too, | before he go to bed. 5.01. 9
go to, go to! 5.01.138
go to, go to! 5.01.138
course of my authority | might go one way, and 5.02. 71
for me? | must i go like a traitor thither? 5.02.131
go break among the press, and find a way out 5.03. 84
not somewhat darker than helen's — well, go to! TRO 1.01. 42 P
come go we then together. 1.01.116
and whither go they? 1.02. 2
why, go to then. 1.02.127 P
go thy way, hector! 1.02.200 P
go thy way, troilus, go thy way! 1.02.235 P
go thy way, troilus, go thy way! 1.02.236 P
yourself shall feast with us before you go, 1.03.308
yet go we under our opinion still | that we have 1.03.382
go we to him straight. 1.03.388
i bade the vile owl go learn me the tenor of the 2.01. 90 P
well, go to, go to. 2.01. 93 P
well, go to, go to. 2.01. 93 P
o, meaning you? i will go learn more of it. 2.01.130
let helen go; 2.02. 17
as you must needs, for you all cried "go, go" — 2.02. 85
as you must needs, for you all cried "go, go" — 2.02. 85
troy burns, or else let helen go. 2.02.112
go and tell him | we come to speak with him, and 2.03.121
go tell him this, and add, | that if he overhold 2.03.132
"bring action hither, this cannot go to war." 2.03.136
let ajax go to him. 2.03.178
dear lord, go you and greet him in his tent. 2.03.179
that ajax makes | when they go from achilles. 2.03.184
this lord go to him! 2.03.198
and say in thunder, "achilles go to him." 2.03.199
if i go to him, with my armed fist | i'll /pash 2.03.202
o no, you shall not go. 2.03.204
let me go to him. 2.03.206
go we to council. 2.03.265
go to, sweet queen, go to — commends himself 3.01. 66 P
to, sweet queen, go to — commends himself most 3.01. 66 P
go to, go to. 3.02. 53 P
go to, go to. 3.02. 53 P
come in, come in, i'll go get a fire. 3.02. 59 P
our head shall go bare till merit /crown /it. 3.02. 92 P
let me go and try. 3.02.147
go to, a bargain made, seal it, seal it, i'll be 3.02.197 P
go call thersites hither, sweet patroclus. 3.03.234
aleven of the clock it will go one way or other. 3.03.296 P
how now, how now, how go maidenheads? 4.02. 23 P
go hang yourself, you naughty mocking uncle! 4.02. 25
good uncle, go and see. 4.02. 35
you know of him, but yet go fetch him hither, go 4.02. 57 P
know of him, but yet go fetch him hither, go. 4.02. 57 P
i will go meet them; 4.02. 70
the young prince will go mad. 4.02. 75 P
o you immortal gods! i will not go. 4.02. 94
i'll go in and weep. 4.02.105
i will not go from troy. 4.02.109
and is it true that i must go from troy? 4.04. 30
go, gentle knight, | stand by our ajax. 4.05. 88
i will go eat with thee and see your knights. 4.05.158
first, all you peers of greece, go to my tent; 4.05.271
fall greeks, fail fame, honor or go or stay, 5.01. 43
we go wrong, we go wrong. 5.01. 67
we go wrong, we go wrong. 5.01. 67
both /at /once, to those | that go or tarry. 5.01. 78
i beseech you go. 5.02. 39
now, good my lord, go off; 5.02. 40
will you go? 5.02. 50
you shall not go. 5.02.100
by all the everlasting gods, i'll go! 5.03. 5
unarm thee, go, and doubt thou not, brave boy, 5.03. 35
come, hector, come, go back. 5.03. 62
ay, but thou shalt not go. 5.03. 70
go in and cheer the town. 5.03. 92
go, wind, to wind, there turn and change 5.03.110
i'll go look on. 5.04. 2 P
go, go, my servant, take thou troilus' horse, 5.05. 1
go, go, my servant, take thou troilus' horse, 5.05. 1
i go, my lord. 5.05. 5
go bear patroclus' body to achilles, | and bid 5.05. 17
till when, go seek thy fortune. 5.06. 19
never go home, here starve we out the night — 5.10. 2
aye be call'd | go in to troy and say /there, 5.10. 17
to troy with comfort go; 5.10. 30
where go you | with bats and clubs? COR 1.01. 55
go get you home, you fragments! 1.01.222
besides, if things go well, | opinion that so 1.01.270
and when he caught it, he let it go again, and 1.03. 61 P
you must go visit the good lady that lies in. 1.03. 77 P
but i cannot go thither. 1.03. 79 P
come, you shall go with us. 1.03. 86 P
in truth la, go with me, and i'll tell you 1.03. 89 P
true, on mine honor, and so i pray go with us. 1.03.101 P
solemnness out a' door, and go along with us. 1.03.108 P
go sound thy trumpet in the market–place; 1.05. 26
i will go wash; 1.09. 68
go we to our tent. 1.09. 92
go you to th' city, | learn how 'tis held, and 1.10. 27
will not you go? 1.10. 29
for the love of juno, let's go. 2.01.101 P
good ladies, let's go. 2.01.133 P
give way there, and go on! 2.01.193
our office may, | during his power, go sleep. 2.01.223
pray you go fit you to the custom, and | take to 2.02.142
me, and i'll direct you how you shall go by him. 2.03. 46 P
let the high office and the honor go | to one 2.03.122
and cannot go without any honest man's voice. 2.03.132 P
let them go on; 2.03.255
it will be dangerous to go on — no further. 3.01. 26
go call the people, in whose name myself 3.01.173
go, get you to /your house; 3.01.229
i'll go to him, and undertake to bring him 3.01.322
go not home. 3.01.329
let go. 3.02. 18
come, go with us, speak fair. 3.02. 70
go to them, with this bonnet in thy hand, | and 3.02. 73
prithee now, | go, and be rul'd; 3.02. 90
prithee now, say you will, and go about it. 3.02. 98
must i go show them my unbarb'd sconce? 3.02. 99
pray you let us go. 3.02.142
go about it. 3.03. 24
go see him out at gates, and follow him, | as he 3.03.138
believe't not lightly — though i go alone, 4.01. 29
my first son, | whither /wilt thou go? 4.01. 34
full | of the wars' surfeits to go rove with one 4.01. 46
i'll tell thee what — yet go! 4.02. 22
pray let's go. 4.02. 36
ere you go, hear this: 4.02. 38
come, let's go. 4.02. 51
well, let us go together. 4.03. 52 P
pray go to the door. 4.05. 8 P
follow your function, go, and batten on cold 4.05. 32 P
o, come, go in, | and take our friendly senators 4.05.131
he'll go, he says, and sowl the porter of rome 4.05.200 P
go see this rumorer whipt. 4.06. 48
go whip him 'fore the people's eyes — his 4.06. 61
go, masters, get you home, be not dismay'd. 4.06.149
go home, | and show no sign of fear. 4.06.151
pray let's go. 4.06.160
no, i'll not go. 5.01. 1
go you that banish'd him | a mile before his 5.01. 4
pray you go to him. 5.01. 39
stand, and go back. 5.02. 1
be it so, go back. 5.02. 12
therefore go back. 5.02. 27 P
therefore go back. 5.02. 33 P
back, i say, go; 5.02. 56 P
nay, go not from us thus. 5.03.131
come, let us go. 5.03.177
i will go meet the ladies. 5.04. 52
go tell the lords a' th' city i am here. 5.06. 1
romans, let us go; TIT 1.01.273
but go thy ways, go give that changing piece 1.01.309
ways, go give that changing piece | to him that 1.01.309
go to; 2.01. 41
him, and i'll go fetch thy sons | to back thy 2.03. 53
what beg'st thou then? fond woman, let me go. 2.03.172
so now go tell, and if thy tongue can speak, 2.04. 1
go home, call for sweet water, wash thy hands. 2.04. 6
and 'twere my cause, i should go hang myself. 2.04. 9
come let us go, and make thy father blind, | for 2.04. 52
nay, come, agree whose hand shall go along, 3.01.174
my hand shall go. 3.01.176
by heaven, it shall not go! 3.01.176
then i'll go fetch an axe. 3.01.184
i go, andronicus, and for thy hand | look by and 3.01.200
as for thee, boy, go get thee from my sight; 3.01.283
somewhither would she have thee go with her. 4.01. 11
sweet aunt, | and, madam, if my uncle marcus go, 4.01. 27
and come, i will go get a leaf of brass, | and 4.01.102
come go with me into mine armory; 4.01.113
lucius and i'll go brave it at the court. 4.01.121
come let us go and pray to all the gods | for 4.02. 46
go to the empress, tell her this i said. 4.02.145
go pack with him, and give the mother gold, 4.02.155
shall | go sound the ocean, and cast your nets; 4.03. 7
go get you gone, and pray be careful all, | and 4.03. 21
and, kinsmen, then we may go pipe for justice. 4.03. 24
come, marcus, let us go. publius, follow me. 4.03.121
go take him away and hang him presently. 4.04. 45
go drag the villain hither by the hair, | nor 4.04. 56
go thou before, to be our ambassador. 4.04.100
then go successantly, and plead to him. 4.04.113
go thou with him, and when it is thy hap | to 5.02.101
go thou with them, and in the emperor's court 5.02.104
go, gentle marcus, to thy nephew lucius; 5.02.122
whiles i go tell my lord the emperor | how i 5.02.138
let me go grind their bones to powder small, 5.02.198
go fetch them hither to us presently. 5.03. 59
go, go into old titus' sorrowful house, | and 5.03.142
go, go into old titus' sorrowful house, | and 5.03.142

thou villain capulet! — hold me not, let me go. ROM 1.01. 79
you, capulet, shall go along with me, | and, 1.01. 99
soft, i will go along; 1.01.195
come go with me. 1.02. 34
go, sirrah, trudge about | through fair verona, 1.02. 34
go thither, and with unattainted eye | compare 1.02. 85
i'll go along no such sight to be shown, | but 1.02.100
go, girl, seek happy nights to happy days. 1.03.105
in going to this mask, | but 'tis no wit to go. 1.04. 49
i say he shall, go to! 1.05. 77
go to! 1.05. 78
go to, go to, | you are a saucy boy. 1.05. 82
go to, go to, | you are a saucy boy. 1.05. 82
you are a princox, go, | be quiet, or — more 1.05. 86
go ask his name. 1.05.134
can i go forward when my heart is here? 2.01. 1
come, shall we go? 2.01. 41
go then, for 'tis in vain | to seek him here 2.01. 41
but come, young waverer, come go with me, | in 2.03. 89
go to, i say you shall. 2.04.184 P
go thy ways, wench, serve god. 2.05. 44 P
have you got leave to go to shrift to–day? 2.05. 66
go, i'll to dinner, hie you to the cell. 2.05. 77
marry, go before to field, he'll be your 3.01. 58
go, villain, fetch a surgeon. 3.01. 94
either thou or i, or both, must go with him. 3.01.129
up, sir, go with me; 3.01.139
and to't they go like lightning, for, ere i 3.01.172
will you go to them? 3.02.129
go get thee to thy love as was decreed, | ascend 3.03.146
go before, nurse; 3.03.155
go hence, good night; 3.03.166
wife, go you to her ere you go to bed, 3.04. 15
wife, go you to her ere you go to bed, 3.04. 15
go you to juliet ere you go to bed; 3.04. 31
go you to juliet ere you go to bed; 3.04. 31
i have more care to stay than will to go. 3.05. 23
to go with paris to saint peter's church, | or i 3.05.154
good prudence, smatter with your gossips, go. 3.05.171
go in, and tell my lady i am gone, | having 3.05.231
go, counsellor, | thou and my bosom henceforth 3.05.239
or bid me go into a new–made grave, | and hide 4.01. 84
go home, be merry, give consent | to marry paris 4.01. 89
sirrah, go hire me twenty cunning cooks. 4.02. 2
go, be gone. 4.02. 9
send for the county, go tell him of this. 4.02. 23
ay, marry, go, i say, and fetch him hither. 4.02. 30
will you go with me into my closet | to help me 4.02. 33
go, nurse, go with her, we'll to church 4.02. 37
nurse, go with her, we'll to church to–morrow. 4.02. 37
go thou to juliet, help to deck up her. 4.02. 41
go, you cot–quean, go, | get you to bed. 4.04. 6
go, you cot–quean, go, | get you to bed. 4.04. 6
go waken juliet, go and trim her up, | i'll go 4.04. 25
go waken juliet, go and trim her up, | i'll go 4.04. 25
and trim her up, | i'll go and chat with paris. 4.04. 26
come, is the bride ready to go to church? 4.05. 33
ready to go, but never to return. 4.05. 34
sir, go you in, and, madam, go with him; 4.05. 91
sir, go you in, and, madam, go with him; 4.05. 91
and go, sir paris. 4.05. 92
and not poison, go with me | to juliet's grave, 5.01. 85
friar john, go hence, | get me an iron crow, and 5.02. 20
brother, i'll go and bring it thee. 5.02. 23
do as i bid thee, go. 5.03. 9
obey and go with me, for thou must die. 5.03. 57
o lord, they fight! i will go call the watch. 5.03. 71
go with me to the vault. 5.03.131
stay then, i'll go alone. 5.03.135
come go, good juliet, i dare no longer stay. 5.03.159
go get thee hence, for i will not away. 5.03.160
go, some of you, whoe'er you find attach. 5.03.173
go tell the prince, run to the capulets, | raise 5.03.177
and she, too desperate, would not go with me, 5.03.263
go hence to have more talk of these sad things; 5.03.307
go not away. TIM 1.01.154
go not you hence | till i have thank'd you. 1.01.244
go, | let him have a table by himself, | for he 1.02. 29
my lord, in heart; and let the health go round. 1.02. 53
i go, sir. 2.01. 33
ay, go, sir; 2.01. 34
go. 2.01. 35
takes no accompt | how things go from him, nor 2.02. 4
go to my steward. 2.02. 18
go, thou wast born a bastard, and thou't die a 2.02. 84 P
fool, i will go with you to lord timon's. 2.02. 89 P
masters, they approach sadly, and go away merry; 2.02.101 P
my master's house merrily, and go away sadly. 2.02.102 P
go to! 2.02.128
go you, sir, to the senators — | of whom, even 2.02.196
go to ventidius. 2.02.220
go, bid all my friends again. | lucius, lucullus 3.04.110
go, i charge thee, invite them all, let in the 3.04.116
grief too, as i understand how all things go. 3.06. 18 P
what, dost thou go? 3.06. 99
his fortune by the arm, | and go along with him. 4.02. 8
thou't go, strong thief, | when gouty keepers of 4.03. 46
go on — here's gold — go on; 4.03.108
go on — here's gold — go on; 4.03.108
go great with tigers, dragons, wolves, and bears 4.03.189
go, suck the subtle blood o' th' grape, | till 4.03.429
to athens go, | break open shops; 4.03.446
go, live rich and happy, | but thus condition'd: 4.03.525
let it go naked, men may see't the better. 5.01. 67
go, live still; 5.01.188
lips, let four words go by and language end! 5.01.220
go, go, good countrymen, and for this fault JC 1.01. 56
go, go, good countrymen, and for this fault 1.01. 56
go you down that way towards the capitol, | this 1.01. 63
will you go see the order of the course? 1.02. 25
i would i might go to hell among the rogues. 1.02.268 P
now, | did i go through a tempest dropping fire. 1.03. 10
let us go, | for it is after midnight, and ere 1.03.162
go to the gate, somebody knocks. 2.01. 60
now, good metellus, go along by him. 2.01.218
why, so i do. good portia, go to bed. 2.01.260
portia, go in a while, | and by and by thy bosom 2.01.304
go bid the priests do present sacrifice, | and 2.02. 5
yet caesar shall go forth; 2.02. 28
and caesar shall go forth. 2.02. 48
do not go forth to–day; 2.02. 50
decius, go tell them caesar will not come. 2.02. 68
give me my robe, for i will go. 2.02.107
good friends, go in, and taste some wine with me 2.02.126
we, like friends, will straightway go together. 2.02.127
i go to take my stand, | to see him pass on to 2.04. 25
i must go in. 2.04. 39
let him go | and presently prefer his suit to 3.01. 27
go to the pulpit, brutus. 3.01. 84
cassius, go you into the other street, | and 3.02. 3
those that will follow cassius, go with him; 3.02. 6
let him go up into the public chair, | we'll 3.02. 63
noble antony, go up. 3.02. 64
and they would go and kiss dead caesar's wounds, 3.02.132
why, friends, you go to do you know not what. 3.02.235
go fetch fire. 3.02.257 P
away, go! 3.03. 38 P
but, lepidus, go you to caesar's house; 4.01. 7
must be taught, and train'd, and bid go forth; 4.01. 35
and let us presently go sit in council, | how 4.01. 45
go to; you are not, cassius. 4.03. 32
go show your slaves how choleric you are, | and 4.03. 43
let me go in to see the generals. 4.03.124
then, with your will, go on; 4.03.224
go and commend me to my brother cassius; 4.03.306
roman, | that ever brutus will go bound to rome; 5.01.111
go, pindarus, get higher on that hill; 5.03. 20
whilst i go to meet | the noble brutus, 5.03. 73
who will go with me? 5.04. 2
go on, | and see whe'er brutus be alive or dead, 5.04. 29
go get him surgeons. MAC 1.02. 44
go pronounce his present death, | and with his 1.02. 64
thus do go, about, about, | thrice to thine, and 1.03. 34
go bid thy mistress, when my drink is ready, 2.01. 31
i go, and it is done; 2.01. 62
go get some water, | and wash this filthy 2.02. 43
go carry them, and smear | the sleepy grooms 2.02. 46
i'll go no more. 2.02. 47
all professions that go the primrose way to th' 2.03. 18 P
god's benison go with you, and with those | that 2.04. 40
go not my horse the better, | i must become a 3.01. 25
now go to the door, and stay there till we call. 3.01. 72
in your nature | that you can let this go? 3.01. 87
ay, in the catalogue ye go for men, | as hounds 3.01. 91
so prithee go with me. 3.02. 56
his horses go about. 3.03. 11
upon the order of your going, | but go at once. 3.04.119
no more, | returning were as tedious as go o'er. 3.04.137
round about the cauldron go; 4.01. 4
never is o'ertook | unless the deed go with it. 4.01.146
come go we to the king, our power is ready, 4.03.236
go to, go to; 5.01. 46 P
go to, go to; 5.01. 46 P
will she go now to bed? 5.01. 69 P
go prick thy face, and over–red thy fear, | thou 5.03. 14
some must go off; 5.09. 2
i do beseech you give him leave to go. HAM 1.02. 61
i pray thee stay with us, go not to wittenberg. 1.02.119
the time invests you, go, your servants tend. 1.03. 83
ay, fashion you may call it. go to, go to. 1.03.112
ay, fashion you may call it. go to, go to. 1.03.112
it beckons you to go away with it, | as if it 1.04. 58
a more removed ground, | but do not go with it. 1.04. 62
it waves me still. — | go on, i'll follow thee. 1.04. 79
you shall not go, my lord. 1.04. 80
be rul'd, you shall not go. 1.04. 81
go on, i'll follow thee. 1.04. 86
speak, i'll go no further. 1.05. 1
is, and for my own poor part, | i will go pray. 1.05.132
let us go in together, | and still your fingers 1.05.186
nay, come, let's go together. 1.05.190
quarrelling, | drabbing — you may go so far. 2.01. 26
that done, he lets me go, | and, with his head 2.01. 93
come, go with me. 2.01. 98
i will go seek the king. 2.01. 98
come, go we to the king. 2.01.114
go some of you, | and bring these gentlemen 2.02. 36
go to your rest, at night we'll feast together. 2.02. 84
but let that go. 2.02. 95
as i am, if like a crab you could go backward. 2.02.204 P
you go to seek the lord hamlet, there he is. 2.02.220 P
go thy ways to a nunn'ry. 3.01.128 P
to a nunn'ry, go, and quickly too. 3.01.139 P
go to, i'll no more on't, it hath made me mad. 3.01.146 P
to a nunn'ry, go. 3.01.149 P
madness in great ones must not /unwatch'd go. 3.01.188
go make you ready. 3.02. 45 P
why, let the strooken deer go weep, | the hart 3.02.271
speak with you in her closet ere you go to bed. 3.02.332 P
why do you go about to recover the wind of me, 3.02.346 P
liege, | i'll call upon you ere you go to bed, 3.03. 34
words without thoughts never to heaven go. 3.03. 98
go, go, you question with a wicked tongue. 3.04. 12
go, go, you question with a wicked tongue. 3.04. 12
you go not till i set you up a glass | where you 3.04. 19
lets go by | th' important acting of your dread 3.04.107
good night, but go not to my uncle's bed — 3.04.159
an't shall go hard | but i will delve one yard 3.04.207
friends both, go join you with some further aid: 4.01. 33
go seek him out, speak fair, and bring the body 4.01. 36
where the body is, and go with us to the king. 4.02. 26 P
you how a king may go a progress through the 4.03. 30 P
shall nose him as you go up the stairs into the 4.03. 36 P
go seek him there. 4.03. 38 P
go, captain, from me greet the danish king. 4.04. 1
go softly on. 4.04. 8
we go to gain a little patch of ground | that 4.04. 18
will't please you go, my lord? 4.04. 30
i'll be with you straight — go a little before. 4.04. 31
trick of fame | go to their graves like beds, 4.04. 62
which bewept to the ground did not go | with 4.05. 39
let him go, gertrude, do not fear our person: 4.05.123
let him go, gertrude. 4.05.127
them so well, | they shall go far with little. 4.05.140
no, no, he is dead, | go to thy death–bed, | he 4.05.193
go but apart, | make choice of whom your wisest 4.05.204
i pray you go with me. 4.05.220
motive, | why to a public count i might not go, 4.07. 17
whose worth, if praises may go back again, 4.07. 27
if the man go to this water and drown himself, 5.01. 16 P
go to. 5.01. 40 P
go get thee in, and fetch me a sup of liquor. 5.01. 59 P
so guildenstern and rosencrantz go to't. 5.02. 56
let go! 5.02.343
go bid the soldiers shoot. 5.02.403
bed, | go to th' creating a whole tribe of fops, LR 1.02. 14
go, sirrah, seek him; 1.02. 77 P
pray ye go, there's my key. 1.02.170 P
if you do stir abroad, go arm'd. 1.02.170 P
me not stay a jot for dinner, go get it ready. 1.04. 8 P
go you and call my fool hither. 1.04. 43 P
go you and tell my daughter i would speak with 1.04. 75 P
go you call hither my fool. 1.04. 77 P
go to, have you wisdom? 1.04. 91 P
should play bo–peep, | and go the /fools among." 1.04.178
go, go, my people. 1.04.272
go, go, my people. 1.04.272
go you before to gloucester with these letters. 1.05. 1 P
be merry, thy wit shall not go slip–shod. 1.05. 12 P
pursue him, ho! go after. by no means what? 2.01. 43
to go out of my dialect, which you discommend so 2.02.109 P
let go thy hold when a great wheel runs down a 2.04. 71 P
go tell the duke, and 's wife, i'ld speak with 2.04.116
i'll go with thee, | thy fifty yet doth double 2.04.258
if only to go warm were gorgeous, | why, nature 2.04.268
o fool, i shall go mad! 2.04.286
i will go seek the king. 3.01. 50
i'll speak a prophecy ere i go: 3.02. 80 P
go to; 3.03. 8 P
go you and maintain talk with the duke, that my 3.03. 15 P
prithee go in thyself, seek thine own ease. 3.04. 23
but i'll go in. 3.04. 25
in, boy, go first. 3.04. 26
go to thy bed, and warm thee. 3.04. 48 P
go in with me; 3.04.148
good my lord, take his offer, go into th' house. 3.04.156
importune him once more to go, my lord, | his 3.04.161
sirrah, come on; go along with us. 3.04.179 P
go with me to the duchess. 3.05. 14 P
we'll go to supper i' th' morning. 3.06. 84 P
and i'll go to bed at noon. 3.06. 85 P
go seek the traitor gloucester, | pinion him 3.07. 22
go thrust him out at gates, and let him smell 3.07. 93
then shall you go no further. 4.02. 11
father, | it is thy business that i go about; 4.04. 24
let go my hand. 4.06. 27
go thou further off: 4.06. 30
go to, they are not men o' their words: 4.06.103 P
let go his arm. 4.06.234
chill not let go, zir, without vurther /cagion. 4.06.235 P
let go, slave, or thou di'st! 4.06.236
good gentleman, go your gait, and let poor voke 4.06.237 P
all my reports go with the modest truth, | nor 4.07. 5
desire him to go in, trouble him no more | till 4.07. 80
sister, you'll go with us? 5.01. 34
'tis most convenient, pray go with us. 5.01. 36
o ho, i know the riddle. — i will go. 5.01. 37
grace go with you, sir! 5.02. 4
go follow them to prison. 5.03. 27
go after her; she's desperate, govern her. 5.03.162
i have a journey, sir, shortly to go: 5.03.322
please | to get good guard and go along with me. OTH 1.01.179
you were best go in. 1.02. 30
a word here in the house, | and go with you. 1.02. 49
marry, to — come, captain, will you go? 1.02. 53
whither will you that i go | to answer this your 1.02. 84
behind, | a moth of peace, and he go to the war, 1.03.256
let me go with him. 1.03.259
why, go to bed and sleep. 1.03.304 P
thy joy than to be drown'd and go without her. 1.03.361 P
thou art sure of me — go make money. 1.03.364 P
traverse, go, provide thy money. 1.03.371 P
go to, farewell. do you hear, roderigo? 1.03.376 P
i pray you, sir, go forth, | and give us truth 2.01. 57
letting go safely by | the divine desdemona. 2.01. 72
you rise to play, and go to bed to work. 2.01.115
iago, | go to the bay and disembark my coffers. 2.01.208
i pray you, after the lieutenant, go. 2.03.137
let me go, sir, or i'll knock you o'er the 2.03.153 P
go out and cry a mutiny. 2.03.157
does't not go well? 2.03.374
retire thee, go where thou art billeted. 2.03.380
go, vanish into air, away! 3.01. 20 P
why, go to then. 3.03.208
come, i'll go in with you. 3.03.288
go, leave me. 3.03.320
by foolish honesty and love), | i will go on. 3.03.413
come go with me apart, i will withdraw | to 3.03.477
go to! where lodges he? 3.04. 7 P
go, and importune her. 3.04.108
i will go meet him. 3.04.138
i will go seek him. 3.04.165
go to, woman! 3.04.183
as he shall smile, othello shall go mad; 4.01.100
go to, well said, well said. 4.01.114
go to; say no more. 4.01.169 P
and yet go on | and turn again; 4.01.253
do but go after, | and mark how he continues. 4.01.280
go. 4.02. 19
have i none | but what should go by water. 4.02.104
you are a fool; go to. 4.02.148
good friend, go to him; 4.02.150
go in, and weep not; 4.02.171
well, go to; very well. 4.02.191 P
go to! 4.02.192 P
i cannot go to, man, nor 'tis not very well. 4.02.192 P
with a harlotry, and thither will i go to him — 4.02.234 P
stand not amaz'd at it, but go along with me; 4.02.239 P
and hath commanded me to go to bed, | and bid me 4.03. 13
that song to–night | will not go from my mind; 4.03. 31
to do | but to go hang my head all at one side 4.03. 32
shall i go fetch your night–gown? 4.03. 34
go know of cassio where he supp'd to–night. 5.01.117
o, did he so? i charge you go with me. 5.01.120

gentlemen, let's go see poor cassio dress'd. 5.01.124
will you go on afore? 5.01.128
with cassio, mistress. go to, charm your tongue. 5.02.183
perchance, iago, i will ne'er go home. 5.02.197
let it go all. 5.02.246
do you go back dismay'd? 5.02.269
where should othello go? 5.02.271
you must forsake this room and go with us. 5.02.330
a word or two before you go. 5.02.338
property | which still should go with antony. ANT 1.01. 59
go, you wild bedfellow, you cannot soothsay. 1.02. 51 P
let him marry a woman that cannot go, sweet isis 1.02. 64 P
we will not look upon him. go with us. 1.02. 87
what, says the married woman you may go? 1.03. 20
for your going, | but bid farewell, and go. 1.03. 33
nilus' slime, i go from hence | thy soldier, 1.03. 69
unpitied folly, | and all the gods go with you! 1.03. 99
let us go. 1.03.101
that the men might go to wars with the women! 2.02. 66 P
go to then — your considerate stone. 2.02.110 P
let us go. 2.02.242
well, go to, i will. 2.05. 36
go get thee hence! 2.05. 95
go to the fellow, good alexas, bid him | report 2.05.111
let him for ever go — let him not, charmian — 2.05.115
go hang, sir, hang! 2.07. 53
would it were all, | that it might go on wheels! 2.07. 93
cup us till the world go round, | cup us till 2.07.117
go round, | cup us till the world go round! 2.07.118
you praise caesar, say "caesar," go no further. 3.02. 13
look, here i have you, thus i let you go, | and 3.02. 63
go to, go to. come hither, sir. 3.03. 2
go to, go to. come hither, sir. 3.03. 2
go, make thee ready, | our letters are prepar'd. 3.03. 37
you requested, | yourself shall go between 's. 3.04. 25
egyptians | and the phoenicians go a–ducking; 3.07. 64
go to him, madam, speak to him, | he's 3.11. 43
caesar, i go. 3.12. 33
go on: right royal. 3.13. 55
go, put on thy defenses. 4.04. 10
love we rise betime, | and go to't with delight. 4.04. 21
go, eros, send his treasure after; 4.05. 12
go forth, agrippa, and begin the fight. 4.06. 1
go charge agrippa | plant those that have 4.06. 7
no, i will go seek | some ditch wherein to die; 4.06. 36
go we to him. 4.09. 27
bring thee word | straight how 'tis like to go. 4.12. 3
mardian, go tell him i have slain myself; 4.13. 7
go. 4.14. 37
bruised pieces, go, | you have been nobly borne. 4.14. 42
o charmian, i will never go from hence. 4.15. 1
they do not go together. 4.15. 47
go to him, dolabella, bid him yield; 5.01. 1
go and say | we purpose her no shame. 5.01. 61
go, | and with your speediest bring us what she 5.01. 66
gallus, go you along. 5.01. 69
go with me to my tent, where you shall see | how 5.01. 73
go with me, and see | what i can show in this. 5.01. 76
thou shalt | go back, i warrant thee; 5.02.156
prithee go hence, | or i shall show the cinders 5.02.172
go put it to the haste. 5.02.196
go fetch | my best attires. 5.02.227
sirrah iras, go. 5.02.229
you shall, at least, | go see my lord aboard. CYM 1.01.178
her beauty and her brain go not together. 1.02. 30 P
you'll go with us? 1.02. 38 P
nay, come, let's go together. 1.02. 40 P
rather shunn'd to go even with what i heard than 1.04. 44 P
make her go back, even to the yielding, had i 1.04.104 P
since doubting things go ill often hurts more 1.06. 95
and i must go up and down like a cock that 2.01. 21 P
come, i'll go see this italian. 2.01. 48 P
go. 2.01. 50 P
who lets go by no vantages that may | prefer you 2.03. 45
go bid my woman | search for a jewel that too 2.03.140
i hope so; go and search. 2.03.149
i will go there and do't, i' th' court, before 2.04.148
to 's execution, man, | could never go so slow. 3.02. 71
go, bid my woman feign a sickness, say | she'll 3.02. 74
go, look after. 3.05. 55
go in and cheer the king, he rages, none | dare 3.05. 67
let it be thy first service, go. 3.05.128 P
to milford go, | and find not her whom thou 3.05.159
boys, we'll go dress our hunt. 3.06. 89
go you to hunting, i'll abide with him. 4.02. 6
we'll leave you for this time, go in, and rest. 4.02. 43
if you'll go fetch him, | we'll say our song 4.02.253
go with me. 4.02.386
by heavens, i'll go. 4.04. 43
go before | this lout as he exceeds our lords, 5.02. 8
you, sir, you know not which way you shall go. 5.04.176 P
does the world go round? 5.05.232
therefore, my lord, go travel for a while, PER 1.02.106
go tell their general we attend him here, | to 1.04. 79
i go, my lord. 1.04. 82
come, thou shalt go home, and we'll have flesh 2.01. 81 P
but, master, i'll go draw up the net. 2.01. 93 P
go search like nobles, like noble subjects, 2.04. 50
along to go. 3.ch. 41
go thy ways, good mariner, | i'll bring the body 3.01. 80
go, i pray you, | walk, and be cheerful once 4.01. 38
care not for me, | i can go home alone. 4.01. 42
well, i will go, | but yet i have no desire to 4.01. 42
let her go! 4.01. 97
but i'll go search the market. 4.02. 25 P
with shame which is her way to go with warrant. 4.02.128 P
pray you, will you go with us? 4.02.150 P
o, go to. 4.03. 19
shall 's go hear the vestals sing? 4.05. 7 P
go thy ways. 4.06. 65 P
did you go to't so young? 4.06. 74 P
will you not go the way of womenkind? 4.06.149 P
go to the wars, would you? 4.06.170 P
whispers in mine ear, "go not till he speak." 5.01. 96
beseech you first, go with me to my house, 5.03. 65
or to go tiptoe | before the street be foul? TNK 1.02. 57
go and find out | the bones of your dead lords, 1.04. 6
go to, leave your pointing. 2.01. 51 P
will ye go forward, cousin? 2.02.126
i will not go. 2.02.267
then i am resolv'd, i will not go. 2.02.269
must i go? 2.02.273
if i go, he has her. 2.03. 20
but that's all one, i'll go through, let her 2.03. 31
go to! 2.03. 42
pray you, whither go you? 2.03. 60
thou wilt not go along? 2.03. 68
emily, i hope | he shall not go afoot. 2.05. 53
go lead the way; 2.05. 59
and i'll go seek him through the world that is 3.04. 23
and i go forward. 3.05. 16
we may go whistle; all the fat's i' th' fire. 3.05. 39
go thy ways, i'll remember thee, i'll fit thee! 3.05. 58
go take her, | and fluently persuade her to a 3.05. 86
well, sir, go forward, we will edify. 3.05. 98
pray go on, sir. 4.01. 65
ask me now, sweet sister — | i may go look! 4.02. 52
come, i'll go visit 'em. 4.02.152
poor wench, go weep, for whosoever wins | loses 4.02.155
too, as ever he may go upon 's legs, for in the 4.03. 14 P
sometime we go to barley–break, we of the 4.03. 30 P
or hang or drown themselves, thither they go — 4.03. 35 P
go with me | before the god of our profession. 5.01. 37
too, | yea, the speed also — to go on, i mean, 5.01. 41
let us go. 5.01. 68
which perish'd should | go to't unsentenc'd. 5.01.157
go, go! 5.02. 27
go, go! 5.02. 27
will you go with me? 5.02. 73
nay, we'll go with you, | i will not lose the 5.02.102
come, sweet, we'll go to dinner, | and then 5.02.107
you must go. 5.03. 28
than humble banks can go to law with waters 5.03. 99
the scene's not for our seeing, go we hence, 5.03.134
let's go off, | and bear us like the time. 5.04.136
as but to banish you, whither would you go? STM II.C 125
go you to france or flanders, | to any german II.C 127
"for shame," he cries, "let go, and let me go, VEN 379
"for shame," he cries, "let go, and let me go, 379
"fie, fie," he says, "you crush me, let me go, 611
their scratch'd ears, bleeding as they go. 924
to those two armies that would let him go, LUC 76
climb | his wonted height, yet ere he go to bed, 776
"go get me hither paper, ink, and pen, | yet 1289
throng her inventions, which shall go before. 1302
tak'st, | 'mongst our mourners shalt thou go. PHT 20
that thou among the wastes of time must go, SON 12.10
wind, | or say with princes if it shall go well, 14. 7
towards thee i'll run, and give him leave to go. 51.14
and that which governs me to go about | doth 113. 2
i grant i never saw a goddess go — | my 130.11
eyes straight, though thy proud heart go wide. 140.14
of city, and had let go by | the swiftest hours, LC 59
GOAD 1 FR 0.0001 REL FR 1 V 0 P
is that temptation that doth goad us on | to sin MM 2.02.181
GOADED 2 FR 0.0002 REL FR 2 V 0 P
and therefore, goaded with most sharp occasions, AWW 5.01. 14
'tis, their own, | which we have goaded onward. COR 2.03.263
GOADS 1 FR 0.0001 REL FR 1 V 0 P
sleep, which being spotted | is goads, thorns, WT 1.02.329
GOAL 4 FR 0.0004 REL FR 4 V 0 P
but to th' goal: WT 1.02. 96
nerves, and can | get goal for goal of youth. ANT 4.08. 22
nerves, and can | get goal for goal of youth. 4.08. 22
then honor be but a goal to my will, | this day PER 2.01.165
GOAT 7 FR 0.0008 REL FR 5 V 2 P
am i ridden with a welsh goat too? WIV 5.05.137 P
thou damned and luxurious mountain goat, H5 4.04. 19
there is one goat for you. 5.01. 29 P
hence, old goat! COR 3.01.176
and feed on curds and whey, and suck the goat, TIT 4.02.178
gall of goat, and slips of yew | sliver'd in the MAC 4.01. 27
exchange me for a goat, | when i shall turn the OTH 3.03.180
GOATISH 1 FR 0.0001 REL FR 0 V 1 P
to lay his goatish disposition on the charge of LR 1.02.127 P
GOATS 9 FR 0.0010 REL FR 7 V 2 P
neither, | as flesh of muttons, beefs, or goats. MV 1.03.167
i will fetch up your goats, audrey. AYL 3.03. 2 P
i am here with thee and thy goats, as the most 3.03. 7 P
the goats ran from the mountains, and the herds 1H4 3.01. 38
wanton as youthful goats, wild as young bulls. 4.01.103
not for cadwallader and all his goats. H5 5.01. 28
were they as prime as goats, as hot as monkeys, OTH 3.03.403
goats and monkeys! 4.01.263
but that of coward hares, hot goats, and venison CYM 4.04. 37
GOBBETS 2 FR 0.0002 REL FR 2 V 0 P
with gobbets of thy /mother's bleeding heart. 2H6 4.01. 85
into as many gobbets will i cut it | as wild 5.02. 58
/GOBBO 6 FR 0.0006 REL FR 0 V 6 P
me, saying to me, "/gobbo, launcelot /gobbo, MV 2.02. 3 P
me, "/gobbo, launcelot /gobbo, good launcelot," 2.02. 4 P
good launcelot," or "good /gobbo," or "good 2.02. 5 P
or "good launcelot /gobbo, use your legs, take 2.02. 5 P
honest launcelot, take heed, honest /gobbo," or, 2.02. 8 P
as aforesaid, "honest launcelot /gobbo, do not 2.02. 9 P
GO–BETWEEN 1 FR 0.0001 REL FR 0 V 1 P
me, her assistant or go–between parted from me. WIV 2.02.263 P
GOBLET 2 FR 0.0002 REL FR 0 V 2 P
concave as a cover'd goblet or a worm–eaten nut. AYL 3.04. 24 P
didst swear to me upon a parcel–gilt goblet, 2H4 2.01. 87 P
GOBLETS 1 FR 0.0001 REL FR 1 V 0 P
gown, | my figur'd goblets for a dish of wood, R2 3.03.150
GOBLIN 2 FR 0.0002 REL FR 2 V 0 P
goblin, lead them up and down. MND 3.02.399
be thou a spirit of health, or goblin damn'd, HAM 1.04. 40
GOBLINS 5 FR 0.0005 REL FR 5 V 0 P
charge my goblins that they grind their joints TMP 4.01.258
we talk with goblins, owls, and sprites; ERR 2.02.190
i have one | of sprites and goblins. WT 2.01. 26
that mouldeth goblins swift as frenzy's thoughts TRO 5.10. 29
with, ho, such bugs and goblins in my life, HAM 5.02. 22
GOD *(also gar, got*)*
/GOD 38 FR 0.0043 REL FR 20 V 18 P
leaving the fear of /god on the left hand, and WIV 2.02. 23 P
/god bless them and make them his servants! 2.02. 52 P
/god /save you, sir! 2.02.154 P
/god be prais'd for my jealousy! 2.02.309 P
/god bless thee, bully–doctor! 2.03. 18 P
/god save you, master doctor caius! 2.03. 19 P
/god save you, good sir hugh! 3.01. 41 P
/god pless you from his mercy sake, all of you! 3.01. 42 P
/afore /god, a mad host. 3.01.112 P
but as we, under /god, are supreme head, | so JN 3.01.155
where /god he knows how we shall answer him; 5.07. 60
/god /save /the /king! R2 4.01.172
/god /save /the /king! 4.01.174
/god /pardon /all /oaths /that /are /broke /to 4.01.214
/god /keep /all /vows /unbroke /are /made /to 4.01.215
/god /save /king /henry, /unking'd /richard 4.01.220
/to /look /upon /the /hideous /god /of /war 2H4 2.03. 35
/god keep me so! H5 4.07.116
i beseech /god on my knees thou mayst be turn'd 2H6 4.10. 58 P
this do i beg of /god, | when i am cold in love R3 2.01. 39
/i /pray /god /he /be /not, /i /say. 3.04. 58
why then, by /god — 4.04.377
/o /god, /i /could /be /bounded /in /a /nutshell HAM 2.02.254 P
and of all christians' souls, /i /pray /god. 4.05.200 P
lieutenant be, | and i (/god bless the mark!) OTH 1.01. 33
'fore /god, they have given me a rouse already. 2.03. 64 P
'fore /god, an excellent song. 2.03. 75 P
'fore /god, this is a more exquisite song than 2.03. 98 P
/god forgive us our sins! 2.03.111 P
marry, /god forbid! 2.03.261 P
o /god, that men should put an enemy in their 2.03.289 P
good /god, the souls of all my tribe defend 3.03.175
in venice they do let /god see the pranks | they 3.03.202
then would to /god that i had never seen't! 3.04. 77
/god save /thee, worthy general! 4.01.216
/god me such uses send, | not to pick bad from 4.03.104
o /god! o heavenly /god! 5.02.218
o /god! o heavenly /god! 5.02.218
GOD 796 FR 0.0899 REL FR 530 V 266 P
had i been any god of power, i would | have sunk TMP 1.02. 10
it would control my dam's god, setebos, | and 1.02.373
and sure it waits upon | some god o' th' island. 1.02.390
that's a brave god, and bears celestial liquor. 2.02.117
i prithee be my god. 2.02.149
ass | was i to take this drunkard for a god, 5.01.297
if this fond love were not a blinded god? TGV 4.04.196
be drunk with those that have the fear of god, WIV 1.01.184 P
how near the god drew to the complexion of a 5.05. 7 P
for god sake hold your hands! ERR 1.02. 93
pray god our cheer | may answer my good will and 3.01. 19
are you a god? 3.02. 39
going to bed and says, "god give you good rest!" 4.03. 32 P
comes that the wenches say, "god damn me," 4.03. 53 P
as much to say, "god make me a light wench." 4.03. 54 P
o husband, god doth know you din'd at home, 4.04. 65
god and the rope–maker bear me witness | that i 4.04. 90
god help, poor souls, how idlely do they talk! 4.04.129
god, for thy mercy! they are loose again. 4.04.144
hold, hurt him not for god sake! 5.01. 33
the chain, | which, god he knows, i saw not; 5.01.229
god help the noble claudio! ADO 1.01. 88 P
i thank god and my cold blood, i am of your 1.01.130 P
god keep your ladyship still in that mind! 1.01.133 P
not so, but indeed, god forbid it should be so." 1.01.217 P
not shortly, god forbid it should be otherwise. 1.01.219 P
to the tuition of god. 1.01.281 P
is said, "god sends a curst cow short horns" — 2.01. 22 P
by being too curst, god will send you no horns. 2.01. 25 P
not till god make men of some other mettle than 2.01. 59 P
for god defend the lute should be like the case! 2.01. 94 P
god match me with a good dancer! 2.01.107 P
and god keep him out of my sight when the dance 2.01.109 P
i would to god some scholar would conjure her, 2.01.256 P
o god, sir, here's a dish i love not, i cannot 2.01.274 P
name the day of marriage, and god give thee joy! 2.01.301 P
cousins, god give you joy! 2.01.336 P
her hair shall be of what color it please god. 2.03. 35 P
and i pray god his bad voice bode no mischief. 2.03. 81 P
o god! 2.03.104 P
god give me patience!" 2.03.148 P
before god! and, in my mind, very wise. 2.03.185 P
if he do fear god, 'a must necessarily keep 2.03.193 P
for the man doth fear god, howsoever it seems 2.03.197 P
o god of love! 3.01. 47
my lord and brother, god save you! 3.02. 80 P
god hath blest you with a good name. 3.03. 13 P
why, give god thanks, and make no boast of it, 3.03. 19 P
together, and thank god you are rid of a knave. 3.03. 30 P
sometime like god bel's priests in the old 3.03.134 P
god give me joy to wear it, for my heart is 3.04. 24 P
i, but god send every one their heart's desire! 3.04. 60 P
o, god help me, god help me, how long have you 3.04. 67 P
o, god help me, god help me, how long have you 3.04. 67 P
and his wits are not so blunt as, god help, i 3.05. 11 P
i thank god i am as honest as any man living 3.05. 13 P
god help us, it is a world to see! 3.05. 35 P
but god is to be worshipp'd; 3.05. 39 P
gifts that god gives. 3.05. 43 P
as freely, son, as god did give her me. 4.01. 26
"true"! o god! 4.01. 68
o, god defend me, how am i beset! 4.01. 77
why then god forgive me! 4.01.281 P
unmitigated rancor — o god, that i were a man! 4.01.306 P
masters, do you serve god? 4.02. 16 P
write down, that they hope they serve god; 4.02. 18 P
and write god first, for god defend but god 4.02. 19 P
for god defend but god should go before such 4.02. 19 P
for god defend but god should go before such 4.02. 19 P
'fore god, they are both in a tale. 4.02. 30 P
god knows i lov'd my niece, | and she is dead, 5.01. 87
god bless me from a challenge! 5.01.144 P
god saw him when he was hid in the garden. 5.01.179 P
their blades, which, god be thank'd, hurt not. 5.01.187 P
and reverent youth, and i praise god for you. 5.01.316 P
god save the foundation! 5.01.318 P
god keep your worship! 5.01.323 P
god restore you to health! 5.01.324 P
a merry meeting may be wish'd, god prohibit it! 5.01.326 P
"the god of love, | that sits above, | and knows 5.02. 26
serve god, love me, and mend. 5.02. 93 P
soever the matter, i hope in god for high words. LLL 1.01.192 P

god grant us patience! 1.01.194 P
in my correction, and god defend the right! 1.01.213 P
dominator of navarre, my soul's earth's god, and 1.01.221 P
i thank god i have as little patience as another 1.02.165 P
assist me, some extemporal god of rhyme, for i 1.02.183 P
god bless my ladies! 2.01. 77
now god save thy life! 2.01.191
i thank your worship, god be wi' you! 3.01.150 P
god dig–you–den all! 4.01. 42 P
god comfort thy capacity! 4.02. 44 P
god give you good morrow, master person. 4.02. 82 P
sir, god save your life! 4.02.144 P
sir, you have done this in the fear of god, very 4.02.147 P
one with a paper, god give him grace to groan! 4.03. 19 P
god amend us, god amend! 4.03. 74
god amend us, god amend! 4.03. 74
god bless the king! 4.03.187
i praise god for you, sir. 5.01. 2 P
they will, they will, god knows, | and leap for 5.02.290
fair sir, god save you! where's the princess? 5.02.310
and utters it again when god doth please. 5.02.316
nor god, nor i, delights in perjur'd men. 5.02.346
white glove (how white the hand, god knows!), 5.02.411
and, to begin, wench — so god help me, law! 5.02.414
god give thee joy of him! 5.02.448
doth this man serve god? 5.02.524 P
'a speaks not like a man of god his making. 5.02.526 P
he's a god or a painter, for he makes faces. 5.02.643 P
god save you, madam! 5.02.716
to you your father should be as a god; MND 1.01. 47
god speed fair helena! whither away? 1.01.180
with /yourselves, to bring in (god shield us!) 3.01. 30 P
a paramour is, god bless us, a thing of naught. 4.02. 14 P
he for a man, god warr'nt us; 5.01.319 P
she for a woman, god bless us. 5.01.320 P
god defend me from these two! MV 1.02. 52 P
god made him, and therefore let him pass for a 1.02. 56 P
and i pray god grant them a fair departure. 1.02.110 P
who, god bless the mark, is a kind of devil; 2.02. 24 P
honest exceeding poor man and, god be thank'd, 2.02. 53 P
marry, god forbid, the boy was the very staff of 2.02. 66 P
me, is my boy, god rest his soul, alive or dead? 2.02. 71 P
him, i will run as far as god has any ground. 2.02.110 P
god bless your worship! 2.02.120 P
you have the grace of god, sir, and he hath 2.02.151 P
some god direct my judgment! 2.07. 13
i thank god, i thank god. 3.01.102 P
i thank god, i thank god. 3.01.102 P
pray god bassanio come | to see me pay his debt, 3.03. 35
of kings, | it is an attribute to god himself; 4.01.195
a halter gratis — nothing else, for god sake. 4.01.379
be bassanio so for me — | but god sort all! 5.01.132
i am helping you to mar that which god made, a AYL 1.01. 33 P
god be with my old master! 1.01. 83 P
and so god keep your worship! 1.01.162 P
god help thee, shallow man! 3.02. 71 P
god make incision in thee! 3.02. 72 P
why, god will send more, if the man will be 3.02.209 P
god buy you, let's meet as little as we can. 3.02.257 P
against it, and i thank god i am not a woman, to 3.02.348 P
god 'ild you for your last company. 3.03. 74 P
nay then god buy you, and you talk in blank 4.01. 31 P
and almost chide god for making you that 4.01. 36 P
will spit, and for lovers lacking (god warn us!) 4.01. 77 P
and in good earnest, and so god mend me, and by 4.01.189 P
"art thou god to shepherd turn'd, | that a 4.03. 40
god ye good ev'n, william. 5.01. 14 P
ay, sir, i thank god. 5.01. 24 P
"thank god" — a good answer. art rich? 5.01. 25 P
god rest you merry, sir. 5.01. 59 P
god save you, brother. 5.02. 17 P
god buy you, and god mend your voices! 5.03. 40 P
god buy you, and god mend your voices! 5.03. 40 P
god 'ild you, sir, i desire you of the like. 5.04. 54 P
honor, and renown | to hymen, god of every town! 5.04.146
whom would to god i had well knock'd at first, SHR 1.02. 34
grumio, mum! god save you, signior gremio. 1.02.162
gentlemen, god save you. 1.02.218
god save you, gentlemen! 2.01. 40 P
god send you joy, petruchio! 2.01.319
a gentleman | and makes a god of such a cullion. 4.02. 20
god give him joy! 4.02. 52
god save you, sir! 4.02. 72
rome, | and so to tripoli, if god lend me life. 4.02. 76
marry, god forbid! 4.02. 78
o mercy, god! 4.03. 87
then, god be blest, it /is the blessed sun, 4.05. 18
the church together, god send 'em good shipping! 5.01. 42 P
no, sir, god forbid, but asham'd to kiss. 5.01.146
pray god, sir, your wife send you not a worse. 5.02. 84
and, being a winner, god give you good night! 5.02.187
i know not what he shall — god send him well! AWW 1.01.176
have the blessing of god till i have issue a' my 1.03. 25 P
would god would serve the world so all the year! 1.03. 83 P
love no god, that would not extend his might 1.03.112 P
god shield you mean it not! 1.03.168
madam, if god have lent a man any manners, he 2.02. 8 P
'fore god, i think so. 2.03. 45 P
fly, | and to imperial love, that god most high, 2.03. 75
who? god? 2.03.247 P
not in heaven, whither god send her quickly! 2.04. 11 P
in earth, from whence god send her quickly! 2.04. 13 P
god save you, captain. 2.05. 31 P
god save you, pilgrim! 3.05. 32 P
now, god delay our rebellion! 4.03. 19 P
god bless you, captain parolles. 4.03.315 P
god save you, noble captain. 4.03.316 P
a bold charter, but i thank my god it holds yet. 4.05. 93 P
god save you, sir. 5.01. 8
me at once both the office of god and the devil? 5.02. 49 P
i praise god for you. 5.02. 55 P
well, god give them wisdom that have it; TN 1.05. 14 P
god bless thee, lady! 1.05. 36 P
god send you, sir, a speedy infirmity, for the 1.05. 78 P
excellently done, if god did all. 1.05.236 P
for the love o' god, peace! 2.03. 85 P
now the melancholy god protect thee, and the 2.04. 73 P
god comfort thee! 3.04. 32 P

pray god he be not bewitch'd! 3.04.101 P
well, and god have mercy upon one of our souls! 3.04.166 P
gentleman, god save thee! 3.04.218 P
pray god defend me! 3.04.302 P
pray god he keep his oath! 3.04.310 P
but o, how vild an idol proves this god! 3.04.365
god buy you, good sir topas. 4.02.100 P
for the love of god, a surgeon! 5.01.172 P
for the love of god, your help! 5.01.176 P
and the fire–rob'd god, | golden apollo, a poor WT 4.04. 29
god shall forgive you cordelion's death | the JN 2.01. 12
and this is geffrey's in the name of god. 2.01.106
but god hath made her sin and her the plague 2.01.185
then god forgive the sin of all those souls 2.01.283
god and our right! 2.01.299
which we, god knows, have turn'd another way, 2.01.549
away, and glister like the god of war | when he 5.01. 54
how god and good men hate so foul a liar. R2 1.01.114
o, god defend my soul from such deep sin! 1.01.187
to god, the widow's champion and defense. 1.02. 43
(which god defend a knight should violate!) 1.03. 18
both to defend my loyalty and truth | to god, my 1.03. 20
and by the grace of god, and this mine arm, | to 1.03. 22
a traitor to my god, my king, and me — | and as 1.03. 24
to god of heaven, king richard, and to me — 1.03. 40
god in thy good cause make thee prosperous! 1.03. 78
however god or fortune cast my lot, | there 1.03. 85
receive thy lance, and god defend the right! 1.03.101
and derby | stands here for god, his sovereign, 1.03.105
a traitor to his god, his king, and him, | and 1.03.108
to god, his sovereign, and to him disloyal, 1.03.114
swear by the duty that y' owe to god | (our part 1.03.180
you never shall, so help you truth and god, 1.03.183
but what thou art, god, thou, and i do know, 1.03.204
a brace of draymen bid god speed him well, | and 1.04. 32
now put it, god, in the physician's mind | to 1.04. 59
pray god we may make haste and come too late! 1.04. 64
now, afore god — god forbid i say true! 2.01.200
now, afore god — god forbid i say true! 2.01.200
now, afore god, 'tis shame such wrongs are borne 2.01.238
god save your majesty! 2.02. 41
now god in heaven forbid! 2.02. 51
god for his mercy, what a tide of woes | comes 2.02. 98
i would to god | (so my untruth had not provok'd 2.02.100
god for his richard hath in heavenly pay | a 3.02. 60
if he serve god, | we'll serve him too, and be 3.02. 98
they break their faith to god as well as us. 3.02.101
show us the hand of god | that hath dismiss'd us 3.03. 77
friends, | yet know, my master, god omnipotent, 3.03. 85
o god, o god, that e'er this tongue of mine 3.03.133
o god, o god, that e'er this tongue of mine 3.03.133
pray god the plants thou graft'st may never grow 3.04.101
marry, god forbid! 4.01.114
would god that any in this noble presence | were 4.01.117
o, forfend it, god, | that in a christian 4.01.129
stirr'd up by god, thus boldly for his king. 4.01.133
whilst all tongues cried, "god save /thee, 5.02. 11
no man cried "god save him!" 5.02. 28
that had not god, for some strong purpose, 5.02. 34
not, | god knows i had as lief be none as one. 5.02. 49
if god prevent not, i purpose so. 5.02. 55
god for his mercy! 5.02. 75
i would to god, my lords, he might be found. 5.03. 4
god save your grace! 5.03. 26
i pardon him as god shall pardon me. 5.03.131
a god on earth thou art. 5.03.136
come, my old son, i pray god make thee new. 5.03.146
as, god save thy grace — majesty i should say, 1H4 1.02. 17 P
i would to god thou and i knew where a commodity 1.02. 82 P
much harm upon me, hal, god forgive thee for it! 1.02. 92 P
god give thee the spirit of persuasion and him 1.02.152 P
guns, and drums, and wounds, god save the mark! 1.03. 56
unhappy king | (whose wrongs in us god pardon!) 1.03.149
behalf | (as both of you — god pardon it! 1.03.174
by god, he shall not have a scot of them, | no, 1.03.214
god forgive me! 1.03.255
nay, by god, soft, i know a trick worth two of 2.01. 36 P
hath abundance of charge too — god knows what. 2.01. 58 P
them is fat and grows old, god help the while! 2.04.132 P
pray god you have not murd'red some of them. 2.04.189 P
sack and sugar be a fault, god help the wicked! 2.04.470 P
and on your eyelids crown the god of sleep, 3.01.214
now god help thee! 3.01.241 P
"as true as i live," and "as god shall mend me," 3.01.249 P
i know not whether god will have it so | for 3.02. 4
god pardon thee! 3.02. 29
and god forgive them that so much have sway'd 3.02.130
this in the name of god i promise here, | the 3.02.153
this two and thirty years, god reward me for it! 3.03. 48 P
what thing? why, a thing to thank god on. 3.03.117 P
i am no thing to thank god on, i would thou 3.03.118 P
nay, and i do, i pray god my girdle break. 3.03.151 P
well, god be thank'd for these rebels, they 3.03.190 P
by god, i cannot flatter, i do defy | the 4.01. 6
pray god my news be worth a welcome, lord. 4.01. 87
and would to god | you were of our determination 4.03. 32
and god defend but still i should stand so, | so 4.03. 38
and when he heard him swear and vow to god | he 4.03. 60
pray god you do. 4.03.113
and god befriend us, as our cause is just! 5.01.120
why, thou owest god a death. 5.01.126 P
did you beg any? god forbid! 5.02. 35
god keep lead out of me! 5.03. 34 P
nay, before god, hal, if percy be alive, thou 5.03. 50 P
and god forbid a shallow scratch should drive 5.04. 11
by god, thou hast deceiv'd me, lancaster, | i 5.04. 17
o god, they did me too much injury | that ever 5.04. 51
and would to god | thy name in arms were now as 5.04. 69
he that rewards me, god reward him! 5.04.163 P
good, and god will! 2H4 1.01. 13
that which i would to god i had not seen, | but 1.01.106
god may finish it when he will, 'tis not a hair 1.02. 23 P
pray god his tongue be hotter! 1.02. 34 P
god give your lordship good time of day. 1.02. 93 P
well, god mend him! 1.02.109 P
well, god send the prince a better companion! 1.02.199 P
god send the companion a better prince! 1.02.201 P
i would to god my name were not so terrible to 1.02.217 P

be honest, and god bless your expedition! 1.02.221 P
i am loath to pawn my plate, so god save me law! 2.01.154 P
before god, i am exceeding weary. 2.02. 1 P
and god knows whether those that /bawl out the 2.02. 23 P
god save your grace! 2.02. 73 P
god send the wench no worse fortune! 2.02.140 P
from a god to a bull? 2.02.173 P
for yours, the god of heaven brighten it! 2.03. 17
god save you, sir john! 2.04.110 P
god let me not live, but i will murther your 2.04.134 P
o thou dull god, why li'st thou with the vile 3.01. 15
o god, that one might read the book of fate, 3.01. 45
(though then, god knows, i had no such intent, 3.01. 72
'fore god, a likely fellow! 3.02.175 P
a man can die but once, we owe god a death. 3.02.235 P
god keep you, master silence, i will not use 3.02.288 P
god prosper your affairs! 3.02.292 P
god send us peace! 3.02.293 P
'fore god, would you would. 3.02.296 P
go to, i have spoke at a word. god keep you! 3.02.297 P
/and either end in peace, which god so frame! 4.01.178
how deep you were within the books of god? 4.02. 17
to us th' /imagin'd voice of god himself, | the 4.02. 19
ta'en up, | under the counterfeited zeal of god, 4.02. 27
god, and not we, hath safely fought to–day. 4.02.121
if god doth give successful end | to this debate 4.04. 1
lo where it sits, | which god shall guard; 4.05. 44
god witness with me, when i here came in, | and 4.05.149
of it, | let god for ever keep it from my head, 4.05.174
god put /it in thy mind to take it hence, | that 4.05.178
god knows, my son, | by what by–paths and 4.05.183
how i came by the crown, o god forgive, | and 4.05.218
laud be to god! 4.05.235
but yet, god forbid, sir, but a knave should 5.01. 44 P
o god, i fear all will be overturn'd! 5.02. 19
good morrow, and god save your majesty! 5.02. 43
state, | and (god consigning to my good intents) 5.02.143
say, | god shorten harry's happy life one day! 5.02.145
'fore god, you have here goodly dwelling and 5.03. 5 P
good cheer, | and praise god for the merry year, 5.03. 18
sir john, god save you! 5.03. 84 P
arrant knave, i would to god that i might die, 5.04. 1 P
but i pray god the fruit of her womb miscarry. 5.04. 13 P
o god, that right should thus overcome might! 5.04. 24 P
god bless thy lungs, good knight. 5.05. 9 P
god save thy grace, king hal! my royal hal! 5.05. 41
god save thee, my sweet boy! 5.05. 43
for god doth know, so shall the world perceive, 5.05. 57
god and his angels guard your sacred throne, H5 1.02. 7
and god forbid, my dear and faithful lord, 1.02. 13
for god doth know how many now in health | shall 1.02. 18
we charge you, in the name of god, take heed; 1.02. 23
but this lies all within the will of god, | to 1.02.289
save those to god, that run before our business. 1.02.303
for, god before, | we'll chide this dolphin at 1.02.307
'fore god, his grace is bold to trust these 2.02. 1
law, | and god acquit them of their practices! 2.02.144
our purposes god justly hath discover'd, | and i 2.02.151
but god be thanked for prevention, | which /i in 2.02.158
beseeching god, and you, to pardon me. 2.02.160
god quit you in his mercy! 2.02.166
the taste whereof god of his mercy give | you 2.02.179
since god so graciously hath brought to light 2.02.185
us deliver | our puissance into the hand of god, 2.02.190
so 'a cried out, "god, god, god!" 2.03. 19 P
so 'a cried out, "god, god, god!" 2.03. 19 P
so 'a cried out, "god, god, god!" 2.03. 19 P
comfort him, bid him 'a should not think of god; 2.03. 20 P
the patterns that by god and by french fathers 2.04. 61
he wills you, in the name of god almighty, 2.04. 77
and upon this charge | cry, "god for harry, 3.01. 34
so god sa' me, 'tis shame to stand still, it is 3.02.110 P
he is not — god be praised and blessed! 3.06. 9 P
ay, i praise god, and i have merited some love 3.06. 23 P
god pless your majesty! 3.06. 87 P
yet, forgive me, god, | that i do brag thus! 3.06.150
yet, god before, tell him we will come on, 3.06.156
god almighty! 4.01. 3
i thank you. god be with you! 4.01. 61 P
men, they have no wings to fly from god. 4.01.169 P
sin to think that, making god so free an offer, 4.01.183 P
what kind of god art thou, that suffer'st more 4.01.241
o god of battles, steel my soldiers' hearts, 4.01.289
god buy you, princes all; 4.03. 6
god be with you all! 4.03. 78
good god, why should they mock poor fellows thus 4.03. 92
as, if god please, they shall — my ransom then 4.03.120
and how thou pleasest, god, dispose the day! 4.03.133
alexander, god knows, and you know, in his rages 4.07. 34 P
praised be god, and not our strength, for it! 4.07. 87
god pless it, and preserve it, as long as it 4.07.108 P
to be ashamed of your majesty, praised be god, 4.07.114 P
and please god of his grace that i might see. 4.07.164 P
of warwick, here is — praised be god for it! 4.08. 21 P
and i pray you to serve god, and keep you out of 4.08. 64 P
o god, thy arm was here; 4.08.106
take it, god, | for it is none but thine! 4.08.111
or take that praise from god | which is his only 4.08.115
this acknowledgment, | that god fought for us. 4.08.120
signal, and ostent | quite from himself to god. 5.pr. 22
god pless you, aunchient pistol! 5.01. 17 P
you scurvy, lousy knave, god pless you! 5.01. 18 P
god buy you, and keep you, and heal your pate. 5.01. 66 P
but, before god, kate, i cannot look greenly, 5.02.142 P
god save your majesty! 5.02.281 P
god, the best maker of all marriages, | combine 5.02.359
god speak this amen! 5.02.368
awe, | more than god or religious churchmen may. 1H6 1.01. 40
thou art no friend to god or to the king. 1.03. 25
here's beauford, that regards nor god nor king, 1.03. 60
good god, these nobles should such stomachs bear 1.03. 90
to celebrate the joy that god hath given us. 1.06. 14
pray god she prove not masculine ere long, | if 2.01. 22
god is our fortress, in whose conquering name 2.01. 26
so help me god, as i dissemble not! 3.01.140
so help me god, as i intend it not! 3.01.141
god speed the parliament! 3.02. 60

god buy, my lord, we came but to tell you | that 3.02. 73
got | first to my god and next unto your grace. 3.04. 12
god save king henry, of that name the sixt! 4.01. 2
this shall ye do, so help you righteous god! 4.01. 8
god and saint george, talbot and england's right 4.02. 55
god comfort him in this necessity! 4.03. 15
o god, that somerset, who in proud heart | doth 4.03. 24
then god take mercy on brave talbot's soul, 4.03. 34
god knows thou art a collop of my flesh, | and 5.04. 18
with "god preserve the good duke humphrey!" 2H6 1.01.162
so god help warwick, as he loves the land | and 1.01.205
this was my dream, what it doth bode god knows. 1.02. 31
but, by the grace of god and hume's advice, 1.02. 72
but god in mercy so deal with my soul | as i in 1.03.157
pray god the duke of york excuse himself! 1.03.178
god is my witness, i am falsely accus'd by the 1.03.188 P
by the eternal god, whose name and power | thou 1.04. 25
to see how god in all his creatures works! 2.01. 7
now god be prais'd, that to believing souls 2.01. 64
god knows, of pure devotion, being call'd | a 2.01. 87
ay, god almighty help me! 2.01. 93
clear as day, i thank god and saint albon. 2.01.105 P
o god, seest thou this, and bearest so long? 2.01.151
o god, what mischiefs work the wicked ones, 2.01.182
in sight of god and us, your guilt is great; 2.03. 2
protector be, and god shall be my hope, | my 2.03. 24
god and king henry govern england's realm. 2.03. 30
here let them end it, and god defend the right! 2.03. 55
o lord bless me, i pray god, for i am never able 2.03. 77 P
fellow, thank god, and the good wine in thy 2.03. 95 P
o god, have i overcome mine enemies in this 2.03. 97 P
and god in justice hath reveal'd to us | the 2.03.102
so help me god, as i have watch'd the night, 3.01.110
i say no more than truth, so help me god! 3.01.120
god forbid any malice should prevail, | that 3.02. 23
pray god he may acquit him of suspicion! 3.02. 25
marry, god forfend! 3.02. 30
o heavenly god! 3.02. 37
true, | but how he died god knows, not henry. 3.02.131
if my suspect be false, forgive me, god, | for 3.02.139
air, | blaspheming god and cursing men on earth. 3.02.372
o god, forgive him! 3.03. 29
o that i were a god, to shoot forth thunder 4.01.104
any | save to the god of heaven and to my king; 4.01.126
god save your majesty! 4.02. 71 P
sir, i thank god, i have been so well brought up 4.02.105 P
for god forbid so many simple souls | should 4.04. 10
come, margaret, god, our hope, will succor us. 4.04. 55
and seeing ignorance is the curse of god, 4.07. 73
god should be so obdurate as yourselves, | how 4.07.115
up his cap, and say, "god save his majesty!" 4.08. 15
god save the king! god save the king! 4.08. 19 P
god save the king! god save the king! 4.08. 19 P
god on our side, doubt not of victory. 4.08. 52
god save the king! god save the king! 4.09. 22 P
god save the king! god save the king! 4.09. 22 P
doornail, i pray god i may never eat grass more. 4.10. 41 P
great god, how just art thou! 5.01. 68
god knows how long it is i have to live, | and 5.03. 17
no; god forbid your grace should be forsworn. 3H6 1.02. 18
child, | lest thou be hated both of god and man. 1.03. 9
me, | lest in revenge thereof, sith god is just, 1.03. 41
my sons, god knows what hath bechanced them; 1.04. 6
but god he knows thy share thereof is small. 1.04.129
open thy gate of mercy, gracious god! 1.04.177
and when thou fail'st (as god forbid the hour!) 2.01.190
god and saint george for us! 2.01.204
withhold revenge, dear god! 2.02. 7
here on my knee i vow to god above | i'll never 2.03. 29
to whom god will, there be the victory! 2.05. 15
o god! 2.05. 21
o god! 2.05. 61
pardon me, god, i knew not what i did! 2.05. 69
o, pity, god, this miserable age! 2.05. 88
and what god will, that let your king perform; 3.01.100
god forbid that, for he'll take vantages. 3.02. 25
god forbid that i should wish them sever'd 4.01. 21
them sever'd | whom god hath join'd together; 4.01. 22
let us be back'd with god, and with the seas, 4.01. 43
so god help montague as he proves true! 4.01.143
warwick and his friends, god and saint george! 4.02. 29
now that god and friends | have shaken edward 4.06. 1
but, warwick, after god, thou set'st me free, 4.06. 16
and chiefly therefore i thank god and thee. 4.06. 17
our dukedom till god please to send the rest. 4.07. 47
"edward the fourth, by the grace of god, king of 4.07. 72 P
if any such be here — as god forbid! 5.04. 48
o, god forgive my sins, and pardon thee! 5.06. 60
which done, god take king edward to his mercy, R3 1.01.151
o god! 1.02. 62
villain, thou know'st nor law of god nor man: 1.02. 70
then god grant me too | thou mayst be damned for 1.02.102
by, | having god, her conscience, and these bars 1.02.234
god make your majesty joyful, as you have been! 1.03. 19
god grant him health! did you confer with him? 1.03. 35
(whom god preserve better than you would wish!) 1.03. 59
god grant we never may have need of you! 1.03. 75
mean time, god grants that i have need of you. 1.03. 76
and less'ned be that small, god i beseech him! 1.03.110
which god revenge! 1.03.136
i would to god my heart were flint, like 1.03.139
and god, not we, hath plagu'd thy bloody deed. 1.03.180
so just is god, to right the innocent. 1.03.181
god, i pray him, | that none of you may live his 1.03.211
o god that seest it, do not suffer it! 1.03.270
god pardon them that are the cause thereof! 1.03.314
tell them that god bids us do good for evil: 1.03.334
o god! 1.04. 69
i will, my lord. god give your grace good rest! 1.04. 75
and like a traitor to the name of god | didst 1.04.205
if god will be avenged for the deed, | o, know 1.04.215
make peace with god, for you must die, my lord. 1.04.249
souls | to counsel me to make my peace with god, 1.04.251
that you will war with god by murd'ring me? 1.04.253
god punish me | with hate in those where i 2.01. 34
i thank my god for my humility. 2.01. 73
i would to god all strifes were well compounded. 2.01. 75
god grant that some, less noble and less loyal, 2.01. 92
o god! 2.01.132
god will revenge it. 2.01.139
god will revenge it, whom i will importune 2.02. 14
god is much displeas'd | that you take with 2.02. 89
god bless thee, and put meekness in thy breast, 2.02.107
for god sake let not us two stay at home; 2.02.147
neighbors, god speed! 2.03. 6
ay, sir, it is too true, god help the while! 2.03. 8
no, no, good friends, god wot, | for then this 2.03. 18
will touch us all too near, if god prevent not. 2.03. 26
but, if god sort it so, | 'tis more than we 2.03. 36
but leave it all to god. 2.03. 45
than of his outward show, which, god he knows, 3.01. 10
god keep you from them, and from such false 3.01. 15
god keep me from false friends! 3.01. 16
god bless your grace with health and happy days! 3.01. 18
on what occasion, god he knows, not i, | the 3.01. 26
god in heaven forbid | we should infringe the 3.01. 40
god knows i will not do it, to the death! 3.02. 55
god keep your lordship in that gracious mind! 3.02. 56
pray god, i say, i prove a needless coward! 3.02. 88
god hold it, to your honor's good content! 3.02.105
god bless the prince from all the pack of you! 3.03. 5
o, remember, god, | to hear her prayer for them, 3.03. 19
be satisfied, dear god, with our true blood, 3.03. 22
which we more hunt for than the grace of god! 3.04. 97
god and our /innocence defend and guard us! 3.05. 20
their country's good | cry, "god save richard, 3.07. 22
no, so god help me, they spake not a word, | but 3.07. 24
some ten voices cried, "god save king richard!" 3.07. 36
marry, god defend his grace should say us nay! 3.07. 81
me, | who, earnest in the service of my god, 3.07.106
which pleaseth god above | and all good men of 3.07.109
but, god be thank'd, there is no need of me, 3.07.165
which god defend that i should wring from him! 3.07.173
for god doth know, and you may partly see, | how 3.07.235
god bless your grace! we see it and will say it. 3.07.237
god give your graces both | a happy and a joyful 4.01. 5
o, would to god that the inclusive verge | of 4.01. 58
and die ere men can say, "god save the queen!" 4.01. 62
wilt thou, o god, fly from such gentle lambs, 4.04. 22
o upright, just, and true–disposing god, | how 4.04. 55
god witness with me, i have wept for thine. 4.04. 60
cancel his bond of life, dear god, i pray, 4.04. 77
and kneels, and says, "god save the queen"? 4.04. 94
ay, i thank god, my father, and yourself. 4.04.156
for thee, | god knows, in torment and in agony. 4.04.164
that god, the law, my honor, and her love | can 4.04.341
it, | and so god give you quiet rest to–night! 5.03. 43
god give us leisure for these rites of love! 5.03.101
god and good angels fight on richmond's side, 5.03.175
god and our good cause fight upon our side; 5.03.240
god will in justice ward you as his soldiers; 5.03.254
then, in the name of god and all these rights, 5.03.263
god and saint george! 5.03.270
god and your arms be prais'd, victorious friends 5.05. 1
great god of heaven, say amen to all! 5.05. 8
and let their heirs (god, if thy will be so) 5.05. 32
that she may long live here, god say amen! 5.05. 41
ask god for temp'rance, that's th' appliance H8 1.01.124
god mend all! 1.02.201
o, god save ye! 2.01. 1
and god forgive me! 2.01.136
pray god he do, he'll never know himself else. 2.02. 22
pray god he be not angry. 2.02. 63
favor | to him that does best, god forbid else. 2.02.114
now i pray god, amen! 2.03. 56
if not, i' th' name of god, | your pleasure be 2.04. 56
nay, before, | or god will punish me. 2.04. 75
but with thanks to god for such | a royal lady, 2.04.153
speak like honest men (pray god ye prove so!), 3.01. 69
full little, god knows, looking | either for 3.01. 75
now god incense him, | and let him cry "ha!" 3.02. 61
ever god bless your highness! 3.02.136
god bless him! 3.02.392
had i but serv'd my god with half the zeal | i 3.02.455
god save you, sir! where have you been broiling? 4.01. 56
than man could give him, he died fearing god. 4.02. 68
god safely quit her of her burthen, and | with 5.01. 70
god and your majesty | protect mine innocence, 5.01.140
the god of heaven | both now and ever bless her! 5.01.164
by some that hate me | (god turn their hearts! 5.02. 15
and that i would not for a cow, god save her! 5.03. 27
god protect thee! 5.04. 10
god shall be truly known, and those about her 5.04. 36
yet god achilles still cries, "excellent! TRO 1.03.169
which is that god in office, guiding men? 1.03.231
to make the service greater than the god, | and 2.02. 57
god buy you, with all my heart. 3.03.293 P
god save your good worships! COR 2.01.144 P
as if that whatsoever god who leads him | were 2.01.219
amen, amen. god save thee, noble consul! 2.03.136 P
you speak a' th' people | as if you were a god, 3.01. 81
he is their god; 4.06. 90
the god of soldiers, | with the consent of 5.03. 70
he wants nothing of a god but eternity and a 5.04. 24 P
name not the god, thou boy of tears! 5.06.100
god give you joy, sir, of your gallant bride! TIT 1.01.400
what god will have discovered for revenge. 4.01. 74
well, god give her good rest! 4.02. 63
brood, | nor great alcides, nor the god of war, 4.02. 95
to effect, | there's not a god left unsolicited. 4.03. 61
why, there it goes, god give his lordship joy! 4.03. 77
god forbid i should be so bold to press to 4.03. 91 P
god be with you, sir, i will. 4.03.120 P
this to apollo, this to the god of war: 4.04. 15
god and saint steven give you god–den. 4.04. 42 P
thou believest no god: 5.01. 71
i know | an idiot holds his bauble for a god, 5.01. 79
and keeps the oath which by that god he swears, 5.01. 80
therefore thou shalt vow | by that same god, 5.01. 82
what god soe'er it be | that thou adorest and 5.01. 82
even by my god i swear to thee i will. 5.01. 86
god gi' god–den. i pray, sir, can you read? ROM 1.02. 57 P
god forbid! 1.03. 4
susan and she — god rest all christian souls! 1.03. 18
well, susan is with god, | she was too good for 1.03. 19
and then my husband — god be with his soul! 1.03. 39
god mark thee to his grace! 1.03. 59
god shall mend my soul, | you'll make a mutiny 1.05. 79
self, | which is the god of my idolatry, | and 2.02.114
god pardon sin! wast thou with rosaline? 2.03. 44
god ye good morrow, gentlemen. 2.04.109 P
god ye good den, fair gentlewoman. 2.04.110 P
gentlewoman, that god hath made, himself to mar. 2.04.115 P
now, afore god, i am so vex'd that every part 2.04.161 P
now god in heaven bless thee! hark you, sir. 2.04.194
o god, she comes! 2.05. 18
go thy ways, wench, serve god. 2.05. 45 P
table, and says, "god send me no need of thee!" 3.01. 7 P
i saw it with mine eyes — | god save the mark! 3.02. 53
o god, did romeo's hand shed tybalt's blood? 3.02. 71
o god, i have an ill–divining soul! 3.05. 54
god pardon /him! 3.05. 82
that god had lent us but this only child, | but 3.05.165
god in heaven bless her! 3.05.168
o god! 3.05.204
god shield i should disturb devotion! 4.01. 41
god join'd my heart and romeo's, thou our hands, 4.01. 55
now, afore god, this reverend holy friar, | all 4.02. 31
god knows when we shall meet again. 4.03. 14
god forgive me! 4.05. 7
traffic's thy god, and thy god confound thee! TIM 1.01.239 P
traffic's thy god, and thy god confound thee! 1.01.239 P
plutus, the god of gold, | is but his steward. 1.01.276
thou visible god, | that sold'rest close 4.03.386
and this man | is now become a god, and cassius JC 1.02.116
he did shake — 'tis true, this god did shake; 1.02.121
art thou some god, some angel, or some devil, 4.03.279
god save the king! MAC 1.02. 47
how you shall bid god 'ield us for your pains, 1.06. 13
one cried, "god bless us!" 2.02. 24
say "amen," | when they did say "god bless us!" 2.02. 27
in the great hand of god i stand, and thence 2.03.130
while then, god be with you! 3.01. 43
now, god help thee, poor monkey! 4.02. 59 P
poor, innocent lamb | t' appease an angry god. 4.03. 17
but god above | deal between thee and me! 4.03.120
good god betimes remove | the means that makes 4.03.162
pray god it be, sir. 5.01. 58 P
god, god, forgive us all! 5.01. 75
god, god, forgive us all! 5.01. 75
and paid his score, | and so god be with him! 5.09. 19
before my god, i might not this believe HAM 1.01. 56
shrill–sounding throat | awake the god of day, 1.01.152
o god, god, | how /weary, stale, flat, and 1.02.132
o god, god, | how /weary, stale, flat, and 1.02.132
o god, a beast, that wants discourse of reason, 1.02.150
o god! 1.05. 24
friending to you, | god willing, shall not lack. 1.05.186
god buy ye, fare ye well. 2.01. 66
with what, i' th' name of god? 2.01. 73
soul, | both to my god and to my gracious king. 2.02. 45
god save you, sir! 2.02.221 P
how like a god! 2.02.307 P
why — "as by lot, god wot," | and then, you 2.02.416
pray god your voice, like a piece of uncurrent 2.02.427 P
'fore god, my lord, well spoken, with good 2.02.466 P
ay, so god buy to you! 2.02.549
god hath given you one face, and you make 3.01.143 P
o god, your only jig–maker. 3.02.125 P
god bless you, sir. 3.02.373 P
where every god did seem to set his seal | to 3.04. 61
god buy you, sir. 4.04. 30
well, god dild you! 4.05. 42 P
god be at your table! 4.05. 44 P
we cast away moan, | god 'a' mercy on his soul!" 4.05.199
god buy you. 4.05.200 P
do you /see this, o god? 4.05.202
god bless you, sir. 4.06. 7 P
one that would circumvent god, might it not? 5.01. 79 P
for love of god, forbear him. 5.01.273
o god, horatio, what a wounded name, | things 5.02.344
you are one of those that will not serve god, if OTH 1.01.109 P
god be with you! 1.03.189
even as her appetite shall play the god | with 2.03.347
god buy you; 3.03.375
what's antony? the god of jupiter. ANT 3.02. 10
he is a god and knows | what is most right. 3.13. 60
that will take rewards | and say "god quit you!" 3.13.124
'tis the god hercules, whom antony lov'd, | now 4.03. 16
he hath fought to–day | as if a god, in hate of 4.08. 25
he sits 'mongst men like a /descended god; CYM 1.06.169
cloys his beak, | as when his god is pleas'd. 5.04.119
and for further grief — god give you joy! PER 2.05. 87
the god of this great vast, rebuke these surges, 3.01. 1
what courage, sir? god save you! 3.01. 38 P
attends the former, | making a man a god. 3.02. 31
she's able to freeze the god priapus, and undo a 4.06. 3 P
striv'd | god neptune's annual feast to keep, 5.ch. 17
the most just god | for every graff would send a 5.01. 59
and thou by some incensed god sent hither | to 5.01.143
no mortal officer | more like a god than you. 5.03. 63
o, i hope some god, | some god hath put his TNK 1.01. 71
some god hath put his mercy in your manhood, 1.01. 72
(better the red–ey'd god of war nev'r /ware), 2.02. 21
do sweetly, | and god knows what may come on't. 2.03. 58
and enforc'd the god | snatch up the goodly boy 4.02. 16
go with me | before the god of our profession. 5.01. 38
before god, that's as true as the gospel. STM II.C 88 P
if i told you all you were in arms 'gainst god. II.C 95
marry, god forbid that! II.C 96 P
for to the king god hath his office lent | of II.C 98
him his own name, | calls him a god on earth. II.C 104
rising 'gainst him that god himself installs, II.C 105
god himself installs, | but rise 'gainst god? II.C 106
and like as if that god | owed not nor made not II.C 135
good god, good god, | that i from such an humble III 5
good god, good god, | that i from such an humble III 5
now, | even by the stern and direful god of war, VEN 98
for mast'ring her that foil'd the god of fight! 114
"o thou clear god, and patron of all light, 860
thou seem'st not what thou art, a god, a king; LUC 601
seely groom, god wot, it was defect | of spirit, 1345
the painter was no god to lend her those, | and 1461
one god is god of both (as poets feign), | one PP 8.13

one god is god of both (as poets feign), | one 8.13
she told the youngling how god mars did try her, 11. 3
quoth she, "the warlike god embrac'd me," | and 11. 5
quoth she, "the warlike god unlac'd me," | as if 11. 7
forgot, | all my lady's love is lost, god wot. 17. 6
that god forbid, that made me first your slave, SON 58. 1
friend, | a god in love, to whom i am confin'd. 110.12
GOD–A–MERCY 6 FR 0.0006 REL FR 2 V 4 P
god–a–mercy, grumio, then he shall have no odds.
SHR 4.03.153 P
"god–a–mercy, fellow!" JN 1.01.185
god–a–mercy, so should i be sure to be 1H4 3.03. 50 P
god–a–mercy, old heart! H5 4.01. 34
god–a–mercy, that thou wilt believe me, but a TRO 5.04. 31 P
well, god–a–mercy. HAM 2.02.172 P
GODDAUGHTER 1 FR 0.0001 REL FR 0 V 1 P
fairest daughter and mine, my goddaughter ellen?
2H4 3.02. 6 P
GODDED 1 FR 0.0001 REL FR 1 V 0 P
measure of a father, | nay, godded me indeed. COR 5.03. 11
GOD–DEN *(also good–en, etc.)*
GOD–DEN 5 FR 0.0005 REL FR 1 V 4 P
god–den to your worship, good captain james. H5 3.02. 84 P
god–den to your worships; COR 2.01. 93 P
god and saint steven give you god–den. TIT 4.04. 43 P
whipt and tormented and — god–den, good fellow.
ROM 1.02. 56
god gi' god–den. i pray, sir, can you read? 1.02. 57 P
GODDESS 37 FR 0.0041 REL FR 34 V 3 P
sure, the goddess | on whom these airs attend! TMP 1.02.422
is she the goddess that hath sever'd us, | and 5.01.187
but, like a thrifty goddess, she determines MM 1.01. 38
pardon, goddess of the night, | those that slew ADO 5.03. 12
thou being a goddess, i forswore not thee. LLL 4.03. 63
makes flesh a deity, | a green goose a goddess; 4.03. 73
too, | i were the fairest goddess on the ground. 5.02. 36
o helen, goddess, nymph, perfect, divine! MND 3.02.137
to call me goddess, nymph, divine and rare, 3.02.226
a guide, a goddess, and a sovereign, | a AWW 1.01.169
she said, was no goddess, that had put such 1.03.111 P
titled goddess, | and worth it, with addition! 4.02. 2
and thou, good goddess nature, which hast made WT 2.03.104
and your fair princess — goddess! 5.01.131
furious fickle wheel, | that goddess blind, H5 3.06. 28
patience herself, what goddess e'er she be, TRO 1.01. 27
a sister were a grace, or a daughter a goddess, 1.02.237 P
now the fair goddess fortune | fall deep in love COR 1.05. 20
this goddess, this semiramis, this nymph, | this TIT 2.01. 22
nature, art my goddess, to thy law | my services LR 1.02. 1
hear, nature, hear, dear goddess, hear! 1.04.275
dear goddess, hear that prayer of the people! ANT 1.02. 70 P
in th' abiliments of the goddess isis | that day 3.06. 17
o thou goddess, | thou divine nature, thou CYM 4.02.169
celestial dian, goddess argentine, | i will obey PER 5.01.250
a maid–child call'd marina, whom, o goddess, 5.03. 6
by heaven, she is a goddess! TNK 2.02.134
do reverence; | she is a goddess, arcite! 2.02.135
her | as she is heavenly and a blessed goddess; 2.02.163
which if the goddess of it grant, she gives 5.01. 71
to the goddess venus | commend we our proceeding 5.01. 74
o, then, most soft sweet goddess, | give me the 5.01.126
let us rise | and bow before the goddess. 5.01.136
earth's sovereign salve, to do a goddess good. VEN 28
thou being a goddess, i forswore not thee: PP 3. 6
chide, | the guilty goddess of my harmful deeds, SON 111. 2
i grant i never saw a goddess go — | my 130.11
GODDESSES 4 FR 0.0004 REL FR 2 V 2 P
wits too dull to reason of such goddesses, /and AYL 1.02. 53 P
sings 'em over as they were gods or goddesses: WT 4.04.208 P
gods and goddesses, | all the whole synod of ANT 3.10. 4
o gods and goddesses! CYM 4.02.295
GODDESS–LIKE 3 FR 0.0003 REL FR 3 V 0 P
poor lowly maid, | most goddess–like prank'd up. WT 4.04. 10
more goddess–like than wife–like, such assaults CYM 3.02. 8
dances | as goddess–like to her admired lays. PER 5.ch. 4
GODFATHER 3 FR 0.0003 REL FR 2 V 1 P
and every godfather can give a name. LLL 1.01. 93
you must be godfather, and answer for her. H8 5.02.197
here will be father, godfather, and all together 5.03. 38 P
GODFATHERS 3 FR 0.0003 REL FR 3 V 0 P
these earthly godfathers of heaven's lights, LLL 1.01. 88
in christ'ning shalt thou have two godfathers: MV 4.01.398
he should for that commit your godfathers. R3 1.01. 48
GODHEAD 3 FR 0.0003 REL FR 3 V 0 P
that was the way to make his godhead wax, | for LLL 5.02. 10
"why, thy godhead laid apart, | warr'st thou AYL 4.03. 44
your low–laid son our godhead will uplift. CYM 5.04.103
GODHEADS 1 FR 0.0001 REL FR 0 V 1 P
for, were your godheads to borrow of men, men TIM 3.06. 74 P
GOD–I–GODEN 1 FR 0.0001 REL FR 1 V 0 P
o, god–i–goden! ROM 3.05.172
GODLIKE 8 FR 0.0009 REL FR 8 V 0 P
ay, that is study's godlike recompense. LLL 1.01. 58
a noble and a true conceit | of godlike amity, MV 3.04. 3
with due observance of /thy godlike seat, TRO 1.03. 31
that capability and godlike reason | to fust in HAM 4.04. 38
rest you said | thou hast been godlike perfit, PER 5.01.206
makest affections bend | to godlike honors; TNK 1.01.230
what godlike power | hast thou not power upon? 5.01. 89
his race | should show i' th' world too godlike. 5.03.118
GODLINESS 2 FR 0.0002 REL FR 1 V 1 P
i warrant you, he will not hear of godliness. TN 3.04.122 P
honor | that, with the little godliness i have, OTH 1.02. 9
GODLY 4 FR 0.0004 REL FR 3 V 1 P
in honest, civil, godly company, for this trick. WIV 1.01.182 P
excellence | to have a godly peace concluded of 1H6 5.01. 5
fie, for godly shame! TRO 2.02. 32
alas, a kind of godly jealousy | (which i 4.04. 80
GOD'S* *(see compounds under 's and 'z)*
GOD'S* *(also got's, 'od's*, 'ud's)*
/GOD'S* 4 FR 0.0004 REL FR 3 V 1 P
/god's wrong is most of all: R3 4.04.377
well, /god's above all; OTH 2.03.102 P
good lieutenant — /god's /will, gentlemen — 2.03.158
/god's /will, lieutenant, /hold! 2.03.162
GOD'S* 124 FR 0.0140 REL FR 90 V 34 P
when 's god's asleep, he'll rob his bottle. TMP 2.02.151 P
will be an old abusing of god's patience and the WIV 1.04. 5 P
for god's sake send some other messenger. ERR 2.01. 77
hold, sir, for god's sake! 2.02. 24
for god's sake take a house! 5.01. 36
but keep your way a' god's name, i have done. ADO 1.01.143 P
i shall lessen god's sending that way, for it is 2.01. 22 P
well, god's a good man; 3.05. 36 P
god's my life, where's the sexton? 4.02. 70 P
and borrows money in god's name, the which he 5.01.310 P
and will lend nothing for god's sake. 5.01.312 P
god's blessing on your beard! LLL 2.01.203
god's my life, stol'n hence, and left me asleep! MND 4.01.203 P
be god's sonties, 'twill be a hard way to hit. MV 2.02. 45 P
and earthly power doth then show likest god's 4.01.196
no, god's my judge, | the clerk will ne'er wear 5.01.157
is he of god's making? AYL 3.02.205 P
for god's sake, a pot of small ale. SHR in.2. 1 P
but if you have a stomach, to't a' god's name; 1.02.194
come on a' god's name! 4.05. 1
god's mercy, maiden! AWW 1.03.149
home | and pray god's blessing into thy attempt. 1.03.254
whiles we, god's wrathful agent, do correct JN 2.01. 87
brought to the field | as god's own soldier, 2.01.566
god's is the quarrel, for god's substitute, R2 1.02. 37
god's is the quarrel, for god's substitute, 1.02. 37
in god's name and the king's, say who thou art 1.03. 11
here do stand in arms | to prove by god's grace, 1.03. 37
but what, a' god's name, doth become of this? 2.01.251
uncle, for god's sake speak comfortable words. 2.02. 76
for god's sake fairly let her be entreated. 3.01. 37
for god's sake let us sit upon the ground | and 3.02.155
a' god's name let it go. 3.03.146
in god's name i'll ascend the regal throne. 4.01.113
them, | and shall the figure of god's majesty, 4.01.125
what ho, my liege! for god's sake let me in. 5.03. 74
god's body, the turkeys in my pannier are quite 1H4 2.01. 26 P
god's me, my horse! 2.03. 94
for god's sake, lords, convey my /tristful queen 2.04.393
should be "by this fire, that/'s god's angel." 3.03. 35 P
god's light, i was never call'd so in mine own 3.03. 62 P
for god's sake, cousin, stay till all come in. 4.03. 29
for god's sake come. 5.04. 16
wilt thou kill god's officers and the king's? 2H4 2.01. 51 P
o yet, for god's sake, go not to these wars! 2.03. 9
god's light, with two points on your shoulder? 2.04.132 P
god's light, these villains will make the word 2.04.147 P
for god's sake be quiet. 2.04.178 P
for god's sake thrust him down stairs. 2.04.188 P
god's blessing of your good heart! 2.04.303 P
grace of york, in god's name then set forward. 4.01.225
by god's liggens, i thank thee. 5.03. 65 P
we well resolv'd, and by god's help | and yours, H5 1.02.222
we will in france, by god's grace, play a set 1.02.262
god's vassals drop and die; 3.02. 8
we are in god's hand, brother, not in theirs. 3.06.169
god's arm strike with us! 4.03. 5
god's will, i pray thee wish not one man more. 4.03. 23
god's peace, i would not lose so great an honor 4.03. 31
god's will, my liege, would you and i alone, 4.03. 74
black shoe trod upon god's ground and his earth, 4.07.142 P
god's will, and his pleasure, captain, i beseech 4.08. 2 P
say very true, scald knave, when god's will is. 5.01. 32 P
cheeks, | god's mother deigned to appear to me, 1H6 1.02. 78
then come a' god's name, i fear no woman. 1.02.102
arms this day against god's peace and the king's 1.03. 75 P
now, by god's will, thou wrong'st him, somerset; 2.04. 82
for god's sake let him have /'em; 4.07. 89
tends to god's glory and my country's weal. 5.01. 27
for god's sake pity my case. 2H6 1.03.213 P
and so i pray you go in god's name, and leave us 1.04. 9 P
now by god's mother, priest, i'll shave your 2.01. 50
soul, god's goodness hath been great to thee. 2.01. 82
such as by god's book are adjudg'd to death. 2.03. 4
a' god's name see the lists and all things fit; 2.03. 54
but god's will be done! 3.01. 86
god's secret judgment. 3.02. 31
peace to his soul, if god's good pleasure be! 3.03. 26
under his tongue, he speaks not a' god's name. 4.07.108 P
and so god's curse light upon you all! 4.08. 32 P
for god's sake, lords, give signal to the fight. 3H6 2.02.100
would i were dead, if god's good will were so; 2.05. 19
we charge you, in god's name and the king's, 3.01. 97
in god's name lead; 3.01. 99
and, by god's mother, i, being but a bachelor, 3.02.103
then in god's name, lords, | be valiant, and 5.04. 81
for god's sake, take away this captive scold. 5.05. 29
foul devil, for god's sake hence, and trouble us R3 1.02. 50
therefore for god's sake entertain good comfort, 1.03. 4
and there awake god's gentle–sleeping peace. 1.03.287
and he to yours, and all of you to god's! 1.03.302
by god's holy mother, | she hath had too much 1.03.305
in god's name, what art thou? 1.04.163
how canst thou urge god's dreadful law to us, 1.04.209
no, no, by god's good grace his son shall reign. 2.03. 10
in god's name speak, when is the royal day? 3.04. 3
blood, | that foul defacer of god's handiwork, 4.04. 51
either thou wilt die by god's just ordinance 4.04.184
in god's name cheerly on, courageous friends, 5.02. 14
then in god's name march! 5.02. 22
one that hath ever been god's enemy. 5.03.252
then if you fight against god's enemy, | god 5.03.253
by god's fair ordinance conjoin together! 5.05. 31
lead on a' god's name. H8 2.01. 78
god's peace be with him! 2.01.111
o, god's will, much better | she ne'er had known 2.03. 12
sacred person — in god's name | turn me away; 2.04. 41
my lord and me — | which god's dew quench! 2.04. 80
at be thy country's, | thy god's, and truth's; 3.02.448
god's blest mother! 5.01.153
by god's lid, it does one's heart good. TRO 1.02.211 P
o god's lady dear! ROM 2.05. 61
god's will, | what simpleness is this? 3.03. 76
god's bread, it makes me mad! 3.05.176
what a god's gold | that he is worshipp'd in a TIM 5.01. 47
who committed treason enough for god's sake, yet
MAC 2.03. 10 P
god's benison go with you, and with those | that 2.04. 40
why then, god's soldier be he! 5.09. 13
for god's love let me hear! HAM 1.02.195
god's bodkin, man, much better: 2.02.529 P
you nickname god's creatures and make your 3.01.145 P
mystery of things | as if we were god's spies; LR 5.03. 17
for they were a mark | worth a god's view. TNK 1.04. 21
god's lid, his richness | and costliness of 5.03. 96
GODS' 1 FR 0.0001 REL FR 1 V 0 P
if sanctimony be the gods' delight, | if there TRO 5.02.140
GODS 362 FR 0.0409 REL FR 308 V 54 P
look down, you gods, | and on this couple drop a TMP 5.01.201
now the hot–bloodied gods assist me! WIV 5.05. 2 P
when gods have hot backs, what shall poor men do 5.05. 11 P
to know, when maidens sue, | men give like gods; MM 1.04. 81
o, had the gods done so, i had not now ERR 1.01. 98
however they have writ the style of gods, | and ADO 5.01. 37
the voice of all the gods | make heaven drowsy LLL 4.03.341
we, hermia, like two artificial gods, | have MND 3.02.203
why then you left me (o, the gods forbid!) 3.02.276
if two gods should play some heavenly match, MV 3.05. 79
truly, i would the gods had made thee poetical. AYL 3.03. 16 P
wish then that the gods had made me poetical? 3.03. 23 P
and therefore i pray the gods make me honest. 3.03. 34 P
not a slut, though i thank the gods i am foul. 3.03. 38 P
well, prais'd be the gods for thy foulness! 3.03. 40 P
well, the gods give us joy! 3.03. 47 P
i pray the gods she may with all my heart! SHR 4.04. 67
dally not with the gods, but get thee gone. 4.04. 68
o immortal gods! 5.01. 66 P
the gods forbid else! AWW 3.05. 74
the gentleness of all the gods go with thee! TN 2.01. 44
and why he left your court, the gods themselves WT 3.02. 75
within, i'll serve you | as i would do the gods. 3.02.207
could not move the gods | to look that way thou 3.02.213
is as a meeting of the petty gods, | and you the 4.04. 4
the gods themselves | (humbling their deities to 4.04. 25
sings 'em over as they were gods or goddesses: 4.04.208 P
sure the gods do this year connive at us, and we 4.04.676 P
the gods | will have fulfill'd their secret 5.01. 35
the blessed gods | purge all infection from our 5.01.168
you gods, look down | and from your sacred vials 5.03.121
kings it makes gods, and meaner creatures kings. R3 5.02. 24
all clinquant, all in gold, like heathen gods, H8 1.01. 19
but pandarus — o gods! TRO 1.01. 94
well, the gods are above, time must friend or 1.02. 77 P
but i attest the gods, your full consent | gave 2.02.132
forget that thou art jove, the king of gods, and 2.03. 11 P
wish'd, my lord? the gods grant — o my lord! 3.02. 62 P
that dwells with gods above. 3.02.157
emulous missions 'mongst the gods themselves, 3.03.189
place with thought and almost, like the gods, 3.03.199
o the gods! what's the matter? 4.02. 84 P
o you immortal gods! i will not go. 4.02. 94
o you gods divine, | make cressid's name the 4.02. 99
in so strain'd a purity | that the blest gods, 4.04. 25
have the gods envy? 4.04. 28
but the just gods gainsay | that any /drop thou 4.05.132
it would discredit the blest gods, proud man, 4.05.247
o all you gods! 5.02. 77
by all the everlasting gods, i'll go! 5.03. 5
be gone, i say, the gods have heard me swear. 5.03. 15
the gods are deaf to hot and peevish vows; 5.03. 16
for th' love of all the gods, | let's leave the 5.03. 44
farewell, the gods with safety stand about thee! 5.03. 94
if in his death the gods have us befriended, 5.09. 9
hector! the gods forbid! 5.10. 3
sit, gods, upon your thrones, and smile at troy! 5.10. 7
but dare all imminence that gods and men 5.10. 13
for the gods know i speak this in hunger for COR 1.01. 23 P
the gods, not the patricians, make it, and 1.01. 73
senate, who | (under the gods) keep you in awe, 1.01.187
that the gods sent not | corn for the rich men 1.01.207
being mov'd, he will not spare to gird the gods. 1.01.256
the gods assist you! 1.02. 36
the roman gods | lead their successes as we wish 1.06. 6
o gods, | he has the stamp of martius, and i 1.06. 22
other's slave, | and the gods doom him after! 1.08. 6
"we thank the gods | our rome hath such a 1.09. 8
the gods begin to mock me. 1.09. 79
o, he is wounded, i thank the gods for't. 2.01.121 P
the gods grant them true! 2.01.141 P
petition'd all the gods | for my prosperity! 2.01.170
now the gods crown thee! 2.01.179
o me, the gods! 2.03. 54
the gods give you joy, sir, heartily! 2.03.111 P
the gods give him joy, and make him good friend 2.03.134 P
we pray the gods he may deserve your loves. 2.03.157
the gods forbid! 3.01.232
now the good gods forbid | that our renowned 3.01.288
i cannot do it to the gods, | must i then do't 3.02. 38
th' honor'd gods | keep rome in safety, and the 3.03. 33
with a voice as free | as i do pray the gods. 3.03. 74
the gods preserve our noble tribunes! 3.03.143
o the gods! 4.01. 37
by the good gods | i'ld with thee every foot. 4.01. 56
the hoarded plague a' th' gods | requite your 4.02. 11
i would the gods had nothing else to do | but to 4.02. 45
you bless me, gods! 4.05.135
the gods preserve you both! 4.06. 20
now the gods keep you! 4.06. 25
the gods have well prevented it, and rome | sits 4.06. 36
the gods be good to us! 4.06.153 P
the glorious gods sit in hourly synod about thy 5.02. 68 P
the good gods assuage thy wrath, and turn the 5.02. 76 P
doves' eyes, | which can make gods forsworn? 5.03. 28
you gods, i /prate, | and the most noble mother 5.03. 48
thou barr'st us | our prayers to the gods, which 5.03.105
of honor, | to imitate the graces of the gods; 5.03.150
and the gods will plague thee | that thou 5.03.166
the gods look down, and this unnatural scene 5.03.184
the gods be good unto us! 5.04. 30 P
in such a case the gods will not be good unto us 5.04. 31 P
first, the gods bless you for your tidings; 5.04. 58
call all your tribes together, praise the gods, 5.05. 2
wilt thou draw near the nature of the gods? TIT 1.01.117
the self–same gods that arm'd the queen of troy 1.01.136
and here i swear by all the roman gods, | sith 1.01.322
the gods of rome forfend | i should be author to 1.01.434
now, by the gods that warlike goths adore, 2.01. 61
a den, | unless the gods delight in tragedies? 4.01. 60

and pray the roman gods confound you both! 4.02. 6
come let us go and pray to all the gods | for 4.02. 46
pray to the devils, the gods have given us over. 4.02. 48
we will solicit heaven and move the gods | to 4.03. 51
my lords, you know, /as /know the mightful gods, 4.04. 5
i call the gods to witness, i will choose | mine TIM 1.01.137
the gods preserve ye! 1.01.162
traffic confound thee, if the gods will not! 1.01.237 P
if traffic do it, the gods do it. 1.01.238 P
it hath pleas'd the gods to remember my father's 1.02. 2
o you gods! 1.02. 39 P
feasts are too proud to give thanks to the gods. 1.02. 61
immortal gods, i crave no pelf, | i pray for no 1.02. 62
but the gods themselves have provided that i 1.02. 88 P
o you gods, think i, what need we have any 1.02. 95 P
so the gods bless me, | when all our offices 2.02.157
you gods, reward them! 2.02.213
o you gods! 3.01. 55
now, before the gods, i am asham'd on't. 3.02. 18 P
servilius, now before the gods, i am not able to 3.02. 49 P
hope, now all are fled, | save only the gods. 3.03. 36
i'm weary of this charge, the gods can witness. 3.04. 25
his debts, | and make a clear way to the gods. 3.04. 76
good gods! 3.04. 76
tear me, take me, and the gods fall upon you! 3.04. 99
now the gods keep you old enough that you may 3.05.103
soldiers should brook as little wrongs as gods. 3.05.116
the gods require our thanks. 3.06. 69 P
to borrow of men, men would forsake the gods. 3.06. 75 P
the rest of your fees, o gods — the senators of 3.06. 79 P
what is amiss in them, you gods, make suitable 3.06. 81 P
religion to the gods, peace, justice, truth, 4.01. 16
the gods confound (hear me, you good gods all) 4.01. 37
the gods confound (hear me, you good gods all) 4.01. 37
let me be recorded by the righteous gods, | i am 4.02. 4
for bounty, that makes gods, do still mar men. 4.02. 41
no, gods, i am no idle votarist; 4.03. 27
ha, you gods! 4.03. 31
what this, you gods? 4.03. 31
if thou wilt not promise, the gods plague thee, 4.03. 74 P
the gods confound them all in thy conquest, 4.03.104
agues | th' immortal gods that hear you. 4.03.139
which the gods grant thee t' attain to! 4.03.327 P
o you gods! 4.03.458
the gods are witness, | nev'r did poor steward 4.03.479
exceptless rashness, | you perpetual–sober gods! 4.03.496
the gods out of my misery | has sent thee 4.03.524
you | to the protection of the prosperous gods, 5.01.183
pray to the gods to intermit the plague | that JC 1.01. 54
for let the gods so speed me as i love | the 1.02. 88
ye gods, it doth amaze me | a man of such a 1.02.128
now in the names of all the gods at once, | upon 1.02.148
or else the world, too saucy with the gods, 1.03. 12
when the most mighty gods by tokens send | such 1.03. 55
therein, ye gods, you make the weak most strong; 1.03. 91
therein, ye gods, you tyrants do defeat; 1.03. 92
let's carve him as a dish fit for the gods, 2.01.173
o ye gods! 2.01.302
by all the gods that romans bow before, | i here 2.01.320
whose end is purpos'd by the mighty gods? 2.02. 27
the gods do this in shame of cowardice; 2.02. 41
the mighty gods defend thee! 2.03. 8 P
judge, o you gods, how dearly caesar lov'd him! 3.02.182
judge me, you gods! 4.02. 38
or, by the gods, this speech were else your last 4.03. 14
o ye gods, ye gods, must i endure all this? 4.03. 41
o ye gods, ye gods, must i endure all this? 4.03. 41
by the gods, | you shall digest the venom of 4.03. 46
be ready, gods, with all your thunderbolts, 4.03. 81
o ye immortal gods! 4.03.157
the gods to–day stand friendly, that we may, 5.01. 93
by your leave, gods! 5.03. 89
the gods defend him from so great a shame! 5.04. 23
all you gods, | in general synod take away her HAM 2.02.493
but if the gods themselves did see her then, 2.02.512
eyes of heaven, | and passion in the gods." 2.02.518
apollo, king, | thou swear'st thy gods in vain. LR 1.01.161
the gods to their dear shelter take thee, maid, 1.01.182
gods, gods! 1.01.254
gods, gods! 1.01.254
now, gods, stand up for bastards! 1.02. 22
now, gods that we adore, whereof comes this? 1.04.290
the /revengive gods | 'gainst parricides did all 2.01. 45
o the blest gods! 2.04.168
you see me here, you gods, a poor old man, | as 2.04.272
let the great gods, | that keep this dreadful 3.02. 49
the gods reward your kindness! 3.06. 5 P
by the kind gods, 'tis most ignobly done | to 3.07. 35
o you gods! 3.07. 70
kind gods, forgive me that, and prosper him! 3.07. 92
o gods! 4.01. 25
as flies to wanton boys are we to th' gods, 4.01. 36
fairies and gods | prosper it with thee! 4.06. 29
o you mighty gods! 4.06. 34
think that the clearest gods, who make them 4.06. 73
but to the girdle do the gods inherit, | beneath 4.06.126
you ever–gentle gods, take my breath from me, 4.06.217
o you kind gods! 4.07. 13
cordelia, | the gods themselves throw incense. 5.03. 21
false to thy gods, thy brother, and thy father, 5.03.135
the gods are just, and of our pleasant vices 5.03.171
the gods defend her! bear him hence awhile. 5.03.257
nay, we must think men are not gods, | nor of OTH 3.04.148
why, sir, give the gods a thankful sacrifice. ANT 1.02.161 P
the gods best know — 1.03. 24
(though you in swearing shake the throned gods), 1.03. 28
unpitied folly, | and all the gods go with you! 1.03. 99
if the great gods be just, they shall assist 2.01. 1
be't as our gods will have't! 2.01. 50
before the gods my knee shall bow my prayers 2.03. 3
the gods confound thee, dost thou hold there 2.05. 92
this great world, | chief factors for the gods: 2.06. 10
so the gods keep you, | and make the hearts of 3.02. 36
thus i let you go, | and give you to the gods. 3.02. 64
the good gods will mock me presently, | when i 3.04. 15
and the high gods, | to do you justice, makes 3.06. 87
gods and goddesses, | all the whole synod of 3.10. 4
thy beck might from the bidding of the gods 3.11. 60
now, gods and devils! 3.13. 89
the wise gods seel our eyes, | in our own filth 3.13.112
the gods forbid! 4.02. 19
i ask no more, | and the gods yield you for't! 4.02. 33
the gods make this a happy day to antony! 4.05. 1
i have liv'd in such dishonor that the gods 4.14. 56
the gods withhold me! 4.14. 69
me | to throw my sceptre at the injurious gods, 4.15. 76
the gods rebuke me, but it is tidings | to wash 5.01. 27
but you gods will give us | some faults to make 5.01. 32
so the gods preserve thee! 5.01. 60
you lie up to the hearing of the gods! 5.02. 95
sir, the gods | will have it thus, my master and 5.02.115
the gods! 5.02.171
the gods forbid! 5.02.213
o the good gods! 5.02.221
i know that a woman is a dish for the gods, if 5.02.274 P
devils do the gods great harm in their women; 5.02.276 P
which the gods give men | to excuse their after 5.02.286
that i may say | the gods themselves do weep! 5.02.300
you gentle gods, give me but this i have, | and CYM 1.01.115
o the gods! | when shall we see again? 1.01.123
the gods protect you, | and bless the good 1.01.128
a thing for sale, and only the gift of the gods. 1.04. 85 P
which the gods have given you? 1.04. 86 P
by the gods, it is one. 1.04.148 P
but | it is an office of the gods to venge it, 1.06. 92
made me to fan you thus, but the gods made you 1.06.177
to your protection i commend me, gods, | from 2.02. 8
you good gods, | let what is here contain'd 3.02. 29
good news, gods! 3.02. 39
all the comfort | the gods will diet me with. 3.04.180
may the gods | direct you to the best! 3.04.192
reckon'd, but of those | who worship dirty gods. 3.06. 55
gods! 3.06. 80
pardon me, gods! 3.06. 86
gods, what lies i have heard! 4.02. 32
displace our heads where (thanks, /ye gods!) 4.02.122
let ord'nance | come as the gods foresay it; 4.02.146
o gods and goddesses! 4.02.295
a drop of pity | as a wren's eye, fear'd gods, a 4.02.305
last night the very gods show'd me a vision | (i 4.02.346
and do | no harm by it, though the gods hear, i 4.02.378
but first, and't please the gods, | i'll hide my 4.02.387
gods, if you | should have ta'en vengeance on my 5.01. 7
gods, put the strength o' th' leonati in me! 5.01. 31
is that we scarce are men and you are gods. 5.02. 10
you good gods, give me | the penitent instrument 5.04. 9
gods are more full of mercy. 5.04. 13
then, jupiter, thou king of gods, | why hast 5.04. 77
you whom the gods have made | preservers of my 5.05. 1
but since the gods | will have it thus, that 5.05. 78
the gods do mean to strike me | to death with 5.05.234
the gods throw stones of sulphur on me, if 5.05.240
o gods! 5.05.243
marry, the gods forefend! 5.05.287
laud we the gods, | and let our crooked smokes 5.05.476
you gods that made me man, and sway in love, PER 1.01. 19
draw heaven down, and all the gods to hearken; 1.01. 83
kings are earth's gods; 1.01.103
the gods of greece protect you! 1.04. 97
now gods forbid't, and i have a gown here! 2.01. 78 P
the which the gods protect thee /from! 2.01.129
d' ye take it, and the gods give thee good an't! 2.01.146 P
for who hates honor hates the gods above. 2.03. 22
princes in this should live like gods above, 2.03. 59
now, by the gods, he could not please me better. 2.03. 72
now, by the gods, i pity his misfortune, | and 2.03. 90
the most high gods not minding longer | to 2.04. 3
by the gods, i have not. 2.05. 51
now, by the gods, i do applaud his courage. 2.05. 58
o you gods! 3.01. 22
now the good gods | throw their best eyes upon't 3.01. 36
o you most potent gods! 3.02. 63
for a fee, | the gods requite his charity!" 3.02. 75
the gods | make up the rest upon you! 3.03. 4
the gods revenge it upon me and mine | to the 3.03. 24
by the holy gods | i cannot rightly say. 3.04. 7
the fitter then the gods should have her. 4.01. 10
for | the gods are quick of ear, and i am sworn 4.01. 69
stand upon with the gods will be strong with us 4.02. 34 P
come, the gods have done their part in you. 4.02. 70 P
the gods defend me! 4.02. 89
if it please the gods to defend you by men, then 4.02. 90 P
the heavens, the gods | do like this worst. 4.03. 20
do swear to th' gods that winter kills the flies 4.03. 50
now the gods to bless your honor! 4.06. 21 P
that the gods | would set me free from this 4.06. 99
way thou goest, | and the gods strengthen thee! 4.06.107
the good gods preserve you! 4.06.107
as it were to stink afore the face of the gods. 4.06.136 P
hark, hark, you gods! 4.06.146 P
that the gods | would safely deliver me from 4.06.179
hail, reverent sir! the gods preserve you! 5.01. 14
the gods preserve you! 5.01. 39
leave her, | and the gods make her prosperous! 5.01. 79
knees, thank the holy gods as loud | as thunder 5.01.198
no more, you gods! 5.03. 40
and who to thank | (besides the gods) for this 5.03. 58
through whom the gods have shown their power; 5.03. 60
the gods can have no mortal officer | more like 5.03. 62
the gods for murder seemed so content | to 5.03. 99
get you and pray the gods | for success and TNK 1.01.208
throats and have not | due audience of the gods. 1.02. 83
but that we fear the gods in him, he brings not 1.02. 94
th' impartial gods, who from the mounted heavens 1.04. 4
and deck the temples of those gods that hate us; 2.02. 23
if the gods please — to hold here a brave 2.02. 59
to close mine eyes, | or prayers to the gods. 2.02. 94
had not the loving gods found this place for us, 2.02.108
bring her fruit | fit for the gods to feed on; 2.02.239
i would make her | so near the gods in nature, 2.02.242
good gods! 2.03. 13
thou kill'st me, | the gods and i forgive thee. 3.06. 98
o all ye gods, despise me then. 3.06.258
the gods comfort her! 4.01. 48
and fights | of gods and such men near 'em. 4.02. 25
and before the gods | tender their holy prayers. 5.01. 1
the all–fear'd gods, bow down your stubborn 5.01. 13
and, as the gods regard ye, fight with justice. 5.01. 15
he whom the gods | do of the two know best, i 5.03. 38
the gods by their divine arbitrement | have 5.03.107
surely the gods | would have him die a bachelor, 5.03.116
we come towards the gods, | young and unwapper'd 5.04. 9
that sure shall please the gods | sooner than 5.04. 11
the gods requite you all, and make her thankful! 5.04. 36
the gods will show their glory in a life | that 5.04. 43
the gods are mighty, arcite. 5.04. 87
acknowledge to the gods | our thanks that you 5.04.100
in the passage | the gods have been most equal. 5.04.115
the gods my justice | take from my hand, and 5.04.120
"then love and fortune be my gods, my guide! LUC 351
for kings like gods should govern every thing. 602
to rouse our roman gods with invocations | that 1831

GODSON 1 FR 0.0001 REL FR 1 V 0 P
what, did my father's godson seek your life? LR 2.01. 91

GOER–BACK 1 FR 0.0001 REL FR 1 V 0 P
a needle, that i might prick | the goer–back. CYM 1.01.169

GOERS 1 FR 0.0001 REL FR 1 V 0 P
would demonstrate them now | but goers backward. AWW 1.02. 48

GOERS–BETWEEN 1 FR 0.0001 REL FR 0 V 1 P
let all pitiful goers–between be call'd to the TRO 3.02.201 P

GOES 180 FR 0.0203 REL FR 132 V 48 P
it goes on, i see, | as my soul prompts it. TMP 1.02.420
silver! there it goes, silver! 4.01.256
and time | goes upright with his carriage. 5.01. 3
for being ignorant to whom it goes, | i writ at TGV 2.01.110
play the cur with him, look you, it goes hard: 4.04. 2 P
and goes me to the fellow that whips the dogs: 4.04. 24 P
love | than hate of eglamour that goes with her. 5.02. 54
now, the report goes she has all the rule of her WIV 1.03. 52 P
on my consent, and my consent goes not that way. 3.02. 77 P
her husband goes this morning a–birding; 3.05. 44 P
of such places, and goes to them by his note. 4.02. 63 P
there is an old tale goes, that herne the hunter 4.04. 28
how it goes with us, and do look to know | what MM 1.01. 57
lion in a cave, | that goes not out to prey. 1.03. 23
the nurse, and quite athwart | goes all decorum. 1.03. 31
and see how he goes about to abuse me! 3.02.203 P
nothing goes right — we would, and we would not 4.04. 34
he that goes in the calve's–skin that was kill'd ERR 4.03. 18 P
thus goes every one to the world but i, and i am ADO 2.01.318 P
time goes on crutches till love have all his 2.01.357 P
valor, | goes foremost in report through italy. 3.01. 97
if it prove so, then loving goes by haps: 3.01.105
'a goes up and down like a gentleman. 3.03.126 P
that goes without a burden. 3.04. 44 P
sir, your wit ambles well, it goes easily. 5.01.158 P
thing man is when he goes in his doublet and 5.01.200 P
now mercy goes to kill, | and shooting well is LLL 4.01. 24
my lady goes to kill horns, but, if thou marry, 4.01.111
then, as she goes, what upward lies | the street 4.03.276
third he caper'd, and cried, "all goes well." 5.02.113
must understand he goes but to see a noise that MND 3.01. 91 P
ay, that way goes the game. 3.02.289
he goes before me and still dares me on. 3.02.413
it goes not forward, doth it? 4.02. 6 P
no heresy, | hanging and wiving goes by destiny. MV 2.09. 83
now he goes, | with no less presence, but with 3.02. 53
thus it goes: AYL 2.05. 49 P
plenty in it, it goes much against my stomach. 3.02. 21 P
there's a girl goes before the priest, and 4.01.140 P
who goes there? SHR 1.02.140 P
yet oftentimes he goes but mean apparell'd. 3.02. 73
good grumio, tell me, how goes the world? 4.01. 33 P
my life, sir? how, i pray? for that goes hard. 4.02. 80
one that goes with him. AWW 1.01. 99
then my dial goes not true. 2.05. 6 P
from the report that goes upon your goodness, 5.01. 13
the story then goes false, you threw it him 5.03.229
glove, my lord, she goes off and on at pleasure. 5.03.278 P
your passion bears | goes on my master's griefs. TN 3.04.207
what's that to us? the time goes by; away! 3.04.364
a good house–keeper goes as fairly as to say a 4.02. 9 P
where goes cesario? 5.01.134
were you a woman, as the rest goes even, | i 5.01.239
who is't that goes with me? WT 2.01.116
as this world goes, to pass for honest. 2.03. 73
howe'er the business goes, you have made fault 3.02.217
a merry heart goes all the day, | your sad tires 4.03.125
that goes to bed wi' th' sun | and with him 4.04.105
a passing merry one and goes to the tune of "two 4.04.288 P
how goes it now, sir? 5.02. 27 P
should say, "look where three–farthings goes!" JN 1.01.143
you are the hare of whom the proverb goes, 2.01.137
how goes all in france? 4.02.109
how goes the day with us? o, tell me, hubert. 5.03. 1
off goes his bonnet to an oyster–wench, | a R2 1.04. 31
and crossly to thy good all fortune goes. 2.04. 24
and all goes worse than i have power to tell. 3.02.120
then whither he goes, thither let me go. 5.01. 85
yet all goes well, yet all our joints are whole. 1H4 4.01. 83
/a fool go with thy soul, whither it goes! 5.03. 22
how goes the field? 5.05. 16
what's he that goes there? 2H4 1.02. 58 P
i hope your lordship goes abroad by advice. 1.02. 96 P
for all the soil of the achievement goes | with 4.05.189
cannon touches, | and down goes all before them. H5 3.pr. 34
their villainy goes against my weak stomach, and 3.02. 52 P
a rogue, that now and then goes to the wars, to 3.06. 68 P
for forth he goes, and visits all his host, 4.pr. 32
who goes there? 4.01. 90 P
what means he now? go ask him whither he goes. 1H6 2.03. 28
when gloucester says the word, king henry goes, 3.01.183
there goes the talbot, with his colors spread, 3.03. 31
thus suffolk hath prevail'd, and thus he goes, 5.05.103
so, there goes our protector in a rage. 2H6 1.01.147
thither goes these news, as fast as horse can 1.04. 74
whither goes vaux so fast? what news, i prithee? 3.02.367
and so much shall you give, or off goes yours. 4.01. 17
then the world goes hard | when clifford cannot 3H6 2.06. 77
trust me, my lord, all hitherto goes well, | the 4.02. 1
who goes there? 4.03. 26
how goes the world with thee? R3 3.02. 96
if i revolt, off goes young george's head; 4.05. 4

clear, 'tis i must snuff it, | then out it goes. H8 3.02. 97
how goes her business? 4.01. 23
well, the voice goes, madam: 4.02. 11
the fruit she goes with | i pray for heartily, 5.01. 20
was harness'd light, | and to the field goes he; TRO 1.02. 9
the noise goes, this: 1.02. 12
hector's, and how he looks, and how he goes! 1.02.234 P
is | that by a pace goes backward with a purpose 1.03.128
ay, sir, when he goes before me. 3.01. 3 P
strait so narrow, | where one but goes abreast. 3.03.155
ever smiles, | and farewell goes out sighing. 3.03.169
ajax goes up and down the field, asking for 3.03.244 P
follow his torch, he goes to calchas' tent. 5.01. 85
pleas'd with this dainty bait, thus goes to bed. 5.08. 20
singularity, he goes | upon this present action. COR 1.01.278
with his mail'd hand then wiping, forth he goes, 1.03. 35
bring me word thither | how the world goes, that 1.10. 32
but when goes this forward? 4.05.213 P
his friends | blush that the world goes well, 4.06. 5
alarbus goes to rest, and we survive | to TIT 1.01.133
why, there it goes, god give his lordship joy! 4.03. 77
revenge now goes | to lay a complot to betray 5.02.146
a weak slave, for the weakest goes to the wall. ROM 1.01. 14 P
love goes toward love as schoolboys from their 2.02.156
that cannot lick his fingers goes not with me. 4.02. 8 P
i have not seen you long, how goes the world? TIM 1.01. 2
how goes the world, that i am thus encount'red 2.02. 36
in all shapes that man goes up and down in from 2.02.113 P
and at length | how goes our reck'ning? 2.02.150
he goes away in a cloud; 3.04. 42
a just and true report that goes of his having. 5.01. 16
this foot of mine as far | as who goes farthest. JC 1.03.120
when think you that the sword goes up again? 5.01. 52
thou seest the world, volumnius, how it goes; 5.05. 22
and when goes hence? MAC 1.05. 59
how goes the night, boy? 2.01. 1
and she goes down at twelve. 2.01. 3
goes the king hence to–day? 2.03. 53
how goes the world, sir, now? 2.04. 21
goes fleance with you? 3.01. 35
this /tune goes manly. 4.03.235
at least, the whisper goes so. HAM 1.01. 80
solemn march | goes slow and stately by them. 1.02.202
than the main voice of denmark goes withal. 1.03. 28
then goes he to the length of all his arm, | and 2.01. 85
to be honest, as this world goes, is to be one 2.02.178 P
and indeed it goes so heavily with my 2.02.297 P
this fear, | which now goes too free–footed. 3.03. 26
and now i'll do't — and so 'a goes to heaven, 3.03. 74
as damn'd and black | as hell, whereto it goes. 3.03. 95
look where he goes, even now, out at the portal! 3.04.136
how dangerous is it that this man goes loose! 4.03. 2
goes it against the main of poland, sir, | or 4.04. 15
it is, will he, nill he, he goes, mark you that. 5.01. 17 P
but goes thy heart with this? LR 1.01.105
till the speed of his rage goes slower; 1.02.167 P
but the great one that goes upward, let him draw 2.04. 74 P
the wren goes to't, and the small gilded fly 4.06.112
the fitchew nor the soiled horse goes to't 4.06.122
in a light, yet you see how this world goes. 4.06.148 P
a man may see how this world goes with no eyes. 4.06.151 P
preferment goes by letter and affection, | and OTH 1.01. 36
/faith, the cry goes that you marry her. 4.01.123 P
he goes into mauritania and taketh away with him 4.02.224 P
how goes it now? he looks gentler than he did. 4.03. 11
that thou, residing here, goes yet with me; ANT 1.03.103
goes to and back, /lackeying the varying tide, 1.04. 46
how goes it with my brave mark antony? 1.05. 38
barber'd ten tines o'er, goes to the feast; 2.02.224
he goes forth gallantly. 4.04. 36
how goes it here? 5.02.329
he goes hence frowning; CYM 3.05. 18
wrote already to the emperor | how it goes here. 3.05. 22
for your bride goes to that with shame which is PER 4.02.127 P
old helicanus goes along. 4.04. 13
with mind assur'd | 'tis bad he goes about? TNK 1.02. 98
woman, | his face, methinks, goes that way. 2.05. 21
i prithee run | and tell me how it goes. 5.03. 71
then it goes hard, i see. ep 5
breaketh his rein, and to her straight goes he. VEN 264
his snout digs sepulchres where e'er he goes; 622
the many musits through the which he goes | are 683
with swift intent he goes | to quench the coal LUC 46
let him have time to mark how slow time goes 990
once set on ringing, with his own weight goes; 1494
onward to troy with the blunt swains he goes, 1504
face | of that black blood a wat'ry rigol goes, 1745
each changing place with that which goes before, SON 60. 3

GOES'T 1 FR 0.0001 REL FR 1 V 0 P
be not a niggard of your speech; how goes't? MAC 4.03.180

GOEST 14 FR 0.0015 REL FR 12 V 2 P
goest about to apply a moral medicine to a ADO 1.03. 11 P
whither goest thou? MV 2.04. 16
come go with me, peruse this as thou goest. 2.04. 38
now thou goest from fortune's office to nature's AYL 1.02. 40 P
or thou goest to th' grange, or mill. WT 4.04.303
then whither goest? 4.04.308
thou goest to coventry, there to behold | our R2 1.02. 45
imagine it | to lie that way thou goest, not 1.03.287
this most wise rebellion, thou goest foremost; COR 1.01.158
than thou owest, | ride more than thou goest, LR 1.04.121
fellow, where goest? 4.01. 29
what, goest thou back? ANT 5.02.155
persever in that clear way thou goest, | and the PER 4.06.106
as thou goest onwards, still will pluck thee SON 126. 6

GOETH 1 FR 0.0001 REL FR 1 V 0 P
his testy master goeth about to take him, | when VEN 319

GOFFE 1 FR 0.0001 REL FR 1 V 0 P
and thither i will send you matthew goffe. 2H6 4.05. 10

GOGS–WOUNS 1 FR 0.0001 REL FR 1 V 0 P
"ay, by gogs–wouns," quoth he, and swore so loud SHR 3.02.160

GOING 104 FR 0.0117 REL FR 64 V 40 P
the sound is going away. TMP 3.02.148 P
you chid at sir proteus for going ungarter'd! TGV 2.01. 73 P
and am going with sir proteus to the imperial's 2.03. 4 P
to my friends, | and i am going to deliver them. 3.01. 54
stay'd so long that going will scarce serve the 3.01.379 P
my daughter takes his going grievously. 3.02. 14
page, trust me, i was going to your house. WIV 2.01. 33 P
and now she's going to my wife, and falstaff's 3.02. 36 P
linen upon him, as if it were going to bucking; 3.03.131 P
at court, and they are going to meet him. 4.03. 3 P
for i am that way going to temptation, | where MM 2.02.158
and i am going with instruction to him. 2.03. 38
i am now going to resolve him. 3.01.189 P
art going to prison, pompey? 3.02. 61 P
i am going to visit the prisoner. fare you well. 3.02.258 P
that thinks a man always going to bed and says, ERR 4.03. 32 P
and never going aright, being a watch, | but LLL 3.01.192
else your memory is bad, going o'er it erewhile. 4.01. 97
do this expediently, and turn him going. AYL 3.01. 18
met your wive's wit going to your neighbor's bed 4.01.168 P
trow you whither i am going? SHR 1.02.164
and i in going, madam, weep o'er my father's AWW 1.01. 3 P
i am going, forsooth. 1.03. 96 P
i take it, to rossillion, | whither i am going. 5.01. 29
at that time that i knew of their going to bed, 5.03.263 P
"i will waylay thee going home, where if it be TN 3.04.159 P
with oaths, | should yet say, "sir, no going." WT 1.02. 49
quarters of a mile hence, unto whom i was going. 4.03. 81 P
when was you going to bed? 4.04.244 P
if | his going i could frame to serve my turn, 4.04.509
kindred, are going to see the queen's picture. 5.02.173 P
more, going to seek the grave | of arthur, whom JN 4.02.164
there are pilgrims going to canterbury with rich 1H4 1.02.126 P
at home and go not, i'll hang you for going. 1.02.135 P
the hill, 'tis going to the king's exchequer. 2.02. 55 P
lie, ye rogue, 'tis going to the king's tavern. 2.02. 56 P
is now going with some charge to the lord john 2H4 1.02. 62 P
i hear you are going with lord john of lancaster 1.02.204 P
i am undone by his going, i warrant you, he's an 2.01. 23 P
and, but my going, nothing can redeem it. 2.03. 8
thou art going to the wars, and whether i shall 2.04. 66 P
are you now going to dispatch this thing? R3 1.03.340
then was i going prisoner to the tower, | by the 3.02.100
upon this french going out, took he upon him H8 1.01. 73
i am glad they are going, | for sure there's no 1.03. 42
she's going away. 2.04.124
view'd in open as his queen, | going to chapel; 3.02.405
she is going, wench. pray, pray. 4.02. 99
it now, for it has been a great while going by. TRO 1.02.169 P
/titled as achilles' is, | by going to achilles. 2.03.194
sense, behold itself, | not going from itself; 3.03.107
mother, i am going to the market–place; COR 3.02.131
look, i am going. 3.02.134
and going | about their functions friendly. 4.06. 8
the nobles in great earnestness are going | all 4.06. 58
lips, | coming and going with thy honey breath. TIT 2.04. 25
i am going with my pigeons to the tribunal plebs 4.03. 92 P
and we mean well in going to this mask, | but ROM 1.04. 48
what's he that now is going out of door? 1.05.130
going to find a barefoot brother out, | one of 5.02. 5
threat'ned me with death, going in the vault, 5.03.276
whither art going? TIM 1.01.191 P
thou art going to lord timon's feast? 1.01.260
i shall unfold to thee, as we are going, | to JC 2.01.330
speak | in the same pulpit whereto i am going, 3.01.250
whither are you going? 3.03. 6 P
whither am i going? 3.03. 13 P
directly, i am going to caesar's funeral. 3.03. 20 P
his name out of his heart, and turn him going. 3.03. 34 P
thou marshal'st me the way that i was going, MAC 2.01. 42
stand not upon the order of your going, | but go 3.04.118
intent | in going back to school in wittenberg, HAM 1.02.113
my lord, he's going to his mother's closet. 3.03. 27
since my young lady's going into france, sir, LR 1.04. 73 P
whither is he going? 2.04.296
to see't, | that going shall be us'd with feet. 3.02. 94
advise the duke, where you are going, to a most 3.07. 9 P
going to put out | the other eye of gloucester. 4.02. 71
bid me farewell, and let me hear thee going. 4.06. 31
their going hence even as their coming hither, 5.02. 10
determine, | either for her stay or going; OTH 1.03.276
and i was going to your lodging, cassio. 3.04.172
if you will watch his going thence (which i will 4.02.235 P
whose quality, going on, | the sides o' th' ANT 1.02.191
nay, pray you, seek no color for your going, 1.03. 32
no going then; 1.03. 34
that which most with you should safe my going, 1.03. 55
provide your going, | choose your own company, 3.04. 36
not more in parting | than greatness going off. 4.13. 6
now my spirit is going, | i can no more. 4.15. 58
i was going, sir, | to give him welcome. CYM 1.06. 54
to whom being going, almost spent with hunger, 3.06. 62
to the king's party there's no going. 4.04. 9
still going? 5.03. 64
want eyes to direct them the way i am going, but 5.04.186 P
thee to desist | for going on death's net, whom PER 1.01. 40
you, there's no going but by their consent. 4.06.197 P
action with you | as that whereto i am going, TNK 1.01.103
ladies, | this is a service, whereto i am going, 1.01.171
prorogue this business we are going about, and 1.01.196
you are going now to gaze upon my mistress, 3.01.117
you are going now to look upon a sun | that 3.01.120
and now 'tis dark, and going i shall fall." VEN 719
since from thee going he went willful–slow, SON 51.13

/GOLD 1 FR 0.0001 REL FR 1 V 0 P
knows almost every /grain /of /pluto's /gold, TRO 3.03.197

GOLD 227 FR 0.0256 REL FR 185 V 42 P
and set it down | with gold on lasting pillars: TMP 5.01.208
the water nectar, and the rocks pure gold. TGV 2.04.171
and seven hundred pounds of moneys, and gold, WIV 1.01. 51 P
she is a region in guiana, all gold and bounty. 1.03. 69 P
vile, | his dove will prove, his gold will hold, 1.03. 98
i warrant you, in silk and gold, and in such 2.02. 67 P
found thee of more value | than stamps in gold, 3.04. 16
a hundred pound in gold more than your loss. 4.06. 5
not with fond sicles of the tested gold, | or MM 2.02.149
where is the gold i gave in charge to thee? ERR 1.02. 70
to me, sir? why, you gave no gold to me. 1.02. 71
he ask'd me for a /thousand marks in gold: 2.01. 61
"my gold!" 2.01. 62
"my gold!" 2.01. 63
"my gold!" 2.01. 64
"my gold!" 2.01. 66
yet the gold bides still | that others touch and 2.01.110
touch and, often touching, will | where gold; 2.01.112
the gold i gave to dromio is laid up | safe at 2.02. 1
you receiv'd no gold? 2.02. 9
home to the centaur with the gold you gave me. 2.02. 16
and charg'd him with a thousand marks in gold, 3.01. 8
the fineness of the gold, and chargeful fashion, 4.01. 29
master, here's the gold you sent me for. 4.03. 12 P
what gold is this? what adam dost thou mean? 4.03. 15 P
and why dost thou deny the bag of gold? 4.04. 96
and, gentle master, i receiv'd no gold; 4.04. 98
you saw they speak us fair, give us gold: 4.04.153 P
cloth a' gold and cuts, and lac'd with silver, ADO 3.04. 19 P
fear not, man, we'll tip thy horns with gold, 5.04. 44
one, her hairs were gold, crystal the other's LLL 4.03.140
be, | in their gold coats spots you see: MND 2.01. 11
turns into yellow gold his salt green streams. 3.02.393
he hath devis'd in these three chests of gold, MV 1.02. 30 P
or is your gold and silver ewes and rams? 1.03. 95
what gold and jewels she is furnish'd with, 2.04. 31
this first, of gold, who this inscription bears, 2.07. 4
let's see once more this saying grav'd in gold: 2.07. 36
being ten times undervalued to tried gold? 2.07. 53
so rich a gem | was set in worse than gold. 2.07. 55
bears the figure of an angel | stamp'd in gold, 2.07. 57
"all that glisters is not gold, | often have you 2.07. 65
gold, silver, and base lead. 2.09. 20
i shall never see my gold again. 3.01.111 P
therefore then, thou gaudy gold, | hard food for 3.02.101
you shall have gold | to pay the petty debt 3.02.306
is thick inlaid with patens of bright gold. 5.01. 59
about a hoop of gold, a paltry ring | that she 5.01.147
beauty provoketh thieves sooner than gold. AYL 1.03.110
here is the gold, | all this i give you, let me 2.03. 45
yond man | if he for gold will give us any food: 2.04. 65
if that love or gold | can in this desert place 2.04. 71
be, | and buy it with your gold right suddenly. 2.04.100
their harness studded all with gold and pearl. SHR in.2. 42
why, give him gold enough, and marry him to a 1.02. 78 P
it is, | i would not wed her for a mine of gold. 1.02. 92
city | is richly furnished with plate and gold, 2.01.347
pearl, | valens of venice gold in needle–work; 2.01.354
what 'cerns it you if i wear pearl and gold? 5.01. 76 P
take this purse of gold, | and let me buy your AWW 3.07. 14
well–weighing sums of gold to corrupt him to a 4.03.180 P
"dian, the count's a fool, and full of gold" — 4.03.211
"when he swears oaths, bid him drop gold, and 4.03.223
need not to ask you if gold will corrupt him to 4.03.277 P
for saying so, there's gold. TN 1.02. 18
shalt not be the worse for me, there's gold. 5.01. 28 P
gold, all gold! WT 3.03.121 P
gold, all gold! 3.03.122 P
this is fairy gold, boy, and 'twill prove so. 3.03.123 P
close with him, give him gold; 4.04.801 P
bear, yet he is oft led by the nose with gold. 4.04.802 P
the business for us, here is that gold i have. 4.04.807 P
gold and a means to do the prince my master good 4.04.833 P
the meagre cloddy earth to glittering gold. JN 3.01. 80
and by the merit of vild gold, dross, dust, 3.01.165
when gold and silver becks me to come on. 3.03. 13
to gild refined gold, to paint the lily, | to 4.02. 11
shall subscribe them for large sums of gold, R2 1.04. 50
as thriftless sons their scraping fathers' gold. 5.03. 69
a purse of gold most resolutely snatch'd on 1H4 1.02. 33 P
brought three hundred marks with him in gold. 2.01. 56 P
boys, hearts of gold, all the titles of good 2.04.278 P
never call a true piece of gold a counterfeit. 2.04.492 P
but i will inset you neither in gold nor silver, 2H4 1.02. 17 P
a good heart's worth gold. 2.04. 32 P
learning a mere hoard of gold kept by a devil, 4.03.115 P
a hoop of gold to bind thy brothers in, | that 4.04. 43
into revolt | when gold becomes her object! 4.05. 66
the cank'red heaps of strange–achieved gold; 4.05. 71
therefore thou best of gold art /worst /of gold. 4.05.160
therefore thou best of gold art /worst /of gold. 4.05.160
the singing masons building roofs of gold, | the H5 1.02.198
that (almost) mightst have coin'd me into gold, 2.02. 98
for me, the gold of france did not seduce, 2.02.155
the king's a bawcock, and a heart of gold, | a 4.01. 44
the intertissued robe of gold and pearl, | the 4.01.262
by jove, i am not covetous for gold, | nor care 4.03. 24
in stead of gold, we'll offer up our arms, 1H6 1.01. 46
in this, | and doth deserve a coronet of gold. 3.03. 89
large sums of gold and dowries with their wives, 2H6 1.01.129
put forth thy hand, reach at the glorious gold. 1.02. 11
hume must make merry with the duchess' gold; 1.02. 87
dame eleanor gives gold to bring the witch; 1.02. 91
gold cannot come amiss, were she a devil. 1.02. 92
yet have i gold flies from another coast — | i 1.02. 93
sort how it will, i shall have gold for all. 1.02.107
are my chests fill'd up with extorted gold? 4.07. 99
this hand was made to handle nought but gold. 5.01. 7
that gold must round engirt these brows of mine, 5.01. 99
give me thy gold — if thou hast any gold — 3H6 2.05. 80
give me thy gold — if thou hast any gold — 2.05. 80
wedges of gold, great anchors, heaps of pearl, R3 1.04. 26
it made me once restore a purse of gold that (by 1.04.140 P
touch, | to try if thou be current gold indeed. 4.02. 9
know'st thou not any whom corrupting gold | will 4.02. 34
gold were as good as twenty orators, | and will, 4.02. 38
all clinquant, all in gold, like heathen gods, H8 1.01. 19
but when the way was made | and pav'd with gold, 1.01.188
the o'er–great cardinal | hath show'd him gold; 1.01.223
me | i'll hide my silver beard in a gold beaver, TRO 1.03.296
chests in corioles, and the gold that's in them. COR 2.01.131 P
i tell you, he does sit in gold, his eye | red 5.01. 63
i will be bright, and shine in pearl and gold, TIT 2.01. 19
i would not for a million of gold | the cause 2.01. 49
i had none, | to bury so much gold under a tree, 2.03. 2
know that this gold must coin a stratagem, 2.03. 5
and so repose, sweet gold, for their unrest, 2.03. 8
my gracious lord, here is the bag of gold. 2.03.280
go pack with him, and give the mother gold, 4.02.155
and hid the gold within that letter mentioned, 5.01.107
eyes, | nor ope her lap to saint–seducing gold. ROM 1.01.214
that in gold clasps locks in the golden story; 1.03. 92
because musicians have no gold for sounding: 4.05.141 P
there is thy gold, worse poison to men's souls, 5.01. 80

for i will /raise her statue in pure gold, 5.03.299
plutus, the god of gold, | is but his steward. TIM 1.01.276
if i want gold, steal but a beggar's dog | and 2.01. 5
and give it timon, why, the dog coins gold. 2.01. 6
and usurers' men, bawds between gold and want! 2.02. 60 P
whilst i have gold, i'll be his steward still. 4.02. 50
gold? 4.03. 26
yellow, glittering, precious gold? 4.03. 26
i have but little gold of late, brave timon, 4.03. 91
here is some gold for thee. 4.03.101
put up thy gold. 4.03.108
go on — here's gold — go on; 4.03.108
there's gold to pay thy soldiers, | make large 4.03.127
hast thou gold yet? 4.03.130
i'll take the gold thou givest me, | not all thy 4.03.130
give us some gold, good timon; hast thou more? 4.03.133
well, more gold — what then? 4.03.149
believe't that we'll do any thing for gold. 4.03.150
there's more gold. 4.03.164
if thou wilt, | tell them there i have gold; 4.03.289
here is no use for gold. 4.03.290
i'll say th' hast gold; 4.03.393
where should he have this gold? 4.03.398 P
the mere want of gold, and the falling–from of 4.03.400 P
rascal thieves, | here's gold. 4.03.429
there's more gold. 4.03.445
i give you, | and gold confound you howsoe'er! 4.03.449
rumor hold for true that he's | so full of gold? 5.01. 4
/phrynia and /timandra had gold of him. 5.01. 5
do so, i have gold for thee. 5.01. 40
what a god's gold | that he is worshipp'd in a 5.01. 47
y' have heard that i have gold, | i am sure you 5.01. 76
look you, i love you well, i'll give you gold, 5.01.100
and come to me, | i'll give you gold enough. 5.01.104
there's gold; 5.01.112
you came for gold, ye slaves. 5.01.112
you are an alcumist, make gold of that. 5.01.114
he shall but bear them as the ass bears gold, JC 4.01. 21
to sell and mart your offices for gold | to 4.03. 11
i did send to you | for certain sums of gold, 4.03. 70
i did send | to you for gold to pay my legions, 4.03. 76
dearer than pluto's mine, richer than gold: 4.03.102
i, that denied thee gold, will give my heart: 4.03.104
like a piece of uncurrent gold, be not crack'd HAM 2.02.428 P
when usurers tell their gold i' th' field, | and LR 3.02. 91
/plate /sin with gold, | and the strong lance of 4.06.165
never lack'd gold, and yet went never gay, OTH 2.01.150
there's a poor piece of gold for thee. 3.01. 24 P
of gold and jewels that i bobb'd from him | as 5.01. 16
the poop was beaten gold, | purple the sails, ANT 2.02.192
she did lie | in her pavilion — cloth of gold, 2.02.199
if thou so yield him, there is gold, and here 2.05. 28
why, there's more gold. 2.05. 31
the gold i give thee will i melt and pour | down 2.05. 34
i'll set thee in a shower of gold, and hail 2.05. 45
there's gold for thee, | thou must not take my 3.03. 34
cleopatra and himself in chairs of gold | were 3.06. 4
i have a ship | laden with gold, take that, 3.11. 5
my turpitude | thou dost so crown with gold! 4.06. 33
i'll give thee, friend, | an armor all of gold; 4.08. 27
i will wage against your gold, gold to it. CYM 1.04.132 P
i will wage against your gold, gold to it. 1.04.132 P
jewel, this your jewel, and my gold are yours — 1.04.153 P
i will fetch my gold and have our two wagers 1.04.167 P
that play with all infirmities for gold | which 1.06.124
this foolish imogen, i should have gold enough. 2.03. 8 P
'tis gold | which buys admittance (oft it doth), 2.03. 67
and 'tis gold | which makes the true man kill'd 2.03. 70
there is gold for you, | sell me your good 2.03. 82
i should have lost the worth of it in gold. 2.04. 42
though i had found | gold strew'd i' th' floor. 3.06. 49
all gold and silver rather turn to dirt, | as 3.06. 53
pieces of gold 'gainst this which then he wore 5.05.183
behold, | here's poison and here's gold; PER 1.01.155
holding out gold that's by the touchstone tried; 2.02. 37
if the sea's stomach be o'ercharg'd with gold, 3.02. 54
begin to part | their fringes of bright gold. 3.02.100
he will line your apron with gold. 4.06. 59 P
hold, here's gold for thee. 4.06.105
hold, here's more gold for thee. 4.06.113
here, here's gold for thee. 4.06.181
you | that for our gold we may provision have, 5.01. 56
and give you gold for such provision | as our 5.01.257
sweeter | than her gold buttons on the boughs, TNK 3.01. 6
he wears a well–steel'd axe, the staff of gold. 4.02.115
but gold that's put to use more gold begets." VEN 768
but gold that's put to use more gold begets." 768
that cedar tops and hills seem burnish'd gold. 858
"the aged man that coffers up his gold | is LUC 855
thy int'rest was not bought | basely with gold, 1068
and often is his gold complexion dimm'd, | and SON 18. 6
as those gold candles fix'd in heaven's air: 21.12
crack'd many a ring of posied gold and bone, LC 45

GOLD–BOUND 1 FR 0.0001 REL FR 1 V 0 P
thou other gold–bound brow, is like the first. MAC 4.01.114

/GOLDEN 1 FR 0.0001 REL FR 1 V 0 P
/now /is /this /golden /crown /like /a /deep R2 4.01.184

GOLDEN 104 FR 0.0117 REL FR 97 V 7 P
govern, sir, | t' excel the golden age. TMP 2.01.169
whose golden touch could soften steel and stones TGV 3.02. 78
sail like my pinnace to these golden shores. WIV 1.03. 80
spread o'er the silver waves thy golden hairs, ERR 3.02. 48
when in the streets he meets such golden gifts. 3.02.183
cut with her golden oars the silver stream, ADO 3.01. 27
facility, and golden cadence of poesy, caret. LLL 4.02.122 P
"so sweet a kiss the golden sun gives not | to 4.03. 25
debtor, | my red dominical, my golden letter: 5.02. 44
bow, | by his best arrow with the golden head, MND 1.01.170
by thy gracious, golden, glittering /gleams, | i 5.01.274
hang on her temples like a golden fleece, MV 1.01.170
a golden mind stoops not to shows of dross. 2.07. 20
but here an angel in a golden bed | lies all 2.07. 58
what says the golden chest? 2.09. 23
so are those crisped snaky golden locks, | which 3.02. 92
a golden mesh t' entrap the hearts of men 3.02.122
carelessly, as they did in the golden world. AYL 1.01.118 P
with silken coats and caps, and golden rings, SHR 4.03. 55
how will she love when the rich golden shaft TN 1.01. 34
his counsel now might do me golden service, 4.03. 8
when that is known and golden time convents, | a 5.01.382
golden apollo, a poor humble swain, | as i seem WT 4.04. 30
golden quoifs and stomachers | for my lads to 4.04.224
and with her golden hand hath pluck'd on france JN 3.01. 57
that it in golden letters should be set | among 3.01. 85
his golden uncontroll'd enfranchisement, | more R2 1.03. 90
and those his golden beams to you here lent 1.03.146
to lift shrewd steel against our golden crown, 3.02. 59
thy stomach, pleasure, and thy golden sleep? 1H4 2.03. 41
thy golden sceptre for a leaden dagger, and thy 2.04.381 P
team | begins his golden progress in the east. 3.01.219
glittering in golden coats like images, | as 4.01.100
him | even at the heels in golden multitudes. 4.03. 73
golden care! 2H4 4.05. 23
that from this golden rigol hath divorc'd | so 4.05. 36
and golden times, and happy news of price. 5.03. 96
i speak of africa and golden joys. 5.03.100
receiv'd the golden earnest of our death; H5 2.02.169
up in the air, crown'd with the golden sun, 2.04. 58
royally, | after this golden day of victory. 1H6 1.06. 31
worthy saint michael, and the golden fleece, 4.07. 69
queen, | to put a golden sceptre in thy hand, 5.03.118
set this diamond safe | in golden palaces, as it 5.03.170
for that's the golden mark i seek to hit. 2H6 1.01.243
to rage | until the golden circuit on my head, 3.01.352
see how the morning opes her golden gates, | and 3H6 2.01. 21
his viands sparkling in a golden cup, | his body 2.05. 52
to cross me from the golden time i look for! 3.02.127
than to accomplish twenty golden crowns! 3.02.152
great albion's queen in former golden days; 3.03. 7
that cropp'd the golden prime of this sweet R3 1.02.247
orator | as if the golden fee for which i plead 3.05. 96
to bear the golden yoke of sovereignty, | which 3.07.146
verge | of golden metal that must round my brow 4.01. 59
his bed | did i enjoy the golden dew of sleep, 4.01. 83
hid'st thou that forehead with a golden crown 4.04.140
th' aspiring flame | of golden sovereignty; 4.04.329
the weary sun hath made a golden set, | and by 5.03. 19
a glist'ring grief | and wear a golden sorrow. H8 2.03. 22
had as lieve helen's golden tongue had commended TRO 1.02.105 P
as when the golden sun salutes the morn, | and, TIT 2.01. 5
(our pastimes done), possess a golden slumber, 2.03. 26
and fill his aged ears | with golden promises, 4.04. 97
peer'd forth the golden window of the east, | a ROM 1.01.119
that in gold clasps locks in the golden story; 1.03. 92
couch his limbs, there golden sleep doth reign. 2.03. 38
thou cut'st my head off with a golden axe, | and 3.03. 22
the learned pate | ducks to the golden fool. TIM 4.03. 18
all that impedes thee from the golden round, MAC 1.05. 28
golden opinions from all sorts of people, 1.07. 33
his silver skin lac'd with his golden blood, 2.03.112
hanging a golden stamp about their necks, | put 4.03.153
this majestical roof fretted with golden fire, HAM 2.02.301 P
when that her golden couplets are disclosed, 5.01.287
all 's golden words are spent. 5.02.130 P
bald crown when thou gav'st thy golden one away. LR 1.04.163 P
and golden phoebus never be beheld | of eyes ANT 5.02.317
mary–buds begin to ope their golden eyes; CYM 2.03. 24
th' chamber | with golden cherubins is fretted. 2.04. 88
put | his brows within a golden crown and call'd 3.01. 60
golden lads and girls all must, | as 4.02.262
that have this golden chance and know not why. 5.04.132
with golden fruit, but dangerous to be touch'd; PER 1.01. 28
hours | shake off the golden slumber of repose. 3.02. 23
in glitt'ring golden characters express | a 4.03. 44
to his bold ends honor and golden ingots, TNK 1.02. 17
then with her windy sighs and golden hairs | to VEN 51
love's golden arrow at him should have fled, 947
the fishes spread on it their golden gills; 1100
dew | against the golden splendor of the sun! LUC 25
that golden hap which their superiors want. 42
which virtue gave the golden age to gild | their 60
survive, | and be an eye–sore in my golden coat; 205
her hair like golden threads play'd with her 400
knit poisonous clouds about his golden head. 777
smear with dust their glitt'ring golden tow'rs; 945
as, but for loss of nestor's golden words, | it 1420
and town, | the golden bullet beats it down. PP 18.18
despite of wrinkles, this thy golden time. SON 3.12
still, | attending on his golden pilgrimage: 7. 8
kissing with golden face the meadows green, 33. 3
before the golden tresses of the dead, | the 68. 5
reserve their character with golden quill | and 85. 3

GOLDENLY 1 FR 0.0001 REL FR 0 V 1 P
and report speaks goldenly of his profit. AYL 1.01. 6 P

GOLD'S 2 FR 0.0002 REL FR 2 V 0 P
villain, thou didst deny the gold's receipt, ERR 2.02. 17
thou know'st not gold's effect. SHR 1.02. 93

GOLDSMITH 9 FR 0.0010 REL FR 9 V 0 P
but soft, i see the goldsmith. ERR 4.01. 19
but neither chain nor goldsmith came to me: 4.01. 24
i see, sir, you have found the goldsmith now. 4.03. 46
thou hast suborn'd the goldsmith to arrest me. 4.04. 82
one angelo, a goldsmith. do you know him? 4.04.132
come, jailer, bring me where the goldsmith is, 4.04.142
that goldsmith there, were he not pack'd with 5.01.219
there did this perjur'd goldsmith swear me down 5.01.227
the goldsmith here | denies that saying. 5.01.274

GOLDSMITH'S 1 FR 0.0001 REL FR 1 V 0 P
while i go to the goldsmith's house, go thou ERR 4.01. 15

GOLDSMITHS' 1 FR 0.0001 REL FR 0 V 1 P
you not been acquainted with goldsmiths' wives, AYL 3.02.271 P

GOLGOTHA 2 FR 0.0002 REL FR 2 V 0 P
the field of golgotha and dead men's skulls. R2 4.01.144
reeking wounds, | or memorize another golgotha, MAC 1.02. 40

GOLIAH 1 FR 0.0001 REL FR 0 V 1 P
/brook, i fear not goliah with a weaver's beam, WIV 5.01. 22 P

GOLIASES 1 FR 0.0001 REL FR 1 V 0 P
for none but samsons and goliases | it sendeth 1H6 1.02. 33

GONDILO *(also gundello)*

GONDILO 1 FR 0.0001 REL FR 1 V 0 P
that in a gondilo were seen together | lorenzo MV 2.08. 8

GONDOLIER *(see gundolier)*

/GONE 4 FR 0.0004 REL FR 3 V 1 P
/and /then /be /gone /and /trouble /you /no R2 4.01.303
/get /thee /gone, | /i /see /thou /art /not /for TIT 3.02. 57
he /gone in triumph, and mercutio slain! ROM 3.01.122
/king /of /france /is /so /suddenly /gone /back, LR 4.03. 1 P

GONE 497 FR 0.0561 REL FR 423 V 74 P
but 'tis gone. TMP 1.02.395
and your affection not gone forth, i'll make you 1.02.449
no, no, he's gone. 2.01.123
he's gone. 2.01.244
when that's gone, | he shall drink nought but 3.02. 65
our remembrances with | a heaviness that's gone. 5.01.200
and the particular accidents gone by | since i 5.01.306
wilt thou be gone? TGV 1.01. 11
go, go, be gone, to save your ship from wrack, 1.01.148
will ye be gone? 1.02. 49
go, get you gone; 1.02. 97
what, gone without a word? 2.02. 16
is gone with her along, and i must after, | for 2.04.176
but, valentine being gone, i'll quickly cross 2.06. 40
no matter who's displeas'd when you are gone: 2.07. 66
for which the youthful lover now is gone, | and 3.01. 41
if she do chide, 'tis not to have you gone, 3.01. 98
for "get you gone," she doth not mean "away!" 3.01.101
be gone! 3.01.168
according to our proclamation, gone? 3.02. 12
gone, my good lord. 3.02. 13
gone to seek his dog, which to–morrow, by his 4.02. 78 P
than hate for silvia, that is gone for love. 5.02. 56
therefore be gone, solicit me no more. 5.04. 40
all his successors (gone before him) hath done't WIV 1.01. 14 P
i pray you be gone. 1.02. 11 P
priest to meddle or make — you may be gone; 1.04.110 P
would have gone to the truth of his words; 2.01. 61 P
be gone, and come when you are call'd. 3.03. 19 P
well, be gone; i will not miss her. 3.05. 55 P
her husband is this morning gone a–birding. 3.05.128 P
woman, a fat woman, gone up into his chamber. 4.05. 11 P
old fat woman even now with me, but she's gone. 4.05. 25 P
they are gone but to meet the duke, villain, do 4.05. 71 P
they had gone down too, but that a wise burgher MM 1.02. 99 P
so long that nineteen zodiacs have gone round 1.02.168
the duke is very strangely gone from hence; 1.04. 50
all hope is gone, | unless you have the grace by 1.04. 68
get you gone, and let me hear no more of you. 2.01.206 P
pray you be gone. 2.02. 66
that now you are come, you will be gone. 3.01.176 P
i know you'ld fain be gone. 5.01.120
but tuesday night last gone, in 's garden–house, 5.01.229
compact with her that's gone, think'st thou thy 5.01.242
is the duke gone? 5.01.299
then is your cause gone too. 5.01.300
if it prove so, i will be gone the sooner. ERR 1.02.103
and from the mart he's somewhere gone to dinner. 2.01. 5
go, get thee gone, fetch me an iron crow. 3.01. 84
time, i think, to trudge, pack, and be gone. 3.02.153
get thee gone, | buy thou a rope, and bring it 4.01. 19
hie thee, slave, be gone! 4.01.107
no evil lost is wail'd when it is gone. 4.02. 24
no, no, the bell, 'tis time that i were gone: 4.02. 53
may we be gone? 4.03. 36 P
i conjure thee to leave me and be gone. 4.03. 67
and i'll be gone, sir, and not trouble you. 4.03. 70
fly, be gone! 5.01.184
thirty–three years have i but gone in travail 5.01.401
likeness of your grace, for trouble being gone, ADO 1.01.100 P
that have gone about | to link my dear friend to 4.01. 64
i am gone, though i am here; 4.01.293 P
thy slander hath gone through and through her 5.01. 68
john is the author of all, who is fled and gone. 5.02. 99 P
nay then will i be gone. LLL 2.01.127
ay, our way to be gone. 2.01.258
will these turtles be gone? 4.03.208
is this your perfectness? be gone, you rogue! 5.02.174
why, that they have, and bid them so be gone. 5.02.182
she says, you have it, and you may be gone. 5.02.183
gone to her tent. 5.02.311
the party is gone" — 5.02.671
fellow hector, she is gone; 5.02.672 P
i'll be gone. MND 2.01. 16
and here my mistress. would that he were gone! 2.01. 59
hence, get thee gone, and follow me no more. 2.01.194
through the forest have i gone, | but athenian 2.02. 66
so awake when i am gone, | for i must now to 2.02. 82
what, out of hearing gone? 2.02.152
if e'er i lov'd her, all that love is gone. 3.02.170
why, get you gone. who is't that hinders you? 3.02.318
get you gone, you dwarf; 3.02.328
burial, | already to their wormy beds are gone. 3.02.384
when i come where he calls, then he is gone. 3.02.414
fairies, be gone, and be /all /ways away. 4.01. 41
our intent | was to be gone from athens, where 4.01.152
if our sport had gone forward, we had all been 4.02. 17 P
how chance moonshine is gone before thisby comes 5.01.312 P
yellow cowslip cheeks, | are gone, are gone! 5.01.333
yellow cowslip cheeks, | are gone, are gone! 5.01.333
as you would say in plain terms, gone to heaven. MV 2.02. 65 P
ay, marry, i'll be gone about it straight. 2.04. 24
than to be under sail, and gone to–night. 2.06. 68
under sail, | with him is gratiano gone along; 2.08. 2
lord, | you must be gone from hence immediately. 2.09. 8
choice, | immediately to leave you, and be gone. 2.09. 16
so be gone, you are sped." 2.09. 72
a diamond gone, cost me two thousand ducats in 3.01. 84 P
the thief gone with so much, and so much to find 3.01. 93 P
o love! dispatch all business, and be gone! 3.02.323
waste no time in words, | but get thee gone. 3.04. 55
well, you are gone both ways. 3.05. 18 P
get thee gone, but do it. 4.01.397
finger | hath not the ring upon it, it is gone. 5.01.188
and seem more virtuous | when she is gone. AYL 1.03. 82
and she believes, where ever they are gone, 2.02. 15
my lord, he is but even now gone hence; 2.07. 3
be gone, i say, | i will not to wedding with 3.03.104
would have gone near | to fall in love with him; 3.05.125
ta'en his bow and arrows and is gone forth — to 4.03. 4 P
sirrah, be gone, or talk not, i advise you. SHR 1.02. 44
o excellent motion! fellows, let's be gone. 1.02.278
farewell, sweet masters both, i must be gone. 3.01. 85
for me, i'll not be gone till i please myself. 3.02.212

faith, he is gone unto the taming–school. 4.02. 54
go get thee gone, thou false deluding slave, 4.03. 31
go get thee gone, i say. 4.03. 35
go take it hence, be gone, and say no more. 4.03.165
dally not with the gods, but get thee gone. 4.04. 68
but now he's gone, and my idolatrous fancy AWW 1.01. 97
get you gone, sirrah. 1.03. 8 P
get you gone, sir, i'll talk with you more anon. 1.03. 64 P
you'll be gone, sir knave, and do as i command 1.03. 90 P
be gone to–morrow, and be sure of this, | what i 1.03.255
is she gone to the king? 2.05. 20 P
madam, my lord is gone, for ever gone. 3.02. 46
madam, my lord is gone, for ever gone. 3.02. 46
madam, he's gone to serve the duke of florence. 3.02. 52
i will be gone. 3.02.122
i will be gone, | that pitiful rumor may report 3.02.126
"i am saint jaques' pilgrim, thither gone. 3.04. 4
when haply he shall hear that she is gone, | he 3.04. 35
lost our labor, they are gone a contrary way. 3.05. 8 P
to acquaint his grace you are gone about it? 3.06. 79 P
my lord that's gone made himself much sport out 4.05. 64 P
i do beseech you, whither is he gone? 5.01. 27
offense, | crying, "that's good that's gone." 5.03. 60
if you be not mad, be gone. TN 1.05.199 P
dear heart, since i must needs be gone." 2.03.102
rudesby, be gone! 4.01. 51
i prithee be gone. 4.02.119 P
i am gone, sir, | and anon, sir, | i'll be with 4.02.120
gone already! WT 1.02.185
'tis far gone, | when i shall gust it last. 1.02.218
i can hook to me — say that she were gone, 2.03. 7
i pray you do not push me, i'll be gone. 2.03.125
farewell, we are gone. 2.03.130
favor, | i do give lost, for i do feel it gone, 3.02. 95
and fear | of the queen's speed, is gone. 3.02.145
how? gone? 3.02.145
what's gone and what's past help | should be 3.02.222
i am gone for ever. 3.03. 58
go see if the bear be gone from the gentleman 3.03.129 P
is it not too far gone? 4.04.344
will't please you, sir, be gone? 4.04.446
he is gone aboard a new ship to purge melancholy 4.04.762 P
we are gone else. 4.04.820 P
is none worthy, | respecting her that's gone. 5.01. 35
time doth boast itself | above a better gone, so 5.01. 97
with all greediness of affection are they gone, 5.02.103 P
my land, | legitimation, name, and all is gone; JN 1.01.248
gone to be married? 3.01. 1
gone to swear a peace? 3.01. 1
gone to be friends? 3.01. 2
fellow, be gone! 3.01. 36
envenom him with words, or get thee gone, | and 3.01. 63
and bloody england into england gone, 3.04. 8
if that young arthur be not gone already, | even 3.04.163
the suit which you demand is gone and dead. 4.02. 84
avaunt, thou hateful villain, get thee gone! 4.03. 77
but are gone | to offer service to your enemy; 5.01. 33
art thou gone so? 5.07. 70
what is six winters? they are quickly gone. R2 1.03.260
well, he is gone, and with him go these thoughts 1.04. 37
york is too far gone with grief, | or else he 2.01.184
your husband, he is gone to save far off, 2.02. 80
my lord, your son was gone before i came. 2.02. 86
is gone to ravenspurgh | to offer service to the 2.03. 31
our countrymen are gone and fled, | as well 2.04. 16
are gone to bullingbrook, dispers'd and fled. 3.02. 74
and salisbury | is gone to meet the king, who 3.03. 3
so, now i have mine own again, be gone, | that i 5.01. 99
away, be gone! 5.02.117
worcester, get thee gone, for i do see | danger 1H4 1.03. 15
who strook this heat up after i was gone? 1.03.139
what ho! is gilliams with the packet gone? 2.03. 65
shall we be gone? 3.01.139
nay, prithee be gone. 3.03.174 P
so be gone; 5.01.112
he's gone /into smithfield to buy your worship a 2H4 1.02. 50 P
we are time's subjects, and time bids be gone. 1.03.110
didst thou not, when she was gone down stairs, 2.01. 99 P
be gone, good ancient. 2.04.172 P
i pray thee, jack, be quiet, the rascal's gone. 2.04.208 P
thou't forget me when i am gone. 2.04.277 P
'tis not ten years gone | since richard and 3.01. 57
i would wart might have gone, sir. 3.02.163 P
nobody to do any thing about her when i am gone, 3.02.231 P
the dangers of the days but newly gone, | whose 4.01. 80
the army is discharged all and gone. 4.03.127
i think he's gone to hunt, my lord, at windsor. 4.04. 14
this door is open, he is gone this way. 4.05. 55
then get thee gone, and dig my grave thyself, 4.05.110
you, | my father is gone wild into his grave; 5.02.123
the fuel is gone that maintain'd that fire. H5 2.03. 43 P
the king will be gone from southampton. 2.03. 45 P
the french is gone off, look you, and there is 3.06. 92 P
as who should say, "when i am dead and gone, 1H6 1.04. 93
guests | are often welcomest when they are gone. 2.02. 56
not to be gone from hence; 3.02. 94
come, dally not, be gone. 4.05. 11
mine own is gone. 4.07. 1
now he is gone, my lord, you need not fear. 5.02. 17
be gone, i say, for, till you do return, | i 5.05. 94
lordings, farewell, and say, when i am gone, | i 2H6 1.01.145
stands on a tickle point now they are gone. 1.01.216
still revelling like lords till all be gone; 1.01.224
come, let's be gone. 1.03. 41 P
and, ten to one, old joan had not gone out. 2.01. 4
when i am dead and gone, | may honorable peace 2.03. 37
what, gone, my lord, and bid me not farewell? 2.04. 85
art thou gone too? 2.04. 87
away, be gone. 3.02. 14
so get thee gone, that i may know my grief, 3.02.346
even now be gone. 3.02.352
ay, marry, will we; therefore get ye gone. 4.02.153
my hope is gone, now suffolk is deceas'd. 4.04. 56
thou hast spoke too much already; get thee gone. 3H6 1.01.258
now thou art gone we have no staff, no stay. 2.01. 69
and now to london all the crew are gone | to 2.01.174
my queen and son are gone to france for aid; 3.01. 28
/is thither gone to crave the french king's 3.01. 30
there's thy reward, be gone. 3.03.233
clarence and somerset both gone to warwick? 4.01.127
i'll leave you to your fortune and be gone | to 4.07. 55
where's richard gone? 5.05. 83
king henry and the prince his son are gone; 5.06. 89
when they are gone, then must i count my gains. R3 1.01.162
therefore be gone. 1.02. 48
son | to be your comforter when he is gone. 1.03. 10
why grow the branches when the root is gone? 2.02. 41
what stay had i but edward? and he's gone. 2.02. 74
what stay had we but clarence? and he's gone. 2.02. 75
what stays had i but they? and they are gone. 2.02. 76
but what, is catesby gone? 3.05. 12
o dorset, speak not to me, get thee gone! 4.01. 38
and be gone | to brecknock while my fearful head 4.02.121
hence both are gone with conscience and remorse 4.03. 20
ay, thou wouldst be gone to join with richmond; 4.04.490
so get thee gone; 4.05. 6
he's gone to th' king; H8 1.01.128
me, | i have no further gone in this than by | a 1.02. 69
thomas lovell's heads | should have gone off. 1.02.186
gone slightly o'er low steps and now are mounted 2.04.112
of the peers | have uncontemn'd gone by him, or 3.02. 10
o, cromwell, | the king has gone beyond me! 3.02.408
are ye all gone? 4.02. 83
be gone. 5.01. 86
get you gone, | and do as i have bid you. 5.01.155
gone between and between, but small thanks for TRO 1.01. 71 P
was hector arm'd and gone ere ye came to ilium? 1.02. 48 P
hector was gone, but helen was not up. 1.02. 50 P
condition i had gone barefoot to india. 1.02. 74 P
ne'er look, ne'er look, the eagles are gone; 1.02.244 P
sith /every action that hath gone before, 1.03. 13
what, are you gone again? 3.02. 43 P
i would be gone. 3.02.150
gone? 4.02. 81 P
thou must be gone, wench, thou must be gone; 4.02. 90 P
thou must be gone, wench, thou must be gone; 4.02. 91 P
must to thy father, and be gone from troilus. 4.02. 92 P
be gone, i say, the gods have heard me swear. 5.03. 15
hector is gone. 5.10. 14
hence to your homes, be gone! COR 1.01.248
'tis not four days gone | since i heard thence; 1.02. 6
against whom cominius the general is gone, with 1.03. 97 P
be gone, away! 3.01.229
get you gone. 3.01.230
be gone, beseech you. 3.01.235
be gone! 3.01.239
pray you be gone. 3.01.249
the people's enemy is gone, is gone! 3.03.136
the people's enemy is gone, is gone! 3.03.136
our enemy is banish'd, he is gone! hoo! hoo! 3.03.137
bid them all home, he's gone; 4.02. 1
say their great enemy is gone, and they | stand 4.02. 6
will you be gone? 4.02. 14
now, pray, sir, get you gone; 4.02. 37
if he had gone forth consul, found it so. 4.06. 35
therefore be gone. 5.02. 87
the volscians are dislodg'd, and martius gone. 5.04. 41
my rage is gone, | and i am struck with sorrow. 5.06.146
t' appease their groaning shadows that are gone. TIT 1.01.126
one, | so trouble me no more, but get you gone. 1.01.367
aaron is gone, and my compassionate heart | will 2.03.217
this way to death my wretched sons are gone, 3.01. 98
for love of her that's gone, | perhaps, she 4.01. 43
you rememb'red, marcus, she's gone, she's fled. 4.03. 5
go get you gone, and pray be careful all, | and 4.03. 21
and talk of them when he was dead and gone. 5.03.166
we'll measure them a measure and be gone. ROM 1.04. 10
'tis gone, 'tis gone, 'tis gone. 1.05. 24
'tis gone, 'tis gone, 'tis gone. 1.05. 24
'tis gone, 'tis gone, 'tis gone. 1.05. 24
away, be gone, the sport is at the best. 1.05.119
nay, gentlemen, prepare not to be gone, | we 1.05.121
come let's away, the strangers all are gone. 1.05.144
'tis almost morning, i would have thee gone — 2.02.176
is he gone and hath nothing? 3.01. 92
romeo, away, be gone! 3.01.132
hence be gone, away! 3.01.135
alack the day, he's gone, he's kill'd, he's dead 3.02. 39
for who is living, if those two are gone? 3.02. 68
tybalt is gone, and romeo banished, | romeo that 3.02. 69
either be gone before the watch be set, | or by 3.03.167
well, get you gone, a' thursday be it then. 3.04. 30
wilt thou be gone? 3.05. 1
i must be gone and live, or stay and die. 3.05. 11
therefore stay yet, thou need'st not to be gone. 3.05. 16
hie hence, be gone, away! 3.05. 26
o, now be gone, more light and light it grows. 3.05. 35
art thou gone so, love — lord, ay, husband, 3.05. 43
go in, and tell my lady i am gone, | having 3.05.231
hold, get you gone. 4.01.122
go, be gone. 4.02. 9
what, is my daughter gone to friar lawrence? 4.02. 11
faith, we may put up our pipes and be gone. 4.05. 97 P
no matter, get thee gone, | and hire those 5.01. 32
in dear employment — therefore hence be gone. 5.03. 32
i will be gone, sir, and not trouble ye. 5.03. 40
fly hence and leave me, think upon these gone, 5.03. 60
o, be gone! 5.03. 63
stay not, be gone; 5.03. 66
my master knows not but i am gone hence, | and 5.03.132
he is gone happy, and has left me rich. TIM 1.02. 4
get you gone, | put on a most importunate aspect 2.01. 27
get you gone. 2.01. 32
answer not, i am gone. 2.02. 87 P
'tis all engag'd, some forfeited and gone, | and 2.02.146
give it in a breath, | how quickly were it gone! 2.02.154
when the means are gone that buy this praise, 2.02.169
the breath is gone whereof this praise is made. 2.02.170
get you gone, sirrah. 3.01. 38 P
so noble a master fall'n, all gone, and not 4.02. 6
i prithee beat thy drum and get thee gone. 4.03. 97
speak not, be gone. 4.03.129
hence, be gone! 4.03.274
get thee gone. 4.03.280
till now you have gone on and fill'd the time 5.04. 3
upon neat's–leather have gone upon my handiwork. JC 1.01. 26 P
be gone! 1.01. 52
and he's gone | to seek you at your house. 1.03.149
stay not to answer me, but get thee gone. 2.04. 2
is caesar yet gone to the capitol? 2.04. 24
ay, caesar, but not gone. 3.01. 2
away, away, be gone! 4.03.138
portia, art thou gone? 4.03.166
this morning are they fled away and gone, | and 5.01. 83
our day is gone, | clouds, dews, and dangers 5.03. 63
her husband's to aleppo gone, master o' th' MAC 1.03. 7
whose care is gone before to bid us welcome: 1.04. 57
nam'd, and gone to scone | to be invested. 2.04. 31
is banquo gone from court? 3.02. 1
get thee gone; 3.04. 30
being gone, | i am a man again. 3.04.106
get you gone, | and at the pit of acheron | meet 3.05. 14
thither macduff | is gone to pray the holy king, 3.06. 30
gone? 4.01.133
'tis gone, and will not answer. HAM 1.01. 52
with martial stalk hath he gone by our watch. 1.01. 66
'tis gone! 1.01.142
which have freely gone | with this affair along. 1.02. 15
'a is far gone. 2.02.189 P
full thirty times hath phoebus' cart gone round 3.02.155
where is he gone? 4.01. 23
"he is dead and gone, lady, | he is dead and 4.05. 29
is dead and gone, lady, | he is dead and gone, 4.05. 30
next, your son gone, and he most violent author 4.05. 80
he is gone, he is gone, | and we cast away moan, 4.05.197
flaxen was his pole, | he is gone, he is gone, 4.05.197
when these are gone, | the woman will be out. 4.07.188
therefore be gone, | without our grace, our love LR 1.01.264
and the king gone to–night? 1.02. 24
the night gone by. 1.02.153 P
get you gone, | and hasten your return. 1.04.339
thy asses are gone about 'em. 1.05. 34 P
winter's not gone yet, if the wild geese fly 2.04. 46 P
if he ask for me, i am ill and gone to bed. 3.03. 17 P
sir, but trouble him not — his wits are gone. 3.06. 87
are gone with him toward dover, where they boast 3.07. 19
good friend, be gone, | thy comforts can do me 4.01. 15
above the rest, be gone. 4.01. 48
edmund, i think, is gone, | in pity of his 4.05. 11
gone, sir; 4.06. 41
she's gone for ever! 5.03.260
i might have sav'd her, now she's gone for ever! 5.03.271
he is gone indeed. 5.03.316
gone she is; OTH 1.01.160
to mourn a mischief that is past and gone | is 1.03.204
there's one gone to the harbor? 2.01.120
you see this fellow that is gone before: 2.03.121
nay, get thee gone. 2.03.382
of years (yet that's not much), | she's gone. 3.03.267
avaunt, be gone! 3.03.335
othello's occupation's gone! 3.03.357
'tis gone. 3.03.446
is't gone? 3.04. 80
when he is gone, | i would on great occasion 4.01. 57
so get thee gone, good night. 4.03. 58
'tis but a man gone. 5.01. 10
she's like a liar gone to burning hell: 5.02.129
he's gone, but his wife's kill'd. 5.02.238
there's a great spirit gone! ANT 1.02.122
she's good, being gone; 1.02.126
i must be gone. 1.02.136
vacancy, | had gone to gaze on cleopatra too, 2.02.217
get thee gone. 2.03. 31
they have dispatch'd with pompey, he is gone; 3.02. 2
but how, when antony is gone, | through whom i 3.03. 5
'tis done already, and the messenger gone. 3.06. 31
been what he knew himself, it had gone well. 3.10. 26
friends, be gone, | i have myself resolv'd upon 3.11. 8
be gone. 3.11. 10
friends, be gone, you shall | have letters from 3.11. 15
kings for messengers | not many moons gone by. 3.12. 6
hence with thy stripes, be gone! 3.13.152
who's gone this morning? 4.05. 6
is he gone? 4.05. 11
bid them all fly, be gone. 4.12. 17
'tis well th' art gone, | if it be well to live; 4.12. 39
o, quick, or i am gone. 4.15. 31
our strength is all gone into heaviness, | that 4.15. 33
the odds is gone, | and there is nothing left 4.15. 66
well, get thee gone, farewell. 5.02.278
you must be gone, | and i shall here abide the CYM 1.01. 88
i am gone. 1.01.130
so, get you gone. 2.03. 27 P
i hope it be not gone to tell my lord | that i 2.03.147
why hast thou gone so far, | to be unbent when 3.04.107
but for her, | where is she gone? 3.05. 60
gone she is | to death or to dishonor, and my 3.05. 62
now i think on thee, | my hunger's gone; 3.06. 16
if he be gone, he'll make his grave a bed. 4.02.216
hast done, | home art gone, and ta'en thy wages. 4.02.261
i have gone all night. 4.02.294
'tis gone. 4.02.312
imogen, | the great part of my comfort, gone; 4.03. 5
her son gone, | so needful for this present! 4.03. 7
i nothing know where she remains, why gone, 4.03. 14
gone! 5.04.126
had it gone with us, | we should not, when the 5.05. 76
but her son | is gone, we know not how, nor 5.05.273
if i discover'd not which way she was gone, | it 5.05.277
the breath is gone, and the sore eyes see clear PER 1.01. 99
does speak sufficiently he's gone to travel. 1.03. 13
how? the king gone? 1.03. 14
but since he's gone, the king's seas must please 1.03. 27
most honor'd cleon, i must needs be gone. 3.03. 1
i have gone through for this piece you see. 4.02. 43 P
dead, | nor none can know, leonine being gone. 4.03. 30
to fetch his daughter home, who first is gone. 4.04. 20
do in such a place as this, she being once gone. 4.05. 3 P
heart | leaps to be gone into my mother's bosom. 5.03. 45
roses, their sharp spines being gone, | not TNK 1.01. 1
'twill take form, the heats are gone to–morrow. 1.01.152
set you forward, | for i will see you gone. 1.01.218
come, let's be gone, lads. 2.03. 73

the /brake i meant, is gone | after his fancy. 3.02. 1
all's char'd when he is gone. 3.02. 21
good night, good night, y' are gone. 3.04. 11
heard her | repeat this often, "palamon is gone, 4.01. 67
is gone to th' wood to gather mulberries. 4.01. 68
if she see him once, she's gone — she's done, 4.01.124
till either gorge be stuff'd, or prey be gone; VEN 58
what bare excuses mak'st thou to be gone! 188
and when from thence he struggles to be gone, 227
my day's delight is past, my horse is gone, 380
therefore no marvel though thy horse be gone. 390
are they not quickly told, and quickly gone? 520
the sheep are gone to fold, birds to their nest, 532
"thou hadst been gone," quoth she, "sweet boy, 613
my sighs are blown away, my salt tears gone, 1071
the wind would blow it off, and being gone, 1089
"o, that is gone for which i sought to live, LUC 1051
of day, | and ere i rose was tarquin gone away. 1281
her maid is gone, and she prepares to write, 1296
and yet the duteous vassal scarce is gone; 1360
and scarce the herd gone to the hedge for shade, PP 6. 2
then how when nature calls thee to be gone, SON 4.11
check'd with frost and lusty leaves quite gone, 5. 7
hung with the trophies of my lovers gone, | who 31.10
leap large lengths of miles when thou art gone, 44.10
for when these quicker elements are gone | in 45. 5
with all these, from these would i be gone, 66.13
moan, | and mock you with me after i am gone. 71.14
though i (once gone) to all the world must die; 81. 6
alas, 'tis true i have gone here and there, 110. 1

/GONERIL 2 FR 0.0002 REL FR 0 V 2 P
/arraign /her /first, /'tis /goneril. LR 3.06. 46 P
/is /your /name /goneril? 3.06. 50 P

GONERIL 9 FR 0.0010 REL FR 7 V 2 P
goneril, | our eldest–born, speak first. LR 1.01. 53
and pleasure, | than that conferr'd on goneril. 1.01. 82
i cannot be so partial, goneril, | to the great 1.04.311
forth | from goneril his mistress salutations; 2.04. 32
o regan, goneril! 3.04. 19
o goneril, | you are not worth the dust which 4.02. 29
goneril with a white beard? 4.06. 96 P
so i would say) affectionate servant, goneril." 4.06.270 P
exasperates, makes mad her sister goneril, | and 5.01. 60

GONZAGO 3 FR 0.0003 REL FR 0 V 3 P
can you play "the murther of gonzago"? HAM 2.02.538 P
gonzago is the duke's name, his wife, baptista. 3.02.239 P
his name's gonzago, the story is extant, and 3.02.262 P

GONZAGO'S 1 FR 0.0001 REL FR 0 V 1 P
the murtherer gets the love of gonzago's wife. HAM 3.02.264 P

GONZALO 9 FR 0.0010 REL FR 9 V 0 P
fresh water, that | a noble neapolitan, gonzalo, TMP 1.02.161
long live gonzalo! 2.01.170
as amply and unnecessarily | as this gonzalo; 2.01.265
hand, do you the like, | to fall it on gonzalo. 2.01.296
heard you this, gonzalo? 2.01.316
sir, "the good old lord gonzalo," | his tears 5.01. 15
holy gonzalo, honorable man, | mine eyes, ev'n 5.01. 62
o good gonzalo, | my true preserver, and a loyal 5.01. 68
i say amen, gonzalo! 5.01.204

GOOD *(also goot, gud)*

/GOOD 25 FR 0.0028 REL FR 20 V 5 P
nay, /good lysander; MND 2.02. 43
/do /that /office /of /thine /own /good /will R2 4.01.177
/good /king, /great /king, /and /yet /not 4.01.263
/great /king, /and /yet /not /greatly /good, 4.01.263
/o, /good! 4.01.317
/o, /my /good /lord /mowbray, | /construe /the 2H4 4.01.101
/now /good /or /bad, /'tis /but /the /chance /of TRO pr 31
/in /good /troth, /it /begins /so. 3.01.114 P
is my day's work done, i'll take /good breath. 5.08. 3
o /good but most unwise patricians! COR 3.01. 91
/good /grandsire, /leave /these /bitter /deep TIT 3.02. 46
'tis not alone my inky cloak, /good mother, HAM 1.02. 77
/what /have /you, /my /good /friends, /deserv'd 2.02.240 P
/for /there /is /nothing /either /good /or /bad, 2.02.250 P
that's good, "/mobled /queen" /is /good. 2.02.504 P
i am to do a /good turn for them. 4.06. 22 P
/but /i /am /very /sorry, /good /horatio, 5.02. 75
/and /the /good /king /his /master | /will LR 2.02.141
come, my /good lord, away. 2.02.151
/i /do, | /if /this /man /come /to /good. 3.07.100
/could /my /good /brother /suffer /you /to /do 4.02. 44
/why, /good /sir? 4.03. 41
/good /sir — 4.06.197
/do, /good /my /friend. in happy time, iago. OTH 3.01. 30
/good troth, i think thou wouldst not. 4.03. 70

GOOD 2960 FR 0.3346 REL FR 1960 V 1000 P
good; TMP 1.01. 3 P
good boatswain, have care. 1.01. 9 P
nay, good, be patient. 1.01. 15 P
good, yet remember whom thou hast aboard. 1.01. 19 P
cheerly, good hearts! 1.01. 26 P
stand fast, good fate, to his hanging, make the 1.01. 30 P
it should the good ship so have swallow'd and 1.02. 12
o, good sir, i do. 1.02. 88
like a good parent, did beget of him | a 1.02. 94
good wombs have borne bad sons. 1.02.120
'tis a good dullness, | and give it way. 1.02.185
had that in't which good natures | could not 1.02.359
and that you will some good instruction give 1.02.425
a word, good sir, | i fear you have done 1.02.443
good things will strive to dwell with't. 1.02.460
then wisely, good sir, weigh | our sorrow with 2.01. 8
of he or adrian, for a good wager, first begins 2.01. 28 P
good lord, how you take it! 2.01. 81 P
why, in good time. 2.01. 96 P
himself with his good arms in lusty stroke | to 2.01.120
it is foul weather in us all, good sir, | when 2.01.142
nay, good my lord, be not angry. 2.01.186 P
your content | tender your own good fortune? 2.01.270
now, good angels | preserve the king! 2.01.306
be not afeard — thy good friend trinculo. 2.02.102 P
by this good light, this is a very shallow 2.02.144 P
well drawn, monster, in good sooth! 2.02.147 P
with much more ease, for my good will is to it, 3.01. 30
more that i may call men than you, good friend, 3.01. 51
in thy life, if thou beest a good moon–calf. 3.02. 22 P
trinculo, keep a good tongue in your head. 3.02. 35 P
thou liv'st, keep a good tongue in thy head. 3.02.112 P
what harmony is this? my good friends, hark! 3.03. 18
of five for one will bring us | good warrant of. 3.03. 49
three | from milan did supplant good prospero, 3.03. 70
so, with good life, | and observation strange, 3.03. 86
more abstenious, | or else good night your vow! 4.01. 54
good my lord, give me thy favor still. 4.01.204
do that good mischief which may make this island 4.01.217
sir, "the good old lord gonzalo," | his tears 5.01. 15
o good gonzalo, | my true preserver, and a loyal 5.01. 68
i will requite you with as good a thing, | at 5.01.169
freshly beheld | our royal, good, and gallant 5.01.237
my bands | with the help of your good hands. ep 10
in thy happiness | when thou dost meet good hap; TGV 1.01. 15
war with good counsel, set the world at nought; 1.01. 68
then thus: of many good i think him best. 1.02. 21
be calm, good wind, blow not a word away | till 1.02.115
'twere good, i think, your lordship sent him 1.03. 29
with other gentlemen of good esteem | are 1.03. 40
good company; 1.03. 43
them shall proteus go — | and in good time! 1.03. 44
madam and mistress, a thousand good morrows. 2.01. 96 P
o, give ye good ev'n! 2.01. 98 P
and so, good morrow, servant. 2.01.134
'twere good you knock'd him. 2.04. 7 P
sir valentine, your father is in good health: 2.04. 50
a letter from your friends | of much good news? 2.04. 52
ay, my good lord, i know the gentleman | to be 2.04. 55
ay, my good lord, a son that well deserves | the 2.04. 59
mind | with all good grace to grace a gentleman. 2.04. 74
beshrew me, sir, but if he make this good, | he 2.04. 75
good proteus, go with me to my chamber, | in 2.04.184
to lesson me and tell me some good mean | how 2.07. 5
that fits as well as "tell me, good my lord, 2.07. 50
else, no worldly good should draw from me. 3.01. 9
but, good my lord, do it so cunningly | that my 3.01. 44
ay, my good lord. 3.01.132
my ears are stopp'd and cannot hear good news, 3.01.206
time is the nurse and breeder of all good. 3.01.245
"item, she brews good ale." 3.01.303 P
"blessing of your heart, you brew good ale." 3.01.305 P
if her liquor be good, she shall; 3.01.346 P
for good things should be prais'd. 3.01.347 P
gone, my good lord. 3.02. 13
proteus, the good conceit i hold of thee | (for 3.02. 17
(for thou hast shown some sign of good desert) 3.02. 18
where your good word cannot advantage him, 3.02. 42
him, | lest it should ravel and be good to none, 3.02. 52
the turn | to give the onset to thy good advice. 3.02. 93
madam, good ev'n to your ladyship. 4.02. 85
and so, good rest. 4.02.132
sir eglamour, a thousand times good morrow. 4.03. 6
thou art not ignorant what dear good will | i 4.03. 14
me, | as much i wish all good befortune you. 4.03. 41
good morrow, gentle lady. 4.03. 45
good morrow, kind sir eglamour. 4.03. 46
you currish thanks is good enough for such a 4.04. 49 P
witness good bringing up, fortune, and truth: 4.04. 69
from me, | to bind him to remember my good will; 4.04. 98
gentlewoman, good day; 4.04.108
it may not be; good madam, pardon me. 4.04.126
go on, good eglamour, | out at the postern by 5.01. 8
o good sir, my master charg'd me to deliver a 5.04. 88 P
they are reformed, civil, full of good, | and 5.04.156
know the young gentlewoman, she has good gifts. WIV 1.01. 63 P
much good do it your good heart! 1.01. 82 P
much good do it your good heart! 1.01. 82 P
how doth good mistress page? 1.01. 83 P
i am glad to see you, good master slender. 1.01. 88 P
'tis a good dog. 1.01. 94 P
he's a good dog, and a fair dog — can there be 1.01. 96 P
he is good, and fair. 1.01. 97 P
i would i could do a good office between you. 1.01.100 P
pauca verba; sir john, good worts. 1.01.120 P
good worts? 1.01.121 P
good cabbage. 1.01.121 P
be avis'd, sir, and pass good humors. 1.01.166 P
by your leave, good mistress. 1.01.193 P
can you carry your good will to the maid? 1.01.231 P
will you, upon good dowry, marry her? 1.01.238 P
his meaning is good. 1.01.256 P
do so, good mine host. 1.03. 12 P
a tapster is a good trade. 1.03. 16 P
the good humor is to steal at a minute's rest. 1.03. 27 P
i ken the wight; he is of substance good. 1.03. 37 P
it is good. 1.03. 56 P
who even now gave me good eyes too, examin'd my 1.03. 60 P
anne is a good girl, and i wish — 1.04. 34 P
run in here, good young man; 1.04. 37 P
good master, be content. 1.04. 70 P
to speak a good word to mistress anne page for 1.04. 83 P
man, i'll do /you your master what good i can; 1.04. 93 P
it is not good you tarry here. 1.04.111 P
how now, good woman, how dost thou? 1.04.134 P
better that it pleases your good worship to ask. 1.04.135 P
shall i do any good, think'st thou? 1.04.142 P
good faith, it is such another nan; 1.04.149 P
and my good man too. 2.01.103 P
'twas a good sensible fellow — well. 2.01.147 P
and i pray, how does good mistress anne? 2.01.164 P
good even and twenty, good master page! 2.01.195 P
good even and twenty, good master page! 2.01.196 P
good mine host o' th' garter, a word with you. 2.01.203 P
the frenchman hath good skill in his rapier. 2.01.222 P
i have grated upon my good friends for three 2.02. 7 P
you were good soldiers and tall fellows; 2.02. 11 P
give your worship good morrow. 2.02. 33 P
good morrow, goodwife. 2.02. 34 P
good maid then. 2.02. 36 P
why, sir, she's a good creature. 2.02. 55 P
be brief, my good she–mercury. 2.02. 79 P
leads a very frampold life with him, good heart. 2.02. 91 P
setting the attraction of my good parts aside, i 2.02.106 P
for 'tis not good that children should know any 2.02.128 P
good body, i thank thee. 2.02.142 P
good master /brook, i desire more acquaintance 2.02.162 P
good sir john, i sue for yours — not to charge 2.02.164 P
money is a good soldier, sir, and will on. 2.02.170 P
speak, good master /brook, i shall be glad to be 2.02.178 P
though i had never so good means as desire to 2.02.182 P
but, good sir john, as you have one eye upon my 2.02.185 P
o good sir! 2.02.256 P
now, good master doctor! 2.03. 20 P
give you good morrow, sir. 2.03. 21 P
adieu, good master doctor. 2.03. 81 P
and i shall procure–a you de good guest: 2.03. 91 P
by gar, 'tis good; vell said. 2.03. 96 P
pray you now, good master slender's servingman, 3.01. 1 P
costard when i have good opportunities for the 3.01. 15 P
good morrow, good sir hugh. 3.01. 36 P
good morrow, good sir hugh. 3.01. 37 P
the dice, and a good studient from his book, and 3.01. 38 P
/god save you, good sir hugh! 3.01. 41 P
we are come to you to do a good office, master 3.01. 49 P
nay, good master parson, keep in your weapon. 3.01. 73 P
so do you, good master doctor. 3.01. 75 P
pray you use your patience in good time. 3.01. 82 P
ay, dat is very good, excellant. 3.01. 99 P
good plots, they are laid, and our revolted 3.02. 38 P
trust me, a good knot. 3.02. 51 P
i have good cheer at home, and i pray you all go 3.02. 51 P
i hope i have your good will, father page. 3.02. 60 P
thou'rt a good boy. 3.03. 33 P
what's the matter, good mistress page? 3.03. 97 P
or bid farewell to your good life for ever. 3.03.119 P
good master ford, be contented. 3.03.166 P
dat is good, by gar; with all my heart! 3.03.241 P
and how does good master fenton? 3.04. 34 P
my uncle can tell you good jests of him. 3.04. 39 P
father stole two geese out of a pen, good uncle. 3.04. 41 P
good master shallow, let him woo for himself. 3.04. 50 P
i thank you for that good comfort. 3.04. 53 P
now, good mistress anne — 3.04. 55 P
good master fenton, come not to my child. 3.04. 72
no, good master fenton. 3.04. 74
good mistress page, for that i love your 3.04. 78
let me have your good will. 3.04. 82
good mother, do not marry me to yond fool. 3.04. 83
good master fenton, | i will not be your friend 3.04. 88
now heaven send thee good fortune! 3.04.101 P
i have promis'd, and i'll be as good as my word, 3.04.108 P
give your worship good morrow. 3.05. 27 P
good heart, that was not her fault. 3.05. 38 P
as good luck would have it, comes in one 3.05. 83 P
to bring this woman to evil for your good. 3.05. 97 P
next, to be compass'd, like a good bilbo, in the 3.05.110 P
in good sadness, sir, i am sorry that for my 3.05.123 P
that is a good william. 4.01. 38 P
and that's a good root. 4.01. 54 P
he is a good sprag memory. 4.01. 82 P
adieu, good sir hugh. 4.01. 84 P
good hearts, devise something; 4.02. 73 P
ay, in good sadness, is he, and talks of the 4.02. 91 P
nay, good, sweet husband! 4.02.180 P
good gentlemen, let him /not strike the old 4.02.180 P
womanhood and the witness of a good conscience, 4.02.207 P
i'll to the doctor, he hath my good will, | and 4.04. 84
i tell you for good will, look you. 4.05. 79 P
i tell you for good will; 4.05. 89 P
mistress ford, good heart, is beaten black and 4.05.112 P
good hearts, what ado here is to bring you 4.05.124 P
hark, good mine host: 4.06. 18
both, my good host, to go along with me. 4.06. 47
i hope good luck lies in odd numbers. 5.01. 2 P
that's good too; 5.02. 8 P
strew good luck, ouphes, on every sacred room, 5.05. 57
now, good sir john, how like you windsor wives? 5.05.106
till thou art able to woo her in good english. 5.05.134 P
seese is not good to give putter; 5.05.140 P
good george, be not angry. 5.05.200 P
pardon, good father! good my mother, pardon! 5.05.216
pardon, good father! good my mother, pardon! 5.05.216
good husband, let us every one go home, | and 5.05.241
now, good my lord, | let there be some more test MM 1.01. 47
qualify the laws | as to your soul seems good. 1.01. 66
and thou the velvet — thou art good velvet; 1.02. 31 P
good counsellors lack no clients. 1.02.106 P
one word, good friend. lucio, a word with you. 1.02.142
if they'll do you any good. 1.02.143
i thank you, good friend lucio. 1.02.192
you do blaspheme the good in mocking me. 1.04. 38
what poor ability's in me | to do him good? 1.04. 76
and makes us lose the good we oft might win, 1.04. 78
good sir, adieu. 1.04. 90
if these be good people in a commonweal that do 2.01. 41 P
in here before your good honor two notorious 2.01. 49 P
in the world that good christians ought to have. 2.01. 55 P
they are not china dishes, but very good dishes. 2.01. 94 P
unless they kept very good diet, as i told you 2.01.112 P
because it is an open room and good for winter. 2.01.132 P
hoping you'll find good cause to whip them all. 2.01.137
good morrow to your lordship. 2.01.138
good master froth, look upon his honor; 2.01.148 P
'tis for a good purpose. 2.01.149 P
good then; 2.01.156 P
marry, i thank your good worship for it. 2.01.182 P
thank you, good pompey; 2.01.244 P
i thank your worship for your good counsel; 2.01.252 P
under your good correction, i have seen | when, 2.02. 10
ay, my good lord, a very virtuous maid, | and to 2.02. 20
become them with one half so good a grace | as 2.02. 62
good, good my lord, bethink you: 2.02. 87
good, good my lord, bethink you: 2.02. 87
good my lord, turn back. 2.02.145
foully for those things | that make her good? 2.02.174
i am the provost. what's your will, good friar? 2.03. 2
is like a good thing, being often read, | grown 2.04. 8
let's write "good angel" on the devil's horn, 2.04. 16
it were as good | to pardon him that hath from 2.04. 42
and that's not good. 2.04. 75
let /me be ignorant, and in nothing good, | but 2.04. 76
what ho! peace here; grace and good company! 3.01. 44
most good, most good indeed. 3.01. 55
most good, most good indeed. 3.01. 55
in good time. 3.01.179 P
hand that hath made you fair hath made you good; 3.01.181 P

o, how much is the good duke deceiv'd in angelo! 3.01.191 P
the love i have in doing good a remedy presents 3.01.198 P
of the lady, and good words went with her name. 3.01.211 P
show me how, good father. 3.01.238 P
fare you well, good father. 3.01.269 P
bless you, good father friar. 3.02. 11 P
and you, good brother father. 3.02. 13 P
him, he were as good go a mile on his errand. 3.02. 37 P
why, 'tis good; 3.02. 58 P
farewell, good pompey. 3.02. 69 P
you will turn good husband now, pompey, you will 3.02. 70 P
i hope, sir, your good worship will be my bail. 3.02. 72 P
yes, in good sooth, the vice is of a great 3.02.101 P
farewell, good friar, i prithee pray for me. 3.02.180 P
good my lord, be good to me, your honor is 3.02.191 P
good my lord, be good to me, your honor is 3.02.191 P
good my lord. 3.02.192 P
good even, good father. 3.02.214 P
good even, good father. 3.02.214 P
which i (by my good leisure) have discredited to 3.02.247 P
'tis good; 4.01. 14
music oft hath such a charm | to make bad good, 4.01. 15
to make bad good, and good provoke to harm. 4.01. 15
what is the news from this good deputy? 4.01. 27
with this maid, | she comes to do you good. 4.01. 51
good friar, i know you do, and have found it. 4.01. 53
pray, sir, by your good favor — for surely, sir 4.02. 32 P
sir, a good favor you have, but that you have a 4.02. 33 P
sir, for your kindness, i owe you a good turn. 4.02. 59 P
who can do good on him? 4.02. 68
of the night | envelop you, good provost! 4.02. 74
good morrow; 4.02.105 P
more than thanks and good fortune, by the saint 4.02.178 P
pardon me, good father, it is against my oath. 4.02.181 P
you must be so good, sir, to rise and be put to 4.03. 27 P
this shall be done, good father, presently. 4.03. 82
but i will keep her ignorant of her good, | to 4.03.109
good morning to you, fair and gracious daughter. 4.03.112
in that good path that i would wish it go, | and 4.03.133
good even. friar, where's the provost? 4.03.149 P
good night. 4.04. 19 P
thank thee, varrius, thou hast made good haste. 4.05. 11
and good supporters are you. 5.01. 18
no, my good lord, | nor wish'd to hold my peace. 5.01. 78
this' a good friar, belike! 5.01.131
good friar, let's hear it. 5.01.162
and, my good lord, | but tuesday night last gone 5.01.228
now, good my lord, give me the scope of justice, 5.01.234
in very good time. 5.01.285 P
here of the fox, | good night to your redress! 5.01.299
then, good prince, | no longer session hold upon 5.01.370
your life, | and choke your good to come. 5.01.422
o my good lord! 5.01.430
no, my good lord; it was by private message. 5.01.460
good my lord, do not recompense me in making me 5.01.516 P
thanks, good friend escalus, for thy much 5.01.528
i have a motion much imports your good, 5.01.535
word, | and go indeed, having so good a mean. ERR 1.02. 18
good sister, let us dine, and never fret; 2.01. 6
in good time, sir: what's that? 2.02. 57 P
sir, learn to jest in good time — there's a 2.02. 64 P
good signior angelo, you must excuse us all, 3.01. 1
may answer my good will and your good welcome 3.01. 20
answer my good will and your good welcome here. 3.01. 20
good meat, sir, is common; 3.01. 24
though my cates be mean, take them in good part; 3.01. 28
good sir, make haste. 3.01.119
as good to wink, sweet love, as look on night. 3.02. 58
i'll fetch my sister to get her good will. 3.02. 70
good signior, take the stranger to my house, 4.01. 36
good lord! 4.01. 48
good sir, say whe'r you'll answer me or no: 4.01. 60
going to bed and says, "god give you good rest!" 4.03. 33 P
good sir, be patient. 4.04. 18
good now, hold thy tongue. 4.04. 21 P
good doctor pinch, you are a conjurer, 4.04. 47
is't good to soothe him in these contraries? 4.04. 79
heart and good will you might, | but surely, 4.04. 85
good master doctor, see him safe convey'd | home 4.04.122
be mad, good master, | cry "the devil!" 4.04.127
good sir, draw near to me, i'll speak to him. 5.01. 12
good people, enter and lay hold on him. 5.01. 91
bed, | to do him all the grace and good i could. 5.01.164
no, my good lord. 5.01.207
then | i hope i shall have leisure to make good, 5.01.376
take it, and much thanks for my good cheer. 5.01.393
he hath done good service, lady, in these wars. ADO 1.01. 48 P
and a good soldier too, lady. 1.01. 53 P
and a good soldier to a lady, but what is he to 1.01. 54 P
do, good friend. 1.01. 92 P
good signior leonato, are you come to meet your 1.01. 96 P
speed of your tongue, and so good a continuer. 1.01.142 P
jack, to tell us cupid is a good hare–finder and 1.01.184 P
as they write "here is good horse to hire," let 1.01.266 P
in the mean time, good signior benedick, repair 1.01.275 P
my liege, your highness now may do me good. 1.01.290
learn | any hard lesson that may do thee good. 1.01.293
are they good? 1.02. 6 P
/event stamps them, but they have a good cover; 1.02. 8 P
a good sharp fellow. 1.02. 18 P
good cousin, have a care this busy time. 1.02. 27 P
with a good leg and a good foot, uncle, and 2.01. 14 P
with a good leg and a good foot, uncle, and 2.01. 14 P
in the world, if 'a could get her good will. 2.01. 17 P
music, cousin, if you be not woo'd in good time. 2.01. 70 P
i have a good eye, uncle, i can see a church by 2.01. 82 P
revellers are ent'ring, brother, make good room. 2.01. 85 P
god match me with a good dancer! 2.01.107 P
and that i had my good wit out of the "hundred 2.01.130 P
in every good thing. 2.01.152 P
grace had got the good will of this young lady, 2.01.216 P
shall find her the infernal ate in good apparel. 2.01.256 P
none, but to desire your good company. 2.01.272 P
with her father, and his good will obtain'd. 2.01.300 P
good lord, for alliance! 2.01.318 P
my lord, to help my cousin to a good husband. 2.01.376 P
have walk'd ten mile afoot to see a good armor, 2.03. 16 P
of good discourse, an excellent musician, and 2.03. 33 P
yea, my good lord. 2.03. 38
o good my lord, tax not so bad a voice | to 2.03. 44
by my troth, a good song. 2.03. 75 P
it were good that benedick knew of it by some 2.03.154 P
were it good, think you? 2.03.172 P
he hath indeed a good outward happiness. 2.03.183 P
let her wear it out with good counsel. 2.03.202 P
to see how much he is unworthy so good a lady. 2.03.209 P
good margaret, run thee to the parlor, | there 3.01. 1
and therefore certainly it were not good | she 3.01. 57
indeed he hath an excellent good name. 3.01. 98
good den, brother. 3.02. 81 P
the word is too good to paint out her wickedness 3.02.109 P
are you good men and true? 3.03. 1 P
that were a punishment too good for them, if 3.03. 4 P
god hath blest you with a good name. 3.03. 14 P
well, masters, good night. 3.03. 84 P
fellows' counsels and your own, and good night. 3.03. 87 P
bids me a thousand times good night — i tell 3.03.148 P
good ursula, wake my cousin beatrice, and desire 3.04. 1 P
no, pray thee, good meg, i'll wear this. 3.04. 8 P
by my troth 's not so good, and i warrant your 3.04. 9 P
good morrow, coz. 3.04. 39 P
good morrow, sweet hero. 3.04. 40 P
help to dress me, good coz, good meg, good 3.04. 98 P
to dress me, good coz, good meg, good ursula. 3.04. 98 P
to dress me, good coz, good meg, good ursula. 3.04. 99 P
what is it, my good friends? 3.05. 8 P
for i hear as good exclamation on your worship 3.05. 25 P
a good old man, sir, he will be talking; 3.05. 33 P
well, god's a good man; 3.05. 36 P
all men are not alike, alas, good neighbor! 3.05. 40 P
go, good partner, go, get you to francis seacole 3.05. 57 P
that is some good. 4.01.211
tarry, good beatrice. by this hand, i love thee. 4.01.324 P
as shall be prov'd upon thee by good witness. 4.02. 79 P
good den, good den. 5.01. 46
good den, good den. 5.01. 46
good day to both of you. 5.01. 46
nay, do not quarrel with us, good old man. 5.01. 50
good day, my lord. 5.01.112 P
i will make it good how you dare, with what you 5.01.146 P
well, i will meet you, so i may have good cheer. 5.01.151 P
"nay," said i, "a good wit." 5.01.163 P
nor i, | and yet, to satisfy this good old man, 5.01.276
but in loving, leander the good swimmer, troilus 5.02. 30 P
will not admit any good part to intermingle with 5.02. 64 P
but for which of my good parts did you first 5.02. 65 P
a good epithite! 5.02. 66 P
that liv'd in the time of good neighbors. 5.02. 77 P
now, unto thy bones good night! 5.03. 22
good morrow, masters, put your torches out. 5.03. 24
good morrow, masters — each his several way. 5.03. 29
signior leonato, truth it is, good signior, 5.04. 21
my will is your good will | may stand with ours, 5.04. 28
in which, good friar, i shall desire your help. 5.04. 31
good morrow to this fair assembly. 5.04. 34
good morrow, prince; 5.04. 35
good morrow, claudio; 5.04. 35
good morrow, benedick. 5.04. 40
you, but, by this good day, i yield upon great 5.04. 94 P
proceeded well, to stop all good proceeding! LLL 1.01. 95
no, my good lord, i have sworn to stay with you; 1.01.111
anthony dull, a man of good repute, carriage, 1.01.268 P
i'll lay my head to any good man's hat, | these 1.01.308
let them be men of good repute and carriage. 1.02. 69 P
he was a man of good carriage, great carriage, 1.02. 70 P
salomon so seduced, and he had a very good wit. 1.02.175 P
good lord boyet, my beauty, though but mean, 2.01. 13
good boyet, | you are not ignorant, all–telling 2.01. 20
for he hath wit to make an ill shape good, | and 2.01. 59
and much too little of that good i saw | is my 2.01. 62
your own good thoughts excuse me, and farewell. 2.01.175
would that do it good? 2.01.187
good sir, be not offended, | she is an heir of 2.01.204
/rosaline, by good hap. 2.01.210
good wits will be jangling, but, gentles, agree: 2.01.225
a good l'envoy, ending in the goose; 3.01. 99 P
sir, your pennyworth is good, and your goose be 3.01.102
o, my good knave costard, exceedingly well met! 3.01.143 P
as thou wilt win my favor, good my knave, | do 3.01.152
here (good my glass), take this for telling true 4.01. 18
he's a good friend of mine. 4.01. 54
stand aside, good bearer. 4.01. 55
from my lord berowne, a good master of mine, 4.01.104
hit it, | thou canst not hit it, my good man. 4.01.126
good night, my good owl. 4.01.139
good night, my good owl. 4.01.139
and done in the testimony of a good conscience. 4.02. 2 P
perge, good master holofernes, perge, so it 4.02. 53 P
but the gift is good in those /in whom it is 4.02. 71 P
you are a good member of the commonwealth. 4.02. 76 P
god give you good morrow, master person. 4.02. 82 P
a good lustre of conceit in a turf of earth; 4.02. 87 P
good master person, be so good as read me this 4.02. 90 P
person, be so good as read me this letter. 4.02. 90 P
ah, good old mantuan! 4.02. 94 P
good costard, go with me. 4.02.144 P
and mine too, good lord! 4.03. 91
amen, so i had mine. is not that a good word? 4.03. 92
ah, good my liege, i pray thee pardon me! 4.03.150
good heart, what grace hast thou thus to reprove 4.03.151
where lies thy grief, o, tell me, good dumaine? 4.03.169
i post from love; good lover, let me go. 4.03.186
'twere good yours did; 4.03.268
and, good berowne, now prove | our loving lawful 4.03.280
my familiar, i do assure ye, very good friend; 5.01. 96 P
your sweet self are good at such eruptions and 5.01.114 P
beauteous as ink — a good conclusion. 5.02. 41
the king was weeping–ripe for a good word. 5.02.274
yes, in good faith. 5.02.280
good madam, if by me you'll be advis'd, | let's 5.02.300
nay, my good lord, let me o'errule you now. 5.02.515
here is like to be a good presence of worthies: 5.02.533 P
proceed, good alexander. 5.02.567
he is a marvellous good neighbor, faith, and a 5.02.582 P
good neighbor, faith, and a very good bowler; 5.02.583 P
stand aside, good pompey. 5.02.587 P
thanks, good egeus. what's the news with thee? MND 1.01. 21
a good persuasion; 1.01.156
my good lysander, | i swear to thee, by cupid's 1.01.168
and good luck grant thee thy demetrius! 1.01.221
first, good peter quince, say what the play 1.02. 8 P
a very good piece of work, i assure you, and a 1.02. 13 P
now, good peter quince, call forth your actors 1.02. 14 P
that i will do any man's heart good to hear me. 1.02. 71 P
do their work, and they shall have good luck. 2.01. 41
so good night, with lullaby. 2.02. 19
we'll rest us, hermia, if you think it good, 2.02. 37
and good night, sweet friend. 2.02. 60
lysander, if you live, good sir, awake. 2.02.102
good troth, you do me wrong (good sooth, you do) 2.02.129
good troth, you do me wrong (good sooth, you do) 2.02.129
you of more acquaintance, good master cobweb. 3.01.182 P
good master peaseblossom, i shall desire you of 3.01.188 P
good master mustardseed, i know your patience 3.01.191 P
/of more acquaintance, good master mustardseed. 3.01.195 P
ah, good demetrius, wilt thou give him me? 3.02. 63
and here, with all good will, with all my heart, 3.02.164
good hermia, do not be so bitter with me. 3.02.306
mounsieur cobweb, good mounsieur, get you your 4.01. 10 P
and, good mounsieur, bring me the honey–bag. 4.01. 12 P
and, good mounsieur, have a care the honey–bag 4.01. 14 P
pray you, leave your curtsy, good mounsieur. 4.01. 20 P
nothing, good mounsieur, but to help cavalery 4.01. 22 P
i have a reasonable good ear in music. 4.01. 28 P
i could munch your good dry oats. 4.01. 32 P
good hay, sweet hay, hath no fellow. 4.01. 33 P
welcome, good robin. 4.01. 46
good morrow, friends. 4.01.139
but, my good lord, i wot not by what power 4.01.164
apparel together, good strings to your beards, 4.02. 36 P
if we offend, it is with our good will. 5.01.108
we come not to offend, | but with good will. 5.01.110
a good moral, my lord: 5.01.120 P
a very gentle beast, and of a good conscience. 5.01.227 P
truly, the moon shines with a good grace. 5.01.268 P
thy mantle good, | what, stain'd with blood? 5.01.282
so, good night unto you all. 5.01.436
good morrow, my good lords. MV 1.01. 65
good morrow, my good lords. 1.01. 65
good signiors both, when shall we laugh? 1.01. 66
come, good lorenzo. 1.01.103
i pray you, good bassanio, let me know it, | and 1.01.135
in the same abundance as your good fortunes are; 1.02. 4 P
good sentences, and well pronounc'd. 1.02. 10 P
do were as easy as to know what were good to do, 1.02. 13 P
it is a good divine that follows his own 1.02. 14 P
easier teach twenty what were good to be done, 1.02. 16 P
o'er the meshes of good counsel the cripple. 1.02. 20 P
holy men at their death have good inspirations; 1.02. 28 P
to his own good parts that he can shoe him 1.02. 42 P
fift welcome with so good heart as i can bid the 1.02.127 P
antonio is a good man. 1.03. 12 P
in saying he is a good man is to have you 1.03. 16 P
rest you fair, good signior, | your worship was 1.03. 59
was this inserted to make interest good? 1.03. 94
three thousand ducats — 'tis a good round sum. 1.03.103
good fortune then! 2.01. 45
launcelot /gobbo, good launcelot," or "good 2.02. 4 P
good launcelot," or "good /gobbo," or "good 2.02. 4 P
or "good /gobbo," or "good launcelot /gobbo, use 2.02. 5 P
to swear upon a book, i shall have good fortune. 2.02.160 P
be a woman, she's a good wench for this gear. 2.02.166 P
i pray thee, good leonardo, think on this: 2.02.169
farewell, good launcelot. 2.03. 15
we have not made good preparation. 2.04. 4
'tis good we do so. 2.04. 27
they in themselves, good sooth, are too too 2.06. 42
let good antonio look he keep his day, | or he 2.08. 25
plain highway of talk, that the good antonio, 3.01. 12 P
o that i had a title good enough to keep his 3.01. 13 P
what's that good for? 3.01. 52 P
i thank thee, good tubal, good news, good news! 3.01.106 P
i thank thee, good tubal, good news, good news! 3.01.106 P
i thank thee, good tubal, good news, good news! 3.01.106 P
go, good tubal, at our synagogue, tubal. 3.01.130 P
and seen our wishes prosper, | to cry good joy. 3.02.188
good joy, my lord and lady! 3.02.188
and do you, gratiano, mean good faith? 3.02.210
i pray you tell me how my good friend doth. 3.02.233
how doth that royal merchant, good antonio? 3.02.239
since i have your good leave to go away, | i 3.02.324
hear me yet, good shylock. 3.03. 3
i never did repent for doing good, | nor shall 3.04. 10
therefore be a' good cheer, for truly i think 3.05. 5 P
is but one hope in it that can do you any good, 3.05. 7 P
and he says you are no good member of the 3.05. 34 P
planted in his memory | an army of good words, 3.05. 67
and now, good sweet, say thy opinion, | how dost 3.05. 71
good cheer, antonio! 4.01.111
repair thy wit, good youth, or it will fall | to 4.01.141
'twere good you do so much for charity. 4.01.261
why then the devil give him good of it! 4.01.345
this ring, good sir, alas, it is a trifle! 4.01.430
good sir, this ring was given me by my wife, 4.01.441
come, good sir, will you show me to this house? 4.02. 19
from my master, with his horn full of good news. 5.01. 47 P
so shines a good deed in a naughty world. 5.01. 91
nothing is good, i see, without respect; 5.01. 99
pardon me, good lady, | for, by these blessed 5.01.219
my clerk hath some good comforts too for you. 5.01.289
you in his will to give me good education. AYL 1.01. 67 P
further offend you than becomes me for my good. 1.01. 80 P
'twill be a good way; 1.01. 93 P
good morrow to your worship. 1.01. 95 P
good monsieur charles, what's the new news at 1.01. 96 P
therefore he gives them good leave to wander. 1.01.103 P
an envious emulator of every man's good parts, a 1.01.144 P
farewell, good charles. 1.01.163 P
but love no man in good earnest, nor no further 1.02. 27 P
us sit and mock the good huswife fortune from 1.02. 31 P
that swore by his honor they were good pancakes, 1.02. 64 P
pancakes were naught and the mustard was good, 1.02. 66 P
fair princess, you have lost much good sport. 1.02. 99 P
i would have told you of good wrestling, which 1.02.110 P

call him hither, good monsieur le beau. 1.02.163 P
good sir, i do in friendship counsel you | to 1.02.261
and pity her for her good father's sake; 1.02.281
o, a good wish upon you! 1.03. 24 P
out of service, let us talk in good earnest. 1.03. 26 P
then, good my liege, mistake me not so much | to 1.03. 64
sermons in stones, and good in every thing. 2.01. 17
o good old man, how well in thee appears | the 2.03. 56
therefore courage, good aliena. 2.04. 8 P
ay, be so, good touchstone. 2.04. 19 P
peace, i say. good even to /you, friend. 2.04. 69
cheerly, good adam! 2.06. 18 P
sun, | and rail'd on lady fortune in good terms, 2.07. 16
in good set terms, and yet a motley fool. 2.07. 17
"good morrow, fool," quoth i. 2.07. 18
what, for a counter, would i do but good? 2.07. 63
or else a rude despiser of good manners, | that 2.07. 92
church, | if ever sat at any good man's feast, 2.07.115
and sat at good men's feasts, and wip'd our eyes 2.07.122
i thank ye, and be blest for your good comfort! 2.07.135
in fair round belly with good capon lin'd, 2.07.154
give us some music, and, good cousin, sing. 2.07.173
if that you were the good sir rowland's son, 2.07.191
good old man, | thou art right welcome as thy 2.07.197
in respect of itself, it is a good life; 3.02. 14 P
and content is without three good friends; 3.02. 26 P
that good pasture makes fat sheep; 3.02. 27 P
art may complain of good breeding or comes of a 3.02. 30 P
wast at court, thou never saw'st good manners; 3.02. 41 P
if thou never saw'st good manners, then thy 3.02. 42 P
those that are good manners at the court are as 3.02. 46 P
in respect of a good piece of flesh indeed! 3.02. 66 P
no man's happiness, glad of other men's good, 3.02. 75 P
and never cried, "have patience, good people!" 3.02.157 P
good my complexion! 3.02.194 P
finding him, and relish it with good observance. 3.02.234 P
give me audience, good madam. 3.02.238 P
but, good faith, i had as lief have been myself 3.02.253 P
farewell, good signior love. 3.02.291 P
adieu, good monsieur melancholy. 3.02.293 P
i would give him some good counsel, for he seems 3.02.364 P
but, in good sooth, are you he that hangs the 3.02.391 P
with all my heart, good youth. 3.02.433 P
come apace, good audrey; 3.03. 1 P
nor a man's good wit seconded with the forward 3.03. 13 P
foul slut were to put good meat into an unclean 3.03. 36 P
many a man has good horns, and knows no end of 3.03. 54 P
good even, good master what–ye–call't; 3.03. 73 P
good even, good master what–ye–call't; 3.03. 73 P
and have a good priest that can tell you what 3.03. 85 P
it will be a good excuse for me hereafter to 3.03. 93 P
farewell, good master oliver: 3.03. 98 P
as good cause as one would desire, therefore 3.04. 5 P
i' faith, his hair is of a good color. 3.04. 10 P
i told him, of as good as he, so he laugh'd and 3.04. 37 P
thank heaven, fasting, for a good man's love; 3.05. 58
why, 'tis good to be sad and say nothing. 4.01. 8 P
why then 'tis good to be a post. 4.01. 9 P
good day and happiness, dear rosalind! 4.01. 30 P
very good orators, when they are out, they will 4.01. 75 P
for, good youth, he went but forth to wash him 4.01.102 P
are you not good? 4.01.121 P
then, can one desire too much of a good thing? 4.01.124 P
by my troth, and in good earnest, and so god 4.01.188 P
good morrow, fair ones. 4.03. 75
be of good cheer, youth. 4.03.163
take a good heart and counterfeit to be a man. 4.03.173 P
good sir, go with us. 4.03.178 P
faith, the priest was good enough, for all the 5.01. 3 P
we that have good wits have much to answer for; 5.01. 11 P
good ev'n, audrey. 5.01. 13 P
god ye good ev'n, william. 5.01. 14 P
and good ev'n to you, sir. 5.01. 15 P
good ev'n, gentle friend. 5.01. 16 P
"thank god" — a good answer. art rich? 5.01. 25 P
"so, so" is good, very good, very excellent good 5.01. 27 P
so" is good, very good, very excellent good; 5.01. 27 P
so" is good, very good, very excellent good; 5.01. 28 P
do, good william. 5.01. 58 P
it shall be to your good; 5.02. 10 P
that i know you are a gentleman of good conceit. 5.02. 53 P
you should bear a good opinion of my knowledge, 5.02. 55 P
draw a belief from you, to do yourself good, and 5.02. 58 P
good shepherd, tell this youth what 'tis to love 5.02. 83
but, my good lord, this boy is forest–born, 5.04. 30
good my lord, bid him welcome. 5.04. 40 P
good my lord, like this fellow. 5.04. 51 P
the book — as you have books for good manners. 5.04. 91 P
he's as good at any thing, and yet a fool. 5.04.105 P
good duke, receive thy daughter, | hymen from 5.04.111
shall share the good of our returned fortune, 5.04.174
if it be true that good wine needs no bush, 'tis ep 3 P
'tis true that a good play needs no epilogue. ep 4 P
yet to good wine they do use good bushes; ep 5 P
yet to good wine they do use good bushes; ep 5 P
and good plays prove the better by the help of ep 6 P
prove the better by the help of good epilogues. ep 7 P
am i in then, that am neither a good epilogue, ep 8 P
insinuate with you in the behalf of a good play! ep 9 P
and i am sure, as many as have good beards, or ep 21 P
as many as have good beards, or good faces, or ep 21 P
how silver made it good | at the hedge–corner, SHR in.1. 19
why, belman is as good as he, my lord; in.1. 22
now lord be thanked for my good amends! in.2. 97
therefore they thought it good you hear a play, in.2. 134
no, my good lord, it is more pleasing stuff. in.2. 139
arm'd | with his good will and thy good company, 1.01. 6
arm'd | with his good will and thy good company, 1.01. 6
only, good master, while we do admire | this 1.01. 29
from all such devils, good lord deliver us! 1.01. 66
and me too, good lord! 1.01. 67
husht, master, here's some good pastime toward; 1.01. 68
that i may soon make good | what i have said, 1.01. 74
and let it not displease thee, good bianca, 1.01. 76
sorry am i that our good will effects | bianca's 1.01. 86
to mine own children in good bringing–up, | and 1.01. 99
your gifts are so good, here's none will hold 1.01.106 P
man, there be good fellows in the world, and a 1.01.128 P
sufficeth my reasons are both good and weighty. 1.01.248
a good matter, surely; 1.01.250 P
and my good friend petruchio! 1.02. 21 P
good hortensio, | i bade the rascal knock upon 1.02. 36
think scolding would do little good upon him. 1.02.109 P
and by good fortune i have lighted well | on 1.02.167
read in poetry | and other books, good ones, i 1.02.170
i'll tell you news indifferent good for either. 1.02.180
me, | and i do hope good days and long to see. 1.02.192
my mind presumes, for his own good and /ours. 1.02.213
i would i were as sure of a good dinner. 1.02.217
the motion's good indeed, and be it so, 1.02.279
good sister, wrong me not, nor wrong yourself, 2.01. 1
good morrow, neighbor baptista. 2.01. 39 P
good morrow, neighbor gremio. 2.01. 40 P
and you, good sir! 2.01. 42
y' are welcome, sir, and he, for your good sake. 2.01. 61
welcome, good cambio. 2.01. 85 P
what, will my daughter prove a good musician? 2.01.144
she's apt to learn and thankful for good turns. 2.01.165
good morrow, kate — for that's your name, i 2.01.182
in good time! 2.01.195
alas, good kate, i will not burthen thee, | for 2.01.202
nay, come again, | good kate; 2.01.219
nay then good night our part! 2.01.301
i'll leave her houses three or four as good, 2.01.366
adieu, good neighbor. 2.01.399
'tis in my head to do my master good. 2.01.406
good master, take it not unkindly, pray, | that 3.01. 57
patience, good katherine, and baptista too. 3.02. 21
good sooth, even thus; 3.02.116
when i should bid good morrow to my bride | and 3.02.122
'twere good methinks to steal our marriage, 3.02.140
a fire, good curtis. 4.01. 16 P
she was, good curtis, before this frost; 4.01. 22 P
i prithee, good grumio, tell me, how goes the 4.01. 33 P
ready, and therefore, good grumio, the news. 4.01. 39 P
let's ha't, good grumio. 4.01. 59 P
nay, good sweet kate, be merry. 4.01.143
then go with me to make the matter good. 4.02.115
'tis passing good, i prithee let me have it. 4.03. 18
i like it well, good grumio, fetch it me. 4.03. 21
much good do it unto thy gentle heart! 4.03. 51
o no, good kate; 4.03.179
'twere good he were school'd. 4.04. 9
i pray you stand good father to me now, | give 4.04. 21
and, for the good report i hear of you, | and 4.04. 28
long, | i am content, in a good father's care, 4.04. 31
good lord, how bright and goodly shines the moon 4.05. 2
good morrow, gentle mistress, where away? 4.05. 27
fair lovely maid, once more good day to thee. 4.05. 33
do, good old grandsire, and withal make known 4.05. 50
she is of good esteem, | her dowry wealthy, and 4.05. 64
the church together, god send 'em good shipping! 5.01. 42 P
while i play the good husband at home, my son 5.01. 68 P
i thank my good father, i am able to maintain it 5.01. 76 P
married my daughter without asking my good will? 5.01.134 P
our stomachs up | after our great good cheer. 5.02. 10
very well mended. kiss him for that, good widow. 5.02. 25
a good swift simile, but something currish. 5.02. 54
i thank thee for that gird, good tranio. 5.02. 58
now, in good sadness, son petruchio, | i think 5.02. 63
now fair befall thee, good petruchio! 5.02.111
'tis a good hearing when children are toward. 5.02.182
and, being a winner, god give you good night! 5.02.187
is at all times good must of necessity hold his AWW 1.01. 8 P
what is it, my good lord, the king languishes of 1.01. 32 P
have those hopes of her good that her education 1.01. 39 P
good my lord, | advise him. 1.01. 71
fear makes in you is a virtue of a good wing, 1.01.204 P
get thee a good husband, and use him as he uses 1.01.214 P
it is the count /rossillion, my good lord, 1.02. 18
much repairs me | to talk of your good father. 1.02. 31
his good remembrance, sir, | lies richer in your 1.02. 48
live" — | this his good melancholy oft began, 1.02. 56
may have your ladyship's good will to go to the 1.03. 18 P
i do beg your good will in this case. 1.03. 21 P
"among nine bad if one be good, | among nine bad 1.03. 77
if one be good, | among nine bad if one be good, 1.03. 78
if one be good, | there's yet one good in ten." 1.03. 79
what, one good in ten? 1.03. 80 P
one good woman in ten, madam, which is a 1.03. 82 P
and we might have a good woman born but /or 1.03. 86 P
good madam, pardon me! 1.03.185
that his good receipt | shall for my legacy be 1.03.244
good sparks and lustrous, a word, good metals: 2.01. 41 P
good sparks and lustrous, a word, good metals: 2.01. 41 P
good faith, across! 2.01. 67
but, my good lord, 'tis thus: 2.01. 68
now, good lafew, | bring in the admiration, that 2.01. 87
ay, my good lord. 2.01.100
but a trifle neither, in good faith, if the 2.02. 34 P
you are too young, too happy, and too good, | to 2.03. 96
yes, my good lord, | but never hope to know why 2.03.109
good alone | is good, without a name; 2.03.128
good alone | is good, without a name; 2.03.129
proud scornful boy, unworthy this good gift, 2.03.151
obey our will, which travails in thy good; 2.03.158
good fortune and the favor of the king | smile 2.03.177
yet art thou good for nothing but taking up, and 2.03.207 P
so, my good window of lettice, fare thee well! 2.03.213 P
yes, good faith, ev'ry dram of it, and i will 2.03.221 P
he is my good lord; 2.03.245 P
good, very good, it is so then. 2.03.265 P
good, very good, it is so then. 2.03.265 P
good, very good, let it be conceal'd awhile. 2.03.265 P
good, very good, let it be conceal'd awhile. 2.03.266 P
sir, i have your good will to have mine own good 2.04. 15 P
your good will to have mine own good /fortunes. 2.04. 16 P
a good knave, i' faith, and well fed. 2.04. 38
and make this haste as your own good proceeding, 2.04. 49
he, sir, 's a good workman, a very good tailor. 2.05. 18 P
he, sir, 's a good workman, a very good tailor. 2.05. 19 P
a good traveller is something at the latter end 2.05. 28 P
at my hand, but we must do good against evil. 2.05. 48 P
i shall not break your bidding, good my lord. 2.05. 88
good my lord, | the reasons of our state i 3.01. 9
boy, | to fly the favors of so good a king, | to 3.02. 29
'save you, good madam. 3.02. 45
all the honor | that good convenience claims. 3.02. 72
there's nothing here that is too good for him 3.02. 80
ay, my good lady, he. 3.02. 86
indeed, good lady, | the fellow has a deal of 3.02. 89
he is too good and fair for death and me, | whom 3.04. 16
i /warr'nt, good creature, wheresoe'er she is, 3.05. 66
nay, good my lord, put him to't; 3.06. 1 P
the owner of no one good quality worthy your 3.06. 11 P
by the good aid that i of you shall borrow, 3.07. 11
good captain, let me be th' interpreter. 4.01. 7 P
language, gabble enough, and good enough. 4.01. 20 P
no, my good lord, diana. 4.02. 2
for shaking off so good a wife and so sweet a 4.03. 7 P
is of a mingled yarn, good and ill together: 4.03. 72 P
in good sadness, i do not know. 4.03.203 P
good morrow, noble captain. 4.03.314 P
good captain, will you give me a copy of the 4.03.319 P
and by the leave of my good lord the king, 4.04. 13
'twas a good lady, 'twas a good lady. 4.05. 13 P
'twas a good lady, 'twas a good lady. 4.05. 13 P
the master i speak of ever keeps a good fire. 4.05. 48 P
since i heard of the good lady's death and that 4.05. 69 P
got, or a noble scar, is a good liv'ry of honor; 4.05. 99 P
i will come after you with what good speed | our 5.01. 34
good master lavatch, give my lord lafew this 5.02. 1 P
who of herself is a good lady and would not have 5.02. 31 P
my name, my good lord, is parolles. 5.02. 39 P
o my good lord, you were the first that found me 5.02. 42 P
offense, | crying, "that's good that's gone." 5.03. 60
good my lord, | ask him upon his oath, if he 5.03.184
he's a good drum, my lord, but a naughty orator. 5.03.253 P
ay, my good lord. 5.03.270
good mother, fetch my bail. 5.03.295
no, my good lord, | 'tis but the shadow of a 5.03.306
o my good lord, when i was like this maid, | i 5.03.309
good tom drum, lend me a handkercher. 5.03.321 P
these clothes are good enough to drink in, and TN 1.03. 11 P
book, and hath all the good gifts of nature. 1.03. 27 P
good mistress accost, i desire better 1.03. 52 P
good mistress mary accost — 1.03. 55 P
art thou good at these kickshawses, knight? 1.03.115 P
therefore, good youth, address thy gait unto her 1.04. 15
make that good. 1.05. 7 P
a good lenten answer. 1.05. 9 P
where, good mistress mary? 1.05. 11 P
away — is not that as good as a hanging to you? 1.05. 17 P
many a good hanging prevents a bad marriage; 1.05. 19 P
apt, in good faith, very apt. 1.05. 26 P
and't be thy will, put me into good fooling! 1.05. 32 P
madonna, that drink and good counsel will amend; 1.05. 43 P
good madonna, give me leave to prove you a fool. 1.05. 57 P
dexteriously, good madonna. 1.05. 60 P
good my mouse of virtue, answer me. 1.05. 62 P
good madonna, why mourn'st thou? 1.05. 66 P
good fool, for my brother's death. 1.05. 67 P
good sir toby! 1.05.122 P
good beauties, let me sustain no scorn; 1.05.174 P
good gentle one, give me modest assurance if you 1.05.179 P
no, good swabber, i am to hull here a little 1.05.203 P
good madam, let me see your face. 1.05.230 P
o good antonio, forgive me your trouble. 2.01. 34 P
she made good view of me; 2.02. 19
'twas very good, i' faith. 2.03. 24 P
you have a love–song, or a song of good life? 2.03. 36 P
ay, ay. i care not for good life. 2.03. 38 P
excellent good, i' faith. 2.03. 45 P
good, good. 2.03. 46 P
good, good. 2.03. 46 P
good, i' faith. come, begin. 2.03. 71 P
nay, good sir toby. 2.03.103 P
'twere as good a deed as to drink when a man's 2.03.126 P
reason for't, but i have reason good enough. 2.03.146 P
good night, penthesilea. 2.03.177 P
before me, she's a good wench. 2.03.178 P
now good morrow, friends. 2.04. 1
now, good cesario, but that piece of song, 2.04. 2
it that always makes a good voyage of nothing. 2.04. 78 P
the unknown belov'd, this, and my good wishes": 2.05. 91 P
sentence is but a chev'ril glove to a good wit. 3.01. 12 P
be not afraid, good youth, i will not have you, 3.01.131
grace and good disposition attend your ladyship! 3.01.135
love sought is good, but given unsought is 3.01.156
and so adieu, good madam, never more | will i my 3.01.161
oft good turns | are shuffled off with such 3.03. 15
good maria, let this fellow be look'd to. 3.04. 60 P
get him to say his prayers, good sir toby, get 3.04.118 P
good, and valiant. 3.04.149 P
a good note, that keeps you from the blow of the 3.04.153 P
very brief, and to exceeding good sense — less. 3.04.158 P
good. 3.04.161 P
good. 3.04.165 P
him out to be of good capacity and breeding; 3.04.186 P
stand here, make a good show on't; 3.04.289 P
o good sir toby, hold! here come the officers. 3.04.319 P
that i promis'd you, i'll be as good as my word. 3.04.323 P
thou hast, sebastian, done good feature shame. 3.04.366
give fools money get themselves a good report — 4.01. 22 P
nor lean enough to be thought a good studient; 4.02. 7 P
an honest man and a good house–keeper goes as 4.02. 8 P
the knave counterfeits well; a good knave. 4.02. 19 P
topas, sir topas, good sir topas, go to my lady. 4.02. 23 P
good sir topas, do not think i am mad; 4.02. 29 P
good fool, as ever thou wilt deserve well at my 4.02. 80 P
ay, good fool. 4.02. 85 P
maintain no words with him, good fellow. 4.02. 99 P
god buy you, good sir topas. 4.02.100 P
good fool, help me to some light and some paper. 4.02.105 P
good fool, some ink, paper, and light; 4.02.109 P
i'll follow this good man, and go with you, 4.03. 32
then lead the way, good father, and heavens so 4.03. 34
good master fabian, grant me another request. 5.01. 2 P
i know thee well; how dost thou, my good fellow? 5.01. 10 P
tertio, is a good play, and the old saying is, 5.01. 36 P
sir, is a good tripping measure, or the bells of 5.01. 38 P
what do you say, cesario? good my lord — 5.01.106
good madam, hear me speak, | and let no quarrel 5.01.355
yet, good deed, leontes, | i love thee not a jar WT 1.02. 42

one good deed dying tongueless | slaughters a 1.02. 92
my last good deed was to entreat his stay; 1.02. 97
ay, my good lord. 1.02.120
no, in good earnest. 1.02.150
ay, my good lord. 1.02.210
at the good queen's entreaty. 1.02.220
"good" should be pertinent, | but so it is, it 1.02.221
good my lord, be cur'd | of this diseas'd 1.02.296
canst with thine eyes at once see good and evil, 1.02.303
i must be the poisoner | of good polixenes, and 1.02.353
good day, camillo. 1.02.366
good camillo, | your chang'd complexions are to 1.02.380
yourself and me | cry lost, and so good night! 1.02.411
on, good camillo. 1.02.411
good expedition be my friend, and comfort | the 1.02.458
good time encounter her! 2.01. 20
let's have that, good sir. 2.01. 26
good my lords, | i am not prone to weeping, as 2.01.107
do not weep, good fools, | there is no cause. 2.01.118
good my lord — 2.01.139
so have we thought it good | from our free 2.01.193
as i take it, | if the good truth were known. 2.01.199
good lady, | no court in europe is too good for 2.02. 2
lady, | no court in europe is too good for thee, 2.02. 3
now, good sir, | you know me, do you not? 2.02. 4
bosom, let't not be doubted | i shall do good. 2.02. 52
he took good rest to–night; 2.03. 10
nay, rather, good my lords, be second to me. 2.03. 27
not so hot, good sir, | i come to bring him 2.03. 32
good my liege, i come; 2.03. 52
i say, i come | from your good queen. 2.03. 58
good queen? 2.03. 59
good queen, my lord, good queen, i say good 2.03. 60
queen, my lord, good queen, i say good queen, 2.03. 60
queen, my lord, good queen, i say good queen, 2.03. 60
and would by combat make her good, so were i | a 2.03. 61
the good queen | (for she is good) hath brought 2.03. 65
the good queen | (for she is good) hath brought 2.03. 66
i am none, by this good light. 2.03. 83
and thou, good goddess nature, which hast made 2.03.104
will never do him good, not one of you. 2.03.129
me word 'tis done | (and by good testimony) or 2.03.137
'tis good speed; 2.03.199
new woo my queen, recall the good camillo, 3.02.156
but that the good mind of camillo tardied | my 3.02.162
what fit is this, good lady? 3.02.174
thou wouldst have poison'd good camillo's honor, 3.02.188
now, good my liege, | sir, royal sir, forgive a 3.02.226
"good antigonus, | since fate (against thy 3.03. 27
good luck, and't be thy will! 3.03. 68 P
come, good boy, the next way home. 3.03.126 P
that's a good deed. 3.03.133 P
a lucky day, boy, and we'll do good deeds on't. 3.03.138 P
all, both joy and terror | of good and bad, that 4.01. 2
i pray thee, good camillo, be no more 4.02. 1 P
(three–man song–men all, and very good ones), 4.03. 42 P
o good sir, tenderly, o! 4.03. 70 P
o good sir, softly, good sir! 4.03. 72 P
o good sir, softly, good sir! 4.03. 72 P
good sir, softly. 4.03. 75 P
no, good sweet sir; 4.03. 79 P
i cannot tell, good sir, for which of his 4.03. 88 P
when my good falcon made her flight across | thy 4.04. 15
as your good flock shall prosper. 4.04. 70
good sooth, she is | the queen of curds and 4.04.160
now in good time! 4.04.163
pray, good shepherd, what fair swain is this 4.04.166
do me no harm, good man" — puts him off, 4.04.199 P
him, with "whoop, do me no harm, good man." 4.04.200 P
ay, good brother, or go about to think. 4.04.217 P
since these good men are pleas'd, let them come 4.04.340 P
no, good sir; 4.04.402
himself a wife, but as good reason | the father 4.04.407
cast your good counsels | upon his passion. 4.04.495
now, good camillo, | i am so fraught with 4.04.513
my good camillo, | she's as forward of her 4.04.579
and what i saw, to my good use i rememb'red. 4.04.604 P
how now, good fellow? 4.04.628 P
a good nose is requisite also, to smell out work 4.04.672 P
comfort, good comfort! 4.04.818 P
he was provided to do us good. 4.04.830 P
and a means to do the prince my master good; 4.04.834 P
took something good | to make a perfect woman, 5.01. 14
now, good now, | say so but seldom. 5.01. 19
not at all, good lady. 5.01. 20
for present comfort, and for future good, | to 5.01. 32
good paulina, | who hast the memory of hermione, 5.01. 49
then, good my lords, bear witness to his oath. 5.01. 72
good madam — 5.01. 75
o my brother, | good gentleman! 5.01.148
good my lord, | she came from libya. 5.01.156
that "once," i see, by your good father's speed, 5.01.210
come, good my lord. 5.01.233
come those i have done good to against my will, 5.02.124 P
and to give me your good report to the prince my 5.02.151 P
ay, and it like your good worship. 5.02.155 P
we'll be thy good masters. 5.02.174 P
o grave and good paulina, the great comfort 5.03. 1
so much to my good comfort as it is | now 5.03. 33
good my lord, forbear. 5.03. 80
turn, good lady, | our perdita is found. 5.03.120
good paulina, | lead us from hence, where we may 5.03.151
silence, good mother, hear the embassy. JN 1.01. 6
a good blunt fellow. 1.01. 71
then, good my liege, let me have what is mine, 1.01.114
in sooth, good friend, your father might have 1.01.123
philip, good old sir robert's wive's eldest son. 1.01.159
brother, adieu, good fortune come to thee! 1.01.180
"good den, sir richard!" 1.01.185
how now, good lady, | what brings you here to 1.01.220
good leave, good philip. 1.01.231
good leave, good philip. 1.01.231
me | upon good friday and ne'er broke his fast. 1.01.235
therefore, good mother, | to whom am i beholding 1.01.238
"knight, knight," good mother, basilisco–like. 1.01.244
then, good my mother, let me know my father; 1.01.249
that supernal judge that stirs good thoughts 2.01.112
there's a good mother, boy, that blots thy 2.01.132
there's a good grandame, boy, that would blot 2.01.133
there's a good grandame. 2.01.163
good my mother, peace. 2.01.163
what other harm have i, good lady, done, | but 3.01. 38
good father cardinal, cry thou amen | to my keen 3.01.181
good reverend father, make my person yours, 3.01.224
and, my good friend, thy voluntary oath | lives 3.03. 23
to say what good respect i have of thee. 3.03. 28
good friend, thou hast no cause to say so yet, 3.03. 30
yet it shall come for me to do thee good. 3.03. 32
good hubert, hubert, hubert, throw thine eye 3.03. 59
patience, good lady, comfort, gentle constance! 3.04. 22
when fortune means to men most good, | she looks 3.04.119
good morrow, hubert. 4.01. 9
good morrow, little prince. 4.01. 9
or "what good love may i perform for you?" 4.01. 49
no, in good sooth; 4.01.105
his youth | the rich advantage of good exercise. 4.02. 60
good lords, although my will to give is living, 4.02. 83
good ground, be pitiful and hurt me not! 4.03. 2
as good to die and go, as die and stay. 4.03. 8
what e'er you think, good words, i think, were 4.03. 28
here's a good world! 4.03.116
away then with good courage! 5.01. 78
be of good comfort; 5.03. 9
and will not let me welcome this good news. 5.03. 15
after such bloody toil, we bid good night, | and 5.05. 6
keep good quarter and good care to–night; 5.05. 20
keep good quarter and good care to–night; 5.05. 20
be of good comfort, prince, for you are born 5.07. 25
here to make good the boist'rous late appeal, R2 1.01. 4
malice, | or worthily, as a good subject should, 1.01. 10
until the heavens, envying earth's good hap, 1.01. 23
speak | my body shall make good upon this earth, 1.01. 37
too good to be so, and too bad to live, | since 1.01. 40
will i make good against thee, arm to arm, 1.01. 76
upon his bad life to make all this good, | that 1.01. 99
how god and good men hate so foul a liar. 1.01.114
good uncle, let this end where it begun; 1.01.158
as much good stay with thee as go with me! 1.02. 57
with all good speed at plashy visit me. 1.02. 66
and what shall good old york there see | but 1.02. 67
god in thy good cause make thee prosperous! 1.03. 78
thy son is banish'd upon good advice, | whereto 1.03.233
no, the apprehension of the good | gives but the 1.03.300
may be a president and witness good | that thou 2.01.130
that their events can never fall out good. 2.01.214
quick is mine ear to hear of good towards him. 2.01.234
no good at all that i can do for him, | unless 2.01.235
for him, | unless you call it good to pity him, 2.01.236
his designs crave haste, his haste good hope. 2.02. 44
less value is my company | than your good words. 2.03. 20
no, my good lord, he hath forsook the court, 2.03. 26
no, my good lord, for that is not forgot | which 2.03. 37
as in a soul rememb'ring my good friends, | and, 2.03. 47
keeps good old york there with his men of war? 2.03. 52
and crossly to thy good all fortune goes. 2.04. 24
the news is very fair and good, my lord: 3.03. 5
take not, good cousin, further than you should, 3.03. 16
yes, my good lord, | it doth contain a king. 3.03. 24
no, good my lord, let's fight with gentle words, 3.03.131
yea, my good lord. 3.03.209
i could weep, madam, would it do you good. 3.04. 21
and i could sing, would weeping do me good, 3.04. 22
to a dear friend of the good duke of york's 3.04. 70
sweet soul to the bosom | of good old abraham! 4.01.104
learn, good soul, | to think our former state a 5.01. 17
good sometimes queen, prepare thee hence for 5.01. 37
with good old folks and let them tell /thee 5.01. 41
and ere thou bid good night, to quite their 5.01. 43
'twere no good part | to take on me to keep and 5.01. 97
good mother, be content, it is no more | than my 5.02. 82
thy overflow of good converts to bad, | and thy 5.03. 64
rise up, good aunt. 5.03. 92
good aunt, stand up. 5.03.111
good aunt, stand up. 5.03.129
good uncle, help to order several powers | to 5.03.140
o would the deed were good! 5.05.114
but neither my good word nor princely favor. 5.06. 42
and let men say we be men of good government, 1H4 1.02. 27 P
knew where a commodity of good names were to be 1.02. 83 P
i see a good amendment of life in thee, from 1.02.102 P
good morrow, ned. 1.02.111 P
good morrow, sweet hal. 1.02.112 P
soul that thou soldest him on good friday last, 1.02.115 P
manhood, nor good fellowship in thee, nor thou 1.02.139 P
now, my good sweet honey lord, ride with us 1.02.160 P
you have good leave to leave us. 1.03. 20
yea, my good lord. 1.03. 22
which many a good tall fellow had destroyed | so 1.03. 62
the circumstance considered, good my lord, 1.03. 70
into the good thoughts of the world again; 1.03.182
if he fall in, good night, or sink or swim. 1.03.194
good cousin, give me audience for a while. 1.03.211
good uncle, tell your tale — i have done. 1.03.256
farewell, good brother, we shall thrive, i trust 1.03.300
and 'twere not as good deed as drink to break 2.01. 29 P
good morrow, carriers, what's a' clock? 2.01. 32 P
good morrow, master gadshill. 2.01. 53 P
and 'twere not as good a deed as drink to turn 2.02. 22 P
i prithee, good prince — hal! 2.02. 40 P
help me to my horse, good king's son. 2.02. 41 P
laughter for a month, and a good jest for ever. 2.02. 96 P
away, good ned. 2.02.108
lord, our plot is a good plot as ever was laid, 2.03. 17 P
a good plot, good friends, and full of 2.03. 18 P
a good plot, good friends, and full of 2.03. 18 P
an excellent plot, very good friends. 2.03. 19 P
o my good lord, why are you thus alone? 2.03. 37
a lad of mettle, a good boy (by the lord, so 2.04. 12 P
i shall command all the good lads in eastcheap. 2.04. 14 P
i am so good a proficient in one quarter of an 2.04. 18 P
if manhood, good manhood, be not forgot upon the 2.04.128 P
there lives not three good men unhang'd in 2.04.130 P
all the titles of good fellowship come to you! 2.04.278 P
well, that rascal hath good mettle in him, he 2.04.349 P
it is like we shall have good trading that way. 2.04.365 P
peace, good pint–pot, peace, good ticklebrain. 2.04.397 P
peace, good pint–pot, peace, good ticklebrain. 2.04.397 P
wherein is he good, but to taste sack and drink 2.04.455 P
no, my good lord, banish peto, banish bardolph, 2.04.474 P
my masters, for a true face and good conscience. 2.04.501 P
good night, my noble lord. 2.04.523
i think it is good morrow, is it not? 2.04.524
me betimes in the morning, and so good morrow, 2.04.549 P
good morrow, good my lord. 2.04.550 P
good morrow, good my lord. 2.04.550 P
sit, cousin percy, sit, good cousin hotspur, 3.01. 7
i | and my good lord of worcester will set forth 3.01. 83
good manners be your speed! 3.01.188
good father, tell her that she and my aunt percy 3.01.194
one that no persuasion can do good upon. 3.01.197
by'r lady, he is a good musician. 3.01.231
not mine, in good sooth. 3.01.246 P
not yours, in good sooth! 3.01.247 P
"not you, in good sooth," and "as true as i live 3.01.248 P
a good mouth–filling oath, and leave "in sooth," 3.01.254
your majesty's good thoughts away from me! 3.02.131
percy is but my factor, good my lord, | to 3.02.147
how now, good blunt? 3.02.162
or four times, liv'd well and in good compass, 3.03. 19 P
i make as good use of it as many a man doth of a 3.03. 29 P
bought me lights as good cheap at the dearest 3.03. 45 P
good my lord, hear me. 3.03. 94 P
darest thou be as good as thy word now? 3.03.143 P
sweet beef, i must still be good angel to thee. 3.03.177 P
i am good friends with my father and may do any 3.03.181 P
were it good | to set the exact wealth of all 4.01. 45
it were not good, for therein should we read 4.01. 49
i press me none but good householders, /yeomen's 4.02. 15 P
my good lord of westmerland, i cry you mercy! 4.02. 51 P
tut, tut, good enough to toss, food for powder, 4.02. 65 P
good cousin, be advis'd, stir not to–night. 4.03. 5
some | envy your great deservings and good name, 4.03. 35
king | have any way your good deserts forgot, 4.03. 46
hie, good sir michael, bear this sealed brief 4.04. 1
my good lord, | i guess their tenor. 4.04. 6
to–morrow, good sir michael, is a day | wherein 4.04. 8
why, my good lord, you need not fear, | there is 4.04. 21
no, good worcester, no, | we love our people 5.01.103
therefore, good cousin, let not harry know, | in 5.02. 24
good, and god will! 2H4 1.01. 13
as good as heart can wish: 1.01. 13
a gentleman well bred and of good name, | that 1.01. 26
now, travers, what good tidings comes with you? 1.01. 33
the water itself was a good healthy water, but, 1.02. 3 P
he hath since done good service at shrewsbury, 1.02. 61 P
am sure he is, to the hearing of any thing good. 1.02. 69 P
my good lord! 1.02. 93 P
god give your lordship good time of day. 1.02. 93 P
our english nation, if they have a good thing, 1.02.215 P
a good wit will make use of any thing. 1.02.247 P
o lord, ay! good master snare. 2.01. 6 P
yea, good master snare, i have ent'red him and 2.01. 9 P
in mine own house, most beastly, in good faith. 2.01. 14 P
good master fang, hold him sure. 2.01. 24 P
good master snare, let him not scape. 2.01. 25 P
good people, bring a rescue or two. 2.01. 56 P
good my lord, be good to me; 2.01. 63 P
good my lord, be good to me; 2.01. 63 P
what man of good temper would endure this 2.01. 81 P
telling us she had a good dish of prawns, 2.01. 96 P
she hath been in good case, and the truth is, 2.01.106 P
come, go along with me, good master gower. 2.01.179
i must wait upon my good lord here, i thank you, 2.01.184 P
my good lord here, i thank you, good sir john. 2.01.185 P
tell me how many good young princes would do so, 2.02. 30 P
faith, and let it be an excellent good thing. 2.02. 33 P
a crown's worth of good interpretation. 2.02. 92 P
deliver'd with good respect. 2.02.101 P
now you are in an excellent good temperality. 2.04. 23 P
you, is as red as any rose, in good truth law! 2.04. 25 P
a good heart's worth gold. 2.04. 31 P
sick of a calm, yea, good faith. 2.04. 36 P
you are both, i' good truth, as rheumatic as two 2.04. 57 P
i am in good name and fame with the very best. 2.04. 75 P
longer ago than wed'sday last, i' good faith — 2.04. 87 P
i'll drink no more than will do me good, for no 2.04.119 P
no, good captain pistol, not here, sweet captain 2.04.138 P
was an excellent good word before it was ill 2.04.149 P
pray thee go down, good ancient. 2.04.151 P
good captain peesel, be quiet, 'tis very late, 2.04.161 P
these be good humors indeed! 2.04.163
be gone, good ancient. 2.04.172 P
peace, good doll, do not speak like a 2.04.234 P
a good shallow young fellow. 2.04.237 P
'a would have made a good pantler, 'a would 'a' 2.04.238 P
they say poins has a good wit. 2.04.239 P
he a good wit? 2.04.240 P
join'd–stools, and swears with a good grace, and 2.04.248 P
god's blessing of your good heart! 2.04.303 P
for the boy, there is a good angel about him, 2.04.335 P
falstaff, good night. 2.04.366
you see, my good wenches, how men of merit are 2.04.375 P
farewell, good wenches, if i be not sent away 2.04.377 P
o, run, doll, run, run, good doll. 2.04.389 P
make good speed. 3.01. 3
many good morrows to your majesty! 3.01. 32
is it good morrow, lords? 3.01. 33
why then good morrow to you all, my lords. 3.01. 35
restored | with good advice and little medicine. 3.01. 43
and how doth my good cousin silence? 3.02. 3 P
good morrow, good cousin shallow. 3.02. 4 P
good morrow, good cousin shallow. 3.02. 4 P
say my cousin william is become a good scholar. 3.02. 10 P
how a good yoke of bullocks at /stamford fair? 3.02. 38 P
'a drew a good bow, and dead! 3.02. 43 P
it would have done a man's heart good to see. 3.02. 48 P
a score of good ewes may be worth ten pounds. 3.02. 50 P
good morrow, honest gentlemen. 3.02. 55 P
what is your good pleasure with me? 3.02. 59 P
i knew him a good backsword man. 3.02. 63 P
how doth the good knight? 3.02. 64 P
it is good, yea indeed is it. 3.02. 69 P
good phrases are surely, and ever were, very 3.02. 70 P
it comes of accommodo, very good, a good phrase. 3.02. 72 P

it comes of accommodo, very good, a good phrase. 3.02. 72 P
and a word of exceeding good command, by heaven. 3.02. 76 P
look, here comes good sir john. 3.02. 81 P
give me your good hand, give me your worship's 3.02. 82 P
good hand, give me your worship's good hand. 3.02. 83 P
welcome, good sir john. 3.02. 84 P
to see you well, good master robert shallow. 3.02. 85 P
good master silence, it well befits you should 3.02. 89 P
your good worship is welcome. 3.02. 91 P
fellow, young, strong, and of good friends. 3.02.103 P
very singular good, in faith, well said, sir 3.02.108 P
i will do my good will, sir, you can have no 3.02.156 P
well said, good woman's tailor! 3.02.158 P
o lord, good my lord captain — 3.02.177 P
good master corporate bardolph, stand my friend, 3.02.220 P
and, good master corporal captain, for my old 3.02.229 P
no man's too good to serve 's prince, and let it 3.02.237 P
well said, th' art a good fellow. 3.02.239 P
very well, go to, very good, exceeding good. 3.02.274 P
very well, go to, very good, exceeding good. 3.02.274 P
well said, i' faith, wart, th' art a good scab. 3.02.276 P
whose learning and good letters peace hath 4.01. 44
then reason will our hearts should be as good. 4.01.155
as chaff, | and good from bad find no partition. 4.01.194
and therefore be assur'd, my good lord marshal, 4.01.218
good day to you, gentle lord archbishop, | and 4.02. 2
good my lord of lancaster, | i am not here 4.02. 30
merry, | but heaviness foreruns the good event. 4.02. 82
to say thus, some good thing comes to–morrow. 4.02. 84
and, good my lord, so please you, let our trains 4.02. 93
go, good lord hastings, | and, ere they be 4.02. 95
good tidings, my lord hastings! 4.02.106
as good a man as he, sir, whoe'er i am. 4.03. 11 P
call in the powers, good cousin westmerland. 4.03. 25
let it do something, my good lord, that may do 4.03. 59 P
my good lord, that may do me good, and call it 4.03. 60 P
court, stand my good lord in your good report. 4.03. 83 P
court, stand my good lord in your good report. 4.03. 83 P
good faith, this same young sober–blooded boy 4.03. 87 P
a good sherris–sack hath a twofold operation in 4.03. 96 P
endeavor of drinking good and good store of 4.03.121 P
of drinking good and good store of fertile 4.03.121 P
no, my good lord, he is in presence here. 4.04. 17
nor lose the good advantage of his grace | by 4.04. 28
wherefore should these good news make me sick? 4.04.102
heard he the good news yet? | tell it him. 4.05. 11
i'll follow you, good master robert shallow. 5.01. 60 P
good morrow, cousin warwick, good morrow. 5.02. 20
good morrow, cousin warwick, good morrow. 5.02. 20
good morrow, cousin. 5.02. 21
o, good my lord, you have lost a friend indeed, 5.02. 27
good morrow, and god save your majesty! 5.02. 43
yet be sad, good brothers, | for, by my faith, 5.02. 49
but entertain no more of it, good brothers, 5.02. 54
state, | and (god consigning to my good intents) 5.02.143
marry, good air. 5.03. 8 P
this davy serves you for good uses, he is your 5.03. 10 P
a good varlet, a good varlet, a very good varlet 5.03. 12 P
a good varlet, a good varlet, a very good varlet 5.03. 12 P
a good varlet, a very good varlet, sir john. 5.03. 12 P
a good varlet. 5.03. 14 P
shall "do nothing but eat, and make good cheer, 5.03. 17
good master silence, i'll give you a health for 5.03. 23 P
master page, good master page, sit. 5.03. 27 P
not the ill wind which blows no man to good. 5.03. 86 P
and shall good news be baffled? 5.03.105
what? i do bring good news? 5.03.128
and withal devise something to do thyself good. 5.03.134 P
god bless thy lungs, good knight. 5.05. 9 P
i beseech you, good sir john, let me have five 5.05. 83 P
sir, i will be as good as my word. 5.05. 85 P
if you look for a good speech now, you undo me, ep 3 P
but a good conscience will make any possible ep 21 P
when my legs are too, i will bid you good night. ep 34 P
H5 six thousand and two hundred good esquires; 1.01. 14
but, my good lord, | how now for mitigation of 1.01. 69
with good acceptance of his majesty; 1.01. 83
send for him, good uncle. 1.02. 2
advis'd by good intelligence | of this most 2.pr. 12
good morrow, lieutenant bardolph. 2.01. 2 P
let't be so, good corporal nym. 2.01. 13 P
good corporal, be patient here. 2.01. 27 P
good lieutenant! 2.01. 39 P
good corporal! 2.01. 39 P
good corporal nym, show thy valor, and put up 2.01. 43 P
i would prick your guts a little in good terms, 2.01. 58 P
good bardolph, put thy face between his sheets, 2.01. 83 P
good husband, come home presently. 2.01. 88 P
the king is a good king, but it must be as it 2.01.125 P
be a' good cheer." 2.03. 18 P
for, my good liege, she is so idly king'd, | her 2.04. 26
good my sovereign, | take up the english short, 2.04. 71
and you, good yeomen, | whose limbs were made in 3.01. 25
good bawcock, bate thy rage; 3.02. 25
these be good humors! 3.02. 26 P
bad words are match'd with as few good deeds; 3.02. 39 P
duke, it is not so good to come to the mines; 3.02. 58 P
god–den to your worship, good captain james. 3.02. 84 P
look you, being as good a man as yourself, both 3.02.129 P
i do not know you so good a man as myself. 3.02.132 P
in good truth, the poet makes a most excellent 3.06. 37 P
would desire the duke to use his good pleasure, 3.06. 55 P
very good. 3.06. 60 P
but that we thought not good to bruise an injury 3.06.122 P
and perfection of a good and particular mistress 3.07. 47 P
you have good judgment in horsemanship. 3.07. 55 P
he will keep that good name still. 3.07.102 P
bids them good morrow with a modest smile, | and 4.pr. 33
good morrow, brother bedford. 4.01. 3
which is both healthful and good husbandry. 4.01. 7
good morrow, old sir thomas erpingham. 4.01. 13
a good soft pillow for that good white head 4.01. 14
a good soft pillow for that good white head 4.01. 14
'tis good for men to love their present pains 4.01. 18
do my good morrow to them, and anon | desire 4.01. 26
no, my good knight; 4.01. 29
as good a gentleman as the emperor. 4.01. 42
fame, | of parents good, of fist most valiant. 4.01. 46
a good old commander and a most kind gentleman. 4.01. 95 P
but if the cause be not good, the king himself 4.01.134 P
good old knight, | collect them all together at 4.01.286
dear lord gloucester, and my good lord exeter, 4.03. 9
farewell, good salisbury, and good luck go with 4.03. 11
good salisbury, and good luck go with thee! 4.03. 11
this story shall the good man teach his son; 4.03. 56
good god, why should they mock poor fellows thus 4.03. 92
good argument, i hope, we will not fly — | and 4.03.113
he is a gentleman of a good house, and for his 4.04. 45 P
the french might have a good prey of us, if he 4.04. 76 P
lives he, good uncle? 4.06. 4
being in his right wits and his good judgments, 4.07. 47 P
tell you there is good men porn at monmouth. 4.07. 52 P
the welshmen did good service in a garden where 4.07. 98 P
for i am welsh, you know, good countryman. 4.07.105
thanks, good my /countryman. 4.07.110
though he be as good a gentleman as the devil is 4.07.137 P
gower is a good captain, and is good knowledge 4.07.149 P
and is good knowledge and literatured in the 4.07.149 P
follow, good cousin warwick. 4.07.175
there is more good toward you peradventure than 4.08. 3 P
in his cap, and i have been as good as my word. 4.08. 32 P
it is with a good will; 4.08. 68 P
your shoes is not so good. 4.08. 70 P
'tis a good silling, i warrant you, or i will 4.08. 71 P
what prisoners of good sort are taken, uncle? 4.08. 75
yes, my conscience, he did us great good. 4.08.121 P
as in good time he may, from ireland coming, 5.pr. 31
will you be so good, scald knave, as eat it? 5.01. 30 P
it is good for your green wound and your ploody 5.01. 42 P
much good do you, scald knave, heartily. 5.01. 53 P
away, the skin is good for your broken coxcomb. 5.01. 54 P
good. 5.01. 57 P
ay, leeks is good. 5.01. 58 P
correction teach you a good english condition. 5.01. 78 P
joy and good wishes | to our most fair and 5.02. 3
of this good day and of this gracious meeting, 5.02. 13
happily a woman's voice may do some good, | when 5.02. 93
she hath good leave. 5.02. 98
a good leg will fall, a straight back will stoop 5.02.159 P
but a good heart, kate, is the sun and the moon, 5.02.162 P
but, good kate, mock me mercifully, the rather, 5.02.201 P
therefore needs prove a good soldier–breeder. 5.02.206 P
thou shalt find the best king of good fellows. 5.02.243 P
perfectly i love her, and that is good english. 5.02.284 P
then, good my lord, teach your cousin to consent 5.02.304 P
1H6 good god, these nobles should such stomachs bear 1.03. 90
improvident soldiers, had your watch been good, 2.01. 58
the law, | good faith, i am no wiser than a daw. 2.04. 18
good master vernon, it is well objected; 2.04. 43
away, away, good william de la pole! 2.04. 80
good master vernon, i am bound to you | that you 2.04.128
therefore, good uncle, for my father's sake, 2.05. 51
mourn not, except thou sorrow for my good, 2.05.111
or make my will th' advantage of my good. 2.05.129
no, my good lords, it is not that offends, | it 3.01. 35
but he shall know i am as good — 3.01. 41
as good? | thou bastard of my grandfather! 3.01. 41
o my good lords, and virtuous henry, | pity the 3.01. 76
good morrow, gallants, want ye corn for bread? 3.02. 41
what will you do, good greybeard? 3.02. 50
employ thee then, sweet virgin, for our good. 3.03. 16
and for these good deserts | we here create you 3.04. 25
why, what is he? as good a man as york. 3.04. 36
pretend some alteration in good will? 4.01. 54
good lord, what madness rules in brain–sick men, 4.01.111
good cousins both, of york and somerset, | quiet 4.01.114
good my lords, be friends. 4.01.133
and, good my lord of somerset, unite | your 4.01.164
well, my good lord, and as the only means | to 5.01. 8
your purpose is both good and reasonable; 5.01. 36
good wishes, praise, and prayers | shall suffolk 5.03.173
yes, my good lord, a pure unspotted heart, 5.03.182
kneel down and take my blessing, good my girl. 5.04. 25
hanging is too good. 5.04. 33
tush, my good lord, this superficial tale | is 5.05. 10
and you, good uncle, banish all offense. 5.05. 96
2H6 him "humphrey, the good duke of gloucester," 1.01.159
with "god preserve the good duke humphrey!" 1.01.162
excepting none but good duke humphrey; 1.01.193
join we together, for the public good, | in what 1.01.199
yes, my good lord, i'll follow presently. 1.02. 60
and will they undertake to do me good? 1.02. 77
the lord protect him, for he's a good man! 1.03. 5 P
against her will, good king? 1.03.144
i have good witness of this; 1.03.200 P
patience, good lady, wizards know their times. 1.04. 15
see you well guerdon'd for these good deserts. 1.04. 46
at your pleasure, my good lord. 1.04. 78
were it not good your grace could fly to heaven? 2.01. 17
good uncle, hide such malice; 2.01. 25
becomes | so good a quarrel and so bad a peer. 2.01. 28
good queen, and whet not on these furious peers, 2.01. 33
good fellow, tell us here the circumstance, 2.01. 72
tell me, good fellow, cam'st thou here by chance 2.01. 85
by good saint albon, who said, "simon, come; 2.01. 89
alas, good master, my wife desired some damsons, 2.01.100
now, my good lords of salisbury and warwick, 2.02. 1
and if thy claim be good, | the nevils are thy 2.02. 7
that virtuous prince, the good duke humphrey. 2.02. 74
farewell, good king; 2.03. 37
ay, good my lord; 2.03. 52
and here's a pot of good double beer, neighbor. 2.03. 64 P
god, and the good wine in thy master's way. 2.03. 96 P
night by night, in studying good for england. 3.01.111
for, good king henry, thy decay i fear. 3.01.194
and yet, good humphrey, is the hour to come 3.01.204
even so myself bewails good gloucester's case 3.01.217
eyes | look after him, and cannot do him good, 3.01.219
and yet herein i judge mine own wit good — 3.01.232
for that is good deceit | which mates him first 3.01.264
no more, good york; 3.01.304
ay, my good lord, he's dead. 3.02. 7
'tis, my good lord. 3.02. 13
than from true evidence of good esteem | he be 3.02. 21
that good duke humphrey traitorously is murd'red 3.02.123
that he is dead, good warwick, 'tis too true, 3.02.130
and you, forsooth, had the good duke to keep. 3.02.183
they say, by him the good duke humphrey died; 3.02.248
come, warwick, come, good warwick, go with me, 3.02.298
peace to his soul, if god's good pleasure be! 3.03. 26
thou that smil'dst at good duke humphrey's death 4.01. 76
more, the king's council are no good workmen. 4.02. 14 P
he was an honest man, and a good bricklayer. 4.02. 40 P
i thank you, good people — there shall be no 4.02. 72 P
be encount'red with a man as good as himself. 4.02.116 P
it is to you, good people, that i speak, | over 4.02.129
and good reason; 4.02.162 P
the tongue of an enemy be a good counsellor, or 4.02.171 P
if we mean to thrive and do good, break open the 4.03. 15 P
cheeks are pale for watching for your good. 4.07. 85
continue still in this so good a mind, | and 4.09. 17
or unto death, to do my country good. 4.09. 43
as all things shall redound unto your good. 4.09. 47
think this word "sallet" was born to do me good; 4.10. 11 P
he were created knight for his good service. 5.01. 77
they come, i'll warrant they'll make it good. 5.01.122
can we outrun the heavens? good margaret, stay. 5.02. 73
good brother, as thou lov'st and honorest arms, 3H6 1.01.116
my title's good, and better far than his. 1.01.130
what good is this to england and himself! 1.01.177
thou art as opposite to every good | as the 1.04.134
heard | the happy tidings of his good escape. 2.01. 7
ay, good my lord, and leave us to our fortune. 2.02. 75
unsheathe your sword, good father; 2.02. 80
how now, my lord, what hap? what hope of good? 2.03. 8
would i were dead, if god's good will were so; 2.05. 19
nay, take me with thee, good sweet exeter; 2.05.137
breathe we, lords, good fortune bids us pause, 2.06. 31
fight closer or, good faith, you'll catch a blow 3.02. 23
ay, good leave have you, for you will have leave 3.02. 34
and would you not do much to do them good? 3.02. 38
to do them good i would sustain some harm. 3.02. 39
then get your husband's lands, to do them good. 3.02. 40
queen, | and yet too good to be your concubine. 3.02. 98
weak, | as may appear by edward's good success, 3.03.146
now for awhile farewell, good duke of york. 4.03. 57
hands | he hath good usage and great liberty, 4.05. 6
true, my good lord, i know you for no less. 4.07. 22
the good old man would fain that all were well, 4.07. 31
thanks, good montgomery; 4.07. 45
i'll do thee service for so good a gift. 5.01. 33
stand we in good array; 5.01. 62
welcome, good clarence, this is brother–like. 5.01.105
as good to chide the waves as speak them fair. 5.04. 24
good clarence, do; 5.05. 73
good day, my lord. what, at your book so hard? 5.06. 1
ay, my good lord — my lord, i should say rather 5.06. 2
'tis sin to flatter, "good" was little better: 5.06. 3
"good gloucester" and "good devil" were alike, 5.06. 4
"good gloucester" and "good devil" were alike, 5.06. 4
therefore, not "good lord." 5.06. 5
brother, good day. R3 1.01. 42
was it not she, and that good man of worship, 1.01. 66
good time of day unto my gracious lord! 1.01.122
as much unto my good lord chamberlain! 1.01.123
as thou dost swallow up this good king's blood, 1.02. 66
which renders good for bad, blessings for curses 1.02. 69
therefore for god's sake entertain good comfort, 1.03. 4
good time of day unto your royal grace! 1.03. 18
the countess richmond, good my lord of derby, 1.03. 20
to your good prayer will scarcely say amen. 1.03. 21
be you, good lord, assur'd | i hate not you for 1.03. 23
madam, good hope, his grace speaks cheerfully. 1.03. 34
good counsel, marry! 1.03.260
i was too hot to do somebody good | that is too 1.03.310
tell them that god bids us do good for evil: 1.03.334
talkers are no good doers. 1.03.350
i will, my lord. god give your grace good rest! 1.04. 75
now have i done a good day's work. 2.01. 1
and in good time, | here comes sir richard 2.01. 45
good morrow to my sovereign king and queen, 2.01. 47
i hate it, and desire all good men's love. 2.01. 62
ay, my good lord, and no man in the presence 2.01. 85
good grandam, tell us, is our father dead? 2.02. 1
for my good uncle gloucester | told me the king, 2.02. 20
and make me die a good old man! 2.02.109
me seemeth good that, with some little train, 2.02.120
good morrow, neighbor, whither away so fast? 2.03. 1
give you good morrow, sir. 2.03. 6
doth the news hold of good king edward's death? 2.03. 7
no, no, by god's good grace his son shall reign. 2.03. 10
no, no, good friends, god wot, | for then this 2.03. 18
why, my good cousin, it is good to grow. 2.04. 9
why, my good cousin, it is good to grow. 2.04. 9
good faith, good faith, the saying did not hold 2.04. 16
good faith, good faith, the saying did not hold 2.04. 16
good madam, be not angry with the child. 2.04. 36
i thank you, good my lord, and thank you all. 3.01. 19
and in good time, here comes the sweating lord. 3.01. 24
good lords, make all the speedy haste you may. 3.01. 60
now in good time, here comes the duke of york. 3.01. 95
myself and my good cousin buckingham | will to 3.01.137
and bid my lord, for joy of this good news, 3.01.184
good catesby, go effect this business soundly. 3.01.186
my good lords both, with all the heed i can. 3.01.187
and at the other is my good friend catesby; 3.02. 22
many good morrows to my noble lord! 3.02. 35
good morrow, catesby, you are early stirring. 3.02. 36
ay, my good lord. 3.02. 42
and thereupon he sends you this good news, 3.02. 48
my lord, good morrow, good morrow, catesby. 3.02. 74
my lord, good morrow, good morrow, catesby. 3.02. 74
go on before, i'll talk with this good fellow. 3.02. 95
god hold it, to your honor's good content! 3.02.105
i thank thee, good sir john, with all my heart. 3.02.109
good faith, and when i met this holy man | the 3.02.116
my noble lords and cousins all, good morrow. 3.04. 22
i saw good strawberries in your garden there. 3.04. 32
when that he bids good morrow with such spirit. 3.04. 50
who builds his hope in air of your good looks 3.04. 98
to murther me and my good lord of gloucester? 3.05. 39
and your good graces both have well proceeded, 3.05. 48
but, my good lord, your grace's words shall 3.05. 62

and so, my good lord mayor, we bid farewell. 3.05. 71
is the indictment of the good lord hastings, 3.06. 1
here's a good world the while! 3.06. 10
i bid them that did love their country's good 3.07. 21
and stand between two churchmen, good my lord — 3.07. 48
return, good catesby, to the gracious duke, 3.07. 65
no less importing than our general good, | are 3.07. 68
he fears, my lord, you mean no good to him. 3.07. 87
should | suspect me that i mean no good to him. 3.07. 89
and all good men of this ungovern'd isle. 3.07.110
which here we waken to our country's good, | the 3.07.124
then, good my lord, take to your royal self 3.07.195
do, good my lord, your citizens entreat you. 3.07.201
as much to you, good sister! whither away? 4.01. 7
and in good time, here the lieutenant comes. 4.01. 12
be of good cheer. mother, how fares your grace? 4.01. 37
thou to richmond, and good fortune guide thee! 4.01. 91
go thou to richard, and good angels tend thee! 4.01. 92
to sanctuary, and good thoughts possess thee! 4.01. 93
gold were as good as twenty orators, | and will, 4.02. 38
mean time, but think how i may do thee good, 4.03. 33
and anne my wife hath bid this world good night. 4.03. 39
good or bad news, that thou com'st in so bluntly 4.03. 45
and brief, good mother, for i am in haste. 4.04.162
lo at their birth good stars were opposite. 4.04.216
as i intend more good to you and yours | than 4.04.238
what good is cover'd with the face of heaven, 4.04.240
heaven, | to be discover'd, that can do me good? 4.04.241
mad'st quick conveyance with her good aunt anne. 4.04.283
be opposite all planets of good luck | to my 4.04.402
ay, if the devil tempt you to do good. 4.04.419
here, my good lord. 4.04.442
o, true, good catesby. 4.04.449
none good, my liege, to please you with the 4.04.457
neither good nor bad! 4.04.459
no, my good lord, therefore mistrust me not. 4.04.478
no, my good lord, my friends are in the north. 4.04.483
but this good comfort bring i to your highness: 4.04.520
no, my good lord, therefore be patient. 5.01. 2
good captain blunt, bear my good–night to him, 5.03. 30
yet one thing more, good captain, do for me — 5.03. 33
blunt, make some good means to speak with him, 5.03. 40
good night, good captain blunt. 5.03. 44
good night, good captain blunt. 5.03. 44
good norfolk, hie thee to thy charge, | use 5.03. 53
who prays continually for richmond's good. 5.03. 84
good lords, conduct him to his regiment. 5.03.103
once more, good night, kind lords and gentlemen. 5.03.107
good angels guard thy battle! 5.03.138
good angels guard thee from the boar's annoy! 5.03.151
god and good angels fight on richmond's side, 5.03.175
for any good | that i myself have done unto 5.03.187
nay, good my lord, be not afraid of shadows. 5.03.215
good morrow, richmond! 5.03.223
god and our good cause fight upon our side; 5.03.240
a good direction, warlike sovereign. 5.03.302
good morrow, and well met. H8 1.01. 1
would by a good discourser lose some life, 1.01. 41
all this was ord'red by the good discretion | of 1.01. 50
my good lord cardinal, they vent reproaches 1.02. 23
take good heed | you charge not in your spleen a 1.02.173
all the good our english | have got by the late 1.03. 5
come, good sir thomas, | we shall be late else, 1.03. 64
as merry | as, first, good company, good wine, 1.04. 6
first, good company, good wine, good welcome, 1.04. 6
first, good company, good wine, good welcome, 1.04. 6
good wine, good welcome, | can make good people. 1.04. 7
my welcome, | and to you all good health. 1.04. 38
good lord chamberlain, | go, give 'em welcome: 1.04. 56
a good digestion to you all; 1.04. 62
see then, | by all your good leaves, gentlemen; 1.04. 85
let's be merry, | good my lord cardinal: 1.04.105
all good people, | you that thus far have come 2.01. 55
dying, | go with me like good angels to my end, 2.01. 75
all good people, | pray for me! 2.01.131
good angels keep it from us! 2.01.142
to the good queen possess'd him with a scruple 2.01.158
good day to both your graces. 2.02. 13
excellence | that angels love good men with; 2.02. 34
thanks, my good lord chamberlain. 2.02. 61
my good lord cardinal? 2.02. 73
my good lord, have great care | i be not found a 2.02. 77
this good man, | this just and learned priest, 2.02. 95
that good fellow, | if i command him, follows my 2.02.132
she | so good a lady that no tongue could ever 2.03. 3
nay, good troth. 2.03. 33
good morrow, ladies. 2.03. 50
my good lord, | not your demand; 2.03. 51
and becoming | the action of good women. 2.03. 55
commends his good opinion of you to you, and 2.03. 61
good lady, | make yourself mirth with your 2.03.100
put me off, | and take your good grace from me? 2.04. 22
present state, | or touch of her good person? 2.04.156
i speak my good lord card'nal to this point, 2.04.167
world against the person | of the good queen, 2.04.225
they should be good men, their affairs as 3.01. 22
o, good my lord, no latin; 3.01. 42
to taint that honor every good tongue blesses, 3.01. 55
way to sorrow — | you have too much, good lady; 3.01. 57
forgetting (like a good man) your late censure 3.01. 64
my lords, i thank you both for your good wills, 3.01. 68
last fit of my greatness — good your graces, 3.01. 78
you turn the good we offer into envy. 3.01.113
madam, you wander from the good we aim at. 3.01.138
why should we, good lady, | upon what cause, 3.01.155
good my lord, | you are full of heavenly stuff, 3.02.136
and 'tis a kind of good deed to say well, | and 3.02.153
to th' good of your most sacred person and | the 3.02.173
that for your highness' good i ever labor'd 3.02.191
as you respect the common good, the state | of 3.02.290
so fare you well, my little good lord cardinal. 3.02.349
so farewell — to the little good you bear me. 3.02.350
when he thinks, good easy man, full surely | his 3.02.356
never so truly happy, my good cromwell; 3.02.377
good cromwell, | neglect him not; 3.02.419
must i needs forgo | so good, so noble, and so 3.02.423
good sir, have patience. 3.02.458
alas, good lady! 4.01. 35

good sir, speak it to us. 4.01. 61
is held no great good lover of the archbishop's, 4.01.104
prithee, good griffith, tell me how he died. 4.02. 9
your highness | to hear me speak his good now? 4.02. 47
yes, good griffith, | i were malicious else. 4.02. 47
he was a scholar, and a ripe and good one; 4.02. 51
unwilling to outlive the good that did it; 4.02. 60
good griffith, | cause the musicians play me 4.02. 77
good wench, let's sit down quiet | for fear we 4.02. 81
madam, such good dreams | possess your fancy. 4.02. 93
and heartily entreats you take good comfort. 4.02.119
o my good lord, that comfort comes too late, 4.02.120
madam, in good health. 4.02.124
a right good husband (let him be a noble), | and 4.02.146
these are the whole contents, and, good my lord, 4.02.154
when i am dead, good wench, | let me be us'd 4.02.167
good hour of night, sir thomas! 5.01. 5
that it may find | good time, and live; 5.01. 22
yet my conscience says | she's a good creature, 5.01. 25
good night, sir thomas. 5.01. 54
alas, good lady! 5.01. 69
and my good mistress will | remember in my 5.01. 77
charles, good night. | well, sir, what follows? 5.01. 78
ay, my good lord. 5.01. 82
my good and gracious lord of canterbury. 5.01. 92
ah, my good lord, i grieve at what i speak, 5.01. 95
and am right glad to catch this good occasion 5.01.109
stand up, good canterbury! 5.01.113
the good i stand on is my truth and honesty. 5.01.122
be of good cheer, | they shall no more prevail 5.01.142
look, the good man weeps! 5.01.152
now good angels | fly o'er thy royal head, and 5.01.159
at least good manners — as not thus to suffer 5.02. 29
my good lord archbishop, i'm very sorry | to sit 5.02. 43
my good lords: 5.02. 67
ah, my good lord of winchester — i thank you, 5.02. 93
i thank you, | you are always my good friend; 5.02. 94
are a little, | by your good favor, too sharp; 5.02.109
good master secretary, | i cry your honor mercy; 5.02.112
stay, good my lords, | i have a little yet to 5.02.132
not only good and wise but most religious; 5.02.151
you were ever good at sudden commendations, 5.02.157
good man, sit down. 5.02.165
this good man (few of you deserve that title), 5.02.173
good man, those joyful tears show thy true 5.02.208
good master porter, i belong to th' larder. 5.03. 4 P
shall be with you presently, good master puppy. 5.03. 29 P
they fell on, i made good my place; 5.03. 54 P
and to your royal grace and the good queen, | my 5.04. 4
thank you, good lord archbishop. 5.04. 8
is, | with all the virtues that attend the good, 5.04. 27
good grows with her; 5.04. 32
to you, my good lord mayor, | and you, good 5.04. 69
and you, good brethren, i am much beholding; 5.04. 70
all the expected good w' are like to hear | for ep 8
in | the merciful construction of good women, ep 10
good pandarus! how now, pandarus? TRO 1.01. 69
hark what good sport is out of town to–day. 1.01.113
good; and what of him? 1.02. 14
good morrow, uncle pandarus. 1.02. 42 P
good morrow, cousin cressid. 1.02. 43 P
good morrow, alexander. 1.02. 44 P
is too flaming a praise for a good complexion. 1.02.104 P
good niece, do, sweet niece cressida. 1.02.179 P
wit, i can tell you, and he's man good enough. 1.02.191 P
it does a /man's heart good. 1.02.204 P
by god's lid, it does one's heart good. 1.02.212 P
why, this will do helen's heart good now, ha? 1.02.216 P
is not birth, beauty, good shape, discourse, 1.02.253 P
good boy, tell him i come. 1.02.275 P
fare ye well, good niece. 1.02.276 P
of a king, | sans check, to good and bad. 1.03. 94
good arms, strong joints, true swords, and, 1.03.238
shall make it good, or do his best to do it: 1.03.274
a scantling | of good or bad unto the general, 1.03.342
nay, good ajax. 2.01. 77 P
good words, thersites. 2.01. 88 P
'a were as good crack a fusty nut with no kernel 2.01.101 P
yes, good sooth. to achilles, to ajax, to — 2.01.109 P
a good riddance. 2.01.120 P
good thersites, come in and rail. 2.03. 23 P
a good quarrel to draw emulous factions and 2.03. 73 P
ay, my good son. 2.03.257
fair prince, here is good broken music. 3.01. 49 P
rude, in sooth, in good sooth, very rude. 3.01. 56 P
ay, good my lord. 3.01. 91 P
ay, good now, love, love, nothing but love. 3.01.113 P
and yet, good faith, i wish'd myself a man, | or 3.02.127
good diomed, | furnish you fairly for this 3.03. 32
it may do good, pride hath no other glass | to 3.03. 47
good day, good day. 3.03. 62
good day, good day. 3.03. 62
good morrow, ajax. 3.03. 66
good morrow. 3.03. 68
ay, and good next day too. 3.03. 69
neither gave to me | good word nor look. 3.03.144
those scraps are good deeds past, which are 3.03.148
i said, "good morrow, ajax"; 3.03.260 P
had i so good occasion to lie long | as /you, 4.01. 4
that's my mind too. good morrow, lord aeneas. 4.01. 7
good morrow, all. 4.01. 51
she hath not given so many good words breath 4.01. 74
good morrow then. 4.02. 6
come, beshrew your heart, you'll ne'er be good, 4.02. 29
good uncle, go and see. 4.02. 35
good morrow, lord, good morrow. 4.02. 44
good morrow, lord, good morrow. 4.02. 44
good, good, my lord, the secrets of neighbor 4.02. 72
good, good, my lord, the secrets of neighbor 4.02. 72
good uncle, i beseech you, on my knees /i 4.02. 88 P
good my brother troilus, | tell you the lady 4.03. 3
nay, good my lord! 4.04. 98
good brother, come you hither, | and bring 4.04. 99
i had good argument for kissing once. 4.05. 26
he was a soldier good, | but, by great mars, the 4.05.197
let me embrace thee, good old chronicle, | that 4.05.202
so now, fair prince of troy, i bid good night. 5.01. 71
thanks and good night to the greeks' general. 5.01. 73

good night, my lord. 5.01. 74
good night, sweet lord menelaus. 5.01. 74
good night and welcome, both /at /once, to those 5.01. 77
good night. 5.01. 79
good night, great hector. 5.01. 83
and so, good night. 5.01. 87
good night. 5.02. 28
no, no, good night, i'll be your fool no more. 5.02. 32
now, good my lord, go off; 5.02. 40
and so, good night. 5.02. 44
good night. 5.02.106
good troilus, chide me for it. 5.03. 39
it be, | great hector was as good a man as he. 5.09. 6
good traders in the flesh, set this in your 5.10. 45 P
one word, good citizens. COR 1.01. 14 P
accounted poor citizens, the patricians good. 1.01. 16 P
could be content to give him good report for't, 1.01. 33 P
masters, my good friends, mine honest neighbors, 1.01. 62
note me this, good friend: 1.01.127
you, my good friends, this says the belly, mark 1.01.141
the senators of rome are this good belly, | and 1.01.148
we have ever your good word. 1.01.166
he that will give good words to thee will 1.01.167
tickled with good success, disdains the shadow 1.01.260
then his good report should have been my son; 1.03. 20 P
none less dear than thine and my good martius, i 1.03. 23 P
my ladies both, good day to you. 1.03. 48 P
a fine spot, in good faith. 1.03. 53 P
i thank your ladyship; well, good madam. 1.03. 54 P
no, good madam, i will not out of doors. 1.03. 71 P
you must go visit the good lady that lies in. 1.03. 77 P
no, good madam, pardon me, indeed i will not 1.03. 87 P
o, good madam, there can be none yet. 1.03. 91 P
give me excuse, good madam, i will obey you in 1.03.102 P
come, good sweet lady. 1.03.107 P
so, the good horse is mine. 1.04. 5
now prove good seconds: 1.04. 43
take | convenient numbers to make good the city, 1.05. 12
make good this ostentation, and you shall 1.06. 86
he that has but effected his good will | hath 1.09. 18
whereof we have ta'en good and good store — of 1.09. 32
whereof we have ta'en good and good store — of 1.09. 32
more cruel to your good report than grateful 1.09. 54
at all times | to undercrest your good addition 1.09. 72
we may articulate | for their own good and ours. 1.09. 78
'twill be deliver'd back on good condition. 1.10. 2
what good condition can a treaty find | i' th' 1.10. 6
good or bad? 2.01. 3 P
make but an interior survey of your good selves! 2.01. 40 P
they lie deadly that tell you have good faces. 2.01. 62 P
you wear out a good wholesome forenoon in 2.01. 69 P
good ladies, let's go. 2.01.133 P
god save your good worships! 2.01.145 P
nay, my good soldier, up; 2.01.171
my head, | the good patricians must be visited, 2.01.196
know, good mother, | i had rather be their 2.01.202
it shall be to him then as our good wills: 2.01.242
'twixt doing them neither good nor harm; 2.02. 18 P
speak, good cominius: 2.02. 48
that's thousand to one good one — when you now 2.02. 79
your good voice, sir, what say you? 2.03. 78 P
him joy, and make him good friend to the people! 2.03.135 P
not having the power to do the good it would, 3.01.160
speak, good sicinius. 3.01.191
by the tribunes' leave, and yours, good people, 3.01.280
now the good gods forbid | that our renowned 3.01.288
our good city | cleave in the midst and perish. 3.02. 27
a good demand. 3.02. 45
in asking their good loves, but thou wilt frame 3.02. 84
can give, | to have't with saying "good morrow." 3.03. 93
my country's good with a respect more tender, 3.03.112
take good cominius | with thee a while. 4.01. 34
by the good gods | i'ld with thee every foot. 4.01. 56
ever thou wise words, | and for rome's good. 4.02. 22
tribe before him, | his good sword in his hand. 4.02. 25
good man, the wounds that he does bear for rome! 4.02. 28
all tending to the good of their adversaries. 4.03. 41 P
a good memory | and witness of the malice and 4.05. 71
general," but he was always good enough for him. 4.05.182 P
we stood to't in good time. is this menenius? 4.06. 10
weaker sort may wish | good martius home again. 4.06. 71
o, you have made good work! 4.06. 80
you have made good work, | you and your 4.06. 95
if they | should say, "be good to rome," they 4.06.112
you have made | good work, you and your cry! 4.06.147
the gods be good to us! 4.06.153 P
and shows good husbandry for the volscian state, 4.07. 22
you have made good work! 5.01. 15
be your country's pleader, your good tongue, 5.01. 36
yet your good will | must have that thanks from 5.01. 45
lip | and hum at good cominius much unhearts me. 5.01. 49
good faith, i'll prove him, | speed how it will. 5.01. 60
good my friends, | if you have heard your 5.02. 8
i have been | the book of his good acts, whence 5.02. 15
the good gods assuage thy wrath, and turn the 5.02. 76 P
now, good aufidius, | were you in my stead, 5.03.191
but, good sir, | what peace you'll make, advise 5.03.196
the gods be good unto us! 5.04. 30 P
such a case the gods will not be good unto us. 5.04. 31 P
good news, good news! 5.04. 40
good news, good news! 5.04. 40
this is good news. 5.04. 51
to strike at him admits | a good construction. 5.06. 20
pius | for many good and great deserts to rome. TIT 1.01. 24
spoils, | returns the good andronicus to rome, 1.01. 37
the good andronicus, | patron of virtue, rome's 1.01. 64
interrupter of the good | that noble–minded 1.01.208
to gratify the good andronicus, | and gratulate 1.01.220
that brought her for this high good turn so far? 1.01.397
'tis good, sir, you are very short with us; 1.01.409
for good lord titus' innocence in all, | whose 1.01.437
take up this good old man, and cheer the heart 1.01.457
and must advise the emperor for his good. 1.01.464
and let it be mine honor, good my lord, | that i 1.01.466
ay, and as good as saturninus may. 2.01. 90
many good morrows to your majesty; 2.02. 11
madam, to you as many and as good. 2.02. 12
long, | good king, to be so mightily abused. 2.03. 87

or, wanting strength to do thee so much good, 2.03.238
shall thy good uncle, and thy brother lucius, 3.01.122
good titus, dry thine eyes. 3.01.138
good aaron, wilt thou help to chop it off? 3.01.161
good aaron, give his majesty my hand. 3.01.193
let fools do good, and fair men call for grace, 3.01.204
for that good hand thou sent'st the emperor. 3.01.235
good uncle marcus, see how swift she comes. 4.01. 3
write thou, good niece, and here display at last 4.01. 73
that we will prosecute by good advice | mortal 4.01. 92
can you hear a good man groan | and not relent, 4.01.123
it did me good, before the palace gate | to 4.02. 35
but me more good to see so great a lord | basely 4.02. 37
good morrow, lords. 4.02. 51
well, god give her good rest! 4.02. 63
no, my good lord, but pluto sends you word, | if 4.03. 38
you are a good archer, marcus; 4.03. 53
you were as good to shoot against the wind. 4.03. 58
good boy, in virgo's lap; 4.03. 65
how now, good fellow, wouldst thou speak with us 4.04. 39
devil | that robb'd andronicus of his good hand; 5.01. 41
too like the sire for ever being good. 5.01. 50
good lord, how like the empress' sons they are! 5.02. 64
good murther, stab him, he's a murtherer. 5.02.100
thee, | good rapine, stab him, he is a ravisher. 5.02.103
but would it please thee, good andronicus, | to 5.02.111
good uncle, take you in this barbarous moor, 5.03. 4
i fear the emperor means no good to us. 5.03. 10
peace, for love, for league, and good to rome. 5.03. 23
we are beholding to you, good andronicus. 5.03. 33
if one good deed in all my life i did, | i do 5.03.189
i serve as good a man as you. ROM 1.01. 55 P
unless good counsel may the cause remove. 1.01.142
good morrow, cousin. 1.01.160
good heart, at what? 1.01.184
at thy good heart's oppression. 1.01.184
a right good mark–man! and she's fair i love. 1.01.206
in good time! 1.02. 44 P
whipt and tormented and — god–den, good fellow. 1.02. 56
susan is with god, | she was too good for me. 1.03. 20
take our good meaning, for our judgment sits 1.04. 46
to bear, | making them women of good carriage. 1.04. 94
when good manners shall lie all in one or two 1.05. 3 P
good thou, save me a piece of marchpane, and, as 1.05. 7 P
nay, sit, nay, sit, good cousin capulet, | for 1.05. 30
good pilgrim, you do wrong your hand too much, 1.05. 97
and a good lady, and a wise and virtuous. 1.05.114
i thank you, honest gentlemen, good night. 1.05.124
call, good mercutio. 2.01. 6
romeo, good night, i'll to my truckle–bed, 2.01. 39
sweet, good night! 2.02.120
good night, good night! 2.02.123
good night, good night! 2.02.123
anon, good nurse! 2.02.137
three words, dear romeo, and good night indeed. 2.02.142
a thousand times good night! 2.02.154
good night, good night! 2.02.184
good night, good night! 2.02.184
that i shall say good night till it be morrow. 2.02.185
but to the earth some special good doth give; 2.03. 18
nor aught so good but, strain'd from that fair 2.03. 19
good morrow, father. 2.03. 31
head | so soon to bid good morrow to thy bed. 2.03. 34
that's my good son, but where hast thou been 2.03. 47
be plain, good son, and homely in thy drift, 2.03. 55
"by jesu, a very good blade! 2.04. 30 P
a very good whore!" 2.04. 30 P
good morrow to you both. 2.04. 46 P
pardon, good mercutio, my business was great, 2.04. 49 P
come between us, good benvolio, my wits faints. 2.04. 67 P
nay, good goose, bite not. 2.04. 78 P
good peter, to hide her face, for her fan's the 2.04.107 P
god ye good morrow, gentlemen. 2.04.109 P
god ye good den, fair gentlewoman. 2.04.110 P
is it good den? 2.04.111 P
an old hare hoar, | is very good meat in lent; 2.04.136
if i see occasion in a good quarrel, and the law 2.04.160 P
good heart, and, i' faith, i will tell her as 2.04.173 P
and stay, good nurse — behind the abbey wall 2.04.187
but she, good soul, had as lieve see a toad, a 2.04.202 P
rosemary, that it would do you good to hear it. 2.04.212 P
now, good sweet nurse — o lord, why lookest 2.05. 21
if good, thou shamest the music of sweet news 2.05. 23
come, i pray thee speak, good, good nurse, speak 2.05. 28
i pray thee speak, good, good nurse, speak. 2.05. 28
is thy news good or bad? 2.05. 35
let me be satisfied, is't good or bad? 2.05. 37
good even to my ghostly confessor. 2.06. 21
i pray thee, good mercutio, let's retire. 3.01. 1
gentlemen, good den, a word with one of you. 3.01. 38
and so, good capulet — which name i tender | as 3.01. 71
good king of cats, nothing but one of your nine 3.01. 77 P
good mercutio! 3.01. 90
arise, one knocks. good romeo, hide thyself. 3.03. 71
here all the night | to hear good counsel. 3.03.160
go hence, good night; 3.03.166
time | every good hap to you that chances here. 3.03.171
farewell, good night. 3.03.172
madam, good night, commend me to your daughter. 3.04. 9
good night. 3.04. 35
good father, i beseech you on my knees, | hear 3.05.158
good prudence, smatter with your gossips, go. 3.05.171
nor what is mine shall never do thee good. 3.05.194
or 'twere as good he were | as living here and 3.05.224
well, he may chance to do some good on her. 4.02. 13
good night. 4.03. 12
look to the bak'd meats, good angelica, | spare 4.04. 5
good /faith, 'tis day. 4.04. 21
honest good fellows, ah, put up, put up, | for 4.05. 98
no, my good lord. 5.01. 32
and be prosperous, and farewell, good fellow. 5.03. 42
good gentle youth, tempt not a desp'rate man. 5.03. 59
tell me, good my friend, | what torch is yond, 5.03.124
come go, good juliet, i dare no longer stay. 5.03.159
this letter doth make good the friar's words, 5.03.286
good day, sir. TIM 1.01. 1
that happy verse | which aptly sings the good." 1.01. 17
'tis a good form. 1.01. 17
'tis a good piece. 1.01. 28
is't good? 1.01. 36
upon his good and gracious nature hanging, 1.01. 56
ay, my good lord, five talents is his debt, 1.01. 95
freely, good father. 1.01.110
ay, my good lord, and she accepts of it. 1.01.135
no, my good lord, he speaks the common tongue 1.01.174
good morrow to thee, gentle apemantus! 1.01.178
i be gentle, stay thou for thy good morrow — 1.01.179
good for their meat, and safer for their lives. 1.02. 45
let it flow this way, my good lord. 1.02. 54
much good dich thy good heart, apemantus! 1.02. 72 P
much good dich thy good heart, apemantus! 1.02. 72 P
o, no doubt, my good friends, but the gods 1.02. 88 P
look you, my good lord, | i must entreat you 1.02.168
is, | being of no power to make his wishes good. 1.02.196
gave | good words the other day of a bay courser 1.02.211
wert not sullen), | i would be good to thee. 1.02.237
good even, varro. what, | you come for money? 2.02. 9
nay, good my lord — 2.02. 26
contain thyself, good friend. 2.02. 26
one varro's servant, my good lord — 2.02. 27
i do beseech you, good my lords, keep on, | i'll 2.02. 34
gramercies, good fool; how does your mistress? 2.02. 67 P
good! gramercy. 2.02. 71 P
as good a trick as ever hangman serv'd thief. 2.02. 94 P
a fool in good clothes, and something like thee. 2.02.108 P
o my good lord, | at many times i brought in my 2.02.132
o my good lord, the world is but a word; 2.02.152
bid him suppose some good necessity | touches 2.02.227
athens, thy very bountiful good lord and master? 3.01. 11 P
alas, good lord! 3.01. 22 P
'tis, if he would not keep so good a house. 3.01. 23 P
good parts in thee! 3.01. 37 P
good boy, wink at me, and say thou saw'st me not 3.01. 43 P
he is my very good friend, and an honorable 3.02. 1 P
see, by good hap, yonder's my lord; 3.02. 25 P
i to disfurnish myself against such a good time, 3.02. 45 P
commend me bountifully to his good lordship, and 3.02. 53 P
good servilius, will you befriend me so far as 3.02. 57 P
i'll look you out a good turn, servilius. 3.02. 60
i'd such a courage to do him good. 3.03. 24
well met, good morrow, titus and hortensius. 3.04. 1
good day at once. 3.04. 7
welcome, good brother. 3.04. 7
good gods! 3.04. 76
my lords, | as you are great, be pitifully good. 3.05. 52
all | my honor to you, upon his good returns. 3.05. 81
the good time of day to you, sir. 3.06. 1 P
ah, my good friend, what cheer? 3.06. 40 P
the gods confound (hear me, you good gods all) 4.01. 37
good fellows all, | the latest of my wealth i'll 4.02. 22
when man's worst sin is, he does too much good! 4.02. 39
give us some gold, good timon; hast thou more? 4.03.133
and wonder of good deeds evilly bestow'd! 4.03.461
i beg of you to know me, good my lord, | t' 4.03.487
good as the best. 5.01. 21
good honest men! 5.01. 80
power, and thy good name | live with authority; 5.01.162
go, go, good countrymen, and for this fault JC 1.01. 56
but let not therefore my good friends be griev'd 1.02. 43
tell me, good brutus, can you see your face? 1.02. 51
therefore, good brutus, be prepar'd to hear; 1.02. 66
if it be aught toward the general good, | set 1.02. 85
where i stood, cried, "alas, good soul!" 1.02.272 P
good, i will expect you. 1.02.293 P
this rudeness is a sauce to his good wit, 1.02.300
good even, casca; 1.03. 1
good night then, casca; 1.03. 39
your ear is good. cassius, what night is this! 1.03. 42
good cinna, take this paper, | and look you lay 1.03.142
'tis good. 2.01. 60
good morrow, brutus, do we trouble you? 2.01. 87
silver hairs | will purchase us a good opinion, 2.01.145
alas, good cassius, do not think of him. 2.01.185
now, good metellus, go along by him. 2.01.218
good gentlemen, look fresh and merrily; 2.01.224
and so good morrow to you every one. 2.01.228
why, so i do. good portia, go to bed. 2.01.260
i but in the suburbs | of your good pleasure? 2.01.286
vouchsafe good morrow from a feeble tongue. 2.01.313
good morrow, worthy caesar, | i come to fetch 2.02. 58
good morrow, caesar. 2.02.109
good morrow, casca. 2.02.111
good morrow, antony. 2.02.117
good friends, go in, and taste some wine with me 2.02.126
and take good note | what caesar doth, what 2.04. 14
at mine own house, good lady. 2.04. 22
caesar | to be so good to caesar as to hear me: 2.04. 29
good morrow to you. 2.04. 33
publius, good cheer, | there is no harm intended 3.01. 89
you in | with all kind love, good thoughts, and 3.01.176
last, not least in love, yours, good trebonius. 3.01.189
our reasons are so full of good regard | that 3.01.224
but speak all good you can devise of caesar, 3.01.246
as i slew my best lover for the good of rome, i 3.02. 45 P
good countrymen, let me depart alone, | and, for 3.02. 55
the good is oft interred with their bones; 3.02. 76
'tis good you know not that you are his heirs, 3.02.145
good friends, sweet friends, let me not stir you 3.02.210
welcome, good messala. 4.03.163
i do not think it good. 4.03.198
good reasons must of force give place to better: 4.03.203
hear me, good brother. 4.03.212
good night. 4.03.229
farewell, good messala. 4.03.231
good night, titinius. 4.03.232
noble cassius, | good night, and good repose. 4.03.233
noble cassius, | good night, and good repose. 4.03.233
good night, my lord. 4.03.237
good night, good brother. 4.03.237
good night, good brother. 4.03.237
good night, lord brutus. 4.03.238
lie down, good sirs, | it may be i shall 4.03.250
bear with me, good boy, i am much forgetful. 4.03.255
if i do live, | i will be good to thee. 4.03.266
gentle knave, good night; 4.03.269
and, good boy, good night. 4.03.272
and, good boy, good night. 4.03.272
good words are better than bad strokes, octavius 5.01. 29
your bad strokes, brutus, you give good words; 5.01. 30
now be a freeman, and with this good sword, 5.03. 41
mistrust of good success hath done this deed. 5.03. 66
come hither, good volumnius; list a word. 5.05. 15
good volumnius, | thou know'st that we two went 5.05. 25
thou art a fellow of a good respect; 5.05. 45
farewell, good strato. 5.05. 50
i kill'd not thee with half so good a will. 5.05. 51
do so, good messala. 5.05. 63
general honest thought | and common good to all, 5.05. 72
who like a good and hardy soldier fought MAC 1.02. 4
good sir, why do you start, and seem to fear 1.03. 51
cannot be good. 1.03.131
if good, why do i yield to that suggestion 1.03.134
this have i thought good to deliver thee, my 1.05. 10 P
good repose the while! 2.01. 29
good morrow, noble sir. 2.03. 44
good morrow, both. 2.03. 44
ha, good father, | thou seest the heavens, as 2.04. 4
here comes the good macduff. 2.04. 20
alas the day, | what good could they pretend? 2.04. 24
and with those | that would make good of bad, 2.04. 41
why, by the verities on thee made good, | may 3.01. 8
ay, my good lord. 3.01. 19
we should have else desir'd your good advice 3.01. 20
ay, my good lord. our time does call upon 's. 3.01. 36
this i made good to you | in our last conference 3.01. 78
to pray for this good man, and for his issue, 3.01. 88
good things of day begin to droop and drowse, 3.02. 52
fly, good fleance, fly, fly, fly! 3.03. 17
yet he's good that did the like for fleance. 3.04. 17
ay, my good lord; 3.04. 25
now good digestion wait on appetite, | and 3.04. 37
here, my good lord. 3.04. 47
what, my good lord? 3.04. 48
think of this, good peers, | but as a thing of 3.04. 95
displac'd the mirth, broke the good meeting, 3.04.108
at once, good night. 3.04.117
good night, and better health | attend his 3.04.119
a kind good night to all! 3.04.120
for mine own good | all causes shall give way. 3.04.134
blood, | then the charm is firm and good. 4.01. 38
what e'er thou art, for thy good caution, thanks 4.01. 73
good! 4.01. 96
ay, my good lord. 4.01.143
it were a good sign that i should quickly have a 4.02. 62 P
to do good sometime | accounted dangerous folly. 4.02. 76
sword, and like good men | bestride our downfall 4.03. 3
a good and virtuous nature may recoil | in an 4.03. 19
quarrels unjust against the good and loyal, 4.03. 83
my thoughts | to thy good truth and honor. 4.03.117
a most miraculous work in this good king, 4.03.147
good god betimes remove | the means that makes 4.03.162
and good men's lives | expire before the flowers 4.03.171
gracious england hath | lent us good siward, and 4.03.190
so good night! 5.01. 77
good night, good doctor. 5.01. 79
good night, good doctor. 5.01. 79
his uncle siward, and the good macduff. 5.02. 2
ay, my good lord; 5.03. 57
it is the cry of women, my good lord. 5.05. 8
well, good night. HAM 1.01. 11
give you good night. 1.01. 16
barnardo hath my place. | give you good night. 1.01. 18
welcome, horatio, welcome, good marcellus. 1.01. 20
good now, sit down, and tell me, he that knows, 1.01. 70
if there be any good thing to be done | that may 1.01.130
and we here dispatch | you, good cornelius, and 1.02. 34
good hamlet, cast thy nighted color off, | and 1.02. 68
it is not, nor it cannot come to good, | but 1.02.158
sir, my good friend — i'll change that name 1.02.163
my good lord! 1.02.166
good even, sir. 1.02.167
a truant disposition, good my lord. 1.02.169
form of the thing, each word made true and good, 1.02.210
i shall the effect of this good lesson keep | as 1.03. 45
but, good my brother, | do not, as some 1.03. 46
good my lord, tell it. 1.05.119
and now, good friends, | as you are friends, 1.05.140
once more remove, good friends. 1.05.163
you shall do marvell's wisely, good reynaldo, 2.01. 3
but, my good lord — 2.01. 35
"good sir," or so, or "friend," or "gentleman," 2.01. 46
very good, my lord. 2.01. 48
good my lord. 2.01. 67
no, my good lord, but, as you did command, | i 2.01.105
good gentlemen, he hath much talk'd of you, 2.02. 19
to show us so much gentry and good will | as to 2.02. 22
th' embassadors from norway, my good lord, | are 2.02. 40
thou still hast been the father of good news. 2.02. 42
i assure my good liege | i hold my duty as i 2.02. 43
welcome, my good friends! 2.02. 58
good madam, stay awhile. 2.02.115
give me leave, | how does my good lord hamlet? 2.02.171
in a dead dog, being a good kissing carrion — 2.02.182 P
my /excellent good friends! 2.02.224 P
good lads, how do you both? 2.02.225 P
i know the good king and queen have sent for you 2.02.281 P
welcome, good friends. 2.02.422 P
what speech, my good lord? 2.02.433 P
spoken, with good accent and good discretion. 2.02.466 P
spoken, with good accent and good discretion. 2.02.467 P
that's good, "/mobled /queen" /is /good. 2.02.504 P
good my lord, will you see the players well 2.02.522 P
my good friends, i'll leave you /till night. 2.02.546 P
good my lord! 2.02.548 P
good gentlemen, give him a further edge, | and 3.01. 26
that your good beauties be the happy cause | of 3.01. 38
good my lord, | how does your honor for this 3.01. 89
that no revenue hast but thy good spirits | to 3.02. 58
did i, my lord, and was accounted a good actor. 3.02.100 P
no, good mother, here's metal more attractive. 3.02.109 P
you are as good as a chorus, my lord. 3.02.245 P
o good horatio, i'll take the ghost's word for a 3.02.286 P
good my lord, voutsafe me a word with you. 3.02.296 P
good my lord, put your discourse into some frame 3.02.308 P

nay, good my lord, this courtesy is not of the 3.02.314 P
good my lord, what is your cause of distemper? 3.02.337 P
almost as bad, good mother, | as kill a king, 3.04. 28
yea, curb and woo for leave to do him good. 3.04.155
good night, but go not to my uncle's bed — 3.04.159
that to the use of actions fair and good | he 3.04.163
once more, good night, | and when you are 3.04.170
so, again, good night. 3.04.177
one word more, good lady. 3.04.180
'twere good you let him know, | for who, that's 3.04.188
mother, good night indeed. 3.04.213
good night, mother. 3.04.217
apprehension kills | the unseen good old man. 4.01. 12
good. 4.03. 46
good sir, whose powers are these? 4.04. 9
if his chief good and market of his time | be 4.04. 34
'twere good she were spoken with, for she may 4.05. 14
of it, and so i thank you for your good counsel. 4.05. 71 P
good night, ladies, good night. 4.05. 72 P
good night, ladies, good night. 4.05. 72 P
sweet ladies, good night, good night. 4.05. 73 P
sweet ladies, good night, good night. 4.05. 73 P
follow her close, give her good watch, i pray 4.05. 74
and whispers | for good polonius' death; 4.05. 83
calmly, good laertes. 4.05.117
good laertes, | if you desire to know the 4.05.140
to his good friends thus wide i'll ope my arms, 4.05.146
speak | like a good child and a true gentleman. 4.05.149
they say 'a made a good end — "for bonny sweet 4.05.186 P
these good fellows will bring thee where i am. 4.06. 27 P
but, good laertes, | will you do this, keep 4.07.128
good. 5.01. 15 P
good. 5.01. 16 P
i like thy wit well, in good faith. 5.01. 45 P
which could say, "good morrow, sweet lord! 5.01. 82 P
good my lord, be quiet. 5.01.265
i pray thee, good horatio, wait upon him. 5.01.293
good gertrude, set some watch over your son. 5.01.296
ay, good my lord. 5.02. 37
no, my good lord. 5.02. 83
nay, good my lord, for my ease, in good faith. 5.02.105 P
nay, good my lord, for my ease, in good faith. 5.02.105 P
nay, good my lord — 5.02.214 P
ay, my good lord. 5.02.266
good madam! 5.02.290
no med'cine in the world can do thee good; 5.02.314
good night, sweet prince, | and flights of 5.02.359
mother fair, there was good sport at his making, LR 1.01. 23 P
good my lord, | you have begot me, bred me, 1.01. 95
ay, my good lord. 1.01.105
good my liege — 1.01.120
bear, | our potency made good, take thy reward. 1.01.172
that good effects may spring from words of love. 1.01.185
if the matter were good, my lord, i durst swear 1.02. 63 P
in the sun and moon portend no good to us. 1.02.104 P
parted you in good terms? 1.02.156 P
man if there be any good meaning toward you. 1.02.173 P
my good intent | may carry through itself to 1.04. 2
i would you would make use of your good wisdom 1.04.219
this man hath had good counsel — a hundred 1.04.322
yes indeed, thou wouldst make a good fool. 1.05. 38 P
you have now the good advantage of the night. 2.01. 22
ay, my good lord. 2.01.109
our good old friend, | lay comforts to your 2.01.125
good dawning to thee, friend. art of this house? 2.02. 1 P
that wouldst be a bawd in way of good service, 2.02. 20 P
sir, in good faith, in sincere verity, | under 2.02.105
a good man's fortune may grow out at heels. 2.02.157
give you good morrow! 2.02.158
good king, that must approve the common saw, 2.02.160
fortune, good night! 2.02.173
well, my good lord, i have inform'd them so. 2.04. 98
ay, my good lord. 2.04.100
good morrow to you both. 2.04.127
good sir, no more; 2.04.157
good sir, to th' purpose. 2.04.181
i have good hope | thou didst not know on't. 2.04.188
and in good time you gave it. 2.04.250
good nuncle, in, ask thy daughters blessing. 3.02. 11 P
a house to put 's head in has a good head–piece. 3.02. 26 P
good my lord, enter, | the tyranny of the open 3.04. 1
good my lord, enter here. 3.04. 4
good my lord, enter. 3.04. 5
good my lord, enter here. 3.04. 22
good my lord, take his offer, go into th' house. 3.04.156
ah, that good kent! 3.04.163
good my lord, soothe him; 3.04.177
come, good athenian. 3.04.180
now, good my lord, lie here and rest awhile. 3.06. 82
good friend, i prithee take him in thy arms; 3.06. 88
good my friends, consider | you are my guests. 3.07. 30
thou shouldst have said, "good porter, turn the 3.07. 64
treasons to us, | who is too good to pity thee. 3.07. 90
o, my good lord, | i have been your tenant, and 4.01. 12
good friend, be gone, | thy comforts can do me 4.01. 15
gone, | thy comforts can do me no good at all; 4.01. 16
poor tom hath been scar'd out of his good wits. 4.01. 57 P
bless thee, good man's son, from the foul fiend! 4.01. 58 P
o my good lord, the duke of cornwall's dead, 4.02. 70
no, my good lord, i met him back again. 4.02. 90
ay, my good lord; 4.02. 92
and remediate | in the good man's /distress! 4.04. 18
now fare ye well, good sir. 4.06. 32
"ay," and "no" too, was no good divinity. 4.06.100 P
good apothecary, | sweeten my imagination. 4.06.130
this' a good block. 4.06.183
now, good sir, what are you? 4.06.220
and feeling sorrows, | am pregnant to good pity. 4.06.223
good gentleman, go your gait, and let poor voke 4.06.237 P
o thou good kent, how shall i live and work | to 4.07. 1
then be't so, my good lord. how does the king? 4.07. 12
be by, good madam, when we do awake him, | i 4.07. 22
be comforted, good madam, the great rage, | you 4.07. 77
the shadow of this tree | for your good host; 5.02. 2
good guard, | until their greater pleasures 5.03. 1
the let–alone lies not in your good will. 5.03. 79
not sure, though hoping, of this good success, 5.03.195
hath mov'd me, | and shall perchance do good: 5.03.201
come | to bid my king and master aye good night. 5.03.236
some good i mean to do, | despite of mine own 5.03.244
o my good master! 5.03.268
with my good biting falchion | i would have made 5.03.277
he's a good fellow, i can tell you that; 5.03.285
no, my good lord, i am the very man — 5.03.287
he, in good time, must his lieutenant be, | and OTH 1.01. 32
patience, good sir. 1.01.104
please | to get good guard and go along with me. 1.01.179
on, good roderigo, i will deserve your pains. 1.01.183
good signior, you shall more command with years 1.02. 60
good your grace, pardon me: 1.03. 52
my very noble and approv'd good masters: 1.03. 77
and found good means | to draw from her a prayer 1.03.151
good brabantio, | take up this mangled matter at 1.03.172
and heaven defend your good souls, that you 1.03.266
what else needful your good grace shall think 1.03.286
good night to every one. 1.03.288
but, good lieutenant, is your general wiv'd? 2.01. 60
good ancient, you are welcome. 2.01. 96
let it not gall your patience, good iago, | that 2.01. 97
very good; 2.01.174 P
i prithee, good iago, | go to the bay and 2.01.207
he is a good one, and his worthiness | does 2.01.210
good michael, look you to the guard to–night. 2.03. 1
michael, good night. 2.03. 7
good night. 2.03. 11
not to–night, good iago, i have very poor and 2.03. 33 P
good faith, a little one; 2.03. 66 P
it's true, good lieutenant. 2.03.105 P
not, or his good nature | prizes the virtue that 2.03.133
nay, good lieutenant; 2.03.151 P
nay, good lieutenant — /god's /will, gentlemen 2.03.158
than to deceive so good a commander with so 2.03.278 P
since it is as it is, mend it for your own good. 2.03.302 P
good wine is a good familiar creature, if it be 2.03.309 P
good wine is a good familiar creature, if it be 2.03.309 P
and, good lieutenant, i think you think i love 2.03.311 P
good night, lieutenant, i must to the watch. 2.03.333 P
good night, honest iago. 2.03.335 P
to this parallel course, | directly to his good? 2.03.350
and by how much she strives to do him good, 2.03.358
and bid "good morrow, general." 3.01. 2
good morrow, good lieutenant. 3.01. 41
good morrow, good lieutenant. 3.01. 41
well, my good lord, i'll do't. 3.02. 4
be thou assur'd, good cassio, i will do | all my 3.03. 1
good madam, do. 3.03. 3
good my lord, | if i have any grace or power to 3.03. 45
good love, call him back. 3.03. 54
good my lord, pardon me: 3.03.133
it were not for your quiet nor your good, | nor 3.03.152
good name in man and woman, dear my lord, | is 3.03.155
but he that filches from me my good name | robs 3.03.159
good /god, the souls of all my tribe defend 3.03.175
a good wench, give it me. 3.03.313
well, my good lady. 3.04. 34
well, my good lord. 3.04. 35
'tis a good hand, | a frank one. 3.04. 43
hath founded his good fortunes on your love, 3.04. 94
how now, good cassio, what's the news with you? 3.04.109
'tis very good; i must be circumstanc'd. 3.04.201
that's not so good now. 4.01. 23
good sir, be a man; 4.01. 65
away, | and laid good 'scuses upon your ecstasy; 4.01. 79
good, good; 4.01.209 P
good, good; 4.01.209 P
very good. 4.01.210 P
excellent good. what trumpet is that same? 4.01.213
and what's the news, good cousin lodovico? 4.01.219
how do you, my good lady? 4.02. 96
good madam, what's the matter with my lord? 4.02. 98
for, in good faith, | i am a child to chiding. 4.02.113
good friend, go to him; 4.02.150
o, pardon me; 'twill do me good to walk. 4.03. 2
madam, good night; i humbly thank your ladyship. 4.03. 3
therefore, good emilia, | give me my nightly 4.03. 15
good /faith, how foolish are our minds! 4.03. 23
so get thee gone, good night. 4.03. 58
good night, good night. 4.03.104
good night, good night. 4.03.104
wear thy good rapier bare, and put it home. 5.01. 2
are you of good or evil? 5.01. 65
patience awhile, good cassio. 5.01. 87
some good man bear him carefully from hence, 5.01. 99
stay you, good gentlemen. 5.01.105
alas, good gentleman! alas, good cassio! 5.01.115
alas, good gentleman! alas, good cassio! 5.01.115
o, good my lord, i would speak a word with you! 5.02. 90
were't good? 5.02. 94
o, good my lord! 5.02.102
o, my good lord, yonder's foul murthers done! 5.02.106
good gentlemen, let me have leave to speak. 5.02.195
should such a fool | do with so good a wife? 5.02.234
that, with this little arm and this good sword, 5.02.262
o thou othello, that was once so good, | fall'n 5.02.291
take but good note, and you shall see in him ANT 1.01. 11
news, my good lord, from rome. 1.01. 18
good sir, give me good fortune. 1.02. 14 P
good sir, give me good fortune. 1.02. 14 P
good now, some excellent fortune! 1.02. 26 P
good isis, hear me this prayer, though thou deny 1.02. 67 P
good isis, i beseech thee! 1.02. 69 P
she's good, being gone; 1.02.126
i know by that same eye there's some good news. 1.03. 19
good now, play one scene | of excellent 1.03. 78
"good friend," quoth he, | "say the firm roman 1.05. 42
him, | note him, good charmian, 'tis the man; 1.05. 54
welcome, my good alexas. 1.05. 66
which the wise pow'rs | deny us for our good; 2.01. 7
good enobarbus, 'tis a worthy deed, | and shall 2.02. 1
say, "agrippa, be it so," | to make this good? 2.02.142
may i never | (to this good purpose, that so 2.02.144
good enobarbus! 2.02.174 P
good enobarbus, make yourself my guest | whilst 2.02.243
good night, sir. 2.03. 4
good night, dear lady. 2.03. 7
good night, sir. 2.03. 8
good night. 2.03. 9
sir, good success! 2.04. 9
and when good will is show'd, though't come too 2.05. 8
good madam, hear me. 2.05. 36
so tart a favor | to trumpet such good tidings! 2.05. 39
"but yet," it does allay | the good precedence; 2.05. 51
matter to mine ear, | the good and bad together: 2.05. 55
for what good turn? 2.05. 58
good madam, patience. 2.05. 62
good madam, keep yourself within yourself, | the 2.05. 75
be honest, it is never good | to bring bad news. 2.05. 85
good your highness, patience. 2.05.106
go to the fellow, good alexas, bid him | report 2.05.111
who at philippi the good brutus ghosted, | there 2.06. 13
villainy, | in thee't had been good service. 2.07. 75
let's ha't, good soldier. 2.07.105
pompey, good night. 2.07.119
good brother, | let me request you /off, our 2.07.119
good night. 2.07.125
good antony, your hand. 2.07.126
i could do more to do antonius good, | but 3.01. 25
good fortune, worthy soldier, and farewell. 3.02. 22
good majesty! 3.03. 2
that's not so good. he cannot like her long. 3.03. 14
the fellow has good judgment. 3.03. 25
one thing more to ask him yet, good charmian — 3.03. 45
o my good lord, | believe not all, or, if you 3.04. 10
the good gods will mock me presently, | when i 3.04. 15
already, will their good thoughts call from him. 3.06. 21
good my lord, | to come thus was i not 3.06. 55
a good rebuke, | which might have well becom'd 3.07. 25
why then good night indeed. 3.10. 29
madam, o good empress! 3.11. 33
good my lord — 3.13.109
when my good stars, that were my former guides, 3.13.145
never anger | made good guard for itself. 4.01. 10
might do you service | so good as you have done. 4.02. 19
well, my good fellows, wait on me to–night. 4.02. 20
like a master | married to your good service, 4.02. 31
brother, good night; to–morrow is the day. 4.03. 1
belike 'tis but a rumor. good night to you. 4.03. 5
well, sir, good night. 4.03. 6
and you. good night, good night. 4.03. 8
and you. good night, good night. 4.03. 8
come, good fellow, put thine iron on. 4.04. 3
seest thou, my good fellow? 4.04. 9
good morrow to thee, welcome. 4.04. 18
the morn is fair. good morrow, general. 4.04. 24
good morrow, general. 4.04. 25
comfort, and tenfold | for thy good valor. 4.07. 16
my good knave eros, now thy captain is | even 4.14. 12
too late, good diomed. call my guard, i prithee. 4.14.128
bear me, good friends, where cleopatra bides, 4.14.131
nay, good my fellows, do not please sharp fate 4.14.135
i have led you oft, carry me now, good friends, 4.14.139
assist, good friends. 4.15. 31
what, what, good cheer! 4.15. 83
good sirs, take heart, | we'll bury him; 4.15. 85
hear me, good friends — | but i will tell you 5.01. 48
bid her have good heart. 5.01. 56
be of good cheer; 5.02. 21
quick, quick, good hands. 5.02. 39
hear me, good madam: 5.02.100
shall bereave yourself | of my good purposes, 5.02.131
here, my good lord. 5.02.136
good queen, let us entreat you. 5.02.158
say, good caesar, | that i some lady trifles 5.02.164
finish, good lady, the bright day is done, | and 5.02.193
adieu, good queen, i must attend on caesar. 5.02.206
o the good gods! 5.02.221
truly, she makes a very good report o' th' worm; 5.02.255 P
very good. 5.02.269 P
yare, yare, good iras; 5.02.283
(i mean, that married her, alack, good man! CYM 1.01. 18
and 'twere good | you lean'd unto his sentence 1.01. 77
and bless the good remainders of the court! 1.01.129
she's a good sign, but i have seen small 1.02. 30 P
but, good pisanio, | when shall we hear from him 1.03. 22
as fair and as good — a kind of hand–in–hand 1.04. 70 P
too fair and too good for any lady in brittany. 1.04. 72 P
it is an earnest of a farther good | that i mean 1.05. 65
but when to my good lord i prove untrue, | i'll 1.05. 86
thanks, good sir, | you're kindly welcome. 1.06. 13
first, a very excellent good conceited thing; 2.03. 17 P
good morrow to your majesty, and to my gracious 2.03. 35 P
son, | when you have given good morning to your 2.03. 61
is gold for you, | sell me your good report. 2.03. 83
how, my good name? 2.03. 84
to report of you | what i shall think is good? 2.03. 85
good morrow, fairest: sister, your sweet hand. 2.03. 86
good morrow, sir. 2.03. 87
she's my good lady, and will conceive, i hope, 2.03.153
their tenure good, i trust. 2.04. 36
or is't not | too dull for your good wearing? 2.04. 41
good sir, we must, | if you keep covenant. 2.04. 49
shall, by the power we hold, be our good deed, 3.01. 57
if it be so to do good service, never | let me 3.02. 14
you good gods, | let what is here contain'd 3.02. 29
good wax, thy leave. 3.02. 35
good news, gods! 3.02. 39
turbands on without | good morrow to the sun. 3.03. 7
alas, good lady! 3.04. 45
now methinks | thy favor's good enough. 3.04. 49
all good seeming, | by thy revolt, o husband, 3.04. 54
good madam, hear me. 3.04. 57
good lady, | hear me with patience. 3.04.111
why, good fellow, | what shall i do the while? 3.04.127
we'll even | all that good time will give us. 3.04.182
leave not the worthy lucius, good my lords, 3.05. 16
and my end | can make good use of either. 3.05. 64
o, good my lord! 3.05. 83
well, my good lord. 3.05.116 P
such a foe, good heavens! 3.06. 27
good masters, harm me not. 3.06. 45
good troth, | i have stol'n nought, nor would 3.06. 47
nor measure our good minds | by this rude place 3.06. 64
so, sir, i yoke me | in my good brother's fault. 4.02. 20
appears he hath had | good ancestors. 4.02. 48

i wish my brother make good time with him, | you 4.02.108
then on good ground we fear, | if we do fear 4.02.143
by good euriphile, our mother. 4.02.234
thersites' body is as good as ajax', | when 4.02.252
good faith, | i tremble still with fear; 4.02.302
nature did) | hath alter'd that good picture? 4.02.365
my master, | a very valiant britain, and a good, 4.02.369
cry out for service, | try many, all good; 4.02.373
'lack, good youth! 4.02.374
say his name, good friend. 4.02.376
ay, good youth, | and rather father thee than 4.02.394
good my liege, | the day that she was missing he 4.03. 16
good my liege, | your preparation can affront no 4.03. 28
every good servant does not all commands; 5.01. 6
therefore, good heavens, | hear patiently my 5.01. 21
made good the passage, cried to those that fled, 5.03. 23
you good gods, give me | the penitent instrument 5.04. 9
since, jupiter, our son is good, | take off his 5.04. 85
most unlike our courtiers, | as good as promise! 5.04.137
so, if i prove a good repast to the spectators, 5.04.155 P
thou bring'st good news, i am call'd to be made 5.04.193 P
we were all of one mind, and one mind good. 5.04.204 P
that their good souls may be appeas'd with 5.05. 72
i do not bid thee beg my life, good lad, | and 5.05.101
your life, good master, | must shuffle for 5.05.104
thou'rt my good youth — my page; 5.05.118
is living, let the time run on | to good or bad. 5.05.129
the good posthumus | (what should i say? 5.05.157
he was too good to be | where ill men were, and 5.05.158
best of all | amongst the rar'st of good ones), 5.05.160
i would not thy good deeds should from my lips 5.05.288
how of descent | as good as we? 5.05.309
but i will prove that two on 's are as good | as 5.05.311
and our good his. 5.05.315
ay, my good lord. 5.05.379
my good master, | i will yet do you service. 5.05.403
good my lord of rome, | call forth your 5.05.425
here, my good lord. 5.05.434
a happy peace to you | and all good men, as PER 1.01. 51
good sooth, i care not for you. 1.01. 86
the which is good in nothing but in sight! 1.01.123
who seem'd my good protector, and, being here, 1.02. 82
the care i had and have of subjects' good | on 1.02.118
was a wise fellow and had good discretion that, 1.03. 4 P
the good in conversation, | to whom i give my 2.ch. 9
good helicane, that stay'd at home, | not to eat 2.ch. 17
he strive | to killen bad, keep good alive, 2.ch. 20
and he, good prince, having all lost, | by waves 2.ch. 33
but if the good king simonides were of my mind 2.01. 43 P
good fellow, what's that? 2.01. 53 P
pentapolis, and our king the good simonides. 2.01.100 P
the good simonides, do you call him? 2.01.101
for his peaceable reign and good government. 2.01.103 P
his subjects the name of good by his government. 2.01.105 P
d' ye take it, and the gods give thee good an't! 2.01.147 P
to make some good, but others to exceed, | and 2.03. 16
we are honor'd much by good simonides. 2.03. 20
good morrow to the good simonides. 2.05. 1
good morrow to the good simonides. 2.05. 1
all fortune to the good simonides! 2.05. 24
the worst of all her scholars, my good lord. 2.05. 31
patience, good sir, do not assist the storm. 3.01. 19
patience, good sir, | even for this charge. 3.01. 26
now the good gods | throw their best eyes upon't 3.01. 36
go thy ways, good mariner, | i'll bring the body 3.01. 80
good morrow. 3.02. 10
good morrow to your lordship. 3.02. 11
'tis a good constraint of fortune it belches 3.02. 55
dead, | who was by good appliance recovered. 3.02. 86
good madam, make me blessed in your care | in 3.03. 31
yet my good will is great, though the gift small 3.04. 18
present murderer does prepare | for good marina, 4.ch. 39
come, come, i know 'tis good for you. 4.01. 44
says, did never fear, | but cried "good seamen!" 4.01. 53
good sooth, it show'd well in you. 4.01. 88
continual action are even as good as rotten. 4.02. 9 P
she has a good face, speaks well, and has 4.02. 47 P
speaks well, and has excellent good clothes; 4.02. 48 P
seldom but that pity begets you a good opinion, 4.02.120 P
fram'd this piece, she meant thee a good turn; 4.02.140 P
i am glad to see your honor in good health. 4.06. 22 P
less than it gives a good report to a number to 4.06. 40 P
make the judgment good | that thought you worthy 4.06. 93
the good gods preserve you! 4.06.107
dost | hear from me, it shall be for thy good. 4.06.116
my fortunes — parentage — good parentage — 5.01. 97
thee — that thou cam'st | from good descending? 5.01.128
patience, good sir! | or here i'll cease. 5.01.144
as my good nurse lychorida hath oft | delivered 5.01.159
but, good sir, | whither will you have me? 5.01.175
no, good faith; 5.01.177
to king pericles, | if good king pericles be. 5.01.179
it is not good to cross him, give him way. 5.01.230
lord cerimon hath letters of good credit, sir, 5.03. 77
and a good play | (whose modest scenes blush on TNK pr 3
how will it shake the bones of that good man, pr 17
this good deed | shall raze you out o' th' book 1.01. 32
sword | that does good turns to th' world; 1.01. 49
i had as lief trace this good action with you 1.01.102
pray have good comfort. 1.01.129
sun, | and were good kings when living. 1.01.147
why, good ladies, | this is a service, whereto i 1.01.170
thus dost thou still make good | the tongue o' 1.01.226
good cheer, ladies! 1.01.233
where every evil | hath a good color; 1.02. 39
good dares not. 1.02. 71
to him, | store never hurts good governors. 1.03. 6
all the good that may | be wish'd upon thy head, 1.04. 2
so adieu, | and heaven's good eyes look on you! 1.04. 13
our good swords now | (better the red–ey'd god 2.02. 20
that's a good wench! 2.02.124
yet, good madam, | sometimes her modesty will 2.02.143
and grasp | our good swords in our hands, i 2.02.209
by this good light, | had i a sword, i would 2.02.264
do, good keeper. 2.02.271
good gods! 2.03. 13
take a new lesson out, and be a good wench. 2.03. 35
"fair gentle maid, good morrow. 2.04. 24
you were call'd | a good knight and a bold. 3.01. 65
a good sword in thy hand, and do but say | that 3.01. 75
if a good title, | i am persuaded this question, 3.01.112
sit down, and, good now, | no more of these vain 3.03. 9
drink a good hearty draught, it breeds good 3.03. 17
a good hearty draught, it breeds good blood, man 3.03. 17
i am glad | you have so good a stomach. 3.03. 21
i am gladder | i have so good meat to't. 3.03. 22
good night, good night, y' are gone. 3.04. 11
good night, good night, y' are gone. 3.04. 11
and are you mad, good woman? 3.05. 77
too | and have done as good boys should do, 3.05.143
with him bring | two swords and two good armors. 3.06. 3
o, good morrow. 3.06. 16
good morrow, noble kinsman. 3.06. 17
me, cousin, | where got'st thou this good armor? 3.06. 54
good cousin, thrust the buckle | through far 3.06. 61
prithee take mine, good cousin. 3.06. 65
that was a very good one, and that day, | i well 3.06. 72
up, and under me | i had a right good horse. 3.06. 77
not made in passion neither, but good heed. 3.06.232
good sir, remember. 4.01. 3
be of good comfort, man; 4.01. 17
i bring you news, | good news. 4.01. 18
ye are a good man | and ever bring good news. 4.01. 24
ye are a good man | and ever bring good news. 4.01. 25
i hope they are good. 4.01. 30
honorable, | how good they'll prove, i know not. 4.01. 31
it, and as good by me | as by another that less 4.01. 43
good ev'n, good men. 4.01.116
good ev'n, good men. 4.01.116
good heaven, | what a sweet face has arcite! 4.02. 6
good friend, be royal. 4.02.154
i were a beast and i'ld call it good sport. 4.03. 53 P
and palamon is sweet, and ev'ry good thing. 4.03. 87 P
this advice i told you done any good upon her? 5.02. 1
sir, my good lord, | your sister will no further 5.03. 10
get herself | some part of a good name, and many 5.03. 27
i did think | good palamon would miscarry, yet i 5.03.101
he is a good one | as ever strook at head. 5.03.108
for he that was thus good | encount'red yet his 5.03.122
so it far'd | good space between these kinsmen; 5.03.129
to live still, | have their good wishes; 5.04. 6
a right good creature, more to me deserving 5.04. 34
thou art a right good man, and while i live, 5.04. 97
gentlemen, good night. ep 18
for what's a sorry parsnip to a good heart? STM II.C 9 P
good masters, hear me speak. II.C 57
th' art a good house–keeper and i thank thy good II.C 58 P
and i thank thy good worship for my brother II.C 59 P
me set up before your thoughts, good friends, II.C 90
good god, good god, | that i from such an humble III 5
good god, good god, | that i from such an humble III 5
earth's sovereign salve, to do a goddess good. VEN 28
thirst for drink than she for this good turn. 92
her, and she by her good will | will never rise, 479
so thou wilt buy, and pay, and use good dealing, 514
light | do summon us to part and bid good night. 534
"now let me say 'good night,' and so say you; 535
"good night," quoth she, and, ere he says "adieu 537
but all in vain, good queen, it will not be; 607
venus salutes him with this fair good morrow: 859
it is as good | to wither in my breast as in his 1181
so guiltless she securely gives good cheer | and LUC 89
and with good thoughts makes dispensation, 248
a little harm done to a great good end | for 528
if all these petty ills shall change thy good, 656
"let my good name, that senseless reputation, 820
we have no good that we can say is ours, | but 873
"o time, thou tutor both to good and bad, 995
the remedy indeed to do me good | is to let 1028
grief grieves most at that would do it good; 1117
her mistress she doth give demure good morrow, 1219
if tears could help, mine own would do me good. 1274
doubt, | till my bad angel fire my good one out. PP 2.14
silly queen, with more than love's good will, 9. 7
beauty is but a vain and doubtful good, | a 13. 1
a doubtful good, a gloss, a glass, a flower, 13. 5
good night, good rest. 14. 1
good night, good rest. 14. 1
she bade good night that kept my rest away, 14. 2
good day, of night now borrow: 14.29
but not to tell of good or evil luck, | of SON 14. 3
now see what good turns eyes for eyes have done: 24. 9
but that i hope some good conceit of thine | in 26. 7
as thou being mine, mine is thy good report. 36.14
and each doth good turns now unto the other: 47. 2
and captive good attending captain ill: 66.12
so thou be good, slander doth but approve | /thy 70. 5
i think good thoughts whilst other write good 85. 5
good thoughts whilst other write good words, 85. 5
as thou being mine, mine is thy good report. 96.14
to leave for nothing all thy sum of good; 109.12
ill, | so you o'er–green my bad, my good allow? 112. 4
in their wills count bad what i think good? 121. 8
yet in good faith some say that thee behold, 131. 5
doubt, | till my bad angel fire my good one out. 144.14
to be forbod the sweets that seems so good | for LC 164

GOOD–EN *(also god–den, etc.)*
GOOD–EN 3 FR 0.0003 REL FR 3 V 0 P
good–en, our neighbors, COR 4.06. 20
good–en to you all, good–en to you all. 4.06. 21
good–en to you all, good–en to you all. 4.06. 21
GOOD–FAC'D 1 FR 0.0001 REL FR 0 V 1 P
no, good–fac'd sir, no, sweet sir. WT 4.03.115 P
GOODFELLOW 1 FR 0.0001 REL FR 1 V 0 P
and knavish sprite | call'd robin goodfellow. MND 2.01. 34
GOOD–FELLOWSHIP 1 FR 0.0001 REL FR 1 V 0 P
true, | even in soul of sound good–fellowship — TRO 4.01. 53
GOOD–JER *(also good–year)*
GOOD–JER 1 FR 0.0001 REL FR 0 V 1 P
what the good–jer! WIV 1.04.122 P
GOODLIER 2 FR 0.0002 REL FR 2 V 0 P
i have no ambition | to see a goodlier man. TMP 1.02.484
if he were honester | he were much goodlier. AWW 3.05. 80
/GOODLIEST 1 FR 0.0001 REL FR 1 V 0 P
/strove | /who /should /express /her /goodliest. LR 4.03. 17
GOODLIEST 2 FR 0.0002 REL FR 2 V 0 P
she is the goodliest woman | that ever lay by H8 4.01. 69
sent by me | the goodliest weapons of his armory TIT 4.02. 11
GOOD–LIMB'D 1 FR 0.0001 REL FR 0 V 1 P
a good–limb'd fellow, young, strong, and of good 2H4 3.02.102 P
/GOODLY 2 FR 0.0002 REL FR 1 V 1 P
/that /threw'st /dust /upon /his /goodly /head 2H4 1.03.103
/a /goodly /one, /in /which /there /are /many HAM 2.02.245 P
GOODLY 85 FR 0.0096 REL FR 65 V 20 P
thou mightst call him | a goodly person. TMP 1.02.417
growing, | plants with goodly burthen bowing; 4.01.113
how many goodly creatures are there here! 5.01.182
which i wear in my head, here's a goodly sight. 5.01.260 P
now, by my modesty, a goodly broker! TGV 1.02. 41
seeing you are beautified | with goodly shape, 4.01. 54
'tis a goodly credit for you. WIV 4.02.189 P
she became | a joyful mother of two goodly sons: ERR 1.01. 50
we are like to prove a goodly commodity, being ADO 3.03.177 P
there's goodly catching of cold. 3.04. 65 P
surely a princely testimony, a goodly count, 4.01.316 P
cheek, | a goodly apple rotten at the heart. MV 1.03.101
o, what a goodly outside falsehood hath! 1.03.102
goodly lord, what a wit–snapper are you! 3.05. 49 P
by my fay, a goodly nap, | but did i never speak SHR in.2. 81
for though you lay here in this goodly chamber, in.2. 84
where did you study all this goodly speech? 2.01.262
frown, | and wherefore gaze this goodly company, 3.02. 94
lord, how bright and goodly shines the moon! 4.05. 2
she says you have some goodly jest in hand. 5.02. 91
make itself two, which is a goodly increase, and AWW 1.01.148 P
if it be so, you have wound a goodly clew; 1.03.182
of melancholy /sold a goodly manor for a song. 3.02. 9 P
velvet knows, but 'tis a goodly patch of velvet. 4.05. 96 P
she is spread of late | into a goodly bulk. WT 2.01. 20
be but about | to say she is a goodly lady, and 2.01. 66
when you have said she's goodly, come between 2.01. 75
a daughter, and a goodly babe, | lusty and like 2.02. 24
now have look'd on, | such goodly things as you? 5.01.178
shall show more goodly and attract more eyes 1H4 1.02.214
a goodly portly man, i' faith, and a corpulent, 2.04.422 P
here's goodly stuff toward! 2H4 2.04.200 P
here's a goodly tumult! 2.04.204 P
off a mile, | in goodly form comes on the enemy, 4.01. 20
god, you have here goodly dwelling and rich. 5.03. 5 P
a goodly prize, fit for the devil's grace! 1H6 5.03. 33
thou, being a king, blest with a goodly son, 3H6 2.02. 23
were it not pity that this goodly boy | should 2.02. 34
is not a dukedom, sir, a goodly gift? 5.01. 31
and somerset another goodly mast? 5.04. 17
not like the fruit of such a goodly tree. 5.06. 52
the heavens have blest you with a goodly son R3 1.03. 9
we have many goodly days to see: 4.04.320
car | gives token of a goodly day to–morrow. 5.03. 21
troy must not be, nor goodly ilion stand. TRO 2.02.109
"o heart," as the goodly saying is, "o heart, 4.04. 15 P
and the goodly transformation of jupiter there, 5.01. 53 P
stand, thou greek, thou art a goodly mark. 5.06. 27
thy goodly armor thus hath cost thy life. 5.08. 2
a goodly medicine for my aching bones! 5.10. 35 P
here's goodly work! COR 3.01.260
a goodly city is this antium. 4.04. 1
a goodly house! 4.05. 5
y' are goodly things, you voices! 4.06.146
a goodly lady, trust me, of the hue | that i TIT 1.01.261
'tis thought you have a goodly gift in horning, 2.03. 67
dismounted from your snow–white goodly steed, 2.03. 76
a goodly humor, is it not, my lords? 4.04. 19
this goodly summer with your winter mix'd. 5.02.171
here's goodly gear! a sail, a sail! ROM 2.04.101 P
your lordship's a goodly villain. TIM 3.03. 27 P
and take our goodly aged men by th' beards, 5.01.172
england have i offer | of goodly thousands. MAC 4.03. 44
i saw him once, 'a was a goodly king. HAM 1.02.186
with my disposition, that this goodly frame, the 2.02.298 P
here's a goodly watch indeed! OTH 2.03.160
was this fair paper, this most goodly book, 4.02. 71
those his goodly eyes, | that o'er the files and ANT 1.01. 2
the ptolomies' pyramises are very goodly things; 2.07. 35 P
a goodly day not to keep house with such | whose CYM 3.03. 1
goodly and gallant shall be false and perjur'd 3.04. 63
like goodly buildings left without a roof | soon PER 2.04. 36
why do you make us love your goodly gifts | and 3.01. 23
i will do't, but yet she is a goodly creature. 4.01. 9
seeing this goodly vessel ride before us, | i 5.01. 18
this was a goodly person, | till the disaster 5.01. 36
is't not a goodly /presence? 5.01. 66
he's goodly, | and like enough the duke hath TNK 2.02.226
i, seeing, thought he was a goodly man; 2.04. 8
the goodly mothers that have groan'd for these, 3.06.245
they are princes | as goodly as your own eyes, 3.06.276
snatch up the goodly boy and set him by him, | a 4.02. 17
their smoothness, like a goodly champaign plain, LUC 1247
boat, | he of tall building and of goodly pride. SON 80.12
set | the goodly objects which abroad they find LC 137
GOODMAN 16 FR 0.0018 REL FR 6 V 10 P
is such a league between my goodman and he! WIV 3.02. 25 P
come hither, goodman bald–pate, do you know me?
MM 5.01.326
goodman verges, sir, speaks a little /off the ADO 3.05. 9 P
/dictynna, goodman dull, /dictynna, goodman dull
LLL 4.02. 36
goodman dull, /dictynna, goodman dull. 4.02. 36
via, goodman dull! 5.01.149 P
i am your goodman. SHR in.2. 105
adieu, goodman devil. TN 4.02.131
the old days of goodman adam to the pupil age of
1H4 2.04. 93 P
lady, i think 'a be, but goodman puff of barson. 2H4 5.03. 89 P
goodman death, goodman bones! 5.04. 28 P
goodman death, goodman bones! 5.04. 28 P
and't please your grace, against john goodman, 2H6 1.03. 17 P
what, goodman boy? ROM 1.05. 77
nay, but hear you, goodman delver — HAM 5.01. 14 P
with you, goodman boy, /and you please! LR 2.02. 45 P
/GOODNESS 1 FR 0.0001 REL FR 1 V 0 P
/wisdom /and /goodness /to /the /vild /seem LR 4.02. 38
GOODNESS 65 FR 0.0073 REL FR 53 V 12 P
which any print of goodness wilt not take, TMP 1.02.352
the goodness that is cheap in beauty makes MM 3.01.181 P

cheap in beauty makes beauty brief in goodness; 3.01.182 P
virtue is bold, and goodness never fearful. 3.01.208 P
bliss and goodness on you! 3.02.215 P
but that there is so great a fever on goodness, 3.02.223 P
and we hear | such goodness of your justice, 5.01. 6
good friend escalus, for thy much goodness, 5.01.528
derives her honesty and achieves her goodness. AWW 1.01. 45 P
and thy goodness | share with thy birthright! 1.01. 63
altogether so great as the first in goodness, 4.03.287 P
from the report that goes upon your goodness, 5.01. 13
but our natural goodness | imparts this; WT 2.01.164
your honor and your goodness is so evident 2.02. 41
i have of thee, thine own goodness hath made. 4.02. 12 P
merits it) with you, | worthy his goodness. 5.01.176
and thy abundant goodness shall excuse | this R2 5.03. 65
there is some soul of goodness in things evil, H5 4.01. 4
for talbot means no goodness by his looks. 1H6 3.02. 72
soul, god's goodness hath been great to thee. 2H6 2.01. 82
therefore, for goodness sake, and as you are H8 pr 23
his end, | goodness and he fill up one monument! 2.01. 94
must now confess, if they have any goodness, 2.02. 90
for goodness sake, consider what you do, | how 3.01.159
and, to confirm his goodness, | tied it by 3.02.249
whilst your great goodness, out of holy pity, 3.02.263
all goodness | is poison to thy stomach. 3.02.282
yes, that goodness | of gleaning all the land's 3.02.283
the goodness of your intercepted packets | you 3.02.286
your goodness, | since you provoke me, shall be 3.02.287
in which i have commended to his goodness | the 4.02.131
from thy endless goodness send prosperous life, 5.04. 1 P
(but few now living can behold that goodness) 5.04. 21
cannot distaste the goodness of a quarrel TRO 2.02.123
were, | to an untirable and continuate goodness; TIM 1.01. 11
recanting goodness, sorry ere 'tis shown; 1.02. 17
low by his own heart, | undone by goodness! 4.02. 38
basis sure, | for goodness dare not check thee; MAC 4.03. 33
and the chance of goodness | be like our 4.03.136
it, | and nothing is at a like goodness still, HAM 4.07.116
for goodness, growing to a plurisy, | dies in 4.07.117
shall i live and work | to match thy goodness? LR 4.07. 2
lord, | you know the goodness i intend upon you: 5.01. 7
the goodness of the night upon you, friends! OTH 1.02. 35
it a vice in her goodness not to do more than 2.03.321 P
and out of her own goodness make the net | that 2.03.361
are | evils enow to darken all his goodness: ANT 1.04. 11
but there's no goodness in thy face, if antony 2.05. 37
for indeed, there is no goodness in the worm. 5.02.267 P
my mistress exceeds in goodness the hugeness of CYM 1.04.144 P
and thy most perfect goodness | her assur'd 1.06.158
towards himself, his goodness forespent on us, 2.03. 59
your very goodness and your company | o'erpays 2.04. 9
your honor and your goodness teach me to't PER 3.03. 26
like a thief, | that robs thee of thy goodness! 4.06.115
fair /one, all goodness that consists in beauty, 5.01. 70
and, of thy boundless goodness, take some note TNK 1.01. 51
certainly | 'tis a main goodness, cousin, that 2.02. 63
may thy goodness | get thee a happy husband!" 2.04. 24
pray observe her goodness. 2.05. 35
both despisers | of thee and of thy goodness. 3.06.138
not to be held ungrateful to her goodness — 4.01. 22
many will not buy | his goodness with this note; 5.04. 53
a healthful state | which, rank of goodness, SON 118.12
which die for goodness, who have liv'd for crime 124.14
GOOD-NIGHT 2 FR 0.0002 REL FR 2 V 0 P
good captain blunt, bear my good-night to him, R3 5.03. 30
bellman, | which gives the stern'st good-night. MAC 2.02. 4
GOOD-NIGHTS 2 FR 0.0002 REL FR 1 V 1 P
sware they were his fancies or his good-nights. 2H4 3.02.319 P
many good-nights, my lord! i rest your servant. H8 5.01. 55
GOODRIG 1 FR 0.0001 REL FR 1 V 0 P
lord talbot of goodrig and urchinfield, | lord 1H6 4.07. 64
GOOD'S 1 FR 0.0001 REL FR 1 V 0 P
where ev'ry seeming good's | a certain evil; TNK 1.02. 39
GOODS 24 FR 0.0027 REL FR 23 V 1 P
dispose, | my goods, my lands, my reputation; TGV 2.07. 87
his goods confiscate to the duke's dispose, ERR 1.01. 20
and /the great care of goods at randon left, 1.01. 42
lest that your goods too soon be confiscate: 1.02. 2
your goods that lay at host, sir, in the centaur 5.01.411
of christian blood, thy lands and goods | are, MV 4.01.310
thou diest, and all thy goods are confiscate. 4.01.332
doth contrive | shall seize one half his goods; 4.01.353
to quit the fine for one half of his goods, | i 4.01.381
is said, "many a man knows no end of his goods."
AYL 3.03. 53 P
crowns in my purse i have, and goods at home, SHR 1.02. 57
me, | left soly heir to all his lands and goods, 2.01.117
she is my goods, my chattels, she is my house, 3.02.230
which for our goods we do no further ask | than JN 4.02. 64
we seize into our hands | his plate, his goods, R2 2.01.210
my father's goods are all distrain'd and sold, 2.03.131
come, we will all put forth, body and goods. 2H4 1.01.186
while as the silly owner of the goods | weeps 2H6 1.01.225
lands, goods, horse, armor, any thing i have 5.01. 52
and all his lands and goods confiscate. 3H6 4.06. 55
and thither bear your treasure and your goods. R3 2.04. 69
attach'd | our merchants' goods at burdeaux. H8 1.01. 96
to forfeit all your goods, lands, tenements, 3.02.342
and as goods lost are seld or never found, | as PP 13. 7
GOODWIFE 2 FR 0.0002 REL FR 0 V 2 P
good morrow, goodwife. WIV 2.02. 34 P
did not goodwife keech, the butcher's wife, come 2H4 2.01. 93 P
GOODWIN 2 FR 0.0002 REL FR 2 V 0 P
are wrack'd three nights ago on goodwin sands; JN 5.03. 11
are cast away, and sunk on goodwin sands. 5.05. 13
GOODWINS 1 FR 0.0001 REL FR 0 V 1 P
the goodwins, i think they call the place, a MV 3.01. 4 P
GOOD-YEAR *(also good-jer)*
GOOD-YEAR 3 FR 0.0003 REL FR 0 V 3 P
what the good-year, my lord! ADO 1.03. 1 P
what the good-year! 2H4 2.04. 59 P
what the good-year, do you think i would deny 2.04.177 P
GOOD-YEARS 1 FR 0.0001 REL FR 1 V 0 P
the good-years shall devour them, flesh and fell LR 5.03. 24
GOOSE 29 FR 0.0032 REL FR 12 V 17 P
swim like a duck, thou art made like a goose. TMP 2.02.132 P
near the god drew to the complexion of a goose! WIV 5.05. 8 P
until the goose came out of door, | and stayed LLL 3.01. 91
until the goose came out of door, | staying the 3.01. 97
a good l'envoy, ending in the goose; 3.01. 99 P
the boy hath sold him a bargain, a goose, that's 3.01.101
your pennyworth is good, and your goose be fat. 3.01.102
a fat l'envoy — ay, that's a fat goose. 3.01.104
boy's fat l'envoy, the goose that you bought, 3.01.109
i smell some l'envoy, some goose, in this. 3.01.122 P
makes flesh a deity, | a green goose a goddess; 4.03. 73
true; and a goose for his discretion. MND 5.01.232 P
his discretion, and the fox carries the goose. 5.01.234 P
for the goose carries not the fox. 5.01.236 P
when every goose is cackling, would be thought MV 5.01.105
why then my taxing like a wild goose flies, AYL 2.07. 86
one side, breaks his staff like a noble goose. 3.04. 45 P
go, ye giddy goose. 1H4 3.01.228 P
winchester goose, i cry, "a rope! 1H6 1.03. 53
some galled goose of winchester would hiss. TRO 5.10. 54
hast more of the wild goose in one of thy wits ROM 2.04. 72 P
was i with you there for the goose? 2.04. 74 P
thing when thou wast not there for the goose. 2.04. 76 P
nay, good goose, bite not. 2.04. 78 P
is it not then well serv'd in to a sweet goose? 2.04. 82 P
which, added to the goose, proves thee far and 2.04. 86 P
goose, proves thee far and wide a broad goose. 2.04. 87 P
come in, tailor, here you may roast your goose. MAC 2.03. 15 P
goose, /and i had you upon sarum plain, | i'ld LR 2.02. 83
GOOSEBERRY 1 FR 0.0001 REL FR 0 V 1 P
age shapes /them, /are not worth a gooseberry. 2H4 1.02.173 P
GOOSE-LOOK 1 FR 0.0001 REL FR 1 V 0 P
where got'st thou that goose-look? MAC 5.03. 12
GOOSE-PEN 1 FR 0.0001 REL FR 0 V 1 P
though thou write with a goose-pen, no matter. TN 3.02. 50 P
//GOOSE-QUILLS 1 FR 0.0001 REL FR 0 V 1 P
/are /afraid /of //goose-quills /and /dare HAM 2.02.344 P
GOOT *(also good, gud)*
GOOT 4 FR 0.0004 REL FR 0 V 4 P
peradventure prings goot discretions with it: WIV 1.01. 44 P
it were a goot motion if we leave our pribbles 1.01. 54 P
pounds, and possibilities, is goot gifts. 1.01. 65 P
fery goot. 1.01.144 P
GORBELLIED 1 FR 0.0001 REL FR 0 V 1 P
hang ye, gorbellied knaves, are ye undone? 1H4 2.02. 88 P
GORBODUC 1 FR 0.0001 REL FR 0 V 1 P
very wittily said to a niece of king gorboduc, TN 4.02. 14 P
GOR'D 7 FR 0.0008 REL FR 6 V 1 P
forked heads | have their round haunches gor'd. AYL 2.01. 25
for me, if i be gor'd with mowbray's spear. R2 1.03. 60
that have before gor'd the gentle bosom of peace H5 4.01.165 P
paris is gor'd with menelaus' horn. TRO 1.01.112
is at stake, | my fame is shrowdly gor'd. 3.03.228
rule in this realm, and the gor'd state sustain. LR 5.03.321
gor'd mine own thoughts, sold cheap what is most
SON 110. 3
GORDIAN 2 FR 0.0002 REL FR 2 V 0 P
the gordian knot of it he will unloose, H5 1.01. 46
as slippery as the gordian knot was hard! CYM 2.02. 34
GORE* 11 FR 0.0012 REL FR 11 V 0 P
lay them in gore, | since you have shore | with MND 5.01.339
with bloodless stroke my heart doth gore; TN 2.05.106
comes to him where in gore he lay insteeped, H5 4.06. 12
wounded steeds | fret fetlock deep in gore, and 4.07. 79
grieve thee more than streams of foreign gore. 1H6 3.03. 55
all bedaub'd in blood, | all in gore blood; ROM 3.02. 56
why, let the war receive't in valiant gore, TIM 3.05. 83
their daggers | unmannerly breech'd with gore. MAC 2.03.116
fire, | and thus o'er-sized with coagulate gore, HAM 2.02.462
with javeling's point a churlish swine to gore, VEN 616
an image like thyself, all stain'd with gore, 664
GORG'D 2 FR 0.0002 REL FR 2 V 0 P
being with his presence glutted, gorg'd, and 1H4 3.02. 84
gorg'd with the dearest morsel of the earth, ROM 5.03. 46
GORGE 9 FR 0.0010 REL FR 6 V 3 P
known | how he hath drunk, he cracks his gorge, WT 2.01. 44
couple a gorge! H5 2.01. 71
tout /a /cette /heure de couper votre gorge. 4.04. 36 P
owy, cuppele gorge, permafoy, | peasant, unless 4.04. 37
and ulcerous sores | would cast the gorge at, TIM 4.03. 41
my gorge rises at it. HAM 5.01.187 P
his generation messes | to gorge his appetite, LR 1.01.118
find itself abus'd, begin to heave the gorge, OTH 2.01.233 P
till either gorge be stuff'd, or prey be gone; VEN 58
GORGED 1 FR 0.0001 REL FR 1 V 0 P
look as the full-fed hound or gorged hawk, LUC 694
GORGEOUS 9 FR 0.0010 REL FR 9 V 0 P
the cloud-capp'd tow'rs, the gorgeous palaces, TMP 4.01.152
at the first op'ning of the gorgeous east, LLL 4.03.219
of beads, | my gorgeous palace for a hermitage, R2 3.03.148
of may, | and gorgeous as the sun at midsummer; 1H4 4.01.102
this new and gorgeous garment, majesty, | sits 2H4 5.02. 44
so seems this gorgeous beauty to mine eyes. 1H6 5.03. 64
deceit should dwell | in such a gorgeous palace! ROM 3.02. 85
if only to go warm were gorgeous, | why, nature LR 2.04.268
nature needs not what thou gorgeous wear'st, 2.04.269
GORGET 1 FR 0.0001 REL FR 1 V 0 P
and, with a palsy fumbling on his gorget, TRO 1.03.174
GORGING 1 FR 0.0001 REL FR 1 V 0 P
gorging and feeding from our soldiers' hands, JC 5.01. 81
GORGON 2 FR 0.0002 REL FR 2 V 0 P
and destroy your sight | with a new gorgon. MAC 2.03. 72
though he be painted one way like a gorgon, ANT 2.05.116
GORMANDIZING *(also gurmandize)*
GORMANDIZING 1 FR 0.0001 REL FR 1 V 0 P
leave gormandizing, know the grave doth gape 2H4 5.05. 53
GORSE *(see goss)*
GORY 3 FR 0.0003 REL FR 3 V 0 P
forbids | a gory emulation 'twixt us twain. TRO 4.05.123
what mean these masterless and gory swords | to ROM 5.03.142
never shake | thy gory locks at me. MAC 3.04. 50
GOSLING 2 FR 0.0002 REL FR 1 V 1 P
i'll never | be such a gosling to obey instinct, COR 5.03. 35
marry, whip the gosling, i think i shall have PER 4.02. 86 P
GOSPEL 1 FR 0.0001 REL FR 0 V 1 P
before god, that's as true as the gospel. STM II.C 88 P
GOSPELL'D 1 FR 0.0001 REL FR 1 V 0 P
are you so gospell'd, | to pray for this good MAC 3.01. 87
GOSPELS 1 FR 0.0001 REL FR 0 V 1 P
but as a madman's epistles are no gospels, so it TN 5.01.288 P
GOSS 1 FR 0.0001 REL FR 1 V 0 P
briers, sharp furzes, pricking goss, and thorns, TMP 4.01.180
GOSSAMERS *(also goss'mer)*
GOSSAMERS 1 FR 0.0001 REL FR 1 V 0 P
a lover may bestride the gossamers | that idles ROM 2.06. 18
GOSSIP 8 FR 0.0009 REL FR 4 V 4 P
what ho, gossip ford! what ho! WIV 4.02. 9 P
with all my heart, i'll gossip at this feast. ERR 5.01.408
if my gossip report be an honest woman of her MV 3.01. 7 P
would she were as lying a gossip in that as ever 3.01. 8 P
and make the babbling gossip of the air | cry TN 1.05.273
wife, come in then and call me gossip quickly? 2H4 2.01. 94 P
guilt of ours, | a long-tongu'd babbling gossip? TIT 4.02.150
speak to my gossip venus one fair word, | one ROM 2.01. 11
GOSSIP'D 1 FR 0.0001 REL FR 1 V 0 P
full often hath she gossip'd by my side, | and MND 2.01.125
GOSSIPING 2 FR 0.0002 REL FR 2 V 0 P
will you walk in to see their gossiping? ERR 5.01.420
full warm of blood, of mirth, of gossiping. JN 5.02. 59
GOSSIP-LIKE 1 FR 0.0001 REL FR 0 V 1 P
i will leave you now to your gossip-like humor. ADO 5.01.186 P
GOSSIP'S 2 FR 0.0002 REL FR 2 V 0 P
and sometime lurk i in a gossip's bowl, | in MND 2.01. 47
utter your gravity o'er a gossip's bowl, | for ROM 3.05.174
GOSSIPS' 1 FR 0.0001 REL FR 1 V 0 P
go to a gossips' feast, and go with me — ERR 5.01.406
GOSSIPS 6 FR 0.0006 REL FR 5 V 1 P
yet 'tis not a maid, for she hath had gossips; TGV 3.01.270 P
christendoms | that blinking cupid gossips. AWW 1.01.175
about some gossips for your highness. WT 2.03. 41
are mighty gossips in our monarchy. R3 1.01. 83
my noble gossips, y' have been too prodigal. H8 5.04. 12
good prudence, smatter with your gossips, go. ROM 3.05.171
GOSS'MER *(also gossamers)*
GOSS'MER 1 FR 0.0001 REL FR 1 V 0 P
hadst thou been aught but goss'mer, feathers, LR 4.06. 49
GO'ST 2 FR 0.0002 REL FR 2 V 0 P
ne'er throughout the year to church thou go'st 1H6 1.01. 42
stay'st thou here, and go'st not to the duke? R3 4.04.446
GOT* *(also gar, gat, god)*
/GOT* 2 FR 0.0002 REL FR 1 V 1 P
was never virgin /got till virginity was first AWW 1.01.128 P
/i /never /got /him. LR 2.01. 78
GOT* 127 FR 0.0143 REL FR 93 V 34 P
got by the devil himself | upon thy wicked dam, TMP 1.02.319
of the isle with four legs, who hath got, as i 2.02. 66 P
i say by sorcery he got this isle; 3.02. 52
from me he got it. 3.02. 53
plot | the means that dusky dis my daughter got, 4.01. 89
let me not, | since i have my dukedom got, | and ep 6
and show thee all the treasure we have got; TGV 4.01. 73
our youth got me to play the woman's part, | and 4.04.160
there is no fear of got in a riot. WIV 1.01. 37 P
shall desire to hear the fear of got, and not to 1.01. 38 P
(got deliver to a joyful resurrections!) 1.01. 52 P
got pless your house here! 1.01. 73 P
so got udge me, that is a virtuous mind. 1.01.185 P
sir john falstaff, serve got, and leave your 5.05.129 P
this is strange. who hath got the right anne? 5.05.211 P
contract | i got possession of julietta's bed. MM 1.02.146
he hath got his friend with child. 1.04. 29
is with child, | and he that got it, sentenc'd; 2.03. 13
the one ne'er got me credit, the other mickle ERR 3.01. 45
what, have you got the picture of old adam new 4.03. 13 P
it one way, for the prince hath got your hero. ADO 2.01.191 P
that your grace had got the good will of this 2.01.216 P
your father got excellent husbands, if a maid 2.01.324 P
and got a calf in that same noble feat | much 5.04. 50
what a beard hast thou got! MV 2.02. 94 P
thou hast got more hair on thy chin than dobbin 2.02. 94 P
i thank your lordship, you have got me one. 3.02.196
i got a promise of this fair one here | to have 3.02.206
may partly hope that your father got you not, 3.05. 11 P
since he hath got the jewel that i loved, | and 5.01.224
till katherine the curst have got a husband. SHR 1.02.128
no doubt but he hath got a quiet catch. 2.01.331
to the english, the french ne'er got 'em. AWW 2.03. 95 P
some hurts, and say i got them in exploit. 4.01. 37 P
your mother was | when your sweet self was got. 4.02. 10
a scar nobly got, or a noble scar, is a good 4.05. 99 P
by what rough enforcement | you got it from her. 5.03.108
she got the ring, | and i had that which any 5.03.217
and at that time he got his wife with child. 5.03.301
which hast made it | so like to him that got it, WT 2.03.105
open air, before | i have got strength of limit. 3.02.106
they were warmer that got this than the poor 3.03. 75 P
when this same lusty gentleman was got. JN 1.01.108
your face hath got five hundred pound a year, 1.01.152
be the hour by night or day | when i was got, 1.01.166
for thou wast got i' th' way of honesty. 1.01.181
but say thou didst not well | when i was got, 1.01.272
got with swearing "lay by," and spent with 1H4 1.02. 35 P
got with much ease. 2.02.104
what never-dying honor hath he got | against 3.02.106
i have got, in exchange of a hundred and fifty 4.02. 13 P
belike then my appetite was not princely got, 2H4 2.02. 10 P
hath got the voice in hell for excellence; H5 2.02.113
that's all the riches i got in his service. 2.03. 44 P
and /swear i got them in the gallia wars. 5.01. 89
he was thinking of civil wars when he got me; 5.02.226 P
ascribes the glory of his conquest got | first 1H6 3.04. 11
his wits, | to keep by policy what henry got? 2H6 1.01. 84
and are the cities that i got with wounds 1.01.121
had henry got an empire by his marriage, | and 1.01.153
thus got the house of lancaster the crown. 2.02. 29
to emblaze the honor that thy master got. 4.10. 71
well, lords, we have not got that which we have: 5.03. 20
henry the fourth by conquest got the crown. 3H6 1.01.132
the army of the queen hath got the field. 1.04. 1
"what my great-grandfather and grandsire got, 2.02. 37
hear | that things ill got had ever bad success? 2.02. 46
whoever got thee, there thy mother stands, | for 2.02.133
the air hath got into my deadly wounds, | and 2.06. 27
i'll tell you how these lands are to be got. 3.02. 42
but when the fox hath once got in his nose, 4.07. 25
that's not my fear, my meed hath got me fame: 4.08. 38
her deity | got my lord chamberlain his liberty. R3 1.01. 77
as being got, your father then in france, | and 3.07. 10
in his unlawful bed, he got | this edward, whom 3.07.190

being now seen possible enough, got credit, H8 1.01. 37
have got by the late voyage is but merely | a 1.03. 6
of fool and feather that they got in france, 1.03. 25
have got a speeding trick to lay down ladies. 1.03. 40
and got your leave | to make this present 2.04.219
sent innumerable substance | (by what means got, 3.02.327
how got they in, and be hang'd? 5.03. 17 P
knew | love got so sweet as when desire did sue. TRO 1.02.291
no sooner got but lost? 4.02. 74 P
has got that same scurvy doting foolish /young 5.04. 3 P
"come on, you cowards, you were got in fear, COR 1.03. 33
they fought together, but aufidius got off. 2.01.128 P
to heal again | than hear say how i got them. 2.02. 70
i got them in my country's service, when | some 2.03. 52
and that the spoil got on the antiates | was 3.03. 4
the plebeians have got your fellow tribune, 5.04. 36
that shone so brightly when this boy was got, TIT 4.02. 90
have you got leave to go to shrift to–day? ROM 2.05. 66
hath got this mortal hurt | in my behalf; 3.01.110
the tears have got small victory by that, | for 4.01. 30
else, | on whom i may confer what i have got. TIM 1.01.122
ye have got a humor there | does not become a 1.02. 26
thou mightst have sooner got another service; 4.03.504
where our desire is got without content; MAC 3.02. 5
has thirty–one | swelt'red venom sleeping got, 4.01. 8
on the instant they got clear of our ship, so i HAM 4.06. 19 P
age dotes on, only got the tune of the time and, 5.02.189 P
tribe of fops, | got 'tween asleep and wake? LR 1.02. 15
got praises of the king | for him attempting who 2.02.121
my daughters | got 'tween the lawful sheets. 4.06.116
the dark and vicious place where thee he got 5.03.173
how got she out? OTH 1.01.169
oft got without merit, and lost without 2.03.269 P
have by their brave instruction got upon me | a ANT 4.14. 98
and i send him | the greatness he has got. 5.02. 30
what got he by that? CYM 2.01. 6 P
now our voices | have got the mannish crack, 4.02.236
only | affected greatness got by you, not you; 5.05. 38
by villainy | i got this ring. 5.05.143
i have got two worlds by't. 5.05.374
me, | whereas no glory's got to overcome. PER 1.04. 70
here's nothing to be got now–a–days unless thou 2.01. 69 P
he's well got sure. TNK 2.05. 24
and got your pardon, and discover'd how | and by 4.01. 19
she stay'd, | and fell, scarce to be got away. 4.01.102
and courtiers that have got maids with child, 4.03. 41 P
alas, poor things, what is it you have got, STM II.C 68
of your opinions cloth'd, | what had you got? II.C 80
lullaby, the learned man hath got the lady gay, PP 15.15
my verse | as every alien pen hath got my use, SON 78. 3
what a mansion have those vices got | which for 95. 9
for my help lies | where cupid got new fire — 153.14
GOTH 4 FR 0.0004 REL FR 4 V 0 P
lascivious goth, and all the bitterest terms TIT 2.03.110
but who comes here, led by a lusty goth? 5.01. 19
"for i must bear thee to a trusty goth, | who, 5.01. 34
o worthy goth, this is the incarnate devil 5.01. 40
GOTHS 28 FR 0.0031 REL FR 27 V 1 P
poet, honest ovid, was among the goths. AYL 3.03. 9 P
from weary wars against the barbarous goths, TIT 1.01. 28
here goths have given me leave to sheathe my 1.01. 85
give us the proudest prisoner of the goths, 1.01. 96
whom your goths beheld | alive and dead, and for 1.01.122
his tent | may favor tamora, the queen of goths 1.01.139
(when goths were goths and tamora was queen), 1.01.140
(when goths were goths and tamora was queen), 1.01.140
can make you greater than the queen of goths. 1.01.269
and therefore, lovely tamora, queen of goths, 1.01.315
speak, queen of goths, dost thou applaud my 1.01.321
if saturnine advance the queen of goths, | she 1.01.330
how comes it that the subtile queen of goths 1.01.392
now, by the gods that warlike goths adore, 2.01. 61
hie to the goths and raise an army there, | and 3.01.285
now will i to the goths and raise a pow'r, | to 3.01.299
mortal revenge upon these traitorous goths, 4.01. 93
now to the goths, as swift as swallow flies, 4.02.172
but /... | join with the goths, and with 4.03. 33
the goths have gathered head, and with a power 4.04. 63
is warlike lucius general of the goths? 4.04. 69
to pluck proud lucius from the warlike goths. 4.04.110
lord lucius, and you princes of the goths, | the 5.01.156
hand, | to scatter and disperse the giddy goths, 5.02. 78
who leads towards rome a band of warlike goths, 5.02.113
thou shalt inquire him out among the goths: 5.02.123
him | some of the chiefest princes of the goths. 5.02.125
welcome, ye warlike goths; 5.03. 27
GOT'S *(also god's*, 'od's*, 'ud's)*
GOT'S 3 FR 0.0003 REL FR 0 V 3 P
here is got's plessing, and your friend, and WIV 1.01. 75 P
nay, got's lords and his ladies! 1.01.235 P
got's will, and his passion of my heart! 3.01. 62 P
GOTS *(also got'st)*
GOTS 1 FR 0.0001 REL FR 1 V 0 P
or by what means gots thou to be releas'd? 1H6 1.04. 25
GOT'ST *(also gots)*
GOT'ST 3 FR 0.0003 REL FR 3 V 0 P
as thou got'st milan, | i'll come by naples. TMP 2.01.291
where got'st thou that goose–look? MAC 5.03. 12
me, cousin, | where got'st thou this good armor? TNK 3.06. 54
GOT/'T 1 FR 0.0001 REL FR 1 V 0 P
this her bracelet | (o cunning, how i got/'t!), CYM 5.05.205
GOTTEN 5 FR 0.0005 REL FR 4 V 1 P
he was gotten in drink. WIV 1.03. 22 P
have gotten leave | to look upon my sometimes R2 5.05. 74
jack cade hath gotten london bridge: 2H6 4.04. 49
lost | all that which henry the fift had gotten? 3H6 3.03. 90
and, that once gotten, doubt not of large pay. 4.07. 88
GOURD 1 FR 0.0001 REL FR 1 V 0 P
for gourd and fullam holds, | and high and low WIV 1.03. 85
GOUT 8 FR 0.0009 REL FR 4 V 4 P
do curse the gout, sapego, and the rheum | for MM 3.01. 31
latin, and a rich man that hath not the gout; AYL 3.02.320 P
but the gout galls the one, and the pox pinches 2H4 1.02.230 P
a pox of this gout! 1.02.243 P
or, a gout of this pox! 1.02.244 P
am i better | than one that's sick o' th' gout, CYM 5.04. 5
the gout had knit his fingers into knots, TNK 5.01.112
beguile | the gout and rheum, that in lag hours 5.04. 8
GOUTS 2 FR 0.0002 REL FR 2 V 0 P
and on thy blade and dudgeon gouts of blood, MAC 2.01. 46
plagu'd with cramps and gouts and painful fits, LUC 856
GOUTY 3 FR 0.0003 REL FR 2 V 1 P
so out of joint that he is a gouty briareus, TRO 1.02. 28 P
when gouty keepers of thee cannot stand. TIM 4.03. 47
than the true gouty landlord which doth owe them LC 140
/GOVERN 1 FR 0.0001 REL FR 1 V 0 P
/stars /above /us, /govern /our /conditions, LR 4.03. 33
GOVERN 28 FR 0.0031 REL FR 24 V 4 P
i would with such perfection govern, sir, | t' TMP 2.01.168
but truer stars did govern proteus' birth: TGV 2.07. 74
let it be as humors and conceits shall govern. MV 3.05. 64 P
distrust | govern the motion of a kingly eye. JN 5.01. 47
and for mine, sir, i will govern it. 2H4 2.02.164 P
he being of age to govern of himself? 2H6 1.01.166
god and king henry govern england's realm. 2.03. 30
wife, let's in, and learn to govern better, 4.09. 48
not fit to govern and rule multitudes, | which 5.01. 94
for how can tyrants safely govern home, | unless 3H6 3.03. 69
alas, how should you govern any kingdom, | that 4.03. 35
no doubt shall then, and till then, govern well. R3 2.03. 15
the duke | shall govern england.'" H8 1.02.171
madam, though venus govern your desires, TIT 2.03. 30
but yet let reason govern thy lament. 3.01.218
in hope thyself should govern rome and me. 4.04. 60
thanks, gentle romans, may i govern so, | to 5.03.147
of some high powers | that govern us below. JC 5.01.107
if such a one be fit to govern, speak. MAC 4.03.101
fit to govern? 4.03.102
govern these ventages with your fingers and HAM 3.02.357 P
go after her; she's desperate, govern her. LR 5.03.162
the heart of brothers govern in our loves, | and ANT 2.02.147
spirit | is all afraid to govern thee near him; 2.03. 30
and be resolved he lives to govern us, | or, PER 2.04. 31
behind | is left to govern it, you bear in mind, 4.04. 14
if he govern the country, you are bound to him 4.06. 55 P
for kings like gods should govern every thing. LUC 602
GOVERNANCE 1 FR 0.0001 REL FR 1 V 0 P
still | under the surly gloucester's governance? 2H6 1.03. 47
GOVERN'D 18 FR 0.0020 REL FR 12 V 6 P
him, master /brook, that ever govern'd frenzy. WIV 5.01. 19 P
off, and now is the whole man govern'd with one; ADO 1.01. 67 P
into a lute–string and now govern'd by stops. 3.02. 60 P
thy currish spirit | govern'd a wolf, who, MV 4.01.134
we be men of good government, being govern'd, as 1H4 1.02. 28 P
doth ebb and flow like the sea, being govern'd, 1.02. 32 P
for you are altogether govern'd by humors. 3.01.233 P
a hare–brain'd hotspur, govern'd by a spleen. 5.02. 19
in equal rank with the best govern'd nation, 2H4 5.02.137
that i, being govern'd by the watery moon, | may R3 2.02. 69
woe to that land that's govern'd by a child! 2.03. 11
how i have govern'd our determin'd jest? TIT 5.02.139
mind he carries | that ever govern'd man. TIM 1.01.281
and we are govern'd with our mothers' spirits; JC 1.03. 83
on, | his corporal motion govern'd by my spirit; 4.01. 33
be govern'd by your knowledge, and proceed | i' LR 4.07. 18
betwixt a father by thy step–dame govern'd, | a CYM 2.01. 58
and govern'd him in strength, though not in lust VEN 42
GOVERNED 1 FR 0.0001 REL FR 1 V 0 P
think | a due sincerity governed his deeds, MM 5.01.446
GOVERNESS 2 FR 0.0002 REL FR 2 V 0 P
therefore the moon, the governess of floods, MND 2.01.103
where their dear governess and lady lies, | do LUC 443
GOVERNMENT 29 FR 0.0032 REL FR 23 V 6 P
study, | the government i cast upon my brother, TMP 1.02. 75
of government the properties to unfold | would MM 1.01. 3
my lips in vain, or discover his government. 3.01.194 P
fact, till now in the government of lord angelo, 4.02.136 P
on a recorder — a sound, but not in government. MND 5.01.123 P
all must be even in our government. R2 3.04. 36
and let men say we be men of good government, 1H4 1.02. 27 P
rage, | defect of manners, want of government, 3.01.182
under whose government come they along? 4.01. 19
afoot, | come underneath the yoke of government. 2H4 4.04. 10
for government, though high, and low, and lower, H5 1.02.180
under the sweet shade of your government. 2.02. 28
kept | as that whereof i had the government, 1H6 2.01. 64
is this the government of britain's isle, | and 2H6 1.03. 44
'tis government that makes them seem divine, 3H6 1.04.132
crown, | i here resign my government to thee, 4.06. 24
hearts, | that no dissension hinder government. 4.06. 40
i mean, in bearing weight of government, | while 4.06. 51
in him there is a hope of government, | which, R3 2.03. 12
and kingly government of this your land: 3.07.132
thy meekness saint–like, wife–like government, H8 2.04.139
each part, depriv'd of supple government, ROM 4.01.102
fear not my government. OTH 3.03.256
him home, | deputing cassio in his government. 4.01.237
quite besides | the government of patience! CYM 2.04.150
this tharsus, o'er which i have the government, PER 1.04. 21
for his peaceable reign and good government. 2.01.103 P
his subjects the name of good by his government. 2.01.105 P
showed deep regard and smiling government. LUC 1400
GOVERNOR 19 FR 0.0021 REL FR 17 V 2 P
be | a horse whereon the governor doth ride, MM 1.02.160
in — but this new governor | awakes me all the 1.02.165
as from her lord, her governor, her king. MV 3.02.165
to wound thy lord, thy king, thy governor. SHR 5.02.138
our uncle york lord governor of england; R2 2.01.220
how yet resolves the governor of the town? H5 3.03. 1
king is, | being ordain'd his special governor, 1H6 1.01.171
now, governor of paris, take your oath: 4.01. 3
lucius, all hail, rome's gracious governor! TIT 5.03.146
i am glad on't; 'tis a worthy governor. OTH 2.01. 30
my hopes do shape him for the governor. 2.01. 55
to you, lord governor, | remains the censure of 5.02.367
where's the lord governor? PER 1.04. 56
lord governor, for so we hear you are, | let not 1.04. 85
next, he's the governor of this country, and a 4.06. 53 P
parts, and are the governor of this place. 4.06. 81 P
and in it is lysimachus the governor, | who 5.01. 4
i am the governor of this place you lie before. 5.01. 21
sir, 'tis the governor of meteline, | who, 5.01.219
GOVERNOR'S 1 FR 0.0001 REL FR 1 V 0 P
and thou shalt find me at the governor's. 1H6 1.04. 20
GOVERNORS 2 FR 0.0002 REL FR 2 V 0 P
lord, and picardy | hath slain their governors, 2H6 4.01. 89
to him, | store never hurts good governors. TNK 1.03. 6
GOVERNS 3 FR 0.0003 REL FR 3 V 0 P
governs lord angelo, a man whose blood | is very MM 1.04. 57
who governs here? TN 1.02. 24
and that which governs me to go about | doth SON 113. 2
GOWER 14 FR 0.0015 REL FR 4 V 10 P
now, master gower, what news? 2H4 2.01.133
come, go along with me, good master gower. 2.01.179
master gower, shall i entreat you with me to 2.01.182 P
will you sup with me, master gower? 2.01.188 P
master gower, if they become me not, he was a 2.01.191 P
i tell you what, captain gower: H5 3.06. 82 P
ay, he was porn at monmouth, captain gower. 4.07. 12 P
under captain gower, my liege. 4.07.148 P
gower is a good captain, and is good knowledge 4.07.149 P
know'st thou gower? 4.07.165 P
stand away, captain gower, i will give treason 4.08. 13 P
i will tell you asse my friend, captain gower: 5.01. 5 P
was sung, | from ashes ancient gower is come, PER 1.ch. 2
pardon old gower — this long's the text. 2.ch. 40
GOWN 49 FR 0.0055 REL FR 22 V 27 P
put off that gown, trinculo. TMP 4.01.227 P
by this hand, i'll have that gown. 4.01.228 P
part, | and i was trimm'd in madam julia's gown, TGV 4.04.161
pray you give me my gown, or else keep it in WIV 3.01. 34 P
there is no woman's gown big enough for him; 4.02. 70 P
the fat woman of brainford, has a gown above. 4.02. 76 P
put on the gown the while. 4.02. 83 P
kneel down before him, hang upon his gown; MM 2.02. 44
by order of law a furr'd gown to keep him warm; 3.02. 7 P
the duchess of milan's gown that they praise so. ADO 3.04. 16 P
i'll change my black gown for a faithful friend. LLL 5.02.834
lay forth the gown. SHR 4.03. 62
thy gown? 4.03. 86
i see she's like to have neither cap nor gown. 4.03. 93
i never saw a better fashion'd gown, | more 4.03.101
i tell thee, i, that thou hast marr'd her gown. 4.03.114
the gown is made | just as my master had 4.03.115
i bid thy master cut out the gown, but i did not 4.03.126 P
"inprimis, a loose–bodied gown" — 4.03.134 P
if ever i said loose–bodied gown, sew me in the 4.03.135 P
i said a gown. 4.03.137 P
well, sir, in brief, the gown is not for me. 4.03.155
take up my mistress' gown for thy master's use! 4.03.159 P
take up my mistress' gown to his master's use! 4.03.162
tailor, i'll pay thee for thy gown to–morrow, 4.03.166
of humility over the black gown of a big heart. AWW 1.03. 95 P
officers about me, in my branch'd velvet gown; TN 2.05. 48 P
i prithee put on this gown and this beard, make 4.02. 1 P
the first that ever dissembled in such a gown. 4.02. 6 P
have done this without thy beard and gown, he 4.02. 65 P
my gay apparel for an almsman's gown, | my R2 3.03.149
hangs about me like an old lady's loose gown; 1H4 3.03. 4 P
well, you shall have it, though i pawn my gown. 2H4 2.01.159 P
come, thou shalt go to the wars in a gown. 3.02.184 P
the very train of her worst wearing gown | was 2H6 1.03. 85
why, that's well said. what color is my gown of? 2.01.109
for i cannot | put on the gown, stand naked, and COR 2.02.137
here he comes, and in the gown of humility, mark 2.03. 40 P
i may be consul, i have here the customary gown. 2.03. 87 P
i have lost my gown. TIM 3.06.110 P
here lies my gown. 3.06.117 P
my gown. JC 4.03.231
give me the gown. 4.03.239
i put it in the pocket of my gown. 4.03.253
for shame, put on your gown; OTH 1.01. 86
now gods forbid't, and i have a gown here! PER 2.01. 79 P
shalt have my best gown to make thee a pair; 2.01.163 P
i'll have a gown full of 'em — and of these: TNK 2.02.128
where's my wedding gown? 4.01.109
GOWN'S 1 FR 0.0001 REL FR 0 V 1 P
and your gown's a most rare fashion, i' faith. ADO 3.04. 14 P
GOWNS 5 FR 0.0005 REL FR 3 V 2 P
and one that hath two gowns, and every thing ADO 4.02. 85 P
but cloaks and gowns, before this day, a many. 2H6 2.01.113
and wrap our bodies in black mourning gowns, 3H6 2.01.161
robes and furr'd gowns hide all. LR 4.06.165
nor for measures of lawn, nor for gowns, OTH 4.03. 74 P
/GRAC'D 1 FR 0.0001 REL FR 1 V 0 P
/on | /and /bless'd /and /grac'd /and /did, 2H4 4.01.137
GRAC'D 13 FR 0.0014 REL FR 12 V 1 P
tunis was never grac'd before with such a TMP 2.01. 75 P
have done the time more benefit and grac'd WT 5.01. 22
and grac'd thy poor sire with his bridal day, 3H6 2.02.155
and we are grac'd with wreaths of victory. 5.03. 2
name | that ever grac'd me with thy company? R3 4.04.175
had grac'd the tender temples of my child, | and 4.04.383
aims, | in whom already he's well grac'd, cannot COR 1.01.264
and manners, to intrude where i am grac'd, | and TIT 2.01. 27
were the grac'd person of our banquo present, MAC 3.04. 40
a tavern or a brothel | than a grac'd palace. LR 1.04.246
place, and grac'd | the thankings of a king. CYM 5.05.406
the powerful venus well hath grac'd her altar, TNK 5.04.105
not his grace, but were all grac'd by him. LC 119
/GRACE 2 FR 0.0002 REL FR 2 V 0 P
/how /fares /your /grace? 2H4 4.05. 49
/am /thus /bold /to /put /your /grace /in /mind R3 4.02.110
GRACE 601 FR 0.0679 REL FR 516 V 85 P
did quarrel with the noblest grace she ow'd, TMP 3.01. 45
heavens rain grace | on that which breeds 3.01. 75
a grace it had, devouring. 3.03. 84
thee leave these, and with her sovereign grace, 4.01. 72
thy grace shall have it. 4.01.229 P
steal by line and level, and't like your grace. 4.01.240 P
of whose soft grace | for the like loss i have 5.01.142
that swear'st grace o'erboard, not an oath on 5.01.219
i'll be wise hereafter, | and seek for grace. 5.01.296
truth hath better deeds than words to grace it. TGV 2.02. 18
mind | with all good grace to grace a gentleman. 2.04. 74
mind | with all good grace to grace a gentleman. 2.04. 74
please it your grace, there is a messenger 3.01. 52
cannot your grace win her to fancy him? 3.01. 67
what would your grace have me to do in this? 3.01. 80
do curse the grace that with such grace hath 3.01.146

the grace that with such grace hath blest them, 3.01.146
longer than i prove loyal to your grace | let me 3.02. 20
grace | let me not live to look upon your grace. 3.02. 21
we'll wait upon your grace till after supper, 3.02. 95
the heaven such grace did lend her, | that she 4.02. 42
your grace is welcome to a man disgrac'd, 5.04.123
i thank your grace; 5.04.148
with our discourse to make your grace to smile. 5.04.163
i think the boy hath grace in him; he blushes. 5.04.165
i warrant you, my lord — more grace than boy. 5.04.166
i will not be absence at the grace. WIV 1.01.265 P
they have not so little grace, i hope. 2.02.112 P
worth | to undergo such ample grace and honor, MM 1.01. 23
i think thou never wast where grace was said. 1.02. 19 P
grace is grace, despite of all controversy; 1.02. 24 P
grace is grace, despite of all controversy; 1.02. 24 P
art a wicked villain, despite of all grace. 1.02. 26 P
may your grace speak of it? 1.03. 6
it rested in your grace | to unloose this 1.03. 31
unless you have the grace by your fair prayer 1.04. 69
become them with one half so good a grace | as 2.02. 62
grace go with you, benedicite! 2.03. 39
what ho! peace here; grace and good company! 3.01. 44
but grace, being the soul of your complexion, 3.01.183 P
to know, | grace to stand, and virtue go; 3.02.264
grace of the duke, revenges to your heart, | and 4.03.135
alack, when once our grace we have forgot, 4.04. 33
happy return be to your royal grace! 5.01. 3
that's i, and't like your grace. 5.01. 74
heaven shield your grace from woe, | as i, thus 5.01.118
for certain words he spake against your grace 5.01.129
blessed be your royal grace! 5.01.137
yet | did, as he vouches, misreport your grace. 5.01.148
when i perceive your grace, like pow'r divine, 5.01.369
and sequent death, | is all the grace i beg. 5.01.374
his company must do his minions grace, | whilst ERR 2.01. 87
in your knowledge and your grace you show not 3.02. 31
possess'd with such a gentle sovereign grace, 3.02.160
have won his grace to come in person hither, 5.01.116
may it please your grace, antipholus, my husband 5.01.136
bed, | to do him all the grace and good i could. 5.01.164
and immediately | ran hither to your grace, whom 5.01.252
as sure, my liege, as i do see your grace. 5.01.280
to my house in the likeness of your grace, for ADO 1.01.100 P
please it your grace lead on? 1.01.159 P
i would your grace would constrain me to tell. 1.01.206 P
and he hath ta'en you newly into his grace, 1.03. 22 P
be a canker in a hedge than a rose in his grace, 1.03. 28 P
that your grace had got the good will of this 2.01.216 P
will your grace command me any service to the 2.01.263 P
therefore your grace may well say i have lost it 2.01.281 P
his grace hath made the match, and all grace say 2.01.303 P
made the match, and all grace say amen to it. 2.01.304 P
hath your grace ne'er a brother like you? 2.01.323 P
your grace is too costly to wear every day. 2.01.328 P
but i beseech your grace pardon me, i was born 2.01.329 P
one woman, one woman shall not come in my grace. 2.03. 30 P
is, | as hush'd on purpose to grace harmony! 2.03. 39
thou seest that all the grace that she hath left 4.01.171
and then grace us in the disgrace of death; LLL 1.01. 3
i only swore to study with your grace, | and 1.01. 51
a maid of grace and complete majesty — | about 1.01.136
not by might mast'red, but by special grace. 1.01.152
be now as prodigal of all dear grace | as nature 2.01. 9
/importunes personal conference with his grace. 2.01. 32
and shape to win grace though he had no wit. 2.01. 60
i hear your grace hath sworn out house–keeping: 2.01.104
so please your grace, the packet is not come 2.01.163
health and fair desires consort your grace! 2.01.177
a most acute juvenal, volable and free of grace! 3.01. 66
please you to gratify the table with a grace, i 4.02.155 P
one with a paper, god give him grace to groan! 4.03. 20 P
thy grace being gain'd cures all disgrace in me. 4.03. 65
what grace hast thou thus to reprove | these 4.03.151
i beseech your grace let this letter be read: 4.03.191
your grace needs not fear it. 4.03.197
for i must tell thee it will please his grace 5.01.102 P
gracious, though few have the grace to do it. 5.01.140 P
and wit's own grace to grace a learned fool. 5.02. 72
and wit's own grace to grace a learned fool. 5.02. 72
where's her grace? 5.02. 80
and not a man of them shall have the grace, 5.02.128
nor to their penn'd speech render we no grace, 5.02.147
have not the grace to grace it with such show. 5.02.320
have not the grace to grace it with such show. 5.02.320
sin, | thus purifies itself and turns to grace. 5.02.776
no, no, my lord, your grace is perjur'd much, 5.02.790
whose influence is begot of that loose grace 5.02.859
be it so she will not here before your grace MND 1.01. 39
i do entreat your grace to pardon me. 1.01. 58
but i beseech your grace that i may know | the 1.01. 62
the more my prayer, the lesser is my grace. 2.02. 89
what though i be not so in grace as you, | so 3.02.232
if you have any pity, grace, or manners, | you 3.02.241
intent, | came here in grace of our solemnity. 4.01.134
so please your grace, the prologue is address'd. 5.01.106
think what thou wilt, i am thy lover's grace; 5.01.195
truly, the moon shines with a good grace. 5.01.268 P
hand in hand, with fairy grace, | will we sing, 5.01.399
you have the grace of god, sir, and he hath MV 2.02.150 P
nay more, while grace is saying, hood mine eyes 2.02.193
two, | and wear my dagger with the braver grace, 3.04. 65
i think the best grace of wit will shortly turn 3.05. 44 P
ready, so please your grace. 4.01. 2
your grace hath ta'en great pains to qualify 4.01. 7
i have possess'd your grace of what i purpose, 4.01. 35
from both, my lord. bellario greets your grace. 4.01.120
"your grace shall understand that at the receipt 4.01.150 P
i humbly do desire your grace of pardon, | i 4.01.402
or if he do not mightily grace himself on thee, AYL 1.01.149 P
no, i warrant your grace, you shall not entreat 1.02.205 P
yes, i beseech your grace, i am not yet well 1.02.217 P
i do beseech your grace | let me the knowledge 1.03. 45
words, | they are as innocent as grace itself. 1.03. 54
happy is your grace, | that can translate the 2.01. 18
at whom so oft | your grace was wont to laugh, 2.02. 9
but yet have the grace to consider that tears do 3.04. 2 P
is my love, | and in such a poverty of grace, 3.05.100
you, to do yourself good, and not to grace me. 5.02. 58 P
i know the boy will well usurp the grace, SHR in.1. 131
now shall my friend petruchio do me grace, | and 1.02.131
bless you with such grace | as 'longeth to a 4.02. 44
and these great tears grace his remembrance more AWW 1.01. 80
i will tell truth, by grace itself i swear. 1.03.220
to return | and find your grace in health. 2.01. 7
the greatest grace lending grace, | ere twice 2.01.160
the greatest grace lending grace, | ere twice 2.01.160
but i hope your own grace will keep you where 3.05. 26 P
i will grace the attempt for a worthy exploit. 3.06. 68 P
bold to acquaint his grace you are gone about it 3.06. 78 P
i duly am inform'd | his grace is at marsellis, 4.04. 9
of the sallet, or rather the herb of grace. 4.05. 17 P
my lord, to bring me in some grace, for you did 5.02. 47 P
one brings thee in grace and the other brings 5.02. 50 P
vanquish'd thereto by the fair grace and speech 5.03.133
her /inf'nite /cunning, with her modern grace, 5.03.216
he does it with a better grace, but i do it more TN 2.03. 82 P
grace and good disposition attend your ladyship! 3.01.135
put your grace in your pocket, sir, for this 5.01. 32 P
grace to boot! WT 1.02. 80
o, would her name were grace! 1.02. 99
'tis grace indeed. 1.02.105
but beseech your grace | be plainer with me, let 1.02.264
action i now go on | is for my better grace. 2.01.122
came to your court, how i was in your grace, 3.02. 47
now grown in grace | equal with wond'ring. 4.01. 24
grace and remembrance be to you both, | and 4.04. 76
to offer to have his daughter come into grace! 4.04.778 P
wink of an eye some new grace will be born. 5.02.110 P
it is a surplus of your grace, which never | my 5.03. 7
for she was as tender | as infancy and grace. 5.03. 27
out of your grace devise, ordain, impose | some JN 3.01.250
your grace shall stay behind | so strongly 3.03. 1
enemies may not have this | to grace occasions, 4.02. 62
cause — | to grace the gentry of a land remote, 5.02. 31
your grace shall pardon me, i will not back. 5.02. 78
and by the grace of god, and this mine arm, | to R2 1.03. 22
here do stand in arms | to prove by god's grace, 1.03. 37
did grace our hollow parting with a tear. 1.04. 9
words by you, | here comes his grace in person. 2.03. 82
grace me no grace, nor uncle me no uncle. 2.03. 87
grace me no grace, nor uncle me no uncle. 2.03. 87
and that word "grace" | in an ungracious mouth 2.03. 88
i beseech your grace | look on my wrongs with an 2.03.115
it stands your grace upon to do him right. 2.03.138
but we must win your grace to go with us | to 2.03.163
how brooks your grace the air | after your late 3.02. 2
comfort, my liege, why looks your grace so pale? 3.02. 75
your grace mistakes; 3.03. 10
to come at traitors' calls and do them grace. 3.03.181
should grace the triumph of great bullingbrook? 3.04. 99
i'll set a bank of rue, sour herb of grace. 3.04.105
i do beseech your grace to pardon me. 5.02. 60
god save your grace! 5.03. 26
to have some conference with your grace alone. 5.03. 27
ill mayst thou thrive if thou grant any grace! 5.03. 99
march sadly after, grace my mournings here, | in 5.06. 51
as, god save thy grace — majesty i should say, 1H4 1.02. 17 P
i should say, for grace thou wilt have none — 1.02. 18 P
are content to do the profession some grace, 2.01. 71 P
and the fire of grace be not quite out of thee, 2.04.383 P
thou art violently carried away from grace, 2.04.447 P
i would your grace would take me with you. 2.04.460 P
whom means your grace? 2.04.461 P
and that's the dearest grace it renders you — 3.01.180
the archbishop's grace of york, douglas, 3.02.119
my lord, and i said i heard your grace say so; 3.03.106 P
i would you would accept of grace and love. 4.03.112
to grace this latter age with noble deeds. 5.01. 92
and, will they take the offer of our grace, 5.01.106
and chid his truant youth with such a grace | as 5.02. 62
cheerly, my lord, how fares your grace? 5.04. 44
for my part, if a lie may do thee grace, | i'll 5.04.157
ill–spirited worcester, did not we send grace, 5.05. 2
and i beseech your grace | i may dispose of him. 5.05. 23
i thank your grace for this high courtesy, 5.05. 32
gan vail his stomach and did grace the shame 2H4 1.01.129
he may keep his own grace, but he's almost out 1.02. 28 P
most worshipful lord, and't please your grace, i 2.01. 70 P
this is the right fencing grace, my lord, tap 2.01.193 P
god save your grace! 2.02. 73 P
and swears with a good grace, and wears his 2.04.248 P
o, the lord preserve thy grace! 2.04.291 P
what says your grace? 2.04.349 P
his grace says that which his flesh rebels 2.04.350 P
please it your grace | to go to bed. 3.01. 98
gaultree forest, and't shall please your grace. 4.01. 2
unto your grace do i in chief address | the 4.01. 31
of the speech of peace that bears such grace, 4.01. 48
to tell you from his grace | that he will give 4.01.140
to meet his grace just distance 'tween our 4.01.224
your grace of york, in god's name then set 4.01.225
before, and greet his grace. 4.01.226
opener and intelligencer | between the grace, 4.02. 21
/employ the countenance and grace of heav'n, 4.02. 24
i sent your grace | the parcels and particulars 4.02. 35
pleaseth your grace to answer them directly 4.02. 52
word, | and thereupon i drink unto your grace. 4.02. 68
i pledge your grace, and, if you knew what pains 4.02. 73
and i beseech your grace let it be book'd with 4.03. 46 P
nor lose the good advantage of his grace | by 4.04. 28
by which his grace must mete the lives of other, 4.04. 77
will't please your grace to go along with us? 4.05. 19
though no man be assur'd what grace to find, 5.02. 30
shallow, i will make the king do you grace. 5.05. 6 P
god save thy grace, king hal! my royal hal! 5.05. 41
make less thy body (hence) and more thy grace, 5.05. 52
the king is full of grace and fair regard. H5 1.01. 22
which is a wonder how his grace should glean it, 1.01. 53
which i have open'd to his grace at large, | as 1.01. 78
as i perceiv'd his grace would fain have done, 1.01. 85
they know your grace hath cause, and means, and 1.02.125
unto whose grace our passion is as subject | as 1.02.242
we will in france, by god's grace, play a set 1.02.262
and by their hands this grace of kings must die, 2.pr. 28
god, his grace is bold to trust these traitors. 2.02. 1
with hope | to do your grace incessant services. 2.02. 38
question your grace the late embassadors, | with 2.04. 31
whiles yet the cool and temperate wind of grace 3.03. 30
doute point d'apprendre, par la grace de dieu, 3.04. 40 P
saying our grace is only in our heels, | and 3.05. 34
to grace himself at his return into london under 3.06. 68 P
shall i attend your grace? 4.01. 29
as long as it pleases his grace, and his majesty 4.07.109 P
it is necessary, look your grace, that he keep 4.07.139 P
your grace doo's me as great honors as can be 4.07.160 P
and please god of his grace that i might see. 4.07.164 P
that, look your grace, has strook the glove 4.08. 26 P
pleaseth your grace | to appoint some of your 5.02. 78
oui, vraiment, sauf votre grace, ainsi dit–il. 5.02.112 P
a base wallon, to win the dolphin's grace, 1H6 1.01.137
town, | something i must do to procure me grace. 1.04. 7
one eye thou hast to look to heaven for grace; 1.04. 83
i muse we met not with the dolphin's grace, 2.02. 19
we grace the yeoman by conversing with him. 2.04. 81
is not his grace protector to the king? 3.01. 60
lord, we know your grace to be a man | just and 3.01. 94
and if your grace mark every circumstance, | you 3.01.152
your grace may starve, perhaps, before that time 3.02. 48
got | first to my god and next unto your grace. 3.04. 12
writ to your grace from th' duke of burgundy. 4.01. 12
what means his grace, that he hath chang'd his 4.01. 50
we institute your grace | to be our regent in 4.01.162
and york as fast upon your grace exclaims, 4.04. 30
how doth your grace affect their motion? 5.01. 7
proffers his only daughter to your grace | in 5.01. 19
a goodly prize, fit for the devil's grace! 5.03. 33
what answer makes your grace unto my suit? 5.03.150
your grace shall well and quietly enjoy. 5.03.159
from above, | by inspiration of celestial grace, 5.04. 40
because you want the grace that others have, 5.04. 46
not whom we will, but whom his grace affects, 5.05. 57
to marry princess margaret for your grace; 2H6 1.01. 4
her sight did ravish, but her grace in speech, 1.01. 32
my lord protector, so it please your grace, 1.01. 39
we here discharge your grace from being regent 1.01. 66
what say'st thou? majesty? i am but grace. 1.02. 71
but, by the grace of god and hume's advice, 1.02. 72
as by your grace shall be propounded him. 1.02. 81
mine is, and't please your grace, against john 1.03. 16 P
under the wings of our protector's grace, 1.03. 38
whether your grace be worthy, yea or no, 1.03.107
what needs your grace | to be protector of his 1.03.118
your grace shall give me leave, my lord of york, 1.04. 76
were it not good your grace could fly to heaven? 2.01. 17
born blind, and't please your grace. 2.01. 75
at berwick in the north, and't like your grace. 2.01. 81
yes, my lord, if it please your grace. 2.01.135
as more at large your grace shall understand. 2.01.173
so please your grace, we'll take her from the 2.04. 17
i summon your grace to his majesty's parliament, 2.04. 70
and't please your grace, here my commission 2.04. 76
am i given in charge, may't please your grace. 2.04. 80
'twill make them cool in zeal unto your grace. 3.01.177
say we intend to try his grace to–day, | if he 3.02. 16
what answer makes your grace to the rebels' 4.04. 7 P
and calls your grace usurper, openly, | and vows 4.04. 30
please it your grace to be advertised | the duke 4.09. 23
king, | seditious to his grace and to the state. 5.01. 37
lo, i present your grace a traitor's head, | the 5.01. 66
and not to grace an aweful princely sceptre. 5.01. 98
obey, audacious traitor, kneel for grace. 5.01.108
and in my conscience do repute his grace | the 5.01.177
but is your grace dead, my lord of somerset? 3H6 1.01. 18
and kneel for grace and mercy at my feet: 1.01. 75
victory /from the field | i'll see your grace; 1.01.262
about that which concerns your grace and us: 1.02. 8
no; god forbid your grace should be forsworn. 1.02. 18
what would your grace have done unto him now? 1.04. 65
now, perjur'd henry, wilt thou kneel for grace, 2.02. 81
clifford, ask mercy and obtain no grace. 2.06. 69
why then i will do what your grace commands. 3.02. 49
'twill grieve your grace my sons should call you 3.02.100
and yet methinks your grace hath not done well 4.01. 51
your grace hath still been fam'd for virtuous, 4.06. 26
yet in this one thing let me blame your grace, 4.06. 30
"edward the fourth, by the grace of god, king of 4.07. 71 P
no, exeter, these graces challenge grace; 4.08. 48
what will your grace have done with margaret? 5.07. 37
this armed guard | that waits upon your grace? R3 1.01. 43
i do beseech your grace to pardon me, and withal 1.01.103
and cheer his grace with quick and merry eyes. 1.03. 5
good time of day unto your royal grace! 1.03. 18
madam, good hope, his grace speaks cheerfully. 1.03. 34
they love his grace but lightly | that fill his 1.03. 45
to who in all this presence speaks your grace? 1.03. 54
to thee, that hast nor honesty nor grace: 1.03. 55
his royal grace | (whom god preserve better than 1.03. 58
and for your grace, and yours, my gracious lord. 1.03.320
we wait upon your grace. 1.03.322
why looks your grace so heavily to–day? 1.04. 1
i will, my lord. god give your grace good rest! 1.04. 75
buckingham doth turn his hate | upon your grace, 2.01. 33
to take our brother clarence to your grace. 2.01. 77
of you | had so much grace to put it in my mind. 2.01.121
we wait upon your grace. 2.01.141
i do cry you mercy, | i did not see your grace. 2.02.105
i marvel that her grace did leave it out. 2.02.111
no, no, by god's good grace his son shall reign. 2.03. 10
king | had virtuous uncles to protect his grace. 2.03. 21
"small herbs have grace, great weeds do grow 2.04. 13
i could have given my uncle's grace a flout, 2.04. 24
i'll resign unto your grace | the seal i keep, 2.04. 70
your grace attended to their sug'red words, 3.01. 13
god bless your grace with health and happy days! 3.01. 18
would fain have come with me to meet your grace, 3.01. 29
will your grace | persuade the queen to send the 3.01. 32
it is too heavy for your grace to wear. 3.01.120
uncle, your grace knows how to bear with him. 3.01.127
your grace, we think, should soonest know his 3.04. 9
i thank his grace, i know he loves me well; 3.04. 14
his grace looks cheerfully and smooth this 3.04. 48
the tender love i bear your grace, my lord, 3.04. 63

and i myself secure, in grace and favor. 3.04. 91
o momentary grace of mortal men, | which we more 3.04. 96
which we more hunt for than the grace of god! 3.04. 97
offices | at any time to grace my stratagems. 3.05. 11
he doth entreat your grace, my noble lord, | to 3.07. 59
are come to have some conference with his grace. 3.07. 69
take on his grace the sovereignty thereof, | but 3.07. 79
marry, god defend his grace should say us nay! 3.07. 81
now, catesby, what says his grace? 3.07. 83
his grace not being warn'd thereof before: 3.07. 86
and so once more return and tell his grace. 3.07. 91
see where his grace stands, 'tween two clergymen 3.07. 95
i do beseech your grace to pardon me, | who, 3.07.105
would it might please your grace, | on our 3.07.114
in this just cause come i to move your grace. 3.07.140
my lord, this argues conscience in your grace, 3.07.174
god bless your grace! we see it and will say it. 3.07.237
to-morrow then we will attend your grace, | and 3.07.244
and i'll salute your grace of york as mother 4.01. 29
be of good cheer. mother, how fares your grace? 4.01. 37
your grace may do your pleasure. 4.02. 21
that call'd your grace | to breakfast once, 4.04.176
true — when avoided grace makes destiny: 4.04.219
if grace had blest thee with a fairer life. 4.04.221
what from your grace i shall deliver to him. 4.04.448
i'll muster up my friends and meet your grace 4.04.488
have i pluck'd off to grace thy brows withal. 5.05. 6
i thank your grace: H8 1.01. 2
whose grace | chalks successors their way, nor 1.01. 59
like it your grace, | the state takes notice of 1.01.100
ay, please your grace. 1.01.117
every shire, | of the king's grace and pardon. 1.02.104
a general welcome from his grace | salutes ye 1.04. 1
his grace is ent'ring. 1.04. 21
your grace is noble. 1.04. 38
i told your grace they would talk anon. 1.04. 49
thus they pray'd | to tell your grace, that, 1.04. 66
they have done my poor house grace; 1.04. 73
your grace? 1.04. 77
which they would have your grace | find out, and 1.04. 83
i am glad | your grace is grown so pleasant. 1.04. 90
an't please your grace, sir thomas bullen's 1.04. 92
your grace, | i fear, with dancing is a little 1.04. 99
i do beseech your grace, for charity, | if ever 2.01. 79
commend me to his grace; 2.01. 86
to th' water side i must conduct your grace; 2.01. 95
i would your grace would give us but an hour 2.02. 79
your grace has given a president of wisdom 2.02. 85
your grace must needs deserve all strangers' 2.02.101
but to be commanded | for ever by your grace, 2.02.119
annual support, | out of his grace he adds. 2.03. 65
put me off, | and take your good grace from me? 2.04. 22
his grace | hath spoken well and justly; 2.04. 64
and't please your grace, the two great cardinals 3.01. 16
zeal and obedience he still bore your grace, 3.01. 63
i would your grace | would leave your griefs, 3.01. 91
if your grace | could but be brought to know our 3.01.153
let his grace go forward, | and dare us with his 3.02.281
how does your grace? 3.02.376
king has cur'd me, | i humbly thank his grace; 3.02.381
i am glad your grace has made that right use of 3.02.386
while her grace sate down | to rest a while, 4.01. 65
at length her grace rose, and with modest paces 4.01. 82
how does your grace? 4.02. 1
but i /think your grace, | out of the pain you 4.02. 7
how much her grace is alter'd on the sudden? 4.02. 96
and't like your grace — 4.02.100
first, mine own service to your grace, the next, 4.02.115
that his noble grace would have some pity | upon 4.02.139
of his great grace | and princely care 5.01. 48
your grace must wait till you be call'd for. 5.02. 7
i'll show your grace the strangest sight — 5.02. 20
the high promotion of his grace of canterbury, 5.02. 23
chief cause concerns his grace of canterbury. 5.02. 38
your grace may enter now. 5.02. 42
may it please your grace — 5.02.169
may it like your grace | to let my tongue excuse 5.02.183
and to your royal grace and the good queen, | my 5.04. 4
had i a sister were a grace, or a daughter a TRO 1.02.236 P
shapes, | severals and generals of grace exact, 1.03.180
you are in the state of grace? 3.01. 15 P
grace? 3.01. 16 P
but i can tell that in each grace of these 4.04. 89
your soldiers use him as the grace 'fore meat, COR 4.07. 3
to grace him only | that thought he could do 5.03. 15
rather to show a noble grace to both parts 5.03.121
thou think | i'll grace thee with that robbery, 5.06. 88
match | i hold me highly honored of your grace, TIT 1.01.245
only thus much i give your grace to know: 1.01.413
kneel in the streets and beg for grace in vain. 1.01.455
the tribune and his nephews kneel for grace, | i 1.01.480
horn and hound we'll give your grace bon jour. 1.01.494
to serve, and to deserve my mistress' grace, 2.01. 34
i promised your grace a hunter's peal. 2.02. 13
no grace? 2.03.182
let fools do good, and fair men call for grace, 3.01.204
deliver an oration to the emperor with a grace? 4.03. 99 P
sir, i could never say grace in all my life. 4.03.100 P
can you with a grace deliver up a supplication? 4.03.106 P
no, not a word, how can i grace my talk, 5.02. 17
villains, for shame you could not beg for grace. 5.02.179
god mark thee to his grace! ROM 1.03. 59
o, mickle is the powerful grace that lies | in 2.03. 15
in man as well as herbs, grace and rude will; 2.03. 28
doth grace for grace and love for love allow; 2.03. 86
doth grace for grace and love for love allow; 2.03. 86
how this grace | speaks his own standing! TIM 1.01. 30
her, | whose present grace to present slaves and 1.01. 71
you have done our pleasures much grace, fair 1.02.146
e'en so thou outrun'st grace. 2.02. 88 P
base | to sue and be denied such common grace. 3.05. 94
to grace in captive bonds his chariot-wheels? JC 1.01. 34
and we will grace his heels | with the most 3.01.120
do grace to caesar's corpse, and grace his 3.02. 57
and grace his speech | tending to caesar's 3.02. 57
my noble partner | you greet with present grace, MAC 1.03. 55
renown and grace is dead, | the wine of life is 2.03. 94
highness | to grace us with your royal company? 3.04. 44
and bear | his hopes 'bove wisdom, grace, and 3.05. 31
of the most pious edward with such grace | that 3.06. 27
all things foul would wear the brows of grace, 4.03. 23
brows of grace, | yet grace must still look so. 4.03. 24
about his throne | that speak him full of grace. 4.03.159
that calls upon us, by the grace of grace, | we 5.09. 38
that calls upon us, by the grace of grace, | we 5.09. 38
that may to thee do ease, and grace to me, HAM 1.01.131
sits smiling to my heart, in grace whereof, | no 1.02.124
a double blessing is a double grace, | occasion 1.03. 53
his virtues else, be they as pure as grace, | as 1.04. 33
angels and ministers of grace defend us! 1.04. 39
so grace and mercy at your most need help you. 1.05.180
thyself do grace to them, and bring them in. 2.02. 53
and that your grace hath screen'd and stood 3.04. 3
act | that blurs the grace and blush of modesty, 3.04. 41
see what a grace was seated on this brow: 3.04. 55
mother, for love of grace, | lay not that 3.04.144
conscience and grace, to the profoundest pit! 4.05.133
we may call it herb of grace a' sundays. 4.05.182 P
your grace has laid the odds a' th' weaker side. 5.02.261
no less than life, with grace, health, beauty, LR 1.01. 58
and nothing more, may fitly like your grace, 1.01.200
that hath depriv'd me of your grace and favor, 1.01.229
without our grace, our love, our benison. 1.01.265
him, | but yet, alas, stood i within his grace, 1.01.273
"fools had ne'er less grace in a year, | for 1.04.166
for him i thank your grace. 2.01.117
against the grace and person of my master, 2.02.131
let me beseech your grace not to do so. 2.02.140
hail to your grace! 2.04.127
dwells in the /fickle grace of her he follows. 2.04.186
what means your grace? 2.04.187
marry, here's grace and a codpiece — that's a 3.02. 40 P
and cry | these dreadful summoners grace. 3.02. 59
how fares your grace? 3.04.125
what, hath your grace no better company? 3.04.142
i do beseech your grace — 3.04.171
if e'er your grace had speech with man so poor, 5.01. 38
grace go with you, sir! 5.02. 4
that's as we list to grace him. 5.03. 61
in his own grace he doth exalt himself, | more 5.03. 67
good your grace, pardon me: OTH 1.03. 52
humbly i thank your grace. 1.03. 70
and therefore little shall i grace my cause | in 1.03. 88
please it your grace, on to the state affairs. 1.03.190
so please your grace, my ancient; 1.03.283
what else needful your good grace shall think 1.03.286
and the grace of heaven, | before, behind thee, 2.01. 85
if i have any grace or power to move you, | his 3.03. 46
o grace! 3.03.373
unpin me — have grace and favor /in /them. 4.03. 21
and though we have some grace, | yet have we 4.03. 92
crime | unreconcil'd as yet to heaven and grace, 5.02. 27
me have thy hand | further this act of grace; ANT 2.02.146
for her heirs, | now hazarded to thy grace. 3.12. 19
give me grace to lay | my duty on your hand. 3.13. 81
grace grow where those drops fall, my hearty 4.02. 38
sharp fate | to grace it with your sorrows. 4.14.136
who is so full of grace that it flows over | on 5.02. 24
for kindness | where he for grace is kneel'd to. 5.02. 28
another antony | in her strong toil of grace. 5.02.348
past grace? obedience? CYM 1.01.136
past hope, and in despair, that way past grace. 1.01.137
but i beseech your grace, without offense | (my 1.05. 6
t' entreat your grace but in a small request, 1.06.181
on purpose and on promise | to see your grace. 1.06.203
madam, all joy befall your grace, and you! 3.05. 9
nature hath meal and bran, contempt and grace. 4.02. 27
can find him, if | our grace can make him so. 5.05. 7
boy, | thou hast look'd thyself into my grace, 5.05. 94
or, by our greatness and the grace of it 5.05.132
of face | as heaven had lent her all his grace; PER 1.ch. 24
your grace is welcome to our town and us. 1.04.106
marshal, the rest, as they deserve their grace. 2.03. 19
we thank your grace. 2.03. 52
he thanks your grace; 2.03. 86
but think | your grace, that fed my country with 3.03. 18
we'll bring your grace e'en to the edge a' th' 3.03. 35
on whose grace | you may depend hereafter. 3.03. 40
who hath gain'd | of education all the grace, 4.ch. 9
to grace thy marriage-day, i'll beautify. 5.03. 76
humane grace | affords them dust and shadow. TNK 1.01.144
to speak, before thy noble grace, this tenner; 3.05.123
your petition of grace and acceptance into her 4.03. 89 P
take to thy grace | me thy vow'd soldier, who do 5.01. 94
he look'd all grace and success, and he is 5.03. 69
to arcite gave | the grace of the contention. 5.04.108
and give grace unto | the funeral of arcite, in 5.04.125
and calls it heavenly moisture, air of grace, VEN 64
mixed, | which to her oratory adds more grace. LUC 564
flesh being proud, desire doth fight with grace, 712
sighs and groans and tears may grace the fashion 1319
grace and majesty | you might behold triumphing 1387
thy grace being gain'd cures all disgrace in me. PP 3. 8
a lily pale, with damask dye to grace her, 7. 5
truth, and rarity, | grace in all simplicity, PHT 54
yet eyes this cunning want to grace their art, SON 24.13
and dost him grace when clouds do blot the 28.10
lascivious grace, in whom all ill well shows, 40.13
in all external grace you have some part, | but 53.13
he live, | and with his presence grace impiety, 67. 2
wing, | and given grace a double majesty. 78. 8
aid, | my verse alone had all thy gentle grace, 79. 2
some say thy grace is youth and gentle sport; 96. 2
both grace and faults are lov'd of more and less 96. 3
to mourn for me, since mourning doth thee grace, 132.11
swear that brightness doth not grace the day? 150. 4
a youthful suit — it was to gain my grace — LC 79
his real habitude gave life and grace | to 114
yet their purpos'd trim | piec'd not his grace, 119
/nun, | who, disciplin'd, ay, dieted in grace, 261
o, how the channel to the stream gave grace! 285
"thus merely with the garment of a grace, | the 316

GRACED 3 FR 0.0003 REL FR 3 V 0 P
well-belov'd | and daily graced by the emperor; TGV 1.03. 58
her virtues, graced with external gifts, | do 1H6 5.05. 3
and arts with thy sweet graces graced be; SON 78.12

GRACEFUL 6 FR 0.0006 REL FR 5 V 1 P
a fine, quaint, graceful, and excellent fashion, ADO 3.04. 22 P
a graceful gentleman, against whose person | (so WT 5.01.171
human powers, | and gave him graceful posture. COR 2.01.221
could not with graceful eyes attend those wars ANT 2.02. 60
with such a graceful courtesy delivered? PER 2.02. 41
this so darks | in philoten all graceful marks, 4.ch. 36

GRACELESS 6 FR 0.0006 REL FR 6 V 0 P
her | will not so graceless be to be ingrate. SHR 1.02.268
and graceless traitor to her loving lord? 5.02.160
work, | the graceless action of a heavy hand — JN 4.03. 58
graceless, wilt thou deny thy parentage? 1H6 5.04. 14
o graceless men! they know not what they do. 2H6 4.04. 38
thus, graceless, holds he disputation | 'tween LUC 246

GRACE'S 22 FR 0.0024 REL FR 15 V 7 P
always obedient to your grace's will, | i come MM 1.01. 25
now that is your grace's part. ADO 1.01.212 P
i cry you mercy, uncle. by your grace's pardon. 2.01.339 P
his own person, for i am his grace's farborough; LLL 1.01.184 P
of punishment, by thy sweet grace's officer, 1.01.267 P
i do adore thy sweet grace's slipper. 5.02.667 P
to fill up your grace's request in my stead. MV 4.01.160 P
the well-lost life of mine on his grace's cure AWW 1.03.248
holy seems the quarrel | upon your grace's part; 3.01. 5
and exactly begg'd | your grace's pardon, and i R2 1.01.141
he heard of your grace's coming to town. 2H4 2.02. 99 P
john your son doth kiss your grace's hand. 4.04. 83
your grace's title shall be multiplied. 2H6 1.02. 73
i | in england work your grace's full content. 1.03. 67
i think i should have told your grace's tale. 3.01. 44
so might your grace's person be in danger. 4.04. 45
i'll claim that promise at your grace's hand. R3 3.01.197
your grace's words shall serve | as well as i 3.05. 62
leaving this, what is your grace's pleasure? 3.07.108
what's your grace's will? MAC 4.01.135
i am at your grace's pleasure. PER 2.03.111
it is your grace's pleasure to commend, | not my 2.05. 29

GRACES 51 FR 0.0057 REL FR 46 V 5 P
i will be king and queen — 'save our graces! TMP 3.02.107 P
i will pay thy graces | home both in word and 5.01. 70
flatter and praise, commend, extol their graces; TGV 3.01.102
heaven give thee moving graces! MM 2.02. 36
graces will appear, and there's an end. ADO 2.01.123 P
but till all graces be in one woman, one woman 2.03. 29 P
if half thy outward graces had been placed 4.01.101
grace | as nature was in making graces dear, LLL 2.01. 10
o then, what graces in my love do dwell, | that MND 1.01.206
in graces, and in qualities of breeding; MV 2.07. 33
commend | the parts and graces of the wrastler AYL 2.02. 13
of men | their graces serve them but as enemies? 2.03. 11
this roof | the enemy of all your graces lives. 2.03. 18
be fill'd | with all graces wide-enlarg'd. 3.02.143
if you will lead these graces to the grave | and TN 1.05.242
and from your sacred vials pour your graces WT 5.03.122
/and natural graces that extinguish art; 1H6 5.03.192
no, exeter, these graces challenge grace; 3H6 4.08. 48
i beseech your graces both to pardon me: R3 1.01. 84
and your good graces both have well proceeded, 3.05. 48
god give your graces both | a happy and a joyful 4.01. 5
hath into monstrous habits put the graces | that H8 1.02.122
good day to both your graces. 2.02. 13
pray their graces | to come near. 3.01. 18
your graces find me here part of a huswife | (i 3.01. 24
last fit of my greatness — good your graces, 3.01. 78
inventory | of your best graces in your mind; 3.02.138
i confess your royal graces | show'r'd on me 3.02.166
for your great graces | heap'd upon me, poor 3.02.174
all princely graces | that mould up such a 5.04. 25
of honor, | to imitate the graces of the gods; COR 5.03.150
and shall continue our graces towards him. MAC 1.06. 30
these are portable, | with other graces weigh'd. 4.03. 90
the king-becoming graces, | as justice, verity, 4.03. 91
and thy best graces spend it at thy will! HAM 1.02. 63
convert his gyves to graces, so that my arrows, 4.07. 21
your graces are right welcome. LR 2.01.129
what means your graces? 3.07. 30
mark, and /denotement of her parts and graces. OTH 2.03.318 P
whose virtue and whose general graces speak ANT 2.02.129
which, by their graces, i will keep. CYM 1.04. 87 P
but 'tis your graces | that from my mutest 1.06.115
thus adjourn'd | the graces for his merits due, 5.04. 79
graces her subjects, and her thoughts the king PER 1.01. 13
and here the graces of our youths must wither TNK 2.02. 27
all jointly list'ning, but with several graces, LUC 1410
and in fresh numbers number all your graces, SON 17. 6
and arts with thy sweet graces graced be; 78.12
slow, | they rightly do inherit heaven's graces, 94. 5
thou mak'st faults graces that to thee resort. 96. 4
than of your graces and your gifts to tell; 103.12

GRACING 1 FR 0.0001 REL FR 1 V 0 P
gracing the scroll that tells of this war's loss JN 2.01.348

/GRACIOUS 2 FR 0.0002 REL FR 2 V 0 P
/my /gracious /liege, | you won it, wore it, 2H4 4.05.220
/a /father, /and /a /gracious /aged /man, LR 4.02. 41

GRACIOUS 195 FR 0.0220 REL FR 184 V 11 P
how fares my gracious sir? TMP 5.01.253
my gracious lord, that which i would discover TGV 3.01. 4
but when i call to mind your gracious favors 3.01. 6
why, that word makes the faults gracious. 3.01.368 P
hath made him that gracious denial which he is MM 3.01.165 P
do no stain to your own gracious person; 3.01.202 P
i am a brother | of gracious order, late come 3.02.219
good morning to you, fair and gracious daughter. 4.03.112
o gracious duke, | harp not on that; 5.01. 63
to try her gracious fortune with lord angelo, 5.01. 76
o my most gracious lord, | i hope you will not 5.01.416
therefore, most gracious duke, with thy command ERR 5.01.159
justice, most gracious duke, o, grant me justice 5.01.190
i came from corinth, my most gracious lord — 5.01.366
of harm, | and never shall it more be gracious. ADO 4.01.108
delivers in such apt and gracious words | that LLL 2.01. 73
my love (her mistress) is a gracious moon, | she 4.03.226
that is the way to make an offense gracious, 5.01.140 P
i thank you, gracious lords, | for all your fair 5.02.729
and, my gracious duke, | this man hath bewitch'd MND 1.01. 26
and, my gracious duke, | be it so she will not 1.01. 38
to make it the more gracious, i shall sing it at 4.01.218 P

for, by thy gracious, golden, glittering /gleams 5.01.274
but, being season'd with a gracious voice, MV 3.02. 76
i leave him to your gracious acceptance, whose 4.01.164 P
there is but one sham'd that was never gracious; AYL 1.02.188 P
pardon, my gracious lord; AWW 2.03.167
me, | commend the paper to his gracious hand, 5.01. 31
my gracious sovereign, | howe'er it pleases you 5.03. 87
gracious sovereign, | whether i have been to 5.03.128
and the shape of nature | a gracious person. TN 1.05.262
thou wast in very gracious fooling last night, 2.03. 22 P
gracious olivia — 5.01.105
the entreaties | of our most gracious mistress. WT 1.02.233
my gracious lord, | i may be negligent, foolish, 1.02.249
and comfort | the gracious queen, part of his 1.02.459
come, my gracious lord, | shall i be your 2.01. 2
dear gentlewoman, | how fares our gracious lady? 2.02. 19
a gracious innocent soul, | more free than he is 2.03. 29
and gracious be the issue! 3.01. 22
and foolish sire | blemish'd his gracious dam; 3.02.198
their issue not being gracious, than they are in 4.02. 27 P
sir, my gracious lord, | to chide at your 4.04. 5
the gracious mark o' th' land, you have obscur'd 4.04. 8
gracious my lord, | you know /your father's 4.04.466
which is | your gracious self, embrace but my 4.04.523
begetting wonder, as | you, gracious couple, do; 5.01.134
my gracious liege, when that my father liv'd, JN 1.01. 95
there was not such a gracious creature born. 3.04. 81
words, | remembers me of all his gracious parts, 3.04. 96
of happy days befall | my gracious sovereign, my R2 1.01. 21
'tis nothing but conceit, my gracious lady. 2.02. 33
my gracious lord, i tender you my service, 2.03. 41
from the most gracious regent of this land, 2.03. 77
my gracious uncle — 2.03. 85
my gracious uncle, let me know my fault, | on 2.03.106
nor near nor farther off, my gracious lord, 3.02. 64
that spring from one most gracious head, | and 3.03.108
with all the gracious utterance thou hast 3.03.125
my gracious lord — 3.03.189
my gracious lord, i come but for mine own. 3.03.196
this match'd with other did, my gracious lord, 1H4 1.01. 49
one of them is well known, my gracious lord, | a 2.04.510
i come with gracious offers from the king, | if 4.03. 30
will, | for he is gracious if he be observ'd, 2H4 4.04. 30
my gracious lord, you look beyond him quite: 4.04. 67
my gracious lord! 4.05. 34
where is my gracious lord of canterbury? H5 1.02. 1
then hear me, gracious sovereign, and you peers, 1.02. 33
gracious lord, | stand for your own, unwind your 1.02.100
they of those marches, gracious sovereign, 1.02.140
hath dull'd and cloy'd with gracious favors — 2.02. 9
were now the general of our gracious empress, 5.pr. 30
of this good day and of this gracious meeting, 5.02. 13
our gracious brother, i will go with them. 5.02. 92
my gracious lords, to add to your laments, 1H6 1.01.103
heaven and our lady gracious hath it pleas'd 1.02. 74
mean time look gracious on thy prostrate thrall. 1.02.117
heaven, be thou gracious to none alive, | if 1.04. 85
accept this scroll, most gracious sovereign, 3.01.148
my gracious prince, and honorable peers, 3.04. 1
my gracious sovereign, as i rode from callice, 4.01. 9
grant me the combat, gracious sovereign. 4.01. 78
royal name, | as deputy unto that gracious king, 5.03.161
in the queen | to your most gracious hands, that 2H6 1.01. 13
great king of england, and my gracious lord, 1.01. 24
pardon me, gracious lord, | some sudden qualm 1.01. 53
all health unto my gracious sovereign! 3.01. 82
ah, gracious lord, these days are dangerous: 3.01.142
how fares my gracious lord? 3.02. 37
comfort, my sovereign! gracious henry, comfort! 3.02. 38
come hither, gracious sovereign, view this body. 3.02.149
my gracious lord, entreat him, speak him fair. 4.01.120
my gracious lord, retire to killingworth, 4.04. 39
my gracious lord, here in the parliament | let 3H6 1.01. 64
farewell, my gracious lord, i'll to my castle. 1.01.206
open thy gate of mercy, gracious god! 1.04.177
who crown'd the gracious duke in high despite, 2.01. 59
my gracious liege, this too much lenity | and 2.02. 9
my gracious father, by your kingly leave, | i'll 2.02. 63
right gracious lord, i cannot brook delay. 3.02. 18
three, my most gracious lord. 3.02. 29
no, gracious lord, except i cannot do it. 3.02. 47
'tis better said than done, my gracious lord. 3.02. 90
my gracious lord, henry your foe is taken, | and 3.02.118
those gracious words revive my drooping thoughts 3.03. 21
and, gracious madam, in our king's behalf | i am 3.03. 59
but is he gracious in the people's eye? 3.03.117
ay, gracious sovereign, they are so link'd in 4.01.116
yet, gracious madam, bear it as you may: 4.04. 14
good time of day unto my gracious lord! R3 1.01.122
may | but beg one favor at thy gracious hand, 1.02.207
nothing that i respect, my gracious lord. 1.03.295
and for your grace, and yours, my gracious lord. 1.03.320
if his rule were true, he should be gracious. 2.04. 20
and no doubt he is, my gracious madam. 2.04. 21
is all unknown to me, my gracious lord. 2.04. 48
my gracious lady, go, | and thither bear your 2.04. 68
he did, my gracious lord, begin that place, 3.01. 70
upon record, my gracious lord. 3.01. 74
what, my gracious lord? 3.01. 90
god keep your lordship in that gracious mind! 3.02. 56
'tis a vile thing to die, my gracious lord, 3.02. 62
his gracious pleasure any way therein. 3.04. 17
return, good catesby, to the gracious duke, 3.07. 65
famous plantagenet, most gracious prince, | lend 3.07.100
your gracious self to take on you the charge 3.07.131
my gracious sovereign? 4.02. 2
prove me, my gracious lord. 4.02. 68
virtuous and fair, royal and gracious. 4.04.205
my gracious sovereign, now in devonshire, | as i 4.04.498
here, most gracious liege. 5.03. 4
myself, | look on my forces with a gracious eye; 5.03.109
abate the edge of traitors, gracious lord, 5.05. 35
a gracious king that pardons all offenses H8 2.02. 67
i do beseech | you, gracious madam, to unthink 2.04.104
most gracious sir, | in humblest manner i 2.04.144
protection, | he's loving and most gracious. 3.01. 94
my good and gracious lord of canterbury. 5.01. 92
in this most gracious lady | heaven ever laid up 5.04. 6

honors all engag'd | to make it gracious. TRO 2.02.125
my gracious silence, hail! COR 2.01.175
so his gracious nature | would think upon you 2.03.187
from him pluck'd | either his gracious promise, 2.03.193
son, | were gracious in the eyes of royal rome, TIT 1.01. 11
gracious lavinia, rome's rich ornament, | that i 1.01. 52
rome, be as just and gracious unto me | as i am 1.01. 60
stand gracious to the rites that we intend! 1.01. 78
gracious conqueror, | victorious titus, rue the 1.01.104
gracious triumpher in the eyes of rome! 1.01.170
were gracious in those princely eyes of thine, 1.01.429
of a year or two | makes me less gracious, or 2.01. 32
how now, dear sovereign and our gracious mother? 2.03. 89
my gracious lord, here is the bag of gold. 2.03.280
my gracious lord, no tribune hears you speak. 3.01. 32
o gracious emperor! 3.01.157
my gracious lord, my lovely saturnine, | lord of 4.04. 27
then, gracious auditory, be it known to you 5.03. 96
lucius, all hail, rome's gracious governor! 5.03.146
or, if thou wilt, swear by thy gracious self, ROM 2.02.113
upon his good and gracious nature hanging, TIM 1.01. 56
these are gracious drops. JC 3.02.194
for them the gracious duncan have i murther'd, MAC 3.01. 65
the gracious duncan | was pitied of macbeth; 3.06. 3
for donalbain | to kill their gracious father? 3.06. 10
and here from gracious england have i offer | of 4.03. 43
gracious england hath | lent us good siward, and 4.03.189
what's your gracious pleasure? 5.03. 30
gracious my lord, | i should report that which i 5.05. 29
so hallowed, and so gracious is that time. HAM 1.01.164
and bow them to your gracious leave and pardon. 1.02. 56
soul, | both to my god and to my gracious king. 2.02. 45
gracious, so please you, | we will bestow 3.01. 42
what would your gracious figure? 3.04.104
thy state is the more gracious, for 'tis a vice 5.02. 84 P
gracious my lord, hard by here is a hovel, LR 3.02. 61
the ottomites, reverend and gracious, | steering OTH 1.03. 33
yet (by your gracious patience) | i will a round 1.03. 89
most gracious duke, | to my unfolding lend your 1.03.243
yes, gracious madam. ANT 1.05. 13
by your most gracious pardon, | i sing but after 1.05. 72
gracious madam, | i that do bring the news made 2.05. 66
give to a gracious message | an host of tongues, 2.05. 86
most gracious majesty! 3.03. 7
to your majesty, and to my gracious mother! CYM 2.03. 36 P
o gracious lady! 3.04. 98
but, gracious sir, | here are your sons again, 5.05.347
did relieve me | to see this gracious season. 5.05.401
o, seek not to entrap me, gracious lord, | a PER 2.05. 45
i hope she's pleas'd, | her signs were gracious. TNK 5.01.173
lo in the orient when the gracious light | lifts SON 7. 1
be as thy presence is gracious and kind, | or to 10.11
methinks no face so gracious is as mine, | no 62. 5
but now my gracious numbers are decay'd, | and 79. 3
shall will in others seem right gracious, | and 135. 7

GRACIOUSLY 6 FR 0.0006 REL FR 5 V 1 P
good, | but graciously to know i am no better. MM 2.04. 77
since god so graciously hath brought to light H5 2.02.185
son | did graciously plead for his funerals; TIT 1.01.381
then at my suit look graciously on him; 1.01.439
what he will do graciously, i will thankfully PER 4.06. 60 P
points on me graciously with fair aspect, | and SON 26.10

GRADATION 2 FR 0.0002 REL FR 2 V 0 P
by cold gradation and weal–balanc'd form, | we MM 4.03.100
and not by old gradation, where each second OTH 1.01. 37

GRAFF 4 FR 0.0004 REL FR 2 V 2 P
i'll graff it with you, and then i shall graff AYL 3.02.117 P
you, and then i shall graff it with a medlar. 3.02.117 P
god | for every graff would send a caterpillar, PER 5.01. 60
this bastard graff shall never come to growth. LUC 1062

GRAFFING 1 FR 0.0001 REL FR 0 V 1 P
eat a last year's pippin of mine own graffing, 2H4 5.03. 3 P

GRAFT 2 FR 0.0002 REL FR 2 V 0 P
and noble stock | was graft with crab–tree slip, 2H6 3.02.214
/her royal stock graft with ignoble plants, R3 3.07.127

GRAFTED 5 FR 0.0005 REL FR 5 V 0 P
he scatter'd not in ears, but grafted them, | to AWW 1.02. 54
counted | a servant grafted in my serious trust WT 1.02.246
as thou art match'd withal and grafted to, 1H4 3.02. 15
home that will not | be grafted to your relish. COR 2.01.189
all the particulars of vice so grafted | that, MAC 4.03. 51

GRAFTERS 1 FR 0.0001 REL FR 1 V 0 P
into the clouds | and overlook their grafters? H5 3.05. 9

GRAFT'ST 1 FR 0.0001 REL FR 1 V 0 P
god the plants thou graft'st may never grow. R2 3.04.101

/GRAIN 1 FR 0.0001 REL FR 1 V 0 P
knows almost every /grain /of /pluto's /gold, TRO 3.03.197

GRAIN 17 FR 0.0019 REL FR 14 V 3 P
sir, 'tis in grain, noah's flood could not do it ERR 3.02.106 P
'tis in grain, sir, 'twill endure wind and TN 1.05.237 P
there's not a grain of it the face to sweeten WT 2.01.156
a grain, a dust, a gnat, a wandering hair, | any JN 4.01. 92
now he weighs time | even to the utmost grain; H5 2.04.138
in july when | we see each grain of gravel, i do H8 1.01.155
infects the sound pine and diverts his grain TRO 1.03. 8
and their store–houses cramm'd with grain; COR 1.01. 81 P
they say there's grain enough? 1.01.196
made you against the grain | to voice him consul 2.03.233
pent to linger | but with a grain a day, i would 3.03. 90
for one poor grain or two, to leave unburnt 5.01. 27
for one poor grain or two? 5.01. 28
and say which grain will grow, and which will MAC 1.03. 59
his pernicious soul | rot half a grain a day! OTH 5.02.156
upon the slime and ooze scatters his grain, ANT 2.07. 22
a grain of honor | they not o'erweigh us. TNK 5.04. 18

/GRAINED* 1 FR 0.0001 REL FR 1 V 0 P
and there i see such black and /grained spots HAM 3.04. 90

GRAINED* 3 FR 0.0003 REL FR 3 V 0 P
though now this grained face of mine be hid | in ERR 5.01.312
my grained ash an hundred times hath broke, COR 4.05.108
so slides he down upon his grained bat, | and LC 64

GRAINS 3 FR 0.0003 REL FR 2 V 1 P
for thou exists on many a thousand grains | that MM 3.01. 20
reasons are as two grains of wheat hid in two MV 1.01.116 P
we are the grains, | you are the musty chaff, COR 5.01. 30

GRAMERCIES 3 FR 0.0003 REL FR 2 V 1 P
gramercies, tranio, well dost thou advise. SHR 1.01. 41
gramercies, lad. 1.01.163

gramercies, good fool; how does your mistress? TIM 2.02. 67 P

GRAMERCY 5 FR 0.0005 REL FR 3 V 2 P
gramercy! wouldst thou aught with me? MV 2.02.121 P
gramercy, fellow. there, drink that for me. R3 3.02.106
be it so, titus, and gramercy too. TIT 1.01.495
gramercy, lovely lucius. what's the news? 4.02. 7
good! gramercy. TIM 2.02. 71 P

GRAMMAR 2 FR 0.0002 REL FR 1 V 1 P
youth of the realm in erecting a grammar school; 2H6 4.07. 33 P
it well, | i read it in the grammar long ago. TIT 4.02. 23

GRAND 14 FR 0.0015 REL FR 11 V 3 P
refusing her grand hests, she did confine thee, TMP 1.02.274
find this grand liquor that hath gilded 'em? 5.01.280
me dat you make grand preparation for a duke de WIV 4.05. 87 P
to saint jaques le grand. AWW 3.05. 34
is a pilgrimage to saint jaques le grand; 4.03. 49 P
the grand conspirator, abbot of westminster, R2 5.06. 19
suivez–vous le grand capitaine. H5 4.04. 66 P
that excellent grand tyrant of the earth | that R3 4.04. 52
produce the grand sum of his sins, the articles H8 3.02.293
manners, to /unseal | their grand commission; HAM 5.02. 18
so thy grand captain, antony, | shall set thee ANT 3.01. 9
morn–dew on the myrtle leaf | to his grand sea. 3.12. 10
whilst we dispatch | this grand act of our life, TNK 1.01.164
thou grand decider | of dusty and old titles, 5.01. 63

GRANDAM 19 FR 0.0021 REL FR 15 V 4 P
like a young wench that had buried her grandam; TGV 2.01. 24 P
why, my grandam, having no eyes, look you, wept 2.03. 12 P
she might 'a' been /a grandam ere she died. LLL 5.02. 17
studied in a sad ostent | to please his grandam, MV 2.02.197
that the soul of our grandam might happily TN 4.02. 52 P
lest thou dispossess the soul of thy grandam. 4.02. 60 P
grandam, i will not wish thy wishes thrive: JN 3.01.334
at your birth | our grandam earth, having this 1H4 3.01. 33
iwis your grandam had a worser match. R3 1.03.101
good grandam, tell us, is our father dead? 2.02. 1
then you conclude, my grandam, he is dead. 2.02. 12
grandam, we can; 2.02. 20
think you my uncle did dissemble, grandam? 2.02. 31
grandam, one night as we did sit at supper, | my 2.04. 10
grandam, this would have been a biting jest. 2.04. 30
grandam, his nurse. 2.04. 32
my grandam told me he was murd'red there. 3.01.145
him that my lady | was fairer than his grandam, TRO 1.03.299
at a winter's fire, | authoriz'd by her grandam. MAC 3.04. 65

GRANDAME 9 FR 0.0010 REL FR 9 V 0 P
i am thy grandame, richard, call me so. JN 1.01.168
there's a good grandame, boy, that would blot 2.01.133
come to thy grandame, child. 2.01.159
do, child, go to it grandame, child, | give 2.01.160
give grandame kingdom, and it grandame will 2.01.161
kingdom, and it grandame will | give it a plum, 2.01.161
there's a good grandame. 2.01.163
thy grandame loves thee, and thy uncle will | as 3.03. 3
grandame, i will pray | (if ever i remember to 3.03. 14

GRANDAME'S 1 FR 0.0001 REL FR 1 V 0 P
his grandame's wrongs, and not his mother's JN 2.01.168

GRANDAM'S 2 FR 0.0002 REL FR 2 V 0 P
a woman's will, a cank'red grandam's will! JN 2.01.194
a grandam's name is little less in love | than R3 4.04.299

GRANDCHILD 1 FR 0.0001 REL FR 1 V 0 P
and in her hand | the grandchild to her blood. COR 5.03. 24

GRANDE 1 FR 0.0001 REL FR 0 V 1 P
/je /m'en vois a la cour — la grande affaire. WIV 1.04. 52 P

/GRANDEUR 1 FR 0.0001 REL FR 0 V 1 P
vous abaissez votre /grandeur en baisant la main H5 5.02.254 P

GRANDFATHER 13 FR 0.0014 REL FR 10 V 3 P
marry, the son of my grandfather. TGV 3.01.295 P
he is cupid's grandfather, and learns news of LLL 2.01.255
was ajax, call'd so from his grandfather. SHR 3.01. 53
indeed i am not john of gaunt, your grandfather, 1H4 2.02. 67 P
your grandfather of famous memory, an't please H5 4.07. 92 P
his grandfather was lionel duke of clarence, 1H6 2.04. 83
henry the fourth, grandfather to this king, 2.05. 63
as good? | thou bastard of my grandfather! 3.01. 42
thy grandfather, roger mortimer, earl of march: 3H6 1.01.106
old, | my father and my grandfather were kings; 3.01. 77
thy famous grandfather | doth live again in thee 5.04. 52
ay, some mad message from his mad grandfather. TIT 4.02. 3
thy tailor, rascal, | who is thy grandfather! CYM 4.02. 82

GRANDFATHER'S 2 FR 0.0002 REL FR 0 V 2 P
a seal–ring of my grandfather's worth forty mark 1H4 3.03. 82 P
a–piece, and a seal–ring of my grandfather's. 3.03.102 P

GRAND–GUARD 1 FR 0.0001 REL FR 1 V 0 P
you care not for a grand–guard? TNK 3.06. 58

GRANDJURORS 1 FR 0.0001 REL FR 0 V 1 P
you are grandjurors, are ye? 1H4 2.02. 91 P

GRAND–JURYMEN 1 FR 0.0001 REL FR 0 V 1 P
they have been grand–jurymen since before noah TN 3.02. 16 P

GRANDMOTHER 4 FR 0.0004 REL FR 2 V 2 P
sin | to think but nobly of my grandmother. TMP 1.02.119
it was the son of thy grandmother. TGV 3.01.297 P
"with a child of our grandmother eve, a female; LLL 1.01.263 P
that fair queen isabel, his grandmother, | was H5 1.02. 81

GRANDPRE 3 FR 0.0003 REL FR 2 V 1 P
beaumont, grandpre, roussi, and faulconbridge, H5 3.05. 44
the lord grandpre. 3.07.128 P
grandpre and roussi, faulconbridge and foix, 4.08. 99

/GRANDSIRE 1 FR 0.0001 REL FR 1 V 0 P
/good /grandsire, /leave /these /bitter /deep TIT 3.02. 46

GRANDSIRE 23 FR 0.0026 REL FR 20 V 3 P
silver, is her grandsire upon his death's–bed WIV 1.01. 51 P
did her grandsire leave her seven hundred pound? 1.01. 58 P
sit like his grandsire cut in alablaster? MV 1.01. 84
do, good old grandsire, and withal make known SHR 4.05. 50
for that my grandsire was an englishman, JN 5.04. 42
o, had thy grandsire with a prophet's eye | seen R2 2.01.104
wherein my grandsire and my father sat? 3H6 1.01.125
"what my great–grandfather and grandsire got, 2.02. 37
that was a man | when hector's grandsire suck'd. TRO 1.03.292
i knew thy grandsire, | and once fought with him 4.05.196
help, grandsire, help! TIT 4.01. 1
for i have heard my grandsire say full oft, 4.01. 18
grandsire, 'tis ovid's metamorphosis, | my 4.01. 42
ay, with my dagger in their bosoms, grandsire. 4.01.118
my grandsire, well advis'd, hath sent by me 4.02. 10
thy grandsire lov'd thee well. 5.03.161

o grandsire, grandsire, ev'n with all my heart 5.03.172
o grandsire, grandsire, ev'n with all my heart 5.03.172
for i am proverb'd with a grandsire phrase, ROM 1.04. 37
is not this a lamentable thing, grandsire, that 2.04. 31 P
hellish pyrrhus | old grandsire priam seeks." HAM 2.02.464
or else the devil will make a grandsire of you. OTH 1.01. 91
thou hast been a grandsire and begot | a father CYM 5.04.123
/GRANDSIRE'S 1 FR 0.0001 REL FR 1 V 0 P
/weep /to /see /his /grandsire's /heaviness. TIT 3.02. 49
GRANDSIRE'S 1 FR 0.0001 REL FR 1 V 0 P
that stands upon your royal grandsire's bones, R2 3.03.106
GRANDSIRES 2 FR 0.0002 REL FR 1 V 1 P
guarded with grandsires, babies, and old women, H5 3.pr. 20
mouldy ere /your grandsires had nails /on /their TRO 2.01.105 P
GRANGE 3 FR 0.0003 REL FR 2 V 1 P
there, at the moated grange, resides this MM 3.01.264 P
or thou goest to th' grange, or mill. WT 4.04.303
my house is not a grange. OTH 1.01.106
/GRANT 1 FR 0.0001 REL FR 1 V 0 P
/you, /lords, /to /grant /the /commons' /suit? R2 4.01.154
GRANT 118 FR 0.0133 REL FR 95 V 23 P
being once perfected how to grant suits, | how TMP 1.02. 79
will you grant with me | that ferdinand is 2.01.243
i grant, sweet love, that i did love a lady; TGV 4.02.105
to grant one boon that i shall ask of you. 5.04.150
i grant it, for thine own, what e'er it be. 5.04.151
heaven grant us its peace, but not the king of MM 1.02. 4 P
i grant; 1.02. 29 P
for what obscured light the heavens did grant ERR 1.01. 66
most gracious duke, o, grant me justice, | even 5.01.190
that then i lost for thee, now grant me justice. 5.01.194
the fairest grant is the necessity. ADO 1.01.317
god grant us patience! LLL 1.01.194 P
so you grant pasture for me. 2.01.222
minute of the hour, | grant us your loves. 5.02.788
and good luck grant thee thy demetrius! MND 1.01.221
i grant you, friends, if you should fright the 1.02. 79 P
than my faint means would grant continuance. MV 1.01.125
and i pray god grant them a fair departure. 1.02.110 P
the duke shall grant me justice. 3.03. 8
duke | will never grant this forfeiture to hold. 3.03. 25
grant me two things, i pray you, | not to deny 4.01.423
and ask me what you will, i will grant it. AYL 4.01.114 P
and wooing, she should grant? 5.02. 4 P
and grant it. AWW 2.03. 77
which great love grant, and so i take my leave. 2.03. 85
heaven delights to hear | and loves to grant, 3.04. 28
grant it me, o king, in you it best lies; 5.03.145 P
good master fabian, grant me another request. TN 5.01. 2 P
well, grant it then, | and tell me, in the 5.01.334
't may — i grant. WT 1.02.114
a death to grant this. 4.02. 3 P
my father will grant precious things as trifles. 5.01.222
o, if thou grant my need, | which only lives but JN 3.01.211
i will both hear and grant you your requests. 4.02. 46
we grant thou canst outscold us. 5.02.160
ill mayst thou thrive if thou grant any grace! R2 5.03. 99
i grant ye, upon instinct. 1H4 2.04.356 P
i grant you i was down and out of breath, and so 5.04.146 P
and yet in some respects i grant i cannot go. 2H4 1.02.167 P
grant that our hopes (yet likely of fair birth) 1.03. 63
grant that, my poor virtue, grant that. 2.04. 46 P
grant that, my poor virtue, grant that. 2.04. 46 P
with grant of our most just and right desires, 4.02. 40
and grant it may with thee in true peace live! 4.05.219
i grant your worship that he is a knave, sir; 5.01. 43 P
do not, in grant of all demands at large, H5 2.04.121
grant him there; 5.pr. 7
any occasion to write for matter of grant, shall 5.02.338 P
grant me the combat, gracious sovereign. 1H6 4.01. 78
and me, my lord, grant me the combat too. 4.01. 79
pay recompense, if you will grant my suit. 5.03. 19
your highness shall do well to grant her suit; 3H6 3.02. 8
i see the lady hath a thing to grant, | before 3.02. 12
before the king will grant her humble suit. 3.02. 13
be pitiful, dread lord, and grant it then. 3.02. 32
my mind will never grant what i perceive | your 3.02. 67
if thou vouchsafe to grant | that virtuous lady 3.03. 55
heavens grant that warwick's words bewitch him 3.03.112
your grant, or your denial, shall be mine. 3.03.130
it was my will and grant, | and for this once my 4.01. 49
i grant ye. R3 1.02.101
dost grant me, hedgehog? 1.02.102
then god grant me too | thou mayst be damned for 1.02.102
reasons, i beseech you, | grant me this boon. 1.02.218
god grant him health! did you confer with him? 1.03. 35
god grant we never may have need of you! 1.03. 75
god grant that some, less noble and less loyal, 2.01. 92
and i, unjustly too, must grant it you. 2.01.126
o, make them joyful, grant their lawful suit! 3.07.203
wish'd, my lord? the gods grant — o my lord! TRO 3.02. 62 P
what should they grant? 3.02. 64 P
and cupid grant all tongue–tied maidens here 3.02.210
the gods grant them true! COR 2.01.141 P
grant that, and tell me | in peace what each of 3.02. 43
by the entreaty and grant of the whole table. 4.05.199 P
the thing i have forsworn to grant may never 5.03. 80
you have said you will not grant us any thing; 5.03. 87
they pray — grant thou, lest faith turn to ROM 1.05.104
do not move, though grant for prayers' sake. 1.05.105
grant i may never prove so fond, | to trust man TIM 1.02. 64
to kill, i grant, is sin's extremest gust, | but 3.05. 54
and grant, as timon grows, his hate may grow 4.01. 39
which the gods grant thee t' attain to! 4.03.327 P
grant i may ever love, and rather woo | those 4.03.467
and then i grant we put a sting in him | that at JC 2.01. 16
i grant i am a woman; 2.01.292
i grant i am a woman; 2.01.294
brutus hath a suit | that caesar will not grant. 2.04. 43
grant that, and then is death a benefit; 3.01.103
that business, | if you would grant the time. MAC 2.01. 24
i grant him bloody, | luxurious, avaricious, 4.03. 57
mad let us grant him then, and now remains HAM 2.02.100
the duke must grant me that. LR 2.01. 81
marry, before your ladyship, i grant, | she puts OTH 2.01.105
whereon, i do beseech thee, grant me this, | to 3.03. 84
i grant indeed it hath not appear'd; 4.02.210 P
let's grant it is not | amiss to tumble on the ANT 1.04. 16
i grieving grant | did you too much disquiet. 2.02. 69
for what i have conquer'd, | i grant him part; 3.06. 35
demands | thou mean'st to have him grant thee. 5.02. 11
and i think | he'll grant the tribute, send th' CYM 2.04. 13
home, i grant | we were to question farther; 2.04. 51
grant, heavens, that which i fear | prove false! 3.05. 52
thy words, i grant, are bigger; 4.02. 78
brain of britain, | by whom, i grant, she lives. 5.05. 15
require a little space for prayer, | i grant it. PER 4.01. 68
if you grant not | my sister her petition, in TNK 1.01.200
i grant your wish, for, to say true, your cousin 3.06.180
which if the goddess of it grant, she gives 5.01. 71
or else grant | the file and quality i hold i 5.01.160
although we grant you get the thing you seek? STM II.C 69
grant them removed and grant that this your II.C 72
them removed and grant that this your noise II.C 72
as well to hear as grant what he hath said. LUC 915
grant, if thou wilt, thou art belov'd of many, SON 10. 3
i grant, sweet love, thy lovely argument 79. 5
i grant thou wert not married to my muse, | and 82. 1
i grant i never saw a goddess go — | my 130.11
GRANTED 31 FR 0.0035 REL FR 27 V 4 P
this being granted in course — and now follows MM 3.01.249 P
but is there no quick recreation granted? LLL 1.01.161
come on, thou /art granted space. AWW 4.01. 88
it must be granted i am duke of lancaster. R2 2.03.124
and lands restor'd again be freely granted. 3.03. 41
knees, | which on thy royal party granted once, 3.03.115
written, be assur'd | will easily be granted. 1H4 1.03.264
must needs be granted to be much at one. H5 5.02.192 P
the king hath granted every article: 5.02.332
at, | and the offender granted scope of speech, 2H6 3.01.176
before i would have granted to that act. 3H6 1.01.245
her suit is granted for her husband's lands. 3.02.117
the benefit thereof is always granted | to those R3 3.01. 48
whereby his suit was granted | ere it was ask'd H8 1.01.186
which if granted | (as he made semblance of his 1.02.197
let this be granted, and achilles' horse | makes TRO 1.03.211
and a petition granted them — a strange one, COR 1.01.210
what is granted them? 1.01.214
when we granted that, | here was "i thank you 2.03.170
or granted less, aufidius? 5.03.193
that granted, how canst thou believe an oath? TIT 5.01. 72
sir, this granted (as it is a most pregnant and OTH 2.01.235 P
difficult weight, | and fearful to be granted. 3.03. 83
which soon he granted, | being an abstract ANT 3.06. 60
requires to live in egypt, which not granted, 3.12. 12
you are a fool granted, therefore your issues, CYM 2.01. 46 P
let it be granted you have seen all this (and 2.04. 92
him | and his succession granted rome a tribute, 3.01. 8
you their captives, which ourself have granted; 5.05. 73
they prevail'd, had their suits fairly granted: TNK 4.01. 27
consents bewitch'd, ere he desire, have granted, LC 131
GRANTETH 1 FR 0.0001 REL FR 1 V 0 P
but his heart granteth | no penetrable entrance LUC 558
GRANTING 4 FR 0.0004 REL FR 4 V 0 P
swear), | i am so far from granting thy request, TGV 4.02.101
you granting of my suit, | if that be sin, i'll MM 2.04. 70
fit for my modest suit and your free granting. TNK 3.06.235
for how do i hold thee but by thy granting, SON 87. 5
GRANTS 3 FR 0.0003 REL FR 3 V 0 P
that love which virtue begs and virtue grants. 3H6 3.02. 63
mean time, god grants that i have need of you. R3 1.03. 76
and his sword | grants scarce distinction. ANT 3.01. 29
/GRANT'ST 1 FR 0.0001 REL FR 1 V 0 P
then, if thou /grant'st th' art a man, i have TIM 4.03.474
GRANT'ST 1 FR 0.0001 REL FR 1 V 0 P
thou grant'st no time for charitable deeds: LUC 908
GRAPE 6 FR 0.0006 REL FR 4 V 2 P
when he had a desire to eat a grape, would open AYL 5.01. 34 P
there's one grape yet; AWW 2.03. 99 P
go, suck the subtle blood o' th' grape, | till TIM 4.03.429
the juice of egypt's grape shall moist this lip. ANT 5.02.282
his complexion | is, as a ripe grape, ruddy. TNK 4.02. 96
for one sweet grape who will the vine destroy? LUC 215
GRAPES 9 FR 0.0010 REL FR 5 V 4 P
'twas in the bunch of grapes, where indeed you MM 2.01.129 P
with purple grapes, green figs, and mulberries; MND 3.01.167
meaning thereby that grapes were made to eat and
AYL 5.01. 35 P
o, will you eat | no grapes, my royal fox? AWW 2.01. 70
but you will | my noble grapes, and if my royal 2.01. 71
the tartness of his face sours ripe grapes. COR 5.04. 18 P
the wine she drinks is made of grapes. OTH 2.01.252 P
drown'd, | with thy grapes our hairs be crown'd! ANT 2.07.116
so poor birds, deceiv'd with painted grapes, VEN 601
GRAPPLE *(also gripple)*
GRAPPLE 8 FR 0.0009 REL FR 7 V 1 P
i was as willing to grapple as he was to board. LLL 2.01.218
with which such scathful grapple did he make TN 5.01. 56
and grapple with him ere he come so nigh. JN 5.01. 61
from the north to south, | and let them grapple. 1H4 1.03.197
grapple your minds to sternage of this navy, H5 3.pr. 18
york, | to grapple with the house of lancaster; 2H6 1.01.257
grapple them unto thy soul with hoops of steel, HAM 1.03. 63
valor, and in the grapple i boarded them. 4.06. 18 P
GRAPPLES 1 FR 0.0001 REL FR 1 V 0 P
off, | grapples you to the heart and love of us, MAC 3.01.105
GRAPPLING 1 FR 0.0001 REL FR 1 V 0 P
the grappling vigor and rough frown of war | is JN 3.01.104
GRASP 3 FR 0.0003 REL FR 3 V 0 P
thy hand is made to grasp a palmer's staff | and 2H6 5.01. 97
the whole space that's in the tyrant's grasp, MAC 4.03. 36
to be one hour at liberty and grasp | our good TNK 2.02.208
GRASP'D 3 FR 0.0003 REL FR 3 V 0 P
as one that grasp'd | and tugg'd for life, and 2H6 3.02.172
and bloody steel grasp'd in their ireful hands, 3H6 2.05.132
those hands, that grasp'd the heaviest club, ANT 4.12. 46
GRASPED 1 FR 0.0001 REL FR 1 V 0 P
for so much trash as may be grasped thus? JC 4.03. 26
GRASPS 2 FR 0.0002 REL FR 2 V 0 P
as he would fly | grasps in the comer. TRO 3.03.168
but flies the grasps of love | with wings more 4.02. 13
/GRASS 1 FR 0.0001 REL FR 0 V 1 P
sir, i have not much skill in /grass. AWW 4.05. 21 P
GRASS 22 FR 0.0024 REL FR 17 V 5 P
how lush and lusty the grass looks! how green! TMP 2.01. 53 P
'tis true she rides me and i long for grass. ERR 2.02.200
to tread a measure with her on this grass. LLL 5.02.185
to tread a measure with you on this grass. 5.02.187
decking with liquid pearl the bladed grass | (a MND 1.01.211
plucking the grass to know where sits the wind, MV 1.01. 18
the grass whereon thou tread'st the presence R2 1.03.289
her pasters' grass with faithful english blood. 3.03.100
grew like the summer grass, fastest by night, H5 1.01. 65
mowing like grass | your fresh fair virgins and 3.03. 13
where biting cold would never let grass grow, 2H6 3.02.337
and in cheapside shall my palfrey go to grass; 4.02. 69 P
into this garden, to see if i can eat grass, or 4.10. 8 P
doornail, i pray god i may never eat grass more. 4.10. 41 P
with frost, or grass beat down with storms. TIT 4.04. 71
we cannot live on grass, on berries, water, | as TIM 4.03.422
sir, but "while the grass grows" — the proverb HAM 3.02.343 P
sweet bottom grass and high delightful plain, VEN 236
for on the grass she lies as she were slain, 473
the grass stoops not, she treads on it so light, 1028
no flow'r was nigh, no grass, herb, leaf, or 1055
white | show'd like an april daisy on the grass, LUC 395
GRASS–GREEN 1 FR 0.0001 REL FR 1 V 0 P
dead and gone, | at his head a grass–green turf, HAM 4.05. 31
GRASSHOPPERS 1 FR 0.0001 REL FR 1 V 0 P
legs, | the cover of the wings of grasshoppers, ROM 1.04. 63
GRASS–PLOT 1 FR 0.0001 REL FR 1 V 0 P
here on this grass–plot, in this very place, TMP 4.01. 73
GRASSY 1 FR 0.0001 REL FR 1 V 0 P
we march | upon the grassy carpet of this plain. R2 3.03. 50
GRATE* 5 FR 0.0005 REL FR 4 V 1 P
or else you had look'd through the grate, like a WIV 2.02. 9 P
turn'd, | or a dry wheel grate on the axle–tree, 1H4 3.01.130
what peer hath been suborn'd to grate on you? 2H4 4.01. 90
/wont through a secret grate of iron bars | in 1H6 1.04. 10
here, through this grate, i count each one, 1.04. 60
GRATED 2 FR 0.0002 REL FR 1 V 1 P
i have grated upon my good friends for three WIV 2.02. 7 P
and mighty states characterless are grated | to TRO 3.02.188
GRATEFUL 5 FR 0.0005 REL FR 3 V 2 P
this is a gift very grateful, i am sure of it. SHR 2.01. 76 P
i cannot give thee less, to be call'd grateful. AWW 2.01.129
more cruel to your good report than grateful COR 1.09. 54
as in grateful virtue i am bound | to your free TIM 1.02. 5
odors which are grateful to the sense. TNK 4.03. 85 P
GRATES 2 FR 0.0002 REL FR 2 V 0 P
grates me, the sum. ANT 1.01. 18
the threshold grates the door to have him heard, LUC 306
GRATIANO 16 FR 0.0018 REL FR 14 V 2 P
most noble kinsman, | gratiano, and lorenzo. MV 1.01. 58
i hold the world but as the world, gratiano, | a 1.01. 77
wise men, | for gratiano never lets me speak. 1.01.107
gratiano speaks an infinite deal of nothing, 1.01.114 P
and desire gratiano to come anon to my lodging. 2.02.117 P
gratiano! 2.02.176
but hear thee, gratiano: 2.02.180
meet me and gratiano | at gratiano's lodging 2.04. 25
fie, fie, gratiano, where are all the rest? 2.06. 62
under sail, | with him is gratiano gone along; 2.08. 2
and do you, gratiano, mean good faith? 3.02.210
go, gratiano, run and overtake him; 4.01.452
now, in faith, gratiano, | you give your wife 5.01.174
and pardon me, my gentle gratiano, | for that 5.01.260
signior gratiano? OTH 5.01. 93
gratiano, keep the house, | and seize upon the 5.02.365
GRATIANO'S 1 FR 0.0001 REL FR 1 V 0 P
at gratiano's lodging some hour hence. MV 2.04. 26
GRATIFY 9 FR 0.0010 REL FR 8 V 1 P
it shall please you to gratify the table with a LLL 4.02.155 P
antonio, gratify this gentleman, | for in my MV 4.01.406
you must, as we do, gratify this gentleman, | to SHR 1.02.271
to gratify his noble service that | hath thus COR 2.02. 40
to gratify the good andronicus, | and gratulate TIT 1.01.220
of his armory | to gratify your honorable youth, 4.02. 12
and she did gratify his amorous works | with OTH 5.02.213
fear'd /hopes | i barely gratify your love; CYM 2.04. 7
the which when any shall not gratify, | or pay PER 1.04.101
GRATII 1 FR 0.0001 REL FR 0 V 1 P
lodowick, and gratii, two hundred fifty each; AWW 4.03.164 P
GRATILLITY 1 FR 0.0001 REL FR 0 V 1 P
i did impeticos thy gratillity; TN 2.03. 26 P
GRATING 2 FR 0.0002 REL FR 2 V 0 P
bray, | and grating shock of wrathful iron arms, R2 1.03.136
grating so harshly all his days of quiet | with HAM 3.01. 3
GRATIS 10 FR 0.0011 REL FR 7 V 3 P
think'st thou i'll endanger my soul gratis? WIV 2.02. 16 P
in low simplicity | he lends out money gratis, MV 1.03. 44
this is the fool that lent out money gratis! 3.03. 2
a halter gratis — nothing else, for god sake. 4.01.379
gavest thyself away gratis, and i thank thee for 2H4 4.03. 69 P
when corn was given them gratis, you repin'd, COR 3.01. 43
give forth | the corn a' th' store–house gratis, 3.01.114
kind of service | did not deserve corn gratis. 3.01.125
the lover shall not sigh gratis, the humorous HAM 2.02.322 P
he gratis comes, and thou art well apaid, | as LUC 914
GRATITUDE 4 FR 0.0004 REL FR 3 V 1 P
which gratitude | through flinty tartar's bosom AWW 4.04. 6
whose gratitude | towards her deserved children COR 3.01.289
effects of courtesy, dues of gratitude: LR 2.04.179
thou canst not, in the course of gratitude, but CYM 3.05.120 P
GRATUITY *(see gratillity)*
GRATULATE *(also congratulate)*
GRATULATE 4 FR 0.0004 REL FR 4 V 0 P
there's more behind that is more gratulate. MM 5.01.529
to gratulate the gentle princes there. R3 4.01. 10
and gratulate his safe return to rome, | the TIT 1.01.221
come freely | to gratulate thy plenteous bosom. TIM 1.02.125
GRAV'D* 3 FR 0.0003 REL FR 3 V 0 P
let's see once more this saying grav'd in gold: MV 2.07. 36
and lie full low, grav'd in the hollow ground. R2 3.02.140
his brow | is grav'd, and seems to bury what it TNK 5.03. 46
/GRAVE* 2 FR 0.0002 REL FR 2 V 0 P
/are /now /become /enamor'd /on /his /grave. 2H4 1.03.102
/neck, | /have /talk'd /of /monmouth's /grave. 2.03. 45
GRAVE* 191 FR 0.0216 REL FR 177 V 14 P
all hail, great master, grave sir, hail! TMP 1.02.189
where | every third thought shall be my grave. 5.01.312
being unprevented, to your timeless grave. TGV 3.01. 21
for in /his grave | assure thyself my love is 4.02.113
go to thy lady's grave and call hers thence, 4.02.116

upon whose grave thou vow'dst pure chastity. 4.03. 21
more grave and wrinkled than the aims and ends MM 1.03. 5
there my father's grave | did utter forth a 3.01. 85
may seem as shy, as grave, as just, as absolute 5.01. 54
and dwell upon your grave when you are dead; ERR 3.01.104
faster and faster, till he sink into his grave. ADO 2.01. 80 P
to rib her cerecloth in the obscure grave. MV 2.07. 51
and that it should lie with you in your grave. 5.01.154
here lie i down, and measure out my grave. AYL 2.06. 2 P
pisa, renowned for grave citizens, | gave me my SHR 1.01. 10
and thou return unexperienc'd to thy grave. 4.01. 84 P
often been, | pisa renowned for grave citizens. 4.02. 95
on every tomb, on every grave | a lying trophy, AWW 2.03.138
spoken it, 'tis dead, and i am the grave of it. 4.03. 13 P
not knowing them until we know their grave. 5.03. 62
he would quickly have the gift of a grave. TN 1.03. 33 P
youth | than in a nuntio's of more grave aspect. 1.04. 28
if you will lead these graces to the grave | and 1.05.242
o, where | sad true lover never find my grave, 2.04. 65
toward my grave | i have travell'd but two hours 5.01.162
a part, whose issue | will hiss me to my grave: WT 1.02.189
if it be so, | we need no grave to bury honesty, 2.01.155
them) and the reverence | of the grave wearers. 3.01. 6
and my near'st of kin | cry fie upon my grave! 3.02. 54
one grave shall be for both; 3.02.236
but for some other reasons, my grave sir, 4.04.411
that thought to fill his grave in quiet; 4.04.454
as my antigonus to break his grave | and come 5.01. 42
so must thy grave | give way to what's seen now! 5.01. 97
o grave and good paulina, the great comfort 5.03. 1
i'll fill your grave up. 5.03.101
in vain, said many | a prayer upon her grave. 5.03.141
by this brave duke came early to his grave; JN 2.01. 5
i would that i were low laid in my grave, | i am 2.01.164
a grave. 3.03. 66
a grave unto a soul, | holding th' eternal 3.04. 17
child, | his little kingdom of a forced grave. 4.02. 98
more, going to seek the grave | of arthur, whom 4.02.164
or, when he doom'd this beauty to a grave, 4.03. 39
found it too precious–princely for a grave. 4.03. 40
despite of death that lives upon my grave, | to R2 1.01.168
that words seem'd buried in my sorrow's grave. 1.04. 15
mind | to help him to his grave immediately! 1.04. 60
gaunt am i for the grave, gaunt as a grave, 2.01. 82
gaunt am i for the grave, gaunt as a grave, 2.01. 82
convey me to my bed, then to my grave; 2.01.137
for both hast thou, and both become the grave. 2.01.140
and my large kingdom for a little grave, | a 3.03.153
a little little grave, an obscure grave — | or 3.03.154
a little little grave, an obscure grave — | or 3.03.154
hath yielded up his body to the grave; 5.06. 21
thy ignominy sleep with thee in the grave, | but 1H4 5.04.100
then get thee gone, and dig my grave thyself, 2H4 4.05.110
you, | my father is gone wild into his grave; 5.02.123
know the grave doth gape | for thee thrice wider 5.05. 53
speak freely of our acts, or else our grave, H5 1.02.231
the grave doth gape, and doting death is near, 2.01. 61
seem they grave and learned? 2.02.128
break up their drowsy grave, and newly move 4.01. 22
year | with profitable labor to his grave: 4.01.277
and here will talbot mount, or make his grave. 1H6 2.01. 34
wear, | until it wither with me to my grave, 2.04.110
swift–winged with desire to get a grave, | as 2.05. 15
thy grave admonishments prevail with me. 2.05. 98
to bid his young son welcome to his grave? 4.03. 40
now my old arms are young john talbot's grave. 4.07. 32
for clothing me in these grave ornaments. 5.01. 54
long, | or sell my title for a glorious grave. 2H6 3.01. 92
that is to see how deep my grave is made, | for 3.02.150
air, | thy grave is digg'd already in the earth. 4.10. 52
unto a dunghill, which shall be thy grave, | and 4.10. 81
wilt thou go dig a grave to find out war, | and 5.01.169
me | that bows unto the grave with mickle age. 5.01.174
and either victory, or else a grave. 3H6 2.02.174
would bring white hairs unto a quiet grave. 2.05. 40
your brother richard mark'd him for the grave, 2.06. 40
for who liv'd king, but i could dig his grave? 5.02. 21
and wet his grave with my repentant tears) | i R3 1.02.215
but first i'll turn yon fellow in his grave, 1.02.260
drown desperate sorrow in dead edward's grave, 2.02. 99
famously enrich'd | with politic grave counsel; 2.03. 20
cousin of buckingham, and sage grave men, 3.07.227
i to my grave, where peace and rest lie with me! 4.01. 94
that thou wouldst as soon afford a grave | as 4.04. 31
no black envy | shall make my grave. H8 2.01. 86
of life to't than | the grave does to th' dead; 2.04.192
weep for me, | almost no grave allow'd me. 3.01.151
may know | i was a chaste wife to my grave. 4.02.170
your most grave belly was deliberate, | not rash COR 1.01.128
you shall not be | the grave of your deserving; 1.09. 20
with those that say you are reverend grave men, 2.01. 61 P
not so honorable a grave as to stuff a botcher's 2.01. 88 P
every gash was an enemy's grave. 2.01.156 P
most reverend and grave elders, to desire | the 2.02. 42
you grave but reakless senators, have you thus 3.01. 92
your judgments, my grave lords, | must give this 5.06.105
him, that | must bear my beating to his grave — 5.06.108
and shall she carry this unto her grave? TIT 2.03.127
womb | of this deep pit, poor bassianus' grave. 2.03.240
do thou so much as dig the grave for him: 2.03.270
hear me, grave fathers! 3.01. 1
grave tribunes, once more i entreat of you — 3.01. 31
me, | and, were they but attired in grave weeds, 3.01. 43
of age, | grave witnesses of true experience, 5.03. 78
out, | and sent her enemies unto the grave. 5.03.103
bid him farewell, commit him to the grave, | do 5.03.170
and give him burial in his fathers' grave. 5.03.192
cast by their grave beseeming ornaments | to ROM 1.01. 93
my grave is like to be my wedding–bed. 1.05.135
what is her burying grave, that is her womb; 2.03. 10
not in a grave, | to lay one in, another out to 2.03. 83
me to–morrow, and you shall find me a grave man. 3.01. 98 P
do now, | taking the measure of an unmade grave. 3.03. 70
wilt thou wash him from his grave with tears? 3.05. 70
i would the fool were married to her grave! 3.05.140
or bid me go into a new–made grave, | and hide 4.01. 84
to follow this fair corse unto her grave. 4.05. 93
go with me | to juliet's grave, for there must i 5.01. 86
nightly shall be to strew thy grave and weep. 5.03. 17
i'll bury thee in a triumphant grave. 5.03. 83
a grave? 5.03. 84
this, | to press before thy father to a grave? 5.03.215
to help to take her from her borrowed grave, 5.03.248
he came with flowers to strew his lady's grave, 5.03.281
creatures as | of grave and austere quality, TIM 1.01. 54
pluck the grave wrinkled senate from the bench, 4.01. 5
large–handed robbers your grave masters are, 4.01. 11
from our companion thrown into his grave, | so 4.02. 9
let this damn you, | and ditches grave you all! 4.03.166
then, timon, presently prepare thy grave; 4.03.377
dead, sure, and this his grave. 5.03. 5
vast neptune weep for aye | on thy low grave, on 5.04. 79
still hath been both grave and prosperous) | in MAC 3.01. 21
whose heavy hand hath bow'd you to the grave, 3.01. 89
duncan is in his grave; 3.02. 22
it cannot | be call'd our mother, but our grave; 4.03.166
he cannot come out on 's grave. 5.01. 64 P
my lord, come from the grave | to tell us this. HAM 1.05.125
into my grave. 2.02.207 P
is now most still, most secret, and most grave, 3.04.214
and in his grave rain'd many a tear" — | fare 4.05.167
thee she is, therefore make her grave straight. 5.01. 3 P
sweet maid, | and not have strew'd thy grave. 5.01.246
to outface me with leaping in her grave? 5.01.278
this grave shall have a living monument. 5.01.297
so be my grave my peace, as here i give | her LR 1.01.125
thou wert better in a grave than to answer with 3.04.101 P
you do me wrong to take me out o' th' grave: 4.07. 44
most grave brabantio, | in simple and pure soul OTH 1.01.106
most potent, grave, and reverend signiors, | my 1.03. 76
so justly to your grave ears i'll present | how 1.03.124
the tyrant custom, most grave senators, | hath 1.03.229
still as the grave. 5.02. 94
worst of all follow him laughing to his grave, ANT 1.02. 67 P
this grave charm, | whose eye beck'd forth my 4.12. 25
a ditch in egypt | be gentle grave unto me! 5.02. 58
no grave upon the earth shall clip in it | a 5.02.359
mother, | and every day do honor to her grave. CYM 3.03.105
the secrets of the grave | this viperous slander 3.04. 38
if he be gone, he'll make his grave a bed. 4.02.216
live here, fidele, | i'll sweeten thy sad grave. 4.02.220
to th' grave! 4.02.233
consummation have, | and renowned be thy grave! 4.02.281
wood–leaves and weeds i ha' strew'd his grave, 4.02.390
make him with our pikes and partisans | a grave. 4.02.400
and having thrown him from your wat'ry grave, PER 2.01. 10
he's both their parent, and he is their grave, 2.03. 46
if in his grave he rest, we'll find him there; 2.04. 30
i time | to give thee hallow'd to thy grave, but 3.01. 59
shall as a carpet hang upon thy grave | while 4.01. 16
thou art a grave and noble counsellor, | most 5.01.182
you were at wars when she the grave enrich'd, TNK 1.03. 51
funeral path brings to your household's grave: 1.05. 11
the best way is, the next way to a grave; 3.02. 33
if she refuse me, yet my grave will wed me, 3.06.284
being steel'd, soft sighs can never grave it. VEN 376
"what is thy body but a swallowing grave, 757
clepes him king of graves and grave for kings, 995
whose downward eye still looketh for a grave, 1106
o foul dishonor to my household's grave! LUC 198
thou their fair life, and they thy fouler grave; 661
and grave, like water that doth eat in steel, 755
there pleading might you see grave nestor stand, 1401
to eat the world's due, by the grave and thee. SON 1.14
thou art the grave where buried love doth live, 31. 9
the earth can yield me but a common grave, 81. 7

GRAVEL 3 FR 0.0003 REL FR 2 V 1 P
o gravel heart! MM 4.03. 64
in july when | we see each grain of gravel, i do H8 1.01.155
/catarrhs, loads a' gravel in the back, TRO 5.01. 19 P

GRAVEL–BLIND 1 FR 0.0001 REL FR 0 V 1 P
being more than sand–blind, high gravel–blind, MV 2.02. 37 P

GRAVELESS 1 FR 0.0001 REL FR 1 V 0 P
lie graveless, till the flies and gnats of nile ANT 3.13.166

GRAVELL'D 1 FR 0.0001 REL FR 0 V 1 P
and when you were gravell'd for lack of matter, AYL 4.01. 74 P

GRAVELY 1 FR 0.0001 REL FR 0 V 1 P
if thou dost it half so gravely, so majestically 1H4 2.04.435 P

GRAVE–MAKER 2 FR 0.0002 REL FR 0 V 2 P
ask'd this question next, say "a grave–maker": HAM 5.01. 58 P
how long hast thou been grave–maker? 5.01.142 P

GRAVE–MAKERS 1 FR 0.0001 REL FR 0 V 1 P
but gard'ners, ditchers, and grave–makers; HAM 5.01. 30 P

GRAVE–MAKING 1 FR 0.0001 REL FR 0 V 1 P
'a sings in grave–making. HAM 5.01. 66 P

GRAVEN 1 FR 0.0001 REL FR 1 V 0 P
survey, | if time have any wrinkle graven there; SON 100.10

GRAVENESS 1 FR 0.0001 REL FR 1 V 0 P
and his weeds, | importing health and graveness. HAM 4.07. 81

GRAVER 6 FR 0.0006 REL FR 5 V 1 P
my lord, | and leave you to your graver steps. WT 1.02.173
him — let some graver eye | pierce into that — H8 1.01. 67
against a graver bench | than ever frown'd in COR 3.01.106
our graver business | frowns at this levity. ANT 2.07.120
and to the graver | a child that guided dotards. CYM 1.01. 49
you bear a graver purpose, i hope. 1.04.139 P

GRAVE'S 2 FR 0.0002 REL FR 1 V 1 P
world's shame, grave's due by life usurp'd, R3 4.04. 27
whose grave's this, sirrah? HAM 5.01.118 P

GRAVES 35 FR 0.0039 REL FR 34 V 1 P
graves at my command | have wak'd their sleepers TMP 5.01. 48
graves, yawn and yield your dead, | till death ADO 5.03. 19
now it is the time of night | that the graves, MND 5.01.380
let's talk of graves, of worms, and epitaphs, R2 3.02.145
till they have fretted us a pair of graves 3.03.167
kinsmen digg'd their graves with weeping eyes. 3.03.169
turning your books to graves, your ink to blood, 2H4 4.01. 50
our bodies shall no doubt | find native graves; H5 4.03. 96
spirits walk, and ghosts break up their graves, 2H6 1.04. 19
and flagging wings | cleep dead men's graves, 4.01. 6
no, if i digg'd up thy forefathers' graves | and 3H6 1.03. 27
thy womb let loose to chase us to our graves. R3 4.04. 54
untimely smoth'red in their dusky graves. 4.04. 70
deep and dead, poor infants, in their graves. 4.04.363
build their evils on the graves of great men, H8 2.01. 67
her two hands, and she | sleep in their graves. 5.01. 32
which show | like graves i' th' holy churchyard. COR 3.03. 51
oft have i digg'd up dead men from their graves, TIT 5.01.135
being loose, unfirm, with digging up of graves, ROM 5.03. 6
to–night | have my old feet stumbled at graves! 5.03.122
dies that bears not one spurn to their graves TIM 1.02.141
graves only be men's works, and death their gain 5.01.222
about | to find ourselves dishonorable graves. JC 1.02.138
lightens, opens graves, and roars | as doth the 1.03. 74
and graves have yawn'd and yielded up their dead 2.02. 18
as from your graves rise up, and walk like MAC 2.03. 79
if charnel–houses and our graves must send 3.04. 70
the graves stood /tenantless and the sheeted HAM 1.01.115
trick of fame | go to their graves like beds, 4.04. 62
disorders follow us disquietly to our graves. LR 1.02.114 P
o' th' night | are strewings fitt'st for graves. CYM 4.02.285
look | like patience gazing on kings' graves, PER 5.01.138
you comfort | to give your dead lords graves; TNK 1.01.149
clepes him king of graves and grave for kings, VEN 995
show, | of mouthed graves will give thee memory; SON 77. 6

GRAVEST 1 FR 0.0001 REL FR 1 V 0 P
the generous and gravest citizens | have hent MM 4.06. 13

GRAVE–STONE 3 FR 0.0003 REL FR 3 V 0 P
of the sea may beat | thy grave–stone daily; TIM 4.03.379
come, | and let my grave–stone be your oracle. 5.01.219
and on his grave–stone this insculpture, which 5.04. 67

GRAVITIES 1 FR 0.0001 REL FR 1 V 0 P
eyes, | have misbecom'd our oaths and gravities, LLL 5.02.768

GRAVITY 15 FR 0.0017 REL FR 10 V 5 P
odds with his own gravity and patience that ever WIV 3.01. 54 P
i never heard a man of his place, gravity, and 3.01. 57 P
yea, my gravity, | wherein (let no man hear me) MM 2.04. 9
how ill agrees it with your gravity | to ERR 2.02.168
be dress'd in an opinion | of wisdom, gravity, MV 1.01. 92
'tis not for gravity to play at cherry–pit with TN 3.04.116 P
what doth gravity out of his bed at midnight? 1H4 2.04.294 P
your face but should have his effect of gravity. 2H4 1.02.161 P
wit, | and to such men of gravity and learning, H8 3.01. 73
utter your gravity o'er a gossip's bowl, | for ROM 3.05.174
whit appear, | but all be buried in his gravity. JC 2.01.149
the gravity and stillness of your youth | the OTH 2.03.191
what a bold gravity, and yet inviting, | has TNK 4.02. 41
vassal, and induce | stale gravity to dance; 5.01. 85
was | shall reasons find of settled gravity — SON 49. 8

GRAVITY'S 1 FR 0.0001 REL FR 1 V 0 P
excess | as gravity's revolt to /wantonness. LLL 5.02. 74

GRAVY 3 FR 0.0003 REL FR 0 V 3 P
his effect of gravy, gravy, gravy. 2H4 1.02.162 P
his effect of gravy, gravy, gravy. 1.02.162 P
his effect of gravy, gravy, gravy. 1.02.162 P

GRAY *(see grey*, etc.)*

GRAYMALKIN 1 FR 0.0001 REL FR 1 V 0 P
i come, graymalkin! MAC 1.01. 8

GRAY'S 1 FR 0.0001 REL FR 0 V 1 P
stockfish, a fruiterer, behind gray's inn. 2H4 3.02. 33 P

GRAZ'D 2 FR 0.0002 REL FR 2 V 0 P
when jacob graz'd his uncle laban's sheep — MV 1.03. 71
a reverend man that graz'd his cattle nigh, LC 57

GRAZE* 8 FR 0.0009 REL FR 6 V 2 P
when beasts most graze, birds best peck, and men LLL 1.01.236 P
and do not shear the fleeces that i graze. AYL 2.04. 79
pride is to see my ewes graze and my lambs suck. 3.02. 77 P
graze where you will, you shall not house with ROM 3.05.188
ass) to shake his ears | and graze in commons. JC 4.01. 27
dart of chance | could neither graze nor pierce? OTH 4.01.268
so graze, as you find pasture. CYM 5.04. 2
graze on my lips, and if those hills be dry, VEN 233

GRAZING *(also crasing)*

GRAZING 1 FR 0.0001 REL FR 1 V 0 P
i should leave grazing, were i of your flock, WT 4.04.109

GREASE 7 FR 0.0008 REL FR 1 V 6 P
fire of lust have melted him in his own grease. WIV 2.01. 68 P
clothes that fretted in their own grease. 3.05.114 P
(when i was more than half stew'd in grease, 3.05.119 P
she's the kitchen wench and all grease, and i ERR 3.02. 96 P
and is not the grease of a mutton as wholesome AYL 3.02. 56 P
grease that's sweaten | from the murderer's MAC 4.01. 65
put in a cauldron of lead and usurers' grease, TNK 4.03. 37 P

GREASES 1 FR 0.0001 REL FR 1 V 0 P
and morsels unctious, greases his pure mind, TIM 4.03.195

GREASILY 1 FR 0.0001 REL FR 1 V 0 P
come, you talk greasily, your lips grow foul. LLL 4.01.137

GREASY 10 FR 0.0011 REL FR 6 V 4 P
consult together against this greasy knight. WIV 2.01.108 P
socks, foul stockings, greasy napkins, that, 3.05. 91 P
note, | while greasy joan doth keel the pot. LLL 5.02.920
note, | while greasy joan doth keel the pot. 5.02.929
"sweep on, you fat and greasy citizens, | 'tis AYL 2.01. 55
our ewes, and their fells you know are greasy. 3.02. 54 P
thou whoreson, obscene, greasy tallow–catch — 1H4 2.04.228 P
the bits and greasy relics | of her o'er–eaten TRO 5.02.159
cast | your stinking greasy caps in hooting at COR 4.06.131
mechanic slaves | with greasy aprons, rules, and ANT 5.02.210

/GREAT 6 FR 0.0006 REL FR 5 V 1 P
/good /king, /great /king, /and /yet /not R2 4.01.263
/for /thy /great /bounty, /that /not /only 4.01.300
/being /so /great, /i /have /no /need /to /beg. 4.01.309
/gasping /for /life /under /great /bullingbrook, 2H4 1.01.208
/much /more, /in /this /great /work | (/which 1.03. 48
/lords /and /great /men /will /not /let /me; LR 1.04.152 P

GREAT 946 FR 0.1069 REL FR 734 V 212 P
i have great comfort from this fellow. TMP 1.01. 28 P
in its contrary, as great | as my trust was, 1.02. 95
all hail, great master, grave sir, hail! 1.02.189
ship wrack'd, | and his great person perish. 1.02.237
sir, you may thank yourself for this great loss, 2.01.124
out of that no hope | what great hope have you! 2.01.240
their great guilt | (like poison given to work a 3.03.104
(like poison given to work a great time after) 3.03.105
great juno, comes, i know her by her gait. 4.01.102
the solemn temples, the great globe itself, 4.01.153
at which my nose is in great indignation. 4.01.200 P
as great to me as late, and, supportable | to 5.01.145
now, trust me, 'tis an office of great worth, TGV 1.02. 44
which would be great impeachment to his age, 1.03. 15
and all our house in a great perplexity, yet did 2.03. 8 P
to me | with commendation from great potentates, 2.04. 79

kiss, | and, of so great a favor growing proud, 2.04.161
there's some great matter she'ld employ me in. 4.03. 3
and fit for great employment, worthy lord. 5.04.157
the cause with as great discreetly as we can. WIV 1.01.146 P
never come in mine own great chamber again else, 1.01.154 P
but if there be no great love in the beginning, 1.01.246 P
does he not wear a great round beard, like a 1.04. 20 P
'tis a great charge to come under one body's 1.04. 98 P
you shall find it a great charge; 1.04.101 P
well, farewell, i am in great haste now. 1.04.161 P
to thy great comfort in this mystery of ill 2.01. 71 P
admirable discourse, of great admittance, 2.02.226 P
you have yourself been a great fighter, though 2.03. 43 P
i have a great dispositions to cry. 3.01. 22 P
he doth object i am too great of birth, | and 3.04. 4
i like not when a oman has a great peard. 4.02.193 P
i spy a great peard under his muffler. 4.02.194 P
round about an oak, with great ragg'd horns, 4.04. 31
sight, | we two in great amazedness will fly; 4.04. 56
fat falstaff | hath a great scene; 4.06. 17
little chiding than a great deal of heart–break. 5.03. 10 P
anne page, and she's a great lubberly boy. 5.05.184 P
before so noble and so great a figure | be MM 1.01. 49
i have great hope in that; 1.02.182
sir, she came in great with child; 2.01. 89 P
the beastliest sense you are pompey the great. 2.01.219 P
alas, it hath been great pains to you. 2.01.265 P
this, | no ceremony that to great ones 'longs, 2.02. 59
could great men thunder | as jove himself does, 2.02.110
great men may jest with saints; 2.02.127
whose credit with the judge, or own great place, 2.04. 92
in corporal sufferance finds a pang as great 3.01. 79
the great soldier who miscarried at sea? 3.01.210 P
in good sooth, the vice is of a great kindred; 3.02.101 P
but that there is so great a fever on goodness, 3.02.222 P
with the stroke and line of his great justice. 4.02. 80
o, death's a great disguiser, and you may add to 4.02.174 P
and brave master shoe–tie the great traveller, 4.03. 17 P
forty more — all great doers in our trade, and 4.03. 18 P
and that by great injunctions i am bound | to 4.03. 96
respect to your great place! 5.01.292
and /the great care of goods at randon left, ERR 1.01. 42
but to our honor's great disparagement, | yet 1.01.148
so great a charge from thine own custody? 1.02. 61
it seems he hath great care to please his wife. 2.01. 56
small cheer and great welcome makes a merry 3.01. 26
mole in my neck, the great wart on my left arm, 3.02.143 P
great pails of puddled mire to quench the hair; 5.01.173
this day, great duke, she shut the doors upon me 5.01.204
for these deep shames and great indignities. 5.01.254
in great measure. ADO 1.01. 25 P
fair praise, and too little for a great praise; 1.01.173 P
and in such great letters as they write "here is 1.01.265 P
for indeed he hath made great preparation. 1.01.278 P
i came yonder from a great supper. 1.03. 42 P
let us to the great supper, their cheer is the 1.03. 71 P
that i was duller than a great thaw, huddling 2.01.244 P
fetch you a hair off the great cham's beard, do 2.01.268 P
for either he avoids them with great discretion, 2.03.191 P
to her wit, nor no great argument of her folly, 2.03.234 P
that would be as great a soil in the new gloss 3.02. 5 P
there to–morrow, there is a great coil to–night. 3.03. 93 P
i am now in great haste, as it may appear unto 3.05. 50 P
"no," said i, "a great wit." 5.01.162 P
"right," says she, "a great gross one." 5.01.162 P
by this good day, i yield upon great persuasion, 5.04. 95 P
"great deputy, the welkin's vicegerent, and sole LLL 1.01.219 P
what sign is it when a man of great spirit grows 1.02. 1 P
a great sign, sir, that he will look sad. 1.02. 3 P
what great men have been in love? 1.02. 65 P
he was a man of good carriage, great carriage, 1.02. 71 P
and that's great marvel, loving a light wench. 1.02.123 P
(which is a great argument of falsehood) if i 1.02.170 P
i saw | is my report to his great worthiness. 2.01. 63
sole imperator and great general | of trotting 3.01.185
to see great hercules whipping a gig, | and 4.03.165
they have been at a great feast of languages, 5.01. 37 P
designs, and of great import indeed too — but 5.01.100 P
this swain, because of his great limb or joint, 5.01.128 P
limb or joint, shall pass pompey the great; 5.01.128 P
great reason: for past care is still past cure. 5.02. 28
but as fair as yours, | my favor were as great: 5.02. 33
one man in one poor man, pompion the great, sir. 5.02.502 P
them to think me worthy of pompey the great; 5.02.506 P
when great things laboring perish in their birth 5.02.520
the swain, pompey the great; 5.02.535 P
"the great." 5.02.551
it is "great," sir. 5.02.552
"pompey surnam'd the great, | that oft in field 5.02.552
great thanks, great pompey. 5.02.557 P
great thanks, great pompey. 5.02.557 P
i made a little fault in "great." 5.02.559 P
pompey the great — 5.02.570 P
"great hercules is presented by this imp, 5.02.588
greater than great, great, great, great pompey! 5.02.685 P
greater than great, great, great, great pompey! 5.02.685 P
greater than great, great, great, great pompey! 5.02.685 P
greater than great, great, great, great pompey! 5.02.685 P
thanks | for my great suit so easily obtain'd. 5.02.739
of great revenue, and she hath no child. MND 1.01.158
you leave a casement of the great chamber window 3.01. 57 P
we must have a wall in the great chamber; 3.01. 63 P
play | intended for great theseus' nuptial day. 3.02. 12
methinks i have a great desire to a bottle of 4.01. 32 P
three, | we'll hold a feast in great solemnity. 4.01.185
and grows to something of great constancy; 5.01. 26
great clerks have purposed | to greet me with 5.01. 93
what harm a wind too great might do at sea. MV 1.01. 24
is to come fairly off from the great debts 1.01.128
my little body is a–weary of this great world. 1.02. 2 P
and he makes it a great appropriation to his own 1.02. 41 P
he hath a great infection, sir, as one would say 2.02.125 P
your grace hath ta'en great pains to qualify 4.01. 7
to do a great right, do a little wrong, | and 4.01.216
you that, in the great heap of your knowledge? AYL 1.02. 68 P
foolery that wise men have makes a great show. 1.02. 90 P
and that a great cause of the night is lack of 3.02. 28 P
'tis a word too great for any mouth of this 3.02.226 P
man more dead than a great reckoning in a little 3.03. 15 P
by my faith, you have great reason to be sad. 4.01. 21 P
there is too great testimony in your complexion 4.03.169 P
though there was no great matter in the ditty, 5.03. 35 P
uncle, | whom he reports to be a great magician, 5.04. 33
wedding is great juno's crown, | o blessed bond 5.04.141
men of great worth resorted to this forest, 5.04.155
you to your land, and love, and great allies; 5.04.189
since for the great desire i had | to see fair SHR 1.01. 1
lombardy, | the pleasant garden of great italy, 1.01. 4
a merchant of great traffic through the world, 1.01. 12
their love is not so great, hortensio, but we 1.01.107 P
that made great jove to humble him to her hand, 1.01.169
have i not heard great ord'nance in the field, 1.02.203
that gives not half so great a blow to hear | as 1.02.208
yea, leave that labor to great hercules, | and 1.02.255
if you accept them, then their worth is great. 2.01.101
though little fire grows great with little wind, 2.01.134
father hath no less | than three great argosies, 2.01.378
and have prepar'd great store of wedding cheer, 3.02.186
our stomachs up | after our great good cheer. 5.02. 10
too little payment for so great a debt. 5.02.154
my heart as great, my reason haply more, | to 5.02.171
whose skill was almost as great as his honesty; AWW 1.01. 19 P
and it was his great right to be so — gerard de 1.01. 27 P
and these great tears grace his remembrance more 1.01. 80
think him a great way fool, soly a coward; 1.01.101
madam — in great friends, for the knaves come 1.03. 42 P
to give great charlemain a pen in 's hand | and 2.01. 77
to dissever so | our great self and our credit, 2.01.123
great floods have flown | from simple sources; 2.01.139
and great seas have dried | when miracles have 2.01.140
and debile minister, great power, great 2.03. 34 P
great power, great transcendence, which should 2.03. 34 P
which great love grant, and so i take my leave. 2.03. 85
where great additions swell 's, and virtue none, 2.03.127
what great creation and what dole of honor 2.03.169
believing thee a vessel of too great a burthen. 2.03.205 P
nothing, is to be a great part of your title, 2.04. 26 P
the great prerogative and rite of love, | which, 2.04. 41
you, my lord, he is very great in knowledge, and 2.05. 8 P
stars have fail'd | to equal my great fortune. 2.05. 76
my haste is very great. 2.05. 77
whose great decision hath much blood let forth 3.01. 3
man | that the great figure of a council frames 3.01. 12
we, | great in our hope, lay our best love and 3.03. 2
day, | great mars, i put myself into thy file; 3.03. 9
or to the worth | of the great count himself, 3.05. 60
four or five, to great saint jaques bound, 3.05. 95
he might at some great and trusty business in a 3.06. 15 P
for a week escape a great deal of discoveries, 3.06. 92 P
which well approves | y' are great in fortune. 3.07. 14
and great ones i dare not give; 4.01. 39 P
three great oaths would scarce make that be 4.01. 59 P
if i should swear by jove's great attributes | i 4.02. 25
sir, so should i be a great deal of his act. 4.03. 46 P
the great dignity that his valor hath here 4.03. 68 P
not altogether so great as the first in goodness 4.03.287 P
in goodness, but greater a great deal in evil. 4.03.287 P
if my heart were great, | 'twould burst at this. 4.03.330
i am no great nebuchadnezzar, sir, i have not 4.05. 20 P
you, i can serve as great a prince as you are. 4.05. 37 P
sir, that always lov'd a great fire, and the 4.05. 48 P
that leads to the broad gate and the great fire. 4.05. 55 P
the nature of his great offense is dead, | and 5.03. 23
strikes some scores away | from the great compt; 5.03. 57
to the great sender turns a sour offense, 5.03. 59
come, or sent it us | upon her great disaster. 5.03.112
great king, i am no strumpet, by my life; 5.03.292
what great ones do the less will prattle of) TN 1.02. 33
lady, takes great exceptions to your ill hours. 1.03. 5 P
that he's a fool, he's a great quarreller; 1.03. 30 P
but i am a great eater of beef and i believe 1.03. 85 P
well penn'd, i have taken great pains to con it. 1.05.174 P
alas, i took great pains to study it, and 'tis 1.05.194 P
of great estate, of fresh and stainless youth; 1.05.259
mine eye too great a flatterer for my mind. 1.05.309
without book and utters it by great swarths; 2.03.149 P
hath for your love as great a pang of heart | as 2.04. 90
and her t's, and thus makes she her great p's. 2.05. 88 P
some are /born great, some /achieve greatness, 2.05.145 P
the matter, i hope, is not great, sir — begging 3.01. 54 P
this was a great argument of love in her toward 3.02. 11 P
bears in his visage no great presage of cruelty. 3.02. 65 P
do, he'll smile, and take't for a great favor. 3.02. 83 P
belike you slew great number of his people? 3.03. 29
"some are born great" — 3.04. 41 P
that word of some great man and now applies it 4.01. 13 P
i am afraid this great lubber, the world, will 4.01. 14 P
as to say a careful man and a great scholar. 4.02. 10 P
then thou art | as great as that thou fear'st. 5.01.150
the letter at sir toby's great importance, | in 5.01.363
why, "some are born great, some achieve 5.01.370 P
a great while ago the world begun, | /with hey 5.01.405
great difference betwixt our bohemia and your WT 1.01. 3 P
you pay a great deal too dear for what's given 1.01. 17 P
camillo, this great sir will yet stay longer. 1.02.212
as she's rare, | must it be great; 1.02.453
by his great authority, | which often hath no 2.01. 53
violence, in the which three great ones suffer, 2.01.128
as well as one so great and so forlorn | may 2.02. 20
no lady living | so meet for this great errand. 2.02. 44
is | by law and process of great nature thence 2.02. 58
foretells | the great apollo suddenly will have 2.03.200
great apollo | turn all to th' best! 3.01. 14
(thus by apollo's great divine seal'd up) 3.01. 19
this sessions (to our great grief we pronounce) 3.02. 1
a moi'ty of the throne, a great king's daughter, 3.02. 39
the hand deliver'd | of great apollo's priest; 3.02.128
now blessed be the great apollo! 3.02.137
my great profaneness 'gainst thine oracle! 3.02.154
quit his fortunes here | (which you knew great), 3.02.168
a million of beating may come to a great matter. 4.03. 60 P
piedness shares | with great creating nature. 4.04. 88
this cannot be but a great courtier. 4.04.748 P
a great man, i'll warrant; 4.04.752 P
which though it be great pity, yet it is 4.04.775 P
he seems to be of great authority. 4.04.800 P
great alexander | left his to th' worthiest; 5.01. 47
please you, great sir, | bohemia greets you from 5.01.180
thought she had some great matter there in hand, 5.02.104 P
the great comfort | that i have had of thee! 5.03. 1
kneel thou down philip, but rise more great, JN 1.01.161
arthur, that great forerunner of thy blood, 2.01. 2
from whom hast thou this great commission, 2.01.110
of him | as great alcides' /shows upon an ass. 2.01.144
in us, that are our own great deputy, | and bear 2.01.365
hear us, great kings! 2.01.416
become thy great birth nor deserve a crown. 3.01. 50
nature and fortune join'd to make thee great. 3.01. 52
to me and to the state of my great grief | let 3.01. 70
for my grief's so great | that no supporter but 3.01. 71
thou little valiant, great in villainy! 3.01.116
head, | so under him that great supremacy, 3.01.156
having so great a title | to be more prince, as 4.01. 10
be great in act, as you have been in thought. 5.01. 45
that borrow their behaviors from the great, 5.01. 51
grow great by your example and put on | the 5.01. 52
and great affections wrastling in thy bosom 5.02. 41
and with a great heart heave away this storm. 5.02. 55
church, | the great metropolis and see of rome; 5.02. 72
for the great supply, | that was expected by the 5.03. 9
even to our ocean, to our great king john. 5.04. 57
it must be great that can inherit us | so much R2 1.01. 85
with too great a court | and liberal largess, 1.04. 43
i mock my name, great king, to flatter thee. 2.01. 87
wert thou not brother to great edward's son, 2.01.121
and, for these great affairs do ask some charge, 2.01.159
my heart is great, but it must break with 2.01.228
base men by his endowments are made great. 2.03.139
grows strong and great in substance and in power 3.02. 35
a puny subject strikes | at thy great glory. 3.02. 87
strives bullingbrook to be as great as we? 3.02. 97
o that i were as great | as is my grief, or 3.03.136
had he done so to great and growing men, | they 3.04. 61
but in the balance of great bullingbrook, 3.04. 87
should grace the triumph of great bullingbrook? 3.04. 99
great duke of lancaster, i come to thee | from 4.01.107
then, as i said, the duke, great bullingbrook, 5.02. 7
a woman, and thy aunt, great king, 'tis i. 5.03. 76
great king, within this coffin i present | thy 5.06. 30
and that it was great pity, so it was, | this 1H4 1.03. 59
did lead to fight | against that great magician, 1.03. 83
in changing hardiment with great glendower. 1.03.101
imagination of some great exploit | drives him 1.03.199
along with company, for they have great charge. 2.01. 46 P
and tranquility, burgomasters and great oney'rs, 2.01. 76 P
for the counterpoise of so great an opposition." 2.03. 13 P
their breath | on some great sudden hest. 2.03. 62
instinct is a great matter; 2.04.272 P
had his great name profaned with their scorns, 3.02. 64
whose hot incursions and great name in arms, 3.02.108
in his enterprises | discomfited great douglas, 3.02.114
it lends a lustre and more great opinion, | a 4.01. 77
a larger dare to our great enterprise, | than if 4.01. 78
the powers of us may serve so great a day. 4.01.132
being men of such great leading as you are, 4.03. 17
some | envy your great deservings and good name, 4.03. 35
grew by our feeding to so great a bulk | that 5.01. 62
the odds | of his great name and estimation, 5.01. 98
thy name in arms were now as great as mine! 5.04. 70
fare thee well, great heart! 5.04. 87
if i do grow great, i'll grow less, for i'll 5.04.163 P
you are too great to be by me gainsaid, | your 2H4 1.01. 91
truth is, sir john, you live in great infamy. 1.02.137 P
means are very slender, and your waste is great. 1.02.141 P
i am the fellow with the great belly, and he my 1.02.146 P
or the other plays the rogue with my great toe. 1.02.245 P
largely in the hope | of great northumberland, 1.03. 13
so, with great imagination | proper to madmen, 1.03. 31
thou art a great fool. 2.01.195 P
as thou hast not done a great while, because the 2.02. 21 P
than in the perfum'd chambers of the great, 3.01. 12
since richard and northumberland, great friends, 3.01. 58
a perfect guess | that great northumberland, 3.01. 89
foeman may with as great aim level at the edge 3.02.266 P
me the spare men, and spare me the great ones. 3.02.270 P
my friends and brethren in these great affairs, 4.01. 6
who, great and puff'd up with this retinue, doth 4.03.111 P
with a great power of english and of scots, 4.04. 98
with such a deep demeanor in great sorrow | that 4.05. 84
how might a prince of my great hopes forget | so 5.02. 68
forget | so great indignities you laid upon me? 5.02. 69
that the great body of our state may go | in 5.02.136
i will be the man yet that shall make you great. 5.05. 80 P
scaffold to bring forth | so great an object. H5 pr 11
and let us, ciphers to this great accompt, | on pr 17
where charles the great, having subdu'd the 1.02. 46
and charles the great | subdu'd the saxons, and 1.02. 61
of the true line and stock of charles the great, 1.02. 71
and lewis the son | of charles the great. 1.02. 77
the which marriage the line of charles the great 1.02. 84
in the right | of your great predecessor, king 1.02.248
we therefore have great cause of thankfulness, 2.02. 32
sir, | you show great mercy if you give him life 2.02. 50
with what great state he heard their embassy, 2.04. 32
be merciful, great duke, to men of mould. 3.02. 22
thy manly rage, | abate thy rage, great duke! 3.02. 24
and of great expedition and knowledge in th' 3.02. 77 P
are yet not ready | to raise so great a siege. 3.03. 47
therefore, great king, | we yield our town and 3.03. 47
high dukes, great princes, barons, lords, and 3.05. 46
for your great seats now quit you of great 3.05. 47
your great seats now quit you of great shames. 3.05. 47
this becomes the great. 3.05. 55
are perfit in the great commanders' names, and 3.06. 70 P
of th' athversary hath been very great, 3.06. 99 P
hath been very great, reasonable great. 3.06. 99 P
give them great meals of beef and iron and steel 3.07.149 P
'tis true that we are in great danger, | the 4.01. 1
but to examine the wars of pompey the great, you 4.01. 69 P
but we have no great cause to desire the 4.01. 87 P
o, be sick, great greatness, | and bid thy 4.01.251
i would not lose so great an honor | as one man 4.03. 31
alexander the great. 4.07. 14 P
why, i pray you, is not "pig" great? 4.07. 15 P

the pig, or the great, or the mighty, or the 4.07. 16 P
i think alexander the great was born in macedon. 4.07. 19 P
the fat knight with the great belly doublet. 4.07. 48 P
no, great king; 4.07. 70
o, give us leave, great king, | to view the 4.07. 81
may be his enemy is a gentleman of great sort, 4.07.136 P
grace doo's me as great honors as can be desir'd 4.07.160 P
great master of france, the brave sir guichard 4.08. 95
was ever known so great and little loss, | on 4.08.110
yes, my conscience, he did us great good. 4.08.121 P
by whom this great assembly is contriv'd, | we 5.02. 6
great kings of france and england: 5.02. 24
o kate, nice customs cur'sy to great kings. 5.02.268 P
or the loss of those great towns | will make him 1H6 1.01. 63
to keep our great saint george's feast withal. 1.01.154
out of a great deal of old iron i chose forth. 1.02.101
helen, the mother of great constantine, | nor 1.02.142
so great fear of my name 'mongst them were 1.04. 50
is come with a great power to raise the siege. 1.04.103
by me entreats, great lord, thou wouldst 2.02. 40
and therefore tell her i return great thanks, 2.02. 51
great is the rumor of this dreadful knight, 2.03. 7
to feast so great a warrior in my house. 2.03. 82
great lords and gentlemen, what means this 2.04. 1
reign, | before whose glory i was great in arms, 2.05. 24
now declare, sweet stem from york's great stock, 2.05. 41
as in this haughty great attempt | they labored 2.05. 79
that malice was a great and grievous sin; 3.01.128
you have great reason to do richard right, 3.01.153
town | great cordelion's heart was buried, | so 3.02. 83
then judge, great lords, if i have done amiss; 4.01. 27
feeds in the bosom of such great commanders, 4.03. 48
talbot dead, great york might bear the name. 4.04. 9
your loss is great, so your regard should be; 4.05. 22
none, | dizzy–ey'd fury and great rage of heart 4.07. 11
but where's the great alcides of the field, 4.07. 60
great earl of washford, waterford, and valence, 4.07. 63
great marshal to henry the sixt | of all his 4.07. 70
charles, | a man of great authority in france, 5.01. 18
our great progenitors had conquered? 5.04.110
and of such great authority in france | as his 5.05. 41
of that great shadow i did represent: 2H6 1.01. 14
great king of england, and my gracious lord, 1.01. 24
we thank you all for this great favor done | in 1.01. 71
and no great friend, i fear me, to the king. 1.01.150
why doth the great duke humphrey knit his brows, 1.02. 3
and from the great and new–made duke of suffolk; 1.02. 95
if they were known, as the suspect is great, 1.03.136
great is his comfort in this earthly vale, 2.01. 68
soul, god's goodness hath been great to thee. 2.01. 82
and would ye not think /his cunning to be great, 2.01.130
in sight of god and us, your guilt is great; 2.03. 2
but great men tremble when the lion roars, | and 3.01. 19
levy great sums of money through the realm | for 3.01. 61
that these great lords, and margaret our queen, 3.01.207
henry my lord is cold in great affairs, | too 3.01.224
great lords, from ireland am i come amain, | to 3.01.282
for, being green, there is great hope of help. 3.01.287
say that he thrive, as 'tis great like he will, 3.01.379
me, | i have great matters to impart to thee. 3.02.299
by devilish policy art thou grown great | and, 4.01. 83
great men oft die by vild besonians: 4.01.134
savage islanders | pompey the great; 4.01.138
great men have reaching hands; 4.07. 81
i seek not to wax great by others' /waning, | or 4.10. 20
and swallow my sword like a great pin, ere thou 4.10. 29 P
to entertain great england's lawful king! 5.01. 4
should raise so great a power without his leave, 5.01. 21
scarce can i speak, my choler is so great. 5.01. 23
great god, how just art thou! 5.01. 68
it is great sin to swear unto a sin, | but 5.01.182
whereat the great lord of northumberland, 3H6 1.01. 4
and now in england to our heart's great sorrow, 1.01.128
though the odds be great, | i doubt not, uncle, 1.02. 71
but how is it that great plantagenet | is 1.04. 99
can my tongue unload my heart's great burthen, 2.01. 81
great lord of warwick, if we should recompt 2.01. 96
with promise of high pay and great rewards; 2.01.134
ay, now methinks i hear great warwick speak. 2.01.186
the great commanding warwick | /is thither gone 3.01. 29
great albion's queen in former golden days; 3.03. 7
unless abroad they purchase great alliance? 3.03. 70
then warwick disannuls great john of gaunt, 3.03. 81
hands | he hath good usage and great liberty, 4.05. 6
nor much oppress'd them with great subsidies, 4.08. 45
thou art no atlas for so great a weight; 5.01. 36
away, away, to meet the queen's great power! 5.02. 50
great lords, wise men ne'er sit and wail their 5.04. 1
while great promotions | are daily given to R3 1.03. 79
maid | than a great queen with this condition, 1.03.107
king, | i was a pack–horse in his great affairs: 1.03.121
wedges of gold, great anchors, heaps of pearl, 1.04. 26
my stranger soul | was my great father–in–law, 1.04. 49
shall never wake until the great judgment day. 1.04.103 P
the great king of kings | hath in the table of 1.04.195
when great leaves fall, then winter is at hand; 2.03. 33
herbs have grace, great weeds do grow apace." 2.04. 13
trust | my absence doth neglect no great design, 3.04. 24
were't not that by great preservation | we live 3.05. 36
in deep designs, in matter of great moment, | no 3.07. 67
home | to high promotions and great dignity. 4.04.314
and be not peevish/–fond in great designs. 4.04.417
and who is england's king but great york's heir? 4.04.472
my lord, the army of great buckingham — 4.04.506
crew, | and many other of great name and worth; 4.05. 16
great reason why — | lest i revenge. 5.03.185
a thousand hearts are great within my bosom. 5.03.347
great god of heaven, say amen to all! 5.05. 8
think you see them great, | and follow'd with H8 pr 27
and the limbs | of this great sport together, as 1.01. 47
such | to whom as great a charge as little honor 1.01. 77
laying manors on 'em | for this great journey. 1.01. 85
heart of it, | thanks you for this great care. 1.02. 2
that your subjects | are in great grievance: 1.02. 20
that he may furnish and instruct great teachers 1.02.113
this night he makes a supper, and a great one, 1.03. 52
but few now give so great ones. 1.03. 63
as great embassadors | from foreign princes. 1.04. 55
(out of the great respect they bear to beauty) 1.04. 69
shall become | of the great duke of buckingham. 2.01. 3
the great duke | came to the bar; 2.01. 11
build their evils on the graves of great men, 2.01. 67
us and the emperor (the queen's great nephew), 2.02. 25
lord, have great care | i be not found a talker. 2.02. 77
the two great cardinals | wait in the presence. 3.01. 16
yet will i add an honor — a great patience. 3.01.137
for your great graces | heap'd upon me, poor 3.02.174
you | to render up the great seal presently 3.02.229
whilst your great goodness, out of holy pity, 3.02.263
bold | to carry into flanders the great seal. 3.02.319
weeps to see him | so little of his great self. 3.02.336
about the giving–back the great seal to us, 3.02.347
thy spirit wonder | a great man should decline? 3.02.375
is held no great good lover of the archbishop's, 4.01.104
however, yet there is no great breach; 4.01.106
that the great child of honor, cardinal wolsey, 4.02. 6
and if there be | no great offense belongs to't, 5.01. 12
they say in great extremity, and fear'd | she'll 5.01. 19
of his great grace | and princely care 5.01. 48
oppos'd, and with a malice | of as great size. 5.01.135
the council pray'd me | to make great haste. 5.02. 3
the cause betwixt her and this great offender. 5.02.156
and one as great as you are? 5.02.175
indian with the great tool come to court, the 5.03. 34 P
we shall have | great store of room, no doubt, 5.03. 73
you great fellow, | stand close up, or i'll make 5.03. 87
heir | as great in admiration as herself, | so 5.04. 42
star–like rise as great in fame as she was, 5.04. 46
it now, for it has been a great while going by. TRO 1.02.168 P
but the protractive trials of great jove | to 1.03. 20
great agamemnon, nestor shall apply | thy latest 1.03. 32
thou great commander, nerves and bone of greece, 1.03. 55
thou great, and wise, to hear ulysses speak. 1.03. 69
and the great hector's sword had lack'd a master 1.03. 76
great agamemnon, | this chaos, when degree is 1.03.124
the great achilles, whom opinion crowns | the 1.03.142
sometime, great agamemnon, | thy topless 1.03.151
for the great swinge and rudeness of his poise, 1.03.207
is this great agamemnon's tent, i pray you? 1.03.216
joints, true swords, and, great jove's accord, 1.03.238
we have, great agamemnon, here in troy | a 1.03.260
dry enough), will, with great speed of judgment, 1.03.329
man, | for that will physic the great myrmidon, 1.03.377
a great deal of your wit, too, lies in your 2.01. 98 P
hector shall have a great catch, and /'a knock 2.01.100 P
of a king | so great as our dread father's, in a 2.02. 27
bear the great sway of his affairs with reason, 2.02. 35
disgrace to your great worths, and shame to me, 2.02.151
and that great minds, of partial indulgence | to 2.02.178
yours, | you valiant offspring of great priamus. 2.02.207
i was advertis'd their great general slept, 2.02.211
o thou great thunder–darter of olympus, forget 2.03. 10 P
folly and ignorance, be thine in great revenue! 2.03. 29 P
he burns | with entertaining great hyperion. 2.03.197
please it our great general | to call together 2.03.259
all the island kings — disarm great hector. 3.01.154
desir'd my cressid in right great exchange, 3.03. 21
let him be sent, great princes, | and he shall 3.03. 27
now, great thetis' son! 3.03. 94
brave hector's breast | and great troy shriking. 3.03.141
then marvel not, thou great and complete man, 3.03.181
themselves, | and drave great mars to faction. 3.03.190
sing, | "great hector's sister did achilles win, 3.03.212
but our great ajax bravely beat down him." 3.03.213
and your great love to me restrains you thus. 3.03.221
to see great hector in his weeds of peace, | to 3.03.239
jove bless great ajax! 3.03.280 P
it is great morning, and the hour prefix'd | for 4.03. 1
whiles others fish with craft for great opinion, 4.04.103
i with great truth catch mere simplicity; 4.04.104
though the great bulk achilles be thy guard, 4.04.128
may pierce the head of the great combatant | and 4.05. 5
and great deal misprising | the knight oppos'd. 4.05. 74
in the extremity of great and little, | valor 4.05. 78
did in great ilion thus translate him to me. 4.05.112
thou art, great lord, my father's sister's son, 4.05.120
son, | a cousin–german to great priam's seed; 4.05.121
hence | a great addition earned in thy death. 4.05.141
and great achilles | doth long to see unarm'd 4.05.152
great agamemnon comes to meet us here. 4.05.159
from heart of very heart, great hector, welcome. 4.05.171
but, by great mars, the captain of us all, 4.05.198
breach whereout | hector's great spirit flew. 4.05.246
that this great soldier may his welcome know. 4.05.276
from my great purpose in to–morrow's battle. 5.01. 38
good night, great hector. 5.01. 83
you flow to great /distraction. 5.02. 41
great achilles | is arming, weeping, cursing, 5.05. 30
eye, | it is decreed hector the great must die. 5.07. 8
it be, | great hector was as good a man as he. 5.09. 6
great troy is ours, and our sharp wars are ended 5.09. 10
think, | you, the great toe of this assembly? COR 1.01.155
i the great toe! why the great toe? 1.01.156
i the great toe! why the great toe? 1.01.156
the dearth is great, | the people mutinous; 1.02. 10
to keep your great pretenses veil'd till when 1.02. 20
and her great charms | misguide thy opposers' 1.05. 21
is | able to bear against the great aufidius | a 1.06. 79
where great patricians shall attend and shrug, 1.09. 4
why, 'tis no great matter; 2.01. 28 P
will rob you of a great deal of patience. 2.01. 29 P
faith, there hath been many great men that have 2.02. 7 P
son, | who after great hostilius here was king; 2.03.240
twice being censor, | was his great ancestor. 2.03.245
break out, | and sack great rome with romans. 3.01.314
those whose great power must try him — even 3.03. 80
say their great enemy is gone, and they | stand 4.02. 6
appear well in these wars, his great opposer, 4.03. 35 P
if it be your will, | where great aufidius lies. 4.04. 8
to all the volsces, | great hurt and mischief; 4.05. 67
denied but peace is a great maker of cuckolds. 4.05.229 P
the nobles in great earnestness are going | all 4.06. 58
of intercession which | great nature cries, 5.03. 33
and stick i' th' wars | like a great sea–mark, 5.03. 74
thou know'st, great son, | the end of war's 5.03.140
we have all | great cause to give great thanks. 5.04. 60
we have all | great cause to give great thanks. 5.04. 60
we'll deliver you | of your great danger. 5.06. 14
sold the blood and labor | of our great action; 5.06. 47
but still subsisting | under your great command. 5.06. 73
made my heart | too great for what contains it. 5.06.103
the great danger | which this man's life did owe 5.06.136
takes from aufidius a great part of blame. 5.06.145
pius | for many good and great deserts to rome. TIT 1.01. 24
thou great defender of this capitol, | stand 1.01. 77
create | lord saturninus rome's great emperor, 1.01.232
no more, great empress, bassianus comes. 2.03. 52
great reason that my noble lord be rated | for 2.03. 81
and might not gain so great a happiness | as 2.04. 20
for all my blood in rome's great quarrel shed, 3.01. 4
but me more good to see so great a lord | basely 4.02. 37
nor great alcides, nor the god of war, | shall 4.02. 95
frantic wretch, that holp'st to make me great, 4.04. 59
i have received letters from great rome | which 5.01. 2
therefore, great lords, be as your titles 5.01. 5
brave slip, sprung from the great andronicus, 5.01. 9
my master is the great rich capulet, and if you ROM 1.02. 79 P
too great oppression for a tender thing. 1.04. 24
ask'd for and sought for, in the great chamber. 1.05. 13 P
a montague, | the only son of your great enemy. 1.05.137
good mercutio, my business was great, and in 2.04. 50 P
love is like a great natural that runs lolling 2.04. 91 P
we'll keep no great ado — a friend or two, 3.04. 23
in this rage, with some great kinsman's bone, 4.03. 53
a great suspicion. stay the friar too. 5.03.187
some work, some dedication | to the great lord. TIM 1.01. 20
this confluence, this great flood of visitors. 1.01. 42
so they come by great bellies. 1.01.206 P
great men should drink with harness on their 1.02. 52
he commands us to provide, and give great gifts, 1.02.192
my master is awak'd by great occasion | to call 2.02. 21
of your estate | and your great flow of debts. 2.02.142
great timon! 2.02.168
whose death he's stepp'd | into a great estate. 2.02.224
having great and instant occasion to use fifty 3.01. 18 P
a little part, and undo a great deal of honor! 3.02. 48 P
such may rail against great buildings. 3.04. 65 P
my lords, | as you are great, be pitifully good. 3.05. 52
you great benefactors, sprinkle our society with 3.06. 70 P
thy great fortunes | are made thy chief 4.02. 43
can bear great fortune | but by contempt of 4.03. 7
forgetting thy great deeds when neighbor states, 4.03. 95
go great with tigers, dragons, wolves, and bears 4.03.189
and with his great attraction | robs the vast 4.03.436
poor straggling soldiers with | great quantity. 5.01. 7
which argues a great sickness in his judgment 5.01. 29
have travail'd in the great show'r of your gifts 5.01. 70
and enter in our ears like great triumphers | in 5.01.196
shall sit and pant in your great chairs of ease, 5.04. 11
nor are they such | that these great tow'rs, 5.04. 25
when they are in great danger, i recover them. JC 1.01. 24 P
to see great pompey pass the streets of rome; 1.01. 42
of mine hath buried | thoughts of great value, 1.02. 50
i, as aeneas, our great ancestor, | did from the 1.02.112
our caesar feed | that he is grown so great? 1.02.150
when went there by an age since the great flood 1.02.152
he is a great observer, and he looks | quite 1.02.202
all tending to the great opinion | that rome 1.02.318
him and his worth, and our great need of him, 1.03.161
which is a great way growing on the south, 2.01.107
and that great vow | which did incorporate and 2.01.272
signifies that from you great rome shall suck 2.02. 87
and that great men shall press | for tinctures, 2.02. 88
there | speak to great caesar as he comes along. 2.04. 38
read it, great caesar. 3.01. 7
to sound more sweetly in great caesar's ear 3.01. 50
great caesar — 3.01. 75
of the matter, | caesar has had great wrong. 3.02.110
all the while ran blood) great caesar fell. 3.02.189
and now, octavius, | listen great things. 4.01. 41
did not great julius bleed for justice' sake? 4.03. 19
even so great men great losses should endure. 4.03.193
even so great men great losses should endure. 4.03.193
he bears too great a mind. 5.01.112
the gods defend him from so great a shame! 5.04. 23
he, | did that they did in envy of great caesar; 5.05. 70
from fife, great king, | where the norweyan MAC 1.02. 48
great happiness! 1.02. 58
and great prediction | of noble having and of 1.03. 55
thy praises in his kingdom's great defense, 1.03. 99
thou wouldst be great, | art not without 1.05. 18
thou'ldst have, great glamis, | that which cries 1.05. 22
give him tending, | he brings great news. 1.05. 38
great glamis! 1.05. 54
this night's great business into my dispatch, 1.05. 68
and his great love, sharp as his spur, hath holp 1.06. 23
hath been | so clear in his great office, that 1.07. 18
who shall bear the guilt | of our great quell? 1.07. 72
and | sent forth great largess to your offices. 2.01. 14
of hurt minds, great nature's second course, 2.02. 36
will all great neptune's ocean wash this blood 2.02. 57
drink, sir, is a great provoker of three things. 2.03. 25 P
up, up, and see | the great doom's image! 2.03. 78
in the great hand of god i stand, and thence 2.03.130
it had been as a gap in our great feast, | and 3.01. 12
hand | cancel and tear to pieces that great bond 3.02. 49
denies his person | at our great bidding? 3.04.128
great business must be wrought ere noon: 3.05. 22
until | great birnan wood to high dunsinane hill 4.01. 93
that this great king may kindly say | our duties 4.01.131
great tyranny, lay thou thy basis sure, | for 4.03. 32
their malady convinces | the great assay of art; 4.03.143
let's make us med'cines of our great revenge 4.03.214
a great perturbation in nature, to receive at 5.01. 9 P
great dunsinane he strongly fortifies. 5.02. 12
by this great clatter, one of greatest note 5.07. 21
see, | so great a day as this is cheaply bought. 5.09. 3
but the great cannon to the clouds shall tell, HAM 1.02.126
my news shall be the fruit to that great feast. 2.02. 52
that great baby you see there is not yet out of 2.02.382 P
and enterprises of great pitch and moment | with 3.01. 85
madness in great ones must not /unwatch'd go. 3.01.188
then there's hope a great man's memory may 3.02.132 P
where love is great, the littlest doubts are 3.02.171

where little fears grow great, great love grows 3.02.172
little fears grow great, great love grows there. 3.02.172
the great man down, you mark his favorite flies, 3.02.204
your mother, in most great affliction of spirit, 3.02.311 P
as my great power thereof may give thee sense, 4.03. 59
rightly to be great | is not to stir without 4.04. 53
great | is not to stir without great argument, 4.04. 54
each toy seems prologue to some great amiss, 4.05. 18
where th' offense is, let the great axe fall. 4.05.219
is the great love the general gender bear him, 4.07. 18
and the more pity that great folk should have 5.01. 27 P
might be in 's time a great buyer of land, with 5.01.104 P
or, if 'a do not, 'tis no great matter there. 5.01.151 P
trade that 'a will keep out water a great while, 5.01.171 P
and, but that great command o'ersways the order, 5.01.228
and many such–like /as's of great charge, | that 5.02. 43
you that 'a has laid a great wager on your head. 5.02.102 P
of very soft society, and great showing; 5.02.108 P
i take him to be a soul of great article, and 5.02.117 P
great rivals in our youngest daughter's love, LR 1.01. 46
as my great patron thought on in my prayers — 1.01.142
for you, great king, | i would not from your 1.01.208
it would make a great gap in your own honor and 1.02. 84 P
there's a great abatement of kindness appears as 1.04. 60 P
goneril, | to the great love i bear you — 1.04.312
under th' allowance of your great aspect, 2.02.106
go thy hold when a great wheel runs down a hill, 2.04. 72 P
but the great one that goes upward, let him draw 2.04. 73 P
and danger | speak 'gainst so great a number? 2.04.240
that their great stars | thron'd and set high? 3.01. 22
let the great gods, | that keep this dreadful 3.02. 49
the realm of albion | come to great confusion. 3.02. 86
bending his sword | to his great master, who, 4.02. 75
therefore great france | my mourning and 4.04. 25
it was great ignorance, gloucester's eyes being 4.05. 9
shake patiently my great affliction off. 4.06. 36
to quarrel with your great opposeless wills, 4.06. 38
this great world | shall so wear out to nought. 4.06.134
mightst behold the great image of authority: 4.06.158 P
that we are come | to this great stage of fools. 4.06.183
cure this great breach in his abused nature, 4.07. 14
be comforted, good madam, the great rage, | you 4.07. 77
a wall'd prison, packs and sects of great ones, 5.03. 18
thy great employment | will not bear question; 5.03. 32
great thing of us forgot! 5.03.237
what comfort to this great decay may come 5.03.298
three great ones of the city, | in personal suit OTH 1.01. 8
forsooth, a great arithmetician, | one michael 1.01. 19
and little of this great world can i speak 1.03. 86
i will your serious and great business scant 1.03.267
that i spake of, our great captain's captain, 2.01. 74
great jove, othello guard, | and swell his sail 2.01. 77
the great contention of /the sea and skies 2.01. 92
as this will i ensnare as great a fly as cassio. 2.01.169 P
it gives me wonder great as my content | to see 2.01.183
cyprus, | i have found great love amongst them. 2.01.205
she loves him, 'tis apt and of great credit. 2.01.287
i stand accomptant for as great a sin), | but 2.01.293
and 'tis great pity that the noble moor | should 2.03.138
and your name is great | in mouths of wisest 2.03.192
that he you hurt is of great fame in cyprus, 3.01. 45
of great fame in cyprus, | and great affinity; 3.01. 46
for sure he fills it up with great ability — 3.03.247
yet 'tis the plague /of great ones, 3.03.273
things, | though great ones are their object. 3.04.145
i would on great occasion speak with you. 4.01. 58
it is a great price | for a small vice. 4.03. 69
i have no great devotion to the deed, | and yet 5.01. 8
my great revenge | had stomach for them all. 5.02. 74
for he was great of heart. 5.02.361
which in the scuffles of great fights hath burst ANT 1.01. 7
he comes too short of that great property 1.01. 58
there's a great spirit gone! 1.02.122
though, between them and a great cause, they 1.02.139 P
throw | pompey the great and all his dignities 1.02.188
natural vice to hate | /our great competitor. 1.04. 3
we do bear | so great weight in his lightness. 1.04. 25
that i might sleep out this great gap of time 1.05. 5
and great pompey | would stand and make his eyes 1.05. 31
that great med'cine hath | with his tinct gilded 1.05. 36
"say the firm roman to great egypt sends | this 1.05. 43
if the great gods be just, they shall assist 2.01. 1
that which combin'd us was most great, and let 2.02. 18
great mark antony | is now a widower. 2.02.119
all little jealousies, which now seem great, 2.02.131
and all great fears, which now import their 2.02.132
in our loves, | and sway our great designs! 2.02.148
for he hath laid strange courtesies and great 2.02.154
great, and increasing; 2.02.162
she made great caesar lay his sword to bed; 2.02.227
the world and my great office will sometimes 2.03. 1
three, | the senators alone of this great world, 2.06. 9
you have been a great thief by sea. 2.06. 92 P
it is to have a name in great men's fellowship. 2.07. 11 P
we bid a loud farewell | to these great fellows. 2.07.133
place, note well, | may make too great an act. 3.01. 13
you take from me a great part of myself; 3.02. 24
our great navy's rigg'd. 3.05. 19
great media, parthia, and armenia | he gave to 3.06. 14
though you fled | from that great face of war, 3.13. 5
say to great caesar this in /deputation: 3.13. 74
when one so great begins to rage, he's hunted 4.01. 7
determine this great war in single fight! 4.04. 37
great herod to incline himself to caesar | and 4.06. 13
to this great fairy i'll commend thy acts, 4.08. 12
smiling from | the world's great snare uncaught? 4.08. 18
had our great palace the capacity | to camp this 4.08. 32
wouldst thou be window'd in great rome, and see 4.14. 72
farewell, great chief. shall i strike now? 4.14. 93
must be as great | as that which makes it. 4.15. 5
o sun, | burn the great sphere thou mov'st in! 4.15. 10
had i great juno's power, | the strong–wing'd 4.15. 34
the breaking of so great a thing should make | a 5.01. 14
and it is great | to do that thing that ends all 5.02. 4
your loss is as yourself, great; 5.02.101
devils do the gods great harm in their women; 5.02.276 P
that i might hear thee call great caesar ass 5.02.307
see | high order in this great solemnity. 5.02.366
been the fall of an ass, which is no great hurt. CYM 1.02. 37 P
him, i doubt not, a great deal from the matter. 1.04. 16 P
you are a great deal abus'd in too bold a 1.04.114 P
that our great king himself doth woo me oft 1.05. 14
thou art then | as great as is thy master — 1.05. 51
queen, and you | recoil from your great stock. 1.06.128
honor'd with confirmation your great judgment 1.06.174
of rich and exquisite form, their values great, 1.06.190
t' enjoy thy banish'd lord and this great land! 2.01. 65
one of your great knowing | should learn, being 2.03. 97
this, your king | hath heard of great augustus. 2.04. 11
be false and perjur'd | from thy great fail. 3.04. 64
in a great pool a swan's nest. 3.04.139
trims, wherein | you made great juno angry. 3.04.165
but our great court | made me to blame in memory 3.05. 50
great men, | that had a court no bigger than 3.06. 81
it is great morning. come away! — who's there? 4.02. 61
great griefs, i see, med'cine the less; 4.02.243
fear no more the frown o' th' great, | thou art 4.02.264
imogen, | the great part of my comfort, gone; 4.03. 5
great the slaughter is | here made by th' roman; 5.03. 78
great the answer be | britains must take. 5.03. 79
great jupiter be prais'd! 5.03. 84
and so, great pow'rs, | if you will take this 5.04. 26
great nature, like his ancestry, | moulded the 5.04. 48
praise o' th' world, | as great sicilius' heir. 5.04. 51
let us with care perform his great behest. 5.04.122
hail, great king! 5.05. 25
thou hadst, great king, a subject who | was 5.05.316
methought | great jupiter, upon his eagle back'd 5.05.427
and in the temple of great jupiter | our peace 5.05.482
antiochus the great | built up this city for his PER 1.ch. 17
that would be son to great antiochus. 1.01. 26
great king, | few love to hear the sins they 1.01. 91
the great antiochus, | 'gainst whom i am too 1.02. 16
since he's so great can make his will his act, 1.02. 18
all poverty was scorn'd, and pride so great, 1.04. 30
the great ones eat up the little ones. 2.01. 28 P
to express | my commendations great, whose 2.02. 9
our hearts nor outward eyes | /envied the great, 2.03. 26
for though | this king were great, his greatness 2.04. 14
the contrary) | as great in blood as i myself. 2.05. 80
the god of this great vast, rebuke these surges, 3.01. 1
yet my good will is great, though the gift small 3.04. 18
he will repent the breadth of his great voyage, 4.01. 36
roguing thieves serve the great pirate valdes, 4.01. 96
advanc'd in time to great and high estate. 4.04. 16
i am great with woe, and shall deliver weeping. 5.01.106
lest this great sea of joys rushing upon me 5.01.192
great sir, they shall be brought you to my house 5.03. 26
(besides the gods) for this great miracle. 5.03. 58
and wish great juno would | resume her ancient TNK 1.02. 21
leaden–footed | till his great rage be off him. 1.02. 85
repeat my wishes | to our great lord, of whose 1.03. 2
whose speed | the great bellona i'll solicit; 1.03. 13
observ'd him | since our great lord departed? 1.03. 34
in and kneel, with great assurance | that we, 1.03. 94
men of great quality, as may be judg'd | by 1.04. 14
and great apollo's mercy, all our best | their 1.04. 46
the prison i keep, though it be for great ones, 2.01. 3 P
and ignorance | the virtues of the great ones? 2.02.107
at whose great feet i offer up my penner. 3.05.124
off | this great adventure to a second trial. 3.06.119
be'st, | as thou art spoken, great and virtuous, 3.06.152
a great likelihood | of both their pardons; 4.01. 6
in the great lake that lies behind the palace, 4.01. 53
yet a great deal short, | methinks, of him 4.02. 89
but of a tough soul, seeming | as great as any. 4.02.118
they show | great and fine art in nature. 4.02.123
in great hope she had fix'd her liking on this 4.03. 64 P
would account i had a great penn'worth on't to 4.03. 67 P
make the number more i have great hope in this. 4.03. 98 P
force and great feat | must put my garland on, 5.01. 43
give me, great mars, | some token of thy 5.01. 60
o great corrector of enormous times, | shaker of 5.01. 62
i never at great feasts | sought to betray a 5.01.102
bless me with a sign | of thy great pleasure. 5.01.129
arise, great sir, and give the tidings ear 5.04. 46
our country is a great eating country, argo they STM II.C 5 P
so much come too short of your great trespass II.C 124
to be great | is, when the thread of hazard is III 19
spun, | a bottom great wound up, greatly undone. III 21
or what great danger dwells upon my suit? VEN 206
the sovereignty of either being so great | that LUC 69
and when great treasure is the meed proposed, 132
the guilt being great, the fear doth still 229
a little harm done to a great good end | for 528
"o opportunity, thy guilt is great! 876
wilt thou sort an hour great strifes to end? 899
great grief grieves most at that would do it 1117
in great commanders, grace and majesty | you 1387
then must the love be great 'twixt thee and me, PP 8. 3
ditty, | that to hear it was great pity. 20.12
once do frown, | then farewell his great renown; 20.46
why dost thou use | so great a sum of sums, yet SON 4. 8
great princes' favorites their fair leaves 25. 5
duty so great, which wit so poor as mine | may 26. 5
o no, thy love, though much, is not so great, 61. 9
was it the proud full sail of his great verse, 86. 1
so thy great gift, upon misprision growing, 87.11
and my great mind most kingly drinks it up: 114.10
all | wherein i should your great deserts repay, 117. 2
honoring, | or laid great bases for eternity, 125. 3
in things of great receipt with ease we prove 136. 7

GREAT–BELLIED 2 FR 0.0002 REL FR 1 V 1 P

with child, and being great–bellied, and longing MM 2.01. 98 P
great–bellied women, | that had not half a week H8 4.01. 76

/GREATER 1 FR 0.0001 REL FR 1 V 0 P

/i /am /greater /than /a /king; R2 4.01.305

GREATER 96 FR 0.0108 REL FR 76 V 20 P

a full poor cell, | and thy no greater father. TMP 1.02. 21
youth | of greater time than i shall show to be. TGV 2.07. 48
than the wit, for the greater hides the less. 3.01.362 P
of yours, and therefore the gift the greater. 4.04. 58 P
i will do a greater thing than that, upon your WIV 1.01.240 P
the greater file of the subject held the duke to MM 3.02.136 P
is no greater forfeit to the law than angelo who 4.02.158 P
you make my bonds still greater. 5.01. 8
their cheer is the greater that i am subdu'd. ADO 1.03. 72 P
but on this travail look for greater birth: 4.01.213
beg a greater matter, | thou now requests but LLL 5.02.207
greater than great, great, great, great pompey! 5.02.685 P
can you do me greater harm than hate? MND 3.02.271
the greater throw | may turn by fortune from the MV 2.01. 33
so doth the greater glory dim the less: 5.01. 93
no greater heart in thee? AYL 2.06. 4 P
ay, and greater wonders than that. 5.02. 28 P
do i labor for a greater esteem than may in some 5.02. 56 P
in padua | of greater sums than i have promised. SHR 3.02.135
to my heel with no greater a run but my head and 4.01. 15 P
greater than shows itself at the first view | to AWW 2.05. 68
in goodness, but greater a great deal in evil. 4.03.287 P
yet, for a greater confirmation | (for in an act WT 2.01.180
(which never tender lady hath borne greater) 2.02. 22
but smacks of something greater than herself, 4.04.158
a greater pow'r than we denies all this, | and JN 2.01.368
gives but the greater feeling to the worse. R2 1.03.301
greater he shall not be; 3.02. 98
i'll make it greater ere i part from thee, | and 1H4 5.04. 71
i would my means were greater and my waist 2H4 1.02.143 P
would of that seed grow to a greater falseness, 3.01. 90
revives two greater in the heirs of life; 4.01.198
to give a greater sum | than ever at one time H5 1.01. 79
the greater therefore should our courage be. 4.01. 2
the fewer men, the greater share of honor. 4.03. 22
what were it but to make my sorrow greater? 2H6 3.02.148
a sin, | but greater sin to keep a sinful oath. 5.01.183
i am resolv'd to bear a greater storm | than any 5.01.198
blows, | commanded always by the greater gust, 3H6 3.01. 88
the harder match'd, the greater victory: 5.01. 70
a greater gift than that i'll give my cousin. R3 3.01.115
a greater gift? o, that's the sword to it. 3.01.116
ensuing evil, if it fall, | greater than this. H8 2.01.142
to endure more miseries and greater far | than 3.02.389
never greater, | nor, i'll assure you, better 4.01. 11
and, to add greater honors to his age | than man 4.02. 67
to make the service greater than the god, | and TRO 2.02. 57
in self–assumption greater | than in the note of 2.03.124
sail swift, though greater hulks draw deep. 2.03.266
upon power, and throw forth greater themes | for COR 1.01.220
their hate with greater devotion than they can 2.02. 19 P
that's no matter, the greater part carries it, i 2.03. 37 P
in hazard | than stay, past doubt, for greater. 2.03.257
we are the greater pole, and in true fear | they 3.01.134
their obedience fails | to th' greater bench. 3.01.166
but a greater soldier than he, you wot one. 4.05.162 P
but i take him to be the greater soldier. 4.05.168 P
can make you greater than the queen of goths. TIT 1.01.269
a greater power than we can contradict | hath ROM 5.03.153
fortunes, | the greater scorns the lesser. TIM 4.03. 6
whiles they behold a greater than themselves, JC 1.02.209
the greater part, the horse in general, | are 4.02. 29
but brutus makes mine greater than they are. 4.03. 87
lesser than macbeth, and greater. MAC 1.03. 65
and for an earnest of a greater honor, | he bade 1.03.104
greater than both, by the all–hail hereafter! 1.05. 55
but where the greater malady is fix'd, | the LR 3.04. 8
until their greater pleasures first be known 5.03. 2
canst thou to damnation add | greater than that. OTH 3.03.373
which i have greater reason to believe now than 4.02.213 P
they are greater storms and tempests than ANT 1.02.148 P
how lesser enmities may give way to greater. 2.01. 43
but small to greater matters must give way. 2.02. 11
caesar and he are greater friends than ever. 2.05. 48
but it raises the greater war between him and 2.07. 9 P
the greater cantle of the world is lost | with 3.10. 6
so great a thing should make | a greater crack. 5.01. 15
art then | as great as is thy master — greater, CYM 1.05. 51
yet 'tis greater skill | in a true hate, to pray 2.05. 33
which attends | in place of greater state. 3.03. 78
therein false strook, can take no greater wound, 3.04.114
virtue and cunning were endowments greater PER 3.02. 27
whereto i am going, | greater than any /war. TNK 1.01.172
two greater and two better never yet | made 4.02. 62
is a prince too, | and, if it may be, greater; 4.02. 92
her pleading hath deserv'd a greater fee; VEN 609
to wink, being blinded with a greater light: LUC 375
unto a greater uproar tempts his veins. 427
abide, | and with the wind in greater fury fret. 648
the lesser thing should not the greater hide: 663
leaving his spoil perplex'd in greater pain. 733
that lose half with greater patience bear it 1158
than | retire again, till meeting greater ranks, 1441
and yet love knows it is a greater grief | to SON 40.11
doth but approve | /thy worth the greater, being 70. 6
fairer than at first, more strong, far greater. 119.12

GREATEST 53 FR 0.0060 REL FR 42 V 11 P

and your bum is the greatest thing about you, so MM 2.01.217 P
the greatest note of it is his melancholy. ADO 3.02. 54 P
which is the greatest lady, the highest? LLL 4.01. 46 P
this is the greatest error of all the rest. MND 5.01.246 P
and the magnificoes | of greatest port, have all MV 3.02.281
and the greatest of my pride is to see my ewes AYL 3.02. 76 P
that can assure my daughter greatest dower SHR 2.01.343
he that of greatest works is finisher | oft does AWW 2.01.136
the greatest grace lending grace, | ere twice 2.01.160
him from the wrath | of greatest justice. 3.04. 29
my greatest grief, | though little he do feel it 3.04. 32
which were the greatest obloquy i' th' world 4.02. 44
which were the greatest obloquy i' th' world 4.02. 48
the last was the greatest, but that i have not 4.03. 91 P
one of the greatest in the christian world 4.04. 2
but to himself | the greatest wrong of all. 5.03. 15
is a gentleman of the greatest promise that ever WT 1.01. 36 P
one must prove greatest. JN 2.01.332
lies | the mightiest of thy greatest enemies, R2 5.06. 32
upon enforcement flies with greatest speed, | so 2H4 1.01.120
art now one of the greatest men in this realm. 5.03. 87 P
it is the greatest admiration in the universal H5 4.01. 66 P
"the empty vessel makes the greatest sound." 4.04. 69 P
or else reproach be talbot's greatest fame! 1H6 3.02. 76
the greatest miracle that e'er ye wrought! 5.04. 66
hath won the greatest favor of the commons, 2H6 1.01.192
and so says york — for he hath greatest cause. 1.01.207
the greatest man in england but the king. 2.02. 82
thy greatest help is quiet, gentle nell. 2.04. 67

our earl of warwick, edward's greatest friend. 3H6 3.03. 45
which did subdue the greatest part of spain; 3.03. 82
the greatest strength and power that he can make R3 4.04.450
that when the greatest stroke of fortune falls H8 2.02. 35
the greatest monarch now alive may glory | in 5.02.198
where i know | our greatest friends attend us. COR 1.01.245
but that which gives my soul the greatest spurn TIT 3.01.101
i am the greatest, able to do least, | yet most ROM 5.03.223
the greatest of your having lacks a half | to TIM 2.02.144
i count it one of my greatest afflictions, say, 3.02. 56 P
your greatest want is, you want much of meat. 4.03.416
the greatest is behind. MAC 1.03.117
clatter, one of greatest note | seems bruited. 5.07. 21
the greatest discords be | that e'er our hearts OTH 2.01.198
or thou, the greatest soldier of the world, ANT 1.03. 38
of the world, | art turn'd the greatest liar. 1.03. 39
were't twenty of the greatest tributaries | that 3.13. 96
like the greatest spot | of all thy sex; 4.12. 35
i liv'd, the greatest prince o' th' world, | the 4.15. 54
be it known that we, the greatest, are 5.02.176
last, and greatest, | i would be thought a TNK 2.05. 14
for greatest scandal waits on greatest state. LUC 1006
for greatest scandal waits on greatest state. 1006
most worthy comfort, now my greatest grief, SON 48. 6
GREAT–EY'D 1 FR 0.0001 REL FR 1 V 0 P
arch'd like the great–ey'd juno's, but far TNK 4.02. 20
GREAT–GRANDFATHER
3 FR 0.0003 REL FR 3 V 0 P
deriv'd from edward, his great–grandfather. H5 1.01. 89
for you shall read that my great–grandfather 1.02.146
"what my great–grandfather and grandsire got, 3H6 2.02. 37
GREAT–GRANDSIRE 1 FR 0.0001 REL FR 1 V 0 P
a little time before | that our great–grandsire, 2H4 4.04.128
GREAT–GRANDSIRE'S
1 FR 0.0001 REL FR 1 V 0 P
my dread lord, to your great–grandsire's tomb, H5 1.02.103
GREAT–GROWN 1 FR 0.0001 REL FR 1 V 0 P
and take the great–grown traitor unawares. 3H6 4.08. 63
/GREATLY 1 FR 0.0001 REL FR 1 V 0 P
/great /king, /and /yet /not /greatly /good, R2 4.01.263
GREATLY 12 FR 0.0013 REL FR 9 V 3 P
i greatly fear my money is not safe. ERR 1.02.105
their daughters profit very greatly under you. LLL 4.02. 75 P
well, we cannot greatly condemn our success. AWW 3.06. 55 P
madam, i know not, nor i greatly care not, | god R2 5.02. 48
but in that small most greatly lived | this star H5 ep 5
it skills not greatly who impugns our doom. 2H6 3.01.281
for though they cannot greatly sting to hurt, 3H6 2.06. 94
and wonder greatly that man's face can fold | in TIT 2.03.266
but greatly to find quarrel in a straw | when HAM 4.04. 55
to hear music the general does not greatly care. OTH 3.01. 17 P
you, but | i do not greatly care to be deceiv'd, ANT 5.02. 14
spun, | a bottom great wound up, greatly undone. STM III 21
GREATNESS' 1 FR 0.0001 REL FR 1 V 0 P
on greatness' favor dream as i have done, | wake CYM 5.04.128
GREATNESS 80 FR 0.0090 REL FR 61 V 19 P
if thy greatness will | revenge it on him — for TMP 3.02. 53
i do beseech thy greatness, give him blows, 3.02. 64
no might nor greatness in mortality | can MM 3.02.185
o place and greatness! 4.01. 59
it pleaseth his greatness to impart to armado, a LLL 5.01.107 P
but, most esteemed greatness, will you hear the 5.02.885 P
the greatness whereof i cannot enough commend, MV 4.01.158 P
and in the greatness of my word, you die. AYL 1.03. 89
to you what further becomes his greatness, even AWW 3.06. 70 P
i am above thee, but be not afraid of greatness. TN 2.05.144 P
some are /born great, some /achieve greatness, 2.05.145 P
and some have greatness thrust upon 'em. 2.05.146 P
"be not afraid of greatness": 'twas well writ. 3.04. 39 P
"some achieve greatness" — 3.04. 43 P
"and some have greatness thrust upon them." 3.04. 45 P
"some are born great, some achieve greatness, 5.01.371 P
and some have greatness thrown upon them." 5.01.371 P
your greatness | hath not been us'd to fear. WT 4.04. 17
he comes not | like to his father's greatness. 5.01. 89
art perjur'd too, | and sooth'st up greatness. JN 3.01.121
that greatness should so grossly offer it. 4.02. 94
rage, forget | your worth, your greatness, and 4.03. 86
pope, | your sovereign greatness and authority. 5.01. 4
the scourge of greatness to be us'd on it, | and 1H4 1.03. 11
and that same greatness too which our own hands 1.03. 12
though sometimes it show greatness, courage, 3.01.179
to, | accompany the greatness of thy blood, 3.02. 16
which oft the ear of greatness needs must hear 3.02. 24
he presently, as greatness knows itself, | steps 4.03. 74
and such a flood of greatness fell on you, 5.01. 48
complexion of my greatness to acknowledge it. 2H4 2.02. 5 P
make me out of love with my greatness. 2.02. 12 P
that i and greatness were compell'd to kiss), 3.01. 74
he set abroach | in shadow of such greatness? 4.02. 15
between his greatness and thy other brethren. 4.04. 26
thou seek'st the greatness that will overwhelm 4.05. 97
that would deliver up his greatness so | into 5.02.111
and show my sail of greatness | when i do rouse H5 1.02.274
model to thy inward greatness, | like little 2.pr. 16
that day to see his greatness and to teach 4.01.184 P
twin–born with greatness, subject to the breath 4.01.234
o, be sick, great greatness, | and bid thy 4.01.251
and greatness of his place be grief to us, | yet 2H6 1.01.173
as for words, whose greatness answers words, 4.10. 53
that i would rather hide me from my greatness — R3 3.07.161
than in my greatness covet to be hid | and in 3.07.163
as suits | the greatness of his person. H8 2.01.100
for i feel | the last fit of my greatness — 3.01. 78
touch'd the highest point of all my greatness, 3.02.223
a long farewell to all my greatness! 3.02.351
full surely | his greatness is a–ripening, nips 3.02.357
knowing she will not lose her wonted greatness, 4.02.102
and by those claim their greatness, not by blood 5.04. 38
his honor and the greatness of his name | shall 5.04. 51
sides but even now | corrivall'd greatness? TRO 1.03. 44
o'er–wrested seeming | he acts thy greatness in; 1.03.158
full of envy at his greatness as cerberus is at 2.01. 33 P
did move your greatness and this noble state 2.03.109
possess'd he is with greatness, | and speaks not 2.03.170
'tis certain, greatness, once fall'n out with 3.03. 75
who deserves greatness | deserves your hate; COR 1.01.176
we are shent for keeping your greatness back? 5.02. 99 P
th' abuse of greatness is when it disjoins JC 2.01. 18
thee, my dearest partner of greatness, that thou MAC 1.05. 11 P
ignorant of what greatness is promis'd thee. 1.05. 13 P
many | as will to greatness dedicate themselves, 4.03. 75
his greatness weigh'd, his will is not his own, HAM 1.03. 17
as by your safety, greatness, wisdom, all things 4.07. 8
mine honesty | shall not make poor my greatness, ANT 2.02. 93
next, cleopatra does confess thy greatness, 3.12. 16
not more in parting | than greatness going off. 4.13. 6
lest, in her greatness, by some mortal stroke 5.01. 64
and i send him | the greatness he has got. 5.02. 30
some squeaking cleopatra boy my greatness | i' 5.02.220
breed of greatness! CYM 4.02. 25
only | affected greatness got by you, not you; 5.05. 38
or, by our greatness and the grace of it 5.05.132
let it suffice the greatness of your powers | to PER 2.01. 8
his greatness was no guard | to bar heaven's 2.04. 14
of such a virtuous greatness that this lady, TNK 2.02.257
GREAT–SIZ'D 2 FR 0.0002 REL FR 2 V 0 P
a great–siz'd monster of ingratitudes. TRO 3.03.147
and, thou great–siz'd coward, | no space of 5.10. 26
GREAT'ST 8 FR 0.0009 REL FR 7 V 1 P
far surpasseth sycorax | as great'st does least. TMP 3.02.103
which was the great'st | of his profession, that AWW 1.03.243
when miracles have by the great'st been denied. 2.01.141
that he has taken their great'st commander, and 3.05. 5 P
worse than the great'st infection | that e'er WT 1.02.423
her thanks | in the great'st humbleness, and H8 5.01. 65
the great'st taste | most palates theirs. COR 3.01.103
empery | would make the great'st king double — CYM 1.06.121
GREAT–UNCLE 1 FR 0.0001 REL FR 0 V 1 P
and your great–uncle edward the plack prince of H5 4.07. 93 P
GREAT–UNCLE'S 1 FR 0.0001 REL FR 1 V 0 P
and your great–uncle's, edward the black prince, H5 1.02.105
GRECE *(see grise, grize)*
GRECIAN 23 FR 0.0026 REL FR 21 V 2 P
and sigh'd his soul toward the grecian tents, MV 5.01. 5
had his brains dash'd out with a grecian club, AYL 4.01. 98 P
and look how many grecian tents do stand TRO 1.03. 79
troy, | to rouse a grecian that is true in love. 1.03.279
the grecian dames are sunburnt, and not worth 1.03.282
but if there be not in our grecian /mould | a 1.03.293
when helenus beholds | a grecian and his sword, 2.02. 43
he brought a grecian queen, whose youth and 2.02. 78
to see these grecian lords! 3.03.138
the grecian diomed, and our antenor | deliver'd 4.02. 62
i'll bring her to the grecian presently; 4.03. 6
i will corrupt the grecian sentinels, | to give 4.04. 72
the grecian youths are full of quality; 4.04. 76
and bring aeneas and the grecian with you. 4.04.100
grecian, thou dost not use me courteously, | to 4.04.121
thou couldst say, "this hand is grecian all, 4.05.125
desire | my famous cousin to our grecian tents. 4.05.151
stone will cost | a drop of grecian blood. 4.05.224
when many times the captive grecian falls, 5.03. 40
hold thy whore, grecian! 5.04. 24 P
a retire upon our grecian part. 5.08. 15
when it spit forth blood | at grecian sword, COR 1.03. 43
set, | and you in grecian tires are painted new; SON 53. 8
GRECIAN'S 1 FR 0.0001 REL FR 1 V 0 P
her bawdy veins, | a grecian's life hath sunk; TRO 4.01. 71
GRECIANS' 1 FR 0.0001 REL FR 1 V 0 P
wars since you refus'd | the grecians' cause. TRO 4.05.268
GRECIANS 6 FR 0.0006 REL FR 5 V 1 P
quoth she, | "why the grecians sacked troy? AWW 1.03. 71
the grecians keep our aunt. TRO 2.02. 80
i must then to the grecians? 4.04. 55
all, | to which the grecians are most prompt and 4.04. 88
you wisest grecians, pardon me this brag. 4.05.257
whereupon the grecians began to proclaim 5.04. 16 P
'GREE *(also agree, etc.)*
'GREE 1 FR 0.0001 REL FR 0 V 1 P
how 'gree you now? MV 2.02.101 P
/GREECE* 1 FR 0.0001 REL FR 1 V 0 P
/from /isles /of /greece | /the /princes TRO pr 1
GREECE* 21 FR 0.0023 REL FR 16 V 5 P
hector of greece, my boy! WIV 2.03. 34 P
five summers have i spent in farthest greece, ERR 1.01.132
as stephen sly, and old john naps of greece, SHR in.2. 93
as did the youthful paris once to greece, | with 1H6 5.05.104
helen of greece was fairer far than thou, 3H6 2.02.146
a man as troilus than agamemnon and all greece. TRO 1.02.246 P
thou great commander, nerves and bone of greece, 1.03. 55
as agamemnon and the hand of greece | should 1.03. 63
if there be one among the fair'st of greece 1.03.265
so shall each lord of greece, from tent to tent. 1.03.307
the plague of greece upon thee, thou mongrel 2.01. 12 P
would make thee the loathsomest scab in greece. 2.01. 29 P
troilus had rather troy were borne to greece 4.01. 47
i tell thee, lord of greece, | she is as far 4.04.123
hail, all the state of greece! 4.05. 65
first, all you peers of greece, go to my tent; 4.05.271
a graver bench | than ever frown'd in greece. COR 3.01.107
gratis, as 'twas us'd | sometime in greece — 3.01.115
the gods of greece protect you! PER 1.04. 97
in our country of greece gets more with begging 2.01. 64 P
before the which is drawn the power of greece, LUC 1368
'GREED 5 FR 0.0005 REL FR 5 V 0 P
means | plotted and 'greed on for my happiness. TGV 2.04.183
between you 'greed concerning her observance? MM 4.01. 41
your dowry 'greed on; SHR 2.01.270
we have 'greed so well together | that upon 2.01.297
this 'greed upon, | to part with unhack'd edges ANT 2.06. 37
GREEDILY 1 FR 0.0001 REL FR 1 V 0 P
and greedily devour the treacherous bait; ADO 3.01. 28
GREEDINESS 4 FR 0.0004 REL FR 1 V 3 P
thither with all greediness of affection are WT 5.02.102 P
th' unsatiate greediness of his desire, | and R3 3.07. 7
the wolf, thy greediness would afflict thee, and TIM 4.03.334 P
fox in stealth, wolf in greediness, dog in LR 3.04. 93 P
GREEDY 7 FR 0.0008 REL FR 6 V 1 P
o'er my exteriors with such a greedy intention, WIV 1.03. 66 P
of man | so keen and greedy to confound a man. MV 3.02.276
so many greedy looks of young and old | through R2 5.02. 13
stopping my greedy ear with their bold deeds, 2H4 1.01. 78
and with a greedy ear | devour up my discourse. OTH 1.03.149
to the greedy touch | of common–kissing titan, CYM 3.04.162
rolling his greedy eyeballs in his head. LUC 368
'GREEING 1 FR 0.0001 REL FR 1 V 0 P
eye well knows what with his gust is 'greeing, SON 114.11
/GREEK 1 FR 0.0001 REL FR 1 V 0 P
/on /one /and /other /side, /troyan /and /greek, TRO pr 21
GREEK 26 FR 0.0029 REL FR 21 V 5 P
'tis a greek invocation, to call fools into a AYL 2.05. 59 P
long studying at rheims, as cunning in greek, SHR 2.01. 81 P
and this small packet of greek and latin books. 2.01.100
i prithee, foolish greek, depart from me. TN 4.01. 18
then she's a merry greek indeed. TRO 1.02.109 P
ay, greek, that is my name. 1.03.246
and every greek of mettle, let him know, | what 1.03.258
truer, | than ever greek did couple in his arms, 1.03.276
a valiant greek, aeneas, take his hand, 4.01. 8
'twas to bring this greek | to calchas' house, 4.01. 37
for her delivery to this valiant greek | comes 4.03. 2
entreat her fair, and, by my soul, fair greek, 4.04.113
this blended knight, half troyan and half greek. 4.05. 86
were thy commixtion greek and troyan so | that 4.05.124
the sinews of this leg | all greek, and this all 4.05.127
there's many a greek and troyan dead | since 4.05.214
sweet honey greek, tempt me no more to folly. 5.02. 18
bid me do any thing but that, sweet greek. 5.02. 27
guardian! why, greek! 5.02. 47
ay, greek, and that shall be divulged well | in 5.02.163
hark, greek: 5.02.167
what art /thou, greek? 5.04. 26
stand, thou greek, thou art a goodly mark. 5.06. 27
i am unarm'd, forgo this vantage, greek. 5.08. 9
ay, he spoke greek. JC 1.02.279 P
but, for mine own part, it was greek to me. 1.02.284 P
GREEKISH 9 FR 0.0010 REL FR 8 V 1 P
knit all the greekish ears | to his experienc'd TRO 1.03. 67
'fore all the greekish heads, which with one 1.03.221
the edge of steel | or force of greekish sinews. 3.01.153
and all the greekish girls shall tripping sing, 3.03.211
thou shouldst not bear from me a greekish member 4.05.130
cruel way | through ranks of greekish youth, and 4.05.185
and diomed | in ilion, on your greekish embassy. 4.05.216
i'll heat his blood with greekish wine to–night, 5.01. 1
might send that greekish whoremasterly villain 5.04. 7 P
GREEKS' 1 FR 0.0001 REL FR 1 V 0 P
thanks and good night to the greeks' general. TRO 5.01. 73
/GREEKS 1 FR 0.0001 REL FR 1 V 0 P
/fresh /and /yet /unbruised /greeks /do /pitch TRO pr 14
GREEKS 28 FR 0.0031 REL FR 26 V 2 P
caesars and with cannibals | and troiant greeks? 2H4 2.04.167
against the greeks that would have ent'red troy. 3H6 2.01. 52
the greeks are strong, and skillful to their TRO 1.01. 7
stay behind her father, let her to the greeks; 1.01. 81 P
there is among the greeks | a lord of troyan 1.02. 12
there is amongst the greeks achilles, a better 1.02.247 P
hector, in view of troyans and of greeks, 1.03.273
thus once again says nestor from the greeks: 2.02. 2
though no man lesser fears the greeks than i 2.02. 8
paris should do some vengeance on the greeks. 2.02. 73
for an old aunt whom the greeks held captive, 2.02. 77
the dull and factious nobles of the greeks 2.02.209
that all the greeks begin to worship ajax; 3.03.182
as for her greeks and troyans suff'red death. 4.01. 75
a woeful cressid 'mongst the merry greeks! 4.04. 56
most dearly welcome to the greeks, sweet lady. 4.05. 18
when that a ring of greeks have /hemm'd thee in, 4.05.193
fall greeks, fail fame, honor or go or stay, 5.01. 43
and i do stand engag'd to many greeks, | even in 5.03. 68
and there the strawy greeks, ripe for his edge, 5.05. 24
come both you cogging greeks, have at you both! 5.06. 11
the greeks upon advice did bury ajax | that slew TIT 1.01.379
when subtile greeks surpris'd king priam's troy. 5.03. 84
he finds him | striking too short at greeks. HAM 2.02.469
all curses madded hecuba gave the greeks, | and CYM 4.02.313
gazing upon the greeks with little lust. LUC 1384
as 'twere encouraging the greeks to fight, 1402
eyes | of all the greeks that are thine enemies. 1470
/GREEN 3 FR 0.0003 REL FR 1 V 2 P
turn'd my daughter into /green; WIV 5.05.201 P
why? did you take her in /green? 5.05.208 P
ourself and bushy, /bagot /here /and /green, R2 1.04. 23
GREEN 97 FR 0.0109 REL FR 76 V 21 P
how lush and lusty the grass looks! how green! TMP 2.01. 54 P
with an eye of green in't. 2.01. 56 P
summon'd me hither, to this short–grass'd green? 4.01. 83
and on this green land | answer your summons; 4.01.130
by moonshine do the green sour ringlets make, 5.01. 37
and 'twixt the green sea and the azur'd vault 5.01. 43
urchins, ouphes, and fairies, green and white, WIV 4.04. 50
that quaint in green she shall be loose enrob'd, 4.06. 41
master doctor, my daughter is in green. 5.03. 2 P
fairies, black, grey, green, and white, | you 5.05. 37
th' expressure that it bears, green let it be, 5.05. 67
an oak but with one green leaf on it would have ADO 2.01.240 P
spring is near when green geese are a–breeding. LLL 1.01. 97
of the sea–water green, sir. 1.02. 82 P
green indeed is the color of lovers; 1.02. 86 P
it was so, sir, for she had a green wit. 1.02. 89 P
makes flesh a deity, | a green goose a goddess; 4.03. 73
lark to shepherd's ear | when wheat is green, MND 1.01.185
fairy queen, | to dew her orbs upon the green. 2.01. 9
and now they never meet in grove or green, | by 2.01. 28
and the green corn | hath rotted ere his youth 2.01. 94
and the quaint mazes in the wanton green | for 2.01. 99
this green plot shall be our stage, this 3.01. 3 P
with purple grapes, green figs, and mulberries; 3.01.167
turns into yellow gold his salt green streams. 3.02.393
his eyes were green as leeks. 5.01.335
unto the green holly, | most friendship is AYL 2.07.180
a shrunk panel, and like green timber warp, warp 3.03. 88 P
a green and gilded snake had wreath'd itself, 4.03.108
that o'er the green corn–field did pass, | in 5.03. 18
you may be jogging whiles your boots are green. SHR 3.02.211
sun, | that every thing i look on seemeth green; 4.05. 47
and with a green and yellow melancholy | she sat TN 2.04.113
saw myself unbreech'd | in my green velvet coat, WT 1.02.156
boys, too green and idle | for girls of nine), o 3.02.181
the green neptune | a ram and bleated; 4.04. 28
that yon green boy shall have no sun to ripe JN 2.01.472
how green you are and fresh in this old world! 3.04.145
so, green, thou art the midwife to my woe, | and R2 2.02. 62

bushy and green, i will not vex your souls — 3.01. 2
where is green? 3.02.123
is bushy, green, and the earl of wiltshire dead? 3.02.141
the fresh green lap of fair king richard's land, 3.03. 47
i mean the earl of wiltshire, bushy, green. 3.04. 53
that strew the green lap of the new-come spring? 5.02. 47
knaves in kendal green came at my back and let 1H4 2.04.222 P
these men in kendal green when it was so dark 2.04.232 P
i told thee they were ill for a green wound? 2H4 2.01. 98 P
peter bullcalf o' th' green! 3.02.172 P
i remember at mile-end green, when i lay at 3.02.279 P
art not firm enough, since griefs are green, 4.05.203
sharp as a pen, and 'a /babbl'd of green fields. H5 2.03. 17 P
it is good for your green wound and your ploody 5.01. 42 P
the freckled cowslip, burnet, and green clover, 5.02. 49
for, being green, there is great hope of help. 2H6 3.01.287
how much the estate is green and yet ungovern'd. R3 2.02.127
yet, since it is but green, it should be put 2.02.135
and't had been a green hair, i should have TRO 1.02.152 P
were your days | as green as ajax', and your 2.03.254
thou green sarcenet flap for a sore eye, thou 5.01. 31 P
the fields are fragrant and the woods are green. TIT 2.02. 2
the green leaves quiver with the cooling wind 2.03. 14
her vestal livery is but sick and green, | and ROM 2.02. 8
hath not so green, so quick, so fair an eye | as 3.05.220
where bloody tybalt, yet but green in earth, 4.03. 42
green earthen pots, bladders, and musty seeds, 5.01. 46
convert o' th' instant, green virginity! TIM 4.01. 7
and wakes it now to look so green and pale | at MAC 1.07. 37
seas incarnadine, | making the green one red. 2.02. 60
our dear brother's death | the memory be green, HAM 1.02. 2
you speak like a green girl, | unsifted in such 1.03.101
drinks the green mantle of the standing pool; LR 3.04.133 P
in him that folly and green minds look after; OTH 2.01.247 P
by a sycamore tree, | sing all a green willow; 4.03. 41
"sing all a green willow must be my garland. 4.03. 51
when i was green in judgment, cold in blood, ANT 1.05. 74
and o'er green neptune's back | with ships made 4.14. 58
a withered branch, that's only green at top; PER 2.02. 43
of her weed | to strow thy green with flowers. 4.01. 14
better lads nev'r danc'd | under green tree; TNK 2.03. 39
"for i'll cut my green coat a foot above my knee 3.04. 19
sing to her such green songs of love as she says 4.03. 81 P
power hast turn'd | green neptune into purple, 5.01. 50
with that thy rare green eye — which never yet 5.01.144
ear, | or like a fairy, trip upon the green, VEN 146
mellow plum doth fall, the green sticks fast, 527
say, | the text is old, the orator too green, 806
on the green coverlet, whose perfect white LUC 394
with young adonis, lovely, fresh, and green, PP 4. 2
and stood stark naked on the brook's green brim. 6.10
like a green plum that hangs upon a tree, | and 10. 5
not, | green plants bring not forth their dye; 17.26
and summer's green all girded up in sheaves SON 12. 7
kissing with golden face the meadows green, 33. 3
and they shall live, and he in them still green. 63.14
and true, | making no summer of another's green, 68.11
first i saw you fresh, which yet are green. 104. 8
GREEN-A 2 FR 0.0002 REL FR 0 V 2 P
/une /boite /en verd, a box, a green-a box. WIV 1.04. 46 P
a green-a box. 1.04. 47 P
GREEN-DROPPING 1 FR 0.0001 REL FR 1 V 0 P
and in the breach appears | green-dropping sap, VEN 1176
GREENER 1 FR 0.0001 REL FR 1 V 0 P
between the promise of his greener days | and H5 2.04.136
GREEN-EY'D 1 FR 0.0001 REL FR 1 V 0 P
it is the green-ey'd monster which doth mock OTH 3.03.166
GREEN-EYED 1 FR 0.0001 REL FR 1 V 0 P
and shudd'ring fear, and green-eyed jealousy! MV 3.02.110
GREENLY 2 FR 0.0002 REL FR 1 V 1 P
kate, i cannot look greenly, nor gasp out my H5 5.02.143 P
and we have done but greenly | in hugger-mugger
HAM 4.05. 83
GREENS 1 FR 0.0001 REL FR 1 V 0 P
in warlike march these greens before your town, JN 2.01.242
GREEN-SICKNESS 4 FR 0.0004 REL FR 2 V 2 P
they fall into a kind of male green-sickness, 2H4 4.03. 93 P
out, you green-sickness carrion! ROM 3.05.156
says, is troubled | with the green-sickness. ANT 3.02. 6
now the pox upon her green-sickness for me! PER 4.06. 13 P
GREEN-SLEEVES 2 FR 0.0002 REL FR 0 V 2 P
hundred psalms to the tune of "green-sleeves." WIV 2.01. 63 P
let it thunder to the tune of "green-sleeves," 5.05. 19 P
GREEN-SORD 1 FR 0.0001 REL FR 1 V 0 P
low-born lass that ever | ran on the green-sord. WT 4.04.157
GREENWICH 1 FR 0.0001 REL FR 1 V 0 P
being at greenwich, | after your highness had H8 1.02.188
GREENWOOD 1 FR 0.0001 REL FR 1 V 0 P
under the greenwood tree | who loves to lie with AYL 2.05. 1
GREET 45 FR 0.0050 REL FR 45 V 0 P
other of our friends | will greet us here anon. MM 4.05. 13
with visages display'd, to talk and greet. LLL 5.02.144
when we greet, | with eyes best seeing, heaven's 5.02.374
to greet me with premeditated welcomes; MND 5.01. 94
along by him | and never stays to greet him. AYL 2.01. 54
a friend, not a friend greet | my poor corpse, TN 2.04. 61
father | to greet him and to give him comforts. WT 4.04.557
to greet a man not worth her pains, much less 5.01.155
so weeping, smiling, greet i thee, my earth, R2 3.02. 10
before, and greet his grace. 2H4 4.01.226
let him greet england with our sharp defiance. H5 3.05. 37
for there the sun shall greet them, | and draw 4.03.100
that sund'red friends greet in the hour of death 1H6 4.03. 42
i do greet your excellence | with letters of 5.04. 94
york, if thou meanest well, i greet thee well. 2H6 5.01. 14
to greet mine own land with my wishful sight. 3H6 3.01. 14
the first that there did greet my stranger soul R3 1.04. 48
my lord, the mayor of london comes to greet you. 3.01. 17
pure heart's love, to greet the tender prince. 4.01. 4
dear lord, go you and greet him in his tent. TRO 2.03.179
let us to priam's hall | to greet the warriors. 3.01.149
so do each lord, and either greet him not, | or 3.03. 52
a merrier day did never yet greet rome, | no, COR 5.04. 42
there greet in silence, as the dead are wont, TIT 1.01. 90
i may, | i greet your honors from andronicus — 4.02. 5
and secretly to greet the empress' friends. 4.02.174
greet him from me, | bid him suppose some good TIM 2.02.226
two of their most reverend senate, greet thee. 5.01.129
the senators of athens greet thee, timon. 5.01.136
and with his former title greet macbeth. MAC 1.02. 65
my noble partner | you greet with present grace, 1.03. 55
go, captain, from me greet the danish king. HAM 4.04. 1
we will greet the time. LR 5.01. 54
the duke does greet you, general, | and he OTH 1.02. 36
i greet thy love, | not with vain thanks, but 3.03.469
the duke and the senators of venice greet you. 4.01.217
caesar and antony shall well greet together: ANT 2.01. 39
dignity | as we greet modern friends withal, and 5.02.167
if you please | to greet your lord with writing, CYM 1.06.206
why so sadly | greet you our victory? 5.05. 24
i pray greet him fairly. PER 5.01. 10
the regent made in metelin, | to greet the king. 5.02. 9
and scarcely greet me with that sun, thine eye, SON 49. 6
when i was wont to greet it with my lays, | as 102. 6
gentle doom, | and taught it thus anew to greet: 145. 8
GREETED 1 FR 0.0001 REL FR 1 V 0 P
what part of the world | i should be greeted, if HAM 4.06. 6
GREETETH 1 FR 0.0001 REL FR 1 V 0 P
lord | of that unworthy wife that greeteth thee, LUC 1304
GREETING 24 FR 0.0027 REL FR 20 V 4 P
ere twice the sun hath made his journal greeting MM 4.03. 88
salutation and greeting to you all! AYL 5.04. 39 P
fellow, you — and thus much for greeting. SHR 4.01.112 P
what greeting will you to my lord lafew? AWW 4.03.317 P
thus, after greeting, speaks the king of france JN 1.01. 2
do i turn to thee, | and mark my greeting well; R2 1.01. 36
that thou returnest no greeting to thy friends? 1.03.254
his father, harry prince of wales, greeting." 2H4 2.02.120 P
health and fair greeting from our general, | the 4.01. 27
for we hear | your greeting is from him, not H5 1.02.236
here, | to whom expressly i bring greeting too. 2.04.112
humphrey of buckingham, i accept thy greeting. 2H6 5.01. 15
this is the most despiteful gentle greeting, TRO 4.01. 33
let me confirm my princely brother's greeting: 4.05.174
my flesh tremble in their different greeting. ROM 1.05. 90
the appertaining rage | to such a greeting. 3.01. 64
i pray you do my greeting. TIM 5.01.212
time | to bear my greeting to the senators, JC 2.02. 61
you stop our way | with such prophetic greeting? MAC 1.03. 78
for bearers of this greeting to old norway, HAM 1.02. 35
they give /their greeting to the citadel. OTH 2.01. 94
he shall have every day a several greeting, | or ANT 1.05. 77
every stage | with an augmented greeting. 3.06. 55
caesar sends greeting to the queen of egypt, 5.02. 9
GREETINGS 8 FR 0.0009 REL FR 8 V 0 P
and my loving greetings | to those of mine in AWW 1.03.252
from him | give you all greetings that a king, WT 5.01.140
take special care my greetings be delivered. R2 3.01. 39
first, to do greetings to thy royal person, 3H6 3.03. 52
from whom i have receiv'd not only greetings, COR 2.01.197
no opportunity | that may convey my greetings, ROM 3.05. 50
most fair return of greetings and desires. HAM 2.02. 60
(i will subscribe) gentle adieus and greetings; ANT 4.05. 14
GREETS 13 FR 0.0014 REL FR 11 V 2 P
gentle and fair, your brother kindly greets you. MM 1.04. 24
from both, my lord. bellario greets your grace. MV 4.01.120
my mother greets me kindly. is she well? AWW 2.04. 1 P
sir, | bohemia greets you from himself by me; WT 5.01.181
the appellant in all duty greets your highness, R2 1.03. 52
he greets me well, sir. 2H4 3.02. 63 P
from him, and thus he greets your majesty: H5 2.04. 76
goths, | the roman emperor greets you all by me, TIT 5.01.157
he greets me well. JC 4.02. 6
this diamond he greets your wife withal, | by MAC 2.01. 15
is in safety | and greets your highness dearly. CYM 1.06. 13
find | it greets me as an enterprise of kindness PER 4.03. 38
and wordless so greets heaven for his success. LUC 112
GREGORY 6 FR 0.0006 REL FR 3 V 3 P
where is nathaniel, gregory, philip? SHR 4.01.122
were none fine but adam, rafe, and gregory; 4.01.136
turk gregory never did such deeds in arms as i 1H4 5.03. 45 P
sent a large commission | to gregory de cassado, H8 3.02.321
gregory, on my word, we'll not carry coals. ROM 1.01. 1 P
gregory, remember thy washing blow. 1.01. 62 P
GREGORY'S 1 FR 0.0001 REL FR 1 V 0 P
at saint gregory's well. TGV 4.02. 84
GREMIO 23 FR 0.0026 REL FR 17 V 6 P
or, signior gremio, you, know any such, | prefer SHR 1.01. 96
so will i, signior gremio. 1.01.113 P
tush, gremio; 1.01.126 P
how say you, signior gremio? 1.01.141 P
grumio, mum! god save you, signior gremio. 1.02.162
gremio, 'tis now no time to vent our love; 1.02.178
that she's the choice love of signior gremio. 1.02.234
you will have gremio to keep you fair. 2.01. 17
good morrow, neighbor gremio. 2.01. 40 P
you wrong me, signior gremio, give me leave. 2.01. 46
pardon me, signior gremio, i would fain be doing 2.01. 74
a thousand thanks, signior gremio. 2.01. 84 P
say, signior gremio, what can you assure her? 2.01.345
as any one | old signior gremio has in padua, 2.01.368
what, have i pinch'd you, signior gremio? 2.01.371
gremio, 'tis known my father hath no less | than 2.01.377
gremio is outvied. 2.01.385
if not, to signior gremio. 2.01.397
we'll overreach the greybeard, gremio, | the 3.02.145
signior gremio, came you from the church? 3.02.149
besides, old gremio is heark'ning still, | and 4.04. 53
talk not, signior gremio; 5.01. 96 P
how likes gremio these quick-witted folks? 5.02. 38
/GREW 1 FR 0.0001 REL FR 1 V 0 P
/his /grief /grew /puissant /and /the /strings LR 5.03.217
GREW 37 FR 0.0041 REL FR 33 V 4 P
and to my state grew stranger, being transported TMP 1.02. 76
how her acquaintance grew with this lewd fellow. ADO 5.01.332
that the rude sea grew civil at her song, | and MND 2.01.152
so we grew together, | like to a double cherry, 3.02.208
but that his beard grew thin and hungerly, | and SHR 3.02.175
and grew a twenty years removed thing | while TN 5.01. 89
ballads and all men's ears grew to his tunes. WT 4.04.185 P
man) grew so in love with the wenches' song, 4.04.606 P
grew a companion to the common streets, 1H4 3.02. 68
grew by our feeding to so great a bulk | that 5.01. 62
which daily grew to quarrel and to bloodshed, 2H4 4.05.194
grew like the summer grass, fastest by night, H5 1.01. 65
hence grew the general wrack and massacre; 1H6 1.01.135
some words there grew 'twixt somerset and me; 2.05. 46
my uncle grew so fast | that he could gnaw a R3 2.04. 27
heart | grossly grew captive to his honey words, 4.01. 79
in their embracement, as they grew together, H8 1.01. 10
he fell sick suddenly and grew so ill | he could 4.02. 15
had witchcraft in't, he grew unto his seat, HAM 4.07. 85
whereupon she grew round-womb'd, and had indeed,
LR 1.01. 14 P
speak yet, how grew your quarrel? 2.02. 61 P
up kisses by the roots | that grew upon my lips; OTH 3.03.424
julius caesar | grew fat with feasting there. ANT 2.06. 65
/autumn it was | that grew the more by reaping. 5.02. 88
his strange absence, | grew shameless desperate; CYM 5.05. 58
which fear so grew in me, i hither fled, | under PER 1.02. 80
great, | the name of help grew odious to repeat. 1.04. 31
rings she made | of rushes that grew by, and to TNK 4.01. 89
plunges | disroot his rider whence he grew, but 5.04. 75
grew kinder, and his fury was assuag'd. VEN 318
grew i not faint? 645
which should example where your equal grew? SON 84. 4
making their tomb the womb wherein they grew? 86. 4
from their proud lap pluck them where they grew; 98. 8
the ills that were not, grew to faults assured, 118.10
and grew a seething bath, which yet men prove 153. 7
heard where his plants in others' orchards grew, LC 171
GREW'ST 2 FR 0.0002 REL FR 2 V 0 P
i would thou grew'st unto the shores o' th' CYM 1.03. 1
one half so well | as when thou grew'st thyself. 4.02.203
/GREY* 1 FR 0.0001 REL FR 0 V 1 P
/purr /the /cat /is /grey. LR 3.06. 45 P
GREY* 42 FR 0.0047 REL FR 34 V 8 P
her eyes are grey as glass, and so are mine; TGV 4.04.192
fairies, black, grey, green, and white, | you WIV 5.05. 37
and, with grey hairs and bruise of many days, ADO 5.01. 65
dapples the drowsy east with spots of grey. 5.03. 27
and the lark, | the plain-song cuckoo grey, MND 3.01.131
for if but once thou show me thy grey light, 3.02.419
"it was the friar of orders grey, | as he forth SHR 4.01.145
item, two grey eyes, with lids to them; TN 1.05.248 P
slip, and i'll give him my horse, grey capilet. 3.04.286 P
so sure as this beard's grey — what will you WT 2.03.162
that reverent vice, that grey iniquity, that 1H4 2.04.453 P
him as the sun | in the grey vault of heaven, 2H4 2.03. 19
sir thomas grey, knight, of northumberland, H5 2.pr. 25
scroop, and grey, in their dear care | and 2.02. 58
grey of northumberland, this same is yours: 2.02. 68
treason, by the name of thomas grey, knight, of 2.02.150 P
and these grey locks, the pursuivants of death, 1H6 2.05. 5
field | this lady's husband, sir richard grey, 3H6 3.02. 2
has your king married the lady grey? 3.03.174
you | of this new marriage with the lady grey? 4.01. 2
tell me some reason why the lady grey | should 4.01. 25
my lady grey his wife, clarence, 'tis she | that R3 1.01. 64
in all which time you and your husband grey 1.03.126
me | to be reveng'd on rivers, dorset, grey. 1.03.332
lord rivers and lord grey are sent to pomfret, 2.04. 42
so falls it out | with rivers, vaughan, grey; 3.02. 65
come, grey, come, vaughan, let us here embrace. 3.03. 25
th' adulterate hastings, rivers, vaughan, grey, 4.04. 69
where is the gentle rivers, vaughan, grey? 4.04.147
and edward's children, grey and rivers, | holy 5.01. 3
think upon grey, and let thy soul despair! 5.03.141
the hunt is up, the /morn is bright and grey, TIT 2.02. 1
hildings and harlots, thisby a grey eye or so, ROM 2.04. 42 P
i'll say yon grey is not the morning's eye, 3.05. 19
and yon grey lines | that fret the clouds are JC 2.01.103
rogue says here that old men have grey beards, HAM 2.02.197 P
life i have spar'd at suit of his grey beard — LR 2.02. 63 P
spare my grey beard, you wagtail? 2.02. 67 P
girl, though grey | do something mingle with our ANT 4.08. 19
that in lag hours attend | for grey approachers; TNK 5.04. 9
mine eyes are grey, and bright, and quick in VEN 140
better becomes the grey cheeks of th' east, SON 132. 6
GREYBEARD 3 FR 0.0003 REL FR 3 V 0 P
greybeard, thy love doth freeze. SHR 2.01.338
we'll overreach the greybeard, gremio, | the 3.02.145
what will you do, good greybeard? 1H6 3.02. 50
GREYBEARDS 2 FR 0.0002 REL FR 2 V 0 P
this word "love," which greybeards call divine, 3H6 5.06. 81
to be afeard to tell greybeards the truth? JC 2.02. 67
GREY-COATED 1 FR 0.0001 REL FR 1 V 0 P
film, | her waggoner a small grey-coated gnat, ROM 1.04. 67
GREY-EY'D 2 FR 0.0002 REL FR 2 V 0 P
the grey-ey'd morn smiles on the frowning night, ROM 2.03. 1
he's grey-ey'd, | which yields compassion where TNK 4.02.131
GREYHOUND 7 FR 0.0008 REL FR 4 V 3 P
how does your fallow greyhound, sir? WIV 1.01. 89 P
ay, and hector's a greyhound. LLL 5.02.659 P
o, sir, lucentio slipp'd me like his greyhound, SHR 5.02. 52
this fawning greyhound then did proffer me! 1H4 1.03.252
may stroke him as gently as a puppy greyhound. 2H4 2.04. 98 P
even like a fawning greyhound in the leash, | to COR 1.06. 38
mastiff, greyhound, mongrel grim, | hound or LR 3.06. 68
GREYHOUND'S 1 FR 0.0001 REL FR 0 V 1 P
thy wit is as quick as the greyhound's mouth — ADO 5.02. 11 P
GREYHOUNDS 5 FR 0.0005 REL FR 4 V 1 P
thy greyhounds are as swift | as breathed stags; SHR in.2. 47
i see you stand like greyhounds in the slips, H5 3.01. 31
like a brace of greyhounds | having the fearful 3H6 2.05.129
and has sent your honor two brace of greyhounds.
TIM 1.02.189 P
as hounds and greyhounds, mungrels, spaniels, MAC 3.01. 92
/GRIEF 10 FR 0.0011 REL FR 9 V 1 P
/very /true, /my /grief /lies /all /within, R2 4.01.295
/are /merely /shadows /to /the /unseen /grief 4.01.297
/of /any /ground | /to /build /a /grief /on. 2H4 4.01.108
/and /cannot /passionate /our /tenfold /grief TIT 3.02. 6
/poor /man, /grief /has /so /wrought /on /him, 3.02. 79
/the /bravery /of /his /grief /did /put /me HAM 5.02. 79
/when /grief /hath /mates, /and /bearing LR 3.06.107
/the /queen /to /any /demonstration /of /grief? 4.03. 10 P
/she /started | /to /deal /with /grief /alone. 4.03. 32
/his /grief /grew /puissant /and /the /strings 5.03.217
GRIEF 242 FR 0.0273 REL FR 230 V 12 P
but he's something stain'd | with grief (that's TMP 1.02.416
when every grief is entertain'd that's offer'd, 2.01. 16
eye, | who hath cause to wet the grief on't. 2.01.128
let grief and sorrow still embrace his heart 5.01.214

a little time, my lord, will kill that grief. TGV 3.02. 15
say | no grief did ever come so near thy heart 4.03. 19
but think upon my grief, a lady's grief, | and 4.03. 28
but think upon my grief, a lady's grief, | and 4.03. 28
i now begin with grief and shame to utter. MM 5.01. 96
grief hath chang'd me since you saw me last, ERR 5.01.298
with me — | after so long grief, such nativity! 5.01.407
that know love's grief by his complexion! ADO 1.01.313
one /can master a grief but he that has it. 3.02. 28 P
being that i flow in grief, | the smallest twine 4.01.249
and upon the grief of this suddenly died. 4.02. 63 P
and 'tis not wisdom thus to second grief 5.01. 2
as thus for thus, and such a grief for such, 5.01. 13
patch grief with proverbs, make misfortune drunk 5.01. 17
can counsel and speak comfort to that grief 5.01. 21
and they thy glory through my grief will show. LLL 4.03. 36
that in love's grief desir'st society: 4.03.126
where lies thy grief, o, tell me, good dumaine? 4.03.169
honest plain words best pierce the ear of grief, 5.02.753
you give your wife too unkind a cause of grief; MV 5.01.175
if you do sorrow at my grief in love, | by AYL 3.05. 87
your sorrow and my grief | were both extermin'd. 3.05. 88
i that our good will effects | bianca's grief. SHR 1.01. 87
she is not for your turn, the more my grief. 2.01. 63
dead, excessive grief the enemy to the living. AWW 1.01. 56 P
if the living be enemy to the grief, the excess 1.01. 57 P
i have felt so many quirks of joy and grief 3.02. 49
my greatest grief, | though little he do feel it 3.04. 32
grief would have tears, and sorrow bids me speak 3.04. 42
of her nature became as a prey to her grief; 4.03. 52 P
like patience on a monument, | smiling at grief. TN 2.04.115
that honorable grief lodg'd here which burns WT 2.01.111
this sessions (to our great grief we pronounce) 3.02. 1
i prize it | as i weigh grief, which i would 3.02. 43
and what's past help | should be past grief. 3.02.223
thou must know the king is full of grief. 4.04.765 P
pow'r | to take off so much grief from you as he 5.03. 55
for grief is proud and makes his owner stoop. JN 3.01. 69
to me and to the state of my great grief | let 3.01. 70
o, this will make my mother die with grief! 3.03. 5
o, if i could, what grief should i forget! 3.04. 50
for, being not mad, but sensible of grief, | my 3.04. 53
/friends | do glue themselves in sociable grief, 3.04. 65
you hold too heinous a respect of grief. 3.04. 90
you are as fond of grief as of your child. 3.04. 92
grief fills the room up of my absent child, 3.04. 93
then, have i reason to be fond of grief? 3.04. 98
and "where lies your grief?" 4.01. 48
the fire is dead with grief, | being create for 4.01.105
but there is little reason in your grief; 4.03. 30
brother's wife | with her companion, grief, must R2 1.02. 55
grief boundeth where /it falls, | not with the 1.02. 58
thy grief is but thy absence for a time. 1.03.258
joy absent, grief is present for that time. 1.03.259
to men in joy, but grief makes one hour ten. 1.03.261
else | but that i was a journeyman to grief? 1.03.274
to counterfeit oppression of such grief | that 1.04. 14
within me grief hath kept a tedious fast; 2.01. 75
york is too far gone with grief, | or else he 2.01.184
why i should welcome such a guest as grief, 2.02. 7
each substance of a grief hath twenty shadows, 2.02. 14
which shows like grief itself, but is not so; 2.02. 15
find shapes of grief, more than himself, to wail 2.02. 22
is still deriv'd | from some forefather grief; 2.02. 35
so, | for nothing hath begot my something grief, 2.02. 36
nothing lives but crosses, cares, and grief. 2.02. 79
you, feel want, | taste grief, need friends: 3.02.176
o that i were as great | as is my grief, or 3.03.137
sorrow and grief of heart | makes him speak 3.03.184
when my poor heart no measure keeps in grief; 3.04. 8
or if of grief, being altogether had, | it adds 3.04. 15
why should hard–favor'd grief be lodg'd in thee, 5.01. 14
join not with grief, fair woman, do not so, | to 5.01. 16
wedding it, there is such length in grief. 5.01. 94
smiles, | the badges of his grief and patience, 5.02. 33
out of my grief and my impatience | answer'd 1H4 1.03. 51
a plague of sighing and grief, it blows a man up 2.04.332 P
or take away the grief of a wound? 5.01.132 P
the big year, swoll'n with some other grief, 2H4 in 13
weak'ned with grief, being now enrag'd with 1.01.144
with grief, being now enrag'd with grief, | are 1.01.144
this present grief had wip'd it from my mind. 1.01.211
it hath it original from much grief, from study, 1.02.115 P
the parcels and particulars of our grief, | the 4.02. 36
therefore my grief | stretches itself beyond the 4.04. 56
ere you with grief had spoke and i had heard 4.05.141
weak shoulders, overborne with burthening grief, 1H6 2.05. 10
roan hangs her head for grief | that such a 3.02.124
i foresee with grief | the utter loss of all the 5.04.111
company, | i may revolve and ruminate my grief. 5.05.101
ay, grief, i fear me, both at first and last. 5.05.102
to you duke humphrey must unload his grief, 2H6 1.01. 76
your grief, the common grief of all the land. 1.01. 77
your grief, the common grief of all the land. 1.01. 77
for grief that they are past recovery; 1.01.116
and greatness of his place be grief to us, | yet 1.01.173
sorrow and grief have vanquish'd all my powers; 2.01.179
mine eyes are full of tears, my heart of grief. 2.03. 17
be patient, gentle nell, forget this grief. 2.04. 26
my heart is drown'd with grief, | whose flood 3.01.198
so get thee gone, that i may know my grief, 3.02.346
oft have i heard that grief softens the mind, 4.04. 1
no, warwick, i remember it to my grief, | and, 3H6 1.01. 93
and i with grief and sorrow to the court. 1.01.210
and when with grief he wept, | the ruthless 2.01. 60
to weep is to make less the depth of grief: 2.01. 85
for what is in this world but grief and woe? 2.05. 20
with tears, and break o'ercharg'd with grief. 2.05. 78
grief more than common grief! 2.05. 94
grief more than common grief! 2.05. 94
she, poor wretch, for grief can speak no more; 3.01. 47
be plain, queen margaret, and tell thy grief; 3.03. 19
these news i must confess are full of grief, 4.04. 13
and, after many length'ned hours of grief, | die R3 1.03.207
ay, brother, to our grief, as it is yours. 3.01. 98
and being but a toy, which is no grief to give. 3.01.114
or i with grief and extreme age shall perish 4.04.186
but that still use of grief makes wild grief 4.04.230
that still use of grief makes wild grief tame, 4.04.230
the subject's grief | comes through commissions, H8 1.02. 56
than to be perk'd up in a glist'ring grief | and 2.03. 21
killing care and grief of heart | fall asleep, 3.01. 13
what grief hath set these jaundies o'er your TRO 1.03. 2
the grief is fine, full, perfect, that i taste, 4.04. 3
the like allayment could i give my grief: 4.04. 8
no more my grief, in such a precious loss. 4.04. 10
here, tamora, though griev'd with killing grief. TIT 2.03.260
my grief was at the height before thou cam'st, 3.01. 70
for at your grief | see how my wretched sister 3.01.136
to thee sent back — | thy grief their sports! 3.01.238
witness these trenches made by grief and care, 5.02. 23
steel, | nor can i utter all our bitter grief, 5.03. 89
doth add more grief to too much of mine own. ROM 1.01.189
one desperate grief cures with another's 1.02. 48
who is already sick and pale with grief | that 2.02. 5
to cease thy /suit, and leave me to my grief. 2.02.152
it were a grief, so brief to part with thee. 3.03.174
some grief shows much of love, | but much of 3.05. 72
but much of grief shows still some want of wit. 3.05. 73
clouds, | that sees into the bottom of my grief? 3.05.197
o juliet, i already know thy grief, | it strains 4.01. 46
with which grief | it is supposed the fair 5.03. 50
grief of my son's exile hath stopp'd her breath. 5.03.211
you, to remove that siege of grief from her, 5.03.237
i am sick of that grief too, as i understand how TIM 3.06. 17 P
eye, i will present | my honest grief unto him; 4.03.470
nev'r did poor steward wear a truer grief | for 4.03.480
t' accept my grief, and whilst this poor wealth 4.03.488
hands from whom | you have receiv'd your grief; 5.04. 24
but, o grief, | where hast thou led me? JC 1.03.111
make me acquainted with your cause of grief. 2.01.256
when grief and blood ill–temper'd vexeth him? 4.03.115
and grief that young octavius with mark antony 4.03.153
now is that noble vessel full of grief, | that 5.05. 13
what's the newest grief? MAC 4.03.174
the grief that does not speak | whispers the 4.03.209
our great revenge | to cure this deadly grief. 4.03.215
of your sword, let grief | convert to anger; 4.03.228
it us befitted | to bear our hearts in grief, HAM 1.02. 3
with all forms, moods, /shapes of grief, | that 1.02. 82
of impious stubbornness, 'tis unmanly grief, 1.02. 94
might move | more grief to hide, than hate to 2.01.116
the origin and commencement of his grief 3.01.177
all alone entreat him | to show his grief. 3.01.183
the violence of either grief or joy | their own 3.02.196
where joy most revels, grief doth most lament; 3.02.198
grief /joys, joy grieves, on slender accident. 3.02.199
o, this is the poison of deep grief, it springs 4.05. 75
death, | and am most sensibly in grief for it, 4.05.151
laertes, i must commune with your grief, | or 4.05.203
what is he whose grief | bears such an emphasis, 5.01.254
as full of grief as age, wretched in both. LR 2.04.273
to tell thee, | the grief hath craz'd my wits. 3.04.170
'twixt two extremes of passion, joy and grief, 5.03.199
for my particular grief | is of so flood–gate OTH 1.03. 55
he robs himself that spends a bootless grief. 1.03.209
sentence and the sorrow | that, to pay grief, 1.03.215
that he hath left part of his grief with me | to 3.03. 53
whilst you were here o'erwhelmed with your grief 4.01. 76
thought so then — i'll kill myself for grief — 5.02.192
and pure grief | shore his old thread in twain. 5.02.205
this grief is crown'd with consolation: ANT 1.02.167 P
which, being dried with grief, will break to 4.09. 17
a grief that /smites | my very heart at root. 5.02.104
my supreme crown of grief, and those repeated CYM 1.06. 4
whose remembrance | is yet fresh in their grief. 2.04. 15
proof as strong as my grief and as certain as i 3.04. 24 P
fear not, 'tis empty of all things but grief. 3.04. 69
i do note | that grief and patience, rooted in 4.02. 57
and let the stinking elder, grief, untwine | his 4.02. 59
toys, | is jollity for apes, and grief for boys. 4.02.194
to my grief, i am | the heir of his reward, 5.05. 12
the tomb where grief should sleep, can breed me PER 1.02. 5
and for further grief — god give you joy! 2.05. 87
taken sustenance | but to prorogue his grief. 5.01. 26
but the main grief springs from the loss | of a 5.01. 29
be, hath endur'd a grief | might equal yours, if 5.01. 87
o grief and time, | fearful consumers, you will TNK 1.01. 69
set down in ice, which, by hot grief uncandied, 1.01.107
stand up, | your grief is written in your cheek. 1.01.110
t' instruct me 'gainst a capital grief indeed — 1.01.123
but when could grief | cull forth, as unpang'd 1.01.168
honor) lastly | children of grief and ignorance. 2.02. 55
in me hath grief slain fear, and, but for one 3.02. 5
make them droop with grief and hang the head. VEN 666
and now his grief may be compared well | to one 701
impostumes, grief, and damn'd despair | swear 743
as striving who should best become her grief; 968
grief hath two tongues, and never woman yet 1007
"my tongue cannot express my grief for one, 1069
for every little grief to wet his eyes; 1179
frantic with grief thus breathes she forth her LUC 762
my talk with tears, my grief with groans, | poor 797
thy honey turns to gall, thy joy to grief! 889
true grief is fond and testy as a child, | who 1094
sometime her grief is dumb and hath no words, 1105
grief best is pleas'd with grief's society; 1111
great grief grieves most at that would do it 1117
grief dallied with nor law nor limit knows. 1120
if thou dost weep for grief of my sustaining, 1272
conceit and grief an eager combat fight, | what 1298
so i commend me from our house in grief, | my 1308
short schedule collatine may know | her grief, 1313
to give her so much grief, and not a tongue. 1463
(as if with grief or travail he had fainted), 1543
being from the feeling of her own grief brought 1578
and tell thy grief, that we may give redress. 1603
blow | the grief away that stops his answer so; 1664
to push grief on, and back the same grief draw. 1673
to push grief on, and back the same grief draw. 1673
help wounds, or grief help grievous deeds? 1822
thus of every grief in heart | he with thee doth PP 20.53
nor can thy shame give physic to my grief, SON 34. 9
and yet love knows it is a greater grief | to 40.11
that thou hast her, it is not all my grief, 42. 1
most worthy comfort, now my greatest grief, 48. 6
my grief lies onward and my joy behind. 50.14
likewise lent me | of grief and blushes, aptly LC 200

GRIEF'S 4 FR 0.0004 REL FR 4 V 0 P

for my grief's so great | that no supporter but JN 3.01. 71
grief best is pleas'd with grief's society; LUC 1111
her grief, but not her grief's true quality. 1313
doth nightly make grief's length seem stronger. SON 28.14

/GRIEFS 6 FR 0.0006 REL FR 6 V 0 P

/drinking /my /griefs, /whilst /you /mount /up R2 4.01.189
/i /am, /but /still /my /griefs /are /mine. 4.01.191
/my /state /depose, | /but /not /my /griefs; 4.01.193
/and /find /our /griefs /heavier /than /our 2H4 4.01. 69
/and /have /the /summary /of /all /our /griefs 4.01. 73
/are /wrong'd /and /would /unfold /our /griefs, 4.01. 77

GRIEFS 62 FR 0.0070 REL FR 61 V 1 P

know then, i here forget all former griefs, TGV 5.04.142
impos'd | than i to speak my griefs unspeakable: ERR 1.01. 32
my griefs cry louder than advertisement. ADO 5.01. 32
how shall she know my griefs? LLL 4.03. 41
i understand you not, my griefs are double. 5.02.752
these griefs and losses have so bated me | that MV 3.03. 32
to bear your griefs yourself, and leave me out; AYL 1.03.103
if thou engrossest all the griefs are thine, AWW 3.02. 65
your passion bears | goes on my master's griefs. TN 3.04.207
on her frights and griefs | (which never tender WT 2.02. 21
our griefs, and not our manners, reason now. JN 4.03. 29
since it hath been beforehand with our griefs. 5.07.111
ere thou bid good night, to quite their griefs, R2 5.01. 43
hath sent to know | the nature of your griefs, 1H4 4.03. 42
he bids you name your griefs, and with all speed 4.03. 48
from our princely general | to know your griefs, 2H4 4.01.140
these griefs shall be with speed redress'd, 4.02. 59
art not firm enough, since griefs are green, 4.05.203
more | of mortal griefs than do thy worshippers? H5 4.01.242
shall change all griefs and quarrels into love. 5.02. 20
my mildness hath allay'd their swelling griefs, 3H6 4.08. 42
i am the mother of these griefs: R3 2.02. 80
and let my griefs frown on the upper hand. 4.04. 37
i would your grace | would leave your griefs, H8 3.01. 92
whose fury not dissembled speaks his griefs. TIT 1.01.438
dissemble all your griefs and discontents. 1.01.443
ah, now no more will i control thy griefs. 3.01.259
lives | but in oblivion and hateful griefs. 3.01.295
oft, | extremity of griefs would make men mad; 4.01. 19
griefs of mine own lie heavy in my breast, ROM 1.01.186
these griefs, these woes, these sorrows make me 3.02. 89
and needly will be rank'd with other griefs, 3.02.117
"when griping griefs the heart doth wound, 4.05.126
'twas time and griefs | that fram'd him thus. TIM 5.01.122
tell them that, to ease them of their griefs, 5.01.198
when thy first griefs were but a mere conceit, 5.04. 14
though thou abhorr'dst in us our human griefs, 5.04. 75
be factious for redress of all these griefs, JC 1.03.118
what private griefs they have, alas, i know not, 3.02.213
cassius, be content, | speak your griefs softly; 4.02. 42
then in my tent, cassius, enlarge your griefs, 4.02. 46
o cassius, i am sick of many griefs. 4.03.144
as we shall make our griefs and clamor roar MAC 1.07. 78
liberty if you deny your griefs to your friend. HAM 3.02.339 P
so should my thoughts be sever'd from my griefs, LR 4.06.282
the griefs are ended | by seeing the worst, OTH 1.03.202
to enforce no further | the griefs between ye: ANT 2.02.100
some griefs are med'cinable, that is one of them CYM 3.02. 33
great griefs, i see, med'cine the less; 4.02.243
such griefs as you yourself do lay upon yourself PER 1.02. 66
here, | and by relating tales of others' griefs, 1.04. 2
o my distressed lord, even such our griefs are; 1.04. 7
know that our griefs are risen to the top, | and 2.04. 23
your griefs, for what? 2.04. 25
that thou thoughts' thy griefs might equal mine, 5.01.131
what griefs our beds, | that our dear lords have TNK 1.01.140
and the enjoying of our griefs together. 2.02. 60
those joys, griefs, angers, fears, my friend 2.02.188
pleas'd | to show in generous terms your griefs, 3.01. 54
and such griefs sustain | that they prove LUC 139
for her griefs, so lively shown, | made me think PP 20.17
when other petty griefs have done their spite, SON 90.10

GRIEF–SHOT 1 FR 0.0001 REL FR 1 V 0 P

friend, grief–shot | with his unkindness? COR 5.01. 44

GRIEVANCE 6 FR 0.0006 REL FR 6 V 0 P

commend thy grievance to my holy prayers, | for TGV 1.01. 17
well become such sweet–complaining grievance. 3.02. 85
that your subjects | are in great grievance: H8 1.02. 20
i'll know his grievance, or be much denied. ROM 1.01.157
or put upon you what restraint or grievance OTH 1.02. 15
sat, | her grievance with his hearing to divide: LC 67

GRIEVANCES 7 FR 0.0008 REL FR 7 V 0 P

madam, i pity much your grievances, | which TGV 4.03. 37
i told him gently of our grievances, | of his 1H4 5.02. 36
for this contains our general grievances: 2H4 4.01.167
weary | of dainty and such picking grievances, 4.01.196
i promis'd you redress of these same grievances 4.02.113
place, | or reason coldly of your grievances, ROM 3.01. 52
then can i grieve at grievances foregone, | and SON 30. 9

/GRIEV'D 1 FR 0.0001 REL FR 1 V 0 P

/that /nothing /have, /with /nothing /griev'd, R2 4.01.216

GRIEV'D 13 FR 0.0014 REL FR 12 V 1 P

griev'd i, i had but one? ADO 4.01.127
i have too griev'd a heart | to take a tedious MV 2.07. 76
charge thee be not thou more griev'd than i am. AYL 1.03. 92
was ever gentleman thus griev'd as i? SHR 2.01. 37
are not you griev'd that arthur is his prisoner? JN 3.04.123
was ever king so griev'd for subjects' woe? 3H6 2.05.111
him a foreign man still, which so griev'd him, H8 2.02.128
here, tamora, though griev'd with killing grief. TIT 2.03.260
i have heard, and griev'd, | how cursed athens, TIM 4.03. 93
but let not therefore my good friends be griev'd JC 1.02. 43
whereat griev'd, | that so his sickness, age, HAM 2.02. 65
it griev'd my heart to hear what pitiful cries PER 2.01. 20 P
no more be griev'd at that which thou hast done: SON 35. 1

/GRIEVE 1 FR 0.0001 REL FR 1 V 0 P

/you /shall /not /grieve | /lending /me /this LR 4.03. 53

GRIEVE 41 FR 0.0046 REL FR 37 V 4 P

and neither heaven nor man grieve at the mercy. MM 2.02. 50
thou, that hast no unkind mate to grieve thee, ERR 2.01. 38
would it not grieve a woman to be overmaster'd ADO 2.01. 60 P
yet do not suddenly, for it may grieve him. MV 2.08. 34
grieve not that i am fall'n to this for you; 4.01.266

sir, grieve not you, you are welcome 5.01.239
being but a moonish youth, grieve, be effeminate AYL 3.02.410 P
him that has most cause to grieve it should be) WT 2.01. 77
how will this grieve you, | when you shall come 2.01. 96
he shall not need to grieve | at knowing of thy 4.04.415
or something hath the nothing that i grieve — R2 2.02. 37
but i shall grieve you to report the rest. 2.02. 95
do not you grieve at this, i shall be sent for 2H4 5.05. 77 P
i grieve to hear what torments you endur'd, 1H6 1.04. 57
nor grieve that roan is so recovered: 3.03. 2
should grieve thee more than streams of foreign 3.03. 55
but wherefore grieve i at an hour's poor loss, 2H6 3.02.381
i prithee grieve, to make me merry, york. 3H6 1.04. 86
how it doth grieve me that thy head is here! 2.02. 55
'twill grieve your grace my sons should call you 3.02.100
the cause | he may a little grieve at. H8 2.01. 39
would it not grieve an able man to leave | so 2.02.141
ah, my good lord, i grieve at what i speak, 5.01. 95
but it must grieve young pyrrhus now at home TRO 3.03.209
doth that grieve thee? | o withered truth! 5.02. 45
and grieve his spirit that dares not challenge 5.02. 94
and grieve to hear't. COR 5.06. 62
and yet no man like he doth grieve my heart. ROM 3.05. 83
shall it not grieve thee dearer than thy death, JC 3.01.196
how it did grieve macbeth! MAC 3.06. 11
show his eyes, and grieve his heart; 4.01.110
laugh, cannot but make the judicious grieve; HAM 3.02. 26 P
as we dearly grieve | for that which thou hast 4.03. 41
let that grieve him: CYM 3.02. 32
and i grieve myself | to think, when thou shalt 3.04. 92
italy annoy us, but | we grieve at chances here. 4.03. 35
and — which more may grieve thee, | as it doth 5.05.144
i shall, | unless thou wouldst grieve quickly. 5.05.170
thought it princely charity to grieve for them. PER 1.02.100
it shall no longer grieve without reproof. 2.04. 19
then can i grieve at grievances foregone, | and SON 30. 9

GRIEVED 7 FR 0.0008 REL FR 7 V 0 P
brother, and this grieved count | did see her, ADO 4.01. 89
wonder not, | nor be not grieved; SHR 4.05. 64
and is't not pity, o my grieved friends, | that JN 5.02. 24
a trespass that doth vex my grieved soul; R2 1.01.138
glasses of thine eyes | i see thy grieved heart. 1.03.209
the grieved commons | hardly conceive of me; H8 1.02.104
for war, acquainted | my grieved ear withal; ANT 3.06. 59

GRIEVES 24 FR 0.0027 REL FR 20 V 4 P
but yet so false that he grieves my very TGV 4.02. 61 P
it grieves me for the death of claudio — | but MM 2.01.280
it, adam, that grieves me, and the spirit of my AYL 1.01. 22 P
lord, | the melancholy jaques grieves at that, 2.01. 26
how it grieves me to see thee wear thy heart in 5.02. 19 P
it grieves me | much more for what i cannot do TN 3.04.335
o, it grieves my soul, | that i must draw this JN 5.02. 15
at some thing it grieves, | more than with R2 2.02. 12
grieves at heart | so many of his shadows thou 1H4 5.04. 29
it grieves his highness. 1H6 4.01.133
it grieves my soul to leave thee unassail'd. 2H6 5.02. 18
cry "content" to that which grieves my heart, 3H6 3.02.183
that grieves me when i see my shame in him. R3 2.02. 54
such news, my lord, as grieves me to report. 2.04. 39
it grieves many. H8 1.02.110
who grieves much for your weakness, and by me 4.02.117
her blood, | when she does praise me grieves me. COR 1.09. 15
a fly, | and nothing grieves me heartily indeed, TIT 5.01.143
it grieves me to see so many dip their meat in TIM 1.02. 40 P
grief /joys, joy grieves, on slender accident. HAM 3.02.199
i warrant it grieves my husband | as if the OTH 3.03. 3
he grieves much, | and me as much to see his TNK 2.04. 27
thy coward heart with false bethinking grieves." VEN 1024
great grief grieves most at that would do it LUC 1117

GRIEVEST 1 FR 0.0001 REL FR 1 V 0 P
thou grievest my gall. LLL 5.02.237

GRIEVING 6 FR 0.0006 REL FR 5 V 1 P
therefore i will die a woman with grieving. ADO 4.01.323 P
unworthier may attain, | and die with grieving. MV 2.01. 38
th' effects of his fond jealousies so grieving WT 4.01. 18
honest iago, that looks dead with grieving, OTH 2.03.177
i grieving grant | did you too much disquiet. ANT 2.02. 69
grieving themselves to guess at others' smarts, LUC 1238

GRIEVINGLY 1 FR 0.0001 REL FR 1 V 0 P
grievingly i think | the peace between the H8 1.01. 87

/GRIEVOUS 2 FR 0.0002 REL FR 2 V 0 P
/and /these /grievous /crimes | /committed /by R2 4.01.223
/dear /blood /shed /for /our /grievous /sins, R3 1.04.190

GRIEVOUS 26 FR 0.0029 REL FR 23 V 3 P
if lost, why then a grievous labor won; TGV 1.01. 33
else would stand under grievous imposition, as MM 1.02.188 P
a grievous fault! say, woman, didst thou so? ERR 5.01.206
been this day acquitted | of grievous penalties, MV 4.01.410
old john of gaunt is grievous sick, my lord, R2 1.04. 54
but the commons hath he pill'd with grievous taxes, 2.01.246
the complaints i hear of thee are grievous. 1H4 2.04.442 P
he cannot come, my lord, he is grievous sick. 4.01. 16
why then let grievous, ghastly, gaping wounds 2H4 2.04.198
girding with grievous siege castles and towns; H5 1.02.152
that malice was a great and grievous sin; 1H6 3.01.128
and torture him with grievous ling'ring death. 2H6 3.02.247
for suddenly a grievous sickness took him, 3.02.370
'tis very grievous to be thought upon. R3 1.01.141
if heaven have any grievous plague in store 1.03.216
i lay unto the grievous charge of others. 1.03.325
i wash my hands | of this most grievous murther! 1.04.273
that anne, my wife, is very grievous sick; 4.02. 51
a grievous burthen was thy birth to me, | tetchy 4.04.168
therefore take with thee my most grievous curse, 4.04.188
of late | heard many grievous — i do say, my H8 5.01. 98
say, my lord, | grievous — complaints of you; 5.01. 99
if it were so, it was a grievous fault, | and JC 3.02. 79
hath seen a grievous wrack and sufferance | on OTH 2.01. 23
in troth, a very grievous punishment, as one TNK 4.03. 45 P
help wounds, or grief help grievous deeds? LUC 1822

GRIEVOUSLY 6 FR 0.0006 REL FR 4 V 2 P
my daughter takes his going grievously. TGV 3.02. 14
and has been grievously peaten as an old oman. WIV 4.04. 21 P
i will tell you — he beat me grievously, in the 5.01. 20 P
i do suspect thee very grievously. JN 4.03.134
fault, | and grievously hath caesar answer'd it. JC 3.02. 80
what are you here that cry so grievously? OTH 5.01. 53

GRIFFIN 2 FR 0.0002 REL FR 2 V 0 P
the dove pursues the griffin; MND 2.01.232
a clip-wing'd griffin and a moulten raven, | a 1H4 3.01.150

GRIFFITH 10 FR 0.0011 REL FR 10 V 0 P
o griffith, sick to death! H8 4.02. 1
didst thou not tell me, griffith, as thou ledst 4.02. 5
prithee, good griffith, tell me how he died. 4.02. 9
yet thus far, griffith, give me leave to speak 4.02. 32
yes, good griffith, | i were malicious else. 4.02. 47
but such an honest chronicler as griffith. 4.02. 72
good griffith, | cause the musicians play me 4.02. 77
and brought me garlands, griffith, which i feel 4.02. 91
admit him entrance, griffith; 4.02.107
griffith, farewell. 4.02.165

GRIM 22 FR 0.0024 REL FR 22 V 0 P
kinsman to grim and comfortless despair, | and ERR 5.01. 80
like her mother, for her father is but grim. LLL 2.01.256
so should a murtherer look — so dead, so grim. MND 3.02. 57
grim death, how foul and loathsome is thine SHR in.1. 35
if thou that bid'st me be content wert grim, JN 3.01. 43
to grim necessity, and he and i | will keep a R2 5.01. 21
for his grim aspect | and large proportion of 1H6 2.03. 20
iron | and hemm'd about with grim destruction. 4.03. 21
murderous tyranny | sits in grim majesty, to 2H6 3.02. 50
but, with thy grim looks and | the thunder–like COR 1.04. 58
thou hast a grim appearance, and thy face 4.05. 60
would to the bleeding and the grim alarm MAC 5.02. 4
mastiff, greyhound, mongril grim, | hound or LR 3.06. 68
cherubin — | ay, here, look grim as hell! OTH 4.02. 64
i know this act shows horrible and grim. 5.02.203
wight did die, | as yon grim looks do testify. PER 1.ch. 40
another flap–mouth'd mourner, black and grim, VEN 920
"but this foul, grim, and urchin–snouted boar, 1105
as the grim lion fawneth o'er his prey, | sharp LUC 421
whose grim aspect sets every joint a–shaking; 452
grim cave of death! 769
ruin, beauty's wrack, and grim care's reign; 1451

GRIME 2 FR 0.0002 REL FR 1 V 1 P
a man may go over shoes in the grime of it. ERR 3.02.104 P
my face i'll grime with filth, | blanket my LR 2.03. 9

GRIM–GRINNING 1 FR 0.0001 REL FR 1 V 0 P
"grim–grinning ghost, earth's worm, what dost VEN 933

GRIM–LOOK'D 1 FR 0.0001 REL FR 1 V 0 P
o grim–look'd night! MND 5.01.170

GRIMLY 2 FR 0.0002 REL FR 2 V 0 P
the skies look grimly | and threaten present WT 3.03. 3
they know not, they cannot tell, look grimly, ANT 4.12. 5

GRIM–VISAG'D 1 FR 0.0001 REL FR 1 V 0 P
grim–visag'd war hath smooth'd his wrinkled R3 1.01. 9

GRIN 7 FR 0.0008 REL FR 7 V 0 P
come, grin on me, and i will think thou smil'st, JN 3.04. 34
small curs are not regarded when they grin, 2H6 3.01. 18
see how the pangs of death do make him grin! 3.03. 24
against the senseless winds shall grin in vain, 4.01. 77
what valor were it, when a cur doth grin, | for 3H6 1.04. 56
and to grin like lions | upon the pikes o' th' CYM 5.03. 38
or as the wolf doth grin before he barketh, | or VEN 459

GRIND 6 FR 0.0006 REL FR 6 V 0 P
charge my goblins that they grind their joints TMP 4.01.258
they to dust should grind it | and throw't COR 3.02.103
hark, villains, i will grind your bones to dust, TIT 5.02.186
let me go grind their bones to powder small, 5.02.198
thou hast, | they'll grind /th' /one the other. ANT 3.05. 15
mine appetite i never more will grind | on newer SON 110.10

GRINDING 3 FR 0.0003 REL FR 1 V 2 P
a cake out of the wheat must tarry the grinding. TRO 1.01. 15 P
ay, the grinding; 1.01. 17 P
no, not to stay the grinding of the axe, | my HAM 5.02. 24

GRINDSTONE 1 FR 0.0001 REL FR 0 V 1 P
let the porter let in susan grindstone and nell. ROM 1.05. 9 P

GRINNING 4 FR 0.0004 REL FR 2 V 2 P
scoffing his state and grinning at his pomp, R2 3.02.163
i like not such grinning honor as sir walter 1H4 5.03. 59 P
not one now to mock your own grinning — quite HAM 5.01.192 P
showing the sun his teeth, grinning at the moon, TNK 1.01.100

GRIP'D 2 FR 0.0002 REL FR 2 V 0 P
we live not to be grip'd by meaner persons. H8 2.02.135
stood his spear, | grip'd in an armed hand; LUC 1425

GRIPE 10 FR 0.0011 REL FR 9 V 1 P
let vultures gripe thy guts! WIV 1.03. 85
he that speaks doth gripe the hearer's wrist, JN 4.02.190
seek you to seize and gripe into your hands R2 2.01.189
can gripe the sacred handle of our sceptre, 3.03. 80
to gripe the general sway into your hand, 1H4 5.01. 57
and, with a feeble gripe, says, "dear my lord, H5 4.06. 22
crown, | and put a barren sceptre in my gripe, MAC 3.01. 61
and then, sir, would he gripe and wring my hand; OTH 3.03.421
we have yet many among us can gripe as hard as CYM 3.01. 40 P
gripe not at earthly joys as erst they did; PER 1.01. 49

GRIPE'S 1 FR 0.0001 REL FR 1 V 0 P
like a white hind under the gripe's sharp claws, LUC 543

GRIPES 3 FR 0.0003 REL FR 3 V 0 P
him, | to see how inly sorrow gripes his soul. 3H6 1.04.171
take my cause | out of the gripes of cruel men, H8 5.02.135
join gripes with hands | made hard with hourly CYM 1.06.106

GRIPING 2 FR 0.0002 REL FR 2 V 0 P
"when griping griefs the heart doth wound, ROM 4.05.126
and griping it, the needle his finger pricks, LUC 319

GRIPPLE *(also grapple)*

/GRIPPLE 1 FR 0.0001 REL FR 1 V 0 P
thyself, | and /gripple thee unto a pagan shore, JN 5.02. 36

GRISE *(also grize)*

GRISE 2 FR 0.0002 REL FR 1 V 1 P
which, as a grise or step, may help these lovers OTH 1.03.200
they stand a grise above the reach of report. TNK 2.01. 28 P

GRISL'D *(also grisled, grizzled)*

GRISL'D 1 FR 0.0001 REL FR 1 V 0 P
his beard was grisl'd, no? HAM 1.02.239

GRISLED 1 FR 0.0001 REL FR 1 V 0 P
the grisled north | disgorges such a tempest PER 3.ch. 47

GRISLY 3 FR 0.0003 REL FR 3 V 0 P
this grisly beast, which lion hight by name, MND 5.01.139
my grisly countenance made others fly, | none 1H6 1.04. 47
swift subtle post, carrier of grisly care, LUC 926

GRISSEL 1 FR 0.0001 REL FR 1 V 0 P
for patience she will prove a second grissel, SHR 2.01.295

GRIZE *(also grise)*

GRIZE 2 FR 0.0002 REL FR 2 V 0 P
no, not a grize; TN 3.01.124
for every grize of fortune | is smooth'd by that TIM 4.03. 16

GRIZZLE 1 FR 0.0001 REL FR 1 V 0 P
be | when time hath sow'd a grizzle on thy case? TN 5.01.165

GRIZZLED *(also grisl'd, grisled)*

GRIZZLED 1 FR 0.0001 REL FR 1 V 0 P
to the boy caesar send this grizzled head, | and ANT 3.13. 17

GROAN 42 FR 0.0047 REL FR 39 V 3 P
when he should groan, | patch grief with ADO 5.01. 16
assist our moan, | help us to sigh and groan, 5.03. 17
i would you heard it groan. LLL 2.01.183
i will love, write, sigh, pray, sue, groan: 3.01.204
one with a paper, god give him grace to groan! 4.03. 20 P
or groan for joan, or spend a minute's time | in 4.03.180
you ne'er oppress'd me with a mother's groan, AWW 1.03.147
in fine, made a groan of her last breath, and 4.03. 52 P
and future ages groan for this foul act. R2 4.01.138
twice for one step i'll groan, the way being 5.01. 91
that i may strive to kill it with a groan. 5.01.100
hear, hear how dying salisbury doth groan! 1H6 1.04.104
i will weep, and 'twixt each groan | say, "who's 2H6 3.01.221
would curses kill, as doth the mandrake's groan, 3.02.310
a deadly groan, like life and death's departing. 3H6 2.06. 43
i well might hear, delivered with a groan, | "o, 5.02. 46
that blood will make 'em one day groan for't. H8 2.01.106
'fore my wars | have i heard groan and drop. COR 4.04. 4
can you hear a good man groan | and not relent, TIT 4.01.123
what, shall i groan and tell thee? ROM 1.01.200
groan? why, no; | but sadly tell me, who? 1.01.200
i did hear him groan; JC 1.02.124
horses /did neigh, and dying men did groan, 2.02. 23
gold, | to groan and sweat under the business, 4.01. 22
did the king sigh, but /with a general groan. HAM 3.03. 23
two or three groan. OTH 5.01. 42
the strong conception | that i do groan withal. 5.02. 56
then in the midst a tearing groan did break ANT 4.14. 31
could not find death where i did hear him groan, CYM 5.03. 69
rather | groan so in perpetuity than be cur'd 5.04. 6
at the proclamation, but he made a groan at it, PER 4.02.108 P
some say, | groan under such a mast'ry. TNK 1.01.231
made her groan a month for't; 3.03. 35
no, lady, no, my heart longs not to groan, | but VEN 785
what may a heavy groan advantage thee? 950
by their suggestion gives a deadly groan. 1044
(and there she stay'd | till after a deep groan) LUC 1276
for now 'tis stale to sigh, to weep, and groan. 1362
hide, | which heavily he answers with a groan, SON 50.11
for that same groan doth put this in my mind: 50.13
thy face hath not the power to make love groan; 131. 6
beshrew that heart that makes my heart to groan 133. 1

GROAN'D 4 FR 0.0004 REL FR 4 V 0 P
under my burthen groan'd, which rais'd in me TMP 1.02.156
hadst thou groan'd for him | as i have done, R2 5.02.102
fair for which love groan'd for and would die, ROM 2.pr. 3
the goodly mothers that have groan'd for these, TNK 3.06.245

GROANING 9 FR 0.0010 REL FR 6 V 3 P
shall be done, sir, with the groaning juliet? MM 2.02. 15
and still converse | with groaning wretches; LLL 5.02.852
every minute and groaning every hour would AYL 3.02.303 P
and that gave to me | many a groaning throe. H8 2.04.200
t' appease their groaning shadows that are gone. TIT 1.01.126
is not this better now than groaning for love? ROM 2.04. 88 P
and groaning underneath this age's yoke, | have JC 1.02. 61
earth | with carrion men, groaning for burial. 3.01.275
it would cost you a groaning to take off mine HAM 3.02.249 P

/GROANS 1 FR 0.0001 REL FR 1 V 0 P
/with /sighing, /girl, /kill /it /with /groans; TIT 3.02. 15

GROANS 41 FR 0.0046 REL FR 38 V 3 P
where thou didst vent thy groans | as fast as TMP 1.02.280
thy groans | did make wolves howl, and penetrate 1.02.287
be in love — where scorn is bought with groans; TGV 1.01. 29
me | with bitter fasts, with penitential groans, 2.04.131
sad sighs, deep groans, nor silver–shedding 3.01.232
th' anointed sovereign of sighs and groans, LLL 3.01.182
of sighs, of groans, of sorrow, and of teen! 4.03.162
with the clamors of their own dear groans, 5.02.864
than my heart cool with mortifying groans. MV 1.01. 82
the wretched animal heav'd forth such groans AYL 2.01. 36
and cost me the dearest groans of a mother, i AWW 4.05. 11 P
with groans that thunder love, with sighs of TN 1.05.256
and what hear there for welcome but my groans? R2 1.02. 70
go count thy way with sighs, i mine with groans. 5.01. 89
tells what hour it is | are clamorous groans, 5.05. 56
and tears, and groans | show minutes, times, and 5.05. 57
fields, and blows, and groans applaud our sport! 1H4 1.03.302
the dead men's blood, the privy maidens' groans, H5 2.04.107
to see my tears and hear my deep–fet groans. 2H6 2.04. 33
might liquid tears or heart–offending groans 3.02. 60
i would be blind with weeping, sick with groans, 3.02. 62
save for a night of groans | endur'd of her, for R3 4.04.303
groans out for ha, ha, ha! TRO 3.01.126
or if you cannot weep, yet give some groans, 5.10. 49
his revenges with the easy groans of old women, COR 5.02. 42 P
thy old groans yet ringing in mine ancient ears; ROM 2.03. 74
not i, unless the breath of heart–sick groans 3.03. 72
religion groans at it. TIM 3.02. 76
where sighs, and groans, and shrieks that rent MAC 4.03.168
i have not art to reckon my groans, but that i HAM 2.02.121 P
such groans of roaring wind and rain, i never LR 3.02. 47
then love's deep groans i never shall regard, VEN 377
and now she beats her heart, whereat it groans, 829
children's tears nor mothers' groans respecting, LUC 431
be moved with my tears, my sighs, my groans. 588
my talk with tears, my grief with groans, | poor 797
afflict him in his bed with bedred groans; 975
tear, | and with deep groans the diapason bear; 1132
when sighs and groans and tears may grace the 1319
a thousand groans, but thinking on thy face, SON 131.10
it break, with bleeding groans they pine, | and LC 275

GROAT 6 FR 0.0006 REL FR 3 V 3 P
a half–fac'd groat five hundred pound a year! JN 1.01. 94
hold you, there is a groat to heal your pate. H5 5.01. 58 P
me a groat! 5.01. 60 P
i take thy groat in earnest of revenge. 5.01. 63
the king, | or any groat i hoarded to my use, 2H6 3.01.113
will not see a red herring at a harry groat, STM II.C 2 P

GROATS 5 FR 0.0005 REL FR 2 V 3 P
again else, of seven groats in mill–sixpences, WIV 1.01.155 P
as fit as ten groats is for the hand of an AWW 2.02. 21 P

the cheapest of us is ten groats too dear. R2 5.05. 68
seven groats and two pence. 2H4 1.02.235 P
things created | to buy and sell with groats, to COR 3.02. 10
GROIN 2 FR 0.0002 REL FR 1 V 1 P
are you not hurt i' th' groin? 2H4 2.04.210 P
sheath'd unaware the tusk in his soft groin. VEN 1116
GROOM 21 FR 0.0023 REL FR 21 V 0 P
'tis a groom indeed, | a grumbling groom, and SHR 3.02.152
a grumbling groom, and that the girl shall find. 3.02.153
'tis like you'll prove a jolly surly groom, 3.02.213
i was a poor groom of thy stable, king, | when R2 5.05. 72
am, i yield to thee, | or to the meanest groom. 2H6 2.01.181
must not be shed by such a jaded groom. 4.01. 52
pole | than stand uncover'd to the vulgar groom. 4.01.128
home to your cottages, forsake this groom: 4.02.124
an ordinary groom is for such payment. H8 5.01.172
was a councillor to try him, | not as a groom. 5.02.179
be slave and sumpter | to this detested groom. LR 2.04.217
and in terms like bride and groom | devesting OTH 2.03.180
besides, thou wert too base | to be his groom. CYM 2.03.127
i should woo hard, but be your groom in honesty: 3.06. 69
and prostitute me to the basest groom | that PER 4.06.190
is with me, i met your groom | by mars's altar. TNK 1.01. 61
thee | unto the base bed of some rascal groom, LUC 671
charging the sour-fac'd groom to hie as fast 1334
when, seely groom, god wot, it was defect | of 1345
"'for some hard-favor'd groom of thine,' quoth 1632
th' adulterate death of lucrece and her groom. 1645
GROOMS 8 FR 0.0009 REL FR 8 V 0 P
you loggerheaded and unpolish'd grooms! SHR 4.01.125
shall i be flouted thus by dunghill grooms? 1H6 1.03. 14
councillor, | 'mong boys, grooms, and lackeys. H8 5.02. 18
the fields are near, and you are gallant grooms. TIT 4.02.164
and the surfeited grooms | do mock their charge MAC 2.02. 5
them, and smear | the sleepy grooms with blood. 2.02. 47
i'll gild the faces of the grooms withal, | for 2.02. 53
poor grooms are sightless night, kings glorious LUC 1013
GROP'D 1 FR 0.0001 REL FR 1 V 0 P
in the dark | grop'd i to find out them, had my HAM 5.02. 14
GROPING 1 FR 0.0001 REL FR 0 V 1 P
groping for trouts in a peculiar river. MM 1.02. 90 P
GROS 1 FR 0.0001 REL FR 0 V 1 P
de son mauvais, corruptible, gros, et impudique, H5 3.04. 53 P
GROSS 60 FR 0.0067 REL FR 49 V 11 P
unwholesome humidity, this gross wat'ry pumpion.
WIV 3.03. 41 P
i never saw him so gross in his jealousy till 3.03.189 P
matter to prevent so gross o'erreaching as this? 5.05.136 P
with character too gross is writ on juliet. MM 1.02.155
than we do minister | to our gross selves? 2.02. 87
to be received plain, i'll speak more gross: 2.04. 82
lay open to my earthy, gross conceit, ERR 3.02. 34
"right," says she, "a great gross one." ADO 5.01.162 P
he throws upon the gross world's baser slaves; LLL 1.01. 30
you know how much the gross sum of deuce-ace 1.02. 46 P
tongue proves dainty bacchus gross in taste. 4.03.336
well-liking wits they have — gross gross, fat 5.02.268
well-liking wits they have — gross gross, fat 5.02.268
and we that sell by gross, the lord doth know, 5.02.319
i cannot instantly raise up the gross | of full MV 1.03. 55
it were too gross | to rib her cerecloth in the 2.07. 50
which, to term in gross, | is an unlesson'd girl 3.02.158
here shall he see | gross fools as he, | and if AYL 2.05. 56
that may be chosen out of the gross band of the 4.01.195 P
now to all sense 'tis gross: AWW 1.03.172
sir toby, i will wash off gross acquaintance, i TN 2.05.162 P
pronounce thee a gross lout, a mindless slave, WT 1.02.301
(which was as gross as ever touch'd conjecture, 2.01.176
a gross hag! 2.03.108
that could conceive a gross and foolish sire 3.02.197
handle, though they come to him by th' gross; 4.04.207 P
in gross rebellion and detested treason. R2 2.03.109
whilst my gross flesh sinks downward, here to 5.05.112
father that begets them, gross as a mountain, 1H4 2.04.226 P
well known, my gracious lord, | a gross fat man. 2.04.511
what is the gross sum that i owe thee? 2H4 2.01. 84 P
so, like gross terms, | the prince will in the 4.04. 73
though the truth of it stands off as gross | as H5 2.02.103
free from gross passion, or of mirth or anger, 2.02.132
but in gross brain little wots | what watch the 4.01.282
o gross and miserable ignorance! 2H6 4.02.168
of those gross taunts that oft i have endur'd. R3 1.03.105
who is so gross | that cannot see this palpable 3.06. 10
they say, it were a very gross kind of behavior, ROM 2.04.166 P
you cannot make gross sins look clear; TIM 3.05. 38
know his gross patchery, love him, feed him, 5.01. 96
toward thee forgetfulness too general gross; 5.01.144
but, in the gross and scope of mine opinion, HAM 1.01. 68
things rank and gross in nature | possess it 1.02.136
examples gross as earth exhort me: 4.04. 46
hour | he flashes into one gross crime or other LR 1.03. 4
midway air | show scarce so gross as beetles. 4.06. 14
to the gross clasps of a lascivious moor — | if OTH 1.01.126
leave), | i say again, hath made a gross revolt, 1.01.134
judge me the world, if 'tis not gross in sense, 1.02. 72
and fools as gross | as ignorance made drunk. 3.03.404
do abuse their husbands | in such gross kind? 4.03. 63
most heathenish and most gross! 5.02.313
rank of gross diet, shall we be enclouded, | and ANT 5.02.212
the circuit of my breast any gross stuff | to TNK 3.01. 46
not gross to sink, but light, and will aspire. VEN 150
lest he should hold it her own gross abuse, LUC 1315
though my gross blood be stain'd with this abuse 1655
and their gross painting might be better us'd SON 82.13
my nobler part to my gross body's treason; 151. 6
GROSSER 5 FR 0.0005 REL FR 5 V 0 P
the grosser manner of these world's delights LLL 1.01. 29
be copy now to /men of grosser blood, | and H5 3.01. 24
hitting a grosser quality, is cried up | for our H8 1.02. 84
that liberal shepherds give a grosser name, HAM 4.07.170
speech | to grosser issues nor to larger reach OTH 3.03.219
GROSSLY 20 FR 0.0022 REL FR 17 V 3 P
let them say 'tis grossly done, so it be fairly WIV 2.02.142 P
oft provok'st, yet grossly fear'st | thy death, MM 3.01. 18
should slip so grossly, both in the heat of 5.01.472
to counterfeit thus grossly with your slave, ERR 2.02.169
vesture of decay | doth grossly close it in, we MV 5.01. 65
speak not so grossly, you are all amaz'd. 5.01.266
eyes | see it so grossly shown in thy behaviors AWW 1.03.178
but am in that dimension grossly clad | which TN 5.01.237
are led so grossly by this meddling priest, JN 3.01.163
though you, and all the rest so grossly led, 3.01.168
that greatness should so grossly offer it. 4.02. 94
hostess, and he slanders thee most grossly. 1H4 3.03.132 P
working so grossly in /a natural cause | that H5 2.02.107
heart | grossly grew captive to his honey words, R3 4.01. 79
'a took my father grossly, full of bread, | with HAM 3.03. 80
he hath now cast her off appears too grossly. LR 1.01.292 P
would you, the /supervisor, grossly gape on? OTH 3.03.395
for our flight, | most grossly, by his own! ANT 3.10. 28
corrupted, | grossly engirt with daring infamy: LUC 1173
in my love's veins thou hast too grossly dy'd. SON 99. 5
GROSSNESS 6 FR 0.0006 REL FR 4 V 2 P
drove the grossness of the foppery into a WIV 5.05.124 P
and i will purge thy mortal grossness so, | that MND 3.01.160
text, | hiding the grossness with fair ornament? MV 3.02. 80
believe such impossible passages of grossness. TN 3.02. 73 P
weigh it but with the grossness of this age, R3 3.01. 46
whose grossness little characters sum up; TRO 1.03.325
GROUND* *(also grund)*
/GROUND* 1 FR 0.0001 REL FR 1 V 0 P
/you /should /have /an /inch /of /any /ground 2H4 4.01.107
GROUND* 180 FR 0.0203 REL FR 149 V 31 P
furlongs of sea for an acre of barren ground, TMP 1.01. 66 P
the ground indeed is tawny. 2.01. 55 P
lead off this ground, and let's make further 2.01.323
went on four legs cannot make him give ground"; 2.02. 62 P
beat the ground | for kissing of their feet; 4.01.173
if the ground be overcharg'd, you were best TGV 1.01.101 P
her chamber is aloft, far from the ground, | and 3.01.114
like a fair house built on another man's ground, WIV 2.02.216 P
to the ground, mistress. MM 1.02.103 P
having waste ground enough, | shall we desire to 2.02.169
but one, the wicked'st caitiff on the ground, 5.01. 53
then is he the ground | of my defeatures. ERR 2.01. 97
lapwing, runs | close by the ground, to hear our ADO 3.01. 25
now for the ground which? LLL 1.01.239 P
i do affect the very ground (which is base) 1.02.167 P
kisses the base ground with obedient breast? 4.03.221
have found the ground of study's excellence 4.03.296
they are the ground, the books, the academes, 4.03.299
too, | i were the fairest goddess on the ground. 5.02. 36
with that they all did tumble on the ground, 5.02.115
sleeping sound, | on the dank and dirty ground. MND 2.02. 75
on the ground? 2.02.100
follow me then | to plainer ground. 3.02.404
on the ground | sleep sound; 3.02.448
and rock the ground whereon these sleepers be. 4.01. 86
was found | with these mortals on the ground. 4.01.102
stand'st between her father's ground and mine! 5.01.175
so i will not rest till i have run some ground. MV 2.02.104 P
him, i will run as far as god has any ground. 2.02.111 P
kind of fruit | drops earliest to the ground, 4.01.116
to see such a sight, it well becomes the ground. AYL 3.02.243 P
lay couching, head on ground, with cat-like 4.03.115
we will bestrow the ground. SHR in.2. 40
"gamouth i am, the ground of all accord: 3.01. 73
that barefoot plod i the cold ground upon, AWW 3.04. 6
as your feet hits the ground they step on. TN 3.04.278 P
give ground if you see him furious. 3.04.304 P
though i confess, on base and ground enough, 5.01. 75
and my ground to do't | is the obedience to a WT 1.02.353
did lack than i, my lord, | upon this ground; 2.01.159
and you shall help to put him i' th' ground. 3.03.137 P
made her flight across | thy father's ground. 4.04. 16
whose sons lie scattered on the bleeding ground. JN 2.01.304
and lay this angiers even with the ground, 2.01.399
and when that we have dash'd them to the ground, 2.01.405
well, | made to run even upon even ground, 2.01.576
i strike my foot | upon the bosom of the ground, 4.01. 3
good ground, be pitiful and hurt me not! 4.03. 2
when english measure backward their own ground 5.05. 3
on some known ground of treachery in him? R2 1.01. 11
or any other ground inhabitable | where ever 1.01. 65
then england's ground, farewell, sweet soil, 1.03.306
dar'd once to touch a dust of england's ground? 2.03. 91
look not to the ground, | ye favorites of a king 3.02. 87
and lie full low, grav'd in the hollow ground. 3.02.140
save our deposed bodies to the ground? 3.02.150
for god's sake let us sit upon the ground | and 3.02.155
the blood of english shall manure the ground, 4.01.137
an' never will i rise up from the ground | till 5.02.116
knees still kneel till to the ground they grow; 5.03.106
so proudly as if he disdain'd the ground. 5.05. 83
and like bright metal on a sullen ground, | my 1H4 1.02.212
where fadom-line could never touch the ground, 1.03.204
yards of uneven ground is threescore and ten 2.02. 25 P
lay thine ear close to the ground, and list if 2.02. 32 P
began to give me ground; 2.04.216 P
no man so potent breathes upon the ground | but 4.01. 11
rise from the ground like feathered mercury, 4.01.106
dead, | breathless and bleeding on the ground. 5.04.134
mare, if i have any vantage of ground to get up. 2H4 2.01. 79 P
by this heavenly ground i tread on, i must be 2.01.140 P
if they get ground and vantage of the king, 2.03. 53
which should not find a ground to root upon 3.01. 91
thus do the hopes we have in him touch ground 4.01. 17
and, by the ground they hide, i judge their 4.01. 21
till that his passions, like a whale on ground, 4.04. 40
who on the french ground play'd a tragedy, H5 1.02.106
we shall your tawny ground with your red blood 3.06.161
who hath measur'd the ground? 3.07.127 P
black shoe trod upon god's ground and his earth, 4.07.142 P
hedges | they pitched in the ground confusedly, 1H6 1.01.118
with my nails digg'd stones out of the ground 1.04. 45
my words | on any plot of ground in christendom. 2.04. 89
that droops his sapless branches to the ground. 2.05. 12
roan, i'll shake thy bulwarks to the ground. 3.02. 17
as to vouchsafe one glance unto the ground. 2H6 1.02. 16
a spirit rais'd from depth of under ground, 1.02. 79
raising up wicked spirits from under ground, 2.01.170
will bring thy head with sorrow to the ground! 2.03. 19
be'st found | on any ground that i am ruler of, 3.02.296
now, by the ground that i am banish'd from, 3.02.334
that kiss'd the queen shall sweep the ground, 4.01. 75
may that ground gape, and swallow me alive, 3H6 1.01.161
and give no foot of ground!" 1.04. 15
body | might in the ground be closed up in rest! 2.01. 76
did, | giving no ground unto the house of york, 2.06. 16
down, | and with dishonor laid me on the ground, 3.03. 9
whereof the root was fix'd in virtue's ground, 3.03.125
blood of lancaster | sink in the ground? 5.06. 62
makes him to send, that he may learn the ground.
R3 1.03. 68
for on that ground i'll make a holy descant — 3.07. 49
let us survey the vantage of the ground. 5.03. 15
i would these dewy tears were from the ground. 5.03.284
stops on a sudden, looks upon the ground, | then H8 3.02.114
unspotted lily shall she pass | to th' ground, 5.04. 62
know not why, they hate upon no better a ground.
COR 2.02. 11 P
on fair ground | i could beat forty of them. 3.01.241
while i remain above the ground, you shall 4.01. 51
like to a bowl upon a subtle ground, | i have 5.02. 20
and the ground shrinks before his treading. 5.04. 19 P
full well i wot the ground of all this grudge. TIT 2.01. 48
should the empress know | this discord's ground, 2.01. 70
but hope to pluck a dainty doe to ground. 2.02. 26
and make a checker'd shadow on the ground. 2.03. 15
throw your mistempered weapons to the ground, ROM 1.01. 87
lead | so stakes me to the ground i cannot move. 1.04. 16
and fall upon the ground, as i do now, | taking 3.03. 69
there on the ground, with his own tears made 3.03. 83
lifts me above the ground with cheerful thoughts 5.01. 5
holding thy ear close to the hollow ground, | so 5.03. 4
the ground is bloody, search about the 5.03.172
we see the ground whereon these woes do lie, 5.03.179
but the true ground of all these piteous woes 5.03.180
with man's blood paint the ground, gules, gules. TIM 4.03. 60
my credit now stands on such slippery ground JC 3.01.191
their charges off | a little from this ground. 4.02. 49
the people 'twixt philippi and this ground | do 4.03.204
is not that he that lies upon the ground? 5.03. 57
profound, | i'll catch it ere it come to ground; MAC 3.05. 25
to kiss the ground before young malcolm's feet, 5.08. 28
friends to this ground. HAM 1.01. 15
action | it waves you to a more removed ground, 1.04. 61
then we'll shift our ground. 1.05.156
neptune's salt wash and tellus' orbed ground, 3.02.156
we go to gain a little patch of ground | that 4.04. 18
which bewept to the ground did not go | with 4.05. 39
to think they would lay him i' th' cold ground. 4.05. 70 P
how the knave jowls it to the ground, as if 5.01. 76 P
upon what ground? 5.01.160 P
she should in ground unsanctified been lodg'd 5.01.229
millions of acres on us, till our ground, 5.01.281
'tis on such ground and to such wholesome end LR 2.04.144
methinks the ground is even. 4.06. 3
when thou wast here above the ground, i was | a ANT 1.05. 30
he added to your having, gave you some ground. CYM 1.02. 19 P
how long a fool you were upon the ground. 1.02. 24 P
i should get ground of your fair mistress; 1.04.104 P
whiles yet the dew's on ground, gather those 1.05. 1
he on the ground, my speech of insultment ended 3.05.140 P
nights together | have made the ground my bed. 3.06. 3
then on good ground we far, | if we do fear 4.02.143
got the mannish crack, sing him to th' ground, 4.02.236
the ground that gave them first has them again: 4.02.289
we have th' advantage of the ground, | the lane 5.02. 11
what fairies haunt this ground? 5.04.133
nobler sir ne'er liv'd | 'twixt sky and ground. 5.05.146
let's quit this ground, | and smoke the temple 5.05.397
i have ground the axe myself, | do but you PER 1.02. 58
she were a thornier piece of ground than she is, 4.06.144 P
upon what ground is his distemperature? 5.01. 27
and make him cry from under ground, "o, fan TNK pr 18
but touch the ground for us no longer time 1.01. 97
theirs has more ground, is more maturely 1.03. 56
where there is a path of ground i'll venture, 2.06. 33
a bolder traitor never trod thy ground, | a 3.06.141
shall grow to th' ground but i'll get mercy. 3.06.192
what seest thou in the ground? VEN 118
now gazeth she on him, now on the ground; 224
clapping their proud tails to the ground below, 923
to wash the foul face of the sluttish ground, 983
as when the wind imprison'd in the ground, 1046
and in his blood that on the ground lay spill'd, 1167
my sable ground of sin i will not paint, | to LUC 1074
my soul and body to the skies and ground, | my 1199
then jointly to the ground their knees they bow, 1846
as flowers dead lie withered on the ground, | as PP 13. 9
how sighs resound through heartless ground, 17.23
or as sweet-season'd showers are to the ground; SON 75. 2
my mistress when she walks treads on the ground. 130.12
in a cold valley-fountain of that ground; 153. 4
GROUNDED 5 FR 0.0005 REL FR 5 V 0 P
grounded upon no other argument | but that the AYL 1.02.279
from wayward sickness and no grounded malice. R3 1.03. 29
how grounded he his title to the crown | upon H8 1.02.144
remedy, | it is so grounded inward in my heart. SON 62. 4
hate of my sin, grounded on sinful loving: 142. 2
GROUNDLINGS 1 FR 0.0001 REL FR 0 V 1 P
to split the ears of the groundlings, who for HAM 3.02. 11 P
GROUND-PIECE 1 FR 0.0001 REL FR 1 V 0 P
you were | the ground-piece of some painter, i TNK 1.01.122
GROUND'S 2 FR 0.0002 REL FR 2 V 0 P
our ground's the lowest, and we are half way PER 1.04. 78
or know what ground's made happy by his breath. 2.04. 28
GROUNDS 10 FR 0.0011 REL FR 9 V 1 P
myself in my incertain grounds to fail | as AWW 3.01. 15
but i shall lose the grounds i work upon. 3.07. 3
that it is his grounds of faith that all that TN 2.03.151 P
but when we know the grounds and authors of it, 5.01.353
and like a thief to come to rob my grounds, 2H6 4.10. 34
i'll have grounds | more relative than this — HAM 2.02.603
and on /other grounds | christen'd and heathen, OTH 1.01. 29
but that i did proceed upon just grounds | to 5.02.138
the boy he should not pass those grounds. PP 9. 8
in brief the grounds and motives of her woe. LC 63
GROVE 18 FR 0.0020 REL FR 18 V 0 P
and now they never meet in grove or green, | by MND 2.01. 28
thou shalt not from this grove | till i torment 2.01.146
ere he do leave this grove, | thou shalt fly him 2.01.245
thou some of it, and seek through this grove: 2.01.259

what night–rule now about this haunted grove? 3.02. 5
did ever dian so become a grove | as kate this SHR 2.01.258
amongst a grove the very straightest plant, 1H4 1.01. 82
he that breaks a stick of gloucester's grove 2H6 1.02. 33
this evening, on the east side of the grove. 2.01. 42
are ye advis'd? the east side of the grove. 2.01. 47
their sweetest shade a grove of cypress trees! 3.02.323
i am attended at the cypress grove. COR 1.10. 30
underneath the grove of sycamore | that westward ROM 1.01.121
i say, a moving grove. MAC 5.05. 37
this said, she hasteth to a myrtle grove, VEN 865
make thy sad grove in my dishevell'd hair; LUC 1129
in men, as in a rough–grown grove, remain 1249
pleasant shade, | which a grove of myrtles made, PP 20. 4

GROVEL 2 FR 0.0002 REL FR 1 V 1 P
if so, gaze on, and grovel on thy face, | until 2H6 1.02. 9
be you prostrate and grovel on the earth. 1.04. 11 P

GROVELLING 1 FR 0.0001 REL FR 1 V 0 P
many a widow's husband grovelling lies, | coldly JN 2.01.305

GROVES 5 FR 0.0005 REL FR 5 V 0 P
of hills, brooks, standing lakes, and groves, TMP 5.01. 33
the groves may tread | even till the eastern MND 3.02.390
for, besides the groves, | the skies, the 4.01.115
who hath abandoned her holy groves | to see the TIT 2.03. 58
but like to groves, being topp'd, they higher PER 1.04. 9

/GROW 4 FR 0.0004 REL FR 2 V 2 P
/how /comes /it? /do /they /grow /rusty? HAM 2.02.337 P
/if /they /should /grow /themselves /to /common 2.02.348 P
whose heads | /do /grow beneath their shoulders. OTH 1.03.145
his steerage shall your thoughts /grow /on — PER 4.04. 19

GROW 150 FR 0.0169 REL FR 119 V 31 P
i prithee let me bring thee where crabs grow; TMP 2.02.167
heavens let fall | to make this contract grow; 4.01. 19
another tale, if matters grow to your likings. WIV 1.01. 78 P
i hope, upon familiarity will grow more content. 1.01.250 P
as those that feed grow full, as blossoming time MM 1.04. 41
and i trust it will grow to a most prosperous 3.01.260 P
on angelo, | to weed my vice and let his grow! 3.02.270
shall love, in /building, grow so /ruinous? ERR 3.02. 4
grow this to what adverse issue it can, i will ADO 2.02. 51 P
paid that now men grow hard–hearted and will 5.01.311 P
weeds the corn and still lets grow the weeding. LLL 1.01. 96
such short–liv'd wits do wither as they grow. 2.01. 54
come, you talk greasily, your lips grow foul. 4.01.137
nay then two treys, and if you grow so nice, 5.02.232
then die a calf, before your horns do grow. 5.02.253
so will i grow, so live, so die, my lord, | ere MND 1.01. 79
and so grow to a point. 1.02. 10 P
and grow big–bellied with the wanton wind; 2.01.129
so sorrow's heaviness doth heavier grow | for 3.02. 84
thy lips, those kissing cherries, tempting grow! 3.02.140
you grow exceeding strange. MV 1.01. 67
fare you well! i'll grow a talker for this gear. 1.01.110
father did something smack, something grow to, 2.02. 18 P
have all miscarried, my creditors grow cruel, my 3.02.316 P
if we grow all to be pork–eaters, we shall not 3.05. 24 P
i shall grow jealious of you shortly, launcelot, 3.05. 29 P
and discourse grow commendable in none only but 3.05. 45 P
begin you to grow upon me? AYL 1.01. 85 P
thus men may grow wiser every day. 1.02.137 P
if he, compact of jars, grow musical, | we shall 2.07. 5
which otherwise would grow into extremes. SHR in.1. 138
fiddler, forbear, you grow too forward, sir. 3.01. 1
to grow there and to bear — "let me not live" AWW 1.02. 55
i grow to you, and our parting is a tortur'd 2.01. 36 P
thine honor where | we please to have it grow. 2.03.157
be bold you do so grow in my requital | as 5.01. 5
there thy fixed foot shall grow | till thou have TN 1.04. 17
besides, you grow dishonest. 1.05. 42 P
to die, even when they to perfection grow! 2.04. 41
though i would not have it grow on my chin. 3.01. 47 P
or will not else thy craft so quickly grow, 5.01.166
how should this grow? WT 1.02.431
one | he chides to hell and bids the other grow 4.04.553
grow great by your example and put on | the JN 5.01. 52
mine honor is my life, both grow in one, | take R2 1.01.182
to ear the land that hath some hope to grow, 3.02.212
base court, where kings grow base, | to come at 3.03.180
god the plants thou graft'st may never grow. 3.04.101
for ever may my knees grow to the earth, | my 5.03. 30
knees still kneel till to the ground they grow; 5.03.106
that blood should sprinkle me to make me grow. 5.06. 46
they grow like hydra's heads. 1H4 5.04. 25
if i do grow great, i'll grow less, for i'll 5.04.163 P
if i do grow great, i'll grow less, for i'll 5.04.164 P
sooner have a beard grow in the palm of my hand 2H4 1.02. 21 P
our present musters grow upon the file | to five 1.03. 10
that it may grow and sprout as high as heaven, 2.03. 60
this will grow to a brawl anon. 2.04.172 P
how foul it is, what rank diseases grow, | and 3.01. 39
would of that seed grow to a greater falseness, 3.01. 90
your part, bullcalf, grow till you come unto it. 3.02.252 P
limb united, | grow stronger for the breaking. 4.01.221
if you grow foul with me, pistol, i will scour H5 2.01. 56 P
good service in a garden where leeks did grow, 4.07. 99 P
defective in their natures, grow to wildness. 5.02. 55
but grow like savages — as soldiers will | that 5.02. 59
will turn white, a curl'd pate will grow bald, a 5.02.161 P
my lord of gloucester, now ye grow too hot: 2H6 1.01.137
the winds grow high, so do your stomachs, lords. 2.01. 53
betime, | before the wound do grow uncurable; 3.01.286
where biting cold would never let grass grow, 3.02.337
when we grow stronger, then we'll make our claim 3H6 4.07. 59
why grow the branches when the root is gone? R3 2.02. 41
why, my good cousin, it is good to grow. 2.04. 9
my uncle rivers talk'd how i did grow | more 2.04. 11
herbs have grace, great weeds do grow apace." 2.04. 13
and since, methinks i would not grow so fast, 2.04. 14
they that my trust must grow to, live not here. H8 3.01. 89
or felt the flatteries that grow upon it! 3.01.144
utterly | grow from the king's acquaintance, by 3.01.161
but to stubborn spirits | they swell and grow, 3.01.164
mine eyes grow dim. 4.02.164
so i grow stronger, you more honor gain. 5.02.215
they grow still too; 5.03. 68
shall then be his, and like a vine grow to him. 5.04. 49
grow in the veins of actions highest rear'd, TRO 1.03. 6
how doth pride grow? 2.03.152 P
and i'll grow friend with danger. 4.04. 70
let grow thy sinews till their knots be strong, 5.03. 33
or else your actions would grow wondrous single; COR 2.01. 36 P
friends, | i' th' war do grow together; 3.02. 43
shall grow dear friends | and interjoin their 4.04. 21
here grow no damned drugs, here are no storms, TIT 1.01.154
ay, boy, grow ye so brave? 2.01. 45
who marks the waxing tide grow wave by wave, 3.01. 95
could we but learn from whence his sorrows grow, ROM 1.01.154
no less! nay, bigger: women grow by men. 1.03. 95
till strange love grow bold, | think true love 3.02. 15
his hate may grow | to the whole race of mankind TIM 4.01. 39
hatch'd, would as his kind grow mischievous, JC 2.01. 33
o, i grow faint. 2.04. 43
and say which grain will grow, and which will MAC 1.03. 59
there if i grow, | the harvest is your own. 1.04. 32
for nature crescent does not grow alone | in HAM 1.03. 11
and you, my sinows, grow not instant old, | but 1.05. 94
sir, shall grow old as i am, if like a crab you 2.02.203 P
where little fears grow great, great love grows 3.02.172
my spirits grow dull, and fain i would beguile 3.02.226
hazard so near 's as doth hourly grow | out of 3.03. 6
defeat | does by their own insinuation grow. 5.02. 59
i grow, i prosper: LR 1.02. 21
his knights grow riotous, and himself upbraids 1.03. 6
have found a safe redress, but now grow fearful, 1.04.206
a good man's fortune may grow out at heels. 2.02.157
and all the idle weeds that grow | in our 4.04. 5
why then your other senses grow imperfect | by 4.06. 5
should increase | even as our days do grow! OTH 2.01.195
of your love shall grow stronger than it was 2.03.325 P
though other things grow fair against the sun, 2.03.376
would stand and make his eyes grow in my brow; ANT 1.05. 32
terms, | nor curstness grow to th' matter. 2.02. 25
labor when i wash my brain | and it grow fouler. 2.07.100
but when we in our viciousness grow hard | (o 3.13.111
grace grow where those drops fall, my hearty 4.02. 38
to live, | the loathness to depart would grow. CYM 1.01.108
grow, /patience! 4.02. 58
they grow, | and set them on lud's–town. 4.02.122
be jointed to the old stock, and freshly grow, 5.04.143 P
be jointed to the old stock, and freshly grow; 5.05.440 P
fence the roots they grow by and defend them — PER 1.02. 31
decrease not, but grow faster than the years; 1.02. 85
the vine shall grow, but we shall never see it; TNK 2.02. 43
the gall of hazard, so they grow together, 2.02. 66
my knees shall grow to th' ground but i'll get 3.06.192
a virgin flow'r, | must grow alone, unpluck'd. 5.01.168
my palamon i hope will grow too, finely, | now 5.02. 95
of dung — as you know they grow in dung — have STM II.C 13 P
my beauty as the spring doth yearly grow, | my VEN 141
to grow unto himself was his desire, | and so 1180
and as their captain, so their pride doth grow, LUC 298
sing, | trees did grow and plants did spring; PP 20. 6
itself confounded, | saw division grow together, PHT 42
and die as fast as they see others grow, | and SON 12.12
i send them back again and straight grow sad. 45.14
the /soil is this, that thou dost common grow. 69.14
speaking of worth, what worth in you doth grow. 83. 8
how like eve's apple doth thy beauty grow, | if 93.13
give full growth to that which still doth grow. 115.14
if hairs be wires, black wires grow on her head. 130. 4
for if i should despair, i should grow mad, 140. 9

GROWETH 1 FR 0.0001 REL FR 1 V 0 P
deceiv'd, | our fine musician groweth amorous. SHR 3.01. 63

GROWING 33 FR 0.0037 REL FR 32 V 1 P
hence his ambition growing — | dost thou hear? TMP 1.02.105
vines with clust'ring bunches growing, | plants 4.01.112
kiss, | and, of so great a favor growing proud, TGV 2.04.161
lest, growing ruinous, the building fall | and 5.04. 9
do owe to you | is growing to me by antipholus, ERR 4.01. 8
things growing are not ripe until their season, MND 2.02.117
and give my scene such growing | as you had WT 4.01. 16
sir, the year growing ancient, | not yet on 4.04. 79
virgin branches yet | your maidenheads growing. 4.04.116
cut off the heads of /too fast growing sprays, R2 3.04. 34
had he done so to great and growing men, | they 3.04. 61
he is retir'd, to ripe his growing fortunes, 2H4 4.01. 13
on, and sickness growing | upon our soldiers, we H5 3.03. 55
were growing time once ripened to my will. 1H6 2.04. 99
or bath'd thy growing with our heated bloods. 3H6 2.02.169
when dying clouds contend with growing light, 2.05. 2
well dispos'd, the mind growing once corrupt, H8 1.02.116
still growing in a majesty and pomp, the which 2.03. 7
which ever has and ever shall be growing, | till 3.02.178
this growing image of thy fiend–like face? TIT 5.01. 45
these growing feathers pluck'd from caesar's JC 1.01. 72
which is a great way growing on the south, 2.01.107
and will labor | to make thee full of growing. MAC 1.04. 29
still, | for goodness, growing to a plurisy, HAM 4.07.117
of the north | shakes all our buds from growing. CYM 1.03. 37
head, which now is growing upon thy shoulders, 4.01. 16 P
oxlips in their cradles growing, | marigolds on TNK 1.01. 10
things growing to themselves are growth's abuse. VEN 166
i know what thorns the growing rose defends, | i LUC 492
adonis made | under an osier growing by a brook, PP 6. 5
my friend's muse grown with this growing age, SON 32.10
so thy great gift, upon misprision growing, 87.11
growing a bath and healthful remedy | for men 154.11

GROWN 59 FR 0.0066 REL FR 52 V 7 P
who with age and envy | was grown into a hoop? TMP 1.02.259
being often read, | grown /sere and tedious; MM 2.04. 9
why are you grown so rude? MND 3.02.262
and are you grown so high in his esteem, 3.02.294
my master is grown quarrelsome. SHR 1.02. 13
without words, and words are grown so false, i TN 3.01. 24 P
avoid what's grown than question how 'tis born. WT 1.02.433
now grown in grace | equal with wond'ring. 4.01. 24
neighbors, is grown into an unspeakable estate. 4.02. 40 P
more, | is not your father grown incapable | of 4.04.397
and liberal largess, are grown somewhat light, R2 1.04. 44
the /king's grown bankrout, like a broken man. 2.01.257
eleven buckrom men grown out of two. 1H4 2.04.219 P
the english army is grown weak and faint; 1H6 1.01.158
grown to this faction in the temple garden, 2.04.125
this late dissension grown betwixt the peers 3.01.188
such as were grown to credit by the wars; 4.01. 36
is your priesthood grown peremptory? 2H6 2.01. 23
by devilish policy art thou grown great | and, 4.01. 83
is the man grown mad? 5.01.131
the world is grown so bad | that wrens make prey R3 1.03. 69
i hope he is much grown since last i saw him. 2.04. 5
physic, their diseases | are grown so catching. H8 1.03. 37
i am glad | your grace is grown so pleasant. 1.04. 90
(though he be grown so desperate to be honest), 3.01. 86
ajax is grown self–will'd, and bears his head TRO 1.03.188
dull and long–continued truce | is resty grown. 1.03.263
my thoughts were like unbridled children grown 3.02.122
a woman impudent and mannish grown | is not more 3.03.217
he's grown a very land–fish, languageless, a 3.03.263 P
he is grown | too proud to be so valiant. COR 1.01.258
o, he is grown most kind of late. 4.06. 11
this martius is grown from man to dragon: 5.04. 13 P
are you so desperate grown to threat your TIT 2.01. 40
and quench the fire, the room is grown too hot. ROM 1.05. 28
but my true love is grown to such excess | i 2.06. 33
our caesar feed | that he is grown so great? JC 1.02.150
what a blunt fellow is this grown to be! 1.02.295
me, | in personal action, yet prodigious grown, 1.03. 77
for he is superstitious grown of late, | quite 2.01.195
there the grown serpent lies; MAC 3.04. 28
as if increase of appetite had grown | by what HAM 1.02.144
none, my lord, but the world's grown honest. 2.02.237 P
diseases desperate grown | by desperate 4.03. 9
the age is grown so pick'd that the toe of the 5.01.140 P
in a year, | for wise men are grown foppish, LR 1.04.167
is grown so vild | that it doth hate what gets 3.04.195
the hated, grown to strength, | are newly grown ANT 1.03. 48
grown to strength, | are newly grown to love; 1.03. 49
and quietness, grown sick of rest, would purge 1.03. 53
i have told him lepidus was grown too cruel, 3.06. 32
those that would die or e'er resist are grown CYM 5.03. 50
me, i was grown so low | and crestfall'n with my TNK 3.06. 6
lord, how y' are grown! 5.02. 94
the peace wherein you have till now grown up STM II.C 65
"had my friend's muse grown with this growing SON 32.10
and sweets grown common lose their dear delight. 102.12
who hast by waning grown, and therein show'st 126. 3
now this ill–wresting world is grown so bad, 140.11

GROWS 83 FR 0.0093 REL FR 67 V 16 P
and as with age his body uglier grows, | so his TMP 4.01.191
the more it grows, and fawneth on her still. TGV 4.02. 15
to recover his hair that grows bald by nature. ERR 2.02. 73 P
and, knowing how the debt grows, i will pay it. 4.04.121
say, how grows it due? 4.04.134
your light grows dark by losing of your eyes. LLL 1.01. 79
but like of each thing that in season grows. 1.01.107
it when a man of great spirit grows melancholy? 1.02. 2 P
sing, boy, my spirit grows heavy in love. 1.02.122 P
glory grows guilty of detested crimes, | when, 4.01. 31
it grows dark, he may stumble. 5.02.630
which withering on the virgin thorn | grows, MND 1.01. 78
where oxlips and the nodding violet grows, 2.01.250
and grows to something of great constancy; 5.01. 26
prove the weeping philosopher when he grows old, MV 1.02. 49 P
the hebrew will turn christian, he grows kind. 1.03.178
seem then that dobbin's tail grows backward. 2.02. 96 P
the spirit of my father grows strong in me, and AYL 1.01. 70 P
and mine, but it grows something stale with me. 2.04. 62 P
of all opinion that grows rank in them | that i 2.07. 46
sirs, | if you should smile, he grows impatient. SHR in.1. 99
no profit grows where is no pleasure ta'en. 1.01. 39
than at home, | where small experience grows. 1.02. 52
why, how now, dame, whence grows this insolence? 2.01. 23
though little fire grows great with little wind, 2.01.134
see, sir, how your fooling grows old, and people TN 1.05.110 P
the man grows mad, away with him! 3.04.371
yet indirection thereby grows direct, | and JN 3.01.276
now, by my life, this day grows wondrous hot; 3.02. 1
grows strong and great in substance and in power R2 3.02. 35
and one of them is fat and grows old, god help 1H4 2.04.132 P
the more it is trodden on, the faster it grows, 2.04.401 P
i lay aside that which grows to me? 2H4 1.02. 88 P
come, it grows late, we'll to bed. 2.04.276 P
the strawberry grows underneath the nettle, H5 1.01. 60
that grows not in a fair consent with ours; 2.02. 22
and, now the matter grows to compremise, 1H6 5.04.149
the more we stay, the stronger grows our foe. 3H6 3.03. 40
high–reaching buckingham grows circumspect. R3 4.02. 31
to the rebels, and their power grows strong. 4.04.505
for it grows again | fresher than e'er it was, H8 2.01.154
lute, wench, my soul grows sad with troubles. 3.01. 1
good grows with her; 5.04. 32
grows to an envious fever | of pale and TRO 1.03.133
grows dainty of his worth, and in his tent 1.03.145
barbarism, and policy grows into an ill opinion. 5.04. 17 P
when steel grows soft as the parasite's silk, COR 1.09. 45
it is a purpos'd thing, and grows by plot, | to 3.01. 38
hie you, make haste, for it grows very late. ROM 3.03.164
o, now be gone, more light and light it grows. 3.05. 35
it wears, sir, as it grows. TIM 1.01. 3
and nature, as it grows again toward earth, | is 2.02.218
and grant, as timon grows, his hate may grow 4.01. 39
i have a tree, which grows here in my close, 5.01.205
when marcus brutus grows so covetous | to lock JC 4.03. 79
he grows worse and worse, | question enrages him MAC 3.04.116
there grows | in my most ill–compos'd affection 4.03. 76
deeper, grows with more pernicious root | than 4.03. 85
'tis an unweeded garden | that grows to seed, HAM 1.02.136
of the mind and soul | grows wide withal. 1.03. 14
little fears grow great, great love grows there. 3.02.172
but "while the grass grows" — the proverb is 3.02.343 P
there is a willow grows askaunt the brook, 4.07.166
what grows of it, no matter. LR 1.03. 23
thou sayest the king grows mad, i'll tell thee, 3.04.165
my sickness grows upon me. 5.03.105
high supper–time, and the night grows to waste. OTH 4.02.242 P
quat almost to the sense, | and he grows angry. 5.01. 12
out of tune, | and sweet revenge grows harsh. 5.02.116

but his whole action grows | not in the power ANT 3.07. 68
not born where't grows, | but worn a bait for CYM 3.04. 56
that wildly grows in them but yields a crop | as 4.02.180
what being more known grows worse, to smother it PER 1.01.106
grows elder now, and cares it be not done. 1.02. 15
here comes that which grows to the stalk, never 4.06. 41 P
the sun grows high, let's walk in. TNK 2.02.148
plighted with | a love that grows as you decay. 5.03.111
incorporate then they seem, face grows to face. VEN 540
hasty spring still blasts and ne'er grows old! LUC 49
when i consider every thing that grows | holds SON 15. 1
grows fairer than at first, more strong, far 119.12
that it nor grows with heat nor drowns with 124.12
root pity in thy heart, that, when it grows, 142.11
GROW'ST 3 FR 0.0003 REL FR 3 V 0 P
fast as thou shalt wane, so fast thou grow'st, SON 11. 1
when in eternal lines to time thou grow'st. 18.12
thy lovers withering as thy sweet self grow'st; 126. 4
GROWTH 17 FR 0.0019 REL FR 13 V 4 P
and three or four more of their growth, we'll WIV 4.04. 49
gain nothing under him but growth, for the which AYL 1.01. 14 P
young men, of excellent growth and presence. 1.02.122 P
let me stay the growth of his beard, if thou 3.02.210 P
o'er sixteen years and leave the growth untried WT 4.01. 6
say of wax, my growth would approve the truth. 2H4 1.02.159 P
whose want gives growth to th' imperfections H5 5.02. 69
york | has almost overta'en him in his growth. R3 2.04. 7
to touch his growth nearer than he touch'd mine. 2.04. 25
you said that idle weeds are fast in growth: 3.01.103
to stop all hopes whose growth may damage me. 4.02. 59
tortive and errant from his course of growth. TRO 1.03. 9
thy rose, | i cannot give it vital growth again, OTH 5.02. 14
this bastard graff shall never come to growth. LUC 1062
in pride of all his growth | a vengeful canker SON 99.12
and stops /her pipe in growth of riper days: 102. 8
to give full growth to that which still doth 115.14
GROWTH'S 1 FR 0.0001 REL FR 1 V 0 P
things growing to themselves are growth's abuse. VEN 166
GRUB 3 FR 0.0003 REL FR 1 V 2 P
is difference between a grub and a butterfly, COR 5.04. 11 P
and a butterfly, yet your butterfly was a grub. 5.04. 12 P
made by the joiner squirrel or old grub, | time ROM 1.04. 60
GRUBB'D 1 FR 0.0001 REL FR 1 V 0 P
stock, sir thomas, | i wish it grubb'd up now. H8 5.01. 23
GRUBS 1 FR 0.0001 REL FR 1 V 0 P
lends his light | to grubs and eyeless skulls? ROM 5.03.126
GRUDG'D 1 FR 0.0001 REL FR 1 V 0 P
for they have grudg'd us contribution. JC 4.03.206
GRUDGE 11 FR 0.0012 REL FR 11 V 0 P
serv'd | without or grudge or grumblings. TMP 1.02.249
cancel all grudge, repeal thee home again, TGV 5.04.143
i will feed fat the ancient grudge i bear him. MV 1.03. 47
that grudge one thought against your majesty! 1H6 3.01.175
your private grudge, my lord of york, will out, 4.01.109
if ever any grudge were lodg'd between us; R3 2.01. 66
full well i wot the ground of all this grudge. TIT 2.01. 48
from ancient grudge break to new mutiny, | where ROM pr 3
there is some grudge between 'em; JC 4.03.125
'tis not in thee | to grudge my pleasures, to LR 2.04.174
nor shall he grudge to fall, | nor think he dies TNK 3.06.297
GRUDGES 1 FR 0.0001 REL FR 1 V 0 P
my noble queen, let former grudges pass, | and 3H6 3.03.195
GRUDGING 3 FR 0.0003 REL FR 2 V 1 P
of his heart he eats his meat without grudging; ADO 3.04. 89 P
how will their grudging stomachs be provok'd 1H6 4.01.141
by heaven, my soul is purg'd from grudging hate, R3 2.01. 9
GRUEL 1 FR 0.0001 REL FR 1 V 0 P
by a drab, | make the gruel thick and slab. MAC 4.01. 32
GRUMBLE 2 FR 0.0002 REL FR 1 V 1 P
what, do you grumble? SHR 4.01.167
art thou that dost grumble there i' th' straw? LR 3.04. 44 P
GRUMBLEST 1 FR 0.0001 REL FR 0 V 1 P
thou grumblest and railest every hour on TRO 2.01. 32 P
GRUMBLING 3 FR 0.0003 REL FR 3 V 0 P
a grumbling groom, and that the girl shall find. SHR 3.02.153
somerset, buckingham, | and grumbling york; 2H6 1.03. 70
boy, that with his grumbling voice | was wont to 3H6 1.04. 76
GRUMBLINGS 1 FR 0.0001 REL FR 1 V 0 P
serv'd | without or grudge or grumblings. TMP 1.02.249
GRUMIO 22 FR 0.0024 REL FR 12 V 10 P
here, sirrah grumio, knock, i say. SHR 1.02. 5
my old friend grumio! 1.02. 21 P
rise, grumio, rise, we will compound this 1.02. 27
first, | then had not grumio come by the worst. 1.02. 35
your ancient, trusty, pleasant servant grumio. 1.02. 47
peace, grumio, it is the rival of my love. 1.02.141
grumio, mum! god save you, signior gremio. 1.02.162
grumio, my horse. 3.02.204
grumio, | draw forth thy weapon, we are beset 3.02.235
is my master and his wife coming, grumio? 4.01. 18 P
i prithee, good grumio, tell me, how goes the 4.01. 33 P
ready, and therefore, good grumio, the news. 4.01. 40 P
let's ha't, good grumio. 4.01. 59 P
welcome home, grumio! 4.01.106 P
how now, grumio? 4.01.107 P
what, grumio! 4.01.108 P
fellow grumio! 4.01.109 P
i like it well, good grumio, fetch it me. 4.03. 21
mustard, | or else you get no beef of grumio. 4.03. 28
grumio gave order how it should be done. 4.03.117
god–a–mercy, grumio, then he shall have no odds. 4.03.153 P
sirrah grumio, go to your mistress, | say i 5.02. 95
GRUMIO'S 1 FR 0.0001 REL FR 1 V 0 P
petruchio, patience, i am grumio's pledge. SHR 1.02. 45
GRUND *(also ground*)*
GRUND 1 FR 0.0001 REL FR 0 V 1 P
de gud service, or i'll lig i' the grund for it; H5 3.02.116 P
GRUNT 2 FR 0.0002 REL FR 2 V 0 P
and neigh, and bark, and grunt, and roar, and MND 3.01.110
bear, | to grunt and sweat under a weary life, HAM 3.01. 76
GUALTIER 2 FR 0.0002 REL FR 2 V 0 P
thy name is gualtier, being rightly sounded. 2H6 4.01. 37
gualtier or walter, which it is, i care not. 4.01. 38
/GUARD 1 FR 0.0001 REL FR 1 V 0 P
king | to some retention /and /appointed /guard, LR 5.03. 47
GUARD 91 FR 0.0102 REL FR 86 V 5 P
will guard your person while you take your rest, TMP 2.01.197
'tis best we stand upon our guard, | or that we 2.01.321
and your ways, whose wraths to guard you from — 3.03. 79
stands at a guard with envy; MM 1.03. 51
he broke from those that had the guard of him, ERR 5.01.149
guard with halberds! 5.01.185
though argus were her eunuch and her guard. LLL 3.01.199
left in the fearful guard | of an unthrifty MV 1.03.175
but she is arm'd for him and keeps her guard AWW 3.05. 73
look you now, he's out of his guard already. TN 1.05. 86 P
ladyship were best to have some guard about you, 3.04. 12 P
life at any price, betake you to your guard; 3.04.231 P
heaven guard my mother's honor, and my land! JN 1.01. 70
pomp, | to guard a title that was rich before, 4.02. 10
guard it, i pray thee, with a lurking adder, R2 3.02. 20
that art a guard too wanton for the head | which 2H4 1.01.148
some guard /these /traitors to the block of 4.02.122
lead him hence, and see you guard him sure. 4.03. 75
lo where it sits, | which god shall guard; 4.05. 44
the crown immortally | long guard it yours! 4.05.144
the heavens thee guard and keep, most royal imp 5.05. 42
god and his angels guard your sacred throne, H5 1.02. 7
my army but a weak and sickly guard; 3.06.155
of it, for there is none to guard it but boys. 4.04. 77 P
i'll be your guard. 1H6 1.02.127
abominable gloucester, guard thy head, | for i 1.03. 87
wherefore a guard of chosen shot i had | that 1.04. 53
let us have knowledge at the court of guard. 2.01. 4
tut, holy joan was his defensive guard. 2.01. 49
sirs, take away the duke, and guard him sure. 2H6 3.01.188
set | to guard the chicken from a hungry kite, 3.01.249
that they will guard you, whe'er you will or no, 3.02.265
and disorder wounds | where it should guard. 5.02. 33
about, | and but attended by a simple guard, 3H6 4.02. 16
at unawares may beat down edward's guard, | and 4.02. 23
wherefore else guard we his royal tent | but to 4.03. 21
this is his tent, and see where stand his guard. 4.03. 23
either betray'd by falsehood of his guard | or 4.04. 8
and, often but attended with weak guard, 4.05. 7
what means this armed guard | that waits upon R3 1.01. 42
god and our /innocence defend and guard us! 3.05. 20
bid my guard watch; 5.03. 76
good angels guard thy battle! 5.03.138
good angels guard thee from the boar's annoy! 5.03.151
let some o' th' guard be ready there. H8 5.02.130
to guard a thing not ours nor worth to us | (had TRO 2.02. 22
though the great bulk achilles be thy guard, 4.04.128
henceforth guard thee well, | for i'll not kill 4.05.253
ajax commands the guard to tend on you. 5.01. 72
my will and all offenses | a guard of patience. 5.02. 54
ajax, your guard, stays to conduct you home. 5.02.184
to your bands, | let us alone to guard corioles. COR 1.02. 27
were it | at home, upon my brother's guard, even 1.10. 25
let a guard | attend us through the city. 3.03.140
you guard like men, 'tis well. 5.02. 2
where is the emperor's guard? TIT 1.01.283
be employ'd | now to guard sure their master. TIM 3.03. 39
let /lucilius and titinius guard our door. JC 4.02. 52
have you had quiet guard? HAM 1.01. 10
let them guard the door. 4.05. 98
nation | he swore had neither motion, guard, nor 4.07.101
my father hath set guard to take my brother, LR 2.01. 16
no place | that guard and most unusual vigilance 2.03. 4
good guard, | until their greater pleasures 5.03. 1
transported with no worse nor better guard | but OTH 1.01.124
please | to get good guard and go along with me. 1.01.179
great jove, othello guard, | and swell his sail 2.01. 77
to–night watches on the court of guard. 2.01.218 P
good michael, look you to the guard to–night. 2.03. 1
in night, and on the court and guard of safety? 2.03.216
come guard the door without; 5.02.241
never anger | made good guard for itself. ANT 4.01. 10
the messenger | came on my guard, and at thy 4.06. 22
hour, | we must return to th' court of guard. 4.09. 2
let us bear him | to th' court of guard; 4.09. 31
the guard, ho! 4.14.104
too late, good diomed. call my guard, i prithee. 4.14.128
the emperor's guard! 4.14.129
the guard, what ho! 4.14.129
monument, | his guard have brought him thither. 4.15. 9
guard her till caesar come. 5.02. 36
for the queen, | i'll take her to my guard. 5.02. 67
to that destruction which i'll guard them from 5.02.132
and the tempters of the night | guard me, CYM 2.02. 10
oppose and she | should from encounter guard. 2.05. 19
his greatness was no guard | to bar heaven's PER 2.04. 14
my cause and honor guard me! TNK 3.06. 92
put thyself | upon thy present guard — 3.06.122
draw not thy sword to guard iniquity, | for it LUC 626
to guard the lawful reasons on thy part: SON 49.12
whoe'er keeps me, let my heart be his guard, 133.11
GUARDAGE 1 FR 0.0001 REL FR 1 V 0 P
run from her guardage to the sooty bosom | of OTH 1.02. 70
GUARDANT 2 FR 0.0002 REL FR 1 V 1 P
but when my angry guardant stood alone, 1H6 4.07. 9
that a jack guardant cannot office me from my COR 5.02. 62 P
GUARDED 13 FR 0.0014 REL FR 12 V 1 P
discourse is sometime guarded with fragments, ADO 1.01.286 P
him a livery | more guarded than his fellows'; MV 2.02.155
grace shall stay behind | so strongly guarded. JN 3.03. 2
led on by bloody youth, guarded with rage, | and 2H4 4.01. 34
guarded with grandsires, babies, and old women, H5 3.pr. 20
sure they found some place | but weakly guarded, 1H6 2.01. 74
see them guarded | and safely brought to dover, 5.01. 48
in a long motley coat guarded with yellow, H8 pr 16
so, let the ports be guarded; COR 1.07. 1
my lord, guarded, to know your pleasure. HAM 4.03. 14
so slackly guarded, and the search so slow, CYM 1.01. 64
advantage of the ground, | the lane is guarded. 5.02. 12
i think the honey guarded with a sting: LUC 493
GUARDIAN 5 FR 0.0005 REL FR 4 V 1 P
just cause, being her uncle and her guardian. ADO 2.03.167 P
that judge hath made me guardian to this boy, JN 2.01.115
now, my sweet guardian! hark, a word with you. TRO 5.02. 7
guardian! why, greek! 5.02. 47
his predecessors | and guardian of their bones. MAC 2.04. 35
GUARDIANS 1 FR 0.0001 REL FR 1 V 0 P
made you my guardians, my depositaries, | but LR 2.04.251
GUARDS 9 FR 0.0010 REL FR 8 V 1 P
body to invest and cover | in prenzie guards! MM 3.01. 96
and the guards are but slightly basted on ADO 1.01.287 P
o, rhymes are guards on wanton cupid's hose: LLL 4.03. 56
must fall, for heaven still guards the right. R2 3.02. 62
that guards the peace and safety of your person? 2H4 5.02. 88
o'er me with your wings, | you heavenly guards! HAM 3.04.104
and quench the guards of th' ever–fixed pole; OTH 2.01. 15
when we are guarded | and both upon our guards, TNK 3.06. 29
shook off my sober guards and civil fears; LC 298
GUD *(also good, goot)*
GUD 6 FR 0.0006 REL FR 0 V 6 P
i say gud day, captain fluellen. H5 3.02. 83 P
it sall be vary gud, gud feith, gud captens bath 3.02.102 P
it sall be vary gud, gud feith, gud captens bath 3.02.102 P
gud feith, gud captens bath, and i sall quit you 3.02.102 P
and i sall quit you with gud leve, as i may pick 3.02.103 P
themselves to slomber, ay'll de gud service, or 3.02.115 P
GUDGEON 1 FR 0.0001 REL FR 1 V 0 P
this melancholy bait | for this fool gudgeon, MV 1.01.102
GUERDON *(also gardon)*
GUERDON 2 FR 0.0002 REL FR 2 V 0 P
death, in guerdon of her wrongs, | gives her ADO 5.03. 5
there's thy guerdon; LLL 3.01.169
GUERDON'D 2 FR 0.0002 REL FR 2 V 0 P
see you well guerdon'd for these good deserts. 2H6 1.04. 46
and am i guerdon'd at the last with shame? 3H6 3.03.191
/GUERRA 1 FR 0.0001 REL FR 0 V 1 P
put it, as they say, to fortuna de la /guerra. LLL 5.02.531 P
GUESS 54 FR 0.0061 REL FR 49 V 5 P
well — i guess the sequel; TGV 2.01.116
i guess not. MM 4.04. 7 P
but i guess, it stood in her chin, by the salt ERR 3.02.127 P
we may guess by this what you are, being a man. ADO 1.01.110 P
thus, | like muscovites or russians, as i guess. LLL 5.02.121
store, | and, by the near guess of my memory, MV 1.03. 54
i partly guess; for i have lov'd ere now. AYL 2.04. 24
no, corin, being old, thou canst not guess, 2.04. 25
but, as i guess | by the stern brow and waspish 4.03. 8
words can witness, or your thoughts can guess. SHR 2.01.336
as 'tis with us that square our guess by shows; AWW 2.01.150
for i can guess that by thy honest aid | thou 5.03.329
what incidency thou dost guess of harm | is WT 1.02.403
(which i do guess | you do not purpose to him) 4.04.468
it is my lord of berkeley, as i guess. R2 2.03. 68
my good lord, | i guess their tenor. 1H4 4.04. 7
king richard might create a perfect guess | that 2H4 3.01. 88
which i could with a ready guess declare, H5 1.01. 96
better far, i guess, | that we do make our 1H6 2.01. 29
that was, | for i am ignorant and cannot guess. 2.05. 60
me their words as near as thou canst guess them. 3H6 4.01. 90
guess thou the rest; 4.04. 28
and, by thy guess, how nigh is clarence now? 5.01. 8
to london, all in post, and, as i guess, | to 5.05. 84
you cannot guess who caus'd your father's death. R3 2.02. 19
but canst thou guess that he doth aim at it? 3.02. 45
no farther than the tower, and, as i guess, 4.01. 8
i know not, mighty sovereign, but by guess. 4.04.465
well, as you guess? 4.04.466
unless for that, my liege, i cannot guess. 4.04.474
you cannot guess wherefore the welshman comes. 4.04.476
of this great sport together, as you guess? H8 1.01. 47
you may guess quickly what. 2.01. 7
now by thy looks | i guess thy message. 5.01.162
we might guess they reliev'd us humanely; COR 1.01. 18 P
as i guess, martius, | their bands i' th' vaward 1.06. 52
guess but /by my entertainment with him if thou 5.02. 63 P
here, | that he thereby may have a likely guess, TIT 2.03.207
canst thou not guess wherefore she plies thee 4.01. 15
my lord, i know not, i, nor can i guess, 4.01. 16
of the stars | give guess how near to day. JC 2.01. 3
humh! i guess at it. MAC 4.03.203
here is the guess of their true strength and LR 5.01. 52
ay, so i thought. how many, as you guess? OTH 1.03. 36
though i perchance am vicious in my guess | (as 3.03.145
guess at her years, i prithee. ANT 3.03. 26
though you can guess what temperance should be, 3.13.121
and to this hour no guess in knowledge | which CYM 1.01. 60
you must guess | i have an office there. TNK 3.01.109
i guess he is a prince too, | and, if it may be, 4.02. 91
grieving themselves to guess at others' smarts, LUC 1238
friend, | i guess one angel in another's hell: PP 2.12
and that, in guess, they measure by thy deeds, SON 69.10
friend, | i guess one angel in another's hell. 144.12
GUESS'D 3 FR 0.0003 REL FR 3 V 0 P
him he knew well, and guess'd that it was she, TGV 5.02. 39
grounds to fail | as often as i guess'd. AWW 3.01. 16
well guess'd, believe me, for that was my 3H6 4.05. 22
GUESSE *(also guests)*
GUESSE 1 FR 0.0001 REL FR 0 V 1 P
look to thy servants, cherish thy guesse. 1H4 3.03.172 P
GUESSES 1 FR 0.0001 REL FR 1 V 0 P
throw your vild guesses in the devil's teeth, OTH 3.04.184
GUESSINGLY 1 FR 0.0001 REL FR 1 V 0 P
i have a letter guessingly set down, | which LR 3.07. 47
/GUEST 1 FR 0.0001 REL FR 1 V 0 P
to be made | /for /such /a /guest /is /meet." HAM 5.01.121
GUEST 38 FR 0.0043 REL FR 34 V 4 P
now, my young guest, methinks you're allycholly; TGV 4.02. 26 P
but first, master guest, and master page, and WIV 2.03. 74 P
and i shall procure–a you de good guest: 2.03. 92 P
ay, to a niggardly host and more sparing guest: ERR 3.01. 27
i would not yield to be your house's guest: LLL 5.02.354
see | lorenzo, who is thy new master's guest, MV 2.03. 6
am bold to show myself a forward guest | within SHR 2.01. 51
to keep you as a prisoner, | not like a guest: WT 1.02. 53
or my guest? 1.02. 55
your guest then, madam. 1.02. 56
to my kingly guest | unclasp'd my practice, quit 3.02.166
is at the nuptial of his son a guest | that best 4.04.395
why i should welcome such a guest as grief, R2 2.02. 7
save bidding farewell to so sweet a guest | as 2.02. 8
when triumph is become an alehouse guest? 5.01. 15
a feast | fits a dull fighter and a keen guest. 1H4 4.02. 80
to–night in harflew will we be your guest; H5 3.03. 57
your lordship is a guest too. H8 1.03. 51
slightly shakes his parting guest by th' hand, TRO 3.03.166
smells well, but i | appear not like a guest. COR 4.05. 6

tell my master what a strange guest he has here. 4.05. 35 P
you are my guest, lavinia, and your friends. TIT 1.01.490
feast, | whereto i have invited many a guest, ROM 1.02. 21
it fits when such a villain is a guest. 1.05. 75
feast | whereat a villain's not a welcome guest. TIM 3.06.103
this guest of summer, | the temple-haunting MAC 1.06. 3
and noble hostess, | we are your guest to-night. 1.06. 25
here's our chief guest. 3.01. 11
clay for to be made | for such a guest is meet." HAM 5.01. 97
it should be better he became her guest; ANT 2.02.221
make yourself my guest | whilst you abide here. 2.02.243
/be /my so us'd a guest as not an hour | in the PER 1.02. 3
but you, my knight and guest, | to whom this 2.03. 9
lest jealousy, that sour unwelcome guest, VEN 449
and reverend welcome to her princely guest, LUC 90
comparing him to that unhappy guest | whose deed 1565
another time mine eye is my heart's guest, | and SON 47. 7
and thither hied, a sad distemper'd guest; 153.12

GUEST-CAVALIER 1 FR 0.0001 REL FR 0 V 1 P
no suit against my knight, my guest-cavalier? WIV 2.01.213 P

GUEST-JUSTICE 1 FR 0.0001 REL FR 0 V 1 P
pardon, guest-justice. WIV 2.03. 57 P

GUESTS *(also guesse)*

/GUESTS 1 FR 0.0001 REL FR 1 V 0 P
/to /know | /what /guests /were /in /her /eyes, LR 4.03. 21

GUESTS 18 FR 0.0020 REL FR 13 V 5 P
i have turn'd away my other guests; WIV 4.03. 11 P
healthful welcome to their shipwrack'd guests, ERR 1.01.114
provide the feast, father, and bid the guests, SHR 2.01.316
your guests are coming: WT 4.04. 48
see, your guests approach, | address yourself to 4.04. 52
must be tittle-tattling before all our guests? 4.04.246 P
look to the guests within. 1H4 2.04. 81 P
on, therefore take heed what guests you receive. 2H4 2.04. 93 P
unbidden guests | are often welcomest when they 1H6 2.02. 55
y' are welcome, my fair guests. H8 1.04. 35
to th' court, and there ye shall be my guests; 4.01.115
madam, the guests are come, supper serv'd up, ROM 1.03.100 P
my soul, | you'll make a mutiny among my guests! 1.05. 80
so many guests invite as here are writ. 4.02. 1
be bright and jovial among your guests to-night. MAC 3.02. 28
good my friends, consider | you are my guests. LR 3.07. 31
you are princes and my guests. PER 2.03. 8
a woeful hostess brooks not merry guests. LUC 1125

GUEST-WISE 1 FR 0.0001 REL FR 1 V 0 P
my heart to her but as guest-wise sojourn'd, MND 3.02.171

GUIANA 1 FR 0.0001 REL FR 0 V 1 P
she is a region in guiana, all gold and bounty. WIV 1.03. 69 P

GUICHARD 1 FR 0.0001 REL FR 1 V 0 P
of france, the brave sir guichard dolphin, H5 4.08. 95

GUIDE 28 FR 0.0031 REL FR 24 V 4 P
some heavenly power guide us | out of this TMP 5.01.105
wilt thou aspire to guide the heavenly car, TGV 3.01.154
heaven guide him to thy husband's cudgel; WIV 4.02. 88 P
and the devil guide his cudgel afterwards! 4.02. 89 P
be, | to guide our measure round about the tree. 5.05. 79
love, the heavens themselves do guide the state; 5.05.232
you, if my instructions may be your guide. MM 4.02.170 P
a guide, a goddess, and a sovereign, | a AWW 1.01.169
do what you will, your wisdom be your guide. 2H4 2.03. 6
my stay, my guide, and lanthorn to my feet; 2H6 2.03. 25
thou to richmond, and good fortune guide thee! R3 4.01. 91
who did guide — | i mean, who set the body and H8 1.01. 45
of their souls | by reason guide his execution. TRO 1.03.210
desires, in all fair measure, fairly guide them! 3.01. 44 P
yet gives he not till judgment guide his bounty, 4.05.102
here comes himself to guide you. 5.01. 69
if souls guide vows, if vows be sanctimonies, 5.02.139
guide, if thou canst, | this after me. TIT 4.01. 69
heaven guide thy pen to print thy sorrows plain, 4.01. 75
come, bitter conduct, come, unsavory guide! ROM 5.03.116
pray entertain them, give them guide to us. TIM 1.01.243
is cover'd, as 'tis now, | guide thou the sword. JC 5.03. 45
he hath a wisdom that doth guide his valor | to MAC 3.01. 52
became his guide, | led him, begg'd for him, LR 5.03.191
and that you'd guide me to your sovereign's PER 2.01.140
and aesculapius guide us! 3.02.110
them, | wishing adonis had his team to guide, VEN 179
"then love and fortune be my gods, my guide! LUC 351

GUIDED 5 FR 0.0005 REL FR 3 V 2 P
(which is baser) guided by her foot (which is LLL 1.02.168 P
we have been guided by thee hitherto, | and of 1H6 3.03. 9
more after our commandment than as guided | by COR 2.03.230
and to the graver | a child that guided dotards. CYM 1.01. 50
every action to be guided by others' experiences 1.04. 45 P

GUIDER 1 FR 0.0001 REL FR 1 V 0 P
our guider, come, to th' roman camp conduct us. COR 1.07. 7

GUIDERIUS 3 FR 0.0003 REL FR 3 V 0 P
who | the king his father call'd guiderius — CYM 3.03. 88
most worthy prince, as yours, is true guiderius; 5.05.358
guiderius had | upon his neck a mole, a sanguine 5.05.363

GUIDES 9 FR 0.0010 REL FR 7 V 2 P
lest the devil that guides him should aid him, i WIV 3.05.147 P
or, by the affection that now guides me most, MM 2.04.168
all's brave that youth mounts and folly guides. AYL 3.04. 46 P
discomfort guides my tongue | and bids me speak R2 3.02. 65
my blood begins my safer guides to rule, | and OTH 2.03.205
when my good stars, that were my former guides, ANT 3.13.145
his body, | and guides his arm to brave things. TNK 4.02.102
that guides this hand to give this wound to me." LUC 1722
till whatsoever star that guides my moving SON 26. 9

GUIDING 3 FR 0.0003 REL FR 3 V 0 P
ever whilst i live, | into your guiding power. AWW 2.03.104
jove send her | a better guiding spirit! WT 2.03.127
which is that god in office, guiding men? TRO 1.03.231

/GUIDON 1 FR 0.0001 REL FR 1 V 0 P
i stay but for my /guidon; H5 4.02. 60

GUIENNE 1 FR 0.0001 REL FR 1 V 0 P
guienne, champaigne, rheims, orleance, | paris, 1H6 1.01. 60

GUILDENSTERN 9 FR 0.0010 REL FR 6 V 3 P
welcome, dear rosencrantz and guildenstern! HAM 2.02. 1
thanks, rosencrantz and gentle guildenstern. 2.02. 33
thanks, guildenstern and gentle rosencrantz. 2.02. 34
how dost thou, guildenstern? 2.02.225 P
hark you, guildenstern, and you too — at each 2.02.381 P
ho, guildenstern! 4.01. 32
rosencrantz and guildenstern hold their course 4.06. 28 P
so guildenstern and rosencrantz go to't. 5.02. 56
that rosencrantz and guildenstern are dead. 5.02.371

GUILDERS 2 FR 0.0002 REL FR 2 V 0 P
who, wanting guilders to redeem their lives, ERR 1.01. 8
to persia, and want guilders for my voyage: 4.01. 4

GUILDFORD *(see guilford, etc.)*

GUILDHALL 2 FR 0.0002 REL FR 2 V 0 P
the mayor towards guildhall hies him in all post R3 3.05. 73
look for the news that the guildhall affords. 3.05.102

GUILE 4 FR 0.0004 REL FR 4 V 0 P
should be found such false dissembling guile? 1H6 4.01. 63
treacherous, and full of guile | be he unto me! R3 2.01. 38
poor clarence, by thy guile betray'd to death! 5.03.133
cannot be," quoth she, "that so much guile" — LUC 1534

GUILED 1 FR 0.0001 REL FR 1 V 0 P
thus ornament is but the guiled shore | to a MV 3.02. 97

GUILEFUL 2 FR 0.0002 REL FR 2 V 0 P
by guileful fair words peace may be obtain'd. 1H6 1.01. 77
i train'd thy brethren to that guileful hole, TIT 5.01.104

GUILES 1 FR 0.0001 REL FR 1 V 0 P
the wiles and guiles that women work, PP 18.37

GUILFORD 2 FR 0.0002 REL FR 2 V 0 P
to, with sir henry guilford | this night to be H8 1.03. 66
you are young, sir harry guilford. 1.04. 9

GUILFORDS 1 FR 0.0001 REL FR 1 V 0 P
in kent, my liege, the guilfords are in arms, R3 4.04.503

GUILT 33 FR 0.0037 REL FR 32 V 1 P
thy conscience | is so possess'd with guilt. TMP 1.02.472
their great guilt | (like poison given to work a 3.03.104
my shame and guilt confounds me. TGV 5.04. 73
a murd'rous guilt shows not itself more soon TN 3.01.147
course, | even to the guilt or the purgation. WT 3.02. 7
hear, | although apparent guilt be seen in them, R2 4.01.124
my guilt be on my head, and there an end. 5.01. 69
the guilt of conscience take thou for thy labor, 5.06. 41
england shall double gild his treble guilt, 2H4 4.05.128
have for the gilt of france (o guilt indeed!) H5 2.pr. 26
have on them the guilt of premeditated and 4.01.162 P
in sight of god and us, your guilt is great; 2H6 2.03. 2
for by his death we do perceive his guilt, | and 2.03.101
me, | nor store of treasons to augment my guilt. 3.01.169
his guilt should be but idly posted over, 3.01.255
but that the guilt of murther bucklers thee, 3.02.216
that laid their guilt upon my guiltless R3 1.02. 98
that, his apparent open guilt omitted — | i 3.05. 30
let them not speak a word, the guilt is plain, TIT 2.03.301
the old man hath found their guilt, | and sends 4.02. 26
shall she live to betray this guilt of ours, | a 4.02.149
who shall bear the guilt | of our great quell? MAC 1.07. 71
grooms withal, | for it must seem their guilt. 2.02. 54
if his occulted guilt | do not itself unkennel HAM 3.02. 80
my stronger guilt defeats my strong intent, 3.03. 40
amiss, | so full of artless jealousy is guilt, 4.05. 19
the heaviness and guilt within my bosom | takes CYM 5.02. 1
the guilt being great, the fear doth still LUC 229
this guilt would seem death-worthy in thy 635
for they their guilt with weeping will unfold, 754
"o opportunity, thy guilt is great! 876
but they whose guilt within their bosoms lie 1342
lest my bewailed guilt should do thee shame, SON 36.10

GUILTIAN 1 FR 0.0001 REL FR 0 V 1 P
guiltian, cosmo, lodowick, and gratii, two AWW 4.03.163 P

GUILTIER 2 FR 0.0002 REL FR 2 V 0 P
a thief or two | guiltier than him they try. MM 2.01. 21
lord, | i should be guiltier than my guiltiness, 5.01.367

GUILTILY 1 FR 0.0001 REL FR 1 V 0 P
bloody and guilty, guiltily awake, | and in a R3 5.03.154

GUILTINESS 9 FR 0.0010 REL FR 8 V 1 P
not fairies, and yet the guiltiness of my mind, WIV 5.05.123 P
confess | a natural guiltiness such as is his, MM 2.02.139
lord, | i should be guiltier than my guiltiness, 5.01.367
her blush is guiltiness, not modesty. ADO 4.01. 42
full of dear guiltiness, and therefore this: LLL 5.02.791
and die in terror of thy guiltiness! R3 5.03.170
they vanish tongue-tied in their guiltiness. JC 1.01. 62
nay, guiltiness will speak, | though tongues OTH 5.01.109
fear i know not, | since guiltiness i know not; 5.02. 39

GUILTLESS 25 FR 0.0028 REL FR 24 V 1 P
as fast lock'd up in sleep as guiltless labor MM 4.02. 66
if this sweet lady lie not guiltless here ADO 4.01.169
pardon me, | i am but as a guiltless messenger. AYL 4.03. 12
to be generous, guiltless, and of free TN 1.05. 92 P
whose guiltless drops | are every one a woe, a H5 1.02. 25
stain'd with the guiltless blood of innocents, 1H6 5.04. 44
and all to make away my guiltless life. 2H6 3.01.167
by shameful murther of a guiltless king | and 4.01. 95
hands are free from guiltless blood-shedding, 4.07.102
laid their guilt upon my guiltless shoulders. R3 1.02. 98
o, spare my guiltless wife and my poor children! 1.04. 72
because i will be guiltless from the meaning. 1.04. 94
we give to thee our guiltless blood to drink. 3.03. 14
for then my guiltless blood must cry against 'em H8 2.01. 68
if the duke be guiltless, | 'tis full of woe; 2.01.139
that i am guiltless of your father's death, HAM 4.05.150
i am guiltless as i am ignorant | of what hath LR 1.04.273
traitors ensteep'd to enclog the guiltless keel, OTH 2.01. 70
dames even thus, | all guiltless, meet reproach. 4.01. 47
a guiltless death i die. 5.02.122
a mistress, expectation | most guiltless on't. TNK 3.01. 15
his success, but i | am guiltless of election. 5.01.154
so guiltless she securely gives good cheer | and LUC 89
to burn the guiltless casket where it lay! 1057
let guiltless souls be freed from guilty woe: 1482

GUILTS 1 FR 0.0001 REL FR 1 V 0 P
close pent-up guilts, | rive your concealing LR 3.02. 57

GUILTY 85 FR 0.0096 REL FR 76 V 9 P
with whispering and most guilty diligence, | in MM 4.01. 38
but, lest myself be guilty to self-wrong, | i'll ERR 3.02.163
whilst upon me the guilty doors were shut, | and 4.04. 63
the world was very guilty of such a ballet some LLL 1.02.111 P
glory grows guilty of detested crimes, | when, 4.01. 31
i heard your guilty rhymes, observ'd your 4.03.137
guilty, my lord, guilty! 4.03.201
guilty, my lord, guilty! 4.03.201
of breath — your gentleness | was guilty of it. 5.02.736
i am not guilty of lysander's blood; MND 3.02. 75
again, | no bed shall e'er be guilty of my stay, MV 3.02.326
i confess me much guilty to deny so fair and AYL 1.02.184 P
truth that e'er thine own tongue was guilty of. AWW 4.01. 33 P
because he's guilty, and he is not guilty. 5.03.289
because he's guilty, and he is not guilty. 5.03.289
have answer'd heaven | boldly, "not guilty"; WT 1.02. 74
he who shall speak for her is afar off guilty 2.01.104
party to | the anger of the king, nor guilty of 2.02. 60
liege, | he is not guilty of her coming hither. 2.03.145
it shall scarce boot me | to say "not guilty." 3.02. 26
but as th' unthought-on accident is guilty | to 4.04.538
be guilty of the stealing that sweet breath JN 4.03.136
if guilty dread have left thee so much strength R2 1.01. 73
along | the clogging burthen of a guilty soul. 1.03.200
his hands were guilty of no kinred blood, | but 2.01.182
and darts his light through every guilty hole, 3.02. 43
world, | aumerle is guilty of my true appeal; 4.01. 79
to wash this blood off from my guilty hand. 5.06. 50
or misprision | is guilty of this fault, and not 1H4 1.03. 28
i'll be no longer guilty of this sin. 2.04.241 P
or, guilty in defense, be thus destroy'd? H5 3.03. 43
no more is the king guilty of their damnation 4.01.174 P
than he was before guilty of those impieties for 4.01.175 P
his trespass yet lives guilty in thy blood, 1H6 2.04. 94
and shall my youth be guilty of such blame? 4.05. 47
wherein am i guilty? 2H6 3.01.103
to-day, | if he be guilty, as 'tis published. 3.02. 17
as guilty of duke humphrey's timeless death. 3.02.187
unless i find him guilty, he shall not die. 4.02. 96 P
my mild entreaty shall not make you guilty. 3H6 3.01. 91
for somerset, off with his guilty head. 5.05. 3
suspicion always haunts the guilty mind; 5.06. 11
not | how that the guilty kindred of the queen R3 2.01.136
this land | would i be guilty of so deep a sin. 3.01. 43
within the guilty closure of thy walls | richard 3.03. 11
that ever yet this land was guilty of. 4.03. 3
men, | to fight against this guilty homicide. 5.02. 18
and with guilty fear | let fall thy lance. 5.03.142
bloody and guilty, guiltily awake, | and in a 5.03.154
throng to the bar, crying all, "guilty! 5.03.199
guilty!" 5.03.199
is he found guilty? H8 2.01. 7
his accusations | he pleaded still not guilty, 2.01. 13
have found him guilty of high treason. 2.01. 27
i dare not make myself so guilty | to give up 3.01.139
if you can blush, and cry "guilty," cardinal, 3.02.305
and find out /murderers in their guilty /caves; TIT 5.02. 52
the basin that receives your guilty blood. 5.02.183
like damned guilty deeds to sinners' minds: ROM 3.02.111
hour | is guilty of this lamentable chance! 5.03.146
nobly bears, | is guilty of a several bastardy, JC 2.01.138
and then it started like a guilty thing | upon a HAM 1.01.148
as in their birth, wherein they are not guilty 1.04. 25
crimes | the youth you breathe of guilty, be 2.01. 44
make mad the guilty, and appall the free, 2.02.564
heard | that guilty creatures sitting at a play 2.02.589
he that is not guilty of his own death shortens 5.01. 19 P
we make guilty of our disasters the sun, the LR 1.02.120 P
dares any | so noble bear a guilty business? TNK 3.01. 90
many a murther | set off whereto she's guilty. 5.03. 28
this said, his guilty hand pluck'd up the latch, LUC 358
decays, | the guilty rebel for remission prays. 714
behind, | and he the burthen of a guilty mind. 735
he faintly flies, sweating with guilty fear; 740
since thou art guilty of my cureless crime, 772
"yet am i guilty of thy honor's wrack, | yet for 841
"guilty thou art of murther and of theft, 918
of theft, | guilty of perjury and subornation, 919
guilty of treason, forgery, and shift, | guilty 920
and shift, | guilty of incest, that abomination; 921
be guilty of my death, since of my crime. 931
let guiltless souls be freed from guilty woe: 1482
so | that blushing red no guilty instance gave, 1511
chide, | the guilty goddess of my harmful deeds, SON 111. 2
lest guilty of my faults thy sweet self prove: 151. 4

GUILTY-LIKE 1 FR 0.0001 REL FR 1 V 0 P
it, | that he would steal away so guilty-like, OTH 3.03. 39

GUINEA 1 FR 0.0001 REL FR 0 V 1 P
would drown myself for the love of a guinea hen, OTH 1.03.315 P

GUINOVER 1 FR 0.0001 REL FR 0 V 1 P
was a woman when queen guinover of britain was a LLL 4.01.123 P

GUISE 5 FR 0.0005 REL FR 4 V 1 P
my lord of suffolk, say, is this the guise, | is 2H6 1.03. 42
how rarely does it meet with this time's guise, TIM 4.03.465
this is her very guise, and, upon my life, fast MAC 5.01. 19 P
to shame the guise o' th' world, i will begin CYM 5.01. 32
quoth she, "this was thy father's guise — VEN 1177

GULES 3 FR 0.0003 REL FR 3 V 0 P
with man's blood paint the ground, gules, gules. TIM 4.03. 60
with man's blood paint the ground, gules, gules. 4.03. 60
head to foot | now is he total gules, horridly HAM 2.02.457

GULF 10 FR 0.0011 REL FR 10 V 0 P
fall | a drop of water in the breaking gulf, ERR 2.02.126
as fierce | as waters to the sucking of a gulf. H5 2.04. 10
for certainly thou art so near the gulf, | thou 4.03. 82
whose envious gulf did swallow up his life. 3H6 5.06. 25
and almost should'red in the swallowing gulf R3 3.07.128
that only like a gulf it did remain | i' th' COR 1.01. 98
follow thine enemy in a fiery gulf | than 3.02. 91
maw and gulf | of the ravin'd salt-sea shark, MAC 4.01. 23
but, like a gulf, doth draw | what's near it HAM 3.03. 16
a swallowing gulf that even in plenty wanteth. LUC 557

GULFS 1 FR 0.0001 REL FR 1 V 0 P
wash me in steep-down gulfs of liquid fire! OTH 5.02.280

GULL* 9 FR 0.0010 REL FR 4 V 5 P
i should think this a gull, but that the ADO 2.03.118 P
if i do not gull him into an ayword, and make TN 2.03.134 P
yond gull malvolio is turn'd heathen, a very 3.02. 69 P
coxcomb and a knave, a thin-fac'd knave, a gull! 5.01.207 P
and made the most notorious geck and gull | that 5.01.343
by us you us'd us so | as that ungentle gull, 1H4 5.01. 60
why, 'tis a gull, a fool, a rogue, that now and H5 3.06. 67 P
wing, | lord timon will be left a naked gull, TIM 2.01. 31
o gull, o dolt, | as ignorant as dirt! OTH 5.02.163

GULL-CATCHER 1 FR 0.0001 REL FR 0 V 1 P
here comes my noble gull-catcher. TN 2.05.187 P

GULL'D 1 FR 0.0001 REL FR 1 V 0 P
if that same demon that hath gull'd thee thus H5 2.02.121

GULLS 2 FR 0.0002 REL FR 2 V 0 P
darkness, | i do beweep to many simple gulls — R3 1.03.327

which nightly gulls him with intelligence, | as SON 86.10
/GUM 1 FR 0.0001 REL FR 1 V 0 P
our poesy is as a /gum, which /oozes | from TIM 1.01. 21
GUM 3 FR 0.0003 REL FR 2 V 1 P
the gum down-roping from their pale-dead eyes, H5 4.02. 48
eyes purging thick amber and plum-tree gum, and HAM 2.02.199 P
as the arabian trees | their medicinable gum. OTH 5.02.351
GUMM'D 1 FR 0.0001 REL FR 0 V 1 P
horse, and he frets like a gumm'd velvet. 1H4 2.02. 2 P
GUMS* 2 FR 0.0002 REL FR 2 V 0 P
have pluck'd my nipple from his boneless gums, MAC 1.07. 57
balms, and gums, and heavy cheers, | sacred TNK 1.05. 4
GUN 5 FR 0.0005 REL FR 5 V 0 P
sword, pike, knife, gun, or need of any engine, TMP 2.01.162
is that lead slow which is fir'd from a gun? LLL 3.01. 62
or like an overcharged gun, recoil, | and turns 2H6 3.02.331
name, | shot from the deadly level of a gun, ROM 3.03.103
staineth, | or like the deadly bullet of a gun, VEN 461
GUNDELLO *(also gondilo)*
GUNDELLO 1 FR 0.0001 REL FR 0 V 1 P
i will scarce think you have swam in a gundello. AYL 4.01. 38 P
GUNDOLIER 1 FR 0.0001 REL FR 1 V 0 P
but with a knave of common hire, a gundolier, OTH 1.01.125
GUNNER 3 FR 0.0003 REL FR 3 V 0 P
the boatswain, and i, | the gunner and his mate, TMP 2.02. 47
and the nimble gunner | with linstock now the H5 3.pr. 32
chief master gunner am i of this town, 1H6 1.04. 6
GUNPOWDER 3 FR 0.0003 REL FR 2 V 1 P
i am afraid of this gunpowder percy though he be 1H4 5.04.121 P
work as strong | as aconitum or rash gunpowder. 2H4 4.04. 48
and, touch'd with choler, hot as gunpowder, H5 4.07.180
GUN'S 1 FR 0.0001 REL FR 1 V 0 P
sort, | rising and cawing at the gun's report, MND 3.02. 22
GUNS 2 FR 0.0002 REL FR 2 V 0 P
talk so like a waiting-gentlewoman | of guns, 1H4 1.03. 56
and but for these vile guns | he would himself 1.03. 63
GUN-STONES 1 FR 0.0001 REL FR 1 V 0 P
of his | hath turn'd his balls to gun-stones, H5 1.02.282
GURMANDIZE *(also gormandizing)*
GURMANDIZE 1 FR 0.0001 REL FR 1 V 0 P
thou shalt not gurmandize, | as thou hast done MV 2.05. 3
GURNET 1 FR 0.0001 REL FR 0 V 1 P
asham'd of my soldiers, i am a sous'd gurnet. 1H4 4.02. 12 P
GURNEY 1 FR 0.0001 REL FR 1 V 0 P
james gurney, wilt thou give us leave a while? JN 1.01.230
GUSH 1 FR 0.0001 REL FR 1 V 0 P
shall gush pure streams to purge my impure tale. LUC 1078
GUST* 7 FR 0.0008 REL FR 6 V 1 P
gift of a coward to allay the gust he hath in TN 1.03. 31 P
'tis far gone, | when i shall gust it last. WT 1.02.219
as doth a sail, fill'd with a fretting gust, 3H6 2.06. 35
blows, | commanded always by the greater gust, 3.01. 88
to kill, i grant, is sin's extremest gust, | but TIM 3.05. 54
earth's dark womb some gentle gust doth get, LUC 549
eye well knows what with his gust is 'greeing, SON 114.11
GUSTS 8 FR 0.0009 REL FR 8 V 0 P
when they are fretten with the gusts of heaven; MV 4.01. 77
yet extreme gusts will blow out fire and all; SHR 2.01.135
heart, | and like as rigor of tempestuous gusts 1H6 5.05. 5
what did i then, but curs'd the gentle gusts, 2H6 3.02. 88
by interims and conveying gusts we have heard COR 1.06. 5
scatter'd by winds and high tempestuous gusts, TIT 5.03. 69
gusts and foul flaws to herdmen and to herds. VEN 456
against the stormy gusts of winter's day | and SON 13.11
GUSTY 1 FR 0.0001 REL FR 1 V 0 P
for once, upon a raw and gusty day, | the JC 1.02.100
GUTS 12 FR 0.0013 REL FR 2 V 10 P
let vultures gripe thy guts! WIV 1.03. 85
as sure as his guts are made of puddings. 2.01. 31 P
strange that sheep's guts should hale souls out ADO 2.03. 59 P
why, thou clay-brain'd guts, thou knotty-pated 1H4 2.04.227 P
falstaff, you carried your guts away as nimbly, 2.04.258 P
that stuff'd cloak-bag of guts, that roasted 2.04.452 P
should, how would thy guts fall about thy knees! 3.03.152 P
it is all fill'd up with guts and midriff. 3.03.155 P
i would prick your guts a little in good terms, H5 2.01. 58 P
his wit in his belly and his guts in his head, TRO 2.01. 73 P
i'll lug the guts into the neighbor room. HAM 3.04.212
may go a progress through the guts of a beggar. 4.03. 31 P
GUTS-GRIPING 1 FR 0.0001 REL FR 0 V 1 P
rotten diseases of the south, the guts-griping, TRO 5.01. 18 P
GUTTER'D 1 FR 0.0001 REL FR 1 V 0 P
the gutter'd rocks and congregated sands, OTH 2.01. 69
GUY 1 FR 0.0001 REL FR 1 V 0 P
i am not sampson, nor sir guy, nor colbrand, H8 5.03. 22
GUYNES 1 FR 0.0001 REL FR 1 V 0 P
'twixt guynes and arde — | i was then present, H8 1.01. 7
GUYSORS 1 FR 0.0001 REL FR 1 V 0 P
paris, guysors, poictiers, are all quite lost. 1H6 1.01. 61
GYVE 1 FR 0.0001 REL FR 0 V 1 P
i will gyve thee in thine own courtship. OTH 2.01.170 P
GYVES 8 FR 0.0009 REL FR 6 V 2 P
assist him, it shall redeem you from your gyves; MM 4.02. 11 P
wide betwixt the legs, as if they had gyves on, 1H4 4.02. 41 P
like a poor prisoner in his twisted gyves, | and ROM 2.02.179
convert his gyves to graces, so that my arrows, HAM 4.07. 21
i repent, | i cannot do it better than in gyves, CYM 5.04. 14
quit me of these cold gyves, give me a sword, TNK 3.01. 72
run, the jingling of his gyves | might call fell 3.02. 14
playing patient sports in unconstrained gyves? LC 242
H 2 FR 0.0002 REL FR 1 V 1 P
for the letter that begins them all, h. ADO 3.04. 56 P
that was like a t, | but now 'tis made an h. ANT 4.07. 8
HA' *(also 'a', ave, have)*
HA' 25 FR 0.0028 REL FR 11 V 14 P
i ha' told them over and over, they lack no WIV 3.03. 18 P
i would not ha' your distemper in this kind for 3.03.216 P
i ha' married oon garsoon, a boy; 5.05.205 P
ha' ta'en a couple of as arrant knaves as any in ADO 3.05. 31 P
therefore ha' done with words; SHR 3.02.116
spoke like an officer. ha' to thee, lad! 5.02. 37
ha' not you seen, camillo | (but that's past WT 1.02.267
i'll ha' thee burnt. 2.03.114
you ha' done me a charitable office. 4.03. 76 P
ran from the battle ha' done this slaughter. H5 4.07. 6 P
come then, away, let's ha' no more ado. 3H6 4.05. 27
by this light, i'll ha' more. H8 5.01.171
then we shall ha' means to vent | our musty COR 1.01.225
with apemantus, let's ha' some sport with 'em. TIM 2.02. 47 P
many a time and often i ha' din'd with him, and 3.01. 23 P
i ha' told him on't, but i could ne'er get him 3.01. 28 P
time, when i might ha' shown myself honorable! 3.02. 45 P
besides — i ha' not since put up my sword — JC 1.03. 19
will you ha' the truth an't? HAM 5.01. 23 P
and chud ha' bin zwagger'd out of my life, LR 4.06.238 P
life, 'twould not ha' bin zo long as 'tis by a 4.06.239 P
much, but i ha' prais'd ye | when you have well ANT 2.06. 76
yet ha' we | a brain that nourishes our nerves, 4.08. 20
wood-leaves and weeds i ha' strew'd his grave, CYM 4.02.390
ha' you done? PER 4.06. 62 P
HA *(also hah)*
/HA 1 FR 0.0001 REL FR 1 V 0 P
/ha, /let's /see. R2 4.01.294
HA 188 FR 0.0212 REL FR 100 V 88 P
ha, ha, ha! TMP 2.01. 36 P
ha, ha, ha! 2.01. 36 P
ha, ha, ha! 2.01. 36 P
ha? 2.02. 59 P
ha, ha, ha! 3.02. 82 P
ha, ha, ha! 3.02. 82 P
ha, ha, ha! 3.02. 82 P
ha, ha! 5.01.263
ha, ha! 5.01.263
ha? TGV 2.01. 3
ha! WIV 1.01. 40 P
ha, thou mountain-foreigner! 1.01.161
ha, ha! 2.01. 8 P
ha, ha! 2.01. 8 P
ah, ha! 2.02.152 P
ha, bully? 2.03. 28 P
ha? 2.03. 29 P
ha, do i perceive dat? 3.01.115 P
have you make-a de sot of us, ha, ha? 3.01.116 P
have you make-a de sot of us, ha, ha? 3.01.116 P
ha? 3.05.139 P
ha? 4.05. 15 P
am i a woodman, ha? 5.05. 27 P
the tempter, or the tempted, who sins most, ha? MM 2.02.163
ha? 2.04. 42
ha? 2.04.149
ha? 3.02. 47 P
ha? 3.02. 49 P
ha? 3.02. 55 P
does bridget paint still, pompey? ha? 3.02. 79 P
ha, no, no, faith, thou sing'st well enough for ADO 2.03. 77 P
ha! 2.03.257 P
ha, ah ha! 3.03. 84 P
ha, ah ha! 3.03. 84 P
why then, some be of laughing, as, ah, ha, he! 4.01. 22 P
ha! not for the wide world. 4.01.290 P
ha, ha? what sayest thou? LLL 3.01. 53 P
ha, ha? what sayest thou? 3.01. 53 P
what says that fool of hagar's offspring, ha? MV 2.05. 44
ha! 2.09. 23
ha, what sayest thou? 3.01. 16 P
ha, ha! 3.01.107 P
ha, ha! 3.01.107 P
sola, sola! wo ha, ho! sola, sola! 5.01. 39 P
ha! SHR 1.01.104
ha! 1.02.140 P
ha, higher! TN 1.03.141 P
ha, ha, excellent! 1.03.141 P
ha, ha, excellent! 1.03.141 P
ha? 3.04. 42 P
ah ha, does she so? 3.04. 94 P
"she loves another" — who calls, ha? 4.02. 79 P
in his rage and his wrath, | cries, ah, ha! 4.02.128
ha? WT 1.02.230
and straight | the shrug, the hum or ha (these 2.01. 71
ha, ha, what a fool honesty is! 4.04.595 P
ha, ha, what a fool honesty is! 4.04.595 P
ha, majesty! JN 2.01.350
ha? 4.03.120
ha, ha, keep time! R2 5.05. 42
ha, ha, keep time! 5.05. 42
ha, cousin, is it not? 1H4 1.01. 75
and of york, | to join with mortimer, ha? 1.03.281
ha, you shall see now in very sincerity of fear 2.03. 29 P
ha? 2H4 1.01. 48
ha? 2.04.283 P
ha, ha, ha! 3.02.107 P
ha, ha, ha! 3.02.107 P
ha, ha, ha! 3.02.107 P
ha, ha, ha! 3.02.146 P
ha, ha, ha! 3.02.146 P
ha, ha, ha! 3.02.146 P
ha, 'twas a merry night. 3.02.198 P
ha, cousin silence, that thou hadst seen that 3.02.211 P
ha, sir john, said i well? 3.02.212 P
you'll crack a quart together, ha, will you not, 5.03. 63 P
ca, ha! H5 3.07. 13 P
montez /a cheval! my horse, varlot lackey! ha! 4.02. 2
and dout them with superfluous courage, ha! 4.02. 11
ha, art thou bedlam? 5.01. 19
ha, ha, ha! 1H6 2.03. 43
ha, ha, ha! 2.03. 43
ha, ha, ha! 2.03. 43
ha? 3H6 4.01.112
ha! R3 1.03.233
ah ha, my lord, this prince is not an edward! 3.07. 71
ha? am i king? 'tis so — but edward lives. 4.02. 14
norfolk, we must have knocks. ha, must we not? 5.03. 5
ha? H8 1.01.115
ha? 1.02.186
ah ha, | there's mischief in this man. 1.02.186
who's there? ha? 2.02. 63
ha? 2.02. 66
ha? 2.02. 72
i do assure you | the king cried "ha!" 3.02. 61
now god incense him, | and let him cry "ha!" 3.02. 62
ha? 5.01. 66
ha? canterbury? 5.01. 81
ha? 5.01. 86
ha? 5.02. 25
why, this will do helen's heart good now, ha? TRO 1.02.216 P
to ha, ha, he! 3.01.123
to ha, ha, he! 3.01.123
a while, but ha, ha, ha! 3.01.125
a while, but ha, ha, ha! 3.01.125
a while, but ha, ha, ha! 3.01.125
groans out for ha, ha, ha! 3.01.126
groans out for ha, ha, ha! 3.01.126
groans out for ha, ha, ha! 3.01.126
ha? 3.03. 67
ha? known? 3.03.194
ha? 3.03.283 P
ha? 3.03.291 P
ha, ha! 4.02. 31 P
ha, ha! 4.02. 31 P
ha, ha! 4.02. 38
ha, ha! 4.02. 38
ha! 4.05.208
ha, art thou there? 5.06. 8
now do i see thee, ha! have at thee, hector! 5.06. 13
ha? martius coming home? COR 2.01.102 P
ha? 5.03. 19
ha? 5.06.100
ha, ha, ha! TIT 3.01.264
ha, ha, ha! 3.01.264
ha, ha, ha! 3.01.264
ha, ha! 4.03. 68
ha, ha! 4.03. 68
ha, banishment? ROM 3.03. 12
ha, ha! 3.04. 19
ha, ha! 3.04. 19
mass, and well said, a merry whoreson, ha! 4.04. 20
ha? TIM 3.01. 49 P
ha? 3.02. 31 P
ha! 3.04. 41
ha, you gods! 4.03. 31
ha? 4.03. 45
ha? who calls? JC 1.02. 13
ha, ha! how vildly doth this cynic rhyme! 4.03.133
ha, ha! how vildly doth this cynic rhyme! 4.03.133
ha? portia? 4.03.148
ha! 4.03.275
ha, good father, | thou seest the heavens, as MAC 2.04. 4
ha, ha, boy, say'st thou so? HAM 1.05.150
ha, ha, boy, say'st thou so? 1.05.150
ha, ha! are you honest? 3.01.102 P
ha, ha! are you honest? 3.01.102 P
ah, ha! 3.02.291 P
ha, have you eyes? 3.04. 67
and must th' inheritor himself have no more, ha? 5.01.112 P
ha? say'st thou so? LR 1.04. 63 P
weakens, his discernings | are lethargied — ha! 1.04.229
ha? 1.04.305
ha, ha, ha! 1.05. 13 P
ha, ha, ha! 1.05. 13 P
ha, ha, ha! 1.05. 13 P
ha? | mak'st thou this shame thy pastime? 2.04. 5
hah, ha, he wears cruel garters. 2.04. 7 P
ha? 3.04.105 P
ha! 4.06. 96 P
ha! 5.03.272
ha? OTH 3.03.165
ha, ha, false to me? 3.03.333
ha, ha, false to me? 3.03.333
ha? wherefore? 3.04. 78
ha, ha, ha! 4.01.117 P
ha, ha, ha! 4.01.117 P
ha, ha, ha! 4.01.117 P
ha, ha, ha! 4.01.121 P
ha, ha, ha! 4.01.121 P
ha, ha, ha! 4.01.121 P
ha, ha, ha! 4.01.140 P
ha, ha, ha! 4.01.140 P
ha, ha, ha! 4.01.140 P
ha, ha! | give me to drink mandragora. ANT 1.05. 3
ha, ha! | give me to drink mandragora. 1.05. 3
them every one an antony, | and say, "ah, ha! 2.05. 15
ha, my brave emperor! 2.07.103
ha? 3.13.105
ha? CYM 2.01. 11 P
ha, come and bring away the nets! PER 2.01. 13 P
ha, bots on't, 'tis come at last, and 'tis 2.01.118 P
"ha!" 4.01. 61
hum, ha! 5.01. 83
ha! TNK 2.02.134
and /ye know what wenches, ha? 2.03. 39
ha, boys, heigh for the weavers! 2.03. 49
ah ha, my friend, my friend! 5.04. 23
HABERDASHER'S 1 FR 0.0001 REL FR 0 V 1 P
there was a haberdasher's wife of small wit near H8 5.03. 47 P
HABERDEPOIS 1 FR 0.0001 REL FR 0 V 1 P
hair will turn scales between their haberdepois. 2H4 2.04.254 P
HABILIMENT 1 FR 0.0001 REL FR 1 V 0 P
thus, in this strange and sad habiliment, | i TIT 5.02. 1
HABILIMENTS *(also abiliments)*
HABILIMENTS 3 FR 0.0003 REL FR 3 V 0 P
my riches are these poor habiliments, | of which TGV 4.01. 13
even in these honest mean habiliments, SHR 4.03.170
hither | thus plated in habiliments of war, R2 1.03. 28
HABIT 35 FR 0.0039 REL FR 28 V 7 P
but in what habit will you go along? TGV 2.07. 39
how use doth breed a habit in a man! 5.04. 1
o proteus, let this habit make thee blush! 5.04.104
and in that habit, when slender sees his time WIV 4.06. 36
therefore i prithee | supply me with the habit, MM 1.03. 46
how often dost thou with thy case, thy habit, 2.04. 13
my mind promises with my habit, no loss shall 3.01.178 P
not changing heart with habit, i am still 5.01.384
here she comes in the habit of a light wench; ERR 4.03. 52 P
shall come apparell'd in more precious habit, ADO 4.01.227
confronted were with four | in russian habit; LLL 5.02.368
dance, | nor never more in russian habit wait. 5.02.401
a better bad habit of frowning than the count MV 1.02. 59 P
if i do not put on a sober habit, | talk with 2.02.190
but in such a habit | that they shall think we 3.04. 60
and under that habit play the knave with him. AYL 3.02.296 P
fie, doff this habit, shame to your estate, | an SHR 3.02.100
clouds, | so honor peereth in the meanest habit. 4.03.174
seem a sober ancient gentleman by your habit; 5.01. 74 P

a slow tongue, in the habit of some sir of note, TN 3.04. 73 P
one face, one voice, one habit, and two persons, 5.01.216
and not alone in habit and device, | exterior JN 1.01.210
you know me by my habit. H5 3.06.114
matron, | it is her habit only that is honest, TIM 4.03.114
this slave-like habit? 4.03.205
if thou didst put this sour cold habit on | to 4.03.239
costly thy habit as thy purse can buy, | but not HAM 1.03. 70
or by some habit, that too much o'er-leavens 1.04. 29
my father, in his habit as he lived! 3.04.135
of the time and, out of an habit of encounter, a 5.02.190 P
and in this habit | met i my father with his LR 5.03.189
there was a fourth man, in a silly habit, | that CYM 5.03. 86
us scan | the outward habit by the inward man. PER 2.02. 57
but now he throws that shallow habit by, LUC 1814
o, love's best habit is in seeming trust, | and SON 138.11

/HABITATION 1 FR 0.0001 REL FR 1 V 0 P
/an /habitation /giddy /and /unsure | /hath /he 2H4 1.03. 89

HABITATION 4 FR 0.0004 REL FR 3 V 1 P
that dost this habitation where thou keep'st MM 3.01. 10
to aery nothing | a local habitation and a name. MND 5.01. 17
to eat of the habitation which your prophet the MV 1.03. 33 P
got | which for their habitation chose out thee, SON 95.10

HABITED 2 FR 0.0002 REL FR 2 V 0 P
she shall be habited as it becomes | the partner WT 4.04.546
or is it dian habited like her, | who hath TIT 2.03. 57

HABIT'S 1 FR 0.0001 REL FR 1 V 0 P
o, love's best habit's in a soothing tongue, PP 1.11

HABITS 11 FR 0.0012 REL FR 9 V 2 P
these four will change habits, and present the LLL 5.02.539
full of straying shapes, of habits, and of forms 5.02.763
drives me to these habits of her liking. TN 2.05.169 P
but when in other habits you are seen, 5.01.387
for most it caught me, the celestial habits WT 3.01. 4
they will know us by our horses, by our habits, 1H4 1.02.175 P
hath into monstrous habits put the graces | that H8 1.02.122
if ye be any thing but churchmen's habits) | put 3.01.117
of habits devil, is angel yet in this, | that to HAM 3.04.162
than these thin habits and poor likelihoods | of OTH 1.03.108
men know | more valor in me than my habits show. CYM 5.01. 30

HABITUDE 1 FR 0.0001 REL FR 1 V 0 P
his real habitude gave life and grace | to LC 114

HAC (*also hag**)

HAC 2 FR 0.0002 REL FR 1 V 1 P
he teaches him to "hic" and to "hac," which WIV 4.01. 66 P
"in hac spe vivo." PER 2.02. 44

HACK* 5 FR 0.0005 REL FR 2 V 3 P
these knights will hack, and so thou shouldst WIV 2.01. 52 P
keep their limbs whole and hack our english. 3.01. 77 P
a slave art thou to hack thy sword as thou hast 1H4 2.04.261 P
hew them to pieces, hack their bones asunder, 1H6 4.07. 47
to cut the head off and then hack the limbs — JC 2.01.163

HACK'D 11 FR 0.0012 REL FR 7 V 4 P
is hack'd down, and his summer leaves all faded, R2 1.02. 20
and through, my sword hack'd like a hand-saw — 1H4 2.04.168 P
in earnest, how came falstaff's sword so hack'd? 2.04.304 P
why, he hack'd it with his dagger, and said he 2.04.305 P
richard the second here was hack'd to death; R3 3.03. 12
though we leave it with a root, thus hack'd, H8 1.02. 97
and his helm more hack'd than hector's, and how TRO 1.02.233 P
handless, hack'd and chipp'd, come to him, 5.05. 34
hack'd one another in the sides of caesar. JC 5.01. 40
fight, till from my bones my flesh be hack'd. MAC 5.03. 32
bear our hack'd targets like the men that owe ANT 4.08. 31

HACKET 2 FR 0.0002 REL FR 1 V 1 P
ask marian hacket, the fat ale-wife of wincot, SHR in.2. 21 P
sometimes you would call out for cicely hacket. in.2. 89

HACKNEY 1 FR 0.0001 REL FR 0 V 1 P
is but a colt, and your love perhaps a hackney. LLL 3.01. 32 P

HACKS 2 FR 0.0002 REL FR 0 V 2 P
look you what hacks are on his helmet! TRO 1.02.205 P
there be hacks! 1.02.208 P

H'AD 1 FR 0.0001 REL FR 1 V 0 P
worth of thrice the sum | h'ad sent to me first, TIM 3.03. 23

HAD (*also 'ad*)

/HAD 19 FR 0.0021 REL FR 16 V 3 P
/i /thought /you /had /been /willing /to /resign R2 4.01.190
/my /lord /your /son /had /only /but /the 2H4 1.01.192
/word, /rebellion, /it /had /froze /them /up, 1.01.199
/till /we /had /his /assistance /by /the /hand. 1.03. 21
/he /had /no /legs /that /practic'd /not /his 2.03. 23
/had /my /sweet /harry /had /but /half /their 2.03. 43
/had /my /sweet /harry /had /but /half /their 2.03. 43
/thing, /in /honor, /had /my /father /lost, 4.01.111
/if /your /father /had /been /victor /there, 4.01.132
/he /ne'er /had /borne /it /out /of /coventry; 4.01.133
"/these /wounds /i /had /on /crispin's /day." H5 4.03. 48
as if those organs /had /deceptious functions, TRO 5.02.123
/as /if /we /should /forget /we /had /no /hands, TIT 3.02. 32
/how /if /that /fly /had /a /father /and /mother 3.02. 60
/why, /he /had /none. HAM 5.01. 34 P
/if /i /had /a /monopoly /out, /they /would LR 1.04.153 P
/be /false /persuaded | /i /had /daughters. 1.04.234
who hath /had three suits to his back, six 3.04.135 P
/i /had /rather /lose /the /battle /than /that 5.01. 18

HAD 1536 FR 0.1736 REL FR 1109 V 427 P
a brave vessel | (who had, no doubt, some noble TMP 1.02. 7
had i been any god of power, i would | have sunk 1.02. 10
had i not | four, or five, women once that 1.02. 46
what foul play had we, that we came from thence? 1.02. 60
was | the ivy which had hid my princely trunk, 1.02. 86
as my trust was, which had indeed no limit, | a 1.02. 96
some food we had, and some fresh water, that | a 1.02.160
would't had been done! 1.02.349
i had peopled else | this isle with calibans. 1.02.350
had that in't which good natures | could not 1.02.359
as if it had lungs, and rotten ones. 2.01. 48 P
what if he had said "widower aeneas" too? 2.01. 80 P
would i had never | married my daughter there! 2.01.108
had i plantation of this isle, my lord — 2.01.144
and it had not fall'n flat-long. 2.01.181 P
(as once i was) and had but this fish painted, 2.02. 28 P
for she had a tongue with a tang, | would cry to 2.02. 50
says such baseness | had never like executor. 3.01. 13
i would the lightning had | burnt up those logs 3.01. 16
i had rather crack my sinews, break my back, 3.01. 26
that, if i then had wak'd after long sleep, 3.02.139
whose throats had hanging at 'em | wallets of 3.03. 45
a grace it had, devouring. 3.03. 84
i had forgot that foul conspiracy | of the beast 4.01.139
father | for his advice, nor thought i had one. 5.01.191
one) had plotted with them | to take my life. 5.01.273
he is drunk now. where had he wine? 5.01.278
and yet i would i had o'erlook'd the letter; TGV 1.02. 50
when willingly i would have had her here! 1.02. 61
to walk alone, like one that had the pestilence; 2.01. 21 P
to sigh, like a schoolboy that had lost his abc; 2.01. 22 P
like a young wench that had buried her grandam; 2.01. 23 P
o, that you had mine eyes, or your own eyes had 2.01. 70 P
or your own eyes had the lights they were wont 2.01. 71 P
i would have had them writ more movingly. 2.01.128
should i have wish'd a thing, it had been he. 2.04. 82
i told your ladyship | had come along with me, 2.04. 88
know | that i had any light from thee of this. 3.01. 49
yet 'tis not a maid, for she hath had gossips; 3.01.270 P
if crooked fortune had not thwarted me. 4.01. 22
me happy, | or else i often had been miserable. 4.01. 35
if i had not had more wit than he, to take a 4.04. 13 P
if i had not had more wit than he, to take a 4.04. 13 P
he did, i think verily he had been hang'd for't; 4.04. 15 P
sure as i live, he had suffer'd for't. 4.04. 15 P
he had not been there (bless the mark!) 4.04. 18 P
he hath stol'n, otherwise he had been executed; 4.04. 31 P
he hath kill'd, otherwise he had suffer'd for't. 4.04. 33 P
as if the garment had been made for me; 4.04.163
if i had such a tire, this face of mine | were 4.04.185
eyes, | for i had rather wink than look on them. 5.02. 14
had i been seized by a hungry lion, | i would 5.04. 33
by this hat, then he in the red face had it; WIV 1.01.170 P
i say the gentleman had drunk himself out of his 1.01.175 P
i had rather than forty shillings i had my book 1.01.198 P
than forty shillings i had my book of songs and 1.01.198 P
i had rather walk here, i thank you. 1.01.282 P
if he had found the young man, he would have 1.04. 49 P
if he had been throughly mov'd, you should have 1.04. 90 P
we had an hour's talk of that wart. 1.04.151 P
i had rather be a giantess, and lie under mount 2.01. 79 P
my merry host hath had the measuring of their 2.01.207 P
i had rather hear them scold than fight. 2.01.231 P
or else you had look'd through the grate, like a 2.02. 8 P
i had myself twenty angels given me this morning 2.02. 71 P
though i had never so good means as desire to 2.02.182 P
my desires had instance and argument to commend 2.02.247 P
i had as lief you would tell me of a mess of 3.01. 63 P
whether had you rather lead mine eyes, or eye 3.02. 3 P
i had rather, forsooth, go before you like a man 3.02. 5 P
where had you this pretty weathercock? 3.02. 18 P
the dickens his name is my husband had him of. 3.02. 20 P
i had rather than a thousand pound he were out 3.03.123 P
never stand "you had rather" and "you had rather 3.03.125 P
stand "you had rather" and "you had rather." 3.03.126 P
i had a father, mistress anne; 3.04. 38 P
alas, i had rather be set quick i' th' earth, 3.04. 86
but yet i would my master had mistress anne; 3.04.104 P
or i would master slender had her; 3.04.105 P
or, in sooth, i would master fenton had her. 3.04.106 P
i had been drown'd, but that the shore was 3.05. 14 P
should i have been when i had been swell'd! 3.05. 17 P
as cold as if i had swallow'd snowballs for 3.05. 22 P
i have had ford enough. 3.05. 35 P
instant of our encounter, after we had embrac'd, 3.05. 73 P
once or twice what they had in their basket. 3.05.102 P
truly, i thought there had been one number more, 4.01. 23 P
basket too, howsoever he hath had intelligence. 4.02. 92 P
i hope not, i had lief as bear so much lead. 4.02.113 P
they have had my /house a week at command. 4.03. 9 P
beguil'd him of a chain, had the chain or no. 4.05. 33 P
i had other things to have spoken with her too 4.05. 40 P
the knave constable had set me i' th' stocks, i' 4.05.119 P
sir, as you told me you had appointed? 5.01. 14 P
sir john, we have had ill luck; 5.05.116 P
if it had not been i' th' church, i would have 5.05.184 P
if i did not think it had been anne page, would 5.05.186 P
if i had been married to him (for all he was in 5.05.191 P
in woman's apparel) i would not have had him. 5.05.193 P
she cried "budget," as anne and i had appointed, 5.05.198 P
of us, 'twere all alike | as if we had them not. MM 1.01. 35
i had as lief be a list of an english kersey as 1.02. 32 P
near to the speech we had to such a purpose. 1.02. 78 P
they had gone down too, but that a wise burgher 1.02. 99 P
i had as lief have the foppery of freedom as the 1.02.133 P
hide our love | till time had made them for us. 1.02.153
whom i would save, had a most noble father! 2.01. 7
had time coher'd with place, or place with 2.01. 11
whether you had not sometime in your life 2.01. 14
his offense | for i have had such faults; 2.01. 28
who, if she had been a woman cardinally given, 2.01. 79 P
sir, we had but two in the house, which at that 2.01. 91 P
hath she had any more than one husband? 2.01.201 P
the office, you had continu'd in it some time. 2.01.262 P
i had a brother then. 2.02. 42
if he had been as you, and you as he, | you 2.02. 64
i would to heaven i had your potency, | and you 2.02. 67
those many had not dar'd to do that evil | if 2.02. 91
th' edict infringe | had answer'd for his deed. 2.02. 93
you had marr'd all else. 2.02.148
which had you rather, that the most just law 2.04. 52
this, | i had rather give my body than my soul. 2.04. 56
had he twenty heads to tender down | on twenty 2.04.180
/though all the world's vastidity you had, | to 3.01. 68
angelo had never the purpose to corrupt her; 3.01.161 P
i had rather my brother die by the law than my 3.01.189 P
images newly made woman to be had now, for 3.02. 46 P
he had some feeling of the sport; 3.02.119 P
the duke had crotchets in him. 3.02.127 P
yet had he fram'd to himself (by the instruction 3.02.244 P
wish | you had not found me here so musical. 4.01. 11
it that the absent duke had not either deliver'd 4.02.132 P
he hath evermore had the liberty of the prison; 4.02.147 P
duke of dark corners had been at home, he had 4.03.157 P
of dark corners had been at home, he had liv'd. 4.03.158 P
would yet he had liv'd! 4.04. 32
but he's more, | had i more name for badness. 5.01. 59
if he had so offended, | he would have weigh'd 5.01.110
had he been lay, my lord, | for certain words he 5.01.128
in your retirement, i had swing'd him soundly. 5.01.130
i would he had some cause | to prattle for 5.01.181
a time | when i'll depose i had him in mine arms 5.01.198
my brother had but justice, | in that he did the 5.01.448
had you a special warrant for the deed? 5.01.459
but i had rather it would please you i might be 5.01.506 P
for me, | and by me, had not our hap been bad: ERR 1.01. 38
bear) | had made provision for her following me, 1.01. 47
there had she not been long but she became | a 1.01. 49
a league from epidamium had we sail'd | before 1.01. 62
had fast'ned him unto a small spare mast, | such 1.01. 79
whilst i had been like heedful of the other. 1.01. 82
o, had the gods done so, i had not now 1.01. 98
i had not now | worthily term'd them merciless 1.01. 98
fortune had left to both of us alike | what to 1.01.105
at length, another ship had seiz'd on us, | and, 1.01.112
had not their /bark been very slow of sail; 1.01.116
there is your money that i had to keep. 1.02. 8
sixpence that i had a' we'nsday last | to pay 1.02. 55
the saddler had it, sir, i kept it not. 1.02. 57
leave battering, i had rather have it a head. 2.02. 36 P
told me what privy marks i had about me, as, the 3.02.142 P
think, if my breast had not been made of faith, 3.02.145
she had transform'd me to a curtal dog, and made 3.02.146
nor now i had not, but that i am bound | to 4.01. 3
that i met with you | he had of me a chain. 4.01. 10
consent to pay thee that i never had! 4.01. 74
first he denied you had in him no right. 4.02. 7
and show'd me silks that he had bought for me, 4.03. 8
give me the ring of mine you had at dinner, | or 4.03. 68
where would you had remain'd until this time, 4.04. 66
due for a chain your husband had of him. 4.04.135
he did bespeak a chain for me, but had it not. 4.04.136
you, | but i protest he had the chain of me, 5.01. 2
had hoisted sail and put to sea to-day. 5.01. 21
this chain you had of me, can you deny it? 5.01. 22
i think i had, i never did deny it. 5.01. 23
husband, | who i made lord of me and all i had, 5.01.137
that here and there his fury had committed. 5.01.147
he broke from those that had the guard of him, 5.01.149
but had he such a chain of thee, or no? 5.01.257
he had, my lord, and when he ran in here, 5.01.258
heard you confess you had the chain of him, 5.01.261
'tis true, my liege, this ring i had of her. 5.01.278
that is the chain, sir, which you had of me. 5.01.378
you had musty victual, and he hath holp to eat ADO 1.01. 50 P
find in my heart that i had not a hard heart, 1.01.126 P
i had rather hear my dog bark at a crow than a 1.01.131 P
i would my horse had the speed of your tongue, 1.01.141 P
trust myself, though i had sworn the contrary, 1.01.195 P
from my house — if i had it — 1.01.282 P
but had a rougher task in hand | than to drive 1.01.299
i had rather be a canker in a hedge than a rose 1.03. 27 P
if i had my mouth, i would bite; 1.03. 34 P
if i had my liberty, i would do my liking. 1.03. 35 P
on his face, i had rather lie in the woollen! 2.01. 30 P
and that i had my good wit out of the "hundred 2.01.129 P
i would he had boarded me. 2.01.143 P
that your grace had got the good will of this 2.01.216 P
yet it had not been amiss the rod had been made, 2.01.227 P
yet it had not been amiss the rod had been made, 2.01.227 P
she told me, not thinking i had been myself, 2.01.243 P
with all that adam had left him before he 2.01.252 P
and now had he rather hear the tabor and the 2.03. 14 P
and he had been a dog that should have howl'd 2.03. 79 P
i had as live have heard the night-raven, come 2.03. 81 P
thought her spirit had been invincible against 2.03.114 P
i would have sworn it had, my lord, especially 2.03.116 P
o, when she had writ it, and was reading it over 2.03.136 P
i would she had bestow'd this dotage on me, i 2.03.168 P
if it had been painful, i would not have come. 2.03.251 P
his excellence did earn it, ere he had it. 3.01. 99
did confirm any slander that don john had made, 3.03.159 P
confess'd the vile encounters they have had | a 4.01. 93
if half thy outward graces had been placed 4.01.101
griev'd i, i had but one? 4.01.127
why had i one? 4.01.129
why had i not with charitable hand | took up a 4.01.131
mourn, | if ever love had interest in his liver, 4.01.231
liver, | and wish he had not so accused her — 4.01.232
or that i had any friend would be a man for my 4.01.318 P
that he had receiv'd a thousand ducats of don 4.02. 47 P
and a fellow that hath had losses, and one that 4.02. 84 P
o that i had been writ down an ass! 4.02. 86 P
we had lik'd to have had our two noses snapp'd 5.01.115 P
we had lik'd to have had our two noses snapp'd 5.01.115 P
had we fought, i doubt we should have been too 5.01.118 P
which i had rather seal with my death than 5.01.240 P
men, | a third is fled, that had a hand in it. 5.01.267
the sight whereof i think you had from me, 5.04. 25
bull jove, sir, had an amiable low, | and some 5.04. 48
i had well hop'd thou wouldst have denied 5.04.112 P
i had rather pray a month with mutton and LLL 1.01.302 P
color, methinks sampson had small reason for it. 1.02. 87 P
it was so, sir, for she had a green wit. 1.02. 89 P
so tempted, and he had an excellent strength; 1.02.174 P
salomon so seduced, and he had a very good wit. 1.02.175 P
and shape to win grace though he had no wit. 2.01. 60
navarre had notice of your fair approach, | and 2.01. 81
which we much rather had depart withal, | and 2.01.146
almost i had. 3.01. 34 P
o that i had my wish! 4.03. 90
and i had mine! 4.03. 90
amen, so i had mine. is not that a good word? 4.03. 92
and i had but one penny in the world, thou 5.01. 71 P
is the very remuneration i had of thy master, 5.01. 73 P
had she been light, like you, | of such a merry, 5.02. 15
i should have fear'd her had she been a devil." 5.02.106
had he been adam, he had tempted eve. 5.02.322
had he been adam, he had tempted eve. 5.02.322
we have had pastimes here and pleasant game. 5.02.360
would say, "thanks, pompey," i had done. 5.02.556
she never had so sweet a changeling. MND 2.01. 23
but if i had wit enough to get out of this wood, 3.01.149 P
i had rather give his carcass to my hounds. 3.02. 64
i had no judgment when to her i swore. 3.02.134
sides, voices, and minds | had been incorporate. 3.02.208

i would i had your bond, for i perceive | a weak 3.02.267
the man | by the athenian garments he had on? 3.02.349
i had rather have a handful or two of dried peas 4.01. 37 P
for she his hairy temples then had rounded 4.01. 51
when i had at my pleasure taunted her, | and she 4.01. 57
i have had a most rare vision. 4.01.204 P
i have had a dream, past the wit of man to say 4.01.205 P
methought i was, and methought i had — but man 4.01.209 P
if he will offer to say what methought i had. 4.01.211 P
if our sport had gone forward, we had all been 4.02. 17 P
had gone forward, we had all been made men. 4.02. 17 P
and the duke had not given him sixpence a day 4.02. 21 P
that had in it a crannied hole or chink, 5.01.158
if he that writ it had play'd pyramus and hang'd 5.01.358 P
believe me, sir, had i such venture forth, | the MV 1.01. 15
i would have stay'd till i had made you merry, 1.01. 60
if worthier friends had not prevented me. 1.01. 61
in my school–days, when i had lost one shaft, 1.01.140
than if you had made waste of all i have. 1.01.157
had i but the means | to hold a rival place with 1.01.173
what were good to do, chapels had been churches, 1.02. 13 P
i had rather be married to a death's–head with a 1.02. 50 P
i had rather he should shrive me than wive me. 1.02.130 P
i had forgot — three months — you told me so. 1.03. 67
but if my father had not scanted me, | and 2.01. 17
something grow to, he had a kind of taste — 2.02. 18 P
indeed, if you had your eyes, you might fail of 2.02. 75 P
i am sure he had more hair of his tail than i 2.02. 97 P
had you been as wise as bold, | young in limbs, 2.07. 70
old, | your answer had not been inscroll'd. 2.07. 72
o that i had a title good enough to keep his 3.01. 13 P
whether antonio have had any loss at sea or no? 3.01. 43 P
me a ring that he had of your daughter for a 3.01.118 P
turkis, i had it of leah when i was a bachelor. 3.01.121 P
make me wish a sin, | that i had been forsworn. 3.02. 14
love | had been the very sum of my confession. 3.02. 36
i would you had won the fleece that he hath lost 3.02.242
i freely told you all the wealth i had | ran in 3.02.254
that if he had | the present money to discharge 3.02.272
wish, for all that, that i had not kill'd them; 3.04. 73
be judge | whether bassanio had not once a love. 4.01.277
had been her husband rather than a christian! 4.01.297
had i been judge, thou shouldst have had ten 4.01.399
i been judge, thou shouldst have had ten more, 4.01.399
would he were gelt that had it, for my part, 5.01.144
will ne'er wear hair on 's face that had it. 5.01.158
if you had known the virtue of the ring, | or 5.01.199
if you had pleas'd to have defended it | with 5.01.204
i'll die for't but some woman had the ring! 5.01.208
no woman had it, but a civil doctor, | which did 5.01.210
even he that had held up the very life | of my 5.01.214
had you been there, i think you would have 5.01.221
which, but for him that had your husband's ring, 5.01.250
had your husband's ring, | had quite miscarried. 5.01.251
i had it of him. 5.01.258
whether till the next night she had rather stay, 5.01.302
throat till this other had pull'd out thy tongue AYL 1.01. 60 P
i had myself notice of my brother's purpose 1.01.139 P
i had as lief thou didst break his neck as his 1.01.146 P
thy banish'd father, had banish'd thy uncle, the 1.02. 10 P
by our beards (if we had them) thou art. 1.02. 74 P
by my knavery (if i had it) then i were. 1.02. 75 P
swearing by his honor, for he never had any; 1.02. 78 P
or if he had, he had sworn it away before ever 1.02. 78 P
he had sworn it away before ever he saw those 1.02. 79 P
if i had a thunderbolt in mine eye, i can tell 1.02.214 P
had i before known this young man his son, | i 1.02.237
else had she with her father rang'd along. 1.03. 68
that from the hunter's aim had ta'en a hurt, 2.01. 34
thy sum of more | to that which had too /much." 2.01. 49
part, i had rather bear with you than bear you. 2.04. 11 P
dugs that her pretty chopp'd hands had milk'd; 2.04. 50 P
i thought that all things had been savage here, 2.07.107
so had you need, | i scarce can speak to thank 2.07.169
for some of them had in them more feet than the 3.02.165 P
faith, i had as lief have been myself alone. 3.02.254 P
and so had i; 3.02.255 P
had not that been as proper? 3.02.306 P
truly, i would the gods had made thee poetical. 3.03. 16 P
wish then that the gods had made me poetical? 3.03. 23 P
duke yesterday, and had much question with him. 3.04. 35 P
i had rather hear you chide than this man woo. 3.05. 65
had they mark'd him | in parcels as i did, would 3.05.124
him, | for what had he to do to chide at me? 3.05.129
i had rather have a fool to make me merry than 4.01. 27 P
i had as lief be woo'd of a snail. 4.01. 52 P
troilus had his brains dash'd out with a grecian 4.01. 97 P
many a fair year though hero had turn'd nun, if 4.01.101 P
if it had not been for a hot midsummer night; 4.01.102 P
a man that had a wife with such a wit, he might 4.01.165 P
a green and gilded snake had wreath'd itself, 4.03.108
tears our recountments had most kindly bath'd, 4.03.140
his arm | the lioness had torn some flesh away, 4.03.147
flesh away, | which all this while had bled; 4.03.148
when he had a desire to eat a grape, would open 5.01. 33 P
i thought thy heart had been wounded with the 5.02. 22 P
that would i, had i kingdoms to give with her. 5.04. 8
undone three tailors, i have had four quarrels, 5.04. 46 P
kiss as many of you as had beards that pleas'd ep 19 P
since for the great desire i had | to see fair SHR 1.01. 1
but i had as lief take her dowry with this 1.01.131 P
and would i had given him the best horse in 1.01.142 P
her face, | such as the daughter of agenor had, 1.01.168
so had you need. 1.01.210
that lucentio indeed had baptista's youngest 1.01.240
whom would to god i had well knock'd at first, 1.02. 34
first, | then had not grumio come by the worst. 1.02. 35
fair leda's daughter had a thousand wooers, 1.02.242
terms, | as had she studied to misuse me so. 2.01.159
had i a glass, i would. 2.01.233
would katherine had never seen him though! 3.02. 26
he, as if | he had been aboard, carousing to his 3.02.171
a fool, | if she had not a spirit to resist. 3.02.221
would all the world but he had quite forsworn! 4.02. 35
gown is made | just as my master had direction. 4.03.116
and i had thee in place where, thou shouldst 4.03.149 P
for she is chang'd, as she had never been. 5.02.115
this young gentlewoman had a father — o, that AWW 1.01. 17 P
father — o, that "had," how sad a passage 'tis! 1.01. 18 P
had it stretch'd so far, would have made nature 1.01. 19 P
that wishing well had not a body in't, | which 1.01.181
i would i had that corporal soundness now | as 1.02. 24
youth | he had the wit which i can well observe 1.02. 32
his equal had awak'd them, and his honor, 1.02. 38
madam, the care i have had to even your content, 1.03. 3 P
that had put such difference betwixt their two 1.03.111 P
had you not lately an intent — speak truly — 1.03.218
madam, i had. 1.03.219
and manifest experience had collected | for 1.03.223
king, | had from the conversation of my thoughts 1.03.234
i would you had kneel'd, my lord, to ask me 2.01. 64
i would i had, so i had broke thy pate, | and 2.01. 66
i would i had, so i had broke thy pate, | and 2.01. 66
i ne'er had worse luck in my life in my "o lord, 2.02. 57 P
not one of those but had a noble father. 2.03. 62
i had rather be in this choice than throw 2.03. 78 P
she had her breeding at my father's charge — 2.03.114
you had my prayers to lead them on, and to keep 2.04. 17 P
so that you had her wrinkles and i her money, i 2.04. 20 P
this had been truth, sir. 2.04. 31 P
it hath happen'd all as i would have had it, 3.02. 1 P
i know a man that had this trick of melancholy 3.02. 8 P
had i spoke with her, | i could have well 3.04. 20
madam, | if i had given you this at overnight, 3.04. 23
for the king had married him | against his 3.05. 53
have prevented, if he had been there to command. 3.06. 53 P
some dishonor we had in the loss of that drum, 3.06. 56 P
and knowing i had no such purpose? 4.01. 36 P
i would i had any drum of the enemy's. 4.01. 61 P
he had sworn to marry me | when his wife's dead; 4.02. 71
who had even tun'd his bounty to sing happiness 4.03. 9 P
so curiously he had set this counterfeit. 4.03. 34 P
he weeps like a wench that had shed her milk. 4.03.107 P
that had the whole theoric of war in the knot of 4.03.142 P
in that country he had the honor to be the 4.03.269 P
but women were that had receiv'd so much shame, 4.03.327 P
you never had a servant to whose trust | your 4.04. 15
your daughter–in–law had been alive at this hour 4.05. 4 P
i would i had not known him; 4.05. 8 P
that ever nature had praise for creating. 4.05. 10 P
if she had partaken of my flesh, and cost me the 4.05. 10 P
i had talk of you last night; 5.02. 52 P
the main consents are had, and here we'll stay 5.03. 69
had you that craft to reave her | of what should 5.03. 86
but when i had subscrib'd | to mine own fortune, 5.03. 96
course of honor | as she had made the overture, 5.03. 99
if he does think | he had not my virginity. 5.03.186
and i had that which any inferior might | at 5.03.218
tricks he hath had in him, which gentlemen have. 5.03.239 P
that strain again, it had a dying fall; TN 1.01. 4
world | till i had made mine own occasion mellow 1.02. 43
i would i had bestow'd that time in the tongues 1.03. 92 P
o, had i but follow'd the arts! 1.03. 93 P
then hadst thou had an excellent head of hair. 1.03. 95 P
if the heavens had been pleas'd, would we had so 2.01. 20 P
heavens had been pleas'd, would we had so ended! 2.01. 20 P
that methought her eyes had lost her tongue, 2.02. 20
i had rather than forty shillings i had such a 2.03. 20 P
rather than forty shillings i had such a leg, 2.03. 20 P
o fellow, come, the song we had last night. 2.04. 42
my father had a daughter lov'd a man, | as it 2.04.107
ay, and you had any eye behind you, you might 2.05.136 P
i would therefore my sister had had no name, sir 3.01. 16 P
i would therefore my sister had had no name, sir 3.01. 16 P
i had rather hear you to solicit that | than 3.01.109
i had as lief be a brownist as a politician. 3.02. 31 P
i am one that had rather go with sir priest than 3.04.271 P
i had a pass with him, rapier, scabbard, and all 3.04.274 P
plague on't, and i thought he had been valiant, 3.04.283 P
which i had recommended to his use | not half an 5.01. 91
why should i not (had i the heart to do it), 5.01.117
i had rather than forty pound i were at home. 5.01.177 P
but if he had not been in drink, he would have 5.01.193 P
but, had it been the brother of my blood, | i 5.01.210
i never had a brother; 5.01.226
i had a sister, | whom the blind waves and 5.01.228
my father had a mole upon his brow. 5.01.242
and so had mine. 5.01.243
from her birth | had numb'red thirteen years. 5.01.245
parts | we had conceiv'd against him. 5.01.362
with toss–pots still had drunken heads, | for 5.01.403
if the king had no son, they would desire to WT 1.01. 45 P
desire to live on crutches till he had one. 1.01. 46 P
i had thought, sir, to have held my peace until 1.02. 28
you had drawn oaths from him not to stay. 1.02. 29
had we pursu'd that life, | and our weak spirits 1.02. 71
your precious self had then not cross'd the eyes 1.02. 79
three crabbed months had sour'd themselves to 1.02.102
you had much ado to make his anchor hold, | when 1.02.213
if i | had servants true about me, that bare 1.02.309
of thousands that had struck anointed kings 1.02.358
as he had lost some province and a region 1.02.369
as he had seen't or been an instrument | to vice 1.02.415
but i'ld say he had not; 2.01. 62
and i had rather glib myself than they | should 2.01.149
i had rather you did lack than i, my lord, 2.01.158
you had only in your silent judgment tried it, 2.01.171
will bring all, whose spiritual counsel had, 2.01.186
though a present death | had been more merciful. 2.03.185
which not to have done i think had been in me 3.02. 67
and toward your friend, whose love had spoke, 3.02. 69
you had a bastard by polixenes, | and i but 3.02. 83
which had been done, | but that the good mind of 3.02.161
would i had been by, to have help'd the old man! 3.03.107 P
i would you had been by the ship side, to have 3.03.109 P
scene such growing | as you had slept between. 4.01. 17
better not to have had thee than thus to want 4.02. 13 P
if you had but look'd big and spit at him, he'ld 4.03.106 P
i would i had some flow'rs o' th' spring that 4.04.113
he utters them as he had eaten ballads and all 4.04.185 P
we had the tune on't a month ago. 4.04.294 P
had force and knowledge | more than was ever 4.04.374
as if my trinkets had been hallow'd and brought 4.04.601 P
his pettitoes till he had both tune and words, 4.04.607 P
and had not the old man come in with a whoobub 4.04.615 P
i had not left a purse alive in the whole army. 4.04.617 P
indeed i have had earnest, but i cannot with 4.04.645 P
what an exchange had this been, without boot! 4.04.675 P
and then your blood had been the dearer by i 4.04.704 P
your worship had like to have given us one, if 4.04.727 P
if you had not taken yourself with the manner. 4.04.728 P
if i had a mind to be honest, i see fortune 4.04.831 P
o that ever i | had squar'd me to thy counsel! 5.01. 52
had she such power, | she had just cause. 5.01. 60
had she such power, | she had just cause. 5.01. 61
she had, and would incense me | to murther her i 5.01. 61
is colder than that theme, "she had not been, 5.01.100
had our prince, | jewel of children, seen this 5.01.115
this hour, he had pair'd | well with this lord; 5.01.116
he had himself | the lands and waters 'twixt 5.01.143
they look'd as they had heard of a world 5.02. 14 P
she had one eye declin'd for the loss of her 5.02. 74 P
could have seen't, the woe had been universal. 5.02. 92 P
had he himself eternity and could put breath 5.02. 97 P
i thought she had some great matter there in 5.02.104 P
now, had i not the dash of my former life in me, 5.02.113 P
for had i been the finder–out of this secret, it 5.02.121 P
the great comfort | that i have had of thee! 5.03. 2
if i had thought the sight of my poor image 5.03. 57
would not cease | till she had kindled france, JN 1.01. 33
had of your father claim'd this son for his? 1.01.122
and if my brother had my shape | and i had his, 1.01.138
and if my brother had my shape | and i had his, 1.01.139
if thou hadst said him nay, it had been sin. 1.01.275
their fixed beds of lime | had been dishabited, 2.01.220
i had a thing to say, | but i will fit it with 3.03. 25
i had a thing to say, but let it go. 3.03. 33
had bak'd thy blood and made it heavy, thick, 3.03. 43
well could i bear that england had this praise, 3.04. 15
he talks to me that never had a son. 3.04. 91
had you such a loss as i, | i could give better 3.04. 99
if you had won it, certainly you had. 3.04.118
if you had won it, certainly you had. 3.04.118
handkercher about your brows | (the best i had, 4.01. 43
but you at your sick service had a prince. 4.01. 52
done, | what we so fear'd he had a charge to do. 4.02. 75
haste | had falsely thrust upon contrary feet, 4.02.198
i had a mighty cause | to wish him dead, but 4.02.205
no had, my lord? why, did you not provoke me? 4.02.207
shame, | this murther had not come into my mind; 4.02.223
deep shame had struck me dumb, made me break off 4.02.235
therefore 'twere reason you had manners now. 4.03. 31
the earth had not a hole to hide this deed. 4.03. 36
we had a kind of light what would ensue. 4.03. 61
be said, | they saw we had a purpose of defense. 5.01. 76
than had i seen the vaulty top of heaven 5.02. 52
that hand which had the strength, even at your 5.02.137
when we were happy we had other names. 5.04. 8
time | than if you had at leisure known of this. 5.06. 27
which else would post until it had return'd R2 1.01. 56
three parts of that receipt i had for callice 1.01.126
your grace's pardon, and i hope i had it. 1.01.141
the part i had in woodstock's blood | doth more 1.02. 1
by this time, had the king permitted us, | one 1.03.194
us, | one of our souls had wand'red in the air, 1.03.195
but i had rather | you would have bid me argue 1.03.237
had i thy youth and cause, i would not stay. 1.03.305
he should have had a volume of farewells; 1.04. 18
but since it would not, he had none of me. 1.04. 19
well, | and had the tribute of his supple knee, 1.04. 33
o, had thy grandsire with a prophet's eye | seen 2.01.104
which his triumphant father's hand had won. 2.01.181
richly in both, if justice had her right. 2.01.227
perhaps they had ere this, but that they stay 2.01.289
my lord, i had forgot to tell your lordship: 2.02. 93
god | (so my untruth had not provok'd him to it) 2.02.101
the king had cut off my head with my brother's. 2.02.102
i had thought, my lord, to have learn'd his 2.03. 24
what power the duke of york had levied there, 2.03. 34
had you first died, and he been thus trod down, 2.03.126
i have had feeling of my cousin's wrongs, | and 2.03.141
i had forgot myself, am i not king? 3.02. 83
me rather had my heart might feel your love 3.03.192
or if of grief, being altogether had, | it adds 3.04. 15
that he had not so trimm'd and dress'd his land 3.04. 56
had he done so to great and growing men, | they 3.04. 61
had he done so, himself had borne the crown, 3.04. 65
had he done so, himself had borne the crown, 3.04. 65
i heard you say that you had rather refuse | the 4.01. 15
under whose colors he had fought so long. 4.01.100
beasts, | i had been still a happy king of men. 5.01. 36
walls | with painted imagery had said at once, 5.02. 16
that had not god, for some strong purpose, 5.02. 34
not, | god knows i had as lief be none as one. 5.02. 49
had not an ear to hear my true time broke. 5.05. 48
that some night–tripping fairy had exchang'd 1H4 1.01. 87
else he had been damn'd for cozening the devil. 1.02.122 P
which many a good tall fellow had destroyed | so 1.03. 62
what e'er lord harry percy then had said | to 1.03. 71
o lord, i would it had been two! 2.04. 60 P
both which i have had, but their date is out, 2.04.503 P
at the same season if your mother's cat had 3.01. 18
kitten'd, though yourself had never been born. 3.01. 19
i had rather be a kitten and cry mew | than one 3.01.127
i had rather hear a brazen canstick turn'd, | or 3.01.129
i had rather live | with cheese and garlic in a 3.01.159
i had rather hear lady, my brach, howl in irish. 3.01.235 P
had i so lavish of my presence been, | so 3.02. 39
the crown, | had still kept loyal to possession, 3.02. 43
had his great name profaned with their scorns, 3.02. 64
so when he had occasion to be seen, | he was but 3.02. 74
he had his part of it, let him pay. 3.03. 75 P
here behind the arras and had my pocket pick'd. 3.03. 98 P
i would it had been of horse. 3.03.187 P
i would the state of time had first been whole 4.01. 25
whole | ere he by sickness had been visited, 4.01. 26
but yet i would your father had been here. 4.01. 60
such as had been ask'd twice on the banes, such 4.02. 16 P
as had as lieve hear the devil as a drum, such 4.02. 18 P
you would think that i had a hundred and fifty 4.02. 34 P
me on the way and told me i had unloaded all the 4.02. 36 P
wide betwixt the legs, as if they had gyves on, 4.02. 41 P
for indeed i had the most of them out of prison. 4.02. 41 P
i thought your honor had already been at 4.02. 53 P

i know not where they had that, and for their 4.02. 71 P
the seeming sufferances that you had borne, 5.01. 51
thus, | i never had triumph'd upon a scot. 5.03. 15
hot termagant scot had paid me scot and lot too. 5.04.114 P
many a creature else | had been alive this hour, 5.05. 8
he told me that rebellion had bad luck, | and 2H4 1.01. 41
that rebellion | had met ill luck? 1.01. 51
he was some hilding fellow that had stol'n | the 1.01. 57
that which i would to god i had not seen, | but 1.01.106
had three times slain th' appearance of the king 1.01.128
this present grief had wip'd it from my mind. 1.01.211
be crowing as if he had writ man ever since his 1.02. 26 P
i had as live they would put ratsbane in my 1.02. 41 P
aside, i had lied in my throat if i had said so. 1.02. 81 P
aside, i had lied in my throat if i had said so. 1.02. 82 P
telling us she had a good dish of prawns, 2.01. 96 P
i had thought weariness durst not have attach'd 2.02. 2 P
'a had him from me christian, and look if the 2.02. 70 P
eyes, and methought he had made two holes in the 2.02. 82 P
therefore captains had need look to't. 2.04.150 P
(though then, god knows, i had no such intent, 3.01. 72
you had not four such swingebucklers in all the 3.02. 21 P
bona /robas were and had the best of them all at 3.02. 24 P
you may, but if he had been a man's tailor, he'd 3.02.152 P
and had robin nightwork by old nightwork before 3.02.208 P
very truth, sir, i had as live be hang'd, sir, 3.02.222 P
john a' gaunt as if he had been sworn brother to 3.02.321 P
lords | had not been here to dress the ugly form 4.01. 39
this had been cheerful after victory. 4.02. 88
and i had but a belly of any indifferency, i 4.03. 20 P
had they been rul'd by me, | you should have won 4.03. 66
i would you had the wit, 'twere better than your 4.03. 86 P
if i had a thousand sons, the first humane 4.03.122 P
had found some months asleep and leapt them over 4.04.124
i had forestall'd this dear and deep rebuke 4.05.140
ere you with grief had spoke and i had heard 4.05.141
ere you with grief had spoke and i had heard 4.05.141
that had before my face murdered my father, 4.05.167
and i had many living to upbraid | my gain of it 4.05.192
and had a purpose now | to lead out many to the 4.05.209
sir, a new link to the bucket must needs be had; 5.01. 23 P
if i had a suit to master shallow, i would humor 5.01. 71 P
do with a fellow that never had the ache in his 5.01. 83 P
i would his majesty had call'd me with him; 5.02. 6
o that the living harry had the temper | of he, 5.02. 15
we meet like men that had forgot to speak. 5.02. 22
not think master silence had been a man of this 5.03. 37 P
o, if i had had time to have made new liveries, 5.05. 11 P
o, if i had had time to have made new liveries, 5.05. 11 P
this doth infer the zeal i had to see him. 5.05. 14 P
was like, and had indeed against us pass'd, H5 1.01. 3
had nobles richer and more loyal subjects, 1.02.127
and went away and it had been any christom child 2.03. 11 P
by french fathers | had twenty years been made. 2.04. 62
i had rather have my horse to my mistress. 3.07. 57 P
i had as live have my mistress a jade. 3.07. 59 P
a boast as that, if i had a sow to my mistress. 3.07. 62 P
if the english had any apprehension, they would 3.07.135 P
for if their heads had any intellectual armor, 3.07.137 P
sleep, | had the forehand and vantage of a king. 4.01.280
o that we now had here | but one ten thousand of 4.03. 16
bardolph and nym had ten times more valor than 4.04. 70 P
stopp'd, | but i had not so much of man in me, 4.06. 30
for had you been as i took you for, i made no 4.08. 54 P
thou wouldst think i had sold my farm to buy my 5.02.125 P
whose state so many had the managing, | that ep 11
england ne'er had a king until his time: 1H6 1.01. 8
virtue he had, deserving to command; 1.01. 9
had not churchmen pray'd, | his thread of life 1.01. 33
his thread of life had not so soon decay'd. 1.01. 34
no leisure had he to enrank his men; 1.01.115
here had the conquest fully been seal'd up, | if 1.01.130
if sir john falstaff had not play'd the coward. 1.01.131
so you had need, for orleance is besieg'd; 1.01.157
suppose | they had such courage and audacity? 1.02. 36
the earl of bedford had a prisoner | call'd the 1.04. 27
if i now had him brought into my power. 1.04. 37
wherefore a guard of chosen shot i had | that 1.04. 53
improvident soldiers, had your watch been good, 2.01. 58
had all your quarters been as safely kept | as 2.01. 63
kept | as that whereof i had the government, 2.01. 64
we had not been thus shamefully surpris'd. 2.01. 65
and what a terror he had been to france. 2.02. 17
arms, | this loathsome sequestration have i had; 2.05. 25
tongue, | else with the like i had requited him. 2.05. 50
and of thy cunning had no diffidence; 3.03. 10
for, had the passions of thy heart burst out, 4.01.183
he might have sent, and had the horse. 4.04. 33
and had the maidenhood | of thy first fight, i 4.06. 17
had death been french, then death had died 4.07. 28
death been french, then death had died to–day. 4.07. 28
had york and somerset brought rescue in, | we 4.07. 33
and yet a dispensation may be had. 5.03. 86
had been a little ratsbane for thy sake! 5.04. 29
i wish some ravenous wolf had eaten thee! 5.04. 31
i never had to do with wicked spirits. 5.04. 42
it dies, and if it had a thousand lives. 5.04. 75
our great progenitors had conquered? 5.04.110
dame | (had i sufficient skill to utter them) 5.05. 13
i had in charge at my depart for france, | as 2H6 1.01. 2
the mutual conference that my mind hath had, 1.01. 25
france, | undoing all, as all had never been! 1.01.103
i never read but england's kings have had 1.01.128
had henry got an empire by his marriage, | and 1.01.153
for i had hope of france, | even as i have of 1.01.237
i thought king henry had resembled thee | in 1.03. 53
ask what thou wilt. that i had said, and done! 1.04. 28
and, ten to one, old joan had not gone out. 2.01. 4
had not your man put up the fowl so suddenly, 2.01. 44
the fowl so suddenly, | we had had more sport. 2.01. 45
the fowl so suddenly, | we had had more sport. 2.01. 45
edward the third, my lords, had seven sons: 2.02. 10
from whose line | i claim the crown, had issue, 2.02. 35
edmund had issue, roger earl of march; 2.02. 37
roger had issue, edmund, anne, and eleanor. 2.02. 38
and, but for owen glendower, had been king, 2.02. 41
fellow, | which he had thought to have murther'd 2.03.104
and had i twenty times so many foes, | and each 2.04. 60
and each of them had twenty times their power, 2.04. 61
and, had i first been put to speak my mind, | i 3.01. 43
for i had hope of france | as firmly as i hope 3.01. 87
pay, | nor ever had one penny bribe from france. 3.01.109
myself had notice of your conventicles — | and 3.01.166
as if she had suborned some to swear | false 3.01.180
witness the fortune he hath had in france. 3.01.292
had been the regent there in stead of me, | he 3.01.294
myself and beauford had him in protection, | and 3.02.180
and you, forsooth, had the good duke to keep. 3.02.183
and had i not been cited so by them, | yet did i 3.02.281
had i but said, i would have kept my word; 3.02.293
enough, | so suffolk had thy heavenly company: 3.02.361
so he had need, for 'tis threadbare. 4.02. 7 P
for his father had never a house but the cage. 4.02. 52 P
by her he had two children at one birth. 4.02.139
i fear me, love, if that i had been dead, | thou 4.04. 23
our forefathers had no other books but the score 4.07. 34 P
these arms till you had recover'd your ancient 4.08. 26 P
my brain–pan had been cleft with a brown bill; 4.10. 12 P
he durst not sit there, had your father liv'd. 3H6 1.01. 63
would i had died a maid | and never seen thee, 1.01.216
had i been there, which am a silly woman, | the 1.01.243
henry had none, but did usurp the place. 1.02. 25
had i thy brethren here, their lives and thine 1.03. 25
in blood of those that had encount'red him. 1.04. 13
till our king henry had shook hands with death. 1.04.102
had he been slaughter–man to all my kin, | i 1.04.169
had he been ta'en, we should have heard the news 2.01. 4
had he been slain, we should have heard the news 2.01. 5
or had he scap'd, methinks we should have heard 2.01. 6
but all in vain, they had no heart to fight, 2.01.135
hear | that things ill got had ever bad success? 2.02. 46
and would my father had left me no more! 2.02. 50
and had he match'd according to his state, | he 2.02.152
hadst thou been meek, our title still had slept, 2.02.160
king, | had slipp'd our claim until another age. 2.02.162
thy burning car never had scorch'd the earth. 2.06. 13
they never then had sprung like summer flies; 2.06. 17
had left no mourning widows for our death, | and 2.06. 19
to tell you plain, i had rather lie in prison. 3.02. 70
brothers, you muse what chat we two have had. 3.02.109
lost | all that which henry the fift had gotten? 3.03. 90
had he none else to make a stale but me? 3.03.260
and meaner than myself have had like fortune. 4.01. 71
she had the wrong. 4.01.102
alas, that warwick had no more forecast, | but, 5.01. 42
i had rather chop this hand off at a blow, | and 5.01. 50
my parks, my walks, my manors that i had, | even 5.02. 24
ah, that thy father had been so resolv'd! 5.05. 22
if you had, | the thought of them would have 5.05. 63
had i not reason, think ye, to make haste, | and 5.06. 72
cursed the heart that had the heart to do it! R3 1.02. 15
that all the standers–by had wet their cheeks 1.02.162
iwis your grandam had a worser match. 1.03.101
i had rather be a country servant maid | than a 1.03.106
i had rather be a pedlar: 1.03.148
she hath had too much wrong, and i repent | my 1.03.306
for had i curs'd now, i had curs'd myself. 1.03.318
for had i curs'd now, i had curs'd myself. 1.03.318
methoughts that i had broken from the tower 1.04. 9
of york and lancaster, | that had befall'n us. 1.04. 16
had you such leisure in the time of death | to 1.04. 34
methought i had, and often did i strive | to 1.04. 36
/'zounds, he dies! i had forgot the reward. 1.04.125 P
i would he knew that i had sav'd his brother! 1.04.276
when oxford had me down, he rescued me, | and 2.01.113
of you | had so much grace to put it in my mind. 2.01.121
sorrow | as i had title in thy noble husband! 2.02. 48
what stay had i but edward? and he's gone. 2.02. 74
what stay had we but clarence? and he's gone. 2.02. 75
what stays had i but they? and they are gone. 2.02. 76
was never widow had so dear a loss. 2.02. 77
were never orphans had so dear a loss. 2.02. 78
was never mother had so dear a loss. 2.02. 79
king | had virtuous uncles to protect his grace. 2.03. 21
now, by my troth, if i had been rememb'red, | i 2.04. 23
he dreamt the boar had rased off his helm. 3.02. 11
and they indeed had no cause to mistrust; 3.02. 85
had you not come upon your cue, my lord, 3.04. 26
william lord hastings had pronounc'd your part 3.04. 27
for, were he, he had shown it in his looks. 3.04. 57
that the subtile traitor | this day had plotted, 3.05. 38
had he done so? 3.05. 40
yet had we not determin'd he should die | until 3.05. 52
i would have had you heard | the traitor speak, 3.05. 56
words shall serve | as well as i had seen, and 3.05. 63
my princely father, then had wars in france, 3.05. 88
when he had done, some followers of mine own, 3.07. 34
please you; | but i had rather kill two enemies. 4.02. 71
i had an edward, till a richard kill'd him; 4.04. 40
i had a /harry, till a richard kill'd him: 4.04. 41
i had a richard too, and thou didst kill him; 4.04. 44
i had a rutland too, thou /holp'st to kill him. 4.04. 45
that had his teeth before his eyes | to worry 4.04. 49
if grace had blest thee with a fairer life. 4.04.221
you speak as if that i had slain my cousins! 4.04.222
had grac'd the tender temples of my child, | and 4.04.383
and both the princes had been breathing here, 4.04.384
methought the souls of all that i had murther'd 5.03.204
a drowsy head | have i since your departure had, 5.03.229
had rather have us win than him they follow: 5.03.244
want of means, poor rats, had hang'd themselves. 5.03.331
which had they, what four thron'd ones could H8 1.01. 11
what had he | to do in these fierce vanities? 1.01. 53
seal | he solemnly had sworn that what he spoke 1.02.165
that, had the king in his last sickness fail'd, 1.02.184
after your highness had reprov'd the duke 1.02.189
quoth he, "i for this had been committed — | as 1.02.193
directly | their very noses had been councillors 1.03. 9
he had a black mouth that said other of him. 1.03. 58
had the cardinal | but half my lay–thoughts in 1.04. 10
i had it from my father. 1.04. 27
i had my trial, | and must needs say a noble one 2.01.118
your lordship sent for, with all the care i had, 2.02. 2 P
we had need pray, | and heartily, for our 2.02. 44
will, much better | she ne'er had known pomp! 2.03. 13
would i had no being | if this salute my blood a 2.03.102
mine | that had to him deriv'd your anger did i 2.04. 32
the wisest prince that there had reign'd by many 2.04. 49
that they had gather'd a wise council to them 2.04. 51
who had been hither sent on the debating | /a 2.04.174
the smile of heaven, who had | commanded nature, 2.04.188
or shortly after | this world had air'd them. 2.04.194
the daring'st counsel which i had to doubt, 2.04.216
and showers | there had made a lasting spring. 3.01. 8
believe me, she has had much wrong. 3.01. 48
would i had never trod this english earth, | or 3.01.143
would he had! 3.02. 42
since i had my office, | i have kept you next my 3.02.156
i had rather want those than my head. 3.02.309
had i but serv'd my god with half the zeal | i 3.02.455
had i not known those customs | i should have 4.01. 20
which when the people | had the full view of, 4.01. 71
flew up, and had their faces | been loose, this 4.01. 74
faces | been loose, this day they had been lost. 4.01. 75
that had not half a week to go, like rams | in 4.01. 77
she had all the royal makings of a queen, | as 4.01. 87
that gentle physic given in time had cur'd me; 4.02.122
if heaven had pleas'd to have given me longer 4.02.152
life | and able means, we had not parted thus. 4.02.153
i had thought | they had parted so much honesty 5.02. 27
they had parted so much honesty among 'em — 5.02. 28
has he had knowledge of it? 5.02. 39
he had better starve | than but once think his 5.02.167
i had thought i had had men of some 5.02.170
i had thought i had had men of some 5.02.170
i had thought i had had men of some 5.02.170
would try him to the utmost had ye mean, | which 5.02.181
but if i spar'd any | that had a head to hit, 5.03. 24
would i had known no more! 5.04. 59
her, but i would somebody had heard her talk TRO 1.01. 45 P
i have had my labor for my travail; 1.01. 70 P
condition i had gone barefoot to india. 1.02. 74 P
i had as lieve helen's golden tongue had 1.02.104 P
helen's golden tongue had commended troilus for 1.02.105 P
and't had been a green hair, i should have 1.02.152 P
had i a sister were a grace, or a daughter a 1.02.236 P
i had rather be such a man as troilus than 1.02.244 P
troy, yet upon his bases, had been down, | and 1.03. 75
the great hector's sword had lack'd a master, 1.03. 76
agamemnon, how if he had biles — full, all over 2.01. 2 P
and i had the scratching of thee, i would make 2.01. 28 P
ere /your grandsires had nails /on /their /toes, 2.01.105 P
not ours nor worth to us | (had it our name) the 2.02. 23
and had as ample power as i have will, | paris 2.02.140
man, | or that we women had men's privilege | of 3.02.128
all the commerce that you have had with troy 3.03.205
i had rather be a tick in a sheep than such a 3.03.311 P
had i so good occasion to lie long | as /you, 4.01. 4
troilus had rather troy were borne to greece 4.01. 47
i would they had broke 's neck! 4.02. 76 P
i had good argument for kissing once. 4.05. 26
wherein my sword had not impressure made | /of 4.05.131
we have had pelting wars since you refus'd | the 4.05.267
had she no lover there | that wails her absence? 4.05.288
i had your heart before, this follows it. 5.02. 83
think we had mothers, do not give advantage | to 5.02.130
wife hath dreamt, thy mother hath had visions, 5.03. 63
much more a fresher man, | had i expected thee. 5.06. 21
they have had inkling this fortnight what we COR 1.01. 58 P
of martius, "o, if he | had borne the business!" 1.01.270
to bodily act ere rome | had circumvention? 1.02. 6
now in first seeing he had prov'd himself a man. 1.03. 17 P
but had he died in the business, madam, how then 1.03. 18 P
had i a dozen sons, each in my love alike, and 1.03. 22 P
i had rather had eleven die nobly for their 1.03. 24 P
i had rather had eleven die nobly for their 1.03. 24 P
he had rather see the swords and hear a drum 1.03. 55 P
wheel | three or four miles about, else had i, 1.06. 20
which told me they had beat you to your trenches 1.06. 40
emulation | hath not that honor in't it had; 1.10. 13
and he had stay'd by him, i would not have been 2.01.130 P
he had, before this last expedition, twenty–five 2.01.153 P
thou have laugh'd had i come coffin'd home, 2.01.176
i had rather be their servant in my way | than 2.01.203
he did not care whether he had their love or no, 2.02. 16 P
i would you rather had been silent. 2.02. 61
i had rather have my wounds to heal again | than 2.02. 69
i had rather have one scratch my head i' th' sun 2.02. 75
he had rather venture all his limbs for honor 2.02. 80
as if i had receiv'd them for the hire | of 2.02.149
he said he had wounds, which he could show in 2.03.166
when he had no power, | but was a petty servant 2.03.177
had touch'd his spirit | and tried his 2.03.191
as cause had call'd you up, have held him to; 2.03.194
why, had your bodies | no heart among you? 2.03.203
or had you tongues to cry | against the 2.03.204
say you ne'er had done't | (harp on that still) 2.03.251
tullus aufidius then had made new head? 3.01. 1
he had, my lord, and that it was which caus'd 3.01. 2
against the volsces for they had so vildly 3.01. 10
how often he had met you, sword to sword; 3.01. 13
i wish i had a cause to seek him there, | to 3.01. 19
have i had children's voices? 3.01. 30
though there the people had more absolute pow'r, 3.01.116
have we not had a taste of his obedience — 3.01.316
i would have had you put your power well on 3.02. 17
your power well on | before you had worn it out. 3.02. 18
lesser had been | the /thwartings of your 3.02. 20
you had not show'd them how ye were dispos'd 3.02. 22
to say, | if you had been the wife of hercules, 4.01. 17
i would i had the power | to say so to my 4.02. 15
i would he had continued to his country | as he 4.02. 30
i would he had. 4.02. 32
"i would he had"? 4.02. 33
i would the gods had nothing else to do | but to 4.02. 45
you had more beard when i last saw you, but your 4.03. 8 P
for if | i had fear'd death, of all the men i' 4.05. 81
and i had purpose | once more to hew thy target 4.05.119
had we no other quarrel else to rome but that 4.05.127
i had thought to have strooken him with a cudgel 4.05.149 P
he had, sir, a kind of face, methought — i 4.05.155 P
he had so, looking as it were — would i were 4.05.157 P
i had as live be a condemn'd man. 4.05.176 P
and he had been cannibally given, he might have 4.05.188 P

blush that the world goes well, who rather had, 4.06. 5
we wish'd coriolanus | had lov'd you as we did. 4.06. 25
if he had gone forth consul, found it so. 4.06. 35
as those should do that had deserv'd his hate, 4.06.113
you had not | join'd in commission with him; 4.07. 13
of yourself, or else | to him had left it soly. 4.07. 16
till he had forg'd himself a name a' th' fire 5.01. 14
of a state | to one whom they had punish'd. 5.01. 21
he was not taken well, he had not din'd: 5.01. 50
if you had told as many lies in his behalf as 5.02. 24 P
an evident calamity, though we had | our wish, 5.03.112
this fellow had a volscian to his mother; 5.03.178
his countenance as if | i had been mercenary. 5.06. 40
when he had carried rome and that we look'd 5.06. 42
post, | and had no welcomes home, but he returns 5.06. 50
o that i had him, | with six aufidiuses, or more 5.06.127
sons, | half of the number that king priam had, TIT 1.01. 80
would you had hit it too! 2.01. 97
he that had wit would think that i had none, 2.03. 1
he that had wit would think that i had none, 2.03. 1
had i the pow'r that some say dian had, | thy 2.03. 61
had i the pow'r that some say dian had, | thy 2.03. 61
moor, | if foul desire had not conducted you? 2.03. 79
no sooner had they told this hellish tale, | but 2.03.105
and had you not by wondrous fortune come, | this 2.03.112
come, | this vengeance on me had they executed: 2.03.113
had the monster seen those lily hands | tremble 2.04. 44
had he heard the heavenly harmony | which that 2.04. 48
hath hurt me more than had he kill'd me dead: 3.01. 92
had i but seen thy picture in this plight, | it 3.01.103
had she a tongue to speak, now would she say 3.01.144
hunt | (o, had we never, never hunted there!), 4.01. 56
had he not reason, lord demetrius? 4.02. 39
i would we had a thousand roman dames | at such 4.02. 41
rome never had more cause. 4.04. 62
had nature lent thee but thy mother's look, 5.01. 29
trim sport for them which had the doing of it. 5.01. 96
that codding spirit had they from their mother, 5.01. 99
wherein i had no stroke of mischief in it? 5.01.110
and when i had it, drew myself apart, | and 5.01.112
when, for his hand, he had his two sons' heads, 5.01.115
ay, that i had not done a thousand more. 5.01.124
well are you fitted, had you but a moor. 5.02. 85
it were convenient you had such a devil. 5.02. 90
now judge what /cause had titus to revenge 5.03.125
for i had then laid wormwood to my dug, ROM 1.03. 26
and yet i warrant it had upon it brow | a bump 1.03. 52
till she had laid it and conjur'd it down. 2.01. 26
had i it written, i would tear the word. 2.02. 57
(marry, she had a better love to berhyme her), 2.04. 40 P
if i had, my weapon should quickly have been out 2.04.158 P
good soul, had as lieve see a toad, a very toad, 2.04.202 P
had she affections and warm youthful blood, 2.05. 12
romeo, | who had but newly entertain'd revenge, 3.01.171
o tybalt, tybalt, the best friend i had! 3.02. 61
death | was woe enough if it had ended there; 3.02.115
that we have had no time to move our daughter. 3.04. 2
o, now i would they had chang'd voices too, 3.05. 32
that god had lent us but this only child, | but 3.05.165
and yourself | had part in this fair maid, now 4.05. 67
looks, | sharp misery had worn him to the bones; 5.01. 41
and if you had the strength | of twenty men, it 5.01. 78
romeo | hath had no notice of these accidents; 5.02. 27
breath, | hath had no power yet upon thy beauty: 5.03. 93
that i had no angry wit to be a lord. TIM 1.01.234 P
you had rather be at a breakfast of enemies than 1.02. 76 P
how had you been my friends else? 1.02. 90 P
joy had the like conception in our eyes, | and 1.02.110
'tis pity bounty had not eyes behind, | that man 1.02.163
would i had a rod in my mouth, that i might 2.02. 76 P
had you not fully laid my state before me, 2.02.125
have rated my expense | as i had leave of means. 2.02.127
that had, give't these fellows | to whom 'tis 2.02.229
yet, had he mistook him and sent to me, i should 3.02. 22 P
not, for the wealth of athens, i had done't now. 3.02. 52 P
carriage, | had his necessity made use of me, 3.02. 82
was above mine, | else surely his had equall'd. 3.04. 32
spent, | as if he had but prov'd an argument. 3.05. 23
if you had sent but two hours before — 3.06. 45 P
thou saw'st them, when i had prosperity. 4.03. 78
i had rather be alone. 4.03.100
myself, | who had the world as my confectionary, 4.03.260
i had rather be a beggar's dog than apemantus. 4.03.356 P
i never had honest men about me, i; 4.03.477
had i a steward | so true, so just, and now so 4.03.490
that you had power and wealth | to requite me by 4.03.521
/phrynia and /timandra had gold of him. 5.01. 5
ere thou hadst power or we had cause of fear, 5.04. 15
have wish'd that noble brutus had his eyes. JC 1.02. 62
i had as lief not be as live to be | in awe of 1.02. 95
he had a fever when he was in spain, | and when 1.02.119
brutus had rather be a villager | than to repute 1.02.172
i should not then ask casca what had chanc'd. 1.02.220
that, to my thinking, he would fain have had it. 1.02.240 P
because caesar refus'd the crown, that it had, 1.02.247 P
and i had been a man of any occupation, if i 1.02.266 P
he said, if he had done or said any thing amiss, 1.02.269 P
if caesar had stabb'd their mothers, they would 1.02.274 P
doth wish | you had but that opinion of yourself 2.01. 92
and what men to–night | have had resort to you; 2.01.276
had you a healthful ear to hear of it. 2.01.319
your best friends shall wish i had been further. 2.02.125
i would have had thee there and here again | ere 2.04. 4
had i as many eyes as thou hast wounds, 3.01.200
had you rather caesar were living, and die all 3.02. 22 P
who, though he had no hand in his death, shall 3.02. 42 P
of the matter, | caesar has had great wrong. 3.02.110
belike they had some notice of the people, | how 3.02.270
notice of the people, | how i had mov'd them. 3.02.271
i had rather be a dog, and bay the moon, | than 4.03. 27
i had rather coin my heart | and drop my blood 4.03. 72
had you your letters from your wife, my lord? 4.03.181
this tongue had not offended so to–day, | if 5.01. 46
i had rather have | such men my friends than 5.04. 28
thy life hath had some smatch of honor in it. 5.05. 46
no sooner justice had, with valor arm'd, MAC 1.02. 29
a sailor's wife had chestnuts in her lap, | and 1.03. 4
would they had stay'd! 1.03. 82
as one that had been studied in his death, | to 1.04. 9
one of my fellows had the speed of him, | who, 1.05. 35
had scarcely more | than would make up his 1.05. 36
heels, and had a purpose | to be his purveyor; 1.06. 21
out, had i so sworn as you | have done to this. 1.07. 58
had he not resembled | my father as he slept, i 2.02. 12
resembled | my father as he slept, i had done't. 2.02. 13
as they had seen me with these hangman's hands. 2.02. 25
i had most need of blessing, and "amen" | stuck 2.02. 29
i had thought to have let in some of all 2.03. 17 P
had i but died an hour before this chance, | i 2.03. 91
this chance, | i had liv'd a blessed time; 2.03. 92
those of his chamber, as it seem'd, had done't. 2.03.101
that had a heart to love, and in that heart 2.03.117
if he had been forgotten, | it had been as a gap 3.01. 11
it had been as a gap in our great feast, | and 3.01. 12
which you thought had been | our innocent self? 3.01. 77
nought's had, all's spent, | where our desire is 3.02. 4
i had else been perfect, | whole as the marble, 3.04. 20
here had we now our country's honor roof'd, 3.04. 39
think | that, had he duncan's sons under his key 3.06. 18
had i three ears, i'ld hear thee. 4.01. 78
what had he done, to make him fly the land? 4.02. 1
he had none; 4.02. 2
shall have more vices than it had before, | more 4.03. 47
nay, had i pow'r, i should | pour the sweet milk 4.03. 97
the old man to have had so much blood in him? 5.01. 40 P
the thane of fife had a wife; 5.01. 42 P
the which no sooner had his prowess confirm'd 5.09. 7
had he his hurts before? 5.09. 12
had i as many sons as i have hairs, | i would 5.09. 14
have you had quiet guard? HAM 1.01. 10
had made his course t' illume that part of 1.01. 37
such was the very armor he had on | when he the 1.01. 60
which had /return'd | to the inheritance of 1.01. 91
of fortinbras, | had he been vanquisher; 1.01. 93
or that the everlasting had not fix'd | his 1.02.131
as if increase of appetite had grown | by what 1.02.144
had left the flushing in her galled eyes, | she 1.02.155
would i had met my dearest foe in heaven | or 1.02.182
foe in heaven | or ever i had seen that day, 1.02.183
two nights together had these gentlemen, 1.02.196
where, as they had delivered, both in time, 1.02.209
i would i had been there. 1.02.234
purport | as if he had been loosed out of hell 2.01. 80
better heed and judgment | i had not coted him. 2.01.109
when i had seen this hot love on the wing — 2.02.132
think, | if i had play'd the desk or table–book, 2.02.136
what a treasure had he, my lord? 2.02.405 P
"but who, ah woe, had seen the mobled queen" — 2.02.502
who this had seen, with tongue in venom steep'd, 2.02.510
had he the motive and /the /cue for passion 2.02.561
that it were better my mother had not borne me: 3.01.123 P
do, i had as live the town–crier spoke my lines. 3.02. 3 P
some of nature's journeymen had made men, and 3.02. 34 P
alack, | i had forgot. 'tis so concluded on. 3.04.201
it had been so with us had we been there. 4.01. 13
it had been so with us had we been there. 4.01. 13
but this gallant | had witchcraft in't, he grew 4.07. 85
as had he been incorps'd and demi–natur'd | with 4.07. 87
of their nation | he swore had neither motion, 4.07.101
how much i had to do to calm his rage! 4.07.192
if this had not been a gentlewoman, she should 5.01. 23 P
into the land, | as if i had never been such." 5.01. 74
that skull had a tongue in it, and could sing 5.01. 75 P
fine revolution, and we had the trick to see't. 5.01. 90 P
dark | grop'd i to find out them, had my desire, 5.02. 14
to my brains, | they had begun the play. 5.02. 31
i had my father's signet in my purse, | which 5.02. 49
must be edified by the margent ere you had done. 5.02.156 P
had i but time — as this fell sergeant, death, 5.02.336
had it th' ability of life to thank you. 5.02.373
stage, | for he was likely, had he been put on, 5.02.397
i thought the king had more affected the duke of LR 1.01. 1 P
whereupon she grew round–womb'd, and had indeed, 1.01. 14 P
for her cradle ere she had a husband for her bed 1.01. 15 P
had he a hand to write this? 1.02. 56 P
i am, had the maidenl'est star in the firmament 1.02.132 P
would i had two coxcombs and two daughters! 1.04.105 P
"fools had ne'er less grace in a year, | for 1.04.166
i had rather be any kind o' thing than a fool, 1.04.185 P
i had thought, by making this well known unto 1.04.205
that /it had it head bit off by it young." 1.04.216
this man hath had good counsel — a hundred 1.04.322
if i had thee in lipsbury pinfold, i would make 2.02. 9 P
though they had been but two years o' th' trade. 2.02. 59 P
goose, /and i had you upon sarum plain, | i'ld 2.02. 83
whose welcome i perceiv'd had poison'd mine — 2.04. 39
i had rather break mine own. 3.04. 5
reserv'd a blanket, else we had been all sham'd. 3.04. 65 P
i had a son, | now outlaw'd from my blood; 3.04.166
sir, what letters had you late from france? 3.07. 42
if wolves had at thy gate howl'd that /dearn 3.07. 63
thee in my touch, | i'ld say i had eyes again. 4.01. 24
and told me i had turn'd the wrong side out. 4.02. 9
madam, i had rather — 4.05. 22
had he been where he thought, | by this had 4.06. 44
he thought, | by this had thought been past. 4.06. 45
he had a thousand noses, | horns welk'd and 4.06. 70
and told me i had the white hairs in my beard 4.06. 97 P
i am only sorry | he had no other deathsman. 4.06.258
had you not been their father, these white 4.07. 29
though he had bit me, should have stood that 4.07. 36
life and wits at once | had not concluded all. 4.07. 41
if e'er your grace had speech with man so poor, 5.01. 38
whose age had charms in it, whose title more, 5.03. 48
have been demanded | ere you had spoke so far. 5.03. 63
on, | you look as you had something more to say. 5.03.202
had i your tongues and eyes, i'ld use them so 5.03.259
who hast had my purse | as if the strings were OTH 1.01. 2
but he, sir, had th' election; 1.01. 27
of whom his eyes had seen the proof | at rhodes, 1.01. 28
o, would you had had her! 1.01.175
o, would you had had her! 1.01.175
i had thought t' have yerk'd him here under the 1.02. 5
since these arms of mine had seven years' pith, 1.03. 83
whereof by parcels she had something heard, 1.03.154
she wish'd she had not heard it, yet she wish'd 1.03.162
wish'd | that heaven had made her such a man. 1.03.163
and bade me, if i had a friend that lov'd her, 1.03.164
she lov'd me for the dangers i had pass'd, | and 1.03.167
i had rather to adopt a child than get it. 1.03.191
if the /beam of our lives had not one scale of 1.03.327 P
h'as had most favorable and happy speed: 2.01. 67
had tongue at will, and yet was never loud, 2.01.149
it had been better you had not kiss'd your three 2.01.172 P
it had been better you had not kiss'd your three 2.01.173 P
if she had been bless'd, she would never have 2.01.252 P
but now | (as if some planet had unwitted men), 2.03.182
and would in action glorious i had lost | those 2.03.186
though he had twinn'd with me, both at a birth, 2.03.212
i had rather have this tongue cut from my mouth 2.03.221
i had thought you had receiv'd some bodily wound 2.03.266 P
i had thought you had receiv'd some bodily wound 2.03.266 P
what had he done to you? 2.03.285 P
i could heartily wish this had not befall'n; 2.03.301 P
had i as many mouths as hydra, such an answer 2.03.304 P
the day had broke | before we parted. 3.01. 32
i did not think he had been acquainted with her. 3.03. 99
of her revolt, | for she had eyes, and chose me. 3.03.189
i had rather be a toad | and live upon the vapor 3.03.270
what sense had i in her stol'n hours of lust? 3.03.338
i had been happy, if the general camp, | pioners 3.03.345
pioners and all, had tasted her sweet body, | so 3.03.346
tasted her sweet body, | so i had nothing known. 3.03.347
o, that the slave had forty thousand lives! 3.03.442
me, i had rather have lost my purse | full of 3.04. 25
that had numb'red in the world | the sun to 3.04. 70
then would to /god that i had never seen't! 3.04. 77
but now i find i had suborn'd the witness, | and 3.04.153
house, | boding to all) he had my handkerchief. 4.01. 22
if i had said i had seen him do you wrong? 4.01. 24
if i had said i had seen him do you wrong? 4.01. 24
he had one yesterday. 4.01. 51
wheresoever you had it, i'll take out no work 4.01.155 P
had it pleas'd heaven | to try me with 4.02. 47
had they rain'd | all kind of sores and shames 4.02. 48
the jewels you have had from me to deliver 4.02.186 P
i would you had never seen him! 4.03. 18
my mother had a maid call'd barbary; 4.03. 26
she had a song of "willow," | an old thing 'twas 4.03. 28
i think i should, and undo't when i had /done't. 4.03. 72 P
that thrust had been mine enemy indeed, | but 5.01. 24
had all his hairs been lives, my great revenge 5.02. 74
my great revenge | had stomach for them all. 5.02. 75
i had forgot thee. 5.02.103
/nay, had she been true, | if heaven would make 5.02.143
this did i fear, but thought he had no weapon; 5.02.360
i had rather heat my liver with drinking. ANT 1.02. 24 P
if every of your wishes had a womb, | and 1.02. 38
but soon that war had end, and the time's state 1.02. 91
would i had never seen her! 1.02.152
you had then left unseen a wonderful piece of 1.02.153 P
women but fulvia, then had you indeed a cut, and 1.02.166 P
would she had never given you leave to come! 1.03. 21
i would i had thy inches, thou shouldst know 1.03. 40
or | /vouchsaf'd to think he had partners. 1.04. 8
i would you had her spirit in such another; 2.02. 62
would we had all such wives, that the men might 2.02. 65 P
three kings i had newly feasted, and did want 2.02. 76
and then when poisoned hours had bound me up 2.02. 90
that truth should be silent i had almost forgot. 2.02.108 P
would we had spoke together! 2.02.164
we had much more monstrous matter of feast, 2.02.181 P
vacancy, | had gone to gaze on cleopatra too, 2.02.217
would i had never come from thence, nor you 2.03. 11 P
if our eyes had authority, here they might take 2.06. 95 P
i had as live have a reede that will do me no 2.07. 12 P
villainy, | in thee't had been good service. 2.07. 75
but i had rather fast from all, four days, 2.07.102
him of letters he had formerly wrote to pompey; 3.05. 10 P
we had not rated him | his part o' th' isle. 3.06. 25
fainted, | longing for what it had not; 3.06. 48
had our general | been what he knew himself, it 3.10. 25
been what he knew himself, it had gone well. 3.10. 26
and no practice had | in the brave squares of 3.11. 39
which had superfluous kings for messengers | not 3.12. 5
spirits | to hear from me you had left antony, 3.13. 70
birthday, | i had thought t' have held it poor; 3.13.185
and chides as he had power | to beat me out of 4.01. 1
thou and those thy scars had once prevail'd | to 4.05. 2
had we done so at first, we had droven them home 4.07. 5
we had droven them home | with clouts about 4.07. 5
i had a wound here that was like a t, | but now 4.07. 7
cause, but as't had been | each man's like mine; 4.08. 6
of mankind, had | destroyed in such a shape. 4.08. 25
had our great palace the capacity | to camp this 4.08. 32
whose heart i thought i had, for she had mine — 4.14. 16
whose heart i thought i had, for she had mine — 4.14. 16
which whilst it was mine had annex'd unto't | a 4.14. 17
she had a prophesying fear | of what hath come 4.14.120
you did suspect | she had dispos'd with caesar, 4.14.123
had i great juno's power, | the strong–wing'd 4.15. 34
had my lips that power, | thus would i wear them 4.15. 39
equal theirs | till they had stol'n our jewel. 4.15. 78
i had rather seel my lips than to my peril 5.02.146
i'll catch thine eyes | though they had wings. 5.02.157
if they had swallow'd poison, 'twould appear 5.02.345
but had his titles by tenantius, whom | he CYM 1.01. 31
and had (besides this gentleman in question) 1.01. 34
he had two sons (if this be worth your hearing, 1.01. 57
that mightst have had the sole son of my queen! 1.01.138
play'd than fought | and had no help of anger. 1.01.163
i would they had not come between us. 1.02. 22 P
till you had measur'd how long a fool you were 1.02. 23 P
would there had been some hurt done! 1.02. 34 P
not so, unless it had been the fall of an ass, 1.02. 36 P
of space had pointed him sharp as my needle; 1.03. 19
nay, followed him till he had melted from | the 1.03. 20
of him, but had | most pretty things to say. 1.03. 25
give him that parting kiss which i had set 1.03. 34
of his endowments had been tabled by his side, 1.04. 6 P
we had very many there could behold the sun with 1.04. 11 P
it had been pity you should have been put 1.04. 39 P
had been something too fair and too good for any 1.04. 71 P
even to the yielding, had i admittance, and 1.04.105 P

would i had put my estate and my neighbor's on 1.04.123 P
had i been thief–stol'n, | as my two brothers, 1.06. 5
had i this cheek | to bathe my lips upon; 1.06. 99
i had almost forgot | t' entreat your grace but 1.06.180
was there ever man had such luck? 2.01. 1 P
i had a hundred pound on't; 2.01. 2 P
if his wit had been like him that broke it, it 2.01. 8 P
would he had been one of my rank! 2.01. 15 P
i had rather not be so noble as i am. 2.01. 18 P
which i had rather | you felt than make't my 2.03.110
had i not brought | the knowledge of your 2.04. 50
you had of her pure honor gains or loses | your 2.04. 59
but profess | had that was well worth watching), 2.04. 68
her andirons | (i had forgot them) were two 2.04. 89
by jupiter, i had it from her arm. 2.04.121
o, that i had her here, to tear her limb–meal! 2.04.147
which then they had to take from 's, to resume 3.01. 15
here is a box, i had it from the queen, | what's 3.04.188
would i had wings to follow it! 3.05.155 P
though i had found | gold strew'd i' th' floor. 3.06. 48
it on the board so soon | as i had made my meal, 3.06. 51
fault, i should | have died had i not made it. 3.06. 57
would it had been so, that they | had been my 3.06. 75
that they | had been my father's sons, then had 3.06. 76
my father's sons, then had my prize | been less, 3.06. 76
that had a court no bigger than this cave, 3.06. 82
that did attend themselves and had the virtue 3.06. 83
appears he hath had | good ancestors. 4.02. 47
as juno had been sick | and he her dieter. 4.02. 50
he had not apprehension | of roaring terrors; 4.02.110
have knock'd out his brains, for he had none. 4.02.115
this, the fool had borne | my head as i do his. 4.02.116
i had no mind | to hunt this day; 4.02.147
would i had done't! 4.02.156
but yields a crop | as if it had been sow'd. 4.02.181
i had rather | have skipp'd from sixteen years 4.02.198
thus smiling, as some fly had tickled slumber, 4.02.210
horse, save one that had | a rider like myself, 4.04. 38
my faults, i never | had liv'd to put on this; 5.01. 9
so had you saved | the noble imogen to repent, 5.01. 9
who had not now been drooping here, if seconds 5.03. 90
drooping here, if seconds | had answer'd him. 5.03. 91
since he had rather | groan so in perpetuity 5.04. 5
prevented it, she had | ta'en off by poison. 5.05. 46
she did confess she had | for you a mortal 5.05. 49
time | (when she had fitted you with her craft), 5.05. 55
it had been vicious | to have mistrusted her; 5.05. 65
had it gone with us, | we should not, when the 5.05. 76
never master had | a page so kind, so duteous, 5.05. 85
gentleman may render | of whom he had this ring. 5.05.136
i had rather thou shouldst live while nature 5.05.151
o, would | our viands had been poison'd, or at 5.05.156
lord in love and one | that had a royal lover, 5.05.172
he spake of her, as dian had hot dreams, | and 5.05.180
so, had it been a carbuncle | of phoebus' wheel; 5.05.189
safely, had it | been all the worth of 's car. 5.05.190
i had it from the queen. 5.05.242
youth, i blame ye not, | you had a motive for't. 5.05.268
accident | i had a feigned letter of my master's 5.05.279
that headless man | i thought had been my lord. 5.05.300
than a band of clotens | had ever scar for. 5.05.305
guiderius had | upon his neck a mole, a sanguine 5.05.363
i had you down and might | have made you finish. 5.05.411
of face | as heaven had lent her all his grace; PER 1.ch. 24
heaven, that i had thy head! 1.01.109
from whence we had our being and our birth. 1.02.114
the care i had and have of subjects' good | on 1.02.118
was a wise fellow and had good discretion that, 1.03. 4 P
now do i see he had some reason for't; 1.03. 7 P
and doubting lest he had err'd or sinn'd, | to 1.03. 21
master, if i had been the sexton, i would have 2.01. 36 P
me too, and when i had been in his belly, i 2.01. 40 P
you'll remember from whence you had them. 2.01.152 P
he had need mean better than his outward show 2.02. 48
had princes sit like stars about his throne, 2.03. 39
had not a show might countervail his worth. 2.03. 56
withhold the vengeance that they had in store, 2.04. 4
to bar heaven's shaft, but sin had his reward. 2.04. 15
sir, say if you had, who takes offense | at that 2.05. 71
who, if it had conceit, would die, as i | am 3.01. 16
for a more blusterous birth had never babe. 3.01. 28
a terrible child–bed hast thou had, my dear, 3.01. 56
of an egyptian | that had nine hours lien dead, 3.02. 85
that the strict fates had pleas'd you had 3.03. 8
fates had pleas'd you had brought her hither 3.03. 8
had not o'erboard thrown me | for to seek my 4.02. 66
well, if we had of every nation a traveller, we 4.02.113 P
i had rather than twice the worth of her she had 4.06. 1 P
twice the worth of her she had ne'er come here. 4.06. 2 P
and she were a rose indeed, if she had but — 4.06. 35 P
had i brought hither a corrupted mind, | thy 4.06.104
a corrupted mind, | thy speech had altered it. 4.06.105
would she had never come within my doors. 4.06.148 P
name | was given me by one that had some power, 5.01.148
but in no wise | till he had done his sacrifice, 5.02. 12
when fame | had spread his cursed deed, the 5.03. 96
more power on him | than ever he had on thee, TNK 1.01. 88
i had as lief trace this good action with you 1.01.102
ingots, | which, though he won, he had not; 1.02. 18
she would long | till she had such another, and 1.03. 69
had mine ear | stol'n some new air, or at 1.03. 74
had they been taken | when their last hurts were 1.04. 25
but forty thousand fold we had rather have 'em 1.04. 36
they would have look'd had they been victors, 2.01. 32 P
what had we been, old in the court of creon, 2.02.105
had not the loving gods found this place for us, 2.02.108
we had died as they do, ill old men, unwept, 2.02.109
and had their epitaphs, the people's curses. 2.02.110
but say that one | had rather combat me? 2.02.197
false–self and thy friend had but this fortune 2.02.207
good light, | had i a sword, i would kill thee. 2.02.265
and yet he had a cousin, fair as he too; 2.04. 16
had i a sword, | and these house–clogs away — 3.01. 42
the wolves would jaw me, so | he had this file. 3.02. 8
the marshal's sister | had her share too, as i 3.03. 37
and i could wish i had not said i lov'd her, 3.06. 40
i had not said i lov'd her, | though i had died; 3.06. 41
up, and under me | i had a right good horse. 3.06. 77
you had indeed, | a bright bay, i remember. 3.06. 77
scorn us, | and say we had a noble difference, 3.06.116
they prevail'd, had their suits fairly granted: 4.01. 27
rushes and the reeds | had so encompass'd it. 4.01. 62
y' had best look to her, | for, if she see him 4.01.123
i'll warrant ye he had not so few last night 4.01.137
and had in her | the coy denials of young maids, 4.02. 10
an eye as heavy | as if he had lost his mother; 4.02. 28
for, if my brother but even now had ask'd me 4.02. 47
me | whether i lov'd, i had run mad for arcite; 4.02. 48
i had rather both, | so neither for my sake 4.02. 68
in great hope she had fix'd her liking on this 4.03. 64 P
and would account i had a great penn'worth on't 4.03. 66 P
none — would not, | had i kenn'd all that were. 5.01.100
and have hotly ask'd them | if they had mothers; 5.01.106
i had one, a woman, | and women 'twere they 5.01.106
aged cramp | had screw'd his square foot round, 5.01.111
the gout had knit his fingers into knots, 5.01.112
his globy eyes | had almost drawn their spheres, 5.01.114
this anatomy | had by his young fair fere a boy, 5.01.116
twenty times had been far better, | for there 5.02. 7
i had rather see a wren hawk at a fly | than 5.03. 2
i had no end in't else; 5.03. 75
palamon | had the best–boding chance. 5.03. 77
they said that palamon had arcite's body 5.03. 79
had there such fellows liv'd when you were babes STM II.C 63
till now grown up | had been ta'en from you, and II.C 66
of your opinions cloth'd, | what had you got? II.C 80
you had taught | how insolence and strong hand II.C 80
had ta'en his last leave of the weeping morn, VEN 2
for where they lay the shadow had forsook them, 176
them, | wishing adonis had his team to guide, 179
o, had thy mother borne so hard a mind, | she 203
she had not brought forth thee, but died unkind. 204
his eyes saw her eyes as they had not seen them, 357
and all this dumb play had his acts made plain 359
o, would thou hadst not, or i had no hearing! 428
i had my load before, now press'd with bearing: 430
"had i no eyes but ears, my ears would love 433
had not his clouded with his brow's repine; 490
but for thy piteous lips no more had seen. 504
when he did frown, o, had she then gave over, 571
such nectar from his lips she had not suck'd. 572
"hadst thou but bid beware, then he had spoke, 943
and, hearing him, thy power had lost his power. 944
upon the wide wound that the boar had trench'd 1052
if he had spoke, the wolf would leave his prey, 1097
"had i been tooth'd like him, i must confess, 1117
what priceless wealth the heavens had him lent LUC 17
when heavy sleep had clos'd up mortal eyes. 163
sin | to wish that i their father had not been. 210
"had collatinus kill'd my son or sire, | or lain 232
that had narcissus seen her as she stood, 265
self–love had never drown'd him in the flood. 266
o, had they in that darksome prison died, | then 379
then had they seen the period of their ill! 380
eyes like marigolds had sheath'd their light, 397
back, | for it had been dishonor to disdain him. 844
lamenting philomele had ended | the well–tun'd 1079
this plot of death when sadly she had laid, 1212
ere she with blood had stain'd her stain'd 1316
such sweet observance in this work was had, 1385
in her the painter had anatomiz'd | time's ruin, 1450
the spring that those shrunk pipes had fed, 1455
had doting priam check'd his son's desire, 1490
troy had been bright with fame, and not with 1491
(as if with grief or travail he had fainted), 1543
that my poor beauty had purloin'd his eyes, 1651
when they had sworn to this advised doom, | they 1849
scarce had the sun dried up the dewy morn, | and PP 6. 1
for his approach that often there had been. 6. 8
ah, that i had my lady at this bay: 11.13
"had women been so strong as men, | in faith, 18.35
as men, | in faith, you had not had it then." 18.36
as men, | in faith, you had not had it then." 18.36
as love in twain | had the essence but in one, PHT 26
you know | you had a father, let your son say so SON 13.14
"had my friend's muse grown with this growing 32.10
a dearer birth than this his love had brought 32.11
being had, to triumph, being lack'd, to hope. 52.14
to show what wealth she had | in days long since 67.13
save what is had or must from you be took. 75.12
aid, | my verse alone had all thy gentle grace, 79. 2
thus have i had thee as a dream doth flatter: 87.13
and buds of marjerom had stol'n thy hair; 99. 7
a third, nor red nor white, had stol'n of both, 99.10
and to his robb'ry had annex'd thy breath, | but 99.11
but sweet or color it had stol'n from thee. 99.15
they had not still enough your worth to sing: 106.12
past reason hunted, and no sooner had, | past 129. 6
had, having, and in quest to have, extreme, | a 129.10
which many legions of true hearts had warm'd, 154. 6
time had not scythed all that youth begun, | nor LC 12
eyne, | which on it had conceited characters, 16
brine | that seasoned woe had pelleted in tears, 18
of folded schedules had she many a one, | which 43
of city, and had let go by | the swiftest hours, 59
myself, if i had self–applied | love to myself, 76
weep, | he had the dialect and different skill, 125
"'my parts had pow'r to charm a sacred /nun, 260

HADE 1 FR 0.0001 REL FR 0 V 1 P
sir, shall we sow the hade land with wheat? 2H4 5.01. 14 P

HADST 107 FR 0.0121 REL FR 81 V 26 P
thou hadst; TMP 1.02. 48
rock, | who hadst deserv'd more than a prison. 1.02.362
thou nothing bated | in what thou hadst to say; 3.03. 86
fan, i took't upon mine honor thou hadst it not. WIV 2.02. 13 P
hadst thou not fifteen pence? 2.02. 14
o boy, thou hadst a father! 3.04. 37 P
hadst thou not order? MM 2.02. 8
i would thou hadst done so by claudio. 5.01.468
where is the thousand marks thou hadst of me? ERR 1.02. 81
if thou hadst been dromio to–day in my place, 3.01. 46
the man | that hadst a wife once call'd aemilia, 5.01.343
what a hero hadst thou been, | if half thy ADO 4.01.100
i said thou hadst a fine wit. 5.01.160 P
berowne, read it over. where hadst thou it? LLL 4.03.193
where hadst thou it? 4.03.194
thou call'dst me dog before thou hadst a cause, MV 3.03. 6
my father, so thou hadst been still with me, i AYL 1.02. 11 P
i would thou hadst been son to some man else: 1.02.224
deed | hadst thou descended from another house. 1.02.228
i would thou hadst told me of another father. 1.02.230
but hadst thou not cross'd me, thou shouldst SHR 4.01. 72 P
hadst thou not the privilege of antiquity upon AWW 2.03.209 P
thou tell'st me where thou hadst this ring, 5.03.283
then hadst thou had an excellent head of hair. TN 1.03. 95 P
hadst it? 2.03. 25 P
thou hadst need send for more money. 2.03.182 P
whether hadst thou rather be a faulconbridge, JN 1.01.134
if thou hadst said him nay, it had been sin. 1.01.275
wish him dead, but thou hadst none to kill him. 4.02.206
hadst not thou been by, | a fellow by the hand 4.02.220
hadst thou but shook thy head or made a pause 4.02.231
hadst thou groan'd for him | as i have done, R2 5.02.102
thou hadst fire and sword on thy side, and yet 1H4 2.04.316 P
what instinct hadst thou for it? 2.04.318 P
i did not think thou hadst been an ignis fatuus 3.03. 39 P
o douglas, hadst thou fought at holmedon thus, 5.03. 14
if like a christian thou hadst truly borne 5.05. 9
that thou hadst seen that that this knight and i 2H4 3.02.211 P
thou wert better thou hadst strook thy mother, 5.04. 10 P
thou never hadst renown, nor canst not lose it. 1H6 4.05. 40
hadst thou been his mother, thou couldst have 2H6 2.01. 79
if thou hadst been born blind, | thou mightst as 2.01.124
thy fortune, york, hadst thou been regent there, 3.01.305
thyself as if thou hadst been in thine own 4.03. 4 P
hadst thou but lov'd him half so well as i, | or 3H6 1.01.220
hadst thou been meek, our title still had slept, 2.02.160
hadst thou never given consent | that phaeton 2.06. 11
henry, hadst thou sway'd as kings should do, 2.06. 14
and thou this day hadst kept thy chair in peace. 2.06. 20
than if thou never hadst deserv'd our hate. 5.01.104
hadst thou been kill'd when first thou didst 5.06. 35
thou hadst not liv'd to kill a son of mine. 5.06. 36
teeth hadst thou in thy head when thou wast born 5.06. 53
thou hadst but power over his mortal body, | his R3 1.02. 47
that thou hadst call'd me all these bitter names 1.03.235
i thought thou hadst been resolute. 1.04.113 P
thou hadst an edward, till a richard kill'd him; 4.04. 42
thou hadst a richard, till a richard kill'd him. 4.04. 43
thou hadst a clarence too, and richard kill'd 4.04. 46
king my husband made | thou hadst not broken, 4.04.380
if thou hadst fear'd to break an oath by him, 4.04.381
would thou hadst ne'er been born! TRO 4.02. 85 P
hadst thou beheld — COR 1.09. 13
although i know thou hadst rather | follow thine 3.02. 90
hadst thou foxship | to banish him that strook 4.02. 18
even at thy teat thou hadst thy tyranny; TIT 2.03.145
hadst thou in person ne'er offended me, | even 2.03.161
if thou hadst hands to help thee knit the cord. 2.04. 10
if thou hadst, thou hadst been poor–john. ROM 1.01. 30 P
if thou hadst, thou hadst been poor–john. 1.01. 31 P
i would say thou hadst suck'd wisdom from thy 1.03. 68
i would thou hadst my bones, and i thy news. 2.05. 27
what hadst thou to do in hell | when thou didst 3.02. 80
hadst thou no poison mix'd, no sharp–ground 3.03. 44
hadst thou wealth again, | rascals should have't TIM 4.03.217
hadst thou like us from our first swath 4.03.252
if thou hadst not been born the worst of men, 4.03.275
of men, | thou hadst been a knave and flatterer. 4.03.276
and th' hadst hated meddlers sooner, thou 4.03.309 P
thou hadst some means to keep a dog. 4.03.316 P
ere thou hadst power or we had cause of fear, 5.04. 15
would thou hadst less deserv'd, | that the MAC 1.04. 18
if th' hadst rather hear it from our mouths, 4.01. 62
judge of israel, what a treasure hadst thou! HAM 2.02.404 P
sun, | and thou hadst not come to my bed.'" 4.05. 66
hadst thou thy wits and didst persuade revenge, 4.05.169
hadst not been born than not t' have pleas'd me LR 1.01.234
thou hadst little wit in thy bald crown when 1.04.162 P
fellow when thou hadst no need to care for her 1.04.191 P
not have been old till thou hadst been wise. 1.05. 45 P
and thou hadst been set i' th' stocks for that 2.04. 64 P
hadst thou been aught but goss'mer, feathers, 4.06. 49
as if thou then hadst shut up in thy brain OTH 3.03.114
thou hadst been better have been born a dog 3.03.362
aches at thee, would thou hadst never been born! 4.02. 69
the blow thou hadst | shall make thy peace for ANT 2.05. 69
hadst thou narcissus in thy face, to me | thou 2.05. 96
hadst thou done so, | the kings that have 4.05. 3
would, polydore, thou hadst not done't! CYM 4.02.155
thou hadst, great king, a subject who | was 5.05.316
if thou hadst drunk to him, 't 'ad been a PER 4.03. 11
thou hadst been toss'd from wrong to injury, 5.01.130
o, would thou hadst not, or i had no hearing! VEN 428
"thou hadst been gone," quoth she, "sweet boy, 613
"hadst thou but bid beware, then he had spoke, 943
what hast thou then more than thou hadst before? SON 40. 2
all mine was thine, before thou hadst this more. 40. 4

HAD'T 1 FR 0.0001 REL FR 1 V 0 P
o, had't been a stranger, not my child, | to R2 1.03.239

HAEC 1 FR 0.0001 REL FR 0 V 1 P
singulariter, nominativo, hic, haec, hoc. WIV 4.01. 41 P

HAG* *(also hac)*

HAG* 8 FR 0.0009 REL FR 6 V 2 P
this blue–ey'd hag was hither brought with child TMP 1.02.269
nominativo, hig, hag, hog; WIV 4.01. 42 P
come down, you witch, you hag you, come down, i 4.02.179 P
a gross hag! WT 2.03.108
foul fiend of france, and hag of all despite, 1H6 3.02. 52
fell banning hag, enchantress, hold thy tongue! 5.03. 42
have done thy charm, thou hateful with'red hag. R3 1.03.214
this is the hag, when maids lie on their backs, ROM 1.04. 92

HAGAR'S 1 FR 0.0001 REL FR 1 V 0 P
what says that fool of hagar's offspring, ha? MV 2.05. 44

HAG–BORN 1 FR 0.0001 REL FR 1 V 0 P
a freckled whelp, hag–born) not honor'd with | a TMP 1.02.283

HAGGARD 4 FR 0.0004 REL FR 4 V 0 P
another way i have to man my haggard, | to make SHR 4.01.193
as i have lov'd this proud disdainful haggard. 4.02. 39
and, like the haggard, check at every feather TN 3.01. 64
if i do prove her haggard, | though that her OTH 3.03.260

HAGGARDS 1 FR 0.0001 REL FR 1 V 0 P
are as coy and wild | as haggards of the rock. ADO 3.01. 36

HAGGISH 1 FR 0.0001 REL FR 1 V 0 P
long, | but on us both did haggish age steal on, AWW 1.02. 29
HAGGLED 1 FR 0.0001 REL FR 1 V 0 P
suffolk first died, and york, all haggled over, H5 4.06. 11
HAGS 4 FR 0.0004 REL FR 4 V 0 P
and wedded be thou to the hags of hell, | for 2H6 4.01. 79
how now, you secret, black, and midnight hags? MAC 4.01. 48
filthy hags, | why do you show me this? 4.01.115
no, you unnatural hags, | i will have such LR 2.04.278
HAG–SEED 1 FR 0.0001 REL FR 1 V 0 P
hag–seed, hence! TMP 1.02.365
HAH *(also ha)*
HAH 14 FR 0.0015 REL FR 11 V 3 P
hah, it may be i go under that title because i ADO 2.01.205 P
hah! 2.03. 35 P
hah! what say'st thou, silvius? AYL 3.05. 83
hah! R3 1.02.238
hah? what is that? COR 3.01. 25
hah, let me see her. ROM 4.05. 25
hah! MAC 2.02. 56
hah, 'swounds, i should take it; HAM 2.02.576
hah, ha, he wears cruel garters. LR 2.04. 7 P
hah? i like not that. OTH 3.03. 35
hah? 3.03.303
hah, no more moving? 5.02. 93
hah? 5.02.158
hah? | no harm, i trust, is done? CYM 1.01.160
/HAIL* 1 FR 0.0001 REL FR 1 V 0 P
/did /they /not /sometimes /cry "/all /hail!" R2 4.01.169
HAIL* 75 FR 0.0084 REL FR 73 V 2 P
all hail, great master, grave sir, hail! TMP 1.02.189
all hail, great master, grave sir, hail! 1.02.189
hail, many–colored messenger, that ne'er | dost 4.01. 76
tune of "green–sleeves," hail kissing–comfits, WIV 5.05. 20 P
hail, virgin, if you be, as those cheek–roses MM 1.04. 16
hail to you, provost! so i think you are. 2.03. 1
"all hail, the richest beauties on the earth!" LLL 5.02.158
all hail, sweet madam, and fair time of day! 5.02.339
"fair" in "all hail" is foul, as i conceive. 5.02.340
and when this hail some heat from hermia felt, MND 1.01.244
hail, mortal! 3.01.175
hail! 3.01.176
hail! 3.01.177
hail! 3.01.178
for thou mayst see a sunshine and a hail | in me AWW 5.03. 33
hail, most royal sir! WT 1.02.366
hail, you anointed deputies of heaven! JN 3.01.136
hail, noble prince of france! 5.02. 68
hail, royal prince! R2 5.05. 67
all hail, my lords! 1H6 2.02. 34
judas kiss'd his master, | and cried "all hail!" 3H6 5.07. 34
hail, all the state of greece! TRO 4.05. 65
hail, noble martius! COR 1.01.163
my gracious silence, hail! 2.01.175
hail, sir! 4.06. 12
hail to you both! 4.06. 12
hail, lords! 5.06. 70
hail, rome, victorious in thy mourning weeds! TIT 1.01. 70
lucius, all hail, rome's royal emperor! 5.03.141
lucius, all hail, rome's gracious governor! 5.03.146
hail to thee, worthy timon, and to all | that of TIM 1.02.122
hail, worthy timon! 5.01. 55
caesar, all hail! JC 2.02. 58
hail, caesar! read this schedule. 3.01. 3
hail, caesar!" 5.01. 32
hail, brave friend! MAC 1.02. 5
all hail, macbeth, hail to thee, thane of glamis 1.03. 48
hail, macbeth, hail to thee, thane of glamis! 1.03. 48
all hail, macbeth, hail to thee, thane of cawdor 1.03. 49
hail, macbeth, hail to thee, thane of cawdor! 1.03. 49
all hail, macbeth, that shalt be king hereafter! 1.03. 50
hail! 1.03. 62
hail! 1.03. 63
hail! 1.03. 64
so all hail, macbeth and banquo! 1.03. 68
banquo and macbeth, all hail! 1.03. 69
and in which addition, hail, most worthy thane, 1.03.106
referr'd me to the coming on of time with 'hail, 1.05. 9 P
hail, king! 5.09. 20
hail, king of scotland! 5.09. 25
hail, king of scotland! 5.09. 25
hail to your lordship! HAM 1.02.160
hail to thee, noble master! LR 2.04. 4
hail to your grace! 2.04.127
hail, gentle sir. 4.06.208
hail to thee, lady! OTH 2.01. 85
sovereign of egypt, hail! ANT 1.05. 34
of gold, and hail | rich pearls upon thee. 2.05. 45
hail, caesar, and my lord! 3.06. 39
hail, most dear caesar! 3.06. 39
from my cold heart let heaven engender hail, 3.13.159
hail, thou fair heaven! CYM 3.03. 7
hail, heaven! 3.03. 9
hail, heaven! 3.03. 9
hail, great king! 5.05. 25
hail, reverent sir! the gods preserve you! PER 5.01. 14
sir king, all hail! 5.01. 39
hail, royal sir! 5.01. 40
hail, sir! my lord, lend ear. 5.01. 82
hail, dian! 5.03. 1
hail, madam, and my queen! 5.03. 49
thou doughty duke, all hail! TNK 3.05.100
all hail, sweet ladies! 3.05.100
hail, sovereign queen of secrets, who hast power 5.01. 77
could scape the hail of his all–hurting aim, LC 310
HAIL'D* 4 FR 0.0004 REL FR 4 V 0 P
he hail'd down oaths that he was only mine; MND 1.01.243
they hail'd him father to a line of kings. MAC 3.01. 59
"well hail'd, well hail'd, you jolly gallants! TNK 3.05. 63
"well hail'd, well hail'd, you jolly gallants! 3.05. 63
HAILSTONE 1 FR 0.0001 REL FR 1 V 0 P
of fire upon the ice, | or hailstone in the sun. COR 1.01.174
HAILSTONES 1 FR 0.0001 REL FR 1 V 0 P
rogues, hence, avaunt, vanish like hailstones; WIV 1.03. 81
/HAIR 1 FR 0.0001 REL FR 1 V 0 P
might change or cease, /tears /his /white /hair, LR 3.01. 7
HAIR 119 FR 0.0134 REL FR 67 V 52 P
not so much perdition as an hair | betid to any TMP 1.02. 30
with hair up–staring (then like reeds, not hair) 1.02.213
hair up–staring (then like reeds, not hair), 1.02.213
not a hair perish'd; 1.02.217
you are like to lose your hair, and prove a bald 4.01.237 P
why then your ladyship must cut your hair. TGV 2.07. 44
there's not a hair on 's head but 'tis a 3.01.191 P
"item, she hath more hair than wit, and more 3.01.353 P
"item, she hath more hair than wit" — 3.01.358 P
more hair than wit? 3.01.359 P
the hair that covers the wit is more than the 3.01.361 P
her hair is auburn, mine is perfect yellow: 4.04.189
she has brown hair, and speaks small like a WIV 1.01. 47 P
you go against the hair of your professions. 2.03. 40 P
for a man to recover his hair that grows bald by ERR 2.02. 73 P
and recover the lost hair of another man. 2.02. 76 P
why is time such a niggard of hair, being, as it 2.02. 77 P
hath scanted /men in hair he hath given them in 2.02. 80 P
but there's many a man hath more hair than wit. 2.02. 83 P
of those but he hath the wit to lose his hair. 2.02. 85 P
/e'en no time to recover hair lost by nature. 2.02.103 P
a rush, a hair, a drop of blood, a pin, | a nut, 4.03. 72
great pails of puddled mire to quench the hair; 5.01.173
fetch you a hair off the great cham's beard, do ADO 2.01.268 P
and her hair shall be of what color it please 2.03. 34 P
sobs, beats her heart, tears her hair, prays, 2.03.147 P
excellently, if the hair were a thought browner; 3.04. 14 P
it mourns that painting /and usurping hair LLL 4.03.255
as bright apollo's lute, strung with his hair. 4.03.340
cutting a smaller hair than may be seen; 5.02.258
of her fantasy | with bracelets of thy hair, MND 1.01. 33
some of your french crowns have no hair at all; 1.02. 97 P
or bear, | pard, or boar with bristled hair, 2.02. 31
such a tender ass, if my hair do but tickle me, 4.01. 25 P
would you desire lime and hair to speak better? 5.01.165 P
stones with lime and hair knit /up /in /thee. 5.01.191
thou hast got more hair on thy chin than dobbin MV 2.02. 94 P
i am sure he had more hair of his tail than i 2.02. 97 P
shall lose a hair through bassanio's fault. 3.02.302
scale do turn | but in the estimation of a hair, 4.01.331
clerk will ne'er wear hair on 's face that had 5.01.158
his very hair is of the dissembling color. AYL 3.04. 7 P
i' faith, his hair is of a good color. 3.04. 10 P
'tis not your inky brows, your black silk hair, 3.05. 46
he said mine eyes were black and my hair black, 3.05.130
a wretched ragged man, o'ergrown with hair, 4.03.106
and not presume to touch a hair of my master's SHR 4.01. 93 P
and ev'ry hair that's on't, helen, that's dead, AWW 5.03. 77
then hadst thou had an excellent head of hair. TN 1.03. 96 P
why, would that have mended my hair? 1.03. 97 P
in his next commodity of hair, send thee a beard 3.01. 44 P
so that there be not | too much hair there, but WT 2.01. 10
that have made themselves all men of hair. 4.04.326 P
this hair i tear is mine, | my name is constance JN 3.04. 45
a grain, a dust, a gnat, a wandering hair, | any 4.01. 92
are turned to one thread, one little hair. 5.07. 54
geese, i'll never wear hair on my face more. 1H4 2.04.139 P
ye me, | i'll cavil on the ninth part of a hair. 3.01.138
the /tithe of a hair was never lost in my house 3.03. 58 P
bardolph was shav'd and lost many a hair, and 3.03. 60 P
the quality and hair of our attempt | brooks no 4.01. 61
it when he will, 'tis not a hair amiss yet. 2H4 1.02. 24 P
there is not a white hair in your face but 1.02.160 P
i perceiv'd the first white hair of my chin. 1.02.242 P
the weight of a hair will turn scales between 2.04.254 P
chin is but enrich'd | with one appearing hair, H5 3.pr. 23
thee, constable, my mistress wears his own hair. 3.07. 61 P
like prisoners wildly overgrown with hair, | put 5.02. 43
his hair uprear'd, his nostrils stretch'd with 2H6 3.02.171
look, on the sheets his hair, you see, is 3.02.174
mine hair be fix'd an end, as one distract; 3.02.318
comb down his hair; 3.03. 15
old salisbury, shame to thy silver hair, | thou 5.01.162
this hand, fast wound about thy coal–black hair, 3H6 5.01. 54
my hair doth stand an end to hear her curses. R3 1.03.303
an angel, with bright hair | dabbled in blood, 1.04. 53
bound together) | weigh'd not a hair of his. H8 3.02.259
and her hair were not somewhat darker than TRO 1.01. 41 P
the open ulcer of my heart | her eyes, her hair, 1.01. 54
without cause, and merry against the hair; 1.02. 27 P
takes upon her to spy a white hair on his chin. 1.02.139 P
at the white hair that helen spied on troilus' 1.02.150 P
and't had been a green hair, i should have 1.02.152 P
not so much at the hair as at his pretty answer. 1.02.154 P
that white hair is my father, and all the rest 1.02.162 P
to a hair. 3.01.144 P
if i be false, or swerve a hair from truth, 3.02.184
tear my bright hair and scratch my praised 4.02.107
see him pluck aufidius down by th' hair; COR 1.03. 30
and not a hair upon a soldier's head | which 4.06.133
my fleece of woolly hair that now uncurls, TIT 2.03. 34
rent off thy silver hair, thy other hand 3.01.260
go drag the villain hither by the hair, | nor 4.04. 56
desirest me to stop in my tale against the hair. ROM 2.04. 96 P
a man that hath a hair more or a hair less in 3.01. 17 P
hath a hair more or a hair less in his beard 3.01. 18 P
thou speak, then mightst thou tear thy hair, 3.03. 68
yea, beg a hair of him for memory, | and, dying, JC 3.02.134
that mak'st my blood cold, and my hair to stare? 4.03.280
whose horrid image doth unfix my hair | and make MAC 1.03.135
and thy hair, | thou other gold–bound brow, is 4.01.113
and my fell of hair | would at a dismal treatise 5.05. 11
and each particular hair to stand an end, | like HAM 1.05. 19
your bedded hair, like life in excrements, 3.04.121
that curl'd my hair; LR 3.04. 86 P
which, like the courser's hair, hath yet but ANT 1.02.193
let him not leave out | the color of her hair. 2.05.114
her hair, what color? 3.03. 32
/unscissor'd shall this hair of mine remain, PER 3.03. 29
you the marks of her, the color of her hair, 4.02. 58 P
for me, a hair shall never fall of these men. TNK 3.06.287
his hair hangs long behind him, black and 4.02. 83
or like a nymph, with long dishevelled hair, VEN 147
her hair like golden threads play'd with her LUC 400
"let him have time to tear his curled hair, 981
make thy sad grove in my dishevell'd hair; 1129
and buds of marjerom had stol'n thy hair; SON 99. 7
her hair, nor loose nor tied in formal plat, LC 29
"'and lo behold these talents of their hair, 204
HAIR–BREADTH 1 FR 0.0001 REL FR 1 V 0 P
of hair–breadth scapes i' th' imminent deadly OTH 1.03.136
HAIRLESS 2 FR 0.0002 REL FR 2 V 0 P
have arm'd their thin and hairless scalps R2 3.02.112
whose beams upon his hairless face are fix'd, VEN 487
HAIR'S 1 FR 0.0001 REL FR 0 V 1 P
and i profess requital to a hair's breadth, not WIV 4.02. 3 P
HAIRS 35 FR 0.0039 REL FR 24 V 11 P
and more faults than hairs, and more wealth than TGV 3.01.354 P
"and more faults than hairs" — 3.01.364 P
spread o'er the silver waves thy golden hairs, ERR 3.02. 48
and, with grey hairs and bruise of many days, ADO 5.01. 65
her amber hairs for foul hath amber coted. LLL 4.03. 85
one, her hairs were gold, crystal the other's 4.03.140
superfluity comes sooner by white hairs, but MV 1.02. 9 P
here in her hairs | the painter plays the spider 3.02.120
note | in the fair multitude of those her hairs! JN 3.04. 62
bind up your hairs. 3.04. 68
as they have given these hairs their liberty!" 3.04. 72
more the pity, his white hairs do witness it, 1H4 2.04.468 P
how ill white hairs becomes a fool and jester! 2H4 5.05. 48
from the earth, as if his entrails were hairs; H5 3.07. 14 P
would bring white hairs unto a quiet grave. 3H6 2.05. 40
has not past three or four hairs on his chin — TRO 1.02.112 P
"here's but two and fifty hairs on your chin — 1.02.157 P
"two and fifty hairs," quoth he, "and one white. 1.02.161 P
she, "which of these hairs is paris my husband?" 1.02.163 P
and bakes the /elf–locks in foul sluttish hairs, ROM 1.04. 90
for his silver hairs | will purchase us a good JC 2.01.144
had i as many sons as i have hairs, | i would MAC 5.09. 14
blanket my loins, elf all my hairs in knots, LR 2.03. 10
these hairs which thou dost ravish from my chin 3.07. 38
me i had the white hairs in my beard ere the 4.06. 98 P
had all his hairs been lives, my great revenge OTH 5.02. 74
drown'd, | with thy grapes our hairs be crown'd! ANT 2.07.116
my very hairs do mutiny; 3.11. 13
in my respect than all the hairs above thee, CYM 2.03.135
cried her almost to the number of her hairs, i PER 4.02. 95 P
never to wash his face, nor cut his hairs; 4.04. 28
then with her windy sighs and golden hairs | to VEN 51
i'll make a shadow for thee of my hairs; 191
fanning the hairs, who wave like feath'red wings 306
if hairs be wires, black wires grow on her head. SON 130. 4
HAIR–WORTH 1 FR 0.0001 REL FR 1 V 0 P
owing | not a hair–worth of white, which some TNK 5.04. 51
HAIRY 6 FR 0.0006 REL FR 3 V 3 P
why, thou didst conclude hairy men plain dealers ERR 2.02. 86 P
methinks i am marvail's hairy about the face; MND 4.01. 24 P
for she his hairy temples then had rounded 4.01. 51
and thus the hairy fool, | much marked of the AYL 2.01. 40
you are rough and hairy. WT 4.04.722 P
"his brawny sides, with hairy bristles armed, VEN 625
HAL 42 FR 0.0047 REL FR 2 V 40 P
now, hal, what time of day is it, lad? 1H4 1.02. 1 P
indeed you come near me now, hal, for we that 1.02. 13 P
well, hal, well, and in some sort it jumps with 1.02. 69 P
but, hal, i prithee trouble me no more with 1.02. 81 P
thou hast done much harm upon me, hal, god 1.02. 92 P
before i knew thee, hal, i knew nothing, and now 1.02. 93 P
why, hal, 'tis my vocation, hal, 'tis no sin for 1.02.104 P
'tis my vocation, hal, 'tis no sin for a man to 1.02.104 P
good morrow, sweet hal. 1.02.112 P
hal, wilt thou make one? 1.02.137 P
where's poins, hal? 2.02. 7 P
hal! 2.02. 20 P
i prithee, good prince — hal! 2.02. 40 P
gaunt, your grandfather, but yet no coward, hal. 2.02. 68 P
where hast been, hal? 2.04. 3 P
i tell thee what, hal, if i tell thee a lie, 2.04.193 P
four, hal, i told thee four. 2.04.198 P
dost thou hear me, hal? 2.04.209 P
for it was so dark, hal, that thou couldest not 2.04.223 P
ah, no more of that, hal, and thou lovest me! 2.04.283 P
when i was about thy years, hal, i was not an 2.04.330 P
but tell me, hal, art not thou horrible afeard? 2.04.366 P
dost thou hear, hal? 2.04.491 P
wilt thou believe me, hal, three or four bonds 3.03.101 P
a thousand pound, hal? 3.03.136 P
why, hal! 3.03.145 P
dost thou hear, hal? 3.03.164 P
now, hal, to the news at court for the robbery, 3.03.174 P
what, hal? 4.02. 50 P
mine, hal, mine. 4.02. 63 P
hal, if thou see me down in the battle and 5.01.121 P
i would 'twere bed–time, hal, and all well. 5.01.125 P
o hal, i prithee give me leave to breathe a 5.03. 44 P
nay, before god, hal, if percy be alive, thou 5.03. 50 P
ay, hal, 'tis hot, 'tis hot. 5.03. 53 P
well said, hal! 5.04. 75 P
to it, hal! 5.04. 75 P
no abuse, hal, a' mine honor, no abuse. 2H4 2.04.313 P
no abuse, hal. 2.04.316 P
no abuse, hal; 2.04.323 P
god save thy grace, king hal! my royal hal! 5.05. 41
god save thy grace, king hal! my royal hal! 5.05. 41
HALBERD 1 FR 0.0001 REL FR 1 V 0 P
advance thy halberd higher than my breast, | or, R3 1.02. 40
HALBERDS 2 FR 0.0002 REL FR 2 V 0 P
guard with halberds! ERR 5.01.185
unless our halberds did shut up his passage. 3H6 4.03. 20
HALCYON 1 FR 0.0001 REL FR 1 V 0 P
and turn their halcyon beaks | with every gale LR 2.02. 78
HALCYONS' 1 FR 0.0001 REL FR 1 V 0 P
expect saint martin's summer, halcyons' days, 1H6 1.02.131
HAL'D 3 FR 0.0003 REL FR 2 V 1 P
thus strangers may be hal'd and abus'd. SHR 5.01.108 P
it most innocent mouth) | hal'd out to murther; WT 3.02.101
hal'd thither | by most mechanical and dirty 2H4 5.05. 35
HALE 9 FR 0.0010 REL FR 7 V 2 P
that sheep's guts should hale souls out of men's ADO 2.03. 59 P
oxen and wain–ropes cannot hale them together. TN 3.02. 60 P
i'll hale the dolphin headlong from his throne, 1H6 1.01.149
womb, | although ye hale me to a violent death. 5.04. 64
hale him away, and let him talk no more. 2H6 4.01.131
of the great combatant | and hale him hither. TRO 4.05. 6
and hale him up and down, all swearing, if | the COR 5.04. 37
jet, | to hale thy vengeful waggon swift away, TIT 5.02. 51

and hither hale that misbelieving moor | to be 5.03.143
HALED 1 FR 0.0001 REL FR 1 V 0 P
even like a man new haled from the rack, | so 1H6 2.05. 3
/HALES 1 FR 0.0001 REL FR 0 V 1 P
so /hales and pulls me. OTH 4.01.140 P
HALES 1 FR 0.0001 REL FR 0 V 1 P
name of henry the fift hales them to an hundred 2H6 4.08. 57 P
HALF *(also hauf)*
/HALF 1 FR 0.0001 REL FR 1 V 0 P
/sweet /harry /had /but /half /their /numbers, 2H4 2.03. 43
HALF 226 FR 0.0255 REL FR 177 V 49 P
and now farewell | till half an hour hence. TMP 3.01. 91
lie, being but half a fish and half a monster? 3.02. 29 P
lie, being but half a fish and half a monster? 3.02. 29 P
within this half hour will he be asleep. 3.02.113
take all, or half, for easing me of the carriage WIV 2.02.173 P
coming, with half windsor at his heels, to 3.03.114 P
i am half afraid he will have need of washing, 3.03.182 P
(when i was more than half stew'd in grease, 3.05.119 P
seven year and a half, sir. MM 2.01.260 P
and a half, sir. 2.01.264 P
become them with one half so good a grace | as 2.02. 62
even now, even here, not half an hour since. ERR 2.02. 14
you know i gave it you half an hour since. 4.01. 65
then half signior benedick's tongue in count ADO 2.01. 11 P
and half count john's melancholy in signior 2.01. 12 P
all other respects, and made her half myself. 2.03.170 P
if half thy outward graces had been placed 4.01.101
and speak /off half a dozen dang'rous words, 5.01. 97
and make a dark night too of half the day — LLL 1.01. 45
being but the one half of an entire sum 2.01.130
but that one half which is unsatisfied, | we 2.01.138
nor shines the silver moon one half so bright 4.03. 29
half, "hauf"; 5.01. 22 P
the letter is too long by half a mile. 5.02. 54
i thought to close mine eyes some half an hour; 5.02. 90
twice to your visor, and half once to you. 5.02.227
there's half a dozen sweets. 5.02.234
and would afford my speechless vizard half. 5.02.246
no, i'll not be your half. 5.02.249
with half that wish the wisher's eyes be press'd MND 2.02. 65
name, and half his face must be seen through the 3.01. 36 P
shall reply amazedly, | half sleep, half waking; 4.01.147
shall reply amazedly, | half sleep, half waking; 4.01.147
i am half afeard | thou wilt say anon he is some MV 2.09. 96
disgrac'd me, and hind'red me half a million, 3.01. 55 P
one half of me is yours, the other half yours — 3.02. 16
one half of me is yours, the other half yours — 3.02. 16
with leave, bassanio, i am half yourself, | and 3.02.248
and i must freely have the half of any thing 3.02.249
axe, bear half the keenness | of thy sharp envy. 4.01.125
doth contrive | shall seize one half his goods; 4.01.353
the other half | comes to the privy coffer of 4.01.353
for half thy wealth, it is antonio's; 4.01.370
the other half comes to the general state, 4.01.371
to quit the fine for one half of his goods, | i 4.01.381
so he will let me have | the other half in use, 4.01.383
or half her worthiness that gave the ring, | or 5.01.200
for you'll be rotten ere you be half ripe, and AYL 3.02.120 P
iwis it is not half way to her heart; SHR 1.01. 62
may perhaps call him half a score knaves or so. 1.02.110 P
that gives not half so great a blow to hear | as 1.02.208
after my death the one half of my lands, | and 2.01.121
regard, | to wish me wed to one half lunatic, 2.01.287
son, i'll be your half, bianca comes. 5.02. 78
half of the which dare not shake the snow from AWW 4.03.167 P
half won is match well made; 4.03.225
left cheek is a cheek of two pile and a half, 4.05. 98 P
by mine honor, half drunk. TN 1.05.116 P
behavior to his own shadow this half hour. 2.05. 17 P
not have him miscarry for the half of my dowry. 3.04. 63 P
hold, there's half my coffer. 3.04.347
i snatch'd one half out of the jaws of death, 3.04.360
to his use | not half an hour before. 5.01. 92
do't, and thou hast the one half of my heart; WT 1.02.348
water, nor the bear half din'd on the gentleman. 3.03.106 P
i think there is not half a kiss to choose | who 4.04.175
but jumps twelve foot and a half by th' squier. 4.04.339 P
the gentleman is half /flea'd already. 4.04.641 P
with half that face would he have all my land — JN 1.01. 93
he is the half part of a blessed man, | left to 2.01.437
match, | the sea enraged is not half so deaf, 2.01.451
himself | in mortal fury half so peremptory, 2.01.454
and, now it is half conquer'd, must i back 5.02. 95
tell thee, hubert, half my power this night, 5.06. 39
who half an hour since came from the dolphin, 5.07. 83
though he divide the realm and give thee half, R2 5.01. 60
old sir john with half a dozen more are at the 1H4 2.04. 82 P
if thou dost it half so gravely, so majestically 2.04.435 P
of death or death's hand for this one half year. 4.01.136
not a shirt and a half in all my company, and 4.02. 42 P
and the half shirt is two napkins tack'd 4.02. 43 P
that not a horse is half the half of himself. 4.03. 24
that not a horse is half the half of himself. 4.03. 24
and would have told him half his troy was burnt; 2H4 1.01. 73
his power to build it, who, half thorough, 1.03. 59
shaft a fourteen and fourteen and a half, that 3.02. 48 P
you provided me here half a dozen sufficient men 3.02. 93 P
yet not so sound, and half so deeply sweet, | as 4.05. 26
heart | to stab at half an hour of my life. 4.05.108
what, canst thou not forbear me half an hour? 4.05.109
us, | we lose the better half of our possession; H5 1.01. 8
with half their forces the full pride of france, 1.02.112
and let another half stand laughing by, | all 1.02.113
compound a boy, half french, half english, that 5.02.208 P
boy, half french, half english, that shall go to 5.02.208 P
arms, | of england's coat one half is cut away. 1H6 1.01. 81
sheep run not half so treacherous from the wolf, 1.05. 30
age, | and twit with cowardice a man half dead? 3.02. 55
with more than half the gallian territories, 5.04.139
not all these lords do vex me half so much | as 2H6 1.03. 75
not half so bad as thine to england's king, 1.04. 47
within this half hour, hath receiv'd his sight, 2.01. 62
hadst thou but lov'd him half so well as i, | or 3H6 1.01.220
that you stand pensive as half malecontent? 4.01. 10
fear | my joy of liberty is half eclips'd. 4.06. 63
and half our sailors swallow'd in the flood? 5.04. 5
into this breathing world, scarce half made up, R3 1.01. 21
now thy proud neck bears half my burthen'd yoke, 4.04.111
his regiment lies half a mile at least | south 5.03. 37
half your suit | never name to us; H8 1.02. 10
you have half our power. 1.02. 11
the cardinal | but half my lay–thoughts in him, 1.04. 11
i have half a dozen healths | to drink to these 1.04.105
pray tell him | you met him half in heaven. 2.01. 88
i will not wish ye half my miseries, | i have 3.01.108
had i but serv'd my god with half the zeal | i 3.02.455
down | to rest a while, some half an hour or so, 4.01. 66
that had not half a week to go, like rams | in 4.01. 77
and has done half an hour, to know your 5.02. 41
would you were half so honest! 5.02.117
and 'twould, you'd carry half. TRO 2.03.219 P
divide eternity in twain, | and give him half; 2.03.246
i would not for half troy have you seen here. 4.02. 41
this ajax is half made of hector's blood, | in 4.05. 83
in love whereof, half hector stays at home; 4.05. 84
half heart, half hand, half hector comes to seek 4.05. 85
half heart, half hand, half hector comes to seek 4.05. 85
half hector comes to seek | this blended knight, 4.05. 85
this blended knight, half troyan and half greek. 4.05. 86
this blended knight, half troyan and half greek. 4.05. 86
half stints their strife before their strokes 4.05. 93
my prophecy is but half his journey yet, | for 4.05.218
may worthy troilus be half attached | with that 5.02.161
your eyes, half out, weep out at pandar's fall; 5.10. 48
were half to half the world by th' ears, and he COR 1.01.233
were half to half the world by th' ears, and he 1.01.233
half all cominius' honors are to martius, 1.01.273
upon him a' we'nsday half an hour together; 1.03. 59 P
lend you him i will | for half a hundred years. 1.04. 7
within this mile and half. 1.04. 8
i, sir, | half an hour since brought my report. 1.06. 21
i am half through: 2.03.123
throat, | and wak'd half dead with nothing. 4.05.126
take | th' one half of my commission, and set 4.05.138
and but one half of what he was yesterday; 4.05.198 P
for the other has half by the entreaty and grant 4.05.199 P
would half my wealth | would buy this for a lie! 4.06.159
sons, | half of the number that king priam had, TIT 1.01. 80
was never scythia half so barbarous. 1.01.131
renowmed titus, more than half my soul — 1.01.373
gain so great a happiness | as half thy love? 2.04. 21
and that you'll say ere half an hour pass. 3.01.191
"peace, tawny slave, half me and half thy dame. 5.01. 27
"peace, tawny slave, half me and half thy dame. 5.01. 27
not half so big as a round little worm | prick'd ROM 1.04. 68
in half an hour she promised to return. 2.05. 2
excess | i cannot sum up sum of half my wealth. 2.06. 34
therefore we'll have some half a dozen friends, 3.04. 27
full half an hour. 5.03.130
which was not half so beautiful and kind; TIM 1.02.148
the greatest of your having lacks a half | to 2.02.144
i should not urge it half so faithfully. 3.02. 41
and the best half should have return'd to him, 3.02. 84
who then dares to be half so kind again? 4.02. 40
and half their faces buried in their cloaks, JC 2.01. 74
that you unfold to me, yourself, your half, 2.01.274
of half that worth as those your swords, made 3.01.155
i kill'd not thee with half so good a will. 5.05. 51
now o'er the one half world | nature seems dead, MAC 2.01. 49
might | to half a soul and to a notion craz'd 3.01. 82
we have lost | best half of our affair. 3.03. 21
man's memory may outlive his life half a year, HAM 3.02.132 P
half a share. 3.02.279 P
it, | and /live the purer with the other half. 3.04.158
things in doubt | that carry but half sense. 4.05. 7
in thee there is not half an hour's life. 5.02.315
my plight shall carry | half my love with him, LR 1.01.102
half my love with him, half my care and duty. 1.01.102
him, you should enjoy half his revenue for ever, 1.02. 53 P
i wake him, you should enjoy half his revenue." 1.02. 56 P
stew'd in his haste, half breathless, /panting 2.04. 31
she hath abated me of half my train; 2.04.159
thy half o' th' kingdom hast thou not forgot, 2.04.180
dismissing half your train, come then to me. 2.04.204
fathom and half, fathom and half! poor tom! 3.04. 37 P
fathom and half, fathom and half! poor tom! 3.04. 37 P
if thou shouldst dally half an hour, his life, 3.06. 93
half way down | hangs one that gathers sampire, 4.06. 14
until some half hour past, when i was arm'd. 5.03.194
heart is burst, you have lost half your soul; OTH 1.01. 87
if she confess that she was half the wooer, 1.03.176
faith, half asleep. 4.02. 97
desdemona would half have corrupted a votarist. 4.02.187 P
but half an hour! 5.02. 82
his pernicious soul | rot half a grain a day! 5.02.156
thou hast not half that pow'r to do me harm | as 5.02.162
be tales, | where now half tales be truths. ANT 2.02.134
half the heart of caesar, worthy maecenas! 2.02.172 P
so half my egypt were submerg'd and made | a 2.05. 94
half afeard to come. 3.03. 1
with half the bulk o' th' world play'd as i 3.11. 64
when half to half the world oppos'd, he being 3.13. 9
when half to half the world oppos'd, he being 3.13. 9
you were half blasted ere i knew you; 3.13.105
say, shall never be sav'd by half that they do. 5.02.257 P
about some half hour hence, | pray you speak CYM 1.01.176
half all /men's hearts are his. 1.06.168
a minute old, for one | not half so old as that. 2.05. 32
my brother wears thee not the one half so well 4.02.202
ground's the lowest, and we are half way there. PER 1.04. 78
give them life whom hunger starv'd half dead. 1.04. 96
they say they're half fish, half flesh. 2.01. 25 P
they say they're half fish, half flesh. 2.01. 25 P
marry, sir, half a day's journey. 2.01.107 P
half the flood | hath their keel cut. 3.ch. 45
walk half an hour, leonine, at the least. 4.01. 45
half his own heart, set in too, that i hope TNK 4.01. 14
i half suspected | what you told me. 4.01. 47
on't to give half my state that both she and i 4.03. 67 P
have half persuaded her that i am palamon. 5.02. 3
within this half hour she came smiling to me 5.02. 4
lust's winter comes ere summer half be done; VEN 802
they that lose half with greater patience bear LUC 1158
hides your life, and shows not half your parts. SON 17. 4
thou canst not, love, disgrace me half so ill, 89. 5
even | doth half that glory to the sober west, 132. 8
HALF–ACHIEVED 1 FR 0.0001 REL FR 1 V 0 P
i will not leave the half–achieved harflew H5 3.03. 8
HALF–BLOODED 1 FR 0.0001 REL FR 1 V 0 P
half–blooded fellow, yes. LR 5.03. 80
HALF–BLOWN 1 FR 0.0001 REL FR 1 V 0 P
lilies boast, | and with the half–blown rose. JN 3.01. 54
HALF–CAN 1 FR 0.0001 REL FR 0 V 1 P
traveller, and wild half–can that stabb'd pots, MM 4.03. 17 P
HALF–CAPS 1 FR 0.0001 REL FR 1 V 0 P
with certain half–caps and cold–moving nods, TIM 2.02.212
HALF–CHEEK 1 FR 0.0001 REL FR 0 V 1 P
saint george's half–cheek in a brooch. LLL 5.02.616 P
HALF–CHEEK'D 1 FR 0.0001 REL FR 0 V 1 P
and with a half–cheek'd bit and a head–stall of SHR 3.02. 57 P
HALF–FAC'D 4 FR 0.0004 REL FR 3 V 1 P
a half–fac'd groat five hundred pound a year! JN 1.01. 94
but out upon this half–fac'd fellowship! 1H4 1.03.208
and this same half–fac'd fellow, shadow, give me 2H4 3.02.264 P
hopeful colors | advance our half–fac'd sun, 2H6 4.01. 98
HALF–FACE 1 FR 0.0001 REL FR 1 V 0 P
because he hath a half–face like my father! JN 1.01. 92
HALF–KIRTLES 1 FR 0.0001 REL FR 0 V 1 P
you be not swing'd, i'll forswear half–kirtles. 2H4 5.04. 21 P
HALF–MOON 3 FR 0.0003 REL FR 2 V 1 P
a semicircle, | or a half–moon made with a pen. WT 2.01. 11
score a pint of bastard in the half–moon," or so 1H4 2.04. 27 P
from the best of all my land | a huge half–moon, 3.01. 99
HALF–PART 2 FR 0.0002 REL FR 0 V 2 P
half–part, mates, half–part. PER 4.01. 94 P
half–part, mates, half–part. 4.01. 94 P
HALFPENCE 3 FR 0.0003 REL FR 0 V 3 P
she tore the letter into a thousand halfpence; ADO 2.03.140 P
they were all like one another as halfpence are, AYL 3.02.354 P
twelve leagues, and sold it for three halfpence. H5 3.02. 44 P
HALFPENNY 7 FR 0.0008 REL FR 0 V 7 P
he cannot creep into a halfpenny purse, nor into WIV 3.05.146 P
marry, sir, halfpenny farthing. LLL 3.01.148 P
had of thy master, thou halfpenny purse of wit, 5.01. 74 P
my hat to a halfpenny, pompey proves the best 5.02.560 P
be in england seven halfpenny loaves sold for a 2H6 4.02. 66 P
friends, my thanks are too dear a halfpenny. HAM 2.02.274 P
by a halfpenny loaf a day, troy weight. STM II.C 7 P
HALF–PENNYWORTH 1 FR 0.0001 REL FR 0 V 1 P
but one half–pennyworth of bread to this 1H4 2.04.540 P
HALF–PINT 1 FR 0.0001 REL FR 0 V 1 P
lest i let forth your half–pint of blood. COR 5.02. 56 P
HALF–SIGHTS 1 FR 0.0001 REL FR 1 V 0 P
half–sights saw | that arcite was no babe. TNK 5.03. 95
HALF–SUPP'D 1 FR 0.0001 REL FR 1 V 0 P
my half–supp'd sword, that frankly would have TRO 5.08. 19
HALF–SWORD 1 FR 0.0001 REL FR 0 V 1 P
if i were not at half–sword with a dozen of them 1H4 2.04.164 P
HALF–WORKERS 1 FR 0.0001 REL FR 1 V 0 P
for men to be, but women | must be half–workers? CYM 2.05. 2
HALF–YARD 1 FR 0.0001 REL FR 1 V 0 P
thou yard, three–quarters, half–yard, quarter, SHR 4.03.108
HALIDOM *(also holidam, holidame)*
HALIDOM 1 FR 0.0001 REL FR 0 V 1 P
by my halidom, i was fast asleep. TGV 4.02.135 P
HALING 1 FR 0.0001 REL FR 1 V 0 P
galling | his kingly hands haling ropes, | and, PER 4.01. 54
HALL 15 FR 0.0017 REL FR 13 V 2 P
and tom bears logs into the hall | and milk LLL 5.02.914
that light we see is burning in my hall. MV 5.01. 89
meet me to–morrow in the temple hall | at two 1H4 3.03.199
'tis merry in hall when beards wags all, | and 2H4 5.03. 34
within the temple hall we were too loud, | the 1H6 2.04. 3
at lower end of the hall, hurl'd up their caps, R3 3.07. 35
ev'n to the hall, to hear what shall become | of H8 2.01. 2
let us to priam's hall | to greet the warriors. TRO 3.01.148
how some men creep in skittish fortune's hall, 3.03.134
as many as be here of pandar's hall, | your eyes 5.10. 47
a hall, a hall! ROM 1.05. 26
a hall, a hall! 1.05. 26
readiness, | and meet i' th' hall together. MAC 2.03.134
sir, i will walk here in the hall. HAM 5.02.173 P
back to him that you attend him in the hall. 5.02.197 P
HALLOW* *(also alow, holla, hollo, hollow*, etc., 'loo, loo)*
HALLOW* 5 FR 0.0005 REL FR 5 V 0 P
hallow your name to the reverberate hills, | and TN 1.05.272
sword, i will hallow thee for this thy deed, 2H6 4.10. 67
with their echoes, | no more now must we hallow; TNK 2.02. 48
i cannot hallow. 3.02. 9
this, far off, she hears some huntsman hallow; VEN 973
HALLOW'D* 6 FR 0.0006 REL FR 3 V 3 P
have the cudgel hallow'd and hung o'er the altar WIV 4.02.204 P
he hallow'd but even now. WT 3.03. 77 P
if my trinkets had been hallow'd and brought a 4.04.601 P
we will make fast within a hallow'd verge. 2H6 1.04. 22
i time | to give thee hallow'd to thy grave, but PER 3.01. 59
what if i hallow'd for him? TNK 3.02. 8
/HALLOWED 1 FR 0.0001 REL FR 1 V 0 P
/hallowed with sighs that burning lungs did LC 228
HALLOWED 6 FR 0.0006 REL FR 6 V 0 P
not a mouse | shall disturb this hallowed house. MND 5.01.388
nor my prayers | are not words duly hallowed, H8 2.03. 68
so hallowed, and so gracious is that time. HAM 1.01.164
the worms were hallowed that did breed the silk, OTH 3.04. 73
in hallowed clouds commend their swelling TNK 5.01. 4
even as when first i hallowed thy fair name. SON 108. 8
HALLOWING 2 FR 0.0002 REL FR 1 V 1 P
what hallowing and what stir is this to–day? TGV 5.04. 13
i have lost it with hallowing and singing of 2H4 1.02.190 P
HALLOWMAS *(also hollowmas)*
HALLOWMAS 3 FR 0.0003 REL FR 0 V 3 P
to speak puling, like a beggar at hallowmas. TGV 2.01. 26 P
whose father died at hallowmas. MM 2.01.124 P
was't not at hallowmas, master froth? 2.01.124 P
HALT 11 FR 0.0012 REL FR 9 V 2 P
all praise | and make it halt behind her. TMP 4.01. 11
thou dost not halt. SHR 2.01.256
and yet you halt not. 3.02. 89
'tis no matter if i do halt, i have the wars for 2H4 1.02.245 P
that dogs bark at me as i halt by them — | why, R3 1.01. 23
that their limbs may halt | as lamely as their TIM 4.01. 24
freely, or the /blank verse shall halt for't. HAM 2.02.325 P

i'll halt after. ANT 4.07. 16
lame, blind, halt, creep, cry out for thee, LUC 902
smell — | a cripple soon can find a halt — PP 18.10
speak of my lameness, and i straight will halt, SON 89. 3
HALTER 7 FR 0.0008 REL FR 4 V 3 P
give him a halter. MV 2.02.105 P
a halter gratis — nothing else, for god sake. 4.01.379
no, if rightly taken, halter. 1H4 2.04.325 P
as soon be strangled with a halter as another. 2.04.498 P
a halter, soldiers! TIT 5.01. 47
the slaughter, | if my cap would buy a halter, LR 1.04.320
a halter pardon him! OTH 4.02.136
HALTER'D 1 FR 0.0001 REL FR 1 V 0 P
a halter'd neck which does the hangman thank ANT 3.13.130
HALTERS 2 FR 0.0002 REL FR 1 V 1 P
and humbly thus, with halters on their necks, 2H6 4.09. 11
knives under his pillow, and halters in his pew, LR 3.04. 54 P
HALTING 7 FR 0.0008 REL FR 4 V 3 P
conflict four of his five wits went halting off, ADO 1.01. 66 P
hand, | a halting sonnet of his own pure brain, 5.04. 87
here comes sir toby halting — you shall hear TN 5.01.192 P
(not trusting to this halting legate here, JN 5.02.174
for to serve bravely is to come halting off, you 2H4 2.04. 49 P
no farther halting. CYM 3.05. 92
not halting under crimes | many and stale. TNK 5.04. 10
HALTS 3 FR 0.0003 REL FR 3 V 0 P
on me, that halts and am misshapen thus? R3 1.02.250
my free drift | halts not particularly, but TIM 1.01. 46
bang'd the turks, | that their designment halts. OTH 2.01. 22
HALVES 1 FR 0.0001 REL FR 1 V 0 P
i'll have no halves; SHR 5.02. 79
HAMES 1 FR 0.0001 REL FR 1 V 0 P
away with oxford to hames castle straight; 3H6 5.05. 2
/HAMLET 5 FR 0.0005 REL FR 2 V 3 P
/hamlet! /lord /hamlet! HAM 4.02. 2 P
/hamlet! /lord /hamlet! 4.02. 2 P
/letters, /my /lord, /from /hamlet: 4.07. 36
/hamlet." 4.07. 48 P
/hamlet, thou art slain. 5.02.313
HAMLET 72 FR 0.0081 REL FR 62 V 10 P
in which our valiant hamlet | (for so this side HAM 1.01. 84
of the article /design'd, | his fell to hamlet. 1.01. 95
what we have seen to–night | unto young hamlet, 1.01.170
though yet of hamlet our dear brother's death 1.02. 1
but now, my cousin hamlet, and my son — 1.02. 64
good hamlet, cast thy nighted color off, | and 1.02. 68
sweet and commendable in your nature, hamlet, 1.02. 87
let not thy mother lose her prayers, hamlet, | i 1.02.118
this gentle and unforc'd accord of hamlet | sits 1.02.123
for hamlet, and the trifling of his favor, 1.03. 5
please you, something touching the lord hamlet. 1.03. 89
for lord hamlet, | believe so much in him, that 1.03.123
as to give words or talk with the lord hamlet. 1.03.134
i'll call thee hamlet, | king, father, royal 1.04. 44
now, hamlet, hear: 1.05. 34
o hamlet, what /a falling–off was there | from 1.05. 47
lord hamlet! 1.05.113
and what so poor a man as hamlet is | may do, t' 1.05.184
lord hamlet, with his doublet all unbrac'd, | no 2.01. 75
and bring these gentlemen where hamlet is. 2.02. 37
came this from hamlet to her? 2.02.114
lady, whilst this machine is to him, hamlet." 2.02.124 P
"lord hamlet is a prince out of thy star; 2.02.141
give me leave, | how does my good lord hamlet? 2.02.171
you go to seek the lord hamlet, there he is. 2.02.220 P
for we have closely sent for hamlet hither, 3.01. 29
you need not tell us what lord hamlet said, | we 3.01.179
how fares our cousin hamlet? 3.02. 92 P
i have nothing with this answer, hamlet, these 3.02. 96 P
come hither, my dear hamlet, sit by me. 3.02.108 P
hamlet, thou hast thy father much offended. 3.04. 9
why, how now, hamlet? 3.04. 13
o hamlet, speak no more! 3.04. 88
no more, sweet hamlet! 3.04. 96
bodies strongest works, | speak to her, hamlet. 3.04.115
o hamlet, thou hast cleft my heart in twain. 3.04.156
what, gertrude? how does hamlet? 4.01. 6
hamlet in madness hath polonius slain, | and 4.01. 34
who calls on hamlet? 4.02. 3 P
now, hamlet, where's polonius? 4.03. 16 P
hamlet, this deed, for thine especial safety — 4.03. 40
ay, hamlet. 4.03. 46
thy loving father, hamlet. 4.03. 50
to that effect, | the present death of hamlet. 4.03. 65
i should be greeted, if not from lord hamlet. 4.06. 6
/he that thou knowest thine, hamlet." 4.06. 31 P
from hamlet? who brought them? 4.07. 38
of his | did hamlet so envenom with his envy 4.07.103
hamlet comes back. 4.07.124
hamlet return'd shall know you are come home. 4.07.130
that our last king hamlet overcame fortinbras. 5.01.144 P
was that very day that young hamlet was born — 5.01.147 P
this is i, | hamlet the dane! 5.01.258
hamlet, hamlet! 5.01.264
hamlet, hamlet! 5.01.264
come, hamlet, come, and take this hand from me. 5.02.225
was't hamlet wrong'd laertes? 5.02.233
never hamlet! 5.02.233
if hamlet from himself be ta'en away, | and when 5.02.234
then hamlet does it not, hamlet denies it. 5.02.236
then hamlet does it not, hamlet denies it. 5.02.236
so, | hamlet is of the faction that is wronged, 5.02.238
cousin hamlet, | you know the wager? 5.02.259
if hamlet give the first or second hit, | or 5.02.268
to earth, | "now the king drinks to hamlet." 5.02.278
hamlet, this pearl is thine, | here's to thy 5.02.282
here, hamlet, take my napkin, rub thy brows. 5.02.288
the queen carouses to thy fortune, hamlet. 5.02.289
no, the drink, the drink — o my dear hamlet — 5.02.309
it is here, hamlet. 5.02.313
exchange forgiveness with me, noble hamlet. 5.02.329
let four captains | bear hamlet, like a soldier, 5.02.396
HAMLET'S 8 FR 0.0009 REL FR 8 V 0 P
have you heard | of hamlet's transformation; HAM 2.02. 5
have found | the very cause of hamlet's lunacy. 2.02. 49
be the happy cause | of hamlet's wildness. 3.01. 39
'tis hamlet's character. 4.07. 51
and that in hamlet's hearing, for a quality 4.07. 72
hop'd thou shouldst have been my hamlet's wife. 5.01.244
wronged, | his madness is poor hamlet's enemy. 5.02.239
the king shall drink to hamlet's better breath, 5.02.271
HAMMER 4 FR 0.0004 REL FR 2 V 2 P
i saw a smith stand with his hammer, thus, | the JN 4.02.193
yet i'll hammer it out. R2 5.05. 5
you with the motion of a pewterer's hammer, come 2H4 3.02.263 P
and, will, thou shalt have my hammer; 2H6 2.03. 75 P
HAMMER'D 2 FR 0.0002 REL FR 2 V 0 P
are you more stubborn–hard than hammer'd iron? JN 4.01. 67
to spoil antiquities of hammer'd steel, | and LUC 951
HAMMERED 2 FR 0.0002 REL FR 2 V 0 P
offer, | who but to–day hammered of this design, WT 2.02. 47
unless my nerves were brass or hammered steel. SON 120. 4
HAMMERING 3 FR 0.0003 REL FR 3 V 0 P
that | whereon this month i have been hammering. TGV 1.03. 18
and wilt thou still be hammering treachery, | to 2H6 1.02. 47
blood and revenge are hammering in my head. TIT 2.03. 39
HAMMERS 3 FR 0.0003 REL FR 3 V 0 P
knights, | with busy hammers closing rivets up, H5 4.pr. 13
and never did the cyclops' hammers fall | on HAM 2.02.489
rules, and hammers, shall | uplift us to the ANT 5.02.210
HAMPER 1 FR 0.0001 REL FR 1 V 0 P
she'll hamper thee, and dandle thee like a baby. 2H6 1.03.145
/HAMPTON 1 FR 0.0001 REL FR 1 V 0 P
seen | the well–appointed king at /hampton pier H5 3.pr. 4
HAMPTON 1 FR 0.0001 REL FR 1 V 0 P
of france | to kill us here in hampton. H5 2.02. 91
HAMS 3 FR 0.0003 REL FR 0 V 3 P
as yours constrains a man to bow in the hams. ROM 2.04. 53 P
lack of wit, together with most weak hams; HAM 2.02.200 P
know the french knight that cow'rs i' the hams? PER 4.02.105 P
HAMSTRING 1 FR 0.0001 REL FR 1 V 0 P
whose conceit | lies in his hamstring, and doth TRO 1.03.154
HANC *(see hang*)*
/HAND 8 FR 0.0009 REL FR 4 V 4 P
/give /me /thy /hand, /terrestrial; WIV 3.01.105 P
/on /this /side /my /hand, /and /on /that /side R2 4.01.183
/and /this /unwieldy /sceptre /from /my /hand, 4.01.205
/till /we /had /his /assistance /by /the /hand. 2H4 1.03. 21
/this /poor /right /hand /of /mine | /is /left TIT 3.02. 7
is my right hand, and this is my left /hand. OTH 2.03.115 P
and, /by /this /hand, falls me thus about my 4.01.135 P
/by /this /hand, i think it is scurvy, and begin 4.02.193 P
HAND 883 FR 0.0998 REL FR 724 V 159 P
of the present, we will not hand a rope more. TMP 1.01. 23 P
lend thy hand, | and pluck my magic garment from 1.02. 23
and when i rear my hand, do you the like, | to 2.01.295
here's my hand. 3.01. 89
trouble him any more in 's tale, by this hand, i 3.02. 49 P
and, by this hand, i'll turn my mercy out o' 3.02. 69 P
give me thy hand. 3.02.111 P
who once again | i tender to thy hand. 4.01. 5
give me thy hand. 4.01.220 P
by this hand, i'll have that gown. 4.01.227 P
here is her hand, the agent of her heart; TGV 1.03. 46
here is my hand for my true constancy; 2.02. 8
when one's right hand | is perjured to the bosom 5.04. 67
come, come, a hand from either. 5.04.116
a great charge to come under one body's hand. WIV 1.04. 99 P
the very hand; 2.01. 83 P
we have sport in hand. 2.01.197 P
my hand, bully; 2.01.217 P
leaving the fear of /god on the left hand, and 2.02. 24 P
i come to her with any detection in my hand, my 2.02.246 P
next, give me your hand; 2.02.253 P
give me thy hand, celestial; 3.01.106 P
your husband's here at hand, bethink you of some 3.03.127 P
he should be a cuckold) held his hand. 3.05.105 P
come, mother prat, come give me your hand. 4.02.183 P
time | to take her by the hand and bid her go, 4.06. 37
to pinch her by the hand, and, on that token, 4.06. 44
and i will deliver his wife into your hand. 5.01. 29 P
strange things in hand, master /brook! 5.01. 29 P
when you see your time, take her by the hand, 5.03. 2 P
pray you lock hand in hand; 5.05. 77
pray you lock hand in hand; 5.05. 77
give me your hand, | i'll privily away. MM 1.01. 66
being one) | in hand, and hope of action; 1.04. 52
by this hand, sir, his wife is a more respected 2.01.165 P
the hand that hath made you fair hath made you 3.01.180 P
had now, for putting the hand in the pocket and 3.02. 46 P
take then this your companion by the hand, | who 4.01. 54
you, sir, here is the hand and seal of the duke; 4.02.192 P
give /me your hand, | and let the subject see, 5.01. 13
you must walk by us on our other hand; 5.01. 17
this is the hand which, with a vow'd contract, 5.01.209
friar, advise him, | i leave him to your hand. 5.01.486
give me your hand and say you will be mine, | he 5.01.492
say, is your tardy master now at hand? ERR 2.01. 44
beshrew his hand, i scarce could understand it. 2.01. 49
that never touch well welcome to thy hand, 2.02.116
and from my false hand cut the wedding–ring, 2.02.137
beat me at the mart, i have your hand to show; 3.01. 12
if by strong hand you offer to break in | now in 3.01. 98
give me thy hand. 3.02. 69
by the barrenness, hard in the palm of the hand. 3.02.121 P
give me your hand, and let me feel your pulse. 4.04. 52
there is my hand, and let it feel your ear. 4.04. 53
and careful hours with time's deformed hand 5.01.299
and now let's go hand in hand, not one before 5.01.426
and now let's go hand in hand, not one before 5.01.426
your hand, leonato, we will go together. ADO 1.01.160 P
but had a rougher task in hand | than to drive 1.01.299
marry, it is your brother's right hand. 1.03. 49 P
and claudio, hand in hand in sad conference. 1.03. 60 P
and claudio, hand in hand in sad conference. 1.03. 60 P
here's his dry hand up and down. 2.01.118 P
thee, | taming my wild heart to thy loving hand. 3.01.112
take not away thy heavy hand, | death is the 4.01.115
why had i not with charitable hand | took up a 4.01.131
bear her in hand until they come to take hands, 4.01.304 P
tarry, good beatrice. by this hand, i love thee. 4.01.324 P
i will kiss your hand, and so i leave you. 4.01.332 P
by this hand, claudio shall render me a dear 4.01.333 P
nay, never lay thy hand upon thy sword, | i fear 5.01. 54
marry, beshrew my hand, | if it should give your 5.01. 55
in faith, my hand meant nothing to my sword. 5.01. 57
men, | a third is fled, that had a hand in it. 5.01.267
no, that you shall not till you take her hand, 5.04. 56
give me your hand before this holy friar — | i 5.04. 58
her, | for here's a paper written in his hand, 5.04. 86
and here's another | writ in my cousin's hand, 5.04. 89
that his own hand may strike his honor down LLL 1.01. 20
mean time receive such welcome at my hand | as 2.01.168
and to her white hand see thou do commend | this 3.01.168
a giving hand, though foul, shall have fair 4.01. 23
i' faith, your hand is out. 4.01.133
and if my hand be out, then belike your hand is 4.01.135
if my hand be out, then belike your hand is in. 4.01.135
to see him kiss his hand! 4.01.146
"to the snow–white hand of the most beauteous 4.02.132 P
this paper into the royal hand of the king; 4.02.141 P
my hand is sworn | ne'er to pluck thee from thy 4.03.109
when shall you hear that i | will praise a hand, 4.03.182
then homeward every man attach the hand | of his 4.03.372
ladies, withdraw; the gallants are at hand. 5.02.308
is he | that kiss'd his hand away in courtesy; 5.02.324
by this white glove (how white the hand, god 5.02.411
the sudden hand of death close up mine eye! 5.02.815
of hell, | to die upon the hand i love so well. MND 2.01.244
of our fairy band, | helena is here at hand, 3.02.111
turns to a crow | when thou hold'st up thy hand. 3.02.143
get you your weapons in your hand, and kill me a 4.01. 11 P
hath not seen, man's hand is not able to taste, 4.01.212 P
what revels are in hand? 5.01. 36
here repent you, | the actors are at hand; 5.01.116
hand in hand, with fairy grace, | will we sing, 5.01.399
hand in hand, with fairy grace, | will we sing, 5.01.399
and the blots of nature's hand | shall not in 5.01.409
but sway'd and fashion'd by the hand of heaven. MV 1.03. 93
may turn by fortune from the weaker hand: 2.01. 34
turn up on your right hand at the next turning, 2.02. 41 P
at the very next turning, turn of no hand, but 2.02. 43 P
i know the hand; 2.04. 12
in faith, 'tis a fair hand, | and whiter than 2.04. 12
paper it writ on | is the fair hand that writ. 2.04. 14
and weigh thy value with an even hand. 2.07. 25
turning his face, he put his hand behind him, 2.08. 47
wondrous sensible | he wrung bassanio's hand, 2.08. 49
sweet, | to show how costly summer was at hand, 2.09. 94
your hand, salerio. 3.02.238
i have work in hand | that you yet know not of. 3.04. 57
give me your hand. 4.01.169
give me your hand, bassanio, fare you well! 4.01.265
do not draw back your hand, i'll take no more, 4.01.428
stood dido with a willow in her hand | upon the 5.01. 10
within the house, your mistress is at hand, 5.01. 52
your husband is at hand, i hear his trumpet. 5.01.122
now, by this hand, | i gave it to a youth, | a 5.01.161
why, i were best to cut my left hand off, | and 5.01.177
i would not take this hand from thy throat till AYL 1.01. 60 P
could give more, but that her hand lacks means. 1.02.247
a boar–spear in my hand, and — in my heart 1.03.118
give me your hand, | and let me all your 2.07.199
youth, by the white hand of rosalind, i am that 3.02.394 P
even a toy in hand here, sir. 3.03. 76 P
by this hand, it will not kill a fly. 4.01.111 P
give me your hand, orlando. 4.01.125 P
i saw her hand, she has a leathern hand, | a 4.03. 24
i saw her hand, she has a leathern hand, | a 4.03. 24
has a leathern hand, | a freestone–colored hand. 4.03. 25
she has a huswive's hand — but that's no matter 4.03. 27
this is a man's invention and his hand. 4.03. 29
left on your right hand brings you to the place. 4.03. 80
give me your hand. art thou learned? 5.01. 38 P
that thou mightst join /her hand with his 5.04.114
the rather for i have some sport in hand, SHR in.1. 91
that made great jove to humble him to her hand, 1.01.169
master, for my hand, | both our inventions meet 1.01.189
all books of love, see that at any hand — | and 1.02.146
not her that chides, sir, at any hand, i pray. 1.02.225
us, | that covenants may be kept on either hand. 2.01.127
and bow'd her hand to teach her fingering; 2.01.150
give me thy hand, kate, i will unto venice | to 2.01.314
to give my hand oppos'd against my heart | unto 3.02. 9
i complain on thee to our mistress, whose hand 4.01. 30 P
whose hand (she being now at hand) thou shalt 4.01. 30 P
e'en at hand, alighted by this; 4.01.117 P
i tell you, sir, she bears me fair in hand. 4.02. 3
here is my hand, and here i firmly vow | never 4.02. 28
she says you have some goodly jest in hand. 5.02. 91
please, | my hand is ready, may it do him ease. 5.02.179
and at this time | his tongue obey'd his hand. AWW 1.02. 41
to give great charlemain a pen in 's hand | and 2.01. 77
then shalt thou give me with thy kingly hand 2.01.193
here is my hand, the premises observ'd, | thy 2.01.201
put off 's cap, kiss his hand, and say nothing, 2.02. 10 P
as ten groats is for the hand of an attorney, as 2.02. 21 P
very hand of heaven. 2.03. 31 P
and with this healthful hand, whose banish'd 2.03. 48
be not afraid that i your hand should take, 2.03. 89
here, take her hand, | proud scornful boy, 2.03.150
take her by the hand, | and tell her she is 2.03.173
i take her hand. 2.03.176
give me thy hand. 2.03.215 P
you than you have or will to deserve at my hand, 2.05. 48 P
and, after some dispatch in hand at court, 3.02. 54
'tis but the boldness of his hand, haply, 3.02. 77
and that with his own hand he slew the duke's 3.05. 6 P
let him fetch off his drum in any hand. 3.06. 43 P
by the hand of a soldier, i will undertake it. 3.06. 72 P
me, | commend the paper to his gracious hand, 5.01. 31
give me your hand. 5.02. 41 P
you give away this hand, and that is mine; 5.03.170
by this hand, they are scoundrels and TN 1.03. 34 P
fair lady, do you think you have fools in hand? 1.03. 65 P
sir, i have not you by th' hand. 1.03. 66 P
marry, but you shall have — and here's my hand. 1.03. 68 P
i pray you bring your hand to th' butt'ry–bar, 1.03. 70 P
i am not such an ass but i can keep my hand dry. 1.03. 75 P
marry, now i let go your hand, i am barren. 1.03. 79 P
i hold the olive in my hand; 1.05.210 P

nature's own sweet and cunning hand laid on. 1.05.240
my lady has a white hand, and the mermidons are 2.03. 27 P
she shall know of it, by this hand. 2.03.124 P
i extend my hand to him thus, quenching my 2.05. 65 P
by my life, this is my lady's hand. 2.05. 86 P
it is, in contempt of question, her hand. 2.05. 88 P
"if this fall into thy hand, revolve. 2.05.143 P
give me your hand, sir. 3.01. 94 P
this was look'd for at your hand, and this was 3.02. 24 P
write it in a martial hand, be curst and brief. 3.02. 42 P
i think we do know the sweet roman hand. 3.04. 28 P
dost thou smile so, and kiss thy hand so oft? 3.04. 33 P
by my troth, thou hast an open hand. 4.01. 21 P
let go thy hand. 4.01. 37
as ever thou wilt deserve well at my hand, help 4.02. 81 P
by this hand, i am. 4.02.109 P
give me thy hand, | and let me see thee in thy 5.01.272
here is my hand — you shall from this time be 5.01.325
you must not now deny it is your hand; 5.01.331
write from it, if you can, in hand or phrase, 5.01.332
but out of question 'tis maria's hand. 5.01.347
ere i could make thee open thy white hand | /and WT 1.02.103
give me thy hand, | be pilot to me, and thy 1.02.447
makes but trifles of his eyes | first hand me. 2.03. 64
the very mould and frame of hand, nail, finger. 2.03.103
by the hand deliver'd | of great apollo's priest 3.02.127
the heavens with that we have in hand are angry, 3.03. 5
lend me thy hand, i'll help thee. 4.03. 68 P
come, lend me thy hand. 4.03. 69 P
your hand, my perdita. 4.04.154
i take thy hand, this hand, | as soft as dove's 4.04.362
i take thy hand, this hand, | as soft as dove's 4.04.362
swain seems to wash | the hand was fair before! 4.04.367
come, your hand; | and, daughter, yours. 4.04.390
a quick eye, and a nimble hand, is necessary for 4.04.671 P
inside of your purse to the outside of his hand, 4.04.804 P
toward the sea-side, go on the right hand, i 4.04.825 P
thought she had some great matter there in hand, 5.02.105 P
for the king's son took me by the hand, and 5.02.141 P
give me thy hand: 5.02.156 P
yet you look'd upon | or hand of man hath done; 5.03. 17
but began, | give me that hand of yours to kiss. 5.03. 46
indeed, descend, | and take you by the hand; 5.03. 89
nay, present your hand. 5.03.107
and take her by the hand, whose worth and 5.03.144
and put the same into young arthur's hand, | thy JN 1.01. 14
by the honor-giving hand | of cordelion knighted 1.01. 53
brother by th' mother's side, give me your hand; 1.01.163
nor keep his princely heart from richard's hand. 1.01.267
i give you welcome with a powerless hand, | but 2.01. 15
till your strong hand shall help to give him 2.01. 33
they are at hand, | to parley or to fight, 2.01. 77
and the hand of time | shall draw this brief 2.01.102
arthur of britain, yield thee to my hand, | and 2.01.156
than e'er the coward hand of france can win. 2.01.158
lo in this right hand, whose protection | is 2.01.236
who by the hand of france this day hath made 2.01.302
who are at hand, triumphantly displayed, | to 2.01.309
and by this hand i swear, | that sways the earth 2.01.343
holds hand with any princess of the world. 2.01.494
not that i have the power to clutch my hand 2.01.589
but for my hand, as unattempted yet, | like a 2.01.591
what means that hand upon that breast of thine? 3.01. 21
and with her golden hand hath pluck'd on france 3.01. 57
without th' assistance of a mortal hand. 3.01.158
and meritorious shall that hand be call'd, 3.01.176
a curse, | let go the hand of that arch-heretic, 3.01.192
do not let go thy hand. 3.01.195
this royal hand and mine are newly knit, | and 3.01.226
keep in peace that hand which thou dost hold. 3.01.261
i may disjoin my hand, but not my faith. 3.01.262
i am with both, each army hath a hand, | and in 3.01.328
so i kiss your hand. 3.03. 16
give me thy hand. 3.03. 25
a sceptre snatch'd with an unruly hand | must be 3.04.135
and with my hand at midnight held your head; 4.01. 45
we cannot hold mortality's strong hand. 4.02. 82
who, with his shears and measure in his hand, 4.02.196
thy hand hath murd'red him. 4.02.205
here is your hand and seal for what i did. 4.02.215
then shall this hand and seal | witness against 4.02.217
by, | a fellow by the hand of nature mark'd, 4.02.221
and consequently thy rude hand to act | the deed 4.02.240
this hand of mine | is yet a maiden and an 4.02.251
of mine | is yet a maiden and an innocent hand, 4.02.252
work, | the graceless action of a heavy hand — 4.03. 58
hand — | if that it be the work of any hand. 4.03. 59
if that it be the work of any hand? 4.03. 60
it is the shameful work of hubert's hand, | the 4.03. 62
till i have set a glory to this hand, | by 4.03. 71
a thousand businesses are brief in hand, | and 4.03.158
thus have i yielded up into your hand | the 5.01. 1
take again | from this my hand, as holding of 5.01. 3
by some damn'd hand was robb'd and ta'en away. 5.01. 41
we cannot deal but with the very hand | of stern 5.02. 22
for thou shalt thrust thy hand as deep | into 5.02. 60
to give us warrant from the hand of heaven, 5.02. 66
war, | that, like a lion fostered up at hand, 5.02. 75
that hand which had the strength, even at your 5.02.137
shall that victorious hand be feebled here, 5.02.146
and even at hand a drum is ready brac'd | that 5.02.169
for at hand | (not trusting to this halting 5.02.173
faded, | by envy's hand and murder's bloody axe. R2 1.02. 21
let me kiss my sovereign's hand | and bow my 1.03. 46
and craves to kiss your hand and take his leave. 1.03. 53
who can hold a fire in his hand | by thinking on 1.03.294
shall furnish us | for our affairs in hand. 1.04. 47
herself | against infection and the hand of war, 2.01. 44
his noble hand | did win what he did spend, and 2.01.179
which his triumphant father's hand had won. 2.01.181
this covenant makes, my hand thus seals it. 2.03. 50
over | to execution and the hand of death. 3.01. 30
barkloughly castle call they this at hand? 3.02. 1
dear earth, i do salute thee with my hand, 3.02. 6
on both his knees doth kiss king richard's hand, 3.03. 36
show us the hand of god | that hath dismiss'd us 3.03. 77
for well we know no hand of blood and bone | can 3.03. 79
harry bullingbrook, doth humbly kiss thy hand, 3.03.104
head, | and by the buried hand of warlike gaunt, 3.03.109
yields | to the possession of thy royal hand. 4.01.110
ay, hand from hand, my love, and heart from 5.01. 82
ay, hand from hand, my love, and heart from 5.01. 82
but heaven hath a hand in these events, | to 5.02. 37
stay thy revengeful hand, thou hast no cause to 5.03. 42
my heart is not confederate with my hand. 5.03. 53
it was, villain, ere thy hand did set it down. 5.03. 54
pardon is all the suit i have in hand. 5.03.130
that jade hath eat bread from my royal hand, 5.05. 85
this hand hath made him proud with clapping him. 5.05. 86
thy own hand yields thy death's instrument, | go 5.05.106
that hand shall burn in never-quenching fire 5.05.108
thy fierce hand | hath with the king's blood 5.05.109
a deed of slander with thy fatal hand | upon my 5.06. 35
to wash this blood off from my guilty hand. 5.06. 50
sedgy bank, | in single opposition hand to hand, 1H4 1.03. 99
sedgy bank, | in single opposition hand to hand, 1.03. 99
i'll keep them, by this hand. 1.03.216
at hand, quoth pick-purse. 2.01. 48 P
that's even as far as — at hand, quoth the 2.01. 49 P
give me thy hand. 2.01. 91 P
some heavy business hath my lord in hand, | and 2.03. 63
room, and lend me thy hand to laugh a little. 2.04. 2 P
even now into my hand by an under-skinker, one 2.04. 23 P
came in, foot and hand, and with a thought seven 2.04.217 P
dark, hal, that thou couldest not see thy hand. 2.04.224 P
it was so dark thou couldst not see thy hand? 2.04.233 P
some private conference, but be near at hand, 3.02. 2
they are, | if promises be kept on every hand, 3.02.168
of death or death's hand for this one half year. 4.01.136
to meet you on the way, and kiss your hand, 5.01. 36
to gripe the general sway into your hand, 5.01. 57
alone | the insulting hand of douglas over you, 5.04. 54
but that the earthy and cold hand of death 5.04. 84
both the blunts | kill'd by the hand of douglas, 2H4 1.01. 17
now with joints of steel | must glove this hand; 1.01.147
now let not nature's hand | keep the wild flood 1.01.153
in the palm of my hand than he shall get one /of 1.02. 21 P
to bear a gentleman in hand, and then stand upon 1.02. 37 P
have you not a moist eye, a dry hand, a yellow 1.02.181 P
and harry prince of wales | are near at hand. 2.01.135
by this hand, thou thinkest me as far in the 2.02. 45 F
to pluto's damned lake, by this hand, to th' 2.04.157 P
and were these inward wars once out of hand, 3.01.107
come on, come on, give me your hand, sir, give 3.02. 2 P
give me your hand, sir, give me your hand, sir. 3.02. 2 P
give me your good hand, give me your worship's 3.02. 82 P
good hand, give me your worship's good hand. 3.02. 83 P
put me a caliver into wart's hand, bardolph. 3.02.270 P
beard the silver hand of peace hath touch'd, 4.01. 43
to lay a heavy and unequal hand | upon our 4.01.100
the prince is here at hand. 4.01.223
and a hand | open as day for /meting charity; 4.04. 31
john your son doth kiss your grace's hand. 4.04. 83
unless some dull and favorable hand | will 4.05. 2
but as an honor snatch'd with boist'rous hand, 4.05.191
give me your hand, master bardolph. 5.01. 55 P
for which i do commit into your hand | th' 5.02.113
there is my hand. 5.02.117
in which you, father, shall have foremost hand. 5.02.140
thither | by most mechanical and dirty hand. 5.05. 36
and in regard of causes now in hand, | which i H5 1.01. 77
while that the armed hand doth fight abroad, 1.02.178
my rightful hand in a well-hallow'd cause. 1.02.293
give me thy hand. 2.01.113
and shall forget the office of our hand | sooner 2.02. 33
us deliver | our puissance into the hand of god, 2.02.190
i put my hand into the bed and felt them, and 2.03. 23 P
and all our princes captiv'd by the hand | of 2.04. 55
by my hand i swear, and my father's soul, the 3.02. 90 P
by my hand, 'tish ill done! 3.02. 93 P
shame to stand still, it is shame, by my hand; 3.02.111 P
in liberty of bloody hand, shall range, | with 3.03. 12
if your pure maidens fall into the hand | of hot 3.03. 20
the blind and bloody soldier with foul hand 3.03. 34
la main? elle est appelee de hand. 3.04. 7 P
de hand. et les doigts? 3.04. 8 P
la main, de hand; 3.04. 12 P
de hand, de fingres, et de nailes. 3.04. 18 P
d' hand, de fingre, de nailes, d' arma, de 3.04. 28 P
d' hand, de fingre, de mailes — 3.04. 45 P
d' hand, de fingre, de nailes, d' arma, d' elbow 3.04. 58 P
we are in god's hand, brother, not in theirs. 3.06.169
by the white hand of my lady, he's a gallant 3.07. 93 P
by this hand i will take thee a box on the ear. 4.01.215 P
candlesticks, | with torch-staves in their hand; 4.02. 46
and with his cap in hand | like a base pander 4.05. 13
he smil'd me in the face, raught me his hand, 4.06. 21
and something lean to cutpurse of quick hand. 5.01. 86
the looks of an empress, take me by the hand, 5.02.236 P
upon that i kiss your hand, and i call you my 5.02.251 P
he ne'er lift up his hand but conquered. 1H6 1.01. 16
be not dismay'd, for succor is at hand: 1.02. 50
accursed fatal hand | that hath contriv'd this 1.04. 76
he beckons with his hand and smiles on me, | as 1.04. 92
now, by this maiden blossom in my hand, | i 2.04. 75
here, winchester, i offer thee my hand. 3.01.126
love for thy love and hand for hand i give. 3.01.135
love for thy love and hand for hand i give. 3.01.135
but gather we our forces out of hand, | and set 3.02.102
on either hand thee there are squadrons pitch'd, 4.02. 23
my hand would free her, but my heart says no. 5.03. 61
queen, | to put a golden sceptre in thy hand, 5.03.118
give thee her hand, for sign of plighted faith. 5.03.162
and here at hand the dolphin and his train 5.04.100
put forth thy hand, reach at the glorious gold. 2H6 1.02. 11
but to the matter that we have in hand. 1.03.159
that time best fits the work we have in hand. 1.04. 20
where it best fits to be, in henry's hand. 2.03. 44
and charity chas'd hence by rancor's hand; 3.01.144
here is my hand, the deed is worthy doing. 3.01.278
then, noble york, take thou this task in hand. 3.01.318
the king and all the peers are here at hand. 3.02. 10
and with my fingers feel his hand unfeeling. 3.02.145
give me thy hand, | that i may dew it with my 3.02.339
o, could this kiss be printed in thy hand, 3.02.343
hold up thy hand, make signal of thy hope. 3.03. 28
thou not kiss'd thy hand and held my stirrup? 4.01. 53
this hand of mine hath writ in thy behalf, | and 4.01. 63
brutus' bastard hand | stabb'd julius caesar; 4.01.136
no better sign of a brave mind than a hard hand. 4.02. 20 P
being burnt i' th' hand for stealing of sheep. 4.02. 63 P
thy hand is but a finger to my fist, | thy leg a 4.10. 48
this hand was made to handle nought but gold. 5.01. 7
thy hand is made to grasp a palmer's staff | and 5.01. 97
here is a hand to hold a sceptre up, | and with 5.01.102
for one to thrust his hand between his teeth, 3H6 1.04. 57
arms, | yet parted but the shadow with his hand. 1.04. 69
to thee | as now i reap at thy too cruel hand! 1.04.166
for hand to hand he would have vanquish'd thee. 2.01. 73
for hand to hand he would have vanquish'd thee. 2.01. 73
thou shalt know this strong right hand of mine 2.01.152
whose hand is that the forest bear doth lick? 2.02. 13
darraign your battle, for they are at hand. 2.02. 72
brother, give me thy hand, and gentle warwick, 2.03. 44
this is the hand that stabb'd thy father york, 2.04. 6
and this the hand that slew thy brother rutland, 2.04. 7
this man whom hand to hand i slew in fight | may 2.05. 56
this man whom hand to hand i slew in fight | may 2.05. 56
if this right hand would buy two hours' life 2.06. 80
rail at him, | this hand should chop it off; 2.06. 82
unless my hand and strength could equal them. 3.02.145
humbly to kiss your hand, and with my tongue 3.03. 61
yet shall you have all kindness at my hand 3.03.149
therefore delay not, give thy hand to warwick, 3.03.246
and, with thy hand, thy faith irrevocable | that 3.03.247
and here, to pledge my vow, i give my hand. 3.03.250
hath pawn'd an open hand in sign of love; 4.02. 9
his hand to wield a sceptre, and himself 4.06. 73
brother, we will proclaim you out of hand, | the 4.07. 63
in sign of truth, i kiss your highness' hand. 4.08. 26
then clarence is at hand, i hear his drum. 5.01. 11
they are at hand, and you shall quickly know. 5.01. 15
i had rather chop this hand off at a blow, | and 5.01. 50
this hand, fast wound about thy coal-black hair, 5.01. 54
if thou be there, sweet brother, take my hand, 5.02. 34
prepare you, lords, for edward is at hand, 5.04. 60
by the self-same hand that made these wounds! R3 1.02. 11
o, cursed be the hand that made these holes! 1.02. 14
and even with the word | this hand, which for 1.02.189
may | but beg one favor at thy gracious hand, 1.02.207
and then deny her aiding hand therein | and lay 1.03. 95
i'll kiss thy hand | in sign of league and amity 1.03.279
for he holds vengeance in his hand, | to hurl 1.04.199
/hastings and rivers, take each other's hand, 2.01. 7
and with my hand i seal my true heart's love. 2.01. 10
love lord hastings, let him kiss your hand, 2.01. 21
which with a bounteous hand was kindly lent; 2.02. 93
when great leaves fall, then winter is at hand; 2.03. 33
i'll claim that promise at your grace's hand. 3.01.197
your honor hath no shriving work in hand. 3.02.115
which in a set hand fairly is engross'd | that 3.06. 2
the mayor is here at hand. 3.07. 45
and look you get a prayer-book in your hand, 3.07. 47
and see, a book of prayer in his hand — | true 3.07. 98
led in the hand of her kind aunt of gloucester? 4.01. 2
give me thy hand. 4.02. 3
and let my griefs frown on the upper hand. 4.04. 37
but at hand, at hand, | ensues his piteous and 4.04. 73
but at hand, at hand, | ensues his piteous and 4.04. 73
whose hand soever lanch'd their tender hearts, 4.04.225
i kiss his hand. 4.05. 19
if not to heaven, then hand in hand to hell. 5.03.313
if not to heaven, then hand in hand to hell. 5.03.313
stretch'd him, and, with one hand on his dagger, H8 1.02.204
a hand as fruitful as the land that feeds us; 1.03. 56
the fairest hand i ever touch'd! 1.04. 75
to your highness' hand | i tender my commission; 2.02.102
give me your hand. 2.02.117
ever by your grace, whose hand has rais'd me. 2.02.119
to his own hand, in 's bedchamber. 3.02. 77
that, as my hand has open'd bounty to you, | my 3.02.184
more | on you than any, so your hand and heart, 3.02.186
and your master) with his own hand gave me; 3.02.247
those articles, my lord, are in the king's hand: 3.02.299
still in thy right hand carry gentle peace | to 3.02.445
what that contains, | that paper in your hand? 4.01. 14
th' archbishop | is the king's hand and tongue, 5.01. 38
come, come, give me your hand. 5.01. 94
give me thy hand, stand up; 5.01.115
y' have made a fine hand, fellows! 5.03. 70
into whose hand i give thy life. 5.04. 11
handlest in thy discourse, o, that her hand, TRO 1.01. 55
and puts me her white hand to his cloven chin — 1.02.119 P
indeed she has a marvell's white hand, i must 1.02.136 P
as agamemnon and the hand of greece | should 1.03. 63
and esteem no act | but that of hand. 1.03.200
they place before his hand that made the engine, 1.03.208
fair lord aeneas, let me touch your hand; 1.03.304
and on the cause and question now in hand | have 2.02.164
what exploit's in hand? where sups he to-night? 3.01. 81 P
here i hold your hand, here my cousin's. 3.02.198 P
slightly shakes his parting guest by th' hand, 3.03.166
a valiant greek, aeneas, take his hand, 4.01. 8
by venus' hand i swear, | no man alive can love 4.01. 23
there is at hand | paris your brother, and 4.02. 60
we must give up to diomedes' hand | the lady 4.02. 65
they are at hand and ready to effect it. 4.02. 68
and to his hand when i deliver her, | think it 4.03. 7
at the port, lord, i'll give her to thy hand, 4.04.111
lady, give me your hand, and, as we walk, | to 4.04.138
half heart, half hand, half hector comes to seek 4.05. 85
his heart and hand both open and both free, 4.05.100
thou couldst say, "this hand is grecian all, 4.05.125
give me thy hand, my cousin. 4.05.157
that hast so long walk'd hand in hand with time. 4.05.203
that hast so long walk'd hand in hand with time. 4.05.203
thy hand upon that match. 4.05.270
give me your hand. 5.01. 84
nor the hand of mars | beck'ning with fiery 5.03. 52
what work's, my countrymen, in hand? COR 1.01. 55
bloody brow | with his mail'd hand then wiping, 1.03. 35
would i | wash my fierce hand in 's heart. 1.10. 27
your hand, and yours! 2.01.194
son, | go to them, with this bonnet in thy hand, 3.02. 73

give me thy hand. | come. 4.01. 57
tribe before him, | his good sword in his hand. 4.02. 25
your hand; 4.05.147
by my hand, i had thought to have strooken him 4.05.149 P
sanctifies himself with 's hand, and turns up 4.05.195 P
dismiss'd me | thus, with his speechless hand. 5.01. 67
and in her hand | the grandchild to her blood. 5.03. 23
o, bless me here with thy victorious hand, TIT 1.01.163
with his own hand did slay his youngest son, 1.01.418
my lords, a solemn hunting is in hand, | there 2.01.112
vengeance is in my heart, death in my hand, 2.03. 38
your mother's hand shall right your mother's 2.03.121
o brother, help me with thy fainting hand — 2.03.233
reach me thy hand, that i may help thee out, 2.03.237
thy hand once more; 2.03.243
what accursed hand | hath made thee handless in 3.01. 66
chop off your hand | and send it to the king; 3.01.153
with all my heart i'll send the emperor my hand. 3.01.160
stay, father, for that noble hand of thine, 3.01.162
my hand will serve the turn. 3.01.164
my hand hath been but idle, let it serve | to 3.01.171
nay, come, agree whose hand shall go along, 3.01.174
my hand shall go. 3.01.176
agree between you, i will spare my hand. 3.01.183
lend me thy hand, and i will give thee mine. 3.01.187
good aaron, give his majesty my hand. 3.01.193
tell him it was a hand that warded him | from 3.01.194
and for thy hand | look by and by to have thy 3.01.200
o, here i lift this one hand up to heaven, | and 3.01.206
for that good hand thou sent'st the emperor. 3.01.235
and here's thy hand, in scorn to thee sent back 3.01.237
thy warlike hand, thy mangled daughter here, 3.01.255
hair, thy other hand | gnawing with thy teeth, 3.01.260
head, | and in this hand the other will i bear; 3.01.280
bear thou my hand, sweet wench, between thy 3.01.282
my name, | without the help of any hand at all. 4.01. 71
i'll be at hand, sir, see you do it bravely. 4.03.112 P
devil | that robb'd andronicus of his good hand; 5.01. 41
i play'd the cheater for thy father's hand, 5.01.111
when, for his hand, he had his two sons' heads, 5.01.115
talk, | wanting a hand to give/'t that accord? 5.02. 18
is not thy coming for my other hand? 5.02. 27
i'll find some cunning practice out of hand, 5.02. 77
death, | my hand cut off and made a merry jest; 5.02.174
this one hand yet is left to cut your throats, 5.02.181
the trumpets show the emperor is at hand. 5.03. 16
to slay his daughter with his own right hand, 5.03. 37
of that true hand that fought rome's quarrel out 5.03.102
will hand in hand all headlong hurl ourselves, 5.03.132
will hand in hand all headlong hurl ourselves, 5.03.132
shall, | lo hand in hand lucius and i will fall. 5.03.136
shall, | lo hand in hand lucius and i will fall. 5.03.136
and bring our emperor gently in thy hand, 5.03.138
what lady's that which doth enrich the hand | of ROM 1.05. 41
and, touching hers, make blessed my rude hand. 1.05. 51
if i profane with my unworthiest hand | this 1.05. 93
good pilgrim, you do wrong your hand too much, 1.05. 97
see how she leans her cheek upon her hand! 2.02. 23
o that i were a glove upon that hand, | that i 2.02. 24
it is nor hand nor foot, | nor arm nor face, 2.02. 40
bird, | that lets it hop a little from his hand, 2.02.178
for the bawdy hand of the dial is now upon the 2.04.112 P
all men's, and for a hand and a foot and a body, 2.05. 41 P
tybalt, here slain, whom romeo's hand did slay! 3.01.152
scorn, with one hand beats | cold death aside, 3.01.161
o god, did romeo's hand shed tybalt's blood? 3.02. 71
what sorrow craves acquaintance at my hand, 3.03. 5
on the white wonder of dear juliet's hand, | and 3.03. 36
her, as that name's cursed hand | murder'd her 3.03.104
hold thy desperate hand! 3.03.108
give me thy hand. 3.03.172
thursday is near, lay hand on heart, advise. 3.05.190
and ere this hand, by thee to romeo's seal'd, 4.01. 56
my dreams presage some joyful news at hand. 5.01. 2
o, give me thy hand, | one writ with me in sour 5.03. 81
than with that hand that cut thy youth in twain 5.03. 99
a cup clos'd in my true love's hand? 5.03.161
o brother montague, give me thy hand. 5.03.296
whom fortune with her ivory hand wafts to her, TIM 1.01. 70
my hand to thee, mine honor on my promise. 1.01.148
give me your hand. 1.01.163
master" and the cap | plays in the right hand, 2.01. 19
pray'd you | to hold your hand more close. 2.02.139
time, with his fairer hand, | offering the 5.01.123
you bear too stubborn and too strange a hand JC 1.02. 35
come on my right hand, for this ear is deaf, 1.02.213
he put it by with the back of his hand thus, and 1.02.223 P
held up his left hand, which did flame and burn 1.03. 16
and yet his hand, | not sensible of fire, 1.03. 17
so every bondman in his own hand bears | the 1.03.101
hold, my hand. 1.03.117
/in favor's like the work we have in hand, 1.03.129
thy full petition at the hand of brutus! 2.01. 58
but with an angry wafter of your hand | gave 2.01.246
if brutus have in hand | any exploit worthy the 2.01.316
such an exploit have i in hand, ligarius, | had 2.01.318
casca, you are the first that rears your hand. 3.01. 30
i kiss thy hand, but not in flattery, caesar; 3.01. 52
let each man render me his bloody hand. 3.01.184
next, caius cassius, do i take your hand; 3.01.186
else shall you not have any hand at all | about 3.01.248
woe to the hand that shed this costly blood! 3.01.258
lend me your hand. 3.01.297
who, though he had no hand in his death, shall 3.02. 42 P
he is at hand, and pindarus is come | to do you 4.02. 4
but if he be at hand | i shall be satisfied. 4.02. 9
but hollow men, like horses hot at hand, | make 4.02. 23
do you confess so much? give me your hand. 4.03.117
their battles are at hand; 5.01. 4
on | upon the left hand of the even field. 5.01. 17
upon the right hand i, keep thou the left. 5.01. 18
give me thy hand, messala. 5.01. 72
give me your hand first. fare you well, my lord. 5.05. 49
the weird sisters, hand in hand, | posters of MAC 1.03. 32
the weird sisters, hand in hand, | posters of 1.03. 32
the eye wink at the hand; 1.04. 52
welcome in your eye, | your hand, your tongue; 1.05. 65
give me your hand. 1.06. 28
i see before me, | the handle toward my hand? 2.01. 34
and wash this filthy witness from your hand. 2.02. 44
ocean wash this blood | clean from my hand? 2.02. 58
this my hand will rather | the multitudinous 2.02. 58
in the great hand of god i stand, and thence 2.03.130
thence to be wrench'd with an unlineal hand, 3.01. 62
how you were borne in hand, how cross'd, the 3.01. 80
whose heavy hand hath bow'd you to the grave, 3.01. 89
and with thy bloody and invisible hand | cancel 3.02. 48
things i have in head, that will to hand, 3.04.138
our suffering country | under a hand accurs'd! 3.06. 49
my heart shall be | the firstlings of my hand. 4.01.148
such sanctity hath heaven given his hand, | they 4.03.144
of arabia will not sweeten this little hand. 5.01. 51 P
come, come, come, come, give me your hand. 5.01. 67 P
i hope the days are near at hand | that chambers 5.04. 1
of us, by strong hand | and terms compulsatory, HAM 1.01.102
the hand more instrumental to the mouth, | than 1.02. 48
that it went hand in hand even with the vow | i 1.05. 49
that it went hand in hand even with the vow | i 1.05. 49
i, sleeping, by a brother's hand | of life, of 1.05. 74
and, with his other hand thus o'er his brow, 2.01. 86
and impotence | was falsely borne in hand, sends 2.02. 67
nor do not saw the air too much with your hand, 3.02. 5 P
what if this cursed hand | were thicker than 3.03. 43
offense's gilded hand may /shove by justice, 3.03. 58
if by direct or by collateral hand | they find 4.05.207
know you the hand? 4.07. 51
the hand of little employment hath the daintier 5.01. 69 P
the corse they follow did with desp'rate hand 5.01.220
hold off thy hand! 5.01.263
come, hamlet, come, and take this hand from me. 5.02.225
no, by this hand. 5.02.258
the treacherous instrument is in /thy hand, 5.02.316
that lord whose hand must take my plight shall LR 1.01.101
and here i take cordelia by the hand, | duchess 1.01.243
had he a hand to write this? 1.02. 57 P
it is his hand, my lord; 1.02. 67 P
o regan, will you take her by the hand? 2.04.194
why not by th' hand, sir? 2.04.195
give me your hand. have you no more to say? 3.01. 51
hide thee, thou bloody hand; 3.02. 53
is it not as this mouth should tear this hand 3.04. 15
give me thy hand. who's there? 3.04. 41 P
false of heart, light of ear, bloody of hand; 3.04. 92 P
foot out of brothels, thy hand out of plackets, 3.04. 96 P
be certain, you have mighty business in hand. 3.05. 16 P
hold your hand, my lord! 3.07. 72
and more convenient is he for my hand | than for 4.05. 31
give me your hand. 4.06. 25
let go my hand. 4.06. 27
o, let me kiss that hand! 4.06.132
thou rascal beadle, hold thy bloody hand! 4.06.160
lay hand upon him. 4.06.188
give me your hand, | i'll lead you to some 4.06.223
now let thy friendly hand | put strength enough 4.06.230
give me your hand; 4.06.284
and hold your hand in benediction o'er me. 4.07. 57
away, old man, give me thy hand, away! 5.02. 5
give me thy hand; 5.02. 7
before, behind thee, and on every hand, OTH 2.01. 86
not see her paddle with the palm of his hand? 2.01.254 P
lechery, by this hand; 2.01.257 P
hard at hand comes the master and main exercise, 2.01.262 P
this is my ancient, this is my right hand, and 2.03.114 P
i pray you, sir, hold your hand. 2.03.152 P
you cannot, if my heart were in your hand, | nor 3.03.163
and then, sir, would he gripe and wring my hand; 3.03.421
spotted with strawberries in your wive's hand? 3.03.435
give me your hand. this hand is moist, my lady. 3.04. 36
give me your hand. this hand is moist, my lady. 3.04. 36
this hand of yours requires | a sequester from 3.04. 39
'tis a good hand, | a frank one. 3.04. 43
for 'twas that hand that gave away my heart. 3.04. 45
a liberal hand. 3.04. 46
yours, by this hand. 4.01.175 P
i strike it, and it hurts my hand. 4.01.183 P
and put in every honest hand a whip | to lash 4.02.142
give me thy hand, roderigo. 4.02.206 P
her hand on her bosom, her head on her knee, 4.03. 42
be near at hand, i may miscarry in't. 5.01. 6
here, at thy hand; be bold, and take thy stand. 5.01. 7
by heaven, i saw my handkerchief in 's hand. 5.02. 62
i saw it in his hand; 5.02.215
of one whose hand, | like the base /indian, 5.02.346
show him your hand. ANT 1.02. 11
the hand could pluck her back that shov'd her on 1.02.127
let me have thy hand | further this act of grace 2.02.145
there's my hand. 2.02.148
to kiss — a hand that kings | have lipp'd, and 2.05. 29
lie they upon thy hand, | and be undone by 'em! 2.05.105
let me have your hand. 2.06. 48
let me shake thy hand, | i never hated thee. 2.06. 73
but give me your hand, menas; 2.06. 95 P
good antony, your hand. 2.07.126
and shall, sir, give 's your hand. 2.07.127
i kiss his conqu'ring hand. 3.13. 75
give me grace to lay | my duty on your hand. 3.13. 82
them | so saucy with the hand of she here — 3.13. 98
be familiar with | my playfellow, your hand, 3.13.125
the white hand of a lady fever thee, | shake 3.13.138
give me thy hand, | thou hast been rightly 4.02. 10
give me thy hand; 4.08. 11
man, | commend unto his lips thy /favoring hand. 4.08. 23
give me thy hand. 4.08. 29
the hand of death hath raught him. 4.09. 29
what thou wouldst do | is done unto thy hand; 4.14. 29
souls do couch on flowers, we'll hand in hand, 4.14. 51
souls do couch on flowers, we'll hand in hand, 4.14. 51
but that self hand | which writ his honor in the 5.01. 21
y' are fall'n into a princely hand, fear nothing 5.02. 22
o' th' time | died with their swords in hand; CYM 1.01. 36
they were parted | by gentlemen at hand. 1.01.164
your hand — a covenant. 1.04.164 P
this hand, whose touch | (whose every touch) 1.06.100
good morrow, fairest: sister, your sweet hand. 2.03. 86
tasted her in bed, my hand | and ring is yours; 2.04. 57
but i have a hand. 3.01. 41 P
came from horse, the place | was near at hand. 3.04. 2
my husband's hand! 3.04. 14
thou shalt not damn my hand. 3.04. 74
and if i do not by thy hand, thou art | no 3.04. 75
so divine | that cravens my weak hand. 3.04. 78
your hand, my lord. 3.05. 12
it is posthumus' hand, i know't. 3.05.108 P
give me thy hand, here's my purse. 3.05.123 P
fortune put them into my hand! 4.01. 23 P
when i have slain thee with my proper hand, 4.02. 97
with his own single hand he'ld take us in, 4.02.121
this is his hand, | his foot mercurial, his 4.02.309
whom she bore in hand to love | with such 5.05. 43
no, no, alack, | there's other work in hand. 5.05.103
wrought by th' hand | of his queen mother, which 5.05.361
on her and hers, | have laid most heavy hand. 5.05.465
a city on whom plenty held full hand, | for PER 1.04. 22
the fift, an hand environed with clouds, 2.02. 36
scorn now their hand should give them burial. 2.04. 12
or my hand subscribe | to any syllable that made 2.05. 69
to dangle't in my hand, or to go tiptoe | before TNK 1.02. 57
who is at hand to seal | the promise of his 1.02. 92
but | playing o'er business in his hand, another 1.03. 31
the hand of war hurts none here, nor the seas 2.02. 87
without your noble hand to close mine eyes, | or 2.02. 93
kiss her fair hand, sir. 2.05. 37
of prisonment were off me and this hand | but 3.01. 32
a good sword in thy hand, and do but say | that 3.01. 75
give me your hand, farewell. 3.01. 98
i would be sorry else. | give me your hand. 3.05. 78
my sword | is in my hand, and, if thou kill'st 3.06. 97
give me thy noble hand. 3.06.101
this hand shall never more | come near thee with 3.06.102
that fair hand, and that honest heart you gave 3.06.197
the same breath smil'd, and kiss'd her hand. 4.01. 93
tickle't up | in two hours, if his hand be in. 4.01.139
in his hand | he bears a charging–staff emboss'd 4.02.139
they have a noble work in hand will honor | the 5.01. 6
with hand armipotent from forth blue clouds 5.01. 54
a very fair hand, and casts himself th' accounts 5.02. 58
yes, by this fair hand, will i. 5.02. 86
at this instant are | hand to hand at it. 5.03. 84
at this instant are | hand to hand at it. 5.03. 84
reach thy hand; 5.04. 91
the gods my justice | take from my hand, and 5.04.121
how insolence and strong hand should prevail, STM II.C 81
with self–same hand, self reasons, and self II.C 85
and by her fair immortal hand she swears | from VEN 80
my smooth moist hand, were it with thy hand felt 143
smooth moist hand, were it with thy hand felt, 143
can thy right hand seize love upon thy left? 158
sometime she shakes her head, and then his hand, 223
with one fair hand she heaveth up his hat, | her 351
her other tender hand his fair cheek feels: 352
full gently now she takes him by the hand, | a 361
"give me my hand," saith he, "why dost thou feel 373
"you hurt my hand with wringing, let us part, 421
in hand with all things, nought at all effecting 912
she takes him by the hand, and that is cold, 1124
her joy with heav'd–up hand she doth express, LUC 111
quoth he, "she took me kindly by the hand, | and 253
"and how her hand, in my hand being lock'd, 260
"and how her hand, in my hand being lock'd, 260
this said, his guilty hand pluck'd up the latch, 358
which gives the watch–word to his hand full soon 370
her lily hand her rosy cheek lies under, 386
without the bed her other fair hand was, | on 393
eye, | his eye commends the leading to his hand; 436
his hand, as proud of such a dignity, | smoking 437
ranks of blue veins, as his hand did scale, 440
his hand, that yet remains upon her breast 463
beating her bulk, that his hand shakes withal. 467
"poor hand, why quiver'st thou at this decree? 1030
yield to my hand, my hand shall conquer thee: 1210
yield to my hand, my hand shall conquer thee: 1210
weeps, the other takes in hand | no cause, but 1235
fight, | making such sober action with his hand, 1403
here one man's hand lean'd on another's head, 1415
stood his spear, | grip'd in an armed hand; 1425
a hand, a foot, a face, a leg, a head | stood 1427
at last he takes her by the bloodless hand, 1597
that guides this hand to give this wound to me." 1722
this said, he strook his hand upon his breast, 1842
my hand hath sworn | ne'er to pluck thee from PP 16.11
then let not winter's ragged hand deface | in SON 6. 1
a woman's face with nature's own hand painted 20. 1
and this my hand against myself uprear, | to 49.11
or at your hand th' account of hours to crave, 58. 3
praising thy worth, despite his cruel hand. 60.14
with time's injurious hand crush'd and o'erworn, 63. 2
when i have seen by time's fell hand defaced 64. 1
or what strong hand can hold his swift foot back 65.11
remember not | the hand that writ it, for i love 71. 6
the lily i condemned for thy hand, | and buds of 99. 6
ah, yet doth beauty, like a dial hand, | steal 104. 9
of hand, of foot, of lip, of eye, of brow, | i 106. 6
to what it works in, like the dyer's hand. 111. 7
for since each hand hath put on nature's power, 127. 5
leap | to kiss the tender inward of thy hand, 128. 6
those lips that love's own hand did make 145. 1
but in her maiden hand | the fairest votary took 154. 4
desire | was sleeping by a virgin hand disarm'd. 154. 8
proclaim'd in her a careless hand of pride; LC 30
"so many have, that never touch'd his hand, 141
"'o, then advance of yours that phraseless hand, 225

HANDED 2 FR 0.0002 REL FR 2 V 0 P
and handed love as you do, i was wont | to load WT 4.04.348
(as poisonous tongu'd as handed) hath prevail'd CYM 3.02. 5

HAND–FAST 2 FR 0.0002 REL FR 1 V 1 P
if that shepherd be not in hand–fast, let him WT 4.04.768 P
of her to hold | the hand–fast to her lord. CYM 1.05. 78

HANDFUL 2 FR 0.0002 REL FR 1 V 1 P
his page a' t'other side, that handful of wit! LLL 4.01.147
i had rather have a handful or two of dried peas MND 4.01. 37 P

HANDICRAFT 1 FR 0.0001 REL FR 0 V 1 P
the best wit of any handicraft man in athens. MND 4.02. 10 P

HANDICRAFTS 1 FR 0.0001 REL FR 0 V 1 P
much advantage the poor handicrafts of the city. STM II.C 71 P

HANDICRAFTS–MEN 1 FR 0.0001 REL FR 0 V 1 P
virtue is not regarded in handicrafts–men. 2H6 4.02. 11 P
HAND–IN–HAND 1 FR 0.0001 REL FR 0 V 1 P
as good — a kind of hand–in–hand comparison — CYM 1.04. 70 P
HANDIWORK 3 FR 0.0003 REL FR 2 V 1 P
we know his handiwork. JN 1.01.238
blood, | that foul defacer of god's handiwork, R3 4.04. 51
upon neat's–leather have gone upon my handiwork. JC 1.01. 26 P
HANDKERCHER 5 FR 0.0005 REL FR 3 V 2 P
why, and where | this handkercher was stain'd. AYL 4.03. 97
to sound when he show'd me your handkercher? 5.02. 26 P
good tom drum, lend me a handkercher. AWW 5.03.321 P
i knit my handkercher about your brows | (the JN 4.01. 42
a handkercher, which, say to her, did drain R3 4.04.276
HANDKERCHERS 2 FR 0.0002 REL FR 1 V 1 P
pockets as their gloves or their handkerchers; H5 3.02. 48 P
ladies and maids their scarfs and handkerchers, COR 2.01.264
/HANDKERCHIEF 1 FR 0.0001 REL FR 1 V 0 P
/the /handkerchief! OTH 3.04. 93
HANDKERCHIEF 30 FR 0.0034 REL FR 23 V 7 P
but a handkerchief and rings of his that paulina WT 5.02. 66 P
you give me now | for that same handkerchief? OTH 3.03.306
what handkerchief? 3.03.306
what handkerchief? 3.03.307
have you not sometimes seen a handkerchief 3.03.434
but such a handkerchief | (i am sure it was your 3.03.437
where should i lose the handkerchief, emilia? 3.04. 23
lend me thy handkerchief. 3.04. 52
that handkerchief | did an egyptian to my mother 3.04. 55
fetch me the handkerchief, my mind misgives. 3.04. 89
the handkerchief! 3.04. 92
the handkerchief! 3.04. 96
sure, there's some wonder in this handkerchief; 3.04.101
but if i give my wife a handkerchief — 4.01. 10
but, for the handkerchief — 4.01. 18
house, | boding to all) he had my handkerchief. 4.01. 22
handkerchief — confessions — handkerchief! 4.01. 37 P
handkerchief — confessions — handkerchief! 4.01. 37 P
handkerchief? 4.01. 43 P
mean by that same handkerchief you gave me even 4.01.149 P
by heaven, that should be my handkerchief! 4.01.158 P
and did you see the handkerchief? 4.01.173 P
that handkerchief which i so lov'd, and gave 5.02. 48
by heaven, i saw my handkerchief in 's hand. 5.02. 62
i saw the handkerchief. 5.02. 66
it was a handkerchief, an antique token | my 5.02.216
that handkerchief thou speak'st of | i found by 5.02.225
by that handkerchief | that was my wive's? 5.02.319
then wav'd his handkerchief? CYM 1.03. 6
with glove or hat or handkerchief | still waving 1.03. 11
/HANDLE 1 FR 0.0001 REL FR 1 V 0 P
/o, /handle /not /the /theme, /to /talk /of TIT 3.02. 29
HANDLE 11 FR 0.0012 REL FR 4 V 7 P
mistress bridget lost the handle of her fan, i WIV 2.02. 12 P
to question, you shall see how i'll handle her. MM 5.01.272 P
all the lawyers in bohemia can learnedly handle, WT 4.04.206 P
can gripe the sacred handle of our sceptre, R2 3.03. 80
abuse, and then i know how to handle you. 2H4 2.04.312 P
'a did in some sort, indeed, handle women; H5 2.03. 37 P
he could not therefore handle an english cudgel. 5.01. 77 P
and not to wear, handle, or use any sword, 1H6 1.03. 78 P
this hand was made to handle nought but gold. 2H6 5.01. 7
sheath, | till you know better how to handle it. TIT 2.01. 42
i see before me, | the handle toward my hand? MAC 2.01. 34
HANDLED 4 FR 0.0004 REL FR 3 V 1 P
i think, if you handled her privately, she would MM 5.01.275 P
how wert thou handled, being prisoner? 1H6 1.04. 24
said | a stouter champion never handled sword. 3.04. 19
untouch'd or slightly handled in discourse. R3 3.07. 19
HANDLES 1 FR 0.0001 REL FR 0 V 1 P
that fellow handles his bow like a crow–keeper; LR 4.06. 87 P
HANDLESS 2 FR 0.0002 REL FR 2 V 0 P
that noseless, handless, hack'd and chipp'd, TRO 5.05. 34
hath made thee handless in thy father's sight? TIT 3.01. 67
HANDLEST 1 FR 0.0001 REL FR 1 V 0 P
handlest in thy discourse, o, that her hand, TRO 1.01. 55
HANDLING 5 FR 0.0005 REL FR 3 V 2 P
why, we are still handling our ewes, and their AYL 3.02. 53 P
a rotten case abides no handling. 2H4 4.01.159
and then they will endure handling, which before H5 5.02.310 P
mulberry | that will not hold the handling: COR 3.02. 80
a wild bird being tam'd with too much handling, VEN 560
HANDMAID 4 FR 0.0004 REL FR 4 V 0 P
but from her handmaid do return this answer: TN 1.01. 24
stay, let thy humble handmaid speak to thee. 1H6 3.03. 42
as from a blushing handmaid, to his highness; H8 2.03. 72
goths, | she will a handmaid be to his desires, TIT 1.01.331
HANDMAIDS 2 FR 0.0002 REL FR 2 V 0 P
fear and niceness | (the handmaids of all women, CYM 3.04.156
her twinkling handmaids too (by him defil'd) LUC 787
HAND'S 1 FR 0.0001 REL FR 1 V 0 P
tend'rer cheek receives her soft hand's print, VEN 353
/HANDS 13 FR 0.0014 REL FR 12 V 1 P
/little /look'd /for /at /your /helping /hands. R2 4.01.161
/with /mine /own /hands /i /give /away /my 4.01.208
/of /you, /with /pilate, /wash /your /hands, 4.01.239
/want /our /hands | /and /cannot /passionate TIT 3.02. 5
/such /violent /hands /upon /her /tender /life. 3.02. 22
/what /violent /hands /can /she /lay /on /her 3.02. 25
/dost /thou /urge /the /name /of /hands, | /to 3.02. 26
/handle /not /the /theme, /to /talk /of /hands, 3.02. 29
/as /if /we /should /forget /we /had /no /hands, 3.02. 32
/marcus /did /not /name /the /word /of /hands! 3.02. 33
mountain's top | even on their knees and /hands, TIM 1.01. 87
/deserv'd /at /the /hands /of /fortune, /that HAM 2.02.240 P
/to /let /these /hands /obey /my /blood, | /they LR 4.02. 64
HANDS 317 FR 0.0358 REL FR 260 V 57 P
unto these yellow sands, | and then take hands: TMP 1.02.376
of a tree with mine own hands since i was cast 2.02.123 P
give me your hands. 5.01.213
my bands | with the help of your good hands. ep 10
o hateful hands, to tear such loving words! TGV 1.02.102
our cat wringing her hands, and all our house in 2.03. 8 P
wringing her hands, whose whiteness so became 3.01.229
but neither bended knees, pure hands held up, 3.01.231
you, a sweet virtue in a maid with clean hands. 3.01.279 P
is as tall a man of his hands as any is between WIV 1.04. 26 P
troth, sir, all is in his hands above. 1.04.144 P
no promise of satisfaction at her hands? 2.02.210 P
on their heads, | and rattles in their hands. 4.04. 52
hold up your hands, say nothing; MM 5.01.438
for god sake hold your hands! ERR 1.02. 93
nay, he's at two hands with me, and that my two 2.01. 45 P
nay, rather persuade him to hold his hands. 4.04. 23 P
and have nothing at his hands for my service but 4.04. 32 P
and it shall privilege him from your hands 5.01. 95
to be a thief, shall we not lay hands on him? ADO 3.03. 55 P
but truth of her, | these hands shall tear her; 4.01.191
bear her in hand until they come to take hands, 4.01.304 P
let them be in the hands — 4.02. 68 P
deserve well at my hands by helping me to the 5.02. 2 P
here's our own hands against our hearts. 5.04. 91 P
or your hands in your pocket like a man after LLL 3.01. 20 P
therefore of all hands must we be forsworn. 4.03.215
ay, or i would these hands might never part. 5.02. 57
take hands. 5.02.219
why take we hands then? 5.02.220
if this thou do deny, let our hands part, 5.02.811
into the hands of one that loves you not; MND 2.01.216
when at your hands did i deserve this scorn? 2.02.124
as if our hands, our sides, voices, and minds 3.02.207
your hands than mine are quicker for a fray; 3.02.342
come, my queen, take hands with me, | and rock 4.01. 85
come, come to me, | with hands as pale as milk; 5.01.338
give me your hands, if we be friends, | and 5.01.437
hath not a jew hands, organs, dimensions, senses MV 3.01. 59 P
i commit into your hands | the husbandry and 3.04. 24
see thou render this | into my /cousin's hands, 3.04. 50
on forfeit of my hands, my head, my heart. 4.01.212
wilt thou lay hands on me, villain? AYL 1.01. 55 P
dugs that her pretty chopp'd hands had milk'd; 2.04. 50 P
worth seizure do we seize into our hands, | till 3.01. 10
salute not at the court but you kiss your hands; 3.02. 49 P
why, do not your courtier's hands sweat? 3.02. 55 P
besides, our hands are hard. 3.02. 59 P
the courtier's hands are perfum'd with civet. 3.02. 64 P
nothing, is to have rich eyes and poor hands. 4.01. 25 P
her old gloves were on, but 'twas her hands; 4.03. 26
and they shook hands and swore brothers. 5.04.102 P
here's eight that must take hands | to join in 5.04.128
"will't please your lordship cool your hands?" SHR in.1. 58
please your mightiness to wash your hands? in.2. 76
that till the father rid his hands of her, 1.01.181
unbind my hands, i'll pull them off myself, 2.01. 4
i prithee, sister kate, untie my hands. 2.01. 21
i know not what to say, but give me your hands. 2.01.318
basins and ewers to lave her dainty hands; 2.01.348
master's horse–tail till they kiss their hands. 4.01. 94 P
lay hands on the villain. 5.01. 38 P
and craves no other tribute at thy hands | but 5.02.152
and place your hands below your husband's foot; 5.02.177
and say nothing, has neither leg, hands, lip, AWW 2.02. 11 P
by your leave, hold your hands — though i know 4.03.189 P
your gentle hands lend us, and take our hearts. ep 6
we can hardly make distinction of our hands. TN 2.03.161 P
thy fates open their hands, let thy blood and 2.05.147 P
it did come to his hands, and commands shall be 3.04. 27 P
confirm'd by mutual joinder of your hands, 5.01.157
shook hands, as over a vast; WT 1.01. 30 P
for ever | unvenerable be thy hands, if thou 2.03. 78
what needs these hands? 2.03.127
the bastard brains with these my proper hands 2.03.140
five justices' hands at it, and witnesses more 4.04.283 P
take hands, a bargain! 4.04.383
kisses the hands | of your fresh princess; 4.04.550
was casting up of eyes, holding up of hands, 5.02. 47 P
a tall fellow of thy hands and that thou wilt 5.02.164 P
no tall fellow of thy hands and that thou wilt 5.02.166 P
thou wouldst be a tall fellow of thy hands. 5.02.168 P
our colors do return in those same hands | that JN 2.01.319
our lusty english, all with purpled hands, 2.01.322
command thy son and daughter to join hands. 2.01.532
close your hands. 2.01.533
and, by disjoining hands, hell lose a soul. 3.01.197
no longer than we well could wash our hands | to 3.01.234
and shall these hands, so lately purg'd of blood 3.01.239
"o that these hands could so redeem my son | as 3.04. 71
but since correction lieth in those hands R2 1.02. 4
air, | have i deserved at your highness' hands. 1.03.158
put into his hands | that knows no touch to tune 1.03.164
lay on our royal sword your banish'd hands; 1.03.179
his hands were guilty of no kinred blood, | but 2.01.182
seek you to seize and gripe into your hands 2.01.189
you will, we seize into our hands | his plate, 2.01.209
affairs | thus disorderly thrust into my hands, 2.02.110
to wash your blood | from off my hands, here in 3.01. 6
earth, | and do thee favors with my royal hands. 3.02. 11
peace is made | with heads, and not with hands. 3.02.138
that lift your vassal hands against my head, 3.03. 89
uncle, give me your hands; 3.03.202
and if i do not, may my hands rot off, | and 4.01. 49
where rude misgoverned hands from windows' tops 5.02. 5
and interchangeably set down their hands, | to 5.02. 98
was by the rude hands of that welshman taken, 1H4 1.01. 41
and that same greatness too which our own hands 1.03. 12
dozen of scots at a breakfast, washes his hands, 2.04.104 P
our hands are full of business, let's away, 3.02.179
thou doest, and do it with unwash'd hands too. 3.03.184 P
i cannot rid my hands of him. 2H4 1.02.202 P
and that i am a proper fellow of my hands, and 2.02. 68 P
will fortune never come with both hands full, 4.04.103
his greatness so | into the hands of justice." 5.02.112
and by their hands this grace of kings must die, H5 2.pr. 28
god, and i have merited some love at his hands. 3.06. 24 P
who twice a day their wither'd hands hold up 4.01.299
there is not work enough for all our hands, 4.02. 19
happy that he hath fall'n into the hands of one 4.04. 61 P
you have enschedul'd briefly in your hands. 5.02. 73
i' faith, do, and so clap hands and a bargain. 5.02.130 P
stay, stay thy hands! 1H6 1.02.104
my heart and hands thou hast at once subdu'd. 1.02.109
alive, | if salisbury wants mercy at thy hands! 1.04. 86
hold your slaught'ring hands and keep the peace. 3.01. 87
a letter was deliver'd to my hands, | writ to 4.01. 11
much, when sceptres are in children's hands; 4.01.192
ye both be suddenly surpris'd | by bloody hands, 5.03. 41
for i will touch thee but with reverend hands. 5.03. 47
in the queen | to your most gracious hands, that 2H6 1.01. 13
clapping their hands, and crying with loud voice 1.01.160
weeps over them, and wrings his hapless hands, 1.01.226
till france be won into the dolphin's hands. 1.03.170
lay hands upon these traitors and their trash. 1.04. 41
you put sharp weapons in a madman's hands. 3.01.347
lay not thy hands on me; 3.02. 46
some violent hands were laid on humphrey's life! 3.02.138
i do believe that violent hands were laid | upon 3.02.156
his hands abroad display'd, as one that grasp'd 3.02.172
when have i aught exacted at your hands, | /but 4.07. 69
great men have reaching hands; 4.07. 81
these hands are free from guiltless 4.07.102
i wonder how the king escap'd our hands. 3H6 1.01. 1
ah, whither shall i fly to scape their hands? 1.03. 1
hold you his hands whilest i do set it on. 1.04. 95
till our king henry had shook hands with death. 1.04.102
by many hands your father was subdu'd, | but 2.01. 56
your legs did better service than your hands. 2.02.104
i throw my hands, mine eyes, my heart to thee, 2.03. 36
and cheers these hands that slew thy sire and 2.04. 9
and i, who at his hands receiv'd my life, | have 2.05. 67
life, | have by my hands of life bereaved him. 2.05. 68
and bloody steel grasp'd in their ireful hands, 2.05.132
for at their hands i have deserv'd no pity. 2.06. 26
why linger we? let us lay hands upon him. 3.01. 26
too, | unless they seek for hatred at my hands; 4.01. 80
at whose hands | he hath good usage and great 4.05. 5
warwick and clarence, give me both your hands. 4.06. 38
now join your hands, and with your hands your 4.06. 39
your hands, and with your hands your hearts, 4.06. 39
call edward king and at his hands beg mercy? 5.01. 23
that, to deserve well at my brother's hands, | i 5.01. 93
if heaven will take the present at our hands. R3 1.01.120
nay, he is dead, and slain by edward's hands. 1.02. 92
we go to use our hands, and not our tongues. 1.03.351
the noble duke of clarence to your hands. 1.04. 92
that you depart, and lay no hands on me. 1.04.191
would i wash my hands | of this most grievous 1.04.272
and pluck'd two crutches from my feeble hands, 2.02. 58
i never look'd for better at his hands | after 3.05. 50
scarce the blood was well wash'd from his hands 4.01. 67
that at her hands which the king's king forbids. 4.04.346
put in their hands thy bruising irons of wrath, 5.03.110
consent proceeded | under your hands and seals. H8 2.04.223
put my sick cause into his hands that hates me? 3.01.118
up the great seal presently | into our hands, 3.02.230
into your own hands, card'nal, by extortion; 3.02.285
cromwell, her two hands, and she | sleep in 5.01. 31
pace 'em not in their hands to make 'em gentle, 5.02. 57
she be not, she has the mends in her own hands. TRO 1.01. 68 P
he is a gouty briareus, many hands and no use, 1.02. 29 P
that do contrive how many hands shall strike 1.03.201
you must needs, for you all clapp'd your hands, 2.02. 87
ag'd sir, hands off. COR 3.01.177
lay hands upon him, | and bear him to the rock. 3.01.221
lay hands upon him. 3.01.226
down the tarpeian rock | with rigorous hands. 3.01.266
are the people's mouths, | and we their hands. 3.01.271
in thy hands clutch'd as many millions, in | thy 3.03. 71
and take our friendly senators by th' hands, 4.05.132
you have made fair hands, | you and your crafts! 4.06.117
but kneels and holds up hands for fellowship, 5.03.175
that saidst i begg'd the empire at thy hands. TIT 1.01.307
and wash their hands in bassianus' blood. 2.03. 45
and with thine own hands kill me in this place! 2.03.169
go home, call for sweet water, wash thy hands. 2.04. 6
she hath no tongue to call, nor hands to wash, 2.04. 7
if thou hadst hands to help thee knit the cord. 2.04. 10
what stern ungentle hands | hath lopp'd and 2.04. 16
had the monster seen those lily hands | tremble 2.04. 44
give me a sword, i'll chop off my hands too, 3.01. 72
'tis well, lavinia, that thou hast no hands, 3.01. 79
for hands to do rome service is but vain. 3.01. 80
thou hast no hands to wipe away thy tears, | nor 3.01.106
or shall we cut away our hands like thine? 3.01.130
which of your hands hath not defended rome, 3.01.167
shall seize this prey out of his father's hands. 4.02. 96
by me thou shalt have justice at his hands. 4.03.104
and cut her hands, and trimm'd her as thou 5.01. 93
caius and valentine, lay hands on them. 5.02.158
both her sweet hands, her tongue, and that more 5.02.175
and that more dear | than hands or tongue, her 5.02.176
where civil blood makes civil hands unclean. ROM pr 4
from those bloody hands | throw your mistempered 1.01. 86
to wield old partisans, in hands as old, 1.01. 94
manners shall lie all in one or two men's hands, 1.05. 4 P
for saints have hands that pilgrims' hands do 1.05. 99
saints have hands that pilgrims' hands do touch, 1.05. 99
o then, dear saint, let lips do what hands do, 1.05.103
do thou but close our hands with holy words, 2.06. 6
ay me, what news? why dost thou wring thy hands? 3.02. 36
ay, madam, from the reach of these my hands. 3.05. 85
and see how he will take it at your hands. 3.05.125
god join'd my heart and romeo's, thou our hands, 4.01. 55
for i am sure you have your hands full all, | in 4.03. 11
nay, put out all your hands. TIM 4.02. 28
i'll beat thee, but i should infect my hands. 4.03.364
were not erected by their hands from whom | you 5.04. 23
and clapp'd their chopp'd hands, and threw up JC 1.02.245 P
in several hands, in at his windows throw, | as 1.02.316
give me your hands all over, one by one. 2.01.112
it shall be said his judgment rul'd our hands; 2.01.147
came smiling and did bathe their hands in it. 2.02. 79
speak hands for me! 3.01. 76
and let us bathe our hands in caesar's blood 3.01.106
whilst your purpled hands do reek and smoke, 3.01.158
as by our hands and this our present act | you 3.01.166
act | you see we do, yet see you but our hands, 3.01.167
therefore i took your hands, but was indeed 3.01.218
their infants quartered with the hands of war; 3.01.268
from the hard hands of peasants their vile trash 4.03. 74
caesar, thou canst not die by traitors' hands, 5.01. 56
gorging and feeding from our soldiers' hands, 5.01. 81
which nev'r shook hands, nor bade farewell to MAC 1.02. 21

as they had seen me with these hangman's hands. 2.02. 25
what hands are here? 2.02. 56
my hands are of your color; 2.02. 61
their hands and faces were all badg'd with blood 2.03.102
there would be hands uplifted in my right; 4.03. 42
look how she rubs her hands. 5.01. 27 P
action with her, to seem thus washing her hands. 5.01. 29 P
what, will these hands ne'er be clean? 5.01. 43 P
wash your hands, put on your night–gown, look 5.01. 62 P
his secret murthers sticking on his hands; 5.02. 17
by self and violent hands | took off her life; 5.09. 36
your father, | these hands are not more like. HAM 1.02.212
hold off your hands. 1.04. 80
i hold it fit that we shake hands and part, 1.05.128
and lay your hands again upon my sword. 1.05.158
your hands? 2.02.371 P
since love our hearts and hymen did our hands 3.02.159
thoughts black, hands apt, drugs fit, and time 3.02.255
leave wringing of your hands. 3.04. 34
ears without hands or eyes, smelling sans all, 3.04. 79
caps, hands, and tongues applaud it to the 4.05.108
as many | as there are tongues, are hands, are 4.07.121
with robber's hands my hospitable favors | you LR 3.07. 40
to whose hands you have sent the lunatic king — 3.07. 46
and give the distaff | into my husband's hands. 4.02. 18
i will not swear these are my hands. 4.07. 54
hold your hands, | both you of my inclining, and OTH 1.02. 81
weapons rather use | than their bare hands. 1.03.175
doth give up | the execution of his wit, hands, 3.03.466
the hearts of old gave hands; 3.04. 46
but our new heraldry is hands, not hearts. 3.04. 47
breath, indeed, these hands have newly stopp'd. 5.02.202
if it lay in their hands to make me a cuckold, ANT 1.02. 76 P
our lives upon to use our strongest hands. 2.01. 51
with the touches of those flower–soft hands, 2.02.210
these hands do lack nobility that they strike 2.05. 82
faces are true, whatsome'er their hands are. 2.06. 98 P
come, let's all take hands, | till that the 2.07.106
all take hands. 2.07.108
antony part here, even here | do we shake hands. 4.12. 20
and with those hands, that grasp'd the heaviest 4.12. 46
my resolution and my hands i'll trust, | none 4.15. 49
quick, quick, good hands. 5.02. 39
join gripes with hands | made hard with hourly CYM 1.06.106
what | if i do line one of their hands? 2.03. 67
let thine own hands take away her life. 3.04. 27 P
due fall on me by | the hands of romans! 4.04. 47
lay hands on him; 5.03. 91
a war did cease | (ere bloody hands were wash'd) 5.05.485
poison and treason are the hands of sin, | ay, PER 1.01.139
then you love us, we you, and we'll clasp hands: 2.04. 57
nay, come, your hands and lips must seal it too; 2.05. 85
lend me your hands. 3.02.107
galling | his kingly hands haling ropes, | and, 4.01. 54
you are light into my hands, where you are like 4.02. 72 P
fault | to scape his hands where i was to die. 4.02. 75
do but you hold out | your helping hands, and we TNK pr 26
dowagers, take hands, | let us be widows to our 1.01.165
our hands advanc'd before our hearts, what will 1.02.112
these hands shall never draw 'em out like 2.02. 24
and grasp | our good swords in our hands, i 2.02.209
with these hands | void of appointment, that 3.01. 39
come shake hands again then, | and take heed, as 3.06.302
give me your hands. 5.03.109
and those same hands | that you like rebels lift STM II.C 108
nor thy soft hands, sweet lips, and crystal eyne VEN 633
theirs whose desperate hands themselves do slay, 765
"to thee, to thee, my heav'd–up hands appeal, LUC 638
such wretched hands such wretched blood should 999
do in consent shake hands to torture me, | the SON 28. 6
it might unused stay | from hands of falsehood, 48. 4
or monarch's hands that lets not bounty fall LC 41

HAND–SAW* 2 FR 0.0002 REL FR 0 V 2 P

my sword hack'd like a hand–saw — ecce signum! 1H4 2.04.168 P
wind is southerly i know a hawk from a hand–saw. HAM 2.02.379 P

HANDSOME 20 FR 0.0022 REL FR 11 V 9 P

looks handsome in three hundred pounds a year! WIV 3.04. 33
cousin, let him be a handsome fellow, or else ADO 2.01. 54 P
two gowns, and every thing handsome about him. 4.02. 85 P
'a shall wear nothing handsome about him. 5.04.104 P
is't not a handsome gentleman? AWW 3.05. 80
ever i dress myself handsome till thy return — 2H4 2.04.279 P
a bachelor, and a handsome stripling too: R3 1.03.100
they were young and handsome, and of the best H8 2.02. 3 P
an' a courteous, and a kind, and a handsome, ROM 2.05. 56
sweet, and by very much more handsome than fine. HAM 2.02.445 P
besides, the knave is handsome, young, and hath OTH 2.01.245 P
a very handsome man. 4.03. 36
to see a handsome man loose–wiv'd, so it is a ANT 1.02. 71 P
now, afore me, a handsome fellow! PER 2.01. 80 P
vow'd her maidenhead | to a young handsome man. TNK 2.04. 14
his mother was a wondrous handsome woman, | his 2.05. 20
their knees | begg'd with such handsome pity, 4.01. 9
to bury you, | and see the house made handsome. 4.01. 79
two such young handsome men | shall never fall 4.02. 3
he that has | lov'd a young handsome wench then, ep 6

HANDSOMELY 3 FR 0.0003 REL FR 2 V 1 P

look | to have my pardon, trim it handsomely. TMP 5.01.294
are rich, but he wears them not handsomely. WT 4.04.750 P
"and if we miss to meet him handsomely, | sweet TIT 2.03.268

HANDSOMENESS 1 FR 0.0001 REL FR 0 V 1 P

i will beat thee into handsomeness. TRO 2.01. 15 P

HANDWRITING 1 FR 0.0001 REL FR 1 V 0 P

your own handwriting would tell you what i think ERR 3.01. 14

HANDY–DANDY 1 FR 0.0001 REL FR 0 V 1 P

places, and, handy–dandy, which is the justice, LR 4.06.153 P

/HANG* 1 FR 0.0001 REL FR 1 V 0 P

/how /would /he /hang /his /slender /gilded TIT 3.02. 61

HANG* 178 FR 0.0201 REL FR 106 V 72 P

hang, cur! TMP 1.01. 43 P
hang, you whoreson, insolent noisemaker! 1.01. 43 P
hence! hang not on my garments. 1.02.475
with a tang, | would cry to a sailor, 'go hang!' 2.02. 51
then to sea, boys, and let her go hang!" 2.02. 54
and even with such–like valor men hang and drown 3.03. 59
come, hang /them /on this line. 4.01.193
"hang him up," says the duke. TGV 4.04. 22 P
hang the trifle, woman! WIV 2.01. 46 P
hang 'em, slaves! 2.01.173 P
at a word, hang no more about me, i am no gibbet 2.02. 16 P
hang him, poor cuckoldly knave! 2.02.270 P
hang him, mechanical salt–butter rogue! 2.02.278 P
it shall hang like a meteor o'er the cuckold's 2.02.280 P
and as idle as she may hang together, for want 3.02. 13 P
hang him, dishonest rascal! 3.03.185 P
accusativo, /hung, hang, hog. 4.01. 47 P
hang him, dishonest varlet! 4.02.102 P
hang her, witch! 4.02.191 P
draw you, master froth, and you will hang them. MM 2.01.206 P
if you head and hang all that offend that way 2.01.238 P
kneel down before him, hang upon his gown; 2.02. 44
if you will hang me for it, you may; 5.01.505 P
"hang up thy mistress! ERR 2.01. 67
o lord, he will hang upon him like a disease; ADO 1.01. 86 P
or hang my bugle in an invisible baldrick, all 1.01.241 P
pen and hang me up at the door of a 1.01.253 P
if i do, hang me in a bottle like a cat, and 1.01.257 P
and he should, it were an alms to hang him. 2.03.158 P
hang him, truant! 3.02. 18 P
hang it! 3.02. 23 P
you must hang it first, and draw it afterwards. 3.02. 24 P
truly, i would not hang a dog by my will, much 3.03. 63 P
love, | and on my eyelids shall conjecture hang, 4.01.106
family's old monument | hang mournful epitaphs, 4.01.207
invention, | hang her an epitaph upon her tomb, 5.01.284
hang thou there upon the tomb, | praising her 5.03. 9
hang me by the neck if horns that year miscarry. LLL 4.01.112
if i do, hang me; 4.03. 8 P
they not, think you, hang themselves to–night? 5.02.270
to make judas hang himself. 5.02.604 P
when icicles hang by the wall | and dick the 5.02.912
and that were enough to hang us all. MND 1.02. 76 P
that would hang us, every mother's son. 1.02. 78 P
would have no more discretion but to hang us; 1.02. 81 P
here, | and hang a pearl in every cowslip's ear. 2.01. 15
hang off, thou cat, thou bur! 3.02.260
for they shall hang out for the lion's claws. 4.02. 41 P
hang on her temples like a golden fleece, MV 1.01.170
beg that thou mayst have leave to hang thyself, 4.01.364
hang there, my verse, in witness of my love, AYL 3.02. 1
tongues i'll hang on every tree, | that shall 3.02.127
and hang it round with all my wanton pictures. SHR in.1. 47
will he woo her? ay — or i'll hang her. 1.02.197
be mad and merry, or go hang yourselves; 3.02.226
i know that knave, hang him! AWW 3.05. 16 P
marry, hang you! 3.05. 91 P
general's looks, we shall be fain to hang you. 4.03.240 P
let them hang themselves in their own straps. TN 1.03. 12 P
my lady will hang thee for thy absence. 1.05. 3 P
let her hang me! 1.05. 5 P
marry, hang thee, brock! 2.05.103 P
opinion, where you will hang like an icicle on a 3.02. 27 P
hang him, foul collier! 3.04.117 P
go hang yourselves all! 3.04.123 P
the tenth of mankind | would hang themselves. WT 1.02.200
hang all the husbands | that cannot do that feat 2.03.110
hang him, he'll be made an example. 4.04.817 P
and hang a calve's–skin on those recreant limbs. JN 3.01.129
and hang a calve's–skin on those recreant limbs. 3.01.131
and hang a calve's–skin on those recreant limbs. 3.01.133
and hang a calve's–skin on his recreant limbs. 3.01.199
do so, king philip, hang no more in doubt. 3.01.219
hang nothing but a calve's–skin, most sweet lout 3.01.220
woes, | and teaches me to kill or hang myself. 3.04. 56
a rush will be a beam | to hang thee on; 4.03.130
if any plague hang over us, 'tis he. R2 5.03. 3
do not thou, when thou art king, hang a thief. 1H4 1.02. 62 P
at home and go not, i'll hang you for going. 1.02.135 P
if i hang, i'll make a fat pair of gallows; 2.01. 67 P
for if i hang, old sir john hangs with me, and 2.01. 67 P
hang thyself in thine own heir–apparent garters! 2.02. 43 P
hang ye, gorbellied knaves, are ye undone? 2.02. 88 P
hang him! 2.03. 34 P
hang me up by the heels for a rabbit–sucker or a 2.04.436 P
hang in the air a thousand leagues from hence, 3.01.224
if thou get'st any leave of me, hang me; 2H4 1.02. 89 P
hang yourself, you muddy cunger, hang yourself! 2.04. 53 P
hang yourself, you muddy cunger, hang yourself! 2.04. 53 P
hang him, swaggering rascal! 2.04. 71 P
hang him, rogue! 2.04.146 P
hang him, baboon! 2.04.240 P
let us not hang like roping icicles | upon our H5 3.05. 23
which i am sure will hang upon my tongue like a 5.02.179 P
signior, hang! 1H6 3.02. 68
you to break your necks or hang yourselves! 5.04. 91
hang up your ensigns, let your drums be still, 5.04.174
my lord, hang me if ever i spake the words. 2H6 1.03.197 P
till the axe of death | hang over thee, as sure 2.04. 50
no, it will hang upon my richest robes, | and 2.04.108
hang him with his pen and inkhorn about his neck 4.02.109 P
and hang thee o'er my tomb when i am dead. 4.10. 68
make | no excuse current but to hang thyself. R3 1.02. 84
and flourish'd, | i'll hang my head and perish. H8 3.01.153
beaten corn, | and hang their heads with sorrow. 5.04. 32
to have done is to hang | quite out of fashion, TRO 3.03.151
go hang yourself, you naughty mocking uncle! 4.02. 25
hang ye! COR 1.01.181
hang 'em! 1.01.190
hang 'em! 1.01.204
as they would hang them on the horns a' th' moon 1.01.213
no better than picture–like to hang by th' wall, 1.03. 11 P
hang 'em, | i would they would forget me, like 2.03. 56
let them hang! 3.02. 23
the blame | may hang upon your hardness, 5.03. 91
and 'twere my cause, i should go hang myself. TIT 2.04. 9
go take him away and hang him presently. 4.04. 45
me, and i hang the head | as flowers with frost, 4.04. 70
hang him on this tree, | and by his side his 5.01. 47
first hang the child, that he may see it sprawl 5.01. 51
hang up philosophy! ROM 3.03. 57
hang thee, young baggage! 3.05.160
and you be not, hang, beg, starve, die in the 3.05.192
hang him, jack! 4.05.145 P
lips, | haply some poison yet doth hang on them, 5.03.165
hang thyself! TIM 1.01.267 P
hang him, he'll abuse us. 2.02. 48 P
hang thee, monster! 4.03. 88
will o'er some high–vic'd city hang his poison 4.03.110
up in thee, | i'ld give thee leave to hang it. 4.03.280
hang them, or stab them, drown them in a draught 5.01.102
my tree hath felt the axe, | and hang himself. 5.01.212
night nor day | hang upon his penthouse lid; MAC 1.03. 20
who must hang them? 4.02. 54 P
enow to beat the honest men and hang up them. 4.02. 58 P
and sundry blessings hang about his throne 4.03.158
does he feel his title | hang loose about him, 5.02. 21
country round, | hang those that talk of fear. 5.03. 36
hang out our banners on the outward walls, | the 5.05. 1
upon the next tree shall thou hang alive, | till 5.05. 38
how is it that the clouds still hang on you? HAM 1.02. 66
why, she should hang on him | as if increase of 1.02.143
boughs her crownet weeds | clamb'ring to hang, 4.07.173
in this world to drown or hang themselves, more 5.01. 28 P
air | hang fated o'er men's faults light on thy LR 3.04. 68
hang him instantly. 3.07. 4 P
restoration hang | thy medicine on my lips, and 4.07. 25
wife and me | to hang cordelia in the prison, 5.03.254
would teach me tyranny, | to hang clogs on them. OTH 1.03.198
bear no hinge nor loop | to hang a doubt on; 3.03.366
hang her, i do but say what she is. 4.01.187 P
to do | but to go hang my head all at one side 4.03. 32
your diver | did hang a salt–fish on his hook, ANT 2.05. 17
go hang, sir, hang! 2.07. 53
go hang, sir, hang! 2.07. 53
whom | he may at pleasure whip, or hang, or 3.13.150
rebel to my will, | may hang no longer on me. 4.09. 15
pyramides my gibbet, | and hang me up in chains! 5.02. 62
conquest, shall | hang in what place you please. 5.02.136
and, for i am richer than to hang by th' walls, CYM 3.04. 52
hang there like fruit, my soul, | till the tree 5.05.263
shall as a carpet hang upon thy grave | while PER 4.01. 16
marry, hang her up for ever! 4.06.137 P
marry, hang you! 4.06.148 P
about, and hang | your shield afore your heart, TNK 1.01.196
and hang for't afterward! 2.02.264
hang him, plum porridge! 2.03. 72
lest i should drown, or stab, or hang myself! 3.02. 30
if one be mad, or hang or drown themselves, 4.03. 35 P
his head, | seem'd with strange art to hang. 5.04. 79
make them droop with grief and hang the head. VEN 666
over one shoulder doth she hang her head; 1058
thy kinsmen hang their heads at this disdain, LUC 521
cross their arms and hang their heads with mine, 793
hang on such thorns, and play as wantonly, SON 54. 7
and hang more praise upon deceased i | than 72. 7
do hang | upon those boughs which shake against 73. 2
"his browny locks did hang in crooked curls, LC 85

HANG'D 84 FR 0.0095 REL FR 31 V 53 P

if he be not born to be hang'd, our case is TMP 1.01. 33 P
he'll be hang'd yet, | though every drop of 1.01. 58
that a man is never undone till he be hang'd, TGV 2.05. 5 P
he did, i think verily he had been hang'd for't; 4.04. 15 P
ay, or else i would i might be hang'd, la! WIV 1.01.258 P
would i were hang'd la, else! 5.05.181 P
ere he would have hang'd a man for the getting a MM 3.02.117 P
i'll be hang'd first; 3.02.168 P
should be in hanging, if i should be hang'd, i 4.02. 40 P
you must rise and be hang'd, master barnardine! 4.03. 22 P
all night, and is hang'd betimes in the morning, 4.03. 46 P
your sheep–biting face, and be hang'd an hour! 5.01.354 P
whipt first, sir, and hang'd after. 5.01.507
nuptial finish'd, | let him be whipt and hang'd. 5.01.513
have howl'd thus, they would have hang'd him, ADO 2.03. 80 P
well follow'd: judas was hang'd on an elder. LLL 5.02.606 P
is quick by him and hang'd for pompey that is 5.02.681 P
a day for playing pyramus, i'll be hang'd. MND 4.02. 23 P
play'd pyramus and hang'd himself in thisby's 5.01.358 P
a wolf, who, hang'd for human slaughter, | even MV 4.01.134
thou must be hang'd at the state's charge. 4.01.367
thy name should be hang'd and carv'd upon these AYL 3.02.173 P
i'll see thee hang'd on sunday first. SHR 2.01.299
she says she'll see thee hang'd first. 2.01.300
he that is well hang'd in this world needs to TN 1.05. 5 P
yet you will be hang'd for being so long absent, 1.05. 16 P
and, lozel, thou art worthy to be hang'd, | that WT 2.03.109
hang'd in the frowning wrinkle of her brow! JN 2.01.505
that, hang'd and drawn and quarter'd, there 2.01.508
i shall yield up my crown, let him be hang'd. 4.02.157
if you will not, tarry at home and be hang'd. 1H4 1.02.133 P
an' it be not four by the day, i'll be hang'd. 2.01. 2 P
come away and be hang'd! 2.01. 22 P
come, and be hang'd! 2.01. 31 P
marry, i'll see thee hang'd first. 2.01. 40 P
poins! poins, and be hang'd! poins! 2.02. 4 P
medicines to make me love him, i'll be hang'd. 2.02. 19 P
you rogues, give me my horse, and be hang'd! 2.02. 30 P
to be hang'd. 2.02. 59 P
now cannot i strike him, if i should be hang'd. 2.02. 73 P
thou tak'st leave, thou wert better be hang'd. 2H4 1.02. 90 P
and you do not make him hang'd among you, the 2.02. 96 P
very truth, sir, i had as live be hang'd, sir, 3.02.223 P
that i might die, that i might have thee hang'd. 5.04. 2 P
thou dar'st as well be hang'd. H5 4.01.218 P
with a wooden dagger, and they are both hang'd, 4.04. 73 P
sirrah, or you must fight, or else be hang'd. 2H6 1.03.217
be hang'd up for example at their doors. 4.02.180
they could not read, thou hast hang'd them, when 4.07. 44 P
will you needs be hang'd with your pardons about 4.08. 22 P
better do so than tarry and be hang'd. 3H6 4.05. 26
want of means, poor rats, had hang'd themselves. R3 5.03.331
belong to th' gallows, and be hang'd, ye rogue! H8 5.03. 6 P
how got they in, and be hang'd? 5.03. 17 P
i will see you hang'd like clatpoles ere i come TRO 2.01.117 P
would i were hang'd but i thought there was more COR 4.05.158 P
the man must not be hang'd till the next week. TIT 4.03. 83 P
come, sirrah, you must be hang'd. 4.04. 47
hang'd! 4.04. 48 P
but i'll be hang'd, sir, if he wear your livery. ROM 3.01. 57
ho, ho, confess'd it? hang'd it, have you not? TIM 1.02. 22

learning die then that day thou art hang'd. 2.02. 83 P
burthens of the dead — some that were hang'd, 4.03.146
speak and be hang'd. 5.01.131
i can as well be hang'd as tell the manner of it JC 1.02.235 P
that hang'd himself on th' expectation of plenty MAC 2.03. 4 P
that does so is a traitor, and must be hang'd. 4.02. 50 P
and must they all be hang'd that swear and lie? 4.02. 51 P
and my poor fool is hang'd! LR 5.03.306
thou rather to be hang'd in compassing thy joy OTH 1.03.360 P
to confess, and be hang'd for his labor — first 4.01. 38 P
be hang'd for his labor — first to be hang'd, 4.01. 39 P
i will be hang'd if some eternal villain, | some 4.02.130
i will be hang'd else. 4.02.133
sound and be hang'd, sound out! ANT 2.07.133
for this pains | caesar hath hang'd him. 4.06. 15
it was hang'd | with tapestry of silk and silver CYM 2.04. 68
i'll be hang'd then. 5.04.195 P
if i do it not, i am sure to be hang'd at home. PER 1.03. 3 P
i perceive | i shall not be hang'd now, although 1.03. 26
i'll be hang'd though, | if he dare venture. TNK 2.03. 71
my father's to be hang'd for his escape; 3.02. 22
besides, my father must be hang'd to–morrow, 5.02. 80
and daff'd me to a cabin hang'd with care, | to PP 14. 3
HANGED 1 FR 0.0001 REL FR 1 V 0 P
he hath stol'n a pax, and hanged must 'a be — H5 3.06. 40
/HANGERS 1 FR 0.0001 REL FR 0 V 1 P
with their assigns, as girdle, /hangers, and so. HAM 5.02.150 P
HANGERS 2 FR 0.0002 REL FR 0 V 2 P
the /carriages, sir, are the hangers. HAM 5.02.157 P
i would it /might /be hangers till then. 5.02.160 P
HANGETH 2 FR 0.0002 REL FR 1 V 1 P
who now hangeth like a jewel in the ear of caelo LLL 4.02. 4 P
reproach and dissolution hangeth over him. R2 2.01.258
HANG–HOG 1 FR 0.0001 REL FR 0 V 1 P
"hang–hog" is latin for bacon, i warrant you. WIV 4.01. 48 P
/HANGING 2 FR 0.0002 REL FR 1 V 1 P
/might /i, /hanging /on /hotspur's /neck, 2H4 2.03. 44
in a chain, /hanging at his /brother's leg — to TRO 5.01. 56 P
HANGING 40 FR 0.0045 REL FR 22 V 18 P
good fate, to his hanging, make the rope of his TMP 1.01. 31 P
whose throats had hanging at 'em | wallets of 3.03. 45
bear | unto a ragged, fearful, hanging rock, TGV 1.02.118
the picture that is hanging in your chamber; 4.02.121
it is but heading and hanging. MM 2.01.237 P
but that you have a hanging look — do you call, 4.02. 33 P
but what mystery there should be in hanging, if 4.02. 39 P
this may prove worse than hanging. 5.01.360 P
is pressing to death, whipping, and hanging. 5.01.523 P
wears a key in his ear and a lock hanging by it, ADO 5.01.309 P
conscience, hanging about the neck of my heart, MV 2.02. 13 P
no heresy, | hanging and wiving goes by destiny. 2.09. 83
away — is not that as good as a hanging to you? TN 1.05. 18 P
many a good hanging prevents a bad marriage; 1.05. 19 P
he that wears her like her medal hanging | about WT 1.02.307
beating and hanging are terrors to me. 4.03. 29 P
i am sorry that by hanging thee i can | but 4.04.421
if they have overheard me now — why, hanging. 4.04.627 P
session, hanging, yields a careful man work. 4.04.685 P
mean thou shalt have the hanging of the thieves, 1H4 1.02. 67 P
this, if i scape hanging for killing that rogue. 2.02. 14 P
eye, and a foolish hanging of thy nether lip, 2.04.404 P
curling their monstrous heads and hanging them 2H4 3.01. 23
hanging is too good. 1H6 5.04. 33
hanging the head at ceres' plenteous load? 2H6 1.02. 2
some dreadful story hanging on thy tongue? 3H6 2.01. 44
if thou stand'st not i' th' state of hanging, or COR 5.02. 65 P
not die | so sweet a death as hanging presently. TIT 5.01.146
some consequence yet hanging in the stars ROM 1.04.107
upon his good and gracious nature hanging, TIM 1.01. 56
your blood to froth, | and so scape hanging. 4.03.431
hanging a golden stamp about their necks, | put MAC 4.03.153
creatures as | we count not worth the hanging CYM 1.05. 20
hanging is the word, sir. 5.04.153 P
by night | that seek out silent hanging. TNK 3.05.127
his braided hanging mane | upon his compass'd VEN 271
she sinketh down, still hanging by his neck, 593
woes, | for sorrow, like a heavy hanging bell, LUC 1493
which in my bosom's shop is hanging still, SON 24. 7
hat, | hanging her pale and pined cheek beside; LC 32
HANGING'S 1 FR 0.0001 REL FR 0 V 1 P
i am sure hanging's the way of winking. CYM 5.04.190 P
HANGINGS 3 FR 0.0003 REL FR 3 V 0 P
my hangings all of tyrian tapestry; SHR 2.01.349
him, | and like rich hangings in a homely house, 2H6 5.03. 12
shook down my mellow hangings, nay, my leaves, CYM 3.03. 63
HANGMAN 17 FR 0.0019 REL FR 5 V 12 P
yet i will be content to be a lawful hangman. MM 4.02. 16 P
for i do find your hangman is a more penitent 4.02. 49 P
your friends, sir — the hangman. 4.03. 26 P
and the little hangman dare not shoot at him. ADO 3.02. 11 P
some hangman must put on my shroud and lay me WT 4.04.457
fifty times) shall all come under the hangman; 4.04.775 P
of the thieves, and so become a rare hangman. 1H4 1.02. 68 P
whereof the hangman hath no lean wardrobe. 1.02. 72 P
the cords, the ladder, or the hangman rather? 1.03.166
it, i pray thee keep that for the hangman, for i 2.01. 64 P
what talkest thou to me of the hangman? 2.01. 66 P
as good a trick as ever hangman serv'd thief. TIM 2.02. 94 P
by heaven, i rather would have been his hangman. OTH 1.01. 34
a halter'd neck which does the hangman thank ANT 3.13.130
your sleep, and a hangman to help him to bed, i CYM 5.04.174 P
off, or the common hangman shall execute it. PER 4.06.128 P
serve by indenture to the common hangman: 4.06.176
HANGMAN'S 3 FR 0.0003 REL FR 2 V 1 P
was stol'n from me by the hangman's boys in the TGV 4.04. 56 P
can, | no, not the hangman's axe, bear half the MV 4.01.125
as they had seen me with these hangman's hands. MAC 2.02. 25
HANGMEN 2 FR 0.0002 REL FR 1 V 1 P
doublets that hangmen would | bury with those COR 1.05. 6
some of the best of 'em were hereditary hangmen. 2.01. 93 P
HANGS 43 FR 0.0048 REL FR 29 V 14 P
under the blossom that hangs on the bough. TMP 5.01. 94
well, thereby hangs a tale. WIV 1.04.149 P
shape of love's tyburn that hangs up simplicity. LLL 4.03. 52
what passion hangs these weights upon my tongue? AYL 1.02.257
and thereby hangs a tale." 2.07. 28
hangs odes upon hawthorns and elegies on 3.02.361 P
are you he that hangs the verses on the trees, 3.02.392 P
saddles into the dirt, and thereby hangs a tale. SHR 4.01. 58 P
he that hangs himself is a virgin; AWW 1.01.138 P
it hangs like flax on a distaff; TN 1.03.102 P
she hangs about his neck. WT 5.03.112
now, by the sky that hangs above our heads, | i JN 2.01.397
suppose | devouring pestilence hangs in our air, R2 1.03.284
what seal is that, that hangs without thy bosom? 5.02. 56
for if i hang, old sir john hangs with me, and 1H4 2.01. 68 P
my skin hangs about me like an old lady's loose 3.03. 3 P
up | and hangs resolv'd correction in the arm 2H4 4.01.211
to me, | for in my gallery thy picture hangs; 1H6 2.03. 37
roan hangs her head for grief | that such a 3.02.124
droops this lofty pine and hangs his sprays, 2H6 2.03. 45
hangs on the cutting short that fraudful man. 3.01. 81
and mark how well the sequel hangs together: R3 3.06. 4
is that poor man that hangs on princes' favors! H8 3.02.367
not for the worth that hangs upon our quarrel. TRO 2.03.207
he hangs the lip at something. 3.01.139 P
from purest snow | and hangs on dian's temple — COR 5.03. 67
it seems she hangs upon the cheek of night | as ROM 1.05. 45
contempt and beggary hangs upon thy back; 5.01. 71
there's the fool hangs on your back already. TIM 2.02. 55 P
night hangs upon mine eyes, my bones would rest, JC 5.05. 41
the moon | there hangs a vap'rous drop profound, MAC 3.05. 24
half way down | hangs one that gathers sampire, LR 4.06. 15
the usurer hangs the cozener. 4.06.163
o, thereby hangs a tail. OTH 3.01. 8 P
whereby hangs a tale, sir? 3.01. 9 P
so hangs, and lolls, and weeps upon me; 4.01.139 P
nay, sometime hangs both thief and true man. CYM 2.03. 72
here's a fish hangs in the net, like a poor PER 2.01.116 P
and thick slumber | hangs upon mine eyes. 5.01.235
and thereby hangs a tale. TNK 3.03. 41
his hair hangs long behind him, black and 4.02. 83
at last she calls to mind where hangs a piece LUC 1366
like a green plum that hangs upon a tree, | and PP 10. 5
HANG'ST 1 FR 0.0001 REL FR 1 V 0 P
him, fellow, wherefore hang'st thou upon him? 2H4 2.01. 68
HANNIBAL 4 FR 0.0004 REL FR 2 V 2 P
o thou wicked hannibal! MM 2.01.175 P
prove this, thou wicked hannibal, or i'll have 2.01.178 P
"this hector far surmounted hannibal. LLL 5.02.670
a witch by fear, not force, like hannibal, 1H6 1.05. 21
/HAP 1 FR 0.0001 REL FR 1 V 0 P
/what /will /hap /more //to–night, /safe /scape LR 3.06.114
HAP 26 FR 0.0029 REL FR 24 V 2 P
for the mischance of the hour, if it so hap. TMP 1.01. 26 P
in thy happiness | when thou dost meet good hap; TGV 1.01. 15
for me, | and by me, had not our hap been bad: ERR 1.01. 38
and, knowing whom it was their hap to save, 1.01.113
/rosaline, by good hap. LLL 2.01.210
whose hap shall be to have her | will not so SHR 1.02.267
hap what hap may, i'll roundly go about her; 4.04.107
hap what hap may, i'll roundly go about her; 4.04.107
what else may hap, to time i will commit, | only TN 1.02. 60
until the heavens, envying earth's good hap, R2 1.01. 23
more blessed hap did ne'er befall our state. 1H6 1.06. 10
some, | and try your hap against the irishmen? 2H6 3.01.314
how now, my lord, what hap? what hope of good? 3H6 2.03. 8
our hap is loss, our hope but sad despair, | our 2.03. 9
more direful hap betide that hated wretch | that R3 1.02. 17
from that contented hap which i enjoy'd, | i 1.03. 83
for 'tis ill hap | if they hold when their H8 ep 13
this hint | when we shall hap to give't them. COR 3.03. 24
and when it is thy hap | to find another that is TIT 5.02.101
his help to crave, and my dear hap to tell. ROM 2.02.189
time | every good hap to you that chances here. 3.03.171
see, by good hap, yonder's my lord; TIM 3.02. 25 P
and whatsomever else shall hap to–night, | give HAM 1.02.248
be it art or hap, | he hath spoken true. ANT 2.03. 33
that golden hap which their superiors want. LUC 42
if thou issueless shalt hap to die, | the world SON 9. 3
HAPLESS 8 FR 0.0009 REL FR 8 V 0 P
if happ'ly won, perhaps a hapless gain; TGV 1.01. 32
o my dear silvia! hapless valentine! 3.01.262
hapless egeon, whom the fates have mark'd | to ERR 1.01.140
his days may finish ere that hapless time. 1H6 3.01.200
weeps over them, and wrings his hapless hands, 2H6 1.01.226
see, ruthless queen, a hapless father's tears! 3H6 1.04.156
and i, the hapless male to one sweet bird, 5.06. 15
in vain | some happy mean to end a hapless life. LUC 1045
HAPLY *(also happily, happ'ly)*
HAPLY 32 FR 0.0036 REL FR 32 V 0 P
haply when they have judg'd me fast asleep, TGV 3.01. 25
haply, in private. ERR 5.01. 60
haply i see a friend will save my life, | and 5.01.284
haply my presence | may well abate the SHR in.1. 136
here let us breathe and haply institute | a 1.01. 8
my heart as great, my reason haply more, | to 5.02.171
'tis but the boldness of his hand, haply, AWW 3.02. 77
when haply he shall hear that she is gone, | he 3.04. 35
haply thou mayst inform | something to save thy 4.01. 82
for such disguise as haply shall become | the TN 1.02. 54
haply your eye shall light upon some toy | you 3.03. 44
more than he haply may retail from me. 2H4 1.01. 32
favor | may haply purchase him a box a' th' ear. H5 4.07.173
the commons haply rise, to save his life; 2H6 3.01.240
but if we haply scape | (as well we may, if not 5.02. 79
and i, that, haply, take them from him now, 3H6 2.05. 58
which haply by much company might be urg'd; R3 2.02.137
who haply may | misconster us in him and wail 3.05. 60
you might haply think | tongue–tied ambition, 3.07.144
then haply will she weep. 4.04.273
lips, | haply some poison yet doth hang on them, ROM 5.03.165
haply the seas and countries different | with HAM 3.01.171
and haply one as kind | for husband shalt thou 3.02.176
haply, for i am black, | and have not those soft OTH 3.03.263
so haply are they friends to antony. ANT 3.13. 48
haply you shall not see me more, or if, | a 4.02. 26
haply despair hath seiz'd her; CYM 3.05. 60
a dangerous speech, | though haply well for you. 5.05.314
haply so long until | the follow'd make pursuit? TNK 1.02. 51
haply i think on thee, and then my state | (like SON 29.10
wrong, | and haply of our old acquaintance tell. 89.12
wilt thou not haply say, | "truth needs no color 101. 5
HAPP'D 1 FR 0.0001 REL FR 1 V 0 P
and tell my lord and lady what hath happ'd. OTH 5.01.127
HAPPEN 8 FR 0.0009 REL FR 6 V 2 P
if this should ever happen, thou wouldst be ADO 1.01.269 P
in the loss that may happen, it concerns you AWW 1.03.120 P
to effect | what ever i shall happen to devise. R2 4.01.330
yet am i arm'd against the worst can happen; 3H6 4.01.128
(i would be all) against the worst may happen. H8 3.01. 25
what can happen | to me above this wretchedness? 3.01.122
more mischance | on plots and errors happen. HAM 5.02.395
shall be punish'd | with what shall happen — TNK 5.03. 8
HAPPEN'D 3 FR 0.0003 REL FR 2 V 1 P
probable) of every | these happen'd accidents; TMP 5.01.250
it hath happen'd all as i would have had it, AWW 3.02. 1 P
pray speak what has happen'd. H8 2.01. 6
HAPPENED 2 FR 0.0002 REL FR 2 V 0 P
and, if you will, tell what hath happened: SHR 4.04. 64
behold | what ruin happened in revenge of him, 1H6 2.02. 11
HAPPIER 18 FR 0.0020 REL FR 16 V 2 P
you are the happier woman. WIV 2.01.106 P
happier than this, | she is not bred so dull but MV 3.02.161
happier the man whom favorable stars | allots SHR 4.05. 40
happily met, the happier for thy son. 4.05. 59
what his happier affairs may be, are to me WT 4.02. 30 P
house, | against the envy of less happier lands; R2 2.01. 49
me | a little happier than my wretched father. H8 2.01.120
this is a happier and more comely time | than COR 4.06. 27
happier is he that has no friend to feed | than TIM 1.02.203
not so happy, yet much happier. MAC 1.03. 66
that i am wretched | makes thee the happier; LR 4.01. 66
senseless linen, happier therein than i! CYM 1.03. 7
some falls are means the happier to arise. 4.02.403
and happier much by his affliction made. 5.04.108
thou think'st thyself the happier thing to be TNK 3.01. 25
thee, | or ten times happier be it ten for one; SON 6. 8
ten times thyself were happier than thou art, 6. 9
rhyme, | exceeded by the height of happier men. 32. 8
HAPPIES 1 FR 0.0001 REL FR 1 V 0 P
which happies those that pay the willing loan; SON 6. 6
HAPPIEST 5 FR 0.0005 REL FR 5 V 0 P
happiest of all, is that her gentle spirit MV 3.02.163
i'll gild it with the happiest terms i have. 1H4 5.04.158
the happiest youth, viewing his progress through 2H4 3.01. 54
the happiest gift that ever marquess gave, | the 2H6 1.01. 15
the first and happiest hearers of the town, | be H8 pr 24
HAPPILY *(also haply, happ'ly)*
HAPPILY 40 FR 0.0045 REL FR 34 V 6 P
but that he writes | how happily he lives, how TGV 1.03. 57
happily | you something know, yet i believe MM 4.02. 95
parts that become thee happily enough | and in MV 2.02.182
happily to wive and thrive as best i may. SHR 1.02. 56
if wealthily, then happily in padua. 1.02. 76
this gentleman is happily arriv'd, | my mind 1.02.212
signior baptista, you are happily met. 4.04. 19
still, | and happily we might be interrupted. 4.04. 54
happily met, the happier for thy son. 4.05. 59
and happily i have arrived at the last | unto 5.01.127
of my thoughts | happily been absent then. AWW 1.03.235
my lord, and i wish it happily effected. 4.05. 79 P
of our grandam might happily inhabit a bird. TN 4.02. 52 P
here comes a gentleman that happily knows more. WT 5.02. 20 P
will post | to consummate this business happily. JN 5.07. 95
and happily may your sweet self put on | the 5.07.101
which elder years | may happily bring forth. R2 5.03. 22
shall happily meet | to bear our fortunes in our 1H4 1.03.297
happily a woman's voice may do some good, | when H5 5.02. 93
might happily have prov'd far worse than his. 2H6 3.01.306
he stepp'd before me happily | for my example. H8 4.02. 10
i am happily come hither. 5.01. 85
i am glad | i came this way so happily; 5.02. 9
read | his fame unparallel'd, happily amplified; COR 5.02. 16
in rome, | a roman now adopted happily, | and TIT 1.01.463
happily you may catch her in the sea; 4.03. 8
shall happily make thee there a joyful bride. ROM 3.05.115
happily met, my lady and my wife! 4.01. 18
the king hath happily receiv'd, macbeth, | the MAC 1.03. 89
which, happily, foreknowing may avoid, | o speak HAM 1.01.134
happily he is the second time come to them, for 2.02.384 P
happily, when i shall wed, | that lord whose LR 1.01.100
in choler, and happily may strike at you — OTH 2.01.273 P
with her country forms, | and happily repent. 3.03.238
if happily you my father do suspect | an 4.02. 44
happily, amen! ANT 2.02.152
yea, happily, near | the residence of posthumus; CYM 3.04.147
who may (happily) be a little angry for my so 4.01. 19 P
you happily may think | are like the troyan PER 1.04. 92
though happily her careless /wear) i followed TNK 1.03. 73
/HAPPINESS 1 FR 0.0001 REL FR 1 V 0 P
/to /diet /rank /minds /sick /of /happiness, 2H4 4.01. 64
HAPPINESS 62 FR 0.0070 REL FR 49 V 13 P
wish me partaker in thy happiness | when thou TGV 1.01. 14
all happiness bechance to thee in milan. 1.01. 61
to seal our happiness with their consents! 1.03. 49
means | plotted and 'greed on for my happiness. 2.04.183
one feast, one house, one mutual happiness. 5.04.173
lead forth and bring you back in happiness! MM 1.01. 74
me, sorrow abides and happiness takes his leave. ADO 1.01.102 P
a dear happiness to women, they would else have 1.01.128 P
he hath indeed a good outward happiness. 2.03.183 P
saith the text, is the happiness of life. LLL 4.02.162 P
it is no mean happiness, therefore, to be seated MV 1.02. 7 P
owe no man hate, envy no man's happiness, glad AYL 3.02. 75 P
good day and happiness, dear rosalind! 4.01. 30 P
it is to look into happiness through another 5.02. 44 P
will i apply that treats of happiness | by SHR 1.01. 19
all | that happiness and prime can happy call. AWW 2.01.182
even tun'd his bounty to sing happiness to him. 4.03. 10 P
all days of glory, joy, and happiness. JN 3.04.117
each day still better other's happiness | until R2 1.01. 22
more health and happiness betide my liege | than 3.02. 91
first, to thy sacred state wish i all happiness. 5.06. 6
and new happiness | added to that that i am to 2H4 4.04. 81
health, peace, and happiness to my royal father! 4.05.226
thou bring'st me happiness and peace, son john, 4.05.227

those tears | by number into hours of happiness. 5.02. 61
look pale | with envy of each other's happiness, H5 5.02.351
general, | and happiness to his accomplices! 1H6 5.02. 9
long live queen margaret, england's happiness! 2H6 1.01. 37
all happiness unto my lord the king! 3.01. 93
health and all happiness to my lord the king! 5.01.124
thou dost confirm his happiness for ever. R3 1.02.208
i fear our happiness is at the height. 1.03. 41
thing you gave in charge | beget your happiness, 4.03. 26
compare dead happiness with living woe; 4.04.119
of ten times double gain of happiness. 4.04.324
in her consists my happiness and thine; 4.04.406
his overthrow heap'd happiness upon him; H8 4.02. 64
they promis'd me eternal happiness, | and 4.02. 90
she shall be, to the happiness of england, | an 5.04. 56
pomp, | that hath aspir'd to solon's happiness, TIT 1.01.177
and might not gain so great a happiness | as 2.04. 20
tongue | unfold the imagin'd happiness that both ROM 2.06. 28
back, | happiness courts thee in her best array, 3.03.142
the steepy mount | to climb his happiness, would TIM 1.01. 76
all happiness to your honor! 1.01.109
might we but have that happiness, my lord, that 1.02. 84 P
the best of happiness, | honor, and fortunes, 1.02.228
great happiness! MAC 1.02. 58
a happiness that often madness hits on, which HAM 2.02.209 P
well — happiness to their sheets! OTH 2.03. 29 P
and lo the happiness! 3.04.108
for, in my sense, 'tis happiness to die. 5.02.290
unstate his happiness and be stag'd to th' show ANT 3.13. 30
so he wishes you all happiness, that remains CYM 3.02. 45 P
happiness! 3.05. 17
to sour your happiness, i must report | the 5.05. 26
will, | to compass such a /boundless happiness! PER 1.01. 24
of all 'say'd yet, i wish thee happiness! 1.01. 60
and crown you king of this day's happiness. 2.03. 11
what happiness has palamon! TNK 2.03. 13
and happiness prefer me to a place | where i may 2.03. 81
o happiness enjoy'd but of a few, | and, if LUC 22

HAPP'LY *(also haply, happily)*

HAPP'LY 5 FR 0.0005 REL FR 4 V 1 P
when thou, happ'ly, seest | some rare noteworthy TGV 1.01. 12
if happ'ly won, perhaps a hapless gain; 1.01. 32
happ'ly i do. 2.04. 11 P
happ'ly this life is best, | if quiet life be CYM 3.03. 29
happ'ly that name of "chaste" unhapp'ly set LUC 8

HAPP'NED 1 FR 0.0001 REL FR 0 V 1 P
how unluckily it happ'ned that i should purchase TIM 3.02. 46 P

/HAPPY 2 FR 0.0002 REL FR 2 V 0 P
/free /things /and /happy /shows /behind, | /but LR 3.06.105
/those /happy /smilets | /that /play'd /on /her 4.03. 19

HAPPY 215 FR 0.0243 REL FR 198 V 17 P
thankful | to any happy messenger from thence. TGV 2.04. 53
my health and happy being at your court. 3.01. 57
my youthful travel therein made me happy, | or 4.01. 34
lady, a happy evening! 5.01. 7
but, by my coming, i have made you happy. 5.04. 30
let me be blest to make this happy close; 5.04.117
the gift hath made me happy. 5.04.148
if not, happy man be his dole! WIV 3.04. 64 P
happy thou art not, | for what thou hast not, MM 3.01. 21
happy return be to your royal grace! 5.01. 3
it your comfort, | so happy is your brother. 5.01.399
born, and wed | unto a woman, happy but for me, ERR 1.01. 37
my life, | and happy were i in my timely death, 1.01.138
be happy, lady, for you are like an honorable ADO 1.01.111 P
i were but little happy, if i could say how much 2.01.307 P
happy are they that hear their detractions and 2.03.229 P
you have stay'd me in a happy hour, i was about 4.01.283 P
they did not bless us with one happy word. LLL 5.02.370
four happy days bring in | another moon; MND 1.01. 2
happy be theseus, our renowned duke! 1.01. 20
but earthlier happy is the rose distill'd, 1.01. 76
demetrius loves your fair, o happy fair! 1.01.182
how happy some o'er other some can be! 1.01.226
happy is hermia, wheresoe'er she lies, | for she 2.02. 90
o most happy hour! 4.02. 28 P
o happy torment, when my torturer | doth teach MV 3.02. 37
happy in this, she is not yet so old | but she 3.02.160
fair thoughts and happy hours attend on you! 3.04. 41
she kneels and prays | for happy wedlock hours. 5.01. 32
all promise, | your mistress shall be happy. AYL 1.02.245
happy is your grace, | that can translate the 2.01. 18
think my brother happy in having what he wishes 5.02. 47 P
and after, every of this happy number, | that 5.04.172
well, you are come to me in happy time, | the SHR in.1. 90
fair mistress and be happy rivals in bianca's 1.01.117 P
happy man be his dole! 1.01.139 P
what happy gale | blows you to padua here from 1.02. 48
well mayst thou woo, and happy be thy speed! 2.01.138
happy the parents of so fair a child! 4.05. 39
to be short, what not, that's sweet and happy. 5.02.110
all | that happiness and prime can happy call. AWW 2.01.182
you are too young, too happy, and too good, | to 2.03. 96
in happy time! 5.01. 6
for they shall yet belie thy happy years, | that TN 1.04. 30
i thank my stars, i am happy. 2.05.170 P
if nothing lets to make us happy both | but this 5.01.249
i shall have share in this most happy wrack. 5.01.266
why, happy man be 's dole! WT 1.02.163
happy star reign now! 1.02.363
least if you make a care | of happy holding her. 4.04.356
now were i happy if | his going i could frame to 4.04.508
happy be you! | all that you speak shows fair. 4.04.622
cull forth | out of one side her happy minion, JN 2.01.392
pains | will bring this labor to an happy end. 3.02. 10
now happy he whose cloak and center can | hold 4.03.155
me, | and i have made a happy peace with him, 5.01. 63
when we were happy we had other names. 5.04. 8
and happy newness, that intends old right. 5.04. 61
many years of happy days befall | my gracious R2 1.01. 20
take from my mouth the wish of happy years. 1.03. 94
are to a wise man ports and happy havens. 1.03.276
this happy breed of men, this little world, 2.01. 45
my life, | how happy then were my ensuing death! 2.01. 68
whom fair befall in heaven 'mongst happy souls, 2.01.129
i count myself in nothing else so happy | as in 2.03. 46
a happy gentleman in blood and lineaments, | by 3.01. 9
hath clouded all thy happy days on earth. 3.02. 68
soul, | to think our former state a happy dream, 5.01. 18
beasts, | i had been still a happy king of men. 5.01. 36
mine age, | and rob me of a happy mother's name? 5.02. 93
knees, | and never see day that the happy sees, 5.03. 94
o happy vantage of a kneeling knee! 5.03.132
now, my masters, happy man be his dole, say i, 1H4 2.02. 76 P
disgrac'd me in my happy victories, | sought to 4.03. 97
then (happy) low, lie down! 2H4 3.01. 30
you wish me health in very happy season, | for i 4.02. 79
i should rejoice now at this happy news, | and 4.04.109
be happy, he will trouble you no more. 4.05.127
"happy am i, that have a man so bold, | that 5.02.108
and not less happy, having such a son | that 5.02.110
say, | god shorten harry's happy life one day! 5.02.145
and golden times, and happy news of price. 5.03. 96
divide your happy england into four, | whereof H5 1.02.214
omit no happy hour | that may give furth'rance 1.02.300
wherein thou art less happy, being fear'd, 4.01.248
we few, we happy few, we band of brothers; 4.03. 60
and he esteems himself happy that he hath fall'n 4.04. 60 P
where ne'er from france arriv'd more happy men. 4.08.126
so happy be the issue, brother /england, | of 5.02. 12
us, | this happy night the frenchmen are secure, 1H6 2.01. 11
saint denis bless this happy stratagem! 3.02. 18
this is the happy wedding torch | that joineth 3.02. 26
would you not suppose | your bondage happy, to 5.03.111
you, | if happy england's royal king be free. 5.03.115
thanks, reignier, happy for so sweet a child, 5.03.148
and you yourself shall steer the happy helm. 2H6 1.03.100
or count them happy that enjoys the sun? 2.04. 39
and if my death might make this island happy, 3.01.148
and thought thee happy when i shook my head? 4.01. 55
this happy day | is not itself, nor have we won 5.03. 5
you are come to sandal in a happy hour; 3H6 1.02. 63
heard | the happy tidings of his good escape. 2.01. 7
and happy always was it for that son | whose 2.02. 47
methinks it were a happy life | to be no better 2.05. 21
'tis a happy thing | to be the father unto many 3.02.104
and all at once, once more a happy farewell. 4.08. 31
my mind presageth happy gain and conquest. 5.01. 71
for thou hast made the happy earth thy hell, R3 1.02. 51
long die thy happy days before thy death, | and, 1.03.206
though 'twere to buy a world of happy days — 1.04. 6
allies, | and make me happy in your unity. 2.01. 31
and, princely peers, a happy time of day! 2.01. 48
happy indeed, as we have spent the day. 2.01. 49
god bless your grace with health and happy days! 3.01. 18
to-morrow then i judge a happy day. 3.04. 6
in happy time, here comes the duke himself. 3.04. 21
myself, | no doubt we bring it to a happy issue. 3.07. 54
happy were england, would this virtuous prince 3.07. 78
and make (no doubt) us happy by his reign. 3.07.170
me, | the right and fortune of his happy stars, 3.07.172
graces both | a happy and a joyful time of day! 4.01. 6
kind tyrrel, am i happy in thy news? 4.03. 24
in charge | beget your happiness, be happy then, 4.03. 26
for happy wife, a most distressed widow; 4.04. 98
heaven and fortune bar me happy hours! 4.04.400
and be a happy mother by the deed. 4.04.427
live and beget a happy race of kings! 5.03.152
sleep, | dream of success and happy victory! 5.03.165
and all | that made me happy, at one stroke has H8 2.01.117
i care not (so much i am happy | above a number) 3.01. 33
may you be happy in your wish, my lord, | for i 3.02. 43
never so truly happy, my good cromwell! 3.02.377
those men are happy, and so are all are near her 4.01. 50
sure those men are happy that shall have 'em. 4.02.147
long, and ever happy, to the high and mighty 5.04. 2 P
heaven ever laid up to make parents happy | may 5.04. 7
before | this happy child, did i get any thing. 5.04. 65
be happy that my arms are out of use; TRO 5.06. 16
of daily fortune ever taints | the happy man; COR 4.07. 39
you have won a happy victory to rome; 5.03.186
when with a happy storm they were surpris'd, TIT 2.03. 23
o happy man, they have befriended thee! 3.01. 52
how happy art thou then, | from these devourers 3.01. 56
lords, was't not a happy star | led us to rome, 4.02. 32
i would thou wert so happy by thy stay | to hear ROM 1.01.158
these happy masks that kiss fair ladies' brows, 1.01.230
younger than she are happy mothers made. 1.02. 12
go, girl, seek happy nights to happy days. 1.03.105
go, girl, seek happy nights to happy days. 1.03.105
for this alliance may so happy prove | to turn 2.03. 91
there art thou happy. 3.03.137
there art thou happy. 3.03.138
there art thou happy. 3.03.140
madam, in happy time, what day is that? 3.05.111
i think you are happy in this second match, 3.05.222
o happy dagger, | this is thy sheath; 5.03.169
it stains the glory in that happy verse | which TIM 1.01. 16
the senators of athens, happy men! 1.01. 40
he is gone happy, and has left me rich. 1.02. 4
now lord timon's happy hours are done and past, 3.02. 6 P
go, live rich and happy, | but thus condition'd: 4.03.525
and you are come in very happy time | to bear my JC 2.02. 60
thou never com'st unto a happy birth, | but 5.03. 70
away, | to part the glories of this happy day. 5.05. 81
not so happy, yet much happier. MAC 1.03. 66
as happy prologues to the swelling act | of the 1.03.128
th' untimely emptying of the happy throne, | and 4.03. 68
happy, in that we are not /over-happy, on HAM 2.02.228 P
that your good beauties be the happy cause | of 3.01. 38
in happy time. 5.02.205 P
and by the happy hollow of a tree | escap'd the LR 2.03. 2
therefore, thou happy father, | think that the 4.06. 72
most happy! 4.06.226
about it, and write happy when th' hast done. 5.03. 35
whether a maid so tender, fair, and happy, | so OTH 1.02. 66
h'as had most favorable and happy speed: 2.01. 67
were now to die, | 'twere now to be most happy; 2.01.190
/do, /good /my /friend. in happy time, iago. 3.01. 30
i had been happy, if the general camp, | pioners 3.03.345
chaste, and true, | there's no man happy; 4.02. 18
rest you happy! ANT 1.01. 62
o happy horse, to bear the weight of antony! 1.05. 21
adieu, be happy! 3.02. 64
the gods make this a happy day to antony! 4.05. 1
been thief-stol'n, | as my two brothers, happy! CYM 1.06. 6
o happy leonatus! 1.06.156
tell me how wales was made so happy as | t' 3.02. 60
tell him | wherein you're happy — which will 3.04.174
he shall be happy that can find him, if | our 5.05. 6
happy be you! 5.05.404
so i bequeath a happy peace to you | and all PER 1.01. 50
he is a happy king, since he gains from his 2.01.104 P
with me? and welcome. happy day, my lords. 2.04. 22
or know what ground's made happy by his breath. 2.04. 28
happy what follows! 3.01. 31
she is all happy as the fairest of all, | and, 5.01. 49
do't, and happy, by my silver bow! 5.01.248
either way, i am happy: TNK 2.03. 22
may thy goodness | get thee a happy husband!" 2.04. 25
your father | sure is a happy sire then. 2.05. 9
and now the happy season once more fits | that VEN 327
unlock'd the treasure of his happy state; LUC 16
but happy monarchs still are fear'd for love; 611
in vain | some happy mean to end a hapless life. 1045
resembling sire, and child, and happy mother, SON 8.11
now stand you on the top of happy hours, | and 16. 5
then happy i, that love and am beloved | where i 25.13
how can i then return in happy plight | that am 28. 1
this wish i have, then ten times happy me! 37.14
how would thy shadow's form form happy show | to 43. 6
save where you are how happy you make those. 57.12
o, what a happy title do i find, | happy to have 92.11
i find, | happy to have thy love, happy to die! 92.12
i find, | happy to have thy love, happy to die! 92.12
since saucy jacks so happy are in this, | give 128.13

HAPS 5 FR 0.0005 REL FR 5 V 0 P
if it prove so, then loving goes by haps: ADO 3.01.105
or how haps it i seek not to advance | or raise 1H6 3.01. 31
how haps it in this smooth discourse | you told 3H6 3.03. 88
how e'er my haps, my joys /were ne'er /begun. HAM 4.03. 68
desire, | /sends /word of all that haps in tyre: PER 2.ch. 22

HARBINGER 5 FR 0.0005 REL FR 5 V 0 P
apparel vice like virtue's harbinger; ERR 3.02. 12
fast, | and yonder shines aurora's harbinger, MND 3.02.380
i'll be myself the harbinger and make joyful MAC 1.04. 45
child of ver, | merry spring-time's harbinger, TNK 1.01. 8
but thou shriking harbinger, | foul precurrer of PHT 5

HARBINGERS 2 FR 0.0002 REL FR 2 V 0 P
those clamorous harbingers of blood and death. MAC 5.06. 10
as harbingers preceding still the fates | and HAM 1.01.122

HARBOR 22 FR 0.0024 REL FR 21 V 1 P
safely in harbor | is the king's ship, in the TMP 1.02.226
dare you presume to harbor wanton lines? TGV 1.02. 42
"my thoughts do harbor with my silvia nightly, 3.01.140
that they should harbor where their lord should 3.01.149
why i desire thee | to give me secret harbor, MM 1.03. 4
i will not harbor in this town to-night. ERR 3.02.149
though so denied fair harbor in my house. LLL 2.01.174
argosies | are richly come to harbor suddenly. MV 5.01.277
where shame doth harbor, even in mowbray's face. R2 1.01.195
man, | and find no harbor in a royal heart. 2H6 3.01.336
where shall it find a harbor in the earth? 5.01.168
o monstrous fault, to harbor such a thought! 3H6 3.02.164
now, for this night, let's harbor here in york; 4.07. 79
either to harbor fled, | or made a toast for TRO 1.03. 44
shall make their harbor in our town till we TIM 5.04. 53
harbor more craft and more corrupter ends | than LR 2.02.102
there's one gone to the harbor? OTH 2.01.120
do thou meet me presently at the harbor. 2.01.214 P
my treasure's in the harbor; ANT 3.11. 11
sluggish /crare | mightst easil'est harbor in? CYM 4.02.206
nature of your error | should give you harbor? STM II.C 127
dark harbor for defame! LUC 768

HARBORAGE 2 FR 0.0002 REL FR 2 V 0 P
craves harborage within your city walls. JN 2.01.234
and harborage for ourself, our ships, and men. PER 1.04.100

HARBOR'D 1 FR 0.0001 REL FR 1 V 0 P
were harbor'd in their rude circumference. JN 2.01.262

HARBORING 1 FR 0.0001 REL FR 1 V 0 P
this breast from harboring foul deceitful 2H6 4.07.103

HARBORS 3 FR 0.0003 REL FR 2 V 1 P
or that, or any place that harbors men. ERR 1.01.136
you that, though she harbors you as her kinsman, TN 2.03. 96 P
and in his simple show he harbors treason. 2H6 3.01. 54

/HARD 1 FR 0.0001 REL FR 1 V 0 P
/will /not /allow, | /stand /in /hard /cure. LR 3.06.100

HARD 179 FR 0.0202 REL FR 134 V 45 P
and here you sty me | in this hard rock, whiles TMP 1.02.343
alas, now pray you | work not so hard. 3.01. 16
my father | is hard at study; 3.01. 20
it shall go hard but i'll prove it by another. TGV 1.01. 85 P
and being so hard to me that brought your mind, 1.01.138 P
fear she'll prove as hard to you in telling your 1.01.139 P
no token but stones, for she's as hard as steel. 1.01.140 P
now, daughter silvia, you are hard beset. 2.04. 49
wrong, | to bear a hard opinion of his truth: 2.07. 81
play the cur with him, look you, it goes hard: 4.04. 2 P
robert, be ready here hard by in the brew-house, WIV 3.03. 10 P
hard by, at street end; he will be here anon. 4.02. 39 P
your master is hard at door. 4.02.109 P
are all couch'd in a pit hard by herne's oak, 5.03. 13 P
i have been drinking hard all night, and i will MM 4.03. 53 P
unkindness blunts it more than marble hard. ERR 2.01. 93
master, knock the door hard. 3.01. 58
by the barrenness, hard in the palm of the hand. 3.02.120 P
/one whose hard heart is button'd up with steel; 4.02. 34
find in my heart that i had not a hard heart, ADO 1.01.127 P
learn | any hard lesson that may do thee good. 1.01.293
for "scorn," "horn," a hard rhyme; 5.02. 38 P
o, these are barren tasks, too hard to keep, LLL 1.01. 47
butt-shaft is too hard for hercules' club, and 1.02.176 P
you are too hard for me. 2.01.258
was that the king that spurr'd his horse so hard 4.01. 1
she's too hard for you at pricks, sir, challenge 4.01.138
hard lodging and thin weeds | nip not the gaudy 5.02.801
but there is two hard things: MND 3.01. 47 P
is it not hard, nerissa, that i cannot choose MV 1.02. 25 P
whose own hard dealings teaches them suspect 1.03.161
my conscience is but a kind of hard conscience, 2.02. 29 P
be god's sonties, 'twill be a hard way to hit. 2.02. 45 P
and it shall go hard but i will better the 3.01. 72 P
hard food for midas, i will none of thee; 3.02.102

deny not, | it will go hard with poor antonio. 3.02.290
you may as well do any thing most hard, | as 4.01. 78
he attendeth here hard by | to know your answer, 4.01.145
since nought so stockish, hard, and full of rage 5.01. 81
indeed there is fortune too hard for nature, AYL 1.02. 48 P
punish me not with your hard thoughts, wherein i 1.02.183 P
i have by hard adventure found mine own. 2.04. 45
besides, our hands are hard. 3.02. 59 P
lord, it is a hard matter for friends to meet; 3.02.184 P
he trots hard with a young maid between the 3.02.313 P
time's pace is so hard that it seems the length 3.02.316 P
heart th' accustom'd sight of death makes hard, 3.05. 4
'tis at the tuft of olives here hard by. 3.05. 75
shepherd, ply her hard. 3.05. 76
have you heard, but something hard of hearing: SHR 2.01.183
my life, sir? how, i pray? for that goes hard. 4.02. 80
it shall go hard if cambio go without her. 4.04.108
this is hard and undeserv'd measure, my lord. AWW 2.03.257 P
'tis hard! 2.03.297
'tis a hard bondage to become the wife | of a 3.05. 64
that were hard to compass, | because she will TN 1.02. 44
the count himself here hard by woos her. 1.03.107 P
not i, | it is too hard a knot for me t' untie! 2.02. 41
under your hard construction must i sit, | to 3.01.115
you'll kiss me hard and speak to me as if | i WT 2.01. 5
this ballad against the hard hearts of maids. 4.04.278 P
or else 'twere hard luck, being in so 5.02.147 P
made hard with kneeling, i do pray to thee, JN 3.01.310
making the hard way sweet and delectable. R2 2.03. 7
your fearful land | with hard bright steel, and 3.02.111
"it is as hard to come as for a camel | to 5.05. 16
thorough the flinty ribs | of this hard world, 5.05. 21
yea, but i doubt they will be too hard for us. 1H4 1.02.181 P
who bears hard | his brother's death at bristow, 1.03.270
here, hard by. stand close. 2.02. 75 P
hark how hard he fetches breath. 2.04.530 P
their courage with hard labor tame and dull, 4.03. 23
after him came spurring hard | a gentleman, 2H4 1.01. 36
after you have labor'd so hard, you should talk 2.02. 29 P
return, and't shall go hard but i'll make him a 3.02.329 P
already 'a be kill'd with your hard opinions; ep 31 P
hold hard the breath, and bend up every spirit H5 3.01. 16
the flesh'd soldier, rough and hard of heart, 3.03. 11
o hard condition, | twin-born with greatness, 4.01.233
what is this castle call'd that stands hard by? 4.07. 88
lord, a hard condition for a maid to consign to. 5.02.298 P
was, | again, in pity of my hard distress, 1H6 2.05. 87
because thy flinty heart, more hard than they, 2H6 3.02. 99
no better sign of a brave mind than a hard hand. 4.02. 20 P
'twill go hard with you. 4.02.101 P
humphrey stafford and his brother are hard by, 4.02.114 P
for he is fierce and cannot brook hard language. 4.09. 45
she is hard by with twenty thousand men; 3H6 1.02. 51
then, clifford, were thy heart as hard as steel, 2.01.201
then the world goes hard | when clifford cannot 2.06. 77
he plies her hard, and much rain wears the 3.02. 50
good day, my lord. what, at your book so hard? 5.06. 1
spur your proud horses hard, and ride in blood; R3 5.03.340
or else you suffer | too hard an exclamation. H8 1.02. 52
hearts of most hard temper | melt and lament for 2.03. 11
strikes his breast hard, and anon he casts | his 3.02.117
my mind's not on't, you are too hard for me. 5.01. 57
spirit of sense | hard as the palm of ploughman. TRO 1.01. 59
the hard and soft, seem all affin'd and kin; 1.03. 25
blunt wedges rive hard knots; 1.03.316
why was my cressid then so hard to win? 3.02.116
hard to seem won; 3.02.117
the great aufidius | a shield as hard as his. COR 1.06. 80
he was ever too hard for him; 4.05.184 P
he was too hard for him, directly to say the 4.05.185 P
o, be to me, though thy hard heart say no, TIT 2.03.155
is soft as wax, tribunes more hard than stones; 3.01. 45
in penalty alike, and 'tis not hard, i think, ROM 1.02. 2
the orchard walls are high and hard to climb, 2.02. 63
who knocks so hard? 3.03. 78
distasteful looks, and these hard fractions, TIM 2.02.211
hard fate! 3.05. 74
in sufferance, time | hath made thee hard in't. 4.03.269
o you hard hearts, you cruel men of rome, | knew JC 1.01. 36
know | that i do fawn on men and hug them hard, 1.02. 75
rome | under these hard conditions as this time 1.02.174
caesar doth bear me hard, but he loves brutus. 1.02.313
caius ligarius doth bear caesar hard, | who 2.01.215
how hard it is for women to keep counsel! 2.04. 9
i do beseech ye, if you bear me hard, | now, 3.01.157
from the hard hands of peasants their vile trash 4.03. 74
(whereto the rather shall his day's hard journey MAC 1.07. 62
is the initiate fear that wants hard use: 3.04.142
things at once | 'tis hard to reconcile. 4.03.139
last | upon his will i seal'd my hard consent. HAM 1.02. 60
indeed, my lord, it followed hard upon. 1.02.179
he took me by the wrist, and held me hard, 2.01. 84
what, have you given him any hard words of late? 2.01.104
an't shall go hard | but i will delve one yard 3.04.207
i have watch'd and travell'd hard: LR 2.02.155
'tis hard, almost impossible. 2.04.242
or the hard rein which both of them hath borne 3.01. 27
gracious my lord, hard by here is a hovel, 3.02. 61
repose you there, while i to this hard house 3.02. 63
t' obey in all your daughters' hard commands. 3.04.149
any cause in nature that make these hard hearts? 3.06. 78 P
hard, hard. o filthy traitor! 3.07. 32
hard, hard. o filthy traitor! 3.07. 32
godliness i have, | i did full hard forbear him. OTH 1.02. 10
venetian be not too hard for my wits and all the 1.03.356 P
hard at hand comes the master and main exercise, 2.01.261 P
let me but bind it hard, within this hour | it 3.03.286
then kiss me hard, | as if he pluck'd up kisses 3.03.422
but when we in our viciousness grow hard | (o ANT 3.13.111
take to you no hard thoughts. 5.02.117
from this practice but make hard your heart; CYM 1.05. 24
with hands | made hard with hourly falsehood 1.06.107
as slippery as the gordian knot was hard! 2.02. 34
the stone's too hard to come by. 2.04. 46
many among us can gripe as hard as cassibelan. 3.01. 40 P
art o' th' court, | as hard to leave as keep; 3.03. 47
how hard it is to hide the sparks of nature! 3.03. 79
outcraftied him, | and he's at some hard point. 3.04. 16
when resty sloth | finds the down pillow hard. 3.06. 35
i should woo hard, but be your groom in honesty: 3.06. 69
the certainty of this hard life, aye hopeless 4.04. 27
like fragments in hard voyages, became | the 5.03. 44
should from my lips | pluck a hard sentence. 5.05.289
for death-like dragons here affright thee hard. PER 1.01. 29
retain anew | her charitable heart, now hard, TNK 1.02. 25
no hard oppressor | dare take this from us; 2.02. 84
yet pardon me hard language. 3.01.106
i spurr'd hard to come up, and under me | i had 3.06. 76
he was kept down with hard meat and ill lodging, 5.02. 97
then it goes hard, i see. ep 5
"art thou obdurate, flinty, hard as steel? VEN 199
o, had thy mother borne so hard a mind, | she 203
the bearing earth with his hard hoof he wounds, 267
o, give it me, lest thy hard heart do steel it, 375
because adonis' heart hath made mine hard." 378
for where a heart is hard they make no batt'ry." 426
he bends her fingers, holds her pulses hard, 476
eyes' shrowd tutor, that hard heart of thine, 500
hot, faint, and weary, with her hard embracing, 559
fearing some hard news from the warlike band LUC 255
deep impression bears | of hard misfortune, 1713
the wind, | faithful friends are hard to find: PP 20.32
my deepest sense, how hard true sorrow hits, SON 120.10
why, 'twas beautiful and hard, | whereto his LC 211

HARD-A-KEEPING 1 FR 0.0001 REL FR 1 V 0 P
or, having sworn too hard-a-keeping oath, LLL 1.01. 65

HARD-BELIEVING 1 FR 0.0001 REL FR 1 V 0 P
o hard-believing love, how strange it seems! VEN 985

HARDEN 1 FR 0.0001 REL FR 1 V 0 P
tears harden lust, though marble /wear with LUC 560

HARDER 13 FR 0.0014 REL FR 11 V 2 P
seek to soften that — than which what's harder? MV 4.01. 79
and make itself a pastime | to harder bosoms! WT 1.02.153
hard bright steel, and hearts harder than steel. R2 3.02.111
the harder match'd, the greater victory: 3H6 5.01. 70
thinking it harder for our mistress to devise TRO 3.02. 79 P
(more harder than the stones whereof 'tis rais'd LR 3.02. 64
harder, harder — so. 4.06.173
harder, harder — so. 4.06.173
whither your costard or my ballow be the harder. 4.06.242 P
cheek, | exposing it (but o, the harder heart! CYM 3.04.161
o, if no harder than a stone thou art, | melt at LUC 593
him with hard'ned hearts, harder than stones, 978
and my next self thou harder hast engrossed: SON 133. 6

HARDEST 2 FR 0.0002 REL FR 1 V 1 P
style, and the hardest voice of her behavior (to WIV 1.03. 47 P
the hardest knife ill us'd doth lose his edge. SON 95.14

HARDEST-TIMBER'D 1 FR 0.0001 REL FR 1 V 0 P
hews down and fells the hardest-timber'd oak. 3H6 2.01. 55

HARD-FAVOR'D 8 FR 0.0009 REL FR 6 V 2 P
is she not hard-favor'd, sir? TGV 2.01. 48 P
no, truly, unless thou wert hard-favor'd; AYL 3.03. 29 P
why should hard-favor'd grief be lodg'd in thee, R2 5.01. 14
disguise fair nature with hard-favor'd rage; H5 3.01. 8
is that devil's butcher, | hard-favor'd richard? 3H6 5.05. 78
"were i hard-favor'd, foul, or wrinkled old, VEN 133
"hard-favor'd tyrant, ugly, meagre, lean, 931
"'for some hard-favor'd groom of thine,' quoth LUC 1632

HARD-FAVORED 1 FR 0.0001 REL FR 1 V 0 P
o thou whose wounds become hard-favored death,
1H6 4.07. 23

HARD-HAIR'D 1 FR 0.0001 REL FR 1 V 0 P
hard-hair'd, and curl'd, thick twin'd like TNK 4.02.104

HARD-HANDED 1 FR 0.0001 REL FR 1 V 0 P
hard-handed men that work in athens here, MND 5.01. 72

HARD-HEARTED 8 FR 0.0009 REL FR 6 V 2 P
that now men grow hard-hearted and will lend ADO 5.01.311 P
you draw me, you hard-hearted adamant; MND 2.01.195
o, sir, i will not be so hard-hearted; TN 1.05.244 P
o king, believe not this hard-hearted man! R2 5.03. 87
ah, my sour husband, my hard-hearted lord, 5.03.121
hard-hearted clifford, take me from the world, 3H6 1.04.167
why, that same pale hard-hearted wench, that ROM 2.04. 4
or were they all hard-hearted? TNK 2.02.122

HARDIEST 1 FR 0.0001 REL FR 1 V 0 P
and when the hardiest warriors did retire, 3H6 1.04. 14

HARDIMENT 3 FR 0.0003 REL FR 3 V 0 P
in changing hardiment with great glendower. 1H4 1.03.101
now, | for thus popp'd paris in his hardiment, TRO 4.05. 28
like hardiment posthumus hath | to cymbeline CYM 5.04. 75

HARDINESS 2 FR 0.0002 REL FR 2 V 0 P
nation lose | the name of hardiness and policy. H5 1.02.220
hardness ever | of hardiness is mother. CYM 3.06. 22

/HARDLY 1 FR 0.0001 REL FR 1 V 0 P
/i /hardly /yet /have /learn'd | /to /insinuate, R2 4.01.164

HARDLY 40 FR 0.0045 REL FR 25 V 15 P
truly, sir, i think you'll hardly win her. TGV 1.01.133 P
i look on you, i can hardly think you my master. 2.01. 31 P
now trust me, madam, it came hardly off; 2.01.109
i can hardly believe that, since you know not MM 3.02.153 P
me | that i shall hardly spare a pound of flesh MV 3.03. 33
i was an irish rat, which i can hardly remember. AYL 3.02.177 P
it stands so that i may hardly tarry so long. SHR in.2. 125 P
that mortal ears might hardly endure the din? 1.01.173
hardly serve. AWW 4.01. 54 P
matter we can hardly make distinction of our TN 2.03.160 P
i can hardly forbear hurling things at him. 3.02. 81 P
i could hardly entreat him back. 3.04. 58 P
you'll leave yourself | hardly one subject. WT 2.03.112
and as hardly | will he endure your sight as yet 4.04.469
myself, well mounted, hardly have escap'd. JN 5.06. 42
days, | and hardly kept our countrymen together, R2 2.04. 2
very hardly, upon such a subject. 2H4 2.02. 44 P
you shall not hardly offend her. 2.04.116 P
that can hardly be, master shallow. 5.05. 76 P
her husband's neck, hardly to be shook off. H5 5.02.180 P
supply, | and hardly keeps his men from mutiny, 1H6 1.01.160
that hardly we escap'd the pride of france. 3.02. 40
have done, for more i hardly can endure. 2H6 1.04. 38
these oracles | are hardly attain'd, and hardly 1.04. 71
are hardly attain'd, and hardly understood. 1.04. 71
with me, | knowing how hardly i can brook abuse? 5.01. 92
so | that hardly can i check my eyes from tears. 3H6 1.04.151
have aught committed that is hardly borne | /by R3 2.01. 58
the grieved commons | hardly conceive of me; H8 1.02.105
so | that we shall hardly in our ages see COR 3.01. 7
i was hardly mov'd to come to thee; 5.02. 72 P
and what remains will hardly stop the mouth | of TIM 2.02.147
and he that's once denied will hardly speed. 3.02. 62
profit again should hardly draw me here. MAC 5.03. 62
goneril, | and hardly shall i carry out my side, LR 5.01. 61
hardly gave audience, or | /vouchsaf'd to think ANT 1.04. 7
see | how hardly i was drawn into this war, 5.01. 74
yet use thee not so hardly | as prouder livers CYM 3.03. 8
'twill hardly come out. PER 2.01.117 P
till heavens did | make hardly one the winner. TNK 5.03.130

HARD'NED 2 FR 0.0002 REL FR 2 V 0 P
hard'ned be the hearts | of all that hear me, WT 3.02. 52
stone him with hard'ned hearts, harder than LUC 978

HARDNESS 6 FR 0.0006 REL FR 6 V 0 P
the blame | may hang upon your hardness, COR 5.03. 91
and prompt alacrity | i find in hardness; OTH 1.03.233
o, hardness to dissemble! 3.04. 34
against the flint and hardness of my fault, ANT 4.09. 16
hardness ever | of hardiness is mother. CYM 3.06. 21
whose containing | is so from sense in hardness, 5.05.431

HARD'NING 1 FR 0.0001 REL FR 1 V 0 P
of my brains | (and hard'ning of my brows). WT 1.02.146

HARDOCKS 1 FR 0.0001 REL FR 1 V 0 P
with hardocks, hemlock, nettles, cuckoo-flow'rs, LR 4.04. 4

HARD-RUL'D 1 FR 0.0001 REL FR 1 V 0 P
lie i' th' bosom of | our hard-rul'd king. H8 3.02.101

HARDY 9 FR 0.0010 REL FR 8 V 1 P
that you be never so hardy to come again in his TN 2.02. 9 P
/renown'd | for hardy and undoubted champions; 3H6 5.07. 6
how now, my hardy, stout, resolved mates, | are R3 1.03.339
and buckingham, back'd with the hardy welshmen, 4.03. 47
who like a good and hardy soldier fought MAC 1.02. 4
this body | as hardy as the nemean lion's nerve. HAM 1.04. 83
thing, nor be so hardy | ever to take a husband. TNK 1.01.204
the hardy youths strive for the games of honor, 2.02. 10
which shows him hardy, fearless, proud of 4.02. 80

HARE 19 FR 0.0021 REL FR 13 V 6 P
cold decree — such a hare is madness the youth, MV 1.02. 19 P
her love is not the hare that i do hunt; AYL 4.03. 18
paltry boy, and more a coward than a hare. TN 3.04.386 P
you are the hare of whom the proverb goes, JN 2.01.137
what sayest thou to a hare, or the melancholy of 1H4 1.02. 77 P
stirs | to rouse a lion than to start a hare! 1.03.198
heels for a rabbit-sucker or a poulter's hare. 2.04.437 P
having the fearful flying hare in sight, | with 3H6 2.05.130
manhood and honor | should have hare hearts, TRO 2.02. 48
if i fly, martius, | hollow me like a hare. COR 1.08. 7
no hare, sir, unless a hare, sir, in a lenten ROM 2.04.132 P
no hare, sir, unless a hare, sir, in a lenten 2.04.132 P
an old hare hoar, | and an old hare hoar, | is 2.04.134
an old hare hoar, | and an old hare hoar, | is 2.04.135
but a hare that is hoar | is too much for a 2.04.137
or the hare the lion. MAC 1.02. 35
comes i' th' nick, as mad as a march hare. TNK 3.05. 73
by me, | uncouple at the timorous flying hare, VEN 674
"and when thou hast on foot the purblind hare, 679

HAREBELL 1 FR 0.0001 REL FR 1 V 0 P
nor | the azur'd harebell, like thy veins; CYM 4.02.222

HARE-BRAIN'D 2 FR 0.0002 REL FR 2 V 0 P
a hare-brain'd hotspur, govern'd by a spleen. 1H4 5.02. 19
this town, for they are hare-brain'd slaves, 1H6 1.02. 37

HARE-FINDER 1 FR 0.0001 REL FR 0 V 1 P
us cupid is a good hare-finder and vulcan a rare ADO 1.01.184 P

HARE-LIP 2 FR 0.0002 REL FR 1 V 1 P
never mole, hare-lip, nor scar, | nor mark MND 5.01.411
pin, /squinies the eye, and makes the hare-lip; LR 3.04.118 P

HARES 4 FR 0.0004 REL FR 3 V 1 P
have the voice of lions and the act of hares, TRO 3.02. 88 P
where he should find you lions, finds you hares; COR 1.01.171
and snatch 'em up, as we take hares, behind: ANT 4.07. 13
but that of coward hares, hot goats, and venison CYM 4.04. 37

HARFLEW 8 FR 0.0009 REL FR 7 V 1 P
majestical, | holding due course to harflew. H5 3.pr. 17
with fatal mouths gaping on girded harflew. 3.pr. 27
i will not leave the half-achieved harflew 3.03. 8
therefore, you men of harflew, | take pity of 3.03. 27
come, uncle exeter, | go you and enter harflew; 3.03. 52
to-night in harflew will we be your guest; 3.03. 57
with pennons painted in the blood of harflew. 3.05. 49
tell him we could have rebuk'd him at harflew, 3.06.121 P

/HA'RFORD-WEST 1 FR 0.0001 REL FR 1 V 0 P
at pembroke or at /ha'rford-west in wales. R3 4.05. 10

/HARK 1 FR 0.0001 REL FR 1 V 0 P
/hark, /marcus, /what /she /says; TIT 3.02. 35

HARK 159 FR 0.0179 REL FR 130 V 29 P
my quaint ariel, | hark in thine ear. TMP 1.02.318
hark, hark! 1.02.381
hark, hark! 1.02.381
hark, hark, i hear | the strain of strutting 1.02.385
hark, hark, i hear | the strain of strutting 1.02.385
hark now i hear them — ding-dong bell. 1.02.405
hark what thou else shalt do me. 1.02.496
what harmony is this? my good friends, hark! 3.03. 18
hark, hark! 4.01.257
hark, hark! 4.01.257
hark, they roar! 4.01.261
but hark thee: TGV 3.01.127
hark, hark! 4.02. 36 P
hark, hark! 4.02. 36 P
hark, what fine change is in the music. 4.02. 68 P
whither go you, george, hark you? WIV 2.01.149 P
hark, i will tell you what our sport shall be. 2.01.210 P
cannot attain it, why then hark you hither! 3.04. 21
hark ye, master slender would speak a word with 3.04. 29 P
hark, good mine host: 4.06. 18
and, in requital of your prophecy, hark you: MM 2.01.245 P
hark how i'll bribe you. 2.02.145
but hark, what noise? 4.02. 69
hark how the villain would close now, after his 5.01.342 P
hark, hark, i hear him, mistress; ERR 5.01.184
hark, hark, i hear him, mistress; 5.01.184
hark, slave, it is but this: LLL 3.01.162 P
but hark, a voice! MND 3.01. 86
"lower"? hark again. 3.02.305
but hark, i hear the footing of a man. MV 5.01. 24
music, hark! 5.01. 97
hark, apollo plays, | and twenty caged SHR in.2. 35
hark, tranio, thou mayst hear minerva speak. 1.01. 84

hark you, sir, i'll have them very fairly bound 1.02.145
hortensio, hark. 1.02.211
hark you, sir, you mean not her to — 1.02.223
hark, petruchio, she says she'll see thee hang'd 2.01.300
hark, hark, i hear the minstrels play. 3.02.183
hark, hark, i hear the minstrels play. 3.02.183
hark! AWW 3.05. 8 P
hark you, they come this way. 3.05. 38
hark ye, | the queen your mother rounds apace: WT 2.01. 15
ancientry, stealing, fighting — hark you now! 3.03. 63 P
hark, perdita! | i'll hear you by and by. 4.04.506
hark, the kings and the princes, our kindred, 5.02.172 P
come hither, little kinsman, hark, a word. JN 3.03. 18
but hark you, kate, | i must not have you 1H4 2.03.102
but hark you, kate, | whither i go, thither 2.03.114
nay, but hark you, francis: 2.04. 58 P
but hark ye, what cunning match have you made 2.04. 89 P
hark how hard he fetches breath. 2.04.530 P
hark thee hither, mistress doll. 2H4 2.04.152 P
hark how they shout! 4.02. 87
hark you, the king is coming, and i must speak H5 3.06. 85 P
hark how our steeds for present service neigh! 4.02. 8
but hark, what new alarum is this same? 4.06. 35
hark, countrymen, either renew the fight, | or 1H6 1.05. 27
hark, by the sound of drum you may perceive 3.03. 29
hark ye; not so; in witness, take ye that. 3.04. 37
hark, hark, the dolphin's drum, a warning bell, 4.02. 39
hark, hark, the dolphin's drum, a warning bell, 4.02. 39
but hark you, margaret, | no princely 5.03.175
and hark ye, sirs: 5.04. 55
ah, hark, the fatal followers do pursue, | and i 3H6 1.04. 22
hark, hark, my lord, what shouts are these? 4.08. 51
hark, hark, my lord, what shouts are these? 4.08. 51
i cannot think it. hark, what noise is this? R3 2.02. 33
hark, a drum. 3.05. 16
hark, come hither, tyrrel. 4.02. 78
hark, i hear their drum. 5.03.337
hark, the trumpets sound; H8 5.03. 82
hark what good sport is out of town to–day. TRO 1.01.113
hark, they are coming from the field. 1.02.177 P
hark, do you not hear the people cry "troilus"? 1.02.224 P
that string, | and hark what discord follows. 1.03.110
hark, there's one up. 4.02. 18
hark, you are call'd. 4.04. 50
hark, hector's trumpet! 4.04.140
now, my sweet guardian! hark, a word with you. 5.02. 7
hark a word in your ear. 5.02. 34
hark, greek: 5.02.167
hark how troy roars! 5.03. 83
they are at it, hark! 5.03. 95
hark! 5.08. 15
hark, hark, what /shout is this? 5.09. 1
hark, hark, what /shout is this? 5.09. 1
hark, our drums | are bringing forth our youth. COR 1.04. 15
hark you, far off! 1.04. 19
and hark, what noise the general makes! 1.05. 9
hark, the trumpets. 2.01.156 P
why, hark you! 5.04. 48
hark you! 5.04. 51
hark, how they joy! 5.04. 57
but hark! 5.06. 48
why, hark ye, hark ye, and are you such fools TIT 2.01. 99
hark ye, hark ye, and are you such fools | to 2.01. 99
hark, tamora, the empress of my soul, | which 2.03. 40
hark how her sighs doth /blow! 3.01.225
hark ye, lords, you see i have given her physic, 4.02.162
hark, wretches, how i mean to martyr you. 5.02.180
hark, villains, i will grind your bones to dust, 5.02.186
now god in heaven bless thee! hark you, sir. ROM 2.04.194
hark ye, your romeo will be here at night. 3.02.140
hark how they knock! 3.03. 74
for hark you, tybalt being slain so late, | it 3.04. 24
hark, hark, one knocks. JC 2.01.304
hark, hark, one knocks. 2.01.304
hark, boy, what noise is that? 2.04. 16
hark, he is arriv'd. 4.02. 30
ho, lucilius, hark, a word with you. 5.01. 69
and hark, they shout for joy. 5.03. 32
hark thee, clitus. 5.05. 5
hark thee, dardanius. 5.05. 8
hark! MAC 2.02. 2
hark! 2.02. 11
hark! who lies i' th' second chamber? 2.02. 17
hark, more knocking. 2.02. 66
hark, i hear horses. 3.03. 8
hark, i am call'd; 3.05. 34
hark, she speaks. 5.01. 32 P
hark you, guildenstern, and you too — at each HAM 2.02.381 P
hark, the duke's trumpets! LR 2.01. 79
horrible steep. | hark, do you hear the sea? 4.06. 4
hark in thine ear: 4.06.152 P
hark. 5.03. 26
but hark! OTH 2.01. 93
but hark, what noise? 2.03.144
hark how these instruments summon to supper! 4.02.169
hark, who is't that knocks? 4.03. 53 P
hark! 5.01. 40
hark! 5.01. 46
hark, canst thou hear me? 5.02.247
hark, ventidius. ANT 2.02. 16
widow? charmian, hark. 3.03. 27
hark, the land bids me tread no more upon't, 3.11. 1
hark! 4.03. 13
peace! | hark further. 4.09. 11
hark, the drums | demurely wake the sleepers. 4.09. 29
but hark thee, charmian. 5.02.192
hark thee, a word. CYM 1.05. 32
hark, hark, the lark at heaven's gate sings, 2.03. 20
hark, hark, the lark at heaven's gate sings, 2.03. 20
hark you, he swears; 2.04.122
hark, the game is rous'd! 3.03. 98
hark, boys. 3.06. 80
my ingenious instrument | (hark, polydore), it 4.02.187
hark! 4.02.188
the rest (hark in thine ear) as black as incest, PER 1.02. 76
hark you, my friend. you said you could not beg? 2.01. 85 P
hark you, sir; do you know where ye are? 2.01. 96 P
ay, but hark you, my friend, 'twas we that made 2.01.148 P
hark, hark, you gods! 4.06.146 P
hark, hark, you gods! 4.06.146 P
shall be discover'd, please you sit and hark. 5.ch. 24
but hark, what music? 5.01.223
hark, sir, they call | the scatter'd to the TNK 3.01.108
hark, 'tis a wolf! 3.02. 4
hark how yon spurs to spirit do incite | the 5.03. 56
hark, "arcite! 5.03. 93

HARLOT 7 FR 0.0008 REL FR 7 V 0 P
and tear the stain'd skin off my harlot brow, ERR 2.02.136
dissembling harlot, thou art false in all, | and 4.04.101
for the harlot king | is quite beyond mine arm, WT 2.03. 4
consorted with that harlot, strumpet shore, R3 3.04. 71
or a harlot for her weeping, | or a dog that TIM 1.02. 66
more, | portia is brutus' harlot, not his wife. JC 2.01.287
to my father, brands the harlot | even here, HAM 4.05.119

HARLOTRY 4 FR 0.0004 REL FR 2 V 2 P
like one of these harlotry players as ever i see 1H4 2.04.395 P
desperate here, a peevish self–will'd harlotry, 3.01.196
a peevish self/–will'd harlotry it is. ROM 4.02. 14
he sups to–night with a harlotry, and thither OTH 4.02.233 P

HARLOT'S 2 FR 0.0002 REL FR 2 V 0 P
and possess me | some harlot's spirit! COR 3.02.112
the harlot's cheek, beautied with plast'ring art HAM 3.01. 50

HARLOTS 3 FR 0.0003 REL FR 2 V 1 P
while she with harlots feasted in my house. ERR 5.01.205
helen and hero hildings and harlots, thisby a ROM 2.04. 42 P
as thine is now, held with a brace of harlots. TIM 4.03. 80

/HARM 1 FR 0.0001 REL FR 1 V 0 P
/mouth, | /thy /sheep /shall /take /no /harm." LR 3.06. 44

HARM 97 FR 0.0109 REL FR 76 V 21 P
tell your piteous heart | there's no harm done. TMP 1.02. 15
no harm: 1.02. 15
doth your honor see any harm in his face? MM 2.01.153 P
master froth do the constable's wife any harm? 2.01.158 P
more lenity to lechery would do no harm in him. 3.02. 98 P
but indeed i can do you little harm; 3.02.166 P
to make bad good, and good provoke to harm. 4.01. 15
deep | gave any tragic instance of our harm: ERR 1.01. 64
here this night, they will surely do us no harm. 4.04.152 P
is there any harm in "the heavier for a husband" ADO 3.04. 34 P
to turn all beauty into thoughts of harm, | and 4.01.107
yet bend not all the harm upon yourself; 5.01. 39
when i was wont to think no harm all night, LLL 1.01. 44
most power to do most harm, least knowing ill; 2.01. 58
mislead night–wanderers, laughing at their harm? MND 2.01. 39
never harm, | nor spell, nor charm, | come our 2.02. 16
seem to say we will do no harm with our swords, 3.01. 18 P
although i hate her, i'll not harm her so. 3.02.270
can you do me greater harm than hate? 3.02.271
be not afraid; she shall not harm thee, helena. 3.02.321
what harm a wind too great might do at sea. MV 1.01. 24
glad of other men's good, content with my harm, AYL 3.02. 76 P
if that be all, masters, i hear no harm. SHR 1.02.188
it shall do you no harm to learn. AWW 2.02. 36 P
and in his sleep he does little harm, save to 4.03.256 P
of beef and i believe that does harm to my wit. TN 1.03. 85 P
what incidency thou dost guess of harm | is WT 1.02.403
to answer, "whoop, do me no harm, good man" — 4.04.199 P
him, with "whoop, do me no harm, good man." 4.04.200 P
fear not, man, here's no harm intended to thee. 4.04.629 P
what other harm have i, good lady, done, | but JN 3.01. 38
but spoke the harm that is by others done? 3.01. 39
which harm within itself so heinous is | as it 3.01. 40
i doubt | my uncle practices more harm to me. 4.01. 20
but for containing fire to harm mine eye. 4.01. 66
for the instrument is cold, | and would not harm me. 4.01.104
that speaks thy words again to do thee harm! R2 2.01.231
that any harm should stain so fair a show! 3.03. 71
thou hast done much harm upon me, hal, god 1H4 1.02. 92 P
to say i know more harm in him than in myself, 2.04.466 P
why, sir john, my face does you no harm. 3.03. 28 P
no harm. what more? 4.01. 90
he never did harm, that i heard of. H5 3.07.100 P
follow, and see there be no harm between them. 4.07.182
dare presume, sweet prince, he thought no harm. 1H6 4.01.179
doth york intend no harm to us | that thus he 2H6 5.01. 56
i never did thee harm; why wilt thou slay me? 3H6 1.03. 38
to do them good i would sustain some harm. 3.02. 39
what may befall him, to his harm and ours. 4.06. 95
when as he meant all harm. 5.07. 34
no other harm but loss of such a lord. R3 1.03. 7
cannot a plain man live and think no harm, | but 1.03. 51
lest to thy harm thou move our patience. 1.03.247
as well the fear of harm, as harm apparent, | in 2.02.130
as well the fear of harm, as harm apparent, | in 2.02.130
glory, | to feed my humor wish thyself no harm. 4.01. 64
you know an enemy intends you harm; TRO 2.02. 39
and reason flies the object of all harm. 2.02. 41
why, 'tis this naming of him does him harm. 2.03.228
you | (like one that means his proper harm) in COR 1.09. 57
what harm can your beesom conspectuities glean 2.01. 64 P
'twixt doing them neither good nor harm; 2.02. 18 P
the which shall turn you to no further harm 3.01.282
it shall find | the harm of unscann'd swiftness, 3.01.311
she loves thee, boy, too well to do thee harm. TIT 4.01. 6
i never did thee harm. TIM 4.03.172
call'st thou that harm? 4.03.173
for here it sleeps, and does no hired harm. 4.03.291
there is no harm intended to your person, | nor JC 3.01. 90
'twere best he speak no harm of brutus here! 3.02. 68
and oftentimes, to win us to our harm, | the MAC 1.03.123
for none of woman born | shall harm macbeth. 4.01. 81
i have done no harm. 4.02. 74
world — where to do harm | is often laudable, 4.02. 75
womanly defense, | to say i have done no harm? 4.02. 79
he shall never more | be fear'd of doing harm. LR 2.01.111
a satisfaction of my thought, | no further harm. OTH 3.03. 98
in bed | an hour, or more, not meaning any harm? 4.01. 4
naked in bed, iago, and not mean harm? 4.01. 5
but then i saw no harm, and then i heard | each 4.02. 4
thou hast not half that pow'r to do me harm | as 5.02.162
devils do the gods great harm in their women; ANT 5.02.276 P
sir, | harm not yourself with your vexation, | i CYM 1.01.134
hah? | no harm, i trust, is done? 1.01.161
suspect you, madam, | but you shall do no harm. 1.05. 32
good masters, harm me not. 3.06. 45
no exorciser harm thee! 4.02.276
if i do lie and do | no harm by it, though the 4.02.378
he hath done no britain harm, | though he have 5.05. 90
that i suffer'd | was all the harm i did. 5.05.336
/one | that fears not to do harm; TNK 1.02. 71
better never born | than minister to such harm! 5.03. 66
the heat i have from thence doth little harm, VEN 195
whose inward ill no outward harm express'd. LUC 91
one sweetly flatters, th' other feareth harm, 172
a little harm done to a great good end | for 528
harm have i done to them, but ne'er was harmed, LC 194

HARM'D 4 FR 0.0004 REL FR 4 V 0 P
though yet he never harm'd me, here i quit him. AWW 5.03.299
she hath been then more fear'd than harm'd, my H5 1.02.155
than ever you /or yours by me were harm'd! R3 4.04.239
it harm'd not me. OTH 3.03.339

HARM–DOING 1 FR 0.0001 REL FR 1 V 0 P
she never knew harm–doing — o, now after | so H8 2.03. 5

HARMED 2 FR 0.0002 REL FR 2 V 0 P
his short thick neck cannot be easily harmed; VEN 627
harm have i done to them, but ne'er was harmed, LC 194

HARMFUL 10 FR 0.0011 REL FR 10 V 0 P
is | as it makes harmful all that speak of it. JN 3.01. 41
eyes, ears, and harmful sound of words — | then 3.03. 51
peace, | and be no further harmful than in show. 5.02. 77
lest, being suffer'd in that harmful slumber, 2H6 3.02.262
lenity | and harmful pity must be laid aside. 3H6 2.02. 10
more mild, but yet more harmful — kind in R3 4.04.173
of wisdom | than prais'd for harmful mildness. LR 1.04.344
but not without that harmful stroke which since 4.02. 77
in her harmless breast | a harmful knife, that LUC 1724
chide, | the guilty goddess of my harmful deeds, SON 111. 2

/HARMLESS 1 FR 0.0001 REL FR 1 V 0 P
/poor /harmless /fly, | /that, /with /his TIT 3.02. 63

HARMLESS 18 FR 0.0020 REL FR 15 V 3 P
which you say is a harmless fairy, has done TMP 4.01.196 P
yet this is your harmless fairy, monster! 4.01.212 P
why he, a harmless necessary cat; MV 4.01. 55
out of the bowels of the harmless earth, | which 1H4 1.03. 61
harmless richard was murthered traitorously. 2H6 2.02. 27
as is the sucking lamb or harmless dove. 3.01. 71
do seek subversion of thy harmless life? 3.01.208
looking the way her harmless young one went, 3.01.215
a napkin steeped in the harmless blood | of 3H6 2.01. 62
dens, | poor harmless lambs abide their enmity. 2.05. 75
so first the harmless sheep doth yield his 5.06. 8
i took him for the plainest harmless creature R3 3.05. 25
and she (like harmless lightning) throws her eye CYM 5.05.394
she is continually in a harmless distemper, TNK 4.03. 3 P
his insulting falchion lies | harmless lucretia, LUC 510
such harmless creatures have a true respect | to 1347
and give the harmless show | an humble gait, 1507
even here she sheathed in her harmless breast 1723

HARMONIOUS 2 FR 0.0002 REL FR 2 V 0 P
majestic vision, and | harmonious charmingly. TMP 4.01.119
uttering such dulcet and harmonious breath MND 2.01.151

HARMONY 21 FR 0.0023 REL FR 19 V 2 P
th' harmony of their tongues hath into bondage TMP 3.01. 41
what harmony is this? my good friends, hark! 3.03. 18
is, | as hush'd on purpose to grace harmony! ADO 2.03. 39
tongue | doth ravish like enchanting harmony. LLL 1.01.167
the gods | make heaven drowsy with the harmony. 4.03.342
the night | become the touches of sweet harmony. MV 5.01. 57
such harmony is in immortal souls, | but whilst 5.01. 63
this is | the patroness of heavenly harmony. SHR 3.01. 5
and while i pause, serve in your harmony. 3.01. 14
hands | that knows no touch to tune the harmony. R2 1.03.165
dying men | enforce attention like deep harmony. 2.01. 6
when such strings jar, what hope of harmony? 2H6 2.01. 55
at last by notes of household harmony | they 3H6 4.06. 14
meditating | on that celestial harmony i go to. H8 4.02. 80
nell, he is full of harmony. TRO 3.01. 53 P
had he heard the heavenly harmony | which that TIT 2.04. 48
cannot i command to any utt'rance of harmony. HAM 3.02.362 P
above do tune | the harmony of this peace. CYM 5.05.467
fed | with such delightful pleasing harmony. PER 2.05. 28
she questionless with her sweet harmony, | and 5.01. 45
"lest the deceiving harmony should run | into VEN 781

HARM'S 1 FR 0.0001 REL FR 1 V 0 P
know'st thou any harm's intended towards him? JC 2.04. 31

HARMS 19 FR 0.0021 REL FR 19 V 0 P
which bars a thousand harms and lengthens life. SHR in.2. 136
my spirit can no longer bear these harms. 1H6 4.07. 30
arms | of the most bloody nurser of his harms! 4.07. 46
but cheerly seek how to redress their harms. 3H6 5.04. 2
the loss of such a lord includes all harms. R3 1.03. 8
but none can help our harms by wailing them. 2.02.103
this league | peep'd harms that menac'd him — H8 1.01.183
to heal rome's harms, and wipe away her woe! TIT 5.03.148
your charms, | the close contriver of all harms, MAC 3.05. 7
being compar'd | with my confineless harms. 4.03. 55
whose nature is so far from doing harms | that LR 1.02.180
let me still take away the harms i fear, | not 1.04.329
repair those violent harms that my two sisters 4.07. 27
ten thousand harms, more than the ills i know, ANT 1.02.129
beg often our own harms, which the wise pow'rs 2.01. 6
are weakly fortress'd from a world of harms. LUC 28
o impious act, including all foul harms! 199
their oaths, should right poor ladies' harms." 1694
for fear of harms that preach in our behoof. LC 165

HARNESS 6 FR 0.0006 REL FR 6 V 0 P
their harness studded all with gold and pearl. SHR in.2. 42
he doth fill fields with harness in the realm, 1H4 3.02.101
faith, young troilus, doff thy harness, youth, TRO 5.03. 31
men should drink with harness on their throats. TIM 1.02. 52
at least we'll die with harness on our back. MAC 5.05. 51
through proof of harness to my heart, and there ANT 4.08. 15

HARNESS'D 2 FR 0.0002 REL FR 2 V 0 P
this harness'd masque and unadvised revel, JN 5.02.132
before the sun rose he was harness'd light, TRO 1.02. 8

HARP 8 FR 0.0009 REL FR 7 V 1 P
his word is more than the miraculous harp. TMP 2.01. 87 P
o gracious duke, | harp not on that; MM 5.01. 64
to be sung | by an athenian eunuch to the harp." MND 5.01. 45
me no more | than an unstringed viol or a harp, R2 1.03.162
i framed to the harp | many an english ditty 1H4 3.01.121
harp not on that string, madam, that is past. R3 4.04.364
harp on it still shall i till heart–strings 4.04.365
say you ne'er had done't | (harp on that still) COR 2.03.252

HARP'D 1 FR 0.0001 REL FR 1 V 0 P
thou hast harp'd my fear aright. MAC 4.01. 74
HARPER'S 1 FR 0.0001 REL FR 1 V 0 P
nor woo in rhyme, like a blind harper's song! LLL 5.02.405
HARPIER 1 FR 0.0001 REL FR 1 V 0 P
harpier cries, "'tis time, 'tis time." MAC 4.01. 3
HARPING 2 FR 0.0002 REL FR 1 V 1 P
still harping on my daughter. HAM 2.02.187 P
proud and disdainful, harping on what i am, ANT 3.13.142
HARPY 3 FR 0.0003 REL FR 2 V 1 P
bravely the figure of this harpy hast thou TMP 3.03. 83
hold three words' conference with this harpy. ADO 2.01.271 P
thou art like the harpy, | which, to betray, PER 4.03. 46
HARRIED 1 FR 0.0001 REL FR 1 V 0 P
i repent me much | that so i harried him. ANT 3.03. 40
HARROW 2 FR 0.0002 REL FR 2 V 0 P
let the volsces | plough rome and harrow italy, COR 5.03. 34
whose lightest word | would harrow up thy soul, HAM 1.05. 16
/HARROWS 1 FR 0.0001 REL FR 1 V 0 P
most like; it /harrows me with fear and wonder. HAM 1.01. 44
/HARRY 2 FR 0.0002 REL FR 2 V 0 P
/had /my /sweet /harry /had /but /half /their 2H4 2.03. 43
i had a /harry, till a richard kill'd him: R3 4.04. 41
HARRY 107 FR 0.0121 REL FR 89 V 18 P
when, harry? R2 1.01.162
my lord aumerle, is harry herford arm'd? 1.03. 1
harry of herford, lancaster, and derby | am i, 1.03. 35
harry of herford, lancaster, and derby, 1.03.100
harry of herford, lancaster, and derby | stands 1.03.104
and holds you dear | as harry duke of herford, 2.01.144
and is not harry true? 2.01.192
intelligence | that harry duke of herford, 2.01.279
lord northumberland, his son young harry percy, 2.02. 53
it is my son, young harry percy, | sent from my 2.03. 21
harry, how fares your uncle? 2.03. 23
welcome, harry. 3.03. 20
harry bullingbrook, doth humbly kiss thy hand, 3.03.104
young harry percy, and brave archibald, | that 1H4 1.01. 53
and dishonor stain the brow | of my young harry. 1.01. 86
then would i have his harry and he mine. 1.01. 90
which harry percy here at holmedon took, | were, 1.03. 24
what e'er lord harry percy then had said | to 1.03. 71
and "gentle harry percy" and "kind cousin" — 1.03.254
i'll know your business, harry, that i will. 2.03. 80
in faith, i'll break thy little finger, harry, 2.03. 87
yet no farther wise | than harry percy's wife; 2.03.108
"o my sweet harry," says she, "how many hast 2.04.105 P
harry, i do not only marvel where thou spendest 2.04.398 P
there is a thing, harry, which thou hast often 2.04.411 P
for, harry, now i do not speak to thee in drink 2.04.414 P
for, harry, i see virtue in his looks. 2.04.427 P
now, harry, whence come you? 2.04.440 P
yet let me wonder, harry, | at thy affections, 3.02. 29
and in that very line, harry, standest thou, 3.02. 85
why, harry, do i tell thee of my foes, | which 3.02.122
and your unthought–of harry chance to meet. 3.02.141
on wednesday next, harry, you shall set forward, 3.02.173
and, harry, you shall march | through 3.02.175
i saw young harry with his beaver on, | his 4.01.104
harry to harry shall, hot horse to horse, | meet 4.01.122
harry to harry shall, hot horse to horse, | meet 4.01.122
and quick–raised power | meets with lord harry; 4.04. 13
but there is mordake, vernon, lord harry percy, 4.04. 24
therefore, good cousin, let not harry know, | in 5.02. 24
short breath to–day | but i and harry monmouth! 5.02. 49
thy likeness, for in stead of thee, king harry, 5.03. 8
harry, withdraw thyself, thou bleedest too much. 5.04. 2
if i mistake not, thou art harry monmouth. 5.04. 59
my name is harry percy. 5.04. 61
reign | of harry percy and the prince of wales. 5.04. 67
/nor shall it, harry, for the hour is come | to 5.04. 68
o, harry, thou hast robb'd me of my youth! 5.04. 77
myself and you, son harry, will towards wales, 5.05. 39
to noise abroad that harry monmouth fell | under 2H4 in 29
prince harry slain outright, and both the blunts 1.01. 16
and harry monmouth's brawn, the hulk sir john, 1.01. 19
and that young harry percy's spur was cold. 1.01. 42
said he young harry percy's spur was cold? 1.01. 49
to harry monmouth, whose swift wrath beat down 1.01.109
against the welsh, himself and harry monmouth; 1.03. 83
and harry prince of wales | are near at hand. 2.01.134
king nearest his father, harry prince of wales, 2.02.120 P
when your own percy, when my heart's dear harry, 2.03. 12
and here's four harry ten shillings in french 3.02.221 P
hereof comes it that prince harry is valiant, 4.03.117 P
come hither to me, harry. 4.05. 89
thy wish was father, harry, to that thought: 4.05. 92
harry the fift is crown'd! 4.05.119
for the fift harry from curb'd license plucks 4.05.130
come hither, harry, sit thou by my bed, | and 4.05.181
therefore, my harry, | be it thy course to busy 4.05.212
i'll lie, | in that jerusalem shall harry die. 4.05.240
to keep prince harry in continual laughter the 5.01. 79 P
here come the heavy issue of dead harry. 5.02. 14
o that the living harry had the temper | of he, 5.02. 15
amurath an amurath succeeds, | but harry harry. 5.02. 49
amurath an amurath succeeds, | but harry harry. 5.02. 49
but harry lives, that shall convert those tears 5.02. 60
under king harry. 5.03.114
harry the fourth, or fift? 5.03.114
harry the fourth. 5.03.115
harry the fift's the man. 5.03.117
then should the warlike harry, like himself, H5 pr 5
coronets, | promis'd to harry and his followers. 2.pr. 11
think we king harry strong; 2.04. 48
embassadors from harry king of england | do 2.04. 65
back, | tells harry that the king doth offer him 3.pr. 29
and upon this charge | cry, "god for harry, 3.01. 34
bar harry england, that sweeps through our land 3.05. 48
say thou to harry of england, though we seem'd 3.06.118 P
alas, poor harry of england! 3.07.130 P
define, | a little touch of harry in the night. 4.pr. 47
the lord in heaven bless thee, noble harry! 4.01. 33
harry le roy. 4.01. 49 P
harry the king, bedford and exeter, | warwick 4.03. 53
once more i come to know of thee, king harry, 4.03. 79
i shall, king harry. 4.03.126
well, harry of monmouth's life is come after it 4.07. 32 P
so also harry monmouth, being in his right wits 4.07. 46 P
and much more cause, | did they this harry. 5.pr. 35
hand, and say, "harry of england, i am thine"; 5.02.237 P
sooner persuade harry of england than a general 5.02.278 P
servant in arms to harry king of england, | and 1H6 4.02. 4
no, harry, harry, 'tis no land of thine; 3H6 3.01. 15
no, harry, harry, 'tis no land of thine; 3.01. 15
when holy harry died, and my sweet son. R3 4.04. 25
harry the sixt bids thee despair and die. 5.03.127
harry, that prophesied thou shouldst be king, 5.03.129
you are young, sir harry guilford. H8 1.04. 9
sir harry, | place you that side, i'll take the 1.04. 19
will not see a red herring at a harry groat, STM II.C 1 P
HARRY'S 8 FR 0.0009 REL FR 6 V 2 P
been | a banish'd woman from my harry's bed? 1H4 2.03. 39
falstaff, banish not him thy harry's company, 2.04.478 P
company, banish not him thy harry's company — 2.04.479 P
i run before king harry's victory, | who in a 2H4 in 23
yet weep that harry's dead, and so will i, | but 5.02. 59
say, | god shorten harry's happy life one day! 5.02.145
till harry's back–return again to france. H5 5.pr. 41
o harry's wife, triumph not in my woes! R3 4.04. 59
HARSH 31 FR 0.0035 REL FR 29 V 2 P
and mar the concord with too harsh a descant: TGV 1.02. 91
mine, | for they are harsh, untuneable, and bad. 3.01.209
be | they will digest this harsh indignity. LLL 5.02.289
words of mercury are harsh after the songs of 5.02.930 P
not on thy sole, but on thy soul, harsh jew, MV 4.01.123
tedious it were to tell, and harsh to hear — SHR 3.02.105
but a harsh hearing when women are froward. 5.02.183
a most harsh one, and not to be understood AWW 2.03.190 P
how dares thy harsh rude tongue sound this R2 3.04. 74
yet oftentimes it doth present harsh rage, 1H4 3.01.181
into the harsh and boist'rous tongue of war? 2H4 4.01. 49
as curst, as harsh, and horrible to hear, 2H6 3.02.312
that clarence is so harsh, so blunt, unnatural, 3H6 5.01. 86
plain and not honest is too harsh a style. R3 4.04.360
music leave, | they are harsh and heavy to me. H8 4.02. 95
the cygnet's down is harsh and spirit of sense TRO 1.01. 58
volscians' ears, | and harsh in sound to thine. COR 4.05. 59
straining harsh discords and unpleasing sharps. ROM 3.05. 28
like sweet bells jangled, out of time and harsh; HAM 3.01.158
and in this harsh world draw thy breath in pain 5.02.348
out of tune, | and sweet revenge grows harsh. OTH 5.02.116
not confound the time with conference harsh; ANT 1.01. 45
what counts harsh fortune casts upon my face, 2.06. 54
nor no more ado | with that harsh, noble, simple CYM 3.04.132
upon a valiant race thy harsh | and potent 5.04. 83
time, | hell only danceth at so harsh a chime. PER 1.01. 85
loud music is too harsh for ladies' heads, 2.03. 97
i have been harsh | to large confessors, and TNK 5.01.104
ill–nurtur'd, crooked, churlish, harsh in voice, VEN 134
melodious discord, heavenly tune harsh sounding, 431
harsh, featureless, and rude, barrenly perish: SON 11.10
HARSHER 1 FR 0.0001 REL FR 1 V 0 P
hard, and harsher | than strife or war could be. TNK 1.02. 25
HARSHLY 3 FR 0.0003 REL FR 2 V 1 P
i tell you, 'twill sound harshly in her ears. ERR 4.04. 7
if they will fare so harshly o' th' trumpet's TIM 3.06. 34 P
grating so harshly all his days of quiet | with HAM 3.01. 3
HARSHNESS 3 FR 0.0003 REL FR 3 V 0 P
and he's compos'd of harshness. TMP 3.01. 9
(which is due to me) | to stubborn harshness. MND 1.01. 38
nature shall not give | thee o'er to harshness. LR 2.04.172
HARSH–RESOUNDING
1 FR 0.0001 REL FR 1 V 0 P
with harsh–resounding trumpets' dreadful bray, R2 1.03.135
HARSH–SOUNDING 1 FR 0.0001 REL FR 1 V 0 P
to whom he sung, in rude harsh–sounding rhymes,
JN 4.02.150
HART 9 FR 0.0010 REL FR 8 V 1 P
if a hart do lack a hind, | let him seek out AYL 3.02.101
the hart. TN 1.01. 16
that instant was i turn'd into a hart, | and my 1.01. 20
should leave me at the white hart in southwark? 2H6 4.08. 25 P
the hart achilles | keeps thicket. TRO 2.03.258
to hunt the panther and the hart with me, | with TIT 1.01.493
here wast thou bay'd, brave hart, | here didst JC 3.01.204
thou wast the forest to this hart, | and this 3.01.207
strooken deer go weep, | the hart ungalled play, HAM 3.02.272
HARTS 2 FR 0.0002 REL FR 2 V 0 P
the swiftest harts have posted you by land, CYM 2.04. 27
"our britain's harts die flying, not our men. 5.03. 24
HARUM 1 FR 0.0001 REL FR 0 V 1 P
/genitivo, horum, harum, horum. WIV 4.01. 61 P
HARVEST 18 FR 0.0020 REL FR 16 V 2 P
at the farthest | in the very end of harvest! TMP 4.01.115
that you frame the season for your own harvest. ADO 1.03. 25 P
scarce show a harvest of their heavy toil; LLL 4.03.323
after the man | that the main harvest reaps. AYL 3.05.103
and yet, when wit and youth is come to harvest, TN 3.01.132
and make thee curse the harvest of that corn. 1H6 3.02. 47
and reap the harvest which that rascal sow'd. 2H6 3.01.381
i'll blast his harvest, /and your head were laid 3H6 5.07. 21
right, as snow in harvest. R3 1.04.242
though we have spent our harvest of this king, 2.02.115
king, | we are to reap the harvest of his son. 2.02.116
to reap the harvest of perpetual peace | by this 5.02. 15
there if i grow, | the harvest is your own. MAC 1.04. 33
his grain, | and shortly comes to harvest. ANT 2.07. 23
minist'red, | and in 's spring became a harvest; CYM 1.01. 46
is, and thou hast the harvest out of thine own PER 4.02.141 P
and useless barns the harvest of his wits; LUC 859
my poor lips, which should that harvest reap, SON 128. 7
HARVEST–HOME 2 FR 0.0002 REL FR 1 V 1 P
rogue's coffer, and there's my harvest–home. WIV 2.02.275 P
show'd like a stubble–land at harvest–home. 1H4 1.03. 35
HARVEST–MAN 1 FR 0.0001 REL FR 1 V 0 P
like to a harvest–man /that's task'd to mow | or COR 1.03. 36
/H'AS 1 FR 0.0001 REL FR 1 V 0 P
that 'twixt my sheets | /h'as done my office. OTH 1.03.388
H'AS 24 FR 0.0027 REL FR 12 V 12 P
h'as censur'd him | already, and, as i hear, the MM 1.04. 72
but h'as left me here behind to expound the SHR 4.04. 78 P
module, h'as deceiv'd me like a double–meaning AWW 4.03. 99 P
him forth, h'as sat i' th' stocks all night, 4.03.101 P
h'as led the drum before the english tragedians. 4.03.266 P
h'as been told so; TN 1.05.147 P
h'as broke my head across and has given sir toby 5.01.175 P
h'as hurt me, and there's th' end on't. 5.01.196 P
h'as here writ a letter to you; 5.01.285 P
h'as a book in his pocket with red letters in't. 2H6 4.02. 90 P
he may, my lord, h'as wherewithal: H8 1.03. 59
alas, h'as banish'd me his bed already, | his 3.01.119
day, no man think | h'as business at his house; 5.04. 75
h'as such a confirm'd countenance. COR 1.03. 59 P
h'as said enough. 3.01.161
h'as spoken like a traitor, and shall answer 3.01.162
h'as only sent his present occasion now, my lord TIM 3.02. 34 P
h'as much disgrac'd me in't, i'm angry at him, 3.03. 13
why, /i say, my lords, h'as done fair service, 3.05. 62
h'as almost charm'd me from my profession, by 4.03.450 P
h'as caught me in his eye, i will present | my 4.03.469
h'as had most favorable and happy speed: OTH 2.01. 67
h'as done no more than other knights have done, PER 2.03. 34
knights have done, | h'as broken a staff or so; 2.03. 35
HA'S 1 FR 0.0001 REL FR 1 V 0 P
itself), these shrugs, these hums and ha's, WT 2.01. 74
HAS (*also 'as*)
/HAS 7 FR 0.0008 REL FR 4 V 3 P
/has /sorrow /made /thee /dote /already? TIT 3.02. 23
/poor /man, /grief /has /so /wrought /on /him, 3.02. 79
/there /has /been /much /to /do /on /both /sides HAM 2.02.352 P
/o, /there /has /been /much /throwing /about /of 2.02.358 P
/him /even /o'er /the /time /he /has /lost. LR 4.07. 79
that /has an eye can stamp and counterfeit OTH 2.01.243 P
and command what cost | your heart /has mind to.
ANT 3.04. 38
HAS 402 FR 0.0454 REL FR 246 V 156 P
entertainment till | mine enemy has more pow'r. TMP 1.02.467
ca–caliban | has a new master, get a new man. 2.02.185
he has brave utensils (for so he calls them) 3.02. 96
which, when he has a house, he'll deck withal. 3.02. 97
her waspish–headed son has broke his arrows, 4.01. 99
has done little better than play'd the jack with 4.01.197 P
o brave new world | that has such people in't! 5.01.184
stone, and has no more pity in him than a dog. TGV 2.03. 10 P
she dreams on him that has forgot her love; 4.04. 81
if he has a quarter of your coat, there is but WIV 1.01. 28 P
she has brown hair, and speaks small like a 1.01. 47 P
know the young gentlewoman, she has good gifts. 1.01. 62 P
now, the report goes she has all the rule of her 1.03. 52 P
but nobody but has his fault — but let that 1.04. 14 P
yet there has been knights, and lords, and 2.02. 63 P
of them all, and yet there has been earls, nay 2.02. 76 P
has ford's wife and page's wife acquainted each 2.02.108 P
her husband has a marvellous infection to the 2.02.114 P
by gar, he has save his soul, dat he is no come; 2.03. 6 P
he has pray his pible well, dat he is no come. 2.03. 7 P
he has no more knowledge in hibocrates and galen 3.01. 65 P
he has made us his vlouting–stog. 3.01.117 P
has page any brains? 3.02. 30 P
he capers, he dances, he has eyes of youth; 3.02. 67 P
and has threat'ned to put me into everlasting 3.03. 30 P
the fat woman of brainford, has a gown above. 4.02. 76 P
i like not when a oman has a great peard. 4.02.193 P
you say he has been thrown in the rivers, and 4.04. 20 P
and has been grievously peaten as an old oman. 4.04. 21 P
cozen–germans that has cozen'd all the hosts of 4.05. 77 P
ere she sleep, has thrice her prayers said, 5.05. 50
impiety has made a feast of thee. MM 1.02. 57 P
now, which of your hips has the most profound 1.02. 58 P
well; what has he done? 1.02. 87 P
has he affections in him, | that thus can make 3.01.107
the deputy, sir, he has given him warning. 3.02. 34 P
th' one has my pity; 4.02. 61
one /can master a grief but he that has it. ADO 3.02. 29 P
(for she has been too long a–talking of), the 3.02.103 P
'a has been a vile thief this seven year; 3.03.126 P
chin than dobbin my fill–horse has on his tail. MV 2.02. 95 P
him, i will run as far as god has any ground. 2.02.110 P
many a man has good horns, and knows no end of
AYL 3.03. 54 P
i saw her hand, she has a leathern hand, | a 4.03. 24
she has a huswive's hand — but that's no matter 4.03. 27
and therefore has he closely mew'd her up, SHR 1.01.183
has my fellow tranio stol'n your clothes? 1.01.223 P
is there any man has rebus'd your worship? 1.02. 7 P
he that has the two fair daughters? 1.02.221
as any one | old signior gremio has in padua, 2.01.368
well, petruchio, this has put me in heart. 4.05. 77
'a has a little gall'd me, i confess; 5.02. 60
here's a man stands that has brought his pardon. AWW 2.01. 63
hand, and say nothing, has neither leg, hands, 2.02. 11 P
thou not, bertram, | what she has done for me? 2.03.109
thou know'st she has rais'd me from my sickly 2.03.111
the king has done you wrong; 2.03.300
she is not well, but yet she has her health. 2.04. 2 P
lady, | the fellow has a deal of that too much, 3.02. 90
nothing in france, until he has no wife! 3.02.100
might you not know she would do as she has done 3.04. 2
say the french count has done most honorable 3.05. 3 P
it is reported that he has taken their great'st 3.05. 5 P
of yours | that has done worthy service. 3.05. 48
look, he has spied us. 3.05. 90 P
he says he has a stratagem for't. 3.06. 35 P
this has no holding, | to swear by him whom i 4.02. 27
he has much worthy blame laid upon him for 4.03. 6 P
nothing of me, has 'a? 4.03.112 P
he has every thing that an honest man should not 4.03.259 P
what an honest man should have, he has nothing. 4.03.261 P
marry, in coming on he has the cramp. 4.03.291 P
that has a knot on't yet. 4.03.324 P
sir, 'a has an english /name, but his fisnomy is 4.05. 39 P
for his sauciness, and indeed he has no pace, 4.05. 67 P
that has fall'n into the unclean fishpond of her 5.02. 20 P
i think she has. 5.03.210
why, he has three thousand ducats a year. TN 1.03. 22 P
wit than a christian or an ordinary man has; 1.03. 84 P
an ordinary fool that has no more brain than a 1.05. 85 P
one of thy kin has a most weak pia mater. 1.05.115 P
by my troth, the fool has an excellent breast. 2.03. 19 P
and so sweet a breath to sing, as the fool has. 2.03. 21 P
my lady has a white hand, and the mermidons are 2.03. 27 P
he has been yonder i' the sun practicing 2.05. 16 P
what dish a' poison has she dress'd him! 2.05.112 P

no, indeed, sir, the lady olivia has no folly. 3.01. 32 P
and that no woman has, nor never none | shall 3.01.159
they say he has been fencer to the sophy. 3.04.278 P
but he has promis'd me, as he is a gentleman and 3.04.307 P
he has heard that word of some great man and now 4.01. 12 P
my head across and has given sir toby a bloody 5.01.175 P
who has done this, sir andrew? 5.01.179 P
it has an elder sister, | or i mistake you. WT 1.02. 98
that little thinks she has been sluic'd in 's 1.02.194
i have seen a lady's nose | that has been blue, 2.01. 15
he has discover'd my design, and i | remain a 2.01. 50
for 'tis polixenes | has made thee swell thus. 2.01. 62
(from him that has most cause to grieve it 2.01. 77
shall know your mistress | has deserv'd prison, 2.01.120
that forced baseness | which he has put upon't! 2.03. 80
this has been some stair–work, some trunk–work, 3.03. 73 P
a footman by the garments he has left with thee. 4.03. 67 P
he has the prettiest love–songs for maids, so 4.04.193 P
has he any unbraided wares? 4.04.203 P
may be he has paid you more, which will shame 4.04.240 P
here has been too much homely foolery already. 4.04.332 P
he has his health, and ampler strength indeed 4.04.403
your flesh and blood has not offended the king, 4.04.694 P
secret things, all but what she has with her. 4.04.697 P
has the old man e'er a son, sir, do you hear, 4.04.781 P
he has a son, who shall be flay'd alive; 4.04.783 P
for has not the divine apollo said, | is't not 5.01. 37
the other, when she has obtain'd your eye, 5.01.105
desires you to attach his son, who has | (his 5.01.182
camillo has betray'd me; 5.01.193
who now | has these poor men in question. 5.01.198
has the king found his heir? 5.02. 29 P
shepherd's son, who has not only his innocence 5.02. 64 P
would be thence that has the benefit of access? 5.02.109 P
which has | my evils conjur'd to remembrance, 5.03. 39
the fixure of her eye has motion in't, | as we 5.03. 67
for this affliction has a taste as sweet | as 5.03. 76
ay, and make it manifest where she has liv'd, 5.03.114
i have inquir'd, so has my husband, man by man, 1H4 3.03. 56 P
how has he the leisure to be sick | in such a 4.01. 17
has not the boy profited? 2H4 2.02. 84 P
that, as oft as he has occasion to name himself; 2.02.110 P
they say poins has a good wit. 2.04.239 P
and such other gambol faculties 'a has, that 2.04.251 P
she has nobody to do any thing about her when i 3.02.230 P
for him, a court, and now has he land and beefs! 3.02.327 P
"be merry, be merry, my wife has all, | for 5.03. 32
the king has kill'd his heart. H5 2.01. 88 P
he has no more directions in the true 3.02. 71 P
what he has spoke to me, that is well, i warrant 3.06. 65 P
the duke of exeter has very gallantly maintain'd 3.06. 91 P
has strook the glove which your majesty is take 4.08. 26 P
the fellow has mettle enough in his belly. 4.08. 62 P
duke humphrey has done a miracle to–day. 2H6 2.01.157
with him, he has a familiar under his tongue, he 4.07.107 P
has your king married the lady grey? 3H6 3.03.174
york | has almost overta'en him in his growth. R3 2.04. 7
whence has he that? H8 1.01. 69
or has given all before, and he begins | a new 1.01. 71
but our count–cardinal | has done this, and 'tis 1.01.173
lo you, my lord, | the net has fall'n upon me! 1.01.203
free pardon to each man that has denied | the 1.02.100
a french song and a fiddle has no fellow. 1.03. 41
bevy, has brought with her | one care abroad. 1.04. 4
pray speak what has happen'd. 2.01. 6
't has done, upon the premises, but justice; 2.01. 63
at one stroke has taken | for ever from the 2.01.117
heaven has an end in all; 2.01.124
wife | has crept too near his conscience. 2.02. 17
conscience | has crept too near another lady. 2.02. 18
now he has crack'd the league | between us and 2.02. 24
a jewel, has hung twenty years | about his neck, 2.02. 31
excuse me, | the king has sent me otherwhere. 2.02. 59
this priest has no pride in him? 2.02. 81
your grace has given a president of wisdom 2.02. 85
i know your majesty has always lov'd her | so 2.02.109
ever by your grace, whose hand has rais'd me. 2.02.119
that man i' th' world who shall report he has 2.04.135
and like her true nobility she has | carried 2.04.143
believe me, she has had much wrong. 3.01. 48
and to that woman (when she has done most) | yet 3.01.136
he has my heart yet and shall have my prayers 3.01.180
has the king this? 3.02. 37
has left the cause o' th' king unhandled, and 3.02. 58
he has, and we shall see him | for it an 3.02. 73
which ever has and ever shall be growing, | till 3.02.178
that, as my hand has open'd bounty to you, | my 3.02.184
take notice, lords, he has a loyal breast, | for 3.02.200
upon the daring huntsman that has gall'd him; 3.02.207
this paper has undone me. 3.02.210
at length broke under me, and now has left me, 3.02.362
the king has cur'd me, | i humbly thank his 3.02.380
i am glad your grace has made that right use of 3.02.386
when he has run his course and sleeps in 3.02.398
o, cromwell, | the king has gone beyond me! 3.02.408
our king has all the indies in his arms, | and 4.01. 45
the king has made him master | o' th' jewel 4.01.110
he has strangled | his language in his tears. 5.01.156
has he had knowledge of it? 5.02. 39
and has done half an hour, to know your 5.02. 41
shall this lady, | when she has so much english. 5.04. 14
this oracle of comfort has so pleas'd me | that 5.04. 66
she be not, she has the mends in her own hands. TRO 1.01. 68 P
so he has. 1.02.100 P
and you know he has not past three or four hairs 1.02.112 P
indeed she has a marvell's white hand, i must 1.02.136 P
it now, for it has been a great while going by. 1.02.168 P
he has a shrowd wit, i can tell you, and he's 1.02.190 P
bobb'd his brain more than he has beat my bones. 2.01. 70 P
has not so much wit — 2.01. 78 P
see he is his argument that has his argument, 2.03. 96 P
a very horse, | that has he knows not what. 3.03.127
howsoever, he shall pay for me ere he has me. 3.03.297 P
be in him when hector has knock'd out his brains 3.03.302 P
for what he has he gives, what thinks he shows, 4.05.101
quails, but he has not so much brain as ear–wax; 5.01. 52 P
has got that same scurvy doting foolish /young 5.04. 3 P
the bull has the game, ware horns ho! 5.07. 12 P
you what services he has done for his country? COR 1.01. 30 P
he has no equal. 1.01.253
say, has our general met the enemy? 1.04. 3
gods, | he has the stamp of martius, and i have 1.06. 23
mother, | who has a charter to extol her blood, 1.09. 14
he that has but effected his good will | hath 1.09. 18
has he disciplin'd aufidius soundly? 2.01.126 P
the senate has letters from the general, wherein 2.01.134 P
he has more cause to be proud. 2.01.145 P
the true knowledge he has in their disposition, 2.02. 13 P
wherein every one of us has a single honor, in 2.03. 44 P
he has done nobly, and cannot go without any 2.03.132 P
he has it now; 2.03.151
he has our voices, sir. 2.03.156
nor has coriolanus | deserv'd this so dishonor'd 3.01. 59
this man has marr'd his fortune. 3.01.253
o, he's a limb that has but a disease: 3.01.294
what has he done to rome that's worthy death? 3.01.296
he has been bred i' th' wars | since 'a could 3.01.318
the warlike service he has done, consider; 3.03. 49
for that he has | (as much as in him lies) from 3.03. 93
has the porter his eyes in his head, that he 4.05. 11 P
tell my master what a strange guest he has here. 4.05. 35 P
what an arm he has! 4.05.152 P
for the other has half by the entreaty and grant 4.05.199 P
you, sir, he has as many friends as enemies; 4.05.206 P
but he has a merit | to choke it in the 4.07. 48
has he din'd, canst thou tell? 5.02. 34 P
our general has sworn you out of reprieve and 5.02. 49 P
has cluck'd thee to the wars, and safely home 5.03.163
he has wings, he's more than a creeping thing. 5.04. 13 P
perfidiously | he has betray'd your business, 5.06. 91
he is gone happy, and has left me rich. TIM 1.02. 4
and has sent your honor two brace of greyhounds. 1.02.188 P
happier is he that has no friend to feed | than 1.02.203
i think no usurer but has a fool to his servant; 2.02. 98 P
every man has his fault, and honesty is his. 3.01. 27 P
has friendship such a faint and milky heart, 3.01. 54
unto his honor has my lord's meat in him; 3.01. 57
what has he sent? 3.02. 31 P
and what has he sent now? 3.02. 33 P
my knowing, timon has been this lord's father, 3.02. 67
timon's money | has paid his men their wages. 3.02. 70
has ventidius and lucullus denied him, | and 3.03. 8
broader than he that has no house to put his 3.04. 64 P
his comfortable temper has forsook him, he's 3.04. 71 P
he has made too much plenty with /'em. 3.05. 66
he has a sin that often | drowns him and takes 3.05. 67
fury | he has been known to commit outrages 3.05. 71
i cannot think but your age has forgot me, | it 3.05. 92
other day, and now he has beat it out of my hat. 3.06.113 P
nor has he with him to | supply his life, or 4.02. 46
seek to thrive | by that which has undone thee; 4.03.211
how has the ass broke the wall, that thou art 4.03.349 P
in their rough power | has uncheck'd theft. 4.03.444
an alteration of honor has desp'rate want made! 4.03.462
gods out of my misery | has sent thee treasure. 4.03.525
of his | has been but a try for his friends? 5.01. 9
yond cassius has a lean and hungry look, | he JC 1.02.194
of the matter, | caesar has had great wrong. 3.02.110
has he, masters? 3.02.110
the earth hath bubbles, as the water has, | and MAC 1.03. 79
he has almost supp'd. 1.07. 29
know you not he has? 1.07. 30
our knocking has awak'd him; 2.03. 43
the night has been unruly. 2.03. 54
treason has done his worst; 3.02. 24
the /time has been, | that when the brains were 3.04. 77
he has borne all things well, and i do think 3.06. 17
cold stone | days and nights has thirty–one 4.01. 7
he has kill'd me, mother: 4.02. 84
smacking of every sin | that has a name; 4.03. 60
the tyrant has not batter'd at their peace? 4.03.178
he has no children. 4.03.216
she has light by her continually, 'tis her 5.01. 22 P
she has spoke what she should not, i am sure of 5.01. 48 P
heaven knows what she has known. 5.01. 49 P
my mind she has mated, and amaz'd my sight. 5.01. 78
the time has been, my senses would have cool'd 5.05. 10
your son, my lord, has paid a soldier's debt. 5.09. 5
what, has this thing appear'd again to–night? HAM 1.01. 21
look whe'er he has not turn'd his color and has 2.02.519 P
not turn'd his color and has tears in 's eyes. 2.02.520 P
act | that has no relish of salvation in't — 3.03. 92
has this fellow no feeling of his business? 5.01. 65 P
signify to you that 'a has laid a great wager on 5.02.102 P
horses, against the which he has impawn'd, as i 5.02.148 P
thus has he, and many more of the same breed 5.02.188 P
your grace has laid the odds a' th' weaker side. 5.02.261
lights | on fortinbras, he has my dying voice. 5.02.356
has he never before sounded you in this business LR 1.02. 69 P
this fellow has banish'd two on 's daughters, 1.04.102 P
a fox, when one has caught her, | and such a 1.04.317
but i can tell why a snail has a house. 1.05. 27 P
he that has a house to put 's head in has a good 3.02. 25 P
a house to put 's head in has a good head–piece. 3.02. 25 P
that will house | before the head has any, | the 3.02. 28
seeming | has practic'd on man's life! 3.02. 57
"he that has and a little tine wit — | with 3.02. 74
has his daughters brought him to this pass? 3.04. 63
he's a yeoman that has a gentleman to his son; 3.06. 12 P
he has some reason, else he could not beg. 4.01. 31
who has the office? 5.03.249
she has deceiv'd her father, and may thee. OTH 1.03.293
who has put in? 2.01. 65
alas! she has no speech. 2.01.102
what an eye she has! 2.03. 22 P
who has that breast so pure | /but /some 3.03.138
mine, 'tis his, and has been slave to thousands; 3.03.158
/i' /faith, i fear it has. 3.03.215
i take no pleasure | in aught an eunuch has. ANT 1.05. 10
but there is never a fair woman has a true face. 2.06. 99 P
he has a cloud in 's face. 3.02. 51
the fellow has good judgment. 3.03. 25
he has done all this and more | in alexandria. 3.06. 1
caesar has taken toryne. 3.07. 55
o, /he has given example for our flight, | most 3.10. 27
upon a course | which has no need of you. 3.11. 10
he needs as many, sir, as caesar has, | or needs 3.13. 49
and what is done, tell him he has | hipparchus, 3.13.148
the soldier | that has this morning left thee, 4.05. 5
his chests and treasure | he has not with him. 4.05. 11
caesar himself has work, and our oppression 4.07. 2
we'll spill the blood | that has to–day escap'd. 4.08. 4
he has deserv'd it, were it carbuncled | like 4.08. 28
give him hope and fear | of what he has, and has 4.12. 9
him hope and fear | of what he has, and has not. 4.12. 9
she, eros, has | pack'd cards with caesar's, and 4.14. 18
she has robb'd me of my sword. 4.14. 23
be paid but once, | and that she has discharg'd. 4.14. 28
confin'd in all she has, her monument, | of thy 5.01. 53
and i send him | the greatness he has got. 5.02. 30
who has the note of them? CYM 1.05. 2
she doth think she has | strange ling'ring 1.05. 33
those she has | will stupefy and dull the sense 1.05. 36
nor has no friends | so much as but to prop him? 1.05. 59
my lord, i fear, | has forgot britain. 1.06.113
the ground that gave them first has them again: 4.02.289
your death has eyes in 's head then; 5.04.178 P
who has a book of all that monarchs do, | he's PER 1.01. 94
he has found the meaning. 1.01.109
your lord has /betook himself to unknown travels 1.03. 34
the king my father, sir, has drunk to you — 2.03. 75
or council has respect with him but he. 2.04. 18
your honor has through ephesus pour'd forth 3.02. 43
boult, has she any qualities? 4.02. 46 P
she has a good face, speaks well, and has 4.02. 47 P
speaks well, and has excellent good clothes; 4.02. 47 P
instruct her what she has to do, that she may 4.02. 55 P
of our profession, she has me her quirks, her 4.06. 7 P
she has here spoken holy words to the lord 4.06.132 P
here our play has ending. 5.03.102
i am sure | it has a noble breeder and a pure, TNK pr 10
and reason has no manners | to say it is not you 1.03. 48
theirs has more ground, is more maturely 1.03. 56
like old importment's bastard) has this end, 1.03. 80
till she for shame see what a wrong she has done 2.02. 39
this garden has a world of pleasures in't. 2.02.118
what happiness has palamon! 2.03. 13
he has a tongue will tame tempests, | and make 2.03. 16
if i go, he has her. 2.03. 20
this fellow has a vengeance trick o' th' hip. 2.03. 70
driven to | when fifteen once has found us! 2.04. 7
he has as much to please a woman in him | (if he 2.04. 9
and yet he has not thank'd me | for what i have 2.06. 21
the duke has lost hippolyta; 3.01. 1
he has mistook the /brake i meant, is gone 3.02. 1
he has no weapons, | he cannot run, the jingling 3.02. 13
spare it not, | the duke has more, coz. eat now. 3.03. 20
the sun has seen my folly. 3.04. 3
faith, very little. love has us'd you kindly. 3.06. 67
lo, cousin, lo, our folly has undone us. 3.06.107
your cousin | has ten times more offended, for i 3.06.181
kill this cousin, | on any piece the earth has. 3.06.263
palamon has clear'd you, | and got your pardon, 4.01. 18
has given a sum of money to her marriage, | a 4.01. 23
all these must be boys, | he has the trick on't; 4.01.132
good heaven, | what a sweet face has arcite! 4.02. 7
and quick sweetness, | has this young prince! 4.02. 14
and yet inviting, | has this brown manly face! 4.02. 42
my virgin's faith has fled me; 4.02. 46
his show | has all the ornament of honor in't. 4.02. 93
he has felt | without doubt what he fights for, 4.02. 96
red and white, for yet no beard has blest him; 4.02.107
their fame has fir'd me so — till they appear. 4.02.153
i think she has a perturb'd mind, which i cannot 4.03. 59 P
best loves me | and has the truest title in't, 5.01.159
has this advice i told you done any good upon 5.02. 1
will be honest, | she has the path before her. 5.02. 23
and has done this long hour, to visit you. 5.02. 42
you know | the chestnut mare the duke has? 5.02. 61
what dowry has she? 5.02. 64
my cousin palamon | has made so fair a choice. 5.02. 92
palamon | has a most menacing aspect, his brow 5.03. 45
then he has won. 5.03. 68
conquer'd triumphs, | the victor has the loss; 5.04.114
he that has | lov'd a young handsome wench then, ep 5
nay, it has infected it with the palsy, for STM II.C 12 P

/HAST 8 FR 0.0009 REL FR 7 V 1 P

/hast smutch'd thy nose? WT 1.02.121
/with /all /pleas'd, /that /hast /all /achiev'd! R2 4.01.217
/and /thou /hast /kill'd /him. TIT 3.02. 65
/for /thou /hast /done /a /charitable /deed. 3.02. 70
/thy /other /titles /thou /hast /given /away, LR 1.04.149 P
/justicer, /why /hast /thou /let /her /scape? 3.06. 56
thou by that small hurt /hast cashier'd cassio. OTH 2.03.375
/world, thou /hast a pair of chaps — no more, ANT 3.05. 13

HAST 619 FR 0.0699 REL FR 506 V 113 P

good, yet remember whom thou hast aboard. TMP 1.01. 19 P
hast thou, spirit, | perform'd to point the 1.02.193
the mariners, say how thou hast dispos'd, | and 1.02.225
let me remember thee what thou hast promis'd, 1.02.243
hast thou forgot | the foul witch sycorax, who 1.02.257
hast thou forgot her? 1.02.259
thou hast. where was she born? speak. tell me. 1.02.260
once in a month recount what thou hast been, 1.02.262
till | thou hast howl'd away twelve winters. 1.02.296
thou hast slept well, | awake! 1.02.305
and hast put thyself | upon this island as a spy 1.02.455
thou hast done well, fine ariel! 1.02.495
o stephano, hast any more of this? 2.02.133 P
hast thou not dropp'd from heaven? 2.02.137 P
honest lord, | thou hast said well; 3.03. 35
bravely the figure of this harpy hast thou 3.03. 83
of my instruction hast thou nothing bated | in 3.03. 85
love, and thou | hast strangely stood the test. 4.01. 7
hast thou, which art but air, a touch, a feeling 5.01. 21
how thou hast met us here, whom three hours 5.01.136
hast thou no mouth by land? 5.01.220
thou, julia, thou hast metamorphis'd me, | made TGV 1.01. 66
well hast thou advis'd; 1.03. 34
hast thou observ'd that? even she, i mean. 2.01. 44 P
because thou hast not so much charity in thee as 2.05. 57 P
o sweet–suggesting love, if thou hast sinn'd, 2.06. 7
whose sovereignty so oft thou hast preferr'd 2.06. 15
as thou hast lent me wit to plot this drift. 2.06. 43

that which thyself hast now disclos'd to me. 3.01. 32
for thou hast stay'd so long that going will 3.01.378 P
(for thou hast shown some sign of good desert) 3.02. 18
this discipline shows thou hast been in love. 3.02. 87
that hast deceiv'd so many with thy vows? 4.02. 98
thyself hast lov'd, and i have heard thee say 4.03. 18
thou hast entertain'd | a fox to be the shepherd 4.04. 91
thou hast no faith left now, unless thou'dst two 5.04. 50
treacherous man, | thou hast beguil'd my hopes! 5.04. 64
how oft hast thou with perjury cleft the root? 5.04.103
to make such means for her as thou hast done, 5.04.137
thou thy silvia, for thou hast deserv'd her. 5.04.147
thou hast prevail'd, i pardon them and thee; 5.04.158
faith, thou hast some crotchets in thy head now. WIV 2.01.154 P
hast thou no suit against my knight, my 2.01.212 P
thou hast the right arch'd beauty of the brow 3.03. 56 P
hast thou no understandings for thy cases and 4.01. 69 P
yes, that thou hast; MM 1.02. 42 P
for what thou hast not, still thou striv'st to 3.01. 22
to get, | and what thou hast, forget'st. 3.01. 23
friend hast thou none, | for thine own bowels, 3.01. 28
thou hast nor youth nor age, | but as it were an 3.01. 32
thou hast neither heat, affection, limb, nor 3.01. 37
thank thee, varrius, thou hast made good haste. 4.05. 11
is't not enough thou hast suborn'd these women 5.01.306
hast thou or word, or wit, or impudence, | that 5.01.363
if thou hast, | rely upon it till my tale be 5.01.364
try all the friends thou hast in ephesus; ERR 1.01.152
and tell me how thou hast dispos'd thy charge. 1.02. 73
what mistress, slave, hast thou? 1.02. 87
thou, that hast no unkind mate to grieve thee, 2.01. 38
thou hast thine own form. 2.02.198
thou hast stol'n both mine office and my name: 3.01. 44
luce — luce, thou hast answer'd him well. 3.01. 53
thou hast no husband yet, nor i no wife. 3.02. 68
how hast thou lost thy breath? 4.02. 30
thou hast suborn'd the goldsmith to arrest me. 4.04. 82
hast thou delight to see a wretched man | do 4.04.115
hast thou so crack'd and splitted my poor tongue 5.01.309
dromio, what stuff of mine hast thou embark'd? 5.01.410
too, that thou hast shifted out of thy tale into ADO 3.03.142 P
thou hast so wrong'd mine innocent child and me 5.01. 63
i say thou hast belied mine innocent child! 5.01. 67
thou hast kill'd my child. 5.01. 78
thou hast mettle enough in thee to kill care. 5.01.133 P
thou the slave that with thy breath hast kill'd 5.01.263
thou hast frighted the word out of his right 5.02. 55 P
how hast thou purchased this experience? LLL 3.01. 26 P
thou hast no feeling of it, moth. 3.01.114 P
thou hast mistaken his letter. 4.01.106
thou hast thump'd him with thy bird–bolt under 4.03. 23 P
what grace hast thou thus to reprove | these 4.03.151
what present hast thou there? 4.03.187
go to, thou hast it ad dunghill, at the fingers' 5.01. 77 P
thou hast spoken no word all this while. 5.01.149 P
because thou hast no face. 5.02.608 P
thou, lysander, thou hast given her rhymes, MND 1.01. 28
thou hast by moonlight at her window sung | with 1.01. 30
with cunning hast thou filch'd my daughter's 1.01. 36
in that same place thou hast appointed me 1.01.177
when thou hast stolen away from fairy land, 2.01. 65
with thy brawls thou hast disturb'd our sport. 2.01. 87
hast thou the flower there? 2.01.247
but hast thou yet latch'd the athenian's eyes 3.02. 36
for thou, i fear, hast given me cause to curse. 3.02. 46
if thou hast slain lysander in his sleep, 3.02. 47
it cannot be but thou hast murd'red him; 3.02. 56
hast thou slain him then? 3.02. 66
and hast thou kill'd him sleeping? 3.02. 70
what hast thou done? 3.02. 88
thou hast mistaken quite, | and laid the 3.02. 88
o wall, full often hast thou heard my moans, 5.01.188
what a beard hast thou got! MV 2.02. 94 P
thou hast got more hair on thy chin than dobbin 2.02. 94 P
i know thee well, thou hast obtain'd thy suit. 2.02.144
as thou hast done with me — what, jessica! 2.05. 4
hast thou found my daughter? 3.01. 80 P
husband | hast thou of me as she is for /a wife. 3.05. 84
no, none that thou hast wit enough to make. 4.01.127
thou hast contrived against the very life | of 4.01.360
and thou hast incurr'd | the danger formerly by 4.01.361
state, | thou hast not left the value of a cord; 4.01.366
thou hast rail'd on thyself. AYL 1.01. 61 P
thou hast not, cousin, | prithee be cheerful. 1.03. 93
hast thou been drawn to by thy fantasy? 2.04. 31
did make thee run into, | thou hast not lov'd; 2.04. 36
or if thou hast not sat as i do now, | wearing 2.04. 37
in thy mistress' praise, | thou hast not lov'd; 2.04. 39
or if thou hast not broke from company 2.04. 40
my passion now makes me, | thou hast not lov'd. 2.04. 42
for thou thyself hast been a libertine, | as 2.07. 65
that thou with license of free foot hast caught, 2.07. 68
hast any philosophy in thee, shepherd? 3.02. 21 P
thou hast my love; is not that neighborly? 3.05. 90
thou hast hawks will soar | above the morning SHR in.2. 43
thou hast a lady far more beautiful | than any in.2. 62
thou hast hit it; come sit on me. 2.01.198
nor hast thou pleasure to be cross in talk; 2.01.249
what hast thou to do? 3.02.216
what, hast thou din'd? 4.03. 59
i tell thee, i, that thou hast marr'd her gown. 4.03.114
thou hast fac'd many things. 4.03.122 P
thou hast brav'd many men, brave not me; 4.03.124 P
but hast thou done thy errand to baptista? 4.04. 14
too, | hast thou beheld a fresher gentlewoman? 4.05. 29
then hast thou taught hortensio to be untoward. 4.05. 79
how hast thou offended? | where is lucentio? 5.01.113
i think thou hast the veriest shrew of all. 5.02. 64
the wager thou hast won, and i will add | unto 5.02.112
now go thy ways, thou hast tam'd a curst shrow. 5.02.188
when thou hast leisure, say thy prayers; AWW 1.01.212 P
when thou hast none, remember thy friends. 1.01.213 P
whose banish'd sense | thou hast repeal'd, a 2.03. 49
thou hast power to choose, and they none to 2.03. 56
for thou hast to pull at a smack a' th' contrary 2.03.224 P
thou hast a son shall take this disgrace off me, 2.03.235 P
then hast thou all again. 3.02.102
but what linsey–woolsey hast thou to speak to us 4.01. 11 P

thou hast spoken all already, unless thou canst 5.03.267 P
wherefore hast thou accus'd him all this while? 5.03.288
i will believe thou hast a mind that suits TN 1.02. 50
either tell me where thou hast been, or i will 1.05. 1 P
thou hast spoke for us, madonna, as if thy 1.05.112 P
if thou hast her not i' th' end, call me cut. 2.03.186 P
why, thou hast put him in such a dream, that 2.05.193 P
for that i woo, thou therefore hast no cause; 3.01.154
that defense thou hast, betake thee to't. 3.04.220 P
what nature the wrongs are thou hast done him, i 3.04.221 P
thou hast, sebastian, done good feature shame. 3.04.366
by my troth, thou hast an open hand. 4.01. 21 P
bloody and so dear, | hast made thine enemies? 5.01. 72
hast thou forgot thyself? 5.01.141
little faith, though thou hast too much fear. 5.01.171
thou hast said to me a thousand times | thou 5.01.267
priest–like, thou | hast cleans'd my bosom: WT 1.02.238
do't, and thou hast the one half of my heart; 1.02.348
i will seem friendly, as thou hast advis'd me. 1.02.350
which hast made it | so like to him that got it, 2.03.104
it, if thou hast | the ordering of the mind too, 2.03.105
thou, traitor, hast set on thy wife to this. 2.03.131
thou, that hast | a heart so tender o'er it, 2.03.132
hast thou read truth? 3.02.138
what studied torments, tyrant, hast for me? 3.02.175
away with thee the very services thou hast done; 4.02. 17 P
thou hast need of more rags to lay on thee, 4.03. 54 P
what hast here? ballads? 4.04.259 P
thou hast sworn my love to be. 4.04.306
thou hast sworn it more to me: 4.04.307
what advocate hast thou to him? 4.04.740 P
age, thou hast lost thy labor. 4.04.760 P
good paulina, | who hast the memory of hermione, 5.01. 50
me, mine own, | where hast thou been preserv'd? 5.03.124
thou hast found mine, | but how, is to be 5.03.138
go, faulconbridge, now hast thou thy desire, | a JN 1.01.176
hast thou conspired with thy brother too, | that 1.01.241
hast thou denied thyself a faulconbridge? 1.01.251
till angiers, and the right thou hast in france, 2.01. 22
that thou hast under–wrought his lawful king, 2.01. 95
from whom hast thou this great commission, 2.01.110
france, hast thou yet more blood to cast away? 2.01.334
thou hast not sav'd one drop of blood | in this 2.01.341
and if thou hast the mettle of a king, | being 2.01.401
it is not so, thou hast misspoke, misheard; 3.01. 4
hast thou not spoke like thunder on my side? 3.01.124
for that which thou hast sworn to do amiss | is 3.01.270
kept, | but thou hast sworn against religion, 3.01.280
against the blood that thou hast married? 3.01.301
good friend, thou hast no cause to say so yet, 3.03. 30
a fearful eye thou hast. 4.02.106
thou hast made me giddy | with these ill tidings 4.02.131
what a noble combat hast /thou fought | between 5.02. 43
thou hast a perfect thought. 5.06. 6
hast thou, according to thy oath and band, R2 1.01. 2
tell me, moreover, hast thou sounded him, | if 1.01. 8
since thou hast far to go, bear not along | the 1.03.199
why, uncle, thou hast many years to live. 1.03.225
and therein fasting, hast thou made me gaunt. 2.01. 81
hast thou tapp'd out and drunkenly carous'd. 2.01.127
for both hast thou, and both become the grave. 2.01.140
his face thou hast, for even so look'd he, 2.01.176
thou hast said enough. 3.02.203
with all the gracious utterance thou hast 3.03.125
'tis well that thou hast cause, | but thou 3.04. 19
and will maintain what thou hast said is false 4.01. 27
thou hast a traitor in thy presence there. 5.03. 40
thy revengeful hand, thou hast no cause to fear. 5.03. 42
that horse that thou so often hast bestrid, 5.05. 79
more than thou hast, and with it joy thy life. 5.06. 26
for though mine enemy thou hast ever been, 5.06. 28
for thou hast wrought | a deed of slander with 5.06. 34
that thou hast forgotten to demand that truly 1H4 1.02. 4 P
what a devil hast thou to do with the time of 1.02. 6 P
thou hast call'd her to a reckoning many a time 1.02. 49 P
give thee thy due, thou hast paid all there. 1.02. 52 P
thou hast the most unsavory /similes and art 1.02. 79 P
o, thou hast damnable iteration, and art indeed 1.02. 90 P
thou hast done much harm upon me, hal, god 1.02. 91 P
hast thou never an eye in thy head? 2.01. 27 P
hast no faith in thee? 2.01. 31 P
why hast thou lost the fresh blood in thy cheeks 2.03. 44
and thou hast talk'd | of sallies and retires, 2.03. 50
where hast been, hal? 2.04. 3 P
thou hast lost much honor that thou wert not 2.04. 20 P
how long hast thou to serve, francis? 2.04. 41 P
says she, "how many hast thou kill'd to–day?" 2.04.106 P
welcome, jack, where hast thou been? 2.04.113 P
again, and when thou hast tir'd thyself in base 2.04.250 P
art thou to hack thy sword as thou hast done, 2.04.262 P
let's hear, jack, what trick hast thou now? 2.04.265 P
and ever since thou hast blush'd extempore. 2.04.316 P
harry, which thou hast often heard of, and it is 2.04.411 P
tell me, where hast thou been this month? 2.04.432 P
what hast thou found? 2.04.532 P
thy place in council thou hast rudely lost, 3.02. 32
for thou hast lost thy princely privilege | with 3.02. 86
thou hast sav'd me a thousand marks in links and 3.03. 42 P
but the sack that thou hast drunk me would have 3.03. 44 P
what letters hast thou there? 4.01. 13
a borrowed title hast thou bought too dear. 5.03. 23
by god, thou hast deceiv'd me, lancaster, | i 5.04. 17
so many of his shadows thou hast met | and not 5.04. 30
thou hast redeem'd thy lost opinion, | and 5.04. 48
in this fair rescue thou hast brought to me. 5.04. 50
o, harry, thou hast robb'd me of my youth! 5.04. 77
than those proud titles thou hast won of me. 5.04. 79
full bravely hast thou flesh'd | thy maiden 5.04.130
thou hast a sigh to blow away this praise, 2H4 1.01. 80
note how many pair of silk stockings thou hast, 2.02. 15 P
as thou hast not done a great while, because the 2.02. 21 P
what the devil hast thou brought there? 2.04. 1 P
battle as thou hast done in a woman's petticoat? 3.02.154 P
what disease hast thou? 3.02.180 P
thou hast a better place in his affection | than 4.04. 22
thou hast stol'n that which after some few hours 4.05.101
my death | thou hast seal'd up my expectation. 4.05.103
whom thou hast whetted on thy stony heart | to 4.05.107

most renown'd, | hast eat thy bearer up." 4.05.164
thou hast drawn my shoulder out of joint. 5.04. 2 P
nym, thou hast spoke the right. H5 2.01.123
o, how hast thou with jealousy infected | the 2.02.126
why, now thou hast unwish'd five thousand men; 4.03. 76
and thou hast given me most bitter terms. 4.08. 42
thou hast me, if thou hast me, at the worst; 5.02.231 P
thou hast me, if thou hast me, at the worst; 5.02.232 P
thou hast astonish'd me with thy high terms. 1H6 1.02. 93
my heart and hands thou hast at once subdu'd. 1.02.109
one eye thou hast to look to heaven for grace; 1.04. 83
sir thomas gargrave, hast thou any life? 1.04. 88
that hast by tyranny these many years | wasted 2.03. 40
in prison hast thou spent a pilgrimage, | and 2.05.116
or thou shouldst find thou hast dishonor'd me. 3.01. 9
which thou thyself hast given her woeful breast. 3.03. 51
i come to know what prisoners thou hast ta'en, 4.07. 56
hast not a tongue? 5.03. 68
fond man, remember that thou hast a wife, | then 5.03. 81
hast thou by secret means | us'd intercession to 5.04.147
for thou hast given me in this beauteous face 2H6 1.01. 21
hast thou not worldly pleasure at command 1.02. 45
hast thou as yet conferr'd | with margery jordan 1.02. 74
the commons hast thou rack'd, the clergy's bags 1.03.128
hast thou been long blind and now restor'd? 2.01. 74
how long hast thou been blind? 2.01. 95
o peter, thou hast prevail'd in right! 2.03. 98 P
although thou hast been conduct of my shame. 2.04.101
no, not to lose it all, as thou hast done. 3.01.296
hast thou not spirit to curse thine enemy? 3.02.308
hast thou not kiss'd thy hand and held my 4.01. 53
how often hast thou waited at my cup, | fed from 4.01. 56
how in our voiding lobby hast thou stood | and 4.01. 61
thou hast hit it; 4.02. 19 P
or hast thou a mark to thyself, like a honest 4.02.103 P
thou hast most traitorously corrupted the youth 4.07. 32 P
the tally, thou hast caus'd printing to be us'd, 4.07. 35 P
and dignity, thou hast built a paper–mill. 4.07. 37 P
to thy face that thou hast men about thee that 4.07. 38 P
thou hast appointed justices of peace, to call 4.07. 41 P
moreover, thou hast put them in prison, and 4.07. 43 P
they could not read, thou hast hang'd them, when 4.07. 44 P
king | unto the commons, whom thou hast misled, 4.08. 8
shall fight with all the strength thou hast, 4.10. 50
false king, why hast thou broken faith with me, 5.01. 91
or wherefore dost abuse it if thou hast it? 5.01.172
hast thou not sworn allegiance unto me? 5.01.179
call buckingham, and all the friends thou hast, 5.01.193
now, by my sword, well hast thou fought to–day; 5.03. 15
well hast thou spoken, cousin, be it so. 3H6 1.01. 66
what title hast thou, traitor, to the crown? 1.01.104
talk not of france, sith thou hast lost it all. 1.01.110
how hast thou injur'd both thyself and us! 1.01.179
seeing thou hast prov'd so unnatural a father! 1.01.218
thou hast undone thyself, thy son, and me, | and 1.01.232
thou hast spoke too much already; get thee gone. 1.01.258
thou hast one son, for his sake pity me, | lest 1.03. 40
then let me die, for now thou hast no cause. 1.03. 45
why, now thou hast thy wish: 1.04.143
why, now thou hast thy will: 1.04.144
thou hast slain | the flow'r of europe for his 2.01. 70
and treacherously hast thou vanquish'd him, 2.01. 72
as thou hast shown it flinty by thy deeds, | i 2.01.202
for, well i wot, thou hast thy mother's tongue. 2.02.134
ah, warwick, why hast thou withdrawn thyself? 2.03. 14
give me thy gold — if thou hast any gold — 2.05. 80
how many children hast thou, widow? tell me. 3.02. 26
thou art a widow, and thou hast some children, 3.02.102
and all the trouble thou hast turn'd me to? 5.05. 16
for thou hast made the happy earth thy hell, R3 1.02. 51
to thee, that hast nor honesty nor grace: 1.03. 55
but repetition of what thou hast marr'd, | that 1.03.164
when thou hast broke it in such dear degree? 1.04.210
and hast the comfort of thy children left; 2.02. 56
a cockatrice hast thou hatch'd to the world, 4.01. 54
than thou hast made me by my dear lord's death!" 4.01. 76
why, /there thou hast it; 4.02. 72
all the slaughters, wretch, that thou hast done! 4.04.139
then by something that thou hast not wrong'd. 4.04.373
that thou hast wronged in the time o'erpast; 4.04.388
live whose fathers thou hast slaughter'd, 4.04.391
parents live whose children thou hast butcher'd, 4.04.393
to come, for that thou hast | misus'd ere us'd, 4.04.395
courageous richmond, well hast thou acquit thee. 5.05. 3
to this point hast thou heard him | at any time H8 1.02.145
but thou hast forc'd me | (out of thy honest 3.02.429
thou hast the sweetest face i ever look'd on. 4.01. 43
whom i most hated living, thou hast made me, 4.02. 73
sure | thou hast a cruel nature and a bloody. 5.02.164
lord archbishop, | thou hast made me now a man! 5.04. 64
thou hast no more brain than i have in mine TRO 2.01. 43 P
why hast thou not serv'd thyself in to my table 2.03. 41 P
fellow, thou hast not seen the lady cressid. 3.01. 37 P
troth, sweet /lord, thou hast a fine forehead. 3.01.108 P
hast not slept to–night? 4.02. 32 P
by him that thunders, thou hast lusty arms! 4.05.136
when thou hast hung /thy advanced sword i' th' 4.05.188
that hast so long walk'd hand in hand with time. 4.05.203
sword, thou hast thy fill of blood and death. 5.08. 4
so often hast thou beat me; COR 1.10. 8
hast not the soft way which, thou dost confess, 3.02. 82
theirs, so far | as thou hast power and person. 3.02. 86
as thou hast said | my praises made thee first a 3.02.107
perform a part | thou hast not done before. 3.02.110
and thou hast oft beheld | heart–hard'ning 4.01. 24
thou hast years upon thee, and thou art too full 4.01. 45
blows for rome | than thou hast spoken words? 4.02. 20
thou hast a grim appearance, and thy face 4.05. 60
then if thou hast | a heart of wreak in thee, 4.05. 84
each word thou hast spoke hath weeded from my 4.05.102
thou hast beat me out | twelve several times, 4.05.121
thou hast affected the /fine strains of honor, 5.03.149
thou hast never in thy life | show'd thy dear 5.03.160
with more strength | than thou hast to deny't. 5.03.177
i am glad thou hast set thy mercy and thy honor 5.03.200
thou hast made my heart | too great for what 5.06.102
thou hast done a deed whereat valor will weep. 5.06.132
how many sons hast thou of mine in store, | that TIT 1.01. 94

that hast thus lovingly reserv'd | the cordial 1.01.165
whose friend in justice thou hast ever been, 1.01.180
o, see what thou hast done! 1.01.341
even thou hast strook upon my crest, | and with 1.01.364
with these boys mine honor thou hast wounded. 1.01.365
whom thou in triumph long | hast prisoner held, 2.01. 15
what, hast not thou full often strook a doe, 2.01. 93
aaron, thou hast hit it. 2.01. 97
away, for thou hast stay'd us here too long. 2.03.181
brother, hast thou hurt thee with the fall? 2.03.203
to prove thou hast a true–divining heart, 2.03.214
a craftier tereus, cousin, hast thou met, | and 2.04. 41
'tis well, lavinia, that thou hast no hands, 3.01. 79
thou hast no hands to wipe away thy tears, | nor 3.01.106
thou, poor man, hast drown'd it with thine own. 3.01.141
o, would thou wert as thou tofore hast been! 3.01.293
villain, what hast thou done? 4.02. 73
thou hast undone our mother. 4.02. 75
and therein, hellish dog, thou hast undone her. 4.02. 77
publius, publius, what hast thou done? 4.03. 69
see, thou hast shot off one of taurus' horns. 4.03. 70
sirrah, hast thou a knife? 4.03.115
for /then hast made it like an humble suppliant. 4.03.117
and when thou hast given it the emperor, | knock 4.03.118
and hast a thing within thee called conscience, 5.01. 75
it be | that thou adorest and hast in reverence, 5.01. 83
and what not done, that thou hast cause to rue, 5.01.109
thou hast the odds of me, therefore no more. 5.02. 19
well hast thou lesson'd us, this shall we do. 5.02.110
what hast thou done, unnatural and unkind? 5.03. 48
why hast thou slain thine only daughter thus? 5.03. 55
this love that thou hast shown | doth add more ROM 1.01.188
thou wilt fall backward when thou hast more wit, 1.03. 42
for that which thou hast heard me speak to–night 2.02. 87
my good son, but where hast thou been then? 2.03. 47
thou hast most kindly hit it. 2.04. 55 P
this jest now, till thou hast worn out thy pump, 2.04. 62 P
for thou hast more of the wild goose in one of 2.04. 72 P
what hast thou found? 2.04.131 P
hast thou met with him? 2.05. 19
when thou hast breath | to say to me that thou 2.05. 31
more or a hair less in his beard than thou hast. 3.01. 18 P
other reason but because thou hast hazel eyes. 3.01. 20 P
thou hast quarrell'd with a man for coughing in 3.01. 24 P
excuse the injuries | that thou hast done me, 3.01. 67
what hast thou there? 3.02. 34
how hast thou the heart, | being a divine, a 3.03. 48
beast in seeming both, | thou hast amaz'd me! 3.03.114
hast thou slain tybalt? 3.03.116
that love which thou hast vow'd to cherish; 3.03.129
well, well, thou hast a careful father, child, 3.05.107
hast thou not a word of joy? 3.05.211
well, thou hast comforted me marvellous much. 3.05.230
thy face is mine, and thou hast sland'red it. 4.01. 35
o, shut the door, and when thou hast done so, 4.01. 44
thou hast the strength of will to /slay thyself, 4.01. 72
get thee to bed and rest, for thou hast need. 4.03. 13
hast thou no letters to me from the friar? 5.01. 31
i sell thee poison, thou hast sold me none. 5.01. 83
thou hast a servant nam'd lucilius. TIM 1.01.111
where thou hast feign'd him a worthy fellow. 1.01.223 P
and all the lands thou hast | lie in a pitch'd 1.02.224
and what hast thou there under thy cloak, pretty 3.01. 14 P
and thee after, when thou hast conquer'd! 4.03.105
hast thou gold yet? 4.03.130
give us some gold, good timon; hast thou more? 4.03.133
thou hast cast away thyself, being like thyself, 4.03.220
what hast thou given? 4.03.270
i'll say th' hast gold; 4.03.393
thou hast painfully discover'd; 5.02. 1
rome, thou hast lost the breed of noble bloods! JC 1.02.151
but, o grief, | where hast thou led me? 1.03.112
thou hast no figures nor no fantasies, | which 2.01.231
hast conjur'd up | my mortified spirit. 2.01.323
thou hast wrong'd caius ligarius. 2.03. 4 P
come hither, fellow; which way hast thou been? 2.04. 21
thou hast some suit to caesar, hast thou not? 2.04. 27
thou hast some suit to caesar, hast thou not? 2.04. 27
had i as many eyes as thou hast wounds, 3.01.200
thou hast describ'd | a hot friend cooling. 4.02. 18
alas, thou hast misconstrued every thing! 5.03. 84
strato, thou hast been all this while asleep; 5.05. 32
that thou hast prov'd lucilius' saying true. 5.05. 59
where hast thou been, sister? MAC 1.03. 1
that hast no less deserv'd, nor must be known 1.04. 30
thou hast it now: 3.01. 1
thou hast no speculation in those eyes | which 3.04. 94
thou hast harp'd my fear aright. 4.01. 74
and let the angel whom thou still hast serv'd 5.08. 14
if thou hast any sound, or use of voice, | speak HAM 1.01.128
or if thou hast uphoarded in thy life | extorted 1.01.136
those friends thou hast, and their adoption 1.03. 62
if thou hast nature in thee, bear it not, | let 1.05. 81
thou still hast been the father of good news. 2.02. 42
thee | that no revenue hast but thy good spirits 3.02. 58
for thou hast been | as one in suff'ring all 3.02. 65
and rewards | hast ta'en with equal thanks; 3.02. 68
hamlet, thou hast thy father much offended. 3.04. 9
o me, what hast thou done? 3.04. 25
o hamlet, thou hast cleft my heart in twain. 3.04.156
no life to breathe | what thou hast said to me. 3.04.199
dearly grieve | for that which thou hast done — 4.03. 42
too much of water hast thou, poor ophelia, | and 4.07.185
how long hast thou been grave–maker? 5.01.142 P
princes at a shot | so bloodily hast strook? 5.02.367
that thou hast sought to make us break our /vow LR 1.01.168
that justly think'st and hast most rightly said! 1.01.183
thou hast her, france, let her be thine, for we 1.01.262
thou hast par'd thy wit o' both sides, and left 1.04.187 P
that thou hast power to shake my manhood thus, 1.04.297
thy half o' th' kingdom hast thou not forgot, 2.04.180
wretch | that hast within thee undivulged crimes 3.02. 52
what hast thou been? 3.04. 84 P
where hast thou sent the king? 3.07. 50
the wretch that thou hast blown unto the worst 4.01. 8
who hast not in thy brows an eye discerning 4.02. 52
hast heavy substance, bleed'st not, speak'st, 4.06. 52
altitude | which thou hast perpendicularly fell. 4.06. 54
thou hast seen a farmer's dog bark at a beggar? 4.06.154 P
thou hast /one daughter | who redeems nature 4.06.205
slave, thou hast slain me. 4.06.246
about it, and write happy when th' hast done. 5.03. 35
what art thou | that hast this fortune on me? 5.03.166
if more, the more th' hast wrong'd me. 5.03.169
th' hast spoken right, 'tis true. 5.03.174
who hast had my purse | as if the strings were OTH 1.01. 2
in honest plainness thou hast heard me say | my 1.01. 97
foul thief, where hast thou stow'd my daughter? 1.02. 62
damn'd as thou art, thou hast enchanted her, 1.02. 63
that thou hast practic'd on her with foul charms 1.02. 73
all my heart | which, but thou hast already, 1.03.194
look to her, moor, if thou hast eyes to see; 1.03.292
what miserable praise hast thou for her that's 2.01.139 P
of wine, if thou hast no name to be known by, 2.03.282 P
hast stol'n it from her? 3.03.310
thou hast set me on the rack. 3.03.335
thou hast taken against me a most just exception 4.02.207 P
but, roderigo, if thou hast that in thee indeed, 4.02.212 P
that hast such noble sense of thy friend's wrong 5.01. 32
thou hast not half that pow'r to do me harm | as 5.02.162
thou hast done a deed — | i care not for thy 5.02.164
for thou hast kill'd the sweetest innocent 5.02.199
thou hast no weapon, and perforce must suffer. 5.02.256
hast thou affections? ANT 1.05. 12
thou hast a sister by the mother's side, 2.02.118
rogue, thou hast liv'd too long. 2.05. 73
merchandise which thou hast brought from rome 2.05.104
which if thou hast considered, let us know | if 2.06. 5
thou hast serv'd me with much faith; 2.07. 58
hast thou drunk well? 2.07. 65
thou hast, ventidius, that | without the which a 3.01. 27
and throw between them all the food thou hast, 3.05. 14
thou hast forespoke my being in these wars, 3.07. 3
o, whither hast thou led me, egypt? 3.11. 51
caesar, thou hast subdu'd | his judgment too. 3.13. 36
since | thou hast been whipt for following him. 3.13.137
where hast thou been, my heart? 3.13.172
thou hast been rightly honest — so hast thou — 4.02. 11
thou hast been rightly honest — so hast thou — 4.02. 11
'tis thou | hast sold me to this novice, and my 4.12. 14
thou hast seen these signs, | they are black 4.14. 7
which thou hast worn | most useful for thy 4.14. 79
do at once | the thing why thou hast drawn it. 4.14. 89
die when thou hast liv'd, | quicken with kissing 4.15. 38
hast thou no care of me? 4.15. 60
what thou hast done thy master caesar knows, 5.02. 65
and when thou hast done this chare, i'll give 5.02.231
hast thou the pretty worm of nilus there, | that 5.02.243
hast thou not learn'd me how | to make perfumes? CYM 1.05. 12
on, but think | thou hast thy mistress still; 1.05. 69
why hast thou abus'd | so many miles with a 3.04.102
why hast thou gone so far, | to be unbent when 3.04.107
to be unbent when thou hast ta'en thy stand, 3.04.108
and constantly thou hast stuck to the bare 3.05.118 P
hast any of thy late master's garments in thy 3.05.123 P
what hast thou done? 4.02.117
envy much | thou hast robb'd me of this deed. 4.02.159
rages, | thou thy worldly task hast done, | home 4.02.260
thou hast finish'd joy and moan. 4.02.273
why hast thou thus adjourn'd | the graces for 5.04. 78
thou hast been a grandsire and begot | a father 5.04.123
and thou hast created | a mother and two 5.04.124
boy, | thou hast look'd thyself into my grace, 5.05. 94
o imogen, | thou hast lost by this a kingdom. 5.05.373
helicanus, thou | hast mov'd us. PER 1.02. 51
thou hast bewitch'd my daughter, and thou art 2.05. 49
and thou that hast | upon the winds command, 3.01. 2
thou hast as chiding a nativity | as fire, air, 3.01. 32
a terrible child–bed hast thou had, my dear, 3.01. 56
thou hast a heart | that ever cracks for woe! 3.02. 76
thy oath remember, thou hast sworn to do't. 4.01. 1
sir, hast thou cried her through the market? 4.02. 93 P
is, and thou hast the harvest out of thine own 4.02.141 P
whom thou hast pois'ned too. 4.03. 10
rest you said | thou hast been godlike perfit, 5.01.206
that hast slain | the scythe–tusk'd boar; TNK 1.01. 78
hast much more power on him | than ever he had 1.01. 87
lady, | if ever thou hast felt what sorrow was, 2.02.276
thou hast the start now; 2.03. 8
hast likewise blest a /place | with thy sole 3.01. 10
me language such | as thou hast show'd me feat! 3.01. 45
i will forgive | the trespass thou hast done me, 3.01. 77
thou hast well describ'd him. 4.02. 89
that with thy power hast turn'd | green neptune 5.01. 49
who hast power | to call the fiercest tyrant 5.01. 77
that hast the might, | even with an eye–glance, 5.01. 79
what godlike power | hast thou not power upon? 5.01. 90
poor servant, thou hast lost. 5.03. 72
but, more, the more thou hast | either of honor, STM III 14
quoth she, "hast thou a tongue? VEN 427
"and when thou hast on foot the purblind hare, 679
o yes, it may, thou hast no eyes to see, | but 939
why hast thou cast into eternal sleeping | those 951
"alas, poor world, what treasure hast thou lost! 1075
with such black payment as thou hast pretended; LUC 576
hast thou put on his shape to do him shame? 597
"hast thou command? 624
life was mine which thou hast here deprived. 1752
o, from thy cheeks my image thou hast torn, 1762
friend, | whilst thou hast wherewith to spend; PP 20.34
that thou no form of thee hast left behind, SON 9. 6
face with nature's own hand painted | hast thou, 20. 2
and thou (all they) hast all the all of me. 31.14
no more be griev'd at that which thou hast done: 35. 1
what hast thou then more than thou hadst before? 40. 2
that thou hast her, it is not all my grief, 42. 1
to leave poor me thou hast the strength of laws, 49.13
thou hast pass'd by the ambush of young days, 70. 9
so then thou hast but lost the dregs of life, 74. 9
in my love's veins thou hast too grossly dy'd. 99. 5
who hast by waning grown, and therein show'st 126. 3
and my next self thou harder hast engrossed: 133. 6
him have i lost, thou hast both him and me, | he 134.13
whoever hath her wish, thou hast thy will, | and 135. 1
why of eyes' falsehood hast thou forged hooks, 137. 7
o, from what pow'r hast thou this pow'rful might 150. 1
whence hast thou this becoming of things ill, 150. 5

HASTE 175 FR 0.0197 REL FR 164 V 11 P

he is in haste; TGV 1.03. 89
will you make haste? 2.04.190
bid him make haste and meet me at the north–gate 3.01.260
well, farewell, i am in great haste now. WIV 1.04.161 P
trudge with it in all haste, and carry it among 3.03. 14 P
i am in haste, go along with me, i'll tell you 5.01. 23 P
our haste from hence is of so quick condition MM 1.01. 53
my haste may not admit it, | nor need you, on 1.01. 62
haste you speedily to angelo; 3.01.261 P
break off thy song, and haste thee quick away. 4.01. 7
i shall attend your leisure, but make haste, 4.01. 56
that spirit's possess'd with haste | that wounds 4.02. 88
thank thee, varrius, thou hast made good haste. 4.05. 11
haste still pays haste, and leisure answers 5.01.410
haste still pays haste, and leisure answers 5.01.410
claudio stoop'd to death, and with like haste. 5.01.415
that in such haste i sent to seek his master? ERR 2.01. 2
good sir, make haste. 3.01.119
/sweat now, make haste! 4.02. 29
you, | by dromio here, who came in haste for it. 4.04. 84
i am now in great haste, as it may appear unto ADO 3.05. 50 P
we have some haste, leonato. 5.01. 47
some haste, my lord! 5.01. 48
i leave you too, for here comes one in haste. 5.02. 94 P
haste, signify so much, while we attend, | like LLL 2.01. 33
did stumble with haste in his eyesight to be; 2.01.239
wings, and no eyes, figure unheedy haste; MND 1.01.237
my fairy lord, this must be done with haste, 3.02.378
but, notwithstanding, haste, make no delay; 3.02.394
return in haste, for i do feast to–night | my MV 2.02.171
your good leave to go away, | i will make haste; 3.02.325
and therefore haste away, | for we must measure 3.04. 83
soft, no haste. 4.01.321
away, make haste. 4.01.454
away, make haste. 4.02. 18
mistress, dispatch you with your safest haste, AYL 1.03. 41
this dispatch'd with all the haste thou canst; SHR in.1. 129
signior baptista, my business asketh haste, 2.01.114
who woo'd in haste, and means to wed at leisure. 3.02. 11
but so it is, my haste doth call me hence, | and 3.02.187
that will not be in haste. 4.03. 72
frank nature, rather curious than in haste, AWW 1.02. 20
this haste hath wings indeed. 2.01. 93
haste you again. 2.02. 71 P
and make this haste as your own good proceeding, 2.04. 49
my haste is very great. 2.05. 77
i pray you stay not, but in haste to horse. 2.05. 87
hence, it requires haste of your lordship. 4.03. 94 P
night, and with more haste | than is his use. 5.01. 23
ay, that's the theme, | to her in haste. TN 2.04.123
blame not this haste of mine. 4.03. 22
make your best haste, and go not | too far i' WT 3.03. 10
but who comes in such haste in riding–robes? JN 1.01.217
blood | that hot rash haste so indirectly shed. 2.01. 49
go we, as well as haste will suffer us, | to 2.01.559
haste before, | and ere our coming see thou 3.03. 6
nay, but make haste; 4.02.170
which his nimble haste | had falsely thrust upon 4.02.197
o, haste thee to the peers, | throw this report 4.02.260
the angry lords with all expedient haste. 4.02.268
lords, i am hot with haste in seeking you. 4.03. 74
in haste whereof, most heartily i pray | your R2 1.01.150
pray god we may make haste and come too late! 1.04. 64
for his designs crave haste, his haste good hope 2.02. 44
his designs crave haste, his haste good hope. 2.02. 44
bloody with spurring, fiery–red with haste. 2.03. 58
the treason that my haste forbids me show. 5.03. 50
my liege, this haste was hot in question, | and 1H4 1.01. 34
i'll haste the writer, and withal | break with 3.01.141
but, sirrah, make haste, percy is already in the 4.02. 74 P
brief | with winged haste to the lord marshal, 4.04. 2
how much they do import, you would make haste. 4.04. 5
therefore make haste. 4.04. 40
therefore, lord constable, haste on montjoy, H5 3.05. 61
from a trumpet take, | and use it for my haste. 4.02. 62
i'll to the tower with all the haste i can, | to 1H6 1.01.167
and therefore haste i to the parliament, 2.05.127
whither away, sir john falstaff, in such haste? 3.02.104
from callice, | to haste unto your coronation, 4.01. 10
then let's make haste away, and look unto the 2H6 1.01.208
why com'st thou in such haste? 4.04. 26
in haste, post–haste, are come to join with you; 3H6 2.01.139
and haste is needful in this desp'rate case. 4.01.129
brother, the time and case requireth haste, 4.05. 18
it is his policy | to haste thus fast, to find 5.04. 63
had i not reason, think ye, to make haste, | and 5.06. 72
sweet flow'rs are slow and weeds make haste. R3 2.04. 15
good lords, make all the speedy haste you may. 3.01. 60
make haste, the hour of death is expiate. 3.03. 24
which now the loving haste of these our friends, 3.05. 54
come, madam, come, i in all haste was sent. 4.01. 56
and brief, good mother, for i am in haste. 4.04.162
i will, my lord, with all convenient haste. 4.04.443
earl surrey was sent thither, and in haste too, H8 2.01. 43
of my glory, | i haste now to my setting. 3.02.225
highness' pardon, | my haste made me unmannerly. 4.02.105
it seems you are in haste. 5.01. 11
the council pray'd me | to make great haste. 5.02. 3
in all swift haste. TRO 1.01.116
or, if you please, | haste there before us. 4.01. 41
she is to do, | and haste her to the purpose. 4.03. 5
injurious time now with a robber's haste | crams 4.04. 42
haste we, diomed, | to reinforcement, or we 5.05. 15
have the spirit, will haste | to help cominius. COR 1.05. 13
and with our fair entreaties haste them on. 5.01. 74
o, let us hence, i stand on sudden haste. ROM 2.03. 93
jesu, what haste! 2.05. 29
make haste, lest mine be about your ears ere it 3.01. 81 P
let romeo hence in haste, | else, when he is 3.01.194
hie you, make haste, for it grows very late. 3.03.164
do you like this haste? 3.04. 22
i wonder at this haste, that i must wed | ere he 3.05.118
so, | and i am nothing slow to slack his haste. 4.01. 3
now do you know the reason of this haste. 4.01. 15
make haste, make haste. 4.04. 16

make haste, make haste. 4.04. 16
hie, make haste, | make haste, the bridegroom he 4.04. 26
make haste, the bridegroom he is come already, 4.04. 27
he is come already, | make haste, i say. 4.04. 28
get on your cloak and haste you to lord timon; TIM 2.01. 15
to stop affliction, let him take his haste, 5.01.210
those that with haste will make a mighty fire JC 1.03.107
close a while, for here comes one in haste. 1.03.131
cinna, where haste you so? 1.03.133
leave me with haste. 2.01.309
what a haste looks through his eyes! MAC 1.02. 46
come, let's make haste, she'll soon be back 3.05. 36
wisdom plucks me | from over–credulous haste. 4.03.120
the rivals of my watch, bid them make haste. HAM 1.01. 13
that this sweaty haste | doth make the night 1.01. 77
farewell, and let your haste commend your duty. 1.02. 39
and at the sound it shrunk in haste away | and 1.02.219
one with moderate haste might tell a hundreth. 1.02.237
haste me to know't, that i, with wings as swift 1.05. 29
bid the players make haste. 3.02. 49 P
we will haste us. 3.03. 26
i pray you haste in this. 4.01. 37
pray you make haste. 4.03. 57
eats not the flats with more impiteous haste 4.05.101
let us haste to hear it, | and call the noblest 5.02.386
coming hither, now i' th' night, i' th' haste, LR 2.01. 24
resolve me with all modest haste which way 2.04. 25
stew'd in his haste, half breathless, /panting 2.04. 31
discovery, but your haste | is now urg'd on you. 5.01. 53
haste thee, for thy life. 5.03.252
which ever as she could with haste dispatch, OTH 1.03.148
th' affair cries haste, | and speed must answer 1.03.276
i must with haste from hence. ANT 1.02.132
haste we for it, | yet, ere we put ourselves in 2.02.164
with what haste | the weight we must convey with 3.01. 35
make your soonest haste; 3.04. 27
go put it to the haste. 5.02.196
make haste. CYM 1.05. 2
that both mine ears | must not in haste abuse), 1.06.131
your breath cool yourself, telling your haste. PER 1.01.159
out thy sorrows which /thou bring'st in haste, 1.04. 58
and then with what haste you can, get you to bed 2.05. 93
ear, and i am sworn | to do my work with haste. 4.01. 70
since that our theme is haste, | i stamp this TNK 1.01.215
each thing | our haste does leave imperfect. 1.04. 12
but why all this haste, sir? 4.01. 51
it is a cursed haste you made | if you have done 5.04. 41
shaking her wings, devouring all in haste, VEN 57
and all in haste she coasteth to the cry. 870
her more than haste is mated with delays, | like 909
and in her haste unfortunately spies | the foul 1029
return again in haste, | thou seest our LUC 321
so his unhallowed haste her words delays, | and 552
with their fresh falls' haste | add to his flow, 650
the cause craves haste, and it will soon be writ 1295
"at ardea to my lord with more than haste." 1332
outruns the eye that doth behold his haste, 1668
weary with toil, i haste me to my bed, | the SON 27. 1
where thou art, why should i haste me thence? 51. 3
lie, | made more or less by thy continual haste. 123.12

HASTED 1 FR 0.0001 REL FR 0 V 1 P
but let it be so hasted that supper be ready at MV 2.02.114 P

HASTEN 9 FR 0.0010 REL FR 6 V 3 P
shall be employ'd | to hasten on his expedition. TGV 1.03. 77
too far in anger, lest thou hasten thy trial; AWW 2.03.212 P
lady, | and bid her hasten all the house to bed, ROM 3.03.156
will you two help to hasten them? HAM 3.02. 50 P
get you gone, | and hasten your return. LR 1.04.340
hasten his musters and conduct his pow'rs. 4.02. 16
pray you hasten | your generals after. ANT 2.04. 1
and hasten the success, which doubt not will TNK 4.03.100 P
shore, | so do our minutes hasten to their end, SON 60. 2

HASTE–POST–HASTE 1 FR 0.0001 REL FR 1 V 0 P
he requires your haste–post–haste appearance, OTH 1.02. 37

HASTES 2 FR 0.0002 REL FR 2 V 0 P
and in his wisdom hastes our marriage, | to stop ROM 4.01. 11
the mutiny he there hastes t' oppress, | says to PER 3.ch. 29

HASTETH 2 FR 0.0002 REL FR 2 V 0 P
away he springs, and hasteth to his horse. VEN 258
this said, she hasteth to a myrtle grove, 865

HASTILY 4 FR 0.0004 REL FR 3 V 1 P
and hearing how hastily you are to depart, i am MM 4.03. 51 P
here comes the prince and claudio hastily. ADO 5.01. 45
hastily lead away. WT 5.03.155
what brings you here to court so hastily? JN 1.01.221

HASTING 2 FR 0.0002 REL FR 2 V 0 P
are both landed, | hasting to th' court. WT 2.03.197
hasting to feed her fawn hid in some brake. VEN 876

HASTINGS' 2 FR 0.0002 REL FR 2 V 0 P
mean | of my lord hastings' late imprisonment. R3 1.03. 90
is lighted on poor hastings' wretched head! 3.04. 93

/HASTINGS 1 FR 0.0001 REL FR 1 V 0 P
/hastings and rivers, take each other's hand, R3 2.01. 7

HASTINGS 46 FR 0.0052 REL FR 46 V 0 P
the question then, lord hastings, standeth thus: 2H4 1.03. 15
and so to you, lord hastings, and to all. 4.02. 3
you are too shallow, hastings, much too shallow, 4.02. 50
go, good lord hastings, | and, ere they be 4.02. 95
good tidings, my lord hastings! 4.02.106
mowbray, the bishop scroop, hastings, and all, 4.04. 84
for this one speech lord hastings well deserves 3H6 4.01. 47
but, ere i go, hastings and montague, | resolve 4.01.134
and hastings as he favors edward's cause! 4.01.144
'tis the lord hastings, the king's chiefest 4.03. 11
richard and hastings. 4.03. 29
now, my lord hastings and sir william stanley, 4.05. 1
brother of gloucester, lord hastings, and the 4.05. 16
and the lord hastings, who attended him | in 4.06. 82
brother richard, lord hastings, and the rest, 4.07. 1
that made him send lord hastings to the tower, R3 1.01. 68
lord hastings was /to /her /for /his delivery? 1.01. 75
the new–delivered hastings? 1.01.121
and so wast thou, lord hastings, when my son 1.03.210
namely, to derby, hastings, buckingham — | and 1.03.328
and i, as i love hastings with my heart! 2.01. 17
wife, love lord hastings, let him kiss your hand 2.01. 21
there, hastings, i will never more remember 2.01. 23
hastings, love lord marquess. 2.01. 25
come, hastings, help me to my closet. 2.01.134
fie, what a slug is hastings, that he comes not 3.01. 22
if she deny, lord hastings, go with him, | and 3.01. 35
come on, lord hastings, will you go with me? 3.01. 58
to make william lord hastings of our mind | for 3.01.162
he will do all in all as hastings doth. 3.01.168
sound thou lord hastings | how he doth stand 3.01.170
lord hastings will not yield to our complots? 3.01.192
when she exclaim'd on hastings, you, and i, 3.03. 16
she buckingham, | then curs'd she hastings. 3.03. 19
lord hastings, you and he are near in love. 3.04. 13
william lord hastings had pronounc'd your part 3.04. 27
than my lord hastings no man might be bolder, 3.04. 29
catesby hath sounded hastings in our business, 3.04. 36
the dangerous and unsuspected hastings. 3.05. 23
is the indictment of the good lord hastings, 3.06. 1
and yet within these five hours hastings liv'd, 3.06. 8
o, let me think on hastings, and be gone | to 4.02.121
th' adulterate hastings, rivers, vaughan, grey, 4.04. 69
where is kind hastings? 4.04.148
hastings, and edward's children, grey and rivers 5.01. 3
think on lord hastings. 5.03.156

HAST'NING 1 FR 0.0001 REL FR 1 V 0 P
to your court | whiles he was hast'ning (in the WT 5.01.189

HASTY 20 FR 0.0022 REL FR 17 V 3 P
the first suit is hot and hasty, like a scotch ADO 2.01. 75 P
are you so hasty now? 5.01. 49
take no unkindness of his hasty words. SHR 4.03.167
or teach thy hasty spleen to do me shame, | i'll JN 4.03. 97
ire, | in rage, deaf as the sea, hasty as fire. R2 1.01. 19
being upon hasty employment in the king's 2H4 2.01.127 P
is he so hasty that he doth suppose | my sleep 4.05. 60
yet hasty marriage seldom proveth well. 3H6 4.01. 18
with hasty germans and blunt hollanders, | hath 4.08. 2
art thou so hasty? R3 4.04.163
be not so hasty to confound my meaning: 4.04.262
and something spoke in choler, ill, and hasty. H8 2.01. 34
hasty and tinder–like upon too trivial motion; COR 2.01. 50 P
in the repeal, as hasty | to expel him thence. 4.07. 32
of breath | as violently as hasty powder fir'd ROM 5.01. 64
fire, | who, much enforced, shows a hasty spark, JC 4.03.112
have to use you did provoke | our hasty sending. HAM 2.02. 4
to bandy hasty words, to scant my sizes, | and LR 2.04.175
i'll stay | till hasty polydore return, and CYM 4.02.165
thy hasty spring still blasts and ne'er grows LUC 49

HASTY–FOOTED 1 FR 0.0001 REL FR 1 V 0 P
when we have chid the hasty–footed time | for MND 3.02.200

HASTY–WITTED 1 FR 0.0001 REL FR 1 V 0 P
an hasty–witted body | would say your head and SHR 5.02. 40

HA'T 11 FR 0.0012 REL FR 6 V 5 P
let's ha't, good grumio. SHR 4.01. 59 P
well, go thy ways, old lad, for thou shalt ha't. 5.02.181
come, you shall ha't; AWW 5.02. 38 P
it is no matter now i ha't again. TRO 5.02. 72
kindly, sir, i pray let me ha't. COR 2.03. 76 P
you shall ha't, worthy sir. 2.03. 79 P
we'll ha't to–morrow night. HAM 2.02.540 P
a solemn wager on your cunnings — | i ha't! 4.07.156
by heaven, i'll ha't! 5.02.343
or sky inclips, | is thine, if thou wilt ha't. ANT 2.07. 69
let's ha't, good soldier. 2.07.105

HAT 34 FR 0.0038 REL FR 18 V 16 P
ariel, | fetch me the hat and rapier in my cell. TMP 5.01. 84
this hat is nan, our maid. TGV 2.03. 21 P
by this hat, then he in the red face had it; WIV 1.01.170 P
otherwise he might put on a hat, a muffler, and 4.02. 71 P
there's her thrumm'd hat and her muffler too. 4.02. 78 P
wears his faith but as the fashion of his hat: ADO 1.01. 76 P
'a brushes his hat a' mornings; 3.02. 41 P
knowest that the fashion of a doublet, or a hat, 3.03.118 P
i'll lay my head to any good man's hat, | these LLL 1.01.308
with your hat penthouse–like o'er the shop of 3.01. 17 P
my hat to a halfpenny, pompey proves the best 5.02.560 P
hood mine eyes | thus with my hat, and sigh and MV 2.02.194
is his head worth a hat? AYL 3.02.206 P
take my color'd hat and cloak. SHR 1.01.207
is coming in a new hat and an old jerkin; 3.02. 43 P
an old hat, and the humor of forty fancies 3.02. 68 P
there was no link to color peter's hat, | and 4.01.134
hose, a scarlet cloak, and a copatain hat! 5.01. 67 P
take your sweetheart's hat | and pluck it o'er WT 4.04.650
nay, you shall have no hat. 4.04.658
more sir johns, and, putting off his hat, said, 2H4 2.04. 7 P
i'll canvass thee in thy broad cardinal's hat, 1H6 1.03. 36
under my feet i stamp thy cardinal's hat; 1.03. 49
your holy hat to be stamp'd on the king's coin. H8 3.02.325
choice is rather to have my hat than my heart, i COR 2.03. 99 P
and with his hat, thus waving it in scorn, | "i 2.03.167
other day, and now he has beat it out of my hat. TIM 3.06.113 P
what, man, ne'er pull your hat upon your brows; MAC 4.03.208
no hat upon his head, his stockins fouled, HAM 2.01. 76
by his cockle hat and staff, | and his sandal 4.05. 25
with glove or hat or handkerchief | still waving CYM 1.03. 11
('tis in my cloak–bag) doublet, hat, hose, all 3.04.169
with one fair hand she heaveth up his hat, | her VEN 351
for some, untuck'd, descended her sheav'd hat, LC 31

HATCH* 9 FR 0.0010 REL FR 9 V 0 P
thee from the door, or sit down at the hatch: ERR 3.01. 33
in at the window, or else o'er the hatch. JN 1.01.171
to cudgel you and make you take the hatch, | to 5.02.138
such things become the hatch and brood of time, 2H4 3.01. 86
'tis true, the raven doth not hatch a lark, TIT 2.03.149
and i do doubt the hatch and the disclose | will HAM 3.01.166
head, | dogs leapt the hatch, and all are fled. LR 3.06. 73
than the ills i know, | my idleness doth hatch. ANT 1.02.130
or hateful cuckoos hatch in sparrows' nests? LUC 849

HATCH'D* 9 FR 0.0010 REL FR 8 V 1 P
and so in progress to be hatch'd and born, | are MM 2.02. 97
folly, in wisdom hatch'd, | hath wisdom's LLL 5.02. 70
'tis hatch'd, and shall be so. SHR 1.01.206
a cockatrice hast thou hatch'd to the world, R3 4.01. 54
again | as venerable nestor, hatch'd in silver, TRO 1.03. 65
egg, | which, hatch'd, would as his kind grow JC 2.01. 33
events | new hatch'd to th' woeful time. MAC 2.03. 59
the evils she hatch'd were not effected; CYM 5.05. 60
'twere not amiss to keep our door hatch'd. PER 4.02. 33 P

HATCHES 8 FR 0.0009 REL FR 6 V 2 P
the mariners all under hatches stowed, | who, TMP 1.02.230
find the mariners asleep | under the hatches. 5.01. 99
and (how we know not) all clapp'd under hatches, 5.01.231
if he come under my hatches, i'll never to sea WIV 2.01. 92 P
back, | i stood upon the hatches in the storm; 2H6 3.02.103
my cabin tempted me to walk | upon the hatches. R3 1.04. 13
along | upon the giddy footing of the hatches, 1.04. 17
we have a chest beneath the hatches, caulk'd and PER 3.01. 70 P

HATCHET 1 FR 0.0001 REL FR 0 V 1 P
a hempen /caudle then, and the help of hatchet. 2H6 4.07. 91 P

HATCHING 1 FR 0.0001 REL FR 1 V 0 P
must show themselves, which in the hatching, COR 1.02. 21

HATCHMENT 1 FR 0.0001 REL FR 1 V 0 P
no trophy, sword, nor hatchment o'er his bones, HAM 4.05.215

/HATE 2 FR 0.0002 REL FR 2 V 0 P
/a /general /voice | /cried /hate /upon /him; 2H4 4.01.135
my birthplace /hate i, and my love's upon | this COR 4.04. 23

HATE 183 FR 0.0206 REL FR 162 V 21 P
shall make me chide thee, if not hate thee. TMP 1.02.477
they all do hate him | as rootedly as i. 3.02. 94
but barren hate, | sour–ey'd disdain, and 4.01. 19
weeds so loathly | that you shall hate it both. 4.01. 22
to plead for love deserves more fee than hate. TGV 1.02. 48
for love of you, not hate unto my friend, | hath 3.01. 46
if she do frown, 'tis not in hate of you, | but 3.01. 96
three things that women highly hold in hate. 3.02. 33
ay, but she'll think that it is spoke in hate. 3.02. 34
to hate young valentine and love my friend. 3.02. 65
love | than hate of eglamour that goes with her. 5.02. 54
more to cross that love | than hate for silvia, 5.02. 56
i something do excuse the thing i hate, | for MM 2.04.119
refuse me, hate me, torture me to death! ADO 4.01.184
all that, and if she did not hate him deadly, 5.01.177 P
so much i hate a breaking cause to be | of LLL 5.02.355
the more i hate, the more he follows me. MND 1.01.198
can you not hate me, as i know you do, | but you 3.02.149
when i am sure you hate me with your hearts. 3.02.154
the hate i bare thee made me leave thee so? 3.02.190
although i hate her, i'll not harm her so. 3.02.270
can you do me greater harm than hate? 3.02.271
hate me, wherefore? 3.02.272
no jest | that i do hate thee and love helena. 3.02.281
jealousy | to sleep by hate and fear no enmity? 4.01.145
i hate him for he is a christian; MV 1.03. 42
but yet i'll go in hate, to feed upon | the 2.05. 14
yourself, | hate counsels not in such a quality. 3.02. 6
more than a lodg'd hate and a certain loathing 4.01. 60
every offense is not a hate at first. 4.01. 68
by this kind of chase, i should hate him, for my AYL 1.03. 33 P
yet i hate not orlando. 1.03. 34 P
no, faith, hate him not, for my sake. 1.03. 35 P
get that i wear, owe no man hate, envy no man's 3.02. 74 P
for my part, | i love him not, nor hate him not; 3.05.127
have more cause to hate him than to love him, 3.05.128
let not your hate encounter with my love | for AWW 1.03.208
both my revenge and hate | loosing upon thee, in 2.03.164
house, | acquaint my mother with my hate to her, 2.03.287
that can such sweet use make of what they hate, 4.04. 22
while shameful hate sleeps out the afternoon. 5.03. 66
thou didst hate her deadly, | and she is dead, 5.03.117
i hate it as an unfill'd can. TN 2.03. 6 P
way, it must be with valor, for policy i hate. 3.02. 31 P
i hate ingratitude more in a man | than lying, 3.04.354
i hate a drunken rogue. 5.01.201 P
i say thou liest, camillo, and i hate thee, WT 1.02.300
judge, | that i can find should merit any hate. JN 2.01.520
night, | thou hate and terror to prosperity, 3.04. 28
prince, | and free from other misbegotten hate, R2 1.01. 33
how god and good men hate so foul a liar. 1.01.114
the swelling difference of your settled hate. 1.01.201
and for our eyes do hate the dire aspect | of 1.03.127
this low'ring tempest of your home–bred hate, 1.03.187
merely in hate, 'gainst any of us all, | that 2.01.243
is near the hate of those love not the king. 2.02.128
by so much fills their hearts with deadly hate. 2.02.131
turns to the sourest and most deadly hate. 3.02.136
i'll hate him everlastingly | that bids me be of 3.02.207
that fear to hate, and hate turns one or both 5.01. 67
and hate turns one or both | to worthy danger 5.01. 67
i hate the murtherer, love him murthered. 5.06. 40
i hate it. 1H4 2.02. 47 P
they hate us youth. 2.02. 85 P
your majesty hath no just cause to hate me. 2H4 5.02. 66
rose, | as cognizance of my blood–drinking hate, 1H6 2.04.108
and suffolk's cloudy brow his stormy hate; 2H6 3.01.155
teeth, | with full as many signs of deadly hate, 3.02.314
alas, poor york, but that i hate thee deadly, 3H6 1.04. 84
these words have turn'd my hate to love, | and i 3.03.199
than if thou never hadst deserv'd our hate. 5.01.104
and hate the idle pleasures of these days. R3 1.01. 31
king | in deadly hate the one against the other; 1.01. 35
to take her in her heart's extremest hate, 1.02.231
i hate not you for her proud arrogance. 1.03. 24
live each of you the subjects to his hate, | and 1.03.301
/o, if you love my brother, hate not me! 1.04.226
on | to do this deed will hate you for the deed. 1.04.255
by heaven, my soul is purg'd from grudging hate, 2.01. 9
when ever buckingham doth turn his hate | upon 2.01. 32
with hate in those where i expect most love! 2.01. 35
made peace of enmity, fair love of hate, 2.01. 51
i hate it, and desire all good men's love. 2.01. 62
that they which brought me in my master's hate, 3.02. 58
can lesser hide his love or hate than he, | for 3.04. 52
nay then indeed she cannot choose but hate thee, 4.04.289
alas, i rather hate myself | for hateful deeds 5.03.189
all the commons | hate him perniciously, and, o' H8 2.01. 50
vain pomp and glory of this world, i hate ye! 3.02.365
last, cherish those hearts that hate thee; 3.02.443
this is of purpose laid by some that hate me 5.02. 14
i do hate a proud man, as i do hate the TRO 2.03.158 P
man, as i do hate the engend'ring of toads. 2.03.158 P
love, | so much by weight hate i her diomed. 5.02.168
who deserves greatness | deserves your hate; COR 1.01.177
and call him noble, that was now your hate; 1.01.183
there is the man of my soul's hate, aufidius, 1.05. 10
none but thee, for i do hate thee | worse than a 1.08. 1
we hate alike: 1.08. 2
that with the fusty plebeians hate thine honors, 1.09. 7
and custom 'gainst | my hate to martius. 1.10. 24

know not why, they hate upon no better a ground. 2.02. 11 P
whether they love or hate him manifests the true 2.02. 13 P
but he seeks their hate with greater devotion 2.02. 18 P
enforce his pride, | and his old hate unto you; 2.03.220
after the inveterate hate he bears you. 2.03.226
whose breath i hate | as reek a' th' rotten fens 3.03.120
since i have ever followed thee with hate, 4.05. 98
ay, and it makes men hate one another. 4.05.230 P
as those should do that had deserv'd his hate, 4.06.113
then you should hate rome, as he does. 5.02. 38 P
rome | which signifies what hate they bear their TIT 5.01. 3
i hate the word | as i hate hell, all montagues, ROM 1.01. 70
i hate the word | as i hate hell, all montagues, 1.01. 71
cank'red with peace, to part your cank'red hate; 1.01. 95
here's much to do with hate, but more with love. 1.01.175
o loving hate! 1.01.176
my only love sprung from my only hate! 1.05.138
my life were better ended by their hate, | than 2.02. 77
/lives, | by doing damned hate upon thyself? 3.03.118
swear | it shall be romeo, whom you know i hate, 3.05.122
proud can i never be of what i hate, | but 3.05.147
but thankful even for hate that is meant love. 3.05.148
see what a scourge is laid upon your hate, 5.03.292
hate a lord with my heart. TIM 1.01.229 P
i hate not to be banish'd, | it is a cause 3.05.111
his hate may grow | to the whole race of mankind 4.01. 39
i am misanthropos, and hate mankind. 4.03. 54
yield him who all the human sons do hate, | from 4.03.185
i hate thee worse. 4.03.234
why shouldst thou hate men? 4.03.269
on what i hate i feed not. 4.03.306 P
dost hate a medlar? 4.03.307 P
hate all, curse all, show charity to none, | but 4.03.527
i, timon, who, alive, all living men did hate; 5.04. 72
when thou didst hate him worst, thou lovedst him JC 4.03.106
beg nor fear | your favors nor your hate. MAC 1.03. 61
others that lesser hate him | do call it valiant 5.02. 13
more grief to hide, than hate to utter love. HAM 2.01.116
she owes, | unfriended, new adopted to our hate, LR 1.01.203
make such a stray | to match you where i hate; 1.01.210
grown so vild | that it doth hate what gets it. 3.04.146
that thy strange mutations make us hate thee, 4.01. 11
heart, if ever i | did hate thee or thy father. 5.03.179
thou toldst me thou didst hold him in thy hate. OTH 1.01. 7
though i do hate him as i do hell–pains, | yet, 1.01.154
i retell thee again and again, i hate the moor. 1.03.366 P
i hate the moor, | and it is thought abroad that 1.03.386
crown and hearted throne | to tyrannous hate! 3.03.449
for nought i did in hate, but all in honor. 5.02.295
in time we hate that which we often fear. ANT 1.03. 12
it is not caesar's natural vice to hate | /our 1.04. 2
i cannot hate thee worser than i do, | if thou 2.05. 90
fought to–day | as if a god, in hate of mankind, 4.08. 25
lack of charity | to accuse myself i hate you; CYM 2.03.110
yet 'tis greater skill | in a true hate, to pray 2.05. 34
i love and hate her; 3.05. 70
and in that point | i will conclude to hate her, 3.05. 78
we hate the prince | of tyre, and thou must kill PER 1.01.155
and deck the temples of those gods that hate us; TNK 2.02. 23
uses of this place | that all men hate so much? 2.02. 70
to make thee hate the hunting of the boar, VEN 711
i hate not love, but your device in love, | that 789
there is no hate in loving; LUC 240
yield to my love, if not, enforced hate, | in 668
time's office is to fine the hate of foes, | to 936
that makes him honor'd, or begets him hate; 1005
for thou art so possess'd with murd'rous hate, SON 10. 5
shall hate be fairer lodg'd than gentle love? 10.10
such civil war is in my love and hate, | that i 35.12
for i must ne'er love him whom thou dost hate. 89.14
then hate me when thou wilt, if ever, now, | now 90. 1
but shoot not at me in your wakened hate: 117.12
as subject to time's love, or to time's hate, 124. 3
love is my sin, and thy dear virtue hate, | hate 142. 1
hate of my sin, grounded on sinful loving: 142. 2
breath'd forth the sound that said "i hate" | to 145. 2
"i hate" she alter'd with an end | that follow'd 145. 9
"i hate" from hate away she threw, | and sav'd 145.13
"i hate" from hate away she threw, | and sav'd 145.13
but, love, hate on, for now i know thy mind: 149.13
the more i hear and see just cause of hate? 150.10
in vowing new hate after new love bearing. 152. 4

HATED 29 FR 0.0032 REL FR 26 V 3 P
are hated most of those they did deceive, | so MND 2.02.140
heresy, | of all be hated, but the most of me! 2.02.142
and from thy hated presence part i /so: 3.02. 80
o hated potion, hence! 3.02.264
hate him, for my father hated his father dearly; AYL 1.03. 33 P
silvius, the time was that i hated thee; 3.05. 92
nay, hated too, worse than the great'st WT 1.02.423
o sir, i shall be hated to report it! 3.02.143
if to be fat be to be hated, then pharaoh's 1H4 2.04.473 P
to no further use | but to be known and hated. 2H4 4.04. 73
child, | lest thou be hated both of god and man. 3H6 1.03. 9
more direful hap betide that hated wretch | that R3 1.02. 17
whom i most hated living, thou hast made me, H8 4.02. 73
enemy | (who is of rome worse hated than of you) COR 1.02. 13
that of all things upon the earth he hated 3.01. 14
made him fear'd, | so hated, and so banish'd; 4.07. 48
despis'd, distressed, hated, martyr'd, kill'd! ROM 4.05. 59
henceforth hated be | of timon man and all TIM 3.06.104
and th' hadst hated meddlers sooner, thou 4.03.309 P
how fain would i have hated all mankind, | and 4.03.499
hated by one he loves, brav'd by his brother, JC 4.03. 96
and on the sixt to turn thy hated back | upon LR 1.01.175
if fortune brag of two she lov'd and hated, 5.03.281
the hated, grown to strength, | are newly grown ANT 1.03. 48
let me shake thy hand, | i never hated thee. 2.06. 74
and hated | for being preferr'd so well. CYM 2.03.130
pitied nor hated, to the face of peril | myself 5.01. 28
not, | let me find that my father ever hated — TNK 2.05. 58
past reason hated as a swallowed bait | on SON 129. 7

HATEFUL 46 FR 0.0052 REL FR 45 V 1 P
o hateful hands, to tear such loving words! TGV 1.02.102
which is as hateful to me as the reek of a WIV 3.03. 78 P
and shamed life a hateful. MM 3.01.116
against his honor | in hateful practice. 5.01.107
you'll not be perjur'd, 'tis a hateful thing; LLL 4.03.155
eyes, | and make her full of hateful fantasies. MND 2.01.258
seeking sweet favors for this hateful fool, | i 4.01. 49
undo | this hateful imperfection of her eyes. 4.01. 63
away by any secret course | thy hateful life. JN 3.01.179
merriment — | a passion hateful to my purposes; 3.03. 47
avaunt, thou hateful villain, get thee gone! 4.03. 77
will the hateful commons perform for us, R2 2.02.138
with haughty arms this hateful name in us. 1H4 5.02. 40
where hateful death put on his ugliest mask | to 2H4 1.01. 66
and in thy hateful lungs, yea, in thy maw, perdy H5 2.01. 49
and nothing teems | but hateful docks, rough 5.02. 52
gloucester, hide thee from their hateful looks, 2H6 2.04. 23
for he's disposed as the hateful raven. 3.01. 76
but left that hateful office unto thee. 3.02. 93
reveng'd may she be on that hateful duke, 3H6 1.01.266
have done thy charm, thou hateful with'red hag. R3 1.03.214
urge his hateful luxury | and bestial appetite 3.05. 80
myself | for hateful deeds committed by myself. 5.03.190
the noblest hateful love, that e'er i heard of. TRO 4.01. 34
a hateful truth. 4.04. 31
as hateful as /cocytus' misty mouth. TIT 2.03.236
shows | pass the remainder of our hateful days? 3.01.132
lives | but in oblivion and hateful griefs. 3.01.295
small, | and with this hateful liquor temper it, 5.02.199
my name, dear saint, is hateful to myself, ROM 2.02. 55
tell me, that i may sack | the hateful mansion. 3.03.108
accurs'd, unhappy, wretched, hateful day! 4.05. 43
o day, o day, o day, o hateful day! 4.05. 52
is man so hateful to thee, | that art thyself a TIM 4.03. 52
o hateful error, melancholy's child, | why dost JC 5.03. 67
pronounce a title | more hateful to mine ear. MAC 5.07. 9
in my fancy pluck | upon my hateful life. LR 4.02. 86
shall upon record | bear hateful memory: ANT 4.09. 9
wooer | more hateful than the foul expulsion is CYM 2.01. 60
hateful divorce of love" — thus chides she VEN 932
now she adds honors to his hateful name; 994
to sland'rous tongues and wretched hateful days? LUC 161
hateful it is: 240
"o hateful, vaporous, and foggy night! 771
or hateful cuckoos hatch in sparrows' nests? 849
longing to hear the hateful foe bewray'd. 1698

HATEFULLY 1 FR 0.0001 REL FR 1 V 0 P
to see, | but hatefully at randon dost thou hit. VEN 940

HATER 1 FR 0.0001 REL FR 1 V 0 P
prove | a lover of thy drum, hater of love. AWW 3.03. 11

HATERS 1 FR 0.0001 REL FR 1 V 0 P
and i wore my life | to spend upon his haters. ANT 5.01. 9

HATE'S 1 FR 0.0001 REL FR 1 V 0 P
to be her love's wrong than hate's known injury. SON 40.12

HATES 23 FR 0.0026 REL FR 20 V 3 P
on thurio, whom your gentle daughter hates, TGV 3.01. 14
our radiant queen hates sluts and sluttery. WIV 5.05. 46
i will never love that which my friend hates. ADO 5.02. 71 P
wherefore speaks he this | to her he hates? MND 3.02.228
he hates our sacred nation, and he rails, | even MV 1.03. 48
therefore he hates me. 3.03. 24
hates any man the thing he would not kill? 4.01. 67
(yet i know not why) hates nothing more than he. AYL 1.01.165 P
by your simp'ring, none of you hates them), that ep 16 P
with her that hateth thee and hates us all, 2H6 2.04. 52
are deceiv'd, your brother gloucester hates you. R3 1.04.232
the broken rancor of your high–swoll'n hates, 2.02.117
besides, he hates me for my father warwick, 4.01. 85
put my sick cause into his hands that hates me? H8 3.01.118
no space of earth shall sunder our two hates. TRO 5.10. 27
but when i tell him he hates flatterers | he JC 2.01.207
thou call'st on him that hates thee. LR 3.07. 88
he hates him | that would upon the rack of this 5.03.314
is, and hates the slime | that sticks on filthy OTH 5.02.148
for who hates honor hates the gods above. PER 2.03. 22
for who hates honor hates the gods above. 2.03. 22
be as that cursed man that hates his country, TNK 2.02.199
he scowls and hates himself for his offense, LUC 738

HATETH 5 FR 0.0005 REL FR 5 V 0 P
the more i love, the more he hateth me. MND 1.01.199
with her that hateth thee and hates us all, 2H6 2.04. 52
lord say, the traitors hateth thee, | therefore 4.04. 43
who hateth him and honors not his father, 4.08. 16
who hateth thee that i do call my friend? SON 149. 5

HATFIELD 2 FR 0.0002 REL FR 2 V 0 P
the second, william of hatfield; 2H6 2.02. 12
but william of hatfield died without an heir. 2.02. 33

'HATH 2 FR 0.0002 REL FR 2 V 0 P
him, 'hath commanded | to–morrow morning to the H8 5.01. 50
'hath set a mark which nature could not reach to TNK 1.04. 43

H'ATH 1 FR 0.0001 REL FR 1 V 0 P
h'ath, my lord, wrung from me my slow leave | by HAM 1.02. 58

/HATH 15 FR 0.0017 REL FR 14 V 1 P
/hath /sorrow /struck | /so /many /blows /upon R2 4.01.277
/soon /my /sorrow /hath /destroy'd /my /face. 4.01.291
/the /shadow /of /your /sorrow /hath /destroy'd 4.01.292
/what /hath /then /befall'n? 2H4 1.01.177
/their //over–greedy /love /hath /surfeited. 1.03. 88
/hath /he /that /buildeth /on /the /vulgar 1.03. 90
/authorities | /that /he /hath /given /away! LR 1.03. 18
/sorrow | /the /king /hath /cause /to /plain. 3.01. 39
"/her /boat /hath /a /leak, | /and /she /must 3.06. 26
/when /grief /hath /mates, /and /bearing 3.06.107
/who /hath /he /left /behind /him /general? 4.03. 7 P
/the /friend /hath /lost /his /friend, | /and 5.03. 55
pompeius | /hath given the dare to caesar, and ANT 1.02.184
/hath stuff'd the hollow vessels with their PER 1.04. 67
our master mars | /hath vouch'd his oracle, and TNK 5.04.107

HATH 2054 FR 0.2321 REL FR 1586 V 468 P
methinks he hath no drowning mark upon him, his TMP 1.01. 29 P
tell me, that | hath kept with thy remembrance. 1.02. 44
lady) hath mine enemies | brought to this shore; 1.02.179
have follow'd it, | or it hath drawn me rather. 1.02.395
it eats and sleeps and hath such senses | as we 1.02.413
he hath lost his fellows, | and strays about to 1.02.417
he hath rais'd the wall, and houses too. 2.01. 88 P
what strange fish | hath made his meal on thee? 2.01.114
eye, | who hath cause to wet the grief on't. 2.01.128
when he is earth'd, hath here almost persuaded 2.01.234
say this were death | that now hath seiz'd them, 2.01.261
that hath lately suffer'd by a thunderbolt. 2.02. 36 P
for it hath been said, "as proper a man as ever 2.02. 60 P
of the isle with four legs, who hath got, as i 2.02. 66 P
he shall pay for him that hath him, and that 2.02. 77 P
th' harmony of their tongues hath into bondage 3.01. 41
my man–monster hath drown'd his tongue in sack. 3.02. 12 P
man a coward that hath drunk so much sack as i 3.02. 27 P
that by his cunning hath | cheated me of the 3.02. 43
nor hath not | one spirit to command: 3.02. 93
that hath to instrument this lower world | and 3.03. 54
sea | hath caus'd to belch up you; 3.03. 56
expos'd unto the sea (which hath requit it) 3.03. 71
why hath thy queen | summon'd me hither, to this 4.01. 82
is she the goddess that hath sever'd us, | and 5.01.187
find this grand liquor that hath gilded 'em? 5.01.280
why, he, of all the rest, hath never mov'd me. TGV 1.02. 27
some love of yours hath writ to you in rhyme. 1.02. 76
heavy? belike it hath some burden then? 1.02. 82
excuse | hath he excepted most against my love. 1.03. 83
how long hath she been deform'd? 2.01. 64 P
and she hath taught her suitor, | he being her 2.01.137
why, she hath not writ to me? 2.01.151 P
she, when she hath made you write to yourself? 2.01.152 P
why, she hath given you a letter. 2.01.159 P
and that letter hath she deliver'd, and there an 2.01.161 P
herself hath taught her love himself to write 2.01.168
for truth hath better deeds than words to grace 2.02. 18
it is so, it is so — it hath the worser sole. 2.03. 17 P
that hath more mind to feed on your blood than 2.04. 27 P
hath he not a son? 2.04. 58
yet hath sir proteus (for that's his name) 2.04. 67
belike that now she hath enfranchis'd them 2.04. 90
why, lady, love hath twenty pair of eyes. 2.04. 95
they say that love hath not an eye at all. 2.04. 96
love hath chas'd sleep from my enthralled eyes, 2.04.134
and hath so humbled me as i confess | there is 2.04.137
and that hath dazzled my reason's light; 2.04.210
less shall she that hath love's wings to fly, 2.07. 11
hath made me publisher of this pretense. 3.01. 47
upon advice, hath drawn my love from her, | and, 3.01. 73
that man that hath a tongue, i say is no man, 3.01.104
of men, | that no man hath access by day to her. 3.01.109
that no man hath recourse to her by night. 3.01.112
the grace that with such grace hath blest them, 3.01.146
so much of bad already hath possess'd them. 3.01.207
hath she forsworn me? 3.01.213
and she hath offered to the doom | (which, 3.01.224
yet 'tis not a maid, for she hath had gossips; 3.01.270 P
she hath more qualities than a water–spaniel, 3.01.272 P
"item, she hath many nameless virtues." 3.01.317 P
"item, she hath a sweet mouth." 3.01.327 P
"item, she hath no teeth." 3.01.340 P
well, the best is, she hath no teeth to bite. 3.01.344 P
"item, she hath more hair than wit, and more 3.01.353 P
"item, she hath more hair than wit" — 3.01.358 P
he hath stay'd for a better man than thee. 3.01.375 P
since his exile she hath despis'd me most, 3.02. 3
but it hath been the longest night | that e'er i 4.02.139
sat in the stocks for puddings he hath stol'n, 4.04. 31 P
stood on the pillory for geese he hath kill'd, 4.04. 33 P
belike she thinks that proteus hath forsook her? 4.04.146
she hath been fairer, madam, than she is: 4.04.149
the air hath starv'd the roses in her cheeks, 4.04.154
being nimble–footed, he hath outrun us, | but 5.03. 7
and julia herself hath brought it hither. 5.04. 99
the gift hath made me happy. 5.04.148
i think the boy hath grace in him; he blushes. 5.04.165
that you will wonder what hath fortuned. 5.04.169
his successors (gone before him) hath done't; WIV 1.01. 14 P
he hath wrong'd me, master page. 1.01.102 P
he hath wrong'd me, indeed he hath, at a word he 1.01.105 P
he hath wrong'd me, indeed he hath, at a word he 1.01.106 P
wrong'd me, indeed he hath, at a word he hath. 1.01.106 P
he hath studied her /well, and translated her 1.03. 49 P
he hath a /legion of angels. 1.03. 53 P
he hath but a little /whey–face, with a little 1.04. 22 P
he hath fought with a warrener. 1.04. 26 P
an unweigh'd behavior hath this flemish drunkard 2.01. 23 P
why, he hath not been thrice in my company! 2.01. 26 P
i warrant he hath a thousand of these letters, 2.01. 74 P
till he hath pawn'd his horses to mine host of 2.01. 96 P
he hath wrong'd me in some humors. 2.01.129 P
my merry host hath had the measuring of their 2.01.207 P
i think, hath appointed them contrary places; 2.01.208 P
have heard the frenchman hath good skill in his 2.01.222 P
marry, she hath receiv'd your letter — for the 2.02. 81 P
mistress page hath her hearty commendations to 2.02. 95 P
and hath sent your worship a morning's draught 2.02.146 P
the which hath something embold'ned me to this 2.02.167 P
i have pursu'd her as love hath pursu'd me, 2.02.201 P
which hath been on the wing of all occasions. 2.02.201 P
rate, and that hath taught me to say this: 2.02.205 P
the jealous wittolly knave hath masses of money, 2.02.272 P
my wife hath sent to him, the hour is fix'd, the 2.02.289 P
the devil himself hath not such a name. 2.02.300 P
and sir hugh hath shown himself a wise and 2.03. 54 P
hath he any eyes? 3.02. 30 P
hath he any thinking? 3.02. 31 P
sure they sleep, he hath no use of them. 3.02. 31 P
i think my husband hath some special suspicion 3.03.187 P
your father and my uncle hath made motions. 3.04. 63 P
a kind heart he hath. 3.04.102 P
you come to know what hath pass'd between me and 3.05. 62 P
ford, your sorrow hath eaten up my sufferance. 4.02. 1 P
and hath drawn him and the rest of their company 4.02. 34 P
but he hath an abstract for the remembrance of 4.02. 62 P
her my house, and hath threat'ned to beat her. 4.02. 87 P
basket too, howsoever he hath had intelligence. 4.02. 92 P
that hath the jealious fool to her husband! 4.02.131 P
it hath done meritorious service. 4.02.205 P
i'll to the doctor, he hath my good will, | and 4.04. 84
one that hath taught me more wit than ever i 4.05. 59 P
and how my transformation hath been wash'd and 4.05. 96 P
who mutually hath answer'd my affection | (so 4.06. 10
fat falstaff | hath a great scene; 4.06. 17
her father hath commanded her to slip | away 4.06. 23
she hath consented. 4.06. 25
hath appointed | that he shall likewise shuffle 4.06. 28

likewise hath | made promise to the doctor. 4.06. 33
her mother hath intended | (the better to 4.06. 38
the maid hath given consent to go with him. 4.06. 45
hath the finest mad devil of jealousy in him, 5.01. 18 P
it hath strook ten a' clock. 5.02. 10 P
the windsor bell hath strook twelve; 5.05. 1 P
he hath enjoy'd nothing of ford's but his 5.05.112 P
her master slender hath married her daughter. 5.05.173 P
this is strange. who hath got the right anne? 5.05.211 P
th' offense is holy that she hath committed, 5.05.225
to strike at me, that your arrow hath glanc'd. 5.05.235 P
in | as art and practice hath enriched any MM 1.01. 12
she hath prosperous art | when she will play 1.02.184
hath a purpose | more grave and wrinkled than 1.03. 4
he hath got his friend with child. 1.04. 29
law, | as mice by lions) hath pick'd out an act, 1.04. 64
the provost hath | a warrant for 's execution. 1.04. 73
elbow's wife, that he hath cause to complain of? 2.01.116 P
because he hath some offenses in him that thou 2.01.185 P
hath she had any more than one husband? 2.01.201 P
alas, it hath been great pains to you. 2.01.265 P
alas, | he hath but as offended in a dream! 2.02. 4
judgment hath | repented o'er his doom. 2.02. 11
hath he a sister? 2.02. 19
who is it that hath died for this offense? 2.02. 88
the law hath not been dead, though it hath slept 2.02. 90
law hath not been dead, though it hath slept. 2.02. 90
others, | hath yet a kind of medicine in itself, 2.02.135
of her own youth, | hath blister'd her report. 2.03. 12
as that the sin hath brought you to this shame, 2.03. 31
heaven hath my empty words, | whilst my 2.04. 2
to pardon him that hath from nature stol'n | a 2.04. 43
sweet uncleanness | as she that he hath stain'd? 2.04. 55
i know your virtue hath a license in't, | which 2.04.145
though he hath fall'n by prompture of the blood, 2.04.178
yet hath he in him such a mind of honor | that, 2.04.179
i have overheard what hath pass'd between you 3.01.160 P
only he hath made an assay of her virtue to 3.01.162 P
hath made him that gracious denial which he is 3.01.164 P
the hand that hath made you fair hath made you 3.01.180 P
hand that hath made you fair hath made you good; 3.01.181 P
the assault that angelo hath made to you, 3.01.184 P
you, fortune hath convey'd to my understanding; 3.01.185 P
but that frailty hath examples for his falling, 3.01.186 P
this forenam'd maid hath yet in her the 3.01.239 P
all reason should have quench'd her love) hath 3.01.242 P
what offense hath this man made you, sir? 3.02. 14 P
marry, sir, he hath offended the law; 3.02. 15 P
sir, she hath eaten up all her beef, and she is 3.02. 56 P
of his life, and the business he hath helm'd, 3.02.143 P
so please you, this friar hath been with him, 3.02.212 P
that he hath forc'd me to tell him he is indeed 3.02.253 P
if he chance to fail, he hath sentenc'd himself. 3.02.257 P
hath often still'd my brawling discontent. 4.01. 9
though music oft hath such a charm | to make bad 4.01. 14
me, hath any body inquir'd for me here to–day? 4.01. 16 P
he hath a garden circummur'd with brick, | whose 4.01. 28
the hand, | who hath a story ready for your ear. 4.01. 55
he hath been a bawd. 4.02. 27 P
of justice | lord angelo hath to the public ear 4.02. 99
my lord hath sent you this note, and by me this 4.02.102 P
hence hath offense his quick celerity, | when it 4.02.110
strangely, for he hath not us'd it before. 4.02.117 P
hath he borne himself penitently in prison? 4.02.140 P
he hath evermore had the liberty of the prison; 4.02.147 P
it hath not mov'd him at all. 4.02.152 P
to the law than angelo who hath sentenc'd him. 4.02.158 P
angelo hath seen them both, and will discover 4.02.172 P
ere twice the sun hath made his journal greeting 4.03. 88
hath yet the deputy sent my brother's pardon? 4.03.114
he hath releas'd him, isabel, from the world, 4.03.115
already he hath carried | notice to escalus and 4.03.129
every letter he hath writ hath disvouch'd other. 4.04. 1 P
every letter he hath writ hath disvouch'd other. 4.04. 1 P
she hath been a suitor to me for her brother, 5.01. 34
her madness hath the oddest frame of sense, 5.01. 61
some one hath set you on; 5.01.112
hath this woman | most wrongfully accus'd your 5.01.139
hath set the women on to this complaint. 5.01.251
and one that hath spoke most villainous speeches 5.01.263 P
like pow'r divine, | hath look'd upon my passes. 5.01.370
whose salt imagination yet hath wrong'd | your 5.01.401
and us, | it hath in solemn synods been decreed, ERR 1.01. 13
the clock hath strucken twelve upon the bell: 1.02. 45
perhaps some merchant hath invited him, | and 2.01. 4
heaven's eye | but hath his bound in earth, in 2.01. 17
it seems he hath great care to please his wife. 2.01. 56
hath homely age th' alluring beauty took | from 2.01. 89
then he hath wasted it. 2.01. 90
and no man that hath a name | by falsehood and 2.01.112
for they say, every why hath a wherefore. 2.02. 44 P
and what he hath scanted /men in hair he hath 2.02. 80 P
scanted /men in hair he hath given them in wit. 2.02. 80 P
but there's many a man hath more hair than wit. 2.02. 82 P
a man of those but he hath the wit to lose his 2.02. 84 P
some other mistress hath thy sweet aspects: 2.02.111
desert) | hath oftentimes upbraided me withal: 3.01.113
shame hath a bastard fame, well managed; 3.02. 19
he gains by death that hath such means to die: 3.02. 51
hath almost made me traitor to myself; 3.02.162
a devil in an everlasting garment hath him; 4.02. 33
hath he not reason to turn back an hour in a day 4.02. 62
a ring he hath of mine worth forty ducats, | and 4.03. 83
i think, when he hath lam'd me, i shall beg with 4.04. 38 P
how long hath this possession held the man? 5.01. 44
this week he hath been heavy, sour, sad, | and 5.01. 45
hath he not lost much wealth by wrack of sea? 5.01. 49
hath not else his eye | stray'd his affection in 5.01. 50
hath scar'd thy husband from the use of wits. 5.01. 86
it cannot be that she hath done thee wrong. 5.01.135
that hath abused and dishonored me, | even in 5.01.199
that she this day hath shameless thrown on me. 5.01.202
grief hath chang'd me since you saw me last, 5.01.298
up, | yet hath my night of life some memory, 5.01.315
o, my old master! who hath bound him here? 5.01.339
it shall not need, thy father hath his life. 5.01.391
here that don /pedro hath bestow'd much honor on ADO 1.01. 10 P

he hath borne himself beyond the promise of his 1.01. 13 P
he hath indeed better bett'red expectation than 1.01. 15 P
he hath an uncle here in messina will be very 1.01. 18 P
how many hath he kill'd and eaten in these wars? 1.01. 43 P
but how many hath he kill'd? 1.01. 44 P
he hath done good service, lady, in these wars. 1.01. 48 P
had musty victual, and he hath holp to eat it. 1.01. 50 P
trencherman, he hath an excellent stomach. 1.01. 51 P
all the wealth that he hath left to be known a 1.01. 70 P
he hath every month a new sworn brother. 1.01. 72 P
her mother hath many times told me so. 1.01.105 P
should die while she hath such meet food to feed 1.01.121 P
my dear friend leonato hath invited you all. 1.01.148 P
hath not the world one man but he will wear his 1.01.197 P
what secret hath held you here, that you 1.01.204 P
for indeed he hath made great preparation. 1.01.277 P
hath leonato any son, my lord? 1.01.294
hath he provided this music? 1.02. 2 P
hath the fellow any wit that told you this? 1.02. 17 P
and he hath ta'en you newly into his grace, 1.03. 22 P
that young start–up hath all the glory of my 1.03. 67 P
you may light on a husband that hath no beard. 2.01. 32 P
he that hath a beard is more than a youth, and 2.01. 36 P
and he that hath no beard is less than a man; 2.01. 37 P
amorous on hero and hath withdrawn her father to 2.01.156 P
it one way, for the prince hath got your hero. 2.01.191 P
the lady beatrice hath a quarrel to you. 2.01.236 P
his grace hath made the match, and all grace say 2.01.303 P
hath your grace ne'er a brother like you? 2.01.323 P
she hath often dreamt of unhappiness and wak'd 2.01.345 P
to tell him that he hath wrong'd his honor in 2.02. 23 P
your brother's honor, who hath made this match, 2.02. 37 P
after he hath laugh'd at such shallow follies in 2.03. 9 P
see you where benedick hath hid himself? 2.03. 40
whom she hath in all outward behaviors seem'd 2.03. 97 P
he hath ta'en th' infection. hold it up. 2.03.121 P
hath she made her affection known to benedick? 2.03.123 P
and the ecstasy hath so much overborne her that 2.03.151 P
ten proofs to one that blood hath the victory. 2.03.165 P
(as you know all) hath a contemptible spirit. 2.03.180 P
he hath indeed a good outward happiness. 2.03.183 P
indeed he hath an excellent good name. 3.01. 98
he hath twice or thrice cut cupid's bow–string, 3.02. 10 P
he hath a heart as sound as a bell, and his 3.02. 12 P
it be a fancy that he hath to strange disguises 3.02. 32 P
a fancy to this foolery, as it appears he hath, 3.02. 38 P
hath any man seen him at the barber's? 3.02. 43 P
but the barber's man hath been seen with him, 3.02. 45 P
old ornament of his cheek hath already stuff'd 3.02. 46 P
in dearness of heart hath holp to effect your 3.02. 98 P
god hath blest you with a good name. 3.03. 13 P
much more a man who hath any honesty in him. 3.03. 64 P
who hath indeed, most like a liberal villain, 4.01. 92
hath no man's dagger here a point for me? 4.01.109
hath drops too few to wash her clean again, 4.01.141
and in her eye there hath appear'd a fire | to 4.01.162
thou seest that all the grace that she hath left 4.01.171
time hath not yet so dried this blood of mine, 4.01.193
in the height a villain, that hath slander'd, 4.01.302 P
your soul the count claudio hath wrong'd hero? 4.01.329 P
go to, and a fellow that hath had losses, and 4.02. 84 P
hath had losses, and one that hath two gowns, 4.02. 85 P
thy slander hath gone through and through her 5.01. 68
he hath bid me to a calve's–head and a capon, 5.01.154 P
"nay," said i, "he hath the tongues." 5.01.166 P
and hath challeng'd thee? 5.01.197 P
by this time our sexton hath reform'd signior 5.01.254 P
my brother hath a daughter, | almost the copy of 5.01.288
but always hath been just and virtuous | in any 5.01.302
the which he hath us'd so long and never paid 5.01.310 P
call beatrice to you, who i think hath legs. 5.02. 24 P
with knowing what hath pass'd between you and 5.02. 48 P
prov'd my lady hero hath been falsely accus'd, 5.02. 97 P
mile of my court" — hath this been proclaim'd? LLL 1.01.120 P
and when it hath the thing it hunteth most, 1.01.145
that hath a mint of phrases in his brain; 1.01.165
which each to other hath so strongly sworn. 1.01.307
doth noise abroad, navarre hath made a vow, 2.01. 22
whose edge hath power to cut, whose will still 2.01. 50
for he hath wit to make an ill shape good, | and 2.01. 59
that every one her own hath garnished | with 2.01. 78
i hear your grace hath sworn out house–keeping: 2.01.104
of that which hath so faithfully been paid. 2.01.156
she hath but one for herself, to desire that 2.01.200
that in words which his eye hath disclos'd. 2.01.251
obscure precedence that hath tofore been sain. 3.01. 82
the boy hath sold him a bargain, a goose, that's 3.01.101
he hath never fed of the dainties that are bred 4.02. 24
he hath not eat paper, as it were; 4.02. 25 P
he hath not drunk ink; 4.02. 25 P
and here he hath framed a letter to a sequent of 4.02.138 P
or by the way of progression, hath miscarried. 4.02.140 P
love, and it hath taught me to rhyme and to be 4.03. 12 P
well, she hath one a' my sonnets already: 4.03. 15 P
bore it, the fool sent it, and the lady hath it: 4.03. 16 P
her amber hairs for foul hath amber coted. 4.03. 85
what zeal, what fury, hath inspir'd thee now? 4.03.225
i marvel thy master hath not eaten thee for a 5.01. 39 P
a man of travel, that hath seen the world; 5.01.108 P
for he hath been five thousand year a boy. 5.02. 11
o, he hath drawn my picture in his letter! 5.02. 38
hath wisdom's warrant and the help of school, 5.02. 71
that well by heart hath conn'd his embassage. 5.02. 98
and quick berowne hath plighted faith to me. 5.02.283
full merrily | hath this brave /manage, this 5.02.482
alas, poor machabeus, how hath he been baited! 5.02.631 P
pompey hath made the challenge. 5.02.706 P
hath much deformed us, fashioning our humors 5.02.757
and what in us hath seem'd ridiculous — | as 5.02.759
jack hath not gill. 5.02.875
lord, | this man hath my consent to marry her. MND 1.01. 25
this man hath bewitch'd the bosom of my child. 1.01. 27
scornful lysander, true, he hath my love; 1.01. 95
and ere a man hath power to say "behold!" 1.01.147
of great revenue, and she hath no child. 1.01.158
that he hath turn'd a heaven unto a hell! 1.01.207
nor hath love's mind of any judgment taste; 1.01.236
because that she as her attendant hath | a 2.01. 21

hath every pelting river made so proud | that 2.01. 91
the ox hath therefore stretch'd his yoke in vain 2.01. 93
hath rotted ere his youth attain'd a beard. 2.01. 95
full often hath she gossip'd by my side, | and 2.01.125
the wildest hath not such a heart as you. 2.01.229
the man | by the athenian garments he hath on. 2.01.264
for she hath blessed and attractive eyes. 2.02. 91
so hath thy breath, my dearest thisby dear. 3.01. 85
giant–like ox–beef hath devour'd many a 3.01.193 P
you your kindred hath made my eyes water ere now 3.01.194 P
now i perceive that she hath made compare 3.02.290
she hath urg'd her height, | and with her 3.02.291
height, forsooth, she hath prevail'd with him. 3.02.293
but he hath chid me hence and threat'ned me | to 3.02.312
whose liquor hath this virtuous property, | to 3.02.367
good hay, sweet hay, hath no fellow. 4.01. 33 P
flower | hath such force and blessed power. 4.01. 74
the eye of man hath not heard, the ear of man 4.01.211 P
hath not heard, the ear of man hath not seen, 4.01.212 P
"bottom's dream," because it hath no bottom; 4.01.216 P
he hath simply the best wit of any handicraft 4.02. 9 P
thus hath he lost sixpence a day during his life 4.02. 19 P
i will tell you is, that the duke hath din'd. 4.02. 35 P
such tricks hath strong imagination, | that, if 5.01. 18
he hath rid his prologue like a rough colt; 5.01.119 P
indeed he hath play'd on this prologue like a 5.01.122 P
since lion vild hath here deflow'r'd my dear; 5.01.292
she hath spied him already with those sweet eyes 5.01.321 P
the iron tongue of midnight hath told twelve. 5.01.363
this palpable–gross play hath well beguil'd 5.01.367
nature hath fram'd strange fellows in her time: MV 1.01. 51
something too prodigal | hath left me gag'd. 1.01.130
the lott'ry that he hath devis'd in these three 1.02. 29 P
he hath a horse better than the neapolitan's, a 1.02. 58 P
he hath neither latin, french, nor italian, and 1.02. 69 P
that he hath a neighborly charity in him, for he 1.02. 79 P
he hath an argosy bound to tripolis, another to 1.03. 18 P
upon the rialto, he hath a third at mexico, a 1.03. 20 P
and other ventures he hath, squand'red abroad. 1.03. 21 P
o, what a goodly outside falsehood hath! 1.03.102
should i not say, | "hath a dog money? 1.03.121
this aspect of mine | hath fear'd the valiant; 2.01. 9
he hath a great infection, sir, as one would say 2.02.125 P
and hath preferr'd thee, if it be preferment 2.02.146
have the grace of god, sir, and he hath enough. 2.02.151 P
she hath directed | how i shall take her from 2.04. 29
with, | what page's suit she hath in readiness. 2.04. 32
and true she is, as she hath prov'd herself; 2.06. 55
chooseth me must give and hazard all he hath." 2.07. 9
chooseth me must give and hazard all he hath." 2.07. 16
many a man his life hath sold | but my outside 2.07. 67
she hath the stones upon her, and the ducats." 2.08. 22
and for the jew's bond which he hath of me, 2.08. 41
the prince of arragon hath ta'en his oath, | and 2.09. 2
chooseth me must give and hazard all he hath." 2.09. 21
thus hath the candle sing'd the moth. 2.09. 79
that antonio hath a ship of rich lading wrack'd 3.01. 3 P
why, the end is, he hath lost a ship. 3.01. 17 P
he hath disgrac'd me, and hind'red me half a 3.01. 54 P
hath not a jew eyes? 3.01. 59 P
hath not a jew hands, organs, dimensions, senses 3.01. 59 P
hath an argosy cast away, coming from tripolis. 3.01.100 P
and yet a maiden hath no tongue but thought — 3.02. 8
what demigod | hath come so near creation? 3.02.116
and hath woven | a golden mesh t' entrap the 3.02.121
that thinks he hath done well in people's eyes, 3.02.142
would you had won the fleece that he hath lost. 3.02.242
hath all his ventures fail'd? 3.02.267
by my husband, he hath made me a christian! 3.05. 19 P
the fool hath planted in his memory | an army of 3.05. 66
for the poor rude world | hath not her fellow. 3.05. 83
your grace hath ta'en great pains to qualify 4.01. 7
why he hath made the ewe bleak for the lamb; 4.01. 74
the law, your exposition | hath been most sound. 4.01.238
of the law | hath full relation to the penalty, 4.01.248
he hath refus'd it in the open court; 4.01.338
jew, | the law hath yet another hold on you. 4.01.347
upon more advice | hath sent you here this ring, 4.02. 7
the man that hath no music in himself, | nor is 5.01. 83
you see my finger | hath not the ring upon it, 5.01.188
since he hath got the jewel that i loved, | and 5.01.224
my clerk hath some good comforts too for you. 5.01.289
hath a disposition to come in disguis'd against AYL 1.01.125 P
leave thee till he hath ta'en thy life by some 1.01.152 P
you know my father hath no child but i, nor none 1.02. 17 P
for what he hath taken away from thy father 1.02. 19 P
when nature hath made a fair creature, may she 1.02. 43 P
though nature hath given us wit to flout at 1.02. 45 P
hath not fortune sent in this fool to cut off 1.02. 46 P
/and hath sent this natural for our whetstone; 1.02. 53 P
but his will hath in it a more modest working. 1.02.202 P
hath ta'en displeasure 'gainst his gentle niece, 1.02.278
know'st thou not the duke | hath banish'd me, 1.03. 95
that he hath not. 1.03. 95
no, hath not? 1.03. 96
something that hath a reference to my state: 1.03.127
hath not old custom made this life more sweet 2.01. 2
than doth your brother that hath banish'd you. 2.01. 28
hath heard your praises, and this night he means 2.03. 22
he hath been all this day to look you. 2.05. 32 P
me not fool till heaven hath sent me fortune." 2.07. 19
one that hath been a courtier, | and says, if 2.07. 36
a voyage, he hath strange places cramm'd | with 2.07. 40
let me see wherein | my tongue hath wrong'd him; 2.07. 84
it do him right, | then he hath wrong'd himself. 2.07. 85
of bare distress hath ta'en from me the show 2.07. 95
of drops that sacred pity hath engend'red; 2.07.123
who after me hath many a weary step | limp'd in 2.07.130
that he that hath learn'd no wit by nature nor 3.02. 29 P
sweetest nut hath sourest rind, | such a nut is 3.02.109
trow you who hath done this? 3.02.179 P
nay, he hath but a little beard. 3.02.208 P
latin, and a rich man that hath not the gout; 3.02.320 P
giddy offenses as he hath generally tax'd their 3.02.349 P
who hath promis'd to meet me in this place of 3.03. 44 P
the noblest deer hath them as huge as the rascal 3.03. 57 P
as the ox hath his bow, sir, the horse his curb, 3.03. 79 P
the falcon her bells, so man hath his desires; 3.03. 80 P

he hath bought a pair of cast lips of diana. 3.04. 15 P
now show the wound mine eye hath made in thee. 3.05. 20
and he hath bought the cottage and the bounds 3.05.107
said of him that cupid hath clapp'd him o' th' 4.01. 48 P
but he hath a rosalind of a better leer than you 4.01. 66 P
world what the bird hath done to her own nest. 4.01.204 P
my affection hath an unknown bottom, like the 4.01.208 P
he hath ta'en his bow and arrows and is gone 4.03. 4 P
turn'd, | that a maiden's heart hath burn'd?" 4.03. 41
her (for i see love hath made thee a tame snake) 4.03. 70 P
he hath no interest in me in the world. 5.01. 8 P
the boy | can do all this that he hath promised? 5.04. 2
and hath been tutor'd in the rudiments | of many 5.04. 31
he hath been a courtier, he swears. 5.04. 42 P
the duke hath put on a religious life, | and 5.04.181
he hath. 5.04.183
persuade him that he hath been lunatic, | and SHR in.1. 63
such as he hath observ'd in noble ladies | unto in.1. 111
who for this seven years hath esteemed him | no in.1. 122
and till the tears that she hath shed for thee in.2. 64
too much sadness hath congeal'd your blood, in.2. 132
whose sudden sight hath thrall'd my wounded eye. 1.01.220
he hath the jewel of my life in hold, | his 1.02.119
therefore this order hath baptista ta'en, | that 1.02.126
hath promis'd me to help /me to another, | a 1.02.172
no, sir, but hear i do that he hath two: 1.02.251
scholar, that hath been long studying at rheims, 2.01. 80 P
why no, for she hath broke the lute to me. 2.01.148
your father hath consented | that you shall be 2.01.269
no doubt but he hath got a quiet catch. 2.01.331
'tis known my father hath no less | than three 2.01.377
than hath been taught by any of my trade; 3.01. 69
yet never means to wed where he hath woo'd. 3.02. 17
hath been often burst and now repair'd with 3.02. 59 P
which hath two letters for her name fairly set 3.02. 61 P
hath all so long detain'd you from your wife, 3.02.103
he hath some meaning in his mad attire. 3.02.124
for it hath tam'd my old master and my new 4.01. 24 P
why, she hath a face of her own. 4.01.100 P
which hath as long lov'd me | as i have lov'd 4.02. 38
him, | hath publish'd and proclaim'd it openly. 4.02. 85
and, if you will, tell what hath happened: 4.04. 64
my master hath appointed me to go to saint 4.04.102 P
gentlewoman, | thy son by this hath married. 4.05. 63
for our first merriment hath made thee jealous. 4.05. 76
o, he hath murd'red his master! 5.01. 87 P
ay, mistress bride, hath that awakened you? 5.02. 42
she hath prevented me. 5.02. 49
confess, confess, hath he not hit you here? 5.02. 59
hath cost me /a hundred crowns since supper–time 5.02.128
my mind hath been as big as one of yours, | my 5.02.170
he hath abandon'd his physicians, madam, under AWW 1.01. 13 P
whose practices he hath persecuted time with 1.01. 14 P
the wars hath so kept you under that you must 1.01.195 P
and do suppose | what hath been cannot be. 1.01.226
he hath arm'd our answer, | and florence is 1.02. 11
than in haste, | hath well compos'd thee. 1.02. 21
my fear hath catch'd your fondness! 1.03.170
my love hath in't a bond | whereof the world 1.03.188
hath amaz'd me more | than i dare blame my 2.01. 84
this haste hath wings indeed. 2.01. 93
so holy writ in babes hath judgment shown, 2.01.138
moist hesperus hath quench'd her sleepy lamp, 2.01.164
hath told the thievish minutes how they pass, 2.01.166
rate | worth name of life in thee hath estimate: 2.01.180
of wonder that hath shot out in our latter times 2.03. 8 P
heaven hath through me restor'd the king to 2.03. 64
whose great decision hath much blood let forth 3.01. 3
it hath happen'd all as i would have had it, 3.02. 1 P
she hath recover'd the king, and undone me. 3.02. 20 P
ambitious love hath so in me offended | that 3.04. 5
her intents, | which thus she hath prevented. 3.04. 22
many a maid hath been seduc'd by them, and the 3.05. 20 P
too far in his virtue, which he hath not, he 3.06. 14 P
that downward hath succeeded in his house | from 3.07. 23
now he hath a smack of all neighboring languages 4.01. 15 P
but my heart hath the fear of mars before it, 4.01. 29 P
soul, | in your fine frame hath love no quality? 4.02. 4
especially he hath incurr'd the everlasting 4.03. 8 P
he hath perverted a young gentlewoman here in 4.03. 14 P
he hath given her his monumental ring, and 4.03. 17 P
hath the count all this intelligence? 4.03. 60 P
that his valor hath here acquir'd for him shall 4.03. 69 P
sir, of whom he hath taken a solemn leave. 4.03. 77 P
the duke hath offer'd him letters of 4.03. 78 P
he hath confess'd himself to morgan, whom he 4.03.108 P
and what think you he hath confess'd? 4.03.111 P
he hath out–villain'd villainy so far, that the 4.03.273 P
hath brought me up to be your daughter's dower, 4.04. 19
as it hath fated her to be my motive | and 4.04. 20
his highness hath promis'd me to do it, and, to 4.05. 74 P
up the displeasure he hath conceiv'd against 4.05. 75 P
that in such intelligence hath seldom fail'd. 4.05. 83 P
i am a man whom fortune hath cruelly scratch'd. 5.02. 26 P
all that he is hath reference to your highness. 5.03. 29
hath not in nature's mystery more science | than 5.03.103
who hath for four or five removes come short 5.03.131
th' sequent issue, | hath it been owed and worn. 5.03.198
she hath that ring of yours. 5.03.209
my master hath been an honorable gentleman. 5.03.238 P
tricks he hath had in him, which gentlemen have. 5.03.239 P
lord, | who hath abus'd me, as he knows himself, 5.03.298
he knows himself my bed he hath defil'd, | and 5.03.300
o, she that hath a heart of that fine frame | to TN 1.01. 32
hath kill'd the flock of all affections else 1.01. 35
she hath abjur'd the /company | and /sight of 1.02. 40
book, and hath all the good gifts of nature. 1.03. 27 P
he hath indeed, almost natural; 1.03. 29 P
and but that he hath the gift of a coward to 1.03. 31 P
coward to allay the gust he hath in quarrelling, 1.03. 31 P
he hath known you but three days, and already 1.04. 3 P
the rudeness that hath appear'd in me have i 1.05.214 P
present mirth hath present laughter; 2.03. 48
eye | hath stay'd upon some favor that it loves. 2.04. 24
hath it not, boy? 2.04. 25
the parts that fortune hath bestow'd upon her, 2.04. 83
hath for your love as great a pang of heart | as 2.04. 90
my matter hath no voice, lady, but to your own 3.01. 88 P
his very genius hath taken the infection of the 3.04.129 P
refuse it not, it hath no tongue to vex you; 3.04.209
no man hath any quarrel to me. 3.04.226 P
for your opposite hath in him what youth, 3.04.231 P
souls and bodies hath he divorc'd three, and his 3.04.237 P
he hath better bethought him of his quarrel, and 3.04.297 P
fruitless pranks | this ruffian hath botch'd up, 4.01. 56
it hath bay windows transparent as barricadoes, 4.02. 36 P
three months this youth hath tended upon me, 5.01. 99
hath newly pass'd between this youth and me. 5.01.155
since when, my watch hath told me, toward my 5.01.162
be | when time hath sow'd a grizzle on thy case? 5.01.165
who hath made this havoc with them? 5.01.202 P
by that | i do perceive it hath offended you. 5.01.213
hath been between this lady and this lord. 5.01.258
me first on shore | hath my maid's garments. 5.01.275
this practice hath most shrewdly pass'd upon 5.01.352
in recompense whereof he hath married her. 5.01.364
he hath been most notoriously abus'd. 5.01.379
he hath not told us of the captain yet. 5.01.381
hath been royally attorney'd with interchange of WT 1.01. 27 P
nine changes of the wat'ry star hath been | the 1.02. 1
the king hath on him such a countenance | as he 1.02.368
make known | how he hath drunk, he cracks his 2.01. 44
which often hath no less prevail'd than so | on 2.01. 54
(which never tender lady hath borne greater) 2.02. 22
madam — he hath not slept to–night, commanded 2.03. 31
is good) hath brought you forth a daughter — 2.03. 66
tongue, who late hath beat her husband, | and 2.03. 92
sir, their speed | hath been beyond accompt. 2.03.198
for, as she hath | been publicly accus'd, so 2.03.203
as it hath been to us rare, pleasant, speedy, 3.01. 13
my past life | hath been as continent, as chaste 3.02. 34
for as | thy brat hath been cast out, like to 3.02. 87
our ship hath touch'd upon | the deserts of 3.03. 1
hath made thy person for the thrower–out | of my 3.03. 29
i do believe | hermione hath suffer'd death, and 3.03. 42
from the gentleman and how much he hath eaten. 3.03.130 P
my master, hath sent for me, to whose feeling 4.02. 7 P
i have of thee, thine own goodness hath made. 4.02. 12 P
exercises than formerly he hath appear'd. 4.02. 33 P
a man, who hath a daughter of most rare note. 4.02. 41 P
but my father hath made her mistress of the 4.03. 39 P
she hath made me four and twenty nosegays for 4.03. 41 P
horseman's coat, it hath seen very hot service. 4.03. 68 P
he hath been since an ape–bearer, then a 4.03. 95 P
your greatness | hath not been us'd to fear. 4.04. 18
he hath songs for man or woman, of all sizes; 4.04.191 P
he hath ribbons of all the colors i' th' rainbow 4.04.204 P
he hath promis'd you more than that, or there be 4.04.237 P
he hath paid you all he promis'd you. 4.04.239 P
own report, sir, hath danc'd before the king; 4.04.338 P
whom, it should seem, | hath sometime lov'd! 4.04.362
hath not my gait in it the measure of the court? 4.04.732 P
so much | that heirless it hath made my kingdom, 5.01. 10
hath something seiz'd | his wish'd ability, he 5.01.142
and hath he too | expos'd this paragon to th' 5.01.152
pow'r no jot | hath she to change our loves. 5.01.218
my liege, | your eye hath too much youth in't. 5.01.225
so near to hermione hath done hermione that they 5.02.100 P
for she hath privately twice or thrice a day, 5.02.105 P
yet you look'd upon | or hand of man hath done; 5.03. 17
why, what a madcap hath heaven lent us here! JN 1.01. 84
he hath a trick of cordelion's face, | the 1.01. 85
mine eye hath well examined his parts, | and 1.01. 89
because he hath a half–face like my father! 1.01. 92
your face hath got five hundred pound a year, 1.01.152
hath she no husband | that will take pains to 1.01.218
your just demands, | hath put himself in arms. 2.01. 57
that judge hath made me guardian to this boy, 2.01.115
but god hath made her sin and her the plague 2.01.185
who is it that hath warn'd us to the walls? 2.01.201
save in aspect, hath all offense seal'd up; 2.01.250
who by the hand of france this day hath made 2.01.302
blood hath bought blood, and blows have answer'd 2.01.329
that hath been forward first | to speak unto 2.01.482
whole, | hath willingly departed with a part, 2.01.563
hath drawn him from his own determin'd aid, 2.01.584
but for because he hath not woo'd me yet: 2.01.588
this news hath made thee a most ugly man. 3.01. 37
and with her golden hand hath pluck'd on france 3.01. 57
what hath this day deserv'd? 3.01. 84
what hath it done, | that it in golden letters 3.01. 84
and our oppression hath made up this league. 3.01.106
there is no tongue hath power to curse him right 3.01.183
i am with both, each army hath a hand, | and in 3.01.328
wrath, | a rage whose heat hath this condition, 3.01.341
what he hath won, that hath he fortified. 3.04. 10
what he hath won, that hath he fortified. 3.04. 10
who hath read or heard | of any kindred action 3.04. 13
where but by chance a silver drop hath fall'n, 3.04. 63
and bitter shame hath spoil'd the sweet word's 3.04.110
strange to think how much king john hath lost 3.04.121
as heartily as he is glad he hath him. 3.04.124
john hath seiz'd arthur, and it cannot be | that 3.04.131
he hath a stern look, but a gentle heart. 4.01. 87
the breath of heaven hath blown his spirit out, 4.01.109
o, where hath our intelligence been drunk? 4.02.116
where hath it slept? 4.02.117
thy hand hath murd'red him. 4.02.205
ship–boy's semblance hath disguis'd me quite. 4.03. 4
the king hath dispossess'd himself of us. 4.03. 23
sir, sir, impatience hath his privilege. 4.03. 32
murther, as hating what himself hath done, 4.03. 37
arthur doth live, the king hath sent for you. 4.03. 75
all kent hath yielded; 5.01. 30
london hath receiv'd, | like a kind host, the 5.01. 31
the legate of the pope hath been with me, | and 5.01. 62
and he hath promis'd to dismiss the powers | led 5.01. 64
my heart hath melted at a lady's tears, | being 5.02. 47
king john hath reconcil'd | himself to rome, his 5.02. 69
and come ye now to tell me john hath made | his 5.02. 91
because that john hath made his peace with rome? 5.02. 96
what penny hath rome borne? 5.02. 97
whom he hath us'd rather for sport than need) 5.02.175
this fever, that hath troubled me so long, 5.03. 3
say king john, sore sick, hath left the field. 5.04. 6
thus hath he sworn, | and i with him, and many 5.04. 16
to be so sad to–night | as this hath made me. 5.05. 16
at whose request the king hath pardon'd them, 5.06. 35
which he hath left so shapeless and so rude. 5.07. 27
ay, marry, now my soul hath elbow–room; 5.07. 28
my heart hath one poor string to stay it by, 5.07. 55
as it on earth hath been thy servant still. 5.07. 73
for many carriages he hath dispatch'd | to the 5.07. 90
since it hath been beforehand with our griefs. 5.07.111
that mowbray hath receiv'd eight thousand nobles R2 1.01. 88
the which he hath detain'd for lewd employments, 1.01. 90
hath love in thy old blood no living fire? 1.02. 10
hath caus'd his death, the which if wrongfully, 1.02. 39
truth hath a quiet breast. 1.03. 96
stay, the king hath thrown his warder down. 1.03.118
with that dear blood which it hath fostered; 1.03.126
hath from the number of his banish'd years 1.03.210
ere the six years that he hath to spend | can 1.03.219
for gnarling sorrow hath less power to bite 1.03.292
and hath sent post–haste | to entreat your 1.04. 55
hath made a shameful conquest of itself. 2.01. 66
within me grief hath kept a tedious fast; 2.01. 75
words, life, and all, old lancaster hath spent. 2.01.150
call in the letters–patents that he hath | by 2.01.202
the commons hath he pill'd with grievous taxes, 2.01.246
the nobles hath he fin'd | for ancient quarrels, 2.01.247
wars hath not wasted it, for warr'd he hath not, 2.01.252
wars hath not wasted it, for warr'd he hath not, 2.01.252
more hath he spent in peace than they in wars. 2.01.255
the earl of wiltshire hath the realm in farm. 2.01.256
he hath not money for these irish wars, | his 2.01.259
each substance of a grief hath twenty shadows, 2.02. 14
so, | for nothing hath begot my something grief, 2.02. 36
or something hath the nothing that i grieve — 2.02. 37
who strongly hath set footing in this land: 2.02. 48
the earl of worcester | hath broken his staff, 2.02. 59
now hath my soul brought forth her prodigy, 2.02. 64
is my kinsman, whom the king hath wrong'd, 2.02.114
and yet your fair discourse hath been as sugar, 2.03. 6
hath very much beguil'd | the tediousness and 2.03. 11
as mine hath done | by sight of what i have, 2.03. 17
no, my good lord, he hath forsook the court, 2.03. 26
the noble duke hath been too much abused. 2.03.137
the noble duke hath sworn his coming is | but 2.03.148
hath power to keep you king in spite of all. 3.02. 28
who all this while hath revell'd in the night, 3.02. 48
for every man that bullingbrook hath press'd 3.02. 58
god for his richard hath in heavenly pay | a 3.02. 60
hath clouded all thy happy days on earth. 3.02. 68
side, | for time hath set a blot upon my pride. 3.02. 81
york | hath power enough to serve our turn. 3.02. 90
my father hath a power, inquire of him, | and 3.02.186
my tongue hath but a heavier tale to say. 3.02.197
to ear the land that hath some hope to grow, 3.02.212
richard not far from hence hath hid his head. 3.03. 6
the time hath been, | would you have been so 3.03. 11
that hath dismiss'd us from our stewardship, 3.03. 78
his coming hither hath no further scope | than 3.03.112
he that hath suffered this disordered spring 3.04. 48
hath now himself met with the fall of leaf. 3.04. 49
bullingbrook | hath seiz'd the wasteful king. 3.04. 55
waste of idle hours hath quite thrown down. 3.04. 66
hath suggested thee | to make a second fall of 3.04. 75
scorns to unsay what once it hath delivered. 4.01. 9
in all this presence that hath mov'd me so. 4.01. 32
many a time hath banish'd norfolk fought | for 4.01. 92
hath bullingbrook depos'd | thine intellect? 5.01. 27
hath he been in thy heart? 5.01. 28
but heaven hath a hand in these events, | to 5.02. 37
hath held his current and defil'd himself! 5.03. 63
your mother well hath pray'd, and prove you true 5.03.145
for now hath time made me his numb'ring clock: 5.05. 50
that jade hath eat bread from my royal hand, 5.05. 85
this hand hath made him proud with clapping him. 5.05. 86
hath with the king's blood stain'd the king's 5.05.110
hath yielded up his body to the grave; 5.06. 21
and he hath brought us smooth and welcome news. 1H4 1.01. 66
which he in this adventure hath surpris'd | to 1.01. 93
whereof the hangman hath no lean wardrobe. 1.02. 73 P
than that which hath no foil to set it off. 1.02.215
my blood hath been too cold and temperate, 1.03. 1
which hath been smooth as oil, soft as young 1.03. 7
hath willfully betray'd | the lives of those 1.03. 81
hear, that earl of march | hath lately married. 1.03. 85
brother, the king hath made your nephew mad. 1.03.138
till he hath found a time to pay us home. 1.03.288
in the wild of kent hath brought three hundred 2.01. 55 P
one that hath abundance of charge too — god 2.01. 58 P
she will, she will, justice hath liquor'd her. 2.01. 85 P
the rascal hath remov'd my horse, and tied him i 2.02. 11 P
thy spirit within thee hath been so at war, 2.03. 56
and thus hath so bestirr'd thee in thy sleep, 2.03. 57
some heavy business hath my lord in hand, | and 2.03. 63
hath butler brought those horses from the 2.03. 67
a weasel hath not such a deal of spleen | as you 2.03. 78
and hath sent for you | to line his enterprise, 2.03. 82
well, that rascal hath good mettle in him, he 2.04.349 P
cry | hath followed certain men unto this house. 2.04.508
which calls me pupil or hath read to me? 3.01. 45
three times hath henry bullingbrook made head 3.01. 63
the archdeacon hath divided it | into three 3.01. 71
my youth | hath faulty wand'red and irregular, 3.02. 27
save mine, which hath desir'd to see thee more, 3.02. 89
he hath more worthy interest to the state | than 3.02. 98
what never–dying honor hath he got | against 3.02.106
thrice hath this hotspur, mars in swathling 3.02.112
so hath the business that i come to speak of. 3.02.163
lord mortimer of scotland hath sent word | that 3.02.164
villainous company, hath been the spoil of me. 3.03. 10 P
he? alas, he is poor, he hath nothing. 3.03. 76 P
in my heart's love hath no man than yourself. 4.01. 8
no eye hath seen such scarecrows. 4.02. 38 P
for thy theft hath already made thee butter. 4.02. 61 P
the king hath sent to know | the nature of your 4.03. 41
but yet the king hath drawn | the special head 4.04. 27
us, | for he hath heard of our confederacy, 4.04. 38
honor hath no skill in surgery then? 5.01.133 P

who hath it? 5.01.136 P
it hath the excuse of youth and heat of blood, 5.02. 17
the lord of stafford dear to–day hath bought 5.03. 7
thee, king harry, | this sword hath ended him. 5.03. 9
the king hath many marching in his coats. 5.03. 25
like not such grinning honor as sir walter hath. 5.03. 59 P
sir nicholas gawsey hath for succor sent, | and 5.04. 45
hath for succor sent, | and so hath clifton. 5.04. 46
death hath not strook so fat a deer to–day, 5.04.107
of a man who hath not the life of a man; 5.04.117 P
hath beaten down young hotspur and his troops, 2H4 in 25
full of high feeding, madly hath broke loose, 1.01. 10
flood | hath left a witness'd usurpation. 1.01. 63
see what a ready tongue suspicion hath! 1.01. 84
hath by instinct knowledge from others' eyes 1.01. 86
of unwelcome news | hath but a losing office, 1.01.101
the sum of all | is that the king hath won, and 1.01.132
and hath sent out | a speedy power to encounter 1.01.132
thee like a sow that hath overwhelm'd all her 1.02. 11 P
in security, for he hath the horn of abundance, 1.02. 46 P
my lord, but he hath since done good service at 1.02. 61 P
it hath it original from much grief, from study, 1.02.115 P
the young prince hath misled me. 1.02.145 P
service at shrewsbury hath a little gilded over 1.02.148 P
well, the king hath sever'd you. 1.02.203 P
he hath eaten me out of house and home, he hath 2.01. 74 P
he hath put all my substance into that fat belly 2.01. 75 P
she hath been in good case, and the truth is, 2.01.106 P
and the truth is, poverty hath distracted her. 2.01.107 P
company as thou art hath in reason taken from me 2.02. 49 P
him to the heart, but he hath forgot that. 2.04. 9 P
bardolph hath brought word. 2.04. 18 P
the wither'd elder hath not his pole claw'd like 2.04.258 P
the fiend hath prick'd down bardolph 2.04.332 P
your majesty hath been this fortnight ill, | and 3.01.104
same starv'd justice hath done nothing but prate 3.02.304 P
and the feats he hath done about turnbull street 3.02.306 P
beard the silver hand of peace hath touch'd, 4.01. 43
learning and good letters peace hath tutor'd, 4.01. 44
now) | hath put us in these ill–beseeming arms, 4.01. 84
what peer hath been suborn'd to grate on you? 4.01. 90
but he hath forc'd us to compel this offer, 4.01.145
hath the prince john a full commission, | in 4.01.160
for he hath found to end one doubt by death 4.01.197
that hath enrag'd him on to offer strokes, | as 4.01.209
the king hath wasted all his rods | on late 4.01.213
who hath not heard it spoken | how deep you were 4.02. 16
the which hath been with scorn shov'd from the 4.02. 37
god, and not we, hath safely fought to–day. 4.02.121
a good sherris–sack hath a twofold operation in 4.03. 96 P
he did naturally inherit of his father, he hath, 4.03.119 P
he hath a tear for pity, and a hand | open as 4.04. 31
for when his headstrong riot hath no curb, 4.04. 62
the manner how this action hath been borne 4.04. 88
hath wrought the mure that should confine it in 4.04.119
the river hath thrice flowed, no ebb between, 4.04.125
that from this golden rigol hath divorc'd | so 4.05. 36
the prince hath ta'en it hence. 4.05. 59
depending | hath fed upon the body of my father; 4.05.159
for all my reign hath been but as a scene 4.05.197
it hath been prophesied to me many years, | i 4.05.236
his life | hath left me open to all injuries. 5.02. 8
well, peace be with him that hath made us heavy! 5.02. 25
dead, | and tell him who hath sent me after him. 5.02. 41
your majesty hath no just cause to hate me. 5.02. 66
who hath writ me down | after my seeming. 5.02.128
in me | hath proudly flow'd in vanity till now; 5.02.130
there hath been a man or two kill'd about her. 5.04. 6 P
he hath intent his wonted followers | shall all 5.05. 98
the king hath call'd his parliament, my lord. 5.05.103
he hath. 5.05.104
the flat unraised spirits that hath dar'd | on H5 pr 9
you would say it hath been all in all his study; 1.01. 42
they know your grace hath cause, and means, and 1.02.125
so hath your highness. 1.02.126
who hath been still a giddy neighbor to us; 1.02.145
hath shook and trembled at th' ill neighborhood. 1.02.154
she hath been then more fear'd than harm'd, my 1.02.155
when all her chevalry hath been in france, | and 1.02.157
she hath herself not only well defended | but 1.02.159
tell him he hath made a match with such a 1.02.264
of his | hath turn'd his balls to gun–stones, 1.02.282
see, thy fault france hath in thee found out, 2.pr. 20
the king hath run bad humors on the knight, 2.01.121 P
the king hath note of all that they intend, | by 2.02. 6
whom he hath dull'd and cloy'd with gracious 2.02. 9
and this man | hath, for a few light crowns, 2.02. 89
to us | than cambridge is, hath likewise sworn. 2.02. 93
hath got the voice in hell for excellence; 2.02.113
if that same demon that hath gull'd thee thus 2.02.121
and thus thy fall hath left a kind of blot | to 2.02.138
our purposes god justly hath discover'd, | and i 2.02.151
since god so graciously hath brought to light 2.02.185
the kindred of him hath been flesh'd upon us; 2.04. 50
base | that hath not noble lustre in your eyes. 3.01. 30
he hath a killing tongue and a quiet sword; 3.02. 34 P
he hath heard that men of few words are the best 3.02. 36 P
our expectation hath this day an end. 3.03. 44
'tis certain he hath pass'd the river somme. 3.05. 1
and of buxom valor, hath, by cruel fate, | and 3.06. 26
for he hath stol'n a pax, and hanged must 'a be 3.06. 40
but exeter hath given the doom of death | for 3.06. 44
of th' athversary hath been very great, 3.06. 98 P
my part, i think the duke hath lost never a man, 3.06.100 P
for conclusion, he hath betray'd his followers, 3.06.134 P
your air of france | hath blown that vice in me. 3.06.152
nay, the man hath no wit that cannot, from the 3.07. 31 P
who hath measur'd the ground? 3.07.127 P
no note | how dread an army hath enrounded him; 4.pr. 36
he hath not told his thought to the king? 4.01. 99 P
the king himself hath a heavy reckoning to make, 4.01.135 P
that he which hath no stomach to this fight, 4.03. 35
who hath sent thee now? 4.03. 88
fly — | and time hath worn us into slovenry. 4.03.114
himself happy that he hath fall'n into the hands 4.04. 60 P
disorder, that hath spoil'd us, friend us now! 4.05. 17
hath caus'd every soldier to cut his prisoner's 4.07. 9 P
would fain see the man, that hath but two legs, 4.07.162 P
so swift a pace hath thought that even now | you 5.pr. 15
since then my office hath so far prevail'd, 5.02. 29
alas, she hath from france too long been chas'd, 5.02. 38
the king hath heard them; 5.02. 74
she hath good leave. 5.02. 98
because he hath not the gift to woo in other 5.02.155 P
with maiden walls that war hath /never ent'red. 5.02.322 P
the king hath granted every article: 5.02.332
only he hath not yet subscribed this: 5.02.335
our bending author hath pursu'd the story, | in ep 2
which oft our stage hath shown; ep 13
each hath his place and function to attend: 1H6 1.01.173
gall — | nor men nor money hath he to make war. 1.02. 17
hath the late overthrow wrought this offense? 1.02. 49
the spirit of deep prophecy she hath, 1.02. 55
this means shall we sound what skill she hath. 1.02. 63
heaven and our lady gracious hath it pleas'd 1.02. 74
hath here distrain'd the tower to his use. 1.03. 61
chance is this that suddenly hath cross'd us? 1.04. 72
hand | that hath contriv'd this woeful tragedy! 1.04. 77
thus joan de pucelle hath perform'd her word. 1.06. 3
to celebrate the joy that god hath given us. 1.06. 14
the french | she carry armor as she hath begun. 2.01. 24
there hath at least five frenchmen died to–night 2.02. 9
that she may boast she hath beheld the man 2.02. 42
yet hath a woman's kindness overrul'd; 2.02. 50
long time thy shadow hath been thrall to me, 2.03. 36
i find thou art no less than fame hath bruited, 2.03. 68
what you have done hath not offended me; 2.03. 76
between two dogs, which hath the deeper mouth, 2.04. 12
two girls, which hath the merriest eye — | i 2.04. 15
hath not thy rose a canker, somerset? 2.04. 68
hath not thy rose a thorn, plantagenet? 2.04. 69
and even since then hath richard been obscur'd, 2.05. 26
me | and hath detain'd me all my flow'ring youth 2.05. 56
which somerset hath offer'd to my house, | i 2.05.125
it is not that that hath incens'd the duke: 3.01. 36
too, | hath been enacted through your enmity. 3.01.116
duke | hath banish'd moody discontented fury, 3.01.123
the bishop hath a kindly gird. 3.01.131
hath wrought this hellish mischief unawares, 3.02. 39
either she hath bewitch'd me with her words, 3.03. 58
when talbot hath set footing once in france 3.03. 64
pucelle hath bravely play'd her part in this, 3.03. 88
that hath reclaim'd | to your obedience fifty 3.04. 5
that hath so long been resident in france? 3.04. 14
means his grace, that he hath chang'd his style? 4.01. 50
hath he forgot he is his sovereign? 4.01. 52
with him, my lord, for he hath done me wrong. 4.01. 85
and i with him, for he hath done me wrong. 4.01. 86
hath sullied all his gloss of former honor | by 4.04. 6
hath now entrapp'd the noble–minded talbot: 4.04. 37
the regent hath with talbot broke his word, 4.06. 2
the sword of orleance hath not made me smart; 4.06. 42
to know who hath obtain'd the glory of the day. 4.07. 52
the turk, that two and fifty kingdoms hath, 4.07. 73
hath gain'd thy daughter princely liberty. 5.03.140
this argues what her kind of life hath been, 5.04. 15
take her away, for she hath liv'd too long, | to 5.04. 34
joan of aire hath been | a virgin from her 5.04. 49
it's sign she hath been liberal and free. 5.04. 82
of beauteous margaret hath astonish'd me. 5.05. 2
thus suffolk hath prevail'd, and thus he goes, 5.05.103
the mutual conference that my mind hath had, 2H6 1.01. 25
some sudden qualm hath struck me at the heart, 1.01. 54
or hath mine uncle beauford and myself, | with 1.01. 88
and hath his highness in his infancy | crowned 1.01. 93
hath given the duchy of anjou, and maine, | unto 1.01.110
hath won the greatest favor of the commons, 1.01.192
and so says york — for he hath greatest cause. 1.01.207
whose bookish rule hath pull'd fair england down 1.01.259
the commonwealth hath daily run to wrack, | the 1.03.124
the dolphin hath prevail'd beyond the seas, 1.03.125
in execution | upon offenders hath exceeded law, 1.03.133
for he hath witness of his servant's malice. 1.03.209
within this half hour, hath receiv'd his sight, 2.01. 62
soul, god's goodness hath been great to thee. 2.01. 82
but still remember what the lord hath done. 2.01. 84
my lords, saint albon here hath done a miracle; 2.01.129
news, i think, hath turn'd your weapon's edge; 2.01.176
that hath dishonored gloucester's honest name. 2.01.195
father, the duke hath told the truth; 2.02. 28
eleanor, the law, thou seest, hath judged thee; 2.03. 15
my master, he hath learnt so much fence already. 2.03. 78 P
and god in justice hath reveal'd to us | the 2.03.102
thus sometimes hath the brightest day a cloud, 2.04. 1
by flattery hath he won the commons' hearts; 3.01. 28
well hath your highness seen into this duke; 3.01. 42
by means whereof his highness hath lost france. 3.01.106
hath he not twit our sovereign lady here | with 3.01.178
'tis york that hath more reason for his death. 3.01.245
witness the fortune he hath had in france. 3.01.292
crafty kern, | hath he conversed with the enemy, 3.01.368
thrice is he arm'd that hath his quarrel just; 3.02.233
but all the honor salisbury hath won | is, that 3.02.275
he hath no eyes, the dust hath blinded them. 3.03. 14
he hath no eyes, the dust hath blinded them. 3.03. 14
this hand of mine hath writ in thy behalf, | and 4.01. 63
first let my words stab him, as he hath me. 4.01. 66
lord, and picardy | hath slain their governors, 4.01. 89
he hath confess'd! 4.02.107 P
cade, the duke of york hath taught you this. 4.02.154
that that lord say hath gelded the commonwealth, 4.02.165 P
hath this lovely face | rul'd like a wandering 4.04. 15
lord say, jack cade hath sworn to have thy head. 4.04. 19
hath given them heart and courage to proceed. 4.04. 35
jack cade hath gotten london bridge: 4.04. 49
i think he hath a very fair warning. 4.06. 10 P
this tongue hath parley'd unto foreign kings 4.07. 77
hath made me full of sickness and diseases. 4.07. 89
hath my sword therefore broke through london 4.08. 23 P
alas, he hath no home, no place to fly to; 4.08. 38
henry hath money, you are strong and manly; 4.08. 51
it hath serv'd me instead of a quart pot to 4.10. 13 P
famine and no other hath slain me. 4.10. 60 P
tell kent from me, she hath lost her best man, 4.10. 73 P
the king hath sent him sure; 5.01. 13
end, | the king hath yielded unto thy demand: 5.01. 40
hath clapp'd his tail between his legs and cried 5.01.154
why, warwick, hath thy knee forgot to bow? 5.01.161
thus war hath given thee peace, for thou art 5.02. 29
is truly dedicate to war | hath no self–love; 5.02. 38
hath not essentially but by circumstance | the 5.02. 39
hath made the wizard famous in his death. 5.02. 69
and it hath pleas'd him that three times to–day 5.03. 18
richard hath best deserv'd of all my sons. 3H6 1.01. 17
hath made us by–words to our enemies. 1.01. 42
hath he deserv'd to lose his birthright thus? 1.01.219
hath made her break out into terms of rage! 1.01.265
that hath authority over him that swears. 1.02. 24
france | when as the enemy hath been ten to one; 1.02. 74
hath stopp'd the passage where thy words should 1.03. 22
thy father hath. 1.03. 39
the army of the queen hath got the field. 1.04. 1
my sons, god knows what hath bechanced them; 1.04. 6
now phaeton hath tumbled from his car, | and 1.04. 33
whose frown hath made thee faint and fly ere 1.04. 48
hath thy fiery heart so parch'd thine entrails 1.04. 87
hath that poor monarch taught thee to insult? 1.04.124
his name that valiant duke hath left with thee; 2.01. 89
who hath not seen them, even with those wings 2.02. 29
full well hath clifford play'd the orator, 2.02. 43
the queen hath best success when you are absent. 2.02. 74
for what hath broach'd this tumult but thy pride 2.02.159
and though the edge hath something hit ourselves 2.02.166
brother's blood the thirsty earth hath drunk, 2.03. 15
till either death hath clos'd these eyes of mine 2.03. 31
thou that so stoutly hath resisted me, | give me 2.05. 79
and hath bereft thee of thy life too late. 2.05. 93
the air hath got into my deadly wounds, | and 2.06. 27
you are the king king edward hath depos'd; 3.01. 69
i see the lady hath a thing to grant, | before 3.02. 12
the ghostly father now hath done his shrift. 3.02.107
but now mischance hath trod my title down, | and 3.03. 8
scotland hath will to help, but cannot help; 3.03. 34
hath plac'd thy beauty's image and thy virtue. 3.03. 64
you told not how henry the sixt hath lost | all 3.03. 89
mine ear hath tempted judgment to desire. 3.03.133
tell him from me that he hath done me wrong, 3.03.231
hath not our brother made a worthy choice? 4.01. 3
them sever'd | whom god hath join'd together; 4.01. 22
which he hath giv'n for fence impregnable, | and 4.01. 44
and yet methinks your grace hath not done well 4.01. 51
"tell him from me that he hath done me wrong, 4.01.110
hath pawn'd an open hand in sign of love; 4.02. 9
for he hath made a solemn vow | never to lie and 4.03. 4
warwick may lose, that now hath won the day. 4.04. 15
(for trust not him that hath once broken faith), 4.04. 30
hands | he hath good usage and great liberty, 4.05. 6
your grace hath still been fam'd for virtuous, 4.06. 26
but when the fox hath once got in his nose, 4.07. 25
hath pass'd in safety through the narrow seas, 4.08. 3
methinks the power that edward hath in field 4.08. 35
that's not my fear, my meed hath got me fame: 4.08. 38
my pity hath been balm to heal their wounds, 4.08. 41
my mildness hath allay'd their swelling griefs, 4.08. 42
the queen from france hath brought a puissant 5.02. 31
montague hath breath'd his last, | and to the 5.02. 40
hath rais'd in gallia have arriv'd our coast, 5.03. 8
give more strength to that which hath too much, 5.04. 9
and take his thanks that yet hath nothing else. 5.04. 59
by this, i hope, she hath a son for me. 5.05. 90
what scene of death hath roscius now to act? 5.06. 10
the bird that hath been limed in a bush, | with 5.06. 13
france | hath pawn'd the sicils and jerusalem, 5.07. 39
grim–visag'd war hath smooth'd his wrinkled R3 1.01. 9
hath appointed | this conduct to convey me to 1.01. 44
belike his majesty hath some intent | that you 1.01. 49
hath mov'd his highness to commit me now. 1.01. 61
his majesty hath straitly given in charge | that 1.01. 85
we say that shore's wife hath a pretty foot, | a 1.01. 93
how hath your lordship brook'd imprisonment? 1.01.125
o, he hath kept an evil diet long, | and 1.01.139
intent, | clarence hath not another day to live: 1.01.150
which his hell–govern'd arm hath butchered! 1.02. 67
the better for the king of heaven that hath him. 1.02.105
thy beauty hath, and made them blind with 1.02.166
to him that hath most cause to be a mourner, 1.02.211
hath she forgot already that brave prince, 1.02.239
and god, not we, hath plagu'd thy bloody deed. 1.03.180
wrath | hath in eternal darkness folded up. 1.03.268
she hath had too much wrong, and i repent | my 1.03.306
that word "judgment" hath bred a kind of remorse 1.04.107 P
and he that hath commanded is our king. 1.04.194
kings | hath in the table of his law commanded 1.04.196
but his red color hath forsook his cheeks. 2.01. 86
but death hath snatch'd my husband from my arms, 2.02. 57
why, so hath this, both by his father and mother 2.03. 22
who hath committed them? 2.04. 44
the tiger now hath seiz'd the gentle hind; 2.04. 50
the weary way hath made you melancholy. 3.01. 3
hath not yet div'd into the world's deceit; 3.01. 8
this prince hath neither claim'd it nor deserv'd 3.01. 51
which by his death hath lost much majesty. 3.01.100
the prince my brother hath outgrown me far. 3.01.104
he hath, my lord. 3.01.105
your honor hath no shriving work in hand. 3.02.115
catesby hath sounded hastings in our business, 3.04. 36
thee | that ever wretched age hath look'd upon. 3.04.105
saith the duke, thus hath the duke inferr'd" — 3.07. 32
the royal tree hath left us royal fruit, | which 3.07.167
the king hath strictly charg'd the contrary. 4.01. 17
hath he set bounds between their love and me? 4.01. 20
which hitherto hath held /my eyes from rest; 4.01. 81
whom envy hath immur'd within your walls — 4.01. 99
hath he so long held out with me untir'd, | and 4.02. 44
the chaplain of the tower hath buried them, 4.03. 29
and anne my wife hath bid this world good night. 4.03. 39
hath dimm'd your infant morn to aged night. 4.04. 16
ah, who hath any cause to mourn but we? 4.04. 34
from forth the kennel of thy womb hath crept | a 4.04. 47
thus hath the course of justice whirl'd about, 4.04.105
and not be richard that hath done all this. 4.04.287
and when this arm of mine hath chastised | the 4.04.331
george, profan'd, hath lost his lordly honor; 4.04.369
thy life hath it dishonor'd. 4.04.376

thy broken faith hath made the prey for worms. 4.04.386
hath any well–advised friend proclaim'd | reward 4.04.515
such proclamation hath been made, my lord. 4.04.517
say that the queen hath heartily consented | he 4.05. 7
hath turn'd my feigned prayer on my head, | and 5.01. 21
wrong hath but wrong, and blame the due of blame 5.01. 29
he hath no friends but what are friends for fear 5.02. 20
who hath descried the number of the traitors? 5.03. 9
the weary sun hath made a golden set, | and by 5.03. 19
my conscience hath a thousand several tongues, 5.03.193
cock | hath twice done salutation to the morn, 5.03.210
one that made means to come by what he hath, 5.03.248
one that hath ever been god's enemy. 5.03.252
england hath long been mad and scarr'd herself: 5.05. 23
i cannot tell | what heaven hath given him — H8 1.01. 67
for france hath flaw'd the league, and hath 1.01. 95
and hath attach'd | our merchants' goods at 1.01. 95
and i know his sword | hath a sharp edge; 1.01.110
the o'er–great cardinal | hath show'd him gold; 1.01.223
'em, which hath flaw'd the heart | of all their 1.02. 21
hath into monstrous habits put the graces | that 1.02.122
"hath sent to me, wishing me to permit | john de 1.02.161
self, hath sent | one general tongue unto us: 2.02. 94
approve the fair conceit | the king hath of you. 2.03. 75
it hath already publicly been read, | and on all 2.04. 3
hath my behavior given to your displeasure, 2.04. 20
his grace | hath spoken well and justly; 2.04. 65
for he hath a witchcraft | over the king in 's 3.02. 18
the king hath found | matter against him that 3.02. 20
the king already | hath married the fair lady. 3.02. 42
is stol'n away to rome, hath ta'en no leave, 3.02. 57
fellow, and hath ta'en much pain | in the king's 3.02. 72
one | hath crawl'd into the favor of the king, 3.02.103
what piles of wealth hath he accumulated | to 3.02.107
whom the king hath in secrecy long married, 3.02.403
it hath strook. 5.01. 1
who hath so far | given ear to our complaint, of 5.01. 47
let him to field, troilus, alas, hath none. TRO 1.01. 5
lay'st in every gash that love hath given me 1.01. 62
hath robb'd many beasts of their particular 1.02. 19 P
man into whom nature hath so crowded humors that 1.02. 22 P
there is no man hath a virtue that he hath not a 1.02. 24 P
man hath a virtue that he hath not a glimpse of, 1.02. 24 P
he hath the joints of every thing, but every 1.02. 27 P
and shame whereof hath ever since kept hector 1.02. 35 P
why, paris hath color enough. 1.02. 99 P
what grief hath set these jaundies o'er your 1.03. 2
sith /every action that hath gone before, 1.03. 13
and what hath mass or matter, by itself | lies 1.03. 29
the herd hath more annoyance by the breeze 1.03. 48
the specialty of rule hath been neglected, | and 1.03. 78
goes backward with a purpose | it hath to climb. 1.03.129
most wisely hath ulysses here discover'd | the 1.03.138
why, this hath not a finger's dignity. 1.03.204
he hath a lady, wiser, fairer, truer, | than 1.03.275
that means not, hath not, or is not in love! 1.03.288
if then one is, or hath, /or means to be, | that 1.03.289
/mould | a noble man that hath no spark of fire 1.03.294
pride | that hath to this maturity blown up | in 1.03.317
call some knight to arms | that hath a stomach, 2.01.125
thousand dismes, | hath been as dear as helen; 2.02. 20
because your speech hath none that tell him so? 2.02. 36
whose price hath launch'd above a thousand ships 2.02. 82
which hath our several honors all engag'd | to 2.02.124
paris should ne'er retract what he hath done, 2.02.141
for 'tis a cause that hath no mean dependance 2.02.192
achilles hath inveigled his fool from him. 2.03. 91 P
the elephant hath joints, but none for courtesy; 2.03.105 P
much attribute he hath, and much the reason 2.03.116
when time is old /and hath forgot itself, | when 3.02.185
whom troy hath still denied, but this antenor, 3.03. 22
pride hath no other glass | to show itself but 3.03. 47
hath any honor, but honor for those honors 3.03. 81
cannot make boast to have that which he hath, 3.03. 98
till it hath travell'd and is /mirror'd there 3.03.110
time hath, my lord, a wallet at his back, 3.03.145
for emulation hath a thousand sons | that one by 3.03.156
which hath an operation more divine | than 3.03.203
like an hostess that hath no arithmetic but her 3.03.253 P
her bawdy veins, | a grecian's life hath sunk; 4.01. 71
carrion weight, | a troyan hath been slain. 4.01. 73
she hath not given so many good words breath 4.01. 74
wak'd by the lark, hath rous'd the ribald crows, 4.02. 9
night hath been too brief. 4.02. 11
why, my negation hath no taste of madness. 5.02.127
what hath she done, prince, that can /soil our 5.02.134
hath nothing been but shapes and forms of 5.03. 12
thy wife hath dreamt, thy mother hath had 5.03. 63
wife hath dreamt, thy mother hath had visions, 5.03. 63
the fierce polydamas | hath beat down menon; 5.05. 7
bastard margarelon | hath doreus prisoner, | and 5.05. 8
ajax hath lost a friend, | and foams at mouth, 5.05. 35
who hath done to–day | mad and fantastic 5.05. 37
ajax hath ta'en aeneas! 5.06. 22
thy goodly armor thus hath cost thy life. 5.08. 2
"achilles hath the mighty hector slain!" 5.08. 14
till he hath lost his honey and his sting; 5.10. 42
i say unto you, what he hath done famously, he COR 1.01. 36 P
he hath faults (with surplus) to tire in 1.01. 45 P
agrippa, one that hath always lov'd the people. 1.01. 51 P
thy exercise hath been too violent for | a 1.05. 15
my work hath yet not warm'd me. 1.05. 17
thank the gods | our rome hath such a soldier." 1.09. 9
his good will | hath overta'en mine act. 1.09. 19
emulation | hath not that honor in't it had; 1.10. 13
the state hath another, his wife another, and, i 2.01.108 P
he hath in this action outdone his former deeds 2.01.135 P
where he hath won, | with fame, a name to 2.01.163
and end, but will | lose those he hath won. 2.01.226
people in what hatred | he still hath held them; 2.01.246
faith, there hath been many great men that have 2.02. 7 P
he hath deserv'd worthily of his country, and 2.02. 24 P
but he hath so planted his honors in their eyes 2.02. 28 P
service that | hath thus stood for his country; 2.02. 41
the people than | he hath hereto priz'd them at. 2.02. 60
we do, sir, tell us what hath brought you to't. 2.03. 63 P
bruising to you | when he hath power to crush? 2.03.203
that hath beside well in his person wrought | to 2.03.246
hath he not pass'd the noble and the common? 3.01. 29
he hath resisted law, | and therefore law shall 3.01.266
killing our enemies, the blood he hath lost 3.01.297
(which, i dare vouch, is more than that he hath, 3.01.298
bend like his | that hath receiv'd an alms! 3.02.120
straight, he hath been us'd | ever to conquer, 3.03. 25
but since he hath | serv'd well for rome — 3.03. 82
as he hath follow'd you, with all despite; 3.03.139
there hath been in rome strange insurrections; 4.03. 13 P
hath been! 4.03. 16 P
martius, who hath done | to thee particularly, 4.05. 65
have all forsook me, hath devour'd the rest, 4.05. 76
this extremity | hath brought me to thy hearth; 4.05. 79
word thou hast spoke hath weeded from my heart 4.05.102
my grained ash an hundred times hath broke, 4.05.108
can, | and three examples of the like hath been 4.06. 51
yet he hath left undone | that which shall break 4.07. 24
as he hath spices of them all — not all, | for 4.07. 46
hath not a tomb so evident as a chair | t' extol 4.07. 52
evident as a chair | t' extol what it hath done. 4.07. 53
you hear what he hath said | which was sometime 5.01. 1
lots to blanks | my name hath touch'd your ears: 5.02. 11
who like a block hath denied my access to thee. 5.02. 78 P
he that hath a will to die by himself fears it 5.02.104 P
young boy | hath an aspect of intercession which 5.03. 32
and my true lip | hath virgin'd it e'er since. 5.03. 48
i accuse | the city ports by this hath enter'd, 5.06. 6
whose children he hath slain, their base throats 5.06. 52
the highest degree | he hath abus'd your powers. 5.06. 85
city he | hath widowed and unchilded many a one, 5.06.151
hath yok'd a nation strong, train'd up in arms. TIT 1.01. 30
five times he hath return'd | bleeding to rome, 1.01. 33
lo, as the bark that hath discharg'd his fraught 1.01. 71
pomp, | that hath aspir'd to solon's happiness, 1.01.177
though /chance of war hath wrought this change 1.01.264
whose wisdom hath her fortune conquered. 1.01.336
the deed | that hath dishonored all our family: 1.01.345
this monument five hundreth years hath stood, 1.01.350
that hath express'd himself in all his deeds | a 1.01.422
rise, titus, rise, my empress hath prevail'd. 1.01.459
that he hath breath'd in my dishonor here. 2.01. 56
but dawning day new comfort hath inspir'd. 2.02. 10
who hath abandoned her holy groves | to see the 2.03. 58
if fear hath made thee faint, as me it hath — 2.03.234
if fear hath made thee faint, as me it hath — 2.03.234
she hath no tongue to call, nor hands to wash, 2.04. 7
stern ungentle hands | hath lopp'd and hew'd, 2.04. 17
but sure some tereus hath deflow'red thee, | and 2.04. 26
and he hath cut those pretty fingers off | that 2.04. 42
harmony | which that sweet tongue hath made, 2.04. 49
hath made thee handless in thy father's sight? 3.01. 67
what fool hath added water to the sea? 3.01. 68
speak, gentle sister, who hath mart'red thee? 3.01. 81
o, say thou for her, who hath done this deed? 3.01. 87
deer | that hath receiv'd some unrecuring wound. 3.01. 90
hath hurt me more than had he kill'd me dead: 3.01. 92
nor tongue to tell me who hath mart'red thee. 3.01.107
because the law hath ta'en revenge on them. 3.01.117
thine, | that hath thrown down so many enemies, 3.01.163
which of your hands hath not defended rome, 3.01.167
my hand hath been but idle, let it serve | to 3.01.171
more hath it merited, that let it have. 3.01.196
where life hath no more interest but to breathe! 3.01.249
even in their throats that hath committed them. 3.01.274
read to her sons than she hath read to thee 4.01. 13
o, do ye read, my lord, what she hath writ? 4.01. 77
thy father hath full oft | for his ungrateful 4.01.110
that hath more scars of sorrow in his heart 4.01.126
of lucius, | he hath some message to deliver us. 4.02. 2
hath sent by me | the goodliest weapons of his 4.02. 10
the old man hath found their guilt, | and sends 4.02. 26
belike for joy the emperor hath a son. 4.02. 50
what hath he sent her? 4.02. 63
he says that he hath taken them down again, for 4.03. 81 P
in the people's ears, there nought hath pass'd, 4.04. 7
whose loss hath pierc'd him deep and scarr'd his 4.04. 31
myself hath often heard them say, | when i have 4.04. 74
and wherein rome hath done you any scath, | let 5.01. 7
show me a villain that hath done a rape, | and i 5.02. 94
show me a thousand that hath done thee wrong, 5.02. 96
what, hath the firmament moe suns than one? 5.03. 17
titus | hath ordain'd to an honorable end, | for 5.03. 22
whereof their mother daintily hath fed, | eating 5.03. 61
eating the flesh that she herself hath bred. 5.03. 62
tell us what sinon hath bewitch'd our ears, | or 5.03. 85
or who hath brought the fatal engine in | that 5.03. 86
many a story hath he told to thee, | and bid 5.03.164
how many thousand times hath these poor lips, 5.03.167
that hath been breeder of these dire events. 5.03.178
many a morning hath he there been seen, | with ROM 1.01.131
hit | with cupid's arrow, she hath dian's wit; 1.01.209
then she hath sworn that she will still live 1.01.217
she hath, and in that sparing /makes huge waste; 1.01.218
she hath forsworn to love, and in that vow | do 1.01.223
she hath not seen the change of fourteen years; 1.02. 9
earth hath swallowed all my hopes but she; 1.02. 14
what names the writing person hath here writ. 1.02. 43 P
verona's summer hath not such a flower. 1.03. 77
o then i see queen mab hath been with you. 1.04. 53
but he that hath the steerage of my course 1.04.112
that makes dainty, | she i'll swear hath corns. 1.05. 20
and, on my life, hath stol'n him home to bed. 2.01. 4
he hath hid himself among these trees | to be 2.01. 30
love, | which the dark night hath so discovered. 2.02.106
poison hath residence and medicine power; 2.03. 24
our romeo hath not been in bed to–night. 2.03. 42
where on a sudden one hath wounded me | that's 2.03. 50
hath wash'd thy sallow cheeks for rosaline! 2.03. 70
hath sent a letter to his father's house. 2.04. 7
gentlewoman, that god hath made, himself to mar. 2.04.115 P
and she hath the prettiest sententious of it, of 2.04.211 P
and therefore hath the wind–swift cupid wings. 2.05. 8
with a man that hath a hair more or a hair less 3.01. 17 P
and yet thy head hath been beaten as addle as an 3.01. 23 P
because he hath waken'd thy dog that hath lain 3.01. 26 P
waken'd thy dog that hath lain asleep in the sun 3.01. 26 P
the prince expressly hath | forbid this bandying 3.01. 88
is he gone and hath nothing? 3.01. 92
hath got this mortal hurt | in my behalf; 3.01.110
tybalt, that an hour | hath been my cousin! 3.01.113
juliet, | thy beauty hath made me effeminate, 3.01.114
that gallant spirit hath aspir'd the clouds, 3.01.117
to an impatient child that hath new robes | and 3.02. 30
hath romeo slain himself? 3.02. 45
"banished," | hath slain ten thousand tybalts. 3.02.114
for exile hath more terror in his look, | much 3.03. 13
taking thy part, hath rush'd aside the law, 3.03. 26
upon his body that hath slaughter'd him! 3.05.102
hath sorted out a sudden day of joy, | that thou 3.05.109
still my care hath been | to have her match'd; 3.05.177
hath not so green, so quick, so fair an eye | as 3.05.220
green, so quick, so fair an eye | as paris hath. 3.05.221
which she hath prais'd him with above compare 3.05.238
subtilly hath minist'red to have me dead, | lest 4.03. 25
not, | for he hath still been tried a holy man. 4.03. 29
the second cock hath crowed, | the curfew–bell 4.04. 3
the curfew–bell hath rung, 'tis three a' clock. 4.04. 4
the county paris hath set up his rest | that you 4.05. 6
that hath ta'en her hence to make me wail, 4.05. 31
thy wedding–day | hath death lain with thy wife. 4.05. 36
death is my heir, | my daughter he hath wedded. 4.05. 39
and cruel death hath catch'd it from my sight! 4.05. 48
had part in this fair maid, now heaven hath all, 4.05. 67
marry, sir, because silver hath a sweet sound. 4.05.131 P
romeo | hath had no notice of these accidents; 5.02. 27
death, that hath suck'd the honey of thy breath, 5.03. 92
breath, | hath had no power yet upon thy beauty: 5.03. 93
how long hath he been there? 5.03.130
we can contradict | hath thwarted our intents. 5.03.154
poison, i see, hath been his timeless end. 5.03.162
dead, | who here hath lain this two days buried. 5.03.176
this dagger hath mista'en, for lo his house | is 5.03.203
grief of my son's exile hath stopp'd her breath. 5.03.211
spirits thy power | hath conjur'd to attend. TIM 1.01. 7
this gentleman of mine hath serv'd me long; 1.01.142
sir, your jewel | hath suffered under praise. 1.01.165
it hath pleas'd the gods to remember my father's 1.02. 2
hath presented to you | four milk–white horses, 1.02.182
he hath put me off | to the succession of new 2.02. 19
room | hath blaz'd with lights and bray'd with 2.02.161
no villainous bounty yet hath pass'd my heart; 2.02.173
something hath been amiss — a noble nature 2.02.208
hath sent to your lordship to furnish him, 3.01. 19 P
may it please your honor, my lord hath sent — 3.02. 30 P
i know my lord hath spent of timon's wealth, 3.04. 26
who in hot blood | hath stepp'd into the law, 3.05. 12
he hath sent me an earnest inviting, which many 3.06. 9 P
but he hath conjur'd me beyond them, and i must 3.06. 11 P
hath in her more destruction than thy sword, 4.03. 63
hath doubtfully pronounc'd the throat shall cut, 4.03.122
face | hath to the marbled mansion all above 4.03.191
hath a distracted and most wretched being, 4.03.246
in sufferance, time | hath made thee hard in't. 4.03.269
it is nois'd he hath a mass of treasure. 4.03.402 P
behold, the earth hath roots; 4.03.417
aid, hath /sense withal | of it own fall, 5.01.147
come hither, ere my tree hath felt the axe, 5.01.211
timon hath made his everlasting mansion | upon 5.01.215
sun, hide thy beams, timon hath done his reign. 5.01.223
"timon is dead, who hath outstretch'd his span: 5.03. 3
our captain hath in every figure skill, | an 5.03. 7
cunning in excess, | hath broke their hearts. 5.04. 29
by means whereof this breast of mine hath buried JC 1.02. 49
you | what hath proceeded worthy note to–day. 1.02.181
tell us what hath chanc'd to–day | that caesar 1.02.217
'tis very like, he hath the falling sickness. 1.02.254
no, caesar hath it not; 1.02.255
that heaven hath infus'd them with these spirits 1.03. 69
of any promise that hath pass'd from him. 2.01.140
the clock hath stricken three. 2.01.192
which sometime hath his hour with every man. 2.01.251
as it hath much prevail'd on your condition, | i 2.01.254
thrice hath calphurnia in her sleep cried out, 2.02. 2
a lioness hath whelped in the streets, | and 2.02. 17
hath begg'd that i will stay at home to–day. 2.02. 82
as that same ague which hath made you lean. 2.02.113
brutus hath a suit | that caesar will not grant. 2.04. 42
how caesar hath deserv'd to lie in death, | mark 3.01.132
so pity pity — | hath done this deed on caesar. 3.01.172
back with speed, and tell him what hath chanc'd. 3.01.287
brutus | hath told you caesar was ambitious; 3.02. 78
fault, | and grievously hath caesar answer'd it. 3.02. 80
he hath brought many captives home to rome, 3.02. 88
when that the poor have cried, caesar hath wept; 3.02. 91
wherein hath caesar thus deserv'd your loves? 3.02.236
moreover, he hath left you all his walks, | his 3.02.247
he hath left them you, | and to your heirs for 3.02.249
hath given me some worthy cause to wish | things 4.02. 8
friendly conference, | as he hath us'd of old. 4.02. 18
brutus hath riv'd my heart. 4.03. 85
hath cassius liv'd | to be but mirth and 4.03.113
mistrust of my success hath done this deed. 5.03. 65
mistrust of good success hath done this deed. 5.03. 66
the ghost of caesar hath appear'd to me | two 5.05. 17
tongue | hath almost ended his live's history. 5.05. 40
thy life hath had some smatch of honor in it. 5.05. 46
and no man else hath honor by his death. 5.05. 57
what he hath lost, noble macbeth hath won. MAC 1.02. 67
what he hath lost, noble macbeth hath won. 1.02. 67
the earth hath bubbles, as the water has, | and 1.03. 79
the king hath happily receiv'd, macbeth, | the 1.03. 89
ill, | why hath it given me earnest of success, 1.03.132
think upon what hath chanc'd; 1.03.153
this castle hath a pleasant seat, the air 1.06. 1
hath made his pendant bed and procreant cradle. 1.06. 8
his spur, hath holp him | to his home before us. 1.06. 23
this duncan | hath borne his faculties so meek, 1.07. 17
meek, hath been | so clear in his great office, 1.07. 17
hath he ask'd for me? 1.07. 30
he hath honor'd me of late, and i have bought 1.07. 32
hath it slept since? 1.07. 36
he hath been in unusual pleasure, and | sent 2.01. 13
that which hath made them drunk hath made me 2.02. 1
which hath made them drunk hath made me bold; 2.02. 1
what hath quench'd them hath given me fire. 2.02. 2
what hath quench'd them hath given me fire. 2.02. 2

"glamis hath murther'd sleep, and therefore 2.02. 39
your constancy | hath left you unattended. 2.02. 66
confusion now hath made his masterpiece! 2.03. 66
most sacrilegious murther hath broke ope | the 2.03. 67
shaft that's shot | hath not yet lighted, and 2.03.142
this sore night | hath trifled former knowings. 2.04. 4
those that macbeth hath slain. 2.04. 23
(which still hath been both grave and prosperous 3.01. 21
he hath a wisdom that doth guide his valor | to 3.01. 52
whose heavy hand hath bow'd you to the grave, 3.01. 89
which bounteous nature | hath in him clos'd; 3.01. 98
world | hath so incens'd that i am reckless what 3.01.109
ere the bat hath flown | his cloister'd flight, 3.02. 40
drowsy hums | hath rung night's yawning peal, 3.02. 43
hath nature that in time will venom breed, | no 3.04. 29
is often thus, | and hath been from his youth. 3.04. 53
blood hath been shed ere now, i' th' olden time, 3.04. 74
you have done | hath been but for a wayward son, 3.05. 11
report | hath so exasperate /the king that he 3.06. 38
thrice the brinded cat hath mew'd. 4.01. 1
sow's blood, that hath eaten | her nine farrow; 4.01. 64
he hath not touch'd you yet. 4.03. 14
it hath been | th' untimely emptying of the 4.03. 67
and it hath been | the sword of our slain kings. 4.03. 86
scotland hath foisons to fill up your will | of 4.03. 88
upon thyself | hath banish'd me from scotland. 4.03.113
hath from my soul | wip'd the black scruples, 4.03.115
by many of these trains hath sought to win me 4.03.118
such sanctity hath heaven given his hand, | they 4.03.144
virtue, | he hath a heavenly gift of prophecy, 4.03.157
gracious england hath | lent us good siward, and 4.03.189
so, | for it hath cow'd my better part of man! 5.08. 18
by his worth, for then | it hath no end. 5.09. 12
who hath reliev'd you? HAM 1.01. 17
barnardo hath my place. | give you good night. 1.01. 17
with martial stalk hath he gone by our watch. 1.01. 66
hath in the skirts of norway here and there 1.01. 97
to some enterprise | that hath a stomach in't, 1.01.100
no fairy takes, nor witch hath power to charm, 1.01.163
yet so far hath discretion fought with nature 1.02. 5
he hath not fail'd to pester us with message 1.02. 22
is death of fathers, and who still hath cried, 1.02.104
what is't, ophelia, he hath said to you? 1.03. 88
he hath very oft of late | given private time to 1.03. 91
he hath, my lord, of late made many tenders | of 1.03. 99
he hath importun'd me with love | in honorable 1.03.110
and hath given countenance to his speech, my 1.03.113
hath op'd his ponderous and marble jaws | to 1.04. 50
you, | for every man hath business and desire, 1.05.130
that hath made him mad. 2.01.107
death, that thus hath put him | so much from th' 2.02. 8
good gentlemen, he hath much talk'd of you, 2.02. 19
trail of policy so sure | as it hath us'd to do, 2.02. 48
he hath found | the head and source of all your 2.02. 54
duty and obedience, mark, | hath given me this. 2.02.108
this in obedience hath my daughter shown me, 2.02.125
me, | and more /above, hath his solicitings, 2.02.126
but how hath she | receiv'd his love? 2.02.128
hath there been such a time — i would fain know 2.02.153
hath now this dread and black complexion smear'd 2.02.455
and the /dev'l hath power | t' assume a pleasing 2.02.599
god hath given you one face, and you make 3.01.143 P
go to, i'll no more on't, it hath made me mad. 3.01.146 P
sh' hath seal'd thee for herself, for thou hast 3.02. 65
full thirty times hath phoebus' cart gone round 3.02.155
now what my /love is, proof hath made you know, 3.02.169
great affliction of spirit, hath sent me to you. 3.02.312 P
your behavior hath strook her into amazement and 3.02.326 P
it hath the primal eldest curse upon't, | a 3.03. 37
and that your grace hath screen'd and stood 3.04. 3
that thus hath cozen'd you at hoodman–blind? 3.04. 77
but heaven hath pleas'd it so | to punish me 3.04.173
to draw apart the body he hath kill'd, | o'er 4.01. 24
hamlet in madness hath polonius slain, | and 4.01. 34
from his mother's closet hath he dragg'd him. 4.01. 35
how now, what hath befall'n? 4.03. 11
may fish with the worm that hath eat of a king, 4.03. 27 P
and eat of the fish that hath fed of that worm. 4.03. 28 P
ground | that hath in it no profit but the name. 4.04. 19
thought which quarter'd hath but one part wisdom 4.04. 42
how long hath she been thus? 4.05. 67
that he which hath your noble father slain 4.07. 4
and hath abatements and delays as many | as 4.07.120
the crowner hath sate on her, and finds it 5.01. 4 P
argues an act, and an act hath three branches — 5.01. 11 P
custom hath made it in him a property of 5.01. 67 P
of little employment hath the daintier sense. 5.01. 70 P
stealing steps | hath clawed me in his clutch, 5.01. 72
his clutch, | and hath shipped me into the land, 5.01. 73
here's a skull now hath lien you i' th' earth 5.01.173 P
he hath bore me on his back a thousand times. 5.01.186 P
he that hath kill'd my king and whor'd my mother 5.02. 64
he hath much land, and fertile; 5.02. 85 P
sir, hath wager'd with him six barbary horses, 5.02.147 P
the king, sir, hath laid, sir, that in a dozen 5.02.165 P
he hath laid on twelve for nine, and it would 5.02.167 P
the foul practice | hath turn'd itself on me. 5.02.318
his breeding, sir, hath been at my charge. LR 1.01. 9 P
he hath been out nine years, and away he shall 1.01. 32 P
with this king | hath rivall'd for our daughter. 1.01.191
i crave no more than hath your highness offer'd, 1.01.194
that hath depriv'd me of your grace and favor, 1.01.229
not to have it | hath lost me in your liking. 1.01.233
lord, who hath receiv'd you | at fortune's alms. 1.01.277
we have made of it hath /not been little. 1.01.289 P
with what poor judgment he hath now cast her off 1.01.291 P
yet he hath ever but slenderly known himself. 1.01.293 P
and soundest of his time hath been but rash; 1.01.295 P
quality of nothing hath not such need to hide 1.02. 34 P
who sways, not as it hath power, but as it is 1.02. 50 P
life for him that he hath writ this to feel my 1.02. 86 P
some little time hath qualified the heat of his 1.02.161 P
some villain hath done me wrong. 1.02.165 P
into france, sir, the fool hath much pin'd away. 1.04. 74 P
as i am ignorant | of what hath moved you. 1.04.274
this man hath had good counsel — a hundred 1.04.322
what he hath utter'd i have writ my sister; 1.04.331
my father hath set guard to take my brother, 2.01. 16
our father he hath writ, so hath our sister, 2.01.122
our father he hath writ, so hath our sister, 2.01.122
yes, sir, but anger hath a privilege. 2.02. 70
who hath most fortunately been inform'd | of my 2.02.167
what's he that hath so much thy place mistook 2.04. 12
regan, she hath tied | sharp–tooth'd unkindness, 2.04.134
she hath abated me of half my train; 2.04.159
'tis his own blame hath put himself from rest, 2.04.290
what hath been seen, | either in snuffs and 3.01. 25
or the hard rein which both of them hath borne 3.01. 27
whom the foul fiend hath led through fire and 3.04. 52 P
that hath laid knives under his pillow, and 3.04. 54 P
he hath no daughters, sir. 3.04. 69
who hath /had three suits to his back, six 3.04.135 P
what, hath your grace no better company? 3.04.142
to tell thee, | the grief hath craz'd my wits. 3.04.170
or false, it hath made thee earl of gloucester. 3.05. 17 P
my lord of gloucester hath convey'd him hence. 3.07. 15
poor tom hath been scar'd out of his good wits. 4.01. 57 P
stroke which since | hath pluck'd him after. 4.02. 78
my mourning and importun'd tears hath pitied. 4.04. 26
he hath slept long. 4.07. 17
your business of the world hath so an end, | and 5.01. 45
king lear hath lost, he and his daughter ta'en. 5.02. 6
this speech of yours hath mov'd me, | and shall 5.03.200
he hath commission from thy wife and me | to 5.03.253
the wonder is, he hath endur'd so long, | he but 5.03.317
the oldest hath borne most; 5.03.326
leave), | i say again, hath made a gross revolt, OTH 1.01.134
and hath in his effect a voice potential | as 1.02. 13
the senate hath sent about three several quests 1.02. 46
faith, he to–night hath boarded a land carract. 1.02. 50
hath rais'd me from my bed, nor doth the general 1.03. 54
hath thus beguil'd your daughter of herself, 1.03. 66
for the state affairs | hath hither brought. 1.03. 73
and front of my offending | hath this extent, no 1.03. 81
hath made the flinty and steel /couch of war 1.03.230
thine hath no less reason. 1.03.367 P
he hath a person and a smooth dispose | to be 1.03.397
methinks the wind hath spoke aloud at land, | a 2.01. 5
if it hath ruffian'd so upon the sea, | what 2.01. 7
the desperate tempest hath so bang'd the turks, 2.01. 21
hath seen a grievous wrack and sufferance | on 2.01. 23
he hath achiev'd a maid | that paragons 2.01. 61
i fear | my soul hath her content so absolute 2.01.191
and hath all those requisites in him that folly 2.01.246 P
knave, and the woman hath found him already. 2.01.248 P
the lusty moor | hath leap'd into my seat; 2.01.296
iago hath direction what to do; 2.03. 4
he hath not yet made wanton the night with her; 2.03. 16 P
with that which he hath drunk to–night already, 2.03. 49
whom love hath turn'd almost the wrong side out, 2.03. 52
to desdemona hath to–night carous'd | potations 2.03. 53
that | which heaven hath forbid the ottomites? 2.03.171
stillness of your youth | the world hath noted, 2.03.192
it hath pleas'd the devil drunkenness to give 2.03.296 P
for that he hath devoted and given up himself to 2.03.316 P
cassio hath beaten thee, | and thou by that 2.03.374
that he hath left part of his grief with me | to 3.03. 53
hath ta'en your part — to have so much to do 3.03. 73
i see this hath a little dash'd your spirits. 3.03.214
my wayward husband hath a hundred times | woo'd 3.03.292
it /yet hath felt no age nor known no sorrow. 3.04. 37
hath founded his good fortunes on your love, 3.04. 94
when it hath blown his ranks into the air, | and 3.04.135
cyprus to him, | hath puddled his clear spirit; 3.04.143
hath he said any thing? 4.01. 29
he hath, my lord, but be you well assur'd, | no 4.01. 30
what hath he said? 4.01. 31
and when | he hath, and is again to cope your 4.01. 86
she gave it him, and he hath giv'n it his whore. 4.01.177 P
o, the world hath not a sweeter creature! 4.01.184 P
in her bed, even the bed she hath contaminated. 4.01.208 P
alas, iago, my lord hath so bewhor'd her, 4.02.115
hath she forsook so many noble matches? 4.02.125
you have told me she hath receiv'd them and 4.02.188 P
it hath not appear'd. 4.02.209 P
i grant indeed it hath not appear'd; 4.02.210 P
and hath commanded me to go to bed, | and bid me 4.03. 13
and yet he hath given me satisfying reasons. 5.01. 9
he hath a daily beauty in his life | that makes 5.01. 19
cassio hath here been set on in the dark | by 5.01.112
and tell my lord and lady what hath happ'd. 5.01.127
he hath confess'd. 5.02. 68
that he hath us'd thee. 5.02. 70
honest iago hath ta'en order for't. 5.02. 72
hath kill'd a young venetian | call'd roderigo. 5.02.112
o, who hath done this deed? 5.02.123
o mistress, villainy hath made mocks with love! 5.02.151
the moor hath kill'd my mistress! 5.02.167
that she with cassio hath the act of shame | a 5.02.211
the woman falls; sure he hath kill'd his wife. 5.02.236
this wretch hath part confess'd his villainy. 5.02.296
why he hath thus ensnar'd my soul and body? 5.02.302
sir, you shall understand what hath befall'n, 5.02.307
which in the scuffles of great fights hath burst ANT 1.01. 7
on the sudden | a roman thought hath strook him. 1.02. 83
hath with his parthian force | extended asia; 1.02.100
act upon her, she hath such a celerity in dying. 1.02.144 P
the business she hath broached in the state 1.02.171
like the courser's hair, hath yet but life, 1.02.193
it hath been taught us from the primal state 1.04. 41
that great med'cine hath | with his tinct gilded 1.05. 36
for he hath laid strange courtesies and great 2.02.154
be it art or hap, | he hath spoken true. 2.03. 34
and that is it | hath made me rig my navy, at 2.06. 20
itself, and it is as broad as it hath breadth. 2.07. 43 P
e'er thy tongue | hath so betray'd thine act. 2.07. 78
that the conquering wine hath steep'd our sense 2.07.107
the wild disguise hath almost | antick'd us all. 2.07.124
the man hath seen some majesty, and should know. 3.03. 42
hath he seen majesty? 3.03. 43
but he hath wag'd | new wars 'gainst pompey; 3.04. 3
their lust | since then hath made between them. 3.06. 8
sister, cleopatra | hath nodded him to her. 3.06. 66
he hath given his empire | up to a whore, who 3.06. 66
he hath assembled | bocchus, the king of libya; 3.06. 68
so hath my lord dar'd him to single fight. 3.07. 30
oft | (when he hath mus'd of taking kingdoms in) 3.13. 83
our force by land | hath nobly held; 3.13.170
my messenger | he hath whipt with rods, dares me 4.01. 3
for this pains | caesar hath hang'd him. 4.06. 15
antony | hath after thee sent all thy treasure, 4.06. 20
he hath fought to–day | as if a god, in hate of 4.08. 24
the hand of death hath raught him. 4.09. 29
this foul egyptian hath betrayed me. 4.12. 10
my fleet hath yielded to the foe, and yonder 4.12. 11
hath at fast and loose | beguil'd me to the very 4.12. 28
to the young roman boy she hath sold me, and i 4.12. 48
she hath betray'd me, and shall die the death. 4.14. 26
a prophesying fear | of what hath come to pass; 4.14.121
work, hath sent | me to proclaim the truth, and 4.14.125
not caesar's valor hath o'erthrown antony, | but 4.15. 14
antony, | but antony's hath triumph'd on itself. 4.15. 15
which writ his honor in the acts it did | hath, 5.01. 23
caesar knows, | and he hath sent for thee. 5.02. 66
caesar hath sent — 5.02.321
tells me | she hath pursu'd conclusions infinite 5.02.355
hath referr'd herself | unto a poor but worthy CYM 1.01. 6
he that hath lost her too; 1.01. 11
hath a heart that is not | glad at the thing 1.01. 14
he that hath miss'd the princess is a thing 1.01. 16
and he that hath her | (i mean, that married her 1.01. 17
hath charg'd you should not speak together. 1.01. 83
this hath been | your faithful servant. 1.01.173
the violence of action hath made you reek as a 1.02. 2 P
so worthy as since he hath been allow'd the name 1.04. 3 P
which hath the king | five times redeem'd from 1.05. 62
a wedded lady | that hath her husband banish'd. 1.06. 3
hath nature given them eyes | to see this 1.06. 32
us, he hath a court | he little cares for and a 1.06.153
the credit that thy lady hath of thee | deserves 1.06.157
he hath a kind of honor sets him off, | more 1.06.170
which hath | honor'd with confirmation your 1.06.173
since | my lord hath interest in them, i will 1.06.195
every jack slave hath his bellyful of fighting, 2.01. 20 P
sleep hath seiz'd me wholly. 2.02. 7
she hath been reading late | the tale of tereus; 2.02. 44
is too new, | she hath not yet forgot him. 2.03. 42
garment | that ever hath but clipt his body, is 2.03.134
a jewel that too casually | hath left mine arm. 2.03.142
this, your king | hath heard of great augustus. 2.04. 11
being corrupted, | hath stol'n it from her? 2.04.117
no, he hath enjoy'd her. 2.04.126
she hath bought the name of whore thus dearly. 2.04.128
never talk on't: | she hath been colted by him. 2.04.133
the present wrath | he hath against himself. 2.04.152
use the sword of caesar | hath too much mangled, 3.01. 56
that hath moe kings his servants than | thyself 3.01. 63
hath prevail'd | on thy too ready hearing? 3.02. 5
and hath as oft a sland'rous epitaph | as record 3.03. 52
that drug–damn'd italy hath outcraftied him, 3.04. 15
pisanio, hath play'd the strumpet in my bed; 3.04. 21 P
she hath my letter for the purpose; 3.04. 29 P
sword, the paper | hath cut her throat already! 3.04. 33
mother was her painting) hath betray'd him. 3.04. 50
art, hath done you both | this cursed injury. 3.04.121
whose love–suit hath been to me | as fearful as 3.04.133
hath britain all the sun that shines? 3.04.136
my emperor hath wrote i must from hence, | and 3.05. 2
lucius hath wrote already to the emperor | how 3.05. 21
the pow'rs that he already hath in gallia | will 3.05. 24
that it would be thus | hath made us forward. 3.05. 29
she hath not appear'd | before the roman, nor to 3.05. 30
nor to us hath tender'd | the duty of the day. 3.05. 31
of posthumus, most retir'd | hath her life been; 3.05. 37
he hath a drug of mine; 3.05. 57
haply despair hath seiz'd her; 3.05. 60
and that she hath all courtly parts more 3.05. 71
from every one | the best she hath, and she, of 3.05. 73
on his dead body, and when my lust hath din'd 3.05.141 P
she hath despis'd me rejoicingly, and i'll be 3.05.144 P
nature hath meal and bran, contempt and grace. 4.02. 27
appears he hath had | good ancestors. 4.02. 47
those runagates, that villain | hath mock'd me. 4.02. 63
but time hath nothing blurr'd those lines of 4.02.104
if we do fear this body hath a tail | more 4.02.144
howsoe'er, | my brother hath done well. 4.02.147
occasion | hath cadwal now to give it motion? 4.02.188
to th' east, | my father hath a reason for't. 4.02.256
devil cloten, | hath here cut off my lord. 4.02.316
damn'd pisanio | hath with his forged letters 4.02.318
the senate hath stirr'd up the confiners | and 4.02.337
nature did) | hath alter'd that good picture? 4.02.365
friends, | the boy hath taught us manly duties. 4.02.397
hath not deserv'd my service nor your loves, 4.04. 25
or hath moe ministers than we | that draw his 5.03. 72
hath my poor boy done aught but well, | whose 5.04. 35
like hardiment posthumus hath | to cymbeline 5.04. 75
profit, but my wish hath a preferment in't. 5.04.206 P
he hath been search'd among the dead and living; 5.05. 11
he hath done no britain harm, | though he have 5.05. 90
and hath | more of thee merited than a band of 5.05.303
he it is that hath | assum'd this age: 5.05.318
who hath upon him still that natural stamp. 5.05.366
abridgment | hath to it circumstantial branches, 5.05.383
this hath some seeming. 5.05.452
it hath been sung at festivals, | on ember–eves PER 1.ch. 5
who hath taught | my frail mortality to know 1.01. 41
he hath found the meaning, | for which we mean 1.01.143
men should be, | till he hath pass'd necessity. 2.ch. 6
alas, the seas hath cast me on the rocks, 2.01. 5
may see the sea hath cast upon your coast — 2.01. 56
hath made the ball | for them to play upon, 2.01. 60
and i'll tell you, he hath a fair daughter, and 2.01.108 P
it hath been a shield | 'twixt me and death" — 2.01.126
which shows that beauty hath his power and will, 2.02. 34
in framing an artist, art hath thus decreed, 2.03. 15
the which hath fire in darkness, none in light: 2.03. 44
she hath so strictly tied | her to her chamber, 2.05. 8
this by the eye of cynthia hath she vowed, | and 2.05. 11
now sleep yslacked hath the rout, | no din but 3.ch. 1
hymen hath brought the bride to bed, | where, by 3.ch. 9
half the flood | hath their keel cut. 3.ch. 46
fear the flaw, | it hath done to me the worst. 3.01. 40
with us at sea it hath been still observ'd, and 3.01. 51 P

hath built lord cerimon | such strong renown as 3.02. 47
she hath not been | entranc'd above five hours. 3.02. 93
heavenly jewels | which pericles hath lost, 3.02. 99
who hath gain'd | of education all the grace, 4.ch. 8
our cleon hath | one daughter, and a full–grown 4.ch. 15
dead, | and cursed dionyza hath | the pregnant 4.ch. 43
on whom foul death hath made this slaughter. 4.04. 37
hath thetis' birth–child on the heavens bestowed 4.04. 41
hath your principal made known unto you who i am 4.06. 82 P
i doubt not but thy training hath been noble. 4.06.112
as hath been belch'd on by infected lungs. 4.06.169
since my master and mistress hath bought you, 4.06.196 P
a man who for this three months hath not spoken 5.01. 24
be, hath endur'd a grief | might equal yours, if 5.01. 87
kings, | but time hath rooted out my parentage, 5.01. 92
as my good nurse lychorida hath oft | delivered 5.01.159
is like to be, | that thus hath made me weep. 5.01.185
lord cerimon hath letters of good credit, sir, 5.03. 77
now for the love of him whom jove hath mark'd TNK 1.01. 29
some god hath put his mercy in your manhood, 1.01. 72
where every evil | hath a good color; 1.02. 39
appalls) hath sent | deadly defiance to him, and 1.02. 90
of our fate, | who hath bounded our last minute. 1.02.103
yet fate hath brought them off. 1.03. 41
and like enough the duke hath taken notice 2.02.227
strong note of me, | hath made me near her; 3.01. 18
in me hath grief slain fear, and, but for one 3.02. 5
surfeit of her eye hath distemper'd the other 4.03. 70 P
of love as she says palamon hath sung in prison. 4.03. 82 P
there's many a man alive that hath outliv'd 5.04. 1
what | hath wak'd us from our dream? 5.04. 48
the powerful venus well hath grac'd her altar, 5.04.105
your kinsman hath confess'd the right o' th' 5.04.116
hath chid down all the majesty of england, STM II.C 73
for to the king god hath his office lent | of II.C 98
hath bid him rule, and will'd you to obey; II.C 100
he hath not only lent the king his figure, | his II.C 102
saith that the world hath ending with thy life. VEN 12
yet hath he been my captive, and my slave, | and 101
"over my altars hath he hung his lance, | his 103
and for my sake hath learn'd to sport and dance, 105
the heart hath treble wrong | when it is barr'd 329
because adonis' heart hath made mine hard." 378
the sea hath bounds, but deep desire hath none, 389
the sea hath bounds, but deep desire hath none, 389
but, when his glutton eye so full hath fed, 399
thy mermaid's voice hath done me double wrong: 429
hath taught them scornful tricks, and such 501
his day's hot task hath ended in the west; 530
now quick desire hath caught the yielding prey, 547
she hath assay'd as much as may be prov'd. 608
her pleading hath deserv'd a greater fee; 609
"on his bow–back he hath a battle set | of 619
beauty hath nought to do with such foul fiends. 638
"and therefore hath she brib'd the destinies 733
under whose simple semblance he hath fed | upon 795
hath dropp'd a precious jewel in the flood, | or 824
for who hath she to spend the night withal, 847
when he hath ceas'd his ill–resounding noise, 919
now she unweaves the web that she hath wrought: 991
he, foul creature, that hath done thee wrong, 1005
grief hath two tongues, and never woman yet 1007
to recreate himself when he hath song, | the 1095
he thought to kiss him, and hath kill'd him so. 1110
in that high task hath done her beauty wrong, LUC 80
this siege that hath engirt his marriage, | this 221
hath barr'd him from the blessed thing he sought 340
so from himself impiety hath wrought, | that for 341
love's fire fear's frost hath dissolution. 355
that thinks she hath beheld some ghastly sprite, 451
thy beauty hath ensnar'd thee to this night, 485
only he hath an eye to gaze on beauty, | and 496
the wolf hath seiz'd his prey, the poor lamb 677
but she hath lost a dearer thing than life, 687
and he hath won what he would lose again; 688
a captive victor that hath lost in gain, 730
in thy weak hive a wand'ring wasp hath crept, 839
and scarce hath eyes his treasure to behold, 857
"so then he hath it when he cannot use it, | and 862
free that soul which wretchedness hath chained? 900
as well to hear as grant what he hath said. 915
"why hath thy servant opportunity | betray'd the 932
of that true type hath tarquin rifled me. 1050
for day hath nought to do what's done by night." 1092
sometime her grief is dumb and hath no words, 1105
chide rough winter that the flow'r hath kill'd; 1255
when more is felt than one hath power to tell. 1288
so woe hath wearied woe, moan tired moan, | that 1363
and rail on pyrrhus that hath done him wrong, 1467
alone | upon his head that hath transgressed so; 1481
whose deed hath made herself herself detest. 1566
which all this time hath overslipp'd her thought 1576
that she with painted images hath spent, | being 1577
he hath no power to ask her how she fares. 1594
"what uncouth ill event | hath thee befall'n, 1599
love, what spite hath thy fair color spent? 1600
"then be this all the task it hath to say: 1618
but she, that yet her sad task hath not said, 1699
hath serv'd a dumb arrest upon his tongue, | who 1780
which she too early and too late hath spill'd." 1801
i owed her, and 'tis mine that she hath kill'd." 1803
her lips to mine how often hath she joined, PP 7. 7
how many tales to please me hath she coined, 7. 9
heart hath his hope, and eyes their wished sight 14.22
lullaby, the learned man hath got the lady gay, 15.15
my hand hath sworn | ne'er to pluck thee from 16.11
i, | love hath forlorn me, living in thrall; 17.14
when as thine eye hath chose the dame, | and 18. 1
when craft hath taught her thus to say: 18.34
love hath reason, reason none, | if what parts, PHT 47
but beauty's waste hath in the world an end, SON 9.11
let those whom nature hath not made for store, 11. 9
and summer's lease hath all too short a date; 18. 4
than that tongue that more hath more express'd. 23.12
o, learn to read what silent love hath writ: 23.13
mine eye hath play'd the painter and hath 24. 1
eye hath play'd the painter and hath /stell'd 24. 1
that hath his windows glazed with thine eyes. 24. 8
thy merit hath my duty strongly knit, | to thee 26. 2
hath dear religious love stol'n from mine eye 31. 6
the region ·loud hath mask'd him from me now. 33.12
that she hath thee, is of my wailing chief, | a 42. 3
and losing her, my friend hath found that loss; 42.10
when as thy love hath cast his utmost sum, 49. 3
since every one hath, every one, one shade, 53. 3
but that which is | hath been before, how are 59. 2
morn | hath travell'd on to age's steepy night, 63. 5
decay, | ruin hath taught me thus to ruminate, 64.11
veins, | for she hath no exchequer now but his, 67.11
by seeing farther than the eye hath shown. 69. 8
away, | my life hath in this line some interest, 74. 3
my verse | as every alien pen hath got my use, 78. 3
you still shall live (such virtue hath my pen) 81.13
do not, when my heart hath scap'd this sorrow, 90. 5
and every humor hath his adjunct pleasure, 91. 5
when in the least of them my life hath end; 92. 6
how like a winter hath my absence been | from 97. 1
hath put a spirit of youth in every thing, 98. 3
than when it hath my added praise beside. 103. 4
hath motion, and mine eye may be deceiv'd; 104.12
the mortal moon hath her eclipse endur'd, | and 107. 5
which hath not figur'd to thee my true spirit? 108. 2
of his quick objects hath the mind no part, 113. 7
what wretched errors hath my heart committed, 119. 5
whilst it hath thought itself so blessed never? 119. 6
for since each hand hath put on nature's power, 127. 5
sweet beauty hath no name, no holy bow'r, | but 127. 7
that music hath a far more pleasing sound; 130.10
thy face hath not the power to make love groan; 131. 6
me from myself thy cruel eye hath taken, | and 133. 5
whoever hath her wish, thou hast thy will, | and 135. 1
hath left me, and i desperate now approve 147. 7
what eyes hath love put in my head, | which have 148. 1
old, | not age, but sorrow, over me hath power; LC 74
the one a palate hath that needs will taste, 167
nature hath charg'd me that i hoard them not, 220
in thee hath neither sting, knot, nor confine, 265
both fire from hence and chill extincture hath. 294

HATING 2 FR 0.0002 REL FR 2 V 0 P
murther, as hating what himself hath done, JN 4.03. 37
vain, | as hating thee, /are rising up in arms; 2H6 4.01. 93

HATRED 17 FR 0.0019 REL FR 17 V 0 P
tempt not too much the hatred of my spirit, MND 2.01.211
that hatred is so far from jealousy | to sleep 4.01.144
with immodest hatred | the child–bed privilege WT 3.02.102
other's happiness, | may cease their hatred; H5 5.02.352
too, | unless they seek for hatred at my hands; 3H6 4.01. 80
to urge his hatred more to clarence | with lies R3 1.01.147
eyes, | the bleeding witness of my hatred by, 1.02.233
aiming, belike, at your interior hatred, | that 1.03. 65
and turn you all your hatred now on me? 1.03.189
dissemble not your hatred, swear your love. 2.01. 8
i will never more remember | our former hatred, 2.01. 24
mild, but yet more harmful — kind in hatred. 4.04.173
what his high hatred would effect wants not | a H8 1.01.107
we must suggest the people in what hatred | he COR 2.01.245
to seek him there, | to oppose his hatred fully. 3.01. 20
i bear no hatred, blessed man, for lo | my ROM 2.03. 53
for there can live no hatred in thine eye, SON 93. 5

HATS 6 FR 0.0006 REL FR 5 V 1 P
your rye–straw hats put on, | and these fresh TMP 4.01.136
some sleeves, some hats, from yielders all MND 3.02. 30
there's a dozen of 'em, with delicate fine hats, AWW 4.05.105 P
some that have accus'd them wear their hats. R3 3.02. 93
hats, cloaks | (doublets, i think) flew up, and H8 4.01. 73
sir, their hats are pluck'd about their ears, JC 2.01. 73

HAT'ST 1 FR 0.0001 REL FR 1 V 0 P
if thou hat'st curses, | stay not; TIM 4.03.534

HAUD 4 FR 0.0004 REL FR 0 V 4 P
sir nathaniel, haud credo. LLL 4.02. 11 P
'twas not a haud credo, 'twas a pricket. 4.02. 12 P
to insert again my haud credo for a deer. 4.02. 19 P
i said the deer was not a haud credo, 'twas a 4.02. 20 P

HAUF *(also half)*

HAUF 1 FR 0.0001 REL FR 0 V 1 P
half, "hauf"; LLL 5.01. 22 P

/HAUGHT 1 FR 0.0001 REL FR 1 V 0 P
/lord /of /thine, /thou /haught /insulting /man, R2 4.01.254

HAUGHT 2 FR 0.0002 REL FR 2 V 0 P
with clifford and the haught northumberland, 3H6 2.01.169
the queen's sons and brothers haught and proud! R3 2.03. 28

HAUGHTINESS 1 FR 0.0001 REL FR 1 V 0 P
pride, haughtiness, opinion, and disdain, | the 1H4 3.01.183

HAUGHTY 14 FR 0.0015 REL FR 14 V 0 P
with haughty arms this hateful name in us. 1H6 5.02. 40
arrogant winchester, that haughty prelate, 1H6 1.03. 23
this cardinal's more haughty than the devil. 1.03. 85
as in this haughty great attempt | they labored 2.05. 79
these haughty words of hers | have batt'red me 3.03. 78
valiant and virtuous, full of haughty courage, 4.01. 35
to us, | yet let us watch the haughty cardinal; 2H6 1.01.174
oft have i seen the haughty cardinal, | more 1.01.185
beside the haughty protector, have we beauford 1.03. 68
whose haughty spirit, winged with desire, | will 3H6 1.01.267
whose humble means match not his haughty spirit.
R3 4.02. 37
sir edward courtney and the haughty prelate, 4.04.500
thee never, nor thy traitorous haughty sons, TIT 1.01.302
this is that banish'd haughty montague, | that ROM 5.03. 49

HAUNCH 2 FR 0.0002 REL FR 1 V 1 P
divide me like a brib'd–buck, each a haunch. WIV 5.05. 24 P
which ever in the haunch of winter sings | the 2H4 4.04. 92

HAUNCHES 1 FR 0.0001 REL FR 1 V 0 P
forked heads | have their round haunches gor'd. AYL 2.01. 25

HAUNT 18 FR 0.0020 REL FR 17 V 1 P
you wrong me, sir, thus still to haunt my house. WIV 3.04. 69
and held in idle price to haunt assemblies MM 1.03. 9
i charge thee hence, and do not haunt me thus. MND 2.02. 85
and this our life, exempt from public haunt, AYL 2.01. 15
and i do haunt thee in the battle thus | because 1H4 5.03. 4
that did haunt me in my sleep | to undertake the R3 1.02.122
and, when thou wed'st, let sorrow haunt thy bed; 4.01. 73
week by days, | did haunt you in the field. TRO 4.01. 11
i'll haunt thee like a wicked conscience still, 5.10. 28
we talk here in the public haunt of men. ROM 3.01. 50
where they /most breed and haunt, i have MAC 1.06. 9
wife and children's ghosts will haunt me still. 5.07. 16
and out of haunt | this mad young man. HAM 4.01. 18
i have charg'd thee not to haunt about my doors. OTH 1.01. 96
let the devil and his dam haunt you! 4.01.148 P
shall want troops, | and all the haunt be ours. ANT 4.14. 54
what fairies haunt this ground? CYM 5.04.133
of fortune, though they haunt you mortally, PER 3.03. 6

HAUNTED 7 FR 0.0008 REL FR 6 V 1 P
our court you know is haunted | with a refined LLL 1.01.162
we are haunted. MND 3.01.104 P
what night–rule now about this haunted grove? 3.02. 5
some haunted by the ghosts they have deposed, R2 3.02.158
strain | that haunted us in our familiar paths. H5 2.04. 52
with female fairies will his tomb be haunted, CYM 4.02.217
in personal duty, following where he haunted. LC 130

HAUNTING 2 FR 0.0002 REL FR 1 V 1 P
the least of which haunting a nobleman | loseth 1H4 3.01.184
what do you mean by this haunting of me? OTH 4.01.147 P

/HAUNTS 1 FR 0.0001 REL FR 0 V 1 P
/the /foul /fiend /haunts /poor /tom /in /the LR 3.06. 29 P

HAUNTS 8 FR 0.0009 REL FR 3 V 5 P
one that claims me, one that haunts me, one that ERR 3.02. 82 P
if not, shun me, and i will spare your haunts. MND 2.01.142
there is a man haunts the forest, that abuses AYL 3.02.359 P
he haunts wakes, fairs, and bear–baitings. WT 4.03.102 P
there is a devil haunts thee in the likeness of 1H4 2.04.447 P
sequestration | from open haunts and popularity. H5 1.01. 59
suspicion always haunts the guilty mind; 3H6 5.06. 11
she haunts me in every place. OTH 4.01.132 P

HAUTBOY *(see hoboy)*

HAVE *(also 'a', ave, ha')*

/HAVE 53 FR 0.0060 REL FR 43 V 10 P

HAVE 6229 FR 0.7041 REL FR 4497 V 1732 P

HAVEN 7 FR 0.0008 REL FR 7 V 0 P
at the last | unto the wished haven of my bliss. SHR 5.01.128
from ravenspurgh haven before the gates of york, 3H6 4.07. 8
sea is given, | they have put forth the haven — ANT 4.10. 7
would not suffer me | to bring him to the haven; CYM 1.01.171
would thou grew'st unto the shores o' th' haven, 1.03. 1
was made so happy as | t' inherit such a haven. 3.02. 61
what shipping and what lading's in our haven, PER 1.02. 49

HAVENS 1 FR 0.0001 REL FR 1 V 0 P
are to a wise man ports and happy havens. R2 1.03.276

HAVER 1 FR 0.0001 REL FR 1 V 0 P
chiefest virtue, and | most dignifies the haver; COR 2.02. 85

HAVERFORD–WEST *(see ha'rford–west)*

HAVE'S 1 FR 0.0001 REL FR 1 V 0 P
and what strength i have's mine own, | which is TMP ep 2

HAVE'T 8 FR 0.0009 REL FR 7 V 1 P
i have't in my nose too. TN 2.03.163 P
nay, let me have't; WT 1.02.101
can give, | to have't with saying "good morrow." COR 3.03. 93
thou wealth again, | rascals should have't. TIM 4.03.218
i'll have't disputed on, | 'tis probable, and OTH 1.02. 75
i have't. 1.03.403
will give you satisfaction, you might have't. 3.03.408
be't as our gods will have't! ANT 2.01. 50

/HAVING 1 FR 0.0001 REL FR 1 V 0 P
/who, /having /seen /me /in /my /worst /estate, LR 5.03.210

HAVING 177 FR 0.0200 REL FR 137 V 40 P
having both the key | of officer and office, set TMP 1.02. 83
like one | who having into truth, by telling of 1.02.100
shapes as he, | having seen but him and caliban. 1.02.480
burns, | 'twill weep for having wearied you. 3.01. 19
brain him, | having first seiz'd his books; 3.02. 89
having nothing but the word "noddy" for my pains
TGV 1.01.124 P
wrack, | which cannot perish having thee aboard, 1.01.149
age, | in having known no travel in his youth. 1.03. 16
why, my grandam, having no eyes, look you, wept 2.03. 12 P
and i as rich in having such a jewel | as twenty 2.04.169
i, having been acquainted with the smell before, 4.04. 22 P
see the hell of having a false woman! WIV 2.02.292 P
belike having receiv'd wrong by some person, is 3.01. 53 P
the gentleman is of no having. 3.02. 72 P
ford, having an honest man to your husband, to 3.03. 99 P
having bound up the threat'ning twigs of birch, MM 1.03. 24
and having but two in the dish (as i said), 2.01.100 P
this very man, having eaten the rest (as i said) 2.01.101 P
having waste ground enough, | shall we desire to 2.02.169
lord angelo, having affairs to heaven, | intends 3.01. 56
she (having the truth of honor in her) hath made 3.01.164 P
having in that perish'd vessel the dowry of his 3.01.217 P
how may i do it, having the hour limited, and an 4.02.165 P
word, | and go indeed, having so good a mean. ERR 1.02. 18
you have no stomach, having broke your fast: 1.02. 50
woo hero for himself, and having obtain'd her, ADO 1.03. 63 P
having so swift and excellent a wit | as she is 3.01. 89
or, having sworn too hard–a–keeping oath, LLL 1.01. 65
having once this juice, | i'll watch titania MND 2.01.176
not fear, lady, the having any of these lords. MV 1.02.100 P
truth is that the jew, having done me wrong, 2.02.133 P
having made one, | methinks it should have power 3.02.124
life, | for, having such a blessing in his lady, 3.05. 75
and having that do choke their service up | even AYL 2.03. 61
choke their service up | even with the having. 2.03. 62
for simply your having in beard is a younger 3.02.377 P
my brother happy in having what he wishes for. 5.02. 47 P
having no other reason | but that his beard grew SHR 3.02.174
having come to padua | to gather in some debts, 4.04. 24
that, having this obtain'd, you presently AWW 2.04. 52
vanity, | having vainly fear'd too little. 5.03.123
having been three months married to her, sitting TN 2.05. 44 P
having come from a day–bed, where i have left 2.05. 48 P
my fortunes, having cast me on your niece, give 2.05. 69 P
my having is not much; 3.04.345
and, having sworn truth, ever will be true. 4.03. 33
to think that my desire of having is the sin of 5.01. 47 P
i shall incur to pass it, | having no warrant. WT 2.02. 56
having made me businesses which none without 4.02. 14 P
and, having flown over many knavish professions, 4.03. 98 P
of what having? 4.04.719 P
having both their country quitted | with this 5.01.192
having no external thing to lose | but the word JN 2.01.571
and in their rage, i having hold of both, | they 3.01.329
no, no, i will not, having breath to cry. 3.04. 37
having so great a title | to be more prince, as 4.01. 10
that, having our fair order written down, | both 5.02. 4

death, having prey'd upon the outward parts, 5.07. 15
having my freedom, boast of nothing else | but R2 1.03.273
our grandam earth, having this distemp'rature, 1H4 3.01. 33
wind | bated like eagles having lately bath'd, 4.01. 99
having been well, that would have made me sick, 2H4 1.01.138
you speak as having power to do wrong, but 2.01.129 P
the leaders, having charge from you to stand, 4.02. 99
were, | i spake unto this crown as having sense, 4.05.157
having such a son | that would deliver up his 5.02.110
charles the great, having subdu'd the saxons, H5 1.02. 46
things, having full reference | to one consent, 1.02.205
that, having neither the voice nor the heart of 5.02.287 P
having any occasion to write for matter of grant 5.02.337 P
having full scarce six thousand in his troop, 1H6 1.01.112
cowardly fled, not having struck one stroke. 1.01.134
secure, | having all day carous'd and banqueted: 2.01. 12
a triumph, having vow'd | to try his strength, 5.05. 31
cost and charges, without having any dowry." 2H6 1.01. 61 P
mine, | and, having both together heav'd it up, 1.02. 13
having neither subject, wealth, nor diadem. 4.01. 82
like to a ship that, having scap'd a tempest, 4.09. 32
who having pinch'd a few and made them cry, 3H6 2.01. 16
/e'en for the loss of thee, having no more, | as 2.05.119
having the fearful flying hare in sight, | with 2.05.130
and, having france thy friend, thou shalt not 2.06. 92
where having nothing, nothing can he lose. 3.03.152
we, having now the best at barnet field, | will 5.03. 20
having my country's peace and brothers' loves. 5.07. 36
by, | having god, her conscience, and these bars R3 1.02.234
not to kill him, having a warrant, but to be 1.04.110 P
having no more but thought of what thou wast 4.04.107
having bought love with such a bloody spoil. 4.04.290
you having lands, and blest with beauteous wives 5.03.321
having heard by fame | of this so noble and so H8 1.04. 66
his highness having liv'd so long with her, and 2.03. 2
our content | is our best having. 2.03. 23
having here | no judge indifferent, nor no more 2.04. 16
having brought the queen | to a prepar'd place 4.01. 63
he having color enough, and the other higher, is TRO 1.02.103 P
host, | having his ear full of his airy fame, 1.03.144
how much in having, or without or in, | cannot 3.03. 97
of this feast, | having fully din'd before. COR 1.09. 11
having been supple and courteous to the people, 2.02. 26 P
having determin'd of the volsces and | to send 2.02. 37
not having the power to do the good it would, 3.01.160
and thus far having stretch'd it (here be with 3.02. 74
back, that's the utmost of your having, back! 5.02. 57 P
and bear the palm for having bravely shed | thy 5.03.117
having read it, | bid them repair to th' 5.06. 2
and, having gilt the ocean with his beams, TIT 2.01. 6
is not my sorrow deep, having no bottom? 3.01.216
not having that which, having, makes them short. ROM 1.01.164
not having that which, having, makes them short. 1.01.164
by having him, making yourself no less. 1.03. 94
having some business, /do entreat her eyes | to 2.02. 16
having no other reason but because thou hast 3.01. 19 P
much, | and that we have a curse in having her. 3.05.167
and having now provided | a gentleman of noble 3.05.178
having displeas'd my father, to lawrence' cell, 3.05.232
the greatest of your having lacks a half | to TIM 2.02.144
having great and instant occasion to use fifty 3.01. 18 P
a just and true report that goes of his having. 5.01. 16
sir, | having often of your open bounty tasted, 5.01. 58
and having brought our treasure where we will, JC 4.01. 24
early, | who, having some advantage on octavius, 5.03. 6
prediction | of noble having and of royal hope, MAC 1.03. 56
the interim having weigh'd it, let us speak 1.03.154
any one, having no witness to confirm my speech. 5.01. 17 P
having ever seen in the prenominate crimes | the HAM 2.01. 43
neither having th' accent of christians nor the 3.02. 31 P
fellow | who, having been prais'd for bluntness, LR 2.02. 96
having more man than wit about me, drew. 2.04. 42
as having sense of beauty, do omit | their OTH 2.01. 71
and passion, having my best judgment collied, 2.03.206
who having, by their own importunate suit, | or 4.01. 26
and having the world for your labor, 'tis a 4.03. 81 P
us, | or scant our former having in despite: 4.03. 91
against my stomach, | having alike your cause? ANT 2.02. 51
and having lost her breath, she spoke, and 2.02.230
having a son and friends, since julius caesar, 2.06. 12
having made use of him in the wars 'gainst 3.05. 7 P
having in sicily | sextus pompeius spoil'd, we 3.06. 24
own, but he added to your having, gave you some CYM 1.02. 18 P
having thus far proceeded | (unless thou 1.05. 15
you, having proceeded but | by both your wills. 2.04. 55
but my mother, having power of his testiness, 4.01. 21 P
having work | more plentiful than tools to do't 5.03. 8
having found the back door open | of the 5.03. 45
quite crack'd, | i having ta'en the forfeit. 5.05.208
having receiv'd the punishment before | for that 5.05.343
split, | and he, good prince, having all lost, PER 2.ch. 33
and having thrown him from your wat'ry grave, 2.01. 10
and for his sake i wish the having of it; 2.01.139
will you, not having my consent, | bestow your 2.05. 76
in brass, | having call'd them from the deep! 3.01. 4
your lordship, having | rich tire about you, 3.02. 21
and having wooed | a villain to attempt it, who 5.01.172
villain to attempt it, who having drawn to do't, 5.01.173
where, having bound things scatter'd, we will TNK 1.04. 48
us not, | having our ancient reputation with us, 3.03. 11
that, having two fair gauds of equal sweetness, 4.02. 53
having these virtues, | i think he might be 5.02. 55
but having no defects, why dost abhor me? VEN 138
that the star-gazers, having writ on death, 509
and having felt the sweetness of the spoil, 553
but having thee at vantage (wondrous dread!) 635
do burn themselves for having so offended." 810
having lost the fair discovery of her way. 828
having no fair to lose, you need not fear, | the 1083
eye, | which having all, all could not satisfy; LUC 96
in having much, torments us with defect | of 151
having solicited th' eternal power | that his 345
having no other pleasure of his gain | but 860
conclusion | who, having two sweet babes, when 1161
for having traffic with thyself alone, | thou of SON 4. 9
and having climb'd the steep-up heavenly hill, 7. 5
and having thee, of all men's pride i boast: 91.12
that, having such a scope to show her pride, 103. 2
had, having, and in quest to have, extreme, | a 129.10
why so large cost, having so short a lease, 146. 5

HAVINGS 2 FR 0.0002 REL FR 2 V 0 P
but par'd my present havings, to bestow | my H8 3.02.159
whose rarest havings made the blossoms dote, LC 235

HAVIOR 6 FR 0.0006 REL FR 5 V 1 P
i will keep the havior of reputation. WIV 1.03. 78 P
with the same havior that your passion bears TN 3.04.206
a' gaunt, | even in the lusty havior of his son. R2 1.03. 77
eye, | nor the dejected havior of the visage, HAM 1.02. 81
and sith so neighbored to his youth and havior, 2.02. 12
put thyself | into a havior of less fear, ere CYM 3.04. 9

HAVOC 10 FR 0.0011 REL FR 9 V 1 P
nor fortune made such havoc of my means, | nor ADO 4.01.195
who hath made this havoc with them? TN 5.01.202 P
and wide havoc made | for bloody power to rush JN 2.01.220
cry "havoc," kings! 2.01.357
for a time | of pell-mell havoc and confusion. 1H4 5.01. 82
cat, | to 'tame and havoc more than she can eat. H5 1.02.173
do not cry havoc where you should but hunt COR 3.01.273
confines with a monarch's voice | cry "havoc," JC 3.01.273
this quarry cries on havoc. HAM 5.02.364
whose havoc in vast field | unearthed skulls TNK 5.01. 51

HAWK* 10 FR 0.0011 REL FR 6 V 4 P
i have a fine hawk for the bush. WIV 3.03.231 P
for a hawk, a horse, or a husband? ADO 3.04. 55 P
i'll venture so much of my hawk or hound, | but SHR 5.02. 72
when i bestride him, i soar, i am a hawk; H5 3.07. 15 P
where as the king and queen do mean to hawk. 2H6 1.02. 58
wind is southerly i know a hawk from a hand-saw. HAM 2.02.379 P
i could have kept a hawk, and well have hollow'd TNK 2.05. 11
he said may, | the third he said it was a hawk, 3.05. 70
i had rather see a wren hawk at a fly | than 5.03. 2
look as the full-fed hound or gorged hawk, LUC 694

HAWK'D 1 FR 0.0001 REL FR 1 V 0 P
was by a mousing owl hawk'd at, and kill'd. MAC 2.04. 13

HAWKING* 4 FR 0.0004 REL FR 3 V 1 P
without hawking or spitting or saying we are AYL 5.03. 12 P
dost thou love hawking? SHR in.2. 43
and draw | his arched brows, his hawking eye, AWW 1.01. 94
talking of hawking; 2H6 2.01. 49

HAWKS 5 FR 0.0005 REL FR 5 V 0 P
thou hast hawks will soar | above the morning SHR in.2. 43
between two hawks, which flies the higher pitch, 1H6 2.04. 11
my lord protector's hawks do tow'r so well; 2H6 2.01. 10
some in their hawks and hounds, some in their SON 91. 4
cost, | of more delight than hawks or horses be; 91.11

HAWTHORN 7 FR 0.0008 REL FR 3 V 4 P
like a many of these lisping hawthorn buds, that WIV 3.03. 71 P
when wheat is green, when hawthorn buds appear. MND 1.01.185
our stage, this hawthorn brake our tiring-house, 3.01. 4 P
gives not the hawthorn bush a sweeter shade | to 3H6 2.05. 42
"through the sharp hawthorn blow the /cold winds LR 3.04. 47 P
still through the hawthorn blows the cold wind: 3.04. 98 P
again betake you to your hawthorn house. TNK 3.01. 82

HAWTHORNS 1 FR 0.0001 REL FR 0 V 1 P
hangs odes upon hawthorns and elegies on AYL 3.02.361 P

HAY* 10 FR 0.0011 REL FR 5 V 5 P
to the worthies, and let them dance the hay. LLL 5.01.154
i have a great desire to a bottle of hay. MND 4.01. 33 P
good hay, sweet hay, hath no fellow. 4.01. 33 P
good hay, sweet hay, hath no fellow. 4.01. 33 P
my aunts, | while we lie tumbling in the hay. WT 4.03. 12
cold biting winter mars our hop'd-for hay. 3H6 4.08. 61
immortal passado, the punto reverso, the hay! ROM 2.04. 26 P
i'll drain him dry as hay: MAC 1.03. 18
in pure kindness to his horse, butter'd his hay. LR 2.04.126 P
th' accounts | of all his hay and provender. TNK 5.02. 59

HAYSTALKS 1 FR 0.0001 REL FR 1 V 0 P
set fire on barns and haystalks in the night, TIT 5.01.133

/HAZARD 1 FR 0.0001 REL FR 1 V 0 P
/sets /all /on /hazard — /and /hither /am /i TRO pr 22

HAZARD 46 FR 0.0052 REL FR 41 V 5 P
climb it | without apparent hazard of his life. TGV 3.01.116
to hazard life, and rescue you from him | that 5.04. 21
of my cunning, i will lay myself in hazard. MM 4.02.156 P
both | or bring your latter hazard back again, MV 1.01.151
after dinner | your hazard shall be made. 2.01. 45
chooseth me must give and hazard all he hath." 2.07. 9
chooseth me must give and hazard all he hath." 2.07. 16
hazard for lead? 2.07. 17
men that hazard all | do it in hope of fair 2.07. 18
i'll then nor give nor hazard aught for lead. 2.07. 21
that comes to hazard for my worthless self. 2.09. 18
chooseth me must give and hazard all he hath." 2.09. 21
you shall look fairer ere i give or hazard. 2.09. 22
pause a day or two | before you hazard, for in 3.02. 2
thou this to hazard needs must intimate | skill AWW 2.01.183
worthy sake | to th' extreme edge of hazard. 3.03. 6
and to the hazard of | all incertainties himself WT 3.02.168
backs, | to make a hazard of new fortunes here. JN 2.01. 71
my heart, | albeit i make a hazard of my head. 1H4 1.03.128
main | on the nice hazard of one doubtful hour? 4.01. 48
that your attempts may overlive the hazard | and 2H4 4.01. 15
shall strike his father's crown into the hazard. H5 1.02.263
who will go to hazard with me for twenty 3.07. 85 P
you must first go yourself to hazard, ere you 3.07. 87 P
to hazard all our lives in one small boat! 1H6 4.06. 33
all these, and more, we hazard by thy stay; 4.06. 40
cast, | and i will stand the hazard of the die. R3 5.04. 10
this mutiny were better put in hazard | than COR 2.03.256
to your fortune and | the hazard of much blood. 3.02. 61
that which shall break his neck, or hazard mine, 4.07. 25
kill, | what folly 'tis to hazard life for ill! TIM 3.05. 37
oft thou shouldst hazard thy life for thy dinner 4.03.335 P
we stand much hazard if they bring not timon. 5.02. 5
and by the hazard of the spotted die | let die 5.04. 34
the storm is up, and all is on the hazard. JC 5.01. 68
endure | hazard so near 's as doth hourly grow HAM 3.03. 6
should hazard such a place as his own second OTH 2.03.139
give up yourself merely to chance and hazard, ANT 3.07. 47
would hazard the winning both of first and last. CYM 1.04. 93 P
the hazard therefore due fall on me by | the 4.04. 46
think death no hazard in this enterprise. PER 1.01. 5
let 'em suffer | the gall of hazard, so they TNK 2.02. 66
and in this madness if i hazard thee | and take 2.02.202
do make my cause | your personal hazard. 5.01. 74
is, when the thread of hazard is once spun, | a STM III 20
such hazard now must doting tarquin make, LUC 155

HAZARDED 2 FR 0.0002 REL FR 2 V 0 P
to see, | i hazarded the loss of whom i lov'd. ERR 1.01.131
for her heirs, | now hazarded to thy grace. ANT 3.12. 19

HAZARDS 4 FR 0.0004 REL FR 4 V 0 P
which fault lies on the hazards of all husbands JN 1.01.119
i will upon all hazards well believe | thou art 5.06. 7
well | my hazards still have been your solace, COR 4.01. 28
thorough the hazards of this untrod state | with JC 3.01.136

HAZEL 1 FR 0.0001 REL FR 0 V 1 P
other reason but because thou hast hazel eyes. ROM 3.01. 20 P

HAZEL-NUT 1 FR 0.0001 REL FR 1 V 0 P
her chariot is an empty hazel-nut, | made by the ROM 1.04. 59

HAZEL-NUTS 1 FR 0.0001 REL FR 1 V 0 P
and as brown in hue | as hazel-nuts, and sweeter SHR 2.01.255

HAZEL-TWIG 1 FR 0.0001 REL FR 1 V 0 P
kate like the hazel-twig | is straight and SHR 2.01.253

HE* *(also 'a)*

/HE* 42 FR 0.0047 REL FR 33 V 9 P

HE* 6683 FR 0.7554 REL FR 4692 V 1991 P

/HEAD 6 FR 0.0006 REL FR 4 V 2 P
have operations /in /my /head which be humors of WIV 1.03. 89 P
/like /herne, /with /huge /horns /on /his /head. 4.04. 43
/give /this /heavy /weight /from /off /my /head, R2 4.01.204
/before /you /said, | "/let /us /make /head." 2H4 1.01.168
/that /threw'st /dust /upon /his /goodly /head 1.03.103
/i /mean, /my /head /upon /your /lap? HAM 3.02.114 P

HEAD 512 FR 0.0578 REL FR 396 V 116 P
his bold head | 'bove the contentious waves he TMP 2.01.118
sees a crown | dropping upon thy head. 2.01.209
it did before, i know not where to hide my head. 2.02. 23 P
thy eyes are almost set in thy head. 3.02. 9 P
trinculo, keep a good tongue in your head. 3.02. 35 P
where thou mayst knock a nail into his head. 3.02. 61
thou liv'st, keep a good tongue in thy head. 3.02.112 P
now does my project gather to a head: 5.01. 1
if these be true spies which i wear in my head, 5.01.260 P
his head unmellowed, but his judgment ripe; TGV 2.04. 70
it, heap on your head | a pack of sorrows which 3.01. 19
not a hair on 's head but 'tis a valentine. 3.01.192 P
slender, i broke your head; WIV 1.01.122 P
sir, i have matter in my head against you, and 1.01.123 P
his hands as any is between this and his head. 1.04. 26 P
does he not hold up his head, as it were, and 1.04. 29 P
page, i shall turn your head out of my door. 1.04.124 P
faith, thou hast some crotchets in thy head now. 2.01.155 P
of her than sharp words, let it lie on my head. 2.01.184 P
i would have nothing lie on my head. 2.01.187 P
of a peck, hilt to point, heel to head; 3.05.112 P
come hither, william; hold up your head; come. 4.01. 17 P
hold up your head. 4.01. 19 P
page and i will look some linen for your head. 4.02. 81 P
with ribands pendant, flaring 'bout her head; 4.06. 42
i say, time wears, hold up your head and mince. 5.01. 7 P
out of our hearts by the head and shoulders, and 5.05.148 P
these three days his head to be chopp'd off. MM 1.02. 69 P
and thy head stands so tickle on thy shoulders 1.02.172 P
if you head and hang all that offend that way 2.01.238 P
none, but such remedy as, to save a head, | to 3.01. 61
and deliberate word | nips youth i' th' head, 3.01. 90
can you cut off a man's head? 4.02. 2 P
if he be a married man, he's his wive's head, 4.02. 4 P
head, and i can never cut off a woman's head. 4.02. 5 P
let me have claudio's head sent me by five. 4.02.123 P
to deliver his head in the view of angelo? 4.02.167 P
morning executed, and his head borne to angelo. 4.02.171 P
shave the head, and tie the beard, and say it 4.02.175 P
executioner, and off with barnardine's head. 4.02.207 P
his beard and head | just of his color. 4.03. 72
quick, dispatch, and send the head to angelo. 4.03. 92
here is the head, i'll carry it myself. 4.03.102
the world, | his head is off and sent to angelo. 4.03.116
and to the head of angelo | accuse him home and 4.03.142
i dare not for my head fill my belly; 4.03.154 P
upon the act of fornication | to lose his head, 5.01. 71
he sends a warrant | for my poor brother's head. 5.01.103
should have died when claudio lost his head — 5.01.488
you home | the head of ragozine for claudio's, 5.01.533
between you, i shall have a holy head. ERR 2.01. 80
leave battering, i had rather have it a head. 2.02. 36 P
i must get a sconce for my head, and insconce it 2.02. 37 P
no longer from head to foot than from hip to hip 3.02.113 P
and thereof comes it that his head is light. 5.01. 72
would not have his head on her shoulders for all ADO 1.01.114 P
me like an old cuckold with horns on his head, 2.01. 45 P
i know you by the waggling of your head. 2.01.115 P
come, you shake the head at so long a breathing, 2.01.362 P
from the crown of his head to the sole of his 3.02. 9 P
know, claudio, to thy head, | thou hast so 5.01. 62
bull's horns on the sensible benedick's head? 5.01.182 P
i'll lay my head to any good man's hat, | these LLL 1.01.308
pray you, which is the head lady? 4.01. 43 P
i assure ye it was a buck of the first head. 4.02. 10 P
bows not his vassal head and, strooken blind, 4.03.220
when the suspicious head of theft is stopp'd. 4.03.333
a word, for thou art not so long by the head as 5.01. 40 P
spell'd backward, with the horn on his head? 5.01. 48 P
i beseech thee apparel thy head; 5.01. 99 P
with libbard's head on knee. 5.02.548
the head of a bodkin. 5.02.611 P
hide thy head, achilles — here comes hector in 5.02.632 P
demetrius, i'll avouch it to his head, | made MND 1.01.106
bow, | by his best arrow with the golden head, 1.01.170
for i upon this bank will rest my head. 2.02. 40
take, | an ass's nole i fixed on his head. 3.02. 17
where dost thou hide thy head? 3.02.406
and stick musk-roses in thy sleek smooth head, 4.01. 3
scratch my head, peaseblossom. 4.01. 7 P
from off the head of this athenian swain, | that 4.01. 65
robin, take off this head. 4.01. 80
i beg the law, the law, upon his head. 4.01.155
he should have worn the horns on his head. 5.01.241 P
i have ne'er a tongue in my head, well! MV 2.02.157 P

nor thrust your head into the public street | to 2.05. 32
whose ambitious head | spets in the face of 2.07. 44
did i deserve no more than a fool's head? 2.09. 59
you will to bed, | i will ever be your head. 2.09. 71
with one fool's head i came to woo, | but i go 2.09. 75
who dare scarce show his head on the rialto; 3.01. 45 P
is fancy bred, | or in the heart or in the head? 3.02. 64
often known | to be the dowry of a second head, 3.02. 95
a soft and dull–ey'd fool | to shake the head, 3.03. 15
i never knew so young a body with so old a head. 4.01.164 P
my deeds upon my head! 4.01.206
on forfeit of my hands, my head, my heart. 4.01.212
wears yet a precious jewel in his head; AYL 2.01. 14
is his head worth a hat? 3.02.206 P
the matter's in my head and in my heart. 3.05.137
comes slowly, he carries his house on his head; 4.01. 55 P
your doublet and hose pluck'd over your head, 4.01.203 P
do well to set the deer's horns upon his head, 4.02. 5 P
who with her head nimble in threats approach'd 4.03.109
lay couching, head on ground, with cat–like 4.03.115
cover thy head, cover thy head; 5.01. 16 P
cover thy head, cover thy head; 5.01. 17 P
balm his foul head in warm distilled waters, SHR in.1. 48
and with declining head into his bosom, | bid in.1. 119
or an old trot with ne'er a tooth in her head, 1.02. 80 P
sir, give him head, i know he'll prove a jade. 1.02.247
and with that word she strook me on the head, 2.01.153
'tis in my head to do my master good. 2.01.406
with no greater a run but my head and my neck. 4.01. 16 P
head, and butt! 5.02. 40
would say your head and butt were head and horn. 5.02. 41
would say your head and butt were head and horn. 5.02. 41
thy life, thy keeper, | thy head, thy sovereign; 5.02.147
and my prayers pluck down, | fall on thy head! AWW 1.01. 70
/loneliness, and find | your salt tears' head. 1.03.172
the better whilst i have a tooth in my head. 2.03. 42 P
to pluck his indignation on thy head | by the 3.02. 30
come, headsman, off with his head. 4.03.308 P
and most courteous feathers, which bow the head, 4.05.106 P
then hadst thou had an excellent head of hair. TN 1.03. 95 P
though now you have no sea–cap on your head. 3.04.330
h'as broke my head across and has given sir toby 5.01.175 P
you broke my head for nothing, and that that i 5.01.185 P
knee–deep, o'er head and ears a fork'd one! WT 1.02.186
sometimes her head on one side, some another — 3.03. 20
what maids lack from head to heel. 4.04.227
any toys for your head | of the new'st and 4.04.319
with honey, set on the head of a wasp's nest; 4.04.784 P
life in me, would preferment drop on my head. 5.02.114 P
pour your graces | upon my daughter's head! 5.03.123
or no, | that still i lay upon my mother's head, JN 1.01. 76
makes it take head from all indifferency, | from 2.01.579
what dost thou mean by shaking of thy head? 3.01. 19
but as we, under /god, are supreme head, | so 3.01.155
and raise the power of france upon his head, 3.01.193
i will denounce a curse upon his head. 3.01.319
austria's head lie there, | while philip 3.02. 3
i will not keep this form upon my head | when 3.04.101
when your head did but ache, | i knit my 4.01. 41
and with my hand at midnight held your head; 4.01. 45
out, | and strew'd repentant ashes on his head. 4.01.110
not seek to stuff | my head with more ill news, 4.02.134
then let the worst unheard fall on your head. 4.02.136
hadst thou but shook thy head or made a pause 4.02.231
before i drew this gallant head of war, | and 5.02.113
from false mowbray their first head and spring. R2 1.01. 97
lift me up | to reach at victory above my head, 1.03. 72
whose compass is no bigger than thy head, | and 2.01.101
this tongue that runs so roundly in thy head 2.01.122
head | should run thy head from thy unreverent 2.01.123
you pluck a thousand dangers on your head, | you 2.01.205
the king had cut off my head with my brother's. 2.02.102
richard not far from hence hath hid his head. 3.03. 6
when such a sacred king should hide his head! 3.03. 9
for taking so the head, your whole head's length 3.03. 14
that lift your vassal hands against my head, 3.03. 89
that spring from one most gracious head, | and 3.03.108
may hourly trample on their sovereign's head; 3.03.157
i live, | and buried once, why not upon my head? 3.03.159
as far as callice, to mine uncle's head?" 4.01. 13
ere foul sin gathering head | shall break into 5.01. 58
my guilt be on my head, and there an end. 5.01. 69
threw dust and rubbish on king richard's head. 5.02. 6
but dust was thrown upon his sacred head, 5.02. 30
hand | upon my head and all this famous land. 5.06. 36
and never show thy head by day nor light. 5.06. 44
rob them, cut this head off from my shoulders. 1H4 1.02.166 P
and hid his crisp head in the hollow bank 1.03.106
my heart, | albeit i make a hazard of my head. 1.03.128
the crown | upon the head of this forgetful man, 1.03.161
speed, | to save our heads by raising of a head, 1.03.284
hast thou never an eye in thy head? 2.01. 28 P
three times hath henry bullingbrook made head 3.01. 63
down, | and rest your gentle head upon her lap, 3.01.212
quick, quick, that i may lay my head in thy lap. 3.01.227 P
wouldst thou have thy head broken? 3.01.237 P
turns head against the lion's armed jaws, | and, 3.02.102
i will redeem all this on percy's head, | and in 3.02.132
and on my head | my shames redoubled! 3.02.143
a mighty and a fearful head they are, | if 3.02.167
if we without his help can make a head | to push 4.01. 80
drove us to seek out | this head of safety, and 4.03.103
of worcester, and a head | of gallant warriors, 4.04. 25
the special head of all the land together: 4.04. 28
it rain'd down fortune show'ring on your head, 5.01. 47
out of your sight and raise this present head, 5.01. 66
this present enterprise set off his head, | i do 5.01. 88
all his offenses live upon my head | and on his 5.02. 20
what honor dost thou seek | upon my head? 5.03. 3
hold up thy head, vile scot, or thou art like 5.04. 39
i'll crop, to make a garland for my head. 5.04. 73
stoop'd his anointed head as low as death. 2H4 in 32
with that he gave his able horse the head, | and 1.01. 43
thou shak'st thy head, and hold'st it fear or 1.01. 95
that art a guard too wanton for the head | which 1.01.148
with a white head and something a round belly. 1.02.188 P
can peep out his head but i am thrust upon it. 1.02.213 P
may hold up head without northumberland? 1.03. 17
dinner to the lubber's head in lumbert street, 2.01. 28 P
cut me off the villain's head, throw the quean 2.01. 47 P
the prince broke thy head for liking his father 2.01. 89 P
uneasy lies the head that wears a crown. 3.01. 31
time will come, that foul sin, gathering head, 3.01. 76
see him break scoggin's head at the court–gate, 3.02. 30 P
him well, and betted much money on his head. 3.02. 45 P
with a head fantastically carv'd upon it with a 3.02.311 P
and then he burst his head for crowding among 3.02.323 P
hearse | be drops of balm to sanctify thy head; 4.05.114
royal liege, | accusing it, i put it on my head, 4.05.165
of it, | let god for ever keep it from my head, 4.05.174
well | how troublesome it sate upon my head. 4.05.186
then, pistol, lay thy head in furies' lap. 5.03.106
the sin upon my head, dread sovereign! H5 1.02. 97
th' advised head defends itself at home; 1.02.179
act | for which we have in head assembled them? 2.02. 18
turn head, and stop pursuit; 2.04. 69
them know | of what a monarchy you are the head. 2.04. 73
and on your head | turning the widows' tears, 2.04.105
let it pry through the portage of the head 3.01. 10
for 'a never broke any man's head but his own, 3.02. 40 P
so chrish save me, i will cut off your head. 3.02.133 P
let him cry, "praise and glory on his head!" 4.pr. 31
a good soft pillow for that good white head 4.01. 14
the ill upon his own head, the king is not to 4.01.187 P
abominable gloucester, guard thy head, | for i 1H6 1.03. 87
my lord, my lord, the french have gather'd head. 1.04.100
the shame hereof will make me hide my head. 1.05. 39
my father, earl of cambridge, lost his head. 2.05. 54
roan hangs her head for grief | that such a 3.02.124
lord bishop, set the crown upon his head. 4.01. 1
and let her head fall into england's lap. 5.03. 26
hand, | and set a precious crown upon thy head, 5.03.119
and shakes his head, and trembling stands aloof, 2H6 1.01.227
fist, | nor wear the diadem upon his head, 1.01.246
hanging the head at ceres' plenteous load? 1.02. 2
face, | until thy head be circled with the same. 1.02. 10
grove | shall lose his head for his presumption. 1.02. 34
to me, | and on my head did set the diadem. 1.02. 40
and set the triple crown upon his head — | that 1.03. 63
would make thee quickly hop without thy head. 1.03.137
i'll have thy head for this thy traitor's speech 1.03.194
the ringleader and head of all this rout, | have 2.01.166
will bring thy head with sorrow to the ground! 2.03. 19
causeless have laid disgraces on my head, | and 3.01.162
to rage | until the golden circuit on my head, 3.01.352
a thousand crowns, or else lay down your head. 4.01. 16
and thought thee happy when i shook my head? 4.01. 55
on our longboat's side | strike off his head. 4.01. 69
no, rather let my head | stoop to the block than 4.01.124
there let his head and liveless body lie, 4.01.142
have the lord say's head for selling the dukedom 4.02.161 P
no, no, and therefore we'll have his head. 4.02.173 P
here may his head lie on my throbbing breast; 4.04. 5
lord say, jack cade hath sworn to have thy head. 4.04. 19
but get you to smithfield and gather head, | and 4.05. 9
i'll see if his head will stand steadier on a 4.07. 95 P
i say, and strike off his head presently, and 4.07.109 P
sir james cromer, and strike off his head, and 4.07.111 P
realm shall not wear a head on his shoulders, 4.07.120 P
him, | and he that brings his head unto the king 4.08. 66
crowns of the king by carrying my head to him, 4.10. 28 P
and there cut off thy most ungracious head, 4.10. 82
and pluck the crown from feeble henry's head. 5.01. 2
lo, i present your grace a traitor's head, | the 5.01. 66
head, | the head of cade, whom i in combat slew. 5.01. 67
the head of cade! 5.01. 68
for thousand yorks he shall not hide his head, 5.01. 85
that head of thine doth not become a crown: 5.01. 96
if it be banish'd from the frosty head, | where 5.01.167
thus do i hope to shake king henry's head. 3H6 1.01. 20
father, tear the crown from the usurper's head. 1.01.114
sweet father, do so, set it on your head. 1.01.115
and giv'n unto the house of york such head | as 1.01.233
and will you pale your head in henry's glory, 1.04.103
and, with the crown, his head, | and, whilest we 1.04.107
off with his head, and set it on york gates, 1.04.179
they took his head, and on the gates of york 2.01. 65
you were, | making another head to fight again. 2.01.141
can pluck the diadem from faint henry's head, 2.01.153
shall for the fault make forfeit of his head. 2.01.197
yonder's the head of that arch–enemy | that 2.02. 2
how it doth grieve me that thy head is here! 2.02. 55
for grace, | and set thy diadem upon my head, 2.02. 82
if thou deny, their blood upon thy head, | for 2.02.129
from off the gates of york fetch down the head, 2.06. 52
your father's head, which clifford placed there; 2.06. 53
off with the traitor's head, | and rear it in 2.06. 85
my crown is in my heart, not on my head; 3.01. 62
until my misshap'd trunk that bears this head 3.02.170
to set the crown once more on henry's head. 4.04. 27
warwick, although my head still wear the crown, 4.06. 23
his head by nature fram'd to wear a crown, | his 4.06. 72
what is the body when the head is off? 5.01. 41
shall, whiles thy head is warm and new cut off, 5.01. 55
for somerset, off with his guilty head. 5.05. 3
he's sudden, if a thing comes in his head. 5.05. 86
hadst thou in thy head when thou wast born, | to 5.06. 53
blast his harvest, /and your head were laid, 5.07. 21
why do you look on us, and shake your head, R3 2.02. 5
chop off his head! 3.01.193
for they account his head upon the bridge. 3.02. 70
that he will lose his head ere give consent 3.04. 38
off with his head! 3.04. 76
is lighted on poor hastings' wretched head! 3.04. 93
make a short shrift, he longs to see your head. 3.04. 95
bear him my head. 3.04.106
here is the head of that ignoble traitor, | the 3.05. 22
gone | to brecknock while my fearful head is on! 4.02.122
from which even here i slip my /weary head, 4.04.112
thy head (all indirectly) gave direction. 4.04.226
th' imperial metal, circling now thy head, | had 4.04.382
if i revolt, off goes young george's head; 4.05. 4
hath turn'd my feigned prayer on my head, | and 5.01. 21
to–morrow's vengeance on the head of richard. 5.03.206
that ever ent'red in a drowsy head | have i 5.03.228
draw, archers, draw your arrows to the head! 5.03.339
off with his son george's head! 5.03.344
who first rais'd head against usurping richard, H8 2.01.108
and flourish'd, | i'll hang my head and perish. 3.01.153
i had rather want those than my head. 3.02.309
now good angels | fly o'er thy royal head, and 5.01.160
but if i spar'd any | that had a head to hit, 5.03. 24
fire–drake did i hit three times on the head, 5.03. 44 P
me till her pink'd porringer fell off her head, 5.03. 48 P
stand close up, or i'll make your head ache. 5.03. 88
an addle egg as well as you love an idle head, TRO 1.02.134 P
and bears his head | in such a rein, in full as 1.03.188
one voice | call agamemnon head and general. 1.03.222
i would thou didst itch from head to foot; 2.01. 27 P
his wit in his belly and his guts in his head, 2.01. 74 P
but, by my head, 'tis pride. 2.03. 88 P
if you do, our melancholy upon your head! 3.01. 69 P
our head shall go bare till merit /crown /it. 3.02. 91 P
as who should say there were wit in this head, 3.03.255 P
would he were knock'd i' th' head! 4.02. 34
this brave shall oft make thee to hide thy head. 4.04.137
air | may pierce the head of the great combatant 4.05. 5
you fillip me a' th' head. 4.05. 45
stand fast, and wear a castle on thy head! 5.02.187
troilus, thou coward troilus, show thy head! 5.06. 1
the kingly–crowned head, the vigilant eye, | the COR 1.01.115
he'll beat aufidius' head below his knee, | and 1.03. 46
ere in our own house i do shade my head, | the 2.01.195
i had rather have one scratch my head i' th' sun 2.02. 75
when tarquin made a head for rome, he fought 2.02. 88
tullus aufidius then had made new head? 3.01. 1
more learned than the ears), waving thy head, 3.02. 77
has the porter his eyes in his head, that he 4.05. 12 P
and not a hair upon a soldier's head | which 4.06.133
on, | and help to set a head on headless rome. TIT 1.01.186
a better head her glorious body fits | than his 1.01.187
blood and revenge are hammering in my head. 2.03. 39
come, brother, take a head, | and in this hand 3.01.279
the goths have gathered head, and with a power 4.04. 63
me, and i hang the head | as flowers with frost, 4.04. 70
of me, | as true a dog as ever fought at head. 5.01.102
he swung about his head and cut the winds, | who ROM 1.01.111
what if her eyes were there, they in her head? 2.02. 18
as glorious to this night, being o'er my head, 2.02. 27
it argues a distempered head | so soon to bid 2.03. 33
lord, how my head aches! 2.05. 48
what a head have i! 2.05. 48
thy head is as full of quarrels as an egg is 3.01. 22 P
and yet thy head hath been beaten as addle as an 3.01. 23 P
by my head, here comes the capulets. 3.01. 35 P
thou cut'st my head off with a golden axe, | and 3.03. 22
i have a head, sir, that will find out logs, 4.04. 18
thee, youth, | put not another sin upon my head, 5.03. 62
and know their spring, their head, their true 5.03.218
the sun, for sorrow, will not show his head. 5.03.306
bowing his head against the steepy mount | to TIM 1.01. 75
mean eyes have seen | the foot above the head. 1.01. 94
bid me | return so much, i have shook my head, 2.02.137
what heart, head, sword, force, means, but is 2.02.167
than he that has no house to put his head in? 3.04. 64 P
and set quarrelling | upon the head of valor; 3.05. 28
to cut the head off and then hack the limbs — JC 2.01.163
than caesar's arm | when caesar's head is off. 2.01.183
then you scratch'd your head, | and too 2.01.243
we must straight make head; 4.01. 42
and chastisement doth therefore hide his head. 4.03. 16
and fix'd his head upon our battlements. MAC 1.02. 23
the spring, the head, the fountain of your blood 2.03. 98
upon my head they plac'd a fruitless crown, 3.01. 60
with twenty trenched gashes on his head, | the 3.04. 26
strange things i have in head, that will to hand 3.04.138
when i shall tread upon the tyrant's head, | or 4.03. 45
behold where stands | th' usurper's cursed head: 5.09. 21
and the chief head | of this post–haste and HAM 1.01.106
the head is not more native to the heart, | the 1.02. 47
methought | it lifted up it head and did address 1.02.216
my lord, from head to foot. 1.02.228
yielding of that body | whereof he is the head. 1.03. 24
account | with all my imperfections on my head. 1.05. 79
no hat upon his head, his stockins fouled, 2.01. 76
and thrice his head thus waving up and down, 2.01. 90
and, with his head over his shoulder turn'd, 2.01. 94
the head and source of all your son's distemper. 2.02. 55
head to foot | now is he total gules, horridly 2.02.456
which was declining on the milky head | of 2.02.478
a clout upon that head | where late the diadem 2.02.506
dead and gone, | at his head a grass–green turf, 4.05. 31
haste | than young laertes, in a riotous head, 4.05.102
'a pour'd a flagon of rhenish on my head once. 5.01.180 P
woe | fall ten times /treble on that cursed head 5.01.247
pelion, or the skyish head | of blue olympus. 5.01.253
of the axe, | my head should be strook off. 5.02. 25
your bonnet to his right use, 'tis for the head. 5.02. 93 P
you that 'a has laid a great wager on your head. 5.02.103 P
lapwing runs away with the shell on his head. 5.02.186 P
that /it had it head bit off by it young." LR 1.04.216
why, to put 's head in, not to give it away to 1.05. 30 P
thunderbolts, | singe my white head! 3.02. 6
your high–engender'd battles 'gainst a head | so 3.02. 23
he that has a house to put 's head in has a good 3.02. 25 P
that will house | before the head has any, | the 3.02. 28
the head has any, | the head and he shall louse: 3.02. 29
tom will throw his head at them. 3.06. 64 P
and wail, | for, with throwing thus my head, 3.06. 72
the sea, with such a storm as his bare head | in 3.07. 59
whose high and bending head | looks fearfully in 4.01. 73
decline your head: 4.02. 22
bear'st a cheek for blows, a head for wrongs, 4.02. 51
methinks he seems no bigger than his head. 4.06. 16
and does shake the head | to hear of pleasure's 4.06.120
no eyes in your head, nor no money in your purse 4.06.146 P
that eyeless head of thine was first fram'd 4.06.227
and from th' extremest upward of thy head | to 5.03.137
back do i toss these treasons to thy head, 5.03.147
the very head and front of my offending | hath OTH 1.03. 80
destruction on my head if my bad blame | light 1.03.177
adversities | make head against my estimation! 1.03.274
to change the cod's head for the salmon's tail; 2.01.155
on horror's head horrors accumulate; 3.03.370

have you not hurt your head? 4.01. 59
if any wretch have put this in your head, | let 4.02. 15
all kind of sores and shames on my bare head, 4.02. 49
to do | but to go hang my head all at one side 4.03. 32
her hand on her bosom, her head on her knee, 4.03. 42
let antony look over caesar's head | and speak ANT 2.02. 5
i'll unhair thy head, | thou shalt be whipt with 2.05. 64
chariots, and | put garlands on thy head. 3.01. 11
that herod's head | i'll have; 3.03. 4
from th' head of /actium | beat th' approaching 3.07. 51
to the boy caesar send this grizzled head, | and 3.13. 17
that head, my lord? 3.13. 19
now from head to foot | i am marble–constant; 5.02.239
arm me, audacity, from head to foot, | or, like CYM 1.06. 19
him know | if that his head have ear in music; 3.04.175
hath in gallia | will soon be drawn to head, 3.05. 25
posthumus, thy head, which now is growing upon 4.01. 15 P
this, the fool had borne | my head as i do his. 4.02.117
cut off one cloten's head, | son to the queen 4.02.118
and in time | may make some stronger head, the 4.02.139
body hath a tail | more perilous than the head. 4.02.145
my throat, i have ta'en | his head from him. 4.02.151
below the violet, | not wagging his sweet head; 4.02.173
nay, cadwal, we must lay his head to th' east, 4.02.255
o posthumus, alas, | where is thy head? 4.02.321
thee at the heart | and left this head on. 4.02.323
your death has eyes in 's head then; 5.04.178 P
or at least | those which i heav'd to head! 5.05.157
i cut off 's head, | and am right glad he is not 5.05.295
then give my tongue like leave to love my head. PER 1.01.108
heaven, that i had thy head! 1.01.109
meaning, | for which we mean to have his head. 1.01.144
dead, | my heart can lend no succor to my head. 1.01.169
and knowing this kingdom is without a head — 2.04. 35
the men of tyrus on the head | of helicanus 3.ch. 26
a pillow for his head. 5.01.236
another | directing in his head, his mind nurse TNK 1.03. 32
on my head no toy | but was her pattern, her 1.03. 71
all the good that may | be wish'd upon thy head, 1.04. 3
put but thy head out of this window more, | and, 2.02.212
put my head out? 2.02.215
the other lose his head, | and all his friends; 3.06.296
that you must lose your head to–morrow morning, 4.01. 77
about his head he wears the winner's oak, | and 4.02.137
he is a good one | as ever strook at head. 5.03.109
that arcite's legs, being higher than his head, 5.04. 78
victor's wreath | even then fell off his head; 5.04. 80
should step as 'twere up to my country's head STM III 7
and rein his proud head to the saddle–bow; VEN 14
hold up thy head, | look in mine eyeballs, there 118
sometime she shakes her head, and then his hand, 223
breast, full eye, small head, and nostril wide, 296
make them droop with grief and hang the head. 666
fled | into the deep–dark cabins of her head, 1038
over one shoulder doth she hang her head; 1058
she bows her head, the new–sprung flow'r to 1171
rolling his greedy eyeballs in his head. LUC 368
between whose hills her head entombed is; 390
wears | he pens her piteous clamors in her head, 681
knit poisonous clouds about his golden head. 777
here one man's hand lean'd on another's head, 1415
a head | stood for the whole to be imagined. 1427
alone | upon his head that hath transgressed so; 1481
where thou wast wont to rest thy weary head, 1621
with head declin'd, and voice damm'd up with woe 1661
take counsel of some wiser head, | neither too PP 18. 5
the gracious light | lifts up his burning head, SON 7. 2
not show my head where thou mayst prove me. 26.14
but then begins a journey in my head | to work 27. 3
away, | to live a second life on second head; 68. 7
if hairs be wires, black wires grow on her head. 130. 4
what eyes hath love put in my head, | which have 148. 1
upon her head a platted hive of straw, | which LC 8

HEADED 1 FR 0.0001 REL FR 1 V 0 P
and all th' embossed sores and headed evils, AYL 2.07. 67

HEADIER 1 FR 0.0001 REL FR 1 V 0 P
and am fallen out with my more headier will, LR 2.04.110

HEADING 1 FR 0.0001 REL FR 0 V 1 P
it is but heading and hanging. MM 2.01.237 P

HEADLAND *(see hade)*

HEADLESS 5 FR 0.0005 REL FR 5 V 0 P
a hog, a headless bear, sometime a fire, | and MND 3.01.109
and smooth my way upon their headless necks; 2H6 1.02. 65
on, | and help to set a head on headless rome. TIT 1.01.186
a headless man? CYM 4.02.308
that headless man | i thought had been my lord. 5.05.299

HEADLONG 7 FR 0.0008 REL FR 7 V 0 P
and throw the rider headlong in the lists, | a R2 1.02. 52
to pluck him headlong from the usurped throne. 5.01. 65
i'll hale the dolphin headlong from his throne, 1H6 1.01.149
hence will i drag thee headlong by the heels 2H6 4.10. 80
will hand in hand all headlong hurl ourselves, TIT 5.03.132
and the deficient sight | topple down headlong. LR 4.06. 24
or stop the headlong fury of his speed. LUC 501

//HEAD–LUGG'D 1 FR 0.0001 REL FR 1 V 0 P
/even /the //head–lugg'd /bear /would /lick, LR 4.02. 42

HEADLY 1 FR 0.0001 REL FR 1 V 0 P
and contagious clouds | of headly murther, spoil H5 3.03. 32

HEAD–PIECE 2 FR 0.0002 REL FR 1 V 1 P
by some severals | of head–piece extraordinary? WT 1.02.227
a house to put 's head in has a good head–piece. LR 3.02. 26 P

HEAD–PIECES 1 FR 0.0001 REL FR 0 V 1 P
they could never wear such heavy head–pieces. H5 3.07.139 P

HEAD'S 5 FR 0.0005 REL FR 5 V 0 P
taking so the head, your whole head's length. R2 3.03. 14
or else his head's assurance is but frail. R3 4.04.496
her head's declin'd, and death will seize her, ANT 3.11. 47
a dove's motion when the head's pluck'd off; TNK 1.01. 98
his head's yellow, | hard–hair'd, and curl'd, 4.02.103

/HEADS 1 FR 0.0001 REL FR 1 V 0 P
rocks, /and hills whose /heads touch heaven, OTH 1.03.141

HEADS 109 FR 0.0123 REL FR 88 V 21 P
such men | whose heads stood in their breasts? TMP 3.03. 47
else falls | upon your heads — is nothing but 3.03. 81
with rounds of waxen tapers on their heads, WIV 4.04. 51
be glad to give out a commission for more heads. MM 2.01.240 P
had he twenty heads to tender down | on twenty 2.04.180
her, fellow, by the rest that have no heads. LLL 4.01. 45 P
or hide your heads like cowards, and fly hence. 5.02. 86
and their heads are hung | with ears that sweep MND 4.01.120
should in their own confines with forked heads AYL 2.01. 24
how the young folks lay their heads together! SHR 1.02.139 P
let their heads be slickly comb'd, their blue 4.01. 91 P
sever'd in religion, their heads are both one: AWW 1.03. 53 P
with toss–pots still had drunken heads, | for TN 5.01.403
and how she long'd to eat adders' heads, and WT 4.04.265 P
now, by the sky that hangs above our heads, | i JN 2.01.397
when they talk of him, they shake their heads, 4.02.188
the pains you take | by cutting off your heads. 5.04. 16
will rain hot vengeance on offenders' heads. R2 1.02. 8
if we prevail, their heads shall pay for it. 3.02.126
their peace is made | with heads, and not with 3.02.138
ay, all of them at bristow lost their heads. 3.02.142
cover your heads, and mock not flesh and blood 3.02.171
lest you mistake the heavens are over our heads. 3.03. 17
cut off the heads of /too fast growing sprays, 3.04. 34
i have to london sent | the heads of salisbury, 5.06. 8
the heads of brocas and sir bennet seely, | two 5.06. 14
speed, | to save our heads by raising of a head, 1H4 1.03.284
in their bellies no bigger than pins' heads, and 4.02. 22 P
cut me off the heads | of all the favorites that 4.03. 85
o, would the quarrel lay upon our heads, | and 5.02. 47
they grow like hydra's heads. 5.04. 25
reward valor bear the sin upon their own heads. 5.04.150 P
that the blunt monster with uncounted heads, 2H4 in 18
as the times do brawl, | /are in three heads: 1.03. 71
to melt | and drop upon our bare unarmed heads. 2.04.365
curling their monstrous heads and hanging them 3.01. 23
element (which show like pins' heads to her), 4.03. 53 P
their most reverend heads dash'd to the walls; H5 3.03. 37
for if their heads had any intellectual armor, 3.07.137 P
bear and have their heads crush'd like rotten 3.07.144 P
and arms, and heads, chopp'd off in a battle, 4.01.136 P
and their poor jades | lob down their heads, 4.02. 47
gay new coats o'er the french soldiers' heads 4.03.118
turn on the bloody hounds with heads of steel, 1H6 4.02. 51
we'll both together lift our heads to heaven, 2H6 1.02. 14
were plac'd the heads of edmund duke of somerset 1.02. 29
heaping confusion on their own heads thereby! 2.01.183
giddy multitude do point | and nod their heads, 2.04. 22
ay, all of you have laid your heads together — 3.01.165
take your houses over your heads, ravish your 4.08. 30 P
i see them lay their heads together to surprise 4.08. 58 P
my soul to heaven, my blood upon your heads! 3H6 1.04.168
to hurl upon their heads that break his law. R3 1.04.200
might better wear their heads | than some that 3.02. 92
now margaret's curse is fall'n upon our heads, 3.03. 15
up to some scaffold, there to lose their heads. 4.04.243
the cardinal's and sir thomas lovell's heads H8 1.02.185
too many curses on their heads | that were the 2.01.138
of the sea, | hung their heads, and then lay by. 3.01. 11
the heads of all thy brother cardinals | (with 3.02.257
i'll scratch your heads; 5.03. 9 P
and on your heads | clap round fines for neglect 5.03. 79
beaten corn, | and hang their heads with sorrow. 5.04. 32
'fore all the greekish heads, which with one TRO 1.03.221
for which we lose our heads to gild his horns! 4.05. 31
so of many, not that our heads are some brown, COR 2.03. 19 P
groats, to show bare heads | in congregations, 3.02. 10
the beast | with many heads butts me away. 4.01. 2
you lords and heads a' th' state, perfidiously 5.06. 90
their heads, i mean. TIT 3.01.202
here are the heads of thy two noble sons, | and 3.01.236
see thy two sons' heads, | thy warlike hand, thy 3.01.254
for these two heads do seem to speak to me, 3.01.271
when, for his hand, he had his two sons' heads, 5.01.115
and when thy car is loaden with their heads, | i 5.02. 53
and make two pasties of your shameful heads, 5.02.189
and in that paste let their vile heads be bak'd. 5.02.200
i will cut off their heads. ROM 1.01. 23 P
the heads of the maids? 1.01. 24 P
ay, the heads of the maids, or their maidenheads 1.01. 25 P
soul | is but a little way above our heads, 3.01.127
the vaulty heaven so high above our heads. 3.05. 22
but they do shake their heads, and i am here TIM 2.02.202
let's shake our heads, and say, | as 'twere a 4.02. 25
stout men's pillows from below their heads. 4.03. 33
smil'd at one another, and shook their heads; JC 1.02.283 P
and, waving our red weapons o'er our heads, 3.01.109
and kites | fly o'er our heads, and downward 5.01. 85
yet, countrymen! o, yet, hold up your heads! 5.04. 1
though castles topple on their warders' heads; MAC 4.01. 56
do slope | their heads to their foundations; 4.01. 58
in fine together, | and wager o'er your heads. HAM 4.07.134
mistook | fall'n on th' inventors' heads: 5.02.385
horses are tied by the heads, dogs and bears by LR 2.04. 8 P
that keep this dreadful pudder o'er our heads, 3.02. 50
how shall your houseless heads and unfed sides, 3.04. 30
and men whose heads | /do /grow beneath their OTH 1.03.144
let our best heads | know that to–morrow the ANT 4.01. 10
them home | with clouts about their heads. 4.07. 6
and on the gates of lud's–town set your heads. CYM 4.02. 99
displace our heads where (thanks, /ye gods!) 4.02.122
covering heavens | fall on their heads like dew! 5.05.351
whose towers bore heads so high they kiss'd the PER 1.04. 24
loud music is too harsh for ladies' heads, 2.03. 97
that for our crowned heads we have no roof TNK 1.01. 52
require him he advance it o'er our heads; 1.01. 93
with chaplets on their heads of daffadillies, 4.01. 73
thy kinsmen hang their heads at this disdain, LUC 521
cross their arms and hang their heads with mine, 793

HEADSHAKE 1 FR 0.0001 REL FR 1 V 0 P
with arms encumb'red thus, or this headshake, HAM 1.05.174

HEADSMAN 1 FR 0.0001 REL FR 0 V 1 P
come, headsman, off with his head. AWW 4.03.308 P

HEAD–STALL 1 FR 0.0001 REL FR 0 V 1 P
bit and a head–stall of sheep's leather which, SHR 3.02. 57 P

HEADSTRONG 10 FR 0.0011 REL FR 10 V 0 P
(the needful bits and curbs to headstrong weeds) MM 1.03. 20
why, headstrong liberty is lash'd with woe: ERR 2.01. 15
and thus i'll curb her mad and headstrong humor. SHR 4.01.209
i charge thee tell these headstrong women | what 5.02.130
but such a headstrong potent fault it is | that TN 3.04.204
for when his headstrong riot hath no curb, 2H4 4.04. 62
peace, headstrong warwick! 2H6 1.03.175
i have seduc'd a headstrong kentishman, | john 3.01.356
grown | too headstrong for their mother. TRO 3.02.123
how now, my headstrong, where have you been ROM 4.02. 16

HEADY 2 FR 0.0002 REL FR 2 V 0 P
slain, | and all the currents of a heady fight; 1H4 2.03. 55
in a flood | with such a heady currance, H5 1.01. 34

HEADY–RASH 1 FR 0.0001 REL FR 1 V 0 P
nor heady–rash, provok'd with raging ire, ERR 5.01.216

HEAL 13 FR 0.0014 REL FR 10 V 3 P
expense, | i seek to heal it only by his wealth. WIV 3.04. 6
it is a rupture that you may easily heal; MM 3.01.235 P
did make offense, his eye did heal it up. AYL 3.05.117
we will heal up all, | for we'll create young JN 2.01.550
and heal the inveterate canker of one wound | by 5.02. 14
hold you, there is a groat to heal your pate. H5 5.01. 59 P
god buy you, and keep you, and heal your pate. 5.01. 67 P
my pity hath been balm to heal their wounds, 3H6 4.08. 41
those wounds heal ill that men do give TRO 3.03.229
i had rather have my wounds to heal again | than COR 2.02. 69
to heal rome's harms, and wipe away her woe! TIT 5.03.148
but must not break my back to heal his finger. TIM 2.01. 24
what wound did ever heal but by degrees? OTH 2.03.371

HEAL'D 2 FR 0.0002 REL FR 1 V 1 P
lodge thee till thy wound be throughly heal'd; TGV 1.02.112
to the same diseases, heal'd by the same means, MV 3.01. 62 P

HEALETH 1 FR 0.0001 REL FR 1 V 0 P
bearing away the wound that nothing healeth, LUC 731

HEALING 2 FR 0.0002 REL FR 2 V 0 P
royalty he leaves | the healing benediction. MAC 4.03.156
loud, we do commit | murther in healing wounds. ANT 2.02. 22

HEALS 1 FR 0.0001 REL FR 1 V 0 P
such a salve can speak | that heals the wound, SON 34. 8

HEAL'ST 1 FR 0.0001 REL FR 1 V 0 P
that heal'st with blood | the earth when it is TNK 5.01. 64

/HEALTH 2 FR 0.0002 REL FR 1 V 1 P
day | to seek thy /health by beneficial help. ERR 1.01.151
/tameness /of /a /wolf, /a /horse's /health, /a LR 3.06. 19 P

HEALTH 108 FR 0.0122 REL FR 91 V 17 P
sir valentine, your father is in good health: TGV 2.04. 50
i left them all in health. 2.04.124
my health and happy being at your court. 3.01. 57
thine own confession, learn to begin thy health; MM 1.02. 38 P
god restore you to health! ADO 5.01.324 P
sweet health and fair desires consort your grace LLL 2.01.177
a beard, fair health, and honesty; 5.02.824
but, as in health, come to my natural taste, MND 4.01.174
to see her noble lord restor'd to health, | who SHR in.1. 121
and quaff carouses to our mistress' health, 1.02.275
"a health!" 3.02.170
dine with my father, drink a health to me, | for 3.02.196
therefore a health to all that shot and miss'd. 5.02. 51
to return | and find your grace in health. AWW 2.01. 7
health, at your bidding, serve your majesty! 2.01. 18
health shall live free, and sickness freely die. 2.01.168
hath through me restor'd the king to health. 2.03. 64
she is not well, but yet she has her health. 2.04. 2 P
he has his health, and ampler strength indeed WT 4.04.403
even in the instant of repair and health, | the JN 3.04.113
that, for the health and physic of our right, 5.02. 21
i am in health, i breathe, and see thee ill. R2 2.01. 92
my lord, to have learn'd his health of you. 2.03. 24
more health and happiness betide my liege | than 3.02. 91
his health was never better worth than now. 1H4 4.01. 27
your loving complices | /lean on /your health, 2H4 1.01.164
lordship to have a reverend care of your health. 1.02.100 P
in bodily health, sir. 2.02.103 P
health and fair greeting from our general, | the 4.01. 27
health to my lord, and gentle cousin, mowbray. 4.02. 78
you wish me health in very happy season, | for i 4.02. 79
health to my sovereign, and new happiness 4.04. 81
and no food — | such are the poor, in health; 4.04.106
health, peace, and happiness to my royal father! 4.05.226
but health, alack, with youthful wings is flown 4.05.228
silence, i'll give you a health for that anon. 5.03. 24 P
health and long life to you, master silence. 5.03. 52 P
for god doth know how many now in health | shall H5 1.02. 18
who when they were in health, i tell thee, 3.06.148
the beggar's knee, | command the health of it? 4.01.257
to our sister, | health and fair time of day; 5.02. 3
princes french, and peers, health to you all! 5.02. 8
my honorable lords, health to you all! 1H6 1.01. 57
all health unto my gracious sovereign! 2H6 3.01. 82
health and glad tidings to your majesty! 4.09. 7
health and all happiness to my lord the king! 5.01.124
will soon recover his accustom'd health. R3 1.03. 2
god grant him health! did you confer with him? 1.03. 35
well, madam, and in health. 2.04. 40
god bless your grace with health and happy days! 3.01. 18
most fit | for your best health and recreation. 3.01. 67
all health, my sovereign lord! 4.03. 23
my welcome, | and to you all good health. H8 1.04. 38
a health, gentlemen! 1.04. 96
health to your lordships. 2.02. 61
whose health and royalty i pray for. 2.03. 73
madam, in good health. 4.02.124
but for your health and your disgestion sake, TRO 2.03.111
health to you, valiant sir, | during all 4.01. 11
bloods are now in calm, and, so long, health! 4.01. 16
it gives me an estate of seven years' health, in COR 2.01.115 P
know that justice lives | in saturninus' health, TIT 4.04. 24
of lead, bright smoke, cold fire, sick health, ROM 1.01.180
my lord, in heart; and let the health go round. TIM 1.02. 53
of whom, even to the state's best health, i have 2.02.197
his health is well, sir. 3.01. 12 P
i am right glad that his health is well, sir; 3.01. 13 P
temper has forsook him, he's much out of health, 3.04. 72 P
and, if it be so far beyond his health, 3.04. 74
honor, health, and compassion to the senate! 3.05. 5
of health and living now begins to mend, | and 5.01.187
it is not for your health thus to commit | your JC 2.01.235
i am not well in health, and that is all. 2.01.257
brutus is wise, and, were he not in health, | he 2.01.258
have mind upon your health; 4.03. 36
who wear our health but sickly in his life, MAC 3.01.106
wait on appetite, | and health on both! 3.04. 38
come, love and health to all, | then i'll sit 3.04. 86
night, and better health | attend his majesty! 3.04.119
and purge it to a sound and pristine health, | i 5.03. 52

no jocund health that denmark drinks to–day, HAM 1.02.125
the safety and health of this whole state, | and 1.03. 21
be thou a spirit of health, or goblin damn'd, 1.04. 40
and his weeds, | importing health and graveness. 4.07. 81
importing denmark's health and england's too, 5.02. 21
this pearl is thine, | here's to thy health! 5.02.283
no less than life, with grace, health, beauty, LR 1.01. 58
all office | whereto our health is bound; 2.04.107
have a measure to the health of black othello. OTH 2.03. 32 P
to the health of our general! 2.03. 86 P
wine enough, | cleopatra's health to drink. ANT 1.02. 13
in state of health thou say'st, and thou say'st 2.05. 56
i have a health for you. 2.06.133 P
sit — and some wine! a health to lepidus! 2.07. 29 P
with the health that pompey gives him, else he 2.07. 51 P
this health to lepidus! 2.07. 84
continues well my lord? his health, beseech you? CYM 1.06. 56
of my lord's health, of his content — yet not 3.02. 31
you health. so please you, sir. 4.02. 31
mistress' lips — | we drink this health to you. PER 2.03. 52
i am glad to see your honor in good health. 4.06. 22 P
blood we venture | should be as for our health, TNK 1.02.110
to your health, etc. 3.03. 12
and ev'ry day discourse you into health, | as i 3.06. 38
was she in health? 4.01. 34
wife that greeteth thee, | health to thy person; LUC 1305
assured | of /thy fair health, recounting it to SON 45.12
no news but health from their physicians know; 140. 8

HEALTHFUL 10 FR 0.0011 REL FR 10 V 0 P
gave healthful welcome to their shipwrack'd ERR 1.01.114
and with this healthful hand, whose banish'd AWW 2.03. 48
which is both healthful and good husbandry. H5 4.01. 7
healthful, and ever since a fresh admirer | of H8 1.01. 3
had you a healthful ear to hear of it. JC 2.01.319
keep time, | and makes as healthful music. HAM 3.04.141
our other healthful members even to a sense | of OTH 3.04.147
if antony | be free and healthful — so tart a ANT 2.05. 38
and brought to medicine a healthful state SON 118.11
growing a bath and healthful remedy | for men 154.11

HEALTH–GIVING 1 FR 0.0001 REL FR 0 V 1 P
most wholesome physic of thy health–giving air; LLL 1.01.234 P

HEALTHS 4 FR 0.0004 REL FR 2 V 2 P
with drinking healths to my niece. TN 1.03. 38 P
i have half a dozen healths | to drink to these H8 1.04.105
spanish blades, | of healths five fadom deep; ROM 1.04. 85
those healths will make thee and thy state look TIM 1.02. 56 P

HEALTHSOME 1 FR 0.0001 REL FR 1 V 0 P
whose foul mouth no healthsome air breathes in, ROM 4.03. 34

HEALTHY 2 FR 0.0002 REL FR 0 V 2 P
nay, not, as one would say, healthy; MM 1.02. 55 P
the water itself was a good healthy water, but, 2H4 1.02. 4 P

HEAP 11 FR 0.0012 REL FR 10 V 1 P
it, heap on your head | a pack of sorrows which TGV 3.01. 19
you that, in the great heap of your knowledge? AYL 1.02. 68 P
hence, heap of wrath, foul indigested lump, | as 2H6 5.01.157
among this princely heap, if any here | by false R3 2.01. 54
alas, why would you heap this care on me? 3.07.204
all on a heap, like to a slaughtered lamb, | in TIT 2.03.223
your potent and infectious fevers heap | on TIM 4.01. 22
when i have laid proud athens on a heap — 4.03.102
drawn | upon a heap a hundred ghastly women, JC 1.03. 23
presumes to reach, all the whole heap must die. PER 1.01. 33
i know mine own is but a heap of ruins, | and no TNK 2.03. 19

HEAP'D 8 FR 0.0009 REL FR 8 V 0 P
with measure heap'd in joy, to th' measures fall AYL 5.04.179
and heap'd sedition on his crown at home. 3H6 2.02.158
for your great graces | heap'd upon me, poor H8 3.02.175
his overthrow heap'd happiness upon him; 4.02. 64
and mountainous error be too highly heap'd | for COR 2.03.120
if the measure of thy joy | be heap'd like mine, ROM 2.06. 25
for some new honors that are heap'd on caesar. JC 1.02.134
old, | and the late dignities heap'd up to them, MAC 1.06. 19

HEAPING 2 FR 0.0002 REL FR 1 V 1 P
and my profit therein the heaping friendships. WT 4.02. 19 P
heaping confusion on their own heads thereby! 2H6 2.01.183

HEAPS 7 FR 0.0008 REL FR 7 V 0 P
the cank'red heaps of strange–achieved gold; 2H4 4.05. 71
let us on heaps go offer up our lives. H5 4.05. 18
and all her husbandry doth lie on heaps, 5.02. 39
wedges of gold, great anchors, heaps of pearl, R3 1.04. 26
when they charge on heaps | the enemy flying. TRO 3.02. 28
distinctly ranges, | in heaps and piles of ruin. COR 3.01.206
even such heaps and sums of love and wealth | as TIM 5.01.152

HEAP'ST 1 FR 0.0001 REL FR 1 V 0 P
my youth, thou heap'st | a year's age on me. CYM 1.01.132

/HEAR 8 FR 0.0009 REL FR 6 V 2 P
the hours come back! that did i never /hear. ERR 4.02. 55
/hear other things: MV 3.04. 23
is it not news to /hear of petruchio's coming? SHR 3.02. 33 P
/hear /me /more /plainly. 2H4 4.01. 66
last night, i /hear, they lay at stony–stratford R3 2.04. 1
/we /shall /hear /music, /wit, /and /oracle. TRO 1.03. 74
/no /more /of /drowning, /do /you /hear? OTH 1.03.378 P
i /hear him coming. 5.01. 22

HEAR 929 FR 0.1050 REL FR 702 V 227 P
do you not hear him? TMP 1.01. 13 P
hence his ambition growing — | dost thou hear? 1.02.106
hear a little further, | and then i'll bring 1.02.135
sit still, and hear the last of our sea–sorrow: 1.02.170
i hear | the strain of strutting chanticleer: 1.02.385
hark now i hear them — ding–dong bell. 1.02.405
i hear it now above me. 1.02.408
that wonders | to hear thee speak of naples. 1.02.434
he does hear me, | and that he does i weep. 1.02.434
go sleep, and hear us. 2.01.190 P
do you not hear me speak? 2.01.210
his spirits hear me, | and yet i needs must 2.02. 3
storm brewing, i hear it sing i' th' wind. 2.02. 19 P
hear my soul speak: 3.01. 63
do not approach | till thou dost hear me call. 4.01. 50
that the blind mole may not | hear a foot fall; 4.01.195
do you hear, monster? 4.01.201 P
that rejoice | to hear the solemn curfew: 5.01. 40
i long | to hear the story of your life, which 5.01.313
to milan let me hear from thee by letters | of TGV 1.01. 57
but dost thou hear? 1.01. 94 P
hear sweet discourse, converse with noblemen, 1.03. 31
if this be he you oft have wish'd to hear from. 2.04.103
when you have done, we look to hear from you. 2.04.120
i will not hear thy vain excuse, | but, as thou 3.01.168
my ears are stopp'd and cannot hear good news, 3.01.206
peace! we'll hear him. 4.01. 9
bring you where you shall hear music and see the 4.02. 31 P
but shall i hear him speak? 4.02. 33 P
ay; but peace, let's hear 'em. 4.02. 38 P
i likewise hear that valentine is dead. 4.02.112
to mantua, where i hear he makes abode; 4.03. 23
to hear me speak the message i am sent on. 4.04.112
i see, and hear — | love, lend me patience to 5.04. 26
'tis your penance but to hear | the story of 5.04.170
the council shall hear it, it is a riot. WIV 1.01. 35 P
it is not meet the council hear a riot; 1.01. 36 P
look you, shall desire to hear the fear of got, 1.01. 38 P
to hear the fear of got, and not to hear a riot. 1.01. 39 P
we three to hear it and end it between them. 1.01.142 P
you hear all these matters denied, gentlemen; 1.01.186 P
you hear it. 1.01.187 P
hear the truth of it: 1.04. 75 P
did you ever hear the like? 2.01. 69 P
for, believe me, i hear the parson is no jester. 2.01.209 P
i had rather hear them scold than fight. 2.01.231 P
sir, i hear you are a scholar (i will be brief 2.02.180 P
eye upon my follies, as you hear them unfolded, 2.02.186 P
hear mine host of the garter. 3.01.100 P
a man may hear this show'r sing in the wind. 3.02. 37 P
sir, will you hear me? 3.04. 74
i marvel i hear not of master /brook; 3.05. 57 P
you shall hear. 3.05. 83 P
nay, you shall hear, master /brook, what i have 3.05. 95 P
i hear not of him in the court. 4.03. 5 P
you shall hear how things go, and, i warrant, to 4.05.122 P
yet hear me speak. 4.06. 3
i will hear you, master fenton, and i will (at 4.06. 6 P
hear the truth of it. 5.05.220
and, as i hear, the provost hath | a warrant for MM 1.04. 73
do you hear how he misplaces? 2.01. 88 P
get you gone, and let me hear no more of you. 2.01.206 P
to your honor, | please but your honor hear me. 2.02. 28
her, | that i desire to hear her speak again? 2.02.177
your partner, as i hear, must die to–morrow, 2.03. 37
wherein (let no man hear me) i take pride, 2.04. 10
nay, but hear me, | your sense pursues not mine. 2.04. 73
bring /me to hear /them speak, where i may be 3.01. 52 P
nay, hear me, isabel. 3.01.147
o hear me, isabella! 3.01.150
let me hear you speak farther. 3.01.205 P
as it is, | you shall hear more ere morning. 4.02. 95
pray you let's hear. 4.02.119 P
"whatsoever you may hear to the contrary, let 4.02.120 P
he will hear none. 4.02.147 P
i hear his straw rustle. 4.03. 35 P
but hear you — 4.03. 61
and we hear | such goodness of your justice, 5.01. 5
hear me yourself; 5.01. 30
hear me, o hear me, here. 5.01. 32
hear me, o hear me, here. 5.01. 32
her shall you hear disproved to her eyes, | till 5.01.161
good friar, let's hear it. 5.01.162
whom it concerns to hear this matter forth, | do 5.01.255
'tis he should hear me speak. 5.01.294
and we will hear you speak. 5.01.295
we bid be quiet when we hear it cry; ERR 2.01. 35
let's hear it. 2.02. 71 P
shouldst thou but hear i were licentious, | and 2.02.131
or sleep i now and think i hear all this? 2.02.183
do you hear, you minion? 3.01. 54
you hear how he importunes me — the chain! 4.01. 53
i do arrest you, sir: you hear the suit. 4.01. 79
do you not hear it ring? 4.02. 51
these ears of mine thou know'st did hear thee; 5.01. 26
hark, hark, i hear him, mistress; 5.01.184
left, | my dull deaf ears a little use to hear: 5.01.317
good, | if this be not a dream i see and hear. 5.01.377
and hear at large discoursed all our fortunes; 5.01.396
i had rather hear my dog bark at a crow than a ADO 1.01.131 P
you hear, count claudio, i can be secret as a 1.01.209 P
you should hear reason. 1.03. 5 P
for hear me, hero: 2.01. 72 P
but hear these ill news with the ears of claudio 2.01.173
she cannot endure to hear tell of a husband. 2.01.347 P
her chamber–window, hear me call margaret hero, 2.02. 43 P
margaret hero, hear margaret term me claudio; 2.02. 44 P
and now had he rather hear the tabor and the 2.03. 14 P
come, shall we hear this music? 2.03. 37
come, balthasar, we'll hear that song again. 2.03. 43
yea, marry, dost thou hear, balthasar? 2.03. 84 P
tell benedick of it, and hear what 'a will say. 2.03.171 P
we will hear further of it by your daughter, let 2.03.205 P
i hear how i am censur'd; 2.03.224 P
happy are they that hear their detractions and 2.03.229 P
close by the ground, to hear our conference. 3.01. 25
yet tell her of it, hear what she will say. 3.01. 81
for the which i hear what they say of him. 3.02. 58 P
to you, which these hobby–horses must not hear. 3.02. 73 P
yet count claudio may hear, for what i would 3.02. 86 P
if you hear a child cry in the night, you must 3.03. 65 P
how if the nurse be asleep and will not hear us? 3.03. 68 P
the ewe that will not hear her lamb when it baes 3.03. 71 P
well, masters, we hear our charge. 3.03. 88 P
didst thou not hear somebody? 3.03.128 P
for i hear as good exclamation on your worship 3.05. 25 P
i be but a poor man, i am glad to hear it. 3.05. 27 P
leonato, | i am sorry you must hear. 4.01. 88
and this grieved count | did see her, hear her, 4.01. 90
hear me a little, | for i have only been silent 4.01.155
the proudest of them shall well hear of it. 4.01.192
when he shall hear she died upon his words, 4.01.223
hear me, beatrice — 4.01.308 P
as you hear of me, so think of me. 4.01.334 P
hear you, my lords — 5.01. 47
i will not hear you. 5.01.107
let me hear from you. 5.01.149 P
do you hear me, and let this count kill me. 5.01.231 P
and either i must shortly hear from him, or i 5.02. 58 P
will you go hear this news, signior? 5.02.101 P
not, i, | but i protest i love to hear him lie, LLL 1.01.175
to hear, or forbear hearing? 1.01.196 P
to hear meekly, sir, and to laugh moderately; 1.01.197 P
will you hear this letter with attention? 1.01.215 P
as we would hear an oracle. 1.01.216 P
did you hear the proclamation? 1.01.284 P
i am less proud to hear you tell my worth | than 2.01. 17
hear me, dear lady: i have sworn an oath. 2.01. 97
i hear your grace hath sworn out house–keeping: 2.01.104
do you hear, my mad wenches? 2.01.257
thus dost thou hear the nemean lion roar 4.01. 88
did you ever hear better? 4.01. 95
will you hear an extemporal epitaph on the death 4.02. 50 P
let me hear a staff, a stanze, a verse; 4.02.104
what will berowne say when that he shall hear 4.03.143
when shall you hear that i | will praise a hand, 4.03.181
him to passion, and therefore let's hear it. 4.03.198
a lover's ear will hear the lowest sound, | when 4.03.332
you hear his learning. 5.01. 50 P
but will you hear? 5.02.282
will hear your idle scorns, continue then, | and 5.02.865
will you hear the dialogue that the two learned 5.02.885 P
ever read, | could ever hear by tale or history, MND 1.01.133
therefore hear me, hermia: 1.01.156
that i will do any man's heart good to hear me. 1.02. 71 P
their spheres, | to hear the sea–maid's music? 2.01.154
speak, and if you hear; 2.02.153
will sing, that they shall hear i am not afraid. 3.01.123 P
hear my excuse, | my love, my life, my soul, 3.02.245
what, wilt thou hear some music, my sweet love? 4.01. 27
i do hear the morning lark. 4.01. 94
my love shall hear the music of my hounds. 4.01.106
never did i hear | such gallant chiding; 4.01.114
judge when you hear. 4.01.127
of this discourse we more will hear anon. 4.01.178
let us hear, sweet bottom. 4.02. 33 P
and i do not doubt but to hear them say, it is a 4.02. 44 P
and we will hear it. 5.01. 76
i will hear that play; 5.01. 81
chink, | to spy and i can hear my thisby's face. 5.01.193
walls are so willful to hear without warning. 5.01.209 P
or to hear a bergomask dance between two of our 5.01.353 P
shylock, do you hear? MV 1.03. 52
and let me see — but hear you, | methoughts you 1.03. 68
of usance for my moneys, and you'll not hear me. 1.03.141
but hear thee, gratiano: 2.02.180
signior bassanio, hear me: 2.02.189
hear you me, jessica: 2.05. 28
doors, and when you hear the drum | and the vile 2.05. 29
you were best to tell antonio what you hear, 2.08. 33
do you hear whether antonio have had any loss at 3.01. 42 P
i often came where i did hear of her, but cannot 3.01. 81 P
but let me hear the letter of your friend. 3.02.314
hear me yet, good shylock. 3.03. 3
i pray thee hear me speak. 3.03. 11
i will not hear thee speak. 3.03. 12
time the court shall hear bellario's letter. 4.01.149
you hear the learn'd bellario, what he writes, 4.01.167
if she were by to hear you make the offer. 4.01.289
but hark, i hear the footing of a man. 5.01. 24
doth grossly close it in, we cannot hear it. 5.01. 65
i am never merry when i hear sweet music. 5.01. 69
if they but hear perchance a trumpet sound, | or 5.01. 75
your husband is at hand, i hear his trumpet. 5.01.122
for, as i hear, he was much bound for you. 5.01.137
nay, but hear me. 5.01.246
and thou shalt hear how he will shake me up. AYL 1.01. 27 P
you shall hear me. 1.01. 66 P
dear sovereign, hear me speak. 1.03. 66
i cannot hear of any that did see her. 2.02. 4
when i did hear | the motley fool thus moral on 2.07. 28
didst thou hear these verses? 3.02.163 P
but didst thou hear without wondering how thy 3.02.172 P
do you hear, forester? 3.02.297 P
i had rather hear you chide than this man woo. 3.05. 65
he that speaks them pleases those that hear. 3.05.112
will you hear the letter? 4.03. 36
did you ever hear such railing? 4.03. 46 P
to her that is not here, nor doth not hear. 5.02.108
it but time lost to hear such a foolish song. 5.03. 40 P
there is a lord will hear you play to–night; SHR in.1. 93
i long to hear him call the drunkard husband, in.1. 133
i see, i hear, i speak; in.2. 70
therefore they thought it good you hear a play, in.2. 134
hark, tranio, thou mayst hear minerva speak. 1.01. 84
if that be all, masters, i hear no harm. 1.02.188
that gives not half so great a blow to hear | as 1.02.208
hear me with patience. 1.02.237
no, sir, but hear i do that he hath two: 1.02.251
morrow, kate — for that's your name, i hear. 2.01.182
nay, hear you, kate. in sooth you scape not so. 2.01.240
let's hear. o fie, the treble jars. 3.01. 39
"hic steterat priami," take heed he hear us not, 3.01. 44 P
and yet we hear not of our son–in–law. 3.02. 3
tedious it were to tell, and harsh to hear — 3.02.105
hark, hark, i hear the minstrels play. 3.02.183
this 'tis to feel a tale, not to hear a tale. 4.01. 63 P
do you hear, ho? 4.01. 98 P
i hear my master. 4.01.118 P
and, for the good report i hear of you, | and 4.04. 28
you, | signior baptista, of whom i hear so well. 4.04. 37
do you hear, sir? 5.01. 26 P
but do you hear, sir? 5.01.133 P
would always say — | methinks i hear him now; AWW 1.02. 53
i will now hear. 1.03. 1 P
i must not hear thee, fare thee well, kind maid! 2.01.145
sir, will you hear my suit? 2.03. 76
do you hear, monsieur? a word with you. 2.03.184 P
whilst i can shake my sword or hear the drum. 2.05. 91
you shall hear i am run away; 3.02. 22 P
say i, madam, if he run away, as i hear he does. 3.02. 40 P
for my part, i only hear your son was run away. 3.02. 43 P
whom heaven delights to hear | and loves to 3.04. 27
when haply he shall hear that she is gone, | he 3.04. 35
which you hear him so confidently undertake to 3.06. 20 P
and by midnight look to hear further from me. 3.06. 77 P
you shall hear one anon. 4.01. 63 P
keep him muffled | till we do hear from them. 4.01. 91
i'll order take my mother shall not hear. 4.02. 55

in the mean time, what hear you of these wars? 4.03. 37 P
i hear there is an overture of peace. 4.03. 39 P
not ended, as fearing to hear of it hereafter. 4.03. 97 P
you are, you must have the patience to hear it. 4.03.115 P
we shall hear of your /lordship anon. 4.03.195 P
i beseech your honor to hear me one single word. 5.02. 35 P
do you not hear, fellows? take away the lady. TN 1.05. 39 P
we'll once more hear orsino's embassy. 1.05.166
rather to wonder at you than to hear you. 1.05.199 P
us the place alone, we will hear this divinity. 1.05.218 P
o, stay and hear, your true-love's coming, 2.03. 40
to hear by the nose, it is dulcet in contagion. 2.03. 56 P
i had rather hear you to solicit that | than 3.01.109
so, let me hear you speak. 3.01.122
i warrant you, he will not hear of godliness. 3.04.121 P
and hear thou there how many fruitless pranks 4.01. 55
that sometime savors nobly), but hear me this: 5.01.120
comes sir toby halting — you shall hear more. 5.01.192 P
good madam, hear me speak, | and let no quarrel 5.01.355
i would not be a stander-by to hear | my WT 1.02.279
dost thou hear, camillo, | i conjure thee, by 1.02.399
it softly, | yond crickets shall not hear it. 2.01. 31
la you now, you hear! 2.03. 50
and i beseech you hear me, who professes 2.03. 53
and honor 'fore | who please to come and hear. 3.02. 42
hard'ned be the hearts | of all that hear me, 3.02. 53
but yet hear this — mistake me not; 3.02.109
if you did but hear the pedlar at the door, you 4.04.181 P
if thou'lt bear a part, thou shalt hear; 4.04.293 P
o, hear me breathe my life | before this ancient 4.04.360
let me hear | what you profess. 4.04.368
hear? 4.04.399
hark, perdita! | i'll hear you by and by. 4.04.507
i understand the business, i hear it. 4.04.670 P
nay, but hear me. 4.04.690 P
nay — but hear me. 4.04.691 P
e'er a son, sir, do you hear, and't like you, 4.04.781 P
that even your ears | should rift to hear me, 5.01. 66
that which you hear you'll swear you see, there 5.02. 31 P
what to speak, | i am content to hear; 5.03. 93
shall be holy, as | you hear my spell is lawful. 5.03.105
for thou shalt hear that i, | knowing by paulina 5.03.125
silence, good mother, hear the embassy. JN 1.01. 6
none but heaven, and you, and i, shall hear. 1.01. 43
hear the crier. 2.01.134
let us hear them speak | whose title they admit, 2.01.199
for our advantage — therefore hear us first: 2.01.206
o, tremble! for you hear the lion roar. 2.01.294
hear us, great kings! 2.01.416
persever not, but hear me, mighty kings. 2.01.421
speak on with favor, we are bent to hear. 2.01.422
hear me, o, hear me! 3.01.112
hear me, o, hear me! 3.01.112
o husband, hear me! 3.01.305
hear me without thine ears, and make reply 3.03. 49
which cannot hear a lady's feeble voice, | which 3.04. 41
now hear me speak with a prophetic spirit; 3.04.126
o sir, when he shall hear of your approach, | if 3.04.162
nay, hear me, hubert, drive these men away, 4.01. 78
i will both hear and grant you your requests. 4.02. 46
be drawn in france, | and she not hear of it? 4.02.119
and, as i hear, my lord, | the lady constance in 4.02.121
but if you be afeard to hear the worst, | then 4.02.135
do but hear me, sir. 4.03.119
your nobles will not hear you, but are gone | to 5.01. 33
now hear our english king, | for thus his 5.02.128
which then our leisure would not let us hear, R2 1.01. 5
brow, ourselves will hear | the accuser and the 1.01. 16
and what hear there for welcome but my groans? 1.02. 70
though richard my live's counsel would not hear, 2.01. 15
quick is mine ear to hear of good towards him. 2.01.234
but, lords, we hear this fearful tempest sing, 2.01.263
and yet we hear no tidings from the king, 2.04. 3
thieves are not judg'd but they are by to hear, 4.01.123
sweet york, be patient. hear me, gentle liege. 5.03. 91
i never long'd to hear a word till now, | say 5.03.115
music do i hear? 5.05. 41
had not an ear to hear my true time broke. 5.05. 48
the latest news we hear | is that the rebels 5.06. 1
but whether they be ta'en or slain we hear not. 5.06. 4
then let me hear | of you, my gentle cousin 1H4 1.01. 30
hear ye, yedward, if i tarry at home and go not, 1.02.134 P
whose daughter, as we hear, that earl of march 1.03. 84
let me not hear you speak of mortimer. 1.03.119
or you shall hear in such a kind from me | as 1.03.121
send us your prisoners, or you will hear of it. 1.03.124
he did, myself did hear it. 1.03.157
hear you, cousin, a word. 1.03.227
pismires, when i hear | of this vile politician, 1.03.240
canst not hear? 2.01. 28 P
list if thou canst hear the tread of travellers. 2.02. 33 P
stand close, i hear them coming. 2.02. 97 P
but hear you, my lord. 2.03. 73
away, you rogue, dost thou not hear them call? 2.04. 78 P
dost thou hear me, hal? 2.04.209 P
in base comparisons, hear me speak but this — 2.04.251 P
come, let's hear, jack, what trick hast thou now 2.04.265 P
why, hear you, my masters, was it for me to kill 2.04.268 P
before, i blush'd to hear his monstrous devices. 2.04.313 P
the complaints i hear of thee are grievous. 2.04.442 P
dost thou hear, hal? 2.04.491 P
i had rather hear a brazen canstick turn'd, | or 3.01.129
with all my heart i'll sit and hear her sing. 3.01.220
ye thief, and hear the lady sing in welsh. 3.01.234 P
i had rather hear lady, my brach, howl in irish. 3.01.235 P
which oft the ear of greatness needs must hear 3.02. 24
my lord, i pray you hear me. 3.03. 91 P
good my lord, hear me. 3.03. 94 P
dost thou hear, hal? 3.03.164 P
on fire | to hear this rich reprisal is so nigh, 4.01.118
that's the worst tidings that i hear of /yet. 4.01.127
as had as lieve hear the devil as a drum, such 4.02. 18 P
tut, i came not to hear this. 4.03. 89
hear me, my liege. 5.01. 22
and so i hear he doth account me too; 5.01. 95
doth he hear it? 5.01.137 P
life | did hear a challenge urg'd more modestly, 5.02. 52
never did i hear | of any prince so wild a 5.02. 70
scroop, | who, as we hear, are busily in arms. 5.05. 38
i hear for certain and dare speak the truth, 2H4 1.01.188
and, as i hear, is now going with some charge to 1.02. 62 P
i hear his majesty is return'd with some 1.02.103 P
and i hear, moreover, his highness is fall'n 1.02.107 P
the disease, for you hear not what i say to you. 1.02.119 P
i hear you are going with lord john of lancaster 1.02.203 P
well spoke on, i can hear it with mine own ears. 2.02. 65 P
mistress tearsheet would fain hear some music. 2.04. 12 P
dost thou hear, hostess? 2.04. 79 P
dost thou hear? it is mine ancient. 2.04. 82 P
you would bless you to hear what he said. 2.04. 95 P
didst thou hear me? 2.04.305 P
to hear and absolutely to determine | of what 4.01.162
encircled you to hear with reverence | your 4.02. 6
will not go off until they hear you speak. 4.02.100
lords, | i hear the king my father is sore sick. 4.03. 77
i never thought to hear you speak again. 4.05. 91
and hear (i think) the very latest counsel 4.05.182
a son, | hear your own dignity so much profan'd, 5.02. 93
when thou dost hear i am as i have been, 5.05. 60
and, as we hear you do reform yourselves, | we 5.05. 68
i cannot now speak, i will hear you soon. 5.05. 94
gently to hear, kindly to judge, our play. H5 pr 34
hear him but reason in divinity, | and, 1.01. 38
hear him debate of commonwealth affairs, | you 1.01. 41
and you shall hear | a fearful battle rend'red 1.01. 43
save that there was not time enough to hear, 1.01. 84
i'll wait upon you, and i long to hear it. 1.01. 98
before we hear him, of some things of weight 1.02. 5
for we will hear, note, and believe in heart, 1.02. 30
then hear me, gracious sovereign, and you peers, 1.02. 33
for hear her but exampled by herself: 1.02.156
for we hear | your greeting is from him, not 1.02.235
dukedoms that you claim | hear no more of you. 1.02.257
hear me, hear me what i say. 2.01. 63 P
hear me, hear me what i say. 2.01. 63 P
hear your sentence. 2.02.166
hear the shrill whistle which doth order give 3.pr. 9
go speak, the duke will hear thy voice; 3.06. 46
why, the enemy is loud, you hear him all night. 4.01. 75 P
thou never shalt hear herald any more. 4.03.127
your majesty hear now, saving your majesty's 4.08. 33 P
i will be glad to hear you confess it brokenly 5.02.106 P
lieutenant, is it you whose voice i hear? 1H6 1.03. 16
i grieve to hear what torments you endur'd, 1.04. 57
hear, hear how dying salisbury doth groan! 1.04.104
hear, hear how dying salisbury doth groan! 1.04.104
when they shall hear how we have play'd the men. 1.06. 16
this is my servant, hear him, noble prince. 4.01. 80
he fables not, i hear the enemy. 4.02. 42
i were best to leave him, for he will not hear. 5.03. 83
hear ye, captain? are you not at leisure? 5.03. 97
away from me, and let me hear no more! 2H6 1.02. 50
we'll hear more of your matter before the king. 1.03. 35 P
will her ladyship behold and hear our exorcisms? 1.04. 4 P
sorry i am to hear what i have heard. 2.01.189
my lord, i long to hear it at full. 2.02. 6
to see my tears and hear my deep-fet groans. 2.04. 33
didst ever hear a man so penitent? 3.02. 4
until they hear the order of his death. 3.02.129
as curst, as harsh, and horrible to hear, 3.02.312
let me hear from thee; 3.02.405
words as no christian ear can endure to hear. 4.07. 41 P
hear me but speak, and bear me where you will. 4.07. 59
what noise is this i hear? 4.08. 3 P
for, as i hear, the king is fled to london, | to 5.03. 24
hear him, lords, | and be you silent and 3H6 1.01.121
my lord of warwick, hear but one word: 1.01.170
i cannot stay to hear these articles. 1.01.180
i shame to hear thee speak. 1.01.231
stay, gentle margaret, and hear me speak. 1.01.257
prove the contrary, if you'll hear me speak. 1.02. 20
i hear their drums. 1.02. 69
sweet clifford, hear me speak before i die: 1.03. 18
nay, stay, let's hear the orisons he makes. 1.04.110
say how he died, for i will hear it all. 2.01. 49
nor now my scandal, richard, dost thou hear; 2.01.151
ay, now methinks i hear great warwick speak. 2.01.186
didst thou never hear | that things ill got had 2.02. 45
for, as i hear, | you that are king, though he 2.02. 89
done with words, my lords, and hear me speak. 2.02.117
forbear awhile, we'll hear a little more. 3.01. 27
and, as i hear, the great commanding warwick 3.01. 29
with remorse | to hear and see her plaints, her 3.01. 41
why stops my lord? shall i not hear my task? 3.02. 52
bona, hear me speak | before you answer warwick. 3.03. 65
now, sister, let us hear your firm resolve. 3.03.129
i hear, yet say not much, but think the more. 4.01. 83
men well inclin'd to hear what thou command'st; 4.08. 16
then clarence is at hand, i hear his drum. 5.01. 11
that we could hear no news of his repair? 5.01. 20
but at last | i well might hear, delivered with 5.02. 46
and, as we hear, march on to fight with us. 5.03. 9
go bear them hence, i will not hear them speak. 5.05. 4
bring forth the gallant, let us hear him speak. 5.05. 12
ere ye come there, be sure to hear some news. 5.05. 48
didst thou not hear me swear i would not do it? 5.05. 74
i'll hear no more; 5.06. 57
ghost | to hear the lamentations of poor anne, R3 1.02. 9
one place else, if you will hear me name it. 1.02.110
to hear the piteous moan that rutland made 1.02.157
hear me, you wrangling pirates, that fall out 1.03.157
stay, dog, for thou shalt hear me. 1.03.215
my hair doth stand an end to hear her curses. 1.03.303
withal obdurate, do not hear him plead; 1.03.346
i am afraid, methinks, to hear you tell it. 1.04. 65
i will not rise, unless your highness hear me. 2.01. 98
pale when they did hear of clarence' death? 2.01.137
hear you the news abroad? 2.03. 3
but i hear no; 2.04. 6
how, my young york? i prithee let me hear it. 2.04. 26
shall we hear from you, catesby, ere we sleep? 3.01.188
to hear her prayer for them, as now for us! 3.03. 20
yet witness what you hear we did intend. 3.05. 70
the marquess dorset, as i hear, is fled | to 4.02. 48
i hear the news, my lord. 4.02. 86
aery wings | and hear your mother's lamentation! 4.04. 14
let not the heavens hear these tell-tale women 4.04.150
then patiently hear my impatience. 4.04.157
do then, but i'll not hear. 4.04.160
i prithee hear me speak. 4.04.180
hear me a word; 4.04.181
prepare her ears to hear a wooer's tale; 4.04.327
hark, i hear their drum. 5.03.337
only they | that come to hear a merry, bawdy H8 pr 14
i am sorry | to hear this of him; 1.01.194
person | i'll hear him his confessions justify, 1.02. 6
sit by us, you shall hear | (this was his 1.02.124
we cannot feel too little, hear too much. 1.02.128
hour | to hear from him a matter of some moment; 1.02.163
i hear of none but the new proclamation | that's 1.03. 17
to hear what shall become | of the great duke of 2.01. 2
again to th' bar, to hear | his knell rung out, 2.01. 31
hear what i say, and then go home and lose me. 2.01. 57
yet, you that hear me, | this from a dying man 2.01.124
did you not of late days hear | a buzzing of a 2.01.147
pray hear me. 3.01.142
i should be glad to hear such news as this 3.02. 24
so i hear. 3.02. 74
speedily i wish | to hear from rome. 3.02. 90
hear the king's pleasure, cardinal! 3.02.228
till you hear further from his highness. 3.02.232
lords, | can ye endure to hear this arrogance? 3.02.278
and thus far hear me, cromwell, | and when i am 3.02.431
your highness | to hear me speak his good now? 4.02. 47
hear me, sir thomas, y' are a gentleman | of 5.01. 27
we shall hear more anon. 5.02. 35
his royal self in judgment comes to hear | the 5.02.155
but know i come not | to hear such flattery now, 5.02.159
do you hear, master porter? 5.03. 28 P
others, to hear the city | abus'd extremely, and ep 5
all the expected good w' are like to hear | for ep 8
hark, do you not hear the people cry "troilus"? TRO 1.02.224 P
should be shut up, hear what ulysses speaks. 1.03. 58
thou great, and wise, to hear ulysses speak. 1.03. 69
it rich | to hear the wooden dialogue and sound 1.03.155
thou bitch-wolf's son, canst thou not hear? 2.01. 10 P
thought | unfit to hear moral philosophy. 2.02.167
ay, the heavens hear me! 2.03. 36 P
hear you, patroclus: 2.03.112
shall not hedge us out, we'll hear you sing, 3.01. 60 P
come, i'll hear no more of this, i'll sing you a 3.01.105 P
i long to hear how they sped to-day. 3.01.141 P
hear me, paris: 4.01. 69
hear me, love. be thou but true of heart — 4.04. 58
hear why i speak it, love. 4.04. 75
do you hear, my lord? do you hear? 5.03. 97 P
do you hear, my lord? do you hear? 5.03. 97 P
now, | but thou anon shalt hear of me again; 5.06. 18
fate, hear me what i say! 5.06. 25
but hear you, hear you! 5.10. 32 P
but hear you, hear you! 5.10. 32 P
before we proceed any further, hear me speak. COR 1.01. 1 P
well, i'll hear it, sir; 1.01. 93 P
where th' other instruments | did see and hear, 1.01.102
patience awhile, you'st hear the belly's answer. 1.01.126
hence, and hear | how the dispatch is made, and 1.01.276
hear me profess sincerely: 1.03. 21 P
methinks i hear hither your husband's drum; 1.03. 29
see the swords and hear a drum than look upon 1.03. 55 P
then shall we hear their 'larum, and they ours. 1.04. 9
be frighted | and, gladly quak'd, hear more; 1.09. 6
what you have done, before our army hear me. 1.09. 27
and they smart | to hear themselves rememb'red. 1.09. 29
to see him, and | the blind to hear him speak. 2.01.263
please you | to hear cominius speak? 2.02. 62
never shame to hear | what you have nobly done. 2.02. 67
to heal again | than hear say how i got them. 2.02. 70
than idly sit | to hear my nothings monster'd. 2.02. 77
for honor | than /one /on /'s ears to hear it? 2.02. 81
hear you this triton of the minnows? 3.01. 89
hear me, people, peace! 3.01.191
let's hear our tribune; 3.01.192
hear me one word, | beseech you, tribunes, hear 3.01.214
beseech you, tribunes, hear me but a word. 3.01.215
hear me speak! 3.01.275
we'll hear no more. 3.01.306
they are prepar'd | with accusations, as i hear, 3.02.140
and when they hear me say, "it shall be so | i' 3.03. 13
first hear me speak. 3.03. 41
hear me, my masters, and my common friends — 3.03.108
that thou mayst hear of us | and we of thee; 4.01. 39
you shall | hear from me still, and never of me 4.01. 52
that's worthily | as any ear can hear. 4.01. 54
if that i could for weeping, you should hear — 4.02. 13
should hear — | nay, and you shall hear some. 4.02. 14
ere you go, hear this: 4.02. 38
i am joyful to hear of their readiness, and am 4.03. 46 P
we hear not of him, neither need we fear him; 4.06. 1
where is he, hear you? 4.06. 17
nay, i hear nothing; 4.06. 18
his mother and his wife | hear nothing from him. 4.06. 19
faith, we hear fearful news. 4.06.139
you hear what he hath said | which was sometime 5.01. 1
if he coy'd | to hear cominius speak, i'll keep 5.01. 7
do you hear? 5.01. 8
i think he'll hear me. 5.01. 48
he'll never hear him. 5.01. 62
who, as i hear, mean to solicit him | for mercy 5.01. 72
our general | will no more hear from thence. 5.02. 6
word, menenius, | i will not hear thee speak. 5.02. 92
do you hear how we are shent for keeping your 5.02. 98 P
may hang upon your hardness, therefore hear us. 5.03. 91
for we'll | hear nought from rome in private. 5.03. 93
he approaches, you shall hear him. 5.06. 69
peace both, and hear me speak. 5.06.110
my noble masters, hear me speak. 5.06.131
then hear me speak indifferently for all; TIT 1.01.430
terms | that ever ear did hear to such effect, 2.03.111
i will not hear her speak, away with her! 2.03.137
sweet lords, entreat her hear me but a word. 2.03.138
hear me, grave fathers! 3.01. 1
the tribunes hear you not, no man is by, | and 3.01. 28
if they did hear, | they would not mark me; 3.01. 33
dear heart, for heaven shall hear our prayers, 3.01.210

can you hear a good man groan | and not relent, 4.01.123
that highly may advantage thee to hear. 5.01. 56
'twill vex thy soul to hear what i shall speak: 5.01. 62
ruthful to hear, yet piteously perform'd. 5.01. 66
to that which thou shalt hear of me anon. 5.01. 90
but let them hear what fearful words i utter. 5.02.168
while i stand by and weep to hear him speak. 5.03. 95
neighbor–stained steel — | will they not hear? ROM 1.01. 83
and hear the sentence of your moved prince. 1.01. 88
wert so happy by thy stay | to hear true shrift. 1.01.159
hear all, all see; 1.02. 30
i have rememb'red me, thou s' hear our counsel. 1.03. 9
and if he hear thee, thou wilt anger him. 2.01. 22
shall i hear more, or shall i speak at this? 2.02. 37
i hear some noise within; 2.02.136
nurse, that loves to hear himself talk, and will 2.04.147 P
did you ne'er hear say, | "two may keep counsel, 2.04.196
rosemary, that it would do you good to hear it. 2.04.212 P
of us, look to hear nothing but discords. 3.01. 47 P
/thou fond mad man, hear me a little speak. 3.03. 52
here all the night | to hear good counsel. 3.03.160
i must hear from thee every day in the hour, 3.05. 44
o, how my heart abhors | to hear him nam'd, and 3.05.100
hear me with patience but to speak a word. 3.05.159
i hear thou must, and nothing may prorogue it, 4.01. 48
things that, to hear them told, have made me 4.01. 86
i hear him near. 4.04. 23
digging up of graves, | but thou shalt hear it. 5.03. 7
i hear some noise, lady. 5.03.151
nay, sir, but hear me on: TIM 1.01. 77
lord timon, hear me speak. 1.01.110
i thank you, you shall hear from me anon. 1.01.153
wait attendance | till you hear further from me. 1.01.162
why then another time i'll hear thee. 1.02.178
thou wilt not hear me now, thou shalt not then. 1.02.247 P
what shall be done, he will not hear, till feel. 2.02. 7
you would not hear me; 2.02.127
though you hear now (too late), yet now's a time 2.02.143
my lord, and which i hear from common rumors, 3.02. 5 P
do you hear, sir? 3.04. 43
business, but he would not hear my excuse. 3.06. 14 P
alcibiades is banish'd: hear you of it? 3.06. 53 P
the gods confound (hear me, you good gods all) 4.01. 37
hear you, master steward, where's our master? 4.02. 1
agues | th' immortal gods that hear you. 4.03.139
ay, and you hear him cog, see him dissemble, 5.01. 95
banks | to hear the replication of your sounds JC 1.01. 46
i hear a tongue shriller than all the music 1.02. 16
speak, caesar is turn'd to hear. 1.02. 17
therefore, good brutus, be prepar'd to hear; 1.02. 66
i did hear him groan; 1.02.124
you have to say | i will with patience hear, and 1.02.169
both meet to hear and answer such high things. 1.02.170
for he loves to hear | that unicorns may be 2.01.203
had you a healthful ear to hear of it. 2.01.319
i hear none, madam. 2.04. 17
sooth, madam, i hear nothing. 2.04. 20
caesar | to be so good to caesar as to hear me: 2.04. 29
those that will hear me speak, let 'em stay here 3.02. 5
i will hear brutus speak. 3.02. 8
i will hear cassius, and compare their reasons, 3.02. 9
reasons, | when severally we hear them rendered. 3.02. 10
and lovers, hear me for my cause, and be silent, 3.02. 13 P
for my cause, and be silent, that you may hear. 3.02. 14 P
stay ho, and let us hear mark antony. 3.02. 62
go up into the public chair, | we'll hear him. 3.02. 64
peace, let us hear what antony can say. 3.02. 71
peace ho, let us hear him. 3.02. 72
let but the commons hear this testament — 3.02.130
we'll hear the will. read it, mark antony. 3.02.138
the will, the will! we will hear caesar's will. 3.02.139
read the will, we'll hear it, antony. 3.02.147
peace there, hear the noble antony. 3.02.207 P
we'll hear him, we'll follow him, we'll die with 3.02.208 P
yet hear me, countrymen, yet hear me speak. 3.02.233
yet hear me, countrymen, yet hear me speak. 3.02.233
peace ho, hear antony, most noble antony! 3.02.234 P
let's stay and hear the will. 3.02.239
hear me with patience. 3.02.245
hear me, for i will speak. 4.03. 38
why ask you? hear you aught of her in yours? 4.03.185
hear me, good brother. 4.03.212
didst thou not hear their shouts? 5.03. 83
hear not my steps, which /way /they walk, for MAC 2.01. 57
hear it not, duncan, for it is a knell, | that 2.01. 63
didst thou not hear a noise? 2.02. 14
i hear a knocking | at the south entry. 2.02. 62
'tis not for you to hear what i can speak: 2.03. 84
we hear our bloody cousins are bestow'd | in 3.01. 29
hark, i hear horses. 3.03. 8
to–morrow | we'll hear ourselves again. 3.04. 31
i hear it by the way; 3.04.129
any heart alive | to hear the men deny't. 3.06. 16
feast, i hear | macduff lives in disgrace. 3.06. 22
if th' hadst rather hear it from our mouths, 4.01. 62
hear his speech, but say thou nought. 4.01. 70
had i three ears, i'ld hear thee. 4.01. 78
i did hear | the galloping of horse. 4.01.139
royal preparation | makes us hear something. 5.03. 58
would have cool'd | to hear a night–shriek, and 5.05. 11
thou'lt be afraid to hear it. 5.07. 5
i think i hear them. stand ho! who is there? HAM 1.01. 14
down, | and let us hear barnardo speak of this. 1.01. 34
i would not hear your enemy say so, | nor shall 1.02.170
for god's love let me hear! 1.02.195
do not sleep, | but let me hear from you. 1.03. 4
speak, i am bound to hear. 1.05. 6
so art thou to revenge, when thou shalt hear. 1.05. 7
now, hamlet, hear: 1.05. 34
come on, you hear this fellow in the cellarage, 1.05.151
o, speak of that, that do i long to hear. 2.02. 50
but you shall hear. 2.02.112 P
do you hear, let them be well us'd, for they are 2.02.523 P
him, friends, we'll hear a play to–morrow. 2.02.535 P
dost thou hear me, old friend? 2.02.537 P
did seem in him a kind of joy | to hear of it. 3.01. 19
your majesties | to hear and see the matter. 3.01. 23
doth much content me | to hear him so inclin'd. 3.01. 25

i hear him coming. withdraw, my lord. 3.01. 54
it offends me to the soul to hear a robustious 3.02. 9 P
will the king hear this piece of work? 3.02. 46 P
dost thou hear? 3.02. 62
arras i'll convey myself | to hear the process. 3.03. 29
withdraw, | i hear him coming. 3.04. 7
nor did you nothing hear? 3.04.133
and they shall hear and judge 'twixt you and me. 4.05.206
you shortly shall hear more. 4.07. 33
laertes, you shall hear them. 4.07. 41
nay, but hear you, goodman delver — 5.01. 14 P
hear you, sir, | what is the reason that you use 5.01.288
but wilt thou hear now how i did proceed? 5.02. 27
i cannot live to hear the news from england, 5.02.354
so shall you hear | of carnal, bloody, and 5.02.380
let us haste to hear it, | and call the noblest 5.02.386
hear me, recreant, | on thine allegiance, hear LR 1.01.166
me, recreant, | on thine allegiance, hear me! 1.01.167
you where you shall hear us confer of this, and 1.02. 91 P
i will fitly bring you to hear my lord speak. 1.02.169 P
shall i hear from you anon? 1.02.177 P
he's coming, madam, i hear him. 1.03. 11
hear, nature, hear, dear goddess, hear! 1.04.275
hear, nature, hear, dear goddess, hear! 1.04.275
hear, nature, hear, dear goddess, hear! 1.04.275
when she shall hear this of thee, with her nails 1.04.307
i hear my father coming. 2.01. 28
i hear that you have shown your father | a 2.01.105
bid them come forth and hear me, | or at their 2.04.117
hear me, my lord: 2.04.260
ere long you are like to hear | (if you dare 4.02. 19
soon may i hear and see him! 4.04. 29
if you do chance to hear of that blind traitor, 4.05. 37
horrible steep. | hark, do you hear the sea? 4.06. 4
bid me farewell, and let me hear thee going. 4.06. 31
hear you, sir! 4.06. 46
shake the head | to hear of pleasure's name — 4.06.121
do you hear aught, sir, of a battle toward? 4.06.209
far off methinks i hear the beaten drum. 4.06.285
had speech with man so poor, | hear me one word. 5.01. 39
and hear poor rogues | talk of court news; 5.03. 13
stay yet, hear reason. 5.03. 82
/'sblood, but you'll not hear me. OTH 1.01. 4
these things to hear | would desdemona seriously 1.03.145
i pray you hear her speak. 1.03.175
i never yet did hear | that the bruis'd heart 1.03.218
go to, farewell. do you hear, roderigo? 1.03.376 P
what shall we hear of this? 2.01. 9
to hear music the general does not greatly care. 3.01. 16 P
dost thou hear, mine honest friend? 3.01. 21 P
no, i hear not your honest friend; i hear you. 3.01. 22 P
no, i hear not your honest friend; i hear you. 3.01. 22 P
why, stay, and hear me speak. 3.03. 31
i am sorry to hear this. 3.03.344
within these three days let me hear thee say 3.03.472
dost thou hear, iago, | i will be found most 4.01. 89
but (dost thou hear) most bloody. 4.01. 91
do you hear, cassio? 4.01.113
you shall hear more by midnight. 4.01.212 P
will you hear me, roderigo? 4.02.181 P
i will hear further reason for this. 4.02.244 P
/did not you hear a cry? 5.01. 49
nay, /an' you stare, we shall hear more anon. 5.01.107
hark, canst thou hear me? 5.02.247
nay, hear them, antony. ANT 1.01. 19
is come from caesar, therefore hear it, antony. 1.01. 27
hear the ambassadors. 1.01. 48
nay, hear him. 1.02. 25 P
good isis, hear me this prayer, though thou deny 1.02. 68 P
dear goddess, hear that prayer of the people! 1.02. 70 P
tale lie death, | i hear him as he flatter'd. 1.02. 99
hear me, queen: 1.03. 41
not now to hear thee sing. 1.05. 9
you may, when you hear no more words of pompey, 2.02.104 P
let me hear agrippa further speak. 2.02.123
good madam, hear me. 2.05. 36
will't please you hear me? 2.05. 41
thee, captain, | and hear me speak a word. 2.07. 39
if for the sake of merit thou wilt hear me, 2.07. 55
let neptune hear we bid a loud farewell | to 2.07.132
sweet octavia, | you shall hear from me still; 3.02. 60
didst hear her speak? 3.03. 12
who's his lieutenant, hear you? 3.07. 77
hear it apart. 3.13. 47
spirits | to hear from me you had left antony, 3.13. 70
from his all–obeying breath i hear | the doom of 3.13. 77
dost thou hear, lady? 3.13.172
see if other watchmen | do hear what we do. 4.03. 18
how now? | how now? do you hear this? 4.03. 19
do you hear, masters? do you hear? 4.03. 20
do you hear, masters? do you hear? 4.03. 20
to daff't for our repose, shall hear a storm. 4.04. 13
he shall not hear thee, or from caesar's camp 4.05. 8
let's hear him, for the things he speaks | may 4.09. 24
hear you, sir? 4.09. 28
gentle, hear me: 4.15. 47
hear me, good friends — | but i will tell you 5.01. 48
we'll hear him what he says. 5.01. 51
hear me, good madam: 5.02.100
methinks i hear | antony call; 5.02.283
i hear him mock | the luck of caesar, which the 5.02.285
that i might hear thee call great caesar ass 5.02.307
good pisanio, | when shall we hear from him? CYM 1.03. 23
to be by | and hear him mock the frenchman. 1.06. 76
let me hear no more. 1.06.117
did you hear of a stranger that's come to court 2.01. 32 P
and you shall hear | the legion now in gallia 2.04. 17
will you hear more? 2.04.141
when we shall hear | the rain and wind beat dark 3.03. 36
good madam, hear me. 3.04. 57
good lady, | hear me with patience. 3.04.112
thief, | hear but my name, and tremble. 4.02. 87
and do | no harm by it, though the gods hear, i 4.02.378
can affront no less | than what you hear of. 4.03. 30
nor hear i from my mistress, who did promise 4.03. 38
that when they hear their roman horses neigh, 4.04. 17
good heavens, | hear patiently my purpose: 5.01. 22
rather to wonder at the things you hear | than 5.03. 54

could not find death where i did hear him groan, 5.03. 69
wilt thou hear more, my lord? 5.05.146
while nature will | than die ere i hear more. 5.05.152
peace, my lord, hear, hear — 5.05.227
peace, my lord, hear, hear — 5.05.227
when shall i hear all through? 5.05.382
and that to hear an old man sing | may to your PER 1.ch. 13
few love to hear the sins they love to act; 1.01. 92
should let their ears hear their faults hid! 1.02. 62
intend my travel, where i'll hear from thee, 1.02.116
with their superfluous riots, hear these tears! 1.04. 54
lord governor, for so we hear you are, | let not 1.04. 85
griev'd my heart to hear what pitiful cries they 2.01. 21 P
therefore hear you, mistress, either frame 2.05. 81
your will to mine — and you, sir, hear you — 2.05. 82
live, and make | us weep to hear your fate, fair 3.02.103
did you ever hear the like? 4.05. 1 P
shall 's go hear the vestals sing? 4.05. 7 P
i hear say you're of honorable parts, and are 4.06. 80 P
if thou dost | hear from me, it shall be for thy 4.06.116
i'll hear you more, to th' bottom of your story, 5.01.164
my lord, i hear none. 5.01.227
rarest sounds! do ye not hear? 5.01.231
music, my lord, i hear. 5.01.232
now do i long to hear how you were found, | how 5.03. 56
do our longing stay | to hear the rest untold. 5.03. 84
and the first sound this child hear be a hiss, TNK pr 16
you shall hear | scenes, though below his art, pr 27
and true gentility's, | hear and respect me! 1.01. 26
thrive with fair ones, | hear and respect me! 1.01. 28
hear nothing but the clock that tells our woes; 2.02. 42
i would hear you still. 2.02.111
to hear him | sing in an evening, what a heaven 2.04. 18
of another | you would not hear me doubted, but 3.01. 61
you hear the horns: 3.01. 96
i'll hear no more. 3.03. 53
i hear the horns. 3.05. 93
next hear my prayers. 3.06.210
hear you no more? 4.01. 1
which you'll hear of | at better time. 4.01. 29
pray did you ever hear | of one young palamon? 4.01.116
to hear there a proud lady and a proud city–wife 4.03. 51 P
the which there is | no deafing — but to hear, 5.03. 9
peace, hear me! STM II.C 1 P
the noble earl of shrewsbury, let's hear him. II.C 30 P
we'll hear the earl of surrey. II.C 31 P
we'll hear both. II.C 33 P
we'll not hear my lord of surrey, no, no, no, no II.C 38 P
shall we hear shrieve more speak? II.C 41 P
let's hear him. II.C 42 P
let's hear shrieve more. II.C 43 P
good masters, hear me speak. II.C 57
though neither eyes nor ears to hear nor see, VEN 437
and that i could not see, nor hear, nor touch, 440
anon their loud alarums he doth hear, | and now 700
"lie quietly, and hear a little more, | nay, do 709
the tiger would be tame and gently hear him; 1096
until her husband's welfare she did hear; LUC 263
trembling fear, as fowl hear falcons' bells. 511
quoth he, "by heaven, i will not hear thee. 667
as well to hear as grant what he hath said. 915
o, hear me then, injurious, shifting time! 930
she hoards, to spend when he is by to hear her, 1318
see sad sights moves more than hear them told, 1324
'tis but a part of sorrow that we hear: 1328
with sad attention long to hear her words. 1610
longing to hear the hateful foe bewray'd. 1698
thou lov'st to hear the sweet melodious sound PP 8. 9
i fear — | lest that my mistress hear my song; 18.50
be it said, | to hear her secrets so bewray'd. 18.54
ditty, | that to hear it was great pity. 20.12
that to hear her so complain, | scarce i could 20.15
senseless trees they cannot hear thee, 20.21
music to hear, why hear'st thou music sadly? SON 8. 1
to hear with eyes belongs to love's fine wit. 23.14
dead | than you shall hear the surly sullen bell 71. 2
for fear of which, hear this, thou age unbred: 104.13
i love to hear her speak, yet well i know | that 130. 9
the more i hear and see just cause of hate? 150.10
"'how mighty then you are, o, hear me tell! LC 253

/HEARD 4 FR 0.0004 REL FR 3 V 1 P

/heard in genoa? MV 3.01.107 P
/and /cornwall's /powers /you /heard /not? LR 4.03. 48
you /heard her say herself, it was not i. OTH 5.02.127
mine ears, that /heard her flattery, nor my CYM 5.05. 64

HEARD 365 FR 0.0412 REL FR 264 V 101 P

when i arriv'd and heard thee, that made gape TMP 1.02.292
wert thou, if the king of naples heard thee? 1.02.432
now, we heard a hollow burst of bellowing | like 2.01.311
i heard nothing. 2.01.313
heard you this, gonzalo? 2.01.316
sir, i heard a humming | (and that a strange one 2.01.317
milan, | of whom so often i have heard renown, 5.01.193
excellent device, was there ever heard a better, TGV 2.01.139
he heard not that. 4.02.118
and i have heard thee say | no grief did ever 4.03. 18
for i have heard him say a thousand times | his 4.04.134
i heard say he was outrun on cotsall. WIV 1.01. 90 P
i think there are, sir, i heard them talk'd of. 1.01.288 P
mov'd, you should have heard him so loud and so 1.04. 91 P
i never heard such a drawling, affecting rogue. 2.01.141 P
you heard what this knave told me, did you not? 2.01.169 P
yes, and you heard what the other told me? 2.01.171 P
i have heard the frenchman hath good skill in 2.01.222 P
i never heard a man of his place, gravity, and 3.01. 57 P
heard you that? 3.03.201 P
you have heard of such a spirit, and well you 4.04. 35
i never heard any soldier dislike it. MM 1.02. 17 P
you have not heard of the proclamation, have you 1.02. 93 P
have you not heard speak of mariana, the sister 3.01.209 P
i have heard of the lady, and good words went 3.01.211 P
i never heard the absent duke much detected for 3.02.121 P
painting, sir, i have heard say, is a mystery; 4.02. 36 P
i have heard it was ever his manner to do so. 4.02.134 P
till you have heard me in my true complaint 5.01. 24
of thing on thing, | as e'er i heard in madness. 5.01. 63
lord, and i have heard | your royal ear abus'd. 5.01.138
spake with her, saw her, nor heard from her, 5.01.223

thou hast, | rely upon it till my tale be heard, 5.01.365
(as i have heard him swear himself there's one 5.01.510
thus have you heard me sever'd from my bliss, ERR 1.01.118
have you not heard men say, | that time comes 4.02. 59
who heard me to deny it or forswear it? 5.01. 25
heard you confess you had the chain of him, 5.01.261
and when i have heard it, what blessing brings ADO 1.03. 6 P
and there heard it agreed upon that the prince 1.03. 61 P
i heard him swear his affection. 2.01.168 P
for i have heard my daughter say, she hath often 2.01.344 P
i had as live have heard the night–raven, come 2.03. 82 P
sit you — you heard my daughter tell you how. 2.03.111 P
and when you have seen more, and heard more, 3.02.122 P
what heard you him say else? 4.02. 46 P
no? come, brother, away! i will be heard. 5.01.108
also, the watch heard them talk of one deformed. 5.01.307 P
her | upon the error that you heard debated. 5.04. 3
as i look'd for, but the best that ever i heard. LLL 1.01.280 P
so i heard you say. 1.02.142 P
was there with him, if i have heard a truth. 2.01. 65
i do protest i never heard of it; 2.01.157
i would you heard it groan. 2.01.183
her mother's, i have heard. 2.01.202
i heard your guilty rhymes, observ'd your 4.03.137
oft have i heard of you, my lord berowne, 5.02.841
i must confess that i have heard so much, | and MND 1.01.111
and heard a mermaid on a dolphin's back 2.01.150
he goes but to see a noise that he heard, and is 3.01. 91 P
i never heard | so musical a discord, such sweet 4.01.117
the eye of man hath not heard, the ear of man 4.01.211 P
he cannot be heard of. 4.02. 3 P
i have heard it over, | and it is nothing, 5.01. 77
wittiest partition that ever i heard discourse, 5.01.167 P
o wall, full often hast thou heard my moans, 5.01.188
this is the silliest stuff that ever i heard. 5.01.210 P
have you heard any imputation to the contrary? MV 1.03. 13 P
is not gold, | often have you heard that told; 2.07. 66
i never heard a passion so confus'd, | so 2.08. 12
antonio, as i heard in genoa — 3.01. 98 P
your daughter spent in genoa, as i heard, one 3.01.108 P
when i was with him i have heard him swear | to 3.02.284
i have heard | your grace hath ta'en great pains 4.01. 6
he is not, nor we have not heard from him. 5.01. 35
time that ever i heard breaking of ribs was AYL 1.02.138 P
hath heard your praises, and this night he means 2.03. 22
o yes, i heard them all, and more, too, for some 3.02.164 P
i have heard him read many lectures against it, 3.02.347 P
you have heard him swear downright he was. 3.04. 29 P
so please you, for i never heard it yet; 4.03. 37
yet heard too much of phebe's cruelty. 4.03. 38
o, i have heard him speak of that same brother, 4.03.121
if i heard you rightly, | the duke hath put on a 5.04.180
there is much matter to be heard and learn'd. 5.04.185
(for yet his honor never heard a play), | you SHR in.1. 96
have i not in my time heard lions roar? 1.02.200
have i not heard the sea, puff'd up with winds, 1.02.201
have i not heard great ord'nance in the field, 1.02.203
have i not in a pitched battle heard | loud 1.02.205
of that report which i so oft have heard. 2.01. 53
well have you heard, but something hard of 2.01.183
/old /news, and such news as you never heard of! 3.02. 31 P
thou shouldst have heard how her horse fell and 4.01. 73 P
thou shouldst have heard in how miry a place, 4.01. 75 P
i have often heard | of your entire affection to 4.02. 22
you might have heard it else proclaim'd about. 4.02. 87
i know him not, but i have heard of him; 4.02. 97
i heard not of it before. AWW 1.01. 35 P
the complaints i have heard of you i do not all 1.03. 9 P
of sorrow that e'er i heard virgin exclaim in, 1.03.118 P
with, should be once heard and thrice beaten. 2.05. 31 P
so that from point to point now have you heard 3.01. 1
honesty, and that | i have not heard examin'd. 3.05. 63
since i heard of the good lady's death and that 4.05. 69 P
i have heard my father name him. TN 1.02. 28
i heard my lady talk of it yesterday; 1.03. 15 P
i have heard her swear't. 1.03.111 P
i heard you were saucy at my gates, and allow'd 1.05.197 P
of messaline, whom i know you have heard of. 2.01. 18 P
that old and antique song we heard last night; 2.04. 3
me, and i have heard herself come thus near, 2.05. 24 P
i have heard of some kind of men that put 3.04.243 P
than you have heard him brag to you he will. 3.04.317
he has heard that word of some great man and now 4.01. 12 P
or heard | (for to a vision so apparent rumor WT 1.02.269
infection | that e'er was heard or read! 1.02.424
shall i be heard? 2.01.115
i ne'er heard yet | that any of these bolder 3.02. 54
i have heard (but not believ'd) the spirits o' 3.03. 16
i have heard, sir, of such a man, who hath a 4.02. 41 P
for i have heard it said, | there is an art 4.04. 86
i think | you have heard of my poor services, i' 4.04.516
heard the old shepherd deliver the manner how he 5.02. 4 P
methought, i heard the shepherd say, he found 5.02. 7 P
look'd as they had heard of a world ransom'd, or 5.02. 14 P
i never heard of such another encounter, which 5.02. 56 P
told him i heard them talk of a farthel and i 5.02.116 P
the thunder of my cannon shall be heard. JN 1.01. 26
country to be judg'd by you | that e'er i heard. 1.01. 46
lay, | as i have heard my father speak himself, 1.01.107
who hath read or heard | of any kindred action 3.04. 13
i have heard you say | that we shall see and 3.04. 76
indeed we heard how near his death he was 4.02. 87
but this from rumor's tongue | i idly heard — 4.02.124
or have you read, or heard, or could you think? 4.03. 42
again | after they heard young arthur was alive? 5.01. 38
have i not heard these islanders shout out 5.02.103
then all too late comes counsel to be heard, R2 2.01. 27
mann'd with three hundred men, as i have heard, 2.03. 54
i heard you say, "is not my arm of length, 4.01. 11
i heard you say that you had rather refuse | the 4.01. 15
i heard thee say, and vauntingly thou spak'st it 4.01. 36
i heard the banished norfolk say | that thou, 4.01. 80
he was, i heard the proclamation. 1H4 1.03.147
i heard him tell it to one of his company last 2.01. 56 P
and heard thee murmur tales of iron wars, 2.03. 48
still run and roar'd, as ever i heard bull–calf. 2.04.260 P
which thou hast often heard of, and it is known 2.04.411 P
as the cuckoo is in june, | heard, not regarded; 3.02. 76
o jesu, i have heard the prince tell him, i know 3.03. 83 P
my lord, and i said i heard your grace say so; 3.03.105 P
and when he heard him swear and vow to god | he 4.03. 60
us, | for he hath heard of our confederacy, 4.04. 38
this is the strangest tale that ever i heard. 5.04.154
i heard say your lordship was sick, i hope your 2H4 1.02. 95 P
thus have you heard our cause and known our 1.03. 1
i have heard better news. 2.01.166
he heard of your grace's coming to town. 2.02. 99 P
pardon, sir, i have heard the word. 3.02. 73 P
we have heard the chimes at midnight, master 3.02.214 P
huswives that he heard the carmen whistle, and 3.02.317 P
who hath not heard it spoken | how deep you were 4.02. 16
heard he the good news yet? | tell it him. 4.05. 11
ere you with grief had spoke and i had heard 4.05.141
this that you heard was but a color. 5.05. 86 P
i heard a bird so sing, | whose music, to my 5.05.107
no, with no more than if we heard that england H5 2.04. 24
with what great state he heard their embassy, 2.04. 32
he hath heard that men of few words are the best 3.02. 36 P
i wad full fain heard some question 'tween you 3.02.118 P
i have heard a sonnet begin so to one's mistress 3.07. 41 P
he never did harm, that i heard of. 3.07.100 P
i myself heard the king say he would not be 4.01.190 P
the king hath heard them; 5.02. 74
ne'er heard i of a warlike enterprise | more 1H6 2.01. 44
and i have heard it said, unbidden guests | are 2.02. 55
i have heard you preach | that malice was a 3.01.127
but when they heard he was thine enemy, | they 3.03. 71
a proper jest, and never heard before, | that 2H6 1.01.132
i have heard her reported to be a woman of an 1.04. 6 P
oft | myself have heard a voice to call him so. 2.01. 92
sorry i am to hear what i have heard. 2.01.189
strange tortures for offenders, never heard of, 3.01.122
oft have i heard that grief softens the mind, 4.04. 1
the most complete champion that ever i heard! 4.10. 56 P
cade, | who since i heard to be discomfited. 5.01. 63
he been ta'en, we should have heard the news; 3H6 2.01. 4
he been slain, we should have heard the news; 2.01. 5
methinks we should have heard | the happy 2.01. 6
wondrous strange, the like yet never heard of. 2.01. 33
o, speak no more, for i have heard too much. 2.01. 48
for in the marches here we heard you were, 2.01.140
oft have i heard his praises in pursuit, | but 2.01.149
like to a dismal clangor heard from far, 2.03. 18
myself have often heard him say, and swear, 3.03.123
when i have heard your king's desert recounted, 3.03.132
for i have heard that she was there in place. 4.01.103
even now we heard the news. 5.02. 32
should, if a coward heard her speak these words, 5.04. 40
and, if the rest be true which i have heard, 5.06. 55
for i have often heard my mother say | i came 5.06. 70
heard you not what an humble suppliant | lord R3 1.01. 74
and the most merciless, that e'er was heard of! 1.03.183
oft have i heard of sanctuary men, | but 3.01. 55
i would have had you heard | the traitor speak, 3.05. 56
as well as i had seen, and heard him speak; 3.05. 63
words | i've heard him utter to his son–in–law, H8 1.02.136
to this point hast thou heard him | at any time 1.02.145
having heard by fame | of this so noble and so 1.04. 66
for when the king once heard it, out of anger 2.01.150
have you heard it? 2.03. 92
do not deliver | what here y' have heard to her. 2.03.107
their arguments | be now produc'd and heard. 2.04. 68
every thing that heard him play, | even the 3.01. 9
where no mention | of me more must be heard of, 3.02.434
of late | heard many grievous — i do say, my 5.01. 98
and to have heard you | without indurance 5.01.120
i would somebody had heard her talk yesterday, TRO 1.01. 45 P
the noblest hateful love, that e'er i heard of. 4.01. 34
be gone, i say, the gods have heard me swear. 5.03. 15
it may be you have heard it, | but, since it COR 1.01. 90
'tis not four days gone | since i heard thence; 1.02. 7
i heard a senator speak it. 1.03. 95 P
by interims and conveying gusts we have heard 1.06. 5
briefly we heard their drums. 1.06. 16
i heard him swear, | were he to stand for consul 2.01.231
reproof and rebuke from every ear that heard it. 2.02. 34 P
battles thrice six | i have seen, and heard of; 2.03.129
forget that ever | he heard the name of death. 3.01.259
i may be heard, i would crave a word or two, 3.01.281
i have heard you say | honor and policy, like 3.02. 41
what you have seen him do, and heard him speak, 3.03. 77
i have heard it said, the fittest time to 4.03. 32 P
'fore my wars | have i heard groan and drop. 4.04. 4
i have heard him say so himself. 4.05.184 P
before you punish him, where he heard this, 4.06. 53
if you have heard your general talk of rome 5.02. 9
my stead, would you have heard | a mother less? 5.03.192
horns, | as if a double hunt were heard at once, TIT 2.03. 19
yet have i heard — o, could i find it now! 2.03.150
o tamora, was ever heard the like? 2.03.276
had he heard the heavenly harmony | which that 2.04. 48
for i have heard my grandsire say full oft, 4.01. 18
myself hath often heard them say, | when i have 4.04. 74
i heard a child cry underneath a wall. 5.01. 24
when soon i heard | the crying babe controll'd 5.01. 25
oft have you heard me wish for such an hour, 5.02.159
now have you heard the truth, what say you, 5.03.128
yet tell me not, for i have heard it all: ROM 1.01.174
that which thou hast heard me speak to–night. 2.02. 87
i have heard in some sort of thy miseries. TIM 4.03. 77
i have heard, and griev'd, | how cursed athens, 4.03. 93
y' have heard that i have gold, | i am sure you 5.01. 76
the enemy's drum is heard, and fearful scouring 5.02. 15
i have heard | where many of the best respect in JC 1.02. 58
you and i have heard our fathers say | there was 1.02.158
besides the things that we have heard and seen, 2.02. 15
of all the wonders that i yet have heard, | it 2.02. 34
i have, when you have heard what i can say; 2.02. 92
i heard a bustling rumor, like a fray, | and the 2.04. 18
sure the boy heard me. 2.04. 42
i heard him say, brutus and cassius | are rid 3.02.268
the moon is down; i have not heard the clock. MAC 2.01. 2
i heard the owl scream and the crickets cry. 2.02. 15
i stood and heard them; 2.02. 21
methought i heard a voice cry, "sleep no more! 2.02. 32
and, as they say, | lamentings heard i' th' air; 2.03. 56
the heaviest sound | that ever yet they heard. 4.03.203
what, at any time, have you heard her say? 5.01. 13 P
upon the stage, | and then is heard no more. 5.05. 26
i have heard | the cock, that is the trumpet to HAM 1.01.149
so have i heard and do in part believe it. 1.01.165
i heard it not. 1.04. 5
never to speak of this that you have heard. 1.05.160
something have you heard | of hamlet's 2.02. 4
i heard thee speak me a speech once, but it was 2.02.434 P
i have heard | that guilty creatures sitting at 2.02.588
i have heard of your paintings, well enough. 3.01.142 P
us what lord hamlet said, | we heard it all. 3.01.180
i have seen play — and heard others /praise, 3.02. 29 P
have you heard the argument? 3.02.232 P
cry to be heard, as 'twere from heaven to earth, 4.05.217
sith you have heard, and with a knowing ear, 4.07. 3
and you must needs have heard, how i am punish'd 5.02.229
but i have heard him oft maintain it to be fit LR 1.02. 71 P
i have told you what i have seen and heard; 1.02.174 P
you have heard of the news abroad, i mean the 2.01. 6 P
have you heard of no likely wars toward, 'twixt 2.01. 10 P
i can call but now) i have heard /strange /news. 2.01. 87
i heard myself proclaim'd, | and by the happy 2.03. 1
wind and rain, i never | remember to have heard. 3.02. 48
i have heard more since. 4.01. 35
idle pebble chafes, | cannot be heard so high. 4.06. 22
lark so far | cannot be seen or heard. 4.06. 59
sir, this i heard: 5.01. 21
in honest plainness thou hast heard me say | my OTH 1.01. 97
neither my place, nor aught i heard of business, 1.03. 53
whereof by parcels she had something heard, 1.03.154
she wish'd she had not heard it, yet she wish'd 1.03.162
for that i heard the clink and fall of swords, 2.03.234
if you have any music that may not be heard, 3.01. 15 P
i heard thee say even now, thou lik'st not that, 3.03.109
in sleep i heard him say, "sweet desdemona, 3.03.419
or heard him say — as knaves be such abroad, 4.01. 25
nor ever heard — nor ever did suspect. 4.02. 2
and then i heard | each syllable that breath 4.02. 4
/faith, i have heard too much; 4.02.182 P
i have heard it said so. 4.03. 60
what's amiss, | may it be gently heard. ANT 2.02. 20
if cleopatra heard you, your /reproof | were 2.02.121
whom ne'er the word of "no" woman heard speak, 2.02.223
i have heard it, pompey, | and am well studied 2.06. 46
i have heard that julius caesar | grew fat with 2.06. 64
you have heard much. 2.06. 65
then so much have i heard; 2.06. 67
and i have heard, apollodorus carried — 2.06. 68
i have heard the ptolomies' pyramises are very 2.07. 34 P
without contradiction, i have heard that. 2.07. 36 P
madam, i heard her speak; she is low–voic'd. 3.03. 13
you have heard on't, sweet? 3.07. 23
heard you of nothing strange about the streets? 4.03. 3
most noble empress, you have heard of me? 5.02. 71
no matter, sir, what i have heard or known. 5.02. 73
i heard of one of them no longer than yesterday, 5.02.250 P
to go even with what i heard than in my every CYM 1.04. 44 P
this, your king | hath heard of great augustus. 2.04. 11
and this you might have heard of here, by me, 2.04. 77
i have heard of riding wagers, | where horses 3.02. 71
true honest men being heard, like false aeneas, 3.04. 58
i have heard i am a strumpet, and mine ear, 3.04.113
i love this youth, and i have heard you say, 4.02. 21
gods, what lies i have heard! 4.02. 32
i have heard of such. 4.02. 72
it may be heard at court that such as we | cave 4.02.137
i heard no letter from my master since | i wrote 4.03. 36
heard you all this, her women? 5.05. 61
we have heard your miseries as far as tyre, PER 1.04. 88
such whales have i heard on a' th' land, who 2.01. 32 P
and i have heard you knights of tyre | are 2.03.101
i heard of an egyptian | that had nine hours 3.02. 84
o, you have heard something of my power, and so 4.06. 86 P
you have heard me say, when i did fly from tyre, 5.03. 50
in antiochus and his daughter you have heard 5.03. 85
i have heard the fortunes | of your dead lords, TNK 1.01. 56
i heard them reported in the battle to be the 2.01. 29 P
i have heard | strange howls this livelong night 3.02. 11
and i have heard some call him arcite, and — 3.03. 32
and for a preface, | i never heard a better. 3.05.151
methought i heard a dreadful clap of thunder 3.06. 83
nothing that i heard, | for i came home before 4.01. 3
neither heard i one question | of your name or 4.01. 15
sport, | i heard a voice, a shrill one; 4.01. 56
only i heard her | repeat this often, "palamon 4.01. 66
as ever you heard, but say nothing. 4.01.135
thine ear | (which nev'r heard scurril term, 5.01.147
i have heard | two emulous philomels beat the 5.03.123
i heard she was not well; 5.04. 26
it, | for i have heard it is a life in death, VEN 413
as if they heard the woeful words she told; 1126
the threshold grates the door to have him heard, LUC 306
have heard the cause of my untimely death, 1178
have you not heard it said full oft, | a woman's PP 18.41
than think that we before have heard them told. SON 123. 8
heard where his plants in others' orchards grew, LC 171

HEARDST 2 FR 0.0002 REL FR 1 V 1 P
creature in the vessel | which thou heardst cry, TMP 1.02. 32
the blackest news that ever thou heardst. TGV 3.01.286 P

HEARER 5 FR 0.0005 REL FR 3 V 2 P
and tire the hearer with a book of words. ADO 1.01.307
lamented, pitied, and excus'd | of every hearer; 4.01.217
wearing thy hearer in thy mistress' praise, AYL 2.04. 38
duer paid to the hearer than the turk's tribute. 2H4 3.02.307 P
and you too — at each ear a hearer — that HAM 2.02.382 P

HEARER'S 1 FR 0.0001 REL FR 1 V 0 P
he that speaks doth gripe the hearer's wrist, JN 4.02.190

HEARERS 11 FR 0.0012 REL FR 9 V 2 P
i love you the better; the hearers may cry amen. ADO 2.01.105 P
which shallow laughing hearers give to fools. LLL 5.02.860
and send the hearers weeping to their beds. R2 5.01. 45
upon my soul, the hearers will shed tears; 3H6 1.04.161
for, gentle hearers, know, | to rank our chosen H8 pr 17
the first and happiest hearers of the town, | be pr 24
to the hearers, sir. TRO 3.01. 22 P
filling their hearers | with strange invention. MAC 3.01. 31
use of it doth move | the hearers to collection. HAM 4.05. 9

makes them stand | like wonder–wounded hearers? 5.01.257
will tie the hearers to attend each line, | how LUC 818
HEAREST 3 FR 0.0003 REL FR 3 V 0 P
tell me not, friar, that thou hearest of this, ROM 4.01. 50
as signal that thou hearest something approach. 5.03. 8
what e'er thou hearest or seest, stand all aloof 5.03. 26
HEARETH 1 FR 0.0001 REL FR 1 V 0 P
he heareth not, he stirreth not, he moveth not, ROM 2.01. 15
HEARING 96 FR 0.0108 REL FR 75 V 21 P
and sorceries terrible | to enter human hearing, TMP 1.02.265
out o' your wits, and hearing too? 3.02. 79 P
she is not within hearing, sir. TGV 2.01. 8 P
fair woman, and i'll vouchsafe thee the hearing. WIV 2.02. 43 P
tell you, sir, if you will give me the hearing. 2.02.177 P
and leave you to the hearing of the cause, MM 2.01.136
he's hearing of a cause; 2.02. 1
whilst my invention, hearing not my tongue, 2.04. 3
ever return to have hearing of this business. 3.01.204 P
and hearing how hastily you are to depart, i am 4.03. 50 P
and take her hearing prisoner with the force ADO 1.01.324
to hear, or forbear hearing? LLL 1.01.196 P
i do confess much of the hearing it, but little 1.01.285 P
child, make passionate my sense of hearing. 3.01. 2 P
royalty, bestow on me the sense of hearing. 5.02.664 P
what, out of hearing gone? MND 2.02.152
sense, | it pays the hearing double recompense. 3.02.180
and, hearing our intent, | came here in grace of 4.01.133
almost damn those ears | which, hearing them, MV 1.01. 99
eyes, | hearing applause and universal shout, 3.02.143
and in the hearing of these many friends | i 5.01.241
here was he merry, hearing of a song. AYL 2.07. 4
hearing how that every day | men of great worth 5.04.154
your honor's players, hearing your amendment, SHR in.2. 129
sir, | that, hearing of her beauty and her wit, 2.01. 48
have you heard, but something hard of hearing: 2.01.183
hearing thy mildness prais'd in every town, 2.01.191
'tis a good hearing when children are toward. 5.02.182
but a harsh hearing when women are froward. 5.02.183
hearing your high majesty is touch'd | with that AWW 2.01.110
hearing so much, will speed her foot again, 3.04. 37
garden door be shut, and leave me to my hearing.
TN 3.01. 93 P
no hearing, no feeling, but my sir's song, and WT 4.04.612 P
the princess hearing of her mother's statue, 5.02. 94 P
for all the welshmen, hearing thou wert dead, R2 3.02. 73
speak to his gentle hearing kind commends. 3.03.126
hearing how our plaints and prayers do pierce, 5.03.127
king, | if you vouchsafe me hearing and respect. 1H4 4.03. 31
the vent of hearing when loud rumor speaks? 2H4 in 2
am sure he is, to the hearing of any thing good. 1.02. 68 P
so, i did not think thou wast within hearing. 2.04.310 P
he alt'red much upon the hearing it. 4.05. 13
hour, i think, is come | to give him hearing. H5 1.01. 93
for, hearing this, i must perforce compound 4.06. 33
beds, | hearing alarums at our chamber–doors. 1H6 2.01. 42
to give me hearing what i shall reply. 3.01. 28
peers, | hearing of your arrival in this realm, 3.04. 2
sweet madam, give me hearing in a cause. 5.03.106
good, my liege, to please you with the hearing, R3 4.04.457
they are | most pestilent to th' hearing, and, H8 1.02. 49
his plain–song | and have an hour of hearing, 1.03. 46
you to declare, in hearing | of all these ears 2.04.146
and grief of heart | fall asleep, or hearing, 3.01. 14
more in joy at first hearing he was a man–child COR 1.03. 16 P
wholesome forenoon in hearing a cause between an 2.01. 70 P
when you are hearing a matter between party and 2.01. 73 P
bleeding, the more entangled by your hearing. 2.01. 78 P
he's sentenc'd; no more hearing. 3.03.109
who, hearing of our martius' banishment, 4.06. 43
offenses to us | shall have judicious hearing. 5.06.126
as any mortal body hearing it | should straight TIT 2.03.103
to brave the tribune in his brother's hearing. 4.02. 36
that living mortals, hearing them, run mad — ROM 4.03. 48
or am i mad, hearing him talk of juliet, | to 5.03. 80
i have | deserv'd this hearing — bid 'em send TIM 2.02.198
ever at the best, hearing well of your lordship. 3.06. 27 P
on the dying deck, | hearing the surges threat; 4.02. 21
hearing you were retir'd, your friends fall'n 5.01. 59
and, being men, hearing the will of caesar, | it JC 3.02.143
the hearing of my wife with your approach; MAC 1.04. 46
air, | where hearing should not latch them. 4.03.195
but lend thy serious hearing | to what i shall HAM 1.05. 5
your clemency, | we beg your hearing patiently. 3.02.151
fit, | behind the arras hearing something stir, 4.01. 9
and that in hamlet's hearing, for a quality 4.07. 72
ears are senseless that should give us hearing, 5.02.369
am almost ready to dissolve, | hearing of this. LR 5.03.205
hearing that you prepar'd for war, acquainted ANT 3.06. 58
you lie up to the hearing of the gods! 5.02. 95
he had two sons (if this be worth your hearing, CYM 1.01. 57
rather than story him in his own hearing. 1.04. 34 P
to ears and tongues | be theme and hearing ever) 3.01. 4
hath prevail'd | on thy too ready hearing? 3.02. 6
counsellor should fill the bores of hearing, 3.02. 57
make some stronger head, the which he hearing 4.02.139
spirits of region low, | offend our hearing; 5.04. 94
in private, if you please | to give me hearing. 5.05.116
hearing us praise our loves of italy | for 5.05.161
who, hearing of your melancholy state, | did PER 5.01.220
make the world think, when it comes to hearing, TNK 3.06. 11
it is enough my hearing shall be punish'd | with 5.03. 7
o, would thou hadst not, or i had no hearing! VEN 428
and, hearing him, thy power had lost his power. 944
and in my hearing be you mute and dumb, | my LUC 1123
hearing you prais'd, i say, "'tis so, 'tis true, SON 85. 9
sat, | her grievance with his hearing to divide: LC 67
HEARINGS 1 FR 0.0001 REL FR 1 V 0 P
and younger hearings are quite ravished, | so LLL 2.01. 75
HEARKEN 8 FR 0.0009 REL FR 3 V 5 P
thou be pleas'd to hearken once again to the TMP 3.02. 39 P
ay, but hearken, sir; TGV 2.01.172 P
hearken after their offense, my lord. ADO 5.01.212 P
simplicity of man to hearken after the flesh. LLL 1.01.217 P
the youngest daughter, whom you hearken for, SHR 1.02.258
till thy return — well, hearken a' th' end. 2H4 2.04.280 P
draw heaven down, and all the gods to hearken; PER 1.01. 83
ear, | to hearken if his foes pursue him still. VEN 699
HEARKEN'D 1 FR 0.0001 REL FR 0 V 1 P
as they would have hearken'd to their father's PER 4.02. 99 P
HEARKENS 3 FR 0.0003 REL FR 3 V 0 P
to me inveterate, hearkens my brother's suit, TMP 1.02.122
he hearkens after prophecies and dreams, | and R3 1.01. 54
she hearkens for his hounds and for his horn; VEN 868
HEARK'NED 1 FR 0.0001 REL FR 1 V 0 P
that ever said i heark'ned for your death. 1H4 5.04. 52
HEARK'NING 1 FR 0.0001 REL FR 1 V 0 P
besides, old gremio is heark'ning still, | and SHR 4.04. 53
HEARS 35 FR 0.0039 REL FR 31 V 4 P
he hears with ears. WIV 1.01.148
"he hears with ear"? 1.01.150 P
i warrant thee, nobody hears — mine own people, 2.02. 50 P
she hears herself. LLL 5.02.195
bleat softly then, the butcher hears you cry. 5.02.255
lies in the ear | of him that hears it, never in 5.02.862
he hears merry tales and smiles not. MV 1.02. 47 P
but by the ear, that hears most nobly of him. AWW 3.05. 50
whilst he that hears makes fearful action | with JN 4.02.191
may move and what he hears may be believ'd, that
1H4 1.02.154 P
as oft as he hears | owen glendower spoke of. 3.01. 11
and he nor sees nor hears us what we say. 3H6 2.06. 63
and fled (as he hears since) to burgundy. 4.06. 79
the drum your honor hears marcheth from warwick. 5.01. 13
what traitor hears me, and says not amen? R3 5.05. 22
may be he hears the king | does whet his anger H8 3.02. 91
he hears nought privately that comes from troy. TRO 1.03.249
my gracious lord, no tribune hears you speak. TIT 3.01. 32
he hears no music; JC 1.02.204
scarcely hears | of this his nephew's purpose — HAM 1.02. 29
fadoms to the sea | and hears it roar beneath. 1.04. 78
says she hears | there's tricks i' th' world, 4.05. 4
and when your mistress hears thus much from you,
LR 4.05. 34
every one hears that, | which can distinguish 4.06.210
but the free comfort which from thence he hears; OTH 1.03.213
he, when he hears of her, cannot restrain | from 4.01. 98
not till he hears how antony is touch'd | with ANT 2.02.139
he hears, and nods, and hums, | and then cries, TNK 3.05. 15
to one sore sick that hears the passing bell. VEN 702
and yet she hears no tidings of her love. 867
anon she hears them chaunt it lustily, | and all 869
by this she hears the hounds are at a bay, 877
this, far off, she hears some huntsman hallow; 973
even at this word she hears a merry horn, 1025
but will is deaf and hears no heedful friends; LUC 495
HEARSAY 2 FR 0.0002 REL FR 2 V 0 P
arrow made, | that only wounds by hearsay. ADO 3.01. 23
let them say more that like of hearsay well, | i SON 21.13
HEARS'D 1 FR 0.0001 REL FR 0 V 1 P
would she were hears'd at my foot, and the MV 3.01. 89 P
HEARSE 5 FR 0.0005 REL FR 4 V 1 P
let all the tears that should bedew my hearse 2H4 4.05.113
wherewith you now bedew king henry's hearse, | i 1H6 1.01.104
if honor may be shrouded in a hearse — | whilst R3 1.02. 2
stand from the hearse, stand from the body. JC 3.02.165 P
we wept after her hearse, | and yet we mourn. PER 4.03. 41
HEARSED 2 FR 0.0002 REL FR 2 V 0 P
why thy canoniz'd bones, hearsed in death, HAM 1.04. 47
thy sea within a puddle's womb is hearsed, | and LUC 657
HEAR'ST 9 FR 0.0010 REL FR 7 V 2 P
hear'st thou, biondello? SHR 4.04. 98 P
hear'st thou the news abroad, who are arriv'd? JN 4.02.160
stand'st thou still, and hear'st such a calling? 1H4 2.04. 80 P
stain to thy countrymen, thou hear'st thy doom! 1H6 4.01. 45
hear'st thou, mars? COR 5.06. 99
hear'st thou of them? MAC 5.03. 56
hear'st thou, pisanio? CYM 3.02. 48
boar, | unlike myself thou hear'st me moralize, VEN 712
music to hear, why hear'st thou music sadly? SON 8. 1
HEAR'T 3 FR 0.0003 REL FR 2 V 1 P
and grieve to hear't. COR 5.06. 62
will you hear't again? OTH 2.03.100 P
the hollow mine of earth | and will not hear't. 4.02. 80
/HEART 10 FR 0.0011 REL FR 10 V 0 P
/pride /of /kingly /sway /from /out /my /heart; R2 4.01.206
/he /that /buildeth /on /the /vulgar /heart. 2H4 1.03. 90
man, those joyful tears show thy true /heart. H8 5.02.208
/who, /when /my /heart, /all /mad /with /misery, TIT 3.02. 9
/when /thy /poor /heart /beats /with /outrageous 3.02. 13
/just /against /thy /heart /make /thou /a /hole, 3.02. 17
/thou /kill'st /my /heart! 3.02. 54
/what /store /her /heart /is /made /an. LR 3.06. 54
/forth, /as /if /it /press'd /her /heart; 4.03. 26
which makes /her both th' /heart and place | of PER 4.ch. 10
HEART 1066 FR 0.1205 REL FR 878 V 188 P
o, the cry did knock | against my very heart. TMP 1.02. 9
tell your piteous heart | there's no harm done. 1.02. 14
o, my heart bleeds | to think o' th' teen that i 1.02. 63
awake, dear heart, awake! 1.02.305
i could find in my heart to beat him — 2.02.156 P
you, did | my heart fly to your service, there 3.01. 65
ay, with a heart as willing | as bondage e'er of 3.01. 88
and mine, with my heart in't. 3.01. 90
sir, | the white cold virgin snow upon my heart 4.01. 55
let grief and sorrow still embrace his heart 5.01.214
wit with musing weak, heart sick with thought. TGV 1.01. 69
when inward joy enforc'd my heart to smile! 1.02. 63
here is her hand, the agent of her heart; 1.03. 46
my heart accords thereto, | and yet a thousand 1.03. 90
his tears pure messengers sent from his heart, 2.07. 77
his heart as far from fraud as heaven from earth 2.07. 78
"blessing of your heart, you brew good ale." 3.01.305 P
sacrifice your tears, your sighs, your heart; 3.02. 73
who, in my mood, i stabb'd unto the heart. 4.01. 49
it makes me have a slow heart. 4.02. 65 P
madam, if your heart be so obdurate, | vouchsafe 4.02.119
no grief did ever come so near thy heart | as 4.03. 19
even from a heart | as full of sorrows as the 4.03. 32
him | that with his very heart despiseth me? 4.04. 94
read over julia's heart (thy first best love), 5.04. 46
and entertain'd 'em deeply in her heart. 5.04.102
much good do it your good heart! WIV 1.01. 82 P
and i thank you always with my heart, la! 1.01. 84 P
with my heart. 1.01. 85 P
'tis the heart, master page, 'tis here, 'tis 2.01.226 P
fairest, that would have won any woman's heart; 2.02. 70 P
leads a very frampold life with him, good heart. 2.02. 91 P
blessing on your heart for't! 2.02.107 P
now, sir john, here is the heart of my purpose: 2.02.224 P
my heart is ready to crack with impatience. 2.02.288 P
my heart of elder? 2.03. 29 P
got's will, and his passion of my heart! 3.01. 62 P
by gar, with all my heart. 3.01.122 P
dat is good, by gar; with all my heart! 3.03.241 P
a kind heart he hath. 3.04.102 P
through fire and water for such a kind heart. 3.04.104 P
good heart, that was not her fault. 3.05. 38 P
it, that it would yearn your heart to see it. 3.05. 44 P
blessing of his heart! 4.01. 13 P
how now, sweet heart! 4.02. 12 P
not follow the imaginations of your own heart. 4.02.156 P
mistress ford, good heart, is beaten black and 4.05.112 P
mistress page is come with me, sweet heart. 5.05. 23 P
start, | it is the flesh of a corrupted heart. 5.05. 87
fed in heart, whose flames aspire, | as thoughts 5.05. 97
my heart misgives me. 5.05.213 P
mercy in vienna | live in thy tongue and heart. MM 1.01. 45
tongue far from heart — play with all virgins 1.04. 33
if so your heart were touch'd with that remorse 2.02. 54
and ask your heart what it doth know | that's 2.02.137
and in my heart the strong and swelling evil 2.04. 6
why does my blood thus muster to my heart, 2.04. 20
to save a head, | to cleave a heart in twain. 3.01. 62
o gravel heart! 4.03. 64
grace of the duke, revenges to your heart, | and 4.03.135
waters from your eyes | with a light heart; 4.03.147
i am pale at mine heart to see thine eyes so red 4.03.151 P
ay, with my heart, | and punish them to your 5.01.239
not changing heart with habit, i am still 5.01.384
your brother's death i know sits at your heart; 5.01.389
and so deep sticks it in my penitent heart 5.01.475
cheer may you have, but not with better heart. ERR 3.01. 29
a fair presence, though your heart be tainted; 3.02. 13
eye's clear eye, my dear heart's dearer heart, 3.02. 62
not been made of faith, and my heart of steel, 3.02.145
my tongue, though not my heart, shall have his 4.02. 18
my heart prays for him, though my tongue do 4.02. 28
/one whose hard heart is button'd up with steel; 4.02. 34
heart and good will you might, | but surely, 4.04. 85
me, i could find in my heart to stay here still, 4.04.155 P
with all my heart, i'll gossip at this feast. 5.01.408
i could find in my heart that i had not a hard ADO 1.01.126 P
find in my heart that i had not a hard heart, 1.01.127 P
he is no hypocrite, but prays from his heart. 1.01.152 P
and in her bosom i'll unclasp my heart, | and 1.01.323
you have lost the heart of signior benedick. 2.01.277 P
use for it, a double heart for his single one. 2.01.279 P
in faith, lady, you have a merry heart. 2.01.313 P
tells him in his ear that he is in her heart. 2.01.316 P
weeps, sobs, beats her heart, tears her hair, 2.03.147 P
impossible, she may wear her heart out first. 2.03.204 P
but nature never fram'd a woman's heart | of 3.01. 49
thee, | taming my wild heart to thy loving hand. 3.01.112
he hath a heart as sound as a bell, and his 3.02. 12 P
is the clapper, for what his heart thinks, his 3.02. 13 P
and in dearness of heart hath holp to effect 3.02. 98 P
joy to wear it, for my heart is exceeding heavy. 3.04. 24 P
carduus benedictus, and lay it to your heart; 3.04. 74 P
if i would think my heart out of thinking, that 3.04. 84 P
yet now in despite of his heart he eats his meat 3.04. 89 P
i could find in my heart to bestow it all of 3.05. 22 P
about thy thoughts and counsels of thy heart! 4.01.102
and do it with all thy heart. 4.01.285 P
with so much of my heart that none is left to 4.01.286 P
i would eat his heart in the market–place. 4.01.307 P
slander hath gone through and through her heart, 5.01. 68
my heart is sorry for your daughter's death; 5.01.103
pluck up, my heart, and be sad. 5.01.204 P
in spite of your heart, i think. 5.02. 68 P
alas, poor heart, if you spite it for my sake, i 5.02. 69 P
i will live in thy heart, die in thy lap, and be 5.02.102 P
my heart is with your liking. 5.04. 32
as you shall deem yourself lodg'd in my heart, LLL 2.01.173
lady, i will commend you to /mine /own heart. 2.01.180 P
sick at the heart. 2.01.185
his heart, like an agot, with your print 2.01.236
negligent student! learn her by heart. 3.01. 35 P
by heart and in heart, boy. 3.01. 36 P
by heart and in heart, boy. 3.01. 36 P
and out of heart, master; 3.01. 37 P
by heart you love her, because your heart cannot 3.01. 41 P
love her, because your heart cannot come by her; 3.01. 42 P
in heart you love her, because your heart is in 3.01. 42 P
her, because your heart is in love with her; 3.01. 43 P
and out of heart you love her, being out of 3.01. 44 P
being out of heart that you cannot enjoy her. 3.01. 44 P
of trotting paritors — o my little heart! 3.01.186
we bend to that the working of the heart; 4.01. 33
poor deer's blood, that my heart means no ill. 4.01. 35
on thy picture, and my heart on thy every part. 4.01. 85 P
persuade my heart to this false perjury? 4.03. 60
his loving bosom to keep down his heart. 4.03.134
good heart, what grace hast thou thus to reprove 4.03.151
but, sweet heart, let that pass. 5.01.105 P
is — but, sweet heart, i do implore secrety — 5.01.109 P
for a light heart lives long. 5.02. 18
dost thou not wish in heart | the chain were 5.02. 55
that well by heart hath conn'd his embassage. 5.02. 98
that contempt will kill the speaker's heart, 5.02.149
lord longaville said i came o'er his heart, 5.02.278
a blister on his sweet tongue, with my heart, 5.02.335
and that 'a wears next his heart for a favor. 5.02.715 P
a heavy heart bears not a humble tongue. 5.02.737
part, | neither intitled in the other's heart. 5.02.812
hence /hermit then — my heart is in thy breast. 5.02.816
behold the window of my heart, mine eye, | what 5.02.838
cunning hast thou filch'd my daughter's heart, MND 1.01. 36
art | you sway the motion of demetrius' heart. 1.01.193
that i will do any man's heart good to hear me. 1.02. 71 P
set your heart at rest; 2.01.121
draw not iron, for my heart | is true as steel. 2.01.196
the wildest hath not such a heart as you. 2.01.229
one heart, one bed, two bosoms, and one troth. 2.02. 42
i mean, that my heart unto yours /is knit, | so 2.02. 47

knit, | so that but one heart we can make of it; 2.02. 48
that through thy bosom makes me see thy heart. 2.02.105
methought a serpent eat my heart away, | and you 2.02.149
i, | pierc'd through the heart with your stern 3.02. 59
and here, with all good will, with all my heart, 3.02.164
my heart to her but as guest-wise sojourn'd, 3.02.171
so, with two seeming bodies but one heart, | two 3.02.212
by night | and stol'n my love's heart from him? 3.02.284
a foolish heart, that i leave here behind. 3.02.319
and all the faith, the virtue of my heart, | the 4.01.169
his tongue to conceive, nor his heart to report, 4.01.213 P
beshrew my heart, but i pity the man. 5.01.290 P
ay, that left pap, | where heart doth hop. 5.01.299
than my heart cool with mortifying groans. MV 1.01. 82
fift welcome with so good heart as i can bid the 1.02.128 P
cheek, | a goodly apple rotten at the heart. 1.03.101
outbrave the heart most daring on the earth, 2.01. 28
hanging about the neck of my heart, says very 2.02. 14 P
i have too griev'd a heart | to take a tedious 2.07. 76
i will have the heart of him if he forfeit, for, 3.01.127 P
is fancy bred, | or in the heart or in the head? 3.02. 64
with all my heart, so thou canst get a wife. 3.02.195
madam, with all my heart, | i shall obey you in 3.04. 35
his jewish heart! 4.01. 80
with all my heart. 4.01.147
on forfeit of my hands, my head, my heart. 4.01.212
by him cut off | nearest the merchant's heart. 4.01.233
"nearest his heart," those are the very words. 4.01.254
i'll pay it instantly with all my heart. 4.01.281
since you do take it, love, so much at heart. 5.01.145
i could not for my heart deny it him. 5.01.165
even so void is your false heart of truth. 5.01.189
and indeed so much in the heart of the world, AYL 1.01.169 P
and envious disposition | sticks me at heart. 1.02.242
these burs are in my heart. 1.03. 17 P
in my heart | lie there what hidden woman's fear 1.03.118
i could find in my heart to disgrace my man's 2.04. 4 P
no greater heart in thee? 2.06. 4 P
o that your highness knew my heart in this! 3.01. 13
distill'd | helen's cheek, but not /her heart, 3.02.145
tripp'd up the wrastler's heels, and your heart, 3.02.213 P
o, ominous! he comes to kill my heart. 3.02.246 P
just as high as my heart. 3.02.269 P
your liver as clean as a sound sheep's heart, 3.02.423 P
with all my heart, good youth. 3.02.433 P
if he were of a fearful heart, stagger in this 3.03. 49 P
quite traverse, athwart the heart of his lover, 3.04. 43 P
whose heart th' accustom'd sight of death makes 3.05. 4
now i do frown on thee with all my heart, | and 3.05. 15
phebe, with all my heart. 3.05.136
the matter's in my head and in my heart. 3.05.137
turn'd, | that a maiden's heart hath burn'd?" 4.03. 41
apart, | warr'st thou with a woman's heart?" 4.03. 45
after some small space, being strong at heart, 4.03.151
you lack a man's heart. 4.03.164
take a good heart and counterfeit to be a man. 4.03.173 P
me to see thee wear thy heart in a scarf! 5.02. 20 P
i thought thy heart had been wounded with the 5.02. 22 P
rosalind so near the heart as your gesture cries 5.02. 62 P
i do desire it with all my heart; 5.03. 3 P
hand with his | whose heart within his bosom is. 5.04.115
you and you are heart in heart; 5.04.132
you and you are heart in heart; 5.04.132
with all my heart. SHR in.1. 83
iwis it is not half way to her heart; 1.01. 62
now, | affection is not rated from the heart. 1.01.160
and could not get him for my heart to do it. 1.02. 38
to give my hand oppos'd against my heart | unto 3.02. 9
to the roof of my mouth, my heart in my belly, 4.01. 8 P
you, sweet dear, prove mistress of my heart! 4.02. 10
much good do it unto thy gentle heart! 4.03. 51
my tongue will tell the anger of my heart, | or 4.03. 77
or else my heart concealing it will break, | and 4.03. 78
i pray the gods she may with all my heart! 4.04. 67
well, petruchio, this has put me in heart. 4.05. 77
my heart as great, my reason haply more, | to 5.02.171
never approaches her heart but the tyranny of AWW 1.01. 50 P
heart too capable | of every line and trick of 1.01. 95
a man may draw his heart out ere 'a pluck one. 1.03. 88 P
of humility over the black gown of a big heart. 1.03. 95 P
and yet my heart | will not confess he owes the 2.01. 8
ay, with all my heart, and thou art worthy of it 2.03.218 P
what's the matter, sweet heart? 2.03.268 P
what, what, sweet heart? 2.03.271 P
since i cannot yet find in my heart to repent. 2.05. 12 P
haply, | which his heart was not consenting to. 3.02. 78
my heart is heavy, and mine age is weak; 3.04. 41
wheresoe'er she is, | her heart weighs sadly. 3.05. 67
with all my heart, my lord. 3.06.117
but my heart hath the fear of mars before it, 4.01. 29 P
how he would woo, | as if she sate in 's heart. 4.02. 70
if my heart were great, | 'twould burst at this. 4.03.330
ere my heart | durst make too bold a herald of 5.03. 45
o, she that hath a heart of that fine frame | to TN 1.01. 32
when liver, brain, and heart, | these sovereign 1.01. 36
taurus? that/'s sides and heart. 1.03.139 P
no, my profound heart; 1.05.183 P
and then show you the heart of my message. 1.05.191 P
answer by the method, in the first of his heart. 1.05.227 P
love make his heart of flint that you shall love 1.05.286
"farewell, dear heart, since i must needs be 2.03.102
so sways she level in her husband's heart. 2.04. 31
hath for your love as great a pang of heart | as 2.04. 90
strong a passion | as love doth give my heart; 2.04. 95
no woman's heart | so big, to hold so much; 2.04. 95
in faith, they are as true of heart as we. 2.04.106
with bloodless stroke my heart doth gore; 2.05.106
thoughts | that tyrannous heart can think? 3.01.120
a cypress, not a bosom, | hides my heart. 3.01.122
i have one heart, one bosom, and one truth, 3.01.158
for thou perhaps mayst move | that heart, which 3.01.164
your dormouse valor, to put fire in your heart, 3.02. 20 P
to bed? ay, sweet heart, and i'll come to thee. 3.04. 30 P
ill of the devil, how he takes it at heart! 3.04.101 P
i have said too much unto a heart of stone, 3.04.201
he started one poor heart of mine, in thee. 4.01. 59
why should i not (had i the heart to do it), 5.01.117
love, | to spite a raven's heart within a dove. 5.01.131
my heart dances, | but not for joy; WT 1.02.110
and my young rover, he's | apparent to my heart. 1.02.177
with all the nearest things to my heart, as well 1.02.236
'shrew my heart, | you never spoke what did 1.02.281
do't, and thou hast the one half of my heart; 1.02.348
i saw his heart in 's face. 1.02.447
that hast | a heart so tender o'er it, take it 2.03.133
she lives | my heart will be a burthen to me. 2.03.206
even pushes 'gainst our heart — the party tried 3.02. 2
her heart is but o'ercharg'd; 3.02.150
o, cut my lace, lest my heart, cracking it, 3.02.173
cleft the heart | that could conceive a gross 3.02.196
he is touch'd | to th' noble heart. 3.02.222
i am glad at heart | to be so rid o' th' 3.03. 14
weep i cannot, | but my heart bleeds; 3.03. 52
me no money, i pray you, that kills my heart. 4.03. 83 P
i am false of heart that way, and that he knew, 4.03.108 P
a merry heart goes all the day, | your sad tires 4.03.125
your heart is full of something that does take 4.04.346
from me are pack'd and lock'd | up in my heart, 4.04.359
o, my heart! 4.04.424
bosom there, | and speak his very heart. 4.04.564
whose fresh complexion and whose heart together 4.04.574
break the back of man, the heart of monster. 4.04.770 P
as if she would pin her to her heart, that she 5.02. 78 P
for i am sure my heart wept blood. 5.02. 89 P
needs must you lay your heart at his dispose, JN 1.01.263
nor keep his princely heart from richard's hand. 1.01.267
with all my heart i thank thee for my father! 1.01.270
richard, that robb'd the lion of his heart, 2.01. 3
hand, | but with a heart full of unstained love. 2.01. 16
and quarter'd in her heart! 2.01.506
have you the heart? 4.01. 41
he hath a stern look, but a gentle heart. 4.01. 87
with all my heart, my liege. 4.02.180
yea, without stop, didst let thy heart consent, 4.02.239
my heart hath melted at a lady's tears, | being 5.02. 47
and with a great heart heave away this storm. 5.02. 55
yea, thrust this enterprise into my heart, | and 5.02. 90
o, my heart is sick! 5.03. 4
beshrew thy very heart! 5.05. 14
the tackle of my heart is crack'd and burn'd, 5.07. 52
my heart hath one poor string to stay it by, 5.07. 55
as low as to thy heart | through the false R2 1.01.124
never did captive with a freer heart | cast off 1.03. 88
glasses of thine eyes | i see thy grieved heart. 1.03.209
to breathe the abundant dolor of the heart. 1.03.257
my heart will sigh when i miscall it so, | which 1.03.263
for my heart disdained that my tongue | should 1.04. 12
my heart is great, but it must break with 2.01.228
my heart this covenant makes, my hand thus seals 2.03. 50
show me thy humble heart, and not thy knee, 2.03. 83
mine ear is open, and my heart prepar'd, | the 3.02. 93
in my heart-blood warm'd, that sting my heart! 3.02.131
and sends allegiance and true faith of heart 3.03. 37
and his heart | to faithful service of your 3.03.117
swell'st thou, proud heart? 3.03.140
for on my heart they tread now whilst i live, 3.03.158
sorrow and grief of heart | makes him speak 3.03.184
me rather had my heart might feel your love 3.03.192
up, cousin, up, your heart is up, i know, | thus 3.03.194
when my poor heart no measure keeps in grief; 3.04. 8
and i will turn thy falsehood to thy heart, 4.01. 39
hath he been in thy heart? 5.01. 28
hand from hand, my love, and heart from heart. 5.01. 82
hand from hand, my love, and heart from heart. 5.01. 82
and piece the way out with a heavy heart. 5.01. 92
thus give i mine, and thus take i thy heart. 5.01. 96
part | to take on me to keep and kill thy heart. 5.01. 98
my heart is not confederate with my hand. 5.03. 53
a serpent that will sting thee to the heart. 5.03. 58
we pray with heart and soul, and all beside; 5.03.104
or in thy piteous heart plant thou thine ear, 5.03.126
with all my heart | i pardon him. 5.03.135
that would divorce this terror from my heart" — 5.04. 9
clamorous groans, which strike upon my heart, 5.05. 56
yet blessing on his heart that gives it me! 5.05. 64
how it ern'd my heart when i beheld | in london 5.05. 76
my tongue dares not, that my heart shall say. 5.05. 97
and tell him so, for i will ease my heart, 1H4 1.03.127
of fear and cold heart will he to the king, and 2.03. 31 P
books in england, i could find in my heart — 2.04. 50 P
marry, | and i am glad of it with all my heart. 3.01.126
with all my heart i'll sit and hear her sing. 3.01.220
heart, you swear like a comfit-maker's wife: 3.01.247 P
with all my heart. 3.01.266
and hold their level with thy princely heart? 3.02. 17
or i will tear the reckoning from his heart. 3.02.152
i shall be out of heart shortly, and then i 3.03. 6 P
as heart can think. 4.01. 84
well, | you speak it out of fear and cold heart. 4.03. 7
zeal, | my father, in kind heart and pity mov'd, 4.03. 64
grieves at heart | so many of his shadows thou 5.04. 29
fare thee well, great heart! 5.04. 87
with all my heart. 5.05. 24
as good as heart can wish: 2H4 1.01. 13
that, each heart being set | on bloody courses, 1.01.158
my heart bleeds inwardly that my father is so 2.02. 48 P
beshrew your heart, | fair daughter, you do draw 2.03. 45
it ang'red him to the heart, but he hath forgot 2.04. 9 P
i' faith, sweet heart, methinks now you are in 2.04. 22 P
beats as extraordinarily as heart would desire, 2.04. 24 P
me some sack, and, sweet heart, lie thou there. 2.04.183
do, and thou dar'st for thy heart. 2.04.224 P
troth, i kiss thee with a most constant heart. 2.04.270 P
god's blessing of your good heart! 2.04.303 P
if my heart be not ready to burst — well, sweet 2.04.379 P
and with what danger, near the heart of it. 3.01. 40
it would have done a man's heart good to see. 3.02. 48 P
by the mass, i could anger her to th' heart. 3.02.204 P
that man that sits within a monarch's heart 4.02. 11
muster me all to their captain, the heart, who, 4.03.111 P
the blood weeps from my heart when i do shape, 4.04. 58
whom thou hast whetted on thy stony heart | to 4.05.107
your majesty, | how cold it strook my heart! 4.05.151
i thank thee with my heart, kind master bardolph 5.01. 57 P
put the fashion on | and wear it in my heart. 5.02. 53
there's a merry heart! 5.03. 23 P
leman mine, | and a merry heart lives long-a." 5.03. 48
any thing, and wilt not call, beshrew thy heart. 5.03. 56 P
my king! my jove! i speak to thee, my heart! 5.05. 46
for we will hear, note, and believe in heart, H5 1.02. 30
like little body with a mighty heart, | what 2.pr. 17
the king has kill'd his heart. 2.01. 88 P
ah, poor heart! 2.01.118 P
his heart is fracted and corroborate. 2.01.124
we carry not a heart with us from hence | that 2.02. 21
for my manly heart doth ern. 2.03. 3
the flesh'd soldier, rough and hard of heart, 3.03. 11
he'll drop his heart into the sink of fear, 3.05. 59
i love and honor with my soul, and my heart, and 3.06. 8 P
bardolph, a soldier firm and sound of heart, 3.06. 25
god-a-mercy, old heart! 4.01. 34
the king's a bawcock, and a heart of gold, | a 4.01. 44
so full a voice issue from so empty a heart; 4.04. 68 P
all offenses, my lord, come from the heart. 4.08. 46 P
her vine, the merry cheerer of the heart, 5.02. 41
and plead his love-suit to her gentle heart? 5.02.101
you will love me soundly with your french heart, 5.02.105 P
but a good heart, kate, is the sun and the moon, 5.02.162 P
those parts in me that you love with your heart. 5.02.201 P
the thoughts of your heart with the looks of an 5.02.235 P
the voice nor the heart of flattery about me, i 5.02.288 P
my heart and hands thou hast at once subdu'd. 1H6 1.02.109
but o, the treacherous falstaff wounds my heart, 1.04. 35
bed, | ready they were to shoot me to the heart. 1.04. 56
it irks his heart he cannot be reveng'd. 1.04.105
with all my heart, and think me honored | to 2.03. 81
or durst not for his craven heart say thus. 2.04. 87
from envious malice of thy swelling heart. 3.01. 26
or i would see his heart out ere the priest 3.01.120
ay, but, i fear me, with a hollow heart. 3.01.136
town | great cordelion's heart was buried, | so 3.02. 83
burgundy | enshrines thee in his heart, and 3.02.119
a gentler heart did never sway in court; 3.02.135
and with submissive loyalty of heart | ascribes 3.04. 10
lord, in heart desiring still | you may behold 4.01. 76
bewray'd the faintness of my master's heart. 4.01.107
for, had the passions of thy heart burst out, 4.01.183
who in proud heart | doth stop my cornets, were 4.03. 24
it warm'd thy father's heart with proud desire 4.06. 11
words of yours draw life-blood from my heart. 4.06. 43
none, | dizzy-ey'd fury and great rage of heart 4.07. 11
my hand would free her, but my heart says no. 5.03. 61
yes, my good lord, a pure unspotted heart, 5.03.182
joan, this kills thy father's heart outright! 5.04. 2
do breed love's settled passions in my heart, 5.05. 4
lend me a heart replete with thankfulness! 2H6 1.01. 20
affords | and overjoy of heart doth minister. 1.01. 31
some sudden qualm hath struck me at the heart, 1.01. 54
france should have torn and rent my very heart 1.01.126
thy late exploits done in the heart of france 1.01.196
burnt | unto the prince's heart of calydon. 1.01.235
back, | and in her heart she scorns our poverty. 1.03. 81
o lord, my heart! 1.03.216 P
beat on a crown, the treasure of thy heart, 2.01. 20
how irksome is this music to my heart! 2.01. 54
such as my heart doth tremble to unfold: 2.01.162
ambitious churchman, leave to afflict my heart. 2.01.178
my heart assures me that the earl of warwick 2.02. 78
mine eyes are full of tears, my heart of grief. 2.03. 17
i pray thee sort thy heart to patience, | these 2.04. 68
a heart unspotted is not easily daunted. 3.01.100
the envious load that lies upon his heart; 3.01.157
my heart is drown'd with grief, | whose flood 3.01.198
but that my heart accordeth with my tongue, 3.01.269
man, | and find no harbor in a royal heart. 3.01.336
because thy flinty heart, more hard than they, 3.02. 99
a heart it was, bound in with diamonds, | and 3.02.107
it, | and so i wish'd thy body might my heart. 3.02.109
and bid mine eyes be packing with my heart, 3.02.111
being all descended to the laboring heart, | who 3.02.163
which with the heart there cools and ne'er 3.02.166
that shall be scoured in his rancorous heart 3.02.199
stronger breastplate than a heart untainted! 3.02.232
and even now my burthen'd heart would break, 3.02.320
and take my heart with thee. 3.02.408
with gobbets of thy /mother's bleeding heart. 4.01. 85
hath given them heart and courage to proceed. 4.04. 35
wives be as free as heart can wish or tongue can 4.07.125 P
will he conduct you through the heart of france, 4.08. 36
and let thy tongue be equal with thy heart. 5.01. 89
at this sight | my heart is turn'd to stone; 5.02. 50
heart, be wrathful still: 5.02. 70
my heart for anger burns, i cannot brook it. 3H6 1.01. 60
far be the thought of this from henry's heart, 1.01. 70
o clifford, how thy words revive my heart! 1.01.163
the loss of those three lords torments my heart; 1.01.270
even in the lukewarm blood of henry's heart. 1.02. 34
it could not slake mine ire nor ease my heart. 1.03. 29
to prick thy finger, though to wound his heart. 1.04. 55
hath thy fiery heart so parch'd thine entrails 1.04. 87
o tiger's heart wrapp'd in a woman's hide! 1.04.137
serves to quench my furnace-burning heart; 2.01. 80
but all in vain, they had no heart to fight, 2.01.135
then, clifford, were thy heart as hard as steel, 2.01.201
doth not the object cheer your heart, my lord? 2.02. 4
steel thy melting heart | to hold thine own and 2.02. 41
the execution of my big-swoll'n heart | upon 2.02.111
to let thy tongue detect thy base-born heart? 2.02.143
his father revell'd in the heart of france, 2.02.150
i throw my hands, mine eyes, my heart to thee, 2.03. 36
and here's the heart that triumphs in their 2.04. 8
blown with the windy tempest of my heart | upon 2.05. 86
upon thy wounds, that kills mine eye and heart! 2.05. 87
my heart, sweet boy, shall be thy sepulchre, 2.05.115
for from my heart thine image ne'er shall go; 2.05.116
her tears will pierce into a marble heart; 3.01. 38
my crown is in my heart, not on my head; 3.01. 62
my eye's too quick, my heart o'erweens too much, 3.02.144
cry "content" to that which grieves my heart, 3.02.183
my tongue, while heart is drown'd in cares. 3.03. 14
to tell the passion of my sovereign's heart, 3.03. 62
mine such as fill my heart with unhop'd joys. 3.03.172
to rest mistrustful where a noble heart | hath 4.02. 8
did glad my heart with hope of this young 4.06. 93

so doth my heart misgive me, in these conflicts 4.06. 94
blood, my want of strength, my sick heart shows, 5.02. 8
this cheers my heart, to see your forwardness. 5.04. 65
no, no, my heart will burst and if i speak, 5.05. 59
and i will speak, that so my heart may burst. 5.05. 60
cursed the heart that had the heart to do it! R3 1.02. 15
cursed the heart that had the heart to do it! 1.02. 15
fouler than heart can think thee, thou canst 1.02. 83
my proud heart sues, and prompts my tongue to 1.02.170
if thy revengeful heart cannot forgive, | lo 1.02.173
i would i knew thy heart. 1.02.192
even so thy breast encloseth my poor heart: 1.02.204
with all my heart, and much it joys me too, | to 1.02.219
i would to god my heart were flint, like 1.03.139
far be it from my heart, the thought thereof! 1.03.149
when he shall split thy very heart with sorrow, 1.03.299
and i, as i love hastings with my heart! 2.01. 17
is this thy vow unto my sickly heart. 2.01. 42
i long with all my heart to see the prince. 2.04. 4
knows, | seldom or never jumpeth with the heart. 3.01. 11
my dagger, little cousin? with all my heart. 3.01.111
with a heavy heart, | thinking on them, go i 3.01.149
i thank thee, good sir john, with all my heart. 3.02.109
marry, and will, my lord, with all my heart. 3.04. 34
by his face straight shall you know his heart. 3.04. 53
what of his heart perceive you in his face | by 3.04. 54
even where his raging eye or savage heart, 3.05. 83
as well we know your tenderness of heart | and 3.07.210
that my pent heart may have some scope to beat, 4.01. 34
my woman's heart | grossly grew captive to his 4.01. 78
poor heart, adieu, i pity thy complaining. 4.01. 87
help nothing else, yet do they ease the heart. 4.04.131
till it was whetted on thy stone–hard heart | to 4.04.228
madam, with all my heart. 4.04.270
put in her tender heart th' aspiring flame | of 4.04.328
look your heart be firm, | or else his head's 4.04.495
quoth she, "shall split thy heart with sorrow, 5.01. 26
my heart is ten times lighter than my looks. 5.03. 3
but cheer thy heart, and be thou not dismay'd. 5.03.174
(and take it from a heart that wishes towards H8 1.01.103
my life itself, and the best heart of it, 1.02. 1
'em, which hath flaw'd the heart | of all their 1.02. 21
sweet heart, | i were unmannerly to take you out 1.04. 94
if ever any malice in your heart | were hid 2.01. 80
speaks 'em, | and every true heart weeps for't. 2.02. 39
her | so dear in heart not to deny her that | a 2.02.110
too, a woman's heart, which ever yet | affected 2.03. 28
but your heart | is cramm'd with arrogancy, 2.04.109
killing care and grief of heart | fall asleep, 3.01. 13
he has my heart yet and shall have my prayers 3.01.180
fret the string, | the master–cord on 's heart! 3.02.106
i have kept you next my heart, have not alone 3.02.157
my heart dropp'd love, my pow'r rain'd honor, 3.02.185
more | on you than any, so your hand and heart, 3.02.186
my heart weeps to see him | so little of his 3.02.335
i feel my heart new open'd. 3.02.366
(i speak it with a single heart, my lords) | a 5.02. 73
pray heaven the king may never find a heart 5.02. 77
with a true heart | and brother–love i do it. 5.02.205
each troyan that is master of his heart, | let TRO 1.01. 4
i was about to tell thee — when my heart, | as 1.01. 34
pourest in the open ulcer of my heart | her eyes 1.01. 53
well, i would my heart were in her body. 1.02. 78 P
it does a /man's heart good. 1.02.204 P
by god's lid, it does one's heart good. 1.02.212 P
why, this will do helen's heart good now, ha? 1.02.216 P
heart of our numbers, soul and only sprite | in 1.03. 56
great jove's accord, | nothing so full of heart. 1.03.239
what heart receives from hence a conquering part 1.03.352
spirit on our party | without a heart to dare, 2.02.157
yes, lion–sick, sick of proud heart. 2.03. 86 P
my heart beats thicker than a feverous pulse, 3.02. 36
boldness comes to me now, and brings me heart. 3.02.113
let them say, to stick the heart of falsehood, 3.02.195
god buy you, with all my heart. 3.03.293 P
fare ye well, with all my heart. 3.03.299 P
as heart can think or courage execute. 4.01. 14
come, beshrew your heart, you'll ne'er be good, 4.02. 29
my clear voice with sobs and break my heart 4.02.108
a priest there off'ring to it his own heart. 4.03. 9
"o heart," as the goodly saying is, "o heart, 4.04. 15 P
as the goodly saying is, "o heart, heavy heart, 4.04. 16
as the goodly saying is, "o heart, heavy heart, 4.04. 16
or my heart will be blown up by /th' /root. 4.04. 54 P
hear me, love. be thou but true of heart — 4.04. 58
that there is no maculation in thy heart; 4.04. 64
half heart, half hand, half hector comes to seek 4.05. 85
his heart and hand both open and both free, 4.05.100
from heart of very heart, great hector, welcome. 4.05.171
from heart of very heart, great hector, welcome. 4.05.171
he that takes that doth take my heart withal. 5.02. 82
i had your heart before, this follows it. 5.02. 83
but with my heart the other eye doth see. 5.02.108
sith yet there is a credence in my heart, | an 5.02.120
well | in characters as red as mars his heart 5.02.164
words, mere words, no matter from the heart; 5.03.108
here lies thy heart, thy sinews, and thy bone. 5.08. 12
the counsellor heart, the arm our soldier, | our COR 1.01.116
even to the court, the heart, to th' seat o' th' 1.01.136
to break the heart of generosity | and make bold 1.01.211
in heart | as merry as when our nuptial day was 1.06. 30
o'er them aufidius, | their very heart of hope. 1.06. 55
but cannot make my heart consent to take | a 1.09. 37
would i | wash my fierce hand in 's heart. 1.10. 27
no more of this, it does offend my heart; 2.01.168
a curse begin at very root on 's heart, | that 2.01.185
choice is rather to have my hat than my heart, i 2.03. 99 P
by his looks, methinks, | 'tis warm at 's heart. 2.03.152
with a proud heart he wore his humble weeds. 2.03.153
why, had your bodies | no heart among you? 2.03.204
i have a heart as little apt as yours, | but yet 3.02. 29
nor by th' matter which your heart prompts you, 3.02. 54
which often thus correcting thy stout heart, 3.02. 78
with my base tongue give to my noble heart | a 3.02.100
for i mock at death | with as big heart as thou. 3.02.128
then he speaks | what's in his heart, and that 3.03. 29
make invincible | the heart that conn'd them. 4.01. 11
it would unclog my heart | of what lies heavy 4.02. 47

the nobles receive so to heart the banishment of 4.03. 22 P
whose double bosoms seems to wear one heart, 4.04. 13
then if thou hast | a heart of wreak in thee, 4.05. 85
word thou hast spoke hath weeded from my heart 4.05.102
more dances my rapt heart | than when i first my 4.05.116
whom with a crack'd heart i have sent to rome, 5.03. 9
him, and men of heart | look'd wond'ring each at 5.06. 98
thou hast made my heart | too great for what 5.06.102
the cordial of mine age to glad my heart! TIT 1.01.166
rome's royal mistress, mistress of my heart, 1.01.241
these words are razors to my wounded heart. 1.01.314
nor with sour looks afflict his gentle heart. 1.01.441
and cheer the heart | that dies in tempest of 1.01.457
sweet heart, look back. 1.01.481
aaron, arm thy heart, and fit thy thoughts, | to 2.01. 12
vengeance is in my heart, death in my hand, 2.03. 38
but be your heart to them | as unrelenting flint 2.03.140
o, be to me, though thy hard heart say no, 2.03.155
ne'er let my heart know merry cheer indeed 2.03.188
that ever eye with sight made heart lament! 2.03.205
my heart suspects more than mine eye can see. 2.03.213
to prove thou hast a true–divining heart, 2.03.214
and my compassionate heart | will not permit 2.03.217
o, that i knew thy heart, and knew the beast, 2.04. 34
doth burn the heart to cinders where it is. 2.04. 37
weep, | or, if not so, thy noble heart to break: 3.01. 60
with all my heart i'll send the emperor my hand. 3.01.160
do then, dear heart, for heaven shall hear our 3.01.210
sicily, | and be my heart an ever–burning hell! 3.01.242
alas, poor heart, that kiss is comfortless | as 3.01.250
curs'd be that heart that forc'd us to this 4.01. 72
that hath more scars of sorrow in his heart 4.01.126
the close enacts and counsels of thy heart! 4.02.118
hath pierc'd him deep and scarr'd his heart, 4.04. 31
that, were his heart | almost impregnable, his 4.04. 97
yet should both ear and heart obey my tongue. 4.04. 99
and almost broke my heart with extreme laughter. 5.01.113
and on them shalt thou ease thy angry heart. 5.02.119
the venomous malice of my swelling heart! 5.03. 13
and if your highness knew my heart, you were. 5.03. 34
my heart is not compact of flint nor steel, 5.03. 88
ev'n with all my heart | would i were dead, so 5.03.172
good heart, at what? ROM 1.01.184
but woo her, gentle paris, get her heart, | my 1.02. 16
let wantons light of heart | tickle the 1.04. 35
did my heart love till now? 1.05. 52
can i go forward when my heart is here? 2.01. 1
come to thy heart as that within my breast! 2.02.124
being tasted, stays all senses with the heart. 2.03. 26
the very pin of his heart cleft with the blind 2.04. 15 P
good heart, and, i' faith, i will tell her as 2.04.173 P
beshrew your heart for sending me about | to 2.05. 51
o, break, my heart, poor bankrout, break at once 3.02. 57
o serpent heart, hid with a flow'ring face! 3.02. 73
how hast thou the heart, | being a divine, a 3.03. 48
i do with all my heart; 3.05. 82
and yet no man like he doth grieve my heart. 3.05. 83
is my poor heart, so for a kinsman vex'd. 3.05. 95
o, how my heart abhors | to hear him nam'd, and 3.05. 99
thursday is near, lay hand on heart, advise. 3.05.190
beshrow my very heart, | i think you are happy 3.05.221
speak'st thou from thy heart? 3.05.226
god join'd my heart and romeo's, thou our hands, 4.01. 55
or my true heart with treacherous revolt | turn 4.01. 58
my heart is wondrous light, | since this same 4.02. 46
sweet heart! 4.05. 3
because my heart itself plays "my heart is full. 4.05.106 P
my heart itself plays "my heart is full." 4.05.107 P
"when griping griefs the heart doth wound, 4.05.126
hate a lord with my heart. TIM 1.01.230 P
he outgoes | the very heart of kindness. 1.01.275
grateful virtue i am bound | to your free heart, 1.02. 6
my lord, in heart; and let the health go round. 1.02. 53
much good dich thy good heart, apemantus! 1.02. 72 P
my heart is ever at your service, my lord. 1.02. 75 P
did not you chiefly belong to my heart? 1.02. 92 P
this, | to show him what a beggar his heart is, 1.02.195
and your several visitations | so kind to heart, 1.02.219
what heart, head, sword, force, means, but is 2.02.167
no villainous bounty yet hath pass'd my heart; 2.02.173
secure thy heart; 2.02.176
has friendship such a faint and milky heart, 3.01. 54
return'd to him, | so much i love his heart. 3.02. 85
it is against my heart. 3.04. 21
now | (like all mankind) show me an iron heart? 3.04. 83
cut my heart in sums. 3.04. 92
and ne'er prefer his injuries to his heart, | to 3.05. 34
with all my heart, gentlemen both; 3.06. 25 P
poor honest lord, brought low by his own heart, 4.02. 37
the canker gnaw thy heart, | for showing me 4.03. 50
lend me a fool's heart and a woman's eyes, | and 5.01.157
so thou wilt send thy gentle heart before, | to 5.04. 48
are the ruddy drops | that visit my sad heart. JC 2.01.290
bosom shall partake | the secrets of my heart. 2.01.306
foot, | and with a heart new–fir'd i follow you, 2.01.332
they could not find a heart within the beast. 2.02. 40
caesar should be a beast without a heart | if he 2.02. 42
the heart of brutus earns to think upon! 2.02.129
my heart laments that virtue cannot live | out 2.03. 13
set a huge mountain 'tween my heart and tongue! 2.04. 7
how weak a thing | the heart of woman is! 2.04. 40
cimber throws before thy seat | an humble heart. 3.01. 35
and this indeed, o world, the heart of thee. 3.01.208
thy heart is big; 3.01.282
my heart is in the coffin there with caesar, 3.02.106
then burst his mighty heart, | and, in his 3.02.186
pluck but his name out of his heart, and turn 3.03. 34 P
fret till your proud heart break; 4.03. 42
i had rather coin my heart | and drop my blood 4.03. 72
brutus hath riv'd my heart. 4.03. 85
within, a heart | dearer than pluto's mine, 4.03.101
i, that denied thee gold, will give my heart: 4.03.104
and my heart too. 4.03.118
my heart is thirsty for that noble pledge. 4.03.160
now i have taken heart thou vanishest. 4.03.287
witness the hole you made in caesar's heart, 5.01. 31
he lies not like the living. o my heart! 5.03. 58
come, cassius' sword, and find titinius' heart. 5.03. 90

my heart doth joy that yet in all my life | i 5.05. 34
and make my seated heart knock at my ribs, MAC 1.03.136
let me infold thee | and hold thee to my heart. 1.04. 32
lay it to thy heart, and farewell." 1.05. 13 P
face must hide what the false heart doth know. 1.07. 82
but i shame | to wear a heart so white. 2.02. 62
tongue nor heart | cannot conceive nor name thee 2.03. 64
that had a heart to love, and in that heart 2.03.117
and in that heart | courage to make 's love 2.03.117
off, | grapples you to the heart and love of us, 3.01.105
friends, | for my heart speaks they are welcome. 3.04. 8
for 'twould have anger'd any heart alive | to 3.06. 15
yet my heart | throbs to know one thing: 4.01.100
show his eyes, and grieve his heart; 4.01.110
the very firstlings of my heart shall be | the 4.01.147
not speak | whispers the o'er–fraught heart, and 4.03.210
blunt not the heart, enrage it. 4.03.229
the heart is sorely charg'd. 5.01. 53 P
would not have such a heart in my bosom for the 5.01. 55 P
the mind i sway by, and the heart i bear, 5.03. 9
i am sick at heart | when i behold — seyton, i 5.03. 19
which the poor heart would fain deny, and dare 5.03. 28
perilous stuff | which weighs upon the heart? 5.03. 45
'tis bitter cold, | and i am sick at heart. HAM 1.01. 9
the head is not more native to the heart, | the 1.02. 47
a heart unfortified, or mind impatient, | an 1.02. 96
we in our peevish opposition | take it to heart? 1.02.101
accord of hamlet | sits smiling to my heart, in 1.02.124
but break my heart, for i must hold my tongue. 1.02.159
or lose your heart, or your chaste treasure open 1.03. 31
this good lesson keep | as watchman to my heart. 1.03. 46
o, fie, hold, hold, my heart, | and you, my 1.05. 93
say you then, would heart of man once think it? 1.05.121
or given my heart a /winking, mute and dumb, 2.02.137
must, like a whore, unpack my heart with words, 2.02.585
with all my heart, and it doth much content me 3.01. 24
this something–settled matter in his heart, 3.01.173
in my heart's core, ay, in my heart of heart, 3.02. 73
in my heart's core, ay, in my heart of heart, 3.02. 73
you would pluck out the heart of my mystery, you 3.02.366 P
o heart, lose not thy nature! 3.02.393
stubborn knees, and heart, with strings of steel 3.03. 70
and let me wring your heart, for so i shall, 3.04. 35
o hamlet, thou hast cleft my heart in twain. 3.04.156
i' th' world, and hems, and beats her heart, 4.05. 5
and you must put me in your heart for friend, 4.07. 2
it warms the very sickness in my heart | that i 4.07. 55
painting of a sorrow, | a face without a heart? 4.07.109
in my heart there was a kind of fighting | that 5.02. 4
not think how ill all's here about my heart — 5.02.213 P
if thou didst ever hold me in thy heart, 5.02.346
now cracks a noble heart. 5.02.359
in my true heart | i find she names my very deed LR 1.01. 70
i am, i cannot heave | my heart into my mouth. 1.01. 92
but goes thy heart with this? 1.01.105
and as a stranger to my heart and me | hold thee 1.01.115
as here i give | her father's heart from her. 1.01.126
though the fork invade | the region of my heart; 1.01.145
a heart and brain to breed it in? 1.02. 57 P
but i hope his heart is not in the contents. 1.02. 67 P
and shake in pieces the heart of his obedience. 1.02. 85 P
drew from my heart all love, | and added to the 1.04.269
i know his heart. 1.04.330
o madam, my old heart is crack'd, it's crack'd! 2.01. 90
o, how this mother swells up toward my heart! 2.04. 56
o me, my heart! my rising heart! but down! 2.04.121
o me, my heart! my rising heart! but down! 2.04.121
most serpent–like, upon the very heart. 2.04.161
but this heart | shall break into a hundred 2.04.284
makes his toe | what he his heart should make 3.02. 32
i have one part in my heart | that's sorry yet 3.02. 72
wilt break my heart? 3.04. 4
old kind father, whose frank heart gave all — 3.04. 20
by his porridge, made him proud of heart, to 3.04. 56 P
spouse, set not thy sweet heart on proud array. 3.04. 82 P
proud in heart and mind; 3.04. 85 P
lust of my mistress' heart and did the act of 3.04. 87 P
false of heart, light of ear, bloody of hand; 3.04. 92 P
of silks betray thy poor heart to woman. 3.04. 95 P
in a wild field were like an old lecher's heart, 3.04.112 P
that in the fury of his heart, when the foul 3.04.131 P
see what breeds about her heart. 3.06. 77 P
which came from one that's of a neutral heart, 3.07. 48
yet, poor old heart, he holp the heavens to rain 3.07. 62
with all my heart. 4.06. 32
it is, | and my heart breaks at it. 4.06.142
i'll make it on thy heart, | ere i taste bread, 5.03. 93
that, if my speech offend a noble heart, | thy 5.03.127
thy valor, and thy heart, thou art a traitor; 5.03.134
best spirits are bent | to prove upon thy heart, 5.03.141
with the hell–hated lie o'erwhelm thy heart, 5.03.148
let sorrow split my heart, if ever i | did hate 5.03.178
when 'tis told, o, that my heart would burst! 5.03.183
but his flaw'd heart | (alack, too weak the 5.03.197
it came even from the heart of — o, she's dead! 5.03.225
break, heart, i prithee break! 5.03.313
the native act and figure of my heart | in OTH 1.01. 62
after | but i will wear my heart upon my sleeve 1.01. 64
your heart is burst, you have lost half your 1.01. 87
to draw from her a prayer of earnest heart 1.03.152
i here do give thee that with all my heart 1.03.193
with all my heart | i would keep from thee. 1.03.194
that the bruis'd heart was pierced through the 1.03.219
with all my heart. 1.03.278
what say'st thou, noble heart? 1.03.302 P
she puts her tongue a little in her heart, | and 2.01.106
prating — let not thy discreet heart think it. 2.01.225 P
they're close dilations, working from the heart, 3.03.123
you cannot, if my heart were in your hand, | nor 3.03.163
up | the execution of his wit, hands, heart, 3.03.466
this argues fruitfulness and liberal heart; 3.04. 38
for 'twas that hand that gave away my heart. 3.04. 45
love | whom i, with all the office of my heart, 3.04.113
no, my heart is turn'd to stone; 4.01.182 P
with all my heart, sir. 4.01.216
but there, where i have garner'd up my heart, 4.02. 57
/forth of my heart those charms, thine eyes, are 5.01. 35
amen, with all my heart! 5.02. 34

o perjur'd woman, thou dost stone my heart, 5.02. 63
he lies to th' heart. 5.02.156
speak, for my heart is full. 5.02.175
for he was great of heart. 5.02.361
state | this heavy act with heavy heart relate. 5.02.371
his captain's heart, | which in the scuffles of ANT 1.01. 6
shouldst know | there were a heart in egypt. 1.03. 41
but my full heart | remains in use with you. 1.03. 43
to bear such idleness so near the heart | as 1.03. 94
his speech sticks in my heart. 1.05. 41
the heart of brothers govern in our loves, | and 2.02.147
half the heart of caesar, worthy maecenas! 2.02.172 P
she purs'd up his heart upon the river of cydnus 2.02.187 P
and for his ordinary pays his heart | for what 2.02.225
can settle | the heart of antony, octavia is | a 2.02.241
she never come, | to make my heart her vassal. 2.06. 56
her tongue will not obey her heart, nor can 3.02. 47
nor can | her heart inform her tongue — the 3.02. 48
and command what cost | your heart /has mind to. 3.04. 38
that have my heart parted betwixt two friends 3.06. 77
cheer your heart, | be you not troubled with the 3.06. 81
each heart in rome does love and pity you; 3.06. 92
take from his heart, take from his brain, from 3.07. 11
my heart was to thy rudder tied by th' strings, 3.11. 57
from my cold heart let heaven engender hail, 3.13.159
where hast thou been, my heart? 3.13.172
in our captain's brain | restores his heart. 3.13.198
thou art | the armorer of my heart. 4.04. 7
this blows my heart. 4.06. 33
through proof of harness to my heart, and there 4.08. 15
throw my heart | against the flint and hardness 4.09. 15
novice, and my heart | makes only wars on thee. 4.12. 14
loose | beguil'd me to the very heart of loss. 4.12. 29
whose heart i thought i had, for she had mine — 4.14. 16
it was divided | between her heart and lips. 4.14. 33
of ajax cannot keep | the battery from my heart. 4.14. 39
heart, once be stronger than thy continent, 4.14. 40
good sirs, take heart, | we'll bury him; 4.15. 85
with the courage which the heart did lend it, 5.01. 23
the heart did lend it, | splitted the heart. 5.01. 24
and the heart | where mine his thoughts did 5.01. 45
bid her have good heart. 5.01. 56
a grief that /smites | my very heart at root. 5.02.105
i think the king | be touch'd at very heart. CYM 1.01. 10
hath a heart that is not | glad at the thing 1.01. 14
take it, heart, | but keep it till you woo 1.01.112
sir, with all my heart. 1.04.100 P
from this practice but make hard your heart; 1.05. 24
but even the very middle of my heart | is warm'd 1.06. 27
your cause doth strike my heart | with pity that 1.06.118
(as i have such a heart that both mine ears 1.06.130
cannot take two from twenty, for his heart, 2.01. 55
that i, which know my heart, do here pronounce 2.03.107
with all my heart. 2.04.152
hit | the innocent mansion of my love, my heart. 3.04. 68
come, here's my heart: 3.04. 78
you shall no more | be stomachers to my heart. 3.04. 84
cheek, | exposing it (but o, the harder heart! 3.04.161
i'll have this secret from thy heart, or rip 3.05. 86
from thy heart, or rip | thy heart to find it. 3.05. 87
(the bitterness of it i now belch from my heart) 3.05.134 P
a heart as big? 4.02. 77
pisanio might have kill'd thee at the heart 4.02.322
to taint his nobler heart and brain | with 5.04. 65
woe is my heart | that the poor soldier that so 5.05. 2
to you, the liver, heart, and brain of britain, 5.05. 14
ears, that /heard her flattery, nor my heart, 5.05. 64
a roman with a roman's heart can suffer. 5.05. 81
ay, with all my heart, | and lend my best 5.05.116
for whom my heart drops blood, and my false 5.05.148
dead, | my heart can lend no succor to my head. PER 1.01.169
it griev'd my heart to hear what pitiful cries 2.01. 20 P
i am glad on't with all my heart. 2.05. 74
thou hast a heart | that ever cracks for woe! 3.02. 76
your lady | take from my heart all thankfulness! 3.03. 4
and yourself, | with more than foreign heart. 4.01. 33
your looks foreshow | you have a gentle heart. 4.01. 86
with all my heart, and, when you come ashore, 5.01.260
my heart | leaps to be gone into my mother's 5.03. 44
him lead his line | to catch one at my heart. TNK 1.01.117
a counter–reflect 'gainst | my brother's heart, 1.01.128
and hang | your shield afore your heart, about 1.01.197
and retain anew | her charitable heart, now hard 1.02. 25
pieces, keep enthron'd | in your dear heart! 1.03. 11
possess | the high throne in his heart. 1.03. 96
but in my heart was palamon, and there, | lord, 2.04. 17
sister, beshrew my heart, you have a servant 2.05. 62
the athenians pay it | to th' heart of ceremony. 3.01. 4
take twenty, domine. — how does my sweet heart? 3.05.148
fair hand, and that honest heart you gave me — 3.06.197
half his own heart, set in too, that i hope 4.01. 14
nav'l, and in ice up to th' heart, and there th' 4.03. 43 P
being laid unto | mine innocent true heart, arms 5.01.134
yes, sweet heart, | and i am glad my cousin 5.02. 90
on the sinister side the heart lies; 5.03. 76
if thy heart, | thy worthy, manly heart, be yet 5.04. 87
thy worthy, manly heart, be yet unbroken, | give 5.04. 88
for what's a sorry parsnip to a good heart? STM II.C 9 P
"is thine own heart to thine own face affected? VEN 157
the heart hath treble wrong | when it is barr'd 329
my heart all whole as thine, thy heart my wound! 370
my heart all whole as thine, thy heart my wound! 370
"give me my heart," saith she, "and thou shalt 374
o, give it me, lest thy hard heart do steel it, 375
because adonis' heart hath made mine hard." 378
else, suffer'd, it will set the heart on fire: 388
remove your siege from my unyielding heart, | to 423
for where a heart is hard they make no batt'ry." 426
eyes' shrowd tutor, that hard heart of thine, 500
that they have murd'red this poor heart of mine, 502
"a thousand kisses buys my heart from me, | and 517
bids him farewell, and look well to her heart, 580
for my sick heart commands mine eyes to watch. 584
my boding heart pants, beats, and takes no rest, 647
knocks at my heart, and whispers in mine ear, 659
thought of it doth make my faint heart bleed, 669
for know, my heart stands armed in mine ear, 779
and then my little heart were quite undone, | in 783
no, lady, no, my heart longs not to groan, | but 785
my face is full of shame, my heart of teen, 808
and now she beats her heart, whereat it groans, 829
through which it enters to surprise her heart, 890
mistakes that aim and cleaves an infant's heart. 942
thy coward heart with false bethinking grieves." 1024
and never wound the heart with looks again, 1042
mine eyes are turn'd to fire, my heart to lead: 1072
my throbbing heart shall rock thee day and night 1186
eyes forgo their light, my false heart bleed? LUC 228
thrives not in the heart that shadows dreadeth, 270
my heart shall never countermand mine eye. 276
but with a pure appeal seeks to the heart, 293
but his hot heart, which fond desire doth scorch 314
by their high treason is his heart misled, 369
anon his beating heart, alarum striking, | gives 433
his drumming heart cheers up his burning eye, 435
on her bare breast, the heart of all her land; 439
may feel her heart (poor citizen!) 465
but his heart granteth | no penetrable entrance 558
beat at thy rocky and wrack–threat'ning heart, 590
from a pure heart command thy rebel will; 625
she wakes her heart by beating on her breast, 759
against my heart | will fix a sharp knife to 1137
faint not, faint heart, but stoutly say, 'so be 1209
the face of either cipher'd either's heart, 1396
and then against my heart he set his sword, 1640
here with a sigh, as if her heart would break, 1716
do not steep thy heart | in such relenting dew 1828
persuade my heart to this false perjury? PP 3. 3
to win his heart she touch'd him here and there 4. 7
my heart doth charge the watch; 14.14
heart hath his hope, and eyes their wished sight 14.22
heart is bleeding, all help needing, | o cruel 17.15
thus of every grief in heart | he with thee doth 20.53
a woman's gentle heart, but not acquainted SON 20. 3
thee | is but the seemly raiment of my heart, 22. 6
bearing thy heart, which i will keep so chary 22.11
presume not on thy heart when mine is slain, 22.13
strength's abundance weakens his own heart, | so 23. 4
thy beauty's form in table of my heart; 24. 2
they draw but what they see, know not the heart. 24.14
when i am sometime absent from thy heart, | thy 41. 2
mine eye and heart are at a mortal war, | how to 46. 1
mine eye my heart /thy picture's sight would bar 46. 3
my heart mine eye the freedom of that right. 46. 4
my heart doth plead that thou in him dost lie 46. 5
a quest of thoughts, all tenants to the heart, 46.10
and my heart's right /thy inward love of heart. 46.14
betwixt mine eye and heart a league is took, 47. 1
or heart in love with sighs himself doth smother 47. 4
and to the painted banquet bids my heart; 47. 6
awakes my heart to heart's and eye's delight. 47.14
but you like none, none you, for constant heart. 53.14
remedy, | it is so grounded inward in my heart. 62. 4
do not, when my heart hath scap'd this sorrow, 90. 5
thy looks with me, thy heart in other place. 93. 4
take heed, dear heart, of this large privilege, 95.13
o, never say that i was false of heart, | though 109. 1
these blenches gave my heart another youth, 110. 7
for it no form delivers to the heart | of bird, 113. 5
what wretched errors hath my heart committed, 119. 5
so long as brain and heart | have faculty by 122. 5
no, let me be obsequious in thy heart, | and 125. 9
for well thou know'st to my dear doting heart 131. 3
me, | knowing thy heart torment me with disdain, 132. 2
let it then as well beseem thy heart | to mourn 132.10
beshrew that heart that makes my heart to groan 133. 1
beshrew that heart that makes my heart to groan 133. 1
prison my heart in thy steel bosom's ward, | but 133. 9
but then my friend's heart let my poor heart 133.10
then my friend's heart let my poor heart bail; 133.10
whoe'er keeps me, let my heart be his guard, 133.11
whereto the judgment of my heart is tied? 137. 8
why should my heart think that a several plot, 137. 9
which my heart knows the wide world's common 137.10
things right true my heart and eyes have erred, 137.13
wrong | that thy unkindness lays upon my heart, 139. 2
dear heart, forbear to glance thine eye aside; 139. 6
eyes straight, though thy proud heart go wide. 140.14
but 'tis my heart that loves what they despise, 141. 3
dissuade one foolish heart from serving thee, 141.10
root pity in thy heart, that, when it grows, 142.11
state, | straight in her heart did mercy come, 145. 5
might | with insufficiency my heart to sway, 150. 2
sweetly suppos'd them mistress of his heart. LC 142
and bastards of his foul adulterate heart. 175
not one whose flame my heart so much as warmed, 191
eyes | what rocky heart to water will not wear? 291
"that not a heart which in his level came 309
o, that forc'd thunder from his heart did fly, 325

HEART–ACHE 1 FR 0.0001 REL FR 1 V 0 P
the heart–ache and the thousand natural shocks HAM 3.01. 61

HEART–BLOOD 7 FR 0.0008 REL FR 6 V 1 P
the which no balm can cure but his heart–blood R2 1.01.172
snakes, in my heart–blood warm'd, that sting my 3.02.131
thou hast said is false | in thy heart–blood, 4.01. 28
thy heart–blood i will have for this day's work. 1H6 1.03. 83
with heart–blood of the house of lancaster; 2H6 2.02. 66
wouldst have left thy dearest heart–blood there 3H6 1.01.223
the mortal venus, the heart–blood of beauty, TRO 3.01. 32 P

HEART–BREAK 1 FR 0.0001 REL FR 0 V 1 P
little chiding than a great deal of heart–break. WIV 5.03. 10 P

HEART–BREAKING 1 FR 0.0001 REL FR 0 V 1 P
as it is a heart–breaking to see a handsome man ANT 1.02. 71 P

HEART–BURN'D 1 FR 0.0001 REL FR 0 V 1 P
can see him but i am heart–burn'd an hour after. ADO 2.01. 4 P

HEART–BURNING 1 FR 0.0001 REL FR 0 V 1 P
of devoted and heart–burning heat of duty, don LLL 1.01.277 P

HEART–BURNT 1 FR 0.0001 REL FR 0 V 1 P
so should i be sure to be heart–burnt. 1H4 3.03. 50 P

HEART–DEEP 1 FR 0.0001 REL FR 1 V 0 P
lord is taken | heart–deep with your distress. TNK 1.01.105

HEART–EASING 1 FR 0.0001 REL FR 1 V 0 P
or keep him from heart–easing words so long, LUC 1782

HEARTED 3 FR 0.0003 REL FR 2 V 1 P
my cause is hearted; OTH 1.03.366 P
thy crown and hearted throne | to tyrannous hate 3.03.448
i will be treble–sinew'd, hearted, breath'd, ANT 3.13.177

HEARTEN 1 FR 0.0001 REL FR 1 V 0 P
and hearten those that fight in your defense. 3H6 2.02. 79

HEARTENS 1 FR 0.0001 REL FR 1 V 0 P
and therein heartens up his servile powers, LUC 295

HEART–GRIEF 1 FR 0.0001 REL FR 1 V 0 P
that sits in heart–grief and uneasiness | under H5 2.02. 27

HEARTH 3 FR 0.0003 REL FR 2 V 1 P
let me but stand, i will not hurt your hearth. COR 4.05. 24 P
this extremity | hath brought me to thy hearth; 4.05. 79
being banish'd for't, he came unto my hearth, 5.06. 29

HEART–HARD'NING 1 FR 0.0001 REL FR 1 V 0 P
hast oft beheld | heart–hard'ning spectacles; COR 4.01. 25

HEART–HEAVINESS 1 FR 0.0001 REL FR 0 V 1 P
i to–morrow be at the height of heart–heaviness, AYL 5.02. 46 P

HEARTHS 1 FR 0.0001 REL FR 1 V 0 P
fires thou find'st unrak'd and hearths unswept, WIV 5.05. 44

HEARTILY 39 FR 0.0044 REL FR 24 V 15 P
no, i thank you, forsooth, heartily; WIV 1.01.267 P
i beseech you heartily, some of you go home with 3.02. 79 P
and he heartily prays some occasion may detain ADO 1.01.149 P
the which she wept heartily and said she car'd 5.01.174 P
i cry your worships mercy, heartily. MND 3.01.179 P
beshrow me but i love her heartily, | for she is MV 2.06. 52
most heartily i do beseech the court | to give 4.01.243
i am heartily glad i came hither to you. AYL 1.01.159 P
o, thou didst then never love so heartily! 2.04. 33
and when a man thanks me heartily, methinks i 2.05. 28 P
come, kate, and wash, and welcome heartily. SHR 4.01.154
i am heartily sorry that he'll be glad of this. AWW 4.03. 63 P
pray heartily he be at' palace. WT 4.04.711 P
as heartily as he is glad he hath him. JN 3.04.124
heartily request | th' enfranchisement of arthur 4.02. 51
most heartily i pray | your highness to assign R2 1.01.150
which /i in sufferance heartily will rejoice, H5 2.02.159
i peseech you heartily, scurvy, lousy knave, at 5.01. 22 P
much good do you, scald knave, heartily. 5.01. 53 P
we heartily solicit | your gracious self to take R3 3.07.130
say that the queen hath heartily consented | he 4.05. 7
yes, heartily beseech you. H8 1.02.176
be what they will, i heartily forgive 'em; 2.01. 65
and heartily, for our deliverance, | or this 2.02. 45
and heartily entreats you take good comfort. 4.02.119
the fruit she goes with | i pray for heartily, 5.01. 21
your highness | most heartily to pray for her. 5.01. 66
i thank ye heartily; 5.04. 13
and therefore give you our voices heartily. COR 2.03.105 P
the gods give you joy, sir, heartily! 2.03.111 P
sir, heartily well met, and most glad of your 4.03. 48 P
and laugh'd so heartily | that both mine eyes TIT 5.01.116
a fly, | and nothing grieves me heartily indeed, 5.01.143
we doubt it nothing, heartily farewell. HAM 1.02. 41
i am sorry they offend you, heartily, | yes, 1.05.134
offend you, heartily, | yes, faith, heartily. 1.05.135
i could heartily wish this had not befall'n; OTH 2.03.301 P
two creatures heartily. CYM 1.06. 83
and learn of him, i heartily beseech thee, | to VEN 404

HEARTINESS 1 FR 0.0001 REL FR 1 V 0 P
derive a liberty | from heartiness, from bounty, WT 1.02.113

HEART–INFLAMING 1 FR 0.0001 REL FR 1 V 0 P
laid by his side his heart–inflaming brand, SON 154. 2

HEARTLESS 4 FR 0.0004 REL FR 4 V 0 P
art thou drawn among these heartless hinds? ROM 1.01. 66
begin | to sound a parley to his heartless foe, LUC 471
which heartless peasants did so well resemble, 1392
how sighs resound through heartless ground, PP 17.23

HEARTLINGS 1 FR 0.0001 REL FR 0 V 1 P
'od's heartlings, that's a pretty jest indeed! WIV 3.04. 57 P

HEARTLY 1 FR 0.0001 REL FR 0 V 1 P
pray heartly pardon me. WIV 3.03.227 P

HEART–OFFENDING 1 FR 0.0001 REL FR 1 V 0 P
might liquid tears or heart–offending groans 2H6 3.02. 60

HEART–PIERC'D 1 FR 0.0001 REL FR 1 V 0 P
indeed — | such heart–pierc'd demonstration! TNK 1.01.124

HEART'S 57 FR 0.0064 REL FR 48 V 9 P
your heads — is nothing but heart's sorrow, TMP 3.03. 81
made them watchers of mine own heart's sorrow. TGV 2.04.135
one, lady, if you knew his pure heart's truth, 4.02. 88
the valiant heart's not whipt out of his trade. MM 2.01.256
eye's clear eye, my dear heart's dearer heart, ERR 3.02. 62
/of his heart's meteors tilting in his face? 4.02. 6
i, but god send every one their heart's desire! ADO 3.04. 61 P
by the heart's still rhetoric disclosed with LLL 2.01.229
fortune now | to my heart's hope! MV 2.09. 20
i wish your ladyship all heart's content. 3.04. 42
your heart's desires be with you! AYL 1.02.199 P
in our heart's table — heart too capable | of AWW 1.01. 95
if heart's presages be not vain, | we three here R2 2.02.142
in my heart's love hath no man than yourself. 1H4 4.01. 8
when your own percy, when my heart's dear harry, 2H4 2.03. 12
a good heart's worth gold. 2.04. 31 P
in drink, but you must bear, the heart's all. 5.03. 29 P
such is the fullness of my heart's content. 2H6 1.01. 35
red sparkling eyes blab his heart's malice, 3.01.154
heart's discontent and sour affliction | be 3.02.301
but that my heart's on future mischief set, | i 5.02. 84
and now in england to our heart's great sorrow, 3H6 1.01.128
can my tongue unload my heart's great burthen, 2.01. 81
mine full of sorrow and heart's discontent. 3.03.173
to take her in her heart's extremest hate, R3 1.02.231
and with my hand i seal my true heart's love. 2.01. 10
on pure heart's love, to greet the tender prince 4.01. 4
and from my heart's love i do thank thee for it. 4.04.261
to my proceeding, if with dear heart's love, 4.04.403
then though my heart's content firm love doth TRO 1.02.294
his heart's his mouth; COR 3.01.256
in the dust i write | my heart's deep languor, TIT 3.01. 13
at thy good heart's oppression. ROM 1.01.184
if my heart's dear love — 2.02.115
then plainly know my heart's dear love is set 2.03. 57
i have an interest in your heart's proceeding; 3.01.188
o, musicians, "heart's ease, heart's ease"! 4.05.102 P
o, musicians, "heart's ease, heart's ease"! 4.05.103 P
and you will have me live, play "heart's ease." 4.05.104 P
why "heart's ease"? 4.05.105 P
alcibiades, your heart's in the field now. TIM 1.02. 73 P
such men as he be never at heart's ease | whiles JC 1.02.208

and i will wear him | in my heart's core, ay, in HAM 3.02. 73
my heart's subdu'd | even to the very quality of OTH 1.03.250
which rips my bosom | almost to th' heart's — TNK 1.02. 62
but when the heart's attorney once is mute, VEN 335
sweet music, and heart's deep sore wounding. 432
heavy heart's lead, melt at mine eyes' red fire! 1073
words, so thick come in his poor heart's aid, LUC 1784
defying, | heart's denying, causer of this. PP 17. 4
clear eye's moiety and the dear heart's part — SON 46.12
and my heart's right /thy inward love of heart. 46.14
another time mine eye is my heart's guest, | and 47. 7
awakes my heart to heart's and eye's delight. 47.14
in many's looks the false heart's history | is 93. 7
e'er thy thoughts or thy heart's workings be, 93.11
thy proud heart's slave and vassal wretch to be: 141.12

HEARTS' 1 FR 0.0001 REL FR 1 V 0 P
they encounter thee with their hearts' thanks. MAC 3.04. 9

/HEARTS 1 FR 0.0001 REL FR 1 V 0 P
/with /all /our /hearts. R3 2.02.145

HEARTS 182 FR 0.0205 REL FR 155 V 27 P
heigh, my hearts! TMP 1.01. 5 P
cheerly, cheerly, my hearts! 1.01. 6 P
cheerly, good hearts! 1.01. 26 P
set all hearts i' th' state | to what tune 1.02. 84
what they think in their hearts they may effect, WIV 2.02.307 P
will break their hearts but they will effect. 2.02.308 P
your hearts are mighty, your skins are whole, 3.01.108 P
farewell, my hearts. 3.02. 87 P
good hearts, devise something; 4.02. 73 P
can find in their hearts the poor unvirtuous fat 4.02.217 P
good hearts, what ado here is to bring you 4.05.124 P
marrying, | to give our hearts united ceremony. 4.06. 51
thrust virtue out of our hearts by the head and 5.05.147 P
therefore all hearts in love use their own ADO 2.01.177
here's our own hands against our hearts. 5.04. 92 P
may lighten our own hearts and our wives' heels. 5.04.119 P
sweet hearts, we shall be rich ere we depart, LLL 5.02. 1
curtsy, sweet hearts — and so the measure ends. 5.02.221
they are infected, in their hearts it lies; 5.02.420
as it should pierce a hundred thousand hearts; MND 2.01.160
when i am sure you hate me with your hearts. 3.02.154
where are these lads? where are these hearts? 4.02. 26 P
and fresh days of love | accompany your hearts! 5.01. 30
you, whose gentle hearts do fear | the smallest 5.01.219
whose hearts are all as false | as stairs of MV 3.02. 83
a golden mesh t' entrap the hearts of men 3.02.122
from brassy bosoms and rough hearts of flints, 4.01. 31
sway, | it is enthroned in the hearts of kings, 4.01.194
was devis'd, | of many faces, eyes, and hearts, AYL 3.02.151
but that our soft conditions and our hearts SHR 5.02.167
howsome'er their hearts are sever'd in religion, AWW 1.03. 53 P
our hearts receive your warnings. 2.01. 22
dear perfection hearts that scorn'd to serve 5.03. 18
your gentle hands lend us, and take our hearts. ep 6
in women's waxen hearts to set their forms! TN 2.02. 30
how now, my hearts? 2.03. 16 P
physics the subject, makes old hearts fresh. WT 1.01. 39 P
the justice of your hearts will thereto add 2.01. 67
hard'ned be the hearts | of all that hear me, 3.02. 52
this ballad against the hard hearts of maids. 4.04.278 P
he that perforce robs lions of their hearts JN 1.01.268
fifteen thousand hearts of england's breed — 2.01.275
this act so evilly borne shall cool the hearts 3.04.149
and then the hearts | of all his people shall 3.04.164
to sound the purposes of all their hearts, 4.02. 48
and their gentle hearts | to fierce and bloody 5.02.157
how he did seem to dive into their hearts | with R2 1.04. 25
you lose a thousand well–disposed hearts, | and 2.01.206
grievous taxes, | and quite lost their hearts; 2.01.247
ancient quarrels, and quite lost their hearts. 2.01.248
by so much fills their hearts with deadly hate. 2.02.131
hard bright steel, and hearts harder than steel. 3.02.111
your hearts of sorrow, and your eyes of tears. 4.01.332
steel'd | the hearts of men, they must perforce 5.02. 35
boys, hearts of gold, all the titles of good 1H4 2.04.278 P
loseth men's hearts and leaves behind a stain 3.01.185
and art almost an alien to the hearts | of all 3.02. 34
that i did pluck allegiance from men's hearts, 3.02. 52
with hearts in their bellies no bigger than 4.02. 21 P
win | the hearts of all that he did angle for; 4.03. 84
then reason will our hearts should be as good. 2H4 4.01.155
whose hearts have left their bodies here in H5 1.02.128
you | with hearts create of duty and of zeal. 2.02. 31
for if you hide the crown | even in your hearts, 2.04. 98
o god of battles, steel my soldiers' hearts, 4.01.289
opposed numbers | pluck their hearts from them. 4.01.292
but, by the mass, our hearts are in the trim; 4.03.115
as can be desir'd in the hearts of his subjects. 4.07.161 P
combine your hearts in one, your realms in one! 5.02.360
your hearts i'll stamp out with my horse's heels 1H6 1.04.108
to join your hearts in love and amity. 3.01. 68
methinks i should revive the soldiers' hearts, 3.02. 97
will nothing turn your unrelenting hearts? 5.04. 59
not his smoothing words | bewitch your hearts. 2H6 1.01.157
and stol'st away the ladies' hearts of france, 1.03. 52
by flattery hath he won the commons' hearts; 3.01. 28
in your breasts, will sting your hearts. 3.01.344
reigns in the hearts of all our present parts. 5.02. 87
and let our hearts and eyes, like civil war, 3H6 2.05. 77
your hands, and with your hands your hearts, 4.06. 39
may move your hearts to pity if you mark him. R3 1.03.348
you scarcely have the hearts to tell me so, 1.04.175
and therefore cannot have the hearts to do it. 1.04.176
truly, the hearts of men are full of fear. 2.03. 38
but look'd not on the poison of their hearts. 3.01. 14
for our hearts, | he knows no more of mine than 3.04. 10
whose hand soever lanch'd their tender hearts, 4.04.225
slew her brothers | a pair of bleeding hearts; 4.04.272
a thousand hearts are great within my bosom. 5.03.347
and cold hearts freeze | allegiance in them; H8 1.02. 61
you make friends | and give your hearts to, when 2.01.128
hearts of most hard temper | melt and lament for 2.03. 11
but cardinal sins and hollow hearts i fear ye. 3.01.104
angels' faces, but heaven knows your hearts. 3.01.145
the hearts of princes kiss obedience, | so much 3.01.162
bear witness, all that have not hearts of iron, 3.02.424
last, cherish those hearts that hate thee; 3.02.443
by some that hate me | (god turn their hearts! 5.02. 15
manhood and honor | should have hare hearts, TRO 2.02. 48
you shall fight your hearts out ere i part you 3.02. 52 P
now put your shields before your hearts, and COR 1.04. 24
and fight | with hearts more proof than shields. 1.04. 25
shall say against their hearts, "we thank the 1.09. 8
eyes for th' time, | but hearts for the event. 2.01.270
and his actions in their hearts that for their 2.02. 30 P
and have hearts | inclinable to honor and 2.02. 55
as she speaks, why, their hearts were yours; 3.02. 87
cog their hearts from them, and come home 3.02.133
let every feeble rumor shake your hearts! 3.03.125
eyes flow with joy, hearts dance with comforts, 5.03. 99
rather than rob me of the people's hearts! TIT 1.01.207
i will restore to thee | the people's hearts, 1.01.211
well said, my hearts! ROM 1.05. 86
cheerly, my hearts! 1.05. 88
love then lies | not truly in their hearts, but 2.03. 68
to his love and tendance | all sorts of hearts; TIM 1.01. 58
that you would once use our hearts, whereby we 1.02. 85 P
methinks false hearts should never have sound 1.02.234
and try the argument of hearts by borrowing, 2.02.178
up | my discontented troops, and lay for hearts. 3.05.114
yet do our hearts wear timon's livery, | that 4.02. 17
the eyes, and hearts of men | at duty, more than 4.03.261
o thou touch of hearts, | think thy slave man 4.03.389
cunning in excess, | hath broke their hearts. 5.04. 29
o you hard hearts, you cruel men of rome, | knew JC 1.01. 36
and stemming it with hearts of controversy; 1.02.109
and forgave him with all their hearts. 1.02.273 P
o, he sits high in all the people's hearts; 1.03.157
and let our hearts, as subtle masters do, | stir 2.01.175
with the most boldest and best hearts of rome. 3.01.121
our hearts you see not, they are pitiful; 3.01.169
of malice, and our hearts | of brothers' temper, 3.01.174
stir | your hearts and minds to mutiny and rage, 3.02.122
i come not, friends, to steal away your hearts. 3.02.216
and some that smile have in their hearts, i fear 4.01. 50
let us speak | our free hearts each to other. MAC 1.03.155
and make our faces vizards to our hearts, 3.02. 34
things, | whose hearts are absent too. 5.04. 14
it us befitted | to bear our hearts in grief, HAM 1.02. 3
since love our hearts and hymen did our hands 3.02.159
if it be you that stirs these daughters' hearts LR 2.04.274
any cause in nature that make these hard hearts? 3.06. 78 P
he arrives he moves | all hearts against us. 4.05. 11
to know our enemies' minds, we rip their hearts, 4.06.260
keep yet their hearts attending on themselves, OTH 1.01. 51
discords be | that e'er our hearts shall make! 2.01.199
yet wild, the people's hearts brimful of fear, 2.03.214
the hearts of old gave hands; 3.04. 46
but our new heraldry is hands, not hearts. 3.04. 47
the skillful | conserv'd of maidens' hearts. 3.04. 75
upon her, | that true hearts cannot bear it. 4.02.117
into the hearts of such as have not thrived ANT 1.03. 51
caesar gets money where | he loses hearts. 2.01. 14
and to knit your hearts | with an unslipping 2.02.125
her live | to join our kingdoms and our hearts, 2.02.151
no slander, they steal hearts. 2.06.101 P
hoo, hearts, tongues, /figures, scribes, bards, 3.02. 16
and make the hearts of romans serve your ends! 3.02. 37
this kingly seal | and plighter of high hearts! 3.13.126
know, my hearts, | i hope well of to–morrow, and 4.02. 41
the hearts | that /spannell'd me at heels, to 4.12. 20
with tears as sovereign as the blood of hearts, 5.01. 41
half all /men's hearts are his. CYM 1.06.168
look thorough a casement to allure false hearts, 2.04. 34
the back door open | of the unguarded hearts, 5.03. 46
have neither in our hearts nor outward eyes PER 2.03. 25
our hands advanc'd before our hearts, what will TNK 1.02.112
our hearts | are in his army, in his tent. 1.03. 16
come weigh, my hearts, cheerly! 4.01.146
there | require of him the hearts of lions and 5.01. 39
for by our ears our hearts oft tainted be; LUC 38
stone him with hard'ned hearts, harder than 978
they drown their eyes or break their hearts. 1239
nor ashy pale the fear that false hearts have. 1512
hearts remote, yet not asunder; PHT 29
thy bosom is endeared with all hearts, | which i SON 31. 1
nothing that the thought of hearts can mend; 69. 2
then thou alone kingdoms of hearts shouldst owe. 70.14
which many legions of true hearts had warm'd, 154. 6
kept hearts in liveries, but mine own was free, LC 195
encamp'd in hearts, but fighting outwardly. 203
"'now all these hearts that do on mine depend, 274

HEART'S–EASE 1 FR 0.0001 REL FR 1 V 0 P
what infinite heart's–ease | must kings neglect, H5 4.01.236

HEART–SICK 2 FR 0.0002 REL FR 2 V 0 P
not i, unless the breath of heart–sick groans ROM 3.03. 72
i am sick still, heart–sick. CYM 4.02. 37

HEART–SORE 2 FR 0.0002 REL FR 2 V 0 P
coy looks with heart–sore sighs; TGV 1.01. 30
with nightly tears, and daily heart–sore sighs, 2.04.132

HEART–SORROWING 1 FR 0.0001 REL FR 1 V 0 P
you cloudy princes and heart–sorrowing peers R3 2.02.112

HEART–STRING 1 FR 0.0001 REL FR 1 V 0 P
and from heart–string | i love the lovely bully. H5 4.01. 47

HEART–STRINGS 4 FR 0.0004 REL FR 3 V 1 P
so false that he grieves my very heart–strings. TGV 4.02. 62 P
on it still shall i till heart–strings break. R3 4.04.365
that her jesses were my dear heart–strings, OTH 3.03.261
shall tune our heart–strings to true LUC 1141

HEART–STROOK 1 FR 0.0001 REL FR 1 V 0 P
labors to outjest | his heart–strook injuries. LR 3.01. 17

HEART–WHOLE 1 FR 0.0001 REL FR 0 V 1 P
th' shoulder, but i'll warrant him heart–whole. AYL 4.01. 49 P

HEART–WISH'D 1 FR 0.0001 REL FR 1 V 0 P
when he most burnt in heart–wish'd luxury, | he LC 314

HEARTY 10 FR 0.0011 REL FR 9 V 1 P
thee and thy company i bid | a hearty welcome. TMP 5.01.111
if hearty sorrow | be a sufficient ransom for TGV 5.04. 74
page hath her hearty commendations to you too; WIV 2.02. 96 P
many and hearty thankings to you both. MM 5.01. 4
and concludes in hearty prayers | that your 2H4 4.01. 14
and, lords, accept this hearty kind embrace. 1H6 3.03. 82
at first | and last, the hearty welcome. MAC 3.04. 2
hearty thanks; LR 4.06.224
grow where those drops fall, my hearty friends! ANT 4.02. 38
drink a good hearty draught, it breeds good TNK 3.03. 17

/HEAT 1 FR 0.0001 REL FR 1 V 0 P
/and /the /best /quarrels, /in /the /heat, /are LR 5.03. 56

HEAT 77 FR 0.0087 REL FR 67 V 10 P
even as one heat another heat expels, | or as TGV 2.04.192
even as one heat another heat expels, | or as 2.04.192
which with an hour's heat | dissolves to water, 3.02. 7
of that — that am as subject to heat as butter; WIV 3.05.115 P
thou hast neither heat, affection, limb, nor MM 3.01. 37
both in the heat of blood | and lack of temper'd 5.01.472
she knows the heat of a luxurious bed; ADO 4.01. 41
of devoted and heart–burning heat of duty, don LLL 1.01.277 P
change not your offer made in heat of blood; 5.02.800
and when this hail some heat from hermia felt, MND 1.01.244
and let my liver rather heat with wine | than my MV 1.01. 81
then farewell heat, and welcome frost! 2.07. 75
of color, weight, and heat, pour'd all together, AWW 2.03.119
the element itself, till seven years' heat, TN 1.01. 25
one draught above heat makes him a fool, the 1.05.132 P
furlongs ere | with spur we heat an acre. WT 1.02. 96
heat outwardly or breath within, i'll serve you 3.02.206
wrath, | a rage whose heat hath this condition, JN 3.01.341
heat me these irons hot, and look thou stand 4.01. 1
the iron of itself, though heat red–hot, 4.01. 61
i can heat it, boy. 4.01.104
snow | by thinking on fantastic summer's heat? R2 1.03.299
in the very heat | and pride of their contention 1H4 1.01. 59
who strook this heat up after i was gone? 1.03.139
it hath the excuse of youth and heat of blood, 5.02. 17
took fire and heat away | from the best–temper'd 2H4 1.01.114
you do measure the heat of our livers with the 1.02.175 P
all to a merriment, if you take not the heat. 2.04.299 P
the heat is past, follow no further now; 4.03. 24
sit | like a rich armor worn in heat of day, 4.05. 30
decoct their cold blood to such valiant heat? H5 3.05. 20
and of the heat of the ginger. 3.07. 20 P
and to sun's parching heat display'd my cheeks, 1H6 1.02. 77
in winter's cold and summer's parching heat, 2H6 1.01. 81
nay, we shall heat you thoroughly anon. 5.01.159
heed, lest by your heat you burn yourselves. 5.01.160
went all afoot in summer's scalding heat, | that 3H6 5.07. 18
heat not a furnace for your foe so hot | that it H8 1.01.140
heat them, and they retort that heat again | to TRO 3.03.101
and they retort that heat again | to the first 3.03.101
and renders back | his figure and his heat. 3.03.123
but he in heat of action | is more vindicative 4.05.106
i'll heat his blood with greekish wine to–night, 5.01. 1
not in this heat, sir, now. COR 3.01. 63
to come upon them in the heat of their division. 4.03. 18 P
till i find the stream | to cool this heat, a TIT 2.01.134
that almost freezes up the heat of life. ROM 4.03. 16
to see meat fill knaves, and wine heat fools. TIM 1.01.261
words to the heat of deeds too cold breath gives MAC 2.01. 61
giving more light than heat, extinct in both HAM 1.03.118
screen'd and stood between | much heat and him. 3.04. 4
son, | upon the heat and flame of thy distemper 3.04.123
o heat, dry up my brains! 4.05.155
we must do something, and i' th' heat. LR 1.01.308 P
time hath qualified the heat of his displeasure, 1.02.161 P
it is a business of some heat. OTH 1.02. 40
nor to comply with heat (the young affects | in 1.03.263
i know not where is that promethean heat | that 5.02. 12
i had rather heat my liver with drinking. ANT 1.02. 24 P
you'll heat my blood; no more. 1.03. 80
fear no more the heat o' th' sun, | nor the CYM 4.02.258
that /blast gives heat and stronger glowing; PER 1.02. 41
to give my tongue that heat to ask your help; 2.01. 75
pray walk softly, do not heat your blood. 4.01. 48
never did passenger in summer's heat | more VEN 91
them, | and titan, tired in the midday heat, 177
shall cool the heat of this descending sun: 190
the heat i have from thence doth little harm, 195
at his love, and scorns the heat he feels, 311
o rash false heat, wrapp'd in repentant cold, LUC 48
no exclamation | can curb his heat, or rein his 706
that knows not parching heat nor freezing cold, 1145
thy heat of lust, fond paris, did incur | this 1473
which erst from heat did canopy the herd, | and SON 12. 6
it nor grows with heat nor drowns with show'rs. 124.12
this holy fire of love | a dateless lively heat, 153. 6
which from love's fire took heat perpetual, 154.10

HEATED 6 FR 0.0006 REL FR 5 V 1 P
cool'd my friends, heated mine enemies; MV 3.01. 57 P
that robb'd my soldiers of their heated spleen; 3H6 2.01.124
or bath'd thy growing with our heated bloods. 2.02.169
i fear, with dancing is a little heated. H8 1.04.100
mass, | with heated visage, as against the doom; HAM 3.04. 50
within him, | and as a heated lion so he looks; TNK 4.02. 82

HEATH 3 FR 0.0003 REL FR 2 V 1 P
of sea for an acre of barren ground, long heath, TMP 1.01. 66 P
upon the heath. MAC 1.01. 6
why | upon this blasted heath you stop our way 1.03. 77

/HEATHEN 1 FR 0.0001 REL FR 0 V 1 P
/what, /art /a /heathen? HAM 5.01. 35 P

HEATHEN 4 FR 0.0004 REL FR 2 V 2 P
the heathen philosopher, when he had a desire to AYL 5.01. 33 P
yond gull malvolio is turn'd heathen, a very TN 3.02. 70 P
all clinquant, all in gold, like heathen gods, H8 1.01. 19
and on /other grounds | christen'd and heathen, OTH 1.01. 30

HEATHENISH 1 FR 0.0001 REL FR 1 V 0 P
most heathenish and most gross! OTH 5.02.313

HEATING 2 FR 0.0002 REL FR 1 V 1 P
the making of the cake, the heating the oven, TRO 1.01. 25 P
disorder breeds by heating of the blood; VEN 742

HEAT–OPPRESSED 1 FR 0.0001 REL FR 1 V 0 P
proceeding from the heat–oppressed brain? MAC 2.01. 39

HEATS 3 FR 0.0003 REL FR 2 V 1 P
when i am cold, he heats me with beating; ERR 4.04. 33 P
'twill take form, the heats are gone to–morrow. TNK 1.01.152
love's fire heats water, water cools not love. SON 154.14

HEAT'ST 1 FR 0.0001 REL FR 0 V 1 P
thou heat'st my blood. LLL 1.02. 30 P

/HEAV'D 1 FR 0.0001 REL FR 1 V 0 P
/or /twice /she /heav'd /the /name /of "/father" LR 4.03. 25

HEAV'D 6 FR 0.0006 REL FR 5 V 1 P
play (as thou say'st) were we heav'd thence, TMP 1.02. 62
of sack which the sailors heav'd o'erboard — by 2.02.122 P
the wretched animal heav'd forth such groans AYL 2.01. 36
mine, | and, having both together heav'd it up, 2H6 1.02. 13

one heav'd a–high, to be hurl'd down below; R3 4.04. 86
or at least | those which i heav'd to head! CYM 5.05.157
HEAV'D–UP 2 FR 0.0002 REL FR 2 V 0 P
her joy with heav'd–up hand she doth express, LUC 111
"to thee, to thee, my heav'd–up hands appeal, 638
HEAVE 12 FR 0.0013 REL FR 9 V 3 P
didst thou see me heave up my leg and make water TGV 4.04. 37 P
and with a great heart heave away this storm. JN 5.02. 55
seen, | heave him away upon your winged thoughts H5 5.pr. 8
to heave the traitor somerset from hence, | and 2H6 5.01. 61
this shoulder was ordain'd so thick to heave, 3H6 5.07. 23
and heave it shall some weight, or break my back 5.07. 24
i am, i cannot heave | my heart into my mouth. LR 1.01. 91
find itself abus'd, begin to heave the gorge, OTH 2.01.233 P
me no service as a partisan i could not heave. ANT 2.07. 13 P
from this fair throne to heave the owner out. LUC 413
sighs like whirlwinds labor hence to heave thee. 586
oft did she heave her napkin to her eyne, LC 15
HEAVED 1 FR 0.0001 REL FR 1 V 0 P
hast, | and if mine arm be heaved in the air, 2H6 4.10. 51
/HEAVEN 17 FR 0.0019 REL FR 15 V 2 P
ay, by my sceptre and my hopes of /heaven. AWW 2.01.192
/yet /amen, /if /heaven /do /think /him /me. R2 4.01.175
/a /blot, /damn'd /in /the /book /of /heaven. 4.01.236
/derives /from /heaven /his /quarrel /and /his 2H4 1.01.206
/didst /thou /beat /heaven /with /blessing 1.03. 92
/not /sigh, /nor /hold /thy /stumps /to /heaven, TIT 3.02. 42
/heaven /and /earth! LR 1.02. 97 P
/now /heaven /help /him! 3.07.107
/and /bellowed /out | /as /he'd /burst /heaven, 5.03.214
pray /heaven he be; OTH 2.01. 34
/heaven bless the isle of cyprus and our noble 2.02. 10 P
/by /heaven, thou echo'st me, | as if there were 3.03.106
/by /heaven, i'll know thy thoughts. 3.03.162
/heaven bless us! 3.04. 81
o /heaven, that such companions thou'dst unfold, 4.02.141
no — yes, sure — /o /heaven, roderigo! 5.01. 90
thy unprepared spirit, | no, /heaven forefend! 5.02. 32
HEAVEN 638 FR 0.0721 REL FR 577 V 61 P
smile, | infused with a fortitude from heaven, TMP 1.02.154
hast thou not dropp'd from heaven? 2.02.137 P
o heaven, o earth, bear witness to this sound, 3.01. 68
here, afore heaven, | i ratify this my rich gift 4.01. 7
and silvia (witness heaven, that made her fair) TGV 2.06. 25
heart as far from fraud as heaven from earth. 2.07. 78
by heaven, my wrath shall far exceed the love 3.01.166
the heaven such grace did lend her, | that she 4.02. 42
which heaven and fortune still rewards with 4.03. 31
but yet so coldly | as, heaven it knows, i would 4.04.107
o, heaven be judge how i love valentine, | whose 5.04. 36
o heaven! 5.04. 59
is not satisfied | is nor of heaven nor earth, 5.04. 80
o heaven! 5.04.110
bear witness, heaven, i have my wish for ever. 5.04.119
o heaven! this is mistress anne page. WIV 1.01.190 P
yet heaven may decrease it upon better 1.01.246 P
well, heaven send anne page no worse fortune! 1.04. 32 P
can do more than i do with her, i thank heaven. 1.04.130 P
you that by the way, i praise heaven for it. 1.04.141 P
heaven forgive me! 2.01. 28 P
well — heaven forgive you, and all of us, i 2.02. 56 P
to whose falls —" | heaven prosper the right! 3.01. 30 P
well, heaven knows how i love you, and you shall 3.03. 80 P
pray heaven it be not so, that you have such a 3.03.112 P
heaven make you better than your thoughts! 3.03.204 P
heaven forgive my sins at the day of judgment! 3.03.212 P
no, heaven so speed me in my time to come! 3.04. 12
i ne'er made my will yet, i thank heaven. 3.04. 58 P
such a sickly creature, i give heaven praise. 3.04. 59 P
now heaven send thee good fortune! 3.04.101 P
heaven guide him to thy husband's cudgel; 4.02. 88 P
pray heaven it be not full of knight again. 4.02.112 P
heaven be my witness you do, /and if you suspect 4.02.133 P
one of you does not serve heaven well, that you 4.05.125 P
heaven prosper our sport! 5.02. 12 P
heaven forgive our sins! 5.05. 31 P
fenton, heaven give thee joy! 5.05.236
fenton, | heaven give you many, many merry days! 5.05.240
heaven doth with us as we with torches do, | not MM 1.01. 32
heaven grant us its peace, but not the king of 1.02. 4 P
for our offense by weight | the words of heaven: 1.02.122
heaven forgive him! 2.01. 37
whom i detest before heaven and your honor — 2.01. 69 P
ay, sir; whom i thank heaven is an honest woman. 2.01. 72 P
heaven give thee moving graces! 2.02. 36
heaven keep your honor! 2.02. 42
and neither heaven nor man grieve at the mercy. 2.02. 50
i would to heaven i had your potency, | and you 2.02. 67
shall we serve heaven | with less respect than 2.02. 85
officer | would use his heaven for thunder, 2.02.113
merciful heaven, | thou rather with thy sharp 2.02.114
plays such fantastic tricks before high heaven 2.02.121
pray heaven she win him! 2.02.125
with such gifts that heaven shall share with you 2.02.147
that shall be up at heaven and enter there | ere 2.02.152
heaven keep your honor safe! 2.02.157
sorrow is always toward ourselves, not heaven, 2.03. 32
showing we would not spare heaven as we love it, 2.03. 33
heaven hath my empty words, | whilst my 2.04. 2
heaven in my mouth, | as if i did but only chew 2.04. 4
even so. heaven keep your honor! 2.04. 34
'tis set down so in heaven, but not in earth. 2.04. 50
his life, if it be sin, | heaven let me bear it! 2.04. 70
help heaven! 2.04.127
lord angelo, having affairs to heaven, | intends 3.01. 56
heaven shield my mother play'd my father fair! 3.01.140
he who the sword of heaven will bear | should be 3.02.261
heaven give your spirits comfort! 4.02. 70
o, 'tis an accident that heaven provides! 4.03. 77
forbear it therefore, give your cause to heaven. 4.03.124
madness, pray heaven his wisdom be not tainted! 4.04. 4 P
for yourself, pray heaven you then | be perfect. 5.01. 81
by heaven, fond wretch, thou know'st not what 5.01.105
heaven shield your grace from woe, | as i, thus 5.01.118
o heaven, the vanity of wretched fools! 5.01.164
as there comes light from heaven, and words from 5.01.225
am i in earth, in heaven, or in hell? ERR 2.02.212
my sole earth's heaven, and my heaven's claim. 3.02. 64
i conjure thee by all the saints in heaven! 4.04. 57
i never saw the chain, so help me heaven; 5.01.268
his head, and say, "get you to heaven, beatrice, ADO 2.01. 45 P
beatrice, get you to heaven, here's no place for 2.01. 46 P
a high hope for a low heaven. LLL 1.01.194 P
ay, and, by heaven, one that will do the deed 3.01.198
"by heaven, that thou art fair, is most 4.01. 60 P
the welkin, the heaven, and anon falleth like a 4.02. 6 P
by heaven, i do love, and it hath taught me to 4.03. 12 P
shot, by heaven! 4.03. 22 P
by heaven, the wonder in a mortal eye! 4.03. 83
the sea will ebb and flow, heaven show his face; 4.03.212
eye | dares look upon the heaven of her brow, 4.03.223
by heaven, thy love is black as ebony. 4.03.243
the gods | make heaven drowsy with the harmony. 4.03.342
by heaven, all dry–beaten with pure scoff! 5.02.263
by heaven, you did; 5.02.452
like to a silver bow | /new bent in heaven, MND 1.01. 10
in a spleen, unfolds both heaven and earth; 1.01.146
that he hath turn'd a heaven unto a hell! 1.01.207
i'll follow thee and make a heaven of hell, | to 2.01.243
doth glance from heaven to earth, from earth to 5.01. 13
from heaven to earth, from earth to heaven; 5.01. 13
but sway'd and fashion'd by the hand of heaven. MV 1.03. 93
as you would say in plain terms, gone to heaven. 2.02. 65 P
if e'er the jew her father come to heaven, | it 2.04. 33
heaven and thy thoughts are witness that thou 2.06. 32
ambitious head | spets in the face of heaven, is 2.07. 45
i have toward heaven breath'd a secret vow | to 3.04. 27
no mercy for me in heaven because i am a jew's 3.05. 33 P
he finds the joys of heaven here on earth; 3.05. 76
it, | in reason he should never come to heaven! 3.05. 78
when they are fretten with the gusts of heaven; 4.01. 77
it droppeth as the gentle rain from heaven 4.01.185
an oath, an oath, i have an oath in heaven! 4.01.228
i would she were in heaven, so she could 4.01.291
look how the floor of heaven | is thick inlaid 5.01. 58
by heaven, i will ne'er come in your bed | until 5.01.190
by heaven, it is the same i gave the doctor! 5.01.257
fare you well! pray heaven i be deceiv'd in you! AYL 1.02.197 P
for, by this heaven, now at our sorrows pale, 1.03.104
and little reaks to find the way to heaven | by 2.04. 81
as many matters as he, but i give heaven thanks, 2.05. 36 P
me not fool till heaven hath sent me fortune." 2.07. 19
of every sprite | heaven would in little show. 3.02.140
therefore heaven nature charg'd | that one body 3.02.141
heaven would that she these gifts should have, 3.02.153
and thank heaven, fasting, for a good man's love 3.05. 58
then is there mirth in heaven, | when earthly 5.04.108
thy daughter, | hymen from heaven brought her, 5.04.112
heaven cease this idle humor in your honor! SHR in.2. 13
what stars do spangle heaven with such beauty, 4.05. 31
what heaven more will, | that thee may furnish, AWW 1.01. 68
heaven bless him! | farewell, bertram. 1.01. 73
ourselves do lie, | which we ascribe to heaven. 1.01.217
i care no more for than i do for heaven, | so i 1.03.164
as heaven shall work in me for thine avail, | to 1.03.184
here on my knee, before high heaven and you, 1.03.192
that before you, and next unto high heaven, | i 1.03.193
be sanctified | by th' luckiest stars in heaven, 1.03.246
by heaven, i'll steal away. 2.01. 33
the help of heaven we count the act of men. 2.01.152
of heaven, not me, make an experiment. 2.01.154
very hand of heaven. 2.03. 31 P
heaven hath through me restor'd the king to 2.03. 64
we understand it, and thank heaven for you. 2.03. 65
one, that she's not in heaven, whither god send 2.04. 11 P
whom heaven delights to hear | and loves to 3.04. 27
a heaven on earth i have won by wooing thee. 4.02. 66
for which live long to thank both heaven and me! 4.02. 67
of her last breath, and now she sings in heaven. 4.03. 53 P
my husband hies him home, where, heaven aiding, 4.04. 12
doubt not but heaven | hath brought me up to be 4.04. 18
which better than the first, o dear heaven, 5.03. 71
i know his soul is in heaven, fool. TN 1.05. 69 P
mourn for your brother's soul being in heaven. 1.05. 71 P
too old, by heaven. 2.04. 29
heaven restore thee! 3.04. 46 P
comes the countess, now heaven walks on earth. 5.01. 97
and whom, by heaven i swear, i tender dearly, 5.01.126
blood, we should have answer'd heaven | boldly, WT 1.02. 73
plainly as heaven sees earth and earth sees 1.02.315
as heaven sees earth and earth sees heaven, 1.02.315
by each particular star in heaven and | by all 1.02.425
spotless | i' th' eyes of heaven and to you — i 2.01.132
that 'twixt heaven and earth | might thus have 5.01.132
father's bless'd | (as he from heaven merits it) 5.01.175
the heaven sets spies upon us, will not have 5.01.203
which none but heaven, and you, and i, shall JN 1.01. 43
i put you o'er to heaven and to my mother. 1.01. 62
heaven guard my mother's honor, and my land! 1.01. 70
i give heaven thanks i was not like to thee! 1.01. 83
why, what a madcap hath heaven lent us here! 1.01. 84
heaven, lay not my transgression to my charge 1.01.256
the peace of heaven is theirs that lift their 2.01. 35
not, bleed france, and peace ascend to heaven, 2.01. 86
proud contempt that beats his peace to heaven. 2.01. 88
which heaven shall take in nature of a fee; 2.01.170
with these crystal beads heaven shall be brib'd 2.01.171
thou monstrous slanderer of heaven and earth! 2.01.173
thou monstrous injurer of heaven and earth, 2.01.174
against th' /invulnerable clouds of heaven, 2.01.252
by heaven, these scroyles of angiers flout you, 2.01.373
make work upon ourselves, for heaven or hell. 2.01.407
by heaven, lady, you shall have no cause | to 3.01. 96
hail, you anointed deputies of heaven! 3.01.136
of peace, | heaven knows they were besmear'd and 3.01.236
so jest with heaven? 3.01.242
let thy vow | first made to heaven, first be to 3.01.266
made to heaven, first be to heaven perform'd, 3.01.266
alter not the doom | forethought by heaven! 3.01.312
by heaven, hubert, i am almost asham'd | to say 3.03. 27
the sun is in the heaven, and the proud day, 3.03. 34
adjunct to my act, | by heaven, i would do it. 3.03. 58
i am not mad, i would to heaven i were! 3.04. 48
we shall see and know our friends in heaven. 3.04. 77
when i shall meet him in the court of heaven | i 3.04. 87
abortives, presages, and tongues of heaven, 3.04.158
and i would to heaven | i were your son, so you 4.01. 23
if heaven be pleas'd that you must use me ill, 4.01. 55
for heaven sake, hubert, let me not be bound! 4.01. 77
o heaven! 4.01. 91
the breath of heaven hath blown his spirit out, 4.01.109
o heaven! i thank you, hubert. 4.01.131
to seek the beauteous eye of heaven to garnish, 4.02. 15
o, when the last accompt 'twixt heaven and earth 4.02.216
heaven take my soul, and england keep my bones! 4.03. 10
by heaven, i think my sword's as sharp as yours. 4.03. 82
and truth of all this realm | is fled to heaven; 4.03.145
and heaven itself doth frown upon the land. 4.03.159
than had i seen the vaulty top of heaven 5.02. 52
to give us warrant from the hand of heaven, 5.02. 66
the sun of heaven, methought, was loath to set, 5.05. 1
withhold thine indignation, mighty heaven, | and 5.06. 37
and then my soul shall wait on thee to heaven, 5.07. 72
first, heaven be the record to my speech, | in R2 1.01. 30
earth, | or my divine soul answer it in heaven. 1.01. 38
put we our quarrel to the will of heaven, | who, 1.02. 6
let heaven revenge, for i may never lift | an 1.02. 40
oath, | as so defend thee heaven and thy valor! 1.03. 15
me — | and as i truly fight, defend me heaven! 1.03. 25
speak like a true knight, so defend thee heaven! 1.03. 34
to god of heaven, king richard, and to me — 1.03. 40
me — | and as i truly fight, defend me heaven! 1.03. 41
and i from heaven banish'd as from hence! 1.03.203
all places that the eye of heaven visits | are 1.03.275
whom fair befall in heaven 'mongst happy souls, 2.01.129
now god in heaven forbid! 2.02. 51
comfort's in heaven, and we are on the earth, 2.02. 78
and meteors fright the fixed stars of heaven, 2.04. 9
my comfort is, that heaven will take our souls, 3.01. 33
else heaven would, | and we will not. 3.02. 30
that when the searching eye of heaven is hid 3.02. 37
must fall, for heaven still guards the right. 3.02. 62
by heaven, i'll hate him everlastingly | that 3.02.207
at meeting tears the cloudy cheeks of heaven. 3.03. 57
the king of heaven forbid our lord the king 3.03.101
by heaven, i'll throw at all! 4.01. 57
as false, by heaven, as heaven itself is true. 4.01. 64
as false, by heaven, as heaven itself is true. 4.01. 64
but heaven hath a hand in these events, | to 5.02. 37
which, like the meteors of a troubled heaven, 1H4 1.01. 10
by heaven, methinks it were an easy leap, | to 1.03.201
the blessed sun of heaven prove a micher and eat 2.04.408 P
with | a rising sigh he wisheth you in heaven. 3.01. 10
the front of heaven was full of fiery shapes 3.01. 14
the front of heaven was full of fiery shapes, 3.01. 37
for the hot vengeance, and the rod of heaven, 3.02. 10
and then i stole all courtesy from heaven, | and 3.02. 50
for, heaven to earth, some of us never shall | a 5.02. 99
adieu, and take thy praise with thee to heaven! 5.04. 99
let heaven kiss earth! 2H4 1.01.153
for yours, the god of heaven brighten it! 2.03. 17
him as the sun | in the grey vault of heaven, 2.03. 19
that it may grow and sprout as high as heaven, 2.03. 60
and begin to patch up thine old body for heaven? 2.04.233 P
by heaven, poins, i feel me much to blame | so 2.04.361
a tall gentleman, by heaven, and a most gallant 3.02. 61 P
and a word of exceeding good command, by heaven. 3.02. 77 P
between the grace, the sanctities of heaven, 4.02. 21
and both against the peace of heaven and him 4.02. 29
for me, by heaven (i bid you be assur'd), | i'll 5.02. 56
ascend | the brightest heaven of invention! H5 pr 2
therefore doth heaven divide | the state of man 1.02.183
wheresome'er he is, either in heaven or in hell! 2.03. 8 P
the borrowed glories that by gift of heaven, 2.04. 79
the lord in heaven bless thee, noble harry! 4.01. 33
their wither'd hands hold up | toward heaven, to 4.01.300
if we no more meet till we meet in heaven, 4.03. 7
and draw their honors reeking up to heaven, 4.03.101
my soul shall thine keep company to heaven; 4.06. 16
which by a vision sent to her from heaven 1H6 1.02. 52
heaven and our lady gracious hath it pleas'd 1.02. 74
one eye thou hast to look to heaven for grace; 1.04. 83
heaven, be thou gracious to none alive, | if 1.04. 85
now, quiet soul, depart when heaven please, 3.02.110
and soul with soul from france to heaven fly. 4.05. 55
will cry for vengeance at the gates of heaven. 5.04. 53
now heaven forfend, the holy maid with child? 5.04. 65
we'll both together lift our heads to heaven, 2H6 1.02. 14
were it not good your grace could fly to heaven? 2.01. 17
thy heaven is on earth, thine eyes and thoughts 2.01. 19
madam, for myself, to heaven i do appeal, | how 2.01.186
shall blow ten thousand souls to heaven or hell; 3.01.350
nor let the rain of heaven wet this place | to 3.02.341
any | save to the god of heaven and to my king; 4.01.126
knowledge the wing wherewith we fly to heaven, 4.07. 74
then, heaven, set ope thy everlasting gates | to 4.09. 13
how much thou wrong'st me, heaven be my judge. 4.10. 76
by heaven, thou shalt rule no more | o'er him 5.01.104
o'er him whom heaven created for thy ruler. 5.01.105
thou dispense with heaven for such an oath? 5.01.181
if not in heaven, you'll surely sup in hell. 5.01.216
peace with his soul, heaven, if it be thy will! 5.02. 30
the last day | knit earth and heaven together! 5.02. 42
i vow by heaven these eyes shall never close. 3H6 1.01. 24
and in that hope i throw mine eyes to heaven, 1.04. 37
my soul to heaven, my blood upon your heads! 1.04.168
in this the heaven figures some event. 2.01. 32
must edward fall, which peril heaven forefend! 2.01.191
smile, gentle heaven! 2.03. 6
yet that thy brazen gates of heaven may ope 2.03. 40
where e'er it be, in heaven or in earth. 2.03. 43
o, pity, pity, gentle heaven, pity! 2.05. 96
i'll make my heaven in a lady's lap, | and deck 3.02.148
i'll make my heaven to dream upon the crown, 3.02.168
king lewis, i here protest in sight of heaven, 3.03.181
bids you all farewell, to meet in heaven. 5.02. 49
by heaven, brat, i'll plague ye for that word. 5.05. 27
by heaven, i will not do thee so much ease. 5.05. 72
by heaven, i think there is no man /is secure R3 1.01. 71
that i will shortly send thy soul to heaven, 1.01.119
if heaven will take the present at our hands. 1.01.120
george be pack'd with post–horse up to heaven. 1.01.146

the better for the king of heaven that hath him. 1.02.105
he is in heaven, where thou shalt never come. 1.02.106
by heaven, i will acquaint his majesty | of 1.03.104
york's dread curse prevail so much with heaven 1.03.190
can curses pierce the clouds and enter heaven? 1.03.194
if heaven have any grievous plague in store 1.03.216
this earth's thralldom to the joys of heaven. 1.04.248
and more /in peace my soul shall part to heaven, 2.01. 5
by heaven, my soul is purg'd from grudging hate, 2.01. 9
all–seeing heaven, what a world is this! 2.01. 83
much more to be thus opposite with heaven, | for 2.02. 94
god in heaven forbid | we should infringe the 3.01. 40
farewell, until we meet again in heaven. 3.03. 26
by heaven, we come to him in perfit love, | and 3.07. 90
what good is cover'd with the face of heaven, 4.04.240
as long as heaven and nature lengthens it. 4.04.353
heaven and fortune bar me happy hours! 4.04.400
for the self–same heaven | that frowns on me 5.03.286
if not to heaven, then hand in hand to hell. 5.03.313
great god of heaven, say amen to all! 5.05. 8
smile heaven upon this fair conjunction, | that 5.05. 20
a gift that heaven gives for him, which buys | a H8 1.01. 65
i cannot tell | what heaven hath given him — 1.01. 67
the will of heaven be done, and the king's 1.01.215
master — | whose honor heaven shield from soil! 1.02. 26
where this heaven of beauty | shall shine at 1.04. 59
by heaven, she is a dainty one. 1.04. 94
yet, heaven bear witness, | and if i have a 2.01. 59
sweet sacrifice, | and lift my soul to heaven. 2.01. 78
pray tell him | you met him half in heaven. 2.01. 88
heaven has an end in all; 2.01.124
heaven keep me from such counsel! 2.02. 37
heaven will one day open | the king's eyes, that 2.02. 41
no, not for all the riches under heaven. 2.03. 35
heaven witness, | i have been to you a true and 2.04. 22
methought | i stood not in the smile of heaven, 2.04.188
heaven is above all yet; 3.01.100
angels' faces, but heaven knows your hearts. 3.01.145
heaven forgive me! 3.02.135
my pray'rs to heaven for you, my loyalty, 3.02.177
too heavy for a man that hopes for heaven! 3.02.385
and my integrity to heaven, is all | i dare now 3.02.453
my hopes in heaven do dwell. 3.02.459
heaven bless thee! 4.01. 42
and saint–like | cast her fair eyes to heaven, 4.01. 84
his blessed part to heaven, and slept in peace. 4.02. 30
heaven comfort her! 4.02. 99
the dews of heaven fall thick in blessings on 4.02.133
sake that lov'd him | heaven knows how dearly. 4.02.138
if heaven had pleas'd to have given me longer 4.02.152
by heaven, i will, | or let me lose the fashion 4.02.158
the god of heaven | both now and ever bless her! 5.01.164
pray heaven he sound not my disgrace! 5.02. 13
pray heaven the king may never find a heart 5.02. 77
how much are we bound to heaven | in daily 5.02.149
and let heaven | witness how dear i hold this 5.02.206
heaven, from thy endless goodness send 5.04. 1 P
lady | heaven ever laid up to make parents happy 5.04. 7
let me speak, sir, | for heaven now bids me; 5.04. 15
royal infant — heaven still move about her! 5.04. 17
(when heaven shall call her from this cloud of 5.04. 44
where ever the bright sun of heaven shall shine, 5.04. 50
children | shall see this, and bless heaven. 5.04. 55
me | that when i am in heaven i shall desire 5.04. 67
strong as the axle–tree | on which heaven rides, TRO 1.03. 67
heaven bless thee from a tutor, and discipline 2.03. 29 P
as many farewells as be stars in heaven, | with 4.04. 44
the lustre in your eye, heaven in your cheek, 4.04.118
who neither looks upon the heaven nor earth, 4.05.281
cressid is mine, tied with the bonds of heaven. 5.02.154
strong as heaven itself: 5.02.155
the bonds of heaven are slipp'd, dissolv'd, and 5.02.156
fool's play, by heaven, hector. 5.03. 43
no, by the flame of yonder glorious heaven, | he 5.06. 23
strike at the heaven with your staves as lift COR 1.01. 68
or, by the fires of heaven, i'll leave the foe 1.04. 39
as i can of those mysteries which heaven | will 4.02. 35
by the jealous queen of heaven, that kiss | i 5.03. 46
of a god but eternity and a heaven to throne in. 5.04. 24 P
and here in sight of heaven to rome i swear, TIT 1.01.329
do, and vow to heaven and to his highness | that 1.01.474
never hopes more heaven than rests in thee, 2.03. 41
by heaven, it shall not go! 3.01.176
o, here i lift this one hand up to heaven, | and 3.01.206
dear heart, for heaven shall hear our prayers, 3.01.210
when heaven doth weep, doth not the earth 3.01.221
or else to heaven she heaves them for revenge. 4.01. 40
heaven guide thy pen to print thy sorrows plain, 4.01. 75
he thinks, with jove in heaven, or some where 4.03. 41
we will solicit heaven and move the gods | to 4.03. 51
news, news from heaven! 4.03. 78
why, didst thou not come from heaven? 4.03. 89
from heaven! 4.03. 90 P
be so bold to press to heaven in my young days. 4.03. 91 P
and now he writes to heaven for his redress. 4.04. 13
stars that make dark heaven light. ROM 1.02. 25
two of the fairest stars in all the heaven, 2.02. 15
her /eyes in heaven | would through the airy 2.02. 20
as is a winged messenger of heaven | unto the 2.02. 28
the sun not yet thy sighs from heaven clears, 2.03. 73
now god in heaven bless thee! hark you, sir. 2.04.194
away to heaven, respective lenity, | and 3.01.123
and he will make the face of heaven so fine 3.02. 23
can heaven be so envious? 3.02. 40
romeo can, | though heaven cannot. 3.02. 41
heaven is here | where juliet lives, and every 3.03. 29
live here in heaven and may look on her, | but 3.03. 32
the heaven and earth? 3.03.119
since birth, and heaven, and earth, all three do 3.03.120
the vaulty heaven so high above our heads. 3.05. 22
god in heaven bless her! 3.05.168
my husband is on earth, my faith in heaven; 3.05.205
unless that husband send it me from heaven | by 3.05.207
that heaven should practice stratagems | upon so 3.05.209
heaven and yourself | had part in this fair maid 4.05. 66
had part in this fair maid, now heaven hath all, 4.05. 67
but heaven keeps his part in eternal life. 4.05. 70
for 'twas your heaven she should be advanc'd, 4.05. 72
above the clouds, as high as heaven itself? 4.05. 74
by heaven, i will tear thee joint by joint, 5.03. 35
by heaven, i love thee better than myself, | for 5.03. 64
and bear this work of heaven with patience. 5.03.261
that heaven finds means to kill your joys with 5.03.293
i'll lock thy heaven from thee. TIM 1.02.248 P
with all th' abhorred births below crisp heaven 4.03.183
live in all the spite | of wreakful heaven, 4.03.229
that which i show, heaven knows, is merely love, 4.03.515
not all the whips of heaven are large enough — 5.01. 61
either there is a civil strife in heaven, | or JC 1.03. 11
lightning seem'd to open | the breast of heaven, 1.03. 51
that heaven hath infus'd them with these spirits 1.03. 69
nor heaven nor earth have been at peace to–night 2.02. 1
by heaven, i had rather coin my heart | and drop 4.03. 72
nor heaven peep through the blanket of the dark MAC 1.05. 53
there's husbandry in heaven, | their candles are 2.01. 4
knell, | that summons thee to heaven or to hell. 2.01. 64
god's sake, yet could not equivocate to heaven. 2.03. 11 P
if it find heaven, must find it out to–night. 3.01.141
key | (as, and't please heaven, he shall not), 3.06. 19
heaven preserve you! 4.02. 72
new sorrows | strike heaven on the face, that it 4.03. 6
such sanctity hath heaven given his hand, | they 4.03.144
how he solicits heaven, | himself best knows; 4.03.149
merciful heaven! 4.03.207
did heaven look on, | and would not take their 4.03.223
heaven rest them now! 4.03.227
if he scape, | heaven forgive him too! 4.03.235
heaven knows what she has known. 5.01. 49 P
made his course t' illume that part of heaven HAM 1.01. 37
by heaven i charge thee speak! 1.01. 49
have heaven and earth together demonstrated 1.01.124
it shows a will most incorrect to heaven, | a 1.02. 95
fie, 'tis a fault to heaven, | a fault against 1.02.101
the king's rouse the heaven shall bruit again, 1.02.127
that he might not beteem the winds of heaven 1.02.141
heaven and earth, | must i remember? 1.02.142
would i had met my dearest foe in heaven | or 1.02.182
show me the steep and thorny way to heaven, 1.03. 48
lord, | with almost all the holy vows of heaven. 1.03.114
bring with thee airs from heaven, or blasts from 1.04. 41
by heaven, i'll make a ghost of him that lets me 1.04. 85
heaven will direct it. 1.04. 91
though lewdness court it in a shape of heaven, 1.05. 54
leave her to heaven, | and to those thorns that 1.05. 86
o all you host of heaven! 1.05. 92
yes, by heaven! 1.05.104
not i, my lord, by heaven. 1.05.120
ay, by heaven, /my /lord. 1.05.122
there are more things in heaven and earth, 1.05.166
as oft as any passions under heaven | that does 2.01.102
by heaven it is as proper to our age | to cast 2.01.111
is nearer to heaven than when i saw you last, by 2.02.426 P
and bowl the round nave down the hill of heaven 2.02.496
have made milch the burning eyes of heaven, 2.02.517
prompted to my revenge by heaven and hell, 2.02.584
as i do crawling between earth and heaven? 3.01.128 P
nor earth to me give food, nor heaven light, 3.02.216
o, my offense is rank, it smells to heaven, | it 3.03. 36
and now i'll do't — and so 'a goes to heaven, 3.03. 74
sole son, do this same villain send | to heaven. 3.03. 78
and how his audit stands who knows save heaven? 3.03. 82
trip him, that his heels may kick at heaven, 3.03. 93
words without thoughts never to heaven go. 3.03. 98
confess yourself to heaven, | repent what's past 3.04.149
but heaven hath pleas'd it so | to punish me 3.04.173
in heaven, send thither to see; 4.03. 33 P
by heaven, thy madness shall be paid with weight 4.05.157
cry to be heard, as 'twere from heaven to earth, 4.05.217
why, even in that was heaven ordinant. 5.02. 48
the cannons to the heavens, the heaven to earth, 5.02.277
heaven make thee free of it! 5.02.332
by heaven, i'll ha't! 5.02.343
o, let me not be mad, not mad, sweet heaven! LR 1.05. 46
all the stor'd vengeances of heaven fall | on 2.04.162
and broke them in the sweet face of heaven: 3.04. 89 P
the bounty and the benison of heaven | to boot, 4.06.225
that parts us shall bring a brand from heaven, 5.03. 22
by heaven, i rather would have been his hangman. OTH 1.01. 34
heaven is my judge, not i for love and duty, 1.01. 59
o heaven! 1.01.169
as truly as to heaven | i do confess the vices 1.03.122
rocks, /and hills whose /heads touch heaven, 1.03.141
wish'd | that heaven had made her such a man. 1.03.163
vouch with me, heaven, i therefore beg it not 1.03.261
and heaven defend your good souls, that you 1.03.266
i cannot, 'twixt the heaven and the main, 2.01. 3
and the grace of heaven, | before, behind thee, 2.01. 85
and duck again as low | as hell's from heaven! 2.01.189
that | which heaven hath forbid the ottomites? 2.03.171
now, by heaven, | my blood begins my safer 2.03.204
if she be false, /o, /then heaven /mocks itself! 3.03.278
what he will do with it | heaven knows, not i; 3.03.298
do deeds to make heaven weep, all earth amaz'd; 3.03.371
o heaven forgive me! 3.03.373
all my fond love thus do i blow to heaven. 3.03.445
now, by yond marble heaven, | in the due 3.03.460
pray heaven it be state matters, as you think, 3.04.155
heaven keep the monster from othello's mind! 3.04.163
their virtue tempts, and they tempt heaven. 4.01. 8
by heaven, i would most gladly have forgot it. 4.01. 19
i mock you not, by heaven. 4.01. 60
by heaven, that should be my handkerchief! 4.01.158 P
he might he is not, | i would to heaven he were! 4.01.272
let heaven requite it with the serpent's curse! 4.02. 16
lest, being like one of heaven, the devils 4.02. 36
heaven doth truly know it. 4.02. 38
heaven truly knows that thou art false as hell. 4.02. 39
had it pleas'd heaven | to try me with 4.02. 47
heaven stops the nose at it, and the moon winks; 4.02. 77
by heaven, you do me wrong. 4.02. 81
o, heaven forgive us! 4.02. 88
nay, heaven doth know. 4.02.129
if any such there be, heaven pardon him! 4.02.135
for, by this light of heaven, | i know not how i 4.02.150
here, here! for heaven sake, help me! 5.01. 50
marry, heaven forbid! 5.01. 72
crime | unreconcil'd as yet to heaven and grace, 5.02. 27
then heaven | have mercy on me! 5.02. 33
but with such general warranty of heaven | as i 5.02. 60
by heaven, i saw my handkerchief in 's hand. 5.02. 62
if heaven would make me such another world | of 5.02.144
this deed of thine is no more worthy heaven 5.02.160
let heaven and men and devils, let them all, 5.02.221
by heaven, i do not, i do not, gentlemen. 5.02.232
are there no stones in heaven | but what serves 5.02.234
look of thine will hurl my soul from heaven, 5.02.274
then must thou needs find out new heaven, new ANT 1.01. 17
our parts so poor | but was a race of heaven. 1.03. 37
his faults, in him, seem as the spots of heaven, 1.04. 12
should have ascended to the roof of heaven, 3.06. 49
from my cold heart let heaven engender hail, 3.13.159
that heaven and earth may strike their sounds 4.08. 38
spend that kiss | which is my heaven to have. 5.02.303
heaven restore me! CYM 1.01.148
with orisons, for then | i am in heaven for him; 1.03. 33
hail, thou fair heaven! 3.03. 7
hail, heaven! 3.03. 9
hail, heaven! 3.03. 9
more pious debts to heaven than in all | the 3.03. 72
heaven and my conscience knows | thou didst 3.03. 99
be | yet left in heaven as small a drop of pity 4.02.304
but his jovial face — | murther in heaven? 4.02.312
(in despite | of heaven and men) her purposes; 5.05. 59
heaven mend all! 5.05. 68
they are worthy | to inlay heaven with stars. 5.05.352
of face | as heaven had lent her all his grace; PER 1.ch. 24
her face, like heaven, enticeth thee to view 1.01. 30
as sick men do | who know the world, see heaven, 1.01. 48
that gives heaven countless eyes to view men's 1.01. 73
would draw heaven down, and all the gods to 1.01. 83
blind mole casts | copp'd hills towards heaven, 1.01.101
heaven, that i had thy head! 1.01.109
how dares the plants look up to heaven, from 1.02. 55
and heaven forbid | that kings should let their 1.02. 61
if heaven slumber while their creatures want, 1.04. 16
but see what heaven can do by this our change: 1.04. 33
the curse of heaven and men succeed their evils! 1.04.104
yet cease your ire, you angry stars of heaven! 2.01. 1
are | a model which heaven makes like to itself. 2.02. 11
him, | a fire from heaven came and shrivell'd up 2.04. 9
these surges, | which wash both heaven and hell; 3.01. 2
and heaven can make | to herald thee from the 3.01. 33
neptune and | the gentlest winds of heaven. 3.03. 37
led on by heaven, and crown'd with joy at last. 5.03. 90
whose successes | makes heaven unfear'd, and TNK 1.02. 64
both heaven and earth | friend thee for ever! 1.04. 1
by heaven, she is a goddess! 2.02.134
him | sing in an evening, what a heaven it is! 2.04. 19
your attendance | cannot please heaven, and i 3.01.111
by heaven and earth, | there's nothing in thee 3.03. 45
he's in heaven. 3.04. 4
o heaven, | what more than man is this! 3.06.156
pray heaven it hold so! 4.01. 16
or as iris | newly dropp'd down from heaven. 4.01. 88
heaven forbid, man! 4.01.140
good heaven, | what a sweet face has arcite! 4.02. 6
as from a promontory | pointed in heaven, should 4.02. 23
the blissful dew of heaven does arrouse you. 5.04.104
it is in heaven that i am thus and thus, | and STM III 1
sun that shines from heaven shines but warm, VEN 193
quoth she, "in earth or heaven, | or in the 493
stealing moulds from heaven that were divine, 730
"call it not love, for love to heaven is fled, 793
and wordless so greets heaven for his success. LUC 112
that shuts him from the heaven of his thought, 338
the eye of heaven is out, and misty night 356
by heaven and earth, and all the power of both, 572
to all the host of heaven i complain me: 598
quoth he, "by heaven, i will not hear thee. 667
when both were kept for heaven and collatine? 1166
as heaven (it seem'd) to kiss the turrets bow'd. 1372
there is no heaven, /be holy then, | when time PP 18.45
go well, | by oft predict that i in heaven find: SON 14. 8
though yet, heaven knows, it is but as a tomb 17. 3
sometime too hot the eye of heaven shines, | and 18. 5
who heaven itself for ornament doth use, | and 21. 3
dost him grace when clouds do blot the heaven; 28.10
and trouble deaf heaven with my bootless cries, 29. 3
but heaven in thy creation did decree | that in 93. 9
then give me welcome, next my heaven the best, 110.13
to shun the heaven that leads men to this hell. 129.14
and yet, by heaven, i think my love as rare | as 130.13
and truly not the morning sun of heaven | better 132. 5
a fiend | from heaven to hell is flown away: 145.12
the sun itself sees not till heaven clears. 148.12

HEAVEN–BRED 1 FR 0.0001 REL FR 1 V 0 P
ay, much is the force of heaven–bred poesy. TGV 3.02. 71

HEAVEN–HU'D 1 FR 0.0001 REL FR 1 V 0 P
the heaven–hu'd sapphire and the opal blend LC 215

/HEAVEN–KISSING 1 FR 0.0001 REL FR 1 V 0 P
mercury | new lighted on a /heaven–kissing hill, HAM 3.04. 59

/HEAVENLY 1 FR 0.0001 REL FR 1 V 0 P
/the /holy /water /from /her /heavenly /eyes, LR 4.03. 30

HEAVENLY 70 FR 0.0079 REL FR 66 V 4 P
tell me, heavenly bow, | if venus or her son, as TMP 4.01. 86
and when i have requir'd | some heavenly music 5.01. 52
some heavenly power guide us | out of this 5.01.105
o heavenly julia! TGV 1.03. 50
even she; and is she not a heavenly saint? 2.04.145
wilt thou aspire to guide the heavenly car, 3.01.154
i claim the promise for her heavenly picture. 4.04. 87
"have i caught thee, my heavenly jewel?" WIV 3.03. 43
to make her heavenly comforts of despair, | when MM 4.03.110
"did not the heavenly rhetoric of thine eye, LLL 4.03. 58
my vow was earthly, thou a heavenly love; 4.03. 64
who sees the heavenly rosaline, | that, like a 4.03.217
"out of your favors, heavenly spirits, vouchsafe 5.02.166
hate a breaking cause to be | of heavenly oaths, 5.02.356
love | put on by us, if, in your heavenly eyes, 5.02.767
those heavenly eyes, that look into these faults 5.02.769
of these three contains her heavenly picture. MV 2.07. 48
if two gods should play some heavenly match, 3.05. 79
but heavenly rosalind! AYL 1.02.289

of many parts | by heavenly synod was devis'd, 3.02.150
wakes, | to make a dulcet and a heavenly sound; SHR in.1. 51
this is | the patroness of heavenly harmony. 3.01. 5
as those two eyes become that heavenly face? 4.05. 32
"a showing of a heavenly effect in an earthly AWW 2.03. 23 P
god for his richard hath in heavenly pay | a R2 3.02. 60
by this heavenly ground i tread on, i must be 2H4 2.01.140 P
o heavenly god! 2H6 3.02. 37
enough, | so suffolk had thy heavenly company: 3.02.361
and by the hope i have of heavenly bliss, | that 3H6 3.03.182
but 'twas thy heavenly face that set me on. R3 1.02.182
you are full of heavenly stuff, and bear the H8 3.02.137
holy and heavenly thoughts still counsel her. 5.04. 29
nothing but heavenly business | should rob my TRO 4.01. 5
had he heard the heavenly harmony | which that TIT 2.04. 48
but romeo's name speaks heavenly eloquence. ROM 3.02. 33
into strong shudders and to heavenly agues | th' TIM 4.03.138
virtue, | he hath a heavenly gift of prophecy, MAC 4.03.157
heavenly powers, restore him! HAM 3.01.141 P
o'er me with your wings, | you heavenly guards! 3.04.104
on necessity, fools by heavenly compulsion, LR 1.02.122 P
they do suggest at first with heavenly shows, OTH 2.03.352
no, by this heavenly light! 4.03. 65
nor i neither by this heavenly light; 4.03. 66
this sorrow's heavenly, | it strikes where it 5.02. 21
o, she was heavenly true! 5.02.135
o /god! o heavenly /god! 5.02.218
from the possession of this heavenly sight! 5.02.278
o heavenly mingle! ANT 1.05. 59
though this a heavenly angel, hell is here. CYM 2.02. 50
flow, flow, | you heavenly blessings, on her! 3.05.161
cases to those heavenly jewels | which pericles PER 3.02. 98
most heavenly music! 5.01.233
her | as she is heavenly and a blessed goddess; TNK 2.02.163
and if she be not heavenly, i would make her 2.02.241
narcissus was a sad boy, but a heavenly. 4.02. 32
port even where | the heavenly limiter pleases. 5.01. 30
the heavenly fires | did scorch his mortal son, 5.01. 91
o all you heavenly powers, where is /your mercy? 5.03.139
o you heavenly charmers, | what things you make 5.04.131
and calls it heavenly moisture, air of grace, VEN 64
done, | between this heavenly and earthly sun. 198
melodious discord, heavenly tune harsh sounding, 431
and backward drew | the heavenly moisture, that 542
within his thought her heavenly image sits, LUC 288
did not the heavenly rhetoric of thine eye, PP 3. 1
my vow was earthly, thou a heavenly love; 3. 7
whose heavenly touch | upon the lute doth ravish 8. 5
and having climb'd the steep–up heavenly hill, SON 7. 5
such heavenly touches ne'er touch'd earthly 17. 8
gilding pale streams with heavenly alcumy; 33. 4
HEAVENLY–HARNESS'D 1 FR 0.0001 REL FR 1 V 0 P
the hour before the heavenly–harness'd team 1H4 3.01.218
HEAVEN–MOVING 1 FR 0.0001 REL FR 1 V 0 P
draws those heaven–moving pearls from his poor JN 2.01.169
HEAVEN'S 40 FR 0.0045 REL FR 40 V 0 P
saucy sweetness that do coin heaven's image | in MM 2.04. 45
there's nothing situate under heaven's eye | but ERR 2.01. 16
my sole earth's heaven, and my heaven's claim. 3.02. 64
study is like the heaven's glorious sun, | that LLL 1.01. 84
these earthly godfathers of heaven's lights, 1.01. 88
that sings heaven's praise with such an earthly 4.02.118
with eyes best seeing, heaven's fiery eye, | by 5.02.375
and heaven's artillery thunder in the skies? SHR 1.02.204
you give away heaven's vows, and those are mine; AWW 5.03.171
heaven's offer we refuse, | the proffered means R2 3.02. 31
card'nal, if thou think'st on heaven's bliss, 2H6 3.03. 27
take heed, for heaven's sake take heed, lest at H8 3.01.110
it's heaven's will! 3.02.128
serve your lust, shadowed from heaven's eye, TIT 2.01.130
o, that which i would hide from heaven's eye, 4.02. 59
or dost thou not, heaven's curse upon thee! TIM 4.03.132
that the heaven's breath | smells wooingly here; MAC 1.06. 5
striding the blast, or heaven's cherubin, hors'd 1.07. 22
heaven's face does glow | o'er this solidity and HAM 3.04. 48
thou out of heaven's benediction com'st | to the LR 2.02.161
use them so | that heaven's vault should crack. 5.03.260
but yet heaven's bounty towards him might | be CYM 1.06. 78
azure lac'd | with blue of heaven's own tinct. 2.02. 23
hark, hark, the lark at heaven's gate sings, 2.03. 20
greatness was no guard | to bar heaven's shaft, PER 2.04. 15
so adieu, | and heaven's good eyes look on you! TNK 1.04. 13
for heaven's sake save their lives, and banish 3.06.251
hollow womb resounds like heaven's thunder; VEN 268
and coal–black clouds that shadow heaven's light 533
she fram'd thee in high heaven's despite, | to 731
mortal stars as bright as heaven's beauties, LUC 13
by heaven's fair sun that breeds the fat earth's 1837
to sing heaven's praise with such an earthly PP 5.14
that heaven's air in this huge rondure hems. SON 21. 8
as those gold candles fix'd in heaven's air: 21.12
from sullen earth) sings hymns at heaven's gate, 29.12
the world may stain when heaven's sun staineth. 33.14
a crow that flies in heaven's sweetest air. 70. 4
slow, | they rightly do inherit heaven's graces, 94. 5
all quit, but, spite of heaven's fell rage, LC 13
HEAVENS' 3 FR 0.0003 REL FR 3 V 0 P
to death, | /wish'd himself the heavens' breath. LLL 4.03.106
by the heavens' assistance and your strength, 3H6 5.04. 68
to death, | wish'd himself the heavens' breath. PP 16. 8
/HEAVENS 2 FR 0.0002 REL FR 2 V 0 P
by /heavens, the duke shall know how slack you R3 1.04.275
/if /that /the /heavens /do /not /their /visible LR 4.02. 46
HEAVENS 155 FR 0.0175 REL FR 136 V 19 P
o the heavens! TMP 1.02. 59
o the heavens! 1.02.116
heavens thank you for't! 1.02.175
heavens! 1.02.429
heavens keep him from these beasts! 2.01.324
heavens rain grace | on that which breeds 3.01. 75
give us kind keepers, heavens! what were these? 3.03. 20
no sweet aspersion shall the heavens let fall 4.01. 18
o heavens, that they were living both in naples, 5.01.149
heavens defend me from that welsh fairy, lest he WIV 5.05. 81 P
love, the heavens themselves do guide the state; 5.05.232
the heavens give safety to your purposes! MM 1.01. 73
o heavens! 2.04. 19
o heavens, it cannot be. 3.01. 98
o heavens, what stuff is here? 3.02. 4 P
you have paid the heavens your function, and the 3.02.249 P
for what obscured light the heavens did grant ERR 1.01. 66
for the heavens, he shows me where the bachelors ADO 2.01. 48 P
ah, heavens, it is /a most pathetical nit! LLL 4.01.148
o heavens, i have my wish! 4.03. 79
and beauty's crest becomes the heavens well. 4.03.252
and the heavens were so pleas'd that thou wert 5.01. 75 P
heavens shield lysander, if they mean a fray! MND 3.02.447
"for the heavens, rouse up a brave mind," says MV 2.02. 12 P
o heavens, this is my true–begotten father, who, 2.02. 35 P
o heavens! SHR 1.02. 39 P
the heavens have thought well on thee, lafew, AWW 5.03.150
if the heavens had been pleas'd, would we had so TN 2.01. 20 P
lady, the heavens rain odors on you! 3.01. 84 P
o heavens themselves! 3.04.357
malvolio, thy wits the heavens restore! 4.02. 95 P
and heavens so shine | that they may fairly note 4.03. 34
the heavens continue their loves! WT 1.01. 31 P
i must be patient till the heavens look | with 2.01.106
and the heavens themselves | do strike at my 3.02.146
the heavens with that we have in hand are angry, 3.03. 5
i never saw | the heavens so dim by day. 3.03. 56
he, and men — the earth, the heavens, and all: 4.04.371
to be made, but by | (as heavens forefend!) 4.04.530
at the last | do as the heavens have done, 5.01. 5
my lord should to the heavens be contrary, 5.01. 45
for which the heavens, taking angry note, | have 5.01.173
and son unto the king, whom heavens directing, 5.03.150
arm, you heavens, against these perjur'd kings! JN 3.01.107
be husband to me, heavens! 3.01.108
better other's happiness | until the heavens, R2 1.01. 23
the means that heavens yield must be embrac'd, 3.02. 29
lest you mistake the heavens are over our heads. 3.03. 17
the heavens were all on fire, the earth did 1H4 3.01. 23
then the earth shook to see the heavens on fire, 3.01. 24
thou pourest down from these swelling heavens 3.01.199
from enemies heavens keep your majesty, | and, 2H4 4.04. 94
the heavens thee guard and keep, most royal imp 5.05. 42
hung be the heavens with black, yield day to 1H6 1.01. 1
combat with adverse planets in the heavens! 1.01. 54
mars his true moving, even as in the heavens, 1.02. 1
what tumult's in the heavens? 1.04. 98
heavens, can you suffer hell so to prevail? 1.05. 9
if not of hell, the heavens sure favor him. 2.01. 47
heavens keep old bedford safe! 3.02.100
yet heavens have glory for this victory! 3.02.117
o thou eternal mover of the heavens, | look with 2H6 3.03. 19
and heavens and honor be witness that no want of 4.08. 62 P
whom angry heavens do make their minister, 5.02. 34
can we outrun the heavens? good margaret, stay. 5.02. 73
if i be not, heavens be reveng'd on me! 3H6 1.01. 57
heavens grant that warwick's words bewitch him 3.03.112
then, since the heavens have shap'd my body so, 5.06. 78
the heavens have blest you with a goodly son R3 1.03. 9
let not the heavens hear these tell–tale women 4.04.150
the heavens themselves, the planets, and this TRO 1.03. 85
now heavens forfend such scarcity of /youth! 1.03.302
ay, the heavens hear me! 2.03. 36 P
thank the heavens, lord, thou art of sweet 2.03.240
o heavens, what have i done! 3.02.138
heavens, what a man is there! 3.03.126
o heavens, what some men do, | while some men 3.03.132
o heavens, "be true" again? 4.04. 74
o heavens, you love me not. 4.04. 82
tell me, you heavens, in which part of his body 4.05.242
answer me, heavens! 4.05.246
no notes of sally, for the heavens, sweet 5.03. 14
frown on, you heavens, effect your rage with 5.10. 6
heavens bless my lord from fell aufidius! COR 1.03. 45
o heavens! o heavens! 4.01. 12
o heavens! o heavens! 4.01. 12
o blessed heavens! 4.02. 20
behold, the heavens do ope, | the gods look down 5.03.183
sent by the heavens for prince saturnine, TIT 1.01.335
(whether by device or no, the heavens can tell). 1.01.395
rome and the righteous heavens be my judge, 1.01.426
till the heavens | reveal the damn'd contriver 4.01. 35
o heavens, can you hear a good man groan | and 4.01.123
revenge the heavens for old andronicus! 4.01.129
so smile the heavens upon this holy act, | that ROM 2.06. 1
to move the heavens to smile upon my state, 4.03. 4
the heavens do low'r upon you for some ill; 4.05. 94
o heavens! 5.03.202
heavens, that i were a lord! TIM 1.01.227 P
heavens, have i said, the bounty of this lord! 2.02.164
roots, you clear heavens! 4.03. 28
who ever knew the heavens menace so? JC 1.03. 44
but wherefore did you so much tempt the heavens? 1.03. 53
to see the strange impatience of the heavens; 1.03. 61
the heavens themselves blaze forth the death of 2.02. 31
the heavens speed thee in thine enterprise! 2.04. 41
thou seest the heavens, as troubled with man's MAC 2.04. 5
but, gentle heavens, | cut short all 4.03.231
heavens secure him! HAM 1.05.113
heavens make our presence and our practices 2.02. 38
a silence in the heavens, the rack stand still, 2.02.484
o, help him, you sweet heavens! 3.01.133 P
o heavens, die two months ago, and not forgotten 3.02.130 P
is there not rain enough in the sweet heavens 3.03. 45
o heavens, is't possible a young maid's wits 4.05.160
the cannons to the heavens, the heaven to earth, 5.02.277
o heavens! LR 2.04.189
you heavens, give me that patience, patience i 2.04.271
to them, | and show the heavens more just. 3.04. 36
o heavens! 3.05. 12 P
poor old heart, he holp the heavens to rain. 3.07. 62
heavens, deal so still! 4.01. 66
this judgment of the heavens, that makes us 5.03.232
let the heavens | give him defense against the OTH 2.01. 44
the heavens forbid | but that our loves and 2.01.193
o heavens forefend! 5.02.186
our worser thoughts heavens mend! ANT 1.02. 62 P
let him breathe between the heavens and earth, 3.12. 14
no more obey the heavens than our courtiers' CYM 1.01. 2
but heavens know | some men are much to blame. 1.06. 76
the heavens hold firm | the walls of thy dear 2.01. 62
gate | instructs you how t' adore the heavens, 3.03. 3
grant, heavens, that which i fear | prove false! 3.05. 52
such a foe, good heavens! 3.06. 27
heavens, | how deeply you at once do touch me! 4.03. 3
the heavens still must work. 4.03. 41
by heavens, i'll go. 4.04. 43
therefore, good heavens, | hear patiently my 5.01. 21
for all was lost | but that the heavens fought; 5.03. 4
door open | of the unguarded hearts, heavens, 5.03. 46
the benediction of these covering heavens | fall 5.05.350
whom heavens, in justice, both on her and hers, 5.05.464
the heavens, | through you, increase our wonder, PER 3.02. 95
of all the faults beneath the heavens, the gods 4.03. 20
heavens forgive it! 4.03. 39
thetis' birth–child on the heavens bestowed; 4.04. 41
o heavens bless my girl! 5.01.223
heavens make a star of him! 5.03. 79
those best affections that the heavens infuse TNK 1.03. 9
who from the mounted heavens | view us their 1.04. 4
heavens lend | a thousand differing ways to one 1.05. 13
o you heavens, dares any | so noble bear a 3.01. 89
till heavens did | make hardly one the winner. 5.03.129
what priceless wealth the heavens had him lent LUC 17
as if the heavens should countenance his sin. 343
HEAVES 2 FR 0.0002 REL FR 2 V 0 P
or else to heaven she heaves them for revenge. TIT 4.01. 40
matter in these sighs, these profound heaves — HAM 4.01. 1
HEAVETH 1 FR 0.0001 REL FR 1 V 0 P
with one fair hand she heaveth up his hat, | her VEN 351
/HEAVIER 1 FR 0.0001 REL FR 1 V 0 P
/find /our /griefs /heavier /than /our /offenses 2H4 4.01. 69
HEAVIER 14 FR 0.0015 REL FR 11 V 3 P
then was your sin of heavier kind than his. MM 2.03. 28
a heavier task could not have been impos'd ERR 1.01. 31
'twill be heavier soon by the weight of a man. ADO 3.04. 26 P
there any harm in "the heavier for a husband"? 3.04. 35 P
so sorrow's heaviness doth heavier grow | for MND 3.02. 84
for they are heavier | than all thy woes can WT 3.02.208
norfolk, for thee remains a heavier doom, R2 1.03.148
woe doth the heavier sit | where it perceives it 1.03.280
my tongue hath but a heavier tale to say. 3.02.197
peace be with us, lest we be heavier! 2H4 5.02. 26
i weigh it lightly, were it heavier. R3 3.01.121
more, | but he as he, the heavier for a whore. TRO 4.01. 67
the brain the heavier for being too light, the CYM 5.04.164 P
of roses, yet is heavier | than lead itself, TNK 5.01. 96
HEAVIEST 7 FR 0.0008 REL FR 7 V 0 P
that e'er i watch'd, and the most heaviest. TGV 4.02.140
the heaviest and the worst | is your displeasure H8 3.02.391
servant, or endure | your heaviest censure. COR 5.06.141
to your public laws | at heaviest answer. TIM 5.04. 63
which shall possess them with the heaviest sound MAC 4.03.202
those hands, that grasp'd the heaviest club, ANT 4.12. 46
us, | and which is heaviest, palamon, unmarried. TNK 2.02. 29
HEAVILY 12 FR 0.0013 REL FR 9 V 3 P
but mark how heavily this befell to the poor MM 3.01.218 P
help us to sigh and groan, | heavily, heavily. ADO 5.03. 18
help us to sigh and groan, | heavily, heavily. 5.03. 18
till death be uttered, | heavily, heavily. 5.03. 21
till death be uttered, | heavily, heavily. 5.03. 21
thou shalt be heavily punished. LLL 1.02.150 P
why looks your grace so heavily to–day? R3 1.04. 1
man | that looks not heavily and full of dread. 2.03. 40
which i have heavily borne, there ran a rumor MAC 4.03.182
indeed it goes so heavily with my disposition, HAM 2.02.297 P
and heavily from woe to woe tell o'er | the sad SON 30.10
hide, | which heavily he answers with a groan, 50.11
/HEAVINESS 1 FR 0.0001 REL FR 1 V 0 P
/weep /to /see /his /grandsire's /heaviness. TIT 3.02. 49
HEAVINESS 16 FR 0.0018 REL FR 15 V 1 P
strangeness of your story put | heaviness in me. TMP 1.02.307
our remembrances with | a heaviness that's gone. 5.01.200
so sorrow's heaviness doth heavier grow | for MND 3.02. 84
and quicken his embraced heaviness | with some MV 2.08. 52
to lay aside life–harming heaviness | and R2 2.02. 3
charming your blood with pleasing heaviness, 1H4 3.01.215
merry, | but heaviness foreruns the good event. 2H4 4.02. 82
i am here, brother, full of heaviness. 4.05. 8
to–night she's mewed up to her heaviness. ROM 3.04. 11
one who, to put thee from thy heaviness, | hath 3.05.108
in the heaviness of sleep | we put fresh LR 4.07. 20
our strength is all gone into heaviness, | that ANT 4.15. 33
the heaviness and guilt within my bosom | takes CYM 5.02. 1
the purse too light, being drawn of heaviness. 5.04.165 P
she would request to know your heaviness." LUC 1283
unmask, dear dear, this moody heaviness, | and 1602
HEAVING 2 FR 0.0002 REL FR 1 V 1 P
the heaving of my lungs provokes me to LLL 3.01. 76 P
than the performance of our heaving spleens, | i TRO 2.02.196
HEAVINGS 1 FR 0.0001 REL FR 1 V 0 P
him and do sigh | at each his needless heavings, WT 2.03. 35
HEAV'N 7 FR 0.0008 REL FR 7 V 0 P
pray heav'n he prove so when you come to him! TGV 2.07. 79
but, heav'n be thank'd, it is but voluntary. JN 5.01. 29
/employ the countenance and grace of heav'n, 2H4 4.02. 24
either heav'n with lightning strike the R3 1.02. 64
the will of heav'n | be done in this and all H8 1.01.209
lov'd him next heav'n? 3.01.130
'tis the right ring, by heav'n! 5.02.138
HEAV'NLY 2 FR 0.0002 REL FR 2 V 0 P
and heav'nly blessings | follow such creatures. H8 2.03. 57
have deaf'd | the ears of heav'nly justice. TNK 1.02. 81
HEAV'N'S 1 FR 0.0001 REL FR 1 V 0 P
heav'n's peace be with him! H8 2.02.129
HEAV'NS' 1 FR 0.0001 REL FR 1 V 0 P
thou whom the heav'ns' plagues | have humbled to LR 4.01. 64
HEAV'NS 3 FR 0.0003 REL FR 3 V 0 P
yet heav'ns are just, and time suppresseth 3H6 3.03. 77
to whom the heav'ns in thy nativity | adjudg'd 4.06. 33
his face was as the heav'ns, and therein stuck ANT 5.02. 79
/HEAVY 3 FR 0.0003 REL FR 3 V 0 P
/i /give /this /heavy /weight /from /off /my R2 4.01.204
/alack /the /heavy /day, | /that /i /have /worn 4.01.257
/most /just /and /heavy /causes /make /oppose. LR 5.01. 27
HEAVY 184 FR 0.0208 REL FR 162 V 22 P

will you laugh me asleep, for i am very heavy? TMP 2.01.189 P
you, sir, | do not omit the heavy offer of it. 2.01.194
thank you. wondrous heavy. 2.01.198
mean task | would be as heavy to me as odious, 3.01. 5
it is too heavy for so light a tune. TGV 1.02. 81
heavy? belike it hath some burden then? 1.02. 82
for she is lumpish, heavy, melancholy, | and, 3.02. 62
master fenton, talk not to me, my mind is heavy; WIV 4.06. 2 P
under whose heavy sense your brother's life MM 1.04. 65
thou bear'st thy heavy riches but a journey, 3.01. 27
there have i made my promise upon the heavy 4.01. 34
this week he hath been heavy, sour, sad, | and ERR 5.01. 45
hour | my heavy burthen /ne'er delivered. 5.01.403
sing no moe, | of dumps so dull and heavy; ADO 2.03. 71
indeed that tells a heavy tale for him. 3.02. 61 P
joy to wear it, for my heart is exceeding heavy. 3.04. 25 P
otherwise 'tis light, and not heavy. 3.04. 37 P
take not away thy heavy hand, | death is the 4.01.115
lady, and her death shall fall heavy on you. 5.01.149 P
i would bend under any heavy weight | that he'll 5.01.277
sing, boy, my spirit grows heavy in love. LLL 1.02.122 P
is not lead a metal heavy, dull, and slow? 3.01. 59
scarce show a harvest of their heavy toil; 4.03.323
he made her melancholy, sad, and heavy, | and so 5.02. 14
for the news i bring | is heavy in my tongue. 5.02.719
a heavy heart bears not a humble tongue. 5.02.737
hath well beguil'd | the heavy gait of night. MND 5.01.368
whilst the heavy ploughman snores, | all with 5.01.373
as makes it light or heavy in the substance | or MV 4.01.328
for a light wife doth make a heavy husband, 5.01.130
knowing no burthen of heavy tedious penury. AYL 3.02.324 P
why, this' a heavy chance 'twixt him and you, SHR 1.02. 46
and yet as heavy as my weight should be. 2.01.205
trust him not in matter of heavy consequence; AWW 2.05. 45 P
yonder is heavy news within between two soldiers 3.02. 33 P
it is | a charge too heavy for my strength, but 3.03. 4
let every word weigh heavy of her worth, | that 3.04. 31
my heart is heavy, and mine age is weak; 3.04. 41
ceas'd | in heavy satisfaction and would never 5.03.100
heavy matters, heavy matters! WT 3.03.112 P
heavy matters, heavy matters! 3.03.112 P
what wit can make heavy and vengeance bitter; 4.04.773 P
is purchase of a heavy curse from rome, | or the JN 3.01.205
so heavy as thou shalt not shake them off, | but 3.01.296
had bak'd thy blood and made it heavy, thick, 3.03. 43
still and anon cheer'd up the heavy time, 4.01. 47
work, | the graceless action of a heavy hand — 4.03. 58
hath troubled me so long, | lies heavy on me. 5.03. 4
be mowbray's sins so heavy in his bosom | that R2 1.02. 50
a heavy sentence, my most sovereign liege, | and 1.03.154
and so heavy sad, | as, /though on thinking on no 2.02. 30
makes me with heavy nothing faint and shrink. 2.02. 32
with the eyes of heavy mind | i see thy glory 2.04. 18
so may you by my dull and heavy eye: 3.02.196
alack the heavy day | when such a sacred king 3.03. 8
to drive away the heavy thought of care? 3.04. 2
that lie shall lie so heavy on my sword, | that 4.01. 66
the heavy accent of thy moving tongue, | and in 5.01. 47
and piece the way out with a heavy heart. 5.01. 92
came | a post from wales loaden with heavy news, 1H4 1.01. 37
some heavy business hath my lord in hand, | and 2.03. 63
that lie too heavy on the commonwealth, | cries 4.03. 80
i am as hot as molten lead, and as heavy too. 5.03. 34 P
i should have a heavy miss of thee | if i were 5.04.105
turn'd on themselves, like dull and heavy lead. 2H4 1.01.118
and as the thing that's heavy in itself | upon 1.01.119
so did our men, heavy in hotspur's loss, | lend 1.01.121
a heavy descension! 2.02.173 P
of these times | to lay a heavy and unequal hand 4.01.100
thine's too heavy to mount. 4.03. 56 P
me | is tears and heavy sorrows of the blood, 4.05. 38
here come the heavy issue of dead harry. 5.02. 14
argument | is all too heavy to admit much talk. 5.02. 24
well, peace be with him that hath made us heavy! 5.02. 25
in | their heavy burthens at his narrow gate, H5 1.02.201
me | are heavy orisons 'gainst this poor wretch! 2.02. 53
they could never wear such heavy head–pieces. 3.07.138 P
the king himself hath a heavy reckoning to make, 4.01.135 P
bell, | sings heavy music to thy timorous soul, 1H6 4.02. 40
and let thy suffolk take his heavy leave. 2H6 3.02.306
go tell this heavy message to the king. 3.02.379
nothing so heavy as these woes of mine. 5.02. 65
and if thou tell'st the heavy story right, 3H6 1.04.160
whose heavy looks foretell | some dreadful story 2.01. 43
o heavy times, begetting such events! 2.05. 63
whose soul is that which takes her heavy leave? 2.06. 42
and, as thou seest, ourselves in heavy plight. 3.03. 37
thou slander of thy heavy mother's womb! R3 1.03.230
england, | and cited up a thousand heavy times, 1.04. 14
my soul is heavy, and i fain would sleep. 1.04. 74
that bear this heavy mutual load of moan, | now 2.02.113
have made it tedious, wearisome, and heavy. 3.01. 5
it is too heavy for your grace to wear. 3.01.120
with a heavy heart, | thinking on them, go i 3.01.149
now thy heavy curse | is lighted on poor 3.04. 92
thus margaret's curse falls heavy on my neck: 5.01. 25
look that my staves be sound, and not too heavy. 5.03. 65
that they may crush down with a heavy fall | the 5.03.111
let me sit heavy on thy soul to–morrow! 5.03.118
let me sit heavy in thy soul to–morrow, | i that 5.03.131
let me sit heavy in thy soul to–morrow, | rivers 5.03.139
too heavy for a man that hopes for heaven! H8 3.02.385
music leave, | they are harsh and heavy to me. 4.02. 95
not wrong, | but makes it much more heavy. TRO 2.02.188
as the goodly saying is, "o heart, heavy heart, 4.04. 16
what troyan is that same that looks so heavy? 4.05. 95
i am light, and heavy. COR 2.01.184
would unclog my heart | of what lies heavy to't. 4.02. 48
you heavy people, circle me about, | that i may TIT 3.01.276
o publius, is not this a heavy case, | to see 4.03. 25
care, | witness the tiring day and heavy night, 5.02. 24
and day by day i'll do this heavy task, | so 5.02. 58
a while, | for nature puts me to a heavy task. 5.03.150
bed, | away from light steals home my heavy son, ROM 1.01.137
o heavy lightness, serious vanity, | misshapen 1.01.178
griefs of mine own lie heavy in my breast, 1.01.186
being but heavy, i will bear the light. 1.04. 12
under love's heavy burthen do i sink. 1.04. 22
love from love, toward school with heavy looks. 2.02.157
dead, | unwieldy, slow, heavy, and pale as lead. 2.05. 17
and thou and romeo press /one heavy bier! 3.02. 60
bed, | which heavy sorrow makes them apt unto. 3.03.157
look, look! o heavy day! 4.05. 18
is fashion'd for the journey, dull and heavy. TIM 2.02.219
it pleases time and fortune to lie heavy | upon 3.05. 10
weigh them, it is as heavy; JC 1.02.146
why you are heavy, and what men to–night | have 2.01.275
canst thou hold up thy heavy eyes awhile, | and 4.03.256
but under heavy judgment bears that life | which MAC 1.03.110
of my ingratitude even now | was heavy on me. 1.04. 16
a heavy summons lies like lead upon me, | and 2.01. 6
whose heavy hand hath bow'd you to the grave, 3.01. 89
seneca cannot be too heavy, nor plautus too HAM 2.02.400 P
o heavy burthen! 3.01. 53
and course of thought | 'tis heavy with him. 3.03. 84
o heavy deed! 4.01. 12
till that her garments, heavy with their drink, 4.07.181
this is too heavy; let me see another. 5.02.264
take vantage, heavy eyes, not to behold | this LR 2.02.171
hast heavy substance, bleed'st not, speak'st, 4.06. 52
your eyes are in a heavy case, your purse in a 4.06.147 P
and i a heavy interim shall support | by his OTH 1.03.258
o heavy ignorance! 2.01.143 P
alas the heavy day! 4.02. 42
thrown such despite and heavy terms upon her, 4.02.116
'tis heavy night; 5.01. 42
o heavy hour! 5.02. 98
state | this heavy act with heavy heart relate. 5.02.371
state | this heavy act with heavy heart relate. 5.02.371
their ships are yare, yours heavy. ANT 3.07. 38
most heavy day! 4.14.134
how heavy weighs my lord! 4.15. 32
a heavy sight! 4.15. 40
discourse is heavy, fasting; CYM 3.06. 90
a heavy reckoning for you, sir. 5.04.157 P
but now my heavy conscience sinks my knee, | as 5.05.413
on her and hers, | have laid most heavy hand. 5.05.465
but to relieve them of their heavy load; PER 1.04. 91
what e'er it be, | 'tis wondrous heavy. 3.02. 53
his daughter's woe and heavy well–a–day | in her 4.04. 49
of heavy pericles think this his bark; 5.ch. 22
balms, and gums, and heavy cheers, | sacred TNK 1.05. 4
is't not too heavy? 3.06. 56
of an eye as heavy | as if he had lost his 4.02. 27
be | that thou should think it heavy unto thee? VEN 156
and with a heavy, dark, disliking eye, | his 182
her heavy anthem still concludes in woe, | and 839
what may a heavy groan advantage thee? 950
heavy heart's lead, melt at mine eyes' red fire! 1073
cold, | she whispers in his ears a heavy tale, 1125
bed, | intending weariness with heavy sprite; LUC 121
when heavy sleep had clos'd up mortal eyes. 163
with heavy eye, knit brow, and strengthless pace 709
he thence departs a heavy convertite, | she 743
the ear | the heavy motion that it doth behold, 1326
bright things stain'd) a kind of heavy fear. 1435
woes, | for sorrow, like a heavy hanging bell, 1493
though woe be heavy, yet it seldom sleeps, | and 1574
through heavy sleep on sightless eyes doth stay! SON 43.12
/nought by elements so slow | but heavy tears, 44.14
how heavy do i journey on the way, | when what i 50. 1
keep open | my heavy eyelids to the weary night? 61. 2
to sing, | and heavy ignorance aloft to fly, 78. 6
that heavy saturn laugh'd and leapt with him. 98. 4

HEAVY–GAITED 1 FR 0.0001 REL FR 1 V 0 P
and heavy–gaited toads lie in their way, | doing R2 3.02. 15

HEAVY–HEADED 1 FR 0.0001 REL FR 1 V 0 P
this heavy–headed revel east and west | makes us HAM 1.04. 17

HEBONA 1 FR 0.0001 REL FR 1 V 0 P
stole, | with juice of cursed hebona in a vial, HAM 1.05. 62

HEBREW *(also ebrew)*

HEBREW 3 FR 0.0003 REL FR 2 V 1 P
if not, thou art an hebrew, a jew, and not worth TGV 2.05. 54 P
tubal, a wealthy hebrew of my tribe, | will MV 1.03. 57
the hebrew will turn christian, he grows kind. 1.03.178

HECAT 2 FR 0.0002 REL FR 2 V 0 P
why, how now, hecat? you look angerly. MAC 3.05. 1
sun, | the /mysteries of hecat and the night; LR 1.01.110

HECATE 1 FR 0.0001 REL FR 1 V 0 P
i speak not to that railing hecate, | but unto 1H6 3.02. 64

HECAT'S 4 FR 0.0004 REL FR 4 V 0 P
that do run | by the triple hecat's team | from MND 5.01.384
witchcraft celebrates | pale hecat's off'rings; MAC 2.01. 52
ere to black hecat's summons | the shard–borne 3.02. 41
with hecat's ban thrice blasted, thrice HAM 3.02.258

HECKFER *(also heifer, etc.)*

HECKFER 1 FR 0.0001 REL FR 1 V 0 P
and yet the steer, the heckfer, and the calf WT 1.02.124

HECKFERS 1 FR 0.0001 REL FR 0 V 1 P
kin as the parish heckfers are to the town bull. 2H4 2.02.157 P

HECTIC 1 FR 0.0001 REL FR 1 V 0 P
for like the hectic in my blood he rages, | and HAM 4.03. 66

/HECTOR 1 FR 0.0001 REL FR 1 V 0 P
/hector /is /dead; TRO 5.10. 22

HECTOR 127 FR 0.0143 REL FR 86 V 41 P
said i well, bully hector? WIV 1.03. 11 P
hector of greece, my boy! 2.03. 33 P
as hector, i assure you, and in the managing of ADO 2.03.189 P
he presents hector of troy; LLL 5.02.534 P
thy head, achilles — here comes hector in arms. 5.02.632 P
hector was but a troyan in respect of this. 5.02.636 P
but is this hector? 5.02.637 P
i think hector was not so clean–timber'd. 5.02.638 P
this cannot be hector. 5.02.642 P
of lances the almighty, | gave hector a gift" — 5.02.645
gave hector a gift, the heir of ilion; 5.02.652
give it the rein, for it runs against hector. 5.02.658 P
speak, brave hector, we are much delighted. 5.02.665 P
"this hector far surmounted hannibal. 5.02.670
fellow hector, she is gone; 5.02.672 P
then shall hector be whipt for jaquenetta that 5.02.680 P
hector trembles. 5.02.687 P
hector will challenge him. 5.02.690 P
was not that hector? 5.02.880
thou art as valorous as hector of troy, worth 2H4 2.04.219 P
a second hector, for his grim aspect | and large 1H6 2.03. 20
farewell, my hector, and my troy's true hope. 3H6 4.08. 25
lest hector or my father should perceive me, | i TRO 1.01. 36
hector, whose patience | is as a virtue fix'd, 1.02. 4
a lord of troyan blood, nephew to hector, | they 1.02. 13
man, that makes me smile, make hector angry? 1.02. 32 P
say he yesterday cop'd hector in the battle and 1.02. 33 P
hath ever since kept hector fasting and waking. 1.02. 35 P
was hector arm'd and gone ere ye came to ilium? 1.02. 48 P
hector was gone, but helen was not up. 1.02. 50 P
e'en so; hector was stirring early. 1.02. 51 P
what, not between troilus and hector? 1.02. 63 P
say as i say, for i am sure he is not hector. 1.02. 68 P
no, nor hector is not troilus in some degrees. 1.02. 69 P
he is not hector. 1.02. 75 P
no, hector is not a better man than troilus. 1.02. 79 P
hector shall not have his /wit this year. 1.02. 85 P
three pound, lift as much as his brother hector. 1.02.116 P
and hector laugh'd. 1.02.148 P
that's hector, that, that, look you, that; 1.02.199 P
go thy way, hector! 1.02.200 P
o brave hector! 1.02.201 P
here in troy | a prince call'd hector — priam 1.03.261
hector, in view of troyans and of greeks, 1.03.273
if any come, hector shall honor him; 1.03.280
hath, /or means to be, | that one meets hector; 1.03.290
this challenge that the gallant hector sends, 1.03.321
that can from hector bring those honors off, 1.03.334
he that meets hector issues from our choice, 1.03.347
therefore 'tis meet achilles meet not hector. 1.03.357
consent | that ever hector and achilles meet, 1.03.362
what glory our achilles shares from hector, 1.03.366
of his eyes, | should he scape hector fair. 1.03.371
ajax draw | the sort to fight with hector; 1.03.375
hector shall have a great catch, and /'a knock 2.01. 99 P
that hector, by the /fift hour of the sun, 2.01.122
hector, what say you to't? 2.02. 7
than hector is. 2.02. 14
why, brother hector, | we may not think the 2.02.118
but, worthy hector, | she is a theme of honor 2.02.198
for i presume brave hector would not lose | so 2.02.203
hector, deiphobus, helenus, antenor, and all the 3.01.135 P
i must woo you | to help unarm our hector. 3.01.150
all the island kings — disarm great hector. 3.01.154
withal bring word if hector will to–morrow | be 3.03. 34
much | to throw down hector than polyxena. 3.03.208
shall ajax fight with hector? 3.03.225
to see great hector in his weeds of peace, | to 3.03.239
he must fight singly to–morrow with hector, and 3.03.248 P
for if hector break not his neck i' th' combat, 3.03.258 P
the /most valorous hector to come unarm'd to my 3.03.275 P
desires you to invite hector to his tent — 3.03.285 P
will be in him when hector has knock'd out his 3.03.302 P
thou blowest for hector. 4.05. 11
hector bade ask. 4.05. 71
which way would hector have it? 4.05. 71
'tis done like hector. 4.05. 73
valor and pride excel themselves in hector, 4.05. 79
in love whereof, half hector stays at home; 4.05. 84
half hector comes to seek | this blended knight, 4.05. 85
manly as hector, but more dangerous, | for 4.05.104
for hector in his blaze of wrath subscribes | to 4.05.105
a second hope, as fairly built as hector. 4.05.109
hector, thou sleep'st, | awake thee! 4.05.114
as hector pleases. 4.05.119
hector would have them fall upon him thus. 4.05.137
i thank thee, hector. 4.05.138
a thought of added honor torn from hector. 4.05.145
doth long to see unarm'd the valiant hector. 4.05.153
from heart of very heart, great hector, welcome. 4.05.171
most gentle and most valiant hector, welcome! 4.05.227
now, hector, i have fed mine eyes on thee; 4.05.231
i have with exact view perus'd thee, hector, 4.05.232
you may have every day enough of hector, | if 4.05.263
dost thou entreat me, hector? 4.05.268
welcome, brave hector, welcome, princes all. 5.01. 70
diomed, | keep hector company an hour or two. 5.01. 81
good night, great hector. 5.01. 83
rather leave to see hector than not to dog him. 5.01. 95 P
hector, by this, is arming him in troy; 5.02.183
where is my brother hector? 5.03. 7
unarm, sweet hector. 5.03. 25
fool's play, by heaven, hector. 5.03. 43
hector, then 'tis wars. 5.03. 49
come, hector, come, go back. 5.03. 62
o, farewell, dear hector! 5.03. 80
antics, one another meet, | and all cry, hector! 5.03. 87
o hector! 5.03. 87
hector, i take my leave. 5.03. 89
and chipp'd, come to him, | crying on hector. 5.05. 35
where is this hector? 5.05. 44
hector, where's hector? 5.05. 47
hector, where's hector? 5.05. 47
i will none but hector. 5.05. 47
now do i see thee, ha! have at thee, hector! 5.06. 13
and when i have the bloody hector found, 5.07. 4
eye, | it is decreed hector the great must die. 5.07. 8
look, hector, how the sun begins to set, | how 5.08. 5
"achilles hath the mighty hector slain!" 5.08. 14
it be, | great hector was as good a man as he. 5.09. 6
starve we out the night — | hector is slain. 5.10. 3
hector! the gods forbid! 5.10. 3
hector is gone. 5.10. 14
when she did suckle hector, look'd not lovelier COR 1.03. 41
wert thou the hector | that was the whip of your 1.08. 11
when their brave hope, bold hector, march'd to LUC 1430
here manly hector faints, here troilus sounds, 1486

/HECTOR'S 1 FR 0.0001 REL FR 1 V 0 P
/us /address /to /tend /on /hector's /heels. TRO 4.04.146

HECTOR'S 23 FR 0.0026 REL FR 19 V 4 P
his leg is too big for hector's. LLL 5.02.639
ay, and hector's a greyhound. 5.02.659
weep what it foresaw | in hector's wrath. TRO 1.02. 11
hector's a gallant man. 1.02. 39
and his helm more hack'd than hector's, and how 1.02.233 P
and the great hector's sword had lack'd a master 1.03. 76
that was a man | when hector's grandsire suck'd. 1.03.292
find hector's purpose | pointing on him. 1.03.330
hector's opinion | is this in way of truth; 2.02.188

as if his foot were on brave hector's breast 3.03.140
sing, | "great hector's sister did achilles win, 3.03.212
hark, hector's trumpet! 4.04.140
this ajax is half made of hector's blood, | in 4.05. 83
breach whereout | hector's great spirit flew. 4.05.246
as hector's leisure and your bounties shall 4.05.273
hector's dead! 5.03. 87
art thou for hector's match? 5.04. 26
to close the day up, hector's life is done. 5.08. 8
achilles! achilles! hector's slain! achilles! 5.09. 3
the bruit is, hector's slain, and by achilles. 5.09. 4
go in to troy and say /there, "hector's dead!" 5.10. 17
than hector's forehead when it spit forth blood COR 1.03. 42
and kneel, sweet boy, the roman hector's hope, TIT 4.01. 88
HECTORS 2 FR 0.0002 REL FR 2 V 0 P
there is a thousand hectors in the field: TRO 5.05. 19
you have shown all hectors. ANT 4.08. 7
/HECUBA 1 FR 0.0001 REL FR 1 V 0 P
what's hecuba to him, or he to /hecuba, | that HAM 2.02.559
HECUBA 14 FR 0.0015 REL FR 12 V 2 P
queen hecuba and helen. TRO 1.02. 1
queen hecuba laugh'd that her eyes ran o'er. 1.02.142 P
here is a letter from queen hecuba, | a token 5.01. 39
my retire, | not priamus and hecuba on knees, 5.03. 54
how hecuba cries out! 5.03. 83
who shall tell priam so, or hecuba? 5.10. 15
the breasts of hecuba, | when she did suckle COR 1.03. 40
and i have read that hecuba of troy | ran mad TIT 4.01. 20
say on, come to hecuba. HAM 2.02.501 P
for hecuba! 2.02.558
what's hecuba to him, or he to /hecuba, | that 2.02.559
all curses madded hecuba gave the greeks, | and CYM 4.02.313
dwell'd, | till she despairing hecuba beheld, LUC 1447
"lo here weeps hecuba, here priam dies, | here 1485
/HE'D 1 FR 0.0001 REL FR 1 V 0 P
/and /bellowed /out | /as /he'd /burst /heaven, LR 5.03.214
HE'D 3 FR 0.0003 REL FR 2 V 1 P
he'd sow't with nettle-seed. TMP 2.01.145
had been a man's tailor, he'd 'a' prick'd you. 2H4 3.02.153 P
to show his sorrow, he'd correct himself; PER 1.03. 22
HEDG'D 2 FR 0.0002 REL FR 2 V 0 P
and hedg'd me by his wit to yield myself | his MV 2.01. 18
even till that england, hedg'd in with the main, JN 2.01. 26
/HEDGE 1 FR 0.0001 REL FR 1 V 0 P
or /hedge aside from the direct forthright, TRO 3.03.158
HEDGE 13 FR 0.0014 REL FR 6 V 7 P
am fain to shuffle, to hedge, and to lurch; WIV 2.02. 25 P
be a canker in a hedge than a rose in his grace, ADO 1.03. 27 P
the white sheet bleaching on the hedge, | with WT 4.03. 5
i will but look upon the hedge and follow you. 4.04.826 P
sirrah jack, thy horse stands behind the hedge; 1H4 2.02. 71 P
one, they'll find linen enough on every hedge. 4.02. 48 P
honorable, and there was he born, under a hedge; 2H6 4.02. 51 P
nay, this shall not hedge us out, we'll hear you TRO 3.01. 60 P
you forget yourself | to hedge me in. JC 4.03. 30
there's such divinity doth hedge a king | that HAM 4.05.124
deign | the roughest berry on the rudest hedge; ANT 1.04. 64
face the lion walk'd along | behind some hedge, VEN 1094
and scarce the herd gone to the hedge for shade, PP 6. 2
HEDGE–BORN 1 FR 0.0001 REL FR 1 V 0 P
like a hedge–born swain | that doth presume to 1H6 4.01. 43
HEDGE–CORNER 2 FR 0.0002 REL FR 1 V 1 P
how silver made it good | at the hedge–corner, SHR in.1. 20
can come no other way but by this hedge–corner. AWW 4.01. 2 P
HEDGEHOG 1 FR 0.0001 REL FR 1 V 0 P
dost grant me, hedgehog? R3 1.02.102
HEDGEHOGS 2 FR 0.0002 REL FR 2 V 0 P
then like hedgehogs which | lie tumbling in my TMP 2.02. 10
thorny hedgehogs, be not seen, | newts and MND 2.02. 10
HEDGE–PIG 1 FR 0.0001 REL FR 1 V 0 P
thrice, and once the hedge–pig whin'd. MAC 4.01. 2
HEDGE–PRIEST 1 FR 0.0001 REL FR 0 V 1 P
the braggart, the hedge–priest, the fool, and LLL 5.02.542 P
HEDGES 5 FR 0.0005 REL FR 5 V 0 P
her fruit–trees all unprun'd, her hedges ruin'd, R2 3.04. 45
her hedges even–pleach'd, | like prisoners H5 5.02. 42
all our vineyards, fallows, meads, and hedges, 5.02. 54
stead whereof sharp stakes pluck'd out of hedges 1H6 1.01.117
him, how he coasts | and hedges his own way. H8 3.02. 39
HEDGE–SPARROW 1 FR 0.0001 REL FR 1 V 0 P
"the hedge–sparrow fed the cuckoo so long, LR 1.04.215
HEED 57 FR 0.0064 REL FR 40 V 17 P
you | must be so too, if heed me; TMP 2.01.220
therefore take heed, | as hymen's lamps shall 4.01. 22
take heed, have open eye, for thieves do foot by WIV 2.01.122
take heed, ere summer comes or cuckoo–birds do 2.01.123
the warrant's for yourself; take heed to't. MM 5.01. 83
and teach your ears to list me with more heed. ERR 4.01.101
who dazzling so, that eye shall be his heed, LLL 1.01. 82
take heed the queen come not within his sight; MND 2.01. 19
take heed, honest launcelot, take heed, honest MV 2.02. 7 P
honest launcelot, take heed, honest /gobbo," or, 2.02. 7 P
"hic steterat priami," take heed he hear us not, SHR 3.01. 44 P
take heed, signior baptista, lest you be 5.01. 98 P
those girls of italy, take heed of them. AWW 2.01. 19
well, diana, take heed of this french earl. 3.05. 11 P
to take heed of the allurement of one count 4.03.214 P
alas the day, take heed of him! 2H4 2.01. 13 P
on, therefore take heed what guests you receive. 2.04. 93 P
therefore let men take heed of their company. 5.01. 77 P
therefore take heed how you impawn our person, H5 1.02. 21
we charge you, in the name of god, take heed; 1.02. 23
once more, with better heed | to re–survey them, 5.02. 80
take heed, be wary how you place your words, 1H6 3.02. 3
hume, if you take not heed, you shall go near 2H6 1.02.102
take heed, my lord, the welfare of us all 3.01. 80
take heed, lest by your heat you burn yourselves 5.01.160
o buckingham, take heed of yonder dog! R3 1.03.288
take heed; 1.04.199
take heed you dally not before your king, | lest 2.01. 12
my good lords both, with all the heed i can. 3.01.187
take good heed | you charge not in your spleen a H8 1.02.173
i say, take heed; 1.02.175
give heed to't: 2.04.170
take heed, for heaven's sake take heed, lest at 3.01.110
for heaven's sake take heed, lest at once | the 3.01.110
a heed | was in his countenance. 3.02. 80
let them take heed of troilus; TRO 1.02. 58 P
take heed, the quarrel's most ominous to us. 5.07. 20 P
have you with heed perused | what i have written COR 5.06. 61
take heed, take heed, for such die miserable. ROM 3.03.145
take heed, take heed, for such die miserable. 3.03.145
i take no heed of thee; TIM 1.02. 35 P
is past depth | to those that, without heed, do 3.05. 13
but there's no heed to be taken of them; JC 1.02.273 P
take heed of cassius; 2.03. 1 P
rank | as may dishonor him, take heed of that, HAM 2.01. 21
i am sorry that with better heed and judgment 2.01.108
take heed, sirrah — the whip. LR 1.04.110 P
take heed o' th' foul fiend. 3.04. 80 P
and take heed on't, | make it a darling like OTH 3.04. 65
sweet soul, take heed, | take heed of perjury, 5.02. 50
take heed of perjury, thou art on thy death–bed. 5.02. 51
take heed you fall not. ANT 2.07.129
but take heed to your kindness though! TNK 2.02.125
not made in passion neither, but good heed. 3.06.232
and take heed, as you are gentlemen, this 3.06.303
take heed: 4.03. 34 P
take heed, dear heart, of this large privilege, SON 95.13
HEEDED 1 FR 0.0001 REL FR 1 V 0 P
take thou no care, it shall be heeded. ANT 5.02.268
HEEDFUL 7 FR 0.0008 REL FR 7 V 0 P
whilst i had been like heedful of the other. ERR 1.01. 82
and the heedful slave | is wand'red forth, in 2.02. 2
be heedful. JN 4.01. 5
where fame, late ent'ring at his heedful ears, 3H6 3.03. 63
give him heedful note, | for i mine eyes will HAM 3.02. 84
so heedful fear | is almost chok'd by unresisted LUC 281
but will is deaf and hears no heedful friends; 495
HEEDFULL'ST 1 FR 0.0001 REL FR 1 V 0 P
me | in heedfull'st reservation to bestow them, AWW 1.03.225
HEEDFULLY 4 FR 0.0004 REL FR 4 V 0 P
sir, most heedfully. TMP 1.02. 78
unheedful vows may heedfully be broken, | and he TGV 2.06. 11
and wretched fools' secrets heedfully o'er–eye. LLL 4.03. 78
heedfully doth view | the sight which makes LUC 454
HEEDLESS 2 FR 0.0002 REL FR 2 V 0 P
you heedless joltheads and unmanner'd slaves! SHR 4.01.166
o, negligent and heedless discipline! 1H6 4.02. 44
HEEL 16 FR 0.0018 REL FR 10 V 6 P
rapier, and come after my heel to the court. WIV 1.04. 60 P
of a peck, hilt to point, heel to head; 3.05.112 P
my shoulder to my heel with no greater a run but SHR 4.01. 15 P
gabr'el's pumps were all unpink'd i' th' heel; 4.01.133
began, | on the catastrophe and heel of pastime, AWW 1.02. 57
what maids lack from head to heel. WT 4.04.227
thou use to beat me, i will begin at thy heel, TRO 2.01. 48 P
nor heel the high lavolt, nor sweeten talk, 4.04. 86
when well–apparell'd april on the heel | of ROM 1.02. 27
by my heel, i care not. 3.01. 36 P
one woe doth tread upon another's heel, | so HAM 4.07.163
peasant comes so near the heel of the courtier, 5.01.141 P
consuls, at thy heel | did famine follow, whom ANT 1.04. 58
at heel of that, defy him. 2.02.157
who ne'er wore rowel | nor iron on his heel! CYM 4.04. 40
took heel to do't, | and yet died too! 5.03. 67
/HEELS 2 FR 0.0002 REL FR 2 V 0 P
/after /th' /admired /heels /of /bullingbrook, 2H4 1.03.105
/us /address /to /tend /on /hector's /heels. TRO 4.04.146
HEELS 72 FR 0.0081 REL FR 44 V 28 P
close at the heels of her virtues. TGV 3.01.322 P
well, sirs, i am almost out at heels. WIV 1.03. 31 P
follow my heels, rugby. 1.04.125 P
sir actaeon he, with ringwood at thy heels — 2.01.118
come at my heels, jack rugby. 2.03. 98 P
lead mine eyes, or eye your master's heels? 3.02. 4 P
with half windsor at his heels, to search for 3.03.114 P
and at his heels a rabble of his companions, 3.05. 75 P
nay, and you will not, sir, i'll take my heels. ERR 1.02. 94
you would keep from my heels, and beware of an 3.01. 18
and at her heels a huge infectious troop | of 5.01. 81
ye light o' love with your heels! ADO 3.04. 47 P
i scorn that with my heels. 3.04. 51 P
may lighten our own hearts and our wives' heels. 5.04.119 P
do not run, scorn running with thy heels." MV 2.02. 9 P
my heels are at your commandement, i will run. 2.02. 31 P
that tripp'd up the wrastler's heels, and your AYL 3.02.213 P
i think 'twas made of atalanta's heels. 3.02.277 P
where death and danger dogs the heels of worth. AWW 3.04. 15
no matter, his heels have deserv'd it, in 4.03.103 P
detraction at your heels than fortunes before TN 2.05.137 P
and looks pale, as if a bear were at his heels. 3.04.295 P
away from his father with his clog at his heels. WT 4.04.679 P
with many hundreds treading on his heels; JN 4.02.149
be mercury, set feathers to thy heels, | and fly 4.02.174
the dolphin rages at our very heels. 5.07. 80
straight shall dog them at the heels. R2 5.03.139
show it a fair pair of heels and run from it? 1H4 2.04. 48 P
hang me up by the heels for a rabbit–sucker or a 2.04.437 P
to dog his heels and curtsy at his frowns, | to 3.02.127
him | even at the heels in golden multitudes. 4.03. 73
and bending forward strook his armed heels 2H4 1.01. 44
to be worn in my cap than to wait at my heels. 1.02. 16 P
to punish you by the heels would amend the 1.02.123 P
back unarm'd, | they baying him at the heels. 1.03. 80
assume the port of mars, and at his heels H5 pr 6
with winged heels, as english mercuries. 2.pr. 7
saying our grace is only in our heels, | and 3.05. 34
yerk out their armed heels at their dead masters 4.07. 80
follow fluellen closely at the heels. 4.07.171
with the plebeians swarming at their heels, | go 5.pr. 27
hearts i'll stamp out with my horse's heels, 1H6 1.04.108
be dragg'd at my horse heels till i do come to 2H6 4.03. 13 P
treasons, makes me betake me to my heels. 4.08. 64 P
hence will i drag thee headlong by the heels 4.10. 80
death and destruction dogs thee at thy heels; R3 4.01. 39
i'll lay ye all | by th' heels, and suddenly; H8 5.03. 79
the very wings of reason to his heels | and fly TRO 2.02. 44
how ugly night comes breathing at his heels; 5.08. 6
following the fliers at the very heels, | with COR 1.04. 49
will (too late) | tie leaden pounds to 's heels. 3.01.312
death on the wheel, or at wild horses' heels, 3.02. 2
and pull her out of acheron by the heels. TIT 4.03. 45
tickle the senseless rushes with their heels. ROM 1.04. 36
upon the heels of my presentment, sir. TIM 1.01. 27
i will fly, like a dog, the heels a' th' ass. 1.01.272 P
page thy heels | and skip when thou point'st out 4.03.224
the throng that follows caesar at the heels, JC 2.04. 34
and we will grace his heels | with the most 3.01.120
these skipping kerns to trust their heels, | but MAC 1.02. 30
we cours'd him at the heels, and had a purpose 1.06. 21
is there no sequel at the heels of this mother's HAM 3.02.329 P
trip him, that his heels may kick at heaven, 3.03. 93
a grass–green turf, | at his heels a stone." 4.05. 32
if a man's brains were in 's heels, were't not LR 1.05. 8 P
is it two days since i tripp'd up thy heels, and 2.02. 30 P
a good man's fortune may grow out at heels. 2.02.157
this very night at one another's heels; OTH 1.02. 42
thee, would have still | followed thy heels. ANT 4.05. 6
the hearts | that /spannell'd me at heels, to 4.12. 21
sir, | i'll follow you at heels; TNK 1.01.221
beating his kind embracements with her heels. VEN 312
HEFTS 1 FR 0.0001 REL FR 1 V 0 P
his gorge, his sides, | with violent hefts. WT 2.01. 45
HEIFER *(also heckfer, etc.)*
HEIFER 1 FR 0.0001 REL FR 1 V 0 P
who finds the heifer dead and bleeding fresh, 2H6 3.02.188
HEIFER'S 1 FR 0.0001 REL FR 1 V 0 P
as fox to lamb, or wolf to heifer's calf, | pard TRO 3.02.193
/HEIGH 1 FR 0.0001 REL FR 1 V 0 P
with heigh, /with /heigh, the thrush and the jay WT 4.03. 10
HEIGH 6 FR 0.0006 REL FR 3 V 3 P
heigh, my hearts! TMP 1.01. 5 P
to peer, | with heigh, the doxy over the dale! WT 4.03. 2
with heigh, /with /heigh, the thrush and the jay 4.03. 10
heigh, heigh! 1H4 2.04.487 P
heigh, heigh! 2.04.487 P
ha, boys, heigh for the weavers! TNK 2.03. 49
HEIGH–HO 11 FR 0.0012 REL FR 6 V 5 P
in a corner and cry "heigh–ho for a husband!" ADO 2.01.320 P
heigh–ho! 3.04. 54 P
heigh–ho! MND 4.01.202 P
heigh–ho, sing heigh–ho! AYL 2.07.180
heigh–ho, sing heigh–ho! 2.07.180
/then heigh–ho, the holly! 2.07.182
heigh–ho, sing, etc. 2.07.190
heigh–ho! 4.03.168 P
heigh–ho! 1H4 2.01. 1 P
with heigh–ho, the wind and the rain — | must LR 3.02. 75
heigh–ho! TNK 3.03. 42
HEIGHT *(also heighth, highth)*
HEIGHT 34 FR 0.0038 REL FR 29 V 5 P
therefore i know she is about my height. TGV 4.04.164
and in the height of this bath (when i was more WIV 3.05.118 P
and punish them to your height of pleasure. MM 5.01.240
me, | even in the strength and height of injury: ERR 5.01.200
is 'a not approv'd in the height a villain, that ADO 4.01.301 P
she hath urg'd her height, | and with her MND 3.02.291
her height, forsooth, she hath prevail'd with 3.02.293
and bid the main flood bate his usual height; MV 4.01. 72
i to–morrow be at the height of heart–heaviness, AYL 5.02. 46 P
now put you to the height of your breeding. AWW 2.02. 2 P
or with pale beggar–fear impeach my height R2 1.01.189
as with the tide swell'd up unto his height, 2H4 2.03. 63
and bend up every spirit | to his full height. H5 3.01. 17
grave, | or flourish to the height of my degree. 1H6 2.04.111
i fear our happiness is at the height. R3 1.03. 41
by him that rais'd me to this careful height 1.03. 82
seduc'd the pitch and height of his degree | to 3.07.188
unto the dignity and height of fortune, | the 4.04.244
and richard falls in height of all his pride! 5.03.176
by day and night, | he's traitor to th' height. H8 1.02.214
whose height commands as subject all the vale, TRO 1.02. 3
patroclus, let us feast him to the height. 5.01. 3
but to your wishes' height advance you both. TIT 2.01.125
my grief was at the height before thou cam'st, 3.01. 70
so, | captives, to be advanced to this height? 4.02. 34
urge it no more | on height of our displeasure. TIM 3.05. 86
we, at the height, are ready to decline. JC 4.03.217
our achievements, though perform'd at height, HAM 1.04. 21
by th' height, the lowness, or the mean, if ANT 2.07. 19
even in the height and pride of all his glory, PER 2.04. 6
color of her hair, complexion, height, her age, 4.02. 58 P
permit the sun to climb | his wonted height, yet LUC 776
vaunt in their youthful sap, at height decrease, SON 15. 7
rhyme, | exceeded by the height of happier men. 32. 8
HEIGHTEN'D 1 FR 0.0001 REL FR 1 V 0 P
who being so heighten'd, | he watered his new COR 5.06. 21
HEIGHTH *(also height, highth)*
HEIGHTH 2 FR 0.0002 REL FR 2 V 0 P
the heighth, the crest, or crest unto the crest, JN 4.03. 46
leaving the fight in heighth, flies after her. ANT 3.10. 20
/HEINOUS 1 FR 0.0001 REL FR 1 V 0 P
/shouldst /thou /find /one /heinous /article, R2 4.01.233
HEINOUS 18 FR 0.0020 REL FR 18 V 0 P
what heinous sin is it in me | to be ashamed to MV 2.03. 16
which harm within itself so heinous is | as it JN 3.01. 40
you hold too heinous a respect of grief. 3.04. 90
the image of a wicked heinous fault | lives in 4.02. 71
a jest, | exampled by this heinous spectacle. 4.03. 56
climate souls refin'd | should show so heinous, R2 4.01.131
if on the first, how heinous e'er it be, | to 5.03. 34
o heinous, strong, and bold conspiracy! 5.03. 59
if thou delight to view thy heinous deeds, R3 1.02. 53
which rome reputes to be a heinous sin, | yield TIT 1.01.448
i do remit these young men's heinous faults. 1.01.484
sons of tamora | performers of this heinous, 4.01. 80
art thou not sorry for these heinous deeds? 5.01.123
to join with him and right his heinous wrongs. 5.02. 4
appear to prove upon thy person | thy heinous, LR 5.03. 92
in store, | due to this heinous capital offense, PER 2.04. 5
thy heinous hours wait on them as their pages. LUC 910
but i forbid thee one most heinous crime, | o, SON 19. 8
HEINOUSLY 1 FR 0.0001 REL FR 0 V 1 P
i am heinously unprovided. 1H4 3.03.189 P
/HEIR 2 FR 0.0002 REL FR 2 V 0 P
/son /and /heir /to /th' /earl /of /arundel, R2 2.01.280
one nickname for her purblind son and /heir, ROM 2.01. 12
HEIR 109 FR 0.0123 REL FR 98 V 11 P
and his only heir | and princess no worse issued TMP 1.02. 58
o thou mine heir | of naples and of milan, what 2.01.112
then tell me, | who's the next heir of naples? 2.01.245

's queen of tunis, | so is she heir of naples; 2.01.256
/an heir, and /near allied unto the duke. TGV 4.01. 47
arm'd and reverted, making war against her heir. ERR 3.02.124 P
no child but hero, she's his only heir. ADO 1.01.295
one hero, the daughter and heir of leonato. 1.03. 54 P
dead, | and she alone is heir to both of us. 5.01.290
between lord perigort and the beauteous heir LLL 2.01. 41
the heir of alanson, /katherine her name. 2.01.195
not offended, | she is an heir of falconbridge. 2.01.205
gave hector a gift, the heir of ilion; 5.02.652
and truly, when he dies, thou shalt be his heir; AYL 1.02. 19 P
that calling | to be adopted heir to frederick. 1.02.234
no, let my father seek another heir. 1.03. 99
me, | left soly heir to all his lands and goods, SHR 2.01.117
i am my father's heir and only son. 2.01.364
is mine only son, and heir to the lands of me, 5.01. 85 P
fair, | in these to nature she's immediate heir; AWW 2.03.132
and the king shall live without an heir, if that WT 3.02.135 P
thou, a sceptre's heir, | that thus affects a 4.04.419
wipe me, father, i | am heir to my affection. 4.04.481
that king leontes shall not have an heir | till 5.01. 39
not for issue, | the crown will find an heir. 5.01. 47
has the king found his heir? 5.02. 29 P
the son and heir to that same faulconbridge. JN 1.01. 56
is that the elder, and art thou the heir? 1.01. 57
my mother's son did get your father's heir; 1.01.128
your father's heir must have your father's land. 1.01.129
and, to his shape, were heir to all this land, 1.01.144
were he my brother, nay, my kingdom's heir, | as R2 1.01.116
did not the one deserve to have an heir? 2.01.193
is not his heir a well–deserving son? 2.01.194
woe, | and bullingbrook my sorrow's dismal heir. 2.02. 63
though you are old enough to be my heir. 3.03.205
who with willing soul | adopts /thee heir, and 4.01.109
not here apparent that thou art heir apparent — 1H4 1.02. 58 P
my brother edmund mortimer | heir to the crown? 1.03.157
and heir from heir shall hold his quarrel up 2H4 4.02. 48
and heir from heir shall hold his quarrel up 4.02. 48
send to prison | th' immediate heir of england! 5.02. 71
did, as heir general, being descended | of H5 1.02. 66
sole heir male | of the true line and stock of 1.02. 70
himself as th' heir to th' lady lingare, 1.02. 74
tenth, | who was sole heir to the usurper capet, 1.02. 78
you are their heir, you sit upon their throne; 1.02.117
the first–begotten and the lawful heir | of 1H6 2.05. 65
remov'd, | leaving no heir begotten of his body) 2.05. 72
they labored to plant the rightful heir, | i 2.05. 80
thou art my heir; 2.05. 96
the duke of york was rightful heir to the crown. 2H6 1.03. 27 P
of york say he was rightful heir to the crown? 1.03. 29 P
york | was rightful heir unto the english crown 1.03.184
the eldest son and heir of john of gaunt, 2.02. 22
for richard, the first son's heir, being dead, 2.02. 31
but william of hatfield died without an heir. 2.02. 33
anne, | my mother, being heir unto the crown, 2.02. 44
she was heir | to roger earl of march, who was 2.02. 47
as next the king he was successive heir, | and 3.01. 49
reign, | for i am rightful heir unto the crown. 4.02.131
the rightful heir to england's royal seat. 5.01.178
tell me, may not a king adopt an heir? 3H6 1.01.135
whose heir my father was, and i am his. 1.01.140
but that the next heir should succeed and reign. 1.01.146
than have made that savage duke thine heir, 1.01.224
now you are heir, therefore enjoy it now. 1.02. 12
chair, | and this is he was his adopted heir. 1.04. 98
i was adopted heir by his consent. 2.02. 88
with this my son, prince edward, henry's heir, 3.03. 31
to have the heir of the lord hungerford. 4.01. 48
to give the heir and daughter of lord scales 4.01. 52
or else you would not have bestow'd the heir 4.01. 56
edward's fruit, true heir to th' english crown. 4.04. 24
to save, at least, the heir of edward's right; 4.04. 32
the view, | and that be heir to his unhappiness! R3 1.02. 25
he would make his son | heir to the crown — 3.05. 78
what heir of york is there alive but we? 4.04.471
and who is england's king but great york's heir? 4.04.472
(well worthy the best heir o' th' world) should H8 2.04.196
to the gladding of | your highness with an heir! 5.01. 72
her ashes new create another heir | as great in 5.04. 41
many an heir | of these fair edifices 'fore my COR 4.04. 2
here within as if he were son and heir to mars; 4.05.192 P
fall of either | makes the survivor heir of all. 5.06. 18
that touches this my first–born son and heir! TIT 4.02. 92
and be received for the emperor's heir, | and 4.02.158
the son and heir of old tiberio. ROM 1.05.129
lie, | and young affection gapes to be his heir; 2.pr. 2
death is my son–in–law, death is my heir, | my 4.05. 38
up | to see thy son and heir now /early down. 5.03.209
and my estate deserves an heir more rais'd TIM 1.01.119
mine heir from forth the beggars of the world, 1.01.138
thousand natural shocks | that flesh is heir to; HAM 3.01. 62
pandar, and the son and heir of a mungril bitch; LR 2.02. 22 P
where each second | stood heir to th' first. OTH 1.01. 38
for even her folly help'd her to an heir. 2.01.137
his daughter, and the heir of 's kingdom (whom CYM 1.01. 4
the heir of cymbeline and britain, who | the 3.03. 87
praise o' th' world, | as great sicilius' heir. 5.04. 51
i am | the heir of his reward, which i will add 5.05. 13
took a peer, | who died and left a female heir, PER 1.ch. 22
one sorrow never comes but brings an heir | that 1.04. 63
the heir of kingdoms, and another /life | to 5.01.207
i am your heir, and you are mine; TNK 2.02. 83
are you his heir? 2.05. 8
his tender heir might bear his memory: SON 1. 4
be death's conquest and make worms thine heir. 6.14
but now is black beauty's successive heir, | and 127. 3

HEIR–APPARENT 5 FR 0.0005 REL FR 2 V 3 P
hang thyself in thine own heir–apparent garters! 1H4 2.02. 43 P
was it for me to kill the heir–apparent? 2.04.269 P
thou being heir–apparent, could the world pick 2.04.366 P
blood, | and heir–apparent to the english crown. 2H6 1.01.152
claps can sound, | "our heir–apparent is a king! PER 3.ch. 37

HEIRLESS 1 FR 0.0001 REL FR 1 V 0 P
so much | that heirless it hath made my kingdom, WT 5.01. 10

HEIRS' 1 FR 0.0001 REL FR 1 V 0 P
for this is thine and not king henry's heirs'. 3H6 1.01. 27

HEIRS 23 FR 0.0026 REL FR 23 V 0 P
of night, | you orphan heirs of fixed destiny, WIV 5.05. 39
keen edge, | and make us heirs of all eternity. LLL 1.01. 7
marry them to your heirs! MV 4.01. 94
these your contracted | heirs of your kingdoms, WT 5.03. 6
us, our lives, our children, and our heirs. R2 2.01.245
gave him their heirs as pages, followed him 1H4 4.03. 72
revives two greater in the heirs of life; 2H4 4.01.198
unfather'd heirs and loathly births of nature. 4.04.122
'longs | to him and to his heirs, namely, the H5 2.04. 81
confirm the crown to me and to mine heirs, | and 3H6 1.01.172
the crown to thee and to thine heirs for ever, 1.01.195
to entail him and his heirs unto the crown, 1.01.235
g | of edward's heirs the murtherer shall be. R3 1.01. 40
to bar my master's heirs in true descent — 3.02. 54
the wronged heirs of york do pray for thee. 5.03.137
and in record left them the heirs of shame. 5.03.335
and let their heirs (god, if thy will be so) 5.05. 32
'neither the king nor 's heirs | (tell you the H8 1.02.168
'tis good you know not that you are his heirs, JC 3.02.145
and to your heirs for ever — common pleasures, 3.02.250
the circle of the ptolomies for her heirs, | now ANT 3.12. 18
those rich–left heirs that let their fathers lie CYM 4.02.226
careless heirs | may the two latter darken and PER 3.02. 28

HE'LD 8 FR 0.0009 REL FR 7 V 1 P
on twenty bloody blocks, he'ld yield them up, MM 2.04.181
but look'd big and spit at him, he'ld have run. WT 4.03.106 P
what then? | he'ld make an end of thy posterity. COR 4.02. 26
when all's spent, he'ld be cross'd then, and he TIM 1.02.162
that horrid act | of the divorce he'ld make. CYM 2.01. 62
he'ld lay the future open. 3.02. 29
with his own single hand he'ld take us in, 4.02.121
might break out and swear | he'ld fetch us in; 4.02.141

HELD *(also hild)*

HELD 89 FR 0.0100 REL FR 81 V 8 P
amends, with which | i fear a madness held me. TMP 5.01.116
wherewith my brother held you in the cloister? TGV 1.03. 2
but neither bended knees, pure hands held up, 3.01.231
i was, and held me glad of such a doom. 4.01. 32
he should be a cuckold) held his hand. WIV 3.05.105 P
where there was no proportion held in love. 5.05.222
and held in idle price to haunt assemblies MM 1.03. 9
file of the subject held the duke to be wise. 3.02.136 P
and i, to blame, have held him here too long. ERR 4.01. 47
how long hath this possession held the man? 5.01. 44
what secret hath held you here, that you ADO 1.01.204 P
yourself, held precious in the world's esteem, LLL 2.01. 4
voice, | the other must be held the worthier. MND 1.01. 55
modesty | to urge the thing held as a ceremony? MV 5.01.206
even he that had held up the very life | of my 5.01.214
which i held my duty speedily to acquaint you AWW 1.03.118 P
such pestiferous reports of men very nobly held, 4.03.306 P
you, when i have held familiarity with fresher 5.02. 3 P
well held out, i' faith! TN 4.01. 5 P
sir, to have held my peace until | you had drawn WT 1.02. 28
thou dost make possible things not so held, 1.02.139
as if you held a brow of much distraction. 1.02.149
and with my hand at midnight held your head; JN 4.01. 45
deed, which both our tongues held vild to name. 4.02.241
castle, which they say is held | by bushy, bagot R2 2.03.164
and told him of those triumphs held at oxford. 5.03. 14
hath held his current and defil'd himself! 5.03. 63
and 'twixt his finger and his thumb he held | a 1H4 1.03. 37
he held me last night at least nine hours | in 3.01.154
and the contrarious winds that held the king 5.01. 52
is held from falling with so weak a wind | that 2H4 4.05. 99
crown and kingdom, indirectly held | from him, H5 2.04. 94
and say withal, i think he held the right. 1H6 2.04. 38
false, | the argument you held was wrong in you; 2.04. 57
thou not kiss'd thy hand and held my stirrup? 2H6 4.01. 53
so will the queen, that living held him dear. 4.01.147
which held thee dearly as his soul's redemption, 3H6 2.01.102
for all the rest is held at such a rate | as 2.02. 51
courtesy, | i must be held a rancorous enemy. R3 1.03. 50
and the nobility | held in contempt, while great 1.03. 79
which hitherto hath held /my eyes from rest; 4.01. 81
hath he so long held out with me untir'd, | and 4.02. 44
and, by'r lady, | held current music too. H8 1.03. 47
yes, but it held not; 2.01.149
and held for certain | the king will venture at 2.01.155
was he not held a learned man? 2.02.123
held a late court at dunstable — six miles off 4.01. 27
again | to york–place, where the feast is held. 4.01. 94
is held no great good lover of the archbishop's, 4.01.104
for an old aunt whom the greeks held captive, TRO 2.02. 77
i might have still held off, | and then you 4.02. 17
better be held nor more attain'd than by | a COR 1.01.265
spies of the volsces | held me in chase, that i 1.06. 19
learn how 'tis held, and what they are that must 1.10. 28
people in what hatred | he still hath held them; 2.01.246
it is held | that valor is the chiefest virtue, 2.02. 83
as cause had call'd you up, have held him to; 2.03.194
to grant may never | be held by you denials. 5.03. 81
upright he held it, lords, that held it last. TIT 1.01.200
upright he held it, lords, that held it last. 1.01.200
whom thou in triumph long | hast prisoner held, 2.01. 15
in bootless prayer have they been held up, | and 3.01. 75
being held a foe, he may not have access | to ROM 2.pr. 9
it may be thought we held him carelessly, 3.04. 25
as thine is now, held with a brace of harlots. TIM 4.03. 80
held up his left hand, which did flame and burn JC 1.03. 16
quite from the main opinion he held once | of 2.01.196
you know that i held epicurus strong, | and his 5.01. 76
i held the sword, and he did run on it. 5.05. 65
that it was he in the times past which held you MAC 3.01. 76
wherein the spirit held his wont to walk. HAM 1.04. 6
he took me by the wrist, and held me hard, 2.01. 84
my life i never held but as /a pawn | to wage LR 1.01.155
he held them sixpence all too dear, | with that OTH 2.03. 91
i have ever held my cap off to thy fortunes. ANT 2.07. 57
the loyalty well held to fools does make | our 3.13. 42
our force by land | hath nobly held; 3.13.170
birthday, | i had thought t' have held it poor; 3.13.185
that she held the very garment of posthumus in CYM 3.05.134 P
we are held as outlaws. 4.02. 67
a city on whom plenty held full hand, | for PER 1.04. 22
whilest ours was blurted at and held a mawkin 4.03. 34
not to be held ungrateful to her goodness — TNK 4.01. 22
fee, | he held such petty bondage in disdain, VEN 394
her blood, in poor revenge, held it in chase; LUC 1736
held back his sorrow's tide, to make it more; 1789
will be a totter'd weed, of small worth held: SON 2. 4
my body is the frame wherein 'tis held, | and 24. 3
"and long upon these terms i held my city, LC 176

/HELEN 1 FR 0.0001 REL FR 1 V 0 P
/whose /strong /immures | /the /ravish'd /helen, TRO pr 9

HELEN 53 FR 0.0060 REL FR 35 V 18 P
helen, to you our minds we will unfold: MND 1.01.208
and might | to honor helen and to be her knight. 2.02.144
o helen, goddess, nymph, perfect, divine! 3.02.137
and now to helen is it home return'd, | there to 3.02.172
helen, it is not so. 3.02.173
helen, i love thee, by my life, i do! 3.02.251
my lord, fair helen told me of their stealth, 4.01.160
and i, like helen, till the fates me kill. 5.01.197
little helen, farewell. AWW 1.01.188 P
you, madam, that he bid helen come to you. 1.03. 66 P
my gentlewoman i would speak with her — helen, 1.03. 69 P
the business is for helen to come hither. 1.03. 96 P
you know, helen, | i am a mother to you. 1.03.137
yes, helen, you might be my daughter–in–law. 1.03.167
but think you, helen, | if you should tender 1.03.235
why, helen, thou shalt have my leave and love, 1.03.251
give helen this, | and urge her to a present 2.02. 63
mort du vinaigre! is not this helen? 2.03. 44 P
you must not marvel, helen, at my course, 2.05. 58
and ev'ry hair that's on't, helen, that's dead, 5.03. 77
this ring was mine, and, when i gave it helen, 5.03. 83
i am afeard the life of helen, lady, | was 5.03.153
thy doll, and helen of thy noble thoughts, | is 2H4 5.05. 33
helen, the mother of great constantine, | nor 1H6 1.02.142
helen of greece was fairer far than thou, 3H6 2.02.146
kin to me, therefore she's not so fair as helen. TRO 1.01. 75 P
be as fair a' friday as helen is on sunday. 1.01. 76 P
fools on both sides, helen must needs be fair, 1.01. 90
queen hecuba and helen. 1.02. 1
helen was not up, was she? 1.02. 49 P
hector was gone, but helen was not up. 1.02. 50 P
helen herself swore th' other day that troilus, 1.02. 92 P
you, i think helen loves him better than paris. 1.02.107 P
but to prove to you that helen loves him: 1.02.118 P
but to prove to you that helen loves troilus — 1.02.128 P
the white hair that helen spied on troilus' chin 1.02.150 P
and helen so blush'd, and paris so chaf'd, and 1.02.166 P
paris is dirt to him, and i warrant helen, to 1.02.239 P
"deliver helen, and all damage else — | as 2.02. 3
let helen go; 2.02. 17
thousand dismes, | hath been as dear as helen; 2.02. 20
a helen and a woe! 2.02.111
troy burns, or else let helen go. 2.02.112
or sword to draw, | when helen is defended; 2.02.158
or death unfam'd, | where helen is the subject. 2.02.160
if helen then be wife to sparta's king, | as it 2.02.183
to you | in resolution to keep helen still, 2.02.191
no, sir, helen. 3.01. 35 P
sweet helen, i must woo you | to help unarm our 3.01.149
who, in your thoughts, deserves fair helen best, 4.01. 54
me a kiss | when helen is a maid again and his. 4.05. 50
a gipsy, helen and hero hildings and harlots, ROM 2.04. 42 P
who's there? my woman? helen? CYM 2.02. 1

HELENA 25 FR 0.0028 REL FR 23 V 2 P
head, | made love to nedar's daughter, helena, MND 1.01.107
(where i did meet thee once with helena | to do 1.01.166
keep promise, love. look, here comes helena. 1.01.179
god speed fair helena! whither away? 1.01.180
his folly, helena, is no fault of mine. 1.01.200
helena, adieu: 1.01.224
transparent helena, nature shows art, | that 2.02.104
not hermia but helena i love. 2.02.113
the wind, | and helena of athens look thou find. 3.02. 95
of our fairy band, | helena is here at hand, 3.02.111
and now both rivals, to mock helena. 3.02.156
and yours of helena to me bequeath, | whom i do 3.02.166
that would not let him bide — | fair helena! 3.02.187
stay, gentle helena; 3.02.245
my love, my life, my soul, fair helena! 3.02.246
no jest | that i do hate thee and love helena. 3.02.281
be not afraid; she shall not harm thee, helena. 3.02.321
speak not of helena, | take not her part. 3.02.332
right, | of thine or mine, is most in helena. 3.02.337
demetrius is, | this helena, old nedar's helena. 4.01.130
demetrius is, | this helena, old nedar's helena. 4.01.130
them, | fair helena in fancy following me. 4.01.163
and the pleasure of mine eye, | is only helena. 4.01.171
no more of this, helena; AWW 1.01. 52 P
lucio and the lively helena." ROM 1.02. 70 P

HELEN'S 10 FR 0.0011 REL FR 6 V 4 P
sees helen's beauty in a brow of egypt. MND 5.01. 11
nature presently distill'd | helen's cheek, but AYL 3.02.145
be this sweet helen's knell, and now forget her. AWW 5.03. 67
'twas mine, 'twas helen's, | whoever gave it you 5.03.104
hair were not somewhat darker than helen's — TRO 1.01. 42 P
i had as lieve helen's golden tongue had 1.02.105 P
why, this will do helen's heart good now, ha? 1.02.216 P
as will stop the eye of helen's needle, for whom 2.01. 80 P
greece, | for helen's rape the city to destroy, LUC 1369
on helen's cheek all art of beauty set, | and SON 53. 7

HELENUS 8 FR 0.0009 REL FR 1 V 7 P
that's helenus. TRO 1.02.219 P
that's helenus. 1.02.220 P
that's helenus. 1.02.221 P
can helenus fight, uncle? 1.02.222 P
helenus? 1.02.223 P
helenus is a priest. 1.02.225 P
when helenus beholds | a grecian and his sword, 2.02. 42
hector, deiphobus, helenus, antenor, and all the 3.01.135 P

/HELIAS 1 FR 0.0001 REL FR 1 V 0 P
/dardan /and /timbria, /helias, /chetas, /troien TRO pr 16

HELICANE 5 FR 0.0005 REL FR 5 V 0 P
good helicane, that stay'd at home, | not to eat PER 2.ch. 17
follow me then. lord helicane, a word. 2.04. 21
wrong not yourself then, noble helicane; 2.04. 26
live, noble helicane! 2.04. 40
and since lord helicane enjoineth us, | we with 2.04. 55

HELICANUS 14 FR 0.0015 REL FR 14 V 0 P
helicanus, thou | hast mov'd us. PER 1.02. 50
thou speak'st like a physician, helicanus, 1.02. 67
of tyrus on the head | of helicanus would set on 3.ch. 27

old helicanus goes along. 4.04. 13
whom helicanus late | advanc'd in time to great 4.04. 15
where is lord helicanus? 5.01. 1
ho, helicanus! 5.01.180
o helicanus, strike me, honored sir, | give me a 5.01.190
o helicanus, | down on thy knees, thank the holy 5.01.197
mine own, helicanus — | she is not dead at 5.01.214
tell helicanus, my marina, tell him | o'er, 5.01.224
helicanus! 5.01.251
'twas helicanus then. 5.03. 53
in helicanus may you well descry | a figure of 5.03. 91
HELICONS 1 FR 0.0001 REL FR 1 V 0 P
shall dunghill curs confront the helicons? 2H4 5.03.104
HE'LL 124 FR 0.0140 REL FR 90 V 34 P
he'll be hang'd yet, | though every drop of TMP 1.01. 58
when 's god's asleep, he'll rob his bottle. 2.02.151 P
which, when he has a house, he'll deck withal. 3.02. 97
from toe to crown he'll fill our skins with 4.01.233
ay me, he'll find the young man there, and be WIV 1.04. 65 P
for he swears he'll turn me away. 3.03. 32 P
nay, but he'll be here presently. 4.02. 97 P
fie, fie, he'll never come. 4.04. 18 P
well, let it not be doubted but he'll come, 4.04. 44
he'll tell me all his purpose. 4.04. 77
sure he'll come. 4.04. 77
he'll speak like an anthropophaginian unto thee. 4.05. 9 P
benedick too much, but he'll be meet with you, i ADO 1.01. 47 P
do, he'll but break a comparison or two on me, 2.01.146 P
of her love, 'tis very possible he'll scorn it, 2.03.179 P
any heavy weight | that he'll enjoin me to. 5.01.278
our lady help my lord! he'll be forsworn. LLL 2.01. 98
must shoot nearer, or he'll ne'er hit the clout. 4.01.134
he'll sound! 5.02.392
he'll | seem to break loose — take on as you MND 3.02.257
he'll go along o'er the wide world with me; AYL 1.03.132
he'll make a proper man. 3.05.115
he begin once, he'll rail in his rope–tricks. SHR 1.02.112 P
sir, give him head, i know he'll prove a jade. 1.02.247
he'll woo a thousand, 'point the day of marriage 3.02. 15
i' faith, he'll have a lusty widow now, | that 4.02. 50
ay, and he'll tame her. 4.02. 53
i am heartily sorry that he'll be glad of this. AWW 4.03. 63 P
am i or that or this for what he'll utter, 5.03.208
he knows i am no maid, and he'll swear to't; 5.03.290
but he'll have but a year in all these ducats. TN 1.03. 23 P
and he says he'll stand at your door like a 1.05.147 P
supporter to a bench, but he'll speak with you. 1.05.149 P
he'll speak with you, will you or no. 1.05.153 P
if she do, he'll smile, and take't for a great 3.02. 82 P
he says he'll come. 3.04. 1
he'll stay, my lord. WT 1.02. 87
moon | upon the water as he'll stand and read 4.04.173
hang him, he'll be made an example. 4.04.817 P
transported that | he'll think anon it lives. 5.03. 70
and meagre as an ague's fit, | and so he'll die; JN 3.04. 86
he flatly says he'll not lay down his arms. 5.02.126
he'll breed revengement and a scourge for me; 1H4 3.02. 7
and yet he'll be crowing as if he had writ man 2H4 1.02. 26 P
paul's, and he'll buy me a horse in smithfield; 1.02. 52 P
he'll not swagger with a barbary hen, if her 2.04. 99 P
from him, give him air, he'll straight be well. 4.04.116
be sick with joy, he'll recover without physic. 4.05. 14 P
he'll yield the crow a pudding one of these days H5 2.01. 87 P
he'll call you to so hot an answer of it | that 2.04.123
he'll make your paris louvre shake for it, 2.04.132
he'll drop his heart into the sink of fear, 3.05. 59
but he'll remember with advantages | what feats 4.03. 50
fast | before he'll buy again at such a rate. 1H6 3.02. 43
he'll make his cap co–equal with the crown." 5.01. 33
if gloucester be displac'd, he'll be protector. 2H6 1.01.177
he'll wrest the sense and hold us here all day. 3.01.186
be wise, he'll never call ye jack cade more. 4.06. 9 P
god forbid that, for he'll take vantages. 3H6 3.02. 25
nay then whip me; he'll rather give her two. 3.02. 28
saying, he'll lade it dry to have his way: 3.02.139
tell him, in hope he'll prove a widower shortly, 3.03.227
him, in hope he'll prove a widower shortly, 4.01. 99
he'll soon find means to make the body follow. 4.07. 26
no, he'll say 'twas done cowardly when he wakes. R3 1.04.101 P
why, then he'll say we stabb'd him sleeping. 1.04.105 P
which i presume he'll take in gentle part. 3.04. 20
he'll carry it so | to make the sceptre his. H8 1.02.134
pray god he do, he'll never know himself else. 2.02. 22
he'll lay about him to–day, i can tell them that TRO 1.02. 55 P
yes, he'll fight indifferent well. 1.02.223 P
if none, he'll say in troy when he retires, 1.03.281
'tis like he'll question me | why such 3.03. 42
th' combat, he'll break't himself in vainglory. 3.03.259 P
why, he'll answer nobody; 3.03.268 P
he cares not, he'll obey conditions. 4.05. 72
that sleeve is mine that he'll bear on his helm. 5.02.169
he'll tickle it for his concupy. 5.02.177 P
he'll beat aufidius' head below his knee, | and COR 1.03. 46
to say he'll turn your current in a ditch, | and 3.01. 96
he'll go, he says, and sowl the porter of rome 4.05.200 P
he'll shake | your rome about your ears. 4.06. 98
sir, i beseech you, think you he'll carry rome? 4.07. 27
i think he'll be to rome | as is the aspray to 4.07. 33
i think he'll hear me. 5.01. 48
he'll never hear him. 5.01. 62
he'll so awake as he in fury shall | cut off the TIT 4.04. 25
go before to field, he'll be your follower; ROM 3.01. 58
in your bed, | he'll fright you up, i' faith. 4.05. 11
he'll spare none. TIM 1.01.177
hang him, he'll abuse us. 2.02. 48 P
he'll think your mother chides, and leave you so JC 4.03.123
show, he'll not shame to tell you what it means. HAM 3.02.145 P
he'll shape his old course in a country new. LR 1.01.187
he'll not feel wrongs | which tie him to an 4.02. 13
he'll strike, and quickly too. 5.03.286
and i dare think he'll prove to desdemona | a OTH 2.01.290
he'll be as full of quarrel and offense | as my 2.03. 50
he'll watch the horologe a double set | if drink 2.03.130
you well assur'd, | no more than he'll unswear. 4.01. 31
he'll come anon — "sing all a green willow must 4.03. 50 P
he'll never yield to that. ANT 3.06. 37
now he'll outstare the lightning: 3.13.194
he'll lead me then in triumph? 5.02.109
he'll make demand of her, and spend that kiss 5.02.302
and i think | he'll grant the tribute, send th' CYM 2.04. 13
the sword like me, he'll scarcely look on't. 3.06. 26
if he be gone, he'll make his grave a bed. 4.02.216
he'll then instruct us of this body. 4.02.360
for if he'll do as he is made to do, | i know 5.03. 61
i know he'll quickly fly my friendship too. 5.03. 62
he'll stop the course by which it might be known PER 1.02. 23
with hostile forces he'll o'erspread the land, 1.02. 24
lop that doubt, he'll fill this land with arms, 1.02. 90
here to have death in peace is all he'll crave. 2.01. 11
whereto he'll infuse pow'r and press you forth TNK 1.01. 73
twenty to one, he'll come to speak to her, | and 2.03. 14
he'll eat a horn–book ere he fail. 2.03. 42
"his shackles will betray him, he'll be taken, 4.01. 70
he'll tickle't up | in two hours, if his hand be 4.01.138
he'll dance the morris twenty mile an hour, 5.02. 51
twenty strike of oats, but he'll ne'er have her. 5.02. 65
a miller's mare, he'll be the death of her. 5.02. 67
do you think he'll have me? 5.02. 92
/HELL 1 FR 0.0001 REL FR 1 V 0 P
/thou /torments /me /ere /i /come /to /hell! R2 4.01.270
HELL 170 FR 0.0192 REL FR 145 V 25 P
cried, "hell is empty, | and all the devils are TMP 1.02.214
if i would but go to hell for an eternal moment WIV 2.01. 49 P
i am damn'd in hell for swearing to gentlemen my 2.02. 10 P
see the hell of having a false woman! 2.02.291 P
/and the bottom were as deep as hell, i should 3.05. 13 P
the oil that's in me should set hell on fire; 5.05. 35 P
have given ourselves without scruple to hell, 5.05.149 P
cast, he would appear | a pond as deep as hell. MM 3.01. 93
o, 'tis the cunning livery of hell, | the 3.01. 94
am i in earth, in heaven, or in hell? ERR 2.02.212
no, he's in tartar limbo, worse than hell: 4.02. 32
before the judgment carries poor souls to hell. 4.02. 40
of the berrord, and lead his apes into hell. ADO 2.01. 41 P
well then, go you into hell. 2.01. 42 P
man may live as quiet in hell as in a sanctuary, 2.01.258 P
black is the badge of hell, | the hue of LLL 4.03.250
o hell! to choose love by another's eyes. MND 1.01.140
that he hath turn'd a heaven unto a hell! 1.01.207
i'll follow thee and make a heaven of hell, | to 2.01.243
o hell! 3.02.145
one sees more devils than vast hell can hold; 5.01. 9
our house is hell, and thou, a merry devil, MV 2.03. 2
o hell! 2.07. 62
it so, | let fortune go to hell for it, not i. 3.02. 21
up, | signior baptista, for this fiend of hell, SHR 1.01. 88
any man is so very a fool to be married to hell? 1.01.125 P
and for your love to her lead apes in hell. 2.01. 34
i think his soul is in hell, madonna. TN 1.05. 68 P
if all the devils of hell be drawn in little, 3.04. 85 P
a fiend like thee might bear my soul to hell. 3.04.217
as hell, sir topas. 4.02. 35 P
though ignorance were as dark as hell; 4.02. 46 P
one | he chides to hell and bids the other grow WT 4.04.553
when i was got, i'll send his soul to hell. JN 1.01.272
make work upon ourselves, for heaven or hell. 2.01.407
and, by disjoining hands, hell lose a soul. 3.01.197
clamors of hell, be measures to our pomp? 3.01.304
you shall think the devil is come from hell. 4.03.100
there is not yet so ugly a fiend of hell | as 4.03.123
let hell want pains enough to torture me. 4.03.138
within me is a hell, and there the poison | is 5.07. 46
and plague injustice with the pains of hell. R2 3.01. 34
terrible hell | make war upon their spotted 3.02.133
seal of death, | that marks thee out for hell. 4.01. 26
fitzwater, thou art damn'd to hell for this. 4.01. 43
go thou and fill another room in hell. 5.05.107
says that this deed is chronicled in hell. 5.05.116
what hole in hell were hot enough for him? 1H4 1.02.108 P
and you in hell, as oft as he hears | owen 3.01. 11
for one of them, she's in hell already, and 2H4 2.04.338 P
die, | if hell and treason hold their promises, H5 2.pr. 29
hath got the voice in hell for excellence; 2.02.113
wheresome'er he is, either in heaven or in hell! 2.03. 8 P
nay sure, he's not in hell; 2.03. 9 P
and 'a said it was a black soul burning in hell? 2.03. 42 P
with conscience wide as hell, mowing like grass 3.03. 13
never sees horrid night, the child of hell; 4.01.271
all hell shall stir for this. 5.01. 68
hundreds he sent to hell, and none durst stand 1H6 1.01.123
heavens, can you suffer hell so to prevail? 1.05. 9
to join with witches and the help of hell! 2.01. 18
i think this talbot be a fiend of hell. 2.01. 46
if not of hell, the heavens sure favor him. 2.01. 47
hell our prison is. 4.07. 58
and hell too strong for me to buckle with: 5.03. 28
to ashes, | thou foul accursed minister of hell! 5.04. 93
for what is wedlock forced, but a hell, | an age 5.05. 62
to think upon my pomp shall be my hell. 2H6 2.04. 41
shall blow ten thousand souls to heaven or hell; 3.01.350
give thee thy hire and send thy soul to hell, 3.02.225
all the foul terrors in dark–seated hell — 3.02.328
and wedded be thou to the hags of hell, | for 4.01. 79
in despite of the devils and hell, have through 4.08. 61 P
so wish i, i might thrust thy soul to hell. 4.10. 79
if not in heaven, you'll surely sup in hell. 5.01.216
o war, thou son of hell, | whom angry heavens do 5.02. 33
line, | and leave not one alive, i live in hell. 3H6 1.03. 33
whose father for his hoarding went to hell? 2.02. 48
whiles i live, t' account this world but hell, 3.02.169
down, down to hell, and say i sent thee thither 5.06. 67
let hell make crook'd my mind to answer it. 5.06. 79
avaunt, thou dreadful minister of hell! R3 1.02. 46
for thou hast made the happy earth thy hell, 1.02. 51
and thou unfit for any place, but hell. 1.02.109
hie thee to hell for shame, and leave this world 1.03.142
affrights thee with a hell of ugly devils! 1.03.226
the slave of nature and the son of hell! 1.03.229
death, and hell have set their marks on him, 1.03.292
could not believe but that i was in hell, | such 1.04. 62
and live with richmond, from the reach of hell. 4.01. 42
earth gapes, hell burns, fiends roar, saints 4.04. 75
thou cam'st on earth to make the earth my hell. 4.04.167
as long as hell and richard likes of it. 4.04.354
if not to heaven, then hand in hand to hell. 5.03.313
if not from hell, the devil is a niggard, | or H8 1.01. 70
before, and he begins | a new hell in himself. 1.01. 72
is become as black | as if besmear'd in hell. 1.02.124
with such a hell of pain and world of charge; TRO 4.01. 58
wights she stays | as tediously as hell, but 4.02. 13
by hell and all hell's torments, | i will not 5.02. 43
pluto and hell! COR 1.04. 36
the fires i' th' lowest hell fold in the people! 3.03. 68
andronicus, would thou were shipp'd to hell, TIT 1.01.206
sicily, | and be my heart an ever–burning hell! 3.01.242
if you will have revenge from hell, you shall. 4.03. 39
and, sith there's no justice in earth nor hell, 4.03. 50
fire, | so i might have your company in hell, 5.01.149
could not all hell afford you such a devil? 5.02. 86
i hate the word | as i hate hell, all montagues, ROM 1.01. 71
this torture should be roar'd in dismal hell. 3.02. 44
what hadst thou to do in hell | when thou didst 3.02. 80
walls, | but purgatory, torture, hell itself. 3.03. 18
o friar, the damned use that word in hell; 3.03. 47
i would i might go to hell among the rogues. JC 1.02.268 P
with ate by his side come hot from hell, | shall 3.01.271
and pall thee in the dunnest smoke of hell, MAC 1.05. 51
knell, | that summons thee to heaven or to hell. 2.01. 64
if a man were porter of hell gate, he should 2.03. 2 P
but this place is too cold for hell. 2.03. 17 P
of horrid hell can come a devil more damn'd | in 4.03. 56
pour the sweet milk of concord into hell, 4.03. 98
hell is murky! 5.01. 36 P
thyself a hotter name | than any is in hell. 5.07. 7
though hell itself should gape | and bid me hold HAM 1.02.244
with thee airs from heaven, or blasts from hell, 1.04. 41
and shall i couple hell? 1.05. 93
as if he had been loosed out of hell | to speak 2.01. 80
prompted to my revenge by heaven and hell, 2.02.584
churchyards yawn and hell itself /breathes out 3.02.389
his soul may be as damn'd and black | as hell, 3.03. 95
rebellious hell, | if thou canst mutine in a 3.04. 82
to hell, allegiance! 4.05.132
thought and afflictions, passion, hell itself, 4.05.188
there's hell, there's darkness, | there is the LR 4.06.127
to find out practices of cunning hell | why this OTH 1.03.102
too hard for my wits and all the tribe of hell, 1.03.357 P
hell and night | must bring this monstrous birth 1.03.403
divinity of hell! 2.03.350
arise, black vengeance, from the hollow hell! 3.03.447
o, 'tis the spite of hell, the fiend's arch–mock 4.01. 70
heaven truly knows that thou art false as hell. 4.02. 39
cherubin — | ay, here, look grim as hell! 4.02. 64
to saint peter, | and keeps the gate of hell! 4.02. 92
and hell gnaw his bones! 4.02.136
she's like a liar gone to burning hell: 5.02.129
o, i were damn'd beneath all depth in hell | but 5.02.137
and shot their fires | into th' abysm of hell. ANT 3.13.147
that all the plagues of hell should at one time CYM 1.06.111
though this a heavenly angel, hell is here. 2.02. 50
and all the fiends of hell | divide themselves 2.04.129
another stain, as big as hell can hold, | were 2.04.140
all faults that name, nay, that hell knows, 2.05. 27
time, | hell only danceth at so harsh a chime. PER 1.01. 85
these surges, | which wash both heaven and hell; 3.01. 2
fiend | of hell would not in reputation change. 4.06.164
"o comfort–killing night, image of hell! LUC 764
with slow sad gait descended | to ugly hell, 1082
and that deep torture may be call'd a hell, 1287
"such devils steal effects from lightless hell, 1555
to win me soon to hell, my female evil PP 2. 5
friend, | i guess one angel in another's hell: 2.12
i am to wait, though waiting so be hell, | not SON 58.13
distill'd from limbecks foul as hell within, 119. 2
as i by yours, y' have pass'd a hell of time, 120. 6
to shun the heaven that leads men to this hell. 129.14
to win me soon to hell, my female evil 144. 5
friend, | i guess one angel in another's hell. 144.12
a fiend | from heaven to hell is flown away: 145.12
who art as black as hell, as dark as night. 147.14
what a hell of witchcraft lies | in the small LC 288
HELL–BLACK 1 FR 0.0001 REL FR 1 V 0 P
as his bare head | in hell–black night endur'd, LR 3.07. 60
HELL–BORN 1 FR 0.0001 REL FR 1 V 0 P
or blot with hell–born sin such saint–like forms LUC 1519
HELL–BROTH 1 FR 0.0001 REL FR 1 V 0 P
trouble, | like a hell–broth boil and bubble. MAC 4.01. 19
HELLESPONT 4 FR 0.0004 REL FR 3 V 1 P
how young leander cross'd the hellespont. TGV 1.01. 22
love, | and yet you never swom the hellespont. 1.01. 26
to wash him in the hellespont and being taken AYL 4.01.103 P
due on | to the propontic and the hellespont, OTH 3.03.456
HELL–FIRE 1 FR 0.0001 REL FR 0 V 1 P
but i think upon hell–fire and dives that liv'd 1H4 3.03. 31 P
HELL–GOVERN'D 1 FR 0.0001 REL FR 1 V 0 P
which his hell–govern'd arm hath butchered! R3 1.02. 67
HELL–HATED 1 FR 0.0001 REL FR 1 V 0 P
with the hell–hated lie o'erwhelm thy heart, LR 5.03.148
HELL–HOUND 2 FR 0.0002 REL FR 2 V 0 P
a hell–hound that doth hunt us all to death: R3 4.04. 48
turn, hell–hound, turn! MAC 5.08. 3
HELL–HOUNDS 1 FR 0.0001 REL FR 1 V 0 P
a pair of cursed hell–hounds and their dame. TIT 5.02.144
HELLISH 8 FR 0.0009 REL FR 8 V 0 P
soul, | from out the state of hellish cruelty! MV 3.04. 21
only sin | and hellish obstinacy tie thy tongue, AWW 1.03.180
hath wrought this hellish mischief unawares, 1H6 3.02. 39
upon my body with their hellish charms? R3 3.04. 62
no sooner had they told this hellish tale, | but TIT 2.03.105
and therein, hellish dog, thou hast undone her. 4.02. 77
the hellish pyrrhus | old grandsire priam seeks. HAM 2.02.463
remains the censure of this hellish villain, OTH 5.02.368
HELL–KITE 1 FR 0.0001 REL FR 1 V 0 P
o hell–kite! MAC 4.03.217
HELL–PAINS 2 FR 0.0002 REL FR 1 V 1 P
i would it were hell–pains for thy sake, and my AWW 2.03.232 P
though i do hate him as i do hell–pains, | yet, OTH 1.01.154
HELL'S 3 FR 0.0003 REL FR 3 V 0 P
richard yet lives, hell's black intelligencer, R3 4.04. 71
by hell and all hell's torments, | i will not TRO 5.02. 43
and duck again as low | as hell's from heaven! OTH 2.01.189
/HELM* 2 FR 0.0002 REL FR 2 V 0 P
/with /plumed /helm /thy /state /begins /to LR 4.02. 57
/with /this /thin /helm? 4.07. 35

HELM* 17 FR 0.0019 REL FR 14 V 3 P
and fortune play upon thy prosperous helm | as AWW 3.03. 7
for every honor sitting on his helm | would they 1H4 3.02.142
together, i pluck'd this glove from his helm. H5 4.07.156 P
and you yourself shall steer the happy helm. 2H6 1.03.100
is't meet that he | should leave the helm and, 3H6 5.04. 7
we will not from the helm to sit and weep, | but 5.04. 21
he dreamt the boar had rased off his helm. R3 3.02. 11
fortune and victory sit on thy helm! 5.03. 79
and his helm more hack'd than hector's, and how TRO 1.02.233 P
but, by the forge that /stithied mars his helm, 4.05.255
to–morrow will i wear it on my helm, | and 5.02. 93
that sleeve is mine that he'll bear on his helm. 5.02.169
/young knave's sleeve of troy there in his helm. 5.04. 4 P
let housewives make a skillet of my helm, | and OTH 1.03.272
amorous surfeiter would have donn'd his helm ANT 2.01. 33
at the helm | a seeming mermaid steers; 2.02.208
by th' helm of mars, i saw them in the war, TNK 1.04. 17
HELM'D 1 FR 0.0001 REL FR 0 V 1 P
his life, and the business he hath helm'd, must, MM 3.02.143 P
HELMET 6 FR 0.0006 REL FR 4 V 2 P
steel | over the glittering helmet of my foe! R2 4.01. 51
from helmet to the spur all blood he was. H5 4.06. 6
majesty is take out of the helmet of alanson. 4.08. 27 P
borne | his bruised helmet and his bended sword 5.pr. 18
look you what hacks are on his helmet! TRO 1.02.205 P
die, | not cowardly put off my helmet to | my ANT 4.15. 56
HELMETED 1 FR 0.0001 REL FR 1 V 0 P
unto the helmeted bellona use them | and pray TNK 1.01. 75
HELMETS 4 FR 0.0004 REL FR 4 V 0 P
with unhack'd swords, and helmets all unbruis'd, JN 2.01.254
let them lay by their helmets and their spears, R2 1.03.119
or shall we on the helmets of our foes | tell 3H6 2.01.163
fall | the usurping helmets of our adversaries; R3 5.03.112
HELMS* 5 FR 0.0005 REL FR 5 V 0 P
stanley did dream the boar did /rase our helms, R3 3.04. 82
victory sits on our helms. 5.03.351
and you slander | the helms o' th' state, who COR 1.01. 77
unbuckling helms, fisting each other's throat, 4.05.125
cannot weep | when our friends don their helms, TNK 1.03. 19
/HELP 2 FR 0.0002 REL FR 2 V 0 P
/come /help /to /bear /thy /master; LR 3.06.100
/now /heaven /help /him! 3.07.107
HELP 337 FR 0.0381 REL FR 269 V 68 P
thee, | by help of her more potent ministers, TMP 1.02.275
bottle will recover him, i will help his ague. 2.02. 93 P
and help to celebrate | a contract of true love; 4.01.132
help to bear this away where my hogshead of wine 4.01.250 P
i rather think | you have not sought her help, 5.01.142
my bands | with the help of your good hands. ep 10
and i will help thee to prefer her too: TGV 2.04.157
cease to lament for that thou canst not help, 3.01.243
and study help for that which thou lament'st. 3.01.244
another thing she may, and that cannot i help. 3.01.352 P
her eyes repair, | to help him of his blindness; 4.02. 47
if you will help to bear it, sir john, take all, WIV 2.02.172 P
help me away. 3.03.141 P
help to cover your master, boy. 3.03.143 P
help to search my house this one time. 4.02.160 P
come all to help him, and so stop the air | by MM 2.04. 25
help heaven! 2.04.127
here's a fellow will help you to–morrow in your 4.02. 22 P
what, resists he? help him, lucio. 5.01.350 P
day | to seek thy /health by beneficial help. ERR 1.01.151
so, come, help: 3.01. 56
if a crow help us in, sirrah, we'll pluck a crow 3.01. 83
god help, poor souls, how idly do they talk! 4.04.129
let's call more help | to have them bound again. 4.04.145
him be brought forth, and borne hence for help. 5.01.160
and sure (unless you send some present help) 5.01.176
i never saw the chain, so help me heaven; 5.01.268
god help the noble claudio! ADO 1.01. 88 P
my lord, to help my cousin to a good husband. 2.01.375 P
o, god help me, god help me, how long have you 3.04. 67 P
o, god help me, god help me, how long have you 3.04. 67 P
help to dress me, good coz, good meg, good 3.04. 98 P
and his wits are not so blunt as, god help, i 3.05. 11 P
god help us, it is a world to see! 3.05. 35 P
help, uncle! 4.01.113
assist our moan, | help us to sigh and groan, 5.03. 17
in which, good friar, i shall desire your help. 5.04. 31
and my help. 5.04. 32
our lady help my lord! he'll be forsworn. LLL 2.01. 98
hath wisdom's warrant and the help of school, 5.02. 71
help, hold his brows! 5.02.392
and, to begin, wench — so god help me, law! 5.02.414
help me, lysander, help me! MND 2.02.145
help me, lysander, help me! 2.02.145
help! 3.01.105 P
he murther cries, and help from athens calls. 3.02. 26
but to help cavalery cobweb to scratch. 4.01. 22 P
with the help of a surgeon he might yet recover, 5.01.310 P
well then, it now appears you need my help. MV 1.03.114
to one that i would have him help to waste | his 2.05. 50
and take upon command what help we have | that AYL 2.07.125
god help thee, shallow man! 3.02. 71 P
i will help you if i can. 5.02.111 P
prove the better by the help of good epilogues. ep 6 P
help, /masters, help, my master is mad. SHR 1.02. 18 P
help, /masters, help, my master is mad. 1.02. 18 P
help thee to a wife | with wealth enough, and 1.02. 85
hath promis'd me to help /me to another, | a 1.02.172
and help to dress your sister's chamber up. 3.01. 83
help, help, help! 5.01. 58 P
help, help, help! 5.01. 58 P
help, help, help! 5.01. 58 P
help, son! help, signior baptista! 5.01. 60 P
help, son! help, signior baptista! 5.01. 60 P
he, that they cannot help him, | they, that they AWW 1.03.238
cannot help him, | they, that they cannot help. 1.03.239
what i can help thee to thou shalt not miss. 1.03.256
a senseless help when help past sense we deem. 2.01.124
a senseless help when help past sense we deem. 2.01.124
thou thought'st to help me, and such thanks i 2.01.130
the help of heaven we count the act of men. 2.01.152
fee, | but, if i help, what do you promise me? 2.01.190
give me some help here ho! 2.01.209
me leave to use | the help of mine own eyes. 2.03.108
and let me buy your friendly help thus far, 3.07. 15
we cannot help it. 5.01. 2
this man may help me to his majesty's ear, | if 5.01. 7
her fortunes ever stood | necessitied to help, 5.03. 85
deserve well at my hand, help me to a candle, TN 4.02. 81 P
good fool, help me to some light and some paper. 4.02.105 P
i will help you to't. 4.02.113 P
for the love of god, your help! 5.01.177 P
i'll help you, sir toby, because we'll be 5.01.204 P
will you help? 5.01.206 P
by whose gentle help | i was preserv'd to serve 5.01.255
camillo was his help in this, his pandar. WT 2.01. 46
what's gone and what's past help | should be 3.02.222
he cried to me for help and said his name was 3.03. 96 P
and you shall help to put him i' th' ground. 3.03.136 P
o, help me, help me! 4.03. 52 P
o, help me, help me! 4.03. 52 P
lend me thy hand, i'll help thee. 4.03. 69 P
no hope to help you, | but as you shake off one 4.04.568
your strong hand shall help to give him strength JN 2.01. 33
and by whose help i mean to chastise it. 2.01.117
my arm shall give thee help to bear thee hence, 5.04. 58
but when it first did help to wound itself. 5.07.114
you never shall, so help you truth and god, R2 1.03.183
thou canst help time to furrow me with age, 1.03.229
mind | to help him to his grave immediately! 1.04. 60
uncle, help to order several powers | to oxford, 5.03.140
help, help, help! 5.05.104
help, help, help! 5.05.104
help, help, help! 5.05.104
help me to my horse, good king's son. 1H4 2.02. 40 P
them is fat and grows old, god help the while! 2.04.132 P
sack and sugar be a fault, god help the wicked! 2.04.471 P
nor shall we need his help these fourteen days. 3.01. 87
now god help thee! 3.01.241 P
opinion, that did help me to the crown, | had 3.02. 42
if we without his help can make a head | to push 4.01. 80
with his help | we shall o'erturn it topsy–turvy 4.01. 81
what with our help, what with the absent king, 5.01. 49
i do not need your help, | and god forbid a 5.04. 10
and those two things i confess i cannot help. 2H4 2.02. 69 P
if the cook help to make the gluttony, you help 2.04. 44 P
the gluttony, you help to make the diseases, 2.04. 44 P
gone, and she is old, and cannot help herself. 3.02.232 P
we well resolv'd, and by god's help | and yours, H5 1.02.222
doth rise and help hyperion to his horse, | and 4.01.275
thou dost not wish more help from england, coz? 4.03. 73
without more help, could fight this royal battle 4.03. 75
whoe'er helps thee, 'tis thou that must help me: 1H6 1.02.107
bear hence his body, i will help to bury it. 1.04. 87
help salisbury to make his testament. 1.05. 17
to join with witches and the help of hell! 2.01. 18
so help me god, as i dissemble not! 3.01.140
so help me god, as i intend it not! 3.01.141
those that hurt, and hurt not those that help. 3.03. 53
this shall ye do, so help you righteous god! 4.01. 8
villain | and cannot help the noble chevalier. 4.03. 14
the help of one stands me in little stead. 4.06. 31
now help, ye charming spells and periapts, | and 5.03. 2
help me this once, that france may get the field 5.03. 12
benefit, | so you do condescend to help me now. 5.03. 17
to compass wonders but by help of devils. 5.04. 48
so god help warwick, as he loves the land | and 2H6 1.01.205
come offer at my shrine, and i will help thee." 2.01. 90
ay, god almighty help me! 2.01. 93
thy greatest help is quiet, gentle nell. 2.04. 67
so help me god, as i have watch'd the night, 3.01.110
i say no more than truth, so help me god! 3.01.120
for, being green, there is great hope of help. 3.01.287
help, lords, the king is dead. 3.02. 33
run, go, help, help! o henry, ope thine eyes! 3.02. 35
run, go, help, help! o henry, ope thine eyes! 3.02. 35
a hempen /caudle then, and the help of hatchet. 4.07. 91 P
so let it help me now against thy sword, | as i 5.02. 24
now, if the help of norfolk and myself, | with 3H6 2.01.178
for how can i help them and not myself? 3.01. 21
scotland hath will to help, but cannot help; 3.03. 34
scotland hath will to help, but cannot help; 3.03. 34
but by thy help to this distressed queen? 3.03.213
so god help montague as he proves true! 4.01.143
he | must help you more than you are hurt by me. 4.06. 76
for doubtless burgundy will yield him help, 4.06. 90
seas, | and brought desired help from burgundy. 4.07. 6
to help king edward in his time of storm, | as 4.07. 43
o, welcome, oxford, for we want thy help. 5.01. 66
let him depart before we need his help. 5.04. 49
did it to help thee to a better husband. R3 1.02.139
she may help you to many fair preferments, | and 1.03. 94
to help thee curse this poisonous bunch–back'd 1.03.245
come, hastings, help me to my closet. 2.01.134
give me no help in lamentation, | i am not 2.02. 66
but none can help our harms by wailing them. 2.02.103
ay, sir, it is too true, god help the while! 2.03. 8
no, so god help me, they spake not a word, | but 3.07. 24
and much i need to help you, were there need: 3.07.166
that i should wish for thee to help me curse 4.04. 80
what they will impart | help nothing else, yet 4.04.131
of night come to my tent | and help to arm me. 5.03. 78
those that were the means to help him; 5.03.249
withdraw, my lord, i'll help you to a horse. 5.04. 8
it will help me nothing | to plead mine H8 1.01.207
in haste too, | lest he should help his father. 2.01. 44
now the lord help, | they vex me past my 2.04.130
yes, my lord; | but yet i cannot help you. 5.02. 5
i must woo you | to help unarm our hector. TRO 3.01.150
there is no help. 4.01. 48
and would, as i shall pity, i could help! 4.03. 11
come, come, thersites, help to trim my tent; 5.01. 45
what he cannot help in his nature, you account a COR 1.01. 41 P
and | your knees to them (not arms) must help. 1.01. 74
march from hence | to help our fielded friends! 1.04. 12
have the spirit, will haste | to help cominius. 1.05. 14
no better thought of, a little help will serve; 2.03. 15 P
for conscience' sake to help to get thee a wife. 2.03. 33 P
help, ye citizens! 3.01.179
help martius, help! 3.01.226
help martius, help! 3.01.226
you that be noble, help him, young and old! 3.01.227
rome, such as was never | s' incapable of help. 4.06.120
i cannot help it now, | unless by using means i 4.07. 6
refuse your aid | in this so never–needed help, 5.01. 34
we'll meet them, | and help the joy. 5.04. 62
help, three a' th' chiefest soldiers; 5.06.148
on, | and help to set a head on headless rome. TIT 1.01.186
brothers, help to convey her hence away, | and 1.01.287
help, lucius, help! 1.01.291
help, lucius, help! 1.01.291
why dost not comfort me and help me out | from 2.03.209
o brother, help me with thy fainting hand — 2.03.233
reach me thy hand, that i may help thee out, 2.03.237
nor i no strength to climb without thy help. 2.03.242
if thou hadst hands to help thee knit the cord. 2.04. 10
is that the one will help to cut the other. 3.01. 78
this, | as far from help as limbo is from bliss! 3.01.149
good aaron, wilt thou help to chop it off? 3.01.161
help, grandsire, help! 4.01. 1
help, grandsire, help! 4.01. 1
help her. 4.01. 45
my name, | without the help of any hand at all. 4.01. 71
now help, or woe betide thee evermore! 4.02. 56
sirs, help our uncle to convey him in. 5.03. 15
his help to crave, and my dear hap to tell. ROM 2.02.189
remedies | within thy help and holy physic lies. 2.03. 52
help me into some house, benvolio, | or i shall 3.01.105
weep with me, past hope, past /cure, past help! 4.01. 45
if in thy wisdom thou canst give no help, | do 4.01. 52
and with this knife i'll help it presently. 4.01. 54
and strength shall help afford. 4.01.125
closet | to help me sort such needful ornaments 4.02. 34
go thou to juliet, help to deck up her. 4.02. 41
what, are you busy, ho? need you my help? 4.03. 6
help, help! 4.05. 14
help, help! 4.05. 14
help, help! 4.05. 21
help, help! 4.05. 21
call help. 4.05. 21
sound | with speedy help doth lend redress." 4.05.143
and left no friendly drop | to help me after? 5.03.164
to help to take her from her borrowed grave, 5.03.248
him | a gentleman that well deserves a help, TIM 1.01.102
'tis not enough to help the feeble up, | but to 1.01.107
service, from whose help | i deriv'd liberty. 1.02. 7
provided that i shall have much help from you: 1.02. 89 P
servilius, help! my lord, my lord! 3.04. 78
caesar cried, "help me, cassius, or i sink!" JC 1.02.111
calphurnia in her sleep cried out, | "help, ho! 2.02. 3
but i am faint, my gashes cry for help. MAC 1.02. 42
line the rebel | with hidden help and vantage, 1.03.113
help me hence, ho! 2.03.118
that by the help of these (with him above | to 3.06. 32
now, god help thee, poor monkey! 4.02. 59 P
now is the time of help; 4.03.186
here, as before, never, so help you mercy, | how HAM 1.05.169
so grace and mercy at your most need help you. 1.05.180
o, help him, you sweet heavens! 3.01.133 P
will you two help to hasten them? 3.02. 50 P
help, angels! 3.03. 69
help ho! 3.04. 22
what ho, help! 3.04. 23
the bark is ready, and the wind at help, | th' 4.03. 44
no help? LR 2.01. 36
help ho! murther, help! 2.02. 40 P
help ho! murther, help! 2.02. 40 P
help ho! murther, murther! 2.02. 43 P
help me, help me! 3.04. 40 P
help me, help me! 3.04. 40 P
to live till he be old, | give me some help! 3.07. 70
help, help! o, help! 5.03.223
help, help! o, help! 5.03.223
help, help! o, help! 5.03.223
what kind of help? 5.03.223
we lack'd your counsel and your help to–night. OTH 1.03. 51
may help these lovers | /into /your /favor. 1.03.200
/god's /will, gentlemen — | help ho! 2.03.159
sir — montano — /sir — | help, masters! 2.03.160
there comes a fellow crying out for help, | and 2.03.226
importune her help to put you in your place 2.03.319 P
and this may help to thicken other proofs | that 3.03.430
so help me every spirit sanctified, | as i have 3.04.126
i am maim'd for ever. help ho! murther, murther! 5.01. 27
o, help ho! light! a surgeon! 5.01. 30
o, help! 5.01. 39
to come in to the cry without more help. 5.01. 44
here, here! for heaven sake, help me! 5.01. 50
give me some help. 5.01. 55
come in, and give some help. 5.01. 59
o, help me there! 5.01. 60
help, help ho! 5.02.120
help, help ho! 5.02.120
help! 5.02.120
help, help ho, help! 5.02.166
help, help ho, help! 5.02.166
help, help ho, help! 5.02.166
help me away, dear charmian, i shall fall. ANT 1.03. 15
for that you must | but say i could not help it. 2.02. 71
nay, i'll help too. | what's this for? 4.04. 5
sooth law, i'll help. thus it must be. 4.04. 8
help me, my women! 4.13. 1
help, charmian, help, iras, help; 4.15. 12
help, charmian, help, iras, help; 4.15. 12
help, charmian, help, iras, help; 4.15. 12
help, friends below, let's draw him hither. 4.15. 13
help me, my women — we must draw thee up. 4.15. 30
play'd than fought | and had no help of anger. CYM 1.01.163
look'd on him without the help of admiration, 1.04. 4 P
peep through thy marble mansion, help, | or we 5.04. 87
help, jupiter, or we appeal, | and from thy 5.04. 91
your sleep, and a hangman to help him to bed, i 5.04.174 P
o gentlemen, help | mine and your mistress! 5.05.229
help, help! 5.05.231
help, help! 5.05.231
wanting breath to speak, help me with tears. PER 1.04. 19
great, | the name of help grew odious to repeat. 1.04. 31
what pitiful cries they made to us to help them, 2.01. 21 P
well–a–day, we could scarce help ourselves. 2.01. 22 P
to give my tongue that heat to ask your help; 2.01. 75

help, master, help! 2.01.116 P
help, master, help! 2.01.116 P
what means the /nun? she dies, help, gentlemen! 5.03. 15
o, help now! | our cause cries for your knee. TNK 1.01.199
is blown abroad, help me, thy poor well–willer, 3.05.116
help me, dear sister, in a deed so virtuous 3.06.193
so your help be! 5.01. 14
her help she sees, but help she cannot get, VEN 93
her help she sees, but help she cannot get, 93
for one sweet look thy help i would assure thee, 371
they buy thy help, but sin ne'er gives a fee, LUC 913
let him have time of time's help to despair, 983
since that my case is past the help of law. 1022
poor helpless help, the treasure stol'n away, 1056
if tears could help, mine own would do me good. 1274
the help that thou shalt lend me | comes all too 1685
do wounds help wounds, or grief help grievous 1822
help wounds, or grief help grievous deeds? 1822
but kneel with me and help to bear thy part, 1830
alas, she could not help it! PP 15.12
heart is bleeding, all help needing, | o cruel 17.15
other help for him i see that there is none. 17.36
friend indeed, | he will help thee in thy need: 20.50
without thy help, by me be borne alone. SON 36. 4
your shallowest help will hold me up afloat, 80. 9
i, sick withal, the help of bath desired, | and 153.11
the bath for my help lies | where cupid got new 153.13
HELP'D *(also holp, etc.)*
HELP'D 6 FR 0.0006 REL FR 3 V 3 P
and, being help'd, inhabits there. TGV 4.02. 48
not to be help'd — AWW 2.03. 16 P
would i had been by, to have help'd the old man! WT 3.03.107 P
had been by the ship side, to have help'd her; 3.03.110 P
the first was i that help'd thee to the crown; R3 5.03.167
for even her folly help'd her to an heir. OTH 2.01.137
HELPER 2 FR 0.0002 REL FR 1 V 1 P
executioner, who in his office lacks a helper. MM 4.02. 9 P
her to be my motive | and helper to a husband. AWW 4.04. 21
HELPERS 3 FR 0.0003 REL FR 3 V 0 P
you speedy helpers, that are substitutes | under 1H6 5.03. 5
they may awake their helpers to comfort them. PER 1.04. 17
before the holy altars of your helpers, | the TNK 5.01. 12
HELPFUL 4 FR 0.0004 REL FR 4 V 0 P
our helpful ship was splitted in the midst; ERR 1.01.103
lend friends, and friends their helpful swords. R2 3.03.132
well, | and gave the tongue a helpful ornament, 1H4 3.01.123
and our practices | pleasant and helpful to him! HAM 2.02. 39
/HELPING 1 FR 0.0001 REL FR 1 V 0 P
/little /look'd /for /at /your /helping /hands. R2 4.01.161
HELPING 6 FR 0.0006 REL FR 3 V 3 P
well at my hands by helping me to the speech of ADO 5.02. 2 P
i am helping you to mar that which god made, a AYL 1.01. 32 P
maintain'd till by helping baptista's eldest SHR 1.01.137 P
not helping, death's my fee, | but, if i help, AWW 2.01.189
half, | it is too little, helping him to all; R2 5.01. 61
do but you hold out | your helping hands, and we TNK pr 26
HELPLESS 7 FR 0.0008 REL FR 7 V 0 P
hopeless and helpless doth egeon wend, | but to ERR 1.01.157
with urging helpless patience would relieve me; 2.01. 39
life | i pour the helpless balm of my poor eyes. R3 1.02. 13
as those poor birds that helpless berries saw. VEN 604
upon my cheeks what helpless shame i feel." LUC 756
this helpless smoke of words doth me no right. 1027
poor helpless help, the treasure stol'n away, 1056
HELPS 15 FR 0.0017 REL FR 12 V 3 P
and i, with your two helps, will so practice on ADO 2.01.382 P
conjoins with my disease, | and helps to end me. 2H4 4.05. 64
christ's mother helps me, else i were too weak. 1H6 1.02.106
whoe'er helps thee, 'tis thou that must help me: 1.02.107
and with their helps only defend ourselves: 3H6 4.01. 45
with other muniments and petty helps | in this COR 1.01.118
do very little alone, for your helps are many, 2.01. 36 P
that seem like prudent helps, are very poisonous 3.01.220
where's potpan, that he helps not to take away? ROM 1.05. 1 P
prince's doom, | it helps not, it prevails not. 3.03. 60
for out a' doors he went without their helps, HAM 2.01. 96
is not more ugly to the thing that helps it 3.01. 51
he that helps him take all my outward worth. LR 4.04. 10
be sick, | but that my resolution helps me. CYM 3.06. 4
tree | (or die in th' adventure), be my helps, PER 1.01. 22
HELP'ST 1 FR 0.0001 REL FR 1 V 0 P
what mean'st thou, that thou help'st me not? R3 1.04.274
HELTER–SKELTER 1 FR 0.0001 REL FR 1 V 0 P
and helter–skelter have i rode to thee, | and 2H4 5.03. 94
HEM* 10 FR 0.0011 REL FR 4 V 6 P
stroke his beard, | and, sorrow wag, cry "hem!" ADO 5.01. 16
hem them away. AYL 1.03. 18 P
i would try, if i could cry "hem" and have him. 1.03. 19 P
you breathe in your watering, they cry "hem!" 1H4 2.04. 17 P
better than i was. hem! 2H4 2.04. 30 P
our watch–word was "hem, boys!" 3.02.218 P
hem! TRO 1.02.228 P
now play me nestor, hem, and stroke thy beard, 1.03.165
dead, | entomb'd upon the very hem o' th' sea, TIM 5.04. 66
cough, or cry "hem," if anybody come. OTH 4.02. 29
HEMLOCK 3 FR 0.0003 REL FR 3 V 0 P
her fallow leas | the darnel, hemlock, and rank H5 5.02. 45
shark, | root of hemlock digg'd i' th' dark, MAC 4.01. 25
with hardocks, hemlock, nettles, cuckoo–flow'rs, LR 4.04. 4
/HEMM'D 1 FR 0.0001 REL FR 1 V 0 P
when that a ring of greeks have /hemm'd thee in, TRO 4.05.193
HEMM'D 3 FR 0.0003 REL FR 3 V 0 P
iron | and hemm'd about with grim destruction. 1H6 4.03. 21
"since i have hemm'd thee here | within the VEN 229
as one with treasure laden, hemm'd with thieves; 1022
HEMP 1 FR 0.0001 REL FR 1 V 0 P
free, | and let not hemp his windpipe suffocate. H5 3.06. 43
HEMPEN 3 FR 0.0003 REL FR 2 V 1 P
what hempen home–spuns have we swagg'ring here,
MND 3.01. 77
upon the hempen tackle ship–boys climbing; H5 3.pr. 8
ye shall have a hempen /caudle then, and the 2H6 4.07. 90 P
HEMPSEED 1 FR 0.0001 REL FR 0 V 1 P
do, thou hempseed! 2H4 2.01. 58 P
HEMS* 2 FR 0.0002 REL FR 2 V 0 P
hears | there's tricks i' th' world, and hems, HAM 4.05. 5
that heaven's air in this huge rondure hems. SON 21. 8
HEN 8 FR 0.0009 REL FR 2 V 6 P
of thee than a barbary cock–pigeon over his hen, AYL 4.01.151 P
a combless cock, so kate will be my hen. SHR 2.01.226
which if — lord have mercy on thee for a hen! AWW 2.03.213 P
none, sir; i have no pheasant cock, nor hen. WT 4.04.744 P
how now, dame partlet the hen? 1H4 3.03. 52 P
he'll not swagger with a barbary hen, if her 2H4 2.04. 99 P
when she, poor hen, fond of no second brood, COR 5.03.162
would drown myself for the love of a guinea hen, OTH 1.03.315 P
/HENCE 1 FR 0.0001 REL FR 1 V 0 P
/i /would /breed /from /hence /occasions, /and LR 1.03. 24
HENCE 379 FR 0.0428 REL FR 363 V 16 P
hence! TMP 1.01. 16 P
hence his ambition growing — | dost thou hear? 1.02.105
hence with diligence! 1.02.304
hag–seed, hence! 1.02.365
so, slave, hence! 1.02.374
hence! hang not on my garments. 1.02.475
hence, bashful cunning, | and prompt me, plain 3.01. 81
and now farewell | till half an hour hence. 3.01. 91
hence, and bestow your luggage where you found 5.01.299
but now he parted hence to embark for milan. TGV 1.01. 71
how churlishly i chid lucetta hence, | when 1.02. 60
only, in lieu thereof, dispatch me hence. 2.07. 88
desert, | is privilege for thy departure hence. 3.01.160
as thou lov'st thy life, make speed from hence. 3.01.169
death, | but, fly i hence, i fly away from life. 3.01.187
from hence, from silvia, and from me thy friend. 3.01.220
walk hence with that | and manage it against 3.01.248
thy letters may be here, though thou art hence, 3.01.250
sir, but i do; or else i would be hence. 4.02. 22
grief, | and on the justice of my flying hence, 4.03. 29
go, get thee hence, and find my dog again, | or 4.04. 59
these likelihoods confirm her flight from hence: 5.02. 43
rogues, hence, avaunt, vanish like hailstones; WIV 1.03. 81
our haste from hence is of so quick condition MM 1.01. 53
hence shall we see, | if power change purpose, 1.03. 53
the duke is very strangely gone from hence; 1.04. 50
hence hath offense his quick celerity, | when it 4.02.110
give him leave to escape hence, he would not. 4.02.148 P
therefore hence away! 4.06. 15
woe, | as i, thus wrong'd, hence unbelieved go! 5.01.119
take him hence; 5.01.311
go take her hence, and marry her instantly. 5.01.377
bed would break, | and take her hence in horror. 5.01.436
hence, prating peasant! fetch thy master home. ERR 2.01. 81
you spurn me hence, and he will spurn me hither: 2.01. 84
self–harming jealousy — fie, beat it hence! 2.01.102
i did not see you since you sent me hence | home 2.02. 15
i'll meet you at that place some hour hence. 3.01.122
and therefore 'tis high time that i were hence. 3.02.157
some blessed power deliver us from hence! 4.03. 44
go bear him hence. 4.04.130
to fetch my poor distracted husband hence. 5.01. 39
i will not hence, and leave my husband here; 5.01.109
nor send him forth, that we may bear him hence. 5.01.158
him be brought forth, and borne hence for help. 5.01.160
my dear son, which is hence a just sevennight, ADO 2.01.360 P
but i would have thee hence, and here again. 2.03. 6 P
hence from her, let her die. 4.01.154
come let us hence, and put on other weeds, | and 5.03. 30
to fright them hence with that dread penalty. LLL 1.01.127
hence, sirs, away! 4.03.208
or hide your heads like cowards, and fly hence. 5.02. 86
hence /hermit then — my heart is in thy breast. 5.02.816
/fairies, skip hence — | i have forsworn his MND 2.01. 61
hence, get thee gone, and follow me no more. 2.01.194
then, for the third part of a minute, hence, 2.02. 2
hence, you long–legg'd spinners, hence! 2.02. 21
hence, you long–legg'd spinners, hence! 2.02. 21
hence, away! 2.02. 25
i charge thee hence, and do not haunt me thus. 2.02. 85
o hated potion, hence! 3.02.264
but he hath chid me hence and threat'ned me | to 3.02.312
god's my life, stol'n hence, and left me asleep! 4.01.204 P
at gratiano's lodging some hour hence. MV 2.04. 26
lord, | you must be gone from hence immediately. 2.09. 8
from this finger, then parts life from hence; 3.02.184
for you shall hence upon your wedding–day. 3.02.311
i pray you give me leave to go from hence, | i 4.01.395
no note at all of our being absent hence — 5.01.120
my lord, he is but even now gone hence; AYL 2.07. 3
go hence a little, and i shall conduct you, | if 3.04. 55
if you be a true lover, hence, and not a word; 4.03. 73 P
and from hence i go | to make these doubts all 5.04. 24
hence comes it that your kindred shuns your SHR in.2. 28
house, | as beaten hence by your strange lunacy. in.2. 29
and banish hence these abject lowly dreams. in.2. 32
while i make way from hence to save my life. 1.01.234
if without more words you will get you hence. 1.02.230
him that mov'd you hither | remove you hence. 2.01.196
but so it is, my haste doth call me hence, | and 3.02.187
me, | for i must hence, and farewell to you all. 3.02.197
sirrah, get you hence, | and bid my cousin 4.01.150
hence, make your best of it. 4.03.100
go take it hence, be gone, and say no more. 4.03.165
and therefore frolic, we will hence forthwith, 4.03.182
hence is it that we make trifles of terrors, AWW 2.03. 3 P
my being here it is that holds thee hence. 3.02.123
and this morning your departure hence, it 4.03. 94 P
he hence remov'd last night, and with more haste 5.01. 23
for but a month ago i went from hence, | and TN 1.02. 31
sweet sister, | we will not part from hence. 5.01.385
we should, for perpetuity, | go hence in debt. WT 1.02. 6
stay, | we'll thwack him hence with distaffs. 1.02. 37
my people did expect my hence departure | two 1.02.450
hence! 1.02.462
bear the boy hence, he shall not come about her. 2.01. 59
go, do our bidding; hence! 2.01.125
lest that the treachery of the two fled hence 2.01.195
force her hence. 2.03. 62
hence with her, out o' door! 2.03. 68
hence with it, and together with the dam 2.03. 95
once more, take her hence. 2.03.112
hast | a heart so tender o'er it, take it hence, 2.03.133
that thou carry | this female bastard hence, and 2.03.175
take her hence; 3.02.149
kinsman not past three quarters of a mile hence, 4.03. 81 P
get you hence, for i must go | where it fits not 4.04.297
of antigonus, that carried hence the child? 5.02. 60 P
lead us from hence, where we may leisurely 5.03.152
so hence! JN 1.01. 27
armors, that march'd hence so silver–bright, 2.01.315
hence, and watch. 4.01. 5
this must be answer'd either here or hence. 4.02. 89
that i must die here and live hence by truth? 5.04. 29
i pray you bear me hence | from forth the noise 5.04. 44
my arm shall give thee help to bear thee hence, 5.04. 58
desolate, desolate, will i hence and die: R2 1.02. 73
and i from heaven banish'd as from hence! 1.03.203
com'st thou because the anointed king is hence? 2.03. 96
discharge my followers, let them hence away, 3.02.217
richard not far from hence hath hid his head. 3.03. 6
sometimes queen, prepare thee hence for france. 5.01. 37
hence, villain! 5.02. 86
take hence the rest, and give them burial here. 5.05.118
i'll be sworn i have power to shame him hence. 1H4 3.01. 60
break with your wives of your departure hence. 3.01.142
hang in the air a thousand leagues from hence, 3.01.224
some twelve days hence | our general forces at 3.02.177
of our proceedings kept the earl from hence, 4.01. 65
hence therefore, every leader to his charge, 5.01.118
hence therefore, thou nice crutch! 2H4 1.01.145
and hence, thou sickly coif! 1.01.147
you hunt counter, hence, avaunt! 1.02. 90 P
night, and we must hence and leave it unpick'd. 2.04.368 P
all members of our cause, both here and hence, 4.01.169
fondly brought here and foolishly sent hence. 4.02.119
blunt, lead him hence, and see you guard him 4.03. 75
up, and bear me hence | into some other chamber. 4.04.131
the prince hath ta'en it hence. 4.05. 59
all you sage counsellors, hence! 4.05.120
god put /it in thy mind to take it hence, | that 4.05.178
foreign quarrels, that action, hence borne out, 4.05.214
make less thy body (hence) and more thy grace, 5.05. 52
come, will you hence? 5.05.109
and therefore, living hence, did give ourself H5 1.02.270
so get you hence in peace; 1.02.294
we carry not a heart with us from hence | that 2.02. 21
get you therefore hence, | poor miserable 2.02.177
bear them hence. 2.02.181
speed him hence, | let him greet england with 3.05. 36
let him go hence, and with his cap in hand 4.05. 13
hence! 5.01. 21
hence grew the general wrack and massacre; 1H6 1.01.135
when i have chased all thy foes from hence, 1.02.115
now beat them hence, why do you let them stay? 1.03. 54
thee i'll chase hence, thou wolf in sheep'i 1.03. 55
bear hence his body, i will help to bury it. 1.04. 87
with sweet enlargement doth dismiss me hence. 2.05. 30
but now thy uncle is removing hence, | as 2.05.104
keepers, convey him hence, and i myself | will 2.05.120
not to be gone from hence; 3.02. 94
for i am marching hence. 3.03. 39
that i may bear them hence | and give them 4.07. 85
go take their bodies hence. 4.07. 91
i'll bear them hence; 4.07. 92
then lead me hence; 5.04. 86
till thou speak, thou shalt not pass from hence. 2H6 1.04. 27
you four, from hence to prison back again; 2.03. 5
go, take hence that traitor from our sight, 2.03.100
stanley, i prithee go, and take me hence, | i 2.04. 91
and charity chas'd hence by rancor's hand; 3.01.144
even so remorseless have they borne him hence; 3.01.213
away even now, or i will drag thee hence. 3.02.229
now get thee hence, the king, thou know'st, is 3.02.386
convey him hence, and on our longboat's side 4.01. 68
away, convey him hence. 4.01.103
and so farewell, for i must hence again. 4.05. 12
hence will i drag thee headlong by the heels 4.10. 80
to heave the traitor somerset from hence, | and 5.01. 61
hence, heap of wrath, foul indigested lump, | as 5.01.157
would she break from hence, that this my body 3H6 2.01. 75
foreslow no longer, make we hence amain. 2.03. 56
i'll bear thee hence, where i may weep my fill. 2.05.113
i'll bear thee hence, and let them fight that 2.05.121
are at our backs, and therefore hence amain. 2.05.133
i will not hence, till with my talk and tears 3.03.158
alas, you know, 'tis far from hence to france; 4.01. 4
for i will hence to warwick's other daughter, 4.01.120
now therefore let us hence, and lose no hour, 4.01.148
i'll hence forthwith unto the sanctuary, | to 4.04. 31
but let us hence, my sovereign, to provide | a 4.06. 87
forthwith we'll send him hence to brittany, 4.06. 97
then fare you well, for i will hence again, | i 4.07. 48
seize on the shame–fac'd henry, bear him hence, 4.08. 52
hence with him to the tower, let him not speak. 4.08. 57
how far hence is thy lord, mine honest fellow? 5.01. 2
and do expect him here some two hours hence. 5.01. 10
nay rather, wilt thou draw thy forces hence, 5.01. 25
here pitch our battle, hence we will not budge. 5.04. 66
go bear them hence, i will not hear them speak. 5.05. 4
i'll hence to london on a serious matter. 5.05. 47
away with her, go bear her hence perforce. 5.05. 68
nay, never bear me hence, dispatch me here; 5.05. 69
away, i say, i charge ye bear her hence. 5.05. 81
now march we hence. 5.05. 87
away with her, and waft her hence to france. 5.07. 41
cursed the blood that let this blood from hence! R3 1.02. 16
foul devil, for god's sake hence, and trouble us 1.02. 50
embassage | from my redeemer to redeem me hence; 2.01. 4
but i shall laugh at this a twelvemonth hence, 3.02. 57
let me but meet you, ladies, /an hour hence, 4.01. 28
hence both are gone with conscience and remorse 4.03. 20
to have him suddenly convey'd from hence. 4.04. 76
lash hence these overweening rags of france, 5.03.328
what hence? H8 1.02.192
hence i took a thought | this was a judgment on 2.04.194
other comforts) far hence | in mine own country, 3.01. 90
you, | from hence you be committed to the tower, 5.02. 89
what heart receives from hence a conquering part TRO 1.03.352
when i am hence, | i'll answer to my lust, and 4.04.131
and bear hence | a great addition earned in thy 4.05.140
hence, broker, lackey! 5.10. 33
some two months hence my will shall here be made 5.10. 52
hence to your homes, be gone! COR 1.01.248
let's hence, and hear | how the dispatch is made 1.01.276

that we with smoking swords may march from hence 1.04. 11
hence; 1.07. 6
get you hence instantly, and tell those friends 2.03.213
hence, old goat! 3.01.176
hence, rotten thing! 3.01.178
will you hence | before the tag return, whose 3.01.246
to eject him hence | were but one danger, and to 3.01.285
hence! 4.05. 49 P
therefore let's hence, | and with our fair 5.01. 73
my country's love | than when i parted hence, 5.06. 72
bear from hence his body, | and mourn you for 5.06.141
brothers, help to convey her hence away, | and TIT 1.01.287
i pray you let us hence, | and let her joy her 2.03. 82
drag hence her husband to some secret hole, 2.03.129
now will i hence to seek my lovely moor, | and 2.03.190
on, you thick–lipp'd slave, i'll bear you hence, 4.02.175
this wicked emperor may have shipp'd her hence, 4.03. 23
now will i hence about thy business, | and take 5.02.132
some loving friends convey the emperor hence, 5.03.191
was that my father that went hence so fast? ROM 1.01.162
i must hence to wait; 1.03.103 P
hence will i to my ghostly /sire's close cell, 2.02.188
o, let us hence, i stand on sudden haste. 2.03. 93
then hie you hence to friar lawrence' cell, 2.05. 68
didst consort him here, | shalt with him hence. 3.01.131
hence be gone, away! 3.01.135
offense | immediately we do exile him hence. 3.01.187
let romeo hence in haste, | else, when he is 3.01.194
bear hence this body and attend our will; 3.01.196
hence "banished" is banish'd from the world, 3.03. 19
ascend her chamber, hence and comfort her. 3.03.147
go hence, good night; 3.03.166
or by the break of day /disguis'd from hence. 3.03.168
hie hence, be gone, away! 3.05. 26
hunting thee hence with hunt's–up to the day. 3.05. 34
night | shall romeo bear thee hence to mantua. 4.01.117
that hath ta'en her hence to make me wail, 4.05. 31
i will hence to–night. 5.01. 26
friar john, go hence, | get me an iron crow, and 5.02. 20
hence, and stand aloof. 5.03. 1
in dear employment — therefore hence be gone. 5.03. 32
fly hence and leave me, think upon these gone, 5.03. 60
my master knows not but i am gone hence, | and 5.03.132
go get thee hence, for i will not away. 5.03.160
go hence to have more talk of these sad things; 5.03.307
go not you hence | till i have thank'd you. TIM 1.01.244
away, unpeaceable dog, or i'll spurn thee hence! 1.01.271 P
hence, be gone! 4.03.274
hence, pack! 5.01.112
there's payment, hence! 5.01.113
hence! JC 1.01. 1
some two months hence, up higher toward the 2.01.109
betimes, | and every man hence to his idle bed; 2.01.117
hence! wilt thou lift up olympus? 3.01. 74
run hence, proclaim, cry it about the streets. 3.01. 79
how many ages hence | shall this our lofty scene 3.01.111
hie hence, and tell him so. 3.01.290
get you hence, sirrah; saucy fellow, hence! 4.03.134
get you hence, sirrah; saucy fellow, hence! 4.03.134
companion, hence! 4.03.138
early to–morrow will we rise, and hence. 4.03.230
hence! 5.05. 43
from hence to enverness, | and bind us further MAC 1.04. 42
and when goes hence? 1.05. 59
goes the king hence to–day? 2.03. 53
help me hence, ho! 2.03.118
from hence to th' palace gate | make it their 3.03. 13
hence, horrible shadow! 3.04.105
unreal mock'ry, hence! 3.04.106
hence with your little ones. 4.02. 69
take thy face hence. 5.03. 19
drug, | would scour these english hence? 5.03. 56
there is nor flying hence, nor tarrying here. 5.05. 47
both here and hence pursue me lasting strife, HAM 3.02.222
but we will ship him hence, and this vile deed 4.01. 30
must send thee hence | /with /fiery /quickness; 4.03. 42
delay it not, i'll have him hence to–night. 4.03. 55
hence, and avoid my sight! LR 1.01.124
freedom lives hence, and banishment is here. 1.01.181
i think our father will hence to–night. 1.01.285 P
several messengers | from hence attend dispatch. 2.01.125
my lord of gloucester hath convey'd him hence. 3.07. 15
thou wilt o'ertake us hence a mile or twain | i' 4.01. 42
faith, he is posted hence on serious matter. 4.05. 8
hence, | lest that th' infection of his fortune 4.06.232
their going hence even as their coming hither, 5.02. 10
from heaven, | and fire us hence like foxes. 5.03. 23
the gods defend her! bear him hence awhile. 5.03.257
bear them from hence. 5.03.319
from hence trust not your daughters' minds | by OTH 1.01.170
went he hence now? 3.03. 51
profit, and from hence | i'll love no friend, 3.03.379
he went hence but now; 3.04.132
hence, avaunt! 4.01.260
o, for a chair, | to bear him easily hence! 5.01. 83
some good man bear him carefully from hence, 5.01. 99
i must with haste from hence. ANT 1.02.132
under us require, | our quick remove from hence. 1.02.196
nilus' slime, i go from hence | thy soldier, 1.03. 69
your honor calls you hence, | therefore be deaf 1.03. 97
and i, hence fleeting, here remain with thee. 1.03.104
hence, | horrible villain, or i'll spurn thine 2.05. 62
go get thee hence! 2.05. 95
get thee hence; 2.05.103
lead me from hence; 2.05.109
take hence this jack and whip him. 3.13. 93
take him hence. 3.13.101
hence with thy stripes, be gone! 3.13.152
hence, mardian, | and bring me how he takes my 4.13. 9
hence, saucy eunuch, peace! 4.14. 25
that thou depart'st hence safe | does pay thy 4.14. 36
o charmian, i will never go from hence. 4.15. 1
prithee go hence, | or i shall show the cinders 5.02.172
get thee hence, farewell. 5.02.259
your highness, | i will from hence to–day. CYM 1.01. 80
thou basest thing, avoid hence, from my sight! 1.01.125
about some half hour hence, | pray you speak 1.01.176
but first of all, | how we may steal from hence; 3.02. 62
but first, how get hence. 3.02. 64
hence, vile instrument! 3.04. 73
my emperor hath wrote i must from hence, | and 3.05. 2
he goes hence frowning; 3.05. 18
hence! 4.02. 67
hence then, and thank | the man that gave them 4.02. 84
i'll follow those that even now fled hence, 4.02. 98
he went hence even now. 4.02.189
you snatch some hence for little faults; 5.01. 12
poor shadows of elysium, hence, and rest | upon 5.04. 97
they went hence so soon as they were born. 5.04.126
dangerous fellow, hence! 5.05.237
take him hence, | the whole world shall not save 5.05.320
brief, he must hence depart to tyre: PER 3.ch. 39
the petty wrens of tharsus will fly hence | and 4.03. 22
bird melodious, or bird fair, | is absent hence! TNK 1.01. 18
as before, hence you, | and at the banks of 1.01.211
chances, | were we from hence, would sever us. 2.02. 95
brought him to a little wood | a mile hence. 2.06. 4
i'll come again some two hours hence and bring 3.03. 49
methinks, from hence, as from a promontory 4.02. 22
the scene's not for our seeing, go we hence, 5.03.134
bear this hence. 5.04.109
your spirit | to send him hence forgiven. 5.04.120
i pray you hence, and leave me here alone, | for VEN 382
sighs like whirlwinds labor hence to heave thee. LUC 586
till after a deep groan) "tarquin from hence?" 1276
the turtle fled | in a mutual flame from hence. PHT 24
breed, to brave him when he takes thee hence. SON 12.14
by praising him here who doth hence remain! 39.14
from hence your memory death cannot take, 81. 3
your name from hence immortal life shall have, 81. 5
i teach thee how | to make him seem long hence, 101.14
hence, thou suborn'd informer! 125.13
and controversy hence a question takes, LC 110
both fire from hence and chill extincture hath. 294

HENCEFORTH 43 FR 0.0048 REL FR 36 V 7 P
whereof, henceforth carry your letters yourself: TGV 1.01.145 P
this babble shall not henceforth trouble me. 1.02. 95
meaning henceforth to trouble you no more. 2.01.119
pardon me, wife, henceforth do what thou wilt. WIV 4.04. 6
and dispose | for henceforth of poor claudio. ADO 5.01.295
henceforth my wooing mind shall be express'd LLL 5.02.412
henceforth be never numb'red among men! MND 3.02. 67
from henceforth i will, coz, and devise sports. AYL 1.02. 24 P
wheel, that her gifts may henceforth be bestow'd 1.02. 32 P
henceforth i vow it shall be so for me. SHR 4.05. 15
i will henceforth eat no fish of fortune's AWW 5.02. 7 P
direct thy feet | where thou and i, henceforth, TN 5.01.169
if ever, henceforth, thou | these rural latches WT 4.04.437
from henceforth bear his name whose form thou JN 1.01.160
sure | i will from henceforth rather be myself, 1H4 1.03. 5
henceforth | let me not hear you speak of 1.03.118
i must not have you henceforth question me 2.03.103
henceforth ne'er look on me. 2.04.445 P
floods, | and flow henceforth in formal majesty. 2H4 5.02.133
and henceforth let a welsh correction teach you H5 5.01. 78 P
henceforth we banish thee, on pain of death. 1H6 4.01. 47
henceforth i charge you, as you love our favor, 4.01.135
that henceforth he shall trouble us no more. 2H6 3.01.324
and be henceforth a burying–place to all that do 4.10. 63 P
and will that thou henceforth attend on us. 5.01. 80
henceforth i will not have to do with pity. 5.02. 56
for never henceforth shall i joy again, | never, 3H6 2.01. 77
pass, | and henceforth i am thy true servitor. 3.03.196
for i will henceforth be no more unconstant. 5.01.102
henceforth guard thee well, | for i'll not kill TRO 4.05.253
or be ye not henceforth call'd my children. TIT 2.03.115
henceforth i never will be romeo. ROM 2.02. 51
thou and my bosom henceforth shall be twain. 3.05.240
henceforth be no feast | whereat a villain's not TIM 3.06.102
henceforth hated be | of timon man and all 3.06.104
yes, cassius, and, from henceforth, | when you JC 4.03.121
henceforth be earls, the first that ever MAC 5.09. 29
henceforth i'll bear | affliction till it do cry LR 4.06. 75
you may see, lepidus, and henceforth know, | it ANT 1.04. 1
henceforth | the white hand of a lady fever thee 3.13.137
to write and read | be henceforth treacherous! CYM 4.02.317
from henceforth i'll not dare | to ask you any TNK 1.01.203
"bonnet nor veil henceforth no creature wear! VEN 1081

HENCEFORWARD 6 FR 0.0006 REL FR 3 V 3 P
or dagger, henceforward, upon pain of death. 1H6 1.03. 78 P
and now henceforward it shall be treason for any 2H6 4.06. 5 P
and henceforward all things shall be in common. 4.07. 18 P
henceforward will i bear | upon my target three 3H6 2.01. 39
henceforward do your messages yourself. ROM 2.05. 64
henceforward i am ever rul'd by you. 4.02. 22

HENCE–GOING 1 FR 0.0001 REL FR 1 V 0 P
in time, from our hence–going | and our return, CYM 3.02. 63

HENCHMAN 1 FR 0.0001 REL FR 1 V 0 P
beg a little changeling boy | to be my henchman. MND 2.01.121

HENRI 1 FR 0.0001 REL FR 0 V 1 P
notre tres cher fils henri, roi d'angleterre, H5 5.02.339 P

HENRICUS 1 FR 0.0001 REL FR 0 V 1 P
praeclarissimus filius noster henricus, rex H5 5.02.341 P

/HENRY 4 FR 0.0004 REL FR 3 V 1 P
/state /and /crown | /to /henry /bullingbrook. R2 4.01.180
/god /save /king /henry, /unking'd /richard 4.01.220
/and /then /that /henry /bullingbrook /and /he, 2H4 4.01.115
by the name of /henry lord scroop of masham. H5 2.02.147 P

HENRY 163 FR 0.0184 REL FR 156 V 7 P
greece, | and peter turph, and henry pimpernell, SHR in.2. 94
and brought prince henry in their company, | at JN 5.06. 34
brought hither henry herford thy bold son, R2 1.01. 3
himself and to approve | henry of herford, 1.03.113
henry bullingbrook | on both his knees doth kiss 3.03. 35
him, | and long live henry, fourth of that name! 4.01.112
the devil take henry of lancaster and thee! 5.05.102
three times hath henry bullingbrook made head 1H4 3.01. 63
with all the world | in praise of henry percy. 5.01. 87
henry lord scroop of masham, and the third, H5 2.pr. 24
is thine, and henry plantagenet is thine"; 5.02.240 P
henry the sixt, in infant bands crown'd king ep 9
king henry the fift, too famous to live long! 1H6 1.01. 6
henry is dead, and never shall revive. 1.01. 18
henry the fift, thy ghost i invocate: 1.01. 52
if henry were recall'd to life again, | these 1.01. 66
remember, lords, your oaths to henry sworn: 1.01.162
and then i will proclaim young henry king. 1.01.169
whom henry, our late sovereign, ne'er could 1.03. 24
henry the fift he first train'd to the wars; 1.04. 79
and for the right | of english henry, shall this 2.01. 36
since henry monmouth first began to reign, 2.05. 23
henry the fourth, grandfather to this king, 2.05. 63
long after this, when henry the fift 2.05. 82
o my good lords, and virtuous henry, | pity the 3.01. 76
when gloucester says the word, king henry goes, 3.01.183
which in the time of henry nam'd the fift | was 3.01.195
that henry born at monmouth should win all, 3.01.197
win all, | and henry born at windsor lose all: 3.01.198
i, as sure as english henry lives | and as his 3.02. 80
for there young henry with his nobles lie. 3.02.129
ill, | who then but english henry will be lord, 3.03. 66
god save king henry, of that name the sixt! 4.01. 2
pardon me, princely henry, and the rest. 4.01. 18
and this is mine, sweet henry, favor him. 4.01. 81
ever–living man of memory, | henry the fift. 4.03. 52
great marshal to henry the sixt | of all his 4.07. 70
verified | henry the fift did sometime prophesy: 5.01. 31
let henry fret, and all the world repine. 5.02. 20
henry is youthful and will quickly yield. 5.03. 99
embrace | the christian prince, king henry, were 5.03.172
solicit henry with her wondrous praise; 5.03.190
that, in regard king henry gives consent, | of 5.04.124
intents, | to love and honor henry as her lord. 5.05. 21
and otherwise will henry ne'er presume. 5.05. 22
henry is able to enrich his queen, | and not to 5.05. 51
whom should we match with henry, being a king, 5.05. 66
for henry, son unto a conqueror, | is likely to 5.05. 73
suffolk, ambassador for henry king of england, 2H6 1.01. 45 P
that the said henry shall espouse the lady 1.01. 46 P
did my brother henry spend his youth, | his 1.01. 78
his wits, | to keep by policy what henry got? 1.01. 84
wives, | and our king henry gives away his own, 1.01.130
had henry got an empire by his marriage, | and 1.01.153
and henry was well pleas'd | to change two 1.01.218
till henry, surfeiting in joys of love | with 1.01.251
against my king and nephew, virtuous henry, | be 1.02. 20
where henry and dame margaret kneel'd to me, 1.02. 39
shall king henry be a pupil still | under the 1.03. 46
i thought king henry had resembled thee | in 1.03. 53
the duke yet lives that henry shall depose; 1.04. 30
"the duke yet lives that henry shall depose; 1.04. 59
death reign'd as king | till henry bullingbrook, 2.02. 21
crown'd by the name of henry the fourth, 2.02. 23
henry doth claim the crown from john of gaunt, 2.02. 54
henry will to himself | protector be, and god 2.03. 23
god and king henry govern england's realm. 2.03. 30
here, noble henry, is my staff. 2.03. 32
resign | as ere thy father henry made it mine; 2.03. 34
why, now is henry king and margaret queen, | and 2.03. 39
thus king henry throws away his crutch | before 3.01.189
for, good king henry, thy decay i fear. 3.01.194
henry my lord is cold in great affairs, | too 3.01.224
be, | and henry put apart, the next for me. 3.01.383
run, go, help, help! o henry, ope thine eyes! 3.02. 35
comfort, my sovereign! gracious henry, comfort! 3.02. 38
for henry weeps that thou dost live so long. 3.02.121
true, | but how he died god knows, not henry. 3.02.131
o henry, let me plead for gentle suffolk! 3.02.289
for his father's sake, henry the fift (in whose 4.02.157 P
henry the fift, that made all france to quake, 4.08. 17
is cade the son of henry the fift, | that thus 4.08. 34
henry hath money, you are strong and manly; 4.08. 51
the name of henry the fift hales them to an 4.08. 56 P
and henry, though he be infortunate, | assure 4.09. 18
a messenger from henry, our dread liege, | to 5.01. 17
till henry be more weak and i more strong. 5.01. 31
and let my sovereign, virtuous henry, | command 5.01. 48
and bashful henry depos'd, whose cowardice 3H6 1.01. 41
shall be the war that henry means to use. 1.01. 73
the crown, | in following this usurping henry. 1.01. 81
i am the son of henry the fift, | who made the 1.01.107
peace thou! and give king henry leave to speak. 1.01.120
prove it, henry, and thou shalt be king. 1.01.131
henry the fourth by conquest got the crown. 1.01.132
lords, | resign'd the crown to henry the fourth, 1.01.139
think not that henry shall be so depos'd. 1.01.153
king henry, be thy title right or wrong, | lord 1.01.159
henry of lancaster, resign thy crown. 1.01.164
base, fearful, and despairing henry! 1.01.178
turn this way, henry, and regard them not. 1.01.189
long live king henry! plantagenet, embrace him. 1.01.202
divorce myself | both from thy table, henry, and 1.01.248
mine, boys? not till king henry be dead. 1.02. 10
henry had none, but did usurp the place. 1.02. 25
and trust not simple henry nor his oaths. 1.02. 59
till our king henry had shook hands with death. 1.04.102
now, perjur'd henry, wilt thou kneel for grace, 2.02. 81
what say'st thou, henry, wilt thou yield the 2.02.101
say, henry, shall i have my right, or no? 2.02.126
which, whiles it lasted, gave king henry light. 2.06. 2
impairing henry, strength'ning misproud york. 2.06. 7
and, henry, hadst thou sway'd as kings should do 2.06. 14
that led calm henry, though he were a king, | as 2.06. 34
she, on his left side, craving aid for henry; 3.01. 43
she weeps, and says her henry is depos'd; 3.01. 45
so would you be again to henry, | if he were 3.01. 95
my gracious lord, henry your foe is taken, | and 3.02.118
is clarence, henry, and his son young edward, 3.02.130
that henry, sole possessor of my love, | is, of 3.03. 24
reason may suffice, | that henry liveth still; 3.03. 72
because thy father henry did usurp, | and thou 3.03. 79
and after john of gaunt, henry the fourth, 3.03. 83
and after that wise prince, henry the fift, 3.03. 85
from these our henry lineally descends. 3.03. 87
you told not how henry the sixt hath lost | all 3.03. 89
lost | all that which henry the fift had gotten? 3.03. 90
for shame, leave henry, and call edward king. 3.03.100
the more that henry was unfortunate. 3.03.118
henry now lives in scotland at his ease; 3.03.151
did i put henry from his native right? 3.03.190
him, | i here renounce him and return to henry. 3.03.194
bona, | and replant henry in his former state. 3.03.198
renowned prince, how shall poor henry live, 3.03.214
belike he thinks me henry. 4.01. 96

applaud the name of henry with your leader. 4.02. 27
but henry now shall wear the english crown, 4.03. 49
to do, | to free king henry from imprisonment, 4.03. 63
my liege, it is young henry, earl of richmond. 4.06. 67
for now we owe allegiance unto henry. 4.07. 19
but, master mayor, if henry be your king, | yet 4.07. 20
my right, | and henry but usurps the diadem. 4.07. 66
for well i wot that henry is no soldier. 4.07. 83
thee | to flatter henry and forsake thy brother! 4.07. 85
seize on the shame–fac'd henry, bear him hence, 4.08. 52
and henry is my king, warwick his subject. 5.01. 38
you left poor henry at the bishop's palace, 5.01. 45
henry, your sovereign, | is prisoner to the foe, 5.04. 76
indeed 'tis true that henry told me of; 5.06. 69
king henry and the prince his son are gone; 5.06. 89
room, | and triumph, henry, in thy day of doom. 5.06. 93
of these plantagenets, henry and edward, | as R3 1.02.118
for i did kill king henry — | but 'twas thy 1.02.179
thou kill'dst my husband henry in the tower, 1.03.118
so stood the state when henry the sixt | was 2.03. 16
me, henry the sixt | did prophesy that richmond 4.02. 95
holy king henry and thy fair son edward, 5.01. 4
to, with sir henry guilford | this night to be H8 1.03. 66
my noble father, henry of buckingham, | who 2.01.107
henry the seventh succeeding, truly pitying | my 2.01.112
henry the eight, life, honor, name, and all 2.01.116
say, henry king of england, come into the court. 2.04. 6 P
henry king of england, etc. 2.04. 8 P
HENRY'S 47 FR 0.0053 REL FR 47 V 0 P
thrown | a brave defiance in king henry's teeth, 1H4 5.02. 42
stars | that have consented unto henry's death: 1H6 1.01. 5
since arms avail not now that henry's dead. 1.01. 47
say'st thou, man, before dead henry's corse? 1.01. 62
wherewith you now bedew king henry's hearse, | i 1.01.104
with henry's death the english circle ends, 1.02.136
since henry's death, i fear, there is conveyance 1.03. 2
france were no place for henry's warriors, | nor 3.03. 22
regard, | king henry's peers and chief nobility 4.01.146
i'll undertake to make thee henry's queen, | to 5.03.117
i am unworthy to be henry's wife. 5.03.122
my daughter shall be henry's, if he please. 5.03.156
and i again, in henry's royal name, | as deputy 5.03.160
that, when thou com'st to kneel at henry's feet, 5.03.194
king henry's faithful and anointed queen. 5.05. 91
shall henry's conquest, bedford's vigilance, 2H6 1.01. 96
king henry's diadem, | enchas'd with all the 1.02. 7
demanding of king henry's life and death, | and 2.01.171
where it best fits to be, in henry's hand. 2.03. 44
obscure and lousy swain, king henry's blood, 4.01. 50
and pluck the crown from feeble henry's head. 5.01. 2
thus do i hope to shake king henry's head. 3H6 1.01. 20
for this is thine and not king henry's heirs'. 1.01. 27
far be the thought of this from henry's heart, 1.01. 70
even in the lukewarm blood of henry's heart. 1.02. 34
ay, this is he that took king henry's chair, 1.04. 97
and will you pale your head in henry's glory, 1.04.103
touching king henry's oath and your succession. 2.01.119
can pluck the diadem from faint henry's head, 2.01.153
and who shines now but henry's enemies? 2.06. 10
with this my son, prince edward, henry's heir, 3.03. 31
if that go forward, henry's hope is done. 3.03. 58
yet here prince edward stands, king henry's son. 3.03. 73
before thy coming, lewis was henry's friend. 3.03.143
and joy that thou becom'st king henry's friend. 3.03.201
not that i pity henry's misery, | but seek 3.03.264
but what said henry's queen? 4.01.102
to set the crown once more on henry's head. 4.04. 27
together like a double shadow | to henry's body, 4.06. 50
as henry's late presaging prophecy | did glad my 4.06. 92
my waned state for henry's regal crown. 4.07. 4
open the gates, we are king henry's friends. 4.07. 28
rest you, whiles i lament king henry's corse. R3 1.02. 32
see dead henry's wounds | open their congeal'd 1.02. 55
so much with heaven | that henry's death, my 1.03.191
now | came to me as i follow'd henry's corse, 4.01. 66
king henry's issue, richmond, comforts thee. 5.03.123
HENS 1 FR 0.0001 REL FR 0 V 1 P
a couple of short–legg'd hens, a joint of mutton 2H4 5.01. 27 P
HENT 3 FR 0.0003 REL FR 3 V 0 P
and gravest citizens | have hent the gates, and MM 4.06. 14
foot–path way, | and merrily hent the stile–a; WT 4.03.124
up, sword, and know thou a more horrid hent: HAM 3.03. 88
HENTON 2 FR 0.0002 REL FR 2 V 0 P
to this | by a vain prophecy of nicholas henton. H8 1.02.147
what was that henton? 1.02.148
HEPS 1 FR 0.0001 REL FR 1 V 0 P
the oaks bear mast, the briers scarlet heps; TIM 4.03.419
HER* *(also 'er)*
/HER* 55 FR 0.0062 REL FR 48 V 7 P
HER* 4444 FR 0.5023 REL FR 3432 V 1012 P
HERALD *(also heralt)*
/HERALD 2 FR 0.0002 REL FR 2 V 0 P
/a /herald, /ho, /a /herald! LR 5.03.102
/a /herald, /ho, /a /herald! 5.03.102
HERALD 32 FR 0.0036 REL FR 32 V 0 P
my herald thoughts in thy pure bosom rest them, TGV 3.01.144
my herald is return'd. LLL 3.01. 69
their herald is a pretty knavish page, | that 5.02. 97
a herald, kate? o, put me in thy books! SHR 2.01.224
durst make too bold a herald of my tongue; AWW 5.03. 46
where is montjoy the herald? H5 3.05. 36
when they were in health, i tell thee, herald, 3.06.148
herald, save thou thy labor. 4.03.121
come thou no more for ransom, gentle herald, 4.03.122
thou never shalt hear herald any more. 4.03.127
take a trumpet, herald, | ride thou unto the 4.07. 56
here comes the herald of the french, my liege. 4.07. 66
how now, what means this, herald? 4.07. 68
i tell thee truly, herald, | i know not if the 4.07. 83
now, herald, are the dead numb'red? 4.08. 73
herald, conduct me to the dolphin's tent, | to 1H6 4.07. 51
herald, away, and throughout every town 2H6 4.02.176
wing, | jove's mercury, and herald for a king! R3 4.03. 55
after my death i wish no other herald, | no H8 4.02. 69
may one that is a herald and a prince | do a TRO 1.03.218
as the most noble corse that ever herald | did COR 5.06.143
it was the lark, the herald of the morn, | no ROM 3.05. 6
thanks, | only to herald thee into his sight, MAC 1.03.102
a station like the herald mercury | new lighted HAM 3.04. 58
when time shall serve, let but the herald cry, LR 5.01. 48
a herald, ho! 5.03.102
come hither, herald. 5.03.107
heaven can make | to herald thee from the womb. PER 3.01. 34
the owl (night's herald) shrieks, 'tis very late VEN 531
some loathsome dash the herald will contrive, LUC 206
sole arabian tree, | herald sad and trumpet be, PHT 3
ornament, | and only herald to the gaudy spring, SON 1.10
HERALDRY *(also heraldy)*
HERALDRY 4 FR 0.0004 REL FR 3 V 1 P
two of the first, /like coats in heraldry, | due MND 3.02.213
of your birth and virtue gives you heraldry. AWW 2.03.262 P
but our new heraldry is hands, not hearts. OTH 3.04. 47
this heraldry in lucrece' face was seen, LUC 64
HERALD'S 2 FR 0.0002 REL FR 1 V 1 P
shoulders like a herald's coat without sleeves; 1H4 4.02. 44 P
but thou shalt wear it as a herald's coat, | to 2H6 4.10. 70
HERALDS 8 FR 0.0009 REL FR 8 V 0 P
heralds, from off our tow'rs we might behold, JN 2.01.325
like heralds 'twixt two dreadful battles set: 4.02. 78
our heralds go with him; H5 4.07.116
heralds, wait on us. 1H6 1.01. 45
and night–walking heralds | that trudge betwixt R3 1.01. 72
by their heralds challeng'd | the noble spirits H8 1.01. 34
love's heralds should be thoughts, | which ten ROM 2.05. 4
send | such dreadful heralds to astonish us. JC 1.03. 56
HERALDY *(also heraldry)*
HERALDY 2 FR 0.0002 REL FR 2 V 0 P
compact | well ratified by law and heraldy, HAM 1.01. 87
complexion smear'd | with heraldy more dismal. 2.02.456
HERALT *(also herald)*
HERALT 1 FR 0.0001 REL FR 0 V 1 P
silence is the perfectest heralt of joy; ADO 2.01.306 P
HERB 9 FR 0.0010 REL FR 6 V 3 P
the herb i showed thee once. MND 2.01.169
fetch me this herb, and be thou here again | ere 2.01.173
sight | (as i can take it with another herb), 2.01.184
then crush this herb into lysander's eye; 3.02.366
sallets ere we light on such another herb. AWW 4.05. 15 P
of the sallet, or rather the herb of grace. 4.05. 17 P
i'll set a bank of rue, sour herb of grace. R2 3.04.105
we may call it herb of grace a' sundays. HAM 4.05.182 P
no flow'r was nigh, no grass, herb, leaf, or VEN 1055
HERBERT 2 FR 0.0002 REL FR 2 V 0 P
sir walter herbert, a renowned soldier, | sir R3 4.05. 12
and /you, sir walter herbert — stay with me. 5.03. 28
HERBLETS 1 FR 0.0001 REL FR 1 V 0 P
even so | these herblets shall, which we upon CYM 4.02.287
HERBS 11 FR 0.0012 REL FR 9 V 2 P
medea gathered the enchanted herbs | that did MV 5.01. 13
they are not herbs, you knave, they are AWW 4.05. 18 P
her knots disordered and her wholesome herbs R2 3.04. 46
and choke the herbs for want of husbandry. 2H6 3.01. 33
"small herbs have grace, great weeds do grow R3 2.04. 13
such with'red herbs as these | are meet for TIT 3.01.177
the powerful grace that lies | in plants, herbs, ROM 2.03. 16
encamp them still | in man as well as herbs, 2.03. 28
it with one gender of herbs or distract it with OTH 1.03.323 P
the herbs that have on them cold dew o' th' CYM 4.02.284
herbs for their smell, and sappy plants to bear: VEN 165
HERB–WOMAN 1 FR 0.0001 REL FR 0 V 1 P
why, your herb–woman, she that sets seeds and PER 4.06. 85 P
HERCULEAN 1 FR 0.0001 REL FR 1 V 0 P
how this herculean roman does become | the ANT 1.03. 84
HERCULES' *(also ercles', etc.)*
HERCULES' 2 FR 0.0002 REL FR 0 V 2 P
the interim undertake one of hercules' labors, ADO 2.01.365 P
butt–shaft is too hard for hercules' club, and LLL 1.02.176 P
/HERCULES 1 FR 0.0001 REL FR 0 V 1 P
/my /lord — /hercules /and /his /load /too. HAM 2.02.361 P
HERCULES 34 FR 0.0038 REL FR 21 V 13 P
discard, bully hercules, cashier; WIV 1.03. 6 P
she would have made hercules have turn'd spit, ADO 2.01.253 P
like the shaven hercules in the smirch'd 3.03.136 P
now as valiant as hercules that only tells a lie 4.01.321 P
hercules, master. LLL 1.02. 66 P
most sweet hercules! 1.02. 67 P
to see great hercules whipping a gig, | and 4.03.165
for valor, is not love a hercules, | still 4.03.337
the page, hercules. 5.01.129 P
he shall present hercules in minority; 5.01.134 P
cry, "well done, hercules, now thou crushest the 5.01.138 P
armado's page, hercules; 5.02.536 P
"great hercules is presented by this imp, 5.02.588
i was with hercules and cadmus once, | when in a MND 4.01.112
told my love, | in glory of my kinsman hercules. 5.01. 47
if hercules and lichas play at dice | which is MV 2.01. 32
go, hercules! 3.02. 60
the beards of hercules and frowning mars, | who, 3.02. 85
now hercules be thy speed, young man! AYL 1.02.210 P
yea, leave that labor to great hercules, | and SHR 1.02.255
in breaking 'em he is stronger than hercules. AWW 4.03.253 P
why, thou knowest i am as valiant as hercules; 1H4 2.04.271 P
i thought i should have seen some hercules, | a 1H6 2.03. 19
but hercules himself must yield to odds; 3H6 2.01. 53
to say, | if you had been the wife of hercules, COR 4.01. 17
as hercules | did shake down mellow fruit. 4.06. 99
but no more like my father | than i to hercules. HAM 1.02.153
let hercules himself do what he may, | the cat 5.01.291
by hercules, i think i am i' th' right. ANT 3.07. 67
'tis the god hercules, whom antony lov'd, | now 4.03. 16
not hercules | could have knock'd out his brains CYM 4.02.114
his martial thigh, | the brawns of hercules; 4.02.311
hercules our kinsman | (then weaker than your TNK 1.01. 66
seen, | since hercules, a man of tougher sinews. 2.05. 2
/HERD 1 FR 0.0001 REL FR 1 V 0 P
before he should thus stoop to th' /herd, but COR 3.02. 32
HERD 17 FR 0.0019 REL FR 14 V 3 P
sure it was the roar | of a whole herd of lions. TMP 2.01.316
for do but note a wild and wanton herd, | or MV 5.01. 71
anon a careless herd, | full of the pasture, AYL 2.01. 52
jowl horns together like any deer i' th' herd. AWW 1.03. 55 P
drew the rest of the herd to me that all their WT 4.04.608 P
a little herd of england's timorous deer, 1H6 4.02. 46
troop | as doth a lion in a herd of neat, | or 3H6 2.01. 14
noise of thy cross–bow | will scare the herd, 3.01. 7
the herd hath more annoyance by the breeze TRO 1.03. 48
you herd of — biles and plagues | plaster you COR 1.04. 31
are these your herd? 3.01. 33
he perceiv'd the common herd was glad he refus'd JC 1.02.264 P
the hill of basan, to outroar | the horned herd! ANT 3.13.128
the mounted heavens | view us their mortal herd, TNK 1.04. 5
and sometime sorteth with a herd of deer: VEN 689
and scarce the herd gone to the hedge for shade, PP 6. 2
which erst from heat did canopy the herd, | and SON 12. 6
HERDMEN 1 FR 0.0001 REL FR 1 V 0 P
gusts and foul flaws to herdmen and to herds. VEN 456
HERDS 4 FR 0.0004 REL FR 4 V 0 P
and the herds | were strangely clamorous to the 1H4 3.01. 38
and we in herds thy game, i give thee thanks TNK 5.01.132
gusts and foul flaws to herdmen and to herds. VEN 456
herds stands weeping, flocks all sleeping, PP 17.27
HERDSMAN 1 FR 0.0001 REL FR 1 V 0 P
worthy enough a herdsman, yea, him too, | that WT 4.04.435
HERDSMEN 2 FR 0.0002 REL FR 0 V 2 P
pray let's see these four threes of herdsmen. WT 4.04.336 P
being the herdsmen of the beastly plebeians. COR 2.01. 95 P
/HERE 19 FR 0.0021 REL FR 17 V 2 P
ourself and bushy, /bagot /here /and /green, R2 1.04. 23
/you /that /here /are /under /our /arrest, 4.01.158
/here, /cousin, /seize /the /crown; 4.01.181
/here, /cousin, | /on /this /side /my /hand, 4.01.182
/have /here /deliver'd /me /to /my /sour /cross, 4.01.241
/they /can /see /a /sort /of /traitors /here. 4.01.246
/for /i /have /given /here /my /soul's /consent 4.01.249
/i /have /a /king /here /to /my /flatterer. 4.01.308
/i /take /not /on /me /here /as /a /physician, 2H4 4.01. 60
/here /is /no /drink! TIT 3.02. 35
/melody, | /came /here /to /make /us /merry! 3.02. 65
/peace, /who /comes /here? HAM 5.02. 80
/thy /land, | /come /place /him /here /by /me, LR 1.04.142
/the /one /in /motley /here, | /the /other 1.04.146
/come /sit /thou /here, /most /learned /justicer 3.06. 21
/thou, /sapient /sir, /sit /here. 3.06. 22
/i /here /take /my /oath /before /this 3.06. 46 P
desperate of my fortunes if they check me /here. OTH 2.03.332 P
which i have /here recover'd from the moor. 5.02.240
HERE 2230 FR 0.2520 REL FR 1702 V 528 P
here, master; what cheer? TMP 1.01. 2 P
what do you here? 1.01. 38 P
if thou rememb'rest aught ere thou cam'st here, 1.02. 51
cam'st here, | how thou cam'st here thou mayst. 1.02. 52
here in this island we arriv'd, and here | have 1.02.171
in this island we arriv'd, and here | have i, 1.02.171
here cease more questions. 1.02.184
"hell is empty, | and all the devils are here." 1.02.215
with child, | and here was left by th' sailors. 1.02.270
(save for the son that /she did litter here, | a 1.02.282
and here you sty me | in this hard rock, whiles 1.02.342
foot it featly here and there, | and, sweet 1.02.379
good instruction give | how i may bear me here. 1.02.426
thou dost here usurp | the name thou ow'st not, 1.02.454
for i can here disarm thee with this stick, 1.02.473
the air breathes upon us here most sweetly. 2.01. 47 P
here is every thing advantageous to life. 2.01. 50 P
when he is earth'd, hath here almost persuaded 2.01.234
he's undrown'd, | as he that sleeps here swims. 2.01.238
here lies your brother, | no better than the 2.01.280
while you here do snoring lie, | open–ey'd 2.01.300
whiles we stood here securing your repose, 2.01.310
here comes a spirit of his, and to torment me 2.02. 15
what have we here? 2.02. 24 P
i will here shroud till the dregs of the storm 2.02. 40 P
here shall i die ashore —" | this is a very 2.02. 43
have we devils here? 2.02. 57 P
here is that which will give language to you, 2.02. 82 P
here; swear then how thou escap'dst. 2.02.127 P
here, kiss the book. 2.02.130 P
else being drown'd, we will inherit here. 2.02.175 P
here! 2.02.175 P
even here i will put off my hope, and keep it 3.03. 7
will't please you taste of what is here? 3.03. 42
which here, in this most desolate isle, else 3.03. 80
have given you here a third of mine own life, 4.01. 3
here, afore heaven, | i ratify this my rich gift 4.01. 7
what would my potent master? here i am. 4.01. 34
whom i give thee pow'r) here to this place. 4.01. 38
on his toe, | will be here with mop and mow. 4.01. 47
here on this grass–plot, in this very place, 4.01. 73
here thought they to have done | some wanton 4.01. 94
let me live here ever; 4.01.122
seest thou here, | this is the mouth o' th' cell 4.01.215
look what a wardrobe here is for thee! 4.01.223 P
but this rough magic | i here abjure; 5.01. 51
would here have kill'd your king, i do forgive 5.01. 78
trouble, wonder, and amazement | inhabits here. 5.01.105
how should prospero | be living, and be here? 5.01.120
i here could pluck his highness' frown upon you 5.01.127
how thou hast met us here, whom three hours 5.01.136
here have i few attendants, | and subjects none 5.01.166
arise, and say how thou cam'st here. 5.01.181
how many goodly creatures are there here! 5.01.182
o, look, sir, look, sir, here is more of us. 5.01.216
now 'tis true, | i must be here confin'd by you, ep 4
else | betideth here in absence of thy friend; TGV 1.01. 59
well, sir, here is for your pains. 1.01.131 P
when willingly i would have had her here! 1.02. 61
here is a coil with protestation! 1.02. 96
look, here is writ "kind julia." 1.02.106
and here is writ "love–wounded proteus." 1.02.110
lo, here in one line is his name twice writ, 1.02.120
shall these papers lie like tell–tales here? 1.02.130
yet here they shall not lie, for catching cold. 1.02.133
here is her hand, the agent of her heart; 1.03. 46
here is her oath for love, her honor's pawn: 1.03. 47
peace, here she comes. 2.01. 93 P
here, take you this. 2.02. 6
here is my hand for my true constancy; 2.02. 8
why, he that's tied here, crab, my dog. 2.03. 40 P
here comes my father. 2.04. 47 P
and here he means to spend his time a while. 2.04. 80
have done, have done; here comes the gentleman. 2.04. 99
there is a lady in /milano here | whom i affect; 3.01. 81
what's here? 3.01.137

and here an engine fit for my proceeding! 3.01.138
what's here? 3.01.150
tarry i here, i but attend on death, | but, fly 3.01.186
here if thou stay, thou canst not see thy love; 3.01.246
thy letters may be here, though thou art hence, 3.01.250
here is the cate–log of her condition. 3.01.274 P
here follow her vices. 3.01.321 P
she did, my lord, when valentine was here. 3.02. 27
of which if you should here disfurnish me, | you 4.01. 14
but here comes thurio. 4.02. 16
ay, but i hope, sir, that you love not here. 4.02. 21
here have i brought him back again. 4.04. 52 P
stayest thou to vex me here? 4.04. 61
here, youth, there is my purse; 4.04.176
here is her picture: 4.04.184
here comes the duke. 5.02. 30
here can i sit alone, unseen of any, | and to 5.04. 4
who's this comes here? 5.04. 18
ransom for offense, | i tender't here: 5.04. 76
here 'tis; this is it. 5.04. 91
here she stands: 5.04.129
know then, i here forget all former griefs, 5.04.142
forgive them what they have committed here | and 5.04.154
got pless your house here! WIV 1.01. 73 P
here is got's plessing, and your friend, and 1.01. 75 P
justice shallow, and here young master slender, 1.01. 76 P
is sir john falstaff here? 1.01. 98 P
here comes sir john. 1.01.108 P
word of denial in thy labras here! 1.01.163
i had my book of songs and sonnets here. 1.01.199 P
kind of tender, made afar off by sir hugh here. 1.01.209 P
in his country, simple though i stand here. 1.01.219 P
here comes fair mistress anne. 1.01.259 P
i had rather walk here, i thank you. 1.01.282 P
i have writ me here a letter to her; 1.03. 58 P
and here another to page's wife, who even now 1.03. 59 P
here, take the humor–letter; 1.03. 77 P
here will be an old abusing of god's patience 1.04. 4 P
out alas! here comes my master. 1.04. 36 P
run in here, good young man; 1.04. 37 P
here, sir! 1.04. 57 P
'tis ready, sir, here in the porch. 1.04. 61 P
anne's mind — that's neither here nor there. 1.04.106 P
it is not good you tarry here. 1.04.111 P
here, read, read; 2.01. 54 P
the heart, master page, 'tis here, 'tis here. 2.01.227 P
the heart, master page, 'tis here, 'tis here. 2.01.227 P
here, boys, here, here! shall we wag? 2.01.230 P
here, boys, here, here! shall we wag? 2.01.230 P
here, boys, here, here! shall we wag? 2.01.230 P
and i have a bag of money here troubles me. 2.02.171 P
now, sir john, here is the heart of my purpose: 2.02.224 P
to see thee traverse, to see thee here, to see 2.03. 25 P
here comes doctor caius. 3.01. 72 P
here, set it down. 3.03. 6 P
robert, be ready here hard by in the brew–house, 3.03. 10 P
here comes little robin. 3.03. 21 P
my master knows not of your being here, and has 3.03. 30 P
gentleman that he says is here now in the house, 3.03.108 P
it be not so, that you have such a man here; 3.03.113 P
but if you have a friend here, convey, convey 3.03.117 P
your husband's here at hand, bethink you of some 3.03.126 P
look, here is a basket; 3.03.129 P
of any reasonable stature, he may creep in here, 3.03.130 P
let me creep in here. 3.03.142 P
go take up these clothes here quickly. 3.03.146 P
here, here, here be my keys. 3.03.162 P
here, here, here be my keys. 3.03.162 P
here, here, here be my keys. 3.03.162 P
some special suspicion of falstaff's being here, 3.03.188 P
you may ask your father, here he comes. 3.04. 66 P
what does master fenton here? 3.04. 68
here, sir. 3.05. 2 P
o, here he comes. 3.05. 59 P
i'll but bring my young man here to school. 4.01. 8 P
truly, i am so glad you have nobody here. 4.02. 19 P
i am glad the fat knight is not here. 4.02. 29 P
protests to my husband he is now here, and hath 4.02. 33 P
but i am glad the knight is not here. 4.02. 36 P
hard by, at street end; he will be here anon. 4.02. 40 P
i am undone! the knight is here. 4.02. 41 P
but what make you here? 4.02. 54 P
nay, but he'll be here presently. 4.02. 97 P
well, he's not here i seek for. 4.02.158 P
(sometime a keeper here in windsor forest) 4.04. 29
here, master doctor, in perplexity and doubtful 4.05. 84 P
here is a letter will say somewhat. 4.05.123 P
hearts, what ado here is to bring you together! 4.05.124 P
image of the jest | i'll show you here at large. 4.06. 18
the purpose why, is here; 4.06. 21
and here it rests, that you'll procure the vicar 4.06. 48
for me, i am here a windsor stag, and the 5.05. 12 P
who comes here? 5.05. 15 P
tempest of provocation, i will shelter me here. 5.05. 21 P
here are his horns, master /brook; 5.05.111 P
here comes master fenton. 5.05.213 P
here is no remedy. 5.05.231
and do look to know | what doth befall you here. MM 1.01. 58
what's to do here, thomas tapster? 1.02.112 P
here comes signior claudio, led by the provost 1.02.114 P
my absolute power and place here in vienna, 1.03. 13
here, if it like your honor. 2.01. 33
and do bring in here before your good honor two 2.01. 49 P
prove it before these varlets here, thou 2.01. 86 P
(as i said), master froth here, this very man, 2.01.101 P
i beseech you, look into master froth here, sir; 2.01.123 P
i hope here be truths. 2.01.127 P
why, very well then; i hope here be truths. 2.01.133 P
which is the wiser here: 2.01.172 P
here in vienna, sir. 2.01.194 P
here is the sister of the man condemn'd 2.02. 18
degrees, | but here they live, to end. 2.02. 99
the afflicted spirits | here in the prison. 2.03. 5
look, here comes one; 2.03. 10
what ho! peace here; grace and good company! 3.01. 44
and here, by this is your brother sav'd, your 3.01.253 P
o heavens, what stuff is here? 3.02. 4 P
but who comes here? 3.02.189
here comes a man of comfort, whose advice | hath 4.01. 8
wish | you had not found me here so musical. 4.01. 11
me, hath any body inquir'd for me here to–day? 4.01. 16 P
upon this time have i promis'd here to meet. 4.01. 17 P
i have sat here all day. 4.01. 20 P
here is in our prison a common executioner, who 4.02. 8 P
by the year, and let him abide here with you; 4.02. 24 P
who call'd here of late? 4.02. 74
and here comes claudio's pardon. 4.02.101
but here nurs'd up and bred, one that is a 4.02.130 P
claudio, whom here you have warrant to execute, 4.02.157 P
you, sir, here is the hand and seal of the duke; 4.02.192 P
find, within these two days he will be here. 4.02.199 P
am as well acquainted here as i was in our house 4.03. 1 P
house, for here be many of her old customers. 4.03. 3 P
then is there here one master caper, at the suit 4.03. 9 P
then have we here young dizzy, and young master 4.03. 12 P
look you, sir, here comes your ghostly father. 4.03. 48 P
here in the prison, father, | there died this 4.03. 69
here is the head, i'll carry it myself. 4.03.102
peace, ho, be here! 4.03.106
who's here? 4.03.148
but they say the duke will be here to–morrow. 4.03.155 P
other of our friends | will greet us here anon. 4.05. 13
here is lord angelo shall give you justice; 5.01. 27
hear me, o hear me, here. 5.01. 32
by whose advice | thou cam'st here to complain. 5.01.114
unfold the evil which is here wrapp'd up | in 5.01.117
one that i would were here, friar lodowick. 5.01.125
and to set on this wretched woman here | against 5.01.132
my knees, | or else for ever be confixed here, 5.01.232
scope of justice, | my patience here is touch'd. 5.01.235
would he were here, my lord, for he indeed 5.01.250
shall entreat you to abide here till he come and 5.01.265 P
call that same isabel here once again, i would 5.01.269 P
my lord, here comes the rascal i spoke of, here 5.01.283 P
the rascal i spoke of, here with the provost. 5.01.284 P
come you to seek the lamb here of the fox, 5.01.298
villain's mouth | which here you come to accuse. 5.01.303
his subject am i not, | nor here provincial. 5.01.316
this state | made me a looker–on here in vienna, 5.01.317
which consummate, | return him here again. 5.01.379
for this new–married man approaching here, 5.01.400
but here must end the story of my life, | and ERR 1.01.137
merchant | is apprehended for /arrival here; 1.02. 4
here comes the almanac of my true date: 1.02. 41
we being strangers here, how dar'st thou trust 1.02. 60
here comes your man, now is your husband nigh. 2.01. 43
or else what lets it but he would be here? 2.01.105
see, here he comes. 2.02. 6
even now, even here, not half an hour since. 2.02. 14
answer my good will and your good welcome here. 3.01. 20
nor to–day here you must not, come again when 3.01. 41
here is neither cheer, sir, nor welcome: 3.01. 66
your cake here is warm within: 3.01. 71
you stand here in the cold. 3.01. 71
break any breaking here, and i'll break your 3.01. 74
there's none but witches do inhabit here, | and 3.02.156
i see a man here needs not live by shifts, 3.02.182
and i, to blame, have held him here too long. 4.01. 47
here is thy fee, arrest him, officer. 4.01. 76
then swore he that he was a stranger here. 4.02. 9
here, go: 4.02. 29
wiles, | and lapland sorcerers inhabit here. 4.03. 11
here are the angels that you sent for to deliver 4.03. 40 P
and so am i, | and here we wander in illusions: 4.03. 43
and here she comes in the habit of a light wench 4.03. 52 P
we'll mend our dinner here. 4.03. 59
here comes my man: 4.04. 8
you, | by dromio here, who came in haste for it. 4.04. 84
master, i am here ent'red in bond for you. 4.04.125
faith, stay here this night, they will surely do 4.04.151 P
i could find in my heart to stay here still, and 4.04.155 P
how is the man esteem'd here in the city? 5.01. 4
second to none that lives here in the city: 5.01. 7
therefore depart, and leave him here with me. 5.01.108
i will not hence, and leave my husband here; 5.01.109
behind the ditches of the abbey here. 5.01.122
that here and there his fury had committed. 5.01.147
and here the abbess shuts the gates on us, | and 5.01.156
peace, fool, thy master and his man are here, 5.01.178
even now we hous'd him in the abbey here, | and 5.01.188
he had, my lord, and when he ran in here, 5.01.258
and then you fled into this abbey here, | from 5.01.264
if here you hous'd him, here he would have been; 5.01.272
if here you hous'd him, here he would have been; 5.01.272
the goldsmith here | denies that saying. 5.01.274
saw'st thou him enter at the abbey here? 5.01.279
that here my only son | knows not my feeble key 5.01.310
o, my old master! who hath bound him here? 5.01.339
why, here begins his morning story right: 5.01.357
and this fair gentlewoman, her sister here, 5.01.374
these ducats pawn i for my father here. 5.01.390
the pains | to go with us into the abbey here, 5.01.395
i find here that don /pedro hath bestow'd much ADO 1.01. 9 P
he hath an uncle here in messina will be very 1.01. 18 P
he set up his bills here in messina, and 1.01. 39 P
him we shall stay here at the least a month, and 1.01.149 P
and what secret hath held you here, that you 1.01.204 P
as they write "here is good horse to hire," let 1.01.266 P
"here you may see benedick the married man." 1.01.267 P
who comes here? 1.03. 40 P
was not count john here at supper? 2.01. 1 P
i found him here as melancholy as a lodge in a 2.01.214 P
for certainly, while she is here, a man may live 2.01.257 P
look here she comes. 2.01.262 P
here, claudio, i have woo'd in thy name, and 2.01.298 P
i am here already, sir. 2.03. 5 P
but i would have thee hence, and here again. 2.03. 7 P
here comes beatrice. 2.03.244 P
you are thought here to be the most senseless 3.03. 22 P
let us go sit here upon the church–bench till 3.03. 89 P
here, man, i am at thy elbow. 3.03. 98 P
we have here recover'd the most dangerous piece 3.03.167 P
ask my lady beatrice else, here she comes. 3.04. 38 P
behold how like a maid she blushes here! 4.01. 34
leonato, stand i here? 4.01. 69
hath no man's dagger here a point for me? 4.01.109
could she here deny | the story that is printed 4.01.121
if this sweet lady lie not guiltless here 4.01.169
your daughter here the /princes left for dead, 4.01.202
i am gone, though i am here; 4.01.293 P
o that he were here to write me down as ass! 4.02. 75 P
here comes the prince and claudio hastily. 5.01. 45
see, see, here comes the man we went to seek. 5.01.110
"here dwells benedick the married man"? 5.01.183 P
here, here comes master signior leonato, and the 5.01.257 P
here, here comes master signior leonato, and the 5.01.257 P
here stand a pair of honorable men, | a third is 5.01.266
both, | possess the people in messina here | how 5.01.281
not under white and black, this plaintiff here, 5.01.305 P
i leave you too, for here comes one in haste. 5.02. 94 P
tongues | was the hero that here lies. 5.03. 4
here comes the prince and claudio. 5.04. 33
we here attend you. 5.04. 36
here comes other reck'nings. 5.04. 52
that are recorded in this schedule here. LLL 1.01. 18
that is, to live and study here three years. 1.01. 35
and stay here in your court for three years' 1.01. 52
for well you know here comes in embassy | the 1.01.134
decree, | she must lie here on mere necessity. 1.01.148
the ebon–colored ink which here thou viewest, 1.01.243 P
now here is three studied ere ye'll thrice wink; 1.02. 51 P
here comes boyet. 2.01. 80
like one that comes here to besiege his court, 2.01. 86
here comes navarre. 2.01. 89
your father here doth intimate | the payment of 2.01.128
for here he doth demand to have repaid | a 2.01.142
but here without you shall be so receiv'd | as 2.01.172
navarre and his book–men, for here 'tis abused. 2.01.227
the princess comes to hunt here in the park, 3.01.164
here (good my glass), take this for telling true 4.01. 18
here comes a member of the commonwealth. 4.01. 41
you are the thickest here. 4.01. 51
it importeth none here. 4.01. 57
armado is a spaniard that keeps here in court, 4.01. 98
here, sweet, put up this — 'twill be thine 4.01.107
here are only numbers ratified, but, for the 4.02.121 P
and here he hath framed a letter to a sequent of 4.02.138 P
and here is part of my rhyme, and here my 4.03. 13 P
is part of my rhyme, and here my mallicholy. 4.03. 14 P
here comes one with a paper, god give him grace 4.03. 19 P
who is he comes here? 4.03. 42
like a demigod here sit i in the sky, | and 4.03. 77
what makes treason here? 4.03.188
it is berowne's writing, and here is his name. 4.03.199
i'll prove her fair, or talk till doomsday here. 4.03.270
here comes boyet, and mirth is in his face. 5.02. 79
that by and by disguis'd /they will be here. 5.02. 96
since you are strangers and come here by chance, 5.02.218
immediately they will again be here | in their 5.02.287
let us complain to them what fools were here, 5.02.302
o, you have liv'd in desolation here, | unseen, 5.02.357
we have had pastimes here and pleasant game. 5.02.360
here they stay'd an hour, | and talk'd apace; 5.02.368
here stand i, lady, dart thy skill at me, 5.02.396
i do forswear them, and i here protest, | by 5.02.410
were not you here but even now, disguis'd? 5.02.433
when you then were here, | what did you whisper 5.02.435
here was a consent, | knowing aforehand of our 5.02.460
here is like to be a good presence of worthies: 5.02.533 P
ship is under sail, and here she comes amain. 5.02.546
along this coast, i here am come by chance, 5.02.554
thy head, achilles — here comes hector in arms. 5.02.632 P
be it so she will not here before your grace MND 1.01. 39
in such a presence here to plead my thoughts; 1.01. 61
keep promise, love. look, here comes helena. 1.01.179
is all our company here? 1.02. 1 P
here is the scroll of every man's name, which is 1.02. 4 P
here, peter quince. 1.02. 43 P
here, peter quince. 1.02. 59 P
here, peter quince. 1.02. 62 P
and i hope here is a play fitted. 1.02. 65 P
but masters, here are your parts, and i am to 1.02. 99 P
i must go seek some dewdrops here, | and hang a 2.01. 14
our queen and all her elves come here anon. 2.01. 17
the king doth keep his revels here to–night; 2.01. 18
here comes oberon. 2.01. 58
and here my mistress. would that he were gone! 2.01. 59
why art thou here | come from the farthest steep 2.01. 68
the human mortals want their winter here; 2.01.101
and be thou here again | ere the leviathan can 2.01.173
but who comes here? 2.01.186
and here am i, and wode within this wood, 2.01.192
when all the world is here to look on me? 2.01.226
weaving spiders, come not here; 2.02. 20
here is my bed; 2.02. 64
night and silence — who is here? 2.02. 70
and here the maiden, sleeping sound, | on the 2.02. 74
but who is here? 2.02.100
what a dream was here! 2.02.147
what hempen home–spuns have we swagg'ring here, 3.01. 77
stay thou but here a while, | and by and by i 3.01. 86
a stranger pyramus than e'er played here. 3.01. 88
i will walk up and down here, and i will sing, 3.01.123 P
thou shalt remain here, whether thou wilt or no. 3.01.153
here comes my messenger. 3.02. 4
and, at our stamp, here o'er and o'er one falls; 3.02. 25
here therefore for a while i will remain. 3.02. 83
pay, | if for his tender here i make some stay. 3.02. 87
by some illusion see thou bring her here. 3.02. 98
of our fairy band, | helena is here at hand, 3.02.111
and here, with all good will, with all my heart, 3.02.164
a foolish heart, that i leave here behind. 3.02.319
approach, ghosts, wand'ring here and there, 3.02.381
here comes one. 3.02.400
here, villain, drawn and ready. where art thou? 3.02.402
follow my voice; we'll try no manhood here. 3.02.412
i in dark uneven way, | and here will rest me. 3.02.418
come hither; i am here. 3.02.425
here she comes, curst and sad. 3.02.439
here will i rest me till the break of day. 3.02.446
came this night | that i sleeping here was found 4.01.101
my lord, this' my daughter here asleep, | and 4.01.128
i wonder of their being here together. 4.01.131
intent, | came here in grace of our solemnity. 4.01.134

i swear, | i cannot truly say how i came here. 4.01.148
do not you think | the duke was here, and bid us 4.01.195
here come the lovers, full of joy and mirth. 5.01. 28
here, mighty theseus. 5.01. 38
hard–handed men that work in athens here, 5.01. 72
all for your delight | we are not here. 5.01.115
that you should here repent you, | the actors 5.01.115
at large discourse, while here they do remain. 5.01.151
here come two noble beasts in, a man and a lion. 5.01.217 P
may now perchance both quake and tremble here, 5.01.221
here comes thisby. 5.01.261 P
mark, poor knight, | what dreadful dole is here! 5.01.278
since lion vild hath here deflow'r'd my dear; 5.01.292
here she comes, and her passion ends the play. 5.01.314 P
that you have but slumb'red here | while these 5.01.425
here comes bassanio, your most noble kinsman, MV 1.01. 57
the prince his master will be here to–night. 1.02.126 P
who is he comes here? 1.03. 39 P
the rate of usance here with us in venice. 1.03. 45
here comes the man. 2.02.111 P
i have here a dish of doves that i would bestow 2.02.135 P
edge of a feather–bed, here are simple scapes. 2.02.165 P
hold here, take this. 2.04. 19
here comes lorenzo, more of this hereafter. 2.06. 20
approach, | here dwells my father jew. 2.06. 25
here, catch this casket, it is worth the pains. 2.06. 33
what if i stray'd no farther, but chose here? 2.07. 35
but here an angel in a golden bed | lies all 2.07. 58
here do i choose, and thrive i as i may! 2.07. 60
what have we here? 2.07. 62
this, | and instantly unlock my fortunes here. 2.09. 52
what's here? 2.09. 54
what is here? 2.09. 62
fool i shall appear | by the time i linger here. 2.09. 74
here; what would my lord? 2.09. 85
for here he comes in the likeness of a jew. 3.01. 20 P
here comes another of the tribe; 3.01. 77 P
i would detain you here some month or two 3.02. 9
me more than eloquence, | and here choose i. 3.02.107
what find i here? 3.02.114
here are sever'd lips, | parted with sugar 3.02.118
here in her hairs | the painter plays the spider 3.02.120
for, wooing here until i sweat again, | and 3.02.203
i got a promise of this fair one here | to have 3.02.206
but who comes here? 3.02.218
if that the youth of my new int'rest here | have 3.02.221
my purpose was not to have seen you here, | but 3.02.227
here are a few of the unpleasant'st words | that 3.02.251
here is a letter, lady, | the paper as the body 3.02.263
contemplation, | only attended by nerissa here, 3.04. 29
here he /comes. 3.05. 28 P
he finds the joys of heaven here on earth; 3.05. 76
what, is antonio here? 4.01. 1
for thy three thousand ducats here is six. 4.01. 84
sent for to determine this, | come here to–day. 4.01.107
here stays without | a messenger with letters 4.01.107
i stand here for law. 4.01.142
he attendeth here hard by | to know your answer, 4.01.145
and here, i take it, is the doctor come. 4.01.168
which is the merchant here? 4.01.174
yes, here i tender it for him in the court, 4.01.209
here 'tis, most reverend doctor, here it is. 4.01.226
here 'tis, most reverend doctor, here it is. 4.01.226
i stay here on my bond. 4.01.242
which here appeareth due upon the bond. 4.01.249
are there balance here to weigh | the flesh? 4.01.255
ay, sacrifice them all | here to this devil, to 4.01.287
this bond doth give thee here no jot of blood; 4.01.306
here is the money. 4.01.319
i have it ready for thee, here it is. 4.01.337
here in the court, of all he dies possess'd 4.01.389
recant | the pardon that i late pronounced here. 4.01.392
upon more advice | hath sent you here this ring, 4.02. 7
before the break of day | be here at belmont. 5.01. 30
leave hollowing, man — here. 5.01. 43 P
here! 5.01. 45 P
my master will be here ere morning. 5.01. 48 P
here will we sit, and let the sounds of music 5.01. 55
never to part with it, and here he stands. 5.01.171
here, lord bassanio, swear to keep this ring. 5.01.256
here is a letter, read it at your leisure. 5.01.267
lorenzo here | shall witness i set forth as soon 5.01.270
for here i read for certain that my ships | are 5.01.287
more properly, stays me here at home unkept; AYL 1.01. 8 P
now, sir, what make you here? 1.01. 29 P
o, sir, very well; here in your orchard. 1.01. 41 P
the duke's wrastler, here to speak with me? 1.01. 89 P
so please you, he is here at the door, and 1.01. 91 P
here comes monsieur /le beau. 1.02. 91 P
for the best is yet to do, and here, where you 1.02.115 P
you must if you stay here, for here is the place 1.02.144 P
here, for here is the place appointed for the 1.02.144 P
down, and that which here stands up | is but a 1.02.250
of the duke, | that here was at the wrastling? 1.02.270
and here detain'd by her usurping uncle | to 1.02.274
look, here comes the duke. 1.03. 39 P
here feel we not the penalty of adam, | the 2.01. 5
why, what make you here? 2.03. 4
no matter whither, so you come not here. 2.03. 30
here is the gold, | all this i give you, let me 2.03. 45
years till now almost fourscore | here lived i, 2.03. 72
here lived i, but now live here no more. 2.03. 72
look you, who comes here, a young man and an old 2.04. 20 P
that young swain that you saw here but erewhile, 2.04. 89
here shall he see | no enemy | but winter and 2.05. 6
here shall he see | /no /enemy | /but /winter 2.05. 43
here shall he see | gross fools as he, | and if 2.05. 55
here lie i down, and measure out my grave. 2.06. 2 P
i will here be with thee presently, and if i 2.06. 10 P
here was he merry, hearing of a song. 2.07. 4
but who comes here? 2.07. 87
i thought that all things had been savage here, 2.07.107
here comes young master ganymed, my new 3.02. 86 P
here comes my sister reading, stand aside. 3.02.124
for look here what i found on a palm tree. 3.02.175 P
what makes he here? 3.02.222 P
you bring me out. soft, comes he not here? 3.02.251 P
here in the skirts of the forest, like fringe 3.02.335 P

i am here with thee and thy goats, as the most 3.03. 7 P
for here we have no temple but the wood, no 3.03. 49 P
here comes sir oliver. 3.03. 64 P
will you dispatch us here under this tree, or 3.03. 65 P
is there none here to give the woman? 3.03. 67 P
even a toy in hand here, sir. 3.03. 76 P
he attends here in the forest on the duke your 3.04. 33 P
who comes here? 3.04. 46 P
'tis at the tuft of olives here hard by. 3.05. 75
and here much orlando! 4.03. 2 P
look who comes here. 4.03. 5 P
for here comes more company. 4.03. 74 P
and here upon his arm | the lioness had torn 4.03.146
there is a youth here in the forest lays claim 5.01. 6 P
here comes the man you mean. 5.01. 9 P
a fair name. wast born i' the forest here? 5.01. 23 P
upon you, and here live and die a shepherd. 5.02. 12 P
for look you, here comes my rosalind. 5.02. 16 P
here comes a lover of mine and a lover of hers. 5.02. 75 P
to her that is not here, nor doth not hear. 5.02.108
here come two of the banish'd duke's pages. 5.03. 5 P
rosalind, | you will bestow her on orlando here? 5.04. 7
here comes a pair of very strange beasts, which 5.04. 36 P
i press in here, sir, amongst the rest of the 5.04. 55 P
purposely to take | his brother here, and put 5.04.158
ends | that here were well begun and well begot; 5.04.171
what's here? SHR in.1. 31
(travelling some journey) to repose him here. in.1. 76
for though you lay here in this goodly chamber, in.2. 84
marry, i fare well, for here is cheer enough. in.2. 101
here, noble lord, what is thy will with her? in.2. 103
here let us breathe and haply institute | a 1.01. 8
part, | and be in padua here vincentio's son, 1.01.195
here comes the rogue. 1.01.221
your fellow tranio here, to save my life, | puts 1.01.228
here, sirrah grumio, knock, i say. 1.02. 5
villain, i say, knock me here soundly. 1.02. 8
knock you here, sir? 1.02. 9 P
am i, sir, that i should knock you here, sir? 1.02. 10 P
not these words plain, "sirrah, knock me here; 1.02. 41 P
rap me here; 1.02. 41 P
gale | blows you to padua here from old verona? 1.02. 49
here is a gentleman whom by chance i met, | upon 1.02.181
of all thy suitors here i charge /thee tell 2.01. 8
here i swear | i'll plead for you myself, but 2.01. 14
but who comes here? 2.01. 38
own, | that, being a stranger in this city here, 2.01. 89
daughters, | i here bestow a simple instrument, 2.01. 99
i'll attend her here, | and woo her with some 2.01.168
but here she comes, and now, petruchio, speak. 2.01.181
here comes your father. 2.01.279
and to cut off all strife, here sit we down: 3.01. 21
here, madam: 3.01. 27
when will he be here? 3.02. 39 P
and here and there piec'd with packthread. 3.02. 62 P
and make assurance here in padua | of greater 3.02.134
and therefore here i mean to take my leave. 3.02.188
and here she stands, touch her whoever dare, 3.02.233
here. 4.01. 61 P
here, here, sir, here, sir. 4.01.123 P
here, here, sir, here, sir. 4.01.123 P
here, here, sir, here, sir. 4.01.123 P
here, sir! 4.01.124
here, sir! 4.01.124
here, sir! 4.01.124
here, sir! 4.01.124
here, sir — as foolish as i was before. 4.01.128
as they are, here are they come to meet you. 4.01.138
some water here! 4.01.149
bed, | and here i'll fling the pillow, there the 4.01.201
here is my hand, and here i firmly vow | never 4.02. 28
and here i firmly vow | never to woo her more, 4.02. 28
and here i take the like unfeigned oath, | never 4.02. 32
from florence, and must here deliver them. 4.02. 90
my father is here look'd for every day, | to 4.02.117
'twixt me and one baptista's daughter here. 4.02.119
here, love, thou seest how diligent i am | to 4.03. 39
here, take away this dish. 4.03. 44
here is the cap your worship did bespeak. 4.03. 63
what masquing stuff is here? 4.03. 87
why, here is the note of the fashion to testify. 4.03.129 P
but, sir, here comes your boy; 4.04. 8
here comes baptista; 4.04. 18
your son lucentio here | doth love my daughter, 4.04. 40
send for your daughter by your servant here; 4.04. 58
but h'as left me here behind to expound the 4.04. 78 P
but soft, company is coming here. 4.05. 26
thither must i, and here i leave you, sir. 5.01. 10
i think i shall command your welcome here; 5.01. 12
pisa, and is here at the door to speak with him. 5.01. 28 P
is come from padua and here looking out at the 5.01. 31 P
but who is here? 5.01. 42 P
here, signior tranio, | this bird you aim'd at, 5.02. 49
confess, confess, hath he not hit you here? 5.02. 59
now, by my holidam, here comes katherina! 5.02. 99
here is a wonder, if you talk of a wonder. 5.02.106
who comes here? AWW 1.01. 98
we here receive it | a certainty, vouch'd from 1.02. 4
what's he comes here? 1.02. 17
what does this knave here? 1.03. 8 P
then i confess | here on my knee, before high 1.03.192
i am commanded here, and kept a coil with | "too 2.01. 27
i shall stay here the forehorse to a smock, 2.01. 30
an emblem of war, here on his sinister cheek; 2.01. 43 P
here is my hand, the premises observ'd, | thy 2.01.201
give me some help here ho! 2.01.209
here it is, and all that belongs to't. 2.02. 35 P
here comes the king. 2.03. 39 P
here, take her hand, | proud scornful boy, 2.03.150
that hugs his kicky–wicky here at home, 2.03.280
here he comes. 2.05. 13 P
here comes my clog. 2.05. 53
ease, will day by day | come here for physic. 3.01. 19
what have we here? 3.02. 17 P
here they come will tell you more; 3.02. 42 P
there's nothing here that is too good for him 3.02. 80
my being here it is that holds thee hence. 3.02.123
shall i stay here to do't? 3.02.124

look, here comes a pilgrim. 3.05. 30 P
at the saint francis here beside the port. 3.05. 36
here you shall see a countryman of yours | that 3.05. 47
whatsome'er he is, | he's bravely taken here. 3.05. 52
here he comes. 3.06. 39 P
but couch ho, here he comes, to beguile two 4.01. 22 P
if there be here german, or dane, low dutch, 4.01. 71
here, take my ring! 4.02. 51
perverted a young gentlewoman here in florence, 4.03. 15 P
that his valor hath here acquir'd for him shall 4.03. 69 P
here 'tis, here's a paper. 4.03.206 P
know you any here? 4.03.313 P
alive at this hour, and your son here at home, 4.05. 5 P
by his authority he remains here, which he 4.05. 66 P
'a will be here to–morrow, or i am deceiv'd by 4.05. 82 P
have letters that my son will be here to–night. 4.05. 85 P
the king's not here. 5.01. 22
not here, sir? 5.01. 22
look, here he comes himself. 5.02. 18 P
here is a purr of fortune's, sir, or of 5.02. 19 P
had, and here we'll stay | to see our widower's 5.03. 69
who by this i know | is here attending. 5.03.135
than for to think that i would sink it here. 5.03.181
you saw one here in court could witness it. 5.03.200
by him and by this woman here what know you? 5.03.237
though yet he never harm'd me, here i quit him. 5.03.299
who governs here? TN 1.02. 24
you brought in one night here to be her wooer. 1.03. 16 P
for here comes sir andrew agueface. 1.03. 43 P
the count himself here hard by woos her. 1.03.107 P
i thank you. here comes the count. 1.04. 9 P
on your attendance, my lord, here. 1.04. 11
here comes my lady. 1.05. 29 P
for — here he comes — one of thy kin has a 1.05.114 P
'tis a gentleman here — a plague o' these 1.05.120 P
will you hoist sail, sir? here lies your way. 1.05.202 P
good swabber, i am to hull here a little longer. 1.05.203 P
here, madam, at your service. 1.05.299
here comes the fool, i' faith. 2.03. 15 P
what a caterwauling do you keep here! 2.03. 72 P
he is not here, so please your lordship, that 2.04. 8 P
o' favor with my lady about a bear–baiting here. 2.05. 8 P
here comes the little villain. 2.05. 13 P
for here comes the trout that must be caught 2.05. 22 P
what employment have we here? 2.05. 82 P
soft, here follows prose. 2.05.142 P
here is yet a postscript. 2.05.173 P
here comes my noble gull–catcher. 2.05.187 P
send, | after the last enchantment you did here, 3.01.112
that, were i ta'en here, it would scarce be 3.03. 28
here he is, here he is. how is't with you, sir? 3.04. 87 P
here he is, here he is. how is't with you, sir? 3.04. 87 P
here he comes with your niece. 3.04.197 P
here, wear this jewel for me, 'tis my picture. 3.04.208
stand here, make a good show on't; 3.04.288 P
o good sir toby, hold! here come the officers. 3.04.319 P
for the fair kindness you have show'd me here, 3.04.342
this youth that you see here | i snatch'd one 3.04.359
in leaving his friend here in necessity and 3.04.387 P
they have laid me here in hideous darkness. 4.02. 30 P
they have here propertied me, keep me in 4.02. 91 P
the minister is here. 4.02. 94 P
but here the lady comes. 4.03. 21
let your lady know i am here to speak with her, 5.01. 42 P
here comes the man, sir, that did rescue me. 5.01. 50
here in the streets, desperate of shame and 5.01. 64
here comes the countess, now heaven walks on 5.01. 97
i charge thee by thy reverence | here to unfold, 5.01.152
'od's lifelings, here he is! 5.01.184 P
here comes sir toby halting — you shall hear 5.01.192 P
deity in my nature | of here and every where. 5.01.228
h'as here writ a letter to you; 5.01.286 P
you, | here at my house and at my proper cost. 5.01.319
here is my hand — you shall from this time be 5.01.325
and in such forms which here were presuppos'd 5.01.350
toby | set this device against malvolio here, 5.01.360
they're here with me already, whisp'ring, WT 1.02.217
most understand | bohemia stays here longer. 1.02.230
stays here longer. 1.02.230
here comes bohemia. 1.02.364
methinks | my favor here begins to warp. 1.02.365
which are here | by this discovery lost. 1.02.440
that honorable grief lodg'd here which burns 2.01.111
here 'tis — commends it to your blessing. 2.03. 67
unroosted | by thy dame partlet here. 2.03. 76
i, nor any | but one that's here — and that's 2.03. 84
that the queen | appear in person here in court. 3.02. 10
thou art here accused and arraigned of high 3.02. 13 P
here standing | to prate and talk for life and 3.02. 40
hurried | here to this place, i' th' open air, 3.02.105
tell me what blessings i have here alive, | that 3.02.107
and here beholding | his daughter's trial! 3.02.120
you here shall swear upon this sword of justice, 3.02.124
ay, my lord, even so | as it is here set down. 3.02.139
unclasp'd my practice, quit his fortunes here 3.02.167
of king polixenes) it should here be laid, 3.03. 44
what have we here? 3.03. 69 P
that got this than the poor thing is here. 3.03. 76 P
but look thee here, boy. 3.03.113 P
look thee here, take up, take up, boy; 3.03.116 P
and when i wander here and there, | i then do 4.03. 17
now here, | at upper end o' th' table, now i' 4.04. 58
not thou, man, thou shalt lose nothing here. 4.04.256 P
what hast here? ballads? 4.04.259 P
here has been too much homely foolery already. 4.04.332 P
even here undone! 4.04.441
sea | with her who here i cannot hold on shore; 4.04.499
who have we here? 4.04.623
what a boot is here, with this exchange! 4.04.676 P
aside, here is more matter for a hot brain. 4.04.684 P
to effect your suits, here is man shall do it. 4.04.798 P
the business for us, here is that gold i have. 4.04.807 P
by his command | have i here touch'd sicilia, 5.01.139
and my wife's, in safety | here, where we are. 5.01.168
from our air whilest you | do climate here! 5.01.170
here, in your city; 5.01.186
here comes a gentleman that happily knows more. 5.02. 20 P
here comes the lady paulina's steward, he can 5.02. 26 P

here come those i have done good to against my 5.02.124 P
but here it is; 5.03. 18
and here justified | by us, a pair of kings. 5.03.145
the borrowed majesty, of england here. JN 1.01. 4
here have we war for war and blood for blood, 1.01. 19
here is the strangest controversy | come from 1.01. 44
why, what a madcap hath heaven lent us here! 1.01. 84
what brings you here to court so hastily? 1.01.221
that right in peace which here we urge in war, 2.01. 47
backs, | to make a hazard of new fortunes here. 2.01. 71
sake | with burden of our armor here we sweat. 2.01. 92
look here upon thy brother geffrey's face: 2.01. 99
that are advanced here | before the eye and 2.01.207
which here we came to spout against your town, 2.01.256
know him in us, that here hold up his right. 2.01.364
and bear possession of our person here, | lord 2.01.366
beds, | that here come sacrifices for the field. 2.01.420
here i and sorrows sit; 3.01. 73
here is my throne, bid kings come bow to it. 3.01. 74
here comes the holy legate of the pope. 3.01.135
and from pope innocent the legate here, | do in 3.01.139
law cannot give my child his kingdom here, | for 3.01.187
the devil tempts thee here | in likeness of a 3.01.208
look who comes here! 3.04. 17
and so i would be here, but that i doubt | my 4.01. 19
read here, young arthur. 4.01. 33
give me the iron, i say, and bind him here. 4.01. 74
here once again we sit; 4.02. 1
this must be answer'd either here or hence. 4.02. 89
that thou for truth giv'st out are landed here? 4.02.130
here is your hand and seal for what i did. 4.02.215
this is the prison. what is he lies here? 4.03. 34
remote, | and follow unacquainted colors here? 5.02. 32
what, here? 5.02. 33
have i not here the best cards for the game, 5.02.105
shall that victorious hand be feebled here, 5.02.146
war | plead for our interest and our being here. 5.02.165
(not trusting to this halting legate here, 5.02.174
supply, | that was expected by the dolphin here, 5.03. 10
lead me to the revolts of england here. 5.04. 7
that i must die here and live hence by truth? 5.04. 29
here: what news? 5.05. 9
why, here walk i in the black brow of night, 5.06. 17
let him be brought into the orchard here. 5.07. 10
here to make good the boist'rous late appeal, R2 1.01. 4
let not my cold words here accuse my zeal. 1.01. 47
gage, | disclaiming here the kinred of the king, 1.01. 70
or here or elsewhere to the furthest verge 1.01. 93
i am disgrac'd, impeach'd, and baffled here, 1.01.170
the cause of his arrival here in arms; 1.03. 8
i, who ready here do stand in arms | to prove by 1.03. 36
and derby | stands here for god, his sovereign, 1.03.105
here standeth thomas mowbray, duke of norfolk, 1.03.110
that sun that warms you here shall shine on me, 1.03.145
and those his golden beams to you here lent 1.03.146
dear | as harry duke of herford, were he here. 2.01.144
here comes the duke of york. 2.02. 73
here am i left to underprop his land, | who, 2.02. 82
we three here part that ne'er shall meet again. 2.02.143
lord, | i am a stranger here in gloucestershire. 2.03. 3
but who comes here? 2.03. 20
here come the lords of ross and willoughby, 2.03. 57
but who comes here? 2.03. 67
words by you, | here comes his grace in person. 2.03. 82
and here art come | before the expiration of thy 2.03.110
i am denied to sue my livery here, | and yet my 2.03.129
here in the view of men | i will unfold some 3.01. 6
in murthers and in outrage /boldly here, | but 3.02. 40
but who comes here? 3.02. 90
but who comes here? 3.03. 19
while here we march | upon the grassy carpet of 3.03. 49
what sport shall we devise here in this garden 3.04. 1
but stay, here come the gardeners. 3.04. 24
here did she fall a tear, here in this place 3.04.104
here in this place | i'll set a bank of rue, 3.04.104
rue, even for ruth, here shortly shall be seen, 3.04.106
that norfolk lies, here do i throw down this, 4.01. 84
and who sits here that is not richard's subject? 4.01.122
my lord of herford here, whom you call king, 4.01.134
and mutiny | shall here inhabit, and this land 4.01.143
pains, | of capital treason we arrest you here. 4.01.151
a woeful pageant have we here beheld. 4.01.321
here let us rest, if this rebellious earth 5.01. 5
which our profane hours here have thrown down. 5.01. 25
think i am dead, and that even here thou takest, 5.01. 38
weep thou for me in france, i for thee here; 5.01. 87
here comes my son aumerle. 5.02. 41
what treachery is here! 5.02. 75
a dozen of them here have ta'en the sacrament, 5.02. 97
we'll keep him here, then what is that to him? 5.02.100
but who comes here? 5.03. 22
withdraw yourselves, and leave us here alone. 5.03. 28
peruse this writing here, and thou shalt know 5.03. 49
thou frantic woman, what dost thou make here? 5.03. 89
and here is not a creature but myself, | i 5.05. 4
and here have i the daintiness of ear | to check 5.05. 45
while i stand fooling here, his jack of the 5.05. 60
fellow, give place, here is no longer stay. 5.05. 95
my gross flesh sinks downward, here to die. 5.05.112
take hence the rest, and give them burial here. 5.05.118
appear | at large discoursed in this paper here. 5.06. 10
but here is carlisle living, to abide | thy 5.06. 22
march sadly after, grace my mournings here, | in 5.06. 51
here is /a dear, a true industrious friend, 1H4 1.01. 62
were it not here apparent that thou art heir 1.02. 57 P
which harry percy here at holmedon took, | were, 1.03. 24
here comes your uncle. 1.03.130
he apprehends a world of figures here, | but not 1.03.209
all studies here i solemnly defy, | save how to 1.03.228
peas and beans are as dank here as a dog, and 2.01. 8 P
here, hard by. stand close. 2.02. 75 P
no, ye fat chuffs, i would your store were here! 2.02. 89 P
there be four of us here have ta'en a thousand 2.04.158 P
here i lay, and thus i bore my point. 2.04.195 P
it, yea, and can show it you here in the house; 2.04.257 P
here comes lean jack, here comes bare-bone. 2.04.325 P
here comes lean jack, here comes bare-bone. 2.04.326 P
here was sir john bracy from your father; 2.04.333 P
well, here is my leg. 2.04.388 P
and here is my speech. stand aside, nobility. 2.04.389 P
if then thou be son to me, here lies the point: 2.04.406 P
well, here i am set. 2.04.438 P
and here i stand. judge, my masters. 2.04.439 P
the man, i do assure you, is not here, | for i 2.04.512
no, here it is. 3.01. 6
come, here is the map. 3.01. 69
methinks my moi'ty, north from burton here, | in 3.01. 95
and here the smug and silver trent shall run 3.01.101
indent, | to rob me of so rich a bottom here. 3.01.104
yea, but a little charge will trench him here, 3.01.111
here come our wives, and let us take our leave. 3.01.189
she is desperate here, a peevish self-will'd 3.01.196
from hence, | and straight they shall be here. 3.01.225
this in the name of god i promise here, | the 3.02.153
you owe money here besides, sir john, for your 3.03. 72 P
'sblood, and he were here, i would cudgel him 3.03. 86 P
night i fell asleep here behind the arras and 3.03. 97 P
he writes me here, that inward sickness — | and 4.01. 31
but yet i would your father had been here. 4.01. 60
than if the earl were here, for men must think, 4.01. 79
king | in deputation left behind him here, 4.03. 87
here comes your cousin. 5.02. 27
my lord, here are letters for you. 5.02. 79
each man do his best, and here draw i | a sword, 5.02. 92
done, all's won, here breathless lies the king. 5.03. 16
here. 5.03. 18
scape shot-free at london, i fear the shot here, 5.03. 31 P
but who comes here? 5.03. 39 P
what, stands thou idle here? 5.03. 40
you shall find no boy's play here, i can tell 5.04. 76 P
but soft, whom have we here? 5.04.131
why is rumor here? 2H4 in 22
who keeps the gate here ho? where is the earl? 1.01. 1
that the lord bardolph doth attend him here. 1.01. 3
here comes the earl. 1.01. 6
here comes my servant travers, who i sent | on 1.01. 28
look, here comes more news. 1.01. 59
i do here walk before thee like a sow that hath 1.02. 11 P
sir, here comes the nobleman that committed the 1.02. 55 P
here, here. 2.01. 7 P
here, here. 2.01. 7 P
what is the matter? keep the peace here, ho! 2.01. 61 P
what are you brawling here? 2.01. 65
i must wait upon my good lord here, i thank you, 2.01.184 P
sir john, you loiter here too long, being you 2.01.186 P
by the mass, here comes bardolph. 2.02. 69 P
is your master here in london? 2.02.144 P
here will be the prince and master poins anon, 2.04. 15 P
by the mass, here will be old utis, it will be 2.04. 19 P
lo here comes sir john. 2.04. 32 P
if he swagger, let him not come here. 2.04. 73 P
shut the door, there comes no swaggerers here; 2.04. 77 P
there comes no swaggerers here. 2.04. 81 P
there comes none here. 2.04. 95 P
here, pistol, i charge you with a cup of sack, 2.04.111 P
more, pistol, i would not have you go off here. 2.04.137 P
good captain pistol, not here, sweet captain. 2.04.138 P
have we not hiren here? 2.04.160 P
have we not hiren here? 2.04.175 P
a' my word, captain, there's none such here. 2.04.176 P
come we to full points here? 2.04.184
but speak nothing, 'a shall be nothing here. 2.04.194 P
is thine hostess here of the wicked? 2.04.328 P
here come two of sir john falstaff's men, as i 3.02. 53 P
look, here comes good sir john. 3.02. 81 P
have you provided me here half a dozen 3.02. 93 P
here, and't please you. 3.02.101 P
here, sir. 3.02.125 P
here, sir. 3.02.138 P
here, sir. 3.02.148 P
here, sir. 3.02.174 P
is here all? 3.02.186 P
here is two more call'd than your number, you 3.02.188 P
your number, you must have but four here, sir. 3.02.189 P
here stand, my lords, and send discoverers forth 4.01. 3
here doth he wish his person, with such powers 4.01. 10
what well-appointed leader fronts us here? 4.01. 25
lords | had not been here to dress the ugly form 4.01. 39
of it, | but to establish here a peace indeed, 4.01. 86
here come i from our princely general | to know 4.01.139
all members of our cause, both here and hence, 4.01.169
here is return'd my lord of westmerland. 4.01.222
the prince is here at hand. 4.01.223
you are well encount'red here, my cousin mowbray 4.02. 1
text | /than now to see you here an iron man, 4.02. 8
of heaven and him | have here upswarm'd them. 4.02. 30
i am not here against your father's peace, | but 4.02. 31
and though we here fall down, | we have supplies 4.02. 44
and swear here, by the honor of my blood, | my 4.02. 55
ours, and here between the armies | let's drink 4.02. 62
fondly brought here and foolishly sent hence. 4.02.119
here comes our general. 4.03. 23 P
found'red ninescore and odd posts, and here, 4.03. 36 P
here he is, and here i yield him, and i beseech 4.03. 45 P
here he is, and here i yield him, and i beseech 4.03. 45 P
no, my good lord, he is in presence here. 4.04. 17
who's here? 4.04. 80
here at more leisure may your highness read, 4.04. 89
set me the crown upon my pillow here. 4.05. 5
i am here, brother, full of heaviness. 4.05. 8
no, i will sit and watch here by the king. 4.05. 20
why did you leave me here alone, my lords? 4.05. 50
we left the prince my brother here, my liege, 4.05. 51
he is not here. 4.05. 54
when we withdrew, my liege, we left it here. 4.05. 58
depart the chamber, leave us here alone. 4.05. 90
god witness with me, when i here came in, | and 4.05.149
look, look, here comes my john of lancaster. 4.05.225
here, sir. 5.01. 8 P
here is now the smith's note for shoeing and 5.01. 18 P
here come the heavy issue of dead harry. 5.02. 14
here comes the prince. 5.02. 42
god, you have here goodly dwelling and rich. 5.03. 5 P
and lusty lads roam here and there | so merrily, 5.03. 20
why, here it is, welcome these pleasant days! 5.03.141
stand here by me, master shallow, i will make 5.05. 5 P
come here, pistol, stand behind me. 5.05. 10 P
i was lately here in the end of a displeasing ep 8 P
here i promis'd you i would be, and here i ep 13 P
be, and here i commit my body to your mercies. ep 13 P
all the gentlewomen here have forgiven me; ep 22 P
carry them here and there, jumping o'er times, H5 pr 29
not here in presence. 1.02. 2
hearts have left their bodies here in england, 1.02.128
here comes ancient pistol and his wife. 2.01. 26 P
good corporal, be patient here. 2.01. 27 P
offer nothing here. 2.01. 40 P
my lord of cambridge here, | you know how apt 2.02. 85
of france | to kill us here in hampton. 2.02. 91
unless the dolphin be in presence here, | to 2.04.111
for the dolphin, | i stand here for him. 2.04.116
king | come here himself to question our delay; 2.04.142
show us here | the mettle of your pasture; 3.01. 26
here 'a comes, and the scots captain, captain 3.02. 74 P
here is the man. 3.06. 20 P
go therefore tell thy master here i am; 3.06.153
by him, at all adventures, so we were quit here. 4.01.117 P
then i would he were here alone; 4.01.121 P
you love him not so ill to wish him here alone, 4.01.125 P
so that here men are punish'd for before-breach 4.01.170 P
o that we now had here | but one ten thousand of 4.03. 16
think themselves accurs'd they were not here; 4.03. 65
here comes his majesty. 4.07. 54 P
here comes the herald of the french, my liege. 4.07. 66
fought a most prave pattle here in france. 4.07. 95 P
here, fluellen, wear thou this favor for me and 4.07.153 P
my lord of warwick, here is — praised be god 4.08. 20 P
here is his majesty. 4.08. 22 P
my liege, here is a villain and a traitor, that, 4.08. 25 P
this was my glove, here is the fellow of it; 4.08. 28 P
look, here is the fellow of it. 4.08. 39 P
here, uncle exeter, fill this glove with crowns, 4.08. 57
here is the number of the slaught'red french. 4.08. 74
here was a royal fellowship of death! 4.08.101
o god, thy arm was here; 4.08.106
their huge and proper life | be here presented. 5.pr. 6
why, here he comes, swelling like a turkey-cock. 5.01. 14 P
go with the princes, or stay here with us? 5.02. 91
yet leave our cousin katherine here with us: 5.02. 95
here comes your father. 5.02.279 P
that here i kiss her as my sovereign queen. 5.02.358
that here you maintain several factions; 1H6 1.01. 71
here, there, and every where, enrag'd he slew. 1.01.124
here had the conquest fully been seal'd up, | if 1.01.130
myself | for living idly here in pomp and ease, 1.01.142
i do remember it, and here take my leave, | to 1.01.165
at pleasure here we lie near orleance; 1.02. 6
why live we idly here? 1.02. 13
here is my keen-edg'd sword, | deck'd with /five 1.02. 98
where be these warders, that they wait not here? 1.03. 3
what noise is this? what traitors have we here? 1.03. 15
here by the cheeks i'll drag thee up and down. 1.03. 51
hath here distrain'd the tower to his use. 1.03. 61
and would have armor here out of the tower, | to 1.03. 67
of men assembled here in arms this day against 1.03. 74 P
here, said they, is the terror of the french, 1.04. 42
here, through this grate, i count each one, 1.04. 60
and i here, at the bulwark of the bridge. 1.04. 67
here, here she comes. 1.05. 4
here, here she comes. 1.05. 4
and here will talbot mount, or make his grave. 2.01. 34
here cometh charles, i marvel how he sped. 2.01. 48
here sound retreat, and cease our hot pursuit. 2.02. 3
and here advance it in the market-place, | the 2.02. 5
after that things are set in order here, | we'll 2.02. 32
here is the talbot, who would speak with him? 2.02. 37
belief, | i go to certify her talbot's here. 2.03. 32
you are deceiv'd, my substance is not here; 2.03. 51
i tell you, madam, were the whole frame here, 2.03. 54
he will be here, and yet he is not here. 2.03. 58
he will be here, and yet he is not here. 2.03. 58
too loud, | the garden here is more convenient. 2.04. 4
tut, tut, here is a mannerly forbearance. 2.04. 19
i pluck this pale and maiden blossom here, 2.04. 47
here in my scabbard, meditating that | shall dye 2.04. 60
and here i prophesy: 2.04.124
age, | let dying mortimer here rest himself. 2.05. 2
here dies the dusky torch of mortimer, | chok'd 2.05.122
here, winchester, i offer thee my hand. 3.01.126
see here, my friends and loving countrymen, 3.01.137
here ent'red pucelle and her practisants. 3.02. 20
here is the best and safest passage in? 3.02. 22
we came but to tell you | that we are here. 3.02. 74
lives | and as his father here was conqueror, 3.02. 81
here will i sit before the walls of roan | and 3.02. 91
france, | and not have title of an earldom here. 3.03. 26
deserts | we here create you earl of shrewsbury, 3.04. 26
what's here? 4.01. 55
this fellow here, with envious carping tongue, 4.01. 90
here is sir william lucy, who with me | set from 4.04. 10
here on my knee i beg mortality, | rather than 4.05. 32
and leave my followers here to fight and die? 4.05. 45
then here i take my leave of thee, fair son, 4.05. 52
here, purposing the bastard to destroy, | came 4.06. 25
antic death, which laugh'st us here to scorn, 4.07. 18
stinking and fly-blown lies here at our feet. 4.07. 76
were but his picture left amongst you here, | it 4.07. 83
to keep them here, | they would but stink, and 4.07. 89
is she not here? 5.03. 68
and here i will expect thy coming. 5.03.145
the christian prince, king henry, were he here. 5.03.172
and here at hand the dolphin and his train 5.04.100
still, | for here we entertain a solemn peace. 5.04.175
and here conclude with me | that margaret shall 5.05. 77
here are the articles of contracted peace 2H6 1.01. 40
we here create thee the first duke of suffolk, 1.01. 64
we here discharge your grace from being regent 1.01. 66
here, hume, take this reward. 1.02. 85
here 'a comes, methinks, and the queen with him. 1.03. 6 P
what's here? 1.03. 20 P
my lord of somerset will keep me here | without 1.03.168
because here is a man accused of treason. 1.03.177
we'll see your trinkets here all forthcoming. 1.04. 53
what have we here? 1.04. 58

here comes the townsmen on procession, | to 2.01. 66
good fellow, tell us here the circumstance, 2.01. 72
cam'st thou here by chance | or of devotion, to 2.01. 85
my lords, saint albon here hath done a miracle; 2.01.129
gloucester, see here the tainture of thy nest, 2.01.184
well, for this night we will repose us here; 2.01.196
done, | live in your country here in banishment, 2.03. 12
here, noble henry, is my staff. 2.03. 32
here let them end it, and god defend the right! 2.03. 55
here, neighbor horner, i drink to you in a cup 2.03. 59 P
and here, neighbor, here's a cup of charneco. 2.03. 62 P
here, peter, i drink to thee, and be not afraid. 2.03. 68 P
here, robin, and if i die, i give thee my aporn; 2.03. 74 P
and here, tom, take all the money that i have. 2.03. 76 P
please your grace, here my commission stays; 2.04. 76
must you, sir john, protect my lady here? 2.04. 79
i do arrest thee of high treason here. 3.01. 97
and here commit you to my lord cardinal | to 3.01.137
hath he not twit our sovereign lady here | with 3.01.178
he'll wrest the sense and hold us here all day. 3.01.186
best, | do or undo, as if ourself were here. 3.01.196
here is my hand, the deed is worthy doing. 3.01.278
this devil here shall be my substitute; 3.01.371
here comes my lord. 3.02. 5
the king and all the peers are here at hand. 3.02. 10
it cannot be but he was murd'red here, | the 3.02.177
wrathful weapons drawn | here in our presence? 3.02.238
why, what tumultuous clamor have we here? 3.02.239
if after three days' space thou here be'st found 3.02.295
here could i breathe my soul into the air, | as 3.02.391
here shall they make their ransom on the sand, 4.01. 10
the commons here in kent are up in arms, | and 4.01.100
this villain here, | being captain of a pinnace, 4.01.106
her furr'd pack, she washes bucks here at home. 4.02. 48 P
here i am, thou particular fellow. 4.02.112 P
here, sir. 4.03. 2 P
here may his head lie on my throbbing breast; 4.04. 5
but i am troubled here with them myself; 4.05. 7
and here, sitting upon london stone, i charge 4.06. 2 P
here they be that dare and will disturb thee. 4.08. 6
and here pronounce free pardon to them all 4.08. 9
sword make way for me, for here is no staying. 4.08. 60 P
whom have we here? 5.01. 12
here is a hand to hold a sceptre up, | and with 5.01.102
and here comes clifford to deny their bail. 5.01.123
why, what a brood of traitors have we here! 5.01.141
the queen this day here holds her parliament, 3H6 1.01. 35
by words or blows here let us win our right. 1.01. 37
lord, here in the parliament | let us assail the 1.01. 64
i here entail | the crown to thee and to thine 1.01.194
conditionally that here thou take an oath | to 1.01.196
here comes the queen, whose looks bewray her 1.01.211
i here divorce myself | both from thy table, 1.01.247
intend here to besiege you in your castle. 1.02. 50
had i thy brethren here, their lives and thine 1.03. 25
here must i stay, and here my life must end. 1.04. 26
here must i stay, and here my life must end. 1.04. 26
come make him stand upon this molehill here 1.04. 67
for in the marches here we heard you were, 2.01.140
how it doth grieve me that thy head is here! 2.02. 55
ay, crook–back, here i stand to answer thee, 2.02. 96
the wound that bred this meeting here | cannot 2.02.121
why stand we like soft–hearted women here, 2.03. 25
here on my knee i vow to god above | i'll never 2.03. 29
now, richard, i am with thee here alone: 2.04. 5
here on this molehill will i sit me down. 2.05. 14
here sits a king more woeful than you are. 2.05.124
here burns my candle out; 2.06. 1
ay, here it dies, | which, whiles it lasted, 2.06. 1
here stand we both and aim we at the best; 3.01. 8
here comes a man, let's stay till he be past. 3.01. 12
here in this country where we now remain. 3.01. 75
yet here prince edward stands, king henry's son. 3.03. 73
king lewis, i here protest in sight of heaven, 3.03.181
him, | i here renounce him and return to henry. 3.03.194
and here, to pledge my vow, i give my hand. 3.03.250
here comes the king. 4.01. 6
that with the king here resteth in his tent? 4.03. 10
let them go, here is | the duke. 4.03. 29
yea, brother of clarence, art thou here too? 4.03. 41
is prisoner to the bishop here, at whose hands 4.05. 5
he shall here find his friends with horse and 4.05. 12
crown, | i here resign my government to thee, 4.06. 24
for, till i see them here, by doubtful fear | my 4.06. 62
if you'll not here proclaim yourself our king, 4.07. 54
sound trumpet, edward shall be here proclaim'd. 4.07. 69
now, for this night, let's harbor here in york; 4.07. 79
here at the palace will i rest a while. 4.08. 33
and do expect him here some two hours hence. 5.01. 10
it is not his, my lord, here southam lies; 5.01. 12
look here, i throw my infamy at thee. 5.01. 82
hands, | i here proclaim myself thy mortal foe; 5.01. 94
alas, i am not coop'd here for defense! 5.01.109
why, is not oxford here another anchor? 5.04. 16
i speak not this as doubting any here; 5.04. 43
if any such be here — as god forbid! 5.04. 48
here pitch our battle, hence we will not budge. 5.04. 66
now here a period of tumultuous broils. 5.05. 1
take that, the likeness of this railer here. 5.05. 38
nay, never bear me hence, dispatch me here; 5.05. 69
here sheathe thy sword, i'll pardon thee my 5.05. 70
thou art not here. 5.05. 79
for here i hope begins our lasting joy. 5.07. 46
down to my soul — here clarence comes! R3 1.01. 41
but who comes here? 1.01.121
here. why dost thou spit at me? 1.02.144
lo here i lend thee this sharp–pointed sword, 1.02.174
here /come the /lords of buckingham and derby. 1.03. 17
days, | which here you urge to prove us enemies, 1.03.145
than death can yield me here by my abode. 1.03.168
nor no one here; 1.03.284
but soft, here come my executioners. 1.03.338
well thought upon, i have it here about me. 1.03.343
ho, who's here? 1.04. 84 P
'tis he that sends us to destroy you here. 1.04.243
this interchange of love, i here protest, | upon 2.01. 26
there wanteth now our brother gloucester here 2.01. 43
here comes sir richard ratcliffe and the duke. 2.01. 46
if any here | by false intelligence or wrong 2.01. 54
to–morrow, or next day, they will be here. 2.04. 3
here comes a messenger. what news? 2.04. 38
i want more uncles here to welcome me. 3.01. 6
and in good time, here comes the sweating lord. 3.01. 24
win the duke of york, | anon expect him here; 3.01. 39
now in good time, here comes the duke of york. 3.01. 95
richard the second here was hack'd to death; 3.03. 12
come, grey, come, vaughan, let us here embrace. 3.03. 25
in happy time, here comes the duke himself. 3.04. 21
marry, that with no man here he is offended; 3.04. 56
look back, defend thee, here are enemies! 3.05. 19
here is the head of that ignoble traitor, | the 3.05. 22
and to that end we wish'd your lordship here, 3.05. 67
here is the indictment of the good lord hastings 3.06. 1
and even here brake off, and came away. 3.07. 41
the mayor is here at hand. 3.07. 45
i dance attendance here; 3.07. 56
here catesby comes again. 3.07. 82
which here we waken to our country's good, | the 3.07.124
which fondly you would here impose on me. 3.07.147
and in this resolution here we leave you. 3.07.218
who meets us here? 4.01. 1
and in good time, here the lieutenant comes. 4.01. 12
and here he comes. 4.03. 23
here in these confines slily have i lurk'd, | to 4.04. 3
who comes here? 4.04. 8
then would i hide my bones, not rest them here. 4.04. 33
from which even here i slip my /weary head, 4.04.112
and both the princes had been breathing here, 4.04.384
here, my good lord. 4.04.442
why stay'st thou here, and go'st not to the duke 4.04.446
he makes for england, here to claim the crown. 4.04.468
yet to beat down these rebels here at home. 4.04.530
while we reason here, | a royal battle might be 4.04.535
and here receive we from our father stanley 5.02. 5
here pitch our tent, even here in bosworth field 5.03. 1
pitch our tent, even here in bosworth field. 5.03. 1
here, most gracious liege. 5.03. 4
here will i lie to–night — | but where 5.03. 7
is there a murtherer here? 5.03.184
that you have ta'en a tardy sluggard here. 5.03.225
lo here this long–usurped royalty | from the 5.05. 4
that she may long live here, god say amen! 5.05. 41
those that can pity, here | may (if they think H8 pr 5
they may believe, | may here find truth too. pr 9
here, so please you. 1.01.116
his pomp as well in france | as here at home, 1.01.164
to whisper wolsey), here makes visitation — 1.01.179
here is a warrant from | the king t' attach lord 1.01.216
we should take root here where we sit, or sit 1.02. 87
most liberal, | they are set here for examples. 1.03. 62
none here, he hopes, | in all this noble bevy, 1.04. 3
and so fair assembly | this night to meet here, 1.04. 68
here i'll make | my royal choice. 1.04. 85
we are too open here to argue this; 2.01.168
lo, who comes here? 2.03. 49
a very fresh fish here — fie, fie, fie upon 2.03. 86
do not deliver | what here y' have heard to her. 2.03.107
here. 2.04. 9
having here | no judge indifferent, nor no more 2.04. 16
you have here, lady | (and of your choice), 2.04. 57
again | i do refuse you for my judge, and here, 2.04.118
whereupon we are | now present here together: 2.04.203
to this course | which you are running here. 2.04.218
your graces find me here part of a huswife | (i 3.01. 24
speak it here; 3.01. 29
here are some will thank you, | if you speak 3.01. 46
they that my trust must grow to, live not here. 3.01. 89
that little thought, when she set footing here, 3.01.183
you he bade | attend him here this morning. 3.02. 82
my lord, we have | stood here observing him. 3.02.112
you come to take your stand here, and behold 4.01. 2
and leave me here in wretchedness behind ye? 4.02. 84
madam, we are here. 4.02. 85
but now i am past all comforts here but prayers. 4.02.123
whiles here he liv'd | upon this naughty earth? 5.01.137
i'm very sorry | to sit here at this present, 5.02. 44
do you look for ale and cakes here, you rude 5.03. 11 P
will beget a thousand, here will be father, 5.03. 38 P
mercy o' me, what a multitude are here! 5.03. 67
they are coming, | as if we kept a fair here! 5.03. 69
and here ye lie baiting of bombards, when | ye 5.03. 81
this play can never please | all that are here. ep 2
call here my varlet, i'll unarm again. TRO 1.01. 1
troy, | that find such cruel battle here within? 1.01. 3
who comes here? 1.02. 37 P
so he says here. 1.02. 54 P
shall we stand up here and see them as they pass 1.02.178 P
here, here, here's an excellent place, here we 1.02.181 P
here, here, here's an excellent place, here we 1.02.181 P
excellent place, here we may see most bravely. 1.02.181 P
here comes more. 1.02.240 P
most wisely hath ulysses here discover'd | the 1.03.138
here in troy | a prince call'd hector — priam 1.03.260
for here the troyans taste our dear'st repute 1.03.337
thou art here but to thrash troyans, and thou 2.01. 45 P
i serve here voluntary. 2.01. 94 P
ajax was here the voluntary, and you as under an 2.01. 96 P
here are your reasons: 2.02. 38
look you, who comes here? 2.03. 68 P
here is such patchery, such juggling, and such 2.03. 71 P
let it be known to him that we are here. 2.03. 78
here comes patroclus. 2.03.103 P
here tend the savage strangeness he puts on, 2.03.126
here is a man — but 'tis before his face, | i 2.03.229
there is no tarrying here; 2.03.258
fair prince, here is good broken music. 3.01. 49 P
o, here he comes! how now, how now? 3.02. 5 P
walk here i' th' orchard, i'll bring her 3.02. 16 P
here she is now, swear the oaths now to her that 3.02. 41 P
here i hold your hand, here my cousin's. 3.02.198 P
here i hold your hand, here my cousin's. 3.02.198 P
and cupid grant all tongue–tied maidens here 3.02.210
and here, to do you service, am become | as new 3.03. 11
here is ulysses, | i'll interrupt his reading. 3.03. 92
a strange fellow here | writes me that man, how 3.03. 95
the beauty that is borne here in the face | the 3.03.103
and apprehended here immediately | th' unknown 3.03.124
lords after the combat | to see us here unarm'd. 3.03.237
here lies our way. 4.01. 80
what's all the doors open here? 4.02. 19 P
here, you maid! 4.02. 24 P
i would not for half troy have you seen here. 4.02. 41
is not prince troilus here? 4.02. 47
here, what should he do here? 4.02. 48 P
here, what should he do here? 4.02. 48 P
come, he is here, my lord, do not deny him. 4.02. 49
is he here, say you? 4.02. 51 P
what should he do here? 4.02. 53 P
we met by chance, you did not find me here. 4.02. 71
how now? what's the matter? who was here? 4.02. 78 P
here, here, here he comes. /ah, sweet ducks! 4.04. 11 P
here, here, here he comes. /ah, sweet ducks! 4.04. 11 P
here, here, here he comes. /ah, sweet ducks! 4.04. 11 P
what a pair of spectacles is here! 4.04. 14 P
here is the lady | which for antenor we deliver 4.04.109
here art thou in appointment fresh and fair, 4.05. 1
here is sir diomed. 4.05. 88
there is expectance here from both the sides, 4.05.146
great agamemnon comes to meet us here. 4.05.159
when we have here her base and pillar by us. 4.05.212
here comes thersites. 5.01. 4
here is a letter from queen hecuba, | a token 5.01. 39
honor or go or stay, | my major vow lies here; 5.01. 44
here comes himself to guide you. 5.01. 69
what, are you up here, ho? speak! 5.02. 1
here, diomed, keep this sleeve. 5.02. 66
my soul | of every syllable that here was spoke. 5.02.117
was cressid here? 5.02.125
nor mine, my lord; cressid was here but now. 5.02.128
with that which here his passion doth express? 5.02.162
here, sister, arm'd, and bloody in intent. 5.03. 8
which you do here forbid me, royal priam. 5.03. 75
soft, here comes sleeve and t' other. 5.04. 18 P
now here he fights on galathe his horse | and 5.05. 20
here, there, and every where, he leaves and 5.05. 26
come here about me, you my myrmidons, | mark 5.07. 1
here lies thy heart, thy sinews, and thy bone. 5.08. 12
never go home, here starve we out the night — 5.10. 2
as many as be here of pandar's hall, | your eyes 5.10. 47
two months hence my will shall here be made. 5.10. 52
why stay we prating here? COR 1.01. 48 P
soft, who comes here? 1.01. 50 P
here. what's the matter? 1.01.223
the words — i think | i have the letter here; 1.02. 8
yes, here it is: 1.02. 8
what are you sewing here? 1.03. 52 P
see here these movers that do prize their hours 1.05. 4
if any such be here | (as it were sin to doubt) 1.06. 67
progeny | thou shouldst not scape me here. 1.08. 13
here is the steed, we the caparison. 1.09. 12
i sometime lay here in corioles | at a poor 1.09. 82
have we no wine here? 1.09. 92
two know how you are censur'd here in the city, 2.01. 22 P
some old crab–trees here at home that will not 2.01.188
come, come, they are almost here. 2.02. 1 P
whom | we met here both to thank and to remember 2.02. 47
the common body | to yield what passes here. 2.02. 54
of our proceedings here on th' market–place; 2.02.159
here he comes, and in the gown of humility, mark 2.03. 40 P
so, here comes a brace. 2.03. 61
you know the cause, sir, of my standing here. 2.03. 62
i may be consul, i have here the customary gown. 2.03. 86 P
why in this woolvish /toge should i stand here 2.03.115
here come moe voices. 2.03.125
we stay here for the people. 2.03.150
here was "i thank you for your voices, thank you 2.03.171
son, | who after great hostilius here was king; 2.03.240
thus | given hydra here to choose an officer, 3.01. 93
we do here pronounce, | upon the part o' th' 3.01.208
no, i'll die here. 3.01.222
and to keep him here | our certain death; 3.01.286
thus far having stretch'd it (here be with them) 3.02. 74
here is cominius. 3.02. 92
well, here he comes. 3.03. 30
must all determine here? 3.03. 43
and here defying | those whose great power must 3.03. 79
and here remain with your uncertainty! 3.03.124
dismiss them home. | here comes his mother. 4.02. 8
this lady's husband here — this (do you see?) 4.02. 41
this here before you. 4.04. 11
what service is here? 4.05. 1 P
what have you to do here, fellow? 4.05. 22 P
tell my master what a strange guest he has here. 4.05. 35 P
here, sir. 4.05. 51 P
those my banishers, | stand i before thee here. 4.05. 84
here i cleep | the anvil of my sword, and do 4.05.109
but that i see thee here, | thou noble thing, 4.05.115
who now are here, taking their leaves of me, 4.05.133
he is so made on here within as if he were son 4.05.191 P
here do we make his friends | blush that the 4.06. 4
here come the clusters. 4.06.128
the virtue of your name | is not here passable. 5.02. 13
words in your own, you should not pass here; 5.02. 26 P
if thy captain knew i were here, he would use me 5.02. 51 P
turn the dregs of it upon this varlet here — 5.02. 78 P
yet here he lets me prate | like one i' th' 5.03.159
go tell the lords a' th' city i am here. 5.06. 1
say no more. | here come the lords. 5.06. 59
and we here deliver, | subscrib'd by th' consuls 5.06. 80
that i will here dismiss my loving friends; TIT 1.01. 53
i thank you all and here dismiss you all, | and 1.01. 57
here goths have given me leave to sheathe my 1.01. 85
in peace and honor rest you here, my sons, 1.01.150
readiest champions, repose you here in rest, 1.01.151
here lurks no treason, here no envy swells, 1.01.153
here lurks no treason, here no envy swells, 1.01.153
here grow no damned drugs, here are no storms, 1.01.154
here grow no damned drugs, here are no storms, 1.01.154
in peace and honor rest you here, my sons! 1.01.156
o, bless me here with thy victorious hand, 1.01.163
people of rome, and people's tribunes here, | i 1.01.217
grace, | and here in sight of rome to saturnine, 1.01.246
ransomless here we set our prisoners free. 1.01.274
my lord, you pass not here. 1.01.290

and here i swear by all the roman gods, | sith 1.01.322
and here in sight of heaven to rome i swear, 1.01.329
here none but soldiers and rome's servitors 1.01.352
bury him where you can, he comes not here. 1.01.354
he that would vouch it in any place but here. 1.01.360
inter | his noble nephew here in virtue's nest, 1.01.376
that was thy joy, | be barr'd his entrance here. 1.01.383
rome, | this noble gentleman, lord titus here, 1.01.415
that, on mine honor, here do i protest. 1.01.477
marcus, for thy sake and thy brother's here, 1.01.482
that he hath breath'd in my dishonor here. 2.01. 56
uncouple here and let us make a bay, | and wake 2.02. 3
here comes a parcel of our hopeful booty, 2.03. 49
who have we here? 2.03. 55
here never shines the sun, here nothing breeds, 2.03. 96
here never shines the sun, here nothing breeds, 2.03. 96
they told me, here, at dead time of the night, 2.03. 99
straight they told me they would bind me here 2.03.106
stay, madam, here is more belongs to her: 2.03.122
away, for thou hast stay'd us here too long. 2.03.181
now will i fetch the king to find them here, 2.03.206
again, | till thou art here aloft or i below. 2.03.244
i'll see what hole is here, | and what he is 2.03.246
but out alas, here have we found him dead. 2.03.258
here, tamora, though griev'd with killing grief. 2.03.260
poor bassianus here lies murthered. 2.03.263
that should have murthered bassianus here. 2.03.279
my gracious lord, here is the bag of gold. 2.03.280
kind, | have here bereft my brother of his life. 2.03.282
but who comes with our brother marcus here? 3.01. 58
here stands my other son, a banish'd man, | and 3.01. 99
man, | and here my brother, weeping at my woes; 3.01.100
o, here i lift this one hand up to heaven, | and 3.01.206
here are the heads of thy two noble sons, | and 3.01.236
thy warlike hand, thy mangled daughter here, 3.01.255
pattern'd by that the poet here describes, | by 4.01. 57
sweet girl, for here are none but friends, 4.01. 61
my lord, look here; 4.01. 68
look here, lavinia. 4.01. 68
and here display at last | what god will have 4.01. 73
what's here? 4.02. 18
here lacks but your mother for to say amen. 4.02. 44
soft, who comes here? 4.02. 51
all, | here aaron is, and what with aaron now? 4.02. 54
here is the babe, as loathsome as a toad 4.02. 67
here, "ad apollinem"; 4.03. 54
here, boy, "to pallas"; 4.03. 56
then here is a supplication for you; 4.03.109 P
here, marcus, fold it in the oration, | for 4.03.116
you a letter and a couple of pigeons here. 4.04. 44 P
but who comes here, led by a lusty goth? 5.01. 19
do | see here in bloody lines i have set down: 5.02. 14
see here he comes, and i must ply my theme. 5.02. 80
when he is here, even at thy solemn feast, | i 5.02.115
madam, depart at pleasure, leave us here. 5.02.145
here stands the spring whom you have stain'd 5.02.170
what here shall miss, our toil shall strive to ROM pr 14
tool, here comes /two of the house of montagues. 1.01. 31 P
"better," here comes one of my master's kinsmen. 1.01. 58 P
here were the servants of your adversary, | and 1.01.106
what fray was here? 1.01.173
tut, i have lost myself, i am not here: 1.01.197
find them out whose names are written here! 1.02. 38 P
to find those persons whose names are here writ, 1.02. 42 P
what names the writing person hath here writ. 1.02. 44 P
madam, i am here, | what is your will? 1.03. 5
here in verona, ladies of esteem, | are made 1.03. 70
here are the beetle brows shall blush for me. 1.04. 32
we cannot be here and there too. 1.05. 14 P
town | here in my house do him disparagement; 1.05. 70
am i the master here, or you? 1.05. 78
more torches here! 1.05.125
what's he that follows here, that would not 1.05.132
can i go forward when my heart is here? 2.01. 1
to seek him here that means not to be found. 2.01. 42
thou art, | if any of my kinsmen find thee here. 2.02. 65
i would not for the world they saw thee here. 2.02. 74
and but thou love me, let them find me here; 2.02. 76
let me stand here till thou remember it. 2.02.171
or if not so, then here i hit it right — | our 2.03. 41
holy saint francis, what a change is here! 2.03. 65
lo here upon thy cheek the stain doth sit | of 2.03. 75
here comes romeo, here comes romeo. 2.04. 36 P
here comes romeo, here comes romeo. 2.04. 36 P
here is for thy pains. 2.04.182
here comes the lady. 2.06. 16
by my head, here comes the capulets. 3.01. 35 P
we talk here in the public haunt of men. 3.01. 50
here all eyes gaze on us. 3.01. 53
well, peace be with you, sir, here comes my man. 3.01. 56
which too untimely here did scorn the earth. 3.01.118
here comes the furious tybalt back again. 3.01.121
thou wretched boy, that didst consort him here, 3.01.130
tybalt, here slain, whom romeo's hand did slay! 3.01.152
o, here comes my nurse, | and she brings news; 3.02. 31
here on his manly breast. 3.02. 53
vile earth, to earth resign, end motion here, 3.02. 59
hark ye, your romeo will be here at night. 3.02.140
here from verona art thou banished. 3.03. 15
heaven is here | where juliet lives, and every 3.03. 29
live here in heaven and may look on her, | but 3.03. 32
i could have stay'd here all the night | to hear 3.03.159
here, sir, a ring she bid me give you, sir. 3.03.163
and here stands all your state: 3.03.166
time | every good hap to you that chances here. 3.03.171
bed, | acquaint her here of my son paris' love, 3.04. 16
here comes your father, tell him so yourself; 3.05.124
o'er a gossip's bowl, | for here we need it not. 3.05.175
faith, here it is. 3.05.212
he were | as living here and you no use of him. 3.05.225
look, sir, here comes the lady toward my cell. 4.01. 17
so many guests invite as here are writ. 4.02. 1
by holy lawrence to fall prostrate here | and 4.02. 20
what should she do here? 4.03. 18
the county will be here with music straight, 4.04. 22
what noise is here? 4.05. 17
come, we'll in here, tarry for the mourners, and 4.05.145 P
here lives a caitiff wretch would sell it him." 5.01. 52
me, | here in this city visiting the sick, | and 5.02. 7
i could not send it — here it is again — | nor 5.02. 14
afraid to stand alone | here in the churchyard, 5.03. 11
and here is come to do some villainous shame 5.03. 52
and apprehend thee for a felon here. 5.03. 69
for here lies juliet, and her beauty makes 5.03. 85
keeps | thee here in dark to be his paramour? 5.03.105
here, here will i remain | with worms that are 5.03.108
here will i remain | with worms that are thy 5.03.108
o, here | will i set up my everlasting rest, 5.03.109
as i did sleep under this /yew tree here, | i 5.03.137
what's here? 5.03.161
here lies the county slain, | and juliet 5.03.174
dead, | who here hath lain this two days buried. 5.03.176
here is a friar, that trembles, sighs, and weeps 5.03.184
sovereign, here lies the county paris slain, 5.03.195
here is a friar, and /slaughter'd romeo's man, 5.03.199
and here i stand both to impeach and purge 5.03.226
here untimely lay | the noble paris and true 5.03.258
and here he writes that he did buy a poison | of 5.03.288
i have a jewel here — TIM 1.01. 12
and rich. here is a water, look ye. 1.01. 18
here is a touch; 1.01. 36
attends he here, or no? lucilius! 1.01.114
here, at your lordship's service. 1.01.115
this fellow here, lord timon, this thy creature, 1.01.116
look who comes here; will you be chid? 1.01.176
here, my lord, in readiness. 1.02.166 P
here, my lord, a trifle of our love. 1.02.207
what a coil's here! 1.02.230
here, sir, what is your pleasure? 2.01. 14
here comes the lord. 2.02. 13
my lord, here is a note of certain dues. 2.02. 16
of athens here, my lord. 2.02. 17
stay, here comes the fool with apemantus, let's 2.02. 46 P
look you, here comes my master's page. 2.02. 72 P
aside, aside, here comes lord timon. 2.02.119 P
heads, and i am here | no richer in return. 2.02.202
please your lordship, here is the wine. 3.01. 30 P
we wait for certain money here, sir. 3.04. 46
my lord, here is my bill. 3.04. 85 P
here, my lord. 3.04.109
he sent to me, sir — here he comes. 3.06. 24 P
here 'tis. 3.06.116 P
here lies my gown. 3.06.117 P
what is here? 4.03. 25
here is some gold for thee. 4.03.101
here, i will mend thy feast. 4.03.282
here is no use for gold. 4.03.290
for here it sleeps, and does no hired harm. 4.03.291
to me, thou mightst have hit upon it here. 4.03.347 P
thou singly honest man, | here, take; 4.03.524
here is his cave. 5.01.126
peace and content be here! 5.01.127
i have a tree, which grows here in my close, 5.01.205
here come our brothers. 5.02. 13
who's here? 5.03. 2
"here lies a wretched corse, of wretched soul 5.04. 70
here lie i, timon, who, alive, all living men 5.04. 72
thy fill, but pass and stay not here thy gait." 5.04. 73
here, my lord. JC 1.02. 2
but wherefore do you hold me here so long? 1.02. 83
and land, | in every place, save here in italy. 1.03. 88
close a while, for here comes one in haste. 1.03.131
when it is lighted, come and call me here. 2.01. 8
and no man here | but honors you; 2.01. 90
here lies the east; doth not the day break here? 2.01.101
here lies the east; doth not the day break here? 2.01.101
here, as i point my sword, the sun arises, 2.01.106
east | stands, as the capitol, directly here. 2.01.111
for here have been | some six or seven, who did 2.01.276
giving myself a voluntary wound | here, in the 2.01.301
here is a sick man that would speak with you. 2.01.310
romans bow before, | i here discard my sickness! 2.01.321
calphurnia here, my wife, stays me at home: 2.02. 75
here will i stand till caesar pass along, | and 2.03. 11
i would have had thee there and here again | ere 2.04. 4
art thou here yet? 2.04. 10
here the street is narrow; 2.04. 33
here, quite confounded with this mutiny. 3.01. 86
soft, who comes here? a friend of antony's. 3.01.122
but here comes antony. welcome, mark antony! 3.01.147
as here by caesar, and by you cut off, | the 3.01.162
here wast thou bay'd, brave hart, | here didst 3.01.204
here didst thou fall, and here thy hunters stand 3.01.205
didst thou fall, and here thy hunters stand, 3.01.205
strooken by many princes, | dost thou here lie! 3.01.210
mark antony, here take you caesar's body. 3.01.244
here is a mourning rome, a dangerous rome, | no 3.01.288
that will hear me speak, let 'em stay here; 3.02. 5
who is here so base that would be a bondman? 3.02. 29 P
who is here so rude that would not be a roman? 3.02. 31 P
who is here so vile that will not love his 3.02. 32 P
here comes his body, mourn'd by mark antony, who 3.02. 41 P
and, for my sake, stay here with antony. 3.02. 56
'twere best he speak no harm of brutus here! 3.02. 68
here, under leave of brutus and the rest | (for 3.02. 81
spoke, | but here i am to speak what i do know. 3.02.101
look you here, | here is himself, marr'd as you 3.02.196
here is himself, marr'd as you see with traitors 3.02.197
here is the will, and under caesar's seal: 3.02.240
here was a caesar! 3.02.252
what? shall i find you here? 4.01. 10
or here or at the capitol. 4.01. 11
before the eyes of both our armies here | (which 4.02. 43
pella | for taking bribes here of the sardians; 4.03. 3
there is my dagger, | and here my naked breast; 4.03.101
now sit we close about this taper here, | and 4.03.164
i have here received letters | that young 4.03.167
here in the tent. 4.03.240
here it is, i think. 4.03.274
who comes here? 4.03.275
they mean to warn us at philippi here, 5.01. 5
hands, | who to philippi here consorted us. 5.01. 82
this ensign here of mine was turning back; 5.03. 3
thee up to yonder troops | and here again, that 5.03. 17
i will be here again, even with a thought. 5.03. 19
here, take thou the hilts, | and when my face is 5.03. 43
here comes the general. 5.04. 17
and, this last night, here in philippi fields. 5.05. 19
fly, fly, my lord, there is no tarrying here. 5.05. 30
who comes here? MAC 1.02. 45
here i have a pilot's thumb, | wrack'd as 1.03. 28
were such things here as we do speak about? 1.03. 83
to th' self–same tune and words. who's here? 1.03. 88
the king comes here to–night. 1.05. 31
that tend on mortal thoughts, unsex me here, 1.05. 41
my dearest love, | duncan comes here to–night. 1.05. 59
that the heaven's breath | smells wooingly here; 1.06. 6
might be the be–all and the end–all — here, 1.07. 5
but here, upon this bank and /shoal of time, 1.07. 6
in these cases | we still have judgment here, 1.07. 8
he's here in double trust: 1.07. 12
what hands are here? 2.02. 56
napkins enow about you, here you'll sweat for't. 2.03. 6 P
come in, tailor, here you may roast your goose. 2.03. 14 P
here he comes. 2.03. 43
here lay duncan, | his silver skin lac'd with 2.03.111
what should be spoken here, where our fate, 2.03.121
here comes the good macduff. 2.04. 20
here i'll sit i' th' midst. 3.04. 10
here had we now our country's honor roof'd, 3.04. 39
here is a place reserv'd, sir. 3.04. 45
here, my good lord. 3.04. 47
if i stand here, i saw him. 3.04. 73
would he were here! 3.04. 90
'shall not be long but i'll be here again. 4.02. 23
take a homely man's advice, | be not found here; 4.02. 69
and here from gracious england have i offer | of 4.03. 43
o my breast, | thy hope ends here! 4.03.114
here abjure | the taints and blames i laid upon 4.03.123
see who comes here. 4.03.159
lo you, here she comes! 5.01. 19 P
profit again should hardly draw me here. 5.03. 62
here let them lie | till famine and the ague eat 5.05. 3
there is nor flying hence, nor tarrying here. 5.05. 47
and underwrit, | "here may you see the tyrant." 5.08. 27
here comes newer comfort. 5.09. 19
hath in the skirts of norway here and there HAM 1.01. 97
'tis here! 1.01.141
'tis here! 1.01.141
we have here writ | to norway, uncle of young 1.02. 27
and we here dispatch | you, good cornelius, and 1.02. 33
here in the cheer and comfort of our eye, | our 1.02.116
i stay too long — but here my father comes. 1.03. 52
yet here, laertes? 1.03. 55
though i am native here | and to the manner born 1.04. 14
touching this vision here, | it is an honest 1.05.137
here, as before, never, so help you mercy, | how 1.05.169
that you voutsafe your rest here in our court 2.02. 13
and here give up ourselves, in the full bent, 2.02. 30
or my dear majesty your queen here, think, | if 2.02.135
walks four hours together | here in the lobby. 2.02.161
satirical rogue says here that old men have grey 2.02.197 P
is it not monstrous that this player here, | but 2.02.551
they are here about the court, | and, as i think 3.01. 19
'twere by accident, may here | affront ophelia. 3.01. 30
ophelia, walk you here. 3.01. 42
o, what a noble mind is here o'erthrown! 3.01.150
here, sweet lord, at your service. 3.02. 53
our tragedy, | here stooping to your clemency, 3.02.150
both here and hence pursue me lasting strife, 3.02.222
sweet, leave me here a while, | my spirits grow 3.02.225
of jove himself, and now reigns here | a very, 3.02.283
i'll silence me even here; 3.04. 4
look here upon this picture, and on this, | the 3.04. 53
here is your husband, like a mildewed ear, 3.04. 64
o, here they come. 4.02. 4 P
alas, look here, my lord. 4.05. 37
brands the harlot | even here, between the 4.05.120
and in a postscript here, he says, "alone." 4.07. 52
months since | here was a gentleman of normandy: 4.07. 82
for here lies the point: 5.01. 10 P
here lies the water; 5.01. 15 P
here stands the man; 5.01. 16 P
why, here in denmark. 5.01.161 P
i have been sexton here, man and boy, thirty 5.01.162 P
here hung those lips that i have kiss'd i know 5.01.188 P
here comes the king, | the queen, the courtiers. 5.01.217
yet here she is allow'd her virgin crants, | her 5.01.232
dost /thou come here to whine? 5.01.277
sir, here is newly come to court laertes, 5.02.106 P
sir, i will walk here in the hall. 5.02.173 P
not think how ill all's here about my heart — 5.02.212 P
roughly awake, i here proclaim was madness. 5.02.232
here, hamlet, take my napkin, rub thy brows. 5.02.288
it is here, hamlet. 5.02.313
lo here i lie, | never to rise again. 5.02.318
here, thou incestious /murd'rous, damned dane, 5.02.325
is /thy /union here? 5.02.326
are here arrived, give order that these bodies 5.02.377
becomes the field, but here shows much amiss. 5.02.402
amorous sojourn, | and here are to be answer'd. LR 1.01. 48
here i disclaim all my paternal care, 1.01.113
as here i give | her father's heart from her. 1.01.125
freedom lives hence, and banishment is here. 1.01.181
and here i take cordelia by the hand, | duchess 1.01.243
thee and thy virtues here i seize upon, | be it 1.01.252
thou losest here, a better where to find. 1.01.261
here comes one o' the parings. 1.04.188 P
does any here know me? 1.04.226
here do you keep a hundred knights and squires, 1.04.241
his duchess will be here with him this night. 2.01. 4 P
the duke be here to–night? 2.01. 14
light, ho, here! 2.01. 31
here stood he in the dark, his sharp sword out, 2.01. 38
weapons? arms? what's the matter here? 2.02. 47 P
of this /dread exploit, | drew on me here again. 2.02.124
so much thy place mistook | to set thee here? 2.04. 13
and meeting here the other messenger, | whose 2.04. 38
worth | the shame which here it suffers. 2.04. 45
with the earl, sir, here within. 2.04. 59
follow me not, | stay here. 2.04. 60
wherefore | should he sit here? 2.04.113
sharp–tooth'd unkindness, like a vulture, here. 2.04.135
her letter, | that she would soon be here. 2.04.184

who comes here? 2.04.189
you see me here, you gods, a poor old man, | as 2.04.272
here i stand your slave, | a poor, infirm, weak, 3.02. 19
alas, sir, are you here? 3.02. 42
gracious my lord, hard by here is a hovel, 3.02. 61
here is the place, my lord; 3.04. 1
good my lord, enter here. 3.04. 4
good my lord, enter here. 3.04. 22
come not in here, nuncle, here's a spirit. 3.04. 39 P
come, unbutton here. 3.04.109 P
look, here comes a walking fire. 3.04.114 P
here is better than the open air, take it 3.06. 1 P
now, good my lord, lie here and rest awhile. 3.06. 82
here, sir, but trouble him not — his wits are 3.06. 87
but who comes here? 4.01. 9
here, take this purse, thou whom the heav'ns' 4.01. 64
madam, here comes my lord. 4.02. 28
he is not here. 4.02. 89
and at her late being here | she gave strange 4.05. 24
here, friend, 's another purse; 4.06. 28
as i stood here below, methought his eyes | were 4.06. 69
but who comes here? 4.06. 80
o, here he is: 4.06.188
though that the queen on special cause is here, 4.06.215
here, in the sands, | thee i'll rake up, the 4.06.273
particular broils | are not the question here. 5.01. 31
here is the guess of their true strength and 5.01. 52
here, father, take the shadow of this tree | for 5.02. 1
no further, sir, a man may rot even here. 5.02. 8
that i create thee here | my lord and master. 5.03. 77
nothing less | than i have here proclaim'd thee. 5.03. 95
here is mine: 5.03.128
the wheel is come full circle, i am here. 5.03.175
here comes kent. 5.03.230
is he not here? 5.03.237
that's but a trifle here. 5.03.296
here is her father's house, i'll call aloud. OTH 1.01. 74
and wheeling stranger | of here and every where. 1.01.137
thought t' have yerk'd him here under the ribs. 1.02. 5
i will but spend a word here in the house, | and 1.02. 48
ancient, what makes he here? 1.02. 49
here comes another troop to seek for you. 1.02. 54
whose messengers are here about my side, | upon 1.02. 89
so was i bid report here to the state | by 1.03. 15
here is more news. 1.03. 32
here comes brabantio and the valiant moor. 1.03. 47
here is the man — this moor, whom now, it seems 1.03. 71
here comes the lady; 1.03.170
father, | i do perceive here a divided duty: 1.03.181
i here do give thee that with all my heart 1.03.193
at nine i' th' morning here we'll meet again. 1.03.279
the ship is here put in. 2.01. 25
and is in full commission here for cyprus. 2.01. 29
whose footing here anticipates our thoughts | a 2.01. 76
but that he's well and will be shortly here. 2.01. 90
great as my content | to see you here before me. 2.01.184
enough of this content, | it stops me here; 2.01.197
'tis here; 2.01.311
and here without are a brace of cyprus gallants 2.03. 30 P
too — and behold what innovation it makes here. 2.03. 41 P
here, at the door; i pray you call them in. 2.03. 46 P
but here they come. 2.03. 61
what is the matter here? 2.03.164
i do follow here in the chase, not like a hound 2.03.363 P
masters, play here, i will content your pains; 3.01. 1
before emilia here, | i give thee warrant of thy 3.03. 19
madam, here comes my lord. 3.03. 29
i have been talking with a suitor here, | a man 3.03. 42
i have a pain upon my forehead, here. 3.03.284
how now? what do you here alone? 3.03.300
and, to th' advantage, i, being here, took't up. 3.03.312
look, here 'tis. 3.03.313
look here, iago, | all my fond love thus do i 3.03.444
of a sacred vow | i here engage my words. 3.03.462
witness that here iago doth give up | the 3.03.465
for me to devise a lodging and say he lies here, 3.04. 12 P
for here's a young and sweating devil here 3.04. 42
here, my lord. 3.04. 52
made demonstrable here in cyprus to him, | hath 3.04.142
i do attend here on the general, | and think it 3.04.193
way that i can bring you, | for i attend here; 3.04.200
whilst you were here o'erwhelmed with your grief 4.01. 76
bade him anon return and here speak with me, 4.01. 80
here he comes. 4.01. 99
she was here even now; 4.01.132 P
cherubin — | ay, here, look grim as hell! 4.02. 64
here i kneel: 4.02.151
his abode be ling'red here by some accident; 4.02.226 P
no, unpin me here. 4.03. 34
'tis neither here nor there. 4.03. 59
here, stand behind this /bulk, straight will he 5.01. 1
here, at thy hand; be bold, and take thy stand. 5.01. 7
here, here! for heaven sake, help me! 5.01. 50
here, here! for heaven sake, help me! 5.01. 50
what are you here that cry so grievously? 5.01. 53
he that lies slain here, cassio, | was my dear 5.01.101
cassio hath here been set on in the dark | by 5.01.112
my mistress here lies murthered in her bed — 5.02.185
the ice–brook's temper — | o, here it is. 5.02.254
here is my journey's end, here is my butt | and 5.02.267
here is my butt | and very sea–mark of my utmost 5.02.267
that's he that was othello; here i am. 5.02.284
here is a letter | found in the pocket of the 5.02.308
of the slain roderigo, | and here another. 5.02.310
you must not stay here longer, your dismission ANT 1.01. 26
here is my space, | kingdoms are clay; 1.01. 34
hush, here comes antony. 1.02. 79
was he not here? 1.02. 80
here, at your service. my lord approaches. 1.02. 86
you have broach'd here cannot be without you, 1.02.173 P
but here comes antony. 1.03. 13
let her not say 'tis i that keep you here, | i 1.03. 22
look here, and at thy sovereign leisure read 1.03. 60
that thou, residing here, goes yet with me; 1.03.103
and i, hence fleeting, here remain with thee. 1.03.104
when thou wast here above the ground, i was | a 1.05. 30
here comes | the noble antony. 2.02. 13
if we compose well here, to parthia. 2.02. 15
no more than my residing here at rome | might be 2.02. 37
at mine intent | by what did here befall me. 2.02. 42
to have me out of egypt, made wars here; 2.02. 95
make yourself my guest | whilst you abide here. 2.02.244
is gold, and here | my bluest veins to kiss — a 2.05. 28
much tall youth | that else must perish here. 2.06. 8
then | i came before you here a man prepar'd 2.06. 40
i did not think, sir, to have met you here. 2.06. 49
well met here. 2.06. 56
here they might take two thieves kissing. 2.06. 95 P
we look'd not for mark antony here. 2.06.108 P
he married but his occasion here. 2.06.131 P
here they'll be, man. 2.07. 1 P
we will here part. 3.02. 38
look, here i have you, thus i let you go, | and 3.02. 63
the glory of the action, and not resting here, 3.05. 10 P
nay, i have done, | here comes the emperor. 3.07. 20
see you here, sir? 3.11. 30
them | so saucy with the hand of she here — 3.13. 98
here we. 4.03. 9
i had a wound here that was like a t, | but now 4.07. 7
fortune and antony part here, even here | do we 4.12. 19
antony part here, even here | do we shake hands. 4.12. 19
here i am antony, | yet cannot hold this visible 4.14. 13
only | i here importune death awhile, until | of 4.15. 19
here, my good lord. 5.02.136
here, madam. 5.02.141
this, | that thou, vouchsafing here to visit me, 5.02.160
here is a rural fellow | that will not be denied 5.02.233
what work is here, charmian? is this well done? 5.02.325
how goes it here? 5.02.329
here, on her breast, | there is a vent of blood, 5.02.348
here comes the gentleman, | the queen, and CYM 1.01. 68
and i shall here abide the hourly shot | of 1.01. 89
look here, love, | this diamond was my mother's. 1.01.111
remain, remain thou here, | while sense can keep 1.01.117
here is your servant. 1.01.159
here comes the britain. 1.04. 28 P
let us leave here, gentlemen. 1.04. 99 P
here they are, madam. 1.05. 5
here comes a flattering rascal, upon him | will 1.05. 27
when he was here, | he did incline to sadness, 1.06. 61
wild motion of mine eye, | firing it only here; 1.06.104
and | solicits here a lady that disdains | thee 1.06.147
here the leaf's turn'd down | where philomele 2.02. 45
though this a heavenly angel, hell is here. 2.02. 50
here comes the king. 2.03. 32 P
attend you here the door of our stern daughter? 2.03. 37
do here pronounce | by th' very truth of it, i 2.03.107
here are letters for you. 2.04. 35
and this you might have heard of here, by me, 2.04. 77
here, take this too, | it is a basilisk unto 2.04.106
o, that i had her here, to tear her limb–meal! 2.04.147
a kind of conquest | caesar made here, but made 3.01. 23
here, but made not here his brag | of "came, and 3.01. 23
against all color here | did put the yoke upon 3.01. 50
lo here she comes. 3.02. 22
madam, here is a letter from my lord. 3.02. 25
let what is here contain'd relish of love, | of 3.02. 30
nor here, /nor here, | nor what ensues, but have 3.02. 78
nor here, /nor here, | nor what ensues, but have 3.02. 78
what is here? 3.04. 80
most like, | bringing me here to kill me. 3.04.117
here is a box, i had it from the queen, | what's 3.04.188
wrote already to the emperor | how it goes here. 3.05. 22
for when fools shall — | who is here? 3.05. 80
here is a path to't; 3.06. 18
who's here? 3.06. 22
now peace be here, | poor house, that keep'st 3.06. 35
victuals, i should think | here were a fairy. 3.06. 41
before i enter'd here i call'd, and thought | to 3.06. 46
remain here in the cave, | we'll come to you 4.02. 1
brother, stay here. | are we not brothers? 4.02. 2
pray you trust me here, | i'll rob none but 4.02. 14
so far have rav'd | to bring him here alone; 4.02.136
be heard at court that such as we | cave here, 4.02.138
at court that such as we | cave here, hunt here, 4.02.138
what cloten's being here to us portends, | or 4.02.182
look, here he comes, | and brings the dire 4.02.195
flowers | whilst summer lasts and i live here, 4.02.219
their pleasures here are past, so /is their pain 4.02.290
the dream's here still; 4.02.306
devil cloten, | hath here cut off my lord. 4.02.316
and lucre in them | have laid this woe here. 4.02.325
you here at milford–haven with your ships. 4.02.335
they are here in readiness. 4.02.336
soft ho, what trunk is here? 4.02.353
a good, | that here by mountaineers lies slain. 4.02.370
the day that she was missing he was here; 4.03. 17
italy annoy us, but | we grieve at chances here. 4.03. 35
here is one: 5.03. 56
great the slaughter is | here made by th' roman; 5.03. 79
which neither here i'll keep nor bear again, 5.03. 82
who had not now been drooping here, if seconds 5.03. 90
to tell | what crows have peck'd them here. 5.03. 93
of her it was | that we meet here so strangely; 5.05.272
and am right glad he is not standing here | to 5.05.296
here are your sons again, and i must lose | two 5.05.348
and here the bracelet of the truest princess 5.05.416
here, my good lord. 5.05.476
cymbeline, | which shines here in the west. 5.05.476
for death–like dragons here affright thee hard. PER 1.01. 29
here they stand martyrs, slain in cupid's wars; 1.01. 38
here pleasures court mine eyes, and mine eyes 1.02. 6
whose arm seems far too short to hit me here. 1.02. 8
when signior sooth here does proclaim peace, 1.02. 44
who seem'd my good protector, and, being here, 1.02. 82
here must i kill king pericles, and if i do it 1.03. 1 P
here comes the lords of tyre. 1.03. 9 P
my dionyza, shall we rest us here, | and by 1.04. 1
here they are but felt, and seen with mischief's 1.04. 8
here stands a lord, and there a lady weeping; 1.04. 47
here many sink, yet those which see them fall 1.04. 48
here. 1.04. 57
go tell their general we attend him here, | to 1.04. 79
feast here awhile, | until our stars that frown 1.04.107
here have you seen a mighty king | his child, i 2.ch. 1
and here he comes. 2.ch. 39
here to have death in peace is all he'll crave. 2.01. 11
now gods forbid't, and i have a gown here! 2.01. 79 P
since i have here my father gave in his will. 2.01.134
and our daughter here, | in honor of whose birth 2.02. 4
sits here like beauty's child, whom nature gat 2.02. 6
and here, i hope, is none that envies it. 2.03. 14
daughter, so you are — here take your place. 2.03. 18
here, with a cup that's /stor'd unto the brim — 2.03. 50
here, say we drink this standing–bowl of wine to 2.03. 65
she tells me here, she'll wed the stranger 2.05. 16
soft, here he comes, i must dissemble it. 2.05. 23
what's here? 2.05. 42
here comes my daughter, she can witness it. 2.05. 66
here is a thing too young for such a place, 3.01. 15
we here below | recall not what we give, and 3.01. 24
portage quit | with all thou canst find here. 3.01. 36
here she lies, sir. 3.01. 55
what's here? 3.02. 63
"here i give to understand, | if e'er this 3.02. 68
nam'd so, here | i charge your charity withal; 3.03. 13
here she comes weeping for her only mistress' 4.01. 11
we every day | expect him here: 4.01. 34
but here comes boult. 4.02. 39 P
we shall have him here to–morrow with his best 4.02.102 P
here he does but repair it. 4.02.111 P
"the fairest, sweetest, and best lies here, 4.04. 34
twice the worth of her she had ne'er come here. 4.06. 2 P
here comes the lord lysimachus disguis'd. 4.06. 16 P
we have here one, sir, if she would — but there 4.06. 27 P
here comes that which grows to the stalk, never 4.06. 41 P
she has here spoken holy words to the lord 4.06.132 P
here, here's gold for thee. 4.06.181
here we her place, | and to her father turn our 5.ch. 11
he is arriv'd | here where his daughter dwells, 5.ch. 15
o, here he is. 5.01. 2
expect even here, where is a kingly patient, 5.01. 71
here of these /shores? 5.01.103
patience, good sir! | or here i'll cease. 5.01.145
be a troubler of your peace, | i will end here. 5.01.152
i here confess myself the king of tyre, | who, 5.03. 2
her, and plac'd her | here in diana's temple. 5.03. 25
look who kneels here! 5.03. 46
how she came plac'd here in the temple; 5.03. 67
here our play has ending. 5.03.102
sir, | as i shall here make trial of my pray'rs, TNK 1.01.193
and here to keep in abstinence we shame | as in 1.02. 6
jump | as they are, here were to be strangers, 1.02. 41
spinsters, we | should hold you here for ever. 1.03. 24
i have, sir. here she comes. 2.01. 15 P
your friend and i have chanc'd to name you here, 2.01. 17 P
here we are, | and here the graces of our youths 2.02. 26
and here the graces of our youths must wither 2.02. 27
here age must find us, | and which is heaviest, 2.02. 28
we shall know nothing here but one another, 2.02. 41
but dead–cold winter must inhabit here still. 2.02. 45
of noble minds) | in us two here shall perish; 2.02. 53
gods please — to hold here a brave patience, 2.02. 59
and here being thus together, | we are an 2.02. 78
here, with a little patience, | we shall live 2.02. 85
the hand of war hurts none here, nor the seas 2.02. 87
i find the court here, | i am sure, a more 2.02. 99
blow wind i' th' breech on 's, and here i'll be, 2.03. 47
and there i'll be, for our town, and here again, 2.03. 48
he cannot | be so unmanly as to leave me here. 2.06. 19
night, i will be here | with wholesome viands; 3.01. 83
here, sir, drink — | i know you are faint — 3.03. 6
is't not mad lodging | here in the wild woods, 3.03. 23
here, arcite, to the wenches | we have known in 3.03. 28
tediosity and disensanity | is here among ye! 3.05. 3
for why, here stand i; 3.05. 12
here the duke comes; 3.05. 12
here, my mad boys, have at ye! 3.05. 24
quo usque tandem? here is a woman wanting. 3.05. 38
gave her promise faithfully she would | be here, 3.05. 44
what have we here? 3.05. 96
we are a few of those collected here | that 3.05.103
do here present this machine, or this frame. 3.05.113
here, palamon: 3.06.102
as i have brought my life here to confirm it, 3.06.164
why her eyes command me | stay here to love her; 3.06.170
none here speak for 'em, | for, ere the sun set, 3.06.183
be wise then | and here forget 'em; 3.06.223
before us that are here, can force his cousin 3.06.294
here, cousin arcite, | i am friends again till 3.06.299
when ye return, who wins i'll settle here; 3.06.307
here they are. 4.01.103
here. 4.01.143
here. 4.01.150
were here a mortal woman, and had in her | the 4.02. 10
here love himself sits smiling. 4.02. 14
what stuff's here? poor soul! 4.03. 17 P
i here, thy priest, | am humbled 'fore thine 5.01.142
o mistress, | thou here dischargest me. 5.01.170
make curtsy, here your love comes. 5.02. 69
to marry us, for here they are nice and foolish. 5.02. 79
what do you here? 5.02. 99
i must ev'n leave you here. 5.02.102
i will stay here, | it is enough my hearing 5.03. 6
let it here be done. 5.03.133
which superstition | here finds allowance — on 5.04. 54
ev'n very here | i sund'red you. 5.04. 99
'tis strange if none be here — and, if he will ep 7
not /one of you here present, | had there such STM II.C 62
here come and sit, where never serpent hisses, VEN 17
"since i have hemm'd thee here | within the 229
i pray you hence, and leave me here alone, | for 382
lo here the gentle lark, weary of rest, | from 853
here kennell'd in a brake she finds a hound, 913
and here she meets another sadly scowling, | to 917
here overcome, as one full of despair, | she 955
"since thou art dead, lo here i prophesy, 1135
"here was thy father's bed, here in my breast; 1183
"here was thy father's bed, here in my breast; 1183
here pale with fear he doth premeditate | the LUC 183
here with a cockatrice' dead–killing eye | he 540
here she exclaims against repose and rest, | and 757
yet save that labor, for i have them here. 1290
here folds she up the tenure of her woe, | her 1310

and here and there the painter interlaces | pale 1390
here one man's hand lean'd on another's head, 1415
here one being throng'd bears back, all boll'n 1417
thy eye kindled the fire that burneth here, 1475
and here in troy, for trespass of thine eye, 1476
"lo here weeps hecuba, here priam dies, | here 1485
"lo here weeps hecuba, here priam dies, | here 1485
here manly hector faints, here troilus sounds, 1486
here manly hector faints, here troilus sounds, 1486
here friend by friend in bloody channel lies, 1487
here feelingly she weeps troy's painted woes, 1492
"for even as subtile sinon here is painted, | so 1541
here all enrag'd, such passion her assails 1562
lo here the hopeless merchant of this loss, 1660
here with a sigh, as if her heart would break, 1716
even here she sheathed in her harmless breast 1723
life was mine which thou hast here deprived. 1752
win his heart she touch'd him here and there — PP 4. 7
here in these brakes deep–wounded with a boar, 9.10
in my thigh," quoth she, "here was the sore." 9.12
yet will she blush, here be it said, | to hear 18.53
here the anthem doth commence: PHT 21
all simplicity, | here enclos'd, in cinders lie. 55
no longer yours than you yourself here live: SON 13. 2
by praising him here who doth hence remain! 39.14
against that time do i insconce me here | within 49. 9
alas, 'tis true i have gone here and there, 110. 1
would have seem'd more black and damned here!" LC 54
"'look here what tributes wounded fancies sent 197
what breast so cold that is not warmed here? 292

HEREABOUT 4 FR 0.0004 REL FR 3 V 1 P
there is no other shelter hereabout. TMP 2.02. 39 P
for all this same, i'll hide me hereabout, | his ROM 5.03. 43
cassio, walk hereabout; OTH 3.04.165
i think that one of them is hereabout, | and 5.01. 57

HEREABOUTS 1 FR 0.0001 REL FR 1 V 0 P
and hereabouts 'a dwells — which late i noted ROM 5.01. 38

HEREAFTER 54 FR 0.0061 REL FR 39 V 15 P
and i'll be wise hereafter, | and seek for grace TMP 5.01.295
i will hereafter make known to you why i have WIV 3.03.225 P
if the encounter acknowledge itself hereafter, MM 3.01.252 P
and to deliver us from devices hereafter, which 4.04. 13 P
let that appear hereafter, and aim better at me ADO 3.02. 96 P
here comes lorenzo, more of this hereafter. MV 2.06. 20
hereafter, in a better world than this, | i AYL 1.02.284
sluttishness may come hereafter. 3.03. 41 P
a good excuse for me hereafter to leave my wife. 3.03. 93 P
not ended, as fearing to hear of it hereafter. AWW 4.03. 97 P
which is away — | but more of this hereafter. 4.04. 26
'tis not hereafter; TN 2.03. 47
you shall know more hereafter. 3.04.125 P
o, father, you'll know more of that hereafter. WT 4.04.343
these words hereafter thy tormentors be! R2 2.01.136
i shall hereafter, my thrice–gracious lord, | be 1H4 3.02. 92
to ye | shall show itself more openly hereafter. 2H4 4.02. 76
when you take occasions to see leeks hereafter, H5 5.01. 56 P
'tis hereafter to know, but now to promise. 5.02.212 P
and that hereafter ages may behold | what ruin 1H6 2.02. 10
fault, | and long hereafter say unto his child, 3H6 2.02. 36
that shalt thou know hereafter. R3 1.02.198
a holy day shall this be kept hereafter. 2.01. 74
you live that shall cry woe for this hereafter. 3.03. 7
myself have many tears to wash | hereafter time, 4.04.390
'tis a girl | promises boys hereafter. H8 5.01.166
here's yet in the word "hereafter" the kneading, TRO 1.01. 24 P
madam, i will obey you in every thing hereafter. COR 1.03.103 P
forsooth, hereafter theirs, so far | as thou 3.02. 85
private friends, hereafter | will i lend ear to. 5.03. 18
as you shall use me hereafter, dry–beat the rest ROM 3.01. 79 P
and hereafter say | a madman's mercy bid thee 5.03. 66
noble timon, of whose memory | hereafter more. TIM 5.04. 81
and of these times, | i shall recount hereafter. JC 1.02.165
for he will live, and laugh at this hereafter. 2.01.191
all hail, macbeth, that shalt be king hereafter! MAC 1.03. 50
malcolm, whom we name hereafter | the prince of 1.04. 38
greater than both, by the all–hail hereafter! 1.05. 55
she should have died hereafter; 5.05. 17
as i perchance hereafter shall think meet | to HAM 1.05.171
remember him hereafter as my honorable friend. LR 1.01. 27 P
away, i say, thou shalt know more hereafter. OTH 2.03.381
my news | i might have told hereafter. ANT 3.05. 22
worthy he is i will leave to appear hereafter, CYM 1.04. 33 P
we'll talk of that hereafter. 3.02. 66
shalt hereafter find | it is no act of common 3.04. 90
yet said hereafter | i might know more. 4.02. 41
never say hereafter | but i am truest speaker. 5.05.375
on whose grace | you may depend hereafter. PER 3.03. 41
for all the fortune of my life hereafter, | yon TNK 2.02.235
that's no matter, | we'll argue that hereafter. 3.03. 5
sorrow on love hereafter shall attend; VEN 1136
and bids her eyes hereafter still be blind; LUC 758
"no dame hereafter living | by my excuse shall 1714

HERE–APPROACH 1 FR 0.0001 REL FR 1 V 0 P
whither indeed, before /thy here–approach, | old MAC 4.03.133

HEREBY 3 FR 0.0003 REL FR 2 V 1 P
that's hereby. LLL 1.02.136 P
hereby, upon the edge of yonder coppice, | a 4.01. 9
i will not reason what is meant hereby, R3 1.04. 93

HEREDITARY 8 FR 0.0009 REL FR 7 V 1 P
do so. to ebb | hereditary sloth instructs me. TMP 2.01.223
the imposition clear'd, | hereditary ours. WT 1.02. 75
some of the best of 'em were hereditary hangmen. COR 2.01. 93 P
have their ingratitude in them hereditary: TIM 2.02.215
the /senator shall bear contempt hereditary, 4.03. 10
and compounded thee | poor rogue hereditary. 4.03.274
to thee and thine hereditary ever | remain this LR 1.01. 79
hereditary, | rather than purchas'd; ANT 1.04. 13

HEREFORD *(see herford, etc.)*

HEREIN 28 FR 0.0031 REL FR 25 V 3 P
prison, | and see our pleasure herein executed. MM 5.01.521
herein you war against your reputation, | and ERR 3.01. 86
and yet would herein others' eyes were worse: 4.02. 26
down | that violates the smallest branch herein. LLL 1.01. 21
but herein mean i to enrich my pain, | to have MND 1.01.250
and herein spend but time | to wind about my MV 1.01.153
my best endeavors shall be done herein. 2.02.173
for herein fortune shows herself more kind 4.01.267
myself notice of my brother's purpose herein, AYL 1.01.140 P
herein i see thou lov'st me not with the full 1.02. 8 P
my lord, | before i freely speak my mind herein, R2 4.01.327
herein all breathless lies | the mightiest of 5.06. 31
idleness, | yet herein will i imitate the sun, 1H4 1.02.197
shalt have charge and sovereign trust herein. 3.02.161
and these | herein misled by your suggestion. 4.03. 51
each several article herein redress'd, | all 2H4 4.01.168
and my consent ne'er ask'd herein before? 2H6 2.04. 72
and yet herein i judge mine own wit good — 3.01.232
herein your highness wrongs both them and me. 3H6 3.02. 75
who knows the lord protector's mind herein? R3 3.04. 7
i will resolve you herein presently. 4.02. 26
herein i teach you | how you shall bid god 'ield MAC 1.06. 12
and of the truth herein | this present object HAM 1.01.155
nor have we herein barr'd | your better wisdoms, 1.02. 14
to suppress | his further gait herein, in that 1.02. 31
with an entreaty, herein further shown, | that 2.02. 76
to bar your offense herein too, i durst attempt CYM 1.04.112 P
herein lives wisdom, beauty, and increase, SON 11. 5

HEREOF 5 FR 0.0005 REL FR 4 V 1 P
is, | i long to know the truth hereof at large. ERR 4.04.143
come go along and see the truth hereof, | for SHR 4.05. 75
what will ensue hereof, there's none can tell; R2 2.01.212
hereof comes it that prince harry is valiant, 2H4 4.03.117 P
the shame hereof will make me hide my head. 1H6 1.05. 39

HERE–REMAIN 1 FR 0.0001 REL FR 1 V 0 P
which often, since my here–remain in england, MAC 4.03.148

/HERE'S 1 FR 0.0001 REL FR 1 V 0 P
/and /here's /another, /whose /warp'd /looks LR 3.06. 53

HERE'S 225 FR 0.0254 REL FR 118 V 107 P
here's neither bush nor shrub to bear off any TMP 2.02. 18 P
well, here's my comfort. 2.02. 45 P
but here's my comfort. 2.02. 55 P
here's my hand. 3.01. 89
here's a maze trod indeed | through forth–rights 3.03. 2
here's a garment for't. 4.01.241 P
which i wear in my head, here's a goodly sight. 5.01.260 P
here's too small a pasture for such store of TGV 1.01. 99 P
here's a million of manners. 2.01. 98 P
here's my mother's breath up and down. 2.03. 28 P
and here's the ladder for the purpose. 3.01.152
here's another letter to her. WIV 1.03. 68 P
opinions, here's the twin–brother of thy letter; 2.01. 72 P
here's a fellow frights english out of his wits. 2.01.138 P
sir, here's a woman would speak with you. 2.02. 31 P
forbear; here's company. 2.03. 17 P
here's mistress page at the door, sweating, and 3.03. 85 P
here's mistress quickly, sir, to speak with you. 3.05. 19 P
here's no man. 4.02.152 P
here's a bohemian–tartar tarries the coming down 4.05. 20 P
why, here's a change indeed in the commonwealth! MM 1.02.104 P
this comes off well. here's a wise officer. 2.01. 57 P
look, signior, here's your sister. 3.01. 49
here's a gentleman, and a friend of mine. 3.02. 41 P
here's a fellow will help you to–morrow in your 4.02. 22 P
look, here's the warrant, claudio, for thy death 4.02. 63
first, here's young master rash, he's in for a 4.03. 4 P
here's a gentlewoman denies all that you have 5.01.281 P
and yet here's one in place i cannot pardon. 5.01.499
but here's a villain that would face me down ERR 3.01. 6
here's too much "out upon thee!" 3.01. 78
lo here's the chain. 3.02.166
here's the note | how much your chain weighs to 4.01. 27
master, here's the gold you sent me for. 4.03. 12 P
here's that, i warrant you, will pay them all. 4.04. 10
you to heaven, here's no place for you maids." ADO 2.01. 46 P
here's his dry hand up and down. 2.01.118 P
sir, here's a dish i love not, i cannot endure 2.01.274 P
here's that shall drive some of them to a 3.05. 62 P
call her forth, brother, here's the friar ready. 5.04. 39
her, | for here's a paper written in his hand, 5.04. 86
and here's another | writ in my cousin's hand, 5.04. 88
here's our own hands against our hearts. 5.04. 91 P
here's a costard broken in a shin. LLL 3.01. 70
look, here's thy love; my foot and her face see. 4.03.273
and here's a marvail's convenient place for our MND 3.01. 2 P
here's my son, sir, a poor boy — MV 2.02.122 P
go to, here's a simple line of life! 2.02.160 P
here's a small trifle of wives! 2.02.161 P
here's the scroll, | the continent and summary 3.02.129
here's a young maid with travel much oppressed, AYL 2.04. 74
here's eight that must take hands | to join in 5.04.128
here's — SHR in.2. 25 P
husht, master, here's some good pastime toward; 1.01. 68
gifts are so good, here's none will hold you. 1.01.106 P
here's no knavery! 1.02.138 P
why, here's no crab, and therefore look not sour 2.01.230
here's snip and nip and cut and slish and slash, 4.03. 90
sir, here's the door, this is lucentio's house. 5.01. 8
here's a madman will murder me. 5.01. 58 P
here's lucentio, | right son to the right 5.01.114
here's packing, with a witness, to deceive us 5.01.118 P
then here's a man stands that has brought his AWW 2.01. 63
look on his letter, madam, here's my passport. 3.02. 56
here's his lordship now. 4.03. 83 P
here 'tis, here's a paper. 4.03.206 P
here's a petition from a florentine, | who hath 5.03.130
your ring, | and, look you, here's your letter. 5.03.311
marry, but you shall have — and here's my hand. TN 1.03. 67 P
here's an overweening rogue! 2.05. 29 P
hold, sir, here's my purse. 3.03. 38
here's the challenge, read it. 3.04.143 P
here's ado, to lock up honesty | and honor from WT 2.02. 9
here's such ado to make no stain a stain | as 2.02. 17
here's a sight for thee; 3.03.114 P
here's flow'rs for you: 4.04.103
here's one to a very doleful tune, how a 4.04.262 P
here's the midwive's name to't, one mistress 4.04.269 P
here's another ballad, of a fish that appear'd 4.04.275 P
fear not, man, here's no harm intended to thee. 4.04.629 P
here's nobody will steal that from thee. 4.04.631 P
here's a stay | that shakes the rotten carcass JN 2.01.455
here's a large mouth indeed, | that spits forth 2.01.457
and here's a prophet that i brought with me 4.02.147
here's a good world! 4.03.116
you rogue, here's lime in this sack too. 1H4 2.04.124 P
shot here, here's no scoring but upon the pate. 5.03. 31 P
here's no vanity! 5.03. 33 P
here's goodly stuff toward! 2H4 2.04.200 P
here's a goodly tumult! 2.04.204 P
and here's four harry ten shillings in french 3.02.221 P
here's wart, you see what a ragged appearance it 3.02.260 P
look here's more news. 4.04. 93
here's my glove; give me another of thine. H5 4.01.211 P
the gates, here's gloucester that would enter. 1H6 1.03. 17
here's beauford, that regards nor god nor king, 1.03. 60
here's gloucester, a foe to citizens, | one that 1.03. 62
here's a silly stately style indeed! 4.07. 72
why, here's a girl! 5.04. 80
man, | we are alone, here's none but thee and i. 2H6 1.02. 69
and here, neighbor, here's a cup of charneco. 2.03. 62 P
and here's a pot of good double beer, neighbor. 2.03. 64 P
but here's a vengeful sword, rusted with ease, 3.02.198
here's a villain! 4.02. 89 P
here's the lord say, which sold the towns in 4.07. 20 P
here's the lord of the soil come to seize me for 4.10. 24 P
brother, here's the earl of wiltshire's blood, 3H6 1.01. 14
here's for my oath, here's for my father's death 1.04.175
for my oath, here's for my father's death. 1.04.175
and here's to right our gentle–hearted king. 1.04.176
and here's the heart that triumphs in their 2.04. 8
ay, here's a deer whose skin's a keeper's fee: 3.01. 22
here's a good world the while! R3 3.06. 10
here's to your ladyship, and pledge it, madam, H8 1.04. 47
here's the pang that pinches: 2.03. 1
but here's yet in the word "hereafter" the TRO 1.01. 23 P
"here's but two and fifty hairs on your chin — 1.02.157 P
here, here's an excellent place, here we may see 1.02.181 P
here's nestor, | instructed by the antiquary 2.03.250
and here's a lord — come knights from east to 2.03.263
here's "in witness whereof the parties 3.02. 57 P
of idiot–worshippers, here's a letter for thee. 5.01. 7 P
here's agamemnon, an honest fellow enough, and 5.01. 51 P
here's a letter come from yond poor girl. 5.03. 99 P
without note, here's many else have done — COR 1.09. 49
look, here's a letter from him; 2.01.108 P
here's he that would take from you all your 3.01.181
here's goodly work! 3.01.260
here's no place for you; 4.05. 8 P
here's no place for you. 4.05. 30 P
here's a strange alteration! 4.05.148 P
here's he that was wont to thwack our general, 4.05.178 P
look thee, here's water to quench it. 5.02. 72 P
and here's thy hand, in scorn to thee sent back TIT 3.01.237
demetrius, here's the son of lucius, | he hath 4.02. 1
here's no sound jest! 4.02. 26
here's a young lad fram'd of another leer: 4.02.119
mean while here's money for thy charges. 4.03.105
see, here's to jove, and this to mercury, | this 4.04. 14
and here's the base fruit of her burning lust. 5.01. 43
here's rome's young captain, let him tell the 5.03. 94
here's much to do with hate, but more with love. ROM 1.01.175
o, here's a wit of cheverel, that stretches from 2.04. 83 P
here's goodly gear! a sail, a sail! 2.04.101 P
here's such a coil! come, what says romeo? 2.05. 65
here's my fiddlestick, here's that shall make 3.01. 48 P
fiddlestick, here's that shall make you dance. 3.01. 48 P
here's drink — i drink to thee. 4.03. 58
here's to my love! 5.03.119
here's one, a friend, and one that knows you 5.03.123
here's romeo's man, we found him in the 5.03.182
here's that which is too weak to be a sinner, TIM 1.02. 58
here's my lord. 3.01. 4 P
here's to thee. 3.01. 32 P
here's three solidares for thee; 3.01. 43 P
o, here's servilius; 3.04. 66 P
here's mine. 3.04. 86 P
every man here's so. 3.06. 19 P
here's a noble feast toward. 3.06. 59 P
go on — here's gold — go on; 4.03.108
rascal thieves, | here's gold. 4.03.429
here's decius brutus, he shall tell them so. JC 2.02. 57
but here's a parchment with the seal of caesar, 3.02.128
look, lucius, here's the book i sought for so; 4.03.252
here's a knocking indeed! MAC 2.03. 1 P
here's a farmer, that hang'd himself on th' 2.03. 4 P
faith, here's an equivocator, that could swear 2.03. 8 P
faith, here's an english tailor come hither for 2.03. 13 P
here's our chief guest. 3.01. 11
here's another, | more potent than the first. 4.01. 75
yet here's a spot. 5.01. 31 P
here's the smell of the blood still. 5.01. 50 P
marry, sir, here's my drift, | and i believe it HAM 2.01. 37
no, good mother, here's metal more attractive. 3.02.109 P
there's rue for you, and here's some for me; 4.05.182 P
here's fine revolution, and we had the trick to 5.01. 90 P
here's a skull now hath lien you i' th' earth 5.01.173 P
here's the commission, read it at more leisure. 5.02. 26
this pearl is thine, | here's to thy health! 5.02.283
here's yet some liquor left. 5.02.342
here's france and burgundy, my noble lord. LR 1.01.188
let me hire him too, here's my coxcomb. 1.04. 95 P
here's a night pities neither wise men nor fools 3.02. 12 P
marry, here's grace and a codpiece — that's a 3.02. 40 P
come not in here, nuncle, here's a spirit. 3.04. 39 P
here's three on 's are sophisticated. 3.04.105 P
come on, sir, here's the place; 4.06. 11
but here's my husband; OTH 1.03.185
here's a goodly watch indeed! 2.03.160
but, masters, here's money for you; 3.01. 11 P
for here's a young and sweating devil here 3.04. 42
here's a change indeed! 4.02.106
here's one comes in his shirt, with light and 5.01. 47
i cry you mercy. here's cassio hurt by villains. 5.01. 69
now here's another discontented paper, | found 5.02.314
here's more news. ANT 1.04. 33
here's to thee, menas! 2.07. 86
here's to caesar! 2.07. 98
here's the manner of't: 3.06. 2
here's sport indeed! 4.15. 32
here's my ring. CYM 1.04.145 P
here's a voucher, | stronger than ever law could 2.02. 39
come, here's my heart: 3.04. 78

well then, here's the point: 3.04.153
give me thy hand, here's my purse. 3.05.123 P
here's money for my meat, | i would have left it 3.06. 49
here's a few flow'rs, but 'bout midnight, more: 4.02.283
here's my knee. 5.05.325
behold, | here's poison and here's gold; PER 1.01.155
behold, | here's poison and here's gold; 1.01.155
here's them in our country of greece gets more 2.01. 63 P
for here's nothing to be got now–a–days unless 2.01. 68 P
here's a fish hangs in the net, like a poor 2.01.116 P
sir, here's a lady that wants breathing too, 2.03.100
here's all that is left living of your queen: 3.01. 20
hold, here's gold for thee. 4.06.105
hold, here's more gold for thee. 4.06.113
here, here's gold for thee. 4.06.181
o, here's | the lady that i sent for. 5.01. 64
i know not, but | here's the regent, sir, of 5.01.186
come forth and fear not, here's no theseus. TNK 3.03. 3
here's friz and maudline. 3.05. 25
and here's something | to paint your pole withal 3.05.152
here's one, if it but hold, i ask no more | for 3.06. 91
but here's the joy: SON 42.13
HERES 1 FR 0.0001 REL FR 0 V 1 P
noster henricus, rex angliae, et heres franciae. H5 5.02.342 P
HERESIES 2 FR 0.0002 REL FR 2 V 0 P
or as the heresies that men do leave | are hated MND 2.02.139
which are heresies, | and, not reform'd, may H8 5.02. 53
HERESY 6 FR 0.0006 REL FR 4 V 2 P
o heresy in fair, fit for these days! LLL 4.01. 22
without opinion, and strange without heresy. 5.01. 6 P
deceive, | so thou, my surfeit and my heresy, MND 2.02.141
the ancient saying is no heresy, | hanging and MV 2.09. 82
it is heresy. TN 1.05.228 P
of the loyal leonatus, | all turn'd to heresy? CYM 3.04. 82
HERETIC 6 FR 0.0006 REL FR 5 V 1 P
stand, | in him that was of late an heretic, WIV 4.04. 9
wast ever an obstinate heretic in the despite of ADO 1.01.234 P
it is an heretic that makes the fire, | not she WT 2.03.115
doth revolt | from his allegiance to an heretic, JN 3.01.175
there is sprung up | an heretic, an arch–one, H8 3.02.102
it fears not policy, that heretic, | which works SON 124. 9
HERETICS 2 FR 0.0002 REL FR 2 V 0 P
die, | transparent heretics, be burnt for liars! ROM 1.02. 91
no heretics burn'd, but wenches' suitors; LR 3.02. 84
HERETO 1 FR 0.0001 REL FR 1 V 0 P
the people than | he hath hereto priz'd them at. COR 2.02. 60
HEREUPON 1 FR 0.0001 REL FR 0 V 1 P
i will hereupon confess i am in love; LLL 1.02. 57 P
/HERFORD 5 FR 0.0005 REL FR 5 V 0 P
have you forgot the duke of /herford, boy? R2 2.03. 36
/the /earl /of /herford /was /reputed /then 2H4 4.01.129
/prayers /and /love | /were /set /on /herford, 4.01.136
th' earldom of /herford, and the moveables, R3 4.02. 90
the duke of buckingham and earl | of /herford, H8 1.01.200
HERFORD 24 FR 0.0027 REL FR 24 V 0 P
brought hither henry herford thy bold son, R2 1.01. 3
cousin of herford, what dost thou object 1.01. 28
our cousin herford and fell mowbray fight. 1.02. 46
a caitive recreant to my cousin herford! 1.02. 53
my lord aumerle, is harry herford arm'd? 1.03. 1
against the duke of herford that appeals me, 1.03. 21
harry of herford, lancaster, and derby | am i, 1.03. 35
cousin of herford, as thy cause is right, | so 1.03. 55
harry of herford, lancaster, and derby, 1.03.100
harry of herford, lancaster, and derby | stands 1.03.104
himself and to approve | henry of herford, 1.03.113
you, cousin herford, upon pain of life, | till 1.03.140
how far brought you high herford on his way? 1.04. 2
i brought high herford, if you call him so, 1.04. 3
and holds you dear | as harry duke of herford, 2.01.144
the royalties and rights of banish'd herford? 2.01.190
and doth not herford live? 2.01.191
that thou wouldst speak to the duke of herford? 2.01.232
intelligence | that harry duke of herford, 2.01.279
to offer service to the duke of herford, | and 2.03. 32
my lord of herford, my message is to you. 2.03. 69
as i was banish'd, i was banish'd herford, | but 2.03.113
my lord of herford here, whom you call king, 4.01.134
claim thou of me | the earldom of herford, and R3 3.01.195
HERFORD'S 7 FR 0.0008 REL FR 7 V 0 P
o, /sit my husband's wrongs on herford's spear, R2 1.02. 47
as herford's love, so his, | as theirs, so mine, 2.01.145
gloucester's death, nor herford's banishment, 2.01.165
take herford's rights away, and take from time 2.01.195
if you do wrongfully seize herford's rights, 2.01.201
and will, i fear, revolt on herford's side. 2.02. 89
is a foul traitor to proud herford's king, | and 4.01.135
/HERFORDSHIRE 1 FR 0.0001 REL FR 1 V 0 P
leading the men of /herfordshire to fight 1H4 1.01. 39
HERITAGE 2 FR 0.0002 REL FR 1 V 1 P
service is no heritage, and i think i shall AWW 1.03. 24 P
and though it was mine own, part of my heritage, PER 2.01.123
HERITIER 1 FR 0.0001 REL FR 0 V 1 P
henri, roi d'angleterre, heritier de france; H5 5.02.340 P
HERMES 1 FR 0.0001 REL FR 0 V 1 P
hoof is more musical than the pipe of hermes. H5 3.07. 18 P
HERMIA 36 FR 0.0040 REL FR 36 V 0 P
against my child, my daughter hermia. MND 1.01. 23
what say you, hermia? 1.01. 46
therefore, fair hermia, question your desires, 1.01. 67
relent, sweet hermia, and, lysander, yield | thy 1.01. 91
can be) | i am belov'd of beauteous hermia. 1.01.104
for you, fair hermia, look you arm yourself | to 1.01.117
therefore hear me, hermia: 1.01.156
there, gentle hermia, may i marry thee; 1.01.161
/yours /would i catch, fair hermia, ere i go; 1.01.187
i will, my hermia. 1.01.224
and when this hail some heat from hermia felt, 1.01.244
where is lysander and fair hermia? 2.01.189
this wood, | because i cannot meet my hermia. 2.01.193
we'll rest us, hermia, if you think it good, 2.02. 37
for lying so, hermia, i do not lie. 2.02. 52
pride, | if hermia meant to say lysander lied. 2.02. 55
happy is hermia, wheresoe'er she lies, | for she 2.02. 90
what though he love your hermia? 2.02.109
yet hermia still loves you; 2.02.110
content with hermia? 2.02.111
not hermia but helena i love. 2.02.113
she sees not hermia. 2.02.135
hermia, sleep thou there, | and never mayst thou 2.02.135
he have stolen away | from sleeping hermia? 3.02. 52
you both are rivals, and love hermia; 3.02.155
for you love hermia; 3.02.163
lysander, keep thy hermia; 3.02.169
injurious hermia! 3.02.195
we, hermia, like two artificial gods, | have 3.02.203
am not i hermia? 3.02.273
good hermia, do not be so bitter with me. 3.02.306
i evermore did love you, hermia, | did ever keep 3.02.307
that hermia should give answer of her choice? 4.01.136
me, so it is — | i came with hermia hither. 4.01.151
it is), my love to hermia | (melted as the snow) 4.01.165
my lord, | was i betrothed ere i /saw hermia; 4.01.172
HERMIA'S 7 FR 0.0008 REL FR 7 V 0 P
love, demetrius, | let me have hermia's; MND 1.01. 94
and as he errs, doting on hermia's eyes, | so i, 1.01.230
for ere demetrius look'd on hermia's eyne, | he 1.01.242
i will go tell him of fair hermia's flight; 1.01.246
made me compare with hermia's sphery eyne! 2.02. 99
these vows are hermia's. 3.02.130
in hermia's love i yield you up my part; 3.02.165
HERMIONE 16 FR 0.0018 REL FR 10 V 6 P
well said, hermione. WT 1.02. 33
hermione, my dearest, thou never spok'st | to 1.02. 88
hermione, | how thou lov'st us, show in our 1.02.173
so forcing faults upon hermione, | i little like 3.01. 16
"hermione, queen to the worthy leontes, king of 3.02. 12 P
open, thou, hermione, contrary to the faith and 3.02. 18 P
"hermione is chaste, polixenes blameless, 3.02.132 P
i do believe | hermione hath suffer'd death, and 3.03. 42
good paulina, | who hast the memory of hermione, 5.01. 50
another, | as like hermione as is her picture, 5.01. 74
o hermione, | as every present time doth boast 5.01. 95
he so near to hermione hath done hermione that 5.02.100 P
to hermione hath done hermione that they say one 5.02.101 P
ever since the death of hermione, visited that 5.02.106 P
that i may say indeed | thou art hermione; 5.03. 25
hermione was not so much wrinkled, nothing | so 5.03. 28
HERMIONE'S 1 FR 0.0001 REL FR 0 V 1 P
the mantle of queen hermione's; WT 5.02. 33 P
/HERMIT 1 FR 0.0001 REL FR 1 V 0 P
hence /hermit then — my heart is in thy breast. LLL 5.02.816
HERMIT 5 FR 0.0005 REL FR 4 V 1 P
a wither'd hermit, fivescore winters worn, LLL 4.03.238
none but a holy hermit and her maid. MV 5.01. 33
for, as the old hermit of prague, that never saw TN 4.02. 12 P
and like a hermit overpass'd thy days. 1H6 2.05.117
let's leave the hermit pity with our mother, TRO 5.03. 45
HERMITAGE 2 FR 0.0002 REL FR 2 V 0 P
speed | to some forlorn and naked hermitage, LLL 5.02.795
of beads, | my gorgeous palace for a hermitage, R2 3.03.148
HERMITS' 1 FR 0.0001 REL FR 0 V 1 P
dozen of such bearded hermits' staves as master 2H4 5.01. 63 P
HERMITS *(also ermites)*
/HERMITS 1 FR 0.0001 REL FR 1 V 0 P
/as /begging /hermits /in /their /holy /prayers. TIT 3.02. 41
/HERNE 1 FR 0.0001 REL FR 1 V 0 P
/disguis'd /like /herne, /with /huge /horns /on WIV 4.04. 43
HERNE 5 FR 0.0005 REL FR 4 V 1 P
there is an old tale goes, that herne the hunter WIV 4.04. 28
age | this tale of herne the hunter for a truth. 4.04. 38
speak i like herne the hunter? 5.05. 27 P
round about the oak | of herne the hunter, let 5.05. 76
will none but herne the hunter serve your turn? 5.05.104
HERNE'S 4 FR 0.0004 REL FR 2 V 2 P
in deep of night to walk by this herne's oak. WIV 4.04. 40
to–night at herne's oak, just 'twixt twelve and 4.06. 19
you in the park about midnight, at herne's oak, 5.01. 11 P
are all couch'd in a pit hard by herne's oak, 5.03. 14 P
HERO 59 FR 0.0066 REL FR 22 V 37 P
sworn the contrary, if hero would be my wife. ADO 1.01.196 P
with hero, leonato's short daughter. 1.01.213 P
no child but hero, she's his only heir. 1.01.295
all prompting me how fair young hero is, 1.01.304
if thou dost love fair hero, cherish it, | and i 1.01.308
disguise, | and tell fair hero i am claudio, 1.01.322
marry, one hero, the daughter and heir of 1.03. 54 P
that the prince should woo hero for himself, and 1.03. 62 P
for hear me, hero: 2.01. 73 P
my brother is amorous on hero and hath withdrawn 2.01.155 P
he is enamor'd on hero. 2.01.164 P
farewell therefore hero! 2.01.182
it one way, for the prince hath got your hero. 2.01.192 P
i have woo'd in thy name, and fair hero is won. 2.01.299 P
and you too, gentle hero? 2.01.374 P
of margaret, the waiting–gentlewoman to hero. 2.02. 14 P
to a contaminated stale, such a one as hero. 2.02. 26 P
to vex claudio, to undo hero, and kill leonato. 2.02. 29 P
tell them that you know that hero loves me, 2.02. 35 P
hear me call margaret hero, hear margaret term 2.02. 44 P
fashion the matter that hero shall be absent — 2.02. 47 P
hero thinks surely she will die, for she says 2.03.173 P
they have the truth of this from hero; 2.03.222 P
hero and margaret have by this play'd their 3.02. 76 P
who, hero? 3.02.105 P
even she — leonato's hero, your hero, every 3.02.106 P
leonato's hero, your hero, every man's hero. 3.02.106 P
leonato's hero, your hero, every man's hero. 3.02.107 P
lady hero's gentlewoman, by the name of hero. 3.03.146 P
and thought they margaret was hero? 3.03.153 P
good morrow, sweet hero. 3.04. 40 P
know you any, hero? 4.01. 15 P
is it not hero? 4.01. 80
marry, that can hero, | hero itself can blot out 4.01. 81
hero, | hero itself can blot out hero's virtue. 4.01. 82
o hero! 4.01.100
what a hero hadst thou been, | if half thy 4.01.100
hero, why, hero! 4.01.114
hero, why, hero! 4.01.114
how now, cousin hero? 4.01.117
do not live, hero, do not ope thine eyes; 4.01.123
sweet hero, she is wrong'd, she is sland'red, 4.01.312 P
your soul the count claudio hath wrong'd hero? 4.01.329 P
don john for accusing the lady hero wrongfully. 4.02. 48 P
to disgrace hero before the whole assembly, and 4.02. 54 P
hero was in this manner accus'd, in this very 4.02. 61 P
my soul doth tell me hero is belied, | and that 5.01. 42
brother incens'd me to slander the lady hero, 5.01.236 P
sweet hero, now thy image doth appear | in the 5.01.251
to–night i'll mourn with hero. 5.01.330
it is prov'd my lady hero hath been falsely 5.02. 97 P
tongues | was the hero that here lies. 5.03. 4
another hero! 5.04. 62
one hero died defil'd, but i do live, | and 5.04. 63
the former hero! hero that is dead! 5.04. 65
the former hero! hero that is dead! 5.04. 65
many a fair year though hero had turn'd nun, if AYL 4.01.101 P
of that age found it was — hero of sestos. 4.01.106 P
a gipsy, helen and hero hildings and harlots, ROM 2.04. 42 P
HEROD 6 FR 0.0006 REL FR 3 V 3 P
what a herod of jewry is this! WIV 2.01. 20 P
for o'erdoing termagant, it out–herods herod. HAM 3.02. 14 P
at fifty, to whom herod of jewry may do homage. ANT 1.02. 28 P
herod of jewry dare not look upon you | but when 3.03. 3
herod of jewry; 3.06. 73
great herod to incline himself to caesar | and 4.06. 13
HEROD'S 2 FR 0.0002 REL FR 2 V 0 P
jewry | at herod's bloody–hunting slaughter–men. H5 3.03. 41
that herod's head | i'll have; ANT 3.03. 4
/HEROES 1 FR 0.0001 REL FR 0 V 1 P
/and /outstretch'd /heroes /the /beggars' HAM 2.02.264 P
HEROES 1 FR 0.0001 REL FR 0 V 1 P
noble heroes! AWW 2.01. 40 P
HEROIC 1 FR 0.0001 REL FR 1 V 0 P
being but fourth of that heroic line. 1H6 2.05. 78
HEROICAL 4 FR 0.0004 REL FR 2 V 2 P
have commiseration on thy heroical vassal! LLL 4.01. 64 P
saw his heroical seed, and smil'd to see him, H5 2.04. 59
the reasons are more potent and heroical. TRO 3.03.192
proud of an heroical cudgelling that he raves in 3.03.248 P
HERO'S 8 FR 0.0009 REL FR 4 V 4 P
would serve to scale another hero's tow'r, | so TGV 3.01.119
appear such seeming truth of hero's disloyalty, ADO 2.02. 48 P
would have it at the lady hero's chamber–window. 2.03. 86 P
woo'd margaret, the lady hero's gentlewoman, by 3.03.145 P
is this face hero's? 4.01. 71
hero, | hero itself can blot out hero's virtue. 4.01. 82
and saw me court margaret in hero's garments, 5.01.238 P
i'll tell you largely of fair hero's death. 5.04. 69
/HERRING 1 FR 0.0001 REL FR 0 V 1 P
/in /tom's /belly /for /two /white /herring. LR 3.06. 31 P
HERRING 5 FR 0.0005 REL FR 0 V 5 P
de herring is no dead so as i vill kill him. WIV 2.03. 12 P
face of the earth, then am i a shotten herring. 1H4 2.04.130 P
a puttock, or a herring without a roe, i would TRO 5.01. 62 P
without his roe, like a dried herring: ROM 2.04. 37 P
will not see a red herring at a harry groat, STM II.C 1 P
HERRINGS 2 FR 0.0002 REL FR 0 V 2 P
as like husbands as pilchers are to herrings, TN 3.01. 34 P
or rather, of stealing a cade of herrings. 2H6 4.02. 34 P
/HERS 1 FR 0.0001 REL FR 1 V 0 P
/with /her — /as /far /as /we /call /hers. LR 5.01. 13
HERS 54 FR 0.0061 REL FR 47 V 7 P
i am hers. TMP 5.01.196
and, may i say to thee, this pride of hers, TGV 3.01. 72
go to thy lady's grave and call hers thence, 4.02.116
or, at the least, in hers sepulchre thine. 4.02.117
mine | were full as lovely as is this of hers; 4.04.186
save this of hers, fram'd by thy villainy! ADO 5.01. 71
if so, my eyes are oft'ner wash'd than hers. MND 2.02. 93
between thy flesh and hers than between jet and MV 3.01. 40 P
and mine, to eke out hers. AYL 1.02.196 P
sure it is hers. 4.03. 30
here comes a lover of mine and a lover of hers. 5.02. 76 P
confess, | and if i die to–morrow, this is hers, SHR 2.01.361
hers it was not. AWW 5.03. 80
you to take it so, | the ring was never hers. 5.03. 89
confess 'twas hers, and by what rough 5.03.107
if you shall prove | this ring was ever hers, 5.03.125
my lord, i do confess the ring was hers. 5.03.231
it might be yours or hers, for aught i know. 5.03.280
and if she did play false, the fault was hers, JN 1.01.118
these haughty words of hers | have batt'red me 1H6 3.03. 78
and mine with hers, and thine, and margaret's. 3H6 3.03.218
indirect and peevish course | is this of hers! R3 3.01. 32
and her worth | in other arms than hers — to TRO 1.03.272
herself and hers are highly bound to thee. TIT 4.02.171
'tis the way | to call hers, exquisite, in ROM 1.01.229
and, touching hers, make blessed my rude hand. 1.05. 51
as mine on hers, so hers is set on mine, | and 2.03. 59
as mine on hers, so hers is set on mine, | and 2.03. 59
nature is asham'd | almost t' acknowledge hers. LR 1.01.213
nor shall ever see | that face of hers again. 1.01.264
more, perchance, does mine, nor his, nor hers. 2.02. 91
if it be that, or any /that was hers, | it OTH 3.03.440
why then 'tis hers, my lord, and, being hers, 4.01. 12
why then 'tis hers, my lord, and, being hers, 4.01. 12
nor scar that whiter skin of hers than snow, 5.02. 4
nay, come, tell iras hers. ANT 1.02. 43 P
hers you are. 1.03. 23
thence that honor of hers which you imagine so CYM 1.04.131 P
king as i am bold her honor | will remain hers. 2.04. 3
flattering, hers; 2.05. 23
deceiving, hers; 2.05. 23
lust and rank thoughts, hers, hers; 2.05. 24
lust and rank thoughts, hers, hers; 2.05. 24
revenges, hers; 2.05. 24
that hell knows, | why, hers, in part or all; 2.05. 28
faith be not tainted with the breach of hers. 3.04. 27 P
that man of hers, pisanio, her old servant, | i 3.05. 54
and win this ring | by hers and mine adultery. 5.05.186
whom heavens, in justice, both on her and hers, 5.05.464
these blushes of hers must be quench'd with some
PER 4.02.124 P
your virtues, | and, as your due, y' are hers. TNK 2.05. 37
but hers, which through the crystal tears gave VEN 491
she showed hers, he saw more wounds than one, PP 9.13
hers, by thy beauty tempting her to thee, SON 41.13
/HERSELF 1 FR 0.0001 REL FR 1 V 0 P
/she /that /herself /will /sliver /and LR 4.02. 34
HERSELF 108 FR 0.0122 REL FR 89 V 19 P
us, and the fair soul herself | weigh'd between TMP 2.01.130
herself hath taught her love himself to write TGV 2.01.168
look you, wept herself blind at my parting. 2.03. 13 P

and julia herself did give it me — | and julia 5.04. 98
and julia herself hath brought it hither. 5.04. 99
my ambling gelding, than my wife with herself. WIV 2.02.305 P
i could have spoken with the woman herself. 4.05. 40 P
(so far forth as herself might be her chooser) 4.06. 11
determines | herself the glory of a creditor, MM 1.01. 39
bid herself assay him. 1.02.181
up all her beef, and she is herself in the tub. 3.02. 57 P
to her eyes, | till she herself confess it. 5.01.162
absence was not six months old | before herself ERR 1.01. 45
and did not she herself revile me there? 4.04. 72
sans fable, she herself revil'd you there. 4.04. 73
truly the lady fathers herself. ADO 1.01.111 P
of unhappiness and wak'd herself with laughing. 2.01.346 P
rail'd at herself, that she should be so 2.03.141 P
she will do a desperate outrage to herself. 2.03.153 P
she hath but one for herself, to desire that LLL 2.01.200
but she herself is hit lower. 4.01.118
she hears herself. 5.02.195
and true she is, as she hath prov'd herself; MV 2.06. 55
and therefore, like herself, wise, fair, and 2.06. 56
for herein fortune shows herself more kind 4.01.267
and out of you she sees herself more proper AYL 3.05. 55
let her never nurse her child herself, for she 4.01.175 P
patience herself would startle at this letter, 4.03. 13
to her, | and unsuspected court her by herself. SHR 1.02.137
that, being mad herself, she's madly mated. 3.02.244
father bequeath'd her to me, and she herself, AWW 1.03.102 P
did communicate to herself her own words to her 1.03.108 P
that your dian | was both herself and love, o, 1.03.213
fill the time, | herself most chastely absent. 3.07. 34
who of herself is a good lady and would not have 5.02. 31 P
five removes come short | to tender it herself. 5.03.132
it did concern | your highness with herself. 5.03.138
by thy honest aid | thou kept'st a wife herself, 5.03.330
still the woman take | an elder than herself, so TN 2.04. 30
me, and i have heard herself come thus near, 2.05. 24 P
and in this she manifests herself to my love, 2.05.168 P
and let her sport herself | with that she's big WT 2.01. 60
what she should shame to know herself | but with 2.01. 91
but smacks of something greater than herself, 4.04.158
this fortress built by nature for herself R2 2.01. 43
gone, and she is old, and cannot help herself. 2H4 3.02.232 P
for hear her but exampled by herself: H5 1.02.156
she hath herself not only well defended | but 1.02.159
in complete glory she reveal'd herself; 1H6 1.02. 83
to make this shameless callet know herself. 3H6 2.02.145
the jealous o'erworn widow and herself, | since R3 1.01. 81
herself, the land, and many a christian soul, 4.04.408
england hath long been mad and scarr'd herself: 5.05. 23
nobility she has | carried herself towards me. H8 2.04.144
heir | as great in admiration as herself, | so 5.04. 42
patience herself, what goddess e'er she be, TRO 1.01. 27
helen herself swore th' other day that troilus, 1.02. 92 P
and by herself, i will not tell you whose. 5.02. 92
seeking to hide herself, as doth the deer | that TIT 3.01. 89
herself and hers are highly bound to thee. 4.02.171
and calls herself revenge, and thinks me mad. 5.02.185
eating the flesh that she herself hath bred. 5.03. 62
let rome herself be bane unto herself, | and she 5.03. 73
let rome herself be bane unto herself, | and she 5.03. 73
castaway, | do shameful execution on herself, 5.03. 76
by, | herself pois'd with herself in either eye; ROM 1.02. 95
by, | herself pois'd with herself in either eye; 1.02. 95
which, too much minded by herself alone, | may 4.01. 13
or in my cell there would she kill herself. 5.03.242
me, | but, as it seems, did violence on herself. 5.03.264
she'll close and be herself, whilest our poor MAC 3.02. 14
that she should lock herself from /his resort, HAM 2.02.143
sh' hath seal'd thee for herself, for thou hast 3.02. 65
divided from herself and her fair judgment, 4.05. 85
when down her weedy trophies and herself | fell 4.07.174
unless she drown'd herself in her own defense? 5.01. 6 P
/argal, she drown'd herself wittingly. 5.01. 12 P
she is herself a dowry. LR 1.01.241
poison'd for my sake, | and after slew herself. 5.03.242
upon her own despair, | that she fordid herself. 5.03.256
hath thus beguil'd your daughter of herself, OTH 1.03. 66
and quiet that her motion | blush'd at herself; 1.03. 96
would not invest herself in such shadowing 4.01. 40 P
her desires | buys herself bread and /clothes. 4.01. 95
you /heard her say herself, it was not i. 5.02.127
that she preparedly may frame herself | to th' ANT 5.01. 55
hath referr'd herself | unto a poor but worthy CYM 1.01. 6
to the world, concluded | most cruel to herself. 5.05. 33
yea, and she herself. 5.05.221
lessen'd herself, and in the beams o' th' sun 5.05.472
for riches strew'd herself even in her streets; PER 1.04. 23
her reason to herself is only known, | which 2.05. 5
she | made known herself my daughter. 5.03. 13
other, get herself | some part of a good name, TNK 5.03. 26
nature that made thee with herself at strife, VEN 11
where herself herself beheld | a thousand times, 1129
where herself herself beheld | a thousand times, 1129
where their queen | means to immure herself, and 1194
but cloudy lucrece shames herself to see, | and LUC 1084
views, | and to herself all sorrow doth compare; 1102
out readily, | so with herself is she in mutiny, 1153
whose deed hath made herself herself detest. 1566
whose deed hath made herself herself detest. 1566
to slay herself, that should have slain her foe. 1827
(since rome herself in them doth stand disgraced 1833
then will i swear beauty herself is black, | and SON 132.13
the destin'd ill she must herself assay? LC 156
she that her fame so to herself contrives, | the 243

HERSELF'S 1 FR 0.0001 REL FR 1 V 0 P

habit only that is honest, | herself's a bawd. TIM 4.03.115

/HE'S 3 FR 0.0003 REL FR 1 V 2 P

/he's /follow'd /both /with /body /and /with 2H4 1.01.203
but /he's out of tune thus. TRO 3.03.301 P
/he's /mad /that /trusts /in /the /tameness /of LR 3.06. 18 P

HE'S 337 FR 0.0381 REL FR 224 V 113 P

and, but he's something stain'd | with grief TMP 1.02.415
he's a traitor. 1.02.461
of him, for | he's gentle, and not fearful. 1.02.469
look, he's winding up the watch of his wit, by 2.01. 12 P
no, no, he's gone. 2.01.123
persuaded | (for he's a spirit of persuasion, 2.01.235
alive, | 'tis as impossible that he's undrown'd, 2.01.237
i have no hope | that he's undrown'd. 2.01.239
he's gone. 2.01.244
if he were that which now he's like — that's 2.01.282
he's a present for any emperor that ever trod on 2.02. 69 P
he's in his fit now, and does not talk after the 2.02. 73 P
and he's compos'd of harshness. 3.01. 9
yourself, | he's safe for these three hours. 3.01. 21
your lieutenant if you list, he's no standard. 3.02. 17 P
for without them | he's but a sot, as i am; 3.02. 93
i am right glad that he's so out of hope. 3.03. 11
and this demi-devil | (for he's a bastard one) 5.01.273
when proteus cannot love where he's belov'd! TGV 5.04. 45
he's a good dog, and a fair dog — can there be WIV 1.01. 96 P
he's a justice of peace in his country, simple 1.01.218 P
he's as far from jealousy as i am from giving 2.01.103 P
he's a very jealousy man. 2.02. 89 P
he's welcome. 3.01. 28 P
warrant you, he's the man should fight with him. 3.01. 68 P
he's too big to go in there. what shall i do? 3.03.134 P
he's a-birding, sweet sir john. 4.02. 8 P
you are utterly sham'd, and he's but a dead man. 4.02. 43 P
well, he's not here i seek for. 4.02.158 P
i have done so, but he's not to be found. MM 1.02.175
not to be weary with you, he's in prison. 1.04. 25
he cannot, sir; he's out at elbow. 2.01. 61 P
he's in the right, constable. 2.01.160 P
he's hearing of a cause; 2.02. 1
he's sentenc'd; 'tis too late. 2.02. 55
he's not prepar'd for death. 2.02. 84
most ignorant of what he's most assur'd | (his 2.02.119
he's coming; 2.02.125
he's now past it, yet (and i say to thee) he 3.02.182 P
if he be a married man, he's his wive's head, 4.02. 4 P
he tyrannous, | but this being so, he's just. 4.02. 85
he's in for a commodity of brown paper and old 4.03. 4 P
he's a better woodman than thou tak'st him for. 4.03.162 P
if he be less, he's nothing, but he's more, 5.01. 58
if he be less, he's nothing, but he's more, 5.01. 58
meddler, | as he's reported by this gentleman; 5.01.146
make up full clear, | whensoever he's convented. 5.01.158
by this lord angelo perceives he's safe; 5.01.494
and from the mart he's somewhere gone to dinner. ERR 2.01. 5
nay, he's at two hands with me, and that my two 2.01. 45 P
that's not my fault, he's master of my state. 2.01. 95
no, he's in tartar limbo, worse than hell: 4.02. 32
and owes more than he's worth to season. 4.02. 58
nay, he's a thief too: 4.02. 59
and now he's there, past thought of human reason 5.01.189
o, he's return'd, and as pleasant as ever he was ADO 1.01. 37 P
how well he's read, to reason against reading! LLL 1.01. 94
he's a good friend of mine. 4.01. 54
he's a god or a painter, for he makes faces. 5.02.643 P
yet he's gentle, never school'd and yet learned, AYL 1.01.166 P
sullen fits, | for then he's full of matter. 2.01. 68
peace, fool, he's not thy kinsman. 2.04. 67
he's fall'n in love with your foulness, and 3.05. 66 P
but sure he's proud — and yet his pride becomes 3.05.114
is not very tall — yet for his years he's tall; 3.05.118
he's as good at any thing, and yet a fool. 5.04.104 P
though he be merry, yet withal he's honest. SHR 3.02. 25
i am glad he's come, howsoe'er he comes. 3.02. 74 P
why, he's a devil, a devil, a very fiend. 3.02.155
he's within, sir, but not to be spoken withal. 5.01. 19 P
but now he's gone, and my idolatrous fancy AWW 1.01. 97
if i be his cuckold, he's my drudge. 1.03. 45 P
and he's of a most facinerious spirit that will 2.03. 29 P
why, he's able to lead her a coranto. 2.03. 43 P
madam, he's gone to serve the duke of florence. 3.02. 52
whatsome'er he is, | he's bravely taken here. 3.05. 52
perchance he's hurt i' th' battle. 3.05. 87 P
he's shrewdly vex'd at something. 3.05. 89 P
him as my kinsman, he's a most notable coward, 3.06. 9 P
he's very near the truth in this. 4.03.151 P
before but a cat, and now he's a cat to me. 4.03.238 P
a pox upon him for me, he's more and more a cat. 4.03.264 P
a pox on him, he's a cat still. 4.03.275 P
he's quoted for a most perfidious slave, | with 5.03.205
he's a good drum, my lord, but a naughty orator. 5.03.253 P
because he's guilty, and he is not guilty. 5.03.289
he's as tall a man as any's in illyria. TN 1.03. 20 P
he's a very fool and a prodigal. 1.03. 24 P
for besides that he's a fool, he's a great 1.03. 30 P
that he's a fool, he's a great quarreller; 1.03. 30 P
moreov'r, he's drunk nightly in your company. 1.03. 36 P
he's a coward and a coystrill that will not 1.03. 40 P
look you now, he's out of his guard already. 1.05. 86 P
for he's in the third degree of drink, he's 1.05.135 P
he's in the third degree of drink, he's drown'd. 1.05.135 P
he's fortified against any denial. 1.05.145 P
now he's deeply in. 2.05. 42 P
he's in yellow stockings. 3.02. 73 P
he's coming, madam, but in very strange manner. 3.04. 8 P
consider, he's an enemy to mankind. 3.04. 98 P
my niece is already in the belief that he's mad. 3.04.136 P
man, he's a very devil, i have not seen such a 3.04.273 P
a coward, but he's the very devil incardinate. 5.01.181 P
o, he's drunk, sir toby, an hour agone; 5.01.198 P
then he's a rogue, and a passy-measures /pavin. 5.01.200 P
they say, poor gentleman, he's much distract. 5.01.280
and you smile not, he's gagg'd." 5.01.376 P
say this to him, | he's beat from his best ward. WT 1.02. 33
he's all my exercise, my mirth, my matter; 1.02.166
and my young rover, he's | apparent to my heart. 1.02.176
provided that, when he's remov'd, your highness 1.02.335
he's at it now. 3.03.106 P
he's simple, and tells much. 4.04.345
he's irremovable, | resolv'd for flight. 4.04.507
he's with the king your father. 5.01.196
keep his own grace, but he's almost out of mine, 2H4 1.02. 28 P
he's gone /into smithfield to buy your worship a 1.02. 50 P
you, he's an infinitive thing upon my score. 2.01. 24 P
he's no swagg'rer, hostess, a tame cheater, i' 2.04. 97 P
to sit under, he's like to be a cold soldier. 3.02.122 P
i think he's gone to hunt, my lord, at windsor. 4.04. 14
he's walk'd the way of nature, | and to our 5.02. 4
faith, he's very ill. H5 2.01. 85 P
nay sure, he's not in hell; 2.03. 9 P
he's in arthur's bosom, if ever man went to 2.03. 9 P
he's of the color of the nutmeg. 3.07. 19 P
white hand of my lady, he's a gallant prince. 3.07. 95 P
him, he's a friend of the duke alanson's. 4.08. 17 P
the lord protect him, for he's a good man! 2H6 1.03. 4 P
for he's disposed as the hateful raven. 3.01. 76
for he's inclin'd as is the ravenous wolves. 3.01. 78
ay, my good lord, he's dead. 3.02. 7
he's a villain and a traitor. 4.02.107 P
and wheresoe'er he is, he's surely dead. 3H6 2.06. 41
i know by that he's dead, and, by my soul, | if 2.06. 79
ay, but he's dead. 2.06. 85
me, | he's very likely now to fall from him, 3.03.209
but he's deceiv'd, we are in readiness. 5.04. 64
he's sudden, if a thing comes in his head. 5.05. 86
what stay had i but edward? and he's gone. R3 2.02. 74
what stay had we but clarence? and he's gone. 2.02. 75
i wonder he's so simple | to trust the mock'ry 3.02. 26
you know his nature, | that he's revengeful; H8 1.01.109
he's gone to th' king; 1.01.128
by day and night, | he's traitor to th' height. 1.02.214
no doubt he's noble; 1.03. 57
protection, | he's loving and most gracious. 3.01. 94
no, he's settled | (not to come off) in his 3.02. 22
observe, observe, he's moody. 3.02. 75
he's discontented. 3.02. 91
he's vex'd at something. 3.02.104
but he's a learned man. 3.02.395
he's a rank weed, sir thomas, | and we must root 5.01. 52
he's honest, on mine honor. 5.01.153
he's worthy of it. 5.02.189
a shrewd turn, and he's your friend for ever." 5.02.211
pandar, | and he's as tetchy to be woo'd to woo, TRO 1.01. 96
he's not himself. 1.02. 76 P
he's one of the flowers of troy, i can tell you. 1.02.186 P
wit, i can tell you, and he's man good enough. 1.02.191 P
he's one o' th' soundest judgments in troy, 1.02.191 P
he's not hurt. 1.02.215 P
he's not yet through warm. 2.03.221 P
he's grown a very land-fish, languageless, a 3.03.263 P
anon he's there afoot, | and there they fly or 5.05. 21
he's dead, and at the murtherer's horse's tail, 5.10. 4
he's a very dog to the commonalty. COR 1.01. 28 P
he's one honest enough; 1.01. 53 P
aims, | in whom already he's well grac'd, cannot 1.01.264
him beard to beard, | he's mine, or i am his. 1.10. 12
he's the devil. 1.10. 16
he's a lamb indeed, that baes like a bear. 2.01. 11 P
he's a bear indeed, that lives like a lamb. 2.01. 12 P
he's poor in no one fault, but stor'd with all. 2.01. 18 P
but he's vengeance proud, and loves not the 2.02. 5 P
no more of him, he's a worthy man. 2.02. 35 P
he's right noble. | let him be call'd for. 2.02.129
he's to make his requests by particulars, 2.03. 43 P
he's not confirm'd, we may deny him yet. 2.03.209
that he's your fixed enemy, and revoke | your 2.03.250
he's a disease that must be cut away. 3.01.293
o, he's a limb that has but a disease: 3.01.294
he's coming. 3.03. 6
he's banish'd, and it shall be so. 3.03.107
he's sentenc'd; no more hearing. 3.03.109
bid them all home, he's gone; 4.02. 1
and he's as like to do't as any man i can 4.05.203 P
it) his friends whilest he's in directitude. 4.05.208 P
now he's coming, | and not a hair upon a 4.06.132
ever verified my friends | (of whom he's chief) 5.02. 18
he's the rock, the oak not to be wind-shaken. 5.02.110 P
he has wings, he's more than a creeping thing. 5.04. 13 P
good murther, stab him, he's a murtherer. TIT 5.02.100
this is not romeo, he's some other where. ROM 1.01.198
as all the world — why, he's a man of wax. 1.03. 76
nay, he's a flower, in faith, a very flower. 1.03. 78
o, he's the courageous captain of compliments. 2.04. 19 P
ah, weraday, he's dead, he's dead, he's dead! 3.02. 37
ah, weraday, he's dead, he's dead, he's dead! 3.02. 37
ah, weraday, he's dead, he's dead, he's dead! 3.02. 37
alack the day, he's gone, he's kill'd, he's dead 3.02. 39
the day, he's gone, he's kill'd, he's dead! 3.02. 39
the day, he's gone, he's kill'd, he's dead! 3.02. 39
o, he's a lovely gentleman! 3.05.218
and yet he's but a filthy piece of work. TIM 1.01.199 P
he's opposite to humanity. 1.01.273
o, he's the very soul of bounty! 1.02.209
by whose death he's stepp'd | into a great 2.02.223
and, when he's sick to death, let not that part 3.01. 61
he's ever sending. 3.02. 32 P
no matter what, he's poor, and that's revenge 3.04. 62 P
temper has forsook him, he's much out of health, 3.04. 72 P
he's truly valiant that can wisely suffer | the 3.05. 31
he's a sworn rioter; 3.05. 67
he's but a mad lord, and nought but humors sways 3.06.111 P
he's flung in rage from this ingrateful seat 4.02. 45
no more, i pray — and he's a steward. 4.03.498
does the rumor hold for true that he's | so full 5.01. 3
remain assur'd | that he's a made-up villain. 5.01. 98
before proud athens he's set down by this, 5.03. 9
fear him not, caesar, he's not dangerous, | he JC 1.02.196
and he's gone | to seek you at your house. 1.03.149
tear him to pieces, he's a conspirator. 3.03. 28 P
but he's a tried and valiant soldier. 4.01. 28
he's ta'en. 5.03. 32
he's here in double trust: MAC 1.07. 12
yet he's good that did the like for fleance. 3.04. 17
father'd he is, and yet he's fatherless. 4.02. 27
he's a traitor. 4.02. 82
some say he's mad; 5.02. 13
he's worth more sorrow, | and that i'll spend 5.09. 16
he's worth no more; 5.09. 17
in all denmark — | but he's an arrant knave. HAM 1.05.124
but, if't be he i mean, he's very wild, 2.01. 18
that he's mad, 'tis true, 'tis true 'tis pity, 2.02. 97
say on, he's for a jig or a tale of bawdry, or 2.02.500 P
my lord, he's going to his mother's closet. 3.03. 27
alas, he's mad! 3.04.105
he's lov'd of the distracted multitude, | who 4.03. 4
on him by them, in his meed he's unfellow'd. 5.02.142 P
and when he's not himself does wrong laertes, 5.02.235

he's fat, and scant of breath. 5.02.287
he's coming, madam, i hear him. LR 1.03. 11
be'st as poor for a subject as he's for a king, 1.04. 21 P
he's coming hither, now i' th' night, i' th' 2.01. 24
if not, he's plain. 2.02.100
modo he's call'd, and mahu. 3.04.144 P
he's a yeoman that has a gentleman to his son; 3.06. 12 P
for he's a mad yeoman that sees his son a 3.06. 13 P
he's dead; 4.06.257
he's scarce awake, let him alone a while. 4.07. 50
he's full of alteration | and self–reproving — 5.01. 3
he's a good fellow, i can tell you that; 5.03.285
he's dead and rotten. 5.03.286
for nought but provender, and when he's old, OTH 1.01. 48
for he's embark'd | with such loud reason to the 1.01.149
if it prove lawful prize, he's made for ever. 1.02. 51
he's married. 1.02. 52
nay, in all confidence, he's not for rhodes. 1.03. 31
he's now in florence. 1.03. 45
but that he's well and will be shortly here. 2.01. 90
sir, he's rash and very sudden in choler, and 2.01.272 P
and he's to watch. 2.03. 54
he's a soldier fit to stand by caesar | and give 2.03.122
sue to him again, and he's yours. 2.03.276 P
he's never any thing but your true servant. 3.03. 9
in faith, he's penitent; 3.03. 63
let him not know't, and he's not robb'd at all. 3.03.343
he's a soldier, and for me to say a soldier lies 3.04. 5 P
the witness, | and he's indicted falsely. 3.04.154
he's busy in the paper. 4.01.230
he's that he is; 4.01.270
he's almost slain, and roderigo quite dead. 5.01.114
he's gone, but his wife's kill'd. 5.02.238
he's speaking now, | or murmuring, "where's my ANT 1.05. 24
madam, he's well. 2.05. 46
he's friends with caesar, | in state of health 2.05. 55
he's bound unto octavia. 2.05. 58
madam, he's married to octavia. 2.05. 60
he's married, madam. 2.05. 72
he's married, madam. 2.05. 91
he's married to octavia. 2.05.101
caesar? why, he's the jupiter of men. 3.02. 9
he's very knowing, | i do perceive't. 3.03. 23
he's walking in the garden — thus, and spurns 3.05. 16
speak to him, | he's unqualited with very shame. 3.11. 44
begins to rage, he's hunted | even to falling. 4.01. 7
o, he's more mad | than telamon for his shield; 4.13. 1
for i remember now | how he's employ'd; 5.01. 72
not being fortune, he's but fortune's knave, | a 5.02. 3
he's for his master, | and enemy to my son. CYM 1.05. 28
he's strange and peevish. 1.06. 54
he's a strange fellow himself, and knows it not. 2.01. 35 P
and he's another, whatsoever he be. 2.01. 39 P
outcraftied him, | and he's at some hard point. 3.04. 16
for he's honorable, | and doubling that, most 3.04.176
and tell the fishes he's the queen's son, cloten 4.02.153
he's alive, my lord. 4.02.359
boy, he's preferr'd | by thee to us, and he 4.02.400
i dare be bound he's true and shall perform 4.03. 18
he's father, son, and husband mild; PER 1.01. 68
for he's no man on whom perfections wait | that, 1.01. 79
he's more secure to keep it shut than shown; 1.01. 95
since he's so great can make his will his act, 1.02. 18
he's bound by the indenture of his oath to be 1.03. 8 P
does speak sufficiently he's gone to travel. 1.03. 13
but since he's gone, the king's seas must please 1.03. 27
sure he's a gallant gentleman. 2.03. 32
he's but a country gentleman: 2.03. 33
he's both their parent, and he is their grave, 2.03. 46
to wisdom he's a fool that will not yield; 2.04. 54
me, | this sword shall prove he's honor's enemy. 2.05. 64
next, he's the governor of this country, and a 4.06. 53 P
now he's secure, | not dreams we stand before TNK 1.01.154
he's goodly, | and like enough the duke hath 2.02.226
he's a blessed man! 2.02.247
and if he lose her then, he's a cold coward. 2.02.253
he's excellent i' th' woods, | bring him to th' 2.03. 53
he's well got sure. 2.05. 24
i'll set it down | he's torn to pieces. 3.02. 18
he's in heaven. 3.04. 4
if he fail, | he's neither man nor soldier. 3.06. 4
he's a villain then. 3.06.264
yes, he's a fine man. 4.01.120
he's swarth and meagre, of an eye as heavy | as 4.02. 27
he's somewhat bigger than the knight he spoke of 4.02. 94
and when he's angry, then a settled valor | (not 4.02.100
he's white–hair'd, | not wanton white, but such 4.02.123
he's grey–ey'd, | which yields compassion where 4.02.131
he finds 'em, | he's swift to make 'em his. 4.02.134
he's round–fac'd, and when he smiles | he shows 4.02.135
he's as fantastical, too, as ever he may go upon 4.03. 13 P
he's a kind gentleman, and i am much bound to 5.02. 44
he's a very fair one. 5.02. 46
will grow too, finely, | now he's at liberty. 5.02. 96
i did but act, he's author of thy slander. VEN 1006
and all those beauties whereof now he's king SON 63. 6

HESPERIA *(see hisperia)*

HESPERIDES 2 FR 0.0002 REL FR 2 V 0 P
still climbing trees in the hesperides? LLL 4.03.338
before thee stands this fair hesperides, | with PER 1.01. 27

HESPERUS 1 FR 0.0001 REL FR 1 V 0 P
moist hesperus hath quench'd her sleepy lamp, AWW 2.01.164

HEST 3 FR 0.0003 REL FR 3 V 0 P
o my father, | i have broke your hest to say so! TMP 3.01. 37
brims, | which spungy april at thy hest betrims, 4.01. 65
their breath | on some great sudden hest. 1H4 2.03. 62

HESTS 1 FR 0.0001 REL FR 1 V 0 P
refusing her grand hests, she did confine thee, TMP 1.02.274

/HEURE 1 FR 0.0001 REL FR 0 V 1 P
tout /a /cette /heure de couper votre gorge. H5 4.04. 35 P

HEUREUX 1 FR 0.0001 REL FR 0 V 1 P
et je m'estime heureux que je tombe entre les H5 4.04. 55 P

HEW 9 FR 0.0010 REL FR 9 V 0 P
hew them to pieces, hack their bones asunder, 1H6 4.07. 47
o, i could hew up rocks and fight with flint, 2H6 5.01. 24
myself, | or hew my way out with a bloody axe. 3H6 3.02.181
once more to hew thy target from thy brawn, | or COR 4.05.120
that we may hew his limbs and on a pile | ad TIT 1.01. 97
let's hew his limbs till they be clean consum'd. 1.01.129
with thy smile | than hew to't with thy sword. TIM 5.04. 46
gods, | not hew him as a carcass fit for hounds; JC 2.01.174
let every soldier hew him down a bough, | and MAC 5.04. 4

HEW'D 1 FR 0.0001 REL FR 1 V 0 P
stern ungentle hands | hath lopp'd and hew'd, TIT 2.04. 17

HEWGH 1 FR 0.0001 REL FR 0 V 1 P
i' th' clout, i' th' clout — hewgh! LR 4.06. 92 P

HEWING 1 FR 0.0001 REL FR 1 V 0 P
in hewing rutland when his leaves put forth, 3H6 2.06. 48

HEWN 3 FR 0.0003 REL FR 2 V 1 P
lady, if he be not hewn now, we shall see H5 2.01. 37 P
we'll never leave till we have hewn thee down, 3H6 2.02.168
must by the roots be hewn up yet ere night. 5.04. 69

HEWS 2 FR 0.0002 REL FR 2 V 0 P
hews down and fells the hardest–timber'd oak. 3H6 2.01. 55
fins of lead, | and hews down oaks with rushes. COR 1.01.181

/HEY 2 FR 0.0002 REL FR 2 V 0 P
/hey /non /nonny, /nonny, /hey /nonny, | and in HAM 4.05.166
bier, | /hey /non /nonny, /nonny, /hey /nonny, 4.05.166

HEY 22 FR 0.0024 REL FR 22 V 0 P
hey, mountain, hey! TMP 4.01.255
hey, mountain, hey! 4.01.255
all your sounds of woe | into hey nonny nonny. ADO 2.03. 69
with a hey, and a ho, and a hey nonino, | that AYL 5.03. 17
lass, | with a hey, and a ho, and a hey nonino, 5.03. 17
when birds do sing, hey ding a ding, ding, 5.03. 20
with a hey, and a ho, and a hey nonino, | these 5.03. 23
rye, | with a hey, and a ho, and a hey nonino, 5.03. 23
with a hey, and a ho, and a hey nonino, | how 5.03. 27
hour, | with a hey, and a ho, and a hey nonino, 5.03. 27
with a hey, and a ho, and a hey nonino, | for 5.03. 31
time, | with a hey, and a ho, and a hey nonino, 5.03. 31
"hey, robin, jolly robin, | tell me how thy lady TN 4.02. 72
with hey ho, the wind and the rain, | a foolish 5.01.390
when i came to man's estate, | with hey ho, etc. 5.01.394
when i came, alas, to wive, | with hey ho, etc. 5.01.398
when i came unto my beds, | with hey ho, etc. 5.01.402
while ago the world begun, | /with hey ho, etc. 5.01.406
with hey, the sweet birds, o, how they sing! WT 4.03. 6
hey ho!" TRO 3.01.126
hey, nonny, nonny, nonny. TNK 3.04. 21
hey, nonny, nonny, nonny, nonny." 3.04. 24

HEY–DAY *(also high–day, hoy–day)*

HEY–DAY 1 FR 0.0001 REL FR 0 V 1 P
hey–day! TRO 5.01. 66 P

HEYDAY 1 FR 0.0001 REL FR 1 V 0 P
at your age | the heyday in the blood is tame, HAM 3.04. 69

HIBOCRATES 1 FR 0.0001 REL FR 0 V 1 P
has no more knowledge in hibocrates and galen — WIV 3.01. 65 P

HIC *(also hig)*

HIC 13 FR 0.0014 REL FR 4 V 9 P
singulariter, nominativo, hic, haec, hoc. WIV 4.01. 41 P
he teaches him to "hic" and to "hac," which 4.01. 66 P
"hic ibat simois; SHR 3.01. 28
hic est /sigeia tellus; 3.01. 28
hic steterat priami regia celsa senis." 3.01. 29
"hic ibat," as i told you before, "simois," i am 3.01. 31 P
i am lucentio, "hic est," son unto vincentio of 3.01. 32 P
disguis'd thus to get your love, "hic steterat," 3.01. 34 P
"hic ibat simois," i know you not, "hic est 3.01. 42 P
i know you not, "hic est /sigeia tellus," i 3.01. 42 P
i trust you not, "hic steterat priami," take 3.01. 43 P
i would have that drum or another, or hic jacet. AWW 3.06. 62 P
hic et ubique? HAM 1.05.156

HID 51 FR 0.0057 REL FR 43 V 8 P
was | the ivy which had hid my princely trunk, TMP 1.02. 86
the still–vex'd bermoothes, there she's hid; 1.02.229
i hid me under the dead moon–calf's gaberdine 2.02.110 P
in a rock by th' sea–side, where my wine is hid. 2.02.135 P
yet in this life | lie hid moe thousand deaths; MM 3.01. 40
to make the truth appear where it seems hid, 5.01. 66
though now this grained face of mine be hid | in ERR 5.01.312
see you where benedick hath hid himself? ADO 2.03. 40
god saw him when he was hid in the garden. 5.01.180 P
things hid and barr'd, you mean, from common LLL 1.01. 57
when mistresses from common sense are hid; 1.01. 64
"all hid, all hid," an old infant play. 4.03. 76
"all hid, all hid," an old infant play. 4.03. 76
that hid the worse and show'd the better face. 5.02.388
are as two grains of wheat hid in two bushels of MV 1.01.116 P
murder cannot be hid long; 2.02. 79 P
a day, | such as the day is when the sun is hid. 5.01.126
running brook, | and cytherea all in sedges hid, SHR in.2. 51
wherefore are these things hid? TN 1.03.125 P
more soon | than love that would seem hid: 3.01.148
that when the searching eye of heaven is hid R2 3.02. 37
richard not far from hence hath hid his head. 3.03. 6
and hid his crisp head in the hollow bank 1H4 1.03.106
be not amaz'd, there's nothing hid from me; 1H6 1.02. 68
these five days have i hid me in these woods and 2H6 4.10. 3 P
iron of naples hid with english gilt, | whose 3H6 2.02.139
than in my greatness covet to be hid | and in R3 3.07.163
any malice in your heart | were hid against me, H8 2.01. 81
and hid the gold within that letter mentioned, TIT 5.01.107
he hath hid himself among these trees | to be ROM 2.01. 30
o serpent heart, hid with a flow'ring face! 3.02. 73
i'll to him, he is hid at lawrence' cell. 3.02.141
true; for he bears it not about him, 'tis hid. TIM 4.03.406 P
hid in an auger–hole, may rush and seize us? MAC 2.03.122
and when we have our naked frailties hid, | that 2.03.126
i will find | where truth is hid, though it were HAM 2.02.158
though it were hid indeed | within the centre. 2.02.158
intelligence is given where you are hid; LR 2.01. 21
o lady, lady, shame would have it hid! 2.01. 93
where have you hid yourself? 5.03.180
the object poisons sight, | let it be hid. OTH 5.02.365
fill till the cup be hid. ANT 2.07. 87
should let their ears hear their faults hid! PER 1.02. 62
bent with sin | and hid intent to murder him; 2.ch. 24
could | no more be hid in him than fire in flax, TNK 5.03. 98
hasting to feed her fawn hid in some brake. VEN 876
which, in pale embers hid, lurks to aspire | and LUC 5
then kings' misdeeds cannot be hid in clay. 609
the scalps of many, almost hid behind, | to jump 1413
for precious friends hid in death's dateless SON 30. 6
time's best jewel from time's chest lie hid? 65.10

HIDDEN 11 FR 0.0012 REL FR 9 V 2 P
make rash remonstrance of my hidden pow'r | than MM 5.01.392
lie there what hidden woman's fear there will — AYL 1.03.119
he needs not, it is no hidden virtue in him. H5 3.07.109 P
kings | confound your hidden falsehood and award R3 2.01. 14
turn | your hidden worthiness into your eye, JC 1.02. 57
line the rebel | with hidden help and vantage, MAC 1.03.113
of his salt and most hidden loose affection? OTH 2.01.241 P
mark how his virtue, like a hidden sun, | breaks TNK 2.05. 23
i will no more be hidden, nor put off | this 3.06.118
foul cank'ring rust the hidden treasure frets, VEN 767
but things remov'd that hidden in /thee lie! SON 31. 8

/HIDE* 1 FR 0.0001 REL FR 0 V 1 P
/hide /fox, /and /all /after. HAM 4.02. 30 P

HIDE* 116 FR 0.0131 REL FR 96 V 20 P
it did before, i know not where to hide my head. TMP 2.02. 23 P
and all the more it seeks to hide itself, | the 3.01. 80
if not, to hide what i have said to thee, | that TGV 4.03. 35
i'll go hide me. WIV 3.03. 35 P
come, thou canst not hide it. 3.03. 66 P
in the house you cannot hide him. 3.03.128 P
from whom we thought it meet to hide our love MM 1.02.152
o, what may man within him hide, | though angel 3.02.271
it seems hid, | and hide the false seems true. 5.01. 67
i cannot hide what i am. ADO 1.03. 13 P
can virtue hide itself? 2.01.122 P
i will hide me in the arbor. 2.03. 36 P
knavery cannot sure hide himself in such 2.03.119 P
there will she hide her, | to listen our propose 3.01. 11
or hide your heads like cowards, and fly hence. LLL 5.02. 86
hide thy head, achilles — here comes hector in 5.02.632 P
in your rich wisdom to excuse or hide | the 5.02.732
and i may hide my face, let me play thisby too. MND 1.02. 51 P
creep into acorn–cups and hide them there. 2.01. 31
i'll run from thee and hide me in the brakes, 2.01.227
where dost thou hide thy head? 3.02.406
way | to hide us from pursuit that will be made AYL 1.03.136
in the which hope i blush, and hide my sword. 2.07.119
a vengeance on your crafty withered hide! SHR 2.01.404
ere they can hide their levity in honor. AWW 1.02. 35
o, ransom, ransom! do not hide mine eyes. 4.01. 67
is it a world to hide virtues in? TN 1.03.131 P
pride, | nor wit nor reason can my passion hide. 3.01.152
you, | and 'a may catch your hide and you alone. JN 2.01.136
walls | can hide you from our messengers of war, 2.01.260
i would set an ox–head to your lion's hide, 2.01.292
thou wear a lion's hide! 3.01.128
the earth had not a hole to hide this deed. 4.03. 36
when such a sacred king should hide his head! R2 3.03. 9
wilt thou not hide the trespass of thine own? 5.02. 89
thou now find out to hide thee from this open 1H4 2.04.264 P
go hide thee behind the arras, the rest walk up 2.04.500 P
their date is out, and therefore i'll hide me. 2.04.504 P
but let my favors hide thy mangled face, | and 5.04. 96
and, by the ground they hide, i judge their 2H4 4.01. 21
and rather choose to hide them in a net | than H5 1.02. 93
as gardeners do with ordure hide those roots 2.04. 39
for if you hide the crown | even in your hearts, 2.04. 97
the shame hereof will make me hide my head. 1H6 1.05. 39
good uncle, hide such malice; 2H6 2.01. 25
gloucester, hide thee from their hateful looks, 2.04. 23
hide not thy poison with such sug'red words. 3.02. 45
what, dost thou turn away and hide thy face? 3.02. 74
go bid her hide him quickly from the duke. 5.01. 84
for thousand yorks he shall not hide his head, 5.01. 85
and if thou dost not hide thee from the bear, 5.02. 2
o tiger's heart wrapp'd in a woman's hide! 3H6 1.04.137
if thou please to hide in this true breast, R3 1.02.175
i'll go hide the body in some hole | till that 1.04.280
and with a virtuous visor hide deep vice! 2.02. 28
can lesser hide his love or hate than he, | for 3.04. 52
that i would rather hide me from my greatness — 3.07.161
then would i hide my bones, not rest them here. 4.04. 33
of a rude stream that must for ever hide me. H8 3.02.364
they are too thin and base to hide offenses. 5.02.160
me | i'll hide my silver beard in a gold beaver, TRO 1.03.296
and dreaming night will hide our joys no longer, 4.02. 10
this brave shall oft make thee to hide thy head. 4.04.137
why then fly on, i'll hunt thee for thy hide. 5.06. 31
hope of revenge shall hide our inward woe. 5.10. 31
to hide your doings, and to silence that | which COR 1.09. 23
them th' unaching scars which i should hide, 2.02.148
this is the hole where aaron bid us hide him. TIT 2.03.186
seeking to hide herself, as doth the deer | that 3.01. 89
for why my bowels cannot hide her woes, | but 3.01.230
o, that which i would hide from heaven's eye, 4.02. 59
being black, puts us in mind they hide the fair. ROM 1.01.231
for fair without the fair within to hide. 1.03. 90
i have night's cloak to hide me from their eyes, 2.02. 75
lolling up and down to hide his bable in a hole. 2.04. 92 P
good peter, to hide her face, for her fan's the 2.04.107 P
arise, one knocks. good romeo, hide thyself. 3.03. 71
bears, | or hide me nightly in a charnel–house, 4.01. 81
and hide me with a dead man in his /shroud — 4.01. 85
for all this same, i'll hide me hereabout, | his 5.03. 43
sun, hide thy beams, timon hath done his reign. TIM 5.01.223
hide it in smiles and affability; JC 2.01. 82
were dim enough | to hide thee from prevention. 2.01. 85
who did hide their faces | even from darkness. 2.01.277
if caesar hide himself, shall they not whisper, 2.02.100
and chastisement doth therefore hide his head. 4.03. 16
and hide thy spurs in him | till he have brought 5.03. 15
seek to hide themselves | in drops of sorrow. MAC 1.04. 34
stars, hide your fires, | let not light see my 1.04. 50
false face must hide what the false heart doth 1.07. 82
let the earth hide thee! 3.04. 92
might move | more grief to hide, than hate to HAM 2.01.116
from a bat, a gib, | such dear concernings hide? 3.04.191
tomb enough and continent | to hide the slain? 4.04. 65
his hide is so tann'd with his trade that 'a 5.01.170 P
of nothing hath not such need to hide itself. LR 1.02. 34 P
hide thee, thou bloody hand; 3.02. 53
thou ow'st the worm no silk, the beast no hide, 3.04.104 P
robes and furr'd gowns hide all. 4.06.165
let us be wary, let us hide our loves"; OTH 3.03.420
to hide me from the radiant sun, and solace | i' CYM 1.06. 86

if caesar can hide the sun from us with a 3.01. 43 P
how hard it is to hide the sparks of nature! 3.03. 79
i'll hide my master from the flies, as deep | as 4.02.388
he tumbled down upon his /nemean hide, | and TNK 1.01. 68
mane, thick tail, broad buttock, tender hide; VEN 298
the lesser thing should not the greater hide: LUC 663
to mask their brows and hide their infamy, | but 794
but little stars may hide them when they list. 1008
to hide the truth of this false night's abuses. 1075
painter labor'd with his skill | to hide deceit, 1507
and from the forlorn world his visage hide, SON 33. 7
on | that sometimes anger thrusts into his hide, 50.10
or as the wardrobe which the robe doth hide, 52.10
not once vouchsafe to hide my will in thine? 135. 6
if thou dost seek to have what thou dost hide, 142.13

/HIDEOUS 1 FR 0.0001 REL FR 1 V 0 P
/to /look /upon /the /hideous /god /of /war 2H4 2.03. 35

HIDEOUS 23 FR 0.0026 REL FR 20 V 3 P
a chain | in a most hideous and dreadful manner. WIV 4.04. 34
which have for long run by the hideous law, | as MM 1.04. 63
all proportions | to a most hideous object. AWW 5.03. 52
sure you have some hideous matter to deliver, TN 1.05.206 P
it) into a most hideous opinion of his rage, 3.04.194 P
they have laid me here in hideous darkness. 4.02. 30 P
presented thee more hideous than thou art. JN 4.02.266
have i not hideous death within my view, 5.04. 22
howl'd, and hideous tempest shook down trees; 3H6 5.06. 46
such hideous cries that with the very noise | i, R3 1.04. 60
after the hideous storm that follow'd, was | a H8 1.01. 90
environed with all these hideous fears, | and ROM 4.03. 50
is | like a phantasma or a hideous dream. JC 2.01. 65
that such a hideous trumpet calls to parley MAC 2.03. 82
making night hideous, and we fools of nature HAM 1.04. 54
base, and with a hideous crash | takes prisoner 2.02.476
consideration check | this hideous rashness. LR 1.01.151
more hideous when thou show'st thee in a child 1.04.260
in thy thought | too hideous to be shown. OTH 3.03.108
that breaking out in hideous violence | would STM II.C 132
shape every bush a hideous shapeless devil. LUC 973
on | to hideous winter and confounds him there, SON 5. 6
and see the brave day sunk in hideous night; 12. 2

HIDEOUSLY 1 FR 0.0001 REL FR 1 V 0 P
which cannot look more hideously upon me | than 2H4 5.02. 12

HIDEOUSNESS 1 FR 0.0001 REL FR 1 V 0 P
go anticly, and show outward hideousness, | and ADO 5.01. 96

HIDES* 16 FR 0.0018 REL FR 14 V 2 P
the cover of the salt hides the salt, and TGV 3.01.360 P
than the wit, for the greater hides the less. 3.01.362 P
but creep in crannies, when he hides his beams: ERR 2.02. 31
a cypress, not a bosom, | hides my heart. TN 3.01.122
court | hides not his visage from our cottage, WT 4.04.445
or the profound seas hides | in unknown fadoms, 4.04.490
wipe off the dust that hides our sceptre's gilt, R2 2.01.294
and hides a sword, from hilts unto the point, H5 2.pr. 9
mount them, and make incision in their hides, 4.02. 9
down their heads, dropping the hides and hips, 4.02. 47
brutus, this sober form of yours hides wrongs, JC 4.02. 40
time shall unfold what plighted cunning hides, LR 1.01.280
'tis strange he hides him in fresh cups, soft CYM 5.03. 71
and with his bonnet hides his angry brow, VEN 339
to draw the cloud that hides the silver moon. LUC 371
it is but as a tomb | which hides your life, and SON 17. 4

/HID–FOX 1 FR 0.0001 REL FR 1 V 0 P
we'll fit the /hid–fox with a pennyworth. ADO 2.03. 42

HIDING 11 FR 0.0012 REL FR 7 V 4 P
hand, and hiding mine honor in my necessity, am WIV 2.02. 24 P
there is no hiding you in the house. 4.02. 64 P
text, | hiding the grossness with fair ornament? MV 3.02. 80
obscuring and hiding from me all gentleman–like AYL 1.01. 69 P
hiding his bitter jests in blunt behavior; SHR 3.02. 13
breach | discredit more in hiding of the fault JN 4.02. 33
unless it swell past hiding, and then it's past TRO 1.02.269 P
nay, what hope | have we in hiding us? CYM 4.04. 4
estate, | hiding base sin in pleats of majesty; LUC 93
in his dim mist th' aspiring mountains hiding, 548
way, | hiding thy brav'ry in their rotten smoke? SON 34. 4

HID'ST 2 FR 0.0002 REL FR 2 V 0 P
thou hid'st a thousand daggers in thy thoughts, 2H4 4.05.106
hid'st thou that forehead with a golden crown R3 4.04.140

HIE 52 FR 0.0058 REL FR 51 V 1 P
this, | that presently you hie you home to bed. TGV 4.02. 94
your message done, hie home unto my chamber, 4.04. 88
and prays that you will hie you home to dinner. ERR 1.02. 90
go hie thee presently, post to the road, | and 3.02.147
to adriana, villain, hie thee straight: 4.01.102
hie thee, slave, be gone! 4.01.107
my way is now to hie home to his house, | and 4.03. 92
to what end did i bid thee hie thee home? 4.04. 15
and to thy state of darkness hie thee straight: 4.04. 56
hie therefore, robin, overcast the night; MND 3.02.355
hie thee, gentle jew. MV 1.03.177
hie thee, go. 2.02.172
cambio, hie you home, | and bid bianca make her SHR 4.04. 62
hie home. AWW 2.05. 77
war | my dearest master, your dear son, may hie. 3.04. 9
hie thee, malvolio. TN 1.05.306
no more than he that threats. to arms let's hie! JN 3.01.347
hie thee to france, | and cloister thee in some R2 5.01. 22
hie, good sir michael, bear this sealed brief 1H4 4.04. 1
hie thee, captain. 2H4 4.02. 71
not fail with me, | but thither would i hie." H5 3.02. 17
more sharper than your swords, hie to the field! 3.05. 39
hie thee to hell for shame, and leave this world R3 1.03.142
go hie thee, hie thee from this slaughter–house, 4.01. 43
go hie thee, hie thee from this slaughter–house, 4.01. 43
well, hie thee to thy lord; 4.05. 19
good norfolk, hie thee to thy charge, | use 5.03. 53
take your commission, hie you to your bands, COR 1.02. 26
hie to the goths and raise an army there, | and TIT 3.01.285
then hie you hence to friar lawrence' cell, ROM 2.05. 68
hie you to church, i must another way, | to 2.05. 72
go, i'll to dinner, hie you to the cell. 2.05. 77
hie to high fortune! honest nurse, farewell. 2.05. 78
hie to your chamber. 3.02.138
hie you, make haste, for it grows very late. 3.03.164
hie hence, be gone, away! 3.05. 26
hie, make haste, | make haste, the bridegroom he 4.04. 26
well, i will hie, | and so bestow these papers JC 1.03.150
hie hence, and tell him so. 3.01.290
hie you, messala, | and i will seek for pindarus 5.03. 78
hie thee hither, | that i may pour my spirits in MAC 1.05. 25
hie you to horse; 3.01. 34
"— willow, willow" — | prithee hie thee; OTH 4.03. 50 P
but yet hie you to egypt again. ANT 2.03. 15
hie thee again. 5.02.194
to dorothy my woman hie thee presently, CYM 2.03.138
hie thee, whiles i say | a priestly farewell to PER 3.01. 68
my temple stands in ephesus, hie thee thither, 5.01.240
as they were mad, unto the wood they hie them, VEN 323
charging the sour–fac'd groom to hie as fast LUC 1334
no, | and forth with bashful innocence doth hie. 1341
o, sweet shepherd, hie thee, | for methinks thou PP 12.11

HIED 2 FR 0.0002 REL FR 2 V 0 P
rose–cheek'd adonis hied him to the chase; VEN 3
and thither hied, a sad distemper'd guest; SON 153.12

HIEMS' 1 FR 0.0001 REL FR 1 V 0 P
and on old hiems' /thin and icy crown | an MND 2.01.109

HIEMS 1 FR 0.0001 REL FR 0 V 1 P
this side is hiems, winter; LLL 5.02.891 P

HIES 7 FR 0.0008 REL FR 7 V 0 P
my husband hies him home, where, heaven aiding, AWW 4.04. 12
mayor towards guildhall hies him in all post. R3 3.05. 73
th' extravagant and erring spirit hies | to his HAM 1.01.154
dear lies dead, | and your unblest fate hies. OTH 5.01. 34
and to him in his barge with fervor hies. PER 5.ch. 20
thus weary of the world, away she hies, | and VEN 1189
whose swift obedience to her mistress hies; LUC 1215

HIG *(also hic)*

HIG 1 FR 0.0001 REL FR 0 V 1 P
nominativo, hig, hag, hog; WIV 4.01. 42 P

/HIGH 3 FR 0.0003 REL FR 3 V 0 P
/my /griefs, /whilst /you /mount /up /on /high. R2 4.01.189
/orgillous, /their /high /blood /chaf'd, | /have TRO pr 2
/mark /the /high /noises, /and /thyself /bewray LR 3.06.111

HIGH 254 FR 0.0287 REL FR 228 V 26 P
way, is | another way so high a hope that even TMP 2.01.241
my high charms work, | and these, mine enemies, 3.03. 88
though with their high wrongs i am strook to th' 5.01. 25
a most high miracle! 5.01.177
i cannot reach so high. TGV 1.02. 84
too low a mistress for so high a servant. 2.04.106
whose high imperious thoughts have punish'd me 2.04.130
she shall be dignified with this high honor — 2.04.158
ay, but her forehead's low, and mine's as high. 4.04.193
and high and low beguiles the rich and poor. WIV 1.03. 86
he woos both high and low, both rich and poor, 2.01.113
he is of too high a region, he knows too much. 3.02. 73 P
plays such fantastic tricks before high heaven MM 2.02.121
celerity, | when it is borne in high authority. 4.02.111
and therefore 'tis high time that i were hence. ERR 3.02.157
methinks she's too low for a high praise, too ADO 1.01.172 P
record it with your high and worthy deeds. 5.01.269
in so high a style, margaret, that no man living 5.02. 6 P
soever the matter, i hope in god for high words. LLL 1.01.193 P
a high hope for a low heaven. 1.01.194 P
like humble/–visag'd suitors, his high will. 2.01. 34
the roof of this court is too high to be yours, 2.01. 92 P
o cross! too high to be enthrall'd to /low. MND 1.01.136
love | (and yet a place of high respect with me) 2.01.209
that pure congealed white, high taurus' snow, 3.02.141
and are you grown so high in his esteem, 3.02.294
vailing her high top lower than her ribs | to MV 1.01. 28
being more than sand–blind, high gravel–blind, 2.02. 36 P
rich, | that only to stand high in your account, 3.02.155
to wag their high tops and to make no noise 4.01. 76
albeit you have deserv'd | high commendation, AYL 1.02.263
just as high as my heart. 3.02.269 P
with age | and high top bald with dry antiquity: 4.03.105
every town, | high wedlock then be honored. 5.04.144
honor, high honor, and renown | to hymen, god of 5.04.145
of such possessions, and so high esteem, SHR in.2. 15
to be whipt at the high cross every morning. 1.01.132 P
what power is it which mounts my love so high, AWW 1.01.220
here on my knee, before high heaven and you, 1.03.192
that before you, and next unto high heaven, | i 1.03.193
hearing your high majesty is touch'd | with that 2.01.110
if thou proceed | as high as word, my deed shall 2.01.210
fly, | and to imperial love, that god most high, 2.03. 75
which should sustain the bound and high curvet 2.03.282
though my revenges were high bent upon him | and 5.03. 10
letters sent me | that sets him high in fame. 5.03. 31
whose high respect and rich validity | did lack 5.03.192
is fancy | that it alone is high fantastical. TN 1.01. 15
coming, | that can sing both high and low. 2.03. 41
(which on my faith deserves high speech) and WT 2.01. 70
art here accused and arraigned of high treason, 3.02. 14 P
thoughts | (thoughts high for one so tender) 3.02.196
your high self, | the gracious mark o' th' land, 4.04. 7
beheld), desires access | to your high presence. 5.01. 88
the odds for high and low's alike. 5.01.207
to treat of high affairs touching that time. JN 1.01.101
how high thy glory tow'rs | when the rich blood 2.01.350
be set | among the high tides in the calendar? 3.01. 86
and that high royalty was ne'er pluck'd off; 4.02. 5
the wall is high, and yet will i leap down. 4.03. 1
namely, to appeal each other of high treason. R2 1.01. 27
setting aside his high blood's royalty, | and 1.01. 58
king, | and lay aside my high blood's royalty, 1.01. 71
how high a pitch his resolution soars! 1.01.109
and spit it bleeding in his high disgrace, 1.01.194
how far brought you high herford on his way? 1.04. 2
i brought high herford, if you call him so, 1.04. 3
but to the next high way, and there i left him. 1.04. 4
gilt, | and make high majesty look like itself, 2.01.295
these high wild hills and rough uneven ways 2.03. 4
ye favorites of a king, are we not high? 3.02. 88
high be our thoughts. 3.02. 89
so high above his limits swells the rage | of 3.02.109
or i'll be buried in the king's high way, | some 3.03.155
thus high at least, although your knee be low. 3.03.195
and his high sceptre yields | to the possession 4.01.109
to whose high will we bound our calm contents. 5.02. 38
thy seat is up on high, | whilst my gross flesh 5.05.111
high sparks of honor in thee have i seen. 5.06. 29
and by and by in as high a flow as the ridge of 1H4 1.02. 38 P
betwixt my love and your high majesty. 1.03. 69
as high in the air as this unthankful king, | as 1.03.136
he that rides at high speed and with his pistol 2.04.345 P
he holds your temper in a high respect, | and 3.01.168
whose high deeds, | whose hot incursions and 3.02.107
the land is burning, percy stands on high, | and 3.03.203
have taught us how to cherish such high deeds 5.05. 30
i thank your grace for this high courtesy, 5.05. 32
like a horse | full of high feeding, madly hath 2H4 1.01. 10
do now wear nothing but high shoes, and bunches 1.02. 38 P
durst not have attach'd one of so high blood. 2.02. 3 P
that it may grow and sprout as high as heaven, 2.03. 60
wilt thou upon the high and giddy /mast | seal 3.01. 18
court–gate, when 'a was a crack not thus high; 3.02. 31 P
i do arrest thee, traitor, of high treason, 4.02.107
now call we our high court of parliament, | and 5.02.134
whose high, upreared, and abutting fronts | the H5 pr 21
for government, though high, and low, and lower, 1.02.180
i arrest thee of high treason, by the name of 2.02.145 P
i arrest thee of high treason, by the name of 2.02.147 P
i arrest thee of high treason, by the name of 2.02.149 P
well, 'tis not so, my lord high constable; 2.04. 41
and teach lavoltas high and swift corantos, 3.05. 33
charles delabreth, high constable of france, 3.05. 40
high dukes, great princes, barons, lords, and 3.05. 46
my lord of orleance, and my lord high constable, 3.07. 7 P
my lord high constable, the english lie within 3.07.125 P
in high and boastful neighs | piercing the 4.pr. 10
that beats upon the high shore of this world — 4.01.265
the sun is high, and we outwear the day. 4.02. 63
charles delabreth, high constable of france, 4.08. 92
thou hast astonish'd me with thy high terms. 1H6 1.02. 93
transported shall be at high festivals | before 1.06. 26
welcome, high prince, the mighty duke of york! 3.01.176
thou wast installed in that high degree. 4.01. 17
but with a proud majestical high scorn | he 4.07. 39
if with a lady of so high resolve | (as is fair 5.05. 75
as by your high imperial majesty | i had in 2H6 1.01. 1
that doth accuse his master of high treason. 1.03.182
yet, by your leave, the wind was very high, 2.01. 3
yea, man and birds are fain of climbing high. 2.01. 8
the winds grow high, so do your stomachs, lords. 2.01. 53
faults, | yet, by reputing of his high descent, 3.01. 48
heir, | and such high vaunts of his nobility, 3.01. 50
i do arrest thee of high treason here. 3.01. 97
and made a preachment of your high descent? 3H6 1.04. 72
who crown'd the gracious duke in high despite, 2.01. 59
with promise of high pay and great rewards; 2.01.134
and thou, lord bourbon, our high admiral, 3.03.252
women and children of so high a courage, | and 5.04. 50
who finds edward | shall have a high reward, and 5.05. 10
and lay those honors on your high desert. R3 1.03. 96
they that stand high have many blasts to shake 1.03.258
but i was born so high, | our aery buildeth in 1.03.262
the princes both make high account of you — 3.02. 69
my desert | unmeritable shuns your high request. 3.07.155
thus high, by thy advice | and thy assistance, 4.02. 3
match'd not the high perfection of my loss. 4.04. 66
the high imperial type of this earth's glory. 4.04.245
home | to high promotions and great dignity. 4.04.314
say she shall be a high and mighty queen. 4.04.347
that high all–seer, which i dallied with, | hath 5.01. 20
sad, high, and working, full of state and woe: H8 pr 3
call'd upon | for high feats done to th' crown, 1.01. 61
what his high hatred would effect wants not | a 1.01.107
i | arrest thee of high treason, in the name 1.01.201
not friended by his wish, to your high person; 1.02.140
have found him guilty of high treason. 2.01. 27
hither, i was lord high constable | and duke of 2.01.102
and high note's | ta'en of your many virtues, 2.03. 59
honor than | your high profession spiritual; 2.04.117
employ'd you where high profits might come home, 3.02.158
is the first, and claims | to be high steward; 4.01. 18
'tis the same: high steward. 4.01. 41
the high promotion of his grace of canterbury, 5.02. 23
to the high and mighty princess of england, 5.04. 2 P
hand of greece | should hold up high in brass, TRO 1.03. 64
which is the ladder of all high designs, | the 1.03.102
which is the high and mighty agamemnon? 1.03.232
do not these high strains | of divination in our 2.02.113
high birth, vigor of bone, desert in service, 3.03.172
nor heel the high lavolt, nor sweeten talk, 4.04. 86
slaves, as high | as i could pick my lance. COR 1.01.199
let the high office and the honor go | to one 2.03.122
in his person wrought | to be set high in place, 2.03.247
that brought her for this high good turn so far? TIT 1.01.397
high emperor, upon my feeble knee | i beg this 2.03.288
o, none of both but are of high desert. 3.01.170
whose high exploits and honorable deeds 5.01. 11
scatter'd by winds and high tempestuous gusts, 5.03. 69
by her high forehead and her scarlet lip, | by ROM 2.01. 18
the orchard walls are high and hard to climb, 2.02. 63
which to the high top–gallant of my joy | must 2.04.190
hie to high fortune! honest nurse, farewell. 2.05. 78
was, and urg'd withal | your high displeasure; 3.01.155
the vaulty heaven so high above our heads. 3.05. 22
above the clouds, as high as heaven itself? 4.05. 74
move them no more by crossing their high will. 4.05. 95
i have upon a high and pleasant hill | feign'd TIM 1.01. 63
to the whole race of mankind, high and low! 4.01. 40
the other, at high wish. 4.03.245
till the high fever seethe your blood to froth, 4.03.430
from high to low throughout, that whoso please 5.01.209
both meet to hear and answer such high things. JC 1.02.170
o, he sits high in all the people's hearts; 1.03.157
presents his fire, and the high east | stands, 2.01.110
most high, most mighty, and most puissant caesar 3.01. 33
though they do appear | as huge as high olympus. 4.03. 92
to stay the providence of some high powers 5.01.106
fortune nothing | takes from his high respect. MAC 3.06. 29
come high or low; 4.01. 67
great birnan wood to high dunsinane hill | shall 4.01. 93
in the most high and palmy state of rome, | a HAM 1.01.113
walks o'er the dew of yon high eastward hill. 1.01.167
"high and mighty, you shall know i am set naked 4.07. 43 P
bodies | high on a stage be placed to the view, 5.02.378
the king is in high rage. LR 2.04.296

that their great stars | thron'd and set high? 3.01. 23
whose high and bending head | looks fearfully in 4.01. 73
idle pebble chafes, | cannot be heard so high. 4.06. 22
conspirant 'gainst this high illustrious prince, 5.03.136
wind–shak'd surge, with high and monstrous mane,
OTH 2.01. 13
tempests themselves, high seas, and howling 2.01. 68
he was a wight of high renown, | and thou art 2.03. 93
and fall of swords, | and cassio high in oath; 2.03.235
of so high and plenteous wit and invention! 4.01.189 P
it is now high supper–time, and the night grows 4.02.242 P
the noise was high. 5.02. 93
upon his son, who, high in name and power, ANT 1.02.189
who neigh'd so high that what i would have spoke 1.05. 49
thee, is | noble, courageous, high unmatchable, 2.03. 21
it is just so high as it is, and moves with it 2.07. 43 P
acquire too high a fame when him we serve's away 3.01. 15
too cruel, | that he his high authority abus'd, 3.06. 33
and the high gods, | to do you justice, makes 3.06. 87
this kingly seal | and plighter of high hearts! 3.13.126
no, let me speak, and let me rail so high, 4.15. 43
let's do't after the high roman fashion, | and 4.15. 87
make | my country's high pyramides my gibbet, 5.02. 61
high events as these | strike those that make 5.02.360
see | high order in this great solemnity. 5.02.366
are arch'd so high that giants may jet through CYM 3.03. 5
make distinction | of place 'tween high and low. 4.02.249
die, | for by his fall my honor must keep high. PER 1.01.149
towers bore heads so high they kiss'd the clouds 1.04. 24
the most high gods not minding longer | to 2.04. 3
that never aim'd so high to love your daughter, 2.05. 47
that horse and sail and high expense | can stead 3.ch. 20
the sea works high, the wind is loud, and will 3.01. 48 P
advanc'd in time to great and high estate. 4.04. 16
possess | the high throne in his heart. TNK 1.03. 96
the sun grows high, let's walk in. 2.02.148
his nose stands high, a character of honor; 4.02.110
sweet bottom grass and high delightful plain, VEN 236
shows his hot courage and his high desire. 276
high crest, short ears, straight legs and 297
through his mane and tail the high wind sings, 305
vultur thought doth pitch the price so high 551
she fram'd thee in high heaven's despite, | to 731
from his moist cabinet mounts up on high, | and 854
ne'er settled equally, but high or low, | that 1139
reck'ning his fortune at such high proud rate LUC 19
in that high task hath done her beauty wrong, 80
for that he color'd with his high estate, 92
and decks with praises collatine's high name, 108
huge rocks, high winds, strong pirates, shelves 335
by their high treason is his heart misled, 369
she conjures him by high almighty jove, | by 568
some high, some low, the painter was so nice; 1412
if it were fill'd with your most high deserts? SON 17. 2
eyes, that taught the dumb on high to sing, 78. 5
advance | as high as learning my rude ignorance. 78.14
thy love is /better than high birth to me, 91. 9
in clamors of all size, both high and low. LC 21

HIGH–BATTLED 1 FR 0.0001 REL FR 1 V 0 P
high–battled caesar will | unstate his happiness ANT 3.13. 29

HIGH–BLOWN 1 FR 0.0001 REL FR 1 V 0 P
my high–blown pride | at length broke under me, H8 3.02.361

HIGH–BORN 1 FR 0.0001 REL FR 1 V 0 P
i am too high–born to be propertied, | to be a JN 5.02. 79

HIGH–BORNE 1 FR 0.0001 REL FR 1 V 0 P
in high–borne words, the worth of many a knight LLL 1.01.172

HIGH/–COLOR'D 1 FR 0.0001 REL FR 0 V 1 P
lepidus is high/–color'd. ANT 2.07. 4 P

HIGH–DAY *(also hey–day, hoy–day)*

HIGH–DAY 4 FR 0.0004 REL FR 1 V 3 P
freedom, high–day! TMP 2.02.186 P
high–day, freedom! 2.02.186 P
freedom, high–day, freedom! 2.02.186 P
thou spend'st such high–day wit in praising him. MV 2.09. 98

HIGH–ENGENDER'D 1 FR 0.0001 REL FR 1 V 0 P
your high–engender'd battles 'gainst a head | so LR 3.02. 23

HIGHER 38 FR 0.0043 REL FR 32 V 6 P
as thoughts do blow them, higher and higher. WIV 5.05. 98
as thoughts do blow them, higher and higher. 5.05. 98
i pray you come, hold up the jest no higher. 5.05.105
no higher than thyself, the judge's clerk, | a MV 5.01.163
let higher italy | (those bated that inherit but AWW 2.01. 12
will he travel higher, or return again into 4.03. 42 P
ha, higher! TN 1.03.141 P
and our weak spirits ne'er been higher rear'd WT 1.02. 72
the higher pow'rs forbid! 3.02.202
up higher to the plain, where we'll set forth JN 2.01.295
steps me a little higher than his vow | made to 1H4 4.03. 75
among wits of no higher breeding than thine. 2H4 2.02. 35 P
we will our youth lead on to higher fields, 4.04. 3
his affections are higher mounted than ours, yet H5 4.01.106 P
between two hawks, which flies the higher pitch, 1H6 2.04. 11
that mounts no higher than a bird can soar. 2H6 2.01. 14
and swell so much the higher by their ebb. 3H6 4.08. 56
advance thy halberd higher than my breast, | or, R3 1.02. 40
him above, his complexion is higher than his. TRO 1.02.102 P
he having color enough, and the other higher, is 1.02.103 P
should lift their bosoms higher than the shores, 1.03.112
that holds his honor higher than his ease, | and 1.03.266
up higher toward the north | he first presents JC 2.01.109
go, pindarus, get higher on that hill; 5.03. 20
set your entreatments at a higher rate | than a HAM 1.03.122
higher than both in blood and life, stands up ANT 1.02.190
but let us rear | the higher our opinion, that 2.01. 36
say to me, whose fortunes shall rise higher, 2.03. 16
the higher nilus swells, | the more it promises; 2.07. 20
on cats and dogs, | then afterward up higher; CYM 1.05. 39
we'll higher to the mountains, there secure us. 4.04. 8
throws down one mountain to cast up a higher. PER 1.04. 6
like to groves, being topp'd, they higher rise. 1.04. 9
higher than all the rest, spreads like a plane TNK 2.06. 5
their contentious throats, now one the higher, 5.03.125
that arcite's legs, being higher than his head, 5.04. 78
turns not, but swells the higher by this let. LUC 646
to jump up higher seem'd, to mock the mind. 1414

HIGHEST 16 FR 0.0018 REL FR 12 V 4 P
highest queen of state, | great juno, comes, i TMP 4.01.101
thy substance, valued at the highest rate, ERR 1.01. 23
which is the greatest lady, the highest? LLL 4.01. 46 P
his life and in the highest compulsion of base AWW 3.06. 29 P
misprision in the highest degree! TN 1.05. 55 P
fool, i'll requite it in the highest degree. 4.02.118 P
brother, let us to the highest of the field, 1H4 5.04.160
perjury, perjury, in the highest degree; R3 5.03.196
i have touch'd the highest point of all my H8 3.02.223
grow in the veins of actions highest rear'd, TRO 1.03. 6
friend no less | than those she placeth highest! COR 1.05. 24
revenge | wrench up thy power to th' highest. 1.08. 11
in the highest degree | he hath abus'd your 5.06. 84
chase, | and climb the highest promontory top. TIT 2.02. 22
athens again, and flourish | with the highest. TIM 5.01. 11
fix'd on the summit of the highest mount, | to HAM 3.03. 18

HIGHEST–PEERING 1 FR 0.0001 REL FR 1 V 0 P
and overlooks the highest–peering hills: TIT 2.01. 8

HIGH–GROWN 1 FR 0.0001 REL FR 1 V 0 P
search every acre in the high–grown field, | and LR 4.04. 7

HIGH–JUDGING 1 FR 0.0001 REL FR 1 V 0 P
nor tell tales of thee to high–judging jove. LR 2.04.228

HIGH–LONE 1 FR 0.0001 REL FR 1 V 0 P
years, | for then she could stand high–lone; ROM 1.03. 36

HIGHLY 15 FR 0.0017 REL FR 13 V 2 P
three things that women highly hold in hate. TGV 3.02. 33
sir, | of credit infinite, highly belov'd, ERR 5.01. 6
her wit | values itself so highly that to her ADO 3.01. 53
i will show myself highly fed and lowly taught. AWW 2.02. 3 P
makes welsh as sweet as ditties highly penn'd, 1H4 3.01.206
wherein thyself shalt highly be employ'd. R3 3.01.180
and mountainous error be too highly heap'd | for COR 2.03.120
match | i hold me highly honored of your grace, TIT 1.01.245
and highly mov'd to wrath | to be controll'd in 1.01.419
herself and hers are highly bound to thee. 4.02.171
it highly us concerns | by day and night t' 4.03. 27
that highly may advantage thee to hear. 5.01. 56
what thou wouldst highly, | that wouldst thou MAC 1.05. 20
conduct me to mine host, we love him highly, 1.06. 29
and heard others /praise, and that highly — not HAM 3.02. 30 P

HIGH–MINDED 1 FR 0.0001 REL FR 1 V 0 P
but i will chastise this high–minded strumpet. 1H6 1.05. 12

HIGHMOST 2 FR 0.0002 REL FR 2 V 0 P
now is the sun upon the highmost hill | of this ROM 2.05. 9
but when from highmost pitch, with weary car, SON 7. 9

HIGHNESS' 47 FR 0.0053 REL FR 46 V 1 P
i here could pluck his highness' frown upon you TMP 5.01.127
it is his highness' pleasure that the queen WT 3.02. 9
what dangers, by his highness' fail of issue, 5.01. 27
is sad and passionate at your highness' tent. JN 2.01.544
in name of lendings for your highness' soldiers, R2 1.01. 89
disburs'd i duly to his highness' soldiers; 1.01.127
and all unlook'd for from your highness' mouth. 1.03.155
air, | have i deserved at your highness' hands. 1.03.158
for their advantage and your highness' loss. 1.04. 41
those prisoners in your highness' name demanded,
1H4 1.03. 23
to make against your highness' claim to france H5 1.02. 36
and do submit me to your highness' mercy. 2.02. 77
charge and command you, in his highness' name, 1H6 1.03. 76 P
lets fall his sword before your highness' feet, 3.04. 9
'tis his highness' pleasure | you do prepare to 2H6 1.02. 56
his highness' pleasure is to talk with him. 2.01. 71
and other of your highness' privy council, | as 2.01.172
or be admitted to your highness' council. 3.01. 27
i do arrest you in his highness' name, | and 3.01.136
and equity exil'd your highness' land. 3.01.146
they say, in him they fear your highness' death; 3.02.249
expect your highness' doom, of life or death. 4.09. 12
we twain will go into his highness' tent. 5.01. 55
so shall you bind me to your highness' service. 3H6 3.02. 43
in sign of truth, i kiss your highness' hand. 4.08. 26
mighty liege, tell me your highness' pleasure, R3 4.04.447
'tis his highness' pleasure | you shall to th' H8 1.01.206
viscount rochford — one of her highness' women. 1.04. 93
to your highness' hand | i tender my commission; 2.02.102
you have, by fortune and his highness' favors, 2.04.111
a known friend, 'gainst his highness' pleasure 3.01. 85
that for your highness' good i ever labor'd 3.02.191
may he continue | long in his highness' favor, 3.02.396
i humbly do entreat your highness' pardon, | my 4.02.104
he attends your highness' pleasure. 5.01. 83
is my duty | t' attend your highness' pleasure. 5.01. 91
'tis his highness' pleasure | and our consent, 5.02. 87
they shall be ready at your highness' will, | to TIT 2.03.297
implor'd your highness' pardon, and set forth MAC 1.04. 6
your highness' part | is to receive our duties; 1.04. 23
to make their audit at your highness' pleasure, 1.06. 27
alone felicitate | in your dear highness' love. LR 1.01. 76
i did commend your highness' letters to them, 2.04. 28
what's your highness' pleasure? ANT 1.05. 8
i crave your highness' pardon. 2.05. 98
that will not be denied your highness' presence. 5.02.234
queen, madam, | desires your highness' company. CYM 1.03. 38

HIGHNESS 144 FR 0.0162 REL FR 133 V 11 P
i do well believe your highness, and did it to TMP 2.01.172 P
i invite your highness and your train | to my 5.01.301
i beseech your highness do not marry me to a MM 5.01.514 P
your highness said even now i made you a duke; 5.01.515 P
but she tells to your highness simple truth! ERR 5.01.211
my liege, your highness now may do me good. ADO 1.01.290
amaz'd, my lord? why looks your highness sad? LLL 5.02.391
choice of which your highness will see first. MND 5.01. 43
a thought unborn | did i offend your highness. AYL 1.03. 52
so was i when your highness took his dukedom, 1.03. 59
so was i when your highness banish'd him. 1.03. 60
o that your highness knew my heart in this! 3.01. 13
i shall beseech your highness, | in such a AWW 2.03.106
his highness hath promis'd me to do it, and, to 4.05. 74 P
his highness comes post from marsellis, of as 4.05. 80 P
all that he is hath reference to your highness. 5.03. 29
it did concern | your highness with herself. 5.03.138
let your highness | lay a more noble thought 5.03.179
to satisfy your highness and the entreaties | of WT 1.02.232
your highness | will take again your queen as 1.02.335
please your highness | to take the urgent hour. 1.02.464
beseech your highness | my women may be with me, 2.01.116
beseech your highness call the queen again. 2.01.126
about some gossips for your highness. 2.03. 41
beseech your highness, give us better credit. 2.03.147
please' your highness, posts | from those you 2.03.193
then, till the fury of his highness settle, 4.04.471
such receiving | as shall become your highness, 4.04.527
my father gave me | for visiting your highness. 5.01.163
her highness is in safety, fear you not. JN 3.02. 8
i leave your highness. 3.03. 14
"once again" (but that your highness pleas'd) 4.02. 3
but it pleas'd your highness | to overbear it, 4.02. 36
doth make a stand at what your highness will. 4.02. 39
your highness should deliver up your crown. 4.02.152
his highness yet doth speak, and holds belief 5.07. 6
danger seen in him | aim'd at your highness, no R2 1.01. 14
the fair reverence of your highness curbs me 1.01. 54
i pray | your highness to assign our trial day. 1.01.151
the appellant in all duty greets your highness, 1.03. 52
glad am i that your highness is so arm'd | to 3.02.104
his highness is fall'n into this same whoreson 2H4 1.02.107 P
your highness knows, comes to no further use 4.04. 72
here at more leisure may your highness read, 4.04. 89
fits | are with his highness very ordinary. 4.04.115
your highness pleased to forget my place, | the 5.02. 77
to bar your highness claiming from the female, H5 1.02. 92
so hath your highness. 1.02.126
will raise your highness such a mighty sum | as 1.02.133
your highness, lately sending into france, | did 1.02.246
so may your highness, and yet punish too. 2.02. 48
your highness bade me ask for it to–day. 2.02. 63
which i beseech your highness to forgive, 2.02.153
and if your father's highness | do not, in grant 2.04.120
i shall deliver so. thanks to your highness. 3.06.167
and what your highness suffer'd under that shape 4.08. 53 P
therefore i beseech your highness pardon me. 4.08. 56 P
of grant, shall name your highness in this form, 5.02.338 P
and then your highness shall command a peace. 1H6 4.01.117
it grieves his highness. 4.01.133
i have inform'd his highness so at large, | as, 5.01. 42
your highness is betroth'd | unto another lady 5.05. 26
and hath his highness in his infancy | crowned 2H6 1.01. 93
to show your highness | a spirit rais'd from 1.02. 78
as i was cause | your highness came to england, 1.03. 66
to present your highness with the man. 2.01. 67
so please your highness to behold the fight. 2.03. 51
well hath your highness seen into this duke; 3.01. 42
by means whereof his highness hath lost france. 3.01.106
what, will your highness leave the parliament? 3.01.197
that if your highness should intend to sleep, 3.02.255
ay, but i hope your highness shall have his. 4.04. 20
york doth present himself unto your highness. 5.01. 59
i would your highness would depart the field, 3H6 2.02. 73
your highness shall do well to grant her suit; 3.02. 8
may it please your highness to resolve me now, 3.02. 19
grant what i perceive | your highness aims at, 3.02. 68
herein your highness wrongs both them and me. 3.02. 75
hath mov'd his highness to commit me now. R3 1.01. 61
i do beseech your highness | to take our brother 2.01. 76
i will not rise, unless your highness hear me. 2.01. 98
your highness shall repose you at the tower; 3.01. 65
what says your highness to my just request? 4.02. 94
your highness told me i should post before. 4.04.455
but this good comfort bring i to your highness: 4.04.520
i would your highness | would give it quick H8 1.02. 65
please your highness note | this dangerous 1.02.138
not long before your highness sped to france, 1.02.151
after your highness had reprov'd the duke 1.02.189
now, madam, may his highness live in freedom, 1.02.200
whom once more i present unto your highness. 2.02. 97
his highness having liv'd so long with her, and 2.03. 2
as from a blushing handmaid, to his highness; 2.03. 72
the which before | his highness shall speak in, 2.04.103
in humblest manner i require your highness 2.04.145
i | did broach this business to your highness, 2.04.150
so please your highness, | the question did at 2.04.212
and did entreat your highness to this course 2.04.217
so please your highness, | the queen being 2.04.231
peace to your highness! 3.01. 23
ever god bless your highness! 3.02.136
and ever may your highness yoke together | (as i 3.02.150
till you hear further from his highness. 3.02.232
a league between his highness and ferrara. 3.02.323
may it please your highness | to hear me speak 4.02. 46
how does his highness? 4.02.124
remember me | in all humility unto his highness. 4.02.161
and desir'd your highness | most heartily to 5.01. 65
to the gladding of | your highness with an heir! 5.01. 72
i wish your highness | a quiet night, and my 5.01. 76
i humbly thank your highness, | and am right 5.01.108
i think your highness saw this many a day. 5.02. 21
do, and vow to heaven and to his highness | that TIT 1.01.474
why doth your highness look so pale and wan? 2.03. 90
to entertain your highness and your empress. 5.03. 32
and if your highness knew my heart, you were. 5.03. 34
will't please your highness feed? 5.03. 54
let your highness | command upon me, to the MAC 3.01. 15
it was, so please your highness. 3.01. 74
may't please your highness sit. 3.04. 38
please't your highness | to grace us with your 3.04. 43
what is't that moves your highness? 3.04. 47
gentlemen, rise, his highness is not well. 3.04. 51
he truly found | it was against your highness. HAM 2.02. 65
i crave no more than hath your highness offer'd, LR 1.01.194
your highness is not entertain'd with that 1.04. 58 P
be silent when i think your highness wrong'd. 1.04. 66 P
display'd so saucily against your highness — 2.04. 41
i am glad to see your highness. 2.04.128
will't please your highness walk? 4.07. 82
good your highness, patience. ANT 2.05.106
please your highness, | i will from hence to–day CYM 1.01. 79
i humbly thank your highness. 1.01.175
pleaseth your highness, ay. 1.05. 5
your highness | shall from this practice but 1.05. 23
is in safety | and greets your highness dearly. 1.06. 13
beseech your highness, | hold me your loyal 4.03. 15
we did, so please your highness. 5.05. 62
which i'll make bold your highness | cannot deny 5.05. 89
i humbly thank your highness. 5.05.100
no more kin to me | than i to your highness; 5.05.113
my breeding was, sir, as | your highness knows. 5.05.340
doth your highness call? PER 1.01.150

so farewell to your highness. 1.01.167
HIGH-PITCH'D 1 FR 0.0001 REL FR 1 V 0 P
did sting | his high-pitch'd thoughts, that LUC 41
HIGH-PLAC'D 1 FR 0.0001 REL FR 1 V 0 P
and our high-plac'd macbeth | shall live the MAC 4.01. 98
HIGH-PROOF 1 FR 0.0001 REL FR 0 V 1 P
for we are high-proof melancholy and would fain ADO 5.01.123 P
HIGH-REACHING 1 FR 0.0001 REL FR 1 V 0 P
high-reaching buckingham grows circumspect. R3 4.02. 31
HIGH-REAR'D 1 FR 0.0001 REL FR 1 V 0 P
like high-rear'd bulwarks, stand before our R3 5.03.242
HIGH-REPENTED 1 FR 0.0001 REL FR 1 V 0 P
my high-repented blames, | dear sovereign, AWW 5.03. 36
HIGH-RESOLVED 1 FR 0.0001 REL FR 1 V 0 P
and with a power | of high-resolved men, bent to TIT 4.04. 64
HIGH-SIGHTED 1 FR 0.0001 REL FR 1 V 0 P
so let high-sighted tyranny range on, | till JC 2.01.118
HIGH-SOARING 1 FR 0.0001 REL FR 1 V 0 P
she is as far high-soaring o'er thy praises | as TRO 4.04.124
HIGH-SPEEDED 1 FR 0.0001 REL FR 1 V 0 P
and this high-speeded pace is but to say | that TNK 1.03. 83
HIGH'ST 1 FR 0.0001 REL FR 1 V 0 P
swear not by, | but take the high'st to witness. AWW 4.02. 24
HIGH-STOMACH'D 1 FR 0.0001 REL FR 1 V 0 P
high-stomach'd are they both and full of ire, R2 1.01. 18
HIGH-SWOLL'N 1 FR 0.0001 REL FR 1 V 0 P
the broken rancor of your high-swoll'n hates, R3 2.02.117
HIGHT 4 FR 0.0004 REL FR 3 V 1 P
this child of fancy, that armado hight, | for LLL 1.01.170
"which, as i remember, hight costard" — 1.01.255 P
this grisly beast, which lion hight by name, MND 5.01.139
this maid | hight philoten, and it is said | for PER 4.ch. 18
HIGHTH *(also height, heighth)*
HIGHTH 1 FR 0.0001 REL FR 1 V 0 P
worth's unknown, although his highth be taken. SON 116. 8
HIGH-VIC'D 1 FR 0.0001 REL FR 1 V 0 P
will o'er some high-vic'd city hang his poison TIM 4.03.110
HIGHWAY 3 FR 0.0003 REL FR 1 V 2 P
prolixity or crossing the plain highway of talk, MV 3.01. 12 P
and knock are too powerful on the highway. WT 4.03. 29 P
he made you for a highway to my bed, | but i, a ROM 3.02.134
HIGHWAYS 2 FR 0.0002 REL FR 1 V 1 P
this is like the mending of highways | in summer MV 5.01.263
and should be buried in highways out of all AWW 1.01.139 P
HIGH-WITTED 1 FR 0.0001 REL FR 1 V 0 P
become | high-witted tamora to gloze with all; TIT 4.04. 35
HIGH-WROUGHT 1 FR 0.0001 REL FR 1 V 0 P
nothing at all, it is a high-wrought flood. OTH 2.01. 2
HILD *(also held)*
HILD 1 FR 0.0001 REL FR 1 V 0 P
o, let it not be hild | poor women's faults that LUC 1257
HILDING 7 FR 0.0008 REL FR 6 V 1 P
for shame, thou hilding of a devilish spirit, SHR 2.01. 26
if your lordship find him not a hilding, hold me AWW 3.06. 3 P
he was some hilding fellow that had stol'n | the 2H4 1.01. 57
to purge this field of such a hilding foe; H5 4.02. 29
out on her, hilding! ROM 3.05.168
a hilding for a livery, a squire's cloth, | a CYM 2.03.123
is that scornful piece, that scurvy hilding, TNK 3.05. 42
HILDINGS 1 FR 0.0001 REL FR 0 V 1 P
a gipsy, helen and hero hildings and harlots, ROM 2.04. 42 P
HILL 40 FR 0.0045 REL FR 31 V 9 P
hard | against the steep-up rising of the hill? LLL 4.01. 2
or mons, the hill. 5.01. 84 P
over hill, over dale, | thorough bush, thorough MND 2.01. 2
met we on hill, in dale, forest, or mead, | by 2.01. 83
inprimis, we came down a foul hill, my master SHR 4.01. 67 P
i spied | an ancient angel coming down the hill, 4.02. 61
so, and at the other hill | command the rest to JN 2.01.298
he is walk'd up to the top of the hill, i'll go 1H4 2.02. 8 P
money of the king's coming down the hill, 'tis 2.02. 54 P
the boy shall lead our horses down the hill. 2.02. 79 P
horse-back-breaker, this huge hill of flesh — 2.04.243 P
runs a' horseback up a hill perpendicular — 2.04.344 P
the sun begins to peer | above yon bulky hill! 5.01. 2
and falling from a hill, he was so bruis'd 5.05. 21
of woncote against clement perkes a' th' hill. 2H4 5.01. 39 P
whiles his most mighty father on a hill | stood H5 1.02.108
when down the hill he holds his fierce career? 3.03. 23
ride thou unto the horsemen on yond hill. 4.07. 57
to sit upon a hill, as i do now, | to carve out 3H6 2.05. 23
i'll stay above the hill, so both may shoot. 3.01. 5
now is the sun upon the highmost hill | of this ROM 2.05. 9
i have upon a high and pleasant hill | feign'd TIM 1.01. 63
throne, this fortune, and this hill, methinks, 1.01. 73
this hill is far enough. JC 5.03. 12
go, pindarus, get higher on that hill; 5.03. 20
with pindarus his bondman, on this hill. 5.03. 56
great birnan wood to high dunsinane hill | shall MAC 4.01. 93
as i did stand my watch upon the hill, | i 5.05. 32
walks o'er the dew of yon high eastward hill. HAM 1.01.167
and bowl the round nave down the hill of heaven 2.02.496
mercury | new lighted on a /heaven-kissing hill, 3.04. 59
go thy hold when a great wheel runs down a hill, LR 2.04. 72 P
when shall i come to th' top of that same hill? 4.06. 1
set we our squadrons on yond side o' th' hill, ANT 3.09. 1
that i were | upon the hill of basan, to outroar 3.13.127
up to yond hill, | your legs are young; CYM 3.03. 10
"by this, poor wat, far off upon a hill, VEN 697
her stand she takes upon a steep-up hill. PP 9. 5
and having climb'd the steep-up heavenly hill, SON 7. 5
from off a hill whose concave womb reworded | a LC 1
HILLO *(also hilloa, illo)*
HILLO 1 FR 0.0001 REL FR 1 V 0 P
hillo, ho, ho, boy! come, /bird, come. HAM 1.05.116
HILLOA 1 FR 0.0001 REL FR 0 V 1 P
hilloa, loa! WT 3.03. 79 P
HILLOCKS 1 FR 0.0001 REL FR 1 V 0 P
round rising hillocks, brakes obscure and rough, VEN 237
HILLS 17 FR 0.0019 REL FR 17 V 0 P
ye elves of hills, brooks, standing lakes, and TMP 5.01. 33
hallow your name to the reverberate hills, | and TN 1.05.272
these high wild hills and rough uneven ways R2 2.03. 4
to climb steep hills | requires slow pace at H8 1.01.131
heels, | or pile ten hills on the tarpeian rock, COR 3.02. 3
and overlooks the highest-peering hills: TIT 2.01. 8
driving back shadows over low'ring hills; ROM 2.05. 6
down, | but keep the hills and upper regions. JC 5.01. 3
rocks, /and hills whose /heads touch heaven, OTH 1.03.141
and let the laboring bark climb hills of seas 2.01.187
our foot | upon the hills adjoining to the city ANT 4.10. 5
blind mole casts | copp'd hills towards heaven, PER 1.01.101
it, | for who digs hills because they do aspire 1.04. 5
graze on my lips, and if those hills be dry, VEN 233
that cedar tops and hills seem burnish'd gold. 858
between whose hills her head entombed is; LUC 390
the pleasures prove | that hills and valleys, PP 19. 3
HILT 3 FR 0.0003 REL FR 1 V 2 P
in the circumference of a peck, hilt to point, WIV 3.05.111 P
out of the town armory, with a broken hilt, and SHR 3.02. 47 P
painted to the hilt | in blood of those that had 3H6 1.04. 12
HILTS 6 FR 0.0006 REL FR 2 V 4 P
seven, by these hilts, or i am a villain else. 1H4 2.04.206 P
and hides a sword, from hilts unto the point, H5 2.pr. 9
i'll run him up to the hilts, as i am a soldier. 2.01. 64 P
him on the costard with the hilts of thy sword, R3 1.04.154 P
here, take thou the hilts, | and when my face is JC 5.03. 43
very responsive to the hilts, most delicate HAM 5.02.152 P
/HIM 59 FR 0.0066 REL FR 53 V 6 P
HIM 5389 FR 0.6091 REL FR 3888 V 1501 P
/HIM'S 1 FR 0.0001 REL FR 1 V 0 P
thou speak'st like /him's untutor'd to repeat: PER 1.04. 74
/HIMSELF 2 FR 0.0002 REL FR 2 V 0 P
/then /threw /he /down /himself /and /all /their 2H4 4.01.125
/for /he /himself /is /subject /to /his /birth: HAM 1.03. 18
HIMSELF 482 FR 0.0544 REL FR 339 V 143 P
the king's son have i landed by himself, | whom TMP 1.02.221
got by the devil himself | upon thy wicked dam, 1.02.319
himself with his good arms in lusty stroke | to 2.01.120
he himself | calls her a nonpareil. 3.02. 99
found a wife | where he himself was lost; 5.01.211
the rest, and let no man take care for himself; 5.01.257 P
well of his wealth; but of himself, so, so. TGV 1.02. 13
scribe, to himself should write the letter? 2.01.140
hath taught her love himself to write unto her 2.01.168
no, the dog is himself, and i am the dog — o! 2.03. 22 P
i care not, though he burn himself in love. 2.05. 53 P
himself would lodge where, senseless, they are 3.01.143
slave, that will thrust himself into secrets. 3.01.383 P
when a cur cannot keep himself in all companies! 4.04. 10 P
he thrusts me himself into the company of three 4.04. 16 P
master parson, who writes himself armigero, in WIV 1.01. 9 P
the gentleman had drunk himself out of his five 1.01.175 P
i am glad he went not in himself; 1.04. 49 P
my master himself is in love with mistress anne 1.04.104 P
pieces with age to show himself a young gallant! 2.01. 22 P
the devil himself hath not such a name. 2.02.300 P
sir hugh hath shown himself a wise and patient 2.03. 54 P
caius, that calls himself doctor of physic? 3.01. 4 P
divulge page himself for a secure and willful 3.02. 42 P
quickly, my kinsman shall speak for himself. 3.04. 23 P
good master shallow, let him woo for himself. 3.04. 51 P
and so buffets himself on the forehead, crying, 4.02. 25 P
the duke himself will be to-morrow at court, and 4.03. 2 P
could great men thunder | as jove himself does, MM 2.02.111
strifes, contended especially to know himself. 3.02.233 P
willingly humbles himself to the determination 3.02.244 P
yet had he fram'd to himself (by the instruction 3.02.245 P
if he chance to fail, he hath sentenc'd himself. 3.02.257 P
pattern in himself to know, | grace to stand, 3.02.263
that in himself which he spurs on his pow'r | to 4.02. 82
such sin | for which the pardoner himself is in. 4.02.109
most manifest, and not denied by himself. 4.02.139 P
hath he borne himself penitently in prison? 4.02.140 P
he should pursue | faults proper to himself. 5.01.110
he would have weigh'd thy brother by himself, 5.01.111
he in time may come to clear himself; 5.01.150
he had some cause | to prattle for himself. 5.01.182
then to glance from him | to th' duke himself, 5.01.310
head — | as like almost to claudio as himself. 5.01.489
(as i have heard him swear himself there's one 5.01.510
(unseen, inquisitive), confounds himself. ERR 1.02. 38
as the plain bald pate of father time himself. 2.02. 70 P
time himself is bald, and therefore, to the 2.02.106 P
is mad, | else would he never so demean himself. 4.03. 82
man | do outrage and displeasure to himself? 4.04.116
when he demean'd himself rough, rude, and wildly 5.01. 88
anon i'm sure the duke himself in person | comes 5.01.119
him, | and with his mad attendant and himself, 5.01.150
he hath borne himself beyond the promise of his ADO 1.01. 13 P
that if he have wit enough to keep himself warm, 1.01. 68 P
for a difference between himself and his horse, 1.01. 69 P
for a fool that betroths himself to unquietness? 1.03. 47 P
that the prince should woo hero for himself, and 1.03. 62 P
'tis certain so, the prince woos for himself. 2.01.174
for the garland he might have worn himself, and 2.01.229 P
see you where benedick hath hid himself? 2.03. 40
cannot sure hide himself in such reverence. 2.03.120 P
i could wish he would modestly examine himself, 2.03.208 P
nay, 'a rubs himself with civet. 3.02. 50 P
yea, or to paint himself? 3.02. 57 P
is to let him show himself what he is and steal 3.03. 59 P
moral when he shall endure | the like himself. 5.01. 31
if he could right himself with quarrelling, 5.01. 51
wise man among twenty that will praise himself. 5.02. 75 P
to death, | /wish'd himself the heavens' breath. LLL 4.03.106
but an ethiop were, | and deny himself for jove, 4.03.117
berowne did swear himself out of all suit. 5.02.275
to make judas hang himself. 5.02.604 P
in himself he is; MND 1.01. 53
lover, that kills himself most gallant for love. 1.02. 23 P
pyramus must draw a sword to kill himself; 3.01. 11 P
lion's neck, and he himself must speak through, 3.01. 38 P
for pyramus therein doth kill himself. 5.01. 67
pyramus and hang'd himself in thisby's garter, 5.01.358 P
his own good parts that he can shoe him himself. MV 1.02. 43 P
when laban and himself were compremis'd | that 1.03. 78
saving your reverence, is the devil himself. 2.02. 26 P
cupid himself would blush | to see me thus 2.06. 38
be match'd, unless the devil himself turn jew. 3.01. 78 P
the duke himself, and the magnificoes | of 3.02.280
shame | as to offend, himself being offended; 4.01. 58
of kings, | it is an attribute to god himself; 4.01.195
dew, | and saw the lion's shadow ere himself, 5.01. 8
the man that hath no music in himself, | nor is 5.01. 83
in both my eyes he doubly sees himself, | in 5.01.244
or if he do not mightily grace himself on thee, AYL 1.01.149 P
it do him right, | then he hath wrong'd himself. 2.07. 85
this, the devil himself will have no shepherds. 3.02. 84 P
foot can fall, he thinks himself too soon there. 3.02.328 P
favor, and bestows himself | like a ripe sister; 4.03. 86
there stripp'd himself, and here upon his arm 4.03.146
but the wise man knows himself to be a fool." 5.01. 32 P
would send me word he cut it to please himself: 5.04. 74 P
would not the beggar then forget himself? SHR in.1. 41
love, | he bear himself with honorable action, in.1. 110
of love between your daughter and himself; 4.04. 27
which runs himself, and catches for his master. 5.02. 53
he that hangs himself is a virgin; AWW 1.01.138 P
or to the worth | of the great count himself, 3.05. 60
of war that caesar himself could not have 3.06. 53 P
he knows is not to be done, damns himself to do, 3.06. 88 P
is that he will steal himself into a man's favor 3.06. 91 P
that so seriously he does address himself unto? 3.06. 95 P
ring, and thinks himself made in the unchaste 4.03. 18 P
nobility in his proper stream o'erflows himself. 4.03. 25 P
how does he carry himself? 4.03.104 P
he hath confess'd himself to morgan, whom he 4.03.108 P
who knows himself a braggart, | let him fear 4.03.334
that's gone made himself much sport out of him. 4.05. 64 P
look, here he comes himself. 5.02. 18 P
but to himself | the greatest wrong of all. 5.03. 14
plutus himself, | that knows the tinct and 5.03.101
lord, | who hath abus'd me, as he knows himself, 5.03.298
he knows himself my bed he hath defil'd, | and 5.03.300
and most provident in peril, bind himself | (courage TN 1.02. 12
the count himself here hard by woos her. 1.03.107 P
bid the dishonest man mend himself: 1.05. 45 P
the best persuaded of himself, so cramm'd (as he 2.03.150 P
he shall find himself most feelingly personated. 2.03.158 P
in little, and legion himself possess'd him, yet 3.04. 86 P
such passion fly | that he believes himself; 3.04.374
that will use the devil himself with courtesy. 4.02. 33 P
sicilia cannot show himself overkind to bohemia. WT 1.01. 21 P
one | who, in rebellion with himself, will have 1.02.355
and a region | lov'd as he loves himself. 1.02.370
fasten'd and fix'd the shame on't in himself, 2.03. 15
in himself too mighty, | and in his parties, his 2.03. 20
any | but one that's here — and that's himself; 2.03. 84
for he | the sacred honor of himself, his 2.03. 85
hazard of | all incertainties himself commended, 3.02.169
so grieving | that he shuts up himself — 4.01. 19
if never, yet that time himself doth say, | he 4.01. 31
and boasts himself | to have a worthy feeding; 4.04.168
reason my son | should choose himself a wife, 4.04.407
that makes himself (but for our honor therein) 4.04.436
the prince himself is about a piece of iniquity: 4.04.678 P
a new ship to purge melancholy and air himself; 4.04.763 P
one that gives out himself prince florizel, 5.01. 85
he had himself | the lands and waters 'twixt 5.01.143
sir, | bohemia greets you from himself by me; 5.01.181
ready to leap out of himself for joy of his 5.02. 49 P
had he himself eternity and could put breath 5.02. 98 P
to be much sea-sick, and himself little better, 5.02.119 P
grief from you as he | will piece up in himself. 5.03. 56
lay, | as i have heard my father speak himself, JN 1.01.107
your just demands, | hath put himself in arms. 2.01. 57
no, not death himself | in mortal fury half so 2.01.453
he doth espy | himself love's traitor. 2.01.507
who in that sale sells pardon from himself; 3.01.167
his head, | unless he do submit himself to rome. 3.01.194
life, | but hold himself safe in his prisonment. 3.04.161
was | before the child himself felt he was sick. 4.02. 88
the king hath dispossess'd himself of us. 4.03. 23
murther, as hating what himself hath done, 4.03. 37
the purse of rich prosperity | as lewis himself; 5.02. 62
king john hath reconcil'd | himself to rome, his 5.02. 70
stands here for god, his sovereign, and himself, R2 1.03.105
both to defend himself and to approve | henry of 1.03.112
direct not him whose way himself will choose, 2.01. 29
the king is not himself, but basely led | by 2.01.241
find shapes of grief, more than himself, to wail 2.02. 22
the banish'd bullingbrook repeals himself, | and 2.02. 49
see, see, king richard doth himself appear, | as 3.03. 62
gaunt, | and by the worth and honor of himself, 3.03.110
hath now himself met with the fall of leaf. 3.04. 49
had he done so, himself had borne the crown, 3.04. 65
in your lord's scale is nothing but himself, 3.04. 85
besides himself, are all the english peers, 3.04. 88
with works of war, retir'd himself | to italy, 4.01. 96
inferior breath, | and he himself not present? 4.01.129
bound to himself! 5.02. 67
hath held his current and defil'd himself! 5.03. 63
which makes him prune himself, and bristle up 1H4 1.01. 98
and the blessed sun himself a fair hot wench in 1.02. 9 P
that, when he please again to be himself, 1.02.200
guns | he would himself have been a soldier. 1.03. 64
and curbs himself even of his natural scope 3.01.169
streets, | enfeoff'd himself to popularity, 3.02. 69
the king himself is to be fear'd as the lion. 3.03.149 P
letters from him! why comes he not himself? 4.01. 15
the king himself in person is set forth, | or 4.01. 91
that not a horse is half the half of himself. 4.03. 24
indeed, | he made a blushing cital of himself, 5.02. 61
semblably furnish'd like the king himself. 5.03. 21
the king himself, who, douglas, grieves at heart 5.04. 29
if not, let him kill the next percy himself. 5.04.142 P
but at the gate, | and he himself will answer. 2H4 1.01. 6
he that buckles himself in my belt cannot live 1.02.138 P
it was, my lord, who lin'd himself with hope, 1.03. 27
flatt'ring himself in project of a power | much 1.03. 29
against the welsh, himself and harry monmouth; 1.03. 83
that, as oft as he has occasion to name himself; 2.02.111 P
see falstaff bestow himself to-night in his true 2.02.169 P
for the prince himself is such another, the 2.04.253 P
to us th' /imagin'd voice of god himself, | the 4.02. 19
is able to speak for himself, when a knave is 5.01. 46 P
then should the warlike harry, like himself, H5 pr 5
convey'd himself as th' heir to th' lady lingare 1.02. 74
was no need to trouble himself with any such 2.03. 21 P
king | come here himself to question our delay; 2.04.142
is digt himself four yard under the countermines 3.02. 62 P
to grace himself at his return into london under 3.06. 68 P
though france himself and such another neighbor 3.06.157

go bid thy master well advise himself. 3.06.159
marry, he told me so himself, and he said he 3.07.107 P
weed, | and make a moral of the devil himself. 4.01. 12
he could wish himself in thames up to the neck; 4.01.115 P
he would not wish himself any where but where he 4.01.119 P
the king himself hath a heavy reckoning to make, 4.01.134 P
to–morrow the king himself will be a clipper. 4.01.228 P
the king himself is rode to view their battle. 4.03. 2
and he esteems himself happy that he hath fall'n 4.04. 60 P
as lucifer and belzebub himself, it is necessary 4.07.138 P
that shall find himself aggrief'd at this glove; 4.07.162 P
signal, and ostent | quite from himself to god. 5.pr. 22
to crown himself king and suppress the prince. 1H6 1.03. 68
that talbot is but shadow of himself? 2.03. 62
age, | let dying mortimer here rest himself. 2.05. 2
must he be then as shadow of himself? 5.04.133
he being of age to govern of himself? 2H6 1.01.166
and demean himself | unlike the ruler of a 1.01.188
if york have ill demean'd himself in france, 1.03.103
the king is old enough himself | to give his 1.03.116
pray god the duke of york excuse himself! 1.03.178
henry will to himself | protector be, and god 2.03. 23
and humphrey duke of gloucester scarce himself, 2.03. 40
with what a majesty he bears himself, | how 3.01. 6
how proud, how peremptory, and unlike himself? 3.01. 8
cade | oppose himself against a troop of kerns, 3.01.361
be encount'red with a man as good as himself. 4.02.116 P
jack cade proclaims himself lord mortimer, 4.04. 28
and vows to crown himself in westminster. 4.04. 31
york doth present himself unto your highness. 5.01. 59
makes him oppose himself against his king. 5.01.133
call buckingham, and bid him arm himself. 5.01.192
nor he that loves himself | hath not essentially 5.02. 38
cheer'd up the drooping army, and himself, 3H6 1.01. 6
what good is this to england and himself! 1.01.177
but hercules himself must yield to odds; 2.01. 53
it seems | as may beseem a monarch like himself. 3.03.122
but most himself if he could see his shame. 3.03.185
shame on himself! 3.03.192
beat down edward's guard, | and seize himself; 4.02. 24
till warwick or himself be quite suppress'd. 4.03. 6
him, | while he himself keeps in the cold field? 4.03. 14
edward will always bear himself as king. 4.03. 45
/comes hunting this way to disport himself. 4.05. 8
and himself | likely in time to bless a regal 4.06. 73
ay, now my sovereign speaketh like himself, 4.07. 67
and make him of like spirit to himself. 5.04. 47
ay, and forswore himself — which jesu pardon! R3 1.03.135
to trust to himself and live without it. 1.04.143 P
even in his /own garments, and did give himself 2.01.117
and may direct his course as please himself, 2.02.129
and, in his full and ripened years, himself, 2.03. 14
uncle, | he prettily and aptly taunts himself: 3.01.134
in happy time, here comes the duke himself. 3.04. 21
but nothing /spake in warrant from himself. 3.07. 33
scatter'd, | and he himself wand'red away alone, 4.04.512
thomas the earl of surrey and himself, | much 5.03. 69
before, and he begins | a new hell in himself. H8 1.01. 72
o' th' combination drew | as himself pleas'd; 1.01.170
and never seek for aid out of himself. 1.02.114
after all this, how did he bear himself? 2.01. 30
but he fell to himself again, and sweetly | in 2.01. 35
pray god he do, he'll never know himself else. 2.02. 22
of nobleness in any person | out of himself? 3.02. 13
strange postures | we have seen him set himself. 3.02.119
it must be himself then. 3.02.251
which he himself | foretold should be his last, 4.02. 26
stomach, ever ranking | himself with princes; 4.02. 35
for then, and not till then, he felt himself, 4.02. 65
'tis just to each of them; he is himself. TRO 1.02. 71 P
himself? alas, poor troilus, i would he were! 1.02. 72 P
himself? 1.02. 76 P
he's not himself. 1.02. 76 P
would 'a were himself! 1.02. 77 P
an universal prey, | and last eat up himself. 1.03.124
if that the prais'd himself bring the praise 1.03.242
troyan, he is awake, | he tells thee so himself. 1.03.256
ay, but that fool knows not himself. 2.01. 66 P
and worthier than himself | here tend the savage 2.03.125
not think he thinks himself a better man than i 2.03.145 P
he that is proud eats up himself. 2.03.154 P
and yet he loves himself. is't not strange? 2.03.160 P
and speaks not to himself but with a pride 2.03.171
in commotion rages, | and batters down himself. 2.03.176
be led | at your request a little from himself. 2.03.181
such as doth revolve | and ruminate himself, 2.03.188
how he describes himself! 2.03.209 P
commends himself most affectionately to you — 3.01. 66 P
nor doth he of himself know them for aught, 3.03.118
goes up and down the field, asking for himself. 3.03.245 P
th' combat, he'll break't himself in vainglory. 3.03.259 P
for i will throw my glove to death himself 4.04. 63
could promise to himself | a thought of added 4.05.144
here comes himself to guide you. 5.01. 69
will 'a swagger himself out on 's own eyes? 5.02.136 P
engaging and redeeming of himself | with such a 5.05. 39
but that he pays himself with being proud. COR 1.01. 33 P
now in first seeing he had prov'd himself a man. 1.03. 17 P
he is himself alone, | to answer all the city. 1.04. 51
and that his country's dearer than himself; 1.06. 72
and to remember | with honors like himself. 2.02. 48
he himself stuck not to call us the many–headed 2.03. 16 P
by jove himself, | it makes the consuls base; 3.01.107
depopulate the city, and | be every man himself? 3.01.264
and not unknit himself | the noble knot he made. 4.02. 31
i have heard him say so himself. 4.05.184 P
our general himself makes a mistress of him, 4.05.194 P
of him, sanctifies himself with 's hand, and 4.05.195 P
he bears himself more proudlier, | even to my 4.07. 8
till he had forg'd himself a name a' th' fire 5.01. 14
hath a will to die by himself fears it not from 5.02.105 P
but stand | as if a man were author of himself, 5.03. 36
people, hoping | to purge himself with words. 5.06. 8
ere he express himself or move the people | with 5.06. 54
he is not with himself, let us withdraw. TIT 1.01.368
upon advice did bury ajax | that slew himself; 1.01.380
that hath express'd himself in all his deeds | a 1.01.422
andronicus himself did take it up. 2.03.294
sons, | the emperor himself and all thy foes, 5.02.117
son, | and private in his chamber pens himself, ROM 1.01.138
out, | and makes himself an artificial night. 1.01.140
is to himself (i will not say how true) | but to 1.01.148
true) | but to himself so secret and so close, 1.01.149
he hath hid himself among these trees | to be 2.01. 30
gentlewoman, that god hath made, himself to mar. 2.04.116 P
"for himself to mar," quoth 'a! 2.04.117 P
nurse, that loves to hear himself talk, and will 2.04.147 P
hath romeo slain himself? 3.02. 45
that cop'st with death himself to scape from it; 4.01. 75
few things loves better | than to abhor himself; TIM 1.01. 60
go, | let him have a table by himself, | for he 1.02. 30
thou disease of a friend, and not himself! 3.01. 53
he cross'd himself by't; 3.03. 29 P
how full of valor did he bear himself | in the 3.05. 64
his semblable, yea, himself, timon disdains; 4.03. 22
the quality of flesh | and not believes himself. 4.03.157
it must be a personating of himself; 5.01. 34
for he is set so only to himself, | that nothing 5.01.117
that nothing but himself which looks like man 5.01.118
my tree hath felt the axe, | and hang himself. 5.01.212
than that poor brutus, with himself at war, JC 1.02. 46
villager | than to repute himself a son of rome 1.02.173
smiles in such a sort | as if he mock'd himself, 1.02.206
what said he when he came unto himself? 1.02.262
when he came to himself again, he said, if he 1.02.269 P
all that he can do | is to himself — take 2.01.187
if caesar hide himself, shall they not whisper, 2.02.100
i shall beseech him to befriend himself. 2.04. 30
sake | he finds himself beholding to us all. 3.02. 67
here is himself, marr'd as you see with traitors 3.02.197
doing himself offense, whilst we, lying still, 4.03.201
for the death | which he did give himself — i 5.01.102
he will be found like brutus, like himself. 5.04. 25
for brutus only overcame himself, | and no man 5.05. 56
norway himself, with terrible numbers, MAC 1.02. 51
the raven himself is hoarse | that croaks the 1.05. 38
that hang'd himself on th' expectation of plenty 2.03. 5 P
sir, can you tell | where he bestows himself? 3.06. 24
in a place | from whence himself does fly? 4.02. 8
how he solicits heaven, | himself best knows; 4.03.150
therein the patient | must minister to himself. 5.03. 46
the devil himself could not pronounce a title 5.07. 8
carve for himself, for on his choice depends HAM 1.03. 20
himself the primrose path of dalliance treads, 1.03. 50
him | so much from th' understanding of himself, 2.02. 9
he does confess he feels himself distracted, 3.01. 5
action we do sugar o'er | the devil himself. 3.01. 48
when he himself might his quietus make | with a 3.01. 74
beating puts him thus | from fashion of himself. 3.01.175
this realm dismantled was | of jove himself, and 3.02.283
voice of the king himself for your succession in 3.02.342 P
hyperion's curls, the front of jove himself, 3.04. 56
feeds on this wonder, keeps himself in clouds, 4.05. 89
if the man go to this water and drown himself, 5.01. 17 P
to him and drown him, he drowns not himself; 5.01. 19 P
and must th' inheritor himself have no more, ha? 5.01.112 P
let hercules himself do what he may, | the cat 5.01.291
but to know a man well were to know himself. 5.02.140 P
/'a does well to commend it himself, there are 5.02.184 P
if hamlet from himself be ta'en away, | and when 5.02.234
and when he's not himself does wrong laertes, 5.02.235
served, | it is a poison temper'd by himself. 5.02.328
yet he hath ever but slenderly known himself. LR 1.01.294 P
and himself upbraids us | on every trifle. 1.03. 6
general dependants as in the duke himself also, 1.04. 61 P
'tis his own blame hath put himself from rest, 2.04.290
'tis best to give him way, he leads himself. 2.04.298
set a–work by a reprovable badness in himself. 3.05. 8 P
himself in person there? 4.05. 2
i am the king himself. 4.06. 84 P
in his own grace he doth exalt himself, | more 5.03. 67
himself; what say'st thou to him? 5.03.126
the duke himself, | or any of my brothers of the OTH 1.02. 95
he robs himself that spends a bootless grief. 1.03.209
i never found man that knew how to love himself. 1.03.314 P
the moor himself at sea, | and is in full 2.01. 28
fleet, every man put himself into triumph; 2.02. 4 P
that he hath devoted and given up himself to the 2.03.317 P
than what he found himself was apt and true. 5.02.177
and he himself confess'd it but even now, | that 5.02.321
antony | will be himself. ANT 1.01. 43
i shall entreat him | to answer like himself. 2.02. 4
but since the cuckoo builds not for himself, 2.06. 28
not he that himself is not so; 2.06.125 P
them to his entreaty, and himself to th' drink. 2.07. 8 P
cleopatra and himself in chairs of gold | were 3.06. 4
had our general | been what he knew himself, it 3.10. 26
may seem to spend his fury | upon himself. 4.06. 10
great herod to incline himself to caesar | and 4.06. 13
caesar himself has work, and our oppression 4.07. 2
set before him, | he needs must see himself. 5.01. 35
but i know the devil himself will not eat a 5.02.273 P
i see him rouse himself | to praise my noble act 5.02.284
i do extend him, sir, within himself, | crush CYM 1.01. 25
that our great king himself doth woo me oft 1.05. 14
in himself, 'tis much; 1.06. 79
and himself. 1.06.113
he's a strange fellow himself, and knows it not. 2.01. 35 P
and towards himself, his goodness forespent on 2.03. 59
the present wrath | he hath against himself. 2.04.152
a golden crown and call'd | himself a king. 3.01. 61
and puts himself in posture | that acts my words 3.03. 94
us, | play judge and executioner all himself, 4.02.128
the king himself | of his wings destitute, the 5.03. 4
as a lion's whelp shall, to himself unknown, 5.04.138 P
as a lion's whelp shall, to himself unknown, 5.05.436 P
a bride | for embracements even of jove himself; PER 1.01. 7
to show his sorrow, he'd correct himself; 1.03. 22
so puts himself unto the shipman's toil, | with 1.03. 23
lord has /betook himself to unknown travels; 1.03. 34
man, of pelf, | ne aught escapend but himself; 2.ch. 36
who is the first that doth prefer himself? 2.02. 17
who is the second that presents himself? 2.02. 23
last, the which the knight himself | with such a 2.02. 40
names himself pericles, | a gentleman of tyre, 2.03. 86
i think | theseus cannot be umpire to himself, TNK 1.03. 45
the duke himself came privately in the night, 2.01. 46 P
fair boy certain, but a fool | to love himself. 2.02.121
might not a man well lose himself and love her? 2.02.155
if he dare make himself a worthy lover, | yet in 2.02.251
how bravely may he bear himself to win her, | if 2.02.254
where he himself will edify the duke | most 2.03. 52
the duke himself | will be in person there. 2.03. 65
here love himself sits smiling. 4.02. 14
and casts himself th' accounts | of all his hay 5.02. 58
rising 'gainst him that god himself installs, STM II.C 105
narcissus so himself himself forsook, | and died VEN 161
narcissus so himself himself forsook, | and died 161
love made those hollows, if himself were slain, 243
doth call himself affection's sentinel, | gives 650
to recreate himself when he hath song, | the 1095
since he himself is reft from her by death. 1174
to grow unto himself was his desire, | and so 1180
fight, | and every one to rest himself betakes, LUC 125
lust, | and for himself himself he must forsake: 157
lust, | and for himself himself he must forsake: 157
just | when he himself himself confounds, 160
just | when he himself himself confounds, 160
so from himself impiety hath wrought, | that for 341
dead–killing eye | he rouseth up himself, and 541
till, like a jade, self–will himself doth tire. 707
for now against himself he sounds this doom, 717
he scowls and hates himself for his offense, 738
let him have time against himself to rave, | let 982
mad, | himself himself seek every hour to kill! 998
mad, | himself himself seek every hour to kill! 998
himself behind | was left unseen, save to the 1425
himself on her self–slaught'red body threw, 1733
drown'd | when as himself to singing he betakes. PP 8.12
to death, | wish'd himself the heavens' breath. 16. 8
an ethiope were, | and deny himself for jove, 16.17
that on himself such murd'rous shame commits. SON 9.14
heart in love with sighs himself doth smother, 47. 4
accomplish'd in himself, not in his case; LC 116

HINC 1 FR 0.0001 REL FR 0 V 1 P
accusativo, hinc. WIV 4.01. 45 P

/HINCKLEY 1 FR 0.0001 REL FR 0 V 1 P
wages, about the sack he lost at /hinckley fair? 2H4 5.01. 24 P

HIND* 11 FR 0.0012 REL FR 9 V 2 P
thou want'st breaking, out upon thee, hind! ERR 3.01. 77
took in the park with the rational hind costard. LLL 1.02.118 P
the mild hind | makes speed to catch the tiger MND 2.01.232
if a hart do lack a hind, | let him seek out AYL 3.02.101
the hind that would be mated by the lion | must AWW 1.01. 91
you are a shallow, cowardly hind, and you lie. 1H4 2.03. 15 P
the tiger now hath seiz'd the gentle hind; R3 2.04. 50
pard to the hind, or step–dame to her son, | yea TRO 3.02.194
but yield me to the veriest hind that shall CYM 5.03. 77
legs, on his hind hoofs | /... on end he stands, TNK 5.04. 76
like a white hind under the gripe's sharp claws, LUC 543

HINDER 14 FR 0.0015 REL FR 13 V 1 P
and hinder them from what this ecstasy | may now TMP 3.03.108
then let me go, and hinder not my course: TGV 2.07. 33
these be the stops that hinder study quite, LLL 1.01. 70
of laughter, hinder not the honor of his design. AWW 3.06. 41 P
which to hinder | were (in your love) a whip to WT 1.02. 24
who shall hinder me? R2 2.02. 67
lurking in our way | to hinder our beginnings. H5 2.02.187
till then fair hope must hinder live's decay; 3H6 4.04. 16
hearts, | that no dissension hinder government. 4.06. 40
who shall hinder me to wail and weep, | to chide R3 2.02. 34
from your affairs | i hinder you too long. H8 5.01. 54
oppos'd to hinder me, should stop my way, | /but TRO 5.03. 57
let me not hinder, cassius, your desires; JC 1.02. 30
dreaded act which thou | so sought'st to hinder. ANT 5.02.332

HINDERED 1 FR 0.0001 REL FR 1 V 0 P
but when his fair course is not hindered, | he TGV 2.07. 27

HINDER–LEGS 1 FR 0.0001 REL FR 1 V 0 P
stands on his hinder–legs with list'ning ear, VEN 698

HINDERS 1 FR 0.0001 REL FR 1 V 0 P
why, get you gone. who is't that hinders you? MND 3.02.318

/HINDMOST 1 FR 0.0001 REL FR 1 V 0 P
they all rush by | and leave you /hindmost; TRO 3.03.160

HINDMOST 2 FR 0.0002 REL FR 2 V 0 P
'tis not his wont to be the hindmost man, | what 2H6 3.01. 2
whose love to you | (though words come hindmost) SON 85.12

HIND'RED 7 FR 0.0008 REL FR 5 V 2 P
and then were you hind'red by the sergeant to ERR 4.03. 39 P
i am sorry, sir, that i have hind'red you, | but 5.01. 1
seems his sleeps were hind'red by thy railing, 5.01. 71
say'st his sports were hind'red by thy brawls: 5.01. 77
disgrac'd me, and hind'red me half a million, MV 3.01. 55 P
if we be hind'red, | we shall your tawny ground H5 3.06.160
but oft have hind'red, oft, | the passages made H8 2.04.165

HIND'RING 2 FR 0.0002 REL FR 2 V 0 P
you minimus, of hind'ring knot–grass made; MND 3.02.329
hind'ring their present fall by this dividing; LUC 551

HINDS* 7 FR 0.0008 REL FR 5 V 2 P
a couple of ford's knaves, his hinds, were WIV 3.05. 98 P
he lets me feed with his hinds, bars me the AYL 1.01. 19 P
'tis like the commons, rude unpolish'd hinds, 2H6 3.02.271
rebellious hinds, the filth and scum of kent, 4.02.122
is a ragged multitude | of hinds and peasants, 4.04. 33
art thou drawn among these heartless hinds? ROM 1.01. 66
he were no lion, were not romans hinds. JC 1.03.106

HINGE 2 FR 0.0002 REL FR 2 V 0 P
hinge thy knee, | and let his very breath whom TIM 4.03.211
that the probation bear no hinge nor loop | to OTH 3.03.365

HINGES 2 FR 0.0002 REL FR 2 V 0 P
like strengthless hinges, buckle under life, 2H4 1.01.141
and crook the pregnant hinges of the knee HAM 3.02. 61

HINT 8 FR 0.0009 REL FR 8 V 0 P
it is a hint | that wrings mine eyes to't. TMP 1.02.134
our hint of woe | is common: 2.01. 3
and ready for this hint | when we shall hap to COR 3.03. 23
it was my hint to speak — such was my process OTH 1.03.142
upon this hint i spake: 1.03.166
when the best hint was given him, he not /took't ANT 3.04. 9
take the hint | which my despair proclaims: 3.11. 18
and one | that had a royal lover, took his hint, CYM 5.05.172

HIP 11 FR 0.0012 REL FR 5 V 6 P
quarters, will not measure her from hip to hip. ERR 3.02.111 P

quarters, will not measure her from hip to hip. 3.02.111 P
longer from head to foot than from hip to hip: 3.02.114 P
longer from head to foot than from hip to hip: 3.02.114 P
and a spaniard from the hip upward, no doublet. ADO 3.02. 36 P
if i can catch him once upon the hip, | i will MV 1.03. 46
now, infidel, i have you on the hip. 4.01.334
on, | i'll have our michael cassio on the hip, OTH 2.01.305
there | that does command my rapier from my hip, TNK 1.02. 56
this fellow has a vengeance trick o' th' hip. 2.03. 70
you would have us upon th' hip, would you? STM II.C 18 P

HIPPARCHUS 1 FR 0.0001 REL FR 1 V 0 P
tell him he has | hipparchus, my enfranched ANT 3.13.149

HIPP'D 1 FR 0.0001 REL FR 0 V 1 P
his horse hipp'd, with an old mothy saddle and SHR 3.02. 48 P

HIPPOCRATES *(see hibocrates)*

HIPPOLYTA 10 FR 0.0011 REL FR 10 V 0 P
now, fair hippolyta, our nuptial hour | draws on MND 1.01. 1
hippolyta, i woo'd thee with my sword, | and won 1.01. 16
come, my hippolyta; 1.01.122
titania, | glance at my credit with hippolyta, 2.01. 75
come, hippolyta. 4.01.186
and hippolyta. 4.01.196
honored hippolyta, | most dreaded amazonian, TNK 1.01. 77
the duke has lost hippolyta; 3.01. 1
for hippolyta, | and fair-ey'd emily, upon their 4.01. 7
hippolyta, | i see one eye of yours conceives a 5.03.136

HIPS *(see heps)*

HIPS 5 FR 0.0005 REL FR 4 V 1 P
now, which of your hips has the most profound MM 1.02. 58 P
then the whole quire hold their hips and loff, MND 2.01. 55
of the ocean | too wide for neptune's hips; 2H4 3.01. 51
down their heads, dropping the hides and hips, H5 4.02. 47
each leaning on their elbows and their hips. VEN 44

HIR'D 6 FR 0.0006 REL FR 5 V 1 P
all this wrong, | hir'd to it by your brother. ADO 5.01.300
manage, and to that end riders dearly hir'd; AYL 1.01. 13 P
if you are hir'd for meed, go back again, | and R3 1.04.228
whose arms | are hir'd to bear their staves; MAC 5.07. 18
of no more trust | than love that's hir'd! ANT 5.02.155
with tomboys hir'd with that self exhibition CYM 1.06.122

/HIRE 1 FR 0.0001 REL FR 1 V 0 P
why, this is /hire /and /salary, not revenge. HAM 3.03. 79

HIRE 17 FR 0.0019 REL FR 15 V 2 P
a ship you sent me to, to hire waftage. ERR 4.01. 95
as they write "here is good horse to hire," let ADO 1.01.266 P
streak'd and pied | should fall as jacob's hire, MV 1.03. 80
the thrifty hire i sav'd under your father, AYL 2.03. 39
may it be possible that foreign hire | could out H5 2.02.100
give thee thy hire and send thy soul to hell, 2H6 3.02.225
country's fat shall pay your pains the hire; R3 5.03.258
a threepence bow'd would hire me, | old as i am, H8 2.03. 36
/that's task'd to mow | or all or lose his hire. COR 1.03. 37
as if i had receiv'd them for the hire | of 2.02.149
than crave the hire which first we do deserve. 2.03.114
sirrah, go hire me twenty cunning cooks. ROM 4.02. 2
get me ink and paper, | and hire post-horses; 5.01. 26
matter, get thee gone, | and hire those horses; 5.01. 33
let me hire him too, here's my coxcomb. LR 1.04. 95 P
better guard | but with a knave of common hire, OTH 1.01.125
there, take thy hire, and all the fiends of hell CYM 2.04.129

HIRED 3 FR 0.0003 REL FR 3 V 0 P
humor, | have hired me to undermine the duchess, 2H6 1.02. 98
for here it sleeps, and does no hired harm. TIM 4.03.291
nor by a hired knife, but that self hand | which ANT 5.01. 21

HIREN 2 FR 0.0002 REL FR 0 V 2 P
have we not hiren here? 2H4 2.04.159 P
have we not hiren here? 2.04.175 P

HIRTIUS 1 FR 0.0001 REL FR 1 V 0 P
where thou slew'st | hirtius and pansa, consuls, ANT 1.04. 58

HIS *(also 's*)*

/HIS 75 FR 0.0084 REL FR 64 V 11 P

HIS 7210 FR 0.8150 REL FR 5739 V 1471 P

HISPERIA 1 FR 0.0001 REL FR 1 V 0 P
hisperia, the princess' gentlewoman, | confesses AYL 2.02. 10

HISS 13 FR 0.0014 REL FR 10 V 3 P
with cloven tongues | do hiss me into madness. TMP 2.02. 14
i warrant thee, if i do not act it, hiss me. WIV 3.03. 38 P
so, if any of the audience hiss, you may cry, LLL 5.01.138 P
when roasted crabs hiss in the bowl, | then 5.02.925
a part, whose issue | will hiss me to my grave: WT 1.02.189
their music frightful as the serpent's hiss, 2H6 3.02.326
who in contempt shall hiss at thee again; 4.01. 78
some galled goose of winchester would hiss. TRO 5.10. 54
tag-rag people did not clap him and hiss him, JC 1.02.259 P
that of an hour's age doth hiss the speaker; MAC 4.03.175
and the first sound this child hear be a hiss, TNK pr 16
he will | against his conscience, let him hiss, ep 8
sun doth scorn you and the wind doth hiss you. VEN 1084

HISS'D 1 FR 0.0001 REL FR 1 V 0 P
who, nothing hurt withal, hiss'd him in scorn. ROM 1.01.112

HISSES 3 FR 0.0003 REL FR 2 V 1 P
he leers than i will a serpent when he hisses. TRO 5.01. 90 P
here come and sit, where never serpent hisses, VEN 17
the adder hisses where the sweet birds sing, LUC 871

HISSING 2 FR 0.0002 REL FR 1 V 1 P
a thousand fiends, a thousand hissing snakes, TIT 2.03.100
frying, boiling, hissing, howling, chatt'ring, TNK 4.03. 33 P

HISSING-HOT 1 FR 0.0001 REL FR 0 V 1 P
think of that — hissing-hot — think of that, WIV 3.05.121 P

HIST 2 FR 0.0002 REL FR 2 V 0 P
hist, romeo, hist! ROM 2.02.158
hist, romeo, hist! 2.02.158

HISTORICAL-PASTORAL 1 FR 0.0001 REL FR 0 V 1 P
pastoral, pastoral-comical, historical-pastoral, HAM 2.02.398 P

HISTORY 22 FR 0.0024 REL FR 19 V 3 P
that to th' observer doth thy history | fully MM 1.01. 28
ever read, | could ever hear by tale or history, MND 1.01.133
all, | that ends this strange eventful history, AYL 2.07.164
it is a kind of history. SHR in.2. 141
and what's her history? TN 2.04.109
which is more | than history can pattern, though WT 3.02. 36
there is a history in all men's lives, 2H4 3.01. 80
that may repeat and history his loss | to new 4.01.201
which supply, | admit me chorus to this history; H5 pr 32
either our history shall with full mouth | speak 1.02.230
point | than can my ears that tragic history. 3H6 5.06. 28
the history of all her secret thoughts. R3 3.05. 28
tongue | hath almost ended his live's history. JC 5.05. 40
either for tragedy, comedy, history, pastoral, HAM 2.02.397 P
sir, a whole history. 3.02.298 P
which often leaves the history unspoke | that it LR 1.01.236
thence | and portance in my /travel's history; OTH 1.03.139
obscure prologue to the history of lust and foul 2.01.258 P
think that man, who knows | by history, report, CYM 1.06. 70
this paper is the history of my knowledge 3.05. 99
if i should tell my history, it would seem PER 5.01.118
in many's looks the false heart's history | is SON 93. 7

/HIT 2 FR 0.0002 REL FR 1 V 1 P
pray you let us /hit together; LR 1.01.303 P
find a white that shall her blackness /hit. OTH 2.01.133

HIT 61 FR 0.0069 REL FR 47 V 14 P
he, he — i can never hit on 's name. WIV 3.02. 24 P
not, | nor by what wonder you do hit of mine — ERR 3.02. 30
yours as blunt as the fencer's foils, which hit, ADO 5.02. 14 P
but she herself is hit lower. LLL 4.01.118
have i hit her now? 4.01.118
france was a little boy, as touching the hit it? 4.01.121 P
was a little wench, as touching the hit it. 4.01.124 P
thou canst not hit it, hit it, hit it, | thou 4.01.125
thou canst not hit it, hit it, hit it, | thou 4.01.125
thou canst not hit it, hit it, hit it, | thou 4.01.125
hit it, | thou canst not hit it, my good man. 4.01.126
marvellous well shot, for they both did hit /it. 4.01.130
must shoot nearer, or he'll ne'er hit the clout. 4.01.134
of this purple dye, | hit with cupid's archery, MND 3.02.103
be god's sonties, 'twill be a hard way to hit. MV 2.02. 46 P
what, not one hit? 3.02.267
he that a fool doth very wisely hit | doth very AYL 2.07. 53
thou hast hit it; come sit on me. SHR 2.01.198
this bird you aim'd at, though you hit her not; 5.02. 50
confess, confess, hath he not hit you here? 5.02. 59
'twas i won the wager, though you hit the white, 5.02.186
he blushes, and 'tis hit. AWW 5.03.195
o, for a stone-bow, to hit him in the eye! TN 2.05. 46 P
your father's image is so hit in you | (his very WT 5.01.127
you have hit it. 1H4 2.04.347 P
princes, flesh'd with conquest, aim to hit. 2H4 1.01.149
for that's the golden mark i seek to hit. 2H6 1.01.243
thou hast hit it; 4.02. 19 P
though the edge hath something hit ourselves, 3H6 2.02.166
and therefore level not to hit their lives. R3 4.04.203
i think you have hit the mark; H8 2.01.165
but if i spar'd any | that had a head to hit, 5.03. 24
that fire-drake did i hit three times on the 5.03. 44 P
i miss'd the meteor once, and hit that woman, 5.03. 50 P
if i cannot ward what i would not have hit, i TRO 1.02.268 P
but, hit or miss, | our project's life this 1.03.383
nice conjecture | where thou wilt hit me dead? 4.05.251
aaron, thou hast hit it. TIT 2.01. 97
would you had hit it too! 2.01. 97
a right fair mark, fair coz, is soonest hit. ROM 1.01.207
well, in that hit you miss: 1.01.208
she'll not be hit | with cupid's arrow, she hath 1.01.208
if love be blind, love cannot hit the mark. 2.01. 33
or if not so, then here i hit it right — | our 2.03. 41
thou hast most kindly hit it. 2.04. 55 P
an envious thrust from tybalt hit the life | of 3.01.168
to me, thou mightst have hit upon it here. TIM 4.03.347 P
my former speeches have but hit your thoughts, MAC 3.06. 1
may miss our name, | and hit the woundless air. HAM 4.01. 44
if hamlet give the first or second hit, | or 5.02.268
a hit, a very palpable hit. 5.02.281
a hit, a very palpable hit. 5.02.281
another hit; 5.02.285
my lord, i'll hit him now. 5.02.295
kiss'd the jack upon an up-cast, to be hit away! CYM 2.01. 2 P
their thoughts do hit | the roofs of palaces, 3.03. 83
it, and hit | the innocent mansion of my love, 3.04. 67
whose arm seems far too short to hit me here. PER 1.02. 8
as ever hit my nostril. 3.02. 62
to see, | but hatefully at randon dost thou hit. VEN 940
or as the snail, whose tender horns being hit, 1033

/HITHER 8 FR 0.0009 REL FR 5 V 3 P
/fetch /hither /richard, /that /in /common /view R2 4.01.155
/do /what /service /am /i /sent /for /hither? 4.01.176
/let /it /command /a /mirror /hither /straight, 4.01.265
/all /on /hazard — /and /hither /am /i /come, TRO pr 22
/come /hither /purposely /to /poison /me. TIT 3.02. 73
/that /she /sends /you /to /prison /hither? HAM 2.02.241 P
/come /hither, /mistress. LR 3.06. 49 P
come /hither. OTH 2.01.214 P

HITHER 300 FR 0.0339 REL FR 234 V 66 P
we heav'd thence, | but blessedly holp hither. TMP 1.02. 63
blue-ey'd hag was hither brought with child, 1.02.269
go take this shape | and hither come in't. 1.02.304
how cam'st thou hither? 2.02.120 P
swear by this bottle how thou cam'st hither — i 2.02.121 P
why hath thy queen | summon'd me hither, to this 4.01. 83
come hither from the furrow and be merry. 4.01.135
the trumpery in my house, go bring it hither, 4.01.186
chalk'd forth the way | which brought us hither. 5.01.204
say, how came you hither? 5.01.228
from them, | and were brought moping hither. 5.01.240
come hither, spirit. 5.01.251
i will send him hither to you presently. TGV 2.04. 86
his worth is warrant for his welcome hither, 2.04.102
and julia herself hath brought it hither. 5.04. 99
come hither. WIV 2.01.108 P
your husband's coming hither, woman, with all 3.03.106 P
cannot attain it, why then hark you hither! 3.04. 21
come hither, william; hold up your head; come. 4.01. 17 P
come hither, mistress ford, mistress ford, the 4.02.129 P
call hither, | i say, bid come before us angelo. MM 1.01. 14
come hither to me, master froth. 2.01.203 P
come you hither to me, master tapster. 2.01.212 P
come hither to me, master elbow; 2.01.257 P
come hither, master constable. 2.01.258 P
come hither, sirrah; 4.02. 1 P
call hither barnardine and claudio. 4.02. 60 P
sirrah, bring barnardine hither. 4.03. 20 P
if yet her brother's pardon be come hither. 4.03.108
who knew of your intent and coming hither? 5.01.124
intended 'gainst lord angelo, came i hither, 5.01.154
come hither, goodman bald-pate, do you know me? 5.01.326
come hither, mariana. 5.01.374
come hither, isabel, | your friar is now your 5.01.381
go fetch him hither, let me look upon him. 5.01.469
you spurn me hence, and he will spurn me hither: ERR 2.01. 84
at the door, master, bid them welcome hither. 3.01. 68
be quiet, people. wherefore throng you hither? 5.01. 38
have won his grace to come in person hither, 5.01.116
and immediately | ran hither to your grace, whom 5.01.252
go call the abbess hither. 5.01.281
bring it hither to me in the orchard. ADO 2.03. 4 P
come hither, leonato. 2.03. 89 P
i came hither to tell you, and, circumstances 3.02.102 P
come hither, neighbor seacole. 3.03. 13 P
and bid her come hither. 3.04. 4 P
you come hither, my lord, to marry this lady. 4.01. 4 P
you come hither to be married to this count. 4.01. 9 P
come you hither, sirrah; 4.02. 26 P
and when i send for you, come hither masked. 5.04. 12
or vainly comes th' admired princess hither. LLL 1.01.140
to the swain, bring him festinately hither. 3.01. 6 P
fetch hither the swain, he must carry me a 3.01. 49 P
come hither, come hither. 3.01.105
come hither, come hither. 3.01.105
if to come hither you have measur'd miles, | and 5.02.191
my gentle puck, come hither. MND 2.01.148
if you think i come hither as a lion, it were 3.01. 42 P
come hither; i am here. 3.02.425
me, so it is — | i came with hermia hither. 4.01.151
of this their purpose hither to this wood, | and 4.01.161
this wood, | and i in fury hither followed them, 4.01.162
that came hither in company of the marquis of MV 1.02.114 P
lorenzo and salerio, welcome hither, | if that 3.02.220
to you, i came hither to acquaint you withal, AYL 1.01.132 P
i am heartily glad i came hither to you. 1.01.159 P
are you crept hither to see the wrastling? 1.02.156 P
call him hither, good monsieur le beau. 1.02.163 P
fetch that gallant hither. 2.02. 17
throat, | come hither, come hither, come hither! 2.05. 5
throat, | come hither, come hither, come hither! 2.05. 5
throat, | come hither, come hither, come hither! 2.05. 5
gets, | come hither, come hither, come hither! 2.05. 42
gets, | come hither, come hither, come hither! 2.05. 42
gets, | come hither, come hither, come hither! 2.05. 42
living in your face, | be truly welcome hither. 2.07.195
he sent me hither, stranger as i am, | to tell 4.03.152
heaven brought her, | yea, brought her hither, 5.04.113
well, bring our lady hither to our sight, | and SHR in.2. 74
you, know any such, | prefer them hither; 1.01. 97
sirrah, come hither, 'tis no time to jest, | and 1.01.226
why came i hither but to that intent? 1.02.198
let him that mov'd you hither | remove you hence 2.01.195
wife, | and sent you hither so unlike yourself? 3.02.104
and bid my cousin ferdinand come hither; 4.01.151
away, away, for he is coming hither. 4.01.187
come hither, crack-hemp. 5.01. 45 P
come hither, you rogue. 5.01. 48 P
go fetch them hither. 5.02.103
away, i say, and bring them hither straight. 5.02.105
the business is for helen to come hither. AWW 1.03. 97 P
farewell. — come hither to me. 2.01. 23
speed her foot again, | led hither by pure love. 3.04. 38
well, call him hither, | we are reconcil'd, and 5.03. 20
come hither, count, do you know these women? 5.03.165
find him, and bring him hither. 5.03.204
were you sent hither to praise me? TN 1.05.249 P
a moderate pace i have since arriv'd but hither. 2.02. 4 P
come hither, boy. 2.04. 15
go call him hither. 3.04. 14
come hither, knight; 3.04.377 P
come hither, fabian; 3.04.377 P
a witchcraft drew me hither: 5.01. 76
fetch malvolio hither. 5.01.278
see him deliver'd, fabian, bring him hither. 5.01.315
liege, | he is not guilty of her coming hither. WT 2.03.145
you, sir, come you hither: 2.03.158
on when thou art dead and rotten, come hither. 3.03. 81 P
welcome hither, | as is the spring to th' earth. 5.01.151
at our importance hither is he come | to spread JN 2.01. 7
embrace him, love him, give him welcome hither. 2.01. 11
some trumpet summon hither to the walls | these 2.01.198
have hither march'd to your endamagement. 2.01.209
hither return all gilt with frenchmen's blood. 2.01.316
come hither, little kinsman, hark, a word. 3.03. 18
come hither, hubert. 3.03. 19
but as i travell'd hither through the land, | i 4.02.143
brought hither henry herford thy bold son, R2 1.01. 3
who hither come engaged by my oath | (which god 1.03. 17
both who he is and why he cometh hither | thus 1.03. 27
and wherefore com'st thou hither | before king 1.03. 31
are making hither with all due expedience, | and 2.01.287
hither come | even at his feet to lay my arms 3.03. 38
his coming hither hath no further scope | than 3.03.112
his noble cousin is right welcome hither, | and 3.03.122
pomp | she came adorned hither like sweet may, 5.01. 79
and how comest thou hither, | where no man never 5.05. 69
richard of burdeaux, by me hither brought. 5.06. 33
come hither, francis. 1H4 2.04. 39 P
thou have power to raise him, bring him hither, 3.01. 59
and since your coming hither have done enough 3.01.176
'tis catching hither, even to our camp. 4.01. 30
who is it like should lead his forces hither? 2H4 1.03. 81
come hither, hostess. 2.01.132 P
let him not come hither. 2.04. 72 P
hark thee hither, mistress doll. 2.04.152 P
cousin, that comes hither anon about soldiers? 3.02. 27 P
i have speeded hither with the very extremest 4.03. 34 P
but as my betters are | that led me hither. 4.03. 66
find him, my lord of warwick, chide him hither. 4.05. 62
he is coming hither. 4.05. 87
come hither to me, harry. 4.05. 89
come hither, harry, sit thou by my bed, | and 4.05.181
yea, marry, william cook, bid him come hither. 5.01. 11 P
what wind blew you hither, pistol? 5.03. 85 P
come hither, boy, ask me this slave in french H5 4.04. 23
call yonder fellow hither. 4.07.118
call him hither to me, soldier. 4.07.151 P
a holy maid hither with me i bring, | which by a 1H6 1.02. 51

come hither, captain. 2.02. 59
come hither, you that would be combatants: 4.01.134
and therefore, as we hither came in peace, | so 4.01.160
sirrah, go fetch the beadle hither straight. 2H6 2.01.137
now fetch me a stool hither by and by. 2.01.138 P
masters, i am come hither, as it were, upon my 2.03. 85 P
come hither, gracious sovereign, view this body. 3.02.149
come hither, sirrah, i must examine thee. 4.02. 97 P
head, and bring them both upon two poles hither. 4.07.112 P
the cause why i have brought this army hither 5.01. 35
call hither clifford, bid him come amain, | to 5.01.114
call hither to the stake my two brave bears, 5.01.144
i will, | for hither we have broken in by force. 3H6 1.01. 29
leave off to wonder why i drew you hither | into 4.05. 2
come hither, england's hope. 4.06. 68
in, | for hither will our friends repair to us. 4.07. 15
come hither, bess, and let me kiss my boy. 5.07. 15
and hither have they sent it for her ransom. 5.07. 40
and how cam'st thou hither? R3 1.04. 85
with clarence, and i came hither on my legs. 1.04. 87 P
who sent you hither? 1.04.171
provoke us hither now to slaughter thee. 1.04.225
the young prince be fet | hither to london, to 2.02.122
come hither, catesby. 3.01.157
go call him hither, boy. 4.02. 41
come hither, catesby. 4.02. 50
hark, come hither, tyrrel. 4.02. 78
/ratcliffe, come hither. 4.04.444
and hither make, as great embassadors | from H8 1.04. 55
my lord chamberlain, | prithee come hither. 1.04. 91
when i came hither, i was lord high constable 2.01.102
come hither, gardiner. 2.02.120
who had been hither sent on the debating | /a 2.04.174
i am happily come hither. 5.01. 85
"bring action hither, this cannot go to war." TRO 2.03.136
bear him, | and bring us cressid hither; 3.03. 31
go call thersites hither, sweet patroclus. 3.03.234
know of him, but yet go fetch him hither, go. 4.02. 57 P
good brother, come you hither, | and bring 4.04. 99
of the great combatant | and hale him hither. 4.05. 6
you brace of warlike brothers, welcome hither. 4.05.175
in faith, i do not. come hither once again. 5.02. 49
your passion draws ears hither. 5.02.181
methinks i hear hither your husband's drum; COR 1.03. 29
call him hither. 1.06. 41
that our best water brought by conduits hither, 2.03.242
assemble presently the people hither; 3.03. 12
than all living women | are we come hither; 5.03. 98
steed, | and wand'red hither to an obscure plot, TIT 2.03. 77
these two have 'ticed me hither to this place: 2.03. 92
brought hither in a most unlucky hour, | to find 2.03.251
will send thee hither both thy sons alive, | and 3.01.155
come hither, aaron. 3.01.186
sirrah, come hither, make no more ado, | but 4.03.102
go drag the villain hither by the hair, | nor 4.04. 56
they hither march amain, under conduct | of 4.04. 65
and brought him hither | to use as you think 5.01. 38
publius, come hither! 5.02.151
go fetch them hither to us presently. 5.03. 59
and hither hale that misbelieving moor | to be 5.03.143
come hither, boy, come, come, and learn of us 5.03.160
what dares the slave | come hither, cover'd with ROM 1.05. 56
a villain that is hither come in spite | to 1.05. 62
come hither, nurse. what is yond gentleman? 1.05.128
how camest thou hither, tell me, and wherefore? 2.02. 62
what unaccustom'd cause procures her hither? 3.05. 67
and hither shall he come, an' he and i | will 4.01.115
ay, marry, go, i say, and fetch him hither. 4.02. 30
come hither, man. 5.01. 58
i must indeed, and therefore came i hither. 5.03. 58
for i come hither arm'd against myself. 5.03. 65
hold him in safety till the prince come hither. 5.03.183
that he should hither come as this dire night 5.03.247
the little casket bring me hither. TIM 1.02.158
come hither. 2.02. 35
i was directed hither. 4.03.198
we are hither come to offer you our service. 5.01. 72
come hither, ere my tree hath felt the axe, 5.01.211
he is welcome hither. JC 2.01. 94
send him but hither, and i'll fashion him. 2.01.220
come hither, fellow; which way hast thou been? 2.04. 21
fetch the will hither, and we shall determine 4.01. 8
come hither, sirrah. 5.03. 36
come hither, good volumnius; list a word. 5.05. 15
welcome hither! MAC 1.04. 27
hie thee hither, | that i may pour my spirits in 1.05. 25
english tailor come hither for stealing out of a 2.03. 13 P
my ever gentle cousin, welcome hither. 4.03.161
when i came hither to transport the tidings, 4.03.181
come hither, gentlemen, | and lay your hands HAM 1.05.157
and hither are they coming to offer you service. 2.02.317 P
the actors are come hither, my lord. 2.02.392 P
for we have closely sent for hamlet hither, 3.01. 29
come hither, my dear hamlet, sit by me. 3.02.108 P
i will forestall their repair hither, and say 5.02.218 P
why does the drum come hither? 5.02.361
go you and call my fool hither. LR 1.04. 43 P
go you call hither my fool. 1.04. 77 P
o, you, sir, you, come you hither, sir. 1.04. 78 P
he's coming hither, now i' th' night, i' th' 2.01. 24
since i came hither | (which i can call but now) 2.01. 86
come hither, friend; 3.06. 86
come hither, fellow. 4.01. 53
come with my lady hither. 4.02. 89
come hither, friend, | tell me what more thou 4.02. 96
we came crying hither. 4.06.178
their going hence even as their coming hither, 5.02. 10
come hither, captain; 5.03. 26
come hither, herald. 5.03.107
/you are welcome hither. 5.03.290
for the state affairs | hath hither brought. OTH 1.03. 73
fetch desdemona hither. 1.03.120
come hither, gentle mistress. 1.03.178
come hither, moor: 1.03.192
if she will stir hither, i shall seem to notify 3.01. 28 P
seek him, bid him come hither. 3.04. 18 P
/unsuiting such a man), | cassio came hither. 4.01. 78
bid her come hither; 4.02. 19
pray you, chuck, come hither. 4.02. 24
and call thy husband hither. 4.02.106
send for him hither; 5.02. 67
seek him, and bring him hither. where's alexas? ANT 1.02. 85
come hither, sir. 2.05. 84
that call'd me timelier than my purpose hither; 2.06. 51
we came hither to fight with you. 2.06.102 P
go to, go to. come hither, sir. 3.03. 2
welcome hither! 3.06. 78
friends, come hither: 3.11. 2
when hither | he sends so poor a pinion of his 3.12. 3
help, friends below, let's draw him hither. 4.15. 13
come hither, proculeius. 5.01. 61
come hither, come! 5.02. 47
come hither. CYM 3.05. 81
service thou dost me, fetch that suit hither. 3.05.128 P
pray you fetch him hither. 4.02.251
i am brought hither | among th' italian gentry, 5.01. 17
which fear so grew in me, i hither fled, | under PER 1.02. 80
the sum of this, | brought hither to pentapolis, 3.ch. 34
fetch hither all my boxes in my closet. 3.02. 81
fates had pleas'd you had brought her hither 3.03. 8
well, as for him, he brought his disease hither; 4.02.111 P
pray you come hither a while. 4.02.115 P
had i brought hither a corrupted mind, | thy 4.06.104
and thou by some incensed god sent hither | to 5.01.143
o, come hither, | thou that beget'st him that 5.01.194
that he can hither come so soon | is by your 5.02. 19
makes morris, and the cause that we came hither. TNK 3.05.120
them with her | and hither came to tell you. 4.01.103
come hither, you are a wise man. 4.01.141
and in a desp'rate rage | post hither, this vile LUC 220
"go get me hither paper, ink, and pen, | yet 1289

HITHERTO 9 FR 0.0010 REL FR 9 V 0 P
england, from trent and severn hitherto, | by 1H4 3.01. 73
which hitherto have borne in them | against the H5 5.02. 15
we have been guided by thee hitherto, | and of 1H6 3.03. 9
trust me, my lord, all hitherto goes well, | the 3H6 4.02. 1
which hitherto hath held /my eyes from rest; R3 4.01. 81
hitherto, in all the progress | both of my life H8 5.02. 67
if you have hitherto conceal'd this sight, | let HAM 1.02.246
and hitherto doth love on fortune tend, | for 3.02.206
i am hitherto your daughter. OTH 1.03.185

HITHERWARD 6 FR 0.0006 REL FR 6 V 0 P
the dolphin is preparing hitherward, | where JN 5.07. 59
kerns | is marching hitherward in proud array, 2H6 4.09. 27
by this at dunsmore, marching hitherward. 3H6 5.01. 3
power are forth already, | and only hitherward. COR 1.02. 33
the british pow'rs are marching hitherward. LR 4.04. 21
shore, | a portly sail of ships make hitherward. PER 1.04. 61

HITHERWARDS 2 FR 0.0002 REL FR 2 V 0 P
is marching hitherwards, with him prince john. 1H4 4.01. 89
set forth, | or hitherwards intended speedily, 4.01. 92

HITS 11 FR 0.0012 REL FR 5 V 6 P
and shoot at me, and he that hits me, let him be ADO 1.01.258 P
o, o, petruchio, tranio hits you now. SHR 5.02. 57
and oft it hits | where hope is coldest and AWW 2.01.143
surely as your feet hits the ground they step on TN 3.04.278 P
why, this hits right; TIM 3.01. 6 P
a happiness that often madness hits on, which HAM 2.02.210 P
and him, he shall not exceed you three hits. 5.02.167 P
will gain nothing but my shame and the odd hits. 5.02.178 P
a strange invisible perfume hits the sense | of ANT 2.02.212
from a well-experienc'd archer hits the mark PER 1.01.162
my deepest sense, how hard true sorrow hits, SON 120.10

HITTING 2 FR 0.0002 REL FR 2 V 0 P
hitting a grosser quality, is cried up | for our H8 1.02. 84
her master, hitting | each object with a joy; CYM 5.05.395

HIVE 8 FR 0.0009 REL FR 8 V 0 P
drones hive not with me, | therefore i part with MV 2.05. 48
home, | i quickly were dissolved from my hive, AWW 1.02. 66
we bring it to the hive, and, like the bees, 2H4 4.05. 77
like an angry hive of bees | that want their 2H6 3.02.125
when that the general is not like the hive | to TRO 1.03. 81
in thy weak hive a wand'ring wasp hath crept, LUC 839
the old bees die, the young possess their hive: 1769
upon her head a platted hive of straw, | which LC 8

HIVES 1 FR 0.0001 REL FR 1 V 0 P
are from their hives and houses driven away. 1H6 1.05. 24

HIZZING 1 FR 0.0001 REL FR 1 V 0 P
red burning spits | come hizzing in upon 'em — LR 3.06. 16

/HO 3 FR 0.0003 REL FR 2 V 1 P
ware pencils /ho! LLL 5.02. 43
/a /herald, /ho, /a /herald! LR 5.03.102
what /ho, pilch! PER 2.01. 12 P

HO 207 FR 0.0234 REL FR 162 V 45 P
what ho! TMP 1.02.313
o ho, o ho! 1.02.349
o ho, o ho! 1.02.349
why, how now, ho! 2.01.308
o, ho, monster! 4.01.225 P
what ho! TGV 1.02. 66
what ho! WIV 1.01. 72 P
who's within there, ho? 1.04.131 P
what ho, gossip ford! what ho! 4.02. 9 P
what ho, gossip ford! what ho! 4.02. 10 P
what ho, mistress page! 4.02.166 P
whoa ho, ho! father page! 5.05.177 P
whoa ho, ho! father page! 5.05.177 P
ho! peace be in this place! MM 1.04. 6
what ho! peace here; grace and good company! 3.01. 44
what ho, within! 4.01. 49
what ho, abhorson! where's abhorson, there? 4.02. 19 P
what ho, barnardine! 4.03. 23 P
peace, ho, be here! 4.03.106
ho, by your leave! 4.03.111
who talks within there? ho, open the door! ERR 3.01. 38
ho! ADO 2.01.198 P
a caudle ho! LLL 4.03.172
ho, ho, ho! coward, why com'st thou not? MND 3.02.421
ho, ho, ho! coward, why com'st thou not? 3.02.421
ho, ho, ho! coward, why com'st thou not? 3.02.421
music, ho, music, such as charmeth sleep! 4.01. 83
ho, no, no, no, no! MV 1.03. 15 P
ho! 2.06. 25
sola, sola! wo ha, ho! sola, sola! 5.01. 39 P
come ho, and wake diana with a hymn, | with 5.01. 66
peace ho! 5.01.109
a quarrel ho already! what's the matter? 5.01.146
with a hey, and a ho, and a hey nonino, | that AYL 5.03. 17
with a hey, and a ho, and a hey nonino, | these 5.03. 23
with a hey, and a ho, and a hey nonino, | how 5.03. 27
with a hey, and a ho, and a hey nonino, | for 5.03. 31
peace ho! 5.04.125
holla, ho, curtis! SHR 4.01. 11 P
ho, boy!" 4.01. 41 P
do you hear, ho? 4.01. 98 P
what ho! 4.01.149
o ho, entreat her! 5.02. 87
give me some help here ho! AWW 2.01.209
but couch ho, here he comes, to beguile two 4.01. 22 P
who saw cesario, ho? TN 1.04. 10
what ho, malvolio! 1.05.299
sweet lady, ho, ho. 3.04. 17 P
sweet lady, ho, ho. 3.04. 17 P
o ho, do you come near me now? 3.04. 64 P
what ho, i say! peace in this prison! 4.02. 18 P
with hey ho, the wind and the rain, | a foolish 5.01.390
when i came to man's estate, | with hey ho, etc. 5.01.394
when i came, alas, to wive, | with hey ho, etc. 5.01.398
when i came unto my beds, | with hey ho, etc. 5.01.402
while ago the world begun, | /with hey ho, etc. 5.01.406
/what noise there, ho? WT 2.03. 39
on toward callice, ho! JN 3.03. 73
speak ho! 5.06. 1
ho! R2 5.02. 74
what ho, my liege! for god's sake let me in. 5.03. 74
what ho! chamberlain! 1H4 2.01. 47 P
what ho! is gilliams with the packet gone? 2.03. 65
who keeps the gate here ho? where is the earl? 2H4 1.01. 1
what is the matter? keep the peace here, ho! 2.01. 62 P
look who's at door there ho! 5.03. 71 P
who's within there, ho? 2H6 1.04. 78
ho, who's here? R3 1.04. 84 P
ho! H8 5.02. 3
what ho! TRO 2.03. 21 P
these lovers cry, o ho, they die! 3.01.121
which seems the wound to kill, | doth turn o ho! 3.01.123
o ho! 3.01.125
o ho! 3.01.126
hey ho!" 3.01.126
see, ho! who is that there? 4.01. 1
what, are you up here, ho! speak! 5.02. 1
ho! bid my trumpet sound! 5.03. 13
the bull has the game, ware horns ho! 5.07. 12 P
stand ho! yet are we masters of the field. 5.10. 1
their noise be our instruction. ladders ho! COR 1.04. 22
the aediles ho! let him be apprehended. 3.01.172
what ho! 3.01.185
well, say. peace ho! 3.03. 41
peace ho! 5.06.123
ho, the gibbet-maker? TIT 4.03. 81 P
what noise is this? give me my long sword ho! ROM 1.01. 75
what ho, you men, you beasts! 1.01. 83
come, we burn daylight, ho! 1.04. 43
a bawd, a bawd, a bawd! so ho! 2.04.130 P
light to my chamber ho! 3.04. 33
ho, daughter, are you up? 3.05. 64
what ho! 4.02. 43
what, are you busy, ho? need you my help? 4.03. 6
what ho! 4.04. 24
some aqua-vitae ho! 4.05. 16
peace ho, for shame! 4.05. 65
what ho, apothecary! 5.01. 57
holy franciscan friar! brother, ho! 5.02. 1
ho, ho, confess'd it? hang'd it, have you not? TIM 1.02. 22
ho, ho, confess'd it? hang'd it, have you not? 1.02. 22
ho, ho! i laugh to think that babe a bastard. 1.02.112 P
ho, ho! i laugh to think that babe a bastard. 1.02.112 P
caphis ho! 2.01. 13
speak ho! 5.03. 2
peace ho, caesar speaks. JC 1.02. 1
what, lucius, ho! 2.01. 1
calphurnia in her sleep cried out, | "help, ho! 2.02. 3
peace ho! 3.02. 54
stay ho, and let us hear mark antony. 3.02. 62
peace ho, let us hear him. 3.02. 72
peace ho, hear antony, most noble antony! 3.02.234 P
peace ho! 3.02.246 P
come, brands ho, fire-brands! 3.03. 35 P
stand ho! 4.02. 1
give the word ho! and stand. 4.02. 2
stand ho! 4.02. 32
stand ho! speak the word along. 4.02. 33
ho, lucilius, hark, a word with you. 5.01. 69
come ho, away! 5.01.125
i am the son of marcus cato, ho! 5.04. 4
i am the son of marcus cato, ho! 5.04. 6
room ho! tell antony, brutus is ta'en. 5.04. 16
who's there? what ho! MAC 2.02. 8
help me hence, ho! 2.03.118
give us a light there, ho! 3.03. 9
i think i hear them. stand ho! who is there? HAM 1.01. 14
illo, ho, ho, my lord! 1.05.115
illo, ho, ho, my lord! 1.05.115
hillo, ho, ho, boy! come, /bird, come. 1.05.116
hillo, ho, ho, boy! come, /bird, come. 1.05.116
what ho, horatio! 3.02. 52 P
o ho, do you mark that? 3.02.111 P
help ho! 3.04. 22
what ho, help! 3.04. 23
ho, guildenstern! 4.01. 32
ho, bring in the lord. 4.03. 15
o ho! 4.05. 33 P
with, ho, such bugs and goblins in my life, 5.02. 22
look to the queen there ho! 5.02.303
ho, let the door be lock'd! 5.02.311
dinner, ho, dinner! LR 1.04. 42 P
ho! 1.04. 47 P
what, oswald, ho! 1.04.313
light, ho, here! 2.01. 31
pursue him, ho! go after. by no means what? 2.01. 43
help ho! murther, help! 2.02. 40 P
help ho! murther, murther! 2.02. 43 P
o, ho! 3.02. 24
ho, you, sir! 4.06. 46

o ho, are you there with me? 4.06.145 P
o ho, i know the riddle. — i will go. 5.01. 37
a herald, ho! 5.03.102
what ho! brabantio, signior brabantio, ho! OTH 1.01. 78
what ho! brabantio, signior brabantio, ho! 1.01. 78
what ho, brabantio! 1.01. 79
strike on the tinder, ho! 1.01.140
get weapons, ho! 1.01.181
what ho, what ho, what ho! 1.03. 12
what ho, what ho, what ho! 1.03. 12
what ho, what ho, what ho! 1.03. 12
let's to the sea–side, ho! 2.01. 36
some wine ho! 2.03. 68 P
and your swag–bellied hollander — drink ho! 2.03. 78 P
some wine ho! 2.03. 97 P
/god's /will, gentlemen — | help ho! 2.03.159
diablo, ho! 2.03.161
hold ho! 2.03.166
why, how now ho? 2.03.169
what ho! 4.01. 47
i am maim'd for ever. help ho! murther, murther! 5.01. 27
o, help ho! light! a surgeon! 5.01. 30
what ho! no watch? no passage? murther, murther! 5.01. 37
ho, murther, murther! 5.01. 64
what is the matter ho? who is't that cried? 5.01. 74
my lord, my lord! what ho! my lord, my lord! 5.02. 85
what ho! my lord, my lord! 5.02. 89
help, help ho! 5.02.120
help, help ho, help! 5.02.166
the music, ho! ANT 2.05. 2
strike the vessels ho! 2.07. 97
ho, noble captain, come. 2.07.135
of late, when i cried "ho!" 3.13. 90
ho, ho, ho! 4.02. 36
ho, ho, ho! 4.02. 36
ho, ho, ho! 4.02. 36
eros, ho! 4.12. 42
eros, ho! 4.12. 49
the guard, ho! 4.14.104
what ho! 4.14.129
the guard, what ho! 4.14.129
approach ho, all's not well; caesar's beguil'd. 5.02.323
what ho, pisanio! CYM 1.06.139
what ho, pisanio! 1.06.148
what ho, pisanio! 1.06.155
by your leave ho! 2.03. 65
ho! 3.06. 22
ho! 3.06. 24
soft ho, what trunk is here? 4.02.353
philemon, ho! PER 3.02. 1
ho, gentlemen! my lord calls. 5.01. 7
ho, helicanus! 5.01.180
i should be near the place. ho, cousin palamon! TNK 3.03. 1
shall we dance ho? 3.05. 81
ho there, doctor! 5.02. 18
hold ho! 5.04. 41
peace ho, peace, i charge you keep the peace! STM II.C 28

/HOAR 1 FR 0.0001 REL FR 1 V 0 P
nor | the boding raven, nor /chough /hoar, | nor TNK 1.01. 20

HOAR 6 FR 0.0006 REL FR 5 V 1 P
is something stale and hoar ere it be spent. ROM 2.04.133 P
an old hare hoar, | and an old hare hoar, | is 2.04.134
an old hare hoar, | and an old hare hoar, | is 2.04.135
but a hare that is hoar | is too much for a 2.04.137
make the hoar leprosy ador'd, place thieves, TIM 4.03. 36
hoar the flamen, | that /scolds against the 4.03.155

HOARD 4 FR 0.0004 REL FR 3 V 1 P
fairy that shall seek | the squirrel's hoard, MND 4.01. 36
o, to what purpose dost thou hoard thy words, R2 1.03.253
and learning a mere hoard of gold kept by a 2H4 4.03.115 P
nature hath charg'd me that i hoard them not, LC 220

HOARDED 2 FR 0.0002 REL FR 2 V 0 P
the king, | or any groat i hoarded to my use, 2H6 3.01.113
the hoarded plague a' th' gods | requite your COR 4.02. 11

HOARDING 2 FR 0.0002 REL FR 2 V 0 P
see thou shake the bags | of hoarding abbots, JN 3.03. 8
whose father for his hoarding went to hell? 3H6 2.02. 48

HOARDS 1 FR 0.0001 REL FR 1 V 0 P
life and feeling of her passion | she hoards, to LUC 1318

HOARS 1 FR 0.0001 REL FR 1 V 0 P
for a score, | when it hoars ere it be spent. ROM 2.04.139

HOARSE 6 FR 0.0006 REL FR 5 V 1 P
hawking or spitting or saying we are hoarse, AYL 5.03. 12 P
warwick is hoarse with calling thee to arms. 2H6 5.02. 7
bondage is hoarse, and may not speak aloud, ROM 2.02.160
and make her airy tongue more hoarse than /mine, 2.02.162
the raven himself is hoarse | that croaks the MAC 1.05. 38
and make him, to the scorn of his hoarse throat, TNK 5.01. 88

HOARSELY 1 FR 0.0001 REL FR 1 V 0 P
with untun'd tongue she hoarsely calls her maid, LUC 1214

HOARY 1 FR 0.0001 REL FR 1 V 0 P
that shows his hoary leaves in the glassy stream HAM 4.07.167

HOARY–HEADED 1 FR 0.0001 REL FR 1 V 0 P
hoary–headed frosts | fall in the fresh lap of MND 2.01.107

HOB* 2 FR 0.0002 REL FR 1 V 1 P
hob, nob, is his word; TN 3.04.240 P
should i stand here | to beg of hob and dick, COR 2.03.116

/HOBBIDIDENCE 1 FR 0.0001 REL FR 0 V 1 P
/hobbididence, /prince /of /dumbness; LR 4.01. 60 P

/HOBBY–HORSE 1 FR 0.0001 REL FR 1 V 0 P
then say | my wife's a /hobby–horse, deserves a WT 1.02.276

HOBBY–HORSE 7 FR 0.0008 REL FR 1 V 6 P
"the hobby–horse is forgot." LLL 3.01. 29 P
call'st thou my love "hobby–horse"? 3.01. 30 P
master, the hobby–horse is but a colt, and your 3.01. 31 P
'a suffer not thinking on, with the hobby–horse, HAM 3.02.134 P
is, "for o, for o, the hobby–horse is forgot." 3.02.135 P
there, give it your hobby–horse. OTH 4.01.154 P
and that will founder the best hobby–horse | (if TNK 5.02. 52

HOBBY–HORSES 1 FR 0.0001 REL FR 0 V 1 P
to you, which these hobby–horses must not hear. ADO 3.02. 73 P

HOBGOBLIN 2 FR 0.0002 REL FR 2 V 0 P
crier hobgoblin, make the fairy oyes. WIV 5.05. 41
those, that hobgoblin call you, and sweet puck, MND 2.01. 40

HOBNAILS 2 FR 0.0002 REL FR 0 V 2 P
we shall buy maidenheads as they buy hobnails, 1H4 2.04.363 P
on my knees thou mayst be turn'd to hobnails. 2H6 4.10. 59 P

HOBOY 1 FR 0.0001 REL FR 0 V 1 P
the case of a treble hoboy was a mansion for him 2H4 3.02.326 P

HOC *(also hog*)*

HOC 2 FR 0.0002 REL FR 0 V 2 P
singulariter, nominativo, hic, haec, hoc. WIV 4.01. 41 P
'tis "semper idem," for "obsque hoc nihil est." 2H4 5.05. 28 P

HODGE–PUDDING 1 FR 0.0001 REL FR 0 V 1 P
what, a hodge–pudding? a bag of flax? WIV 5.05.151 P

HOG* *(also hoc)*

HOG* 6 FR 0.0006 REL FR 3 V 3 P
nominativo, hig, hag, hog; WIV 4.01. 42 P
accusativo, /hung, hang, hog. 4.01. 47 P
a hog, a headless bear, sometime a fire, | and MND 3.01.109
like horse, hound, hog, bear, fire, at every 3.01.111
thou elvish–mark'd, abortive, rooting hog! R3 1.03.227
hog in sloth, fox in stealth, wolf in greediness LR 3.04. 93 P

HOGS 2 FR 0.0002 REL FR 0 V 2 P
of christians will raise the price of hogs. MV 3.05. 24 P
shall i keep your hogs and eat husks with them? AYL 1.01. 37 P

HOGSHEAD 5 FR 0.0005 REL FR 0 V 5 P
to bear this away where my hogshead of wine is, TMP 4.01.251 P
he that is likel'est to a hogshead. LLL 4.02. 86 P
of piercing a hogshead! 4.02. 87 P
froth, as you'ld thrust a cork into a hogshead. WT 3.03. 94 P
empty vessel bear such a huge full hogshead? 2H4 2.04. 63 P

HOGSHEADS 1 FR 0.0001 REL FR 0 V 1 P
amongst three or four score hogsheads. 1H4 2.04. 5 P

HOIS'D 1 FR 0.0001 REL FR 1 V 0 P
hois'd sail, and made his course again for R3 4.04.527

HOISE 1 FR 0.0001 REL FR 1 V 0 P
we'll quickly hoise duke humphrey from his seat. 2H6 1.01.169

HOIST 6 FR 0.0006 REL FR 5 V 1 P
there they hoist us, | to cry to th' sea, that TMP 1.02.148
will you hoist sail, sir? here lies your way. TN 1.05.202 P
to have the enginer | hoist with his own petar, HAM 3.04.207
and hoist thee up to the shouting plebeians! ANT 4.12. 34
shall they hoist me up, | and show me to the 5.02. 55
so hoist we | the sails that must these vessels TNK 5.01. 28

HOISTED 2 FR 0.0002 REL FR 2 V 0 P
had hoisted sail and put to sea to–day. ERR 5.01. 21
that i have hoisted sail to all the winds SON 117. 7

HOISTS 1 FR 0.0001 REL FR 1 V 0 P
like a cow in /june — | hoists sails and flies. ANT 3.10. 15

HOLBORN 1 FR 0.0001 REL FR 1 V 0 P
my lord of ely, when i was last in holborn, | i R3 3.04. 31

/HOLD* 6 FR 0.0006 REL FR 5 V 1 P
and this worm–eaten /hold of ragged stone, 2H4 in 35
/to /hold /your /honor /more /precise /and /nice 2.03. 40
/not /sigh, /nor /hold /thy /stumps /to /heaven, TIT 3.02. 42
/and /i /hold /ambition /of /so /airy /and HAM 2.02.261 P
/god's /will, lieutenant, /hold! OTH 2.03.162
yet, if you please to /hold him off awhile, 3.03.248

HOLD* 493 FR 0.0557 REL FR 395 V 98 P
hold notwithstanding their freshness and glosses TMP 2.01. 63 P
do now let loose my opinion, hold it no longer: 2.02. 35 P
did hold his eyes lock'd in her crystal looks. TGV 2.04. 89
and valentine i'll hold an enemy, | aiming at 2.06. 29
proteus, the good conceit i hold of thee | (for 3.02. 17
three things that women highly hold in hate. 3.02. 33
that they may hold excus'd our lawless lives; 4.01. 52
there, hold! 4.04.127
but better indeed, when you hold /your peace. 5.02. 18
if once again, | /milan shall not hold thee. 5.04.129
i hold him but a fool that will endanger | his 5.04.133
divers philosophers hold that the lips is parcel WIV 1.01.229 P
hold, sirrah, bear you these letters tightly; 1.03. 79
vile, | his dove will prove, his gold will hold, 1.03. 98
does he not hold up his head, as it were, and 1.04. 29 P
hold, there's money for thee. 1.04.155 P
come hither, william; hold up your head; come. 4.01. 17 P
hold up your head. 4.01. 19 P
prithee hold thy peace. 4.01. 73 P
hold it out. 4.02.135 P
go, i'll hold. 5.01. 1 P
i say, time wears, hold up your head and mince. 5.01. 7 P
i pray you come, hold up the jest no higher. 5.05.105
to master /brook you yet shall hold your word, 5.05.244
hold therefore, angelo: MM 1.01. 42
i hold you as a thing enskied, and sainted, | by 1.04. 34
if this law hold in vienna ten year, i'll rent 2.01.240 P
hold you there! 3.01.173 P
and hold you ever to our special drift, | though 4.05. 4
no, my good lord, | nor wish'd to hold my peace. 5.01. 79
lay hold on him. 5.01.359
till my tale be heard, | and hold no longer out. 5.01.366
prince, | no longer session hold upon my shame, 5.01.371
hold up your hands, say nothing; 5.01.438
for god sake hold your hands! ERR 1.02. 93
hold, take thou that, and that. 2.02. 23
hold, sir, for god's sake! 2.02. 24
i hold your dainties cheap, sir, and your 3.01. 21
o, soft, sir, hold you still; 3.02. 69
i cannot, nor i will not, hold me still, | my 4.02. 17
good now, hold thy tongue. 4.04. 21 P
nay, rather persuade him to hold his hands. 4.04. 22 P
hold, hurt him not for god sake! 5.01. 33
good people, enter and lay hold on him. 5.01. 91
i will hold friends with you, lady. ADO 1.01. 91 P
we will hold it as a dream till it appear itself 1.02. 20 P
and truly i hold it a sin to match in my kinred. 2.01. 64 P
rather than hold three words' conference with 2.01.270 P
whose estimation do you mightily hold up — to a 2.02. 25 P
come, | or, if thou wilt hold longer argument, 2.03. 53
he hath ta'en th' infection. hold it up. 2.03.121 P
be, when they hold one an opinion of another's 2.03.216 P
to burn the errors that these princes hold 4.01.163
hold you content. 5.01. 92
i'll hold my mind were she an ethiope. 5.04. 38
and hold fair friendship with his majesty. LLL 2.01.140
do not curst wives hold that self–sovereignty 4.01. 36
ah, never faith could hold, if not to beauty 4.02.106
'gainst whom the world cannot hold argument, 4.03. 59
i that hold it sin | to break the vow i am 4.03.175
i never knew man hold vile stuff so dear. 4.03.272
hold, there is the very remuneration i had of 5.01. 72 P
hold, rosaline, this favor thou shalt wear, 5.02.130
hold, take thou this, my sweet, and give me 5.02.132
if you deny to dance, let's hold more chat. 5.02.228
this field shall hold me, and so hold your vow: 5.02.345
this field shall hold me, and so hold your vow: 5.02.345
help, hold his brows! 5.02.392
can any face of brass hold longer out? 5.02.395
he swore that he did hold me dear | as precious 5.02.444
to jaquenetta to hold the plough for her sweet 5.02.883 P
enough; hold, or cut bow–strings. MND 1.02.111 P
then the whole quire hold their hips and loff, 2.01. 55
or let him hold his fingers thus, and through 3.01. 69 P
wink each at other, hold the sweet jest up; 3.02.239
three, | we'll hold a feast in great solemnity. 4.01.185
one sees more devils than vast hell can hold; 5.01. 9
a fortnight hold we this solemnity, | in nightly 5.01.369
i hold the world but as the world, gratiano, | a MV 1.01. 77
means | to hold a rival place with one of them, 1.01.174
hold here, take this. 2.04. 19
what, must i hold a candle to my shames? 2.06. 41
this, | and hold your fortune for your bliss, 3.02.136
duke | will never grant this forfeiture to hold. 3.03. 25
i'll hold thee any wager, | when we are both 3.04. 62
in my faith | to hold opinion with pythagoras, 4.01.131
jew, | the law hath yet another hold on you. 4.01.347
she would not hold out enemy for ever | for 4.01.447
we should hold day with the antipodes, | if you 5.01.127
if with myself i hold intelligence, | or have AYL 1.03. 47
and you that will not, hold your tongues. 2.05. 30 P
hold death a while at the arm's end. 2.06. 9 P
we cannot hold. 5.01. 12 P
comedy, | for so your doctors hold it very meet, SHR in.2. 131
gifts are so good, here's none will hold you. 1.01.106 P
that love should of a sudden take such hold? 1.01.147
he hath the jewel of my life in hold, | his 1.02.119
iron may hold with her, but never lutes. 2.01.146
nay, by saint jamy, | i hold you a penny, | a 3.02. 83
door | to hold my stirrup nor to take my horse? 4.01.121
well, and hold your own in any case | with such 4.04. 6
hold thee that to drink. 4.04. 17
lay hold on him, i charge you, in the duke's 5.01. 88 P
'tis thought your deer does hold you at a bay. 5.02. 56
good must of necessity hold his virtue to you, AWW 1.01. 8 P
lady, | you must hold the credit of your father. 1.01. 78
i have a desire to hold my acquaintance with 2.03.227 P
will this capriccio hold in thee, art sure? 2.03.293
in the world, i will hold a long distance. 3.02. 24 P
i am the caitiff that do hold him to't; 3.02.114
not a hilding, hold me no more in your respect. 3.06. 4 P
by your leave, hold your hands — though i know 4.03.189 P
hold thee, there's my purse. 4.05. 44 P
i saw him hold acquaintance with the waves | so TN 1.02. 16
that if one break, the other will hold; 1.05. 24 P
who of my people hold him in delay? 1.05.104 P
i hold the olive in my hand; 1.05.209 P
with his lord, | nor hold him up with hopes: 1.05.304
"hold thy peace, thou knave," knight? 2.03. 65 P
it begins, "hold thy peace." 2.03. 68 P
i shall never begin if i hold my peace. 2.03. 70 P
or thy affection cannot hold the bent; 2.04. 37
her, | tell her, i hold as giddily as fortune; 2.04. 84
no woman's heart | so big, to hold so much; 2.04. 96
hold, there's expenses for thee. 3.01. 43 P
hold, sir, here's my purse. 3.03. 38
prithee hold thy peace, this is not the way. 3.04.108 P
therefore, if you hold your life at any price, 3.04.230 P
fabian can scarce hold him yonder. 3.04.282 P
o good sir toby, hold! here come the officers. 3.04.319 P
hold, there's half my coffer. 3.04.347
hold, sir, or i'll throw your dagger o'er the 4.01. 28 P
come on, sir, hold! 4.01. 32 P
hold, toby, on thy life i charge thee hold! 4.01. 45
hold, toby, on thy life i charge thee hold! 4.01. 45
thou shalt hold th' opinion of pythagoras ere i 4.02. 58 P
hold little faith, though thou hast too much 5.01.171
you had much ado to make his anchor hold, | when WT 1.02.213
hold your peaces. 2.01.139
one so great and so forlorn | may hold together. 2.02. 21
if the springe hold, the cock's mine. 4.03. 35 P
your resolution cannot hold when 'tis | oppos'd 4.04. 36
it, and witnesses more than my pack will hold. 4.04.284 P
should hold some counsel | in such a business. 4.04.409
not hold thee of our blood, no, not our kin, 4.04.430
sea | with her who here i cannot hold on shore; 4.04.499
what course i mean to hold | shall nothing 4.04.502
for my visitation shall i | hold up before him? 4.04.556
on his side be the worst, yet hold thee, there's 4.04.636 P
i hold it the more knavery to conceal it; 4.04.681 P
for him, and in his right, we hold this town. JN 2.01.268
we for the worthiest hold the right from both. 2.01.282
weigh so even, | we hold our town for neither; 2.01.333
know him in us, that here hold up his right. 2.01.364
but the huge firm earth | can hold it up. 3.01. 73
france, thou mayst hold a serpent by the tongue, 3.01.258
keep in peace that hand which thou dost hold. 3.01.261
and in their rage, i having hold of both, | they 3.01.329
you hold too heinous a respect of grief. 3.04. 90
makes nice of no vild hold to stay him up. 3.04.138
life, | but hold himself safe in his prisonment. 3.04.161
is this your promise? go to, hold your tongue. 4.01. 96
let me not hold my tongue, let me not, hubert; 4.01. 99
if what in rest you have in right you hold, 4.02. 55
we cannot hold mortality's strong hand. 4.02. 82
of all this isle, | three foot of it doth hold; 4.02.100
cloak and center can | hold out this tempest. 4.03.156
we hold our time too precious to be spent | with 5.02.161
in their throng and press to that last hold, 5.07. 19
who can hold a fire in his hand | by thinking on R2 1.03.294
hold out my horse, and i will first be there. 2.01.300
hold, take my ring. 2.02. 92
hold thy peace. 3.04. 47
that seem'd in eating him to hold him up, | are 3.04. 51
he is in the mighty hold | of bullingbrook; 3.04. 83
do these justs and triumphs hold? 5.02. 52
next our council we | will hold at windsor, so 1H4 1.01.104
for i shall never hold that man my friend 1.03. 90
arms, | which now we hold at much uncertainty. 1.03.299
and great oney'rs, such as can hold in, such as 2.01. 77 P
will she hold out water in foul way? 2.01. 84 P
come a hot june and this civil buffeting hold, 2.04.362 P
of art, | and hold me pace in deep experiments. 3.01. 48

and hold their level with thy princely heart? 3.02. 17
which do hold a wing | quite from the flight of 3.02. 30
i hold as little counsel with weak fear | as you 4.03. 11
i saw him hold lord percy at the point, | with 5.04. 21
hold up thy head, vile scot, or thou art like 5.04. 39
or thou art like | never to hold it up again! 5.04. 40
may hold up head without northumberland? 2H4 1.03. 17
good master fang, hold him sure. 2.01. 25 P
but many thousand reasons hold me back. 2.03. 66
have not seen a hulk better stuff'd in the hold. 2.04. 65 P
hold hook and line, say i. 2.04.158 P
doth she hold her own well? 3.02.205 P
hold, wart, traverse! thas, thas, thas. 3.02.272 P
hold, there's a tester for thee. 3.02.276 P
as might hold sortance with his quality, | the 4.01. 11
to a fangless lion, | may offer, but not hold. 4.01.217
to this monstrous form | to hold our safety up. 4.02. 35
and heir from heir shall hold his quarrel up 4.02. 48
no, no, he cannot long hold out these pangs. 4.04.117
how many nobles then should hold their places, 5.02. 17
can this cockpit hold | the vasty fields of H5 pr 11
to hold in right and title of the female; 1.02. 89
they would hold up this salique law | to bar 1.02. 91
die, | if hell and treason hold their promises, 2.pr. 29
fight, but i will wink and hold out mine iron. 2.01. 8 P
i have, and i will hold, the quondam quickly 2.01. 78
hold hard the breath, and bend up every spirit 3.01. 16
what rein can hold licentious wickedness | when 3.03. 22
who twice a day their wither'd hands hold up 4.01.299
and hold their manhoods cheap whiles any speaks 4.03. 66
hand | like a base pander hold the chamber–door 4.05. 14
hold, there is twelvepence for you, and i pray 4.08. 63 P
hold you, there is a groat to heal your pate. 5.01. 58 P
else ne'er could they hold out so as they do. 1H6 1.02. 43
plantagenet, i see, must hold his tongue, | lest 3.01. 61
to hold your slaught'ring hands and keep the 3.01. 87
yet, pucelle, hold thy peace, | if talbot do but 3.02. 58
o, hold me not with silence over–long! 5.03. 13
fell banning hag, enchantress, hold thy tongue! 5.03. 42
nor hold the sceptre in his childish fist, | nor 2H6 1.01.245
image of pride, why should i hold my peace? 1.03.176
which now they hold by force and not by right; 2.02. 30
hold, peter, hold! i confess, i confess treason. 2.03. 93 P
hold, peter, hold! i confess, i confess treason. 2.03. 93 P
he'll wrest the sense and hold us here all day. 3.01.186
hold up thy hand, make signal of thy hope. 3.03. 28
men shall hold of me in capite; 4.07.123 P
here is a hand to hold a sceptre up, | and with 5.01.102
hold, warwick; 5.02. 14
sword, hold thy temper; 5.02. 70
and therefore fortify your hold, my lord. 3H6 1.02. 52
hold, valiant clifford! 1.04. 51
hold, clifford, do not honor him so much | to 1.04. 54
hold you his hands whilest i do set it on. 1.04. 95
to hold thine own and leave thine own with him. 2.02. 42
northumberland, i hold thee reverently. 2.02.109
defy them then, or else hold close thy lips. 2.02.118
for death doth hold us in pursuit. 2.05.127
no way to fly, nor strength to hold out flight. 2.06. 24
but if you mind to hold your true obedience, 4.01.140
i hold it cowardice | to rest mistrustful where 4.02. 7
thou shalt be the third, /and this sword hold. 5.01. 75
that they do hold their course toward tewksbury. 5.03. 19
hold, richard, hold, for we have done too much. 5.05. 43
hold, richard, hold, for we have done too much. 5.05. 43
i can no longer hold me patient. R3 1.03.156
it was wont to hold me but while one tells 1.04.119 P
intelligence or wrong surmise | hold me a foe — 2.01. 56
i fear thy justice will take hold | on me and 2.01.132
doth the news hold of good king edward's death? 2.03. 7
the saying did not hold | in him that did object 2.04. 16
for we to–morrow hold divided councils, 3.01.179
i hold my life as dear as /you /do yours, | and 3.02. 78
god hold it, to your honor's good content! 3.02.105
you have no cause to hold my friendship doubtful 4.04.492
my son george stanley is frank'd up in hold; 4.05. 3
for when they hold 'em, you would swear directly H8 1.03. 8
let me have such a bowl may hold my thanks, 1.04. 39
you hold a fair assembly; 1.04. 87
i hold my most malicious foe, and think not | at 2.04. 83
and all the fellowship i hold now with him | is 3.01.121
witness how dear i hold this confirmation. 5.02.207
a marshalsea shall hold ye play these two months 5.03. 86
if they hold when their ladies bid 'em clap. ep 14
yet hold i off. TRO 1.02.286
hand of greece | should hold up high in brass, 1.03. 64
nay, i must hold you. 2.01. 79 P
i will hold my peace when achilles' /brach bids 2.01.114 P
of that we hold an idol more than he? 2.03.189
sweet, bid me hold my tongue, | for in this 3.02.129
here i hold your hand, here my cousin's. 3.02.198 P
but we in silence hold this virtue well — 4.01. 78
now, ajax, hold thine own! 4.05.114
i prithee do not hold me to mine oath, | bid me 5.02. 26
hold, patience! 5.02. 29
vow, | but vows to every purpose must not hold; 5.03. 24
hold you still, i say; 5.03. 25
lay hold upon him, priam, hold him fast, | he is 5.03. 59
lay hold upon him, priam, hold him fast, | he is 5.03. 59
hold thy whore, grecian! 5.04. 24 P
than have him hold that purpose and to put it COR 2.01.240
stay, hold, peace! 3.01.187
therefore lay hold of him; 3.01.211
that it shall hold companionship in peace | with 3.02. 49
mulberry | that will not hold the handling: 3.02. 80
if you do hold the same intent wherein | you 5.06. 12
hold, hold, hold, hold! 5.06.130
hold, hold, hold, hold! 5.06.130
hold, hold, hold, hold! 5.06.130
hold, hold, hold, hold! 5.06.130
match | i hold me highly honored of your grace, TIT 1.01.245
hold, hold; 4.03.105
hold, hold; 4.03.105
will hold thee dearly for thy mother's sake." 5.01. 36
and whilst i at a banket hold him sure, | i'll 5.02. 76
whiles that lavinia 'tween her stumps doth hold 5.02.182
thou villain capulet! — hold me not, let me go. ROM 1.01. 79
this night i hold an old accustom'd feast, 1.02. 20
enough of this, i pray thee hold thy peace. 1.03. 49
kin, | to strike him dead i hold it not a sin. 1.05. 59
he that can lay hold of her | shall have the 1.05.116
walls, | for stony limits cannot hold love out, 2.02. 67
hold, tybalt! 3.01. 90
romeo he cries aloud, | "hold, friends! 3.01.165
hold thy desperate hand! 3.03.108
hold your tongue, | good prudence, smatter with 3.05.170
hold, daughter! 4.01. 68
hold then. 4.01. 89
hold, get you gone. 4.01.122
hold, take these keys and fetch more spices, 4.04. 1
hold, there is forty ducats; 5.01. 59
hold, take this letter; 5.03. 23
hold him in safety till the prince come hither. 5.03.183
malice | infects one comma in the course i hold, TIM 1.01. 48
mine eyes cannot hold out water, methinks. 1.02.106 P
the worst is filthy, and would not hold taking, 1.02.154 P
it cannot hold, it will not. 2.01. 4
it cannot hold, no reason | can sound his state 2.01. 12
pray'd you | to hold your hand more close. 2.02.139
will't hold? will't hold? 3.06. 62 P
will't hold? will't hold? 3.06. 62 P
bankrupts, hold fast; 4.01. 8
hold up, you sluts, | your aprons mountant. 4.03.135
does the rumor hold for true that he's | so full 5.01. 3
to all the rout, then hold me dangerous. JC 1.02. 78
but wherefore do you hold me here so long? 1.02. 83
ay, if i be alive, and your mind hold, and your 1.02.291 P
hold, my hand. 1.03.117
augurers | may hold him from the capitol to–day. 2.01.201
but there's but one in all doth hold his place. 3.01. 65
canst thou hold up thy heavy eyes awhile, | and 4.03.256
i will not hold thee long. 4.03.265
ill spirit, i would hold more talk with thee. 4.03.288
but hold thee, take this garland on thy brow; 5.03. 85
yet, countrymen! o, yet, hold up your heads! 5.04. 1
i prithee | hold thou my sword–hilts, whilest i 5.05. 28
hold then my sword, and turn away thy face, 5.05. 47
let me infold thee | and hold thee to my heart. MAC 1.04. 32
through the blanket of the dark | to cry, "hold, 1.05. 54
the blanket of the dark | to cry, "hold, hold!" 1.05. 54
hold, take my sword. 2.01. 4
why do we hold our tongues, | that most may 2.03.119
to–night we hold a solemn supper, sir, | and 3.01. 14
thou marvel'st at my words, but hold thee still: 3.02. 54
t' hold what distance | his wisdom can provide. 3.06. 44
when we hold rumor | from what we fear, yet know 4.02. 19
let us rather | hold fast the mortal sword, and 4.03. 3
and damn'd be him that first cries, "hold, 5.08. 34
and will not let belief take hold of him HAM 1.01. 24
but break my heart, for i must hold my tongue. 1.02.159
hold you the watch to–night? 1.02.225
itself should gape | and bid me hold my peace. 1.02.245
favor, | hold it a fashion and a toy in blood, 1.03. 6
hold off your hands. 1.04. 80
o, fie, hold, hold, my heart, | and you, my 1.05. 93
o, fie, hold, hold, my heart, | and you, my 1.05. 93
i hold it fit that we shake hands and part, 1.05.128
good liege | i hold my duty as i hold my soul, 2.02. 44
good liege | i hold my duty as i hold my soul, 2.02. 44
yet i hold it not honesty to have it thus set 2.02.202 P
if you love me, hold not off. 2.02.291 P
do they hold the same estimation they did when i 2.02.334 P
but, if you hold it fit, after the play | let 3.01.181
first and now, was and is, to hold, as 'twere, 3.02. 22 P
/for women's fear and love hold quantity, | in 3.02.167
and with th' incorporal air do hold discourse? 3.04.118
and guildenstern hold their course for england, 4.06. 28 P
that might hold | if this did blast in proof. 4.07.153
venom'd stuck, | our purpose may hold there. 4.07.162
they hold up adam's profession. 5.01. 31 P
corses, that will scarce hold the laying in — 5.01.166 P
hold off the earth a while, | till i have caught 5.01.249
hold off thy hand! 5.01.263
i once did hold it, as our statists do, | a 5.02. 33
willing, and the king hold his purpose, i will 5.02.176 P
know if your pleasure hold to play with laertes, 5.02.198 P
if thou didst ever hold me in thy heart, 5.02.346
my heart and me | hold thee from this for ever. LR 1.01.116
when she was dear to us, we did hold her so, 1.01.196
straight to my sister | to hold my /very course. 1.03. 26
yes, forsooth, i will hold my tongue; 1.04.195 P
their pow'rs, | and hold our lives in mercy. 1.04.327
no contraries hold more antipathy | than i and 2.02. 87
let go thy hold when a great wheel runs down a 2.04. 72 P
will you yet hold? 2.04.198
many people under two commands | hold amity? 2.04.242
and let this tyrannous night take hold upon you, 3.04.151
fellows, hold the chair, | upon these eyes of 3.07. 67
hold your hand, my lord! 3.07. 72
i never done you | than now to bid you hold. 3.07. 75
thou rascal beadle, hold thy bloody hand! 4.06.160
of his fortune take | like hold on thee. 4.06.234
and hold your hand in benediction o'er me. 4.07. 57
know of the duke if his last purpose hold, | or 5.01. 1
t' appear | where you shall hold your session. 5.03. 54
i hold you but a subject of this war, | not as a 5.03. 60
hold, sir. 5.03.156
if there be more, more woeful, hold it in, | for 5.03.203
thou toldst me thou didst hold him in thy hate. OTH 1.01. 7
yet do i hold it very stuff o' th' conscience 1.02. 2
lay hold upon him, if he do resist | subdue him 1.02. 80
hold your hands, | both you of my inclining, and 1.02. 81
nor doth the general care | take hold on me; 1.03. 55
the trust, the office i do hold of you, | not 1.03.118
mountains melt on them, | can hold the mortise? 2.01. 9
that hold their honors in a wary distance, | the 2.03. 56
for i hold him to be unworthy of his place that 2.03.101 P
i pray you, sir, hold your hand. 2.03.151 P
hold, for your lives! 2.03.165
hold ho! 2.03.166
hold! 2.03.168
hold, for shame! 2.03.168
and hold her free, i do beseech your honor. 3.03.255
my father's eye | should hold her loathed, and 3.04. 62
/'zounds, hold your peace. 5.02.219
that can torment him much, and hold him long, 5.02.334
you do not hold the method to enforce | the like ANT 1.03. 7
what hoop should hold us staunch from edge to 2.02.115
to hold you in perpetual amity, | to make you 2.02.124
gods confound thee, dost thou hold there still? 2.05. 92
things to destiny | hold unbewail'd their way. 3.06. 85
our nineteen legions thou shalt hold by land, 3.07. 58
to the vales, | and hold our best advantage. 4.11. 4
yet cannot hold this visible shape, my knave. 4.14. 14
hold, worthy lady, hold! 5.02. 39
hold, worthy lady, hold! 5.02. 39
my ring i hold dear as my finger, 'tis part of CYM 1.04.133 P
will this hold, think you? 1.04.170 P
and the remembrancer of her to hold | the 1.05. 77
can my sides hold, to think that man, who knows 1.06. 69
the heavens hold firm | the walls of thy dear 2.01. 62
another stain, as big as hell can hold, | were 2.04.140
and franchise | shall, by the power we hold, be 3.01. 57
the sharded beetle in a safer hold | than is the 3.03. 20
'tis some savage hold. 3.06. 18
your highness, | hold me your loyal servant. 4.03. 16
thou art my brother, so we'll hold thee ever. 5.05.399
in your imagination hold | this stage the ship, PER 3.ch. 58
cleon, for the babe | cannot hold out to tyrus. 3.01. 79
i hold it ever | virtue and cunning were 3.02. 26
hold, villain! 4.01. 92 P
hold, here's gold for thee. 4.06.105
hold, here's more gold for thee. 4.06.113
to take from you the jewel you hold so dear. 4.06.154 P
do but you hold out | your helping hands, and we TNK pr 25
spinsters, we | should hold you here for ever. 1.03. 24
gods please — to hold here a brave patience, 2.02. 59
do we all hold against the maying? 2.03. 36
hold? | what should ail us? 2.03. 36
away, boys, and hold! 2.03. 59
pray hold your promise; 3.01.100
by th' tail | and with thy teeth thou hold, will 3.05. 50
he refuses, | if it but hold, i kill him with. 3.06. 15
take my sword, i hold it better. 3.06. 89
here's one, if it but hold, i ask no more | for 3.06. 91
hold thy word, theseus. 3.06.136
in your anger, | your reason will not hold it. 3.06.228
till the hour prefix'd, and hold your course. 3.06.304
pray heaven it hold so! 4.01. 16
the file and quality i hold i may | continue in 5.01.161
hold, hold! o, hold, hold, hold! 5.04. 40
hold, hold! o, hold, hold, hold! 5.04. 40
hold, hold! o, hold, hold, hold! 5.04. 40
hold, hold! o, hold, hold, hold! 5.04. 40
hold, hold! o, hold, hold, hold! 5.04. 40
hold ho! 5.04. 41
hold, in the king's name hold! STM II.C 26
hold, in the king's name hold! II.C 26
plague on them, they will not hold their peace. II.C 53 P
hold up thy head, | look in mine eyeballs, there VEN 118
if so, the world will hold thee in disdain, 761
and hold it for no sin | to wish that i their LUC 209
to hold their cursed–blessed fortune long. 866
lest he should hold it her own gross abuse, 1315
these contraries such unity do hold | only to 1558
'gainst whom the world could not hold argument, PP 3. 2
o, never faith could hold, if not to beauty 5. 2
so should that beauty which you hold in lease SON 13. 5
how with this rage shall beauty hold a plea, 65. 3
o, how shall summer's honey breath hold out 65. 5
what strong hand can hold his swift foot back? 65.11
and for the peace of you i hold such strife | as 75. 3
your shallowest help will hold me up afloat, 80. 9
for how do i hold thee but by thy granting, 87. 5
therefore, like her, i sometime hold my tongue, 102.13
that poor retention could not so much hold, 122. 9
in thy power | dost hold time's fickle glass, 126. 2
for nothing hold me, so it please thee hold 136.11
me, so it please thee hold | that nothing me, a 136.11
no want of conscience hold it that i call | her 151.13

HOLD–DOOR 1 FR 0.0001 REL FR 1 V 0 P
brethren and sisters of the hold–door trade, TRO 5.10. 51

HOLDEN 1 FR 0.0001 REL FR 1 V 0 P
holden at bury the first of this next month. 2H6 2.04. 71

HOLDETH 1 FR 0.0001 REL FR 1 V 0 P
thy wife is proud, she holdeth thee in awe, 1H6 1.01. 39

HOLD–FAST 2 FR 0.0002 REL FR 2 V 0 P
and hold–fast is the only dog, my duck; H5 2.03. 52
while in his hold–fast foot the weak mouse LUC 555

HOLDING 22 FR 0.0024 REL FR 18 V 4 P
it lies much in your holding up. MM 3.01.261 P
the fire, | holding a trencher, jesting merrily? LLL 5.02.477
things base and vile, holding no quantity, MND 1.01.232
fate o'errules, that, one man holding troth, | a 3.02. 92
this has no holding, | to swear by him whom i AWW 4.02. 27
least if you make a care | of happy holding her. WT 4.04.356
was casting up of eyes, holding up of hands, 5.02. 47 P
holding th' eternal spirit, against her will, JN 3.04. 18
from this my hand, as holding of the pope, 5.01. 3
holding in disdain the german women | for some H5 1.02. 48
majestical, | holding due course to harflew. 3.pr. 17
holding corioles in the name of rome, | even COR 1.06. 37
the rest will serve | for a short holding. 1.07. 4
dispropertied their freedoms, holding them, | in 2.01.248
holding thy ear close to the hollow ground, | so ROM 5.03. 4
holding a weak supposal of our worth, | or HAM 1.02. 18
and sometimes i am whipt for holding my peace. LR 1.04.185 P
the holding every man shall /bear as loud | as ANT 2.07.111
if in the holding or loss of that you term her CYM 1.04. 96 P
holding out gold that's by the touchstone tried; PER 2.02. 37
holding their course to paphos, where their VEN 1193
the dispers'd air, who, holding lucrece' life, LUC 1805

HOLDING–ANCHOR 1 FR 0.0001 REL FR 1 V 0 P
the cable broke, the holding–anchor lost, | and 3H6 5.04. 4

/HOLDS 2 FR 0.0002 REL FR 0 V 2 P
/and /the /nation /holds /it /no /sin /to /tarre HAM 2.02.353 P
/holds /it /true, /sir, /that /the /duke /of LR 4.07. 84 P

HOLDS 84 FR 0.0095 REL FR 68 V 16 P
sure, i think she holds them prisoners still. TGV 2.04. 92
for gourd and fullam holds, | and high and low WIV 1.03. 85
put them in secret holds, both barnardine and MM 4.03. 87
for my brother, i think he holds you well, and ADO 3.02. 97 P
th' allusion holds in the exchange. LLL 4.02. 41 P
indeed, the collusion holds in the exchange. 4.02. 42 P

i say, th' allusion holds in the exchange. 4.02. 45 P
and i say, the pollution holds in the exchange, 4.02. 46 P
that holds his poll–axe sitting on a close–stool 5.02.577 P
apollo flies, and daphne holds the chase; MND 2.01.231
bond, for i perceive | a weak bond holds you. 3.02.268
now she holds me not; 3.02.335
that ever holds. MV 2.06. 8
that holds this present question in the court? 4.01.172
hymen's bands, | if truth holds true contents. AYL 5.04.130
which holds not color with the time, nor does AWW 2.05. 59
that too much, | which holds him much to have. 3.02. 91
my being here it is that holds thee hence. 3.02.123
this ring he holds | in most rich choice; 3.07. 25
a bold charter, but i thank my god it holds yet. 4.05. 93 P
he holds belzebub at the stave's end as well as TN 5.01.284 P
how she holds up the neb! WT 1.02.183
while i speak this) holds his wife by th' arm, 1.02.193
that holds in chase mine honor up and down? JN 1.01.223
divinely vow'd upon the right | of him it holds, 2.01.238
holds hand with any princess of the world. 2.01.494
why holds thine eye that lamentable rheum, 3.01. 22
for he that holds his kingdom holds the law; 3.01.188
for he that holds his kingdom holds the law; 3.01.188
nothing there holds out | but dover castle. 5.01. 30
yet doth speak, and holds belief | that, being 5.07. 6
by, | which holds but till thy news be uttered, 5.07. 56
look what thy soul holds dear, imagine it | to R2 1.03.286
and holds you dear | as harry duke of herford, 2.01.143
thou sayest well, and it holds well too, for the 1H4 1.02. 30 P
it holds current that i told you yesternight: 2.01. 53 P
o, the father, how he holds his countenance! 2.04.392 P
he holds your temper in a high respect, | and 3.01.168
holds from all soldiers chief majority | and 3.02.109
with me as my dog, and he holds his place, for 2H4 2.02.107 P
holds his infant up | and hangs resolv'd 4.01.210
when down the hill he holds his fierce career? H5 3.03. 23
who, in the conflict that it holds with death, 2H6 3.02.164
with a staff, but that my puissance holds it up. 4.02.164 P
the queen this day here holds her parliament, 3H6 1.01. 35
best, | the proudest he that holds up lancaster, 1.01. 46
for he holds vengeance in his hand, | to hurl R3 1.04.199
he loves me and he holds me dear. 1.04.233
the fear of that holds off my present aid. 4.05. 5
who holds his state at door 'mongst pursuivants, H8 5.02. 24
that holds his honor higher than his ease, | and TRO 1.03.266
it holds his estimate and dignity | as well 2.02. 54
worth | holds in his blood such swoll'n and hot 2.03.173
'tis said he holds you well, and will be led 2.03.180
troy holds him very dear. 3.03. 19
wars and lechery, nothing else holds fashion. 5.02.195 P
life every man holds dear, but the dear man 5.03. 27
holds honor far more precious–dear than life. 5.03. 28
but kneels and holds up hands for fellowship, COR 5.03.175
i know | an idiot holds his bauble for a god, TIT 5.01. 79
more rais'd | than one which holds a trencher. TIM 1.01.120
the great opinion | that rome holds of his name; JC 1.02.319
but one | that unassailable holds on his rank, 3.01. 69
(from whom this tyrant holds the due of birth) MAC 3.06. 25
effect | holds such an enmity with blood of man HAM 1.05. 65
whiles memory holds a seat | in this distracted 1.05. 96
nature her custom holds, | let shame say what it 4.07.187
he holds me well, | the better shall my purpose OTH 1.03.390
carve for his own rage | holds his soul light; 2.03.174
she holds it a vice in her goodness not to do 2.03.321 P
that your royalty | holds idleness your subject, ANT 1.03. 92
she holds her virtue still, and i my mind. CYM 1.04. 64 P
sea, | this jewel holds his building on my arm. PER 2.01.156
he loves you well that holds his life of you. 2.02. 22
blazon, holds me to | this gentleness of answer: TNK 3.01. 47
nigh, | for all askance he holds her in his eye. VEN 342
he bends her fingers, holds her pulses hard, 476
holds he disputation | 'tween frozen conscience LUC 246
holds disputation with each thing she views, 1101
grows | holds in perfection but a little moment; SON 15. 2
my tongue–tied muse in manners holds her still, 85. 1
words come hindmost) holds his rank before. 85.12
nor his own vision holds what it doth catch; 113. 8
whilst her neglected child holds her in chase, 143. 5
HOLD'ST 4 FR 0.0004 REL FR 4 V 0 P
turns to a crow | when thou hold'st up thy hand. MND 3.02.143
and hold'st it fear or sin | to speak a truth. 2H4 1.01. 95
england, if my love thou hold'st at aught — HAM 4.03. 58
thou hold'st a place for which the pained'st PER 4.06.163
/HOLE 1 FR 0.0001 REL FR 1 V 0 P
/just /against /thy /heart /make /thou /a /hole, TIT 3.02. 17
HOLE 25 FR 0.0028 REL FR 18 V 7 P
this shoe, with the hole in it, is my mother, TGV 2.03. 18 P
there's a hole made in your best coat, master WIV 3.05.141 P
of wrong through the little hole of discretion, LLL 5.02.724 P
that had in it a crannied hole or chink, MND 5.01.158
o, kiss me through the hole of this vild wall! 5.01.200
i kiss the wall's hole, not your lips at all. 5.01.201
spit in the hole, man, and tune again. SHR 3.01. 40
a morris for may–day, as the nail to his hole, AWW 2.02. 25 P
the earth had not a hole to hide this deed. JN 4.03. 36
and darts his light through every guilty hole, R2 3.02. 43
what hole in hell were hot enough for him? 1H4 1.02.107 P
if i find a hole in his coat, i will tell him my H5 3.06. 84 P
i'll go hide the body in some hole | till that R3 1.04.280
drag hence her husband to some secret hole, TIT 2.03.129
this is the hole where aaron bid us hide him. 2.03.186
what subtile hole is this, | whose mouth is 2.03.198
from this /unhallow'd and blood–stained hole? 2.03.210
a precious ring that lightens all this hole, 2.03.227
i'll see what hole is here, | and what he is 2.03.246
i train'd thy brethren to that guileful hole, 5.01.104
lolling up and down to hide his bable in a hole. ROM 2.04. 93 P
witness the hole you made in caesar's heart, JC 5.01. 31
clay, | might stop a hole to keep the wind away. HAM 5.01.214
coal, | now couches from the mouse's hole; PER 3.ch. 6
if in this blemish'd fort i make some hole LUC 1175
HOLES 8 FR 0.0009 REL FR 5 V 3 P
he had made two holes in the ale–wive's 2H4 2.02. 82 P
thou make as many holes in an enemy's battle as 3.02.153 P
o, cursed be the hand that made these holes! R3 1.02. 14
and, in the holes | where eyes did once inhabit, 1.04. 29
body | by thee was punched full of deadly holes. 5.03.125
and bears with glasses, elephants with holes, JC 2.01.205
move in't, are the holes where eyes should be, ANT 2.07. 15 P
stop no more holes but what you should. TNK 3.05. 83
HOLIDAM *(also halidom, holidame)*
HOLIDAM 2 FR 0.0002 REL FR 2 V 0 P
now, by my holidam, here comes katherina! SHR 5.02. 99
and, by my holidam, | the pretty wretch left ROM 1.03. 43
HOLIDAME 1 FR 0.0001 REL FR 1 V 0 P
now, by my holidame, | what manner of man are H8 5.01.116
HOLIDAY 12 FR 0.0013 REL FR 6 V 6 P
not a holiday fool there but would give a piece TMP 2.02. 29 P
make holiday; 4.01.136
he writes verses, he speaks holiday, he smells WIV 3.02. 68 P
cousin, thrown upon thee in holiday foolery; AYL 1.03. 14 P
for now i am in a holiday humor, and like enough 4.01. 69 P
a while to work, and after holiday. R2 3.01. 44
with many holiday and lady terms | he questioned 1H4 1.03. 46
being holiday, the beggar's shop is shut. ROM 5.01. 56
is this a holiday? JC 1.01. 2
sir, we make holiday to see caesar, and to 1.01. 30 P
and do you now cull out a holiday? 1.01. 49
it is a holiday to look on them. TNK 2.01. 53 P
/HOLIDAYS 1 FR 0.0001 REL FR 0 V 1 P
and we'll have flesh for /holidays, fish for PER 2.01. 81 P
HOLIDAYS 1 FR 0.0001 REL FR 1 V 0 P
if all the year were playing holidays, | to 1H4 1.02.204
HOLIDAY–TIME 1 FR 0.0001 REL FR 0 V 1 P
love–letters in the holiday–time of my beauty, WIV 2.01. 2 P
HOLIER 2 FR 0.0002 REL FR 2 V 0 P
what holier than, for royalty's repair, | for WT 5.01. 31
profess'd, that you work not | in holier shapes; TIM 4.03.427
HOLIEST 1 FR 0.0001 REL FR 1 V 0 P
a nun, | or sister sanctified, of holiest note, LC 233
HOLILY 3 FR 0.0003 REL FR 2 V 1 P
how holily he works in all his business! H8 2.02. 23
thou wouldst highly, | that wouldst thou holily; MAC 1.05. 21
their sleep who have died holily in their beds. 5.01. 61 P
HOLINESS 13 FR 0.0014 REL FR 12 V 1 P
/see, | in special business from his holiness. MM 3.02.220
and ill it doth beseem your holiness | to ERR 5.01.110
shall give a holiness, a purity, | to the yet JN 4.03. 53
and from his holiness use all your power | to 5.01. 6
should be delivered to his holiness | for 1H6 5.01. 53
but all his mind is bent to holiness, | to 2H6 1.03. 55
that were a state fit for his holiness. 1.03. 64
with such holiness can you do it? 2.01. 26
to bring my whole cause 'fore his holiness, H8 2.04.120
back her appeal | she intends unto his holiness. 2.04.236
how that the cardinal did entreat his holiness 3.02. 32
with all the business | i writ to 's holiness. 3.02.222
i shall sooner rail thee into wit and holiness, TRO 2.01. 16 P
HOLLA *(also alow, hallow*, etc., hollo, hollow*, etc.,'loo, loo)*
HOLLA 12 FR 0.0013 REL FR 8 V 4 P
holla! LLL 5.02.890 P
holla, dennis! AYL 1.01. 87 P
holla! you clown! 2.04. 66
cry "holla" to /thy tongue, i prithee; 3.02.244 P
holla, within! SHR 2.01.108
holla, ho, curtis! 4.01. 11 P
holla, barnardo! HAM 1.01. 18
he that first lights on him | holla the other. LR 3.01. 55
holla, holla! 5.03. 71
holla, holla! 5.03. 71
holla, stand there! OTH 1.02. 56
his flattering "holla," or his "stand, i say"? VEN 284
HOLLAND 2 FR 0.0002 REL FR 0 V 2 P
a true woman, holland of eight shillings an ell. 1H4 3.03. 71 P
have /made /a /shift /to eat up thy holland. 2H4 2.02. 22 P
HOLLANDER 2 FR 0.0002 REL FR 0 V 2 P
and your swag–bellied hollander — drink ho! OTH 2.03. 78 P
he gives your hollander a vomit ere the next 2.03. 84 P
HOLLANDERS 1 FR 0.0001 REL FR 1 V 0 P
with hasty germans and blunt hollanders, | hath 3H6 4.08. 2
HOLLO *(also alow, hallow*, etc., holla, hollow*, etc.,'loo, loo)*
HOLLO 1 FR 0.0001 REL FR 1 V 0 P
hollo, what storm is this? TIT 2.01. 25
HOLLOW* *(also alow, hallow*, etc., holla, hollo, 'loo, loo)*
/HOLLOW* 2 FR 0.0002 REL FR 2 V 0 P
/purely /from /all /hollow //bias–drawing, TRO 4.05.169
/beats /in /this /hollow /prison /of /my /flesh, TIT 3.02. 10
HOLLOW* 51 FR 0.0057 REL FR 45 V 6 P
now, we heard a hollow burst of bellowing | like TMP 2.01.311
that search'd a hollow walnut for his wive's WIV 4.02.164 P
but so sound as things that are hollow. MM 1.02. 56 P
thy bones are hollow; 1.02. 56 P
to view with hollow eye and wrinkled brow | an MV 4.01.270
break–promise, and the most hollow lover, and AYL 4.01.193 P
and fetch shrill echoes from the hollow earth. SHR in.2. 46
lo, how hollow the fiend speaks within him! TN 3.04. 91 P
yea, faith itself to hollow falsehood change! JN 3.01. 95
cheek, | and he will look as hollow as a ghost, 3.04. 84
did grace our hollow parting with a tear. R2 1.04. 9
whose hollow womb inherits nought but bones. 2.01. 83
even through the hollow eyes of death | i spy 2.01.270
and lie full low, grav'd in the hollow ground. 3.02.140
for within the hollow crown | that rounds the 3.02.160
and hid his crisp head in the hollow bank 1H4 1.03.106
asleep, | and in his ear i'll hollow "mortimer!" 1.03.222
and by his hollow whistling in the leaves 5.01. 5
sound | with hollow poverty and emptiness. 2H4 1.03. 75
pack–horses | and hollow pamper'd jades of asia, 2.04.164
his eye is hollow, and he changes much. 4.05. 6
a nest of hollow bosoms, which he fills | with H5 2.pr. 21
face will wither, a full eye will wax hollow; 5.02.162 P
ay, but, i fear me, with a hollow heart. 1H6 3.01.136
the hollow passage of my poison'd voice, | by 5.04.121
wren, | by crying comfort from a hollow breast, 2H6 3.02. 43
for it is known we were but hollow friends? 3.02. 66
i rather wish you foes than hollow friends. 3H6 4.01.139
deep, hollow, treacherous, and full of guile R3 2.01. 38
but cardinal sins and hollow hearts i fear ye. H8 3.01.104
grecian tents do stand | hollow upon this plain, TRO 1.03. 80
hollow upon this plain, so many hollow factions. 1.03. 80
if i fly, martius, | hollow me like a hare. COR 1.08. 7
descend | into this gaping hollow of the earth? TIT 2.03.249
is torn from forth that pretty hollow cage, 3.01. 84
there's not a hollow cave or lurking–place, | no 5.02. 35
thy dear love sworn but hollow perjury, ROM 3.03.128
that pierc'd the fearful hollow of thine ear; 3.05. 3
holding thy ear close to the hollow ground, | so 5.03. 4
to set a gloss on faint deeds, hollow welcomes, TIM 1.02. 16
consumptions sow | in hollow bones of man, 4.03.152
but hollow men, like horses hot at hand, | make JC 4.02. 23
and who in want a hollow friend doth try, HAM 3.02.208
and by the happy hollow of a tree | escap'd the LR 2.03. 2
arise, black vengeance, from the hollow hell! OTH 3.03.447
is hush'd within the hollow mine of earth | and 4.02. 79
our cheeks and hollow eyes do witness it. PER 1.04. 51
/hath stuff'd the hollow vessels with their 1.04. 67
whose hollow womb resounds like heaven's thunder VEN 268
lo in this hollow cradle take thy rest, | my 1185
within your hollow swelling feathered breasts, LUC 1122
HOLLOW'D 2 FR 0.0002 REL FR 2 V 0 P
a cry more tuneable | was never hollow'd to, nor MND 4.01.125
and well have hollow'd | to a deep cry of dogs; TNK 2.05. 11
HOLLOWED 1 FR 0.0001 REL FR 1 V 0 P
lies | as may be hollowed in thy treacherous ear R2 4.01. 54
HOLLOW–EY'D 1 FR 0.0001 REL FR 1 V 0 P
a needy, hollow–ey'd, sharp–looking wretch, | a ERR 5.01.241
HOLLOW–HEARTED 1 FR 0.0001 REL FR 1 V 0 P
throng many doubtful hollow–hearted friends, R3 4.04.435
HOLLOWING 1 FR 0.0001 REL FR 0 V 1 P
leave hollowing, man — here. MV 5.01. 43 P
HOLLOWLY 2 FR 0.0002 REL FR 2 V 0 P
if hollowly, invert | what best is boded me to TMP 3.01. 70
penitence, if it be sound, | or hollowly put on. MM 2.03. 23
HOLLOWMAS *(also hallowmas)*
HOLLOWMAS 1 FR 0.0001 REL FR 1 V 0 P
sent back like hollowmas or short'st of day. R2 5.01. 80
HOLLOWNESS 3 FR 0.0003 REL FR 2 V 1 P
not with the empty hollowness, but weight. R2 1.02. 59
whose low sounds | reverb no hollowness. LR 1.01.154
machinations, hollowness, treachery, and all 1.02.113 P
HOLLOWS 1 FR 0.0001 REL FR 1 V 0 P
love made those hollows, if himself were slain, VEN 243
HOLLY 2 FR 0.0002 REL FR 2 V 0 P
unto the green holly, | most friendship is AYL 2.07.180
/then heigh–ho, the holly! 2.07.182
HOLMEDON 4 FR 0.0004 REL FR 4 V 0 P
and approved scot, | at holmedon met, | where 1H4 1.01. 55
betwixt that holmedon and this seat of ours; 1.01. 65
which harry percy here at holmedon took, | were, 1.03. 24
o douglas, hadst thou fought at holmedon thus, 5.03. 14
HOLMEDON'S 1 FR 0.0001 REL FR 1 V 0 P
did sir walter see | on holmedon's plains. 1H4 1.01. 70
HOLOFERNES 2 FR 0.0002 REL FR 0 V 2 P
truly, master holofernes, the epithites are LLL 4.02. 8 P
perge, good master holofernes, perge, so it 4.02. 53 P
HOLP *(also help'd, holp'st)*
/HOLP 1 FR 0.0001 REL FR 1 V 0 P
thou art my warrior, | i /holp to frame thee. COR 5.03. 63
HOLP 16 FR 0.0018 REL FR 14 V 2 P
we heav'd thence, | but blessedly holp hither. TMP 1.02. 63
a man is well holp up that trusts to you: ERR 4.01. 22
had musty victual, and he hath holp to eat it. ADO 1.01. 50 P
of heart hath holp to effect your ensuing 3.02. 98 P
sir robert never holp to make this leg. JN 1.01.240
for though it have holp mad men to their wits, R2 5.05. 62
our own hands | have holp to make so portly. 1H4 1.03. 13
three times to–day i holp him to his horse, 2H6 5.03. 8
let him thank me that holp to send him thither; R3 1.02.107
that you | have holp to make this rescue? COR 3.01.275
you have holp to ravish your own daughters, and 4.06. 81
holp to reap the fame | which he did end all his 5.06. 35
turn giddy, and be holp by backward turning; ROM 1.02. 47
his spur, hath holp him | to his home before us. MAC 1.06. 23
poor old heart, he holp the heavens to rain. LR 3.07. 62
you holp us, sir, | as you did mean indeed to be CYM 5.05.422
/HOLP'ST 1 FR 0.0001 REL FR 1 V 0 P
i had a rutland too, thou /holp'st to kill him. R3 4.04. 45
HOLP'ST 1 FR 0.0001 REL FR 1 V 0 P
frantic wretch, that holp'st to make me great, TIT 4.04. 59
/HOLY 3 FR 0.0003 REL FR 3 V 0 P
/sincere /and /holy /in /his /thoughts, | /he's 2H4 1.01.202
/as /begging /hermits /in /their /holy /prayers. TIT 3.02. 41
/the /holy /water /from /her /heavenly /eyes, LR 4.03. 30
HOLY 205 FR 0.0231 REL FR 198 V 7 P
and prompt me, plain and holy innocence! TMP 3.01. 82
i' th' name of something holy, sir, why stand 3.03. 94
may | with full and holy rite be minist'red, 4.01. 17
holy gonzalo, honorable man, | mine eyes, ev'n 5.01. 62
commend thy grievance to my holy prayers, | for TGV 1.01. 17
and seal the bargain with a holy kiss. 2.02. 7
but silvia is too fair, too true, too holy, | to 4.02. 5
holy, fair, and wise is she; 4.02. 41
cell, | where i intend holy confession. 4.03. 44
th' offense is holy that she hath committed, WIV 5.05.225
holy father, throw away that thought; MM 1.03. 1
my holy sir, none better knows than you | how i 1.03. 7
most holy sir, i thank you. 3.01. 47
heaven will bear | should be as holy as severe; 3.02.262
he doth with holy abstinence subdue | that in 4.02. 81
the better, given me by so holy a man. 4.03.113
trust not my holy order | if i pervert your 4.03.147
i know him for a man divine and holy, | not 5.01.144
then | advertising and holy to your business, 5.01.383
between you, i shall have a holy head. ERR 2.01. 80
teach sin the carriage of a holy saint; 3.02. 14
'tis holy sport to be a little vain, | when the 3.02. 27
man, | to yield possession to my holy prayers, 4.04. 55
with wholesome syrups, drugs, and holy prayers, 5.01.104
thee | to bind our loves up in a holy band; ADO 3.01.114
give me your hand before this holy friar — | i 5.04. 58
when after that the holy rites are ended, | i'll 5.04. 68
"a holy parcel of the fairest dames | that ever LLL 5.02.160
the holy suit which fain it would convince, 5.02.746
to church | and see the holy edifice of stone, MV 1.01. 30
virtuous, and holy men at their death have good 1.02. 27 P
this jacob from our holy abram was | (as his 1.03. 72
an evil soul producing holy witness | is like a 1.03. 99
and by our holy sabaoth have i sworn | to have 4.01. 36
she doth stray about | by holy crosses, where 5.01. 31
none but a holy hermit and her maid. 5.01. 33
are sanctified and holy traitors to you. AYL 2.03. 13
and have with holy bell been knoll'd to church, 2.07.121
as full of sanctity as the touch of holy bread. 3.04. 14 P

so holy and so perfect is my love, | and in such 3.05. 99
madam, i desire your holy wishes. AWW 1.01. 59 P
madam, i have other holy reasons, such as they 1.03. 32 P
so holy writ in babes hath judgment shown, 2.01.138
holy seems the quarrel | upon your grace's part; 3.01. 4
if you will tarry, holy pilgrim, | but till the 3.05. 39
what is not holy, that we swear not by, | but 4.02. 23
love is holy, | and my integrity ne'er knew the 4.02. 32
which holy undertaking with most austere 4.03. 49 P
now go with me and with this holy man | into the TN 4.03. 23
call forth the holy father. 5.01.142
hands, | attested by the holy close of lips, 5.01.158
you have not dar'd to break the holy seal | nor WT 3.02.129
what were more holy | than to rejoice the former 5.01. 29
you have a holy father, | a graceful gentleman, 5.01.170
her actions shall be holy, as | you hear my 5.03.104
that e'er i put between your holy looks | my ill 5.03.148
heart, | and fought the holy wars in palestine, JN 2.01. 4
day about | shall never see it but a holy day. 3.01. 82
a wicked day, and not a holy day! 3.01. 83
here comes the holy legate of the pope. 3.01.135
to thee, king john, my holy errand is: 3.01.137
why thou against the church, our holy mother, 3.01.141
archbishop | of canterbury, from that holy see? 3.01.144
this, in our foresaid holy father's name, | pope 3.01.145
o holy sir, | my reverend father, let it not be 3.01.248
i will pray | (if ever i remember to be holy) 3.03. 15
thou art /not holy to belie me so, | i am not 3.04. 44
excellence | the incense of a vow, a holy vow, 4.03. 67
now keep your holy word, go meet the french, 5.01. 5
look where the holy legate comes apace, | to 5.02. 65
set the name of right | with holy breath. 5.02. 68
in, | that so stood out against the holy church, 5.02. 71
my holy lord of milan, from the king | i come to 5.02.120
besides a clergyman | of holy reverence, who, i R2 3.03. 29
you holy clergymen, is there no plot | to rid 4.01.324
our holy lives must win a new world's crown, 5.01. 24
i'll make a voyage to the holy land, | to wash 5.06. 49
to chase these pagans in those holy fields, 1H4 1.01. 24
brake off our business for the holy land. 1.01. 48
we must neglect | our holy purpose to jerusalem. 1.01.102
we would, dear lords, unto the holy land. 2H4 3.01.108
your exposition on the holy text | /than now to 4.02. 7
purpose now | to lead out many to the holy land, 4.05.210
which vainly i suppos'd the holy land. 4.05.238
and a true lover of the holy church. H5 1.01. 23
do we all holy rites: 4.08.122
a holy maid hither with me i bring, | which by a 1H6 1.02. 51
join'd, | a holy prophetess new risen up, | is 1.04.102
tut, holy joan was his defensive guard. 2.01. 49
yes, when his holy state is touch'd so near. 3.01. 58
state holy or unhallow'd, what of that? 3.01. 59
if holy churchmen take delight in broils? 3.01.111
we'll set thy statue in some holy place, | and 3.03. 14
virtuous and holy, chosen from above, | by 5.04. 39
now heaven forfend, the holy maid with child? 5.04. 65
his weapons holy saws of sacred writ, | his 2H6 1.03. 58
faith, holy uncle, would't were come to that! 2.01. 37
by chance | or of devotion, to this holy shrine? 2.01. 86
i'll send some holy bishop to entreat; 4.04. 9
now in his life, against your holy oath? 3H6 1.04.105
joy, | to him forthwith in holy wedlock bands. 3.03.243
perhaps thou wilt object my holy oath: 5.01. 89
poor key–cold figure of a holy king, | pale R3 1.02. 5
come now towards chertsey with your holy load, 1.02. 29
by holy paul, they love his grace but lightly 1.03. 45
by god's holy mother, | she hath had too much 1.03.305
with odd old ends stol'n forth of holy writ, 1.03.336
have you that holy feeling in your souls | to 1.04.250
a holy day shall this be kept hereafter. 2.01. 74
we should infringe the holy privilege | of 3.01. 41
you may jest on, but, by the holy rood, | i do 3.02. 75
and when i met this holy man | the men you talk 3.02.116
now, by the holy mother of our lord, | the 3.07. 2
for on that ground i'll make a holy descant — 3.07. 49
be mov'd, | to draw him from his holy exercise. 3.07. 64
when holy and devout religious men | are at 3.07. 92
his hand — | true ornaments to know a holy man. 3.07. 99
come, let us to our holy work again. 3.07.246
when holy harry died, and my sweet son. 4.04. 25
no, by the holy rood, thou know'st it well, 4.04.166
love, | immaculate devotion, holy thoughts, | i 4.04.404
holy king henry and thy fair son edward, 5.01. 4
virtuous and holy, be thou conqueror! 5.03.128
the prayers of holy saints and wronged souls, 5.03.241
this holy fox, | or wolf, or both (for he is H8 1.01.158
certain words | spoke by a holy monk "that oft," 1.02.160
and thank the holy conclave for their loves; 2.02. 99
holy men i thought ye, | upon my soul, two 3.01.102
sir, | for holy offices i have a time; 3.02.144
whilst your great goodness, out of holy pity, 3.02.263
your holy hat to be stamp'd on the king's coin. 3.02.325
as holy oil, edward confessor's crown, | the rod 4.01. 88
by holy mary, butts, there's knavery. 5.02. 33
and, to strengthen | that holy duty, out of dear 5.02.154
by all that's holy, he had better starve | than 5.02.167
holy and heavenly thoughts still counsel her. 5.04. 29
disguise the holy strength of their command, TRO 2.03.127
humbly as they us'd to creep | to holy altars. 3.03. 74
do not count it holy | /to /hurt /by /being 5.03. 19
which show | like graves i' th' holy churchyard. COR 3.03. 51
more holy and profound, than mine own life, | my 3.03.113
gods, | sith priest and holy water are so near, TIT 1.01.323
who hath abandoned her holy groves | to see the 2.03. 58
with my unworthiest hand | this holy shrine, the ROM 1.05. 94
touch, | and palm to palm is holy palmers' kiss. 1.05.100
have not saints lips, and holy palmers too? 1.05.101
remedies | within thy help and holy physic lies. 2.03. 52
save what thou must combine | by holy marriage. 2.03. 61
holy saint francis, what a change is here! 2.03. 65
so smile the heavens upon this holy act, | that 2.06. 1
do thou but close our hands with holy words, 2.06. 6
alone | till holy church incorporate two in one. 2.06. 37
o holy friar, o tell me, holy friar, | where's 3.03. 81
o holy friar, o tell me, holy friar, | where's 3.03. 81
by my holy order, | i thought thy disposition 3.03.114
are you at leisure, holy father, now, | or shall 4.01. 37
till then adieu, and keep this holy kiss. 4.01. 43
by holy lawrence to fall prostrate here | and 4.02. 20
now, afore god, this reverend holy friar, | all 4.02. 31
not, | for he hath still been tried a holy man. 4.03. 29
holy franciscan friar! brother, ho! 5.02. 1
it doth so, holy sir, and there's my master, 5.03.128
of thee | among a sisterhood of holy nuns. 5.03.157
we still have known thee for a holy man. 5.03.270
nor sight of priests in holy vestments bleeding, TIM 4.03.126
giving our holy virgins to the stain | of 5.01.173
say, | the barren, touched in this holy chase, JC 1.02. 8
we'll burn his body in the holy place, | and 3.02.254
thither macduff | is gone to pray the holy king, MAC 3.06. 30
some holy angel | fly to the court of england, 3.06. 45
put on with holy prayers, and 'tis spoken, | to 4.03.154
lord, | with almost all the holy vows of heaven. HAM 1.03.114
most holy and religious fear it is | to keep 3.03. 8
oft bite the holy cords a–twain | which are t' LR 2.02. 74
confirmations strong | as proofs of holy writ; OTH 3.03.324
that the holy priests | bless her when she is ANT 2.02.238
octavia is of a holy, cold, and still 2.06.122 P
it, were it carbuncled | like holy phoebus' car. 4.08. 29
but nothing | (always reserv'd my holy duty) CYM 1.01. 87
such a holy witch | that he enchants societies 1.06.166
and bows you | to a morning's holy office. 3.03. 4
sinon's weeping | did scandal many a holy tear, 3.04. 60
he's honorable, | and doubling that, most holy. 3.04.177
i am asham'd | to look upon the holy sun, to 4.04. 41
the holy eagle | stoop'd, as to foot us. 5.04.115
my tears that fall | prove holy water on thee! 5.05.269
by the holy gods | i cannot rightly say. PER 3.04. 7
she has here spoken holy words to the lord 4.06.133 P
knees, thank the holy gods as loud | as thunder 5.01.198
that, after holy tie and first night's stir, TNK pr 6
from the blest eye | of holy phoebus, but 1.01. 46
wrinching our holy begging in our eyes | to make 1.01.156
let's think this prison holy sanctuary | to keep 2.02. 71
and before the gods | tender their holy prayers. 5.01. 2
before the holy altars of your helpers, | the 5.01. 12
to my petition, | season'd with holy fear. 5.01.149
out from the bowels of her holy altar | with 5.01.164
by holy human law, and common troth, | by heaven LUC 571
decay, | the impious breach of holy wedlock vow; 809
there is no heaven, /be holy then, | when time PP 18.45
how many a holy and obsequious tear | hath dear SON 31. 5
in him those holy antique hours are seen, 68. 9
sweet beauty hath no name, no holy bow'r, | but 127. 7
which borrow'd from this holy fire of love | a 153. 5
pity | and be not of my holy vows afraid. LC 179

HOLY/–ALES 1 FR 0.0001 REL FR 1 V 0 P
at festivals, | on ember–eves and holy/–ales; PER 1.ch. 6

HOLY–CRUEL 1 FR 0.0001 REL FR 1 V 0 P
be not so holy–cruel. AWW 4.02. 32

HOLY–DAY 1 FR 0.0001 REL FR 1 V 0 P
this little one shall make it holy–day. H8 5.04. 76

HOLY–ROOD 1 FR 0.0001 REL FR 1 V 0 P
on holy–rood day, the gallant hotspur there, 1H4 1.01. 52

HOLY–THISTLE 1 FR 0.0001 REL FR 0 V 1 P
i meant plain holy–thistle. ADO 3.04. 80 P

HOLY–THOUGHTED 1 FR 0.0001 REL FR 1 V 0 P
and holy–thoughted lucrece to their sight | must LUC 384

HOLY–WATER 1 FR 0.0001 REL FR 0 V 1 P
court holy–water in a dry house is better than LR 3.02. 10 P

HOMAGE 17 FR 0.0019 REL FR 14 V 3 P
to give him annual tribute, do him homage, TMP 1.02.113
of homage, and i know not how much tribute, 1.02.124
we'll do thee homage and be rul'd by thee, TGV 4.01. 64
i know his eye doth homage otherwise, | or else ERR 2.01.104
of mine, | nor to her bed no homage do i owe: 3.02. 43
when they do homage to this simple peasant. SHR in.1. 135
bring no overture of war, no taxation of homage; TN 1.05.209 P
sue | his livery, and deny his off'red homage, R2 2.01.204
a monarch, and his countenance enforces homage. H5 3.07. 29 P
drink'st thou oft, in stead of homage sweet, 4.01.250
yours, | and do him homage as obedient subjects, 1H6 4.02. 7
and after all this fearful homage done, | give 2H6 3.02.224
do faithful homage and receive free honors; MAC 3.06. 36
and thy free awe | pays homage to us — thou HAM 4.03. 62
have lin'd their coats, | do themselves homage. OTH 1.01. 54
at fifty, to whom herod of jewry may do homage. ANT 1.02. 29 P
eye | doth homage to his new–appearing sight, SON 7. 3

HOMAGER 1 FR 0.0001 REL FR 1 V 0 P
and that blood of thine | is caesar's homager; ANT 1.01. 31

HOME 350 FR 0.0395 REL FR 271 V 79 P
float | bound sadly home for naples, | supposing TMP 1.02.235
he will carry this island home in his pocket, 2.01. 91 P
i'll bring my wood home faster. 2.02. 72 P
did lie, | though fools at home condemn 'em. 3.03. 27
pay thy graces | home both in word and deed. 5.01. 71
than (living dully sluggardiz'd at home) | wear TGV 1.01. 7
as much to you at home; and so farewell. 1.01. 62
would suffer him to spend his youth at home, 1.03. 5
you | to let him spend his time no more at home, 1.03. 14
i'll leave you to confer of home affairs; 2.04.119
if you think so, then stay at home and go not. 2.07. 62
this, | that presently you hie you home to bed. 4.02. 94
your message done, hie home unto my chamber, 4.04. 88
cancel all grudge, repeal thee home again, 5.04.143
i doubt he be not well, that he comes not home. WIV 1.04. 42 P
get you home; 2.01.153 P
master ford her husband will be from home. 2.02. 88 P
worship that her husband is seldom from home, 2.02.101 P
doctor caius, i am come to fetch you home. 2.03. 52 P
truly, sir, to see your wife. is she at home? 3.02. 12 P
is your wife at home indeed? 3.02. 26 P
i have good cheer at home, and i pray you all go 3.02. 52 P
heartily, some of you go home with me to dinner. 3.02. 80 P
go home, john rugby, i come anon. 3.02. 86 P
get you home, boy. 4.01. 85 P
who's at home besides yourself? 4.02. 12 P
the spirit, | and mock him home to windsor. 4.04. 65
good husband, let us every one go home, | and 5.05.241
who may, in th' ambush of my name, strike home, MM 1.03. 41
i pray you home to dinner with me. 2.01.278 P
shall witness to him i am near at home; 4.03. 95
the duke comes home to–morrow — nay, dry your 4.03.127
the head of angelo | accuse him home and home. 4.03.143
the head of angelo | accuse him home and home. 4.03.143
duke of dark corners had been at home, he had 4.03.157 P
that brought you home | the head of ragozine for 5.01.532
why thou departedst from thy native home, | and ERR 1.01. 29
boys, | made daily motions for our home return: 1.01. 59
the meat is cold, because you come not home: 1.02. 48
you come not home, because you have no stomach: 1.02. 49
and strike you home without a messenger. 1.02. 67
to fetch you from the mart | home to your house, 1.02. 75
she that doth fast till you come home to dinner; 1.02. 89
and prays that you will hie you home to dinner. 1.02. 90
till he come home again, i would forbear. 2.01. 31
but say, i prithee, is he coming home? 2.01. 55
when i desir'd him to come home to dinner, | he 2.01. 60
i thank him, i bare home upon my shoulders: 2.01. 73
go back again, thou slave, and fetch him home. 2.01. 75
go back again, and be new beaten home? 2.01. 76
hence, prating peasant! fetch thy master home. 2.01. 81
whilst i at home starve for a merry look: 2.01. 88
deer, he breaks the pale, | and feeds from home; 2.01.101
your mistress sent to have me home to dinner? 2.02. 10
home to the centaur with the gold you gave me. 2.02. 16
she sent for you by dromio home to dinner. 2.02.154
and that to–morrow you will bring it home. 3.01. 5
get you home | and fetch the chain; 3.01.114
go home with it, and please your wife withal, 3.02.173
buy thou a rope, and bring it home to me. 4.01. 20
and bring thy master home immediately. 4.02. 64
my way is now to hie home to his house, | and 4.03. 92
to what end did i bid thee hie thee home? 4.04. 15
driven out of doors with it when i go from home, 4.04. 36 P
from home, welcom'd home with it when i return; 4.04. 36 P
o husband, god doth know you din'd at home, 4.04. 65
din'd at home? thou villain, what sayest thou? 4.04. 68
sir, sooth to say, you did not dine at home. 4.04. 69
see him safe convey'd | home to my house. 4.04.123
him fast, | and bear him home for his recovery. 5.01. 41
namely, some love that drew him oft from home. 5.01. 56
and therefore let me have him home with me. 5.01.101
once did i get him bound, and sent him home, 5.01.145
and sent my peasant home | for certain ducats; 5.01.231
and in a dark and dankish vault at home | there 5.01.248
that he din'd not at home, but was lock'd out. 5.01.256
you say he din'd at home; 5.01.274
when the achiever brings home full numbers. ADO 1.01. 9 P
and send her home again without a husband. 3.03.163 P
come to your uncle, yonder's old coil at home. 5.02. 96 P
well, sit you out; go home, berowne; adieu. LLL 1.01.110
venue of wit — snip, snap, quick and home. 5.01. 60 P
though my mocks come home by me, i will now be 5.02.634 P
the hall | and milk comes frozen home in pail; 5.02.915
and now to helen is it home return'd, | there to MND 3.02.172
here and there, | troop home to churchyards. 3.02.382
is he come home yet? 4.02. 2 P
which is indeed to return to their home, and to MV 1.02.103 P
my ships come home a month before the day. 1.03.181
sir, i entreat you home with me to dinner. 4.01.401
and be a day before our husbands home. 4.02. 3
mistress' ear, | and draw her home with music. 5.01. 68
dear lady, welcome home! 5.01.113
you are welcome home, my lord. 5.01.132
lie not a night from home. 5.01.230
for my part, he keeps me rustically at home, or, AYL 1.01. 7 P
more properly, stays me here at home unkept; 1.01. 8 P
your praise is come too swiftly home before you. 2.03. 9
when i was at home, i was in a better place, but 2.04. 17 P
then sing him home. 4.02. 12
i would i were at home. 4.03.161
call home thy ancient thoughts from banishment, SHR in.2. 31
master, your love must live a maid at home, 1.01.182
to seek their fortunes farther than at home, 1.02. 51
crowns in my purse i have, and goods at home, 1.02. 57
come, where be these gallants? who's at home? 3.02. 87
and is the bride and bridegroom coming home? 3.02.151
of you all shall find when he comes home. 4.01. 88 P
welcome home, grumio! 4.01.106 P
go hop me over every kennel home, | for you 4.03. 98
cambio, hie you home, | and bid bianca make her 4.04. 62
but they may chance to need thee at home, 5.01. 3 P
while i play the good husband at home, my son 5.01. 69 P
why then let's home again. 5.01.147
whilst thou li'st warm at home, secure and safe; 5.02.151
too, | since i nor wax nor honey can bring home, AWW 1.02. 65
i'll stay at home | and pray god's blessing into 1.03.253
that hugs his kicky–wicky here at home, 2.03.280
you | that presently you take your way for home, 2.05. 64
hie home. 2.05. 77
go thou toward home, where i will never come 2.05. 90
no, come thou home, rossillion, | whence honor 3.02.120
bless him at home in peace, whilst i from far 3.04. 10
three hours 'twill be time enough to go home. 4.01. 25 P
for him shall at home be encount'red with a 4.03. 69 P
my husband hies him home, where, heaven aiding, 4.04. 12
and your son here at home, more advanc'd by the 4.05. 5 P
that my lord your son was upon his return home, 4.05. 71 P
lack'd the sense to know | her estimation home. 5.03. 4
send for your ring, i will return it home, | and 5.03.223
wait on me home, i'll make sport with thee. 5.03.322 P
i'll ride home to–morrow, sir toby. TN 1.03. 89 P
faith, i'll home to–morrow, sir toby. 1.03.105 P
church in a galliard and come home in a coranto? 1.03.128 P
i am sick, or not at home — what you will, to 1.05.109 P
"i will waylay thee going home, where if it be 3.04.159 P
i had rather than forty pound i were at home. 5.01.178 P
that may blow | no sneaping winds at home, to WT 1.02. 13
if at home, sir, | he's all my exercise, my 1.02.165
hold, | when you cast out, it still came home. 1.02.214
or else a fool | that seest a game play'd home, 1.02.248
home, home, the next way. 3.03.124 P
home, home, the next way. 3.03.124 P
come, good boy, the next way home. 3.03.127 P
mistress (let my prophecy | come home to ye!), 4.04.649
all my services | you have paid home; 5.03. 4
that to my home i will no more return | till JN 2.01. 21
will i not think of home, but follow arms. 2.01. 31
we will bear home that lusty blood again | which 2.01.255
sirrah, were i at home, | at your den, sirrah, 2.01.290

now powers from home and discontents at home 4.03.151
now powers from home and discontents at home 4.03.151
and welcome home again discarded faith. 5.04. 12
now these her princes are come home again, 5.07.115
be ready to direct these home alarms. R2 1.01.205
return with welcome home from banishment. 1.03.212
to set | the precious jewel of thy home return. 1.03.267
when time shall call him home from banishment, 1.04. 21
our substitutes at home shall have blank 1.04. 48
renowned for their deeds as far from home, | for 2.01. 53
whilst others come to make him lose at home. 2.02. 81
go, fellow, get thee home, provide some carts, 2.02.106
come home with me to supper, i'll lay | a plot 4.01.333
no joyful tongue gave him his welcome home, 5.02. 29
if you will not, tarry at home and be hang'd. 1H4 1.02.132 P
ye, yedward, if i tarry at home and go not, i'll 1.02.134 P
well, come what will, i'll tarry at home. 1.02.145 P
then | be emptied to redeem a traitor home? 1.03. 86
penny cost | to ransom home revolted mortimer. 1.03. 92
till he hath found a time to pay us home. 1.03.288
him | bootless home and weather–beaten back. 3.01. 66
home without boots, and in foul weather too! 3.01. 67
a rendezvous, a home to fly unto, | if that the 4.01. 57
and low, | a poor unminded outlaw sneaking home, 4.03. 58
that brought you home, and boldly did outdare 5.01. 40
all you that kiss my lady peace at home, that 2H4 1.02.208 P
he hath eaten me out of house and home, he hath 2.01. 74 P
who then persuaded you to stay at home? 2.03. 15
mouldy, stay at home till you are past service; 3.02.251 P
that all their eyes may bear those tokens home 4.02. 64
each hurries toward his home and sporting–place. 4.02.105
which i beseech you to let me have home with me. 5.05. 75 P
if like an ill venture it come unluckily home, i ep 12 P
it follows then the cat must stay at home, | yet H5 1.02.174
th' advised head defends itself at home; 1.02.179
where some, like magistrates, correct at home; 1.02.191
which pillage they with merry march bring home 1.02.195
if we, with thrice such powers left at home, 1.02.217
that men are merriest when they are from home. 1.02.272
good husband, come home presently. 2.01. 89 P
as manhood shall compound. push home. 2.01. 98
he that outlives this day, and comes safe home, 4.03. 41
invites the king of england's stay at home; 5.pr. 37
than bring a burthen of dishonor home | by 2H6 3.01.298
and so will i, and write home for it straight. 4.01. 24
and sent the ragged soldiers wounded home. 4.01. 90
her furr'd pack, she washes bucks here at home. 4.02. 48 P
home to your cottages, forsake this groom: 4.02.124
that will forsake thee and go home in peace. 4.08. 10
alas, he hath no home, no place to fly to; 4.08. 38
and heap'd sedition on his crown at home. 3H6 2.02.158
for many lives stand between me and home; 3.02.173
for how can tyrants safely govern home, | unless 3.03. 69
will not fight for such a hope | go home to bed, 5.04. 56
no news so bad abroad as this at home: R3 1.01.135
for god sake let not us two stay at home; 2.02.147
this fair alliance quickly shall call home | to 4.04.313
yet to beat down these rebels here at home. 4.04.530
your wives shall welcome home the conquerors; 5.03.260
his pomp as well in france | as here at home, H8 1.01.164
hear what i say, and then go home and lose me. 2.01. 57
employ'd you where high profits might come home, 3.02.158
that paris is returned home and hurt. TRO 1.01.109
better at home, if "would i might" were "may." 1.01.114
who said he came hurt home to–day? 1.02.215 P
soul in such a kind, | we left them all at home. 1.03.286
you'll confess /he brought home worthy prize — 2.02. 86
but it must grieve young pyrrhus now at home 3.03.209
in love whereof, half hector stays at home; 4.05. 84
desire them home. 4.05.157
ajax, your guard, stays to conduct you home. 5.02.184
never go home, here starve we out the night — 5.10. 2
go get you home, you fragments! COR 1.01.222
mend and charge home, | or, by the fires of 1.04. 38
him, were it | at home, upon my brother's guard, 1.10. 25
ha? martius coming home? 2.01.102 P
martius coming home! 2.01.106 P
and, i think, there's one at home for you. 2.01.110 P
he was wont to come home wounded. 2.01.119 P
comes the third time home with the oaken garland 2.01.125 P
martius is coming home; 2.01.145 P
thou have laugh'd had i come coffin'd home, 2.01.176
o, welcome home; 2.01.181
some old crab–trees here at home that will not 2.01.188
corioles, let me say, | i cannot speak him home. 2.02.103
welcome home. 3.01. 20
i prithee, noble friend, home to thy house; 3.01.233
go not home. 3.01.329
and come home belov'd | of all the trades in 3.02.133
in this point charge him home, that he affects 3.03. 1
when most strook home, being gentle wounded, 4.01. 8
bid them all home, he's gone; 4.02. 1
bid them home. 4.02. 5
dismiss them home. | here comes his mother. 4.02. 7
you have told them home, | and, by my troth, you 4.02. 48
business, and i will merrily accompany you home. 4.03. 39 P
weaker sort may wish | good martius home again. 4.06. 71
go, masters, get you home, be not dismay'd. 4.06.149
go home, | and show no sign of fear. 4.06.151
come, masters, let's home. 4.06.154 P
so did we all. but come, let's home. 4.06.156 P
to hear cominius speak, i'll keep at home. 5.01. 7
you know the way home again. 5.02. 97 P
the wars, and safely home | loaden with honor. 5.03.163
so we will home to rome, | and die among our 5.03.172
if | the roman ladies bring not comfort home, 5.04. 38
post, | and had no welcomes home, but he returns 5.06. 50
you are most welcome home. 5.06. 60
our spoils we have brought home | doth more than 5.06. 76
he by the senate is accited home | from weary TIT 1.01. 27
these that i bring unto their latest home, 1.01. 83
and strike her home by force, if not by words; 2.01.118
this for me, struck home to show my strength. 2.03.117
go home, call for sweet water, wash thy hands. 2.04. 6
look ye draw home enough, and 'tis there 4.03. 3
bed, | away from light steals home my heavy son, ROM 1.01.137
and, on my life, hath stol'n him home to bed. 2.01. 4
forget, | forgetting any other home but this. 2.02.175
came he not home to–night? 2.04. 2
what, have you din'd at home? 2.05. 45 P
go home, be merry, give consent | to marry paris 4.01. 89
if timon stay at home. TIM 2.02. 91 P
women are more valiant | that stay at home, if 3.05. 48
home, you idle creatures, get you home! JC 1.01. 1
home, you idle creatures, get you home! 1.01. 1
what conquest brings he home? 1.01. 32
to speak with me, | i will come home to you; 1.02.305
come home to me, and i will wait for you. 1.02.306
brought you caesar home? 1.03. 1
if he should stay at home to–day for fear. 2.02. 43
well, | and, for thy humor, i will stay at home. 2.02. 56
calphurnia here, my wife, stays me at home: 2.02. 75
hath begg'd that i will stay at home to–day. 2.02. 82
bring him with triumph home unto his house. 3.02. 49
he hath brought many captives home to rome, 3.02. 88
that, trusted home, | might yet enkindle you MAC 1.03.120
his spur, hath holp him | to his home before us. 1.06. 24
to feed were best at home; 3.04. 34
beard to beard, | and beat them backward home. 5.05. 7
as calling home our exil'd friends abroad | that 5.09. 32
most welcome home! HAM 2.02. 85
at home, my lord. 3.01.130 P
i'll warrant she'll tax him home, | and, as you 3.03. 29
look you lay home to him. 3.04. 1
hamlet return'd shall know you are come home. 4.07.130
and the bringing home | of bell and burial. 5.01.233
with his prepared sword he charges home | my LR 2.01. 51
best /thought it fit | to answer from our home; 2.01.124
plain, | i'ld drive ye cackling home to camelot. 2.02. 84
strange that they should so depart from home, 2.04. 1
my lord, when at their home | i did commend your 2.04. 27
i am now from home, and out of that provision 2.04.205
the king now bears will be reveng'd home; 3.03. 12 P
but i will punish home. 3.04. 16
i must change names at home, and give the 4.02. 17
lord edmund spake not with your lord at home? 4.05. 4
he speaks home, madam. OTH 2.01.165 P
i shall not dine at home; 3.03. 58
what make you from home? 3.04.169
for, as i think, they do command him home, 4.01.236
i am commanded home. 4.01.258
wear thy good rapier bare, and put it home. 5.01. 2
what, are you mad? i charge you, get you home. 5.02.194
perchance, iago, i will ne'er go home. 5.02.197
be wise, and get you home. 5.02.223
speak to me home, mince not the general tongue; ANT 1.02.105
friends in rome | petition us at home. 1.02.183
we had droven them home | with clouts about 4.07. 5
eye beck'd forth my wars and call'd them home, 4.12. 26
it seems, much loves | a gallian girl at home. CYM 1.06. 66
brought | the knowledge of your mistress home, i 2.04. 51
a sickness, say | she'll home to her father; 3.02. 75
th' nest, nor /know not | what air's from home. 3.03. 29
satisfy me home, | what is become of her? 3.05. 92
court i'll knock her back, foot her home again. 3.05.144 P
and all this done, spurn her home to her father, 4.01. 19 P
is he at home? 4.02.189
hast done, | home art gone, and ta'en thy wages. 4.02.261
that confirms it home. 4.02.328
if i do it not, i am sure to be hang'd at home. PER 1.03. 3 P
good helicane, that stay'd at home, | not to eat 2.ch. 17
come, thou shalt go home, and we'll have flesh 2.01. 81 P
pericles | come not home in twice six moons, 3.ch. 31
care not for me, | i can go home alone. 4.01. 42
o, take her home, mistress, take her home. 4.02.123 P
o, take her home, mistress, take her home. 4.02.123 P
i'll bring home some to–night. 4.02.144 P
to fetch his daughter home, who first is gone. 4.04. 20
take me home again | and prostitute me to the 4.06.189
i'll warrant thee, i'll strike home. TNK 3.06. 68
urge it home, brave lady. 3.06.233
for i came home before the business | was fully 4.01. 4
so, | and when your fit comes, fit her home, and 5.02. 11
please her appetite, | and do it home; 5.02. 37
the merchant fears, ere rich at home he lands." LUC 336
back, | brings home his lord and other company, 1584
met far from home, wond'ring each other's chance 1596
thee | so far from home into my deeds to pry, SON 61. 6
comes home again, on better judgment making. 87.12
that is my home of love, if i have rang'd, 109. 5

HOME–BRED 3 FR 0.0003 REL FR 3 V 0 P
this low'ring tempest of your home–bred hate, R2 1.03.187
foreign storms than any home–bred marriage. 3H6 4.01. 38
a mischief worse than civil home–bred strife, VEN 764

HOME–KEEPING 1 FR 0.0001 REL FR 1 V 0 P
home–keeping youth have ever homely wits. TGV 1.01. 2

HOMELY 16 FR 0.0018 REL FR 13 V 3 P
home–keeping youth have ever homely wits. TGV 1.01. 2
upon a homely object love can wink. 2.04. 98
hath homely age th' alluring beauty took | from ERR 2.01. 89
sir, you can eat none of this homely meat. AWW 2.02. 46 P
wherein toward me my homely stars have fail'd 2.05. 75
seldom from the house of a most homely shepherd, WT 4.02. 38 P
here has been too much homely foolery already. 4.04.333 P
briers and made | more homely than thy state. 4.04.426
as he whose brow with homely biggen bound 2H4 4.05. 27
him, | and like rich hangings in a homely house, 2H6 5.03. 12
life | to be no better than a homely swain, | to 3H6 2.05. 22
and to conclude, the shepherd's homely curds, 2.05. 47
be plain, good son, and homely in thy drift, ROM 2.03. 55
if you will take a homely man's advice, | be not MAC 4.02. 68
our stomachs | will make what's homely savory; CYM 3.06. 33
the homely villain cur'sies to her low, | and, LUC 1338

HOMES 2 FR 0.0002 REL FR 2 V 0 P
have sold their fortunes at their native homes, JN 2.01. 69
hence to your homes, be gone! COR 1.01.248

HOME–SPUNS 1 FR 0.0001 REL FR 1 V 0 P
what hempen home–spuns have we swagg'ring here, MND 3.01. 77

HOMEWARD 6 FR 0.0006 REL FR 6 V 0 P
and therefore homeward did they bend their ERR 1.01.117
asia, | and, coasting homeward, came to ephesus; 1.01.134
then homeward every man attach the hand | of his LLL 4.03.372
my affairs | do even drag me homeward; WT 1.02. 24
thumb, | wrack'd as homeward he did come. MAC 1.03. 29
and homeward through the dark laund runs apace, VEN 813

HOMEWARDS 1 FR 0.0001 REL FR 0 V 1 P
pray you draw homewards. AYL 4.03.178 P

HOMICIDE 4 FR 0.0004 REL FR 4 V 0 P
salisbury is a desperate homicide, | he fighteth 1H6 1.02. 25
if i thought that, i tell thee, homicide, R3 1.02.125
men, | to fight against this guilty homicide. 5.02. 18
gentlemen, | a bloody tyrant and a homicide; 5.03.246

HOMICIDES 1 FR 0.0001 REL FR 1 V 0 P
i am with child, ye bloody homicides! 1H6 5.04. 62

HOMILY 1 FR 0.0001 REL FR 0 V 1 P
what tedious homily of love have you wearied AYL 3.02.155 P

/HOMINEM 1 FR 0.0001 REL FR 0 V 1 P
novi /hominem tanquam te. LLL 5.01. 9

HOMMES 1 FR 0.0001 REL FR 0 V 1 P
les langues des hommes sont pleines de H5 5.02.115 P

HOMO 1 FR 0.0001 REL FR 0 V 1 P
go to, homo is a common name to all men. 1H4 2.01. 95 P

/HONEST 2 FR 0.0002 REL FR 1 V 1 P
/to /speak /to /you /like /an /honest /man, /i HAM 2.02.268 P
/where /i /could /not /be /honest, | /i /never LR 5.01. 23

HONEST 301 FR 0.0340 REL FR 174 V 127 P
honest lord, | thou hast said well; TMP 3.03. 34
proteus, i thank thee for thine honest care, TGV 3.01. 22
and once again i do receive thee honest. 5.04. 78
well, let us see honest master page. WIV 1.01. 66 P
be drunk whilst i live again, but in honest, 1.01.182 P
my honest lads, i will tell you what i am about. 1.03. 38 P
an honest, willing, kind fellow as ever servant 1.04. 10 P
the young man is an honest man. 1.04. 72 P
what shall de honest man do in my closet? 1.04. 73 P
dere is no honest man dat shall come in my 1.04. 74 P
to desire this honest gentlewoman, your maid, to 1.04. 82 P
sir, and she is pretty, and honest, and gentle, 1.04.139 P
i detest, an honest maid as ever broke bread. 1.04.150 P
truly, an honest gentleman; 1.04.163 P
if i find her honest, i lose not my labor; 2.01.238 P
and truly master page is an honest man. 2.02.116 P
some say that, though she appear honest to me, 2.02.222 P
i will to my honest knight falstaff, and drink 3.02. 87 P
ford, having an honest man to your husband, to 3.03.100 P
your wife is as honest a omans as i will desires 3.03.220 P
by gar, i see 'tis an honest woman. 3.03.222 P
do, | wives may be merry, and yet honest too: 4.02.105
behold what honest clothes you send forth to 4.02.120 P
mistress ford, the honest woman, the modest wife 4.02.130 P
admirable pleasures and fery honest knaveries. 4.04. 81 P
germans are honest men. 4.05. 72 P
ay, sir; whom i thank heaven is an honest woman. MM 2.01. 72 P
if it be honest you have spoke, you have courage 3.02.156 P
sir, your company is fairer than honest. 4.03.175 P
honest in nothing but in his clothes, and one 5.01.262 P
with words that in an honest suit might move. ERR 4.02. 14
you have done wrong to this my honest friend, 5.01. 19
liv'st | to walk where any honest men resort. 5.01. 28
do you question me, as an honest man should do, ADO 1.01.166 P
i cannot be said to be a flattering honest man) 1.03. 31 P
you may do the part of an honest man in it. 2.01.166 P
why, that's spoken like an honest drovier; 2.01.194 P
the purpose (like an honest man and a soldier), 2.03. 19 P
and truly i'll devise some honest slanders | to 3.01. 84
one word more, honest neighbors. 3.03. 91 P
what would you with me, honest neighbor? 3.05. 1 P
in faith, honest as the skin between his brows. 3.05. 12 P
i thank god i am as honest as any man living 3.05. 13 P
an honest soul, i' faith, sir, by my troth he is 3.05. 38 P
as i am an honest man, he looks pale. 5.01.130 P
i thank thee for thy care and honest pains. 5.01.314
minime, honest master, or rather, master, no. LLL 3.01. 60
i that am honest, i that hold it sin | to break 4.03.175
most dull, honest dull! to our sport; away! 5.01.155
in russet yeas and honest kersey noes. 5.02.413
a foolish mild man, an honest man, look you, and 5.02.581 P
unless you play the honest troyan, the poor 5.02.675 P
honest plain words best pierce the ear of grief, 5.02.753
the pity that some honest neighbors will not MND 3.01.145 P
your name, honest gentleman? 3.01.184 P
and, as i am an honest puck, | if we have 5.01.431
take heed, honest launcelot, take heed, honest MV 2.02. 7 P
honest launcelot, take heed, honest /gobbo," or, 2.02. 8 P
as aforesaid, "honest launcelot /gobbo, do not 2.02. 8 P
very wisely to me, "my honest friend launcelot, 2.02. 15 P
friend launcelot, being an honest man's son" — 2.02. 15 P
man's son" — or rather an honest woman's son, 2.02. 16 P
i say't, is an honest exceeding poor man and, 2.02. 52 P
your worship shall know by this honest old man, 2.02.138 P
my gossip report be an honest woman of her word. 3.01. 7 P
that the good antonio, the honest antonio — o 3.01. 13 P
but if she be less than an honest woman, she is 3.05. 41 P
that she makes fair she scarce makes honest, and AYL 1.02. 38 P
and those that she makes honest she makes very 1.02. 38 P
as the most capricious poet, honest ovid, was 3.03. 8 P
is it honest in deed and word? 3.03. 18 P
for thou swear'st to me thou art honest. 3.03. 26 P
would you not have me honest? 3.03. 28 P
and therefore i pray the gods make me honest. 3.03. 34 P
well met, honest gentleman. 5.03. 7 P
though he be merry, yet withal he's honest. SHR 3.02. 25
and, honest company, i thank you all | that have 3.02.193
even in these honest mean habiliments; 4.03.170
clerk, and some sufficient honest witnesses. 4.04. 95 P
and wander we to see thy honest son, | who will 4.05. 69
sour, | and not obedient to his honest will, 5.02.158
bosom, and i thank you for your honest care. AWW 1.03.127 P
my friends were poor, but honest, so's my love. 1.03.195
'tis pity he is not honest. 3.05. 82
but you say she's honest. 3.06.111
she then was honest. 4.02. 11
was very honest in the behalf of the maid; 4.03.218 P
every thing that an honest man should not have; 4.03.259 P
what an honest man should have, he has nothing. 4.03.260 P
held, can serve the world for no honest use; 4.03.307 P
for i can guess that by thy honest aid | thou 5.03.159
but to be said an honest man and a good TN 4.02. 8 P
mine honest friend, | will you take eggs for WT 1.02.160

go play, mamillius, thou'rt an honest man. 1.02.211
thou art not honest; 1.02.242
will thereto add | 'tis pity she's not honest — 2.01. 68
come between | ere you can say she's honest: 2.01. 76
honest as either, to purge him of that humor 2.03. 38
and no less honest | than you are mad; 2.03. 71
as this world goes, to pass for honest. 2.03. 73
know of it | is that camillo was an honest man; 3.02. 74
and five or six honest wives that were present. 4.04.270 P
father died, | to lie close by his honest bones; 4.04.456
who, i may say, is no honest man, neither to his 4.04.700 P
though i am not naturally honest, i am so 4.04.712 P
tell me (for you seem to be honest plain men) 4.04.794 P
if i had a mind to be honest, i see fortune 4.04.831 P
prince thou art as honest a true fellow as any 5.02.157 P
some honest christian trust me with a gage — R2 4.01. 83
i love him well, he is an honest man. 1H4 3.03. 93 P
i am an honest man's wife, and, setting thy 3.03.119 P
charge an honest woman with picking thy pocket! 3.03.155 P
shalt find me tractable to any honest reason; 3.03.173 P
a man is through with them in honest taking up, 2H4 1.02. 40 P
why, sir, did i say you were an honest man? 1.02. 80 P
if you say i am any other than an honest man. 1.02. 86 P
well, be honest, be honest, and god bless your 1.02.221 P
well, be honest, be honest, and god bless your 1.02.221 P
marry, if thou wert an honest man, thyself and 2.01. 85 P
says he, "you are an honest woman, and well 2.04. 92 P
i will bar no honest man my house, nor no 2.04.102 P
you speak of me /even now before this honest, 2.04.302 P
no abuse, ned, i' th' world, honest ned, none. 2.04.318 P
or honest bardolph, whose zeal burns in his nose 2.04.329 P
good morrow, honest gentlemen. 3.02. 55 P
an honest man, sir, is able to speak for himself 5.01. 45 P
quarter bear out a knave against an honest man, 5.01. 49 P
the knave is mine honest friend, sir, therefore 5.01. 50 P
honest bardolph, welcome. 5.03. 55 P
honest gentleman, i know not your breeding. 5.03.107 P
god, so long as your majesty is an honest man. H5 4.07.114 P
do not cast away an honest man for a villain's 2H6 1.03.202 P
that hath dishonored gloucester's honest name. 2.01.195
to prove him a knave and myself an honest man; 2.03. 87 P
he was an honest man, and a good bricklayer. 4.02. 40 P
to thyself, like a honest plain–dealing man? 4.02.103 P
for they are thrifty honest men, and such | as 4.02.186
not from edward's well–meant honest love, | but 3H6 3.03. 67
how far hence is thy lord, mine honest fellow? 5.01. 2
an honest tale speeds best being plainly told. R3 4.04.358
plain and not honest is too harsh a style. 4.04.360
travel, | and understand again like honest men, H8 1.03. 32
now | an honest country lord, as i am, beaten 1.03. 44
and to deliver | (like free and honest men) our 3.01. 60
ye speak like honest men (pray god ye prove so!) 3.01. 69
(though he be grown so desperate to be honest), 3.01. 86
but be brought to know our ends are honest, 3.01.154
thou hast forc'd me | (out of thy honest truth) 3.02.430
but such an honest chronicler as griffith. 4.02. 72
i thank you, honest lord. 4.02.160
he's honest, on mine honor. 5.01.153
would you were half so honest! 5.02.117
this honest man, wait like a lousy footboy | at 5.02.174
here's agamemnon, an honest fellow enough, and TRO 5.01. 51 P
he's one honest enough; COR 1.01. 53 P
masters, my good friends, mine honest neighbors, 1.01. 62
and cannot go without any honest man's voice. 2.03.133 P
thou art not honest, and the gods will plague 5.03.166
if that be call'd deceit, i will be honest, TIT 3.01.188
i thank you, honest gentlemen, good night. ROM 1.05.124
my invocation | is fair and honest; 2.01. 28
your love says, like an honest gentleman, | an' 2.05. 55
"your love says, like an honest gentleman, 2.05. 60
hie to high fortune! honest nurse, farewell. 2.05. 78
o courteous tybalt, honest gentleman, | that 3.02. 62
honest good fellows, ah, put up, put up, | for 4.05. 98
the man is honest. TIM 1.01.128
thou art timon's dog, and these knaves honest. 1.01.180
to knock out an honest athenian's brains. 1.01.192 P
time to be honest. 1.01.257
o, by no means, | honest ventidius. 1.02. 9
honest water, which ne'er left man i' th' mire. 1.02. 59
thus honest fools lay out their wealth on 1.02.235
mine honest friend, | i prithee but repair to me 2.02. 24
(prithee be not sad, | thou art true and honest; 2.02.221
flaminius, honest flaminius, you are very 3.01. 7 P
draw nearer, honest flaminius. 3.01. 39 P
poor honest lord, brought low by his own heart, 4.02. 37
matron, | it is her habit only that is honest, 4.03.114
eye, i will present | my honest grief unto him; 4.03.470
an honest poor servant of yours. 4.03.475
i never had honest men about me, i; 4.03.477
i do proclaim | one honest man — mistake me not 4.03.497
methinks thou art more honest now than wise; 4.03.502
thou singly honest man, | here, take; 4.03.523
have i once liv'd to see two honest men? 5.01. 56
you that are honest, by being what you are 5.01. 68
ay, you are honest /men. 5.01. 71
most honest men! 5.01. 73
y' are honest men; 5.01. 76
speak truth, y' are honest men. 5.01. 77
good honest men! 5.01. 80
every putting–by mine honest neighbors shouted. JC 1.02.231 P
and honest casca, we have the falling sickness. 1.02.256
a very pleasing night to honest men. 1.03. 43
brutus is noble, wise, valiant, and honest; 3.01.126
only in a general honest thought | and common 5.05. 71
win us with honest trifles, to betray 's | in MAC 1.03.125
why, the honest men. 4.02. 55 P
enow to beat the honest men and hang up them. 4.02. 57 P
blister our tongues, | was once thought honest; 4.03. 13
no mind that's honest | but in it shares some 4.03.197
o, farewell, honest /soldier. HAM 1.01. 16
it is an honest ghost, that let me tell you. 1.05.138
then i would you were so honest a man. 2.02.176 P
honest, my lord? 2.02.177 P
ay, sir, to be honest, as this world goes, is to 2.02.178 P
none, my lord, but the world's grown honest. 2.02.237 P
of affection, but call'd it an honest method, as 2.02.444 P
ha, ha! are you honest? 3.01.102 P
that if you be honest and fair, /your /honesty 3.01.106 P
i am myself indifferent honest, but yet i could 3.01.121 P
and my shape as true, | as honest madam's issue? LR 1.02. 9
i am no honest man if there be any good meaning 1.02.173 P
to love him that is honest, to converse with him 1.04. 15 P
i can keep honest counsel, ride, run, mar a 1.04. 32 P
an honest mind and plain, he must speak truth! 2.02. 99
whip me such honest knaves. OTH 1.01. 49
in honest plainness thou hast heard me say | my 1.01. 97
honest iago, | my desdemona must i leave to thee 1.03.294
that thinks men honest that but seem to be so, 1.03.400
pegs that make this music, | as honest as i am. 2.01.201
iago is most honest. 2.03. 6
it were an honest action to say | so to the moor 2.03.141
honest iago, that looks dead with grieving, 2.03.177
as i am an honest man, i had thought you had 2.03.266 P
in the sincerity of love and honest kindness. 2.03.327 P
good night, honest iago. 2.03.335 P
when this advice is free i give, and honest, 2.03.337
desdemona to subdue | in any honest suit; 2.03.341
for whiles this honest fool | plies desdemona to 2.03.353
dost thou hear, mine honest friend? 3.01. 21 P
no, i hear not your honest friend; i hear you. 3.01. 22 P
i never knew a florentine more kind and honest. 3.01. 40
o, that's an honest fellow. 3.03. 5
cunning, | i have no judgment in an honest face. 3.03. 50
is he not honest? 3.03.103
honest, my lord? 3.03.103
honest? ay, honest. 3.03.104
honest? ay, honest. 3.03.104
i dare be sworn i think that he is honest. 3.03.125
why then i think cassio's an honest man. 3.03.129
i do not think but desdemona's honest. 3.03.225
this honest creature, doubtless, | sees and 3.03.242
o world, | to be direct and honest is not safe. 3.03.378
nay, stay. thou shouldst be honest. 3.03.381
i think my wife be honest, and think she is not; 3.03.384
she may be honest yet. 3.03.433
i durst, my lord, to wager she is honest; 4.02. 12
for, if she be not honest, chaste, and true, 4.02. 17
swear thou art honest. 4.02. 38
i hope my noble lord esteems me honest. 4.02. 65
and put in every honest hand a whip | to lash 4.02.142
o brave iago, honest and just, | that hast such 5.01. 31
but of life as honest | as you that thus abuse 5.01.122
honest iago hath ta'en order for't. 5.02. 72
an honest man he is, and hates the slime | that 5.02.148
my friend, thy husband, honest, honest iago. 5.02.154
my friend, thy husband, honest, honest iago. 5.02.154
nothing | but what indeed is honest to be done; ANT 1.05. 16
th' art an honest man. 2.05. 47
though it be honest, it is never good | to bring 2.05. 85
and what | made all–honor'd, honest, roman 2.06. 16
thou hast been rightly honest — so hast thou — 4.02. 11
and thou art honest too. 4.02. 15
mine honest friends, | i turn you not away, but, 4.02. 29
o, my fortunes have | corrupted honest men! 4.05. 17
draw that thy honest sword, which thou hast worn 4.14. 79
no longer than yesterday, a very honest woman — 5.02.251 P
how mean soe'er, that have their honest wills, CYM 1.06. 8
where i have liv'd at honest freedom, paid 3.03. 71
true honest men being heard, like false aeneas, 3.04. 58
come, fellow, be thou honest, | do thou thy 3.04. 64
but if i were as wise as honest, then | my 3.04.118
and truly, i would think thee an honest man. 3.05.113 P
dishonestly afflicted, but yet honest. 4.02. 40
a cave–keeper, | and cook to honest creatures. 4.02.299
wherein i am false, i am honest; 4.03. 42
to an ancient soldier | (an honest one, i 5.03. 16
true nor modest, | unless i add, we are honest. 5.05. 19
confess'd, | which must approve thee honest. 5.05.245
peace be at your labor, honest fishermen. PER 2.01. 52
honest! 2.01. 53 P
how well this honest mirth becomes their labor! 2.01. 95
an honest woman, or not a woman. 4.02. 85
innocent | and for an honest attribute cry out, 4.03. 18
but amongst honest /women. 4.06.194
and chances | into an honest house, our story 5.ch. 2
now, honest keeper? TNK 2.02.220
and so fair, | let honest men ne'er love again. 2.02.231
by your leaves, honest friends: 2.03. 60
nor none so honest, arcite. 3.03. 4
and earth, | there's nothing in thee honest. 3.03. 46
then as i am an honest man, and love | with all 3.06. 50
fair hand, and that honest heart you gave me — 3.06.197
then if she will be honest, | she has the path 5.02. 22
why, do you think she is not honest, sir? 5.02. 30
(for to that honest purpose it was meant ye), ep 14
but honest fear, bewitch'd with lust's foul LUC 173
of the worn–out age | pawn'd honest looks, but 1351
thee, | and all my honest faith in thee is lost; SON 152. 8

HONESTER 5 FR 0.0005 REL FR 1 V 4 P
that is an old man and no honester than i. ADO 3.05. 14 P
if he were honester | he were much goodlier. AWW 3.05. 79
but an honester and truer–hearted man — well, 2H4 2.04.383 P
when honester men than thou go in their hose and 2H6 4.07. 50 P
'tis an honester service than to meddle with thy COR 4.05. 47 P

HONESTEST 1 FR 0.0001 REL FR 1 V 0 P
him and keeps her guard | in honestest defense. AWW 3.05. 74

HONEST–HEARTED 2 FR 0.0002 REL FR 1 V 1 P
a very honest–hearted fellow, and as poor as the LR 1.04. 19 P
some honest–hearted maids, will sing my dirge, TNK 2.06. 15

HONESTLY 7 FR 0.0008 REL FR 1 V 6 P
and (as i say) paying for them very honestly; MM 2.01.102 P
your saying, by my faith you say honestly. ADO 2.01.235 P
not honestly, my lord, but so covertly that no 2.02. 9 P
you have discharg'd this honestly, keep it to AWW 1.03.122 P
that live honestly by the prick of their needles H5 2.01. 34 P
ye say honestly, rest you merry! ROM 1.02. 62 P
it will show honestly in us, | and is very TIM 5.01. 13

HONEST–NATUR'D 1 FR 0.0001 REL FR 1 V 0 P
but for all this, my honest–natur'd friends, | i TIM 5.01. 86

HONEST–TRUE 1 FR 0.0001 REL FR 1 V 0 P
as i have ever found thee honest–true, | so let MV 3.04. 46

/HONESTY 1 FR 0.0001 REL FR 0 V 1 P
/your /honesty should admit no discourse to your HAM 3.01.107 P

HONESTY 93 FR 0.0105 REL FR 56 V 37 P
launce, by mine honesty, welcome to /milan. TGV 2.05. 1 P
her will, out of honesty into english. WIV 1.03. 50 P
almost ready to wrangle with mine own honesty. 2.01. 85 P
that may not sully the chariness of our honesty. 2.01.100 P
sort, as they say) but in the way of honesty; 2.02. 74 P
amiable siege to the honesty of this ford's wife 2.02.234 P
in your brow, provost, honesty and constancy; MM 4.02.154 P
by mine honesty, | if she be mad — as i believe 5.01. 59
i'll prove mine honor and mine honesty | against ERR 5.01. 30
of approv'd valor, and confirm'd honesty. ADO 2.01.380 P
with them, why, the more is for your honesty. 3.03. 53 P
much more a man who hath any honesty in him. 3.03. 64 P
a beard, fair health, and honesty; LLL 5.02.824
i pray thee, if it stand with honesty, | buy AYL 2.04. 91
for honesty coupled to beauty is to have honey a 3.03. 30 P
and to cast away honesty upon a foul slut were 3.03. 35 P
or i should think my honesty ranker than my wit. 4.01. 84 P
rich honesty dwells like a miser, sir, in a poor 5.04. 60 P
whose skill was almost as great as his honesty; AWW 1.01. 19 P
she derives her honesty and achieves her 1.01. 45 P
though honesty be no puritan, yet it will do no 1.03. 93 P
her name, and no legacy is so rich as honesty. 3.05. 13 P
all her deserving | is a reserved honesty, and 3.05. 62
what his valor, honesty, and expertness in wars; 4.03.178 P
what is his honesty? 4.03.249 P
but little more to say, sir, of his honesty. 4.03.259 P
for this description of thine honesty? 4.03.263 P
let death and honesty | go with your impositions 4.04. 28
manners, nor honesty, but to gabble like tinkers TN 2.03. 87 P
me and as mine honesty puts it to utterance. WT 1.01. 20 P
which hoxes honesty behind, restraining | from 1.02.244
are such allow'd infirmities that honesty | is 1.02.263
sigh (a note infallible | of breaking honesty)? 1.02.288
if therefore you dare trust my honesty, | that 1.02.434
if it be so, | we need no grave to bury honesty, 2.01.155
to lock up honesty | and honor from th' access 2.02. 9
i needs must think it honesty. 4.04.487
ha, ha, what a fool honesty is! 4.04.595 P
it were a piece of honesty to acquaint the king 4.04.680 P
whose honor and whose honesty till now | endur'd 5.01.194
hand, whose worth and honesty | is richly noted; 5.03.144
for thou wast got i' th' way of honesty. JN 1.01.181
there's neither honesty, manhood, nor good 1H4 1.02.139 P
truth, nor honesty in this bosom of thine; 3.03.154 P
there is no honesty in such dealing, unless a 2H4 2.01. 36 P
why then mine honesty shall be my dower, | for 3H6 3.02. 72
proveth edward's love and warwick's honesty. 3.03.180
to thee, that hast nor honesty nor grace: R3 1.03. 55
belong to worship and affect | in honor honesty, H8 1.01. 40
tell you | you have as little honesty as honor, 3.02.271
cardinal, | you'll show a little honesty. 3.02.306
corruption wins not more than honesty. 3.02.444
of the soul, | for honesty and decent carriage, 4.02.145
the good i stand on is my truth and honesty. 5.01.122
they had parted so much honesty among 'em — 5.02. 28
whose honesty the devil | and his disciples only 5.02.146
upon my secrecy, to defend mine honesty, my mask TRO 1.02.262 P
enjoy | that nice–preserved honesty of yours. TIT 2.03.135
no faith, no honesty in men, all perjur'd, | all ROM 3.02. 86
his honesty rewards him in itself, | it must not TIM 1.01.130
off, | and say you /found them in mine honesty. 2.02.135
every man has his fault, and honesty is his. 3.01. 27 P
other oath | than honesty to honesty engag'd JC 2.01.127
other oath | than honesty to honesty engag'd 2.01.127
for i am arm'd so strong in honesty | that they 4.03. 67
yet i hold it not honesty to have it thus set HAM 2.02.202 P
my lord, have better commerce than with honesty? 3.01.109 P
sooner transform honesty from what it is to a 3.01.111 P
than the force of honesty can translate beauty 3.01.112 P
his offense, honesty! LR 1.02.117 P
on whose foolish honesty | my practices ride 1.02.181
should wear a sword, | who wears no honesty. 2.02. 73
a man he is of honesty and trust. OTH 1.03.284
thy honesty and love doth mince this matter, 2.03.247
for i know thou'rt full of love and honesty, 3.03.118
nor for my manhood, honesty, and wisdom, | to 3.03.153
this fellow's of exceeding honesty, | and knows 3.03.258
that lov'st to make thine honesty a vice! 3.03.376
(prick'd to't by foolish honesty and love), | i 3.03.412
it is not honesty in me to speak | what i have 4.01.277
but why should honor outlive honesty? 5.02.245
but mine honesty | shall not make poor my ANT 2.02. 92
mine honesty and i begin to square. 3.13. 41
woman should not do but in the way of honesty — 5.02.253 P
i should woo hard, but be your groom in honesty: CYM 3.06. 69
honor and honesty | i cherish and depend on, TNK 3.01. 50
you | by all the honesty and honor in you, | no 3.03. 14
first, by your leave, | i' th' way of honesty. 5.02. 20
nev'r cast your child away for honesty. 5.02. 21
her honesty! 5.02. 28
yours to command i' th' way of honesty. 5.02. 71
thou smother'st honesty, thou murth'rest troth, LUC 885
tarquin armed to beguild | with outward honesty, 1545

HONESTY'S 1 FR 0.0001 REL FR 1 V 0 P
for honesty's a fool | and loses that it works OTH 3.03.382

HONEY 38 FR 0.0043 REL FR 32 V 6 P
to feed on such sweet honey | and kill the bees TGV 1.02.103
honey, and milk, and sugar: there is three. LLL 5.02.231
my fair, sweet, honey monarch, for, i protest, 5.02.527 P
to beauty is to have honey a sauce to sugar. AYL 3.03. 30 P
and now, my honey love, | will we return unto SHR 4.03. 52
too, | since i nor wax nor honey can bring home, AWW 1.02. 65
then 'nointed over with honey, set on the head WT 4.04.784 P
as the honey of hybla, my old lad of the castle. 1H4 1.02. 41 P
now, my good sweet honey lord, ride with us 1.02.160 P
they surfeited with honey and began | to loathe 3.02. 71
/thighs pack'd with wax, our mouths with honey, 2H4 4.05. 76
the civil citizens kneading up the honey, | the H5 1.02.199
enemies | have steep'd their galls in honey, and 2.02. 30
thus may we gather honey from the weed, | and 4.01. 11
heart | grossly grew captive to his honey words, R3 4.01. 79
that for ever mars | the honey of his language. H8 3.02. 22
shall all repair, | what honey is expected? TRO 1.03. 83
you have the honey still, but these the gall; 2.02.144
sweet honey greek, tempt me no more to folly. 5.02. 18
till he hath lost his honey and his sting; 5.10. 42
sweet honey and sweet notes together fail. 5.10. 44
but when ye have the honey we desire, | let not TIT 2.03.131

lips, | coming and going with thy honey breath. 2.04. 25
o honey nurse, what news? ROM 2.05. 18
the sweetest honey | is loathsome in his own 2.06. 11
death, that hath suck'd the honey of thy breath, 5.03. 92
that suck'd the honey of his /music vows, | now HAM 3.01.156
honey, you shall be well desir'd in cyprus, | i OTH 2.01.204
not to eat honey like a drone | from others' PER 2.ch. 18
of these drones, that rob the bee of her honey. 2.01. 47 P
meed | a thousand honey secrets shalt thou know. VEN 16
which to his speech did honey passage yield, 452
"adieu," | the honey fee of parting tend'red is: 538
i think the honey guarded with a sting: LUC 493
my honey lost, and i, a drone-like bee, | have 836
and suck'd the honey which thy chaste bee kept. 840
thy honey turns to gall, thy joy to grief! 889
o, how shall summer's honey breath hold out SON 65. 5
HONEY-BAG 3 FR 0.0003 REL FR 0 V 3 P
and, good mounsieur, bring me the honey-bag. MND 4.01. 13 P
mounsieur, have a care the honey-bag break not, 4.01. 15 P
loath to have you overflowen with a honey-bag, 4.01. 16 P
HONEY-BAGS 1 FR 0.0001 REL FR 1 V 0 P
the honey-bags steal from the humble-bees, | and MND 3.01.168
HONEY-BEES 1 FR 0.0001 REL FR 1 V 0 P
for so work the honey-bees, | creatures that by H5 1.02.187
HONEYCOMB 1 FR 0.0001 REL FR 1 V 0 P
thou shalt be pinch'd | as thick as honeycomb, TMP 1.02.329
HONEY-DEW 1 FR 0.0001 REL FR 1 V 0 P
as doth the honey-dew | upon a gath'red lily TIT 3.01.112
HONEY-DROPS 1 FR 0.0001 REL FR 1 V 0 P
wings upon my flow'rs | diffusest honey-drops, TMP 4.01. 79
HONEYED 1 FR 0.0001 REL FR 1 V 0 P
ears | to steal his sweet and honeyed sentences; H5 1.01. 50
HONEY-HEAVY 1 FR 0.0001 REL FR 1 V 0 P
matter, | enjoy the honey-heavy dew of slumber. JC 2.01.230
HONEYING 1 FR 0.0001 REL FR 1 V 0 P
honeying and making love | over the nasty sty! HAM 3.04. 93
HONEYLESS 1 FR 0.0001 REL FR 1 V 0 P
rob the hybla bees, | and leave them honeyless. JC 5.01. 35
HONEY-MOUTH'D 1 FR 0.0001 REL FR 1 V 0 P
if i prove honey-mouth'd, let my tongue blister; WT 2.02. 31
HONEYSEED 2 FR 0.0002 REL FR 0 V 2 P
ah, thou honeyseed rogue! 2H4 2.01. 52 P
thou art a honeyseed, a man-queller, and a 2.01. 52 P
HONEY-STALKS 1 FR 0.0001 REL FR 1 V 0 P
than baits to fish, or honey-stalks to sheep, TIT 4.04. 91
HONEYSUCKLE 2 FR 0.0002 REL FR 1 V 1 P
so doth the woodbine the sweet honeysuckle MND 4.01. 42
ah, thou honeysuckle villain! 2H4 2.01. 50 P
HONEYSUCKLES 1 FR 0.0001 REL FR 1 V 0 P
where honeysuckles, ripened by the sun, | forbid ADO 3.01. 8
HONEY-SWEET 3 FR 0.0003 REL FR 0 V 3 P
prithee, honey-sweet husband, let me bring thee H5 2.03. 1 P
my lord pandarus, honey-sweet lord — TRO 3.01. 65 P
not i, honey-sweet queen. 3.01.141 P
HONEY-TONGUED 1 FR 0.0001 REL FR 1 V 0 P
debt | pay him the due of honey-tongued boyet. LLL 5.02.334
HONI 1 FR 0.0001 REL FR 1 V 0 P
and "honi soit qui mal y pense" write | in WIV 5.05. 69
HONNEUR 5 FR 0.0005 REL FR 0 V 5 P
sauf votre honneur, en verite, vous prononcez H5 3.04. 37 P
sauf votre honneur, d' elbow. 3.04. 48 P
et non pour les dames de honneur d'user. 3.04. 54 P
sauf votre honneur, me understand well. 5.02.131 P
sauf votre honneur, le francois que vous parlez, 5.02.188 P
/HONOR 4 FR 0.0004 REL FR 4 V 0 P
/to /hold /your /honor /more /precise /and /nice 2H4 2.03. 40
/what /thing, /in /honor, /had /my /father /lost 4.01.111
it is an /honor that i dream not of. ROM 1.03. 66
an /honor! 1.03. 67
HONOR 681 FR 0.0769 REL FR 576 V 105 P
didst seek to violate | the honor of my child. TMP 1.02.348
upon mine honor, sir, i heard a humming | (and 2.01.317
else i' th' world, | do love, prize, honor you. 3.01. 73
how does thy honor? 3.02. 23 P
ay, on mine honor. 3.02.114
shall never melt | mine honor into lust, to take 4.01. 28
honor, riches, marriage-blessing, | long 4.01.106
whose honor cannot | be measur'd or confin'd. 5.01.121
he after honor hunts, i after love: TGV 1.01. 63
the honor and regard of such a father. 2.04. 60
she shall be dignified with this high honor — 2.04.158
good mean | how with my honor i may undertake 2.07. 6
upon mine honor, he shall never know | that i 3.01. 48
company, | upon whose faith and honor i repose. 4.03. 26
that would have forc'd your honor and your love. 5.04. 22
now, by the honor of my ancestry, | i do applaud 5.04.139
trifling respect, i could come to such honor! WIV 2.01. 45 P
take the honor. 2.01. 47 P
fan, i took't upon mine honor thou hadst it not. 2.02. 13 P
you stand upon your honor! 2.02. 20 P
i can do to keep the terms of my honor precise. 2.02. 22 P
hand, and hiding mine honor in my necessity, am 2.02. 24 P
oaths, under the shelter of your honor! 2.02. 28 P
so securely on the excellency of her honor, that 2.02.243 P
now doth thy honor stand, | in him that was of 4.04. 8
worth | to undergo such ample grace and honor, MM 1.01. 23
nor need you, on mine honor, have to do | with 1.01. 63
i'll wait upon your honor. 1.01. 83
let but your honor know | (whom i believe to be 2.01. 8
here, if it like your honor. 2.01. 33
if it please your honor, i am the poor duke's 2.01. 47 P
in here before your good honor two notorious 2.01. 50 P
if it please your honor, i know not well what 2.01. 53 P
whom i detest before heaven and your honor — 2.01. 70 P
sir, if it please your honor, this is not so. 2.01. 85 P
sir, your honor cannot come to that yet. 2.01.119 P
i beseech your honor, ask me. 2.01.145 P
good master froth, look upon his honor; 2.01.148 P
doth your honor mark his face? 2.01.149 P
doth your honor see any harm in his face? 2.01.153 P
i would know that of your honor. 2.01.159 P
'save your honor! 2.02. 25
i am a woeful suitor to your honor, | please but 2.02. 27
to your honor, | please but your honor hear me. 2.02. 28
heaven keep your honor! 2.02. 42
heaven keep your honor safe! 2.02.157
'save your honor! 2.02.161
even so. heaven keep your honor! 2.04. 34
believe me, on mine honor, | my words express my 2.04.147
little honor to be much believ'd, | and most 2.04.149
yet hath he in him such a mind of honor | that, 2.04.179
would bark your honor from that trunk you bear, 3.01. 71
winters more respect | than a perpetual honor. 3.01. 76
she (having the truth of honor in her) hath made 3.01.164 P
is your brother sav'd, your honor untainted, the 3.01.253 P
to me, your honor is accounted a merciful man. 3.02.192 P
years' continuance, may it please your honor. 3.02.197 P
revenges to your heart, | and general honor. 4.03.136
i warrant your honor. 5.01. 82
my sisterly remorse confutes mine honor, | and i 5.01.100
or else thou art suborn'd against his honor | in 5.01.106
nor heard from her, | upon my faith and honor. 5.01.224
yet hath wrong'd | your well-defended honor, you 5.01.402
consenting to the safeguard of your honor, | i 5.01.419
upon mine honor, thou shalt marry her. 5.01.518
of suspect | th' unviolated honor of your wife. ERR 3.01. 88
i'll prove mine honor and mine honesty | against 5.01. 30
hath bestow'd much honor on a young florentine ADO 1.01. 10 P
that he hath wrong'd his honor in marrying the 2.02. 23 P
as in love of your brother's honor, who hath 2.02. 37 P
would better fit your honor to change your mind. 3.02.116 P
she's but the sign and semblance of her honor. 4.01. 33
upon mine honor, | myself, my brother, and this 4.01. 88
two of them have the very bent of honor, | and 4.01.186
if they wrong her honor, | the proudest of them 4.01.191
yet, by mine honor, i will deal in this | as 4.01.247
but, on my honor, she was charg'd with nothing 5.01.104
that honor which shall bate his scythe's keen LLL 1.01. 6
that his own hand may strike his honor down 1.01. 20
time receive such welcome at my hand | as honor 2.01.169
at my hand | as honor (without breach of honor) 2.01.169
for the best ward of mine honor is rewarding my 3.01.132 P
now by my maiden honor, yet as pure | as the 5.02.351
upon mine honor, no. 5.02.439
and might | to honor helen and to be her knight. MND 2.02.144
within the eye of honor, be assur'd | my purse, MV 1.01.137
and that clear honor | were purchas'd by the 2.09. 42
then be gleaned | from the true seed of honor? 2.09. 47
and how much honor | pick'd from the chaff and 2.09. 47
i thank your honor. 3.02.226
in whom | the ancient roman honor more appears 3.02.295
but if you knew to whom you show this honor, 3.04. 5
o wise young judge, how i do honor thee! 4.01.224
ring, | or your own honor to contain the ring, 5.01.201
no, by my honor, madam, by my soul, | no woman 5.01.209
my honor would not let ingratitude | so much 5.01.218
now, by mine honor, which is yet mine own, 5.01.232
him, as i must for my own honor if he come in; AYL 1.01.130 P
by mine honor, i will, and when i break that 1.02. 21 P
a pure blush thou mayst in honor come off again. 1.02. 29 P
no, by mine honor, but i was bid to come for you 1.02. 60 P
that swore by his honor they were good pancakes, 1.02. 64 P
and swore by his honor the mustard was naught. 1.02. 65 P
no more was this knight, swearing by his honor, 1.02. 78 P
my father's love is enough to honor him enough. 1.02. 83 P
if you outstay the time, upon mine honor, | and 1.03. 88
jealous in honor, sudden, and quick in quarrel, 2.07.151
honor, high honor, and renown | to hymen, god of 5.04.145
honor, high honor, and renown | to hymen, god of 5.04.145
you to your former honor i bequeath, | your 5.04.186
say, "what is it your honor will command?" SHR in.1. 54
an't please your honor, players | that offer in.1. 77
we thank your honor. in.1. 80
i think 'twas soto that your honor means. in.1. 88
(for yet his honor never heard a play), | you in.1. 96
and say, "what is't your honor will command, in.1. 115
will't please your honor taste of these in.2. 3
what raiment will your honor wear to-day? in.2. 4
sly, call not me honor nor lordship. in.2. 5 P
heaven cease this idle humor in your honor! in.2. 13
clouds, | so honor peereth in the meanest habit. 4.03.174
ere they can hide their levity in honor. AWW 1.02. 35
his equal had awak'd them, and his honor, 1.02. 38
whose aged honor cites a virtuous youth, | did 1.03.210
and, would your honor | but give me leave to try 1.03.246
see that you come | not to woo honor, but to wed 2.01. 15
till honor be bought up, and no sword worn | but 2.01. 32
there's honor in the theft. 2.01. 34
now, by my faith and honor, | if seriously i may 2.01. 80
with that malignant cause wherein the honor | of 2.01.111
the honor, sir, that flames in your fair eyes, 2.03. 80
's, and virtue none, | it is a dropsied honor. 2.03.128
and these breed honor. 2.03.133
honor and wealth from me. 2.03.144
it is in us to plant thine honor where | we 2.03.156
what great creation and what dole of honor 2.03.169
by mine honor, if i were but two hours younger, 2.03.253 P
he wears his honor in a box unseen, | that hugs 2.03.279
the duke will lay upon him all the honor | that 3.02. 71
sword can never win | the honor that he loses. 3.02. 94
whence honor but of danger wins a scar, | as oft 3.02.121
the honor of a maid is her name, and no legacy 3.05. 12 P
a suit | corrupt the tender honor of a maid. 3.05. 72
of laughter, hinder not the honor of his design. 3.06. 42 P
this instrument of honor again into his native 3.06. 66 P
it is an honor 'longing to our house, 4.02. 42
brings in the champion honor on my part, 4.02. 50
my house, mine honor, yea, my life, be thine, 4.02. 52
he fleshes his will in the spoil of her honor. 4.03. 17 P
country he had the honor to be the officer at a 4.03.269 P
i would do the man what honor i can, but of this 4.03.271 P
got, or a noble scar, is a good liv'ry of honor; 4.05.100 P
i beseech your honor to hear me one single word. 5.02. 35 P
i could not answer in that course of honor | as 5.03. 98
thou speak'st it falsely, as i love mine honor, 5.03.113
whose age and honor | both suffer under this 5.03.162
lay a more noble thought upon mine honor | than 5.03.180
fairer prove your honor | than in my thought it 5.03.183
by mine honor, half drunk. TN 1.05.116 P
have you not set mine honor at the stake, | and 3.01.118
by maidhood, honor, truth, and every thing, | i 3.01.150
stone, | and laid mine honor too unchary on't. 3.04.202
deny, | that honor, sav'd, may upon asking give? 3.04.212
how with mine honor may i give him that | which 3.04.214
tongue of loss | cried fame and honor on him. 5.01. 59
it then, | and tell me, in the modesty of honor, 5.01.335
eyes | to see alike mine honor as their profits WT 1.02.310
i'll give no blemish to her honor, none. 1.02.341
the parts of man | which honor does acknowledge, 1.02.401
since i am charg'd in honor and by him | that i 1.02.407
for, by the honor of my parents, i | have 1.02.442
by mine honor, | i'll geld 'em all; 2.01.146
me | to have her honor true than your suspicion, 2.01.160
for a worthy lady, | and one who much i honor. 2.02. 6
and honor from th' access of gentle visitors. 2.02. 10
your honor and your goodness is so evident 2.02. 41
but durst not tempt a minister of honor, | lest 2.02. 48
upon mine honor, i | will stand betwixt you and 2.02. 63
commit me for committing honor — trust it, | he 2.03. 49
for he | the sacred honor of himself, his 2.03. 85
to prate and talk for life and honor 'fore | who 3.02. 41
for honor, | 'tis a derivative from me to mine, 3.02. 43
if one jot beyond | the bound of honor, or in 3.02. 51
confess | i lov'd him as in honor he requir'd 3.02. 63
(i prize it not a straw), but for mine honor, 3.02.110
he (most humane | and fill'd with honor) to my 3.02.166
himself commended, | no richer than his honor. 3.02.170
thou wouldst have poison'd good camillo's honor, 3.02.188
since my desires | run not before mine honor, 4.04. 34
that makes himself (but for our honor therein) 4.04.436
save him from danger, do him love and honor, 4.04.510
on mine honor, | i'll point you where you shall 4.04.525
i know, in honor, o that ever i | had squar'd me 5.01. 51
whose honor and whose honesty till now | endur'd 5.01.194
your honor not o'erthrown by your desires, | i 5.01.230
o paulina, | we honor you with trouble; 5.03. 9
and wound her honor with this diffidence. JN 1.01. 65
heaven guard my mother's honor, and my land! 1.01. 70
my father gave me honor, yours gave land. 1.01.164
a foot of honor better than i was, | but many a 1.01.182
for new-made honor doth forget men's names; 1.01.187
that holds in chase mine honor up and down? 1.01.223
for thine own gain shouldst defend mine honor? 1.01.242
that she is bound in honor still to do | what 2.01.522
upholdeth him that thee upholds, | his honor. 3.01.316
o, thine honor, lewis, thine honor! 3.01.316
o, thine honor, lewis, thine honor! 3.01.316
i, by the honor of my marriage-bed, | after 5.02. 93
peace | as we with honor and respect may take, 5.07. 85
mine honor is my life, both grow in one, | take R2 1.01.182
one, | take honor from me, and my life is done. 1.01.183
then, dear my liege, mine honor let me try; 1.01.184
shall wound my honor with such feeble wrong, 1.01.191
go, say i sent thee forth to purchase honor, 1.03.282
love they to live that love and honor have. 2.01.138
which honor and allegiance cannot think. 2.01.208
meaning | to rase one title of your honor out. 2.03. 75
gaunt, | and by the worth and honor of himself, 3.03.110
or have mine honor soil'd | with the attainder 4.01. 23
his honor is as true | in this appeal as thou 4.01. 44
this, | if he may be repeal'd to try his honor. 4.01. 85
thou map of honor, thou king richard's tomb, 5.01. 12
now, | whose state and honor i for aye allow. 5.02. 40
now, by mine honor, by my life, by my troth, | i 5.02. 78
takes on the point of honor to support | so 5.03. 11
an' he shall spend mine honor with his shame, 5.03. 68
mine honor lives when his dishonor dies, | or my 5.03. 70
high sparks of honor in thee have i seen. 5.06. 29
so honor cross it from the north to south, | and 1H4 1.03.196
to pluck bright honor from the pale-fac'd moon, 1.03.202
and pluck up drowned honor by the locks, | so he 1.03.205
thou hast lost much honor that thou wert not 2.04. 20 P
what never-dying honor hath he got | against 3.02.106
that this same child of honor and renown, | this 3.02.139
for every honor sitting on his helm | would they 3.02.142
thou art the king of honor. 4.01. 10
i thought your honor had already been at 4.02. 52 P
my life, | if well-respected honor bid me on, 4.03. 10
well, 'tis no matter, honor pricks me on. 5.01.129 P
but how if honor prick me off when i come on? 5.01.130 P
can honor set to a leg? 5.01.131 P
honor hath no skill in surgery then? 5.01.133 P
what is honor? 5.01.134 P
what is in that word honor? 5.01.134 P
what is that honor? 5.01.135 P
i'll none of it, honor is a mere scutcheon. 5.01.140 P
what honor dost thou seek | upon my head? 5.03. 2
there's honor for you! 5.03. 32 P
like not such grinning honor as sir walter hath. 5.03. 59 P
if not, honor comes unlook'd for, and there's an 5.03. 60 P
if your father will do me any honor, so; 5.04.141 P
please it your honor knock but at the gate, 2H4 1.01. 5
upon mine honor, for a silken point | i'll give 1.01. 53
sweet earl, divorce not wisdom from your honor, 1.01.162
alas, sweet wife, my honor is at pawn, | and, 2.03. 7
no abuse, hal, a' mine honor, no abuse. 2.04.313 P
upon mine honor, all too confident | to give 4.01.150
and swear here, by the honor of my blood, | my 4.02. 55
whereof you did complain, which, by mine honor, 4.02.114
it shall not force | this lineal honor from me. 4.05. 46
england shall give him office, honor, might; 4.05.129
it more | than as your honor and as your renown, 4.05.145
but as an honor snatch'd with boist'rous hand, 4.05.191
sweet princes, what i did, i did in honor, | led 5.02. 35
as much as would maintain, to the king's honor, H5 1.01. 12
what mightst thou do, that honor would thee do, 2.pr. 18
with all appertinents | belonging to his honor; 2.02. 88
your honor wins bad humors. 3.02. 26 P
o, for honor of our land, | let us not hang like 3.05. 22
by faith and honor, | our madams mock at us, and 3.05. 27
with spirit of honor edged | more sharper than 3.05. 38
and a man that i love and honor with my soul, 3.06. 7 P
and 'twere more honor some were away. 3.07. 75 P
the fewer men, the greater share of honor. 4.03. 22
but if it be a sin to covet honor, | i am the 4.03. 28
i would not lose so great an honor | as one man 4.03. 31
i wear it for a memorable honor; 4.07.104
and wear it for an honor in thy cap | till i do 4.08. 59
and from my weary limbs | honor is cudgell'd. 5.01. 85
by mine honor, in true english, i love thee, 5.02.221 P
by which honor i dare not swear thou lovest me, 5.02.222 P
now for the honor of the forlorn french! 1H6 1.02. 19
how shall i honor thee for this success? 1.06. 5

and stands upon the honor of his birth, | if he 2.04. 28
obscur'd, | depriv'd of honor and inheritance. 2.05. 27
father's sake, | in honor of a true plantagenet, 2.05. 52
of which, my lord, your honor is the last. 2.05. 93
house, | i doubt not but with honor to redress. 2.05.126
vow, burgundy, by honor of thy house, | prick'd 3.02. 77
this is a double honor, burgundy; 3.02.116
that i wear | in honor of my noble lord of york, 3.04. 30
sirrah, thy lord i honor as he is. 3.04. 35
farewell talbot, france, and england's honor! 4.03. 23
hath sullied all his gloss of former honor | by 4.04. 6
his false hopes, the trust of england's honor, 4.04. 20
flight cannot stain the honor you have won, 4.05. 26
say, that i may honor thee. 5.03. 50
consent, and for thy honor give consent, | thy 5.03.136
command in anjou what your honor pleases. 5.03.147
intents, | to love and honor henry as her lord. 5.05. 21
and not deface your honor with reproach? 5.05. 29
that dims the honor of this warlike isle! 2H6 1.01.125
thyself | from top of honor to disgrace's feet? 1.02. 49
thou ran'st a–tilt in honor of my love | and 1.03. 51
but if she have forgot | honor and virtue, and 2.01.191
with honor of his birthright to the crown. 2.02. 62
born, | despoiled of your honor in your life, 2.03. 10
this staff of honor raught, there let it stand, 2.03. 43
in thy face i see | the map of honor, truth, and 3.01.203
but all the honor salisbury hath won | is, that 3.02.275
far be it we should honor such as these | with 4.01.123
the man is a proper man, of mine honor; 4.02. 96 P
mayor craves aid of your honor from the tower to 4.05. 4 P
have i affected wealth or honor? 4.07. 98
and heavens and honor be witness that no want of 4.08. 62 P
to emblaze the honor that thy master got. 4.10. 71
upon thine honor, is he prisoner? 5.01. 42
upon mine honor, he is prisoner. 5.01. 43
in whose cold blood no spark of honor bides. 3H6 1.01.184
i live | to honor me as thy king and sovereign, 1.01.198
but thou prefer'st thy life before thine honor; 1.01.246
do not honor him so much | to prick thy finger, 1.04. 54
thereon i pawn my credit and mine honor. 3.03.116
for my desert is honor; 3.03.192
and to repair my honor lost for him, | i here 3.03.193
for matching more for wanton lust than honor, 3.03.210
'tis the more honor, because more dangerous. 4.03. 15
i like it better than a dangerous honor. 4.03. 17
honor now or never! 4.03. 24
while he enjoys the honor and his ease. 4.06. 52
the drum your honor hears marcheth from warwick. 5.01. 13
if honor may be shrouded in a hearse — | whilst R3 1.02. 2
thy honor, state, and seat is due to me. 1.03.111
thou rag of honor! 1.03.232
your fire–new stamp of honor is scarce current. 1.03.255
glories, | an outward honor for an inward toil, 1.04. 79
his honor and myself are at the one, | and at 3.02. 21
i thank your honor. 3.02.107
well met, my lord, i am glad to see your honor. 3.02.108
your honor hath no shriving work in hand. 3.02.115
for which your honor and your faith is pawn'd, 4.02. 89
tell me, what state, what dignity, what honor, 4.04.247
the law, my honor, and her love | can make seem 4.04.341
george, profan'd, hath lost his lordly honor; 4.04.369
belong to worship and affect | in honor honesty, H8 1.01. 40
to whom as great a charge as little honor | he 1.01. 77
wishes towards you | honor and plenteous safety) 1.01.104
and from a mouth of honor quite cry down | this 1.01.137
does buy and sell his honor as he pleases, | and 1.01.192
not unconsidered leave your honor nor | the 1.02. 15
master — | whose honor heaven shield from soil! 1.02. 26
in trust) of him | things to strike honor sad. 1.02.126
henry the eight, life, honor, name, and all 2.01.116
and | does purpose honor to you no less flowing 2.03. 62
beauty and honor in her are so mingled | that 2.03. 76
and prove it too, against mine honor aught — 2.04. 39
you tender more your person's honor than | your 2.04.116
yea, upon mine honor, | i free you from't. 2.04.157
on my honor, | i speak my good lord card'nal to 2.04.166
to taint that honor every good tongue blesses, 3.01. 55
in such a point of weight, so near mine honor 3.01. 71
both for your honor better and your cause; 3.01. 95
yet will i add an honor — a great patience. 3.01.137
the honor of it | does pay the act of it, as i' 3.02.181
my heart dropp'd love, my pow'r rain'd honor, 3.02.185
tell you | you have as little honesty as honor, 3.02.271
a load would sink a navy — too much honor. 3.02.383
and sounded all the depths and shoals of honor, 3.02.436
day with shows, | pageants, and sights of honor. 4.01. 11
they that bear | the cloth of honor over her, 4.01. 48
that the great child of honor, cardinal wolsey, 4.02. 6
undoubtedly | was fashion'd to much honor. 4.02. 50
actions | to keep mine honor from corruption, 4.02. 71
truth and modesty, | now in his ashes honor. 4.02. 75
dead, good wench, | let me be us'd with honor; 4.02.168
he's honest, on mine honor. 5.01.153
sought their malice) | to quench mine honor; 5.02. 16
is this the honor they do one another? 5.02. 26
easiness and childish pity | to one man's honor, 5.02. 61
good master secretary, | i cry your honor mercy; 5.02.113
makes the church | the chief aim of his honor, 5.02.153
monarch now alive may glory | in such an honor; 5.02.199
so i grow stronger, you more honor gain. 5.02.215
that i was fain to draw mine honor in, and let 5.03. 57 P
and't please your honor, | we are but men; 5.03. 74
from her shall read the perfect /ways of honor, 5.04. 37
who from the sacred ashes of her honor | shall 5.04. 45
his honor and the greatness of his name | shall 5.04. 51
i have receiv'd much honor by your presence, 5.04. 71
that holds his honor higher than his ease, | and TRO 1.03.266
if any come, hector shall honor him; 1.03.280
for both our honor and our shame in this | are 1.03.363
as honor, loss of time, travail, expense, 2.02. 4
weigh you the worth and honor of a king | so 2.02. 26
manhood and honor | should have hare hearts, 2.02. 47
to blench from this and to stand firm by honor. 2.02. 68
hector, | she is a theme of honor and renown, 2.02.199
i hope i shall know your honor better! 3.01. 13 P
honor and lordship are my titles. 3.01. 16 P
hath any honor, but honor for those honors 3.03. 81
but honor for those honors | that are without 3.03. 81
dear my lord, | keeps honor bright; 3.03.151
way, | for honor travels in a strait so narrow, 3.03.154
ay, and perhaps receive much honor by him. 3.03.226
but in mine emulous honor let him die, | with 4.01. 29
so," | i speak it in my spirit and honor, "no." 4.04.135
cousin, all honor to thee! 4.05.138
a thought of added honor torn from hector. 4.05.145
me, of what honor was | this cressida in troy? 4.05.287
fall greeks, fail fame, honor or go or stay, 5.01. 43
sweet sir, you honor me. 5.01. 86
mine honor keeps the weather of my fate. 5.03. 26
holds honor far more precious–dear than life. 5.03. 28
art thou of blood and honor? 5.04. 27
wherein he won honor than in the embracements of COR 1.03. 4 P
considering how honor would become such a person 1.03. 10 P
this is true, on mine honor, and so i pray go 1.03.101 P
emulation | hath not that honor in't it had; 1.10. 13
these | in honor follows coriolanus. 2.01.165
and | by deed–achieving honor newly nam'd — 2.01.173
have hearts | inclinable to honor and advance 2.02. 56
he had rather venture all his limbs for honor 2.02. 80
predecessors have, | your honor with your form. 2.02.144
to our noble consul | wish we all joy and honor. 2.02.153
to coriolanus come all joy and honor! 2.02.154
wherein every one of us has a single honor, in 2.03. 44 P
let the high office and the honor go | to one 2.03.122
i have heard you say | honor and policy, like 3.02. 42
if it be honor in your wars to seem | the same 3.02. 46
shall hold companionship in peace | with honor, 3.02. 50
at stake requir'd | i should do so in honor. 3.02. 64
do't, | lest i surcease to honor mine own truth, 3.02.121
i | will answer in mine honor. 3.02.144
might condemn us, | as poisonous of your honor. 5.03.135
thou hast affected the /fine strains of honor, 5.03.149
the wars, and safely home | loaden with honor. 5.03.164
i am glad thou hast set thy mercy and thy honor 5.03.200
him, and i pawn'd | mine honor for his truth; 5.06. 21
made peace | with no less honor to the antiates 5.06. 79
let us entreat by honor of his name, | whom TIT 1.01. 39
right, | whom you pretend to honor and adore, 1.01. 42
and so i love and honor thee and thine, | thy 1.01. 49
with honor and with fortune is return'd, | from 1.01. 67
in peace and honor rest you here, my sons, 1.01.150
in peace and honor rest you here, my sons! 1.01.156
in peace and honor live lord titus long! 1.01.157
give me a staff of honor for mine age, | but not 1.01.198
thee, | but honor thee, and will do till i die. 1.01.213
to him that, for your honor and your state, 1.01.259
with these boys mine honor thou hast wounded. 1.01.365
nest, | that died in honor and lavinia's cause. 1.01.377
here, | is in opinion and in honor wrong'd, 1.01.416
but on mine honor dare i undertake | for good 1.01.436
and let it be mine honor, good my lord, | that i 1.01.466
tend'ring our sister's honor and our own. 1.01.476
that, on mine honor, here do i protest. 1.01.477
upon her wit doth earthly honor wait, | and 2.01. 10
doth make your honor of his body's hue, 2.03. 73
hair, | nor age nor honor shall shape privilege; 4.04. 57
now, by the stock and honor of my kin, | to ROM 1.05. 58
for 'tis a throne where honor may be crown'd 3.02. 93
and art | could to no issue of true honor bring. 4.01. 65
all happiness to your honor! TIM 1.01.109
lord, | pawn me to this your honor, she is his. 1.01.147
my hand to thee, mine honor on my promise. 1.01.148
i must entreat you honor me so much | as to 1.02.169
i beseech your honor, | vouchsafe me a word, it 1.02.176
may it please your honor, lord lucius | (out of 1.02.181
and has sent your honor two brace of greyhounds. 1.02.188 P
honor, and fortunes, keep with you, lord timon! 1.02.229
i love and honor him, | but must not break my 2.01. 23
of long since due debts, | against my honor? 2.02. 39
lucullus you — i hunted with his honor to–day; 2.02.189 P
behalf, i come to entreat your honor to supply; 3.01. 17 P
unto his honor has my lord's meat in him; 3.01. 57
there was very little honor show'd in't. 3.02. 19 P
i have sweat to see his honor. 3.02. 26 P
may it please your honor, my lord hath sent — 3.02. 30 P
a little part, and undo a great deal of honor! 3.02. 48 P
and i hope his honor will conceive the fairest 3.02. 53 P
who bates mine honor shall not know my coin. 3.03. 26
honor, health, and compassion to the senate! 3.05. 5
(/an honor in him which buys out his fault), 3.05. 17
all | my honor to you, upon his good returns. 3.05. 81
'tis honor with most lands to be at odds; 3.05.115
contempt hereditary, | the beggar native honor. 4.03. 11
what an alteration of honor has desp'rate want 4.03.462
beseech your honor | to make it known to us. 5.01. 89
thy glove, | or any token of thine honor else, 5.04. 50
set honor in one eye and death i' th' other, JC 1.02. 86
love | the name of honor more than i fear death. 1.02. 89
well, honor is the subject of my story: 1.02. 92
in hand | any exploit worthy the name of honor. 2.01.317
say, i love brutus, and i honor him; 3.01.128
and, by my honor, | depart untouch'd. 3.01.141
believe me for mine honor, and have respect to 3.02. 15 P
and have respect to mine honor, that you may 3.02. 15 P
as he was valiant, i honor him; 3.02. 26 P
honor for his valor; 3.02. 28 P
such as he is, full of regard and honor. 4.02. 12
a peevish schoolboy, worthless of such honor, 5.01. 61
thy life hath had some smatch of honor in it. 5.05. 46
and no man else hath honor by his death. 5.05. 57
thee as thy wounds, | they smack of honor both. MAC 1.02. 44
and for an earnest of a greater honor, | he bade 1.03.104
every thing | safe toward your love and honor. 1.04. 27
which honor must | not unaccompanied invest him 1.04. 39
when 'tis, | it shall make honor for you. 2.01. 26
here had we now our country's honor roof'd, 3.04. 39
though in your state of honor i am perfect. 4.02. 66
my thoughts | to thy good truth and honor. 4.03.117
as honor, love, obedience, troops of friends, 5.03. 25
that ever scotland | in such an honor nam'd. 5.09. 30
our duty to your honor. HAM 1.02.252
then weigh what loss your honor may sustain | if 1.03. 29
as it behooves my daughter and your honor. 1.03. 97
upon my honor — 2.02.394 P
use them after your own honor and dignity — the 2.02.531 P
lord, | how does your honor for this many a day? 3.01. 90
i warrant your honor. 3.02. 15 P
i have done | that might your nature, honor, and 5.02.231
but in my terms of honor | i stand aloof, and 5.02.246
till by some elder masters of known honor | i 5.02.248
than life, with grace, health, beauty, honor; LR 1.01. 58
fit, | obey you, love you, and most honor you. 1.01. 98
great gap in your own honor and shake in pieces 1.02. 84 P
writ this to feel my affection to your honor, 1.02. 87 P
if your honor judge it meet, i will place you 1.02. 90 P
body never spring | a babe to honor her! 1.04.281
as i have life and honor, | there shall he sit 2.02.133
eye discerning | thine honor from thy suffering, 4.02. 53
no, by mine honor, madam. 5.01. 14
i will maintain | my truth and honor firmly. 5.03.101
scurvy and provoking terms | against your honor OTH 1.02. 8
which, when i know that boasting is an honor, 1.02. 20
i would i might entreat your honor | to scan 3.03.244
and hold her free, i do beseech your honor. 3.03.255
all the office of my heart, | entirely honor. 3.04.114
she is protectress of her honor too; 4.01. 14
her honor is an essence that's not seen; 4.01. 16
your honor is most welcome. 4.03. 4
but why should honor outlive honesty? 5.02.245
for nought i did in hate, but all in honor. 5.02.295
rich in his father's honor, creeps apace | into ANT 1.03. 50
and let it look | like perfect honor. 1.03. 80
your honor calls you hence, | therefore be deaf 1.03. 97
(it wounds thine honor that i speak it now) 1.04. 69
that sleep and feeding may prorogue his honor 2.01. 26
the honor is sacred which he talks on now, 2.02. 85
do | so far ask pardon as befits mine honor | to 2.02. 97
'tis not my profit that does lead mine honor; 2.07. 76
mine honor, it. 2.07. 77
he could not | but pay me terms of honor, cold 3.04. 7
if i lose mine honor, | i lose myself; 3.04. 22
manhood, honor, ne'er before | did violate so 3.10. 22
the scars upon your honor, therefore, he | does 3.13. 58
mine honor was not yielded, | but conquer'd 3.13. 61
or bathe my dying honor in the blood | shall 4.02. 6
expect victorious life | than death and honor. 4.02. 44
shall acquire no honor | demuring upon me. 4.15. 28
of caesar seek your honor, with your safety. 4.15. 46
hand | which writ his honor in the acts it did 5.01. 22
doing the honor of thy lordliness | to one so 5.02.161
who did join his honor | against the romans with CYM 1.01. 29
i honor him | even out of your report. 1.01. 54
i dare lay mine honor | he will remain so. 1.01.174
should not betray | mine interest and his honor; 1.03. 30
a courtier to convince the honor of my mistress, 1.04. 95 P
from thence that honor of hers which you imagine 1.04.131 P
and leave her in such honor as you have trust in 1.04.152 P
is as far | from thy report as thou from honor, 1.06.146
he hath a kind of honor sets him off, | more 1.06.170
and pawn mine honor for their safety. 1.06.194
heavens hold firm | the walls of thy dear honor; 2.01. 63
the lock and ta'en | the treasure of her honor. 2.02. 42
him | according to the honor of his sender, 2.03. 58
to win the king as i am bold her honor | will 2.04. 2
i now | profess myself the winner of her honor, 2.04. 53
you had of her pure honor gains or loses | your 2.04. 59
so they must, | or do your honor injury. 2.04. 80
this is her honor! 2.04. 91
let there be no honor | where there is beauty; 2.04.108
of him i gather'd honor, | which he to seek of 3.01. 70
i' th' name of fame and honor which dies i' th' 3.03. 51
false oaths prevail'd | before my perfect honor, 3.03. 67
mother, | and every day do honor to her grave. 3.03.105
the due of honor in no point omit. 3.05. 11
them | to royalty unlearn'd, honor untaught, 4.02.178
and tenantius' right | with honor to maintain. 5.04. 74
and the grace of it | (which is our honor), 5.05.133
no lesser of her honor confident | than i did 5.05.187
and with oath to violate | my lady's honor. 5.05.285
be | as doth befit our honor and your worth. PER 1.01.120
die, | for by his fall my honor must keep high. 1.01.149
nor boots it me to say i honor /him, | if he 1.02. 20
then honor be but a goal to my will, | this day 2.01.165
in honor of whose birth these triumphs are, 2.02. 5
'tis now your honor, daughter, to entertain 2.02. 14
which, to preserve mine honor, i'll perform. 2.02. 16
honor we love, | for who hates honor hates the 2.03. 21
for who hates honor hates the gods above. 2.03. 22
give to every one that come | to honor them; 2.03. 61
and on her virgin honor will not break it. 2.05. 12
daughter, | but bent all offices to honor her. 2.05. 48
we give, and therein may | use honor with you. 3.01. 26
than to be thirsty after tottering honor, | or 3.02. 40
your honor has through ephesus pour'd forth 3.02. 43
your honor and your goodness teach me to't 3.03. 26
madam, | by bright diana, whom we honor, all 3.03. 28
now the gods to bless your honor! 4.06. 21 P
i am glad to see your honor in good health. 4.06. 22 P
your honor knows what 'tis to say well enough. 4.06. 31 P
i beseech your honor give me leave a word, and 4.06. 46 P
come, we will leave his honor and her together. 4.06. 65 P
if you were born to honor, show it now; 4.06. 92
i beseech your honor one piece for me. 4.06.117 P
and shake to lose his honor) is like her | that, TNK pr 5
whom jove hath mark'd | the honor of your bed, 1.01. 30
born to uphold creation in that honor | first 1.01. 82
to his bold ends honor and golden ingots, 1.02. 17
he | a quarter carrier of that honor which | his 1.02.108
lords, and honor them | with treble ceremony — 1.04. 7
the hardy youths strive for the games of honor, 2.02. 10
shall we two exercise, like twins of honor, 2.02. 18
(which is the curse of honor) lastly | children 2.02. 54
we are young and yet desire the ways of honor, 2.02. 73
a maid, if she have any honor, would be loath 2.02.145
and let mine honor down, and never charge? 2.02.195
of all the world, | dwells fair–ey'd honor. 2.05. 29
all dues | fit for the honor you have won; 2.05. 61
the /void'st of honor | that ev'r bore gentle 3.01. 36
honor and honesty | i cherish and depend on, 3.01. 50
you | by all the honesty and honor in you, | no 3.03. 14
cousin, | is but a debt to honor, and my duty. 3.06. 19
my cause and honor guard me! 3.06. 92
a place prepar'd for those that sleep in honor, 3.06. 99

me, | the law will have the honor of our ends. 3.06.130
by your own spotless honor — 3.06.196
hourly bring your honor | in public question 3.06.221
bow not my honor. 3.06.226
think how you maim your honor | (for now i am 3.06.237
yet i'll preserve | the honor of affection, and 3.06.269
and, by mine honor, once again it stands, | or 3.06.289
fame and honor, | methinks, from hence, as from 4.02. 21
his show | has all the ornament of honor in't. 4.02. 93
his nose stands high, a character of honor; 4.02.110
they are all the sons of honor. 4.02.141
they have a noble work in hand will honor | the 5.01. 6
honor crown the worthiest! 5.01. 17
she shall see deeds of honor in their kind 5.03. 12
a grain of honor | they not o'erweigh us. 5.04. 18
and i to honor. 5.04. 98
the more thou hast | either of honor, office, STM III 15
honor and beauty, in the owner's arms, | are LUC 27
his honor, his affairs, his friends, his state, 45
of all is but to nurse the life | with honor, 142
as life for honor in fell battle's rage, | honor 145
honor for wealth, and oft that wealth doth cost 146
make, | pawning his honor to obtain his lust, 156
to kill thine honor with thy live's decay; 516
and stoop to honor, not to foul desire. 574
thou wrong'st his honor, wound'st his princely 599
"if, collatine, thine honor lay in me, | from me 834
wrack, | yet for thy honor did i entertain him; 842
honor thyself to rid me of this shame, | for if 1031
shame, | for if i die, my honor lives in thee, 1032
"my honor i'll bequeath unto the knife | that 1184
'tis honor to deprive dishonor'd life, | the one 1186
my shame so dead, mine honor is new born. 1190
mine honor be the knife's that makes my wound, 1201
know | her honor is ta'en prisoner by the foe, 1608
dispense, | my low–declined honor to advance? 1705
which husbandry in honor might uphold | against SON 13.10
stars | of public honor and proud titles boast, 25. 2
bars, | unlook'd for joy in that i honor most. 25. 4
foil'd, | is from the book of honor rased quite, 25.11
shame, | nor thou with public kindness honor me, 36.11
me, | unless thou take that honor from thy name. 36.12
and gilded honor shamefully misplac'd, | and 66. 5
finding myself in honor so forbid, | with safest LC 150
with safest distance i mine honor shielded. 151

/HONORABLE 1 FR 0.0001 REL FR 0 V 1 P
/my /oath /before /this /honorable /assembly, LR 3.06. 47 P

HONORABLE 127 FR 0.0143 REL FR 88 V 39 P
holy gonzalo, honorable man, | mine eyes, ev'n TMP 5.01. 62
and sure the match | were rich and honorable; TGV 3.01. 64
it's an honorable kind of thievery. 4.01. 39
he bears an honorable mind, | and will not use a 5.03. 13
my chambers are honorable. WIV 4.05. 22 P
before these varlets here, thou honorable man, MM 2.01. 87 P
to a man, stuff'd with all honorable virtues. ADO 1.01. 57 P
lady, for you are like an honorable father. 1.01.112 P
is not marriage honorable in a beggar? 3.04. 30 P
is not your lord honorable without marriage? 3.04. 31 P
here stand a pair of honorable men, | a third is 5.01.266
conjoin'd | in the state of honorable marriage, 5.04. 30
at tables, chides the dice | in honorable terms; LLL 5.02.327
and be honorable | without the stamp of merit? MV 2.09. 38
lies, | how honorable ladies sought my love, 3.04. 70
commend me to your honorable wife, | tell her 4.01.273
the world esteem'd thy father honorable, | but i AYL 1.02.225
shepherd, let us make an honorable retreat, 3.02.160 P
a married man more honorable than the bare brow 3.03. 60 P
love, | he bear himself with honorable action, SHR in.1. 110
mine honorable mistress. AWW 1.03.139
with lords and honorable personages than the 2.03.261 P
french count has done most honorable service. 3.05. 4 P
you need but plead your honorable privilege. 4.05. 90 P
my master hath been an honorable gentleman. 5.03.239 P
the honorable lady of the house, which is she? TN 1.05.167 P
mistress | (so sovereignly being honorable). WT 1.02.323
in honor and by him | that i think honorable. 1.02.408
add | 'tis pity she's not honest — honorable. 2.01. 68
that honorable grief lodg'd here which burns 2.01.111
of the young prince, whose honorable thoughts 3.02.195
his mind) to find thee | an honorable husband. 5.03.143
an honorable conduct let him have. JN 1.01. 29
from a resolv'd and honorable war | to a most 2.01.585
and there | where honorable rescue and defense 5.02. 18
let me wipe off this honorable dew, | that 5.02. 45
of lancaster, | the honorable father to my foe, R2 1.01.136
and by the honorable tomb he swears | that 3.03.105
that honorable day shall never be seen. 4.01. 91
and is not this an honorable spoil? 1H4 1.01. 74
a dish of skim–milk with so honorable an action! 2.03. 33 P
to the wars, and thy place shall be honorable. 2.04.545 P
to you | this honorable bounty shall belong. 5.05. 26
you call honorable boldness impudent sauciness; 2H4 2.01.123 P
"i will imitate the honorable romans in brevity. 2.02.123 P
is this proceeding just and honorable? 4.02.110
his cause being just and his quarrel honorable. H5 4.01.128 P
know, to this hour is an honorable badge of the 4.07.101 P
tradition, /begun upon an honorable respect, and 5.01. 71 P
my honorable lords, health to you all! 1H6 1.01. 57
my gracious prince, and honorable peers, 3.04. 1
knight, | profaning this most honorable order, 4.01. 41
confirm it so, mine honorable lord. 4.01.122
and whiles the honorable captain there | drops 4.04. 17
dishonor not her honorable name | to make a 4.05. 14
gone, | may honorable peace attend thy throne! 2H6 2.03. 38
blood, | the honorable blood of lancaster, 4.01. 51
therefore am i of an honorable house. 4.02. 49 P
by my faith, the field is honorable, and there 4.02. 50 P
war, | and shame thine honorable age with blood? 5.01.170
set down, set down your honorable load — | if R3 1.02. 1
but you, my honorable lords, may name the time, 3.04. 18
letter, | the honorable board of council out, H8 1.01. 79
with all their honorable points of ignorance 1.03. 26
fair rape | wip'd off, in honorable keeping her. TRO 2.02.149
deserve not so honorable a grave as to stuff a COR 2.01. 88 P
honorable menenius, my boy martius approaches. 2.01.100 P
think'st thou it honorable for a noble man 5.03.154
to men | of noble minds is honorable meed. TIT 1.01.216
to advance | thy name and honorable family, 1.01.239
of his armory | to gratify your honorable youth, 4.02. 12
whose high exploits and honorable deeds 5.01. 11
titus | hath ordain'd to an honorable end, | for 5.03. 22
of honorable reckoning are you both, | and pity ROM 1.02. 4
if that thy bent of love be honorable, | thy 2.02.143
a /damned saint, an honorable villain! 3.02. 79
more honorable state, more courtship lives | in 3.03. 34
stuff'd, as they say, with honorable parts, 3.05.181
your honorable letter he desires | to those have TIM 1.01. 97
my lord, that honorable gentleman, lord lucullus 1.02.186 P
you are honorable, | but yet they could have 2.02.206
and how does that honorable, complete, 3.01. 9 P
my very good friend, and an honorable gentleman. 3.02. 2 P
denied that honorable man? 3.02. 18 P
well, commend me to thy honorable virtuous lord, 3.02. 28 P
time, when i might ha' shown myself honorable! 3.02. 46 P
i cannot pleasure such an honorable gentleman. 3.02. 57 P
illustrious virtue, | and honorable carriage, 3.02. 81
i think this honorable lord did but try us this 3.06. 2 P
my most honorable lord, i am e'en sick of shame 3.06. 41 P
yet i see | thy honorable mettle may be wrought JC 1.02.309
you are my true and honorable wife, | as dear to 2.01.288
brave son, deriv'd from honorable loins! 2.01.322
and the rest | (for brutus is an honorable man, 3.02. 82
so are they all, all honorable men), | come i to 3.02. 83
was ambitious, | and brutus is an honorable man. 3.02. 87
was ambitious, | and brutus is an honorable man. 3.02. 94
ambitious, | and sure he is an honorable man. 3.02. 99
wrong, | who (you all know) are honorable men. 3.02.124
and you, | than i will wrong such honorable men. 3.02.127
i fear i wrong the honorable men | whose daggers 3.02.151
they were traitors; honorable men! 3.02.153
they that have done this deed are honorable. 3.02.212
they are wise and honorable, | and will no doubt 3.02.214
young man, thou couldst not die more honorable. 5.01. 60
importun'd me with love | in honorable fashion. HAM 1.03.111
as of a man faithful and honorable. 2.02.130
remember him hereafter as my honorable friend. LR 1.01. 28 P
let's teach ourselves that honorable stop, | not OTH 2.03. 2
he knows not yet of his honorable fortune. 4.02.234 P
an honorable murderer, if you will; 5.02.294
to his love, which stands | an honorable trial. ANT 1.03. 75
my honorable friend, agrippa! 2.02.173 P
have entertainment, but | no honorable trust. 4.06. 17
how honorable and how kindly we | determine for 5.01. 58
though he be honorable — 5.02.108
if thou wert honorable, | thou wouldst have told CYM 1.06.142
her attendants are | all sworn and honorable. 2.04.125
for he's honorable, | and doubling that, most 3.04.176
he did not flow | from honorable courses. PER 4.03. 28
i would have you note, this is an honorable man. 4.06. 50 P
to him indeed, but how honorable he is in that, 4.06. 56 P
i hear say you're of honorable parts, and are 4.06. 81 P
such most | that, sweating in an honorable toil, TNK 1.02. 33
anger, | as you love any thing that's honorable. 3.06. 27
they are honorable, | how good they'll prove, i 4.01. 30
"shall plight your honorable faiths to me | with LUC 1690

HONORABLE–DANGEROUS 1 FR 0.0001 REL FR 1 V 0 P
enterprise | of honorable–dangerous consequence; JC 1.03.124

/HONORABLY 1 FR 0.0001 REL FR 1 V 0 P
lords, use her /honorably. 3H6 3.02.123

HONORABLY 6 FR 0.0006 REL FR 5 V 1 P
of speaking honorably? ADO 3.04. 29 P
lord | most honorably doth uphold his word. LLL 5.02.449
ay, edward will use women honorably. 3H6 3.02.124
with all his covent honorably receiv'd him; H8 4.02. 19
aemilius, do this message honorably, | and if he TIT 4.04.104
lie, | most like a soldier, ordered honorably. JC 5.05. 79

HONORATO 1 FR 0.0001 REL FR 0 V 1 P
ben venuto, molto honorato signor mio petruchio. SHR 1.02. 25 P

HONOR'D 44 FR 0.0049 REL FR 42 V 2 P
hag–born) not honor'd with | a human shape. TMP 1.02.283
may prosperous be, | and honor'd in their issue. 4.01.105
days | to the sweet glances of thy honor'd love, TGV 1.01. 4
be sometime honor'd for his burning throne! MM 5.01.293
oblivion is the tomb | of honor'd bones indeed. AWW 2.03.141
my honor'd lady, | i have forgiven and forgotten 5.03. 8
you have ever been my father's honor'd friend, WT 4.04.493
yourself, assisted with your honor'd friends, 5.01.113
that noble honor'd lord, is fear'd and lov'd? 5.01.158
i honor'd him, i lov'd him, and will weep | my JN 4.03.105
thou, most fine, most honor'd, most renown'd, 2H4 4.05.163
have made thee fear'd and honor'd of the people; 2H6 1.01.198
my honor'd lord. H8 2.03. 80
most honor'd madam, | my lord of york, out of 3.01. 61
by mingling them with us, the honor'd number, COR 3.01. 72
when he did love his country, | it honor'd him. 3.01.304
th' honor'd gods | keep rome in safety, and the 3.03. 33
then the honor'd mould | wherein this trunk was 5.03. 22
my honor'd lord — TIM 3.02. 26 P
pity not honor'd age for his white beard, | he 4.03.112
and believe it, | my most honor'd lord, | for 4.03.518
i fear'd caesar, honor'd him, and lov'd him. JC 3.01.129
and mayst be honor'd, being cato's son. 5.04. 11
kill brutus, and be honor'd in his death. 5.04. 14
see, see, our honor'd hostess! MAC 1.06. 10
he hath honor'd me of late, and i have bought 1.07. 32
as i do live, my honor'd lord, 'tis true, | and HAM 1.02.221
more honor'd in the breach than the observance. 1.04. 16
my honor'd lord! 2.02.222 P
my honor'd lord, you know right well you did, 3.01. 96
honor'd, belov'd, and haply one as kind | for 3.02.176
lear, | whom i have ever honor'd as my king, LR 1.01.140
in honor'd love. 5.01. 9
wounds, and kiss | the honor'd gashes whole. ANT 4.08. 11
honor'd with confirmation your great judgment CYM 1.06.174
which then he wore | upon his honor'd finger, to 5.05.184
mine honor'd lady! 5.05.232
to an honor'd triumph strangely furnished. PER 2.02. 53
we are honor'd much by good simonides. 2.03. 20
most honor'd cleon, | it must needs be gone. 3.03. 1
the honor'd name | of pericles to rage the city 5.03. 96
you have honor'd her fair birthday with your TNK 2.05. 36
honor'd friend, | to you i give the field; 4.02.149
mightier is the thing | that makes him honor'd, LUC 1005

HONORED 10 FR 0.0011 REL FR 10 V 0 P
feast shall be much honored in your marriage. MV 3.02.212
every town, | high wedlock then be honored. AYL 5.04.144
i am from humble, he from honored name; AWW 1.03.156
and think me honored | to feast so great a 1H6 2.03. 81
match | i hold me highly honored of your grace, TIT 1.01.245
judge, | how i have lov'd and honored saturnine! 1.01.427
most honored timon, | it hath pleas'd the gods TIM 1.02. 1
o helicanus, strike me, honored sir, | give me a PER 5.01.190
honored hippolyta, | most dreaded amazonian, TNK 1.01. 77
they knew, | and him by oath they truly honored: LUC 410

HONOREST 1 FR 0.0001 REL FR 1 V 0 P
good brother, as thou lov'st and honorest arms, 3H6 1.01.116

HONOR–FLAW'D 1 FR 0.0001 REL FR 1 V 0 P
be she honor–flaw'd, | i have three daughters: WT 2.01.143

HONOR–GIVING 1 FR 0.0001 REL FR 1 V 0 P
by the honor–giving hand | of cordelion knighted JN 1.01. 53

HONORIFICABILITUDINITATIBUS 1 FR 0.0001 REL FR 0 V 1 P
long by the head as honorificabilitudinitatibus: LLL 5.01. 41 P

HONORING 2 FR 0.0002 REL FR 2 V 0 P
being on shore, honoring of neptune's triumphs, PER 5.01. 17
canopy, | with my extern the outward honoring, SON 125. 2

HONOR–OWING 1 FR 0.0001 REL FR 1 V 0 P
side | (yoke–fellow to his honor–owing wounds) H5 4.06. 9

HONOR'S 30 FR 0.0034 REL FR 27 V 3 P
here is her oath for love, her honor's pawn: TGV 1.03. 47
but you shall come to it, by your honor's leave. MM 2.01.121 P
i crave your honor's pardon. 2.02. 14
but to our honor's great disparagement, | yet ERR 1.01.148
your honor's players, hearing your amendment, SHR in.2. 129
that is honor's scorn, | which challenges itself AWW 2.03.133
which challenges itself as honor's born, | and 2.03.134
my honor's at the stake, which to defeat, | i 2.03.149
mine honor's such a ring, | my chastity's the 4.02. 45
are forfeited to me, and my honor's paid to him. 5.03.143 P
the gentleman will, for his honor's sake, have TN 3.04.306 P
much strength | as to take up mine honor's pawn, R2 1.01. 74
there is my honor's pawn, | engage it to the 4.01. 55
in proof whereof, there is my honor's pawn, 4.01. 70
a son who is the theme of honor's tongue, 1H4 1.01. 81
and honor's thought | reigns solely in the H5 2.pr. 3
god hold it, to your honor's good content! R3 3.02.105
honor's train | is longer than his foreskirt. H8 2.03. 97
and now at last, laden with honor's spoils, TIT 1.01. 36
and triumphs over chance in honor's bed. 1.01.178
owe, | mine honor's ensigns humbled at thy feet. 1.01.252
wept, | because they died in honor's lofty bed. 3.01. 11
quarrel in a straw | when honor's at the stake. HAM 4.04. 56
to plainness honor's bound, | when majesty falls LR 1.01.148
try honor's cause; PER 2.04. 41
i came unto your court for honor's cause, | and 2.05. 61
me, | this sword shall prove he's honor's enemy. 2.05. 64
for honor's sake, and safely presently | into TNK 3.06.110
forgetting shame's pure blush and honor's wrack. VEN 558
"yet am i guilty of thy honor's wrack, | yet for LUC 841

HONORS' 2 FR 0.0002 REL FR 1 V 1 P
and longing (saving your honors' reverence) for MM 2.01. 90 P
your honors' pardon; COR 2.02. 68

HONORS 81 FR 0.0091 REL FR 77 V 4 P
fair milan | with all the honors on my brother; TMP 1.02.127
therefore take your honors. MM 1.01. 52
threepence — your honors have seen such dishes; 2.01. 93 P
some certain special honors it pleaseth his LLL 5.01.106 P
and when your honors mean to solemnize | the MV 3.02.192
honors thrive, | when rather from our acts we AWW 2.03.135
and all the honors that can fly from us | shall 3.01. 20
your honors all, | i do refer me to the oracle: WT 3.02.114
bed and make her rich | in titles, honors, and JN 2.01.492
his thin bestained cloak | with our pure honors, 4.03. 25
your banish'd honors and restore yourselves 1H4 1.03.181
and all the budding honors on thy crest | i'll 5.04. 72
there were two honors lost, yours and your son's 2H4 2.03. 16
and bloody insurrection | with your fair honors. 4.01. 41
lay a heavy and unequal hand | upon our honors? 4.01.101
that thou wilt needs invest thee with my honors 4.05. 95
sword, | and i do wish your honors may increase, 5.02.104
and all wide–stretched honors that pertain | by H5 2.04. 82
speculation — | but that our honors must not. 4.02. 32
and draw their honors reeking up to heaven, 4.03.101
doo's me as great honors as can be desir'd in 4.07.160 P
let not sloth dim your honors new begot. 1H6 1.01. 79
woman, do what thou canst to save our honors; 1.02.147
will not your honors bear me company? 2.02. 53
your honors shall perceive how i will work | to 3.03. 27
lives, honors, lands, and all, hurry to loss. 4.03. 53
and shall these labors and these honors die? 2H6 1.01. 95
enchas'd with all the honors of the world? 1.02. 8
who hateth him and honors not his father, 4.08. 16
to london | to see these honors in possession. 3H6 2.06.110
but as this title honors me and mine, | so your 4.01. 72
and lay those honors on your high desert. R3 1.03. 96
a most royal prince | restor'd me to my honors; H8 2.01.114
all men's honors | lie like one lump before him, 2.02. 47
bade me enjoy it, with the place and honors, 3.02.248
and bears his blushing honors thick upon him; 3.02.354
no sun shall ever usher forth mine honors, | or 3.02.410
he gave his honors to the world again, | his 4.02. 29
and, to add greater honors to his age | than man 4.02. 67
please your honors, | the chief cause concerns 5.02. 37
that can from hector bring those honors off, TRO 1.03.334
which hath our several honors all engag'd | to 2.02.124
but honor for those honors | that are without 3.03. 81
half all cominius' honors are to martius, COR 1.01.273
and all his faults | to martius shall be honors, 1.01.275
i leave your honors. 1.02. 33
and keep your honors safe! 1.02. 37
that with the fusty plebeians hate thine honors, 1.09. 7
greetings, | but with them change of honors. 2.01.198
he cannot temp'rately transport his honors 2.01.224
with the least cause these his new honors, which 2.01.229
hath so planted his honors in their eyes and his 2.02. 29 P
and to remember | with honors like himself. 2.02. 48
he cannot but with measure fit the honors 2.02.123
them, but he could not | carry his honors even. 4.07. 37
please it your honors | to call me to your 5.06.138
rome, | then let my father's honors live in me, TIT 1.01. 7

proclaim our honors, lords, with trump and drum. 1.01.275
i may, | i greet your honors from andronicus — 4.02. 5
for some new honors that are heap'd on caesar. JC 1.02.134
and no man here | but honors you; 2.01. 91
and though we lay these honors on this man | to 4.01. 19
the name of cassius honors this corruption, 4.03. 15
and sell the mighty space of our large honors 4.03. 25
new honors come upon him, | like our strange MAC 1.03.144
against those honors deep and broad wherewith 1.06. 17
must lave our honors in these flattering streams 3.02. 33
do faithful homage and receive free honors; 3.06. 36
to his wonted way again, | to both your honors. HAM 3.01. 41
who make them honors | of men's impossibilities, LR 4.06. 73
is my privilege, | the privilege of mine honors, 5.03.130
and such addition as your honors | have more 5.03.302
and to his honors and his valiant parts | did i OTH 1.03.253
that hold their honors in a wary distance, | the 2.03. 56
his taints and honors | wag'd equal with him. ANT 5.01. 30
but it honors us | that we have given him cause. CYM 3.05. 18
knighthoods and honors, borne | as i wear mine, 5.02. 6
to-day how many would have given their honors 5.03. 66
makest affections bend | to godlike honors; TNK 1.01.230
how dangerous, if we will keep our honors, | it 1.02. 37
now she adds honors to his hateful name; VEN 994
HOO 6 FR 0.0006 REL FR 5 V 1 P
hoo! COR 2.01.106 P
our enemy is banish'd, he is gone! hoo! hoo! 3.03.137
our enemy is banish'd, he is gone! hoo! hoo! 3.03.137
hoo, says 'a. there's my cap. ANT 2.07.134
hoo, hearts, tongues, /figures, scribes, bards, 3.02. 16
think, speak, cast, write, sing, number, hoo! 3.02. 17
HOOD* 8 FR 0.0009 REL FR 7 V 1 P
is saying, hood mine eyes | thus with my hat, MV 2.02.193
now, by my hood, a gentle, and no jew. 2.06. 51
they live like the old robin hood of england. AYL 1.01.116 P
"and robin hood, scarlet, and john." 2H4 5.03.103
hood my unmann'd blood, bating in my cheeks, ROM 3.02. 14
a jealous hood, a jealous hood! 4.04. 13
a jealous hood, a jealous hood! 4.04. 13
my fam'd works makes lighter | than robin hood!"
TNK pr 21
HOODED 2 FR 0.0002 REL FR 0 V 2 P
lying rascal, you must be hooded, must you? MM 5.01.352 P
'tis a hooded valor, and when it appears, it H5 3.07.111 P
HOODMAN 1 FR 0.0001 REL FR 0 V 1 P
hush, hush! hoodman comes! portotartarossa. AWW 4.03.118 P
HOODMAN-BLIND 1 FR 0.0001 REL FR 1 V 0 P
that thus hath cozen'd you at hoodman-blind? HAM 3.04. 77
HOOD'S 1 FR 0.0001 REL FR 1 V 0 P
by the bare scalp of robin hood's fat friar, TGV 4.01. 36
HOODS 1 FR 0.0001 REL FR 1 V 0 P
but all hoods make not monks. H8 3.01. 23
HOODWINK 3 FR 0.0003 REL FR 2 V 1 P
bring thee to | shall hoodwink this mischance; TMP 4.01.206
we will bind and hoodwink him so, that he shall AWW 3.06. 25 P
and yet seem cold, the time you may so hoodwink.
MAC 4.03. 72
HOODWINK'D 3 FR 0.0003 REL FR 3 V 0 P
and, hoodwink'd as thou art, will lead thee on AWW 4.01. 81
we'll have no cupid hoodwink'd with a scarf, ROM 1.04. 4
the disorder's such | as war were hoodwink'd. CYM 5.02. 16
HOOF 3 FR 0.0003 REL FR 2 V 1 P
plod away i' th' hoof! WIV 1.03. 82
basest horn of his hoof is more musical than the H5 3.07. 17 P
the bearing earth with his hard hoof he wounds, VEN 267
HOOFS 6 FR 0.0006 REL FR 6 V 0 P
rebels wound thee with their horses' hoofs. R2 3.02. 7
nor bruise her flow'rets with the armed hoofs 1H4 1.01. 8
and stiff | under the hoofs of vaunting enemies, 5.03. 42
printing their proud hoofs i' th' receiving H5 pr 27
as 'twere to th' music | his own hoofs made (for TNK 5.04. 60
legs, on his hind hoofs | /... on end he stands, 5.04. 76
HOOK 10 FR 0.0011 REL FR 5 V 5 P
catch a saint, | with saints dost bait thy hook! MM 2.02.180
bait the hook well, this fish will bite. ADO 2.03.108 P
but she | i can hook to me — say that she were WT 2.03. 7
true liegeman upon the cross of a welsh hook — 1H4 2.04.339 P
go with her, with her, hook on, hook on. 2H4 2.01.162 P
go with her, with her, hook on, hook on. 2.01.162 P
hold hook and line, say i. 2.04.158 P
my bended hook shall pierce | their slimy jaws; ANT 2.05. 12
your diver | did hang a salt-fish on his hook, 2.05. 17
loves woman for, besides that hook of wiving, CYM 5.05.167
HOOKING 1 FR 0.0001 REL FR 1 V 0 P
hooking both right and wrong to th' appetite, MM 2.04.176
HOOK-NOS'D 1 FR 0.0001 REL FR 0 V 1 P
justly say, with the hook-nos'd fellow of rome, 2H4 4.03. 41 P
HOOKS 4 FR 0.0004 REL FR 4 V 0 P
to cast up, with a pair of anchoring hooks, TGV 3.01.118
she steal love's sweet bait from fearful hooks. ROM 2.pr. 8
touch'd no unknown baits, nor fear'd no hooks, LUC 103
why of eyes' falsehood hast thou forged hooks, SON 137. 7
HOOP* *(also whoop, etc.)*
/HOOP* 1 FR 0.0001 REL FR 1 V 0 P
or /hoop his body more with thy embraces, | i WT 4.04.439
HOOP* 6 FR 0.0006 REL FR 6 V 0 P
who with age and envy | was grown into a hoop? TMP 1.02.259
and wear his colors like a tumbler's hoop! LLL 3.01.188
about a hoop of gold, a paltry ring | that she MV 5.01.147
a hoop of gold to bind thy brothers in, | that 2H4 4.04. 43
cause | that admiration did not hoop at them; H5 2.02.108
what hoop should hold us staunch from edge to ANT 2.02.115
HOOP'D 1 FR 0.0001 REL FR 1 V 0 P
th' voice of slaves to be | hoop'd out of rome. COR 4.05. 78
HOOPING 1 FR 0.0001 REL FR 0 V 1 P
wonderful, and after that, out of all hooping! AYL 3.02.193 P
HOOPS 2 FR 0.0002 REL FR 1 V 1 P
the three-hoop'd pot shall have ten hoops, and i 2H6 4.02. 67 P
grapple them unto thy soul with hoops of steel, HAM 1.03. 63
HOOT 1 FR 0.0001 REL FR 1 V 0 P
clusters, | who did hoot him out o' th' city. COR 4.06.123
HOOTED *(also howted, etc.)*
HOOTED 1 FR 0.0001 REL FR 1 V 0 P
you, should be hooted at | like an old tale; WT 5.03.116
HOOTING 1 FR 0.0001 REL FR 1 V 0 P
cast | your stinking greasy caps in hooting at COR 4.06.131
HOOTS 1 FR 0.0001 REL FR 1 V 0 P
that nightly hoots and wonders | at our quaint MND 2.02. 6
HOP 8 FR 0.0009 REL FR 8 V 0 P
hop in his walks and gambol in his eyes; MND 3.01.165
ay, that left pap, | where heart doth hop. 5.01.299
fairy sprite | hop as light as bird from brier, 5.01.394
go hop me over every kennel home, | for you SHR 4.03. 98
for you shall hop without my custom, sir. 4.03. 99
would make thee quickly hop without thy head. 2H6 1.03.137
bird, | that lets it hop a little from his hand, ROM 2.02.178
hop forty paces through the public street; ANT 2.02.229
HOP'D 4 FR 0.0004 REL FR 2 V 2 P
i had well hop'd thou wouldst have denied ADO 5.04.112 P
'tis hop'd his sickness is discharg'd. WT 2.03. 11
i hop'd there was no need to trouble himself H5 2.03. 21 P
i hop'd thou shouldst have been my hamlet's wife HAM 5.01.244
HOPDANCE *(see hoppedance)*
HOP'D-FOR 2 FR 0.0002 REL FR 2 V 0 P
cold biting winter mars our hop'd-for hay. 3H6 4.08. 61
us, | that there's no hop'd-for mercy with the 5.04. 35
/HOPE 2 FR 0.0002 REL FR 2 V 0 P
/lives /so /in /hope, /as /in /an /early /spring 2H4 1.03. 38
/fruit | /hope /gives /not /so /much /warrant, 1.03. 40
HOPE 383 FR 0.0433 REL FR 287 V 96 P
i have no hope | that he's undrown'd. TMP 2.01.238
out of that no hope | what great hope have you! 2.01.239
out of that no hope | what great hope have you! 2.01.240
no hope, that way, is | another way so high a 2.01.240
another way so high a hope that even | ambition 2.01.241
i hope now thou art not drown'd. 2.02.109 P
even here i will put off my hope, and keep it 3.03. 7
i am right glad that he's so out of hope. 3.03. 11
as i hope | for quiet days, fair issue, and long 4.01. 23
where i have hope to see the nuptial | of these 5.01.309
hope is a lover's staff; TGV 3.01.248
the least whereof would quell a lover's hope, 4.02. 13
ay, but i hope, sir, that you love not here. 4.02. 21
i hope thou wilt. 4.04. 43
i hope my master's suit will be but cold, 4.04.181
i hope we shall drink down all unkindness. WIV 1.01.196 P
i hope, sir, i will do as it shall become one 1.01.233 P
i hope, upon familiarity will grow more content. 1.01.249 P
the best way were to entertain him with hope, 2.01. 67 P
and that, i hope, is an unmeasurable distance. 2.01.104 P
well, i hope it be not so. 2.01.109 P
hope is a curtal dog in some affairs. 2.01.110
they have not so little grace, i hope. 2.02.112 P
i hope i have your good will, father page. 3.02. 60 P
'tis not so, i hope. 3.03.111 P
and give him another hope, to betray him to 3.03.195 P
i hope not, i had lief as bear so much lead. 4.02.113 P
i hope good luck lies in odd numbers. 5.01. 2 P
i have great hope in that; MM 1.02.182
being one) | in hand, and hope of action; 1.04. 52
all hope is gone, | unless you have the grace by 1.04. 68
i hope here be truths. 2.01.127 P
why, very well then; i hope here be truths. 2.01.133 P
so then you hope of pardon from lord angelo? 3.01. 1
have no other medicine | but only hope: 3.01. 3
i have hope to live, and am prepar'd to die. 3.01. 4
i hope, sir, your good worship will be my bail. 3.02. 72 P
o, you hope the duke will return no more; 3.02.164 P
and i hope, if you have occasion to use me for 4.02. 56 P
i hope it is some pardon or reprieve | for the 4.02. 71
there's some in hope. 4.02. 78
i hope you will not mock me with a husband! 5.01.417
but longer did we not retain much hope; ERR 1.01. 65
of whom i hope to make much benefit; 1.02. 25
for which, i hope, thou felt'st i was displeas'd 2.02. 19
you'll let us in, i hope? 3.01. 54
and if i have not, sir, i hope you have: 4.01. 43
she is too big, i hope, for me to compass. 4.01.111
i hope you do not mean to cheat me so? 4.03. 78
then | i hope i shall have leisure to make good, 5.01.376
but i hope you have no intent to turn husband, ADO 1.01.193 P
i hope to see you one day fitted with a husband. 2.01. 57 P
i hope he be in love. 3.02. 17 P
yea, sir, we hope. 4.02. 17 P
write down, that they hope they serve god; 4.02. 18 P
term, | which i hope well is not enrolled there; LLL 1.01. 38
the which i hope is not enrolled there; 1.01. 41
which i hope well is not enrolled there. 1.01. 46
soever the matter, i hope in god for high words. 1.01.192 P
a high hope for a low heaven. 1.01.194 P
sir, i hope when i do it i shall do it on a full 1.02.148 P
in love, i hope — sweet fellowship in shame. 4.03. 47
sir, under correction, sir, i hope it is not so. 5.02.489
i hope, sir, three times thrice, sir — 5.02.491
but i hope i was perfect. 5.02.558 P
and i hope here is a play fitted. MND 1.02. 65 P
therefore be out of hope, of question, of doubt; 3.02.279
i hope she will be brief. 5.01.317 P
i hope i shall make shift to go without him. MV 1.02. 90 P
as my father, being, i hope, an old man, shall 2.02.134 P
hazard all | do it in hope of fair advantages; 2.07. 19
fortune now | to my heart's hope! 2.09. 20
there is but one hope in it that can do you any 3.05. 6 P
and that is but a kind of bastard hope neither. 3.05. 7 P
and what hope is that, i pray thee? 3.05. 9 P
you may partly hope that your father got you not 3.05. 10 P
that were a kind of bastard hope indeed; 3.05. 13 P
how shalt thou hope for mercy, rend'ring none? 4.01. 88
which speed, we hope, the better for our words. 5.01.115
not that, i hope, which you receiv'd of me. 5.01.185
i hope i shall see an end of him; AYL 1.01.164 P
ribs, that there is little hope of life in him. 1.02.128 P
in the which hope i blush, and hide my sword. 2.07.119
nay, i hope. 3.02. 36 P
a poet, i might have some hope thou didst feign. 3.03. 27 P
no, faith, proud mistress, hope not after it. 3.05. 45
i hope so. 4.01.122 P
and i hope it is no dishonest desire to desire 5.03. 3 P
as those that fear they hope, and know they fear 5.04. 4
i hope this reason stands for my excuse. SHR in.2. 124
me, | and i do hope good days and long to see. 1.02.192
one, | though paris came in hope to speed alone. 1.02.245
so shall you quietly enjoy your hope, | and 3.02.136
reign, | and 'tis my hope to end successfully. 4.01.189
why, how now, kate, i hope thou art not mad. 4.05. 42
i hope i may choose, sir. 5.01. 47 P
out of hope of all but my share of the feast. 5.01.141
i hope better. 5.02. 85
what hope is there of his majesty's amendment? AWW 1.01. 11 P
practices he hath persecuted time with hope, and 1.01. 15 P
the process but only the losing of hope by time. 1.01. 16 P
and i hope to have friends for my wive's sake. 1.03. 39 P
i know i love in vain, strive against hope; 1.03.201
'tis our hope, sir, | after well-ent'red 2.01. 5
so stain our judgment, or corrupt our hope, | to 2.01.120
where hope is coldest and despair most /fits. 2.01.144
but never hope to know why i should marry her. 2.03.110
i hope, sir, i have your good will to have mine 2.04. 15 P
but i hope your lordship thinks not him a 2.05. 1 P
we, | great in our hope, lay our best love and 3.03. 2
gone, | he will return, and hope i may that she, 3.04. 36
i hope i need not to advise you further, but i 3.05. 24 P
but i hope your own grace will keep you where 3.05. 25 P
i hope so. 3.05. 30 P
a wife of me, though there my hope be done. 4.02. 65
and truly, as i hope to live. 4.03.128 P
my reputation and credit and as i hope to live. 4.03.134 P
me, that i hope i shall see him ere i die. 4.05. 84 P
(courage and hope both teaching him the practice
TN 1.02. 13
mine own escape unfoldeth to my hope, | whereto 1.02. 19
and i hope to see a huswife take thee between 1.03.103 P
and o shall end, i hope. 2.05.132 P
the matter, i hope, is not great, sir — begging 3.01. 54 P
i hope, sir, you are, and i am yours. 3.01. 73 P
may have mercy upon mine, but my hope is better, 3.04.168 P
a wrack past hope he was. 5.01. 79
and, acting this in an obedient hope, | why have 5.01.340
in hope it shall not, | most freely i confess, 5.01.358
i hope so, sir, for i have about me many parcels WT 4.04.257 P
no hope to help you, | but as you shake off one 4.04.568
wherein my hope is i shall so prevail | to force 4.04.664
one, i hope i shall not be flay'd out of it. 4.04.815 P
would speak to her and stand in hope of answer. 5.02.102 P
that the oracle | gave hope thou wast in being, 5.03.127
some proper man, i hope. JN 1.01.250
i hope your warrant will bear out the deed. 4.01. 6
and look'd upon, i hope, with cheerful eyes. 4.02. 2
be glorified | as to my ample hope was promised 5.02.112
what surety of the world, what hope, what stay, 5.07. 68
your grace's pardon, and i hope i had it. R2 1.01.141
strong as a tower in hope, i cry amen. 1.03.102
his, | and he our subjects' next degree in hope. 1.04. 36
i hope the king is not yet shipp'd for ireland. 2.02. 42
'tis better hope he is, | for his designs crave 2.02. 43
his designs crave haste, his haste good hope. 2.02. 44
then wherefore dost thou hope he is not shipp'd? 2.02. 45
that he, our hope, might have retir'd his power, 2.02. 46
and driven into despair an enemy's hope, | who 2.02. 47
despair, and be at enmity | with cozening hope. 2.02. 69
life, | which false hope lingers in extremity. 2.02. 72
but theirs is sweet'ned with the hope to have 2.03. 13
and hope to joy is little less in joy | than 2.03. 15
joy is little less in joy | than hope enjoyed. 2.03. 16
to ear the land that hath some hope to grow, 3.02.212
through both | i see some sparks of better hope, 5.03. 21
i hope i shall as soon be strangled with a 1H4 2.04.498 P
and our induction full of prosperous hope. 3.01. 2
the hope and expectation of thy time | is ruin'd 3.02. 36
we read | the very bottom and the soul of hope, 4.01. 50
we may boldly spend upon the hope of what | /is 4.01. 54
i hope no less, yet needful 'tis to fear, | and, 4.04. 34
day, | england did never owe so sweet a hope, 5.02. 67
i hope your lordship goes abroad by advice. 2H4 1.02. 95 P
but i hope he that looks upon me will take me 1.02.166 P
and our supplies live largely in the hope | of 1.03. 12
it was, my lord, who lin'd himself with hope, 1.03. 27
to lay down likelihoods and forms of hope. 1.03. 35
i hope you'll come to supper. 2.01.159 P
i hope, my lord, all's well. 2.01.170 P
i hope, not dead. 5.02. 4
we hope no otherwise from your majesty. 5.02. 62
i hope to see london once ere i die. 5.03. 60 P
we hope to make the sender blush at it. H5 1.02.299
and labor shall refresh itself with hope | to do 2.02. 37
i hope they will not come upon us now. 3.06.168
some of them will fall to-morrow, i hope. 3.07. 72 P
would share from me, | for the best hope i have. 4.03. 33
good argument, i hope, we will not fly — | and 4.03.113
i hope your majesty is pear me testimony and 4.08. 35 P
the venom of such looks we fairly hope | have 5.02. 18
if we have entrance, as i hope we shall, | and 1H6 3.02. 6
brave burgundy, undoubted hope of france, | stay 3.03. 41
where i hope ere long | to be presented, by your 4.01.171
there is no hope that ever i will stay, | if the 4.05. 30
no hope to have redress? 5.03. 18
seen) | will answer our hope in issue of a king; 5.05. 72
such fierce alarums both of hope and fear, | as 5.05. 85
with hope to find the like event in love, | but 5.05.105
for, were there hope to conquer them again, | my 2H6 1.01.117
for i had hope of france, | even as i have of 1.01.237
york, | to be the post, in hope of his reward. 1.04. 77
when such strings jar, what hope of harmony? 2.01. 55
protector be, and god shall be my hope, | my 2.03. 24
for i had hope of france | as firmly as i hope 3.01. 87
as firmly as i hope for fertile england. 3.01. 88
'tis my special hope | that you will clear 3.01.139
for, being green, there is great hope of help. 3.01.287
and we, i hope, sir, are no murtherers. 3.02.181
hold up thy hand, make signal of thy hope. 3.03. 28
over whom, in time to come, i hope to reign, 4.02.130
ay, but i hope your highness shall have his. 4.04. 20
come, margaret, god, our hope, will succor us. 4.04. 55
my hope is gone, now suffolk is deceas'd. 4.04. 56
which makes me hope you are not void of pity. 4.07. 64
such hope have all the line of john of gaunt! 3H6 1.01. 19
thus do i hope to shake king henry's head. 1.01. 20
the hope thereof makes clifford mourn in steel. 1.01. 58
and i, i hope, shall reconcile them all. 1.01.273
and in that hope i throw mine eyes to heaven, 1.04. 37
as the hope of troy | against the greeks that 2.01. 51
and we, in them, no hope to win the day, | so 2.01.136
how now, my lord, what hap? what hope of good? 2.03. 8
our hap is loss, our hope but sad despair, | our 2.03. 9

breasts, | for yet is hope of life and victory. 2.03. 55
and if thou fail us, all our hope is done. 3.03. 33
if that go forward, henry's hope is done. 3.03. 58
i hope all's for the best. 3.03.170
and by the hope i have of heavenly bliss, | that 3.03.182
tell him, in hope he'll prove a widower shortly, 3.03.227
him, in hope he'll prove a widower shortly, 4.01. 99
till then fair hope must hinder live's decay; 4.04. 16
my fear to hope, my sorrows unto joys, | at our 4.06. 4
come hither, england's hope. 4.06. 68
glad my heart with hope of this young richmond, 4.06. 93
farewell, my hector, and my troy's true hope. 4.08. 25
and he that will not fight for such a hope | go 5.04. 55
by this, i hope, she hath a son for me. 5.05. 90
and yet brought forth less than a mother's hope, 5.06. 50
for here i hope begins our lasting joy. 5.07. 46
he cannot live, i hope, and must not die | till R3 1.01.145
i hope so. 1.02.114
but shall i live in hope? 1.02.199
all men, i hope, live so. 1.02.200
madam, good hope, his grace speaks cheerfully. 1.03. 34
i hope this passionate humor of mine will change 1.04.117 P
you, as you hope /to /have /redemption | /by 1.04.189
i hope the king made peace with all of us, | and 2.02.132
in him there is a hope of government, | which, 2.03. 12
i hope he is much grown since last i saw him. 2.04. 5
i hope he is, but yet let mothers doubt. 2.04. 22
nor none that live, i hope. 3.01.147
and if they live, i hope i need not fear. 3.01.148
who builds his hope in air of your good looks 3.04. 98
even that (i hope) which pleaseth god above 3.07.109
true hope is swift and flies with swallow's 5.02. 23
i died for hope ere i could lend thee aid, | but 5.03.173
give | their money out of hope they may believe, H8 pr 8
no more, i hope? 1.01.220
for further life in this world i ne'er hope, 2.01. 69
there is hope | all will be well. 2.03. 55
no friends, no hope, no kindred weep for me, 3.01.150
he falls like lucifer, | never to hope again. 3.02.372
i hope i have. 3.02.387
(the image of his maker) hope to win by it? 3.02.442
i hope she will deserve well — and a little 4.02.136
i hope i am not too late, and yet the gentleman 5.02. 1
let me ne'er hope to see a chine again, | and 5.03. 26
her succor, which were the hope o' th' strond, 5.03. 52 P
and this sailing pandar | our doubtful hope, our TRO 1.01.104
the ample proposition that hope makes | in all 1.03. 3
i hope i shall know your honor better! 3.01. 13 P
and on him erect | a second hope, as fairly 4.05.109
hope of revenge shall hide our inward woe. 5.10. 31
o'er them aufidius, | their very heart of hope. COR 1.06. 55
sir, i hope | my words disbench'd you not? 2.02. 70
we give you any thing, we hope to gain by you. 2.03. 72 P
we hope to find you our friend; 2.03.104 P
and hope to come upon them in the heat of their 4.03. 18 P
not out of hope | (mistake me not) to save my 4.05. 79
i hope to see romans as cheap as volscians. 4.05.232 P
so that all hope is vain, | unless his noble 5.01. 70
finger, there is some hope the ladies of rome, 5.04. 5 P
but i say there is no hope in't; 5.04. 7 P
but hope withal | the self–same gods that arm'd TIT 1.01.135
lord saturnine, whose virtues will, i hope, 1.01.225
choice, | lavinia is thine elder brother's hope. 2.01. 74
this way, or not at all, stand you in hope. 2.01.119
but hope to pluck a dainty doe to ground. 2.02. 26
and with that painted hope braves your 2.03.126
and kneel, sweet boy, the roman hector's hope, 4.01. 88
youth, | the hope of rome, for so he bid me say; 4.02. 13
in hope thyself should govern rome and me. 4.04. 60
for then i hope thou wilt not keep him long, ROM 3.05. 63
and then i hope thou wilt be satisfied. 3.05. 92
come weep with me, past hope, past /cure, past 4.01. 45
i do spy a kind of hope, | which craves as 4.01. 68
and i hope his honor will conceive the fairest TIM 3.02. 53 P
this was my lord's best hope, now all are fled, 3.03. 35
i hope it is not so low with him as he made it 3.06. 5 P
i hope it remains not unkindly with your 3.06. 36 P
if i hope well, i'll never see thee more. 4.03.171
either in hope or present, i'd exchange | for 4.03.520
our hope in him is dead. 5.01.226
that i hope i may use with a safe conscience, JC 1.01. 13 P
upon this hope, that you shall give me reasons 3.01.221
so i hope; 5.01. 57
prediction | of noble having and of royal hope, MAC 1.03. 56
do you not hope your children shall be kings, 1.03.118
was the hope drunk | wherein you dress'd 1.07. 35
be my oracles as well, | and set me up in hope? 3.01. 10
i hope, in no place so unsanctified | where such 4.02. 81
o my breast, | thy hope ends here! 4.03.114
i hope the days are near at hand | that chambers 5.04. 1
'tis his main hope; 5.04. 10
promise to our ear, | and break it to our hope. 5.08. 22
a while | for the supply and profit of our hope, HAM 2.02. 24
so shall i hope your virtues | will bring him to 3.01. 39
i hope we have reform'd that indifferently with 3.02. 36 P
for what advancement may i hope from thee | that 3.02. 57
then there's hope a great man's memory may 3.02.131 P
night, | to desperation turn my trust and hope, 3.02.218
i hope all will be well. 4.05. 68 P
and that, i hope, will teach you to imagine — 4.07. 35
i hope, for my brother's justification, he wrote LR 1.02. 44 P
but i hope his heart is not in the contents. 1.02. 67 P
i have hope | you less know how to value her 2.04.138
i have good hope | thou didst not know on't. 2.04.188
nor any man of quality — i hope to be sav'd. OTH 2.03.107 P
i hope you will consider what is spoke | comes 3.03.216
lord on his behalf, and hope all will be well. 3.04. 19 P
i hope my noble lord esteems me honest. 4.02. 65
suppliest me with the least advantage of hope. 4.02.178 P
if you say /so, i hope you will not kill me. 5.02. 35
but yet i hope, i hope, | they do not point on 5.02. 45
but yet i hope, i hope, | they do not point on 5.02. 45
but i will hope | of better deeds to–morrow. ANT 1.01. 61
and my auguring hope | says it will come to th' 2.01. 10
i cannot hope | caesar and antony shall well 2.01. 38
i hope so, lepidus. 2.06. 57
there's hope in't yet. 3.13.176
i hope well of to–morrow, and will lead you 4.02. 42
i have an absolute hope | our landmen will stand 4.03. 10
his fretted fortunes give him hope and fear | of 4.12. 8
past hope, and in despair, that way past grace. CYM 1.01.137
you bear a graver purpose, i hope. 1.04.139 P
is he dispos'd to mirth? i hope he is. 1.06. 58
not he, i hope. 1.06. 77
i hope it be not gone to tell my lord | that i 2.03.147
i hope so; go and search. 2.03.149
she's my good lady, and will conceive, i hope, 2.03.153
i hope the briefness of your answer made | the 2.04. 30
i hope you know that we | must not continue 2.04. 48
very true, | and so i hope he came by't. 2.04.118
i hope i dream; 4.02.297
the gods hear, i hope | they'll pardon it. 4.02.378
it strikes me, past | the hope of comfort. 4.03. 9
nay, what hope | have we in hiding us? 4.04. 3
being thus quench'd | of hope, not longing, mine 5.05.196
yet hope, succeeding from so fair a tree | as PER 1.01.114
that were to blow at fire in hope to quench it, 1.04. 4
when — the which i hope shall ne'er be seen — 1.04.105
i hope, sir, if you thrive, you'll remember from 2.01.151 P
and here, i hope, is none that envies it. 2.03. 14
you will not do't for all the world, i hope. 4.01. 84
there's no hope she will return. 4.01. 98
o, i hope some god, | some god hath put his TNK 1.01. 71
delay | commends us to a famishing hope. 1.01.167
or entertain'st a hope to blast my wishes, 2.02.170
emily, i hope | he shall not go afoot. 2.05. 52
i hope too wise for that, sir. 2.05. 64
yet i hope, | when he considers more, this love 2.06. 26
set in too, that i hope | all shall be well. 4.01. 14
i hope they are good. 4.01. 30
in great hope she had fix'd her liking on this 4.03. 64 P
make the number more i have great hope in this. 4.03. 98 P
i hope she's pleas'd, | her signs were gracious. 5.01.172
my palamon i hope will grow too, finely, | now 5.02. 95
things out of hope are compass'd oft with VEN 567
sith in thy pride so fair a hope is slain. 762
follow | this sound of hope doth labor to expel, 976
despair and hope makes thee ridiculous: 988
full of foul hope and full of fond mistrust; LUC 284
if in thy hope thou dar'st do such outrage, 605
king, | to shame his hope with deeds degenerate; 1003
when their brave hope, bold hector, march'd to 1430
and to their hope they such odd action yield, 1433
heart hath his hope, and eyes their wished sight PP 14.22
but that i hope some good conceit of thine | in SON 26. 7
wishing me like to one more rich in hope, 29. 5
being had, to triumph, being lack'd, to hope. 52.14
and yet to times in hope my verse shall stand, 60.13
me | but hope of orphans and unfathered fruit, 97.10
but if thou catch thy hope, turn back to me, 143.11

HOPEFUL 9 FR 0.0010 REL FR 9 V 0 P
to th' hopeful execution do i leave you | of MM 1.01. 59
his hopeful son's, his babe's, betrays to WT 2.03. 86
the mother to a hopeful prince, here standing 3.02. 40
whose hopeful colors | advance our half–fac'd 2H6 4.01. 97
from his loins no hopeful branch may spring, 3H6 3.02.126
may fright the hopeful mother at the view, | and R3 1.02. 24
not to let | thy hopeful service perish too. H8 3.02.419
here comes a parcel of our hopeful booty, TIT 2.03. 49
she's the hopeful lady of my earth. ROM 1.02. 15

HOPELESS 10 FR 0.0011 REL FR 10 V 0 P
hopeless to find, yet loath to leave unsought ERR 1.01.135
hopeless and helpless doth egeon wend, | but to 1.01.157
the hopeless word of "never to return" | breathe R2 1.03.152
desperate thieves, all hopeless of their lives, 3H6 1.04. 42
alas, i am a woman, friendless, hopeless! H8 3.01. 80
pawn his fortunes | to hopeless restitution, so COR 3.01. 16
aye hopeless | to have the courtesy your cradle CYM 4.04. 27
to marry him is hopeless; TNK 2.04. 4
she there remains a hopeless castaway; LUC 744
lo here the hopeless merchant of this loss, 1660

HOPE'S 1 FR 0.0001 REL FR 1 V 0 P
my food, my fortune, and my sweet hope's aim, ERR 3.02. 63

/HOPES 1 FR 0.0001 REL FR 1 V 0 P
in these fear'd /hopes | i barely gratify your CYM 2.04. 6

HOPES 61 FR 0.0069 REL FR 55 V 6 P
and all the fair effects of future hopes. TGV 1.01. 50
treacherous man, | thou hast beguil'd my hopes! 5.04. 64
from home, but she hopes there will come a time. WIV 2.02.102 P
your resolution with hopes that are fallible, MM 3.01.168 P
my affections would | be with my hopes abroad. MV 1.01. 17
in the place i go to, | and lose my hopes. 2.02.189
how much unlike my hopes and my deservings! 2.09. 57
it shall become to serve all hopes conceiv'd, SHR 1.01. 15
i have those hopes of her good that her AWW 1.01. 39 P
ay, by my sceptre and my hopes of /heaven. 2.01.192
with his lord, | nor hold him up with hopes: TN 1.05.304
between me and the full prospect of my hopes. 3.04. 82 P
i very well agree with you in the hopes of him; WT 1.01. 37 P
companion that e'er man | bred his hopes out of. 5.01. 12
fled from his father, from his hopes, and with 5.01.184
lest that their hopes prodigiously be cross'd; JN 3.01. 91
by all my hopes, most falsely doth he lie. R2 1.01. 68
i am, | by so much shall i falsify men's hopes, 1H4 1.02.211
by my hopes, | this present enterprise set off 5.01. 87
all | speak plainly your opinions of our hopes. 2H4 1.03. 3
grant that our hopes (yet likely of fair birth) 1.03. 63
thus do the hopes we have in him touch ground 4.01. 17
how might a prince of my great hopes forget | so 5.02. 68
and so farewell, and fair be all thy hopes, 1H6 2.05.113
you, his false hopes, the trust of england's 4.04. 20
in yours they will, in you all hopes are lost. 4.05. 25
shall all thy mother's hopes lie in one tomb? 4.05. 34
the scatt'red foe that hopes to rise again; 3H6 2.06. 93
and shamefully my hopes, by you, are butcher'd. R3 1.03.275
and hopes to find you forward | upon his party 3.02. 46
to stop all hopes whose growth may damage me. 4.02. 59
none here, he hopes, | in all this noble bevy, H8 1.04. 3
fears, | your hopes and friends are infinite. 3.01. 82
he puts forth | the tender leaves of hopes, 3.02.353
too heavy for a man that hopes for heaven! 3.02.385
farewell | the hopes of court! 3.02.459
my hopes in heaven do dwell. 3.02.459
when i do tell thee there my hopes lie drown'd, TRO 1.01. 49
he hopes it is no other | but for your health 2.03.110
and let not discontent | daunt all your hopes. TIT 1.01.268
which never hopes more heaven than rests in thee 2.03. 41
earth hath swallowed all my hopes but she; ROM 1.02. 14
now, antony, our hopes are answered. JC 5.01. 1
death, and bear | his hopes 'bove wisdom, grace, MAC 3.05. 31
i have lost my hopes. 4.03. 24
thoughts speculative their unsure hopes relate, 5.04. 19
popp'd in between th' election and my hopes, HAM 5.02. 65
seeing the worst, which late on hopes depended. OTH 1.03.203
wilt thou be fast to my hopes, if i depend on 1.03.362 P
therefore my hopes (not surfeited to death) 2.01. 50
my hopes do shape him for the governor. 2.01. 55
given to captivity me and my utmost hopes, | i 4.02. 51
this forwardness | makes our hopes fair. CYM 4.02.343
he hopes by you his fortunes yet may flourish. PER 2.02. 47
and being join'd, i'll thus your hopes destroy, 2.05. 86
palamon, | those hopes are prisoners with us. TNK 2.02. 26
it but hold, i ask no more | for all my hopes. 3.06. 92
all the fair hopes of what he undertakes, | and 4.02. 99
though weak–built hopes persuade him to LUC 130
applying fears to hopes, and hopes to fears, SON 119. 3
applying fears to hopes, and hopes to fears, 119. 3

HOPEST 1 FR 0.0001 REL FR 1 V 0 P
why hopest thou so? R2 2.02. 43

HOPING 8 FR 0.0009 REL FR 7 V 1 P
hoping you'll find good cause to whip them all. MM 2.01.137
question, hoping to be the wiser by your answer. AWW 2.02. 39 P
hoping the consequence | will prove as bitter, R3 4.04. 6
people, hoping | to purge himself with words. COR 5.06. 7
withal | hoping it was but an effect of humor, JC 2.01.250
not sure, though hoping, of this good success, LR 5.03.195
thus hoping that adonis is alive, | her rash VEN 1009
and so by hoping more they have but less, | or, LUC 137

HOPKINS 2 FR 0.0002 REL FR 2 V 0 P
o, /nicholas hopkins? H8 1.01.221
devil monk, | hopkins, that made this mischief. 2.01. 22

/HOPPEDANCE 1 FR 0.0001 REL FR 0 V 1 P
/hoppedance /cries /in /tom's /belly /for /two LR 3.06. 30 P

HOP'ST 2 FR 0.0002 REL FR 2 V 0 P
within what space | hop'st thou my cure? AWW 2.01.160
be that thou hop'st to be, or what thou art 2H6 3.01.333

HORACE 3 FR 0.0003 REL FR 2 V 1 P
or rather, as horace says in his — what, my LLL 4.02.102 P
o, 'tis a verse in horace, i know it well, | i TIT 4.02. 22
ay, just — a verse in horace, right, you have 4.02. 24

/HORATIO 1 FR 0.0001 REL FR 1 V 0 P
/but /i /am /very /sorry, /good /horatio, HAM 5.02. 75

HORATIO 30 FR 0.0034 REL FR 22 V 8 P
if you do meet horatio and marcellus, | the HAM 1.01. 12
say — | what, is horatio there? 1.01. 19
welcome, horatio, welcome, good marcellus. 1.01. 20
horatio says 'tis but our fantasy, | and will 1.01. 23
thou art a scholar, speak to it, horatio. 1.01. 42
looks 'a not like the king? mark it, horatio. 1.01. 43
speak to it, horatio. 1.01. 45
how now, horatio? 1.01. 53
horatio — or i do forget myself. 1.02.161
and what make you from wittenberg, horatio? 1.02.164
thrift, thrift, horatio! 1.02.180
heaven | or ever i had seen that day, horatio! 1.02.183
in my mind's eye, horatio. 1.02.185
yes, by saint patrick, but there is, horatio, 1.05.136
are more things in heaven and earth, horatio, 1.05.166
what ho, horatio! 3.02. 52 P
horatio, thou art e'en as just a man | as e'er 3.02. 54
o good horatio, i'll take the ghost's word for a 3.02.286 P
bound for england — if your name be horatio, as 4.06. 12 P
"horatio, when thou shalt have overlook'd this, 4.06. 13 P
by the lord, horatio, this three years i have 5.01.139 P
i knew him, horatio, a fellow of infinite jest, 5.01.184 P
prithee, horatio, tell me one thing. 5.01.195 P
to what base uses we may return, horatio! 5.01.202 P
i pray thee, good horatio, wait upon him. 5.01.293
where i found, horatio — | ah, royal knavery! 5.02. 18
i am dead, horatio. 5.02.333
horatio, i am dead, | thou livest. 5.02.338
o god, horatio, what a wounded name, | things 5.02.344
o, i die, horatio, | the potent poison quite 5.02.352

HORIZON 1 FR 0.0001 REL FR 1 V 0 P
his car | above the border of this horizon, 3H6 4.07. 81

HORN 33 FR 0.0037 REL FR 18 V 15 P
the horn, i say. WIV 2.01.121
let's write "good angel" on the devil's horn, MM 2.04. 16
well, a horn for my money, when all's done. ADO 2.03. 60 P
for "scorn," "horn," a hard rhyme; 5.02. 38 P
staff more reverent than one tipp'd with horn. 5.04.124 P
spell'd backward, with the horn on his head? LLL 5.01. 47 P
ba, pueritia, with a horn added. 5.01. 49 P
ba, most silly sheep, with a horn. 5.01. 50 P
lend me your horn to make one, and i will whip 5.01. 68 P
infamy, /manu cita — a gig of a cuckold's horn. 5.01. 70 P
was never hollow'd to, nor cheer'd with horn, MND 4.01.125
from my master, with his horn full of good news. MV 5.01. 47 P
by so much is a horn more precious than to want. AYL 3.03. 63 P
take thou no scorn to wear the horn, | it was a 4.02. 13
the horn, the horn, the lusty horn | is not a 4.02. 17
the horn, the horn, the lusty horn | is not a 4.02. 17
the lusty horn | is not a thing to laugh to 4.02. 17
why, thy horn is a foot, and so long am i at the SHR 4.01. 27 P
would say your head and butt were head and horn. 5.02. 41
the nail to his hole, the cuckold to his horn, AWW 2.02. 25 P
eye–glass | is thicker than a cuckold's horn), WT 1.02.269
that will take pains to blow a horn before her? JN 1.01.219
in security, for he hath the horn of abundance, 2H4 1.02. 46 P
the basest horn of his hoof is more musical than H5 3.07. 17 P
paris is gor'd with menelaus' horn. TRO 1.01.112
it were no match, your nail against his horn. 4.05. 46
wert thou the devil, and wor'st it on thy horn, 5.02. 95
being but | the horn and noise o' th' monster's, COR 3.01. 95
with horn and hound we'll give your grace bon TIT 1.01.494
poor tom, thy horn is dry. LR 3.06. 75 P
she hearkens for his hounds and for his horn; VEN 868
even at this word she hears a merry horn, 1025
anon adonis comes with horn and hounds; PP 9. 6

HORN–BEASTS 1 FR 0.0001 REL FR 0 V 1 P
but the wood, no assembly but horn–beasts. AYL 3.03. 50 P

HORN–BOOK 2 FR 0.0002 REL FR 1 V 1 P
yes, yes, he teaches boys the horn–book. LLL 5.01. 46 P
he'll eat a horn–book ere he fail. TNK 2.03. 42

HORNED 4 FR 0.0004 REL FR 4 V 0 P
this lanthorn doth the horned moon present — MND 5.01.239
this lanthorn doth the horned moon present; 5.01.244
a horned man's a monster and a beast. OTH 4.01. 62
the hill of basan, to outroar | the horned herd! ANT 3.13.128
HORNER 2 FR 0.0002 REL FR 0 V 2 P
against my master, thomas horner, for saying 2H6 1.03. 26 P
here, neighbor horner, i drink to you in a cup 2.03. 59 P
HORNING 1 FR 0.0001 REL FR 1 V 0 P
'tis thought you have a goodly gift in horning, TIT 2.03. 67
HORN–MAD 5 FR 0.0005 REL FR 2 V 3 P
the young man, he would have been horn–mad. WIV 1.04. 50 P
i'll be horn–mad. 3.05.152 P
why, mistress, sure my master is horn–mad. ERR 2.01. 57
horn–mad, thou villain! 2.01. 58
should ever happen, thou wouldst be horn–mad. ADO 1.01.270 P
HORN–MAKER 1 FR 0.0001 REL FR 0 V 1 P
virtue is no horn–maker; AYL 4.01. 63 P
HORNPIPES 1 FR 0.0001 REL FR 0 V 1 P
amongst them, and he sings psalms to hornpipes. WT 4.03. 44 P
HORN–RING 1 FR 0.0001 REL FR 0 V 1 P
bracelet, horn–ring, to keep my pack from WT 4.04.599 P
/HORNS 1 FR 0.0001 REL FR 1 V 0 P
/like /herne, /with /huge /horns /on /his /head. WIV 4.04. 43
HORNS 49 FR 0.0055 REL FR 23 V 26 P
why then my horns are his horns, whether i wake TGV 1.01. 79 P
why then my horns are his horns, whether i wake 1.01. 79 P
hang like a meteor o'er the cuckold's horns. WIV 2.02.281 P
if i have horns to make one mad, let the proverb 3.05.151 P
round about an oak, with great ragg'd horns, 4.04. 31
i'll do what i can to get you a pair of horns. 5.01. 6 P
the devil, and we shall know him by his horns. 5.02. 14 P
a bull for thy europa, love set on thy horns. 5.05. 4 P
walk — and my horns i bequeath your husbands. 5.05. 26 P
here are his horns, master /brook; 5.05.111 P
pluck off the bull's horns and set them in my ADO 1.01.263 P
"god sends a curst cow short horns" — but to a 2.01. 23 P
by being too curst, god will send you no horns. 2.01. 26 P
me like an old cuckold with horns on his head, 2.01. 44 P
we set the savage bull's horns on the sensible 5.01.182 P
fear not, man, we'll tip thy horns with gold, 5.04. 44
my lady goes to kill horns, but, if thou marry, LLL 4.01.111
hang me by the neck if horns that year miscarry. 4.01.112
if we choose by the horns, yourself come not 4.01.115
than are the tender horns of cockled snails. 4.03.335
horns. 5.01. 65 P
will you give horns, chaste lady? 5.02.252
then die a calf, before your horns do grow. 5.02.253
go, bid the huntsmen wake them with their horns. MND 4.01.138
he should have worn the horns on his head. 5.01.240 P
crescent, and his horns are invisible within the 5.01.242 P
as horns are odious, they are necessary. AYL 3.03. 51 P
many a man has good horns, and knows no end of 3.03. 54 P
horns? 3.03. 56 P
why, horns! 4.01. 59 P
do well to set the deer's horns upon his head, 4.02. 4 P
his leather skin and horns to wear. 4.02. 11
they may jowl horns together like any deer i' AWW 1.03. 54 P
for which we lose our heads to gild his horns! TRO 4.05. 31
the bull has the game, ware horns ho! 5.07. 12 P
they would hang them on the horns a' th' moon, COR 1.01.213
thrusts forth his horns again into the world, 4.06. 44
replying shrilly to the well–tun'd horns, | as TIT 2.03. 18
whiles hounds and horns and sweet melodious 2.03. 27
should be planted presently | with horns, as was 2.03. 63
see, thou hast shot off one of taurus' horns. 4.03. 70
down fell both the ram's horns in the court, 4.03. 73
daughters, and leave his horns without a case. LR 1.05. 31 P
horns welk'd and waved like the /enridged sea. 4.06. 71
you say, must change his horns with garlands! ANT 1.02. 5 P
let me lodge lichas on the horns o' th' moon, 4.12. 45
you hear the horns: TNK 3.01. 96
i hear the horns. 3.05. 93
or as the snail, whose tender horns being hit, VEN 1033
HOROLOGE 1 FR 0.0001 REL FR 1 V 0 P
he'll watch the horologe a double set | if drink OTH 2.03.130
HORRIBLE 26 FR 0.0029 REL FR 24 V 2 P
and moe diversity of sounds, all horrible, | we TMP 5.01.234
thought | imagine howling — 'tis too horrible! MM 3.01.127
him, draw, and, as thou draw'st, swear horrible; TN 3.04.179 P
which being so horrible, so bloody, must | lead WT 2.03.152
your vild intent must needs seem horrible. JN 4.01. 95
black, fearful, comfortless, and horrible. 5.06. 20
but tell me, hal, art not thou horrible afeard? 1H4 2.04.366 P
as curst, as harsh, and horrible to hear, 2H6 3.02.312
he did discharge a horrible oath, whose tenor H8 1.02.206
like | the horrible conceit of death and night, ROM 4.03. 37
writ, | but set them down horrible traitors. TIM 4.03.119
fears | are less than horrible imaginings: MAC 1.03.138
hence, horrible shadow! 3.04.105
horrible sight! 4.01.122
and there assume some other horrible form, HAM 1.04. 72
o, horrible, o, horrible, most horrible! 1.05. 80
o, horrible, o, horrible, most horrible! 1.05. 80
o, horrible, o, horrible, most horrible! 1.05. 80
and with this horrible object, from low farms, LR 2.03. 17
then let fall | your horrible pleasure. 3.02. 19
horrible steep. | hark, do you hear the sea? 4.06. 3
shut up in thy brain | some horrible conceit. OTH 3.03.115
what horrible fancy's this? 4.02. 26
i know this act shows horrible and grim. 5.02.203
horrible villain, or i'll spurn thine eyes ANT 2.05. 63
you shall perceive how horrible a shape | your STM II.C 92
HORRIBLY 8 FR 0.0009 REL FR 2 V 6 P
folly, for i will be horribly in love with her. ADO 2.03.235 P
he is as horribly conceited of him; TN 3.04.294 P
art thou not horribly afraid? 1H4 2.04.369 P
thou wilt be horribly chid to–morrow when thou 2.04.373 P
by this leek, i will most horribly revenge — i H5 5.01. 47 P
my niece is horribly in love with a thing you TRO 3.01. 97 P
horribly stuff'd with epithites of war, | /and, OTH 1.01. 14
she is horribly in love with him, poor beast, TNK 5.02. 62
HORRID 17 FR 0.0019 REL FR 15 V 2 P
the while upon some horrid message for a TN 3.04.199 P
general's cut and a horrid suit of the camp will H5 3.06. 77 P
unto the gazing moon | so many horrid ghosts. 4.pr. 28
never sees horrid night, the child of hell; 4.01.271
make 'em, and | appear in forms more horrid), H8 3.02.196
break his wind | with fear and horrid flight. TIM 5.04. 13
recounts most horrid sights seen by the watch. JC 2.02. 16
whose horrid image doth unfix my hair | and make MAC 1.03.135
air, | shall blow the horrid deed in every eye, 1.07. 24
of horrid hell can come a devil more damn'd | in 4.03. 56
and cleave the general ear with horrid speech, HAM 2.02.563
up, sword, and know thou a more horrid hent: 3.03. 88
sheets of fire, such bursts of horrid thunder, LR 3.02. 46
the sparks of nature, | to quit this horrid act. 3.07. 87
/shows not in the fiend | so horrid as in woman. 4.02. 61
than that horrid act | of the divorce he'ld make CYM 2.01. 61
to themselves | been death's most horrid agents, TNK 1.01.144
HORRIDER 1 FR 0.0001 REL FR 1 V 0 P
that we the horrider may seem to those | which CYM 4.02.331
HORRIDLY 2 FR 0.0002 REL FR 2 V 0 P
of nature | so horridly to shake our disposition HAM 1.04. 55
gules, horridly trick'd | with blood of fathers, 2.02.457
HORROR 16 FR 0.0018 REL FR 14 V 2 P
whose very comfort | is still a dying horror! MM 2.03. 42
bed would break, | and take her hence in horror. 5.01.436
so indeed all disquiet, horror, and perturbation ADO 2.01.260 P
and outface the brow | of bragging horror; JN 5.01. 50
disorder, horror, fear, and mutiny | shall here R2 4.01.142
and take the present horror from the time, MAC 2.01. 59
o horror, horror, horror! 2.03. 64
o horror, horror, horror! 2.03. 64
o horror, horror, horror! 2.03. 64
walk like sprites, | to countenance this horror! 2.03. 80
nothing like the image and horror of it. LR 1.02.175 P
or image of that horror? 5.03.265
inevitable prosecution of | disgrace and horror, ANT 4.14. 66
these thoughts of horror further than you shall 5.02. 63
with horror, madly dying, like her life, | which CYM 5.05. 31
which ever was | the dam of horror, who does TNK 5.03. 23
HORROR'S 1 FR 0.0001 REL FR 1 V 0 P
on horror's head horrors accumulate; OTH 3.03.370
HORRORS 4 FR 0.0004 REL FR 4 V 0 P
frights, changes, horrors, | divert and crack, TRO 1.03. 98
i have supp'd full with horrors; MAC 5.05. 13
been loosed out of hell | to speak of horrors — HAM 2.01. 81
on horror's head horrors accumulate; OTH 3.03.370
HORS'D 4 FR 0.0004 REL FR 3 V 1 P
with joyful tidings, and, being better hors'd, 2H4 1.01. 35
in the stews, i were mann'd, hors'd, and wiv'd. 1.02. 54 P
and ridges hors'd | with variable complexions, COR 2.01.211
hors'd | upon the sightless couriers of the air, MAC 1.07. 22
/HORSE 1 FR 0.0001 REL FR 1 V 0 P
/or, /like /a /gallant /horse /fall'n /in /first TRO 3.03.161
HORSE 234 FR 0.0264 REL FR 155 V 79 P
but a team of horse shall not pluck that from me TGV 3.01.267 P
why, a horse can do no more; 3.01.276 P
nay, a horse cannot fetch, but only carry, 3.01.276 P
be | a horse whereon the governor doth ride, MM 1.02.160
such claim as you would lay to your horse, and ERR 3.02. 86 P
for a difference between himself and his horse, ADO 1.01. 70 P
i would my horse had the speed of your tongue, 1.01.141 P
as they write "here is good horse to hire," let 1.01.266 P
for a hawk, a horse, or a husband? 3.04. 55 P
and two men ride of a horse, one must ride 3.05. 37 P
in two words, the dancing horse will tell you. LLL 1.02. 53 P
a horse to be embassador for an ass. 3.01. 51 P
you must send the ass upon the horse, for he is 3.01. 55 P
was that the king that spurr'd his horse so hard 4.01. 1
the ape his keeper, the tired horse his rider. 4.02.127 P
smile | when i a fat and bean–fed horse beguile, MND 2.01. 45
as true as truest horse, that yet would never 3.01. 96
o — "as true as truest horse, that yet would 3.01.102
sometime a horse i'll be, sometime a hound, | a 3.01.108
like horse, hound, hog, bear, fire, at every 3.01.111
for he doth nothing but talk of his horse, and MV 1.02. 41 P
he hath a horse better than the neapolitan's, a 1.02. 58 P
where is the horse that doth untread again | his 2.06. 10
bow, sir, the horse his curb, and the falcon her AYL 3.03. 79 P
tilter, that spurs his horse but on one side, 3.04. 44 P
and both in a tune, like two gipsies on a horse. 5.03. 15 P
another tell him of his hounds and horse, | and SHR in.1. 61
given him the best horse in padua to begin his 1.01.143 P
his horse hipp'd, with an old mothy saddle and 3.02. 48 P
for all the world caparison'd like the horse; 3.02. 66 P
sir, i say his horse comes, with him on his back 3.02. 79 P
a horse and a man | is more than one, | and yet 3.02. 84
grumio, my horse. 3.02.204
barn, | my horse, my ox, my ass, my any thing; 3.02.232
first, know my horse is tir'd, my master and 4.01. 54 P
both of one horse? 4.01. 69 P
why, a horse. 4.01. 71 P
have heard how her horse fell and she under her 4.01. 73 P
how her horse fell and she under her horse; 4.01. 74 P
how he left her with the horse upon her, how he 4.01. 76 P
how he beat me because her horse stumbled, how 4.01. 77 P
door | to hold my stirrup nor to take my horse? 4.01.121
it shall be seven ere i go to horse. 4.03.191
i pray you stay not, but in haste to horse. AWW 2.05. 87
the general of our horse thou art, and we, 3.03. 1
to charge in with our horse upon our own wings, 3.06. 49 P
of him, how many horse the duke is strong." 4.03.130 P
"five or six thousand horse," i said — i will 4.03.148 P
and the captain of his horse, count rossillion. 4.03.294 P
we must to horse again. 5.01. 37
my purpose is indeed a horse of that color. TN 2.03.167 P
and your horse now would make him an ass. 2.03.168 P
slip, and i'll give him my horse, grey capilet. 3.04.286 P
i'll ride your horse as well as i ride you. 3.04.290 P
i have his horse to take up the quarrel. 3.04.292 P
to horse, to horse! R2 2.01.299
to horse, to horse! 2.01.299
hold out my horse, and i will first be there. 2.01.300
how fondly dost thou spur a forward horse! 4.01. 72
saddle my horse. 5.02. 74
give me my boots, i say, saddle my horse. 5.02. 77
mount thee upon his horse, | spur post, and get 5.02.111
that horse that thou so often hast bestrid, 5.05. 79
that horse that i so carefully have dress'd! 5.05. 80
forgiveness, horse! 5.05. 90
i was not made a horse, | and yet i bear a 5.05. 92
and pride of their contention did take horse, 1H4 1.01. 60
sir walter blunt, new lighted from his horse, 1.01. 63
the new chimney, and yet our horse not pack'd. 2.01. 3 P
i have remov'd falstaff's horse, and he frets 2.02. 2 P
the rascal hath remov'd my horse, and tied him i 2.02. 11 P
give me my horse, you rogues, give me my horse, 2.02. 29 P
you rogues, give me my horse, and be hang'd! 2.02. 30 P
help me to my horse, good king's son. 2.02. 41 P
sirrah jack, thy horse stands behind the hedge; 2.02. 70 P
let us share, and then to horse before day. 2.02. 99 P
now merrily to horse. 2.02.104
one horse, my lord, he brought even now. 2.03. 68
what horse? roan? a crop–ear, is it not? 2.03. 69
why, my horse, my love, my horse. 2.03. 76
why, my horse, my love, my horse. 2.03. 76
god's me, my horse! 2.03. 94
"give my roan horse a drench," says he, and 2.04.107 P
tell thee a lie, spit in my face, call me horse. 2.04.194 P
behind the arras, and snorting like a horse. 2.04.529 P
he is as tedious | as a tired horse, a railing 3.01.158
we'll but seal, | and then to horse immediately. 3.01.266
is made of, i am a peppercorn, a brewer's horse. 3.03. 9 P
up gadshill in the night to catch my horse, if i 3.03. 38 P
i would it had been of horse. 3.03.187 P
go, peto, to horse, to horse, for thou and i 3.03.197
to horse, to horse, for thou and i | have thirty 3.03.197
come let me taste my horse, | who is to bear me 4.01.119
harry to harry shall, hot horse to horse, | meet 4.01.122
harry to harry shall, hot horse to horse, | meet 4.01.122
certain horse | of my cousin vernon's are not 4.03. 19
that not a horse is half the half of himself. 4.03. 24
contention, like a horse | full of high feeding, 2H4 1.01. 9
stopp'd by me to breathe his bloodied horse. 1.01. 38
with that he gave his able horse the head, | and 1.01. 43
fellow that had stol'n | the horse he rode on, 1.01. 58
/into smithfield to buy your worship a horse. 1.02. 51 P
paul's, and he'll buy me a horse in smithfield; 1.02. 53 P
no, fifteen hundred foot, five hundred horse, 2.01.173
saddle my horse. 5.03.122 P
they sell the pasture now to buy the horse, H5 2.pr. 5
but let my horse have his due. 3.07. 3 P
it is the best horse of europe. 3.07. 5 P
high constable, you talk of horse and armor? 3.07. 8 P
i will not change my horse with any that treads 3.07. 12 P
he is indeed a horse, and all other jades you 3.07. 24 P
lord, it is a most absolute and excellent horse. 3.07. 26 P
tongues, and my horse is argument for them all. 3.07. 35 P
to my courser, for my horse is my mistress. 3.07. 44 P
i had rather have my horse to my mistress. 3.07. 58 P
yet do i not use my horse for my mistress, or 3.07. 67 P
ev'n as your horse bears your praises, who would 3.07. 76 P
doth rise and help hyperion to his horse, | and 4.01.275
montez /a cheval! my horse, varlot lackey! ha! 4.02. 2
to horse, you gallant princes! 4.02. 15
straight to horse! 4.02. 15
for my love, or bound my horse for her favors, i 5.02.140 P
the wolf, | or horse or oxen from the leopard, 1H6 1.05. 31
he might have sent, and had the horse. 4.04. 33
therefore, dear boy, mount on my swiftest horse, 4.05. 9
the coward horse that bears me fall and die! 4.06. 47
as market men for oxen, sheep, or horse. 5.05. 54
these news, as fast as horse can carry them — 2H6 1.04. 74
be dragg'd at my horse heels till i do come to 4.03. 13 P
then linger not, my lord, away, take horse. 4.04. 54
thou oughtst not to let thy horse wear a cloak, 4.07. 49 P
lands, goods, horse, armor, any thing i have 5.01. 52
three times to–day i holp him to his horse, 5.03. 8
that beggars mounted run their horse to death. 3H6 1.04.127
i'll kill my horse, because i will not fly. 2.03. 24
shall here find his friends with horse and men 4.05. 12
your horse stands ready at the park–corner. 4.05. 19
but yet i run before my horse to market: R3 1.01.160
where every horse bears his commanding rein 2.02.128
if you will presently take horse with him, | and 3.02. 16
times to–day my foot–cloth horse did stumble, 3.04. 84
give me another horse! 5.03.177
caparison my horse! 5.03.289
length, | consisting equally of horse and foot; 5.03.294
shall have the leading of this foot and horse. 5.03.297
shall be well winged with our chiefest horse. 5.03.300
his horse is slain, and all on foot he fights, 5.04. 4
a horse, a horse! my kingdom for a horse! 5.04. 7
a horse, a horse! my kingdom for a horse! 5.04. 7
a horse, a horse! my kingdom for a horse! 5.04. 7
withdraw, my lord, i'll help you to a horse. 5.04. 8
a horse, a horse! 5.04. 13
a horse, a horse! 5.04. 13
my kingdom for a horse! 5.04. 13
anger is like | a full hot horse, who being H8 1.01.133
the two moist elements, | like perseus' horse. TRO 1.03. 42
and achilles' horse | makes many thetis' sons. 1.03.211
but i think thy horse will sooner con an oration 2.01. 17 P
a very horse, | that has he knows not what. 3.03.126
let me bear another to his horse, for that's the 3.03.306 P
go, go, my servant, take thou troilus' horse, 5.05. 1
now here he fights on galathe his horse | and 5.05. 20
and pay thy life thou owest me for my horse. 5.06. 7
my horse to yours, no. COR 1.04. 2
so, the good horse is mine. 1.04. 5
his mother now than an eight–year–old horse. 5.04. 17 P
come on then, horse and chariots let us have, TIT 2.02. 18
and i have horse will follow where the game 2.02. 23
chiron, we hunt not, we, with horse nor hound, 2.02. 25
'tis alcibiades, and some twenty horse, | all of TIM 1.01.241
if i would sell my horse and buy twenty moe 2.01. 7
better than he, why, give my horse to timon, 2.01. 8
paint till a horse may mire upon your face: 4.03.148
a bear, thou wouldst be kill'd by the horse; 4.03.338 P
wert thou a horse, thou wouldst be seiz'd by the 4.03.339 P
so is my horse, octavius, and for that | i do JC 4.01. 29
the greater part, the horse in general, | are 4.02. 29
mount thou my horse, and hide thy spurs in him 5.03. 15
therefore to horse, | and let us not be dainty MAC 2.03.143
go not my horse the better, | i must become a 3.01. 25
hie you to horse; 3.01. 34
i did hear | the galloping of horse. 4.01.140
when he lay couched in th' ominous horse, | hath HAM 2.02.454
and to such wondrous doing brought his horse, 4.07. 86
that prais'd my lord such–a–one's horse, when 'a 5.01. 85 P

not an ass know when the cart draws the horse? LR 1.04.224 P
take you some company, and away to horse. 1.04.336
summon'd up their meiny, straight took horse, 2.04. 35
in pure kindness to his horse, butter'd his hay. 2.04.126 P
he calls to horse, but will i know not whither. 2.04.297
six shirts to his body — horse to ride, and 3.04.137
the fitchew nor the soiled horse goes to't 4.06.122
stratagem, to shoe | a troop of horse with felt. 4.06.185
why should a dog, a horse, a rat, have life, 5.03.307
have your daughter cover'd with a barbary horse, OTH 1.01.112 P
or is he on his horse? ANT 1.05. 20
o happy horse, to bear the weight of antony! 1.05. 21
do bravely, horse, for wot'st thou whom thou 1.05. 22
the ne'er–yet–beaten horse of parthia | we have 3.01. 33
this is to horse. 3.02. 21
he were the worse for that, were he a horse; 3.02. 52
the neighs of horse to tell of her approach, 3.06. 45
we should serve with horse and mares together, 3.07. 7
mares together, | the horse were merely lost; 3.07. 8
the mares would bear | a soldier and his horse. 3.07. 9
hold by land, | and our twelve thousand horse. 3.07. 59
keep by land | the legions and the horse whole, 3.07. 71
caesar will i render | my legions and my horse: 3.10. 33
that which is now a horse, even with a thought 4.14. 9
o, for a horse with wings! CYM 3.02. 48
thou toldst me, when we came from horse, the 3.04. 1
my horse is tied up safe; 4.01. 22 P
never bestrid a horse, save one that had | a 4.04. 38
are like the troyan horse was stuff'd within PER 1.04. 93
diligence | that horse and sail and high expense 3.ch. 20
when i spur | my horse, i chide him /not; TNK 3.01.107
up, and under me | i had a right good horse. 3.06. 77
did you nev'r see the horse he gave me? 5.02. 45
what think you of this horse? 5.02. 55
on this horse is arcite | trotting the stones of 5.04. 54
for the horse | would make his length a mile, 5.04. 56
i comment not — the hot horse, hot as fire, 5.04. 65
courageously to pluck him from his horse. VEN 30
away he springs, and hasteth to his horse. 258
so did this horse excel a common one, | in shape 293
look what a horse should have he did not lack, 299
with her the horse, and left adonis there. 322
my day's delight is past, my horse is gone, 380
therefore no marvel though thy horse be gone. 390
on thy well–breath'd horse keep with thy hounds. 678
then can no horse with my desire keep pace; SON 51. 9
in their hawks and hounds, some in their horse; 91. 4
'that horse his mettle from his rider takes; LC 107
whether the horse by him became his deed, | or 111

HORSEBACK 6 FR 0.0006 REL FR 4 V 2 P
sits on 's horseback at mine hostess' door, JN 2.01.289
and when i am a' horseback, i will swear | i 1H4 2.03.101
that runs a' horseback up a hill perpendicular 2.04.343 P
a' horseback, ye cuckoo, but afoot he will not 2.04.353 P
was then present, saw them salute on horseback, H8 1.01. 8
and they can well on horseback, but this gallant HAM 4.07. 84

HORSE–BACK–BREAKER 1 FR 0.0001 REL FR 0 V 1 P
this bed–presser, this horse–back–breaker, this 1H4 2.04.242 P

HORSE–DRENCH 1 FR 0.0001 REL FR 0 V 1 P
of no better report than a horse–drench. COR 2.01.118 P

HORSEHAIRS 1 FR 0.0001 REL FR 0 V 1 P
in her ears, which horsehairs and calves'–guts, CYM 2.03. 29 P

HORSE–LEECHES 1 FR 0.0001 REL FR 1 V 0 P
let us to france, like horse–leeches, my boys, H5 2.03. 55

HORSEMAN 2 FR 0.0002 REL FR 1 V 1 P
what, by a horseman, or a footman? WT 4.03. 64 P
and because you say | you are a horseman, i must TNK 2.05. 45

HORSEMAN'S 1 FR 0.0001 REL FR 0 V 1 P
if this be a horseman's coat, it hath seen very WT 4.03. 67 P

HORSEMANSHIP 3 FR 0.0003 REL FR 2 V 1 P
and witch the world with noble horsemanship. 1H4 4.01.110
you have good judgment in horsemanship. H5 3.07. 55 P
i dare not praise | my feat in horsemanship, yet TNK 2.05. 13

HORSEMEN 11 FR 0.0012 REL FR 11 V 0 P
the horsemen sit like fixed candlesticks, | with H5 4.02. 45
ride thou unto the horsemen on yond hill. 4.07. 57
no, | for yet a many of your horsemen peer | and 4.07. 85
to keep the horsemen off from breaking in. 1H6 1.01.119
your troops of horsemen with his bands of foot, 4.01.165
out, some light horsemen, and peruse their wings 4.02. 43
thus delays my promised supply | of horsemen, 4.03. 11
come go, i will dispatch the horsemen straight; 4.04. 40
while we pursu'd the horsemen of the north, | he 3H6 1.01. 2
is enclosed round about | with horsemen, that JC 5.03. 29
our chariots and our horsemen be in readiness. CYM 3.05. 23

HORSE–PISS 1 FR 0.0001 REL FR 0 V 1 P
monster, i do smell all horse–piss, at which my TMP 4.01.199 P

/HORSE'S 1 FR 0.0001 REL FR 0 V 1 P
/tameness /of /a /wolf, /a /horse's /health, /a LR 3.06. 19 P

HORSE'S 3 FR 0.0003 REL FR 3 V 0 P
hearts i'll stamp out with my horse's heels, 1H6 1.04.108
come, tie his body to my horse's tail, | along TRO 5.08. 21
he's dead, and at the murtherer's horse's tail, 5.10. 4

HORSES' 4 FR 0.0004 REL FR 4 V 0 P
rebels wound thee with their horses' hoofs. R2 3.02. 7
what, will you have them weep our horses' blood? H5 4.02. 12
death on the wheel, or at wild horses' heels, COR 3.02. 2
our horses' labor? CYM 3.04.104

HORSES 63 FR 0.0071 REL FR 39 V 24 P
he hath pawn'd his horses to mine host of the WIV 2.01. 96 P
/germans /desire to have three of your horses. 4.03. 2 P
they shall have my horses, but i'll make them 4.03. 8 P
where be my horses? 4.05. 64 P
maidenhead, of colebrook, of horses and money. 4.05. 79 P
his horses are arrested for it, master /brook. 5.05.114 P
his horses are bred better, for, besides that AYL 1.01. 11 P
thy horses shall be trapp'd, | their harness SHR in.2. 41
have as many diseases as two and fifty horses. 1.02. 81 P
the oats have eaten the horses. 3.02.206 P
how i cried, how the horses ran away, how her 4.01. 80 P
him, | and bring our horses unto long–lane end; 4.03.185
go on, and fetch our horses back again. 4.05. 9
ere twice the horses of the sun shall bring AWW 2.01.161
given order for our horses, and to–night, | when 2.05. 25
go thy ways, let my horses be well look'd to, 4.05. 58 P
fresh horses! WT 3.01. 21
you have horses for yourselves. 1H4 1.02.128 P
'tis like that they will know us by our horses, 1.02.175 P
tut, our horses they shall not see — i'll tie 1.02.177 P
the boy shall lead our horses down the hill. 2.02. 79 P
butler brought those horses from the sheriff? 2.03. 67
your uncle worcester's horses came but to–day, 4.03. 21
so are the horses of the enemy | in general 4.03. 25
bardolph, look to our horses. 2H4 5.01. 61 P
let us take any man's horses, the laws of 5.03.136 P
think, when we talk of horses, that you see them H5 pr 26
and give their fasting horses provender, | and 4.02. 58
between two horses, which doth bear him best, 1H6 2.04. 14
spur your proud horses hard, and ride in blood; R3 5.03.340
"my lord, the horses your lordship sent for, H8 2.02. 1 P
for those that tame wild horses | pace 'em not 5.02. 56
of all the horses — | whereof we have ta'en COR 1.09. 31
that plats the manes of horses in the night, ROM 1.04. 89
matter, get thee gone, | and hire those horses; 5.01. 33
our horses! TIM 1.02.167
hath presented to you | four milk–white horses, 1.02.183
it him, it foals me straight | and able horses. 2.01. 10
horses /did neigh, and dying men did groan, JC 2.02. 23
but hollow men, like horses hot at hand, | make 4.02. 23
and duncan's horses (a thing most strange and MAC 2.04. 14
i wish your horses swift and sure of foot; 3.01. 37
hark, i hear horses. 3.03. 8
his horses go about. 3.03. 11
send out moe horses, skirr the country round, 5.03. 35
sir, hath wager'd with him six barbary horses, HAM 5.02.148 P
six barb'ry horses against six french swords, 5.02.161 P
saddle my horses; LR 1.04.253
prepare my horses. 1.04.258
be my horses ready? 1.05. 33 P
how now, are the horses ready? 1.05. 48 P
where may we set our horses? 2.02. 4 P
horses are tied by the heads, dogs and bears by 2.04. 7 P
get horses for your mistress. 3.07. 20
the stale of horses and the gilded puddle ANT 1.04. 62
where horses have been nimbler than the sands CYM 3.02. 72
that when they hear their roman horses neigh, 4.04. 17
and exclaim'd against | the horses of the sun, TNK 1.02. 87
and feel our fiery horses | like proud seas 2.02. 19
that were a shame, sir, | while i have horses. 2.05. 54
the year) presents me with | a brace of horses; 3.01. 20
no, no, we'll use no horses. 3.06. 59
cost, | of more delight than hawks or horses be; SON 91.11

HORSE–SHOE 1 FR 0.0001 REL FR 0 V 1 P
glowing–hot, in that surge, like a horse–shoe; WIV 3.05.121 P

HORSE–STEALER 1 FR 0.0001 REL FR 0 V 1 P
he is not a pick–purse nor a horse–stealer, but AYL 3.04. 23 P

HORSE–TAIL 1 FR 0.0001 REL FR 0 V 1 P
of my master's horse–tail till they kiss their SHR 4.01. 94 P

HORSE–WAY 1 FR 0.0001 REL FR 0 V 1 P
both stile and gate, horse–way and foot–path. LR 4.01. 56 P

HORSING 1 FR 0.0001 REL FR 1 V 0 P
horsing foot on foot? WT 1.02.288

HORTENSIO 29 FR 0.0032 REL FR 27 V 2 P
there, there, hortensio, will you any wife? SHR 1.01. 56
if you, hortensio, | or, signior gremio, you, 1.01. 95
their love is not so great, hortensio, but we 1.01.107 P
think'st thou, hortensio, though her father be 1.01.123 P
best beloved and approved friend, | hortensio; 1.02. 4
signior hortensio, come you to part the fray? 1.02. 23
good hortensio, | i bade the rascal knock upon 1.02. 36
signior hortensio, thus it stands with me: 1.02. 53
signior hortensio, 'twixt such friends as we 1.02. 65
hortensio, peace! 1.02. 93
i will not sleep, hortensio, till i see her, 1.02.103
and you are well met, signior hortensio. 1.02.163
hortensio, have you told him all her faults? 1.02.186
hortensio, hark. 1.02.211
that she's the chosen of signior hortensio. 1.02.235
hortensio, to what end are all these words? 1.02.248
minion, thou liest. is't not hortensio? 2.01. 13
yet read the gamouth of hortensio. 3.01. 72
hortensio will be quit with thee by changing. 3.01. 92
know, sir, that i am call'd hortensio. 4.02. 21
signior hortensio, i have often heard | of your 4.02. 22
love, | and have forsworn you with hortensio. 4.02. 47
eat it up all, hortensio, if thou lovest me. 4.03. 50
hortensio, say thou wilt see the tailor paid. 4.03.164
then hast thou taught hortensio to be untoward. 4.05. 79
and thou, hortensio, with thy loving widow, 5.02. 7
now, for my life, hortensio fears his widow. 5.02. 16
i mean hortensio is afeard of you. 5.02. 19
conceives by me! how likes hortensio that? 5.02. 23

HORTENSIO'S 2 FR 0.0002 REL FR 2 V 0 P
a re, to plead hortensio's passion; SHR 3.01. 74
where is your sister, and hortensio's wife? 5.02.101

HORTENSIUS 1 FR 0.0001 REL FR 1 V 0 P
well met, good morrow, titus and hortensius. TIM 3.04. 1

HORUM 3 FR 0.0003 REL FR 0 V 3 P
/genitivo, horum, harum, horum. WIV 4.01. 61 P
/genitivo, horum, harum, horum. 4.01. 61 P
fast enough of themselves, and to call "horum," 4.01. 67 P

HOSE 22 FR 0.0024 REL FR 4 V 18 P
being in love, could not see to garter his hose; TGV 2.01. 77 P
being in love, cannot see to put on your hose. 2.01. 78 P
a round hose, madam, now's not worth a pin, 2.07. 55
and youthful still, in your doublet and hose, WIV 3.01. 46 P
thee and shall make thee a new doublet and hose. 3.03. 35 P
in his doublet and hose and leaves off his wit! ADO 5.01.200 P
o, rhymes are guards on wanton cupid's hose: LLL 4.03. 56
his doublet in italy, his round hose in france, MV 1.02. 75 P
vessel, as doublet and hose ought to show itself AYL 2.04. 6 P
his youthful hose, well sav'd, a world too wide 2.07.160
i have a doublet and hose in my disposition? 3.02.196 P
day, what shall i do with my doublet and hose? 3.02.220 P
revenue — then your hose should be ungarter'd, 3.02.378 P
have your doublet and hose pluck'd over your 4.01.202 P
a silken doublet, a velvet hose, a scarlet cloak SHR 5.01. 67 P
dost make hose of thy sleeves? AWW 2.03.250 P
through the doublet, four through the hose, my 1H4 2.04.167 P
down fell their hose. 2.04.215 P
like a kern of ireland, your french hose off, H5 3.07. 53 P
men than thou go in their hose and doublets. 2H6 4.07. 51 P
come hither for stealing out of a french hose. MAC 2.03. 14 P
doublet, hat, hose, all | that answer to them. CYM 3.04.169

HOSPITABLE 3 FR 0.0003 REL FR 3 V 0 P
than the constraint of hospitable zeal | in the JN 2.01.244
against the hospitable canon, would i | wash my COR 1.10. 26
with robber's hands my hospitable favors | you LR 3.07. 40

HOSPITAL 1 FR 0.0001 REL FR 1 V 0 P
i'll jest a twelvemonth in an hospital. LLL 5.02.871

HOSPITALITY 2 FR 0.0002 REL FR 2 V 0 P
way to heaven | by doing deeds of hospitality. AYL 2.04. 82
she, "reward not hospitality | with such black LUC 575

HOST* 70 FR 0.0079 REL FR 40 V 30 P
marry, mine host, because i cannot be merry. TGV 4.02. 28 P
but, host, doth this sir proteus that we talk on 4.02. 73
host, will you go? 4.02.134 P
is (lastly and finally) mine host of the garter. WIV 1.01.140 P
mine host of the garter! 1.03. 1 P
truly, mine host, i must turn away some of my 1.03. 4 P
do so, good mine host. 1.03. 12 P
and i have appointed mine host of de jarteer to 1.04.118 P
pawn'd his horses to mine host of the garter. 2.01. 96 P
look where my ranting host of the garter comes. 2.01.189 P
how now, mine host! 2.01.192 P
i follow, mine host, i follow. 2.01.195 P
good mine host o' th' garter, a word with you. 2.01.203 P
my merry host hath had the measuring of their 2.01.207 P
have with you, mine host. 2.01.221 P
jack rugby — mine host de jarteer — have i not 3.01. 91 P
i'll be judgment by mine host of the garter. 3.01. 96 P
hear mine host of the garter. 3.01.100 P
/afore /god, a mad host. 3.01.112 P
cogging companion, the host of the garter. 3.01.120 P
to–morrow on the lousy knave, mine host. 3.03.240 P
it is thine host, thine ephesian, calls. 4.05. 18 P
how now, mine host? 4.05. 19 P
there was, mine host, an old fat woman even now 4.05. 24 P
that there was, mine host, one that hath taught 4.05. 59 P
where is mine host? 4.05. 73 P
vere is mine host de jarteer? 4.05. 83 P
hark, good mine host: 4.06. 18
both, my good host, to go along with me. 4.06. 47
go bear it to the centaur, where we host, | and ERR 1.02. 9
ay, to a niggardly host and more sparing guest: 3.01. 27
your goods that lay at host, sir, in the centaur 5.01.411
i will bring you | where you shall host. AWW 3.05. 94
of smiling peace to march a bloody host, | and JN 3.01.246
like a kind host, the dolphin and his powers. 5.01. 32
then many an old host that i know is damn'd. 1H4 2.04.472 P
the truth, stol'n from my host at saint albons, 4.02. 46 P
how now, mine host pistol? H5 2.01. 28 P
base tike, call'st thou me host? 2.01. 29
mine host pistol, you must come to my master, 2.01. 81 P
rush on his host, as doth the melted snow | upon 3.05. 50
for forth he goes, and visits all his host, 4.pr. 32
big mars seems bankrout in their beggar'd host, 4.02. 43
proclaim it, westmerland, through my host, 4.03. 34
there's not a piece of feather in our host — 4.03.112
and be it death proclaimed through our host | to 4.08.114
swearing that you withhold his levied host, 1H6 4.04. 31
done, | to send me packing with an host of men: 2H6 3.01.342
me | the queen is coming with a puissant host, 3H6 2.01.207
crowns | the sinow and the forehand of our host, TRO 1.03.143
this, sir, is proclaim'd through all our host: 2.01.121
for time is like a fashionable host | that 3.03.165
my lord, you do discomfort all the host. 5.10. 10
with all th' applause and clamor of the host, COR 1.09. 64
i request you | to give my poor host freedom. 1.09. 87
the walls of rome to–morrow | set down our host. 5.03. 2
conduct me to mine host, we love him highly, MAC 1.06. 29
then, as his host, | who should against his 1.07. 14
mingle with society, | and play the humble host. 3.04. 4
shall we shadow | the numbers of our host, and 5.04. 6
o all you host of heaven! HAM 1.05. 92
i am your host, | with robber's hands my LR 3.07. 39
the shadow of this tree | for your good host; 5.02. 2
give to a gracious message | an host of tongues, ANT 2.05. 87
best you saf'd the bringer | out of the host; 4.06. 26
great palace the capacity | to camp this host, 4.08. 33
my divination) | success to th' roman host. CYM 4.02.352
then mine host | and his fat spouse, that TNK 3.05.127
lust–breathed tarquin leaves the roman host, LUC 3
to all the host of heaven i complain me: 598

HOSTAGE 3 FR 0.0003 REL FR 3 V 0 P
and if he stand /on hostage for his safety, TIT 4.04.105
his body's hostage | for his return. CYM 4.02.185
in't will | take hostage of thee for a hundred, TNK 1.01.184

HOSTAGES 4 FR 0.0004 REL FR 3 V 1 P
you know now your hostages: TRO 3.02.107 P
what they are that must | be hostages for rome. COR 1.10. 29
house, | willing you to demand your hostages, TIT 5.01.160
your hostages i have, so have you mine; ANT 2.06. 1

HOSTESS' 1 FR 0.0001 REL FR 1 V 0 P
sits on 's horseback at mine hostess' door, JN 2.01.289

HOSTESS 30 FR 0.0034 REL FR 12 V 18 P
shot be paid and the hostess say "welcome." TGV 2.05. 7 P
but to spite my wife) | upon mine hostess there. ERR 3.01.119
door, | and rail upon the hostess of the house, SHR in.2. 86
the rather for i think i know your hostess | as AWW 3.05. 42
not your jailer then, | but your kind hostess. WT 1.02. 60
one and not | the hostess of the meeting. 4.04. 64
and is not my hostess of the tavern a most sweet 1H4 1.02. 40 P
pox have i to do with my hostess of the tavern? 1.02. 48 P
hostess, clap to the doors! 2.04.276 P
how now, my lady the hostess! 2.04.285 P
ye lie, hostess, bardolph was shav'd and lost 3.03. 59 P
thou say'st true, hostess, and he slanders thee 3.03.131 P
hostess, i forgive thee. 3.03.170 P
hostess, my breakfast, come! 3.03.205
come hither, hostess. 2H4 2.01.132 P
dost thou hear, hostess? 2.04. 79 P
he's no swagg'rer, hostess, a tame cheater, i' 2.04. 97 P
so you do, hostess. 2.04.107 P
cup of sack, do you discharge upon mine hostess. 2.04.113 P
is thine hostess here of the wicked? 2.04.328 P
farewell, hostess, farewell, doll. 2.04.374 P
you must come to my master, and your hostess. H5 2.01. 82 P
farewell, hostess. 2.03. 59 P
ruminates like an hostess that hath no TRO 3.03.252 P
see, see, our honor'd hostess! MAC 1.06. 10
fair and noble hostess, | we are your guest 1.06. 24

by your leave, hostess. 1.06. 31
by the name of most kind hostess, and shut up 2.01. 16
our hostess keeps her state, but in best time 3.04. 5
a woeful hostess brooks not merry guests. LUC 1125
HOSTESS–SHIP 1 FR 0.0001 REL FR 1 V 0 P
should take on me | the hostess–ship o' th' day. WT 4.04. 72
HOSTILE 5 FR 0.0005 REL FR 5 V 0 P
with the armed hoofs | of hostile paces. 1H4 1.01. 9
i in my dangerous affairs | of hostile arms! R3 4.04.399
as now at last | given hostile strokes, and that COR 3.03. 97
their fears of hostile strokes, their aches, TIM 5.01.199
with hostile forces he'll o'erspread the land, PER 1.02. 24
HOSTILITY 4 FR 0.0004 REL FR 4 V 0 P
hostility and civil tumult reigns | between my JN 4.02.247
the breast of civil peace | such bold hostility, 1H4 4.03. 44
are daily seen | by our proceeding in hostility, 1H6 5.04.162
and neither by treason nor hostility | to seek 3H6 1.01.199
HOSTILIUS 2 FR 0.0002 REL FR 2 V 0 P
son, | who after great hostilius here was king; COR 2.03.240
do you observe this, hostilius? TIM 3.02. 63
HOSTLER *(also ostler, etc.)*
HOSTLER 2 FR 0.0002 REL FR 2 V 0 P
ay, as an hostler, that /for /th' poorest piece COR 3.03. 32
that hostler | must rise betime that cozens him. TNK 5.02. 59
HOST'S 1 FR 0.0001 REL FR 1 V 0 P
by computation and mine host's report, | i could ERR 2.02. 4
HOSTS* 2 FR 0.0002 REL FR 1 V 1 P
that has cozen'd all the hosts of readins, of WIV 4.05. 78 P
the battles of the lord of hosts he fought; 1H6 1.01. 31
HOT 170 FR 0.0192 REL FR 119 V 51 P
in vain, | mars's hot minion is return'd again; TMP 4.01. 98
i tell thee, my master is become a hot lover. TGV 2.05. 51 P
i do not seek to quench your love's hot fire, 2.07. 21
come, we have a hot venison pasty to dinner. WIV 1.01.195 P
i cannot abide the smell of hot meat since. 1.01.286 P
with liver burning hot. 2.01.117
when gods have hot backs, what shall poor men do 5.05. 11 P
be not so hot. MM 5.01.313
she is so hot, because the meat is cold: ERR 1.02. 47
but i felt it hot in her breath. 3.02.131 P
their rich aspect to the hot breath of spain, 3.02.136 P
no, not till a hot january. ADO 1.01. 94 P
the first suit is hot and hasty, like a scotch 2.01. 75 P
your wit's too hot, it speeds too fast, 'twill LLL 2.01.119
two hot sheeps, marry. 2.01.219
that is hot ice and wondrous strange snow. MND 5.01. 59
but a hot temper leaps o'er a cold decree — MV 1.02. 18 P
which is the hot condition of their blood, | if 5.01. 74
apply | hot and rebellious liquors in my blood, AYL 2.03. 49
if it had not been for a hot midsummer night; 4.01.102 P
she is not hot, but temperate as the morn; SHR 2.01.294
were not i a little pot and soon hot, my very 4.01. 6 P
is she so hot a shrew as she's reported? 4.01. 21 P
cold comfort, for being slow in thy hot office? 4.01. 32 P
ay, but the mustard is too hot a little. 4.03. 25
anne, and ginger shall be hot i' th' mouth too. TN 2.03.117 P
too hot, too hot! WT 1.02.108
too hot, too hot! 1.02.108
not so hot, good sir, | i come to bring him 2.03. 32
horseman's coat, it hath seen very hot service. 4.03. 68 P
your purse is not hot enough to purchase your 4.03.119 P
hot lavender, mints, savory, marjorum, | the 4.04.104
aside, here is more matter for a hot brain. 4.04.684 P
with aqua–vitae or some other hot infusion; 4.04.787 P
blood | that hot rash haste so indirectly shed. JN 2.01. 49
approach, | commander of this hot malicious day. 2.01.314
in this hot trial more than we of france, 2.01.342
now, by my life, this day grows wondrous hot; 3.02. 1
so hot a speed with such advice dispos'd, | such 3.04. 11
heat me these irons hot, and look thou stand 4.01. 1
must you with hot irons burn out both mine eyes? 4.01. 39
and with hot irons must i burn them out. 4.01. 59
lords, i am hot with haste in seeking you. 4.03. 74
there is so hot a summer in my bosom | that all 5.07. 30
the salt in them is hot. 5.07. 45
the blood is hot that must be cool'd for this. R2 1.01. 51
will rain hot vengeance on offenders' heads. 1.02. 8
for young hot colts being rag'd do rage the more 2.01. 70
were i but now lord of such hot youth | as when 2.03. 99
mounted upon a hot and fiery steed, | which his 5.02. 8
my liege, this haste was hot in question, | and 1H4 1.01. 34
sun himself a fair hot wench in flame–color'd 1.02. 9 P
what hole in hell were hot enough for him? 1.02.108 P
hot livers and cold purses. 2.04.323 P
is like, if there come a hot june and this civil 2.04.361 P
as slow | as hot lord percy is on fire to go. 3.01.264
thou art only mark'd | for the hot vengeance, 3.02. 10
whose hot incursions and great name in arms, 3.02.108
war | all hot and bleeding will we offer them. 4.01.115
harry to harry shall, hot horse to horse, | meet 4.01.122
i am as hot as molten lead, and as heavy too. 5.03. 33 P
ay, hal, 'tis hot, 'tis hot. 5.03. 53 P
ay, hal, 'tis hot, 'tis hot. 5.03. 53 P
or that hot termagant scot had paid me scot and 5.04.113 P
at home, that our armies join not in a hot day! 2H4 1.02.208 P
if it be a hot day, and i brandish any thing but 1.02.210 P
the room where they supp'd is too hot, they'll 2.04. 14 P
fie, this is hot weather, gentlemen. 3.02. 92 P
sherris, that he is become very hot and valiant. 4.03.122 P
when rage and hot blood are his counsellors, 4.04. 63
galling the gleaned land with hot assays, H5 1.02.151
he'll call you to so hot an answer of it | that 2.04.123
the knocks are too hot; 3.02. 4 P
the humor of it is too hot, that is the very 3.02. 5 P
the day is hot, and the weather, and the wars, 3.02.106 P
into the hand | of hot and forcing violation? 3.03. 21
that their hot blood may spin in english eyes, 4.02. 10
and, touch'd with choler, hot as gunpowder, 4.07.180
moral ties me over to time and a hot summer; 5.02.312 P
here sound retreat, and cease our hot pursuit. 1H6 2.02. 3
are ye so hot, sir? 3.02. 58
now, sir, to you, that were so hot at sea, 3.04. 28
my sword should shed hot blood, mine eyes no 2H6 1.01.118
my lord of gloucester, now ye grow too hot: 1.01.137
churchmen so hot? 2.01. 25
lords, cold snow melts with the sun's hot beams: 3.01.223
amiss to cool a man's stomach this hot weather. 4.10. 9 P
oft have i seen a hot o'erweening cur | run back 5.01.151
bosoms of our part | hot coals of vengeance! 5.02. 36
the sun shines hot, and, if we use delay, | cold 3H6 4.08. 60
i was too hot to do somebody good | that is too R3 1.03.310
and finds the testy gentleman so hot | that he 3.04. 37
anger is like | a full hot horse, who being H8 1.01.133
heat not a furnace for your foe so hot | that it 1.01.140
now, | while 'tis hot, i'll put it to the issue. 5.01.176
in hot digestion of this cormorant war — TRO 2.02. 6
so madly hot that no discourse of reason, | nor 2.02.116
to the hot passion of distemp'red blood | than 2.02.169
in his blood such swoll'n and hot discourse 2.03.173
love, and that breeds hot blood, and hot blood 3.01.129 P
hot blood, and hot blood begets hot thoughts, 3.01.129 P
hot blood, and hot blood begets hot thoughts, 3.01.129 P
hot thoughts, and hot thoughts beget hot deeds, 3.01.130 P
and hot thoughts beget hot deeds, and hot deeds 3.01.130 P
thoughts beget hot deeds, and hot deeds is love. 3.01.130 P
is this the generation of love — hot blood, hot 3.01.131 P
love — hot blood, hot thoughts, and hot deeds? 3.01.131 P
love — hot blood, hot thoughts, and hot deeds? 3.01.132 P
as hot as perseus, spur thy phrygian steed, 4.05.186
the gods are deaf to hot and peevish vows; 5.03. 16
that loves a cup of hot wine with not a drop of COR 2.01. 48 P
now let hot aetna cool in sicily, | and be my TIT 3.01.241
and quench the fire, the room is grown too hot. ROM 1.05. 28
are you so hot? 2.05. 62
the day is hot, the capels /are abroad, | and if 3.01. 2
for now, these hot days, is the mad blood 3.01. 4
thou art as hot a jack in thy mood as any in 3.01. 11 P
who, all as hot, turns deadly point to point, 3.01.160
you are too hot. 3.05.175
like those that under hot ardent zeal would set TIM 3.03. 32 P
who in hot blood | hath stepp'd into the law, 3.05. 11
with ate by his side come hot from hell, | shall JC 3.01.271
thou hast describ'd | a hot friend cooling. 4.02. 19
but hollow men, like horses hot at hand, | make 4.02. 23
fortinbras, | of unimproved mettle hot and full, HAM 1.01. 96
when i had seen this hot love on the wing — 2.02.132
now could i drink hot blood, | and do such 3.02.390
when in your motion you are hot and dry — | as 4.07.157
i thank your lordship, it is very hot. 5.02. 94 P
it is very /sultry and hot /for my complexion. 5.02. 98 P
that these hot tears, which break from me LR 1.04.298
tell the hot duke that — | no, but not yet, may 2.04.104
hot questrists after him, met him at gate, | who 3.07. 17
not so hot. 5.03. 66
'tis hot, it smokes, | it came even from the 5.03.224
were they as prime as goats, as hot as monkeys, OTH 3.03.403
hot, hot, and moist. 3.04. 39
hot, hot, and moist. 3.04. 39
many hot inroads | they make in italy; ANT 1.04. 50
th' year between the extremes | of hot and cold, 1.05. 52
you are most hot and furious when you win. CYM 2.03. 5 P
but to be still hot summer's tanlings and | the 4.04. 29
but that of coward hares, hot goats, and venison 4.04. 37
he spake of her, as dian had hot dreams, | and 5.05.180
not too hot. 5.05.321
if fires be hot, knives sharp, or waters deep, PER 4.02.146
set down in ice, which, by hot grief uncandied, TNK 1.01.107
i comment not — the hot horse, hot as fire, 5.04. 65
i comment not — the hot horse, hot as fire, 5.04. 65
she red and hot as coals of glowing fire, | he VEN 35
shows his hot courage and his high desire. 276
his day's hot task hath ended in the west; 530
hot, faint, and weary, with her hard embracing, 559
her champion mounted for the hot encounter: 596
the hot scent–snuffing hounds are driven to 692
which the hot tyrant stains, and soon bereaves, 797
so shall i die by drops of hot desire. 1074
'tween frozen conscience and hot burning will, LUC 247
but his hot heart, which fond desire doth scorch 314
gives the hot charge, and bids them do their 434
cooling his hot face in the chastest tears 682
this hot desire converts to cold disdain; 691
and in that cold, hot burning fire doth dwell; 1557
hot was the day, she hotter that did look | for PP 6. 7
youth is hot and bold, age is weak and cold, 12. 7
sometime too hot the eye of heaven shines, | and SON 18. 5
three april perfumes in three hot junes burn'd, 104. 7
and so the general of hot desire | was sleeping 154. 7
"'lo all these trophies of affections hot, | of LC 218
cold modesty, hot wrath, | both fire from hence 293
HOT–BLOODIED 2 FR 0.0002 REL FR 1 V 1 P
now the hot–bloodied gods assist me! WIV 5.05. 2 P
why, the hot–bloodied france, that dowerless LR 2.04.212
HOT–BLOODS 1 FR 0.0001 REL FR 0 V 1 P
about all the hot–bloods between fourteen and ADO 3.03.132 P
HOT–HOUSE 1 FR 0.0001 REL FR 0 V 1 P
and now she professes a hot–house; MM 2.01. 66 P
HOTLY 8 FR 0.0009 REL FR 8 V 0 P
you see this chase is hotly followed, friends. H5 2.04. 68
do contest | as hotly and as nobly with thy love COR 4.05.111
thou hotly lusts to use her in that kind | for LR 4.06.162
you have been hotly call'd for; OTH 1.02. 44
and have hotly ask'd them | if they had mothers; TNK 5.01.105
with burning eye did hotly overlook them, VEN 178
burneth more hotly, swelleth with more rage; 332
rome, | who this accomplishment so hotly chased, LUC 716
HOTSPUR 10 FR 0.0011 REL FR 9 V 1 P
on holy–rood day, the gallant hotspur there, 1H4 1.01. 52
hotspur took | mordake earl of fife and eldest 1.01. 70
yet of percy's mind, the hotspur of the north, 2.04.102 P
sit, cousin percy, sit, good cousin hotspur, 3.01. 7
thrice hath this hotspur, mars in swathling 3.02.112
this gallant hotspur, this all–praised knight, 3.02.140
the douglas and the hotspur both together | are 5.01.116
a hare–brain'd hotspur, govern'd by a spleen. 5.02. 19
hath beaten down young hotspur and his troops, 2H4 in 25
of hotspur, coldspur? 1.01. 50
/HOTSPUR'S 2 FR 0.0002 REL FR 2 V 0 P
/nothing /but /the /sound /of /hotspur's /name 2H4 2.03. 37
/might /i, /hanging /on /hotspur's /neck, 2.03. 44
HOTSPUR'S 4 FR 0.0004 REL FR 4 V 0 P
fell | under the wrath of noble hotspur's sword, 2H4 in 30
/where hotspur's father, old northumberland, in 36
so did our men, heavy in hotspur's loss, | lend 1.01.121
it was young hotspur's cause at shrewsbury. 1.03. 26
HOTTER 7 FR 0.0008 REL FR 5 V 2 P
his fisnomy is more hotter in france than there. AWW 4.05. 40 P
honor, nor my lusts | burn hotter than my faith. WT 4.04. 35
pray god his tongue be hotter! 2H4 1.02. 35 P
though thou call'st thyself a hotter name | than MAC 5.07. 6
of cneius pompey's — besides what hotter hours, ANT 3.13.118
phoebus thou | add'st flames, hotter than his; TNK 5.01. 91
she hotter that did look | for his approach that PP 6. 7
HOTTEST 2 FR 0.0002 REL FR 1 V 1 P
as he is (and in the hottest day prognostication WT 4.04.788 P
like stinging bees in hottest summer's day, TIT 5.01. 14
HOUND 15 FR 0.0017 REL FR 12 V 3 P
a hound that runs counter, and yet draws ERR 4.02. 39
so doth the hound his master, the ape his keeper LLL 4.02.126 P
sometime a horse i'll be, sometime a hound, | a MND 3.01.108
like horse, hound, hog, bear, fire, at every 3.01.111
i'll venture so much of my hawk or hound, | but SHR 5.02. 72
o hound of crete, think'st thou my spouse to get H5 2.01. 73
his mouth and promise, like brabbler the hound, TRO 5.01. 92 P
"boy," false hound! COR 5.06.112
with horn and hound we'll give your grace bon TIT 1.01.494
chiron, we hunt not, we, with horse nor hound, 2.02. 25
hound or spaniel, brach or /lym, | or bobtail LR 3.06. 69
here in the chase, not like a hound that hunts, OTH 2.03.363 P
of law in lyam | to slip him like a hound; STM II.C 122
here kennell'd in a brake she finds a hound, VEN 913
look as the full–fed hound or gorged hawk, LUC 694
HOUNDS 27 FR 0.0030 REL FR 27 V 0 P
i had rather give his carcass to my hounds. MND 3.02. 64
my love shall hear the music of my hounds. 4.01.106
confusion | of hounds and echo in conjunction. 4.01.111
they bay'd the bear | with hounds of sparta. 4.01.114
my hounds are bred out of the spartan kind; 4.01.119
i charge thee, tender well my hounds | (brach SHR in.1. 16
another tell him of his hounds and horse, | and in.1. 61
thy hounds shall make the welkin answer them in.2. 45
and my desires, like fell and cruel hounds, TN 1.01. 21
heels | (leash'd in, like hounds) should famine, H5 pr 7
turn on the bloody hounds with heads of steel, 1H6 4.02. 51
and whilst the babbling echo mocks the hounds, TIT 2.03. 17
whiles hounds and horns and sweet melodious 2.03. 27
and the hounds | should drive upon thy 2.03. 63
jove shield your husband from his hounds to–day! 2.03. 70
gods, | not hew him as a carcass fit for hounds; JC 2.01.174
your /teeth like apes, and fawn'd like hounds, 5.01. 41
as hounds and greyhounds, mungrels, spaniels, MAC 3.01. 92
to our theban hounds, | that shook the aged TNK 2.02. 46
on thy well–breath'd horse keep with thy hounds. VEN 678
to make the cunning hounds mistake their smell, 686
hot scent–snuffing hounds are driven to doubt, 692
she hearkens for his hounds and for his horn; 868
by this she hears the hounds are at a bay, 877
even so the timorous yelping of the hounds 881
anon adonis comes with horn and hounds; PP 9. 6
some in their hawks and hounds, some in their SON 91. 4
HOUR 330 FR 0.0373 REL FR 277 V 53 P
in your cabin for the mischance of the hour, if TMP 1.01. 26 P
wherefore did they not | that hour destroy us? 1.02.139
taught thee each hour | one thing or other. 1.02.354
to any business that | we say befits the hour. 2.01.290
and now farewell | till half an hour hence. 3.01. 91
within this half hour will he be asleep. 3.02.113
one phoenix | at this hour reigning there. 3.03. 24
at this hour | lies at my mercy all mine enemies 4.01.262
on the sixt hour, at which time, my lord, | you 5.01. 4
and when that hour o'erslips me in the day TGV 2.02. 9
the next ensuing hour some foul mischance 2.02. 11
'twill be this hour ere i have done weeping; 2.03. 1 P
nay more, our marriage hour, | with all the 2.04.179
this is the hour that madam silvia | entreated 4.03. 1
and now it is about the very hour | that silvia 5.01. 2
as my mother was, the first hour i was born. WIV 2.02. 38
my wife hath sent to him, the hour is fix'd, the 2.02.290 P
eleven o' clock the hour. 2.02.310 P
'tis past the hour, sir, that sir hugh promis'd 2.03. 4 P
o this blessed hour! 3.03. 46 P
i was at her house the hour she appointed me. 3.05. 65 P
'twixt eight and nine is the hour, master /brook 3.05.130 P
within a quarter of an hour. 4.04. 5 P
and ask him why, that hour of fairy revel, | in 4.04. 59
the hour draws on. to the oak, to the oak! 5.03. 23 P
she's very near her hour. MM 2.02. 16
at what hour to–morrow | shall i attend your 2.02.159
how may i do it, having the hour limited, and an 4.02.165 P
the hour draws on | prefix'd by angelo. 4.03. 78
we proclaim it in an hour before his ent'ring, 4.04. 8 P
your sheep–biting face, and be hang'd an hour! 5.01.355 P
it claudio was beheaded | at an unusual hour? 5.01.458
that very hour, and in the self–same inn, | a ERR 1.01. 53
within this hour it will be dinner–time; 1.02. 11
reserve them till a merrier hour than this: 1.02. 69
even now, even here, not half an hour since. 2.02. 14
i'll meet you at that place some hour hence. 3.01.122
the hour steals on, i pray you, sir, dispatch. 4.01. 52
you know i gave it you half an hour since. 4.01. 65
yes, if any hour meet a sergeant, 'a turns back 4.02. 56
he not reason to turn back an hour in a day? 4.02. 62
i brought you word an hour since that the bark 4.03. 37 P
serv'd him from the hour of my nativity to this 4.04. 30 P
within this hour i was his bondman, sir, | but 5.01.289
and till this present hour | my heavy burthen 5.01.402
can see him but i am heart–burn'd an hour after. ADO 2.01. 4 P
out a' question, you were born in a merry hour. 2.01.333 P
find me a meet hour to draw don pedro and the 2.02. 33 P
i talk'd with no man at that hour, my lord. 4.01. 86
at that hour last night | talk with a ruffian at 4.01. 90
you have stay'd me in a happy hour, i was about 4.01.283 P
thus did she an hour together trans–shape thy 5.01.170 P
why, an hour in clamor and a quarter in rheum; 5.02. 82 P
the prince and claudio promis'd by this hour 5.04. 13
about the sixt hour; LLL 1.01.236 P
you may do it in an hour, sir. 1.02. 37 P
the hour that fools should ask. 2.01.122
i thought to close mine eyes some half an hour; 5.02. 90
here they stay'd an hour, | and talk'd apace; 5.02.368
and in that hour, my lord, | they did not bless 5.02.369
now, at the latest minute of the hour, | grant 5.02.787
hippolyta, our nuptial hour | draws on apace. MND 1.01. 1
swear | a merrier hour was never wasted there. 2.01. 57

while she was in her dull and sleeping hour, | a 3.02. 8
o most happy hour! 4.02. 28 P
play | to ease the anguish of a torturing hour? 5.01. 37
us at my lodging, and return | all in an hour. MV 2.04. 3
at gratiano's lodging some hour hence. 2.04. 26
his hour is almost past. 2.06. 2
and it is marvel he out–dwells his hour, | for 2.06. 3
fashion of thy malice | to the last hour of act, 4.01. 19
that you would wear it till your hour of death, 5.01.153
'tis but an hour ago since it was nine, | and AYL 2.07. 24
and after one hour more 'twill be eleven, | and 2.07. 25
and so, from hour to hour, we ripe and ripe, 2.07. 26
and so, from hour to hour, we ripe and ripe, 2.07. 26
and then, from hour to hour, we rot and rot; 2.07. 27
and then, from hour to hour, we rot and rot; 2.07. 27
laugh sans intermission | an hour by his dial. 2.07. 33
and groaning every hour would detect the lazy 3.02.303 P
rosalind, i come within an hour of my promise. 4.01. 42 P
two a' clock is your hour? 4.01.186 P
or come one minute behind your hour, i will 4.01.191 P
but at this hour the house doth keep itself, 4.03. 81
left a promise to return again | within an hour, 4.03.100
this carol they began that hour, | with a hey, 5.03. 26
that will i, should i die the hour after. 5.04. 12
and when in music we have spent an hour, | your SHR 3.01. 7
to see him every hour, to sit and draw | his AWW 1.01. 93
on his grace's cure | by such a day an' hour. 1.03.249
to make the coming hour o'erflow with joy | and 2.04. 46
remain there but an hour, nor speak to me. 4.02. 58
i have deliv'red it an hour since. 4.03. 3 P
for he is dieted to his hour. 4.03. 30 P
if i were to live this present hour, i will tell 4.03.161 P
daughter–in–law had been alive at this hour, and 4.05. 5 P
hadst this ring, | thou diest within this hour. 5.03.284
him myself and a sister, both born in an hour. TN 2.01. 19 P
for some hour before you took me from the breach 2.01. 21 P
being once display'd, doth fall that very hour. 2.04. 39
behavior to his own shadow this half hour. 2.05. 18 P
your purse–bearer and leave you | for an hour. 3.03. 48
to his use | not half an hour before. 5.01. 92
o, he's drunk, sir toby, an hour agone; 5.01.198 P
come | taint the condition of this present hour, 5.01.357
please your highness | to take the urgent hour. WT 1.02.465
within this hour bring me word 'tis done | (and 2.03.136
you sent to th' oracle are come | an hour since. 2.03.195
law, and in one self–born hour | to plant and 4.01. 8
if i might die within this hour, i have liv'd 4.04.461
and which he shall know within this hour, if i 4.04.758 P
jewel of children, seen this hour, he had pair'd 5.01.116
out within this hour that ballad–makers cannot 5.02. 24 P
now blessed be the hour by night or day | when i JN 1.01.165
thou shalt rue this hour within this hour. 3.01.323
thou shalt rue this hour within this hour. 3.01.323
the misplac'd john should entertain an hour, 3.04.133
and like the watchful minutes to the hour, 4.01. 46
'tis not an hour since i left him well. 4.03.104
/were born to see so sad an hour as this, 5.02. 26
king john did fly an hour or two before | the 5.05. 17
who half an hour since came from the dolphin, 5.07. 83
to men in joy, but grief makes one hour ten. R2 1.03.261
now comes the sick hour that his surfeit made, 2.02. 84
an hour before i came, the duchess died. 2.02. 97
now, by my soul, i would it were this hour. 4.01. 42
sir, the sound that tells what hour it is | are 5.05. 55
where they did spend a sad and bloody hour, | as 1H4 1.01. 56
he did confound the best part of an hour | in 1.03.100
he is, my lord, an hour ago. 2.03. 66
so good a proficient in one quarter of an hour, 2.04. 18 P
he, and answers, "some fourteen," an hour after; 2.04.108 P
the hour before the heavenly–harness'd team 3.01.218
as thou art to this hour was richard then | when 3.02. 94
not above once in a quarter — of an hour, paid 3.03. 17 P
main | on the nice hazard of one doubtful hour? 4.01. 48
point, | still ending at the arrival of an hour. 5.02. 84
for the hour is come | to end the one of us, and 5.04. 68
and fought a long hour by shrewsbury clock. 5.04.148 P
many a creature else | had been alive this hour, 5.05. 8
the ragged'st hour that time and spite dare 2H4 1.01.151
my poorest subjects | are at this hour asleep! 3.01. 5
to the wet //sea–boy in an hour so rude, | and 3.01. 27
stretches itself beyond the hour of death. 4.04. 57
thee with my honors | before thy hour be ripe? 4.05. 96
heart | to stab at half an hour of my life. 4.05.108
what, canst thou not forbear me half an hour? 4.05.109
and the hour, i think, is come | to give him H5 1.01. 92
omit no happy hour | that may give furth'rance 1.02.300
than i do at this hour joy o'er myself, 2.02.163
up the town, so chrish save me law, in an hour! 3.02. 92 P
and the third hour of drowsy morning /name. 4.pr. 16
fly o'er them all, impatient for their hour. 4.02. 52
thrice within this hour | i saw him down; 4.06. 4
know, to this hour is an honorable badge of the 4.07.101 P
faintly besiege us one hour in a month. 1H6 1.02. 8
talbot, farewell, thy hour is not yet come. 1.05. 13
to run, | finish the process of his sandy hour, 4.02. 36
sund'red friends greet in the hour of death. 4.03. 42
stay, | if the first hour i shrink and run away. 4.05. 31
within this half hour, hath receiv'd his sight, 2H6 2.01. 62
'tis like, my lord, you will not keep your hour. 2.01.177
ten is the hour that was appointed me | to watch 2.04. 6
is the hour to come | that e'er i prov'd thee 3.01.204
you are come to sandal in a happy hour; 3H6 1.02. 63
and when thou fail'st (as god forbid the hour!) 2.01.190
how many makes the hour full complete, | how 2.05. 26
now therefore let us hence, and lose no hour, 4.01.148
that if about this hour he make this way, 4.05. 10
shall rue the hour that ever thou wast born. 5.06. 43
so i might live one hour in your sweet bosom. R3 1.02.124
make haste, the hour of death is expiate. 3.03. 24
meet me within this hour at baynard's castle. 3.05.105
let me but meet you, ladies, /an hour hence, 4.01. 28
for never yet one hour in his bed | did i enjoy 4.01. 82
what comfortable hour canst thou name | that 4.04.174
none, but humphrey hour, that call'd your grace 4.04.176
and every hour more competitors | flock to the 4.04.504
do through the clouds behold this present hour, 5.01. 8
and by the second hour in the morning | desire 5.03. 31
wife, | that never slept a quiet hour with thee, 5.03.160
he should have brav'd the east an hour ago. 5.03.279
could not find | his hour of speech a minute — H8 1.02.121
a choice hour | to hear from him a matter of 1.02.162
his plain–song | and have an hour of hearing, 1.03. 46
and entreat | an hour of revels with 'em. 1.04. 72
the last hour | of my long weary life is come 2.01.132
is this an hour for temporal affairs? 2.02. 72
i would your grace would give us but an hour 2.02. 79
when was the hour | i ever contradicted your 2.04. 27
to hear such news as this | once every hour. 3.02. 25
and what expense by th' hour | seems to flow 3.02.108
down | to rest a while, some half an hour or so, 4.01. 66
about the hour of eight, which he himself 4.02. 26
good hour of night, sir thomas! 5.01. 5
and has done half an hour, to know your 5.02. 41
the wind, | it is not agamemnon's sleeping hour. TRO 1.03.254
grumblest and railest every hour on achilles, 2.01. 32 P
that hector, by the /fift hour of the sun, 2.01.122
ere the first sacrifice, within this hour, | we 4.02. 64
and the hour prefix'd | for her delivery to this 4.03. 1
diomed, | keep hector company an hour or two. 5.01. 81
what, shall i come? the hour — 5.02.104
i have been seeking you this hour, my lord. 5.02.182
should not sell him an hour from her beholding; COR 1.03. 9 P
upon him a' we'nsday half an hour together; 1.03. 59 P
above an hour, my lord. 1.06. 15
how couldst thou in a mile confound an hour, 1.06. 17
i, sir, | half an hour since brought my report. 1.06. 21
advanc'd and darts, | we prove this very hour. 1.06. 62
in a better hour, | let what is meet be said it 3.01.168
i am so dishonor'd that the very hour | you take 3.03. 60
in love | unseparable, shall within this hour, 4.04. 16
a one, | which to this hour bewail the injury, 5.06.152
brought hither in a most unlucky hour, | to find TIT 2.03.251
'tis not an hour since i left them there. 2.03.256
and that you'll say ere half an hour pass. 3.01.191
why dost thou laugh? it fits not with this hour. 3.01.265
oft have you heard me wish for such an hour, 5.02.159
an hour before the worshipp'd sun | peer'd forth ROM 1.01.118
faith, i can tell her age unto an hour. 1.03. 11
by the hour of nine. 2.02.168
within this hour my man shall be with thee, 2.04.188
in half an hour she promised to return. 2.05. 2
fee–simple of my life for an hour and a quarter. 3.01. 32 P
tybalt, that an hour | hath been my cousin! 3.01.112
else, when he is found, that hour is his last. 3.01.195
an hour but married, tybalt murdered, | doting 3.03. 66
company, | i would have been a–bed an hour ago. 3.04. 7
i must hear from thee every day in the hour, 3.05. 44
most miserable hour that e'er time saw | in 4.05. 44
full half an hour. 5.03.130
ah, what an unkind hour | is guilty of this 5.03.145
all alone, | at the prefixed hour of her waking, 5.03.253
life | be sacrific'd some hour before his time, 5.03.268
power | to expel sickness, but prolong his hour! TIM 3.01. 63
what do you think the hour? 3.04. 8
to repair some other hour, i should derive much 3.04. 69 P
i have been up this hour, awake all night. JC 2.01. 88
by the eight hour; is that the uttermost? 2.01.213
which sometime hath his hour with every man. 2.01.251
about the ninth hour, lady. 2.04. 23
there is no hour so fit | as caesar's death's 3.01.153
is no hour so fit | as caesar's death's hour, 3.01.154
i know my hour is come. 5.05. 20
that have but labor'd to attain this hour. 5.05. 42
time and the hour runs through the roughest day. MAC 1.03.147
yet when we can entreat an hour to serve, | we 2.01. 22
timely on him, | i have almost slipp'd the hour. 2.03. 47
had i but died an hour before this chance, | i 2.03. 91
of the night | for a dark hour or twain. 3.01. 27
within this hour, at most, | i will advise you 3.01.127
must embrace the fate | of that dark hour. 3.01.137
let this pernicious hour | stand aye accursed in 4.01.133
known her continue in this a quarter of an hour. 5.01. 30 P
that struts and frets his hour upon the stage, 5.05. 25
you come most carefully upon your hour. HAM 1.01. 6
thus twice before, and jump at this dead hour, 1.01. 65
take thy fair hour, laertes, time be thine, 1.02. 62
what hour now? 1.04. 3
my hour is almost come, | when i to sulph'rous 1.05. 2
upon my secure hour thy uncle stole, | with 1.05. 61
an hour of quiet /shortly shall we see, | till 5.01.298
we have this hour a constant will to publish LR 1.01. 43
every hour | he flashes into one gross crime or 1.03. 3
if thou shouldst dally half an hour, his life, 3.06. 93
fourscore and upward, not an hour more nor less; 4.07. 60
until some half hour past, when i was arm'd. 5.03.194
took once a pliant hour, and found good means OTH 1.03.151
desdemona, i have but an hour | of love, of 1.03.298
from this present hour of five till the bell 2.02. 10 P
not this hour, lieutenant; 2.03. 13 P
it hard, within this hour | it will be well. 3.03.286
or to be naked with her friend in bed | an hour, 4.01. 4
but half an hour! 5.02. 82
o heavy hour! 5.02. 98
thy biddings have been done, and every hour, ANT 1.04. 34
mark antony is every hour in rome | expected. 2.01. 29
and from this hour | the heart of brothers 2.02.146
ere the ninth hour, i drunk him to his bed; 2.05. 21
if we be not reliev'd within this hour, | we 4.09. 1
shall embattle | by th' second hour i' th' morn. 4.09. 4
our hour | is fully out. 4.09. 31
and to this hour no guess in knowledge | which CYM 1.01. 60
about some half hour hence, | pray you speak 1.01.176
at the sixt hour of morn, at noon, at midnight, 1.03. 31
what hour is it? 2.02. 2
this yellow jachimo, in an hour — was't not? 2.05. 14
of miles may we well rid | 'twixt hour and hour? 3.02. 68
of miles may we well rid | 'twixt hour and hour? 3.02. 68
thy shoulders, shall within this hour be off, 4.01. 17 P
'tis the ninth hour o' th' morn. 4.02. 30
unhappy was the clock | that strook the hour! 5.05.154
/be /my so us'd a guest as not an hour | in the PER 1.02. 3
walk half an hour, leonine, at the least. 4.01. 45
every hour in't will | take hostage of thee for TNK 1.01.183
keep the feast full, bate not an hour on't. 1.01.220
have patiently | laid up my hour to come. 2.02. 6
fortune | to be one hour at liberty and grasp 2.02.208
within this hour the whoobub | will be all o'er 2.06. 35
about this hour my cousin gave his faith | to 3.06. 1
or i will make th' advantage of this hour | mine 3.06.123
arcite, | i am friends again till that hour. 3.06.300
this quarrel | sleep till the hour prefix'd, and 3.06.304
gone — she's done, | and undone in an hour. 4.01.125
love, this only | from this hour is complexion. 4.02. 43
lay by your anger for an hour, and dove–like, 5.01. 11
within this half hour she came smiling to me 5.02. 4
well she knew | what hour my fit would take me. 5.02. 10
and has done this long hour, to visit you. 5.02. 42
he'll dance the morris twenty mile an hour, 5.02. 51
i have told my last hour; 5.04. 92
for whom an hour, | but one hour since, i was as 5.04.128
but one hour since, i was as dearly sorry | as 5.04.129
a summer's day will seem an hour but short, VEN 23
what hour is this? 495
and in a peaceful hour doth cry, 'kill, kill!' 652
there shall not be one minute in an hour 1187
let, | till every minute pays the hour his debt. LUC 329
and they would stand auspicious to the hour, 347
wilt thou sort an hour great strifes to end? 899
dread night, wouldst thou one hour come back, 965
mad, | himself himself seek every hour to kill! 998
that he may vow, in that sad hour of mine, 1179
lost, vaded, broken, dead within an hour. PP 13. 6
but out, alack, he was but one hour mine, | the SON 33.11
the which he will not ev'ry hour survey, | for 52. 3
nor dare i chide the world–without–end hour, 57. 5
dost hold time's fickle glass, his sickle, hour; 126. 2
you behold | the injury of many a blasting hour, LC 72

HOUR–GLASS 2 FR 0.0002 REL FR 2 V 0 P
i should not see the sandy hour–glass run | but MV 1.01. 25
of many years | into an hour–glass: H5 pr 31

HOURLY 25 FR 0.0028 REL FR 22 V 3 P
sea–nymphs hourly ring his knell: TMP 1.02.403
and increasing, | hourly joys be still upon you! 4.01.108
habitation where thou keep'st | hourly afflict. MM 3.01. 11
this is an accident of hourly proof, | which i ADO 2.01.181
might tend upon | and call her hourly mistress. AWW 3.02. 83
and endless liar, an hourly promise–breaker, the 3.06. 10 P
sh' adulterates hourly with thine uncle john, JN 3.01. 56
may hourly trample on their sovereign's head; R2 3.03.157
forsworn his company hourly any time this two 1H4 2.02. 16 P
my thoughts do hourly prophesy | mischance unto 2H6 3.02.283
to make parents happy | may hourly fall upon ye! H8 5.04. 8
the glorious gods sit in hourly synod about thy COR 5.02. 68 P
although she lave them hourly in the flood. TIT 4.02.103
hazard so near 's as doth hourly grow | out of HAM 3.03. 6
insolent retinue | do hourly carp and quarrel, LR 1.04.203
the main descry | stands on the hourly thought. 4.06.214
that we the pain of death would hourly die 5.03.186
i hourly learn | a doctrine of obedience, and ANT 5.02. 30
and i shall here abide the hourly shot | of CYM 1.01. 89
with hands | made hard with hourly falsehood 1.06.107
a mother hourly coining plots, a wooer | more 2.01. 59
report should render him hourly to your ear | as 3.04.150
where's hourly trouble for a minute's ease. PER 2.04. 44
hourly bring your honor | in public question TNK 3.06.221
or as those bars which stop the hourly dial, LUC 327

HOUR'S 14 FR 0.0015 REL FR 10 V 4 P
the hour's now come, | the very minute bids thee TMP 1.02. 36
which with an hour's heat | dissolves to water, TGV 3.02. 7
we had an hour's talk of that wart. WIV 1.04.151 P
we have an hour's talk with you. 2.01.167 P
mirth, | i never spent an hour's talk withal. LLL 2.01. 68
break an hour's promise in love! AYL 4.01. 44 P
who, when they see the hour's ripe on earth, R2 1.02. 7
but wherefore grieve i at an hour's poor loss, 2H6 3.02.381
and each hour's joy wrack'd with a week of teen. R3 4.01. 96
and to be on foot at an hour's warning. COR 4.03. 45 P
one hour's storm will drown the fragrant meads, TIT 2.04. 54
i have an hour's talk in store for you; JC 2.02.121
that of an hour's age doth hiss the speaker; MAC 4.03.175
in thee there is not half an hour's life. HAM 5.02.315

HOURS' 4 FR 0.0004 REL FR 4 V 0 P
not three hours' travel from this very place. TN 1.02. 23
if this right hand would buy two hours' life 3H6 2.06. 80
is now the two hours' traffic of our stage; ROM pr 12
art, may yet appear | worth two hours' travail. TNK pr 29

/HOURS 1 FR 0.0001 REL FR 1 V 0 P
/and /with /our /surfeiting /and /wanton /hours 2H4 4.01. 55

HOURS 145 FR 0.0164 REL FR 126 V 19 P
can, that have more time | for vainer hours, and TMP 1.02.174
yourself, | he's safe for these three hours. 3.01. 21
whom three hours since | were wrack'd upon this 5.01.136
your eld'st acquaintance cannot be three hours. 5.01.186
we have convers'd and spent our hours together, TGV 2.04. 63
she will not fail, for lovers break not hours, 5.01. 4
better three hours too soon than a minute too WIV 2.02.312 P
two, tree hours for him, and he is no come. 2.03. 36 P
a thousand irreligious cursed hours | which 5.05.229
he promis'd to meet me two hours since, and he MM 1.02. 75 P
within two hours. 1.02.193
love, | and make a common of my serious hours. ERR 2.02. 29
in ephesus i am but two hours old, | as strange 2.02.148
my wife is shrewish when i keep not hours: 3.01. 2
the hours come back! that did i never /hear. 4.02. 55
and careful hours with time's deformed hand 5.01.299
well, you will temporize with the hours. ADO 1.01.275 P
any man with me convers'd | at hours unmeet, or 4.01.182
and then, to sleep but three hours in the night, LLL 1.01. 42
masks, and merry hours | forerun fair love, 4.03.376
the sisters' vows, the hours that we have spent, MND 3.02.199
o long and tedious night, | abate thy hours! 3.02.432
to wear away this long age of three hours 5.01. 33
of clock, we have two hours | to furnish us. MV 2.04. 8
fair thoughts and happy hours attend on you! 3.04. 41
she kneels and prays | for happy wedlock hours. 5.01. 32
or go to bed now, being two hours to day. 5.01.303
lose and neglect the creeping hours of time; AYL 2.07.112
for these two hours, rosalind, i will leave thee 4.01.177 P
alas, dear love, i cannot lack thee two hours! 4.01.179 P
what, shall i be appointed hours, as though, SHR 1.01.103
i'll not be tied to hours nor 'pointed times, 3.01. 19
luke's church is at your command at all hours. 4.04. 89 P
by mine honor, if i were but two hours younger, AWW 2.03.253 P
here he comes, to beguile two hours in a sleep, 4.01. 22 P

within these three hours 'twill be time enough 4.01. 24 P
lady, takes great exceptions to your ill hours. TN 1.03. 6 P
my grave | i have travell'd but two hours. 5.01.163
how have the hours rack'd and tortur'd me, 5.01.219
hours, minutes? WT 1.02.290
ay, and have been so any time these four hours. 5.02.137 P
let not the hours of this ungodly day | wear out JN 3.01.109
slow hours shall not determinate | the dateless R2 1.03.150
would the word "farewell" have length'ned hours 1.04. 16
accomplish'd with /the number of thy hours; 2.01.177
you have in manner with your sinful hours | made 3.01. 11
which waste of idle hours hath quite thrown down 3.04. 66
which our profane hours here have thrown down. 5.01. 25
the time shall not be many hours of age | more 5.01. 57
and groans | show minutes, times, and hours; 5.05. 58
unless hours were cups of sack, and minutes 1H4 1.02. 7 P
o, let the hours be short, | till fields, and 1.03.301
i must leave you within these two hours. 2.03. 36
with a dozen of them two hours together. 2.04.165 P
he held me last night at least nine hours | in 3.01.154
i'll away within these two hours, and so come in 3.01.261 P
the lag end of my life | with quiet hours; 5.01. 25
and these unseasoned hours perforce must add 2H4 3.01.105
thou hast stol'n that which after some few hours 4.05.101
those tears | by number into hours of happiness. 5.02. 61
his hours fill'd up with riots, banquets, sports H5 1.01. 56
whose hours the peasant best advantages. 4.01.284
more than three hours the fight continued, 1H6 1.01.120
who two hours since | i met in travel toward his 4.03. 35
within six hours they will be at his aid. 4.04. 41
complete, | how many hours brings about the day, 3H6 2.05. 27
so many hours must i tend my flock, | so many 2.05. 31
my flock, | so many hours must i take my rest, 2.05. 32
my rest, | so many hours must i contemplate, 2.05. 33
so many hours must i sport myself, | so many 2.05. 34
so minutes, hours, days, months, and years, 2.05. 38
and do expect him here some two hours hence. 5.01. 10
and, after many length'ned hours of grief, | die R3 1.03.207
sorrow breaks seasons and reposing hours, 1.04. 76
that he could gnaw a crust at two hours old; 2.04. 28
eleven hours i have spent to write it over, 3.06. 5
and yet within these five hours hastings liv'd, 3.06. 8
which, mellow'd by the stealing hours of time, 3.07.168
take all the swift advantage of the hours. 4.01. 48
with the sweet silent hours of marriage joys; 4.04.330
heaven and fortune bar me happy hours! 4.04.400
the silent hours steal on, | and flaky darkness 5.03. 85
away their shilling | richly in two short hours. H8 pr 13
within these forty hours surrey durst better 3.02.253
these should be hours for necessities, | not for 5.01. 2
after so many hours, lives, speeches spent, TRO 2.02. 1
see here these movers that do prize their hours COR 1.05. 4
within these three hours, tullus, | alone i 1.08. 7
whose hours, whose bed, whose meal and exercise 4.04. 14
i have been broad awake two hours and more. TIT 2.02. 17
ay me, sad hours seem long. ROM 1.01.161
it was. what sadness lengthens romeo's hours? 1.01.163
from nine till twelve | is /three long hours, 2.05. 11
death | thou shalt continue two and forty hours, 4.01.105
at some hours in the night spirits resort — 4.03. 44
within this three hours will fair juliet wake. 5.02. 25
now lord timon's happy hours are done and past, TIM 3.02. 6 P
if you had sent but two hours before — 3.06. 45 P
make use of thy salt hours, season the slaves 4.03. 86
i have seen | hours dreadful and things strange; MAC 2.04. 3
you know sometimes he walks four hours together HAM 2.02.160
looks, and my father died within 's two hours. 3.02.127 P
ay, two hours together. LR 1.02.155 P
these weeds are memories of those worser hours; 4.07. 7
pleasure and action make the hours seem short. OTH 2.03.379
what sense had i in her stol'n hours of lust? 3.03.338
eightscore eight hours? 3.04.174
and lovers' absent hours, | more tedious than 3.04.174
now for the love of love, and her soft hours, ANT 1.01. 44
and then when poisoned hours had bound me up 2.02. 90
of cneius pompey's — besides what hotter hours, 3.13.118
for when mine hours | were nice and lucky, men 3.13.178
tend me to-night two hours, i ask no more, | and 4.02. 32
how i would think on him at certain hours | such CYM 1.03. 27
be, will 's free hours languish for | assured 1.06. 72
i have read three hours then. 2.02. 3
shall we discourse | the freezing hours away? 3.03. 39
you, should at these early hours | shake off the PER 3.02. 22
death may usurp on nature many hours, | and yet 3.02. 82
of an egyptian | that had nine hours lien dead, 3.02. 85
she hath not been | entranc'd above five hours. 3.02. 94
i'll come again some two hours hence and bring TNK 3.03. 49
we shall find | too many hours to die in, gentle 3.06.112
he'll tickle't up | in two hours, if his hand be 4.01.139
that in lag hours attend | for grey approachers; 5.04. 8
for lovers' hours are long, though seeming short VEN 842
stuff up his lust, as minutes fill up hours; LUC 297
thy heinous hours wait on them as their pages. 910
betray'd the hours thou gav'st me to repose? 933
to ruinate proud buildings with thy hours, | and 944
"disturb his hours of rest with restless trances 974
soon, | but now are minutes added to the hours; PP 14.26
those hours that with gentle work did frame SON 5. 1
now stand you on the top of happy hours, | and 16. 5
o, carve not with thy hours my love's fair brow, 19. 9
doth it steal sweet hours from love's delight. 36. 8
tend | upon the hours and times of your desire? 57. 2
or at your hand th' account of hours to crave, 58. 3
pry, | to find out shames and idle hours in me, 61. 7
when hours have drain'd his blood and fill'd his 63. 3
in him those holy antique hours are seen, 68. 9
love alters not with his brief hours and weeks, 116.11
which works on leases of short-numb'red hours, 124.10
buy terms divine in selling hours of dross; 146.11
and had let go by | the swiftest hours, observed LC 60

HOUS'D 4 FR 0.0004 REL FR 4 V 0 P

for ever hous'd where it gets possession. ERR 3.01.106
i charge thee, sathan, hous'd within this man, 4.04. 54
even now we hous'd him in the abbey here, | and 5.01.188
if here you hous'd him, here he would have been; 5.01.272

/HOUSE 3 FR 0.0003 REL FR 2 V 1 P

they have had my /house a week at command. WIV 4.03. 9 P
/when /we /see /the /figure /of /the /house, 2H4 1.03. 43
rout, | no din but snores /the /house /about, PER 3.ch. 2

HOUSE 414 FR 0.0468 REL FR 286 V 128 P

by any other house, or person? TMP 1.02. 42
if the ill spirit have so fair a house, | good 1.02.459
which, when he has a house, he'll deck withal. 3.02. 97
the trumpery in my house, go bring it hither, 4.01.186
hands, and all our house in a great perplexity, TGV 2.03. 8 P
marry, at my house. 4.02.137 P
one feast, one house, one mutual happiness. 5.04.173
got pless your house here! WIV 1.01. 73 P
and ask of doctor caius' house which is the way; 1.02. 2 P
and find any body in the house, here will be an 1.04. 4 P
as ever servant shall come in house withal; 1.04. 11 P
him my master, look you, for i keep his house; 1.04. 95 P
come near the house, i pray you. 1.04.132 P
page, trust me, i was going to your house. 2.01. 34 P
she was in his company at page's house; 2.01.236 P
be absence from his house between ten and eleven 2.02. 84 P
like a fair house built on another man's ground, 2.02.215 P
gentleman that he says is here now in the house, 3.03.108 P
than a thousand pound he were out of the house. 3.03.124 P
in the house you cannot hide him. 3.03.128 P
if there be any pody in the house, and in the 3.03.210 P
you to-morrow morning to my house to breakfast; 3.03.230 P
you wrong me, sir, thus still to haunt my house. 3.04. 69
i was at her house the hour she appointed me. 3.05. 65 P
to search his house for his wive's love. 3.05. 77 P
he is at my house. 3.05.145 P
there is no hiding you in the house. 4.02. 64 P
he swears she's a witch, forbade her my house, 4.02. 87 P
one convey'd out of my house yesterday in this 4.02.146 P
in my house i am sure he is. 4.02.148 P
help to search my house this one time. 4.02.160 P
have i not forbid her my house? 4.02.173 P
there's his chamber, his house, his castle, his 4.05. 6 P
thou shalt eat a posset to-night at my house, 5.05.171 P
whose house, sir, was (as they say) pluck'd down MM 2.01. 64 P
which, i think, is a very ill house too. 2.01. 66 P
as well as she, that this house, if it be not a 2.01. 76 P
if it be not a bawd's house, it is pity of her 2.01. 76 P
is pity of her life, for it is a naughty house. 2.01. 77 P
we had but two in the house, which at that very 2.01. 91 P
and it like you, the house is a respected house; 2.01.162 P
and it like you, the house is a respected house; 2.01.163 P
year, i'll rent the fairest house in it after 2.01.241 P
to your worship's house, sir? 2.01.274 P
to my house. 2.01.275 P
husband now, pompey, you will keep the house. 3.02. 71 P
here as i was in our house of profession. 4.03. 2 P
think it were mistress overdone's own house, for 4.03. 3 P
his company | at mariana's house to-night. 4.03.140
i'll call you at your house. 4.04. 16 P
go call at flavio's house, | and tell him where 4.05. 6
to fetch you from the mart | home to your house, ERR 1.02. 75
"i know," quoth he, "no house, no wife, no 2.01. 71
my house was at the phoenix? 2.02. 11
denied my house for his, me for his wife. 2.02.159
gold, | and that i did deny my wife and house. 3.01. 9
thou that keep'st me out from the house i owe? 3.01. 42
you, to the porpentine, | for there's the house. 3.01.117
pleaseth you walk with me down to his house, | i 4.01. 12
while i go to the goldsmith's house, go thou 4.01. 15
good signior, take the stranger to my house, 4.01. 36
my way is now to hie home to his house, | and 4.03. 92
he rush'd into my house, and took perforce | my 4.03. 94
face | revel and feast it at my house to-day, 4.04. 62
were shut, | and i denied to enter in my house? 4.04. 64
see him safe convey'd | home to my house. 4.04.123
husband all in rage to-day | came to my house, 4.04.138
bind dromio too, and bear them to my house. 5.01. 35
for god's sake take a house! 5.01. 36
no, not a creature enters in my house. 5.01. 92
while she with harlots feasted in my house. 5.01.205
officer | to go in person with me to my house. 5.01.234
there is a fat friend at your master's house, 5.01.415
came trouble to my house in the likeness of your ADO 1.01. 99 P
from my house — if i had it — 1.01.281 P
is philemon's roof, within the house is jove. 2.01. 97 P
no, 'twas the vane on the house. 3.03.129 P
to-morrow morning come you to my house, | and 5.01.286
climb o'er the house to unlock the little gate. LLL 1.01.109
oath, | to let you enter his /unpeopled house. 2.01. 88
though so denied fair harbor in my house. 2.01.174
shut | my woeful self up in a mourning house, 5.02.808
from athens is her house remote seven leagues; MND 1.01.159
steal forth thy father's house to-morrow night; 1.01.164
hath devour'd many a gentleman of your house. 3.01.193 P
dance in duke theseus' house triumphantly, | and 4.01. 89
have you sent to bottom's house? 4.02. 1 P
not a mouse | shall disturb this hallowed house. 5.01.388
through the house give glimmering light | by the 5.01.391
of day, | through this house each fairy stray. 5.01.402
see to my house, left in the fearful guard | of MV 1.03.175
but turn down indirectly to the jew's house. 2.02. 44 P
our house is hell, and thou, a merry devil, 2.03. 2
how i shall take her from her father's house, 2.04. 30
jessica, my girl, | look to my house. 2.05. 16
sound of shallow fopp'ry enter | my sober house. 2.05. 36
why then to thee, thou silver treasure house! 2.09. 34
antonio is at his house and desires to speak 3.01. 75 P
this house, these servants, and this same myself 3.02.170
the husbandry and manage of my house | until my 3.04. 25
what if my house be troubled with a rat, | and i 4.01. 44
the wish would make else an unquiet house. 4.01.294
you take my house when you do take the prop 4.01.375
do take the prop | that doth sustain my house; 4.01.376
him, if thou canst, | unto antonio's house. 4.01.454
inquire the jew's house out, give him this deed, 4.02. 1
i pray you show my youth old shylock's house. 4.02. 11
come, good sir, will you show me to this house? 4.02. 19
some welcome for the mistress of the house. 5.01. 38
within the house, your mistress is at hand, 5.01. 52
it is your music, madam, of the house. 5.01. 98
sir, you are very welcome to our house. 5.01.139
let not that doctor e'er come near my house. 5.01.223
i have not yet | enter'd my house. 5.01.273
deed | hadst thou descended from another house. AYL 1.02.228
this is no place, this house is but a butchery; 2.03. 27
make an extent upon his house and lands. 3.01. 17
as well a dark house and a whip as madmen do; 3.02.401 P
worse than jove in a thatch'd house! 3.03. 11 P
if you will know my house, | 'tis at the tuft of 3.05. 74
comes slowly, he carries his house on his head; 4.01. 55 P
but at this hour the house doth keep itself, 4.03. 81
you | the owner of the house i did inquire for? 4.03. 89
for my father's house and all the revenue that 5.02. 10 P
sir, in a poor house, as your pearl in your foul 5.04. 60 P
let them want nothing that my house affords. SHR in.1. 104
comes it that your kindred shuns your house, in.2. 28
door, | and rail upon the hostess of the house, in.2. 86
ay, the woman's maid of the house. in.2. 90
why, sir, you know no house nor no such maid, in.2. 91
schoolmasters will i keep within my house, | fit 1.01. 94
wed her, and bed her, and rid the house of her! 1.01.145 P
keep house and ply his book, welcome his friends 1.01.196
we have not yet been seen in any house, | nor 1.01.199
keep house and port and servants, as i should. 1.01.203
and i trow this is his house. 1.02. 4
way | to the house of signior baptista minola? 1.02.220
show myself a forward guest | within your house, 2.01. 52
my house within the city | is richly furnished 2.01.346
things that belongs | to house or house-keeping. 2.01.356
she is my goods, my chattels, she is my house, 3.02.230
is supper ready, the house trimm'd, rushes 4.01. 46 P
and in my house you shall be friendly lodg'd. 4.02.108
love, | will we return unto thy father's house, 4.03. 53
brav'd in mine own house with a skein of thread? 4.03.110
to feast and sport us at thy father's house. 4.03.183
/sir, this is the house, please it you that i 4.04. 1
not in my house, lucentio, for you know 4.04. 51
list, | or ere i journey to your father's house. 4.05. 8
sir, here's the door, this is lucentio's house. 5.01. 8
feast with the best, and welcome to my house. 5.02. 8
i'll send her to my house, | acquaint my mother AWW 2.03.286
to the dark house and the /detested wife. 2.03.292
the air of paradise did fan the house | and 3.02.125
i know she will lie at my house; 3.05. 31 P
great saint jaques bound, | already at my house. 3.05. 96
now will i lead you to the house, and show you 3.06.110
that downward hath succeeded in his house | from 3.07. 23
it is an honor 'longing to our house, 4.02. 42
a ring, | my chastity's the jewel of our house, 4.02. 46
my house, mine honor, yea, my life, be thine, 4.02. 52
wife some two months since fled from his house. 4.03. 48 P
i am for the house with the narrow gate, which i 4.05. 50 P
the honorable lady of the house, which is she? TN 1.05.167 P
you tell me if this be the lady of the house, 1.05.172 P
assurance if you be the lady of the house, that 1.05.180 P
are you the lady of the house? 1.05.185 P
gate, | and call upon my soul within the house; 1.05.269
do ye make an alehouse of my lady's house, that 2.03. 89 P
your misdemeanors, you are welcome to the house; 2.03. 99 P
he is about the house. 2.04. 13 P
i am all the daughters of my father's house, 2.04.120
for i do live at my house, and my house doth 3.01. 6 P
my house, and my house doth stand by the church. 3.01. 6 P
will you encounter the house? 3.01. 74 P
the house will be the quieter. 3.04.134 P
will return again into the house and desire some 3.04.241 P
back you shall not to the house, unless you 3.04.248 P
sir, or i'll throw your dagger o'er the house. 4.01. 29 P
go with me to my house, | and hear thou there 4.01. 54
say'st thou that house is dark? 4.02. 34 P
mad, sir topas, i say to you this house is dark. 4.02. 41 P
i say this house is as dark as ignorance, though 4.02. 45 P
so, | she could not sway her house, command her 4.03. 17
you, | here at my house and at my proper cost. 5.01.319
kept in a dark house, visited by the priest, 5.01.342
he is seldom from the house of a most homely WT 4.02. 37 P
not at your father's house these seven years 4.04.578
the medicine of our house, how shall we do? 4.04.587
death of hermione, visited that remov'd house. 5.02.107 P
heirs of your kingdoms, my poor house to visit, 5.03. 6
to break within the bloody house of life, | and JN 4.02.210
at ely house. R2 1.04. 58
of a wall, | or as /a moat defensive to a house, 2.01. 48
bid him repair to us to ely house | to see this 2.01.216
uncle, you say the queen is at your house, | for 3.01. 36
o, if you raise this house against this house, 4.01.145
o, if you raise this house against this house, 4.01.145
and cloister thee in some religious house. 5.01. 23
our house, my sovereign liege, little deserves 1H4 1.03. 10
this house is turn'd upside down since robin 2.01. 10 P
the most villainous house in all london road for 2.01. 14 P
in respect of the love i bear your house." 2.03. 3 P
in the respect of the love he bears our house: 2.03. 4 P
his own barn better than he loves our house. 2.03. 6 P
it, yea, and can show it you here in the house; 2.04.258 P
at the door, they are come to search the house. 2.04.490 P
cry | hath followed certain men unto this house. 2.04.508
and so let me entreat you leave the house. 2.04.518
a railing wife, | worse than a smoky house. 3.01.159
talk to me | in any summer house in christendom. 3.01.162
do you think i keep thieves in my house? 3.03. 55 P
of a hair was never lost in my house before. 3.03. 58 P
i was never call'd so in mine own house before. 3.03. 63 P
this house is turn'd bawdy-house, they pick 3.03. 98 P
looks | of favor from myself and all our house, 5.01. 31
like /one that draws the model of an house 2H4 1.03. 58
he stabb'd me in mine own house, most beastly, 2.01. 14 P
he hath eaten me out of house and home, he hath 2.01. 74 P
i will bar no honest man my house, nor no 2.04.103 P
i'll forswear keeping house afore i'll be in 2.04.205 P
for suffering flesh to be eaten in thy house, 2.04.344 P
at your return visit our house, let our old 3.02.294 P
he is a gentleman of a good house, and for his H5 4.04. 45 P
and for that cause i train'd thee to my house. 1H6 2.03. 35
to feast so great a warrior in my house. 2.03. 82
this blot that they object against your house 2.04.116
strong fixed is the house of lancaster, | and 2.05.102
which somerset hath offer'd to my house, | i 2.05.125
give | that doth belong unto the house of york, 3.01.164
vow, burgundy, by honor of thy house, | prick'd 3.02. 77
york, | to grapple with the house of lancaster; 2H6 1.01.257

my lord cardinal's man, for keeping my house, 1.03. 18 P
thus got the house of lancaster the crown. 2.02. 29
with heart–blood of the house of lancaster; 2.02. 66
how they affect the house and claim of york. 3.01.375
go, get you to my house, | i will reward you for 3.02. 8
and now the house of york, thrust from the crown 4.01. 94
therefore am i of an honorable house. 4.02. 49 P
for his father had never a house but the cage. 4.02. 52 P
he made a chimney in my father's house, and the 4.02.148 P
descended from the duke of clarence' house, 4.04. 29
and then break into his son–in–law's house, sir 4.07.110 P
to all that do dwell in this house, because the 4.10. 64 P
meet i an infant of the house of york, | into as 5.02. 57
come, thou new ruin of old clifford's house: 5.02. 61
him, | and like rich hangings in a homely house, 5.03. 12
which now the house of lancaster usurps, | i vow 3H6 1.01. 23
arm'd as we are, let's stay within this house. 1.01. 38
to make a shambles of the parliament house! 1.01. 71
by his soul, thou and thy house shall rue it. 1.01. 94
york, | or i will fill the house with armed men, 1.01.167
be thou a prey unto the house of york, | and die 1.01.185
and giv'n unto the house of york such head | as 1.01.233
disgrace, | and utter ruin of the house of york. 1.01.254
by giving the house of lancaster leave to 1.02. 13
my drift, | nor any of the house of lancaster? 1.02. 47
the sight of any of the house of york | is as a 1.03. 30
may make against the house of lancaster. 2.01.176
did, | giving no ground unto the house of york, 2.06. 16
bring forth that fatal screech–owl to our house 2.06. 56
because in quarrel of the house of york | the 3.02. 6
arm, | this arm upholds the house of lancaster. 3.03.107
and i the house of york. 3.03.108
did i forget that by the house of york | my 3.03.186
have sold their lives unto the house of york, 5.01. 74
i will not ruinate my father's house, | who gave 5.01. 83
from those that wish the downfall of our house! 5.06. 65
and all the clouds that low'r'd upon our house R3 1.01. 3
king, | pale ashes of the house of lancaster, 1.02. 6
mourner, | and presently repair to crosby house; 1.02.212
grey | were factious for the house of lancaster; 1.03.127
now fair befall thee and thy noble house! 1.03.281
to fight | in quarrel of the house of lancaster. 1.04.204
i see the ruin of my house: 2.04. 49
at crosby house, there shall you find us both. 3.01.190
heir to the crown — meaning indeed his house, 3.05. 78
birth, | the lineal glory of your royal house, 3.07.121
to the disgrace and downfall of your house; 3.07.217
thou offspring of the house of lancaster, | the 5.03.136
the true succeeders of each royal house, | by 5.05. 30
they have done my poor house grace; H8 1.04. 73
king has made him master | o' th' jewel house, 4.01.111
beside that of the jewel house, is made master 5.01. 34
well contented | to make your house our tow'r. 5.01.106
day, no man think | h'as business at his house; 5.04. 75
at your own house, there he unarms him. TRO 1.02.274 P
'twas to bring this greek | to calchas' house, 4.01. 38
walk into her house. 4.03. 5
lay here in corioles | at a poor man's house; COR 1.09. 83
i will make my very house reel to–night. 2.01.111 P
ere in our own house i do shade my head, | the 2.01.195
springs of — | the noble house o' th' martians; 2.03.238
of the same house publius and quintus were, 2.03.241
go, get you to /your house; 3.01.229
i prithee, noble friend, home to thy house; 3.01.233
pursue him to his house and pluck him thence, 3.01.307
the capitol exceed | the meanest house in rome, 4.02. 40
nobles of the state | at his house this night. 4.04. 10
which is his house, beseech you? 4.04. 10
a goodly house! 4.05. 5
i cannot get him out o' th' house. 4.05. 21 P
pray you avoid the house. 4.05. 23 P
if he were putting to my house the brand | that 4.06.115
if you'ld save your life, fly to your house. 5.04. 35
the emperor's court is like the house of fame, TIT 2.01.126
marcus, look to my house, | lucius and i'll go 4.01.120
the meeting | even at his father's house, the 4.04.103
he craves a parley at your father's house, 5.01.159
welcome, dread fury, to my woeful house; 5.02. 82
and bid him come and banquet at thy house, 5.02.114
emperor and the empress too | feast at my house, 5.02.128
the villain is alive in titus' house, | and as 5.03.123
souls, | and make a mutual closure of our house. 5.03.134
go, go into old titus' sorrowful house, | and 5.03.142
a dog of the house of montague moves me. ROM 1.01. 8 P
a dog of that house shall move me to stand! 1.01. 11 P
tool, here comes /two of the house of montagues. 1.01. 32 P
at my poor house look to behold this night 1.02. 24
buds shall you this night | inherit at my house; 1.02. 30
my house and welcome on their pleasure stay. 1.02. 37
to our house. 1.02. 74 P
whose house? 1.02. 75 P
and if you be not of the house of montagues, i 1.02. 79 P
town | here in my house do him disparagement; 1.05. 70
bachelor, | her mother is the lady of the house, 1.05.113
hath sent a letter to his father's house. 2.04. 7
a gentleman of the very first house, of the 2.04. 25 P
help me into some house, benvolio, | or i shall 3.01.105
lady, | and bid her hasten all the house to bed, 3.03.156
where you will, you shall not house with me. 3.05.188
for venus smiles not in a house of tears. 4.01. 8
as i remember, this should be the house. 5.01. 55
suspecting that we both were in a house | where 5.02. 9
for lo his house | is empty on the back of 5.03.203
thy creature, | by night frequents my house. TIM 1.01.117
but they enter my master's house merrily, and go 2.02.101 P
'tis, if he would not keep so good a house. 3.01. 23 P
who cannot keep his wealth must keep his house. 3.03. 41
than he that has no house to put his head in? 3.04. 64 P
free, and must my house | be my retentive enemy? 3.04. 80
burn, house! 3.06.104
such a house broke? 4.02. 5
all broken implements of a ruin'd house. 4.02. 16
and he's gone | to seek you at your house. JC 1.03.150
i will yet, ere day, | see brutus at his house. 1.03.154
you shall not stir out of your house to–day. 2.02. 9
call it my fear | that keeps you in the house, 2.02. 51
at mine own house, good lady. 2.04. 22
fled to his house amaz'd. 3.01. 96
bring him with triumph home unto his house. 3.02. 49
we'll bring him to his house | with shouts and 3.02. 52
we'll burn the house of brutus. 3.02.231
he and lepidus are at caesar's house. 3.02.264
some to decius' house, and some to casca's; 3.03. 37 P
but, lepidus, go you to caesar's house; 4.01. 7
broad wherewith | your majesty loads our house. MAC 1.06. 18
to all the house; 2.02. 38
calls to parley | the sleepers of the house? 2.03. 83
woe, alas! | what, in our house? 2.03. 88
there's not a one of them but in his house | i 3.04.130
desire his jewels, and this other's house, | and 4.03. 80
"i saw him enter such a house of sale," HAM 2.01. 58
may play the fool no where but in 's own house. 3.01.132 P
that i have shot my arrow o'er the house | and 5.02.243
but i can tell why a snail has a house. LR 1.05. 28 P
that if they come to sojourn at my house, | i'll 2.01.103
good dawning to thee, friend. art of this house? 2.02. 2 P
he rais'd the house with loud and coward cries. 2.04. 43
do you but mark how this becomes the house! 2.04.153
how in one house | should many people under two 2.04.240
to follow in a house where twice so many | have 2.04.262
this house is little, the old man and 's people 2.04.288
holy–water in a dry house is better than this 3.02. 10 P
he that has a house to put 's head in has a good 3.02. 25 P
the codpiece that will house | before the head 3.02. 27
repose you there, while i to this hard house 3.02. 63
they took from me the use of mine own house, 3.03. 4 P
good my lord, take his offer, go into th' house. 3.04.156
i will have my revenge ere i depart his house. 3.05. 1 P
him, | and quit the house on purpose that their 4.02. 93
here is her father's house, i'll call aloud. OTH 1.01. 74
look to your house, your daughter, and your bags 1.01. 80
my house is not a grange. 1.01.106
if she be in her chamber or your house, | let 1.01.138
at every house i'll call | (i may command at 1.01.180
i will but spend a word here in the house, | and 1.02. 48
but still the house affairs would draw her 1.03.147
indeed, sweet love, i was coming to your house. 3.04.171
as doth the raven o'er the infectious house, 4.01. 21
he supp'd at my house, but i therefore shake not 5.01.119
gratiano, keep the house, | and seize upon the 5.02.365
thou dost o'er–count me of my father's house; ANT 2.06. 27
you have my /father's house — but what, we are 2.07.128
sir, look well to my husband's house; and — 3.02. 45
to rush into the secret house of death | ere 4.15. 81
this mortal house i'll ruin, | do caesar what he 5.02. 51
a goodly day not to keep house with such | whose CYM 3.03. 1
we house i' th' rock, yet use thee not so hardly 3.03. 8
be here, | poor house, that keep'st thyself! 3.06. 36
should house him safe is wrack'd and split, PER 2.ch. 32
surprise and fear | made me to quit the house. 3.02. 18
the house you dwell in proclaims you to be a 4.06. 77 P
do you know this house to be a place of such 4.06. 79 P
your house, but for this virgin that doth prop 4.06.119
basest groom | that doth frequent your house. 4.06.191
and chances | into an honest house, our story 5.ch. 2
sir, they shall be brought you to my house, 5.03. 26
beseech you first, go with me to my house, 5.03. 65
again betake you to your hawthorn house. TNK 3.01. 82
to bury you, | and see the house made handsome. 4.01. 79
"her house is sack'd, her quiet interrupted, LUC 1170
so i commend me from our house in grief, | my 1308
who lets so fair a house fall to decay, | which SON 13. 9

HOUSE–CLOGS 1 FR 0.0001 REL FR 1 V 0 P
had i a sword, | and these house–clogs away — TNK 3.01. 43

HOUSE–EAVES 1 FR 0.0001 REL FR 0 V 1 P
sparrows must not build in his house–eaves, MM 3.02.176 P

/HOUSEHOLD 2 FR 0.0002 REL FR 2 V 0 P
/that /every /day /under /his /household /roof R2 4.01.282
might i but know thee by thy /household badge. 2H6 5.01.201

HOUSEHOLD 14 FR 0.0015 REL FR 12 V 2 P
what, household stuff? SHR in.2. 140 P
a kate | conformable as other household kates. 2.01.278
my household stuff, my field, my barn, | my 3.02.231
and ring these fingers with thy household worms, JN 3.04. 31
and all the household servants fled with him R2 2.02. 60
and dispers'd | the household of the king. 2.03. 28
from my own windows torn my household coat, 3.01. 24
body to anatomize | among my household? 2H4 in 22
familiar in his mouth as household words, H5 4.03. 52
you of my household, leave this peevish broil, 1H6 3.01. 92
at last by notes of household harmony | they 3H6 4.06. 14
rich stuffs, and ornaments of household, which H8 3.02.126
call forth my household servants, let's to–night ANT 4.02. 9
shall undo a whole household, let me be gelded PER 4.06.124 P

HOUSEHOLDER 1 FR 0.0001 REL FR 0 V 1 P
and, which is more, a householder, and, which is ADO 4.02. 81 P

HOUSEHOLDERS 1 FR 0.0001 REL FR 0 V 1 P
i press me none but good householders, /yeomen's 1H4 4.02. 15 P

HOUSEHOLD'S 4 FR 0.0004 REL FR 4 V 0 P
in thee thy mother dies, our household's name, 1H6 4.06. 38
be closed in our household's monument. TIT 5.03.194
funeral path brings to your household's grave: TNK 1.05. 11
o foul dishonor to my household's grave! LUC 198

HOUSEHOLDS' 1 FR 0.0001 REL FR 1 V 0 P
to turn your households' rancor to pure love. ROM 2.03. 92

HOUSEHOLDS 1 FR 0.0001 REL FR 1 V 0 P
two households, both alike in dignity, | in fair ROM pr 1

HOUSE–KEEPER 3 FR 0.0003 REL FR 1 V 2 P
man and a good house–keeper goes as fairly as to TN 4.02. 9 P
the house–keeper, the hunter, every one, MAC 3.01. 96
th' art a good house–keeper and i thank thy good STM II.C 58 P

HOUSE–KEEPERS 1 FR 0.0001 REL FR 0 V 1 P
you are manifest house–keepers. COR 1.03. 51 P

HOUSE–KEEPING 3 FR 0.0003 REL FR 3 V 0 P
i hear your grace hath sworn out house–keeping: LLL 2.01.104
things that belongs | to house or house–keeping. SHR 2.01.356
thy deeds, thy plainness, and thy house–keeping, 2H6 1.01.191

HOUSELESS 2 FR 0.0002 REL FR 2 V 0 P
you houseless poverty, | nay, get thee in. LR 3.04. 26
how shall your houseless heads and unfed sides, 3.04. 30

HOUSE'S 4 FR 0.0004 REL FR 4 V 0 P
i would not yield to be your house's guest: LLL 5.02.354
but stop my house's ears, i mean my casements; MV 2.05. 34
son, in whom my house's name | must be digested; AWW 5.03. 73
secrecy, | unpeg the basket on the house's top, HAM 3.04.193

HOUSES' 1 FR 0.0001 REL FR 1 V 0 P
like roping icicles | upon our houses' thatch, H5 3.05. 24

HOUSES 22 FR 0.0024 REL FR 14 V 8 P
he hath rais'd the wall, and houses too. TMP 2.01. 88 P
all houses in the suburbs of vienna must be MM 1.02. 95 P
but shall all our houses of resort in the 1.02.101 P
nothing but use their abuses in common houses, i 2.01. 43 P
in ransom and free pardon | are of two houses: 2.04.112
to the citizens | by rushing in their houses, ERR 5.01.143
i'll leave her houses three or four as good, SHR 2.01.366
and the mermidons are no bottle–ale houses. TN 2.03. 28 P
even so our houses, and ourselves, and children, H5 5.02. 56
are from their hives and houses driven away. 1H6 1.05. 24
the citizens fly and forsake their houses; 2H6 4.04. 50
with burthens, take your houses over your heads, 4.08. 29 P
face, | the fatal colors of our striving houses; 3H6 2.05. 98
a plague a' both houses! ROM 3.01. 91
a plague a' both your houses! 3.01.100 P
a plague a' both your houses! 3.01.106
your houses! 3.01.108
run to your houses, fall upon your knees, | pray JC 1.01. 53
and with the brands fire the traitors' houses. 3.02.255
the houses he makes lasts till doomsday. HAM 5.01. 59 P
as houses are defil'd for want of use, | they PER 1.04. 37
them, cut their throats, possess their houses, STM II.C 120

HOUSEWIFERY *(see huswifery)*

HOUSEWIVES *(also huswife, etc.)*

HOUSEWIVES 1 FR 0.0001 REL FR 1 V 0 P
let housewives make a skillet of my helm, | and OTH 1.03.272

HOVEL 5 FR 0.0005 REL FR 5 V 0 P
gracious my lord, hard by here is a hovel, LR 3.02. 61
come, your hovel. 3.02. 71
true, boy. come bring us to this hovel. 3.02. 78
in, fellow, there, into th' hovel; 3.04.174
to hovel thee with swine and rogues forlorn | in 4.07. 38

HOVEL–POST 1 FR 0.0001 REL FR 0 V 1 P
do i look like a cudgel or a hovel–post, a staff MV 2.02. 68 P

HOVER 5 FR 0.0005 REL FR 5 V 0 P
hover about me with your aery wings | and hear R3 4.04. 13
hover about her; 4.04. 15
yet, | to hover on the dreadful shore of styx? TIT 1.01. 88
is fair, | hover through the fog and filthy air. MAC 1.01. 12
save me, and hover o'er me with your wings, HAM 3.04.103

HOVER'D 1 FR 0.0001 REL FR 1 V 0 P
which like a cherubin above them hover'd. LC 319

HOVERING 2 FR 0.0002 REL FR 2 V 0 P
or else a hovering temporizer, that | canst with WT 1.02.302
first hovering o'er the paper with her quill. LUC 1297

HOVERS 1 FR 0.0001 REL FR 1 V 0 P
some aery devil hovers in the sky | and pours JN 3.02. 2

/HOW 19 FR 0.0021 REL FR 15 V 4 P
/now /mark /me /how /i /will /undo /myself: R2 4.01.203
/how /soon /my /sorrow /hath /destroy'd /my 4.01.291
/me /the /way | /how /to /lament /the /cause. 4.01.302
/how /able /such /a /work /to /undergo, | /to 2H4 1.03. 54
/how /fares /your /grace? 4.05. 49
/how /chance /the /prophet /could /not /at /that R3 4.02.100
/how /now! TIT 3.02. 23
/how /troy /was /burnt /and /he /made /miserable 3.02. 28
/fie, /how /franticly /i /square /my /talk, 3.02. 31
/how /if /that /fly /had /a /father /and /mother 3.02. 60
/how /would /he /hang /his /slender /gilded 3.02. 61
/how /comes /it? /do /they /grow /rusty? HAM 2.02.337 P
/how /are /they /escoted? 2.02.346 P
hope, will teach you to imagine — | /how /now? 4.07. 36
/how /dost /thou /understand /the /scripture? 5.01. 35 P
/how /long /have /you /been /a /sectary LR 1.02.150 P
/of /how /unnatural /and /bemadding /sorrow 3.01. 38
/how /do /you, /sir? 3.06. 33
/how /light /and /portable /my /pain /seems /now 3.06.108

HOW 2309 FR 0.2610 REL FR 1668 V 641 P
but how is it | that this lives in thy mind? TMP 1.02. 48
cam'st here, | how thou cam'st here thou mayst. 1.02. 52
being once perfected how to grant suits, | how 1.02. 79
how to deny them, who t' advance, and who | to 1.02. 80
of homage, and i know not how much tribute, 1.02.124
i, not rememb'ring how i cried out then, | will 1.02.133
how came we ashore? 1.02.158
the mariners, say how thou hast dispos'd, | and 1.02.225
how now? moody? | what is't thou canst demand? 1.02.244
and teach me how | to name the bigger light, and 1.02.334
to name the bigger light, and how the less, 1.02.335
and my profit on't | is, i know how to curse. 1.02.364
lord, how it looks about! 1.02.411
good instruction give | how i may bear me here. 1.02.426
how? 1.02.431
how lush and lusty the grass looks! how green! 2.01. 53 P
how lush and lusty the grass looks! how green! 2.01. 53 P
how came that widow in? 2.01. 78 P
good lord, how you take it! 2.01. 81 P
i'll teach you how to flow. 2.01.222
if you but knew how you the purpose cherish 2.01.224
how, in stripping it, | you more invest it! 2.01.225
how say you? 2.01.254
"how shall that claribel | measure us back to 2.01.258
and how does your content | tender your own good 2.01.269
and look how well my garments sit upon me, 2.01.272
why, how now, ho! 2.01.308
how cam'st thou to be the siege of this 2.02.105 P
how didst thou scape? 2.02.119 P
how cam'st thou hither? 2.02.119 P
swear by this bottle how thou cam'st hither — i 2.02.120 P
here; swear then how thou escap'dst. 2.02.127 P
how now, moon–calf? 2.02.135 P
how does thine ague? 2.02.136 P
and instruct thee how | to snare the nimble 2.02.169
how features are abroad | i am skilless of; 3.01. 52
how does thy honor? 3.02. 23 P
lo, how he mocks me! wilt thou let him, my lord? 3.02. 30 P
how now shall this be compass'd? 3.02. 58 P
how does my bounteous sister? 4.01.103
spirit, | how fares the king and 's followers? 5.01. 7
but how should prospero | be living, and be here 5.01.119
how thou hast met us here, whom three hours 5.01.136
(how sharp the point of this remembrance is!) 5.01.138
arise, and say how thou cam'st here. 5.01.181
how many goodly creatures are there here! 5.01.182

how beauteous mankind is! 5.01.183
o, how oddly will it sound that i | must ask my 5.01.197
say, how came you hither? 5.01.228
and (how we know not) all clapp'd under hatches, 5.01.231
how fares my gracious sir? 5.01.253
how fine my master is! 5.01.262
how cam'st thou in this pickle? 5.01.281
why, how now, stephano? 5.01.285 P
how young leander cross'd the hellespont. TGV 1.01. 22
why, sir, how do you bear with me? 1.01.122 P
how now? what means this passion at his name? 1.02. 16
fie, fie, how wayward is this foolish love, 1.02. 57
how churlishly i chid lucetta hence, | when 1.02. 60
how angerly i taught my brow to frown, | when 1.02. 62
let's see your song. how now, minion? 1.02. 85
of time, | and how he cannot be a perfect man, 1.03. 20
lordship is not ignorant | how his companion, 1.03. 26
and that thou mayst perceive how well i like it, 1.03. 35
how now? what letter are you reading there? 1.03. 51
but that he writes | how happily he lives, how 1.03. 57
how well-belov'd | and daily graced by the 1.03. 57
and how stand you affected to his wish? 1.03. 60
o, how this spring of love resembleth | the 1.03. 84
how now, sirrah? 2.01. 7 P
why, how know you that i am in love? 2.01. 17 P
how painted? and how out of count? 2.01. 58 P
how painted? and how out of count? 2.01. 58 P
how esteem'st thou me? i account of her beauty. 2.01. 61 P
how long hath she been deform'd? 2.01. 64 P
how now, sir? 2.01.141 P
but see how i lay the dust with my tears. 2.03. 32 P
and how quote you my folly? 2.04. 18 P
how? 2.04. 22 P
how could he see his way to seek out you? 2.04. 94
now tell me: how do all from whence you came? 2.04.122
and how do yours? 2.04.124
how does your lady, and how thrives your love? 2.04.125
how does your lady, and how thrives your love? 2.04.125
determin'd of — how i must climb her window, 2.04.181
how shall i dote on her with more advice, | that 2.04.207
how did thy master part with madam julia? 2.05. 11 P
how then? shall he marry her? 2.05. 16 P
why then, how stands the matter with them? 2.05. 20 P
how say'st thou that my master is become a 2.05. 41 P
than how? 2.05. 44 P
good mean | how with my honor i may undertake 2.07. 6
how will the world repute me | for undertaking 2.07. 59
a mean | how he her chamber-window will ascend, 3.01. 39
how and which way i may bestow myself | to be 3.01. 87
how shall i best convey the ladder thither? 3.01.128
how shall i fashion me to wear a cloak? 3.01.135
how now, signior launce? 3.01.280 P
why, man? how black? 3.01.287 P
how now, sir proteus? 3.02. 11
thou know'st how willingly i would effect | the 3.02. 22
ignorant | how she opposes her against my will? 3.02. 26
she bids me think how i have been forsworn | in 4.02. 10
how now, sir proteus, are you crept before us? 4.02. 18
how now? 4.02. 54 P
how do you, man? 4.02. 55 P
how, out of tune on the strings? 4.02. 60 P
nor how my father would enforce me marry | vain 4.03. 16
how many masters would do this for his servant? 4.04. 29 P
how now, you whoreson peasant, | where have you 4.04. 43
how many women would do such a message? 4.04. 90
how tall was she? 4.04.157
alas, how love can trifle with itself! 4.04.183
how likes she my discourse? 5.02. 15
how now, sir proteus? 5.02. 31
how now, thurio? 5.02. 31
have learn'd me how to brook this patiently. 5.03. 4
how use doth breed a habit in a man! 5.04. 1
how like a dream is this! 5.04. 26
o, heaven be judge how i love valentine, | whose 5.04. 36
how now? 5.04. 86 P
how? 5.04. 92
but how cam'st thou by this ring? 5.04. 96
how? julia? 5.04.100
how oft hast thou with perjury cleft the root? 5.04.103
how doth good mistress page? WIV 1.01. 83 P
how does your fallow greyhound, sir? 1.01. 89 P
how now, mephostophilus? 1.01.130
how now, mistress ford? 1.01.191 P
how now, simple, where have you been? 1.01.200 P
and i to /ford shall eke unfold | how falstaff, 1.03. 97
how say you? 1.04. 28 P
how now, good woman, how dost thou? 1.04.134 P
how now, good woman, how dost thou? 1.04.134 P
what news? how does pretty mistress anne? 1.04.137 P
how shall i be reveng'd on him? 2.01. 30 P
perceive how i might be knighted. 2.01. 55 P
how shall i be reveng'd on him? 2.01. 66 P
how now, meg? 2.01.148 P
how now, sweet frank, why art thou melancholy? 2.01.150 P
and i pray, how does good mistress anne? 2.01.164 P
how now, master ford! 2.01.168 P
how now, mine host! 2.01.191 P
how now, bully-rook! 2.01.193 P
wife acquainted each other how they love me? 2.02.109 P
i know not how i may deserve to be your porter. 2.02.174 P
sith you yourself know how easy it is to be such 2.02.189 P
you to me at night, you shall know how i speed. 2.02.267 P
jack, i vill tell you how i vill kill him. 2.03. 13 P
how full of chollors i am and trempling of mind! 3.01. 11 P
how melancholies i am! 3.01. 13 P
how now, master parson? 3.01. 36 P
how now, my eyas-musket, what news with you? 3.03. 22 P
i see how thine eye would emulate the diamond. 3.03. 55 P
well, heaven knows how i love you, and you shall 3.03. 80 P
how now? 3.03. 93 P
how am i mistook in you! 3.03.104 P
o, how have you deceiv'd me! 3.03.128 P
look how you drumble! 3.03.147 P
how now? 3.03.151 P
alas, how then? 3.04. 3
and how does good master fenton? 3.04. 34 P
mistress anne the jest how my father stole two 3.04. 40 P
they can tell you how things go better than i 3.04. 65 P
why, how now? 3.04. 68
my daughter will i question how she loves you, 3.04. 90
how now? 3.05. 32 P
how so, sir? did she change her determination? 3.05. 68 P
and how long lay you there? 3.05. 94 P
leisure, and you shall know how i speed; 3.05.135 P
how now, sir hugh, no school to-day? 4.01. 10 P
william, how many numbers is in nouns? 4.01. 21 P
how now, sweet heart! 4.02. 12 P
how near is he, mistress page? 4.02. 38 P
how should i bestow him? 4.02. 46 P
how might we disguise him? 4.02. 68 P
we tell our husbands how we have serv'd him? 4.02.213 P
how? 4.04. 17 P
devise but how you'll use him when he comes, 4.04. 26
how now, mine host? 4.05. 19 P
ear of the court, how i have been transform'd, 4.05. 95 P
and how my transformation hath been wash'd and 4.05. 96 P
you shall hear how things go, and, i warrant, to 4.05.122 P
how now, master /brook? 5.01. 9 P
and we have a nay-word how to know one another. 5.02. 5 P
how near the god drew to the complexion of a 5.05. 7 P
now, good sir john, how like you windsor wives? 5.05.106
see now how wit may be made a jack-a-lent, when 5.05.126 P
son? how now? how now, son? have you dispatch'd? 5.05.178 P
son? how now? how now, son? have you dispatch'd? 5.05.178 P
did not i tell you how you should know my 5.05.195 P
how now, master fenton? 5.05.215 P
how chance you went not with master slender? 5.05.217 P
how it goes with us, and do look to know | what MM 1.01. 57
how now, which of your hips has the most 1.02. 58 P
how now? 1.02. 85 P
why, how now, claudio? 1.02.124
you | how i have ever lov'd the life removed, 1.03. 8
instruct me | how i may formally in person bear 1.03. 47
how now, sir, what's your name? 2.01. 45 P
how know you that? 2.01. 68 P
how? thy wife? 2.01. 71 P
how dost thou know that, constable? 2.01. 78 P
do you hear how he misplaces? 2.01. 88 P
how could master froth do the constable's wife 2.01.157 P
how would you live, pompey? 2.01.224 P
how long have you been in this place of 2.01.258 P
how would you be | if he, which is the top of 2.02. 75
hark how i'll bribe you. 2.02.145
how? bribe me? 2.02.146
when men were fond, i smil'd and wond'red how. 2.02.186
i'll teach you how you shall arraign your 2.03. 21
how often dost thou with thy case, thy habit, 2.04. 13
how now? 2.04. 17
how now, fair maid? 2.04. 30
how say you? 2.04. 58
how will you do to content this substitute, and 3.01.187 P
o, how much is the good duke deceiv'd in angelo! 3.01.191 P
but mark how heavily this befell to the poor 3.01.218 P
but how out of this can she avail? 3.01.233 P
show me how, good father. 3.01.238 P
how now, noble pompey? 3.02. 43 P
or how? 3.02. 51 P
how doth my dear morsel, thy mistress? 3.02. 54 P
or how? 3.02. 64 P
how should he be made then? 3.02.107 P
and see how he goes about to abuse me! 3.02.202 P
and let me desire to know how you find claudio 3.02.239 P
how may likeness made in crimes, | making 3.02.273
welcome, how agreed? 4.01. 64
how now? 4.02. 88
how came it that the absent duke had not either 4.02.132 P
how seems he to be touch'd? 4.02.141 P
alack, how may i do it, having the hour limited, 4.02.165 P
into amazement how these things should be; 4.02.204 P
how now, abhorson? what's the news with you? 4.03. 39 P
and hearing how hastily you are to depart, i am 4.03. 50 P
now, sir, how do you find the prisoner? 4.03. 66
and how shall we continue claudio, | to save me 4.03. 84
her maiden loss, | how might she tongue me! 4.04. 25
how i persuaded, how i pray'd, and kneel'd, 5.01. 93
how i persuaded, how i pray'd, and kneel'd, 5.01. 93
how he refell'd me, and how i replied | (for 5.01. 94
how he refell'd me, and how i replied | (for 5.01. 94
to question, you shall see how i'll handle her. 5.01.271 P
how! know you where you are? 5.01.291
hark how the villain would close now, after his 5.01.342 P
how came it claudio was beheaded | at an unusual 5.01.457
how chance thou art return'd so soon? ERR 1.02. 42
how dar'st thou trust | so great a charge from 1.02. 60
and tell me how thou hast dispos'd thy charge. 1.02. 73
how if your husband start some other where? 2.01. 30
fie, how impatience low'reth in your face! 2.01. 86
how many fond fools serve mad jealousy? 2.01.116
how now, sir, is your merry humor alter'd? 2.02. 7
how comes it now, my husband, o, how comes it, 2.02.119
how comes it now, my husband, o, how comes it, 2.02.119
how dearly would it touch thee to the quick, 2.02.130
fie, brother, how the world is chang'd with you: 2.02.152
how can she thus then call us by our names, 2.02.166
how ill agrees it with your gravity | to 2.02.168
teach me, dear creature, how to think and speak: 3.02. 33
not mad, but mated — how, i do not know. 3.02. 54
why, how now, dromio, where run'st thou so fast? 3.02. 71 P
what woman's man, and how besides thyself? 3.02. 79 P
how dost thou mean a fat marriage? 3.02. 94 P
how much your chain weighs to the utmost charect 4.01. 28
you hear how he importunes me — the chain! 4.01. 53
consider how it stands upon my credit. 4.01. 68
how now? 4.01. 93
how hast thou lost thy breath? 4.02. 30
how fondly dost thou reason! 4.02. 57
how now, sir? 4.04. 9
how say you now? is not your husband mad? 4.04. 45
alas, how fiery, and how sharp, he looks! 4.04. 50
alas, how fiery, and how sharp, he looks! 4.04. 50
mark, how he trembles in his ecstasy! 4.04. 51
ay me, poor man, how pale and wan he looks! 4.04.108
and, knowing how the debt grows, i will pay it. 4.04.121
god help, poor souls, how idlely do they talk! 4.04.129
say, how grows it due? 4.04.134
how is the man esteem'd here in the city? 5.01. 4
how long hath this possession held the man? 5.01. 44
discover how, and thou shalt find me just. 5.01.203
that's a question; how shall we try it? 5.01.422
how many gentlemen have you lost in this action? ADO 1.01. 5 P
than you must expect of me to tell you how. 1.01. 17 P
how much better is it to weep at joy than to joy 1.01. 27 P
how many hath he kill'd and eaten in these wars? 1.01. 42 P
but how many hath he kill'd? 1.01. 44 P
i pray thee tell me truly how thou lik'st her. 1.01.178 P
mark how short his answer is: 1.01.213 P
that i neither feel how she should be lov'd nor 1.01.230 P
be lov'd nor know how she should be worthy, is 1.01.231 P
teach it but how, | and thou shalt see how apt 1.01.291
and thou shalt see how apt it is to learn | any 1.01.292
all prompting me how fair young hero is, 1.01.304
how sweetly you do minister to love, | that know 1.01.312
how now, brother, where is my cousin, your son? 1.02. 1 P
how came you to this? 1.03. 56 P
how tartly that gentleman looks! 2.01. 3 P
how know you he loves her? 2.01.167 P
why, how now, count, wherefore are you sad? 2.01.288 P
how then? sick? 2.01.291 P
were but little happy, if i could say how much! 2.01.307 P
i will teach you how to humor your cousin, that 2.01.380 P
how canst thou cross this marriage? 2.02. 7 P
show me briefly how. 2.02. 11 P
since, how much i am in the favor of margaret, 2.02. 13 P
seeing how much another man is a fool when he 2.03. 8 P
how still the evening is, | as hush'd on purpose 2.03. 38
sit you — you heard my daughter tell you how. 2.03.111 P
how, how, i pray you? 2.03.113 P
how, how, i pray you? 2.03.113 P
to see how much he is unworthy so good a lady. 2.03.208 P
i hear how i am censur'd; 2.03.224 P
my talk to thee must be how benedick | is sick 3.01. 20
how wise, how noble, young, how rarely featur'd, 3.01. 60
how wise, how noble, young, how rarely featur'd, 3.01. 60
how wise, how noble, young, how rarely featur'd, 3.01. 60
know | how much an ill word may empoison liking. 3.01. 86
how if 'a will not stand? 3.03. 27 P
for i cannot see how sleeping should offend; 3.03. 40 P
how if they will not? 3.03. 44 P
how if the nurse be asleep and will not hear us? 3.03. 67 P
how giddily 'a turns about all the hot-bloods 3.03.131 P
i should first tell thee how the prince, claudio 3.03.149 P
why, how now? do you speak in the sick tune? 3.04. 41 P
me, how long have you profess'd apprehension? 3.04. 67 P
and how you may be converted i know not, but 3.04. 90 P
how now! 4.01. 21 P
behold how like a maid she blushes here! 4.01. 34
o, god defend me, how am i beset! 4.01. 77
why, how now, cousin, wherefore sink you down? 4.01.110
how doth the lady? 4.01.113
how now, cousin hero? 4.01.117
how much might the man deserve of me that would 4.01.261 P
how answer you for yourselves? 4.02. 22 P
how they might hurt their enemies — if they 5.01. 98
if he be, he knows how to turn his girdle. 5.01.142 P
i will make it good how you dare, with what you 5.01.146 P
i'll tell thee how beatrice prais'd thy wit the 5.01.159 P
how now? 5.01.210 P
confessing to this man how don john your brother 5.01.235 P
how you were brought into the orchard and saw me 5.01.237 P
how you disgrac'd her when you should marry her. 5.01.238 P
i know not how to pray your patience, | yet i 5.01.271
people in messina here | how innocent she died, 5.01.282
how her acquaintance grew with this lewd fellow. 5.01.332
me, and knows me, | how pitiful i deserve" — 5.02. 29
and how long is that, think you? 5.02. 81 P
and now tell me, how doth your cousin? 5.02. 88 P
and how do you? 5.02. 91 P
how dost thou, benedick, the married man? 5.04. 99
study me how to please the eye indeed | by LLL 1.01. 80
how well he's read, to reason against reading! 1.01. 94
how follows that? 1.01. 98
how well this yielding rescues thee from shame! 1.01.118
how you delight, my lords, i know not, i, | but 1.01.174
how low soever the matter, i hope in god for 1.01.192 P
how canst thou part sadness and melancholy, my 1.02. 7 P
how mean you, sir? 1.02. 19 P
how many is one thrice told? 1.02. 39 P
i am sure you know how much the gross sum of 1.02. 45 P
and how easy it is to put "years" to the word 1.02. 51 P
lord, how wise you are! 1.02.138 P
and how can that be true love, which is falsely 1.02.171 P
how needless was it then | to ask the question? 2.01.116
how meanest thou? brawling in french? 3.01. 10 P
how hast thou purchased this experience? 3.01. 26 P
how did this argument begin? 3.01.105
me, how was there a costard broken in a shin? 3.01.111 P
how much carnation ribbon may a man buy for a 3.01.145 P
by my troth, most pleasant. how both did fit it! 4.01.129
lord, how the ladies and i have put him down! 4.01.141
and how most sweetly 'a will swear! 4.01.146
monster ignorance, how deformed dost thou look! 4.02. 23
be a claw, look how he claws him with a talent. 4.02. 63 P
make me forsworn, how shall i swear to love? 4.02.105
how far dost thou excel | no thought can think, 4.03. 39
how shall she know my griefs? 4.03. 41
once more i'll mark how love can vary wit. 4.03. 98
how will he scorn! 4.03.145
how will he spend his wit! 4.03.145
how will he triumph, leap, and laugh at it! 4.03.146
how now, what is in you? why dost thou tear it? 4.03.196
o, some authority how to proceed; 4.03.283
tricks, some quillets, how to cheat the devil. 4.03.284
how i would make him fawn, and beg, and seek, 5.02. 62
ask them how many inches | is in one mile: 5.02.188
tell | how many inches doth fill up one mile. 5.02.193
how many weary steps | of many weary miles you 5.02.195
will you not dance? how come you thus estranged? 5.02.213
look how you butt yourself in these sharp mocks! 5.02.251
how blow? how blow? speak to be understood. 5.02.294
how blow? how blow? speak to be understood. 5.02.294
how, madam? russians? 5.02.362
by this white glove (how white the hand, god 5.02.411
it is not so, for how can this be true, | that 5.02.426

how much is it? 5.02.498 P
sport best pleases that doth /least know how: 5.02.516
alas, you see how 'tis — a little o'erparted. 5.02.584 P
a kissing traitor. how art thou prov'd judas? 5.02.600 P
alas, poor machabeus, how hath he been baited! 5.02.631 P
how fares your majesty? 5.02.726
o, methinks, how slow | this old moon /wanes! MND 1.01. 3
made bold, | nor how it may concern my modesty, 1.01. 60
how now, my love? 1.01.128
how chance the roses there do fade so fast? 1.01.129
o, teach me how you look, and with what art 1.01.192
how happy some o'er other some can be! 1.01.226
how now, spirit, whither wander you? 2.01. 1
how canst thou thus for shame, titania, | glance 2.01. 74
how long within this wood intend you stay? 2.01.138
then how can it be said i am alone, | when all 2.01.225
how came her eyes so bright? 2.02. 92
how fit a word | is that vile name to perish on 2.02.106
lysander, look how i do quake with fear. 2.02.148
how answer you that? 3.01. 12 P
how now, mad spirit? 3.02. 4
i go, i go, look how i go, | swifter than arrow 3.02.100
how can these things in me seem scorn to you, 3.02.126
o, how ripe in show | thy lips, those kissing 3.02.139
how low am i, thou painted maypole? 3.02.296
how low am i? 3.02.297
you see how simple and how fond i am. 3.02.317
you see how simple and how fond i am. 3.02.317
o, how i love thee! 4.01. 45
how i dote on thee! 4.01. 45
how came these things to pass? 4.01. 78
o, how mine eyes do loathe his visage now! 4.01. 79
in our flight | tell me how it came this night 4.01.100
how comes this gentle concord in the world, 4.01.143
i swear, | i cannot truly say how i came here. 4.01.148
some fear, | how easy is a bush suppos'd a bear! 5.01. 22
how shall we beguile | the lazy time, if not 5.01. 40
there is a brief how many sports are ripe. 5.01. 42
how shall we find the concord of this discord? 5.01. 60
how is it else the man i' th' moon? 5.01.247 P
how can it be? 5.01.280
how chance moonshine is gone before thisby comes 5.01.312 P
but how i caught it, found it, or came by it, MV 1.01. 3
antonio, | how much i have disabled mine estate, 1.01.123
how to get clear of all the debts i owe. 1.01.134
how say you by the french lord, monsieur le /bon 1.02. 54 P
how oddly he is suited! 1.02. 73 P
how like you the young german, the duke of 1.02. 84 P
how now, what news? 1.02.122 P
how like a fawning publican he looks! 1.03. 41
but soft, how many months | do you desire? 1.03. 58
is he yet possess'd | how much ye would? 1.03. 65
why, look you how you storm! 1.03.137
lord, how art thou chang'd! 2.02. 99 P
how dost thou and thy master agree? 2.02. 99 P
how 'gree you now? 2.02.101 P
how i shall take her from her father's house, 2.04. 30
how like a younger or a prodigal | the scarfed 2.06. 14
how like the prodigal doth she return, | with 2.06. 17
how shall i know if i do choose the right? 2.07. 10
how many then should cover that stand bare? 2.09. 44
how many be commanded that command? 2.09. 45
how much low peasantry would then be gleaned 2.09. 46
and how much honor | pick'd from the chaff and 2.09. 47
how much unlike art thou to portia! 2.09. 56
how much unlike my hopes and my deservings! 2.09. 57
sweet, | to show how costly summer was at hand, 2.09. 94
how now, shylock, what news among the merchants? 3.01. 22 P
how now, tubal! 3.01. 79 P
i could teach you | how to choose right, but 3.02. 11
how begot, how nourished? 3.02. 65
how begot, how nourished? 3.02. 65
how many cowards, whose hearts are all as false 3.02. 83
how all the other passions fleet to air, | as 3.02.108
but her eyes — | how could he see to do them? 3.02.124
yet look how far | the substance of my praise 3.02.126
i pray you tell me how my good friend doth. 3.02.233
how doth that royal merchant, good antonio? 3.02.239
you shall see | how much i was a braggart. 3.02.258
honor, | how true a gentleman you send relief, 3.04. 6
how dear a lover of my lord your husband, | i 3.04. 7
how little is the cost i have bestowed | in 3.04. 19
lies, | how honorable ladies sought my love, 3.04. 70
how every fool can play upon the word! 3.05. 43 P
o dear discretion, how his words are suited! 3.05. 65
how cheer'st thou, jessica? 3.05. 70
how dost thou like the lord bassanio's wife? 3.05. 72
how shalt thou hope for mercy, rend'ring none? 4.01. 88
o wise young judge, how i do honor thee! 4.01.224
how much more elder art thou than thy looks! 4.01.251
say how i lov'd you, speak me fair in death; 4.01.275
you teach me how a beggar should be answer'd. 4.01.440
and know how well i have deserv'd this ring, 4.01.446
how sweet the moonlight sleeps upon this bank! 5.01. 54
look how the floor of heaven | is thick inlaid 5.01. 58
how far that little candle throws his beams! 5.01. 90
how many things by season season'd are | to 5.01.107
the ring, | and how unwillingly i left the ring, 5.01.196
how you do leave me to mine own protection. 5.01.235
how now, lorenzo? 5.01.288
yet i know no wise remedy how to avoid it. AYL 1.01. 25 P
and thou shalt hear how he will shake me up. 1.01. 27 P
you must not learn me how to remember any 1.02. 6 P
how now, wit, whither wander you? 1.02. 56 P
how prove you that, in the great heap of your 1.02. 68 P
what color, madam? how shall i answer you? 1.02.102 P
how now, daughter and cousin? 1.02.155 P
how dost thou, charles? 1.02.219
o, how full of briers is this working–day world! 1.03. 12 P
therefore devise with me how we may fly, 1.03.100
yet this i will not do, do how i can. 2.03. 35
how well in thee appears | the constant service 2.03. 56
o jupiter, how /weary are my spirits! 2.04. 1 P
o corin, that thou knew'st how i do love her! 2.04. 23
how many actions most ridiculous | hast thou 2.04. 30
why, how now, adam? 2.06. 4 P
why, how now, monsieur, what a life is this, 2.07. 9
thus we may see," quoth he, "how the world wags. 2.07. 23
how then? 2.07. 83
and how like you this shepherd's life, master 3.02. 11 P
i cannot see else how thou shouldst scape. 3.02. 85 P
how brief the life of man | runs his erring 3.02.129
how now? 3.02.158 P
hear without wondering how thy name should be 3.02.172 P
how look'd he? 3.02.221 P
how parted he with thee? 3.02.223 P
term, and then they perceive not how time moves. 3.02.333 P
he taught me how to know a man in love; 3.02.370 P
neither rhyme nor reason can express how much. 3.02.398 P
and how, audrey? 3.03. 2 P
and by how much defense is better than no skill, 3.03. 61 P
how do you, sir? 3.03. 74 P
why, how now, orlando, where have you been all 4.01. 39 P
how if the kiss be denied? 4.01. 78 P
now tell me how long you would have her after 4.01.143 P
that thou didst know how many fathom deep i am 4.01.206 P
are out, let him be judge how deep i am in love. 4.01.215 P
'tis no matter how it be in tune, so it make 4.02. 8 P
how say you now? 4.03. 1 P
mark how the tyrant writes. 4.03. 39
how then might your prayers move? 4.03. 55
my love deny, | and then i'll study how to die." 4.03. 63
if you will know of me | what man i am, and how, 4.03. 96
as how i came into that desert place — | /in 4.03.141
why, how now, ganymed, sweet ganymed? 4.03.157
you tell your brother how well i counterfeited. 4.03.167 P
bear answer back | how you excuse my brother, 4.03.180
how old are you, friend? 5.01. 17 P
how it grieves me to see thee wear thy heart in 5.02. 19 P
did your brother tell you how i counterfeited to 5.02. 25 P
how bitter a thing it is to look into happiness 5.02. 43 P
by how much i shall think my brother happy in 5.02. 46 P
hey nonino, | how that a life was but a flower, 5.03. 28
and how was that ta'en up? 5.04. 48 P
how seventh cause? 5.04. 51 P
how did you find the quarrel on the seventh 5.04. 66 P
and how oft did you say his beard was not well 5.04. 83 P
reason wonder may diminish | how thus we met, 5.04.140
hearing how that every day | men of great worth 5.04.154
how silver made it good | at the hedge–corner, SHR in.1. 19
o monstrous beast, how like a swine he lies! in.1. 34
death, how foul and loathsome is thine image! in.1. 35
how now? in.1. 77
and how my men will stay themselves from in.1. 134
look how thy servants do attend on thee, | each in.2. 33
maid, | and how she was beguiled and surpris'd, in.2. 55
o how we joy to see your wit restor'd! in.2. 77
how fares my noble lord? in.2. 100
for how i firmly am resolv'd you know: 1.01. 49
mates, maid, how mean you that? 1.01. 59
how say you, signior gremio? 1.01.140 P
mark'd you not how her sister | began to scold 1.01.171
nay, how now, where are you? 1.01.222 P
i'll try how you can sol, fa, and sing it. 1.02. 17
how now, what's the matter? 1.02. 20 P
how do you all at verona? 1.02. 22 P
how the young folks lay their heads together! 1.02.139 P
why, how now, dame, whence grows this insolence? 2.01. 23
how now, my friend, why dost thou look so pale? 2.01.142
o, how i long to have some chat with her! 2.01.162
petruchio, how speed you with my daughter? 2.01.281
how but well, sir? 2.01.282
how but well? 2.01.282
why, how now, daughter katherine, in your dumps? 2.01.284
incredible to believe | how much she loves me. 2.01.307
'tis a world to see | how tame, when men and 2.01.312
how fiery and forward our pedant is! 3.01. 48
is it new and old too? how may that be? 3.02. 32 P
how does my father? 3.02. 93
but yet not stay, entreat me how you can. 3.02.203
shall sweet bianca practice how to bride it? 3.02.251
good grumio, tell me, how goes the world? 4.01. 33 P
how? 4.01. 56 P
shouldst have heard how her horse fell and she 4.01. 73 P
thou shouldst have heard in how miry a place, 4.01. 75 P
heard in how miry a place, how she was bemoil'd, 4.01. 75 P
how he left her with the horse upon her, how he 4.01. 76 P
her, how he beat me because her horse stumbled, 4.01. 77 P
how she waded through the dirt to pluck him off 4.01. 77 P
how he swore, how she pray'd that never pray'd 4.01. 79 P
swore, how she pray'd that never pray'd before; 4.01. 79 P
how i cried, how the horses ran away, how her 4.01. 80 P
how i cried, how the horses ran away, how her 4.01. 80 P
the horses ran away, how her bridle was burst; 4.01. 81 P
how i lost my crupper, with many things of 4.01. 81 P
how now, grumio? 4.01.107 P
how now, old lad? 4.01.110 P
how now, you; 4.01.111 P
all things is ready. how near is our master? 4.01.115 P
how durst you, villains, bring it from the 4.01.163
he that knows better how to tame a shrew, | now 4.01.210
see how they kiss and court! 4.02. 27
see how beastly she doth court him! 4.02. 34
my life, sir? how, i pray? for that goes hard. 4.02. 80
but i, who never knew how to entreat, | nor 4.03. 7
how say you to a fat tripe finely broil'd? 4.03. 20
how fares my kate? what, sweeting, all amort? 4.03. 36
thou seest how diligent i am | to dress thy meat 4.03. 39
grumio gave order how it should be done. 4.03.117
but how did you desire it should be made? 4.03.119
and how she's like to be lucentio's wife. 4.04. 66
lord, how bright and goodly shines the moon! 4.05. 2
why, how now, kate, i hope thou art not mad. 4.05. 42
why, how now, gentleman? 5.01. 35 P
how now, what's the matter? 5.01. 71 P
how hast thou offended? | where is lucentio? 5.01.113
mistress, how mean you that? 5.02. 21
conceives by me! how likes hortensio that? 5.02. 23
how likes gremio these quick–witted folks? 5.02. 38
how now, what news? 5.02. 80
how? 5.02. 82
father — o, that "had," how sad a passage 'tis! AWW 1.01. 18 P
how call'd you the man you speak of, madam? 1.01. 24 P
how understand we that? 1.01. 60 P
how may we barricado it against him? 1.01.112 P
no military policy how virgins might blow up men 1.01.121 P
how might one do, sir, to lose it to her own 1.01.150 P
how long is't, count, | since the physician at 1.02. 69
him, | yet never know how that desert should be. 1.03.200
how shall they credit | a poor unlearned virgin, 1.03.239
off thine | by wond'ring how thou took'st it. 2.01. 90
hath told the thievish minutes how they pass, 2.01.166
from whence thou cam'st, how tended on, but rest 2.01.207
o, my knave, how does my old lady? 2.04. 18 P
i know not how i have deserv'd to run into my 2.05. 34 P
i have told my neighbor how you have been 3.05. 14 P
how do you mean? 3.05. 68
how now, monsieur? 3.06. 44 P
i know not how i shall assure you further | but 3.07. 2
as we'll direct her how 'tis best to bear it. 3.07. 20
instruct my daughter how she shall persever, 3.07. 37
how deep? 4.01. 57 P
how have i sworn! 4.02. 20
my mother told me just how he would woo, | as if 4.02. 69
how is this justified? 4.03. 54 P
how mightily sometimes we make us comforts of 4.03. 65 P
and how mightily some other times we drown our 4.03. 67 P
how now? 4.03. 75 P
how now, my lord, is't not after midnight? 4.03. 83 P
how does he carry himself? 4.03.104 P
of him, how many horse the duke is strong." 4.03.129 P
the sacrament on't, how and which way you will. 4.03.136 P
how does your ladyship like it? 4.05. 77 P
lord, how we lose our pains! 5.01. 24
how does your drum? 5.02. 41 P
and therefore know how far i may be pitied. 5.03.161
faith, sir, he did love her, but how? 5.03.243 P
how, i pray you? 5.03.244 P
how is that? 5.03.247 P
of all these ways, | how could you give it him? 5.03.276
o spirit of love, how quick and fresh art thou, TN 1.01. 9
how now, what news from her? 1.01. 22
how will she love when the rich golden shaft 1.01. 34
sir toby belch! how now, sir toby belch? 1.03. 44 P
how say you to that, malvolio? 1.05. 82 P
see, sir, how your fooling grows old, and people 1.05.110 P
how now, sot? 1.05.121 P
how have you come so early by this lethargy? 1.05.123 P
how does he love me? 1.05.254
come to me again | to tell me how he takes it. 1.05.282
how now? 1.05.294
how easy is it for the proper–false | in women's 2.02. 29
how will this fadge? 2.02. 33
how now, my hearts? 2.03. 16 P
i do not, never trust me, take it how you will. 2.03.188 P
how dost thou like this tune? 2.04. 20
how now, my metal of india? 2.05. 13 P
how he jets under his advanc'd plumes! 2.05. 31 P
look how imagination blows him. 2.05. 42 P
how quickly the wrong side may be turn'd outward 3.01. 12 P
o world, how apt the poor are to be proud! 3.01.127
how much the better | to fall before the lion 3.01.128
it is no matter how witty, so it be eloquent and 3.02. 43 P
how shall i feast him? 3.04. 2
how now, malvolio? 3.04. 16 P
why, how dost thou, man? 3.04. 24 P
how do you, malvolio? 3.04. 34 P
and consequently sets down the manner how: 3.04. 72 P
here he is, here he is. how is't with you, sir? 3.04. 87 P
how is't with you, man? 3.04. 88 P
lo, how hollow the fiend speaks within him! 3.04. 91 P
how do you, malvolio? 3.04. 96 P
how is't with you? 3.04. 97 P
ill of the devil, how he takes it at heart! 3.04.100 P
how now, mistress? 3.04.106 P
why, how now, my bawcock? how dost thou, chuck? 3.04.112 P
why, how now, my bawcock? how dost thou, chuck? 3.04.112 P
how with mine honor may i give him that | which 3.04.214
make me tell them how much i lack of a man. 3.04.303 P
but o, how vild an idol proves this god! 3.04.365
and hear thou there how many fruitless pranks 4.01. 55
how runs the stream? 4.01. 60
how vexest thou this man! 4.02. 25 P
voice, and bring me word how thou find'st him. 4.02. 67 P
jolly robin, | tell me how thy lady does." 4.02. 73
alas, sir, how fell you besides your five wits? 4.02. 86 P
i know thee well; how dost thou, my good fellow? 5.01. 10 P
how can that be? 5.01. 16 P
how can this be? 5.01. 92
ay me, detested! how am i beguil'd! 5.01.139
how now, gentleman? how is't with you? 5.01.195 P
how now, gentleman? how is't with you? 5.01.195 P
how have the hours rack'd and tortur'd me, 5.01.219
how have you made division of yourself? 5.01.222
how does he, sirrah? 5.01.283 P
how now, art thou mad? 5.01.293 P
ay, my lord, this same. | how now, malvolio? 5.01.328
how with a sportful malice it was follow'd | may 5.01.365
alas, poor fool, how have they baffled thee! 5.01.369
how say you? WT 1.02. 54
how now, you wanton calf, | art thou my calf? 1.02.126
communicat'st with dreams (how can this be?), 1.02.140
how? my lord? 1.02.147
what cheer? how is't with you, best brother? 1.02.148
how sometimes nature will betray its folly! 1.02.151
how like, methought, i then was to this kernel, 1.02.159
how thou lov'st us, show in our brother's 1.02.174
though you perceive me not how i give line. 1.02.181
how she holds up the neb! 1.02.183
how now, boy? 1.02.207
how came't, camillo, | that he did stay? 1.02.219
how i am gall'd — mightst bespice a cup, | to 1.02.316
how, dare not? 1.02.377
how caught of me? 1.02.387
how far off, how near, | which way to be 1.02.404
how far off, how near, | which way to be 1.02.404
if not, how best to bear it. 1.02.406
how should this grow? 1.02.431
avoid what's grown than question how 'tis born. 1.02.433
how blest am i | in my just censure! 2.01. 36
how accurs'd | in being so blest! 2.01. 38
make known | how he hath drunk, he cracks his 2.01. 44
how came the posterns | so easily open? 2.01. 52
how will this grieve you, | when you shall come 2.01. 96

your suspicion, | be blam'd for't how you might. 2.01.161
how could that be? 2.01.172
dear gentlewoman, | how fares our gracious lady? 2.02. 19
how he may soften at the sight o' th' child: 2.02. 38
how does the boy? 2.03. 10
go, | see how he fares. 2.03. 18
how? 2.03. 41
how ceremonious, solemn, and unearthly | it was 3.01. 7
came to your court, how i was in your grace, 3.02. 47
how i was in your grace, | how merited to be so; 3.02. 48
i know not how it tastes, though it be dish'd 3.02. 72
tastes, though it be dish'd | for me to try how. 3.02. 73
i do feel it gone, | but know not how it went. 3.02. 96
how? gone? 3.02.145
how now there? 3.02.147
how he glisters | through my rust! 3.02.170
and how his piety | does my deeds make the 3.02.171
why, boy, how is it? 3.03. 87 P
i would you did but see how it chafes, how it 3.03. 88 P
you did but see how it chafes, how it rages, how 3.03. 88 P
chafes, how it rages, how it takes up the shore! 3.03. 89 P
to see how the bear tore out his shoulder–bone, 3.03. 95 P
how he cried to me for help and said his name 3.03. 96 P
the ship, to see how the sea flap–dragon'd it; 3.03. 98 P
first, how the poor souls roar'd, and the sea 3.03. 99 P
and how the poor gentleman roar'd, and the bear 3.03.100 P
from the gentleman and how much he hath eaten. 3.03.130 P
with hey, the sweet birds, o, how they sing! 4.03. 6
how now? canst stand? 4.03. 74 P
how do you now? 4.03.110 P
how would he look to see his work, so noble, 4.04. 21
or how | should i, in these my borrowed flaunts, 4.04. 22
have i not told thee how i was cozen'd by the 4.04.251 P
how a usurer's wife was brought to bed of twenty 4.04.262 P
and how she long'd to eat adders' heads, and 4.04.264 P
how now, fair shepherd? 4.04.345
how prettily th' young swain seems to wash | the 4.04.366
why, how now, father? | speak ere thou diest. 4.04.450
how often have i told you 'twould be thus! 4.04.474
how often said my dignity would last | but till 4.04.475
how, camillo, | may this (almost a miracle) be 4.04.533
the medicine of our house, how shall we do? 4.04.587
how now, good fellow? 4.04.628 P
had been the dearer by i know how much an ounce. 4.04.705 P
how now, rustics, whither are you bound? 4.04.714 P
how blessed are we that are not simple men! 4.04.745
which who knows how that may turn back to my 4.04.835 P
how? not women? 5.01.109
old shepherd deliver the manner how he found it; 5.02. 4 P
how goes it now, sir? 5.02. 27 P
death (with the manner how she came to't bravely 5.02. 85 P
how attentiveness wounded his daughter, till, 5.02. 86 P
how if it be false, son? 5.02.161 P
if i do not wonder how thou dar'st venture to be 5.02.171 P
she has liv'd, | or how stol'n from the dead. 5.03.115
how found | thy father's court? 5.03.124
hast found mine, | but how, is to be question'd; 5.03.139
how that ambitious constance would not cease JN 1.01. 32
your tale must be how he employ'd my mother. 1.01. 98
where how he did prevail i shame to speak. 1.01.104
tell me, how if my brother, | who, as you say, 1.01.120
how now, good lady, | what brings you here to 1.01.220
how much unlook'd for is this expedition! 2.01. 79
by how much unexpected, by so much | we must 2.01. 80
how comes it then that thou art call'd a king, 2.01.107
how high thy glory tow'rs | when the rich blood 2.01.350
how like you this wild counsel, mighty states? 2.01.395
mark how they whisper. 2.01.475
england, how may we content | this widow lady? 2.01.547
teach thou this sorrow how to make me die, | and 3.01. 30
how can the law forbid my tongue to curse? 3.01.190
and tell me how you would bestow yourself. 3.01.225
ay, alack, how new | is "husband" in my mouth! 3.01.305
reason | how i may be deliver'd of these woes, 3.04. 55
'tis strange to think how much king john hath 3.04.121
how green you are and fresh in this old world! 3.04.145
how now, foolish rheum? 4.01. 33
and well shall you perceive how willingly | i 4.02. 45
indeed we heard how near his death he was 4.02. 87
how goes all in france? 4.02.109
how wildly then walks my estate in france! 4.02.128
how i have sped among the clergymen | the sums i 4.02.141
how oft the sight of means to do ill deeds 4.02.219
how easy dost thou take all england up | from 4.03.142
you taught me how to know the face of right, 5.02. 88
i come to learn how you have dealt for him; 5.02.121
how goes the day with us? o, tell me, hubert. 5.03. 1
badly, i fear. how fares your majesty? 5.03. 2
how did he take it? who did taste to him? 5.06. 28
how fares your majesty? 5.07. 34
where /god he knows how we shall answer him; 5.07. 60
and knows not how to do it but with tears. 5.07.109
how high a pitch his resolution soars! R2 1.01.109
how god and good men hate so foul a liar. 1.01.114
teaching stern murder how to butcher thee. 1.02. 32
how long a time lies in one little word! 1.03.213
how far brought you high herford on his way? 1.04. 2
how he did seem to dive into their hearts | with 1.04. 25
so it be new, there's no respect how vile — 2.01. 25
my life, | how happy then were my ensuing death! 2.01. 68
how fares our noble uncle lancaster? 2.01. 71
what comfort, man? how is't with aged gaunt? 2.01. 72
o, how that name befits my composition! 2.01. 73
seen how his son's son should destroy his sons, 2.01.105
how long shall i be patient? 2.01.163
ah, how long | shall i tender duty make me suffer 2.01.163
for how art thou a king | but by fair sequence 2.01.198
say | how near the tidings of our comfort is. 2.01.272
how shall we do for money for these wars? 2.02.104
i | know how or which way to order these affairs 2.02.109
how far is it, my lord, to berkeley now? 2.03. 1
harry, how fares your uncle? 2.03. 23
how far is it to berkeley? 2.03. 51
o, then how quickly should this arm of mine, 2.03.103
how brooks your grace the air | after your late 3.02. 2
how far off lies your power? 3.02. 63
how some have been depos'd, some slain in war, 3.02.157
thus, | how can you say to me i am a king? 3.02.177
how far off from the mind of bullingbrook | it 3.03. 45
march on, and mark king richard how he looks. 3.03. 61
how dare thy joints forget | to pay their aweful 3.03. 75
how dares thy harsh rude tongue sound this 3.04. 74
say, where, when, and how, | /cam'st thou by 3.04. 79
how blest this land would be | in this your 4.01. 18
how fondly dost thou spur a forward horse! 4.01. 72
if on the first, how heinous e'er it be, | to 5.03. 34
tell us how near is danger | that we may arm us 5.03. 47
say "pardon," king, let pity teach thee how. 5.03.116
hearing how our plaints and prayers do pierce, 5.03.127
i have been studying how i may compare | this 5.05. 1
how these vain weak nails | may tear a passage 5.05. 19
how sour sweet music is | when time is broke, 5.05. 42
and how comest thou hither, | where no man never 5.05. 69
how it ern'd my heart when i beheld | in london 5.05. 76
tell me, gentle friend, | how went he under him? 5.05. 82
how now, what means death in this rude assault? 5.05.105
well, how then? come, roundly, roundly. 1H4 1.02. 22 P
how now, how now, mad wag? 1.02. 44 P
how now, how now, mad wag? 1.02. 44 P
how agrees the devil and thee about thy soul 1.02.114 P
how shall we part with them in setting forth? 1.02.167 P
at supper, how thirty at least he fought with, 1.02.188 P
by how much better than my word i am, | by so 1.02.210
save how to gall and pinch this bullingbrook, 1.03.229
and see already how he doth begin | to make us 1.03.289
thou layest the plot how. 2.01. 52 P
how many be there of them? 2.02. 63 P
how the fat rogue roar'd! 2.02.111 P
how now, kate? 2.03. 36
how! so far? 2.03.113
how long hast thou to serve, francis? 2.04. 41 P
how old art thou, francis? 2.04. 53 P
says she, "how many hast thou kill'd to–day?" 2.04.106 P
how now, wool–sack, what mutter you? 2.04.135 P
speak, sirs, how was it? 2.04.173 P
how couldst thou know these men in kendal green 2.04.231 P
mark now how a plain tale shall put you down. 2.04.255 P
how now, my lady the hostess! 2.04.285 P
in earnest, how came falstaff's sword so hack'd? 2.04.303 P
how now, my sweet creature of bumbast, how long 2.04.326 P
my sweet creature of bumbast, how long is't ago, 2.04.327 P
o, the father, how he holds his countenance! 2.04.392 P
thy time, but also how thou art accompanied; 2.04.399 P
hark how hard he fetches breath. 2.04.530 P
how scapes he agues, in the devil's name? 3.01. 68
see how this river comes me cranking in, | and 3.01. 97
but | mark how he bears his course, and runs me 3.01.107
fie, cousin percy, how you cross my father! 3.01.145
frowns, | to show how much thou art degenerate. 3.02.128
how now, good blunt? 3.02.162
how now, dame partlet the hen? 3.03. 52 P
how? 3.03. 77 P
heard the prince tell him, i know not how oft, 3.03. 84 P
how? 3.03. 85 P
how now, lad? 3.03. 88 P
how doth thy husband? 3.03. 92 P
should, how would thy guts fall about thy knees! 3.03.152 P
for the robbery, lad, how is that answer'd? 3.03.175 P
how has he the leisure to be sick | in such a 4.01. 17
on, | to see how fortune is dispos'd to us, 4.01. 38
and think how such an apprehension | may turn 4.01. 66
how now, blown jack? how now, quilt? 4.02. 49 P
how now, blown jack? how now, quilt? 4.02. 49 P
how now, mad wag? 4.02. 50 P
if you knew | how much they do import, you would 4.04. 5
how bloodily the sun begins to peer | above yon 5.01. 1
how now, my lord of worcester? 5.01. 9
you have not sought it, how comes it then? 5.01. 27
but how if honor prick me off when i come on? 5.01.130 P
how then? 5.01.131 P
look how we can, or sad or merrily, 5.02. 12
tell me, tell me, | how show'd his tasking? 5.02. 50
cheerly, my lord, how fares your grace? 5.04. 44
ill–weav'd ambition, how much art thou shrunk! 5.04. 88
how if he should counterfeit too and rise? 5.04.122 P
lord, lord, how this world is given to lying! 5.04.145 P
how goes the field? 5.05. 16
have taught us how to cherish such high deeds 5.05. 30
how is this deriv'd? 2H4 1.01. 23
how doth my son and brother? 1.01. 67
the name of rebellion can tell how to make it. 1.02. 77 P
but how i should be your patient to follow your 1.02.128 P
how in our means we should advance ourselves 1.03. 7
how now, whose mare's dead? what's the matter? 2.01. 43 P
how now, sir john? 2.01. 65
how comes this, sir john? 2.01. 80 P
or to take note how many pair of silk stockings 2.02. 14 P
how ill it follows, after you have labor'd so 2.02. 28 P
tell me how many good young princes would do so, 2.02. 29 P
and how doth thy master, bardolph? 2.02. 98 P
and how doth the martlemas, your master? 2.02.101 P
he holds his place, for look you how he writes. 2.02.107 P
"how comes that?" 2.02.114 P
how might we see falstaff bestow himself 2.02.169 P
how do you now? 2.04. 28 P
how now, mistress doll? 2.04. 35 P
feel, masters, how i shake, look you, i warrant 2.04.105 P
alas, poor ape, how thou sweat'st! 2.04.217 P
how? you fat fool, i scorn you. 2.04.296 P
how vildly did you speak of me /even now before 2.04.300 P
abuse, and then i know how to handle you. 2.04.312 P
peto, how now, what news? 2.04.354 P
how now, what's the matter? 2.04.370 P
good wenches, how men of merit are sought after. 2.04.375 P
how many thousand of my poorest subjects | are 3.01. 4
nature's soft nurse, how have i frighted thee, 3.01. 6
the body of our kingdom | how foul it is, what 3.01. 39
how chance's mocks | and changes fill the cup of 3.01. 51
and how doth my good cousin silence? 3.02. 3 P
and how doth my cousin, your bedfellow? 3.02. 5 P
and to see how many of my old acquaintance are 3.02. 34 P
how a good yoke of bullocks at /stamford fair? 3.02. 38 P
how a score of ewes now? 3.02. 49 P
how doth the good knight? 3.02. 64 P
may i ask how my lady his wife doth? 3.02. 65 P
tell me, master shallow, how to choose a man? 3.02.257 P
how swiftly will this feeble the woman's tailor 3.02.268 P
how subject we old men are to this vice of lying 3.02.303 P
how deep you were within the books of god? 4.02. 17
how far forth you do like their articles. 4.02. 53
hark how they shout! 4.02. 87
i know not how they sold themselves, but thou, 4.03. 68 P
how now, bardolph? 4.03.126 P
and how accompanied? 4.04. 15
how chance thou art not with the prince thy 4.04. 20
and how accompanied? /canst /thou /tell /that? 4.04. 52
the manner how this action hath been borne 4.04. 88
how now, rain within doors, and none abroad? 4.05. 9
how doth the king? 4.05. 10
how quickly nature falls into revolt | when gold 4.05. 65
your majesty, | how cold it strook my heart! 4.05.151
well | how troublesome it sate upon my head. 4.05.186
how i came by the crown, o god forgive, | and 4.05.218
how now, my lord chief justice, whither away? 5.02. 1
how doth the king? 5.02. 2
how many nobles then should hold their places, 5.02. 17
how might a prince of my great hopes forget | so 5.02. 68
how now, pistol? 5.03. 83 P
how ill white hairs becomes a fool and jester! 5.05. 48
i cannot perceive how, unless you give me your 5.05. 81 P
but how, my lord, shall we resist it now? H5 1.01. 6
which is a wonder how his grace should glean it, 1.01. 53
admit the means | how things are perfected. 1.01. 69
how now for mitigation of this bill | urg'd by 1.01. 70
how did this offer seem receiv'd, my lord? 1.01. 82
for god doth know how many now in health | shall 1.02. 18
therefore take heed how you impawn our person, 1.02. 21
how you awake our sleeping sword of war — | we 1.02. 22
how he comes o'er us with our wilder days, | not 1.02.267
how now, mine host pistol? 2.01. 28 P
how smooth and even they do bear themselves! 2.02. 3
at, how shall we stretch our eye | when capital 2.02. 55
why, how now, gentlemen? 2.02. 71
look ye how they change! 2.02. 73
you know how apt our love was to accord | to 2.02. 86
o, how hast thou with jealousy infected | the 2.02.126
"how now, sir john?" 2.03. 17 P
how well supplied with noble counsellors, | how 2.04. 33
how modest in exception, and withal | how 2.04. 34
withal | how terrible in constant resolution, 2.04. 35
of grosser blood, | and teach them how to war. 3.01. 25
how now, captain macmorris, have you quit the 3.02. 86 P
how yet resolves the governor of the town? 3.03. 1
how now, captain fluellen, come you from the 3.06. 1 P
how now, fluellen, cam'st thou from the bridge? 3.06. 88 P
by how much "a fool's bolt is soon shot." 3.07.121 P
no note | how dread an army hath enrounded him; 4.pr. 36
for how can they charitably dispose of any thing 4.01.142 P
and to teach others how they should prepare. 4.01.185 P
how shall i know thee again? 4.01.207 P
quarrels enow, if you could tell how to reckon. 4.01.223 P
hark how our steeds for present service neigh! 4.02. 8
how shall we then behold their natural tears? 4.02. 13
and how thou pleasest, god, dispose the day! 4.03.133
how now, what means this, herald? 4.07. 68
how now, sir? you villain! 4.08. 11 P
how now, how now, what's the matter? 4.08. 19 P
how now, how now, what's the matter? 4.08. 19 P
how now, what's the matter? 4.08. 24 P
how canst thou make me satisfaction? 4.08. 45
please your majesty, to tell how many is kill'd? 4.08.118 P
how london doth pour out her citizens! 5.pr. 24
sword, | how many would the peaceful city quit, 5.pr. 33
how say you, lady? 5.02.130 P
how answer you, la plus belle katherine du monde 5.02.216 P
my fair cousin, how perfectly i love her, and 5.02.284 P
how were they lost? what treachery was us'd? 1H6 1.01. 68
how may i reverently worship thee enough? 1.02.145
how now, ambitious /humphrey, what means this? 1.03. 29
sirrah, thou know'st how orleance is besieg'd, 1.04. 1
and how the english have the suburbs won. 1.04. 2
espials have informed me | how the english, in 1.04. 9
and thence discover how with most advantage 1.04. 12
how wert thou handled, being prisoner? 1.04. 24
yet tell'st thou not how thou wert entertain'd. 1.04. 38
one, | and view the frenchmen how they fortify. 1.04. 61
how far'st thou, mirror of all martial men? 1.04. 74
hear, hear how dying salisbury doth groan! 1.04.104
how shall i honor thee for this success? 1.06. 5
when they shall hear how we have play'd the men. 1.06. 16
coward of france, how much he wrongs his fame, 2.01. 16
appear | how much in duty i am bound to both. 2.01. 37
how now, my lords? what, all unready so? 2.01. 39
here cometh charles, i marvel how he sped. 2.01. 48
then how, or which way, should they first break 2.01. 71
no further of the case, | how or which way. 2.01. 73
how can these contrarieties agree? 2.03. 59
how say you, madam? 2.03. 61
how i am brav'd, and must perforce endure it! 2.04.115
as he will have me, how am i so poor? 3.01. 30
or how haps it i seek not to advance | or raise 3.01. 31
o, how this discord doth afflict my soul! 3.01.106
how joyful am i made by this contract! 3.01.143
take heed, be wary how you place your words, 3.02. 3
how will she specify | here is the best and 3.02. 21
your honors shall perceive how i will work | to 3.03. 27
powers, | and seek how we may prejudice the foe. 3.03. 91
i do remember how my father said | a stouter 3.04. 18
how say you, my lord? 4.01. 70
let him perceive how ill we brook his treason, 4.01. 74
how will their grudging stomachs be provok'd 4.01.141
how are we park'd and bounded in a pale, | a 4.02. 45
how now, sir william, whither were you sent? 4.04. 12
and i'll direct thee how thou shalt escape | by 4.05. 10
how dost thou fare? 4.06. 27
how the young whelp of talbot's, raging wood, 4.07. 35
how doth your grace affect their motion? 5.01. 7
see how the ugly witch doth bend her brows, | as 5.03. 34
how canst thou tell she will deny thy suit, 5.03. 75
a wife, | then how can margaret be thy paramour? 5.03. 82
how say you, madam, are ye so content? 5.03.126
how say'st thou, charles? 5.04.165
how shall we then dispense with that contract, 5.05. 28
uncle, how now? 2H6 1.01. 53

how france and frenchmen might be kept in awe, 1.01. 92
but how now, sir john hume? 1.02. 88
sort how it will, i shall have gold for all. 1.02.107
how now, fellow? wouldst any thing with me? 1.03. 10 P
how now, sir knave? 1.03. 22 P
and listen after humphrey, how he proceeds. 1.03.149
to see how god in all his creatures works! 2.01. 7
ay, my lord cardinal, how think you by that? 2.01. 16
how now, my lords? 2.01. 43
why, how now, uncle gloucester? 2.01. 48
how irksome is this music to my heart! 2.01. 54
how cam'st thou so? 2.01. 94
how long hast thou been blind? 2.01. 95
how i have lov'd my king and commonweal; 2.01.187
and, for my wife, i know not how it stands. 2.01.188
look how they gaze! 2.04. 20
see how the giddy multitude do point | and nod 2.04. 21
laugh, | and bid me be advised how i tread. 2.04. 36
and, fly thou how thou canst, they'll tangle 2.04. 55
robes, | and show itself, attire me how i can. 2.04.109
himself, | how insolent of late he is become, 3.01. 7
how proud, how peremptory, and unlike himself? 3.01. 8
how proud, how peremptory, and unlike himself? 3.01. 8
and do not stand on quillets how to slay him; 3.01.261
sleeping, or waking, 'tis no matter how, | so he 3.01.263
how they affect the house and claim of york. 3.01.375
how now? 3.02. 27
how fares my lord? 3.02. 33
how fares my gracious lord? 3.02. 37
what know i how the world may deem of me, | for 3.02. 65
how often have i tempted suffolk's tongue | (the 3.02.114
true, | but how he died god knows, not henry. 3.02.131
that is to see how deep my grave is made, | for 3.02.150
see how the blood is settled in his face. 3.02.160
nest | but may imagine how the bird was dead, 3.02.192
why, how now, lords? 3.02.237
to show how quaint an orator you are; 3.02.274
how fares my lord? 3.03. 1
see how the pangs of death do make him grin! 3.03. 24
how now? 4.01. 32
how often hast thou waited at my cup, | fed from 4.01. 56
how in our voiding lobby hast thou stood | and 4.01. 61
how now? 4.02. 84 P
how now, madam? 4.04. 21
how now? 4.04. 26
how now? is jack cade slain? 4.05. 1
how would it fare with your departed souls? 4.07.116
nor knows he how to live but by the spoil, 4.08. 39
and show'd how well you love your prince and 4.09. 16
how much thou wrong'st me, heaven be my judge. 4.10. 76
let them obey that knows not how to rule; 5.01. 6
great god, how just art thou! 5.01. 68
how art thou call'd? and what is thy degree? 5.01. 73
how now? 5.01. 87
with me, | knowing how hardly i can brook abuse? 5.01. 92
how now, my noble lord? 5.02. 8
god knows how long it is i have to live, | and 5.03. 17
i wonder how the king escap'd our hands. 3H6 1.01. 1
clifford, how i scorn his worthless threats! 1.01.101
o clifford, how thy words revive my heart! 1.01.163
how hast thou injur'd both thyself and us! 1.01.179
how love to me and to her son | hath made her 1.01.264
why, how now, sons and brother, at a strife? 1.02. 4
how began it first? 1.02. 5
think | how sweet a thing it is to wear a crown, 1.02. 29
more, | but that i seek occasion how to rise, 1.02. 45
how now? 1.03. 10
but how is it that great plantagenet | is 1.04. 99
how ill-beseeming is it in thy sex | to triumph 1.04.113
how couldst thou drain the life-blood of the 1.04.138
him, | to see how inly sorrow gripes his soul. 1.04.171
i wonder how our princely father scap'd; 2.01. 1
how fares my brother? 2.01. 8
and watch'd him how he singled clifford forth. 2.01. 12
see how the morning opes her golden gates, | and 2.01. 21
how well resembles it the prime of youth, 2.01. 23
say how he died, for i will hear it all. 2.01. 49
how now, fair lords? 2.01. 95
how now? what news? 2.01.205
how it doth grieve me that thy head is here! 2.02. 55
why, how now, long-tongu'd warwick, dare you 2.02.102
how now, my lord, what hap? what hope of good? 2.03. 8
thereby to see the minutes how they run: 2.05. 25
how many makes the hour full complete, | how 2.05. 26
complete, | how many hours brings about the day, 2.05. 27
day, | how many days will finish up the year, 2.05. 28
year, | how many years a mortal man may live. 2.05. 29
how sweet! 2.05. 41
how lovely! 2.05. 41
how fell? 2.05. 89
how butcherly? 2.05. 89
how will my mother for a father's death | take 2.05.103
how will my wife for slaughter of my son | shed 2.05.105
how will the country for these woeful chances 2.05.107
for how can i help them and not myself? 3.01. 21
he knows the game; how true he keeps the wind! 3.02. 14
how many children hast thou, widow? tell me. 3.02. 26
i'll tell you how these lands are to be got. 3.02. 42
and yet i know not how to get the crown, | for 3.02.172
not knowing how to find the open air | but 3.02.177
for how can tyrants safely govern home, | unless 3.03. 69
how haps it in this smooth discourse | you told 3.03. 88
you told not how henry the sixt hath lost | all 3.03. 89
nay, mark how lewis stamps as he were nettled. 3.03.169
how shall bona be reveng'd | but by thy help to 3.03.212
renowned prince, how shall poor henry live, 3.03.214
how could he stay till warwick made return? 4.01. 5
brother of clarence, how like you our choice, 4.01. 9
alas, how should you govern any kingdom, | that 4.03. 35
kingdom, | that know not how to use embassadors, 4.03. 36
nor how to be contented with one wife, | nor how 4.03. 37
wife, | nor how to use your brothers brotherly, 4.03. 38
nor how to study for the people's welfare, | nor 4.03. 39
nor how to shroud yourself from enemies? 4.03. 40
unsavory news! but how made he escape? 4.06. 80
how evil it beseems thee | to flatter henry and 4.07. 84
how far hence is thy lord, mine honest fellow? 5.01. 2
how far off is our brother montague? 5.01. 4
and, by thy guess, how nigh is clarence now? 5.01. 8
see how the surly warwick mans the wall! 5.01. 17
where slept our scouts, or how are they seduc'd, 5.01. 19
sail how thou canst, have wind and tide thy 5.01. 53
and, live we how we can, yet die we must. 5.02. 28
but cheerly seek how to redress their harms. 5.04. 2
how sweet a plant have you untimely cropp'd! 5.05. 62
and see our gentle queen how well she fares. 5.05. 89
see how my sword weeps for the poor king's death 5.06. 63
how say you, sir? R3 1.01. 96
how hath your lordship brook'd imprisonment? 1.01.125
look how my ring encompasseth thy finger, | even 1.02.203
but since you teach me how to flatter you, 1.02.223
how now, my hardy, stout, resolved mates, | are 1.03.339
for edward's sake, and see how he requites me! 1.04. 68
and how cam'st thou hither? 1.04. 85
how dost thou feel thyself now? 1.04.120 P
how darkly and how deadly dost thou speak! 1.04.169
how darkly and how deadly dost thou speak! 1.04.169
how canst thou urge god's dreadful law to us, 1.04.209
how fain, like pilate, would i wash my hands 1.04.272
how now? 1.04.274
the duke shall know how slack you have been! 1.04.275
who told me how the poor soul did forsake | the 2.01.110
how he did lap me | even in his /own garments, 2.01.116
not | how that the guilty kindred of the queen 2.01.136
how can we aid you with our kindred tears? 2.02. 63
by how much the estate is green and yet 2.02.127
my uncle rivers talk'd how i did grow | more 2.04. 11
how, my young york? i prithee let me hear it. 2.04. 26
how doth the prince? 2.04. 40
days, | how many of you have mine eyes beheld! 2.04. 56
richard of york, how fares our loving brother? 3.01. 96
how fares our cousin, noble lord of york? 3.01.101
how? 3.01.124
uncle, your grace knows how to bear with him. 3.01.127
how he doth stand affected to our purpose, | and 3.01.171
how? wear the garland? dost thou mean the crown? 3.02. 41
but yet you see how soon the day o'ercast. 3.02. 86
how now, sirrah? 3.02. 96
how goes the world with thee? 3.02. 96
look how i am bewitch'd; 3.04. 68
how mine enemies | to-day at pomfret bloodily 3.04. 89
tell them how edward put to death a citizen 3.05. 76
and mark how well the sequel hangs together: 3.06. 4
how now, how now, what say the citizens? 3.07. 1
how now, how now, what say the citizens? 3.07. 1
see, | how far i am from the desire of this. 3.07.236
how doth the prince and my young son of york? 4.01. 14
be of good cheer. mother, how fares your grace? 4.01. 37
how now, lord stanley, what's the news? 4.02. 46
look how thou dream'st! 4.02. 56
mean time, but think how i may do thee good, 4.03. 33
how do i thank thee that this carnal cur | preys 4.04. 56
and teach me how to curse mine enemies! 4.04.117
revolving this will teach thee how to curse. 4.04.123
even so. how think you of it? 4.04.267
how canst thou woo her? 4.04.268
but how long shall that title "ever" last? 4.04.350
but how long fairly shall her sweet life last? 4.04.352
how now? 4.04.432
tell me, how fares our loving mother? 5.03. 82
think how thou stab'st me in my prime of youth 5.03.119
o coward conscience, how dost thou afflict me! 5.03.179
how have you slept, my lord? 5.03.226
how far into the morning is it, lords? 5.03.234
see | how soon this mightiness meets misery; H8 pr 30
how have ye done | since last we saw in france? 1.01. 1
lighted, how they clung | in their embracement, 1.01. 9
till you know | how he determines further. 1.01.214
how grounded he his title to the crown | upon 1.02.144
how know'st thou this? 1.02.150
how now? 1.03. 15
faith, how easy? 1.04. 17
how now, what is't? 1.04. 53
but pray how pass'd it? 2.01. 10
after all this, how did he bear himself? 2.01. 30
say something that is sad, | speak how i fell. 2.01.136
how is the king employ'd? 2.02. 14
how holily he works in all his business! 2.02. 23
how sad he looks! sure he is much afflicted. 2.02. 62
how dare you thrust yourselves | into my private 2.02. 64
how? of me? 2.02.125
how you do talk! 2.03. 44
how tastes it? 2.03. 89
how far i have proceeded, | or how far further 2.04. 90
or how far further shall, is warranted | by a 2.04. 91
him | that i gainsay my deed, how may he wound, 2.04. 96
remember | how under my oppression i did reek 2.04.209
yourself to say | how far you satisfied me. 2.04.212
how now? 3.01. 15
how you stand minded in the weighty difference 3.01. 58
but how to make ye suddenly an answer | in such 3.01. 70
how, sir? 3.01. 92
how you may hurt yourself — ay, utterly | grow 3.01.160
how came | his practices to light? 3.02. 28
o, how? how? 3.02. 29
o, how? how? 3.02. 29
how that the cardinal did entreat his holiness 3.02. 32
him, how he coasts | and hedges his own way. 3.02. 38
how, i' th' name of thrift, | does he rake this 3.02.109
how have i reap'd it? 3.02.204
how eagerly ye follow my disgraces | as if it 3.02.240
and how sleek and wanton | ye appear in every 3.02.241
how innocent i was | from any private malice in 3.02.267
how much, methinks, i could despise this man, 3.02.297
you to your meditations | how to live better. 3.02.346
o, how wretched | is that poor man that hangs on 3.02.366
why, how now, cromwell? 3.02.372
how does your grace? 3.02.376
i have told him | what, and how true, thou art; 3.02.416
how can man then | (the image of his maker) hope 3.02.441
how goes her business? 4.01. 23
how was it? 4.01. 60
how does your grace? 4.02. 1
prithee, good griffith, tell me how he died. 4.02. 9
how much her grace is alter'd on the sudden? 4.02. 96
how long her face is drawn! 4.02. 97
how pale she looks, | and of an earthy cold! 4.02. 97
how does his highness? 4.02.124
sake that lov'd him | heaven knows how dearly. 4.02.138
how now, my lord? 5.01. 89
you not | how your state stands i' th' world, 5.01.127
along, | how earnestly he cast his eyes upon me! 5.02. 12
how much more is his life in value with him! 5.02.143
how much are we bound to heaven | in daily 5.02.149
how may i deserve it, | that am a poor and 5.02.199
witness how dear i hold this confirmation. 5.02.207
how got they in, and be hang'd? 5.03. 17 P
alas, i know not, how gets the tide in? 5.03. 18
reply not in how many fadoms deep | they lie TRO 1.01. 50
good pandarus! how now, pandarus? 1.01. 69
how do you plague me! 1.01. 94
how now, prince troilus, wherefore not a-field? 1.01.105
but how should this man, that makes me smile, 1.02. 31 P
how do you, cousin? 1.02. 44 P
juno have mercy! how came it cloven? 1.02.120 P
but laugh to think how she tickled his chin. 1.02.135 P
look how he looks! 1.02.201 P
look you how his sword is bloodied, and his helm 1.02.232 P
more hack'd than hector's, and how he looks, and 1.02.234 P
hector's, and how he looks, and how he goes! 1.02.234 P
can watch you for telling how i took the blow — 1.02.268 P
how many shallow bauble boats dare sail | upon 1.03. 35
and look how many grecian tents do stand 1.03. 79
how could communities, | degrees in schools, and 1.03.103
how rank soever rounded in with danger. 1.03.196
that do contrive how many hands shall strike 1.03.201
how may | a stranger to those most imperial 1.03.223
how? 1.03.225
well, and how? 1.03.320
agamemnon, how if he had biles — full, all over 2.01. 2 P
why, how now, ajax, wherefore do ye thus? 2.01. 55
how now, thersites, what's the matter, man? 2.01. 56
how may i avoid | (although my will distaste 2.02. 65
how now, thersites? 2.03. 1 P
how doth pride grow? 2.03.151 P
and how his silence drinks up his applause! 2.03.201
how he describes himself! 2.03.209 P
how chance my brother troilus went not? 3.01.137 P
i long to hear how they sped to-day. 3.01.141 P
how now, where's thy master? 3.02. 1 P
o, here he comes! how now, how now? 3.02. 5 P
o, here he comes! how now, how now? 3.02. 5 P
the day, how loath you are to offend daylight! 3.02. 48 P
how now? 3.02. 50 P
o cressid, how often have i wish'd me thus! 3.02. 61 P
how were i then uplifted! 3.02.168
how do you? how do you? 3.03. 63
how do you? how do you? 3.03. 63
how now, patroclus! 3.03. 65
how now, ulysses? 3.03. 94
writes me that man, how dearly ever parted, 3.03. 96
how much in having, or without or in, | cannot 3.03. 97
how some men creep in skittish fortune's hall, 3.03.134
how one man eats into another's pride, | while 3.03.136
how so? 3.03.246 P
how can that be? 3.03.250 P
wherein | you told how diomed, a whole week by 4.01. 10
how now, how now, how go maidenheads? 4.02. 23 P
how now, how now, how go maidenheads? 4.02. 23 P
how now, how now, how go maidenheads? 4.02. 23 P
how earnestly they knock! 4.02. 40
how now, what's the matter? 4.02. 43 P
how now, what's the matter? 4.02. 58
how my achievements mock me! 4.02. 69
how now? what's the matter? who was here? 4.02. 78 P
how can i moderate it? 4.04. 5
how now, lambs? 4.04. 23 P
crams his rich thiev'ry up, he knows not how. 4.04. 43
i true? how now? what wicked deem is this? 4.04. 59
how novelty may move, and parts with /person, 4.04. 79
how have we spent this morning! 4.04.140
i wonder now how yonder city stands | when we 4.05.211
how now, thou /core of envy? 5.01. 4
ah, how the poor world is pest'red with such 5.01. 33 P
how now, my charge? 5.02. 6
how now, troyan? 5.02. 30
how now, my lord? 5.02. 46
how the devil luxury, with his fat rump and 5.02. 55 P
but if i tell how these two did //co-act, 5.02.118
how now, young man, meanest thou to fight to-day 5.03. 29
how now? how now? 5.03. 44
how now? how now? 5.03. 44
look how thou diest! 5.03. 81
look how thy eye turns pale! 5.03. 81
look how thy wounds do bleed at many vents! 5.03. 82
hark how troy roars! 5.03. 83
how hecuba cries out! 5.03. 83
how poor andromache shrills her dolors forth! 5.03. 84
how now, my brother? 5.06. 21
look, hector, how the sun begins to set, | how 5.08. 5
how ugly night comes breathing at his heels; 5.08. 6
and bawds, how earnestly are you set a-work, and 5.10. 37 P
are you set a-work, and how ill requited! 5.10. 38 P
it was an answer. how apply you this? COR 1.01.147
and hear | how the dispatch is made, and in what 1.01.277
in our counsels, | and know how we proceed. 1.02. 3
considering how honor would become such a person 1.03. 10 P
had he died in the business, madam, how then? 1.03. 18 P
how do you both? 1.03. 51 P
how does your little son? 1.03. 53 P
or whether his fall enrag'd him, or how 'twas, 1.03. 64 P
o, i warrant, how he mammock'd it! 1.03. 65 P
how far off lie these armies? 1.04. 8
how have you run | from slaves that apes would 1.04. 35
how long is't since? 1.06. 14
how couldst thou in a mile confound an hour, 1.06. 17
of warriors, | how is't with titus lartius? 1.06. 33
but how prevail'd you? 1.06. 45
how lies their battle? 1.06. 51
learn how 'tis held, and what they are that must 1.10. 28
bring me word thither | how the world goes, that 1.10. 32
do you two know how you are censur'd here in the 2.01. 21 P
why? how are we censur'd? 2.01. 24 P
how now, my as fair as noble ladies — and the 2.01. 97 P

how many stand for consulships? 2.02. 1 P
to heal again | than hear say how i got them. 2.02. 70
your multiplying spawn how can he flatter — 2.02. 78
you see how he intends to use the people. 2.02.155
me, and i'll direct you how you shall go by him. 2.03. 46 P
how, not your own desire? 2.03. 68 P
how now, my masters, have you chose this man? 2.03.155
humble weed, | how in his suit he scorn'd you; 2.03.222
how youngly he began to serve his country, | how 2.03.236
how long continued, and what stock he springs of 2.03.237
how? what? 3.01. 12
how often he had met you, sword to sword; 3.01. 13
how? i inform them? 3.01. 47
how? 3.01. 75
how soon confusion | may enter 'twixt the gap of 3.01.110
how shall this bosom multiplied digest | the 3.01.131
how comes't that you | have holp to make this 3.01.274
you had not show'd them how ye were dispos'd 3.02. 22
how is it less or worse | that it shall hold 3.02. 48
show our general louts | how you can frown, than 3.02. 67
how accompanied? 3.03. 6
how? traitor? 3.03. 67
how, sir? do you meddle with my master? 4.05. 46 P
face, methought — i cannot tell how to term it. 4.05.156 P
look you, one cannot tell how to say that. 4.05.169 P
how probable i do not know — that martius, 4.06. 66
how? 4.06.121
i minded him how royal 'twas to pardon | when it 5.01. 18
good faith, i'll prove him, | speed how it will. 5.01. 61
how? away? 5.02. 81 P
shall poison rather | than pity note how much. 5.02. 87
do you hear how we are shent for keeping your 5.02. 98 P
lords, how plainly | i have borne this business. 5.03. 3
how more unfortunate than all living women | are 5.03. 97
for how can we, | alas! 5.03.106
how can we, for our country pray, | whereto we 5.03.107
hark, how they joy! 5.04. 57
how is it with our general? 5.06. 9
"traitor"? how now? 5.06. 86
how fair the tribune speaks to calm my thoughts! TIT 1.01. 46
how many sons hast thou of mine in store, | that 1.01. 94
father, how we have perform'd | our roman rites. 1.01.142
how proud i am of thee and of thy gifts | rome 1.01.254
how, sir? are you in earnest then, my lord? 1.01.277
how comes it that the subtile queen of goths 1.01.392
judge, | how i have lov'd and honored saturnine! 1.01.427
sheath, | till you know better how to handle it. 2.01. 42
full well shalt thou perceive how much i dare. 2.01. 44
why, how now, lords? 2.01. 45
and think you not how dangerous | it is to jet 2.01. 63
in rome | how furious and impatient they be, 2.01. 76
to achieve her how? 2.01. 81
lavinia, how say you? 2.02. 16
how now, dear sovereign and our gracious mother? 2.03. 89
how these were they that made away his brother. 2.03.208
if it be dark, how dost thou know 'tis he? 2.03.225
how easily murder is discovered! 2.03.287
see how with signs and tokens she can scrowl. 2.04. 5
how happy art thou then, | from these devourers 3.01. 56
or make some sign how i may do thee ease. 3.01.121
how they are stain'd like meadows yet not dry, 3.01.125
see how my wretched sister sobs and weeps. 3.01.137
o, how this villainy | doth fat me with the very 3.01.202
hark how her sighs doth /blow! 3.01.225
good uncle marcus, see how swift she comes. 4.01. 3
see, lucius, see, how much she makes of thee; 4.01. 10
how now, lavinia? 4.01. 30
brother, see, note how she cotes the leaves. 4.01. 50
'tis sure enough, and you knew how, | but if you 4.01. 95
age | to keep mine own, excuse it how she can. 4.02.105
look how the black slave smiles upon the father, 4.02.120
how many women saw this child of his? 4.02.135
but say again, how many saw the child? 4.02.140
and how by this their child shall be advanc'd, 4.02.157
publius, how now? 4.03. 36
how now, my masters? 4.03. 36
how now, good fellow, wouldst thou speak with us 4.04. 39
how much money must i have? 4.04. 46 P
and how desirous of our sight they are. 5.01. 4
that granted, how canst thou believe an oath? 5.01. 72
no, not a word, how can i grace my talk, 5.02. 17
good lord, how like the empress' sons they are! 5.02. 64
how like the empress and her sons you are! 5.02. 84
how i have govern'd our determin'd jest? 5.02.139
tell us, old man, how shall we be employ'd? 5.02.149
hark, wretches, how i mean to martyr you. 5.02.180
o, let me teach you how to knit again | this 5.03. 70
how many thousand times hath these poor lips, 5.03.167
how, turn thy back and run? ROM 1.01. 35 P
is to himself (i will not say how true) | but to 1.01.148
o, teach me how i should forget to think. 1.01.226
how now, who calls? 1.03. 5
how long is it now | to lammas–tide? 1.03. 14
to see now how a jest shall come about! 1.03. 45
how stands your dispositions to be married? 1.03. 65
and see how one another lends content; 1.03. 84
how long is't now since last yourself and i 1.05. 32
why, how now, kinsman, wherefore storm you so? 1.05. 60
see how she leans her cheek upon her hand! 2.02. 23
a name | i know not how to tell thee who i am. 2.02. 54
how camest thou hither, tell me, and wherefore? 2.02. 62
how silver–sweet sound lovers' tongues by night, 2.02.165
there, | rememb'ring how i love thy company. 2.02.173
when and where and how | we met, we woo'd, and 2.03. 61
how much salt water thrown away in waste, | to 2.03. 71
will answer the letter's master, how he dares, 2.04. 11 P
o flesh, flesh, how art thou fishified! 2.04. 38 P
fie, how my bones ache! 2.05. 26
how art thou out of breath, when thou hast 2.05. 31
simple choice, you know not how to choose a man. 2.05. 39 P
lord, how my head aches! 2.05. 48
how oddly thou repliest! 2.05. 59
bid him bethink | how nice the quarrel was, and 3.01.154
and learn me how to lose a winning match, 3.02. 12
how hast thou the heart, | being a divine, a 3.03. 48
how should they when that wise men have no eyes? 3.03. 62
hark how they knock! 3.03. 74
how is it with her? 3.03. 93
and how doth she? 3.03. 97
how well my comfort is reviv'd by this! 3.03.165
how is't, my soul? 3.05. 25
why, how now, juliet? 3.05. 68
o, how my heart abhors | to hear him nam'd, and 3.05. 99
and see how he will take it at your hands. 3.05.125
how now, a conduit, girl? 3.05.129
how now, wife? 3.05.137
how, will she none? 3.05.142
how how, how how, chopp'd logic! 3.05.149
how how, how how, chopp'd logic! 3.05.149
how how, how how, chopp'd logic! 3.05.149
how how, how how, chopp'd logic! 3.05.149
o nurse, how shall this be prevented? 3.05.204
how shall that faith return again to earth, 3.05.206
unless thou tell me how i may prevent it. 4.01. 51
how canst thou try them so? 4.02. 5
how now, my headstrong, where have you been 4.02. 16
how if, when i am laid into the tomb, | i wake 4.03. 30
how sound is she asleep! 4.05. 8
ah me, how sweet is love itself possess'd, 5.01. 10
how now, balthasar? 5.01. 12
how doth my lady? 5.01. 14
how doth my juliet? 5.01. 15
how oft when men are at the point of death 5.03. 88
o, how may i | call this a lightning? 5.03. 90
how oft to–night | have my old feet stumbled at 5.03.121
how long hath he been there? 5.03.130
seek, and know how this foul murder comes. 5.03.198
o wife, look how our daughter bleeds! 5.03.202
i have not seen you long, how goes the world? TIM 1.01. 2
how this grace | speaks his own standing! 1.01. 30
how big imagination | moves in this lip! 1.01. 32
how this lord is followed! 1.01. 39
how shall i understand you? 1.01. 51
you see how all conditions, how all minds, | as 1.01. 52
you see how all conditions, how all minds, | as 1.01. 52
how shall she be endowed, | if she be mated with 1.01.139
how lik'st thou this picture, apemantus? 1.01.195 P
how dost thou like this jewel, apemantus? 1.01.210 P
not worth my thinking. how now, poet? 1.01.214 P
how now, philosopher? 1.01.215 P
how had you been my friends else? 1.02. 90 P
what means that trump? how now? 1.02.115
you see, my lord, how ample y' are belov'd. 1.02.130
i scarce know how. 1.02.180
how now? 1.02.185
that he will neither know how to maintain it, 2.02. 2
takes no accompt | how things go from him, nor 2.02. 4
how goes the world, that i am thus encount'red 2.02. 36
how dost, fool? 2.02. 50 P
how do you, gentlemen? 2.02. 66 P
gramercies, good fool; how does your mistress? 2.02. 67 P
why, how now, captain, what do you in this wise 2.02. 73 P
how dost thou, apemantus? 2.02. 74 P
and at length | how goes our reck'ning? 2.02.150
give it in a breath, | how quickly were it gone! 2.02.154
how many prodigal bits have slaves and peasants 2.02.165
you shall perceive how you | mistake my fortunes 2.02.183
and how does that honorable, complete, 3.01. 9 P
how? 3.02. 15 P
how shall i thank him, think'st thou? 3.02. 32 P
how unluckily it happ'ned that i should purchase 3.02. 46 P
how? 3.03. 7
how fairly this lord strives to appear foul! 3.03. 31 P
i'll show you how t' observe a strange event. 3.04. 17
mark how strange it shows, | timon in this 3.04. 21
how? what does his cashier'd worship mutter? 3.04. 60 P
how full of valor did he bear himself | in the 3.05. 64
how? 3.05. 90
grief too, as i understand how all things go. 3.06. 18 P
and how fare you? 3.06. 25 P
how do you? what's the news? 3.06. 52 P
how? how? 3.06. 56 P
how? how? 3.06. 56 P
how now, my lords? 3.06.106 P
how came the noble timon to this change? 4.03. 67
how cursed athens, mindless of thy worth, 4.03. 94
how dost thou pity him whom thou dost trouble? 4.03. 99
how has the ass broke the wall, that thou art 4.03.349 P
he covetously reserve it, how shall 's get it? 4.03.405 P
how rarely does it meet with this time's guise, 4.03.465
how fain would i have hated all mankind, | and 4.03.499
why, how shall i requite you? 5.01. 73
him, i did mark | how he did shake — 'tis true, JC 1.02.121
how i have thought of this, and of these times, 1.02.164
of the stars | give guess how near to day. 2.01. 3
how that might change his nature, there's the 2.01. 13
caius ligarius, how? 2.01.312
how foolish do your fears seem now, calphurnia! 2.02.105
how hard it is for women to keep counsel! 2.04. 9
how weak a thing | the heart of woman is! 2.04. 39
look how he makes to caesar; mark him. 3.01. 18
how many ages hence | shall this our lofty scene 3.01.111
how many times shall caesar bleed in sport, 3.01.114
how caesar hath deserv'd to lie in death, | mark 3.01.132
how like a deer, strooken by many princes, 3.01.209
know you how much the people may be mov'd | by 3.01.234
how the people take | the cruel issue of these 3.01.293
it is not meet you know how caesar lov'd you: 3.02.141
mark how the blood of caesar followed it, | as 3.02.178
judge, o you gods, how dearly caesar lov'd him! 3.02.182
how now, fellow? 3.02.261
notice of the people, | how i had mov'd them. 3.02.271
how to cut off some charge in legacies. 4.01. 9
how covert matters may be best disclos'd, | and 4.01. 46
a word, lucilius, | how he receiv'd you; 4.02. 14
and if not so, how should i wrong a brother? 4.02. 39
go show your slaves how choleric you are, | and 4.03. 43
how now? what's the matter? 4.03.129
ha, ha! how vildly doth this cynic rhyme! 4.03.133
how scap'd i killing when i cross'd you so? 4.03.150
how ill this taper burns! 4.03.275
which he did give himself — i know not how, 5.01.102
apace, | and see how i regarded caius cassius. 5.03. 88
octavius' tent | how every thing is chanc'd. 5.04. 32
thou seest the world, volumnius, how it goes; 5.05. 22
how died my master, strato? 5.05. 64
how far is't call'd to /forres? MAC 1.03. 39
know i am thane of glamis, | but how of cawdor? 1.03. 72
look how our partner's rapt. 1.03.142
how you shall bid god 'ield us for your pains, 1.06. 13
itself, | and falls on th' other — how now? 1.07. 28
how tender 'tis to love the babe that milks me; 1.07. 55
how goes the night, boy? 2.01. 1
how is't with me, when every noise appalls me? 2.02. 55
how easy is it then! 2.02. 65
how goes the world, sir, now? 2.04. 21
how you were borne in hand, how cross'd, the 3.01. 80
how you were borne in hand, how cross'd, the 3.01. 80
how now, my lord, why do you keep alone, | of 3.02. 8
well, let's away, and say how much is done. 3.03. 22
how say you? 3.04. 68
how say'st thou, that macduff denies his person 3.04.127
why, how now, hecat? you look angerly. 3.05. 1
how did you dare | to trade and traffic with 3.05. 3
how monstrous | it was for malcolm and for 3.06. 8
how it did grieve macbeth! 3.06. 11
how now, you secret, black, and midnight hags? 4.01. 48
you profess | (how e'er you come to know it), 4.01. 51
how will you live? 4.02. 31
yes, he is dead. how wilt thou do for a father? 4.02. 38
nay, how will you do for a husband? 4.02. 39
but how wilt thou do for a father? 4.02. 60 P
poor prattler, how thou talk'st! 4.02. 64 P
how he solicits heaven, | himself best knows; 4.03.149
how does my wife? 4.03.176
be not a niggard of your speech; how goes't? 4.03.180
how came she by that light? 5.01. 21 P
look how she rubs her hands. 5.01. 26 P
how does your patient, doctor? 5.03. 37
which i say i saw, | but know not how to do't. 5.05. 31
how now, horatio? HAM 1.01. 53
how is it that the clouds still hang on you? 1.02. 66
how /weary, stale, flat, and unprofitable | seem 1.02.133
how prodigal the soul | lends the tongue vows. 1.03.116
how is't, my noble lord? 1.05.117
how say you then, would heart of man once think 1.05.121
how strange or odd some'er i bear myself — | as 1.05.170
and how, and who, what means, and where they 2.01. 8
farewell! how now, ophelia, what's the matter? 2.01. 71
but how hath she | receiv'd his love? 2.02.128
how may we try it further? 2.02.159
give me leave, | how does my good lord hamlet? 2.02.171
how say you by that? 2.02.187 P
how pregnant sometimes his replies are! 2.02.208 P
how dost thou, guildenstern? 2.02.224 P
good lads, how do you both? 2.02.226 P
how noble in reason! 2.02.304 P
how infinite in faculties, in form and moving! 2.02.304 P
how express and admirable in action! 2.02.305 P
how like an angel in apprehension! 2.02.306 P
how like a god! 2.02.306 P
how chances it they travel? 2.02.329 P
how smart a lash that speech doth give my 3.01. 49
lord, | how does your honor for this many a day? 3.01. 90
how now, ophelia? 3.01.178
how now, my lord? 3.02. 46 P
how fares our cousin hamlet? 3.02. 92 P
for look you how cheerfully my mother looks, and 3.02.126 P
madam, how like you this play? 3.02.229 P
marry, how? 3.02.237 P
you shall see anon how the murtherer gets the 3.02.263 P
how fares my lord? 3.02.267 P
how can that be, when you have the voice of the 3.02.341 P
you now, how unworthy a thing you make of me! 3.02.363 P
how in my words somever she be shent, | to give 3.02.398
and how his audit stands who knows save heaven? 3.03. 82
why, how now, hamlet? 3.04. 13
how now? a rat? dead, for a ducat, dead! 3.04. 24
how is it with you, lady? 3.04.115
alas, how is't with you, | that you do bend your 3.04.116
look you how pale he glares! 3.04.125
look how it steals away! 3.04.134
what, gertrude? how does hamlet? 4.01. 6
alas, how shall this bloody deed be answer'd? 4.01. 16
how dangerous is it that this man goes loose! 4.03. 2
how now, what hath befall'n? 4.03. 11
but to show you how a king may go a progress 4.03. 30 P
how e'er my haps, my joys /were ne'er /begun. 4.03. 68
how purpos'd, sir, i pray you? 4.04. 11
how all occasions do inform against me, | and 4.04. 32
how stand i then, | that have a father kill'd, a 4.04. 56
how now, ophelia? 4.05. 22
"how should i your true–love know | from another 4.05. 23
how do you, pretty lady? 4.05. 41
how long hath she been thus? 4.05. 67
how cheerfully on the false trail they cry! 4.05.110
how came he dead? 4.05.131
how now, what noise is that? 4.05.154
o, how the wheel becomes it! 4.05.172 P
it be so, laertes — | as how should it be so? 4.07. 58
how otherwise? 4.07. 58
how much i had to do to calm his rage! 4.07.192
how can that be, unless she drown'd herself in 5.01. 6 P
but how does it well? 5.01. 46 P
how the knave jowls it to the ground, as if 5.01. 76 P
how dost thou, sweet lord?" 5.01. 83 P
how absolute the knave is! 5.01.137 P
how long hast thou been grave–maker? 5.01.142 P
how long is that since? 5.01.145 P
how came he mad? 5.01.156 P
how strangely? 5.01.158 P
how long will a man lie i' th' earth ere he rot? 5.01.163 P
and now how abhorr'd in my imagination it is! 5.01.187 P
lips that i have kiss'd i know not how oft. 5.01.189 P
shapes our ends, | rough–hew them how we will — 5.02. 11
but wilt thou hear now how i did proceed? 5.02. 27
and labor'd much | how to forget that learning, 5.02. 35
how was this seal'd? 5.02. 47
very sultry — as 'twere — i cannot tell how. 5.02.101 P
how if i answer no? 5.02.170 P
thou wouldst not think how ill all's here about 5.02.212 P
how i am punish'd | with a sore distraction. 5.02.229
they bleed on both sides. how is it, my lord? 5.02.304
how is't, laertes? 5.02.305

how does the queen? 5.02.308
unknowing world | how these things came about. 5.02.380
how, how, cordelia? LR 1.01. 94
how, how, cordelia? 1.01. 94
you see how full of changes his age is; 1.01.288 P
edmund, how now? 1.02. 26
how now, brother edmund, what serious 1.02.138 P
how now, what art thou? 1.04. 9 P
how old art thou? 1.04. 36 P
how now? 1.04. 49 P
how now, my pretty knave, how dost thou? 1.04. 96 P
how now, my pretty knave, how dost thou? 1.04. 96 P
how now, nuncle? 1.04.104 P
foppish, | and know not how their wits to wear, 1.04.168
how now, daughter? 1.04.189 P
fault, | how ugly didst thou in cordelia show! 1.04.267
feel | how sharper than a serpent's tooth it is 1.04.288
when i have show'd th' unfitness — how now, 1.04.333
how far your eyes may pierce i cannot tell: 1.04.345
canst tell how an oyster makes his shell? 1.05. 25 P
how now, are the horses ready? 1.05. 48 P
how comes that? 2.01. 5 P
with how manifold and strong a bond | the child 2.01. 47
seeing how loathly opposite i stood | to his 2.01. 49
how now, my noble friend? 2.01. 86
how dost, my lord? 2.01. 89
own purpose, | how in my strength you please. 2.01.112
how now, what's the matter? part! 2.02. 44 P
speak yet, how grew your quarrel? 2.02. 61 P
how fell you out? say that. 2.02. 86
o, how this mother swells up toward my heart! 2.04. 56
how chance the king comes with so small a number 2.04. 63
how unremovable and fix'd he is | in his own 2.04. 93
not believe | with how deprav'd a quality — o 2.04.137
hope | you less know how to value her desert 2.04.139
say? how is that? 2.04.140
do you but mark how this becomes the house! 2.04.153
how have i offended? 2.04.195
how came my man i' th' stocks? 2.04.198
how in one house | should many people under two 2.04.240
how dost, my boy? 3.02. 68
how shall your houseless heads and unfed sides, 3.04. 30
how fares your grace? 3.04.125
how to prevent the fiend, and to kill vermin. 3.04.159 P
how, my lord, i may be censur'd, that nature 3.05. 2 P
how malicious is my fortune, that i must repent 3.05. 9 P
how now? 3.07. 14 P
how now, you dog? 3.07. 75
how is't, my lord? 3.07. 94
how look you? 3.07. 94
how now? who's there? 4.01. 24
how should this be? 4.01. 37
you do climb up it now. look how we labor. 4.06. 2
how fearful | and dizzy 'tis, to cast one's eyes 4.06. 11
and yet i know not how conceit may rob | the 4.06. 42
how is't? 4.06. 65
when i do stare, see how the subject quakes. 4.06.108
in a light, yet you see how this world goes. 4.06.147 P
a man may see how this world goes with no eyes. 4.06.150 P
see how yond justice rails upon yond simple 4.06.152 P
but, by your favor, | how near's the other army? 4.06.212
how stiff is my vild sense | that i stand up, 4.06.279
kent, how shall i live and work | to match thy 4.07. 1
then be't so, my good lord. how does the king? 4.07. 12
how does my royal lord? how fares your majesty? 4.07. 43
how does my royal lord? how fares your majesty? 4.07. 43
how have you known the miseries of your father? 5.03.181
(how ever this may gall him with some check) OTH 1.01.148
how didst thou know 'twas she? 1.01.165
how got she out? 1.01.169
how may the duke be therewith satisfied, | whose 1.02. 88
how? 1.02. 93
how say you by this change? 1.03. 17
ay, so i thought. how many, as you guess? 1.03. 36
how i did thrive in this fair lady's love, | and 1.03.125
i should but teach him how to tell my story, 1.03.165
education both do learn me | how to respect you; 1.03.184
i never found man that knew how to love himself. 1.03.314 P
to plume up my will | in double knavery — how? 1.03.394
how? 1.03.394
how? is this true? 2.01. 25
how now? 2.01. 65
o, but i fear — how lost you company? 2.01. 91
come, how wouldst thou praise me? 2.01.124
well prais'd! how if she be black and witty? 2.01.131
how if fair and foolish? 2.01.135
how say you, cassio? 2.01.163 P
how does my old acquaintance of this isle? 2.01.203
how now, roderigo? 2.03.136
why, how now ho? 2.03.169
how comes it, michael, you are thus forgot? 2.03.188
give me to know | how this foul rout began; 2.03.210
how came you thus recover'd? 2.03.294 P
how am i then a villain, | to counsel cassio to 2.03.348
and by how much she strives to do him good, 2.03.358
how now, roderigo? 2.03.362
how poor are they that have not patience! 2.03.370
how, sir? how? 3.01. 5 P
how, sir? how? 3.01. 5 P
how now, my lord? 3.03. 41
and yet how nature erring from itself — 3.03.227
how now, my dear othello? 3.03.279
how now? what do you here alone? 3.03.300
why, how now, general? no more of that. 3.03.334
how now, my lord? 3.03.337
but how? 3.03.394
how satisfied, my lord? 3.03.394
how then? 3.03.400
how is't with you, my lord? 3.04. 33
how do you, desdemona? 3.04. 35
how? 3.04. 84
how now, good cassio, what's the news with you? 3.04.109
how is't with you, my most fair bianca? 3.04.170
how now, cassio? 4.01. 48
how is it, general? 4.01. 59
where, how, how oft, how long ago, and when | he 4.01. 85
where, how, how oft, how long ago, and when | he 4.01. 85
how, how oft, how long ago, and when | he hath, 4.01. 85
how do you /now, lieutenant? 4.01.103
bianca's /pow'r, | how quickly should you speed! 4.01.108
look how he laughs already! 4.01.109
now he tells how she pluck'd him to my chamber. 4.01.141 P
how now, my sweet bianca? how now? how now? 4.01.156 P
how now, my sweet bianca? how now? how now? 4.01.156 P
how now, my sweet bianca? how now? how now? 4.01.156 P
how shall i murther him, iago? 4.01.170 P
did you perceive how he laugh'd at his vice? 4.01.171 P
and to see how he prizes the foolish woman your 4.01.175 P
i thank you. how does lieutenant cassio? 4.01.222
do but go after, | and mark how he continues. 4.01.281
to whom, my lord? with whom? how am i false? 4.02. 40
how do you, madam? 4.02. 96
how do you, my good lady? 4.02. 96
how have i been behav'd, that he might stick 4.02.108
what is your pleasure, madam? how is't with you? 4.02.110
how comes this trick upon him? 4.02.129
light of heaven, | i know not how i lost him. 4.02.151
hark how these instruments summon to supper! 4.02.169
how now, roderigo? 4.02.172 P
how do you mean, removing him? 4.02.228 P
how goes it now? he looks gentler than he did. 4.03. 11
good /faith, how foolish are our minds! 4.03. 23
how silent is this town! 5.01. 64
how is't, brother? 5.01. 71
how do you, cassio? o, a chair, a chair! 5.01. 96
how? unlawfully? 5.02. 70
why, how should she be murd'red? 5.02.126
what is the matter? how now, general? 5.02.168
now — how dost thou look now? 5.02.272
how came you, cassio, by that handkerchief 5.02.319
how he upbraids iago, that he made him | brave 5.02.325
if it be love indeed, tell me how much. ANT 1.01. 14
i'll set a bourn how far to be belov'd. 1.01. 16
how, my love? 1.01. 24
prithee, how many boys and wenches must i have? 1.02. 36 P
but how, but how? give me particulars. 1.02. 56 P
but how, but how? give me particulars. 1.02. 56 P
from sicyon how the news? speak there! 1.02.113
how now, enobarbus? 1.02.130
we see how mortal an unkindness is to them; 1.02.134 P
how now, lady? 1.03. 39
in fulvia's death, how mine receiv'd shall be. 1.03. 65
how this herculean roman does become | the 1.03. 84
shalt thou have report | how 'tis abroad. 1.04. 36
how much unlike art thou mark antony! 1.05. 35
how goes it with my brave mark antony? 1.05. 38
honor | even till a lethe'd dullness — how now, 2.01. 27
how lesser enmities may give way to greater. 2.01. 43
but how the fear of us | may cement their 2.01. 47
how intend you, practic'd? 2.02. 40
not till he hears how antony is touch'd | with 2.02.139
bid you alexas | bring me word how tall she is. 2.05.118
thou know'st | how much we do o'er-count thee. 2.06. 26
how you take | the offers we have sent you. 2.06. 30
i know thee now: how far'st thou, soldier? 2.06. 71
how should that be? 2.07. 63
how, with his banners and his well-paid ranks, 3.01. 32
a very fine one. o, how he loves caesar! 3.02. 7
nay, but how dearly he adores mark antony! 3.02. 8
spake you of caesar? how, the nonpareil! 3.02. 11
but how, when antony is gone, | through whom i 3.03. 5
how now, friend eros? 3.05. 1 P
till we perceiv'd both how you were wrong led 3.06. 80
how now, worthy soldier? 3.07. 60
how appears the fight? 3.10. 8
see | how i convey my shame out of thine eyes 3.11. 52
you did know | how much you were my conqueror, 3.11. 66
observe how antony becomes his flaw, | and what 3.12. 34
how now, masters? 4.03. 18
how now? | how now? do you hear this? 4.03. 18
how now? | how now? do you hear this? 4.03. 19
let's see how it will give off. 4.03. 22
how wouldst thou have paid | my better service, 4.06. 31
bring thee word | straight how 'tis like to go. 4.12. 3
mardian, | and bring me how he takes my death. 4.13. 10
how, not dead? 4.14.103
but, fearing since how it might work, hath sent 4.14.125
how now? 4.15. 6
how heavy weighs my lord! 4.15. 32
how do you, women? 4.15. 82
why, how now, charmian? 4.15. 83
how honorable and how kindly we | determine for 5.01. 58
how honorable and how kindly we | determine for 5.01. 58
us what she says, | and how you find of her. 5.01. 68
for i remember now | how he's employ'd; 5.01. 72
see | how hardly i was drawn into this war, 5.01. 74
how calm and gentle i proceeded still | in all 5.01. 75
you see how easily she may be surpris'd. 5.02. 35
o, behold, | how pomp is followed! 5.02.151
of honesty — how she died of the biting of it, 5.02.253 P
how goes it here? 5.02.329
her own price | proclaims how she esteem'd him; CYM 1.01. 52
how long is this ago? 1.01. 61
how fine this tyrant | can tickle where she 1.01. 84
incur i know not | how much of his displeasure. 1.01.103
how, how? 1.01.114
how, how? 1.01.114
how now, sir? 1.01.159
till you had measur'd how long a fool you were 1.02. 24 P
could best express how slow his soul sail'd on, 1.03. 13
slow his soul sail'd on, | how swift his ship. 1.03. 14
him | how i would think on him at certain hours 1.03. 27
but how comes it he is to sojourn with you? 1.04. 23 P
how creeps acquaintance? 1.04. 24 P
how worthy he is i will leave to appear 1.04. 32 P
hast thou not learn'd me how | to make perfumes? 1.05. 12
how now, pisanio? 1.05. 29
tell thy mistress how | the case stands with her 1.05. 66
how mean soe'er, that have their honest wills, 1.06. 8
how should i be reveng'd? 1.06.129
if it be true, | how should i be reveng'd? 1.06.132
cytherea, | how bravely thou becom'st thy bed! 2.02. 15
rubies unparagon'd, | how dearly they do't! 2.02. 18
how, my good name? 2.03. 84
how now, pisanio? 2.03.136
how? 3.02. 1
how? 3.02. 11
how look i | that i should seem to lack humanity 3.02. 15
how now, pisanio? 3.02. 24
read, and tell me | how far 'tis thither. 3.02. 50
how far it is | to this same blessed milford. 3.02. 58
th' way | tell me how wales was made so happy as 3.02. 60
but first of all, | how we may steal from hence; 3.02. 62
but first, how get hence. 3.02. 64
how many /score of miles may we well rid 3.02. 67
gate | instructs you how t' adore the heavens, 3.03. 3
the rain and wind beat dark december, how, | in 3.03. 37
how you speak! 3.03. 44
how hard it is to hide the sparks of nature! 3.03. 79
on, how thy memory | will then be pang'd by me. 3.04. 94
how live? 3.04.128
wrote already to the emperor | how it goes here. 3.05. 22
how | can her contempt be answer'd? 3.05. 41
how now, my son? 3.05. 66
alas, my lord, | how can she be with him? 3.05. 90
how long is't since she went to milford-haven? 3.05.148 P
how fit his garments serve me! 4.01. 2 P
how much the quantity, the weight as much, | as 4.02. 17
what? how? how? 4.02. 18
what? how? how? 4.02. 18
this youth, how e'er distress'd, appears he hath 4.02. 47
how angel-like he sings! 4.02. 48
how found you him? 4.02.209
pray how far thither? 4.02.292
how? 4.02.312
how should this be? 4.02.323
how? 4.02.355
how came't? 4.02.366
and bring me word how 'tis with her. 4.03. 1
heavens, | how deeply you at once do touch me! 4.03. 4
how many | must murther wives much better than 5.01. 3
heavens, how they wound | some slain before, 5.03. 46
to-day how many would have given their honors 5.03. 66
how dare you ghosts | accuse the thunderer, 5.04. 94
and how you shall speed in your journey's end, i 5.04.182 P
how ended she? 5.05. 30
upon your finger, say | how came it yours? 5.05.138
how? me? 5.05.140
this her bracelet | (o cunning, how i got/'t!), 5.05.205
how comes these staggers on me? 5.05.233
how fares my mistress? 5.05.235
how now, my flesh? 5.05.264
but her son | is gone, we know not how, nor 5.05.273
how of descent | as good as we? 5.05.308
a banish'd man, | i know not how a traitor. 5.05.320
how? my issue? 5.05.331
i know not how to wish | a pair of worthier sons 5.05.355
how liv'd you? 5.05.384
how parted with your /brothers? 5.05.386
how first met them? 5.05.386
with | i know not how much more, should be 5.05.389
how they may be, and yet in two, | as you will PER 1.01. 70
how courtesy would seem to cover sin, | when 1.01.121
how durst thy tongue move anger to our face? 1.02. 54
how dares the plants look up to heaven, from 1.02. 55
air | how many worthy princes' bloods were shed 1.02. 88
how i might stop this tempest ere it came, | and 1.02. 98
how? the king gone? 1.03. 14
how thaliard came full bent with sin | and hid 2.ch. 23
look how thou stir'st now! 2.01. 16 P
when i saw the porpas how he bounc'd and tumbled 2.01. 24 P
master, i marvel how the fishes live in the sea. 2.01. 27 P
how from the /finny subject of the sea | these 2.01. 48
how well this honest mirth becomes their labor! 2.01. 95
how far is his court distant from this shore? 2.01.105 P
how? | do as i bid you, or you'll move me else. 2.03. 70
that best know how to rule and how to reign, 2.04. 38
that best know how to rule and how to reign, 2.04. 38
nay, how absolute she's in't, | not minding 2.05. 19
o, how, lychorida! 3.01. 6
how does my queen? 3.01. 7
how? how, lychorida? 3.01. 18
how? how, lychorida? 3.01. 18
to the pothecary, | and tell me how it works. 3.02. 10
how close 'tis caulk'd and /bitum'd! 3.02. 56
to-night, | for look how fresh she looks! 3.02. 79
how thou stir'st, thou block! 3.02. 90
see how she gins | to blow into life's flower 3.02. 94
how now, marina, why do you keep alone? 4.01. 21
how chance my daughter is not with you? 4.01. 22
lord, how your favor's chang'd | with this 4.01. 24
how have i offended, | wherein my death might 4.01. 79
how dost thou find the inclination of the people 4.02. 96 P
strain you are, | and of how coward a spirit. 4.03. 25
yet none does know but you how she came dead, 4.03. 29
see how belief may suffer by foul show! 4.04. 23
how now? how a dozen of virginities? 4.06. 20 P
how now? how a dozen of virginities? 4.06. 20 P
how now? 4.06. 24 P
to him indeed, but how honorable he is in that, 4.06. 56 P
one, how long have you been at this trade? 4.06. 66 P
how long have you been of this profession? 4.06. 72 P
how now, what's the matter? 4.06.131 P
and how achiev'd you these endowments which 5.01.116
how lost thou /them? 5.01.140
thou little know'st how thou dost startle me 5.01.146
how, a king's daughter? | and call'd marina? 5.01.149
how came you in these parts? 5.01.169
seems to dote, | how sure you are my daughter. 5.01.226
reveal how thou at sea didst lose thy wife. 5.01.244
now do i long to hear how you were found, | how 5.03. 56
how possibly preserved, and who to thank 5.03. 57
will you deliver | how this dead queen relives? 5.03. 64
how she came plac'd here in the temple; 5.03. 67
how will it shake the bones of that good man, TNK pr 17
that best knowest | how to draw out, fit to this 1.01.160
how dangerous, if we will keep our honors, | it 1.02. 37
how his longing | follows his friend: 1.03. 26
i marvel how they would have look'd had they 2.01. 32 P
how do you, noble cousin? 2.02. 1
how do you, sir? 2.02. 1
how, gentle cousin? 2.02. 70
cousin, cousin! how do you, sir? why, palamon! 2.02.131
how modestly she blows, and paints the sun 2.02.139

we'll see how near art can come near their 2.02.149
how i would spread, and fling my wanton arms 2.02.237
how now, keeper? 2.02.243
how bravely may he bear himself to win her, | if 2.02.254
hast felt what sorrow was, | dream how i suffer! 2.02.277
mark how his body's made for't. 2.03. 71
how do you like him, lady? 2.05. 17
mark how his virtue, like a hidden sun, | breaks 2.05. 23
emily my sovereign), how far | i may be proud. 3.01. 16
you have been well advertis'd | how much i dare; 3.01. 59
how stand i then? 3.02. 20
how tastes your victuals? 3.03. 24
how they cry! 3.04. 8
and "how?" 3.05. 7
take twenty, domine. — how does my sweet heart? 3.05.148
how do i look? 3.06. 66
compassion to 'em both, how would you place it? 3.06.213
think how you maim your honor | (for now i am 3.06.237
how their lives | might breed the ruin of my 3.06.239
and discover'd how | and by whose means he 4.01. 19
how was it ended? 4.01. 25
honorable, | how good they'll prove, i know not. 4.01. 31
how he looks! 4.01. 33
how now, sir? 4.02. 55
how prettily she's amiss! 4.03. 28 P
how her brain coins! 4.03. 40 P
how she continues this fancy! 4.03. 48 P
seen it approv'd, how many times i know not, but 4.03. 97 P
then from this gather | how i should tender you. 5.01. 25
pray bring her in | and let's see how she is. 5.02. 25
how old is she? 5.02. 31
how do you like him? 5.02. 46
pretty soul, | how do ye? 5.02. 70
how far is't now to th' end o' th' world, my 5.02. 72
lord, how y' are grown! 5.02. 94
how did you like her? 5.02.103
hark how yon spurs to spirit do incite | the 5.03. 56
i prithee run | and tell me how it goes. 5.03. 71
pray, how does she? 5.04. 25
how do things fare? 5.04. 45
i would now ask ye how ye like the play, | but, ep 1
how say you now, /prentices? STM II.C 22 P
how insolence and strong hand should prevail, II.C 81
how /order should be quell'd, and by this II.C 82
mark | you shall perceive how horrible a shape II.C 92
or how can well that proclamation sound | when II.C 117
nimbly she fastens (o, how quick is love!); VEN 38
look how a bird lies tangled in a net, | so 67
look how he can, she cannot choose but love, 79
how want of love tormenteth? 202
being mad before, how doth she now for wits? 249
his love, perceiving how he was enrag'd, | grew 317
view | how she came stealing to the wayward boy! 344
hue, | how white and red each other did destroy! 346
care, | is how to get my palfrey from the mare." 384
"how like a jade he stood, tied to the tree, 391
how he outruns the wind, and with what care | he 681
look how a bright star shooteth from the sky, 815
how love makes young men thrall and old men dote 837
how love is wise in folly, foolish witty. 838
look how the world's poor people are amazed | at 925
o, how her eyes and tears did lend and borrow! 961
o hard–believing love, how strange it seems! 985
"how much a fool was i | to be of such a weak 1015
contrive, | to cipher me how fondly i did dote; LUC 207
o, how her fear did make her color rise! 257
"and how her hand, in my hand being lock'd, 260
fact, | how can they then assist me in the act? 350
"how will thy shame be seeded in thine age, 603
thy princely office how canst thou fulfill, 628
"think but how vile a spectacle it were | to 631
o, how are they wrapp'd in with infamies | that 636
to ask the spotted princess how she fares. 721
and my true eyes have never practic'd how | to 748
that know not how | to cipher what is writ in 810
line, | how tarquin wronged me, i collatine. 819
afar, | how he in peace is wounded, not in war. 831
alas, how many bear such shameful blows, | which 832
how comes it then, vile opportunity, | being so 895
let him have time to mark how slow time goes 990
and how swift and short | his time of folly and 991
how tarquin must be us'd, read it in me: 1195
how was i overseen that thou shalt see it! 1206
"look, look how list'ning priam wets his eyes, 1548
and they that watch see time how slow it creeps. 1575
he hath no power to ask her how she fares. 1594
"o, teach me how to make mine own excuse, | or 1653
"how may this forced stain be wip'd from me? 1701
make me forsworn, how shall i swear to love? PP 5. 1
her lips to mine how often hath she joined, 7. 7
how many tales to please me hath she coined, 7. 9
she told the youngling how god mars did try her, 11. 3
lord, how mine eyes throw gazes to the east! 14.13
how sighs resound through heartless ground, 17.23
"how true a twain | seemeth this concordant one! PHT 45
how much more praise deserv'd thy beauty's use, SON 2. 9
then how when nature calls thee to be gone, 4.11
mark how one string, sweet husband to another, 8. 9
how can i then be elder than thou art? 22. 8
then may i dare to boast how i do love thee, 26.13
how can i then return in happy plight | that am 28. 1
the other to complain | how far i toil, still 28. 8
how many a holy and obsequious tear | hath dear 31. 5
how can my muse want subject to invent | while 38. 1
o, how thy worth with manners may i sing, | when 39. 1
and that thou teachest how to make one twain, 39.13
how would thy shadow's form form happy show | to 43. 6
how would (i say) mine eyes be blessed made | by 43. 9
war, | how to divide the conquest of thy sight: 46. 2
how careful was i, when i took my way, | each 48. 1
how heavy do i journey on the way, | when what i 50. 1
o, how much more doth beauty beauteous seem | by 54. 1
save where you are how happy you make those. 57.12
hath been before, how are our brains beguil'd, 59. 2
how with this rage shall beauty hold a plea, 65. 3
o, how shall summer's honey breath hold out 65. 5
thy glass will show thee how thy beauties /wear, 77. 1
thy dial how thy precious minutes waste; 77. 2
o, how i faint when i of you do write, | knowing 80. 1
how far a modern quill doth come too short, 83. 7
for how do i hold thee but by thy granting, 87. 5
how like eve's apple doth thy beauty grow, | if 93.13
how sweet and lovely dost thou make the shame 95. 1
how many lambs might the stern wolf betray, | if 96. 9
how many gazers mightst thou lead away, | if 96.11
how like a winter hath my absence been | from 97. 1
i teach thee how | to make him seem long hence, 101.13
mark how with my neglect i do dispense: 112.12
how have mine eyes out of their spheres been 119. 7
to weigh how once i suffered in your crime. 120. 8
my deepest sense, how hard true sorrow hits, 120.10
how oft, when thou, my music, music play'st 128. 1
no, | how can it? 148. 9
o, how can love's eye be true, | that is so 148. 9
who taught thee how to make me love thee more, 150. 9
saw how deceits were gilded in his smiling, LC 172
by how much of me their reproach contains. 189
"'how mighty then you are, o, hear me tell! 253
how coldly those impediments stand forth | of 269
o, how the channel to the stream gave grace! 285

HOWBEIT 3 FR 0.0003 REL FR 3 V 0 P
howbeit, they would hold up this salique law H5 1.02. 91
howbeit, i thank you. COR 1.09. 70
the moor (howbeit that i endure him not) | is of OTH 2.01.288

/HOWE'ER 1 FR 0.0001 REL FR 1 V 0 P
/howe'er /thou /art /a /fiend, | /a /woman's LR 4.02. 66

HOWE'ER 9 FR 0.0010 REL FR 9 V 0 P
howe'er, i charge thee, | as heaven shall work AWW 1.03.183
not seem too dear, | howe'er repented after. 3.07. 28
howe'er it pleases you to take it so, | the ring 5.03. 88
my fore–past proofs, howe'er the matter fall, 5.03.121
my saying, | howe'er you lean to th' nayward. WT 2.01. 64
howe'er the business goes, you have made fault 3.02.217
well shot, | and i am i, howe'er i was begot. JN 1.01.175
howe'er it be, | i cannot but be sad; R2 2.02. 29
at them, | howe'er unfortunate i miss'd my aim. 1H6 1.04. 4

HOWEVER 11 FR 0.0012 REL FR 11 V 0 P
however — but a folly bought with wit, | or TGV 1.01. 34
however they have writ the style of gods, | and ADO 5.01. 37
for, boy, however we do praise ourselves, | our TN 2.04. 32
night, | and have is have, however men do catch. JN 1.01.173
however god or fortune cast my lot, | there R2 1.03. 85
however, yet there is no great breach; H8 4.01.106
however faulty, yet should find respect | for 5.02.110
sends, | however it is spread in general name, TRO 1.03.322
however these disturbers of our peace | buzz in TIT 4.04. 6
however he puts on this tardy form. JC 1.02.299
i shall serve you, sir, | truly, however else. LR 2.01.117

HOWL 10 FR 0.0011 REL FR 7 V 3 P
thy groans | did make wolves howl, and penetrate TMP 1.02.288
i had rather hear lady, my brach, howl in irish. 1H4 3.01.235 P
the law, for the which i think thou wilt howl. 2H4 2.04.345 P
floods o'erswell, and fiends for food howl on! H5 2.01. 93
time when screech–owls cry and ban–dogs howl, 2H6 1.04. 18
each new morn | new widows howl, new orphans cry MAC 4.03. 5
howl, howl, howl! LR 5.03.258
howl, howl, howl! 5.03.258
howl, howl, howl! 5.03.258
proud lady and a proud city–wife howl together! TNK 4.03. 52 P

HOWL'D 6 FR 0.0006 REL FR 5 V 1 P
till | thou hast howl'd away twelve winters. TMP 1.02.296
he had been a dog that should have howl'd thus, ADO 2.03. 80 P
dogs howl'd, and hideous tempest shook down 3H6 5.06. 46
that would be howl'd out in the desert air, MAC 4.03.194
wolves had at thy gate howl'd that /dearn time, LR 3.07. 63
they howl'd many together, | and then they /fed TNK 3.02. 18

HOWLED 1 FR 0.0001 REL FR 1 V 0 P
me, and howled in mine ears | such hideous cries R3 1.04. 59

HOWLET 1 FR 0.0001 REL FR 1 V 0 P
"there was three fools fell out about an howlet: TNK 3.05. 67

HOWLET'S 1 FR 0.0001 REL FR 1 V 0 P
sting, | lizard's leg and howlet's wing, | for a MAC 4.01. 17

HOWLING 14 FR 0.0015 REL FR 9 V 5 P
a plague upon this howling! TMP 1.01. 36 P
a howling monster; a drunken monster! 2.02.179 P
of roaring, shrieking, howling, jingling chains, 5.01.233
my sister crying, our maid howling, our cat TGV 2.03. 7 P
and uncertain thought | imagine howling — 'tis MM 3.01.127
the virgin tribute paid by howling troy | to the MV 3.02. 56
'tis like the howling of irish wolves against AYL 5.02.109 P
fulsome to mine ear | as howling after music. TN 5.01.110
howling attends it. ROM 3.03. 48
shall my sister be | when thou liest howling. HAM 5.01.242
themselves, high seas, and howling winds, | the OTH 2.01. 68
boiling, hissing, howling, chatt'ring, cursing! TNK 4.03. 33 P
to whom she speaks, and he replies with howling. VEN 918
in howling wise, to see my doleful plight. PP 17.22

HOWL'S 1 FR 0.0001 REL FR 1 V 0 P
whose howl's his watch, thus with his stealthy MAC 2.01. 54

HOWLS 3 FR 0.0003 REL FR 2 V 1 P
whiles the mad mothers with their howls confus'd H5 3.03. 39
have heard | strange howls this livelong night; TNK 3.02. 12
and then howls; 4.03. 55 P

/HOWL'ST 1 FR 0.0001 REL FR 1 V 0 P
/dead /vomit /up, | /and /howl'st /to /find /it. 2H4 1.03.100

HOW'S 5 FR 0.0005 REL FR 3 V 2 P
how's the day? TMP 5.01. 3
how's that? LR 1.05. 43 P
how's this? how's this? some more, be sage. PER 4.06. 95
how's this? how's this? some more, be sage. 4.06. 95
how's this? 4.06.121 P

HOWSOE'ER 5 FR 0.0005 REL FR 4 V 1 P
i am glad he's come, howsoe'er he comes. SHR 3.02. 74 P
but howsoe'er, no simple man that sees | this 1H6 4.01.187
i give you, | and gold confound you howsoe'er! TIM 4.03.449
howsoe'er 'tis strange, | or that the negligence CYM 1.01. 65
howsoe'er, | my brother hath done well. 4.02.146

HOWSOEVER 8 FR 0.0009 REL FR 2 V 6 P
basket too, howsoever he hath had intelligence. WIV 4.02. 92 P
howsoever you color it in being a tapster, are MM 2.01.220 P
god, howsoever it seems not in him by some large ADO 2.03.197 P
but, howsoever, strange and admirable. MND 5.01. 27
in my form, | which, howsoever rude exteriorly, JN 4.02.257
howsoever you speak this to feel other men's H5 4.01.125 P
howsoever, he shall pay for me ere he has me. TRO 3.03.296 P
howsoever you have been his liar, as you say you COR 5.02. 31 P

HOWSOEV'R 2 FR 0.0002 REL FR 2 V 0 P
but, howsoev'r you have | been justled from your TMP 5.01.157
and depend on, howsoev'r | you skip them in me, TNK 3.01. 51

HOWSOME'ER 2 FR 0.0002 REL FR 1 V 1 P
then, howsome'er thou speak'st, 'mong other MV 3.05. 89
howsome'er their hearts are sever'd in religion, AWW 1.03. 52 P

HOWSOMEVER 1 FR 0.0001 REL FR 1 V 0 P
but, howsomever thou pursues this act, | taint HAM 1.05. 84

HOW'T 1 FR 0.0001 REL FR 1 V 0 P
how't tumbles! TNK 3.04. 5

HOWTED *(also hooted)*

HOWTED 1 FR 0.0001 REL FR 0 V 1 P
still as he refus'd it, the rabblement howted, JC 1.02.244 P

HOWTING 1 FR 0.0001 REL FR 1 V 0 P
upon the market–place, | howting and shrieking. JC 1.03. 28

HOXES 1 FR 0.0001 REL FR 1 V 0 P
which hoxes honesty behind, restraining | from WT 1.02.244

HOY 1 FR 0.0001 REL FR 0 V 1 P
by the sergeant to tarry for the hoy delay. ERR 4.03. 40 P

HOY–DAY *(also hey–day, high–day)*

HOY–DAY 2 FR 0.0002 REL FR 2 V 0 P
hoy–day, a riddle! R3 4.04.459
hoy–day, | what a sweep of vanity comes this way TIM 1.02.131

HUBBUB *(see whoobub)*

HUBERT 32 FR 0.0036 REL FR 32 V 0 P
hubert, keep this boy. JN 3.02. 5
come hither, hubert. 3.03. 19
o my gentle hubert, | we owe thee much! 3.03. 19
by heaven, hubert, i am almost asham'd | to say 3.03. 27
good hubert, hubert, hubert, throw thine eye 3.03. 59
good hubert, hubert, hubert, throw thine eye 3.03. 59
hubert, hubert, throw thine eye | on yon young 3.03. 59
hubert, i love thee. 3.03. 67
hubert shall be your man, attend on you | with 3.03. 72
good morrow, hubert. 4.01. 9
i were your son, so you would love me, hubert. 4.01. 24
are you sick, hubert? 4.01. 28
too fairly, hubert, for so foul effect. 4.01. 38
and told me hubert should put out mine eyes, | i 4.01. 69
o, save me, hubert, save me! 4.01. 72
for heaven sake, hubert, let me not be bound! 4.01. 77
nay, hear me, hubert, drive these men away, 4.01. 78
hubert, the utterance of a brace of tongues 4.01. 97
let me not hold my tongue, let me not, hubert; 4.01. 99
or, hubert, if you will, cut out my tongue, | so 4.01.100
and glow with shame of your proceedings, hubert. 4.01.113
o, now you look like hubert! 4.01.125
sleep doubtless and secure | that hubert, for 4.01.130
o heaven! i thank you, hubert. 4.01.131
hubert, what news with you? 4.02. 68
hubert, away with him; 4.02.155
this deed of death, | art thou damn'd, hubert. 4.03.119
that villain hubert told me he did live. 5.01. 42
how goes the day with us? o, tell me, hubert. 5.03. 1
commend me to one hubert with your king; 5.04. 40
hubert, i think. 5.06. 6
i'll tell thee, hubert, half my power this night 5.06. 39

HUBERT'S 2 FR 0.0002 REL FR 2 V 0 P
not have believ'd him — no tongue but hubert's. JN 4.01. 70
it is the shameful work of hubert's hand, | the 4.03. 62

HUDDLED 1 FR 0.0001 REL FR 1 V 0 P
that have of late so huddled on his back, | enow MV 4.01. 28

HUDDLING 1 FR 0.0001 REL FR 0 V 1 P
huddling jest upon jest with such impossible ADO 2.01.244 P

HUE* 31 FR 0.0035 REL FR 29 V 2 P
hue and cry, villain, go! WIV 4.05. 90 P
fly, run, hue and cry, villain! 4.05. 91 P
the hue of dungeons, and the school of night; LLL 4.03.251
and cuckoo–buds of yellow hue | do paint the 5.02.896
"most radiant pyramus, most lily–white of hue, MND 3.01. 93
the woosel cock so black of hue, | with 3.01.125
o night with hue so black! 5.01.170
i would not change this hue, | except to steal MV 2.01. 11
what says the silver with her virgin hue? 2.07. 22
slender, and as brown in hue | as hazel–nuts, SHR 2.01.254
the ice, or add another hue | unto the rainbow, JN 4.02. 13
a hue and cry | hath followed certain men unto 1H4 2.04.507
this palliament of white and spotless hue, | and TIT 1.01.182
me, of the hue | that i would choose were i to 1.01.261
doth make your honor of his body's hue, 2.03. 73
'zounds, ye whore, is black so base a hue? 4.02. 71
coal–black is better than another hue, | in that 4.02. 99
hue, | in that it scorns to bear another hue; 4.02.100
fie, treacherous hue, that will betray with 4.02.117
did not thy hue bewray whose brat thou art, 5.01. 28
and thus the native hue of resolution | is HAM 3.01. 83
royal in their smells alone, | but in their hue; TNK 1.01. 3
to note the fighting conflict of her hue, | how VEN 345
teaching the sheets a whiter hue than white, 398
both favor, savor, hue, and qualities, | whereat 747
a man in hue all hues in his controlling, SON 20. 7
and steal dead seeing of his living hue? 67. 6
thou art as fair in knowledge as in hue, 82. 5
smell | of different flowers in odor and in hue, 98. 6
so your sweet hue, which methinks still doth 104.11
flame through water which their hue encloses. LC 287

HUES 1 FR 0.0001 REL FR 1 V 0 P
a man in hue all hues in his controlling, SON 20. 7

HUG 7 FR 0.0008 REL FR 7 V 0 P
darkness as a bride, | and hug it in mine arms. MM 3.01. 84
to hug with swine, to seek sweet safety out | in JN 5.02.142
when they do hug him in their melting bosoms. TIT 3.01.213
whom this beneath world doth embrace and hug TIM 1.01. 44
hug their diseas'd perfumes, and have forgot 4.03.207
know | that i do fawn on men and hug them hard, JC 1.02. 75
which might accite thee to embrace and hug them, STM III 16

/HUGE 2 FR 0.0002 REL FR 2 V 0 P
/like /herne, /with /huge /horns /on /his /head. WIV 4.04. 43
to whose /huge spokes ten thousand lesser things HAM 3.03. 19

HUGE 38 FR 0.0043 REL FR 29 V 9 P
yond same black cloud, yond huge one, looks like TMP 2.02. 21 P
likes | (only for his possessions are so huge), TGV 2.04.175
and huge leviathans | forsake unsounded deeps to 3.02. 79
and at her heels a huge infectious troop | of ERR 5.01. 81

and the huge army of the world's desires — LLL 1.01. 10
a huge translation of hypocrisy, | vildly 5.02. 51
is of that nature that to your huge store | wise 5.02.377
pompey the huge! 5.02.686 P
the patch is kind enough, but a huge feeder, MV 2.05. 46
noblest deer hath them as huge as the rascal. AYL 3.03. 57 P
shall draw this brief into as huge a volume. JN 2.01.103
that no supporter but the huge firm earth | can 3.01. 72
and now 'tis far too huge to be blown out | with 5.02. 86
horse–back–breaker, this huge hill of flesh — 1H4 2.04.243 P
parcel of dropsies, that huge bombard of sack, 2.04.451 P
the frame and huge foundation of the earth 3.01. 16
from the best of all my land | a huge half–moon, 3.01. 99
empty vessel bear such a huge full hogshead? 2H4 2.04. 62 P
draw the huge bottoms through the furrowed sea, H5 3.pr. 12
or the mighty, or the huge, or the magnanimous, 4.07. 16 P
which cannot in their huge and proper life | be 5.pr. 5
she hath, and in that sparing /makes huge waste; ROM 1.01.218
if i were a huge man, i should fear to drink at TIM 1.02. 49 P
and we petty men | walk under his huge legs, and JC 1.02.137
set a huge mountain 'tween my heart and tongue! 2.04. 7
though they do appear | as huge as high olympus. 4.03. 92
and have ingenious feeling | of my huge sorrows! LR 4.06.281
the world's a huge thing; OTH 4.03. 69
methinks it should be now a huge eclipse | of 5.02. 99
to be call'd into a huge sphere, and not to be ANT 2.07. 14 P
this case of that huge spirit now is cold. 4.15. 89
and with /th' /ostent of war will look so huge, PER 1.02. 25
i never saw so huge a billow, sir, | as toss'd 3.02. 58
huge rocks, high winds, strong pirates, shelves LUC 335
lights are soon blown out, huge fires abide, 647
and waste huge stones with little water–drops. 959
that this huge stage presenteth nought but shows SON 15. 3
that heaven's air in this huge rondure hems. 21. 8
HUGELY 2 FR 0.0002 REL FR 2 V 0 P
doth it not flow as hugely as the sea, | till AYL 2.07. 72
hours, | but all alone stands hugely politic, SON 124.11
HUGENESS 1 FR 0.0001 REL FR 0 V 1 P
in goodness the hugeness of your unworthy CYM 1.04.144 P
HUGG'D 2 FR 0.0002 REL FR 2 V 0 P
bay, | hugg'd and embraced by the strumpet wind! MV 2.06. 16
and hugg'd me in his arms, and swore with sobs R3 1.04.245
HUGGER–MUGGER 1 FR 0.0001 REL FR 1 V 0 P
but greenly | in hugger–mugger to inter him; HAM 4.05. 84
/HUGH 1 FR 0.0001 REL FR 0 V 1 P
her troop of fairies, and the welsh devil /hugh? WIV 5.03. 12 P
HUGH 24 FR 0.0027 REL FR 3 V 21 P
sir hugh, persuade me not; WIV 1.01. 1 P
kind of tender, made afar off by sir hugh here. 1.01.209 P
he came of an errand to me from parson hugh. 1.04. 77 P
sir hugh send–a you? 1.04. 87 P
you jack'nape, give–a this letter to sir hugh. 1.04.108 P
be fought between sir hugh the welsh priest and 2.01.201 P
butter, parson hugh the welshman with my cheese, 2.02.303 P
the hour, sir, that sir hugh promis'd to meet. 2.03. 4 P
and sir hugh hath shown himself a wise and 2.03. 54 P
sir hugh is there, is he? 2.03. 76 P
yonder he is coming, this way, sir hugh. 3.01. 27 P
good morrow, good sir hugh. 3.01. 37 P
/god save you, good sir hugh! 3.01. 41 P
my sir hugh? 3.01.104 P
so shall you, master page, and you, sir hugh. 3.02. 83 P
how now, sir hugh, no school to–day? 4.01. 10 P
sir hugh, my husband says my son profits nothing 4.01. 14 P
adieu, good sir hugh. 4.01. 84 P
well said, fairy hugh. 5.05.131 P
hugh oatcake, sir, or george seacole, for they ADO 3.03. 11 P
hugh capet also, who usurp'd the crown | of H5 1.02. 69
king pepin's title and hugh capet's claim, 1.02. 87
sir john and sir hugh mortimer, mine uncles, 3H6 1.02. 62
/pretty! what say you, hugh rebeck? ROM 4.05.133 P
HUGS 1 FR 0.0001 REL FR 1 V 0 P
that hugs his kicky–wicky here at home, AWW 2.03.280
HUJUS 1 FR 0.0001 REL FR 0 V 1 P
genitivo, hujus. WIV 4.01. 43 P
HULK 3 FR 0.0003 REL FR 2 V 1 P
and harry monmouth's brawn, the hulk sir john, 2H4 1.01. 19
you have not seen a hulk better stuff'd in the 2.04. 64 P
provokes the mightiest hulk against the tide, 1H6 5.05. 6
HULKS 1 FR 0.0001 REL FR 1 V 0 P
sail swift, though greater hulks draw deep. TRO 2.03.266
HULL 2 FR 0.0002 REL FR 1 V 1 P
good swabber, i am to hull here a little longer. TN 1.05.203 P
and there they hull, expecting but the aid | of R3 4.04.438
HULLING 1 FR 0.0001 REL FR 1 V 0 P
thus hulling in | the wild sea of my conscience, H8 2.04.200
HUM* *(also humh)*
HUM* 16 FR 0.0018 REL FR 10 V 6 P
instruments | will hum about mine ears, and TMP 3.02.138
hum! WIV 3.05.139 P
and straight | the shrug, the hum or ha (these WT 2.01. 71
i cried "hum," and "well, go to," | but mark'd 1H4 3.01.156
the sad–ey'd justice, with his surly hum, H5 1.02.202
night, | the hum of either army stilly sounds, 4.pr. 5
hum? TRO 3.03.281 P
hum? 3.03.286 P
lip | and hum at good cominius much unhearts me. COR 5.01. 49
talks like a knell, and his hum is a battery. 5.04. 21 P
must he needs trouble me in't — hum! TIM 3.03. 1
hum, i have heard | that guilty creatures HAM 2.02.588
hum! 5.01.103 P
hum? LR 1.02. 55 P
hum, ha! PER 5.01. 83
for burthen–wise i'll hum on tarquin still, LUC 1133
HUMAN 26 FR 0.0029 REL FR 24 V 2 P
and sorceries terrible | to enter human hearing, TMP 1.02.265
hag–born) not honor'd with | a human shape. 1.02.284
(filth as thou art) with human care, and lodg'd 1.02.346
than of | our human generation you shall find 3.03. 33
mine would, sir, were i human. 5.01. 20
now he's there, past thought of human reason. ERR 5.01.189
the human mortals want their winter here; MND 2.01.101
and touching now the point of human skill, 2.02.119
a wolf, who, hang'd for human slaughter, | even MV 4.01.134
her before your eyes to–morrow, human as she is, AYL 5.02. 67 P
if pow'rs divine | behold our human actions (as WT 3.02. 29
is all as monstrous to our human reason | as my 5.01. 41
all his senses have but human conditions. H5 4.01.104 P
where valiant talbot above human thought 1H6 1.01.121
must die, | for that's the end of human misery. 3.02.137
him | were slily crept into his human powers, COR 2.01.220
holding them, | in human action and capacity, 2.01.249
what may be sworn by, both divine and human, 3.01.141
yield him who all the human sons do hate, | from TIM 4.03.185
though thou abhorr'dst in us our human griefs, 5.04. 75
it is too full o' th' milk of human kindness MAC 1.05. 17
with a learned spirit, | of human dealings. OTH 3.03.260
we count not worth the hanging (but none human), CYM 1.05. 20
sensually subdu'd | we lose our human title. TNK 1.01.233
by holy human law, and common troth, | by heaven LUC 571
touch | upon the lute doth ravish human sense; PP 8. 6
HUMANE 9 FR 0.0010 REL FR 7 V 2 P
courtesy | lie further off, in humane modesty; MND 2.02. 57
but, touch'd with humane gentleness and love, MV 4.01. 25
he (most humane | and fill'd with honor) to my WT 3.02.165
the first humane principle i would teach them 2H4 4.03.123 P
in humane gentleness, | welcome to troy! TRO 4.01. 21
noble tribunes, | it is the humane way. COR 3.01.325
ere humane statute purg'd the gentle weal; MAC 3.04. 75
on the mere form of civil and humane seeming, OTH 2.01.239 P
humane grace | affords them dust and shadow. TNK 1.01.144
HUMANELY 2 FR 0.0002 REL FR 1 V 1 P
humanely taken, all, all lost, quite lost; TMP 4.01.190
we might guess they reliev'd us humanely; COR 1.01. 19 P
/HUMANITY 1 FR 0.0001 REL FR 1 V 0 P
/humanity /must /perforce /prey /on /itself, LR 4.02. 49
HUMANITY 10 FR 0.0011 REL FR 7 V 3 P
part | and least proportion of humanity. 1H6 2.03. 53
what nearer debt in all humanity | than wife is TRO 2.02.175
he's opposite to humanity. TIM 1.01.273
hated be | of timon man and all humanity! 3.06.105
the middle of humanity thou never knewest, but 4.03.300 P
them well, they imitated humanity so abominably. HAM 3.02. 35 P
hen, i would change my humanity with a baboon. OTH 1.03.316 P
a rarer spirit never | did steer humanity; ANT 5.01. 32
that i should seem to lack humanity | so much as CYM 3.02. 16
let fair humanity abhor the deed | that spots LUC 195
HUMBLE 70 FR 0.0079 REL FR 62 V 8 P
my affections | are then most humble; TMP 1.02.483
my mistress, dearest, | and i thus humble ever. 3.01. 87
with them, upon her knees, her humble self, TGV 3.01.228
me up, i likewise give her most humble thanks; ADO 1.01.240 P
this is not generous, not gentle, not humble. LLL 5.02.629
a heavy heart bears not a humble tongue. 5.02.737
what humble suit attends thy answer there. 5.02.839
wherein your lady and your humble wife | may SHR in.1. 116
that made great jove to humble him to her hand, 1.01.169
be so humble | to cast thy wand'ring eyes on 3.01. 89
his humble ambition, proud humility; AWW 1.01.171
i am from humble, he from honored name; 1.03.156
my low and humble name to propagate | with any 2.01.197
above | her that so wishes, and her humble love! 2.03. 83
some that humble themselves may, but the many 4.05. 52 P
to be, cast thy humble slough and appear fresh. TN 2.05.149 P
my duty, madam, and most humble service. 3.01. 95
"cast thy humble slough," says she; 3.04. 68 P
god, | golden apollo, a poor humble swain, | as WT 4.04. 30
hearts | with humble and familiar courtesy, R2 1.04. 26
show me thy humble heart, and not thy knee, 2.03. 83
my lord, my humble duty rememb'red, i will not 2H4 2.01.125 P
but indeed these humble considerations make me 2.02. 11 P
and i will stoop and humble my intents | to your 5.02.120
meat, our humble author will continue the story, ep 27 P
who, prologue–like, your humble patience pray, H5 pr 33
thy humble servant vows obedience | and humble 1H6 3.01.166
and humble service till the point of death. 3.01.167
stay, let thy humble handmaid speak to thee. 3.03. 42
be humble to us, call my sovereign yours, | and 4.02. 6
but with as humble lowliness of mind | she is 5.05. 18
gloucester bears this base and humble mind. 2H6 1.02. 62
should honor such as these | with humble suit. 4.01.124
no humble suitors press to speak for right, | no 3H6 3.01. 19
before the king will grant her humble suit. 3.02. 13
my love till death, my humble thanks, my prayers 3.02. 62
fortune, | and to my humble seat conform myself. 3.03. 11
let me give humble thanks for all at once. 3.03.221
but if an humble prayer may prevail, | i then 4.06. 7
heard you not what an humble suppliant | lord R3 1.01. 74
time | my manly eyes did scorn an humble tear; 1.02.164
thy voice is thunder, but thy looks are humble. 1.04.167
whose humble means match not his haughty spirit. 4.02. 37
born, | and range with humble livers in content, H8 2.03. 20
i have been to you a true and humble wife, | at 2.04. 23
i will, when you are humble; 2.04. 74
though from an humble stock, undoubtedly | was 4.02. 49
it, | that am a poor and humble subject to you? 5.02.200
and, being born, his addition shall be humble. TRO 3.02. 95 P
with a proud heart he wore his humble weeds. COR 2.03.153
with what contempt he wore the humble weed, 2.03.221
now humble as the ripest mulberry | that will 3.02. 79
for /then hast made it like an humble suppliant. TIT 4.03.117
i am an humble suitor to your virtues; TIM 3.05. 7
love | by humble message and by promis'd means. 5.04. 20
(at your best leisure) this his humble suit. JC 3.01. 5
cimber throws before thy seat | an humble heart. 3.01. 35
mingle with society, | and play the humble host. MAC 3.04. 4
the heyday in the blood is tame, it's humble, HAM 3.04. 69
shall nev'r look back, nev'r ebb to humble love, OTH 3.03.458
i must | to the young man send humble treaties, ANT 3.11. 62
my humble thanks. CYM 1.06.180
ones, | and humble with a ferula the tall ones, TNK 3.05.112
than humble banks can go to law with waters 5.03. 99
god, | that i from such an humble bench of birth STM III 6
wilt thou be the humble suppliant's friend, LUC 897
and give the harmless show | an humble gait, 1508
assured trust, | and in thy suit be humble true; PP 18.20
is) | the humble as the proudest sail doth bear, SON 80. 6
the humble salve which wounded bosoms fits! 120.12
HUMBLE–BEE 6 FR 0.0006 REL FR 4 V 2 P
the fox, the ape, and the humble–bee, | were LLL 3.01. 84
the fox, the ape, and the humble–bee, | were 3.01. 89
the fox, the ape, and the humble–bee, | were 3.01. 95
kill me a red–hipp'd humble–bee on the top of a MND 4.01. 12 P
than by that red–tail'd humble–bee i speak of. AWW 4.05. 6 P
full merrily the humble–bee doth sing, | till he TRO 5.10. 41
HUMBLE–BEES 1 FR 0.0001 REL FR 1 V 0 P
the honey–bags steal from the humble–bees, | and MND 3.01.168
HUMBLED 10 FR 0.0011 REL FR 10 V 0 P
scratch the nurse | and presently, all humbled, TGV 1.02. 59
and hath so humbled me as i confess | there is 2.04.137
falls not the axe upon the humbled neck | but AYL 3.05. 5
his humility, | in their poor praise he humbled. AWW 1.02. 45
and her to whom my thoughts are humbled all, TIT 1.01. 51
owe, | mine honor's ensigns humbled at thy feet. 1.01.252
by my advice, all humbled on your knees, | you 1.01.472
heav'ns' plagues | have humbled to all strokes. LR 4.01. 65
so humbled | that he hath left part of his grief OTH 3.03. 52
thy priest, | am humbled 'fore thine altar. TNK 5.01.143
HUMBLE–MOUTH'D 1 FR 0.0001 REL FR 1 V 0 P
y' are meek and humble–mouth'd, | you sign your H8 2.04.107
HUMBLENESS 7 FR 0.0008 REL FR 7 V 0 P
with bated breath and whisp'ring humbleness, MV 1.03.124
state, | which humbleness may drive unto a fine. 4.01.372
all humbleness, all patience, and impatience, AYL 5.02. 97
and my appliance, | with all bound humbleness. AWW 2.01.114
her thanks | in the great'st humbleness, and H8 5.01. 65
plead your deserts in peace and humbleness. TIT 1.01. 45
my lords, with all the humbleness i may, | i 4.02. 4
HUMBLER 3 FR 0.0003 REL FR 3 V 0 P
his eyes are humbler than they us'd to be. H5 4.07. 67
methinks his lordship should be humbler, | it 1H6 3.01. 56
let us seem humbler after it is done | than when COR 4.02. 4
HUMBLES 1 FR 0.0001 REL FR 0 V 1 P
judge, but most willingly humbles himself to the MM 3.02.243 P
HUMBLEST 2 FR 0.0002 REL FR 2 V 0 P
if opportunity and humblest suit | cannot attain WIV 3.04. 20
in humblest manner i require your highness H8 2.04.145
HUMBLE/–VISAG'D 1 FR 0.0001 REL FR 1 V 0 P
like humble/–visag'd suitors, his high will. LLL 2.01. 34
HUMBLING 1 FR 0.0001 REL FR 1 V 0 P
themselves | (humbling their deities to love) WT 4.04. 26
HUMBLY 61 FR 0.0069 REL FR 54 V 7 P
i humbly thank you. MM 1.04. 87
i humbly thank you. 2.01.279 P
i humbly thank you. 3.01. 41
i humbly give you leave to depart, and if a ADO 5.01.325 P
i humbly do desire your grace of pardon, | i MV 4.01.402
sir, to your pleasure humbly i subscribe; SHR 1.01. 81
humbly entreating from your royal thoughts | a AWW 2.01.127
i humbly thank you. 3.05. 96
i humbly thank you, sir. 4.03.156 P
that scorn'd to serve | humbly call'd mistress. 5.03. 19
i humbly beseech you, sir, to pardon me all the WT 5.02.149 P
harry bullingbrook, doth humbly kiss thy hand, R2 3.03.104
and i most humbly beseech your lordship to have 2H4 1.02. 99 P
most humbly on my knee i beg | the leading of H5 4.03.130
i humbly pray them to admit th' excuse | of time 5.pr. 3
they humbly sue unto your excellence | to have a 1H6 5.01. 4
and humbly now upon my bended knee, | in sight 2H6 1.01. 10
i humbly thank your royal majesty. 1.03.211
and humbly thus, with halters on their necks, 4.09. 11
and thus most humbly i do take my leave. 3H6 1.02. 61
and what he will, i humbly yield unto. 3.01.101
humbly to kiss your hand, and with my tongue 3.03. 61
speak gentle words and humbly bend thy knee, 5.01. 22
humbly complaining to her deity | got my lord R3 1.01. 76
stroke, | and humbly beg the death upon my knee. 1.02.178
humbly on my knee | i crave your blessing. 2.02.105
i humbly take my leave. 4.03. 35
for one being sued to, one that humbly sues; 4.04.100
wherefore i humbly | beseech you, sir, to spare H8 2.04. 53
king has cur'd me, | i humbly thank his grace; 3.02.381
i do entreat your highness' pardon, | my 4.02.104
i most humbly pray you to deliver | this to my 4.02.129
i humbly thank your highness, | and am right 5.01.108
to come as humbly as they us'd to creep | to TRO 3.03. 73
tell him i humbly desire the valiant ajax to 3.03.273 P
who most humbly desires you to invite hector to 3.03.284 P
weep, they humbly at my feet | receive my tears, TIT 3.01. 41
i humbly thank him, and i thank you all. 5.01. 18
gentle breath, calm look, knees humbly bowed, ROM 3.01.156
humbly i thank your lordship. TIM 1.01.149
own, and humbly prays you | that with your other 2.02. 22
he humbly prays your speedy payment. 2.02. 28
so humbly take my leave. MAC 1.04. 47
most humbly do i take my leave, my lord. HAM 1.03. 82
i humbly thank you, well, /well, /well. 3.01. 91
i humbly thank you, sir. 4.04. 29
i humbly thank you, sir. 5.02. 82
humbly i thank your grace. OTH 1.03. 70
i humbly beseech you proceed to th' affairs of 1.03.220
most humbly therefore bending to your state, | i 1.03.235
i humbly thank you for't. 3.01. 39
i humbly do beseech you of your pardon | for too 3.03.212
i humbly thank your ladyship. 3.04.168
madam, good night; i humbly thank your ladyship. 4.03. 3
humbly, sir, i thank you. ANT 2.02.244
i'll humbly signify what in his name, | that 3.01. 30
i humbly thank your highness. CYM 1.01.175
i humbly take my leave. 1.05. 45
life is yours, | i humbly set it at your will; 4.03. 13
i humbly thank your highness. 5.05.100
thrive, | with death she humbly doth insinuate; VEN 1012
HUME 6 FR 0.0006 REL FR 4 V 2 P
here, hume, take this reward. 2H6 1.02. 85
hume must make merry with the duchess' gold; 1.02. 87
but how now, sir john hume? 1.02. 88
hume, if you take not heed, you shall go near 1.02.102
master hume, we are therefore provided. 1.04. 3 P
but it shall be convenient, master hume, that 1.04. 8 P
HUME'S 2 FR 0.0002 REL FR 2 V 0 P
but, by the grace of god and hume's advice, 2H6 1.02. 72
hume's knavery will be the duchess' wrack, | and 1.02.105
HUMH *(also hum*)*
HUMH 6 FR 0.0006 REL FR 4 V 2 P
lord lucius and lucullus? humh! TIM 2.02.195 P
humh! 3.03. 9

humh! i guess at it. MAC 4.03.203
humh! LR 3.04. 47 P
humh! OTH 5.02. 36
humh! CYM 3.05.103
HUMIDITY 2 FR 0.0002 REL FR 1 V 1 P
we'll use this unwholesome humidity, this gross WIV 3.03. 41 P
sun, draw from the earth | rotten humidity; TIM 4.03. 2
HUMILITY 16 FR 0.0018 REL FR 12 V 4 P
ears | and plant in tyrants mild humility. LLL 4.03.346
a jew wrong a christian, what is his humility? MV 3.01. 69 P
his humble ambition, proud humility; AWW 1.01.171
low ranks, | making them proud of his humility, 1.02. 44
the surplice of humility over the black gown of 1.03. 95 P
the rod, | and fawn on rage with base humility, R2 5.01. 33
i have sounded the very base–string of humility. 1H4 2.04. 6 P
and dress'd myself in such humility | that i did 3.02. 51
a man | as modest stillness and humility; H5 3.01. 4
in all submission and humility | york doth 2H6 5.01. 58
i thank my god for my humility. R3 2.01. 73
in peace, | your bounty, virtue, fair humility; 3.07. 17
in full seeming, | with meekness and humility; H8 2.04.109
remember me | in all humility unto his highness. 4.02.161
on him put | the napless vesture of humility, COR 2.01.234
and in the gown of humility, mark his behavior. 2.03. 40 P
HUMM'D 1 FR 0.0001 REL FR 1 V 0 P
air, or at adventure humm'd /one | from musical TNK 1.03. 75
HUMMING 2 FR 0.0002 REL FR 2 V 0 P
sir, i heard a humming | (and that a strange one TMP 2.01.317
and humming water must o'erwhelm thy corpse, PER 3.01. 63
/HUMOR 4 FR 0.0004 REL FR 3 V 1 P
falstaff will learn the /humor of the age, WIV 1.03. 83
and cheese /and /there's /the /humor /of /it. 2.01.136 P
though his /humor | was nothing but mutation, ay CYM 4.02.132
you'll find it so. she comes. pray /humor her. TNK 5.02. 40
HUMOR 96 FR 0.0108 REL FR 45 V 51 P
that's my humor. WIV 1.01.133 P
if you run the nuthook's humor on me — that is 1.01.168 P
is not the humor conceited? 1.03. 22 P
the good humor is to steal at a minute's rest. 1.03. 27 P
the anchor is deep. will that humor pass? 1.03. 51 P
the humor rises; 1.03. 56 P
humor me the angels. 1.03. 56 P
i thank thee for that humor. 1.03. 64 P
i will run no base humor. 1.03. 77 P
i will discuss the humor of this love to /page. 1.03. 95 P
my humor shall not cool. 1.03.100 P
of mine is dangerous — that is my true humor. 1.03.103 P
i like not the humor of lying. 2.01.129 P
i love not the humor of bread and cheese /and 2.01.135 P
"the humor of it," quoth 'a! 2.01.138 P
see what humor he is in; 2.03. 77 P
let's obey his humor a little further. 4.02.199 P
lightens my humor with his merry jests. ERR 1.02. 21
i am not in a sportive humor now: 1.02. 58
how now, sir, is your merry humor alter'd? 2.02. 7
saving your merry humor, here's the note | how 4.01. 27
fie, now you run this humor out of breath. 4.01. 57
and my cold blood, i am of your humor for that: ADO 1.01.131 P
when i am merry, and claw no man in his humor. 1.03. 18 P
i will teach you how to humor your cousin, that 2.01.380 P
brain awe a man from the career of his humor? 2.03.242 P
where is but a humor or a worm. 3.02. 27 P
i will leave you now to your gossip–like humor. 5.01.186 P
of wit–crackers cannot flout me out of my humor. 5.04.101 P
the black oppressing humor to the most wholesome LLL 1.01.233 P
my sword against the humor of affection would 1.02. 60 P
feet, humor it with turning up your eyelids, 3.01. 13 P
and, to humor the /ignorant, /call /i the deer 4.02. 51 P
his humor is lofty, his discourse peremptory, 5.01. 9 P
the rest — yet my chief humor is for a tyrant. MND 1.02. 28 P
but say it is my humor, is it answer'd? MV 4.01. 43
a spare life, look you, it fits my humor well; AYL 3.02. 20 P
my suitor from his mad humor of love to a living 3.02.418 P
mad humor of love to a living humor of madness, 3.02.419 P
for now i am in a holiday humor, and like enough 4.01. 69 P
a poor humor of mine, sir, to take that that no 5.04. 58 P
heaven cease this idle humor in your honor! SHR in.2. 13
pray you, sir, let him go while the humor lasts. 1.02.107 P
much more a shrew of /thy impatient humor. 3.02. 29
and the humor of forty fancies prick'd in't for 3.02. 68 P
'tis some odd humor pricks him to this fashion; 3.02. 72
he kills her in her own humor. 4.01.180 P
and thus i'll curb her mad and headstrong humor. 4.01.209
you either fear his humor or my negligence, that TN 1.04. 5 P
and then to have the humor of state; 2.05. 52 P
to purge him of that humor | that presses him WT 2.03. 38
frowns | more upon humor than advis'd respect. JN 4.02.214
this inundation of mistemp'red humor | rests by 5.01. 12
sort it jumps with my humor as well as waiting 1H4 1.02. 70 P
uphold | the unyok'd humor of your idleness, 1.02.196
natural scope | when you come 'cross his humor, 3.01.170
thou must not be in this humor with me, dost not 2H4 2.01.150 P
i would humor his men with the imputation of 5.01. 72 P
i have an humor to knock you indifferently well. H5 2.01. 55 P
terms, as i may, and that's the humor of it. 2.01. 59 P
or other in fair terms, that is the humor of it. 2.01. 70 P
that now i will have: that's the humor of it. 2.01. 97 P
well, then that/'s the humor of't. 2.01.116 P
i cannot kiss, that is the humor of it; 2.03. 60 P
the humor of it is too hot, that is the very 3.02. 5 P
they, knowing dame eleanor's aspiring humor, 2H6 1.02. 97
a bedlam and ambitious humor | makes him oppose 5.01.132
was ever woman in this humor woo'd? R3 1.02.227
was ever woman in this humor won? 1.02.228
hope this passionate humor of mine will change. 1.04.118 P
glory, | to feed my humor wish thyself no harm. 4.01. 64
as one being best acquainted with her humor. 4.04.269
and feed his humor kindly as we may, | till time TIT 4.03. 29
a goodly humor, is it not, my lords? 4.04. 19
yield to his humor, smooth and speak him fair, 5.02.140
weary self, | pursued my humor not pursuing his, ROM 1.01.129
black and portendous must this humor prove, 1.01.141
thy veins shall run | a cold and drowsy humor; 4.01. 96
ye have got a humor there | does not become a TIM 1.02. 26
there is no crossing him in 's humor, | else i 1.02.160
and he were cassius, | he should not humor me. JC 1.02.315
for i can give his humor the true bent, | and i 2.01.210
withal | hoping it was but an effect of humor, 2.01.250
well, | and, for thy humor, i will stay at home. 2.02. 56
i stand and crouch | under your testy humor? 4.03. 46
do what you will, dishonor shall be humor. 4.03.109
when that rash humor which my mother gave me 4.03.120
i'll know his humor, when he knows his time. 4.03.136
know him | were he in favor as in humor alter'd. OTH 3.04.125
'tis but his humor. 4.02.165
except she bend her humor, shall be assur'd | to CYM 1.05. 81
facto | the melancholy humor that infects her. TNK 5.02. 38
call, | soothing the humor of fantastic wits? VEN 850
such childish humor from weak minds proceeds; LUC 1825
and every humor hath his adjunct pleasure, SON 91. 5
than that which on thy humor doth depend. 92. 8
HUMOR'D 2 FR 0.0002 REL FR 1 V 1 P
i should have borne the humor'd letter to her; WIV 2.01.130 P
and humor'd thus, | comes at the last and with a R2 3.02.168
HUMOR–LETTER 1 FR 0.0001 REL FR 0 V 1 P
here, take the humor–letter; WIV 1.03. 78 P
HUMOROUS 12 FR 0.0013 REL FR 9 V 3 P
love's whip, | a very beadle to a humorous sigh, LLL 3.01.175
the duke is humorous — what he is indeed | more AYL 1.02.266
the bonny priser of the humorous duke? 2.03. 8
rumination wraps me in a most humorous sadness. 4.01. 19 P
fight | but when her humorous ladyship is by JN 3.01.119
welsh, | and 'tis no marvel he is so humorous. 1H4 3.01.230
as humorous as winter, and as sudden | as flaws 2H4 4.04. 34
by a vain, giddy, shallow, humorous youth, H5 2.04. 28
an observing kind | his humorous predominance; TRO 2.03.129
i am known to be a humorous patrician, and one COR 2.01. 47 P
trees | to be consorted with the humorous night. ROM 2.01. 31
the humorous man shall end his part in peace, HAM 2.02.322 P
HUMOR'S 1 FR 0.0001 REL FR 0 V 1 P
sirrah, what humor's the prince of? 2H4 2.04.236 P
/HUMORS 2 FR 0.0002 REL FR 1 V 1 P
/in /military /rules, /humors /of /blood, | /he 2H4 2.03. 30
i'll /let his /humors blood. TRO 2.03.212 P
HUMORS 34 FR 0.0038 REL FR 15 V 19 P
be avis'd, sir, and pass good humors. WIV 1.01.166 P
/in /my /head which be humors of revenge. 1.03. 90 P
with both the humors, i. 1.03. 94
he hath wrong'd me in some humors. 2.01.129 P
us not be laughing–stocks to other men's humors. 3.01. 86 P
this is fery fantastical humors and jealousies. 3.03.170 P
and, yielding to him, humors well his frenzy. ERR 4.04. 81
they say so most that most his humors know. LLL 2.01. 53
these are complements, these are humors, these 3.01. 23 P
fashioning our humors | even to the opposed end 5.02.757
let it be as humors and conceits shall govern. MV 3.05. 63 P
and the spirit of humors intimate reading aloud TN 2.05. 84 P
and all th' unsettled humors of the land, | rash JN 2.01. 66
by slaves that take their humors for a warrant 4.02.209
in humors like the people of this world: R2 5.05. 10
i am now of all humors that have show'd 1H4 2.04. 92 P
show'd themselves humors since the old days of 2.04. 93 P
dost thou converse with that trunk of humors, 2.04.449 P
for you are altogether govern'd by humors. 3.01.233 P
and 'twere not for thy humors, there's not a 2H4 2.01.148 P
these be good humors indeed! 2.04.163
the king hath run bad humors on the knight, H5 2.01.121 P
he passes some humors and careers. 2.01.126 P
for humors do abound: 3.02. 7
these be good humors! 3.02. 26 P
your honor wins bad humors. 3.02. 27 P
whose church–like humors fits not for a crown. 2H6 1.01.247
hath so crowded humors that his valor is crush'd TRO 1.02. 22 P
what e'er i forge to feed his brain–sick humors, TIT 5.02. 71
humors! ROM 2.01. 7
but a mad lord, and nought but humors sways him. TIM 3.06.112 P
to walk unbraced and suck up the humors | of the JC 2.01.262
he was born | drew all such humors from him. OTH 3.04. 31
those darker humors that | stick misbecomingly TNK 5.03. 53
/HUMPHREY 1 FR 0.0001 REL FR 1 V 0 P
how now, ambitious /humphrey, what means this? 1H6 1.03. 29
HUMPHREY 37 FR 0.0041 REL FR 36 V 1 P
humphrey, my son of gloucester, | where is the 2H4 4.04. 12
humphrey of gloucester, if thou canst accuse, 1H6 3.01. 3
humphrey of gloucester, thou shalt well perceive 5.01. 58
to you duke humphrey must unload his grief, 2H6 1.01. 76
him, | calling him "humphrey, the good duke of 1.01.159
with "god preserve the good duke humphrey!" 1.01.162
we'll quickly hoise duke humphrey from his seat. 1.01.169
despite duke humphrey or the cardinal. 1.01.179
i never saw but humphrey duke of gloucester 1.01.183
excepting none but good duke humphrey; 1.01.193
and make a show of love to proud duke humphrey, 1.01.241
and humphrey with the peers be fall'n at jars: 1.01.253
why doth the great duke humphrey knit his brows, 1.02. 3
but list to me, my humphrey, my sweet duke: 1.02. 35
till we have brought duke humphrey in disgrace. 1.03. 96
and listen after humphrey, how he proceeds. 1.03.149
duke humphrey has done a miracle to–day. 2.01.157
that virtuous prince, the good duke humphrey. 2.02. 74
ah, humphrey, this dishonor in thine age | will 2.03. 18
stay, humphrey duke of gloucester! 2.03. 22
and go in peace, humphrey, no less belov'd 2.03. 26
and humphrey duke of gloucester scarce himself, 2.03. 40
ah, humphrey, can i bear this shameful yoke? 2.04. 37
and humphrey is no little man in england. 3.01. 20
will bring to light in smooth duke humphrey. 3.01. 65
ah, uncle humphrey, in thy face i see | the map 3.01.202
and yet, good humphrey, is the hour to come 3.01.204
as place duke humphrey for the king's protector? 3.01.250
as humphrey, prov'd by reasons, to my liege. 3.01.260
but now return we to the false duke humphrey. 3.01.322
for humphrey being dead, as he shall be, | and 3.01.382
that good duke humphrey traitorously is murd'red 3.02.123
they say, by him the good duke humphrey died; 3.02.248
sir humphrey stafford and his brother are hard 4.02.113 P
sir humphrey stafford and his brother's death 4.04. 34
humphrey of buckingham, i accept thy greeting. 5.01. 15
none, but humphrey hour, that call'd your grace R3 4.04.176
HUMPHREY'S 14 FR 0.0015 REL FR 14 V 0 P
though humphrey's pride | and greatness of his 2H6 1.01.172
cherish duke humphrey's deeds | while they do 1.01.203
and her attainture will be humphrey's fall. 1.02.106
more like an empress than duke humphrey's wife. 1.03. 78
this is the law, and this duke humphrey's doom. 1.03.210
sometime i'll say, i am duke humphrey's wife, 2.04. 42
like to a duchess, and duke humphrey's lady, 2.04. 98
some violent hands were laid on humphrey's life! 3.02.138
but both of you were vowed duke humphrey's foes, 3.02.182
as guilty of duke humphrey's timeless death. 3.02.187
that i am faulty in duke humphrey's death. 3.02.202
and do some service to duke humphrey's ghost. 3.02.231
sometime he talks as if duke humphrey's ghost 3.02.373
thou that smil'dst at good duke humphrey's death 4.01. 76
HUMS* 4 FR 0.0004 REL FR 4 V 0 P
itself), these shrugs, these hums and ha's, WT 2.01. 74
the shard–borne beetle with his drowsy hums MAC 3.02. 42
and hums, as who should say, "you'll rue the 3.06. 42
he hears, and nods, and hums, | and then cries, TNK 3.05. 15
HUNC *(see hung*)*
HUNDRED *(also hundreth)*
/HUNDRED 1 FR 0.0001 REL FR 1 V 0 P
/it /is, /crack'd /in /an /hundred /shivers. R2 4.01.289
HUNDRED 116 FR 0.0131 REL FR 83 V 33 P
that i have wept a hundred several times. TGV 4.04.145
have done any time these three hundred years. WIV 1.01. 13 P
will desire, and seven hundred pounds of moneys, 1.01. 50 P
did her grandsire leave her seven hundred pound? 1.01. 58 P
seven hundred pounds, and possibilities, is goot 1.01. 64 P
together than the hundred psalms to the tune of 2.01. 63 P
among five thousand, and five hundred too. 3.03.221 P
looks handsome in three hundred pounds a year! 3.04. 33
he will make you a hundred and fifty pounds 3.04. 48 P
a hundred pound in gold more than your loss. 4.06. 5
a hundred! MM 1.02.143
hang'd for the getting a hundred bastards, 3.02.118 P
rate, | cannot amount unto a hundred marks, ERR 1.01. 24
five hundred ducats, villain, for a rope? 4.04. 13
i'll serve you, sir, five hundred at the rate. 4.04. 14
two hundred ducats. 4.04.134
my good wit out of the "hundred merry tales" — ADO 2.01.130 P
the payment of a hundred thousand crowns, LLL 2.01.129
there remains unpaid | a hundred thousand more, 2.01.134
to have repaid | a hundred thousand crowns, and 2.01.143
/on payment of a hundred thousand crowns, | to 2.01.144
of one sore i an hundred make by adding but one 4.02. 61
as it should pierce a hundred thousand hearts; MND 2.01.160
i have five hundred crowns, | the thrifty hire i AYL 2.03. 38
i will kill thee a hundred and fifty ways: 5.01. 57 P
farm | i have a hundred milch–kine to the pail, SHR 2.01.357
what if a man bring him a hundred pound or two, 5.01. 21 P
keep your hundred pounds to yourself, he shall 5.01. 23 P
a hundred marks, my kate does put her down. 5.02. 35
a hundred then. 5.02. 74
hath cost me /a hundred crowns since supper–time 5.02.128
more, more, a hundred of them. AWW 2.02. 42 P
spurio, a hundred and fifty; 4.03.161 P
lodowick, and gratii, two hundred fifty each; 4.03.164 P
vaumond, bentii, two hundred fifty each; 4.03.165 P
fifteen hundred shorn, what comes the wool to? WT 4.03. 33 P
at least from fair five hundred pound a year. JN 1.01. 69
a half–fac'd groat five hundred pound a year! 1.01. 94
your face hath got five hundred pound a year, 1.01.152
mann'd with three hundred men, as i have heard, R2 2.03. 54
refuse | the offer of an hundred thousand crowns 4.01. 16
which fourteen hundred years ago were nail'd 1H4 1.01. 26
hath brought three hundred marks with him in 2.01. 55 P
a hundred upon poor four of us. 2.04.161 P
what, a hundred, man? 2.04.163 P
have in this robbery lost three hundred marks. 2.04.520
and i will die a hundred thousand deaths | ere 3.02.158
a hundred thousand rebels die in this. 3.02.160
in exchange of a hundred and fifty soldiers, 4.02. 13 P
fifty soldiers, three hundred and odd pounds. 4.02. 14 P
think that i had a hundred and fifty totter'd 4.02. 34 P
not three of my hundred and fifty left alive, 5.03. 37 P
a hundred mark is a long one for a poor lone 2H4 2.01. 32 P
no, fifteen hundred foot, five hundred horse, 2.01.173
no, fifteen hundred foot, five hundred horse, 2.01.173
john, let me have five hundred of my thousand. 5.05. 83 P
full fifteen earls and fifteen hundred knights, H5 1.01. 13
six thousand and two hundred good esquires; 1.01. 14
a hundred almshouses right well supplied; 1.01. 17
land | until four hundred one and twenty years 1.02. 57
of our redemption | four hundred twenty–six; 1.02. 61
river sala, in the year | eight hundred five. 1.02. 64
lie within fifteen hundred paces of your tents. 3.07.126 P
ten | we shall have each a hundred englishmen. 3.07.157
five hundred poor i have in yearly pay, | who 4.01.298
his ransom he will give you two hundred crowns. 4.04. 46 P
full fifteen hundred, besides common men. 4.08. 79
there lie dead | one hundred twenty–six; 4.08. 83
gentlemen, | eight thousand and four hundred; 4.08. 85
five hundred were but yesterday dubb'd knights. 4.08. 86
there are but sixteen hundred mercenaries; 4.08. 88
beside five hundred prisoners of esteem, | lets 1H6 3.04. 8
in which assault we lost twelve hundred men; 4.01. 24
being call'd | a hundred times and oft'ner, in 2H6 2.01. 88
loather a hundred times to part than die. 3.02.355
a license to kill for a hundred lacking one. 4.03. 7 P
the fift hales them to an hundred mischiefs, and 4.08. 57 P
ay, with five hundred, father, for a need. 3H6 1.02. 67
for i have bought it with an hundred blows. 2.05. 81
give her an hundred marks. i'll to the queen. H8 5.01.170
an hundred marks? 5.01.171
lend you him i will | for half a hundred years. COR 1.04. 7
a hundred thousand welcomes! 2.01.183
i'll have five hundred voices of that sound. 2.03.211
i twice five hundred, and their friends to piece 2.03.212
my grained ash an hundred times hath broke, 4.05.108
my ears have yet not drunk a hundred words | of ROM 2.02. 58
with twenty hundred thousand times more joy 3.03.153
where for this many hundred years the bones | of 4.03. 40
he cannot want fifty — five hundred talents. TIM 3.02. 38
within this mile break forth a hundred springs; 4.03.418
drawn | upon a heap a hundred ghastly women, JC 1.03. 23
which, like a fountain with an hundred spouts, 2.02. 77
lepidus | have put to death an hundred senators. 4.03.175
a hundred ducats a–piece for his picture in HAM 2.02.366 P
with reservation of an hundred knights | by you LR 1.01.133

here do you keep a hundred knights and squires, 1.04.241
man hath had good counsel — a hundred knights! 1.04.322
to let him keep | at point a hundred knights; 1.04.324
if she sustain him and his hundred knights, 1.04.332
can stay with regan, | i and my hundred knights. 2.04.231
shall break into a hundred thousand flaws | or 2.04.285
you, sir, i entertain for one of my hundred; 3.06. 79 P
my letters say a hundred and seven galleys. OTH 1.03. 3
and mine, a hundred forty. 1.03. 4
and mine, two hundred! 1.03. 4
my wayward husband hath a hundred times | woo'd 3.03.292
world | the sun to course two hundred compasses, 3.04. 71
i had a hundred pound on't; CYM 2.01. 3 P
in't will | take hostage of thee for a hundred, TNK 1.01.184
a hundred black–ey'd maids that love as i do, 4.01. 72
is at least two hundred now with child by him — 4.01.129
some two hundred bottles, | and twenty strike of 5.02. 64
a hundred times. 5.02.109
what is ten hundred touches unto thee? VEN 519
is twenty hundred kisses such a trouble?" 522
HUNDRED–POUND 1 FR 0.0001 REL FR 0 V 1 P
beggarly, three–suited, hundred–pound, filthy LR 2.02. 16 P
HUNDREDS 4 FR 0.0004 REL FR 3 V 1 P
with many hundreds treading on his heels; JN 4.02.149
as they buy hobnails, by the hundreds. 1H4 2.04.363 P
hundreds he sent to hell, and none durst stand 1H6 1.01.123
and hundreds call themselves | your creatures, PER 3.02. 44
HUNDRETH *(also hundred)*
HUNDRETH 3 FR 0.0003 REL FR 3 V 0 P
this monument five hundreth years hath stood, TIT 1.01.350
one with moderate haste might tell a hundreth. HAM 1.02.237
even of five hundreth courses of the sun, | show SON 59. 6
/HUNG* 2 FR 0.0002 REL FR 1 V 1 P
accusativo, /hung, hang, hog. WIV 4.01. 47 P
(/his /own /life /hung /upon /the /staff /he 2H4 4.01.124
HUNG* 26 FR 0.0029 REL FR 21 V 5 P
the cudgel hallow'd and hung o'er the altar; WIV 4.02.204 P
hung by th' wall | so long that nineteen zodiacs MM 1.02.167
so hung upon with love, so fortunate | (but MND 3.02.233
and their heads are hung | with ears that sweep 4.01.120
she hung about my neck, and kiss on kiss | she SHR 2.01.308
which hung so tott'ring in the balance that i AWW 1.03.124 P
hung on our driving boat, i saw your brother, TN 1.02. 11
i would have fil'd keys off that hung in chains. WT 4.04.612 P
but rather drows'd and hung their eyelids down, 1H4 3.02. 81
hung be the heavens with black, yield day to 1H6 1.01. 1
and hung their rotten coffins up in chains, | it 3H6 1.03. 28
our bruised arms hung up for monuments, | our R3 1.01. 6
never hung poison on a fouler toad. 1.02.147
a jewel, has hung twenty years | about his neck, H8 2.02. 31
of the sea, | hung their heads, and then lay by. 3.01. 11
when thou hast hung /thy advanced sword i' th' TRO 4.05.188
and in his needy shop a tortoise hung, | an ROM 5.01. 42
sweet instruments hung up in cases that keeps TIM 1.02. 99 P
let no images | be hung with caesar's trophies. JC 1.01. 69
their bloody sign of battle is hung out, | and 5.01. 14
here hung those lips that i have kiss'd i know HAM 5.01.188 P
hung with the painted favors of their ladies, TNK 2.02. 11
his thigh a sword | hung by a curious baldrick, 4.02. 86
"over my altars hath he hung his lance, | his VEN 103
which, like a jewel hung in ghastly night, SON 27.11
hung with the trophies of my lovers gone, | who 31.10
HUNGARIAN 1 FR 0.0001 REL FR 0 V 1 P
o base hungarian wight! WIV 1.03. 20 P
HUNGARY 1 FR 0.0001 REL FR 0 V 1 P
not to composition with the king of hungary, why MM 1.02. 2 P
HUNGARY'S 1 FR 0.0001 REL FR 0 V 1 P
us its peace, but not the king of hungary's! MM 1.02. 5 P
HUNGER 17 FR 0.0019 REL FR 15 V 2 P
anger, with sickness, or with hunger, my lord, ADO 1.01.249 P
oppress'd with two weak evils, age and hunger, AYL 2.07.132
he roar'd | with sharp constraint of hunger; AWW 3.02.118
dost thou so hunger for mine empty chair | that 2H4 4.05. 94
and hunger will enforce them to be more eager. 1H6 1.02. 38
compell'd by hunger | and lack of other means, H8 1.02. 34
the gods know i speak this in hunger for bread, COR 1.01. 24 P
that hunger broke stone walls, that dogs must 1.01.206
if thy revenges hunger for that food | which TIM 5.04. 32
would be as a sauce | to make me hunger more, MAC 4.03. 82
more fell than anguish, hunger, or the sea! OTH 5.02.362
and it gave me present hunger | to feed again, CYM 2.04.137
to whom being going, almost spent with hunger, 3.06. 62
it, | or can conceal his hunger till he famish? PER 1.04. 12
give them life whom hunger starv'd half dead. 1.04. 96
your hunger needs no sauce, i see. TNK 3.03. 25
prey, | sharp hunger by the conquest satisfied, LUC 422
HUNGERFORD 2 FR 0.0002 REL FR 2 V 0 P
and lord scales with him, and lord hungerford. 1H6 1.01.146
to have the heir of the lord hungerford. 3H6 4.01. 48
HUNGERLY 3 FR 0.0003 REL FR 3 V 0 P
but that his beard grew thin and hungerly, | and SHR 3.02.175
and i feed | most hungerly on your sight. TIM 1.01.253
they eat us hungerly, and when they are full OTH 3.04.105
HUNGER'S 2 FR 0.0002 REL FR 2 V 0 P
now i think on thee, | my hunger's gone; CYM 3.06. 16
so sharp are hunger's teeth, that man and wife PER 1.04. 45
HUNGER–STARVED 1 FR 0.0001 REL FR 1 V 0 P
or lambs pursu'd by hunger–starved wolves. 3H6 1.04. 5
HUNGRY 25 FR 0.0028 REL FR 22 V 3 P
had i been seized by a hungry lion, | i would TGV 5.04. 33
brought one pinch, a hungry lean–fac'd villain, ERR 5.01.238
now the hungry /lion roars, | and the wolf MND 5.01.371
there, | food to the suck'd and hungry lioness? AYL 4.03.126
revolt, | but mine is all as hungry as the sea, TN 2.04.100
they are never curst but when they are hungry. WT 3.03.131 P
of peace | must by the hungry now be fed upon. JN 3.03. 10
or cloy the hungry edge of appetite | by bare R2 1.03.296
on the poor souls for whom this hungry war H5 2.04.104
food, | do rush upon us as their hungry prey. 1H6 1.02. 28
and like a hungry lion did commence | rough 4.07. 7
set | to guard the chicken from a hungry kite, 2H6 3.01.249
but now am i so hungry that, if i might have a 4.10. 5 P
that face of his the hungry cannibals | would 3H6 1.04.152
i am hungry for revenge, | and now i cloy me R3 4.04. 61
as the hungry plebeians would the noble martius. COR 2.01. 9 P
then let the pibbles on the hungry beach 5.03. 58
and strew this hungry churchyard with thy limbs. ROM 5.03. 36
sick of man's unkindness | should yet be hungry! TIM 4.03.177
yond cassius has a lean and hungry look, | he JC 1.02.194
but she makes hungry | where most she satisfies; ANT 2.02.236
the ears she feeds, and makes them hungry, | the PER 5.01.112
i am very hungry: TNK 3.04. 11
fill | thy hungry eyes even till they wink with SON 56. 6
when i have seen the hungry ocean gain 64. 5
HUNGRY–STARVED 1 FR 0.0001 REL FR 1 V 0 P
go, go, cheer up thy hungry–starved men; 1H6 1.05. 16
HUNT 35 FR 0.0039 REL FR 32 V 3 P
let fame, that all hunt after in their lives, LLL 1.01. 1
the princess comes to hunt here in the park, 3.01.164
her love is not the hare that i do hunt; AYL 4.03. 18
them all, | to–morrow i intend to hunt again. SHR in.1. 29
or wilt thou hunt? in.2. 44
will you go hunt, my lord? TN 1.01. 16
nineteen and two–and–twenty hunt this weather? WT 3.03. 65 P
you hunt counter, hence, avaunt! 2H4 1.02. 90 P
i think he's gone to hunt, my lord, at windsor. 4.04. 14
for i myself must hunt this deer to death. 2H6 5.02. 15
for i myself will hunt this wolf to death. 3H6 2.04. 13
which we more hunt for than the grace of god! R3 3.04. 97
a hell–hound that doth hunt us all to death: 4.04. 48
and thou shalt hunt a lion that will fly | with TRO 4.01. 20
why then fly on, i'll hunt thee for thy hide. 5.06. 31
he is a lion | that i am proud to hunt. COR 1.01.236
do not cry havoc where you should but hunt 3.01.273
to hunt the panther and the hart with me, | with TIT 1.01.493
the hunt is up, the /morn is bright and grey, 2.02. 1
chiron, we hunt not, we, with horse nor hound, 2.02. 25
horns, | as if a double hunt were heard at once, 2.03. 19
ay, such a place there is where we did hunt | (o 4.01. 55
but if you hunt these bear–whelps, then beware, 4.01. 96
your company to–morrow to hunt with him, and has TIM 1.02.188 P
i'll hunt with him, and let them be receiv'd, 1.02.190
the happy hollow of a tree | escap'd the hunt. LR 2.03. 3
and his spirits should hunt | after new fancies. OTH 3.04. 62
boys, we'll go dress our hunt. CYM 3.06. 89
at court that such as we | cave here, hunt here, 4.02.138
i had no mind | to hunt this day; 4.02.148
we'll hunt no more to–day, nor seek for danger 4.02.162
to hunt the boar with certain of his friends. VEN 588
that thou toldst me thou wouldst hunt the boar. 614
"but if thou needs wilt hunt, be rul'd by me, 673
"why hunt i then for color or excuses? LUC 267
HUNTED 7 FR 0.0008 REL FR 6 V 1 P
let them be hunted soundly. TMP 4.01.262
'tis well, sir, that you hunted for yourself; SHR 5.02. 55
hunt | (o, had we never, never hunted there!), TIT 4.01. 56
lucullus you — i hunted with his honor to–day; TIM 2.02.189 P
begins to rage, he's hunted | even to falling. ANT 4.01. 7
and with that word she spied the hunted boar, VEN 900
past reason hunted, and no sooner had, | past SON 129. 6
HUNTER 9 FR 0.0010 REL FR 6 V 3 P
there is an old tale goes, that herne the hunter WIV 4.04. 28
age | this tale of herne the hunter for a truth. 4.04. 38
speak i like herne the hunter? 5.05. 28 P
round about the oak | of herne the hunter, let 5.05. 76
will none but herne the hunter serve your turn? 5.05.104
he was furnish'd like a hunter. AYL 3.02.245 P
full of despite, bloody as the hunter, attends TN 3.04.223 P
i'll play the hunter for thy life | with all my TRO 4.01. 18
the house–keeper, the hunter, every one, MAC 3.01. 96
HUNTER'S 3 FR 0.0003 REL FR 3 V 0 P
that from the hunter's aim had ta'en a hurt, AYL 2.01. 34
and rouse the prince, and ring a hunter's peal, TIT 2.02. 5
i promised your grace a hunter's peal. 2.02. 13
HUNTERS' 1 FR 0.0001 REL FR 1 V 0 P
this is not hunters' language. CYM 3.03. 74
HUNTERS 2 FR 0.0002 REL FR 2 V 0 P
didst thou fall, and here thy hunters stand, JC 3.01.205
grin like lions | upon the pikes o' th' hunters. CYM 5.03. 39
HUNTETH 1 FR 0.0001 REL FR 1 V 0 P
and when it hath the thing it hunteth most, LLL 1.01.145
HUNTING 17 FR 0.0019 REL FR 15 V 2 P
the king he is hunting the deer: LLL 4.03. 1 P
worn, | our purpos'd hunting shall be set aside. MND 4.01.183
prodigal, or the german hunting in waterwork, is 2H4 2.01.145 P
the beast liv'd, was kill'd with hunting him. H5 4.03. 94
/comes hunting this way to disport himself. 3H6 4.05. 8
for hunting was his daily exercise. 4.06. 85
my lords, a solemn hunting is in hand, | there TIT 2.01.112
madam, now shall ye see | our roman hunting. 2.02. 20
to see the general hunting in this forest? 2.03. 59
hunting thee hence with hunt's–up to the day. ROM 3.05. 34
be round with him, now he comes from hunting. TIM 2.02. 8
when he returns from hunting, | i will not speak LR 1.03. 7
whom i trace | for his quick hunting, stand the OTH 2.01.304
in the cave, | we'll come to you after hunting. CYM 4.02. 2
go you to hunting, i'll abide with him. 4.02. 6
hunting he lov'd, but love he laugh'd to scorn. VEN 4
to make thee hate the hunting of the boar, 711
HUNTINGTON 1 FR 0.0001 REL FR 1 V 0 P
warwick, and huntington, go with the king, | and H5 5.02. 85
HUNTRESS' 1 FR 0.0001 REL FR 1 V 0 P
thy huntress' name that my full life doth sway. AYL 3.02. 4
HUNTRESS 1 FR 0.0001 REL FR 1 V 0 P
the huntress | all moist and cold, some say, TNK 5.01. 92
HUNTS 3 FR 0.0003 REL FR 2 V 1 P
he after honor hunts, i after love: TGV 1.01. 63
of mine | hunts not the trail of policy so sure HAM 2.02. 47
not like a hound that hunts, but one that fills OTH 2.03.364 P
HUNTSMAN 7 FR 0.0008 REL FR 7 V 0 P
huntsman, i charge thee, tender well my hounds SHR in.1. 16
huntsman, what say'st thou? wilt thou go along? 3H6 4.05. 25
upon the daring huntsman that has gall'd him; H8 3.02.207
sweet huntsman — bassianus 'tis we mean — | do TIT 2.03.269
look, sirs, if you can find the huntsman out, 2.03.278
you are a young huntsman, marcus, let alone; 4.01.101
this, far off, she hears some huntsman hallow; VEN 973
HUNTSMEN 4 FR 0.0004 REL FR 4 V 0 P
go, bid the huntsmen wake them with their horns. MND 4.01.138
and like a jolly troop of huntsmen come | our JN 2.01.321
this way, man, see where the huntsmen stand. 3H6 4.05. 15
and from the bishop's huntsmen rescu'd him; 4.06. 84
HUNT'ST 1 FR 0.0001 REL FR 1 V 0 P
may the stag thou hunt'st stand long, | and thy TNK 3.05.154
HUNT'S–UP 1 FR 0.0001 REL FR 1 V 0 P
hunting thee hence with hunt's–up to the day. ROM 3.05. 34
HURDLE 1 FR 0.0001 REL FR 1 V 0 P
or i will drag thee on a hurdle thither. ROM 3.05.155
HURL 10 FR 0.0011 REL FR 10 V 0 P
me, | and hurl the name of husband in my face, ERR 2.02.135
and interchangeably hurl down my gage | upon R2 1.01.146
ground | to hurl at the beholders of my shame. 1H6 1.04. 46
and then hurl down their indignation | on thee, R3 1.03.219
to hurl upon their heads that break his law. 1.04.200
and that same vengeance doth he hurl on thee 1.04.201
will hand in hand all headlong hurl ourselves, TIT 5.03.132
defiance, traitors, hurl we in your teeth. JC 5.01. 64
look of thine will hurl my soul from heaven, OTH 5.02.274
what our contempts doth often hurl from us, | we ANT 1.02.123
HURL'D 2 FR 0.0002 REL FR 2 V 0 P
at lower end of the hall, hurl'd up their caps, R3 3.07. 35
one heav'd a–high, to be hurl'd down below; 4.04. 86
HURLING 1 FR 0.0001 REL FR 0 V 1 P
i can hardly forbear hurling things at him. TN 3.02. 81 P
HURLS 1 FR 0.0001 REL FR 1 V 0 P
wind | upon his lips their silken parcels hurls. LC 87
HURLY 4 FR 0.0004 REL FR 4 V 0 P
and amid this hurly i intend | that all is done SHR 4.01.203
methinks i see this hurly all on foot; JN 3.04.169
that, with the hurly, death itself awakes? 2H4 3.01. 25
why even your hurly | cannot proceed but by STM II.C 113
HURLY–BURLY 1 FR 0.0001 REL FR 1 V 0 P
elbow at the news | of hurly–burly innovation; 1H4 5.01. 78
HURLY–BURLY'S 1 FR 0.0001 REL FR 1 V 0 P
when the hurly–burly's done, | when the battle's MAC 1.01. 3
HURRICANO 1 FR 0.0001 REL FR 1 V 0 P
spout | which shipmen do the hurricano call, TRO 5.02.172
HURRICANOES 1 FR 0.0001 REL FR 1 V 0 P
you cataracts and hurricanoes, spout | till you LR 3.02. 2
HURRIED 5 FR 0.0005 REL FR 5 V 0 P
the ministers for th' purpose hurried thence TMP 1.02.131
in few, they hurried us aboard a bark, | bore us 1.02.144
that desp'rately he hurried through the street ERR 5.01.140
lastly, hurried | here to this place, i' th' WT 3.02.104
ne'er through an arch so hurried the blown tide, COR 5.04. 47
HURRIES 3 FR 0.0003 REL FR 3 V 0 P
and wild amazement hurries up and down | the JN 5.01. 35
each hurries toward his home and sporting–place. 2H4 4.02.105
which madly hurries her she knows not whither: VEN 904
HURRY 4 FR 0.0004 REL FR 3 V 1 P
lives, honors, lands, and all, hurry to loss. 1H6 4.03. 53
the people, which before | were in wild hurry. COR 4.06. 4
fir'd | doth hurry from the fatal cannon's womb. ROM 5.01. 65
so soon as the court hurry is over, we will have TNK 2.01. 18 P
/HURT 1 FR 0.0001 REL FR 1 V 0 P
not count it holy | /to /hurt /by /being /just; TRO 5.03. 20
HURT 100 FR 0.0113 REL FR 67 V 33 P
thou dost me yet but little hurt; TMP 2.02. 79 P
and sweet airs, that give delight and hurt not. 3.02.136
if you could hurt, | your swords are now too 3.03. 66
hold, hurt him not for god sake! ERR 5.01. 33
alas, poor hurt fowl! ADO 2.01.202 P
how they might hurt their enemies — if they 5.01. 98
their blades, which, god be thank'd, hurt not. 5.01.188 P
as the fencer's foils, which hit, but hurt not. 5.02. 14 P
manly wit, margaret, it will not hurt a woman. 5.02. 16 P
should i hurt her, strike her, kill her dead? MND 3.02.269
you mock me, /gentlemen, | let her not hurt me. 3.02.300
with the same food, hurt with the same weapons, MV 3.01. 61 P
that from the hunter's aim had ta'en a hurt, AYL 2.01. 34
which i have darted at thee, hurt thee not, 3.05. 25
there is no force in eyes | that can do hurt. 3.05. 27
be at woman's command, and yet no hurt done! AWW 1.03. 93 P
honesty be no puritan, yet it will do no hurt; 1.03. 94 P
what i can do can do no hurt to try, | since you 2.01.134
perchance he's hurt i' th' battle. 3.05. 87 P
to fight with him, hurt him in eleven places — TN 3.02. 35 P
he protests he will not hurt you. 3.04.301 P
a gentleman and a soldier, he will not hurt you. 3.04.309 P
i never hurt you. 5.01.187
but i bespake you fair, and hurt you not. 5.01.189
if a bloody coxcomb be a hurt, you have hurt me. 5.01.190 P
if a bloody coxcomb be a hurt, you have hurt me. 5.01.191 P
h'as hurt me, and there's th' end on't. 5.01.196 P
get him to bed, and let his hurt be look'd to. 5.01.208 P
i am sorry, madam, i have hurt your kinsman, 5.01.209
good ground, be pitiful and hurt me not! JN 4.03. 2
'tis true — to hurt his master, no /man else. 4.03. 33
worse than a struck fowl or a hurt wild duck. 1H4 4.02. 20 P
it never yet did hurt | to lay down likelihoods 2H4 1.03. 34
are you not hurt i' th' groin? 2.04.210 P
you have hurt him, sir, i' th' shoulder. 2.04.213 P
any hurt in the world, but keeps the bridge most H5 3.06. 10 P
bleed, | opinion shall be surgeon to my hurt, 1H6 2.04. 53
strike those that hurt, and hurt not those that 3.03. 53
those that hurt, and hurt not those that help. 3.03. 53
for though they cannot greatly sting to hurt, 3H6 2.06. 94
by living low, where fortune cannot hurt me, 4.06. 20
he | must help you more than you are hurt by me. 4.06. 76
how you may hurt yourself — ay, utterly | grow H8 3.01.160
that paris is returned home and hurt. TRO 1.01.109
who said he came hurt home to–day? 1.02.215 P
he's not hurt. 1.02.215 P
i doubt he be hurt. 1.02.276 P
is slain, | amphimachus and thoas deadly hurt, 5.05. 12
or slain, and palamedes | sore hurt and bruised. 5.05. 14
all hurt behind! COR 1.04. 37
you sooth'd not, therefore hurt not; 2.02. 73
let me but stand, i will not hurt your hearth. 4.05. 24 P
to all the volsces, | great hurt and mischief; 4.05. 67
brother, hast thou hurt thee with the fall? TIT 2.03.203
with the dismall'st object hurt | that ever eye 2.03.204
hath hurt me more than had he kill'd me dead: 3.01. 92
who, nothing hurt withal, hiss'd him in scorn. ROM 1.01.112
i am hurt. 3.01. 90
what, art thou hurt? 3.01. 92
courage, man, the hurt cannot be much. 3.01. 95
i was hurt under your arm. 3.01.103 P
hath got this mortal hurt | in my behalf; 3.01.110
balm of hurt minds, great nature's second course MAC 2.02. 36

my arrow o'er the house | and hurt my brother. HAM 5.02.244
o, yet defend me, friends, i am but hurt. 5.02.324
and receiv'd | this hurt you see, striving to LR 2.01.108
leave to ponder | on things would hurt me more. 3.04. 25
i have receiv'd a hurt; 3.07. 95
i bleed apace, | untimely comes this hurt. 3.07. 98
thee they may hurt. 4.01. 17
i bleed still, | i am hurt to th' death. OTH 2.03.165
worthy othello, i am hurt to danger. 2.03.197
what, are you hurt, lieutenant? 2.03.259 P
thou by that small hurt /hast cashier'd cassio. 2.03.375
that he you hurt is of great fame in cyprus, 3.01. 45
have you not hurt your head? 4.01. 59
i cry you mercy. here's cassio hurt by villains. 5.01. 69
that pow'r to do me harm | as i have to be hurt. 5.02.163
spake | (after long seeming dead) iago hurt him, 5.02.328
i will not hurt him. ANT 2.05. 81
have i hurt him? CYM 1.02. 6 P
hurt him? 1.02. 9 P
body's a passable carcass, if he be not hurt; 1.02. 10 P
is a throughfare for steel, if it be not hurt. 1.02. 11 P
upon fools, lest the reflection should hurt her. 1.02. 33 P
would there had been some hurt done! 1.02. 35 P
been the fall of an ass, which is no great hurt. 1.02. 37 P
pass was damm'd | with dead men hurt behind, and 5.03. 12
see clear | to stop the air would hurt them. PER 1.01.100
my troth, | i never did her hurt in all my life. 4.01. 74
law, | i never kill'd a mouse, nor hurt a fly; 4.01. 77
when you caught hurt in parting two that fought; 4.01. 87
may rude wind never hurt thee! TNK 2.02.275
i would have nothing hurt thee but my sword, | a 3.06. 87
but you shall not hurt me. 5.02.111
i might do hurt, for they would glance their 5.03. 61
"you hurt my hand with wringing, let us part, VEN 421
to mend the hurt that his unkindness marr'd: 478
upon his hurt she looks so steadfastly, | that 1063
they that have pow'r to hurt and will do none, SON 94. 1
HURTING 1 FR 0.0001 REL FR 1 V 0 P
which she made more sound | by hurting it; PER 4.ch. 25
HURTLED 1 FR 0.0001 REL FR 1 V 0 P
the noise of battle hurtled in the air; JC 2.02. 22
HURTLESS 1 FR 0.0001 REL FR 1 V 0 P
and the strong lance of justice hurtless breaks; LR 4.06.166
HURTLING 1 FR 0.0001 REL FR 1 V 0 P
in which hurtling | from miserable slumber i AYL 4.03.131
HURTS 16 FR 0.0018 REL FR 11 V 5 P
this nor hurts him, nor profits you a jot. MM 4.03.123
"just," said she, "it hurts nobody." ADO 5.01.164 P
for it hurts not him | that he is lov'd of me. AWW 1.03.196
i must give myself some hurts, and say i got 4.01. 37 P
the repulse of tarquin seven hurts i' th' body. COR 2.01.150 P
interest — i myself | rich only in large hurts. TIM 3.05.108
had he his hurts before? MAC 5.09. 12
a spendthrift's sigh, | that hurts by easing. HAM 4.07.123
wheat, and hurts the poor creature of earth. LR 3.04.119 P
sir, for your hurts, | myself will be your OTH 2.03.253
i strike it, and it hurts my hand. 4.01.183 P
a lover's pinch, | which hurts, and is desir'd. ANT 5.02.296
since doubting things go ill often hurts more CYM 1.06. 95
to him, | store never hurts good governors. TNK 1.03. 6
been taken | when their last hurts were given, 1.04. 26
the hand of war hurts none here, nor the seas 2.02. 87
HUSBAND 305 FR 0.0344 REL FR 225 V 80 P
my husband then? TMP 3.01. 87
voyage | did claribel her husband find at tunis, 5.01.209
o that my husband saw this letter! WIV 2.01.100 P
to notify that her husband will be absence from 2.02. 83 P
master ford her husband will be from home. 2.02. 88 P
worship that her husband is seldom from home, 2.02.101 P
her husband has a marvellous infection to the 2.02.114 P
rascally knave her husband will be forth. 2.02.265 P
the dickens his name is my husband had him of. 3.02. 20 P
i would thy husband were dead. 3.03. 50 P
having an honest man to your husband, to give 3.03.100 P
pleases me better, that my husband is deceiv'd, 3.03.179 P
was he in when your husband ask'd who was in the 3.03.181 P
i think my husband hath some special suspicion 3.03.187 P
i mean it not, i seek you a better husband. 3.04. 84
her husband goes this morning a–birding; 3.05. 44 P
but the peaking cornuto her husband, master 3.05. 71 P
her husband is this morning gone a–birding. 3.05.128 P
my husband says my son profits nothing in the 4.01. 14 P
but are you sure of your husband now? 4.02. 6 P
woman, your husband is in his old lines again. 4.02. 21 P
he so takes on yonder with my husband; 4.02. 23 P
protests to my husband he is now here, and hath 4.02. 33 P
i would my husband would meet him in this shape. 4.02. 84 P
but is my husband coming? 4.02. 90 P
that hath the jealious fool to her husband! 4.02.131 P
my husband will come into the chamber. 4.02.167 P
nay, good, sweet husband! 4.02.180 P
and he my husband best of all affects. 4.04. 87
well, husband your device; 4.06. 52
that same knave ford, her husband, hath the 5.01. 18 P
my husband will not rejoice so much at the abuse 5.03. 7 P
see you these, husband? 5.05.107
good husband, let us every one go home, | and 5.05.241
hath she had any more than one husband? MM 2.01.201 P
you will turn good husband now, pompey, you will 3.02. 70 P
he is your husband on a pre–contract: 4.01. 71
will not show my face | until my husband bid me. 5.01.170
i have known my husband, yet my husband | knows 5.01.186
yet my husband | knows not that ever he knew me. 5.01.186
in self–same manner doth accuse my husband, 5.01.196
no? you say your husband. 5.01.201
my husband bids me, now i will unmask. 5.01.206
i hope you will not mock me with a husband! 5.01.417
it is your husband mock'd you with a husband. 5.01.418
it is your husband mock'd you with a husband. 5.01.418
you with all, | to buy you a better husband. 5.01.425
so may my husband. 5.01.441
neither my husband nor the slave return'd, ERR 2.01. 1
how if your husband start some other where? 2.01. 30
here comes your man, now is your husband nigh. 2.01. 43
how comes it now, my husband, o, how comes it, 2.02.119
me, | and hurl the name of husband in my face, 2.02.135
thou art an elm, my husband, i a vine, | whose 2.02.174
husband, i'll dine above with you to–day, | and 2.02.207
thou hast no husband yet, nor i no wife. 3.02. 68
she that doth call me husband, even my soul 3.02.158
where dowsabel did claim me for her husband: 4.01.110
how say you now? is not your husband mad? 4.04. 45
o husband, god doth know you din'd at home, 4.04. 65
i did not, gentle husband, lock thee forth. 4.04. 97
due for a chain your husband had of him. 4.04.135
when as your husband all in rage to–day | came 4.04.137
to fetch my poor distracted husband hence. 5.01. 39
hath scar'd thy husband from the use of wits. 5.01. 86
then let your servants bring my husband forth. 5.01. 93
i will attend my husband, be his nurse, | diet 5.01. 98
i will not hence, and leave my husband here; 5.01.109
holiness | to separate the husband and the wife. 5.01.111
and take perforce my husband from the abbess. 5.01.117
it please your grace, antipholus, my husband, 5.01.136
long since thy husband serv'd me in my wars, 5.01.161
ay me, it is my husband! 5.01.186
his bonds, | and gain a husband by his liberty. 5.01.341
and are not you my husband? 5.01.371
the duke, my husband, and my children both, 5.01.404
but i hope you have no intent to turn husband, ADO 1.01.193 P
thou wilt never get thee a husband, if thou be 2.01. 19 P
just, if he send me no husband, for the which 2.01. 27 P
i could not endure a husband with a beard on his 2.01. 30 P
you may light on a husband that hath no beard. 2.01. 32 P
i hope to see you one day fitted with a husband. 2.01. 58 P
in a corner and cry "heigh–ho for a husband!" 2.01.320 P
she cannot endure to hear tell of a husband. 2.01.348 P
my lord, to help my cousin to a good husband. 2.01.376 P
is not the unhopefullest husband that i know. 2.01.378 P
and send her home again without a husband. 3.03.163 P
have me say, "saving your reverence, a husband." 3.04. 33 P
there any harm in "the heavier for a husband"? 3.04. 35 P
and it be the right husband and the right wife; 3.04. 36 P
then, if your husband have stables enough, 3.04. 48 P
for a hawk, a horse, or a husband? 3.04. 55 P
for you to give your daughter to her husband. 3.05. 55 P
you will say, she did embrace me as a husband, 4.01. 49
friar — | i am your husband if you like of me. 5.04. 59
and when you lov'd, you were my other husband. 5.04. 61
is not in the fashion to choose me a husband. MV 1.02. 22 P
she wept for the death of a third husband. 3.01. 10 P
how dear a lover of my lord your husband, | i 3.04. 7
here, | until her husband and my lord's return. 3.04. 30
i shall be sav'd by my husband, he hath made me 3.05. 19 P
i'll tell my husband, launcelot, what you say. 3.05. 27 P
even such a husband | hast thou of me as she is 3.05. 83
had been her husband rather than a christian! 4.01.297
your husband is at hand, i hear his trumpet. 5.01.122
for a light wife doth make a heavy husband, 5.01.130
but i do take thee, orlando, for my husband. AYL 4.01.139 P
i'll have no husband, if you be not he; 5.04.123
i long to hear him call the drunkard husband, SHR in.1. 133
are you my wife and will not call me husband? in.2. 104
my husband and my lord, my lord and husband, | i in.2. 106
my husband and my lord, my lord and husband, | i in.2. 106
before i have a husband for the elder. 1.01. 51
marry, sir, to get a husband for her sister. 1.01.120 P
a husband! a devil. 1.01.121 P
i say, a husband. 1.01.122 P
eldest daughter to a husband we set his youngest 1.01.138 P
husband we set his youngest free for a husband, 1.01.138 P
till katherine the curst have got a husband. 1.02.128
she is your treasure, she must have a husband; 2.01. 32
now, kate, i am a husband for your turn, | for 2.01.272
i pray you, husband, be not so disquiet. 4.01.168
while i play the good husband at home, my son 5.01. 69 P
husband, let's follow, to see the end of this 5.01.142
your husband, being troubled with a shrew, 5.02. 28
thy husband is thy lord, thy life, thy keeper, 5.02.146
even such a woman oweth to her husband; 5.02.156
my son from me, i bury a second husband. AWW 1.01. 2 P
you shall find of the king a husband, madam; 1.01. 6 P
get thee a good husband, and use him as he uses 1.01.214 P
hand | what husband in thy power i will command. 2.01.194
body that i am father to, then call me husband; 3.02. 60 P
what angel shall | bless this unworthy husband? 3.04. 26
rinaldo, | to this unworthy husband of his wife. 3.04. 30
give me trust, the count he is my husband, | and 3.07. 8
my husband hies him home, where, heaven aiding, 4.04. 12
her to be my motive | and helper to a husband. 4.04. 21
for my daughter, you are no husband for her. 5.03.177 P
(since you lack virtue, i will lose a husband) 5.03.222
choose thou thy husband, and i'll pay thy dower, 5.03.328
whither, my lord? cesario, husband, stay. TN 5.01.143
husband? 5.01.144
ay, husband. can he that deny? 5.01.144
her husband, sirrah? 5.01.145
the one for ever earn'd a royal husband; WT 1.02.107
boldness of a wife | to her allowing husband! 1.02.185
tongue, who late hath beat her husband, | and 2.03. 92
our sovereign lord the king, thy royal husband: 3.02. 17 P
one eye declin'd for the loss of her husband, 5.02. 75 P
thou shouldst a husband take by my consent, | as 5.03.136
his mind) to find thee | an honorable husband. 5.03.143
hath she no husband | that will take pains to JN 1.01.218
thy son as true | as thine was to thy husband, 2.01.125
many a widow's husband grovelling lies, | coldly 2.01.305
be husband to me, heavens! 3.01.108
o husband, hear me! 3.01.305
ay, alack, how new | is "husband" in my mouth! 3.01.306
husband, i cannot pray that thou mayst win; 3.01.331
your husband, he is gone to save far off, R2 2.02. 80
sweet york, sweet husband, be not of that mind, 5.02.107
ah, my sour husband, my hard–hearted lord, 5.03.121
i have inquir'd, so has my husband, man by man, 1H4 3.03. 56 P
how doth thy husband? 3.03. 93 P
love thy husband, look to thy servants, cherish 3.03.171 P
heaven, | for recordation to my noble husband. 2H4 2.03. 61
uses, he is your servingman and your husband. 5.03. 11 P
good husband, come home presently. H5 2.01. 89 P
prithee, honey–sweet husband, let me bring thee 2.03. 1 P
to tumble down thy husband and thyself | from 2H6 1.02. 48
with him the husband of this lovely lady. 1.04. 73
thou, | although thy husband may be menelaus; 3H6 2.02.147
at saint albons field | this lady's husband, sir 3.02. 2
her husband, knave. wouldst thou betray me? R3 1.01.102
what though i kill'd her husband and her father? 1.01.154
is to become her husband and her father: 1.01.156
i did not kill your husband. 1.02. 91
to be reveng'd on him that kill'd my husband. 1.02.137
he that bereft thee, lady, of thy husband, | did 1.02.138
did it to help thee to a better husband. 1.02.139
i, that kill'd her husband and his father, | to 1.02.230
thou kill'dst my husband henry in the tower, 1.03.118
ere you were queen, ay, or your husband king, 1.03.120
in all which time you and your husband grey 1.03.126
was not your husband | in margaret's battle at 1.03.128
a husband and a son thou ow'st to me — | and 1.03.169
sorrow | as i had title in thy noble husband! 2.02. 48
but death hath snatch'd my husband from my arms, 2.02. 57
ah for my husband, for my dear lord edward! 2.02. 71
my husband lost his life to get the crown, | and 2.04. 57
when he that is my husband now | came to me as i 4.01. 65
which issued from my other angel husband, | and 4.01. 68
where is thy husband now? 4.04. 92
the unity the king my husband made | thou hadst 4.04.379
bring me a constant woman to her husband, | one H8 3.01.134
sure in that | i deem you an ill husband, and am 3.02.142
a right good husband (let him be a noble), | and 4.02.146
she, "which of these hairs is paris my husband?" TRO 1.02.164 P
in all humanity | than wife is to the husband? 2.02.176
if my son were my husband, i should freelier COR 1.03. 3 P
i'll tell you excellent news of your husband. 1.03. 90 P
done, and sav'd | your husband so much sweat. 4.01. 19
would i had the power | to say so to my husband. 4.02. 16
this lady's husband here — this (do you see?) 4.02. 41
wife is when she's fall'n out with her husband. 4.03. 33 P
my lord and husband! 5.03. 37
and child to see | the son, the husband, and the 5.03.102
jove shield your husband from his hounds to–day! TIT 2.03. 70
drag hence her husband to some secret hole, 2.03.129
bring thou her husband; 2.03.185
where is your husband? 2.04. 12
thy husband he is dead, and for his death | thy 3.01.108
she weeps because they kill'd her husband, 3.01.114
if they did kill thy husband, then be joyful, 3.01.116
you kill'd her husband, and for that vild fault 5.02.172
and then my husband — god be with his soul! ROM 1.03. 39
"yea," quoth my husband, "fall'st upon thy face? 1.03. 55
there stays a husband to make you a wife. 2.05. 69
o husband! 3.01.147
shall i speak ill of him that is my husband? 3.02. 97
villain cousin would have kill'd my husband. 3.02.101
my husband lives that tybalt would have slain, 3.02.105
tybalt's dead that would have slain my husband. 3.02.106
thou gone so, love — lord, ay, husband, friend! 3.05. 43
ere he that should be husband comes to woo. 3.05.119
my husband is on earth, my faith in heaven; 3.05.205
unless that husband send it me from heaven | by 3.05.207
thy husband in thy bosom there lies dead; 5.03.155
romeo, there dead, was husband to that juliet, 5.03.231
if she be mated with an equal husband? TIM 1.01.140
my husband! MAC 2.02. 13
but for your husband, | he is noble, wise, 4.02. 15
nay, how will you do for a husband? 4.02. 39
where is your husband? 4.02. 80
haply one as kind | for husband shalt thou — HAM 3.02.177
in second husband let me be accurs'd! 3.02.179
a second time i kill my husband dead, | when 3.02.184
dead, | when second husband kisses me in bed. 3.02.185
so think thou wilt no second husband wed, | but 3.02.214
this was your husband. 3.04. 63
here is your husband, like a mildewed ear, 3.04. 64
and for my means, i'll husband them so well, 4.05.139
her cradle ere she had a husband for her bed. LR 1.01. 15 P
so lost a father | that you must lose a husband. 1.01.247
post speedily to my lord your husband, show him 3.07. 2 P
i marvel our mild husband | not met us on the 4.02. 1
i know your lady does not love her husband, | i 4.05. 23
fear /me not. | she and the duke her husband! 5.01. 17
i carry out my side, | her husband being alive. 5.01. 62
that were the most, if he should husband you. 5.03. 70
and i, her husband, contradict your banes. 5.03. 87
but here's my husband; OTH 1.03.185
learn of him, emilia, though he be thy husband. 2.01.162 P
he'll prove to desdemona | a most dear husband. 2.01.291
joint between you and her husband entreat her to 2.03.323 P
i warrant it grieves my husband | as if the 3.03. 3
my wayward husband hath a hundred times | woo'd 3.03.292
look you, cassio and my husband! 3.04.106
and call thy husband hither. 4.02.106
would not make her husband a cuckold to make him 4.03. 76 P
what is the matter, husband? 5.01.111
ask thy husband else. 5.02.136
thy husband knew it all. 5.02.139
my husband? 5.02.140
thy husband. 5.02.141
my husband? 5.02.146
my husband? 5.02.149
i say thy husband. 5.02.150
my husband say she was false? 5.02.152
i say thy husband; 5.02.153
my friend, thy husband, honest, honest iago. 5.02.154
i found by fortune, and did give my husband; 5.02.226
alas, i found it, | and i did give't my husband. 5.02.231
o, that i knew this husband, which, you say, ANT 1.02. 4 P
no worse a husband than the best of men; 2.02.128
i shall pray, "o, bless my lord and husband!" 3.04. 16
husband win, win brother, | prays, and destroys 3.04. 18
husband, i come! 5.02.287
wedded, | her husband banish'd, she imprison'd: CYM 1.01. 8
my dearest husband, | i something fear my 1.01. 85
the loyall'st husband that did e'er plight troth 1.01. 96
a wedded lady | that hath her husband banish'd. 1.06. 3
o, that husband! 1.06. 3
the foul expulsion is | of thy dear husband, 2.01. 61
by thy revolt, o husband, shall be thought | put 3.04. 55
what comfort, when i am | dead to my husband? 3.04.130
i sought a husband, in which labor | i found PER 1.01. 66
he's father, son, and husband mild; 1.01. 68
(which pleasures fits a husband, not a father), 1.01.129
thing, nor be so hardy | ever to take a husband. TNK 1.01.205
may thy goodness | get thee a happy husband!" 2.04. 25

you | content to take th' other to your husband? 3.06.274
a husband i have 'pointed, | but do not know him 5.01.151
i am like to know your husband 'fore yourself 5.03. 37
"so thy surviving husband shall remain | the LUC 519
"then for thy husband and thy children's sake, 533
"my husband is thy friend, for his sake spare me 582
my resolution, husband, do thou take, | mine 1200
by that her death, to do her husband wrong. 1264
shed for the slaught'red husband by the wife; 1376
which when her sad–beholding husband saw, 1590
dear husband, in the interest of thy bed | a 1619
replies her husband, "do not take away | my 1796
mark how one string, sweet husband to another, SON 8. 9
like a deceived husband, so love's face | may 93. 2
and husband nature's riches from expense; 94. 6
HUSBANDED 4 FR 0.0004 REL FR 3 V 1 P
excellent, | if it be husbanded with modesty. SHR in.1. 68
prove that i husbanded her bed in florence, AWW 5.03.126
manur'd, husbanded, and till'd with excellent 2H4 4.03.119 P
my sex, | being so father'd and so husbanded? JC 2.01.297
HUSBANDLESS 1 FR 0.0001 REL FR 1 V 0 P
a widow, husbandless, subject to fears, | a JN 3.01. 14
HUSBANDRY 15 FR 0.0017 REL FR 14 V 1 P
womb | expresseth his full tilth and husbandry. MM 1.04. 44
hands | the husbandry and manage of my house MV 3.04. 25
yield | in lieu of all thy pains and husbandry. AYL 2.03. 65
for one to do her husbandry and her drudgery. 2H4 3.02.113 P
which is both healthful and good husbandry. H5 4.01. 7
and all her husbandry doth lie on heaps, 5.02. 39
and choke the herbs for want of husbandry. 2H6 3.01. 33
and, like as there were husbandry in war, TRO 1.02. 7
and shows good husbandry for the volscian state, COR 4.07. 22
if you suspect my husbandry or falsehood, | call TIM 2.02.155
there's husbandry in heaven, | their candles are MAC 2.01. 4
and borrowing dulleth /th' edge of husbandry. HAM 1.03. 77
trouble you so early, | 'tis not our husbandry. PER 3.02. 20
womb | disdains the tillage of thy husbandry? SON 3. 6
which husbandry in honor might uphold | against 13.10
/HUSBAND'S 1 FR 0.0001 REL FR 1 V 0 P
in mincing with his sword her /husband's limbs, HAM 2.02.514
HUSBAND'S 41 FR 0.0046 REL FR 30 V 11 P
she has all the rule of her husband's purse. WIV 1.03. 53 P
in this town, her husband's name is ford. 2.02.192 P
your husband's coming hither, woman, with all 3.03.106 P
but 'tis most certain your husband's coming, 3.03.114 P
your husband's here at hand, bethink you of some 3.03.126 P
heaven guide him to thy husband's cudgel; 4.02. 88 P
scrape the figures out of your husband's brains. 4.02.216 P
that you have quite forgot | a husband's office? ERR 3.02. 2
i'll see if i can get my husband's ring, | which MV 4.02. 13
i have, | no, not my body nor my husband's bed. 5.01.228
which, but for him that had your husband's ring, 5.01.250
cannot make her fault her husband's occasion, AYL 4.01.174 P
measures my husband's sorrow by his woe: SHR 5.02. 29
and place your hands below your husband's foot; 5.02.177
so sways she level in her husband's heart. TN 2.04. 31
are to herrings, the husband's the bigger. 3.01. 35 P
as he does, | her children not her husband's! WT 2.03.108
to make room for him in my husband's bed. JN 1.01.255
o, /sit my husband's wrongs on herford's spear, R2 1.02. 47
a new–married wife about her husband's neck, H5 5.02.180 P
then get your husband's lands, to do them good. 3H6 3.02. 40
then, thy husband's lands i freely give thee. 3.02. 55
then thou shalt not have thy husband's lands. 3.02. 71
her suit is granted for her husband's lands. 3.02.117
i have bewept a worthy husband's death, | and R3 2.02. 49
methinks i hear hither your husband's drum; COR 1.03. 29
with patience, | and not my husband's secrets? JC 2.01.302
her husband's to aleppo gone, master o' th' MAC 1.03. 7
are the queen, your husband's brother's wife, HAM 3.04. 15
and give the distaff | into my husband's hands. LR 4.02. 18
a plot upon her virtuous husband's life, | and 4.06.272
not in my husband's nose. ANT 1.02. 61 P
sir, look well to my husband's house; and — 3.02. 45
my husband's hand! CYM 3.04. 14
more of the maid to sight than husband's pains. TNK pr 8
thinks he that her husband's shallow tongue — LUC 78
he stories to her ears her husband's fame, | won 106
until her husband's welfare she did hear; 263
by her untimely tears, her husband's love, | by 570
one of my husband's men | bid thou be ready, by 1291
by children's eyes, her husband's shape in mind. SON 9. 8
HUSBANDS' 2 FR 0.0002 REL FR 2 V 0 P
we have been praying for our husbands' welfare, MV 5.01.114
but i do think it is their husbands' faults | if OTH 4.03. 86
HUSBANDS 25 FR 0.0028 REL FR 17 V 8 P
i think, if your husbands were dead, you two WIV 3.02. 14 P
be sure of that — two other husbands. 3.02. 16 P
shall we tell our husbands how we have serv'd 4.02.213 P
walk — and my horns i bequeath your husbands. 5.05. 27 P
i see two husbands, or mine eyes deceive me. ERR 5.01.332
your father got excellent husbands, if a maid ADO 2.01.324 P
marry him, i should marry twenty husbands. MV 1.02. 63 P
we'll see our husbands | before they think of us 3.04. 58
these be the christian husbands. 4.01.295
and be a day before our husbands home. 4.02. 3
me them soundly forth unto their husbands. SHR 5.02.104
what duty they do owe their lords and husbands. 5.02.131
fools are as like husbands as pilchers are to TN 3.01. 34 P
hang all the husbands | that cannot do that feat WT 2.03.110
which fault lies on the hazards of all husbands JN 1.01.119
this his mock mock out of their dear husbands; H5 1.02.285
for husbands, fathers, and betrothed lovers, 2.04.108
and sent our sons and husbands captivate. 1H6 2.03. 42
men for their sons, wives for their husbands, 3H6 5.06. 41
so you mistake your husbands. HAM 3.02.252 P
why have my sisters husbands, if they say | they LR 1.01. 99
the pranks | they dare not show their husbands; OTH 3.03.203
that there be women do abuse their husbands | in 4.03. 62
let husbands know | their wives have sense like 4.03. 93
both for sweet and sour, | as husbands have. 4.03. 96
HUSH 14 FR 0.0015 REL FR 11 V 3 P
hush! TMP 1.02.478
hush and be mute, | or else our spell is marr'd. 4.01.126
but hush, 'tis so. AWW 2.03.300
hush, hush! hoodman comes! portotartarossa. 4.03.118 P
hush, hush! hoodman comes! portotartarossa. 4.03.118 P
my tongue shall hush again this storm of war, JN 5.01. 20
but hush, no more. MAC 3.01. 10
and the orb below | as hush as death, anon the HAM 2.02.486
no words, no words, hush. LR 3.04.181
hush! ANT 1.02. 22 P
hush, here comes antony. 1.02. 79
hush! CYM 5.04. 94
hush, my gentle neighbors! PER 3.02.106
than when her mournful hymns did hush the night, SON 102.10
HUSH'D 7 FR 0.0008 REL FR 7 V 0 P
speak softly, | all's hush'd as midnight yet. TMP 4.01.207
is, | as hush'd on purpose to grace harmony! ADO 2.03. 39
as to be hush'd and nought at all to say. R2 1.01. 53
and hush'd with buzzing night–flies to thy 2H4 3.01. 11
i am hush'd until our city be afire, | and then COR 5.03.181
is hush'd within the hollow mine of earth | and OTH 4.02. 79
even as the wind is hush'd before it raineth, VEN 458
HUSHERING 1 FR 0.0001 REL FR 1 V 0 P
a mean most meanly and in hushering | mend him LLL 5.02.328
HUSHES 1 FR 0.0001 REL FR 1 V 0 P
my lord would speak, my duty hushes me. TN 5.01.107
HUSHT 2 FR 0.0002 REL FR 1 V 1 P
husht, master, here's some good pastime toward; SHR 1.01. 68
husht! PER 1.03. 9 P
/HUSKS 1 FR 0.0001 REL FR 1 V 0 P
/and /what's /to /come /is /strew'd /with /husks TRO 4.05.166
HUSKS 4 FR 0.0004 REL FR 2 V 2 P
roots, and husks | wherein the acorn cradled. TMP 1.02.464
shall i keep your hogs and eat husks with them? AYL 1.01. 37 P
from swine–keeping, from eating draff and husks. 1H4 4.02. 35 P
leaving them but the shales and husks of men. H5 4.02. 18
HUSWIFE *(also housewives)*
HUSWIFE 14 FR 0.0015 REL FR 11 V 3 P
and bootless make the breathless huswife churn, MND 2.01. 37
and mock the good huswife fortune from her wheel AYL 1.02. 31 P
i play the noble huswife with the time, | to AWW 2.02. 60
and i hope to see a huswife take thee between TN 1.03.103 P
doth fortune play the huswife with me now? H5 5.01. 80
your graces find me here part of a huswife | (i H8 3.01. 24
you play the idle huswife with me this afternoon COR 1.03. 70 P
me alone, | i'll play the huswife for this once. ROM 4.02. 43
the bounteous huswife nature on each bush | lays TIM 4.03.420
a huswife that by selling her desires | buys OTH 4.01. 94
that the false huswife fortune break her wheel, ANT 4.15. 44
costlier than would fit | a franklin's huswife. CYM 3.02. 77
be not sick, | for you must be our huswife. 4.02. 45
lo as a careful huswife runs to catch | one of SON 143. 1
HUSWIFERY 2 FR 0.0002 REL FR 2 V 0 P
let huswifery appear. H5 2.03. 62
players in your huswifery, and huswives in your OTH 2.01.112
HUSWIVE'S 1 FR 0.0001 REL FR 1 V 0 P
she has a huswive's hand — but that's no matter AYL 4.03. 27
HUSWIVES 2 FR 0.0002 REL FR 1 V 1 P
to the overscutch'd huswives that he heard the 2H4 3.02.317 P
in your huswifery, and huswives in your beds. OTH 2.01.112
HYBLA 2 FR 0.0002 REL FR 1 V 1 P
as the honey of hybla, my old lad of the castle. 1H4 1.02. 41 P
but for your words, they rob the hybla bees, JC 5.01. 34
HYDRA 3 FR 0.0003 REL FR 2 V 1 P
court, | whereon this hydra son of war is born, 2H4 4.02. 38
thus | given hydra here to choose an officer, COR 3.01. 93
had i as many mouths as hydra, such an answer OTH 2.03.304 P
HYDRA–HEADED 1 FR 0.0001 REL FR 1 V 0 P
nor never hydra–headed willfulness | so soon did H5 1.01. 35
HYDRA'S 1 FR 0.0001 REL FR 1 V 0 P
they grow like hydra's heads. 1H4 5.04. 25
HYEN 1 FR 0.0001 REL FR 0 V 1 P
i will laugh like a hyen, and that when thou art AYL 4.01.156 P
HYMEN 6 FR 0.0006 REL FR 6 V 0 P
and hymen now with luckier issue speed 's | than ADO 5.03. 32
thy daughter, | hymen from heaven brought her, AYL 5.04.112
'tis hymen peoples every town, | high wedlock 5.04.143
honor, and renown | to hymen, god of every town! 5.04.146
since love our hearts and hymen did our hands HAM 3.02.159
hymen hath brought the bride to bed, | where, by PER 3.ch. 9
HYMENAEUS 1 FR 0.0001 REL FR 1 V 0 P
every thing | in readiness for hymenaeus stand, TIT 1.01.325
HYMEN'S 4 FR 0.0004 REL FR 4 V 0 P
take heed, | as hymen's lamps shall light you. TMP 4.01. 23
shall be paid | till hymen's torch be lighted; 4.01. 97
that must take hands | to join in hymen's bands, AYL 5.04.129
thou bright defiler | of hymen's purest bed! TIM 4.03.383
HYMN 5 FR 0.0005 REL FR 5 V 0 P
now, music, sound, and sing your solemn hymn. ADO 5.03. 11
no night is now with hymn or carol blest. MND 2.01.102
come ho, and wake diana with a hymn, | with MV 5.01. 66
who chaunts a doleful hymn to his own death, JN 5.07. 22
"amen" | to every hymn that able spirit affords SON 85. 7
HYMNS 4 FR 0.0004 REL FR 4 V 0 P
chaunting faint hymns to the cold fruitless moon MND 1.01. 73
our solemn hymns to sullen dirges change; ROM 4.05. 88
from sullen earth) sings hymns at heaven's gate, SON 29.12
than when her mournful hymns did hush the night, 102.10
HYPERBOLES 2 FR 0.0002 REL FR 2 V 0 P
three–pil'd hyperboles, spruce affection, LLL 5.02.407
roaring typhon dropp'd, | would seem hyperboles. TRO 1.03.161
HYPERBOLICAL 2 FR 0.0002 REL FR 1 V 1 P
out, hyperbolical fiend! TN 4.02. 25 P
/shout me forth | in acclamations hyperbolical, COR 1.09. 51
HYPERION 3 FR 0.0003 REL FR 3 V 0 P
doth rise and help hyperion to his horse, | and H5 4.01.275
he burns | with entertaining great hyperion. TRO 2.03.197
hyperion to a satyr, so loving to my mother HAM 1.02.140
/HYPERION'S 1 FR 0.0001 REL FR 1 V 0 P
even from /hyperion's rising in the east, TIT 5.02. 56
HYPERION'S 2 FR 0.0002 REL FR 2 V 0 P
whereon hyperion's quick'ning fire doth shine: TIM 4.03.184
hyperion's curls, the front of jove himself, HAM 3.04. 56
HYPOCRISY 6 FR 0.0006 REL FR 6 V 0 P
now step i forth to whip hypocrisy. LLL 4.03.149
a huge translation of hypocrisy, | vildly 5.02. 51
his prayers are full of false hypocrisy, | ours R2 5.03.107
you | for all this spice of your hypocrisy. H8 2.03. 26
it is hypocrisy against the devil. OTH 4.01. 6
your person | without hypocrisy i may not wish TNK 3.01. 95
HYPOCRITE 8 FR 0.0009 REL FR 4 V 4 P
an hypocrite, a virgin–violator, | is it not MM 5.01. 41
i dare swear he is no hypocrite, but prays from ADO 1.01.151 P
and you be a cursing hypocrite once, you must be 5.01.208 P
i would think thee a most princely hypocrite. 2H4 2.02. 54 P
every man would think me an hypocrite indeed. 2.02. 60 P
out, scarlet hypocrite! 1H6 1.03. 56
calls virtue hypocrite, takes off the rose HAM 3.04. 42
sin, | when what is done is like an hypocrite, PER 1.01.122
HYPOCRITES 1 FR 0.0001 REL FR 1 V 0 P
my tongue and soul in this be hypocrites — HAM 3.02.397
HYRCAN 1 FR 0.0001 REL FR 1 V 0 P
the arm'd rhinoceros, or th' hyrcan tiger, MAC 3.04.100
HYRCANIA 1 FR 0.0001 REL FR 1 V 0 P
o, ten times more, than tigers of hyrcania. 3H6 1.04.155
HYRCANIAN 2 FR 0.0002 REL FR 2 V 0 P
the hyrcanian deserts and the vasty wilds | of MV 2.07. 41
"the rugged pyrrhus, like th' hyrcanian beast — HAM 2.02.450
HYSSOP 1 FR 0.0001 REL FR 0 V 1 P
or sow lettuce, set hyssop and weed up /tine, OTH 1.03.322 P
/HYSTERICA 1 FR 0.0001 REL FR 1 V 0 P
/hysterica passio, down, thou climbing sorrow, LR 2.04. 57
I' *(also in)*
/I' 9 FR 0.0010 REL FR 9 V 0 P
/alone /suffers, /suffers /most /i' /th' /mind, LR 3.06.104
/what, /i' /th' /storm? 4.03. 28
/i' /th' /night? 4.03. 28
/the /poor /distressed /lear's /i' /th' /town, 4.03. 38
/i' /faith, i fear it has. OTH 3.03.215
/i' /faith! is't true? 3.04. 75
/i' /faith, you are to blame. 3.04. 97
poor rogue, i think, /i' /faith, she loves me. 4.01.111
of me, who stand /i' /th' gaps to teach you, PER 4.04. 8
I' 391 FR 0.0442 REL FR 229 V 162 P
set all hearts i' th' state | to what tune TMP 1.02. 84
gates of milan, and, i' th' dead of darkness, 1.02.130
i' th' air, or th' earth? 1.02.388
i' th' commonwealth i would, by contraries, 2.01.148
the man i' th' moon's too slow — till new–born 2.01.249
for he is sure i' th' island. 2.01.325
me with urchin–shows, pitch me i' th' mire, 2.02. 5
storm brewing, i hear it sing i' th' wind. 2.02. 20 P
i was the man i' th' moon, when time was. 2.02.139 P
the man i' th' moon? 2.02.146 P
i, | beyond all limit of what else i' th' world, 3.01. 72
a custom with him | i' th' afternoon to sleep. 3.02. 88
i' th' name of something holy, sir, why stand 3.03. 94
therefore my son i' th' ooze is bedded; 3.03.100
oaths are straw | to th' fire i' th' blood. 4.01. 53
i' th' filthy–mantled pool beyond your cell, 4.01.182
i' faith, i'll eat nothing. WIV 1.01.279 P
be there bears i' th' town? 1.01.287 P
plod away i' th' hoof! 1.03. 82
if he do, i' faith, and find any body in the 1.04. 4 P
i' faith, that we will; 1.04.158 P
alas, i had rather be set quick i' th' earth, 3.04. 86
a blind bitch's puppies, fifteen i' th' litter; 3.05. 11 P
no, i'll come no more i' th' basket. 4.02. 49 P
the knave constable had set me i' th' stocks, i' 4.05.119 P
had set me i' th' stocks, i' th' common stocks, 4.05.120 P
we'll couch i' th' castle–ditch till we see the 5.02. 1 P
stag, and the fattest, i think, i' th' forest. 5.05. 13 P
if it had not been i' th' church, i would have 5.05.185 P
thou'rt i' th' right, girl, more o' that. MM 2.02.129
my vouch against you, and my place i' th' state, 2.04.156
and deliberate word | nips youth i' th' head, 3.01. 90
is't not drown'd i' th' last rain? 3.02. 49 P
what news abroad i' th' world? 3.02.221 P
none but only a repair i' th' dark, | and that i 4.01. 42
you let it be proclaim'd betimes i' th' morn. 4.04. 16 P
but you are i' the wrong | to speak before your 5.01. 86
to a curtal dog, and made me turn i' th' wheel. ERR 3.02.146
why, i' faith, methinks she's too low for a high ADO 1.01.171 P
go to, i' faith, and thou wilt needs thrust thy 1.01.200 P
i' faith, lady, i think your blazon to be true, 2.01.296 P
and your gown's a most rare fashion, i' faith. 3.04. 15 P
well said, i' faith, neighbor verges. 3.05. 35 P
an honest soul, i' faith, sir, by my troth he is 3.05. 38 P
i' faith, i thank him, he hath bid me to a 5.01.154 P
i' faith, your hand is out. LLL 4.01.133
i' faith, i will not. 4.03. 8 P
look what you do, you do it still i' th' dark. 5.02. 24
fine, i' faith! MND 3.02.284
myself the man i' th' moon do seem to be. 5.01.245
how is it else the man i' th' moon? 5.01.248 P
the lanthorn is the moon, i the man i' th' moon, 5.01.258 P
thanks, i' faith, for silence is only MV 1.01.111
monday last at six a' clock i' th' morning, 2.05. 25 P
and others, when the bagpipe sings i' th' nose, 4.01. 49
ambition shun, | and loves to live i' th' sun, AYL 2.05. 39
i met a fool i' th' forest, | a motley fool. 2.07. 12
it will be the earliest fruit i' th' country; 3.02.119 P
i' faith, coz, 'tis he. 3.02.216 P
i' faith, his hair is of a good color. 3.04. 10 P
but, i' faith, i should have been a woman by 4.03.175 P
a fair name. wast born i' the forest here? 5.01. 22 P
we are for you, sit i' th' middle. 5.03. 10 P
i' faith, i' faith, and both in a tune, like two 5.03. 14 P
i' faith, i' faith, and both in a tune, like two 5.03. 14 P
i' faith, sir, you shall never need to fear. SHR 1.01. 61
come, you wasp, i' faith you are too angry. 2.01.209
gabr'el's pumps were all unpink'd i' th' heel; 4.01.133
i' faith, he'll have a lusty widow now, | that 4.02. 50
error i' th' bill, sir, error i' th' bill! 4.03.145 P
error i' th' bill, sir, error i' th' bill! 4.03.145 P
you are i' th' right, sir, 'tis for my mistress. 4.03.156 P
steely bones | looks bleak i' th' cold wind. AWW 1.01.104
what one, i' faith? 1.01.178 P
jowl horns together like any deer i' th' herd. 1.03. 55 P
she's very well, and wants nothing i' th' world; 2.04. 4 P
a good knave, i' faith, and well fed. 2.04. 38
perchance he's hurt i' th' battle. 3.05. 87 P
by this same coxcomb that we have i' th' wind, 3.06.114
us some band of strangers i' th' adversary's 4.01. 15 P
which were the greatest obloquy i' th' world 4.02. 44
which were the greatest obloquy i' th' world 4.02. 48
him forth, h'as sat i' th' stocks all night, 4.03.101 P
instant disaster of his setting i' th' stocks; 4.03.110 P

whether one captain dumaine be i' th' camp, a 4.03.176 P
sir, in a dungeon, i' th' stocks, or any where, 4.03.244 P
natural rebellion, done i' th' blade of youth, 5.03. 6
and boarded her i' th' wanton way of youth. 5.03.211
am a fellow o' th' strangest mind i' th' world; TN 1.03.113 P
here comes the fool, i' faith. 2.03. 15 P
'twas very good, i' faith. 2.03. 25 P
excellent good, i' faith. 2.03. 45 P
very sweet and contagious, i' faith. 2.03. 55 P
good, i' faith. come, begin. 2.03. 71 P
anne, and ginger shall be hot i' th' mouth too. 2.03.117 P
th' art i' th' right. 2.03.119 P
if thou hast her not i' th' end, call me cut. 2.03.187 P
what years, i' faith? 2.04. 27
but let concealment, like a worm i' th' bud, 2.04.111
he has been yonder i' the sun practicing 2.05. 16 P
i' faith, or i either? 2.05.192 P
i saw't i' th' orchard. 3.02. 7 P
like a pedant that keeps a school i' th' church. 3.02. 76 P
well held out, i' faith! 4.01. 5 P
his eyes were set at eight i' th' morning. 5.01.199 P
prithee read i' thy right wits. 5.01.297 P
no tongue that moves, none, none i' th' world, WT 1.02. 20
were as twinn'd lambs that did frisk i' th' sun, 1.02. 67
i' fecks! 1.02.120
you would seek us, | we are yours i' th' garden. 1.02.178
what is the news i' th' court? 1.02.367
spotless | i' th' eyes of heaven and to you — i 2.01.132
these dangerous, unsafe lunes i' th' king, 2.02. 28
solemn, and unearthly | it was i' th' off'ring! 3.01. 8
hurried | here to this place, i' th' open air, 3.02.105
there is no truth at all i' th' oracle. 3.02.140
made fault | i' th' boldness of your speech. 3.02.218
best haste, and go not | too far i' th' land; 3.03. 11
and you shall help to put him i' th' ground. 3.03.136 P
i' th' name of me — 4.03. 51 P
at upper end o' th' table, now i' th' middle; 4.04. 59
hath ribbons of all the colors i' th' rainbow; 4.04.204 P
that must be | i' th' virtue of your daughter. 4.04.387
i' th' love | that i have borne your father? 4.04.516
forgiveness, | as 'twere i' th' father's person; 4.04.550
her breeding as | she is i' th' rear 'our birth. 4.04.581
what's i' th' farthel? 4.04.754 P
for thou wast got i' th' way of honesty. JN 1.01.181
sirrah, look to't, i' faith i will, i' faith. 2.01.140
sirrah, look to't, i' faith i will, i' faith. 2.01.140
i have done, i' faith. 1H4 1.03.258
i know a trick worth two of that, i' faith. 2.01. 37 P
not a whit, i' faith, i lack some of thy 2.04.371 P
o jesu, this is excellent sport, i' faith! 2.04.390 P
a goodly portly man, i' faith, and a corpulent, 2.04.422 P
i'll tickle ye for a young prince, i' faith. 2.04.444 P
is the wind in that door, i' faith? 3.03. 88 P
i' faith, i am loath to pawn my plate, so god 2H4 2.01.154 P
i' faith, sweet heart, methinks now you are in 2.04. 22 P
but, i' faith, you have drunk too much canaries, 2.04. 26 P
you are both, i' good truth, as rheumatic as two 2.04. 57 P
longer ago than wed'sday last, i' good faith — 2.04. 87 P
a tame cheater, i' faith, you may stroke him as 2.04. 97 P
peesel, be quiet, 'tis very late, i' faith. 2.04.162 P
are you not hurt i' th' groin? 2.04.210 P
you have hurt him, sir, i' th' shoulder. 2.04.214 P
i' faith, i love thee. 2.04.218 P
i' faith, and thou follow'dst him like a church. 2.04.230 P
no abuse, ned, i' th' world, honest ned, none. 2.04.318 P
'a would have clapp'd i' th' clout at twelve 3.02. 46 P
most excellent, i' faith! 3.02.107 P
well said, i' faith, wart, th' art a good scab. 3.02.276 P
a friend i' th' court is better than a penny in 5.01. 30 P
puff i' thy teeth, most recreant coward base! 5.03. 92
their proud hoofs i' th' receiving earth; H5 pr 27
an irishman, a very valiant gentleman, i' faith. 3.02. 67 P
de gud service, or i'll lig i' the grund for it; 3.02.116 P
valor than this roaring devil i' th' old play, 4.04. 71 P
news have i that my doll is dead i' th' spittle 5.01. 81
i' faith, kate, my wooing is fit for thy 5.02.122 P
give me your answer, i' faith, do, and so clap 5.02.129 P
from being regent | i' th' parts of france, till 2H6 1.01. 67
let it come, i' faith, and i'll pledge you all, 2.03. 66 P
being burnt i' th' hand for stealing of sheep. 4.02. 63 P
and like a glass | did break i' th' wrenching. H8 1.01.167
i stood i' th' level | of a full-charg'd 1.02. 2
is the banket ready | i' th' privy chamber? 1.04. 99
if not, i' th' name of god, | your pleasure be 2.04. 56
that man i' th' world who shall report he has 2.04.135
i' th' progress of this business, | ere a 2.04.176
for no dislike i' th' world against the person 2.04.224
cause, that she should lie i' th' bosom of | our 3.02.100
how, i' th' name of thrift, | does he rake this 3.02.109
part of business which | i bear i' th' state; 3.02.146
of it, as i' th' contrary | the foulness is the 3.02.182
feel | my sword i' th' life-blood of thee else. 3.02.277
among the crowd i' th' abbey, where a finger 4.01. 57
i' th' presence | he would say untruths, and be 4.02. 37
speak of two | the most remark'd i' th' kingdom. 5.01. 33
you not | how your state stands i' th' world, 5.01.127
receive him, | and see him safe i' th' tower. 5.02.132
you i' th' chamblet, get up o' th' rail, | i'll 5.03. 89
i'll meddle nor make no more i' th' matter. TRO 1.01. 83 P
idle head, you would eat chickens i' th' shell. 1.02.134 P
sweet queen, that's a sweet queen — i' faith — 3.01. 71 P
love? ay, that it shall, i' faith. 3.01.112 P
in love, i' faith, to the very tip of the nose. 3.01.127 P
walk here i' th' orchard, i'll bring her 3.02. 16 P
you draw backward, we'll put you i' th' fills. 3.02. 46 P
as the tercel, for all the ducks i' th' river. 3.02. 53 P
pretty, i' faith. 3.02.135 P
achilles stands i' th' entrance of his tent. 3.03. 38
for if hector break not his neck i' th' combat, 3.03.259 P
would he were knock'd i' th' head! 4.02. 34
thou hast hung /thy advanced sword i' th' air, 4.05.188
sciaticas, lime-kills i' th' palm, incurable 5.01. 22 P
youth, | i am to-day i' th' vein of chivalry. 5.03. 32
a gulf it did remain | i' th' midst a' th' body, COR 1.01. 99
presume to know | what's done i' th' capitol; 1.01.192
their bands i' th' vaward are the /antiates, 1.06. 53
shall attend and shrug, | i' th' end admire; 1.09. 5
trumpets shall | i' th' field prove flatterers, 1.09. 43
a treaty find | i' th' part that is at mercy? 1.10. 7
i' th' shoulder and i' th' left arm. 2.01.147 P
i' th' shoulder and i' th' left arm. 2.01.147 P
the repulse of tarquin seven hurts i' th' body. 2.01.150 P
one i' th' neck, and two i' th' thigh — there's 2.01.151 P
one i' th' neck, and two i' th' thigh — there's 2.01.151 P
never would he | appear i' th' market-place, nor 2.01.233
i had rather have one scratch my head i' th' sun 2.02. 75
and i' th' consul's view | slew three opposers. 2.02. 93
he prov'd best man i' th' field, and for his 2.02. 97
that you bear | i' th' body of the weal; 2.03.181
laid falsely | i' th' plain way of his merit. 3.01. 61
being i' th' war, | their mutinies and revolts, 3.01.125
be meet, | and throw their power i' th' dust. 3.01.170
though calved i' th' porch o' th' capitol! 3.01.239
he has been bred i' th' wars | since 'a could 3.01.318
friends, | i' th' war do grow together; 3.02. 43
i have been i' th' market-place; 3.02. 93
tongue can do | i' th' way of flattery further. 3.02.137
so | i' th' right and strength a' th' commons," 3.03. 14
and power i' th' truth a' th' cause. 3.03. 18
which show | like graves i' th' holy churchyard. 3.03. 51
the fires i' th' lowest hell fold in the people! 3.03. 68
i' th' people's name, | i say it shall be so. 3.03.104
chance | that starts i' th' way before thee. 4.01. 37
doth ever cool | i' th' absence of the needer. 4.01. 44
i' th' city of kites and crows. 4.05. 42 P
i' th' city of kites and crows? 4.05. 43 P
of all the men i' th' world | i would have 4.05. 81
he is simply the rarest man i' th' world. 4.05.161 P
the news is, our general is cut i' th' middle, 4.05.197 P
caius martius was | a worthy officer i' th' war, 4.06. 30
i ever said we were i' th' wrong when we 4.06.154 P
if thou stand'st not i' th' state of hanging, or 5.02. 64 P
sink, my knee, i' th' earth; 5.03. 50
and stick i' th' wars | like a great sea-mark, 5.03. 73
here he lets me prate | like one i' th' stocks. 5.03.160
very well took, i' faith, wisely, wisely. ROM 2.04.125 P
heart, and, i' faith, i will tell her as much. 2.04.173 P
i' faith, i am sorry that thou art not well. 2.05. 53
in your bed, | he'll fright you up, i' faith. 4.05. 11
the fire i' th' flint | shows not till it be TIM 1.01. 22
honest water, which ne'er left man i' th' mire. 1.02. 59
else i should tell him well (i' faith, i should) 1.02.161
his fellowship i' th' cause against your city, 5.02. 12
set honor in one eye and death i' th' other, JC 1.02. 86
you that, i'll ne'er look you i' th' face again. 1.02.282 P
quarters that they know | i' th' shipman's card. MAC 1.03. 17
i' th' name of truth, | are ye fantastical, or 1.03. 52
"i would," | like the poor cat i' th' adage? 1.07. 45
hark! who lies i' th' second chamber? 2.02. 17
who's there, i' th' name of belzebub? 2.03. 4 P
that it did, sir, i' the very throat on me; 2.03. 38 P
and, as they say, | lamentings heard i' th' air; 2.03. 56
readiness, | and meet i' th' hall together. 2.03.134
not i' th' worst rank of manhood, say't, | and i 3.01.102
note of expectation | already are i' th' court. 3.03. 11
here i'll sit i' th' midst. 3.04. 10
blood hath been shed ere now, i' th' olden time, 3.04. 74
at the pit of acheron | meet me i' th' morning; 3.05. 16
got, | boil thou first i' th' charmed pot. 4.01. 9
shark, | root of hemlock digg'd i' th' dark, 4.01. 25
pains, | and every one shall share i' th' gains. 4.01. 40
speak'st with all thy wit, and yet, i' faith, 4.02. 42
said, old mole, canst work i' th' earth so fast? HAM 1.05.162
with what, i' th' name of god? 2.01. 73
let her not walk i' th' sun. 2.02.184 P
am i not i' th' right, old jephthah? 2.02.410 P
of reverent priam, seem'd i' th' air to stick. 2.02.479
gives me the lie i' th' throat | as deep as to 2.02.574
excellent, i' faith — of the chameleon's dish, 3.02. 93 P
my lord, you play'd once i' th' university, you 3.02. 99 P
i was kill'd i' th' capitol; 3.02.103 P
jest, poison in jest — no offense i' th' world. 3.02.235 P
'a poisons him i' th' garden for his estate. 3.02.261 P
not there, seek him i' th' other place yourself. 4.03. 34 P
says she hears | there's tricks i' th' world, 4.05. 5
to think they would lay him i' th' cold ground. 4.05. 70 P
to cut his throat i' th' church. 4.07.126
of /all the days i' th' year, i came to't that 5.01.143 P
how long will a man lie i' th' earth ere he rot? 5.01.163 P
now hath lien you i' th' earth three and twenty 5.01.173 P
alexander look'd a' this fashion i' th' earth? 5.01.198 P
lay her i' th' earth, | and from her fair and 5.01.238
skill shall, like a star i' th' darkest night, 5.02.256
we must do something, and i' th' heat. LR 1.01.308 P
i have cut the egg i' th' middle and eat up the 1.04.158 P
clovest thy /crown i' th' middle and gav'st away 1.04.160 P
o' both sides, and left nothing i' th' middle. 1.04.188 P
you are too much of late i' th' frown. 1.04.190 P
why one's nose stands i' th' middle on 's face? 1.05. 19 P
he's coming hither, now i' th' night, i' th' 2.01. 24
coming hither, now i' th' night, i' th' haste, 2.01. 24
i' th' mire. 2.02. 5 P
and thou hadst been set i' th' stocks for that 2.04. 64 P
to teach thee there's no laboring i' th' winter. 2.04. 68 P
not i' th' stocks, fool. 2.04. 87 P
to the eels when she put 'em i' th' paste alive; 2.04.123 P
who put my man i' th' stocks? 2.04.182
how came my man i' th' stocks? 2.04.198
when usurers tell their gold i' th' field, | and 3.02. 91
sea, | thou'dst meet the bear i' th' mouth. 3.04. 11
art thou that dost grumble there i' th' straw? 3.04. 44 P
we'll go to supper i' th' morning. 3.06. 84 P
i' th' last night's storm i such a fellow saw, 4.01. 32
hence a mile or twain | i' th' way toward dover, 4.01. 43
i' th' clout, i' th' clout — hewgh! 4.06. 91 P
i' th' clout, i' th' clout — hewgh! 4.06. 92 P
and proceed | i' th' sway of your own will. 4.07. 19
we two alone will sing like birds i' th' cage; 5.03. 9
of hair-breadth scapes i' th' imminent deadly OTH 1.03.136
at nine i' th' morning here we'll meet again. 1.03.279
where shall we meet i' th' morning? 1.03.373 P
paradoxes to make fools laugh i' th' alehouse. 2.01.139 P
in naples, that they speak i' th' nose thus? 3.01. 4 P
i might do't as well i' th' dark. 4.03. 67
why, the wrong is but a wrong i' th' world; 4.03. 80 P
kill men i' th' dark? 5.01. 63
time we twain | did show ourselves i' th' field, ANT 1.04. 74
offended, and with you | chiefly i' th' world; 2.02. 33
and did want | of what i was i' th' morning; 2.02. 77
so many mermaids, tended her i' th' eyes, | and 2.02.207
and antony | enthron'd i' th' market-place, did 2.02.215
for my peace, | i' th' east my pleasure lies. 2.03. 41
for the best turn i' th' bed. 2.05. 59
the beds i' th' east are soft, and thanks to you 2.06. 50
the least wind i' th' world will blow them down. 2.07. 2 P
o' th' nile | by certain scales i' th' pyramid; 2.07. 18
who does i' th' wars more than his captain can 3.01. 21
i' th' market-place, on a tribunal silver'd, 3.06. 3
i' th' common show-place, where they exercise. 3.06. 12
a charge we bear i' th' war, | and, as the 3.07. 16
by hercules, i think i am i' th' right. 3.07. 67
i' th' midst o' th' fight, | when vantage like a 3.10. 11
a child as soon | as i' th' command of caesar. 3.13. 25
conquer, | and earns a place i' th' story. 3.13. 46
music i' th' air. 4.03. 13
shall embattle | by th' second hour i' th' morn. 4.09. 4
i would they'ld fight i' th' fire or i' th' air; 4.10. 3
i would they'ld fight i' th' fire or i' th' air; 4.10. 3
and would gladly | look him i' th' face. 5.02. 32
acknowledg'd, | put we i' th' roll of conquest. 5.02.181
boy my greatness | i' th' posture of a whore. 5.02.221
i' th' swathing clothes the other, from their CYM 1.01. 59
it cannot be i' th' eye: 1.06. 39
nor i' th' judgment: 1.06. 41
nor i' th' appetite: 1.06. 43
sun, and solace | i' th' dungeon by a snuff! 1.06. 87
take my pow'r i' th' court for yours. 1.06.179
the crimson drops | i' th' bottom of a cowslip. 2.02. 39
i will go there and do't, i' th' court, before 2.04.148
than the sands | that run i' th' clock's behalf. 3.02. 73
we house i' th' rock, yet use thee not so hardly 3.03. 8
i' th' name of fame and honor which dies i' th' 3.03. 51
name of fame and honor which dies i' th' search, 3.03. 51
up thus meanly | i' th' cave /wherein /they bow, 3.03. 83
i' th' world's volume | our britain seems as of 3.04.137
there is cold meat i' th' cave, we'll browse on 3.06. 38
though i had found | gold strew'd i' th' floor. 3.06. 49
then began | a stop i' th' chaser; 5.03. 40
their friends | o'erborne i' th' former wave. 5.03. 48
to be i' th' field, and ask "what news?" 5.03. 65
than we | that draw his knives i' th' war. 5.03. 73
know the french knight that cow'rs i' the hams? PER 4.02.105 P
thou sayest true, i' faith, so they must: 4.02.126 P
crown a' th' earth | i' th' justice of compare! 4.03. 9
the meanest bird | that flies i' th' purer air! 4.06.102
him, if he i' th' blood-siz'd field lay swoll'n, TNK 1.01. 99
i' th' aid o' th' current were almost to sink, 1.02. 8
or i am none | that draw i' th' sequent trace. 1.02. 60
and power | i' th' least of these was dreadful, 1.03. 39
i' th' mean time, look tenderly to the two 2.01. 19 P
sigh, martyr'd as 'twere i' th' deliverance, 2.01. 41 P
boys in athens | blow wind i' th' breech on 's, 2.03. 47
this must be done i' th' woods. 2.03. 50
he's excellent i' th' woods, | bring him to th' 2.03. 53
should break out, though i' th' sanctuary. 3.01. 62
we may go whistle; all the fat's i' th' fire. 3.05. 39
comes i' th' nick, as mad as a march hare. 3.05. 73
'tis a sore life they have i' th' tother place, 4.03. 32 P
and i' th' self-same place | to seat something i 5.01. 27
first, by your leave, | i' th' way of honesty. 5.02. 20
doctor, | methinks you are i' th' wrong still. 5.02. 27
yours to command i' th' way of honesty. 5.02. 71
and that would be a blot i' th' business. 5.02. 81
are they i' th' field? 5.02.100
this trial is as 'twere i' th' night, and you 5.03. 19
his race | should show i' th' world too godlike. 5.03.118
i' th' self-same state | stands many a father 5.04. 2

I* *(also che*)*
/I* 152 FR 0.0171 REL FR 128 V 24 P
I* 21206 FR 2.3971 REL FR 15005 V 6201 P
IACHIMO *(see jachimo)*
IAGO 60 FR 0.0067 REL FR 46 V 14 P

i take it much unkindly | that thou, iago, who OTH 1.01. 2
were i the moor, i would not be iago. 1.01. 57
for know, iago, | but that i love the gentle 1.02. 24
honest iago, | my desdemona must i leave to thee 1.03.294
iago — 1.03.301 P
'tis one iago, ancient to the general. 2.01. 66
captain, | left in the conduct of the bold iago, 2.01. 75
let it not gall your patience, good iago, | that 2.01. 97
i prithee, good iago, | go to the bay and 2.01.207
iago hath direction what to do; 2.03. 4
iago is most honest. 2.03. 6
welcome, iago; we must to the watch. 2.03. 12 P
not to-night, good iago, i have very poor and 2.03. 33 P
honest iago, that looks dead with grieving, 2.03.177
your officer, iago, can inform you — | while i 2.03.198
iago, who began't? 2.03.217
i know, iago, | thy honesty and love doth mince 2.03.246
iago, look with care about the town, | and 2.03.255
my reputation, iago, my reputation! 2.03.265 P
good night, honest iago. 2.03.335 P
/do, /good /my /friend. in happy time, iago. 3.01. 30
i have made bold, iago, | to send in to your 3.01. 33
these letters give, iago, to the pilot, | and by 3.02. 1
what dost thou say, iago? 3.03. 93
why of thy thought, iago? 3.03. 98
thou dost conspire against thy friend, iago, 3.03.142
no, iago, | i'll see before i doubt; 3.03.189
leave me, iago. 3.03.240
i'll have the work ta'en out, | and give't iago. 3.03.297
look here, iago, | all my fond love thus do i 3.03.444
never, iago. 3.03.453
witness that here iago doth give up | the 3.03.465
think so, iago? 4.01. 1
naked in bed, iago, and not mean harm? 4.01. 5
dost thou hear, iago, | i will be found most 4.01. 89
iago /beckons me; now he begins the story. 4.01.130 P
how shall i murther him, iago? 4.01.170 P
o iago! 4.01.172 P
but yet the pity of it, iago! 4.01.196 P
o iago, the pity of it, iago! 4.01.196 P
o iago, the pity of it, iago! 4.01.196 P
get me some poison, iago, this night. 4.01.204 P

this night, iago. 4.01.206 P
alas, iago, my lord hath so bewhor'd her, 4.02.115
am i that name, iago? 4.02.118
alas, iago, | what shall i do to win my lord 4.02.148
day thou daff'st me with some device, iago, and 4.02.176 P
the voice of cassio! iago keeps his word. 5.01. 28
o brave iago, honest and just, | that hast such 5.01. 31
iago? 5.01. 54
o damn'd iago! o inhuman dog! 5.01. 62
honest iago hath ta'en order for't. 5.02. 72
my friend, thy husband, honest, honest iago. 5.02.154
o, are you come, iago? 5.02.169
perchance, iago, i will ne'er go home. 5.02.197
but yet iago knows | that she with cassio hath 5.02.210
iago in the /nick | came in and satisfied him. 5.02.317
how he upbraids iago, that he made him | brave 5.02.325
spake | (after long seeming dead) iago hurt him, 5.02.328
seeming dead) iago hurt him, | iago set him on. 5.02.329
IBAT 3 FR 0.0003 REL FR 1 V 2 P
"hic ibat simois; SHR 3.01. 28
"hic ibat," as i told you before, "simois," i am 3.01. 31 P
"hic ibat simois," i know you not, "hic est 3.01. 42 P
ICARUS 3 FR 0.0003 REL FR 3 V 0 P
thou thy desp'rate sire of crete, | thou icarus; 1H6 4.06. 55
and there died | my icarus, my blossom, in his 4.07. 16
my poor boy, icarus; 3H6 5.06. 21
ICE* 21 FR 0.0023 REL FR 13 V 8 P
of love is as a figure | trenched in ice, which TGV 3.02. 7
some run from brakes of ice and answer none, MM 2.01. 39
in thrilling region of thick–ribbed ice; 3.01.122
when he makes water his urine is congeal'd ice, 3.02.111 P
that is hot ice and wondrous strange snow. MND 5.01. 59
the very ice of chastity is in them. AYL 3.04. 17 P
and if you break the ice and do this /feat, SHR 1.02.265
a piece of ice. 4.01. 14 P
these boys are boys of ice, they'll none have AWW 2.03. 93 P
to smooth the ice, or add another hue | unto the JN 4.02. 13
to turn the sun to ice with fanning in his face H5 4.01.200 P
tut, thou art all ice, thy kindness freezes. R3 4.02. 22
fool slides o'er the ice that you should break. TRO 3.03.215
no, | than is the coal of fire upon the ice, COR 1.01.173
candied with ice, caudle thy morning taste | to TIM 4.03.226
he smote the sledded /polacks on the ice. HAM 1.01. 63
be thou as chaste as ice, as pure as snow, thou 3.01.135 P
or ice try whither your costard or my ballow be LR 4.06.241 P
o, my petition was | set down in ice, which, by TNK 1.01.107
honorable toil, | are paid with ice to cool 'em. 1.02. 34
up to the nav'l, and in ice up to th' heart, and 4.03. 43 P
ICE–BROOK'S 1 FR 0.0001 REL FR 1 V 0 P
was a sword of spain, the ice–brook's temper — OTH 5.02.253
ICELAND 2 FR 0.0002 REL FR 2 V 0 P
pish for thee, iceland dog! H5 2.01. 42
thou prick–ear'd cur of iceland! 2.01. 42
ICI 1 FR 0.0001 REL FR 0 V 1 P
car ce soldat ici est dispose tout /a /cette H5 4.04. 35 P
ICICLE 2 FR 0.0002 REL FR 1 V 1 P
will hang like an icicle on a dutchman's beard, TN 3.02. 27 P
chaste as the icicle | that's curdied by the COR 5.03. 65
ICICLES 3 FR 0.0003 REL FR 3 V 0 P
when icicles hang by the wall | and dick the LLL 5.02.912
where phoebus' fire scarce thaws the icicles, MV 2.01. 5
let us not hang like roping icicles | upon our H5 3.05. 23
ICY 6 FR 0.0006 REL FR 6 V 0 P
and on old hiems' /thin and icy crown | an MND 2.01.109
as the icy fang | and churlish chiding of the AYL 2.01. 6
come | to thrust his icy fingers in my maw, JN 5.07. 37
if he be leaden, icy, cold, unwilling, | be thou R3 3.01.176
and never learn'd | the icy precepts of respect, TIM 4.03.258
whose icy current and compulsive course | nev'r OTH 3.03.454
I/'D 1 FR 0.0001 REL FR 1 V 0 P
i/'d wish no better choice, and think me rarely PER 5.01. 69
I'D 26 FR 0.0029 REL FR 16 V 10 P
i'd throw it down for your deliverance | as MM 3.01.104
i'd venture | the well–lost life of mine on his AWW 1.03.247
i'd give bay curtal and his furniture, | my 2.03. 59
and they were sons of mine, i'd have them whipt, 2.03. 87 P
if i were but two hours younger, i'd beat thee. 2.03.253 P
not worth another word, else i'd call you knave. 2.03.263 P
i were not a very coward, i'd compel it of you, 4.03.321 P
and i thought that, i'd forswear it. TN 1.03. 88 P
o, if i thought that, i'd beat him like a dog! 2.03.141 P
i'd have seen him damn'd ere i'd have challeng'd 3.04.284 P
seen him damn'd ere i'd have challeng'd him. 3.04.285 P
i'd play incessantly upon these jades, | even JN 2.01.385
ten meals i have lost, and i'd defy them all. 2H6 4.10. 62 P
this white beard, i'd fight with thee to–morrow. TRO 4.05.209
an oracle to tell me so, | i'd not believe thee. 4.05.253
i'd make a quarry | with thousands of these COR 1.01.198
and he | upon my party, i'd revolt, to make 1.01.234
i'd have beaten him like a dog, but for 4.05. 51 P
true," i'd not believe them more | than thee, 4.05.105
of your throats | i'd not have given a doit. 5.04. 57
i'd rather than the worth of thrice the sum TIM 3.03. 22
i'd such a courage to do him good. 3.03. 24
were i like thee, i'd throw away myself. 4.03.219
or present, i'd exchange | for this one wish, 4.03.520
i'd have it come to question. LR 1.03. 13
spacious world, | i'd give it to undo the deed. PER 4.03. 6
IDEA 2 FR 0.0002 REL FR 2 V 0 P
th' idea of her life shall sweetly creep | into ADO 4.01.224
being the right idea of your father, | both in R3 3.07. 13
IDEAS 1 FR 0.0001 REL FR 0 V 1 P
shapes, objects, ideas, apprehensions, motions, LLL 4.02. 67 P
IDEM 1 FR 0.0001 REL FR 0 V 1 P
'tis "semper idem," for "obsque hoc nihil est." 2H4 5.05. 28 P
IDEN 5 FR 0.0005 REL FR 4 V 1 P
that alexander iden, an esquire of kent, | took 2H6 4.10. 43
iden, farewell, and be proud of thy victory. 4.10. 72 P
alexander iden, that's my name, | a poor esquire 5.01. 74
iden, kneel down. 5.01. 78
may iden live to merit such a bounty, | and 5.01. 81
/IDES 1 FR 0.0001 REL FR 1 V 0 P
is not to–morrow, boy, the /ides of march? JC 2.01. 40
IDES 6 FR 0.0006 REL FR 6 V 0 P
beware the ides of march. JC 1.02. 18
a soothsayer bids you beware the ides of march. 1.02. 19
beware the ides of march. 1.02. 23
the ides of march are come. 3.01. 1
remember march, the ides of march remember: 4.03. 18
must end that work the ides of march begun. 5.01.113
IDIOT 8 FR 0.0009 REL FR 6 V 2 P
that slender, though well landed, is an idiot; WIV 4.04. 86
mome, malt–horse, capon, coxcomb, idiot, patch! ERR 3.01. 32
the portrait of a blinking idiot, | presenting MV 2.09. 54
letter will make a contemplative idiot of him. TN 2.05. 19 P
making that idiot, laughter, keep men's eyes JN 3.03. 45
mars his idiot! do, rudeness, do, camel, do, do. TRO 2.01. 53 P
i know | an idiot holds his bauble for a god, TIT 5.01. 79
it is a tale | told by an idiot, full of sound MAC 5.05. 27
IDIOTS 3 FR 0.0003 REL FR 3 V 0 P
whiles others play the idiots in her eyes! TRO 3.03.135
for idiots in this case of favor would | be CYM 1.06. 42
so | as seely jeering idiots are with kings, LUC 1812
IDIOT–WORSHIPPERS 1 FR 0.0001 REL FR 0 V 1 P
thou seemest, and idol of idiot–worshippers, TRO 5.01. 7 P
/IDLE 2 FR 0.0002 REL FR 2 V 0 P
or like /an /idle thresher with a flail, | fell 3H6 2.01.131
/idle /old /man, | /that /still /would /manage LR 1.03. 16
IDLE 69 FR 0.0078 REL FR 56 V 13 P
all men idle, all; TMP 2.01.155
none, man, all idle — whores and knaves. 2.01.167 P
or else for want of idle time, could not again TGV 2.01.166
and though myself have been an idle truant, 2.04. 64
ay, and as idle as she may hang together, for WIV 3.02. 13 P
and held in idle price to haunt assemblies MM 1.03. 9
could i, with boot, change for an idle plume, 2.04. 11
to draw with idle spiders' strings | most 3.02.275
make thee the father of their idle dream | and 4.01. 63
is dross, | usurping ivy, brier, or idle moss, ERR 2.02.178
and shrive you of a thousand idle pranks. 2.02.208
these oaths and laws will prove an idle scorn. LLL 1.01.309
the boys, | and critic timon laugh at idle toys! 4.03.168
will hear your idle scorns, continue then, | and 5.02.865
never did mockers waste more idle breath. MND 3.02.168
as the remembrance of an idle gaud | which in my 4.01.167
and this weak and idle theme, | no more yielding 5.01.427
will weary you then no longer with idle talking. AYL 5.02. 51 P
heaven cease this idle humor in your honor! SHR in.2. 13
o yes, my lord, but very idle words, | for in.2. 83
is peevish, proud, idle, made of self–love, AWW 1.01.144 P
an idle lord, i swear. 2.05. 49 P
yet in his idle fire, | to buy his will, it 3.07. 26
of one count rossillion, a foolish idle boy, but 4.03.215 P
your store | i think is not for idle markets, TN 3.03. 46
you are idle shallow things, i am not of your 3.04.123 P
boys, too green and idle | for girls of nine), o WT 3.02.181
and strain their cheeks to idle merriment — | a JN 3.03. 46
possess'd with rumors, full of idle dreams, 4.02.145
thou idle dreamer, wherefore didst thou so? 4.02.153
doth by the idle comments that it makes 5.07. 4
which waste of idle hours hath quite thrown down R2 3.04. 66
what, stands thou idle here? 1H4 5.03. 40
repent at idle times as thou mayst and so 2H4 2.02.129 P
yea, every idle, nice, and wanton reason, 4.01.189
basis by | took stand for idle speculation — H5 4.02. 31
pointing–stock | to every idle rascal follower. 2H6 2.04. 47
and hate the idle pleasures of these days. R3 1.01. 31
you said that idle weeds are fast in growth: 3.01.103
and therefore is he idle? 3.01.105
not sleeping, to engross his idle body, | but 3.07. 76
an addle egg as well as you love an idle head, TRO 1.02.134 P
thou idle immaterial skein of sleave–silk, thou 5.01. 31 P
i' th' midst a' th' body, idle and unactive, COR 1.01. 99
must have you play the idle huswife with me this 1.03. 70 P
my hand hath been but idle, let it serve | to TIT 3.01.171
which are the children of an idle brain, | begot ROM 1.04. 97
ladies, there is an idle banquet attends you, TIM 1.02.155
no, gods, i am no idle votarist; 4.03. 27
home, you idle creatures, get you home! JC 1.01. 1
betimes, | and every man hence to his idle bed; 2.01.117
honesty | that they pass by me as the idle wind, 4.03. 68
or look'd upon this love with idle sight, | what HAM 2.02.138
i must be idle; 3.02. 90
come, come, you answer with an idle tongue. 3.04. 11
i begin to find an idle and fond bondage in the LR 1.02. 49 P
and all the idle weeds that grow | in our 4.04. 5
that on th' unnumb'red idle pebble chafes, 4.06. 21
mine's not an idle cause. OTH 1.02. 95
wherein of antres vast and deserts idle, | rough 1.03.140
reputation is an idle and most false imposition; 2.03.268 P
if idle talk will once be necessary, | i'll not ANT 5.02. 50
and leave this idle theme, this bootless chat; VEN 422
fall again | into your idle over–handled theme. 770
withal, | but idle sounds resembling parasits, 848
"out, idle words, servants to shallow fools! LUC 1016
doth cite each moving sense from idle rest, PP 14.15
pry, | to find out shames and idle hours in me, SON 61. 7
which shall above that idle rank remain | beyond 122. 3
IDLE–HEADED 1 FR 0.0001 REL FR 1 V 0 P
the superstitious idle–headed eld | receiv'd and WIV 4.04. 36
IDLELY 5 FR 0.0005 REL FR 4 V 1 P
god help, poor souls, how idlely do they talk! ERR 4.04.129
mocking the air with colors idlely spread, | and JN 5.01. 72
i see | i talk but idlely, and you laugh at me. R2 3.03.171
have labor'd so hard, you should talk so idlely! 2H4 2.02. 29 P
a thing slipp'd idlely from me. TIM 1.01. 20
IDLENESS 14 FR 0.0015 REL FR 11 V 3 P
wear out thy youth with shapeless idleness. TGV 1.01. 8
a poor unworthy brother of yours, with idleness. AYL 1.01. 34 P
on, | i found the effect of love in idleness, SHR 1.01.151
sir, for want of other idleness, i'll bide your TN 1.05. 64 P
nor conversant with ease and idleness, | till i JN 4.03. 70
uphold | the unyok'd humor of your idleness, 1H4 1.02.196
now, | from every region, apes of idleness! 2H4 4.05.122
conceives by idleness, and nothing teems | but H5 5.02. 51
to have it sterile with idleness or manur'd with OTH 1.03.324 P
than the ills i know, | my idleness doth hatch. ANT 1.02.130
that your royalty | holds idleness your subject, 1.03. 92
i should take you | for idleness itself. 1.03. 93
labor | to bear such idleness so near the heart 1.03. 94
pompey | thrives in our idleness. 1.04. 76
IDLES 1 FR 0.0001 REL FR 1 V 0 P
gossamers | that idles in the wanton summer air, ROM 2.06. 19
IDLY 12 FR 0.0013 REL FR 12 V 0 P
but see, while idly i stood looking on, | i SHR 1.01.150
but this from rumor's tongue | i idly heard — JN 4.02.124
stage, | are idly bent on him that enters next, R2 5.02. 25
to blame | so idly to profane the precious time, 2H4 2.04.362
idly suppos'd the founder of this law, | who H5 1.02. 59
for, my good liege, she is so idly king'd, | her 2.04. 26
myself | for living idly here in pomp and ease, 1H6 1.01.142
why live we idly here? 1.02. 13
his guilt should be but idly posted over, 2H6 3.01.255
even then when they sit idly in the sun. TRO 3.03.233
when the alarum were struck than idly sit | to COR 2.02. 76
redeem | in gentle numbers time so idly spent; SON 100. 6
IDOL 9 FR 0.0010 REL FR 7 V 2 P
was this the idol that you worship so? TGV 2.04.144
i am very loath to be your idol, sir; 4.02.128
but o, how vild an idol proves this god! TN 3.04.365
and what art thou, thou idol ceremony? H5 4.01.240
of that we hold an idol more than he? TRO 2.03.189
thou seemest, and idol of idiot–worshippers, 5.01. 7 P
"to the celestial and my soul's idol, the most HAM 2.02.109 P
well–painted idol, image dull and dead, | statue VEN 212
idolatry, | nor my beloved as an idol show, SON 105. 2
IDOLATROUS 1 FR 0.0001 REL FR 1 V 0 P
and my idolatrous fancy | must sanctify his AWW 1.01. 97
/IDOLATRY 1 FR 0.0001 REL FR 1 V 0 P
pure, pure /idolatry. LLL 4.03. 73
IDOLATRY 5 FR 0.0005 REL FR 5 V 0 P
and, were there sense in his idolatry, | my TGV 4.04.200
dotes, | devoutly dotes, dotes in idolatry, MND 1.01.109
'tis mad idolatry | to make the service greater TRO 2.02. 56
self, | which is the god of my idolatry, | and ROM 2.02.114
let not my love be call'd idolatry, | nor my SON 105. 1
'IELD *(also 'ild, yield)*
'IELD 1 FR 0.0001 REL FR 1 V 0 P
how you shall bid god 'ield us for your pains, MAC 1.06. 13
/IF 25 FR 0.0028 REL FR 22 V 3 P
IF 3765 FR 0.4256 REL FR 2649 V 1116 P
IFS 1 FR 0.0001 REL FR 1 V 0 P
damned strumpet, | talk'st thou to me of "ifs"? R3 3.04. 75
IF'T 12 FR 0.0013 REL FR 12 V 0 P
madam, if't please the queen to send the babe, WT 2.02. 54
if't be so, | for banquo's issue have i fil'd my MAC 3.01. 63
whom you may say (if't please you) fleance 3.06. 6
let me endure your wrath, if't be not so. 5.05. 35
but, if't be he i mean, he's very wild, HAM 2.01. 18
if't be th' affliction of his love or no | that 3.01. 35
if't be so, | hamlet is of the faction that is 5.02.237
if't be your pleasure and most wise consent OTH 1.01.121
i know not if't be true, | but i, for mere 1.03.388
if't be summer news, | smile to't before; CYM 3.04. 12
yes, if't please your majesty. PER 2.05. 91
if't pleas'd his rider | to put pride in him. TNK 5.04. 57
IGNIS 2 FR 0.0002 REL FR 1 V 1 P
thou hadst been an ignis fatuus or a ball of 1H4 3.03. 39 P
opus exegi, quod nec jovis ira, nec ignis" — TNK 3.05. 88
IGNOBLE 9 FR 0.0010 REL FR 9 V 0 P
to most ignoble stooping. TMP 1.02.116
savors | of tyranny, and will ignoble make you, WT 2.03.120
perish, base prince, ignoble duke of york! 1H6 3.01.177
base ignoble wretch! 5.04. 7
'tis but a base ignoble mind | that mounts no 2H6 2.01. 13
blunt–witted lord, ignoble in demeanor! 3.02.210
all confess | that i was not ignoble of descent, 3H6 4.01. 70
here is the head of that ignoble traitor, | the R3 3.05. 22
/her royal stock graft with ignoble plants, 3.07.127
IGNOBLY 4 FR 0.0004 REL FR 4 V 0 P
ay, noble uncle, thus ignobly us'd, | your 1H6 2.05. 35
but that 'tis shown ignobly and in treason. 2H6 5.02. 23
unwisely, not ignobly, have i given. TIM 2.02.174
'tis most ignobly done | to pluck me by the LR 3.07. 35
IGNOMINIOUS 3 FR 0.0003 REL FR 2 V 1 P
with other vile and ignominious terms: 1H6 4.01. 97
sovereign lady here | with ignominious words, 2H6 3.01.179
my followers' base and ignominious treasons, 4.08. 63 P
IGNOMINY 2 FR 0.0002 REL FR 2 V 0 P
thy ignominy sleep with thee in the grave, | but 1H4 5.04.100
ignominy, shame | pursue thy life, and live aye TRO 5.10. 33
IGNOMY 2 FR 0.0002 REL FR 2 V 0 P
ignomy in ransom and free pardon | are of two MM 2.04.111
i blush to think upon this ignomy. TIT 4.02.115
IGNORANCE 42 FR 0.0047 REL FR 30 V 12 P
fie, what the ignorance is! WIV 1.01.176 P
ignorance itself is a plummet o'er me. 5.05.163 P
were my lord so, his ignorance were wise, LLL 2.01.102
where now his knowledge must prove ignorance. 2.01.103
o thou monster ignorance, how deformed dost thou 4.02. 23
thrust thy sharp wit quite through my ignorance, 5.02.398
and thine ignorance makes thee away. AWW 1.01.211 P
and the careless lapse | of youth and ignorance; 2.03.164
i say there is no darkness but ignorance, in TN 4.02. 43 P
i say this house is as dark as ignorance, though 4.02. 45 P
though ignorance were as dark as hell; 4.02. 46 P
to choke his days | with barbarous ignorance, JN 4.02. 59
and dull unfeeling barren ignorance | is made my R2 1.03.168
o, i am ignorance itself in this! 1H4 3.01.210
o gross and miserable ignorance! 2H6 4.02.168
and seeing ignorance is the curse of god, 4.07. 73
and that you come to reprehend my ignorance. R3 3.07.113
with all their honorable points of ignorance H8 1.03. 26
tear, | tamer than sleep, fonder than ignorance, TRO 1.01. 10
which short–arm'd ignorance itself knows is so 2.03. 14 P
common curse of mankind, folly and ignorance, be 2.03. 28 P
a tick in a sheep than such a valiant ignorance. 3.03.312 P
if he have power, | then vail your ignorance; COR 3.01. 98
but by the yea and no | of general ignorance — 3.01.146
till at length | your ignorance (which finds not 3.03.129
who resists | are mock'd for valiant ignorance, 4.06.104
in a violent popular ignorance, given your enemy 5.02. 41 P
flask, | is set afire by thine own ignorance, ROM 3.03.133
impression | interprets for my poor ignorance. TIM 5.04. 69
let me not burst in ignorance, but tell | why HAM 1.04. 46
and make your wantonness /your ignorance. 3.01.146 P
in mine ignorance | your skill shall, like a 5.02.255
it was great ignorance, gloucester's eyes being LR 4.05. 9
o heavy ignorance! OTH 2.01.143 P
that errs in ignorance and not in cunning, | i 3.03. 49
and fools as gross | as ignorance made drunk. 3.03.405
of the world is lost | with very ignorance, we ANT 3.10. 7

but unto us it is | a cell of ignorance, CYM 3.03. 33
honor) lastly | children of grief and ignorance. TNK 2.02. 55
lust and ignorance | the virtues of the great 2.02.106
to sing, | and heavy ignorance aloft to fly, SON 78. 6
advance | as high as learning my rude ignorance. 78.14
/IGNORANT 1 FR 0.0001 REL FR 0 V 1 P
and, to humor the /ignorant, /call /i the deer LLL 4.02. 52 P
IGNORANT 49 FR 0.0055 REL FR 41 V 8 P
who | art ignorant of what thou art, nought TMP 1.02. 18
thou liest, most ignorant monster, i am in case 3.02. 25 P
begin to chase the ignorant fumes that mantle 5.01. 67
i think your lordship is not ignorant | how his TGV 1.03. 25
for being ignorant to whom it goes, | i writ at 2.01.110
thou art not ignorant | how she opposes her 3.02. 25
thou art not ignorant what dear good will | i 4.03. 14
most ignorant of what he's most assur'd | (his MM 2.02.119
either you are ignorant, | or seem so /craftily; 2.04. 74
let /me be ignorant, and in nothing good, | but 2.04. 76
a very superficial, ignorant, unweighing fellow. 3.02.139 P
but i will keep her ignorant of her good, | to 4.03.109
that mourn'd for fashion, ignorant what to fear, ERR 1.01. 73
you are not ignorant, all–telling fame | doth LLL 2.01. 21
your ladyship is ignorant what it is. 2.01.101
all ignorant that soul that sees thee without 4.02.113
nor is the wide world ignorant of her worth, MV 1.01.167
sciences, | whereof i know she is not ignorant. SHR 2.01. 58
drum, being not ignorant of the impossibility, AWW 4.01. 35 P
being so excellently ignorant, will breed no TN 3.04.188 P
imprison't not | in ignorant concealment. WT 1.02.397
either thou art most ignorant by age, | or thou 2.01.173
whose ignorant credulity will not | come up to 2.01.192
i am as ignorant in that, as you | in so 2.03. 70
(wotting no more than i) are ignorant. 3.02. 76
curtain | that shows the ignorant a kind of fear 1H4 4.01. 74
wise bearing or ignorant carriage is caught, as 2H4 5.01. 76 P
that was, | for i am ignorant and cannot guess. 1H6 2.05. 60
and, ignorant of his birth and parentage, 2H6 4.02.144
if i am | traduc'd by ignorant tongues, which H8 1.02. 72
why either were you ignorant to see't, | or, COR 2.03.174
judgment all revoke | your ignorant election. 2.03.219
and the eyes of th' ignorant | more learned than 3.02. 76
rejoicing by being ignorant of what greatness is MAC 1.05. 12 P
transported me beyond | this ignorant present, 1.05. 57
confound the ignorant, and amaze indeed | the HAM 2.02.565
i know you are not ignorant — 5.02.133 P
you are not ignorant of what excellence laertes 5.02.136 P
i am guiltless as i am ignorant | of what hath LR 1.04.273
for i am mainly ignorant | what place this is, 4.07. 64
alas, what ignorant sin have i committed? OTH 4.02. 70
o gull, o dolt, | as ignorant as dirt! 5.02.164
we, ignorant of ourselves, | beg often our own ANT 2.01. 5
for which myself, the ignorant motive, do | so 2.02. 96
and his shipping | (poor ignorant baubles!) CYM 3.01. 27
i am ignorant in what i am commanded. 3.02. 23
of her departure and | dost seem so ignorant, 4.03. 11
what ignorant and mad malicious traitors | are TNK 3.06.132
all ignorant that soul that sees thee without PP 5. 9
/IL 1 FR 0.0001 REL FR 1 V 0 P
con tutto /il core, ben trovato, may i say. SHR 1.02. 24
IL 8 FR 0.0009 REL FR 0 V 8 P
ma foi, il fait fort /chaud. WIV 1.04. 51 P
il faut que j'apprenne a parler. H5 3.04. 4 P
c'est bien dit, madame, il est fort bon anglois. 3.04. 19 P
il est trop difficile, madame, comme je pense. 3.04. 27 P
il me commande a vous dire que vous faites vous 4.04. 34 P
il est content a vous donner la liberte, le 4.04. 52 P
il est /meilleur que l'anglois lequel je parle. 5.02.189 P
leur noces, il n'est pas la coutume de france. 5.02.259 P
ILBOW *(also bilbow, elbow)*
ILBOW 1 FR 0.0001 REL FR 0 V 1 P
de nailes, de arma, de ilbow. H5 3.04. 47 P
'ILD *(also 'ield, yield)*
'ILD 2 FR 0.0002 REL FR 0 V 2 P
god 'ild you for your last company. AYL 3.03. 75 P
god 'ild you, sir, i desire you of the like. 5.04. 54 P
I'LD 34 FR 0.0038 REL FR 31 V 3 P
sometime i'ld divide, | and burn in many places; TMP 1.02.198
i were well awake, | i'ld strive to tell you. 5.01.230
impression of keen whips i'ld wear as rubies, MM 2.04.101
sick for, ere i'ld yield | my body up to shame. 2.04.103
kings | and flourish'd after, i'ld not do't; WT 1.02.359
but i'ld say he had not; 2.01. 62
you speak, sweet, | i'ld have you do it ever; 4.04.137
when you sing, | i'ld have you buy and sell so; 4.04.138
ghost that walk'd, i'ld bid you mark | her eye, 5.01. 63
then i'ld shriek, that even your ears | should 5.01. 65
would he do so, i'ld beg your precious mistress, 5.01.223
the stone is mine), | i'ld not have show'd it. 5.03. 59
by the good gods | i'ld with thee every foot. COR 4.01. 57
up in thee, | i'ld give thee leave to hang it. TIM 4.03.280
had i three ears, i'ld hear thee. MAC 4.01. 78
all my living, i'ld keep my coxcombs myself. LR 1.04.107 P
i'ld have thee beaten for being old before thy 1.05. 41 P
i'ld turn it all | to thy suggestion, plot, and 2.01. 72
plain, | i'ld drive ye cackling home to camelot. 2.02. 84
i'ld speak with the duke of cornwall and his 2.04. 97
the duke, and 's wife, i'ld speak with them — 2.04.116
upon your chin, | i'ld shake it on this quarrel. 3.07. 77
thee in my touch, | i'ld say i had eyes again. 4.01. 24
i'ld use them so | that heaven's vault should 5.03.259
think'st thou i'ld make a life of jealousy? OTH 3.03.177
i'ld whistle her off, and let her down the wind 3.03.262
chrysolite, | i'ld not have sold her for it. 5.02.146
i am not sorry neither, i'ld have thee live; 5.02.289
and such a welcome as i'ld give to him | (after CYM 3.06. 72
i'ld change my sex to be companion with them, 3.06. 87
who is't shall die, i'ld say | "my father, not 4.02. 23
color | i'ld let a parish of such clotens blood, 4.02.168
i were a beast and i'ld call it good sport. TNK 4.03. 52 P
pardon me, | if i were there, i'ld wink. 5.03. 18
ILIADS *(also eliads)*
ILIADS 1 FR 0.0001 REL FR 0 V 1 P
examin'd my parts with most judicious iliads; WIV 1.03. 61 P
ILION 9 FR 0.0010 REL FR 8 V 1 P
gave hector a gift, the heir of ilion; LLL 5.02.652
up here and see them as they pass toward ilion? TRO 1.02.179 P
troy must not be, nor goodly ilion stand. 2.02.109
life shall be as safe | as priam is in ilion. 4.04.116
did in great ilion thus translate him to me. 4.05.112
first i saw yourself and diomed | in ilion, on 4.05.216
so, ilion, fall thou next! 5.08. 11
threat'ning cloud–kissing ilion with annoy, LUC 1370
burnt the shining glory | of rich–built ilion, 1524
/ILIUM 1 FR 0.0001 REL FR 1 V 0 P
/then /senseless /ilium, | seeming to feel this HAM 2.02.474
ILIUM 3 FR 0.0003 REL FR 1 V 2 P
between our ilium and where she /resides, | let TRO 1.01.101
when were you at ilium? 1.02. 45 P
was hector arm'd and gone ere ye came to ilium? 1.02. 48 P
I'LL *(also ay'll)*
/I'LL 12 FR 0.0013 REL FR 10 V 2 P
/i'll /read /enough, | /when /i /do /see /the R2 4.01.273
/i'll /beg /one /boon, | /and /then /be /gone 4.01.302
/'zounds, /i'll entreat no more. R3 3.07.219
in his head, /i'll tell you what i say of him. TRO 2.01. 74 P
/i'll /to /thy /closet, /and /go /read /with TIT 3.02. 82
/i'll /court /his /favors. HAM 5.02. 78
/i'll /see /their /trial /first, /bring /in LR 3.06. 35
/i'll /never /care /what /wickedness /i /do, 3.07. 99
/i'll /fetch /some /flax /and /whites /of /eggs 3.07.106
/sir, /i'll /bring /you /to /our /master /lear, 4.03. 50
/oats, | /if /it /be /man's /work, /i'll /do't. 5.03. 39
/i'll tell you what you shall do. OTH 2.03.314 P
I'LL 1879 FR 0.2124 REL FR 1413 V 466 P
i'll warrant him for drowning, though the ship TMP 1.01. 46 P
and then i'll bring thee to the present business 1.02.136
what i command, i'll rack thee with old cramps, 1.02.369
i'll free thee | within two days for this. 1.02.421
delicate ariel, | i'll set thee free for this. 1.02.443
gone forth, i'll make you | the queen of naples. 1.02.449
come, | i'll manacle thy neck and feet together. 1.02.462
sir, have pity, | i'll be his surety. 1.02.476
i'll teach you how to flow. 2.01.222
as thou got'st milan, | i'll come by naples. 2.01.292
i'll fall flat, | perchance he will not mind me. 2.02. 16
i'll bring my wood home faster. 2.02. 71 P
i'll pull thee by the lesser legs. 2.02.103 P
i'll swear upon that bottle to be thy true 2.02.125 P
i can swim like a duck, i'll be sworn. 2.02.129 P
i'll show thee every fertile inch o' th' island; 2.02.148
i'll kiss thy foot. 2.02.152
i'll swear myself thy subject. 2.02.152
i'll show thee the best springs; 2.02.160
i'll pluck thee berries; 2.02.160
i'll fish for thee, and get thee wood enough. 2.02.161
i'll bear him no more sticks, but follow thee, 2.02.163
i'll bring thee | to clust'ring filberts, and 2.02.170
and sometimes i'll get thee | young scamels from 2.02.171
no more dams i'll make for fish, | nor fetch in 2.02.180
sit down, | i'll bear your logs the while. 3.01. 24
pray give me that, | i'll carry it to the pile. 3.01. 25
if not, i'll die your maid. 3.01. 84
you may deny me, but i'll be your servant, 3.01. 85
i'll to my book, | for yet ere supper–time must 3.01. 94
i'll not serve him, he is not valiant. 3.02. 24 P
thou shalt be lord of it, and i'll serve thee. 3.02. 57
i'll yield him thee asleep, | where thou mayst 3.02. 60
for i'll not show him | where the quick freshes 3.02. 66
by this hand, i'll turn my mercy out o' doors, 3.02. 70 P
i'll go farther off. 3.02. 72 P
after a little time | i'll beat him too. 3.02. 86
wilt come? i'll follow stephano. 3.02.152 P
i'll believe both; 3.03. 24
come to me, | and i'll be sworn 'tis true. 3.03. 26
i'll seek him deeper than e'er plummet sounded, 3.03.101
at a time, | i'll fight their legions o'er. 3.03.103
i'll be thy second. 3.03.103
a turn or two i'll walk | to still my beating 4.01.162
for the prize i'll bring thee to | shall 4.01.205
by this hand, i'll have that gown. 4.01.228 P
of wine is, or i'll turn you out of my kingdom. 4.01.251 P
my charms i'll break, their senses i'll restore, 5.01. 31
my charms i'll break, their senses i'll restore, 5.01. 31
i'll fetch them, sir. 5.01. 32
this airy charm is for, i'll break my staff, 5.01. 54
did ever plummet sound | i'll drown my book. 5.01. 57
whether this be, | or be not, i'll not swear. 5.01.123
which shall be shortly, single i'll resolve you 5.01.248
and i'll be wise hereafter, | and seek for grace 5.01.295
part of it, i'll waste | with such discourse as, 5.01.303
and in the morn | i'll bring you to your ship, 5.01.308
i'll deliver all, | and promise you calm seas, 5.01.314
upon some book i love i'll pray for thee. TGV 1.01. 20
it shall go hard but i'll prove it by another. 1.01. 85 P
and so, sir, i'll commend you to my master. 1.01.146 P
i'll show my mind | according to my shallow 1.02. 7
i'll kiss each several paper for amends. 1.02.105
to the sweet julia" — that i'll tear away — 1.02.122
please you, i'll write your ladyship another. 2.01.129
i'll warrant you, 'tis as well: 2.01.164 P
nay, i'll show you the manner of it. 2.03. 14 P
well then i'll double your folly. 2.04. 21 P
i'll die on him that says so but yourself. 2.04.114
i'll leave you to confer of home affairs; 2.04.119
must use, | and then i'll presently attend you. 2.04.189
if not, to compass her i'll use my skill. 2.04.214
madcap, i'll to the alehouse with you presently; 2.05. 8 P
look thee, i'll but lean, and my staff 2.05. 29 P
and valentine i'll hold an enemy, | aiming at 2.06. 29
now presently i'll give her father notice | of 2.06. 36
i'll quickly cross | by some sly trick blunt 2.06. 40
i'll be as patient as a gentle stream, | and 2.07. 34
and there i'll rest, as after much turmoil | a 2.07. 37
no, girl, i'll knit it up in silken strings, 2.07. 45
by seven a' clock i'll get you such a ladder. 3.01.126
i'll get me one of such another length. 3.01.133
i'll be so bold to break the seal for once. 3.01.139
why, sir, i'll strike nothing. i pray you — 3.01.203 P
come, i'll convey thee through the city–gate; 3.01.254
purse she shall not, for that i'll keep shut. 3.01.351 P
i'll have her. 3.01.355 P
i'll prove it: 3.01.359 P
well, i'll have her; 3.01.369 P
i'll after, to rejoice in the boy's correction. 3.01.384 P
and thy advice this night i'll put in practice: 3.02. 88
i'll bring you where you shall hear music and 4.02. 30 P
to that i'll speak, to that i'll sigh and weep; 4.02.122
to that i'll speak, to that i'll sigh and weep; 4.02.122
send to me in the morning, and i'll send it; 4.02.131
nay, i'll be sworn, i have sat in the stocks for 4.04. 30 P
in what you please; i'll do what i can. 4.04. 42
his love, | i'll get me such a color'd periwig. 4.04.191
i'll use thee kindly for thy mistress' sake 4.04.202
i'll wear a boot, to make it somewhat rounder. 5.02. 6
i'll after, more to be reveng'd on eglamour 5.02. 51
i'll woo you like a soldier, at arms' end, | and 5.04. 57
i'll force thee yield to my desire. 5.04. 59
please you, i'll tell you as we pass along, 5.04.168
i'll ne'er be drunk whilst i live again, but in WIV 1.01.181 P
i'll be drunk with those that have the fear of 1.01.183 P
i' faith, i'll eat nothing. 1.01.279 P
i'll eat nothing, i thank you, sir. 1.01.302 P
i'll rather be unmannerly than troublesome. 1.01.312 P
tester i'll have in pouch when thou shalt lack, 1.03. 87
i'll go watch. 1.04. 7 P
ay, forsooth, i'll fetch it you. 1.04. 48 P
but i'll ne'er put my finger in the fire, and 1.04. 85 P
man, i'll do /you your master what good i can; 1.04. 92 P
fenton, i'll be sworn on a book she loves you. 1.04.145 P
i'll exhibit a bill in the parliament for the 2.01. 28 P
nay, i'll ne'er believe that; 2.01. 37 P
i'll entertain myself like one that i am not 2.01. 86 P
i'll be sure to keep him above deck. 2.01. 90 P
come under my hatches, i'll never to sea again. 2.01. 93 P
but i'll give you a pottle of burnt sack to give 2.01.214 P
think'st thou i'll endanger my soul gratis? 2.02. 16 P
i'll be sworn, | as my mother was, the first 2.02. 37
fair woman, and i'll vouchsafe thee the hearing. 2.02. 42 P
i'll make more of thy old body than i have done. 2.02.139 P
i'll be judgment by mine host of the garter. 3.01. 95 P
with her for more money than i'll speak of. 3.02. 56 P
i'll make him dance. 3.02. 90 P
ay, i'll be sworn. 3.03. 29 P
i'll go hide me. 3.03. 35 P
i'll speak it before the best lord, i would make 3.03. 50 P
keep in that mind, i'll deserve it. 3.03. 82 P
i'll in, i'll in. 3.03.137 P
i'll in, i'll in. 3.03.137 P
i'll in. 3.03.138 P
i'll never — 3.03.142 P
i'll tell you my dream. 3.03.161 P
i'll warrant we'll unkennel the fox. 3.03.163 P
i'll make a shaft or a bolt on't. 3.04. 24 P
i'll leave you. 3.04. 53 P
i have promis'd, and i'll be as good as my word, 3.04.108 P
i'll have my brains ta'en out and butter'd, and 3.05. 7 P
i'll no pullet–sperm in my brewage. 3.05. 31 P
i'll be horn–mad. 3.05.152 P
i'll be with her by and by; 4.01. 7 P
i'll but bring my young man here to school. 4.01. 7 P
no, i'll come no more i' th' basket. 4.02. 49 P
what shall i do? i'll creep up into the chimney. 4.02. 55 P
i'll go out then. 4.02. 65 P
for i'll appoint my men to carry the basket 4.02. 94 P
i'll first direct my men what they shall do with 4.02. 99 P
go up, i'll bring linen for him straight. 4.02.100 P
i'll prat her. 4.02.184 P
i'll conjure you, i'll fortune–tell you! 4.02.186 P
i'll conjure you, i'll fortune–tell you! 4.02.186 P
i'll have the cudgel hallow'd and hung o'er the 4.02.204 P
i'll warrant they'll have him publicly sham'd, 4.02.220 P
ay, sir; i'll call /them to you. 4.03. 7 P
shall have my horses, but i'll make them pay; 4.03. 8 P
i'll sauce them. 4.03. 9 P
i'll sauce them, come. 4.03. 11 P
i'll go buy them vizards. 4.04. 70
nay, i'll to him again in name of /brook; 4.04. 76
i'll to the doctor, he hath my good will, | and 4.04. 84
i'll be so bold as stay, sir, till she come down 4.05. 12 P
i'll call. 4.05. 16 P
i'll give thee | a hundred pound in gold more 4.06. 4
image of the jest | i'll show you here at large. 4.06. 18
i'll to the vicar. 4.06. 52
besides, i'll make a present recompense. 4.06. 55
go, i'll hold. 5.01. 1 P
i'll provide you a chain, and i'll do what i can 5.01. 5 P
and i'll do what i can to get you a pair of 5.01. 5 P
go along with me, i'll tell you all, master 5.01. 24 P
i'll tell you strange things of this knave ford, 5.01. 27 P
i'll wink and couch; 5.05. 48
i'll make the best in gloucestershire know on't. 5.05.180 P
be–gar, i'll raise all windsor. 5.05.209 P
give me your hand, | i'll privily away. MM 1.01. 67
i'll wait upon your honor. 1.01. 83
i'll be your tapster still. 1.02.108 P
i'll to her. 1.02.191 P
i'll see what i can do. 1.04. 84
i'll send him certain word of my success. 1.04. 89
i'll take my leave, | and leave you to the 2.01.135
i'll be suppos'd upon a book, his face is the 2.01.155 P
or i'll have mine action of batt'ry on thee. 2.01.178 P
year, i'll rent the fairest house in it after 2.01.241 P
i'll tell him of you. 2.02. 2
i'll know | his pleasure, may be he will relent. 2.02. 2
hark how i'll bribe you. 2.02.145
i'll teach you how you shall arraign your 2.03. 21
i'll gladly learn. 2.03. 23
nay, i'll not warrant that; 2.04. 59
to do't, | i'll take it as a peril to my soul, 2.04. 65
i'll make it my morn–prayer | to have it added 2.04. 71
to be received plain, i'll speak more gross: 2.04. 82
an outstretch'd throat i'll tell the world aloud 2.04.153
guides me most, | i'll prove a tyrant to him. 2.04.169
i'll to my brother. 2.04.177
i'll tell him yet of angelo's request, | and fit 2.04.186
dear sir, ere long i'll visit you again. 3.01. 46
i'll pray a thousand prayers for thy death, | no 3.01.145
i'll be hang'd first; 3.02.168 P
him i'll desire | to meet me at the consecrated 4.03. 97
here is the head, i'll carry it myself. 4.03.102
i'll make all speed. 4.03.105
her cause and yours | i'll perfect him withal, 4.03.141
nay, tarry, i'll go along with thee. 4.03.165 P
my troth, i'll go with thee to the lane's end. 4.03.177 P

i'll call you at your house.		4.04. 16 P
cousin angelo, | in this i'll be impartial.		5.01.166
a time | when i'll depose i had him in mine arms		5.01.198
to question, you shall see how i'll handle her.		5.01.272 P
i'll lend you all my life to do you service.		5.01.432
i'll speak all.		5.01.438
i'll utter what my sorrow gives me leave.	ERR	1.01. 35
i'll limit thee this day | to seek thy /health		1.01.150
till that, i'll view the manners of the town,		1.02. 12
please you, i'll meet with you upon the mart,		1.02. 27
nay, and you will not, sir, i'll take my heels.		1.02. 94
i'll to the centaur to go seek this slave;		1.02.104
ere i learn love, i'll practice to obey.		2.01. 29
i'll weep what's left away, and weeping die.		2.01.115
i'll make you amends next, to give you nothing		2.02. 53 P
i'll entertain the /offer'd fallacy.		2.02.186
husband, i'll dine above with you to–day, | and		2.02.207
i'll say as they say, and persever so, | and in		2.02.215
sir, i'll tell you when, and you'll tell me		3.01. 39
go fetch me something: i'll break ope the gate.		3.01. 73
breaking here, and i'll break your knave's pate.		3.01. 74
well, i'll break in: go borrow me a crow.		3.01. 80
i'll knock elsewhere, to see if they'll disdain		3.01.121
i'll meet you at that place some hour hence.		3.01.122
transform me then, and to your pow'r i'll yield.		3.02. 40
and as a /bed i'll take /them, and there lie,		3.02. 49
i'll fetch my sister to get her good will.		3.02. 70
i'll stop mine ears against the mermaid's song.		3.02.164
and soon at supper–time i'll visit you, | and		3.02.174
i'll to the mart and there for dromio stay:		3.02.184
or i'll attach you by this officer.		4.01. 6
if not, i'll leave him to the officer.		4.01. 61
and i'll be gone, sir, and not trouble you.		4.03. 70
i'll give thee, ere i leave thee, so much money,		4.04. 2
i'll serve you, sir, five hundred at the rate.		4.04. 14
but with these nails i'll pluck out these false		4.04.104
good sir, draw near to me, i'll speak to him.		5.01. 12
i'll prove mine honor and mine honesty | against		5.01. 30
with all my heart, i'll gossip at this feast.		5.01.408
and in her bosom i'll unclasp my heart, | and	ADO	1.01.323
no, uncle, i'll none.		2.01. 63 P
know the gentleman, i'll tell him what you say.		2.01.144 P
if it will not be, i'll leave you.		2.01.201 P
well, i'll be reveng'd as i may.		2.01.209 P
to be true, though, i'll be sworn, if he be so,		2.01.297 P
me to an oyster, but i'll take my oath on it,		2.03. 24 P
wise, or i'll none;		2.03. 31 P
virtuous, or i'll never cheapen her;		2.03. 31 P
fair, or i'll never look on her;		2.03. 32 P
i'll make her come, i warrant you, presently.		3.01. 14
and truly i'll devise some honest slanders | to		3.01. 84
in, | i'll show thee some attires, and have thy		3.01.102
i'll bring you thither, my lord, if you'll		3.02. 3 P
no, pray thee, good meg, i'll wear this.		3.04. 8 P
i'll wear none but this.		3.04. 12 P
do not wrest true speaking, i'll offend nobody.		3.04. 34 P
do you sing it, and i'll dance it.		3.04. 45 P
i'll wait upon them, i am ready.		3.05. 56 P
for thee i'll lock up all the gates of love,		4.01.105
i'll prove it on his body, if he dare, | despite		5.01. 74
sir boy, i'll whip you from your foining fence,		5.01. 84
i'll tell thee how beatrice prais'd thy wit the		5.01.159 P
and, i'll warrant you, for the love of beatrice.		5.01.195 P
to–night i'll mourn with hero.		5.01.330
i'll hold my mind were she an ethiope.		5.04. 38
i'll tell you largely of fair hero's death.		5.04. 69
and i'll be sworn upon't that he loves her,		5.04. 85
i'll tell thee what, prince:		5.04.100 P
i'll devise thee brave punishments for him.		5.04.127 P
yet, confident, i'll keep what i have sworn,	LLL	1.01.114
and to the strictest decrees i'll write my name.		1.01.117
i'll lay my head to any good man's hat, | these		1.01.308
and, if you prove it, i'll repay it back, | or		2.01.158
i'll give you aquitaine and all that is his,		2.01.248
"no, i'll give you a remuneration":		3.01.139 P
to myself forsworn, to thee i'll faithful prove;		4.02.107
i'll drop the paper.		4.03. 41
once more i'll read the ode that i have writ.		4.03. 97
once more i'll mark how love can vary wit.		4.03. 98
i'll find a fairer face not wash'd to–day.		4.03.269
i'll prove her fair, or talk till doomsday here.		4.03.270
i'll make one in a dance, or so;		5.01.153
therefore i'll darkly end the argument.		5.02. 23
that same berowne i'll torture ere i go.		5.02. 60
since you can cog, i'll play no more with you.		5.02.235
you, | as much in private, and i'll bid adieu.		5.02.241
no, i'll not be your half.		5.02.249
i'll leave it by degrees.		5.02.418
i'll slash, i'll do it by the sword.		5.02.695 P
i'll slash, i'll do it by the sword.		5.02.695 P
i'll do it in my shirt.		5.02.698 P
since when, i'll be sworn, he wore none but a		5.02.713 P
i'll mark no words that smooth–fac'd wooers say.		5.02.828
then, if i have much love, i'll give you some.		5.02.830
i'll serve thee true and faithfully till then.		5.02.831
i'll change my black gown for a faithful friend.		5.02.834
i'll stay with patience, but the time is long.		5.02.835
i'll jest a twelvemonth in an hospital.		5.02.871
demetrius, i'll avouch it to his head, | made	MND	1.01.106
the rest i'll give to be to you translated.		1.01.191
i'll speak in a monstrous little voice, "thisne!		1.02. 52 P
i'll be gone.		2.01. 16
i'll put a girdle round about the earth | in		2.01.175
juice, | i'll watch titania when she is asleep,		2.01.177
herb), | i'll make her render up her page to me.		2.01.185
the one i'll slay;		2.01.190
i'll run from thee and hide me in the brakes,		2.01.227
i'll follow thee and make a heaven of hell, | to		2.01.243
and with the juice of this i'll streak her eyes,		2.01.257
either death, or you, i'll find immediately.		2.02.156
i'll be an auditor, | an actor too perhaps, if i		3.01. 79
i'll meet thee, pyramus, at ninny's tomb."		3.01. 97
i'll follow you, i'll lead you about a round,		3.01.106
i'll follow you, i'll lead you about a round,		3.01.106
sometime a horse i'll be, sometime a hound, | a		3.01.108
i'll give thee fairies to attend on thee;		3.01.157
i'll believe as soon | this whole earth may be		3.02. 52
i'll charm his eyes against she do appear.		3.02. 99
i'll not trust your word.		3.02.268
although i hate her, i'll not harm her so.		3.02.270
follow? nay; i'll go with thee, cheek by jowl.		3.02.338
i'll to my queen and beg her indian boy;		3.02.375
come, thou child, | i'll whip thee with a rod.		3.02.410
i'll find demetrius and revenge this spite.		3.02.420
i'll apply | /to your eye, | gentle lover,		3.02.450
a day for playing pyramus, i'll be hang'd.		4.02. 22 P
i'll tell thee more of this another time;	MV	1.01.100
a while, | i'll end my exhortation after dinner.		1.01.104
fare you well! i'll grow a talker for this gear.		1.01.110
ripe wants of my friend, | i'll break a custom.		1.03. 64
courtesies | i'll lend you thus much moneys"?		1.03.129
content, in faith, i'll seal to such a bond,		1.03.152
for me, | i'll rather dwell in my necessity.		1.03.155
knave, and presently | i'll be with you.		1.03.177
i'll be sworn, if thou be launcelot, thou art		2.02. 91 P
i'll take my leave of the jew in the twinkling.		2.02.167 P
ay, marry, i'll be gone about it straight.		2.04. 24
but yet i'll go in hate, to feed upon | the		2.05. 14
for wives, | i'll watch as long for you then.		2.06. 24
albeit i'll swear that i do know your tongue.		2.06. 27
i'll then nor give nor hazard aught for lead.		2.07. 21
i'll read the writing.		2.07. 64
i'll keep my oath, | patiently to bear my wroth.		2.09. 77
i'll plague him, i'll torture him.		3.01.116 P
i'll plague him, i'll torture him.		3.01.116 P
promise me life, and i'll confess the truth.		3.02. 34
i'll begin it — ding, dong, bell.		3.02. 71
i'll have my bond, speak not against my bond,		3.03. 4
i'll have my bond;		3.03. 12
i'll have my bond, and therefore speak no more.		3.03. 13
i'll not be made a soft and dull–ey'd fool | to		3.03. 14
i'll have no speaking, i will have my bond.		3.03. 17
i'll follow him no more with bootless prayers.		3.03. 20
i'll hold thee any wager, | when we are both		3.04. 62
i'll prove the prettier fellow of the two, | and		3.04. 64
then i'll repent, | and wish, for all that, that		3.04. 72
and twenty of these puny lies i'll tell, | that		3.04. 74
i'll tell thee all my whole device | when i am		3.04. 81
i'll tell my husband, launcelot, what you say.		3.05. 27 P
well, i'll set you forth.		3.05. 90
i'll not answer that;		4.01. 42
i'll pay it instantly with all my heart.		4.01.281
i'll stay no longer question.		4.01.346
me your gloves, i'll wear them for your sake,		4.01.426
and for your love i'll take this ring from you.		4.01.427
do not draw back your hand, i'll take no more,		4.01.428
i'll see if i can get my husband's ring, | which		4.02. 13
i'll die for't but some woman had the ring!		5.01.208
as you, | i'll not deny him any thing i have,		5.01.227
own, | i'll have that doctor for /my bedfellow.		5.01.233
for if i do, i'll mar the young clerk's pen.		5.01.237
ay, and i'll give them him without a fee.		5.01.290
while i live i'll fear no other thing | so sore,		5.01.306
i'll tell thee, charles, it is the stubbornest	AYL	1.01.141 P
if he come to–morrow, i'll give him his payment.		1.01.160 P
alone again, i'll never wrastle for prize more.		1.01.161 P
kindle the boy thither, which now i'll go about.		1.01.173 P
now i'll stand to it, the pancakes were naught		1.02. 65 P
do so; i'll not be by.		1.02.164 P
with my fortunes, | i'll ask him what he would.		1.02.253
say what thou canst, i'll go along with thee.		1.03.105
i'll put myself in poor and mean attire, | and		1.03.111
i'll have no worse a name than jove's own page,		1.03.124
i'll bring you to him straight.		2.01. 69
i'll make him find him.		2.02. 19
i'll do the service of a younger man | in all		2.03. 54
then, if ever i thank any man, i'll thank you;		2.05. 25 P
well, i'll end the song.		2.05. 31 P
i'll give you a verse to this note, that i made		2.05. 46 P
and i'll sing it.		2.05. 48 P
i'll go sleep, if i can;		2.05. 60 P
i'll rail against all the first–born of egypt.		2.05. 60 P
and i'll go seek the duke, his banket is		2.05. 62 P
look'st cheerly, and i'll be with thee quickly.		2.06. 14 P
and in their barks my thoughts i'll character,		3.02. 6
you have too courtly a wit for me, i'll rest.		3.02. 70 P
i'll rhyme you so eight years together, dinners		3.02. 96 P
i'll graff it with you, and then i shall graff		3.02.117 P
tongues i'll hang on every tree, | that shall		3.02.127
i'll tarry no longer with you.		3.02.291 P
i'll tell you who time ambles withal, who time		3.02.309 P
go with me to it and i'll show it you;		3.02.430 P
proceed, proceed. i'll give her.		3.03. 71 P
say | i'll prove a busy actor in their play.		3.04. 59
looks, i'll sauce her with bitter words.		3.05. 68 P
and i'll employ thee too.		3.05. 96
a scatt'red smile, and that i'll live upon.		3.05.104
i'll write to him a very taunting letter, | and		3.05.134
i'll write it straight;		3.05.136
th' shoulder, but i'll warrant him heart–whole.		4.01. 48 P
i'll tell thee, aliena, i cannot be out of the		4.01.215 P
i'll go find a shadow, and sigh till he come.		4.01.216 P
and i'll sleep.		4.01.218 P
my love deny, | and then i'll study how to die."		4.03. 63
i marry woman, and i'll be married to–morrow.		5.02.114 P
and as i love no woman, i'll meet.		5.02.120 P
i'll not fail, if i live.		5.02.122
i'll have no father, if you be not he;		5.04.122
i'll have no husband, if you be not he;		5.04.123
have | i'll stay to know at your abandon'd cave.		5.04.196
to conjure you, and i'll begin with the women.		ep 11 P
i'll pheeze you, in faith.	SHR	in.1. 1 P
fourth, or fift borough, i'll answer him by law.		in.1. 13 P
i'll not budge an inch, boy;		in.1. 14 P
anon i'll give thee more instructions.		in.1. 130
i'll in to counsel them;		in.1. 136
ne'er ask me what raiment i'll wear, for i have		in.2. 8 P
rap me well, or i'll knock your knave's pate.		1.02. 12
sirrah, and you'll not knock, i'll ring it.		1.02. 16
i'll try how you can sol, fa, and sing it.		1.02. 17
and yet i'll promise thee she shall be rich,		1.02. 62
much my friend, | and i'll not wish thee to her.		1.02. 64
i'll tell you what, sir, and she stand him but a		1.02.112 P
you, sir, i'll have them very fairly bound —		1.02.145
liberality, | i'll mend it with a largess.		1.02.150
to her, i'll plead for you | as for my patron,		1.02.154
i'll tell you news indifferent good for either.		1.02.180
will he woo her? ay — or i'll hang her.		1.02.197
unbind my hands, i'll pull them off myself,		2.01. 4
here i swear | i'll plead for you myself, but		2.01. 15
her silence flouts me, and i'll be reveng'd.		2.01. 29
that dowry, i'll assure her of | her widowhood,		2.01.123
quoth she, "i'll fume with them."		2.01.152
i'll attend her here, | and woo her with some		2.01.168
why then i'll tell her plain | she sings as		2.01.170
i'll say she looks as clear | as morning roses		2.01.172
a word, | then i'll commend her volubility,		2.01.175
if she do bid me pack, i'll give her thanks,		2.01.177
i'll crave the day | when i shall ask the banes,		2.01.179
that i'll try.		2.01.219
i swear i'll cuff you, if you strike again.		2.01.220
i'll see thee hang'd on sunday first.		2.01.299
i'll leave her houses three or four as good,		2.01.366
i'll not be tied to hours nor 'pointed times,		3.01. 19
pedascule, i'll watch you better yet.		3.01. 50
not i, believe me, thus i'll visit her.		3.02.114
i'll after him, and see the event of this.		3.02.127
i'll keep mine own, despite of all the world.		3.02.142
i'll tell you, sir lucentio:		3.02.158
for me, i'll not be gone till i please myself.		3.02.212
i'll bring mine action on the proudest he | that		3.02.234
i'll buckler thee against a million.		3.02.239
i'll be with you straight.		4.01.167
fault | i'll find about the making of the bed,		4.01.200
bed, | and here i'll fling the pillow, there the		4.01.201
and if she chance to nod i'll rail and brawl,		4.01.206
and thus i'll curb her mad and headstrong humor.		4.01.209
my tale, | i'll make him glad to seem vincentio,		4.02. 68
in all these circumstances i'll instruct you;		4.02.120
come, mistress kate, i'll bear you company.		4.03. 49
i'll have no bigger, this doth fit the time,		4.03. 69
i'll none of it;		4.03.100
sew'd up again, and that i'll prove upon thee,		4.03.147 P
tailor, i'll pay thee for thy gown to–morrow,		4.03.166
hap what hap may, i'll roundly go about her;		4.04.107
faith, i'll see the church a' your back, and		5.01. 4 P
i'll slit the villain's nose, that would have		5.01.131 P
my cake is dough, but i'll in among the rest,		5.01.140
but not frighted me, therefore i'll sleep again.		5.02. 43
i'll venture so much of my hawk or hound, | but		5.02. 72
son, i'll be your half, bianca comes.		5.02. 78
i'll have no halves;		5.02. 79
i'll bear it all myself.		5.02. 79
get you gone, sir, i'll talk with you more anon.	AWW	1.03. 64 P
i'll stay at home | and pray god's blessing into		1.03.253
by heaven, i'll steal away.		2.01. 33
i'll see thee to stand up.		2.01. 62
nay, i'll fit you, | and not be all day neither.		2.01. 90
i'll like a maid the better whilst i have a		2.03. 41 P
i'll never do you wrong for your own sake.		2.03. 90
i'll beat him, by my life, if i can meet him		2.03.237 P
i'll have no more pity of his age than i would		2.03.239 P
his age than i would have of — i'll beat him,		2.03.240 P
i'll to the tuscan wars, and never bed her.		2.03.273
i'll send her to my house, | acquaint my mother		2.03.286
i'll send her straight away.		2.03.295
i'll to the wars, she to her single sorrow.		2.03.296
more i'll entreat you | written to bear along.		3.02. 94
for with the dark, poor thief, i'll steal away.		3.02.129
i'll question her.		3.05. 32 P
i'll about it this evening, and i will presently		3.06. 74 P
as't please your lordship. i'll leave you.		3.06.109
her, i'll add three thousand crowns | to what is		3.07. 35
to me, | i'll discover that which shall undo the		4.01. 73
and all the secrets of our camp i'll show,		4.01. 84
nay, i'll speak that | which you will wonder at.		4.01. 85
till then i'll keep him dark and safely lock'd.		4.01. 94
i'll lend it thee, my dear;		4.02. 40
my life, be thine, | and i'll be bid by thee.		4.02. 53
i'll order take my mother shall not hear.		4.02. 55
and on your finger in the night i'll put		4.02. 61
therefore i'll lie with him | when i am buried.		4.02. 72
do, i'll take the sacrament on't, how and which		4.03.136 P
thereabouts," set down, for i'll speak truth.		4.03.149 P
nay, i'll read it first, by your favor.		4.03.217 P
i'll whisper with the general, and know his		4.03.296 P
i'll no more drumming, a plague of all drums!		4.03.298 P
captain i'll be no more, | but i will eat and		4.03.331
i'll after them.		4.03.340
this i'll do for you.		5.01. 35
i'll none of him.		5.03.149 P
which on your just proceeding i'll keep off —		5.03.236
faith, i know more than i'll speak.		5.03.256 P
i'll never tell you.		5.03.284
i'll put in bail, my liege.		5.03.285
i'll swear i am a maid, and he knows not.		5.03.291
i'll love her dearly, ever, ever dearly.		5.03.316
wait on me home, i'll make sport with thee.		5.03.322 P
choose thou thy husband, and i'll pay thy dower,		5.03.328
i prithee (and i'll pay thee bounteously)	TN	1.02. 52
i'll serve this duke;		1.02. 55
be you his eunuch, and your mute i'll be;		1.02. 62
i'll confine myself no finer than i am.		1.03. 10 P
i'll drink to her as long as there is a passage		1.03. 38 P
i'll ride home to–morrow, sir toby.		1.03. 88 P
faith, i'll home to–morrow, sir toby.		1.03.105 P
i'll stay a month longer.		1.03.112 P
i'll do my best | to woo your lady.		1.04. 40
i'll no more of you.		1.05. 41 P
want of other idleness, i'll bide your proof.		1.05. 64 P
i'll be sworn thou art;		1.05.291
tell him i'll none of it.		1.05.302
way to–morrow, | i'll give him reasons for't.		1.05.306
she took the ring of me, i'll none of it.		2.02. 12 P
i'll write thee a challenge, or i'll deliver thy		2.03.129 P
or i'll deliver thy indignation to him by word		2.03.130 P
come, i'll go burn some sack, 'tis too late to		2.03.190 P
i'll pay thy pleasure then.		2.04. 69
nay, i'll come.		2.05. 2 P
ay, or i'll cudgel him, and make him cry o!		2.05.133 P
i'll make one too.		2.05.207 P
and thou pass upon me, i'll no more with thee.		3.01. 42 P
by my troth, i'll tell thee, i am almost sick		3.01. 46 P
i'll get 'em all three all ready.		3.01. 91 P

no, faith, i'll not stay a jot longer. 3.02. 1 P
of a flea, i'll eat the rest of th' anatomy. 3.02. 62 P
i'll be your purse–bearer and leave you | for an 3.03. 47
to bed? ay, sweet heart, and i'll come to thee. 3.04. 30 P
i'll come to him. 3.04. 60 P
himself possess'd him, yet i'll speak to him. 3.04. 86 P
lady would not lose him for more than i'll say. 3.04.105 P
i'll give't him. 3.04.171 P
what shall you ask of me that i'll deny, | that 3.04.211
pox on't, i'll not meddle with him. 3.04.280 P
let the matter slip, and i'll give him my horse, 3.04.286 P
i'll make the motion. 3.04.288 P
i'll ride your horse as well as i ride you. 3.04.290 P
i'll be with you anon. 3.04.320 P
that i promis'd you, i'll be as good as my word. 3.04.323 P
lean and low ability | i'll lend you something. 3.04.345
i'll make division of my present with you. 3.04.346
'slid, i'll after him again and beat him. 3.04.391 P
sir, or i'll throw your dagger o'er the house. 4.01. 28 P
i'll go another way to work with him; 4.01. 33 P
i'll have an action of battery against him, if 4.01. 34 P
i'll call sir toby the whilst. 4.02. 3 P
well, i'll put it on, and i will dissemble 4.02. 4 P
nay, i'll ne'er believe a madman till i see his 4.02.116 P
fool, i'll requite it in the highest degree. 4.02.118 P
sir, | and anon, sir, | i'll be with you again; 4.02.122
i'll follow this good man, and go with you, 4.03. 32
i'll sacrifice the lamb that i do love, | to 5.01.130
i'll help you, sir toby, because we'll be 5.01.204 P
i'll bring you to a captain in this town, 5.01.254
i'll be reveng'd on the whole pack of you. 5.01.378 P
and in that | i'll no gainsaying. WT 1.02. 19
yet of your royal presence i'll adventure | the 1.02. 38
i'll give him my commission | to let him there a 1.02. 40
i'll question you | of my lord's tricks and 1.02. 60
no, my lord, i'll fight. 1.02.162
i'll give no blemish to her honor, none. 1.02.341
i'll do't, my lord. 1.02.349
myself, i'll put | my fortunes to your service, 1.02.439
no, i'll none of you. 2.01. 3
and i'll be sworn you would believe my saying, 2.01. 63
which i'll not call a creature of thy place, 2.01. 83
i'll keep my stables where | i lodge my wife; 2.01.134
i'll go in couples with her; 2.01.135
by mine honor, | i'll geld 'em all; 2.01.147
i'll take't upon me. 2.02. 30
i'll show't the king, and undertake to be | her 2.02. 36
i'll presently | acquaint the queen of your most 2.02. 45
tell her, emilia, | i'll use that tongue i have. 2.02. 50
i'll to the queen. 2.02. 53
on mine own accord i'll off, | but first i'll do 2.03. 64
accord i'll off, | but first i'll do my errand. 2.03. 65
which is enough, i'll warrant, | as this world 2.03. 72
i'll ha' thee burnt. 2.03.114
i'll not call you tyrant; 2.03.116
i pray you do not push me, i'll be gone. 2.03.125
(and by good testimony) or i'll seize thy life, 2.03.137
i'll pawn the little blood which i have left 2.03.166
no! i'll not rear | another's issue. 2.03.192
the level of your dreams, | which i'll lay down. 3.02. 82
i'll reconcile me to polixenes, | new woo my 3.02.155
i'll swear't. 3.02.203
within, i'll serve you | as i would do the gods. 3.02.206
i'll speak of her no more, nor of your children; 3.02.229
i'll not remember you of my own lord, | who is 3.02.230
your patience to you, | and i'll say nothing. 3.02.232
once a day i'll visit | the chapel where they 3.02.238
i'll not be long before | i call upon thee. 3.03. 8
go thou away, | i'll follow instantly. 3.03. 14
i'll take it up for pity — yet i'll tarry till 3.03. 76 P
up for pity — yet i'll tarry till my son come; 3.03. 77 P
i'll go see if the bear be gone from the 3.03.128 P
if there be any of him left, i'll bury it. 3.03.131 P
lend me thy hand, i'll help thee. 4.03. 69 P
i'll be with you at your sheep–shearing too. 4.03.119 P
or i'll be thine, my fair, | or not my father's; 4.04. 42
i'll not put | the dibble in earth to set one 4.04. 99
i'll swear for 'em. 4.04.155
wenches, i'll buy for you both. 4.04.312 P
i'll have thy beauty scratch'd with briers and 4.04.425
being now awake, i'll queen it no inch farther, 4.04.449
hark, perdita! | i'll hear you by and by. 4.04.507
i'll point you where you shall have such 4.04.526
known betwixt us three, i'll write you down, 4.04.560
for this | i'll blush you thanks. 4.04.584
a great man, i'll warrant; 4.04.752 P
consider'd, i'll bring you where he is aboard, 4.04.795 P
i'll make it as much more, and leave this young 4.04.807 P
i'll have no wife, paulina. 5.01. 69
let boors and franklins say it, i'll swear it. 5.02.160 P
and i'll swear to the prince thou art a tall 5.02.163 P
but i'll swear it, and i would thou wouldst be a 5.02.167 P
i'll draw the curtain. 5.03. 68
i'll make the statue move indeed, descend, | and 5.03. 88
i'll fill your grave up. 5.03.101
i'll not seek far | (for him, i partly know his 5.03.141
brother, take you my land, i'll take my chance. JN 1.01.151
madam, i'll follow you unto the death. 1.01.154
and if his name be george, i'll call him peter; 1.01.186
anon i'll tell thee more. 1.01.232
when i was got, i'll send his soul to hell. 1.01.272
i'll smoke your skin–coat and i catch you right. 2.01.139
but, ass, i'll take that burthen from your back, 2.01.145
and out of my dear love i'll give thee more 2.01.157
i'll stir them to it. 2.01.415
i'll tell thee what, my friend, | he is a very 3.03. 60
and i'll keep him so, | that he shall not offend 3.03. 64
well, i'll not say what i intend for thee. 3.03. 68
i'll send those powers o'er to your majesty. 3.03. 70
i fear some outrage, and i'll follow her. 3.04.106
thrust but these men away, and i'll forgive you, 4.01. 82
i'll fill these dogged spies with false reports; 4.01.128
stay yet, lord salisbury, i'll go with thee, 4.02. 96
i'll make a peace between your soul and you. 4.02.250
i am afraid, and yet i'll venture it. 4.03. 5
i'll find a thousand shifts to get away. 4.03. 7
spleen to do me shame, | i'll strike thee dead. 4.03. 98
or i'll so maul you and your toasting–iron 4.03. 99
i'll tell thee what; 4.03.120
i'll to the king. 4.03.157
i am no woman, i'll not swound at it. 5.06. 22
i'll tell thee, hubert, half my power this night 5.06. 39
i'll answer thee in any fair degree | or R2 1.01. 80
come, come, my son, i'll bring thee on thy way; 1.03.304
i'll not be by the while. 2.01.211
come, cousin, i'll dispose of you. 2.02.117
may be i will go with you, but yet i'll pause, 2.03.168
i'll hate him everlastingly | that bids me be of 3.02.207
go to flint castle, there i'll pine away — | a 3.02.209
if not, i'll use the advantage of my power, 3.03. 42
be he the fire, i'll be the yielding water; 3.03. 58
i'll give thee scope to beat, | since foes have 3.03.140
i'll give my jewels for a set of beads, | my 3.03.147
or i'll be buried in the king's high way, | some 3.03.155
what you will have, i'll give, and willing too, 3.03.206
madam, i'll sing. 3.04. 19
here in this place | i'll set a bank of rue, 3.04.105
by heaven, i'll throw at all! 4.01. 57
in god's name i'll ascend the regal throne. 4.01.113
i'll lay | a plot shall show us all a merry day. 4.01.333
twice for one step i'll groan, the way being 5.01. 91
i'll not be long behind; 5.02.114
villain, i'll make thee safe. 5.03. 41
yet i'll hammer it out. 5.05. 5
my brain i'll prove the female to my soul, | my 5.05. 6
this dead king to the living king i'll bear; 5.05.117
i'll make a voyage to the holy land, | to wash 5.06. 49
no, i'll give thee thy due, thou hast paid all 1H4 1.02. 52 P
by the lord, i'll be a brave judge. 1.02. 64 P
i'll be damn'd for never a king's son in 1.02. 97 P
thou wilt, lad, i'll make one, an' i do not, 1.02.100 P
at home and go not, i'll hang you for going. 1.02.135 P
well then, once in my days i'll be a madcap. 1.02.142 P
well, come what will, i'll tarry at home. 1.02.145 P
by the lord, i'll be a traitor then, when thou 1.02.146 P
they shall not see — i'll tie them in the wood; 1.02.177 P
longer than he sees reason, i'll forswear arms. 1.02.185 P
well, i'll go with thee. 1.02.191 P
me to–morrow night in eastcheap, there i'll sup. 1.02.193 P
i'll so offend, to make offense a skill, 1.02.216
yea, on his part i'll empty all these veins, 1.03.133
i'll read you matter deep and dangerous, | as 1.03.190
i'll keep them all! 1.03.213
i'll keep them, by this hand. 1.03.216
asleep, | and in his ear i'll hollow "mortimer!" 1.03.222
i'll have a starling shall be taught to speak 1.03.224
i'll talk to you | when you are better temper'd 1.03.234
i'll steal to glendower and lord mortimer, 1.03.295
an' it be not four by the day, i'll be hang'd. 2.01. 1 P
marry, i'll see thee hang'd first. 2.01. 40 P
nicholas' clerks, i'll give thee this neck. 2.01. 62 P
no, i'll none of it, i pray thee keep that for 2.01. 63 P
if i hang, i'll make a fat pair of gallows; 2.01. 67 P
up to the top of the hill, i'll go seek him. 2.02. 8 P
medicines to make me love him, i'll be hang'd. 2.02. 19 P
i'll starve ere i'll rob a foot further. 2.02. 21 P
i'll starve ere i'll rob a foot further. 2.02. 21 P
i'll not bear my own flesh so far afoot again 2.02. 35 P
if i be ta'en, i'll peach for this. 2.02. 44 P
i'll know your business, harry, that i will. 2.03. 80
in faith, i'll break thy little finger, harry, 2.03. 87
step aside, and i'll show thee a /president. 2.04. 33 P
i'll be sworn upon all the books in england, i 2.04. 49 P
i'll play percy, and that damn'd brawn shall 2.04.109 P
i lead this life long, i'll sew nether–stocks, 2.04.116 P
geese, i'll never wear hair on my face more. 2.04.138 P
ye call me coward, by the lord, i'll stab thee. 2.04.145 P
i'll see thee damn'd ere i call thee coward, but 2.04.146 P
i'll be no longer guilty of this sin. 2.04.241 P
faith, and i'll send him packing. 2.04.297 P
do thou stand for me, and i'll play my father. 2.04.434 P
nay, i'll tickle ye for a young prince, i' faith 2.04.443 P
their date is out, and therefore i'll hide me. 2.04.504 P
i'll to the court in the morning. 2.04.543 P
i'll procure this fat rogue a charge of foot, 2.04.545 P
i'll to dinner. 3.01. 50
and i'll be sworn i have power to shame him 3.01. 60
i'll have the current in this place damm'd up, 3.01.100
i'll have it so, a little charge will do it. 3.01.114
i'll not have it alt'red. 3.01.115
i'll give thrice so much land | to any 3.01.135
ye me, | i'll cavil on the ninth part of a hair. 3.01.138
i'll haste the writer, and withal | break with 3.01.141
with all my heart i'll sit and hear her sing. 3.01.220
come, kate, i'll have your song too. 3.01.245 P
be drawn, i'll away within these two hours, and 3.01.261 P
well, i'll repent, and that suddenly, while i am 3.03. 5 P
do thou amend thy face, and i'll amend my life. 3.03. 24 P
no, i'll be sworn, i make as good use of it as 3.03. 29 P
a hair, and i'll be sworn my pocket was pick'd. 3.03. 60 P
i'll not pay a denier. 3.03. 79 P
dost thou think i'll fear thee as i fear thy 3.03.150 P
twenty, take them all, i'll answer the coinage. 4.02. 8 P
i'll not march through coventry with them, 4.02. 38 P
no, i'll be sworn, unless you call three fingers 4.02. 73 P
man | shall be my friend again, and i'll be his. 5.01.108
therefore i'll none of it. honor is a mere 5.01.140 P
deliver what you will, i'll say 'tis so. 5.02. 26
i'll murder all his wardrop, piece by piece, 5.03. 27
well, if percy be alive, i'll pierce him. 5.03. 56 P
come, my lord, i'll lead you to your tent. 5.04. 9
i'll to clifton straight. 5.04. 46
make up to clifton, i'll to sir nicholas gawsey. 5.04. 58
i'll make it greater ere i part from thee, | and 5.04. 71
all the budding honors on thy crest | i'll crop, 5.04. 73
and even in thy behalf i'll thank myself | for 5.04. 97
i'll give you leave to powder me and eat me too 5.04.111 P
therefore i'll make him sure, yea, and i'll 5.04.124 P
make him sure, yea, and i'll swear i kill'd him. 5.04.125 P
i'll take it upon my death, i gave him this 5.04.150 P
i'll gild it with the happiest terms i have. 5.04.158
i'll follow, as they say, for reward. 5.04.162 P
if i do grow great, i'll grow less, for i'll 5.04.163 P
i'll grow less, for i'll purge and leave sack, 5.04.164 P
my lord, i'll tell you what: 2H4 1.01. 51
honor, for a silken point | i'll give my barony. 1.01. 54
no, nor i neither, i'll be at your elbow. 2.01. 20 P
i'll throw thee in the channel. 2.01. 48 P
i'll tickle your catastrophe. 2.01. 60 P
let it alone, i'll make other shift. 2.01.156 P
i'll steep this letter in sack and make him eat 2.02.135 P
i am your shadow, my lord, i'll follow you. 2.02.159 P
i'll see if i can find out sneak. 2.04. 21 P
come, i'll be friends with thee, jack. 2.04. 65 P
i'll no swaggerers, i am in good name and fame 2.04. 75 P
no, i'll no swagg'rers. 2.04. 96 P
come, i'll drink no proofs nor no bullets. 2.04.118 P
i'll drink no more than will do me good, for no 2.04.119 P
wine, i'll thrust my knife in your mouldy chaps, 2.04.129 P
i'll be reveng'd of her. 2.04.154 P
i'll see her damn'd first, to pluto's damned 2.04.156 P
i'll forswear keeping house afore i'll be in 2.04.204 P
keeping house afore i'll be in these tirrits and 2.04.205 P
i'll canvass thee between a pair of sheets. 2.04.225 P
i'll ne'er bear a base mind. 3.02.235 P
faith, i'll bear no base mind. 3.02.240 P
and i'll be sworn 'a ne'er saw him but once in 3.02.321 P
well, i'll be acquainted with him if i return, 3.02.328 P
shall go hard but i'll make him a philosopher's 3.02.329 P
i'll through gloucestershire, and there will i 4.03.128 P
but bear me to that chamber, there i'll lie, 4.05.239
i'll follow you, good master robert shallow. 5.01. 60 P
me, | i'll to the king my master that is dead, 5.02. 40
i'll be your father and your brother too. 5.02. 57
let me but bear your love, i'll bear your cares. 5.02. 58
silence, i'll give you a health for that anon. 5.03. 24 P
sir, sit, i'll be with you anon, most sweet sir, 5.03. 26 P
i'll be with you straight. 5.03. 44 P
come, | i'll pledge you a mile to th' bottom." 5.03. 54
i'll drink to master bardolph, and to all the 5.03. 58 P
and i'll stick by him, sir. 5.03. 68 P
i'll tell thee what, thou damn'd tripe–visag'd 5.04. 7 P
i'll tell you what, you thin man in a censer, i 5.04. 18 P
you be not swing'd, i'll forswear half–kirtles. 5.04. 21 P
my lord, i'll tell you, that self bill is urg'd H5 1.01. 1
i'll wait upon you, and i long to hear it. 1.01. 98
the first stroke, i'll run him up to the hilts, 2.01. 64 P
he that makes the first thrust, i'll kill him; 2.01.100 P
i'll live by nym, and nym shall live by me. 2.01.110
de gud service, or i'll lig i' the grund for it; 3.02.115 P
and i'll pay't as valorously as i may, that sall 3.02.116 P
i'll assure you, 'a utt'red as prave words at 3.06. 63 P
'tis midnight, i'll go arm myself. 3.07. 89 P
tell him i'll knock his leek about his pate 4.01. 54
i'll be before thee. 4.01.288
i'll to my charge. 4.03. 6
i'll fer him, and firk him, and ferret him. 4.04. 28 P
i'll to the throng: 4.05. 22
i'll tell you there is good men porn at monmouth 4.07. 52 P
do you think i'll be forsworn? 4.08. 12 P
well, bawd i'll turn, | and something lean to 5.01. 85
to england will i steal, and there i'll steal; 5.01. 87
i'll ask them. 5.02.197 P
give me my steeled coat, i'll fight for france. 1H6 1.01. 85
bedford, if thou be slack, i'll fight it out. 1.01. 99
the circumstance i'll tell you more at large. 1.01.109
i'll hale the dolphin headlong from his throne, 1.01.149
four of their lords i'll change for one of ours. 1.01.151
i'll to the tower with all the haste i can, | to 1.01.167
and for his safety there i'll best devise. 1.01.172
only this proof i'll of thy valor make, | in 1.02. 94
and while i live, i'll ne'er fly from a man. 1.02.103
i'll be your guard. 1.02.127
what she says i'll confirm. we'll fight it out. 1.02.128
this night the siege assuredly i'll raise: 1.02.130
break up the gates, i'll be your warrantize. 1.03. 13
open the gates, or i'll shut thee out shortly. 1.03. 26
i'll canvass thee in thy broad cardinal's hat, 1.03. 36
i will not slay thee, but i'll drive thee back. 1.03. 41
i'll use to carry thee out of this place. 1.03. 43
here by the cheeks i'll drag thee up and down. 1.03. 51
thee i'll chase hence, thou wolf in sheep's 1.03. 55
cardinal, i'll be no breaker of the law; 1.03. 80
i'll call for clubs, if you will not away. 1.03. 84
i'll never trouble you, if i may spy them. 1.04. 22
frenchmen, i'll be a salisbury to you. 1.04.106
your hearts i'll stamp out with my horse's heels 1.04.108
i'll have a bout with thee; 1.05. 4
devil or devil's dam, i'll conjure thee. 1.05. 5
my breast i'll burst with straining of my 1.05. 10
a statelier pyramis to her i'll rear | than 1.06. 21
agreed. i'll to yond corner. 2.01. 33
i'll be so bold to take what they have left. 2.01. 78
within their chiefest temple i'll erect | a tomb 2.02. 12
i'll sort some other time to visit you. 2.03. 27
i'll find friends to wear my bleeding roses, 2.04. 72
i'll turn my part thereof into thy throat. 2.04. 79
i'll maintain my words | on any plot of ground 2.04. 88
and that i'll prove on better men than somerset, 2.04. 98
yourself, | i'll note you in my book of memory, 2.04.101
and in that ease, i'll tell thee my disease. 2.05. 44
content, i'll to the surgeon's. 3.01.146
i'll by a sign give notice to our friends, 3.02. 8
roan, i'll shake thy bulwarks to the ground. 3.02. 17
damsel, i'll have a bout with you again, | or 3.02. 56
so farewell, talbot, i'll no longer trust thee. 3.03. 84
but i'll unto his majesty, and crave | i may 3.04. 41
when thou shalt see i'll meet thee to thy cost. 3.04. 43
well, miscreant, i'll be there as soon as you, 3.04. 44
first let me know, and then i'll answer you. 4.01. 88
and i'll withdraw me and my bloody power. 4.02. 8
and i'll direct thee how thou shalt escape | by 4.05. 10
ay, rather than i'll shame my mother's womb. 4.05. 35
i'll bear them hence; 4.07. 92
i'll either make thee stoop and bend thy knee, 5.01. 61
i'll lop a member off and give it you | in 5.03. 15
i'll call for pen and ink, and write my mind. 5.03. 66
i'll win this lady margaret. 5.03. 88
i'll undertake to make thee henry's queen, | to 5.03.117
i'll over then to england with this news, | and 5.03.167
joan, sweet daughter joan, i'll die with thee! 5.04. 6
i'll rather keep | that which i have than, 5.04.144
delay, | i'll to the duke of suffolk presently. 2H6 1.01.171
and force perforce i'll make him yield the crown 1.01.258

i'll lengthen it with mine, | and, having both 1.02. 12
and i'll requite it | with sweet rehearsal of my 1.02. 23
next time i'll keep my dreams unto myself, | and 1.02. 53
yes, my good lord, i'll follow presently. 1.02. 60
it is enough, i'll think upon the questions. 1.02. 82
i'll be the first, sure. 1.03. 7 P
i'll tell thee, suffolk, why i am unmeet: 1.03.165
i'll have thy head for this thy traitor's speech 1.03.194
mother, priest, i'll shave your crown for this, 2.01. 50
i' faith, and i'll pledge you all, and a fig for 2.03. 66 P
and i'll prepare | my tear–stain'd eyes to see 2.04. 15
trowest thou that e'er i'll look upon the world, 2.04. 38
sometime i'll say, i am duke humphrey's wife, 2.04. 42
the deed, | and i'll provide his executioner, 3.01.276
for there i'll ship them all for ireland. 3.01.329
i'll see it truly done, my lord of york. 3.01.330
i'll call him presently, my noble lord. 3.02. 18
unworthy though thou art, i'll cope with thee, 3.02.230
i'll have an iris that shall find thee out. 3.02.407
beest death, i'll give thee england's treasure, 3.03. 2
i'll give a thousand pound to look upon him. 3.03. 13
i'll give it, sir, and therefore spare my life. 4.01. 23
stand, villain, stand, or i'll fell thee down. 4.02.115 P
he shall reign, but i'll be protector over him. 4.02.159 P
i'll send some holy bishop to entreat; 4.04. 9
but stay, i'll read it over once again. 4.04. 14
at us, as who should say, i'll be even with you. 4.07. 94 P
i'll see if his head will stand steadier on a 4.07. 95 P
but i'll bridle it. 4.07.106 P
tell him i'll send duke edmund to the tower; 4.09. 38
lord, | i'll yield myself to prison willingly, 4.09. 42
but i'll make thee eat iron like an ostridge, 4.10. 28 P
on which i'll toss the flow'r–de–luce of france. 5.01. 11
i'll send them all as willing as i live. 5.01. 51
they come, i'll warrant they'll make it good. 5.01.122
and that i'll write upon thy burgonet, | might i 5.01.200
staff, | this day i'll wear aloft my burgonet, 5.01.204
and from thy burgonet i'll rend thy bear, | and 5.01.208
i'll plant plantagenet, root him up who dares. 3H6 1.01. 48
i'll have more lives | than drops of blood were 1.01. 96
farewell, my gracious lord, i'll to my castle. 1.01.206
and i'll keep london with my soldiers. 1.01.207
i'll steal away. 1.01.212
victory /from the field | i'll see your grace; 1.01.262
till then, i'll follow her. 1.01.262
i'll write unto them and entreat them fair; 1.01.271
i'll prove the contrary, if you'll hear me speak 1.02. 20
i'll win them, fear it not. 1.02. 60
i'll open them. 1.03. 11
richard, i bear thy name, i'll venge thy death, 2.01. 87
i'll leave my son my virtuous deeds behind, 2.02. 49
leave, | i'll draw it as apparent to the crown, 2.02. 64
why, that's my fortune too, therefore i'll stay. 2.02. 76
but ere sunset i'll make thee curse the deed. 2.02.116
i'll kill my horse, because i will not fly. 2.03. 24
i vow to god above | i'll never pause again, 2.03. 30
i'll aid thee tear for tear, | and let our 2.05. 76
i'll bear thee hence, where i may weep my fill. 2.05.113
i'll bear thee hence, and let them fight that 2.05.121
i'll away before. 2.05.136
and then to brittany i'll cross the sea | to 2.06. 97
i'll stay above the hill, so both may shoot. 3.01. 5
i'll tell thee what befell me on a day | in this 3.01. 10
command, and i'll obey. 3.01. 93
it were no less, but yet i'll make a pause. 3.02. 10
then i'll warrant you all your lands, | and if 3.02. 21
lords, give us leave. i'll try this widow's wit. 3.02. 33
i'll tell you how these lands are to be got. 3.02. 42
it, | and so, i say, i'll cut the causes off, 3.02.142
i'll make my heaven in a lady's lap, | and deck 3.02.148
i'll make my heaven to dream upon the crown, 3.02.168
i'll drown more sailors than the mermaid shall, 3.02.186
i'll slay more gazers than the basilisk, | i'll 3.02.187
i'll play the orator as well as nestor, 3.02.188
tut, were it farther off, i'll pluck it down. 3.02.195
the more i stay, the more i'll succor thee. 3.03. 41
i'll undertake to land them on our coast, | and 3.03.205
and therefore i'll uncrown him ere't be long. 3.03.232
i'll join mine eldest daughter, and my joy, | to 3.03.242
and i'll be chief to bring him down again; 3.03.263
i'll wear the willow garland for his sake." 4.01.100
and therefore i'll uncrown him ere't be long." 4.01.111
i'll follow you, and tell what answer | lewis 4.03. 55
i'll hence forthwith unto the sanctuary, | to 4.04. 31
be thou sure, i'll well requite thy kindness, 4.06. 10
my liege, i'll knock once more to summon them. 4.07. 16
i'll leave you to your fortune and be gone | to 4.07. 55
if fortune serve me, i'll requite this kindness. 4.07. 78
i'll do thee service for so good a gift. 5.01. 33
for my part, i'll not trouble thee with words. 5.05. 5
by heaven, brat, i'll plague ye for that word. 5.05. 27
i'll hence to london on a serious matter. 5.05. 47
sheathe thy sword, i'll pardon thee my death. 5.05. 70
i'll hear no more; 5.06. 57
and then, to purge his fear, i'll be thy death. 5.06. 88
i'll throw thy body in another room, | and 5.06. 92
i'll blast his harvest, /and your head were laid 5.07. 21
i'll tell you what, i think it is our way, | if R3 1.01. 78
i'll in, to urge his hatred more to clarence 1.01.147
for then i'll marry warwick's youngest daughter. 1.01.153
paul, | i'll make a corse of him that disobeys. 1.02. 37
or, by saint paul, i'll strike thee to my foot, 1.02. 41
i'll have her, but i will not keep her long. 1.02.229
i'll be at charges for a looking–glass, | and 1.02.255
but first i'll turn yon fellow in his grave, 1.02.260
i'll kiss thy hand | in sign of league and amity 1.03.279
i'll to the king and signify to him | that thus 1.04. 96
i'll back to the duke of gloucester and tell him 1.04.115 P
i'll not meddle with it, it makes a man a coward 1.04.134 P
do, | i'll drown you in the malmsey–butt within. 1.04.270
i'll go hide the body in some hole | till that 1.04.280
i'll join with black despair against my soul, 2.02. 36
for, by the way, i'll sort occasion, | as index 2.02.148
and so was i. i'll bear you company. 2.03. 47
i'll resign unto your grace | the seal i keep, 2.04. 70
go, i'll conduct you to the sanctuary. 2.04. 73
i'll tell you what, my cousin buckingham — 3.01. 89
i'll win our ancient right in france again, | or 3.01. 92
a greater gift than that i'll give my cousin. 3.01.115
i'll claim that promise at your grace's hand. 3.01.197
i'll go, my lord, and tell him what you say. 3.02. 34
i'll have this crown of mine cut from my 3.02. 43
before i'll see the crown so foul misplac'd. 3.02. 44
but that i'll give my voice on richard's side 3.02. 53
i'll send some packing that yet think not on't. 3.02. 61
go on before, i'll talk with this good fellow. 3.02. 95
i'll wait upon your lordship. 3.02.112
i'll wait upon your lordship. 3.02.123
and in the duke's behalf i'll give my voice, 3.04. 19
withdraw yourself a while, i'll go with you. 3.04. 41
that i'll acquaint our duteous citizens | with 3.05. 65
i'll play the orator | as if the golden fee for 3.05. 95
for on that ground i'll make a holy descant — 3.07. 49
i'll signify so much unto him straight. 3.07. 70
i'll bear thy blame, | and take thy office from 4.01. 24
and i'll salute your grace of york as mother 4.01. 29
and soon i'll rid you from the fear of them. 4.02. 77
do then, but i'll not hear. 4.04.160
and i'll corrupt her manners, stain her beauty, 4.04.207
to save her life, i'll say she is not so. 4.04.213
to make amends i'll give it to your daughter; 4.04.295
i'll muster up my friends and meet your grace 4.04.488
but i'll not trust thee. 4.04.491
i'll draw the form and model of our battle, 5.03. 24
upon my life, my lord, i'll undertake it, | and 5.03. 42
i'll strive with troubled thoughts to take a nap 5.03.104
under our tents i'll play the ease–dropper, | to 5.03.221
withdraw, my lord, i'll help you to a horse. 5.04. 8
i'll undertake may see away their shilling H8 pr 12
i'll say | a man may weep upon his wedding–day. pr 31
i'll follow and outstare him. 1.01.129
i'll to the king, | and from a mouth of honor 1.01.136
you, and i'll go along | by your prescription; 1.01.150
to th' king i'll say't, and make my vouch as 1.01.157
person | i'll hear him his confessions justify, 1.02. 6
on my soul, i'll speak but truth. 1.02.177
the beauty of this kingdom, i'll assure you. 1.03. 54
you that side, i'll take the charge of this. 1.04. 20
here i'll make | my royal choice. 1.04. 85
are a churchman, or, i'll tell you, cardinal, 1.04. 88
i'll save you | that labor, sir. 2.01. 3
i'll tell you in a little. 2.01. 11
as i am made without him, so i'll stand, | if 2.02. 51
i'll make ye know your times of business. 2.02. 71
if it do, | i'll venture one; have at him! 2.02. 84
i'll to the king, | and say i spoke with you. 2.03. 79
my drops of tears | i'll turn to sparks of fire. 2.04. 73
and flourish'd, | i'll hang my head and perish. 3.01.153
i'll no anne bullens for him, | there's more 3.02. 87
i'll startle you | worse than the sacring bell, 3.02.294
nor, i'll assure you, better taken, sir. 4.01. 12
as i walk thither, | i'll tell ye more. 4.01.117
i'll take my leave. 5.01. 9
i'll not come back, the tidings that i bring 5.01.158
give her an hundred marks. i'll to the queen. 5.01.170
by this light, i'll ha' more. 5.01.171
i'll have more, or else unsay't; 5.01.175
now, | while 'tis hot, i'll put it to the issue. 5.01.176
i'll show your grace the strangest sight — 5.02. 20
i'll scratch your heads; 5.03. 9 P
blame me for't, i'll lay ye all | by th' heels, 5.03. 78
or i'll find | a marshalsea shall hold ye play 5.03. 85
stand close up, or i'll make your head ache. 5.03. 88
th' rail, | i'll peck you o'er the pales else. 5.03. 90
call here my varlet, i'll unarm again. TRO 1.01. 1
my part, i'll not meddle nor make no farther. 1.01. 14 P
faith, i'll not meddle in it, let her be as she 1.01. 66 P
and so i'll tell her the next time i see her. 1.01. 82 P
i'll meddle nor make no more i' th' matter. 1.01. 83 P
i'll be sworn 'tis true. 1.02.173 P
and i'll spring up in his tears an' 'twere a 1.02.175 P
i'll tell you them all by their names as they 1.02.182 P
i'll show you troilus anon. 1.02.193 P
nay, i'll watch you for that; 1.02.266 P
me | i'll hide my silver beard in a gold beaver, 1.03.296
i'll prove this troth with my three drops of 1.03.301
'sfoot, i'll learn to conjure and raise devils, 2.03. 5 P
devils, but i'll see some issue of my spiteful 2.03. 6 P
corse, i'll be sworn and sworn upon't she never 2.03. 32 P
i'll decline the whole question: 2.03. 52 P
come, patroclus, i'll speak with nobody. 2.03. 69 P
my armed fist | i'll /pash him o'er the face. 2.03.203
and he be proud with me, i'll pheese his pride. 2.03.205
i'll /let his /humors blood. 2.03.212 P
i will knead him, i'll make him supple. 2.03.221 P
i'll lay my life, with my disposer cressida. 3.01. 87 P
well, i'll make 's excuse. 3.01. 90 P
come, i'll hear no more of this, i'll sing you a 3.01.105 P
hear no more of this, i'll sing you a song now. 3.01.105 P
here i' th' orchard, i'll bring her straight. 3.02. 16 P
i'll fetch her. 3.02. 33 P
come in, come in, i'll go get a fire. 3.02. 59 P
nay, i'll give my word for her too. 3.02.109 P
in that i'll war with you. 3.02.171
made, seal it, seal it, i'll be the witness. 3.02.197 P
know my mind, i'll fight no more 'gainst troy. 3.03. 56
here is ulysses, | i'll interrupt his reading. 3.03. 93
i'll send the fool to ajax and desire him | t' 3.03.235
i'll play the hunter for thy life | with all my 4.01. 18
then, sweet my lord, i'll call mine uncle down, 4.02. 2
it's more than i know, i'll be sworn. 4.02. 52 P
i'll go in and weep. 4.02.105
i'll bring her to the grecian presently; 4.03. 6
but i'll be true. 4.04. 69
and i'll grow friend with danger. 4.04. 70
at the port, lord, i'll give her to thy hand, 4.04.111
achilles be thy guard, | i'll cut thy throat. 4.04.129
i'll answer to my lust, and know you, lord, 4.04.132
and know you, lord, | i'll nothing do on charge. 4.04.133
i'll tell thee, diomed, | this brave shall oft 4.04.136
i'll begin. 4.05. 22
i'll take that winter from your lips, fair lady; 4.05. 24
i'll have my kiss, sir. lady, by your leave. 4.05. 35
i'll make my match to live, | the kiss you take 4.05. 37
i'll give you boot, i'll give you three for one. 4.05. 40
i'll give you boot, i'll give you three for one. 4.05. 40
no, i'll be sworn. 4.05. 45
lady, a word. i'll bring you to your father. 4.05. 53
for i'll not kill thee there, nor there, nor 4.05.254
i'll kill thee every where, yea, o'er and o'er. 4.05.256
but i'll endeavor deeds to match these words, 4.05.259
i'll heat his blood with greekish wine to–night, 5.01. 1
which with my scimitar i'll cool to–morrow. 5.01. 2
this i'll obey. 5.01. 44
little blood they do, i'll be a curer of madmen. 5.01. 50 P
i'll keep you company. 5.01. 86
i'll after — nothing but lechery! 5.01. 97 P
i'll tell you what — 5.02. 21
no, no, good night, i'll be your fool no more. 5.02. 32
i'll fetch you one. 5.02. 61
i'll give you something else. 5.02. 86
i'll bring you to the gates. 5.02.188
by all the everlasting gods, i'll go! 5.03. 5
i'll stand to–day for thee and me and troy. 5.03. 36
i'll go look on. 5.04. 2 P
i'll seek them. 5.04. 35 P
i'll fight with him alone. stand, diomed. 5.06. 9
i'll be ta'en too, | or bring him off. 5.06. 24
i'll frush it and unlock the rivets all, | but 5.06. 29
the rivets all, | but i'll be master of it. 5.06. 30
why then fly on, i'll hunt thee for thy hide. 5.06. 31
is my day's work done, i'll take /good breath. 5.08. 3
as he dare, | i'll through and through you! 5.10. 26
i'll haunt thee like a wicked conscience still, 5.10. 28
till then i'll sweat and seek about for eases, 5.10. 55
well, i'll hear it, sir; COR 1.01. 93 P
i'll lean upon one crutch, and fight with t' 1.01.242
i'll swear 'tis a very pretty boy. 1.03. 57 P
i'll not over the threshold till my lord return 1.03. 74 P
and i'll tell you excellent news of your husband 1.03. 89 P
i'll buy him of you. 1.04. 5
no, i'll nor sell nor give him; 1.04. 6
he that retires, i'll take him for a volsce, 1.04. 28
i'll leave the foe | and make my wars on you. 1.04. 39
i'll fight with none but thee, for i do hate 1.08. 1
but i'll report it | where senators shall mingle 1.09. 2
true sword to sword, i'll potch at him some way, 1.10. 15
'twas time for him too, i'll warrant him that; 2.01.129 P
i'll be sworn they are true. 2.01.143 P
me, and i'll direct you how you shall go by him. 2.03. 46 P
i'll leave you. 2.03. 59
that i'll straight do; 2.03.147
i'll keep you company. will you along? 2.03.149
i'll have five hundred voices of that sound. 2.03.211
i'll give my reasons, | more worthier than their 3.01.119
no, i'll die here. 3.01.222
i'll try whether my old wit be in request | with 3.01.250
i'll go to him, and undertake to bring him 3.01.322
i'll bring him to you. 3.01.332
i'll mountebank their loves, | cog their hearts 3.02.132
i'll return consul, | or never trust to what my 3.02.135
i'll know no further. 3.03. 87
my wife, my mother, | i'll do well yet. 4.01. 21
i'll follow thee a month, devise with thee 4.01. 38
i'll tell thee what — yet go! 4.02. 22
i'll enter. 4.04. 24
he give me way, | i'll do his country service. 4.04. 26
i'll have you talk'd with anon. 4.05. 17 P
so did i, i'll be sworn. 4.05.160 P
no, i'll not go. 5.01. 1
to hear cominius speak, i'll keep at home. 5.01. 7
no; i'll not meddle. 5.01. 38
i'll undertake't. 5.01. 47
therefore i'll watch him | till he be dieted to 5.01. 56
to my request, | and then i'll set upon him. 5.01. 58
good faith, i'll prove him, | speed how it will. 5.01. 60
i'll say an arrant for you. 5.02. 60 P
i'll never | be such a gosling to obey instinct, 5.03. 34
i'll run away till i am bigger, but then i'll 5.03.128
run away till i am bigger, but then i'll fight. 5.03.128
city be afire, | and then i'll speak a little. 5.03.182
make true wars, | i'll frame convenient peace. 5.03.191
i'll not to rome, i'll back with you, and pray 5.03.198
i'll not to rome, i'll back with you, and pray 5.03.198
out of that i'll work | myself a former fortune. 5.03.201
shall he die, | and i'll renew me in his fall. 5.06. 48
thou think | i'll grace thee with that robbery, 5.06. 88
i'll deliver | myself your loyal servant, or 5.06.139
i'll be one. 5.06.148
and with my sword i'll keep this door safe. TIT 1.01.288
follow, my lord, and i'll soon bring her back. 1.01.289
i'll trust by leisure him that mocks me once, 1.01.301
alone, | i'll find a day to massacre them all, 1.01.450
him, and i'll go fetch thy sons | to back thy 2.03. 53
nay then i'll stop your mouth. 2.03.185
i'll see what hole is here, | and what he is 2.03.246
in summer's drought i'll drop upon thee still, 3.01. 19
in winter with warm tears i'll melt the snow, 3.01. 20
give me a sword, i'll chop off my hands too, 3.01. 72
with all my heart i'll send the emperor my hand. 3.01.160
then i'll go fetch an axe. 3.01.184
i'll deceive them both; 3.01.186
but i'll deceive you in another sort, | and that 3.01.190
lucius, i'll fit thee, and withal my boy | shall 4.01.114
no, boy, not so, i'll teach thee another course. 4.01.119
lucius and i'll go brave it at the court. 4.01.121
i'll broach the tadpole on my rapier's point. 4.02. 85
on, you thick–lipp'd slave, i'll bear you hence, 4.02.175
i'll make you feed on berries and on roots, 4.02.177
i'll dive into the burning lake below, | and 4.03. 44
i'll be at hand, sir, see you do it bravely. 4.03.112 P
for this proud mock i'll be thy slaughter–man, 4.04. 58
if thou do this, i'll show thee wondrous things, 5.01. 55
i'll speak no more but "vengeance rot you all!" 5.01. 58
by that god he swears, | to that i'll urge him: 5.01. 81
and then i'll come and be thy waggoner, | and 5.02. 48
and day by day i'll do this heavy task, | so 5.02. 58
i'll make him send for lucius his son; 5.02. 75
i'll find some cunning practice out of hand, 5.02. 77
show me a murtherer, i'll deal with him. 5.02. 93
me, | or else i'll call my brother back again, 5.02.135
and with your blood and it i'll make a paste, 5.02.187
so, now bring them in, for i'll play the cook, 5.02.204
i'll know his grievance, or be much denied. ROM 1.01.157

i'll pay that doctrine, or else die in debt. 1.01.238
now i'll tell you without asking. 1.02. 78 P
i'll go along no such sight to be shown, | but 1.02.100
i'll lay fourteen of my teeth — | and yet, to 1.03. 12
i'll look to like, if looking liking move; 1.03. 97
phrase, | i'll be a candle–holder and look on: 1.04. 38
that makes dainty, | she i'll swear hath corns. 1.05. 20
the measure done, i'll watch her place of stand, 1.05. 50
i'll not endure him. 1.05. 76
for shame, | i'll make you quiet. 1.05. 88
by my fay, it waxes late, | i'll to my rest. 1.05.127
nay, i'll conjure too. 2.01. 6
romeo, good night, i'll to my truckle–bed, 2.01. 39
my love, | and i'll no longer be a capulet. 2.02. 36
call me but love, and i'll be new baptiz'd; 2.02. 50
i'll frown and be perverse, and say thee nay, 2.02. 96
i'll prove more true | than those that have 2.02.100
the god of my idolatry, | and i'll believe thee. 2.02.115
by one that i'll procure to come to thee, 2.02.145
and all my fortunes at thy foot i'll lay, | and 2.02.147
and i'll still stay, to have thee still forget, 2.02.174
i'll tell thee ere thou ask it me again. 2.03. 48
i'll tell thee as we pass, but this i pray, 2.03. 63
with me, | in one respect i'll thy assistant be; 2.03. 90
and spurs, swits and spurs, or i'll cry a match. 2.04. 69 P
speak any thing against me, i'll take him down, 2.04.150 P
and if i cannot, i'll find those that shall. 2.04.152 P
farewell, be trusty, and i'll quit thy pains. 2.04.192
man, but, i'll warrant you, when i say so, she 2.04.205 P
say either, and i'll stay the circumstance. 2.05. 36
but, i'll warrant him, as gentle as a lamb. 2.05. 44 P
go, i'll to dinner, hie you to the cell. 2.05. 77
but i'll be hang'd, sir, if he wear your livery. 3.01. 57
but i'll amerce you with so strong a fine | that 3.01.190
cords, come, nurse, i'll to my wedding–bed, 3.02.136
i'll find romeo | to comfort you, i wot well 3.02.138
i'll to him, he is hid at lawrence' cell. 3.02.141
i'll give thee armor to keep off that word: 3.03. 54
my lord, i'll tell my lady you will come. 3.03.161
i'll find out your man, | and he shall signify 3.03.169
i'll say yon grey is not the morning's eye, 3.05. 19
farewell, farewell! one kiss, and i'll descend. 3.05. 42
i'll send to one in mantua, | where that same 3.05. 88
find thou the means, and i'll find such a man. 3.05.103
but now i'll tell thee joyful tidings, girl. 3.05.104
to answer, "i'll not wed, i cannot love; 3.05.185
but, and you will not wed, i'll pardon you. 3.05.187
and you be mine, i'll give you to my friend; 3.05.191
for, by my soul, i'll ne'er acknowledge thee, 3.05.193
trust to't, bethink you, i'll not be forsworn. 3.05.195
talk not to me, for i'll not speak a word. 3.05.202
i'll to the friar to know his remedy; 3.05.241
and with this knife i'll help it presently. 4.01. 54
and if thou darest, i'll give thee remedy. 4.01. 76
i'll send a friar with speed | to mantua, with 4.01.123
for i'll try if they can lick their fingers. 4.02. 3 P
i'll have this knot knit up to–morrow morning. 4.02. 24
i'll not to bed to–night; 4.02. 42
me alone, | i'll play the huswife for this once. 4.02. 43
i'll call them back again to comfort me. 4.03. 17
and trim her up, | i'll go and chat with paris. 4.04. 26
i will carry no crotchets, i'll re you, i'll fa 4.05.118 P
carry no crotchets, i'll re you, i'll fa you. 4.05.119 P
i'll be with thee straight. 5.01. 33
brother, i'll go and bring it thee. 5.02. 23
for all this same, i'll hide me hereabout, | his 5.03. 43
and in despite i'll cram thee with more food. 5.03. 48
i'll bury thee in a triumphant grave. 5.03. 83
stay then, i'll go alone. 5.03.135
i'll dispose of thee | among a sisterhood of 5.03.156
then i'll be brief. 5.03.169
i'll pay the debt and free him. TIM 1.01.103
what you bestow, in him i'll counterpoise, | and 1.01.145
away, unpeaceable dog, or i'll spurn thee hence! 1.01.270 P
i'll keep you company. 1.01.283
why then another time i'll hear thee. 1.02.178
i'll hunt with him, and let them be receiv'd, 1.02.190
i'll tell you true, i'll call to you. 1.02.217
i'll tell you true, i'll call to you. 1.02.217
no, i'll nothing; 1.02.238 P
i'll lock thy heaven from thee. 1.02.248 P
lords, keep on, | i'll wait upon you instantly. 2.02. 35
pray you walk near, i'll speak with you anon. 2.02.123
i'll look you out a good turn, servilius. 3.02. 60
of me now, | that i'll requite it last? 3.03. 19
i'll show you how t' observe a strange event. 3.04. 17
i'll have it so. my steward! 3.04.108
i'll once more feast the rascals. 3.04.112
my cook and i'll provide. 3.04.117
ages love | security, i'll pawn my victories, 3.05. 80
i'll cheer up | my discontented troops, and lay 3.05.113
i'll tell you more anon. 3.06. 59 P
nothing i'll bear from thee | but nakedness, 4.01. 32
the latest of my wealth i'll share amongst you. 4.02. 23
i'll follow and inquire him out. 4.02. 48
i'll ever serve his mind with my best will; 4.02. 49
whilst i have gold, i'll be his steward still. 4.02. 50
th' art quick, | but yet i'll bury thee; 4.03. 46
i'll take the gold thou givest me, | not all thy 4.03.130
i'll trust to your conditions, be whores still. 4.03.140
if i thrive well, i'll visit thee again. 4.03.170
if i hope well, i'll never see thee more. 4.03.171
i know not what else to do, i'll see thee again. 4.03.354 P
i'll beat thee, but i should infect my hands. 4.03.364
i'll say th' hast gold; 4.03.393
like workmen, i'll example you with thievery: 4.03.435
i'll believe him as an enemy, and give over my 4.03.454 P
i'll meet you at the turn. 5.01. 47
look you, i love you well, i'll give you gold, 5.01.100
and come to me, | i'll give you gold enough. 5.01.104
and i'll beweep these comforts, worthy senators. 5.01.158
i'll teach them to prevent wild alcibiades' 5.01.203
the character i'll take with wax; 5.03. 6
i'll about, | and drive away the vulgar from the JC 1.01. 69
i'll leave you. 1.02. 31
you that, i'll ne'er look you i' th' face again. 1.02.281 P
send him but hither, and i'll fashion him. 2.01.220
i'll get me to a place more void, and there 2.04. 37
i'll fetch him presently. 3.01.142
brutus, bait not me, | i'll not endure it. 4.03. 29
i'll use you for my mirth, yea, for my laughter, 4.03. 49
i'll know his humor, when he knows his time. 4.03.136
i'll have them sleep on cushions in my tent. 4.03.243
thy instrument, | i'll take it from thee; 4.03.272
i'll tell /the news. 5.04. 17
i'll rather kill myself. 5.05. 7
i'll see it done. MAC 1.02. 66
but in a sieve i'll thither sail, | and, like a 1.03. 8
without a tail, | i'll do, i'll do, and i'll do. 1.03. 10
without a tail, | i'll do, i'll do, and i'll do. 1.03. 10
without a tail, | i'll do, i'll do, and i'll do. 1.03. 10
i'll give thee a wind. 1.03. 11
i'll drain him dry as hay: 1.03. 18
i'll be myself the harbinger and make joyful 1.04. 45
i'll go no more. 2.02. 47
i'll gild the faces of the grooms withal, | for 2.02. 53
i'll devil–porter it no further. 2.03. 17 P
i'll bring you to him. 2.03. 47
i'll make so bold to call, | for 'tis my limited 2.03. 51
i'll to england. 2.03.137
no, cousin, i'll to fife. 2.04. 36
supper, sir, | and i'll request your presence. 3.01. 15
yourselves apart, | i'll come to you anon. 3.01.138
i'll call upon you straight; 3.01.139
here i'll sit i' th' midst. 3.04. 10
love and health to all, | then i'll sit down. 3.04. 87
this night i'll spend | unto a dismal and a 3.05. 20
profound, | i'll catch it ere it come to ground; 3.05. 25
i'll send my prayers with him. 3.06. 49
but yet i'll make assurance double sure, | and 4.01. 83
i'll see no more. 4.01.118
i'll charm the air to give a sound, | while you 4.01.129
this deed i'll do before this purpose cool. 4.01.154
'shall not be long but i'll be here again. 4.02. 23
what i believe, i'll wail, | what know, believe; 4.03. 8
i'll fight, till from my bones my flesh be 5.03. 32
i'll put it on. 5.03. 34
throw physic to the dogs, i'll none of it. 5.03. 47
my sword | i'll prove the lie thou speak'st. 5.07. 11
i'll not fight with thee. 5.08. 22
more sorrow, | and that i'll spend for him. 5.09. 17
i'll cross it, though it blast me. HAM 1.01.127
good friend — i'll change that name with you. 1.02.163
i'll speak to it, though hell itself should gape 1.02.244
'twixt aleven and twelf | i'll visit you. 1.02.252
i'll call thee hamlet, | king, father, royal 1.04. 44
it waves me forth again, i'll follow it. 1.04. 68
it waves me still. — | go on, i'll follow thee. 1.04. 79
heaven, i'll make a ghost of him that lets me! 1.04. 85
go on, i'll follow thee. 1.04. 86
speak, i'll go no further. 1.05. 1
i'll wipe away all trivial fond records, | all 1.05. 99
at such a time i'll loose my daughter to him. 2.02.162
i'll board him presently. 2.02.170
i'll speak to him again. 2.02.190 P
i'll have thee speak out the rest of this soon. 2.02.521 P
my good friends, i'll leave you /till night. 2.02.547 P
i'll have these players | play something like 2.02.594
i'll observe his looks, | i'll tent him to the 2.02.596
observe his looks, | i'll tent him to the quick. 2.02.597
i'll have grounds | more relative than this — 2.02.603
wherein i'll catch the conscience of the king. 2.02.605
marry, i'll give thee this plague for thy dowry: 3.01.134 P
go to, i'll no more on't, it hath made me mad. 3.01.146 P
and i'll be plac'd (so please you) in the ear 3.01.184
wear black, for i'll have a suit of sables. 3.02.130 P
i'll mark the play. 3.02.147 P
i'll take the ghost's word for a thousand pound. 3.02.286 P
behind the arras i'll convey myself | to hear 3.03. 28
i'll warrant she'll tax him home, | and, as you 3.03. 29
liege, | i'll call upon you ere you go to bed, 3.03. 34
then i'll look up. 3.03. 50
and now i'll do't — and so 'a goes to heaven, 3.03. 74
i'll silence me even here; 3.04. 4
i'll /warr'nt you, fear me not. 3.04. 6
nay, then i'll set those to you that can speak. 3.04. 17
to be blest, | i'll blessing beg of you. 3.04.172
i'll lug the guts into the neighbor room. 3.04.212
delay it not, i'll have him hence to–night. 4.03. 55
i'll be with you straight — go a little before. 4.04. 31
indeed without an oath i'll make an end on't. 4.05. 57 P
i'll not be juggled with. 4.05.131
only i'll be reveng'd | most throughly for my 4.05.136
and for my means, i'll husband them so well, 4.05.139
to his good friends thus wide i'll ope my arms, 4.05.146
and, for /that purpose, i'll anoint my sword. 4.07.140
i'll touch my point | with this contagion, that, 4.07.146
i'll have preferr'd him | a chalice for the 4.07.159
i'll put another question to thee. 5.01. 37 P
i'll do't. 5.01.277
and thou'lt mouth, | i'll rant as well as thou. 5.01.284
i'll be your foil, laertes; 5.02.255
i'll play this bout first, set it by a while. 5.02.284
my lord, i'll hit him now. 5.02.295
by heaven, i'll ha't! 5.02.343
from my throat, | i'll tell thee thou dost evil. LR 1.01.166
i'll do't before i speak — that you make known 1.01.226
i'll apprehend him. 1.02. 77 P
i'll not endure it. 1.03. 5
the fault of it i'll answer. 1.03. 10
i'll write straight to my sister | to hold my 1.03. 25
i'll not be strucken, my lord. 1.04. 85 P
thou serv'st me, and i'll love thee. 1.04. 88 P
i'll teach you differences. 1.04. 89 P
sirrah, i'll teach thee a speech. 1.04.115 P
give me an egg, and i'll give thee two crowns. 1.04.156 P
degenerate bastard, i'll not trouble thee; 1.04.254
i'll tell thee. 1.04.296
beweep this cause again, i'll pluck ye out, 1.04.302
that i'll resume the shape which thou dost think 1.04.309
all ports i'll bar, the villain shall not scape; 2.01. 80
boy, i'll work the means | to make thee capable. 2.01. 84
to sojourn at my house, | i'll not be there. 2.01.104
i'll make a sop o' th' moonshine of you, you 2.02. 32 P
you rogue, or i'll so carbonado your shanks! 2.02. 38 P
come, i'll flesh ye, come on, young master. 2.02. 46 P
i'll answer that. 2.02.147
i'll entreat for thee. 2.02.154
time i shall sleep out, the rest i'll whistle. 2.02.156
my face i'll grime with filth, | blanket my 2.03. 9
i'll forbear, | and am fallen out with my more 2.04.109
or at their chamber–door i'll beat the drum 2.04.118
but i'll not chide thee, | let shame come when 2.04.225
i'll go with thee, | thy fifty yet doth double 2.04.258
you think i'll weep: 2.04.282
no, i'll not weep. 2.04.283
a hundred thousand flaws | or ere i'll weep. 2.04.286
for his particular, i'll receive him gladly, 2.04.292
in which your pain | that way, i'll this — he 3.01. 54
i'll speak a prophecy ere i go: 3.02. 80 P
but i'll go in. 3.04. 25
i'll pray, and then i'll sleep. 3.04. 27
i'll pray, and then i'll sleep. 3.04. 27
i'll talk a word with this same learned theban. 3.04.157
thou sayest the king grows mad, i'll tell thee, 3.04.165
and i'll go to bed at noon. 3.06. 85 P
upon these eyes of thine i'll set my foot. 3.07. 68
naked soul, | which i'll entreat to lead me. 4.01. 45
i'll bring him the best 'parel that i have, 4.01. 49
and i'll repair the misery thou dost bear | with 4.01. 76
i'll read, and answer. 4.02. 87
i'll love thee much — | let me unseal the 4.05. 21
i'll look no more, | lest my brain turn, and the 4.06. 22
henceforth i'll bear | affliction till it do cry 4.06. 75
there's my gauntlet, i'll prove it on a giant. 4.06. 90 P
no, do thy worst, blind cupid, i'll not love. 4.06.137 P
does offend, none, i say none, i'll able 'em. 4.06.168
i'll put't in proof, | and when i have stol'n 4.06.185
me your hand, | i'll lead you to some biding. 4.06.224
thee i'll rake up, the post unsanctified | of 4.06.274
come, father, i'll bestow you with a friend. 4.06.286
i'll overtake you. — speak. 5.01. 39
let but the herald cry, | and i'll appear again. 5.01. 49
i return to you again, | i'll bring you comfort. 5.02. 4
i'll kneel down | and ask of thee forgiveness. 5.03. 10
i'll do't, my lord. 5.03. 34
i'll make it on thy heart, | ere i taste bread, 5.03. 93
if not, i'll ne'er trust medicine. 5.03. 96
i'll tell you straight. 5.03.280
i'll see that straight. 5.03.288
here is her father's house, i'll call aloud. OTH 1.01. 74
at every house i'll call | (i may command at 1.01.180
her, | for i'll refer me to all things of sense, 1.02. 64
i'll have't disputed on, | 'tis probable, and 1.02. 75
so justly to your grave ears i'll present | how 1.03.124
i'll be with thee betimes. 1.03.375 P
i'll sell all my land. 1.03.382 P
but i'll set down the pegs that make this music, 2.01.200
for the command, i'll lay't upon you. 2.01.265 P
i'll not be far from you. 2.01.266 P
on, | i'll have our michael cassio on the hip, 2.01.305
and, i'll warrant her, full of game. 2.03. 19 P
our friends — but one cup, i'll drink for you. 2.03. 37 P
i'll do't, but it dislikes me. 2.03. 47 P
and i'll do you justice. 2.03. 87 P
i'll beat the knave into a twiggen bottle. 2.03.147 P
me go, sir, or i'll knock you o'er the mazzard. 2.03.153 P
i'll make thee an example. 2.03.251
i'll pour this pestilence into his ear — | that 2.03.356
cassio to her mistress — | i'll set her on — 2.03.384
put up your pipes in your bag, for i'll away. 3.01. 19 P
i'll send her to you presently; 3.01. 36
and i'll devise a mean to draw the moor | out of 3.01. 37
well, my good lord, i'll do't. 3.02. 4
i'll perform it | to the last article. 3.03. 21
rest, | i'll watch him tame, and talk him out of 3.03. 23
i'll intermingle every thing he does | with 3.03. 25
madam, i'll take my leave. 3.03. 30
my desdemona, i'll come to thee straight. 3.03. 87
/by /heaven, i'll know thy thoughts. 3.03.162
no, iago, | i'll see before i doubt; 3.03.190
i'll not believe't. 3.03.279
come, i'll go in with you. 3.03.288
i'll have the work ta'en out, | and give't iago. 3.03.296
and from hence | i'll love no friend, sith love 3.03.380
i'll have some proof. 3.03.386
or suffocating streams, | i'll not endure it. 3.03.390
i'll tear her all to pieces. 3.03.431
i'll move your suit | and seek to effect it to 3.04.166
but i'll see you soon. 3.04.200
you had it, i'll take out no work on't. 4.01.155 P
i'll not expostulate with her, lest her body and 4.01.204 P
i'll send for you anon. 4.01.259
i'll be at thy elbow. 5.01. 3
i'll bind it with my shirt. 5.01. 73
from hence, | i'll fetch the general's surgeon. 5.01.100
yet i'll not shed her blood, | nor scar that 5.02. 3
i'll smell thee on the tree. 5.02. 15
i care not for thy sword, i'll make thee known, 5.02.165
thought so then — i'll kill myself for grief — 5.02.192
all, all, cry shame against me, yet i'll speak. 5.02.222
i'll after that same villain, | for 'tis a 5.02.242
i'll set a bourn how far to be belov'd. ANT 1.01. 16
i'll seem the fool i am not. 1.01. 42
i'll leave you, lady. 1.03. 86
a several greeting, | or i'll unpeople egypt. 1.05. 78
as i may, | i'll play the penitent to you; 2.02. 92
sister's view, | whither straight i'll lead you. 2.02.168
i'll none now. 2.05. 9
them up, | i'll think them every one an antony, 2.05. 14
i'll set thee in a shower of gold, and hail 2.05. 45
or i'll spurn thine eyes | like balls before me; 2.05. 63
i'll unhair thy head, | thou shalt be whipt with 2.05. 64
nay then i'll run. 2.05. 73
but i'll ne'er out. 2.07. 30 P
i'll never follow thy pall'd fortunes more. 2.07. 82
bear him ashore. i'll pledge it for him, pompey. 2.07. 85
possess it, i'll make answer. 2.07.101
the while i'll place you, then the boy shall 2.07.110
i'll try you on the shore. 2.07.126
menas, i'll not on shore. 2.07.130
i'll humbly signify what in his name, | that 3.01. 30
i'll tell you in your ear. 3.02. 46
i'll wrestle with you in my strength of love. 3.02. 62

that herod's head | i'll have; 3.03. 5
i'll raise the preparation of a war | shall 3.04. 26
i'll fight at sea. 3.07. 48
i'll yet follow | the wounded chance of antony, 3.10. 34
i'll see you by and by. 3.11. 24
i'll write it. 3.13. 28
but now i'll set my teeth, | and send to 3.13.180
and to–night i'll force | the wine peep through 3.13.189
next time i do fight, | i'll make death love me; 3.13.192
soldier, | by sea and land i'll fight; 4.02. 5
i'll strike, and cry, "take all!" 4.02. 8
you | where rather i'll expect victorious life 4.02. 43
nay, i'll help too. | what's this for? 4.04. 5
sooth law, i'll help. thus it must be. 4.04. 8
i'll leave thee | now like a man of steel. 4.04. 32
fight, | follow me close, i'll bring you to't. 4.04. 34
i'll halt after. 4.07. 16
to this great fairy i'll commend thy acts, 4.08. 12
i'll give thee, friend, | an armor all of gold; 4.08. 26
i'll bring thee word | straight how 'tis like to 4.12. 2
my resolution and my hands i'll trust, | none 4.15. 49
me to thee, as i was to him | i'll be to caesar; 5.01. 11
this i'll report, dear lady. 5.02. 32
sir, i will eat no meat, i'll not drink, sir; 5.02. 49
once be necessary, | i'll not sleep neither. 5.02. 51
this mortal house i'll ruin, | do caesar what he 5.02. 51
for the queen, | i'll take her to my guard. 5.02. 67
to that destruction which i'll guard them from 5.02.132
i'll take my leave. 5.02.133
but i'll catch thine eyes | though they had 5.02.156
i'll never see't! 5.02.223
i'll give thee leave | to play till doomsday. 5.02.231
crown's /awry, | i'll mend it, and then play — 5.02.319
i'll fetch a turn about the garden, pitying CYM 1.01. 81
and with mine eyes i'll drink the words you send 1.01.100
yet i'll move him | to walk this way. 1.01.103
i'll place it | upon this fairest prisoner. 1.01.122
come, i'll to my chamber. 1.02. 34 P
i'll attend your lordship. 1.02. 39 P
i'll tell thee on the instant thou art then | as 1.05. 50
i'll move the king | to any shape of thy 1.05. 70
good lord i prove untrue, | i'll choke myself. 1.05. 87
there's all i'll do for you. 1.05. 87
come, i'll go see this italian. 2.01. 48 P
lost to–day at bowls i'll win to–night of him. 2.01. 49 P
i'll attend your lordship. 2.01. 51 P
but i'll never give o'er. 2.03. 16 P
if she be up, i'll speak with her; 2.03. 64
if you'll be patient, i'll no more be mad; 2.03.103
i'll be reveng'd. | "his mean'st garment"! well. 2.03.155
i'll make a journey twice as far, t' enjoy | a 2.04. 43
married | to that your diamond, i'll keep them. 2.04. 98
i'll be sworn. 2.04.143
i'll deny nothing. 2.04.146
i'll do something — 2.04.149
i'll write against them, | detest them, curse 2.05. 32
i'll tread these flats. 3.03. 11
i'll meet you in the valleys. 3.03. 78
i'll wake mine eyeballs /out first. 3.04.101
i'll give but notice you are dead, and send him 3.04.124
i'll have this secret from thy heart, or rip 3.05. 86
i'll write to my lord she's dead, 3.05.104
to ask him one thing, i'll remember't anon.) 3.05.131 P
to the court i'll knock her back, foot her home 3.05.143 P
me rejoicingly, and i'll be merry in my revenge. 3.05.145 P
then i'll enter. 3.06. 24
i'll make't my comfort | he is a man, i'll love 3.06. 70
he is a man, i'll love him as my brother: 3.06. 71
go you to hunting, i'll abide with him. 4.02. 6
i'll rob none but myself, and let me die, 4.02. 15
pisanio, | i'll now taste of thy drug. 4.02. 38
i'll follow those that even now fled hence, 4.02. 98
i'll throw't into the creek | behind our rock, 4.02.151
i'll stay | till hasty polydore return, and 4.02.164
i'll willingly to him. 4.02.167
live here, fidele, | i'll sweeten thy sad grave. 4.02.220
i'll weep, and word it with thee; 4.02.240
faith, i'll lie down and sleep. 4.02.294
i'll follow, sir. 4.02.387
i'll hide my master from the flies, as deep | as 4.02.388
(such as i can) twice o'er, i'll weep and sigh, 4.02.392
to the note o' th' king, or i'll fall in them. 4.03. 44
by this sun that shines, | i'll thither. 4.04. 35
by heavens, i'll go. 4.04. 43
and give me leave, | i'll take the better care; 4.04. 45
that is my bed too, lads, and there i'll lie. 4.04. 52
yea, bloody cloth, i'll keep thee, for i wish'd 5.01. 1
peace, | i'll give no wound to thee. 5.01. 21
i'll disrobe me | of these italian weeds and 5.01. 22
so i'll fight | against the part i come with; 5.01. 24
so i'll die | for thee, o imogen, even for whom 5.01. 25
to the face of peril | myself i'll dedicate. 5.01. 29
who dares not stand his foe, i'll be his friend; 5.03. 60
which neither here i'll keep nor bear again, 5.03. 82
o imogen, | i'll speak to thee in silence. 5.04. 29
like it, which | i'll keep, if but for sympathy. 5.04.150
i'll be hang'd then. 5.04.195 P
which i'll make bold your highness | cannot deny 5.05. 89
fitting my bounty and thy state, i'll give it; 5.05. 98
i'll tell you, sir, in private, if you please 5.05.115
i'll be thy master. 5.05.119
lord, | now fear is from me, i'll speak troth. 5.05.274
i'll make my will then, and, as sick men do PER 1.01. 47
by flight i'll shun the danger which i fear. 1.01.142
my pistol's length, | i'll make him sure enough; 1.01.167
day serves not light more faithful than i'll be. 1.02.110
intend my travel, where i'll hear from thee, 1.02.116
and by whose letters i'll dispose myself. 1.02.117
i'll take thy word for faith, not ask thine oath 1.02.120
he would depart, i'll give some light unto you. 1.03. 17
i'll present myself. 1.03. 29
i'll then discourse our woes, felt several years 1.04. 18
i'll do my best, sir. 1.04. 20
i'll show you those in troubles reign, | losing 2.ch. 7
come away, or i'll fetch th' with a wanton. 2.01. 17 P
then i'll turn craver too, and so i shall scape 2.01. 88 P
but, master, i'll go draw up the net. 2.01. 93 P
why, i'll tell you. 2.01. 99 P
and i'll tell you, he hath a fair daughter, and 2.01.107 P
low fortunes better, | i'll pay your bounties; 2.01.143
i'll show the virtue i have borne in arms. 2.01.145
and i'll bring thee to the court myself. 2.01.163 P
this day i'll rise, or else add ill to ill. 2.01.166
which, to preserve mine honor, i'll perform. 2.02. 16
i'll tame you; 2.05. 75
i'll bring you in subjection. 2.05. 75
either be rul'd by me, or i'll make you — | man 2.05. 83
and being join'd, i'll thus your hopes destroy, 2.05. 86
what's dumb in show i'll plain with speech. 3.ch. 14
there i'll leave it | at careful nursing. 3.01. 79
good mariner, | i'll bring the body presently. 3.01. 81
you, | i'll not bereave you of your servant. 4.01. 31
i'll leave you, my sweet lady, for a while. 4.01. 47
i'll swear she's dead, | and thrown into the sea 4.01. 98
but i'll see further: 4.01. 99
but i'll go search the market. 4.02. 25 P
i'll bring home some to–night. 4.02.144 P
i'll say so. 4.03. 16
your ears unto your eyes i'll reconcile. 4.04. 22
i'll do any thing now that is virtuous, but i am 4.05. 8 P
me leave a word, and i'll have done presently. 4.06. 47 P
with other virtues, which i'll keep from boast, 4.06.184
come, i'll do for thee what i can; 4.06.200 P
patience, good sir! | or here i'll cease. 5.01.145
nay, i'll be patient. 5.01.145
i'll hear you more, to th' bottom of your story, 5.01.164
to my just belief, | i'll well remember you. 5.01.239
eftsoons i'll tell thee why. 5.01.255
to grace thy marriage–day, i'll beautify. 5.03. 76
i'll speak anon. TNK 1.01.106
from henceforth i'll not dare | to ask you any 1.01.203
sir, | i'll follow you at heels; 1.01.221
whose speed | the great bellona i'll solicit; 1.03. 13
i'll offer to her | what i shall be advis'd she 1.03. 15
i'll have a gown full of 'em — and of these: 2.02.128
and, as i have a soul, i'll nail thy life to't! 2.02.213
i'll throw my body out, | and leap the garden, 2.02.215
are dangerous, | i'll clap more irons on you. 2.02.271
i'll shake 'em so, ye shall not sleep, | i'll 2.02.272
ye shall not sleep, | i'll make ye a new morris. 2.02.273
i'll see her and be near her, or no more. 2.03. 23
my masters, i'll be there, that's certain. 2.03. 24
and i'll be there. 2.03. 25
to–day, i'll tickle't out | of the jades' tails 2.03. 28
but that's all one, i'll go through, let her 2.03. 31
blow wind i' th' breech on 's, and here i'll be, 2.03. 47
and there i'll be, for our town, and here again, 2.03. 48
i'll be hang'd though, | if he dare venture. 2.03. 71
i'll venture, | and in some poor disguise be 2.03. 78
and somewhat better than your rank i'll use you. 2.05. 43
i'll see you furnish'd, and because you say 2.05. 44
for use me so he shall, or i'll proclaim him, 2.06. 30
i'll presently | provide him necessaries and 2.06. 31
where there is a path of ground i'll venture, 2.06. 33
by him, like a shadow, | i'll ever dwell. 2.06. 35
i'll prove it in my shackles, with these hands 3.01. 39
them, fair coz, | i'll maintain my proceedings. 3.01. 53
i'll bring you every needful thing. 3.01. 99
i'll set it down | he's torn to pieces. 3.02. 17
are faint — then i'll talk further with you. 3.03. 7
well, sir, i'll pledge you. 3.03. 16
i'll tell you | after a draught or two more. 3.03. 18
then i'll leave you; | you are a beast now. 3.03. 46
i'll come again some two hours hence and bring 3.03. 49
i'll hear no more. 3.03. 53
i'll say never a word. 3.04. 18
"for i'll cut my green coat a foot above my knee 3.04. 19
and i'll clip my yellow locks an inch below mine 3.04. 20
and i'll go seek him through the world that is 3.04. 23
go thy ways, i'll remember thee, i'll fit thee! 3.05. 58
go thy ways, i'll remember thee, i'll fit thee! 3.05. 58
i'll lead. 3.05. 90
and furnish'd with your old strength, i'll stay, 3.06. 37
justice of affection, | i'll pay thee soundly. 3.06. 52
this i'll take. 3.06. 52
that's mine then. | i'll arm you first. 3.06. 53
i'll buckle't close. 3.06. 57
i'll warrant thee, i'll strike home. 3.06. 68
i'll warrant thee, i'll strike home. 3.06. 68
i'll give you cause, sweet cousin. 3.06. 69
and in that i'll bury | thee and all crosses 3.06.126
then take my life, i'll woo thee to't. 3.06.156
shall grow to th' ground but i'll get mercy. 3.06.192
nay then i'll in too. 3.06.201
i'll be cut a–pieces | before i take this oath. 3.06.256
her, yet i'll preserve | the honor of affection, 3.06.268
in this place, | in which i'll plant a pyramid; 3.06.293
i'll give ye | now usage like to princes and to 3.06.305
when ye return, who wins i'll settle here; 3.06.307
who loses, yet i'll weep upon his bier. 3.06.308
to her marriage, | a large one, i'll assure you. 4.01. 24
i'll tell you quickly. 4.01. 52
i'll find him out to–morrow." 4.01. 69
i'll bring a bevy, | a hundred black–ey'd maids 4.01. 71
i'll bring it to–morrow. 4.01.109
i'll warrant ye he had not so few last night 4.01.137
i'll choose, | and end their strife. 4.02. 2
come, i'll go visit 'em. 4.02.152
faith, i'll tell you; 4.03. 30 P
a leprous witch to be rid on't, i'll assure you. 4.03. 47 P
i'll leave you to your prayers, and betwixt ye 5.01. 16
and ill lodging, | but i'll kiss him up again. 5.02. 98
i'll away straight. 5.02.101
i'll warrant you within these three or four days 5.02.104
three or four days | i'll make her right again. 5.02.105
if you do, love, i'll cry. 5.02.112
i'll no step further. 5.03. 1
i'll close thine eyes, prince; 5.04. 96
i'll tell you: STM II.C 80
and being set, i'll smother thee with kisses. VEN 18
i'll sigh celestial breath, whose gentle wind 189
i'll make a shadow for thee of my hairs; 191
they burn too, i'll quench them with my tears. 192
give me one kiss, i'll give it thee again, | and 209
i'll be a park, and thou shalt be my deer: 231
she says, "this night i'll waste in sorrow, 583
i'll beg her love: LUC 241
done, some worthless slave of thine i'll slay, 515
for burthen–wise i'll hum on tarquin still, 1133
my stained blood to tarquin i'll bequeath, 1181
"my honor i'll bequeath unto the knife | that 1184
i'll tune thy woes with my lamenting tongue, 1465
i'll murther straight, and then i'll slaughter 1634
murther straight, and then i'll slaughter thee, 1634
therefore i'll lie with love, and love with me, PP 1.13
to myself forsworn, to thee i'll constant prove; 5. 3
theirs for their style i'll read, his for his SON 32.14
towards thee i'll run, and give him leave to go. 51.14
upon thy side against myself i'll fight, | and 88. 3
as i'll myself disgrace, knowing thy will: 89. 7
for thee, against myself i'll vow debate, | for 89.13
spite of him, i'll live in this poor rhyme, 107.11
myself i'll forfeit, so that other mine | thou 134. 3

/ILL 4 FR 0.0004 REL FR 4 V 0 P

look when i serve him so, he takes it /ill. ERR 2.01. 12
corrects the /ill /aspects /of /planets /evil, TRO 1.03. 92
/or /well /or /ill, /as /this /day's /battle's LR 4.07. 96
hair of mine remain, | though i show /ill in't. PER 3.03. 30

ILL 260 FR 0.0294 REL FR 190 V 70 P

wilt not take, | being capable of all ill! TMP 1.02.353
there's nothing ill can dwell in such a temple. 1.02.458
if the ill spirit have so fair a house, | good 1.02.459
'tis an ill office for a gentleman, | especially TGV 3.02. 40
ill, when you talk of war. 5.02. 16
uncivil touch, | thou friend of an ill fashion! 5.04. 61
i wish'd your venison better, it was ill kill'd. WIV 1.01. 83 P
you look very ill. 2.01. 36 P
great comfort in this mystery of ill opinions, 2.01. 72 P
the sweet woman leads an ill life with him. 2.02. 89 P
to take an ill advantage of his absence. 3.03.109 P
you do ill to teach the child such words. 4.01. 65 P
sir john, we have had ill luck; 5.05.116 P
a jack–a–lent, when 'tis upon ill employment! 5.05.127 P
which, i think, is a very ill house too. MM 2.01. 66 P
how ill agrees it with your gravity | to ERR 2.02.168
ill deeds is doubled with an evil word. 3.02. 20
unquiet meals make ill digestions, | thereof the 5.01. 74
and ill it doth beseem your holiness | to 5.01.110
this ill day | a most outrageous fit of madness 5.01.138
your own sake, for i have many ill qualities. ADO 2.01.102 P
nay, if they lead to any ill, i will leave them 2.01.153 P
but hear these ill news with the ears of claudio 2.01.173
and an ill singer, my lord. 2.03. 76 P
know | how much an ill word may empoison liking. 3.01. 86
yes, and his ill conditions, and, in despite of 3.02. 66 P
surely suit ill spent and labor ill bestow'd. 3.02. 99 P
surely suit ill spent and labor ill bestow'd. 3.02.100 P
by my troth, i am exceeding ill. 3.04. 53 P
very ill. 5.02. 90 P
very ill too. 5.02. 92 P
i am ill at reck'ning, it fitteth the spirit of LLL 1.02. 40 P
nothing becomes him ill that he would well. 2.01. 46
most power to do most harm, least knowing ill; 2.01. 58
for he hath wit to make an ill shape good, | and 2.01. 59
to teach a teacher ill beseemeth me. 2.01.108
kill, | and shooting well is then accounted ill. 4.01. 25
poor deer's blood, that my heart means no ill. 4.01. 35
for as it would ill become me to be vain, 4.02. 30
ill, to example ill, | would from my forehead 4.03.122
ill, to example ill, | would from my forehead 4.03.122
ill met by moonlight, proud titania. MND 2.01. 60
of night | and the ill counsel of a desert place 2.01.218
nought shall go ill; 3.02.462
there is some ill a–brewing towards my rest, MV 2.05. 17
nor no ill luck stirring but what lights a' my 3.01. 94 P
yes, other men have ill luck too. 3.01. 97 P
what, what, what? ill luck, ill luck? 3.01. 99 P
what, what, what? ill luck, ill luck? 3.01. 99 P
for no ill will i bear you. AYL 3.05. 71
marry, ill, to like him that ne'er it likes. AWW 1.01.152 P
one of our french wither'd pears, it looks ill, 1.01.161 P
you believe my oaths | when i did love you ill? 4.02. 27
is of a mingled yarn, good and ill together: 4.03. 72 P
you have them ill to friend | till your deeds 5.03.182
which would derive me ill will to speak of; 5.03.265 P
lady, takes great exceptions to your ill hours. TN 1.03. 6 P
of very ill manner: 1.05.153 P
la you, and you speak ill of the devil, how he 3.04.100 P
o, you give me ill counsel. 5.01. 31 P
there's some ill planet reigns; WT 2.01.105
my lord, and fear | we have landed in ill time: 3.03. 3
if to either, thou dost ill. 4.04.304
put between your holy looks | my ill suspicion. 5.03.149
it ill beseems this presence to cry aim | to JN 2.01.196
this day all things begun come to ill end, | yea 3.01. 94
and being not done, where doing tends to ill, 3.01.272
what can go well, when we have run so ill? 3.04. 5
if heaven be pleas'd that you must use me ill, 4.01. 55
hast made me giddy | with these ill tidings. 4.02.132
not seek to stuff | my head with more ill news, 4.02.134
how oft the sight of means to do ill deeds 4.02.219
of means to do ill deeds | make deeds ill done! 4.02.220
even this ill night your breathing shall expire, 5.04. 36
show me the very wound of this ill news; 5.06. 21
poison'd — ill fare! 5.07. 35
us | so much as of a thought of ill in him. R2 1.01. 86
contrive, or complot any ill | 'gainst us, our 1.03.189
i am in health, i breathe, and see thee ill. 2.01. 92
now he that made me knows i see thee ill, | ill 2.01. 93
ill in myself to see, and in thee, seeing ill. 2.01. 94
ill in myself to see, and in thee, seeing ill. 2.01. 94
because my power is weak and all ill left; 2.03.154
too well, too well thou tell'st a tale so ill. 3.02.121
shall ill become the flower of england's face, 3.03. 97
would not this ill do well? 3.03.170
and how, | /cam'st thou by this ill tidings? 3.04. 80
ill mayst thou thrive if thou grant any grace! 5.03. 99
that rebellion | had met ill luck? 2H4 1.01. 51
young prince up and down, like his ill angel. 1.02.164 P
your ill angel is light, but i hope he that 1.02.165 P
i told thee they were ill for a green wound? 2.01. 98 P
how ill it follows, after you have labor'd so 2.02. 28 P
civil, for," said he, "you are in an ill name." 2.04. 90 P
an excellent good word before it was ill sorted; 2.04.150 P

your majesty hath been this fortnight ill, | and 3.01.104
wherefore do you so ill translate yourself | out 4.01. 47
season, | for i am on the sudden something ill. 4.02. 80
against ill chances men are ever merry, | but 4.02. 81
come near me, now i am much ill. 4.04.111
exceeding ill. 4.05. 11
till his face be like a wet cloak ill laid up. 5.01. 85 P
if the deed were ill, | be you contented, 5.02. 83
not the ill wind which blows no man to good. 5.03. 86 P
how ill white hairs becomes a fool and jester! 5.05. 48
which if like an ill venture it come unluckily ep 11 P
hath shook and trembled at th' ill neighborhood. H5 1.02.154
faith, he's very ill. 2.01. 85 P
by chrish law, 'tish ill done! 3.02. 88 P
and my father's soul, the work ish ill done; 3.02. 90 P
o, 'tish ill done, 'tish ill done; 3.02. 92 P
o, 'tish ill done, 'tish ill done; 3.02. 93 P
by my hand, 'tish ill done! 3.02. 93 P
"ill will never said well." 3.07.113 P
vile and ragged foils | (right ill dispos'd, in 4.pr. 51
you love him not so ill to wish him here alone, 4.01.124 P
'tis certain, every man that dies ill, the ill 4.01.186 P
man that dies ill, the ill upon his own head, 4.01.186 P
that old age, that ill layer–up of beauty, can 5.02.230 P
that never may ill office, or fell jealousy, 5.02.363
cowardly knight, ill fortune follow thee! 1H6 3.02.109
and fashion'd thee that instrument of ill, | who 3.03. 65
was infamous | and ill beseeming any common man, 4.01. 31
let him perceive how ill we brook his treason, 4.01. 74
but that it doth presage some ill event. 4.01.191
when i imagine ill | against my king and nephew, 2H6 1.02. 19
if york have ill demean'd himself in france, 1.03.103
death, i never meant him any ill, nor the king, 2.03. 88 P
nell, ill can thy noble mind abrook | the abject 2.04. 10
hear | that things ill got had ever bad success? 3H6 2.02. 46
ill blows the wind that profits nobody. 2.05. 55
it ill befits thy state | and birth that thou 3.03. 2
ill rest betide the chamber where thou liest! R3 1.02.112
in that you brook it ill, it makes him worse; 1.03. 3
for whose sake did i that ill deed? 1.04.211
ill news, by'r lady — seldom comes the better. 2.03. 4
when such ill dealing must be seen in thought. 3.06. 14
no, to their lives ill friends were contrary. 4.04.217
would show a worse sin than ill doctrine. H8 1.03. 60
and something spoke in choler, ill, and hasty. 2.01. 34
believe me, there's an ill opinion spread then, 2.02.124
sure in that | i deem you an ill husband, and am 3.02.142
he fell sick suddenly and grew so ill | he could 4.02. 15
of his own body he was ill, and gave | the 4.02. 43
he was ill, and gave | the clergy ill example. 4.02. 44
for 'tis ill hap | if they hold when their ep 13
ill thought on of her, and ill thought /on of TRO 1.01. 70 P
thought on of her, and ill thought /on of you; 1.01. 71 P
none so noble | whose life were ill bestow'd, or 2.02.159
within his tent, but ill dispos'd, my lord. 2.03. 77
those wounds heal ill that men do give 3.03.229
barbarism, and policy grows into an ill opinion. 5.04. 17 P
are you set a–work, and how ill requited! 5.10. 38 P
fear | /lesser his person than an ill report; COR 1.06. 70
let me deserve so ill as you, and make me | your 3.01. 51
it would, | for th' ill which doth control't. 3.01.161
sword, and is ill school'd | in bolted language; 3.01.319
ill art thou repaid | for that good hand thou TIT 3.01.234
curse — | wherein i did not some notorious ill: 5.01.127
a word ill urg'd to one that is so ill! ROM 1.01.203
a word ill urg'd to one that is so ill! 1.01.203
truly it were an ill thing to be off'red to any 2.04.169 P
shall i speak ill of him that is my husband? 3.02. 97
you shall have none ill, sir, for i'll try if 4.02. 3 P
sir, 'tis an ill cook that cannot lick his own 4.02. 6 P
you love your child so ill | that you run mad, 4.05. 75
the heavens do low'r upon you for some ill; 4.05. 94
again, | for nothing can be ill if she be well. 5.01. 16
then she is well and nothing can be ill: 5.01. 17
o, pardon me for bringing these ill news, 5.01. 22
o, much i fear some ill unthrifty thing. 5.03.136
healths will make thee and thy state look ill, TIM 1.02. 57 P
kill, | what folly 'tis to hazard life for ill! 3.05. 37
it comes not ill; 3.05.111
you'll take it ill. 5.01. 90
in his own change, or by ill officers, | hath JC 4.02. 7
this was an ill beginning of the night. 4.03.234
how ill this taper burns! 4.03.275
ill spirit, i would hold more talk with thee. 4.03.288
what ill request did brutus make to thee? 5.05. 11
this supernatural soliciting | cannot be ill; MAC 1.03.131
if ill, | why hath it given me earnest of 1.03.131
things bad begun make strong themselves by ill. 3.02. 55
beautified ophelia" — that's an ill phrase, a HAM 2.02.111 P
o dear ophelia, i am ill at these numbers. 2.02.120 P
bad epitaph than their ill report while you live 2.02.526 P
it does well to those that do ill. 5.01. 47 P
now thou dost ill to say the gallows is built 5.01. 47 P
wouldst not think how ill all's here about my 5.02.212 P
no marvel then, though he were ill affected: LR 2.01. 98
or a painter could not have made him so ill, 2.02. 59 P
the king must take it ill | that he, so slightly 2.02.145
duke's to blame in this, 'twill be ill taken. 2.02.159
if he ask for me, i am ill and gone to bed. 3.03. 17 P
what, in ill thoughts again? 5.02. 9
i am very ill at ease, | unfit for mine own OTH 3.03. 32
it were enough | to put him to ill thinking. 3.04. 29
i am quickly ill, and well, | so antony loves. ANT 1.03. 72
i learn you take things ill which are not so — 2.02. 29
only, | lest my remembrance suffer ill report; 2.02.156
but let ill tidings tell | themselves when they 2.05. 87
thy plainness, | it nothing ill becomes thee. 2.06. 79
some o' their plants are ill rooted already, the 2.07. 2 P
thou must not take my former sharpness ill. 3.03. 35
i have done ill, | of which i do accuse myself 4.06. 17
i have done my work ill, friends. 4.14.105
for your ill opinion and th' assault you have CYM 1.04.162 P
since doubting things go ill often hurts more 1.06. 95
many times | doth ill deserve by doing well; 3.03. 54
i am ill, but your being by me | cannot amend me 4.02. 11
well or ill, | i am bound to you. 4.02. 45
nothing ill come near thee! 4.02.279
he was too good to be | where ill men were, and 5.05.159
were not this glorious casket stor'd with ill. PER 1.01. 77
and if jove stray, who dares say jove doth ill? 1.01.104
my shipwrack now's no ill, | since i have here 2.01.133
this day i'll rise, or else add ill to ill. 2.01.166
this day i'll rise, or else add ill to ill. 2.01.166
word, nor did ill turn | to any living creature. 4.01. 75
you thoughten | that i came with no ill intent, 4.06.109
us, envy of ill men | crave our acquaintance; TNK 2.02. 90
we had died as they do, ill old men, unwept, 2.02.109
a fire ill take her! does she flinch now? 3.05. 52
'twas very ill done then. 5.02. 13
he was kept down with hard meat and ill lodging, 5.02. 97
her kind of ill | gave me some sorrow. 5.04. 26
this ill presage advisedly she marketh: VEN 457
whose inward ill no outward harm express'd. LUC 91
so that in vent'ring ill we leave to be | the 148
but as they open, they all rate his ill, | which 304
then had they seen the period of their ill! 380
still | under what color he commits this ill. 476
end thy ill aim before thy shoot be ended; 579
me to curse him that thou taught'st this ill! 996
my blood shall wash the slander of mine ill; 1207
then call them not the authors of their ill, 1244
this is too curious–good, this blunt and ill: 1300
so fair a form lodg'd not a mind so ill: 1530
"what uncouth ill event | hath thee befall'n, 1598
outfacing faults in love with love's ill rest. PP 1. 8
fair), | my worser spirit a woman (color'd ill). 2. 4
as tender nurse her babe from faring ill. SON 22.12
and they are rich, and ransom all ill deeds. 34.14
lascivious grace, in whom all ill well shows, 40.13
(though you do any thing) he thinks no ill. 57.14
not blame your pleasure, be it ill or well. 58.14
and captive good attending captain ill. 66.12
if some suspect of ill mask'd not thy show, 70.13
thou canst not, love, disgrace me half so ill, 89. 5
some in their garments, though new–fangled ill, 91. 3
praise, | naming thy name blesses an ill report. 95. 8
the hardest knife ill us'd doth lose his edge. 95.14
for what care i who calls me well or ill, | so 112. 3
which, rank of goodness, would by ill be cured. 118.12
o benefit of ill! 119. 9
and in my madness might speak ill of thee; 140.10
fair, | the worser spirit a woman color'd ill. 144. 4
feeding on that which doth preserve the ill, 147. 3
whence hast thou this becoming of things ill, 150. 5
the destin'd ill she must herself assay? LC 156
ILL–ANNEXED 1 FR 0.0001 REL FR 1 V 0 P
but ill–annexed opportunity | or kills his life LUC 874
ILL–BESEEMING 4 FR 0.0004 REL FR 4 V 0 P
now) | hath put us in these ill–beseeming arms, 2H4 4.01. 84
how ill–beseeming is it in thy sex | to triumph 3H6 1.04.113
an ill–beseeming semblance for a feast. ROM 1.05. 74
man, | and ill–beseeming beast in seeming both, 3.03.113
ILL–BODING 2 FR 0.0002 REL FR 2 V 0 P
but o malignant and ill–boding stars! 1H6 4.05. 6
and his ill–boding tongue no more shall speak. 3H6 2.06. 59
ILL–BREEDING 1 FR 0.0001 REL FR 1 V 0 P
dangerous conjectures in ill–breeding minds. HAM 4.05. 15
ILL–COMPOS'D 1 FR 0.0001 REL FR 1 V 0 P
grows | in my most ill–compos'd affection such MAC 4.03. 77
ILL–DEALING 1 FR 0.0001 REL FR 1 V 0 P
and't might be, | to dure ill–dealing fortune. TNK 1.03. 5
ILL–DISPERSING 1 FR 0.0001 REL FR 1 V 0 P
o ill–dispersing wind of misery! R3 4.01. 52
ILL–DIVINING 1 FR 0.0001 REL FR 1 V 0 P
o god, i have an ill–divining soul! ROM 3.05. 54
ILL–DOING 1 FR 0.0001 REL FR 1 V 0 P
we knew not | the doctrine of ill–doing, nor WT 1.02. 70
ILLEGITIMATE 2 FR 0.0002 REL FR 0 V 2 P
o illegitimate construction! ADO 3.04. 50 P
bastard in valor, in every thing illegitimate. TRO 5.07. 18 P
ILL–ERECTED 1 FR 0.0001 REL FR 1 V 0 P
the way | to julius caesar's ill–erected tower, R2 5.01. 2
ILL–FAC'D 1 FR 0.0001 REL FR 1 V 0 P
ill–fac'd, worse bodied, shapeless every where; ERR 4.02. 20
//ILL–FAVOR'D 1 FR 0.0001 REL FR 1 V 0 P
/sir, /it /was /a /black //ill–favor'd /fly, TIT 3.02. 66
ILL–FAVOR'D 6 FR 0.0006 REL FR 4 V 2 P
out, out, lucetta, that will be ill–favor'd. TGV 2.07. 54
'em, they are very ill–favor'd rough things. WIV 1.01.299 P
what a world of vild ill–favor'd faults | looks 3.04. 32
makes the world full of ill–favor'd children. AYL 3.05. 53
a poor virgin, sir, an ill–favor'd thing, sir, 5.04. 58 P
and wish thee to a shrewd ill–favor'd wife? SHR 1.02. 60
ILL–FAVOREDLY 4 FR 0.0004 REL FR 1 V 3 P
very ill–favoredly, master /brook. WIV 3.05. 67 P
she makes honest she makes very ill–favoredly. AYL 1.02. 39 P
of my verses with reading them ill–favoredly. 3.02.262 P
bones, | ill–favoredly become the morning field. H5 4.02. 40
ILL–HEADED 1 FR 0.0001 REL FR 1 V 0 P
if tall, a lance ill–headed; ADO 3.01. 64
ILL–INHABITED 1 FR 0.0001 REL FR 0 V 1 P
o knowledge ill–inhabited, worse than jove in a AYL 3.03. 10 P
ILLITERATE 2 FR 0.0002 REL FR 1 V 1 P
o illiterate loiterer! TGV 3.01.296 P
yea, the illiterate, that know not how | to LUC 810
ILLNESS 1 FR 0.0001 REL FR 1 V 0 P
but without | the illness should attend it. MAC 1.05. 20
ILL–NURTUR'D 2 FR 0.0002 REL FR 2 V 0 P
presumptuous dame, ill–nurtur'd eleanor, | art 2H6 1.02. 42
ill–nurtur'd, crooked, churlish, harsh in voice, VEN 134
ILLO (*also hillo, hilloa*)
ILLO 1 FR 0.0001 REL FR 1 V 0 P
illo, ho, ho, my lord! HAM 1.05.115
ILL–RESOUNDING 1 FR 0.0001 REL FR 1 V 0 P
when he hath ceas'd his ill–resounding noise, VEN 919
ILL–ROASTED 1 FR 0.0001 REL FR 0 V 1 P
damn'd, like an ill–roasted egg all on one side. AYL 3.02. 37 P
ILLS 10 FR 0.0011 REL FR 10 V 0 P
and makes us rather bear those ills we have, HAM 3.01. 80
the ills we do, their ills instruct us so. OTH 4.03.103
the ills we do, their ills instruct us so. 4.03.103
still, and our ills told us | is as our earing. ANT 1.02.110
ten thousand harms, more than the ills i know, 1.02.129
you some permit | to second ills with ills, each CYM 5.01. 14
you some permit | to second ills with ills, each 5.01. 14
if all these petty ills shall change thy good, LUC 656
t' anticipate | the ills that were not, grew to SON 118.10
and gain by ills thrice more than i have spent. 119.14
ILL–SEEMING 1 FR 0.0001 REL FR 1 V 0 P
muddy, ill–seeming, thick, bereft of beauty, SHR 5.02.143
ILL–SHAP'D 1 FR 0.0001 REL FR 1 V 0 P
and other skins | of ill–shap'd fishes, and ROM 5.01. 44
ILL–SHEATHED 1 FR 0.0001 REL FR 1 V 0 P
the edge of war, like an ill–sheathed knife, 1H4 1.01. 17
ILL–SPIRITED 1 FR 0.0001 REL FR 1 V 0 P
ill–spirited worcester, did not we send grace, 1H4 5.05. 2
ILL–STARR'D 1 FR 0.0001 REL FR 1 V 0 P
o ill–starr'd wench, | pale as thy smock! OTH 5.02.272
ILL–TA'EN 1 FR 0.0001 REL FR 1 V 0 P
theme, but nothing | of his ill–ta'en suspicion! WT 1.02.460
ILL–TEMPER'D 2 FR 0.0002 REL FR 2 V 0 P
when grief and blood ill–temper'd vexeth him? JC 4.03.115
when i spoke that, i was ill–temper'd too. 4.03.116
ILL–TUNED 1 FR 0.0001 REL FR 1 V 0 P
to cry aim | to these ill–tuned repetitions. JN 2.01.197
ILLUME 1 FR 0.0001 REL FR 1 V 0 P
made his course t' illume that part of heaven HAM 1.01. 37
ILLUMINATE 1 FR 0.0001 REL FR 1 V 0 P
for the base matter to illuminate | so vile a JC 1.03.110
ILLUMIN'D 2 FR 0.0002 REL FR 2 V 0 P
not by her fair influence | foster'd, illumin'd, TGV 3.01.184
sky, | so is her face illumin'd with her eye, VEN 486
ILLUMINETH 1 FR 0.0001 REL FR 0 V 1 P
it illumineth the face, which as a beacon gives 2H4 4.03.107 P
ILL–US'D 1 FR 0.0001 REL FR 1 V 0 P
misus'd ere us'd, by times ill–us'd /o'erpast. R3 4.04.396
ILLUSION 3 FR 0.0003 REL FR 3 V 0 P
by some illusion see thou bring her here. MND 3.02. 98
as by the strength of their illusion | shall MAC 3.05. 28
stay, illusion! HAM 1.01.127
ILLUSIONS 2 FR 0.0002 REL FR 2 V 0 P
and so am i, | and here we wander in illusions: ERR 4.03. 43
by th' devil's illusions | the monk might be H8 1.02.178
ILLUSTRATE 3 FR 0.0003 REL FR 1 V 2 P
and most illustrate king cophetua set eye upon LLL 4.01. 65 P
and this most gallant, illustrate, and learned 5.01.121 P
body | and fiery mind illustrate a brave father. TNK 2.05. 22
ILLUSTRATED 1 FR 0.0001 REL FR 1 V 0 P
and obedient subject is | therein illustrated; H8 3.02.181
ILLUSTRIOUS* 5 FR 0.0005 REL FR 4 V 1 P
armado is a most illustrious wight, | a man of LLL 1.01.177
and most illustrious six–or–seven–times–honor'd TRO 3.03.277 P
for his right noble mind, illustrious virtue, TIM 3.02. 80
conspirant 'gainst this high illustrious prince, LR 5.03.136
an eye | base and illustrious as the smoky light CYM 1.06.109
ILL–UTTERING 1 FR 0.0001 REL FR 1 V 0 P
i melt and pour | down thy ill–uttering throat. ANT 2.05. 35
ILL–WEAV'D 1 FR 0.0001 REL FR 1 V 0 P
ill–weav'd ambition, how much art thou shrunk! 1H4 5.04. 88
ILL–WELL 1 FR 0.0001 REL FR 0 V 1 P
you could never do him so ill–well, unless you ADO 2.01.117 P
ILL–WRESTING 1 FR 0.0001 REL FR 1 V 0 P
now this ill–wresting world is grown so bad, SON 140.11
ILLYRIA 10 FR 0.0011 REL FR 2 V 8 P
this is illyria, lady. TN 1.02. 2
and what should i do in illyria? 1.02. 3
he's as tall a man as any's in illyria. 1.03. 20 P
is a passage in my throat and drink in illyria. 1.03. 40 P
as any man in illyria, whatsoever he be, under 1.03.117 P
simply as strong as any man in illyria. 1.03.124 P
witty a piece of eve's flesh as any in illyria. 1.05. 28 P
possibly have found in any part of illyria. 3.04.268 P
against him, if there be any law in illyria. 4.01. 35 P
i am as well in my wits as any man in illyria. 4.02.107 P
ILLYRIAN 1 FR 0.0001 REL FR 1 V 0 P
more | than bargulus the strong illyrian pirate. 2H6 4.01.108
ILS 1 FR 0.0001 REL FR 0 V 1 P
ils sont les mots de son mauvais, corruptible, H5 3.04. 52 P
I'M 12 FR 0.0013 REL FR 12 V 0 P
anon i'm sure the duke himself in person | comes ERR 5.01.119
that you are well restor'd, my lord, i'm glad. AWW 2.03.147
i'm glad 'tis there. H8 1.03. 21
i'm very sorry | to sit here at this present, 5.02. 43
i'm sure | thou hast a cruel nature and a bloody 5.02.163
to the world than malice, | i'm sure, in me. 5.02.188
h'as much disgrac'd me in't, i'm angry at him, TIM 3.03. 13
i'm weary of this charge, the gods can witness. 3.04. 25
i'm worse than mad. 3.05.105
for i have seen more years, i'm sure, than ye. JC 4.03.132
unmerciful lady as you are, i'm none. LR 3.07. 33
i'm not their father, yet who this should be CYM 4.02. 28
/IMAGE 1 FR 0.0001 REL FR 1 V 0 P
/for /by /the /image /of /my /cause /i /see HAM 5.02. 77
IMAGE 54 FR 0.0061 REL FR 45 V 9 P
of any thing the image, tell me, that | hath TMP 1.02. 43
which, like a waxen image 'gainst a fire, TGV 2.04.201
the image of the jest | i'll show you here at WIV 4.06. 17
saucy sweetness that do coin heaven's image | in MM 2.04. 45
the image of it gives me content already, and i 3.01.259 P
the one is too like an image and says nothing, ADO 2.01. 8 P
hero, now thy image doth appear | in the rare 5.01.251
death, how foul and loathsome is thine image! SHR in.1. 35
with any branch or image of thy state; AWW 2.01.198
save in the constant image of the creature TN 2.04. 19
that when the image of it leaves him he must run 2.05.194 P
and clear from any image of offense done to any 3.04.228 P
and to his image, which methought did promise 3.04.362
your father's image is so hit in you | (his very WT 5.01.127
if i had thought the sight of my poor image 5.03. 57
the image of a wicked heinous fault | lives in JN 4.02. 71
but the true and perfect image of life indeed. 1H4 5.04.119 P
to weeds, | and he, the noble image of my youth, 2H4 4.04. 55
father, | the image of his power lay then in me, 5.02. 74
the image of the king whom i presented, | and 5.02. 79
nay more, to spurn at your most royal image, 5.02. 89
image of pride, why should i hold my peace? 2H6 1.03.176
it, | and make my image but an alehouse sign. 3.02. 81
and to survey his dead and earthy image, | what 3.02.147
look in a glass, and call thy image so. 5.01.142
for from my heart thine image ne'er shall go; 3H6 2.05.116
hath plac'd thy beauty's image and thy virtue. 3.03. 64
live | to bear his image and renew his glories! 5.04. 54
the precious image of our dear redeemer, | you R3 2.01.124
how can man then | (the image of his maker) hope

H8 3.02.442
without some image of th' affected merit. TRO 2.02. 60
i, | even like a stony image, cold and numb. TIT 3.01.258
this growing image of thy fiend–like face? 5.01. 45
whose horrid image doth unfix my hair | and make
MAC 1.03.135
up, up, and see | the great doom's image! 2.03. 78
king, | whose image even but now appear'd to us, HAM 1.01. 81
to show virtue her feature, scorn her own image, 3.02. 23 P
this play is the image of a murther done in 3.02.238 P
nothing like the image and horror of it. LR 1.02.175 P
mightst behold the great image of authority: 4.06.158 P
or image of that horror? 5.03.265
stone, | well–painted idol, image dull and dead, VEN 212
on his back doth lie | an image like thyself, 664
within his thought her heavenly image sits, LUC 288
"o comfort–killing night, image of hell! 764
that for achilles' image stood his spear, 1424
at last she sees a wretched image bound, | that 1501
the well–skill'd workman this mild image drew 1520
if in the child the father's image lies, | where 1753
o, from thy cheeks my image thou hast torn, 1762
die single, and thine image dies with thee. SON 3.14
to find where your true image pictur'd lies, 24. 6
sun, | show me your image in some antique book, 59. 7
is it thy will thy image should keep open | my 61. 1
IMAGERY 1 FR 0.0001 REL FR 1 V 0 P
walls | with painted imagery had said at once, R2 5.02. 16
IMAGES 12 FR 0.0013 REL FR 10 V 2 P
none of pygmalion's images newly made woman to
MM 3.02. 45 P
together, | more witnesseth than fancy's images, MND 5.01. 25
glittering in golden coats like images, | as 1H4 4.01.100
loves | are brazen images of canonized saints. 2H6 1.03. 60
death, | and liv'd with looking on his images; R3 2.02. 50
disrobe the images, | if you do find them deck'd JC 1.01. 64
let no images | be hung with caesar's trophies. 1.01. 68
for pulling scarfs off caesar's images, are put 1.02.286 P
thyself didst make | strange images of death. MAC 1.03. 97
fetches, | the images of revolt and flying off. LR 2.04. 90
that she with painted images hath spent, | being LUC 1577
their images i lov'd i view in thee, | and thou SON 31.13
IMAGINARY 10 FR 0.0011 REL FR 10 V 0 P
sure these are but imaginary wiles, | and ERR 4.03. 10
and foul imaginary eyes of blood | presented JN 4.02.265
which for things true weeps things imaginary. R2 2.02. 27
in forms imaginary, th' unguided days | and 2H4 4.04. 59
great accompt, | on your imaginary forces work. H5 pr 18
divide one man, | and make imaginary puissance; pr 25
th' imaginary relish is so sweet | that it TRO 3.02. 19
all is imaginary she doth prove, | he will not VEN 597
for much imaginary work was there, | conceit LUC 1422
save that my soul's imaginary sight | presents SON 27. 9
/IMAGINATION 1 FR 0.0001 REL FR 1 V 0 P
he waxes desperate with /imagination. HAM 1.04. 87
IMAGINATION 31 FR 0.0035 REL FR 22 V 9 P
thee, and | my strong imagination sees a crown TMP 2.01.208
nor can imagination form a shape, | besides 3.01. 56
spirit, what devil suggests this imagination? WIV 3.03.215 P
whose salt imagination yet hath wrong'd | your MM 5.01.401
beyond imagination is the wrong | that she this ERR 5.01.201
sweetly creep | into his study of imagination, ADO 4.01.225
and the poet | are of imagination all compact. MND 5.01. 8
and as imagination bodies forth | the forms of 5.01. 14
such tricks hath strong imagination, | that, if 5.01. 18
worst are no worse, if imagination amend them. 5.01.212 P
it must be your imagination then, and not theirs 5.01.213 P
my imagination | carries no favor in't but AWW 1.01. 82
look how imagination blows him. TN 2.05. 43 P
not now fool myself, to let imagination jade me; 2.05.164 P
prove true, imagination, o, prove true, | that i 3.04.375
and beyond the imagination of his neighbors, is WT 4.02. 39 P
of appetite | by bare imagination of a feast? R2 1.03.297
imagination of some great exploit | drives him 1H4 1.03.199
so, with great imagination | proper to madmen, 2H4 1.03. 31
how big imagination | moves in this lip! TIM 1.01. 32
to put them in, imagination to give them shape, HAM 3.01.125 P
and now how abhorr'd in my imagination it is! 5.01.187 P
why may not imagination trace the noble dust of 5.01.203 P
good apothecary, | sweeten my imagination. LR 4.06.131
in your imagination hold | this stage the ship, PER 3.ch. 58
but for't, | making, to take our imagination, 4.04. 3
punishment, a death | beyond imagination! TNK 2.03. 5
so indeed, | that tremble at th' imagination? VEN 668
the dire imagination she did follow | this sound 975
conceit | can comprehend in still imagination! LUC 702
like fools that in th' imagination set | the LC 136
IMAGINATIONS 5 FR 0.0005 REL FR 4 V 1 P
not follow the imaginations of your own heart. WIV 4.02.156 P
and for unfelt imaginations | they often feel a R3 1.04. 80
and my imaginations are as foul | as vulcan's HAM 3.02. 83
and woes by wrong imaginations lose | the LR 4.06.283
can be, but our imaginations | may make it ours? TNK 2.02. 77
/IMAGIN'D 1 FR 0.0001 REL FR 1 V 0 P
to us th' /imagin'd voice of god himself, | the 2H4 4.02. 19
IMAGIN'D 7 FR 0.0008 REL FR 7 V 0 P
at thy garden–house | in her imagin'd person. MM 5.01.213
bring them i pray thee with imagin'd speed MV 3.04. 52
thus with imagin'd wing our swift scene flies H5 3.pr. 1
broils, | than yet can be imagin'd or suppos'd. 1H6 4.01.186
imagin'd worth | holds in his blood such swoll'n TRO 2.03.172
tongue | unfold the imagin'd happiness that both ROM 2.06. 28
not imagin'd, felt. CYM 4.02.307
IMAGINE 27 FR 0.0030 REL FR 21 V 6 P
and incertain thought | imagine howling — 'tis MM 3.01.127
or you imagine me too unhurtful an opposite. 3.02.165 P
if i should be hang'd, i cannot imagine. 4.02. 40 P
if we imagine no worse of them than they of MND 5.01.215 P
he was to imagine me his love, his mistress; AYL 3.02.408 P
imagine 'twere the right vincentio. SHR 4.04. 12
that he shuts up himself — imagine me, | gentle WT 4.01. 19
dear, imagine it | to lie that way thou goest, R2 1.03.286
and then imagine me taking your part, | and in 2H4 5.02. 96
even now | you may imagine him upon blackheath;
H5 5.pr. 16
breast, | and what i do imagine, let that rest. 1H6 2.05.119
imagine him a frenchman, and thy foe. 4.07. 26
i did imagine what would be her refuge. 5.04. 69

when i imagine ill | against my king and nephew, 2H6 1.02. 19
nest | but may imagine how the bird was dead, 3.02.192
touches me deeper than you can imagine. R3 1.01.112
you, | imagine i have said farewell already. 1.02.224
would you imagine, or almost believe, | were't 3.05. 35
he's as like to do't as any man i can imagine. COR 4.05.204 P
and that, i hope, will teach you to imagine — HAM 4.07. 35
yet t' imagine | an antony were nature's piece ANT 5.02. 98
honor of hers which you imagine so reserv'd. CYM 1.04.131 P
imagine pericles arriv'd at tyre, | welcom'd and PER 4.ch. 1
imagine that you see the wretched strangers, STM II.C 74
"but if thou fall, o, then imagine this, | the VEN 721
imagine her as one in dead of night | from forth LUC 449
lie | imagine every eye beholds their blame, 1343
IMAGINED 2 FR 0.0002 REL FR 2 V 0 P
a head | stood for the whole to be imagined. LUC 1428
and what wrong else may be imagined | by foul 1622
IMAGINING 1 FR 0.0001 REL FR 1 V 0 P
or in the night, imagining some fear, | how easy MND 5.01. 21
IMAGININGS 1 FR 0.0001 REL FR 1 V 0 P
fears | are less than horrible imaginings: MAC 1.03.138
IMBAR 1 FR 0.0001 REL FR 1 V 0 P
a net | than amply to imbar their crooked titles H5 1.02. 94
IMBECILITY 1 FR 0.0001 REL FR 1 V 0 P
strength should be lord of imbecility, | and the TRO 1.03.114
IMBRUE 2 FR 0.0002 REL FR 2 V 0 P
trusty sword, | come, blade, my breast imbrue! MND 5.01.344
shall we imbrue? 2H4 2.04.196
IMITARI 1 FR 0.0001 REL FR 0 V 1 P
imitari is nothing: LLL 4.02.125 P
IMITATE 13 FR 0.0014 REL FR 11 V 2 P
paints itself black, to imitate her brow. LLL 4.03.261
would imitate, and sail upon the land | to fetch MND 2.01.132
fashion, color, ornament, | for him i imitate. TN 3.04.383
idleness, | yet herein will i imitate the sun, 1H4 1.02.197
"i will imitate the honorable romans in brevity. 2H4 2.02.123 P
ears, | then imitate the action of the tiger; H5 3.01. 6
then did they imitate that which i compos'd to 3.07. 43 P
of honor, | to imitate the graces of the gods; COR 5.03.150
that game, we must not dare | to imitate them; TIM 1.02. 13
dost not keep a dog, | whom i would imitate. 4.03.201
to imitate thee well, against my heart | will LUC 1137
whose waves to imitate the battle sought | with 1438
why should false painting imitate his cheek, SON 67. 5
IMITATED 2 FR 0.0002 REL FR 1 V 1 P
them well, they imitated humanity so abominably.
HAM 3.02. 35 P
the counterfeit | is poorly imitated after you; SON 53. 6
IMITATION 5 FR 0.0005 REL FR 5 V 0 P
apish nation | limps after in base imitation. R2 2.01. 23
action, | which, slanderer, he imitation calls, TRO 1.03.150
and in the imitation of these twain — | who, as 1.03.185
(and with what imitation you can borrow | from CYM 3.04.171
yet a little | i did by imitation. TNK 3.06. 81
IMITATIONS 1 FR 0.0001 REL FR 1 V 0 P
that feeds | on objects, arts, and imitations, JC 4.01. 37
IMMACULATE 7 FR 0.0008 REL FR 5 V 2 P
his love sincere, his thoughts immaculate, | his TGV 2.07. 76
my love is most immaculate white and red. LLL 1.02. 90 P
thou sheer, immaculate, and silver fountain, R2 5.03. 61
have, in my pure and immaculate valor, taken sir 2H4 4.03. 37 P
chaste, and immaculate in very thought, | whose 1H6 5.04. 51
immaculate devotion, holy thoughts, | i tender R3 4.04.404
abuse, | immaculate and spotless is my mind; LUC 1656
IMMANITY 1 FR 0.0001 REL FR 1 V 0 P
unnatural | that such immanity and bloody strife 1H6 5.01. 13
IMMASK 1 FR 0.0001 REL FR 0 V 1 P
the nonce, to immask our noted outward garments.
1H4 1.02.180 P
IMMATERIAL 1 FR 0.0001 REL FR 0 V 1 P
thou idle immaterial skein of sleave–silk, thou TRO 5.01. 31 P
IMMEDIACY 1 FR 0.0001 REL FR 1 V 0 P
person, | the which immediacy may well stand up, LR 5.03. 65
IMMEDIATE 15 FR 0.0017 REL FR 13 V 2 P
immediate sentence then, and sequent death, | is MM 5.01.373
minds | a doubtful warrant of immediate death, ERR 1.01. 68
fair, | in these to nature she's immediate heir; AWW 2.03.132
to beg | enfranchisement immediate on his knees, R2 3.03.114
which, as immediate from thy place and blood, 2H4 4.05. 42
send to prison | th' immediate heir of england! 5.02. 71
immediate are my needs, and my relief | must not TIM 2.01. 25
to me in words, | but find supply immediate. 2.01. 27
may | have an immediate freedom of repeal. JC 3.01. 54
you are the most immediate to our throne, | and HAM 1.02.109
and it would come to immediate trial, if your 5.02.168 P
lord, | is the immediate jewel of their souls. OTH 3.03.156
to that end | assemble /we immediate council. ANT 1.04. 75
amity shall prove the immediate author of their 2.06.129 P
for this immediate levy, he commands | his CYM 3.07. 9
IMMEDIATELY 20 FR 0.0022 REL FR 20 V 0 P
and with him at eton | immediately to marry. WIV 4.06. 25
and bring thy master home immediately. ERR 4.02. 64
and immediately | ran hither to your grace, whom 5.01.251
immediately they will again be here | in their LLL 5.02.287
to our law | immediately provided in that case. MND 1.01. 45
either death, or you, i'll find immediately. 2.02.156
perhaps i will return immediately. MV 2.05. 52
lord, | you must be gone from hence immediately. 2.09. 8
choice, | immediately to leave you, and be gone. 2.09. 16
mind | to help him to his grave immediately! R2 1.04. 60
we'll but seal, | and then to horse immediately. 1H4 3.01.266
courtesy, | which i shall give away immediately. 5.05. 33
look, | immediately he was upon his knee, | that 2H6 3.01. 11
and apprehended here immediately | th' unknown
TRO 3.03.124
and they shall be immediately delivered. TIT 5.01.161
offense | immediately we do exile him hence. ROM 3.01.187
west, | and bring in cloudy night immediately. 3.02. 4
and bring messala with you | immediately to us. JC 4.03.142
out, | and something to be done immediately. 5.01. 15
property | on wholesome life usurps immediately. HAM 3.02.260
IMMINENCE 1 FR 0.0001 REL FR 1 V 0 P
but dare all imminence that gods and men TRO 5.10. 13
IMMINENT 7 FR 0.0008 REL FR 7 V 0 P
beast, | the imminent decay of wrested pomp. JN 4.03.154
you have defended me from imminent death. 2H6 5.03. 19
my lord, to dangers | as infinite as imminent! TRO 4.04. 69
for warnings and portents | and evils imminent, JC 2.02. 81

youth | contagious blastments are most imminent. HAM 1.03. 42
see | the imminent death of twenty thousand men, 4.04. 60
scapes i' th' imminent deadly breach, | of being OTH 1.03.136
IMMODERATE 1 FR 0.0001 REL FR 1 V 0 P
so every scope by the immoderate use | turns to MM 1.02.127
IMMODERATELY 1 FR 0.0001 REL FR 1 V 0 P
immoderately she weeps for tybalt's death, | and ROM 4.01. 6
IMMODEST 6 FR 0.0006 REL FR 5 V 1 P
have took upon me | such an immodest raiment —
TGV 5.04.106
she should be so immodest to write to one that ADO 2.03.141 P
with immodest hatred | the child–bed privilege WT 3.02.102
'tis needful that the most immodest word | be 2H4 4.04. 70
asham'd | with this immodest clamorous outrage 1H6 4.01.126
he saith she is immodest, blames her miss; VEN 53
IMMODESTLY 1 FR 0.0001 REL FR 1 V 0 P
cloak | immodestly lies martyr'd with disgrace. LUC 802
IMMOMENT 1 FR 0.0001 REL FR 1 V 0 P
immoment toys, things of such dignity | as we ANT 5.02.166
IMMORTAL 29 FR 0.0032 REL FR 22 V 7 P
but by immortal providence she's mine. TMP 5.01.189
by your renouncement an immortal spirit, | and MM 1.04. 35
by eight to–morrow | thou must be made immortal. 4.02. 65
such harmony is in immortal souls, | but whilst MV 5.01. 63
o immortal gods! SHR 5.01. 66 P
far, would have made nature immortal, and death
AWW 1.01. 20 P
good hap, | add an immortal title to your crown! R2 1.01. 24
marry, the immortal part needs a physician, but 2H4 2.02.104 P
in bloody field, | doth win immortal fame." H5 3.02. 11
o you immortal gods! i will not go. TRO 4.02. 94
ah, the immortal passado, the punto reverso, the ROM 2.04. 25 P
and steal immortal blessing from her lips, | who 3.03. 37
and her immortal part with angels lives. 5.01. 19
immortal gods, i crave no pelf, | i pray for no TIM 1.02. 62
agues | th' immortal gods that hear you. 4.03.139
best respect in rome | (except immortal caesar), JC 1.02. 60
if thou beest not immortal, look about you; 2.03. 6 P
o ye immortal gods! 4.03.157
do to that, | being a thing immortal as itself? HAM 1.04. 67
i have lost the immortal part of myself, and OTH 2.03.263 P
th' immortal jove's dread clamors counterfeit, 3.03.356
you to touch him, for his biting is immortal; ANT 5.02.247 P
on my crown, i have | immortal longings in me. 5.02.281
prunes the immortal wing and cloys his beak, CYM 5.04.118
she sings like one immortal, and she dances | as PER 5.ch. 3
immortal dian! 5.03. 37
and by her fair immortal hand she swears | from VEN 80
me, | and were i not immortal, life were done, 197
your name from hence immortal life shall have, SON 81. 5
IMMORTALITY 2 FR 0.0002 REL FR 2 V 0 P
but immortality attends the former, | making a PER 3.02. 30
fault brought in subjection | her immortality, LUC 725
IMMORTALIZ'D 1 FR 0.0001 REL FR 1 V 0 P
drive them from orleance and be immortaliz'd. 1H6 1.02.148
IMMORTALLY 1 FR 0.0001 REL FR 1 V 0 P
and he that wears the crown immortally | long 2H4 4.05.143
IMMUR'D 2 FR 0.0002 REL FR 2 V 0 P
or shall i think in silver she's immur'd, MV 2.07. 52
whom envy hath immur'd within your walls — R3 4.01. 99
IMMURE 1 FR 0.0001 REL FR 1 V 0 P
where their queen | means to immure herself, and VEN 1194
IMMURED 3 FR 0.0003 REL FR 2 V 1 P
thou wert immured, restrained, captivated, bound
LLL 3.01.124 P
eyes, | lives not alone immured in the brain, 4.03.325
in whose confine immured is the store | which SON 84. 3
/IMMURES 1 FR 0.0001 REL FR 1 V 0 P
/within /whose /strong /immures | /the /ravish'd TRO pr 8
IMOGEN 23 FR 0.0026 REL FR 22 V 1 P
you woo another wife, | when imogen is dead. CYM 1.01.114
thou divine imogen, what thou endur'st, 2.01. 57
if i could get this foolish imogen, i should 2.03. 8 P
o imogen, | safe mayst thou wander, safe return 3.05.104
imogen, | the great part of my comfort, gone; 4.03. 4
my master since | i wrote him imogen was slain. 4.03. 37
so had you saved | the noble imogen to repent, 5.01. 10
but imogen is your own, do your best wills, 5.01. 16
so i'll die | for thee, o imogen, even for whom 5.01. 26
again, | but end it by some means for imogen. 5.03. 83
o imogen, | i'll speak to thee in silence. 5.04. 28
or fruitful object be | in eye of imogen, that 5.04. 56
cast | from her his dearest one, | sweet imogen? 5.04. 62
he shall be lord of lady imogen, | and happier 5.04.107
o imogen! 5.05.225
o imogen, | imogen, imogen! 5.05.226
o imogen, | imogen, imogen! 5.05.227
o imogen, | imogen, imogen! 5.05.227
posthumus, | you ne'er kill'd imogen till now! 5.05.231
the tune of imogen! 5.05.238
imogen, | thy mother's dead. 5.05.269
o imogen, | thou hast lost by this a kingdom. 5.05.372
see, | posthumus anchors upon imogen; 5.05.393
IMOGEN'S 1 FR 0.0001 REL FR 1 V 0 P
for imogen's dear life take mine, and though CYM 5.04. 22
IMP* 5 FR 0.0005 REL FR 4 V 1 P
is one and the self–same thing, dear imp. LLL 1.02. 5 P
"great hercules is presented by this imp, 5.02.588
imp out our drooping country's broken wing, R2 2.01.292
thee guard and keep, most royal imp of fame! 2H4 5.05. 42
heart of gold, | a lad of life, an imp of fame, H5 4.01. 45
IMPAINT 1 FR 0.0001 REL FR 1 V 0 P
want | such water–colors to impaint his cause, 1H4 5.01. 80
IMPAIR 2 FR 0.0002 REL FR 2 V 0 P
wherein it doth impair the seeing sense, | it MND 3.02.179
dumb, | for i impair not beauty being mute, SON 83.11
IMPAIR'D 1 FR 0.0001 REL FR 0 V 1 P
nothing impair'd, but all disorder'd. MND 5.01.126 P
IMPAIRING 1 FR 0.0001 REL FR 1 V 0 P
impairing henry, strength'ning misproud york. 3H6 2.06. 7
IMPALE *(also empale)*
IMPALE 1 FR 0.0001 REL FR 1 V 0 P
did i impale him with the regal crown? 3H6 3.03.189
IMPALED 1 FR 0.0001 REL FR 1 V 0 P
head | be round impaled with a glorious crown. 3H6 3.02.171
IMPANELLED 1 FR 0.0001 REL FR 1 V 0 P
to /'cide this title is impanelled | a quest of SON 46. 9
IMPARE 1 FR 0.0001 REL FR 1 V 0 P

nor dignifies an impare thought with breath; TRO 4.05.103
IMPART 12 FR 0.0013 REL FR 9 V 3 P
it pleaseth his greatness to impart to armado, a LLL 5.01.107 P
lady, | when i did first impart my love to you, MV 3.02.253
me, | i have great matters to impart to thee. 2H6 3.02.299
intend | as closely to conceal what we impart. R3 3.01.159
though what they will impart | help nothing else 4.04.130
what is it that you would impart to me? JC 1.02. 84
let us impart what we have seen to-night | unto HAM 1.01.169
father bears his son | do i impart toward you. 1.02.112
to me | in dreadful secrecy impart they did, 1.02.207
impart. 3.02.330 P
i should impart a thing to you from his majesty. 5.02. 90 P
i | than niggard truth would willingly impart: SON 72. 8
IMPARTED 1 FR 0.0001 REL FR 1 V 0 P
to pass, | as before imparted to your worship, SHR 3.02.130
IMPARTETH 1 FR 0.0001 REL FR 1 V 0 P
but this no slaughter-house no tool imparteth, LUC 1039
IMPARTIAL *(also unpartial)*
IMPARTIAL 6 FR 0.0006 REL FR 6 V 0 P
cousin angelo, | in this i'll be impartial. MM 5.01.166
mowbray, impartial are our eyes and ears. R2 1.01.115
led by th' impartial conduct of my soul; 2H4 5.02. 36
and impartial spirit | as you have done 'gainst 5.02.116
th' impartial gods, who from the mounted heavens TNK 1.04. 4
whereat th' impartial gazer late did wonder, VEN 748
IMPARTMENT 1 FR 0.0001 REL FR 1 V 0 P
as if it some impartment did desire | to you HAM 1.04. 59
IMPARTS 1 FR 0.0001 REL FR 1 V 0 P
but our natural goodness | imparts this; WT 2.01.165
IMPASTED 1 FR 0.0001 REL FR 1 V 0 P
bak'd and impasted with the parching streets, HAM 2.02.459
IMPATIENCE 19 FR 0.0021 REL FR 16 V 3 P
my heart is ready to crack with impatience. WIV 2.02.288 P
/but /first sheathe thy impatience, throw cold 2.03. 84 P
fie, how impatience low'reth in your face! ERR 2.01. 86
all humbleness, all patience, and impatience, AYL 5.02. 97
sir, sir, impatience hath his privilege. JN 4.03. 32
out of my grief and my impatience | answer'd 1H4 1.03. 51
rough deeds of rage and stern impatience; 1H6 4.07. 8
o, but impatience waiteth on true sorrow. 3H6 3.03. 42
what means this scene of rude impatience? R3 2.02. 38
then patiently hear my impatience. 4.04.157
his own impatience | takes from aufidius a great COR 5.06.144
to see the strange impatience of the heavens; JC 1.03. 61
fearing to strengthen that impatience | which 2.01.248
of his wits have given way to his impatience. LR 3.06. 5 P
made out of her impatience — which not wanted ANT 2.02. 68
but mark antony | put me to some impatience. 2.06. 42
and impatience does | become a dog that's mad. 4.15. 79
no farther with your din | express impatience, CYM 5.04.112
said, impatience chokes her pleading tongue, VEN 217
IMPATIENT 20 FR 0.0022 REL FR 19 V 1 P
it presently, | i am impatient of my tarriance. TGV 2.07. 90
nay, master page, be not impatient. WIV 3.04. 71
his tongue, all impatient to speak and not see, LLL 2.01.238
tear | impatient answers from my gentle tongue? MND 3.02.287
sirs, | if you should smile, he grows impatient. SHR in.1. 99
when, with a most impatient devilish spirit, 2.01.151
much more a shrew of /thy impatient humor. 3.02. 29
england, impatient of your just demands, | hath JN 2.01. 56
what a wasp-stung and impatient fool | art thou 1H4 1.03.236
impatient of his fit, breaks like a fire | out 2H4 1.01.142
a penny, you are too impatient to bear crosses. 1.02.226 P
fly o'er them all, impatient for their hour. H5 4.02. 52
wherefore is charles impatient with his friend? 1H6 2.01. 54
in rome | how furious and impatient they be, TIT 2.01. 76
imperious, and impatient of your wrongs, | and 5.01. 6
to an impatient child that hath new robes | and ROM 3.02. 30
impatient of my absence, | and grief that young JC 4.03.152
a heart unfortified, or mind impatient, | an HAM 1.02. 96
to put my father in impatient thoughts | by OTH 1.03.242
rude and impatient, then, like chastity, | she TNK 2.02.141
IMPATIENTLY 3 FR 0.0003 REL FR 3 V 0 P
know'st, being stopp'd, impatiently doth rage; TGV 2.07. 26
impatiently i burn with thy desire; 1H6 1.02.108
and too impatiently stamp'd with your foot. JC 2.01.244
IMPAWN 1 FR 0.0001 REL FR 1 V 0 P
therefore take heed how you impawn our person, H5 1.02. 21
/IMPAWN'D 1 FR 0.0001 REL FR 0 V 1 P
why is this all /impawn'd, /as you call it? HAM 5.02.164 P
IMPAWN'D 3 FR 0.0003 REL FR 2 V 1 P
trunk which you | shall bear along impawn'd, WT 1.02.436
and let there be impawn'd | some surety for a 1H4 4.03.108
against the which he has impawn'd, as i take it, HAM 5.02.148 P
IMPEACH 10 FR 0.0011 REL FR 10 V 0 P
thou art a villain to impeach me thus: ERR 5.01. 29
why, what an intricate impeach is this! 5.01.270
you do impeach your modesty too much, | to leave MND 2.01.214
and doth impeach the freedom of the state, | if MV 3.02.278
will much impeach the justice of the state, 3.03. 29
boy, | under whose warrant i impeach thy wrong, JN 2.01.116
or with pale beggar-fear impeach my height R2 1.01.189
to do him wrong or any way impeach | what then 1H4 1.03. 75
and ten to one is no impeach of valor. 3H6 1.04. 60
and here i stand both to impeach and purge ROM 5.03.226
IMPEACH'D 2 FR 0.0002 REL FR 2 V 0 P
i am disgrac'd, impeach'd, and baffled here, R2 1.01.170
when most impeach'd stands least in thy control. SON 125.14
IMPEACHMENT 2 FR 0.0002 REL FR 2 V 0 P
which would be great impeachment to his age, TGV 1.03. 15
to march on to callice | without impeachment; H5 3.06.142
IMPEACHMENTS 1 FR 0.0001 REL FR 1 V 0 P
queen, | devis'd impeachments to imprison him; R3 2.02. 22
IMPEDES 1 FR 0.0001 REL FR 1 V 0 P
all that impedes thee from the golden round, MAC 1.05. 28
IMPEDIMENT 15 FR 0.0017 REL FR 7 V 8 P
hath (like an impediment in the current) made it MM 3.01.242 P
cross, any impediment will be med'cinable to me. ADO 2.02. 4 P
if there be any impediment, i pray you discover 3.02. 93 P
know any inward impediment why you should not be 4.01. 12 P
conscience) find no impediment to the contrary, 5.02. 85 P
lack of years be no impediment to let him lack a MV 4.01.162 P
i know not what impediment this complaint may be WT 4.04.709 P
whose passage, vex'd with thy impediment, JN 2.01.336
what was th' impediment that broke this off? H5 1.01. 90
view, | what rub or what impediment there is, 5.02. 33
land | have we march'd on without impediment; R3 5.02. 4
than can ever | appear in your impediment. COR 1.01. 72
that we labor'd | (no impediment between) but 2.03.228
and the impediment most profitably remov'd, OTH 2.01.278 P
that so fairly shows) | dream of impediment! ANT 2.02.145
IMPEDIMENTS 8 FR 0.0009 REL FR 8 V 0 P
as all impediments in fancy's course | are AWW 5.03.214
that you foresee not what impediments | drag 1H4 4.03. 18
tears, | the moist impediments unto my speech, 2H4 4.05.139
all continent impediments would o'erbear | that MAC 4.03. 64
i have made my way through more impediments OTH 5.02.263
these impediments | will i file off; TNK 3.01. 84
the marriage of true minds | admit impediments; SON 116. 2
how coldly those impediments stand forth | of LC 269
IMPENETRABLE 1 FR 0.0001 REL FR 1 V 0 P
it is the most impenetrable cur | that ever kept MV 3.03. 18
IMPERATOR 1 FR 0.0001 REL FR 1 V 0 P
sole imperator and great general | of trotting LLL 3.01.185
IMPERCEIVERANT 1 FR 0.0001 REL FR 0 V 1 P
yet this imperceiverant thing loves him in my CYM 4.01. 14 P
IMPERFECT *(also unperfect)*
/IMPERFECT 1 FR 0.0001 REL FR 0 V 1 P
/something /he /left /imperfect /in /the /state, LR 4.03. 3 P
IMPERFECT 6 FR 0.0006 REL FR 5 V 1 P
to be something imperfect in favoring the first COR 2.01. 49 P
stay, you imperfect speakers, tell me more: MAC 1.03. 70
why then your other senses grow imperfect | by LR 4.06. 5
it is a judgment maim'd, and most imperfect, OTH 1.03. 99
each thing | our haste does leave imperfect. TNK 1.04. 12
when in dead night /thy fair imperfect shade SON 43.11
IMPERFECTION 2 FR 0.0002 REL FR 1 V 1 P
i must very much lay open mine own imperfection; WIV 2.02.185 P
undo | this hateful imperfection of her eyes. MND 4.01. 63
IMPERFECTIONS 4 FR 0.0004 REL FR 3 V 1 P
piece out our imperfections with your thoughts; H5 pr 23
whose want gives growth to th' imperfections 5.02. 69
account | with all my imperfections on my head. HAM 1.05. 79
not alone the imperfections of long-engraff'd LR 1.01.297 P
IMPERFECTLY 1 FR 0.0001 REL FR 1 V 0 P
/then, | from one that so imperfectly /conjects, OTH 3.03.149
IMPERIAL *(also emperial)*
IMPERIAL 24 FR 0.0027 REL FR 23 V 1 P
moon, | and the imperial vot'ress passed on, MND 2.01.163
and to imperial love, that god most high, | do AWW 2.03. 75
bold oxlips, and | the crown imperial; WT 4.04.126
that, were i crown'd the most imperial monarch, 4.04.372
my due from thee is this imperial crown, | which 2H4 4.05. 41
lives, and services | to this imperial throne. H5 1.02. 35
with crowns imperial, crowns and coronets, 2.pr. 10
speak upon our cue, and our voice is imperial: 3.06.124 P
ball, | the sword, the mace, the crown imperial, 4.01.261
to bring your most imperial majesties | unto 5.02. 26
and of it left his son imperial lord. ep 8
as by your high imperial majesty | i had in 2H6 1.01. 1
suffolk's imperial tongue is stern and rough, 4.01.121
the high imperial type of this earth's glory. R3 4.04.245
4.04.382
th' imperial metal, circling now thy head, | had TRO 1.03.187
opinion crowns | with an imperial voice — many 1.03.224
a stranger to those most imperial looks | know TIT 1.01. 6
last | that ware the imperial diadem of rome, 1.01. 14
not dishonor to approach | the imperial seat, to 2.01. 13
to mount aloft with thy imperial mistress, | and MAC 1.03.129
to the swelling act | of the imperial theme. 4.03. 20
nature may recoil | in an imperial charge. HAM 1.02. 9
th' imperial jointress to this warlike state, CYM 5.05.474
th' imperial caesar, should again unite | his
IMPERIAL'S 1 FR 0.0001 REL FR 0 V 1 P
going with sir proteus to the imperial's court. TGV 2.03. 5 P
IMPERIOUS 15 FR 0.0017 REL FR 14 V 1 P
whose high imperious thoughts have punish'd me TGV 2.04.130
so looks the strond whereon the imperious flood 2H4 1.01. 62
brains | in cradle of the rude imperious surge, 3.01. 20
i pray, | but one imperious in another's throne? 1H6 3.01. 44
have we beauford | the imperious churchman, 2H6 1.03. 69
or this imperious man will work us all | from H8 2.02. 46
i thank thee, most imperious agamemnon. TRO 4.05.172
presents well worthy rome's imperious lord: TIT 1.01.250
king, be thy thoughts imperious, like thy name. 4.04. 81
imperious, and impatient of your wrongs, | and 5.01. 6
imperious caesar, dead and turn'd to clay, HAM 5.01.213
offenseless dog to affright an imperious lion. OTH 2.03.275 P
not th' imperious show | of the full-fortun'd ANT 4.15. 23
th' imperious seas breeds monsters; CYM 4.02. 35
kings, | imperious supreme of all mortal things. VEN 996
IMPERIOUSLY 2 FR 0.0002 REL FR 2 V 0 P
who's there, that knocks so imperiously? 1H6 1.03. 5
imperiously he leaps, he neighs, he bounds, VEN 265
IMPERTINENCY 1 FR 0.0001 REL FR 1 V 0 P
o, matter and impertinency mix'd! LR 4.06.174
IMPERTINENT 2 FR 0.0002 REL FR 1 V 1 P
the which this story | were most impertinent. TMP 1.02.138
very brief, the suit is impertinent to myself, MV 2.02.137 P
IMPETICOS 1 FR 0.0001 REL FR 0 V 1 P
i did impeticos thy gratillity; TN 2.03. 26 P
IMPETUOSITY 1 FR 0.0001 REL FR 0 V 1 P
of his rage, skill, fury, and impetuosity. TN 3.04.194 P
/IMPETUOUS 1 FR 0.0001 REL FR 1 V 0 P
/which /the /impetuous /blasts /with /eyeless LR 3.01. 8
IMPIETIES 1 FR 0.0001 REL FR 0 V 1 P
guilty of those impieties for the which they are H5 4.01.175 P
IMPIETY 8 FR 0.0009 REL FR 7 V 1 P
impiety has made a feast of thee. MM 1.02. 57 P
thou pure impiety and impious purity! ADO 4.01.104
to keep that oath were more impiety | than 3H6 5.01. 90
my lord, this is impiety in you. TIT 1.01.355
to be in anger is impiety; TIM 3.05. 56
so from himself impiety hath wrought, | that for LUC 341
then let it not be call'd impiety, | if in this 1174
he live, | and with his presence grace impiety, SON 67. 2
IMPIOUS 8 FR 0.0009 REL FR 8 V 0 P
thou pure impiety and impious purity! ADO 4.01.104
what is it then to me, if impious war, | arrayed H5 3.03. 15
thought | it was both impious and unnatural 1H6 5.01. 12
and york and impious beauford, that false priest 2H6 2.04. 53
is a course | of impious stubbornness, 'tis HAM 1.02. 94
and keep their impious turbands on without CYM 3.03. 6
o impious act, including all foul harms! LUC 199
decay, | the impious breach of holy wedlock vow; 809
IMPITEOUS 1 FR 0.0001 REL FR 1 V 0 P
eats not the flats with more impiteous haste HAM 4.05.101
IMPLACABLE 1 FR 0.0001 REL FR 0 V 1 P
his incensement at this moment is so implacable, TN 3.04.238 P
IMPLEACH'D 1 FR 0.0001 REL FR 1 V 0 P
hair, | with twisted metal amorously impleach'd, LC 205
IMPLEMENTS 2 FR 0.0002 REL FR 2 V 0 P
all broken implements of a ruin'd house. TIM 4.02. 16
and foreign mart for implements of war, | why HAM 1.01. 74
IMPLIES 1 FR 0.0001 REL FR 1 V 0 P
that seeks not to find that her search implies, AWW 1.03.216
/IMPLORATORS 1 FR 0.0001 REL FR 1 V 0 P
show, | but mere /implorators of unholy suits, HAM 1.03.129
IMPLOR'D 2 FR 0.0002 REL FR 2 V 0 P
have earnestly implor'd a general peace 1H6 5.04. 98
implor'd your highness' pardon, and set forth MAC 1.04. 6
IMPLORE 7 FR 0.0008 REL FR 5 V 2 P
implore her, in my voice, that she make friends MM 1.02.180
if you'll implore it, that will free your life, 3.01. 65
sweet heart, i do implore secrety — that the LLL 5.01.109 P
i implore so much expense of thy royal sweet 5.02.522 P
that | i kneel and then implore her blessing. WT 5.03. 44
spain advis'd, whose counsel | i will implore. H8 2.04. 56
and implore | her power unto our party. TNK 5.01. 75
IMPLORING 1 FR 0.0001 REL FR 1 V 0 P
penitence comes after all, | imploring pardon. H5 4.01.305
IMPLY 1 FR 0.0001 REL FR 1 V 0 P
any profit, | or my life imply her any danger? PER 4.01. 81
IMPORT 20 FR 0.0022 REL FR 19 V 1 P
be they of much import? TGV 3.01. 55
designs, and of great import indeed too — but LLL 5.01.100 P
and tell us what occasion of import | hath all SHR 3.02.102
what th' import is, | i know not yet. AWW 2.03.276
to be your prisoner should import offending, WT 1.02. 57
is much more general than these lines import. JN 4.03. 17
came from the north, and thus it did import: 1H4 1.01. 51
if you knew | how much they do import, you would 4.04. 5
quite, | except some petty towns of no import. 1H6 1.01. 91
it doth import him much to speak with me. TRO 4.02. 50
and wild, and do import | some misadventure. ROM 5.01. 28
of dear import, and the neglecting it | may do 5.02. 19
what might import my sister's letter to him? LR 4.05. 6
of quality and respect | as doth import you. OTH 1.03.283
if it be not for some purpose of import, 3.03.316
upon my knee, what doth your speech import? 4.02. 31
all great fears, which now import their dangers, ANT 2.02.132
and thousands more | of semblable import — but 3.04. 3
name, | being leo-natus, doth import so much. CYM 5.05.445
thee | were to import forgetfulness in me. SON 122.14
IMPORTANCE 5 FR 0.0005 REL FR 3 V 2 P
the letter at sir toby's great importance, | in TN 5.01.363
(for in an act of this importance 'twere | most WT 2.01.181
not say if th' importance were joy or sorrow; 5.02. 18 P
at our importance hither is he come | to spread JN 2.01. 7
bore, upon importance of so slight and trivial a CYM 1.04. 41 P
IMPORTANCY 1 FR 0.0001 REL FR 1 V 0 P
consider | th' importancy of cyprus to the turk, OTH 1.03. 20
IMPORTANT 7 FR 0.0008 REL FR 5 V 2 P
at your important letters — this ill day | a ERR 5.01.138
if the prince be too important, tell him there ADO 2.01. 71 P
now his important blood will nought deny | that AWW 3.07. 21
come to what is important in't. TN 1.05.192 P
for request's sake only, | he makes important. TRO 2.03.170
i cannot, lord, i have important business, | the 5.01. 82
by | th' important acting of your dread command? HAM 3.04.108
IMPORTANTLY 1 FR 0.0001 REL FR 1 V 0 P
eyes | and ears so cloy'd importantly as now, CYM 4.04. 19
IMPORTED 1 FR 0.0001 REL FR 1 V 0 P
which imported | his fellowship i' th' cause TIM 5.02. 11
IMPORTETH 2 FR 0.0002 REL FR 2 V 0 P
it importeth none here. LLL 4.01. 57
what else more serious | importeth thee to know, ANT 1.02.121
IMPORTING 8 FR 0.0009 REL FR 7 V 1 P
looks in her | with an importing visage, and she AWW 5.03.136
comets, importing change of times and states, 1H6 1.01. 2
no less importing than our general good, | are R3 3.07. 68
thus importing | the several parcels of his H8 3.02.124
message | importing the surrender of those lands HAM 1.02. 23
and his weeds, | importing health and graveness. 4.07. 81
importing denmark's health and england's too, 5.02. 21
importing the mere perdition of the turkish OTH 2.02. 2 P
/IMPORTLESS 1 FR 0.0001 REL FR 1 V 0 P
/matter /needless, /of /importless /burthen, TRO 1.03. 71
IMPORTMENT'S 1 FR 0.0001 REL FR 1 V 0 P
comes in | like old importment's bastard) has TNK 1.03. 80
/IMPORTS 1 FR 0.0001 REL FR 0 V 1 P
/of, /which /imports /to /the /kingdom /so /much LR 4.03. 4 P
IMPORTS 9 FR 0.0010 REL FR 6 V 3 P
it imports no reason | that with such vehemency MM 5.01.108
i have a motion much imports your good, 5.01.535
belike this show imports the argument of the HAM 3.02.139 P
our sovereign process, which imports at full, 4.03. 63
alas, sweet lady, what imports this song? 4.05. 27
what imports the nomination of this gentleman? 5.02.127 P
his gesture imports it. OTH 4.01.138 P
the one of them imports | the death of cassio to 5.02.310
it more imports me | than all the actions that i TNK 1.01.172
IMPORTUNACY 2 FR 0.0002 REL FR 2 V 0 P
not asham'd | to wrong him with thy importunacy? TGV 4.02.111
your importunacy cease till after dinner, | that TIM 2.02. 41
/IMPORTUNATE 1 FR 0.0001 REL FR 0 V 1 P
and among other /importunate and most serious LLL 5.01. 99 P
IMPORTUNATE 5 FR 0.0005 REL FR 3 V 2 P
pray thee, good camillo, be no more importunate. WT 4.02. 1 P
you gone, | put on a most importunate aspect, TIM 2.01. 28
manner was i in debt to my importunate business, 3.06. 13 P
she is importunate, indeed distract. HAM 4.05. 2
who having, by their own importunate suit, | or OTH 4.01. 26
IMPORTUN'D 8 FR 0.0009 REL FR 7 V 1 P
you were kneel'd to and importun'd otherwise TMP 2.01.129
have you importun'd her to such a purpose? WIV 2.02.212 P
and importun'd me | that his attendant — so his ERR 1.01.126

due, | and since i have not much importun'd you, 4.01. 2
have you importun'd him by any means? ROM 1.01.145
he hath importun'd me with love | in honorable HAM 1.03.110
my mourning and importun'd tears hath pitied. LR 4.04. 26
very oft importun'd me | to temper poisons for CYM 5.05.249
IMPORTUNE 13 FR 0.0014 REL FR 12 V 1 P
and did request me to importune you | to let him TGV 1.03. 13
nor need'st thou much importune me to that 1.03. 17
i, their king, that thither them importune, | do 3.01.145
as time and our concernings shall importune, MM 1.01. 56
against all sense you do importune her. 5.01.433
gentlemen, importune me no farther, | for how i SHR 1.01. 48
whom i will importune | with earnest prayers all R3 2.02. 14
importune him for my moneys, be not ceas'd TIM 2.01. 16
importune him once more to go, my lord, | his LR 3.04.161
importune her help to put you in your place OTH 2.03.319 P
go, and importune her. 3.04.108
only | i here importune death awhile, until | of ANT 4.15. 19
whom thine eyes woo as mine importune thee. SON 142.10
/IMPORTUNES 1 FR 0.0001 REL FR 1 V 0 P
/importunes personal conference with his grace. LLL 2.01. 32
IMPORTUNES 3 FR 0.0003 REL FR 2 V 1 P
you hear how he importunes me — the chain! ERR 4.01. 53
here at the door, and importunes access to you. AYL 1.01. 92 P
now he importunes him | to tell it o'er. OTH 4.01.113
IMPORTUNITY 3 FR 0.0003 REL FR 2 V 1 P
comes with him, at my importunity, to fill up MV 4.01.160 P
treasure open | to his unmast'red importunity. HAM 1.03. 32
with any strong or vehement importunity; OTH 3.03.251
IMPOS'D 4 FR 0.0004 REL FR 2 V 2 P
father, | i have on angelo impos'd the office, MM 1.03. 40
a heavier task could not have been impos'd ERR 1.01. 31
should be impos'd upon his father that sent him; H5 4.01.150 P
than for us to undergo any difficulty impos'd. TRO 3.02. 80 P
IMPOSE 10 FR 0.0011 REL FR 9 V 1 P
according to your ladyship's impose, | i am thus TGV 4.03. 8
impose me to what penance your invention | can ADO 5.01.273
lieu thereof, impose on thee nothing but this: LLL 3.01.129 P
a plague | that cupid will impose for my neglect 3.01.202
impose some service on me for thy love. 5.02.840
my ability may undergo | and nobleness impose; WT 2.03.165
ordain, impose | some gentle order, and then we JN 3.01.250
what fates impose, that men must needs abide; 3H6 4.03. 58
which fondly you would here impose on me. R3 3.07.147
way | thou mightst deserve, or they impose, this LR 2.04. 26
IMPOSITION 9 FR 0.0010 REL FR 5 V 4 P
else would stand under grievous imposition, as MM 1.02.189 P
than your father's imposition depending on the MV 1.02.105 P
i do desire you | not to deny this imposition, 3.04. 33
the imposition clear'd, | hereditary ours. WT 1.02. 74
reproach | attend the sequel of your imposition, R3 3.07.232
mistress to devise imposition enough than for us TRO 3.02. 79 P
reputation is an idle and most false imposition; OTH 2.03.269 P
could not reach to | without some imposition, TNK 1.04. 44
aid, | as bound in knighthood to her imposition, LUC 1697
IMPOSITIONS 1 FR 0.0001 REL FR 1 V 0 P
death and honesty | go with your impositions, i AWW 4.04. 29
IMPOSSIBILITIES 3 FR 0.0003 REL FR 3 V 0 P
off, | flattering me with impossibilities. 3H6 3.02.143
god, | that sold'rest close impossibilities, TIM 4.03.387
who make them honors | of men's impossibilities, LR 4.06. 74
IMPOSSIBILITY 4 FR 0.0004 REL FR 3 V 1 P
and what impossibility would slay | in common AWW 2.01.177
being not ignorant of the impossibility, and 4.01. 36 P
so much | that proof is call'd impossibility. TRO 5.05. 29
murd'ring impossibility, to make | what cannot COR 5.03. 61
IMPOSSIBLE *(also unpossible)*
IMPOSSIBLE 41 FR 0.0046 REL FR 27 V 14 P
what impossible matter will he make easy next? TMP 2.01. 89 P
alive, | 'tis as impossible that he's undrown'd, 2.01.237
if it be a match, as nothing is impossible — TGV 3.01.370 P
and tells me 'tis a thing impossible | i should WIV 3.04. 9
'tis impossible he should; 3.05.145 P
should aid him, i will search impossible places. 3.05.148 P
but it is impossible to extirp it quite, friar, MM 3.02.102 P
make not impossible | that which but seems 5.01. 51
'tis not impossible | but one, the wicked'st 5.01. 52
where it is impossible you should take true root ADO 1.03. 23 P
his gift is in devising impossible slanders. 2.01.138 P
jest with such impossible conveyance upon me 2.01.245 P
nay, that's impossible, she may wear her heart 2.03.203 P
that were impossible — but i pray you both, 5.01.280
impossible. LLL 1.02. 38 P
it cannot be, it is impossible: 5.02.856
in paying it, it is impossible i should live, MV 3.02.318 P
she is driven, and it is not impossible to me, AYL 5.02. 65 P
supposing it a thing impossible, | for those SHR 1.02.123
it were impossible i should speed amiss. 2.01.283
curster than she? why, 'tis impossible. 3.02.154
impossible be strange attempts to those | that AWW 1.01.224
can ever believe such impossible passages of TN 3.02. 72 P
est–il impossible d'echapper la force de ton H5 4.04. 16 P
you judge it straight a thing impossible | to 1H6 5.04. 47
but now it is impossible we should. 2H6 1.01.108
to nominate them all, it is impossible. 2.01.128
it is impossible that i should die | by such a 4.01.110
thou canst not, son; it is impossible. 3H6 1.02. 21
no, 'tis impossible he should escape; 2.06. 38
'tis as much impossible — | unless we sweep 'em H8 5.03. 12
run, | and i will strive with things impossible, JC 2.01.325
it is impossible that ever rome | should breed 5.03.100
'tis hard, almost impossible. LR 2.04.242
it is impossible to bear it out. OTH 2.01. 19
it is impossible you should see this, | were 3.03.402
fie, there is no such man; it is impossible. 4.02.134
like her? o isis! 'tis impossible. ANT 3.03. 15
'tis impossible | strange that his power should 3.07. 56
tied | her to her chamber, that 'tis impossible. PER 2.05. 9
thy relation | to points that seem impossible, 5.01.124
IMPOSTERS *(also impostor, imposture)*
IMPOSTERS 1 FR 0.0001 REL FR 1 V 0 P
flaws and starts | (imposters to true fear) MAC 3.04. 63
IMPOSTHUME *(also impostumes)*
IMPOSTHUME 2 FR 0.0002 REL FR 1 V 1 P
whissing lungs, bladders full of imposthume, TRO 5.01. 21 P
this is th' imposthume of much wealth and peace, HAM 4.04. 27
IMPOSTOR *(also imposters, imposture)*
IMPOSTOR 1 FR 0.0001 REL FR 1 V 0 P
what, | an advocate for an impostor? TMP 1.02.478
IMPOSTUMES *(also imposthume)*
IMPOSTUMES 1 FR 0.0001 REL FR 1 V 0 P
surfeits, impostumes, grief, and damn'd despair VEN 743
IMPOSTURE *(also imposters, impostor)*
IMPOSTURE 2 FR 0.0002 REL FR 2 V 0 P
i am not an imposture that proclaim | myself AWW 2.01.155
it may be | you think me an imposture. PER 5.01.177
IMPOTENCE 1 FR 0.0001 REL FR 1 V 0 P
age, and impotence | was falsely borne in hand, HAM 2.02. 66
IMPOTENT 4 FR 0.0004 REL FR 3 V 1 P
wit | to enforce the pained impotent to smile. LLL 5.02.854
delay /leads impotent and snail–pac'd beggary. R3 4.03. 53
who, impotent and bedred, scarcely hears | of HAM 1.02. 29
o most lame and impotent conclusion! OTH 2.01.161 P
IMPOUNDED 1 FR 0.0001 REL FR 1 V 0 P
defended | but taken and impounded as a stray H5 1.02.160
IMPREGNABLE 4 FR 0.0004 REL FR 4 V 0 P
walls about our life | were brass impregnable; R2 3.02.168
which he hath giv'n for fence impregnable, | and 3H6 4.01. 44
were his heart | almost impregnable, his old TIT 4.04. 98
days, | when rocks impregnable are not so stout, SON 65. 7
IMPRESE 1 FR 0.0001 REL FR 1 V 0 P
ras'd out my imprese, leaving me no sign, | save R2 3.01. 25
IMPRESS* 6 FR 0.0006 REL FR 5 V 1 P
this weak impress of love is as a figure TGV 3.02. 6
here the voluntary, and you as under an impress. TRO 2.01. 97 P
who can impress the forest, bid the tree | unfix MAC 4.01. 95
with thy keen sword impress as make me bleed. 5.08. 10
why such impress of shipwrights, whose sore task HAM 1.01. 75
reapers, people | ingross'd by swift impress. ANT 3.07. 36
IMPRESS'D* 3 FR 0.0003 REL FR 3 V 0 P
love's strong passion is impress'd in youth. AWW 1.03.133
who wears my stripes impress'd upon him, that COR 5.06.107
and turn our impress'd lances in our eyes LR 5.03. 50
IMPRESSED* 2 FR 0.0002 REL FR 2 V 0 P
heart, like an agot, with your print impressed, LLL 2.01.236
cross | we are impressed and engag'd to fight — 1H4 1.01. 21
IMPRESSEST 1 FR 0.0001 REL FR 1 V 0 P
"'when thou impressest, what are precepts worth LC 267
IMPRESSION 13 FR 0.0014 REL FR 13 V 0 P
fire, | bears no impression of the thing it was. TGV 2.04.202
th' impression of keen whips i'ld wear as rubies MM 2.04.101
and stol'n the impression of her fantasy | with MND 1.01. 32
where the impression of mine eye infixing, AWW 5.03. 47
that carries no impression like the dam. 3H6 3.02.162
hell, | such terrible impression made my dream. R3 1.04. 63
of thy deep duty more impression show | than COR 5.03. 51
whose soft impression | interprets for my poor TIM 5.04. 68
/subscrib'd it, gave't th' impression, plac'd it HAM 5.02. 52
and yields at last to every light impression? VEN 566
th' impression of strange kinds | is form'd in LUC 1242
that map which deep impression bears | of hard 1712
your love and pity doth th' impression fill SON 112. 1
IMPRESSURE 3 FR 0.0003 REL FR 2 V 1 P
the cicatrice and capable impressure | thy palm AYL 3.05. 23
and the impressure her lucrece, with which she TN 2.05. 92 P
wherein my sword had not impressure made | /of TRO 4.05.131
IMPRIMENDUM 1 FR 0.0001 REL FR 0 V 1 P
of her, cum privilegio ad imprimendum solum; SHR 4.04. 93 P
IMPRIMIS *(see inprimis)*
IMPRINT 1 FR 0.0001 REL FR 1 V 0 P
the vacant leaves thy mind's imprint will bear, SON 77. 3
IMPRINTED 2 FR 0.0002 REL FR 2 V 0 P
you are but as a form in wax | by him imprinted, MND 1.01. 50
lips, sweet seals in my soft lips imprinted, VEN 511
IMPRISON 3 FR 0.0003 REL FR 2 V 1 P
well, then imprison him. MM 3.02. 66 P
imprison him; JN 4.02.155
queen, | devis'd impeachments to imprison him; R3 2.02. 22
IMPRISON'D 13 FR 0.0014 REL FR 12 V 1 P
within which rift | imprison'd, thou didst TMP 1.02.278
to be imprison'd in the viewless winds | and MM 3.01.123
why have you suffer'd me to be imprison'd, TN 5.01.341
that imprison'd me | and hath detain'd me all my 1H6 2.05. 55
our brother is imprison'd by your means, R3 1.03. 77
imprison'd is he, say you? TIM 1.01. 94
imprison'd, and in scarcity of friends, | i 2.02.225
to tithing, and /stock–punish'd and imprison'd; LR 3.04.135 P
wedded, | her husband banish'd, she imprison'd: CYM 1.01. 8
as when the wind imprison'd in the ground, VEN 1046
fed, | show'd life imprison'd in a body dead. LUC 1456
blest, | by new unfolding his imprison'd pride. SON 52.12
beck) | th' imprison'd absence of your liberty, 58. 6
IMPRISONED 2 FR 0.0002 REL FR 2 V 0 P
abbots, imprisoned angels | set at liberty. JN 3.03. 8
and from your womb where you imprisoned were TIT 4.02.124
IMPRISONING 1 FR 0.0001 REL FR 1 V 0 P
and vex'd | by the imprisoning of unruly wind 1H4 3.01. 29
IMPRISONMENT 16 FR 0.0018 REL FR 11 V 5 P
of freedom as the mortality of imprisonment. MM 1.02.134 P
and imprisonment | can lay on nature is a 3.01.129
if imprisonment be the due of a bawd, why, 'tis 3.02. 66 P
you shall have your full time of imprisonment, 4.02. 12 P
beside the charge, the shame, imprisonment, ERR 5.01. 18
a year's imprisonment to be taken with a wench. LLL 1.01.287 P
the potion of imprisonment to me in respect of 2H4 1.02.127 P
rack, | so fare my limbs with long imprisonment; 1H6 2.05. 4
and this her easy–held imprisonment | hath 5.03.139
to do, | to free king henry from imprisonment, 3H6 4.03. 63
for that it made my imprisonment a pleasure; 4.06. 11
well, your imprisonment shall not be long, | i R3 1.01.114
how hath your lordship brook'd imprisonment? 1.01.125
thanks | that were the cause of my imprisonment. 1.01.128
mean | of my lord hastings' late imprisonment. 1.03. 90
concerning his imprisonment was rather | (if H8 5.02.185
IMPRISON'T 1 FR 0.0001 REL FR 1 V 0 P
imprison't not | in ignorant concealment. WT 1.02.396
IMPROBABLE 1 FR 0.0001 REL FR 0 V 1 P
i could condemn it as an improbable fiction. TN 3.04.128 P
IMPROPER *(also unproper)*
/IMPROPER 1 FR 0.0001 REL FR 1 V 0 P
/did /him /service | /improper /for /a /slave. LR 5.03.222
IMPROPERLY *(see unproperly)*
IMPROVE 1 FR 0.0001 REL FR 1 V 0 P
if he improve them, may well stretch so far | as JC 2.01.159
IMPROVIDENT *(also unprovident)*
IMPROVIDENT 2 FR 0.0002 REL FR 1 V 1 P
who says this is improvident jealousy? WIV 2.02.289 P
improvident soldiers, had your watch been good, 1H6 2.01. 58
IMPUDENCE 4 FR 0.0004 REL FR 4 V 0 P
hast thou or word, or wit, or impudence, | that MM 5.01.363
tax of impudence, | a strumpet's boldness, a AWW 2.01.170
wanted | less impudence to gainsay what they did WT 3.02. 56
since men take women's gifts for impudence. PER 2.03. 69
IMPUDENCY 1 FR 0.0001 REL FR 0 V 1 P
without affection, audacious without impudency, LLL 5.01. 5 P
/IMPUDENT 1 FR 0.0001 REL FR 1 V 0 P
/impudent /strumpet! OTH 4.02. 81
IMPUDENT 8 FR 0.0009 REL FR 4 V 4 P
much shame, you might begin an impudent nation. AWW 4.03.328 P
she's impudent, my lord, | and was a common 5.03.187
why, thou whoreson, impudent, emboss'd rascal, 1H4 3.03.157 P
with such more than impudent sauciness from you, 2H4 2.01.112 P
you call honorable boldness impudent sauciness; 2.01.123 P
made impudent with use of evil deeds, | i would 3H6 1.04.117
peace, impudent and shameless warwick, | proud 3.03.156
a woman impudent and mannish grown | is not more TRO 3.03.217
IMPUDENTLY 1 FR 0.0001 REL FR 1 V 0 P
wilt confess, | or else be impudently negative, WT 1.02.274
IMPUDIQUE 1 FR 0.0001 REL FR 0 V 1 P
gros, et impudique, et non pour les dames de H5 3.04. 54 P
IMPUGN 1 FR 0.0001 REL FR 1 V 0 P
law | cannot impugn you as you do proceed. MV 4.01.179
IMPUGNS 1 FR 0.0001 REL FR 1 V 0 P
it skills not greatly who impugns our doom. 2H6 3.01.281
IMPURE 3 FR 0.0003 REL FR 3 V 0 P
from all the impure blots and stains thereof; R3 3.07.234
and pure perfection with impure defeature, VEN 736
gush pure streams to purge my impure tale." LUC 1078
IMPURITY 1 FR 0.0001 REL FR 1 V 0 P
absolute, | that some impurity doth not pollute. LUC 854
IMPUTATION 7 FR 0.0008 REL FR 3 V 4 P
else imputation, | for that he knew you, might MM 5.01.420
have you heard any imputation to the contrary? MV 1.03. 13 P
his men with the imputation of being near their 2H4 5.01. 72 P
upon the sea, the imputation of his wickedness, H5 4.01.149 P
our imputation shall be oddly pois'd | in this TRO 1.03.339
but in the imputation laid on him by them, in HAM 5.02.141 P
if imputation and strong circumstances | which OTH 3.03.406
IMPUTE 4 FR 0.0004 REL FR 4 V 0 P
impute it not a crime | to me, or my swift WT 4.01. 4
impute his words | to wayward sickliness and age R2 2.01.141
and not impute this yielding to light love, ROM 2.02.105
this silence for my sin you did impute, | which SON 83. 9
IN *(also a'*, en, i')*
/IN 131 FR 0.0148 REL FR 112 V 19 P
IN 11511 FR 1.3012 REL FR 8809 V 2702 P
INACCESSIBLE 2 FR 0.0002 REL FR 1 V 1 P
uninhabitable, and almost inaccessible — TMP 2.01. 38 P
e'er you are | that in this desert inaccessible, AYL 2.07.110
INAIDIBLE 1 FR 0.0001 REL FR 1 V 0 P
never ransom nature | from her inaidible estate; AWW 2.01.119
INAUDIBLE 1 FR 0.0001 REL FR 1 V 0 P
th' inaudible and noiseless foot of time AWW 5.03. 41
INAUSPICIOUS *(also unauspicious)*
INAUSPICIOUS 1 FR 0.0001 REL FR 1 V 0 P
and shake the yoke of inauspicious stars | from ROM 5.03.111
INBARK'D *(also embark'd)*
INBARK'D 1 FR 0.0001 REL FR 1 V 0 P
my necessaries are inbark'd. HAM 1.03. 1
/INCAGED 1 FR 0.0001 REL FR 1 V 0 P
head, | and yet, /incaged in so small a verge, R2 2.01.102
INCAGED 2 FR 0.0002 REL FR 2 V 0 P
ay, such a pleasure as incaged birds | conceive, 3H6 4.06. 12
he carries thence incaged in his breast. VEN 582
INCANTATIONS 1 FR 0.0001 REL FR 1 V 0 P
my ancient incantations are too weak, | and hell 1H6 5.03. 27
INCAPABLE *(also uncapable)*
INCAPABLE 6 FR 0.0006 REL FR 6 V 0 P
temporal royalties | he thinks me now incapable; TMP 1.02.111
more, | is not your father grown incapable | of WT 4.04.397
incapable and shallow innocents, | you cannot R3 2.02. 18
rome, such as was never | s' incapable of help. COR 4.06.120
lauds, | as one incapable of her own distress, HAM 4.07.178
incapable of more, replete with you, | my most SON 113.13
INCARDINATE 1 FR 0.0001 REL FR 0 V 1 P
a coward, but he's the very devil incardinate. TN 5.01.182 P
INCARNADINE 1 FR 0.0001 REL FR 1 V 0 P
rather | the multitudinous seas incarnadine, MAC 2.02. 59
INCARNATE 2 FR 0.0002 REL FR 1 V 1 P
'a did, and said they were dev'ls incarnate. H5 2.03. 32 P
goth, this is the incarnate devil | that robb'd TIT 5.01. 40
INCARNATION 1 FR 0.0001 REL FR 0 V 1 P
certainly the jew is the very devil incarnation, MV 2.02. 27 P
INCENS'D 14 FR 0.0015 REL FR 11 V 3 P
have | incens'd the seas and shores — yea, all TMP 3.03. 74
don john your brother incens'd me to slander the ADO 5.01.236 P
room for the incens'd worthies! LLL 5.02.697 P
i know the knight is incens'd against you, even TN 3.04.260 P
yet notwithstanding, being incens'd, he is flint 2H4 4.04. 33
it is not that that hath incens'd the duke: 1H6 3.01. 36
more incens'd against your majesty | than all 3H6 4.01.108
incens'd the lords o' th' council that he is H8 5.01. 43
if 'gainst yourself you be incens'd, we'll put COR 1.09. 56
the people are incens'd against him. 3.01. 32
'twas you incens'd the rabble; 4.02. 33
world | hath so incens'd that i am reckless what MAC 3.01.109
tell me, laertes, | why thou art thus incens'd. HAM 4.05.127
part them, they are incens'd. 5.02.302
INCENSE* 12 FR 0.0013 REL FR 11 V 1 P
i will incense /page to deal with poison; WIV 1.03.100 P
and would incense me | to murther her i married. WT 5.01. 61
breathless excellence | the incense of a vow, a JN 4.03. 67
i never did incense his majesty | against the R3 1.03. 84
pursues | were to incense the boar to follow us, 3.02. 29
now god incense him, | and let him cry "ha!" H8 3.02. 61
whose smoke like incense doth perfume the sky. TIT 1.01.145
and what they may incense him to, being apt | to LR 2.04.306
cordelia, | the gods themselves throw incense. 5.03. 21
incense her kinsmen, | and, though he in a OTH 1.01. 69
hallowed clouds commend their swelling incense TNK 5.01. 4
offer pure incense to so pure a shrine: LUC 194

INCENSED 7 FR 0.0008 REL FR 7 V 0 P
the fearful difference of incensed kings — JN 3.01.238
throw this report on their incensed rage, | and 4.02.261
bosom burns | with an incensed fire of injuries. 2H4 1.03. 14
york | was not incensed by his subtile mother R3 3.01.152
obedience is a slave | to each incensed will. H8 1.02. 65
between the pass and fell incensed points | of HAM 5.02. 61
and thou by some incensed god sent hither | to PER 5.01.143
INCENSEMENT 1 FR 0.0001 REL FR 0 V 1 P
three, and his incensement at this moment is so TN 3.04.238 P
INCENSES 1 FR 0.0001 REL FR 1 V 0 P
the gods, | incenses them to send destruction. JC 1.03. 13
INCENSING 1 FR 0.0001 REL FR 1 V 0 P
we do bury | th' incensing relics of it. AWW 5.03. 25
INCERTAIN *(also uncertain, etc.)*
/INCERTAIN 1 FR 0.0001 REL FR 1 V 0 P
/of /aids /incertain /should /not /be /admitted. 2H4 1.03. 24
INCERTAIN 5 FR 0.0005 REL FR 5 V 0 P
of those that lawless and incertain thought MM 3.01.126
found | myself in my incertain grounds to fail AWW 3.01. 15
his kingdom and devour | incertain lookers–on. WT 5.01. 29
willing misery | outlives incertain pomp, is TIM 4.03.243
since the affairs of men rests still incertain, JC 5.01. 95
INCERTAINTIES 2 FR 0.0002 REL FR 2 V 0 P
hazard of | all incertainties himself commended, WT 3.02.169
incertainties now crown themselves assur'd, SON 107. 7
INCERTAINTY 1 FR 0.0001 REL FR 1 V 0 P
best," | when i was certain o'er incertainty, SON 115.11
INCESSANT 5 FR 0.0005 REL FR 5 V 0 P
yet the incessant weepings of my wife, | weeping ERR 1.01. 70
th' incessant care and labor of his mind | hath 2H4 4.04.118
with hope | to do your grace incessant services. H5 2.02. 38
or we will plague thee with incessant wars. 1H6 5.04.154
for raging wind blows up incessant showers, 3H6 1.04.145
INCESSANTLY 1 FR 0.0001 REL FR 1 V 0 P
i'd play incessantly upon these jades, | even JN 2.01.385
INCEST 8 FR 0.0009 REL FR 8 V 0 P
is't not a kind of incest, to take life | from MM 3.01.138
be | a couch for luxury and damned incest. HAM 1.05. 83
liking took, | and her to incest did provoke — PER 1.ch. 26
so bad | as with foul incest to abuse your soul; 1.01.126
the rest (hark in thine ear) as black as incest, 1.02. 76
mighty king | his child, i wis, to incest bring; 2.ch. 2
of me, | antiochus from incest lived not free; 2.04. 2
and shift, | guilty of incest, that abomination; LUC 921
INCESTIOUS 3 FR 0.0003 REL FR 3 V 0 P
post | with such dexterity to incestious sheets! HAM 1.02.157
or in th' incestious pleasure of his bed, | at 3.03. 90
here, thou incestious /murd'rous, damned dane, 5.02.325
INCESTUOUS 2 FR 0.0002 REL FR 2 V 0 P
ay, that incestuous, that adulterate beast, HAM 1.05. 42
thou simular of virtue | that art incestuous! LR 3.02. 55
/INCH* 1 FR 0.0001 REL FR 1 V 0 P
/you /should /have /an /inch /of /any /ground 2H4 4.01.107
INCH* 19 FR 0.0021 REL FR 11 V 8 P
i'll show thee every fertile inch o' th' island; TMP 2.02.148
toothpicker now from the furthest inch of asia, ADO 2.01.267 P
one inch of delay more is a south–sea of AYL 3.02.196 P
i'll not budge an inch, boy; SHR in.1. 14 P
for every inch of woman in the world, | ay, WT 2.01.137
being now awake, i'll queen it no inch farther, 4.04.449
my inch of taper will be burnt and done, | and R2 1.03.223
not an inch further. 1H4 2.03.114
with the very extremest inch of possibility; 2H4 4.03. 35 P
beldam, i think we watch'd you at an inch. 2H6 1.04. 42
stretches from an inch narrow to an ell broad! ROM 2.04. 84 P
till he disbursed at saint colme's inch | ten MAC 1.02. 61
and tell her, let her paint an inch thick, to HAM 5.01.194 P
ay, every inch a king! LR 4.06.107
am i not an inch of fortune better than she? ANT 1.02. 58 P
if you were but an inch of fortune better than i 1.02. 59 P
her stature to an inch, as wand–like straight, PER 5.01.109
clip my yellow locks an inch below mine e'e. TNK 3.04. 20
arcite's body | within an inch o' th' pyramid, 5.03. 80
INCHARITABLE *(also uncharitably)*
INCHARITABLE 1 FR 0.0001 REL FR 0 V 1 P
you bawling, blasphemous, incharitable dog! TMP 1.01. 41 P
INCHES 11 FR 0.0012 REL FR 8 V 3 P
i with this obedient steel, three inches of it, TMP 2.01.283
ask them how many inches | is in one mile: LLL 5.02.188
tell | how many inches doth fill up one mile. 5.02.193
am i but three inches? SHR 4.01. 27 P
and tell what thou art by inches, thou thing of TRO 2.01. 49 P
fathomless | with spans and inches so diminutive 2.02. 31
one that knows the youth | even to his inches, 4.05.111
home, | they'll give him death by inches. COR 5.04. 39
i would i had thy inches, thou shouldst know ANT 1.03. 40
as many inches as you have oceans. puppies! CYM 1.02. 20 P
on life, and ling'ring, | by inches waste you. 5.05. 52
INCH–MEAL 1 FR 0.0001 REL FR 1 V 0 P
fall and make him | by inch–meal a disease! TMP 2.02. 3
INCH–THICK 1 FR 0.0001 REL FR 1 V 0 P
inch–thick, knee–deep, o'er head and ears a WT 1.02.186
INCIDENCY 1 FR 0.0001 REL FR 1 V 0 P
declare | what incidency thou dost guess of harm WT 1.02.403
INCIDENT 4 FR 0.0004 REL FR 4 V 0 P
strength (a malady | most incident to maids); WT 4.04.125
plagues incident to men, | your potent and TIM 4.01. 21
love, with other incident throes | that nature's 5.01.200
as mutines are incident, by his name | can still STM II.C 115
INCISION 6 FR 0.0006 REL FR 5 V 1 P
why then incision | would let her out in saucers LLL 4.03. 95
and let us make incision for your love, | to MV 2.01. 6
god make incision in thee! AYL 3.02. 72 P
deep malice makes too deep incision. R2 1.01.155
shall we have incision? 2H4 2.04.196
mount them, and make incision in their hides, H5 4.02. 9
INCITE 6 FR 0.0006 REL FR 6 V 0 P
incite them to quick motion, for i must | bestow TMP 4.01. 39
my kindness shall incite thee | to bind our ADO 3.01.113
of what your reverence shall incite us to. H5 1.02. 20
no blown ambition doth our arms incite, | but LR 4.04. 27
that we do incite | the gentry to this business. CYM 3.07. 6
hark how yon spurs to spirit do incite | the TNK 5.03. 56
INCITES 1 FR 0.0001 REL FR 0 V 1 P
for she incites me to that in the letter. TN 3.04. 67 P
INCIVIL *(also uncivil)*
INCIVIL 1 FR 0.0001 REL FR 1 V 0 P
a most incivil one. CYM 5.05.292
INCIVILITY 1 FR 0.0001 REL FR 1 V 0 P
his incivility confirms no less. ERR 4.04. 46
INCLINABLE 1 FR 0.0001 REL FR 1 V 0 P
have hearts | inclinable to honor and advance COR 2.02. 56
INCLINATION 13 FR 0.0014 REL FR 10 V 3 P
he pieces out his wive's inclination; WIV 3.02. 34 P
as it were, his inclination, after his undressed LLL 4.02. 16 P
hearts | to fierce and bloody inclination. JN 5.02.158
the sky | the state and inclination of the day; R2 3.02.195
base inclination, and the start of spleen, | to 1H4 3.02.125
this merry inclination | accords not with the 3H6 3.02. 76
talk, | and give us notice of his inclination; R3 3.01.178
touch'd his spirit | and tried his inclination; COR 2.03.192
observe his inclination in yourself. HAM 2.01. 68
i not, | though inclination be as sharp as will. 3.03. 39
of octavia, her years, | her inclination; ANT 2.05.113
dost thou find the inclination of the people, PER 4.02. 97 P
an accessary by thine inclination | to all sins LUC 922
INCLIN'D 18 FR 0.0020 REL FR 15 V 3 P
thou art inclin'd to sleep; TMP 1.02.185
pity move my father | to be inclin'd my way! 1.02.448
i find | they are inclin'd to do so. 2.01.193
for women, he was not inclin'd that way. MM 3.02.122 P
this reprobate till he were well inclin'd, | and 4.03. 74
hyen, and that when thou art inclin'd to sleep. AYL 4.01.156 P
when you perceive his blood inclin'd to mirth; 2H4 4.04. 38
for he's inclin'd as is the ravenous wolves. 2H6 3.01. 78
but angry, wrathful, and inclin'd to blood, | if 4.02.126
men well inclin'd to hear what thou command'st; 3H6 4.08. 16
glad, or sorry | as i saw it inclin'd. H8 2.04. 27
out my command, | which men are best inclin'd. COR 1.06. 85
that from my first have been inclin'd to thrift, TIM 1.01.118
dedicate themselves, | finding it so inclin'd. MAC 4.03. 76
doth much content me | to hear him so inclin'd. HAM 3.01. 25
inclin'd to this intelligence, pronounce | the CYM 1.06.114
out her beauty stirs up the lewdly inclin'd. PER 4.02.144 P
that never was inclin'd | to accessary yieldings LUC 1657
INCLINE 11 FR 0.0012 REL FR 9 V 2 P
good, | whereto if you'll a willing ear incline, MM 5.01.536
and he from forage will incline to play. LLL 4.01. 91
doth his majesty | incline to it, or no? H5 1.01. 72
i more incline to somerset than york: 1H6 4.01.154
if he would incline to the people, there was COR 2.03. 38 P
we must incline to the king. LR 3.03. 14 P
to hear | would desdemona seriously incline; OTH 1.03.146
great herod to incline himself to caesar | and ANT 4.06. 13
he did incline to sadness, and oft–times | not CYM 1.06. 62
men lose when they incline to treachery, | and TNK 3.01. 67
divine, | unto a view so false will not incline, LUC 292
INCLINES 1 FR 0.0001 REL FR 1 V 0 P
at the full of tide, | and neither way inclines. ANT 3.02. 50
INCLINING 8 FR 0.0009 REL FR 5 V 3 P
entertainment, your inclining cannot be remov'd. AWW 3.06. 39 P
see good and evil, | inclining to them both. WT 1.02.304
or in act or will | that way inclining, hard'ned 3.02. 52
fifty, or, by'r lady, inclining to threescore; 1H4 2.04.425 P
is it your own inclining? HAM 2.02.275 P
hands, | both you of my inclining, and the rest. OTH 1.02. 82
most easy | th' inclining desdemona to subdue 2.03.340
her mood inclining that way that i spoke of, TNK 5.02. 34
INCLIN'ST 1 FR 0.0001 REL FR 1 V 0 P
if thou inclin'st that way, thou art a coward, WT 1.02.243
INCLIPS 1 FR 0.0001 REL FR 1 V 0 P
what e'er the ocean pales, or sky inclips, | is ANT 2.07. 68
INCLUDE 2 FR 0.0002 REL FR 2 V 0 P
us go, we will include all jars | with triumphs, TGV 5.04.160
then every thing include itself in power, TRO 1.03.119
INCLUDED 1 FR 0.0001 REL FR 1 V 0 P
ends, | dispersed are the glories it included. 1H6 1.02.137
INCLUDES 1 FR 0.0001 REL FR 1 V 0 P
the loss of such a lord includes all harms. R3 1.03. 8
INCLUDING 1 FR 0.0001 REL FR 1 V 0 P
o impious act, including all foul harms! LUC 199
INCLUSIVE 2 FR 0.0002 REL FR 2 V 0 P
as notes whose faculties inclusive were | more AWW 1.03.226
o, would to god that the inclusive verge | of R3 4.01. 58
INCOME 1 FR 0.0001 REL FR 1 V 0 P
pain pays the income of each precious thing: LUC 334
INCOMPARABLE 4 FR 0.0004 REL FR 4 V 0 P
a merchant of incomparable wealth. SHR 4.02. 98
her words doth show her wit incomparable, | all 3H6 3.02. 85
now this masque | was cried incomparable; H8 1.01. 27
a most incomparable man, breath'd, as it were, TIM 1.01. 10
INCOMPREHENSIBLE 1 FR 0.0001 REL FR 0 V 1 P
will be the incomprehensible lies that this same 1H4 1.02.187 P
INCONSIDERATE 2 FR 0.0002 REL FR 1 V 1 P
doth the inconsiderate take salve for l'envoy, LLL 3.01. 78 P
rash, inconsiderate, fiery voluntaries, | with JN 2.01. 67
INCONSTANCY 6 FR 0.0006 REL FR 5 V 1 P
inconstancy falls off ere it begins. TGV 5.04.113
the villainous inconstancy of man's disposition WIV 4.05.109 P
with men like /you, men of inconstancy. LLL 4.03.178
o foul revolt of french inconstancy! JN 3.01.322
tongue | (the agent of thy foul inconstancy) 2H6 3.02.115
for now i see inconstancy | more in women than PP 17.11
INCONSTANT *(also unconstant)*
INCONSTANT 11 FR 0.0012 REL FR 8 V 3 P
upon this spotted and inconstant man. MND 1.01.110
apish, shallow, inconstant, full of tears, full AYL 3.02.412 P
is he inconstant, sir, in his favors? TN 1.04. 7 P
of a fool, inconstant | and damnable ingrateful; WT 3.02.186
a city on th' inconstant billows dancing; H5 3.pr. 15
of it, that she is turning, and inconstant, and 3.06. 34 P
and more inconstant than the wind, who woos ROM 1.04.100
o, swear not by the moon, th' inconstant moon, 2.02.109
if no inconstant toy, nor womanish fear, | abate 4.01.119
then the conceit of this inconstant stay | sets SON 15. 9
thou canst not vex me with inconstant mind, 92. 9
INCONTINENCE 1 FR 0.0001 REL FR 1 V 0 P
in abstinence we shame | as in incontinence; TNK 1.02. 7
INCONTINENCY 3 FR 0.0003 REL FR 3 V 0 P
on him, | that he is open to incontinency — HAM 2.01. 30
the cognizance of her incontinency | is this. CYM 2.04.127
thou didst accuse him of incontinency; 3.04. 47
INCONTINENT* 6 FR 0.0006 REL FR 3 V 3 P
which they will climb incontinent, or else be AYL 5.02. 38 P
or else be incontinent before marriage. 5.02. 39 P
lament, | and put on sullen black incontinent. R2 5.06. 48
all incontinent varlots! TRO 5.01. 98 P
matrons, turn incontinent! TIM 4.01. 3
he says he will return incontinent, | and hath OTH 4.03. 12
INCONTINENTLY 1 FR 0.0001 REL FR 0 V 1 P
i will incontinently drown myself. OTH 1.03.305 P
INCONVENIENCE 1 FR 0.0001 REL FR 1 V 0 P
to intercept this inconvenience, | a piece of 1H6 1.04. 14
INCONVENIENCES 1 FR 0.0001 REL FR 1 V 0 P
peace | should not expel these inconveniences, H5 5.02. 66
INCONVENIENT 1 FR 0.0001 REL FR 0 V 1 P
if it appear not inconvenient to you, to set her AYL 5.02. 66 P
INCONY 2 FR 0.0002 REL FR 2 V 0 P
my sweet ounce of man's flesh, my incony jew! LLL 3.01.135
troth, most sweet jests, most incony vulgar wit! 4.01.142
INCORPORAL 1 FR 0.0001 REL FR 1 V 0 P
and with th' incorporal air do hold discourse? HAM 3.04.118
INCORPORATE 10 FR 0.0011 REL FR 9 V 1 P
strange to me, | that, undividable incorporate, ERR 2.02.122
sides, voices, and minds | had been incorporate. MND 3.02.208
to make divorce of their incorporate league; H5 5.02.366
"true is it, my incorporate friends," quoth he, COR 1.01.130
titus, i am incorporate in rome, | a roman now TIT 1.01.462
alone | till holy church incorporate two in one. ROM 2.06. 37
it is casca, one incorporate | to our attempts. JC 1.03.135
vow | which did incorporate and make us one, 2.01.273
and main exercise, th' incorporate conclusion. OTH 2.01.263 P
incorporate then they seem, face grows to face. VEN 540
INCORPS'D 1 FR 0.0001 REL FR 1 V 0 P
as had he been incorps'd and demi–natur'd | with HAM 4.07. 87
INCORRECT 1 FR 0.0001 REL FR 1 V 0 P
it shows a will most incorrect to heaven, | a HAM 1.02. 95
INCREAS'D 1 FR 0.0001 REL FR 1 V 0 P
our wealth increas'd | by prosperous voyages i ERR 1.01. 39
INCREASE 32 FR 0.0036 REL FR 26 V 6 P
earth's increase, foison plenty, | barns and TMP 4.01.110
i will pray, pompey, to increase your bondage. MM 3.02. 75 P
by their increase, now knows not which is which. MND 2.01.114
loss of virginity is rational increase, and AWW 1.01.128 P
make itself two, which is a goodly increase, and 1.01.148 P
world's pleasure and the increase of laughter. 2.04. 37 P
sword, | and i do wish your honors may increase, 2H4 5.02.104
him, | thou wilt but add increase unto my wrath. 2H6 3.02.292
theirs for the earth's increase, mine for my 3.02.385
and that thy summer bred us no increase, | we 3H6 2.02.164
lest thou increase the number of the dead, | and R3 4.01. 44
to quicken your increase, i will beget | mine 4.04.297
let them not live to taste this land's increase 5.05. 38
the lord increase this business! H8 3.02.161
most that | which would increase his evil. COR 1.01.179
her womb's increase | and treasure of my loins; 3.03.114
is nothing but to rust iron, increase tailors, 4.05.219 P
and your misery increase with your age! 5.02.107 P
like to the earth swallow her own increase. TIT 5.02.191
on him | as if increase of appetite had grown HAM 1.02.144
dry up in her the organs of increase, | and from LR 1.04.279
but that our loves and comforts should increase OTH 2.01.194
drink thou; increase the reels. ANT 2.07. 94
make denials | increase your services; CYM 2.03. 49
through you, increase our wonder, and sets up PER 3.02. 96
"upon the earth's increase why shouldst thou VEN 169
unless the earth with thy increase be fed? 170
you do it for increase: 791
from fairest creatures we desire increase, SON 1. 1
herein lives wisdom, beauty, and increase, 11. 5
when i perceive that men as plants increase, 15. 5
the teeming autumn, big with rich increase, 97. 6
INCREASEFUL 1 FR 0.0001 REL FR 1 V 0 P
to cheer the ploughman with increaseful crops, LUC 958
INCREASES 1 FR 0.0001 REL FR 0 V 1 P
whereupon the world increases, and kinreds are 2H4 2.02. 26 P
INCREASETH 2 FR 0.0002 REL FR 2 V 0 P
is in the field, and still his power increaseth. R3 4.03. 48
the enemy increaseth every day; JC 4.03.216
INCREASING 8 FR 0.0009 REL FR 5 V 3 P
long continuance, and increasing, | hourly joys TMP 4.01.107
infirmity, for the better increasing your folly! TN 1.05. 79 P
beard, a decreasing leg, an increasing belly? 2H4 1.02.182 P
great, and increasing; ANT 2.02.162
loyal to his vow, and your increasing in love. CYM 3.02. 46 P
his perishing root with the increasing vine. 4.02. 60
words are done, her woes the more increasing; VEN 254
increasing store with loss, and loss with store; SON 64. 8
INCREDIBLE 1 FR 0.0001 REL FR 1 V 0 P
i tell you 'tis incredible to believe | how much SHR 2.01.306
INCREDULOUS 2 FR 0.0002 REL FR 1 V 1 P
no incredulous or unsafe circumstance — what TN 3.04. 80 P
and never live to show th' incredulous world 2H4 4.05.153
INCUR 7 FR 0.0008 REL FR 7 V 0 P
charg'd, | in peril to incur your former malady, SHR in.2. 122
i know not what i shall incur to pass it, WT 2.02. 55
and then, in speaking, not to incur the last — R3 3.07.152
would ever have, t' incur a general mock, | run OTH 1.02. 69
not almost a fault | t' incur a private check. 3.03. 67
come, i shall incur i know not | how much of his CYM 1.01.102
did incur | this load of wrath that burning troy LUC 1473
INCURABLE *(also uncurable)*
INCURABLE 4 FR 0.0004 REL FR 1 V 3 P
that gave him out incurable — AWW 2.03. 14 P
be minist'red, | or overthrow incurable ensues. JN 5.01. 16
lingers it out, but the disease is incurable. 2H4 1.02.238 P
lime–kills i' th' palm, incurable bone–ache, and TRO 5.01. 22 P
INCURR'D 4 FR 0.0004 REL FR 3 V 1 P
and thou hast incurr'd | the danger formerly by MV 4.01.361
especially he hath incurr'd the everlasting AWW 4.03. 8 P
incurr'd a traitor's name, expos'd myself | from TRO 3.03. 6
who with best meaning have incurr'd the worst. LR 5.03. 4
INCURSIONS 2 FR 0.0002 REL FR 1 V 1 P
whose hot incursions and great name in arms, 1H4 3.02.108
when thou art forth in the incursions, thou TRO 2.01. 30 P
INDE *(also india, indies)*
INDE 3 FR 0.0003 REL FR 2 V 1 P
tricks upon 's with salvages and men of inde? TMP 2.02. 58 P
that, like a rude and savage man of inde, | at LLL 4.03.218
"from the east to western inde, | no jewel is AYL 3.02. 88
INDEBTED 3 FR 0.0003 REL FR 3 V 0 P
and stand indebted, over and above, | in love MV 4.01.413
are deeply indebted for this piece of pains. 2H6 1.04. 44

sir, we are much indebted to your travel, | nor TNK 2.05. 30
/INDEED 5 FR 0.0005 REL FR 4 V 1 P
/when /i /do /see /the /very /book /indeed R2 4.01.274
/indeed /the /instant /action, /a /cause /on 2H4 1.03. 37
/and /you /shall /say, /indeed, /it /is /the 4.01.103
indeed, /indeed, sirs. HAM 1.02.224
/which /dreams /indeed /are /ambition, /for /the 2.02.257 P
INDEED 447 FR 0.0505 REL FR 238 V 209 P
as my trust was, which had indeed no limit, | a TMP 1.02. 96
he did believe | he was indeed the duke, out o' 1.02.103
dolor comes to him indeed; 2.01. 19 P
the ground indeed is tawny. 2.01. 55 P
it is — which is indeed almost beyond credit — 2.01. 59 P
ebbing men, indeed, | most often, do so near the 2.01.226
and a birth, indeed, | which throes thee much to 2.01.230
thou art very trinculo indeed! 2.02.105 P
admir'd miranda, | indeed the top of admiration! 3.01. 38
were a brave monster indeed if they were set in 3.02. 11 P
here's a maze trod indeed | through forth–rights 3.03. 2
o setebos, these be brave spirits indeed! 5.01.261
indeed a sheep doth very often stray, | and if TGV 1.01. 74
indeed i bid the base for proteus. 1.02. 94
no believing you indeed, sir: 2.01.156 P
indeed, madam, i seem so. 2.04. 9 P
'tis indeed, madam, we thank the giver. 2.04. 35 P
it stands under thee indeed. 2.05. 31 P
no valentine indeed, for sacred silvia. 3.01.212
virtues," that indeed know not their fathers, 3.01.319 P
indeed because you are a banish'd man, 4.01. 57
one that takes upon him to be a dog indeed, to 4.04. 12 P
no indeed did she not; 4.04. 52 P
but better indeed, when you hold /your peace. 5.02. 18
it is marring indeed, if he quarter it. WIV 1.01. 26 P
he hath wrong'd me, indeed he hath, at a word he 1.01.105 P
ay indeed, sir. 1.01.293 P
but women, indeed, cannot abide 'em, they are 1.01.298 P
you do yourself wrong indeed la! 1.01.313 P
indeed i am in the waist two yards about; 1.03. 41 P
yes indeed does he. 1.04. 31 P
this is all indeed la! 1.04. 85 P
but, indeed, she is given too much to allicholy 1.04.153 P
that were a jest indeed! 2.02.111 P
that were a trick indeed! 2.02.112 P
is your wife at home indeed? 3.02. 26 P
indeed she is. 3.02. 27 P
'od's heartlings, that's a pretty jest indeed! 3.04. 58 P
that indeed, sir john, is my business. 3.05. 63 P
indeed? 4.02. 15 P
indeed, master ford, this is not well indeed. 4.02.126 P
indeed, master ford, this is not well indeed. 4.02.127 P
yea and no, i think the oman is a witch indeed. 4.02.193 P
i come to speak with her indeed. 4.05. 14 P
and indeed she is now with the doctor at the 5.05.202 P
and indeed with most painful feeling of thy MM 1.02. 36 P
why, here's a change indeed in the commonwealth! 1.02.104 P
therefore indeed, my father, | i have on angelo 1.03. 39
no indeed, sir, not of a pin; 2.01. 96 P
no indeed. 2.01.105 P
ay, so i did indeed. 2.01.108 P
grapes, where indeed you have a delight to sit, 2.01.129 P
most good, most good indeed. 3.01. 55
indeed, it does stink in some sort, sir; 3.02. 28 P
no indeed will i not, pompey, it is not the wear 3.02. 74 P
but indeed i can do you little harm; 3.02.166 P
hath forc'd me to tell him he is indeed justice. 3.02.254 P
and indeed his fact, till now in the government 4.02.136 P
that's he indeed. 5.01. 77
for he indeed | hath set the women on to this 5.01.250
you indeed spoke so of him, and much more, much 5.01.337 P
word, | and go indeed, having so good a mean. ERR 1.02. 18
if i return, i shall be post indeed, | for she 1.02. 64
i am an ass indeed; 4.04. 29 P
he hath indeed better bett'red expectation than ADO 1.01. 15 P
for indeed i promis'd to eat all of his killing. 1.01. 44 P
it is so indeed, he is no less than a stuff'd 1.01. 58 P
so, nor 'twas not so, but indeed, god forbid it 1.01.217 P
for indeed he hath made great preparation. 1.01.277 P
so indeed all disquiet, horror, and perturbation 2.01.260 P
indeed, my lord, he lent it me awhile, and i 2.01.278 P
she did indeed. 2.03.112 P
'tis true indeed, so your daughter says. 2.03.127 P
she doth indeed, my daughter says so; 2.03.150 P
he hath indeed a good outward happiness. 2.03.183 P
he doth indeed show some sparks that are like 2.03.186 P
indeed he hath an excellent good name. 3.01. 98
indeed he looks younger than he did, by the loss 3.02. 48 P
indeed that tells a heavy tale for him. 3.02. 61 P
for indeed the watch ought to offend no man, and 3.03. 80 P
to think what i can, nor indeed i cannot think, 3.04. 83 P
indeed, neighbor, he comes too short of you. 3.05. 41 P
have indeed comprehended two aspicious persons, 3.05. 45 P
who hath indeed, most like a liberal villain, 4.01. 92
in, | and publish it that she is dead indeed. 4.01.204
of his soul, | than when she liv'd indeed. 4.01.230
he shall kill two of us, and men indeed; 5.01. 80
that dare as well answer a man indeed | as i 5.01. 89
i think he be angry indeed. 5.01.141 P
sir, which indeed is not under white and black, 5.01.304 P
i do suffer love indeed, for i love thee against 5.02. 67 P
study me how to please the eye indeed | by LLL 1.01. 80
green indeed is the color of lovers; 1.02. 86 P
finely put on indeed! 4.01.116
indeed 'a must shoot nearer, or he'll ne'er hit 4.01.134
'tis true indeed, the collusion holds in the 4.02. 42 P
and why indeed "naso," but for smelling out the 4.02.123 P
and of great import indeed too — but let that 5.01.100 P
indeed i weigh not you, and therefore light. 5.02. 26
true, out indeed. 5.02.165
we four indeed confronted were with four | in 5.02.367
swords, and that pyramus is not kill'd indeed; MND 3.01. 19 P
and there indeed let him name his name, and tell 3.01. 44 P
for indeed, who would set his wit to so foolish 3.01.134 P
indeed he hath play'd on this prologue like a 5.01.122 P
ay, that's a colt indeed, for he doth nothing MV 1.02. 40 P
which is indeed to return to their home, and to 1.02.102 P
son, for indeed my father did something smack, 2.02. 17 P
such branches of learning, is indeed deceas'd, 2.02. 64 P
nay, indeed, if you had your eyes, you might 2.02. 75 P
her name is margery indeed. 2.02. 91 P
bassanio, who indeed gives rare new liveries. 2.02.109 P
indeed the short and the long is, i serve the 2.02.127 P
lorenzo, certain, and my love indeed, | for who 2.06. 29
cold indeed, and labor lost: 2.07. 74
for indeed | i have engag'd myself to a dear 3.02.260
that were a kind of bastard hope indeed; 3.05. 13 P
woman, she is indeed more than i took her for. 3.05. 42 P
that begg'd it, and indeed | deserv'd it too; 5.01.180
and indeed so much in the heart of the world, AYL 1.01.168 P
indeed there is fortune too hard for nature, 1.02. 48 P
what he is indeed | more suits you to conceive 1.02.266
but yet indeed the /smaller is his daughter. 1.02.272
indeed, my lord, | the melancholy jaques grieves 2.01. 25
and indeed, my lord, | the wretched animal 2.01. 35
in respect of a good piece of flesh indeed! 3.02. 66 P
but indeed an old religious uncle of mine taught 3.02.343 P
and indeed the sundry contemplation of my 4.01. 17 P
religion than if thou wert indeed my rosalind; 4.01.197 P
life, i am a lord indeed | and not a tinker nor SHR in.2. 72
that lucentio indeed had baptista's youngest 1.01.240
the motion's good indeed, and be it so, 1.02.279
'tis a groom indeed, | a grumbling groom, and 3.02.152
is't so indeed? 5.01. 57 P
and i am mean indeed, respecting you. 5.02. 32
seeming to be most which we indeed least are. 5.02.175
he was excellent indeed, madam. AWW 1.01. 28 P
i do affect a sorrow indeed, but i have it too. 1.01. 54 P
are, and indeed i do marry that i may repent. 1.03. 36 P
son were not my brother — | indeed my mother! 1.03.163
this haste hath wings indeed. 2.01. 93
and indeed such a fellow, to say precisely, were 2.02. 12 P
indeed your "o lord, sir!" 2.02. 53 P
it is indeed; 2.03. 21 P
which should indeed give us a further use to be 2.03. 35 P
oblivion is the tomb | of honor'd bones indeed. 2.03.141
truly, she's very well indeed, but for two 2.04. 8 P
nothing, indeed. 2.05. 83
indeed, good lady, | the fellow has a deal of 3.02. 89
he does indeed, | and brokes with all that can 3.05. 70
for indeed he is not for your lordship's respect 3.06.100 P
indeed, sir, she was the sweet marjorom of the 4.05. 16 P
so you were a knave at his service indeed. 4.05. 29 P
for his sauciness, and indeed he has no pace, 4.05. 67 P
not indeed. 5.01. 22
indeed, sir, if your metaphor stink, i will stop 5.02. 12 P
he lov'd her, for indeed he was mad for her, and 5.03.260 P
he hath indeed, almost natural; TN 1.03. 29 P
indeed so much, | that methought her eyes had 2.02. 19
but shall we make the welkin dance indeed? 2.03. 57 P
my purpose is indeed a horse of that color. 2.03.167 P
was not this love indeed? 2.04.115
more, but indeed | our shows are more than will; 2.04.116
but indeed, words are very rascals since bonds 3.01. 20 P
no, indeed, sir, the lady olivia has no folly. 3.01. 32 P
i am indeed not her fool, but her corrupter of 3.01. 35 P
i did some service, of such note indeed, | that, 3.03. 27
why, we shall make him mad indeed. 3.04.133 P
he is indeed, sir, the most skillful, bloody, 3.04.266 P
then you are mad indeed, if you be no better in 4.02. 89 P
but tell me true, are you not mad indeed, or do 4.02.114 P
a spirit i am indeed, | but am in that dimension 5.01.236
he finished indeed his mortal act | that day 5.01.247
for indeed — WT 1.01. 9 P
one that, indeed, physics the subject, makes old 1.01. 38 P
'tis grace indeed. 1.02.105
(which is indeed | more criminal in thee than it 3.02. 88
done, | and then run mad indeed — stark mad! 3.02.183
(this being indeed the issue | of king polixenes 3.03. 43
indeed, he should be a footman by the garments 4.03. 66 P
very pleasant thing indeed and sung lamentably. 4.04.189 P
and indeed, sir, there are cozeners abroad, 4.04.253 P
and ampler strength indeed | than most have of 4.04.403
indeed i have had earnest, but i cannot with 4.04.645 P
indeed brother–in–law was the farthest off you 4.04.703 P
indeed paid down | more penitence than done 5.01. 3
that i may say indeed | thou art hermione; 5.03. 24
indeed, my lord, | if i had thought the sight of 5.03. 56
i'll make the statue move indeed, descend, | and 5.03. 88
here's a large mouth indeed, | that spits forth JN 2.01.457
indeed i have been merrier. 4.01. 12
no indeed is't not; 4.01. 23
indeed we fear'd his sickness was past cure. 4.02. 86
indeed we heard how near his death he was 4.02. 87
indeed your drums, being beaten, will cry out; 5.02.166
old gaunt indeed, and gaunt in being old. R2 2.01. 74
peace have they made with him indeed, my lord. 3.02.128
a king of beasts indeed — if aught but beasts, 5.01. 35
indeed you come near me now, hal, for we that 1H4 1.02. 13 P
/similes and art indeed the most comparative, 1.02. 80 P
and art indeed able to corrupt a saint. 1.02. 91 P
indeed i am not john of gaunt, your grandfather, 2.02. 67 P
do you not indeed? 2.03. 96
or indeed, francis, when thou wilt. 2.04. 66 P
indeed, my lord, i think it be two a' clock. 2.04.525
thou art altogether given over, and wert indeed, 3.03. 36 P
indeed, sir john, you said so. 3.03.141 P
sores, and such as indeed were never soldiers, 4.02. 27 P
for indeed i had the most of them out of prison. 4.02. 41 P
i think, to steal cream indeed, for thy theft 4.02. 60 P
indeed his king) to be engag'd in wales, | there 4.03. 95
these things indeed you have articulate, 5.01. 72
and, which became him like a prince indeed, | he 5.02. 60
he is indeed, and living to kill thee. 5.03. 48 P
but the true and perfect image of life indeed. 5.04.119 P
deeds, | but in the end, to stop my ear indeed, 2H4 1.01. 79
dram of a scruple, or indeed a scruple itself. 1.02.130 P
for indeed | it was young hotspur's cause at 1.03. 25
but indeed these humble considerations make me 2.02. 11 P
my friend — i could be sad, and sad indeed too. 2.02. 43 P
every man would think me an hypocrite indeed. 2.02. 60 P
he was indeed the glass | wherein the noble 2.03. 21
these be good humors indeed! 2.04.163
indeed, sir, to my cost. 3.02. 12 P
and i would have done any thing indeed too, and 3.02. 18 P
in faith, sir, and it is well said indeed too. 3.02. 69 P
it is good, yea indeed is it. 3.02. 70 P
it is often so indeed, but much of the father's 3.02.130 P
of it, | but to establish here a peace indeed, 4.01. 86
this sleep is sound indeed, this is a sleep 4.05. 35
indeed i think the young king loves you not. 5.02. 9
o, good my lord, you have lost a friend indeed, 5.02. 27
my little tiny thief, and welcome indeed too. 5.03. 58 P
'tis so indeed. 5.05. 30 P
to say is of mine own making, and what indeed (i ep 5 P
i meant indeed to pay you with this, which if ep 10 P
you — but, indeed, to pray for the queen. ep 17 P
was like, and had indeed against us pass'd, H5 1.01. 3
have for the gilt of france (o guilt indeed!) 2.pr. 26
'a did in some sort, indeed, handle women; 2.03. 37 P
for indeed three such antics do not amount to a 3.02. 31 P
he is indeed a horse, and all other jades you 3.07. 23 P
indeed, my lord, it is a most absolute and 3.07. 25 P
indeed the french may lay twenty french crowns 4.01.225 P
'twas i indeed thou promisedst to strike, | and 4.08. 41
i am indeed. 1H6 2.03. 48
here's a silly stately style indeed! 4.07. 72
that's some wrong indeed. 2H6 1.03. 19 P
ay indeed was he. 2.01. 76
no indeed, master. 2.01.120
murther indeed, that bloody sin, i tortur'd 3.01.131
i lose indeed; 3.01.183
she was indeed a pedlar's daughter, and sold 4.02. 45 P
when, indeed, only for that cause they have been 4.07. 45 P
and be true king indeed, thou but the shadow. 3H6 4.03. 50
indeed 'tis true that henry told me of; 5.06. 69
now, by saint john, that news is bad indeed! R3 1.01.138
clarence, who i indeed have cast in darkness, 1.03.326
happy indeed, as we have spent the day. 2.01. 49
dukes, earls, lords, gentlemen — indeed of all. 2.01. 69
it is a reeling world indeed, my lord, | and i 3.02. 38
indeed i am no mourner for that news, | because 3.02. 51
and they indeed had no cause to mistrust; 3.02. 85
heir to the crown — meaning indeed his house, 3.05. 78
indeed, left nothing fitting for your purpose 3.07. 18
kindred | and egally indeed to all estates — 3.07.213
touch, | to try if thou be current gold indeed. 4.02. 9
art thou indeed? 4.02. 68
cousins indeed, and by their uncle cozen'd | of 4.04.223
nay then indeed she cannot choose but hate thee, 4.04.289
he was in the right, and so indeed it is. 5.03.275
queen his aunt | (for 'twas indeed his color, H8 1.01.178
the duke | said, 'twas the fear indeed, and that 1.02.158
ay, marry, | there will be woe indeed, lords; 1.03. 39
that churchman bears a bounteous mind indeed, 1.03. 55
there is indeed, which they would have your 1.04. 83
yes indeed was i. 2.01. 6
but indeed he could not. 2.01. 25
i fear he will indeed. 2.02. 10
(indeed to gain the popedom | and fee my friends 3.02.212
nay, and you weep | i am fall'n indeed. 3.02.376
that's news indeed. 3.02.402
their coronets say so. these are stars indeed. 4.01. 54
and indeed this day, | sir (i may tell it you), 5.01. 41
'tis he indeed. 5.02. 25
then she's a merry greek indeed. TRO 1.02.109 P
indeed a tapster's arithmetic may soon bring his 1.02.113 P
indeed she has a marvell's white hand, i must 1.02.136 P
call them shames which are indeed nought else 1.03. 19
that's to't indeed, sir. 3.01. 30 P
sodden business! there's a stew'd phrase indeed! 3.01. 41 P
be, | when that the wat'ry palates taste indeed 3.02. 21
now, by anchises' life, | welcome indeed! 4.01. 23
true indeed! COR 1.01. 79 P
honors, though indeed | in aught he merit not. 1.01.275
indeed you shall not. 1.03. 28
indeed la, 'tis a noble child. 1.03. 67 P
indeed no, by your patience; 1.03. 74 P
good madam, pardon me, indeed i will not forth. 1.03. 87 P
indeed, madam? 1.03. 94 P
indeed i must not. 1.03.109 P
he's a lamb indeed, that baes like a bear. 2.01. 11 P
he's a bear indeed, that lives like a lamb. 2.01. 12 P
you have not indeed lov'd the common people. 2.03. 92 P
indeed i would be consul. 2.03.131
measure of a father, | nay, godded me indeed. 5.03. 11
ne'er let my heart know merry cheer indeed TIT 2.03.188
as indeed i do not, | yet, for i know thou art 5.01. 73
indeed i was their tutor to instruct them. 5.01. 98
a fly, | and nothing grieves me heartily indeed, 5.01.143
indeed i should have ask'd /thee that before. ROM 1.02. 77
is't so indeed? 1.05. 83
three words, dear romeo, and good night indeed. 2.02.142
tale, and meant indeed to occupy the argument no 2.04.100 P
him on the drawer, when indeed there is no need. 3.01. 9 P
and usest none in that true use indeed | which 3.03.124
indeed i never shall be satisfied | with romeo, 3.05. 93
these are news indeed! 3.05.123
i must indeed, and therefore came i hither. 5.03. 58
affect company, | nor is he fit for't indeed. TIM 1.02. 32
true, as you said, timon is shrunk indeed, | and 3.02. 61
no, indeed he is not. 3.04. 36 P
which indeed | is valor misbegot, and came into 3.05. 28
th' art indeed the best, | thou counterfeit'st 5.01. 81
will you indeed? 5.01. 91
may use with a safe conscience, which is indeed, JC 1.01. 14 P
but withal i am indeed, sir, a surgeon to old 1.01. 23 P
but indeed, sir, we make holiday to see caesar, 1.01. 30 P
so indeed he did. 1.02.106
now is it rome indeed and room enough, | when 1.02.156
indeed, it is a strange–disposed time; 1.03. 33
indeed, they say, the senators to–morrow | mean 1.03. 85
indeed he is not fit. 2.01.153
and this indeed, o world, the heart of thee. 3.01.208
hands, but was indeed | sway'd from the point, 3.01.218
if we do meet again, we'll smile indeed; 5.01.120
or that indeed | which outwardly ye show? MAC 1.03. 53
here's a knocking indeed! 2.03. 1 P
those thoughts which should indeed have died 3.02. 10
no indeed, my lord. 4.01.137
whither indeed, before /thy here–approach, | old 4.03.133
these indeed seem, | for they are actions that a HAM 1.02. 83
indeed, my lord, it followed hard upon. 1.02.179
indeed, /indeed, sirs. 1.02.224
indeed? 1.04. 5
and indeed it takes | from our achievements, 1.04. 20

indeed, upon my sword, indeed. 1.05.148
indeed, upon my sword, indeed. 1.05.148
though it were hid indeed | within the centre. 2.02.158
so he does indeed. 2.02.161
indeed that's out of the air. 2.02.208 P
and indeed it goes so heavily with my 2.02.297 P
no indeed are they not. 2.02.336 P
sir, a' monday morning, 'twas then indeed. 2.02.388 P
and amaze indeed | the very faculties of eyes 2.02.565
indeed, my lord, you made me believe so. 3.01.115 P
by th' mass and 'tis, like a camel indeed. 3.02.378 P
hill, | a combination and a form indeed, | where 3.04. 60
mother, good night indeed. 3.04.213
but if indeed you find him not within this month 4.03. 35 P
she is importunate, indeed distract. 4.05. 2
indeed would make one think there might be 4.05. 12
indeed without an oath i'll make an end on't. 4.05. 57 P
he is the brooch indeed | and gem of all the 4.07. 93
that he cried out 'twould be a sight indeed | if 4.07. 99
to show yourself indeed your father's son | more 4.07.125
no place indeed should murther sanctuarize, 4.07.127
i think it be thine indeed, for thou liest in't. 5.01.122 P
it is indifferent cold, my lord, indeed. 5.02. 97 P
indeed, to speak sellingly of him, he is the 5.02.108 P
i' th' darkest night, | stick fiery off indeed. 5.02.257
whereupon she grew round–womb'd, and had indeed,
LR 1.01. 14 P
yes indeed, thou wouldst make a good fool. 1.05. 38 P
so may it be indeed. 4.06. 6
thus might he pass indeed; 4.06. 47
he is gone indeed. 5.03.316
and sign of love, | which is indeed but sign. OTH 1.01.157
yes, sir, i have indeed. 1.01.174
indeed, they are disproportioned; 1.03. 2
but indeed my invention | comes from my pate as 2.01.125
thou bestow on a deserving woman indeed — one 2.01.145 P
you say true, 'tis so indeed. 2.01.171 P
'tis so indeed. 2.01.176 P
indeed she's a most fresh and delicate creature. 2.03. 20 P
she is indeed perfection. 2.03. 28 P
where indeed they are most potent in potting; 2.03. 76 P
here's a goodly watch indeed! 2.03.160
and indeed the course | to win the moor again? 2.03.338
suit | wherein i mean to touch your love indeed, 3.03. 81
indeed! 3.03.101
indeed? 3.03.102
ay, indeed. 3.03.102
whole course of wooing, thou criedst, "indeed!" 3.03.112
not enriches him, | and makes me poor indeed. 3.03.161
you may, indeed, say so; 3.04. 44
there's matter in't indeed, if he be angry. 3.04.139
indeed, sweet love, i was coming to your house. 3.04.171
indeed? 4.01.238
here's a change indeed! 4.02.106
i will indeed no longer endure it; 4.02.178 P
i grant indeed it hath not appear'd; 4.02.210 P
if thou hast that in thee indeed, which i have 4.02.212 P
that thrust had been mine enemy indeed, | but 5.01. 24
the same indeed, a very valiant fellow. 5.01. 52
nay, stare not, masters, it is true indeed. 5.02.188
whose breath, indeed, these hands have newly 5.02.202
(more than indeed belong'd to such a trifle), 5.02.228
if it be love indeed, tell me how much. ANT 1.01. 14
women but fulvia, then had you indeed a cut, and 1.02.166 P
and indeed the tears live in an onion that 1.02.169 P
(as his composure must be rare indeed | whom 1.04. 22
indeed? 1.05. 14
nothing | but what indeed is honest to be done; 1.05. 16
there she appear'd indeed; 2.02.188 P
at land indeed | thou dost o'er–count me of my 2.06. 26
indeed he plied them both with excellent praises 3.02. 14
that year indeed, he was troubled with a rheum; 3.02. 57
indeed he is so; 3.03. 39
why then good night indeed. 3.10. 29
for indeed i have lost command, | therefore i 3.11. 23
o my brave emperor, this is fought indeed! 4.07. 4
which now | is come indeed, when i should see 4.14. 64
here's sport indeed! 4.15. 32
now, noble charmian, we'll dispatch indeed, 5.02.230
for indeed, there is no goodness in the worm. 5.02.266 P
learn'd indeed were that astronomer | that knew CYM 3.02. 27
is not there, who was indeed | the riches of it. 3.04. 70
point | i will conclude to hate her, nay indeed, 3.05. 78
indeed, sir, he that sleeps feels not the 5.04.172 P
yes indeed do i, fellow. 5.04.177 P
indeed a banish'd man, | i know not how a 5.05.319
i you brothers, | when we were so indeed. 5.05.378
sir, | as you did mean indeed to be our brother; 5.05.423
whose death indeed the strongest in our censure, PER 2.04. 34
yes indeed shall you, and taste gentlemen of all 4.02. 78 P
and she were a rose indeed, if she had but — 4.06. 35 P
you are bound to him indeed, but how honorable 4.06. 56 P
for thou lookest | like one i lov'd indeed. 5.01.125
so indeed i did. 5.01.128
t' instruct me 'gainst a capital grief indeed — TNK 1.01.123
indeed you must, my lord. 2.02.268
you had indeed, | a bright bay, i remember. 3.06. 77
that's fine indeed. 5.02. 50
"what should i do, seeing thee so indeed, | that VEN 667
the remedy indeed to do me good | is to let LUC 1028
he that is thy friend indeed, | he will help PP 20.49
but when my glass shows me myself indeed, SON 62. 9
INDENT 2 FR 0.0002 REL FR 2 V 0 P
and indent with fears, | when they have lost and 1H4 1.03. 87
it shall not wind with such a deep indent, | to 3.01.103
INDENTED 1 FR 0.0001 REL FR 1 V 0 P
and with indented glides did slip away | into a AYL 4.03.112
INDENTING 1 FR 0.0001 REL FR 1 V 0 P
turn, and return, indenting with the way; VEN 704
INDENTURE 4 FR 0.0004 REL FR 2 V 2 P
kiss | as seal to this indenture of my love: JN 2.01. 20
as to play the coward with thy indenture, and 1H4 2.04. 47 P
he's bound by the indenture of his oath to be PER 1.03. 8 P
serve by indenture to the common hangman: 4.06.176
INDENTURES 4 FR 0.0004 REL FR 2 V 2 P
and our indentures tripartite are drawn, | which 1H4 3.01. 79
are the indentures drawn? 3.01.139
and the indentures be drawn, i'll away within 3.01.260 P

the length and breadth of a pair of indentures? HAM 5.01.110 P
INDEX 4 FR 0.0004 REL FR 3 V 1 P
as index to the story we late talk'd of, | to R3 2.02.149
the flattering index of a direful pageant; 4.04. 85
that roars so loud and thunders in the index? HAM 3.04. 52
an index and obscure prologue to the history of OTH 2.01.257 P
INDEXES 1 FR 0.0001 REL FR 1 V 0 P
and in such indexes (although small pricks | to TRO 1.03.343
INDIA *(also inde, indies)*
INDIA 7 FR 0.0008 REL FR 5 V 2 P
here | come from the farthest steep of india? MND 2.01. 69
and england, | from lisbon, barbary, and india, MV 3.02.269
how now, my metal of india? TN 2.05. 14 P
affable, and as bountiful | as mines of india. 1H4 3.01.167
and, to–morrow, they | made britain india: H8 1.01. 21
her bed is india, there she lies, a pearl; TRO 1.01.100
condition i had gone barefoot to india. 1.02. 74 P
/INDIAN 1 FR 0.0001 REL FR 1 V 0 P
like the base /indian, threw a pearl away OTH 5.02.347
INDIAN 7 FR 0.0008 REL FR 5 V 2 P
they will lay out ten to see a dead indian. TMP 2.02. 33 P
hath | a lovely boy stolen from an indian king; MND 2.01. 22
and, in the spiced indian air, by night, | full 2.01.124
i'll to my queen and beg her indian boy; 3.02.375
the beauteous scarf | veiling an indian beauty; MV 3.02. 99
not deck'd with diamonds and indian stones, 3H6 3.01. 63
have we some strange indian with the great tool H8 5.03. 34 P
INDIAN–LIKE 1 FR 0.0001 REL FR 1 V 0 P
thus, indian–like, | religious in mine error, i AWW 1.03.204
INDICT 1 FR 0.0001 REL FR 0 V 1 P
phrase that might indict the author of affection HAM 2.02.443 P
INDICTED 1 FR 0.0001 REL FR 1 V 0 P
the witness, | and he's indicted falsely. OTH 3.04.154
/INDICTMENT 1 FR 0.0001 REL FR 1 V 0 P
/that /by /indictment /and /by /dint /of /sword 2H4 4.01.126
INDICTMENT 3 FR 0.0003 REL FR 2 V 1 P
read the indictment. WT 3.02. 11
marry, there is another indictment upon thee, 2H4 2.04.343 P
here is the indictment of the good lord hastings R3 3.06. 1
INDIES *(also inde, india)*
INDIES 5 FR 0.0005 REL FR 1 V 4 P
they shall be my east and west indies, and i WIV 1.03. 72 P
where america, the indies? ERR 3.02.133 P
argosy bound to tripolis, another to the indies; MV 1.03. 19 P
new map, with the augmentation of the indies; TN 3.02. 80 P
our king has all the indies in his arms, | and H8 4.01. 45
INDIFFERENCY 2 FR 0.0002 REL FR 1 V 1 P
makes it take head from all indifferency, | from JN 2.01.579
and i had but a belly of any indifferency, i 2H4 4.03. 21 P
INDIFFERENT 16 FR 0.0018 REL FR 8 V 8 P
therefore the office is indifferent, | being TGV 3.02. 44
i'll tell you news indifferent good for either. SHR 1.02.180
and their garters of an indifferent knit; 4.01. 92 P
and it does indifferent well in a /dun–color'd TN 1.03.134 P
as, item, two lips, indifferent red; 1.05.247 P
look on my wrongs with an indifferent eye. R2 2.03.116
he seems indifferent; H5 1.01. 72
life is come after it indifferent well, for 4.07. 33 P
having here | no judge indifferent, nor no more H8 2.04. 17
yes, he'll fight indifferent well. TRO 1.02.223 P
indifferent. TIM 1.01. 30
i am arm'd, | and dangers are to me indifferent. JC 1.03.115
as the indifferent children of the earth. HAM 2.02.227 P
i am myself indifferent honest, but yet i could 3.01.121 P
it is indifferent cold, my lord, indeed. 5.02. 97 P
i am indifferent. TNK 3.06. 60
INDIFFERENTLY 5 FR 0.0005 REL FR 2 V 3 P
i have an humor to knock you indifferently well. H5 2.01. 55 P
he wav'd indifferently 'twixt doing them neither COR 2.02. 17 P
then hear me speak indifferently for all; TIT 1.01.430
other, | and i will look on both indifferently; JC 1.02. 87
we have reform'd that indifferently with us, HAM 3.02. 36 P
INDIGENT 1 FR 0.0001 REL FR 1 V 0 P
of indigent faint souls past corporal toil, | a H5 1.01. 16
INDIGEST 2 FR 0.0002 REL FR 2 V 0 P
to set a form upon that indigest | which he hath JN 5.07. 26
to make of monsters and things indigest | such SON 114. 5
INDIGESTED 2 FR 0.0002 REL FR 2 V 0 P
hence, heap of wrath, foul indigested lump, | as 2H6 5.01.157
hope, | to wit, an indigested and deformed lump, 3H6 5.06. 51
INDIGN 1 FR 0.0001 REL FR 1 V 0 P
and all indign and base adversities | make head OTH 1.03.273
INDIGNATION 11 FR 0.0012 REL FR 7 V 4 P
at which my nose is in great indignation. TMP 4.01.200 P
to pluck his indignation on thy head | by the AWW 3.02. 30
i'll deliver thy indignation to him by word of TN 2.03.130 P
his indignation derives itself out of a very 3.04.246 P
their iron indignation 'gainst your walls; JN 2.01.212
and quench /his fiery indignation | even in the 4.01. 63
they burn in indignation. 4.02.103
withhold thine indignation, mighty heaven, | and 5.06. 37
of her maid–pale peace | to scarlet indignation, R2 3.03. 99
and then hurl down their indignation | on thee, R3 1.03.219
to suspend your indignation against my brother LR 1.02. 80 P
INDIGNATIONS 1 FR 0.0001 REL FR 0 V 1 P
and his displeasures, and his indignations, and H5 4.07. 36 P
INDIGNE 1 FR 0.0001 REL FR 0 V 1 P
indigne serviteur. H5 5.02.255 P
INDIGNITIES 4 FR 0.0004 REL FR 4 V 0 P
for these deep shames and great indignities. ERR 5.01.254
temperate, | unapt to stir at these indignities, 1H4 1.03. 2
his glorious deeds for my indignities. 3.02.146
forget | so great indignities you laid upon me? 2H4 5.02. 69
INDIGNITY 6 FR 0.0006 REL FR 4 V 2 P
my subject, and he shall not suffer indignity. TMP 3.02. 37 P
complain unto the duke of this indignity. ERR 5.01.113
be | they will digest this harsh indignity. LLL 5.02.289
my lord, you give me most egregious indignity. AWW 2.03.216 P
in me, | nor wrong mine age with this indignity. TIT 1.01. 8
from him that fled some strange indignity OTH 2.03.245
INDIRECT 8 FR 0.0009 REL FR 7 V 1 P
that by direct or indirect attempts | he seek MV 4.01.350
ta'en thy life by some indirect means or other; AYL 1.01.152 P
though indirect, | yet indirection thereby grows JN 3.01.275
we find | too indirect for long continuance. 1H4 4.03.105
by what by–paths and indirect crook'd ways | i 2H4 4.05.184
he needs no indirect or lawless course | to cut R3 1.04.218
what an indirect and peevish course | is this of 3.01. 31

did you by indirect and forced courses | subdue OTH 1.03.111
INDIRECTION 2 FR 0.0002 REL FR 2 V 0 P
yet indirection thereby grows direct, | and JN 3.01.276
peasants their vile trash | by any indirection. JC 4.03. 75
INDIRECTIONS 1 FR 0.0001 REL FR 1 V 0 P
of bias, | by indirections find directions out. HAM 2.01. 63
INDIRECTLY 8 FR 0.0009 REL FR 7 V 1 P
to speak so indirectly i am loath. MM 4.06. 1
but turn down indirectly to the jew's house. MV 2.02. 44 P
that indirectly, and directly too, | thou hast 4.01.359
blood | that hot rash haste so indirectly shed. JN 2.01. 49
i answered indirectly, as i said, | and i 1H4 1.03. 66
crown and kingdom, indirectly held | from him, H5 2.04. 94
thy head (all indirectly) gave direction. R3 4.04.226
why should poor beauty indirectly seek | roses SON 67. 7
/INDISCREET 1 FR 0.0001 REL FR 1 V 0 P
it would ill become me to be vain, /indiscreet, LLL 4.02. 30
INDISCREET 1 FR 0.0001 REL FR 0 V 1 P
so drunken, and so indiscreet an officer. OTH 2.03.279 P
INDISCRETION 2 FR 0.0002 REL FR 2 V 0 P
know | our indiscretion sometime serves us well HAM 5.02. 8
all's not offense that indiscretion finds | and LR 2.04.196
INDISPOS'D 1 FR 0.0001 REL FR 1 V 0 P
to take the indispos'd and sickly fit | for the LR 2.04.111
INDISPOSITION 1 FR 0.0001 REL FR 1 V 0 P
you took, | when my indisposition put you back, TIM 2.02.130
INDISSOLUBLE 1 FR 0.0001 REL FR 1 V 0 P
my duties | are with a most indissoluble tie MAC 3.01. 17
INDISTINCT 2 FR 0.0002 REL FR 2 V 0 P
main and th' aerial blue | an indistinct regard. OTH 2.01. 40
and makes it indistinct | as water is in water. ANT 4.14. 10
INDISTINGUISHABLE 1 FR 0.0001 REL FR 0 V 1 P
butt, you whoreson indistinguishable cur, no. TRO 5.01. 29 P
INDISTINGUISH'D *(also undistinguish'd)*
INDISTINGUISH'D 1 FR 0.0001 REL FR 1 V 0 P
o indistinguish'd space of woman's will! LR 4.06.271
INDITE 1 FR 0.0001 REL FR 0 V 1 P
she will indite him to some supper. ROM 2.04.129 P
INDITED 2 FR 0.0002 REL FR 1 V 1 P
of feathers is he that indited this letter? LLL 4.01. 94
and he is indited to dinner to the lubber's head 2H4 2.01. 28 P
INDIVIDABLE 1 FR 0.0001 REL FR 0 V 1 P
scene individable, or poem unlimited; HAM 2.02.399 P
INDRENCH'D 1 FR 0.0001 REL FR 1 V 0 P
in how many fadoms deep | they lie indrench'd. TRO 1.01. 51
INDUBITATE 1 FR 0.0001 REL FR 0 V 1 P
the pernicious and indubitate beggar zenelophon; LLL 4.01. 66 P
INDUC'D 5 FR 0.0005 REL FR 3 V 2 P
sir, induc'd by my charity, and hearing how MM 4.03. 50 P
your own letter that induc'd me to the semblance TN 5.01.306 P
i do believe | (induc'd by potent circumstances) H8 2.04. 76
induc'd | as you have been — that's for my COR 1.09. 16
they induc'd to steal it? CYM 2.04.125
INDUCE 5 FR 0.0005 REL FR 5 V 0 P
which might | induce you to the question on't? H8 2.04.152
cannot induce you to attend my words. TIT 5.03. 79
livia and octavia, to induce | their mediation, ANT 5.02.169
make them, | must first induce you to believe; CYM 2.04. 63
vassal, and induce | stale gravity to dance; TNK 5.01. 84
INDUCEMENT 3 FR 0.0003 REL FR 3 V 0 P
a well–derived nature | with his inducement. AWW 3.02. 89
if this inducement move her not to love, | send R3 4.04.279
then mark th' inducement. H8 2.04.170
INDUCTION 2 FR 0.0002 REL FR 2 V 0 P
and our induction full of prosperous hope. 1H4 3.01. 2
a dire induction am i witness to, | and will to R3 4.04. 5
INDUCTIONS 1 FR 0.0001 REL FR 1 V 0 P
plots have i laid, inductions dangerous, | by R3 1.01. 32
INDU'D 2 FR 0.0002 REL FR 1 V 1 P
indu'd with intellectual sense and souls, | of ERR 2.01. 22
no, he is best indu'd in the small. LLL 5.02.641 P
INDUE *(also endue, etc.)*
INDUE 2 FR 0.0002 REL FR 1 V 1 P
now mercury indue thee with leasing, for thou TN 1.05. 97 P
lesser is my fear, | i shall indue you with. JN 4.02. 43
INDUED 2 FR 0.0002 REL FR 2 V 0 P
to /mark /the full–fraught man and best indued H5 2.02.139
or like a creature native and indued | unto that HAM 4.07.179
INDULGENCE 2 FR 0.0002 REL FR 2 V 0 P
pardon'd be, | let your indulgence set me free. TMP ep 20
of partial indulgence | to their benumbed wills, TRO 2.02.178
INDULGENCES 1 FR 0.0001 REL FR 1 V 0 P
thou that giv'st whores indulgences to sin. 1H6 1.03. 35
INDULGENT 1 FR 0.0001 REL FR 1 V 0 P
you are too indulgent. ANT 1.04. 16
INDURANCE *(also endurance)*
INDURANCE 1 FR 0.0001 REL FR 1 V 0 P
to have heard you | without indurance further. H8 5.01.121
INDUSTRIOUS 4 FR 0.0004 REL FR 4 V 0 P
my industrious servant, ariel! TMP 4.01. 33
at your industrious scenes and acts of death. JN 2.01.376
here is /a dear, a true industrious friend, 1H4 1.01. 62
event, and put we on | industrious soldiership. MAC 5.04. 16
INDUSTRIOUSLY 1 FR 0.0001 REL FR 1 V 0 P
if industriously | i play'd the fool, it was my WT 1.02.256
INDUSTRY 9 FR 0.0010 REL FR 5 V 4 P
experience is by industry achiev'd, | and TGV 1.03. 22
in the dearest design of industry, don adriano LLL 4.01. 86 P
his industry is up stairs and down stairs, his 1H4 2.04.100 P
brains with care, | their bones with industry; 2H4 4.05. 69
which industry and courage might have sav'd? 3H6 5.04. 11
with idleness or manur'd with industry — why, OTH 1.03.325 P
have cause to use thee with a serious industry, CYM 3.05.111 P
the sweat of industry would dry and die, | but 3.06. 31
and with a dropping industry they skip | from PER 4.01. 62
INEFFECTUAL *(see uneffectual)*
INEQUALITY 1 FR 0.0001 REL FR 1 V 0 P
nor do not banish reason | for inequality, but MM 5.01. 65
INESTIMABLE 3 FR 0.0003 REL FR 3 V 0 P
inestimable stones, unvalued jewels, | all R3 1.04. 27
clapp'd your hands, | and cried "inestimable!" TRO 2.02. 88
seated in a chariot | of an inestimable value, PER 2.04. 8
INEVITABLE 4 FR 0.0004 REL FR 3 V 1 P
must yield to such inevitable shame | as to MV 4.01. 57
with such a mortal motion that it is inevitable; TN 3.04.276 P
women | 'tis fond to wail inevitable strokes, COR 4.01. 26
see behind me | th' inevitable prosecution of ANT 4.14. 65
INEXECRABLE 1 FR 0.0001 REL FR 1 V 0 P

o, be thou damn'd, inexecrable dog! MV 4.01.128
INEXORABLE 2 FR 0.0002 REL FR 2 V 0 P
but you are more inhuman, more inexorable, | o, 3H6 1.04.154
more fierce and more inexorable far | than empty ROM 5.03. 38
INEXPERIENCED *(see unexperienced, etc.)*
INEXPLICABLE 1 FR 0.0001 REL FR 0 V 1 P
of nothing but inexplicable dumb shows and noise HAM 3.02. 12 P
INFALLIBLE *(also unfallible)*
INFALLIBLE 5 FR 0.0005 REL FR 2 V 3 P
he is a motion generative, that's infallible. MM 3.02.112 P
heaven, that thou art fair, is most infallible; LLL 4.01. 61 P
mothers, which is most infallible disobedience. AWW 1.01.137 P
a sigh (a note infallible | of breaking honesty) WT 1.02.287
which is infallible, to england's crown. 2H6 2.02. 5
INFALLIBLY 2 FR 0.0002 REL FR 0 V 2 P
certes the text most infallibly concludes it. LLL 4.02.163 P
your lordship speaks most infallibly of him. HAM 5.02.121 P
INFAMIES 1 FR 0.0001 REL FR 1 V 0 P
o, how are they wrapp'd in with infamies | that LUC 636
INFAMONIZE 1 FR 0.0001 REL FR 0 V 1 P
dost thou infamonize me among potentates? LLL 5.02.678 P
INFAMOUS 2 FR 0.0002 REL FR 2 V 0 P
this fact was infamous | and ill beseeming any 1H6 4.01. 30
o antony, | nobler than my revolt is infamous, ANT 4.09. 19
INFAMY 21 FR 0.0023 REL FR 19 V 2 P
then never dream on infamy, but go. TGV 2.07. 64
who smirched thus and mir'd with infamy, | i ADO 4.01.133
death | will quench the wonder of her infamy. 4.01.239
and i will whip about your infamy, /manu cita — LLL 5.01. 69 P
truth is, sir john, you live in great infamy. 2H4 1.02.137 P
and from the powd'ring–tub of infamy | fetch H5 2.01. 75
beside, what infamy will there arise, | when 1H6 4.01.143
rather than life preserv'd with infamy. 4.05. 33
to be a queen, and crown'd with infamy! 2H6 3.02. 71
look here, i throw my infamy at thee. 3H6 5.01. 82
/her face defac'd with scars of infamy, | /her R3 3.07.126
bed, | throw over her the veil of infamy. 4.04.209
he must not live to trumpet forth my infamy, PER 1.01.145
that we may nothing share | of his loud infamy; TNK 1.02. 76
enmity, | yet strive i to embrace mine infamy." LUC 504
are nature's faults, not their own infamy." 539
to mask their brows and hide their infamy, | but 794
night, | in vain i cavil with mine infamy, | in 1025
livery, | a dying life to living infamy. 1055
corrupted, | grossly engirt with daring infamy: 1173
act will be | my fame and thy perpetual infamy.' 1638
INFANCY 11 FR 0.0012 REL FR 11 V 0 P
thy nerves are in their infancy again | and have TMP 1.02.485
for from our infancy | we have convers'd and TGV 2.04. 62
sleep she as sound as careless infancy; WIV 5.05. 52
and gives the crutch the cradle's infancy. LLL 4.03.241
for she was as tender | as infancy and grace. WT 5.03. 27
hath been | a virgin from her tender infancy, 1H6 5.04. 50
and hath his highness in his infancy | crowned 2H6 1.01. 93
to me, | tetchy and wayward was thy infancy; R3 4.04.169
night, | and skilless as unpractic'd infancy. TRO 1.01. 12
soft infancy, that nothing canst but cry, | add 2.02.105
and simpler than the infancy of truth. 3.02.170
INFANT 23 FR 0.0026 REL FR 21 V 2 P
define, define, well–educated infant. LLL 1.02. 94 P
"all hid, all hid," an old infant play. 4.03. 76
thou disputes like an infant; go whip thy gig. 5.01. 66 P
at first the infant, | mewling and puking in the AYL 2.07.143
even since it could speak, from an infant, WT 3.02. 70
who, on my life, | did perish with the infant. 5.01. 44
outfaced infant state, and done a rape | upon JN 2.01. 97
draws the sweet infant breath of gentle sleep; R2 1.03.133
which, till my infant fortune comes to years, 2.03. 66
"look when his infant fortune came to age" | and 1H4 1.03.253
this infant warrior, in his enterprises 3.02.113
holds his infant up | and hangs resolv'd 2H4 4.01.210
in infant bands crown'd king | of france and H5 ep 9
meet i an infant of the house of york, | into as 2H6 5.02. 57
more than the infant that is born to–night. R3 2.01. 72
hath dimm'd your infant morn to aged night. 4.04. 16
this royal infant — heaven still move about her H8 5.04. 17
that were the servants to this chosen infant, 5.04. 48
within the infant rind of this weak flower ROM 2.03. 23
yet for the love | of this poor infant, this PER 3.01. 41
leaving her | the infant of your care, 3.03. 15
or like the froward infant still'd with dandling VEN 562
old woes, not infant sorrows, bear them mild; LUC 1096
INFANT–LIKE 1 FR 0.0001 REL FR 0 V 1 P
abilities are too infant–like for doing much COR 2.01. 37 P
INFANT'S 3 FR 0.0003 REL FR 3 V 0 P
whiles warm life plays in that infant's veins, JN 3.04.132
mistakes that aim and cleaves an infant's heart. VEN 942
not prizing her poor infant's discontent; SON 143. 8
INFANTS 11 FR 0.0012 REL FR 11 V 0 P
that bites the first–born infants of the spring. LLL 1.01.101
fresh fair virgins and your flow'ring infants. H5 3.03. 14
your naked infants spitted upon pikes, | whiles 3.03. 38
pranks, | as very infants prattle of thy pride. 1H6 3.01. 16
too deep and dead, poor infants, in their graves R3 4.04.363
to thy senses | as infants empty of all thought! TRO 4.02. 6
and arm the minds of infants to exclaims. TIT 4.01. 86
your infants in your arms, and there have sate JC 1.01. 40
their infants quartered with the hands of war; 3.01.268
the canker galls the infants of the spring | too HAM 1.03. 39
or women | that have sod their infants in (and TNK 1.03. 21
INFECT 22 FR 0.0024 REL FR 18 V 4 P
that this coil | would not infect his reason? TMP 1.02.208
to call brother | would even infect my mouth, i 5.01.131
with intrusion | infect thy sap, and live on thy ERR 2.02.180
near her, she would infect to the north star. ADO 2.01.250 P
why do you infect yourself with them? AYL 3.02.114 P
who does infect her? WT 1.02.306
this sickness doth infect | the very life–blood 1H4 4.01. 28
but if it did infect my blood with joy, | or 2H4 4.05.169
lest in our need he might infect another, | and 3H6 5.04. 46
out of my sight, thou dost infect mine eyes! R3 1.02.148
every day | it would infect his speech — that H8 1.02.133
a pestilence | that does infect the land; 5.01. 46
with an imperial voice — many are infect. TRO 1.03.187
and one infect another | against the wind a mile COR 1.04. 33
more of your conversation would infect my brain, 2.01. 94 P
breath infect breath, | that their society (as TIM 4.01. 30
below thy sister's orb | infect the air! 4.03. 3
i'll beat thee, but i should infect my hands. 4.03.364
and wants not buzzers to infect his ear | with HAM 4.05. 90
infect her beauty, | you fen–suck'd fogs, drawn LR 2.04.166
eyes and 'tis enough to infect the city with the STM II.C 10 P
or toads infect fair founts with venom mud? LUC 850
/INFECTED 2 FR 0.0002 REL FR 2 V 0 P
/our /late /king /richard (/being /infected) 2H4 4.01. 58
hecat's ban thrice blasted, thrice /infected, HAM 3.02.258
INFECTED 21 FR 0.0023 REL FR 18 V 3 P
poor worm, thou art infected! TMP 3.01. 31
eyes, | deceive me not now, navarre is infected. LLL 2.01.230
they are infected, in their hearts it lies; 5.02.420
cleanse the foul body of th' infected world, AYL 2.07. 60
with the lampass, infected with the fashions, SHR 3.02. 52 P
were my wive's liver | infected as her life, she WT 1.02.305
my best blood turn | to an infected jelly, and 1.02.418
no venom (for his knowledge | is not infected), 2.01. 42
the world, | never to be infected with delight, JN 4.03. 69
o, how hast thou with jealousy infected | the H5 2.02.126
thine eyes, sweet lady, have infected mine. R3 1.02.149
no more infected with my country's love | than COR 5.06. 71
this is in thee a nature but infected, | a poor TIM 4.03.202
approach the fold and cull th' infected forth, 5.04. 43
infected be the air whereon they ride, | and MAC 4.01.138
infected minds | to their deaf pillows will 5.01. 72
this our court, infected with their manners, LR 1.04.243
as hath been belch'd on by infected lungs. PER 4.06.169
nay, it has infected it with the palsy, for STM II.C 12 P
you know they grow in dung — have infected us, II.C 13 P
"o, that infected moisture of his eye, | o, that LC 323
INFECTING 1 FR 0.0001 REL FR 1 V 0 P
his mind and place | infecting one another, yea, H8 1.01.162
INFECTION 23 FR 0.0026 REL FR 18 V 5 P
has a marvellous infection to the little page; WIV 2.02.115 P
he hath ta'en th' infection. hold it up. ADO 2.03.121 P
he hath a great infection, sir, as one would say MV 2.02.125 P
genius hath taken the infection of the device, TN 3.04.129 P
find it | and that to the infection of my brains WT 1.02.145
worse than the great'st infection | that e'er 1.02.423
purge all infection from our air whilest you 5.01.169
but such is the infection of the time, | that, JN 5.02. 20
herself | against infection and the hand of war, R2 2.01. 44
he shall not breathe infection in this air | but 2H6 3.02.287
vouchsafe, defus'd infection of /a man, | of R3 1.02. 78
lest his infection, being of catching nature, COR 3.01.308
take thou some new infection to thy eye, | and ROM 1.02. 49
it thee, | so fearful were they of infection. 5.02. 16
what is amiss, plague and infection mend! TIM 5.01.221
lest that th' infection of his fortune take LR 4.06.233
what a strange infection | is fall'n into thy CYM 3.02. 3
and it is our infection will make the city shake STM II.C 14 P
to drive infection from the dangerous year! VEN 508
advice is sporting while infection breeds. LUC 907
ah, wherefore with infection should he live, SON 67. 1
but if that flow'r with base infection meet, 94.11
potions of eisel 'gainst my strong infection, 111.10
INFECTIONS 1 FR 0.0001 REL FR 1 V 0 P
all the infections that the sun sucks up | from TMP 2.02. 1
INFECTIOUS 7 FR 0.0008 REL FR 7 V 0 P
and at her heels a huge infectious troop | of ERR 5.01. 81
his presence | i am barr'd, like one infectious. WT 3.02. 98
where the infectious pestilence did reign, ROM 5.02. 10
your potent and infectious fevers heap | on TIM 4.01. 22
as doth the raven o'er the infectious house, OTH 4.01. 21
the most infectious pestilence upon thee! ANT 2.05. 61
effects will be | both noisome and infectious. CYM 1.05. 26
INFECTIOUSLY 1 FR 0.0001 REL FR 1 V 0 P
to what infectiously itself affects, | without TRO 2.02. 59
INFECTS 7 FR 0.0008 REL FR 7 V 0 P
'twas a fear | which oft infects the wisest: WT 1.02.262
infects the sound pine and diverts his grain TRO 1.03. 8
malice | infects one comma in the course i hold, TIM 1.01. 48
corruption, mining all within, | infects unseen. HAM 3.04.149
the nature of bad news infects the teller. ANT 1.02. 95
but infects the winds | with stench of our slain TNK 1.01. 46
facto | the melancholy humor that infects her. 5.02. 38
INFER 6 FR 0.0006 REL FR 5 V 1 P
that need must needs infer this principle, JN 3.01.213
this doth infer the zeal i had to see him. 2H4 5.05. 14 P
i this infer, | that many things, having full H5 1.02.204
time, | infer the bastardy of edward's children. R3 3.05. 75
withal i did infer your lineaments, | being the 3.07. 12
infer fair england's peace by this alliance. 4.04.343
INFERENCE 1 FR 0.0001 REL FR 1 V 0 P
and /blown surmises, | matching thy inference. OTH 3.03.183
INFERIOR 10 FR 0.0011 REL FR 10 V 0 P
in the world, | and yet she is inferior to none. SHR in.2. 67
and i had that which any inferior might | at AWW 5.03.218
so shall inferior eyes, | that borrow their JN 5.01. 50
be judg'd by subject and inferior breath, | and R2 4.01.128
birth, | inferior to none but to his majesty; 1H6 3.01. 96
i trow, | or be inferior to the proudest peer. 5.01. 57
marriage | i may not prove inferior to yourself. 3H6 4.01.122
the strongest nerves and small inferior veins COR 1.01.138
men's natures wrangle with inferior things, OTH 3.04.144
doth bear, | my saucy bark (inferior far to his) SON 80. 7
INFERIORS 1 FR 0.0001 REL FR 0 V 1 P
is fit i should commit offense to my inferiors. CYM 2.01. 29 P
INFERNAL 3 FR 0.0003 REL FR 1 V 2 P
shall find her the infernal ate in good apparel. ADO 2.01.255 P
by this hand, to th' infernal deep, with erebus 2H4 2.04.157 P
sent from th' infernal kingdom | to ease the TIT 5.02. 30
INFERR'D 3 FR 0.0003 REL FR 3 V 0 P
saith the duke, thus hath the duke inferr'd" — R3 3.07. 32
what shall i say more than i have inferr'd? 5.03.314
'tis inferr'd to us, | his days are foul and his TIM 3.05. 72
INFERRETH 1 FR 0.0001 REL FR 1 V 0 P
wrong, | inferreth arguments of mighty strength, 3H6 3.01. 49
INFERRING 1 FR 0.0001 REL FR 1 V 0 P
orator, | inferring arguments of mighty force. 3H6 2.02. 44
INFEST 1 FR 0.0001 REL FR 1 V 0 P
do not infest your mind with beating on | the TMP 5.01.246
INFIDEL 3 FR 0.0003 REL FR 2 V 1 P
lorenzo and his infidel? MV 3.02.218
now, infidel, i have you on the hip. 4.01.334
an infidel! 1H4 2.03. 29 P
INFIDELS 2 FR 0.0002 REL FR 2 V 0 P
peace shall go sleep with turks and infidels, R2 4.01.139
think you we are turks or infidels? R3 3.05. 41
INFINITE *(also inf'nite)*
/INFINITE 1 FR 0.0001 REL FR 0 V 1 P
/count /myself /a /king /of /infinite /space — HAM 2.02.255 P
INFINITE 37 FR 0.0041 REL FR 26 V 11 P
dishonor in that, monster, but an infinite loss. TMP 4.01.210 P
her beauty is exquisite, but her favor infinite. TGV 2.01. 55 P
his tears, | and instances of infinite of love, 2.07. 70
that i have purchas'd at an infinite rate, and WIV 2.02.205 P
his /givings–out were of an infinite distance MM 1.04. 54
of credit infinite, highly belov'd, | second to ERR 5.01. 6
it is past the infinite of thought. ADO 2.03.101 P
our duty is so rich, so infinite, | that we may LLL 5.02.199
gratiano speaks an infinite deal of nothing, MV 1.01.114 P
skill infinite or monstrous desperate. AWW 2.01.184
notable coward, an infinite and endless liar, an 3.06. 10 P
fear, | among the infinite doings of the world, WT 1.02.253
beyond the infinite and boundless reach | of JN 4.03.117
albeit considerations infinite | do make against 1H4 5.01.102
what infinite heart's–ease | must kings neglect, H5 4.01.236
for these fellows of infinite tongue, that can 5.02.156 P
fears, | your hopes and friends are infinite. H8 3.01. 82
sum | the past–proportion of his infinite, | and TRO 2.02. 29
that the will is infinite and the execution 3.02. 82 P
my lord, to dangers | as infinite as imminent! 4.04. 69
in hector, | the one almost as infinite as all, 4.05. 80
that i should pay | countless and infinite, yet TIT 5.03.159
thee, | the more i have, for both are infinite. ROM 2.02.135
of man and beast the infinite malady | crust you TIM 3.06. 98
whose womb unmeasurable and infinite breast 4.03.178
with a discovery of the infinite flatteries 5.01. 36
pure as grace, | as infinite as man may undergo, HAM 1.04. 34
how infinite in faculties, in form and moving! 2.02.304 P
him, horatio, a fellow of infinite jest, of most 5.01.185 P
in nature's infinite book of secrecy | a little ANT 1.02. 10
her, nor custom stale | her infinite variety. 2.02.235
o infinite virtue, com'st thou smiling from 4.08. 17
she hath pursu'd conclusions infinite | of easy 5.02.355
to your so infinite loss, so in our trifles | i CYM 1.01.120
what an infinite mock is this, that a man should 5.04.188 P
in another, | by your own virtues infinite — TNK 3.06.199
infinite pity | that four such eyes should be so 5.03.144
INFINITELY 6 FR 0.0006 REL FR 4 V 2 P
is antonio, | to whom i am so infinitely bound. MV 5.01.135
i will swear | i love thee infinitely. 1H4 2.03.102
and (as most debtors do) promise you infinitely; 2H4 ep 16 P
so infinitely endear'd — TIM 1.02.227
to whose kindnesses i am most infinitely tied. CYM 1.06. 23 P
extremely lov'd him, infinitely lov'd him; TNK 2.04. 15
INFINITIVE 1 FR 0.0001 REL FR 0 V 1 P
you, he's an infinitive thing upon my score. 2H4 2.01. 24 P
INFIRM *(also unfirm)*
INFIRM 4 FR 0.0004 REL FR 3 V 1 P
what is infirm from your sound parts shall fly, AWW 2.01.167
infirm of purpose! MAC 2.02. 49
waywardness that infirm and choleric years bring LR 1.01.298 P
a poor, infirm, weak, and despis'd old man; 3.02. 20
INFIRMITIES 7 FR 0.0008 REL FR 7 V 0 P
are such allow'd infirmities that honesty | is WT 1.02.263
a friend should bear his friend's infirmities; JC 4.03. 86
will you, with those infirmities she owes, LR 1.01.202
that play with all infirmities for gold | which CYM 1.06.124
gower is come, | assuming man's infirmities, PER 1.ch. 3
sea | these fishers tell the infirmities of men, 2.01. 49
of nature, | to mingle beauty with infirmities, VEN 735
INFIRMITY 18 FR 0.0020 REL FR 13 V 5 P
be not disturb'd with my infirmity. TMP 4.01.160
she speaks this in th' infirmity of sense. MM 5.01. 47
will you be cur'd | of your infirmity? AWW 2.01. 69
infirmity, that decays the wise, doth ever make TN 1.05. 76 P
you, sir, a speedy infirmity, for the better 1.05. 78 P
and, but infirmity, | which waits upon worn WT 5.01.141
then, joan, discover thine infirmity, | that 1H6 5.04. 60
not | a man of their infirmity. COR 3.01. 82
their worships to think it was his infirmity. JC 1.02.271 P
i have a strange infirmity, which is nothing MAC 3.04. 85
'tis the infirmity of his age, yet he hath ever LR 1.01.293 P
infirmity doth still neglect all office 2.04.106
i am infortunate in the infirmity, and dare not OTH 2.03. 41 P
him in, | on some odd time of his infirmity, 2.03.127
own second | with one of an ingraft infirmity; 2.03.140
close, | whereto constrain'd by her infirmity, CYM 3.05. 47
and this ambitious foul infirmity, | in having LUC 150
no posterity, | 'twas not their infirmity, | it PHT 60
INFIXED 1 FR 0.0001 REL FR 1 V 0 P
lov'd myself | till now infixed i beheld myself JN 2.01.502
INFIXING 1 FR 0.0001 REL FR 1 V 0 P
where the impression of mine eye infixing, AWW 5.03. 47
INFLAM'D 4 FR 0.0004 REL FR 4 V 0 P
to stop their marches 'fore we are inflam'd. JN 5.01. 7
as red as mars his heart | inflam'd with venus. TRO 5.02.165
my love should kindle to inflam'd respect. LR 1.01.255
that have inflam'd desire in my breast | to PER 1.01. 20
INFLAME 7 FR 0.0008 REL FR 6 V 1 P
my knight, i will inflame thy noble liver, | and 2H4 5.05. 31
it will inflame you, it will make you mad. JC 3.02.144
/again to inflame it and to give satiety a fresh OTH 2.01.228 P
which can as well inflame as it can kill. PER 2.02. 35
thy /lone bosom | inflame too nicely, nor let 4.01. 6
informs the tapster to inflame the reck'ning. TNK 3.05.130
when thou wilt inflame, | how coldly those LC 268
INFLAMING 2 FR 0.0002 REL FR 2 V 0 P
france, i am burn'd up with inflaming wrath, | a JN 3.01.340
attaint | with any passion of inflaming /love, 1H6 5.05. 82
INFLAMMATION 1 FR 0.0001 REL FR 0 V 1 P
some of us should be too, but for inflammation. 2H4 4.03. 96 P
INFLICT 4 FR 0.0004 REL FR 4 V 0 P
i know no pain they can inflict upon him | will 2H6 3.01.377
a caterpillar, | and so inflict our province. PER 5.01. 61
from all that fortune can inflict upon us, | i TNK 2.02. 57
on thee and thine this night i will inflict, LUC 1630
INFLICTION 1 FR 0.0001 REL FR 1 V 0 P
dead to infliction, to themselves are dead, MM 1.03. 28
INFLUENCE 11 FR 0.0012 REL FR 9 V 2 P
star, whose influence | if now i court not, but TMP 1.02.182
if i be not by her fair influence | foster'd, TGV 3.01.183
whose influence is begot of that loose grace LLL 5.02.859

speak, and move under the influence of the most AWW 2.01. 55 P
star–like nobleness gave life and influence | to TIM 5.01. 63
upon whose influence neptune's empire stands HAM 1.01.119
by an enforc'd obedience of planetary influence; LR 1.02.125 P
whose influence, like the wreath of radiant fire 2.02.107
the beauteous influence that makes him bright, VEN 862
whereon the stars in secret influence comment; SON 15. 4
whose influence is thine, and born of thee: 78.10
INFLUENCES 2 FR 0.0002 REL FR 2 V 0 P
thou art, | servile to all the skyey influences, MM 3.01. 9
star in heaven and | by all their influences, WT 1.02.426
INF'NITE *(also infinite)*
/INF'NITE 1 FR 0.0001 REL FR 1 V 0 P
her /inf'nite /cunning, with her modern grace, AWW 5.03.216
INFOLD *(also enfoldings)*
INFOLD 4 FR 0.0004 REL FR 4 V 0 P
gilded /tombs do worms infold. MV 2.07. 69
mist–like infold me from the search of eyes. ROM 3.03. 73
let me infold thee | and hold thee to my heart. MAC 1.04. 31
sometime her arms infold him like a band: VEN 225
INFORM 23 FR 0.0026 REL FR 22 V 1 P
'tis time | i should inform thee farther. TMP 1.02. 23
he would be drunk too, that let me inform you. MM 3.02.128 P
haply thou mayst inform | something to save thy AWW 4.01. 82
inform on that. 4.01. 93
and inform him | so 'tis our will he should. 5.03. 26
us, inform yourselves | we need no more of your WT 2.01.167
led | by flatterers, and what they will inform, R2 2.01.242
we | will hold at windsor, so inform the lords. 1H4 1.01.104
i must inform you of a dismal fight | betwixt 1H6 1.01.105
let him alone, | he did inform the truth. COR 1.06. 42
we'll inform them | of our proceedings here on 2.02.158
how? i inform them? 3.01. 47
i shall inform them. 3.03. 18
jove, inform | thy thoughts with nobleness, that 5.03. 71
who is't that can inform me? HAM 1.01. 79
how all occasions do inform against me, | and 4.04. 32
inform her full of my particular fear, | and LR 1.04.337
your officer, iago, can inform you — | while i OTH 2.03.198
i shall be furnish'd to inform you rightly ANT 1.04. 77
nor can | her heart inform her tongue — the 3.02. 48
with what patience | your wisdom may inform you.
CYM 1.01. 79
i will inform your father. 2.03.152
inform us of thy fortunes, for it seems | they 4.02.361
INFORMAL 1 FR 0.0001 REL FR 1 V 0 P
perceive | these poor informal women are no more
MM 5.01.236
INFORMATION 2 FR 0.0002 REL FR 1 V 1 P
this is one lucio's information against me. MM 3.02.198 P
lest you shall chance to whip your information, COR 4.06. 54
INFORMATIONS 1 FR 0.0001 REL FR 1 V 0 P
in seeking tales and informations | against this H8 5.02.145
INFORM'D 17 FR 0.0019 REL FR 16 V 1 P
many likelihoods inform'd me of this before, AWW 1.03.123 P
i duly am inform'd | his grace is at marsellis, 4.04. 8
and inform'd her fully | i could not answer in 5.03. 97
behove my knowledge | thereof to be inform'd, WT 1.02.396
i have inform'd his highness so at large, | as, 1H6 5.01. 42
i am inform'd that he comes towards london | to 3H6 4.04. 26
and your chaplains' | (for so we are inform'd) H8 5.02. 52
have you inform'd them sithence? COR 3.01. 47
so, | would have inform'd for preparation. MAC 1.05. 33
from my sister | been well inform'd of them, and LR 2.01.102
who hath most fortunately been inform'd | of my 2.02.167
well, my good lord, i have inform'd them so. 2.04. 98
"inform'd" them? dost thou understand me, man? 2.04. 99
are they "inform'd" of this? 2.04.103
when i inform'd him, then he call'd me sot, 4.02. 8
'twas he inform'd against him, | and quit the 4.02. 92
let rome be thus | inform'd. ANT 3.06. 20
INFORMED 3 FR 0.0003 REL FR 3 V 0 P
i am informed throughly of the cause. MV 4.01.173
the prince's espials have informed me | how the 1H6 1.04. 8
we come to be informed by yourselves | what the 5.04.118
INFORMER 2 FR 0.0002 REL FR 2 V 0 P
"this sour informer, this bate–breeding spy, VEN 655
hence, thou suborn'd informer! SON 125.13
INFORMS 2 FR 0.0002 REL FR 2 V 0 P
it is the bloody business which informs | thus MAC 2.01. 48
informs the tapster to inflame the reck'ning. TNK 3.05.130
INFORTUNATE *(also unfortunate)*
INFORTUNATE 3 FR 0.0003 REL FR 2 V 1 P
son's son, | infortunate in nothing but in thee. JN 2.01.178
a mind, | and henry, though he be infortunate, 2H6 4.09. 18
i am infortunate in the infirmity, and dare not OTH 2.03. 41 P
INFRING'D 1 FR 0.0001 REL FR 1 V 0 P
fault, | nor wittingly have i infring'd my vow. 3H6 2.02. 8
INFRINGE 5 FR 0.0005 REL FR 5 V 0 P
if the first that did th' edict infringe | had MM 2.02. 92
i am not partial to infringe our laws; ERR 1.01. 4
and jove for your love would infringe an oath. LLL 4.03.142
forbid | we should infringe the holy privilege R3 3.01. 41
shall i be tempted to infringe my vow | in the COR 5.03. 20
INFRINGED 2 FR 0.0002 REL FR 2 V 0 P
say when that he shall hear | faith infringed, LLL 4.03.144
so, | to flatter thee with an infringed oath; LUC 1061
INFUS'D 3 FR 0.0003 REL FR 3 V 0 P
in thy unhallowed dam, | infus'd itself in thee; MV 4.01.137
with those clear rays which she infus'd on me 1H6 1.02. 85
that heaven hath infus'd them with these spirits JC 1.03. 69
INFUSE 5 FR 0.0005 REL FR 5 V 0 P
that souls of animals infuse themselves | into MV 4.01.132
words, | infuse his breast with magnanimity, 3H6 5.04. 41
these words, these looks, infuse new life in me. TIT 1.01.461
whereto he'll infuse pow'r and press you forth TNK 1.01. 73
those best affections that the heavens infuse 1.03. 9
INFUSED 2 FR 0.0002 REL FR 2 V 0 P
smile, | infused with a fortitude from heaven, TMP 1.02.154
should be infused with so foul a spirit! SHR in.2. 16
INFUSING 2 FR 0.0002 REL FR 2 V 0 P
infusing him with self and vain conceit, | as if R2 3.02.166
gazed, | infusing them with dreadful prophecies: VEN 928
INFUSION 2 FR 0.0002 REL FR 0 V 2 P
with aqua–vitae or some other hot infusion; WT 4.04.787 P
and his infusion of such dearth and rareness as, HAM 5.02.117 P
INFUSIONS 1 FR 0.0001 REL FR 1 V 0 P
to me and to my aid the blest infusions | that PER 3.02. 35

INGENER *(also enginer)*
/INGENER 1 FR 0.0001 REL FR 1 V 0 P
vesture of creation | does tire the /ingener. OTH 2.01. 65
/INGENIOUS* 1 FR 0.0001 REL FR 0 V 1 P
mehercle, if their sons be /ingenious, they LLL 4.02. 78 P
INGENIOUS* 9 FR 0.0010 REL FR 6 V 3 P
what? that an eel is ingenious? LLL 1.02. 27 P
the meaning, pretty ingenious? 3.01. 58 P
a course of learning and ingenious studies. SHR 1.01. 9
looks like a poor, decay'd, ingenious, foolish, AWW 5.02. 23 P
boy, | bold, quick, ingenious, forward, capable: R3 3.01.155
whose wicked deed thy most ingenious sense HAM 5.01.248
and have ingenious feeling | of my huge sorrows! LR 4.06.280
my ingenious instrument | (hark, polydore), it CYM 4.02.186
thou, king, send out | for torturers ingenious; 5.05.215
INGENIOUSLY 1 FR 0.0001 REL FR 1 V 0 P
ingeniously i speak, | no blame belongs to thee. TIM 2.02.221
INGLORIOUS 1 FR 0.0001 REL FR 1 V 0 P
o inglorious league! JN 5.01. 65
INGOTS 2 FR 0.0002 REL FR 2 V 0 P
for, like an ass whose back with ingots bows, MM 3.01. 26
to his bold ends honor and golden ingots, TNK 1.02. 17
INGRAFT *(also engraff'd, ingrafted)*
INGRAFT 2 FR 0.0002 REL FR 2 V 0 P
own second | with one of an ingraft infirmity; OTH 2.03.140
you, | as he takes from you, i ingraft you new. SON 15.14
INGRAFTED 2 FR 0.0002 REL FR 2 V 0 P
for in the ingrafted love he bears to caesar — JC 2.01.184
sit, | i make my love ingrafted to this store: SON 37. 8
INGRATE *(also ingrateful, ungrateful)*
INGRATE 5 FR 0.0005 REL FR 5 V 0 P
her | will not so graceless be to be ingrate. SHR 1.02.268
to whose ingrate and unauspicious altars | my TN 5.01.113
and you degenerate, you ingrate revolts, | you JN 5.02.151
as this ingrate and cank'red bullingbrook. 1H4 1.03.137
ingrate forgetfulness shall poison rather | than COR 5.02. 86
INGRATEFUL 13 FR 0.0014 REL FR 11 V 2 P
that most ingrateful boy there by your side TN 5.01. 77
of a fool, inconstant | and damnable ingrateful; WT 3.02.187
and you are so strait | and so ingrateful, you JN 5.07. 43
ingrateful, savage, and inhuman creature? H5 2.02. 95
so much were a kind of ingrateful injury; COR 2.02. 31 P
the multitude to be ingrateful were to make a 2.03. 10 P
ingrateful rome requites with foul contempt, TIT 5.01. 12
he's flung in rage from this ingrateful seat TIM 4.02. 45
womb, | let it no more bring out ingrateful man! 4.03.188
whereof ingrateful man, with liquorish draughts 4.03.194
of heaven fall | on her ingrateful top! LR 2.04.163
spill at once | that makes ingrateful man! 3.02. 9
ingrateful fox, 'tis he. 3.07. 28
INGRATITUDE 21 FR 0.0023 REL FR 19 V 2 P
julia, | as in revenge of thy ingratitude, | i TGV 1.02.107
my honor would not let ingratitude | so much MV 5.01.218
thou art not so unkind | as man's ingratitude; AYL 2.07.176
i hate ingratitude more in a man | than lying, TN 3.04.354
both disobedience and ingratitude | to you and WT 3.02. 68
well might they fester 'gainst ingratitude, COR 1.09. 30
ingratitude is monstrous, and for the multitude 2.03. 9 P
part, | and so supplant you for ingratitude, TIT 1.01.447
war | take wreak on rome for this ingratitude, 4.03. 34
have their ingratitude in them hereditary: TIM 2.02.215
and now ingratitude makes it worse than stealth. 3.04. 27
the monstrous bulk of this ingratitude | with 5.01. 65
to wipe out our ingratitude with loves | above 5.04. 17
that needs must light on this ingratitude. JC 1.01. 55
ingratitude, more strong than traitors' arms, 3.02.185
the sin of my ingratitude even now | was heavy MAC 1.04. 15
ingratitude! LR 1.04.259
to take't again perforce! monster ingratitude! 1.05. 39 P
save what beats there — filial ingratitude! 3.04. 14
to scourge th' ingratitude that despiteful rome ANT 2.06. 22
the ingratitude of this seleucus does | even 5.02.153
INGRATITUDES 1 FR 0.0001 REL FR 1 V 0 P
a great–siz'd monster of ingratitudes. TRO 3.03.147
INGREDIENCE 2 FR 0.0002 REL FR 2 V 0 P
commends th' ingredience of our poison'd chalice MAC 1.07. 11
chawdron, | for th' ingredience of our cau'dron. 4.01. 34
INGREDIENT 2 FR 0.0002 REL FR 1 V 1 P
present | th' abhorr'd ingredient to his eye, WT 2.01. 43
cup is unbless'd, and the ingredient is a devil. OTH 2.03.308 P
INGROSS'D *(also engross'd)*
INGROSS'D 1 FR 0.0001 REL FR 1 V 0 P
reapers, people | ingross'd by swift impress. ANT 3.07. 36
INHABIT 11 FR 0.0012 REL FR 10 V 1 P
on this island | where man doth not inhabit — TMP 3.03. 57
o thou that dost inhabit in my breast, | leave TGV 5.04. 7
there's none but witches do inhabit here, | and ERR 3.02.156
wiles, | and lapland sorcerers inhabit here. 4.03. 11
of our grandam might happily inhabit a bird. TN 4.02. 53 P
that i have seen inhabit in those cheeks? JN 4.02.107
and mutiny | shall here inhabit, and this land R2 4.01.143
and, in the holes | where eyes did once inhabit, R3 1.04. 30
if trembling i inhabit then, protest me | the MAC 3.04.104
but dead–cold winter must inhabit here still. TNK 2.02. 45
were born, | or durst inhabit on a living brow; SON 68. 4
INHABITABLE *(also uninhabitable)*
INHABITABLE 1 FR 0.0001 REL FR 1 V 0 P
or any other ground inhabitable | where ever R2 1.01. 65
INHABITANTS 2 FR 0.0002 REL FR 2 V 0 P
peopled with wolves, thy old inhabitants! 2H4 4.05.137
that look not like th' inhabitants o' th' earth, MAC 1.03. 41
INHABITS 4 FR 0.0004 REL FR 4 V 0 P
trouble, wonder, and amazement | inhabits here. TMP 5.01.105
love | inhabits in the finest wits of all. TGV 1.01. 44
and, being help'd, inhabits there. 4.02. 48
strong corruption | inhabits our frail blood. TN 3.04.357
INHEARSE 1 FR 0.0001 REL FR 1 V 0 P
that did my ripe thoughts in my brain inhearse, SON 86. 3
INHEARSED 1 FR 0.0001 REL FR 1 V 0 P
see where he lies inhearsed in the arms | of the 1H6 4.07. 45
INHERENT 1 FR 0.0001 REL FR 1 V 0 P
action teach my mind | a most inherent baseness. COR 3.02.123
INHERIT 16 FR 0.0018 REL FR 12 V 4 P
else being drown'd, we will inherit here. TMP 2.02.175 P
yea, all which it inherit, shall dissolve, | and 4.01.154
this, or else nothing, will inherit her. TGV 3.02. 86
but let thine inherit first, for i protest mine WIV 2.01. 73 P
which, with pain purchas'd, doth inherit pain: LLL 1.01. 73

nothing but fair is that which you inherit. 4.01. 20
father's moral parts | mayst thou inherit too! AWW 1.02. 22
(those bated that inherit but the fall | of the 2.01. 13
it must be great that can inherit us | so much R2 1.01. 85
ruins of thy linen shall inherit his kingdom: 2H4 2.02. 24 P
blood he did naturally inherit of his father, he 4.03.118 P
under a tree, | and never after to inherit it. TIT 2.03. 3
buds shall you this night | inherit at my house; ROM 1.02. 30
but to the girdle do the gods inherit, | beneath LR 4.06.126
was made so happy as | t' inherit such a haven. CYM 3.02. 61
slow, | they rightly do inherit heaven's graces, SON 94. 5
INHERITANCE 13 FR 0.0014 REL FR 12 V 1 P
of his salvation, the inheritance of it, and cut AWW 4.03.279 P
born, | doth he lay claim to thine inheritance? JN 1.01. 72
and find th' inheritance of this poor child, 4.02. 97
my claim | to my inheritance of free descent. R2 2.03.136
let the inheritance | descend unto the daughter. H5 1.02. 99
obscur'd, | depriv'd of honor and inheritance. 1H6 2.05. 27
but all the whole inheritance i give | that doth 3.01.163
heat, | to conquer france, his true inheritance? 2H6 1.01. 82
this small inheritance my father left me 4.10. 18
it was my inheritance, as the earldom was. 3H6 1.01. 78
for the inheritance of their loves and safeguard COR 3.02. 68
/return'd | to the inheritance of fortinbras, HAM 1.01. 92
this place | is our inheritance. TNK 2.02. 84
INHERITED 3 FR 0.0003 REL FR 3 V 0 P
treason is not inherited, my lord, | or, if we AYL 1.03. 61
i have lived | to see inherited my very wishes COR 2.01.199
crimes, like lands, | are not inherited. TIM 5.04. 38
INHERITOR 5 FR 0.0005 REL FR 4 V 1 P
to parley with the sole inheritor | of all LLL 2.01. 5
my father, | the quarrel of a true inheritor. 2H4 4.05.168
do thee good, | and be inheritor of thy desire. R3 4.03. 34
and must th' inheritor himself have no more, ha? HAM 5.01.112 P
an heir | that may succeed as his inheritor; PER 1.04. 64
INHERITORS 2 FR 0.0002 REL FR 2 V 0 P
are pleas'd to breed out your inheritors. TRO 4.01. 65
shall worms, inheritors of this excess, | eat up SON 146. 7
INHERITRIX 1 FR 0.0001 REL FR 1 V 0 P
female | should be inheritrix in salique land; H5 1.02. 51
INHERITS 2 FR 0.0002 REL FR 1 V 1 P
her dispositions she inherits, which makes fair AWW 1.01. 41 P
whose hollow womb inherits nought but bones. R2 2.01. 83
INHIBITED 2 FR 0.0002 REL FR 1 V 1 P
which is the most inhibited sin in the canon. AWW 1.01.145 P
of arts inhibited and out of warrant. OTH 1.02. 79
INHIBITION 1 FR 0.0001 REL FR 0 V 1 P
i think their inhibition comes by the means of HAM 2.02.332 P
INHOOP'D 1 FR 0.0001 REL FR 1 V 0 P
and his quails ever | beat mine, inhoop'd, at ANT 2.03. 39
INHOSPITABLE *(also unhospitable)*
INHOSPITABLE 1 FR 0.0001 REL FR 1 V 0 P
there to strike | the inhospitable cleon, but i PER 5.01.253
INHUMAN 8 FR 0.0009 REL FR 8 V 0 P
answer | a stony adversary, an inhuman wretch, MV 4.01. 4
if it should prove | that thou art so inhuman — AWW 5.03.116
ingrateful, savage, and inhuman creature? H5 2.02. 95
but you are more inhuman, more inexorable, | o, 3H6 1.04.154
thy deeds inhuman and unnatural | provokes this R3 1.02. 60
inhuman traitors, you constrain'd and forc'd. TIT 5.02.177
away, inhuman dog, unhallowed slave! 5.03. 14
o damn'd iago! o inhuman dog! OTH 5.01. 62
INHUMANITY 1 FR 0.0001 REL FR 1 V 0 P
case | and this your /mountainish inhumanity. STM II.C 140
INIQUITIES 1 FR 0.0001 REL FR 0 V 1 P
robbers and die in many irreconcil'd iniquities, H5 4.01.153 P
INIQUITY 12 FR 0.0013 REL FR 6 V 6 P
justice or iniquity? MM 2.01.172 P
the prince himself is about a piece of iniquity: WT 4.04.678 P
that reverent vice, that grey iniquity, that 1H4 2.04.454 P
thus, like the formal vice, iniquity, | i R3 3.01. 82
i lack iniquity | sometime to do me service. OTH 1.02. 3
if you are so fond over her iniquity, give her 4.01.197 P
wholesome iniquity have you, that a man may deal
PER 4.06. 25 P
that sets seeds and roots of shame and iniquity. 4.06. 86 P
draw not thy sword to guard iniquity, | for it LUC 626
sing, | what virtue breeds iniquity devours: 872
die, | for sparing justice feeds iniquity. 1687
self so self–loving were iniquity. SON 62.12
INIQUITY'S 1 FR 0.0001 REL FR 0 V 1 P
an ox, and iniquity's throat cut like a calf. 2H6 4.02. 27 P
INITIATE 1 FR 0.0001 REL FR 1 V 0 P
is the initiate fear that wants hard use: MAC 3.04.142
INJOINTED 1 FR 0.0001 REL FR 1 V 0 P
have there injointed them with an after fleet. OTH 1.03. 35
INJUNCTION 3 FR 0.0003 REL FR 2 V 1 P
and pile them up, | upon a sore injunction. TMP 3.01. 11
and with a kind of injunction drives me to these TN 2.05.169 P
though their injunction be to bar my doors, LR 3.04.150
INJUNCTIONS 2 FR 0.0002 REL FR 2 V 0 P
and that by great injunctions i am bound | to MM 4.03. 96
to these injunctions every one doth swear | that MV 2.09. 17
INJUR'D 3 FR 0.0003 REL FR 3 V 0 P
whom have i injur'd that ye seek my death? 2H6 4.07.101
how hast thou injur'd both thyself and us! 3H6 1.01.179
when have i injur'd thee? R3 1.03. 56
INJURE 1 FR 0.0001 REL FR 1 V 0 P
i fly thee, for i would not injure thee. AYL 3.05. 9
INJURER 1 FR 0.0001 REL FR 1 V 0 P
thou monstrous injurer of heaven and earth, JN 2.01.174
INJURIED 1 FR 0.0001 REL FR 1 V 0 P
i do protest i never injuried thee, | but love ROM 3.01. 68
/INJURIES 1 FR 0.0001 REL FR 1 V 0 P
/not /the /king, /that /doth /you /injuries. 2H4 4.01.104
INJURIES 23 FR 0.0026 REL FR 21 V 2 P
do with your injuries as seems you best, | in MM 5.01.256
out of all eyes, tongues, minds, and injuries. ADO 4.01.243
sword, | and won thy love doing thee injuries; MND 1.01. 17
if that the injuries be justly weigh'd | that TN 5.01.367
me, | have stoop'd my neck under your injuries, R2 3.01. 19
were enrich'd with any other injuries but these, 1H4 3.03.161 P
king, | what with the injuries of a wanton time, 5.01. 50
bosom burns | with an incensed fire of injuries. 2H4 1.03. 14
his life | hath left me open to all injuries. 5.02. 8
and for those wrongs, those bitter injuries, 1H6 2.05.124
but what said warwick to these injuries? 3H6 4.01.107
this shall not excuse the injuries | that thou ROM 3.01. 66

and ne'er prefer his injuries to his heart, | to TIM 3.05. 34
the injuries that they themselves procure | must LR 2.04.303
labors to outjest | his heart-strook injuries. 3.01. 17
these injuries the king now bears will be 3.03. 12 P
saints in your injuries, devils being offended, OTH 2.01.111
the record of what injuries you did us, | though ANT 5.02.118
do him wrong | but he does buy my injuries, to CYM 1.01.105
a valiant race thy harsh | and potent injuries. 5.04. 84
virtuous, | the true decider of all injuries, TNK 3.06.153
on thee, | the injuries that to myself i do, SON 88.11
that they elsewhere might dart their injuries: 139.12
INJURIOUS 17 FR 0.0019 REL FR 17 V 0 P
injurious wasps, to feed on such sweet honey TGV 1.02.103
o injurious love, | that respites me a life MM 2.03. 40
injurious world! 4.03.122
injurious hermia! MND 3.02.195
like a false traitor and injurious villain; R2 1.01. 91
injurious duke, that threatest where's no cause. 2H6 1.04. 48
injurious margaret! 3H6 3.03. 78
call him my king by whose injurious doom | my 3.03.101
injurious time now with a robber's haste | crams TRO 4.04. 42
call me their traitor, thou injurious tribune! COR 3.03. 69
me | to throw my sceptre at the injurious gods, ANT 4.15. 76
till the injurious romans did extort | this CYM 3.01. 47
thou injurious thief, | hear but my name, and 4.02. 86
but robb'd and ransack'd by injurious theft. LUC 838
o, hear me then, injurious, shifting time! 930
injurious distance should not stop my way, | for SON 44. 2
with time's injurious hand crush'd and o'erworn, 63. 2
INJURY 31 FR 0.0035 REL FR 25 V 6 P
conceit — | conceit, my comfort and my injury. ERR 4.02. 66
me, | even in the strength and height of injury: 5.01.200
grove | till i torment thee for this injury. MND 2.01.147
you would not do me thus much injury. 3.02.148
you for it, | though i alone do feel the injury. 3.02.219
the world no injury, for in it i have nothing. AYL 1.02.190 P
for such an injury would vex a very saint, SHR 3.02. 28
derives itself out of a very /competent injury; TN 3.04.247 P
little unthought of, and speak out of my injury. 5.01.310 P
the injury of tongues in courts and kingdoms WT 1.02.338
his injury | her injury, the beadle to her sin JN 2.01.187
his injury | her injury, the beadle to her sin 2.01.188
they did me too much injury | that ever said i 1H4 5.04. 51
good to bruise an injury till it were full ripe. H5 3.06.122 P
gunpowder, | and quickly will return an injury. 4.07.181
you do me shameful injury | falsely to draw me R3 1.03. 87
you do him injury to scorn his corse. 2.01. 81
where injury of chance | puts back leave-taking, TRO 4.04. 33
so much were a kind of ingrateful injury; COR 2.02. 31 P
and his injury | the jailer to his pity. 5.01. 64
a one, | which to this hour bewail the injury, 5.06.152
takes, | patience her injury a mock'ry makes. OTH 1.03.207
distinguish betwixt a benefit and an injury, i 1.03.313 P
this trash | to be a party in this injury. 5.01. 86
so they must, | or do your honor injury. CYM 2.04. 80
art, hath done you both | this cursed injury. 3.04.122
thou hadst been toss'd from wrong to injury, PER 5.01.130
to bear love's wrong than hate's known injury. SON 40.12
each check | without accusing you of injury. 58. 8
case | weighs not the dust and injury of age, 108.10
you behold | the injury of many a blasting hour, LC 72
INJUSTICE *(also unjustice)*
INJUSTICE 9 FR 0.0010 REL FR 8 V 1 P
that if any crave redress of injustice, they MM 4.04. 9 P
to th' duke himself, to tax him with injustice? 5.01.310
heavens themselves | do strike at my injustice. WT 3.02.147
hand | of stern injustice and confused wrong. JN 5.02. 23
and plague injustice with the pains of hell. R2 3.01. 34
whose conscience with injustice is corrupted. 2H6 3.02.235
by underhand corrupted foul injustice, | if that R3 5.01. 6
against you, nor injustice | for you or any. H8 2.04. 89
to chase injustice with revengeful arms: LUC 1693
INK 31 FR 0.0035 REL FR 21 V 10 P
why, as black as ink. TGV 3.01.288 P
write till your ink be dry, and with your tears 3.02. 74
were parchment, and the blows you gave were ink, ERR 3.01. 13
she is fall'n | into a pit of ink, that the wide ADO 4.01.140
pen the ebon-colored ink which here thou viewest LLL 1.01.243 P
he hath not drunk ink; 4.02. 26 P
until his ink were temp'red with love's sighs: 4.03.344
beauteous as ink — a good conclusion. 5.02. 41
taunt him with the license of ink. TN 3.02. 45 P
let there be gall enough in thy ink, though thou 3.02. 49 P
that never saw pen and ink, very wittily said to 4.02. 13 P
help me to a candle, and pen, ink, and paper. 4.02. 81 P
good fool, some ink, paper, and light; 4.02.109 P
i will fetch you light and paper and ink. 4.02.117 P
turning your books to graves, your ink to blood, 2H4 4.01. 50
i'll call for pen and ink, and write my mind. 1H6 5.03. 66
give me some ink and paper in my tent; R3 5.03. 23
give me some ink and paper. 5.03. 49
is ink and paper ready? 5.03. 75
in whose comparison all whites are ink | writing TRO 1.01. 56
give me pen and ink. TIT 4.03.106 P
thou knowest my lodging, get me ink and paper, ROM 5.01. 25
ink and paper, charmian. ANT 1.05. 65
but come, away, | get me ink and paper. 1.05. 76
words you send, | though ink be made of gall. CYM 1.01.101
damn'd paper, | black as the ink that's on thee! 3.02. 20
bid nestor bring me spices, ink and /paper, | my PER 3.01. 65
"go get me hither paper, ink, and pen, | yet LUC 1289
that in black ink my love may still shine bright SON 65.14
what's in the brain that ink may character 108. 1
ink would have seem'd more black and damned here LC 54
INKHORN 3 FR 0.0003 REL FR 1 V 2 P
bid him bring his pen and inkhorn to the jail. ADO 3.05. 58 P
to be disgraced by an inkhorn mate, | we and our 1H6 3.01. 99
him with his pen and inkhorn about his neck. 2H6 4.02.110 P
INKLE 2 FR 0.0002 REL FR 1 V 1 P
"what's the price of this inkle?" LLL 3.01.139 P
her inkle, silk, /twin with the rubied cherry, PER 5.ch. 8
INKLES 1 FR 0.0001 REL FR 0 V 1 P
inkles, caddises, cambrics, lawns. WT 4.04.207 P
INKLING 2 FR 0.0002 REL FR 1 V 1 P
yet i can give you inkling | of an ensuing evil, H8 2.01.140
they have had inkling this fortnight what we COR 1.01. 58 P
INKY 3 FR 0.0003 REL FR 3 V 0 P
'tis not your inky brows, your black silk hair, AYL 3.05. 46
with inky blots and rotten parchment bonds; R2 2.01. 64
'tis not alone my inky cloak, /good mother, HAM 1.02. 77
INLAID 1 FR 0.0001 REL FR 1 V 0 P
is thick inlaid with patens of bright gold. MV 5.01. 59
INLAND 5 FR 0.0005 REL FR 3 V 2 P
as doth an inland brook | into the main of MV 5.01. 96
yet am i inland bred | and know some nurture. AYL 2.07. 96
who was in his youth an inland man, one that 3.02.345 P
vital commoners and inland petty spirits muster 2H4 4.03.110 P
our inland from the pilfering borderers. H5 1.02.142
INLAY 1 FR 0.0001 REL FR 1 V 0 P
they are worthy | to inlay heaven with stars. CYM 5.05.352
INLY 4 FR 0.0004 REL FR 4 V 0 P
i have inly wept, | or should have spoke ere TMP 5.01.200
didst thou but know the inly touch of love, TGV 2.07. 18
watchful fires | sit patiently and inly ruminate H5 4.pr. 24
him, | to see how inly sorrow gripes his soul. 3H6 1.04.171
/INMOST 1 FR 0.0001 REL FR 1 V 0 P
where you may see the /inmost part of you. HAM 3.04. 20
INMOST 1 FR 0.0001 REL FR 1 V 0 P
and pierce the inmost centre of the earth; TIT 4.03. 12
INN 13 FR 0.0014 REL FR 6 V 7 P
that very hour, and in the self-same inn, | a ERR 1.01. 53
and then return and sleep within mine inn, | for 1.02. 14
town, | and then go to my inn and dine with me? 1.02. 23
my team and gives me leave to inn the crop. AWW 1.03. 45 P
thou most beauteous inn, | why should R2 5.01. 13
take mine ease in mine inn but i shall have my 1H4 3.03. 81 P
i was once of clement's inn, where i think they 2H4 3.02. 14 P
stockfish, a fruiterer, behind gray's inn. 3.02. 33 P
by old nightwork before i came to clement's inn. 3.02.209 P
when i lay at clement's inn — i was then sir 3.02.280 P
i do remember him at clement's inn, like a man 3.02.309 P
lated traveller apace | to gain the timely inn, MAC 3.03. 7
with their manners, | shows like a riotous inn. LR 1.04.244
INNKEEPER 1 FR 0.0001 REL FR 0 V 1 P
albons, or the red-nose innkeeper of daventry. 1H4 4.02. 47 P
/INNOCENCE 1 FR 0.0001 REL FR 1 V 0 P
god and our /innocence defend and guard us! R3 3.05. 20
INNOCENCE 23 FR 0.0026 REL FR 21 V 2 P
and prompt me, plain and holy innocence! TMP 3.01. 82
o, take the sense, sweet, of my innocence! MND 2.02. 45
all school-days friendship, childhood innocence? 3.02.202
proof, | because what follows is pure innocence. MV 1.01.145
sooth, | and dallies with the innocence of love, TN 2.04. 47
by innocence i swear, and by my youth, | i have 3.01.157
what we chang'd | was innocence for innocence; WT 1.02. 69
what we chang'd | was innocence for innocence; 1.02. 69
the silence often of pure innocence | persuades 2.02. 39
do), | i doubt not then but innocence shall make 3.02. 30
who has not only his innocence (which seems much 5.02. 65 P
even in the matter of mine innocence; JN 4.01. 64
mine innocence and saint george to thrive! R2 1.03. 84
whose white investments figure innocence, | the 2H4 4.01. 45
the truth and innocence of this poor fellow, 2H6 2.03.103
the trust i have is in mine innocence, | and 4.04. 59
will help me nothing | to plead mine innocence; H8 1.01.208
and spotless shall mine innocence arise | when 3.02.301
god and your majesty | protect mine innocence, 5.01.141
for good lord titus' innocence in all, | whose TIT 1.01.437
the best, for the innocence. TIM 1.01.196 P
must feel war's blow, who spares not innocence: PER 1.02. 93
no, | and forth with bashful innocence doth hie. LUC 1341
INNOCENCY 5 FR 0.0005 REL FR 3 V 2 P
signify that craft, being richer than innocency, MM 3.02. 9 P
it seem | like rivers of remorse and innocency. JN 4.03.110
knowest in the state of innocency adam fell, and 1H4 3.03.165 P
with tears of innocency and terms of zeal, | my 4.03. 63
if truth and upright innocency fail me, | i'll 2H4 5.02. 39
/INNOCENT 1 FR 0.0001 REL FR 1 V 0 P
/a /deed /of /death /done /on /the /innocent TIT 3.02. 56
INNOCENT 57 FR 0.0064 REL FR 51 V 6 P
and women too, but innocent and pure; TMP 2.01.156
all abundance, | to feed my innocent people. 2.01.165
hath requit it) | him, and his innocent child; 3.03. 72
a thousand innocent shames | in angel whiteness ADO 4.01.160
thou hast so wrong'd mine innocent child and me 5.01. 63
i say thou hast belied mine innocent child! 5.01. 67
have among you kill'd a sweet and innocent lady. 5.01.192 P
thy breath hast kill'd | mine innocent child? 5.01.264
people in messina here | how innocent she died, 5.01.282
rhyme to "lady" but "baby," an innocent rhyme; 5.02. 38 P
did i not tell you she was innocent? 5.04. 1
words, | they are as innocent as grace itself. AYL 1.03. 54
cours'd one another down his innocent nose | in 2.01. 39
the shrieve's fool with child, a dumb innocent, AWW 4.03.187 P
"my poor prisoner, | i am innocent as you." WT 2.02. 27
a gracious innocent soul, | more free than he is 2.03. 29
which i have left | to save the innocent — any 2.03.167
(the innocent milk in it most innocent mouth) 3.02.100
(the innocent milk in it most innocent mouth) 3.02.100
tyrant, his innocent babe truly begotten, and 3.02.134 P
and from pope innocent the legate here, | do in JN 3.01.139
name, | pope innocent, i do demand of thee. 3.01.146
with his innocent prate | he will awake my mercy 4.01. 25
of mine | is yet a maiden and an innocent hand, 4.02.252
mind | than to be butcher of an innocent child. 4.02.259
defend | my innocent life against an emperor. 4.03. 89
sluic'd out his innocent soul through streams of R2 1.01.103
dog | shall flesh his tooth on every innocent. 2H4 4.05.132
our kinsman gloucester is as innocent | from 2H6 3.01. 69
my conscience tells me you are innocent. 3.01.141
and kill the innocent gazer with thy sight; 3.02. 53
of the skin of an innocent lamb should be made 4.02. 79 P
ah, clifford, murther not this innocent child, 3H6 1.03. 8
so just is god, to right the innocent. R3 1.03.181
among a world of men | to slay the innocent? 1.04.182
to jut | upon the innocent and aweless throne. 2.04. 52
another | within their alablaster innocent arms. 4.03. 11
unlawfully made drunk with innocent blood! 4.04. 30
how innocent i was | from any private malice in H8 3.02.267
perchance because she knows them innocent. TIT 3.01.115
accuse some innocent, and forswear myself, | set 5.01.130
look like th' innocent flower, | but be the MAC 1.05. 65
does murther sleep" — the innocent sleep, 2.02. 33
which you thought had been | our innocent self? 3.01. 78
be innocent of the knowledge, dearest chuck, 3.02. 45
poor, innocent lamb | t' appease an angry god. 4.03. 16
from the fair forehead of an innocent love | and HAM 3.04. 43
pray, innocent, and beware the foul fiend. LR 3.06. 7 P
for thou hast kill'd the sweetest innocent OTH 5.02.199
yourself within yourself, | the man is innocent. ANT 2.05. 76
and hit | the innocent mansion of my love, my CYM 3.04. 68
unless you play the /pious innocent | and for an PER 4.03. 17
she (i sigh and spoke of) were things innocent, TNK 1.03. 60
and commit it | to the like innocent cradle, 1.03. 70
(which, /ev'ry innocent wots well, comes in 1.03. 79
a fool, | an innocent, and i was very angry. 4.01. 41
being laid unto | mine innocent true heart, arms 5.01.134
INNOCENTS 4 FR 0.0004 REL FR 4 V 0 P
stain'd with the guiltless blood of innocents, 1H6 5.04. 44
if murthering innocents be executing, | why then 3H6 5.06. 32
incapable and shallow innocents, | you cannot R3 2.02. 18
some innocents scape not the thunderbolt. ANT 2.05. 77
INNOVATION 4 FR 0.0004 REL FR 2 V 2 P
elbow at the news | of hurly-burly innovation; 1H4 5.01. 78
comes by the means of the late innovation. HAM 2.02.333 P
too — and behold what innovation it makes here. OTH 2.03. 40 P
how horrible a shape | your innovation bears: STM II.C 93
INNOVATOR 1 FR 0.0001 REL FR 1 V 0 P
myself | attach thee as a traitorous innovator, COR 3.01.174
INNS 3 FR 0.0003 REL FR 0 V 3 P
'a must then to the inns a' court shortly. 2H4 3.02. 13 P
swingebucklers in all the inns a' court again; 3.02. 22 P
others to th' inns of court; 2H6 4.07. 2 P
INNUMERABLE 1 FR 0.0001 REL FR 1 V 0 P
then, that you have sent innumerable substance H8 3.02.326
/INOCULATE 1 FR 0.0001 REL FR 0 V 1 P
virtue cannot so /inoculate our old stock but we HAM 3.01.117 P
INORDINATE 3 FR 0.0003 REL FR 2 V 1 P
else, | could such inordinate and low desires, 1H4 3.02. 12
every inordinate cup is unbless'd, and the OTH 2.03.307 P
that nothing in him seem'd inordinate, | save LUC 94
INPRIMIS 5 FR 0.0005 REL FR 0 V 5 P
"inprimis, she can fetch and carry." TGV 3.01.275 P
"inprimis, she can milk." 3.01.301 P
inprimis, we came down a foul hill, my master SHR 4.01. 66 P
"inprimis, a loose-bodied gown" — 4.03.134 P
"inprimis, it is agreed between the french king 2H6 1.01. 43 P
INQUIR'D 4 FR 0.0004 REL FR 0 V 4 P
me, hath any body inquir'd for me here to-day? MM 4.01. 16 P
you have not been inquir'd after. 4.01. 19 P
have you inquir'd yet who pick'd my pocket? 1H4 3.03. 52 P
i have search'd, i have inquir'd, so has my 3.03. 56 P
INQUIRE *(also inquiry)*
INQUIRE 25 FR 0.0028 REL FR 19 V 6 P
i shall inquire you forth. TGV 2.04.186
go, john, go inquire for my master; WIV 1.04. 40 P
would you buy her, that you inquire after her? ADO 1.01.179 P
go presently inquire, and so will i, | where MV 1.01.183
of thy old master, and inquire | my lodging out. 2.02.153
inquire the jew's house out, give him this deed, 4.02. 1
you | the owner of the house i did inquire for? AYL 4.03. 89
i promis'd to inquire carefully | about a SHR 1.02.165
sirrah, inquire further after me. AWW 5.02. 52 P
there, tell the king, he may inquire us out. JN 4.03.115
my father hath a power, inquire of him, | and R2 3.02.186
inquire at london, 'mongst the taverns there, 5.03. 5
sons, inquire me out contracted bachelors, such 1H4 4.02. 16 P
inquire me out some mean poor gentleman, | whom R3 4.02. 53
where you are bound, you must inquire your way, COR 3.01. 54
thou shalt inquire him out among the goths: TIT 5.02.123
by love, that first did prompt me to inquire; ROM 2.02. 80
told you, my young lady bid me inquire you out; 2.04.163 P
i'll follow and inquire him out. TIM 4.02. 48
visit him, to make inquire | of his behavior. HAM 2.01. 4
inquire me first what danskers are in paris, 2.01. 7
can you inquire him out, and be edified by OTH 3.04. 14 P
i did inquire it, | and have my learning from ANT 2.02. 46
tyre, | fame answering the most strange inquire, PER 3.ch. 22
run and inquire. TNK 5.03. 72
INQUIRED 2 FR 0.0002 REL FR 2 V 0 P
you have oft inquired | after the shepherd that AYL 3.04. 47
/prisoner told me | when i inquired their names? TNK 1.04. 22
INQUIRING 1 FR 0.0001 REL FR 1 V 0 P
custrel that comes inquiring for his tib. PER 4.06.166
INQUIRY *(also inquire)*
INQUIRY 1 FR 0.0001 REL FR 1 V 0 P
we have made inquiry of you, and we hear | such MM 5.01. 5
INQUISITION 2 FR 0.0002 REL FR 2 V 0 P
stopp'd | and left me to a bootless inquisition, TMP 1.02. 35
and let not search and inquisition quail | to AYL 2.02. 20
INQUISITIVE 2 FR 0.0002 REL FR 2 V 0 P
at eighteen years became inquisitive | after his ERR 1.01.125
find his fellow forth | (unseen, inquisitive), 1.02. 38
INROADS 1 FR 0.0001 REL FR 1 V 0 P
many hot inroads | they make in italy; ANT 1.04. 50
INSANE 1 FR 0.0001 REL FR 1 V 0 P
or have we eaten on the insane root | that takes MAC 1.03. 84
/INSANIE 1 FR 0.0001 REL FR 0 V 1 P
it insinuateth me of /insanie: LLL 5.01. 25 P
INSATIATE *(also unsatiate)*
INSATIATE 3 FR 0.0003 REL FR 3 V 0 P
light vanity, insatiate cormorant, | consuming R2 2.01. 38
went with child | of that insatiate edward, R3 3.05. 87
o most insatiate and luxurious woman! TIT 5.01. 88
INSCONCE *(also ensconce)*
INSCONCE 2 FR 0.0002 REL FR 1 V 1 P
get a sconce for my head, and insconce it too, ERR 2.02. 38 P
against that time do i insconce me here | within SON 49. 9
INSCRIB'D 1 FR 0.0001 REL FR 1 V 0 P
"ego et rex meus" | was still inscrib'd; H8 3.02.315
INSCRIPTION 1 FR 0.0001 REL FR 1 V 0 P
this first, of gold, who this inscription bears, MV 2.07. 4
INSCRIPTIONS 1 FR 0.0001 REL FR 1 V 0 P
i will survey th' inscriptions back again. MV 2.07. 14
INSCROLL'D 1 FR 0.0001 REL FR 1 V 0 P
old, | your answer had not been inscroll'd. MV 2.07. 72
INSCRUTABLE 1 FR 0.0001 REL FR 1 V 0 P
o jest unseen, inscrutable; TGV 2.01.135

INSCULP'D 1 FR 0.0001 REL FR 1 V 0 P
stamp'd in gold, but that's insculp'd upon; MV 2.07. 57
INSCULPTURE 1 FR 0.0001 REL FR 1 V 0 P
and on his grave–stone this insculpture, which TIM 5.04. 67
INSENSIBLE 3 FR 0.0003 REL FR 0 V 3 P
insensible of mortality, and desperately mortal. MM 4.02.145 P
'tis insensible then? 1H4 5.01.137 P
/sleepy, insensible, a getter of more bastard COR 4.05.224 P
INSEPARABLE *(also unseparable)*
INSEPARABLE 2 FR 0.0002 REL FR 2 V 0 P
swans, | still we went coupled and inseparable. AYL 1.03. 76
grief, | like true, inseparable, faithful loves, JN 3.04. 66
INSEPARATE 1 FR 0.0001 REL FR 1 V 0 P
that a thing inseparate | divides more wider TRO 5.02.148
INSERT 2 FR 0.0002 REL FR 0 V 2 P
to insert again my haud credo for a deer. LLL 4.02. 19 P
which i would set down and insert in't, could HAM 2.02.542 P
INSERTED 2 FR 0.0002 REL FR 1 V 1 P
was this inserted to make interest good? MV 1.03. 94
objects that are inserted 'tween her mind and TNK 4.03. 79 P
INSET 1 FR 0.0001 REL FR 0 V 1 P
but i will inset you neither in gold nor silver, 2H4 1.02. 17 P
INSHELL'D 1 FR 0.0001 REL FR 1 V 0 P
which were inshell'd when martius stood for rome
COR 4.06. 45
INSIDE 6 FR 0.0006 REL FR 3 V 3 P
kissing with inside lip? WT 1.02.286
show the inside of your purse to the outside of 4.04.803 P
outside or inside, i will not return | till my JN 5.02.110
forgotten what the inside of a church is made of 1H4 3.03. 8 P
the inside of a church! 3.03. 9 P
look'd he | o' th' inside of the paper? H8 3.02. 78
INSINEWED *(see ensinewed)*
/INSINUATE 1 FR 0.0001 REL FR 1 V 0 P
/i /hardly /yet /have /learn'd | /to /insinuate, R2 4.01.165
INSINUATE 5 FR 0.0005 REL FR 2 V 3 P
nor cannot insinuate with you in the behalf of a AYL ep 8 P
think'st thou, for that i insinuate, /that toze WT 4.04.735 P
he would insinuate with thee but to make thee R3 1.04.148 P
a lord | basely insinuate and send us gifts. TIT 4.02. 38
thrive, | with death she humbly doth insinuate; VEN 1012
INSINUATETH 1 FR 0.0001 REL FR 0 V 1 P
it insinuateth me of /insanie: LLL 5.01. 25 P
INSINUATING 4 FR 0.0004 REL FR 3 V 1 P
all color | of base insinuating flattery, | i 1H6 2.04. 35
be abus'd | with silken, sly, insinuating jacks? R3 1.03. 53
will practice the insinuating nod and be off to COR 2.03. 99 P
villain, | some busy and insinuating rogue, OTH 4.02.131
INSINUATION 3 FR 0.0003 REL FR 2 V 1 P
yet a kind of insinuation, as it were in via, in LLL 4.02. 14 P
insinuation, parley, and base truce | to arms JN 5.01. 68
defeat | does by their own insinuation grow. HAM 5.02. 59
INSISTED 1 FR 0.0001 REL FR 1 V 0 P
yet i insisted, yet you answer'd not, | but with JC 2.01.245
INSISTING 1 FR 0.0001 REL FR 1 V 0 P
insisting on the old prerogative | and power i' COR 3.03. 17
INSISTURE 1 FR 0.0001 REL FR 1 V 0 P
insisture, course, proportion, season, form, TRO 1.03. 87
INSOCIABLE 2 FR 0.0002 REL FR 1 V 1 P
such insociable and point–devise companions, LLL 5.01. 18 P
if this austere insociable life | change not 5.02.799
INSOLENCE 15 FR 0.0017 REL FR 15 V 0 P
why, how now, dame, whence grows this insolence?
SHR 2.01. 23
hat, | if thou proceed in this thy insolence. 1H6 1.03. 37
his insolence is more intolerable | than all the 2H6 1.01.175
resign it then and leave thine insolence. 1.03.122
why, suffolk, england knows thine insolence. 2.01. 31
wink at the duke of suffolk's insolence, | at 2.02. 70
cry down | this ipswich fellow's insolence; H8 1.01.138
his insolence draws folly from my lips, | but TRO 4.05.258
wonder | his insolence can brook to be commanded
COR 1.01.262
at some time when his soaring insolence | shall 2.01.254
our senate | the cockle of rebellion, insolence, 3.01. 70
and pursy insolence shall break his wind | with TIM 5.04. 12
the insolence of office, and the spurns | that HAM 3.01. 72
who, queasy with his insolence | already, will ANT 3.06. 20
how insolence and strong hand should prevail, STM II.C 81
INSOLENT 9 FR 0.0010 REL FR 7 V 2 P
hang, you whoreson, insolent noisemaker! TMP 1.01. 43 P
out, insolent, thy bastard shall be king | that JN 2.01.122
himself, | how insolent of late he is become, 2H6 3.01. 7
but he already is too insolent; TRO 1.03.368
a paltry, insolent fellow! 2.03.208 P
was | a worthy officer i' th' war, but insolent, COR 4.06. 30
insolent villain! 5.06.129
but other of your insolent retinue | do hourly LR 1.04.202
of being taken by the insolent foe | and sold to OTH 1.03.137
INSOMUCH 1 FR 0.0001 REL FR 0 V 1 P
of my knowledge, insomuch i say i know you are; AYL 5.02. 55 P
INSPIRATION 2 FR 0.0002 REL FR 2 V 0 P
us by our names, | unless it be by inspiration? ERR 2.02.167
from above, | by inspiration of celestial grace, 1H6 5.04. 40
INSPIRATIONS 1 FR 0.0001 REL FR 0 V 1 P
holy men at their death have good inspirations; MV 1.02. 28 P
INSPIR'D 7 FR 0.0008 REL FR 6 V 1 P
what zeal, what fury, hath inspir'd thee now? LLL 4.03.225
methinks i am a prophet new inspir'd, | and thus R2 2.01. 31
inspir'd with the spirit of putting down kings 2H6 4.02. 35 P
that follow'd, was | a thing inspir'd, and, not H8 1.01. 91
but dawning day new comfort hath inspir'd. TIT 2.02. 10
if | you were inspir'd to do those duties which CYM 2.03. 50
if well inspir'd, this battle shall confound TNK 5.01.166
INSPIRE 3 FR 0.0003 REL FR 3 V 0 P
inspire us with the spleen of fiery dragons! R3 5.03.350
inspire me, that i may this treason find! TIT 4.01. 67
pallas inspire me! TNK 3.05. 94
INSPIRED 3 FR 0.0003 REL FR 3 V 0 P
inspired merit so by breath is barr'd. AWW 2.01.148
was mahomet inspired with a dove? 1H6 1.02.140
thou with an eagle art inspired then. 1.02.141
INSTALL'D *(also stall'd)*
INSTALL'D 4 FR 0.0004 REL FR 4 V 0 P
to redeem | and have install'd me in the diadem. 1H6 2.05. 89
what, is my lord of winchester install'd, | and 5.01. 28
he smiles, and says his edward is install'd; 3H6 3.01. 46
install'd lord archbishop of canterbury. H8 3.02.401

INSTALLED 1 FR 0.0001 REL FR 1 V 0 P
thou wast installed in that high degree. 1H6 4.01. 17
INSTALLMENT 2 FR 0.0002 REL FR 2 V 0 P
each fair installment, coat, and sev'ral crest, WIV 5.05. 63
mind | for the installment of this noble duke R3 3.01.163
INSTALLS 1 FR 0.0001 REL FR 1 V 0 P
rising 'gainst him that god himself installs, STM II.C 105
/INSTANCE 1 FR 0.0001 REL FR 1 V 0 P
/it /sends /some /precious /instance /of /itself HAM 4.05.163
INSTANCE 25 FR 0.0028 REL FR 15 V 10 P
what instance of the contrary? TGV 2.04. 16 P
my desires had instance and argument to commend
WIV 2.02.247 P
and his confessor, | gives me this instance. MM 4.03.129
deep | gave any tragic instance of our harm: ERR 1.01. 64
besides this present instance of his rage, | is 4.03. 87
an old, an old instance, beatrice, that liv'd in ADO 5.02. 76 P
instance, briefly; come, instance. AYL 3.02. 52 P
instance, briefly; come, instance. 3.02. 52 P
a better instance, i say; 3.02. 58 P
a more sounder instance, come. 3.02. 61 P
mend the instance, shepherd. 3.02. 69 P
wherefore, what's the instance? AWW 4.01. 40 P
flood of fortune | so far exceed all instance, TN 4.03. 12
for instance, sir, | that you may know you shall WT 4.04.593
a certain instance that glendower is dead. 2H4 3.01.103
and the examples | of every minute's instance 4.01. 83
up, | gave thee no instance why thou shouldst do H5 2.02.119
what instance gives lord warwick for his vow? 2H6 3.02.159
him his fears are shallow, without instance; R3 3.02. 25
instance, o instance! TRO 5.02.153
instance, o instance! 5.02.153
instance, o instance! 5.02.155
instance, o instance! 5.02.155
what instance for it? 5.10. 40 P
so | that blushing red no guilty instance gave, LUC 1511
INSTANCES 7 FR 0.0008 REL FR 6 V 1 P
his tears, | and instances of infinite of love, TGV 2.07. 70
offer them instances, which shall bear no less ADO 2.02. 41 P
cut, | full of wise saws and modern instances; AYL 2.07.156
by travers | give then such instances of loss? 2H4 1.01. 56
had lack'd a master, | but for these instances: TRO 1.03. 77
enough, | but not with such familiar instances, JC 4.02. 16
the instances that second marriage move | are HAM 3.02.182
/INSTANT 2 FR 0.0002 REL FR 2 V 0 P
and till that /instant shut | my woeful self up LLL 5.02.807
/indeed /the /instant /action, /a /cause /on 2H4 1.03. 37
INSTANT 62 FR 0.0070 REL FR 43 V 19 P
the very instant that i saw you, did | my heart TMP 3.01. 64
comes me in the instant of our encounter, after WIV 3.05. 72 P
he send you both these letters at an instant? 4.04. 4 P
which, at the very instant of falstaff's and our 5.03. 15 P
but at this instant he is sick, my lord, | of a MM 5.01.151
and in the instant that i met with you | he had ERR 4.01. 9
from the hour of my nativity to this instant, 4.04. 31 P
i can, at any unseasonable instant of the night, ADO 2.02. 16 P
upon the instant that she was accus'd, | shall 4.01.215
this, "by, in, and without," upon the instant: LLL 3.01. 41 P
show the whole wealth of thy wit in an instant? MV 3.05. 56 P
but in the instant that your messenger came, in 4.01.152 P
rose at an instant, learn'd, play'd, eat AYL 1.03. 74
heels, and your heart, both in an instant. 3.02.213 P
you will take your instant leave a' th' king, AWW 2.04. 48
to this very instant disaster of his setting i' 4.03.110 P
let's take the instant by the forward top; 5.03. 39
that instant was i turn'd into a hart, | and my TN 1.01. 20
wrack'd the same instant of their master's death WT 5.02. 69 P
even in the instant of repair and health, | the JN 3.04.113
weak | to wage an instant trial with the king. 1H4 4.04. 20
but we rose both at an instant and fought a long 5.04.147 P
the french embassador upon that instant | crav'd H5 1.01. 91
since i came to france | until this instant. 4.07. 56
at this instant | he bores me with some trick. H8 1.01.127
whose figure even this instant cloud puts on 1.01.225
take the instant way, | for honor travels in a TRO 3.03.153
even from this instant, banish him our city, COR 3.03.101
more than the instant army we can make, | might 5.01. 37
in the instant came | the fiery tybalt, with his ROM 1.01.108
and at that instant like a babe sprung up. TIM 1.02.111
bid 'em send o' th' instant | a thousand talents 2.02.198
give't these fellows | to whom 'tis instant due. 2.02.230
having great and instant occasion to use fifty 3.01. 18 P
to supply his instant use with so many talents. 3.02. 35 P
to general filths | convert o' th' instant, 4.01. 7
and i feel now | the future in the instant. MAC 1.05. 58
for, from this instant, | there's nothing 2.03. 92
mine, | and a most instant tetter bark'd about, HAM 1.05. 71
and you, my sinows, grow not instant old, | but 1.05. 94
the instant burst of clamor that she made, 2.02.515
on the instant they got clear of our ship, so i 4.06. 19 P
which at this instant so rageth in him, that LR 1.02.162 P
shame itself doth speak | for instant remedy. 1.04.247
whose virtue and obedience doth this instant 2.01.113
our businesses, | which craves the instant use. 2.01.128
shoulder that i see | before me at this instant. 2.02. 95
this sword of mine shall give them instant way 5.03.150
all three | now marry in an instant. 5.03.230
appearance, | even on the instant. OTH 1.02. 38
and will upon the instant put thee to't: 3.03.471
and even from this instant do build on thee a 4.02.205 P
get you to bed on th' instant, i will be 4.03. 7 P
you borrow one another's love for the instant, ANT 2.02.104 P
i'll tell thee on the instant thou art then | as CYM 1.05. 50
speak, or thy silence on the instant is | thy 3.05. 97
way she was gone, | it was my instant death. 5.05.278
battle, at this instant | is full accomplish'd: 5.05.469
the intelligence of state came in the instant TNK 1.02.106
let 's die together, at one instant, duke. 3.06.177
the two bold titlers at this instant are | hand 5.03. 83
to make some special instant special blest, | by SON 52.11
INSTANTLY 26 FR 0.0029 REL FR 21 V 5 P
go, do it instantly. MM 5.01.253
go take her hence, and marry her instantly. 5.01.377
by the top, and instantly break with you of it. ADO 1.02. 15 P
i cannot instantly raise up the gross | of full MV 1.03. 55
this, | and instantly unlock my fortunes here. 2.09. 52
i'll pay it instantly with all my heart. 4.01.281
love, | who led me instantly unto his cave, AYL 4.03.145

and see it instantly consum'd with fire. WT 2.03.134
go thou away, | i'll follow instantly. 3.03. 14
therefore discase thee instantly (thou must 4.04.633 P
and instantly return with me again | to push JN 5.07. 76
spirit | of teaching and of learning instantly. 1H4 5.02. 64
a dreadful lay! address thee instantly! 2H6 5.02. 27
the card'nal instantly will find employment, H8 2.01. 48
sir, my lord would instantly speak with you. TRO 1.02.272 P
cries "/come" to him that instantly must die. 4.04. 51
get you hence instantly, and tell those friends COR 2.03.213
lords, keep on, | i'll wait upon you instantly. TIM 2.02. 35
delay not, caesar, read it instantly. JC 3.01. 9
and i beseech you instantly to visit | my too HAM 2.02. 35
shall the duke | instantly know, and of that LR 3.03. 22
hang him instantly. 3.07. 4 P
mark, i say instantly, and carry it so | as i 5.03. 36
but the least noise of this, dies instantly; ANT 1.02.141 P
and therefore instantly this prince must die, PER 1.01.148
you perish instantly | for breaking prison, and TNK 3.06.113
INSTATE *(see enstate)*
INSTEAD 3 FR 0.0003 REL FR 1 V 2 P
remember the wooing of a peascod instead of her,
AYL 2.04. 51 P
and now, instead of bullets wrapp'd in fire, JN 2.01.227
it hath serv'd me instead of a quart pot to 2H6 4.10. 14 P
INSTEEPED 1 FR 0.0001 REL FR 1 V 0 P
comes to him where in gore he lay insteeped, H5 4.06. 12
INSTIGATE 2 FR 0.0002 REL FR 2 V 0 P
did instigate the bedlam brain–sick duchess | by 2H6 3.01. 51
but some untimely thought did instigate | his LUC 43
INSTIGATED 1 FR 0.0001 REL FR 0 V 1 P
provok'd and instigated by his distemper, and, WIV 3.05. 76 P
INSTIGATION 3 FR 0.0003 REL FR 2 V 1 P
but rather follow | our forceful instigation? WT 2.01.163
as it were, upon my man's instigation, to prove 2H6 2.03. 86 P
friends, | and by their vehement instigation, R3 3.07.139
INSTIGATIONS 1 FR 0.0001 REL FR 1 V 0 P
such instigations have been often dropp'd JC 2.01. 49
INSTINCT 16 FR 0.0018 REL FR 7 V 9 P
but beware instinct — the lion will not touch 1H4 2.04.271 P
instinct is a great matter; 2.04.272 P
i was now a coward on instinct. 2.04.273 P
you are lions too, you ran away upon instinct, 2.04.300 P
what instinct hadst thou for it? 2.04.318 P
yes, jack, upon instinct. 2.04.355 P
i grant ye, upon instinct. 2.04.356 P
a whit, i' faith, i lack some of thy instinct. 2.04.372 P
and thou a natural coward, without instinct. 2.04.494 P
hath by instinct knowledge from others' eyes 2H4 1.01. 86
and mere instinct of love and loyalty, | free 2H6 3.02.250
by a divine instinct men's minds mistrust R3 2.03. 42
i'll never | be such a gosling to obey instinct, COR 5.03. 35
that an invisible instinct should frame them CYM 4.02.177
o rare instinct! 5.05.381
as if by some instinct the wretch did know | his SON 50. 7
INSTINCTIVELY 1 FR 0.0001 REL FR 1 V 0 P
the very rats | instinctively have quit it. TMP 1.02.148
INSTITUTE 2 FR 0.0002 REL FR 2 V 0 P
here let us breathe and haply institute | a SHR 1.01. 8
we institute your grace | to be our regent in 1H6 4.01.162
INSTITUTIONS 1 FR 0.0001 REL FR 1 V 0 P
our city's institutions, and the terms | for MM 1.01. 10
INSTRUCT 28 FR 0.0031 REL FR 23 V 5 P
and instruct thee how | to snare the nimble TMP 2.02.169
and instruct me | how i may formally in person MM 1.03. 46
come on, bawd, | i will instruct thee in my trade; 4.02. 54 P
within my house, | fit to instruct her youth. SHR 1.01. 95
get her cunning schoolmasters to instruct her? 1.01.187
well seen in music, to instruct bianca, | that 1.02.134
a fine musician to instruct our mistress; 1.02.173
to instruct her fully in those sciences, 2.01. 57
in all these circumstances i'll instruct you; 4.02.120
instruct my daughter how she shall persever, AWW 3.07. 37
mile–end, to instruct for the doubling of files. 4.03.270 P
as your charities | shall best instruct you, WT 2.01.114
powerful spirit instruct the kites and ravens 2.03.186
i will instruct my sorrows to be proud, | for JN 3.01. 68
instruct us, boy, what dream, boy? 2H4 2.02. 88 P
what, shall a child instruct you what to do? 1H6 3.01.133
persuade | than i am able to instruct or teach; 4.01.159
that he may furnish and instruct great teachers H8 1.02.113
vehemency | th' occasion shall instruct you. 5.01.149
did see and hear, devise, instruct, walk, feel, COR 1.01.102
indeed i was their tutor to instruct them. TIT 5.01. 98
our own precedent passions do instruct us | what TIM 1.01.133
very nature will instruct her in it and compel OTH 2.01.234 P
the ills we do, their ills instruct us so. 4.03.103
he'll then instruct us of this body. CYM 4.02.360
take her in, instruct her what she has to do, PER 4.02. 54 P
t' instruct me 'gainst a capital grief indeed — TNK 1.01.123
drum, instruct this day | with military skill, 5.01. 57
INSTRUCTED 6 FR 0.0006 REL FR 3 V 3 P
strength and nature | i am not yet instructed. MM 1.01. 80
the service, and that instructed him to mercy. 3.02.120 P
nestor, | instructed by the antiquary times; TRO 2.03.251
i am bastard begot, bastard instructed, bastard 5.07. 17 P
and let thy soul be instructed. OTH 2.01.221 P
and have instructed cowards | to run and show ANT 3.11. 7
INSTRUCTION 16 FR 0.0018 REL FR 10 V 6 P
and that you will some good instruction give TMP 1.02.425
of my instruction hast thou nothing bated | in 3.03. 85
and i am going with instruction to him. MM 2.03. 38
correction and instruction must both work | ere 3.02. 32
to himself (by the instruction of his frailty) 3.02.245 P
glad to receive some instruction from my fellow 4.02. 17 P
the matter being afoot, keep your instruction, 4.05. 3
be /ingenious, they shall want no instruction; LLL 4.02. 79 P
shall go hard but i will better the instruction. MV 3.01. 73 P
in the which my instruction shall serve to AWW 1.01.208 P
their noise be our instruction. ladders ho! COR 1.04. 22
not by your own instruction, | nor by th' matter 3.02. 53
instruction, manners, mysteries, and trades, TIM 4.01. 18
such shadowing passion without some instruction.
OTH 4.01. 41 P
have by their brave instruction got upon me | a ANT 4.14. 98
monument, | of thy intents desires instruction, 5.01. 54
INSTRUCTIONS 7 FR 0.0008 REL FR 5 V 2 P
you, if my instructions may be your guide. MM 4.02.170 P

a good divine that follows his own instructions; MV 1.02. 15 P
anon i'll give thee more instructions. SHR in.1. 130
under my poor instructions yet must suffer AWW 4.04. 27
i cannot say 'tis pity | she lacks instructions, WT 4.04.582
that we but teach | bloody instructions, which, MAC 1.07. 9
and let instructions enter | where folly now CYM 1.05. 47
INSTRUCTS 5 FR 0.0005 REL FR 3 V 2 P
do so. to ebb | hereditary sloth instructs me. TMP 2.01.223
as my understanding instructs me and as mine WT 1.01. 19 P
she well instructs me. HAM 5.02.208 P
if thou dost | as this instructs thee, thou dost LR 5.03. 29
gate | instructs you how t' adore the heavens, CYM 3.03. 3
INSTRUMENT 40 FR 0.0045 REL FR 35 V 5 P
that hath to instrument this lower world | and TMP 3.03. 54
what, to make thee an instrument, and play false AYL 4.03. 68 P
daughters, | i here bestow a simple instrument, SHR 2.01. 99
and through the instrument my pate made way, 2.01.154
take you your instrument, play you the whiles, 3.01. 22
that will be never, tune your instrument. 3.01. 25
madam, before you touch the instrument, | to 3.01. 64
can bring this instrument of honor again into AWW 3.06. 66 P
but loath am to produce | so bad an instrument. 5.03.202
and that i partly know the instrument | that TN 5.01.122
as he had seen't or been an instrument | to vice WT 1.02.415
we'll make an instrument of this; 4.04.624
lo, by my troth, the instrument is cold, | and JN 4.01.103
or useful servingman and instrument | to any 5.02. 81
a harp, | or like a cunning instrument cas'd up, R2 1.03.163
his tongue is now a stringless instrument, 2.01.149
thy own hand yields thy death's instrument, | go 5.05.106
to pine, | was cursed instrument of his decease. 1H6 2.05. 58
and fashion'd thee that instrument of ill, | who 3.03. 65
he was the author, thou the instrument. 3H6 4.06. 18
come, give me an instrument. TRO 3.01. 95 P
nor no instrument | of half that worth as those JC 3.01.154
where is thy instrument? 4.03.239
and touch thy instrument a strain or two? 4.03.257
if thou dost nod, thou break'st thy instrument, 4.03.271
he thinks he still is at his instrument. 4.03.292
going, | and such an instrument i was to use. MAC 2.01. 43
call me what instrument you will, though you HAM 3.02.371 P
the treacherous instrument is in /thy hand, 5.02.316
sir, by many a wind instrument that i know. OTH 3.01. 10 P
i kiss the instrument of their pleasures. 4.01.218
an instrument of this your calling back, | lay 4.02. 45
what poor an instrument | may do a noble deed! ANT 5.02.236
hence, vile instrument! CYM 3.04. 73
my ingenious instrument | (hark, polydore), it 4.02.186
me | the penitent instrument to pick that bolt, 5.04. 10
dionyza hath | the pregnant instrument of wrath PER 4.ch. 44
to find some desp'rate instrument of death, LUC 1038
these means, as frets upon an instrument, 1140
"poor instrument," quoth she, "without a sound, 1464
INSTRUMENTAL 1 FR 0.0001 REL FR 1 V 0 P
the hand more instrumental to the mouth, | than HAM 1.02. 48
INSTRUMENT'S 1 FR 0.0001 REL FR 1 V 0 P
madam, my instrument's in tune. SHR 3.01. 38
/INSTRUMENTS 3 FR 0.0003 REL FR 3 V 0 P
/fraught /with /the /ministers /and /instruments TRO pr 4
/entertain'd, /limbs /are /his /instruments, 1.03.354
my speculative and offic'd /instruments, | that OTH 1.03.270
INSTRUMENTS 27 FR 0.0030 REL FR 23 V 4 P
sometimes a thousand twangling instruments TMP 3.02.137
to their instruments | tune a deploring dump — TGV 3.02. 83
but instruments of some more mightier member MM 5.01.237
my books and instruments shall be my company, SHR 1.01. 82
she taketh most delight | in music, instruments, 1.01. 93
and see withal | the instruments that feel. WT 2.01.154
so that all the instruments which aided to 5.02. 71 P
sound all the lofty instruments of war, | and by 1H4 5.02. 97
lack | the very instruments of chastisement, 2H4 4.01.215
to bend the fatal instruments of war | against 3H6 5.01. 87
where th' other instruments | did see and hear, COR 1.01.101
may these same instruments, which you profane, 1.09. 41
our instruments to melancholy bells, | our ROM 4.05. 86
with instruments upon them, fit to open | these 5.03.200
resemble sweet instruments hung up in cases that TIM 1.02. 99 P
to make them instruments of fear and warning JC 1.03. 70
the genius and the mortal instruments | are then 2.01. 66
the instruments of darkness tell us truths, MAC 1.03.124
borne in hand, how cross'd, the instruments, 3.01. 80
and the pow'rs above | put on their instruments. 4.03.239
pleasant vices | make instruments to plague us: LR 5.03.172
masters, have your instruments been in naples, OTH 3.01. 3 P
are these, i pray you, wind instruments? 3.01. 6 P
hark how these instruments summon to supper! 4.02.169
forth and levy | our worthiest instruments, TNK 1.01.163
the faculties of other instruments | to his own 1.02. 68
is proclaim'd | by the wind instruments. 5.03. 95
INSUBSTANTIAL *(also unsubstantial)*
INSUBSTANTIAL 1 FR 0.0001 REL FR 1 V 0 P
and, like this insubstantial pageant faded, TMP 4.01.155
INSUFFICIENCE 1 FR 0.0001 REL FR 0 V 1 P
senses (unintelligent of our insufficience) may, WT 1.01. 15 P
INSUFFICIENCY 2 FR 0.0002 REL FR 2 V 0 P
eye, | but you must flout my insufficiency? MND 2.02.128
might | with insufficiency my heart to sway, SON 150. 2
/INSULT 1 FR 0.0001 REL FR 1 V 0 P
/me /thy /knife, /i /will /insult /on /him, TIT 3.02. 71
INSULT 3 FR 0.0003 REL FR 3 V 0 P
that you insult, exult, and all at once, | over AYL 3.05. 36
hath that poor monarch taught thee to insult? 3H6 1.04.124
cause, the other | insult without all reason; COR 3.01.144
INSULTED 1 FR 0.0001 REL FR 1 V 0 P
being down, insulted, rail'd, | and put upon him LR 2.02.119
INSULTER 1 FR 0.0001 REL FR 1 V 0 P
obey, | paying what ransom the insulter willeth; VEN 550
/INSULTING 1 FR 0.0001 REL FR 1 V 0 P
/lord /of /thine, /thou /haught /insulting /man, R2 4.01.254
INSULTING 9 FR 0.0010 REL FR 9 V 0 P
alone | the insulting hand of douglas over you, 1H4 5.04. 54
now am i like that proud insulting ship | which 1H6 1.02.138
to scorn, | anon, from thy insulting tyranny, 4.07. 19
insulting charles, hast thou by secret means 5.04.147
and so he walks, insulting o'er his prey, | and 3H6 1.03. 14
the proud insulting queen, | with clifford and 2.01.168
go rate thy minions, proud insulting boy! 2.02. 84
insulting tyranny begins to jut | upon the R3 2.04. 51
so under his insulting falchion lies | harmless LUC 509
INSULTMENT 1 FR 0.0001 REL FR 0 V 1 P
my speech of insultment ended on his dead body, CYM 3.05.140 P
INSULTS 1 FR 0.0001 REL FR 1 V 0 P
while he insults o'er dull and speechless tribes SON 107.12
INSUPPORTABLE 3 FR 0.0003 REL FR 2 V 1 P
my lord, you do me most insupportable vexation. AWW 2.03.230 P
o insupportable and touching loss! JC 4.03.151
o insupportable! OTH 5.02. 98
INSUPPRESSIVE 1 FR 0.0001 REL FR 1 V 0 P
nor th' insuppressive mettle of our spirits, JC 2.01.134
/INSURRECTION 1 FR 0.0001 REL FR 1 V 0 P
/bishop | /turns /insurrection /to /religion. 2H4 1.01.201
INSURRECTION 4 FR 0.0004 REL FR 4 V 0 P
and never yet did insurrection want | such 1H4 5.01. 79
of base and bloody insurrection | with your fair 2H4 4.01. 40
suffers then | the nature of an insurrection. JC 2.01. 69
says, her subjects with foul insurrection | have LUC 722
INSURRECTION'S 1 FR 0.0001 REL FR 1 V 0 P
greater themes | for insurrection's arguing. COR 1.01.221
INSURRECTIONS 1 FR 0.0001 REL FR 0 V 1 P
there hath been in rome strange insurrections; COR 4.03. 13 P
IN'T 99 FR 0.0112 REL FR 65 V 34 P
go take this shape | and hither come in't. TMP 1.02.304
wouldst give me | water with berries in't, and 1.02.334
had that in't which good natures | could not 1.02.359
with an eye of green in't. 2.01. 56 P
and mine, with my heart in't. 3.01. 90
instrument this lower world | and what is in't, 3.03. 55
o brave new world | that has such people in't! 5.01.184
go fetch me a quart of sack — put a toast in't. WIV 3.05. 4 P
i know your virtue hath a license in't, | which MM 2.04.145
he does well in't. 3.02. 96 P
let the mark have a prick in't, to mete at, if LLL 4.01.132
that there shall not be one spot of love in't. AYL 3.02.424 P
of forty fancies prick'd in't for a feather: SHR 3.02. 69 P
carries no favor in't but bertram's. AWW 1.01. 83
there's little can be said in't, 'tis against 1.01.135 P
that wishing well had not a body in't, | which 1.01.181
my love hath in't a bond | whereof the world 1.03.188
there's something in't | more than my father's 1.03.242
france is a stable, we that dwell in't jades, 2.03.284
lordship sees the bottom of /his success in't, 3.06. 36 P
there is something in't that stings his nature; 4.03. 4 P
if your lordship be in't, as i believe you are, 4.03.114 P
my meaning in't, i protest, was very honest in 4.03.218 P
tut, there's life in't, man. TN 1.03.111 P
come to what is important in't. 1.05.192 P
i shall be constrain'd in't to call thee knave, 2.03. 66 P
i warrant there's vinegar and pepper in't. 3.04.144 P
and i will dissemble myself in't, and i would i 4.02. 5 P
there's something in't | that is deceivable. 4.03. 20
nay, there's comfort in't, | whiles other men WT 1.02.196
then the world and all that's in't is nothing, 1.02.293
the queen receives | much comfort in't; 2.02. 26
'mongst all colors | no yellow in't, lest she 2.03.107
that makes the fire, | not she which burns in't. 2.03.116
fellows, if they please, | can clear me in't. 2.03.144
the fail | of any point in't shall not only be 2.03.171
break the holy seal | nor read the secrets in't. 3.02.130
of gambols, because they are not in't; 4.04.329 P
(thou must think there's a necessity in't) and 4.04.634 P
and tell me for what dull part in't | you chose 5.01. 64
my liege, | your eye hath too much youth in't. 5.01.225
the fixure of her eye has motion in't, | as we 5.03. 67
h'as a book in his pocket with red letters in't. 2H6 4.02. 91 P
could wish he were | something mistaken in't. H8 1.01.195
th' world) should not | be gladded in't by me. 2.04.197
bearing a state of mighty moment in't | and 2.04.214
for him, | there's more in't than fair visage. 3.02. 88
emulation | hath not that honor in't it had; COR 1.10. 13
hot wine with not a drop of allaying tiber in't; 2.01. 49 P
appearance, and thy face | bears a command in't; 4.05. 61
but i say there is no hope in't; 5.04. 7 P
there was very little honor show'd in't. TIM 3.02. 19 P
must he needs trouble me in't — hum! 3.03. 1
h'as much disgrac'd me in't, i'm angry at him, 3.03. 13
dost please thyself in't? 4.03.238
in sufferance, time | hath made thee hard in't. 4.03.269
treatise rouse and stir | as life were in't. MAC 5.05. 13
to some enterprise | that hath a stomach in't, HAM 1.01.100
this be madness, yet there is method in't. 2.02.206 P
one speech in't i chiefly lov'd, 'twas aeneas' 2.02.446 P
which i would set down and insert in't, could 2.02.542 P
is there no offense in't? 3.02.233 P
act | that has no relish of salvation in't — 3.03. 92
but this gallant | had witchcraft in't, he grew 4.07. 85
i think it be thine indeed, for thou liest in't. 5.01.122 P
for my part, i do not lie in't, yet it is mine. 5.01.124 P
thou dost lie in't, to be in't and say it is 5.01.125 P
dost lie in't, to be in't and say it is thine. 5.01.125 P
who is to be buried in't? 5.01.134 P
there is a litter ready, lay him in't, | and LR 3.06. 90
then there's life in't. 4.06.202 P
there's matter in't indeed, if he be angry. OTH 3.04.139
be near at hand, i may miscarry in't. 5.01. 6
serves for the matter that is then born in't. ANT 2.02. 10
not for himself, | remain in't as thou mayst. 2.06. 29
and not to be seen to move in't, are the holes 2.07. 15 P
use me well in't. 3.02. 25
there's hope in't yet. 3.13.176
come on, my queen, | there's sap in't yet. 3.13.191
occupation, thou shouldst see | a workman in't. 4.04. 18
for his bounty, | there was no winter in't; 5.02. 87
is there no derogation in't? CYM 2.01. 43 P
our britain seems as of it, but not in't; 3.04.138
it from the queen, | what's in't is precious. 3.04.189
fool, an empty purse, | there was no money in't. 4.02.114
profit, but my wish hath a preferment in't. 5.04.206 P
and then a mind put in't, either our brags 5.05.176
nay, how absolute she's in't, | not minding PER 2.05. 19
hair of mine remain, | though i show /ill in't. 3.03. 30
who cannot feel nor see the rain, being in't, TNK 1.01.120
every hour in't will | take hostage of thee for 1.01.183
thebes and the temptings in't before we further 1.02. 4
and what they win in't, boot and glory; 1.02. 70
(though in't i know thou dost believe thyself) 1.03. 88
this garden has a world of pleasures in't. 2.02.118
if ye fall in't, | think how you maim your honor 3.06.236
his show | has all the ornament of honor in't. 4.02. 93
best loves me | and has the truest title in't, 5.01.159
i had no end in't else; 5.03. 75
INTEGER 1 FR 0.0001 REL FR 1 V 0 P
"integer vitae, scelerisque purus, | non eget TIT 4.02. 20
INTEGRITAS 1 FR 0.0001 REL FR 0 V 1 P
tanta est erga te mentis integritas, regina H8 3.01. 40 P
/INTEGRITY 1 FR 0.0001 REL FR 1 V 0 P
/bids /thee, /with /most /divine /integrity, TRO 4.05.170
INTEGRITY 18 FR 0.0020 REL FR 17 V 1 P
feeling line | that may discover such integrity: TGV 3.02. 76
that neither my coat, integrity, nor persuasion MM 4.02.189 P
first, his integrity | stands without blemish; 5.01.107
to be | of heavenly oaths, vow'd with integrity. LLL 5.02.356
and my integrity ne'er knew the crafts | that AWW 4.02. 33
but we have been | deceiv'd in thy integrity, WT 1.02.240
mine integrity, | being counted falsehood, shall 3.02. 26
ours of true zeal and deep integrity; R2 5.03.108
men | of singular integrity and learning, | yea, H8 2.04. 59
i am sorry my integrity should breed | (and 3.01. 51
and my integrity to heaven, is all | i dare now 3.02.453
thy truth and thy integrity is rooted | in us, 5.01.114
ye, i see, | more out of malice than integrity, 5.02.180
convince me | that my integrity and truth to you TRO 3.02.165
state | of that integrity which should become't; COR 3.01.159
so i do affy | in thy uprightness and integrity, TIT 1.01. 48
child of integrity, hath from my soul | wip'd MAC 4.03.115
she bore in hand to love | with such integrity, CYM 5.05. 44
INTELLECT 4 FR 0.0004 REL FR 1 V 3 P
his intellect is not replenished; LLL 4.02. 26 P
will look again on the intellect of the letter, 4.02.133 P
it rejoiceth my intellect. 5.01. 60 P
hath bullingbrook depos'd | thine intellect? R2 5.01. 28
INTELLECTS 1 FR 0.0001 REL FR 1 V 0 P
and train our intellects to vain delight. LLL 1.01. 71
INTELLECTUAL 2 FR 0.0002 REL FR 1 V 1 P
indu'd with intellectual sense and souls, | of ERR 2.01. 22
for if their heads had any intellectual armor, H5 3.07.138 P
INTELLIGENCE 28 FR 0.0031 REL FR 17 V 11 P
gives intelligence of ford's approach; WIV 3.05. 84 P
basket too, howsoever he hath had intelligence. 4.02. 92 P
my intelligence is true, my jealousy is 4.02.148 P
and i can give you intelligence of an intended ADO 1.03. 44 P
and for this intelligence | if i have thanks, it MND 1.01.248
if with myself i hold intelligence, | or have AYL 1.03. 47
and deliver all the intelligence in his power AWW 3.06. 31 P
hath the count all this intelligence? 4.03. 60 P
him that in such intelligence hath seldom fail'd 4.05. 83 P
from whom i have this intelligence, that he is WT 4.02. 37 P
that's likewise part of my intelligence; 4.02. 45 P
o, where hath our intelligence been drunk? JN 4.02.116
receiv'd intelligence | that harry duke of R2 2.01.278
so that by this intelligence we learn | the 3.03. 1
sought to entrap me by intelligence, | rated 1H4 4.03. 98
borne | betwixt our armies true intelligence. 5.05. 10
advis'd by good intelligence | of this most H5 2.pr. 12
here | by false intelligence or wrong surmise R3 2.01. 55
us | whereof i shall not have intelligence. 3.02. 24
but | from sincere motions, by intelligence, H8 1.01.153
me any thing for the intelligence of this whore. TRO 5.02.192 P
you will be welcome with this intelligence, COR 4.03. 29 P
from whence | you owe this strange intelligence, MAC 1.03. 76
intelligence is given where you are hid; LR 2.01. 21
inclin'd to this intelligence, pronounce | the CYM 1.06.114
(i fast and pray'd for their intelligence) thus: 4.02.347
the intelligence of state came in the instant TNK 1.02.106
which nightly gulls him with intelligence, | as SON 86.10
INTELLIGENCER 2 FR 0.0002 REL FR 2 V 0 P
the very opener and intelligencer | between the 2H4 4.02. 20
richard yet lives, hell's black intelligencer, R3 4.04. 71
INTELLIGENCING 1 FR 0.0001 REL FR 1 V 0 P
a most intelligencing bawd! WT 2.03. 69
INTELLIGENT 4 FR 0.0004 REL FR 2 V 2 P
be intelligent to me, 'tis thereabouts: WT 1.02.378
and speculations | intelligent of our state. LR 3.01. 25
which approves him an intelligent party to the 3.05. 11 P
posts shall be swift and intelligent betwixt us. 3.07. 11 P
INTELLIGIS 1 FR 0.0001 REL FR 0 V 1 P
ne intelligis, domine? LLL 5.01. 25 P
INTELLIGO 1 FR 0.0001 REL FR 0 V 1 P
laus deo, /bone intelligo. LLL 5.01. 27 P
INTEMPERANCE 2 FR 0.0002 REL FR 2 V 0 P
the long-grown wounds of my intemperance. 1H4 3.02.156
boundless intemperance | in nature is a tyranny; MAC 4.03. 66
INTEMPERATE 2 FR 0.0002 REL FR 2 V 0 P
body | to his concupiscible intemperate lust, MM 5.01. 98
but you are more intemperate in your blood ADO 4.01. 59
INTEMP'RATE 1 FR 0.0001 REL FR 0 V 1 P
that intemp'rate surfeit of her eye hath TNK 4.03. 70 P
INTEND 54 FR 0.0061 REL FR 48 V 6 P
and by and by intend to chide myself | even for TGV 4.02.103
cell, | where i intend holy confession. 4.03. 44
she did intend confession | at patrick's cell 5.02. 41
do intend vat i speak? WIV 1.04. 46 P
if he should intend this voyage toward my wife, 2.01.181 P
me, intend a kind of zeal both to the prince and ADO 2.02. 35 P
nor shall not, if i do as i intend. LLL 5.02.429
how long within this wood intend you stay? MND 2.01.138
if thou dost intend | never so little show of 3.02.333
them all, | to-morrow i intend to hunt again. SHR in.1. 29
do you intend to stay with me to-night? in.1. 81
and amid this hurly i intend | that all is done 4.01.203
are they gone, and there they intend to sup. WT 5.02.103 P
well, i'll not say what i intend for thee. JN 3.03. 68
as i intend to thrive in this new world, R2 4.01. 78
whose temper i intend to stain | with the best 1H4 5.02. 93
the king hath note of all that they intend, | by H5 2.02. 6
the king from eltam i intend to send, | and sit 1H6 1.01.176
thy head, | for i intend to have it ere long. 1.03. 88
so help me god, as i intend it not! 3.01.141
he doth intend she shall be england's queen. 5.01. 45
say we intend to try his grace to-day, | if he 2H6 3.02. 16
that if your highness should intend to sleep, 3.02.255
call false caterpillars, and intend their death. 4.04. 37
doth york intend no harm to us | that thus he 5.01. 56
as i intend, clifford, to thrive to-day, | it 5.02. 17
intend here to besiege you in your castle. 3H6 1.02. 50

him, | for i intend but only to surprise him. 4.02. 25
art sworn as deeply to effect what we intend R3 3.01.158
yet witness what you hear we did intend. 3.05. 70
intend some fear, | be not you spoke with but by 3.07. 45
as i intend more good to you and yours | than 4.04.238
and do intend to make her queen of england. 4.04.264
as i intend to prosper and repent, | so thrive i 4.04.397
we bring | to make that only true we now intend, H8 pr 21
we'll not commend what we intend to sell. TRO 4.01. 79
had inkling this fortnight what we intend to do, COR 1.01. 58 P
stand gracious to the rites that we intend! TIT 1.01. 78
will we acquaint withal what we intend, | and 2.01.122
sons | presents that i intend to send them both. 4.01.116
to pry | in what i farther shall intend to do, ROM 5.03. 34
i know not, gentlemen, what you intend, | who JC 3.01.151
my lord, i did intend it. HAM 2.01. 5
and purpose not, since what i /well intend, LR 1.01.225
if thou didst intend | to make this creature 1.04.276
lord, | you know the goodness i intend upon you: 5.01. 7
do you intend it? OTH 4.01.116
/faith, i intend so. 4.01.165 P
and /mak'st me call what i intend to do | a 5.02. 64
how intend you, practic'd? ANT 2.02. 40
for we intend so to dispose you as | yourself 5.02.186
and to tharsus | intend my travel, where i'll PER 1.02.116
i abide) | intend a zealous pilgrimage to thee, SON 27. 6
as they did batt'ry to the spheres intend; LC 23
INTENDED 18 FR 0.0020 REL FR 14 V 4 P
to cross my friend in his intended drift, | than TGV 3.01. 18
her mother hath intended | (the better to WIV 4.06. 38
was complaint | intended 'gainst lord angelo, MM 5.01.154
give you intelligence of an intended marriage. ADO 1.03. 44 P
the very night before the intended wedding — 2.02. 45 P
so shall we stay, mocking intended game, | and LLL 5.02.155
play | intended for great theseus' nuptial day. MND 3.02. 12
though lately we intended | to keep in darkness TN 5.01.152
fear not, man, here's no harm intended to thee. WT 4.04.629 P
intended, or committed, was this fault? R2 5.03. 33
set forth, | or hitherwards intended speedily, 1H4 4.01. 92
that is intended in the general's name. 2H4 4.01.164
a motive | the sooner to effect what i intended. H5 2.02.157
rome, after the measure | as you intended well. COR 5.01. 47
to blow out the intended fire your city is ready 5.02. 45 P
which so took effect | as i intended, for it ROM 5.03.245
know'st thou any harm's intended towards him? JC 2.04. 31
there is no harm intended to your person, | nor 3.01. 90
INTENDETH 1 FR 0.0001 REL FR 1 V 0 P
of war | when he intendeth to become the field. JN 5.01. 55
INTENDING 3 FR 0.0003 REL FR 3 V 0 P
intending deep suspicion, ghastly looks | are at R3 3.05. 8
and so, intending other serious matters, | after TIM 2.02.210
bed, | intending weariness with heavy sprite; LUC 121
INTENDMENT 3 FR 0.0003 REL FR 1 V 2 P
either you might stay him from his intendment, AYL 1.01.133 P
but fear the main intendment of the scot, | who H5 1.02.144
nothing but what i protest intendment of doing. OTH 4.02.203 P
INTENDMENTS 1 FR 0.0001 REL FR 1 V 0 P
and now her sobs do her intendments break. VEN 222
INTENDS 18 FR 0.0020 REL FR 17 V 1 P
for thurio, he intends, shall wed his daughter; TGV 2.06. 39
this night intends to steal away your daughter; 3.01. 11
heaven, | intends you for his swift ambassador, MM 3.01. 57
and happy newness, that intends old right. JN 5.04. 61
any thing that intends to laughter more than i 2H4 1.02. 8 P
which mates him first that first intends deceit. 2H6 3.01.265
as surely as my soul intends to live | with that 3.02.153
then what intends these forces thou dost bring? 5.01. 60
but love to go | whither the queen intends. 3H6 2.05.139
i speak no more than what my soul intends, | and 3.02. 94
back her appeal | she intends unto his holiness. H8 2.04.236
you know an enemy intends you harm; TRO 2.02. 39
you see how he intends to use the people. COR 2.02.155
and | intends t' appear before the people, 5.06. 7
the history unspoke | that it intends to do? LR 1.01.237
which he intends to lear and to cordelia, | the 5.01. 66
caesar through syria | intends his journey, and ANT 5.02.201
no, to–morrow he intends | to hunt the boar with VEN 587
INTEND'ST 1 FR 0.0001 REL FR 1 V 0 P
or aught intend'st to lay unto my charge, | do 1H6 3.01. 4
INTENIBLE 1 FR 0.0001 REL FR 1 V 0 P
yet in this captious and intenible sieve | i AWW 1.03.202
INTENT 55 FR 0.0062 REL FR 51 V 4 P
accuse him in his intent towards our wives are a WIV 2.01.174 P
who knew of your intent and coming hither? MM 5.01.124
his act did not o'ertake his bad intent, | and 5.01.451
and must be buried but as an intent | that 5.01.452
but i hope you have no intent to turn husband, ADO 1.01.193 P
but in this changing, what is your intent? LLL 5.02.137
the effect of my intent is to cross theirs: 5.02.138
and mock for mock is only my intent. 5.02.140
and, hearing our intent, | came here in grace of MND 4.01.133
our intent | was to be gone from athens, where 4.01.151
as minding to content you, | our true intent is. 5.01.114
for the intent and purpose of the law | hath MV 4.01.247
why came i hither but to that intent? SHR 1.02.198
had you not lately an intent — speak truly — AWW 1.03.218
as haply shall become | the form of my intent. TN 1.02. 55
be every thing and their intent every where, for 2.04. 77 P
from all direction, purpose, course, intent — JN 2.01.580
your vild intent must needs seem horrible. 4.01. 95
fair | when the intent of bearing them is just. 1H4 5.02. 88
(though then, god knows, i had no such intent, 2H4 3.01. 72
their cold intent, tenure, and substance thus: 4.01. 9
he hath intent his wonted followers | shall all 5.05. 98
to–morrow shall you bear our full intent | back H5 2.04.114
conceit | to set a gloss upon his bold intent, 1H6 4.01.103
i have, my lord, and their intent is this: 5.01. 3
and, for a minister of my intent, | i have 2H6 3.01.355
loyalty, | free from a stubborn opposite intent, 3.02.251
norfolk, | and tell him privily of our intent. 3H6 1.02. 39
that she was coming with a full intent | to dash 2.01.117
belike his majesty hath some intent | that you R3 1.01. 49
and, if i fail not in my deep intent, | clarence 1.01.149
as for another secret close intent | by marrying 1.01.158
which since you come too late of our intent, 3.05. 69
achilles shall have word of this intent, | so TRO 1.03.306
here, sister, arm'd, and bloody in intent. 5.03. 8
may they perceive 's intent! COR 2.02.156
if you do hold the same intent wherein | you 5.06. 12
and now be it known to you my full intent. TIT 4.02.151
tell him of an intent | that's coming toward him TIM 5.01. 20
have no spur | to prick the sides of my intent, MAC 1.07. 26
for your intent | in going back to school in HAM 1.02.112
my stronger guilt defeats my strong intent, 3.03. 40
and 'tis our fast intent | to shake all cares LR 1.01. 38
derive from him better testimony of his intent, 1.02. 82 P
my good intent | may carry through itself to 1.04. 2
when i dissuaded him from his intent, | and 2.01. 64
yet to be known shortens my made intent. 4.07. 9
you lords and noble friends, know our intent. 5.03.297
general, be advis'd, | he comes to bad intent. OTH 1.02. 56
you may be pleas'd to catch at mine intent | by ANT 2.02. 41
bent with sin | and hid intent to murder him; PER 2.ch. 24
you thoughten | that i came with no ill intent, 4.06.109
and all amaz'd, brake off his late intent, | for VEN 469
with swift intent he goes | to quench the coal LUC 46
"if collatinus dream of my intent, | will he not 218
INTENTION 2 FR 0.0002 REL FR 1 V 1 P
o'er my exteriors with such a greedy intention, WIV 1.03. 66 P
thy intention stabs the centre. WT 1.02.138
/INTENTIVELY 1 FR 0.0001 REL FR 1 V 0 P
she had something heard, | but not /intentively. OTH 1.03.155
INTENTS 22 FR 0.0024 REL FR 21 V 1 P
are no subjects, | intents but merely thoughts. MM 5.01.454
when she's dispos'd, | told our intents before; LLL 5.02.467
humors | even to the opposed end of our intents; 5.02.758
unless you can find sport in their intents, MND 5.01. 79
but my intents are fix'd and will not leave me. AWW 1.01.229
her, | i could have well diverted her intents, 3.04. 21
in us, to be trumpeters of our unlawful intents? 4.03. 27 P
ere i can perfect mine intents, to kneel. 4.04. 4
only take the sacrament | to bury mine intents, R2 4.01.329
and i will stoop and humble my intents | to your 2H4 5.02.120
state, | and (god consigning to my good intents) 5.02.143
command, i mean, of virtuous chaste intents, 1H6 5.05. 20
the time and my intents are savage–wild, | more ROM 5.03. 37
his looks i fear, and his intents i doubt. 5.03. 44
death | if i did stay to look on his intents. 5.03.134
we can contradict | hath thwarted our intents. 5.03.154
be thy intents wicked, or charitable, | thou HAM 1.04. 42
monument, | of thy intents desires instruction, ANT 5.01. 54
if you apply yourself to our intents, | which 5.02.126
and to conquer | their most absurd intents. 5.02.226
for such provision | as our intents will need? PER 5.01.258
tan sacred beauty, blunt the sharp'st intents, SON 115. 7
INTER 5 FR 0.0005 REL FR 5 V 0 P
inter their bodies as become their births. R3 5.05. 15
a queen, and daughter to a king, inter me. H8 4.02.172
remaineth nought but to inter our brethren, TIT 1.01.146
suffer thy brother marcus to inter | his noble 1.01.375
but greenly | in hugger–mugger to inter him; HAM 4.05. 84
INTERCEPT 4 FR 0.0004 REL FR 4 V 0 P
where, if it please you, you may intercept him. TGV 3.01. 43
to intercept this inconvenience, | a piece of 1H6 1.04. 14
toward saint albons to intercept the queen, 3H6 2.01.114
for that they will not intercept my tale. TIT 3.01. 40
INTERCEPTED 4 FR 0.0004 REL FR 4 V 0 P
from whence he intercepted did return | to be 1H4 1.03.151
o, she that might have intercepted thee, | by R3 4.04.137
the goodness of your intercepted packets | you H8 3.02.286
and, being intercepted in your sport, | great TIT 2.03. 80
INTERCEPTER 1 FR 0.0001 REL FR 0 V 1 P
but thy intercepter, full of despite, bloody as TN 3.04.222 P
INTERCEPTION 1 FR 0.0001 REL FR 1 V 0 P
by interception which they dream not of. H5 2.02. 7
INTERCEPTS 1 FR 0.0001 REL FR 1 V 0 P
who intercepts me in my expedition? R3 4.04.136
INTERCESSION 7 FR 0.0008 REL FR 6 V 1 P
besides, her intercession chaf'd him so, | when TGV 3.01.235
means | us'd intercession to obtain a league, 1H6 5.04.148
that through our intercession this revokement H8 1.02.106
with the palsied intercession of such a decay'd COR 5.02. 44 P
hath an aspect of intercession which | great 5.03. 32
for lo | my intercession likewise steads my foe. ROM 2.03. 54
our intercession then | must be to him that TNK 5.01. 45
INTERCESSORS 1 FR 0.0001 REL FR 1 V 0 P
and sigh, and yield | to christian intercessors. MV 3.03. 16
INTERCHAINED 1 FR 0.0001 REL FR 1 V 0 P
two bosoms interchained with an oath, | so then MND 2.02. 49
INTERCHANG'D 1 FR 0.0001 REL FR 1 V 0 P
and interchang'd love–tokens with my child; MND 1.01. 29
INTERCHANGE 7 FR 0.0008 REL FR 6 V 1 P
royally attorney'd with interchange of gifts, WT 1.01. 28 P
and says that once more i shall interchange | my 3H6 4.07. 3
this interchange of love, i here protest, | upon R3 2.01. 26
love | and ample interchange of sweet discourse 5.03. 99
furnish you fairly for this interchange; TRO 3.03. 33
that oft they interchange each other's seat. LUC 70
when i have seen such interchange of state, | or SON 64. 9
INTERCHANGEABLY 4 FR 0.0004 REL FR 3 V 1 P
and interchangeably hurl down my gage | upon R2 1.01.146
and interchangeably set down their hands, | to 5.02. 98
which being sealed interchangeably | (a business 1H4 3.01. 80
witness whereof the parties interchangeably" — TRO 3.02. 58 P
INTERCHANGEMENT 1 FR 0.0001 REL FR 1 V 0 P
strength'ned by interchangement of your rings, TN 5.01.159
INTERCHANGING 2 FR 0.0002 REL FR 2 V 0 P
and interchanging blows i quickly shed | some of 1H6 4.06. 19
while we were interchanging thrusts and blows, ROM 1.01.113
INTERDICT 1 FR 0.0001 REL FR 1 V 0 P
from this session interdict | every fowl of PHT 9
INTERDICTION 1 FR 0.0001 REL FR 1 V 0 P
throne | by his own interdiction stands accus'd, MAC 4.03.107
INTERESS'D 1 FR 0.0001 REL FR 1 V 0 P
and milk of burgundy | strive to be interess'd, LR 1.01. 85
INTEREST 31 FR 0.0035 REL FR 29 V 2 P
he should give her interest, and she gives it TGV 2.01.102 P
mourn, | if ever love had interest in his liver, ADO 4.01.231
my well–won thrift, | which he calls interest. MV 1.03. 51
and what of him? did he take interest? 1.03. 75
no, not take interest, not, as you would say, 1.03. 76
was this inserted to make interest good? 1.03. 94
he hath no interest in me in the world. AYL 5.01. 8 P
the unowed interest of proud swelling state. JN 4.03.147
acquainted me with interest to this land, | yea, 5.02. 89
war | plead for our interest and our being here. 5.02.165
he hath more worthy interest to the state | than 1H4 3.02. 98
you shall have your desires with interest | and 4.03. 49
you claim no interest | in any of our towns of 1H6 5.04.167
that all your interest in those territories | is 2H6 3.01. 84
so much interest have /i in thy sorrow | as i R3 2.02. 47
advantaging their love with interest | of ten 4.04.323
where life hath no more interest but to breathe! TIT 3.01.249
i have an interest in your heart's proceeding; ROM 3.01.188
he is so kind that he now | pays interest for't; TIM 1.02.200
and let out | their coin upon large interest — 3.05.107
of cawdor shall deceive | our bosom interest. MAC 1.02. 64
interest of territory, cares of state), | which LR 1.01. 50
/sister, | i bar it in the interest of my wife; 5.03. 85
should not betray | mine interest and his honor; CYM 1.03. 30
since | my lord hath interest in them, i will 1.06.195
what's thy interest | in this sad wrack? 4.02.365
nor think he dies with interest in this lady. TNK 3.06.298
in the interest of thy bed | a stranger came, LUC 1619
"do not take away | my sorrow's interest, let no 1797
stol'n from mine eye | as interest of the dead, SON 31. 7
away, | my life hath in this line some interest, 74. 3
INTER'GATORIES *(also inter'gatory, interrogatories)*
INTER'GATORIES 2 FR 0.0002 REL FR 1 V 1 P
in, | and charge us there upon inter'gatories, MV 5.01.298
answer to the particular of the inter'gatories. AWW 4.03.183 P
INTER'GATORY 1 FR 0.0001 REL FR 1 V 0 P
the first inter'gatory | that my nerissa shall MV 5.01.300
INTERIM 9 FR 0.0010 REL FR 7 V 2 P
i will in the interim undertake one of hercules' ADO 2.01.364 P
for interim to our studies shall relate, | in LLL 1.01.171
if the interim be but a se'nnight, time's pace AYL 3.02.315 P
and myself have play'd | the interim, by H5 5.pr. 43
what shall defend the interim? TIM 2.02.149
all the interim is | like a phantasma or a JC 2.01. 64
the interim having weigh'd it, let us speak MAC 1.03.154
and i a heavy interim shall support | by his OTH 1.03.258
bound, | the interim, pray you, all confound. PER 5.02. 14
/INTERIM'S 1 FR 0.0001 REL FR 1 V 0 P
/the /interim's /mine, | /and /a /man's /life's HAM 5.02. 73
INTERIMS 1 FR 0.0001 REL FR 1 V 0 P
by interims and conveying gusts we have heard COR 1.06. 5
INTERIOR 3 FR 0.0003 REL FR 2 V 1 P
which pries not to th' interior, but, like the MV 2.09. 28
aiming, belike, at your interior hatred, | that R3 1.03. 65
and make but an interior survey of your good COR 2.01. 40 P
INTERJECTIONS 1 FR 0.0001 REL FR 0 V 1 P
interjections? ADO 4.01. 21 P
INTERJOIN 1 FR 0.0001 REL FR 1 V 0 P
grow dear friends | and interjoin their issues. COR 4.04. 22
INTERLACES 1 FR 0.0001 REL FR 1 V 0 P
and here and there the painter interlaces | pale LUC 1390
INTERLUDE *(see enterlude)*
INTERMINGLE 3 FR 0.0003 REL FR 1 V 2 P
admit any good part to intermingle with them. ADO 5.02. 64 P
i'll intermingle every thing he does | with OTH 3.03. 25
and still among intermingle your petition of TNK 4.03. 88 P
INTERMISSION 4 FR 0.0004 REL FR 4 V 0 P
for intermission | no more pertains to me, my MV 3.02.199
and i did laugh sans intermission | an hour by AYL 2.07. 32
gentle heavens, | cut short all intermission. MAC 4.03.232
deliver'd letters, spite of intermission, LR 2.04. 33
INTERMISSIVE 1 FR 0.0001 REL FR 1 V 0 P
of eyes, | to weep their intermissive miseries. 1H6 1.01. 88
INTERMIT 1 FR 0.0001 REL FR 1 V 0 P
pray to the gods to intermit the plague | that JC 1.01. 54
INTERMIX'D 2 FR 0.0002 REL FR 2 V 0 P
are intermix'd | with scruples and do set the R2 5.05. 12
but best is best, if never intermix'd"? SON 101. 8
INTERPOSE 2 FR 0.0002 REL FR 2 V 0 P
please you to interpose, fair madam, kneel, WT 5.03.119
what watchful cares do interpose themselves JC 2.01. 98
INTERPOSER 1 FR 0.0001 REL FR 1 V 0 P
stay, | nor rest be interposer 'twixt us twain. MV 3.02.327
/INTERPRET 1 FR 0.0001 REL FR 1 V 0 P
/i /can /interpret /all /her /martyr'd /signs: TIT 3.02. 36
INTERPRET 6 FR 0.0006 REL FR 4 V 2 P
now will he interpret to her. TGV 2.01. 95 P
dumbness of the gesture | one might interpret. TIM 1.01. 34
and yet your beards forbid me to interpret MAC 1.03. 46
your thoughts, | which can interpret farther; 3.06. 2
i could interpret between you and your love, if HAM 3.02.246 P
if it be true that i interpret false, | then PER 1.01.124
INTERPRETATION 5 FR 0.0005 REL FR 4 V 1 P
if your lass | interpretation should abuse, and WT 4.04.353
interpretation will misquote our looks, | and we 1H4 5.02. 13
a crown's worth of good interpretation. 2H4 2.02. 92 P
lie in th' interpretation of the time, | and COR 4.07. 50
which by th' interpretation of full time | may 5.03. 69
INTERPRETED 2 FR 0.0002 REL FR 2 V 0 P
this dream is all amiss interpreted, | it was a JC 2.02. 83
thus | would be interpreted a thing perplex'd CYM 3.04. 7
INTERPRETER 8 FR 0.0009 REL FR 3 V 5 P
concerns | unless it have a false interpreter. TGV 1.02. 75
that, | if thou wert near a lewd interpreter! MV 3.04. 80
us, whom we must produce for an interpreter. AWW 4.01. 6 P
good captain, let me be th' interpreter. 4.01. 7 P
as for you, interpreter, you must seem very 4.01. 21 P
our interpreter does it well. 4.03.209 P
madam my interpreter, what says she? H5 5.02.260 P
an ag'd interpreter, though young in days. TIM 5.03. 8
INTERPRETERS 2 FR 0.0002 REL FR 2 V 0 P
kind, are as interpreters | of my behind–hand WT 5.01.150
by sick interpreters (once weak ones) is | not H8 1.02. 82
INTERPRETS 3 FR 0.0003 REL FR 3 V 0 P
impression | interprets for my poor ignorance. TIM 5.04. 69
o, my fear interprets. what, is he dead? OTH 5.02. 73
for then the eye interprets to the ear | the LUC 1325
INTERR'D 6 FR 0.0006 REL FR 6 V 0 P
at worcester must his body be interr'd, | for so JN 5.07. 99
a tomb, wherein his corpse shall be interr'd; 1H6 2.02. 13
(after i have solemnly interr'd | at chertsey R3 1.02.213
death, lie thou there, by a dead man interr'd. ROM 5.03. 87
wherein we saw thee quietly interr'd, | hath HAM 1.04. 49
us, and he shall be interr'd | as soldiers can. CYM 4.02.401
INTERRED 3 FR 0.0003 REL FR 3 V 0 P
i richard's body have interred new, | and on it H5 4.01.295
load, | taken from paul's to be interred there; R3 1.02. 30
the good is oft interred with their bones; JC 3.02. 76

INTERROGATORIES *(also inter'gatories, etc.)*
INTERROGATORIES 2 FR 0.0002 REL FR 2 V 0 P
what earthy name to interrogatories | can taste JN 3.01.147
nor place | will serve our long interrogatories. CYM 5.05.392
INTERRUPT 5 FR 0.0005 REL FR 4 V 1 P
interrupt the monster one word further, and, by TMP 3.02. 68 P
when lo, to interrupt my purpos'd rest, | toward LLL 5.02. 91
here is ulysses, | i'll interrupt his reading. TRO 3.03. 93
aloof, | and do not interrupt me in my course. ROM 5.03. 27
bottom of your story, | and never interrupt you. PER 5.01.165
INTERRUPTED 4 FR 0.0004 REL FR 4 V 0 P
still, | and happily we might be interrupted. SHR 4.04. 54
up | her presence would have interrupted much. JN 2.01.542
whose rage doth rend | like interrupted waters, COR 3.01.248
"her house is sack'd, her quiet interrupted, LUC 1170
INTERRUPTER 1 FR 0.0001 REL FR 1 V 0 P
interrupter of the good | that noble–minded TIT 1.01.208
INTERRUPTEST 1 FR 0.0001 REL FR 1 V 0 P
but that thou interruptest our merriment. LLL 5.02.717
INTERRUPTION 3 FR 0.0003 REL FR 3 V 0 P
the interruption of their churlish drums | cuts JN 2.01. 76
o'erbearing interruption, spite of france? 3.04. 9
and pardon us the interruption | of thy devotion R3 3.07.102
INTERRUPTS 1 FR 0.0001 REL FR 1 V 0 P
for he that interrupts him shall not live. 3H6 1.01.123
INTERTANGLED 1 FR 0.0001 REL FR 1 V 0 P
to water | their intertangled roots of love, but TNK 1.03. 59
INTERTISSUED 1 FR 0.0001 REL FR 1 V 0 P
the intertissued robe of gold and pearl, | the H5 4.01.262
INTERVALLUMS 1 FR 0.0001 REL FR 0 V 1 P
and 'a shall laugh without intervallums. 2H4 5.01. 81 P
INTERVIEW 5 FR 0.0005 REL FR 5 V 0 P
at which interview | all liberal reason i will LLL 2.01.166
majesties | unto this bar and royal interview, H5 5.02. 27
th' interview | that swallowed so much treasure, H8 1.01.165
his fears were that the interview betwixt 1.01.180
me, | and signify this loving interview | to the TRO 4.05.155
/INTESTATE 1 FR 0.0001 REL FR 1 V 0 P
woes, | aery succeeders of /intestate joys, R3 4.04.128
INTESTINE 2 FR 0.0002 REL FR 2 V 0 P
for since the mortal and intestine jars | 'twixt ERR 1.01. 11
did lately meet in the intestine shock | and 1H4 1.01. 12
INTIMATE 3 FR 0.0003 REL FR 2 V 1 P
your father here doth intimate | the payment of LLL 2.01.128
thou this to hazard needs must intimate | skill AWW 2.01.183
spirit of humors intimate reading aloud to him! TN 2.05. 84 P
INTIMATION 1 FR 0.0001 REL FR 0 V 1 P
most barbarous intimation! LLL 4.02. 13 P
INTITLED *(also entitled)*
INTITLED 1 FR 0.0001 REL FR 1 V 0 P
part, | neither intitled in the other's heart. LLL 5.02.812
INTITULED *(also entit'ling)*
INTITULED 2 FR 0.0002 REL FR 1 V 1 P
a companion of the king's, who is intituled, LLL 5.01. 7 P
in that white intituled | from venus' doves, LUC 57
/INTO 6 FR 0.0006 REL FR 5 V 1 P
he's gone /into smithfield to buy your worship a 2H4 1.02. 50 P
/brought /ourselves /into /a /burning /fever, 4.01. 56
/eyes /let /fall | /may /run /into /that /sink, TIT 3.02. 19
/did /put /me | /into /a /tow'ring /passion. HAM 5.02. 80
/a /power | /into /this /scattered /kingdom, LR 3.01. 31
may help these lovers | /into /your /favor. OTH 1.03.201
INTO 647 FR 0.0731 REL FR 446 V 201 P
like one | who having into truth, by telling of TMP 1.02.100
to swim, to dive into the fire, to ride | on the 1.02.191
who with age and envy | was grown into a hoop? 1.02.259
her most unmitigable rage, | into a cloven pine; 1.02.277
wast thou | deservedly confin'd into this rock, 1.02.361
a sea–change | into something rich and strange. 1.02.402
you cram these words into mine ears against 2.01.107
with cloven tongues | do hiss me into madness. 2.02. 14
th' harmony of their tongues hath into bondage 3.01. 41
where thou mayst knock a nail into his head. 3.02. 61
trinculo, run into no further danger. 3.02. 68 P
shall never melt | mine honor into lust, to take 4.01. 28
and | are melted into air, into thin air, | and, 4.01.150
and | are melted into air, into thin air, | and, 4.01.150
if you be pleas'd, retire into my cell, | and 4.01.161
or else return no more into my sight. TGV 1.02. 47
rock, | and throw it thence into the raging sea. 1.02.119
slave, that will thrust himself into secrets. 3.01.384 P
let us into the city presently | to sort some 3.02. 90
and i came no sooner into the dining–chamber but 4.04. 8 P
he thrusts me himself into the company of three 4.04. 17 P
again, | or ne'er return again into my sight. 4.04. 60
then rend thy faith | into a thousand oaths; 5.04. 48
and all those oaths | descended into perjury, to 5.04. 49
her will, out of honesty into english. WIV 1.03. 50 P
go into this closet. 1.04. 38 P
for he cares not what he puts into the press, 2.01. 78 P
you have brought her into such a canaries as 2.02. 60 P
turn another into the register of your own, that 2.02.187 P
threat'ned to put me into everlasting liberty if 3.03. 31 P
so throwing him into the water will do him a 3.03.183 P
and excuse his throwing into the water, and give 3.03.195 P
rogues slighted me into the river with as little 3.05. 9 P
i was thrown into the ford; 3.05. 36 P
they convey'd me into a buck–basket. 3.05. 86 P
like a dutch dish) to be thrown into the thames, 3.05.120 P
master /brook, i will be thrown into etna, as i 3.05.126 P
be thrown into etna, as i have been into thames, 3.05.127 P
he cannot creep into a halfpenny purse, nor into 3.05.146 P
into a halfpenny purse, nor into a pepper–box. 3.05.147 P
mad about his throwing into the water. 4.01. 5 P
step into th' chamber, sir john. 4.02. 11 P
shall i put him into the basket again? 4.02. 47 P
what shall i do? i'll creep up into the chimney. 4.02. 55 P
creep into the kill–hole. 4.02. 58 P
my husband will come into the chamber. 4.02.167 P
woman, a fat woman, gone up into his chamber. 4.05. 12 P
i was beaten myself into all the colors of the 4.05.115 P
come up into my chamber. 4.05.127 P
and i will deliver his wife into your hand. 5.01. 29 P
go before into the park; 5.03. 4 P
follow me into the pit, and when i give the 5.04. 2 P
grossness of the foppery into a receiv'd belief, 5.05.124 P
turn'd my daughter into /green; 5.05.201 P
me | to look into the bottom of my place. MM 1.01. 78
sense your brother's life | falls into forfeit; 1.04. 66
and i beseech you, look into master froth here, 2.01.122 P
part, i never come into any room in a tap–house, 2.01.209 P
death, perchance entering into some monastery, 4.02.201 P
put not yourself into amazement how these things 4.02.204 P
i would desire you to clap into your prayers; 4.03. 41 P
he rush'd into my house, and took perforce | my ERR 4.03. 94
passion | ne'er brake into extremity of rage. 5.01. 48
who put unluckily into this bay | against the 5.01.125
then they fled | into this abbey, whither we 5.01.155
and then you fled into this abbey here, | from 5.01.264
the pains | to go with us into the abbey here, 5.01.395
we came into the world like brother and brother; 5.01.425
did he break out into tears? ADO 1.01. 24 P
yea, and a case to put it into. 1.01.182 P
and thou wilt needs thrust thy neck into a yoke, 1.01.201 P
and he hath ta'en you newly into his grace, 1.03. 22 P
of the berrord, and lead his apes into hell. 2.01. 41 P
well then, go you into hell. 2.01. 42 P
his bad legs falls into the cinquepace faster 2.01. 78 P
faster and faster, till he sink into his grave. 2.01. 79 P
or not laugh'd at, strikes him into melancholy, 2.01.148 P
against whose charms faith melteth into blood. 2.01.180
now will he creep into sedges. 2.01.203 P
of beatrice that puts the world into her person, 2.01.208 P
and the lady beatrice into a mountain of 2.01.366 P
all your sounds of woe | into hey nonny nonny. 2.03. 69
she tore the letter into a thousand halfpence; 2.03.140 P
he ought to enter into a quarrel with fear and 2.03.194 P
us, | and bid her steal into the pleached bower, 3.01. 7
if i should speak, | she would mock me into air; 3.01. 75
which is now crept into a lute–string and now 3.02. 60 P
out of thy tale into telling me of the fashion? 3.03.142 P
clap 's into "light a' love"; 3.04. 44 P
to turn all beauty into thoughts of harm, | and 4.01.107
she is fall'n | into a pit of ink, that the wide 4.01.140
blushing apparitions | to start into her face, a 4.01.160
sweetly creep | into his study of imagination, 4.01.225
life, | into the eye and prospect of his soul, 4.01.229
but manhood is melted into cur'sies, valor into 4.01.319 P
is melted into cur'sies, valor into compliment, 4.01.319 P
and men are only turn'd into tongue, and trim 4.01.320 P
wilt be condemn'd into everlasting redemption 4.02. 56 P
which falls into mine ears as profitless | as 5.01. 4
how you were brought into the orchard and saw me 5.01.237 P
all, | withdraw into a chamber by yourselves, 5.04. 11
and taken following her into the park, which, LLL 1.01.208 P
deliver this paper into the royal hand of the 4.02.141 P
warily | i stole into a neighbor thicket by, 5.02. 94
heavenly eyes, that look into these faults, 5.02.769
his nail | and tom bears logs into the hall 5.02.914
creep into acorn–cups and hide them there. MND 2.01. 31
and "tailor" cries, and falls into a cough; 2.01. 54
into the hands of one that loves you not; 2.01.216
that is, to bring the moonlight into a chamber; 3.01. 48 P
have spoken your speech, enter into that brake; 3.01. 75 P
then crush this herb into lysander's eye; 3.02.366
turns into yellow gold his salt green streams. 3.02.393
like far–off mountains turned into clouds. 4.01.188
should as lion come in strife | into this place, 5.01.226
the man should be put into the lanthorn. 5.01.247 P
and creep into the jaundies | by being peevish? MV 1.01. 85
and you will come into the court and swear that 1.02. 70 P
prophet the nazarite conjur'd the devil into. 1.03. 35 P
nor thrust your head into the public street | to 2.05. 32
that creep into the dreaming bridegroom's ear, 3.02. 52
i commit into your hands | the husbandry and 3.04. 24
see thou render this | into my /cousin's hands, 3.04. 50
turn two mincing steps | into a manly stride; 3.04. 68
your father, i fall into charybdis, your mother. 3.05. 17 P
launcelot, if you thus get my wife into corners! 3.05. 30 P
grace of wit will shortly turn into silence, and 3.05. 44 P
go one, and call the jew into the court. 4.01. 14
infuse themselves | into the trunks of men. 4.01.133
by the same example | will rush into the state. 4.01.222
hand, | and bring your music forth into the air. 5.01. 53
doth an inland brook | into the main of waters. 5.01. 97
have put themselves into voluntary exile with AYL 1.01.101 P
brook such disgrace well as he shall run into, 1.01.134 P
may she not by fortune fall into the fire? 1.02. 44 P
thus must i from the smoke into the smother, 1.02.287
you should fall into so strong a liking with old 1.03. 27 P
of fortune | into so quiet and so sweet a style. 2.01. 20
o yes, into a thousand similes. 2.01. 45
first, for his weeping into the needless stream: 2.01. 46
into a thousand that i have forgotten. 2.04. 32
folly | that ever love did make thee run into, 2.04. 35
we that are true lovers run into strange capers; 2.04. 54 P
a greek invocation, to call fools into a circle. 2.05. 59 P
i think he be transform'd into a beast, | for i 2.07. 1
wouldst thou disgorge into the general world. 2.07. 69
shifts | into the lean and slipper'd pantaloon, 2.07.158
worth seizure do we seize into our hands, | till 3.01. 10
slut were to put good meat into an unclean dish. 3.03. 36 P
that will divide a minute into a thousand parts, 4.01. 45 P
a fool, | and turn'd into the extremity of love. 4.03. 23
indented glides did slip away | into a bush, 4.03.113
as how i came into that desert place — | /in 4.03.141
open his lips when he put it into his mouth, 5.01. 34 P
being pour'd out of a cup into a glass, by 5.01. 42 P
make thee away, translate thy life into death, 5.01. 53 P
thy life into death, thy liberty into bondage. 5.01. 53 P
a thing it is to look into happiness through 5.02. 44 P
i know into what straits of fortune she is 5.02. 64 P
dignity, | and fall into our rustic revelry. 5.04.177
and thrown into neglect the pompous court? 5.04.182
you break into some merry passion | and so SHR in.1. 97
and with declining head into his bosom, | bid in.1. 119
which otherwise would grow into extremes. in.1. 138
i would be loath to fall into my dreams again. in.2. 126 P
your mouth, | tranio is chang'd into lucentio. 1.01.237
and i have thrust myself into this maze, 1.02. 55
but i have cause to pry into this pedant. 3.01. 87
that by degrees we mean to look into, | and 3.02.143
out of their saddles into the dirt, and thereby 4.01. 57 P
cambio is chang'd into lucentio. 5.01.123
he did look far | into the service of the time, AWW 1.02. 27
home | and pray god's blessing into thy attempt. 1.03.254
that's able to breathe life into a stone, 2.01. 73
ensconcing ourselves into seeming knowledge, 2.03. 4 P
ever whilst i live, | into your guiding power. 2.03.104
ever | into the staggers and the careless lapse 2.03.163
have deserv'd to run into my lord's displeasure. 2.05. 34 P
and all, like him that leapt into the custard; 2.05. 37 P
day, | great mars, i put myself into thy file; 3.03. 9
but that he is carried into the leaguer of the 3.06. 26 P
of honor again into his native quarter, be 3.06. 66 P
put myself into my mortal preparation; 3.06. 76 P
he will steal himself into a man's favor and for 3.06. 91 P
i must put you into a butter–woman's mouth and 4.01. 41 P
mule, if you prattle me into these perils. 4.01. 43 P
reading it he chang'd almost into another man. 4.03. 5 P
he travel higher, or return again into france? 4.03. 42 P
boy the count, have i run into this danger. 4.03.301 P
of power you have | to come into his presence. 5.01. 21
that has fall'n into the unclean fishpond of her 5.02. 20 P
and mak'st /conjectural fears to come into me, 5.03.114
but falls into abatement and low price | even in TN 1.01. 13
that instant was i turn'd into a hart, | and my 1.01. 20
and't be thy will, put me into good fooling! 1.05. 32 P
should put your lord into a desperate assurance 2.02. 8 P
if i do not gull him into an ayword, and make 2.03.135 P
get ye all three into the box–tree; 2.05. 15 P
"if this fall into thy hand, revolve. 2.05.143 P
put thyself into the trick of singularity. 2.05.151 P
it cannot but turn him into a notable contempt. 2.05.203 P
you should have bang'd the youth into dumbness. 3.02. 23 P
you are now sail'd into the north of my lady's 3.02. 26 P
and will laugh yourselves into stitches, follow 3.02. 69 P
does smile his face into more lines than is in 3.02. 79 P
put thyself into the trick of singularity"; 3.04. 71 P
it) into a most hideous opinion of his rage, 3.04.193 P
i will return again into the house and desire 3.04.241 P
me and with this holy man | into the chantry by; 4.03. 24
love) | into the danger of this adverse town, 5.01. 84
though you have put me into darkness, and given 5.01.304 P
greatest promise that ever came into my note. WT 1.01. 36 P
she is spread of late | into a goodly bulk. 2.01. 20
and so, with shrieks, | she melted into air. 3.03. 37
froth, as you'd thrust a cork into a hogshead. 3.03. 94 P
neighbors, is grown into an unspeakable estate. 4.02. 40 P
that's the rogue that put me into this apparel. 4.03.104 P
mischief and break a foul gap into the matter, 4.04.197 P
a woman and was turn'd into a cold fish for she 4.04.279 P
you must retire yourself | into some covert. 4.04.650
to offer to have his daughter come into grace! 4.04.778 P
draw our throne into a sheep–cote! 4.04.779 P
eternity and could put breath into his work, 5.02. 98 P
and put the same into young arthur's hand, | thy JN 1.01. 14
he came into the world | full fourteen weeks 1.01.112
shall draw this brief into as huge a volume. 2.01.103
to look into the blots and stains of right. 2.01.114
will send destruction | into this city's bosom. 2.01.410
mouth | sound on into the drowsy race of night; 3.03. 39
day, | i would into thy bosom pour my thoughts. 3.03. 53
and bloody england into england gone, 3.04. 8
to break into this dangerous argument: 4.02. 54
go | and thrust thyself into their companies; 4.02.167
shame, | this murther had not come into my mind; 4.02.223
thus have i yielded up into your hand | the 5.01. 1
they found him dead and cast into the streets, 5.01. 39
hand as deep | into the purse of rich prosperity 5.02. 61
yea, thrust this enterprise into my heart, | and 5.02. 90
their thimbles into armed gauntlets change, 5.02.156
belief | that, being brought into the open air, 5.07. 7
let him be brought into the orchard here. 5.07. 10
put into his hands | that knows no touch to tune R2 1.03.164
how he did seem to dive into their hearts | with 1.04. 25
that is not quickly buzz'd into his ears? 2.01. 26
seek you to seize and gripe into your hands 2.01.189
you will, we seize into our hands | his plate, 2.01.209
and driven into despair an enemy's hope, | who 2.02. 47
affairs | thus disorderly thrust into my hands, 2.02.110
the breath of parley | into his ruin'd ears, and 3.03. 34
let's step into the shadow of these trees. 3.04. 25
gathering head | shall break into corruption. 5.01. 59
off, | of our two cousins coming into london. 5.02. 3
nothing but some band that he is ent'red into 5.02. 65
into the good thoughts of the world again; 1H4 1.03.182
moon, | or dive into the bottom of the deep, 1.03.203
fool | art thou to break into this woman's mood, 1.03.237
shall secretly into the bosom creep | of that 1.03.266
(if matters should be look'd into) for their own 2.01. 72 P
bid butler lead him forth into the park. 2.03. 72
of sugar, clapp'd even now into my hand by an 2.04. 23 P
look down into the pomgarnet, ralph. 2.04. 37 P
waist, i could have crept into any alderman's 2.04.331 P
divided it | into three limits very equally: 3.01. 72
and vaulted with such ease into his seat | as if 4.01.107
and withal to pry | into his title, the which we 4.03.104
to gripe the general sway into your hand, 5.01. 57
his lordship is walk'd forth into the orchard. 2H4 1.01. 4
if the prince put thee into my service for any 1.02. 13 P
his highness is fall'n into this same whoreson 1.02.108 P
i think you are fall'n into the disease, for you 1.02.118 P
death, | and, winking, leapt into destruction. 1.03. 33
put all my substance into that fat belly of his, 2.01. 75 P
melt itself | into the sea, and other times to 3.01. 49
gathering head, | shall break into corruption": 3.01. 77
put me a caliver into wart's hand, bardolph. 3.02.270 P
thrust him and all his apparel into an eel–skin. 3.02.326 P
into the harsh and boist'rous tongue of war? 4.01. 49
fish–meals, that they fall into a kind of male 4.03. 92 P
it ascends me into the brain, dries me there all 4.03. 97 P
up, and bear me hence | into some other chamber. 4.04.132
let us withdraw into the other room. 4.05. 18
the world's whole strength | into one giant arm, 4.05. 45
how quickly nature falls into revolt | when gold 4.05. 65
the achievement goes | with me into the earth. 4.05.190
if i were saw'd into quantities, i should make 5.01. 62 P
them, is turn'd into a justice–like servingman. 5.01. 68 P
those tears | by number into hours of happiness. 5.02. 61
his greatness so | into the hands of justice." 5.02.112
for which i do commit into your hand | th' 5.02.113
you, | my father is gone wild into his grave; 5.02.123
into a thousand parts divide one man, | and make H5 pr 24

of many years | into an hour–glass: pr 31
flag, | look back into your mighty ancestors; 1.02.102
never went with his forces into france | but 1.02.147
came pouring like the tide into a breach, | with 1.02.149
put into parts, doth keep in one consent, 1.02.181
divide your happy england into four, | whereof 1.02.214
whereof take you one quarter into france, | and 1.02.215
your highness, lately sending into france, | did 1.02.246
you cannot revel into dukedoms there. 1.02.253
shall strike his father's crown into the hazard. 1.02.263
for your own reasons turn into your bosoms, | as 2.02. 82
that (almost) mightst have coin'd me into gold, 2.02. 98
and his whole kingdom into desolation. 2.02.173
us deliver | our puissance into the hand of god, 2.02.190
i put my hand into the bed and felt them, and 2.03. 23 P
take from another's pocket to put into mine; 3.02. 50 P
if your pure maidens fall into the hand | of hot 3.03. 20
spirt up so suddenly into the clouds | and 3.05. 8
and in a captive chariot into roan | bring him 3.05. 54
he'll drop his heart into the sink of fear, 3.05. 59
himself at his return into london under the form 3.06. 69 P
turn the sands into eloquent tongues, and my 3.07. 34 P
so, and ride not warily, fall into foul bogs. 3.07. 57 P
that run winking into the mouth of a russian 3.07.143 P
and crowns for convoy put into his purse. 4.03. 37
break out into a second course of mischief, 4.03.106
fly — | and time hath worn us into slovenry. 4.03.114
happy that he hath fall'n into the hands of one 4.04. 61 P
and all my mother came into mine eyes | and gave 4.06. 31
i will give treason his payment into plows, i 4.08. 14 P
shall change all griefs and quarrels into love. 5.02. 20
which to reduce into our former favor | you are 5.02. 63
or by vauting into my saddle with my armor on my 5.02.137 P
be it spoken, i should quickly leap into a wife. 5.02.139 P
that can rhyme themselves into ladies' favors, 5.02.157 P
and at night, when you come into your closet, 5.02.198 P
the cities turn'd into a maid; 5.02.321 P
and rush'd into the bowels of the battle. 1H6 1.01.129
thrust talbot with a spear into the back, | whom 1.01.138
days, | since i have entered into these wars. 1.02.132
if i now had him brought into my power. 1.04. 37
convey me salisbury into his tent, | and then 1.04.110
it will not be, retire into your trenches. 1.05. 33
pucelle is ent'red into orleance | in spite of 1.05. 36
i'll turn my part thereof into thy throat. 2.04. 79
love, | and will at last break out into a flame: 3.01.190
crossing the sea from england into france, 4.01. 89
into the clust'ring battle of the french; 4.07. 13
o, were mine eyeballs into bullets turn'd, 4.07. 79
that divided was | into two parties, is now 5.02. 12
and let her head fall into england's lap. 5.03. 26
welcome, brave earl, into our territories! 5.03.146
asleep, | to pry into the secrets of the state, 2H6 1.01.250
till france be won into the dolphin's hands. 1.03.170
again, | to look into this business thoroughly, 2.01.198
well hath your highness seen into this duke; 3.01. 42
thy mother took into her blameful bed | some 3.02.212
here could i breathe my soul into the air, | as 3.02.391
soul, | or i should breathe it so into thy body, 3.02.398
lock'd into the woefull'st cask | that ever did 3.02.409
day | is crept into the bosom of the sea; 4.01. 2
beggary | is crept into the palace of our king, 4.01.102
and then break into his son–in–law's house, sir 4.07.110 P
throw them into thames! 4.08. 2 P
on a brick wall have i climb'd into this garden, 4.10. 7 P
is't not enough to break into my garden, | and 4.10. 33
we twain will go into his highness' tent. 5.01. 55
may pass into the presence of a king, | lo, i 5.01. 65
into as many gobbets will i cut it | as wild 5.02. 58
and creep into it far before thy time? 3H6 1.01.237
hath made her break out into terms of rage! 1.01.265
the air hath got into my deadly wounds, | and 2.06. 27
her tears will pierce into a marble heart; 3.01. 38
hither | into this chiefest thicket of the park. 4.05. 3
york, | but that we enter as into our dukedom? 4.07. 9
i came into the world with my legs forward. 5.06. 71
sent before my time | into this breathing world, R3 1.01. 21
wits | and fall something into a slower method: 1.02.116
into the tumbling billows of the main. 1.04. 20
and then throw him into the malmsey–butt in the 1.04.155 P
hath not yet div'd into the world's deceit; 3.01. 8
man | the men you talk of came into my mind. 3.02.117
tumble down | into the fatal bowels of the deep. 3.04.101
me | that look into me with considerate eyes. 4.02. 30
and drop into the rotten mouth of death. 4.04. 2
thus far into the bowels of the land | have we 5.02. 3
and all my armor laid into my tent? 5.03. 51
fall | into the blind cave of eternal night. 5.03. 62
how far into the morning is it, lords? 5.03.234
let some graver eye | pierce into that — but i H8 1.01. 68
not consulting, broke | into a general prophecy: 1.01. 92
hath into monstrous habits put the graces | that 1.02.122
his duty) would | have put his knife into him." 1.02.199
should juggle | men into such strange mysteries? 1.03. 2
'em nobly and conduct 'em | into our presence, 1.04. 59
he dives into the king's soul, and there 2.02. 26
look into these affairs see this main end, | the 2.02. 40
man will work us all | from princes into pages. 2.02. 47
to be fashion'd | into what pitch he please. 2.02. 49
thrust yourselves | into my private meditations? 2.02. 65
most learned reverend sir, into our kingdom, 2.02. 76
say, henry king of england, come into the court. 2.04. 6 P
katherine queen of england, come into the court. 2.04. 11 P
katherine queen of england, come into the court. 2.04.126 P
to withdraw | into your private chamber, we 3.01. 28
put your main cause into the king's protection, 3.01. 93
you turn the good we offer into envy. 3.01.113
ye turn me into nothing! 3.01.114
put my sick cause into his hands that hates me? 3.01.118
a noble spirit | as yours was put into you, ever 3.01.170
one | hath crawl'd into the favor of the king, 3.02.103
straight | springs out into fast gait, then 3.02.116
up the great seal presently | into our hands, 3.02.230
of gleaning all the land's wealth into one, 3.02.284
into your own hands, card'nal, by extortion; 3.02.285
bold | to carry into flanders the great seal. 3.02.319
fall into th' compass of a praemunire — | that 3.02.340
or i fall into | the trap is laid for me! 5.01.141
into whose hand i give thy life. 5.04. 11
and when fair cressid comes into my thoughts — TRO 1.01. 30
a man into whom nature hath so crowded humors 1.02. 22 P
humors that his valor is crush'd into folly, his 1.02. 23 P
to him th' other day into the compass'd window 1.02.111 P
power into will, will into appetite, | and 1.03.120
in power, | power into will, will into appetite, 1.03.120
i will beat thee into handsomeness. 2.01. 15 P
i shall sooner rail thee into wit and holiness, 2.01. 16 P
he would pun thee into shivers with his fist, as 2.01. 39 P
am become | as new into the world, strange, 3.03. 12
how one man eats into another's pride, | while 3.03.136
my lord, come you again into my chamber. 4.02. 36
walk into her house. 4.03. 5
to them, | he fumbles up into a loose adieu; 4.04. 46
barbarism, and policy grows into an ill opinion. 5.04. 17 P
nurse | into a rapture lets her baby cry | while COR 2.01.207
him | were slily crept into his human powers, 2.01.220
to have them at all into their estimation and 2.02. 28 P
made the coward | turn terror into sport; 2.02.105
to put our tongues into those wounds and speak 2.03. 7 P
translate his malice towards you into love, 2.03.189
and from thence | into destruction cast him. 3.01.213
put not your worthy rage into your tongue; 3.01.240
with my drum, into a pipe | small as an eunuch, 3.02.113
and to wind | yourself into a power tyrannical, 3.03. 65
nodding of their plumes, | fan you into despair! 3.03.127
war | into the bowels of ungrateful rome, | like 4.05.130
thrusts forth his horns again into the world, 4.06. 44
you stood, confin'd | into an auger's bore. 4.06. 87
if he could burn us all into one coal, | we have 4.06.137
fall down, and knee | the way into his mercy. 5.01. 6
you know the very road into his kindness, | and 5.01. 59
lust, | and tumble me into some loathsome pit, TIT 2.03.176
heart, | aaron and thou look down into this den, 2.03.215
i may be pluck'd into the swallowing womb | of 2.03.239
and what he is that now is leapt into it. 2.03.247
descend | into this gaping hollow of the earth? 2.03.249
and do not break into these deep extremes. 3.01.215
then into limits could i bind my woes: 3.01.220
come go with me into mine armory; 4.01.113
i'll dive into the burning lake below, | and 4.03. 44
kinsmen, shoot all your shafts into the court, 4.03. 62
this scattered corn into one mutual sheaf, 5.03. 71
sheaf, | these broken limbs again into one body. 5.03. 72
go, go into old titus' sorrowful house, | and 5.03.142
of me, | and stole into the covert of the wood. ROM 1.01.125
help me into some house, benvolio, | or i shall 3.01.105
why should you fall into so deep an o? 3.03. 90
clouds, | that sees into the bottom of my grief? 3.05.197
or bid me go into a new–made grave, | and hide 4.01. 84
will you go with me into my closet | to help me 4.02. 33
how if, when i am laid into the tomb, | i wake 4.03. 30
why i descend into this bed of death | is partly 5.03. 28
that state of fortune fall into my keeping, TIM 1.01.150
of man's bred out | into baboon and monkey. 1.01.251
cold–moving nods, | they froze me into silence. 2.02.213
whose death he's stepp'd | into a great estate. 2.02.224
me, | i would have put my wealth into donation, 3.02. 83
down th' int'rest into their glutt'nous maws. 3.04. 52
who in hot blood | hath stepp'd into the law, 3.05. 12
they labor'd | to bring manslaughter into form, 3.05. 27
and came into the world | when sects and 3.05. 29
to his heart, | to bring it into danger. 3.05. 35
usuring senate | pours into captains' wounds? 3.05.110
from our companion thrown into his grave, | so 4.02. 9
we must all part | into this sea of air. 4.02. 22
into strong shudders and to heavenly agues | th' 4.03.138
by thy virtue | set them into confounding odds, 4.03.391
of his friends, drove him into this melancholy. 4.03.401 P
surge resolves | the moon into salt tears; 4.03.440
lord, | into our city with thy banners spread; 5.04. 30
bring me into your city, | and i will use the 5.04. 81
out their shoes, to get myself into more work. JC 1.01. 30 P
and weep your tears | into the channel, till the 1.01. 59
turn | your hidden worthiness into your eye, 1.02. 57
into what dangers would you lead me, cassius, 1.02. 63
that you would have me seek into myself | for 1.02. 64
now | leap in with me into this angry flood, 1.02.103
and first decree | into the /law of children. 3.01. 39
pardon — | i will myself into the pulpit first, 3.01.236
i have borne this corse | into the market–place. 3.01.292
cassius, go you into the other street, | and 3.02. 3
let him go up into the public chair, | we'll 3.02. 63
and conn'd by rote, | to cast into my teeth. 4.03. 99
brutus, thrusting this report | into his ears; 5.03. 75
if you can look into the seeds of time, | and MAC 1.03. 58
into the air; 1.03. 81
corporal melted, | as breath into the wind. 1.03. 82
thanks, | only to herald thee into his sight, 1.03.102
made themselves air, into which they vanish'd. 1.05. 5 P
this night's great business into my dispatch, 1.05. 68
rather than so, come fate into the list, | and 3.01. 70
the murderer's gibbet throw | into the flame. 4.01. 67
pour the sweet milk of concord into hell, 4.03. 98
trains hath sought to win me | into his power, 4.03.119
since his majesty went into the field, i have 5.01. 4 P
my way of life | is fall'n into the sear, the 5.03. 23
melt, | thaw, and resolve itself into a dew! HAM 1.02.130
cliff | that beetles o'er his base into the sea, 1.04. 71
of reason, | and draw you into madness? 1.04. 74
into every brain | that looks so many fadoms to 1.04. 76
and curd, like eager droppings into milk, | the 1.05. 69
us, | put your dread pleasures more into command 2.02. 28
but, better look'd into, he truly found | it was 2.02. 64
fell into a sadness, then into a fast, | thence 2.02.147
make, | fell into a sadness, then into a fast, 2.02.147
thence to a watch, thence into a weakness, 2.02.148
into the madness wherein now he raves, | and all 2.02.150
into my grave. 2.02.207 P
and drive his purpose into these delights. 3.01. 27
honesty can translate beauty into his likeness. 3.01.112 P
would perhaps plunge him into more choler. 3.02.306 P
my lord, put your discourse into some frame, and 3.02.308 P
hath strook her into amazement and admiration. 3.02.327 P
of me, as if you would drive me into a toil? 3.02.347 P
thou turn'st my /eyes into my /very soul, | and 3.04. 89
i'll lug the guts into the neighbor room. 3.04.212
fair, and bring the body | into the chapel. 4.01. 37
nose him as you go up the stairs into the lobby. 4.03. 37 P
lost, | a sister driven into desp'rate terms, 4.07. 26
his clutch, | and hath shipped me into the land, 5.01. 73
born — he that is mad, and sent into england. 5.01.148 P
ay, marry, why was he sent into england? 5.01.149 P
since he went into france i have been in 5.02.210 P
i am, i cannot heave | my heart into my mouth. LR 1.01. 92
your fore–vouch'd affection | fall into taint; 1.01.221
that terrible dispatch of it into your pocket? 1.02. 33 P
wind me into him, i pray you. 1.02. 98 P
hour | he flashes into one gross crime or other 1.03. 4
since my young lady's going into france, sir, 1.04. 73 P
into her womb convey sterility, | dry up in her 1.04.278
what a man cannot smell out, he may spy into. 1.05. 23 P
this weaves itself perforce into my business. 2.01. 15
one whom i will beat into /clamorous whining, if 2.02. 23 P
i will tread this unbolted villain into mortar, 2.02. 66 P
your blinding flames | into her scornful eyes! 2.04.166
shall break into a hundred thousand flaws | or 2.04.285
bids the wind blow the earth into the sea, | or 3.01. 5
good my lord, take his offer, go into th' house. 3.04.156
in, fellow, there, into th' hovel; 3.04.174
my son | came then into my mind, and yet my mind 4.01. 34
and give the distaff | into my husband's hands. 4.02. 18
would stretch thy spirits up into the air. 4.02. 23
taught me to shift | into a madman's rags, t' 5.03.188
condition | put into circumscription and confine OTH 1.02. 27
shall come into no true taste again but by the 2.01.275 P
the lusty moor | hath leap'd into my seat; 2.01.296
the moor | at least into a jealousy so strong 2.01.301
fleet, every man put himself into triumph; 2.02. 4 P
i'll beat the knave into a twiggen bottle. 2.03.148 P
and applause, transform ourselves into beasts! 2.03.292 P
i'll pour this pestilence into his ear — | that 2.03.356
so will i turn her virtue into pitch, | and out 2.03.360
go, vanish into air, away! 3.01. 20 P
it is my nature's plague | to spy into abuses, 3.03.147
my speech should fall into such vild success 3.03.222
or for i am declin'd | into the vale of years 3.03.266
futurity, | can ransom me into his love again, 3.04.118
when it hath blown his ranks into the air, | and 3.04.135
my lord is fall'n into an epilepsy. 4.01. 50
i will chop her into messes. cuckold me! 4.01.200 P
he goes into mauritania and taketh away with him 4.02.224 P
and pour our treasures into foreign laps; 4.03. 88
the world transform'd | into a strumpet's fool. ANT 1.01. 13
fulvia thy wife first came into the field. 1.02. 88
into the hearts of such as have not thrived 1.03. 51
and that night | i laugh'd him into patience; 2.05. 20
melt egypt into nile! 2.05. 78
to be call'd into a huge sphere, and not to be 2.07. 14 P
come down into the boat. 2.07.129
and shot their fires | into th' abysm of hell. 3.13.147
antony | is come into the field. 4.06. 7
we'll beat 'em into bench–holes. 4.07. 9
but better 'twere | thou fell'st into my fury, 4.12. 41
our strength is all gone into heaviness, | that 4.15. 33
it sin | to rush into the secret house of death 4.15. 81
should have shook lions into civil streets, 5.01. 16
see | how hardly i was drawn into this war, 5.01. 74
y' are fall'n into a princely hand, fear nothing 5.02. 22
let the water–flies | blow me into abhorring! 5.02. 60
witch | that he enchants societies into him; CYM 1.06.167
winning will put any man into courage. 2.03. 7 P
a strange infection | is fall'n into thy ear! 3.02. 4
have done, his spirits fly out | into my story; 3.03. 91
strikes life into my speech and shows much more 3.03. 97
put thyself | into a havior of less fear, ere 3.04. 9
and /make me put into contempt the suits | of 3.04. 89
change | command into obedience; 3.04.155
woman it pretty self) into a waggish courage, 3.04.157
i see into thy end and am almost | a man already 3.04.166
testiness, shall turn all into my commendations. 4.01. 21 P
fortune put them into my hand! 4.01. 23 P
i'll throw't into the creek | behind our rock, 4.02.151
to have turn'd my leaping time into a crutch, 4.02.200
you have put me into rhyme. 5.03. 63
work | her son into th' adoption of the crown; 5.05. 56
boy, | thou hast look'd thyself into my grace, 5.05. 94
those arts they have as i | could put into them. 5.05.339
musings into my mind, with thousand doubts | how PER 1.02. 97
sorrows to sound deep our woes | into the air, 1.04. 14
are coming, we will withdraw | into the gallery. 2.02. 59
take i your wish, i leap into the seas, 2.04. 43
how she gins | to blow into life's flower again! 3.02. 95
swear she's dead, | and thrown into the sea. 4.01. 99
you are light into my hands, where you are like 4.02. 72 P
and chances | into an honest house, our story 5.ch. 2
heart | leaps to be gone into my mother's bosom. 5.03. 45
it in — shrunk thee into | the bound thou wast TNK 1.01. 83
by hot grief uncandied, | melts into drops; 1.01.108
descend again into their throats and have not 1.02. 82
cleaving his conscience into twain and doing 1.03. 46
lead into the city, | where, having bound things 1.04. 47
'gainst thy window, | and let in life into thee; 2.03. 10
and ev'ry day discourse you into health, | as i 3.06. 38
and safely presently | into your bush again, sir 3.06.111
she sows into the births of noble bodies, | were 4.02. 9
petition of grace and acceptance into her favor. 4.03. 89 P
out of square in her into their former law and 4.03. 96 P
power hast turn'd | green neptune into purple, 5.01. 50
'twas thy power | to put life into dust: 5.01.110
the gout had knit his fingers into knots, 5.01.112
into whose port | ne'er ent'red wanton sound) to 5.01.147
were they metamorphis'd | both into one — o, 5.03. 85
fall again | into your idle over–handled theme. VEN 770
run | into the quiet closure of my breast, | and 782
why hast thou cast into eternal sleeping | those 951
fled | into the deep–dark cabins of her head, 1038
stay, | and blows the smoke of it into his face, LUC 312
into the chamber wickedly he stalks, | and 365
and lo there falls into thy boundless flood 653
into so bright a day such black–fac'd storms, 1518
that pour'st into my verse | thine own sweet SON 38. 2
on | that sometimes anger thrusts into his hide, 50.10
thee | so far from home into my deeds to pry, 61. 6

they look into the beauty of thy mind, | and 69. 9
lest the wise world should look into your moan, 71.13
even there resolv'd my reason into tears, LC 296
INTOLERABLE 9 FR 0.0010 REL FR 6 V 3 P
first, an intolerable fright, to be detected WIV 3.05.108 P
cold, wither'd, and of intolerable entrails? 5.05.153 P
is that she is intolerable curst | and shrowd SHR 1.02. 89
o vild, | intolerable, not to be endur'd! 5.02. 94
of bread to this intolerable deal of sack! 1H4 2.04.541 P
a married man! that's most intolerable. 1H6 5.04. 79
his insolence is more intolerable | than all the 2H6 1.01.175
my liege, his railing is intolerable. 3.01.172
despiteful and intolerable wrongs! TIT 4.04. 50
INTO'T 7 FR 0.0008 REL FR 2 V 5 P
well, i will look further into't, and i have a WIV 2.01.237 P
shall we clap into't roundly, without hawking or AYL 5.03. 11 P
you have made shift to run into't, boots and AWW 2.05. 36 P
to those that, without heed, do plunge into't. TIM 3.05. 13
i will look further into't. LR 1.04. 71 P
my death, and run into't | as to a lover's bed. ANT 4.14.100
be a place of such resort, and will come into't? PER 4.06. 80 P
INTOXICATES 1 FR 0.0001 REL FR 0 V 1 P
also being a little intoxicates in his prains, H5 4.07. 37 P
INTRATE 1 FR 0.0001 REL FR 1 V 0 P
intrate, filii; TNK 3.05.137
INTREASURED *(also entreasur'd)*
INTREASURED 1 FR 0.0001 REL FR 1 V 0 P
seeds | and weak beginning lie intreasured. 2H4 3.01. 85
INTRENCHANT 1 FR 0.0001 REL FR 1 V 0 P
as easy mayst thou the intrenchant air | with MAC 5.08. 9
INTRENCH'D *(also entrench'd)*
INTRENCH'D 1 FR 0.0001 REL FR 1 V 0 P
the english, in the suburbs close intrench'd, 1H6 1.04. 9
INT'REST 5 FR 0.0005 REL FR 5 V 0 P
not, as you would say, | directly int'rest. MV 1.03. 77
if that the youth of my new int'rest here | have 3.02.221
and take down th' int'rest into their glutt'nous TIM 3.04. 52
and one for int'rest, if thou wilt have twain. VEN 210
but thou shalt know thy int'rest was not bought LUC 1067
INTRICATE 1 FR 0.0001 REL FR 1 V 0 P
why, what an intricate impeach is this! ERR 5.01.270
INT'RIM 2 FR 0.0002 REL FR 2 V 0 P
no int'rim, not a minute's vacancy, | both day TN 5.01. 95
let this sad int'rim like the ocean be | which SON 56. 9
INTRINSE 1 FR 0.0001 REL FR 1 V 0 P
a–twain | which are t' intrinse t' unloose; LR 2.02. 75
INTRINSICATE 1 FR 0.0001 REL FR 1 V 0 P
with thy sharp teeth this knot intrinsicate | of ANT 5.02.304
INTRUDE 3 FR 0.0003 REL FR 3 V 0 P
and manners, to intrude where i am grac'd, | and TIT 2.01. 27
whereinto foul things | sometimes intrude not? OTH 3.03.138
"why should the worm intrude the maiden bud? LUC 848
INTRUDER 2 FR 0.0002 REL FR 2 V 0 P
go, base intruder! TGV 3.01.157
limbs, | unmannerly intruder as thou art! TIT 2.03. 65
INTRUDING 1 FR 0.0001 REL FR 1 V 0 P
thou wretched, rash, intruding fool, farewell! HAM 3.04. 31
INTRUSION 4 FR 0.0004 REL FR 3 V 1 P
embold'ned me to this unseason'd intrusion; WIV 2.02.168 P
of pruning, with intrusion | infect thy sap, and ERR 2.02.179
that may with foul intrusion enter in, | and 3.01.103
i will withdraw, but this intrusion shall, | now ROM 1.05. 91
INUNDATION 4 FR 0.0004 REL FR 4 V 0 P
this inundation of mistemp'red humor | rests by JN 5.01. 12
a lady's tears, | being an ordinary inundation; 5.02. 48
marriage, | to stop the inundation of her tears, ROM 4.01. 12
but with the inundation of the eyes | what rocky LC 290
INUR'D *(also enur'd)*
INUR'D 1 FR 0.0001 REL FR 1 V 0 P
"this glove to wanton tricks | is not inur'd; LUC 321
INURE 1 FR 0.0001 REL FR 0 V 1 P
to inure thyself to what thou art like to be, TN 2.05.148 P
INVADE 2 FR 0.0002 REL FR 2 V 0 P
we must not only arm t' invade the french, | but H5 1.02.136
though the fork invade | the region of my heart; LR 1.01.144
/INVADES 1 FR 0.0001 REL FR 1 V 0 P
/touches /us, /as /france /invades /our /land, LR 5.01. 25
INVADES 1 FR 0.0001 REL FR 1 V 0 P
this contentious storm | invades us to the skin; LR 3.04. 7
INVASION 2 FR 0.0002 REL FR 2 V 0 P
my towns | with dreadful pomp of stout invasion! JN 4.02.173
that now he vows a league, and now invasion. LUC 287
INVASIVE 1 FR 0.0001 REL FR 1 V 0 P
parley, and base truce | to arms invasive? JN 5.01. 69
INVECTIVELY 1 FR 0.0001 REL FR 1 V 0 P
thus most invectively he pierceth through | the AYL 2.01. 58
INVECTIVES 1 FR 0.0001 REL FR 1 V 0 P
breathe out invectives 'gainst the officers. 3H6 1.04. 43
INVEIGH 1 FR 0.0001 REL FR 1 V 0 P
no man inveigh against the withered flow'r, LUC 1254
INVEIGLED 1 FR 0.0001 REL FR 0 V 1 P
achilles hath inveigled his fool from him. TRO 2.03. 91 P
INVENT 9 FR 0.0010 REL FR 6 V 3 P
i say she never did invent this letter, | this AYL 4.03. 28
is not able to invent any thing that intends to 2H4 1.02. 8 P
laughter more than i invent or is invented on me 1.02. 9 P
i would invent as bitter searching terms, | as 2H6 3.02.311
wish courtesy would invent some other custom of OTH 2.03. 35 P
lives, invent a way | safer than banishment. TNK 3.06.217
any death thou canst invent, duke. 3.06.281
how can my muse want subject to invent | while SON 38. 1
yet what of thee thy poet doth invent | he robs 79. 7
INVENTED 2 FR 0.0002 REL FR 1 V 1 P
more than i invent or is invented on me: 2H4 1.02. 9 P
he lies, for i invented it myself. 2H6 4.02.155
INVENTION 31 FR 0.0035 REL FR 23 V 8 P
in her invention and ford's wive's distraction, WIV 3.05. 85 P
whilst my invention, hearing not my tongue, MM 2.04. 3
blood of mine, | nor age so eat up my invention, ADO 4.01.194
impose me to what penance your invention | can 5.01.273
if your love | can labor aught in sad invention, 5.01.283
flowers of fancy, the jerks of invention? LLL 4.02.125 P
neither savoring of poetry, wit, nor invention. 4.02.159 P
i made yesterday in despite of my invention. AYL 2.05. 47 P
this is a man's invention and his hand. 4.03. 29
could not drop forth such giant–rude invention, 4.03. 34
invention is asham'd, | against the proclamation AWW 1.03.173
but return with an invention and clap upon you 3.06. 98 P
be a very plausive invention that carries it. 4.01. 26 P
witty, so it be eloquent and full of invention. TN 3.02. 44 P
or say 'tis not your seal, not your invention. 5.01.333
geck and gull | that e'er invention play'd on? 5.01.344
ascend | the brightest heaven of invention! H5 pr 2
do it without invention, suddenly, | as i with 1H6 3.01. 5
be appeas'd | by such invention as i can devise? 3H6 4.01. 35
let them accuse me by invention; COR 3.02.143
filling their hearers | with strange invention. MAC 3.01. 32
if this letter speed | and my invention thrive, LR 1.02. 20
but indeed my invention | comes from my pate as OTH 2.01.125
of so high and plenteous wit and invention! 4.01.190 P
add more, | from thine invention, offers. ANT 3.12. 29
what excuse can my invention make | when thou LUC 225
when thou thyself dost give invention light? SON 38. 8
which laboring for invention bear amiss | the 59. 3
the same, | and keep invention in a noted weed, 76. 6
a face | that overgoes my blunt invention quite, 103. 7
and in this change is my invention spent, 105.11
INVENTIONS 4 FR 0.0004 REL FR 4 V 0 P
both our inventions meet and jump in one. SHR 1.01.190
to /change true rules for /odd inventions. 3.01. 81
must have inventions to delight the taste, PER 1.04. 40
throng her inventions, which shall go before. LUC 1302
INVENTOR 1 FR 0.0001 REL FR 1 V 0 P
being taught, return | to plague th' inventor. MAC 1.07. 10
INVENTORIALLY 1 FR 0.0001 REL FR 0 V 1 P
know, to divide him inventorially would dozy th' HAM 5.02.113 P
INVENTORIED 1 FR 0.0001 REL FR 0 V 1 P
it shall be inventoried, and every particle and TN 1.05.246 P
INVENTORS' 1 FR 0.0001 REL FR 1 V 0 P
mistook | fall'n on th' inventors' heads: HAM 5.02.385
INVENTORY 6 FR 0.0006 REL FR 4 V 2 P
once, or to bear the inventory of thy shirts, as 2H4 2.02. 17 P
forsooth, an inventory, thus importing | the H8 3.02.124
and bear the inventory | of your best graces in 3.02.137
there take an inventory of all i have, | to the 3.02.451
is as an inventory to particularize their COR 1.01. 21 P
would testify, t' enrich mine inventory. CYM 2.02. 30
INVERNESS *(see enverness)*
INVERT 2 FR 0.0002 REL FR 2 V 0 P
invert | what best is boded me to mischief! TMP 3.01. 70
that doth invert th' attest of eyes and ears, TRO 5.02.122
INVEST 9 FR 0.0010 REL FR 8 V 1 P
how, in stripping it, | you more invest it! TMP 2.01.226
the damned'st body to invest and cover | in MM 3.01. 95
invest me in my motley; AYL 2.07. 58
for this they have been thoughtful to invest 2H4 4.05. 72
that thou wilt needs invest thee with my honors 4.05. 95
honor must | not unaccompanied invest him only, MAC 1.04. 40
i do invest you jointly with my power, LR 1.01.130
nature would not invest herself in such OTH 4.01. 40 P
but those we will depute which shall invest TNK 1.04. 10
INVESTED 4 FR 0.0004 REL FR 4 V 0 P
our substitutes in absence well invested, | and 2H4 4.04. 6
in th' official marks invested, you | anon do COR 2.03.140
nam'd, and gone to scone | to be invested. MAC 2.04. 32
rights, | by me invested, he compeers the best. LR 5.03. 69
INVESTING 1 FR 0.0001 REL FR 1 V 0 P
investing lank–lean cheeks and war–worn coats, H5 4.pr. 26
INVESTMENTS 2 FR 0.0002 REL FR 2 V 0 P
whose white investments figure innocence, | the 2H4 4.01. 45
not of that dye which their investments show, HAM 1.03.128
INVESTS 1 FR 0.0001 REL FR 1 V 0 P
the time invests you, go, your servants tend. HAM 1.03. 83
INVETERATE 4 FR 0.0004 REL FR 4 V 0 P
being an enemy | to me inveterate, hearkens my TMP 1.02.122
and heal the inveterate canker of one wound | by JN 5.02. 14
aim'd at your highness, no inveterate malice. R2 1.01. 14
after the inveterate hate he bears you. COR 2.03.226
INVINCIBLE 4 FR 0.0004 REL FR 2 V 2 P
spirit had been invincible against all assaults ADO 2.03.114 P
man, | of an invincible unconquer'd spirit! 1H6 4.02. 32
reported to be a woman of an invincible spirit; 2H6 1.04. 7 P
with precepts that would make invincible | the COR 4.01. 10
INVIOLABLE 3 FR 0.0003 REL FR 3 V 0 P
and keep our faiths firm and inviolable. JN 5.02. 7
kiss, | as if they vow'd some league inviolable. 3H6 2.01. 30
protest, | upon my part shall be inviolable. R3 2.01. 27
INVIS'D 1 FR 0.0001 REL FR 1 V 0 P
hard, | whereto his invis'd properties did tend; LC 212
/INVISIBLE 1 FR 0.0001 REL FR 0 V 1 P
dimensions to any thick sight were /invisible. 2H4 3.02.313 P
INVISIBLE 26 FR 0.0029 REL FR 18 V 8 P
and mine, invisible | to every eyeball else. TMP 1.02.302
thy shape invisible retain thou still. 4.01.185
to the king's ship, invisible as thou art; 5.01. 97
invisible, | as a nose on a man's face, or a TGV 2.01.135
witness you, | that he is borne about invisible: ERR 5.01.187
or hang my bugle in an invisible baldrick, all ADO 1.01.242 P
are as keen | as is the razor's edge invisible, LLL 5.02.257
i am invisible, | and i will overhear their MND 2.01.186
crescent, and his horns are invisible within the 5.01.242 P
i would i were invisible, to catch the strong AYL 1.02.211 P
then shall you know the wounds invisible | that 3.05. 30
with an invisible and subtle stealth | to creep TN 1.05.297
sir, i would it would make you invisible. 3.01. 30 P
leaves them invisible, and his siege is now JN 5.07. 16
the receipt of fern–seed, we walk invisible. 1H4 2.01. 87 P
than to fern–seed for your walking invisible. 2.01. 90 P
borne with th' invisible and creeping wind, H5 3.pr. 11
heart–blood of beauty, love's invisible soul. TRO 3.01. 33 P
and with thy bloody and invisible hand | cancel MAC 3.02. 48
puff'd | makes mouths at the invisible event, HAM 4.04. 50
o thou invisible spirit of wine, if thou hast no OTH 2.03.281 P
a strange invisible perfume hits the sense | of ANT 2.02.212
that an invisible instinct should frame them CYM 4.02.177
would love | that inward beauty and invisible, VEN 434
be wreak'd on him, invisible commander; 1004
"o unseen shame, invisible disgrace! LUC 827
INVITATION 1 FR 0.0001 REL FR 0 V 1 P
she carves, she gives the leer of invitation. WIV 1.03. 46 P
INVITE 21 FR 0.0023 REL FR 16 V 5 P
i invite your highness and your train | to my TMP 5.01.301
i do invite you to–morrow morning to my house to
WIV 3.03.229 P
some tender money to me, some invite me; ERR 4.03. 4
sir, i do invite you too, you shall not say me LLL 4.02.164 P
thither will i invite the duke and all 's AYL 5.02. 14 P
make friends, invite, and proclaim the banes, SHR 3.02. 16
invite my lords of salisbury and warwick | to 2H6 1.04. 79
now a blessed troop | invite me to a banquet, H8 4.02. 88
t' invite the troyan lords after the combat | to TRO 3.03.236
the valiant ajax to invite the /most valorous 3.03.274 P
desires you to invite hector to his tent — 3.03.284 P
so many guests invite as here are writ. ROM 4.02. 1
methinks they should invite them without knives: TIM 1.02. 44
i charge thee, invite them all, let in the tide 3.04.116
his day's hard journey | soundly invite him), MAC 1.07. 63
whom we invite to see us crown'd at scone. 5.09. 41
which now to claim my vantage doth invite me. HAM 5.02.390
and do invite you to my sister's view, | whither ANT 2.02.167
aboard my galley i invite you all. 2.06. 80
brought you to my house, | whither i invite you. PER 5.03. 27
till now did ne'er invite, nor never vow. LC 182
INVITED 10 FR 0.0011 REL FR 9 V 1 P
i am invited, sir, to certain merchants, | of ERR 1.02. 24
perhaps some merchant hath invited him, | and 2.01. 4
my dear friend leonato hath invited you all. ADO 1.01.148 P
invited by your noble self, hath sent | one H8 2.02. 94
feast, | whereto i have invited many a guest, ROM 1.02. 21
her father lov'd me, oft invited me; OTH 1.03.128
and the generous islanders | by you invited, do 3.03.281
antony sent to her, | invited her to supper. ANT 2.02.220
maid, | my lord, that ne'er before invited eyes, PER 5.01. 85
desire to be invited | to any sensual feast with SON 141. 7
INVITES 5 FR 0.0005 REL FR 5 V 0 P
passion | invites me in this churlish messenger. TN 2.02. 23
invites the king of england's stay at home; H5 5.pr. 37
but rather one that smiles and still invites TIM 2.01. 11
that mine own use invites me to cut down, | and 5.01.206
the bell invites me. MAC 2.01. 62
INVITING 5 FR 0.0005 REL FR 3 V 2 P
he hath sent me an earnest inviting, which many TIM 3.06. 10 P
an inviting eye; and yet methinks right modest. OTH 2.03. 24 P
the time inviting thee? CYM 3.04.105
what a bold gravity, and yet inviting, | has TNK 4.02. 41
whereto th' inviting time our fashion calls; SON 124. 8
INVITIS 1 FR 0.0001 REL FR 1 V 0 P
under the which is writ, "invitis nubibus." 2H6 4.01. 99
INVOCATE 3 FR 0.0003 REL FR 3 V 0 P
henry the fift, thy ghost i invocate: 1H6 1.01. 52
be it lawful that i invocate thy ghost | to hear R3 1.02. 8
than those old nine which rhymers invocate, SON 38.10
INVOCATION 4 FR 0.0004 REL FR 2 V 2 P
sweet invocation of a child, most pretty and LLL 1.02. 97 P
'tis a greek invocation, to call fools into a AYL 2.05. 59 P
voice, | which scorns a modern invocation. JN 3.04. 42
my invocation | is fair and honest; ROM 2.01. 27
INVOCATIONS 1 FR 0.0001 REL FR 1 V 0 P
to rouse our roman gods with invocations | that LUC 1831
INVOK'D 1 FR 0.0001 REL FR 1 V 0 P
so oft have i invok'd thee for my muse, | and SON 78. 1
INVOKE 1 FR 0.0001 REL FR 1 V 0 P
invoke his warlike spirit, | and your H5 1.02.104
INVULNERABLE *(also unvulnerable)*
/INVULNERABLE 1 FR 0.0001 REL FR 1 V 0 P
against th' /invulnerable clouds of heaven, JN 2.01.252
INVULNERABLE 2 FR 0.0002 REL FR 2 V 0 P
my fellow ministers | are like invulnerable. TMP 3.03. 66
violence, | for it is, as the air, invulnerable, HAM 1.01.145
INWARD 34 FR 0.0038 REL FR 31 V 3 P
(whose inward pinches therefore are most strong)
TMP 5.01. 77
when inward joy enforc'd my heart to smile! TGV 1.02. 63
sir, i was an inward of his. MM 3.02.130 P
of you know any inward impediment why you should
ADO 4.01. 12 P
for what is inward between us, let it pass. LLL 5.01. 97 P
who, inward search'd, have livers white as milk, MV 3.02. 86
but from the inward motion to deliver | sweet, JN 1.01.212
knit, | and the conjunction of our inward souls 3.01.227
me, and my inward soul | with nothing trembles; R2 2.02. 11
but yet my inward soul | persuades me it is 2.02. 28
on earth | was parmaciti for an inward bruise, 1H4 1.03. 58
he writes me here, that inward sickness — | and 4.01. 31
and were these inward wars once out of hand, 2H4 3.01.107
which my most inward true and duteous spirit 4.05.147
with an inward wish | you would desire the king H5 1.01. 39
model to thy inward greatness, | like little 2.pr. 16
glories, | an outward honor for an inward toil, R3 1.04. 79
who is most inward with the noble duke? 3.04. 8
hope of revenge shall hide our inward woe. TRO 5.10. 31
the inward service of the mind and soul | grows HAM 1.03. 13
it, | sith nor th' exterior nor the inward man 2.02. 6
that inward breaks, and shows no cause without 4.04. 28
outward | do draw the inward quality after them, ANT 3.13. 33
breaks that sigh | from th' inward of thee? CYM 3.04. 6
us scan | the outward habit by the inward man. PER 2.02. 57
would love | that inward beauty and invisible, VEN 434
whose inward ill no outward harm express'd. LUC 91
and in his inward mind he doth debate | what 185
honesty, but yet defil'd | with inward vice: 1546
the deep vexation of his inward soul | hath 1779
neither in inward worth nor outward fair | can SON 16.11
and my heart's right /thy inward love of heart. 46.14
remedy, | it is so grounded inward in my heart. 62. 4
leap | to kiss the tender inward of thy hand, 128. 6
INWARDLY 3 FR 0.0003 REL FR 2 V 1 P
fire, | consume away in sighs, waste inwardly. ADO 3.01. 78
my heart bleeds inwardly that my father is so 2H4 2.02. 48 P
i bleed inwardly for my lord. TIM 1.02.205
INWARDNESS 1 FR 0.0001 REL FR 1 V 0 P
and though you know my inwardness and love | is ADO 4.01.245
INWARDS 2 FR 0.0002 REL FR 1 V 1 P
makes it course from the inwards to the parts' 2H4 4.03.107 P
doth, like a poisonous mineral, gnaw my inwards; OTH 2.01.297
IO 1 FR 0.0001 REL FR 1 V 0 P
we'll show thee io as she was a maid, | and how SHR in.2. 54
IONIA 1 FR 0.0001 REL FR 1 V 0 P
shook, from syria | to lydia and to ionia, ANT 1.02.103
IONIAN 1 FR 0.0001 REL FR 1 V 0 P
he could so quickly cut the ionian sea, | and ANT 3.07. 22
IPSE 2 FR 0.0002 REL FR 0 V 2 P
for all your writers do consent that ipse is he: AYL 5.01. 43 P
now, you are not ipse, for i am he. 5.01. 44 P

IPSO 1 FR 0.0001 REL FR 1 V 0 P
it cures her ipso facto | the melancholy humor TNK 5.02. 37
IPSWICH 2 FR 0.0002 REL FR 2 V 0 P
cry down | this ipswich fellow's insolence; H8 1.01.138
that he rais'd in you, | ipswich and oxford! 4.02. 59
IRA 2 FR 0.0002 REL FR 2 V 0 P
my lords, "ira furor brevis est," | but yond man TIM 1.02. 28
"et opus exegi, quod nec jovis ira, nec ignis" TNK 3.05. 88
IRAE 1 FR 0.0001 REL FR 1 V 0 P
tantaene animis caelestibus irae? 2H6 2.01. 24
IRAS 9 FR 0.0010 REL FR 8 V 1 P
nay, come, tell iras hers. ANT 1.02. 43 P
i faint, o iras, charmian! 2.05.110
help, charmian, help, iras, help; 4.15. 12
peace, peace, iras! 4.15. 72
now, iras, what think'st thou? 5.02.207
nay, 'tis most certain, iras. 5.02.214
sirrah iras, go. 5.02.229
yare, yare, good iras; 5.02.283
farewell, kind charmian, iras, long farewell. 5.02.292
IRE 6 FR 0.0006 REL FR 6 V 0 P
nor heady-rash, provok'd with raging ire, ERR 5.01.216
high-stomach'd are they both and full of ire, R2 1.01. 18
mad ire and wrathful fury makes me weep, | that 1H6 4.03. 28
it could not slake mine ire nor ease my heart. 3H6 1.03. 29
yet cease your ire, you angry stars of heaven! PER 2.01. 1
your ire is more than mortal; TNK 5.01. 14
IREFUL 5 FR 0.0005 REL FR 5 V 0 P
each one with ireful passion, with drawn swords, ERR 5.01.151
the ireful bastard orleance, that drew blood 1H6 4.06. 16
but only slaught'red by the ireful arm | of 3H6 2.01. 57
and bloody steel grasp'd in their ireful hands, 2.05.132
being ireful, on the lion he will venter. VEN 628
/IRELAND 1 FR 0.0001 REL FR 1 V 0 P
/because /a /bard /of /ireland /told /me /once R3 4.02.106
IRELAND 30 FR 0.0034 REL FR 26 V 4 P
in what part of her body stands ireland? ERR 3.02.116 P
to ireland, poictiers, anjou, touraine, maine, JN 1.01. 11
england and ireland, /anjou, touraine, maine, 2.01.152
now for the rebels which stand out in ireland, R2 1.04. 38
wants, | for we will make for ireland presently. 1.04. 52
to-morrow next | we will for ireland, and 'tis 2.01.218
the first departing of the king for ireland. 2.01.290
i hope the king is not yet shipp'd for ireland. 2.02. 42
what, are there no posts dispatch'd for ireland? 2.02.103
the wind sits fair for news to go for ireland, 2.02.123
no, i will to ireland to his majesty. 2.02.141
and you rode like a kern of ireland, your french H5 3.07. 53 P
as in good time he may, from ireland coming, 5.pr. 31
"england is thine, ireland is thine, france is 5.02.239 P
and, brother york, thy acts in ireland, | in 2H6 1.01.194
and ireland | bear that proportion to my flesh 1.01.232
great lords, from ireland am i come amain, | to 3.01.282
th' uncivil kerns of ireland are in arms, | and 3.01.310
to ireland will you lead a band of men, 3.01.312
for there i'll ship them all for ireland. 3.01.329
whiles i in ireland nourish a mighty band, | i 3.01.348
in ireland have i seen this stubborn cade 3.01.360
why, then from ireland come i with my strength, 3.01.380
the duke of york is newly come from ireland, 4.09. 24
from ireland thus comes york to claim his right, 5.01. 1
king of england and france, and lord of ireland, 3H6 4.07. 73 P
then deputy of ireland, who remov'd, | earl H8 2.01. 42
you sent me deputy for ireland, | far from his 3.02.260
to ireland, i; MAC 2.03.138
are bestow'd | in england and in ireland, not 3.01. 30
IRIS 4 FR 0.0004 REL FR 4 V 0 P
wet, | the many-color'd iris, rounds thine eye? AWW 1.03.152
i'll have an iris that shall find thee out. 2H6 3.02.407
his crest that prouder than blue iris bends. TRO 1.03.379
or as iris | newly dropp'd down from heaven. TNK 4.01. 87
IRISH 9 FR 0.0010 REL FR 6 V 3 P
since pythagoras' time, that i was an irish rat, AYL 3.02.177 P
like the howling of irish wolves against the 5.02.110 P
to deck our soldiers for these irish wars. R2 1.04. 62
now for our irish wars: 2.01.155
he hath not money for these irish wars, | his 2.01.259
did set forth | upon his irish expedition; 1H4 1.03.150
i had rather hear lady, my brach, howl in irish. 3.01.236 P
here, | when he was personal in the irish war. 4.03. 88
so long in his unlucky irish wars | that all in 5.01. 53
IRISHMAN 2 FR 0.0002 REL FR 0 V 2 P
cheese, an irishman with my aqua-vitae bottle, WIV 2.02.303 P
is altogether directed by an irishman, a very H5 3.02. 66 P
IRISHMEN 1 FR 0.0001 REL FR 1 V 0 P
some, | and try your hap against the irishmen? 2H6 3.01.314
IRKS 3 FR 0.0003 REL FR 3 V 0 P
and yet it irks me the poor dappled fools, AYL 2.01. 22
it irks his heart he cannot be reveng'd. 1H6 1.04.105
to see this sight, it irks my very soul. 3H6 2.02. 6
IRKSOME 3 FR 0.0003 REL FR 3 V 0 P
thy company, which erst was irksome to me, | i AYL 3.05. 95
i know she is an irksome brawling scold. SHR 1.02.187
how irksome is this music to my heart! 2H6 2.01. 54
IRON 49 FR 0.0055 REL FR 40 V 9 P
go, get thee gone, fetch me an iron crow. ERR 3.01. 84
which was before barr'd up with ribs of iron! ADO 4.01.151
not this speech like iron through your blood? 5.01.245
but yet you draw not iron, for my heart | is MND 2.01.196
the iron tongue of midnight hath told twelve. 5.01.363
iron may hold with her, but never lutes. SHR 2.01.146
certain, or forswear to wear iron about you. TN 3.04.252 P
come, my young soldier, put up your iron; 4.01. 39 P
their iron indignation 'gainst your walls; JN 2.01.212
bell | did with his iron tongue and brazen mouth 3.03. 38
ah, none but in this iron age would do it! 4.01. 60
the iron of itself, though heat red-hot, 4.01. 61
are you more stubborn-hard than hammer'd iron? 4.01. 67
give me the iron, i say, and bind him here. 4.01. 74
speak a word, | nor look upon the iron angerly. 4.01. 81
that mercy which fierce fire and iron extends, 4.01.119
with this same very iron to burn them out. 4.01.124
the whilst his iron did on the anvil cool, 4.02.194
bray, | and grating shock of wrathful iron arms, R2 1.03.136
and heard thee murmur tales of iron wars, 1H4 2.03. 48
now bind my brows with iron, and approach | the 2H4 1.01.150
text | /than now to see you here an iron man, 4.02. 8
fight, but i will wink and hold out mine iron. H5 2.01. 8 P
them great meals of beef and iron and steel, 3.07.150 P
with a stubborn outside, with an aspect of iron, 5.02.227 P
out of a great deal of old iron i chose forth. 1H6 1.02.101
/wont through a secret grate of iron bars | in 1.04. 10
in iron walls they deem'd me not secure; 1.04. 49
who now is girdled with a waist of iron | and 4.03. 20
but i'll make thee eat iron like an ostridge, 2H6 4.10. 28 P
iron of naples hid with english gilt, | whose 3H6 2.02.139
strike now, or else the iron cools. 5.01. 49
bear witness, all that have not hearts of iron, H8 3.02.424
as iron to adamant, as earth to th' centre, TRO 3.02.179
this peace is nothing but to rust iron, increase COR 4.05.219 P
i will dry-beat you with an iron wit, and put up ROM 4.05.124 P
you with an iron wit, and put up my iron dagger. 4.05.124 P
get me an iron crow, and bring it straight 5.02. 21
give me that mattock and the wrenching iron. 5.03. 22
now | (like all mankind) show me an iron heart? TIM 3.04. 83
nor airless dungeon, nor strong links of iron, JC 1.03. 94
come, good fellow, put thine iron on. ANT 4.04. 3
who ne'er wore rowel | nor iron on his heel! CYM 4.04. 40
food, for yet | his iron bracelets are not off. TNK 2.06. 8
better have endur'd cold iron than done it. 2.06. 10
as they say, from iron | came music's origin), 5.04. 60
the iron bit he crusheth 'tween his teeth, VEN 269
soft pity enters at an iron gate. LUC 595
softer than wax, and yet as iron rusty: PP 7. 4
IRONS 8 FR 0.0009 REL FR 7 V 1 P
heat me these irons hot, and look thou stand JN 4.01. 1
must you with hot irons burn out both mine eyes? 4.01. 39
and with hot irons must i burn them out. 4.01. 59
put in their hands thy bruising irons of wrath, R3 5.03.110
drawing their massy irons and cutting the web! TRO 2.03. 17 P
irons of a doit, doublets that hangmen would COR 1.05. 6
fellow | loaden with irons wiser than the judge, TIM 3.05. 50
are dangerous, | i'll clap more irons on you. TNK 2.02.271
IRON-WITTED 1 FR 0.0001 REL FR 1 V 0 P
i will converse with iron-witted fools | and R3 4.02. 28
IRRECONCIL'D 1 FR 0.0001 REL FR 0 V 1 P
robbers and die in many irreconcil'd iniquities, H5 4.01.153 P
IRRECOVERABLE 1 FR 0.0001 REL FR 0 V 1 P
fiend hath prick'd down bardolph irrecoverable, 2H4 2.04.332 P
IRREGULAR 3 FR 0.0003 REL FR 3 V 0 P
leaving our rankness and irregular course, JN 5.04. 54
against the irregular and wild glendower, | was 1H4 1.01. 40
my youth | hath faulty wand'red and irregular, 3.02. 27
IRREGULOUS 1 FR 0.0001 REL FR 1 V 0 P
conspir'd with that irregulous devil cloten, CYM 4.02.315
IRRELIGIOUS 3 FR 0.0003 REL FR 3 V 0 P
and shun | a thousand irreligious cursed hours WIV 5.05.229
o cruel, irreligious piety! TIT 1.01.130
delivered, | the issue of an irreligious moor, 5.03.121
IRREMOVABLE 1 FR 0.0001 REL FR 1 V 0 P
he's irremovable, | resolv'd for flight. WT 4.04.507
IRREPARABLE 1 FR 0.0001 REL FR 1 V 0 P
irreparable is the loss, and patience | says, it TMP 5.01.140
IRRESOLUTE 1 FR 0.0001 REL FR 1 V 0 P
as a performance | does an irresolute purpose. H8 1.02.209
IRREVOCABLE 3 FR 0.0003 REL FR 3 V 0 P
firm and irrevocable is my doom | which i have AYL 1.03. 83
but when i swear, it is irrevocable. 2H6 3.02.294
thy faith irrevocable | that only warwick's 3H6 3.03.247
IS *(also ish, 's*)*
/IS 75 FR 0.0084 REL FR 46 V 29 P
--IS 1 FR 0.0001 REL FR 1 V 0 P
—is — now comes in, which being glu'd together TNK 3.05.119
IS 9603 FR 1.0855 REL FR 6806 V 2797 P
ISABEL 24 FR 0.0027 REL FR 22 V 2 P
i had your potency, | and you were isabel! MM 2.02. 68
hearing not my tongue, | anchors on isabel; 2.04. 4
one isabel, a sister, desires access to you. 2.04. 18
he shall not, isabel, if you give me love. 2.04.144
who will believe thee, isabel? 2.04.154
then, isabel, live chaste, and, brother, die; 2.04.184
thanks, dear isabel. 3.01.105
o isabel! 3.01.114
nay, hear me, isabel. 3.01.147
not isabel? 4.02. 76
the tongue of isabel. 4.03.107
he hath releas'd him, isabel, from the world, 4.03.115
wretched isabel! 4.03.121
by my troth, isabel, i lov'd thy brother. 4.03.156 P
the body | that took away the match from isabel, 5.01.211
call that same isabel here once again, i would 5.01.269 P
come hither, isabel, | your friar is now your 5.01.381
you are pardon'd, isabel; 5.01.387
sweet isabel, take my part! 5.01.430
isabel! 5.01.436
sweet isabel, do yet but kneel by me. 5.01.437
o isabel! 5.01.442
dear isabel, | i have a motion much imports your 5.01.534
till satisfied | that fair queen isabel, his H5 1.02. 81
ISABELLA 5 FR 0.0005 REL FR 4 V 1 P
gentle isabella, | turn you the key, and know MM 1.04. 7
stead me | as bring me to the sight of isabella, 1.04. 18
you know | i am that isabella and his sister. 1.04. 23
o hear me, isabella! 3.01.150
o pretty isabella, i am pale at mine heart to 4.03.151 P
ISABEL'S 1 FR 0.0001 REL FR 1 V 0 P
but knows he thinks that he knows isabel's. MM 5.01.204
ISBEL 2 FR 0.0002 REL FR 0 V 2 P
world, isbel the woman and /i will do as we may. AWW 1.03. 18 P
i have no mind to isbel since i was at court. 3.02. 12 P
ISBEL'S 1 FR 0.0001 REL FR 0 V 1 P
in isbel's case and mine own. AWW 1.03. 23 P
ISBELS 2 FR 0.0002 REL FR 0 V 2 P
our old /ling and our isbels a' th' country are AWW 3.02. 13 P
like your old ling and your isbels a' th' court. 3.02. 14 P
ISCARIOT 1 FR 0.0001 REL FR 0 V 1 P
not iscariot, sir. LLL 5.02.597 P
ISH *(also is, 's*)*
ISH 7 FR 0.0008 REL FR 0 V 7 P
the work ish give over, the trompet sound the H5 3.02. 88 P
and my father's soul, the work ish ill done; 3.02. 90 P
it ish give over. 3.02. 91 P
works to be done, and there ish nothing done, so 3.02.112 P
what ish my nation? 3.02.122 P
ish a villain, and a basterd, and a knave, and a 3.02.122 P
what ish my nation? 3.02.124 P
ISIDORE 3 FR 0.0003 REL FR 3 V 0 P
to varro and to isidore | he owes nine thousand, TIM 2.01. 1
it is; and yours too, isidore? 2.02. 11
from isidore; 2.02. 27
ISIS 8 FR 0.0009 REL FR 4 V 4 P
him marry a woman that cannot go, sweet isis, i ANT 1.02. 64 P
good isis, hear me this prayer, though thou deny 1.02. 67 P
good isis, i beseech thee! 1.02. 69 P
therefore, dear isis, keep decorum, and fortune 1.02. 73 P
by isis, i will give thee bloody teeth, | if 1.05. 70
like her? o isis! 'tis impossible. 3.03. 15
isis else defend! 3.03. 43
in th' abiliments of the goddess isis | that day 3.06. 17
ISLAND 27 FR 0.0030 REL FR 23 V 4 P
here in this island we arriv'd, and here | have TMP 1.02.171
then was this island | (save for the son that 1.02.281
you do keep from me | the rest o' th' island. 1.02.344
and sure it waits upon | some god o' th' island. 1.02.390
may know if you remain upon this island, | and 1.02.424
hast put thyself | upon this island as a spy, to 1.02.456
though this island seem to be desert — 2.01. 35 P
he will carry this island home in his pocket, 2.01. 91 P
for he is sure i' th' island. 2.01.325
i'll show thee every fertile inch o' th' island; 2.02.148
the folly of this island! 3.02. 4 P
by his cunning hath | cheated me of the island. 3.02. 44
(for, certes, these are people of the island), 3.03. 30
and on this island | where man doth not inhabit 3.03. 56
do that good mischief which may make this island 4.01.217
if this prove | a vision of the island, one dear 5.01.176
dwell | in this bare island by your spell, | but ep 8
claim | to this fair island and the territories, JN 1.01. 10
that island of england breeds very valiant H5 3.07.140 P
yond island carrions, desperate of their bones, 4.02. 39
and if my death might make this island happy, 2H6 3.01.148
enough to purchase such another island, | so 3.03. 3
like to his island, girt in with the ocean, | or 3H6 4.08. 20
you shall do more | than all the island kings — TRO 3.01.154
time of his infirmity, | will shake this island. OTH 2.03.128
not i, for this fair island. 2.03.142
who, like a late-sack'd island, vastly stood LUC 1740
ISLANDER 1 FR 0.0001 REL FR 0 V 1 P
this is no fish, but an islander, that hath TMP 2.02. 36 P
/ISLANDERS 1 FR 0.0001 REL FR 1 V 0 P
if i should say i saw such /islanders | (for, TMP 3.03. 29
ISLANDERS 4 FR 0.0004 REL FR 4 V 0 P
and coops from other lands her islanders, | even JN 2.01. 25
have i not heard these islanders shout out 5.02.103
savage islanders | pompey the great; 2H6 4.01.137
and the generous islanders | by you invited, do OTH 3.03.280
ISLAND'S 2 FR 0.0002 REL FR 2 V 0 P
this island's mine by sycorax my mother, | which TMP 1.02.331
shelter that abuts against | the island's side. PER 5.01. 52
ISLANDS 4 FR 0.0004 REL FR 3 V 1 P
of it in the sea, bring forth more islands. TMP 2.01. 94 P
some to discover islands far away; TGV 1.03. 9
when fame shall in our islands sound her trump, TRO 3.03.210
realms and islands were | as plates dropp'd from ANT 5.02. 91
ISLE 40 FR 0.0045 REL FR 36 V 4 P
in troops i have dispers'd them 'bout the isle. TMP 1.02.220
in an odd angle of the isle, and sitting, | his 1.02.223
and show'd thee all the qualities o' th' isle, 1.02.337
i had peopled else | this isle with calibans. 1.02.351
had i plantation of this isle, my lord — 2.01.144
this is some monster of the isle with four legs, 2.02. 65 P
they say there's but five upon this isle: 3.02. 5 P
i say by sorcery he got this isle; 3.02. 52
the isle is full of noises, | sounds, and sweet 3.02.135
in this most desolate isle, else falls | upon 3.03. 80
you do yet taste | some subtleties o' th' isle, 5.01.124
prospero, his dukedom | in a poor isle; 5.01.212
you'ld be king o' the isle, sirrah? 5.01.288 P
accidents gone by | since i came to this isle. 5.01.307
fertile the isle, the temple much surpassing WT 3.01. 2
blood which ow'd the breadth of all this isle, JN 4.02. 99
that we, the sons and children of this isle, 5.02. 25
this royal throne of kings, this sceptred isle, R2 2.01. 40
farm | in that nook-shotten isle of albion. H5 3.05. 14
our isle be made a nourish of salt tears, | and 1H6 1.01. 50
that dims the honor of this warlike isle! 2H6 1.01.125
is this the government of britain's isle, | and 1.03. 44
with sir john stanley, in the isle of man. 2.03. 13
now | to take her with him to the isle of man. 2.04. 78
why, madam, that is to the isle of man, | there 2.04. 94
is term'd the civill'st place of all this isle: 4.07. 61
duke | in the seat royal of this famous isle? R3 3.01.164
and all good men of this ungovern'd isle. 3.07.110
the noble isle doth want /her proper limbs; 3.07.125
swine | is now even in the centry of this isle, 5.02. 11
may proceed a gem | to lighten all this isle? H8 2.03. 79
with due course toward the isle of rhodes, OTH 1.03. 34
thanks you, the valiant of /this warlike isle, 2.01. 43
how does my old acquaintance of this isle? 2.01.203
/heaven bless the isle of cyprus and our noble 2.02. 11 P
the very elements of this warlike isle, | have i 2.03. 57
in some action | that may offend the isle. 2.03. 61
bell, it frights the isle | from her propriety. 2.03.175
we had not rated him | his part o' th' isle. ANT 3.06. 26
with | the natural bravery of your isle, which CYM 3.01. 18
/ISLES 1 FR 0.0001 REL FR 1 V 0 P
/from /isles /of /greece | /the /princes TRO pr 1
ISLES 1 FR 0.0001 REL FR 1 V 0 P
upon him) from the western isles | of kerns and MAC 1.02. 12
ISRAEL 1 FR 0.0001 REL FR 0 V 1 P
o jephthah, judge of israel, what a treasure HAM 2.02.403 P
ISSU'D 1 FR 0.0001 REL FR 1 V 0 P
of wilderness | ne'er issu'd from his blood. MM 3.01.142
/ISSUE 2 FR 0.0002 REL FR 2 V 0 P
/what /is /the /issue /of /the /business /there. HAM 5.02. 72
to thine and albany's /issue | be this perpetual LR 1.01. 66
ISSUE 113 FR 0.0127 REL FR 95 V 18 P
as i hope | for quiet days, fair issue, and long TMP 4.01. 24
may prosperous be, | and honor'd in their issue. 4.01.105
that his issue | should become kings of naples? 5.01.205
are whole, and let burnt sack be the issue. WIV 3.01.109 P
him, gentlemen, see the issue of his search. 3.03.174 P
door with pistols, that none shall issue out; 4.02. 52 P
see but the issue of my jealousy. 4.02.196 P

many a thousand grains | that issue out of dust. MM 3.01. 21
look you for any other issue? ADO 2.02. 30 P
grow this to what adverse issue it can, i will 2.02. 51 P
till midnight, and let the issue show itself. 3.02.130 P
hand | took up a beggar's issue at my gates, 4.01.132
and hymen now with luckier issue speed 's | than 5.03. 32
and the issue, there create, | ever shall be MND 5.01.405
nature's hand | shall not in their issue stand; 5.01.410
excuse, | that she is issue to a faithless jew. MV 2.04. 37
come forth to view | the issue of th' exploit. 3.02. 60
blessing of god till i have issue a' my body; AWW 1.03. 25 P
which, as the dearest issue of his practice, 2.01.106
conferr'd by testament to th' sequent issue, 5.03.197
a part, whose issue | will hiss me to my grave: WT 1.02.188
to do a thing, where i the issue doubted, 1.02.259
than they | should not produce fair issue. 2.01.150
free undertaking cannot miss | a thriving issue. 2.02. 43
is none of mine, | it is the issue of polixenes. 2.03. 94
so bloody, must | lead on to some foul issue. 2.03.153
no! i'll not rear | another's issue. 2.03.193
and gracious be the issue! 3.01. 22
(this being indeed the issue | of king polixenes 3.03. 43
no less unhappy, their issue not being gracious, 4.02. 27 P
what dangers, by his highness' fail of issue, 5.01. 27
care not for issue, | the crown will find an 5.01. 46
i would most gladly know the issue of it. 5.02. 8 P
being, have preserv'd | myself to see the issue. 5.03.128
must | with fearful bloody issue arbitrate. JN 1.01. 38
charge | that art the issue of my dear offense, 1.01.257
sin and her the plague | on this removed issue, 2.01.186
lo! now! now see the issue of your peace. 3.04. 21
i fear will issue thence | the foul corruption 4.02. 80
to god, my king, and my succeeding issue, R2 1.03. 20
well, well, i see the issue of these arms. 2.03.152
take horse, | uncertain of the issue any way. 1H4 1.01. 61
come, what's the issue? 2.04. 91 P
here come the heavy issue of dead harry. 2H4 5.02. 14
know so full a voice issue from so empty a heart H5 4.04. 68 P
with /mistful eyes, or they will issue too. 4.06. 34
so happy be the issue, brother /england, | of 5.02. 12
and from her blood raise up | issue to me, that 5.02.349
and thou seest that i no issue have, | and that 1H6 2.05. 94
and strong enough to issue out and fight. 4.02. 20
seen) | will answer our hope in issue of a king; 5.05. 72
the issue of the next son should have reign'd. 2H6 2.02. 32
from whose line | i claim the crown, had issue, 2.02. 35
edmund had issue, roger earl of march; 2.02. 37
roger had issue, edmund, anne, and eleanor. 2.02. 38
if the issue of the elder son | succeed before 2.02. 51
till lionel's issue fails, his should not reign. 2.02. 56
and issue forth and bid them battle straight. 3H6 1.02. 70
point | made issue from the bosom of the boy; 1.04. 81
king, | and raise his issue like a loving sire; 2.02. 22
and all the unlook'd–for issue of their bodies 3.02.131
doubt | will issue out again and bid us battle. 5.01. 63
that by g | his issue disinherited should be; R3 1.01. 57
thou loathed issue of thy father's loins! 1.03.231
time, | found that the issue was not his begot; 3.05. 90
myself, | no doubt we bring it to a happy issue. 3.07. 54
cur | preys on the issue of his mother's body, 4.04. 57
if i have kill'd the issue of your womb, | to 4.04.296
mine issue of your blood upon your daughter. 4.04.298
king henry's issue, richmond, comforts thee. 5.03.123
minister communication of | a most poor issue? H8 1.01. 87
example, in their issue | are to be fear'd. 1.02. 90
that if the king | should without issue die, 1.02.134
for her male issue | or died where they were 2.04.192
now, | while 'tis hot, i'll put it to the issue. 5.01.176
you now | the issue of your proper wisdoms rate, TRO 2.02. 89
devils, but i'll see some issue of my spiteful 2.03. 6 P
the issue is embracement. 4.05.148
i therein would have found issue. COR 1.03. 21 P
they fear us not, but issue forth their city. 1.04. 23
if all our wits were to issue out of one skull, 2.03. 21 P
a joyful issue. TIT 4.02. 65
a joyless, dismal, black, and sorrowful issue! 4.02. 66
delivered, | the issue of an irreligious moor, 5.03.121
and art | could to no issue of true honor bring. ROM 4.01. 65
away, thou issue of a mangy dog! TIM 4.03.366
take | the cruel issue of these bloody men, JC 3.01.294
it as a rich legacy | unto their issue. 3.02.137
so, | for banquo's issue have i fil'd my mind, MAC 3.01. 64
to pray for this good man, and for his issue, 3.01. 88
is this | that rises like the issue of a king, 4.01. 87
much, shall banquo's issue ever | reign in this 4.01.102
since that the truest issue of thy throne | by 4.03.106
but certain issue strokes must arbitrate, 5.04. 20
have after. to what issue will this come? HAM 1.04. 89
fault undone, the issue of it being so proper. LR 1.01. 17 P
and my shape as true, | as honest madam's issue? 1.02. 9
may carry through itself to that full issue 1.04. 3
be fast to my hopes, if i depend on the issue? OTH 1.03.363 P
and i think the issue will be, i shall have so 2.03.366 P
whose better issue in the war from italy, | upon ANT 1.02. 93
and all the unlawful issue that their lust 3.06. 7
then old and fond of issue, took such sorrow CYM 1.01. 37
they are the issue of your loins, my liege, 5.05.330
how? my issue? 5.05.331
whose issue | promises britain peace and plenty. 5.05.457
from whence an issue i might propagate, | are PER 1.02. 73
no issue know us; TNK 2.02. 32
sweet issue of a more sweet–smelling sire — VEN 1178
suggested this proud issue of a king; LUC 37
thy issue blurr'd with nameless bastardy; 522
when your sweet issue your sweet form should SON 13. 8
yet this abundant issue seem'd to me | but hope 97. 9
ISSUED 5 FR 0.0005 REL FR 5 V 0 P
his only heir | and princess no worse issued. TMP 1.02. 59
than from it issued forced drops of blood. H5 4.01.297
swain, | but issued from the progeny of kings; 1H6 5.04. 38
which issued from my other angel husband, | and R3 4.01. 68
the citizens of corioles have issued, | and COR 1.06. 10
ISSUELESS 2 FR 0.0002 REL FR 2 V 0 P
taking angry note, | have left me issueless; WT 5.01.174
if thou issueless shalt hap to die, | the world SON 9. 3
ISSUE'S 1 FR 0.0001 REL FR 1 V 0 P
my realms stood in | by this my issue's fail, H8 2.04.199
/ISSUES 1 FR 0.0001 REL FR 1 V 0 P
/could /not /beget | /such /different /issues. LR 4.03. 35
ISSUES 9 FR 0.0010 REL FR 8 V 1 P
are not finely touch'd | but to fine issues; MM 1.01. 36
it issues from the rancor of a villain, | a R2 1.01.143
the state | of our despis'd nobility, our issues H8 3.02.291
he that meets hector issues from our choice, TRO 1.03.347
and shall, albeit sweet music issues thence. 3.02.134
grow dear friends | and interjoin their issues. COR 4.04. 22
speech | to grosser issues nor to larger reach OTH 3.03.219
you are a fool granted, therefore your issues, CYM 2.01. 47 P
yet do effect | rare issues by their operance, TNK 1.03. 63
ISSUING 4 FR 0.0004 REL FR 4 V 0 P
word in it a gaping wound | issuing life–blood. MV 3.02.266
and with the issuing blood | stifle the villain 3H6 2.06. 82
as from a conduit with /three issuing spouts, TIT 2.04. 30
with purple fountains issuing from your veins — ROM 1.01. 85
/IS'T 3 FR 0.0003 REL FR 2 V 1 P
/is't /possible? HAM 2.02.357 P
/and /is't /not /to /be /damn'd, | /to /let 5.02. 68
/yea, /is't /come /to /this? LR 1.04.304
IS'T 195 FR 0.0220 REL FR 150 V 45 P
how now? moody? | what is't thou canst demand? TMP 1.02.245
what, is't a spirit? 1.02.410
is't near dinner–time? TGV 1.02. 67
what is't that you | took up so gingerly? 1.02. 69
what, is't murder? MM 1.02.137 P
peace and prosperity! who is't that calls? 1.04. 15
what is't your worship's pleasure i shall do 2.01.183 P
what is't i dream on? 2.02.178
is't not a kind of incest, to take life | from 3.01.138
is't not drown'd i' th' last rain? 3.02. 49 P
that angelo's a murtherer, is't not strange? 5.01. 39
is't not enough thou hast suborn'd these women 5.01.306
is't good to soothe him in these contraries? ERR 4.04. 79
is't possible? ADO 1.01. 74 P
is't come to this? 1.01.197 P
is't possible? sits the wind in that corner? 2.03. 98 P
some merry mocking lord belike, is't so? LLL 2.01. 52
is't not enough, is't not enough, young man, MND 2.02.125
is't not enough, is't not enough, young man, 2.02.125
why, get you gone. who is't that hinders you? 3.02.318
is't like that lead contains her? MV 2.07. 49
prithee, who is't that thou mean'st? AYL 1.02. 81 P
i pray you, what is't a' clock? 3.02.299 P
is't possible that on so little acquaintance you 5.02. 1 P
and say, "what is't your honor will command, SHR in.1. 115
is't he you mean? 1.02.221
minion, thou liest. is't not hortensio? 2.01. 13
is't possible you will away to–night? 3.02.189
is't possible, friend litio, that mistress 4.02. 1
is't so indeed? 5.01. 57 P
how long is't, count, | since the physician at AWW 1.02. 69
speak, is't so? 1.03.181
lord, is't i | that chase thee from thy country, 3.02.102
ay, marry, is't. 3.05. 38
is't not a handsome gentleman? 3.05. 80
is't but a drum? 3.06. 47 P
how now, my lord, is't not after midnight? 4.03. 84 P
is't real that i see? 5.03.306
is't not well done? TN 1.05.235 P
is't even so? 2.03.105 P
what kind of woman is't? 2.04. 26
here he is, here he is. how is't with you, sir? 3.04. 87 P
how is't with you, man? 3.04. 88 P
how is't with you? 3.04. 97 P
is't possible? 3.04.126 P
is't so saucy? 3.04.145 P
ay, is't! i warrant him. do but read. 3.04.146 P
is't possible that my deserts to you | can lack 3.04.348
how now, gentleman? how is't with you? 5.01.195 P
what cheer? how is't with you, best brother? WT 1.02.148
not noted, is't, | but of the finer natures? 1.02.225
who is't that goes with me? 2.01.116
is't lawful, pray you, to see her women? 2.02. 11
nor is't directly laid to thee, the death | of 3.02.194
apollo said, | is't not the tenor of his oracle, 5.01. 38
no indeed is't not; JN 4.01. 23
and is't not pity, o my grieved friends, | that 5.02. 24
is't not i | that undergo this charge? 5.02. 99
what comfort, man? how is't with aged gaunt? R2 2.01. 72
what is't, knave? 2.02. 96
what is't that takes from thee | thy stomach, 1H4 2.03. 40
my sweet creature of bumbast, how long is't ago, 2.04.327 P
is't a lusty yeoman? 2H4 2.01. 3 P
is't come to that? 2.02. 2 P
is't such a matter to get a pottle–pot's 2.02. 77 P
is't not so? 5.03. 76 P
is't so? 5.03. 78 P
what is't to me, when you yourselves are cause, H5 3.03. 19
no, faith, is't not, kate; 5.02.190 P
is't so, my lords of england? 5.02.331 P
what? wherein talbot overcame, is't so? 1H6 1.01.107
maid, is't thou wilt do these wondrous feats? 1.02. 64
reignier, is't thou that thinkest to beguile me? 1.02. 65
i cannot blame them all, what is't to them? 2H6 1.01.220
what, is't too short? 1.02. 12
is't not enough to break into my garden, | and 4.10. 33
is't cade that i have slain, that monstrous 4.10. 66
is't meet that he | should leave the helm and, 3H6 5.04. 6
is't for my life? 5.06. 29
what is't a' clock? R3 3.02. 4
what is't a' clock? 5.03. 47
marry, is't. H8 1.01. 97
is't possible the spells of france should juggle 1.03. 1
what is't for? 1.03. 18
how now, what is't? 1.04. 53
but is't not cruel | that she should feel the 2.01.165
it's one a' clock, boy, is't not? 5.01. 1
is't not a brave man? TRO 1.02.202 P
is't not a gallant man too, is't not? 1.02.213 P
is't not a gallant man too, is't not? 1.02.213 P
what is't? 1.03.314
and yet he loves himself. is't not strange? 2.03.160 P
is't possible? 4.02. 74 P
is't possible? 4.04. 32
is't a verdict? COR 1.01. 11 P
how long is't since? 1.06. 14
of warriors, | how is't with titus lartius? 1.06. 33
take't, 'tis yours. what is't? 1.09. 81
who is't can blame him? 4.06.105
is't possible that so short a time can alter the 5.04. 9 P
is't most certain? 5.04. 44
how long is't now since last yourself and i ROM 1.05. 32
is't so indeed? 1.05. 83
let me be satisfied, is't good or bad? 2.05. 37
how is't, my soul? 3.05. 25
who is't that calls? 3.05. 65
is't good? TIM 1.01. 36
what time a' day is't, apemantus? 1.01.256
is't not your business too? 2.02. 10
is't true? can 't be? 2.02.203
is't possible the world should so much differ, 3.01. 46
what is't a' clock? JC 2.02.114
what is't a' clock? 2.04. 23
is't possible? 4.03. 38
how far is't call'd to /forres? MAC 1.03. 39
how is't with me, when every noise appalls me? 2.02. 55
what is't you say — the life? 2.03. 69
is't night's predominance, or the day's shame, 2.04. 8
is't known who did this more than bloody deed? 2.04. 22
is't far you ride? 3.01. 23
what is't that moves your highness? 3.04. 47
what is't you do? 4.01. 49
who is't that can inform me? HAM 1.01. 79
you told us of some suit, what is't, laertes? 1.02. 43
what is't, ophelia, he hath said to you? 1.03. 88
ay, marry, is't, | but to my mind, though i am 1.04. 13
how is't, my noble lord? 1.05.117
what is't, my lord, we will. 1.05.143
what is't but to be nothing else but mad? 2.02. 94
alas, how is't with you, | that you do bend your 3.04.116
dear father, is't writ in your revenge | that, 4.05.142
is't possible a young maid's wits | should be as 4.05.160
ay, marry, is't — crowner's quest law. 5.01. 22 P
is't possible? 5.02. 25
such coz'nage — is't not perfect conscience, 5.02. 67
is't not possible to understand in another 5.02.125 P
he leaves, knows what is't to leave betimes, let 5.02.223 P
how is't, laertes? 5.02.305
who's there? what is't you seek? LR 3.04.127
how is't, my lord? 3.07. 94
who is't can say, "i am at the worst"? 4.01. 25
how is't? 4.06. 65
is't not the king? 4.06.107
what is't thou say'st? 5.03.273
is't possible? OTH 2.03.287 P
who is't you mean? 3.03. 44
is't possible, my lord? 3.03.358
is't come to this? 3.03.363
how is't with you, my lord? 3.04. 33
is't possible? 3.04. 68
/i' /faith! is't true? 3.04. 75
is't lost? 3.04. 80
is't gone? 3.04. 80
speak, is't out o' th' way? 3.04. 80
how is't with you, my most fair bianca? 3.04.170
is't come to this? 3.04.183
is't possible? 4.01. 42 P
is't possible? 4.02. 87
what is your pleasure, madam? how is't with you? 4.02.110
hark, who is't that knocks? 4.03. 53 P
is't frailty that thus errs? 4.03. 99
how is't, brother? 5.01. 71
what is the matter ho? who is't that cried? 5.01. 74
who is't that cried? 5.01. 75
is't you, sir, that know things? ANT 1.02. 8 P
say in mine ear, what is't. 2.07. 37
is't long or round? 3.03. 29
what is't you say? 3.07. 9
o, is't come to this? 3.13.115
ay, is't not strange? 4.03. 19
what is't thou say'st? 5.01. 12
is't not your trick? 5.02. 75
is't not meet | that i did amplify my judgment CYM 1.05. 16
pray, what is't? 1.06.184
it's almost morning, is't not? 2.03. 9 P
or is't not | too dull for your good wearing? 2.04. 40
how long is't since she went to milford–haven? 3.05.148 P
and a demand who is't shall die, i'ld say | "my 4.02. 23
yet is't not probable | to come alone, either he 4.02.141
who is't? 4.02.366
what thing is't that i never | did see man die, 4.04. 35
is't enough i am sorry? 5.04. 11
who is't can read a woman? 5.05. 48
what is't | to me, my father? PER 2.03. 57
is't not a goodly /presence? 5.01. 66
is't said this war's afoot? TNK 1.02.104
is't but a rare one? 2.02.154
is't not mad lodging | here in the wild woods, 3.03. 22
is't not too heavy? 3.06. 56
is't not a fine young gentleman? 4.01.118
is't not a wise course? 4.01.127
how far is't now to th' end o' th' world, my 5.02. 72
and what is't but mine own when i praise thee? SON 39. 4
is't not enough to torture me alone, | but slave 133. 3
what labor is't to leave | the thing we have not LC 239
ISTA 1 FR 0.0001 REL FR 1 V 0 P
dii faciant laudis summa sit ista tuae! 3H6 1.03. 48
IT *(also 't)*
/IT 71 FR 0.0080 REL FR 55 V 16 P
IT 8052 FR 0.9102 REL FR 5703 V 2349 P
ITALIAN 14 FR 0.0015 REL FR 9 V 5 P
french, nor italian, and you will come into the MV 1.02. 70 P
an old italian fox is not so kind, my boy. SHR 2.01.403
shall furnish me to those italian fields | where AWW 2.03.290
italian, or french, let him speak to me, | i'll 4.01. 72
now newly perform'd by that rare italian master, WT 5.02. 97 P
that no italian priest | shall tithe or toll in JN 3.01.153
is extant, and written in very choice italian. HAM 3.02.263 P
there's an italian come, and, 'tis thought, one CYM 2.01. 37 P
come, i'll go see this italian. 2.01. 48 P
what false italian | (as poisonous tongu'd as 3.02. 4
i am brought hither | among th' italian gentry, 5.01. 18
me | of these italian weeds and suit myself | as 5.01. 23
mine italian brain | gan in your duller britain 5.05.196
ay, so thou dost, | italian fiend! 5.05.210

ITALY 35 FR 0.0039 REL FR 28 V 7 P
who is so far from italy removed | i ne'er again TMP 2.01.111
he is the only man of italy, | always excepted ADO 3.01. 92
valor, | goes foremost in report through italy. 3.01. 97
a sigh, thou wast the proper'st man in italy. 5.01.173 P
i think he bought his doublet in italy, his MV 1.02. 74 P
if any man in italy have a fairer table, which 2.02.158 P
appears | than any that draws breath in italy. 3.02.296
lombardy, | the pleasant garden of great italy, SHR 1.01. 4
son, | a man well known throughout all italy. 2.01. 69
let higher italy | (those bated that inherit but AWW 2.01. 12
those girls of italy, take heed of them. 2.01. 19
you were beaten in italy for picking a kernel 2.03.258 P
report of fashions in proud italy, | whose R2 2.01. 21
retir'd himself | to italy, and there at venice 4.01. 97
let the volsces | plough rome and harrow italy, COR 5.03. 34
all the swords | in italy, and her confederate 5.03.208
art as hot a jack in thy mood as any in italy, ROM 3.01. 12 P
and land, | in every place, save here in italy. JC 1.03. 88
strife | shall cumber all the parts of italy; 3.01.264
whose better issue in the war from italy, | upon ANT 1.02. 93
our italy | shines o'er with civil swords; 1.03. 44
many hot inroads | they make in italy; 1.04. 51
o, from italy! 2.05. 23
for italy and caesar. 3.05. 20
him swear | the shes of italy should not betray CYM 1.03. 29
must not so far prefer her 'fore ours of italy. 1.04. 66 P
your italy contains none so accomplish'd a 1.04. 94 P
that drug–damn'd italy hath outcraftied him, 3.04. 15
some jay of italy | (whose mother was her 3.04. 49
i have a kinsman who | is bound for italy; 3.06. 61
up the confiners | and gentlemen of italy, most 4.02.338
we fear not | what can from italy annoy us, but 4.03. 34
did you suffer jachimo, | slight thing of italy, 5.04. 64
hearing us praise our loves of italy | for 5.05.161
fame, | won in the fields of fruitful italy; LUC 107
ITCH 7 FR 0.0008 REL FR 5 V 2 P
might scratch her where e'er she did itch. TMP 2.02. 53
do not, porpentine, do not, my fingers itch. TRO 2.01. 26 P
i would thou didst itch from head to foot; 2.01. 27 P
that rubbing the poor itch of your opinion COR 1.01.165
my fingers itch. ROM 3.05.164
mine eyes do itch; OTH 4.03. 58
the itch of his affection should not then | have ANT 3.13. 7
ITCH'D 1 FR 0.0001 REL FR 0 V 1 P
mass, and my elbow itch'd; ADO 3.03. 99 P
ITCHES 2 FR 0.0002 REL FR 1 V 1 P
i see a sword out, my finger itches to make one. WIV 2.03. 46 P
itches, blains, | sow all th' athenian bosoms, TIM 4.01. 28
ITCHING 2 FR 0.0002 REL FR 2 V 0 P
are much condemn'd to have an itching palm, | to JC 4.03. 10
i, an itching palm? 4.03. 12
ITEM 31 FR 0.0035 REL FR 1 V 30 P
"item, she can milk." TGV 3.01.277 P
"item, she brews good ale." 3.01.303 P
"item, she can sew." 3.01.306 P
"item, she can knit." 3.01.308 P
"item, she can wash and scour." 3.01.311 P
"item, she can spin." 3.01.314 P
"item, she hath many nameless virtues." 3.01.317 P
"item, she is not to be /kiss'd fasting, in 3.01.323 P
"item, she hath a sweet mouth." 3.01.327 P
"item, she doth talk in her sleep." 3.01.329 P
"item, she is slow in words." 3.01.332 P
"item, she is proud." 3.01.337 P
"item, she hath no teeth." 3.01.340 P
"item, she is curst." 3.01.343 P
"item, she will often praise her liquor." 3.01.345 P
"item, she is too liberal." 3.01.348 P
"item, she hath more hair than wit, and more 3.01.353 P
"item, she hath more hair than wit" — 3.01.358 P
"item, that no woman shall come within a mile of LLL 1.01.119 P
"item, if any man be seen to talk with a woman 1.01.129 P
as, item, two lips, indifferent red; TN 1.05.247 P
item, two grey eyes, with lids to them; 1.05.247 P
item, one neck, one chin, and so forth. 1.05.248 P
item, a capon ... 2s.2d.. 1H4 2.04.535 P
item, sauce ... 4d.. 2.04.536 P
item, sack, two gallons ... 5s.8d.. 2.04.537 P
item, anchoves and sack after supper ... 2s.6d.. 2.04.538 P
item, bread ... ob.. 2.04.539 P
item, /it /is /further /agreed /between /them, 2H6 1.01. 49 P
"item, it is further agreed between them, that 1.01. 57 P
item, you sent a large commission | to gregory H8 3.02.320
ITEMS 1 FR 0.0001 REL FR 0 V 1 P
by his side, and i to peruse him by items. CYM 1.04. 7 P
ITERANCE 1 FR 0.0001 REL FR 1 V 0 P
what needs this iterance, woman? OTH 5.02.150
ITERATION 2 FR 0.0002 REL FR 1 V 1 P
o, thou hast damnable iteration, and art indeed 1H4 1.02. 90 P
wants similes, truth tir'd with iteration, | as TRO 3.02.176
/ITHACA 2 FR 0.0002 REL FR 1 V 1 P
/speak, /prince /of /ithaca, /and /be't /of TRO 1.03. 70
absence did but fill /ithaca full of months. COR 1.03. 84 P
IT'S 35 FR 0.0039 REL FR 18 V 17 P
ay, give it me, it's mine: TGV 2.01. 3
and when it's writ, for my sake read it over, 2.01.130
ay, boy, it's for love. 2.04. 4 P
it's no matter for that, so she sleep not in her 3.01.330 P
it's an honorable kind of thievery. 4.01. 39
it's dry, sir. TN 1.03. 73 P
if she be, it's four to one she'll none of me. 1.03.106 P
well, it's all one. 1.05.129 P
i strook him first, yet it's no matter for that. 4.01. 36 P
it's sign she hath been liberal and free. 1H6 5.04. 82
it's supper–time, my lord, | it's /nine a' clock R3 5.03. 47
supper–time, my lord, | it's /nine a' clock. 5.03. 48
it's long, and't may be said | it reaches far, H8 1.01.110
and it's come to pass | this tractable obedience 1.02. 63
madam, | it's fit this royal session do proceed, 2.04. 66
it's heaven's will! 3.02.128
it's one a' clock, boy, is't not? 5.01. 1
and the devil come to him, it's all one. TRO 1.02.211 P
swell past hiding, and then it's past watching. 1.02.270 P
it's more than i know, i'll be sworn. 4.02. 51 P
in earnest, it's true; COR 1.03. 95 P
now it's twenty–seven; 2.01.155 P
nay, it's no matter for that. 4.05.165 P
it's sprightly, /waking, audible, and full of 4.05.222 P
the heyday in the blood is tame, it's humble, HAM 3.04. 69
o madam, my old heart is crack'd, it's crack'd! LR 2.01. 90
it's true, good lieutenant. OTH 2.03.105 P
it's the wind. 4.03. 54 P
it's monstrous labor when i wash my brain | and ANT 2.07. 99
look | our lamp is spent, it's out. 4.15. 85
were one such, | it's past the size of dreaming. 5.02. 97
it's almost morning, is't not? CYM 2.03. 9 P
yet still it's strange | what cloten's being 4.02.181
it's fit it should be so, for princes are | a PER 2.02. 10
is our profession any trade, it's no calling. 4.02. 38 P
ITS 12 FR 0.0013 REL FR 11 V 1 P
did beget of him | a falsehood in its contrary, TMP 1.02. 95
their fury and my passion | with its sweet air; 1.02.394
heaven grant us its peace, but not the king of MM 1.02. 4 P
how sometimes nature will betray its folly! WT 1.02.151
its tenderness! 1.02.152
dagger muzzled | lest it should bite its master, 1.02.157
me, let me know my trespass | by its own visage. 1.02.266
or death, upon the earth | of its right father. 3.03. 46
dying with mother's dug between its lips; 2H6 3.02.393
master, till the last | made former wonders its. H8 1.01. 18
must recompense itself | with its own sweat; TNK 1.01.154
assured | beyond its power there's nothing; 1.02. 65
/ITSELF 5 FR 0.0005 REL FR 4 V 1 P
/a /dream /itself /is /but /a /shadow. HAM 2.02.260 P
/it /sends /some /precious /instance /of /itself 4.05.163
/madness | /allows /itself /to /any /thing. LR 3.07.105
/cannot /be /bordered /certain /in /itself. 4.02. 33
/humanity /must /perforce /prey /on /itself, 4.02. 49
ITSELF 260 FR 0.0294 REL FR 219 V 41 P
and all the more it seeks to hide itself, | the TMP 3.01. 80
the solemn temples, the great globe itself, 4.01.153
that it assaults | mercy itself, and frees all ep 18
for love is still most precious in itself, | and TGV 2.06. 24
alas, how love can trifle with itself! 4.04.183
the folly of my soul dares not present itself; WIV 2.02.244 P
simple of itself; 3.05. 31 P
ignorance itself is a plummet o'er me. 5.05.163 P
of so quick condition | that it prefers itself, MM 1.01. 54
mercy is not itself, that oft looks so; 2.01.283
others, | hath yet a kind of medicine in itself, 2.02.135
to my heart, | making both it unable for itself, 2.04. 21
to appear most bright | when it doth tax itself; 2.04. 79
mercy to thee would prove itself a bawd, | 'tis 3.01.149
i have in doing good a remedy presents itself. 3.01.199 P
if the encounter acknowledge itself hereafter, 3.01.252 P
for claudio's, | th' offense pardons itself. 5.01.534
a victory is twice itself when the achiever ADO 1.01. 8 P
joy could not show itself modest enough without 1.01. 22 P
courtesy itself must convert to disdain, if you 1.01.122 P
will hold it as a dream till it appear itself; 1.02. 21 P
can virtue hide itself? 2.01.122 P
let every eye negotiate for itself, | and trust 2.01.178
her wit | values itself so highly that to her 3.01. 53
till midnight, and let the issue show itself. 3.02.130 P
of truth | can cunning sin cover itself withal! 4.01. 36
hero, | hero itself can blot out hero's virtue. 4.01. 82
this shame derives itself from unknown loins"? 4.01.135
truth itself, that thou art lovely. LLL 4.01. 62 P
than beauteous, truer than truth itself, have 4.01. 63 P
where nothing wants that want itself doth seek. 4.03.233
paints itself black, to imitate her brow. 4.03.261
for charity itself fulfills the law, | and who 4.03.361
and even that falsehood, in itself a sin, | thus 5.02.775
sin, | thus purifies itself and turns to grace. 5.02.776
steal both his | and leave itself unfurnish'd. MV 3.02.126
spirit | commits itself to yours to be directed, 3.02.164
in thy unhallowed dam, | infus'd itself in thee; 4.01.137
a wife | which is as dear to me as life itself, 4.01.283
but life itself, my wife, and all the world, 4.01.284
and then his state | empties itself, as doth an 5.01. 96
words, | they are as innocent as grace itself. AYL 1.03. 54
and hose ought to show itself courageous to 2.04. 7 P
as sensual as the brutish sting itself, | and 2.07. 66
shepherd, in respect of itself, it is a good 3.02. 13 P
but at this hour the house doth keep itself, 4.03. 81
and mark what object did present itself | under 4.03.103
a green and gilded snake had wreath'd itself, 4.03.108
suddenly, | seeing orlando, it unlink'd itself, 4.03.111
and to the other | a land itself at large, a 5.04.169
for she is sweeter than perfume itself | to whom SHR 1.02.152
th' ambition in my love thus plagues itself: AWW 1.01. 90
virginity murthers itself, and should be buried 1.01.139 P
a cheese, consumes itself to the very paring, 1.01.142 P
within /t' /one year it will make itself two, 1.01.147 P
and the principal itself not much the worse. 1.01.148 P
clock to itself, knew the true minute when 1.02. 39
i will tell truth, by grace itself i swear. 1.03.220
doctrine, have left off | the danger to itself? 1.03.242
the gift doth stretch itself as 'tis receiv'd, 2.01. 4
which challenges itself as honor's born, | and 2.03.134
greater than shows itself at the first view | to 2.05. 68
her death itself, which could not be her office 4.03. 57 P
the element itself, till seven years' heat, TN 1.01. 25
a murd'rous guilt shows not itself more soon 3.01.147
than ever proof itself would have earn'd him. 3.04.181 P
his indignation derives itself out of a very 3.04.246 P
and make itself a pastime | to harder bosoms! WT 1.02.152
bears not one, | let villainy itself forswear't. 1.02.361
does, for calumny will sear | virtue itself), 2.01. 74
thy brat hath been cast out, like to itself, 3.02. 87
but | the art itself is nature. 4.04. 97
as every present time doth boast itself | above 5.01. 96
no sorrow | but kill'd itself much sooner. 5.03. 53
england for itself. JN 2.01.202
the world, who of itself is peized well, | made 2.01.575
which harm within itself so heinous is | as it 3.01. 40
yea, faith itself to hollow falsehood change! 3.01. 95
therefore, since law itself is perfect wrong, 3.01.189
the iron of itself, though heat red–hot, 4.01. 61
and heaven itself doth frown upon the land. 4.03.159
but when it first did help to wound itself. 5.07.114
us rue, | if england to itself do rest but true. 5.07.118
consuming means, soon preys upon itself. R2 2.01. 39
hath made a shameful conquest of itself. 2.01. 66
no, misery makes sport to mock itself: 2.01. 85
gilt, | and make high majesty look like itself, 2.01.295
which shows like grief itself, but is not so; 2.02. 15
with too much riches it confound itself; 3.04. 60
as false, by heaven, as heaven itself is true. 4.01. 64
melted, | and barbarism itself have pitied him. 5.02. 36
love loving not itself, none other can. 5.03. 88
that sets the word itself against the word! 5.03.122
with scruples and do set the word itself 5.05. 13
have nam'd uncertain, the time itself unsorted, 1H4 2.03. 12 P
o, i am ignorance itself in this! 3.01.210
do, | make blind itself with foolish tenderness. 3.02. 91
he presently, as greatness knows itself, | steps 4.03. 74
and as the thing that's heavy in itself | upon 2H4 1.01.119
sir, the water itself was a good healthy water, 1.02. 3 P
dram of a scruple, or indeed a scruple itself. 1.02.131 P
that, with the hurly, death itself awakes? 3.01. 25
of solid firmness, melt itself | into the sea, 3.01. 48
if that rebellion | came like itself, in base 4.01. 33
to ye | shall show itself more openly hereafter. 4.02. 76
stretches itself beyond the hour of death. 4.04. 57
thy place and blood, | derives itself to me. 4.05. 43
th' advised head defends itself at home; H5 1.02.179
and labor shall refresh itself with hope | to do 2.02. 37
for peace itself should not so dull a kingdom 2.04. 16
description cannot suit itself in words | to 4.02. 53
in life so liveless as it shows itself. 4.02. 55
water, | which never ceaseth to enlarge itself, 1H6 1.02.134
robes, | and show itself, attire me how i can. 2H6 2.04.109
for where thou art, there is the world itself, 3.02.362
this happy day | is not itself, nor have we won 5.03. 6
knows not montague that of itself | england is 3H6 4.01. 39
itself | england is safe, if true within itself? 4.01. 40
that in your outward action shows itself R3 1.03. 66
single, but now married | to one above itself. H8 1.01. 16
my life itself, and the best heart of it, 1.02. 1
by itself | lies rich in virtue and unmingled. TRO 1.03. 29
then every thing include itself in power, 1.03.119
as well wherein 'tis precious of itself | as in 2.02. 55
to what infectiously itself affects, | without 2.02. 59
ignorance itself knows is so abundant scarce, it 2.03. 14 P
and whatever praises itself but in the deed, 2.03.156 P
that itself will leave | to be another's fool. 3.02.149
when time is old /and hath forgot itself, | when 3.02.185
hath no other glass | to show itself but pride; 3.03. 48
not, but commends itself | to others' eyes; 3.03.104
nor doth the eye itself, | that most pure spirit 3.03.105
that most pure spirit of sense, behold itself, 3.03.106
sense, behold itself, | not going from itself; 3.03.107
for speculation turns not to itself, | till it 3.03.109
is /mirror'd there | where it may see itself. 3.03.111
lest your displeasure should enlarge itself | to 5.02. 37
delight, | if there be rule in unity itself, 5.02.141
that cause sets up, with and against itself, 5.02.143
strong as heaven itself: 5.02.155
miracle — yet, in a sort, lechery eats itself. 5.04. 35 P
and, in a word, | scare troy out of itself. 5.10. 21
for him | shall fly out of itself. COR 1.10. 19
were a malice that, giving itself the lie, would 2.02. 32 P
he covets less | than misery itself would give, 2.02.127
to lose itself in a fog, where being three parts 2.03. 31 P
your territories, | though not for rome itself. 4.05.135
time, | and power, unto itself most commendable, 4.07. 51
virtue itself turns vice, being misapplied, ROM 2.03. 21
walls, | but purgatory, torture, hell itself. 3.03. 18
above the clouds, as high as heaven itself? 4.05. 74
because my heart itself plays "my heart is full. 4.05.106 P
ah me, how sweet is love itself possess'd, 5.01. 10
as will disperse itself through all the veins 5.01. 61
provokes itself and like the current flies TIM 1.01. 24
but moves itself | in a wide sea of wax. 1.01. 46
his honesty rewards him in itself, | it must not 1.01.130
no meed but he repays | sevenfold above itself; 1.01.278
being free itself, it thinks all others so. 2.02.233
feeling in itself | a lack of timon's aid, hath 5.01.146
marrow in the bearer strong | cries (of itself) 5.04. 10
for the eye sees not itself | but by reflection, JC 1.02. 52
bars, | never lacks power to dismiss itself. 1.03. 97
not erebus itself were dim enough | to hide thee 2.01. 84
the loyalty i owe, | in doing it, pays itself. MAC 1.04. 23
nimbly and sweetly recommends itself | unto our 1.06. 2
vaulting ambition, which o'erleaps itself, | and 1.07. 27
death's counterfeit, | and look on death itself! 2.03. 77
warrant in that theft | which steals itself, 2.03.146
shame itself, | why do you make such faces? 3.04. 65
poor country, | almost afraid to know itself! 4.03.165
him does condemn | itself for being there? 5.02. 25
war, | the day almost itself professes yours, 5.07. 27
melt, | thaw, and resolve itself into a dew! HAM 1.02.130
up it head and did address | itself to motion, 1.02.217
though hell itself should gape | and bid me hold 1.02.244
virtue itself scapes not calumnious strokes. 1.03. 38
youth to itself rebels, though none else near. 1.03. 44
for /loan oft loses both itself and friend, 1.03. 76
do to that, | being a thing immortal as itself? 1.04. 67
weed | that roots itself in ease on lethe wharf, 1.05. 33
will /sate itself in a celestial bed | and prey 1.05. 56
love, | whose violent property fordoes itself, 2.01.100
guilt | do not itself unkennel in one speech, 3.02. 81
wisdom should show itself more richer to signify 3.02.304 P
churchyards yawn and hell itself /breathes out 3.02.389
armor of the mind | to keep itself from noyance, 3.03. 13
were thicker than itself with brother's blood, 3.03. 44
and oft 'tis seen the wicked prize itself | buys 3.03. 59
since frost itself as actively doth burn, | and 3.04. 87
times | virtue itself of vice must pardon beg, 3.04.154
a mineral of metals base, | shows itself pure: 4.01. 27
it spills itself in fearing to be spilt. 4.05. 20
thought and afflictions, passion, hell itself, 4.05.188
the foul practice | hath turn'd itself on me. 5.02.318
of nothing hath not such need to hide itself. LR 1.02. 34 P
yet nature finds itself scourg'd by the sequent 1.02.105 P
may carry through itself to that full issue 1.04. 3
the shame itself doth speak | for instant remedy 1.04.246
this weaves itself perforce into my business. 2.01. 15
doth this instant | so much commend itself, you 2.01.114
thou art the thing itself: 3.04.106 P
fool to sorrow, | ang'ring itself and others. 4.01. 39
loathed part of nature should | burn itself out. 4.06. 40

of life, when life itself | yields to the theft. 4.06. 43
depriv'd that benefit, | to end itself by death? 4.06. 62
affliction till it do cry out itself | "enough, 4.06. 76
well stand up, | and call itself your brother. 5.03. 66
other sorrows, | and it is still itself. OTH 1.03. 58
justly put on the vouch of very malice itself? 2.01.147 P
her delicate tenderness will find itself abus'd, 2.01.232 P
though true advantage never present itself; 2.01.244 P
diet, | or breed itself so out of circumstances, 3.03. 16
and yet how nature erring from itself — 3.03.227
if she be false, /o, /then heaven /mocks itself! 3.03.278
it is a monster | begot upon itself, born on 3.04.162
a monster | begot upon itself, born on itself. 3.04.162
a better never did itself sustain | upon a 5.02.260
every passion fully strives | to make itself, in ANT 1.01. 51
low'ring, does become | the opposite of itself. 1.02.126
i should take you | for idleness itself. 1.03. 93
the varying tide, | to rot itself with motion. 1.04. 47
sir, like itself, and it is as broad as it hath 2.07. 42 P
honor, ne'er before | did violate so itself. 3.10. 23
let /that be left | which leaves itself. 3.11. 20
never anger | made good guard for itself. 4.01. 10
very force entangles | itself with strength. 4.14. 49
antony, | but antony's hath triumph'd on itself. 4.15. 15
o'erlabor'd sense | repairs itself by rest. CYM 2.02. 12
britain's a world | by itself, and we will 3.01. 13
and but disguise | that which, t' appear itself, 3.04.145
and true preferment shall tender itself to thee. 3.05.154 P
yet who this should be | doth miracle itself, 4.02. 29
life, good master, | must shuffle for itself. 5.05.105
my punishment | itself, and all my treason: 5.05.335
hath taught | my frail mortality to know itself, PER 1.01. 42
blows dust in others' eyes, to spread itself; 1.01. 97
are | a model which heaven makes like to itself. 2.02. 11
since every worth in show commends itself. 2.03. 6
fell storm | shall for itself itself perform. 3.ch. 54
fell storm | shall for itself itself perform. 3.ch. 54
and that work presents itself to th' doing: TNK 1.01.151
bootless toil must recompense itself | with its 1.01.153
the prison itself is proud of 'em; 2.01. 24 P
yet is heavier | than lead itself, stings more 5.01. 97
title of a kingdom may be tried | out of itself. 5.03. 34
beauty within itself should not be wasted. VEN 130
beauty itself doth of itself persuade | the eyes LUC 29
beauty itself doth of itself persuade | the eyes 29
wounding itself to death, rise up and fall, 466
that jealousy itself could not mistrust | false 1516
the poisoned fountain clears itself again, | and 1707
reason, in itself confounded, | saw division PHT 41
who heaven itself for ornament doth use, | and SON 21. 3
of state, | or state itself confounded to decay, 64.10
achieve, | and lace itself with his society? 67. 4
seen, | without all ornament, itself and true, 68.10
sweet, | though to itself it only live and die, 94.10
whilst it hath thought itself so blessed never? 119. 6
the sun itself sees not till heaven clears. 148.12

I'VE 1 FR 0.0001 REL FR 1 V 0 P
words | i've heard him utter to his son–in–law, H8 1.02.136

IVORY 8 FR 0.0009 REL FR 7 V 1 P
thy flesh and hers than between jet and ivory, MV 3.01. 40 P
in ivory coffers i have stuff'd my crowns; SHR 2.01.350
whom fortune with her ivory hand wafts to her, TIM 1.01. 70
here | within the circuit of this ivory pale, VEN 230
jail of snow, | or ivory in an alablaster band, 363
her breasts like ivory globes circled with blue, LUC 407
(rude ram, to batter such an ivory wall!), 464
like ivory conduits coral cesterns filling: 1234

IVY 5 FR 0.0005 REL FR 4 V 1 P
was | the ivy which had hid my princely trunk, TMP 1.02. 86
usurping ivy, brier, or idle moss, | who, all ERR 2.02.178
the female ivy so | enrings the barky fingers of MND 4.01. 43
them, 'tis by the sea–side, browsing of ivy. WT 3.03. 68 P
a belt of straw and ivy buds, | with coral PP 19.13

IVY/–TODS 1 FR 0.0001 REL FR 1 V 0 P
and curl'd, thick twin'd like ivy/–tods, | not TNK 4.02.104

IWIS 3 FR 0.0003 REL FR 3 V 0 P
there be fools alive, iwis, | silver'd o'er, and MV 2.09. 68
iwis it is not half way to her heart; SHR 1.01. 62
iwis your grandam had a worser match. R3 1.03.101

JACET 1 FR 0.0001 REL FR 0 V 1 P
i would have that drum or another, or hic jacet. AWW 3.06. 63 P

JACHIMO 7 FR 0.0008 REL FR 6 V 1 P
signior jachimo will not from it. CYM 1.04.171 P
see! jachimo! 2.04. 26
this yellow jachimo, in an hour — was't not? 2.05. 14
jachimo, | thou didst accuse him of incontinency 3.04. 46
they come | under the conduct of bold jachimo, 4.02.340
why did you suffer jachimo, | slight thing of 5.04. 63
that i was he, | speak, jachimo. 5.05.411

/JACK 1 FR 0.0001 REL FR 1 V 0 P
/that /like /a /jack /thou /keep'st /the /stroke R3 4.02.114

JACK 80 FR 0.0090 REL FR 18 V 62 P
done little better than play'd the jack with us. TMP 4.01.197 P
you are john rugby, and you are jack rugby. WIV 1.04. 58 P
by gar, i vill kill de jack priest; 1.04.117 P
say'st thou so, old jack? 2.02.138 P
jack rugby! 2.03. 1 P
vat is the clock, jack? 2.03. 3 P
by gar, jack rugby, he is dead already, if he be 2.03. 8 P
take your rapier, jack, i vill tell you how i 2.03. 13 P
by gar, he is de coward jack priest of de vorld; 2.03. 31 P
come at my heels, jack rugby. 2.03. 98 P
gar, you are de coward, de jack dog, john ape. 3.01. 83 P
jack rugby — mine host de jarteer — have i not 3.01. 91 P
or do you play the flouting jack, to tell us ADO 1.01.184 P
jack hath not gill. LLL 5.02.875
jack shall have jill; MND 3.02.461
did call me rascal fiddler | and twangling jack, SHR 2.01.158
lunatic, | a madcap ruffian and a swearing jack, 2.01.288
why, "jack, boy! 4.01. 41 P
i stand fooling here, his jack of the clock. R2 5.05. 60
where shall we take a purse to–morrow, jack? 1H4 1.02. 99 P
jack, how agrees the devil and thee about thy 1.02.114 P
sirrah jack, thy horse stands behind the hedge; 2.02. 70 P
tell me flatly i am no proud jack like falstaff, 2.04. 11 P
welcome, jack, where hast thou been? 2.04.113 P
go thy ways, old jack, die when thou wilt; 2.04.127 P
where is it, jack? where is it? 2.04.160 P
not two or three and fifty upon poor old jack, 2.04.188 P
ay, and mark thee too, jack. 2.04.210 P
come, your reason, jack, your reason. 2.04.235 P
mark, jack. 2.04.252 P
let's hear, jack, what trick hast thou now? 2.04.265 P
prithee do, jack. 2.04.296 P
here comes lean jack, here comes bare–bone. 2.04.326 P
how long is't ago, jack, since thou sawest thine 2.04.327 P
yes, jack, upon instinct. 2.04.355 P
banish poins, but for sweet jack falstaff, kind 2.04.475 P
but for sweet jack falstaff, kind jack falstaff, 2.04.476 P
kind jack falstaff, true jack falstaff, valiant 2.04.476 P
true jack falstaff, valiant jack falstaff, and 2.04.476 P
as he is, old jack falstaff, banish not him thy 2.04.477 P
him thy harry's company — banish plump jack, 2.04.479 P
the prince is a jack, a sneak–up. 3.03. 85 P
what say'st thou, jack? 3.03. 96 P
what didst thou lose, jack? 3.03.100 P
my lord, he call'd you jack, and said he would 3.03.138 P
and what should poor jack falstaff do in the 3.03.166 P
i have procur'd thee, jack, a charge of foot. 3.03.186 P
jack, meet me to–morrow in the temple hall | at 3.03.199
how now, blown jack? how now, quilt? 4.02. 49 P
but tell me, jack, whose fellows are these that 4.02. 61 P
poor jack, farewell! 5.04.103
but if i be not jack falstaff, then am i a jack. 5.04.139 P
but if i be not jack falstaff, then am i a jack. 5.04.139 P
usest him, jack falstaff with my /familiars, 2H4 2.02.132 P
come, i'll be friends with thee, jack. 2.04. 66 P
i pray thee, jack, i pray thee do not draw. 2.04.202 P
i pray thee, jack, be quiet, the rascal's gone. 2.04.208 P
well, sweet jack, have a care of thyself. 2.04.380 P
then was jack falstaff, now sir john, a boy, and 3.02. 25 P
is as arrant a villain and a jack sauce, as ever H5 4.07.141 P
but long i will not be jack out of office. 1H6 1.01.175
thee, jack cade the clothier means to dress the 2H6 4.02. 4 P
jack cade, the duke of york hath taught you this 4.02.154
will parley with jack cade their general. 4.04. 13
lord say, jack cade hath sworn to have thy head. 4.04. 19
jack cade proclaims himself lord mortimer, 4.04. 28
jack cade hath gotten london bridge: 4.04. 49
how now? is jack cade slain? 4.05. 1
jack cade! jack cade! 4.06. 7 P
jack cade! jack cade! 4.06. 7 P
be wise, he'll never call ye jack cade more. 4.06. 10 P
since every jack became a gentleman, | there's R3 1.03. 71
there's many a gentle person made a jack. 1.03. 72
you shall perceive that a jack guardant cannot COR 5.02. 62 P
thou art as hot a jack in thy mood as any in ROM 3.01. 11 P
hang him, jack! 4.05.145 P
take hence this jack and whip him. ANT 3.13. 93
the jack of caesar's shall | bear us an arrant 3.13.103
when i kiss'd the jack upon an up–cast, to be CYM 2.01. 2 P
every jack slave hath his bellyful of fighting, 2.01. 20 P

JACK–A–LENT 2 FR 0.0002 REL FR 0 V 2 P
you little jack–a–lent, have you been true to us WIV 3.03. 27 P
see now how wit may be made a jack–a–lent, when 5.05.127 P

JACK–A–NAPE 1 FR 0.0001 REL FR 0 V 1 P
teach a scurvy jack–a–nape priest to meddle or WIV 1.04.109 P

JACK–AN–APE 1 FR 0.0001 REL FR 0 V 1 P
for he speak for a jack–an–ape to anne page. WIV 2.03. 83 P

JACK–AN–APES 4 FR 0.0004 REL FR 0 V 4 P
and i will be like a jack–an–apes also, to burn WIV 4.04. 68 P
that jack–an–apes with scarfs. AWW 3.05. 85 P
on like a butcher and sit like a jack–an–apes, H5 5.02.142 P
then a whoreson jack–an–apes must take me up for CYM 2.01. 3 P

JACK–DOG 1 FR 0.0001 REL FR 0 V 1 P
scurvy jack–dog priest! WIV 2.03. 63 P

JACK'NAPE 1 FR 0.0001 REL FR 0 V 1 P
you jack'nape, give–a this letter to sir hugh. WIV 1.04.107 P

JACKS* 7 FR 0.0008 REL FR 5 V 2 P
boys, apes, braggarts, jacks, milksops! ADO 5.01. 91
a thousand raw tricks of these bragging jacks, MV 3.04. 77
be the jacks fair within, the gills fair without SHR 4.01. 49 P
be abus'd | with silken, sly, insinuating jacks? R3 1.03. 53
were lustier than he is, and twenty such jacks; ROM 2.04.152 P
do i envy those jacks that nimble leap | to kiss SON 128. 5
since saucy jacks so happy are in this, | give 128.13

JACOB 5 FR 0.0005 REL FR 4 V 1 P
a year and a quarter old come philip and jacob. MM 3.02.202 P
when jacob graz'd his uncle laban's sheep — MV 1.03. 71
this jacob from our holy abram was | (as his 1.03. 72
mark what jacob did: 1.03. 77
this was a venture, sir, that jacob serv'd for, 1.03. 91

JACOB'S 3 FR 0.0003 REL FR 3 V 0 P
streak'd and pied | should fall as jacob's hire, MV 1.03. 80
parti–color'd lambs, and those were jacob's. 1.03. 88
by jacob's staff i swear | i have no mind of 2.05. 36

JACQUES 2 FR 0.0002 REL FR 2 V 0 P
jacques chatillion, rambures, vaudemont, H5 3.05. 43
jacques of chatillion, admiral of france, | the 4.08. 93

JACULIS 1 FR 0.0001 REL FR 1 V 0 P
purus, | non eget mauri jaculis, nec arcu." TIT 4.02. 21

JADE 14 FR 0.0015 REL FR 9 V 5 P
only carry, therefore is she better than a jade. TGV 3.01.277 P
no, no, let carman whip his jade, | the valiant MM 2.01.255
sir, give him head, i know he'll prove a jade. SHR 1.02.247
no such jade as you, if me you mean. 2.01.201
not now fool myself, to let imagination jade me; TN 2.05.164 P
that jade hath eat bread from my royal hand, R2 5.05. 85
poor jade is wrung in the withers, out of all 1H4 2.01. 6 P
against the panting sides of his poor jade | up 2H4 1.01. 45
i had as live have my mistress a jade. H5 3.07. 59 P
let the gall'd jade winch, our withers are HAM 3.02.242 P
and presently | backward the jade comes o'er, TNK 5.04. 81
"how like a jade he stood, tied to the tree, VEN 391
till, like a jade, self–will himself doth tire. LUC 707
but love, for love, thus shall excuse my jade: SON 51.12

JADED 3 FR 0.0003 REL FR 3 V 0 P
must not be shed by such a jaded groom. 2H6 4.01. 52
to be thus jaded by a piece of scarlet, H8 3.02.280
of parthia | we have jaded out o' th' field. ANT 3.01. 34

JADE'S 2 FR 0.0002 REL FR 0 V 2 P
you always end with a jade's trick, i know you ADO 1.01.144 P
a red murrion a' thy jade's tricks! TRO 2.01. 20 P

JADES' 2 FR 0.0002 REL FR 1 V 1 P
'em, sir, they shall be jades' tricks, which are AWW 4.05. 61 P
tickle't out | of the jades' tails to–morrow. TNK 2.03. 29

JADES 11 FR 0.0012 REL FR 8 V 3 P
fie, fie on all tir'd jades, on all mad masters, SHR 4.01. 1 P
france is a stable, we that dwell in't jades, AWW 2.03.284
i'd play incessantly upon these jades, | even JN 2.01.385
phaeton, | wanting the manage of unruly jades. R2 3.03.179
is the next way to give poor jades the bots. 1H4 2.01. 9 P
pack–horses | and hollow pamper'd jades of asia, 2H4 2.04.164
water, | a drench for sur–rein'd jades, their H5 3.05. 19
horse, and all other jades you may call beasts. 3.07. 24 P
and their poor jades | lob down their heads, 4.02. 46
and now loud–howling wolves arouse the jades 2H6 4.01. 3
and like deceitful jades | sink in the trial. JC 4.02. 26

JAD'RY 1 FR 0.0001 REL FR 1 V 0 P
all foul means | of boist'rous and rough jad'ry, TNK 5.04. 72

J'AI 1 FR 0.0001 REL FR 0 V 1 P
j'ai gagne deux mots d'anglois vitement. H5 3.04. 13 P

JAIL 10 FR 0.0011 REL FR 3 V 7 P
bid him bring his pen and inkhorn to the jail. ADO 3.05. 59 P
our excommunication, and meet me at the jail. 3.05. 64 P
carry this mad knave to the jail. SHR 5.01. 92 P
carry me to the jail? 5.01. 94 P
away with the dotard! to the jail with him! 5.01.106 P
nose, that would have sent me to the jail. 5.01.132 P
my jail? TIM 3.04. 81
then am i the prisoner, and his bed my jail; LR 4.06.267 P
the hand, | a lily prison'd in a jail of snow, VEN 362
thou canst not then use rigor in my jail: SON 133.12

JAILER 14 FR 0.0015 REL FR 13 V 1 P
when | the steeled jailer is the friend of men. MM 4.02. 87
jailer, take him to thy custody. ERR 1.01.155
thou jailer, thou, | i am thy prisoner. 4.04.109
come, jailer, bring me where the goldsmith is, 4.04.142
jailer, look to him, tell not me of mercy. MV 3.03. 1
jailer, look to him. 3.03. 3
thou naughty jailer, that thou art so fond | to 3.03. 9
well, jailer, on. 3.03. 35
not your jailer then, | but your kind hostess. WT 1.02. 59
ignorance | is made my jailer to attend on me. R2 1.03.169
and his injury | the jailer to his pity. COR 5.01. 65
"but yet" is as a jailer to bring forth | some ANT 2.05. 52
but | your jailer shall deliver you the keys CYM 1.01. 73
thou shalt be then freer than a jailer; 5.04.196 P

JAILERS 1 FR 0.0001 REL FR 0 V 1 P
there were desolation of jailers and gallowses! CYM 5.04.204 P

JAILS 1 FR 0.0001 REL FR 0 V 1 P
break open the jails and let out the prisoners. 2H6 4.03. 16 P

JAKES 1 FR 0.0001 REL FR 0 V 1 P
mortar, and daub the wall of a jakes with him. LR 2.02. 67 P

JAMANY *(also germany)*

JAMANY 1 FR 0.0001 REL FR 0 V 1 P
you make grand preparation for a duke de jamany. WIV 4.05. 87 P

JAMES 7 FR 0.0008 REL FR 4 V 3 P
james gurney, wilt thou give us leave a while? JN 1.01.230
james, | there's toys abroad; 1.01.231
god–den to your worship, good captain james. H5 3.02. 85 P
into his son–in–law's house, sir james cromer, 2H6 4.07.111 P
james tyrrel, and your most obedient subject. R3 4.02. 67
oxford, redoubted pembroke, sir james blunt, 4.05. 14
/pretty too! what say you, james soundpost? ROM 4.05.136 P

JAMY 3 FR 0.0003 REL FR 1 V 2 P
nay, by saint jamy, | i hold you a penny, | a SHR 3.02. 82
and the scots captain, captain jamy, with him. H5 3.02. 75 P
captain jamy is a marvellous falorous gentleman, 3.02. 76 P

/JANE* 1 FR 0.0001 REL FR 1 V 0 P
coarse frieze capacities, ye /jane judgments, TNK 3.05. 8

JANE* 2 FR 0.0002 REL FR 0 V 2 P
him take that for coming a–night to jane smile; AYL 2.04. 48 P
and is jane nightwork alive? 2H4 3.02.198 P

JANGLED 1 FR 0.0001 REL FR 1 V 0 P
like sweet bells jangled, out of time and harsh; HAM 3.01.158

JANGLING 3 FR 0.0003 REL FR 2 V 1 P
good wits will be jangling, but, gentles, agree: LLL 2.01.225
sort, | as this their jangling i esteem a sport. MND 3.02.353
i would have kept such a jangling of the bells, PER 2.01. 41 P

JANUARY 2 FR 0.0002 REL FR 1 V 1 P
no, not till a hot january. ADO 1.01. 94 P
that blasts of january | would blow you through WT 4.04.111

JANUS 2 FR 0.0002 REL FR 2 V 0 P
now, by two–headed janus, | nature hath fram'd MV 1.01. 50
by janus, i think no. OTH 1.02. 33

JAPHET 1 FR 0.0001 REL FR 0 V 1 P
be kin to us, or they will fetch it from japhet. 2H4 2.02.118 P

J'APPRENNE 1 FR 0.0001 REL FR 0 V 1 P
il faut que j'apprenne a parler. H5 3.04. 4 P

JAQUENETTA 9 FR 0.0010 REL FR 1 V 8 P
matter is to me, sir, as concerning jaquenetta: LLL 1.01.202 P
"for jaquenetta (so is the weaker vessel called) 1.01.272 P
for true it is, i was taken with jaquenetta, and 1.01.312 P
with jaquenetta, and jaquenetta is a true girl, 1.01.312 P
come, jaquenetta, away. 1.02.145 P
this significant to the country maid jaquenetta. 3.01.131 P
it is writ to jaquenetta. 4.01. 58
be whipt for jaquenetta that is quick by him and 5.02.680 P
i have vow'd to jaquenetta to hold the plough 5.02.883 P

JAQUENETTA'S 1 FR 0.0001 REL FR 0 V 1 P
he wore none but a dishclout of jaquenetta's, LLL 5.02.714 P

JAQUES' 1 FR 0.0001 REL FR 1 V 0 P
"i am saint jaques' pilgrim, thither gone. AWW 3.04. 4

JAQUES 13 FR 0.0014 REL FR 8 V 5 P
and the beauteous heir | of jaques falconbridge, LLL 2.01. 42
my brother jaques he keeps at school, and report AYL 1.01. 5 P
lord, | the melancholy jaques grieves at that, 2.01. 26
fool, | much marked of the melancholy jaques, 2.01. 41
but what said jaques? 2.01. 43
"ay," quoth jaques, | "sweep on, you fat and 2.01. 54
it will make you melancholy, monsieur jaques. 2.05. 11 P
what you will, monsieur jaques. 2.05. 20 P
stay, jaques, stay. 5.04.194
to saint jaques le grand. AWW 3.05. 34
four or five, to great saint jaques bound, 3.05. 95
is a pilgrimage to saint jaques le grand; 4.03. 49 P
jaques, so many; 4.03.163 P

JAR 8 FR 0.0009 REL FR 8 V 0 P
i love thee not a jar o' th' clock behind | what WT 1.02. 43
and with sighs they jar | their watches on unto R2 5.05. 51
that two such noble peers as ye should jar! 1H6 3.01. 70

when such strings jar, what hope of harmony? 2H6 2.01. 55
were't not a shame that, whilst you live at jar, 4.08. 41
(between whose endless jar justice resides) TRO 1.03.117
shame, be friends, and join for that you jar. TIT 2.01.103
bow, | who conquers where he comes in every jar, VEN 100
JARRING 4 FR 0.0004 REL FR 4 V 0 P
at last, though long, our jarring notes agree, SHR 5.02. 1
his jarring, concord, and his discord, dulcet; AWW 1.01.172
that sees | this jarring discord of nobility, 1H6 4.01.188
th' untun'd and jarring senses, o, wind up | of LR 4.07. 15
JARS 8 FR 0.0009 REL FR 7 V 1 P
not a whit, when it jars so. TGV 4.02. 67 P
us go, we will include all jars | with triumphs, 5.04.160
for since the mortal and intestine jars | 'twixt ERR 1.01. 11
if he, compact of jars, grow musical, | we shall AYL 2.07. 5
let's hear. o fie, the treble jars. SHR 3.01. 39
base is right, 'tis the base knave that jars. 3.01. 47
cease these jars and rest your minds in peace. 1H6 1.01. 44
and humphrey with the peers be fall'n at jars: 2H6 1.01.253
JARTEER *(also garter)*
JARTEER 3 FR 0.0003 REL FR 0 V 3 P
mine host of de jarteer to measure our weapon. WIV 1.04.118 P
jack rugby — mine host de jarteer — have i not 3.01. 91 P
vere is mine host de jarteer? 4.05. 83 P
JASONS 2 FR 0.0002 REL FR 2 V 0 P
strond, | and many jasons come in quest of her. MV 1.01.172
we are the jasons, we have won the fleece. 3.02.241
JAUNCE 1 FR 0.0001 REL FR 1 V 0 P
what a jaunce have i! ROM 2.05. 26
JAUNCING 2 FR 0.0002 REL FR 2 V 0 P
gall'd, and tir'd by jauncing bullingbrook. R2 5.05. 94
to catch my death with jauncing up and down! ROM 2.05. 52
JAUNDIES 2 FR 0.0002 REL FR 2 V 0 P
and creep into the jaundies | by being peevish? MV 1.01. 85
grief hath set these jaundies o'er your cheeks? TRO 1.03. 2
JAVELING'S 1 FR 0.0001 REL FR 1 V 0 P
with javeling's point a churlish swine to gore, VEN 616
JAVELINS 1 FR 0.0001 REL FR 1 V 0 P
no more shake | our pointed javelins, whilst the TNK 2.02. 49
JAW 2 FR 0.0002 REL FR 1 V 1 P
/an /ape an apple, in the corner of his jaw, HAM 4.02. 18 P
i reak not if the wolves would jaw me, so | he TNK 3.02. 7
JAW–BONE 1 FR 0.0001 REL FR 0 V 1 P
as if 'twere cain's jaw–bone, that did the first HAM 5.01. 77 P
/JAWS 2 FR 0.0002 REL FR 2 V 0 P
/when /rank /thersites /opes /his /mastic /jaws, TRO 1.03. 73
the keen teeth from the fierce tiger's /jaws, SON 19. 3
JAWS 9 FR 0.0010 REL FR 9 V 0 P
the jaws of darkness do devour it up: MND 1.01.148
i snatch'd one half out of the jaws of death, TN 3.04.360
even in the jaws of danger and of death. JN 5.02.116
turns head against the lion's armed jaws, | and, 1H4 3.02.102
for whom this hungry war | opens his vasty jaws; H5 2.04.105
graves, and from their misty jaws | breathe foul 2H6 4.01. 6
earth, | thus i enforce thy rotten jaws to open, ROM 5.03. 47
hath op'd his ponderous and marble jaws | to HAM 1.04. 50
my bended hook shall pierce | their slimy jaws; ANT 2.05. 13
JAY 3 FR 0.0003 REL FR 3 V 0 P
what, is the jay more precious than the lark, SHR 4.03.175
heigh, /with /heigh, the thrush and the jay! WT 4.03. 10
some jay of italy | (whose mother was her CYM 3.04. 49
JAY'S 1 FR 0.0001 REL FR 1 V 0 P
show thee a jay's nest, and instruct thee how TMP 2.02.169
JAYS 1 FR 0.0001 REL FR 0 V 1 P
we'll teach him to know turtles from jays. WIV 3.03. 42 P
/JE 2 FR 0.0002 REL FR 0 V 2 P
/o, /je /m'en vois a la cour — la grande WIV 1.04. 52 P
sur mes genoux /je vous donne mille H5 4.04. 54 P
JE 26 FR 0.0029 REL FR 0 V 26 P
je te prie, m'enseignez; H5 3.04. 4 P
j'oublie les doigts, mais je me souviendrai. 3.04. 10 P
je pense qu'ils sont appeles de fingres, oui, de 3.04. 10 P
je pense que je suis le bon ecolier; 3.04. 13 P
je pense que je suis le bon ecolier; 3.04. 13 P
ecoutez, dites–moi si je parle bien: 3.04. 17 P
je m'en fais la repetition de tous les mots que 3.04. 25 P
il est trop difficile, madame, comme je pense. 3.04. 27 P
o seigneur dieu, je m'en oublie d' elbow. 3.04. 31 P
je ne doute point d'apprendre, par la grace de 3.04. 40 P
vous deja oublie ce que je vous ai enseigne? 3.04. 42 P
non, je reciterai a vous promptement: 3.04. 44 P
je ne voudrais prononcer ces mots devant les 3.04. 55 P
je reciterai une autre fois ma lecon ensemble: 3.04. 57 P
je pense que vous etes le gentilhomme de bonne 4.04. 2 P
o, je vous supplie, pour l'amour de dieu, me 4.04. 40 P
je suis le gentilhomme de bonne maison; 4.04. 41 P
ma vie, et je vous donnerai deux cents ecus. 4.04. 42 P
et je m'estime heureux que je tombe entre les 4.04. 55 P
je m'estime heureux que je tombe entre les mains 4.04. 55 P
tombe entre les mains d'un chevalier, je pense, 4.04. 56 P
que dit–il? que je suis semblable a les anges? 5.02.111 P
je quand sur le possession de france, et quand 5.02.181 P
il est /meilleur que l'anglois lequel je parle. 5.02.189 P
ma foi, je ne veux point que vous abaissez votre 5.02.254 P
excusez–moi, je vous supplie, mon tres puissant 5.02.256 P
JEALIOUS 20 FR 0.0022 REL FR 16 V 4 P
for at that time the jealious rascally knave her WIV 2.02.265 P
be detected with a jealious rotten bell–wether; 3.05.109 P
that hath the jealious fool to her husband! 4.02.131 P
i shall grow jealious of you shortly, launcelot, MV 3.05. 29 P
that my most jealious and too doubtful soul TN 4.03. 27
well strook in years, fair, and not jealious; R3 1.01. 92
'tis not to make me jealious | to say my wife is OTH 3.03.183
wear your eyes thus, not jealious nor secure. 3.03.198
air | are to the jealious confirmations strong 3.03.323
of no such baseness | as jealious creatures are, 3.04. 28
is he not jealious? 3.04. 29
is not this man jealious? 3.04. 99
think, | and no conception nor no jealious toy 3.04.156
but jealious souls will not be answer'd so; 3.04.159
they are not ever jealious for the cause, | but 3.04.160
the cause, | but jealious for they're jealious. 3.04.161
the cause, | but jealious for they're jealious. 3.04.161
you are jealious now | that this is from some 3.04.185
of one not easily jealious, but, being wrought, 5.02.345
nor dare i question with my jealious thought SON 57. 9
JEALOUS 32 FR 0.0036 REL FR 23 V 9 P
but, fearing lest my jealous aim might err, TGV 3.01. 28
they say the jealous wittolly knave hath masses WIV 2.02.272 P
he will trust his wife, he will not be jealous. 2.02.301 P
it is not jealous in france. 3.03.173 P
met the jealous knave their master in the door, 3.05.101 P
let them say of me, "as jealous as ford, that 4.02.163 P
who would be jealous then of such a one? ERR 4.02. 23
the venom clamors of a jealous woman | poisons 5.01. 69
thy jealous fits | hath scar'd thy husband from 5.01. 85
and something of that jealous complexion. ADO 2.01.295 P
and jealous oberon would have the child | knight MND 2.01. 24
what, jealous oberon? 2.01. 61
jealous in honor, sudden, and quick in quarrel, AYL 2.07.151
i will be more jealous of thee than a barbary 4.01.150 P
for our first merriment hath made thee jealous. SHR 4.05. 76
innocent soul, | more free than he is jealous. WT 2.03. 30
a true subject, leontes a jealous tyrant, his 3.02.133 P
my lord, your nobles, jealous of your absence, H5 4.01.285
the jealous o'erworn widow and herself, | since R3 1.01. 81
and from her jealous arms pluck him perforce. 3.01. 36
action | is more vindicative than jealous love. TRO 4.05.107
now, by the jealous queen of heaven, that kiss COR 5.03. 46
a jealous hood, a jealous hood! ROM 4.04. 13
a jealous hood, a jealous hood! 4.04. 13
but if thou, jealous, dost return to pry | in 5.03. 33
and be not jealous on me, gentle brutus: JC 1.02. 71
that you do love me, i am nothing jealous; 1.02.162
blam'd as mine own jealous curiosity than as a LR 1.04. 69 P
each jealous of the other, as the stung | are of 5.01. 56
sure | to have my wife as jealous as a turkey. TNK 2.03. 30
jealous of catching, swiftly doth forsake him, VEN 321
let not the jealous day behold that face, LUC 800
JEALOUSIES 11 FR 0.0012 REL FR 8 V 3 P
this is fery fantastical humors and jealousies. WIV 3.03.170 P
this is jealousies. 4.02.157 P
and leave you your jealousies too, i pray you. 5.05.132 P
sleeping else | but what your jealousies awake), WT 3.02.113
being transported by my jealousies | to bloody 3.02.158
together working with thy jealousies | (fancies 3.02.180
th' effects of his fond jealousies so grieving 4.01. 18
rumor is a pipe | blown by surmises, jealousies, 2H4 in 16
you, | let not my jealousies be your dishonors, MAC 4.03. 29
or else break out in peevish jealousies, OTH 4.03. 89
all little jealousies, which now seem great, ANT 2.02.131
JEALOUSY 41 FR 0.0046 REL FR 30 V 11 P
for love, thou know'st, is full of jealousy. TGV 2.04.177
it would give eternal food to his jealousy. WIV 2.01.101 P
he's as far from jealousy as i am from giving 2.01.103 P
he's a very jealousy man. 2.02. 90 P
who says this is improvident jealousy? 2.02.289 P
/god be prais'd for my jealousy! 2.02.309 P
never saw him so gross in his jealousy till now. 3.03.189 P
dwelling in a continual 'larum of jealousy, 3.05. 72 P
intelligence is true, my jealousy is reasonable. 4.02.149 P
see but the issue of my jealousy. 4.02.196 P
hath the finest mad devil of jealousy in him, 5.01. 18 P
self–harming jealousy — fie, beat it hence! ERR 2.01.102
how many fond fools serve mad jealousy? 2.01.116
that jealousy shall be call'd assurance, and all ADO 2.02. 49 P
these are the forgeries of jealousy; MND 2.01. 81
that hatred is so far from jealousy | to sleep 4.01.144
and shudd'ring fear, and green–eyed jealousy! MV 3.02.110
but jealousy what might befall your travel, TN 3.03. 8
(a savage jealousy | that sometime savors nobly) 5.01.119
this jealousy | is for a precious creature: WT 1.02.451
o, how hast thou with jealousy infected | the H5 2.02.126
that never may ill office, or fell jealousy, 5.02.363
alas, a kind of godly jealousy | (which i TRO 4.04. 80
meant to wrack thee, but beshrow my jealousy! HAM 2.01.110
amiss, | so full of artless jealousy is guilt, 4.05. 19
the moor | at least into a jealousy so strong OTH 2.01.301
and /oft my jealousy | shapes faults that are 3.03.147
o, beware, my lord, of jealousy! 3.03.165
souls of all my tribe defend | from jealousy! 3.03.176
think'st thou i'ld make a life of jealousy? 3.03.177
this — | away at once with love or jealousy! 3.03.192
and his unbookish jealousy must /conster | poor 4.01.101
a season, but our jealousy | does yet depend. CYM 4.03. 22
nobler heart and brain | with needless jealousy, 5.04. 66
resume her ancient fit of jealousy | to get the TNK 1.02. 22
lest jealousy, that sour unwelcome guest, VEN 449
reigns, disturbing jealousy | doth call himself 649
spring, | this carry–tale, dissentious jealousy, 657
it shall be waited on with jealousy, | find 1137
that jealousy itself could not mistrust | false LUC 1516
in me, | the scope and tenure of thy jealousy? SON 61. 8
JEAN *(see jane*)*
JEER 1 FR 0.0001 REL FR 1 V 0 P
yea, dost thou jeer and flout me in the teeth? ERR 2.02. 22
JEERING 2 FR 0.0002 REL FR 2 V 0 P
revenge the jeering and disdain'd contempt | of 1H4 1.03.183
so | as seely jeering idiots are with kings, LUC 1812
JELLY 3 FR 0.0003 REL FR 3 V 0 P
my best blood turn | to an infected jelly, and WT 1.02.418
almost to jelly with the act of fear, | stand HAM 1.02.205
out, vild jelly! LR 3.07. 83
JENNET *(also gennets)*
JENNET 1 FR 0.0001 REL FR 1 V 0 P
a breeding jennet, lusty, young, and proud, VEN 260
JENNY'S *(see jinny's)*
JEOPARDY 1 FR 0.0001 REL FR 1 V 0 P
look to thyself, thou art in jeopardy. JN 3.01.346
JEPHTHAH 4 FR 0.0004 REL FR 1 V 3 P
than jephthah when he sacrific'd his daughter. 3H6 5.01. 91
o jephthah, judge of israel, what a treasure HAM 2.02.403 P
am i not i' th' right, old jephthah? 2.02.410 P
if you call me jephthah, my lord, i have a 2.02.411 P
JERKIN 11 FR 0.0012 REL FR 0 V 11 P
mistress line, is not this my jerkin? TMP 4.01.236 P
now is the jerkin under the line. 4.01.236 P
now, jerkin, you are like to lose your hair, and 4.01.237 P
like to lose your hair, and prove a bald jerkin. 4.01.238 P
i quote it in your jerkin. TGV 2.04. 19 P
my jerkin is a doublet. 2.04. 20 P
an old cloak makes a new jerkin; WIV 1.03. 17 P
is coming in a new hat and an old jerkin; SHR 3.02. 44 P
and is not a buff jerkin a most sweet robe of 1H4 1.02. 42 P
what a plague have i to do with a buff jerkin? 1.02. 46 P
wear it on both sides, like a leather jerkin. TRO 3.03.265 P
JERKINS 2 FR 0.0002 REL FR 0 V 2 P
put on two leathern jerkins and aprons, and wait 2H4 2.02.171 P
they will put on two of our jerkins and aprons, 2.04. 16 P
JERKS 1 FR 0.0001 REL FR 0 V 1 P
flowers of fancy, the jerks of invention? LLL 4.02.125 P
JERONIMY 1 FR 0.0001 REL FR 0 V 1 P
go by, saint jeronimy! SHR in.1. 9 P
JERUSALEM 10 FR 0.0011 REL FR 9 V 1 P
do like the mutines of jerusalem, | be friends JN 2.01.378
we must neglect | our holy purpose to jerusalem. 1H4 1.01.102
'tis call'd jerusalem, my noble lord. 2H4 4.05.234
many years, | i should not die but in jerusalem, 4.05.237
i'll lie, | in that jerusalem shall harry die. 4.05.240
is a king, | the king of naples and jerusalem, 1H6 5.05. 40
sicilia, and jerusalem, and crown her queen of 2H6 1.01. 48 P
of naples, | of both the sicils and jerusalem, 3H6 1.04.122
world, | to meet with joy in sweet jerusalem. 5.05. 8
france | hath pawn'd the sicils and jerusalem, 5.07. 39
JESHU *(also cheshu, jesu)*
/JESHU 1 FR 0.0001 REL FR 0 V 1 P
/jeshu pless my soul! WIV 3.01. 11 P
JESHU 1 FR 0.0001 REL FR 0 V 1 P
by jeshu, i am your majesty's countryman, i care H5 4.07.111 P
JESSES 1 FR 0.0001 REL FR 1 V 0 P
haggard, | though that her jesses were my dear OTH 3.03.261
JESSICA 21 FR 0.0023 REL FR 21 V 0 P
tell gentle jessica | i will not fail her; MV 2.04. 19
was not that letter from fair jessica? 2.04. 28
fair jessica shall be my torch–bearer. 2.04. 39
what, jessica! 2.05. 3
as thou hast done with me — what, jessica! 2.05. 4
and rend apparel out — | why, jessica, i say! 2.05. 6
why, jessica! 2.05. 6
i am bid forth to supper, jessica. 2.05. 11
jessica, my girl, | look to my house. 2.05. 15
hear you me, jessica: 2.05. 28
well, jessica, go in. 2.05. 51
seen together | lorenzo and his amorous jessica. 2.08. 9
and will acknowledge you and jessica | in place 3.04. 38
fare you well, jessica. 3.04. 44
how cheer'st thou, jessica? 3.05. 70
night | did jessica steal from the wealthy jew, 5.01. 15
in such a night | did pretty jessica (like a 5.01. 21
but go we in, i pray thee, jessica, | and 5.01. 36
sit, jessica. 5.01. 58
hence — | nor you, lorenzo — jessica, nor you. 5.01.121
there do i give to you and jessica, | from the 5.01.291
JEST 108 FR 0.0122 REL FR 73 V 35 P
i thank thee for that jest; TMP 4.01.241 P
o jest unseen, inscrutable; TGV 2.01.135
why, do you not perceive the jest? 2.01.154 P
in earnest, they parted very fairly in jest. 2.05. 13 P
tell him my name is /brook — only for a jest. WIV 2.01.216 P
that were a jest indeed! 2.02.111 P
then make sport at me, then let me be your jest, 3.03.151 P
mistress anne the jest how my father stole two 3.04. 40 P
'od's heartlings, that's a pretty jest indeed! 3.04. 58 P
we do not act that often jest and laugh; 4.02.106
methinks there would be no period to the jest, 4.02.222 P
the image of the jest | i'll show you here at 4.06. 17
i pray you come, hold up the jest no higher. 5.05.105
with maids to seem the lapwing, and to jest, MM 1.04. 32
great men may jest with saints; 2.02.127
do we jest now, think you? 4.03. 49 P
i pray you jest, sir, as you sit at dinner. ERR 1.02. 62
as you love strokes, so jest with me again. 2.02. 8
what means this jest? 2.02. 21
think'st thou i jest? 2.02. 23
now your jest is earnest, | upon what bargain do 2.02. 24
you, | your sauciness will jest upon my love, 2.02. 28
if you will jest with me, know my aspect, | and 2.02. 32
sir, learn to jest in good time — there's a 2.02. 64 P
do so. this jest shall cost me some expense. 3.01.123
huddling jest upon jest with such impossible ADO 2.01.244 P
huddling jest upon jest with such impossible 2.01.245 P
i remember a pretty jest your daughter told /us 2.03.135 P
tush, tush, man, never fleer and jest at me; 5.01. 58
i jest not; 5.01.145 P
by yea and nay, sir, then i swore in jest. LLL 1.01. 54
catch | the other turns to a mirth–moving jest, 2.01. 71
not a word with him but a jest. 2.01.216
and every jest but a word. 2.01.216
shall that finish the jest? 2.01.221
too bitter is thy jest. 4.03.172
a pox of that jest! 5.02. 46
this jest is dry to me. 5.02.373
let us confess and turn it to a jest. 5.02.390
rated them | at courtship, pleasant jest, and 5.02.780
our letters, madam, show'd much more than jest. 5.02.785
i'll jest a twelvemonth in an hospital. 5.02.871
i jest to oberon and make him smile | when i a MND 2.01. 44
wink each at other, hold the sweet jest up; 3.02.239
do you not jest? 3.02.265
'tis no jest | that i do hate thee and love 3.02.280
though nestor swear the jest be laughable. MV 1.01. 56
then take him up, and manage well the jest. SHR in.1. 45
sirrah, come hither, 'tis no time to jest, | and 1.01.226
in, | i will continue that i broach'd in jest. 1.02. 84
nay then you jest, and now i well perceive | you 2.01. 19
if that be jest, then all the rest was so. 2.01. 22
tranio, you jest, but have you both forsworn me? 4.02. 48
to break a jest | upon the company you overtake? 4.05. 72
have at you for a /bitter jest or two! 5.02. 45
and, as the jest did glance away from me, | 'tis 5.02. 61
she says you have some goodly jest in hand. 5.02. 91
but they may jest | till their own scorn return AWW 1.02. 33
but what's your jest? TN 1.03. 75 P
a dry jest, sir. 1.03. 76 P
no other dowry with her but such another jest. 2.05.185 P
rich stake drawn, | and tak'st it all for jest. WT 1.02.249
and though thou now confess thou didst but jest, JN 3.01. 16
so jest with heaven? 3.01.242
and prove a deadly bloodshed but a jest, 4.03. 55
as gentle and as jocund as to jest | go i to R2 1.03. 95
eyes do drop no tears, his prayers are in jest, 5.03.101
i have a jest to execute that i cannot manage 1H4 1.02.161 P
the virtue of this jest will be the 1.02.186 P

and in the reproof of this lives the jest. 1.02.190 P
when a jest is so forward, and afoot too! 2.02. 46 P
laughter for a month, and a good jest for ever. 2.02. 96 P
nay, tell me if you speak in jest or no. 2.03. 99
have you made with this jest of the drawer? 2.04. 90 P
what, is it a time to jest and dally now? 5.03. 55 P
a slight oath and a jest with a sad brow will do 2H4 5.01. 82 P
reply not to me with a fool–born jest, | presume 5.05. 55
his jest will savor but of shallow wit, | when H5 1.02.295
a proper jest, and never heard before, | that 2H6 1.01.132
to die by thee were but to die in jest, | from 3.02.400
were play'd in jest by counterfeiting actors? 3H6 2.03. 28
i am a subject fit to jest withal, | but far 3.02. 91
well, jest on, brothers. 3.02.116
then none but i shall turn his jest to sorrow. 3.03.261
or did he make the jest against his will? 5.01. 30
grandam, this would have been a biting jest. R3 2.04. 30
you may jest on, but, by the holy rood, | i do 3.02. 75
a queen in jest, only to fill the scene. 4.04. 91
and given in earnest what i begg'd in jest. 5.01. 22
verily, i do not jest with you; COR 1.03. 92 P
i know thou dost but jest. TIT 2.03.253
here's no sound jest! 4.02. 26
how i have govern'd our determin'd jest? 5.02.139
death, | my hand cut off and made a merry jest; 5.02.174
to see now how a jest shall come about! ROM 1.03. 45
follow me this jest now, till thou hast worn out 2.04. 61 P
single sole of it is worn, the jest may remain, 2.04. 63 P
o single–sol'd jest, soly singular for the 2.04. 65 P
i will bite thee by the ear for that jest. 2.04. 77 P
look to't, think on't, i do not use to jest. 3.05.189
no, no, they do but jest, poison in jest — no HAM 3.02.234 P
they do but jest, poison in jest — no offense 3.02.234 P
a fellow of infinite jest, of most excellent 5.01.185 P
their mirth, and affliction a toy to jest at. TNK 2.01. 35 P
to toy, to wanton, dally, smile, and jest, VEN 106
no," quoth she, "sweet death, i did but jest, 997
but smile and jest at every gentle offer. PP 4.12
't may be she joy'd to jest at my exile, | 't 14. 9
JESTED 1 FR 0.0001 REL FR 1 V 0 P
you have but jested with me all this while. SHR 2.01. 20
JESTER 6 FR 0.0006 REL FR 1 V 5 P
for, believe me, i hear the parson is no jester. WIV 2.01.210 P
why, he is the prince's jester, a very dull fool ADO 2.01.137 P
that i was the prince's jester, that i was 2.01.243 P
feste, the jester, my lord, a fool that the lady TN 2.04. 11 P
how ill white hairs becomes a fool and jester! 2H4 5.05. 48
was, sir, yorick's skull, the king's jester. HAM 5.01.181 P
JESTERS 2 FR 0.0002 REL FR 2 V 0 P
with shallow jesters, and rash bavin wits, 1H4 3.02. 61
jesters do oft prove prophets. LR 5.03. 71
JESTING 5 FR 0.0005 REL FR 2 V 3 P
thou liest, thou jesting monkey thou! TMP 3.02. 45
nay, but his jesting spirit, which is now crept ADO 3.02. 59 P
the fire, | holding a trencher, jesting merrily? LLL 5.02.477
close, in the name of jesting! TN 2.05. 20 P
look you there, there's no jesting; TRO 1.02.206 P
JESTINGS 1 FR 0.0001 REL FR 1 V 0 P
her oaths, her tears, and all were jestings. PP 7.12
JEST'S 1 FR 0.0001 REL FR 1 V 0 P
a jest's prosperity lies in the ear | of him LLL 5.02.861
JESTS 17 FR 0.0019 REL FR 10 V 7 P
my uncle can tell you good jests of him. WIV 3.04. 39 P
while other jests are something rank on foot, 4.06. 22
lightens my humor with his merry jests. ERR 1.02. 21
dromio, come, these jests are out of season, 1.02. 68
when i have cause, and smile at no man's jests; ADO 1.03. 14 P
not in him by some large jests he will make. 2.03.198 P
you break jests as braggards do their blades, 5.01.187 P
o' my troth, most sweet jests, most incony LLL 4.01.142
and make him proud to make me proud that jests! 5.02. 66
but, turning these jests out of service, let us AYL 1.03. 26 P
hiding his bitter jests in blunt behavior; SHR 3.02. 13
he must observe their mood on whom he jests, TN 3.01. 62
and with some excellent jests, fire–new from the 3.02. 22 P
he was full of jests, and gipes, and knaveries, H5 4.07. 49 P
bed the livelong day | breaks scurril jests, TRO 1.03.148
he jests at scars that never felt a wound. ROM 2.02. 1
lucky, men did ransom lives | of me for jests; ANT 3.13.180
JESU *(also cheshu, jeshu)*
JESU 21 FR 0.0023 REL FR 8 V 13 P
for jesu christ in glorious christian field, R2 4.01. 93
had said at once, | "jesu preserve /thee! 5.02. 17
o jesu, my lord the prince! 1H4 2.04.284 P
o jesu, this is excellent sport, i' faith! 2.04.390 P
o jesu, he doth it as like one of these harlotry 2.04.395 P
o jesu, my lord, my lord! 2.04.486 P
o jesu, i have heard the prince tell him, i know 3.03. 83 P
o jesu, are you come from wales? 2H4 2.04.293 P
jesu, jesu, the mad days that i have spent! 3.02. 33 P
jesu, jesu, the mad days that i have spent! 3.02. 33 P
jesu, jesu, dead! 3.02. 43 P
jesu, jesu, dead! 3.02. 43 P
in the name of jesu christ, speak fewer. H5 4.01. 65 P
voice, | "jesu maintain your royal excellence!" 2H6 1.01.161
jesu bless him! 1.03. 5 P
for you shall sup with jesu christ to–night. 5.01.214
ay, and forswore himself — which jesu pardon! R3 1.03.135
have mercy, jesu! 5.03.178
jesu maria, what a deal of brine | hath wash'd ROM 2.03. 69
"by jesu, a very good blade! 2.04. 29 P
jesu, what haste! 2.05. 29
JESUS *(also gis)*
JESUS 4 FR 0.0004 REL FR 2 V 2 P
jesus bless us! 1H4 2.02. 82 P
jesus, the days that we have seen! 2H4 3.02.219 P
jesus preserve your royal majesty! 2H6 1.02. 70
"o, jesus bless us, he is born with teeth!" 3H6 5.06. 75
JET* 8 FR 0.0009 REL FR 7 V 1 P
thy flesh and hers than between jet and ivory, MV 3.01. 40 P
black, forsooth, coal–black as jet. 2H6 2.01.110
why then, thou know'st what color jet is of? 2.01.111
and yet, i think, jet did he never see. 2.01.112
dangerous | it is to jet upon a prince's right? TIT 2.01. 64
provide thee two proper palfreys, black as jet, 5.02. 50
are arch'd so high that giants may jet through CYM 3.03. 5
drew, | of amber, crystal, and of beaded jet, LC 37
JETS 1 FR 0.0001 REL FR 0 V 1 P
how he jets under his advanc'd plumes! TN 2.05. 31 P
JETTED 1 FR 0.0001 REL FR 1 V 0 P
whose men and dames so jetted and adorn'd, PER 1.04. 26
JEW 65 FR 0.0073 REL FR 38 V 27 P
a jew would have wept to have seen our parting; TGV 2.03. 11 P
thou art an hebrew, a jew, and not worth the 2.05. 54 P
if i do not love her, i am a jew. ADO 2.03.263 P
my sweet ounce of man's flesh, my incony jew! LLL 3.01.135
most brisky juvenal and eke most lovely jew, MND 3.01. 95
and say there is much kindness in the jew. MV 1.03.153
hie thee, gentle jew. 1.03.177
will serve me to run from this jew my master. 2.02. 2 P
i should stay with the jew my master, who, god 2.02. 23 P
and, to run away from the jew, i should be rul'd 2.02. 25 P
certainly the jew is the very devil incarnation, 2.02. 27 P
to offer to counsel me to stay with the jew. 2.02. 30 P
my master's a very jew. 2.02.105 P
for i am a jew if i serve the jew any longer. 2.02.112 P
for i am a jew if i serve the jew any longer. 2.02.112 P
the short and the long is, i serve the jew, and 2.02.128 P
the very truth is that the jew, having done me 2.02.132 P
i'll take my leave of the jew in the twinkling. 2.02.168 P
most beautiful pagan, most sweet jew! 2.03. 11 P
bid my old master the jew to sup to–night with 2.04. 17 P
if e'er the jew her father come to heaven, | it 2.04. 33
excuse, | that she is issue to a faithless jew. 2.04. 37
approach, | here dwells my father jew. 2.06. 25
now, by my hood, a gentle, and no jew. 2.06. 51
the villain jew with outcries rais'd the duke, 2.08. 4
as the dog jew did utter in the streets. 2.08. 14
for here he comes in the likeness of a jew. 3.01. 21 P
i am a jew. 3.01. 58 P
hath not a jew eyes? 3.01. 59 P
hath not a jew hands, organs, dimensions, senses 3.01. 59 P
if a jew wrong a christian, what is his humility 3.01. 68 P
if a christian wrong a jew, what should his 3.01. 70 P
be match'd, unless the devil himself turn jew. 3.01. 78 P
he had | the present money to discharge the jew, 3.02.273
what sum owes he the jew? 3.02.297
is very low, my bond to the jew is forfeit; 3.02.317 P
go one, and call the jew into the court. 4.01. 14
we all expect a gentle answer, jew! 4.01. 34
i pray you think you question with the jew: 4.01. 70
let me have judgment and the jew his will. 4.01. 83
the jew shall have my flesh, blood, bones, and 4.01.112
not on thy sole, but on thy soul, harsh jew, 4.01.123
between the jew and antonio the merchant. 4.01.155 P
and which the jew? 4.01.174
then must the jew be merciful. 4.01.182
therefore, jew, | though justice be thy plea, 4.01.197
and lawfully by this the jew may claim | a pound 4.01.231
for if the jew do cut but deep enough, | i'll 4.01.280
entreat some power to change this currish jew. 4.01.292
o upright judge! mark, jew: o learned judge! 4.01.313
o learned judge! mark, jew, a learned judge! 4.01.317
soft, | the jew shall have all justice. 4.01.321
o jew! an upright judge, a learned judge! 4.01.323
a daniel, jew! 4.01.333
why doth the jew pause? take thy forfeiture. 4.01.335
i thank thee, jew, for teaching me that word. 4.01.341
forfeiture, | to be so taken at thy peril, jew. 4.01.344
tarry, jew, | the law hath yet another hold on 4.01.346
art thou contented, jew? what dost thou say? 4.01.393
three thousand ducats, due unto the jew, | we 4.01.411
night | did jessica steal from the wealthy jew, 5.01. 15
from the rich jew, a special deed of gift, 5.01.292
every man of them, or i am a jew else, an ebrew 1H4 2.04.179 P
man of them, or i am a jew else, an ebrew jew. 2.04.179 P
digg'd i' th' dark, | liver of blaspheming jew, MAC 4.01. 26
JEWEL 65 FR 0.0073 REL FR 52 V 13 P
but, by my modesty | (the jewel in my dower), i TMP 3.01. 54
and i as rich in having such a jewel | as twenty TGV 2.04.169
and what says she to my little jewel? 4.04. 47 P
unless experience be a jewel — that i have WIV 2.02.204 P
"have i caught thee, my heavenly jewel?" 3.03. 43
the jewel that we find, we stoop and take't, MM 2.01. 24
i see the jewel best enamelled | will lose his ERR 2.01.109
can the world buy such a jewel? ADO 1.01.181 P
now hangeth like a jewel in the ear of caelo, LLL 4.02. 5 P
i knew her by this jewel on her sleeve. 5.02.455
pardon me, sir, this jewel did she wear, | and 5.02.456
and i have found demetrius like a jewel, | mine MND 4.01.191
since he hath got the jewel that i loved, | and MV 5.01.224
wears yet a precious jewel in his head; AYL 2.01. 14
to western inde, | no jewel is like rosalind. 3.02. 89
he hath the jewel of my life in hold, | his SHR 1.02.119
a ring, | my chastity's the jewel of our house, AWW 4.02. 46
we lost a jewel of her, and our esteem | was 5.03. 1
give her this jewel. TN 2.04.123
up my watch, or play with my — some rich jewel. 2.05. 60 P
here, wear this jewel for me, 'tis my picture. 3.04.208
jewel of children, seen this hour, he had pair'd WT 5.01.116
her jewel about the neck of it; 5.02. 33 P
where the jewel of life | by some damn'd hand JN 5.01. 40
a jewel in a ten–times–barr'd–up chest | is a R2 1.01.180
to set | the precious jewel of thy home return. 1.03.267
you back again to your master for a jewel — the 2H4 1.02. 19 P
bear her this jewel, pledge of my affection. 1H6 5.01. 47
view, | i took a costly jewel from my neck, | a 2H6 3.02.106
a jewel, lock'd into the woefull'st cask | that 3.02.409
a loss of her | that, like a jewel, has hung H8 2.02. 31
king has made him master | o' th' jewel house, 4.01.111
beside that of the jewel house, is made master 5.01. 34
as big as thou art, | were not so rich a jewel. COR 1.04. 56
of night | as a rich jewel in an ethiop's ear — ROM 1.05. 46
i have a jewel here — TIM 1.01. 12
sir, your jewel | hath suffered under praise. 1.01.164
lord, | you mend the jewel by the wearing it. 1.01.172
how dost thou like this jewel, apemantus? 1.01.210 P
you honor me so much | as to advance this jewel; 1.02.170
he gave me a jewel th' other day, and now he has 3.06.112 P
did you see my jewel? 3.06.114 P
and mine eternal jewel | given to the common MAC 3.01. 67
in it a jewel | well worth a poor man's taking. LR 4.06. 28
for your sake, jewel, | i am glad at soul i have OTH 1.03.195
lord, | is the immediate jewel of their souls. 3.03.156
equal theirs | till they had stol'n our jewel. ANT 4.15. 78
but that there is this jewel in the world | that CYM 1.01. 91
such honor as you have trust in, she your jewel, 1.04.153 P
she your jewel, this your jewel, and my gold are 1.04.153 P
my woman | search for a jewel that too casually 2.03.141
be pale, i beg but leave to air this jewel. 2.04. 96
'twas leonatus' jewel, | whom thou didst banish; 5.05.143
sea, | this jewel holds his building on my arm. PER 2.01.156
to take from you the jewel you hold so dear. 4.06.154 P
thou, o jewel | o' th' wood, o' th' world, hast TNK 3.01. 9
he restor'd her | as your stol'n jewel, and 5.04.119
hath dropp'd a precious jewel in the flood, | or VEN 824
of that rich jewel he should keep unknown | from LUC 34
"dear lord of that dear jewel i have lost, 1191
which, like a jewel hung in ghastly night, SON 27.11
shall time's best jewel from time's chest lie 65.10
queen | the basest jewel will be well esteem'd, 96. 6
thou art the fairest and most precious jewel. 131. 4
which remain'd the foil | of this false jewel, LC 154
JEWELLER 2 FR 0.0002 REL FR 2 V 0 P
the jeweller that owes the ring is sent for, AWW 5.03.296
i know them both; th' other's a jeweller. TIM 1.01. 8
JEWEL–LIKE 1 FR 0.0001 REL FR 1 V 0 P
her eyes as jewel–like | and /cas'd as richly, PER 5.01.110
JEWELS 33 FR 0.0037 REL FR 27 V 6 P
dumb jewels often in their silent kind | more TGV 3.01. 90
bearing thence | rings, jewels, any thing his ERR 5.01.144
as jewels in crystal for some prince to buy, LLL 2.01.243
and they shall fetch thee jewels from the deep, MND 3.01.158
what gold and jewels she is furnish'd with, MV 2.04. 31
and jewels, two stones, two rich and precious 2.08. 20
in that, and other precious, precious jewels. 3.01. 87 P
were dead at my foot, and the jewels in her ear! 3.01. 89 P
and get our jewels and our wealth together, AYL 1.03.134
of world | i wander from the jewels that i love. R2 1.03.270
i'll give my jewels for a set of beads, | my 3.03.147
yea, joy, our chains and our jewels. 2H4 2.04. 47 P
of pearl, | inestimable stones, unvalued jewels, R3 1.04. 27
of them | as jewels purchas'd at an easy price, TIT 3.01.198
more jewels yet? TIM 1.02.159
money, plate, jewels, and such–like trifles — 3.02. 21 P
and he wears jewels now of timon's gift, | for 3.04. 19
and e'en as if your lord should wear rich jewels 3.04. 23
desire his jewels, and this other's house, | and MAC 4.03. 80
the jewels of our father, with wash'd eyes LR 1.01.268
the jewels you have had from me to deliver OTH 4.02.186 P
if she will return me my jewels, i will give 4.02.198 P
of gold and jewels that i bobb'd from him | as 5.01. 16
of money, plate, and jewels | i am possess'd of; ANT 5.02.138
device, and jewels | of rich and exquisite form, CYM 1.06.189
as jewels lose their glory if neglected, | so PER 2.02. 12
ink and /paper, | my casket and my jewels; 3.01. 66
cases to those heavenly jewels | which pericles 3.02. 98
this letter and some certain jewels | lay with 3.04. 1
found there rich jewels, recovered her, and 5.03. 24
"torches are made to light, jewels to wear, VEN 163
but thou, to whom my jewels trifles are, | most SON 48. 5
placed are, | or captain jewels in the carcanet. 52. 8
JEWESS' 1 FR 0.0001 REL FR 1 V 0 P
a christian by, | will be worth a jewess' eye. MV 2.05. 43
JEWISH 2 FR 0.0002 REL FR 2 V 0 P
dog, | and spet upon my jewish gaberdine, | and MV 1.03.112
his jewish heart! 4.01. 80
JEWRY 7 FR 0.0008 REL FR 5 V 2 P
what a herod of jewry is this! WIV 2.01. 20 P
as is the sepulchre in stubborn jewry | of the R2 2.01. 55
clouds, as did the wives of jewry | at herod's H5 3.03. 40
at fifty, to whom herod of jewry may do homage. ANT 1.02. 29 P
herod of jewry dare not look upon you | but when 3.03. 3
herod of jewry; 3.06. 73
and went to jewry on | affairs of antony, there 4.06. 11
JEW'S 10 FR 0.0011 REL FR 3 V 7 P
i pray you, which is the way to master jew's? MV 2.02. 34 P
i pray you, which is the way to master jew's? 2.02. 40 P
but turn down indirectly to the jew's house. 2.02. 44 P
but i am launcelot, the jew's man, and i am sure 2.02. 89 P
boy, sir, but the rich jew's man, that would, 2.02.123 P
be preferment | to leave a rich jew's service, 2.02.147
and for the jew's bond which he hath of me, 2.08. 41
you not, that you are not the jew's daughter. 3.05. 11 P
for me in heaven because i am a jew's daughter; 3.05. 33 P
inquire the jew's house out, give him this deed, 4.02. 1
JEWS 1 FR 0.0001 REL FR 0 V 1 P
for in converting jews to christians, you raise MV 3.05. 35 P
JEZEBEL 1 FR 0.0001 REL FR 0 V 1 P
fie on him, jezebel! TN 2.05. 41 P
JIG 8 FR 0.0009 REL FR 2 V 6 P
and repenting, is as a scotch jig, a measure, ADO 2.01. 74 P
first suit is hot and hasty, like a scotch jig, 2.01. 75 P
but to jig off a tune at the tongue's end, LLL 3.01. 11 P
a gig, | and profound salomon to tune a jig, 4.03.166
my very walk should be a jig. TN 1.03.129 P
say on, he's for a jig or a tale of bawdry, or HAM 2.02.500 P
you jig and amble, and you /lisp, you nickname 3.01.144 P
and, for a jig, come cut and long tail to him! TNK 5.02. 49
JIGGING 1 FR 0.0001 REL FR 1 V 0 P
should the wars do with these jigging fools? JC 4.03.137
JIG–MAKER 1 FR 0.0001 REL FR 0 V 1 P
o god, your only jig–maker. HAM 3.02.125 P
JIGS 1 FR 0.0001 REL FR 1 V 0 P
all my merry jigs are quite forgot, | all my PP 17. 5
JILL *(also gill, etc.)*
JILL 1 FR 0.0001 REL FR 1 V 0 P
jack shall have jill; MND 3.02.461
JINGLING 2 FR 0.0002 REL FR 2 V 0 P
of roaring, shrieking, howling, jingling chains, TMP 5.01.233
run, the jingling of his gyves | might call fell TNK 3.02. 14
JINNY'S *(also ginn)*
JINNY'S 1 FR 0.0001 REL FR 0 V 1 P
vengeance of jinny's case! WIV 4.01. 62 P
JOAN 21 FR 0.0023 REL FR 21 V 0 P
some men must love my lady, and some joan. LLL 3.01.205
or groan for joan, or spend a minute's time | in 4.03.180
note, | while greasy joan doth keel the pot. 5.02.920
note, | while greasy joan doth keel the pot. 5.02.929
al'ce madam, or joan madam? SHR in.2. 110
well, now can i make any joan a lady. JN 1.01.184
the dolphin, with one joan de pucelle join'd, 1H6 1.04.101
thus joan de pucelle hath perform'd her word. 1.06. 3
'tis joan, not we, by whom the day is won; 1.06. 17

but joan de pucelle shall be france's saint. 1.06. 29
tut, holy joan was his defensive guard. 2.01. 49
his new–come champion, virtuous joan of /aire, 2.02. 20
then thus it must be, this doth joan devise: 3.03. 17
ah, joan, this kills thy father's heart outright 5.04. 2
ah, joan, sweet daughter joan, i'll die with 5.04. 6
joan, sweet daughter joan, i'll die with thee! 5.04. 6
fie, joan, that thou wilt be so obstacle! 5.04. 17
deny me not, i prithee, gentle joan. 5.04. 20
joan of aire hath been | a virgin from her 5.04. 49
then, joan, discover thine infirmity, | that 5.04. 60
and, ten to one, old joan had not gone out. 2H6 2.01. 4
JOB 2 FR 0.0002 REL FR 0 V 2 P
and as poor as job? WIV 5.05.156 P
i am as poor as job, my lord, but not so patient 2H4 1.02.126 P
JOCKEY 1 FR 0.0001 REL FR 1 V 0 P
"jockey of norfolk, be not so bold, | for dickon R3 5.03.304
JOCUND 9 FR 0.0010 REL FR 9 V 0 P
i am full of pleasure, | let us be jocund. TMP 3.02.117
and i, most jocund, apt, and willingly, | to do TN 5.01.132
as gentle and as jocund as to jest | go i to R2 1.03. 95
were jocund, and suppos'd their states were sure R3 3.02. 84
my soul is very jocund | in the remembrance of 5.03.232
out, and jocund day | stands tiptoe on the misty ROM 3.05. 9
then be thou jocund; MAC 3.02. 40
no jocund health that denmark drinks to–day, HAM 1.02.125
who, flatt'red by their leader's jocund show, LUC 296
JOG 2 FR 0.0002 REL FR 2 V 0 P
jog on, jog on, the foot–path way, | and merrily WT 4.03.123
jog on, jog on, the foot–path way, | and merrily 4.03.123
JOGGING 1 FR 0.0001 REL FR 1 V 0 P
you may be jogging whiles your boots are green. SHR 3.02.211
JOHN 269 FR 0.0304 REL FR 105 V 164 P
if he were twenty sir john falstaffs, he shall WIV 1.01. 3 P
if sir john falstaff have committed 1.01. 31 P
the knight sir john is there, and i beseech you 1.01. 70 P
is sir john falstaff here? 1.01. 97 P
here comes sir john. 1.01.108 P
pauca verba; sir john, good worts. 1.01.120 P
sir john, and master mine, | i combat challenge 1.01.161
what say you, scarlet and john? 1.01.173 P
rightly) is, "i am sir john falstaff's." 1.03. 48 P
what, john rugby! 1.04. 1 P
what, john rugby! 1.04. 39 P
john! 1.04. 40 P
what, john, i say! 1.04. 40 P
go, john, go inquire for my master; 1.04. 40 P
what, john rugby! john! 1.04. 56 P
what, john rugby! john! 1.04. 56 P
you are john rugby, and you are jack rugby. 1.04. 58 P
his might | for thee to fight, | john falstaff." 2.01. 19 P
sir john affects thy wife. 2.01.111
sir john, there's one master /brook below would 2.02.144 P
good sir john, i sue for yours — not to charge 2.02.164 P
if you will help to bear it, sir john, take all, 2.02.172 P
but, good sir john, as you have one eye upon my 2.02.185 P
now, sir john, here is the heart of my purpose: 2.02.224 P
what say you to't, sir john? 2.02.251 P
want no money, sir john, you shall want none. 2.02.258 P
gar, you are de coward, de jack dog, john ape. 3.01. 84 P
sir john falstaff. 3.02. 22 P
sir john falstaff! 3.02. 23 P
go home, john rugby, i come anon. 3.02. 86 P
what, john! what, robert! 3.03. 1 P
as i told you before, john and robert, be ready 3.03. 9 P
my master, sir john, is come in at your back 3.03. 24 P
o sweet sir john! 3.03. 47 P
i your lady, sir john? 3.03. 52 P
a plain kerchief, sir john. 3.03. 59 P
what, sir john falstaff! 3.03.139 P
what, john! 3.03.145 P
john! 3.03.145 P
that my husband is deceiv'd, or sir john. 3.03.179 P
another errand to sir john falstaff from my two 3.04.110 P
that indeed, sir john, is my business. 3.05. 63 P
he's a–birding, sweet sir john. 4.02. 8 P
step into th' chamber, sir john. 4.02. 11 P
you die, sir john — unless you go out disguis'd 4.02. 67 P
run up, sir john. 4.02. 79 P
go, go, sweet sir john. 4.02. 80 P
send quickly to sir john, to know his mind. 4.04. 83
come to speak with sir john falstaff from master 4.05. 4 P
bully sir john! 4.05. 16 P
thou /art clerkly, thou art clerkly, sir john. 4.05. 58 P
sir john? art thou there, my deer? my male deer? 5.05. 16 P
now, good sir john, how like you windsor wives? 5.05.106
sir john, we have had ill luck; 5.05.116 P
sir john falstaff, serve got, and leave your 5.05.129 P
why, sir john, do you think, though we would 5.05.146 P
o'er by a country fire — | sir john and all. 5.05.243
let it be so, sir john, | to master /brook you 5.05.243
was not count john here at supper? ADO 2.01. 1 P
i have earn'd of don john a thousand ducats. 3.03.108 P
and plac'd and possess'd by my master don john, 3.03.151 P
did confirm any slander that don john had made, 3.03.159 P
signior benedick, don john, and all the gallants 3.04. 96 P
the practice of it lives in john the bastard, 4.01.188
said, sir, that don john, the prince's brother, 4.02. 39 P
write down prince john a villain. 4.02. 41 P
ducats of don john for accusing the lady hero 4.02. 48 P
prince john is this morning secretly stol'n away 4.02. 61 P
to this man how don john your brother incens'd 5.01.235 P
abus'd, and don john is the author of all, who 5.02. 98 P
my lord, your brother john is ta'en in flight, 5.04.125
as stephen sly, and old john naps of greece, SHR in.2. 93
if you give him not john drum's entertainment, AWW 3.06. 38 P
of thy unnatural uncle, english john. JN 2.01. 10
father geffrey | than thou and john in manners, 2.01.127
king john, this is the very sum of all: 2.01.151
king john, your king and england's, doth 2.01.313
john, to stop arthur's title in the whole, 2.01.562
sh' adulterates hourly with thine uncle john, 3.01. 56
france is a bawd to fortune and king john, 3.01. 60
that strumpet fortune, that usurping john! 3.01. 61
to thee, king john, my holy errand is: 3.01.137
strange to think how much king john hath lost 3.04.121
john hath seiz'd arthur, and it cannot be | that 3.04.131
the misplac'd john should entertain an hour, 3.04.133
that john may stand, then arthur needs must fall 3.04.139
john lays you plots; 3.04.146
plainly denouncing vengeance upon john. 3.04.159
wrath | out of the bloody fingers' ends of john. 3.04.168
king john hath reconcil'd | himself to rome, his 5.02. 69
and come ye now to tell me john hath made | his 5.02. 91
because that john hath made his peace with rome? 5.02. 96
rather for sport than need) | is warlike john; 5.02.176
they say king john, sore sick, hath left the 5.04. 6
seek out king john and fall before his feet; 5.04. 13
even to our ocean, to our great king john. 5.04. 57
said | king john did fly an hour or two before 5.05. 17
old john of gaunt, time–honored lancaster, R2 1.01. 1
and furbish new the name of john a' gaunt, 1.03. 76
old john of gaunt is grievous sick, my lord, 1.04. 54
sir thomas erpingham, sir john ramston, | sir 2.01.283
sir john norbery, sir robert waterton, and 2.01.284
what says sir john sack and sugar? 1H4 1.02.113 P
sir john stands to his word, the devil shall 1.02.117 P
sir john, i prithee leave the prince and me 1.02.149 P
for if i hang, old sir john hangs with me, and 2.01. 68 P
what, a coward, sir john paunch? 2.02. 66 P
indeed i am not john of gaunt, your grandfather, 2.02. 67 P
old sir john with half a dozen more are at the 2.04. 82 P
here was sir john bracy from your father; 2.04.334 P
with him my son, lord john of lancaster, | for 3.02.171
sir john, you are so fretful you cannot live 3.03. 11 P
you are so fat, sir john, that you must needs be 3.03. 21 P
out of all reasonable compass, sir john. 3.03. 23 P
why, sir john, my face does you no harm. 3.03. 28 P
why, sir john, what do you think, sir john? 3.03. 54 P
why, sir john, what do you think, sir john? 3.03. 54 P
no, sir john, you do not know me, sir john. 3.03. 65 P
no, sir john, you do not know me, sir john. 3.03. 65 P
i know you, sir john, you owe me money, sir john 3.03. 66 P
you owe me money, sir john, and now you pick a 3.03. 66 P
you owe money here besides, sir john, for your 3.03. 72 P
an otter, sir john, why an otter? 3.03.126 P
indeed, sir john, you said so. 3.03.141 P
go bear this letter to lord john of lancaster, 3.03.195
to lord john of lancaster, | to my brother john; 3.03.196
is marching hitherwards, with him prince john. 4.01. 89
faith, sir john, 'tis more than time that i were 4.02. 54 P
but, sir john, methinks they are exceeding poor 4.02. 68 P
he is, sir john. i fear we shall stay too long. 4.02. 77 P
the prince of wales, lord john of lancaster, 4.04. 29
lord john of lancaster, go you with him. 5.04. 3
before, i lov'd thee as a brother, john, | but 5.04. 19
come, brother john, full bravely hast thou 5.04.130
this is the strangest fellow, brother john. 5.04.155
then, brother john of lancaster, to you | this 5.05. 25
you, son john, and my cousin westmerland 5.05. 35
young prince john | and westmerland and stafford 2H4 1.01. 17
and harry monmouth's brawn, the hulk sir john, 1.01. 19
sir john umfrevile turn'd me back | with joyful 1.01. 34
with some charge to the lord john of lancaster. 1.02. 63 P
sir john falstaff! 1.02. 65 P
sir john! 1.02. 71 P
sir john falstaff, a word with you. 1.02. 92 P
sir john, i sent for you before your expedition 1.02.101 P
the truth is, sir john, you live in great infamy 1.02.136 P
fie, fie, fie, sir john! 1.02.186 P
are going with lord john of lancaster against 1.02.204 P
snare, we must arrest sir john falstaff. 2.01. 8 P
how now, sir john? 2.01. 65
how comes this, sir john? 2.01. 80 P
sir john, sir john, i am well acquainted with 2.01.109 P
sir john, sir john, i am well acquainted with 2.01.109 P
pray thee, sir john, let it be but twenty nobles 2.01.153 P
my good lord here, i thank you, good sir john. 2.01.185 P
sir john, you loiter here too long, being you 2.01.186 P
master taught you these manners, sir john? 2.01.190 P
"john falstaff, knight" — every man must know 2.02.109 P
"sir john falstaff, knight, to the son of the 2.02.119 P
/familiars, john with my brothers and sisters, 2.02.133 P
and sisters, and sir john with all europe." 2.02.134 P
thou knowest sir john cannot endure an 2.04. 2 P
and aprons, and sir john must not know of it. 2.04. 17 P
lo here comes sir john. 2.04. 32 P
pray ye pacify yourself, sir john. 2.04. 80 P
tilly–fally, sir john, ne'er tell me; 2.04. 83 P
god save you, sir john! 2.04.110 P
i will discharge upon her, sir john, with two 2.04.114 P
and asking every one for sir john falstaff. 2.04.360
was i, and little john doit of staffordshire, 3.02. 19 P
then was jack falstaff, now sir john, a boy, and 3.02. 25 P
this sir john, cousin, that comes hither anon 3.02. 27 P
the same sir john, the very same. 3.02. 29 P
john a' gaunt lov'd him well, and betted much 3.02. 44 P
here come two of sir john falstaff's men, as i 3.02. 53 P
my captain, sir john falstaff, a tall gentleman, 3.02. 61 P
look, here comes good sir john. 3.02. 82 P
welcome, good sir john. 3.02. 84 P
no, sir john, it is my cousin silence, in 3.02. 87 P
what think you, sir john? 3.02.102 P
in faith, well said, sir john, very well said. 3.02.109 P
for th' other, sir john, let me see: 3.02.120 P
do you like him, sir john? 3.02.132 P
shall i prick him, sir john? 3.02.142 P
o sir john, do you remember since we lay all 3.02.194 P
ha, sir john, said i well? 3.02.212 P
have, that we have, in faith, sir john, we have. 3.02.217 P
come, sir john, which four will you have? 3.02.246 P
sir john, sir john, do not yourself wrong. 3.02.254 P
sir john, sir john, do not yourself wrong. 3.02.254 P
sir john, the lord bless you! 3.02.292 P
as familiarly of john a' gaunt as if he had been 3.02.320 P
it, and told john a' gaunt he beat his own name, 3.02.324 P
the prince, lord john and duke of lancaster. 4.01. 28
hath the prince john a full commission, | in 4.01.160
are not you sir john falstaff? 4.03. 10 P
i think you are sir john falstaff, and in that 4.03. 16 P
valor, taken sir john colevile of the dale, a 4.03. 38 P
prince john your son doth kiss your grace's hand 4.04. 83
look, look, here comes my john of lancaster. 4.05.225
thou bring'st me happiness and peace, son john, 4.05.227
sir john, you shall not be excus'd. 5.01. 11 P
sir john, you shall not be excus'd. 5.01. 20 P
where are you, sir john? 5.01. 53 P
come, sir john. 5.01. 59 P
sir john! 5.01. 86 P
well, you must now speak sir john falstaff fair, 5.02. 33
barren, beggars all, beggars all, sir john! 5.03. 8 P
a good varlet, a very good varlet, sir john. 5.03. 13 P
sir john, god save you! 5.03. 84 P
sir john, i am thy pistol and thy friend, | and 5.03. 93
"and robin hood, scarlet, and john." 5.03.103
sir john, thy tender lambkin now is king; 5.03.116
o the lord, that sir john were come! 5.04. 11 P
marry, sir john, which i beseech you to let me 5.05. 74 P
i beseech you, good sir john, let me have five 5.05. 83 P
a color that i fear you will die in, sir john. 5.05. 87 P
go carry sir john falstaff to the fleet. 5.05. 91
will continue the story, with sir john in it, ep 28 P
you come of women, come in quickly to sir john. H5 2.01.118 P
"how now, sir john?" 2.03. 17 P
brother john bates, is not that the morning 4.01. 85 P
sir john falstaff. 4.07. 51 P
john duke of bourbon, and lord bouciqualt: 4.08. 77
john duke of alanson, anthony duke of brabant, 4.08. 96
if sir john falstaff had not play'd the coward. 1H6 1.01.131
he | from john of gaunt doth bring his pedigree, 2.05. 77
whither away, sir john falstaff, in such haste? 3.02.104
english john talbot, captains, /calls you forth, 4.02. 3
and on his son young john, who two hours since 4.03. 35
o young john talbot, i did send for thee | to 4.05. 1
where is john talbot? 4.06. 4
art thou not weary, john? 4.06. 27
where is valiant john? 4.07. 2
now my old arms are young john talbot's grave. 4.07. 32
sir john! 2H6 1.02. 68
but how now, sir john hume? 1.02. 88
and't please your grace, against john goodman, 1.03. 17 P
john southwell, read you; 1.04. 12 P
next to whom | was john of gaunt, the duke of 2.02. 14
the eldest son and heir of john of gaunt, 2.02. 22
henry doth claim the crown from john of gaunt, 2.02. 54
with sir john stanley, in the isle of man. 2.03. 13
and sir john stanley is appointed now | to take 2.04. 77
must you, sir john, protect my lady here? 2.04. 79
and so, sir john, farewell! 2.04. 84
a headstrong kentishman, | john cade of ashford, 3.01.357
well he can, | under the title of john mortimer. 3.01.359
for that john mortimer, which now is dead, | in 3.01.372
we john cade, so term'd of our suppos'd father 4.02. 31 P
rise up sir john mortimer. 4.02.120 P
nay, john, it will be stinking law, for his 4.07. 11 P
such hope have all the line of john of gaunt! 3H6 1.01. 19
sir john and sir hugh mortimer, mine uncles, 1.02. 62
then warwick disannuls great john of gaunt, 3.03. 81
and after john of gaunt, henry the fourth, 3.03. 83
brother, this is sir john montgomery, | our 4.07. 40
welcome, sir john! but why come you in arms? 4.07. 42
nay, stay, sir john, a while, and we'll debate 4.07. 51
now, by saint john, that news is bad indeed! R3 1.01.138
i thank thee, good sir john, with all my heart. 3.02.109
john duke of norfolk, thomas earl of surrey, 5.03.296
john duke of norfolk, walter lord /ferrers, 5.05. 13
of the duke's confessor, john de la car, | one H8 1.01.218
to me, wishing me to permit | john de la car, my 1.02.162
sir gilbert /perk his chancellor, and john car, 2.01. 20
this same should be the voice of friar john. ROM 5.02. 2
friar john, go hence, | get me an iron crow, and 5.02. 20
but he which bore my letter, friar john, | was 5.03.250
JOHN–A–DREAMS 1 FR 0.0001 REL FR 1 V 0 P
peak | like john–a–dreams, unpregnant of my HAM 2.02.568
JOHN'S 4 FR 0.0004 REL FR 1 V 3 P
signior benedick's tongue in count john's mouth, ADO 2.01. 12 P
and half count john's melancholy in signior 2.01. 12 P
bring you the length of prester john's foot, 2.01.268 P
whose title they admit, arthur's or john's. JN 2.01.200
JOHNS 1 FR 0.0001 REL FR 0 V 1 P
and told him there were five more sir johns, and 2H4 2.04. 6 P
JOIN 58 FR 0.0065 REL FR 53 V 5 P
would i flame distinctly, | then meet and join. TMP 1.02.201
her, i will join with thee to disgrace her. ADO 3.02.127 P
do, | but you must join in souls to mock me too? MND 3.02.150
to join with men in scorning your poor friend? 3.02.216
this fellow will but join you together as they AYL 3.03. 86 P
but join you together as they join wainscot; 3.03. 87 P
that thou mightst join /her hand with his 5.04.114
that must take hands | to join in hymen's bands, 5.04.129
in fortune nature brings | to join like likes, AWW 1.01.223
o, two such silver currents when they join | do JN 2.01.441
command thy son and daughter to join hands. 2.01.532
join with the present sickness that i have, R2 2.01.132
join not with grief, fair woman, do not so, | to 5.01. 16
my soul | want mercy if i do not join with him. 1H4 1.03.132
and of york, | to join with mortimer, ha? 1.03.281
this encounter, | if once they join in trial. 5.01. 85
the prince of wales doth join with all the world 5.01. 86
at home, that our armies join not in a hot day! 2H4 1.02.208 P
then join you with them, like a rib of steel, 2.03. 54
shall join together at the latter day and cry H5 4.01.137 P
to join with witches and the help of hell! 1H6 2.01. 18
to join your hearts in love and amity. 3.01. 68
but join in friendship, as your lords have done. 3.01.145
now let us on, my lords, and join our powers, 3.03. 90
cousin of somerset, join you with me, | and all 2H6 1.01.167
join we together, for the public good, | in what 1.01.199
yet must we join him and with the lords, 1.03. 95
join with the traitor, and they jointly swear 4.04. 52
see, see, they join, embrace, and seem to kiss, 3H6 2.01. 29
should notwithstanding join our lights together, 2.01. 37
in haste, post–haste, are come to join with you; 2.01.139
i'll join mine eldest daughter, and my joy, | to 3.03.242
now join your hands, and with your hands your 4.06. 39
away betimes, before his forces join, | and take 4.08. 62
i'll join with black despair against my soul, R3 2.02. 36
ay, thou wouldst be gone to join with richmond; 4.04.490
march on, join bravely, let us to it pell–mell; 5.03.312
shall join | to thrust the lie unto him. COR 5.06.108
shame, be friends, and join for that you jar. TIT 2.01.103
lords, when we join in league | i am a lamb, but 4.02.136
but /... | join with the goths, and with 4.03. 33
to join with him and right his heinous wrongs. 5.02. 4

tell him revenge is come to join with him, | and 5.02. 7
lord, | join with me to forbid him her resort, TIM 1.01.127
and with their faint reply this answer join: 3.03. 25
take my deserts to his, and join 'em both; 3.05. 78
but who did bid thee join with us? MAC 3.03. 1
and after we will both our judgments join | in HAM 3.02. 86
friends both, go join you with some further aid: 4.01. 33
that will with two pernicious daughters join LR 3.02. 22
let witchcraft join with beauty, lust with both, ANT 2.01. 22
her live | to join our kingdoms and our hearts, 2.02.151
who did join his honor | against the romans with CYM 1.01. 29
join gripes with hands | made hard with hourly 1.06.106
let his virtue join | with my request, which 5.05. 88
then join they all together, | like many clouds VEN 971
they join, and shoot their foam at simois' banks LUC 1442
join with the spite of fortune, make me bow, SON 90. 3
JOIN'D 27 FR 0.0030 REL FR 26 V 1 P
with a charm join'd to their suff'red labor, | i TMP 1.02.231
false blood to false blood join'd! JN 3.01. 2
nature and fortune join'd to make thee great. 3.01. 52
so newly join'd in love, so strong in both, 3.01.240
have woe to woe, sorrow to sorrow join'd. R2 2.02. 66
your uncle york is join'd with bullingbrook, 3.02.200
i am join'd with no foot land–rakers, no 1H4 2.01. 73 P
join'd with an enemy proclaim'd, and from his H5 2.02.168
the bastard of orleance with him is join'd; 1H6 1.01. 93
the dolphin, with one joan de pucelle join'd, 1.04.101
pernicious faction | and join'd with charles, 4.01. 60
which join'd with him and made their march for 4.03. 8
whom i encount'red as the battles join'd. 3H6 1.01. 15
our battles join'd, and both sides fiercely 2.01.121
them sever'd | whom god hath join'd together; 4.01. 22
yet, to have join'd with france in such alliance 4.01. 36
lately splinter'd, knit, and join'd together, R3 2.02.118
york, are join'd with me their servant | in the H8 2.02.105
join'd with aufidius, leads a power 'gainst rome COR 4.06. 67
if martius should be join'd /wi' /th' volscians 4.06. 89
you had not | join'd in commission with him; 4.07. 14
god join'd my heart and romeo's, thou our hands,
ROM 4.01. 55
did flame and burn | like twenty torches join'd; JC 1.03. 17
honor, | join'd with a masker and a reveller! 5.01. 62
yet they are not join'd. ANT 4.12. 1
to the majestic cedar join'd, whose issue CYM 5.05.457
and being join'd, i'll thus your hopes destroy, PER 2.05. 86
JOINDER 1 FR 0.0001 REL FR 1 V 0 P
confirm'd by mutual joinder of your hands, TN 5.01.157
JOIN'D–STOOL *(also join–stool, etc.)*
JOIN'D–STOOL 2 FR 0.0002 REL FR 1 V 1 P
a join'd–stool. SHR 2.01.198
thy state is taken for a join'd–stool, thy 1H4 2.04.380 P
JOIN'D–STOOLS 1 FR 0.0001 REL FR 0 V 1 P
with the boys, and jumps upon join'd–stools, and 2H4 2.04.247 P
JOINED 2 FR 0.0002 REL FR 2 V 0 P
her peerless feature, joined with her birth, 1H6 5.05. 68
her lips to mine how often hath she joined, PP 7. 7
JOINER 4 FR 0.0004 REL FR 2 V 2 P
snug, the joiner, you the lion's part. MND 1.02. 64 P
and tell them plainly he is snug the joiner. 3.01. 46 P
then know that i as snug the joiner am | a lion 5.01.223
made by the joiner squirrel or old grub, | time ROM 1.04. 60
JOINETH 1 FR 0.0001 REL FR 1 V 0 P
torch | that joineth roan unto her countrymen, 1H6 3.02. 27
JOINS 2 FR 0.0002 REL FR 2 V 0 P
and mine, fair lady bona, joins with yours. 3H6 3.03.217
/coigns | which the world together joins, | is PER 3.ch. 18
JOIN'ST 2 FR 0.0002 REL FR 2 V 0 P
who join'st thou with, but with a lordly nation 1H6 3.03. 62
and join'st with them will be thy slaughter–men. 3.03. 75
JOIN–STOOL *(also join'd–stool, etc.)*
//JOIN–STOOL 1 FR 0.0001 REL FR 0 V 1 P
/you /mercy, /i /took /you /for /a //join–stool. LR 3.06. 52 P
JOIN–STOOLS 1 FR 0.0001 REL FR 0 V 1 P
away with the join–stools, remove the ROM 1.05. 6 P
JOINT 22 FR 0.0024 REL FR 15 V 7 P
we'll touze you | joint by joint, but we will MM 5.01.312
we'll touze you | joint by joint, but we will 5.01.312
because of his great limb or joint, shall pass LLL 5.01.128 P
this fest'red joint cut off, the rest rest sound R2 5.03. 85
what's a joint of mutton or two in a whole lent? 2H4 2.04.346 P
couple of short–legg'd hens, a joint of mutton, 5.01. 27 P
than a joint burden laid upon us all. 5.02. 55
thou hast drawn my shoulder out of joint. 5.04. 3 P
ay, every joint should seem to curse and ban; 2H6 3.02.319
every thing so out of joint that he is a gouty TRO 1.02. 28 P
upon our joint and several dignities. 2.02.193
with every joint a wound, and that to–morrow! 4.01. 30
out | at every joint and motive of her body. 4.05. 57
thee, hector, | and quoted joint by joint. 4.05.233
thee, hector, | and quoted joint by joint. 4.05.233
by heaven, i will tear thee joint by joint, ROM 5.03. 35
by heaven, i will tear thee joint by joint, 5.03. 35
they answer, in a joint and corporate voice, TIM 2.02.204
the time is out of joint — o cursed spite, HAM 1.05.188
this broken joint between you and her husband OTH 2.03.322 P
mistress, if i have bargain'd for the joint — PER 4.02.130 P
whose grim aspect sets every joint a–shaking; LUC 452
JOINTED 2 FR 0.0002 REL FR 0 V 2 P
shall after revive, be jointed to the old stock, CYM 5.04.142 P
shall after revive, be jointed to the old stock, 5.05.439 P
JOINTER *(also jointure)*
JOINTER 1 FR 0.0001 REL FR 1 V 0 P
fruitful land, all which shall be her jointer. SHR 2.01.370
JOINTING 1 FR 0.0001 REL FR 1 V 0 P
of them, jointing their force 'gainst caesar, ANT 1.02. 92
JOINT–LABORER 1 FR 0.0001 REL FR 1 V 0 P
doth make the night joint–laborer with the day: HAM 1.01. 78
JOINTLY 6 FR 0.0006 REL FR 6 V 0 P
and they jointly swear | to spoil the city and 2H6 4.04. 52
shall have cause of state | craving us jointly. MAC 3.01. 34
and we shall jointly labor with your soul | to HAM 4.05.212
i do invest you jointly with my power, LR 1.01.130
all jointly list'ning, but with several graces, LUC 1410
then jointly to the ground their knees they bow, 1846
JOINTRESS 1 FR 0.0001 REL FR 1 V 0 P
th' imperial jointress to this warlike state, HAM 1.02. 9
JOINT–RING 1 FR 0.0001 REL FR 0 V 1 P
i would not do such a thing for a joint–ring, OTH 4.03. 73 P

JOINTS 21 FR 0.0023 REL FR 19 V 2 P
i do beseech you | (that are of suppler joints) TMP 3.03.107
charge my goblins that they grind their joints 4.01.258
and clap their female joints | in stiff unwieldy R2 3.02.114
how dare thy joints forget | to pay their aweful 3.03. 75
against them both my true joints bended be. 5.03. 98
his weary joints would gladly rise, i know, 5.03.105
yet all goes well, yet all our joints are whole. 1H4 4.01. 83
and as the wretch whose fever–weak'ned joints, 2H4 1.01.140
a scaly gauntlet now with joints of steel | must 1.01.146
shall have none, i swear, but these my joints; H5 4.03.123
he hath the joints of every thing, but every TRO 1.02. 27 P
good arms, strong joints, true swords, and, 1.03.238
the elephant hath joints, but none for courtesy; 2.03.105 P
a chilling sweat o'erruns my trembling joints, TIT 2.03.212
but fettle your fine joints 'gainst thursday ROM 3.05.153
and madly play with my forefathers' joints, 4.03. 51
her blood is settled, and her joints are stiff; 4.05. 26
aches contract and starve your supple joints! TIM 1.01.248
i fear'd thy fortune, and my joints did tremble. VEN 642
her voice is stopp'd, her joints forget to bow, 1061
not my tongue be mute, my frail joints shake? LUC 227
JOINT–SERVANT 1 FR 0.0001 REL FR 1 V 0 P
made him joint–servant with me; COR 5.06. 31
JOINT–STOOL *(see join'd–stool, etc., join–stool, etc.)*
JOINTURE *(also jointer)*
JOINTURE 4 FR 0.0004 REL FR 2 V 2 P
make you a hundred and fifty pounds jointure. WIV 3.04. 49 P
a better jointure, i think, than you make a AYL 4.01. 55 P
touching the jointure that your king must make, 3H6 3.03.136
this is my daughter's jointure, for no more ROM 5.03.297
JOLLITY 6 FR 0.0006 REL FR 5 V 1 P
yet he loseth it in a kind of jollity. ERR 2.02. 89 P
be | wedded, with theseus, all in jollity. MND 4.01. 92
solemnity, | in nightly revels and new jollity. 5.01.370
apprehend | nothing but jollity. WT 4.04. 25
toys, | is jollity for apes, and grief for boys. CYM 4.02.194
born, | and needy nothing trimm'd in jollity, SON 66. 3
/JOLLY 1 FR 0.0001 REL FR 1 V 0 P
"/sleepest /or /wakest /thou, /jolly /shepherd? LR 3.06. 41
JOLLY 9 FR 0.0010 REL FR 9 V 0 P
this life is most jolly. AYL 2.07.183
'tis like you'll prove a jolly surly groom, SHR 3.02.213
"hey, robin, jolly robin, | tell me how thy lady TN 4.02. 72
and like a jolly troop of huntsmen come | our JN 2.01.321
crown, | to her go i, a jolly thriving wooer. R3 4.03. 43
be jolly, lords. ANT 2.07. 59
through alexandria make a jolly march, | bear 4.08. 30
thick sighs from him, whiles the jolly britain CYM 1.06. 67
"well hail'd, well hail'd, you jolly gallants! TNK 3.05. 63
JOLTHEAD 1 FR 0.0001 REL FR 0 V 1 P
fie on thee, jolthead, thou canst not read. TGV 3.01.290 P
JOLTHEADS 1 FR 0.0001 REL FR 1 V 0 P
you heedless joltheads and unmanner'd slaves! SHR 4.01.166
JORDAN* 4 FR 0.0004 REL FR 1 V 3 P
they will allow us ne'er a jordan, and then we 1H4 2.01. 19 P
arthur first in court" — empty the jordan. 2H4 2.04. 34 P
thou as yet conferr'd | with margery jordan, the 2H6 1.02. 75
mother jordan, be you prostrate and grovel on 1.04. 10 P
JOSEPH 1 FR 0.0001 REL FR 0 V 1 P
call forth nathaniel, joseph, nicholas, philip, SHR 4.01. 89 P
JOSHUA 1 FR 0.0001 REL FR 0 V 1 P
joshua, yourself; LLL 5.01.126 P
JOSTLE *(see justle, etc.)*
JOT 25 FR 0.0028 REL FR 20 V 5 P
not a jot the other, | being a murtherer, though MM 4.02. 61
this nor hurts him, nor profits you a jot. 4.03.123
this bond doth give thee here no jot of blood; MV 4.01.306
dangerous, if you break one jot of your promise, AYL 4.01.190 P
and not a jot of tranio in your mouth, | tranio SHR 1.01.236
no, faith, i'll not stay a jot longer. TN 3.02. 1 P
no, sir, no jot. 3.04.329
if one jot beyond | the bound of honor, or in WT 3.02. 50
pow'r no jot | hath she to change our loves. 5.01.217
nor doth he dedicate one jot of color | unto the H5 4.pr. 37
keep | than in possession any jot of pleasure. 3H6 2.02. 53
with whom my soul is any jot at odds | more than R3 2.01. 71
i had no being | if this salute my blood a jot; H8 2.03.103
neither will they bate | one jot of ceremony. COR 2.02.141
holy vestments bleeding, | shall pierce a jot. TIM 4.03.127
not a jot more, my lord. HAM 5.01.113 P
faith, not a jot, but to follow him thither with 5.01.207 P
let me not stay a jot for dinner, go get it LR 1.04. 8 P
not a jot, not a jot. OTH 3.03.215
not a jot, not a jot. 3.03.215
do it, | detain no jot, i charge thee. ANT 4.05. 13
leave not out a jot | o' th' sacred ceremony. TNK 1.01.130
in him, he brings not | a jot of terror to us. 1.02. 95
which he frets at rather | than any jot obeys; 5.04. 71
if springing things be any jot diminish'd, VEN 417
J'OUBLIE 1 FR 0.0001 REL FR 0 V 1 P
ma foi, j'oublie les doigts, mais je me H5 3.04. 9 P
JOUR 4 FR 0.0004 REL FR 2 V 2 P
bon jour, monsieur le beau. AYL 1.02. 97 P
o seigneur! le jour est perdu, tout est perdu! H5 4.05. 2
horn and hound we'll give your grace bon jour. TIT 1.01.494
signior romeo, bon jour! ROM 2.04. 44 P
JOURDAIN *(see jordan*)*
JOURNAL 2 FR 0.0002 REL FR 2 V 0 P
ere twice the sun hath made his journal greeting MM 4.03. 88
you, leave me, | stick to your journal course: CYM 4.02. 10
JOURNEY 28 FR 0.0031 REL FR 25 V 3 P
may undertake | a journey to my loving proteus. TGV 2.07. 7
me | for undertaking so unstaid a journey? 2.07. 60
if proteus like your journey when you come, | no 2.07. 65
of, | to furnish me upon my longing journey. 2.07. 85
thou bear'st thy heavy riches but a journey, MM 3.01. 27
you | look forward on the journey you shall go. 4.03. 58
gentleman that means | (travelling some journey) SHR in.1. 76
list, | or ere i journey to your father's house. 4.05. 8
if th' event o' th' journey | prove as WT 3.01. 11
for 'twill be | two long days' journey, lords, JN 4.03. 20
and go we to attire you for our journey. 2H6 2.04.106
laying manors on 'em | for this great journey. H8 1.01. 85
the londoners | concerning the french journey. 1.02.155
my prophecy is but half his journey yet, | for TRO 4.05.218
to the pace of it | i may spur on my journey. COR 1.10. 33
you have well sav'd me a day's journey. 4.03. 12 P

upon the highmost hill | of this day's journey, ROM 2.05. 10
is fashion'd for the journey, dull and heavy. TIM 2.02.219
(whereto the rather shall his day's hard journey MAC 1.07. 62
i have a journey, sir, shortly to go: LR 5.03.322
you have a shorter journey to your desires by OTH 2.01.277 P
as i conceive the journey, be at /the mount ANT 2.04. 6
caesar through syria | intends his journey, and 5.02.201
i'll make a journey twice as far, t' enjoy | a CYM 2.04. 43
marry, sir, half a day's journey. PER 2.01.107 P
why, a day's journey, wench. TNK 5.02. 73
but then begins a journey in my head | to work SON 27. 3
how heavy do i journey on the way, | when what i 50. 1
JOURNEY–BATED 1 FR 0.0001 REL FR 1 V 0 P
in general journey–bated and brought low. 1H4 4.03. 26
JOURNEYING 1 FR 0.0001 REL FR 1 V 0 P
esteem | are journeying to salute the emperor, TGV 1.03. 41
JOURNEYMAN 1 FR 0.0001 REL FR 1 V 0 P
else | but that i was a journeyman to grief? R2 1.03.274
JOURNEYMEN 1 FR 0.0001 REL FR 0 V 1 P
some of nature's journeymen had made men, and HAM 3.02. 33 P
JOURNEY'S 2 FR 0.0002 REL FR 1 V 1 P
here is my journey's end, here is my butt | and OTH 5.02.267
and how you shall speed in your journey's end, i CYM 5.04.183 P
JOURNEYS 3 FR 0.0003 REL FR 3 V 0 P
journeys end in lovers meeting, | every wise TN 2.03. 43
my lord, whoever journeys to the prince, | for R3 2.02.146
so many journeys may the sun and moon | make us
HAM 3.02.161
JOUST *(see just*, etc.)*
/JOVE 2 FR 0.0002 REL FR 2 V 0 P
/jove /sometime /went /disguis'd, /and /why /not 2H6 4.01. 48
another wanton ganymede | set /jove afire with, TNK 4.02. 16
JOVE 82 FR 0.0092 REL FR 64 V 18 P
or else, by jove i vow, | i should have TGV 4.04.203
remember, jove, thou wast a bull for thy europa, WIV 5.05. 3 P
fault done first in the form of a beast (o jove, 5.05. 9 P
of a fowl — think on't, jove, a foul fault! 5.05. 11 P
send me a cool rut–time, jove, or who can blame 5.05. 14 P
could great men thunder | as jove himself does, MM 2.02.111
as jove himself does, jove would never be quiet, 2.02.111
is philemon's roof, within the house is jove. ADO 2.01. 97 P
at thee, | as once europa did at lusty jove, 5.04. 46
bull jove, sir, had an amiable low, | and some 5.04. 48
thou for whom jove would swear | juno but an LLL 4.03.115
but an ethiop were, | and deny himself for jove, 4.03.117
says one, "o jove!" 4.03.139
and jove for your love would infringe an oath. 4.03.142
by jove, i always took three threes for nine. 5.02.495 P
jove shield thee well for this! MND 5.01.178
jove, jove! AYL 2.04. 60
jove, jove! 2.04. 60
worse than jove in a thatch'd house! 3.03. 11 P
that made great jove to humble him to her hand, SHR 1.01.169
by jove, if ever i knew man, 'twas you. AWW 5.03.287
whose skull jove cram with brains! TN 1.05.113 P
"jove knows i love, | but who? 2.05. 96
jove and my stars be prais'd! 2.05.172 P
jove, i thank thee. 2.05.178 P
now jove, in his next commodity of hair, send 3.01. 44 P
it is jove's doing, and jove make me thankful! 3.04. 75 P
well, jove, not i, is the doer of this, and he 3.04. 82 P
jove bless thee, master parson. 4.02. 11 P
jove send her | a better guiding spirit! WT 2.03.126
now jove afford you cause! 4.04. 16
my king! my jove! i speak to thee, my heart! 2H4 5.05. 46
in thunder and in earthquake, like a jove, H5 2.04.100
by jove, i am not covetous for gold, | nor care 4.03. 24
but jove was never slain, as thou shalt be. 2H6 4.01. 49
but the protractive trials of great jove | to TRO 1.03. 20
heels | and fly like chidden mercury from jove, 2.02. 45
and jove forbid there should be done amongst us 2.02.127
forget that thou art jove, the king of gods, and 2.03. 11 P
jove bless great ajax! 3.03.280 P
by jove, i'll play the hunter for thy life 4.01. 18
jove, let aeneas live, | if to my sword his fate 4.01. 26
by jove multipotent, | thou shouldst not bear 4.05.129
by jove, | i will be patient. 5.02. 46
by jove, i will not speak a word. 5.02. 52
ay, come — o jove! 5.02.105
midnight sleep, | by jove, 'twould be my mind! COR 3.01. 86
by jove himself, | it makes the consuls base; 3.01.107
his trident, | or jove for 's power to thunder. 3.01.256
with the consent of supreme jove, inform | thy 5.03. 71
jove shield your husband from his hounds to–day!
TIT 2.03. 70
apollo, pallas, jove, or mercury, | inspire me, 4.01. 66
he thinks, with jove in heaven, or some where 4.03. 41
see, here's to jove, and this to mercury, | this 4.04. 14
at lovers' perjuries, | they say, jove laughs. ROM 2.02. 93
be as a planetary plague when jove | will o'er TIM 4.03.109
this realm dismantled was | of jove himself, and HAM 3.02.283
hyperion's curls, the front of jove himself, 3.04. 56
nor tell tales of thee to high–judging jove. LR 2.04.228
great jove, othello guard, | and swell his sail OTH 2.01. 77
and she is sport for jove. 2.03. 17 P
be, she makes a show'r of rain as well as jove. ANT 1.02.151 P
thou art, if thou dar'st be, the earthly jove. 2.07. 67
the jove of power make me most weak, most weak, 3.04. 29
by jove that thunders! 3.13. 85
your emperor | continues still a jove. 4.06. 28
jove — | once more let me behold it. CYM 2.04. 98
the king his father call'd guiderius — jove! 3.03. 88
o jove, i think | foundations fly the wretched: 3.06. 6
jove knows what man thou mightst have made; 4.02.207
a bride | for embracements even of jove himself; PER 1.01. 7
and if jove stray, who dares say jove doth ill? 1.01.104
and if jove stray, who dares say jove doth ill? 1.01.104
by jove, i wonder, that is king of thoughts, 2.03. 28
now for the love of him whom jove hath mark'd TNK 1.01. 29
but, o jove, your actions, | soon as they /move, 1.01.137
able to lock jove from a synod, shall | by 1.01.176
"o jove," quoth she, "how much a fool was i | to VEN 1015
she conjures him by high almighty jove, | by LUC 568
"o jove," quoth she, "why was not i a flood?" PP 6.14
thou for whom jove would swear | juno but an 16.15
an ethiope were, | and deny himself for jove, 16.17
JOVEM 1 FR 0.0001 REL FR 1 V 0 P
"ad jovem," that's for you; TIT 4.03. 54

JOVE'S 18 FR 0.0020 REL FR 15 V 3 P
jove's lightning, the precursors | o' th' TMP 1.02.201
and rifted jove's stout oak | with his own bolt; 5.01. 45
thy eye jove's lightning bears, thy voice his LLL 4.02.115
i'll have no worse a name than jove's own page, AYL 1.03.124
it may well be call'd jove's tree, when it drops 3.02.236 P
if i should swear by jove's great attributes | i AWW 4.02. 25
i have lim'd her, but it is jove's doing, and TN 3.04. 74 P
kin to jove's thunder, so surpris'd my sense, WT 3.01. 10
it was jove's case. 2H4 2.02.174 P
top–branch overpeer'd jove's spreading tree, 3H6 5.02. 14
wing, | jove's mercury, and herald for a king! R3 4.03. 55
joints, true swords, and, great jove's accord, TRO 1.03.238
as to jove's statue, and the commons made | a COR 2.01.266
children is enroll'd | in jove's own book, like 3.01.291
th' immortal jove's dread clamors counterfeit, OTH 3.03.356
fetch thee up, | and set thee by jove's side. ANT 4.15. 36
i saw jove's bird, the roman eagle, wing'd CYM 4.02.348
thine eye jove's lightning seems, thy voice his PP 5.11
JOVIAL 4 FR 0.0004 REL FR 4 V 0 P
be bright and jovial among your guests to–night. MAC 3.02. 28
i will be jovial. LR 4.06.199
but his jovial face — | murther in heaven? CYM 4.02.311
our jovial star reign'd at his birth, and in 5.04.105
JOVIS 1 FR 0.0001 REL FR 1 V 0 P
"et opus exegi, quod nec jovis ira, nec ignis" TNK 3.05. 88
JOWL* 2 FR 0.0002 REL FR 1 V 1 P
follow? nay; i'll go with thee, cheek by jowl. MND 3.02.338
they may jowl horns together like any deer i' AWW 1.03. 54 P
JOWLS 1 FR 0.0001 REL FR 0 V 1 P
how the knave jowls it to the ground, as if HAM 5.01. 76 P
/JOY 1 FR 0.0001 REL FR 1 V 0 P
of sorrow or of /joy? R2 3.04. 11
JOY 215 FR 0.0243 REL FR 188 V 27 P
you have cause | (so have we all) of joy; TMP 2.01. 2
rejoice | beyond a common joy, and set it down 5.01.207
embrace his heart | that doth not wish you joy! 5.01.215
when inward joy enforc'd my heart to smile! TGV 1.02. 63
i know you joy not in a love–discourse. 2.04.127
nor to his service no such joy on earth: 2.04.139
what joy is joy, if silvia be not by? 3.01.175
what joy is joy, if silvia be not by? 3.01.175
fenton, heaven give thee joy! WIV 5.05.236
as it is an evil, | and take the shame with joy. MM 2.03. 36
joy to you, mariana! 5.01.526
with her i liv'd in joy; ERR 1.01. 39
and there appears much joy in him, even so much ADO 1.01. 21 P
him, even so much that joy could not show itself 1.01. 22 P
is it to weep at joy than to joy at weeping! 1.01. 28 P
is it to weep at joy than to joy at weeping! 1.01. 28 P
i wish him joy of her. 2.01.193 P
name the day of marriage, and god give thee joy! 2.01.301 P
silence is the perfectest herald of joy; 2.01.306 P
cousins, god give you joy! 2.01.336 P
god give me joy to wear it, for my heart is 3.04. 24 P
whose joy of her is overwhelm'd like mine, | and 5.01. 9
why should i joy in any abortive birth? LLL 1.01.104
and leap for joy, though they are lame with 5.02.291
god give thee joy of him! 5.02.448
him with flowers, and makes him all her joy. MND 2.01. 27
you come | to give their bed joy and prosperity. 2.01. 73
and kiss thy fair large ears, my gentle joy. 4.01. 4
that, if it would but apprehend some joy, | it 5.01. 19
joy, | it comprehends some bringer of that joy; 5.01. 20
here come the lovers, full of joy and mirth. 5.01. 28
joy, gentle friends, joy and fresh days of love 5.01. 29
joy and fresh days of love | accompany your 5.01. 29
joy be the consequence! MV 3.02.107
in measure rain thy joy, scant this excess! 3.02.112
save of joy | express'd and not express'd. 3.02.182
and seen our wishes prosper, | to cry good joy. 3.02.188
good joy, my lord and lady! 3.02.188
i wish you all the joy that you can wish; 3.02.190
well, the gods give us joy! AYL 3.03. 47 P
i take some joy to say you are, because i would 4.01. 89 P
with measure heap'd in joy, to th' measures fall 5.04.179
o how we joy to see your wit restor'd! SHR in.2. 77
god send you joy, petruchio! 2.01.319
god give him joy! 4.02. 52
done, done fond, | was this king priam's joy?" AWW 1.03. 73
to make the coming hour o'erflow with joy | and 2.04. 46
i have felt so many quirks of joy and grief 3.02. 49
my heart dances, | but not for joy; WT 1.02.111
not joy. 1.02.111
my second joy | and first–fruits of my body, 3.02. 96
try all, both joy and terror | of good and bad, 4.01. 1
father (all whose joy is nothing else | but fair 4.04.408
it should take joy | to see her in your arms. 5.01. 80
not say if th' importance were joy or sorrow; 5.02. 18 P
might you have beheld one joy crown another, so 5.02. 44 P
leave of them, for their joy waded in tears. 5.02. 46 P
out of himself for joy of his found daughter, as 5.02. 50 P
daughter, as if that joy were now become a loss, 5.02. 50 P
combat that 'twixt joy and sorrow was fought in 5.02. 73 P
scarce any joy | did ever so long live; 5.03. 51
my life, my joy, my food, my all the world! JN 3.04.104
there's nothing in this world can make me joy: 3.04.107
all days of glory, joy, and happiness. 3.04.117
joy absent, grief is present for that time. R2 1.03.259
to men in joy, but grief makes one hour ten. 1.03.261
and hope to joy is little less in joy | than 2.03. 15
and hope to joy is little less in joy | than 2.03. 15
and let him never see joy that breaks that oath! 2.03.151
i weep for joy | to stand upon my kingdom once 3.02. 4
for if of joy, being altogether wanting, | it 3.04. 13
had, | it adds more sorrow to my want of joy; 3.04. 16
madam, little joy have i | to breathe this news, 3.04. 81
till thou give joy, until thou bid me joy | by 5.03. 95
until thou bid me joy | by pardoning rutland, my 5.03. 95
runs posting on in bullingbrook's proud joy, 5.05. 59
more than thou hast, and with it joy thy life. 5.06. 26
yea, joy, our chains and our jewels. 2H4 2.04. 47 P
if he be sick with joy, he'll recover without 4.05. 14 P
but if it did infect my blood with joy, | or 4.05.169
than i do at this hour joy o'er myself, H5 2.02.163
joy and good wishes | to our most fair and 5.02. 3
talbot, my life, my joy, again return'd? 1H6 1.04. 23
to celebrate the joy that god hath given us. 1.06. 14
all france will be replete with mirth and joy, 1.06. 15
what joy shall noble talbot have | to bid his 4.03. 39
the treasury of everlasting joy. 2H6 2.01. 18
my joy is death; 2.04. 88
for in the shade of death i shall find joy; 3.02. 54
why then dame /margaret was ne'er thy joy. 3.02. 79
live thou to joy thy life; 3.02.365
myself no joy in nought but that thou liv'st. 3.02.366
and all that poets feign of bliss and joy. 3H6 1.02. 31
i cannot joy, until i be resolv'd | where our 2.01. 9
for never henceforth shall i joy again, | never, 2.01. 77
again, | never, o never, shall i see more joy! 2.01. 78
and he that throws not up his cap for joy 2.01.196
since this earth affords no joy to me | but to 3.02.165
and joy that thou becom'st king henry's friend. 3.03.201
i'll join mine eldest daughter, and my joy, | to 3.03.242
fear | my joy of liberty is half eclips'd. 4.06. 63
world, | to meet with joy in sweet jerusalem. 5.05. 8
for here i hope begins our lasting joy. 5.07. 46
small joy have i in being england's queen. R3 1.03.109
as little joy, my lord, as you suppose | you 1.03.150
as little joy you may suppose in me | that i 1.03.152
a little joy enjoys the queen thereof, | for i 1.03.154
for me to joy and weep their gain and loss; 2.04. 59
and bid my lord, for joy of this good news, 3.01.184
and each hour's joy wrack'd with a week of teen. 4.01. 96
wherein dost thou joy? 4.04. 93
sleep, richmond, sleep in peace and wake in joy. 5.03.150
much joy and favor to you; H8 2.02.117
that ne'er dream'd a joy beyond his pleasure; 3.01.135
now all my joy | trace the conjunction! 3.02. 44
that time offer'd sorrow, | this, general joy. 4.01. 7
stifled | with the mere rankness of their joy. 4.01. 59
such joy | i never saw before. 4.01. 75
and myself thus pray | all comfort, joy, in this 5.04. 6
sounding destruction, or some joy too fine, TRO 3.02. 23
i sprang not more in joy at first hearing he was COR 1.03. 16 P
to our noble consul | wish we all joy and honor. 2.02.153
to coriolanus come all joy and honor! 2.02.154
the gods give you joy, sir, heartily! 2.03.111 P
the gods give him joy, and make him good friend 2.03.135 P
which should | make our eyes flow with joy, 5.03. 99
hark, how they joy! 5.04. 57
we'll meet them, | and help the joy. 5.04. 62
tears of true joy for his return to rome. TIT 1.01. 76
with tears of joy | shed on this earth for thy 1.01.161
let not young mutius then, that was thy joy, 1.01.382
god give you joy, sir, of your gallant bride! 1.01.400
hence, | and let her joy her raven–colored love; 2.03. 83
belike for joy the emperor hath a son. 4.02. 50
why, there it goes, god give his lordship joy! 4.03. 77
although i joy in thee, | i have no joy of this ROM 2.02.116
thee, | i have no joy of this contract to–night, 2.02.117
which to the high top–gallant of my joy | must 2.04.190
it cannot countervail the exchange of joy | that 2.06. 4
if the measure of thy joy | be heap'd like mine, 2.06. 24
to woe, | which you, mistaking, offer up to joy. 3.02.104
now i have stain'd the childhood of our joy 3.03. 95
with twenty hundred thousand times more joy 3.03.153
but that a joy past joy calls out on me, | it 3.03.173
but that a joy past joy calls out on me, | it 3.03.173
and joy comes well in such a needy time. 3.05.105
hath sorted out a sudden day of joy, | that thou 3.05.109
hast thou not a word of joy? 3.05.211
when but love's shadows are so rich in joy! 5.01. 11
joy had the like conception in our eyes, | and TIM 1.02.110
joy for his fortune; JC 3.02. 27 P
and hark, they shout for joy. 5.03. 32
my heart doth joy that yet in all my life | i 5.05. 34
than by destruction dwell in doubtful joy. MAC 3.02. 7
i drink to th' general joy o' th' whole table, 3.04. 88
state, | have we, as 'twere with a defeated joy, HAM 1.02. 10
whereon old norway, overcome with joy, | gives 2.02. 72
and there did seem in him a kind of joy | to 3.01. 18
the violence of either grief or joy | their own 3.02.196
where joy most revels, grief doth most lament; 3.02.198
grief /joys, joy grieves, on slender accident. 3.02.199
each opposite that blanks the face of joy | meet 3.02.220
end — "for bonny sweet robin is all my joy." 4.05.187
now, our joy, | although our last and least, to LR 1.01. 82
breeches, "then they for sudden joy did weep, 1.04.175
'twixt two extremes of passion, joy and grief, 5.03.199
though that his joy be joy, | yet throw such OTH 1.01. 71
though that his joy be joy, | yet throw such 1.01. 71
in compassing thy joy than to be drown'd and go 1.03.360 P
o my soul's joy! 2.01.184
it is too much of joy. 2.01.197
that we should, with joy, pleasance, revel, and 2.03.291 P
his remembrance lay | in egypt with his joy; ANT 1.05. 58
myself so sorely | that i will joy no more. 4.06. 19
i wish you all joy of the worm. 5.02.260 P
yes, forsooth; i wish you joy o' th' worm. 5.02.279 P
for joy whereof | the fam'd cassibelan, who was CYM 3.01. 29
doubtless | with joy he will embrace you; 3.04.176
madam, all joy befall your grace, and you! 3.05. 9
thou hast finish'd joy and moan. 4.02.273
do mean to strike me | to death with mortal joy. 5.05.235
her master, hitting | each object with a joy; 5.05.396
this mercy shows we'll joy in such a son; PER 1.01.118
yet neither pleasure's art can joy my spirits, 1.02. 9
joy and all comfort in your sacred breast! 1.02. 34
shall make the gazer joy to see him tread. 2.01.159
and for further grief — god give you joy! 2.05. 87
will i take me to, | and never more have joy. 3.04. 11
led on by heaven, and crown'd with joy at last. 5.03. 90
evermore attending, | new joy wait on you! 5.03.102
think, | did i not by th' abstaining of my joy, TNK 1.01.189
joy seize on you again! 1.05. 12
and two better never yet | made mothers joy — 4.02. 63
wear the girlond | with joy that you have won. 5.03.131
take emilia, | and with her all the world's joy. 5.04. 91
thee, | to take advantage on presented joy; VEN 405
but now i died, and death was lively joy. 498
annoy, | to clip elysium and to lack her joy. 600
expel, | for now reviving joy bids her rejoice, 977
her joy with heav'd–up hand she doth express, LUC 111
a dream, a breath, a froth of fleeting joy. 212
lucrece to their sight | must sell her joy, her 385
this momentary joy breeds months of pain, | this 690
thy honey turns to gall, thy joy to grief! 889
the little birds that tune their morning's joy 1107
sharing joy | to see their youthful sons bright 1431
that through their light joy seemed to appear 1434
sweets with sweets war not, joy delights in joy. SON 8. 2
sweets with sweets war not, joy delights in joy. 8. 2
bars, | unlook'd for joy in that i honor most. 25. 4
but here's the joy: 42.13
this told, i joy, but then no longer glad, | i 45.13
my grief lies onward and my joy behind. 50.14
wherein it finds a joy above the rest, | but 91. 6
woe, | before, a joy propos'd, behind, a dream. 129.12
JOY'D 4 FR 0.0004 REL FR 3 V 1 P
poor fellow never joy'd since the price of oats 1H4 2.01. 12 P
was ever king that joy'd an earthly throne | and 2H6 4.09. 1
joy'd are we that you are. CYM 5.05.424
't may be she joy'd to jest at my exile, | 't PP 14. 9
JOYFUL 32 FR 0.0036 REL FR 26 V 6 P
(got deliver to a joyful resurrections!) WIV 1.01. 52 P
she became | a joyful mother of two goodly sons: ERR 1.01. 50
what a joyful father wouldest thou make me! LLL 5.01. 76 P
that fault, | right joyful of your reformation. 5.02.869
to–morrow is the joyful day, audrey, to–morrow AYL 5.03. 1 P
with us, | we shall be joyful of thy company. SHR 4.05. 52
no joyful tongue gave him his welcome home, R2 5.02. 29
umfrevile turn'd me back | with joyful tidings, 2H4 1.01. 35
o joyful day! 5.03.126 P
dear nurse of arts, plenties, and joyful births, H5 5.02. 35
how joyful am i made by this contract! 1H6 3.01.143
god make your majesty joyful, as you have been! R3 1.03. 19
o, make them joyful, grant their lawful suit! 3.07.203
graces both | a happy and a joyful time of day! 4.01. 6
for joyful mother, one that wails the name; 4.04. 99
i am joyful | to meet the least occasion that H8 3.02. 6
i am most joyful, madam, such good dreams 4.02. 93
man, those joyful tears show thy true /heart. 5.02.208
i am joyful to hear of their readiness, and am COR 4.03. 46 P
if they did kill thy husband, then be joyful, TIT 3.01.116
a joyful issue. 4.02. 65
lord, lord, she will be a joyful woman. ROM 2.04.174 P
but now i'll tell thee joyful tidings, girl. 3.05.104
shall happily make thee there a joyful bride. 3.05.115
he shall not make me there a joyful bride. 3.05.117
my dreams presage some joyful news at hand. 5.01. 2
i am joyful of your sights. TIM 1.01.246
i'll be myself the harbinger and make joyful MAC 1.04. 45
i know this is a joyful trouble to you; 2.03. 48
feats, whilst they with joyful tears | wash the ANT 4.08. 9
let them be joyful too, | for they shall taste CYM 5.05.402
go we hence, | right joyful, with some sorrow. TNK 5.03.135
JOYFULLY 3 FR 0.0003 REL FR 3 V 0 P
then, joyfully, my noble lord of bedford, | my H5 4.03. 8
grace, | and so most joyfully we take our leave. R3 3.07.245
norway, my good lord, | are joyfully return'd. HAM 2.02. 41
JOYLESS 3 FR 0.0003 REL FR 3 V 0 P
thereof, | for i am she, and altogether joyless. R3 1.03.155
a joyless, dismal, black, and sorrowful issue! TIT 4.02. 66
while with a joyless smile she turns away | the LUC 1711
JOYOUS 2 FR 0.0002 REL FR 2 V 0 P
son, | who will of thy arrival be full joyous. SHR 4.05. 70
right joyous are we to behold your face, | most H5 5.02. 9
JOY'S 2 FR 0.0002 REL FR 1 V 1 P
won are done, joy's soul lies in the doing. TRO 1.02.287
o, joy's e'en made away ere't can be born! TIM 1.02.105 P
/JOYS 1 FR 0.0001 REL FR 1 V 0 P
grief /joys, joy grieves, on slender accident. HAM 3.02.199
JOYS 31 FR 0.0035 REL FR 31 V 0 P
and increasing, | hourly joys be still upon you! TMP 4.01.108
he finds the joys of heaven here on earth; MV 3.05. 76
push) to trouble | your joys with like relation. WT 5.03.130
overthrows thy joys, friends, fortune, and thy R2 3.02. 72
thee, | and tidings do i bring, and lucky joys, 2H4 5.03. 95
i speak of africa and golden joys. 5.03.100
makes me from wond'ring fall to weeping joys, 2H6 1.01. 34
surfeiting in joys of love | with his new bride 1.01.251
so cares and joys abound, as seasons fleet. 2.04. 4
mine such as fill my heart with unhop'd joys. 3H6 3.03.172
doth cloud my joys with danger and with sorrow. 4.01. 74
my fear to hope, my sorrows unto joys, | at our 4.06. 4
with all my heart, and much it joys me too, | to R3 1.02.219
this earth's thralldom to the joys of heaven. 1.04.248
and plant your joys in living edward's throne. 2.02.100
woes, | aery succeeders of /intestate joys, 4.04.128
with the sweet silent hours of marriage joys; 4.04.330
that i shall lose distinction in my joys, | as TRO 3.02. 27
and dreaming night will hide our joys no longer, 4.02. 10
o sacred receptacle of my joys, | sweet cell of TIT 1.01. 92
is dead, | and with my child my joys are buried. ROM 4.05. 64
heaven finds means to kill your joys with love. 5.03.293
my plenteous joys, | wanton in fullness, seek to MAC 1.04. 33
how e'er my haps, my joys /were ne'er /begun. HAM 4.03. 68
myself an enemy to all other joys | which the LR 1.01. 73
briefly die their joys | that place them on the CYM 5.05.106
gripe not at earthly joys as erst they did; PER 1.01. 49
are arms to princes and bring joys to subjects. 1.02. 74
lest this great sea of joys rushing upon me 5.01.192
those joys, griefs, angers, fears, my friend TNK 2.02.188
were kisses all the joys in bed, | one woman PP 18.47
JUBITER *(also jupiter)*
JUBITER 1 FR 0.0001 REL FR 0 V 1 P
sir, i know not jubiter, i never drank with him TIT 4.03. 85 P
/JUDAS 1 FR 0.0001 REL FR 1 V 0 P
/so /judas /did /to /christ; R2 4.01.170
JUD–AS 1 FR 0.0001 REL FR 1 V 0 P
jud–as, away! LLL 5.02.628
JUDAS 15 FR 0.0017 REL FR 6 V 9 P
and this gallant gentleman, judas machabeus; LLL 5.01.127 P
the pedant, judas machabeus; 5.02.536 P
"judas i am" — 5.02.595
a judas! 5.02.596 P
"judas i am, ycliped machabeus." 5.02.598
judas machabeus clipt is plain judas. 5.02.599 P
judas machabeus clipt is plain judas. 5.02.599 P
a kissing traitor. how art thou prov'd judas? 5.02.600 P
"judas i am" — 5.02.601
the more shame for you, judas. 5.02.602 P

to make judas hang himself. 5.02.604 P
well follow'd: judas was hang'd on an elder. 5.02.606 P
a light for monsieur judas! 5.02.630
three judases, each one thrice worse than judas! R2 3.02.132
to say the truth, so judas kiss'd his master, 3H6 5.07. 33
JUDASES 1 FR 0.0001 REL FR 1 V 0 P
three judases, each one thrice worse than judas! R2 3.02.132
JUDAS'S 2 FR 0.0002 REL FR 0 V 2 P
something browner than judas's. AYL 3.04. 8 P
marry, his kisses are judas's own children. 3.04. 9 P
JUDE 2 FR 0.0002 REL FR 2 V 0 P
and so adieu, sweet jude! LLL 5.02.626
for the ass to the jude; 5.02.628
JUDG'D 9 FR 0.0010 REL FR 8 V 1 P
haply when they have judg'd me fast asleep, TGV 3.01. 25
it could not be judg'd, sir. WIV 1.01. 91 P
come from the country to be judg'd by you | that JN 1.01. 45
thieves are not judg'd but they are by to hear, R2 4.01.123
be judg'd by subject and inferior breath, | and 4.01.128
it may be judg'd i made the duke away, | so 2H6 3.02. 67
'fore his holiness, | and to be judg'd by him. H8 2.04.121
some displeasure at him, at least he judg'd so; PER 1.03. 20
as may be judg'd | by their appointment. TNK 1.04. 14
JUDGE *(also udge)*
JUDGE 93 FR 0.0105 REL FR 80 V 13 P
i see things too, although you judge i wink. TGV 1.02.136
you shall judge: 4.04. 16 P
o, heaven be judge how i love valentine, | whose 5.04. 36
his frailty, and then judge of my merit. WIV 3.05. 51 P
judge. MM 1.02. 49 P
for that which, if myself might be his judge, 1.04. 27
i would tell what 'twere to be a judge, | and 2.02. 69
of judgment, should | but judge you as you are? 2.02. 77
whose credit with the judge, or own great place, 2.04. 92
there is a devilish mercy in the judge, | if 3.01. 64
receiv'd no sinister measure from his judge, but 3.02.243 P
be you judge | of your own cause. 5.01.166
judge when you hear. MND 4.01.127
thou shalt see, thy eyes shall be thy judge, MV 2.05. 1
for she is wise, if i can judge of her, | and 2.06. 53
to offend and judge are distinct offices, | and 2.09. 61
that's certain, if the devil may be her judge. 3.01. 33 P
o wise young judge, how i do honor thee! 4.01.224
it doth appear you are a worthy judge; 4.01.236
o noble judge! o excellent young man! 4.01.246
o wise and upright judge! 4.01.250
so says the bond, doth it not, noble judge? 4.01.253
bid her be judge | whether bassanio had not once 4.01.276
most rightful judge! 4.01.301
most learned judge! a sentence! come, prepare! 4.01.304
o upright judge! mark, jew: o learned judge! 4.01.313
o upright judge! mark, jew: o learned judge! 4.01.313
o learned judge! mark, jew, a learned judge! 4.01.317
o learned judge! mark, jew, a learned judge! 4.01.317
o jew! an upright judge, a learned judge! 4.01.323
o jew! an upright judge, a learned judge! 4.01.323
had i been judge, thou shouldst have had ten 4.01.399
no, god's my judge, | the clerk will ne'er wear 5.01.157
his ring away | unto the judge that begg'd it, 5.01.180
neither his daughter, if we judge by manners, AYL 1.02.271
but whether wisely or no, let the forest judge. 3.02.122 P
are out, let him be judge how deep i am in love. 4.01.215 P
thou shalt be both the plaintiff and the judge TN 5.01.354
apollo be my judge! WT 3.02.116
compare our faces, and be judge yourself. JN 1.01. 79
from that supernal judge that stirs good 2.01.112
that judge hath made me guardian to this boy, 2.01.115
thoughts themselves should be your judge, | that 2.01.519
you urg'd me as a judge, but i had rather | you R2 1.03.237
men judge by the complexion of the sky | the 3.02.194
were enough noble to be upright judge | of noble 4.01.118
by the lord, i'll be a brave judge. 1H4 1.02. 65 P
and here i stand. judge, my masters. 2.04.439 P
i judge their number | upon or near the rate of 2H4 4.01. 21
gently to hear, kindly to judge, our play. H5 pr 34
we judge no less. 2.02. 39
as i judge | by his blunt bearing he will keep 4.07.176
judge you, my lord of warwick, then between us. 1H6 2.04. 10
then judge, great lords, if i have done amiss; 4.01. 27
and should (if i were worthy to be judge) | be 4.01. 42
you judge it straight a thing impossible | to 5.04. 47
this doom, my lord, if i may judge: 2H6 1.03.204
and yet herein i judge mine own wit good — 3.01.232
forbear to judge, for we are sinners all. 3.03. 31
how much thou wrong'st me, heaven be my judge. 4.10. 76
his captives blood and death, | i cannot judge: 3H6 2.01.128
o that your young nobility could judge | what R3 1.03.256
their verdict up | unto the frowning judge? 1.04.185
to–morrow then i judge a happy day. 3.04. 6
you, cardinal, | i should judge now unhappily. H8 1.04. 89
having here | no judge indifferent, nor no more 2.04. 17
make my challenge | you shall not be my judge; 2.04. 78
from my soul | refuse you for my judge, whom, 2.04. 82
that again | i do refuse you for my judge, and 2.04.118
there sits a judge | that no king can corrupt. 3.01.100
i shall both find your lordship judge and juror, 5.02. 95
and give it | to a most noble judge, the king my 5.02.136
which way do you judge my wit would fly? COR 2.03. 25 P
that can judge as fitly of his worth | as i can 4.02. 34
rome and the righteous heavens be my judge, TIT 1.01.426
now judge what /cause had titus to revenge 5.03.125
fellow | loaden with irons wiser than the judge, TIM 3.05. 50
your senses, that you may the better judge. JC 3.02. 17 P
judge, o you gods, how dearly caesar lov'd him! 3.02.182
judge me, you gods! 4.02. 38
o jephthah, judge of israel, what a treasure HAM 2.02.403 P
we may of their encounter frankly judge, | and 3.01. 33
and they shall hear and judge 'twixt you and me. 4.05.206
if your honor judge it meet, i will place you LR 1.02. 90 P
be judge yourself | whether i in any just term OTH 1.01. 38
heaven is my judge, not i for love and duty, 1.01. 59
judge me the world, if 'tis not gross in sense, 1.02. 72
us, | play judge and executioner all himself, CYM 4.02.128
they have brought (if we judge by the outside) TNK 4.02. 74
that the sense | could not be judge between 'em. 5.03.128
being judge in love, she cannot right her cause. VEN 220
my bloody judge forbod my tongue to speak, | no LUC 1648
and when the judge is robb'd, the prisoner dies. 1652
JUDGED 1 FR 0.0001 REL FR 1 V 0 P
eleanor, the law, thou seest, hath judged thee; 2H6 2.03. 15
JUDGE'S 4 FR 0.0004 REL FR 4 V 0 P
the marshal's truncheon, nor the judge's robe, MM 2.02. 61
in faith, i gave it to the judge's clerk. MV 5.01.143
gave it a judge's clerk! 5.01.157
no higher than thyself, the judge's clerk, | a 5.01.163
JUDGES 5 FR 0.0005 REL FR 5 V 0 P
have authority | when judges steal themselves. MM 2.02.176
judgment shown, | when judges have been babes; AWW 2.01.139
me but | by learned approbation of the judges. H8 1.02. 71
for which attempt the judges have pronounc'd TIT 3.01. 50
and you, the judges, bear a wary eye. HAM 5.02.279
JUDGEST 2 FR 0.0002 REL FR 1 V 1 P
thou judgest false already. 1H4 1.02. 66 P
o thou that judgest all things, stay my thoughts 2H6 3.02.136
JUDGING 1 FR 0.0001 REL FR 1 V 0 P
in the unpartial judging of this business. H8 2.02.106
JUDGMENT 123 FR 0.0139 REL FR 101 V 22 P
his head unmellowed, but his judgment ripe; TGV 2.04. 70
well, | she, in my judgment, was as fair as you; 4.04.151
i'll be judgment by mine host of the garter. WIV 3.01. 95 P
heaven forgive my sins at the day of judgment! 3.03.212 P
let mine own judgment pattern out my death, MM 2.01. 30
judgment hath | repented o'er his doom. 2.02. 11
which is the top of judgment, should | but judge 2.02. 76
to practice his judgment with the disposition of 3.01.163 P
blood | and lack of temper'd judgment afterward. 5.01.473
one that before the judgment carries poor souls ERR 4.02. 40
man should do, for my simple true judgment? ADO 1.01.167 P
no, i pray thee speak in sober judgment. 1.01.170 P
she cannot be so much without true judgment — 3.01. 88
beauty is bought by judgment of the eye, | not LLL 2.01. 15
rather your eyes must with his judgment look. MND 1.01. 57
nor hath love's mind of any judgment taste; 1.01.236
i had no judgment when to her i swore. 3.02.134
some god direct my judgment! MV 2.07. 13
wise as bold, | young in limbs, in judgment old, 2.07. 71
seven times tried that judgment is, | that did 2.09. 64
let me have judgment and the jew his will. 4.01. 83
what judgment shall i dread, doing no wrong? 4.01. 89
i stand for judgment! 4.01.103
a daniel come to judgment! 4.01.223
a well–deserving pillar, | proceed to judgment. 4.01.240
i do beseech the court | to give the judgment. 4.01.244
or knew yourself with your judgment, the fear of AYL 1.02.176 P
it was not well cut, he disabled my judgment: 5.04. 76 P
i say we must not | so stain our judgment, or AWW 2.01.120
so holy writ in babes hath judgment shown, 2.01.138
upon oath, never trust my judgment in any thing. 3.06. 33 P
sir, upon the oaths of judgment and reason. TN 3.02. 15 P
you had only in your silent judgment tried it, WT 2.01.171
if judgment lie in them, then so do we, R2 2.02.133
than to set me off, why then i have no judgment. 2H4 1.02. 14 P
is, i am only old in judgment and understanding; 1.02.192 P
my judgment is we should not step too far 1.03. 20
and strook me in my very seat of judgment; 5.02. 80
and but in purged judgment trusting neither? H5 2.02.136
you have good judgment in horsemanship. 3.07. 55 P
unto the french the dreadful judgment day | so 1H6 1.01. 29
i have perhaps some shallow spirit of judgment; 2.04. 16
god's secret judgment. 2H6 3.02. 31
god, | for judgment only doth belong to thee. 3.02.140
mine ear hath tempted judgment to desire. 3H6 3.03.133
which are so weak of courage and in judgment 4.01. 12
choosing for yourself, you show'd your judgment; 4.01. 61
shall never wake until the great judgment day. R3 1.04.104 P
of that word "judgment" hath bred a kind of 1.04.107 P
to–morrow, in my judgment, is too sudden, | for 3.04. 43
to hear | his knell rung out, his judgment, he H8 2.01. 32
i have this day receiv'd a traitor's judgment, 2.01. 58
rome, the nurse of judgment, | invited by your 2.02. 93
an excellent | and unmatch'd wit and judgment; 2.04. 47
i took a thought | this was a judgment on me, 2.04.195
holiness | to stay the judgment o' th' divorce; 3.02. 33
his royal self in judgment comes to hear | the 5.02.155
you have no judgment, niece. TRO 1.02. 92 P
dry enough), will, with great speed of judgment, 1.03.329
the dangerous /shores | of will and judgment: 2.02. 65
greater | than in the note of judgment; 2.03.125
yet gives he not till judgment guide his bounty, 4.05.102
a whore fight for a whore, he tempts judgment. 5.07. 22 P
to cry | against the rectorship of judgment? COR 2.03.205
and on a safer judgment all revoke | your 2.03.218
your dishonor | mangles true judgment, and 3.01.158
whether /defect of judgment, | to fail in the 4.07. 39
for our judgment sits | five times in that ere ROM 1.04. 46
a gentler judgment vanish'd from his lips — 3.03. 10
it shows but little love or judgment in him. TIM 3.03. 10
contain thee, | attend our weightier judgment. 3.05.101
which argues a great sickness in his judgment 5.01. 29
it shall be said his judgment rul'd our hands; JC 2.01.147
o judgment! 3.02.104
but under heavy judgment bears that life | which MAC 1.03.110
in these cases | we still have judgment here, 1.07. 8
each man's censure, but reserve thy judgment. HAM 1.03. 69
i am sorry that with better heed and judgment 2.01.108
whose blood and judgment are so well co–meddled, 3.02. 69
and waits upon the judgment, and what judgment 3.04. 70
and what judgment | would step from this to this 3.04. 70
who like not in their judgment, but their eyes, 4.03. 5
divided from herself and her fair judgment, 4.05. 85
it shall as level to your judgment 'pear | as 4.05.152
judgment. 5.02.280
answer my life my judgment, | thy youngest LR 1.01.151
and with what poor judgment he hath now cast her 1.01.291 P
that is wise and says little, to fear judgment, 1.04. 16 P
is, but, to my judgment, your highness is not 1.04. 58 P
let thy folly in | and thy dear judgment out! 1.04.272
this judgment of the heavens, that makes us 5.03.232
nay, it is possible enough to judgment. OTH 1.03. 9
it is a judgment main'd, and most imperfect, 1.03. 99
jealousy so strong | that judgment cannot cure. 2.01.302
and passion, having my best judgment collied, 2.03.206
cunning, | i have no judgment in an honest face. 3.03. 50
her will, recoiling to her better judgment, 3.03.236
your suspicion is not without wit and judgment. 4.02.211 P
present pleasure, | and so rebel to judgment. ANT 1.04. 33
when i was green in judgment, cold in blood, 1.05. 74
yourself | by laying defects of judgment to me; 2.02. 55
the fellow has good judgment. 3.03. 25
caesar, thou hast subdu'd | his judgment too. 3.13. 37
be it but to fortify her judgment, which else an CYM 1.04. 22 P
but upon my mended judgment (if i offend /not to 1.04. 46 P
meet | that i did amplify my judgment in | other 1.05. 17
nor i' th' judgment: 1.06. 41
honor'd with confirmation your great judgment 1.06.174
on | the low posthumus slanders so her judgment 3.05. 76
for defect of judgment | is oft the cause of 4.02.111
to the judgment of your eye | i give my cause, PER 1.ch. 41
make the judgment good | that thought you worthy 4.06. 93
grief | cull forth, as unpang'd judgment can, TNK 1.01.169
more buckled with strong judgment, and their 1.03. 57
and when you bark, do it with judgment. 3.05. 37
not from the stars do i my judgment pluck, | and SON 14. 1
so, till the judgment that yourself arise, | you 55.13
comes home again, on better judgment making. 87.12
yet then my judgment knew no reason why | my 115. 3
whereto the judgment of my heart is tied? 137. 8
or if they have, where is my judgment fled, 148. 3
hour, | let it not tell your judgment i am old, LC 73
o appetite, from judgment stand aloof! 166
JUDGMENT–PLACE 1 FR 0.0001 REL FR 1 V 0 P
to old free–town, our common judgment–place. ROM 1.01.102
JUDGMENT'S 1 FR 0.0001 REL FR 1 V 0 P
thy black is fairest in my judgment's place. SON 131.12
JUDGMENTS 14 FR 0.0015 REL FR 10 V 4 P
which served me as fit, by all men's judgments, TGV 4.04.162
provided that you weed your better judgments AYL 2.07. 45
whose judgments are | mere fathers of their AWW 1.02. 61
he might take a measure of his own judgments, 4.03. 33 P
being in his right wits and his good judgments, H5 4.07. 47 P
he's one o' th' soundest judgments in troy, TRO 1.02.192 P
your judgments, my grave lords, | must give this COR 5.06.105
whose judgments in such matters cried in the top HAM 2.02.438 P
and after we will both our judgments join | in 3.02. 86
of accidental judgments, casual slaughters, | of 5.02.382
i see men's judgments are | a parcel of their ANT 3.13. 31
in our own filth drop our clear judgments, make 3.13.113
very eyes | are sometimes like our judgments, CYM 4.02.302
coarse frieze capacities, ye /jane judgments, TNK 3.05. 8
JUDICIOUS 5 FR 0.0005 REL FR 3 V 2 P
examin'd my parts with most judicious iliads; WIV 1.03. 60 P
offenses to us | shall have judicious hearing. COR 5.06.126
wise, judicious, and best knows | the fits o' MAC 4.02. 16
laugh, cannot but make the judicious grieve; HAM 3.02. 26 P
judicious punishment! LR 3.04. 74
JUG 1 FR 0.0001 REL FR 1 V 0 P
"whoop, jug! LR 1.04.225
JUGGLE 1 FR 0.0001 REL FR 1 V 0 P
is't possible the spells of france should juggle H8 1.03. 1
JUGGLED 1 FR 0.0001 REL FR 1 V 0 P
i'll not be juggled with. HAM 4.05.131
JUGGLER 3 FR 0.0003 REL FR 2 V 1 P
a threadbare juggler and a fortune–teller, | a ERR 5.01.240
o me, you juggler! MND 3.02.282
you basket–hilt stale juggler, you! 2H4 2.04.132 P
JUGGLERS 1 FR 0.0001 REL FR 1 V 0 P
as, nimble jugglers that deceive the eye, ERR 1.02. 98
JUGGLING 5 FR 0.0005 REL FR 3 V 2 P
this juggling witchcraft with revenue cherish, JN 3.01.169
she and the dolphin have been juggling. 1H6 5.04. 68
here is such patchery, such juggling, and such TRO 2.03. 71 P
a juggling trick — to be secretly open. 5.02. 24 P
and be these juggling fiends no more believ'd, MAC 5.08. 19
JUGS 1 FR 0.0001 REL FR 1 V 0 P
she brought stone jugs and no seal'd quarts. SHR in.2. 88
JUICE 7 FR 0.0008 REL FR 7 V 0 P
with juice of balm and every precious flow'r; WIV 5.05. 62
the juice of it on sleeping eyelids laid | will MND 2.01.170
having once this juice, | i'll watch titania 2.01.176
and with the juice of this i'll streak her eyes, 2.01.257
stole, | with juice of cursed hebona in a vial, HAM 1.05. 62
the juice of egypt's grape shall moist this lip. ANT 5.02.282
thick–sighted, barren, lean, and lacking juice, VEN 136
JULE 3 FR 0.0003 REL FR 3 V 0 P
when thou hast more wit, | wilt thou not, jule?" ROM 1.03. 43
"wilt thou not, jule?" 1.03. 47
when thou comest to age, | wilt thou not, jule?" 1.03. 57
JULIA 27 FR 0.0030 REL FR 25 V 2 P
thou, julia, thou hast metamorphis'd me, | made TGV 1.01. 66
gav'st thou my letter to julia? 1.01. 95 P
i fear my julia would not deign my lines, 1.01.152
"to julia" — say, from whom? 1.02. 35
look, here is writ "kind julia." 1.02.106
unkind julia, | as in revenge of thy ingratitude 1.02.106
to the sweet julia" — that i'll tear away — 1.02.122
o heavenly julia! 1.03. 50
have patience, gentle julia. 2.02. 1
me in the day | wherein i sigh not, julia, for 2.02. 10
julia, farewell! 2.02. 16
and so is julia that i love — | that i did love 2.04.199
how did thy master part with madam julia? 2.05. 11 P
to leave my julia, shall i be forsworn; 2.06. 1
julia i lose, and valentine i lose: 2.06. 19
for julia, silvia. 2.06. 22
her fair) | shows julia but a swarthy ethiope. 2.06. 26
i will forget that julia is alive, | rememb'ring 2.06. 27
in breaking faith with julia whom i lov'd; 4.02. 11
one julia, that his changing thoughts forget, 4.04.119
times | his julia gave it him at his departure: 4.04.135
mine shall not do his julia so much wrong. 4.04.137
why, this is the ring i gave to julia. 5.04. 93
at my depart | i gave this unto julia. 5.04. 97
and julia herself did give it me — | and julia 5.04. 98
and julia herself hath brought it hither. 5.04. 99
how? julia? 5.04.100
JULIA'S 5 FR 0.0005 REL FR 5 V 0 P
i fear'd to show my father julia's letter, TGV 1.03. 80
keep this remembrance for thy julia's sake. 2.02. 5
part, | and i was trimm'd in madam julia's gown, 4.04.161
read over julia's heart (thy first best love), 5.04. 46
spy | more fresh in julia's with a constant eye? 5.04.115
JULIET 45 FR 0.0050 REL FR 44 V 1 P
and there's madam juliet. MM 1.02.115 P
with character too gross is writ on juliet. 1.02.155

some one with child by him? my cousin juliet? 1.04. 45
shall be done, sir, with the groaning juliet? 2.02. 15
my brother did love juliet, | and you tell me 2.04.142
what, juliet! ROM 1.03. 4
tell me, daughter juliet, | how stands your 1.03. 64
we follow thee. juliet, the county stays. 1.03.104
with tender juliet /match'd is now not fair. 2.pr. 4
it is the east, and juliet is the sun. 2.02. 3
ah, juliet, if the measure of thy joy | be 2.06. 24
o sweet juliet, | thy beauty hath made me 3.01.113
is father, mother, tybalt, romeo, juliet, | all 3.02.123
heaven is here | where juliet lives, and every 3.03. 30
unless philosophy can make a juliet, | displant 3.03. 58
wert thou as young as i, juliet thy love, | an 3.03. 65
i come from lady juliet. 3.03. 80
spakest thou of juliet? 3.03. 93
thy juliet is alive, | for whose dear sake thou 3.03.135
go you to juliet ere you go to bed; 3.04. 31
juliet wills it so. 3.05. 24
why, how now, juliet? 3.05. 68
juliet, on thursday early will i rouse ye; 4.01. 42
o juliet, i already know thy grief, | it strains 4.01. 46
go thou to juliet, help to deck up her. 4.02. 41
go waken juliet, go and trim her up, | i'll go 4.04. 25
juliet! 4.05. 1
for shame, bring juliet forth, her lord is come. 4.05. 22
how doth my juliet? 5.01. 15
well, juliet, i will lie with thee to–night. 5.01. 34
within this three hours will fair juliet wake. 5.02. 25
merciful, | open the tomb, lay me with juliet. 5.03. 73
he told me paris should have married juliet. 5.03. 78
or am i mad, hearing him talk of juliet, | to 5.03. 80
for here lies juliet, and her beauty makes 5.03. 85
ah, dear juliet, | why art thou yet so fair? 5.03.101
come go, good juliet, i dare no longer stay. 5.03.159
and juliet bleeding, warm, and newly dead, | who 5.03.175
cry "romeo," | some "juliet," and some "paris," 5.03.192
and romeo dead, and juliet, dead before, | warm 5.03.196
romeo, there dead, was husband to that juliet, 5.03.231
for whom, and not for tybalt, juliet pin'd. 5.03.236
came to this vault to die, and lie with juliet. 5.03.290
be set | as that of true and faithful juliet. 5.03.302
of more woe | than this of juliet and her romeo. 5.03.310

JULIET'S 4 FR 0.0004 REL FR 4 V 0 P
on the white wonder of dear juliet's hand, | and ROM 3.03. 36
for juliet's sake, for her sake, rise and stand; 3.03. 89
go with me | to juliet's grave, for there must i 5.01. 86
i brought my master news of juliet's death, 5.03.272

JULIETTA 1 FR 0.0001 REL FR 0 V 1 P
and it is for getting madam julietta with child. MM 1.02. 73 P

JULIETTA'S 1 FR 0.0001 REL FR 1 V 0 P
contract | i got possession of julietta's bed. MM 1.02.146

JULIO 1 FR 0.0001 REL FR 0 V 1 P
by that rare italian master, julio romano, who, WT 5.02. 97 P

JULIUS 16 FR 0.0018 REL FR 15 V 1 P
the way | to julius caesar's ill–erected tower, R2 5.01. 2
soul will make | than julius caesar or bright — 1H6 1.01. 56
brutus' bastard hand | stabb'd julius caesar; 2H6 4.01.137
did julius caesar build that place, my lord? R3 3.01. 69
that julius caesar was a famous man; 3.01. 84
pardon me, julius! JC 3.01.204
did not great julius bleed for justice' sake? 4.03. 19
o julius caesar, thou art mighty yet! 5.03. 94
rome, | a little ere the mightiest julius fell, HAM 1.01.114
i did enact julius caesar. 3.02.103 P
having a son and friends, since julius caesar, ANT 2.06. 12
i have heard that julius caesar | grew fat with 2.06. 64
when antony found julius caesar dead, | he cried 3.02. 54
are men more order'd than when julius caesar CYM 2.04. 21
when julius caesar (whose remembrance yet 3.01. 2
be many caesars, | ere such another julius. 3.01. 12

JULY 2 FR 0.0002 REL FR 1 V 1 P
the sixt of july. your loving friend, benedick. ADO 1.01.283 P
and proofs as clear as founts in july when | we H8 1.01.154

JULY'S 1 FR 0.0001 REL FR 1 V 0 P
he makes a july's day short as december, | and WT 1.02.169

JUMP 15 FR 0.0017 REL FR 13 V 2 P
because i will not jump with common spirits, MV 2.09. 32
both our inventions meet and jump in one. SHR 1.01.190
fortune, do cohere and jump | that i am viola — TN 5.01.252
of dildos and fadings, "jump her and thump her"; WT 4.04.195 P
wish | to jump a body with a dangerous physic COR 3.01.154
/shoal of time, | we'ld jump the life to come. MAC 1.07. 7
thus twice before, and jump at this dead hour, HAM 1.01. 65
but since, so jump upon this bloody question, 5.02.375
but though they jump not on a just accompt | (as OTH 1.03. 5
and bring him jump when he may cassio find 2.03.386
our fortune lies | upon this jump. ANT 3.08. 6
or jump the after–inquiry on your own peril; CYM 5.04.182 P
where not to be ev'n jump | as they are, here TNK 1.02. 40
to jump up higher seem'd, to mock the mind. LUC 1414
for nimble thought can jump both sea and land SON 44. 7

JUMPETH 1 FR 0.0001 REL FR 1 V 0 P
knows, | seldom or never jumpeth with the heart. R3 3.01. 11

JUMPING 1 FR 0.0001 REL FR 1 V 0 P
carry them here and there, jumping o'er times, H5 pr 29

JUMPS 5 FR 0.0005 REL FR 2 V 3 P
put l to sore, then sorel jumps from thicket, LLL 4.02. 58
jumps along by him | and never stays to greet AYL 2.01. 53
of the three but jumps twelve foot and a half by WT 4.04.339 P
and in some sort it jumps with my humor as well 1H4 1.02. 69 P
with the boys, and jumps upon join'd–stools, and 2H4 2.04.247 P

/JUNE 1 FR 0.0001 REL FR 1 V 0 P
the breeze upon her, like a cow in /june — ANT 3.10. 14

JUNE 2 FR 0.0002 REL FR 1 V 1 P
is like, if there come a hot june and this civil 1H4 2.04.362 P
be seen, | he was but as the cuckoo is in june, 3.02. 75

JUNES 1 FR 0.0001 REL FR 1 V 0 P
three april perfumes in three hot junes burn'd, SON 104. 7

JUNIUS 2 FR 0.0002 REL FR 2 V 0 P
one's junius brutus, | sicinius velutus, and i COR 1.01.216
lord junius brutus sware for lucrece' rape, TIT 4.01. 91

JUNKETS 1 FR 0.0001 REL FR 1 V 0 P
you know there wants no junkets at the feast. SHR 3.02.248

JUNO 17 FR 0.0019 REL FR 15 V 2 P
great juno, comes, i know her by her gait. TMP 4.01.102
juno sings her blessings on you. 4.01.109
juno and ceres whisper seriously; 4.01.125
juno does command. 4.01.131
whom jove would swear | juno but an ethiop were, LLL 4.03.116
i, his despiteful juno, sent him forth | from AWW 3.04. 13
juno have mercy! how came it cloven? TRO 1.02.120 P
for the love of juno, let's go. COR 2.01.101 P
by juno, i swear ay. LR 2.04. 22
let me sit down. o juno! ANT 3.11. 28
trims, wherein | you made great juno angry. CYM 3.04.165
as juno had been sick | and he her dieter. 4.02. 50
with mars fall out, with juno chide, | that thy 5.04. 32
by juno, that is queen of marriage, | all viands PER 2.03. 30
and /cas'd as richly, in pace another juno; 5.01.111
and wish great juno would | resume her ancient TNK 1.02. 21
jove would swear | juno but an ethiope were, PP 16.16

JUNO–LIKE 1 FR 0.0001 REL FR 1 V 0 P
and lament as i do, | in anger, juno–like. COR 4.02. 53

JUNO'S 6 FR 0.0006 REL FR 6 V 0 P
and wheresoe'er we went, like juno's swans, AYL 1.03. 75
wedding is great juno's crown, | o blessed bond 5.04.141
but sweeter than the lids of juno's eyes | or WT 4.04.121
had i great juno's power, | the strong–wing'd ANT 4.15. 34
not juno's mantle fairer than your tresses, TNK 1.01. 63
arch'd like the great–ey'd juno's, but far 4.02. 20

JUPITER *(also jubiter)*

JUPITER 35 FR 0.0039 REL FR 27 V 8 P
that ne'er | dost disobey the wife of jupiter; TMP 4.01. 77
you were also, jupiter, a swan for the love of WIV 5.05. 6 P
o jupiter, how /weary are my spirits! AYL 2.04. 1 P
o most gentle jupiter, what tedious homily of 3.02.155 P
jupiter | became a bull and bellow'd; WT 4.04. 27
o jupiter, there's no comparison. TRO 1.02. 62 P
"jupiter," quoth she, "which of these hairs is 1.02.163 P
jupiter forbid, | and say in thunder, "achilles 2.03.198
"lo jupiter is yonder, dealing life!" 4.05.191
and the goodly transformation of jupiter there, 5.01. 53 P
his bloody brow? o jupiter, no blood! COR 1.03. 38
by jupiter, forgot! 1.09. 90
take my cap, jupiter, and i thank thee. 2.01.105 P
if jupiter | should from yond cloud speak divine 4.05.103
the moon, | your letter is with jupiter by this. TIT 4.03. 67
what says jupiter? 4.03. 80
but what says jupiter, i ask thee? 4.03. 84
by jupiter, | this shall not be revok'd. LR 1.01.178
by jupiter, i swear no. 2.04. 21
by jupiter, | were i the wearer of antonio's ANT 2.02. 6
caesar? why, he's the jupiter of men. 3.02. 9
what's antony? the god of jupiter. 3.02. 10
wert thou the son of jupiter, and no more | but CYM 2.03.125
by jupiter, i had it from her arm. 2.04.121
by jupiter he swears. 2.04.122
or, by jupiter, | i will not ask again. 3.05. 84
by jupiter, an angel! 3.06. 42
great jupiter be prais'd! 5.03. 84
then, jupiter, thou king of gods, | why hast 5.04. 77
since, jupiter, our son is good, | take off his 5.04. 85
help, jupiter, or we appeal, | and from thy 5.04. 91
thanks, jupiter! 5.04.119
methought | great jupiter, upon his eagle back'd 5.05.427
and in the temple of great jupiter | our peace 5.05.482
themselves, thither they go — jupiter bless us! TNK 4.03. 36 P

JURE 1 FR 0.0001 REL FR 0 V 1 P
we'll jure ye, faith. 1H4 2.02. 91 P

JUREMENT 1 FR 0.0001 REL FR 0 V 1 P
qu'il est contre son jurement de pardonner aucun H5 4.04. 50 P

JURISDICTION 2 FR 0.0002 REL FR 1 V 1 P
within point–blank of our jurisdiction regal. 2H6 4.07. 26 P
you maim'd the jurisdiction of all bishops. H8 3.02.312

JUROR 1 FR 0.0001 REL FR 1 V 0 P
i shall both find your lordship judge and juror, H8 5.02. 95

JURORS 1 FR 0.0001 REL FR 0 V 1 P
spots of thy kindred were jurors on thy life; TIM 4.03.341 P

JURY 2 FR 0.0002 REL FR 2 V 0 P
i not deny | the jury, passing on the prisoner's MM 2.01. 19
his noble jury and foul cause can witness. H8 3.02.269

/JUST* 6 FR 0.0006 REL FR 6 V 0 P
not count it holy | /to /hurt /by /being /just; TRO 5.03. 20
/than /will /preserve /just /so /much /strength TIT 3.02. 2
/and /just /against /thy /heart /make /thou /a 3.02. 17
/making /just /report | /of /how /unnatural /and LR 3.01. 37
/in /thy /just /proof /repeals /and /reconciles 3.06.113
/most /just /and /heavy /causes /make /oppose. 5.01. 27

JUST* 149 FR 0.0168 REL FR 126 V 23 P
and the merchant | have just our theme of woe; TMP 2.01. 6
as you gave in charge, | just as you left them; 5.01. 9
for all the orld, as just as you will desire, WIV 1.01. 50 P
at herne's oak, just 'twixt twelve and one, 4.06. 19
yet still 'tis just. MM 1.02.123
o just but severe law! 2.02. 41
that the most just law | now took your brother's 2.04. 52
ay, just, perpetual durance — a restraint, 3.01. 67
he tyrannous, | but this being so, he's just. 4.02. 85
his beard and head | just of his color. 4.03. 73
shy, as grave, as just, as absolute | as angelo. 5.01. 54
why, just, my lord, and that is angelo, | who 5.01.202
even just the sum that i do owe to you | is ERR 4.01. 7
discover how, and thou shalt find me just. 5.01.203
man that were made just in the midway between ADO 2.01. 7 P
just, if he send me no husband, for the which 2.01. 27 P
my dear son, which is hence a just sevennight, 2.01.360 P
banquet, just so many strange dishes. 2.03. 21 P
i am sorry for her, as i have just cause, being 2.03.166 P
yea, just so much as you may take upon a knive's 2.03.254 P
who can blot that name | with any just reproach? 4.01. 81
"just," said she, "it hurts nobody." 5.01.163 P
but always hath been just and virtuous | in any 5.01.302
much like to you, for you have just his bleat. 5.04. 51
thou less nor more | but just a pound of flesh. MV 4.01.326
if thou tak'st more | or less than a just pound, 4.01.327
and greasy citizens, | 'tis just the fashion. AYL 2.01. 56
yes, just. 3.02.264 P
just as high as my heart. 3.02.269 P
'twas just the difference | betwixt the constant 3.05.122
and nature, stronger than his just occasion, 4.03.129
gown is made | just as my master had direction. SHR 4.03.116
just like the brooch and the toothpick, which AWW 1.01.157 P
just, you say well; so would i have said. 2.03. 19 P
would in so just a business shut his bosom 3.01. 8
my mother told me just how he would woo, | as if 4.02. 69
which on your just proceeding i'll keep off — 5.03.236
just the contrary: the better for thy friends. TN 5.01. 14 P
how blest am i | in my just censure! WT 2.01. 37
so shall she have | a just and open trial. 2.03.205
this your request | is altogether just; 3.02.117
had she such power, | she had just cause. 5.01. 61
swords | in such a just and charitable war. JN 2.01. 36
england, impatient of your just demands, | hath 2.01. 56
our just and lineal entrance to our own; 2.01. 85
throne, | a loyal, just, and upright gentleman. R2 1.03. 87
was not gaunt just? 2.01.192
for he is just and always loved us well. 2.01.221
this swears he, as he is /a /prince, /is just, 3.03.119
and god befriend us, as our cause is just! 1H4 5.01.120
fair | when the intent of bearing them is just. 5.02. 88
it is very just. 2H4 3.02. 81 P
the just proportion that we gave them out. 4.01. 23
it shall appear that your demands are just, 4.01.142
to meet his grace just distance 'tween our 4.01.224
with grant of our most just and right desires, 4.02. 40
is this proceeding just and honorable? 4.02.110
your majesty hath no just cause to hate me. 5.02. 66
you use the same | with the like bold, just, and 5.02.116
no prince nor peer shall have just cause to say, 5.02.144
as nail in door. the things i speak are just. 5.03.121
is not this just? H5 2.01.111
'a parted ev'n just between twelve and one, ev'n 2.03. 12 P
the plain–song is most just; 3.02. 7
just, just; 3.07.147 P
just, just; 3.07.147 P
his cause being just and his quarrel honorable. 4.01.128 P
bring me just notice of the numbers dead | on 4.07.117
with full accord to all our just demands, 5.02. 71
just death, kind umpire of men's miseries, 1H6 2.05. 29
know your grace to be a man | just and upright; 3.01. 95
to give thee answer of thy just demand. 5.03.144
why, this is just | "aio /te, aeacida, romanos 2H6 1.04. 61
thrice is he arm'd that hath his quarrel just; 3.02.233
great god, how just art thou! 5.01. 68
me, | lest in revenge thereof, sith god is just, 3H6 1.03. 41
am come to crave thy just and lawful aid; 3.03. 32
yet heav'ns are just, and time suppresseth 3.03. 77
and if king edward be as true and just | as i am R3 1.01. 36
it is a quarrel just and reasonable, | to be 1.02.136
so just is god, to right the innocent. 1.03.181
with all your just proceedings in this /cause. 3.05. 66
in this just cause come i to move your grace. 3.07.140
what says your highness to my just request? 4.02. 94
o upright, just, and true–disposing god, | how 4.04. 55
not | usurp the just proportion of my sorrow? 4.04.110
either thou wilt die by god's just ordinance 4.04.184
and part in just proportion our small power. 5.03. 26
just as i do now, | he would kiss you twenty H8 1.04. 29
have any goodness, | the trial just and noble. 2.02. 91
this just and learned priest, card'nal campeius, 2.02. 96
our just opinions | and comforts to /your cause. 3.01. 60
be just, and fear not; 3.02.446
'tis just to each of them; he is himself. TRO 1.02. 71 P
but the just gods gainsay | that any /drop thou 4.05.132
rome, be as just and gracious unto me | as i am TIT 1.01. 60
too, | upon a just survey take titus' part, 1.01.446
but yet so just that he will not revenge. 4.01.128
ay, just — a verse in horace, right, you have 4.02. 24
are, | that my report is just and full of truth. 5.03.115
just opposite to what thou justly seem'st, | a ROM 3.02. 78
even in my mistress' case, | just in her case. 3.03. 85
soul, and just of the same piece | is every TIM 3.02. 64
but in defense, by mercy, 'tis most just. 3.05. 55
'tis most just | that thou turn rascal; 4.03.216
had i a steward | so true, so just, and now so 4.03.491
a just and true report that goes of his having. 5.01. 16
'tis just, | and it is very much lamented, JC 1.02. 54
he was my friend, faithful and just to me; 3.02. 85
and what we have to do, | to the direction just. MAC 3.03. 4
you may be rightly just, | what ever i shall 4.03. 30
let our just censures | attend the true event, 5.04. 14
thou art e'en as just a man | as e'er my HAM 3.02. 54
he most violent author | of his own just remove; 4.05. 81
to them, | and show the heavens more just. LR 3.04. 36
is my fortune, that i must repent to be just! 3.05. 10 P
the gods are just, and of our pleasant vices 5.03.171
yourself | whether i in any just term am affin'd OTH 1.01. 39
but though they jump not on a just accompt | (as 1.03. 5
his vice, | 'tis to his virtue a just equinox, 2.03.124
but in a man that's just | they're close 3.03.122
i think that thou art just, and think thou art 3.03.385
hast taken against me a most just exception; 4.02.207 P
o brave iago, honest and just, | that hast such 5.01. 31
but that i did proceed upon just grounds | to 5.02.138
if the great gods be just, they shall assist ANT 2.01. 1
it is just so high as it is, and moves with it 2.07. 43 P
no bond, but to do just ones. CYM 5.01. 7
parts of the world to just and tourney for her PER 2.01.110 P
show | can any way speak in his just commend; 2.02. 49
the most just god | for every graff would send a 5.01. 59
friends, | if this but answer to my just belief, 5.01.238
to perform thy just command, | i here confess 5.03. 1
of monstrous lust the due and just reward. 5.03. 86
too, for 'tis not scissor'd just | to such a TNK 1.02. 54
lover, | and have as just a title to her beauty, 2.02.180
for none but such dare die in these just trials. 3.06.105
as thou art just, thy noble ear against us; 3.06.174
just such another wanton ganymede | set /jove 4.02. 15
fitted and shap'd just to that strength of STM III 4
now was she just before him as he sat, | and VEN 349
wreath'd up in fatal folds just in his way, 879
and most deceiving when it seems most just; 1156
when shall he think to find a stranger just LUC 159
devil, | he entertain'd a show so seeming just, 1514
just to the time, not with the time exchang'd, SON 109. 7
down, | and on just proof surmise accumulate; 117.10
and the just pleasure lost, which is so deemed 121. 3
the more i hear and see just cause of hate? 150.10

JUST–BORNE 1 FR 0.0001 REL FR 1 V 0 P
before we will lay down our just–borne arms JN 2.01.345

JUSTEIUS 1 FR 0.0001 REL FR 1 V 0 P

marcus octavius, marcus justeius, | publicola, ANT 3.07. 72
JUSTEST 1 FR 0.0001 REL FR 1 V 0 P
they shall assist | the deeds of justest men. ANT 2.01. 2
JUSTICE' 2 FR 0.0002 REL FR 2 V 0 P
and poise the cause in justice' equal scales, 2H6 2.01.200
did not great julius bleed for justice' sake? JC 4.03. 19
/JUSTICE 1 FR 0.0001 REL FR 1 V 0 P
/thou /robed /man /of /justice, /take /thy LR 3.06. 36
JUSTICE 175 FR 0.0197 REL FR 149 V 26 P
grief, | and on the justice of my flying hence, TGV 4.03. 29
of gloucester, justice of peace and coram. WIV 1.01. 5 P
and your friend, and justice shallow, and here 1.01. 76 P
he's a justice of peace in his country, simple 1.01.218 P
a justice of peace sometime may be beholding to 1.01.272 P
cavaleiro justice, i say! 2.01.194 P
tell him, cavaleiro justice; 2.01.198 P
and the terms | for common justice, y' are as MM 1.01. 11
dead, | and liberty plucks justice by the nose; 1.03. 29
unloose this tied-up justice when you pleas'd: 1.03. 32
what's open made to justice, | that justice 2.01. 21
open made to justice, | that justice seizes. 2.01. 22
i do lean upon justice, sir, and do bring in 2.01. 49 P
justice or iniquity? 2.01.172 P
and most desire should meet the blow of justice; 2.02. 30
i show it most of all when i show justice; 2.02.100
humbles himself to the determination of justice; 3.02.244 P
hath forc'd me to tell him he is indeed justice. 3.02.254 P
sith that the justice of your title to him 4.01. 73
with the stroke and line of his great justice. 4.02. 80
upon the very siege of justice | lord angelo 4.02. 98
if the duke avouch the justice of your dealing? 4.02.186 P
and we hear | such goodness of your justice, 5.01. 6
justice, o royal duke! 5.01. 20
me in my true complaint | and given me justice, 5.01. 25
true complaint | and given me justice, justice, 5.01. 25
and given me justice, justice, justice, justice! 5.01. 25
and given me justice, justice, justice, justice! 5.01. 25
here is lord angelo shall give you justice; 5.01. 27
her brother, | cut off by course of justice — 5.01. 35
by course of justice! 5.01. 35
now, good my lord, give me the scope of justice, 5.01.234
my brother had but justice, | in that he did the 5.01.448
justice, most sacred duke, against the abbess! ERR 5.01.133
justice, most gracious duke, o, grant me justice 5.01.190
most gracious duke, o, grant me justice, | even 5.01.190
that then i lost for thee, now grant me justice. 5.01.194
justice, sweet prince, against that woman there! 5.01.197
if justice cannot tame you, she shall ne'er ADO 5.01.206 P
and justice always whirls in equal measure: LLL 4.03.381
justice! MV 2.08. 17
justice! 2.08. 21
of the state, | if they deny him justice. 3.02.279
the envious plea | of forfeiture, of justice, 3.02.283
the duke shall grant me justice. 3.03. 8
will much impeach the justice of the state, 3.03. 29
and for thy life let justice be accus'd. 4.01.129
show likest god's | when mercy seasons justice. 4.01.197
though justice be thy plea, consider this, 4.01.198
that, in the course of justice, none of us 4.01.199
thus much | to mitigate the justice of thy plea, 4.01.203
for, as thou urgest justice, be assur'd | thou 4.01.315
thou shalt have justice more than thou desir'st. 4.01.316
soft, | the jew shall have all justice. 4.01.321
he shall have merely justice and his bond. 4.01.339
and then the justice, | in fair round belly with AYL 2.07.153
time is the old justice that examines all such 4.01.199 P
loosing upon thee, in the name of justice, AWW 2.03.165
him from the wrath | of greatest justice. 3.04. 29
and i follow him to his country for justice. 5.03.144 P
now, justice on the doers! 5.03.154
the justice of your hearts will thereto add WT 2.01. 67
sir, lest your justice | prove violence, in the 2.01.127
it came to us, i do in justice charge thee, | on 2.03.180
since we so openly | proceed in justice, which 3.02. 6
thee than it), so thou | shalt feel our justice; 3.02. 90
you here shall swear upon this sword of justice, 3.02.124
heaven shall be brib'd | to do him justice, and JN 2.01.172
to me for justice and rough chastisement; R2 1.01.106
see | justice design the victor's chivalry. 1.01.203
to swear him in the justice of his cause. 1.03. 10
law, | depose him in the justice of his cause. 1.03. 30
why at our justice seem'st thou then to low'r? 1.03.235
richly in both, if justice had her right. 2.01.227
she will, she will, justice hath liquor'd her. 1H4 2.01. 85 P
this seeming brow of justice, did he win | the 4.03. 83
i beseech you, which is justice shallow? 2H4 3.02. 56 P
i do see the bottom of justice shallow. 3.02.302 P
this same starv'd justice hath done nothing but 3.02.304 P
how now, my lord chief justice, whither away? 5.02. 1
the majesty and power of law and justice, | the 5.02. 78
to pluck down justice from your aweful bench? 5.02. 86
you are right justice, and you weigh this well, 5.02.102
bold, | that dares do justice on my proper son; 5.02.109
his greatness so | into the hands of justice." 5.02.112
my friends, and woe to my lord chief justice! 5.03.138 P
come, you rogue, come bring me to a justice. 5.04. 26 P
my lord chief justice, speak to that vain man. 5.05. 44
the sad-ey'd justice, with his surly hum, H5 1.02.202
and god in justice hath reveal'd to us | the 2H6 2.03.102
justice with favor have i always done; 4.07. 67
as i in justice and true right express it. 5.02. 25
i cheer'd them up with justice of our cause, 3H6 2.01.133
head, | for york in justice puts his armor on. 2.02.130
lands, | which we in justice cannot well deny, 3.02. 5
you fight in justice; 5.04. 81
i fear thy justice will take hold | on me and R3 2.01.132
thus hath the course of justice whirl'd about, 4.04.105
god will in justice ward you as his soldiers; 5.03.254
't has done, upon the premises, but justice; H8 2.01. 63
sir, i desire you do me right and justice, | and 2.04. 13
so give me up | to the sharp'st kind of justice. 2.04. 44
stubborn to justice, apt to accuse it, and 2.04.122
would you have me | (if you have any justice, 3.01.116
sharp enough, | lord, for thy justice! 3.02. 93
favor, and do justice | for truth's sake and his 3.02.396
ever | the justice and the truth o' th' question, 5.01.130
that, in this case of justice, my accusers, | be 5.02. 81
(between whose endless jar justice resides) TRO 1.03.117
lose their names, and so should justice too! 1.03.118
subdues him, | and curse that justice did it. COR 1.01.176
and the chairs of justice | supplied with worthy 3.03. 34
that not in the presence | of dreaded justice, 3.03. 98
if he slay me, | he does fair justice; 4.04. 25
defend the justice of my cause with arms; TIT 1.01. 2
to justice, continence, and nobility; 1.01. 15
whose friend in justice thou hast ever been, 1.01.180
earth, | and ripen justice in this commonweal. 1.01.227
suum /cuique is our roman justice: 1.01.280
this prince in justice seizeth but his own. 1.01.281
without controlment, justice, or revenge? 2.01. 68
yet there's as little justice as at land. 4.03. 9
tell him it is for justice and for aid, | and 4.03. 15
and, kinsmen, then we may go pipe for justice. 4.03. 24
marry, for justice, she is so employ'd, | he 4.03. 40
and, sith there's no justice in earth nor hell, 4.03. 50
to send down justice for to wreak our wrongs. 4.03. 52
shall i have justice? 4.03. 80
by me thou shalt have justice at his hands. 4.03.104
for the extent | of egall justice, us'd in such 4.04. 4
as who would say, in rome no justice were. 4.04. 20
but he and his shall know that justice lives 4.04. 23
i beg for justice, which thou, prince, must give ROM 3.01.180
religion to the gods, peace, justice, truth, TIM 4.01. 16
making your wills | the scope of justice; 5.04. 5
of regular justice in your city's bounds, | but 5.04. 61
his body, that did stab | and not for justice? JC 4.03. 21
no sooner justice had, with valor arm'd, MAC 1.02. 29
this even-handed justice | commends th' 1.07. 10
as justice, verity, temp'rance, stableness, 4.03. 92
offense's gilded hand may /shove by justice, HAM 3.03. 58
thee undivulged crimes | unwhipt of justice! LR 3.02. 53
obey thy parents, keep thy word's justice, swear 3.04. 81 P
upon his life | without the form of justice, yet 3.07. 25
see how yond justice rails upon yond simple 4.06.152 P
handy-dandy, which is the justice, which is the 4.06.154 P
and the strong lance of justice hurtless breaks; 4.06.166
a noble heart, | thy arm may do thee justice; 5.03.128
let loose on me the justice of the state | for OTH 1.01.139
and i'll do you justice. 2.03. 87 P
the justice of it pleases; 4.01.209 P
almost persuade | justice to break her sword! 5.02. 17
to do you justice, makes his ministers | of us ANT 3.06. 88
caesar, | not by a public minister of justice, 5.01. 20
"justice, and your father's wrath, should he CYM 3.02. 40 P
or we appeal, | and from thy justice fly. 5.04. 92
whom heavens, in justice, both on her and hers, 5.05.464
and yet but justice; PER 2.04. 13
crown a' th' earth | i' th' justice of compare! 4.03. 9
for thou lookest | modest as justice, and thou 5.01.121
have deaf'd | the ears of heav'nly justice. TNK 1.02. 81
into twain and doing | each side like justice, 1.03. 47
where sin is justice, lust and ignorance | the 2.02.106
i, and the justice of my love, would make thee 3.01. 34
'tis justice. 3.06. 15
and love | with all the justice of affection, 3.06. 51
do such a justice thou thyself wilt envy. 3.06.155
and, as the gods regard ye, fight with justice. 5.01. 15
give them our present justice, since i know 5.03.132
so the deities | have show'd due justice. 5.04.109
the gods my justice | take from my hand, and 5.04.120
god hath his office lent | of dread, of justice, STM II.C 99
justice is feasting while the widow weeps, LUC 906
no rightful plea might plead for justice there. 1649
die, | for sparing justice feeds iniquity. 1687
JUSTICE-LIKE 1 FR 0.0001 REL FR 0 V 1 P
them, is turn'd into a justice-like servingman. 2H4 5.01. 68 P
/JUSTICER 2 FR 0.0002 REL FR 2 V 0 P
/sit /thou /here, /most /learned /justicer; LR 3.06. 21
/false /justicer, /why /hast /thou /let /her 3.06. 56
JUSTICER 1 FR 0.0001 REL FR 1 V 0 P
or knife, or poison, | some upright justicer! CYM 5.05.214
/JUSTICERS 1 FR 0.0001 REL FR 1 V 0 P
you /justicers, that these our nether crimes LR 4.02. 79
JUSTICES' 1 FR 0.0001 REL FR 0 V 1 P
five justices' hands at it, and witnesses more WT 4.04.283 P
JUSTICES 8 FR 0.0009 REL FR 1 V 7 P
though we are justices and doctors and churchmen WIV 2.03. 46 P
i knew when seven justices could not take up a AYL 5.04. 99 P
let the justices make you and fortune friends; AWW 5.02. 33 P
and one of the king's justices of the peace. 2H4 3.02. 58 P
as i return, i will fetch off these justices. 3.02.302 P
him, do bear themselves like foolish justices; 5.01. 67 P
thou hast appointed justices of peace, to call 2H6 4.07. 41 P
marry, we were sent for to the justices. R3 2.03. 46
JUSTIFICATION 1 FR 0.0001 REL FR 0 V 1 P
for my brother's justification, he wrote this LR 1.02. 44 P
JUSTIFIED 4 FR 0.0004 REL FR 2 V 2 P
how is this justified? AWW 4.03. 54 P
we will be justified in our loves; WT 1.01. 9 P
and here justified | by us, a pair of kings. 5.03.145
but will you be more justified? H8 2.04.163
JUSTIFY 10 FR 0.0011 REL FR 9 V 1 P
frown upon you | and justify you traitors. TMP 5.01.128
this woman, | to justify this worthy nobleman, MM 5.01.159
(which seems much) to justify him, but a WT 5.02. 65 P
i cannot justify whom the law condemns. 2H6 2.03. 16
person | i'll hear him his confessions justify, H8 1.02. 6
more particulars | must justify my knowledge. CYM 2.04. 79
eye | i give my cause, who best can justify. PER 1.ch. 42
and justify in knowledge | she is thy very 5.01.217
place, which well | might justify your manhood; TNK 3.01. 64
o, call not me to justify the wrong | that thy SON 139. 1
JUSTIFYING 1 FR 0.0001 REL FR 1 V 0 P
and justifying my love, i must not fly from't. TNK 3.06. 42
JUSTIFY'T 1 FR 0.0001 REL FR 1 V 0 P
say't and justify't. WT 1.02.278
JUSTLE 2 FR 0.0002 REL FR 1 V 1 P
monster, i am in case to justle a constable. TMP 3.02. 26 P
let not the cloud of sorrow justle it | from LLL 5.02.748
JUSTLED 1 FR 0.0001 REL FR 1 V 0 P
you have | been justled from your senses, know TMP 5.01.158
JUSTLES 1 FR 0.0001 REL FR 1 V 0 P
justles roughly by | all time of pause, rudely TRO 4.04. 34
JUSTLING 1 FR 0.0001 REL FR 1 V 0 P
leisure to be sick | in such a justling time? 1H4 4.01. 18
/JUSTLY 2 FR 0.0002 REL FR 1 V 1 P
/i /have /in /equal /balance /justly /weigh'd 2H4 4.01. 67
/let /us /deal /justly. LR 3.06. 40 P
JUSTLY 29 FR 0.0032 REL FR 24 V 5 P
look you speak justly. MM 5.01.296
in this the madman justly chargeth them. ERR 5.01.213
in this | as secretly and justly as your soul ADO 4.01.248
you do keep your promises in love | but justly, AYL 1.02.244
off a first so noble wife, | may justly diet me. AWW 5.03.221
if that the injuries be justly weigh'd | that TN 5.01.367
bohemia the visitation which he justly owes him. WT 1.01. 7 P
me, and yielded, that i may justly say, with the 2H4 4.03. 40 P
and justly and religiously unfold | why the law H5 1.02. 10
in cash, most justly paid. 2.01.115
our purposes god justly hath discover'd, | and i 2.02.151
his grace | hath spoken well and justly; H8 2.04. 65
by him that justly may | bear his betroth'd from TIT 1.01.285
just opposite to what thou justly seem'st, | a ROM 3.02. 78
man | can justly praise but what he does affect. TIM 1.02.215
come, come, deal justly with me. HAM 2.02.276 P
i am justly kill'd with mine own treachery. 5.02.307
he is justly served, | it is a poison temper'd 5.02.327
that justly think'st and hast most rightly said! LR 1.01.183
so justly to your grave ears i'll present | how OTH 1.03.124
did justly put on the vouch of very malice 2.01.146 P
i do not find that thou deal'st justly with me. 4.02.173 P
are as dear as yours, | can justly boast of. CYM 2.03. 80
and justly too, i think, you fear the tyrant, PER 1.02.103
might equal yours, if both were justly weigh'd. 5.01. 88
to do so, and i dare — | and all this justly. TNK 2.02.206
first bequeathing of the soul to) justly | i am, 3.06.148
and justly thus controls his thoughts unjust: LUC 189
one justly weeps, the other takes in hand | no 1235
JUSTNESS 1 FR 0.0001 REL FR 1 V 0 P
we may not think the justness of each act | such TRO 2.02.119
JUSTS 1 FR 0.0001 REL FR 1 V 0 P
do these justs and triumphs hold? R2 5.02. 52
JUT 1 FR 0.0001 REL FR 1 V 0 P
insulting tyranny begins to jut | upon the R3 2.04. 51
JUTTING-OUT 1 FR 0.0001 REL FR 1 V 0 P
serving of becks and jutting-out of bums! TIM 1.02.231
JUTTY 2 FR 0.0002 REL FR 2 V 0 P
rock | o'erhang and jutty his confounded base, H5 3.01. 13
no jutty, frieze, | buttress, nor coign of MAC 1.06. 6
JUVENAL 7 FR 0.0008 REL FR 2 V 5 P
part sadness and melancholy, my tender juvenal? LLL 1.02. 8 P
why tender juvenal? why tender juvenal? 1.02. 12 P
why tender juvenal? why tender juvenal? 1.02. 12 P
i spoke it tender juvenal as a congruent 1.02. 13 P
a most acute juvenal, volable and free of grace! 3.01. 66
most brisky juvenal and eke most lovely jew, MND 3.01. 95
again to your master for a jewel — the juvenal, 2H4 1.02. 19 P
KAISER *(see keiser)*
KAM 1 FR 0.0001 REL FR 1 V 0 P
this is clean kam. COR 3.01.302
KATE 107 FR 0.0121 REL FR 74 V 33 P
and margery, | but none of us car'd for kate; TMP 2.02. 49
mistress kate keepdown was with child by him in MM 3.02.199 P
o most divine kate! LLL 4.03. 81
i prithee, sister kate, untie my hands. SHR 2.01. 21
us, | or shall i send my daughter kate to you? 2.01.167
good morrow, kate — for that's your name, i 2.01.182
lie, in faith, for you are call'd plain kate, 2.01.185
and bonny kate, and sometimes kate the curst; 2.01.186
and bonny kate, and sometimes kate the curst; 2.01.186
but kate, the prettiest kate in christendom, 2.01.187
but kate, the prettiest kate in christendom, 2.01.187
kate of kate-hall, my super-dainty kate, | for 2.01.188
kate of kate-hall, my super-dainty kate, | for 2.01.188
for dainties are all kates, and therefore, kate, 2.01.189
take this of me, kate of my consolation — 2.01.190
alas, good kate, i will not burthen thee, | for 2.01.202
nay, come again, | good kate; 2.01.219
a herald, kate? o, put me in thy books! 2.01.224
a combless cock, so kate will be my hen. 2.01.226
nay, come, kate, come; 2.01.228
nay, hear you, kate. in sooth you scape not so. 2.01.240
why does the world report that kate doth limp? 2.01.252
kate like the hazel-twig | is straight and 2.01.253
as kate this chamber with her princely gait? 2.01.259
o, be thou dian, and let her be kate, | and then 2.01.260
and then let kate be chaste and dian sportful! 2.01.261
now, kate, i am a husband for your turn, | for 2.01.272
for i am he am born to tame you, kate, | and 2.01.276
kate, | and bring you from a wild kate to a kate 2.01.277
kate, | and bring you from a wild kate to a kate 2.01.277
o, the kindest kate! 2.01.307
give me thy hand, kate, i will unto venice | to 2.01.314
and kiss me, kate, we will be married a' sunday. 2.01.324
but where is kate? 3.02. 92
but where is kate? 3.02.110
'twere well for kate and better for myself. 3.02.120
o kate, content thee, prithee be not angry. 3.02.215
they shall go forward, kate, at thy command. 3.02.222
but for my bonny kate, she must with me. 3.02.227
sweet wench, they shall not touch thee, kate! 3.02.238
are those" — | sit down, kate, and welcome. 4.01.142
nay, good sweet kate, be merry. 4.01.143
be merry, kate. 4.01.149
one, kate, that you must kiss, and be acquainted 4.01.152
come, kate, and wash, and welcome heartily. 4.01.154
come, kate, sit down, i know you have a stomach. 4.01.158
will you give thanks, sweet kate, or else shall 4.01.159
i tell thee, kate, 'twas burnt and dried away, 4.01.170
how fares my kate? what, sweeting, all amort? 4.03. 36
i am sure, sweet kate, this kindness merits 4.03. 41
come, mistress kate, i'll bear you company. 4.03. 49
kate, eat apace. 4.03. 52
come, my kate, we will unto your father's | even 4.03.169
o no, good kate; 4.03.179
tell me, sweet kate, and tell me truly too, 4.05. 28
sweet kate, embrace her for her beauty's sake. 4.05. 34
why, how now, kate, i hope thou art not mad. 4.05. 42
prithee, kate, let's stand aside and see the end 5.01. 61 P
first kiss me, kate, and we will. 5.01.143
come, my sweet kate: 5.01.149
to her, kate! 5.02. 33
a hundred marks, my kate does put her down. 5.02. 35

come on, and kiss me, kate. 5.02.180
come, kate, we'll to bed. 5.02.184
how now, kate? 1H4 2.03. 36
i love thee not, | i care not for thee, kate. 2.03. 91
what say'st thou, kate? 2.03. 95
but hark you, kate, | i must not have you 2.03.102
this evening must i leave you, gentle kate. 2.03.106
and so far will i trust thee, gentle kate. 2.03.112
but hark you, kate, | whither i go, thither 2.03.114
will this content you, kate? 2.03.117
come, kate, thou art perfect in lying down. 3.01.226 P
come, kate, i'll have your song too. 3.01.245 P
swear me, kate, like a lady as thou art, | a 3.01.253
do you like me, kate? H5 5.02.107 P
an angel is like you, kate, and you are like an 5.02.109 P
i' faith, kate, my wooing is fit for thy 5.02.122 P
to verses, or to dance for your sake, kate, why, 5.02.133 P
but, before god, kate, i cannot look greenly, 5.02.142 P
thou canst love a fellow of this temper, kate, 5.02.147 P
and while thou liv'st, dear kate, take a fellow 5.02.153 P
but a good heart, kate, is the sun and the moon, 5.02.162 P
you should love the enemy of france, kate; 5.02.172 P
and, kate, when france is mine and i am yours, 5.02.175 P
no, kate? 5.02.178 P
it is as easy for me, kate, to conquer the 5.02.184 P
no, faith, is't not, kate; 5.02.190 P
but, kate, dost thou understand thus much 5.02.192 P
can any of your neighbors tell, kate? 5.02.196 P
and i know, kate, you will to her dispraise 5.02.199 P
but, good kate, mock me mercifully, the rather, 5.02.201 P
if ever thou beest mine, kate, as i have a 5.02.203 P
do but now promise, kate, you will endeavor for 5.02.213 P
mine honor, in true english, i love thee, kate; 5.02.221 P
but, in faith, kate, the elder i wax, the better 5.02.229 P
nay, it will please him well, kate; 5.02.248 P
it shall please him, kate. 5.02.249 P
then i will kiss your lips, kate. 5.02.257 P
o kate, nice customs cur'sy to great kings. 5.02.268 P
dear kate, you and i cannot be confin'd within 5.02.269 P
we are the makers of manners, kate; 5.02.271 P
you have witchcraft in your lips, kate; 5.02.276 P
shall kate be my wife? 5.02.324 P
now welcome, kate; 5.02.357
then shall i swear to kate, and you to me, | and 5.02.373
go thy ways, kate. H8 2.04.134

KATED 1 FR 0.0001 REL FR 1 V 0 P
i warrant him, petruchio is kated. SHR 3.02.245

KATE–HALL 1 FR 0.0001 REL FR 1 V 0 P
kate of kate–hall, my super–dainty kate, | for SHR 2.01.188

KATES 2 FR 0.0002 REL FR 2 V 0 P
for dainties are all kates, and therefore, kate, SHR 2.01.189
a kate | conformable as other household kates. 2.01.278

KATHERINA 8 FR 0.0009 REL FR 8 V 0 P
if either of you both love katherina, | because SHR 1.01. 52
katherina, you may stay, | for i have more to 1.01.100
her name is katherina minola, | renown'd in 1.02. 99
rehears'd, | that ever katherina will be woo'd. 1.02.125
pray have you not a daughter | call'd katherina, 2.01. 43
i have a daughter, sir, call'd katherina. 2.01. 44
brother petruchio, sister katherina, | and thou, 5.02. 6
now, by my holidam, here comes katherina! 5.02. 99

/KATHERINE 1 FR 0.0001 REL FR 1 V 0 P
the heir of alanson, /katherine her name. LLL 2.01.195

KATHERINE 37 FR 0.0041 REL FR 28 V 9 P
but, katherine, what was sent to you from fair LLL 5.02. 47
till katherine the curst have got a husband. SHR 1.02.128
katherine the curst! 1.02.129
liking, | will undertake to woo curst katherine, 1.02.183
but for my daughter katherine, this i know, 2.01. 62
they call me katherine that do talk of me. 2.01.184
marry, so i mean, sweet katherine, in thy bed; 2.01.267
i must and will have katherine to my wife. 2.01.280
why, how now, daughter katherine, in your dumps? 2.01.284
i will be sure my katherine shall be fine. 2.01.317
know | my daughter katherine is to be married. 2.01.394
her sister katherine welcom'd you withal? 3.01. 3
that katherine and petruchio should be married, 3.02. 2
now must the world point at poor katherine, 3.02. 18
patience, good katherine, and baptista too. 3.02. 21
would katherine had never seen him though! 3.02. 26
should ask if katherine should be his wife, 3.02.159
it is, | and so it shall be so for katherine. 4.05. 22
katherine, that cap of yours becomes you not; 5.02.121
katherine, i charge thee tell these headstrong 5.02.130
make you merry with fair katherine of france, 2H4 ep 29 P
king doth offer him | katherine his daughter, H5 3.pr. 30
to our most fair and princely cousin katherine; 5.02. 4
yet leave our cousin katherine here with us: 5.02. 95
fair katherine, and most fair, | will you 5.02. 98
o fair katherine, if you will love me soundly 5.02.104 P
i said so, dear katherine, and i must not blush 5.02.113 P
answer you, la plus belle katherine du monde, 5.02.216 P
and therefore tell me, most fair katherine, will 5.02.234 P
queen of all, katherine, break thy mind to me in 5.02.245 P
a separation | between the king and katherine? H8 2.01.149
say, katherine queen of england, come into the 2.04. 10 P
katherine queen of england, etc. 2.04. 12 P
katherine queen of england, come into the court. 2.04.126 P
katherine our queen, before the primest creature 2.04.230
katherine no more | shall be call'd queen, but 3.02. 69
but i beseech you, what's become of katherine, 4.01. 22

KATHERINE'S 1 FR 0.0001 REL FR 1 V 0 P
at touraine, in saint katherine's churchyard, 1H6 1.02.100

KECKSIES 1 FR 0.0001 REL FR 1 V 0 P
hateful docks, rough thistles, kecksies, burs, H5 5.02. 52

KEECH 2 FR 0.0002 REL FR 1 V 1 P
did not goodwife keech, the butcher's wife, come 2H4 2.01. 93 P
that such a keech can with his very bulk | take H8 1.01. 55

KEEL* *(also cool)*

KEEL* 4 FR 0.0004 REL FR 4 V 0 P
note, | while greasy joan doth keel the pot. LLL 5.02.920
note, | while greasy joan doth keel the pot. 5.02.929
traitors ensteep'd to enclog the guiltless keel, OTH 2.01. 70
half the flood | hath their keel cut. PER 3.ch. 46

KEELS 1 FR 0.0001 REL FR 1 V 0 P
they ear and wound | with keels of every kind. ANT 1.04. 50

KEEN 25 FR 0.0028 REL FR 23 V 2 P
ay, but yet | let us be keen, and rather cut a MM 2.01. 5
th' impression of keen whips i'ld wear as rubies 2.04.101
honor which shall bate his scythe's keen edge, LLL 1.01. 6
the tongues of mocking wenches are as keen | as 5.02.256
cut me to pieces with thy keen conceit; 5.02.399
wherefore was i to this keen mockery born? MND 2.02.123
o, when she is angry, she is keen and shrewd! 3.02.323
that is some satire, keen and critical, | not 5.01. 54
with that keen appetite that he sits down? MV 2.06. 9
of man | so keen and greedy to confound a man. 3.02.276
soul, harsh jew, | thou mak'st thy knife keen; 4.01.124
thy tooth is not so keen, | because thou art not AYL 2.07.177
wounds invisible | that love's keen arrows make. 3.05. 31
cardinal, cry thou amen | to my keen curses; JN 3.01.182
a feast | fits a dull fighter and a keen guest. 1H4 4.02. 80
to leave this keen encounter of our wits | and R3 1.02.115
that my keen knife see not the wound it makes, MAC 1.05. 52
with thy keen sword impress as make me bleed. 5.08. 10
you are keen, my lord, you are keen. HAM 3.02.248 P
you are keen, my lord, you are keen. 3.02.248 P
although assail'd with fortune fierce and keen, PER 5.03. 88
set | this bateless edge on his keen appetite; LUC 9
pluck the keen teeth from the fierce tiger's SON 19. 3
like as to make our appetites more keen, | with 118. 1
by blunting us to make our wits more keen. LC 161

KEEN–EDG'D 1 FR 0.0001 REL FR 1 V 0 P
here is my keen–edg'd sword, | deck'd with five 1H6 1.02. 98

KEENNESS 1 FR 0.0001 REL FR 1 V 0 P
axe, bear half the keenness | of thy sharp envy. MV 4.01.125

/KEEP 4 FR 0.0004 REL FR 4 V 0 P
/god /keep /all /vows /unbroke /are /made /to R2 4.01.215
/roof | /did /keep /ten /thousand /men? 4.01.283
president of peace | to /keep my name ungor'd. HAM 5.02.250
//belly–pinched /wolf | /keep /their /fur /dry, LR 3.01. 14

KEEP 515 FR 0.0582 REL FR 403 V 112 P
i pray now keep below. TMP 1.01. 11 P
keep your cabins; 1.01. 14 P
he, that caliban | whom now i keep in service. 1.02.286
whiles you do keep from me | the rest o' th' 1.02.343
keep in tunis, | and let sebastian wake." 2.01.259
(for else his project dies) to keep them living. 2.01.299
if of life you keep a care, | shake off slumber, 2.01.303
heavens keep him from these beasts! 2.01.324
if i can recover him, and keep him tame, and get 2.02. 69 P
if i can recover him, and keep him tame, i will 2.02. 76 P
trinculo, keep a good tongue in your head. 3.02. 35 P
thou liv'st, keep a good tongue in thy head. 3.02.112 P
hope, and keep it | no longer for my flatterer. 3.03. 7
flat meads thatch'd with stover, them to keep; 4.01. 63
keep tune there still, so you will sing it out. TGV 1.02. 86
keep this remembrance for thy julia's sake. 2.02. 5
if i keep them, i needs must lose myself; 2.06. 20
purse she shall not, for that i'll keep shut. 3.01.351 P
hence, | to keep me from a most unholy match, 4.03. 30
when a cur cannot keep himself in all companies! 4.04. 10 P
much to do | to keep them from uncivil outrages. 5.04. 17
i keep but three men and a boy yet, till my WIV 1.01.274 P
not i, sir, pray you keep on. 1.01.308 P
i will keep the havior of reputation. 1.03. 78 P
him my master, look you, for i keep his house; 1.04. 95 P
do no more adhere and keep place together than 2.01. 62 P
i'll be sure to keep him above deck. 2.01. 91 P
much as i can do to keep the terms of my honor 2.02. 22 P
give me my gown, or else keep it in your arms. 3.01. 34 P
keep a gamester from the dice, and a good 3.01. 37 P
keep them asunder; 3.01. 71 P
nay, good master parson, keep in your weapon. 3.01. 73 P
let them keep their limbs whole and hack our 3.01. 77 P
nay, keep your way, little gallant; 3.02. 1 P
keep in that mind, i'll deserve it. 3.03. 82 P
and i will (at the least) keep your counsel. 4.06. 7 P
i will keep my sides to myself, my shoulders for 5.05. 25 P
and let it keep one shape, till custom make it MM 2.01. 3
heaven keep your honor! 2.02. 42
heaven keep your honor safe! 2.02.157
even so. heaven keep your honor! 2.04. 34
lose a thing | that none but fools would keep. 3.01. 8
complexion, shall keep the body of it ever fair. 3.01.183 P
by order of law a furr'd gown to keep him warm; 3.02. 7 P
husband now, pompey, you will keep the house. 3.02. 71 P
but i will keep her ignorant of her good, | to 4.03.109
the matter being afoot, keep your instruction, 4.05. 3
would fain proclaim | favors that keep within. 5.01. 16
keep me in patience, and with ripened time 5.01.116
there is your money that i had to keep. ERR 1.02. 8
this servitude makes you to keep unwed. 2.01. 26
so he would keep fair quarter with his bed! 2.01.108
keep then fair league and truce with thy true 2.02.145
dromio, keep the gate. 2.02.206
my wife is shrewish when i keep not hours: 3.01. 2
you would keep from my heels, and beware of an 3.01. 18
error | have suffer'd wrong, go keep us company, 5.01.399
that if he have wit enough to keep himself warm, ADO 1.01. 68 P
god keep your ladyship still in that mind! 1.01.133 P
but keep your way a' god's name, i have done. 1.01.142 P
and god keep him out of my sight when the dance 2.01.109 P
he do fear god, 'a must necessarily keep peace; 2.03.193 P
keep your fellows' counsels and your own, and 3.03. 86 P
god keep your worship! 5.01.323 P
why, shall i always keep below stairs? 5.02. 10 P
and to keep those statutes | that are recorded LLL 1.01. 17
subscribe to your deep oaths, and keep it too. 1.01. 23
o, these are barren tasks, too hard to keep, 1.01. 47
yet, confident, i'll keep what i have sworn, 1.01.114
i am the last that will last keep his oath. 1.01.160
swain, i keep her as a vessel of thy law's fury, 1.01.274 P
duke's pleasure is that you keep costard safe, 1.02.127 P
for this damsel, i must keep her at the park; 1.02.130 P
'tis deadly sin to keep that oath, my lord, 2.01.105
and keep not too long in one tune, but a snip 3.01. 21 P
then thou /wilt keep | my tears for glasses, and 4.03. 37
his loving bosom to keep down his heart. 4.03.134
other slow arts entirely keep the brain; 4.03.321
or else we lose ourselves to keep our oaths. 4.03.359
i will, and therefore keep it. 5.02.442
keep some state in thy exit, and vanish. 5.02.594 P
keep promise, love. look, here comes helena. MND 1.01.179
keep word, lysander; 1.01.222
the king doth keep his revels here to–night; 2.01. 18
coats, and some keep back | the clamorous owl, 2.02. 5
reason and love keep little company together 3.01.144 P
lysander, keep thy hermia; 3.02.169
demetrius, i will keep my word with thee. 3.02.266
did ever keep your counsels, never wrong'd you; 3.02.308
my legs can keep no pace with my desires. 3.02.445
well, keep me company but two years moe, | thou MV 1.01.108
if thou keep promise, i shall end this strife, 2.03. 20
are wont | to keep obliged faith unforfeited! 2.06. 7
let good antonio look he keep his day, | or he 2.08. 25
i'll keep my oath, | patiently to bear my wroth. 2.09. 77
a title good enough to keep his name company! 3.01. 14 P
which i did make him swear to keep for ever. 4.02. 14
and that which you did swear to keep for me, | i 5.01.225
and bid him keep it better than the other. 5.01.255
here, lord bassanio, swear to keep this ring. 5.01.256
shall i keep your hogs and eat husks with them? AYL 1.01. 37 P
and so god keep your worship! 1.01.162 P
nay, if i keep not my rank — 1.02.107 P
if you do keep your promises in love | but 1.02.243
usurping uncle | to keep his daughter company, 1.02.275
nay, you might keep that check for it, till you 4.01.167 P
beware my censure, and keep your promise. 4.01.196 P
but at this hour the house doth keep itself, 4.03. 81
keep you your word, o duke, to give your 5.04. 19
keep you your word, phebe, that you'll marry me, 5.04. 21
keep your word, silvius, that you'll marry her 5.04. 23
schoolmasters will i keep within my house, | fit SHR 1.01. 94
keep house and ply his book, welcome his friends 1.01.196
keep house and port and servants, as i should. 1.01.203
but i will charm him first to keep his tongue. 1.01.209
thee, | for in baptista's keep my treasure is. 1.02.118
you will have gremio to keep you fair. 2.01. 17
yes, keep you warm. 2.01.266
being restrain'd to keep him from stumbling, 3.02. 58 P
hear — | sufficeth i am come to keep my word, 3.02.106
i'll keep mine own, despite of all the world. 3.02.142
and with the clamor keep her still awake. 4.01.207
for me, that i may surely keep mine oath, | i 4.02. 36
keep your hundred pounds to yourself, he shall 5.01. 23 P
and keep thy friend | under thy own life's key. AWW 1.01. 66
keep him out. 1.01.114 P
keep it not, you cannot choose but lose by't. 1.01.145 P
discharg'd this honestly, keep it to yourself. 1.03.122 P
my prayers to lead them on, and to keep them on, 2.04. 18 P
hope your own grace will keep you where you are, 3.05. 26 P
and will keep him muffled | till we do hear from 4.01. 90
till then i'll keep him dark and safely lock'd. 4.01. 94
which on your just proceeding i'll keep off — 5.03.236
which she would keep fresh | and lasting in her TN 1.01. 30
i am not such an ass but i can keep my hand dry. 1.03. 75 P
i pray you keep it in. 1.05.197 P
keep your purse; 1.05.284
not extort from me what i am willing to keep in; 2.01. 14 P
what a caterwauling do you keep here! 2.03. 72 P
we did keep time, sir, in our catches. sneck up! 2.03. 93 P
she will keep no fool, sir, till she be married, 3.01. 33 P
still you keep o' th' windy side of the law; 3.04.164 P
pray god he keep his oath! 3.04.310 P
have here propertied me, keep me in darkness, 4.02. 91 P
note, | what time we will our celebration keep 4.03. 30
both day and night did we keep company. 5.01. 96
cesario, you do not keep promise with me. 5.01.103
intended | to keep in darkness what occasion now 5.01.153
and all those swearings keep as true in soul 5.01.270
force me to keep you as a prisoner, | not like a WT 1.02. 52
feasts, keep with bohemia | and with your queen. 1.02.344
i'll keep my stables where | i lodge my wife; 2.01.134
for the creatures | of prey that keep upon't. 3.03. 13
up with't, keep it close. 3.03.124 P
these keep | seeming and savor all the winter 4.04. 74
horn–ring, to keep my pack from fasting. 4.04.600 P
therefore i keep it | /lonely, apart. 5.03. 17
nor keep his princely heart from richard's hand. JN 1.01.267
unless thou let his silver water keep | a 2.01.339
half so peremptory, | as we to keep this city. 2.01.455
and force perforce | keep stephen langton, 3.01.143
keep my need up, and faith is trodden down! 3.01.216
than keep in peace that hand which thou dost 3.01.261
and most forsworn, to keep what thou dost swear; 3.01.287
hubert, keep this boy. 3.02. 5
keep men's eyes | and strain their cheeks to 3.03. 45
and i'll keep him so, | that he shall not offend 3.03. 64
i will not keep this form upon my head | when 3.04.101
cut out my tongue, | so i may keep mine eyes. 4.01.101
heaven take my soul, and england keep my bones! 4.03. 10
keep the peace, i say. 4.03. 93
now keep your holy word, go meet the french, 5.01. 5
out, | and keep it safe for our remembrance. 5.02. 2
and keep our faiths firm and inviolable. 5.02. 7
keep good quarter and good care to–night; 5.05. 20
to keep the oath that we administer: R2 1.03.182
and i, to keep all this. 1.03.192
hath power to keep you king in spite of all. 3.02. 28
my legs can keep no measure in delight, | when 3.04. 7
a pale | keep law and form and due proportion, 3.04. 41
to serve me last that i may longest keep | thy 3.04. 95
to keep him safely till his day of trial. 4.01.153
and he and i | will keep a league till death. 5.01. 22
part | to take on me to keep and kill thy heart. 5.01. 98
we'll keep him here, then what is that to him? 5.02.100
ha, ha, keep time! 5.05. 42
i'll keep them all! 1H4 1.03.213
i'll keep them, by this hand. 1.03.216
those prisoners you shall keep. 1.03.218
give it him | to keep his anger still in motion. 1.03.226
of it, i pray thee keep that for the hangman, 2.01. 63 P
what a brawling dost thou keep! 2.02. 6 P
him keep with, the rest banish. 2.04.430 P
what there is else, keep close, we'll read it at 2.04.542 P
thus did i keep my person fresh and new, | my 3.02. 55
do you think i keep thieves in my house? 3.03. 55 P
i prithee tell me, doth he keep his bed? 4.01. 21
side | must keep aloof from strict arbitrement, 4.01. 70
the king should keep his word in loving us. 5.02. 5
god keep lead out of me! 5.03. 34 P
two stars keep not their motion in one sphere, 5.04. 65
not all this flesh | keep in a little life? 5.04.103

nature's hand | keep the wild flood confin'd! 2H4 1.01.154
he may keep it still at a face royal, for a 1.02. 24 P
he may keep his own grace, but he's almost out 1.02. 27 P
but since all is well, keep it so, wake not a 1.02.153 P
keep them off, bardolph. 2.01. 54 P
what is the matter? keep the peace here, ho! 2.01. 61 P
god keep you, master silence, i will not use 3.02.288 P
go to, i have spoke at a word. god keep you! 3.02.297 P
clean | and keep no tell–tale to his memory 4.01.200
from enemies heavens keep your majesty, | and, 4.04. 94
of it, | let god for ever keep it from my head, 4.05.174
out of this shallow to keep prince harry in 5.01. 78 P
the heavens thee guard and keep, most royal imp 5.05. 42
capet, | could not keep quiet in his conscience, H5 1.02. 79
put into parts, doth keep in one consent, 1.02.181
but tell the dolphin i will keep my state, | be 1.02.273
nor shall my nell keep lodgers. 2.01. 31
but it will be thought we keep a bawdy–house 2.01. 35 P
why the devil should we keep knives to cut one 2.01. 91 P
keep close, i thee command. 2.03. 62
he will keep that good name still. 3.07.101 P
keep thy word; fare thee well. 4.01.221 P
all's not done — yet keep the french the field. 4.06. 2
my soul shall thine keep company to heaven; 4.06. 16
/god keep me so! 4.07.116
is it fit this soldier keep his oath? 4.07.132 P
your grace, that he keep his vow and his oath. 4.07.139 P
then keep thy vow, sirrah, when thou meet'st the 4.07.144 P
by his blunt bearing he will keep his word, 4.07.177
keep it, fellow, | and wear it for an honor in 4.08. 58
god, and keep you out of prawls and prabbles, 4.08. 64 P
god buy you, and keep you, and heal your pate. 5.01. 66 P
prosper this realm, keep it from civil broils, 1H6 1.01. 53
to keep the horsemen off from breaking in. 1.01.119
to keep our great saint george's feast withal. 1.01.154
and keep me on the side where still i am. 2.04. 54
or raise myself, but keep my wonted calling? 3.01. 32
hold your slaught'ring hands and keep the peace. 3.01. 87
like peasant footboys do they keep the walls, 3.02. 69
heavens keep old bedford safe! 3.02.100
keep off aloof with worthless emulation. 4.04. 21
let not your private discord keep away | the 4.04. 22
to keep them here, | they would but stink, and 4.07. 89
and keep not back your powers in dalliance. 5.02. 5
or else, when thou didst keep my lambs a–field, 5.04. 30
i'll rather keep | that which i have than, 5.04.144
peace, | and keep the frenchmen in allegiance. 5.05. 43
his wits, | to keep by policy what henry got? 2H6 1.01. 84
and we will keep it still. 1.01.106
ay, uncle, we will keep it, if we can; 1.01.107
next time i'll keep my dreams unto myself, | and 1.02. 53
my lord of somerset will keep me here | without 1.03.168
'tis like, my lord, you will not keep your hour. 2.01.177
here commit you to my lord cardinal | to keep, 3.01.138
if those that care to keep your royal person 3.01.173
let pale–fac'd fear keep with the mean–born man, 3.01.335
and you, forsooth, had the good duke to keep. 3.02.183
affliction | be playfellows to keep you company! 3.02.302
a sin, | but greater sin to keep a sinful oath. 5.01.183
to keep thee from the tempest of the field. 5.01.197
and i'll keep london with my soldiers. 3H6 1.01.207
keep thou the napkin and go boast of this, | and 1.04.159
as brings a thousandfold more care to keep 2.02. 52
which if they do, yet will i keep thee safe, 4.01. 81
to keep them back that come to succor you. 4.07. 56
to keep that oath were more impiety | than 5.01. 90
that warwick's bones may keep thine company. 5.02. 4
and with thy lips keep in my soul a while. 5.02. 35
but keep our course (though the rough wind say 5.04. 22
way, | if we will keep in favor with the king, R3 1.01. 79
i'll have her, but i will not keep her long. 1.02.229
o, let them keep it till thy sins be ripe, | and 1.03.218
i'll resign unto your grace | the seal i keep, 2.04. 71
god keep you from them, and from such false 3.01. 15
god keep me from false friends! 3.01. 16
god keep your lordship in that gracious mind! 3.02. 56
but now i tell thee (keep it to thyself) | this 3.02.102
devis'd at first to keep the strong in awe: 5.03.310
beneficial sun, | and keep it from the earth. H8 1.01. 57
to pepin or clotharius, they keep state so. 1.03. 10
my lord sands, you are one will keep 'em waking; 1.04. 23
good angels keep it from us! 2.01.142
heaven keep me from such counsel! 2.02. 37
pray you keep your way; 2.04.129
a brief span | to keep your earthly audit; 3.02.141
actions | to keep mine honor from corruption, 4.02. 71
keep comfort to you, and this morning see | you 5.01.144
keep the door close, sirrah. 5.03. 30 P
i will keep where there is wit stirring, and TRO 2.01.118 P
why keep we her? 2.02. 80
the grecians keep our aunt. 2.02. 80
that we have stol'n what we do fear to keep! 2.02. 93
to you | in resolution to keep helen still, 2.02.191
to keep her constancy in plight and youth, 3.02.161
keep then the path, | for emulation hath a 3.03.155
and you as well to keep her, that defend her, 4.01. 59
in what place of the field doth calchas keep? 4.05.278
both taxing me and gaging me to keep | an oath 5.01. 41
diomed, | keep hector company an hour or two. 5.01. 81
i'll keep you company. 5.01. 86
here, diomed, keep this sleeve. 5.02. 66
i will not keep my word. 5.02. 98
not a stroke, but keep yourselves in breath, 5.07. 3
(under the gods) keep you in awe, which else COR 1.01.187
to keep your great pretenses veil'd till when 1.02. 20
and keep your honors safe! 1.02. 37
keep your duties, | as i have set them down. 1.07. 1
if we lose the field, | we cannot keep the town. 1.07. 5
nay, keep your place. 2.02. 66
wash their faces, | and keep their teeth clean. 2.03. 61
i'll keep you company. will you along? 2.03.149
and to keep him here | our certain death; 3.01.286
th' honor'd gods | keep rome in safety, and the 3.03. 34
they have ta'en note of us; keep on your way. 4.02. 10
now the gods keep you! 4.06. 25
to hear cominius speak, i'll keep at home. 5.01. 7
you keep a constant temper. 5.02. 94
this boy, to keep your name | living to time. 5.03.126
rome, | keep then this passage to the capitol, TIT 1.01. 12
and with my sword i'll keep this door safe. 1.01.288
these lovers will not keep the peace. 2.01. 37
o, keep me from their worse than killing lust, 2.03.175
and keep eternal spring–time /on /thy face, | so 3.01. 21
why, what a caterwauling dost thou keep! 4.02. 57
i am of age | to keep mine own, excuse it how 4.02.105
this maugre all the world will i keep safe, | or 4.02.110
keep there. 4.02.134
two may keep counsel when the third's away. 4.02.144
i do but keep the peace. ROM 1.01. 68
think, | for men so old as we to keep the peace. 1.02. 3
what she bid me say, i will keep to myself. 2.04.164 P
say, | "two may keep counsel, putting one away"? 2.04.197
heads, | staying for thine to keep him company. 3.01.128
did ever dragon keep so fair a cave? 3.02. 74
i'll give thee armor to keep off that word: 3.03. 54
we'll keep no great ado — a friend or two, 3.04. 23
for then i hope thou wilt not keep him long, 3.05. 63
dram | that he shall soon keep tybalt company; 3.05. 91
till then adieu, and keep this holy kiss. 4.01. 43
for no pulse | shall keep his native progress, 4.01. 97
your part in her you could not keep from death, 4.05. 69
and keep her at my cell till romeo come — 5.02. 29
the obsequies that i for thee will keep 5.03. 16
vault, | meaning to keep her closely at my cell, 5.03.255
i'll keep you company. TIM 1.01.283
honor, and fortunes, keep with you, lord timon! 1.02.229
i do beseech you, good my lords, keep on, | i'll 2.02. 34
'tis, if he would not keep so good a house. 3.01. 23 P
who cannot keep his wealth must keep his house. 3.03. 41
who cannot keep his wealth must keep his house. 3.03. 41
many do keep their chambers are not sick; 3.04. 73
now the gods keep you old enough that you may 3.05.103
keep it, i cannot eat it. 4.03.101
'tis, then, because thou dost not keep a dog, 4.03.200
thou hadst some means to keep a dog. 4.03.317 P
love him, feed him, | keep in your bosom; 5.01. 97
descend, and keep your words. 5.04. 64
men, | and keep us all in servile fearfulness. JC 1.01. 75
th' eternal devil to keep his state in rome | as 1.02.160
that noble minds keep ever with their likes; 1.02.311
to keep with you at meals, comfort your bed, 2.01.284
how hard it is for women to keep counsel! 2.04. 9
and constant do remain to keep him so. 3.01. 73
down, | but keep the hills and upper regions. 5.01. 3
upon the right hand i, keep thou the left. 5.01. 18
come now, keep thine oath; 5.03. 40
keep this man safe, | give him all kindness; 5.04. 27
nor keep peace between | th' effect and /it! MAC 1.05. 46
it, but still keep | my bosom franchis'd and 2.01. 27
fortune | shall keep us both the safer. 2.03.139
we will keep ourself | till supper–time alone; 3.01. 42
how now, my lord, why do you keep alone, | of 3.02. 8
pray you keep seat. 3.04. 53
and keep the natural ruby of your cheeks, | when 3.04.114
them but in his house | i keep a servant fee'd. 3.04.131
keep it not from me, quickly let me have it. 4.03.200
all annoyance, | and still keep eyes upon her. 5.01. 77
fancies, | that keep her from her rest. 5.03. 39
that keep the word of promise to our ear, | and 5.08. 21
and keep you in the rear of your affection, HAM 1.03. 34
i shall the effect of this good lesson keep | as 1.03. 45
and you yourself shall keep the key of it. 1.03. 86
how, and who, what means, and where they keep, 2.01. 8
for a state, | but keep a farm and carters. 2.02.167
shall live, the rest shall keep as they are. 3.01.149 P
the players cannot keep /counsel, they'll tell 3.02.142 P
o, but she'll keep her word. 3.02.231 P
fear it is | to keep those many many bodies safe 3.03. 9
armor of the mind | to keep itself from noyance, 3.03. 13
my pulse, as yours, doth temperately keep time, 3.04.140
to keep it from divulging, let it feed | even on 4.01. 22
that i can keep your counsel and not mine own. 4.02. 11 P
i thank you, keep the door. 4.05.116
you do this, keep close within your chamber. 4.07.129
trade that 'a will keep out water a great while, 5.01.171 P
clay, | might stop a hole to keep the wind away. 5.01.214
i can keep honest counsel, ride, run, mar a LR 1.04. 32 P
all my living, i'ld keep my coxcombs myself. 1.04.107 P
thy drink and thy whore, | and keep in a' door, 1.04.125
keep a schoolmaster that can teach thy fool to 1.04.179 P
here do you keep a hundred knights and squires, 1.04.241
'tis politic and safe to let him keep | at point 1.04.323
why, to keep one's eyes of either side 's nose, 1.05. 22 P
keep me in temper, i would not be mad! 1.05. 47
keep peace, upon your lives! 2.02. 48
pension beg | to keep base life afoot. 2.04.215
of the dark, | and make them keep their caves. 3.02. 45
that keep this dreadful pudder o'er our heads, 3.02. 50
obey thy parents, keep thy word's justice, swear 3.04. 81 P
keep thy foot out of brothels, thy hand out of 3.04. 96 P
keep thee warm. 3.04.174
i will keep still with my philosopher. 3.04.176
edmund, keep you our sister company; 3.07. 6 P
keep out, che vor' ye, or ice try whither your 4.06.240 P
keep yet their hearts attending on themselves, OTH 1.01. 51
keep up your bright swords, for the dew will 1.02. 59
'tis a pageant | to keep us in false gaze. 1.03. 19
with all my heart | i would keep from thee. 1.03.195
prithee keep up thy quillets. 3.01. 23 P
or feed on nourishing dishes, or keep you warm, 3.03. 78
keep leets and law–days and in sessions sit 3.03.140
dungeon | than keep a corner in the thing i love 3.03.272
(for he conjur'd her she should ever keep it) 3.03.294
heaven keep the monster from othello's mind! 3.04.163
keep a week away? 3.04.173
that's not amiss, | but yet keep time in all. 4.01. 92
or keep it as a cestern for foul toads | to knot 4.02. 61
i pray you turn the key and keep our counsel. 4.02. 94
gratiano, keep the house, | and seize upon the 5.02.365
dear isis, keep decorum, and fortune him ANT 1.02. 73 P
let her not say 'tis i that keep you here, | i 1.03. 22
and keep the turn of tippling with a slave, | to 1.04. 19
in a field of feasts, | keep his brain fuming; 2.01. 24
good madam, keep yourself within yourself, | the 2.05. 75
lepidus, | keep off them, for you sink. 2.07. 60
to keep it builded, be the ram to batter | the 3.02. 30
so the gods keep you, | and make the hearts of 3.02. 36
you keep by land | the legions and the horse 3.07. 70
but we keep whole by land. 3.07. 74
strike not by land, keep whole, provoke not 3.08. 3
the sevenfold shield of ajax cannot keep | the 4.14. 38
must tell him | that majesty, to keep decorum, 5.02. 17
heart, | but keep it till you woo another wife, CYM 1.01.113
remain thou here, | while sense can keep it on. 1.01.118
him from others, he did keep | the deck, with 1.03. 10
which, by their graces, i will keep. 1.04. 87 P
in them, i will keep them | in my bedchamber. 1.06.195
keep unshak'd | that temple, thy fair mind, that 2.01. 63
ay, | to keep her chamber. 2.03. 82
good sir, we must, | if you keep covenant. 2.04. 50
married | to that your diamond, i'll keep them. 2.04. 98
'tis true — nay, keep the ring — 'tis true. 2.04.123
perforce, | behooves me keep at utterance. 3.01. 72
a goodly day not to keep house with such | whose 3.03. 1
and keep their impious turbands on without 3.03. 6
art o' th' court, | as hard to leave as keep; 3.03. 47
thou need'st | but keep that count'nance still. 3.04. 14
yea, bloody cloth, i'll keep thee, for i wish'd 5.01. 1
which neither here i'll keep nor bear again, 5.03. 82
like it, which | i'll keep, if but for sympathy. 5.04.150
made a law, | to keep her still and men in awe, PER 1.ch. 36
he's more secure to keep it shut than shown; 1.01. 95
/'schew no course to keep them from the light. 1.01.136
then, lest my life be cropp'd to keep you clear, 1.01.141
die, | for by his fall my honor must keep high. 1.01.149
and keep your mind, till you return to us, 1.02. 35
shed | to keep his bed of blackness unlaid ope, 1.02. 89
he strive | to killen bad, keep good alive, 2.ch. 20
come put it on, keep thee warm. 2.01. 79 P
"keep it, my pericles, it hath been a shield 2.01.126
this brace — | "for that it sav'd me, keep it. 2.01.128
how now, marina, why do you keep alone? 4.01. 21
'twere not amiss to keep our door hatch'd. 4.02. 33 P
deep, | untied i still my virgin knot will keep. 4.02.147
with other virtues, which i'll keep from boast, 4.06.184
striv'd | god neptune's annual feast to keep, 5.ch. 17
if this play do not keep | a little dull time TNK pr 30
sweet, keep it as my token. 1.01.217
keep the feast full, bate not an hour on't. 1.01.220
and here to keep in abstinence we shame | as in 1.02. 6
how dangerous, if we will keep our honors, | it 1.02. 37
pieces, keep enthron'd | in your dear heart! 1.03. 10
alas, the prison i keep, though it be for great 2.01. 3 P
to keep us from corruption of worse men. 2.02. 72
keep these flowers, | we'll see how near art can 2.02.148
the schoolmaster, | keep touch, do you think? 2.03. 41
and there he shall keep close | till i provide 2.06. 6
daughters, | and shortly you may keep yourself. 2.06. 39
if he keep touch, he dies for't. 3.03. 53
no, keep it, your life lies on it. 3.06. 90
yet i keep close for all this, | close as a 4.01.130
content, | if we shall keep our wedding there. 5.02. 76
peace ho, peace, i charge you keep the peace! STM II.C 28
"o, let him keep his loathsome cabin still! VEN 637
on thy well–breath'd horse keep with thy hounds. 678
and sometime where earth–delving conies keep, 687
the staring ruffian shall it keep in quiet, 1149
of that rich jewel he should keep unknown | from LUC 34
blind they are, and keep themselves enclosed. 378
keep still possession of thy gloomy place, 803
a thousand crosses keep them from thy aid: 912
thy part | to keep thy sharp woes waking, 1136
or keep him from heart–easing words so long, 1782
keep the obsequy so strict. PHT 12
when every private widow well may keep, | by SON 9. 7
which i will keep so chary | as tender nurse her 22.11
thee, | and keep my drooping eyelids open wide, 27. 7
then can no horse with my desire keep pace; 51. 9
is it thy will thy image should keep open | my 61. 1
the same, | and keep invention in a noted weed, 76. 6
to keep an adjunct to remember thee | were to 122.13
she may detain, but not still keep, her treasure 126.10
many nymphs that vow'd chaste life to keep 154. 3

KEEPDOWN 1 FR 0.0001 REL FR 0 V 1 P
mistress kate keepdown was with child by him in MM 3.02.199 P

KEEPER 18 FR 0.0020 REL FR 16 V 2 P
(sometime a keeper here in windsor forest) WIV 4.04. 29
and don armado shall be your keeper. LLL 1.01.304 P
doth the hound his master, the ape his keeper, 4.02.127 P
thy husband is thy lord, thy life, thy keeper, SHR 5.02.146
the keeper of the prison, call to him; WT 2.02. 1
thou art his keeper. JN 3.03. 64
but tell me, keeper, will my nephew come? 1H6 2.05. 17
i, then in london, keeper of the king, 3H6 2.01.111
ah, keeper, keeper, i have done these things R3 1.04. 66
ah, keeper, keeper, i have done these things 1.04. 66
keeper, i prithee sit by me awhile. 1.04. 73
where art thou, keeper? give me a cup of wine. 1.04.161
seems a–sleeping, | or a keeper with my freedom, TIM 1.02. 68
now, honest keeper? TNK 2.02.220
i am ready, keeper. 2.02.222
how now, keeper? 2.02.243
do, good keeper. 2.02.271
base, | my father the mean keeper of his prison, 2.04. 3

KEEPER–BACK 1 FR 0.0001 REL FR 1 V 0 P
flatterer, | a parasite, a keeper–back of death, R2 2.02. 70

KEEPER'S 6 FR 0.0006 REL FR 5 V 1 P
but not kiss'd your keeper's daughter? WIV 1.01.113 P
to make her come and know her keeper's call, SHR 4.01.194
breaks like a fire | out of his keeper's arms, 2H4 1.01.143
ay, here's a deer whose skin's a keeper's fee: 3H6 3.01. 22
and borne her cleanly by the keeper's nose? TIT 2.01. 94
the keeper's coming. TNK 2.02.218

KEEPERS 6 FR 0.0006 REL FR 6 V 0 P
give us kind keepers, heavens! what were these? TMP 3.03. 20
kind keepers of my weak decaying age, | let 1H6 2.05. 1
keepers, convey him hence, and i myself | will 2.05.120
which their keepers call | a lightning before ROM 5.03. 89
when gouty keepers of thee cannot stand. TIM 4.03. 47
of the prosperous gods, | as thieves to keepers. 5.01.184

KEEPEST 2 FR 0.0002 REL FR 0 V 2 P
doth defile, so doth the company thou keepest; 1H4 2.04.414 P
with thee when thou keepest not racket there; 2H4 2.02. 20 P

KEEPING 20 FR 0.0022 REL FR 10 V 10 P

i am betrayed by keeping company | with men like
LLL 4.03.177
or keeping what is sworn, you will prove fools. 4.03.353
thing | so sore, as keeping safe nerissa's ring. MV 5.01.307
for call you that keeping for a gentleman of my AYL 1.01. 9 P
trust a man again for keeping his sword clean, AWW 4.03.144 P
he professes not keeping of oaths; 4.03.252 P
statue, which is in the keeping of paulina — a WT 5.02. 95 P
art thou damn'd for keeping thy word with the 1H4 1.02.120 P
and keeping such vile company as thou art hath 2H4 2.02. 49 P
i'll forswear keeping house afore i'll be in 2.04.204 P
keeping them prisoner underneath /her wings. 1H6 5.03. 57
my lord cardinal's man, for keeping my house, 2H6 1.03. 17 P
i will take order for her keeping close. R3 4.02. 52
is not worth what she doth cost | the keeping. TRO 2.02. 52
is she worth keeping? 2.02. 81
fair rape | wip'd off, in honorable keeping her. 2.02.149
how we are shent for keeping your greatness back
COR 5.02. 98 P
that state of fortune fall into my keeping, TIM 1.01.150
to be trusted but in the keeping of wise people; ANT 5.02.266 P
she pray'd me to excuse her keeping close, CYM 3.05. 46
/KEEPS 1 FR 0.0001 REL FR 0 V 1 P
/their /endeavor /keeps /in /the /wonted /pace; HAM 2.02.338 P
KEEPS 81 FR 0.0091 REL FR 57 V 24 P
where youth, and cost, witless bravery keeps. MM 1.03. 10
but keeps you from dishonor in doing it. 3.01.236 P
is that at the door that keeps all this noise? ERR 3.01. 61
paradise, but that adam that keeps the prison; 4.03. 18 P
poor fool, it keeps on the windy side of care. ADO 2.01.314 P
what pace is this that thy tongue keeps? 3.04. 93 P
armado is a spaniard that keeps here in court, LLL 4.01. 98
my brother jaques he keeps at school, and report AYL 1.01. 5 P
for my part, he keeps me rustically at home, or, 1.01. 7 P
capable impressure | thy palm some moment keeps; 3.05. 24
her father keeps from all access of suitors, SHR 1.02.259
but she is arm'd for him and keeps her guard AWW 3.05. 73
the master i speak of ever keeps a good fire. 4.05. 48 P
like a pedant that keeps a school i' th' church. TN 3.02. 75 P
note, that keeps you from the blow of the law. 3.04.153 P
keeps good old york there with his men of war? R2 2.03. 52
temples of a king | keeps death his court, and 3.02.162
when my poor heart no measure keeps in grief; 3.04. 8
hath surpris'd | to his own use he keeps, and 1H4 1.01. 94
who keeps the gate here ho? where is the earl? 2H4 1.01. 1
thought in the world keeps the road-way better 2.02. 58 P
'a breaks words, and keeps whole weapons. H5 3.02. 35 P
the world, but keeps the bridge most valiantly, 3.06. 11 P
what watch the king keeps to maintain the peace, 4.01.283
and never changes, but keeps his course truly. 5.02.164 P
supply, | and hardly keeps his men from mutiny, 1H6 1.01.160
shall we disturb him, since he keeps no mean? 1.02.121
as an outlaw in a castle keeps | and useth it to 3.01. 47
man, | what e'er occasion keeps him from us now. 2H6 3.01. 3
that keeps his leaves in spite of any storm, 5.01.206
he knows the game; how true he keeps the wind! 3H6 3.02. 14
and so i chide the means that keeps me from it, 3.02.141
him, | while he himself keeps in the cold field? 4.03. 14
thus far our fortune keeps an upward course, 5.03. 1
it beggars any man that keeps it. R3 1.04.141 P
the earl of pembroke keeps his regiment; 5.03. 29
and 'tis this fever that keeps troy on foot, TRO 1.03.135
keeps his tent like him, | makes factious feasts 1.03.190
the hart achilles | keeps thicket. 2.03.259
dear my lord, | keeps honor bright; 3.03.151
keeps place with thought and almost, like the 3.03.199
who keeps the tent now? 5.01. 10 P
borrows of the moon when diomed keeps his word. 5.01. 94 P
they say he keeps a troyan drab, and uses the 5.01. 96 P
mine honor keeps the weather of my fate. 5.03. 26
and keeps the oath which by that god he swears, TIT 5.01. 80
where they say he keeps | to ruminate strange 5.02. 5
care keeps his watch in every old man's eye, ROM 2.03. 35
he fights as you sing prick-song, keeps time, 2.04. 21 P
but heaven keeps his part in eternal life. 4.05. 70
and that the lean abhorred monster keeps | thee 5.03.104
he keeps his tides well. TIM 1.02. 55 P
hung up in cases that keeps their sounds to 1.02. 99 P
he's much out of health, and keeps his chamber. 3.04. 72 P
alone, | yet an arch-villain keeps him company. 5.01.108
call it my fear | that keeps you in the house, JC 2.02. 51
fleance his son, that keeps him company, | whose MAC 3.01.134
to pieces that great bond | which keeps me pale! 3.02. 50
our hostess keeps her state, but in best time 3.04. 5
the confident tyrant | keeps still in dunsinane, 5.04. 9
keeps wassail, and the swagg'ring up-spring HAM 1.04. 9
but with a crafty madness keeps aloof | when we 3.01. 8
he keeps them, like /an /ape an apple, in the 4.02. 17 P
feeds on this wonder, keeps himself in clouds, 4.05. 89
keeps our fortunes from us till our oldness LR 1.02. 47 P
he that keeps nor crust /nor crumb, | weary of 1.04.198
wear'st, | which scarcely keeps thee warm. 2.04.270
ebb, but keeps due on | to the propontic and the OTH 3.03.455
to saint peter, | and keeps the gate of hell! 4.02. 92
who keeps her company? 4.02.137
the voice of cassio! iago keeps his word. 5.01. 28
that thy spirit which keeps thee, is | noble, ANT 2.03. 20
makes him fine, | yet keeps his book uncross'd. CYM 3.03. 26
and there, | lord, what a coil he keeps! TNK 2.04. 18
'a keeps a plentiful shrievaltry, and 'a made my STM II.C 42 P
love keeps his revels where there are but twain; VEN 123
to give away yourself keeps yourself still, SON 16.13
so is the time that keeps you as my chest, | or 52. 9
it is my love that keeps mine eye awake, | mine 61.10
she keeps thee to this purpose, that her skill 126. 7
whoe'er keeps me, let my heart be his guard, 133.11
/KEEP'ST 2 FR 0.0002 REL FR 2 V 0 P
thou /keep'st me from the light, | but i will 3H6 5.06. 84
/that /like /a /jack /thou /keep'st /the /stroke R3 4.02.114
KEEP'ST 7 FR 0.0008 REL FR 6 V 1 P
that dost this habitation where thou keep'st MM 3.01. 10
what art thou that keep'st me out from the house ERR 3.01. 42
go, fool, and whom thou keep'st command. SHR 2.01.257
that keep'st the ports of slumber open wide | to 2H4 4.05. 24
keep'st from me all conveniency than suppliest OTH 4.02.176 P
be here, | poor house, that keep'st thyself! CYM 3.06. 36
cunning love, with tears thou keep'st me blind, SON 148.13
KEEP'T 1 FR 0.0001 REL FR 1 V 0 P
is not to leave't undone, but keep't unknown. OTH 3.03.204
KEISER 1 FR 0.0001 REL FR 0 V 1 P
an emperor — caesar, keiser, and pheazar. WIV 1.03. 9 P
KEN 7 FR 0.0008 REL FR 6 V 1 P
i ken the wight; he is of substance good. WIV 1.03. 37 P
for lo, within a ken our army lies: 2H4 4.01.149
as far as i could ken thy chalky cliffs, | when 2H6 3.02.101
for losing ken of albion's wished coast. 3.02.113
'tis he, i ken the manner of his gait, | he TRO 4.05. 14
pisanio show'd thee, | thou wast within a ken. CYM 3.06. 6
'tis double death to drown in ken of shore, | he LUC 1114
KENDAL 2 FR 0.0002 REL FR 0 V 2 P
knaves in kendal green came at my back and let 1H4 2.04.222 P
know these men in kendal green when it was so 2.04.232 P
KENILWORTH *(see killingworth)*
KENN'D 1 FR 0.0001 REL FR 1 V 0 P
none — would not, | had i kenn'd all that were. TNK 5.01.100
KENNEL* 6 FR 0.0006 REL FR 4 V 2 P
go to kennel, pompey, go. MM 3.02. 85 P
go hop me over every kennel home, | for you SHR 4.03. 98
maz'd with a yelping kennel of french curs! 1H6 4.02. 47
ay, kennel, puddle, sink, whose filth and dirt 2H6 4.01. 71
from forth the kennel of thy womb hath crept | a R3 4.04. 47
truth's a dog must to kennel, he must be whipt LR 1.04.111 P
KENNELL'D 1 FR 0.0001 REL FR 1 V 0 P
here kennell'd in a brake she finds a hound, VEN 913
KEN'ST 1 FR 0.0001 REL FR 1 V 0 P
what ken'st thou? TNK 4.01.151
/KENT 4 FR 0.0004 REL FR 3 V 1 P
/kent! LR 4.03. 28
/is /with /the /earl /of /kent /in /germany. 4.07. 90 P
/kent, /sir, /the /banish'd /kent, /who /in 5.03.220
/sir, /the /banish'd /kent, /who /in /disguise 5.03.220
KENT 30 FR 0.0034 REL FR 25 V 5 P
that were embattailed and rank'd in kent. JN 4.02.200
all kent hath yielded; 5.01. 30
heads of salisbury, /spencer, blunt, and kent. R2 5.06. 8
in the wild of kent hath brought three hundred 1H4 2.01. 55 P
the commons here in kent are up in arms, | and 2H6 4.01.100
rebellious hinds, the filth and scum of kent, 4.02.122
you men of kent — 4.07. 54
what say you of kent? 4.07. 55 P
kent, in the commentaries caesar writ, | is 4.07. 60
that alexander iden, an esquire of kent, | took 4.10. 43
tell kent from me, she hath lost her best man, 4.10. 73 P
a poor esquire of kent, that loves his king. 5.01. 75
power | of essex, norfolk, suffolk, nor of kent, 3H6 1.01.156
shalt stir up in suffolk, norfolk, and in kent, 4.08. 12
in kent, my liege, the guilfords are in arms, R3 4.04.503
my lord of kent. LR 1.01. 27 P
peace, kent! 1.01.121
be kent unmannerly | when lear is mad. 1.01.145
kent, on thy life, no more. 1.01.154
thus kent, o princes, bids you all adieu, 1.01.186
kent banish'd thus? 1.02. 23
and the noble and true-hearted kent banish'd! 1.02.116 P
now, banish'd kent, | if thou canst serve where 1.04. 4
ah, that good kent! 3.04.163
o thou good kent, how shall i live and work | to 4.07. 1
here comes kent. 5.03.230
seest thou this object, kent? 5.03.239
'tis noble kent, your friend. 5.03.269
this is a dull sight. are you not kent? 5.03.283
your servant kent. 5.03.284
KENTISH 2 FR 0.0002 REL FR 2 V 0 P
these kentish rebels would be soon appeas'd! 2H6 4.04. 42
farewell, my lord, trust not the kentish rebels. 4.04. 57
KENTISHMAN 1 FR 0.0001 REL FR 1 V 0 P
i have seduc'd a headstrong kentishman, | john 2H6 3.01.356
KENTISHMEN 1 FR 0.0001 REL FR 1 V 0 P
with whom the kentishmen will willingly rise; 3H6 1.02. 41
KENT'S 1 FR 0.0001 REL FR 0 V 1 P
to have from him as this of kent's banishment. LR 1.01.301 P
KEPT 112 FR 0.0126 REL FR 93 V 19 P
tell me, that | hath kept with thy remembrance. TMP 1.02. 44
bold head | 'bove the contentious waves he kept, 2.01.119
are founder'd | or night kept chain'd below. 4.01. 31
fire that's closest kept burns most of all. TGV 1.02. 30
tow'r, | the key whereof myself have ever kept; 3.01. 36
worth, | and kept severely from resort of men, 3.01.108
but the doors be lock'd and the keys kept safe, 3.01.111
foster'd, illumin'd, cherish'd, kept alive. 3.01.184
these banish'd men, that i have kept withal, 5.04.152
was like an unskillful singer, he kept not time. WIV 1.03. 26 P
he kept company with the wild prince and poins; 3.02. 72 P
you wot of, unless they kept very good diet, as MM 2.01.111 P
i have kept it myself; 3.02.202 P
the saddler had it, sir, i kept it not. ERR 1.02. 57
shoe, but her face nothing like so clean kept: 3.02.103 P
not that adam that kept the paradise, but that 4.03. 17 P
for dead, | let her awhile be secretly kept in, ADO 4.01.203
most impenetrable cur | that ever kept with men. MV 3.03. 19
should have been respective and have kept it. 5.01.156
let no face be kept in mind | but the fair of AYL 3.02. 94
sir, we kept time, we lost not our time. 5.03. 37 P
us, | that covenants may be kept on either hand. SHR 2.01.127
with oaths kept waking, and with brawling fed; 4.03. 10
by being ever kept, it is ever lost. AWW 1.01.131 P
the longer kept, the less worth. 1.01.154 P
the wars hath so kept you under that you must 1.01.195 P
and kept a coil with | "too young" and "the next 2.01. 27
i have kept of them tame, and know their natures 2.05. 45 P
yes, being kept together and put to use. TN 3.01. 50 P
kept in a dark house, visited by the priest, 5.01.342
friend, your father might have kept | this calf, JN 1.01.123
day | ever in france shall be kept festival. 3.01. 76
it is religion that doth make vows kept, | but 3.01.279
shall our feast be kept with slaughtered men? 3.01.302
so i were out of prison and kept sheep, | i 4.01. 17
within me grief hath kept a tedious fast; R2 2.01. 75
days, | and hardly kept our countrymen together, 2.04. 2
with slow but stately pace kept on his course, 5.02. 10
is | when time is broke, and no proportion kept! 5.05. 43
'twas where the madcap duke his uncle kept — 1H4 1.03.244
the crown, | had still kept loyal to possession, 3.02. 43
they are, | if promises be kept on every hand, 3.02.168
of our proceedings kept the earl from hence, 4.01. 65
o that this blossom could be kept from cankers! 2H4 2.02. 94 P
learning a mere hoard of gold kept by a devil, 4.03.115 P
you won it, wore it, kept it, gave it me; 4.05.221
so will i those that kept me company. 5.05. 59
treason and murther ever kept together, | as two H5 2.02.105
prerogatifes and laws of the wars is not kept. 4.01. 68 P
field | we kept together in our chivalry!" 4.06. 19
well summer'd and warm kept, are like flies at 5.02.308 P
and may our oaths well kept and prosp'rous be! 5.02.374
had all your quarters been as safely kept | as 1H6 2.01. 63
how france and frenchmen might be kept in awe, 2H6 1.01. 92
and would have kept so long as breath did last! 1.01.211
them be clapp'd up close, | and kept asunder. 1.04. 51
king, | who kept him in captivity till he died. 2.02. 42
had i but said, i would have kept my word; 3.02.293
he might have kept that glory to this day. 3H6 2.02.153
and thou this day hadst kept thy chair in peace. 2.06. 20
and kept low shrubs from winter's pow'rful wind. 5.02. 15
o, he hath kept an evil diet long, | and R3 1.01.139
a holy day shall this be kept hereafter. 2.01. 74
must gently be preserv'd, cherish'd, and kept. 2.02.119
late he died that might have kept that title, 3.01. 99
besides, he says there are two councils kept; 3.02. 12
long kept in britain at our mother's cost? 5.03.324
kept him a foreign man still, which so griev'd H8 2.02.128
i have kept you next my heart, have not alone 3.02.157
they are coming, | as if we kept a fair here! 5.03. 69
hath ever since kept hector fasting and waking. TRO 1.02. 35 P
beat for barking | as therefore kept to do so. COR 2.03.217
then have i kept it to a worthy end. TIT 3.01.173
shut up in prison, kept without my food, | whipt ROM 1.02. 55
shouldst have kept one to thyself, for i mean to TIM 1.01.265 P
father, | and kept his credit with his purse; 3.02. 68
i have kept back their foes, | while they have 3.05.105
all | i kept were knaves, to serve in meat to 4.03.478
and i with them the third night kept the watch, HAM 1.02.208
which, being kept close, might move | more grief 2.01.115
us, whose providence | should have kept short, 4.01. 18
o, that that earth which kept the world in awe 5.01.215
but kept a reservation to be followed | with LR 2.04.252
she told her, while she kept it, | 'twould make OTH 3.04. 58
which to the tune of flutes kept stroke, and ANT 2.02.195
i have not kept my square, but that to come 2.03. 6
no, pompey, i have kept me from the cup. 2.07. 66
he at philippi kept | his sword e'en like a 3.11. 35
stuck | a sun and moon, which kept their course, 5.02. 80
what have i kept back? 5.02.147
some nobler token i have kept apart | for livia 5.02.168
send your trunk to me, it shall safe be kept, CYM 1.06.209
i would have kept such a jangling of the bells, PER 2.01. 41 P
it kept where i kept, i so dearly lov'd it, 2.01.130
it kept where i kept, i so dearly lov'd it, 2.01.130
i could have kept a hawk, and well have hollow'd TNK 2.05. 11
the maids that kept her company | have half 5.02. 2
he was kept down with hard meat and ill lodging, 5.02. 97
to disseat | his lord that kept it bravely. 5.04. 73
but that | he kept him 'tween his legs, on his 5.04. 76
were beauty under twenty locks kept fast, | yet VEN 575
saw | shall by a painted cloth be kept in awe." LUC 245
for collatine's dear love be kept unspotted: 821
and suck'd the honey which thy chaste bee kept. 840
likes dumps when time is kept with tears. 1127
when both were kept for heaven and collatine? 1166
she bade good night that kept my rest away, PP 14. 2
end, | and kept unus'd, the user so destroys it: SON 9.12
which three till now never kept seat in one. 105.14
angry that his prescriptions are not kept, 147. 6
kept hearts in liveries, but mine own was free, LC 195
but kept cold distance, and did thence remove 237
KEPT'ST 1 FR 0.0001 REL FR 1 V 0 P
by thy honest aid | thou kept'st a wife herself, AWW 5.03.330
KERCHIEF 3 FR 0.0003 REL FR 1 V 2 P
a plain kerchief, sir john. WIV 3.03. 59 P
a hat, a muffler, and a kerchief, and so escape. 4.02. 71 P
chose out, brave caius, | to wear a kerchief! JC 2.01.315
KERELYBONTO 1 FR 0.0001 REL FR 0 V 1 P
kerelybonto, sir, betake thee to thy faith, for AWW 4.01. 75 P
KERN 2 FR 0.0002 REL FR 1 V 1 P
and gentle, and you rode like a kern of ireland, H5 3.07. 53 P
full often, like a shag-hair'd crafty kern, 2H6 3.01.367
KERNEL 4 FR 0.0004 REL FR 1 V 3 P
italy for picking a kernel out of a pomegranate. AWW 2.03.259 P
there can be no kernel in this light nut; 2.05. 43 P
how like, methought, i then was to this kernel, WT 1.02.159
were as good crack a fusty nut with no kernel. TRO 2.01.102 P
KERNELS 2 FR 0.0002 REL FR 1 V 1 P
and, sowing the kernels of it in the sea, bring TMP 2.01. 93 P
as hazel-nuts, and sweeter than the kernels. SHR 2.01.255
KERNS 7 FR 0.0008 REL FR 7 V 0 P
we must supplant those rough rug-headed kerns, R2 2.01.156
th' uncivil kerns of ireland are in arms, | and 2H6 3.01.310
cade | oppose himself against a troop of kerns, 3.01.361
of gallowglasses and stout kerns | is marching 4.09. 26
isles | of kerns and /gallowglasses is supplied, MAC 1.02. 13
these skipping kerns to trust their heels, | but 1.02. 30
i cannot strike at wretched kerns, whose arms 5.07. 17
KERSEY 3 FR 0.0003 REL FR 1 V 2 P
lief be a list of an english kersey as be pil'd, MM 1.02. 33 P
in russet yeas and honest kersey noes. LLL 5.02.413
on one leg and a kersey boot-hose on the other, SHR 3.02. 67 P
KETH *(also quoth)*
KETH 1 FR 0.0001 REL FR 0 V 1 P
die, keth 'a? PER 2.01. 78 P
KETLY 1 FR 0.0001 REL FR 1 V 0 P
suffolk, | sir richard ketly, davy gam, esquire; H5 4.08.104
KETTLE 1 FR 0.0001 REL FR 1 V 0 P
cups, | and let the kettle to the trumpet speak, HAM 5.02.275
KETTLE-DRUM 1 FR 0.0001 REL FR 1 V 0 P
the kettle-drum and trumpet thus bray out | the HAM 1.04. 11
KEY 30 FR 0.0034 REL FR 24 V 6 P
having both the key | of officer and office, set TMP 1.02. 83
tow'r, | the key whereof myself have ever kept; TGV 3.01. 36
i will use her as the key of the cuckoldly WIV 2.02.274 P
turn you the key, and know his business of him; MM 1.04. 8
that makes his opening with this bigger key. 4.01. 31
give her this key, and tell her, in the desk ERR 4.01.103
son | knows not my feeble key of untun'd cares? 5.01.311
in what key shall a man take you to go in the ADO 1.01.185 P
they say he wears a key in his ear and a lock 5.01.308 P

go, tenderness of years, take this key, give LLL 3.01. 5 P
but i will wed thee in another key, | with pomp, MND 1.01. 18
both warbling of one song, both in one key, | as 3.02.206
or | shall i bend low and in a bondman's key, MV 1.03.123
deliver me the key. 2.07. 59
give me a key for this, | and instantly unlock 2.09. 51
and keep thy friend | under thy own life's key. AWW 1.01. 67
then give me leave that /i may turn the key, R2 5.03. 36
thou that didst bear the key of all my counsels, H5 2.02. 96
and with an accent tun'd in self–same key TRO 1.03. 53
hell gate, he should have old turning the key. MAC 2.03. 3 P
think | that, had he duncan's sons under his key 3.06. 18
and you yourself shall keep the key of it. HAM 1.03. 86
pray ye go, there's my key. LR 1.02.170 P
arrant whore, | ne'er turns the key to th' poor. 2.04. 53
shouldst have said, "good porter, turn the key." 3.07. 64
a closet lock and key of villainous secrets; OTH 4.02. 22
i pray you turn the key and keep our counsel. 4.02. 94
death, who is the key | t' unbar these locks. CYM 5.04. 7
speak't in a woman's key — like such a woman TNK 1.01. 94
so am i as the rich whose blessed key | can SON 52. 1

KEY–COLD 2 FR 0.0002 REL FR 2 V 0 P
poor key–cold figure of a holy king, | pale R3 1.02. 5
and then in key–cold lucrece' bleeding stream LUC 1774

KEY–HOLE 1 FR 0.0001 REL FR 0 V 1 P
shut that, and 'twill out at the key–hole; AYL 4.01.163 P

KEYS 13 FR 0.0014 REL FR 10 V 3 P
but the doors be lock'd and the keys kept safe, TGV 3.01.111
here, here, here be my keys. WIV 3.03.162 P
give up your keys. MM 5.01.462
there are my keys. MV 2.05. 12
to command | the keys of all the posterns. WT 1.02.464
i would have fil'd keys off that hung in chains. 4.04.611 P
shoes, and bunches of keys at their girdles, and 2H4 1.02. 39 P
and when you have done so, bring the keys to me. 1H6 2.03. 2
all, | these counties were the keys of normandy. 2H6 1.01.114
what, fear not, man, but yield me up the keys, 3H6 4.07. 37
there lies the duke asleep, and there the keys. R3 1.04. 95
hold, take these keys and fetch more spices, ROM 4.04. 1
your jailer shall deliver you the keys | that CYM 1.01. 73

KHAM'S *(see cham's)*

KIBE 2 FR 0.0002 REL FR 1 V 1 P
if 'twere a kibe, | 'twould put me to my slipper TMP 2.01.276
the heel of the courtier, he galls his kibe. HAM 5.01.141 P

KIBES 2 FR 0.0002 REL FR 0 V 2 P
why then let kibes ensue. WIV 1.03. 32 P
were in 's heels, were't not in danger of kibes? LR 1.05. 9 P

KICK 3 FR 0.0003 REL FR 3 V 0 P
i should kick, being kick'd, and, being at that ERR 3.01. 17
though she be, she feels her young one kick. AWW 5.03.302
trip him, that his heels may kick at heaven, HAM 3.03. 93

/KICK'D 1 FR 0.0001 REL FR 0 V 1 P
/she /kick'd /the /poor /king /her /father. LR 3.06. 47 P

KICK'D 2 FR 0.0002 REL FR 2 V 0 P
i should kick, being kick'd, and, being at that ERR 3.01. 17
our spoils he kick'd at, | and look'd upon COR 2.02.124

KICKSHAWS 1 FR 0.0001 REL FR 0 V 1 P
and any pretty little tiny kickshaws, tell 2H4 5.01. 28 P

KICKSHAWSES 1 FR 0.0001 REL FR 0 V 1 P
art thou good at these kickshawses, knight? TN 1.03.115 P

KICKY–WICKY 1 FR 0.0001 REL FR 1 V 0 P
that hugs his kicky–wicky here at home, AWW 2.03.280

KIDNEY 1 FR 0.0001 REL FR 0 V 1 P
think of that — a man of my kidney. WIV 3.05.115 P

KILDARE'S 1 FR 0.0001 REL FR 1 V 0 P
first, kildare's attendure, | then deputy of H8 2.01. 41

/KILL 3 FR 0.0003 REL FR 3 V 0 P
/me, /i /being /by, /that /i /should /kill /him? R3 4.02.101
/with /sighing, /girl, /kill /it /with /groans; TIT 3.02. 15
/but /that /between /us /we /can /kill /a /fly 3.02. 77

KILL 225 FR 0.0254 REL FR 178 V 47 P
monster, i will kill this man. TMP 3.02.106 P
stabs | kill the still–closing waters, as 3.03. 64
that you might kill your stomach on your meat, TGV 1.02. 68
and kill the bees that yield it with your stings 1.02.104
a little time, my lord, will kill that grief. 3.02. 15
by gar, i vill kill de jack priest; WIV 1.04.117 P
he knew your worship would kill him if he came. 2.03. 11 P
de herring is no dead so as i vill kill him. 2.03. 13 P
jack, i vill tell you how i vill kill him. 2.03. 14 P
by gar, me vill kill de priest, for he speak for 2.03. 82 P
jarteer — have i not stay for him to kill him? 3.01. 92 P
for our kitchens | we kill the fowl of season. MM 2.02. 85
away, they'll kill us. ERR 4.04.146
between them they will kill the conjurer. 5.01.177
to vex claudio, to undo hero, and kill leonato. ADO 2.02. 29 P
kill claudio. 4.01.289 P
you kill me to deny it. farewell. 4.01.291 P
if you go on thus, you will kill yourself, | and 5.01. 1
if thou kill'st me, boy, thou shalt kill a man. 5.01. 79
he shall kill two of us, and men indeed; 5.01. 80
but that's no matter, let him kill one first. 5.01. 81
thou hast mettle enough in thee to kill care. 5.01.133 P
do you hear me, and let this count kill me. 5.01.231 P
now mercy goes to kill, | and shooting well is LLL 4.01. 24
that more for praise than purpose meant to kill. 4.01. 29
my lady goes to kill horns, but, if thou marry, 4.01.111
that contempt will kill the speaker's heart, 5.02.149
some to kill cankers in the musk–rose buds, MND 2.02. 3
stay, though thou kill me, sweet demetrius. 2.02. 84
pyramus must draw a sword to kill himself; 3.01. 11 P
in blood, plunge in the deep, | and kill me too. 3.02. 49
should i hurt her, strike her, kill her dead? 3.02.269
to strike me, spurn me, nay, to kill me too. 3.02.313
and kill me a red–hipp'd humble–bee on the top 4.01. 11 P
for pyramus therein doth kill himself. 5.01. 67
and i, like helen, till the fates me kill. 5.01.197
do all men kill the things they do not love? MV 4.01. 66
hates any man the thing he would not kill? 4.01. 67
come, shall we go and kill us venison? AYL 2.01. 21
to fright the animals and to kill them up | in 2.01. 62
o, ominous! he comes to kill my heart. 3.02.246 P
if mine eyes can wound, now let them kill thee. 3.05. 16
mind, for i protest her frown might kill me. 4.01.110 P
by this hand, it will not kill a fly. 4.01.111 P
was't you that did so oft contrive to kill him? 4.03.134
or, to wit, i kill thee, make thee away, 5.01. 52 P
i will kill thee a hundred and fifty ways: 5.01. 56 P
this is a way to kill a wife with kindness, SHR 4.01.208
and, though i kill him not, i am the cause | his AWW 3.02.115
and the first view shall kill | all repetition. 5.03. 21
done, that is, kill him whom you have recover'd, TN 2.01. 38 P
home, where if it be thy chance to kill me" — 3.04.160 P
both that they will kill one another by the look 3.04.196 P
and fear to kill a woodcock lest thou dispossess 4.02. 59 P
thief at point of death, | kill what i love? 5.01.119
to have him kill a king — poor trespasses, WT 3.02.189
her die again, for then | you kill her double. 5.03.107
woes, | and teaches me to kill or hang myself. JN 3.04. 56
wish him dead, but thou hadst none to kill him. 4.02.206
as thou shalt be, if thou didst kill this child. 4.03.124
since thou dost seek to kill my name in me, | i R2 2.01. 86
to monarchize, be fear'd, and kill with looks, 3.02.165
part | to take on me to keep and kill thy heart. 5.01. 98
that i may strive to kill it with a groan. 5.01.100
down their hands, | to kill the king at oxford. 5.02. 99
was it for me to kill the heir–apparent? 1H4 2.04.269 P
now, by my sword, i will kill all his coats; 5.03. 26
he is indeed, and living to kill thee. 5.03. 48 P
if not, let him kill the next percy himself. 5.04.141 P
wilt thou kill god's officers and the king's? 2H4 2.01. 51 P
he that makes the first thrust, i'll kill him; H5 2.01.100 P
of france | to kill us here in hampton. 2.02. 91
then every soldier kill his prisoners, | give 4.06. 37
kill the poys and the luggage! 4.07. 1 P
angers, look you, kill his best friend, clytus. 4.07. 38 P
which giveth many wounds when one will kill. 1H6 2.05.110
and kill the innocent gazer with thy sight; 2H6 3.02. 53
be poisonous too, and kill thy forlorn queen. 3.02. 77
would curses kill, as doth the mandrake's groan, 3.02.310
first thing we do, let's kill all the lawyers. 4.02. 76 P
have a license to kill for a hundred lacking one 4.03. 7 P
kill and knock down! 4.08. 2 P
retreat or parley when i command them kill? 4.08. 5 P
is able with the change to kill and cure. 5.01.101
priests pray for enemies, but princes kill. 5.02. 71
kill me with thy sword | and not with such a 3H6 1.03. 16
as thou didst kill our tender brother rutland, 2.02.115
i'll kill my horse, because i will not fly. 2.03. 24
for i have murthered where i should not kill. 2.05.122
o, kill me too! 5.05. 41
ah, kill me with thy weapon, not with words! 5.06. 26
thou hadst not liv'd to kill a son of mine. 5.06. 36
i did not kill your husband. R3 1.02. 91
didst thou not kill this king? 1.02.101
for now they kill me with a living death. 1.02.152
for i did kill king henry — | but 'twas thy 1.02.179
then bid me kill myself, and i will do it. 1.02.186
this hand, which for thy love did kill thy love, 1.02.189
shall for thy love kill a far truer love; 1.02.190
fool, thou whet'st a knife to kill thyself. 1.03.243
not to kill him, having a warrant, but to be 1.04.110 P
at my elbow, persuading me not to kill the duke. 1.04.146 P
dar'st thou resolve to kill a friend of mine? 4.02. 69
please you; | but i had rather kill two enemies. 4.02. 71
i had a richard too, and thou didst kill him; 4.04. 44
i had a rutland too, thou /holp'st to kill him. 4.04. 45
yet thou didst kill my children. 4.04.422
be growing, | till death, that winter, kill it. H8 3.02.179
yet that which seems the wound to kill, | doth TRO 3.01.122
in such a sort | the thing he means to kill, 4.01. 25
sleep kill those pretty eyes, | and give as soft 4.02. 4
i came to kill thee, cousin, and bear hence | a 4.05.140
for i'll not kill thee there, nor there, nor 4.05.254
or i'll kill thee every where, yea, o'er and o'er. 4.05.256
let us kill him, and we'll have corn at our own COR 1.01. 10 P
kill, kill, kill, kill, kill him! 5.06.130
kill, kill, kill, kill, kill him! 5.06.130
kill, kill, kill, kill, kill him! 5.06.130
kill, kill, kill, kill, kill him! 5.06.130
kill, kill, kill, kill, kill him! 5.06.130
and with thine own hands kill me in this place! TIT 2.03.169
if they did kill thy husband, then be joyful, 3.01.116
murtherous villains, will you kill your brother? 4.02. 88
as kill a man, or else devise his death, 5.01.128
things | as willingly as one would kill a fly, 5.01.142
arise, fair sun, and kill the envious moon, ROM 2.02. 4
yet i should kill thee with much cherishing. 2.02.183
have none shortly, for one would kill the other. 3.01. 16 P
and all those twenty could but kill one life. 3.01.179
mercy but murders, pardoning those that kill. 3.01.197
wherefore, villain, didst thou kill my cousin? 3.02.100
ne'er so mean, | but "banished" to kill me? 3.03. 46
tybalt would kill thee, | but thou slewest 3.03.137
or in my cell there would she kill herself. 5.03.242
heaven finds means to kill your joys with love. 5.03.293
draught, is the readiest man to kill him; TIM 1.02. 48 P
that then thou mightst kill 'em — and bid me to 1.02. 82 P
if wrongs be evils and enforce us kill, | what 3.05. 36
to kill, i grant, is sin's extremest gust, | but 3.05. 54
choler does kill me that thou art alive; 4.03.367
if alcibiades kill my countrymen, | let 5.01.169
th' infected forth, | but kill not all together. 5.04. 44
grow mischievous, | and kill him in the shell. JC 2.01. 34
let's kill him boldly, but not wrathfully; 2.01.172
kill! 3.02.204 P
is so much that thou wilt kill me straight: 5.04. 13
kill brutus, and be honor'd in his death. 5.04. 14
i'll rather kill myself. 5.05. 7
to kill him, clitus. look, he meditates. 5.05. 12
do repent me of my fury, | that i did kill them. MAC 2.03.107
for donalbain | to kill their gracious father? 3.06. 10
they should find | what 'twere to kill a father; 3.06. 20
a brute part of him to kill so capital a calf HAM 3.02.105 P
a second time i kill my husband dead, | when 3.02.184
as kill a king, and marry with his brother. 3.04. 29
as kill a king! 3.04. 30
kill thy physician, and /the fee bestow | upon LR 1.01.163
how to prevent the fiend, and to kill vermin. 3.04.159 P
we to th' gods, | they kill us for their sport. 4.01. 37
then kill, kill, kill, kill, kill, kill! 4.06.187
then kill, kill, kill, kill, kill, kill! 4.06.187
then kill, kill, kill, kill, kill, kill! 4.06.187
then kill, kill, kill, kill, kill, kill! 4.06.187
then kill, kill, kill, kill, kill, kill! 4.06.187
then kill, kill, kill, kill, kill, kill! 4.06.187
now, whether he kill cassio, | or cassio him, or OTH 5.01. 12
or cassio him, or each do kill the other, 5.01. 13
kill men i' th' dark? 5.01. 63
and i will kill thee | and love thee after. 5.02. 18
i would not kill thy unprepared spirit, | no, 5.02. 31
i would not kill thy soul. 5.02. 32
if you say /so, i hope you will not kill me. 5.02. 35
o, banish me, my lord, but kill me not! 5.02. 78
kill me to–morrow, let me live to–night! 5.02. 80
thought so then — i'll kill myself for grief — 5.02.192
let him not pass, | but kill him rather. 5.02.242
if that thou be'st a devil, i cannot kill thee. 5.02.287
why then we kill all our women. ANT 1.02.133 P
since my becomings kill me when they do not 1.03. 96
on my command, | thou then wouldst kill me. 4.14. 67
and i will kill thee if thou dost deny | thou'st CYM 2.04.145
and, to kill the marvel, | shall be so ever. 3.01. 10
most like, | bringing me here to kill me. 3.04.117
there, thou villain posthumus, will i kill thee. 3.05.132 P
first kill him, and in her eyes; 3.05.138 P
know, if you kill me for my fault, i should 3.06. 56
for friends kill friends, and the disorder's 5.02. 15
the prince | of tyre, and thou must kill him. PER 1.01.156
here must i kill king pericles, and if i do it 1.03. 2 P
which can as well inflame as it can kill. 2.02. 35
why will you kill me? 4.01. 70
prithee kill me. TNK 2.02.263
good light, | had i a sword, i would kill thee. 2.02.265
and | perfumes to kill the smell o' th' prison; 3.01. 86
may they kill him without lets, | and the ladies 3.05.156
he refuses, | if it but hold, i kill him with. 3.06. 15
that no man but thy cousin's fit to kill thee. 3.06. 44
as i dare kill this cousin that denies it, | so 3.06.166
the misadventure of their own eyes kill 'em; 3.06.190
of love about 'em, | and not kill one another? 3.06.220
for that love must and dare kill this cousin, 3.06.262
conscience, let him hiss, and kill | our market. ep 8
kill them, cut their throats, possess their STM II.C 120
for looks kill love, and love by looks reviveth: VEN 464
"o, thou didst kill me, kill me once again. 499
"o, thou didst kill me, kill me once again. 499
still, | like to a mortal butcher bent to kill. 618
and in a peaceful hour doth cry, 'kill, kill!' 652
and in a peaceful hour doth cry, 'kill, kill!' 652
while lust and murder wakes to stain and kill. LUC 168
which in a moment doth confound and kill | all 250
but they must ope, this blessed league to kill, 383
to kill thine honor with thy live's decay; 516
for it was lent thee all that brood to kill. 627
mad, | himself himself seek every hour to kill! 998
kill both thyself and her for yielding so." 1036
"to kill myself," quoth she, "alack, what were 1156
myself thy friend will kill myself thy foe, 1196
and so did kill | the lechers in their deed. 1636
the master loveless, or kill the gallant knight: PP 15. 6
kill me with spites, yet we must not be foes. SON 40.14
and do not kill | the spirit of love with a 56. 7
may time disgrace and wretched /minutes kill. 126. 8
let no unkind, no fair beseechers kill; 135.13
kill me outright with looks, and rid my pain. 139.14

KILL–COURTESY 1 FR 0.0001 REL FR 1 V 0 P
lie | near this lack–love, this kill–courtesy. MND 2.02. 77

/KILL'D 4 FR 0.0004 REL FR 4 V 0 P
/at /that /that /i /have /kill'd, /my /lord — TIT 3.02. 53
/alas, /my /lord, /i /have /but /kill'd /a /fly. 3.02. 59
/and /thou /hast /kill'd /him. 3.02. 65
/empress' /moor, /therefore /i /kill'd /him. 3.02. 67

KILL'D 127 FR 0.0143 REL FR 94 V 33 P
i took him to be kill'd with a thunder–stroke. TMP 2.02.108 P
would here have kill'd your king, i do forgive 5.01. 78
i kill'd a man, whose death i much repent, | but TGV 4.01. 27
stood on the pillory for geese he hath kill'd, 4.04. 33 P
i wish'd your venison better, it was ill kill'd. WIV 1.01. 83 P
you have beaten my men, kill'd my deer, and 1.01.111 P
i think you have kill'd the poor woman. 4.02.188 P
and young drop–heir that kill'd lusty pudding, MM 4.03. 15 P
calve's–skin that was kill'd for the prodigal; ERR 4.03. 19 P
how many hath he kill'd and eaten in these wars? ADO 1.01. 43 P
but how many hath he kill'd? 1.01. 44 P
thou hast kill'd my child. 5.01. 78
what though care kill'd a cat, thou hast mettle 5.01.133 P
you have kill'd a sweet lady, and her death 5.01.148 P
you have among you kill'd a sweet and innocent 5.01.191 P
thou the slave that with thy breath hast kill'd 5.01.263
that, 'twas a pricket that the princess kill'd. LLL 4.02. 49 P
/call /i the deer the princess kill'd a pricket. 4.02. 52 P
be friends with him, 'a kill'd your sister. 5.02. 13
whose club kill'd cerberus, that three–headed 5.02.589
swords, and that pyramus is not kill'd indeed; MND 3.01. 19 P
and hast thou kill'd him sleeping? 3.02. 70
wish, for all that, that i had not kill'd them; MV 3.04. 73
if kill'd, but one dead that is willing to be so AYL 1.02.188 P
which is he that kill'd the deer? 4.02. 1 P
what shall he have that kill'd the deer? 4.02. 10
ashore | i kill'd a man and fear i was descried. SHR 1.01.232
your son will not be kill'd so soon as i thought AWW 3.02. 37 P
why should he be kill'd? 3.02. 39 P
hath kill'd the flock of all affections else TN 1.01. 35
the better | by my regard, but kill'd none so. WT 1.02.390
woman, she you kill'd | would be unparallel'd. 5.01. 15
kill'd? 5.01. 16
she i kill'd? 5.01. 17
no sorrow | but kill'd itself much sooner. 5.03. 53
whom they say is kill'd to–night | on your JN 4.02.165
who kill'd this prince? 4.03.103
poisoned by their wives, some sleeping kill'd, R2 3.02.159
says she, "how many hast thou kill'd to–day?" 1H4 2.04.106 P
make him sure, yea, and i'll swear i kill'd him. 5.04.125 P
why, percy i kill'd myself, and saw thee dead. 5.04.144
both the blunts | kill'd by the hand of douglas, 2H4 1.01. 17
there hath been a man or two kill'd about her. 5.04. 6 P
unless afraid 'a be kill'd with your hard ep 31 P
the king has kill'd his heart. H5 2.01. 88 P
by your own counsel is suppress'd and kill'd. 2.02. 80
the beast liv'd, was kill'd with hunting him. 4.03. 94
he never kill'd any of his friends. 4.07. 41 P
as alexander kill'd his friend clytus, being in 4.07. 45 P

please your majesty, to tell how many is kill'd? 4.08.118 P
'twas you that kill'd young rutland, was it not? 3H6 2.02. 98
whom in this conflict i, unwares, have kill'd. 2.05. 62
my poor young was lim'd, was caught, and kill'd. 5.06. 17
thy son i kill'd for his presumption. 5.06. 34
hadst thou been kill'd when first thou didst 5.06. 35
what though i kill'd her husband and her father? R3 1.01.154
to be reveng'd on him that kill'd my husband. 1.02.137
i, that kill'd her husband and his father, | to 1.02.230
my brother kill'd no man, his fault was thought, 2.01.105
i had an edward, till a richard kill'd him; 4.04. 40
i had a /harry, till a richard kill'd him: 4.04. 41
thou hadst an edward, till a richard kill'd him; 4.04. 42
thou hadst a richard, till a richard kill'd him. 4.04. 43
hadst a clarence too, and richard kill'd him. 4.04. 46
thy edward he is dead, that kill'd my edward; 4.04. 63
if i have kill'd the issue of your womb, | to 4.04.296
he kill'd my son! COR 5.06.121 P
he kill'd my cousin marcus! 5.06.121 P
he kill'd my father! 5.06.122 P
hath hurt me more than had he kill'd me dead: TIT 3.01. 92
she weeps because they kill'd her husband, 3.01.114
you kill'd her husband, and for that vild fault 5.02.172
kill'd her for whom my tears have made me blind. 5.03. 49
which way ran he that kill'd mercutio? ROM 3.01.137
the day, he's gone, he's kill'd, he's dead! 3.02. 39
romeo that kill'd him, he is banished. 3.02. 70
you speak well of him that kill'd your cousin? 3.02. 96
villain cousin would have kill'd my husband. 3.02.101
despis'd, distressed, hated, martyr'd, kill'd! 4.05. 59
and juliet, dead before, | warm and new kill'd. 5.03.197
a bear, thou wouldst be kill'd by the horse; TIM 4.03.338 P
even with the sword that kill'd thee. JC 5.03. 46
i kill'd not thee with half so good a will. 5.05. 51
was by a mousing owl hawk'd at, and kill'd. MAC 2.04. 13
we have scorch'd the snake, not kill'd it; 3.02. 13
you may say (if't please you) fleance kill'd, 3.06. 6
he has kill'd me, mother: 4.02. 84
and i must be from thence! | my wife kill'd too? 4.03.213
i was kill'd i' th' capitol; HAM 3.02.103 P
brutus kill'd me. 3.02.104 P
none wed the second but who kill'd the first. 3.02.180
to draw apart the body he hath kill'd, | o'er 4.01. 24
that have a father kill'd, a mother stain'd, 4.04. 57
he that hath kill'd my king and whor'd my mother 5.02. 64
i am justly kill'd with mine own treachery. 5.02.307
you see, is kill'd in him, /and /yet /it /is LR 4.07. 78
i kill'd the slave that was a–hanging thee. 5.03.275
hath kill'd a young venetian | call'd roderigo. OTH 5.02.112
roderigo kill'd? | and cassio kill'd? 5.02.113
roderigo kill'd? | and cassio kill'd? 5.02.114
no, cassio is not kill'd. 5.02.114
not cassio kill'd? 5.02.115
'twas i that kill'd her. 5.02.130
the moor hath kill'd my mistress! 5.02.167
for thou hast kill'd the sweetest innocent 5.02.199
the woman falls; sure he hath kill'd his wife. 5.02.236
he's gone, but his wife's kill'd. 5.02.238
i bleed, sir, but not kill'd. 5.02.288
i kiss'd thee ere i kill'd thee. 5.02.358
makes the true man kill'd and saves the thief; CYM 2.03. 71
on that | whilst what we have kill'd be cook'd. 3.06. 39
pisanio might have kill'd thee at the heart 4.02.322
that, britain, i have kill'd thy mistress; 5.01. 20
that kill'd thy daughter — villain–like, i lie 5.05.218
posthumus, | you ne'er kill'd imogen till now! 5.05.231
which make a sound, but kill'd are wond'red at. PER 2.03. 63
why would she have me kill'd now? 4.01. 72
law, | i never kill'd a mouse, nor hurt a fly; 4.01. 77
he thought to kiss him, and hath kill'd him so. VEN 1110
with kissing him i should have kill'd him first, 1118
by this the boy that by her side lay kill'd 1165
lest between them both it should be kill'd, LUC 74
"had collatinus kill'd my son or sire, | or lain 232
chide rough winter that the flow'r hath kill'd; 1255
her lively color kill'd with deadly cares. 1593
i owed her, and 'tis mine that she hath kill'd." 1803
kill'd too soon by death's sharp sting! PP 10. 4
KILL'DST 1 FR 0.0001 REL FR 1 V 0 P
thou kill'dst my husband henry in the tower, R3 1.03.118
KILLEN 1 FR 0.0001 REL FR 1 V 0 P
for though he strive | to killen bad, keep good PER 2.ch. 20
KILLETH 1 FR 0.0001 REL FR 1 V 0 P
him i forgive my death that killeth me, | when 1H6 1.02. 20
KILL–HOLE 2 FR 0.0002 REL FR 0 V 2 P
creep into the kill–hole. WIV 4.02. 58 P
or kill–hole? WT 4.04.245 P
KILLING 23 FR 0.0026 REL FR 17 V 6 P
for indeed i promis'd to eat all of his killing. ADO 1.01. 45 P
i believe we must leave the killing out, when MND 3.01. 14 P
this, if i scape hanging for killing that rogue. 1H4 2.02. 15 P
he hath a killing tongue and a quiet sword; H5 3.02. 34 P
looks pale, | killing their fruit with frowns? 3.05. 18
of mischief, | killing in relapse of mortality. 4.03.107
at their dead masters, | killing them twice. 4.07. 81
bridge, killing all those that withstand them. 2H6 4.05. 3 P
but to be damn'd for killing him, from the which R3 1.04.111 P
killing care and grief of heart | fall asleep, H8 3.01. 13
the third day comes a frost, a killing frost, 3.02.355
killing our enemies, the blood he hath lost COR 3.01.297
summer butterflies, | or butchers killing flies. 4.06. 95
o, keep me from their worse than killing lust, TIT 2.03.175
here, tamora, though griev'd with killing grief. 2.03.260
killing that love which thou hast vow'd to ROM 3.03.129
that, by killing of villains, | thou wast born TIM 4.03.106
how scap'd i killing when i cross'd you so? JC 4.03.150
killing swine. MAC 1.03. 2
talk you of killing? OTH 5.02. 33
but this, | killing myself, to die upon a kiss. 5.02.359
her knowledge only | in killing creatures vild, CYM 5.05.252
eat them) | the brine they wept at killing 'em. TNK 1.03. 22
KILLINGWORTH 2 FR 0.0002 REL FR 2 V 0 P
my gracious lord, retire to killingworth, 2H6 4.04. 39
thee, | therefore away with us to killingworth. 4.04. 44
KILLS 24 FR 0.0027 REL FR 16 V 8 P
striking | kills for faults of his own liking! MM 3.02.268
some cupid kills with arrows, some with traps. ADO 3.01.106
it kills sheep; LLL 4.03. 6 P
it kills me, i a sheep: 4.03. 7 P
lover, that kills himself most gallant for love. MND 1.02. 23 P
when truth kills truth, o devilish–holy fray! 3.02.129
he kills her in her own humor. SHR 4.01.180 P
me no money, i pray you, that kills my heart. WT 4.03. 83 P
he that kills me some six or seven dozen of 1H4 2.04.102 P
and with his pistol kills a sparrow flying. 2.04.346 P
i think he will eat all he kills. H5 3.07. 92 P
joan, this kills thy father's heart outright! 1H6 5.04. 2
upon thy wounds, that kills mine eye and heart! 3H6 2.05. 87
ay me, this object kills me! TIT 3.01. 64
a villain kills my father, and for that | i, his HAM 3.03. 76
and in this brainish apprehension kills | the 4.01. 11
give me the addition | whose want even kills me. OTH 4.01.105
that death's unnatural that kills for loving. 5.02. 42
worm of nilus there, | that kills and pains not? ANT 5.02.244
basilisk unto mine eye, | kills me to look on't. CYM 2.04.108
swear to th' gods that winter kills the flies, PER 4.03. 50
in likely thoughts the other kills thee quickly. VEN 990
or kills his life or else his quality. LUC 875
but ah, thought kills me that i am not thought, SON 44. 9
/KILL'ST 1 FR 0.0001 REL FR 1 V 0 P
/thou /kill'st /my /heart! TIT 3.02. 54
KILL'ST 6 FR 0.0006 REL FR 5 V 1 P
if thou kill'st me, boy, thou shalt kill a man. ADO 5.01. 79
"thou kill'st me like a rogue and a villain." TN 3.04.162 P
thou kill'st me in his life; R2 5.03. 72
but kill'st the mother that engend'red thee! JC 5.03. 71
say so, villain, | thou kill'st thy mistress; ANT 2.05. 27
sword | is in my hand, and, if thou kill'st me, TNK 3.06. 97
KILN–HOLE *(see kill–hole)*
KIMMALTON 1 FR 0.0001 REL FR 1 V 0 P
since which she was remov'd to kimmalton, H8 4.01. 34
KIN 35 FR 0.0039 REL FR 25 V 10 P
mercy | is nothing kin to foul redemption. MM 2.04.113
thou wilt say anon he is some kin to thee, MV 2.09. 97
my sword and yours are kin. AWW 2.01. 40 P
one of thy kin has a most weak pia mater. TN 1.05.115 P
of charity, what kin are you to me? 5.01.230
kin to jove's thunder, so surpris'd my sense, WT 3.01. 10
and my near'st of kin | cry fie upon my grave! 3.02. 53
not hold thee of our blood, no, not our kin, 4.04.430
come, lady, i will show thee to my kin, | and JN 1.01.273
blood, | but bloody with the enemies of his kin. R2 2.01.183
shall kin with kin and kind with kind confound. 4.01.141
shall kin with kin and kind with kind confound. 4.01.141
man may be, | not like to me, or any of my kin, 5.02.109
even like those that are kin to the king, for 2H4 2.02.111 P
nay, they will be kin to us, or they will fetch 2.02.117 P
even such kin as the parish heckfers are to the 2.02.157 P
any such proverb so little kin to the purpose. H5 3.07. 68 P
had he been slaughter–man to all my kin, | i 3H6 1.04.169
because she's kin to me, therefore she's not so TRO 1.01. 74 P
and she were /not kin to me, she would be as 1.01. 75 P
the hard and soft, seem all affin'd and kin; 1.03. 25
one touch of nature makes the whole world kin — 3.03.175
no kin, no love, no blood, no soul so near me 4.02. 98
the combatants being kin | half stints their 4.05. 92
were author of himself, | and knew no other kin. COR 5.03. 37
now, by the stock and honor of my kin, | to ROM 1.05. 58
one only daughter have i, no kin else, | on whom TIM 1.01.121
spare thy athenian cradle and those kin | which 5.04. 40
a little more than kin, and less than kind. HAM 1.02. 65
/compounded it with dust, whereto 'tis kin. 4.02. 6
i marvel what kin thou and thy daughters are. LR 1.04.182 P
your words and performances are no kin together. OTH 4.02.183 P
is he thy kin? CYM 5.05.111
no more kin to me | than i to your highness; 5.05.112
falsest cousin | that ever blood made kin! TNK 3.01. 38
/KIND 1 FR 0.0001 REL FR 1 V 0 P
melted with tenderness and /kind compassion, R3 4.03. 7
KIND 300 FR 0.0339 REL FR 240 V 60 P
my slave, who never | yields us kind answer. TMP 1.02.309
for no kind of traffic | would i admit; 2.01.149
of it own kind, all foison, all abundance, | to 2.01.164
who, in this kind of merry fooling, am nothing 2.01.177 P
a kind of not–of–the–newest poor–john. 2.02. 26 P
and crown what i profess with kind event | if i 3.01. 69
give us kind keepers, heavens! what were these? 3.03. 20
their manners are more gentle, kind, than of 3.03. 32
of tongue) a kind | of excellent dumb discourse. 3.03. 38
one of their kind, that relish all as sharply 5.01. 23
look, here is writ "kind julia." TGV 1.02.106
all the kind of the launces have this very fault 2.03. 2 P
him leave, madam, he is a kind of chameleon. 2.04. 25 P
and ev'n in kind love i do conjure thee, | who 2.07. 2
dumb jewels often in their silent kind | more 3.01. 90
the wit to think my master is a kind of a knave; 3.01.264 P
and, proteus, we dare trust you in this kind, 3.02. 56
it's an honorable kind of thievery. 4.01. 39
is she kind as she is fair? 4.02. 44
good morrow, kind sir eglamour. 4.03. 46
a tender, a kind of tender, made afar off by sir WIV 1.01.208 P
kind fellow as ever servant shall come in house 1.04. 10 P
by day or night, | or any kind of light, | with 2.01. 16
it, for if there be a kind woman in windsor, she 2.02.121 P
distemper in this kind for the wealth of windsor 3.03.216 P
a kind heart he hath. 3.04.102 P
through fire and water for such a kind heart. 3.04.103 P
by my size that i have a kind of alacrity in 3.05. 12 P
there is a kind of character in thy life, | that MM 1.01. 27
i prithee, lucio, do me this kind service: 1.02.176
others, | hath yet a kind of medicine in itself, 2.02.135
then was your sin of heavier kind than his. 2.03. 28
is't not a kind of incest, to take life | from 3.01.138
his love toward her ever most kind and natural; 3.01.220 P
admonition, and still forfeit in the same kind! 3.02.194 P
as dangerous to be ag'd in any kind of course, 3.02.225 P
nay, friar, i am a kind of bur, i shall stick. 4.03.179 P
lend him your kind pains | to find out this 5.01.246
o most kind maid, | it was the swift celerity of 5.01.393
drew me from kind embracements of my spouse; ERR 1.01. 43
yet he loseth it in a kind of jollity. 2.02. 89 P
a kind overflow of kindness. ADO 1.01. 26 P
there is a kind of merry war betwixt signior 1.01. 62 P
if the prince do solicit you in that kind, you 2.01. 67 P
me, intend a kind of zeal both to the prince and 2.02. 36 P
and, for such kind of men, the less you meddle 3.03. 52 P
what kind of catechising call you this? 4.01. 78
but they shall find, awak'd in such a kind, 4.01.197
yet a kind of insinuation, as it were in via, in LLL 4.02. 13 P
but in this kind, wanting your father's voice, MND 1.01. 54
be kind and courteous to this gentleman. 3.01.164
my hounds are bred out of the spartan kind; 4.01.119
he says they can do nothing in this kind. 5.01. 88
the best in this kind are but shadows; 5.01.211 P
wands, | and, in the doing of the deed of kind, MV 1.03. 85
this is kind i offer. 1.03.142
the hebrew will turn christian, he grows kind. 1.03.178
something grow to, he had a kind of taste — 2.02. 18 P
who, god bless the mark, is a kind of devil; 2.02. 24 P
my conscience is but a kind of hard conscience, 2.02. 29 P
the patch is kind enough, but a huge feeder, 2.05. 46
and that is but a kind of bastard hope neither. 3.05. 7 P
that were a kind of bastard hope indeed; 3.05. 13 P
the weakest kind of fruit | drops earliest to 4.01.115
for herein fortune shows herself more kind 4.01.267
a kind of boy, a little scrubbed boy, | no 5.01.162
by this kind of chase, i should hate him, for my AYL 1.03. 32 P
and with a kind of umber smirch my face; 1.03.112
and in that kind swears you do more usurp | than 2.01. 27
to /some kind of men | their graces serve them 2.03. 10
the soil, the profit, and this kind of life, | i 2.04. 98
farewell, kind master. 2.06. 3 P
of what kind should this cock come of? 2.07. 90
if the cat will after kind, | so be sure will 3.02.103
whether that thy youth and kind | will the 4.03. 59
will, for my kind offer, when i make curtsy, bid ep 22 P
and then with kind embracements, tempting kisses SHR in.1. 118
it is a kind of history. in.2. 141
for to cunning men | i will be very kind, and 1.01. 98
manners discreetly in all kind of companies. 1.01.242
an old italian fox is not so kind, my boy. 2.01.403
padua affords nothing but what is kind. 5.02. 14
ay, and a kind one too. 5.02. 83
comes by destiny, | your cuckoo sings by kind. AWW 1.03. 63
behaviors | that in their kind they speak it. 1.03.179
i must not hear thee, fare thee well, kind maid! 2.01.145
was like this maid, | i found you wondrous kind. 5.03.310
because she will admit no kind of suit, | no, TN 1.02. 45
crow so at these set kind of fools no better 1.05. 89 P
what kind o' man is he? 1.05.150 P
marry, sir, sometimes he is a kind of puritan. 2.03.140 P
what kind of woman is't? 2.04. 26
and with a kind of injunction drives me to these 2.05.168 P
and to do that well craves a kind of wit. 3.01. 61
my kind antonio, | i can no other answer make 3.03. 13
i have heard of some kind of men that put 3.04.243 P
tempests are kind and salt waves fresh in love. 3.04.384
not your jailer then, | but your kind hostess. WT 1.02. 60
with such a kind of love as might become | a 3.02. 64
of that kind | our rustic garden's barren, and i 4.04. 83
and make conceive a bark of baser kind | by bud 4.04. 94
so rarely kind, are as interpreters | of my 5.01.150
which trust accordingly, kind citizens, | and JN 2.01.231
unyoke this seizure and this kind regreet? 3.01.241
we had a kind of light what would ensue. 4.03. 61
like a kind host, the dolphin and his powers. 5.01. 32
i have a kind soul that would give thanks, | and 5.07.108
but in this kind to come, in braving arms, | be R2 2.03.143
and you that do abet him in this kind | cherish 2.03.146
tell her i send to her my kind commends; 3.01. 38
speak to his gentle hearing kind commends. 3.03.126
shall kin with kin and kind with kind confound. 4.01.141
shall kin with kin and kind with kind confound. 4.01.141
and in this thought they find a kind of ease, 5.05. 28
kind uncle york, the latest news we hear | is 5.06. 1
or you shall hear in such a kind from me | as 1H4 1.03.121
and "gentle harry percy" and "kind cousin" — 1.03.254
company last night at supper, a kind of auditor, 2.01. 57 P
but for sweet jack falstaff, kind jack falstaff, 2.04.475 P
is with a kind of colic pinch'd and vex'd | by 3.01. 28
and breed a kind of question in our cause. 4.01. 68
that shows the ignorant a kind of fear | before 4.01. 74
the king is kind, and well we know the king 4.03. 52
zeal, | my father, in kind heart and pity mov'd, 4.03. 64
the liberal and kind offer of the king. 5.02. 2
as i take it, is a kind of lethargy, and't 2H4 1.02.111 P
your lordship, a kind of sleeping in the blood, 1.02.112 P
his effects in galen, it is a kind of deafness. 1.02.117 P
but thou, like a kind fellow, gavest thyself 4.03. 69 P
fish–meals, that they fall into a kind of male 4.03. 93 P
the oldest sins the newest kind of ways? 4.05.126
thank thee with my heart, kind master bardolph, 5.01. 57 P
i have long dreamt of such a kind of man, | so 5.05. 49
do, | were all thy children kind and natural! H5 2.pr. 19
fetch forth the lazar kite of cressid's kind, 2.01. 76
lord of cambridge, and my kind lord of masham, 2.02. 13
breed, by his sufferance, more of such a kind. 2.02. 46
and thus thy fall hath left a kind of blot | to 2.02.138
still be kind, | and eche out our performance 3.pr. 34
a good old commander and a most kind gentleman. 4.01. 95 P
what kind of god art thou, that suffer'st more 4.01.241
and my kind kinsman, warriors all, adieu! 4.03. 10
farewell, kind lord; 4.03. 12
daughter, | my wit untrain'd in any kind of art. 1H6 1.02. 73
kind keepers of my weak decaying age, | let 2.05. 1
just death, kind umpire of men's miseries, 2.05. 29
a prince, | so kind a father of the commonweal, 3.01. 98
o loving uncle, kind duke of gloucester, | how 3.01.142
and, lords, accept this hearty kind embrace. 3.03. 82
this argues what her kind of life hath been, 5.04. 15
no kinder sign of love | than this kind kiss. 2H6 1.01. 19
york, i commend this kind submission; 5.01. 54
he was lately sent | from your kind aunt, 3H6 2.01.146
"judgment" hath bred a kind of remorse in me. R3 1.04.108 P
o, do not slander him, for he is kind. 1.04.241
of my kind uncle, that i know will give, | and 3.01.113
your tenderness of heart | and gentle, kind, 3.07.211
but penetrable to your kind entreaties, | albeit 3.07.225
led in the hand of her kind aunt of gloucester? 4.01. 2
kind sister, thanks, we'll enter all together. 4.01. 11
kind tyrrel, am i happy in thy news? 4.03. 24
where is kind hastings? 4.04.148

mild, but yet more harmful — kind in hatred. 4.04.173
once more, good night, kind lords and gentlemen. 5.03.107
i take it, is a kind of puppy | to th' old dam, H8 1.01.175
in what kind, let's know, | is this exaction? 1.02. 53
what kind of my obedience i should tender. 2.03. 66
so give me up | to the sharp'st kind of justice. 2.04. 44
and 'tis a kind of good deed to say well, | and 3.02.153
if none of them have soul in such a kind, | we TRO 1.03.285
and underwrite in an observing kind | his 2.03.128
i have a kind of self resides with you; 3.02.148
alas, a kind of godly jealousy | (which i 4.04. 80
against that dog of as bad a kind, achilles; 5.04. 14 P
with a kind of smile, | which ne'er came from COR 1.01.107
so much were a kind of ingrateful injury; 2.02. 31 P
no, 'tis his kind of speech, he did not mock us. 2.03.161
this kind of service | did not deserve corn 3.01.124
this | so criminal, and in such capital kind, 3.03. 81
he had, sir, a kind of face, methought — i 4.05.155 P
o, he is grown most kind of late. 4.06. 11
farewell, kind neighbors! 4.06. 24
he was a kind of nothing, titleless, | till he 5.01. 13
unto me | as i am confident and kind to thee. TIT 1.01. 61
kind rome, that hast thus lovingly reserv'd 1.01.165
are, | fitted by kind for rape and villainy. 2.01.116
no, | nothing so kind, but something pitiful! 2.03.156
two of thy whelps, fell curs of bloody kind, 2.03.281
'cause they take vengeance of such kind of men. 5.02. 63
and wish his mistress were that kind of fruit ROM 2.01. 35
and from her womb children of divers kind | we 2.03. 11
it were a very gross kind of behavior, as they 2.04.166 P
an' a courteous, and a kind, and a handsome, 2.05. 56
fault our law calls death, but the kind prince, 3.03. 25
i do spy a kind of hope, | which craves as 4.01. 68
is rank'd with all deserts, all kind of natures, TIM 1.01. 65
welcome all, let 'em have kind admittance. 1.02.128
which was not half so beautiful and kind; 1.02.148
accept it and wear it, | kind my lord. 1.02.171
he is so kind that he now | pays interest for't; 1.02.199
and your several visitations | so kind to heart, 1.02.219
never mind | was to be so unwise, to be so kind. 2.02. 6
'tis lack of kindly warmth they are not kind; 2.02.217
of me, because i have no power to be kind. 3.02. 54 P
the like to you, kind varro. 3.04. 2
who then dares to be half so kind again? 4.02. 40
alas, kind lord, | he's flung in rage from this 4.02. 44
but in the plainer and simpler kind of people 5.01. 25
performance is a kind of will or testament 5.01. 28
why birds and beasts from quality and kind, JC 1.03. 64
hatch'd, would as his kind grow mischievous, 2.01. 33
do receive you in | with all kind love, good 3.01.176
kind souls, what weep you when you but behold 3.02.195
th' art kind. MAC 1.03. 12
kind gentlemen, your pains | are regist'red 1.03.150
by the name of most kind hostess, and shut up 2.01. 16
a kind good night to all! 3.04.120
a little more than kin, and less than kind. HAM 1.02. 65
and there is a kind of confession in your looks, 2.02.279 P
and there did seem in him a kind of joy | to 3.01. 18
and haply one as kind | for husband shalt thou 3.02.176
and that shall lend a kind of easiness | to the 3.04.166
i must be cruel, only to be kind. 3.04.178
and, like the kind life-rend'ring pelican, 4.05.147
dear maid, kind sister, sweet ophelia! 4.05.159
a kind of week or snuff that will abate it, 4.07.115
in my heart there was a kind of fighting | that 5.02. 4
habit of encounter, a kind of /yesty collection | 5.02.191 P
foolery, but it is such a kind of /gain-giving, 5.02.215 P
thought to set my rest | on her kind nursery. LR 1.01.124
i had rather be any kind o' thing than a fool, 1.04.186 P
who i am sure is kind and comfortable. 1.04.306
so kind a father! 1.05. 32 P
these kind of knaves i know, which in this 2.02.101
that bear bags | shall see their children kind. 2.04. 51
of them hath borne | against the old kind king; 3.01. 28
your old kind father, whose frank heart gave all 3.04. 20
by the kind gods, 'tis most ignobly done | to 3.07. 35
kind gods, forgive me that, and prosper him! 3.07. 92
thou hotly lusts to use her in that kind | for 4.06.162
o you kind gods! 4.07. 13
kind and dear princess! 4.07. 28
what kind of help? 5.03.223
true, | but i, for mere suspicion in that kind, OTH 1.03.389
she is of so free, so kind, so apt, so bless'd a 2.03.320 P
i never knew a florentine more kind and honest. 3.01. 40
there are a kind of men, so loose of soul, 3.03.416
one of this kind is cassio. 3.03.418
if my offense be of such mortal kind | that nor 3.04.115
all kind of sores and shames on my bare head, 4.02. 49
do abuse their husbands | in such gross kind? 4.03. 63
kind gentlemen, let's go see poor cassio dress'd 5.01.124
commend me to my kind lord. 5.02.125
they ear and wound | with keels of every kind. ANT 1.04. 50
the elements be kind to thee, and make | thy 3.02. 40
most kind messenger, | say to great caesar this 3.13. 73
this, look you, that the worm will do his kind. 5.02.263 P
farewell, kind charmian, iras, long farewell. 5.02.292
may be truly read, | what kind of man he is. CYM 1.01. 54
as good — a kind of hand-in-hand comparison — 1.04. 70 P
he hath a kind of honor sets him off, | more 1.06.170
a kind of conquest | caesar made here, but made 3.01. 22
but in a fainter kind — o, not like me, | for 3.02. 55
these are kind creatures. 4.02. 32
never master had | a page so kind, so duteous, 5.05. 86
to beg of you, kind friends, this coat of worth, PER 2.01.136
take off by treason's knife, | and in this kind: 4.ch. 15
assur'd | came of a gentle kind and noble stock, 5.01. 68
thy name, my most kind virgin? 5.01.140
bear 'em speedily | from our kind air, to them TNK 1.04. 38
farewell, kind window. 2.02.274
to you being enemy, | cannot to me be kind. 3.01. 50
none but arcite | in this kind is so bold. 3.01. 92
wish ye | as kind a kinsman as you force me find 3.06. 21
he's a kind gentleman, and i am much bound to 5.02. 44
she shall see deeds of honor in their kind 5.03. 12
but palamon's sadness is a kind of mirth, | so 5.03. 51
her kind of ill | gave me some sorrow. 5.04. 26
being therein train'd | and of kind manage; 5.04. 69
are sorry, still | are children in some kind. 5.04.134
beating his kind embracements with her heels. VEN 312
i felt a kind of fear | when as i met the boar, 998
not die | till mutual overthrow of mortal kind! 1018
there, | conceit deceitful, so compact, so kind, LUC 1423
bright things stain'd) a kind of heavy fear. 1435
be as thy presence is gracious and kind, | or to SON 10.11
their thoughts (although their eyes were kind) 69.11
cannot dispraise but in a kind of praise, 95. 7
kind is my love to-day, to-morrow kind, | still 105. 5
kind is my love to-day, to-morrow kind, | still 105. 5
"fair," "kind," and "true" is all my argument, 105. 9
"fair," "kind," and "true" varying to other 105.10
"fair," "kind," and "true" have often liv'd 105.13
found a kind of meetness | to be diseas'd ere 118. 7
free, | for thou art covetous, and he is kind; 134. 6
and play the mother's part, kiss me, be kind: 143.12
all kind of arguments and question deep, | all LC 121
be, | where neither party is nor true nor kind: 186
their kind acceptance weepingly beseech'd, 207
showing fair nature is both kind and tame; 311

KINDER 7 FR 0.0008 REL FR 7 V 0 P
the kinder we, to give them thanks for nothing. MND 5.01. 89
a kinder gentleman treads not the earth. MV 2.08. 35
i can express no kinder sign of love | than this 2H6 1.01. 18
he remember | a kinder value of the people than COR 2.02. 59
th' unkindest beast more kinder than mankind. TIM 4.01. 36
son | was kinder to his father than my daughters LR 4.06.115
grew kinder, and his fury was assuag'd. VEN 318

KINDEST 3 FR 0.0003 REL FR 3 V 0 P
the dearest friend to me, the kindest man, | the MV 3.02.292
o, the kindest kate! SHR 2.01.307
we do request your kindest ears, and after, COR 2.02. 52

KIND-HEARTED 1 FR 0.0001 REL FR 1 V 0 P
or to thyself at least kind-hearted prove: SON 10.12

KINDLE 11 FR 0.0012 REL FR 10 V 1 P
thou wouldst as soon go kindle fire with snow TGV 2.07. 19
remains but that i kindle the boy thither, which AYL 1.01.172 P
ever in fear to kindle your dislike, | yea, H8 2.04. 25
will be his fire | to kindle their dry stubble; COR 2.01.258
this is the way to kindle, not to quench. 3.01.196
do) bear fire enough | to kindle cowards, and to JC 2.01.121
my love should kindle to inflam'd respect. LR 1.01.255
heart | where mine his thoughts did kindle — ANT 5.01. 46
and yet the fire of life kindle again | the PER 3.02. 83
the knights must kindle | their valor at your TNK 5.03. 29
she seeks to kindle with continual kissing. VEN 606

KINDLED* 9 FR 0.0010 REL FR 8 V 1 P
a bloody fire, | kindled with unchaste desire, WIV 5.05. 96
cony that you see dwell where she is kindled. AYL 3.02.340 P
would not cease | till she had kindled france, JN 1.01. 33
you equal potents, fiery kindled spirits! 2.01.358
your breath first kindled the dead coal of wars 5.02. 83
soon kindled and soon burnt, carded his state, 1H4 3.02. 62
his kindled duty kindled her mistrust, | that LUC 1352
his kindled duty kindled her mistrust, | that 1352
thy eye kindled the fire that burneth here, 1475

KINDLESS 1 FR 0.0001 REL FR 1 V 0 P
treacherous, lecherous, kindless villain! HAM 2.02.581

KINDLIER 1 FR 0.0001 REL FR 1 V 0 P
as they, be kindlier mov'd than thou art? TMP 5.01. 24

KINDLING 2 FR 0.0002 REL FR 1 V 1 P
is kindling coals that fires all my breast, 3H6 2.01. 83
for kindling such a combustion in the state. H8 5.03. 49 P

KINDLY 39 FR 0.0044 REL FR 26 V 13 P
spends what he borrows kindly in your company. TGV 2.04. 39 P
i'll use thee kindly for thy mistress' sake 4.04.202
gentle and fair, your brother kindly greets you. MM 1.04. 24
by that fatherly and kindly power | that you ADO 4.01. 74
thou shalt find i will most kindly requite. AYL 1.01.138 P
age is as a lusty winter, | frosty, but kindly. 2.03. 53
tears our recountments had most kindly bath'd, 4.03.140
let him come, and kindly. SHR in.1. 15 P
this do, and do it kindly, gentle sirs; in.1. 66
that have been more kindly beholding to you than 2.01. 78 P
my mother greets me kindly. is she well? AWW 2.04. 1 P
we'll take your offer kindly. 3.05.101
olivia, and in my sight she uses thee kindly. TN 3.04.156 P
washing with kindly tears his gentle cheeks, 2H4 4.05. 83
gently to hear, kindly to judge, our play. H5 pr 34
that i may kindly give one fainting kiss. 1H6 2.05. 40
the bishop hath a kindly gird. 3.01.131
i take it kindly. 2H6 3.01.346
and pitied me, and kindly kiss'd my cheek; R3 2.02. 24
which with a bounteous hand was kindly lent; 2.02. 93
where he shall see the boar will use us kindly. 3.02. 33
why, this is kindly done. TRO 3.01. 96 P
nay, we must use expostulation kindly, | for it 4.04. 60
he us'd me kindly. COR 1.09. 83
the price is, to ask it kindly. 2.03. 75 P
kindly, sir, i pray let me ha't. 2.03. 76 P
and feed his humor kindly as we may, | till time TIT 4.03. 29
thou hast most kindly hit it. ROM 2.04. 55 P
'tis lack of kindly warmth they are not kind; TIM 2.02.217
you are kindly met, sir. 3.02. 27 P
that this great king may kindly say | our duties MAC 4.01.131
see thy other daughter will use thee kindly, for LR 1.05. 15 P
and kindly creatures | turn all to serpents! ANT 2.05. 78
how honorable and how kindly we | determine for 5.01. 58
thanks, good sir, | you're kindly welcome. CYM 1.06. 14
more virginal fencing, will you use him kindly? PER 4.06. 58 P
do | what he will with me, so he use me kindly, TNK 2.06. 29
faith, very little. love has us'd you kindly. 3.06. 67
quoth he, "she took me kindly by the hand, | and LUC 253

KINDNESS' 1 FR 0.0001 REL FR 1 V 0 P
last longer telling than thy kindness' date. R3 4.04.255

KINDNESS 58 FR 0.0065 REL FR 48 V 10 P
slave, | whom stripes may move, not kindness! TMP 1.02.345
for beauty lives with kindness. TGV 4.02. 45
sir, for your kindness, i owe you a good turn. MM 4.02. 58 P
her wealth's sake use her with more kindness: ERR 3.02. 6
a kind overflow of kindness. ADO 1.01. 26 P
my kindness shall incite thee | to bind our 3.01.113
this were kindness. MV 1.03.143
this kindness will i show. 1.03.143
and say there is much kindness in the jew. 1.03.153
but kindness, nobler ever than revenge, | and AYL 4.03.128
to express the like kindness, myself, that have SHR 2.01. 77 P
this is a way to kill a wife with kindness, 4.01.208
kindness in women, not their beauteous looks, 4.02. 41
sure, sweet kate, this kindness merits thanks. 4.03. 41
while i with self-same kindness welcome thine. 5.02. 5
padua affords this kindness, son petruchio. 5.02. 13
my bosom is full of kindness, and i am yet so TN 2.01. 39 P
for the fair kindness you have show'd me here, 3.04.342
he did me kindness, sir, drew on my side, | but 5.01. 66
him | 'twixt his unkindness and his kindness: WT 4.04.552
more benefit and grac'd | your kindness better. 5.01. 23
he is as full of valor as of kindness, H5 4.03. 15
yet hath a woman's kindness overrul'd; 1H6 2.02. 50
and i may live to do you kindness if | you do it 2H6 2.04. 83
i come, in kindness and unfeigned love, | first, 3H6 3.03. 51
yet shall you have all kindness at my hand 3.03.149
be thou sure, i'll well requite thy kindness, 4.06. 10
if fortune serve me, i'll requite this kindness. 4.07. 78
and look to have it yielded with all kindness. R3 3.01.198
tut, thou art all ice, thy kindness freezes. 4.02. 22
lest that the process of thy kindness | last 4.04.254
therefore accept such kindness as i can. 4.04.310
yet is the kindness but particular, | 'twere TRO 4.05. 20
you know the very road into his kindness, | and COR 5.01. 59
do them that kindness, and take leave of them. TIT 5.03.171
he outgoes | the very heart of kindness. TIM 1.01.275
is not thy kindness subtle, covetous, | if not a 4.03.508
if not a usuring kindness, and, as rich men deal 4.03.509
uncertain voyage, i will some kindness do them: 5.01.202
keep this man safe, | give him all kindness; JC 5.04. 28
it is too full o' th' milk of human kindness MAC 1.05. 17
a great abatement of kindness appears as well in LR 1.04. 60 P
her brother that, in pure kindness to his horse, 2.04.126 P
the gods reward your kindness! 3.06. 5 P
in the sincerity of love and honest kindness. OTH 2.03.328 P
a conqueror that will pray in aid for kindness ANT 5.02. 27
you o'errate my poor kindness, i was glad i did CYM 1.04. 38 P
equal discourtesy | to your best kindness; 2.03. 97
which labor | i found that kindness in a father. PER 1.01. 67
't 'ad been a kindness | becoming well thy /fact 4.03. 11
find | it greets me as an enterprise of kindness 4.03. 38
and do me the kindness of our profession, she 4.06. 6 P
but since your kindness | we have stretch'd thus 5.01. 54
give me, | for such kindness must relieve me: 5.02. 4
your present kindness | makes my past miseries 5.03. 40
but take heed to your kindness though! TNK 2.02.125
shame, | nor thou with public kindness honor me, SON 36.11
i have sworn deep oaths of thy deep kindness, 152. 9

KINDNESSES 4 FR 0.0004 REL FR 2 V 2 P
some other give me thanks for kindnesses; ERR 4.03. 5
as to upbraid you with those kindnesses | that i TN 3.04.351
i have receiv'd some small kindnesses from him, TIM 3.02. 21 P
to whose kindnesses i am most infinitely tied. CYM 1.06. 23 P

KINDRED *(also kinred, etc.)*

KINDRED 26 FR 0.0029 REL FR 19 V 7 P
in good sooth, the vice is of a great kindred; MM 3.02.102 P
i promise you your kindred hath made my eyes MND 3.01.194 P
good breeding or comes of a very dull kindred. AYL 3.02. 31 P
comes it that your kindred shuns your house, SHR in.2. 28
an old mothy saddle and stirrups of no kindred; 3.02. 49 P
the kings and the princes, our kindred, are WT 5.02.173 P
or heard | of any kindred action like to this? JN 3.04. 14
no more oppos'd | against acquaintance, kindred, 1H4 1.01. 16
the kindred of him hath been flesh'd upon us; H5 2.04. 50
is no man /is secure | but the queen's kindred, R3 1.01. 72
and that the queen's kindred are made 1.01. 95
not | how that the guilty kindred of the queen 2.01.136
how can we aid you with our kindred tears? 2.02. 63
part the queen's proud kindred from the prince. 2.02.150
the kindred of the queen, must die at pomfret. 3.02. 50
which we have noted in you to your kindred | and 3.07.212
cozen'd | of comfort, kingdom, kindred, freedom, 4.04.224
no friends, no hope, no kindred weep for me, H8 3.01.150
our kindred, though they be long ere they be TRO 3.02.110 P
where all the kindred of the capulets lie. ROM 4.01.112
and the spots of thy kindred were jurors on thy TIM 4.03.341 P
raise all my kindred. OTH 1.01.167
with other spritely shows | of mine own kindred. CYM 5.05.429
thus much for law or kindred! TNK 2.04. 32
push your name, your ancient love, our kindred, 5.01. 26
of wealth, of filial fear, law, kindred, fame! LC 270

KINDRED'S 2 FR 0.0002 REL FR 2 V 0 P
i saw her laid low in her kindred's vault, | and ROM 5.01. 20
came i to take her from her kindred's vault, 5.03.254

KINDREDS 1 FR 0.0001 REL FR 1 V 0 P
where are our friends and kindreds? TNK 2.02. 8

KINDS 8 FR 0.0009 REL FR 8 V 0 P
some kinds of baseness | are nobly undergone; TMP 3.01. 2
ministers | their several kinds have done. 3.03. 88
two of both kinds makes up four. MND 3.02.438
lilies of all kinds, | the flow'r-de-luce being WT 4.04.126
did begin | as if you met decays of many kinds. TNK 1.02. 29
stern, sad tunes to change their kinds; LUC 1147
th' impression of strange kinds | is form'd in 1242
all frailties that besiege all kinds of blood, SON 109.10

KIND'ST 1 FR 0.0001 REL FR 1 V 0 P
at your kind'st leisure. MAC 2.01. 24

KINE 1 FR 0.0001 REL FR 0 V 1 P
then pharaoh's /lean kine are to be lov'd. 1H4 2.04.473 P

/KING 37 FR 0.0041 REL FR 32 V 5 P
so thou mayst say, the /king lies by a beggar, TN 3.01. 8 P
/why /am /i /sent /for /to /a /king | /before /i R2 4.01.162
/god /save /the /king! 4.01.172
/god /save /the /king! 4.01.174
/still /am /i /king /of /those. 4.01.193
/god /save /king /henry, /unking'd /richard 4.01.220
/containing /the /deposing /of /a /king, | /and 4.01.234
/t' /undeck /the /pompous /body /of /a /king; 4.01.250
/o, /that /i /were /a /mockery /king /of /snow, 4.01.260
/good /king, /great /king, /and /yet /not 4.01.263
/good /king, /great /king, /and /yet /not 4.01.263
/mark, /silent /king, /the /moral /of /this 4.01.290
/and /i /thank /thee, /king, | /for /thy /great 4.01.299
/i /am /greater /than /a /king; 4.01.305
/for /when /i /was /a /king /my /flatterers 4.01.306
/i /have /a /king /here /to /my /flatterer. 4.01.308
/with /the /blood | /of /fair /king /richard, 2H4 1.01.205
/now, "/o /earth, /yield /us /that /king /again, 1.03.106
/of /which /disease | /our /late /king /richard 4.01. 58
/long /ere /this /we /offer'd /to /the /king, 4.01. 75

/and /not /the /king, /that /doth /you /injuries 4.01.104
/either /from /the /king /or /in /the /present 4.01.106
/the /king /that /lov'd /him, /as /the /state 4.01.113
/when /the /king /did /throw /his /warder /down 4.01.123
/grac'd /and /did, /more /than /the /king — 4.01.137
/count /myself /a /king /of /infinite /space — HAM 2.02.255 P
/and /maledictions /against /king /and /nobles, LR 1.02.147 P
/and /the /good /king /his /master | /will 2.02.141
/sorrow | /the /king /hath /cause /to /plain. 3.01. 39
/she /kick'd /the /poor /king /her /father. 3.06. 48 P
/which /makes /me /bend /makes /the /king /bow: 3.06.109
/hap /more //to–night, /safe /scape /the /king! 3.06.114
/why /the /king /of /france /is /so /suddenly 4.03. 1 P
/sought /to /be /king /o'er /her. 4.03. 15
/was /this /before /the /king /return'd? 4.03. 37
/not /bolds /the /king, /with /others /whom, /i 5.01. 26
/in /disguise | /followed /his /enemy /king, 5.03.221

KING 1338 FR 0.1512 REL FR 1140 V 198 P

what cares these roarers for the name of king? TMP 1.01. 17 P
the king and prince at prayers! 1.01. 54
let's all sink wi' th' king. 1.01. 63
wi' th' king of naples | to give him annual 1.02.112
this king of naples, being an enemy | to me 1.02.121
that you have, | which first was mine own king; 1.02.342
weeping again the king my father's wrack, | this 1.02.391
wert thou, if the king of naples heard thee? 1.02.432
at ebb) beheld | the king my father wrack'd. 1.02.437
fair daughter claribel to the king of tunis. 2.01. 71 P
and were the king on't, what would i do? 2.01.146
yet he would be king on't. 2.01.157
professes to persuade) the king his son's alive, 2.01.236
thou payest, | and i the king shall love thee. 2.01.294
now, good angels | preserve the king! 2.01.307
so, king, go safely on to seek thy son. 2.01.327
the king and all our company else being drown'd, 2.02.174 P
i do think, a king | (i would, not so!), 3.01. 60
his daughter and i will be king and queen — 3.02.107 P
prithee, my king, be quiet. 4.01.215
o king stephano! 4.01.222 P
o king stephano! 4.01.226 P
go unrewarded while i am king of this country. 4.01.242 P
spirit, | how fares the king and 's followers? 5.01. 7
the king, | his brother, and yours, abide all 5.01. 11
would here have kill'd your king, i do forgive 5.01. 78
behold, sir king, | the wronged duke of milan, 5.01.106
both in naples, | the king and queen there! 5.01.150
we have safely found | our king and company; 5.01.222
you'ld be king o' the isle, sirrah? 5.01.288 P
while i, their king, that thither them importune TGV 3.01.145
this fellow were a king for our wild faction! 4.01. 37
thee, | love thee as our commander and our king. 4.01. 65
shallow, you'll complain of me to the king? WIV 1.01.110 P
not to composition with the king of hungary, why MM 1.02. 2 P
why then all the dukes fall upon the king. 1.02. 3 P
us its peace, but not the king of hungary's! 1.02. 5 P
the general subject to a well–wish'd king | quit 2.04. 27
what king so strong | can tie the gall up in the 3.02.187
if i were as tedious as a king, i could find in ADO 3.05. 21 P
not a ballet, boy, of the king and the beggar? LLL 1.02.109 P
consider who the king your father sends, | to 2.01. 2
tell him, the daughter of the king of france, 2.01. 30
if then the king your father will restore | but 2.01.137
you do the king my father too much wrong, | and 2.01.153
dread prince of plackets, king of codpieces, 3.01.184
was that the king that spurr'd his horse so hard 4.01. 1
and most illustrate king cophetua set eye upon 4.01. 65 P
the king. 4.01. 71 P
i am the king, for so stands the comparison; 4.01. 78 P
that was a man when king pippen of france was a 4.01.120 P
berowne is one of the votaries with the king, 4.02.137 P
this paper into the royal hand of the king; 4.02.142 P
the king he is hunting the deer: 4.03. 1 P
o, would the king, berowne, and longaville, 4.03.121
you found his mote, the king your mote did see; 4.03.159
i sat, | to see a king transformed to a gnat! 4.03.164
god bless the king! 4.03.187
sir, the king is a noble gentleman, and my 5.01. 95 P
that the king would have me present the princess 5.01.110 P
look you what i have from the loving king. 5.02. 4
behold address'd | the king and his companions. 5.02. 93
"for," quoth the king, "an angel shalt thou see; 5.02.103
and then the king will court thee for his dear. 5.02.131
the king was weeping–ripe for a good word. 5.02.274
the king is my love sworn. 5.02.282
the king, your father — 5.02.719
and by these badges understand the king. 5.02.754
come when the king doth to my lady come; 5.02.829
the king doth keep his revels here to–night; MND 2.01. 18
hath | a lovely boy stolen from an indian king; 2.01. 22
believe me, king of shadows, i mistook. 3.02.347
fairy king, attend and mark; 4.01. 93
as from her lord, her governor, her king. MV 3.02.165
a substitute shines brightly as a king | until a 5.01. 94
shines brightly as a king | until a king be by, 5.01. 95
that would i, were i of all kingdoms king. AYL 5.04. 10
to wound thy lord, thy king, thy governor. SHR 5.02.138
you shall find of the king a husband, madam; AWW 1.01. 6 P
the king very lately spoke of him admiringly and 1.01. 28 P
is it, my good lord, the king languishes of? 1.01. 32 P
done, done fond, | was this king priam's joy?" 1.03. 73
whereof | the king is render'd lost. 1.03.230
else paris, and the medicine, and the king, 1.03.233
stay the king. 2.01. 49 P
touch | is powerful to araise king pippen, nay, 2.01. 76
to be made than alone the recov'ry of the king, 2.03. 36 P
here comes the king. 2.03. 40 P
hath through me restor'd the king to health. 2.03. 64
base, is now | the praised of the king, who, so 2.03.172
good fortune and the favor of the king | smile 2.03.177
write to the king | that which i durst not speak 2.03.288
the king has done you wrong; 2.03.300
you will take your instant leave a' th' king, 2.04. 48
is she gone to the king? 2.05. 20 P
spoke with the king, and have procur'd his leave 2.05. 55
she hath recover'd the king, and undone me. 3.02. 20 P
boy, | to fly the favors of so good a king, | to 3.02. 29
for the king had married him | against his 3.05. 53
the everlasting displeasure of the king, who had 4.03. 9 P
him letters of commendations to the king. 4.03. 79 P
and by the leave of my good lord the king, 4.04. 13
at home, more advanc'd by the king than by that 4.05. 6 P
home, i mov'd the king my master to speak in the 4.05. 71 P
you | to give this poor petition to the king, 5.01. 19
since you are like to see the king before me, 5.01. 30
grant it me, o king, in you it best lies; 5.03.145 P
great king, i am no strumpet, by my life; 5.03.292
her sweet perfections with one self king! TN 1.01. 38
very wittily said to a niece of king gorboduc, 4.02. 14 P
the king of sicilia means to pay bohemia the WT 1.01. 5 P
if the king had no son, they would desire to 1.01. 45 P
the king hath on him such a countenance | as he 1.02.368
by the king. 1.02.413
these dangerous, unsafe lunes i' th' king, 2.02. 28
i'll show't the king, and undertake to be | her 2.02. 36
not a party to | the anger of the king, nor 2.02. 60
for the harlot king | is quite beyond mine arm, 2.03. 4
the daughter of a king, our wife, and one | of 3.02. 3
queen to the worthy leontes, king of sicilia, 3.02. 13 P
adultery with polixenes, king of bohemia, and 3.02. 15 P
away the life of our sovereign lord the king, 3.02. 17 P
and the king shall live without an heir, if that 3.02.134 P
my lord the king! the king! 3.02.142
my lord the king! the king! 3.02.142
to have him kill a king — poor trespasses, 3.02.189
being indeed the issue | of king polixenes) it 3.03. 44
besides, the penitent king, my master, hath sent 4.02. 7 P
(as thou call'st him) and reconcil'd king, my 4.02. 23 P
edge, | for a quart of ale is a dish for a king. 4.03. 8
(as it must be) by th' pow'r of the king. 4.04. 37
own report, sir, hath danc'd before the king; 4.04.338 P
again of dear sicilia | and that unhappy king, 4.04.512
if you may please to think i love the king | and 4.04.521
sent by the king your father | to greet him and 4.04.556
and those that you'll procure from king leontes? 4.04.621
what i do next shall be to tell the king | of 4.04.662
a piece of honesty to acquaint the king withal, 4.04.680 P
way but to tell the king she's a changeling, and 4.04.688 P
your flesh and blood has not offended the king, 4.04.694 P
i will tell the king all, every word, yea, and 4.04.699 P
let us to the king. 4.04.707 P
my business, sir, is to the king. 4.04.739 P
which none must know but the king, and which he 4.04.757 P
the king is not at the palace. 4.04.762 P
thou must know the king is full of grief. 4.04.765 P
be honest plain men) what you have to the king. 4.04.794 P
be in man besides the king to effect your suits, 4.04.798 P
we must to the king, and show our strange sights 4.04.819 P
they have to the king concerns him nothing, let 4.04.838 P
that king leontes shall not have an heir | till 5.01. 39
from him | give you all greetings that a king, 5.01.140
he's with the king your father. 5.01.196
my lord, | is this the daughter of a king? 5.01.208
i perceiv'd in the king and camillo were very 5.02. 10 P
has the king found his heir? 5.02. 29 P
our king, being ready to leap out of himself for 5.02. 49 P
to't bravely confess'd and lamented by the king) 5.02. 86 P
and son unto the king, whom heavens directing, 5.03.150
speaks the king of france | in my behavior to JN 1.01. 2
most certain of one mother, mighty king — 1.01. 59
th' advantage of his absence took the king, 1.01.102
king richard cordelion was thy father. 1.01.253
corner of the west | salute thee for her king; 2.01. 30
that thou hast under–wrought his lawful king, 2.01. 95
how comes it then that thou art call'd a king, 2.01.107
thy bastard shall be king | that thou mayst be a 2.01.122
king /philip, determine what we shall do 2.01.149
king john, this is the very sum of all: 2.01.151
but on the sight of us, your lawful king, | who 2.01.222
and let us in — your king, whose labor'd 2.01.232
man, | and king o'er him and all that he enjoys. 2.01.240
in brief, we are the king of england's subjects: 2.01.267
acknowledge then the king, and let me in. 2.01.269
but he that proves the king, | to him will we 2.01.270
doth not the crown of england prove the king? 2.01.273
fleet | in dreadful trial of our kingdom's king! 2.01.286
arthur of britain england's king and yours. 2.01.311
king john, your king and england's, doth 2.01.313
king john, your king and england's, doth 2.01.313
speak, citizens, for england. who's your king? 2.01.362
the king of england, when we know the king. 2.01.363
the king of england, when we know the king. 2.01.363
be by some certain king purg'd and depos'd. 2.01.372
then after fight who shall be king of it? 2.01.400
and if thou hast the mettle of a king, | being 2.01.401
france is a bawd to fortune and king john, 3.01. 60
to thee, king john, my holy errand is: 3.01.137
can taste the free breath of a sacred king? 3.01.148
king philip, listen to the cardinal. 3.01.198
the king is mov'd, and answers not to this. 3.01.217
do so, king philip, hang no more in doubt. 3.01.219
strange to think how much king john hath lost 3.04.121
o noble dolphin, | go with me to the king. 3.04.178
i will whet on the king. 3.04.181
if you say ay, the king will not say no. 3.04.183
the color of the king doth come and go | between 4.02. 76
and thou, to be endeared to a king, | made it no 4.02.228
the king by me requests your presence straight. 4.03. 22
the king hath dispossess'd himself of us. 4.03. 23
the practice and the purpose of the king; 4.03. 63
arthur doth live, the king hath sent for you. 4.03. 75
there, tell the king, he may inquire us out. 4.03.115
i'll to the king. 4.03.157
king john hath reconcil'd | himself to rome, his 5.02. 69
from the king | i come to learn how you have 5.02.120
now hear our english king, | for thus his 5.02.128
the king doth smile at, and is well prepar'd 5.02.134
i did not think the king so stor'd with friends. 5.04. 1
they say king john, sore sick, hath left the 5.04. 6
seek out king john and fall before his feet; 5.04. 13
commend me to one hubert with your king; 5.04. 40
even to our ocean, to our great king john. 5.04. 57
said | king john did fly an hour or two before 5.05. 17
the king, i fear, is poison'd by a monk. 5.06. 23
the king | yet speaks, and peradventure may 5.06. 30
at whose request the king hath pardon'd them, 5.06. 35
conduct me to the king; 5.06. 43
but now a king, now thus. 5.07. 66
when this was now a king, and now is clay? 5.07. 69
gage, | disclaiming here the kinred of the king, R2 1.01. 70
defend my loyalty and truth | to god, my king, 1.03. 20
a traitor to my god, my king, and me — | and as 1.03. 24
hither | before king richard in his royal lists? 1.03. 32
to god of heaven, king richard, and to me — 1.03. 40
lives or dies, true to king richard's throne, 1.03. 86
a traitor to his god, his king, and him, | and 1.03.108
stay, the king hath thrown his warder down. 1.03.118
by this time, had the king permitted us, | one 1.03.194
and all too soon, i fear, the king shall rue. 1.03.205
but not a minute, king, that thou canst give. 1.03.226
think not the king did banish thee, | but thou 1.03.279
the king did banish thee, | but thou the king. 1.03.280
purchase honor, | and not the king exil'd thee; 1.03.283
will the king come, that i may breathe my last 2.01. 1
the king is come. 2.01. 69
i mock my name, great king, to flatter thee. 2.01. 87
landlord of england art thou now, not king, 2.01.113
for how art thou a king | but by fair sequence 2.01.198
the king is not himself, but basely led | by 2.01.241
that will the king severely prosecute | 'gainst 2.01.244
his noble kinsman — most degenerate king! 2.01.262
the first departing of the king for ireland. 2.01.290
you promis'd, when you parted with the king, 2.02. 2
to please the king i did, to please myself | i 2.02. 5
more than with parting from my lord the king. 2.02. 13
i hope the king is not yet shipp'd for ireland. 2.02. 42
the king had cut off my head with my brother's. 2.02.102
is my kinsman, whom the king hath wrong'd, 2.02.114
our nearness to the king in love | is near the 2.02.127
is near the hate of those love not the king. 2.02.128
wherein the king stands generally condemn'd. 2.02.132
we, | because we ever have been near the king. 2.02.134
and dispers'd | the household of the king. 2.03. 28
com'st thou because the anointed king is hence? 2.03. 96
why, foolish boy, the king is left behind, | and 2.03. 97
if that my cousin king be king in england, | it 2.03.123
if that my cousin king be king in england, | it 2.03.123
stoop | unto the sovereign mercy of the king; 2.03.157
and yet we hear no tidings from the king, 2.04. 3
the king reposeth all his confidence in thee. 2.04. 6
'tis thought the king is dead; 2.04. 7
as well assured richard their king is dead. 2.04. 17
you have misled a prince, a royal king, | a 3.01. 8
near to the king in blood, and near in love 3.01. 17
ere her native king | shall falter under foul 3.02. 25
that power that made you king | hath power to 3.02. 27
hath power to keep you king in spite of all. 3.02. 28
can wash the balm off from an anointed king; 3.02. 55
i had forgot myself, am i not king? 3.02. 83
ye favorites of a king, are we not high? 3.02. 88
that rounds the mortal temples of a king | keeps 3.02.161
thorough his castle wall, and farewell king! 3.02.170
thus, | how can you say to me i am a king? 3.02.177
a king, woe's slave, shall kingly woe obey. 3.02.210
and salisbury | is gone to meet the king, who 3.03. 3
the lord northumberland | to say king richard. 3.03. 8
when such a sacred king should hide his head! 3.03. 9
royally! | why, it contains no king? 3.03. 24
yes, my good lord, | it doth contain a king. 3.03. 25
king richard lies | within the limits of yon 3.03. 25
on both his knees doth kiss king richard's hand, 3.03. 36
the fresh green lap of fair king richard's land, 3.03. 47
methinks king richard and myself should meet 3.03. 54
march on, and mark king richard how he looks. 3.03. 61
see, see, king richard doth himself appear, | as 3.03. 62
yet looks he like a king! 3.03. 68
because we thought ourself thy lawful king; 3.03. 74
the king of heaven forbid our lord the king 3.03.101
the king of heaven forbid our lord the king 3.03.101
northumberland, say thus the king returns: 3.03.121
what must the king do now? 3.03.143
the king shall do it. 3.03.144
the king shall be contented. 3.03.145
must he lose | the name of king? 3.03.146
northumberland, what says king bullingbrook? 3.03.173
down king! 3.03.182
bullingbrook | hath seiz'd the wasteful king. 3.04. 55
what, think you the king shall be deposed? 3.04. 67
why dost thou say king richard is depos'd? 3.04. 77
king richard, he is in the mighty hold | of 3.04. 83
and with that odds he weighs king richard down. 3.04. 89
meet at london london's king in woe. 3.04. 97
who wrought it with the king, and who perform'd 4.01. 4
what subject can give sentence on his king? 4.01.121
stirr'd up by god, thus boldly for his king. 4.01.133
my lord of herford here, whom you call king, 4.01.134
is a foul traitor to proud herford's king, | and 4.01.135
this way the king will come, this is the way 5.01. 1
thou map of honor, thou king richard's tomb, 5.01. 12
king richard's tomb, | and not king richard; 5.01. 13
which art a lion and the king of beasts? 5.01. 34
a king of beasts indeed — if aught but beasts, 5.01. 35
beasts, | i had been still a happy king of men. 5.01. 36
for the deposing of a rightful king. 5.01. 50
banish us both, and send the king with me. 5.01. 83
threw dust and rubbish on king richard's head. 5.02. 6
truth | and lasting fealty to the new–made king. 5.02. 45
bring me my boots, i will unto the king. 5.02. 84
down their hands, | to kill the king at oxford. 5.02. 99
spur post, and get before him to the king, | and 5.02.112
where is the king? 5.03. 23
open the door, secure, foolhardy king! 5.03. 43
i tore it from the traitor's bosom, king; 5.03. 55
a woman, and thy aunt, great king, 'tis i. 5.03. 76
and now chang'd to "the beggar and the king." 5.03. 80
o king, believe not this hard–hearted man! 5.03. 87
say "pardon," king, let pity teach thee how. 5.03.116
speak it in french, king, say "pardonne moy." 5.03.119
didst thou not mark the king, what words he 5.04. 1
from my heart" — | meaning the king at pomfret. 5.04. 10
sometimes am i king; 5.05. 32
penury | persuades me i was better when a king; 5.05. 35
i was a poor groom of thy stable, king, | when 5.05. 72
of thy stable, king, | when thou wert king; 5.05. 73
who | lately came from the king, commands the 5.05.101

this dead king to the living king i'll bear; 5.05.117
this dead king to the living king i'll bear; 5.05.117
great king, within this coffin i present | thy 5.06. 30
1H4 i prithee, sweet wag, when thou art a king, as, 1.02. 17 P
sweet wag, when thou art king, let not us that 1.02. 23 P
gallows standing in england when thou art king? 1.02. 60 P
do not thou, when thou art king, hang a thief. 1.02. 62 P
i'll be a traitor then, when thou art king. 1.02.147 P
as high in the air as this unthankful king, | as 1.03.136
brother, the king hath made your nephew mad. 1.03.138
and then it was when the unhappy king | (whose 1.03.148
you, did king richard then | proclaim my brother 1.03.155
nay, then i cannot blame his cousin king, | that 1.03.158
wherein you range under this subtile king! 1.03.169
and disdain'd contempt | of this proud king, who 1.03.184
first bow'd my knee | unto this king of smiles, 1.03.246
the king will always think him in our debt, 1.03.286
there is ne'er a king christen could be better 2.01. 17 P
of fear and cold heart will he to the king, and 2.03. 31 P
let him tell the king: 2.03. 34 P
prince of wales, yet i am the king of courtesy, 2.04. 10 P
and when i am king of england i shall command 2.04. 13 P
and i will do it in king cambyses' vein. 2.04.387 P
dost thou speak like a king? 2.04.433 P
even in the presence of the crowned king. 3.02. 54
the skipping king, he ambled up and down, | with 3.02. 60
the king himself is to be fear'd as the lion. 3.03.149 P
thou art the king of honor. 4.01. 10
because the king is certainly possess'd | of all 4.01. 40
the king himself in person is set forth, | or 4.01. 91
the king, i can tell you, looks for us all, we 4.02. 56 P
what, is the king encamp'd? 4.02. 76 P
the number of the king exceedeth our. 4.03. 28
i come with gracious offers from the king, | if 4.03. 30
the king hath sent to know | the nature of your 4.03. 41
if that the king | have any way your good 4.03. 45
the king is kind, and well we know the king 4.03. 52
and well we know the king | knows at what time 4.03. 52
of all the favorites that the absent king | in 4.03. 86
in short time after, he depos'd the king, | soon 4.03. 90
indeed his king) to be engag'd in wales, | there 4.03. 95
shall i return this answer to the king? 4.03.106
go to the king, and let there be impawn'd | some 4.03.108
the king with mighty and quick–raised power 4.04. 12
weak | to wage an instant trial with the king. 4.04. 20
but yet the king hath drawn | the special head 4.04. 27
ere the king | dismiss his power he means to 4.04. 36
what with our help, what with the absent king, 5.01. 49
and the contrarious winds that held the king 5.01. 52
the liberal and kind offer of the king. 5.02. 2
the king should keep his word in loving us. 5.02. 5
know, | in any case, the offer of the king. 5.02. 25
the king will bid you battle presently. 5.02. 30
there is no seeming mercy in the king. 5.02. 34
thrown | a brave defiance in king henry's teeth, 5.02. 42
prince of wales stepp'd forth before the king, 5.02. 45
my lord, prepare, the king comes on apace. 5.02. 89
because some tell me that thou art a king. 5.03. 5
thy likeness, for in stead of thee, king harry, 5.03. 8
and thou shalt find a king that will revenge 5.03. 12
done, all's won, here breathless lies the king. 5.03. 16
semblably furnish'd like the king himself. 5.03. 21
why didst thou tell me that thou wert a king? 5.03. 24
the king hath many marching in his coats. 5.03. 25
piece by piece, | until i meet the king. 5.03. 28
another king? 5.04. 25
thou | that counterfeit'st the person of a king? 5.04. 28
the king himself, who, douglas, grieves at heart 5.04. 29
shadows thou hast met | and not the very king. 5.04. 31
yet, in faith, thou bearest thee like a king. 5.04. 36
2H4 i run before king harry's victory, | who in a in 23
and that the king before the douglas' rage in 31
the king is almost wounded to the death, | and, 1.01. 14
three times slain th' appearance of the king, 1.01.128
the sum of all | is that the king hath won, and 1.01.132
doth not the king lack subjects? 1.02. 74 P
well, the king hath sever'd you. 1.02.203 P
upon the power and puissance of the king. 1.03. 9
even as we are, to equal with the king. 1.03. 67
what, is the king but five and twenty thousand? 1.03. 68
so is the unfirm king | in three divided, and 1.03. 73
the king, my lord, and harry prince of wales 2.01.134
where lay the king to–night? 2.01.168
comes the king back from wales, my noble lord? 2.01.176 P
even like those that are kin to the king, for 2.02.112 P
to the son of the king nearest his father, harry 2.02.119 P
if they get ground and vantage of the king, 2.03. 53
"and was a worthy king." 2.04. 35 P
rather damn them with | king cerberus, and let 2.04.168
the king your father is at westminster, | and 2.04.355
and means to boot, | deny it to a king? 3.01. 30
this | king richard might create a perfect guess 3.01. 88
wherein have you been galled by the king? 4.01. 89
shall to the king taste of this action, | that, 4.01.190
the king is weary | of dainty and such picking 4.01.195
the king hath wasted all his rods | on late 4.01.213
would he abuse the countenance of the king, 4.02. 13
lords, | i hear the king my father is sore sick. 4.03. 77
speak lower, princes, for the king recovers. 4.04.129
how doth the king? 4.05. 10
the king your father is dispos'd to sleep. 4.05. 17
no, i will sit and watch here by the king. 4.05. 20
doth the king call? 4.05. 48
how doth the king? 5.02. 2
indeed i think the young king loves you not. 5.02. 9
me, | i'll to the king my master that is dead, 5.02. 40
the image of the king whom i presented, | and 5.02. 79
and, as you are a king, speak in your state 5.02. 99
why, there spoke a king. 5.03. 69 P
let king cophetua know the truth thereof. 5.03.102
i am, sir, under the king, in some authority. 5.03.112 P
under which king, besonian? speak, or die. 5.03.113
under king harry. 5.03.114
sir john, thy tender lambkin now is king; 5.03.116
what, is the old king dead? 5.03.120 P
i know the young king is sick for me. 5.03.135 P
shallow, i will make the king do you grace. 5.05. 6 P
god save thy grace, king hal! my royal hal! 5.05. 41
my king! my jove! i speak to thee, my heart! 5.05. 46
the king hath call'd his parliament, my lord. 5.05.103
whose music, to my thinking, pleas'd the king. 5.05.108
H5 and to the coffers of the king beside, | a 1.01. 18
the king is full of grace and fair regard. 1.01. 22
his seat (and all at once) | as in this king. 1.01. 37
you would desire the king were made a prelate; 1.01. 40
years | after defunction of king pharamond, 1.02. 58
king pepin, which deposed childeric, | did, as 1.02. 65
blithild, which was daughter to king clothair, 1.02. 67
also, king lewis the tenth, | who was sole heir 1.02. 77
king pepin's title and hugh capet's claim, 1.02. 87
king lewis his satisfaction, all appear | to 1.02. 88
never king of england | had nobles richer and 1.02.126
and impounded as a stray | the king of scots; 1.02.161
to fill king edward's fame with prisoner kings, 1.02.162
they have a king, and officers of sorts, | where 1.02.190
your greeting is from him, not from the king. 1.02.236
we are no tyrant, but a christian king, | unto 1.02.241
your great predecessor, king edward the third. 1.02.248
be like a king, and show my sail of greatness 1.02.274
the king is set from london, and the scene | is 2.pr. 34
but till the king come forth, and not till then, 2.pr. 41
the king has kill'd his heart. 2.01. 88 P
the king hath run bad humors on the knight, 2.01.121 P
the king is a good king, but it must be as it 2.01.125 P
the king is a good king, but it must be as it 2.01.125 P
the king hath note of all that they intend, | by 2.02. 6
you would have sold your king to slaughter, 2.02.170
no king of england, if not king of france! 2.02.193
no king of england, if not king of france! 2.02.193
the king will be gone from southampton. 2.03. 45 P
you are too much mistaken in this king. 2.04. 30
think we king harry strong; 2.04. 48
embassadors from harry king of england | do 2.04. 65
thus says my king: 2.04.120
speed, lest that our king | come here himself to 2.04.141
seen | the well–appointed king at /hampton pier 3.pr. 4
back, | tells harry that the king doth offer him 3.pr. 29
and the wars, and the king, and the dukes; 3.02.107 P
therefore, great king, | we yield our town and 3.03. 47
hark you, the king is coming, and i must speak 3.06. 85 P
thus says my king: 3.06.118 P
so far my king and master; 3.06.136 P
back, | and tell thy king i do not seek him now, 3.06.140
and peevish fellow is this king of england, to 3.07.133 P
since i may say, "now lie i like a king." 4.01. 17
then you are a better than the king. 4.01. 43 P
he hath not told his thought to the king? 4.01. 99 P
speak it to you, i think the king is but a man, 4.01.101 P
troth, i will speak my conscience of the king: 4.01.119 P
our obedience to the king wipes the crime of it 4.01.132 P
the king himself hath a heavy reckoning to make, 4.01.134 P
a black matter for the king that led them to it; 4.01.145 P
the king is not bound to answer the particular 4.01.155 P
besides, there is no king, be his cause never so 4.01.159 P
no more is the king guilty of their damnation 4.01.174 P
upon his own head, the king is not to answer it. 4.01.187 P
i myself heard the king say he would not be 4.01.190 P
and to–morrow the king himself will be a clipper 4.01.228 P
upon the king! 4.01.230
our children, and our sins lay on the king! 4.01.232
i am a king that find thee; 4.01.259
the farced title running 'fore the king, | the 4.01.263
sleep, | had the forehand and vantage of a king. 4.01.280
what watch the king keeps to maintain the peace, 4.01.283
where is the king? 4.03. 1
the king himself is rode to view their battle. 4.03. 2
harry the king, bedford and exeter, | warwick 4.03. 53
once more i come to know of thee, king harry, 4.03. 79
i shall, king harry. 4.03.126
is this the king we sent to for his ransom? 4.05. 9
wherefore the king, most worthily, hath caus'd 4.07. 9 P
o, 'tis a gallant king! 4.07. 10 P
our king is not like him in that; 4.07. 40 P
no, great king; 4.07. 70
o, give us leave, great king, | to view the 4.07. 81
soldier, you must come to the king. 4.07.119 P
i beseech you now, come apace to the king. 4.08. 3 P
charles duke of orleance, nephew to the king, 4.08. 76
now we bear the king | toward callice; 5.pr. 6
which like a mighty whiffler 'fore the king 5.pr. 12
invites the king of england's stay at home; 5.pr. 37
the king hath heard them; 5.02. 74
warwick, and huntington, go with the king, | and 5.02. 85
find me such a plain king that thou wouldst 5.02.124 P
take a soldier, take a king. 5.02.166 P
moi'ty, take the word of a king and a bachelor. 5.02.215 P
if he be not fellow with the best king, thou 5.02.242 P
thou shalt find the best king of good fellows. 5.02.242 P
the king hath granted every article: 5.02.332
your majesty demands, that the king of france, 5.02.336 P
in infant bands crown'd king | of france and ep 9
of france and england, did this king succeed; ep 10
1H6 king henry the fift, too famous to live long! 1.01. 6
england ne'er lost a king of so much worth. 1.01. 7
england ne'er had a king until his time: 1.01. 8
he was a king blest of the king of kings. 1.01. 28
he was a king blest of the king of kings. 1.01. 28
the dolphin charles is crowned king in rheims; 1.01. 92
the dolphin crowned king? 1.01. 96
wherewith you now bedew king henry's hearse, | i 1.01.104
and then i will proclaim young henry king. 1.01.169
to eltam will i, where the young king is, 1.01.170
the king from eltam i intend to send, | and sit 1.01.176
thou art no friend to god or to the king. 1.03. 25
and not protector, of the king or realm. 1.03. 32
here's beauford, that regards nor god nor king, 1.03. 60
to crown himself king and suppress the prince. 1.03. 68
third son to the third edward, king of england. 2.04. 84
henry the fourth, grandfather to this king, 2.05. 63
and the lawful heir | of edward king, the third 2.05. 66
clarence, third son | to king edward the third; 2.05. 76
the king, thy sovereign, is not quite exempt 3.01. 25
he, | no one, but he, should be about the king; 3.01. 38
is not his grace protector to the king? 3.01. 60
compassion on the king commands me stoop, | or i 3.01.119
sweet king! 3.01.131
the presence of a king engenders love | amongst 3.01.180
when gloucester says the word, king henry goes, 3.01.183
and then depart to paris to the king, | for 3.02.128
god save king henry, of that name the sixt! 4.01. 2
that you elect no other king but him; 4.01. 4
no more but plain and bluntly "to the king"? 4.01. 51
with charles, the rightful king of france." 4.01. 60
to trouble and disturb the king and us? 4.01.127
regard, | king henry's peers and chief nobility 4.01.146
because, forsooth, the king of scots is crown'd. 4.01.157
i promise you, the king | prettily, methought, 4.01.174
servant in arms to harry king of england, | and 4.02. 4
margaret my name, and daughter to a king, | the 5.03. 51
king, | the king of naples, whosoe'er thou art. 5.03. 52
why, for my king. 5.03. 89
for though her father be the king of naples, 5.03. 94
you, | if happy england's royal king be free. 5.03.115
thy daughter shall be wedded to my king, | whom 5.03.137
a child, | fit to be made companion with a king. 5.03.149
royal name, | as deputy unto that gracious king, 5.03.161
thanks, | because this is in traffic of a king. 5.03.164
embrace | the christian prince, king henry, were 5.03.172
no princely commendations to my king? 5.03.176
never yet taint with love, i send the king. 5.03.183
presume | to send such peevish tokens to a king. 5.03.186
but reignier, king of naples, that prevail'd. 5.04. 78
with letters of commission from the king. 5.04. 95
that, in regard king henry gives consent, | of 5.04.124
and therein reverenc'd for their lawful king. 5.04.140
usurp'st, | of benefit proceeding from our king, 5.04.152
yes, my lord, her father is a king, | the king 5.05. 39
is a king, | the king of naples and jerusalem, 5.05. 40
disgrace not so your king, | that he should be 5.05. 48
whom should we match with henry, being a king, 5.05. 66
but margaret, that is daughter to a king? 5.05. 67
approves her fit for none but for a king. 5.05. 69
seen) | will answer our hope in issue of a king; 5.05. 72
king henry's faithful and anointed queen. 5.05. 91
margaret shall now be queen, and rule the king; 5.05.107
but i will rule both her, the king, and realm. 5.05.108
2H6 the fairest queen that ever king receiv'd. 1.01. 16
great king of england, and my gracious lord, 1.01. 24
makes me the bolder to salute my king | with 1.01. 29
our sovereign and the french king charles, | for 1.01. 41
it is agreed between the french king charles, 1.01. 44 P
ambassador for henry king of england, that the 1.01. 45 P
daughter unto reignier king of naples, sicilia, 1.01. 47 P
and deliver'd /over to the king her father" — 1.01. 52 P
and deliver'd over to the king her father, and 1.01. 59 P
and she sent over of the king of england's own 1.01. 60 P
unto the poor king reignier, whose large style 1.01.111
wives, | and our king henry gives away his own, 1.01.130
it was the pleasure of my lord the king. 1.01.138
and no great friend, i fear me, to the king. 1.01.150
king henry's diadem, | enchas'd with all the 1.02. 7
when i imagine ill | against my king and nephew, 1.02. 20
where as the king and queen do mean to hawk. 1.02. 58
that he was, and that the king was an usurper. 1.03. 31 P
we'll hear more of your matter before the king. 1.03. 36 P
isle, | and this the royalty of albion's king? 1.03. 45
shall king henry be a pupil still | under the 1.03. 46
i thought king henry had resembled thee | in 1.03. 53
but can do more in england than the king. 1.03. 71
because the king, forsooth, will have it so. 1.03.115
the king is old enough himself | to give his 1.03.116
since thou wert king — as who is king but thou? 1.03.123
since thou wert king — as who is king but thou? 1.03.123
against her will, good king? 1.03.144
my soul | as i in duty love my king and country! 1.03.158
"first of the king: what shall of him become?" 1.04. 29
the king and commonweal | are deeply indebted 1.04. 43
not half so bad as thine to england's king, 1.04. 47
the king is now in progress towards saint albons 1.04. 72
that smooth'st it so with king and commonweal! 2.01. 22
come to the king and tell him what miracle. 2.01. 60
bring him near the king, | his highness' 2.01. 70
demanding of king henry's life and death, | and 2.01.171
how i have lov'd my king and commonweal; 2.01.187
after edward the third's death reign'd as king 2.02. 20
seiz'd on the realm, depos'd the rightful king, 2.02. 24
and, but for owen glendower, had been king, 2.02. 41
son | succeed before the younger, i am king. 2.02. 52
long live our sovereign richard, england's king! 2.02. 63
but i am not your king | till i be crown'd, and 2.02. 64
shall one day make the duke of york a king. 2.02. 79
the greatest man in england but the king. 2.02. 82
than when thou wert protector to thy king. 2.03. 27
i see no reason why a king of years | should be 2.03. 28
god and king henry govern england's realm. 2.03. 30
give up your staff, sir, and the king his realm. 2.03. 31
farewell, good king; 2.03. 37
why, now is henry king and margaret queen, | and 2.03. 39
i never meant him any ill, nor the king, nor the 2.03. 89 P
as next the king he was successive heir, | and 3.01. 49
all happiness unto my lord the king! 3.01. 93
that doit that e'er i wrested from the king, 3.01.112
thus king henry throws away his crutch | before 3.01.189
for, good king henry, thy decay i fear. 3.01.194
the king will labor still to save his life, 3.01.239
the king and all the peers are here at hand. 3.02. 10
help, lords, the king is dead. 3.02. 33
with that dread king that took our state upon 3.02.154
stand apart, the king shall know your mind. 3.02.242
an answer from the king, my lord of salisbury! 3.02.270
sent from a sort of tinkers to the king. 3.02.277
an answer from the king, or we will all break in 3.02.278
once by the king, and three times thrice by thee 3.02.358
sometime he calls the king, | and whispers to 3.02.374
go tell this heavy message to the king. 3.02.379
now get thee hence, the king, thou know'st, is 3.02.386
obscure and lousy swain, king henry's blood, 4.01. 50
lord | unto the daughter of a worthless king, 4.01. 81
by shameful murther of a guiltless king | and 4.01. 95
beggary | is crept into the palace of our king, 4.01.102
any | save to the god of heaven and to my king; 4.01.126
his body will i bear unto the king. 4.01.145
and when i am king, as king i will be — 4.02. 70 P
and when i am king, as king i will be — 4.02. 70 P

the king is merciful, if you revolt. 4.02.125
nay, 'tis too true; therefore he shall be king. 4.02.147
go to, sirrah, tell the king from me, that, for 4.02.156 P
assail them with the army of the king. 4.02.175
fight for your king, your country, and your 4.05. 11
be us'd, and, contrary to the king, his crown, 4.07. 36 P
/but to maintain the king, the realm, and you? 4.07. 70
because my book preferr'd me to the king; 4.07. 72
we come ambassadors from the king | unto the 4.08. 7
who loves the king, and will embrace his pardon, 4.08. 14
god save the king! god save the king! 4.08. 19 P
god save the king! god save the king! 4.08. 19 P
we'll follow the king and clifford. 4.08. 53 P
him, | and he that brings his head unto the king 4.08. 66
a mean | to reconcile you all unto the king. 4.08. 69
was ever king that joy'd an earthly throne | and 4.09. 1
crept out of my cradle | but i was made a king, 4.09. 4
was never subject long'd to be a king | as i do 4.09. 5
god save the king! god save the king! 4.09. 22 P
god save the king! god save the king! 4.09. 22 P
crowns of the king by carrying my head to him, 4.10. 27 P
which i will bear in triumph to the king, 4.10. 83
to entertain great england's lawful king! 5.01. 4
the king hath sent him sure; 5.01. 13
i am far better born than is the king; 5.01. 28
more like a king, more kingly in my thoughts; 5.01. 29
is to remove proud somerset from the king, 5.01. 36
end, | the king hath yielded unto thy demand: 5.01. 40
may pass into the presence of a king, | lo, i 5.01. 65
a poor esquire of kent, that loves his king. 5.01. 75
false king, why hast thou broken faith with me, 5.01. 91
king did i call thee? 5.01. 93
thou art not king; 5.01. 93
of capital treason 'gainst the king and crown. 5.01.107
health and all happiness to my lord the king! 5.01.124
this is my king, york, i do not mistake, | but 5.01.129
makes him oppose himself against his king. 5.01.133
i am thy king, and thou a false–heart traitor. 5.01.143
for, as i hear, the king is fled to london, | to 5.03. 24
3H6 i wonder how the king escap'd our hands. 1.01. 1
thus do i hope to shake king henry's head. 1.01. 20
this is the palace of the fearful king, | and 1.01. 25
for this is thine and not king henry's heirs'. 1.01. 27
and when the king comes, offer him no violence, 1.01. 33
unless plantagenet, duke of york, be king, | and 1.01. 40
neither the king, nor he that loves him best, 1.01. 45
to aspire unto the crown and reign as king. 1.01. 53
whom should he follow but his natural king? 1.01. 82
be duke of lancaster, let him be king. 1.01. 86
he is both king and duke of lancaster, | and 1.01. 87
sound drums and trumpets, and the king will fly. 1.01.118
peace thou! and give king henry leave to speak. 1.01.120
prove it, henry, and thou shalt be king. 1.01.131
'twas by rebellion against his king. 1.01.133
tell me, may not a king adopt an heir? 1.01.135
and if he may, then am i lawful king; 1.01.137
my conscience tells me he is lawful king. 1.01.150
king henry, be thy title right or wrong, | lord 1.01.159
let me for this my life–time reign as king. 1.01.171
farewell, faint–hearted and degenerate king, 1.01.183
i live | to honor me as thy king and sovereign, 1.01.198
long live king henry! plantagenet, embrace him. 1.01.202
if you be king, why should not i succeed? 1.01.227
art thou king, and wilt be forc'd? 1.01.230
mine, boys? not till king henry be dead. 1.02. 10
i will be king, or die. 1.02. 35
rise, | and yet the king not privy to my drift, 1.02. 46
whom we have left protectors of the king, | with 1.02. 57
what, was it you that would be england's king? 1.04. 70
ay, marry, sir, now looks he like a king! 1.04. 96
ay, this is he that took king henry's chair, 1.04. 97
you should not be king | till our king henry had 1.04.101
till our king henry had shook hands with death. 1.04.102
thy father bears the type of king of naples, 1.04.121
and here's to right our gentle–hearted king. 1.04.176
i, then in london, keeper of the king, 2.01.111
queen, | bearing the king in my behalf along; 2.01.115
touching king henry's oath and your succession. 2.01.119
but whether 'twas the coldness of the king, 2.01.122
the king unto the queen; 2.01.137
have wrought the easy–melting king like wax. 2.01.171
for king of england shalt thou be proclaim'd 2.01.194
king edward, valiant richard, montague, | stay 2.01.198
he, but a duke, would have his son a king, | and 2.02. 21
thou, being a king, blest with a goodly son, 2.02. 23
proclaims him king, and many fly to him. 2.02. 71
before thy sovereign and thy lawful king? 2.02. 86
i am his king, and he should bow his knee. 2.02. 87
you that are king, though he do wear the crown, 2.02. 90
tongue, | i am a king, and privileg'd to speak. 2.02.120
whose father bears the title of a king | (as if 2.02.140
by that false woman as this king by thee. 2.02.149
and tam'd the king and made the dolphin stoop; 2.02.151
had slept, | and we, in pity of the gentle king, 2.02.161
since thou deniedst the gentle king to speak. 2.02.172
from london by the king was i press'd forth; 2.05. 64
for these woeful chances | misthink the king, 2.05.108
was ever king so griev'd for subjects' woe? 2.05.111
here sits a king more woeful than you are. 2.05.124
which, whiles it lasted, gave king henry light. 2.06. 2
that led calm henry, though he were a king, | as 2.06. 34
there to be crowned england's royal king; 2.06. 88
this is the quondam king; 3.01. 23
and in conclusion wins the king from her | with 3.01. 50
to strengthen and support king edward's place. 3.01. 52
ay, but thou talk'st as if thou wert a king. 3.01. 59
but, if thou be a king, where is thy crown? 3.01. 61
well, if you be a king crown'd with content, 3.01. 66
you are the king king edward hath depos'd; 3.01. 69
you are the king king edward hath depos'd; 3.01. 69
where did you dwell when i was king of england? 3.01. 74
i was anointed king at nine months old, | my 3.01. 76
for we were subjects but while you were king. 3.01. 81
go where you will, the king shall be commanded; 3.01. 92
we are true subjects to the king, king edward. 3.01. 94
we are true subjects to the king, king edward. 3.01. 94
to henry, | if he were seated as king edward is. 3.01. 96
and what god will, that let your king perform; 3.01.100
before the king will grant her humble suit. 3.02. 13
an easy task, 'tis but to love a king. 3.02. 53
one way or other, she is for a king, | and she 3.02. 87
say that king edward take thee for his queen? 3.02. 89
no, mighty king of france; 3.03. 4
is, of a king, become a banish'd man, | and 3.03. 25
seat | of england's true–anointed lawful king. 3.03. 29
from worthy edward, king of albion, | my lord 3.03. 49
sister, | to england's king in lawful marriage. 3.03. 57
king lewis and lady bona, hear me speak | before 3.03. 65
yet here prince edward stands, king henry's son. 3.03. 73
for shame, leave henry, and call edward king. 3.03.100
call him my king by whose injurious doom | my 3.03.101
upon thy conscience, | is edward your true king? 3.03.114
touching the jointure that your king must make, 3.03.136
that bona shall be wife to the english king. 3.03.139
to edward, but not to the english king. 3.03.140
i make king lewis behold | thy sly conveyance 3.03.159
these from our king unto your majesty. 3.03.165
has your king married the lady grey? 3.03.174
king lewis, i here protest in sight of heaven, 3.03.181
no more my king, for he dishonors me, | but most 3.03.184
and joy that thou becom'st king henry's friend. 3.03.201
if king lewis vouchsafe to furnish us | with 3.03.203
and tell false edward, thy supposed king, | that 3.03.223
seest what's pass'd, go fear thy king withal. 3.03.226
here comes the king. 4.01. 6
your king and warwick's, and must have my will. 4.01. 16
and shall have your will, because our king. 4.01. 17
that king lewis | becomes your enemy, for 4.01. 29
leave me, or tarry, edward will be king, | and 4.01. 65
what answer makes king lewis unto our letters? 4.01. 91
"go tell false edward, the supposed king, | that 4.01. 93
now, brother king, farewell, and sit you fast, 4.01.119
the king by this is set him down to sleep. 4.03. 2
that with the king here resteth in his tent? 4.03. 10
but why commands the king | that his chief 4.03. 12
when we parted, | thou call'dst me king. 4.03. 31
embassade | then i degraded you from being king, 4.03. 33
edward will always bear himself as king. 4.03. 45
then, for his mind, be edward england's king, 4.03. 48
and be true king indeed, thou but the shadow. 4.03. 50
to do, | to free king henry from imprisonment, 4.03. 63
what late misfortune is befall'n king edward? 4.04. 3
or tears i blast or drown | king edward's fruit, 4.04. 24
king edward's friends must down. 4.04. 28
you know our king, my brother, | is prisoner to 4.05. 4
but, master mayor, if henry be your king, | yet 4.07. 20
open the gates, we are king henry's friends. 4.07. 28
to help king edward in his time of storm, | as 4.07. 43
again, | i came to serve a king and not a duke. 4.07. 49
if you'll not here proclaim yourself our king, 4.07. 54
by the grace of god, king of england and france, 4.07. 72 P
and whoso'er gainsays king edward's right, | by 4.07. 74
and once again proclaim us king of england. 4.08. 53
call edward king and at his hands beg mercy? 5.01. 23
thought, at least, he would have said the king, 5.01. 29
and henry is my king, warwick his subject. 5.01. 38
but warwick's king is edward's prisoner. 5.01. 39
the king was slily finger'd from the deck! 5.01. 44
war | against his brother and his lawful king? 5.01. 88
for who liv'd king, but i could dig his grave? 5.02. 21
clarence, excuse me to the king my brother; 5.05. 46
king henry and the prince his son are gone; 5.06. 89
to the king of france | hath pawn'd the sicils 5.07. 38
R3 to set my brother clarence and the king | in 1.01. 34
and if king edward be as true and just | as i am 1.01. 36
'tis not the king that sends you to the tower; 1.01. 63
that trudge betwixt the king and mistress shore. 1.01. 73
way, | if we will keep in favor with the king, 1.01. 79
we say the king | is wise and virtuous, and his 1.01. 90
brother, farewell, i will unto the king, | and 1.01.107
were it to call king edward's widow sister, | i 1.01.109
the king is sickly, weak, and melancholy, | and 1.01.136
which done, god take king edward to his mercy, 1.01.151
poor key–cold figure of a holy king, | pale 1.02. 5
rest you, whiles i lament king henry's corse. 1.02. 32
didst thou not kill this king? 1.02.101
the better for the king of heaven that hath him. 1.02.105
for i did kill king henry — | but 'twas thy 1.02.179
at chertsey monast'ry this noble king, | and wet 1.02.214
but so it must be, if the king miscarry. 1.03. 16
saw you the king to–day, my lord of derby? 1.03. 30
who is it that complains unto the king | that i, 1.03. 43
the king, on his own royal disposition | (and 1.03. 63
marry with a king, | a bachelor, and a handsome 1.03. 99
threat you me with telling of the king? 1.03.112
i will avouch't in presence of the king. 1.03.114
ere you were queen, ay, or your husband king, 1.03.120
we follow'd then our lord, our sovereign king. 1.03.146
so should we you, if you should be our king. 1.03.147
should enjoy, were you this country's king — 1.03.151
though not by war, by surfeit die your king, 1.03.196
king, | as ours by murther, to make him a king! 1.03.197
that stir the king against the duke my brother. 1.03.330
i'll to the king and signify to him | that thus 1.04. 96
offended us you have not, but the king. 1.04.178
and he that hath commanded is our king. 1.04.194
the great king of kings | hath in the table of 1.04.195
take heed you dally not before your king, | lest 2.01. 12
lest he that is the supreme king of kings 2.01. 13
good morrow to my sovereign king and queen, 2.01. 47
and said, "dear brother, live, and be a king"? 2.01.114
o, they did urge it still unto the king! 2.01.138
i do lament the sickness of the king, | as loath 2.02. 9
the king mine uncle is to blame for it. 2.02. 13
children, peace, the king doth love you well. 2.02. 17
for my good uncle gloucester | told me the king, 2.02. 21
edward, my lord, thy son, our king, is dead! 2.02. 40
though we have spent our harvest of this king, 2.02.115
fet | hither to london, to be crown'd our king. 2.02.122
i hope the king made peace with all of us, | and 2.02.132
yes, that the king is dead. 2.03. 3
doth the news hold of good king edward's death? 2.03. 7
then the king | had virtuous uncles to protect 2.03. 20
again, | or die a soldier as i liv'd a king. 3.01. 93
and look when i am king, claim thou of me | the 3.01.194
whereof the king my brother was possess'd. 3.01.196
i mean, your voice for crowning of the king. 3.04. 28
cry, "god save richard, england's royal king!" 3.07. 22
some ten voices cried, "god save king richard!" 3.07. 36
to bona, sister to the king of france. 3.07.182
your brother's son shall never reign our king, 3.07.215
long live richard, england's worthy king! 3.07.240
the king hath strictly charg'd the contrary. 4.01. 17
the king? who's that? 4.01. 18
and thy assistance, is king richard seated; 4.02. 4
why, buckingham, i say i would be king. 4.02. 12
ha? am i king? 'tis so — but edward lives. 4.02. 14
the king is angry, see, he gnaws his lip. 4.02. 27
did prophesy that richmond should be king, 4.02. 96
a king — perhaps — /perhaps — 4.02. 98
made i him king for this? 4.02.120
both, | to bear this tidings to the bloody king. 4.03. 22
wing, | jove's mercury, and herald for a king! 4.03. 55
well then, who dost thou mean shall be her king? 4.04.265
the loss you have is but a son being king, | and 4.04.307
the king, that calls your beauteous daughter 4.04.315
again shall you be mother to a king; 4.04.317
tell her the king, that may command, entreats. 4.04.345
that at her hands which the king's king forbids. 4.04.346
the unity the king my husband made | thou hadst 4.04.379
is the king dead? 4.04.470
and who is england's king but great york's heir? 4.04.472
they have not been commanded, mighty king. 4.04.486
will not king richard let me speak with him? 5.01. 1
holy king henry and thy fair son edward, 5.01. 4
this is the day which, in king edward's time, 5.01. 13
least | south from the mighty power of the king. 5.03. 38
king henry's issue, richmond, comforts thee. 5.03.123
harry, that prophesied thou shouldst be king, 5.03.129
the king enacts more wonders than a man, 5.04. 2
H8 for him, which buys | a place next to the king. 1.01. 66
(without the privity o' th' king) t' appoint 1.01. 74
he's gone to th' king; 1.01.128
i'll to the king, | and from a mouth of honor 1.01.136
to th' king i'll say't, and make my vouch as 1.01.157
suggests the king our master | to this last 1.01.164
let the king know | (as soon he shall by me) 1.01.190
in the name | of our most sovereign king. 1.01.202
the king | is pleas'd you shall to th' tower, 1.01.212
from | the king t' attach lord montacute, and 1.01.217
of these exactions, yet the king our master — 1.02. 25
that if the king | should without issue die, 1.02.133
'neither the king nor 's heirs | (tell you the 1.02.168
that, had the king in his last sickness fail'd, 1.02.184
noted, | and generally, whoever the king favors, 2.01. 47
although the king have mercies | more than i 2.01. 70
a separation | between the king and katherine? 2.01.149
for when the king once heard it, out of anger 2.01.150
held for certain | the king will venture at it. 2.01.156
serv'd before a subject, if not before the king, 2.02. 8 P
how is the king employ'd? 2.02. 14
the king will know him one day. 2.02. 21
and out of all these to restore the king, | he 2.02. 29
stroke of fortune falls | will bless the king. 2.02. 36
him, so i'll stand, | if the king please; 2.02. 52
and with some other business put the king | from 2.02. 56
excuse me, | the king has sent me otherwhere. 2.02. 59
a gracious king that pardons all offenses 2.02. 67
conscience, | thou art a cure fit for a king. 2.02. 75
approve the fair conceit | the king hath of you. 2.03. 75
are so mingled | that they have caught the king; 2.03. 77
i'll to the king, | and say i spoke with you. 2.03. 79
say, henry king of england, come into the court. 2.04. 6 P
henry king of england, etc. 2.04. 8 P
the king, your father, was reputed for | a 2.04. 45
my father, king of spain, was reckon'd one | the 2.04. 48
as to rectify | what is unsettled in the king. 2.04. 64
certain | the daughter of a king, my drops of 2.04. 72
the king is present: 2.04. 95
wherein he might the king his lord advertise 2.04.179
weighty difference | between the king and you, 3.01. 59
there sits a judge | that no king can corrupt. 3.01.101
all my full affections | still met the king? 3.01.130
the king loves you, | beware you lose it not. 3.01.171
if you cannot | bar his access to th' king, 3.02. 17
hath a witchcraft | over the king in 's tongue. 3.02. 19
the king hath found | matter against him that 3.02. 20
and came to th' eye o' th' king, wherein was 3.02. 31
"perceive | my king is tangled in affection to 3.02. 35
has the king this? 3.02. 37
the king in this perceives him, how he coasts 3.02. 38
the king already | hath married the fair lady. 3.02. 41
but will the king | digest this letter of the 3.02. 52
has left the cause o' th' king unhandled, and 3.02. 58
i do assure you | the king cried "ha!" 3.02. 61
which | have satisfied the king for his divorce, 3.02. 65
the packet, cromwell, gave't you the king? 3.02. 76
may be he hears the king | does whet his anger 3.02. 91
lie i' th' bosom of | our hard–rul'd king. 3.02.101
one | hath crawl'd into the favor of the king, 3.02.103
the king, the king! 3.02.106
the king, the king! 3.02.106
main secret in the packet | i sent the king? 3.02.216
seal | you ask with such a violence, the king 3.02.246
the king, that gave it. 3.02.251
far from his succor, from the king, from all 3.02.261
the way of loyalty and truth | toward the king, 3.02.273
packets | you writ to th' pope against the king. 3.02.287
innocence arise | when the king knows my truth. 3.02.302
in which you brought the king | to be your 3.02.315
the knowledge | either of king or council, when 3.02.317
the king shall know it, and, no doubt, shall 3.02.348
the king has cur'd me, | i humbly thank his 3.02.380
the worst | is your displeasure with the king. 3.02.392
whom the king hath in secrecy long married, 3.02.403
o, cromwell, | the king has gone beyond me! 3.02.408
seek the king! 3.02.414
the king shall have my service; 3.02.426
serve the king, and — prithee lead me in. 3.02.450
my god with half the zeal | i serv'd my king, he 3.02.456
our king has all the indies in his arms, | and 4.01. 45
a man in much esteem with th' king, and truly 4.01.109
the king has made him master | o' th' jewel 4.01.110
is staying | a gentleman, sent from the king, to 4.02.106

pray you to deliver | this to my lord the king. 4.02.130
and urge the king | to do me this last right. 4.02.157
yet like | a queen, and daughter to a king, 4.02.172
came you from the king, my lord? 5.01. 6
which they moved | have broken with the king, 5.01. 47
the king | shall understand it presently. 5.02. 9
toward the king first, then his laws, in filling 5.02. 50
pray heaven the king may never find a heart 5.02. 77
it | to a most noble judge, the king my master. 5.02.136
the king will suffer but the little finger | of 5.02.141
if the king blame me for't, i'll lay ye all | by 5.03. 78
and posts, like the commandment of a king, TRO 1.03. 93
weigh you the worth and honor of a king | so 2.02. 26
if helen then be wife to sparta's king, | as it 2.02.183
forget that thou art jove, the king of gods, and 2.03. 11 P
you, that if the king call for him at supper, 3.01. 76 P
i was sent for to the king, but why, i know not. 4.01. 36
son, | who after great hostilius here was king; COR 2.03.240
sons, | half of the number that king priam had, TIT 1.01. 80
if to fight for king and commonweal | were piety 1.01.114
king and commander of our commonweal, | the wide 1.01.247
and give the king this fatal–plotted scroll. 2.03. 47
the king my brother shall have notice of this. 2.03. 85
long, | good king, to be so mightily abused. 2.03. 87
now will i fetch the king to find them here, 2.03.206
where is my lord the king? 2.03.259
andronicus, i will entreat the king. 2.03.304
chop off your hand | and send it to the king; 3.01.154
king, be thy thoughts imperious, like thy name. 4.04. 81
when subtile greeks surpris'd king priam's troy. 5.03. 84
when king cophetua lov'd the beggar–maid! ROM 2.01. 14
good king of cats, nothing but one of your nine 3.01. 77 P
fear the people | choose caesar for their king. JC 1.02. 80
to keep his state in rome | as easily as a king. 1.02.161
to–morrow | mean to establish caesar as a king; 1.03. 86
the tarquin drive when he was call'd a king. 2.01. 54
say to the king the knowledge of the broil | as MAC 1.02. 6
mark, king of scotland, mark! 1.02. 28
god save the king! 1.02. 47
from fife, great king, | where the norweyan 1.02. 48
that now | sweno, the norways' king, craves 1.02. 59
all hail, macbeth, that shalt be king hereafter! 1.03. 50
and to be king | stands not within the prospect 1.03. 73
you shall be king. 1.03. 86
the king hath happily receiv'd, macbeth, | the 1.03. 89
if chance will have me king, why, chance may 1.03.143
let us toward the king. 1.03.152
came missives from the king, who all–hail'd me 1.05. 7 P
on of time with 'hail, king that shalt be!' 1.05. 9 P
the king comes here to–night. 1.05. 31
is the king stirring, worthy thane? 2.03. 45
goes the king hence to–day? 2.03. 53
king, cawdor, glamis, all, | as the weird women 3.01. 1
when first they put the name of king upon me, 3.01. 57
say to the king, i would attend his leisure 3.02. 3
thither macduff | is gone to pray the holy king, 3.06. 30
hath so exasperate /the king that he | prepares 3.06. 38
is this | that rises like the issue of a king, 4.01. 87
that this great king may kindly say | our duties 4.01.131
such | a stanchless avarice that, were i king, 4.03. 78
thy royal father | was a most sainted king; 4.03.109
comes the king forth, i pray you? 4.03.140
a most miraculous work in this good king, 4.03.147
come go we to the king, our power is ready, 4.03.236
hail, king! 5.09. 20
hail, king of scotland! 5.09. 25
hail, king of scotland! 5.09. 25
long live the king! HAM 1.01. 3
in the same figure, like the king that's dead. 1.01. 41
looks 'a not like the king? mark it, horatio. 1.01. 43
is it not like the king? 1.01. 58
our last king, | whose image even but now 1.01. 80
a moi'ty competent | was gaged by our king, 1.01. 91
so like the king | that was and is the question 1.01.110
personal power | to business with the king, more 1.02. 37
so excellent a king, that was, to this, 1.02.139
i saw him once, 'a was a goodly king. 1.02.186
my lord, the king your father. 1.02.191
the king my father? 1.02.191
the king doth wake to–night and takes his rouse, 1.04. 8
call thee hamlet, | king, father, royal dane. 1.04. 45
i will go seek the king. 2.01. 98
come, go we to the king. 2.01.114
soul, | both to my god and to my gracious king. 2.02. 45
i know the good king and queen have sent for you 2.02.281 P
and your secrecy to the king and queen moult no 2.02.294 P
he that plays the king shall be welcome — his 2.02.319 P
very strange, for my uncle is king of denmark, 2.02.363 P
no, not for a king, | upon whose property and 2.02.569
wherein i'll catch the conscience of the king. 2.02.605
will the king hear this piece of work? 3.02. 46 P
there is a play to–night before the king, | one 3.02. 75
this is one lucianus, nephew to the king. 3.02.244 P
the king rises. 3.02.265 P
for if the king like not the comedy, | why then 3.02.293
the king, sir — 3.02.299 P
you have the voice of the king himself for your 3.02.342 P
never alone | did the king sigh, but /with a 3.03. 23
nay, i know not, is it the king? 3.04. 26
as kill a king, and marry with his brother. 3.04. 29
as kill a king! 3.04. 30
a king of shreds and patches — | save me, and 3.04.102
let the bloat king tempt you again to bed, 3.04.182
replication should be made by the son of a king? 4.02. 13 P
such officers do the king best service in the 4.02. 17 P
where the body is, and go with us to the king. 4.02. 26 P
the body is with the king, but the king is not 4.02. 27 P
the king, but the king is not with the body. 4.02. 27 P
the king is a thing — 4.02. 28 P
your fat king and your lean beggar is but 4.03. 23 P
may fish with the worm that hath eat of a king, 4.03. 28 P
but to show you how a king may go a progress 4.03. 30 P
go, captain, from me greet the danish king. 4.04. 1
/they cry, "choose we, laertes shall be king!" 4.05.107
clouds, | "laertes shall be king, laertes king!" 4.05.109
clouds, | "laertes shall be king, laertes king!" 4.05.109
where is this king? sirs, stand you all without. 4.05.113
o thou vile king, | give me my father! 4.05.116

there's such divinity doth hedge a king | that 4.05.124
give these fellows some means to the king, they 4.06. 15 P
let the king have the letters i have sent, and 4.06. 22 P
to't that day that our last king hamlet overcame 5.01.144 P
here comes the king, | the queen, the courtiers. 5.01.217
an earnest conjuration from the king, | as 5.02. 38
why, what a king is this! 5.02. 62
that hath kill'd my king and whor'd my mother, 5.02. 64
the king, sir, hath wager'd with him six barbary 5.02.147 P
the king, sir, hath laid, sir, that in a dozen 5.02.165 P
willing, and the king hold his purpose, i will 5.02.176 P
the king and queen and all are coming down. 5.02.203 P
the king shall drink to hamlet's better breath, 5.02.271
to earth, | "now the king drinks to hamlet." 5.02.278
i can no more — the king, the king's to blame. 5.02.320
i thought the king had more affected the duke of LR 1.01. 1 P
the king is coming. 1.01. 33 P
the name, and all th' addition to a king; 1.01.136
lear, | whom i have ever honor'd as my king, 1.01.140
now, by apollo, king, | thou swear'st thy gods 1.01.160
fare thee well, king; 1.01.180
you, who with this king | hath rivall'd for our 1.01.190
for you, great king, | i would not from your 1.01.208
royal king, | give but that portion which 1.01.241
thy dow'rless daughter, king, thrown to my 1.01.256
and the king gone to–night? 1.02. 24
the king falls from bias of nature; 1.02.111 P
honest–hearted fellow, and as poor as the king. 1.04. 20 P
be'st as poor for a subject as he's for a king, 1.04. 22 P
sung, | that such a king should play bo–peep, 1.04.177
up thy heels, and beat thee before the king? 2.02. 30 P
you come with letters against the king, and take 2.02. 36 P
the messengers from our sister and the king. 2.02. 50 P
it pleas'd the king his master very late | to 2.02.116
got praises of the king | for him attempting who 2.02.121
call not your stocks for me, i serve the king, 2.02.128
the king must take it ill | that he, so slightly 2.02.145
good king, that must approve the common saw, 2.02.160
how chance the king comes with so small a number 2.04. 63
the king would speak with cornwall, the dear 2.04.101
the king is in high rage. 2.04.296
i know you. where's the king? 3.01. 3
of them hath borne | against the old kind king; 3.01. 28
i will go seek the king. 3.01. 50
that when we have found the king — in which 3.01. 53
these injuries the king now bears will be 3.03. 12 P
we must incline to the king. 3.03. 14 P
me), the king my old master must be reliev'd. 3.03. 18 P
thou sayest the king grows mad, i'll tell thee, 3.04.165
if i find him comforting the king, it will stuff 3.05. 20 P
a king, a king! 3.06. 11
a king, a king! 3.06. 11
where is the king my master? 3.06. 86
where's the king? 3.07. 14 P
to whose hands you have sent the lunatic king — 3.07. 46
where hast thou sent the king? 3.07. 50
thank thee for the love thou show'dst the king, 4.02. 95
i am the king himself. 4.06. 84 P
is't not the king? 4.06.107
ay, every inch a king! 4.06.107
come, come, i am a king, | masters, know you 4.06.199
meanest wretch, | past speaking of in a king! 4.06.205
the king is mad; 4.06.279
then be't so, my good lord. how does the king? 4.07. 12
please your majesty | that we may wake the king? 4.07. 17
the king is come to his daughter, | with others 5.01. 21
king lear hath lost, he and his daughter ta'en. 5.02. 6
for thee, oppressed king, i am cast down, 5.03. 5
to send the old and miserable king | to some 5.03. 46
come | to bid my king and master aye good night. 5.03.236
speak, edmund, where's the king? 5.03.238
"king stephen was and–a worthy peer, | his OTH 2.03. 89
he hath assembled | bocchus, the king of libya; ANT 3.06. 69
philadelphos, king | of paphlagonia; 3.06. 70
the thracian king, adallas; 3.06. 71
king manchus of arabia; 3.06. 72
king of pont; 3.06. 72
mithridates, king | of comagena; 3.06. 73
though i think the king | be touch'd at very CYM 1.01. 9
none but the king? 1.01. 10
the king he takes the babe | to his protection, 1.01. 40
you tell me, | is she sole child to th' king? 1.01. 56
so soon as i can win th' offended king, | i will 1.01. 75
though the king | hath charg'd you should not 1.01. 82
if the king come, i shall incur i know not | how 1.01.102
alack, the king! 1.01.124
that our great king himself doth woo me oft 1.05. 14
which hath the king | five times redeem'd from 1.05. 62
i'll move the king | to any shape of thy 1.05. 70
empery | would make the great'st king double — 1.06.121
the king my father shall be made acquainted | of 1.06.149
here comes the king. 2.03. 32 P
you are most bound to th' king, | who lets go by 2.03. 44
so sure | to win the king as i am bold her honor 2.04. 2
this, your king | hath heard of great augustus. 2.04. 10
a golden crown and call'd | himself a king. 3.01. 61
boys know little they are sons to th' king, 3.03. 80
who | the king his father call'd guiderius — 3.03. 88
didst set up my disobedience 'gainst the king 3.04. 88
son, i say, follow the king. 3.05. 53
go in and cheer the king, he rages, none | dare 3.05. 67
even to the note o' th' king, or i'll fall in 4.03. 44
the king | hath not deserv'd my service nor your 4.04. 24
the king himself | of his wings destitute, the 5.03. 4
bring him to th' king. 5.03. 94
then, jupiter, thou king of gods, | why hast 5.04. 77
his manacles, bring your prisoner to the king. 5.04.192 P
hail, great king! 5.05. 25
thou, king, send out | for torturers ingenious; 5.05.214
stay, sir king. 5.05.301
thou hadst, great king, a subject who | was 5.05.316
place, and grac'd | the thankings of a king. 5.05.407
this king unto him took a peer, | who died and PER 1.ch. 21
and her thoughts the king | of every virtue 1.01. 13
great king, | few love to hear the sins they 1.01. 91
they do abuse the king that flatter him, | for 1.02. 38
here must i kill king pericles, and if i do it 1.03. 2 P
being bid to ask what he would of the king, 1.03. 5 P

for if a king bid a man be a villain, he's bound 1.03. 7 P
how? the king gone? 1.03. 14
here have you seen a mighty king | his child, i 2.ch. 1
but if the good king simonides were of my mind 2.01. 43 P
pentapolis, and our king the good simonides. 2.01.100 P
he is a happy king, since he gains from his 2.01.104 P
worth, | for it was sometime target to a king; 2.01.137
and crown you king of this day's happiness. 2.03. 11
by jove, i wonder, that is king of thoughts, 2.03. 28
whereby i see that time's the king of men, 2.03. 45
the king my father, sir, has drunk to you — 2.03. 75
for though | this king were great, his greatness 2.04. 14
you | to forbear the absence of your king; 2.04. 46
even in his throat — unless it be the king — 2.05. 56
to th' court of king simonides | are letters 3.ch. 23
if king pericles | come not home in twice six 3.ch. 30
claps can sound, | "our heir–apparent is a king! 3.ch. 37
i, king pericles, have lost | this queen, worth 3.02. 70
her burying, | she was the daughter of a king. 3.02. 73
but since king pericles, | my wedded lord, i 3.04. 8
i love the king your father, and yourself, 4.01. 32
winds have brought | this king to tharsus — 4.04. 18
sir, | our vessel is of tyre, in it the king, 5.01. 23
sir king, all hail! 5.01. 39
that had some power, | my father, and a king. 5.01.149
my mother was the daughter of a king, | who died 5.01.157
the king my father did in tharsus leave me, 5.01.170
i am the daughter to king pericles, | if good 5.01.178
to king pericles, | if good king pericles be. 5.01.179
the regent made in metelin, | to greet the king. 5.02. 9
the temple see, | our king and all his company. 5.02. 18
i here confess myself the king of tyre, | who, 5.03. 2
the king my father gave you such a ring. 5.03. 39
king capaneus was your lord. TNK 1.01. 59
the king calls for you; 1.02. 84
let's to the king, who, were he | a quarter 1.02.107
they are sisters' children, nephews to the king. 1.04. 16
by east and north–east to the king of pigmies, 3.04. 15
that mayst force the king | to be his subject's 5.01. 83
what say you to the mercy of the king? STM II.C 17
for to the king god hath his office lent | of II.C 98
he hath not only lent the king his figure, | his II.C 102
alas, alas, say now the king, | as he is clement II.C 122
entreat their mediation to the king, | give up II.C 145
she clepes him king of graves and grave for VEN 995
who, like a king perplexed in his throne, | by 1043
but king nor peer to such a peerless dame. LUC 21
suggested this proud issue of a king; 37
thou seem'st not what thou art, a god, a king; 601
what dar'st thou not when once thou art a king? 606
"thou art," quoth she, "a sea, a sovereign king, 652
"so shall these slaves be king, and thou their 659
"the baser is he, coming from a king, | to shame 1002
king pandion, he is dead: PP 20.23
flattering, | "pity but he were a king!" 20.40
tyrant wing, | save the eagle, feath'red king; PHT 11
and all those beauties whereof now he's king SON 63. 6
in sleep a king, but waking no such matter. 87.14

KING–BECOMING 1 FR 0.0001 REL FR 1 V 0 P
the king–becoming graces, | as justice, verity, MAC 4.03. 91

KING–CARDINAL 1 FR 0.0001 REL FR 1 V 0 P
the king–cardinal, | that blind priest, like the H8 2.02. 19

KING'D 2 FR 0.0002 REL FR 2 V 0 P
then am i king'd again, and by and by | think R2 5.05. 36
for, my good liege, she is so idly king'd, | her H5 2.04. 26

/KINGDOM 4 FR 0.0004 REL FR 2 V 2 P
/to /pluck /a /kingdom /down | /and /set 2H4 1.03. 49
/a /power | /into /this /scattered /kingdom, LR 3.01. 31
/imports /to /the /kingdom /so /much /fear /and 4.03. 5 P
/the /powers /of /the /kingdom /approach /apace. 4.07. 92 P

KINGDOM 94 FR 0.0106 REL FR 83 V 11 P
this will prove a brave kingdom to me, where i TMP 3.02.144 P
of wine is, or i'll turn you out of my kingdom. 4.01.252 P
not for thy fairy kingdom. MND 2.01.144
the watery kingdom, whose ambitious head | spets MV 2.07. 44
so much | that heirless it hath made my kingdom, WT 5.01. 10
may drop upon his kingdom and devour | incertain 5.01. 28
give grandame kingdom, and it grandame will JN 2.01.161
law cannot give my child his kingdom here, | for 3.01.187
for he that holds his kingdom holds the law; 3.01.188
child, | his little kingdom of a forced grave. 4.02. 98
this kingdom, this confine of blood and breath, 4.02.246
between this chastis'd kingdom and myself, | and 5.02. 84
but dead, thy kingdom cannot buy my breath. R2 1.03.232
for joy | to stand upon my kingdom once again. 3.02. 5
say, is my kingdom lost? 3.02. 95
and my large kingdom for a little grave, | a 3.03.153
beat thee out of thy kingdom with a dagger of 1H4 2.04.137 P
can make a head | to push against a kingdom, 4.01. 81
a kingdom for it was too small a bound, | but 5.04. 90
ruins of thy linen shall inherit his kingdom: 2H4 2.02. 24 P
then you perceive the body of our kingdom | how 3.01. 38
warning to all the rest of this little kingdom, 4.03.109 P
o my poor kingdom, sick with civil blows! 4.05.133
a kingdom for a stage, princes to act, | and H5 pr 3
but that the scot on his unfurnish'd kingdom 1.02.148
teach | the act of order to a peopled kingdom. 1.02.189
and his whole kingdom into desolation. 2.02.173
for peace itself should not so dull a kingdom 2.04. 16
bids you then resign | your crown and kingdom, 2.04. 94
for when /lenity and cruelty play for a kingdom, 3.06.112 P
the muster of his kingdom too faint a number; 3.06.131 P
to conquer the kingdom as to speak so much more 5.02.185 P
by her i claim the kingdom. 2H6 2.02. 47
enjoy the kingdom after my decease. 3H6 1.01.175
but for a kingdom any oath may be broken: 1.02. 16
for chair and dukedom, throne and kingdom say, 2.01. 93
well, say there is no kingdom then for richard; 3.02.146
that, though i want a kingdom, yet in marriage 4.01.121
alas, how should you govern any kingdom, | that 4.03. 35
'twas i that gave the kingdom to thy brother. 5.01. 34
world, | thou cacodemon, there thy kingdom is. R3 1.03.143
and thou a kingdom — all of you allegiance. 1.03.170
write of, | unto the kingdom of perpetual night. 1.04. 47
to his new kingdom of ne'er–changing night. 2.02. 46
or else my kingdom stands on brittle glass. 4.02. 61
by their uncle cozen'd | of comfort, kingdom, 4.04.224

if i did take the kingdom from your sons, | to 4.04.294
a horse, a horse! my kingdom for a horse! 5.04. 7
my kingdom for a horse! 5.04. 13
there will be | the beauty of this kingdom, i'll H8 1.03. 54
most learned reverend sir, into our kingdom, 2.02. 76
this was a judgment on me, that my kingdom 2.04.195
shipwrack'd upon a kingdom, where no pity, | no 3.01.149
to the mere undoing | of all the kingdom. 3.02.330
by your power legative within this kingdom 3.02.339
with all the choicest music of the kingdom, 4.01. 91
one that by suggestion | tied all the kingdom. 4.02. 36
worms, and my poor name | banish'd the kingdom! 4.02.127
speak of two | the most remark'd i' th' kingdom. 5.01. 33
and a soul | none better in my kingdom. 5.01.155
sent from th' infernal kingdom | to ease the TIT 5.02. 30
like to a little kingdom, suffers then | the JC 2.01. 68
banquo's issue ever | reign in this kingdom? MAC 4.01.103
and our whole kingdom | to be contracted in one HAM 1.02. 3
of a promis'd march | over his kingdom. 4.04. 4
they find us touch'd, we will our kingdom give, 4.05.208
you shall know i am set naked on your kingdom. 4.07. 44 P
i have some rights, of memory in this kingdom, 5.02.389
in the division of the kingdom, it appears not LR 1.01. 4 P
that we have divided | in three our kingdom; 1.01. 38
remain this ample third of our fair kingdom, 1.01. 80
sixt to turn thy hated back | upon our kingdom. 1.01.176
that all the kingdom | may have due note of him, 2.01. 82
thy half o' th' kingdom hast thou not forgot, 2.04.180
i never gave you kingdom, call'd you children; 3.02. 17
with the traitors | late footed in the kingdom? 3.07. 45
in your own kingdom, sir. 4.07. 75
take in that kingdom, and enfranchise that; ANT 1.01. 23
to give a kingdom for a mirth, to sit | and keep 1.04. 18
as the president of my kingdom, will | appear 3.07. 17
keep decorum, must | no less beg than a kingdom. 5.02. 18
his daughter, and the heir of 's kingdom (whom CYM 1.01. 4
to be styl'd | the under–hangman of his kingdom, 2.03.130
our kingdom is stronger than it was at that time 3.01. 35 P
and to fight | against my lady's kingdom. 5.01. 19
o imogen, | thou hast lost by this a kingdom. 5.05.373
and knowing this kingdom is without a head — PER 2.04. 35
when peers thus knit, a kingdom ever stands. 2.04. 58
will in that kingdom spend our following days. 5.03. 81
and life, must he set foot | upon this kingdom. TNK 2.02.247
banish'd the kingdom? 2.03. 1
i will not leave the kingdom. 2.03. 18
the title of a kingdom may be tried | out of 5.03. 33
gain | advantage on the kingdom of the shore, SON 64. 6

KINGDOM'D 1 FR 0.0001 REL FR 1 V 0 P
parts | kingdom'd achilles in commotion rages, TRO 2.03.175

KINGDOM'S 10 FR 0.0011 REL FR 10 V 0 P
fleet | in dreadful trial of our kingdom's king! JN 2.01.286
nor let my kingdom's rivers take their course 5.07. 38
were he my brother, nay, my kingdom's heir, | as R2 1.01.116
for that our kingdom's earth should not be 1.03.125
but we our kingdom's safety must so tender, H5 2.02.175
your kingdom's terror and black nemesis? 1H6 4.07. 78
to make prescription for a kingdom's worth. 3H6 3.03. 94
their kingdom's loss, my woeful banishment, R3 1.03.192
thy praises in his kingdom's great defense, MAC 1.03. 99
i see thee compass'd with thy kingdom's pearl, 5.09. 22

KINGDOMS 27 FR 0.0030 REL FR 27 V 0 P
yes, for a score of kingdoms you should wrangle, TMP 5.01.174
to measure kingdoms with his feeble steps; TGV 2.07. 10
that would i, had i kingdoms to give with her. AYL 5.04. 8
that would i, were i of all kingdoms king. 5.04. 10
the injury of tongues in courts and kingdoms WT 1.02.338
these your contracted | heirs of your kingdoms, 5.03. 6
which now the manage of two kingdoms must | with
JN 1.01. 37
between our kingdoms and our royal selves, | and 3.01.232
through all the kingdoms that acknowledge christ 1H4 3.02.111
for never two such kingdoms did contend H5 1.02. 24
me, that the contending kingdoms | of france and 5.02.349
so be there 'twixt your kingdoms such a spousal, 5.02.362
in between the /paction of these kingdoms, | to 5.02.365
the turk, that two and fifty kingdoms hath, 1H6 4.07. 73
and all the wealthy kingdoms of the west, 2H6 1.01.154
(i mean the learned ones in christian kingdoms) H8 2.02. 92
and she whom mighty kingdoms cur'sy to, | like a TIT 5.03. 74
methinks, i could deal kingdoms to my friends, TIM 1.02.220
here is my space, | kingdoms are clay; ANT 1.01. 35
i will piece | her opulent throne with kingdoms. 1.05. 46
her live | to join our kingdoms and our hearts, 2.02.151
armenia | and other of his conquer'd kingdoms, i 3.06. 36
we have kiss'd away | kingdoms and provinces. 3.10. 8
oft | (when he hath mus'd of taking kingdoms in) 3.13. 83
the heir of kingdoms, and another /life | to PER 5.01.207
show | bravely about the titles of two kingdoms. TNK 4.02.145
then thou alone kingdoms of hearts shouldst owe.
SON 70.14

KING–KILLER 1 FR 0.0001 REL FR 1 V 0 P
o thou sweet king–killer, and dear divorce TIM 4.03.381

/KINGLY 1 FR 0.0001 REL FR 1 V 0 P
/the /pride /of /kingly /sway /from /out /my R2 4.01.206

KINGLY 25 FR 0.0028 REL FR 24 V 1 P
flat treason 'gainst the kingly state of youth. LLL 4.03.289
then shalt thou give me with thy kingly hand AWW 2.01.193
to my kingly guest | unclasp'd my practice, quit WT 3.02.166
distrust | govern the motion of a kingly eye. JN 5.01. 47
a king, woe's slave, shall kingly woe obey. R2 3.02.210
thy kingly doom and sentence of his pride. 5.06. 23
and leavest the kingly couch | a watch–case or a 2H4 3.01. 16
o'er france and all her almost kingly dukedoms, H5 1.02.227
reignier of france, i give thee kingly thanks, 1H6 5.03.163
more like a king, more kingly in my thoughts; 2H6 5.01. 29
thou that i will leave my kingly throne, 3H6 1.01.124
my gracious father, by your kingly leave, | i'll 2.02. 63
blood, | were lik'ned oft to kingly sepulchres; 5.02. 20
that in their chains fetter'd the kingly lion, 5.07. 11
and kingly government of this your land: R3 3.07.132
the lord protect him from that kingly title! 4.01. 19
thy crown, usurp'd, disgrac'd his kingly glory. 4.04.371
lawful, by my life | and kingly dignity, we are H8 2.04.228
a prince | do a fair message to his kingly eyes? TRO 1.03.219
i thrice presented him a kingly crown, | which JC 3.02. 96
shall i beg leave to see your kingly eyes, when HAM 4.07. 45 P
this kingly seal | and plighter of high hearts! ANT 3.13.125
galling | his kingly hands haling ropes, | and, PER 4.01. 54
expect even here, where is a kingly patient, 5.01. 71
and my great mind most kingly drinks it up: SON 114.10

KINGLY–CROWNED 1 FR 0.0001 REL FR 1 V 0 P
the kingly–crowned head, the vigilant eye, | the COR 1.01.115

KINGLY–POOR 1 FR 0.0001 REL FR 1 V 0 P
o poverty in wit, kingly–poor flout! LLL 5.02.269

/KING'S 3 FR 0.0003 REL FR 2 V 1 P
the /king's. LLL 4.01. 75 P
the /king's grown bankrout, like a broken man. R2 2.01.257
/rise /thus /nimbly /by /a /true /king's /fall. 4.01.318

KING'S 148 FR 0.0167 REL FR 103 V 45 P
i boarded the king's ship; TMP 1.02.196
then all afire with me, the king's son, 1.02.212
the king's son have i landed by himself, | whom 1.02.221
of the king's ship, | the mariners, say how thou 1.02.224
safely in harbor | is the king's ship, in the 1.02.227
supposing that they saw the king's ship wrack'd, 1.02.236
at the marriage of the king's fair daughter 2.01. 71 P
to the king's ship, invisible as thou art; 5.01. 97
of god's patience and the king's english. WIV 1.04. 5 P
not the king's crown, nor the deputed sword, MM 2.02. 60
the french king's daughter with yourself to LLL 1.01.135
the king's; 4.01. 77 P
this quondam day with a companion of the king's, 5.01. 7 P
sir, it is the king's most sweet pleasure and 5.01. 87 P
by our /assistance, the king's command, and this 5.01.121 P
one show worse than the king's and his company. 5.02.513
would for the king's sake he were living! AWW 1.01. 22 P
it would be the death of the king's disease. 1.01. 23 P
the king's disease — my project may deceive me, 1.01.228
cannot be too sweet for the king's tartness. 4.03. 82 P
the king's not here. 5.01. 22
the king's coming, i know by his trumpets. 5.02. 51 P
the king's a beggar, now the play is done; ep 1
than one condemn'd by the king's own mouth — WT 1.02.445
and so | the king's will be perform'd! 2.01.115
a moi'ty of the throne, a great king's daughter, 3.02. 39
i mentioned a son o' th' king's, which florizel 4.01. 22
whoobub against his daughter and the king's son, 4.04.616 P
go about to make me the king's brother–in–law. 4.04.702 P
the king's daughter is found. 5.02. 23 P
with all certainty, to be the king's daughter. 5.02. 39 P
for the king's son took me by the hand, and 5.02.140 P
then take my king's defiance from my mouth, JN 1.01. 21
with them a bastard of the king's deceas'd, 2.01. 65
man, | i have a king's oath to the contrary. 3.01. 10
in god's name and the king's, say who thou art R2 1.03. 11
is not the king's name twenty thousand names? 3.02. 85
or i'll be buried in the king's high way, | some 3.03.155
have any resting for her true king's queen. 5.01. 6
i am the king's friend, and will rid his foe. 5.04. 11
hath with the king's blood stain'd the king's 5.05.110
the king's blood stain'd the king's own land. 5.05.110
be damn'd for never a king's son in christendom. 1H4 1.02. 97 P
help me to my horse, good king's son. 2.02. 41 P
there's money of the king's coming down the hill 2.02. 54 P
the hill, 'tis going to the king's exchequer. 2.02. 55 P
lie, ye rogue, 'tis going to the king's tavern. 2.02. 56 P
a king's son! 2.04.136 P
what may the king's whole battle reach unto? 4.01.129
i have misus'd the king's press damnably. 4.02. 12 P
wilt thou kill god's officers and the king's? 2H4 2.01. 51 P
upon hasty employment in the king's affairs. 2.01.128 P
say, "there's some of the king's blood spilt." 2.02.113 P
a /borrower's cap, "i am the king's poor cousin, 2.02.116 P
a bastard son of the king's? 2.04.283 P
and one of the king's justices of the peace. 3.02. 58 P
with ringing in the king's affairs upon his 3.02.182 P
i like this fair proceeding of the king's. 5.05. 97
in th' eleventh year of the last king's reign H5 1.01. 2
as much as would maintain, to the king's honor, 1.01. 12
the king's a bawcock, and a heart of gold, | a 4.01. 44
any where so contented as in the king's company, 4.01.127 P
enough, if we know we are the king's subjects. 4.01.131 P
for before–breach of the king's laws in now the 4.01.171 P
of the king's laws in now the king's quarrel. 4.01.171 P
every subject's duty is the king's, but every 4.01.177 P
do it, though i take thee in the king's company. 4.01.220 P
that play'st so subtilly with a king's repose. 4.01.258
carried away all that was in the king's tent; 4.07. 8 P
this day against god's peace and the king's, we 1H6 1.03. 75 P
for treason executed in our late king's days? 2.04. 91
not her penance exceed the king's commission. 2H6 2.04. 75
as place duke humphrey for the king's protector? 3.01.250
more, the king's council are no good workmen. 4.02. 14 P
his brother are hard by, with the king's forces. 4.02.114 P
and you that be the king's friends, follow me. 4.02.181
thither gone to crave the french king's sister 3H6 3.01. 30
we charge you, in god's name and the king's, 3.01. 97
your king's name be obey'd, | and what god will, 3.01. 99
madam, in our king's behalf | i am commanded, 3.03. 59
when i have heard your king's desert recounted, 3.03.132
the lord hastings, the king's chiefest friend. 4.03. 11
how my sword weeps for the poor king's death! 5.06. 63
as thou dost swallow up this good king's blood, R3 1.02. 66
my voice is now the king's, my looks mine own. 1.04.168
our swift–winged souls may catch the king's, 2.02. 44
that at her hands which the king's king forbids. 4.04.346
besides, the king's name is a tower of strength, 5.03. 12
that he would please to alter the king's course, H8 1.01.189
be done, and the king's pleasure | by me obey'd! 1.01.215
every shire, | of the king's grace and pardon. 1.02.104
would prove perfidious, | to the king's danger. 1.02.157
the king's attorney on the contrary | urg'd on 2.01. 15
my vows and prayers | yet are the king's; 2.01. 89
he dives into the king's soul, and there 2.02. 26
see this main end, | the french king's sister. 2.02. 41
heaven will one day open | the king's eyes, that 2.02. 42
you are the king's now. 2.02.118
the king's majesty | commends his good opinion 2.03. 60
you wrong the king's love with these fears, 3.01. 81
put your main cause into the king's protection, 3.01. 93
utterly | grow from the king's acquaintance, by 3.01.161
hath ta'en much pain | in the king's business. 3.02. 73
duchess of alanson, | the french king's sister; 3.02. 86
hear the king's pleasure, cardinal! 3.02.228
bearing the king's will from his mouth expressly 3.02.235
those articles, my lord, are in the king's hand: 3.02.299
that, without the king's assent or knowledge, 3.02.310
without the king's will or the state's allowance 3.02.322
your holy hat to be stamp'd on the king's coin. 3.02.325
lord cardinal, the king's further pleasure is — 3.02.337
and to be | out of the king's protection. 3.02.344
i have, | to the last penny, 'tis the king's. 3.02.452
not appearance and | the king's late scruple, by 4.01. 31
'tis now the king's, and call'd whitehall. 4.01. 97
newly preferr'd from the king's secretary, | the 4.01.102
the king's request that i would visit you, | who 4.02.116
master | o' th' rolls, and the king's secretary; 5.01. 35
th' archbishop | is the king's hand and tongue, 5.01. 38
'tis butts, | the king's physician. 5.02. 11
there to remain till the king's further pleasure 5.02.125
this is the king's ring. 5.02.137
the king's a–bed. MAC 2.01. 12
malcolm and donalbain, the king's two sons, 2.04. 25
and the king's rouse the heaven shall bruit HAM 1.02.127
such thanks | as fits a king's remembrance. 2.02. 26
sir, that soaks up the king's countenance, his 4.02. 15 P
was, sir, yorick's skull, the king's jester. 5.01.181 P
and his crib shall stand at the king's mess. 5.02. 87 P
to my purposes, they follow the king's pleasure. 5.02.201 P
i can no more — the king, the king's to blame. 5.02.320
bear the king's son's body | before our army. ANT 3.01. 3
it was a king's. 4.08. 27
our courtiers' | still seem as does the king's. CYM 1.01. 3
their faces to the bent | of the king's looks, 1.01. 14
that a king's children should be so convey'd, 1.01. 63
this matter of marrying his king's daughter, 1.04. 14 P
lose it for a revenue | of any king's in europe! 2.03.144
to the king's party there's no going. 4.04. 9
further to question me of your king's departure. PER 1.03. 11
since he's gone, the king's seas must please: 1.03. 27
/yon king's to me like to my father's picture, 2.03. 37
'tis the king's subtilty to have my life. 2.05. 44
she was of tyrus the king's daughter, | on whom 4.04. 36
know at large the cause | of your king's sorrow. 5.01. 63
how, a king's daughter? | and call'd marina? 5.01.149
we accept of the king's mercy, but we will show STM II.C 19 P
hold, in the king's name hold! II.C 26

KINGS' 5 FR 0.0005 REL FR 3 V 2 P
a weather–bitten conduit of many kings' reigns. WT 5.02. 56 P
no word like "pardon" for kings' mouths so meet.
R2 5.03.118
when for a day of kings' entreaties a mother COR 1.03. 8 P
look | like patience gazing on kings' graves, PER 5.01.138
then kings' misdeeds cannot be hid in clay. LUC 609

/KINGS 1 FR 0.0001 REL FR 1 V 0 P
sons /he /there proclaim'd the /kings of kings: ANT 3.06. 13

KINGS 130 FR 0.0147 REL FR 121 V 9 P
that his issue | should become kings of naples? TMP 5.01.206
wherein doth sit the dread and fear of kings; MV 4.01.192
sway, | it is enthroned in the hearts of kings, 4.01.194
of thousands that had struck anointed kings WT 1.02.358
kings are no less unhappy, their issue not being 4.02. 26 P
did you see the meeting of the two kings? 5.02. 40 P
act was worth the audience of kings and princes, 5.02. 80 P
and then the two kings call'd my father brother; 5.02.141 P
hark, the kings and the princes, our kindred, 5.02.172 P
and here justified | by us, a pair of kings. 5.03.146
with slaughter coupled to the name of kings. JN 2.01.349
when the rich blood of kings is set on fire! 2.01.351
of men, | in undetermin'd differences of kings. 2.01.355
cry "havoc," kings! 2.01.357
kings of our fear, until our fears, resolv'd, 2.01.371
these scroyles of angiers flout you, kings, 2.01.373
hear us, great kings! 2.01.416
persever not, but hear me, mighty kings. 2.01.421
two such controlling bounds shall you be, kings, 2.01.444
mad world, mad kings, mad composition! 2.01.561
of kings, of beggars, old men, young men, maids, 2.01.570
since kings break faith upon commodity, | gain, 2.01.597
madam, | i may not go without you to the kings. 3.01. 66
state of my great grief | let kings assemble; 3.01. 71
here is my throne, bid kings come bow to it. 3.01. 74
arm, you heavens, against these perjur'd kings! 3.01.107
set armed discord 'twixt these perjur'd kings! 3.01.111
though you and all the kings of christendom 3.01.162
the fearful difference of incensed kings — 3.01.238
it is the curse of kings to be attended | by 4.02.208
such is the breath of kings. R2 1.03.215
this royal throne of kings, this sceptred isle, 2.01. 40
this nurse, this teeming womb of royal kings, 2.01. 51
these signs forerun the death or fall of kings. 2.04. 15
and tell sad stories of the death of kings: 3.02.156
base court, where kings grow base, | to come at 3.03.180
knowest the way | to plant unrightful kings, 5.01. 63
and if we live, we live to tread on kings, | if 1H4 5.02. 85
rigol hath divorc'd | so many english kings. 2H4 4.05. 37
'tis your thoughts that now must deck our kings, H5 pr 28
so do the kings of france unto this day. 1.02. 90
your brother kings and monarchs of the earth 1.02.122
to fill king edward's fame with prisoner kings, 1.02.162
following the mirror of all christian kings, 2.pr. 6
and by their hands this grace of kings must die, 2.pr. 28
what infinite heart's–ease | must kings neglect, 4.01.237
and what have kings, that privates have not too, 4.01.238
great kings of france and england: 5.02. 24
o kate, nice customs cur'sy to great kings. 5.02.269 P
he was a king blest of the king of kings. 1H6 1.01. 28
before the kings and queens of france. 1.06. 27
but kings and mightiest potentates must die, 3.02.136
swain, | but issued from the progeny of kings; 5.04. 38
in presence of the kings of france and sicil, 2H6 1.01. 6
i never read but england's kings have had 1.01.128
and in that chair where kings and queens were 1.02. 38
the spirit of putting down kings and princes — 4.02. 36 P
fellow kings, i tell you that that lord say hath 4.02.164 P
this tongue hath parley'd unto foreign kings 4.07. 77
thou setter–up and plucker–down of kings, 3H6 2.03. 37
to force that fear their subjects' treachery? 2.05. 45
henry, hadst thou sway'd as kings should do, 2.06. 14
say, what art thou talk'st of kings and queens? 3.01. 55
and men may talk of kings, and why not i? 3.01. 58
a crown it is that seldom kings enjoy. 3.01. 65
old, | my father and my grandfather were kings; 3.01. 77

and be you kings: 3.01. 93
learn a while to serve | where kings command. 3.03. 6
proud setter–up and puller–down of kings! 3.03.157
the great king of kings | hath in the table of R3 1.04.195
lest he that is the supreme king of kings 2.01. 13
kings it makes gods, and meaner creatures kings. 5.02. 24
kings it makes gods, and meaner creatures kings. 5.02. 24
live and beget a happy race of kings! 5.03.152
the two kings, | equal in lustre, were now best, H8 1.01. 28
kings, princes, lords! TRO 1.03.264
ships, | and turn'd crown'd kings to merchants. 2.02. 83
fresh kings are come to troy; 2.03.261
you shall do more | than all the island kings — 3.01.154
his beam, | upon the pashed corses of the kings 5.05. 10
circling shadows kings have sought to sleep in, TIT 2.04. 19
two such opposed kings encamp them still | in ROM 2.03. 27
thou shalt get kings, though thou be none. MAC 1.03. 67
your children shall be kings. 1.03. 86
do you not hope your children shall be kings, 1.03.118
should be the root and father | of many kings. 3.01. 6
they hail'd him father to a line of kings. 3.01. 59
to make them kings — the seeds of banquo kings! 3.01. 69
to make them kings — the seeds of banquo kings! 3.01. 69
of the happy throne, | and fall of many kings. 4.03. 69
and it hath been | the sword of our slain kings. 4.03. 87
of your precedent lord, a vice of kings, | a HAM 3.04. 98
richer than that which four successive kings 5.02.273
let me be married to three kings in a forenoon, ANT 1.02. 27 P
three kings i had newly feasted, and did want 2.02. 76
to kiss — a hand that kings | have lipp'd, and 2.05. 29
sons /he /there proclaim'd the /kings of kings: 3.06. 13
are levying | the kings o' th' earth for war. 3.06. 68
and amyntas, | the kings of mede and lycaonia, 3.06. 75
six kings already | show me the way of yielding. 3.10. 33
which had superfluous kings for messengers | not 3.12. 5
unto a muss, kings would start forth | and cry, 3.13. 91
me well, | and kings have been your fellows. 4.02. 13
the kings that have revolted, and the soldier 4.05. 4
but it is tidings | to wash the eyes of kings. 5.01. 28
a princess | descended of so many royal kings. 5.02.327
the kings your ancestors, together with | the CYM 3.01. 17
that hath moe kings his servants than | thyself 3.01. 63
kings, queens, and states, | maids, matrons, nay 3.04. 37
and falsehood | is worse in kings than beggars. 3.06. 14
kings are earth's gods; PER 1.01.103
fits kings as they are men, for they may err. 1.02. 43
that kings should let their ears hear their 1.02. 62
who stood equivalent with mighty kings, | but 5.01. 91
give us the bones | of our dead kings, that we TNK 1.01. 50
duke, think | what beds our slain kings have! 1.01.140
sun, | and were good kings when living. 1.01.147
think | of rotten kings or blubber'd queens? 1.01.180
might well | be by a pair of kings back'd, in a 3.01. 21
thou wor'st that day the three kings fell, but 3.06. 71
and that you sit as kings in your desires, STM II.C 77
clepes him king of graves and grave for kings, VEN 995
that kings might be espoused to more fame, | but LUC 20
for kings like gods should govern every thing. 602
or kings be breakers of their own behests? 852
"time's glory is to calm contending kings, | to 939
grooms are sightless night, kings glorious day; 1013
so | as seely jeering idiots are with kings, 1812
that then i scorn to change my state with kings. SON 29.14
in 'twixt vows, and change decrees of kings, 115. 6

KINRED *(also kindred, etc.)*

KINRED 4 FR 0.0004 REL FR 3 V 1 P
and truly i hold it a sin to match in my kinred. ADO 2.01. 65 P
gage, | disclaiming here the kinred of the king, R2 1.01. 70
his hands were guilty of no kinred blood, | but 2.01.182
whom conscience and my kinred bids to right. 2.02.115

KINRED'S 1 FR 0.0001 REL FR 1 V 0 P
and make us wade even in our kinred's blood: R2 1.03.138

KINREDS 1 FR 0.0001 REL FR 0 V 1 P
and kinreds are mightily strengthen'd. 2H4 2.02. 26 P

KINSMAN 51 FR 0.0057 REL FR 41 V 10 P
quickly, my kinsman shall speak for himself. WIV 3.04. 22 P
were he my kinsman, brother, or my son, | it MM 2.02. 81
kinsman to grim and comfortless despair, | and ERR 5.01. 80
but in that thou art like to be my kinsman, live ADO 5.04.111 P
told my love, | in glory of my kinsman hercules. MND 5.01. 47
here comes bassanio, your most noble kinsman, MV 1.01. 57
peace, fool, he's not thy kinsman. AYL 2.04. 67
but to speak of him as my kinsman, he's a most AWW 3.06. 9 P
sir toby, madam, your kinsman. TN 1.05.105 P
though she harbors you as her kinsman, she's 2.03. 97 P
do theirs — to ask for my kinsman toby — 2.05. 55 P
be opposite with a kinsman, surly with servants; 2.05.150 P
"be opposite with a kinsman, surly with servants 3.04. 69 P
i am sorry, madam, i have hurt your kinsman. 5.01.209
i have a kinsman not past three quarters of a WT 4.03. 80 P
come hither, little kinsman, hark, a word. JN 3.03. 18
should move you to mew up | your tender kinsman, 4.02. 58
gentle kinsman, go | and thrust thyself into 4.02.166
my lord, your valiant kinsman, faulconbridge, 5.03. 5
and let him be no kinsman to my liege, | i do R2 1.01. 59
whether our kinsman come to see his friends. 1.04. 22
his noble kinsman — most degenerate king! 2.01.262
t' other again | is my kinsman, whom the king 2.02.114
farewell, kinsman! 1H4 1.03.234
to make that worse, suff'red his kinsman march 4.03. 93
and his kinsman too. H5 4.01. 59 P
and my kind kinsman, warriors all, adieu! 4.03. 10
do, | because he is near kinsman unto charles. 1H6 5.05. 45
our kinsman gloucester is as innocent | from 2H6 3.01. 69
but you have power in me as in a kinsman. R3 3.01.109
why, how now, kinsman, wherefore storm you so?
ROM 1.05. 60
tybalt, the kinsman to old capulet, | hath sent 2.04. 6
romeo, | that slew thy kinsman, brave mercutio. 3.01.145
o, the blood is spill'd | of my dear kinsman! 3.01.148
he is a kinsman to the montague, | affection 3.01.176
that name's cursed hand | murder'd her kinsman. 3.03.105
look you, she lov'd her kinsman tybalt dearly, 3.04. 3
being our kinsman, if we revel much: 3.04. 26
is my poor heart, so for a kinsman vex'd. 3.05. 95
mercutio's kinsman, noble county paris! 5.03. 75
it is a peerless kinsman. MAC 1.04. 58
first, as i am his kinsman and his subject, 1.07. 13
i have a kinsman who | is bound for italy; CYM 3.06. 60
hercules our kinsman | (then weaker than your TNK 1.01. 66
so strangely, so unlike a noble kinsman, | to 2.02.190
traitor kinsman, | thou shouldst perceive my 3.01. 30
kinsman, you might as well | speak this, and act 3.01. 69
good morrow, noble kinsman. 3.06. 17
wish ye | as kind a kinsman as you force me find 3.06. 21
your kinsman hath confess'd the right o' th' 5.04.116
but as he is my kinsman, my dear friend, | the LUC 237

KINSMAN'S 3 FR 0.0003 REL FR 2 V 1 P
of you, and pace softly towards my kinsman's. WT 4.03.113 P
misuse the tenor of thy kinsman's trust? 1H4 5.05. 5
in this rage, with some great kinsman's bone, ROM 4.03. 53

KINSMEN 24 FR 0.0027 REL FR 23 V 1 P
commend me to my kinsmen and my son. AWW 2.02. 65
both are my kinsmen: R2 2.02.111
two kinsmen digg'd their graves with weeping 3.03.169
both are my kinsmen, and i love them both. 1H6 4.01.155
thy kinsmen and thy friends, i'll have more 3H6 1.01. 96
i do know | kinsmen of mine, three at the least, H8 1.01. 81
kinsmen, this is the way. TIT 4.03. 1
and, kinsmen, then we may go pipe for justice. 4.03. 24
kinsmen, his sorrows are past remedy, | but /... 4.03. 31
kinsmen, shoot all your shafts into the court, 4.03. 62
"better," here comes one of my master's kinsmen.
ROM 1.01. 59 P
thou art, | if any of my kinsmen find thee here. 2.02. 65
therefore thy kinsmen are no stop to me. 2.02. 69
discords too | have lost a brace of kinsmen. 5.03.295
sons, kinsmen, thanes, | and you whose places MAC 1.04. 35
my thanes and kinsmen, | henceforth be earls, 5.09. 28
incense her kinsmen, | and, though he in a OTH 1.01. 69
whose kinsmen have made suit | that their good CYM 5.05. 71
not his kinsmen | in blood unless in quality. TNK 1.02. 78
knights, kinsmen, lovers, yea, my sacrifices, 5.01. 34
so it far'd | good space between these kinsmen; 5.03.129
my dear kinsmen, | whose lives (for this poor 5.04. 13
and tithe of knees | from elder kinsmen, and him STM III 10
thy kinsmen hang their heads at this disdain, LUC 521

KINSWOMAN 3 FR 0.0003 REL FR 0 V 3 P
slander'd, scorn'd, dishonor'd my kinswoman? ADO 4.01.302 P
sir, and a kinswoman of my master's. 2H4 2.02.155 P
but, for my part, she is my kinswoman; TRO 1.01. 44 P

KIRTLE 2 FR 0.0002 REL FR 1 V 1 P
what stuff wilt have a kirtle of? 2H4 2.04.274 P
and a kirtle | embroidered all with leaves of PP 19.11

KISS 220 FR 0.0248 REL FR 182 V 38 P
here, kiss the book. TMP 2.02.130 P
kiss the book. 2.02.142 P
and i will kiss thy foot. 2.02.149
i'll kiss thy foot. 2.02.152
come, kiss. 2.02.157 P
and presently, all humbled, kiss the rod! TGV 1.02. 59
i'll kiss each several paper for amends. 1.02.105
and thus i search it with a sovereign kiss. 1.02.113
now kiss, embrace, contend, do what you will. 1.02.126
and seal the bargain with a holy kiss. 2.02. 7
now should i kiss my father; 2.03. 26 P
well, i kiss her; 2.03. 28 P
should from her vesture chance to steal a kiss, 2.04.160
giving a gentle kiss to every sedge | he 2.07. 29
stop his mouth with a kiss, and let not him ADO 2.01.311 P
i will kiss your hand, and so i leave you. 4.01.332 P
foul words — and thereupon i will kiss thee. 5.02. 51 P
you give him for my sake but one loving kiss. LLL 2.01.249
to see him kiss his hand! 4.01.146
"so sweet a kiss the golden sun gives not | to 4.03. 25
the stairs, as he treads on them, kiss his feet. 5.02.330
i will kiss thy royal finger, and take leave. 5.02.882 P
o, let me kiss | this princess of pure white, MND 3.02.143
and kiss thy fair large ears, my gentle joy. 4.01. 4
o, kiss me through the hole of this vild wall! 5.01.200
i kiss the wall's hole, not your lips at all. 5.01.201
top lower than her ribs | to kiss her burial. MV 1.01. 29
of the earth they come | to kiss this shrine, 2.07. 40
some there be that shadows kiss, | such have but 2.09. 66
lady is, | and claim her with a loving kiss." 3.02.138
when the sweet wind did gently kiss the trees 5.01. 2
salute not at the court but you kiss your hands; AYL 3.02. 49 P
and would you have us kiss tar? 3.02. 63 P
i would kiss before i spoke. 4.01. 72 P
lack of matter, you might take occasion to kiss. 4.01. 75 P
matter, the cleanliest shift is to kiss. 4.01. 77 P
how if the kiss be denied? 4.01. 78 P
were a woman i would kiss as many of you as had ep 18 P
my neck, and kiss on kiss | she vied so fast, SHR 2.01.308
my neck, and kiss on kiss | she vied so fast, 2.01.308
and kiss me, kate, we will be married a' sunday. 2.01.324
bride | and seal the title with a lovely kiss! 3.02.123
master's horse–tail till they kiss their hands. 4.01. 94 P
kate, that you must kiss, and be acquainted with 4.01.152
see how they kiss and court! 4.02. 27
first kiss me, kate, and we will. 5.01.143
no, sir, god forbid, but asham'd to kiss. 5.01.146
nay, i will give thee a kiss; 5.01.148
very well mended. kiss him for that, good widow. 5.02. 25
come on, and kiss me, kate. 5.02.180
to join like likes, and kiss like native things. AWW 1.01.223
put off 's cap, kiss his hand, and say nothing, 2.02. 10 P
strangers and foes do sunder, and not kiss. 2.05. 86
men are to mell with, boys are not to kiss; 4.03.228
plenty, | then come kiss me, sweet and twenty; TN 2.03. 51
dost thou smile so, and kiss thy hand so oft? 3.04. 33 P
's | with one soft kiss a thousand furlongs ere WT 1.02. 95
you'll kiss me hard and speak to me as if | i 2.01. 5
i think there is not half a kiss to choose | who 4.04.175
they kneel, they kiss the earth; 5.01.199
the stars, i see, will kiss the valleys first; 5.01.206
but began, | give me that hand of yours to kiss. 5.03. 46
let no man mock me, | for i will kiss her. 5.03. 80
you'll mar it if you kiss it; 5.03. 82
upon thy cheek lay i this zealous kiss | as seal JN 2.01. 19
the day, | and kiss him with a glorious victory. 2.01.394
so i kiss your hand. 3.03. 16
and i will kiss thy detestable bones, | and put 3.04. 29
him, | and kiss the lips of unacquainted change, 3.04.166
to make his bleak winds kiss my parched lips 5.07. 40
let me kiss my sovereign's hand | and bow my R2 1.03. 46
and craves to kiss your hand and take his leave. 1.03. 63
on both his knees doth kiss king richard's hand, 3.03. 36
harry bullingbrook, doth humbly kiss thy hand, 3.03.104
take the correction, mildly kiss the rod, | and 5.01. 32
and yet not so, for with a kiss 'twas made. 5.01. 75
one kiss shall stop our mouths, and dumbly part; 5.01. 95
thou never see titan kiss a dish of butter, 1H4 2.04.120 P
to meet you on the way, and kiss your hand, 5.01. 36
let heaven kiss earth! 2H4 1.01.153
pray, all you that kiss my lady peace at home, 1.02.207 P
and didst thou not kiss me, and bid me fetch 2.01.102 P
sweet knight, i kiss thy neaf. 2.04.186 P
kiss me, doll. 2.04.262 P
troth, i kiss thee with a most constant heart. 2.04.269 P
that i and greatness were compell'd to kiss), 3.01. 74
john your son doth kiss your grace's hand. 4.04. 83
i cannot kiss, that is the humor of it; H5 2.03. 60 P
i kiss his dirty shoe, and from heart–string | i 4.01. 47
upon that i kiss your hand, and i call you my 5.02.251 P
then i will kiss your lips, kate. 5.02.257 P
to kiss. 5.02.263 P
maids in france to kiss before they are married, 5.02.266 P
fashion of your country in denying me a kiss: 5.02.274 P
that here i kiss her as my sovereign queen. 5.02.358
that i may kindly give one fainting kiss. 1H6 2.05. 40
i kiss these fingers for eternal peace, | and 5.03. 48
no kinder sign of love | than this kind kiss. 2H6 1.01. 19
o, could this kiss be printed in thy hand, 3.02.343
thus two friends condemn'd | embrace, and kiss, 3.02.354
let them kiss one another, for they lov'd well 4.07.130 P
the streets, and at every corner have them kiss. 4.07.136 P
see, see, they join, embrace, and seem to kiss, 3H6 2.01. 29
humbly to kiss your hand, and with my tongue 3.03. 61
in sign of truth, i kiss your highness' hand. 4.08. 26
come hither, bess, and let me kiss my boy. 5.07. 15
and kiss your princely nephew, brothers both. 5.07. 27
witness the loving kiss i give the fruit. 5.07. 32
i'll kiss thy hand | in sign of league and amity R3 1.03.279
love lord hastings, let him kiss your hand, 2.01. 21
give mistress shore one gentle kiss the more. 3.01.185
bear her my true love's kiss; 4.04.430
i kiss his hand. 4.05. 19
now, | he would kiss you twenty with a breath. H8 1.04. 30
to take you out | and not to kiss you. 1.04. 96
the hearts of princes kiss obedience, | so much 3.01.162
with this kiss take my blessing: 5.04. 10
so, so, rub on and kiss the mistress. TRO 3.02. 49 P
a kiss in fee–farm! 3.02. 50 P
me, | 'twas not my purpose thus to beg a kiss. 3.02.137
and scants us with a single famish'd kiss, 4.04. 47
come kiss, and let us part. 4.04. 98
our general doth salute you with a kiss. 4.05. 19
the first was menelaus' kiss, this, mine; 4.05. 32
paris and i kiss evermore for him. 4.05. 34
i'll have my kiss, sir. lady, by your leave. 4.05. 35
the kiss you take is better than you give; 4.05. 38
therefore no kiss. 4.05. 39
may i, sweet lady, beg a kiss of you? 4.05. 47
give me a kiss | when helen is a maid again and 4.05. 49
never's my day, and then a kiss of you. 4.05. 52
do buss the clouds, | must kiss their own feet. 4.05.221
memorial dainty kisses to it, | as i kiss thee. 5.02. 81
o, a kiss | long as my exile, sweet as my COR 5.03. 44
of heaven, that kiss | i carried from thee, dear 5.03. 46
make the silken strings delight to kiss them, TIT 2.04. 46
gentle lavinia, let me kiss thy lips, | or make 3.01.120
that kiss is comfortless | as frozen water to a 3.01.250
let's kiss and part, for we have much to do. 3.01.287
approach you must kneel, then kiss his foot, 4.03.111 P
o, take this warm kiss on thy pale cold lips, 5.03.153
tear for tear, and loving kiss for kiss, | thy 5.03.156
tear for tear, and loving kiss for kiss, | thy 5.03.156
o now, sweet boy, give them their latest kiss! 5.03.169
these happy masks that kiss fair ladies' brows, ROM 1.01.230
to smooth that rough touch with a tender kiss. 1.05. 96
touch, | and palm to palm is holy palmers' kiss. 1.05.100
you kiss by th' book. 1.05.110
fire and powder, | which as they kiss consume. 2.06. 11
farewell, farewell! one kiss, and i'll descend. 3.05. 42
till then adieu, and keep this holy kiss. 4.01. 43
seal with a righteous kiss | a dateless bargain 5.03.114
thus with a kiss i die. 5.03.120
i will kiss thy lips, | haply some poison yet 5.03.164
i will not kiss thee, then the rot returns | to TIM 4.03. 65
close impossibilities, | and mak'st them kiss! 4.03.388
stream | do kiss the most exalted shores of all. JC 1.01. 60
i kiss thy hand, but not in flattery, caesar; 3.01. 52
and they would go and kiss dead caesar's wounds, 3.02.132
entomb, | when living light should kiss it? MAC 2.04. 10
to kiss the ground before young malcolm's feet, 5.08. 28
this kiss, if it durst speak, | would stretch LR 4.02. 22
o, let me kiss that hand! 4.06.132
and let this kiss | repair those violent harms 4.07. 26
it evermore about her | to kiss and talk to. OTH 3.03.296
then kiss me hard, | as if he pluck'd up kisses 3.03.422
what, | to kiss in private? 4.01. 2
an unauthoriz'd kiss! 4.01. 2
i kiss the instrument of their pleasures. 4.01.218
but this, | killing myself, to die upon a kiss. 5.02.359
mark antony | will e'en but kiss octavia, and ANT 2.04. 3
and here | my bluest veins to kiss — a hand 2.05. 29
give me a kiss. 3.11. 70
i kiss his conqu'ring hand. 3.13. 75
i shall return once more | to kiss these lips, i 3.13.174
this is a soldier's kiss; 4.04. 30
wounds, and kiss | the honor'd gashes whole. 4.08. 10
kiss it, my warrior; 4.08. 24
and spend that kiss | which is my heaven to have 5.02.302
give him that parting kiss which i had set CYM 1.03. 34
but kiss, one kiss! 2.02. 17
but kiss, one kiss! 2.02. 17
gone to tell my lord | that i kiss aught but he. 2.03.148
'tis time to fear when tyrants seems to kiss. PER 1.02. 79
and the brine and cloudy billow kiss the moon, i 3.01. 46 P
the devil, if he should cheapen a kiss of her. 4.06. 10 P
haste, | i stamp this kiss upon thy currant lip. TNK 1.01.216
kiss her fair hand, sir. 2.05. 37
me what i would eat, and when i would kiss her. 5.02. 5

why do you rub my kiss off? 5.02. 88
and ill lodging, | but i'll kiss him up again. 5.02. 98
and shall we kiss too? 5.02.108
one kiss from fair emilia. 5.04. 94
what follows more, she murthers with a kiss. VEN 54
and one sweet kiss shall pay this comptless debt 84
boy, | 'tis but a kiss i beg, why art thou coy? 96
the kiss shall be thine own as well as mine. 117
"art thou asham'd to kiss? 121
and died to kiss his shadow in the brook. 162
what were thy lips the worse for one poor kiss? 207
give me one kiss, i'll give it thee again, | and 209
for men will kiss even by their own direction." 216
will never rise, so he will kiss her still. 480
"long may they kiss each other for this cure! 505
if you will say so, you shall have a kiss." 536
trips, | and all is but to rob thee of a kiss. 723
lest she should steal a kiss and die forsworn. 726
the kiss i gave you is bestow'd in vain, | and 771
some catch her by the neck, some kiss her face, 872
nor sun nor wind will ever strive to kiss you: 1082
why then i know | he thought to kiss him, and 1110
but by a kiss thought to persuade him there; 1114
wherein i will not kiss my sweet love's flow'r." 1188
under, | coz'ning the pillow of a lawful kiss; LUC 387
as heaven (it seem'd) to kiss the turrets bow'd. 1372
between each kiss her oaths of true love PP 7. 8
to kiss and clip me till i run away! 11.14
leap | to kiss the tender inward of thy hand, SON 128. 6
give them /thy fingers, me thy lips to kiss. 128.14
and play the mother's part, kiss me, be kind: 143.12
/KISS'D 2 FR 0.0002 REL FR 1 V 1 P
"item, she is not to be /kiss'd fasting, in TGV 3.01.323 P
and /sigh'd, and /kiss'd, and then | /cried, OTH 3.03.425
KISS'D 34 FR 0.0038 REL FR 28 V 6 P
curtsied when you have, and kiss'd, | the wild TMP 1.02.377
thou shalt be worshipp'd, kiss'd, lov'd, and TGV 4.04.199
but not kiss'd your keeper's daughter? WIV 1.01.113 P
after we had embrac'd, kiss'd, protested, and, 3.05. 73 P
is he | that kiss'd his hand away in courtesy; LLL 5.02.324
my cherry lips have often kiss'd thy stones, MND 5.01.190
when with his knees he kiss'd the cretan strond. SHR 1.01.170
and kiss'd her lips with such a clamorous smack 3.02.178
he threw his wounded arm, and kiss'd his lips, H5 4.06. 25
hast thou not kiss'd thy hand and held my 2H6 4.01. 53
thy lips that kiss'd the queen shall sweep the 4.01. 75
to say the truth, so judas kiss'd his master, 3H6 5.07. 33
and pitied me, and kindly kiss'd my cheek; R3 2.02. 24
/which in their summer beauty kiss'd each other. 4.03. 13
'twere better she were kiss'd in general. TRO 4.05. 21
lips that i have kiss'd i know not how oft. HAM 5.01.188 P
better you had not kiss'd your three fingers so OTH 2.01.173 P
well kiss'd! 2.01.175 P
i kiss'd thee ere i kill'd thee. 5.02.358
he kiss'd — the last of many doubled kisses — ANT 1.05. 40
we have kiss'd away | kingdoms and provinces. 3.10. 7
and kiss'd it, madam. CYM 1.03. 6
when i kiss'd the jack upon an up-cast, to be 2.01. 2 P
i kiss'd it: 2.03.146
and winds of all the corners kiss'd your sails, 2.04. 28
i kiss'd it, and it gave me present hunger | to 2.04.137
bore heads so high they kiss'd the clouds, | and PER 1.04. 24
once he kiss'd me — | i lov'd my lips the TNK 2.04. 25
no, not so much as kiss'd me; 2.06. 22
the same breath smil'd, and kiss'd her hand. 4.01. 93
i told her, presently, and kiss'd her twice. 5.02. 6
even so she kiss'd his brow, his cheek, his chin VEN 59
and kiss'd the fatal knife, to end his vow; LUC 1843
and often kiss'd, and often /gan to tear; LC 51
KISSES 34 FR 0.0038 REL FR 30 V 4 P
but my kisses bring again, bring again, | seals MM 4.01. 5
kisses the base ground with obedient breast? LLL 4.03.221
marry, his kisses are judas's own children. AYL 3.04. 9 P
winter's sisterhood kisses not more religiously, 3.04. 16 P
then with kind embracements, tempting kisses, SHR in.1. 118
ergo, he that kisses my wife is my friend. AWW 1.03. 49 P
that, conclusions to be as kisses, if your four TN 5.01. 21 P
kisses the hands | of your fresh princess; WT 4.04.550
i understand thy kisses, and thou mine, | and 1H4 3.01.202
kisses the gashes | that bloodily did yawn upon H5 4.06. 13
his paly lips | with twenty thousand kisses, and 2H6 3.02.142
distinct breath and consign'd kisses to them, TRO 4.04. 45
patroclus kisses you. 4.05. 33
glove, | and gives memorial dainty kisses to it, 5.02. 80
th' wanton spoil | of phoebus' burning kisses — COR 2.01.218
and for my tidings gave me twenty kisses. TIT 5.01.120
o'er ladies' lips, who straight on kisses dream, ROM 1.04. 74
still blush, as thinking their own kisses sin; 3.03. 39
and breath'd such life with kisses in my lips 5.01. 8
dead, | when second husband kisses me in bed. HAM 3.02.185
and let him, for a pair of reechy kisses, | or 3.04.184
i found not cassio's kisses on her lips. OTH 3.03.341
as if he pluck'd up kisses by the roots | that 3.03.423
the bawdy wind, that kisses all it meets, | is 4.02. 78
he kiss'd — the last of many doubled kisses — ANT 1.05. 40
on that unworthy place, | as it rain'd kisses. 3.13. 85
until | of many thousand kisses the poor last 4.15. 20
loaden with kisses, arm'd with thousand cupids, TNK 2.02. 31
and being set, i'll smother thee with kisses. VEN 18
ten kisses short as one, one long as twenty: 22
he kisses her, and she by her good will | will 479
"a thousand kisses buys my heart from me, | and 517
is twenty hundred kisses such a trouble?" 522
were kisses all the joys in bed, | one woman PP 18.47
KISSING 26 FR 0.0029 REL FR 20 V 6 P
beat the ground | for kissing of their feet; TMP 4.01.174
a kissing traitor. how art thou prov'd judas? LLL 5.02.600 P
and, by this virgin palm now kissing thine, | i 5.02.806
ripe in show | thy lips, those kissing cherries, MND 3.02.140
and i remember the kissing of her batler and the AYL 2.04. 49 P
and his kissing is as full of sanctity as the 3.04. 13 P
kissing with inside lip? WT 1.02.286
marry, garlic, | to mend her kissing with! 4.04.163
to make the base earth proud with kissing it. R2 3.03.191
on the top on't (colevile kissing my foot), to 2H4 4.03. 49 P
for it was made | for kissing, lady, not for R3 1.02.172
when the brown wench | lay kissing in your arms, H8 3.02.296
i had good argument for kissing once. TRO 4.05. 26
but that's no argument for kissing now, | for 4.05. 27
in kissing, do you render or receive? 4.05. 36
and bow'd like bondmen, kissing caesar's feet; JC 5.01. 42
in a dead dog, being a good kissing carrion — HAM 2.02.182 P
that kings | have lipp'd, and trembled kissing. ANT 2.05. 30
here they might take two thieves kissing. 2.06. 96 P
when thou hast liv'd, | quicken with kissing. 4.15. 39
tendance, kissing, to | o'ercome you with her CYM 5.05. 53
i am then | kissing the man they look for. TNK 2.06. 37
and kissing speaks, with lustful language broken VEN 47
she seeks to kindle with continual kissing. 606
with kissing him i should have kill'd him first, 1118
kissing with golden face the meadows green, SON 33. 3
KISSING-COMFITS 1 FR 0.0001 REL FR 0 V 1 P
tune of "green-sleeves," hail kissing-comfits, WIV 5.05. 20 P
KITCHEN 6 FR 0.0006 REL FR 4 V 2 P
sir, she's the kitchen wench and all grease, and ERR 3.02. 95 P
did not her kitchen maid rail, taunt, and scorn 4.04. 74
certes she did, the kitchen vestal scorn'd you. 4.04. 75
the kitchen malkin pins | her richest lockram COR 2.01.208
laura to his lady was a kitchen wench (marry, ROM 2.04. 40 P
our brags | were crak'd of kitchen trulls, or CYM 5.05.177
KITCHEN'D 1 FR 0.0001 REL FR 1 V 0 P
that kitchen'd me for you to-day at dinner: ERR 5.01.416
KITCHENS 2 FR 0.0002 REL FR 2 V 0 P
even for our kitchens | we kill the fowl of MM 2.02. 84
in your parlors, wild-cats in your kitchens, OTH 2.01.110
KITE 7 FR 0.0008 REL FR 6 V 1 P
when the kite builds, look to lesser linen. WT 4.03. 23 P
fetch forth the lazar kite of cressid's kind, H5 2.01. 76
set | to guard the chicken from a hungry kite, 2H6 3.01.249
although the kite soar with unbloodied beak? 3.02.193
is beauford term'd a kite? 3.02.196
detested kite, thou liest. LR 1.04.262
ah, you kite! ANT 3.13. 89
KITES 10 FR 0.0011 REL FR 8 V 2 P
as we watch these kites | that bate and beat and SHR 4.01.195
powerful spirit instruct the kites and ravens WT 2.03.186
and made a prey for carrion kites and crows 2H6 5.02. 11
whiles kites and buzzards /prey at liberty. R3 1.01.133
i' th' city of kites and crows. COR 4.05. 42 P
i' th' city of kites and crows? 4.05. 43 P
crows, and kites | fly o'er our heads, and JC 5.01. 84
our monuments | shall be the maws of kites. MAC 3.04. 72
i should 'a' fatted all the region kites | with HAM 2.02.579
the beaks of ravens, talents of the kites, | and TNK 1.01. 41
KITTEN 1 FR 0.0001 REL FR 1 V 0 P
i had rather be a kitten and cry mew | than one 1H4 3.01.127
KITTEN'D 1 FR 0.0001 REL FR 1 V 0 P
season if your mother's cat had | but kitten'd, 1H4 3.01. 19
KNACK 2 FR 0.0002 REL FR 2 V 0 P
a knack, a toy, a trick, a baby's cap. SHR 4.03. 67
sigh | that thou no more shalt see this knack WT 4.04.428
KNACKS 3 FR 0.0003 REL FR 3 V 0 P
knacks, trifles, nosegays, sweetmeats — MND 1.01. 34
you do, i was wont | to load my she with knacks. WT 4.04.349
th' enamell'd knacks o' th' mead or garden! TNK 3.01. 7
KNAPP'D* 2 FR 0.0002 REL FR 0 V 2 P
in that as ever knapp'd ginger or made her MV 3.01. 9 P
she knapp'd 'em o' th' coxcombs with a stick, LR 2.04.123 P
KNAVE 167 FR 0.0188 REL FR 50 V 117 P
this misshapen knave — | his mother was a witch TMP 5.01.268
the wit to think my master is a kind of a knave; TGV 3.01.264 P
but that's all one, if he be but one knave. 3.01.265 P
vere is dat knave rugby? WIV 1.04. 55 P
you heard what this knave told me, did you not? 2.01.169 P
the jealious rascally knave her husband will be 2.02.265 P
hang him, poor cuckoldly knave! 2.02.270 P
the jealous wittolly knave hath masses of money, 2.02.272 P
ford's a knave, and i will aggravate his style; 2.02.284 P
master /brook, shalt know him for knave, and 2.02.285 P
and galen — and he is a knave besides, a 3.01. 66 P
a cowardly knave as you would desires to be 3.01. 67 P
may be the knave bragg'd of that he could not 3.03.199 P
now remembrance to-morrow on the lousy knave, 3.03.240 P
a lousy knave, to have his gibes and his 3.03.242 P
met the jealous knave their master in the door, 3.05.101 P
lest the lunatic knave would have search'd it; 3.05.103 P
the knave constable had set me i' th' stocks, i' 4.05.119 P
that same knave ford, her husband, hath the 5.01. 17 P
i'll tell you strange things of this knave ford, 5.01. 27 P
master /brook, falstaff's a knave, a cuckoldly 5.05.110 P
/brook, falstaff's a knave, a cuckoldly knave; 5.05.110 P
thou art the first knave that e'er mad'st a duke MM 5.01.356
come on, sir knave, have done your foolishness, ERR 1.02. 72
there, take you that, sir knave. 1.02. 92
your wife, sir knave! go get you from the door. 3.01. 64
went in pain, master, this knave would go sore. 3.01. 65
together, and thank god you are rid of a knave. ADO 3.03. 30 P
i leave an arrant knave with your worship, which 5.01.321 P
o, my good knave costard, exceedingly well met! LLL 3.01.143 P
as thou wilt win my favor, good my knave, | do 3.01.152
in the fearful guard | of an unthrifty knave, MV 1.03.176
a christian do not play the knave and get thee, 2.03. 12 P
and swear by your beards that i am a knave. AYL 1.02. 73 P
and under that habit play the knave with him. 3.02.296 P
ne'er a fantastical knave of them all shall 3.03.106 P
me up for the lying'st knave in christendom. SHR in.2. 24 P
base is right, 'tis the base knave that jars. 3.01. 47
now, for my life, the knave doth court my love: 3.01. 49
where is the foolish knave i sent before? 4.01.127
a whoreson, beetle-headed, flap-ear'd knave! 4.01.157
carry this mad knave to the jail. 5.01. 92 P
what does this knave here? AWW 1.03. 8 P
such friends are thine enemies, knave. 1.03. 41 P
ever be a foul-mouth'd and calumnious knave? 1.03. 57 P
you'll be gone, sir knave, and do as i command 1.03. 90 P
as a scolding quean to a wrangling knave, as the 2.02. 26 P
not worth another word, else i'd call you knave. 2.03.263 P
o, my knave, how does my old lady? 2.04. 18 P
away, th' art a knave. 2.04. 28 P
sir, "before a knave th' art a knave," that's 2.04. 29 P
"before a knave th' art a knave," that's "before 2.04. 30 P
a knave," that's "before me th' art a knave." 2.04. 30 P
a good knave, i' faith, and well fed. 2.04. 38
i know that knave, hang him! 3.05. 16 P
yond's that same knave | that leads him to these 3.05. 82
sat i' th' stocks all night, poor gallant knave. 4.03.102 P
they are not herbs, you knave, they are 4.05. 18 P
dost thou profess thyself — a knave or a fool? 4.05. 22 P
at a woman's service, and a knave at a man's. 4.05. 24 P
so you were a knave at his service indeed. 4.05. 29 P
for thee, thou art both knave and fool. 4.05. 32 P
a shrewd knave and an unhappy. 4.05. 63 P
decay'd, ingenious, foolish, rascally knave. 5.02. 24 P
have you play'd the knave with fortune that she 5.02. 30 P
out upon thee, knave! 5.02. 48 P
though you are a fool and a knave, you shall eat 5.02. 54 P
as thou art a knave, and no knave. 5.03.249 P
as thou art a knave, and no knave. 5.03.249 P
most certain. let our catch be "thou knave." TN 2.03. 64 P
"hold thy peace, thou knave," knight? 2.03. 65 P
i shall be constrain'd in't to call thee knave, 2.03. 66 P
time i have constrain'd one to call me knave. 2.03. 68 P
the knave counterfeits well; a good knave. 4.02. 19 P
the knave counterfeits well; a good knave. 4.02. 19 P
an ass-head and a coxcomb and a knave, a 5.01.207 P
and a coxcomb and a knave, a thin-fac'd knave, a 5.01.207 P
what means this scorn, thou most untoward knave? JN 1.01.243
what is't, knave? R2 2.02. 96
farewell, you muddy knave. 1H4 2.01. 97 P
aside, thou art a knave to call me so. 3.03.120 P
say, what beast, thou knave, thou? 3.03.124 P
or any man knows where to have me, thou knave, 3.03.130 P
a /rascally yea-forsooth knave, to bear a 2H4 1.02. 36 P
a young knave, and begging? 1.02. 72 P
and that arrant malmsey-nose knave, bardolph, 2.01. 39 P
that visor is an arrant knave, on my knowledge. 5.01. 41 P
i grant your worship that he is a knave, sir; 5.01. 43 P
but a knave should have some countenance at his 5.01. 44 P
able to speak for himself, when a knave is not. 5.01. 46 P
a quarter bear out a knave against an honest man 5.01. 49 P
the knave is mine honest friend, sir, therefore 5.01. 50 P
the knave will stick by thee, i can assure thee 5.03. 65 P
no, thou arrant knave, i would to god that i 5.04. 1 P
and a basterd, and a knave, and a rascal. H5 3.02.123 P
arrant, rascally, beggarly, lousy knave it is. 4.08. 35 P
beggarly, lousy, pragging knave, pistol, which 5.01. 6 P
you scurvy, lousy knave, god pless you! 5.01. 18 P
heartily, scurvy, lousy knave, at my desires, 5.01. 22 P
will you be so good, scald knave, as eat it? 5.01. 30 P
you say very true, scald knave, when god's will 5.01. 32 P
much good do you, scald knave, heartily. 5.01. 53 P
go, go, you are a counterfeit cowardly knave. 5.01. 70 P
they say, "a crafty knave does need no broker," 2H6 1.02.100
how now, sir knave? 1.03. 22 P
a subtile knave, but yet it shall not serve. 2.01.102
sit there, the lying'st knave | in christendom. 2.01.123
follow the knave, and take this drab away. 2.01.153
to prove him a knave and myself an honest man; 2.03. 86 P
her husband, knave. wouldst thou betray me? R3 1.01.102
a false-hearted rogue, a most unjust knave. TRO 5.01. 89 P
i am a rascal, a scurvy railing knave, a very 5.04. 28 P
piece | will bear the knave by th' volume. COR 3.03. 33
scurvy knave, i am none of his flirt-gills, i am ROM 2.04.153 P
by too and suffer every knave to use me at his 2.04.155 P
scurvy knave! 2.04.162 P
what a pestilent knave is this same! 4.05.144 P
we may account thee a whoremaster and a knave, TIM 2.02.105 P
what, a knave too? 4.03.238
of men, | thou hadst been a knave and flatterer. 4.03.276
there's never a one of you but trusts a knave 5.01. 93
what trade, thou knave? JC 1.01. 15
thou naughty knave, what trade? 1.01. 15
poor knave, i blame thee not, thou art 4.03.241
gentle knave, good night; 4.03.269
in all denmark — | but he's an arrant knave. HAM 1.05.124
who was in life a foolish prating knave. 3.04.215
how the knave jowls it to the ground, as if 5.01. 76 P
he suffer this mad knave now to knock him about 5.01.101 P
how absolute the knave is! 5.01.137 P
though this knave came something saucily to the LR 1.01. 21 P
where's my knave? 1.04. 42 P
my lord's knave! 1.04. 80 P
now, my friendly knave, i thank thee, there's 1.04. 93 P
how now, my pretty knave, how dost thou? 1.04. 96 P
sir, more knave than fool, after your master. 1.04.314
a knave, a rascal, an eater of broken meats; 2.02. 15 P
hundred-pound, filthy worsted-stocking knave; 2.02. 17 P
and art nothing but the composition of a knave, 2.02. 21 P
you beastly knave, know you no reverence? 2.02. 69
hold more antipathy | than i and such a knave. 2.02. 88
why dost thou call him knave? what is his fault? 2.02. 89
you in a plain accent was a plain knave, which 2.02.112 P
you stubborn ancient knave, you reverent 2.02.126
sir, being his knave, i will. 2.02.137
the knave turns fool that runs away, | the fool 2.04. 84
that runs away, | the fool no knave, perdie. 2.04. 85
poor fool and knave, i have one part in my heart 3.02. 72
many a duteous and knee-crooking knave | that, OTH 1.01. 45
better guard | but with a knave of common hire, 1.01.125
a knave very voluble; 2.01.238 P
a slipper and subtle knave, a finder/-out of 2.01.242 P
a devilish knave. 2.01.245 P
besides, the knave is handsome, young, and hath 2.01.245 P
a pestilent complete knave, and the woman hath 2.01.247 P
a knave teach me my duty? 2.03.147 P
i'll beat the knave into a twiggen bottle. 2.03.147 P
for such things in a false disloyal knave | are 3.03.121
the moor's abus'd by some most villainous knave, 4.02.139
some base notorious knave, some scurvy fellow. 4.02.140
sorrow to behold a foul knave uncuckolded; ANT 1.02. 73 P
o, that his fault should make a knave of thee, 2.05.102
my good knave eros, now thy captain is | even 4.14. 12
yet cannot hold this visible shape, my knave. 4.14. 14
not being fortune, he's but fortune's knave, | a 5.02. 3
a sly and constant knave, | not to be shak'd; CYM 1.05. 75
what a drunken knave was the sea to cast thee in PER 2.01. 57 P
KNAVERIES 4 FR 0.0004 REL FR 1 V 3 P
admirable pleasures and fery honest knaveries. WIV 4.04. 81 P
or else commit'st thy knaveries willfully. MND 3.02.346
ability enough to make such knaveries yours. AWW 1.03. 12 P
of jests, and gipes, and knaveries, and mocks — H5 4.07. 49 P
KNAVERY 16 FR 0.0018 REL FR 5 V 11 P

knavery cannot sure hide himself in such ADO 2.03.119 P
this is a knavery of them to make me afeard. MND 3.01.112 P
i see their knavery. 3.01.120 P
by my knavery (if i had it) then i were. AYL 1.02. 75 P
here's no knavery! SHR 1.02.138 P
why, this is flat knavery, to take upon you 5.01. 36 P
and i, to sound the depth of this knavery. 5.01.137 P
i would we were well rid of this knavery. TN 4.02. 68 P
i hold it the more knavery to conceal it; WT 4.04.682 P
'tis as arrant a piece of knavery, mark you now, H5 4.07. 3 P
hume's knavery will be the duchess' wrack, | and 2H6 1.02.105
by holy mary, butts, there's knavery. H8 5.02. 33
such patchery, such juggling, and such knavery! TRO 2.03. 72 P
must sweep my way, | and marshal me to knavery.
HAM 3.04.205
where i found, horatio — | ah, royal knavery! 5.02. 19
and to plume up my will | in double knavery — OTH 1.03.394
KNAVERY'S 1 FR 0.0001 REL FR 1 V 0 P
knavery's plain face is never seen till us'd. OTH 2.01.312
KNAVE'S 8 FR 0.0009 REL FR 3 V 5 P
urinals about his knave's costard when i have WIV 3.01. 14 P
your /urinals about your knave's cogscomb /for 3.01. 89 P
show your knave's visage, with a pox to you! MM 5.01.353 P
breaking here, and i'll break your knave's pate. ERR 3.01. 74
rap me well, or i'll knock your knave's pate. SHR 1.02. 12
an ass and a beast, to bear every knave's wrong. 2H4 2.01. 38 P
this knave's tongue begins to double. 2H6 2.03. 91
foolish /young knave's sleeve of troy there in TRO 5.04. 4 P
KNAVES' 1 FR 0.0001 REL FR 0 V 1 P
are ambitious for poor knaves' caps and legs. COR 2.01. 68 P
KNAVES 43 FR 0.0048 REL FR 22 V 21 P
none, man, all idle — whores and knaves. TMP 2.01.167 P
the fear of god, and not with drunken knaves. WIV 1.01.184 P
in the basket, a couple of ford's knaves, his 3.05. 98 P
will take order for the drabs and the knaves, MM 2.01.235 P
a couple of as arrant knaves as any in messina. ADO 3.05. 32 P
that you are little better than false knaves, 4.02. 21 P
say to you, it is thought you are false knaves. 4.02. 28 P
and, to conclude, they are lying knaves. 5.01.219 P
may perhaps call him half a score knaves or so. SHR 1.02.111 P
where be these knaves? 4.01.120
and bring along these rascal knaves with thee? 4.01.131
for the knaves come to do that for me which i am AWW 1.03. 43 P
and would not have knaves thrive long under /her 5.02. 32 P
'gainst knaves and thieves men shut their gate, TN 5.01.395
he call'd them untaught knaves, unmannerly, | to 1H4 1.03. 43
bacon-fed knaves! 2.02. 84 P
hang ye, gorbellied knaves, are ye undone? 2.02. 88 P
what, ye knaves, young men must live! 2.02. 90 P
three misbegotten knaves in kendal green came at 2.04.222 P
for they are arrant knaves, and will backbite. 2H4 5.01. 32 P
to call them both a pair of crafty knaves. 2H6 1.02.103
might corrupt minds procure knaves as corrupt H8 5.01.132
these lazy knaves? 5.03. 70
y' are lazy knaves, | and here ye lie baiting of 5.03. 80
their cause is calling both the parties knaves. COR 2.01. 79 P
the smiles of knaves | tent in my cheeks, and 3.02.115
more light, you knaves, and turn the tables up; ROM 1.05. 27
thou art timon's dog, and these knaves honest. TIM 1.01.180
why dost thou call them knaves? 1.01.181
be small love amongest these sweet knaves, | and 1.01.249
ay, to see meat fill knaves, and wine heat fools 1.01.261
'tis not so base as you, | for you serve knaves. 3.04. 59
them all, let in the tide | of knaves once more; 3.04.117
bade welcome) | to knaves and all approachers. 4.03.216
all | i kept were knaves, to serve in meat to 4.03.478
we are arrant knaves, believe none of us. HAM 3.01.128 P
fools by heavenly compulsion, knaves, thieves, LR 1.02.123 P
these kind of knaves i know, which in this 2.02.101
i would have none but knaves follow it, since a 2.04. 76 P
whip me such honest knaves. OTH 1.01. 49
or heard him say — as knaves be such abroad, 4.01. 25
the buffet | with knaves that smells of sweat: ANT 1.04. 21
there are verier knaves desire to live, for all CYM 5.04.200 P
KNAVISH 7 FR 0.0008 REL FR 4 V 3 P
their herald is a pretty knavish page, | that LLL 5.02. 97
or else you are that shrewd and knavish sprite MND 2.01. 33
cupid is a knavish lad, | thus to make poor 3.02.440
having flown over many knavish professions, he WT 4.03. 99 P
and their executors, the knavish crows, | fly H5 4.02. 51
'tis a knavish piece of work, but what of that? HAM 3.02.240 P
of it, a knavish speech sleeps in a foolish ear. 4.02. 23 P
KNAV'RY 1 FR 0.0001 REL FR 1 V 0 P
amber bracelets, beads, and all this knav'ry. SHR 4.03. 58
KNEAD 1 FR 0.0001 REL FR 0 V 1 P
i will knead him, i'll make him supple. TRO 2.03.221 P
KNEADED 1 FR 0.0001 REL FR 1 V 0 P
sensible warm motion to become | a kneaded clod;
MM 3.01.120
KNEADING 2 FR 0.0002 REL FR 1 V 1 P
the civil citizens kneading up the honey, | the H5 1.02.199
here's yet in the word "hereafter" the kneading, TRO 1.01. 24 P
/KNEE 1 FR 0.0001 REL FR 1 V 0 P
/flatter, /bow, /and /bend /my /knee. R2 4.01.165
KNEE 66 FR 0.0074 REL FR 63 V 3 P
buckled below fair knighthood's bending knee: WIV 5.05. 72
will you not lend a knee? MM 5.01.442
with libbard's head on knee. LLL 5.02.548
then i confess | here on my knee, before high AWW 1.03.192
on my knee | i give heaven thanks i was not like JN 1.01. 82
upon my knee i beg, go not to arms | against 3.01.308
o, upon my knee, | made hard with kneeling, i do 3.01.309
to whom with all submission, on my knee, | i do 5.07.103
hand | and bow my knee before his majesty, | for R2 1.03. 47
well, | and had the tribute of his supple knee, 1.04. 33
show me thy humble heart, and not thy knee, 2.03. 83
to watch the fearful bending of thy knee, 3.03. 73
you debase your princely knee | to make the base 3.03.190
thus high at least, although your knee be low. 3.03.195
unto my mother's prayers i bend my knee. 5.03. 97
o happy vantage of a kneeling knee! 5.03.132
where i first bow'd my knee | unto this king of 1H4 1.03.245
ago, jack, since thou sawest thine own knee? 2.04.328 P
my own knee? 2.04.329 P
the more and less came in with cap and knee, 4.03. 68
sit on my knee, doll. 2H4 2.04.227 P
thou, when thou command'st the beggar's knee, H5 4.01.256
most humbly on my knee i beg | the leading of 4.03.130
stoop then and set your knee against my foot, 1H6 3.01.168
here on my knee i beg mortality, | rather than 4.05. 32
when he perceiv'd me shrink and on my knee, 4.07. 5
i'll either make thee stoop and bend thy knee, 5.01. 61
and humbly now upon my bended knee, | in sight 2H6 1.01. 10
look, | immediately he was upon his knee, | that 3.01. 11
eye, | and passeth by with stiff unbowed knee, 3.01. 16
on thy knee | make thee beg pardon for thy 3.02.220
/these | if they can brook i bow a knee to man. 5.01.110
why, warwick, hath thy knee forgot to bow? 5.01.161
in duty bend thy knee to me | that bows unto the 5.01.173
i am his king, and he should bow his knee. 3H6 2.02. 87
here on my knee i vow to god above | i'll never 2.03. 29
o warwick, i do bend my knee with thine, | and 2.03. 33
ere my knee rise from the earth's cold face, | i 2.03. 35
no bending knee will call thee caesar now, | no 3.01. 18
speak gentle words and humbly bend thy knee, 5.01. 22
stroke, | and humbly beg the death upon my knee.
R3 1.02.178
humbly on my knee | i crave your blessing. 2.02.105
he'll beat aufidius' head below his knee, | and COR 1.03. 46
self he met, | and struck him on his knee. 2.02. 95
thy knee bussing the stones (for in such 3.02. 75
fall down, and knee | the way into his mercy. 5.01. 5
sink, my knee, i' th' earth; 5.03. 50
your knee, sirrah. 5.03. 75
emperor, upon my feeble knee | i beg this boon, TIT 2.03.288
many a time he danc'd thee on his knee, | sung 5.03.162
even he drops down | the knee before him, and TIM 1.01. 61
and give them title, knee, and approbation 4.03. 37
hinge thy knee, | and let his very breath whom 4.03.211
let me, upon my knee, prevail in this. JC 2.02. 54
and on her knee | hath begg'd that i will stay 2.02. 81
and crook the pregnant hinges of the knee HAM 3.02. 61
i could as well be brought | to knee his throne, LR 2.04.214
upon my knee, what doth your speech import? OTH 4.02. 31
her hand on her bosom, her head on her knee, 4.03. 42
before the gods my knee shall bow my prayers ANT 2.03. 3
here's my knee. CYM 5.05.325
but now my heavy conscience sinks my knee, | as 5.05.413
lend us a knee; TNK 1.01. 96
o, help now! | our cause cries for your knee. 1.01.200
i'll cut my green coat a foot above my knee, 3.04. 19
and with his knee the door he opens wide. LUC 359
KNEE-CROOKING 1 FR 0.0001 REL FR 1 V 0 P
many a duteous and knee-crooking knave | that, OTH 1.01. 45
KNEE-DEEP 2 FR 0.0002 REL FR 2 V 0 P
inch-thick, knee-deep, o'er head and ears a WT 1.02.186
the place | was knee-deep where she sat; TNK 4.01. 83
/KNEEL 1 FR 0.0001 REL FR 1 V 0 P
/nor /nod, /nor /kneel, /nor /make /a /sign, TIT 3.02. 43
KNEEL 65 FR 0.0073 REL FR 62 V 3 P
i will kneel to him. TMP 2.02.118
kneel, and repeat it. 3.02. 40 P
but when they weep and kneel, | all their MM 1.04. 81
kneel down before him, hang upon his gown; 2.02. 44
speak loud and kneel before him. 5.01. 19
should she kneel down in mercy of this fact, 5.01.434
sweet isabel, do yet but kneel by me. 5.01.437
kneel to the duke before he pass the abbey. ERR 5.01.129
to offer war where they should kneel for peace, SHR 5.02.162
ere i can perfect mine intents, to kneel. AWW 4.04. 4
we all kneel. WT 2.03.153
shall i live on to see this bastard kneel | and 2.03.155
they kneel, they kiss the earth; 5.01.199
that | i kneel and then implore her blessing. 5.03. 44
please you to interpose, fair madam, kneel, 5.03.119
kneel thou down philip, but rise more great, JN 1.01.161
our knees still kneel till to the ground they R2 5.03.106
is | that doth with awe and terror kneel to it! 2H4 4.05.176
and so i kneel down before you — but, indeed, ep 16 P
that, when thou com'st to kneel at henry's feet, 1H6 5.03.194
kneel down and take my blessing, good my girl. 5.04. 25
lord marquess, kneel down. 2H6 1.01. 63
then, father salisbury, kneel we together, | and 2.02. 59
iden, kneel down. 5.01. 78
obey, audacious traitor, kneel for grace. 5.01.108
wouldst have me kneel? 5.01.109
we are thy sovereign, clifford, kneel again; 5.01.127
and kneel for grace and mercy at my feet: 3H6 1.01. 75
where i shall kneel to him that slew my father! 1.01.162
edward, kneel down. 2.02. 60
now, perjur'd henry, wilt thou kneel for grace, 2.02. 81
warwick, take the time, kneel down, kneel down. 5.01. 48
warwick, take the time, kneel down, kneel down. 5.01. 48
resign thy chair, and where i stand kneel thou, 5.05. 19
nay, we must longer kneel; i am a suitor. H8 1.02. 9
go to, kneel. 4.02.103
cushion than the flint | i kneel before thee, COR 5.03. 54
and at thy feet i kneel, with tears of joy TIT 1.01.161
kneel in the streets and beg for grace in vain. 1.01.455
the tribune and his nephews kneel for grace, | i 1.01.480
what, wouldst thou kneel with me? 3.01.209
my lord, kneel down with me, lavinia, kneel, 4.01. 87
my lord, kneel down with me, lavinia, kneel, 4.01. 87
and kneel, sweet boy, the roman hector's hope, 4.01. 88
at the first approach you must kneel, then kiss 4.03.111 P
and at thy mercy shall they stoop and kneel, 5.02.118
kneel not, gentle portia. JC 2.01.278
doth not brutus bootless kneel? 3.01. 75
thus, brutus, did my master bid me kneel; 3.01.123
/no, /sir, you must not kneel. LR 4.07. 58
i'll kneel down | and ask of thee forgiveness. 5.03. 10
and yet she'll kneel and pray; OTH 4.02. 23
here i kneel: 4.02.151
caesar, | kneel down, kneel down, and wonder. ANT 3.02. 19
caesar, | kneel down, kneel down, and wonder. 3.02. 19
to lay my crown at 's feet, and there to kneel. 3.13. 76
mine own as i | will kneel to him with thanks. 5.02. 21
arise, you shall not kneel. 5.02.114
kneel not to me. CYM 5.05.417
when thou shalt kneel, and justify in knowledge PER 5.01.217
pray you kneel not; TNK 1.01. 54
myself to do | that which you kneel to have me. 1.01.207
for whose fortunes | i will now in and kneel, 1.03. 94
to kneel to be forgiven | is safer wars than STM II.C 111
but kneel with me and help to bear thy part, LUC 1830
KNEEL'D 10 FR 0.0011 REL FR 10 V 0 P
you were kneel'd to and importun'd otherwise TMP 2.01.129
how i persuaded, how i pray'd, and kneel'd, MM 5.01. 93
i would you had kneel'd, my lord, to ask me AWW 2.01. 64
where henry and dame margaret kneel'd to me, 2H6 1.02. 39
fed from my trencher, kneel'd down at the board, 4.01. 57
kneel'd /at my feet and bid me be advis'd? R3 2.01.108
paces | came to the altar, where she kneel'd, H8 4.01. 83
i kneel'd before him; COR 5.01. 65
stop their nose | that kneel'd unto the buds. ANT 3.13. 40
for kindness | where he for grace is kneel'd to. 5.02. 28
KNEELING 5 FR 0.0005 REL FR 4 V 1 P
made hard with kneeling, i do pray to thee, JN 3.01.310
soul, | kneeling before this ruin of sweet life, 4.03. 65
o happy vantage of a kneeling knee! R2 5.03.132
his own person kneeling at our feet but a weak H5 3.06.132 P
from the place that showed | my duty kneeling, LR 2.04. 30
KNEELS 5 FR 0.0005 REL FR 5 V 0 P
where she kneels and prays | for happy wedlock MV 5.01. 31
who sues, and kneels, and says, "god save the R3 4.04. 94
but kneels and holds up hands for fellowship, COR 5.03.175
look who kneels here! PER 5.03. 46
sat, | and like a lowly lover down she kneels; VEN 350
KNEES 61 FR 0.0069 REL FR 51 V 10 P
with them, upon her knees, her humble self, TGV 3.01.228
but neither bended knees, pure hands held up, 3.01.231
go to your knees, and make ready. MM 3.01.169 P
true, | let me in safety raise me from my knees. 5.01.231
lend me your knees, and all my life to come 5.01.431
i am at him upon my knees every morning and ADO 2.01. 28 P
then down upon her knees she falls, weeps, sobs, 2.03.146 P
mistress, know yourself, down on your knees, AYL 3.05. 57
when with his knees he kiss'd the cretan strond. SHR 1.01.170
and on our knees we beg | (as recompense of our WT 2.03.149
a thousand knees, | ten thousand years together, 3.02.210
on both his knees doth kiss king richard's hand, R2 3.03. 36
to beg | enfranchisement immediate on his knees, 3.03.114
for ever may my knees grow to the earth, | my 5.03. 30
for ever will i walk upon my knees, | and never 5.03. 93
our knees still kneel till to the ground they 5.03.106
should, how would thy guts fall about thy knees! 1H4 3.03.153 P
then i felt to his knees, and so up'ard and H5 2.03. 24 P
he gives you, upon his knees, a thousand thanks, 4.04. 59 P
and made me almost yield upon my knees. 1H6 3.03. 80
he did vow upon his knees he would be even with 2H6 1.03.200 P
stoop to the block than these knees bow to any 4.01.125
i beseech /god on my knees thou mayst be turn'd 4.10. 58 P
you straight are on your knees for pardon, R3 2.01.125
lewd love-bed, | but on his knees at meditation; 3.07. 73
wind | makes flexible the knees of knotted oaks, TRO 1.03. 50
for supple knees | feed arrogance and are the 3.03. 48
i beseech you, on my knees /i /beseech /you, 4.02. 88 P
and dear petition, | pursue we him on knees; 5.03. 10
my retire, | not priamus and hecuba on knees, 5.03. 54
make it, and | your knees to them (not arms) COR 1.01. 74
make motion through my lips, and my arm'd knees, 3.02.118
our wives, and children, on our knees, | are 4.06. 22
your knees to me? 5.03. 57
let us shame him with our knees. 5.03.169
by my advice, all humbled on your knees, | you TIT 1.01.472
/o'er courtiers' knees, that dream on cur'sies ROM 1.04. 72
gentle breath, calm look, knees humbly bowed, 3.01.156
good father, i beseech you on my knees, | hear 3.05.158
mountain's top | even on their knees and /hands, TIM 1.01. 87
run to your houses, fall upon your knees, | pray JC 1.01. 53
and upon my knees | i charm you, by my once 2.01.270
thee, | oft'ner upon her knees than on her feet, MAC 4.03.110
as his shirt, his knees knocking each other, HAM 2.01. 78
bow, stubborn knees, and heart, with strings of 3.03. 70
on my knees i beg | that you'll vouchsafe me LR 2.04.155
you men of cyprus, let her have your knees. OTH 2.01. 84
come on, away, apart upon our knees. CYM 4.02.288
bow your knees. 5.05. 19
please, | i cannot be much lower than my knees. PER 1.02. 47
her prayers, her knees, that she would make a 4.06. 8 P
down on thy knees, thank the holy gods as loud 5.01.198
no knees to me! TNK 1.01. 35
and suffer'd | your knees to wrong themselves. 1.01. 56
o, no knees, none, widow! 1.01. 74
my knees shall grow to th' ground but i'll get 3.06.192
upon their knees | begg'd with such handsome 4.01. 8
on my knees | i ask thy pardon: 4.02. 36
lift up for peace, and your unreverent knees, STM II.C 110
to take prerogative and tithe of knees | from III 9
then jointly to the ground their knees they bow, LUC 1846
KNELL 13 FR 0.0014 REL FR 12 V 1 P
sea-nymphs hourly ring his knell: TMP 1.02.403
let us all ring fancy's knell. MV 3.02. 70
be this sweet helen's knell, and now forget her. AWW 5.03. 67
contempt and clamor | will be my knell. WT 1.02.190
bar, to hear | his knell rung out, his judgment, H8 2.01. 32
play me that sad note | i nam'd my knell, whilst 4.02. 79
a corslet with his eye, talks like a knell, and COR 5.04. 21 P
as 'twere a knell unto our master's fortunes, TIM 4.02. 26
hear it not, duncan, for it is a knell, | that MAC 2.01. 63
the dead man's knell | is there scarce ask'd for 4.03.170
and so his knell is knoll'd. 5.09. 16
little strength rings out the doleful knell: LUC 1495
no deadly, | my wether's bell rings doleful knell, PP 17.18
/KNEW 1 FR 0.0001 REL FR 1 V 0 P
/you /knew /he /walk'd /o'er /perils, /on /an 2H4 1.01.170
KNEW 168 FR 0.0190 REL FR 107 V 61 P
if you but knew how you the purpose cherish TMP 2.01.224
i would i knew his mind. TGV 1.02. 33
i knew him as myself: 2.04. 62
i never knew him otherwise. 2.05. 43 P
one, lady, if you knew his pure heart's truth, 4.02. 88
with the smell before, knew it was crab, and 4.04. 23 P
him he knew well, and guess'd that it was she, 5.02. 39
i never knew a woman so dote upon a man; WIV 2.02.102 P
i would you knew ford, sir, that you might avoid 2.02.276 P
he knew your worship would kill him if he came. 2.03. 10 P
i knew not what 'twas to be beaten till lately. 5.01. 26 P
i knew of your purpose; 5.05.200 P
he knew the service, and that instructed him to MM 3.02.119 P
who knew of your intent and coming hither? 5.01.124
yet my husband | knows not that ever he knew me. 5.01.187
who thinks he knows that he ne'er knew my body, 5.01.203
in 's garden-house, | he knew me as a wife. 5.01.230

did not you say you knew that friar lodowick to 5.01.260 P
for that he knew you, might reproach your life, 5.01.421
i thought it was a fault, but knew it not, | yet 5.01.463
you, sirrah, that knew me for a fool, a coward, 5.01.500
i knew 'twould be a bald conclusion. ERR 2.02.108 P
i knew he was not in his perfect wits. 5.01. 42
to write to one that she knew would flout her. ADO 2.03.142 P
good that benedick knew of it by some other, if 2.03.154 P
certainly it were not good | she knew his love, 3.01. 58
i knew it would be your answer. 3.03. 18 P
but the devil my master knew she was margaret; 3.03.155 P
nor knew not what she did when she spoke to me, 5.01.301
i never knew man hold vile stuff so dear. LLL 4.03.272
i would you knew. 5.02. 31
o that i knew he were but in by th' week! 5.02. 61
i knew her by this jewel on her sleeve. 5.02.455
if you were civil and knew courtesy, | you would MND 3.02.147
you knew, none so well, none so well as you, of MV 3.01. 24 P
knew the tailor that made the wings she flew 3.01. 26 P
for his own part, knew the bird was fledge, and 3.01. 28 P
but if you knew to whom you show this honor, 3.04. 5
for i never knew so young a body with so old a 4.01.163 P
were you the doctor, and i knew you not? 5.01.280
your eyes, or knew yourself with your judgment, AYL 1.02.176 P
o that your highness knew my heart in this! 3.01. 13
an inland man, one that knew courtship too well, 3.02.345 P
i knew what you would prove; 4.01.182 P
no sooner knew the reason but they sought the 5.02. 36 P
i knew when seven justices could not take up a 5.04. 98 P
o that once more you knew but what you are! SHR in.2. 78
best | put finger in the eye, and she knew why. 1.01. 79
i knew not what to take and what to leave? 1.01.104
not her, | and he knew my deceased father well. 1.02.102
a' my word, and she knew him as well as i do, 1.02.108 P
you knew my father well, and in him me, | left 2.01.116
i knew you at the first | you were a moveable. 2.01.196
if you knew my business, | you would entreat me 3.02.191
but i, who never knew how to entreat, | nor 4.03. 7
i knew a wench married in an afternoon as she 4.04. 99 P
as if i knew not his name! 5.01. 81 P
knew the true minute when | exception bid him AWW 1.02. 39
i knew him. 2.01.102
it were fit you knew him, lest, reposing too far 3.06. 13 P
i would i knew in what particular action to try 3.06. 17 P
and my integrity ne'er knew the crafts | that 4.02. 33
for i knew the young count to be a dangerous and 4.03.219 P
she knew her distance and did angle for me, 5.03.212
at that time that i knew of their going to bed, 5.03.263 P
by jove, if ever i knew man, 'twas you. 5.03.287
i knew 'twas i, for many do call me fool. TN 2.05. 81 P
shameful cunning | which you knew none of yours. 3.01.117
we knew not | the doctrine of ill-doing, nor WT 1.02. 69
would i knew the villain, | i would land-damn 2.01.142
i knew she would. 2.03. 44
you knew of his departure, as you know | what 3.02. 77
quit his fortunes here | (which you knew great), 3.02.168
i knew him once a servant of the prince. 4.03. 87 P
i am false of heart that way, and that he knew, 4.03.108 P
wisest beholder, that knew no more but seeing, 5.02. 17 P
knew you of this fair work? JN 4.03.116
so, on my soul, he did, for aught he knew. 5.01. 43
to god thou and i knew where a commodity of good 1H4 1.02. 82 P
before i knew thee, hal, i knew nothing, and now 1.02. 93 P
i knew thee, hal, i knew nothing, and now am i, 1.02. 93 P
the lord, i knew ye as well as he that made ye. 2.04.267 P
if you knew | how much they do import, you would 4.04. 4
knew that we ventured on such dangerous seas 2H4 1.01.181
i knew of this before, but, to speak truth, 1.01.210
it, he might have moe diseases than he knew for. 1.02. 5 P
yea, and you knew me, as you did when you ran 2.04.306 P
you knew i was at your back, and spoke it on 2.04.307 P
we knew where the bona /robas were and had the 3.02. 23 P
i knew him a good backsword man. 3.02. 63 P
and, if you knew what pains | i have bestowed to 4.02. 73
i never knew yet but rebuke and check was the 4.03. 31 P
his finger's end, i knew there was but one way; H5 2.03. 15 P
i knew by that piece of service the men would 3.02. 46 P
himself, and he said he car'd not who knew it. 3.07.108 P
might have a good prey of us, if he knew of it, 4.04. 76 P
i knew her well, she was a midwife. 2H6 4.02. 43 P
pardon me, god, i knew not what i did! 3H6 2.05. 69
and pardon, father, for i knew not thee! 2.05. 70
if warwick knew in what estate he stands, | 'tis 4.03. 18
i would i knew thy heart. R3 1.02.192
i would he knew that i had sav'd his brother! 1.04.276
o beauty, | till now i never knew thee! H8 1.04. 76
to whom | (if i but knew him) with my love and 1.04. 80
accusers, | that never knew what truth meant. 2.01.105
i knew him, and i know him; 2.02. 54
she never knew harm-doing — o, now after | so 2.03. 5
to love, although i knew | he were mine enemy? 2.04. 30
strangely | with me since first you knew me. 4.02.113
ay, if i ever saw him before and knew him. TRO 1.02. 65 P
that she was never yet that ever knew | love got 1.02.290
otherwise, | he knew his man. 2.01.129
by my troth, | i knew you not. 4.02. 46
i knew thou wouldest be his death. 4.02. 86 P
i knew thy grandsire, | and once fought with him 4.05.196
i knew by his face that there was something in COR 4.05.154 P
sirrah, if thy captain knew i were here, he 5.02. 51 P
were author of himself, | and knew no other kin. 5.03. 37
i care not, i, knew she and all the world, | i TIT 2.01. 71
o, that i knew thy heart, and knew the beast, 2.04. 34
o, that i knew thy heart, and knew the beast, 2.04. 34
'tis sure enough, and you knew how, | but if you 4.01. 95
i knew them all though they suppos'd me mad, 5.02.142
and if your highness knew my heart, you were. 5.03. 34
o that she knew she were! ROM 2.02. 11
she knew well | thy love did read by rote that 2.03. 87
i would i knew not why it should be slowed. 4.01. 16
bold | (for that i knew it the most general way) TIM 2.02.200
the devil knew not what he did when he made man 3.03. 28 P
that never knew but better, is some burthen: 4.03.267
would poison were obedient and knew my mind! 4.03.296 P
you cruel men of rome, | knew you not pompey? JC 1.01. 37
who ever knew the heavens menace so? 1.03. 44
because i knew the man, was slighted off. 4.03. 5
i knew your father, | these hands are not more HAM 1.02.211
yet he knew me not at first, 'a said i was a 2.02.188 P
thieves of mercy, but they knew what they did: 4.06. 21 P
alas, poor yorick, i knew him, horatio, a fellow 5.01.184 P
i knew you must be edified by the margent ere 5.02.155 P
i never found man that knew how to love himself. OTH 1.03.314 P
i never knew a florentine more kind and honest. 3.01. 40
i never knew woman love man so. 4.01.110
yet would i knew | that stroke would prove the 4.01.273
thy husband knew it all. 5.02.139
o, that i knew this husband, which, you say, ANT 1.02. 4 P
doubt not, sir, | i knew it for my bond. 1.04. 84
yet if i knew | what hoop should hold us staunch 2.02.114
had our general | been what he knew himself, it 3.10. 26
you were half blasted ere i knew you; 3.13.105
harping on what i am, | not what he knew i was. 3.13.143
i am loath to tell you what i would you knew. 5.02.107
that knew the stars as i his characters; CYM 3.02. 28
she alone knew this; 5.05. 40
i knew him tyrannous, and tyrants' /fears PER 1.02. 84
yet they that knew me | would say it was my best TNK 2.05. 13
i knew 'twould be so. 4.01. 28
her — one of 'em | i knew to be your brother; 4.01.101
nev'r reveal'd secret, for i knew none — would 5.01. 99
i knew a man | of eighty winters — this i told 5.01.107
for well she knew | what hour my fit would take 5.02. 9
miscarry, yet i knew not | why i did think so. 5.03.101
her, | she answers him, as if she knew his mind; VEN 308
whose precious taste her thirsty lips well knew, 543
save of their lord no bearing yoke they knew, LUC 409
yet then my judgment knew no reason why | my SON 115. 3
sometime a blusterer that the ruffle knew | of LC 58
and knew the patterns of his foul beguiling, 170
knew vows were ever brokers to defiling, 173

KNEWEST 1 FR 0.0001 REL FR 0 V 1 P
the middle of humanity thou never knewest, but TIM 4.03.300 P

KNEW'ST 8 FR 0.0009 REL FR 8 V 0 P
o corin, that thou knew'st how i do love her! AYL 2.04. 23
that knew'st this was the prince, and wouldst WT 4.04.459
that knew'st the very bottom of my soul, | that H5 2.02. 97
so is it, if thou knew'st our purposes. HAM 4.03. 47
thou knew'st too well | my heart was to thy ANT 3.11. 56
my spirit | /thy full supremacy thou knew'st, 3.11. 59
wars to-day, and knew'st | the royal occupation, 4.04. 16
if | thou knew'st my mistress breath'd on me, TNK 3.01. 28

/KNIFE 3 FR 0.0003 REL FR 3 V 0 P
/get /some /little /knife /between /thy /teeth, TIT 3.02. 16
/thou /strike /at, /marcus, /with /thy /knife? 3.02. 52
/give /me /thy /knife, /i /will /insult /on /him 3.02. 71

KNIFE 55 FR 0.0062 REL FR 50 V 5 P
sword, pike, knife, gun, or need of any engine, TMP 2.01.162
a stake, | or cut his wezand with thy knife. 3.02. 91
go — a short knife and a throng! WIV 2.02. 18 P
no point, with my knife. LLL 2.01.190
why dost thou whet thy knife so earnestly? MV 4.01.121
soul, harsh jew, | thou mak'st thy knife keen; 4.01.124
you must prepare your bosom for his knife — 4.01.245
the world like cutler's poetry | upon a knife, 5.01.150
i adore, | but silence, like a lucrece knife, TN 2.05.105
brooch, table-book, ballad, knife, tape, glove, WT 4.04.599 P
the edge of war, like an ill-sheathed knife, 1H4 1.01. 17
wine, i'll thrust my knife in your mouldy chaps, 2H4 2.04.129 P
head fantastically carv'd upon it with a knife. 3.02.312 P
have wash'd his knife | with gentle eye-drops. 4.05. 86
from treason's secret knife and traitors' rage 2H6 3.01.174
where's your knife? 3.02.195
i wear no knife to slaughter sleeping men, | but 3.02.197
but set his murth'ring knife unto the root 3H6 2.06. 49
and next his throat unto the butcher's knife. 5.06. 9
fool, thou whet'st a knife to kill thyself. R3 1.03.243
no doubt the murd'rous knife was dull and blunt 4.04.227
his duty) would | have put his knife into him." H8 1.02.199
after "the duke his father," with the "knife," 1.02.203
his period, | to sheathe his knife in us. 1.02.210
love hath given me | the knife that made it. TRO 1.01. 63
my hearth, | presented to my knife his throat. COR 5.06. 30
he would have dropp'd his knife, and fell asleep TIT 2.04. 50
sirrah, hast thou a knife? 4.03.115
have with my knife carved in roman letters, 5.01.139
one paris, that would fain lay knife aboard; ROM 2.04.202 P
thou no poison mix'd, no sharp-ground knife, 3.03. 44
and with this knife i'll help it presently. 4.01. 54
'twixt my extremes and me this bloody knife 4.01. 62
that my keen knife see not the wound it makes, MAC 1.05. 52
shut the door, | not bear the knife myself. 1.07. 16
so mortal that, but dip a knife in it, | where HAM 4.07.142
what means this bloody knife? LR 5.03.224
ever shall | be brooch'd with me, if knife, ANT 4.15. 25
nor by a hired knife, but that self hand | which 5.01. 21
where's thy knife? CYM 3.04. 96
o, give me cord, or knife, or poison, | some 5.05.213
life | /seeks to take off by treason's knife, PER 4.ch. 14
yet for the self-same purpose seek a knife; LUC 1047
will fix a sharp knife to affright mine eye, 1138
"my honor i'll bequeath unto the knife | that 1184
and with my knife scratch out the angry eyes 1469
in her harmless breast | a harmful knife, that 1724
fountain brutus drew | the murd'rous knife, and, 1735
who pluck'd the knife from lucrece' side, 1807
her wrongs to us, and by this bloody knife, | we 1840
and kiss'd the fatal knife, to end his vow; 1843
fortify | against confounding age's cruel knife, SON 63.10
dead, | the coward conquest of a wretch's knife, 74.11
the hardest knife ill us'd doth lose his edge. 95.14
so thou prevent'st his scythe and crooked knife. 100.14

KNIFE'S *(also knive's)*

KNIFE'S 2 FR 0.0002 REL FR 1 V 1 P
not carve most curiously, say my knife's naught. ADO 5.01.156 P
mine honor be the knife's that makes my wound. LUC 1201

KNIGHT 139 FR 0.0157 REL FR 69 V 70 P
as of a knight well-spoken, neat, and fine; TGV 1.02. 10
the knight sir john is there, and i beseech you WIV 1.01. 70 P
knight, you have beaten my men, kill'd my deer, 1.01.111 P
by me, thine own true knight, | by day or night, 2.01. 14
consult together against this greasy knight. 2.01.108 P
shall be our messenger to this paltry knight. 2.01.159 P
i do not think the knight would offer it; 2.01.173 P
hast thou no suit against my knight, my 2.01.212 P
it is a merry knight. 2.01.219 P
de earl, de knight, de lords, de gentlemen, my 2.03. 92 P
i will to my honest knight falstaff, and drink 3.02. 88 P
are these your letters, knight? 3.03.140 P
you dissembling knight! 3.03.144 P
i am glad the fat knight is not here. 4.02. 29 P
but i am glad the knight is not here. 4.02. 36 P
i am undone! the knight is here. 4.02. 41 P
pray heaven it be not full of knight again. 4.02.112 P
poor unvirtuous fat knight shall be any further 4.02.218 P
and, fairy-like, to pinch the unclean knight; 4.04. 58
also, to burn the knight with my taber. 4.04. 69 P
the knight may be robb'd. 4.05. 15 P
assist me, knight, i am undone! 4.05. 90 P
yet be cheerful, knight. 5.05.170 P
the night, | those that slew thy virgin knight, ADO 5.03. 13
the worth of many a knight | from tawny spain, LLL 1.01.172
a man of fire-new words, fashion's own knight. 1.01.178
"no" in /this, most tender-smelling knight. 5.02.566
the worthy knight of troy. 5.02.881
what is thisby? a wand'ring knight? MND 1.02. 45 P
would have the child | knight of his train, to 2.01. 25
and might | to honor helen and to be her knight. 2.02.144
but mark, poor knight, | what dreadful dole is 5.01.277
of a certain knight, that swore by his honor AYL 1.02. 63 P
was good, and yet was not the knight forsworn. 1.02. 67 P
no more was this knight, swearing by his honor, 1.02. 77 P
lay he, stretch'd along, like a wounded knight. 3.02.241 P
suffer her poor knight surpris'd without rescue AWW 1.03.115 P
and of a foolish knight that you brought in one TN 1.03. 16 P
you mistake, knight. 1.03. 56 P
o knight, thou lack'st a cup of canary. 1.03. 80 P
pourquoi, my dear knight? 1.03. 90 P
art thou good at these kickshawses, knight? 1.03.116 P
what is thy excellence in a galliard, knight? 1.03.120 P
if one knight give a — 2.03. 33 P
a mellifluous voice, as i am true knight. 2.03. 53 P
"hold thy peace, thou knave," knight? 2.03. 65 P
be constrain'd in't to call thee knave, knight. 2.03. 66 P
do't, knight. 2.03.129 P
thy exquisite reason, dear knight? 2.03.144 P
let's to bed, knight. 2.03.182 P
send for money, knight; 2.03.186 P
come, knight, come, knight. 2.03.191 P
come, knight, come, knight. 2.03.192 P
treasure of your time with a foolish knight" — 2.05. 78 P
he is knight, dubb'd with unhatch'd rapier and 3.04.235 P
as to know of the knight what my offense to him 3.04.254 P
i know the knight is incens'd against you, even 3.04.260 P
had rather go with sir priest than sir knight. 3.04.271 P
come hither, knight; 3.04.377 P
a landless knight makes thee a landed squire. JN 1.01.177
"knight, knight," good mother, basilisco-like. 1.01.244
"knight, knight," good mother, basilisco-like. 1.01.244
(which god defend a knight should violate!) R2 1.03. 18
marshal, ask yonder knight in arms, | both who 1.03. 26
speak like a true knight, so defend thee heaven! 1.03. 34
by phoebus, he, "that wand'ring knight so fair." 1H4 1.02. 15 P
this gallant hotspur, this all-praised knight, 3.02.140
thou art the knight of the burning lamp. 3.03. 27 P
a gallant knight he was, his name was blunt, 5.03. 20
twenty yards of satin (as i am a true knight), 2H4 1.02. 44 P
"john falstaff, knight" — every man must know 2.02.110 P
"sir john falstaff, knight, to the son of the 2.02.119 P
sweet knight, i kiss thy neaf. 2.04.186 P
how doth the good knight? 3.02. 64 P
seen that that this knight and i have seen! 3.02.212 P
i am a knight, sir, and my name is colevile of 4.03. 3 P
colevile is your name, a knight is your degree, 4.03. 5 P
dale, a most furious knight and valorous enemy. 4.03. 39 P
"do me right, | and dub me knight, | samingo." 5.03. 74
sweet knight, thou art now one of the greatest 5.03. 87 P
o base assyrian knight, what is thy news? 5.03.101
god bless thy lungs, good knight. 5.05. 9 P
my knight, i will inflame thy noble liver, | and 5.05. 31
sir thomas grey, knight, of northumberland, H5 2.pr. 25
the king hath run bad humors on the knight, 2.01.122 P
let us condole the knight, for, lambkins, we 2.01.127
and you, my gentle knight, give me your thoughts 2.02. 14
and, sir knight, | grey of northumberland, this 2.02. 67
to the which | this knight, no less for bounty 2.02. 92
treason, by the name of thomas grey, knight, of 2.02.150 P
no, my good knight; 4.01. 29
good old knight, | collect them all together at 4.01.286
turn'd away the fat knight with the great belly 4.07. 48 P
i warrant it is to knight you, captain. 4.08. 1 P
great is the rumor of this dreadful knight, 1H6 2.03. 7
cowardly knight, ill fortune follow thee! 3.02.109
i vow'd, base knight, when i did meet thee next, 4.01. 14
much more a knight, a captain, and a leader. 4.01. 32
doth but usurp the sacred name of knight, 4.01. 40
be packing therefore, thou that wast a knight; 4.01. 46
doubtless he would have made a noble knight. 4.07. 44
knight of the noble order of saint george, 4.07. 68
what though i be enthrall'd, he seems a knight, 5.03.101
as thou art knight, never to disobey | nor be 5.04.170
he is but a knight, is 'a? 2H6 4.02.117 P
him, i will make myself a knight presently. 4.02.119 P
he were created knight for his good service. 5.01. 77
rise up a knight. 5.01. 78
edward plantagenet, arise a knight, | and learn 3H6 2.02. 61
to-morrow morning call some knight to arms TRO 2.01.124
and great deal misprising | the knight oppos'd. 4.05. 75
half hector comes to seek | this blended knight, 4.05. 86
go, gentle knight, | stand by our ajax. 4.05. 88
the youngest son of priam, a true knight, | not 4.05. 96
amorous troyan, | and am her knight by proof. 5.05. 5
which doth enrich the hand | of yonder knight? ROM 1.05. 42
give this ring to my true knight, | and bid him 3.02.142
he is very often like a knight; TIM 2.02.112 P
the adventerous knight shall use his foil and HAM 2.02.321 P
no squire in debt, nor no poor knight; LR 3.02. 88
he, true knight, | no lesser of her honor CYM 5.05.186
the labor of each knight in his device. PER 2.02. 15
a knight of sparta, my renowned father, | and 2.02. 18
is an armed knight that's conquered by a lady; 2.02. 26
last, the which the knight himself | with such a 2.02. 40

but you, my knight and guest, | to whom this 2.03. 9
awhile, | yon knight doth sit too melancholy, 2.03. 54
not me | unto a stranger knight to be so bold. 2.03. 67
tells me here, she'll wed the stranger knight, 2.05. 16
a letter that she loves the knight of tyre! 2.05. 43
do you know the french knight that cow'rs i' the 4.02.105 P
seas, | attended on by many a lord and knight, 4.04. 11
you were call'd | a good knight and a bold. TNK 3.01. 65
somewhat bigger than the knight he spoke of, 4.02. 94
divine arbitrement | have given you this knight: 5.03.108
he speaks now of as brave a knight as e'er | did 5.03.115
one knight loves both, and both in thee remain. PP 8.14
the master loveless, or kill the gallant knight: 15. 6
of the two the trusty knight was wounded with 15.11
KNIGHT–ARRANT 1 FR 0.0001 REL FR 0 V 1 P
come, come, you she knight–arrant, come. 2H4 5.04. 22 P
KNIGHTED 5 FR 0.0005 REL FR 3 V 2 P
an eternal moment or so, i could be knighted. WIV 2.01. 50 P
perceive how i might be knighted. 2.01. 55 P
hand | of cordelion knighted in the field. JN 1.01. 54
knighted in field, slain manfully in arms, | in TIT 1.01.196
thy caesar knighted me; CYM 3.01. 69
KNIGHT–ERRANT *(see knight–arrant)*
/KNIGHTHOOD 1 FR 0.0001 REL FR 0 V 1 P
i would not take a /knighthood for my fortune. 2H4 5.03.126 P
KNIGHTHOOD 12 FR 0.0013 REL FR 9 V 3 P
by that, and all the rites of knighthood else, R2 1.01. 75
which gently laid my knighthood on my shoulder, 1.01. 79
speak truly on thy knighthood and thy oath, | as 1.03. 14
and, setting thy knighthood aside, thou art a 1H4 3.03.120 P
setting my knighthood and my soldiership aside, 2H4 1.02. 81 P
then set your knighthood and your soldiership 1.02. 83 P
ought to wear | this ornament of knighthood, yea 1H6 4.01. 29
you promis'd knighthood to our forward son, 3H6 2.02. 58
i might well delay | by rule of knighthood, i LR 5.03.146
"o shame to knighthood and to shining arms! LUC 197
by knighthood, gentry, and sweet friendship's 569
aid, | as bound in knighthood to her imposition, 1697
KNIGHTHOOD'S 1 FR 0.0001 REL FR 1 V 0 P
buckled below fair knighthood's bending knee: WIV 5.05. 72
KNIGHTHOODS 1 FR 0.0001 REL FR 1 V 0 P
knighthoods and honors, borne | as i wear mine, CYM 5.02. 6
KNIGHTLY 6 FR 0.0006 REL FR 6 V 0 P
and when my knightly stomach is suffic'd, | why JN 1.01.191
degree | or chivalrous design of knightly trial; R2 1.01. 81
and why thou comest thus knightly clad in arms, 1.03. 12
base | to stain the temper of my knightly sword. 4.01. 29
garter, blemish'd, pawn'd his knightly virtue; R3 4.04.370
by fair and knightly strength to touch the TNK 3.06.295
KNIGHT'S 3 FR 0.0003 REL FR 1 V 2 P
what do you call your knight's name, sirrah? WIV 3.02. 21 P
beshrew me, the knight's in admirable fooling. TN 2.03. 80 P
a knight's daughter, | to be her mistress' H8 3.02. 94
/KNIGHTS 1 FR 0.0001 REL FR 1 V 0 P
great princes, barons, lords, and /knights, H5 3.05. 46
KNIGHTS 49 FR 0.0055 REL FR 45 V 4 P
these knights will hack, and so thou shouldst WIV 2.01. 52 P
yet there has been knights, and lords, and 2.02. 63 P
ten thousand bold scots, two and twenty knights, 1H4 1.01. 68
three knights upon our party slain to–day, | a 5.05. 6
of these six dry, round, old, wither'd knights." 2H4 2.04. 8 P
full fifteen earls and fifteen hundred knights, H5 1.01. 13
tents | the armorers, accomplishing the knights, 4.pr. 12
of other lords and barons, knights and squires, 4.08. 78
of knights, esquires, and gallant gentlemen, 4.08. 84
five hundred were but yesterday dubb'd knights. 4.08. 86
are princes, barons, lords, knights, squires, 4.08. 89
knights of the garter were of noble birth, 1H6 4.01. 34
the knights and gentlemen to come with thee. 3H6 4.08. 13
lords, knights, and gentlemen, what i should say 5.04. 73
here's a lord — come knights from east to west, TRO 2.03.263
will you the knights | shall to the edge of all 4.05. 67
i will go eat with thee and see your knights. 4.05.158
with reservation of an hundred knights | by you LR 1.01.133
his knights grow riotous, and himself upbraids 1.03. 6
and let his knights have colder looks among you; 1.03. 22
here do you keep a hundred knights and squires, 1.04.241
man hath had good counsel — a hundred knights! 1.04.322
to let him keep | at point a hundred knights; 1.04.324
if she sustain him and his hundred knights, 1.04.332
was he not companion with the riotous knights 2.01. 94
can stay with regan, | i and my hundred knights. 2.04.231
some five or six and thirty of his knights, 3.07. 16
arise my knights o' th' battle. CYM 5.05. 20
are princes and knights come from all parts of PER 2.01.109 P
are the knights ready to begin the triumph? 2.02. 1
but stay, the knights are coming, we will 2.02. 58
knights, | to say you're welcome were 2.03. 1
you are right courteous knights. 2.03. 27
h'as done no more than other knights have done, 2.03. 34
what, are you merry, knights? 2.03. 48
and i have heard you knights of tyre | are 2.03.101
these knights unto their several lodgings! 2.03.109
knights, from my daughter this i let you know, 2.05. 2
are making battle, thus like knights appointed, TNK 3.06.134
accompanied | with three fair knights, appear 3.06.292
the knights are come. 4.02. 56
return'd, | and with them their fair knights. 4.02. 67
from the knights. 4.02. 71
knights, kinsmen, lovers, yea, my sacrifices, 5.01. 34
who to thy female knights | allow'st no more 5.01.140
shall confound | both these brave knights, and i 5.01.167
the knights must kindle | their valor at your 5.03. 29
knights, by their oaths, should right poor LUC 1694
in praise of ladies dead and lovely knights, SON 106. 4
KNIT 37 FR 0.0041 REL FR 31 V 6 P
are all knit up | in their distractions. TMP 3.03. 89
no, girl, i'll knit it up in silken strings, TGV 2.07. 45
"item, she can knit." 3.01.308 P
with a wench, when she can knit him a stock? 3.01.310 P
he shall not knit a knot in his fortunes with WIV 3.02. 74 P
not to knit my soul to an approved wanton. ADO 4.01. 44
i mean, that my heart unto yours /is knit, | so MND 2.02. 47
with us | these couples shall eternally be knit. 4.01.181
stones with lime and hair knit /up /in /thee. 5.01.191
and their garters of an indifferent knit; SHR 4.01. 92 P
france, shall we knit our pow'rs, | and lay this JN 2.01.398
this royal hand and mine are newly knit, | and 3.01.226
i knit my handkercher about your brows | (the 4.01. 42
that knit your sinews to the strength of mine. 5.02. 63
and knit our powers to the arm of peace. 2H4 4.01.1'5
the earl of arminack, near knit to charles, | a 1H6 5.01. 17
why doth the great duke humphrey knit his brows,
2H6 1.02. 3
the last day | knit earth and heaven together! 5.02. 42
thou smiling while he knit his angry brows: 3H6 2.02. 20
but lately splinter'd, knit, and join'd together R3 2.02.118
knit all the greekish ears | to his experienc'd TRO 1.03. 67
if thou hadst hands to help thee knit the cord. TIT 2.04. 10
o, let me teach you how to knit again | this 5.03. 70
i'll have this knot knit up to–morrow morning. ROM 4.02. 24
yellow slave | will knit and break religions, TIM 4.03. 35
with a most indissoluble tie | for ever knit. MAC 3.01. 18
and i confess me knit to thy deserving with OTH 1.03.337 P
and to knit your hearts | with an unslipping ANT 2.02.125
then is caesar and he for ever knit together. 2.06.115 P
our sever'd navy too | have knit again, and 3.13.171
to knit their souls | (on whom there is no more CYM 2.03.117
sit, | to knit in her their best perfections. PER 1.01. 11
when peers thus knit, a kingdom ever stands. 2.04. 58
the gout had knit his fingers into knots, TNK 5.01.112
with heavy eye, knit brow, and strengthless pace LUC 709
knit poisonous clouds about his golden head. 777
thy merit hath my duty strongly knit, | to thee SON 26. 2
KNITS 4 FR 0.0004 REL FR 3 V 1 P
day, | he knits his brow and shows an angry eye, 2H6 3.01. 15
the widow likes him not, she knits her brows. 3H6 3.02. 82
the amity that wisdom knits not, folly may TRO 2.03.101 P
sleep that knits up the ravell'd sleave of care, MAC 2.02. 34
KNITTERS 1 FR 0.0001 REL FR 1 V 0 P
the spinsters and the knitters in the sun, | and TN 2.04. 44
KNITTETH 1 FR 0.0001 REL FR 1 V 0 P
by that which knitteth souls and prospers loves, MND 1.01.172
KNIVE'S *(also knife's)*
KNIVE'S 2 FR 0.0002 REL FR 1 V 1 P
as you may take upon a knive's point and choke a
ADO 2.03.255 P
true, 'tis true, witness my knive's sharp point. TIT 5.03. 63
KNIVES 12 FR 0.0013 REL FR 9 V 3 P
at that time, and some say knives have edges. H5 2.01. 22 P
devil should we keep knives to cut one another's 2.01. 92 P
methinks they should invite them without knives: TIM 1.02. 44
rather than render back, out with your knives, 4.01. 9
take't at worst — for their knives care not, 5.01.178
free from our feasts and banquets bloody knives; MAC 3.06. 35
that hath laid knives under his pillow, and LR 3.04. 54 P
if there be cords, or knives, | poison, or fire, OTH 3.03.388
than we | that draw his knives i' th' war. CYM 5.03. 73
if fires be hot, knives sharp, or waters deep, PER 4.02.146
those that with cords, knives, drams, TNK 1.01.142
whet their detested knives against your throats, STM II.C 134
KNOBS 1 FR 0.0001 REL FR 0 V 1 P
and whelks, and knobs, and flames a' fire, and H5 3.06.103 P
KNOCK 68 FR 0.0076 REL FR 33 V 35 P
o, the cry did knock | against my very heart. TMP 1.02. 8
where thou mayst knock a nail into his head. 3.02. 61
go, knock and call; WIV 4.05. 9 P
knock, i say. 4.05. 10 P
knock there, and ask your heart what it doth MM 2.02.137
master, knock the door hard. ERR 3.01. 58
let him knock till it ache. 3.01. 58
i'll knock elsewhere, to see if they'll disdain 3.01.121
go, some of you, knock at the abbey–gate, | and 5.01.165
here, sirrah grumio, knock, i say. SHR 1.02. 5
knock, sir? 1.02. 6 P
whom should i knock? 1.02. 6 P
villain, i say, knock me here soundly. 1.02. 8
knock you here, sir? 1.02. 9 P
am i, sir, that i should knock you here, sir? 1.02. 10 P
villain, i say, knock me at this gate, | and rap 1.02. 11
rap me well, or i'll knock your knave's pate. 1.02. 12
i should knock you first, | and then i know 1.02. 13
sirrah, and you'll not knock, i'll ring it. 1.02. 16
now, knock when i bid you, sirrah villain! 1.02. 19
he bid me knock him and rap him soundly, sir. 1.02. 30 P
i bade the rascal knock upon your gate, | and 1.02. 37
knock at the gate? 1.02. 39 P
not these words plain, "sirrah, knock me here; 1.02. 40 P
knock me well, and knock me soundly"? 1.02. 41 P
knock me well, and knock me soundly"? 1.02. 41 P
and this cuff was but to knock at your ear, and 4.01. 65 P
they're busy within, you were best knock louder. 5.01. 14 P
when midnight comes, knock at my chamber–window;
AWW 4.02. 54
gallows and knock are too powerful on the WT 4.03. 28 P
please it your honor knock but at the gate, 2H4 1.01. 5
i have an humor to knock you indifferently well. H5 2.01. 55 P
tell him i'll knock his leek about his pate 4.01. 54
cap that day, lest he knock that about yours. 4.01. 57 P
and rulers over roan, | therefore we'll knock. 1H6 3.02. 12
knock him down there. 2H6 4.06. 8 P
kill and knock down! 4.08. 2 P
my liege, i'll knock once more to summon them. 3H6 4.07. 16
let the music knock it. H8 1.04.108
should you do, but knock 'em down by th' dozens? 5.03. 32 P
catch, and /'a knock /out either of your brains; TRO 2.01.100 P
how earnestly they knock! 4.02. 40
whether to knock against the gates of rome, | or COR 4.05.141
gave aries such a knock | that down fell both TIT 4.03. 72
knock at my door, and tell me what he says. 4.03.119
knock at his study, where they say he keeps | to 5.02. 5
a perilous knock — and it cried bitterly. ROM 1.03. 54
come knock and enter, and no sooner in, | but 1.04. 33
hark how they knock! 3.03. 74
to knock out an honest athenian's brains. TIM 1.01.192 P
knock me down with 'em, cleave me to the girdle! 3.04. 90
and make my seated heart knock at my ribs, MAC 1.03.136
knock, knock, knock! 2.03. 3 P
knock, knock, knock! 2.03. 3 P
knock, knock, knock! 2.03. 3 P
knock, knock! 2.03. 7 P
knock, knock! 2.03. 7 P
knock, knock, knock! 2.03. 12 P
knock, knock, knock! 2.03. 12 P
knock, knock, knock! 2.03. 12 P
knock, knock! 2.03. 15 P
knock, knock! 2.03. 15 P
this mad knave now to knock him about the sconce
HAM 5.01.101 P
me go, sir, or i'll knock you o'er the mazzard. OTH 2.03.153 P
to the court i'll knock her back, foot her home CYM 3.05.143 P
ne'er than answering | a slave without a knock. 4.02. 74
knock off his manacles, bring your prisoner to 5.04.191 P
live | to knock thy brains out with my shackles. TNK 2.02.219
KNOCK'D 10 FR 0.0011 REL FR 5 V 5 P
'twere good you knock'd him. TGV 2.04. 7 P
whom would to god i had well knock'd at first, SHR 1.02. 34
the brains of my cupid's knock'd out, and i AWW 3.02. 15 P
have of late knock'd too often at my door. 4.01. 28 P
that many have their giddy brains knock'd out; 1H6 3.01. 83
in him when hector has knock'd out his brains, i TRO 3.03.302 P
would he were knock'd i' th' head! 4.02. 34
resolv'd | if brutus so unkindly knock'd or no; JC 3.02.180
and knock'd about the /mazzard with a sexton's HAM 5.01. 89 P
hercules | could have knock'd out his brains, CYM 4.02.115
KNOCKING 13 FR 0.0014 REL FR 7 V 6 P
and come you now with "knocking at the gate"? SHR 1.02. 42 P
bare–headed, sweating, knocking at the taverns, 2H4 2.04.359
more knocking at the door! 2.04.369 P
a flint, which will not show without knocking. TRO 3.03.257 P
whence is that knocking? MAC 2.02. 54
i hear a knocking | at the south entry. 2.02. 62
hark, more knocking. 2.02. 66
wake duncan with thy knocking! 2.02. 71
here's a knocking indeed! 2.03. 1 P
our knocking has awak'd him; 2.03. 43
there's knocking at the gate. 5.01. 66 P
as his shirt, his knees knocking each other, HAM 2.01. 78
knocking out his brains. OTH 4.02.230 P
KNOCKS 19 FR 0.0021 REL FR 14 V 5 P
gate upon one wooer, another knocks at the door.
MV 1.02.133
what's he that knocks as he would beat down the SHR 5.01. 16 P
who knocks so loud at door? 2H4 2.04.352 P
who knocks? 5.03. 71 P
the knocks are too hot; H5 3.02. 3 P
"knocks go and come; 3.02. 8
who's there, that knocks so imperiously? 1H6 1.03. 5
who knocks? R3 3.02. 2
go, go up to the leads, the lord mayor knocks. 3.07. 55
norfolk, we must have knocks. ha, must we not? 5.03. 5
arise, one knocks. good romeo, hide thyself. ROM 3.03. 71
who knocks so hard? 3.03. 78
go to the gate, somebody knocks. JC 2.01. 60
hark, hark, one knocks. 2.01.304
lucius, who's that knocks? 2.01.309
open, locks, | whoever knocks! MAC 4.01. 47
hark, who is't that knocks? OTH 4.03. 53 P
who's there that knocks? CYM 2.03. 77
knocks at my heart, and whispers in mine ear, VEN 659
KNOG 3 FR 0.0003 REL FR 0 V 3 P
i will knog his urinals about his knave's WIV 3.01. 14 P
i will knog your /urinals about your knave's 3.01. 88 P
and let us knog our prains together to be 3.01.119 P
KNOLL'D 3 FR 0.0003 REL FR 3 V 0 P
if ever been where bells have knoll'd to church, AYL 2.07.114
and have with holy bell been knoll'd to church, 2.07.121
and so his knell is knoll'd. MAC 5.09. 16
KNOLLS 1 FR 0.0001 REL FR 1 V 0 P
that your fame | knolls in the ear o' th' world. TNK 1.01.134
/KNOT 1 FR 0.0001 REL FR 1 V 0 P
/marcus, /unknit /that //sorrow–wreathen /knot; TIT 3.02. 4
KNOT 28 FR 0.0031 REL FR 23 V 5 P
isle, and sitting, | his arms in this sad knot. TMP 1.02.224
trust me, a good knot. WIV 3.02. 51 P
he shall not knit a knot in his fortunes with 3.02. 74 P
o you panderly rascals, there's a knot, a /ging, 4.02.118 P
whole theoric of war in the knot of his scarf, AWW 4.03.142 P
that has a knot on't yet. 4.03.324 P
not i, | it is too hard a knot for me t' untie! TN 2.02. 41
for by this knot thou shalt so surely tie | thy JN 2.01.470
unknit | this churlish knot of all–abhorred war? 1H4 5.01. 16
the gordian knot of it he will unloose, H5 1.01. 46
to effect | and surer bind this knot of amity, 1H6 5.01. 16
to confirm that amity | with nuptial knot, if 3H6 3.03. 55
his ancient knot of dangerous adversaries R3 3.01.182
a knot you are of damned blood–suckers. 3.03. 6
and by that knot looks proudly on the crown, 4.03. 42
and with another knot, /five–finger–tied, | the TRO 5.02.157
and not unknit himself | the noble knot he made. COR 4.02. 32
i'll have this knot knit up to–morrow morning. ROM 4.02. 24
feast never behold, | you knot of mouth–friends! TIM 3.06. 89
so often shall the knot of us be call'd | the JC 3.01.117
cestern for foul toads | to knot and gender in! OTH 4.02. 62
to knit your hearts | with an unslipping knot, ANT 2.02.126
with thy sharp teeth this knot intrinsicate | of 5.02.304
as slippery as the gordian knot was hard! CYM 2.02. 34
but brats and beggary) in self–figur'd knot, 2.03.119
deep, | untied i still my virgin knot will keep. PER 4.02.147
their knot of love | tied, weav'd, entangled, TNK 1.03. 41
in thee hath neither sting, knot, nor confine, LC 265
KNOT–GRASS 1 FR 0.0001 REL FR 1 V 0 P
you minimus, of hind'ring knot–grass made; MND 3.02.329
KNOTS 9 FR 0.0010 REL FR 8 V 1 P
with twenty odd–conceited true–love knots: TGV 2.07. 46
been often burst and now repair'd with knots; SHR 3.02. 59 P
her knots disordered and her wholesome herbs R2 3.04. 46
as knots, by the conflux of meeting sap, TRO 1.03. 7
blunt wedges rive hard knots; 1.03.316
let grow thy sinews till their knots be strong, 5.03. 33
precious motives, those strong knots of love, MAC 4.03. 27
blanket my loins, elf all my hairs in knots, LR 2.03. 10
the gout had knit his fingers into knots, TNK 5.01.112
KNOTTED 2 FR 0.0002 REL FR 2 V 0 P
wind | makes flexible the knees of knotted oaks, TRO 1.03. 50
thy knotted and combined locks to part, | and HAM 1.05. 18
KNOTTY 2 FR 0.0002 REL FR 2 V 0 P
and peg thee in his knotty entrails till | thou TMP 1.02.295
the scolding winds | have riv'd the knotty oaks, JC 1.03. 6
KNOTTY–PATED 1 FR 0.0001 REL FR 0 V 1 P
thou clay–brain'd guts, thou knotty–pated fool, 1H4 2.04.227 P
/KNOW 9 FR 0.0010 REL FR 7 V 2 P
/and /know /not /now /what /name /to /call R2 4.01.259
/question /surveyors, /know /our /own /estate, 2H4 1.03. 53

/lord /mowbray, /now /you /know /not /what. 4.01.128
/still /practice /learn /to /know /thy /meaning. TIT 3.02. 45
my lords, you know, /as /know the mightful gods, 4.04. 5
/nuptial /breaches, /and /i /know /not /what. LR 1.02.149 P
/suddenly /gone /back, /know /you /no /reason? 4.03. 2 P
/on /her /ripe /lip /seem'd /not /to /know 4.03. 20
th' nest, nor /know not | what air's from home. CYM 3.03. 28

KNOW 1751 FR 0.1979 REL FR 1300 V 451 P

more to know | did never meddle with my thoughts TMP 1.02. 21
sit down, | for thou must now know farther. 1.02. 33
of homage, and i know not how much tribute, 1.02.124
know thus far forth: 1.02.177
i know thou canst not choose. 1.02.186
know thine own meaning, but wouldst gabble like 1.02.356
and my profit on't | is, i know how to curse. 1.02.364
may know if you remain upon this island, | and 1.02.424
prospero my lord shall know what i have done. 2.01.326
it did before, i know not where to hide my head. 2.02. 22 P
thou wilt anon, i know it by thy trembling. 2.02. 80 P
i should know that voice; 2.02. 87 P
i do not know | one of my sex; 3.01. 48
revenge it on him — for i know thou dar'st, 3.02. 54
bow, | if venus or her son, as thou dost know, 4.01. 87
great juno, comes, i know her by her gait. 4.01.102
we know what belongs to a frippery. 4.01.225 P
them | that yet looks on me, or would know me! 5.01. 83
to abuse me | (as late i have been), i not know. 5.01.113
my dukedom of thee, which perforce, i know, 5.01.133
know for certain | that i am prospero and that 5.01.158
and (how we know not) all clapp'd under hatches, 5.01.231
two of these fellows you | must know and own, 5.01.275
o, they love least that let men know their love. TGV 1.02. 32
i know it well. 1.03. 28
go to, sir; tell me, do you know madam silvia? 2.01. 14 P
why, how know you that i am in love? 2.01. 17 P
but tell me: dost thou know my lady silvia? 2.01. 42 P
why, sir, i know her not. 2.01. 45 P
dost thou know her by my gazing on her, and yet 2.01. 46 P
sir, i know that well enough. 2.01. 50 P
what dost thou know? 2.01. 51 P
i know it well, sir; 2.04. 31 P
i know it well, sir; 2.04. 43 P
know ye don antonio, your countryman? 2.04. 54
i know the gentleman | to be of worth and worthy 2.04. 55
you know him well? 2.04. 61
i know you joy not in a love–discourse. 2.04.127
didst thou but know the inly touch of love, 2.07. 18
know, worthy prince, sir valentine, my friend, 3.01. 10
i know you have determin'd to bestow her | on 3.01. 13
know, noble lord, they have devis'd a mean | how 3.01. 38
he shall never know | that i had any light from 3.01. 48
i know it well, my lord, and sure the match 3.01. 63
doth silvia know that i am banished? 3.01.223
virtues," that indeed know not their fathers, 3.01.319 P
because we know, on valentine's report, | you 3.02. 57
then know that i have little wealth to lose. 4.01. 11
know, then, that some of us are gentlemen, 4.01. 42
for you know that love | will creep in service 4.02. 19
would quickly learn to know him by his voice. 4.02. 89
silvia | entreated me to call and know her mind. 4.03. 2
i am thus early come to know what service | it 4.03. 9
which since i know they virtuously are plac'd, 4.03. 38
therefore know /thou, for this i entertain thee. 4.04. 70
i know they are stuff'd with protestations, 4.04.129
dost thou know her? 4.04.142
almost as well as i do know myself. 4.04.143
therefore i know she is about my height. 4.04.164
she shall thank you for't, if e'er you know her. 4.04.179
know then, i here forget all former griefs, 5.04.142
i know the young gentlewoman, she has good gifts WIV 1.01. 62 P
the council shall know this. 1.01.117 P
let us command to know that of your mouth, or of 1.01.228 P
and have more occasion to know one another. 1.01.249 P
which of you know ford of this town? 1.03. 36 P
but notwithstanding that, i know anne's mind — 1.04.105 P
no, i know anne's mind for that. 1.04.127 P
for i know anne's mind as well as another does. 1.04.164 P
nay, i know not; 2.01. 84 P
unless he know some strain in me that i know not 2.01. 87 P
know some strain in me that i know not myself, 2.01. 88 P
your passes, stoccadoes, and i know not what. 2.01.226 P
and what they made there, i know not. 2.01.236 P
nay–word, that you may know one another's mind, 2.02.126 P
good that children should know any wickedness. 2.02.129 P
old folks, you know, have discretion, as they 2.02.129 P
discretion, as they say, and know the world. 2.02.130 P
i know not how i may deserve to be your porter. 2.02.174 P
sith you yourself know how easy it is to be such 2.02.188 P
largely to many to know what she would have 2.02.199 P
believe it, for you know it. 2.02.231 P
you to me at night, you shall know how i speed. 2.02.267 P
do you know ford, sir? 2.02.269 P
i know him not. 2.02.270 P
thou shalt know i will predominate over the 2.02.281 P
master /brook, shalt know him for knave, and 2.02.285 P
i think you know him: 3.01. 60 P
we'll teach him to know turtles from jays. 3.03. 42 P
if you know yourself clear, why, i am glad of it 3.03.116 P
i know not which pleases me better, that my 3.03.178 P
and you may know by my size that i have a kind 3.05. 12 P
you come to know what hath pass'd between me and 3.05. 61 P
leisure, and you shall know how i speed; 3.05.135 P
alas the day, i know not! 4.02. 69 P
we do not know what's brought to pass under the 4.02.175 P
we know nothing. 4.02.178 P
a spirit, and well you know | the superstitious 4.04. 35
send quickly to sir john, to know his mind. 4.04. 83
seeing her go thorough the streets, to know, sir 4.05. 31 P
what are they? let us know. 4.05. 42 P
to know if it were my master's fortune to have 4.05. 47 P
dere is no duke that the court is know to come. 4.05. 88 P
beam, because i know also life is a shuttle. 5.01. 23 P
and we have a nay–word how to know one another. 5.02. 5 P
and by that we know one another. 5.02. 7 P
the devil, and we shall know him by his horns. 5.02. 13 P
i know vat i have to do. adieu. 5.03. 5 P
i'll make the best in gloucestershire know on't. 5.05.181 P
tell you how you should know my daughter by her 5.05.195 P
since i am put to know that your own science MM 1.01. 5
for you must know, we have with special soul 1.01. 17
grace's will, | i come to know your pleasure. 1.01. 26
and do look to know | what doth befall you here. 1.01. 57
nay, but i know 'tis so. 1.02. 67 P
besides, you know, it draws something near to 1.02. 77 P
you know the lady; 1.02.147
in the seat, that it may know | he can command, 1.02.161
turn you the key, and know his business of him; 1.04. 8
the rather for i now must make you know | i am 1.04. 22
by those that know the very nerves of state, 1.04. 53
and let him learn to know, when maidens sue, 1.04. 80
let but your honor know | (whom i believe to be 2.01. 8
their abuses in common houses, i know no law. 2.01. 43 P
your honor, i know not well what they are; 2.01. 53 P
how know you that? 2.01. 68 P
how dost thou know that, constable? 2.01. 78 P
for, as you know, master froth, i could not give 2.01.103 P
i would know that of your honor. 2.01.158 P
i'll know | his pleasure, may be he will relent. 2.02. 2
for then i pity those i do not know, | which a 2.02.101
and ask your heart what it doth know | that's 2.02.137
and to make me know | the nature of their crimes 2.03. 6
i am come to know your pleasure. 2.04. 31
that you might know it, would much better please 2.04. 32
good, | but graciously to know i am no better. 2.04. 77
i know your virtue hath a license in't, | which 2.04.145
let me know the point. 3.01. 72
ay, but to die, and go we know not where; 3.01.117
confessor to angelo, and i know this to be true; 3.01.166 P
i know none. can you tell me of any? 3.02. 87 P
i know not where; 3.02. 90 P
urine is congeal'd ice, that i know to be true; 3.02.111 P
the duke, and i believe i know the cause of his 3.02.131 P
sir, i know him, and i love him. 3.02.149 P
come, sir, i know what i know. 3.02.152 P
come, sir, i know what i know. 3.02.152 P
believe that, since you know not what you speak. 3.02.153 P
he shall know you better, sir, if i may live to 3.02.161 P
strifes, contended especially to know himself. 3.02.233 P
and let me desire to know how you find claudio 3.02.239 P
pattern in himself to know, | grace to stand, 3.02.263
for i have made him know | i have a servant 4.01. 44
good friar, i know you do, and have found it. 4.01. 53
happily | you something know, yet i believe 4.02. 96
you know the course is common. 4.02.177 P
you know the character, i doubt not, and the 4.02.192 P
i know them both. 4.02.195 P
she's come to know | if yet her brother's pardon 4.03.107
see, to make them know | that outward courtesies 5.01. 14
i know you'ld fain be gone. 5.01.120
my lord, i know him, 'tis a meddling friar. 5.01.127
know you that friar lodowick that she speaks of? 5.01.143
i know him for a man divine and holy, | not 5.01.144
mouth, what he doth know | is true and false; 5.01.155
not that i know. 5.01.200
know you this woman? 5.01.213
my lord, i must confess i know this woman, | and 5.01.216
how! know you where you are? 5.01.291
joint by joint, but we will know his purpose. 5.01.312
come hither, goodman bald–pate, do you know me? 5.01.326
your brother's death i know sits at your heart; 5.01.389
i have confess'd her, and i know her virtue. 5.01.527
yet behind, that/'s meet you all should know. 5.01.539
but we that know what 'tis to fast and pray, ERR 1.02. 51
o, know he is the bridle of your will. 2.01. 13
i know not thy mistress, out on thy mistress!" 2.01. 68
"i know," quoth he, "no house, no wife, no 2.01. 71
i know his eye doth homage otherwhere, | or else 2.01.104
sister, you know he promis'd me a chain; 2.01.106
you know no centaur? 2.02. 9
if you will jest with me, know my aspect, | and 2.02. 32
dost thou not know? 2.02. 40 P
for know, my love, as easy mayst thou fall | a 2.02.125
i know thou canst, and therefore see thou do it. 2.02.139
i know you not: 2.02.147
until i know this sure uncertainty, | i'll 2.02.185
but i should know her as well as she knows me. 2.02.202
say what you will, sir, but i know what i know: 3.01. 11
say what you will, sir, but i know what i know: 3.01. 11
to know the reason of this strange restraint. 3.01. 97
i know a wench of excellent discourse, | pretty 3.01.109
by this i know 'tis made. 3.01.115
mistress — what your name is else, i know not, 3.02. 29
i, then well i know | your weeping sister is no 3.02. 41
not mad, but mated — how, i do not know. 3.02. 54
do you know me, sir? 3.02. 73 P
and i know not what use to put her to but to 3.02. 96 P
if every one knows us, and we know none, | 'tis 3.02.152
i know it well, sir. 3.02.166
you know since pentecost the sum is due, | and 4.01. 1
come, come, you know i gave it you even now. 4.01. 55
you know i gave it you half an hour since. 4.01. 65
i do not know the matter, he is 'rested on the 4.02. 42
i know not at whose suit he is arrested well; 4.02. 44
mistress, that you know. 4.03. 80
o husband, god doth know you din'd at home, 4.04. 65
i know it by their pale and deadly looks. 4.04. 93
one angelo, a goldsmith. do you know him? 4.04.132
i know the man; what is the sum he owes? 4.04.133
is, | i long to know the truth hereof at large. 4.04.143
why look you strange on me? you know me well. 5.01.296
but tell me yet, dost thou not know my voice? 5.01.301
not know my voice! 5.01.308
the duke, and all that know me in the city, 5.01.324
stay, stand apart, i know not which is which. 5.01.365
i know none of that name, lady. ADO 1.01. 32 P
end with a jade's trick, i know you of old. 1.01.144 P
that she is worthy, i know. 1.01.229 P
she should be lov'd nor know how she should be 1.01.231 P
that know love's grief by his complexion! 1.01.313
i know we shall have revelling to–night; 1.01.320
cousins, you know what you have to do. 1.02. 25 P
solicit you in that kind, you know your answer. 2.01. 67 P
i know you well enough, you are signior antonio. 2.01.112 P
i know you by the waggling of your head. 2.01.115 P
do you think i do not know you by your excellent 2.01.121 P
i am sure you know him well enough. 2.01.133 P
when i know the gentleman, i'll tell him what 2.01.144 P
and that is claudio. i know him by his bearing. 2.01.159 P
you know me well, i am he. 2.01.162 P
how know you he loves her? 2.01.167 P
but that my lady beatrice should know me, and 2.01.204 P
lady beatrice should know me, and not know me! 2.01.204 P
is not the unhopefullest husband that i know. 2.01.378 P
tell them that you know that hero loves me, 2.02. 35 P
i know that, but i would have thee hence, and 2.03. 6 P
scorn it, for the man (as you know all) hath a 2.03.180 P
i know her spirits are as coy and wild | as 3.01. 35
and never to let beatrice know of it. 3.01. 43
i know he doth deserve | as much as may be 3.01. 47
one doth not know | how much an ill word may 3.01. 85
nay, but i know who loves him. 3.02. 63 P
that would i know too. 3.02. 64 P
you know he does. 3.02. 90 P
i know not that, when he knows what i know. 3.02. 91 P
i know not that, when he knows what i know. 3.02. 92 P
trust that you see, confess not that you know. 3.02.120 P
than talk, we know what belongs to a watch. 3.03. 38 P
if we know him to be a thief, shall we not lay 3.03. 54 P
therefore know i have earn'd of don john a 3.03.108 P
i know that deformed; 3.03.125 P
but know that i have to–night woo'd margaret, 3.03.144 P
i know him, 'a wears a lock. 3.03.170 P
and how you may be converted i know not, but 3.04. 90 P
i would fain know what you have to say. 3.05. 29 P
if either of you know any inward impediment why 4.01. 12 P
know you any, hero? 4.01. 15 P
know you any, count? 4.01. 17 P
i know what you would say. 4.01. 48
so attir'd in wonder, | i know not what to say. 4.01.145
they know that do accuse me, i know none. 4.01.177
they know that do accuse me, i know none. 4.01.177
if i know more of any man alive | than that 4.01.178
i know not. 4.01.190
and though you know my inwardness and love | is 4.01.245
as strange as the thing i know not. 4.01.269 P
hero is belied, | and that shall claudio know; 5.01. 43
know, claudio, to thy head, | thou hast so 5.01. 62
i know them, yea, | and what they weigh, even to 5.01. 92
fare you well, boy, you know my mind. 5.01.185 P
if you would know your wronger, look on me. 5.01.262
i know not how to pray your patience, | yet i 5.01.271
virtuous | in any thing that i do know by her. 5.01.303
you know your office, brother: 5.04. 14
what is the end of study, let me know. LLL 1.01. 55
why, that to know which else we should not know. 1.01. 56
why, that to know which else we should not know. 1.01. 56
so, | to know the thing i am forbid to know: 1.01. 60
so, | to know the thing i am forbid to know: 1.01. 60
study knows that which yet it doth not know. 1.01. 68
too much to know is to know nought but fame; 1.01. 92
too much to know is to know nought but fame; 1.01. 92
for well you know here comes in embassy | the 1.01.134
our court you know is haunted | with a refined 1.01.162
how you delight, my lords, i know not, i, | but 1.01.174
then i am sure you know how much the gross sum 1.02. 45 P
or be to blame, | by this you shall not know, 1.02.104
i know where it is situate. 1.02.137 P
his forbidden gates, | to know his pleasure; 2.01. 27
know you the man? 2.01. 39
i know him, madam; 2.01. 40
they say so most that most his humors know. 2.01. 53
i know you did. 2.01.116
by adding a tongue which i know will not lie. 2.01.253
i shall know, sir, when i have done it. 3.01.158 P
why, villain, thou must know first. 3.01.159 P
i know not, but i think it was not he. 4.01. 3
thou shalt know her, fellow, by the rest that 4.01. 44 P
shall i teach you to know? 4.01.108
the deer was, as you know, sanguis, in blood, 4.02. 3 P
be the mark, to know thee shall suffice; 4.02.111
how shall she know my griefs? 4.03. 41
not by two that i know. 4.03. 50
you may look pale, but i should blush, i know, 4.03.127
see, | i would not have him know so much by me. 4.03.148
which they'll know | by favors several which 5.02.124
know their minds, boyet. 5.02.175
know what they would. 5.02.178
i know the reason, lady, why you ask. 5.02.243
i will, and so will she, i know, my lord. 5.02.314
and we that sell by gross, the lord doth know, 5.02.319
do not you know my lady's foot by th' squier, 5.02.474
they would know | whether the three worthies 5.02.485
i can assure you, sir, we know what we know. 5.02.490
i can assure you, sir, we know what we know. 5.02.490
sir, we know whereuntil it doth amount. 5.02.493 P
own part, i know not the degree of the worthy, 5.02.506 P
sport best pleases that doth /least know how: 5.02.516
i know not by what power i am made bold, | nor MND 1.01. 59
but i beseech your grace that i may know | the 1.01. 62
know of your youth, examine well your blood, 1.01. 68
he will not know what all but he do know; 1.01.229
he will not know what all but he do know; 1.01.229
but i know | when thou hast stolen away from 2.01. 64
hippolyta, | knowing i know thy love to theseus? 2.01. 76
i know a bank where the wild thyme blows, 2.01.249
thou shalt know the man | by the athenian 2.01.263
for, you know, pyramus and thisby meet by 3.01. 49 P
master mustardseed, i know your patience well. 3.01.191 P
can you not hate me, as i know you do, | but you 3.02.149
this you know i know. 3.02.163
this you know i know. 3.02.163
disparage not the faith thou dost not know, 3.02.174
could not this make thee know, | the hate i bare 3.02.189
i am amaz'd, and know not what to say. 3.02.344
did not you tell me i should know the man | by 3.02.348
i know you two are rival enemies. 4.01.142
you shall know all, that you are like to know. 5.01.117
you shall know all, that you are like to know. 5.01.117
this man is pyramus, if you would know; 5.01.129
for, if you will know, | by moonshine did these 5.01.136
then know that i as snug the joiner am | a lion 5.01.223
in sooth, i know not why i am so sad; MV 1.01. 1

of me, | that i have much ado to know myself. 1.01. 7
plucking the grass to know where sits the wind, 1.01. 18
i know antonio | is sad to think upon his 1.01. 39
i do know of these | that therefore only are 1.01. 95
thou shalt not know the sound of thine own 1.01.109
i pray you, good bassanio, let me know it, | and 1.01.135
you know me well, and herein spend but time | to 1.01.153
do were as easy as to know what were good to do, 1.02. 12 P
in truth, i know it is a sin to be a mocker, but 1.02. 57 P
you know i say nothing to him, for he 1.02. 68 P
temptation without, i know he will choose it. 1.02. 98 P
shall i know your answer? 1.03. 8 P
do you know me, father? 2.02. 69 P
alack the day, i know you not, young gentleman, 2.02. 70 P
do you not know me, father? 2.02. 73 P
alack, sir, i am sand-blind, i know you not. 2.02. 74 P
i know not what i shall think of that; 2.02. 88 P
as your worship shall know by this honest old 2.02.138 P
i know thee well, thou hast obtain'd thy suit. 2.02.144
i know the hand; 2.04. 12
albeit i'll swear that i do know your tongue. 2.06. 27
how shall i know if i do choose the right? 2.07. 10
so — and i know not what's spent in the search. 3.01. 91 P
i would not lose you, and, you know yourself, 3.02. 5
i know he will be glad of our success; 3.02.240
never did i know | a creature that did bear the 3.02.274
and i know, my lord, | if law, authority, and 3.02.288
his reason well i know: 3.03. 21
i know you would be prouder of the work | than 3.04. 8
my people do already know my mind, | and will 3.04. 37
i have work in hand | that you yet know not of. 3.04. 58
not so, sir, neither, i know my duty. 3.05. 54 P
of good words, and i do know | a many fools, 3.05. 67
he attendeth here hard by | to know your answer, 4.01.146
you know the law, your exposition | hath been 4.01.237
i pray you know me when we meet again; 4.01.419
and know how well i have deserv'd this ring, 4.01.446
if you did know to whom i gave the ring, | if 5.01.193
if you did know for whom i gave the ring, | and 5.01.194
know him i shall, i am well sure of it. 5.01.229
you shall not know by what strange accident | i 5.01.278
though yet i know no wise remedy how to avoid it
AYL 1.01. 25 P
know you where you are, sir? 1.01. 40 P
know you before whom, sir? 1.01. 42 P
i know you are my eldest brother, and in the 1.01. 44 P
gentle condition of blood you should so know me. 1.01. 45 P
for my soul (yet i know not why) hates nothing 1.01.165 P
especially of my own people, who best know him, 1.01.170 P
you know my father hath no child but i, nor none 1.02. 17 P
that time to value her, | but now i know her. 1.03. 72
know you not, master, to /some kind of men 2.03. 10
this i must do, or know not what to do; 2.03. 34
my voice is ragged, i know i cannot please you. 2.05. 15 P
young and fair, | they have the gift to know it; 2.07. 38
yet am i inland bred | and know some nurture. 2.07. 97
and know what 'tis to pity and be pitied, | let 2.07.117
no more but that i know the more one sickens the 3.02. 23 P
our ewes, and their fells you know are greasy. 3.02. 54 P
write, | teaching all that read to know | the 3.02.138
but doth he know that i am in this forest and in 3.02.229 P
do you not know i am a woman? 3.02.249 P
but myself, against whom i know most faults. 3.02.281 P
he taught me how to know a man in love; 3.02.370 P
i do not know what "poetical" is: 3.03. 17 P
then shall you know the wounds invisible | that 3.05. 30
mistress, know yourself, down on your knees, 3.05. 57
if you will know my house, | 'tis at the tuft of 3.05. 74
that thou didst know how many fathom deep i am 4.01.206 P
i know not the contents, but, as i guess | by 4.03. 8
no, i protest, i know not the contents, | phebe 4.03. 21
pray you (if you know) | where in the purlieus 4.03. 75
then should i know you by description — | such 4.03. 84
shame, if you will know of me | what man i am, 4.03. 95
might so do, | for well i know he was unnatural. 4.03.124
ay, i know who 'tis; 5.01. 8 P
o, i know where you are. 5.02. 29 P
know of me then (for now i speak to some purpose 5.02. 52 P
that i know you are a gentleman of good conceit. 5.02. 53 P
of my knowledge, insomuch i say i know you are; 5.02. 55 P
i know into what straits of fortune she is 5.02. 64 P
those that fear they hope, and know they fear. 5.04. 4
have | i'll stay to know at your abandon'd cave. 5.04.196
i know my remedy; SHR in.1. 11 P
i know the boy will well usurp the grace, in.1. 131
the fat ale-wife of wincot, if she know me not. in.2. 22 P
why, sir, you know no house nor no such maid, in.2. 91
i know it well. what must i call her? in.2. 108
for how i firmly am resolv'd you know: 1.01. 49
because i know you well and love you well, 1.01. 53
and for i know she taketh most delight | in 1.01. 92
or, signior gremio, you, know any such, | prefer 1.01. 96
our quarrel yet never brook'd parle, know now, 1.01.115 P
counsel me, tranio, for i know thou canst; 1.01.157
assist me, tranio, for i know thou wilt. 1.01.158
and then i know after who comes by the worst. 1.02. 14
if thou know | one rich enough to be petruchio's 1.02. 66
i know her father, though i know not her, | and 1.02.101
i know her father, though i know not her, | and 1.02.101
you know him not, sir. 1.02.116 P
i know she is an irksome brawling scold. 1.02.187
for this reason, if you'll know, | that she's 1.02.233
sir, give him head, i know he'll prove a jade. 1.02.247
i do, | so well i know my duty to my elders. 2.01. 7
sciences, | whereof i know she is not ignorant. 2.01. 58
but for my daughter katherine, this i know, 2.01. 62
i know him well; you are welcome for his sake. 2.01. 70
may i be so bold to know the cause of your 2.01. 87 P
by report | i know him well. 2.01.105
i know not what to say, but give me your hands. 2.01.318
first, as you know, my house within the city 2.01.346
on sunday next you know | my daughter katherine 2.01.393
far | to know the cause why music was ordain'd! 3.01. 10
"hic ibat simois," i know you not, "hic est 3.01. 42 P
you know to-morrow is the wedding-day. 3.01. 84
though he be blunt, i know him passing wise; 3.02. 24
why, sir, you know this is your wedding-day. 3.02. 97
and after me, i know, the rout is coming. 3.02.181
i know you think to dine with me to-day, | and 3.02.185
you know there wants no junkets at the feast. 3.02.248
first, know my horse is tir'd, my master and 4.01. 54 P
come, kate, sit down, i know you have a stomach. 4.01.158
to make her come and know her keeper's call, 4.01.194
know, sir, that i am call'd hortensio. 4.02. 21
i know not what, but formal in apparel, | in 4.02. 64
know you not the cause? 4.02. 82
among them know you one vincentio? 4.02. 96
i know him not, but i have heard of him; 4.02. 97
had thee in place where, thou shouldst know it. 4.03.150 P
where then do you know best | we be affied and 4.04. 48
lucentio, for you know | pitchers have ears, and 4.04. 51
i know it is the sun that shines so bright. 4.05. 5
i know it is the moon. 4.05. 16
yes, i know thee to be signior lucentio. 5.01.105 P
and now you know my meaning. 5.02. 30
i know her answer. 5.02. 97
his sake, | and yet i know him a notorious liar, AWW 1.01.100
i know not what he shall — god send him well! 1.01.176
for i know you lack not folly to commit them, 1.03. 10 P
may the world know them? 1.03. 34 P
i know, madam, you love your gentlewoman 1.03. 99 P
happen, it concerns you something to know it. 1.03.121 P
you know, helen, | i am a mother to you. 1.03.137
him, | yet never know how that desert should be. 1.03.200
i know i love in vain, strive against hope; 1.03.201
you know my father left me some prescriptions 1.03.221
for that is her demand — and know her business? 2.01. 86
but what at full i know, thou know'st no part, 2.01.132
but know i think, and think i know most sure, 2.01.157
but know i think, and think i know most sure, 2.01.157
thy vassal, whom i know | is free for me to ask, 2.01.199
though more to know could not be more to trust 2.01.206
i know my business is but to the court. 2.02. 4 P
but never hope to know why i should marry her. 2.03.110
i know her well; 2.03.113
that wilt not know | it is in us to plant thine 2.03.155
i may say in the default, "he is a man i know." 2.03.229 P
what th' import is, | i know not yet. 2.03.277
to do nothing, to know nothing, and to have 2.04. 25 P
o, i know him well, i, sir, he, sir, 's a good 2.05. 18 P
i know not how i have deserv'd to run into my 2.05. 34 P
have kept of them tame, and know their natures. 2.05. 46 P
why, do you not know him? 2.05. 51 P
yes, i do know him well, and common speech 2.05. 52
at the first view | to you that know them not. 2.05. 69
you know your places well; 3.01. 21
i know a man that had this trick of melancholy 3.02. 8 P
know it before the report come. 3.02. 23 P
might you not know she would do as she has done 3.04. 2
you may know by their trumpets. 3.05. 8 P
i know that knave, hang him! 3.05. 16 P
i know she will lie at my house; 3.05. 31 P
the rather for i think i know your hostess | as 3.05. 42
the count rossillion. know you such a one? 3.05. 49
his face i know not. 3.05. 51
ay, surely, mere the truth, i know his lady. 3.05. 55
i know not what the success will be, my lord, 3.06. 80 P
i know th' art valiant, and to the possibility 3.06. 82 P
you do not know him, my lord, as we do. 3.06. 90 P
i know not how i shall assure you further | but 3.07. 2
fancy, not to know what we speak one to another; 4.01. 17 P
so we seem to know, is to know straight our 4.01. 18 P
seem to know, is to know straight our purpose: 4.01. 19 P
is it possible he should know what he is, and be 4.01. 44 P
i know you are the muskos' regiment, | and i 4.01. 69
and you shall know them | when back again this 4.02. 59
i will confess what i know without constraint. 4.03.122 P
what do you know of it? 4.03.181 P
do you know this captain dumaine? 4.03.184 P
i know him. 4.03.185 P
though i know his brains are forfeit to the next 4.03.190 P
in good sadness, i do not know. 4.03.203 P
i do not know if it be it or no. 4.03.208 P
count of this, the count's a fool, i know it, 4.03.229
but they know his conditions and lay him in 4.03.257 P
and more of his soldiership i know not, except 4.03.268 P
whisper with the general, and know his pleasure. 4.03.296 P
know you any here? 4.03.313 P
you must know | i am supposed dead. 4.04. 10
the king's coming, i know by his trumpets. 5.02. 51 P
lack'd the sense to know | her estimation home. 5.03. 3
not knowing them until we know their grave. 5.03. 62
then if you know | that you are well acquainted 5.03.105
and yet i know not: 5.03.117
whether i have been to blame or no, i know not. 5.03.129
who by this i know | is here attending. 5.03.134
my suit, as i do understand, you know, | and 5.03.160
and therefore know how far i may be pitied. 5.03.161
come hither, count, do you know these women? 5.03.165
can nor will deny | but that i know them. 5.03.167
know you this ring? this ring was his of late. 5.03.227
by him and by this woman here what know you? 5.03.237
do you know he promis'd me marriage? 5.03.255 P
faith, i know more than i'll speak. 5.03.256 P
and of limbo and of furies and i know not what. 5.03.261 P
therefore i will not speak what i know. 5.03.266 P
it might be yours or hers, for aught i know. 5.03.280
if she, my liege, can make me know this clearly, 5.03.315
let us from point to point this story know, | to 5.03.325
and then 'twas fresh in murmur (as, you know, TN 1.02. 32
i know thy constellation is right apt | for this 1.04. 35
i know his soul is in heaven, fool. 1.05. 69 P
i know not, madam. 1.05.102 P
your lord does know my mind, i cannot love him, 1.05.257
yet i suppose him virtuous, know him noble, | of 1.05.258
i do i know not what, and fear to find | mine 1.05.308
let me yet know of you whither you are bound. 2.01. 9 P
you must know of me then, antonio, my name is 2.01. 16 P
of messaline, whom i know you have heard of. 2.01. 18 P
nay, by my troth, i know not; 2.03. 4 P
but i know, to be up late is to be up late. 2.03. 5 P
meeting, | every wise man's son doth know." 2.03. 44
she shall know of it, by this hand. 2.03.123 P
i know i can do it. 2.03.137 P
i know my physic will work with him. 2.03.172 P
ay, but i know — 2.04.103
what dost thou know? 2.04.104
and all the brothers too — and yet i know not. 2.04.121
you know he brought me out o' favor with my lady 2.05. 7 P
for i know this letter will make a contemplative 2.05. 19 P
telling them i know my place as i would they 2.05. 53 P
no man must know." 2.05. 99
"no man must know." 2.05.100 P
"no man must know." 2.05.101 P
"thou canst not choose but know who i am. 2.05.174 P
i know my lady will strike him. 3.02. 82 P
i think we do know the sweet roman hand. 3.04. 28 P
do you know what you say? 3.04. 99 P
you shall know more hereafter. 3.04.124 P
(as i know his youth will aptly receive it) into 3.04.193 P
the wrongs are thou hast done him, i know not; 3.04.222 P
as to know of the knight what my offense to him 3.04.254 P
pray you, sir, do you know of this matter? 3.04.259 P
i know the knight is incens'd against you, even 3.04.260 P
i know your favor well, | though now you have no 3.04.329
take him away, he knows i know him well. 3.04.331
i know of none, | nor know i you by voice or any 3.04.352
none, | nor know i you by voice or any feature. 3.04.353
i my brother know | yet living in my glass; 3.04.379
no, i do not know you, nor i am not sent to you 4.01. 5 P
i know thee well; how dost thou, my good fellow? 5.01. 10 P
will let your lady know i am here to speak with 5.01. 42 P
i know not what 'twas but distraction. 5.01. 68
and that i partly know the instrument | that 5.01.122
but this your minion, whom i know you love, 5.01.125
what thou dost know | hath newly pass'd between 5.01.154
you wrong me, and the world shall know it. 5.01.303 P
but when we know the grounds and authors of it, 5.01.353
in so rare — i know not what to say — we will WT 1.01. 13 P
me, let me know my trespass | by its own visage. 1.02.265
i dare not know, my lord. 1.02.376
do you know, and dare not? 1.02.377
for, to yourself, what you do know, you must, 1.02.379
if you know aught which does behove my knowledge 1.02.395
i know not; 1.02.432
what she should shame to know herself | but with 2.01. 91
when you shall know your mistress | has deserv'd 2.01.119
dion, whom you know | of stuff'd sufficiency. 2.01.184
satisfied and need no more | than what i know, 2.01.190
now, good sir, | you know me, do you not? 2.02. 5
we do not know | how he may soften at the sight 2.02. 37
i know not what i shall incur to pass it, 2.02. 55
durst not call me so, | if she did know me one. 2.03.124
my lord, best know | (/who least will seem to do 3.02. 32
i know not how it tastes, though it be dish'd 3.02. 72
all i know of it | is that camillo was an honest 3.02. 73
as you know | what you have underta'en to do in 3.02. 77
i do feel it gone, | but know not how it went. 3.02. 96
faults i make, when i shall come to know them, 3.02.219
i know this man well; 4.03. 94 P
bear my part, you must know 'tis my occupation. 4.04.295 P
for i must go | where it fits not you to know. 4.04.298
too rough for some that know little but bowling) 4.04.330 P
i know, sir, we weary you. 4.04.333 P
o, father, you'll know more of that hereafter. 4.04.343
i know | she prizes not such trifles as these 4.04.356
know man from man? 4.04.400
which 'tis not fit you know, i not acquaint | my 4.04.412
whom of force must know | the royal fool thou 4.04.423
if i may ever know thou dost but sigh | that 4.04.427
nor think, | nor dare to know that which i know. 4.04.452
nor think, | nor dare to know that which i know. 4.04.452
my lord, | you know /your father's temper. 4.04.467
this you may know, | and so deliver: 4.04.497
besides, you know, | prosperity's the very bond 4.04.572
i think you know my fortunes | do all lie there. 4.04.590
that you may know you shall not want — one word 4.04.594
i am a poor fellow, sir. i know ye well enough. 4.04.638 P
had been the dearer by i know how much an ounce. 4.04.705 P
i know not what impediment this complaint may be 4.04.709 P
i know not, and't like you. 4.04.741 P
i know by the picking on 's teeth. 4.04.752 P
and box, which none must know but the king, and 4.04.757 P
king, and which he shall know within this hour, 4.04.758 P
thou must know the king is full of grief. 4.04.765 P
he must know 'tis none of your daughter nor my 4.04.819 P
i know, in honor, o that ever i | had squar'd me 5.01. 51
i would most gladly know the issue of it. 5.02. 8 P
with it, which they know to be his character; 5.02. 34 P
them talk of a farthel and i know not what; 5.02.116 P
i know you are now, sir, a gentleman born. 5.02.135 P
but i know thou art no tall fellow of thy hands 5.02.165 P
(for him, i partly know his mind) to find thee 5.03.142
i know not why, except to get the land; JN 1.01. 73
we know his handiwork. 1.01.238
then, good my mother, let me know my father; 1.01.249
the king of england, when we know the king. 2.01.363
know him in us, that here hold up his right. 2.01.364
i know she is not, for this match made up | her 2.01.541
i am perplex'd, and know not what to say. 3.01.221
then know | the peril of our curses light on 3.01.294
do not i know thou wouldst? 3.03. 58
that we shall see and know our friends in heaven 3.04. 77
in the court of heaven | i shall not know him: 3.04. 88
your uncle must not know but you are dead. 4.01.127
i idly heard — if true or false i know not. 4.02.124
to know the meaning | of dangerous majesty, when 4.02.212
there's few or none do know me; 4.03. 3
we know the worst. 4.03. 27
yet i know | our party may well meet a prouder 5.01. 78
may know wherefore we took the sacrament, | and 5.02. 6
you taught me how to know the face of right, 5.02. 88
i do know the scope | and warrant limited unto 5.02.122
know the gallant monarch is in arms, | and like 5.02.148
why, know you not? 5.06. 33
it seems you know not then so much as we. 5.07. 81
but what thou art, god, thou, and i do know, R2 1.03.204
what presence must not know, | from where you do 1.03.249
whereto, when they shall know what men are rich, 1.04. 49
yet i know no cause | why i should welcome such 2.02. 6
i know not what to do. 2.02.100
i | know how or which way to order these affairs 2.02.109
then learn to know him now, this is the duke. 2.03. 40
to know what pricks you on | to take advantage 2.03. 78

my gracious uncle, let me know my fault, | on		2.03.106
i know my uncle york | hath power enough to		3.02. 89
i know it, uncle, and oppose not myself		3.03. 18
for well we know no hand of blood and bone | can		3.03. 79
yet know, my master, god omnipotent, | is		3.03. 85
up, cousin, up, your heart is up, i know, | thus		3.03.194
that know the strong'st and surest way to get.		3.03.201
so, | i speak no more than every one doth know.		3.04. 91
what thou dost know of noble gloucester's death,		4.01. 3
i know your daring tongue | scorns to unsay what		4.01. 8
to plant unrightful kings, wilt know again,		5.01. 63
which his aspiring rider seem'd to know, | with		5.02. 9
madam, i know not, nor i greatly care not, | god		5.02. 48
for aught i know, my lord, they do.		5.02. 53
you will be there, i know.		5.02. 54
but now i know thy mind, thou dost suspect		5.02.104
and thou shalt know | the treason that my haste		5.03. 49
i know she is come to pray for your foul sin.		5.03. 82
his weary joints would gladly rise, i know,		5.03.105
but i will have them if i once know where.		5.03.143
that truly which thou wouldest truly know.	1H4	1.02. 5 P
now shall we know if gadshill have set a match.		1.02.106 P
'tis like that they will know us by our horses,		1.02.174 P
i know them to be as true-bred cowards as ever		1.02.183 P
i know you all, and will a while uphold | the		1.02.195
answer'd neglectingly, i know not what — | he		1.03. 52
think might be, but what i know | is ruminated,		1.03.273
soft, i know a trick worth two of that, i' faith		2.01. 36 P
for i know thou worshippest saint nicholas as		2.01. 64 P
remov'd my horse, and tied him i know not where.		2.02. 12 P
the stony-hearted villains know it well enough.		2.02. 26 P
o, 'tis our setter, i know his voice.		2.02. 51 P
and i must know it, else he loves me not.		2.03. 64
i'll know your business, harry, that i will.		2.03. 80
i know you wise, but yet no farther wise | than		2.03.107
thou wilt not utter what thou dost not know,		2.03.111
i know not what you call all, but if i fought		2.04.185 P
how couldst thou know these men in kendal green		2.04.231 P
noted in thy company, but i know not his name.		2.04.418 P
my lord, the man i know.		2.04.464 P
i know thou dost.		2.04.465 P
but to say i know more harm in him than in		2.04.466 P
than in myself, were to say more than i know.		2.04.467 P
then many an old host that i know is damn'd.		2.04.472 P
and i know his death will be a march of twelve		2.04.546 P
i know not whether god will have it so | for		3.02. 4
go to, i know you well enough.		3.03. 64 P
no, sir john, you do not know me, sir john.		3.03. 65 P
i know you, sir john, you owe me money, sir john		3.03. 66 P
heard the prince tell him, i know not how oft,		3.03. 84 P
to thank god on, i would thou shouldst know it.		3.03.119 P
there shalt thou know thy charge, and there		3.03.201
thought | by some that know not why he is away		4.01. 63
for well you know we of the off'ring side | must		4.01. 69
their poverty, i know not where they had that,		4.02. 70 P
the king hath sent to know | the nature of your		4.03. 41
and well we know the king | knows at what time		4.03. 52
o no, my nephew must not know, sir richard,		5.02. 1
therefore, good cousin, let not harry know, | in		5.02. 24
know then, my name is douglas, | and i do haunt		5.03. 3
no, i know this face full well.		5.03. 19
he that but fears the thing he would not know	2H4	1.01. 85
about it, you know where to find me.		1.02.242 P
not be in this humor with me, dost not know me?		2.01.151 P
come, come, i'know thou wast set on to this.		2.01.151 P
thy name, or to know thy face to-morrow, or to		2.02. 14 P
knight" — every man must know that, as oft as		2.02.110 P
and aprons, and sir john must not know of it.		2.04. 17 P
serve bravely is to come halting off, you know;		2.04. 49 P
i know you, mistress dorothy.		2.04.127 P
know we not galloway nags?		2.04.190 P
abuse, and then i know how to handle you.		2.04.312 P
pantler and bread-chipper, and i know not what?		2.04.315 P
and whether she be damn'd for that, i know not.		2.04.340 P
by this day, i know not the phrase, but i will		3.02. 74 P
peace, stand aside, know you where you are?		3.02.119 P
forth | to know the numbers of our enemies.		4.01. 4
from our princely general | to know your griefs,		4.01.140
i know it will well please them.		4.02. 71
they know their duties.		4.02.101
i know not:		4.03. 45 P
i know not how they sold themselves, but thou,		4.03. 68 P
i do not know, my lord.		4.04. 15
you do know these fits | are with his highness		4.04.114
and i myself know well | how troublesome it sate		4.05.185
i know he doth not, and do arm myself | to		5.02. 10
let king cophetua know the truth thereof.		5.03.102
honest gentleman, i know not your breeding.		5.03.107 P
i know the young king is sick for me.		5.03.135 P
know you what 'tis you speak?		5.05. 45
i know thee not, old man, fall to thy prayers.		5.05. 47
know the grave doth gape | for thee thrice wider		5.05. 53
for god doth know, so shall the world perceive,		5.05. 57
where (for any thing i know) falstaff shall die		ep 30 P
then go we in, to know his embassy;	H5	1.01. 95
for god doth know how many now in health | shall		1.02. 18
they know your grace hath cause, and means, and		1.02.125
now are we well prepar'd to know the pleasure		1.02.234
read them, and know i know your worthiness.		2.02. 69
read them, and know i know your worthiness.		2.02. 69
you know how apt our love was to accord | to		2.02. 86
and let them know | of what a monarchy you are		2.04. 72
that you may know | 'tis no sinister nor no		2.04. 84
to-morrow shall you know our mind at full.		2.04.140
i do not know you so good a man as myself.		3.02.132 P
so bold as to tell you i know the disciplines of		3.02.140 P
send | to know what willing ransom he will give.		3.05. 63
i know him not.		3.06. 19 P
but you must learn to know such slanders of the		3.06. 80 P
one bardolph, if your majesty know the man.		3.06.102 P
you know me by my habit.		3.06.114
well then, i know thee.		3.06.115
what shall i know of thee?		3.06.115
what is thy name? i know thy quality.		3.06.137
i know him to be valiant.		3.07.103 P
that's more than we know.		4.01.129 P
for we know enough, if we know we are the king's		4.01.131 P
enough, if we know we are the king's subjects.		4.01.131 P
how shall i know thee again?		4.01.207 P
and i know | 'tis not the balm, the sceptre, and		4.01.259
i know thy errand, i will go with thee.		4.01.308
you know your places.		4.03. 78
once more i come to know of thee, king harry,		4.03. 79
i do not know the french for fer, and ferret,		4.04. 30 P
i did never know so full a voice issue from so		4.04. 67 P
god knows, and you know, in his rages, and his		4.07. 34 P
herald, | i know not if the day be ours or no,		4.07. 84
which, your majesty know, to this hour is an		4.07.101 P
for i am welsh, you know, good countryman.		4.07.105
majesty's countryman, i care not who know it.		4.07.112 P
for i do know fluellen valiant | and, touch'd		4.07.179
sir, know you this glove?		4.08. 6 P
know the glove? i know the glove is a glove.		4.08. 7 P
know the glove? i know the glove is a glove.		4.08. 7 P
i know this, and thus i challenge it.		4.08. 8 P
the world, know to be no petter than a fellow,		5.01. 7 P
that i may know the let why gentle peace		5.02. 65
i know no ways to mince it in love, but directly		5.02.126 P
come, i know thou lovest me;		5.02.197 P
and i know, kate, you will to her dispraise		5.02.199 P
i do not know dat.		5.02.211 P
'tis hereafter to know, but now to promise.		5.02.212 P
lord, if you will teach her to know my meaning;		5.02.307 P
of old i know them;	1H6	1.02. 39
i know thee well, though never seen before.		1.02. 67
he may mean more than we poor men do know:		1.02.122
father, i know, and oft have shot at them,		1.04. 3
wheel, | i know not where i am, nor what i do.		1.05. 20
to know the cause of your abrupt departure.		2.03. 30
and know us by these colors for thy foes, | for		2.04.105
but he shall know i am as good —		3.01. 41
and know the office that belongs to such.		3.01. 55
lord, we know your grace to be a man | just and		3.01. 94
first let me know, and then i'll answer you.		4.01. 88
yet know, my lord, i was provok'd by him, | and		4.01.104
to know who hath obtain'd the glory of the day.		4.07. 52
i come to know what prisoners thou hast ta'en,		4.07. 56
for know, my lords, the states of christendom,		5.04. 96
you know, my lord, your highness is betroth'd		5.05. 26
i know it will excuse | this sudden execution of		5.05. 98
my lord of winchester, i know your mind.	2H6	1.01.139
patience, good lady, wizards know their times.		1.04. 15
they know their master loves to be aloft, | and		2.01. 11
alas, master, i know not.		2.01.116
i know not.		2.01.118
and, for my wife, i know not how it stands.		2.01.188
where, as all you know, | harmless richard was		2.02. 26
we know your mind at full.		2.02. 77
we know the time since he was mild and affable,		3.01. 9
gloucester, know that thou art come too soon,		3.01. 95
i know their complot is to have my life;		3.01.147
i know no pain they can inflict upon him | will		3.01.377
let him know | we have dispatch'd the duke, as		3.02. 1
what know i how the world may deem of me, | for		3.02. 65
stand apart, the king shall know your mind.		3.02.242
so get thee gone, that i may know my grief,		3.02.346
what is my ransom, master? let me know.		4.01. 15
o graceless men! they know not what they do.		4.04. 38
know, cade, we come ambassadors from the king		4.08. 7
i know thee not, why then should i betray thee?		4.10. 32
to know the reason of these arms in peace;		5.01. 18
i know, ere they will have me go to ward,		5.01.112
might i but know thee by thy /household badge.		5.01.201
i know our safety is to follow them, | for, as i		5.03. 23
ah, know you not the city favors them, | and	3H6	1.01. 67
i know not what to say, my title's weak.		1.01.134
but this i know, they have demean'd themselves		1.04. 7
for thou shalt know this strong right hand of		2.01.152
i know it well, lord warwick, blame me not.		2.01.157
would thy best friends did know | how it doth		2.02. 54
to make this shameless callet know herself.		2.02.145
yet know thou, since we have begun to strike,		2.02.167
clifford, dost thou know who speaks to thee?		2.06. 61
i know by that he's dead, and, by my soul, | if		2.06. 79
ah, simple men, you know not what you swear!		3.01. 83
and come some other time to know our mind.		3.02. 17
i know i am too mean to be your queen, | and yet		3.02. 97
and yet i know not how to get the crown, | for		3.02.172
from whom i know not.		3.03.166
alas, you know, 'tis far from hence to france;		4.01. 4
kingdom, | that know not how to use embassadors,		4.03. 36
you know our king, my brother, | is prisoner to		4.05. 4
true, my good lord, i know you for no less.		4.07. 22
they are at hand, and you shall quickly know.		5.01. 15
father of warwick, know you what this means?		5.01. 81
i know my duty, you are all undutiful.		5.05. 33
but what's the matter, clarence, may i know?	R3	1.01. 51
yea, richard, when i know;		1.01. 52
we know thy charge, brakenbury, and will obey.		1.01.105
i know it pleaseth neither of us well.		1.01.113
lady, you know no rules of charity, | which		1.02. 68
but i know none, and therefore am no beast.		1.02. 72
i know so.		1.02.114
that shalt thou know hereafter.		1.02.198
come, we know your meaning, brother gloucester;		1.03. 73
the deed, | o, know you yet he doth it publicly.		1.04.216
the duke shall know how slack you have been!		1.04.275
i do not know that englishman alive | with whom		2.01. 70
i promise you, i scarcely know myself.		2.03. 2
of my kind uncle, that i know will give, | and		3.01.113
therefore he sends to know your lordship's		3.02. 15
i know they do, and i have well deserv'd it.		3.02. 71
think you, but that i know our state secure, | i		3.02. 81
grace, we think, should soonest know his mind.		3.04. 9
we know each other's faces;		3.04. 10
i thank his grace, i know he loves me well;		3.04. 14
by his face straight shall you know his heart.		3.04. 53
because, my lord, you know my mother lives.		3.05. 94
his hand — | true ornaments to know a holy man.		3.07. 99
know then, it is your fault that you resign		3.07.117
as well we know your tenderness of heart | and		3.07.210
yet know, whe'er you accept our suit or no,		3.07.214
for god doth know, and you may partly see, | how		3.07.235
i know a discontented gentleman | whose humble		4.02. 36
i partly know the man;		4.02. 41
know, my loving lord, | the marquess dorset, as		4.02. 47
but where (to say the truth) i do not know.		4.03. 30
for i know the britain richmond aims | at young		4.03. 40
then know that from my soul i love thy daughter.		4.04.256
i know not, mighty sovereign, but by guess.		4.04.465
where is lord stanley quarter'd, do you know?		5.03. 34
for, gentle hearers, know, | to rank our chosen	H8	pr 17
i do know | kinsmen of mine, three at the least,		1.01. 80
you know his nature, | that he's revengeful;		1.01.108
and i know his sword | hath a sharp edge;		1.01.109
well, we shall then know more, and buckingham		1.01.118
know you not | the fire that mounts the liquor		1.01.143
i do know | to be corrupt and treasonous.		1.01.155
let the king know | (as soon he shall by me)		1.01.190
till you know | how he determines further.		1.01.213
it alike with us, | know you of this taxation?		1.02. 40
i know but of a single part in aught | pertains		1.02. 41
you know no more than others?		1.02. 44
wholesome | to those which would not know them,		1.02. 46
in what kind, let's know, | is this exaction?		1.02. 53
which neither know | my faculties nor person,		1.02. 72
if i know you well, | you were the duke's		1.02.171
the king will know him one day.		2.02. 21
pray god he do, he'll never know himself else.		2.02. 22
i knew him, and i know him;		2.02. 54
in which we come | to know your royal pleasure.		2.02. 70
i'll make ye know your times of business.		2.02. 71
i know your majesty has always lov'd her | so		2.02.109
what were't worth to know | the secret of your		2.03. 50
i do not know | what kind of my obedience i		2.03. 65
time | i know your back will bear a duchess.		2.03. 99
if he know | that i am free of your report, he		2.04. 98
many enemies, that know not | why they are so,		2.04.159
with thy approach, i know, | my comfort comes		2.04.240
set against 'em, | i know my life so even.		3.01. 37
as not to know the language i have liv'd in.		3.01. 44
but to know | how you stand minded in the		3.01. 57
of gravity and learning, | in truth i know not.		3.01. 74
but be brought to know our ends are honest,		3.01.154
i know you have a gentle, noble temper, | a soul		3.01.165
you know i am a woman, lacking wit | to make a		3.01.177
what he deserves of you and me i know;		3.02. 14
what though i know her virtuous | and well		3.02. 97
yet i know her for | a spleeny lutheran, and not		3.02. 98
i know 'twill stir him strongly;		3.02.218
yet i know | a way, if it take right, in spite		3.02.218
(i mean your malice), know, officious lords, | i		3.02.237
the king shall know it, and, no doubt, shall		3.02.348
i know myself now, and i feel within me | a		3.02.378
of me will stir him | (i know his noble nature)		3.02.418
these i know.		4.01. 37
i know it;		4.01. 97
that all the world may know | i was a chaste		4.02.169
i know you wise, religious, | and, let me tell		5.01. 28
th' council that he is | (for so i know he is,		5.01. 44
he is | (for so i know he is, they know he is)		5.01. 44
you do desire to know | wherefore i sent for you		5.01. 89
this morning come before us, where, i know,		5.01.101
for i know | there's none stands under more		5.01.111
know you not | how your state stands i' th'		5.01.126
sure you know me?		5.02. 4
has done half an hour, to know your pleasures.		5.02. 41
you shall know many dare accuse you boldly,		5.02. 91
do not i know you for a favorer | of this new		5.02.115
but know i come not | to hear such flattery now,		5.02.158
alas, i know not, how gets the tide in?		5.03. 18
do, i know within a while | all the best men are		ep 12
i know the cause too.	TRO	1.02. 55 P
do you know a man if you see him?		1.02. 64 P
and you know he has not past three or four hairs		1.02.111 P
why, you know 'tis dimpled.		1.02.121 P
do you know what a man is?		1.02.252 P
and know by measure | of their observant toil		1.03.202
looks | know them from eyes of other mortals?		1.03.225
that thou shalt know, troyan, he is awake, | he		1.03.255
and every greek of mettle, let him know, | what		1.03.258
i know that, fool.		2.01. 65 P
a one that dare | maintain — i know not what,		2.01.126
i know not, 'tis put to lott'ry.		2.01.128
you know an enemy intends you harm;		2.02. 39
you know a sword employ'd is perilous, | and		2.02. 40
'tis our mad sister, i do know her voice.		2.02. 98
well may we fight for her whom, we know well,		2.02.161
of our place, | or know not what we are.		2.03. 83
i know not what pride is.		2.03.152 P
know the whole world, he is as valiant —		2.03.232
you know me, do you not?		3.01. 9 P
friend, know me better, i am the lord pandarus.		3.01. 11 P
i hope i shall know your honor better!		3.01. 13 P
i do but partly know, sir, it is music in parts.		3.01. 18 P
know you the musicians?		3.01. 19 P
you must not know where he sups.		3.01. 86 P
you know all, lord pandarus.		3.01.139 P
you know now your hostages:		3.02.107 P
i know not what i speak.		3.02.151
well know they what they speak that speak so		3.02.152
i know, is such a wrest in their affairs | that		3.03. 23
you know my mind, i'll fight no more 'gainst		3.03. 56
what mean these fellows? know they not achilles?		3.03. 70
nor doth he of himself know them for aught,		3.03.118
hector has knock'd out his brains, i know not;		3.03.303 P
we know each other well.		4.01. 31
we do, and long to know each other worse.		4.01. 32
i was sent for to the king, but why, i know not.		4.01. 36
it's more than i know, i'll be sworn.		4.02. 51 P
do not you know of him, but yet go fetch him		4.02. 56 P
my father, | i know no touch of consanguinity;		4.02. 97
i know what 'tis to love, | and would, as i		4.03. 10
i'll answer to my lust, and know you, lord,		4.04.132
not, for you know 'tis true | that you are odd,		4.05. 43
therefore achilles, but what e'er, know this:		4.05. 77
i know your favor, lord ulysses, well.		4.05.213
that this great soldier may his welcome know.		4.05.276
you know me dutiful, therefore, dear sir, | let		5.03. 72
face, | know what it is to meet achilles angry.		5.05. 46
you know caius martius is chief enemy to the	COR	1.01. 7 P
for the gods know i speak this in hunger for		1.01. 24 P
they shall know we have strong arms too.		1.01. 60 P
and presume to know | what's done i' th' capitol		1.01.191

sicinius velutus, and i know not — 'sdeath, 1.01.217
where i know | our greatest friends attend us. 1.01.244
in our counsels, | and know how we proceed. 1.02. 3
ere (almost) rome | should know we were afoot. 1.02. 25
a' th' town, | where they shall know our mind. 1.05. 28
more than i know the sound of martius' tongue 1.06. 26
know you on which side | they have plac'd their 1.06. 51
rome must know | the value of her own. 1.09. 20
nature teaches beasts to know their friends. 2.01. 6 P
do you two know how you are censur'd here in the 2.01. 21 P
i know you can do very little alone, for your 2.01. 35 P
come, sir, come, we know you well enough. 2.01. 66 P
you know neither me, yourselves, nor any thing. 2.01. 67 P
two i' th' thigh — there's nine that i know. 2.01.152 P
know, rome, that all alone martius did fight 2.01.162
you have, i know, petition'd all the gods | for 2.01.170
i know not where to turn. 2.01.181
know, good mother, | i had rather be their 2.01.202
that they have lov'd, they know not wherefore; 2.02. 9 P
so that, if they love they know not why, they 2.02. 10 P
i know they do attend us. 2.02.160
you know the cause, sir, of my standing here. 2.03. 62
and my soul aches | to know, when two 3.01.109
they know the corn | was not our recompense, 3.01.120
he shall well know | the noble tribunes are the 3.01.269
as i do know the consul's worthiness, | so can i 3.01.276
although i know thou hadst rather | follow thine 3.02. 90
i talk of that, that know it. 3.03. 84
know, i pray you — 3.03. 87
i'll know no further. 3.03. 87
we know your drift. speak what? 3.03.116
which heaven | will not have earth to know. 4.02. 36
i know you well, sir, and you know me. 4.03. 1 P
i know you well, sir, and you know me. 4.03. 1 P
know you me yet? 4.03. 5 P
then know me not, | lest that thy wives with 4.04. 4
i know thee not. thy name? 4.05. 64
know thou first, | i lov'd the maid i married; 4.05.113
tell not me! | i know this cannot be. 4.06. 57
how probable i do not know — that martius, 4.06. 66
i do not know what witchcraft's in him, but 4.07. 2
he would not seem to know me. 5.01. 8
you know the very road into his kindness, | and 5.01. 59
you shall know now that i am in estimation; 5.02. 61 P
wife, mother, child i know not. 5.02. 82
you know the way home again. 5.02. 97 P
do you know this lady? 5.03. 63
as certain as i know the sun is fire. 5.04. 45
i know it; 5.06. 18
you are to know | that prosperously i have 5.06. 73
my lords, when you shall know (as in this rage, 5.06.135
know that the people of rome, for whom we stand TIT 1.01. 20
i know not, marcus, but i know it is | (whether 1.01.394
marcus, but i know it is | (whether by device or 1.01.394
only thus much i give your grace to know: 1.01.413
and make them know what 'tis to let a queen 1.01.454
sheath, | till you know better how to handle it. 2.01. 42
and should the empress know | this discord's 2.01. 69
or know ye not, in rome | how furious and 2.01. 75
it is | of a cut loaf to steal a shive, we know. 2.01. 87
know that this gold must coin a stratagem, 2.03. 5
you shall know, my boys, | your mother's hand 2.03.120
i know not what it means, away with her! 2.03.157
ne'er let my heart know merry cheer indeed 2.03.188
now | was i a child to fear i know not what. 2.03.221
if it be dark, how dost thou know 'tis he? 2.03.225
i know thou dost but jest. 2.03.253
we know not where you left them all alive, | but 2.03.257
follows me every where, i know not why. 4.01. 2
alas, sweet aunt, i know not what you mean. 4.01. 4
my lord, i know not, i, nor can i guess, 4.01. 16
i know my noble aunt | loves me as dear as e'er 4.01. 22
that we may know the traitors and the truth! 4.01. 76
although i know | there is enough written upon 4.01. 83
o, 'tis a verse in horace, i know it well, | i 4.02. 22
sir, i know not jubiter, i never drank with him 4.03. 85 P
my lords, you know, /as /know the mightful gods, 4.04. 5
but he and his shall know that justice lives 4.04. 23
i know from whence this same device proceeds. 4.04. 52
then cheer thy spirit, for know thou, emperor, 4.04. 88
i do not, | yet, for i know thou art religious, 5.01. 74
for that i know | an idiot holds his bauble for 5.01. 78
first know thou, i begot him on the empress. 5.01. 87
if thou didst know me, thou wouldst talk with me 5.02. 20
i am not mad, i know thee well enough. 5.02. 21
that i know thee well | for our proud empress, 5.02. 25
know, thou sad man, i am not tamora; 5.02. 28
well shalt thou know her by thine own proportion 5.02.106
i know thou dost, and, sweet revenge, farewell. 5.02.148
know you these two? 5.02.153
you know your mother means to feast with me, 5.02.184
alas, you know i am no vaunter, i; 5.03.113
for well i know | the common voice do cry it 5.03.139
put up your swords, you know not what you do. ROM 1.01. 65
to know our farther pleasure in this case, | to 1.01.101
my noble uncle, do you know the cause? 1.01.143
i neither know it, nor can learn of him. 1.01.144
grow, | we would as willingly give cure as know. 1.01.155
i'll know his grievance, or be much denied. 1.01.157
ay, if i know the letters and the language. 1.02. 61
i know not, sir. 1.05. 43
i know what: 1.05. 84
i know not. 1.05.133
a name | i know not how to tell thee who i am. 2.02. 54
of thy tongue's uttering, yet i know the sound. 2.02. 59
i know thou wilt say "ay," | and i will take thy 2.02. 90
then plainly know my heart's dear love is set 2.03. 57
no, i know it begins with some other letter — 2.04.210 P
simple choice, you know not how to choose a man. 2.05. 39 P
but all this did i know before. 2.05. 46
till thou shalt know the reason of my love, 3.01. 70
acquaintance at my hand, | that i yet know not? 3.03. 6
let me come in, and you shall know my errant. 3.03. 79
i will, and know her mind early to-morrow; 3.04. 10
yond light is not day-light, i know it, i; 3.05. 12
swear | it shall be romeo, whom you know i hate, 3.05.122
i'll to the friar to know his remedy; 3.05.241
you say you do not know the lady's mind? 4.01. 4
now do you know the reason of this haste. 4.01. 15
o juliet, i already know thy grief, | it strains 4.01. 46
shall romeo by my letters know our drift, | and 4.01.114
things for the cook, sir, but i know not what. 4.04. 15
up, | for well you know this is a pitiful case. 4.05. 99
faith, i know not what to say. 4.05.138 P
seek, and know how this foul murder comes. 5.03.198
and know their spring, their head, their true 5.03.218
then say at once what thou dost know in this. 5.03.228
all this i know, and to the marriage | her nurse 5.03.265
i know the merchant. TIM 1.01. 7
i know them both; th' other's a jeweller. 1.01. 8
i do know him | a gentleman that well deserves a 1.01.101
but you well know, | things of like value 1.01.169
you know me, apemantus? 1.01.185 P
i scarce know how. 1.02.180
nor will he know his purse, or yield me this, 1.02.194
i know, no man | can justly praise but what he 1.02.214
that he will neither know how to maintain it, 2.02. 2
if you did know, my lord, my master's wants — 2.02. 29
ask me what you are, and do not know yourselves. 2.02. 65 P
of these letters, i know not which is which. 2.02. 79 P
yet they could have wish'd — they know not — 2.02.207
we know him for no less, though we are but 3.02. 3 P
i know his lordship is but merry with me; 3.02. 37
who bates mine honor shall not know my coin. 3.03. 26
i know my lord hath spent of timon's wealth, 3.04. 26
now we shall know some answer. 3.04. 66 P
for i know your reverend ages love | security, 3.05. 79
my lords, | i do beseech you know me. 3.05. 89
i know not. 3.06. 87 P
know you the quality of lord timon's fury? 3.06.107 P
i know thee well; 4.03. 56
i know thee too, and more than that i know thee 4.03. 58
and more than that i know thee | i not desire to 4.03. 58
than that i know thee | i not desire to know. 4.03. 59
although i know you'll swear, terribly swear 4.03.137
what man didst thou ever know unthrift that was 4.03.311 P
thou talk'st of, didst thou ever know belov'd? 4.03.314 P
when i know not what else to do, i'll see thee 4.03.353 P
he; i know him. 4.03.410 P
then i know thee not. 4.03.476
i beg of you to know me, good my lord, | t' 4.03.487
know his gross patchery, love him, feed him, 5.01. 96
i know none such, my lord. 5.01. 99
name them, my lord, let's know them. 5.01.105
countrymen, | let alcibiades know this of timon, 5.01.170
then let him know, and tell him timon speaks it, 5.01.175
what, know you not, | being mechanical, you JC 1.01. 2
you know it is the feast of lupercal. 1.01. 67
and since you know you cannot see yourself | so 1.02. 67
that of yourself which you yet know not of. 1.02. 70
if you know | that i do fawn on men and hug them 1.02. 74
or if you know | that i profess myself in 1.02. 76
i know that virtue to be in you, brutus, | as 1.02. 90
as well as i do know your outward favor. 1.02. 91
i do not know the man i should avoid | so soon 1.02.200
i know not what you mean by that, but i am sure 1.02.257 P
a common slave — you know him well by sight — 1.03. 15
i know where i will wear this dagger then; 1.03. 89
if i know this, know all the world besides, 1.03. 98
if i know this, know all the world besides, 1.03. 98
poor man, i know he would not be a wolf, | but 1.03.104
then i know | my answer must be made. 1.03.113
now know you, casca, i have mov'd already | some 1.03.121
and i do know, by this they stay for me | in 1.03.125
'tis cinna, i do know him by his gait, | he is a 1.03.132
i know no personal cause to spurn at him, | but 2.01. 11
i know not, sir. 2.01. 41
do you know them? 2.01. 72
know i these men that come along with you? 2.01. 89
and, you know, his means, | if he improve them, 2.01.158
your condition, | i should not know you brutus. 2.01.255
and virtue of my place, | i ought to know of; 2.01.270
is it excepted i should know no secrets | that 2.01.281
this were true, then should i know this secret. 2.01.291
new-fir'd i follow you, | to do i know not what; 2.01.333
most mighty caesar, let me know some cause, 2.02. 69
because i love you, i will let you know. 2.02. 74
and know it now: 2.02. 93
to know my errand, madam. 2.04. 3
none that i know will be, much that i fear may 2.04. 32
know, caesar doth not wrong, nor without cause 3.01. 47
yet in the number i do know but one | that 3.01. 68
fates, we will know your pleasures. 3.01. 98
that we shall die we know, 'tis but the time, 3.01. 99
i know that we shall have him well to friend. 3.01.143
i know not, gentlemen, what you intend, | who 3.01.151
you know not what you do. 3.01.232
know you how much the people may be mov'd | by 3.01.234
i know not what may fall, i like it not. 3.01.243
spoke, | but here i am to speak what i do know. 3.02.101
wrong, | who (you all know) are honorable men. 3.02.124
it is not meet you know how caesar lov'd you: 3.02.141
'tis good you know not that you are his heirs, 3.02.145
you all do know this mantle. 3.02.170
for brutus, as you know, was caesar's angel. 3.02.181
what private griefs they have, alas, i know not, 3.02.213
but (as you know me all) a plain blunt man 3.02.218
and that they know full well | that gave me 3.02.219
i tell you that which you yourselves do know, 3.02.224
why, friends, you go to do you know not what. 3.02.235
alas, you know not! 3.02.237
i do know you well. 4.02. 42
you know that you are brutus that speaks this, 4.03. 13
for i know, | when thou didst hate him worst, 4.03.105
i'll know his humor, when he knows his time. 4.03.136
i know young bloods look for a time of rest. 4.03.262
my lord, i do not know that i did cry. 4.03.296
their bosoms, and i know | wherefore they do it. 5.01. 7
you know that i held epicurus strong, | and his 5.01. 76
which he did give himself — i know not how, 5.01.102
and whether we shall meet again i know not; 5.01.114
o that a man might know | the end of this day's 5.01.122
know me for brutus! 5.04. 8
i know my hour is come. 5.05. 20
blow, | all the quarters that they know | i' th' MAC 1.03. 16
by sinel's death i know i am thane of glamis, 1.03. 71
he labor'd in his country's wrack, i know not; 1.03.114
know | we will establish our estate upon | our 1.04. 36
know you not he has? 1.07. 30
and know | how tender 'tis to love the babe that 1.07. 54
face must hide what the false heart doth know. 1.07. 82
to know my deed, 'twere best not know myself. 2.02. 70
to know my deed, 'twere best not know myself. 2.02. 70
i know this is a joyful trouble to you; 2.03. 48
most bloody piece of work, | to know it further. 2.03.129
know | that it was he in the times past which 3.01. 75
both of you | know banquo was your enemy. 3.01.114
you know your own degrees, sit down. 3.04. 1
which is nothing | to those that know me. 3.04. 86
for now i am bent to know, | by the worst means, 3.04.133
thither he | will come to know his destiny. 3.05. 17
and you all know, security | is mortals' 3.05. 32
you profess | (how e'er you come to know it), 4.01. 51
yet my heart | throbs to know one thing: 4.01.101
seek to know no more. 4.01.103
let me know. 4.01.105
you know not | whether it was his wisdom or his 4.02. 4
we are traitors, | and do not know ourselves; 4.02. 19
from what we fear, yet know not what we fear, 4.02. 20
what i believe, i'll wail, | what know, believe; 4.03. 9
in whom i know | all the particulars of vice so 4.03. 50
my countryman; but yet i know him not. 4.03.160
i know him now. 4.03.162
poor country, | almost afraid to know itself! 4.03.165
the spirits that know | all mortal consequences 5.03. 4
that will with due decision make us know | what 5.04. 17
which i say i saw, | but know not how to do't. 5.05. 31
in what particular thought to work i know not, HAM 1.01. 67
us, | was, as you know, by fortinbras of norway, 1.01. 82
and i this morning know | where we shall find 1.01.174
now follows that you know young fortinbras, 1.02. 17
nay, it is, i know not "seems." 1.02. 76
but you must know your father lost a father, 1.02. 89
for what we know must be, and is as common | as 1.02. 98
i know you are no truant. 1.02.173
writ down in our duty | to let you know of it. 1.02.223
i do not know, my lord, what i should think. 1.03.104
i do know, | when the blood burns, how prodigal 1.03.115
but know, thou noble youth, | the serpent that 1.05. 38
for your desire to know what is between us, 1.05.139
as "well, well, we know," or "we could, and if 1.05.176
to note | that you know aught of me — this do 1.05.179
drift of question | that they do know my son, 2.01. 11
as thus, "i know his father and his friends, 2.01. 14
ay, my lord, | i would know that. 2.01. 37
"i know the gentleman. 2.01. 53
my lord, i do not know, | but truly i do fear it 2.01. 82
been such a time — i would fain know that — 2.02.153
not that i know. 2.02.155
you know sometimes he walks four hours together 2.02.160
do you know me, my lord? 2.02.173 P
i know the good king and queen have sent for you 2.02.281 P
i have of late — but wherefore i know not — 2.02.296 P
wind is southerly i know a hawk from a hand-saw. 2.02.379 P
wot," | and then, you know, "it came to pass, as 2.02.417 P
if 'a do blench, | i know my course. 2.02.598
have, | than fly to others that we know not of? 3.01. 81
my honor'd lord, you know right well you did, 3.01. 96
for wise men know well enough what monsters you 3.01.138 P
we shall know by this fellow. 3.02.141 P
now what my /love is, proof hath made you know, 3.02.169
for thou dost know, o damon dear, | this realm 3.02.281
i know no touch of it, my lord. 3.02.356 P
play upon me, you would seem to know my stops, 3.02.365 P
ere you go to bed, | and tell you what i know. 3.03. 35
up, sword, and know thou a more horrid hent: 3.03. 88
nay, i know not, is it the king? 3.04. 26
'twere good you let him know, | for who, that's 3.04.188
i must to england, you know that? 3.04.200
and let them know both what we mean to do | and 4.01. 39
my lord, guarded, to know your pleasure. 4.03. 14
till i know 'tis done, | how e'er my haps, my 4.03. 67
you know the rendezvous. 4.04. 4
our duty in his eye, | and let him know so. 4.04. 7
coward — i do not know | why yet i live to say, 4.04. 43
"how should i your true-love know | from another 4.05. 23
lord, we know what we are, but know not what we 4.05. 43 P
know what we are, but know not what we may be. 4.05. 44 P
my brother shall know of it, and so i thank you 4.05. 70 P
if you desire to know the certainty | of your 4.05.141
will you know them then? 4.05.145
i do not know from what part of the world | i 4.06. 5
your name be horatio, as i am let to know it is. 4.06. 12 P
you shall know i am set naked on your kingdom. 4.07. 43 P
know you the hand? 4.07. 51
i know him well. 4.07. 93
father, | but that i know love is begun by time, 4.07.111
hamlet return'd shall know you are come home. 4.07.130
nay, i know not. 5.01.178 P
lips that i have kiss'd i know not how oft. 5.01.188 P
let us know | our indiscretion sometime serves 5.02. 7
wilt thou know | th' effect of what i wrote? 5.02. 36
dost know this water-fly? 5.02. 82
the more gracious, for 'tis a vice to know him. 5.02. 85 P
you, though, i know, to divide him inventorially 5.02.113 P
i know you are not ignorant — 5.02.133 P
but to know a man well were to know himself. 5.02.139 P
but to know a man well were to know himself. 5.02.140 P
the same breed that i know the drossy age dotes 5.02.189 P
he sends to know if your pleasure hold to play 5.02.197 P
cousin hamlet, | you know the wager? 5.02.260
do you know this noble gentleman, edmund? LR 1.01. 24 P
i must love you, and sue to know you better. 1.01. 30 P
know that we have divided | in three our kingdom 1.01. 37
i know no answer. 1.01.201
i know you what you are, | and like a sister am 1.01.269
i know no news, my lord. 1.02. 29 P
you know the character to be your brother's? 1.02. 62 P
i do not well know, my lord. 1.02. 79 P
whose mind and mine, i know, in that are one, 1.03. 15
dost thou know me, fellow? 1.04. 26 P
my lord, i know not what the matter is, but, to 1.04. 57 P
dost thou know the difference, my boy, between a 1.04.137 P

foppish, | and know not how their wits to wear, 1.04.168
for you know, nuncle, | "the hedge–sparrow fed 1.04.214
good wisdom | (whereof i know you are fraught) 1.04.220
may not an ass know when the cart draws the 1.04.223 P
does any here know me? 1.04.226
your age, | which know themselves and you. 1.04.252
parts, | that all particulars of duty know, 1.04.264
never afflict yourself to know more of it, | but 1.04.291
i know his heart. 1.04.330
with any thing you know than comes from her 1.05. 3 P
nay, i know not. 2.01. 6 P
i know not /why he comes. 2.01. 79
i know not, madam. 'tis too bad, too bad. 2.01. 96
you know not why we came to visit you? 2.01.118
why dost thou use me thus? i know thee not. 2.02. 11 P
fellow, i know thee. 2.02. 13 P
what dost thou know me for? 2.02. 14 P
you beastly knave, know you no reverence? 2.02. 69
these kind of knaves i know, which in this 2.02.101
i know, sir, i am no flatterer. 2.02.110 P
i know 'tis from cordelia, | who hath most 2.02.166
lord, | you know the fiery quality of the duke, 2.04. 92
i know what reason | i have to think so. 2.04.129
hope | you less know how to value her desert 2.04.139
i have good hope | thou didst not know on't. 2.04.189
what they are yet, i know not, but they shall be 2.04.281
he calls to horse, but will i know not whither. 2.04.297
i know you. where's the king? 3.01. 3
sir, i do know you, | and dare upon the warrant 3.01. 17
who that fellow is | that yet you do not know. 3.01. 49
shall the duke | instantly know, and of that 3.03. 22
be simple–answer'd, for we know the truth. 3.07. 43
dost thou know dover? 4.01. 71
i know not, lady. 4.05. 7
belike | some things — i know not what. 4.05. 21
i know your lady does not love her husband, | i 4.05. 23
i know you are of her bosom. 4.05. 26
and yet i know not how conceit may rob | the 4.06. 42
i know that voice. 4.06. 95
dost thou know me? 4.06.135
i know thee well enough, thy name is gloucester. 4.06.177
come, i am a king, | masters, know you that? 4.06.200
i know thee well; 4.06.252
to know our enemies' minds, we rip their hearts, 4.06.260
it, that you know me not | till time and i think 4.07. 10
sir, do you know me? 4.07. 47
you are a spirit, i know; /when did you die? 4.07. 48
i know not what to say. 4.07. 53
methinks i should know you, and know this man, 4.07. 63
methinks i should know you, and know this man, 4.07. 63
nor i know not | where i did lodge last night. 4.07. 66
i know you do not love me, for your sisters 4.07. 72
know of the duke if his last purpose hold, | or 5.01. 1
lord, | you know the goodness i intend upon you: 5.01. 7
o ho, i know the riddle. — i will go. 5.01. 37
know thou this, that men | are as the time is: 5.03. 30
know, my name is lost, | by treason's tooth 5.03.121
no tearing, lady, i perceive you know it. 5.03.158
ask me not what i know. 5.03.161
i know when one is dead, and when one lives; 5.03.261
you lords and noble friends, know our intent. 5.03.297
the strings were thine, shouldst know of this. OTH 1.01. 3
i know my price, i am worth no worse a place. 1.01. 11
most reverend signior, do you know my voice? 1.01. 93
this thou shalt answer; i know thee, roderigo. 1.01.119
but if you know not this, my manners tell me 1.01.129
for i do know the state | (how ever this may 1.01.147
how didst thou know 'twas she? 1.01.165
do you know | where we may apprehend her and the 1.01.176
'tis yet to know — | which, when i know that 1.02. 19
which, when i know that boasting is an honor, 1.02. 20
for know, iago, | but that i love the gentle 1.02. 24
you best know the place. 1.03.121
i know not if't be true, | but i, for mere 1.03.388
nor know i aught | but that he's well and will 2.01. 89
i know his trumpet. 2.01.178 P
i do not know. 2.03.179
of all that i do know, nor know i aught | by me 2.03.200
nor know i aught | by me that's said or done 2.03.200
give me to know | how this foul rout began; 2.03.209
i know, iago, | thy honesty and love doth mince 2.03.246
i know not. 2.03.286 P
away, i say, thou shalt know more hereafter. 2.03.381
sir, by many a wind instrument that i know. 3.01. 11 P
nothing, my lord; or if — i know not what. 3.03. 36
when /you woo'd my lady, | know of your love? 3.03. 95
my lord, for aught i know. 3.03.104
my lord, you know i love you. 3.03.117
for i know thou'rt full of love and honesty, 3.03.118
and wisdom, | to let you know my thoughts. 3.03.154
/by /heaven, i'll know thy thoughts. 3.03.162
i know our country disposition well: 3.03.201
if more thou dost perceive, let me know more; 3.03.239
i know not that; 3.03.437
do you know, sirrah, where lieutenant cassio 3.04. 1 P
i know not where he lodges, and for me to devise 3.04. 11 P
i know not, madam. 3.04. 24
love again, | but to know so must be my benefit; 3.04.119
nor should i know him | were he in favor as in 3.04.124
i know not, neither; 3.04.188
/faith, that he did — i know not what he did. 4.01. 32
no, let me know, | and knowing what i am, i know 4.01. 72
and knowing what i am, i know what she shall be. 4.01. 73
in your chamber, and know not who left it there! 4.01.152 P
heaven doth truly know it. 4.02. 38
i do not know; i am sure i am none such. 4.02.123
nay, heaven doth know. 4.02.129
light of heaven, | i know not how i lost him. 4.02.151
i know a lady in venice would have walk'd 4.03. 38 P
let husbands know | their wives have sense like 4.03. 93
else let them know, | the ills we do, their ills 4.03.102
i know his gait, 'tis he. 5.01. 23
we do not know. 5.01. 49
know we this face or no? 5.01. 88
even he, sir; did you know him? 5.01. 92
know him? ay. 5.01. 92
none in the world; nor do i know the man. 5.01.103
go know of cassio where he supp'd to–night. 5.01.117
i know not where is that promethean heat | that 5.02. 12
why i should fear i know not, | since guiltiness 5.02. 38
fear i know not, | since guiltiness i know not; 5.02. 39
i know thou didst not; 5.02.174
i scarce did know you, uncle; 5.02.201
i know this act shows horrible and grim. 5.02.203
what you know, you know: 5.02.303
what you know, you know: 5.02.303
befall'n, | which, as i think, you know not. 5.02.308
is't you, sir, that know things? ANT 1.02. 8 P
we'll know all our fortunes. 1.02. 44 P
what else more serious | importeth thee to know, 1.02.121
ten thousand harms, more than the ills i know, 1.02.129
i know by that same eye there's some good news. 1.03. 19
the gods best know — 1.03. 24
thou shouldst know | there were a heart in egypt 1.03. 40
but be prepar'd to know | the purposes i bear; 1.03. 66
that you know well. 1.03. 89
you may see, lepidus, and henceforth know, | it 1.04. 1
what you shall know mean time | of stirs abroad, 1.04. 81
know, worthy pompey, | that what they do delay, 2.01. 2
i know they are in rome together, | looking for 2.01. 19
i know not, menas, | how lesser enmities may 2.01. 42
bind up | the petty difference, we yet not know. 2.01. 49
i do not know, | maecenas, ask agrippa. 2.02. 16
i know you could not lack, i am certain on't, 2.02. 57
let us know | if 'twill tie up thy discontented 2.06. 5
i do not know | wherefore my father should 2.06. 10
know then | i came before you here a man 2.06. 39
the praise of it by telling, you must know, 2.06. 43
i know not | what counts harsh fortune casts 2.06. 53
i know thee now: how far'st thou, soldier? 2.06. 71
they know, | by th' height, the lowness, or the 2.07. 18
thou must know, | 'tis not my profit that does 2.07. 75
the man hath seen some majesty, and should know. 3.03. 42
well i know the man. 3.07. 78
you did know | how much you were my conqueror, 3.11. 65
know you him? 3.12. 2
for us, you know, | whose he is, we are, and 3.13. 51
temperance should be, | you know not what it is. 3.13.122
not know me yet? 3.13.157
let the old ruffian know | i have many other 4.01. 4
know that to–morrow the last of many battles 4.01. 11
know, my hearts, | i hope well of to–morrow, and 4.02. 41
before, | and let the queen know of our /gests. 4.08. 2
the auguries | say they know not, they cannot 4.12. 5
she soon shall know of us, by some of ours, 5.01. 57
for i know your plight is pitied | of him that 5.02. 33
know, sir, that i | will not wait pinion'd at 5.02. 52
assuredly you know me. 5.02. 72
know you what caesar means to do with me? 5.02.106
know | we will extenuate rather than enforce. 5.02.124
i am so simple but i know the devil himself will 5.02.273 P
i know that a woman is a dish for the gods, if 5.02.273 P
you know the peril. CYM 1.01. 80
come, i shall incur i know not | how much of his 1.01.102
but you know strange fowl light upon neighboring 1.04. 89 P
i do know her spirit, | and will not trust one 1.05. 34
i do not know | what is more cordial. 1.05. 63
but heavens know | some men are much to blame. 1.06. 76
you do seem to know | something of me, or what 1.06. 93
i have spoke this to know if your affiance 1.06.163
of a sir so rare, | which you know cannot err. 1.06.176
no, i know that; 2.01. 28 P
a stranger, and i not know on't? 2.01. 34 P
i know her women are about her; 2.03. 66
that i, which know my heart, do here pronounce 2.03.107
i hope you know that we | must not continue 2.04. 48
was i know not where | when i was stamp'd. 2.05. 4
you must know, | till the injurious romans did 3.01. 46
i know your master's pleasure and he mine: 3.01. 84
did you but know the city's usuries, | and felt 3.03. 45
these boys know little they are sons to th' king 3.03. 80
which will make him know | if that his head have 3.04.174
know, if you kill me for my fault, i should 3.06. 56
i know not why | i love this youth, and i have 4.02. 20
yet said hereafter | i might know more. 4.02. 42
i partly know him, 'tis | cloten, the son o' th' 4.02. 64
not these many years, and yet | i know 'tis he. 4.02. 67
thou shalt know | i am son to th' queen. 4.02. 92
i know the shape of 's leg; 4.02.309
who needs must know of her departure and | dost 4.03. 10
i nothing know where she remains, why gone, 4.03. 14
neither know i | what is betide to cloten, but 4.03. 39
upon our note, | to know from whence we are. 4.04. 21
let me make men know | more valor in me than my 5.01. 29
i know he'll quickly fly my friendship too. 5.03. 62
i know you are more clement than vild men, | who 5.04. 18
accuse the thunderer, whose bolt, you know, 5.04. 95
no care of yours it is, you know 'tis ours. 5.04.100
that have this golden chance and know not why. 5.04.132
you, sir, you know not which way you shall go. 5.04.176 P
be directed by some that take upon them to know, 5.04.180 P
yourself that which i am sure you do not know, 5.04.181 P
i know not why, wherefore, | to say "live, boy." 5.05. 95
my life, good lad, | and yet i know thou wilt. 5.05.102
but her son | is gone, we know not how, nor 5.05.273
what became of him | i further know not. 5.05.286
a banish'd man, | i know not how a traitor. 5.05.320
i know not how to wish | a pair of worthier sons 5.05.355
with | i know not how much more, should be 5.05.389
hath taught | my frail mortality to know itself, PER 1.01. 42
as sick men do | who know the world, see heaven, 1.01. 48
it is enough you know, and it is fit, | what 1.01.105
one sin, i know, another doth provoke: 1.01.137
king, desir'd he might know none of his secrets. 1.03. 6 P
royal antiochus, on what cause i know not, 1.03. 19
to know for what he comes, and whence he comes, 1.04. 80
what i have been i have forgot to know, | but 2.01. 71
hark you, sir; do you know where ye are? 2.01. 96 P
i know it by this mark. 2.01.138
him, we desire to know of him | of whence he is, 2.03. 73
he desires to know of you | of whence you are, 2.03. 79
love, | and that's the mark i know you level at. 2.03.113
no, escanes, know this of me, | antiochus from 2.04. 1
know that our griefs are risen to the top, | and 2.04. 23
or know what ground's made happy by his breath. 2.04. 28
that best know how to rule and how to reign, 2.04. 38
knights, from my daughter this i let you know, 2.05. 2
who, for aught i know, | may be (nor can i think 2.05. 78
know you the character? 3.04. 3
come, come, i know 'tis good for you. 4.01. 44
do you know the french knight that cow'rs i' the 4.02.105 P
i know he will come in our shadow, to scatter 4.02.111 P
yet none does know but you how she came dead, 4.03. 29
dead, | nor none can know, leonine being gone. 4.03. 30
flies, | but yet i know you'll do as i advise. 4.03. 51
but how honorable he is in that, i know not. 4.06. 56 P
do you know this house to be a place of such 4.06. 79 P
us, | i made to it to know of whence you are. 5.01. 19
more | let me entreat to know at large the cause 5.01. 62
i said, my lord, if you did know my parentage, 5.01. 99
i know not, but | here's the regent, sir, of 5.01.185
now i know you better. 5.03. 37
i know you not. 5.03. 49
whom now, i know, hast much more power on him TNK 1.01. 87
he that will all the treasure know o' th' earth 1.01.114
know o' th' earth | must know the centre too; 1.01.115
or let me know | why mine own barber is unblest, 1.02. 52
tell us | when we know all ourselves, and let us 1.02.115
though i know | his ocean needs not my poor 1.03. 6
like the elements | that know not what nor why, 1.03. 62
(though in't i know thou dost believe thyself) 1.03. 88
what the reason of it is, i know not. 2.01. 47 P
no issue know us; 2.02. 32
we shall know nothing here but one another, 2.02. 41
where you should never know it, and so perish 2.02. 92
the cause i know not yet. 2.02.222
be as gentle as she's fair, | i know she's his; 2.03. 16
i know mine own is but a heap of ruins, | and no 2.03. 19
and /ye know what wenches, ha? 2.03. 39
for he does all, ye know. 2.03. 41
yes, 'tis a question | to me that know not. 2.03. 62
where were you bred you know it not? 2.03. 63
what should i do to make him know i love him, 2.04. 29
what | you want at any time, let me but know it. 2.05. 55
i have made him know it. 2.06. 12
and i know your office | unjustly is achiev'd. 3.01.111
have in them | a sense to know a man unarm'd, 3.02. 16
i know you are faint — then i'll talk further 3.03. 7
i know you, y' are a tinker. 3.05. 82
i know your cunning, and i know your cause. 3.06.120
i know your cunning, and i know your cause. 3.06.120
know, weak cousin, | i love emilia, and in that 3.06.125
thou shalt know, palamon, i dare as well | die 3.06.128
to make me their contention, or to know me, | to 3.06.253
honorable, | how good they'll prove, i know not. 4.01. 31
but you must know it, and as good by me | as by 4.01. 43
yes, wench, we know him. 4.01.117
him, tell her so, | for a trick that i know. 4.01.123
does she know him? 4.01.141
now, come ask me, brother — | alas, i know not! 4.02. 51
seen it approv'd, how many times i know not, but 4.03. 97 P
you know my prize | must be dragg'd out of blood 5.01. 42
husband i have 'pointed, | but do not know him. 5.01.152
i think so, but i know not thine own will: 5.01.171
you know | the chestnut mare the duke has? 5.02. 60
do not you know me? 5.02. 82
know, of this war | you are the treasure, and 5.03. 30
i am like to know your husband 'fore yourself 5.03. 37
he whom the gods | do of the two know best, i 5.03. 39
why so, i know not; 5.03. 74
since i know | their lives but pinch 'em. 5.03.132
arm your prize, | i know you will not loose her. 5.03.136
of dung — as you know they grow in dung — have STM II.C 13 P
meed | a thousand honey secrets shalt thou know. VEN 16
never can blab, nor know not what we mean. 126
and whe'er he run or fly they know not whether; 304
"i know not love," quoth he, "nor will not know 409
know not love," quoth he, "nor will not know it, 409
before i know myself, seek not to know me, | no 525
before i know myself, seek not to know me, | no 525
for know, my heart stands armed in mine ear, 779
face, why then i know | he thought to kiss him, 1109
and so 'tis thine, but know, it is as good | to 1181
chin, | the reason of this rash alarm to know, LUC 473
i know what thorns the growing rose defends, | i 492
i know repentant tears ensue the deed, 502
that know not how | to cipher what is writ in 810
thou shalt not know | the stained taste of 1058
but thou shalt know thy int'rest was not bought 1067
know, gentle wench, it small avails my mood; 1273
she would request to know your heaviness." 1283
by this short schedule collatine may know | her 1312
she modestly prepares to let them know | her 1607
i do believe her (though i know she lies) | that PP 1. 2
although i know my years be past the best, | i 1. 6
the truth i shall not know, but live in doubt, 2.13
be the mark, to know thee shall suffice: 5. 7
the cock that treads them shall not know. 18.40
these are certain signs to know | faithful 20.55
dear my love, you know | you had a father, let SON 13.13
they draw but what they see, know not the heart. 24.14
as if by some instinct the wretch did know | his 50. 7
wind, | in winged speed no motion shall i know. 51. 8
and you in every blessed shape we know. 53.12
o, know, sweet love, i always write of you, 76. 9
thou by thy dial's shady stealth mayst know 77. 7
thou mayst be false, and yet i know it not. 92.14
therefore in that i cannot know thy change. 93. 6
to know my shames and praises from your tongue; 112. 6
yet well i know | that music hath a far more 130. 9
they know what beauty is, see where it lies, 137. 3
i do believe her, though i know she lies, 138. 2
no news but health from their physicians know; 140. 8
yet this shall i ne'er know, but live in doubt, 144.13
but, love, hate on, for now i know thy mind: 149.13
love is too young to know what conscience is, 151. 1
age, desires to know | in brief the grounds and LC 62

KNOWER 2 FR 0.0002 REL FR 0 V 2 P
thy knower, patroclus. TRO 2.03. 48 P
achilles is my lord, i am patroclus' knower, and 2.03. 54 P

KNOWEST 24 FR 0.0027 REL FR 12 V 12 P
thou knowest not the duke so well as i do; MM 4.03.161 P

thou knowest that the fashion of a doublet, or a ADO 3.03.118 P
o, thou knowest not what it is. LLL 3.01.157 P
which knowest the way | to plant unrightful R2 5.01. 62
with me, and thou knowest he is no starveling. 1H4 2.01. 68 P
thou knowest my old ward: 2.04.194 P
why, thou knowest i am as valiant as hercules; 2.04.270 P
thou knowest, as thou art but man, i dare, but 3.03.145 P
thou knowest in the state of innocency adam fell 3.03.164 P
thou knowest sir john cannot endure an 2H4 2.04. 2 P
thou knowest the law of arms is such | that 1H6 3.04. 38
thou must tell that knowest. TRO 2.03. 50 P
and may, for aught thou knowest, affected be. TIT 2.01. 28
thou knowest my daughter's of a pretty age. ROM 1.03. 10
thou knowest the mask of night is on my face, 2.02. 85
therefore farewell, i see thou knowest me not. 3.01. 65
which, well thou knowest, is cross and full of 4.03. 5
thou knowest my lodging, get me ink and paper, 5.01. 25
/he that thou knowest thine, hamlet." HAM 4.06. 30 P
what to this was sequent | thou knowest already. 5.02. 55
thou showest, | speak less than thou knowest, LR 1.04.119
varlet art thou, to deny thou knowest me? 2.02. 29 P
thou knowest i have power | to take thy life PER 1.02. 56
artesius, that best knowest | how to draw out, TNK 1.01.159

KNOWING 48 FR 0.0054 REL FR 42 V 6 P

what thou art, nought knowing | of whence i am, TMP 1.02. 18
knowing i lov'd my books, he furnish'd me | from 1.02.166
knowing that tender youth is soon suggested, | i TGV 3.01. 34
knowing my mind, you wrong me, master fenton. WIV 3.04. 76
and, knowing whom it was their hap to save, ERR 1.01.113
and, knowing how the debt grows, i will pay it. 4.04.121
what men daily do, not knowing what they do! ADO 4.01. 20 P
with knowing what hath pass'd between you and 5.02. 48 P
most power to do most harm, least knowing ill; LLL 2.01. 58
a consent, | knowing aforehand of our merriment, 5.02.461
hippolyta, | knowing i know thy love to theseus? MND 2.01. 76
had your eyes, you might fail of the knowing me; MV 2.02. 76 P
the other knowing no burthen of heavy tedious AYL 3.02.324 P
for knowing thee to be but young and light. SHR 2.01.203
my praises towards him, | knowing him is enough. AWW 2.01.104
no part, | i knowing all my peril, thou no art. 2.01.133
and knowing i had no such purpose? 4.01. 36 P
not knowing them until we know their grave. 5.03. 62
not need to grieve | at knowing of thy choice. WT 4.04.416
knowing by paulina that the oracle | gave hope 5.03.126
not knowing what they fear, but full of fear. JN 4.02.146
they, knowing dame eleanor's aspiring humor, 2H6 1.02. 97
knowing that thou wouldst have me drown'd on 3.02. 95
with me, | knowing how hardly i can brook abuse? 5.01. 92
thou not, knowing whence thou art extraught, 3H6 2.02.142
not knowing how to find the open air | but 3.02.177
knowing she will not lose her wonted greatness, H8 4.02.102
and, knowing myself again, | repair to th' COR 2.03.147
knowing that with the shadow of his wings | he TIT 4.04. 85
for, in | my knowing, timon has been this lord's TIM 3.02. 67
sith you have heard, and with a knowing ear, HAM 4.07. 3
that, on the view and knowing of these contents, 5.02. 44
knowing nought (like dogs) but following. LR 2.02. 80
and knowing what i am, i know what she shall be. OTH 4.01. 73
he's very knowing, | i do perceive't. ANT 3.03. 23
knowing all measures, the full caesar will 3.13. 35
gentlemen of your knowing to a stranger of his CYM 1.04. 29 P
to sadness, and oft–times | not knowing why. 1.06. 63
either are past remedies, or, timely knowing, 1.06. 97
one of your great knowing | should learn, being 2.03. 97
on them, knowing 'tis | a punishment or trial? 3.06. 10
perfections wait | that, knowing sin within, PER 1.01. 80
and knowing this kingdom is without a head — 2.04. 35
thought he blush'd, as knowing tarquin's lust, LUC 1354
knowing a better spirit doth use your name, SON 80. 2
thou gav'st, thy own worth then not knowing, 87. 9
as i'll myself disgrace, knowing thy will: 89. 7
me, | knowing thy heart torment me with disdain, 132. 2

KNOWINGLY 2 FR 0.0002 REL FR 2 V 0 P

ay, madam, knowingly. AWW 1.03.250
the city's usuries, | and felt them knowingly; CYM 3.03. 46

KNOWINGS 1 FR 0.0001 REL FR 1 V 0 P

this sore night | hath trifled former knowings. MAC 2.04. 4

/KNOWLEDGE 2 FR 0.0002 REL FR 2 V 0 P

/knowledge, /and /reason, /i /should /be /false LR 1.04.233
/and, /from /some /knowledge /and /assurance, 3.01. 41

KNOWLEDGE 80 FR 0.0090 REL FR 54 V 26 P

some oracle | must rectify our knowledge. TMP 5.01.245
he has no more knowledge in hibocrates and galen
WIV 3.01. 65 P
or, if your knowledge be more, it is much MM 3.02.147 P
love talks with better knowledge, and knowledge 3.02.150 P
knowledge, and knowledge with /dearer love. 3.02.151 P
but shall you on your knowledge find this way? 4.01. 36
being come to knowledge that there was complaint 5.01.153
less in your knowledge and your grace you show ERR 3.02. 31
than for that angel knowledge you can say, | yet LLL 1.01.113
where now his knowledge must prove ignorance. 2.01.103
if knowledge be the mark, to know thee shall 4.02.111
do | that in your knowledge may by me be done, MV 1.01.159
you that, in the great heap of your knowledge? AYL 1.02. 69 P
i shall desire more love and knowledge of you. 1.02.285
let me the knowledge of my fault bear with me: 1.03. 46
if thou delay me not the knowledge of his chin. 3.02.211 P
o knowledge ill–inhabited, worse than jove in a 3.03. 10 P
you should bear a good opinion of my knowledge, 5.02. 55 P
request, | that, upon knowledge of my parentage, SHR 2.01. 95
if knowledge could be set up against mortality. AWW 1.01. 30 P
ensconcing ourselves into seeming knowledge, 2.03. 5 P
acquaintance with thee, or rather my knowledge, 2.03.228 P
he is very great in knowledge, and accordingly 2.05. 9 P
in mine own direct knowledge, without any malice 3.06. 8 P
upon my knowledge, he is, and lousy. 4.03.194 P
you beguile the time and feed your knowledge TN 3.03. 41
sir, i profit in the knowledge of myself, and by 5.01. 19 P
i speak it in the freedom of my knowledge: WT 1.01. 12 P
if you know aught which does behove my knowledge 1.02.395
alack, for lesser knowledge! 2.01. 38
no venom (for his knowledge | is not infected), 2.01. 41
when you shall come to clearer knowledge, that 2.01. 97
let him have knowledge who i am. 2.02. 2
rare | even then will rush to knowledge. 3.01. 21
had force and knowledge | more than was ever 4.04.374
to hold | shall nothing benefit your knowledge, 4.04.503
our absence makes us unthrifty to our knowledge. 5.02.112 P
but for the certain knowledge of that truth | i JN 1.01. 61
would bear thee from the knowledge of thyself, 5.02. 35
to my knowledge, | i never in my life did look R2 2.03. 38
hath by instinct knowledge from others' eyes 2H4 1.01. 86
that visor is an arrant knave, on my knowledge. 5.01. 42 P
expedition and knowledge in th' aunchiant wars, H5 3.02. 78 P
upon my particular knowledge of his directions. 3.02. 79 P
followers so far out of his knowledge! 3.07.134 P
and is good knowledge and literatured in the 4.07.149 P
than is in your knowledge to dream of. 4.08. 4 P
let us have knowledge at the court of guard. 1H6 2.01. 4
knowledge the wing wherewith we fly to heaven, 2H6 4.07. 74
i never did her any to my knowledge. R3 1.03.308
that, without the king's assent or knowledge, H8 3.02.310
that, without the knowledge | either of king or 3.02.316
has he had knowledge of it? 5.02. 39
(or rather call my thought a certain knowledge) TRO 4.01. 42
him manifests the true knowledge he has in their COR 2.02. 13 P
will not seal your knowledge with showing them. 2.03.108 P
i shall ere long have knowledge | of my success. 5.01. 61
say to the king the knowledge of the broil | as MAC 1.02. 6
they have more in them than mortal knowledge. 1.05. 3 P
be innocent of the knowledge, dearest chuck, 3.02. 45
you, as 'twere, some distant knowledge of him, HAM 2.01. 13
imaginations lose | the knowledge of themselves. LR 4.06.284
be govern'd by your knowledge, and proceed | i' 4.07. 18
for i mine own gain'd knowledge should profane OTH 1.03.384
as we rate boys who, being mature in knowledge, ANT 1.04. 31
hours had bound me up | from mine own knowledge. 2.02. 91
leave unexecuted | your own renowned knowledge, 3.07. 45
grimly, | and dare not speak their knowledge. 4.12. 6
and to this hour no guess in knowledge | which CYM 1.01. 60
brought | the knowledge of your mistress home, i 2.04. 51
more particulars | must justify my knowledge. 2.04. 79
this paper is the history of my knowledge 3.05. 99
the satisfaction of her knowledge only | in 5.05.251
which by my knowledge found, the sinful father PER 1.02. 77
and not your knowledge, your personal pain, but 3.02. 46
and justify in knowledge | she is thy very 5.01.217
if knowledge be the mark, to know thee shall PP 5. 7
but from thine eyes my knowledge i derive, | and SON 14. 9
here | within the knowledge of mine own desert, 49.10
thou art as fair in knowledge as in hue, 82. 5

/KNOWN 2 FR 0.0002 REL FR 2 V 0 P

/it /must /be /shortly /known /to /him /from HAM 5.02. 71
/when /i /am /known /aright, /you /shall /not LR 4.03. 53

KNOWN 197 FR 0.0222 REL FR 148 V 49 P

thy purposes | with words that made them known.
TMP 1.02.358
letters should not be known; 2.01.151
age, | in having known no travel in his youth. TGV 1.03. 16
like it, | the execution of it shall make known: 1.03. 36
better for you if it were known in counsel. WIV 1.01.118 P
and you have been a man long known to me, though 2.02.181 P
i will hereafter make known to you why i have 3.03.225 P
the truth being known, | we'll all present 4.04. 63
/brook, the matter will be known to–night, or 5.01. 10 P
sir, my name is lucio, well known to the duke. MM 3.02.159 P
i have not yet made known to mariana | a word of 4.01. 48
difficulties are but easy when they are known. 4.02.206 P
danger that might come | if he were known alive? 4.03. 86
i have known my husband, yet my husband | knows 5.01.186
known unto these, and to myself disguis'd? ERR 2.02.214
he hath left to be known a reasonable creature. ADO 1.01. 71 P
i have known when there was no music with him 2.03. 12 P
i have known when he would have walk'd ten mile 2.03. 15 P
hath she made her affection known to benedick? 2.03.123 P
and she will die ere she make her love known, 2.03.175 P
lechery that ever was known in the commonwealth. 3.03.168 P
if i have known her, | you will say, she did 4.01. 48
white and red, | her faults will ne'er be known, LLL 1.02.100
mock them still, as well known as disguis'd. 5.02.301
be dogg'd with company, and our devices known. MND 1.02.104 P
and the country proverb known, | that every man 3.02.458
which is as brief as i have known a play; 5.01. 62
but where thou art not known, why, there they MV 2.02.184
often known | to be the dowry of a second head, 3.02. 94
if you had known the virtue of the ring, | or 5.01.199
"be it known unto all men by these presents." AYL 1.02.123 P
had i before known this young man his son, | i 1.02.237
may show her duty and make known her love?" SHR in.1. 117
son, | a man well known throughout all italy. 2.01. 69
'tis known my father hath no less | than three 2.01.377
and withal make known | which way thou 4.05. 50
i have known thee already. AWW 2.03.101 P
ay, that would be known. 2.03.278
thirds and uses a known truth to pass a thousand 2.05. 30 P
and a gentleman | which i have sometime known. 3.02. 85
no further danger known but the modesty which is 3.05. 27 P
i would i had not known him; 4.05. 8 P
sir, been better known to you, when i have held 5.02. 2 P
you give away myself, which is known mine; 5.03.172
he hath known you but three days, and already TN 1.04. 3 P
nor no railing in a known discreet man, though 1.05. 95 P
when that is known and golden time convents, | a 5.01.382
courts and kingdoms | known and allied to yours. WT 1.02.339
to his eye, make known | how he hath drunk, he 2.01. 43
but be't known | (from him that has most cause 2.01. 76
as i take it, | if the good truth were known. 2.01.199
time's news | be known when 'tis brought forth. 4.01. 27
fellow, sir, that i have known to go about with 4.03. 86 P
a way to make us better friends, more known. 4.04. 66
my dignity would last | but till 'twere known! 4.04.476
things known betwixt us three, i'll write you 4.04.560
and any thing that is fitting to be known — 4.04.720 P
that they were to be known by garment, not by 5.02. 48 P
that is well known — and, as i think, one JN 1.01. 60
time | than if you had at leisure known of this. 5.06. 27
on some known ground of treachery in him? R2 1.01. 11
but what it is that is not yet known what, | i 2.02. 39
be it known unto you | i do remain as neuter. 2.03.158
and it is known to many in our land by the name 1H4 2.04.412 P
if then the tree may be known by the fruit, as 2.04.428 P
one of them is well known, my gracious lord, | a 2.04.510
this oily rascal is known as well as paul's. 2.04.526 P
have you heard our cause and known our means, 2H4 1.03. 1
and my case so openly known to the world, let 2.01. 31 P
i have known thee these twenty–nine years, come 2.04.382 P
to no further use | but to be known and hated. 4.04. 73
be it known to you, as it is very well, i was ep 7 P
(though war nor no known quarrel were in H5 2.04. 17
was ever known so great and little loss, | on 4.08.110
so in the earth, to this day is not known. 1H6 1.02. 2
my worth unknown, no loss is known in me. 4.05. 23
'tis known already that i am possess'd | with 5.04.138
'tis known to you he is mine enemy; 2H6 1.01.148
if they were known, as the suspect is great, 1.03.136
thou mightst as well have known all our names, 2.01.125
why, 'tis well known that, whiles i was 3.01.124
for it is known we were but hollow friends? 3.02. 66
be it known unto thee by these presence, even 4.07. 29 P
when this is known, then to divide the times: 3H6 2.05. 30
now therefore be it known to noble lewis, | that 3.03. 23
of these known evils, but to give me leave | by R3 1.02. 79
and as you are known | the first and happiest H8 pr 23
but you frame | things that are known alike, 1.02. 45
will, much better | she ne'er had known pomp! 2.03. 13
if it be known to him | that i gainsay my deed, 2.04. 95
or be a known friend, 'gainst his highness' 3.01. 85
had i not known those customs | i should have 4.01. 20
the king's further pleasure | be known unto us. 5.02.126
god shall be truly known, and those about her 5.04. 36
would i had known no more! 5.04. 59
as it is known she is, these moral laws | of TRO 2.02.184
let it be known to him that we are here. 2.03. 78
'tis known, achilles, that you are in love 3.03.193
ha? known? 3.03.194
or do you purpose | a victor shall be known? 4.05. 67
but it is not known | whether for east or west. COR 1.02. 9
therefore be it known, | as to us, to all the 1.09. 58
my noble steed, known to the camp, i give him, 1.09. 61
menenius, you are known well enough too. 2.01. 46 P
i am known to be a humorous patrician, and one 2.01. 47 P
follows it that i am known well enough too? 2.01. 63 P
this character, if i be known well enough too? 2.01. 65 P
have you not known | the worthiest men have 2.03. 48
why this was known before. 3.01. 46
nature, never known before | but to be rough, 5.06. 24
the cause were known to them it most concerns. TIT 2.01. 50
and now be it known to you my full intent. 4.02.151
be it known to you | that chiron and the damn'd 5.03. 96
i am the turned forth, be it known to you, 5.03.109
and 'tis known i am a pretty piece of flesh. ROM 1.01. 29 P
too early seen unknown, and known too late! 1.05.139
we still have known thee for a holy man. 5.03.270
that whiles verona by that name is known, 5.03.300
ay, that's well known; TIM 1.01. 3
angry at him, | that might have known my place. 3.03. 14
fury | he has been known to commit outrages 3.05. 71
what you are | make them best seen and known. 5.01. 69
beseech your honor | to make it known to us. 5.01. 90
those that have known the earth so full of JC 1.03. 45
i have not known when his affections sway'd 2.01. 20
if this be known, | cassius or caesar never 3.01. 20
the day will end, | and then the end is known. 5.01.125
nor must be known | no less to have done so, let MAC 1.04. 30
in that heart | courage to make 's love known? 2.03.118
is't known who did this more than bloody deed? 2.04. 22
you made it known to us. 3.01. 83
stones have been known to move and trees to 3.04.122
i am not to you known, | though in your state of 4.02. 65
i have known her continue in this a quarter of 5.01. 29 P
you have known what you should not. 5.01. 46 P
heaven knows what she has known. 5.01. 49 P
yet i have known those which have walk'd in 5.01. 60 P
so this side of our known world esteem'd him) HAM 1.01. 85
never make known what you have seen to–night. 1.05.144
as are companions noted and most known | to 2.01. 23
this must be known, which, being kept close, 2.01.115
to begin, | antiquity forgot, custom not known, 4.05.105
plac'd it safely, | the changeling never known. 5.02. 53
till by some elder masters of known honor | i 5.02.248
that you make known | it is no vicious blot, LR 1.01.226
yet he hath ever but slenderly known himself. 1.01.294 P
had thought, by making this well known unto you, 1.04.205
one that is neither known of thee nor knows thee 2.02. 26 P
yet better thus, and known to be contemn'd, 4.01. 1
'tis known before; 4.04. 22
who, by the art of known and feeling sorrows, 4.06.222
yet to be known shortens my made intent. 4.07. 9
until their greater pleasures first be known 5.03. 2
how have you known the miseries of your father? 5.03.181
if this be known to you, and your allowance, OTH 1.01.127
i should have known it | without a prompter. 1.02. 83
the fortitude of the place is best known to you; 1.03.223 P
if thou hast no name to be known by, let us call 2.03.282 P
you have known him long, and be you well assur'd 3.03. 11
tasted her sweet body, | so i had nothing known. 3.03.347
it /yet hath felt no age nor known no sorrow. 3.04. 37
in me to speak | what i have seen and known. 4.01.278
i will make myself known to desdemona. 4.02.197 P
i care not for thy sword, i'll make thee known, 5.02.165
till that the nature of your fault be known | to 5.02.336
i should have known no less: ANT 1.04. 40
you and i have known, sir. 2.06. 83 P
pray you | be ever known to patience. 3.06. 98
make it so known. 4.06. 3
no matter, sir, what i have heard or known. 5.02. 73
enough to purchase what you have made known. 5.02.148
be it known that we, the greatest, are 5.02.176
offended king, | i will be known your advocate. CYM 1.01. 76
was a friend, to me | known but by letter; 1.01. 99
you all be better known to this gentleman, whom 1.04. 31 P
sir, we have known together in orleance. 1.04. 35 P
will make known | to their approvers they are 2.04. 24
sweeter to you | that have a sharper known; 3.03. 31
this | she wish'd me to make known; 3.05. 50
newness | of cloten's death (we being not known, 4.04. 10
o, i am known | of many in the army. 4.04. 21
i and my brother are not known; 4.04. 32
the vision | which i made known to lucius, ere 5.05.468
what being more known grows worse, to smother it
PER 1.01.106
and what may make him blush in being known, 1.02. 22
stop the course by which it might be known. 1.02. 23

her reason to herself is only known, | which 2.05. 5
'tis known, i ever | have studied physic; 3.02. 31
'tis but a blow, which never shall be known. 4.01. 2
your principal made known unto you who i am? 4.06. 82 P
she | made known herself my daughter. 5.03. 13
since i have known frights, fury, friends' TNK 1.04. 40
to the wenches | we have known in our days! 3.03. 29
'twill be known. 4.01. 31
ay, if the fact be known; LUC 239
all our pleasure known to us poor swains, | all PP 17.29
to bear love's wrong than hate's known injury. SON 40.12
/KNOWS 1 FR 0.0001 REL FR 1 V 0 P
/who /knows /on /whom /fortune /would /then 2H4 4.01.131
KNOWS 223 FR 0.0252 REL FR 173 V 50 P
what 'fool is she, that knows i am a maid, | and TGV 1.02. 53
he lives not now that knows me to be in love, 3.01.266 P
but yet so coldly | as, heaven it knows, i would 4.04.107
she needs not, when she knows it cowardice. 5.02. 21
a woman in windsor knows more of anne's mind WIV 1.04.128 P
he is of too high a region, he knows too much. 3.02. 74 P
my master knows not of your being here, and has 3.03. 29 P
well, heaven knows how i love you, and you shall 3.03. 80 P
none better knows than you | how i have ever MM 1.03. 7
what knows the laws | that thieves do pass on 2.01. 22
this is a thing that angelo knows not, for he 4.02.199 P
the provost knows our purpose and our plot. 4.05. 2
who knows that lodowick? 5.01.126
yet my husband | knows not that ever he knew me. 5.01.187
who thinks he knows that he ne'er knew my body, 5.01.203
but knows he thinks that he knows isabel's. 5.01.204
but knows he thinks that he knows isabel's. 5.01.204
your provost knows the place where he abides, 5.01.252
but i should know her as well as she knows me. ERR 2.02.202
if every one knows us, and we know none, | 'tis 3.02.152
the chain, | which, god he knows, i saw not; 5.01.229
son | knows not my feeble key of untun'd cares? 5.01.311
i warrant one that knows him not. ADO 3.02. 65 P
i know not that, when he knows what i know. 3.02. 91 P
one on't, with any man that knows the /statues, 3.03. 79 P
she knows the heat of a luxurious bed; 4.01. 41
any is in messina, and one that knows the law, 4.02. 83 P
god knows i lov'd my niece, | and she is dead, 5.01. 87
if he be, he knows how to turn his girdle. 5.01.142 P
and knows me, and knows me, | how pitiful i 5.02. 28
that sits above, | and knows me, and knows me, 5.02. 28
study knows that which yet it doth not know. LLL 1.01. 68
they will, they will, god knows, | and leap for 5.02.290
white glove (how white the hand, god knows!), 5.02.411
smiles his cheek in years and knows the trick 5.02.465
by their increase, now knows not which is which. MND 2.01.114
he knows not the stop. 5.01.120 P
sand–blind, high gravel–blind, knows me not. MV 2.02. 37 P
it is a wise father that knows his own child. 2.02. 77 P
and now who knows | but you, lorenzo, whether i 2.06. 30
he knows me as the blind man knows the cuckoo, 5.01.112
he knows me as the blind man knows the cuckoo, 5.01.112
ay, better than him i am before knows me. AYL 1.01. 43 P
is said, "many a man knows no end of his goods." 3.03. 53 P
a man has good horns, and knows no end of them. 3.03. 54 P
love to thee | little knows this love in me; 4.03. 57
but the wise man knows himself to be a fool." 5.01. 32 P
who knows not where a wasp does wear his sting? SHR 2.01.213
who knows not that? 4.01.101 P
knows not which way to stand, to look, to speak, 4.01.185
he that knows better how to tame a shrew, | now 4.01.210
upon his worshipper, | but knows of him no more. AWW 1.03.207
it is not so with him that all things knows | as 2.01.149
whom i am sure he knows not from the enemy. 3.06. 24 P
this business, which he knows is not to be done, 3.06. 87 P
knows he not thy voice? 4.01. 8 P
the duke knows him for no other but a poor 4.03.198 P
who knows himself a braggart, | let him fear 4.03.334
there be a scar under't or no, the velvet knows, 4.05. 96 P
that knows the tinct and multiplying med'cine, 5.03.102
he knows i am no maid, and he'll swear to't; 5.03.290
i'll swear i am a maid, and he knows not. 5.03.291
lord, | who hath abus'd me, as he knows himself, 5.03.298
he knows himself my bed he hath defil'd, | and 5.03.300
"jove knows i love, | but who? TN 2.05. 96
i care not who knows so much of my mettle. 3.04.272 P
take him away, he knows i know him well. 3.04.331
and one that knows | what she should shame to WT 2.01. 90
knows he of this? 4.04.393
which who knows how that may turn back to my 4.04.835 P
here comes a gentleman that happily knows more. 5.02. 20 P
and rings of his that paulina knows. 5.02. 66 P
and so, ere answer knows what question would, JN 1.01.200
tell me, who knows. 2.01.543
which we, god knows, have turn'd another way, 2.01.549
of peace, | heaven knows they were besmear'd and 3.01.236
where /god he knows how we shall answer him; 5.07. 60
and knows not how to do it but with tears. 5.07.109
hands | that knows no touch to tune the harmony. R2 1.03.165
now he that made me knows i see thee ill, | ill 2.01. 93
belong to me, | and am i last that knows it? 3.04. 94
not, | god knows i had as lief be none as one. 5.02. 49
hath abundance of charge too — god knows what. 1H4 2.01. 58 P
nor flesh, a man knows not where to have her. 3.03.128 P
thou or any man knows where to have me, thou 3.03.130 P
know the king | knows at what time to promise, 4.03. 53
he presently, as greatness knows itself, | steps 4.03. 74
the tennis–court–keeper knows better than i, for 2H4 2.02. 19 P
and god knows whether those that /bawl out the 2.02. 23 P
(though then, god knows, i had no such intent, 3.01. 72
for full well he knows | he cannot so precisely 4.01.202
your highness knows, comes to no further use 4.04. 72
god knows, my son, | by what by–paths and 4.05.183
told that by one that knows him better than you. H5 3.07.104 P
alexander, god knows, and you know, in his rages 4.07. 34 P
fair margaret knows | that suffolk doth not 1H6 5.03.141
not so, | i did beget her, all the parish knows. 5.04. 11
god knows thou art a collop of my flesh, | and 5.04. 18
i think she knows not well | (there were so many 5.04. 80
this was my dream, what it doth bode god knows. 2H6 1.02. 31
why, suffolk, england knows thine insolence. 2.01. 31
god knows, of pure devotion, being call'd | a 2.01. 87
true, | but how he died god knows, not henry. 3.02.131
drudge's words, | that speaks he knows not what? 4.02.152
nor knows he how to live but by the spoil, 4.08. 39
let them obey that knows not how to rule; 5.01. 6
god knows how long it is i have to live, | and 5.03. 17
my sons, god knows what hath bechanced them; 3H6 1.04. 6
but god he knows thy share thereof is small. 1.04.129
he knows the game; how true he keeps the wind! 3.02. 14
knows not montague that of itself | england is 4.01. 39
no beast so fierce but knows some touch of pity. R3 1.02. 71
why, who knows not so? 1.03. 92
who knows not that the gentle duke is dead? 2.01. 80
who knows not he is dead? who knows he is? 2.01. 82
who knows not he is dead? who knows he is? 2.01. 82
than of his outward show, which, god he knows, 3.01. 10
on what occasion, god he knows, not i, | the 3.01. 26
uncle, your grace knows how to bear with him. 3.01.127
god knows i will not do it, to the death! 3.02. 55
who knows the lord protector's mind herein? 3.04. 7
he knows no more of mine than i of yours, | or i 3.04. 11
his lordship knows me well and loves me well. 3.04. 30
for thee, | god knows, in torment and in agony. 4.04.164
wand'red away alone, | no man knows whither. 4.04.513
and who knows yet | but from this lady may H8 2.03. 77
your report, he knows | i am not of your wrong. 2.04. 99
full little, god knows, looking | either for 3.01. 75
angels' faces, but heaven knows your hearts. 3.01.145
innocence arise | when the king knows my truth. 3.02.302
all the land knows that. 4.01.105
sake that lov'd him | heaven knows how dearly. 4.02.138
a woman, a man knows not at what ward you lie. TRO 1.02.258 P
that she belov'd knows nought that knows not 1.02.288
she belov'd knows nought that knows not this: 1.02.288
that knows his valor, and knows not his fear, 1.03.268
that knows his valor, and knows not his fear, 1.03.268
as banks of libya (though, apollo knows, | 'tis 1.03.328
ay, but that fool knows not himself. 2.01. 66 P
more ready to cry out, "who knows what follows?" 2.02. 13
ignorance itself knows is so abundant scarce, it 2.03. 14 P
borne here in the face | the bearer knows not, 3.03.104
a very horse, | that has he knows not what. 3.03.127
knows almost every /grain /of /pluto's /gold, 3.03.197
he knows not me. 3.03.260 P
crams his rich thiev'ry up, he knows not how. 4.04. 43
one that knows the youth | even to his inches, 4.05.110
the shepherd knows not thunder from a tabor COR 1.06. 25
he knows not | what i can urge against him. 4.07. 18
come, my captain knows you not. 5.02. 53 P
why should he despair that knows to court it, TIT 2.01. 91
perchance because she knows them innocent. 3.01.115
who, when he knows thou art the empress' babe, 5.01. 35
god knows when we shall meet again. ROM 4.03. 14
one, a friend, and one that knows you well. 5.03.123
my master knows not but i am gone hence, | and 5.03.132
and one that knows what belongs to reason; TIM 3.01. 36 P
tell him that, he knows you are too diligent. 3.04. 39 P
that which i show, heaven knows, is merely love, 4.03.515
danger knows full well | that caesar is more JC 2.02. 44
trebonius knows his time; 3.01. 25
i'll know his humor, when he knows his time. 4.03.136
he knows thy thought: MAC 4.01. 69
and best knows | the fits o' th' season. 4.02. 16
how he solicits heaven, | himself best knows; 4.03.150
but who knows nothing, is once seen to smile; 4.03.167
what need we fear who knows it, when none can 5.01. 38 P
heaven knows what she has known. 5.01. 49 P
who knows if donalbain be with his brother? 5.02. 7
good now, sit down, and tell me, he that knows, HAM 1.01. 70
and how his audit stands who knows save heaven? 3.03. 82
he leaves, knows what is't to leave betimes, let 5.02.223 P
this presence knows, | and you must needs have 5.02.228
that is neither known of thee nor knows thee? LR 2.02. 26 P
whose disposition, all the world well knows, 2.02.153
old, and so — | but she knows what she does. 2.04.236
knows he the wickedness? 4.02. 91
he knows not what he says, and vain is it | that 5.03.294
nor the division of a battle knows | more than a OTH 1.01. 23
cassio knows you not. 2.01.266 P
sees and knows more, much more, than he unfolds. 3.03.243
and knows all /qualities, with a learned spirit, 3.03.259
what he will do with it | heaven knows, not i; 3.03.298
heaven truly knows that thou art false as hell. 4.02. 39
he knows not yet of his honorable fortune. 4.02.234 P
alas! who knows? 5.02.126
but yet iago knows | that she with cassio hath 5.02.210
or who knows | if the scarce–bearded caesar have ANT 1.01. 20
the people knows it, and have now receiv'd | his 3.06. 22
fortune knows | we scorn her most when most she 3.11. 73
he knows that you embrace not antony | as you 3.13. 56
he is a god and knows | what is most right. 3.13. 60
look'st like him that knows a warlike charge. 4.04. 19
what thou hast done thy master caesar knows, 5.02. 65
hold, to think that man, who knows | by history, CYM 1.06. 69
he's a strange fellow himself, and knows it not. 2.01. 36 P
or | who knows if one her women, being corrupted 2.04.116
all faults that name, nay, that hell knows, 2.05. 27
heaven and my conscience knows | thou didst 3.03. 99
jove knows what man thou mightst have made; 4.02.207
my breeding was, sir, as | your highness knows. 5.05.340
your honor knows what 'tis to say well enough. PER 4.06. 31 P
rain, being in't, | knows neither wet nor dry. TNK 1.01.121
do sweetly, | and god knows what may come on't. 2.03. 58
who knows | whether my brows may not be girt 2.03. 79
for now she knows it is no gentle chase, | but VEN 883
which madly hurries her she knows not whither: 904
which knows no pity, but is still severe; 1000
to the rough beast that knows no gentle right, LUC 545
not themselves but he that gives them knows! 833
grief dallied with nor law nor limit knows. 1120
that knows not parching heat nor freezing cold, 1145
though yet, heaven knows, it is but as a tomb SON 17. 3
and yet love knows it is a greater grief | to 40.11
mine eye well knows what with his gust is 114.11
which is not mix'd with seconds, knows no art, 125.11
all this the world well knows, yet none knows 129.13
yet none knows well | to shun the heaven that 129.13
and will, thy soul knows, is admitted there; 136. 3
which my heart knows the wide world's common 137.10
although she knows my days are past the best, 138. 6
my love well knows | her pretty looks have been 139. 9
yet who knows not conscience is born of love? 151. 2
/KNOW'ST 1 FR 0.0001 REL FR 1 V 0 P
/that /not /know'st | /fools /do /those LR 4.02. 53
KNOW'ST 78 FR 0.0088 REL FR 69 V 9 P
from argier, | thou know'st, was banish'd; TMP 1.02.266
thou best know'st | what torment i did find thee 1.02.286
by my gazing on her, and yet know'st her not? TGV 2.01. 47 P
for love, thou know'st, is full of jealousy. 2.04.177
know'st thou not his looks are my soul's food? 2.07. 15
thou know'st, being stopp'd, impatiently doth 2.07. 26
thou know'st how willingly i would effect | the 3.02. 22
dispose of them as thou know'st their deserts. 5.04.159
in his courses till thou know'st what they are. MM 2.01.187 P
wretch, thou know'st not what thou speak'st, 5.01.105
know'st thou his mind? ERR 2.01. 47
these ears of mine thou know'st did hear thee; 5.01. 26
thou know'st we parted, but perhaps, my son, 5.01.322
thou know'st that all my fortunes are at sea, MV 1.01.177
thou know'st where i will tarry. 4.02. 18
know'st thou not the duke | hath banish'd me, AYL 1.03. 94
know'st thou the youth that spoke to me yerwhile 3.05.105
thou know'st not gold's effect. SHR 1.02. 93
but thou know'st winter tames man, woman, and 4.01. 23 P
but what at full i know, thou know'st no part, AWW 2.01.132
know'st thou not, bertram, | what she has done 2.03.108
thou know'st she has rais'd me from my sickly 2.03.111
but wilt thou not speak all thou know'st? 5.03.257 P
know'st thou this country? TN 1.02. 21
cesario, | thou know'st no less but all. 1.04. 13
betimes, and "deliculo surgere," thou know'st — 2.03. 3 P
thy folly somewhere else, | thou know'st not me. 4.01. 11
be that thou know'st thou art, and then thou art 5.01.149
thou know'st | he dies to me again when talk'd WT 5.01.119
art my friend that know'st my tongue so well. JN 5.06. 8
know'st thou not | that when the searching eye R2 3.02. 36
know'st thou fluellen? H5 4.01. 52
know'st thou not | that i have fin'd these bones 4.07. 68
know'st thou gower? 4.07.165 P
peace, mayor, thou know'st little of my wrongs. 1H6 1.03. 59
sirrah, thou know'st how orleance is besieg'd, 1.04. 1
why then, thou know'st what color jet is of? 2H6 2.01.111
thee hence, the king, thou know'st, is coming. 3.02.386
villain, thou know'st nor law of god nor man: R3 1.02. 70
thou know'st our reasons urg'd upon the way; 3.01.160
i, who (as thou know'st) are dear | to princely 3.02. 67
and supper too, although thou know'st it not. 3.02.122
which, as thou know'st, unjustly must be spilt. 3.03. 23
know'st thou not any whom corrupting gold | will 4.02. 34
no, by the holy rood, thou know'st it well, 4.04.166
how know'st thou this? H8 1.02.150
not yet thou know'st me, and, seeing me, dost COR 4.05. 55
prepare thy brow to frown. know'st thou me yet? 4.05. 63
since thou know'st | thy country's strength and 4.05.139
thou know'st, great son, | the end of war's 5.03.140
thou know'st our meaning. TIT 2.03.271
thou know'st them not. TIM 1.01.181
thou know'st i do, i call'd thee by thy name. 1.01.186 P
but thou art wise, and thou know'st well enough 3.01. 40 P
in thy rags thou know'st none, but art despis'd 4.03.303 P
know'st thou any harm's intended towards him? JC 2.04. 31
thou know'st that we two went to school together 5.05. 26
thou know'st that banquo and his fleance lives. MAC 3.02. 37
thou know'st 'tis common, all that lives must HAM 1.02. 72
thou better know'st | the offices of nature, LR 2.04.177
know'st thou the way to dover? 4.01. 55
friend, | tell me what more thou know'st. 4.02. 97
thou know'st, the first time that we smell the 4.06.179
most monstrous! o! | know'st thou this paper? 5.03.161
thou know'st we work by wit, and not by OTH 2.03.372
but that my coat is better than thou know'st. 5.01. 25
thou know'st | how much we do o'er–count thee. ANT 2.06. 25
thou tak'st up | thou know'st not what; CYM 1.05. 61
villain base, | know'st me not by my clothes? 4.02. 81
know'st thou him thou look'st on? 5.05.110
where, as thou know'st, against the face of PER 1.02. 71
but thou know'st this, | 'tis time to fear when 1.02. 78
thou little know'st how thou dost startle me 5.01.146
thou know'st not what it is | with javeling's VEN 615
dost love her because thou know'st i love her, SON 42. 6
and like enough thou know'st thy estimate; 87. 2
for well thou know'st to my dear doting heart 131. 3
in loving thee thou know'st i am forsworn, | but 152. 1
KNOW'T 19 FR 0.0021 REL FR 16 V 3 P
i fill a place, i know't. AWW 1.02. 69
know't, | it will let in and out the enemy, WT 1.02.204
i know't too well. 2.01. 55
let him know't. 4.04.413
we know't, we know't. COR 1.01. 9 P
we know't, we know't. 1.01. 9 P
'twere well | we let the people know't. 3.01. 83
you are, and do not know't. MAC 2.03. 97
haste me to know't, that i, with wings as swift HAM 1.05. 29
i know't, my sister's. LR 2.04.183
i know't. 4.05. 28
worthy prince, i know't. 5.03.179
i know't; OTH 3.03. 10
to be much abus'd | than but to know't a little. 3.03.337
let him not know't, and he's not robb'd at all. 3.03.343
done the state some service, and they know't — 5.02.339
let her know't. ANT 3.13. 16
madam, he will, i know't. 5.02.110
it is posthumus' hand, i know't. CYM 3.05.108 P
L* 3 FR 0.0003 REL FR 3 V 0 P
put l to sore, then sorel jumps from thicket, LLL 4.02. 58
sore, then l to sore makes fifty sores o' sorel: 4.02. 60
sore i an hundred make by adding but one more l. 4.02. 61
LA* *(also law*)*
/LA* 1 FR 0.0001 REL FR 0 V 1 P
/the /marshal /of /france, /monsieur /la /far. LR 4.03. 8 P
LA* 45 FR 0.0050 REL FR 12 V 33 P
and i thank you always with my heart, la! WIV 1.01. 85 P
ay, or else i would i might be hang'd, la! 1.01.258 P
truly la! 1.01.309 P
you do yourself wrong indeed la! 1.01.313 P
/o, /je /m'en vois a la cour — la grande 1.04. 52 P

/je /m'en vois a la cour — la grande affaire. 1.04. 52 P
this is all indeed la! 1.04. 85 P
surely i think you have charms, la; 2.02.104 P
would i were hang'd la, else! 5.05.181 P
ut, re, sol, la, mi, fa. LLL 4.02.100 P
put it, as they say, to fortuna de la /guerra. 5.02.530 P
e la mi, show pity, or i die." SHR 3.01. 78
la you, and you speak ill of the devil, how he TN 3.04.100 P
la you now, you hear! WT 2.03. 50
comment appelez–vous la main en anglois? H5 3.04. 5 P
la main? elle est appelee de hand. 3.04. 7 P
la main, de hand; 3.04. 12 P
je m'en fais la repetition de tous les mots que 3.04. 25 P
doute point d'apprendre, par la grace de dieu, 3.04. 40 P
comment appelez–vous le pied et la robe? 3.04. 50 P
vomissement, et la /truie lavee au bourbier." 3.07. 65 P
qui vous la? 4.01. 35
impossible d'echapper la force de ton bras? 4.04. 16 P
il est content a vous donner la liberte, le 4.04. 52 P
answer you, la plus belle katherine du monde, 5.02.216 P
votre /grandeur en baisant la main d'une (notre 5.02.255 P
leur noces, il n'est pas la coutume de france. 5.02.259 P
away, away, good william de la pole! 1H6 2.04. 80
qui la? 3.02. 13
paysans, la pauvre gens de france, | poor market 3.02. 14
fie, de la pole, disable not thyself. 5.03. 67
the french king charles, and william de la pole, 2H6 1.01. 44 P
and william de la pole, first duke of suffolk. 1.02. 30
the duke of suffolk, william de la pole. 4.01. 45
la fin couronne les /oeuvres. 5.02. 28
of the duke's confessor, john de la car, | one H8 1.01.218
to me, wishing me to permit | john de la car, my 1.02.162
serve your turn, that shall it not, in truth la! TRO 3.01. 75 P
indeed la, 'tis a noble child. COR 1.03. 67 P
in truth la, go with me, and i'll tell you 1.03. 89 P
la, la, la, la! TIM 3.01. 21 P
la, la, la, la! 3.01. 21 P
la, la, la, la! 3.01. 21 P
la, la, la, la! 3.01. 21 P
fa, sol, la, mi. LR 1.02.137 P
LABAN 1 FR 0.0001 REL FR 1 V 0 P
when laban and himself were compremis'd | that MV 1.03. 78
LABAN'S 1 FR 0.0001 REL FR 1 V 0 P
when jacob graz'd his uncle laban's sheep — MV 1.03. 71
LABEL 2 FR 0.0002 REL FR 2 V 0 P
seal'd, | shall be the label to another deed, ROM 4.01. 57
i wak'd, i found | this label on my bosom, whose CYM 5.05.430
LABELL'D 1 FR 0.0001 REL FR 0 V 1 P
every particle and utensil labell'd to my will: TN 1.05.246 P
LABEO *(see labio)*
LABIENUS 1 FR 0.0001 REL FR 1 V 0 P
labienus | (this is stiff news) hath with his ANT 1.02. 99
LABIO 1 FR 0.0001 REL FR 1 V 0 P
labio and flavio, set our battles on. JC 5.03.108
LABOR 99 FR 0.0112 REL FR 76 V 23 P
you mar our labor. TMP 1.01. 13 P
with a charm join'd to their suff'red labor, | i 1.02.231
and their labor | delight in them /sets off; 3.01. 1
my bottle, though i be o'er ears for my labor. 4.01.214 P
if lost, why then a grievous labor won; TGV 1.01. 33
gave me (a lost mutton) nothing for my labor. 1.01. 98 P
why, if it please you, take it for your labor; 2.01.133
if i find her honest, i lose not my labor; WIV 2.01.239 P
if she be otherwise, 'tis labor well bestow'd. 2.01.239 P
as fast lock'd up in sleep as guiltless labor MM 4.02. 66
you do but lose your labor. 5.01.428
against my soul's pure truth, why labor you, ERR 3.02. 37
that labor may you save; see where he comes. 4.01. 14
wits again, | or lose my labor in assaying it. 5.01. 97
surely suit ill spent and labor ill bestow'd. ADO 3.02.100 P
if your love | can labor aught in sad invention, 5.01.283
skim milk, and sometimes labor in the quern, MND 2.01. 36
cold indeed, and labor lost: MV 2.07. 74
before i come, thou art a mocker of my labor. AYL 2.06. 13 P
he saves my labor by his own approach. 2.07. 8
neither do i labor for a greater esteem than may 5.02. 56 P
love, to labor and effect one thing specially. SHR 1.01.118 P
yea, leave that labor to great hercules, | and 1.02.255
commits his body | to painful labor, both by sea 5.02.149
we have lost our labor, they are gone a contrary AWW 3.05. 7 P
ever a friend whose thoughts more truly labor 4.04. 17
practice | as full of labor as a wise man's art; TN 3.01. 66
her face o' fire | with labor, and the thing she WT 4.04. 61
age, thou hast lost thy labor. 4.04.760 P
pains | will bring this labor to an happy end. JN 3.02. 10
and far surmounts our labor to attain it. R2 2.03. 64
the guilt of conscience take thou for thy labor, 5.06. 41
'tis no sin for a man to labor in his vocation. 1H4 1.02.105 P
not like that paying back, 'tis a double labor. 3.03.180 P
and if it do, take it for thy labor, and if it 4.02. 7 P
their courage with hard labor tame and dull, 4.03. 23
and sav'd the treacherous labor of your son. 5.04. 57
th' incessant care and labor of his mind | hath 2H4 4.04.118
and labor shall refresh itself with hope | to do H5 2.02. 37
there's for thy labor, montjoy. 3.06.158
year | with profitable labor to his grave: 4.01.277
herald, save thou thy labor. 4.03.121
while these do labor for their own preferment, 2H6 1.01.181
behooves it us to labor for the realm. 1.01.182
the king will labor still to save his life, 3.01.239
my thoughts that labor to persuade my soul 3.02.137
and yet it is said, labor in thy vocation; 4.02. 16 P
with bootless labor swim against the tide, | and 3H6 1.04. 20
poor queen and son, your labor is but lost; 3.01. 32
with sobs | that he would labor my delivery. R3 1.04.246
a blessed labor, my most sovereign lord. 2.01. 53
them, that their very labor | was to them as a H8 1.01. 25
i'll save you | that labor, sir. 2.01. 4
the queen's in labor, | they say in great 5.01. 18
and fear'd | she'll with the labor end. 5.01. 20
i have had my labor for my travail; TRO 1.01. 70 P
and between, but small thanks for my labor. 1.01. 72 P
a labor sav'd! 3.03.241
never bearing | like labor with the rest, where COR 1.01.101
'tis not to save labor, nor that i want love. 1.03. 81 P
lies, he sold the blood and labor | of our great 5.06. 46
time saw | in lasting labor of his pilgrimage! ROM 4.05. 45
that labor on the bosom of this sphere | to TIM 1.01. 66
vouchsafe my labor, and long live your lordship! 1.01.152
so thou apprehend'st it, take it for thy labor. 1.01.209 P
worthy of thee, and to pay thee for thy labor. 1.01.226 P
and will labor | to make thee full of growing. MAC 1.04. 28
the rest is labor, which is not us'd for you. 1.04. 44
the labor we delight in physics pain. 2.03. 50
thou losest labor. 5.08. 8
time, we thank you for your well–took labor. HAM 2.02. 83
and we shall jointly labor with your soul | to 4.05.212
you do climb up it now. look how we labor. LR 4.06. 2
deliver me, and supply the place for your labor. 4.06.268 P
and be hang'd for his labor — first to be OTH 4.01. 38 P
and having the world for your labor, 'tis a 4.03. 81 P
for you, mistress, | save you your labor. 5.01.101
'tis sweating labor | to bear such idleness so ANT 1.03. 93
it's monstrous labor when i wash my brain | and 2.07. 99
with news the time's with labor, and throes 3.07. 80
hence safe | does pay thy labor richly; 4.14. 37
now all labor | mars what it does; 4.14. 47
but take it for thy labor. CYM 1.05. 61
hourly falsehood (falsehood, as | with labor); 1.06.108
our horses' labor? 3.04.104
labor be his meed. 3.05.162
in which labor | i found that kindness in a PER 1.01. 66
peace be at your labor, honest fishermen. 2.01. 52
how well this honest mirth becomes their labor! 2.01. 95
the labor of each knight in his device. 2.02. 15
if labor through, | our gain but life and TNK 1.02. 11
with much labor; 1.03. 34
which speaks him prone to labor, never fainting 4.02.129
i am in labor | to push your name, your ancient 5.01. 25
follow | this sound of hope doth labor to expel, VEN 976
sighs like whirlwinds labor hence to heave thee. LUC 586
with too much labor drowns for want of skill. 1099
yet save that labor, for i have them here. 1290
what labor is't to leave | the thing we have not LC 239
LABOR'D 19 FR 0.0021 REL FR 16 V 3 P
i have labor'd for the poor gentleman to the MM 3.02.251 P
which never labor'd in their minds till now; MND 5.01. 73
by underhand means labor'd to dissuade him from AYL 1.01.140 P
let us in — your king, whose labor'd spirits, JN 2.01.232
and labor'd all i could to do him right; R2 2.03.142
ill it follows, after you have labor'd so hard, 2H4 2.02. 28 P
that i have labor'd | with all my wits, my pains H5 5.02. 24
that for your highness' good i ever labor'd H8 3.02.191
both of my life and office, i have labor'd, 5.02. 68
your tribunes, that we labor'd | (no impediment COR 2.03.227
which labor'd after him to the mountain's top TIM 1.01. 86
words have took such pains as if they labor'd 3.05. 26
that have but labor'd to attain this hour. JC 5.05. 42
with both | he labor'd in his country's wrack, i MAC 1.03.114
and labor'd much | how to forget that learning, HAM 5.02. 34
to exceed, | and you are her labor'd scholar. PER 2.03. 17
my rudiments | been labor'd so long with ye, TNK 3.05. 4
yes, but all | was vainly labor'd in me; 3.06. 79
in him the painter labor'd with his skill | to LUC 1506
LABORED 4 FR 0.0004 REL FR 4 V 0 P
whom whilst i labored of a love to see, | i ERR 1.01.130
they labored to plant the rightful heir, | i 1H6 2.05. 80
is more | than others' labored meditance; TNK 1.01.136
tile, | we have been fatuus, and labored vainly. 3.05. 41
LABORER 1 FR 0.0001 REL FR 0 V 1 P
sir, i am a true laborer: AYL 3.02. 73 P
LABORERS 1 FR 0.0001 REL FR 1 V 0 P
from my hive, | to give some laborers room. AWW 1.02. 67
LABORING 17 FR 0.0019 REL FR 14 V 3 P
laboring to save his life, and would not rather MM 5.01.391
when great things laboring perish in their birth LLL 5.02.520
that laboring art can never ransom nature | from AWW 2.01.118
purses than giving direction doth from laboring; 1H4 2.01. 51 P
my brain, more busy than the laboring spider, 2H6 3.01.339
being all descended to the laboring heart, | who 3.02.163
to say as, let the magistrates be laboring men; 4.02. 18 P
even in the birth of our own laboring breath. TRO 4.04. 38
laboring for destiny, make cruel way | through 4.05.184
laboring for nine. TIM 3.04. 8
not walk | upon a laboring day without the sign JC 1.01. 4
to teach thee there's no laboring i' th' winter. LR 2.04. 68 P
and let the laboring bark climb hills of seas OTH 2.01.187
ghosted, | there saw you laboring for him. ANT 2.06. 14
there might you see the laboring pioner LUC 1380
which laboring for invention bear amiss | the SON 59. 3
and laboring in moe pleasures to bestow them LC 139
LABOR'S 2 FR 0.0002 REL FR 2 V 0 P
shall be your love and labor's recompense. R2 2.03. 62
the death of each day's life, sore labor's bath, MAC 2.02. 35
LABORS 14 FR 0.0015 REL FR 13 V 1 P
what's dead, | and makes my labors pleasures. TMP 3.01. 7
these sweet thoughts do even refresh my labors, 3.01. 14
shortly shall all my labors end, and thou 4.01.264
the interim undertake one of hercules' labors, ADO 2.01.365 P
his taken labors bid him me forgive; AWW 3.04. 12
and shall these labors and these honors die? 2H6 1.01. 95
and of our labors thou shalt reap the gain. 3H6 5.07. 20
six of his labors you'ld have done, and sav'd COR 4.01. 18
thou lov'st, | shall find thee full of labors. LR 1.04. 7
fool, who labors to outjest | his heart–strook 3.01. 16
but my muse labors, | and thus she is deliver'd: OTH 2.01.127
to eat honey like a drone | from others' labors; PER 2.ch. 19
whose twelve strong labors crown his memory, TNK 3.06.176
all entertain'd, each passion labors so, | that VEN 969
LABORSOME 2 FR 0.0002 REL FR 2 V 0 P
from my slow leave | by laborsome petition, HAM 1.02. 59
and forget | your laborsome and dainty trims, CYM 3.04.164
LABOR'ST 1 FR 0.0001 REL FR 1 V 0 P
for him thou labor'st by thy flight to shun, MM 3.01. 12
LABRAS 1 FR 0.0001 REL FR 1 V 0 P
word of denial in thy labras here! WIV 1.01.163
LABYRINTH 3 FR 0.0003 REL FR 2 V 1 P
thou mayest not wander in that labyrinth, 1H6 5.03.188
what, lost in the labyrinth of thy fury? TRO 2.03. 2 P
goes | are like a labyrinth to amaze his foes. VEN 684
LAC'D 6 FR 0.0006 REL FR 2 V 4 P
gave your letter to her (a lac'd mutton), and TGV 1.01. 97 P
and she (a lac'd mutton) gave me (a lost mutton) 1.01. 97 P
cloth a' gold and cuts, and lac'd with silver, ADO 3.04. 19 P
been candle–cases, one buckled, another lac'd; SHR 3.02. 46 P
his silver skin lac'd with his golden blood, MAC 2.03.112
white and azure lac'd | with blue of heaven's CYM 2.02. 22
LACE 6 FR 0.0006 REL FR 6 V 0 P
o, cut my lace, lest my heart, cracking it, WT 3.02.173
will you buy any tape, | or lace for your cape, 4.04.316
ah, cut my lace asunder, | that my pent heart R3 4.01. 33
do lace the severing clouds in yonder east. ROM 3.05. 8
cut my lace, charmian, come! ANT 1.03. 71
achieve, | and lace itself with his society? SON 67. 4
LACEDAEMON 2 FR 0.0002 REL FR 2 V 0 P
to lacedaemon did my land extend. TIM 2.02.151
his service done | at lacedaemon and byzantium 3.05. 60
LACES 1 FR 0.0001 REL FR 0 V 1 P
indeed a pedlar's daughter, and sold many laces. 2H6 4.02. 46 P
LACIES 1 FR 0.0001 REL FR 0 V 1 P
my wife descended of the lacies — 2H6 4.02. 44 P
'LACK *(also alack)*
'LACK 2 FR 0.0002 REL FR 2 V 0 P
'lack, good youth! CYM 4.02.374
'lack, to what end? 5.03. 59
LACK 100 FR 0.0113 REL FR 77 V 23 P
the truth you speak doth lack some gentleness, TMP 2.01.138
tester i'll have in pouch when thou shalt lack, WIV 1.03. 87
told them over and over, they lack no direction. 3.03. 19 P
bring you the maid, you shall not lack a priest. 4.06. 53
good counsellors lack no clients. MM 1.02.106 P
save that we do the denunciation lack | of 1.02.148
are not mad | have sure more lack of reason. 5.01. 68
blood | and lack of temper'd judgment afterward. 5.01.473
enough, you'll see he shall lack no barns. ADO 3.04. 49 P
doth warrant, | let all my sins lack mercy! 4.01.180
i fear these stubborn lines lack power to move. LLL 4.03. 53
that i may swear beauty doth beauty lack, | if 4.03.247
green | for lack of tread are undistinguishable. MND 2.01.100
nor doth this wood lack worlds of company, | for 2.01.223
and shall i lack the thought | that such a thing MV 1.01. 37
think we are accomplished | with that we lack. 3.04. 62
i beseech you let his lack of years be no 4.01.161 P
impediment to let him lack a reverend estimation 4.01.162 P
shalt not die for lack of a dinner if there live AYL 2.06. 17 P
a great cause of the night is lack of the sun; 3.02. 28 P
if a hart do lack a hind, | let him seek out 3.02.101
and when you were gravell'd for lack of matter, 4.01. 74 P
alas, dear love, i cannot lack thee two hours! 4.01.179 P
she says i am not fair, that i lack manners; 4.03. 15
you lack a man's heart. 4.03.164
am starv'd for meat, giddy for lack of sleep, SHR 4.03. 9
it wanted rather than lack it where there is AWW 1.01. 10 P
and death should have play for lack of work. 1.01. 21 P
that least lend it you shall lack you first. 1.02. 68
for i know you lack not folly to commit them, 1.03. 11 P
waters of my love | and lack not to lose still. 1.03.204
they say our french lack language to deny | if 2.01. 20
you did never lack advice so much | as letting 3.04. 19
respect and rich validity | did lack a parallel; 5.03.193
i pray you yet | (since you lack virtue, i will 5.03.222
and i, that am sure i lack thee, may pass for a TN 1.05. 34 P
they lack retention. 2.04. 96
make me tell them how much i lack of a man. 3.04.303 P
that my deserts to you | can lack persuasion? 3.04.349
what? lack i credit? WT 2.01.157
i had rather you did lack than i, my lord, 2.01.158
dost lack any money? 4.03. 77 P
o, these i lack, | to make you garlands of, and 4.04.127
what maids lack from head to heel. 4.04.227
and call this | your lack of love or bounty, you 4.04.354
up the heavy time, | saying, "what lack you?" JN 4.01. 48
only you do lack | that mercy which fierce fire 4.01.118
a whit, i' faith, i lack some of thy instinct. 1H4 2.04.371 P
doth not the king lack subjects? 2H4 1.02. 74 P
things that are mouldy lack use. 3.02.108 P
that he now doth lack | the very instruments of 4.01.214
lack nothing, be merry! 5.03. 69 P
that lack of means enforce you not to evils, 5.05. 67
and sheath'd their swords for lack of argument. H5 3.01. 21
that they lack; 3.07.137 P
draw out, | and sheathe for lack of sport. 4.02. 23
let's lack no discipline, make no delay, | for, R3 5.03. 17
compell'd by hunger | and lack of other means, H8 1.02. 35
then will ajax lack matter, if he have lost his TRO 2.03. 94 P
for though abundantly they lack discretion, COR 1.01.202
in corioles wear, | and mothers that lack sons. 2.01.179
i shall lack voice: 2.02. 82
who lack not virtue, no, nor power, but that 3.01. 73
consul, which he lost | by lack of stooping — 5.06. 28
canst thou the conscience lack | to think i TIM 2.02.175
conscience lack | to think i shall lack friends? 2.02.176
'tis lack of kindly warmth they are not kind; 2.02.217
so i shall mend mine own, by th' lack of thine. 4.03.284
feeling in itself | a lack of timon's aid, hath 5.01.147
i do lack some part | of that quick spirit that JC 1.02. 28
worthy lord, | your noble friends do lack you. MAC 3.04. 83
you lack the season of all natures, sleep. 3.04.140
is ready, | our lack is nothing but our leave. 4.03.237
friending to you, | god willing, shall not lack. HAM 1.05.186
for the younger sort | to lack discretion. 2.01.114
gum, and that they have a plentiful lack of wit, 2.02.199 P
and lack gall | to make oppression bitter, or 2.02.577
for who not needs shall never lack a friend, 3.02.207
sir, i lack advancement. 3.02.340 P
to't, luxury, pell–mell, for i lack soldiers. LR 4.06.117
i lack iniquity | sometime to do me service. OTH 1.02. 3
signior, | if virtue no delighted beauty lack, 1.03.289
lady, she'll run mad | when she shall lack it. 3.03.318
the borders maritime | lack blood to think on't, ANT 1.04. 52
i know you could not lack, i am certain on't, 2.02. 57
let us, lepidus, | not lack your company. 2.02.169
these hands do lack nobility that they strike 2.05. 82
condemn myself to lack | the courage of a woman 4.14. 59
and am so near the lack of charity | to accuse CYM 2.03.109
julius caesar | smil'd at their lack of skill, 2.04. 22
that i should seem to lack humanity | so much as 3.02. 16
thou shalt not lack | the flower that's like thy 4.02.220
for what we lack | we laugh, for what we have TNK 5.04.132
look what a horse should have he did not lack, VEN 299
annoy, | to clip elysium and to lack her joy. 600
swan, | lest the requiem lack his right. PHT 16
i sigh the lack of many a thing i sought, | and SON 30. 3

have eyes to wonder, but lack tongues to praise. 106.14
at such who, not born fair, no beauty lack, 127.11
and all they foul that thy complexion lack. 132.14
LACK–BEARD 1 FR 0.0001 REL FR 0 V 1 P
for my lord lack–beard there, he and i shall ADO 5.01.192 P
LACK–BRAIN 1 FR 0.0001 REL FR 0 V 1 P
what a lack–brain is this! 1H4 2.03. 16 P
LACK'D 17 FR 0.0019 REL FR 16 V 1 P
whiles we enjoy it, but being lack'd and lost, ADO 4.01.219
that you three fools lack'd me fool to make up LLL 4.03.203
lack'd the sense to know | her estimation home. AWW 5.03. 3
that lack'd sight only, nought for approbation WT 2.01.177
there your charity would have lack'd footing. 3.03.110 P
'twas men i lack'd, and you will give them me; 2H6 3.01.345
the great hector's sword had lack'd a master, TRO 1.03. 76
dispos'd | ere they lack'd power to cross you. COR 3.02. 23
i shall be lov'd when i am lack'd. 4.01. 15
what he spake, though it lack'd form a little, HAM 3.01.163
we lack'd your counsel and your help to–night. OTH 1.03. 51
never lack'd gold, and yet went never gay, 2.01.150
worth love, | comes /dear'd by being lack'd. ANT 1.04. 44
he talks on now, | supposing that i lack'd it. 2.02. 86
being had, to triumph, being lack'd, to hope. SON 52.14
then lack'd i matter, that enfeebled mine. 86.14
love lack'd a dwelling and made him her place; LC 82
LACKEY 10 FR 0.0011 REL FR 5 V 5 P
i will speak to him like a saucy lackey, and AYL 3.02.296 P
sir, his lackey, for all the world caparison'd SHR 3.02. 65 P
a christian footboy or a gentleman's lackey. 3.02. 71 P
in a retreat he outruns any lackey; AWW 4.03.290 P
never anybody saw it but his lackey. H5 3.07.111 P
but like a lackey, from the rise to set, 4.01.272
montez /a cheval! my horse, varlot lackey! ha! 4.02. 2
a scum of britains and base lackey peasants, R3 5.03.317
hence, broker, lackey! TRO 5.10. 33
"thou ceaseless lackey to eternity, | with some LUC 967
/LACKEYING 1 FR 0.0001 REL FR 1 V 0 P
goes to and back, /lackeying the varying tide, ANT 1.04. 46
LACKEYS 4 FR 0.0004 REL FR 3 V 1 P
several devils' names | that were his lackeys. 1H4 3.01.156
that our superfluous lackeys and our peasants, H5 4.02. 26
i must stay with the lackeys with the luggage of 4.04. 74 P
councillor, | 'mong boys, grooms, and lackeys. H8 5.02. 18
LACKING 7 FR 0.0008 REL FR 4 V 3 P
proud, disobedient, stubborn, lacking duty, TGV 3.01. 69
the one lacking the burthen of lean and wasteful AYL 3.02.322 P
they will spit, and for lovers lacking (god warn 4.01. 76 P
a license to kill for a hundred lacking one. 2H6 4.03. 7 P
lacking wit | to make a seemly answer to such H8 3.01.177
thick–sighted, barren, lean, and lacking juice, VEN 136
hearts, | which i by lacking have supposed dead, SON 31. 2
LACK–LINEN 1 FR 0.0001 REL FR 0 V 1 P
poor, base, rascally, cheating, lack–linen mate! 2H4 2.04.124 P
LACK–LOVE 1 FR 0.0001 REL FR 1 V 0 P
she durst not lie | near this lack–love, this MND 2.02. 77
LACK–LUSTRE 1 FR 0.0001 REL FR 1 V 0 P
poke, | and, looking on it with lack–lustre eye, AYL 2.07. 21
LACKS 16 FR 0.0018 REL FR 14 V 2 P
executioner, who in his office lacks a helper. MM 4.02. 9 P
could give more, but that her hand lacks means. AYL 1.02.247
rosalind lacks then the love | which teacheth 1.03. 96
with a priest that lacks latin, and a rich man 3.02.319 P
"after my flame lacks oil, to be the snuff | of AWW 1.02. 59
my master, not myself, lacks recompense. TN 1.05.285
i cannot say 'tis pity | she lacks instructions, WT 4.04.582
on galathe his horse | and there lacks work; TRO 5.05. 21
here lacks but your mother for to say amen. TIT 4.02. 44
lover, | to beautify him, only lacks a cover. ROM 1.03. 88
the greatest of your having lacks a half | to TIM 2.02.144
bars, | never lacks power to dismiss itself. JC 1.03. 97
i think it lacks of twelf. HAM 1.04. 3
of nature is repose, | the which he lacks; LR 4.04. 13
but altogether lacks th' abilities | that rhodes OTH 1.03. 25
that pupils lacks she none of noble race, | who PER 5.ch. 9
LACK'ST 3 FR 0.0003 REL FR 1 V 2 P
o knight, thou lack'st a cup of canary. TN 1.03. 80 P
'tis breath thou lack'st, and that breath wilt R2 2.01. 30
foolery as i have, so much wit thou lack'st. TIM 2.02.117 P
LAD 29 FR 0.0032 REL FR 17 V 12 P
cupid is a knavish lad, | thus to make poor MND 3.02.440
gramercies, lad. SHR 1.01.163
how now, old lad? 4.01.110 P
spoke like an officer. ha' to thee, lad! 5.02. 37
well, go thy ways, old lad, for thou shalt ha't. 5.02.181
dear lad, believe it; TN 1.04. 29
i have been dear to him, lad, some two thousand 3.02. 54 P
like a mad lad, | pare thy nails, dad. 4.02.129
young lad, come forth; JN 4.01. 8
now, hal, what time of day is it, lad? 1H4 1.02. 1 P
by the lord, thou say'st true, lad. 1.02. 39 P
as the honey of hybla, my old lad of the castle. 1.02. 41 P
'zounds, where thou wilt, lad, i'll make one, 1.02.100 P
but a corinthian, a lad of mettle, a good boy 2.04. 12 P
as merry as crickets, my lad. 2.04. 89 P
by the mass, lad, thou sayest true, it is like 2.04.364 P
how now, lad? 3.03. 88 P
to the news at court for the robbery, lad, how 3.03.175 P
a lad of life, an imp of fame, | of parents good H5 4.01. 45
this pretty lad will prove our country's bliss. 3H6 4.06. 70
should leave the helm and, like a fearful lad, 5.04. 7
untutor'd lad, thou art too malapert. 5.05. 32
thy counsel, lad, smells of no cowardice. TIT 2.01.132
here's a young lad fram'd of another leer: 4.02.119
as who should say, "old lad, i am thine own." 4.02.121
no, lad, teach me. LR 1.04.139 P
i do not bid thee beg my life, good lad, | and CYM 5.05.101
not more resembles that sweet rosy lad | who 5.05.121
did court the lad with many a lovely look, PP 4. 3
LADDER 17 FR 0.0019 REL FR 16 V 1 P
the ladder made of cords, and all the means TGV 2.04.182
this night he meaneth with a corded ladder | to 2.06. 33
and with a corded ladder fetch her down; 3.01. 40
why then a ladder, quaintly made of cords, | to 3.01.117
advise me where i may have such a ladder. 3.01.122
by seven a' clock i'll get you such a ladder. 3.01.126
how shall i best convey the ladder thither? 3.01.128
and here's the ladder for the purpose. 3.01.152
thou ladder wherewithal | the mounting R2 5.01. 55
now in as low an ebb as the foot of the ladder, 1H4 1.02. 37 P
the cords, the ladder, or the hangman rather? 1.03.166
thou ladder by the which | my cousin 2H4 3.01. 70
which is the ladder of all high designs, | the TRO 1.03.102
get me a ladder. TIT 5.01. 53
to fetch a ladder, by the which your love | must ROM 2.05. 73
that lowliness is young ambition's ladder, JC 2.01. 22
round, | he then unto the ladder turns his back, 2.01. 25
LADDERS 1 FR 0.0001 REL FR 1 V 0 P
their noise be our instruction. ladders ho! COR 1.04. 22
LADDER–TACKLE 1 FR 0.0001 REL FR 1 V 0 P
and from the ladder–tackle washes off | a PER 4.01. 60
LADE 1 FR 0.0001 REL FR 1 V 0 P
saying, he'll lade it dry to have his way: 3H6 3.02.139
LADEN *(also loaden)*
LADEN 4 FR 0.0004 REL FR 4 V 0 P
and now at last, laden with honor's spoils, TIT 1.01. 36
i have a ship | laden with gold, take that, ANT 3.11. 5
been laden with like frailties which before 5.02.123
as full of fear | as one with treasure laden, VEN 1022
LADIES' 14 FR 0.0015 REL FR 12 V 2 P
black men are pearls in beauteous ladies' eyes. TGV 5.02. 12
such pearls as put out ladies' eyes, | for i had 5.02. 13
then when ourselves we see in ladies' eyes, LLL 4.03.312
these ladies' courtesy | might well have made 5.02.875
but youth in ladies' eyes that flourisheth. SHR 2.01.340
with ladies' faces and fierce dragons' spleens, JN 2.01. 68
that can rhyme themselves into ladies' favors, H5 5.02.157 P
and stol'st away the ladies' hearts of france, 2H6 1.03. 52
these happy masks that kiss fair ladies' brows, ROM 1.01.230
o'er ladies' lips, who straight on kisses dream, 1.04. 74
if you buy ladies' flesh at a million a dram, CYM 1.04.135 P
loud music is too harsh for ladies' heads, PER 2.03. 97
i should pluck | all ladies' scandal on me. TNK 1.01.192
their oaths, should right poor ladies' harms." LUC 1694
/LADIES 2 FR 0.0002 REL FR 1 V 1 P
/and /ladies, /too, /they /will /not /let /me LR 1.04.154 P
/shame /of /ladies! 4.03. 27
LADIES 110 FR 0.0124 REL FR 80 V 30 P
nay, got's lords and his ladies! WIV 1.01.235 P
but it is certain i am lov'd of all ladies, only ADO 1.01.125 P
the ladies follow her, and but one visor remains 2.01.157 P
sigh no more, ladies, sigh no more, | men were 2.03. 62
not to see ladies, study, fast, not sleep. LLL 1.01. 48
god bless my ladies! 2.01. 77
lord, how the ladies and i have put him down! 4.01.141
for, ladies, we will every one be mask'd, | and 5.02.127
fair ladies mask'd are roses in their bud; 5.02.295
ladies, withdraw; the gallants are at hand. 5.02.308
the ladies call him sweet; 5.02.329
once disclos'd, | the ladies did change favors; 5.02.468
your beauty, ladies, | hath much deformed us, 5.02.756
therefore, ladies, | our love being yours, the 5.02.770
to those that make us both — fair ladies, you; 5.02.774
you would fright the duchess and the ladies, MND 1.02. 75 P
you should fright the ladies out of their wits, 1.02. 80 P
which the ladies cannot abide. 3.01. 11 P
will not the ladies be afeard of the lion? 3.01. 27 P
a lion among ladies, is a most dreadful thing; 3.01. 31 P
"ladies," or "fair ladies, i would wish you," or 3.01. 39 P
"ladies," or "fair ladies, i would wish you," or 3.01. 39 P
is two or three lords and ladies more married. 4.02. 16 P
and take your places, ladies. 5.01. 84
you, ladies, you, whose gentle hearts do fear 5.01.219
lies, | how honorable ladies sought my love, MV 3.04. 70
fair ladies, you drop manna in the way | of 5.01.294
daughter, and never two ladies lov'd as they do. AYL 1.01.112 P
you amaze me, ladies. 1.02.109 P
the sport, monsieur, that the ladies have lost? 1.02.135 P
i heard breaking of ribs was sport for ladies. 1.02.139 P
speak to him, ladies, see if you can move him. 1.02.162 P
to deny so fair and excellent ladies any thing. 1.02.185 P
the ladies, her attendants of her chamber, | saw 2.02. 5
and says, if ladies be but young and fair, 2.07. 37
such as he hath observ'd in noble ladies | unto SHR in.1. 111
madam, and nothing else — so lords call ladies. in.2. 111
talkest thou nothing but of ladies? TN 4.02. 26 P
for your own ladies and pale–visag'd maids JN 5.02.154
the flowers fair ladies, and thy steps no more R2 1.03.290
come, ladies, go | to; 3.04. 96
and in my conduct shall your ladies come, | from 1H4 3.01. 91
that, when i come to woo ladies, i fright them. H5 5.02.228 P
is not be de fashon pour les ladies of france — 5.02.261 P
when ladies crave to be encount'red with. 1H6 2.02. 46
it through the court with troops of ladies, 2H6 1.03. 77
and witch sweet ladies with my words and looks. 3H6 3.02.150
let me but meet you, ladies, /an hour hence, R3 4.01. 28
what a loss our ladies | will have of these trim H8 1.03. 37
have got a speeding trick to lay down ladies. 1.03. 40
and a great one, | to many lords and ladies; 1.03. 53
ladies, a general welcome from his grace 1.04. 1
sweet ladies, will it please you sit? 1.04. 19
pray sit between these ladies. 1.04. 24
by your leave, sweet ladies. 1.04. 25
you, if these fair ladies | pass away frowning. 1.04. 32
ladies, you are not merry. 1.04. 42
nay, ladies, fear not; 1.04. 51
fair conduct | crave leave to view these ladies, 1.04. 71
lead in your ladies, ev'ry one. 1.04.103
a dozen healths | to drink to these fair ladies, 1.04.106
good morrow, ladies. 2.03. 50
the rich stream | of lords and ladies, having 4.01. 63
store of room, no doubt, left for the ladies, 5.03. 73
if they hold when their ladies bid 'em clap. ep 14
my ladies both, good day to you. COR 1.03. 48 P
where ladies shall be frighted | and, gladly 1.09. 5
now, my as fair as noble ladies — and the moon, 2.01. 97 P
good ladies, let's go. 2.01.133 P
ladies and maids their scarfs and handkerchers, 2.01.264
down, ladies; 5.03.169
ladies, you deserve | to have a temple built you 5.03.206
finger, there is some hope the ladies of rome, 5.04. 5 P
if | the roman ladies bring not comfort home, 5.04. 38
the ladies have prevail'd, | the volscians are 5.04. 40
i will go meet the ladies. 5.04. 52
cry, "welcome, ladies, welcome!" 5.05. 6
welcome, ladies, | welcome! 5.05. 6
there will the lovely roman ladies troop; TIT 2.01.113
somewhat too early for new–married ladies. 2.02. 15
then let the ladies tattle what they please. 4.02.168
than you, | here in verona, ladies of esteem, ROM 1.03. 70
lath, | scaring the ladies like a crow–keeper, 1.04. 6
ladies that have their toes | unplagu'd with 1.05. 16
and thou shouldst, thou'dst anger ladies. TIM 1.01.205 P
lord, there are certain ladies most desirous of 1.02.116 P
ladies? what are their wills? 1.02.118 P
have done our pleasures much grace, fair ladies, 1.02.146
ladies, there is an idle banquet attends you, 1.02.155
and i, of ladies most deject and wretched, HAM 3.01.155
good night, ladies, good night. 4.05. 72 P
sweet ladies, good night, good night. 4.05. 73 P
than any the rarest of our ladies in france. CYM 1.04. 61 P
where't grows, | but worn a bait for ladies. 3.04. 57
parts more exquisite | than lady, ladies, woman, 3.05. 72
and lords and ladies in their lives | have read PER 1.ch. 7
of tyre | are excellent in making ladies trip, 2.03.102
dear glass of ladies, | bid him that we, whom TNK 1.01. 90
why, good ladies, | this is a service, whereto i 1.01.170
good cheer, ladies! 1.01.233
hung with the painted favors of their ladies, 2.02. 11
by any means | before the ladies see us, and do 2.03. 57
tail without offense | or scandal to the ladies; 3.05. 35
ladies, sit down, we'll stay it. 3.05. 99
all hail, sweet ladies! 3.05.100
ladies, if we have been merry, | and have 3.05.138
without lets, | and the ladies eat his dowsets! 3.05.157
or the sweet compassion | of those two ladies; 4.01. 12
his red lips, after fights, are fit for ladies. 4.02.111
in praise of ladies dead and lovely knights, SON 106. 4
LADING 2 FR 0.0002 REL FR 1 V 1 P
hath a ship of rich lading wrack'd on the narrow MV 3.01. 3 P
returns with precious lading to the bay | from TIT 1.01. 72
LADING'S 1 FR 0.0001 REL FR 1 V 0 P
what shipping and what lading's in our haven, PER 1.02. 49
/LADS 1 FR 0.0001 REL FR 0 V 1 P
follow me, /lads of peace; WIV 3.01.110 P
LADS 23 FR 0.0026 REL FR 14 V 9 P
company | some few odd lads you remember not. TMP 5.01.255
my honest lads, i will tell you what i am about. WIV 1.03. 38 P
we will thrive, lads, we will thrive. 1.03. 74 P
where are these lads? where are these hearts? MND 4.02. 25 P
two lads that thought there was no more behind WT 1.02. 63
stomachers | for my lads to give their dears; 4.04.225
come buy, | buy, lads, or else your lasses cry: 4.04.229
but, my lads, my lads, to–morrow morning by four
1H4 1.02.124 P
my lads, my lads, to–morrow morning by four a' 1.02.124 P
i shall command all the good lads in eastcheap. 2.04. 14 P
by the lord, lads, i am glad you have the money. 2.04.275 P
gallants, lads, boys, hearts of gold, all the 2.04.277 P
and lusty lads roam here and there | so merrily, 2H4 5.03. 20
i like you, lads, about your business straight. R3 1.03.353
cut me to pieces, volsces, men and lads, | stain COR 5.06.111
good lads, how do you both? HAM 2.02.225 P
news, lads! OTH 2.01. 20
'tis well blown, lads. ANT 4.04. 25
golden lads and girls all must, | as CYM 4.02.262
that is my bed too, lads, and there i'll lie. 4.04. 52
(lads more like to run | the country base than 5.03. 19
and three better lads nev'r danc'd | under green TNK 2.03. 38
come, let's be gone, lads. 2.03. 73
/LADY 1 FR 0.0001 REL FR 1 V 0 P
/by'r /lady, i could do much — OTH 3.03. 74
LADY 655 FR 0.0740 REL FR 450 V 205 P
bountiful fortune | (now my dear lady) hath mine TMP 1.02.179
full many a lady | i have ey'd with best regard, 3.01. 39
ceres, most bounteous lady, thy rich leas | of 4.01. 60
and second father | this lady makes him to me. 5.01.196
but tell me: dost thou know my lady silvia? TGV 2.01. 42 P
yourself, sweet lady, for you gave the fire. 2.04. 37 P
why, lady, love hath twenty pair of eyes. 2.04. 95
sweet lady, entertain him | to be my 2.04.104
not so, sweet lady, but too mean a servant | to 2.04.107
sweet lady, entertain him for your servant. 2.04.110
how does your lady, and how thrives your love? 2.04.125
o, but i love his lady too too much, | and 2.04.205
there is a lady in /milano here | whom i affect; 3.01. 81
banished | for practicing to steal away a lady, 4.01. 46
he must carry for a present to his lady. 4.02. 80 P
one, lady, if you knew his pure heart's truth, 4.02. 88
sir proteus, gentle lady, and your servant. 4.02. 91
i grant, sweet love, that i did love a lady; 4.02.105
sweet lady, let me rake it from the earth. 4.02.115
as many, worthy lady, to yourself. 4.03. 7
heart | as when thy lady and thy true–love died, 4.03. 20
good morrow, gentle lady. 4.03. 45
you as well | as you do love your lady silvia: 4.04. 80
tell my lady | i claim the promise for her 4.04. 86
alas, poor lady, desolate and left! 4.04.174
lady, a happy evening! 5.01. 7
yes, py'r lady. WIV 1.01. 28 P
before the best lord, i would make thee my lady. 3.03. 51 P
i your lady, sir john? 3.03. 52 P
alas, i should be a pitiful lady! 3.03. 53 P
you know the lady; MM 1.02.147
do a poor wrong'd lady a merited benefit; 3.01.200 P
i have heard of the lady, and good words went 3.01.211 P
she is a virtuous and a reverend lady: ERR 5.01.134
and bid the lady abbess come to me: 5.01.166
i know none of that name, lady. ADO 1.01. 32 P
he hath done good service, lady, in these wars. 1.01. 48 P
and a good soldier too, lady. 1.01. 53 P
and a good soldier to a lady, but what is he to 1.01. 54 P
i see, lady, the gentleman is not in your books. 1.01. 78 P
i will hold friends with you, lady. 1.01. 91 P
truly the lady fathers herself. 1.01.111 P
be happy, lady, for you are like an honorable 1.01.111 P
what, my dear lady disdain! are you yet living? 1.01.118 P
is she not a modest young lady? 1.01.165 P
she is the sweetest lady that ever i look'd on. 1.01.187 P
you love her, for the lady is very well worthy. 1.01.221 P
lady, will you walk about with your friend? 2.01. 86 P
but that my lady beatrice should know me, and 2.01.203 P
my lord, i have play'd the part of lady fame. 2.01.214 P
grace had got the good will of this young lady, 2.01.217 P
the lady beatrice hath a quarrel to you. 2.01.236 P

dish i love not, i cannot endure my lady tongue. 2.01.275 P
come, lady, come, you have lost the heart of 2.01.276 P
you have put him down, lady, you have put him 2.01.283 P
i' faith, lady, i think your blazon to be true, 2.01.296 P
lady, as you are mine, i am yours. 2.01.308 P
in faith, lady, you have a merry heart. 2.01.312 P
lady beatrice, i will get you one. 2.01.321 P
will you have me, lady? 2.01.326 P
by my troth, a pleasant-spirited lady. 2.01.341 P
benedick and the lady beatrice into a mountain 2.01.366 P
would have it at the lady hero's chamber-window. 2.03. 86 P
i did never think that lady would have lov'd any 2.03. 93 P
a sport of it, and torment the poor lady worse. 2.03.157 P
she's an excellent sweet lady, and (out of all 2.03.159 P
to see how much he is unworthy so good a lady. 2.03.209 P
they seem to pity the lady. 2.03.223 P
they say the lady is fair; 2.03.231 P
she's a fair lady. 2.03.245 P
too long a-talking of), the lady is disloyal. 3.02.104 P
nay, by'r lady, that i think 'a cannot. 3.03. 77 P
by'r lady, i think it be so. 3.03. 83 P
woo'd margaret, the lady hero's gentlewoman, by 3.03.145 P
i will, lady. 3.04. 3 P
of what, lady? 3.04. 29 P
ask my lady beatrice else, here she comes. 3.04. 37 P
nay, by'r lady, i am not such a fool to think 3.04. 82 P
you come hither, my lord, to marry this lady. 4.01. 5 P
lady, you come hither to be married to this 4.01. 9 P
thus, pretty lady, | i am sorry for thy much 4.01. 98
how doth the lady? 4.01.113
have comfort, lady. 4.01.118
lady, were you her bedfellow last night? 4.01.147
this course of fortune, | by noting of the lady. 4.01.158
if this sweet lady lie not guiltless here 4.01.169
lady, what man is he you are accus'd of? 4.01.176
come, lady, die to live; 4.01.253
lady beatrice, have you wept all this while? 4.01.255 P
don john for accusing the lady hero wrongfully. 4.02. 48 P
you have kill'd a sweet lady, and her death 5.01.148 P
have among you kill'd a sweet and innocent lady. 5.01.192 P
sixt and lastly, they have belied a lady; 5.01.218 P
brother incens'd me to slander the lady hero, 5.01.236 P
the lady is dead upon mine and my master's false 5.01.242 P
i can find out no rhyme to "lady" but "baby," an 5.02. 37 P
it is prov'd my lady hero hath been falsely 5.02. 96 P
which is the lady i must seize upon? 5.04. 53
were all address'd to meet you, gentle lady, LLL 2.01. 83
hear me, dear lady: i have sworn an oath. 2.01. 97
our lady help my lord! he'll be forsworn. 2.01. 98
lady, i will commend you to /mine /own heart. 2.01.179 P
sir, i pray you a word. what lady is that same? 2.01.194
a gallant lady. monsieur, fare you well. 2.01.196
she is a most sweet lady. 2.01.207
park, | and in her train there is a gentle lady: 3.01.165
some men must love my lady, and some joan. 3.01.205
we may afford | to any lady that subdues a lord. 4.01. 40
pray you, which is the head lady? 4.01. 43 P
which is the greatest lady, the highest? 4.01. 46 P
from monsieur berowne to one lady rosaline. 4.01. 53
from my lord to my lady. 4.01.102
from which lord to which lady? 4.01.103
to a lady of france that he call'd rosaline. 4.01.105
my lady goes to kill horns, but, if thou marry, 4.01.111
a mark, says my lady! 4.01.131
see him walk before a lady and to bear her fan! 4.01.145
hand of the most beauteous lady rosaline." 4.02.132 P
bore it, the fool sent it, and the lady hath it: 4.03. 16 P
sweet clown, sweeter fool, sweetest lady! 4.03. 17 P
a lady wall'd about with diamonds! 5.02. 3
fair lady — 5.02.239
fair lord — | take that for your fair lady. 5.02.240
i know the reason, lady, why you ask. 5.02.243
a calf, fair lady! 5.02.248
will you give horns, chaste lady? 5.02.252
my lady (to the manner of the days) | in 5.02.365
here stand i, lady, dart thy skill at me, 5.02.396
troth, | i never swore this lady such an oath. 5.02.451
to make my lady laugh when she's dispos'd, 5.02.466
come when the king doth to my lady come; 5.02.829
studies my lady? 5.02.837
and she, sweet lady, dotes, | devoutly dotes, MND 1.01.108
it is the lady that pyramus must love. 1.02. 46 P
thy thisby dear, and lady dear!" 1.02. 54 P
then i must be thy lady; 2.01. 64
a sweet athenian lady is in love | with a 2.01.260
when the next thing he espies | may be the lady. 2.01.263
spell, nor charm, | come our lovely lady nigh. 2.02. 18
o, that a lady, of one man refus'd, | should of 2.02.133
in show, | you would not use a gentle lady so; 3.02.152
this beauteous lady thisby is certain. 5.01.130
tell me now what lady is the same | to whom you MV 1.01.119
in belmont is a lady richly left, | and she is 1.01.161
i am much afeard my lady his mother play'd false 1.02. 43 P
you need not fear, lady, the having any of these 1.02.100 P
do you not remember, lady, in your father's time 1.02.112 P
look'd upon, was the best deserving a fair lady. 1.02.119 P
i tell thee, lady, this aspect of mine | hath 2.01. 8
when 'a roars for prey, | to win /thee, lady. 2.01. 31
choose wrong | never to speak to lady afterward 2.01. 41
enough | may not extend so far as to the lady; 2.07. 28
why, that's the lady. 2.07. 31
why, that's the lady, all the world desires her. 2.07. 38
where is my lady? 2.09. 85
for your bliss, | turn you where your lady is, 3.02.137
fair lady, by your leave, | i come by note, to 3.02.139
so, thrice-fair lady, stand i, even so, | as 3.02.146
my lord and lady, it is now our time, | that 3.02.186
good joy, my lord and lady! 3.02.188
my lord bassanio and my gentle lady, | i wish 3.02.189
gentle lady, | when i did first impart my love 3.02.252
and yet, dear lady, | rating myself at nothing, 3.02.256
here is a letter, lady, | the paper as the body 3.02.263
life, | for, having such a blessing in his lady, 3.05. 75
dear lady, welcome home! 5.01.113
what should i say, sweet lady? 5.01.215
pardon me, good lady, | for, by these blessed 5.01.219
sweet lady, you have given me life and living, 5.01.286
his malice 'gainst the lady | will suddenly AYL 1.02.282
sun, | and rail'd on lady fortune in good terms, 2.07. 16
wounded it is, but with the eyes of a lady. 5.02. 24 P
i have trod a measure, i have flatt'red a lady, 5.04. 45 P
is not the fashion to see the lady the epilogue; ep 1 P
and that his lady mourns at his disease. SHR in.1. 62
and see him dress'd in all suits like a lady; in.1. 106
wherein your lady and your humble wife | may in.1. 116
o, this it is that makes your lady mourn! in.2. 26
thou hast a lady far more beautiful | than any in.2. 62
am i a lord, and have i such a lady? in.2. 68
well, bring our lady hither to our sight, | and in.2. 74
'tis a very excellent piece of work, madam lady; 1.01.254 P
farewell, pretty lady, | you must hold the AWW 1.01. 77
bless you, my fortunate lady! 2.04. 14 P
o, my knave, how does my old lady? 2.04. 19 P
within between two soldiers and my young lady! 3.02. 34 P
i prithee, lady, have a better cheer; 3.02. 64
ay, my good lady, he. 3.02. 86
indeed, good lady, | the fellow has a deal of 3.02. 89
ay, surely, mere the truth, i know his lady. 3.05. 55
alas, poor lady! 3.05. 63
were i his lady, | i would poison that vile 3.05. 83
shaking off so good a wife and so sweet a lady. 4.03. 7 P
for her, writ to my lady mother i am returning, 4.03. 89 P
'twas a good lady, 'twas a good lady. 4.05. 13 P
'twas a good lady, 'twas a good lady. 4.05. 13 P
lady, of that i have made a bold charter, but i 4.05. 92 P
who of herself is a good lady and would not have 5.02. 31 P
my honor'd lady, | i have forgiven and forgotten 5.03. 8
mother, and his lady | offense of mighty note; 5.03. 13
i am afeard the life of helen, lady, | was 5.03.153
this is illyria, lady. TN 1.02. 2
o that i serv'd that lady, | and might not be 1.02. 41
your cousin, my lady, takes great exceptions to 1.03. 5 P
i heard my lady talk of it yesterday; 1.03. 15 P
fair lady, do you think you have fools in hand? 1.03. 64 P
i'll do my best | to woo your lady. 1.04. 41
my lady will hang thee for thy absence. 1.05. 3 P
here comes my lady. 1.05. 30 P
god bless thee, lady! 1.05. 37 P
do you not hear, fellows? take away the lady. 1.05. 40 P
the lady bade take away the fool, therefore i 1.05. 52 P
lady, "cucullus non facit monachum": 1.05. 55 P
what is to be said to him, lady? 1.05.145 P
gentlewoman, my lady calls. 1.05.164 P
the honorable lady of the house, which is she? 1.05.167 P
you tell me if this be the lady of the house, 1.05.171 P
assurance if you be the lady of the house, that 1.05.180 P
are you the lady of the house? 1.05.185 P
some mollification for your giant, sweet lady. 1.05.204 P
most sweet lady — 1.05.221 P
lady, you are the cruell'st she alive | if you 1.05.241
i am no fee'd post, lady; 1.05.284
a lady, sir, though it was said she much 2.01. 25 P
what means this lady? 2.02. 17
'tis, | poor lady, she were better love a dream. 2.02. 26
my lady has a white hand, and the mermidons are 2.03. 27 P
by'r lady, sir, and some dogs will catch well. 2.03. 62 P
if my lady have not call'd up her steward 2.03. 73 P
lady! 2.03. 78 P
"there dwelt a man in babylon, lady, lady!" 2.03. 79 P
"there dwelt a man in babylon, lady, lady!" 2.03. 79 P
my lady bade me tell you that, though she 2.03. 96 P
youth of the count's was to-day with my lady, 2.03.133 P
i can write very like my lady your niece; 2.03.160 P
a fool that the lady olivia's father took much 2.04. 12 P
say that some lady, as perhaps there is, | hath 2.04. 89
sir, shall i to this lady? 2.04.122
out o' favor with my lady about a bear-baiting 2.05. 8 P
the lady of the strachy married the yeoman of 2.05. 39 P
'tis my lady. 2.05. 93 P
i serve her, she is my lady. 2.05.116 P
reason excites to this, that my lady loves me. 2.05.165 P
sport, mark his first approach before my lady. 2.05.198 P
art not thou the lady olivia's fool? 3.01. 31 P
no, indeed, sir, the lady olivia has no folly. 3.01. 32 P
is thy lady within? 3.01. 48 P
my lady is within, sir. 3.01. 55 P
most excellent accomplish'd lady, the heavens 3.01. 84 P
my matter hath no voice, lady, but to your own 3.01. 88 P
dear lady — 3.01.110
i know my lady will strike him. 3.02. 82 P
sweet lady, ho, ho. 3.04. 17 P
sad, lady? 3.04. 20 P
with this ridiculous boldness before my lady? 3.04. 38 P
toby, my lady prays you to have a care of him. 3.04. 92 P
my lady would not lose him for more than i'll 3.04.104 P
"thou com'st to the lady olivia, and in my sight 3.04.155 P
he is now in some commerce with my lady, and 3.04.174 P
the house and desire some conduct of the lady. 3.04.242 P
nor i am not sent to you by my lady, to bid you 4.01. 6 P
and tell me what i shall vent to my lady. 4.01. 16 P
this will i tell my lady straight; 4.01. 30 P
topas, sir topas, good sir topas, go to my lady. 4.02. 24 P
jolly robin, | tell me how thy lady does." 4.02. 73
"my lady is unkind, perdie." 4.02. 75
and convey what i will set down to my lady. 4.02.111 P
but here the lady comes. 4.03. 21
belong you to the lady olivia, friends? 5.01. 8 P
if you will let your lady know i am here to 5.01. 42 P
you uncivil lady, | to whose ingrate and 5.01.112
hath been between this lady and this lord. 5.01.258
so comes it, lady, you have been mistook; 5.01.259
lady, you have. 5.01.330
o' th' clock behind | what lady she her lord. WT 1.02. 44
o my most sacred lady, | temptations have since 1.02. 76
o miserable lady! 1.02.351
be but about | to say she is a goodly lady, and 2.01. 66
you have mistook, my lady, | polixenes for 2.01. 81
good lady, | no court in europe is too good for 2.02. 2
for a worthy lady, | and one who much i honor. 2.02. 5
dear gentlewoman, | how fares our gracious lady? 2.02. 19
(which never tender lady hath borne greater) 2.02. 22
there is no lady living | so meet for this great 2.02. 43
away with that audacious lady! 2.03. 42
been so tenderly officious | with lady margery, 2.03.160
that we may arraign | our most disloyal lady; 2.03.203
a kind of love as might become | a lady like me; 3.02. 65
what fit is this, good lady? 3.02.174
o lady fortune, | stand you auspicious! 4.04. 51
come, lady, come. 4.04.659
not at all, good lady. 5.01. 20
way | the father of this seeming lady and | her 5.01.191
here comes the lady paulina's steward, he can 5.02. 26 P
lady, | dear queen, that ended when i but began, 5.03. 44
turn, good lady, | our perdita is found. 5.03.120
well, now can i make any joan a lady. JN 1.01.184
how now, good lady, | what brings you here to 1.01.220
come, lady, i will show thee to my kin, | and 1.01.273
a wonder, lady! 2.01. 50
with her her niece, the lady blanch of spain; 2.01. 64
peace, lady, pause, or be more temperate. 2.01.195
that daughter there of spain, the lady blanch, 2.01.423
whose veins bound richer blood than lady blanch? 2.01.431
then, prince dolphin, can you love this lady? 2.01.524
is not the lady constance in this troop? 2.01.540
england, how may we content | this widow lady? 2.01.548
call the lady constance; 2.01.553
what other harm have i, good lady, done, | but 3.01. 38
by heaven, lady, you shall have no cause | to 3.01. 96
lady constance, peace! 3.01.112
there's law and warrant, lady, for my curse. 3.01.184
the lady constance speaks not from her faith, 3.01.210
lady, with me, with me thy fortune lies. 3.01.337
i prithee, lady, go away with me. 3.04. 20
patience, good lady, comfort, gentle constance! 3.04. 22
lady, you utter madness, and not sorrow. 3.04. 43
you, in the right of lady blanch your wife, 3.04.142
the lady constance in a frenzy died | three days 4.02.122
'tis nothing but conceit, my gracious lady. R2 2.02. 33
with many holiday and lady terms | he questioned 1H4 1.03. 46
what say'st thou, my lady? 2.03. 74
no lady closer, for i well believe | thou wilt 2.03.110
by'r lady, a long lease for the clinking of 2.04. 45 P
how now, my lady the hostess! 2.04.285 P
now, sirs, by'r lady, you fought fair, so did 2.04.298 P
fifty, or, by'r lady, inclining to threescore; 2.04.425 P
by'r lady, he is a good musician. 3.01.231
ye thief, and hear the lady sing in welsh. 3.01.234 P
i had rather hear lady, my brach, howl in irish. 3.01.235 P
swear me, kate, like a lady as thou art, | a 3.01.253
all you that kiss my lady peace at home, that 2H4 1.02.207 P
wound, to marry me and make me my lady thy wife. 2.01. 92 P
may i ask how my lady his wife doth? 3.02. 65 P
by'r lady, i think 'a be, but goodman puff of 5.03. 89 P
himself as th' heir to th' lady lingare, H5 1.02. 74
grandmother, | was lineal of the lady ermengare, 1.02. 82
o welliday, lady, if he be not hewn now, we 2.01. 36 P
by the white hand of my lady, he's a gallant 3.07. 93 P
how say you, lady? 5.02.130 P
if i could win a lady at leap-frog, or by 5.02.136 P
heaven and our lady gracious hath it pleas'd 1H6 1.02. 74
the virtuous lady, countess of auvergne, | with 2.02. 38
for my lady craves | to know the cause of your 2.03. 29
be not dismay'd, fair lady, nor misconster | the 2.03. 73
i'll win this lady margaret. 5.03. 88
lady, vouchsafe to listen what i say. 5.03.103
lady, wherefore talk you so? 5.03.108
is betroth'd | unto another lady of esteem. 5.05. 27
if with a lady of so high resolve | (as is fair 5.05. 75
that lady margaret do vouchsafe to come | to 5.05. 89
the said henry shall espouse the lady margaret, 2H6 1.01. 46 P
patience, good lady, wizards know their times. 1.04. 15
with him the husband of this lovely lady. 1.04. 73
countenance and confederacy | of lady eleanor, 2.01.165
means | your lady is forthcoming yet at london. 2.01.175
his lady banish'd, and a limb lopp'd off. 2.03. 42
must you, sir john, protect my lady here? 2.04. 79
like to a duchess, and duke humphrey's lady, 2.04. 98
and you, my sovereign lady, with the rest, 3.01.161
hath he not twit our sovereign lady here | with 3.01.178
if ever lady wrong'd her lord so much, | thy 3.02.211
france, | and ask the lady bona for thy queen. 3H6 2.06. 90
i see the lady hath a thing to grant, | before 3.02. 12
vouchsafe to grant | that virtuous lady bona, 3.03. 56
king lewis and lady bona, hear me speak | before 3.03. 65
disdain, | unless the lady bona quit his pain. 3.03.128
has your king married the lady grey? 3.03.174
i will revenge his wrong to lady bona, | and 3.03.197
and mine, fair lady bona, joins with yours. 3.03.217
you | of this new marriage with the lady grey? 4.01. 2
tell me some reason why the lady grey | should 4.01. 25
him | about the marriage of the lady bona. 4.01. 31
but what said lady bona to my marriage? 4.01. 97
answer | lewis and the lady bona send to him. 4.03. 56
my lady grey his wife, clarence, 'tis she | that R3 1.01. 64
lady, you know no rules of charity, | which 1.02. 68
but, gentle lady anne, | to leave this keen 1.02.114
he that bereft thee, lady, of thy husband, | did 1.02.138
thine eyes, sweet lady, have infected mine. 1.02.149
for it was made | for kissing, lady, not for 1.02.172
ill news, by'r lady — seldom comes the better. 2.03. 4
my gracious lady, go, | and thither bear your 2.04. 68
i did, with his contract with lady lucy, | and 3.07. 5
for first was he contract to lady lucy — | your 3.07.179
th' advancement of your children, gentle lady. 4.04.242
lady mine, proceed. H8 1.02. 17
his hour of speech a minute — he, my lady, 1.02.121
and have an hour of hearing, and, by'r lady, 1.03. 46
that noble lady | or gentleman that is not 1.04. 35
conscience | has crept too near another lady. 2.02. 18
she | so good a lady that no tongue could ever 2.03. 3
alas, poor lady! | she's a stranger now again. 2.03. 16
that you may, fair lady, | perceive i speak 2.03. 58
lady, | i shall not fail t' approve the fair 2.03. 73
knows yet | but from this lady may proceed a gem 2.03. 78
there was a lady once ('tis an old story) | that 2.03. 90
good lady, | make yourself mirth with your 2.03.100
you have here, lady | (and of your choice), 2.04. 57
but with thanks to god for such | a royal lady, 2.04.154
noble lady, | i am sorry my integrity should 3.01. 50
way to sorrow — | you have too much, good lady; 3.01. 57
the cordial that ye bring a wretched lady, | a 3.01.106
what will become of me now, wretched lady? 3.01.146
why should we, good lady, | upon what cause, 3.01.155
a creature of the queen's, lady anne bullen." 3.02. 36

the king already | hath married the fair lady. 3.02. 42
last, that the lady anne, | whom the king hath 3.02.402
behold | the lady anne pass from her coronation? 4.01. 3
alas, good lady! 4.01. 35
and more and richer, when he strains that lady. 4.01. 46
carries up the train | is that old noble lady, 4.01. 52
noble lady, | first, mine own service to your 4.02.114
and, sweet lady, does | deserve our better 5.01. 25
alas, good lady! 5.01. 69
duchess of norfolk | and lady marquess dorset. 5.02.203
in this most gracious lady | heaven ever laid up 5.04. 6
so shall this lady, | when she has so much 5.04. 13
this man, lady, hath robb'd many beasts of their TRO 1.02. 19 P
as may be in the world, lady. 1.02. 40 P
he hath a lady, wiser, fairer, truer, | than 1.03.275
/will tell him that my lady | was fairer than 1.03.298
priam, | there is no lady of more softer bowels, 2.02. 11
fellow, thou hast not seen the lady cressid. 3.01. 38 P
truly, lady, no. 3.01. 54 P
and to make a sweet lady sad is a sour offense. 3.01. 72 P
you have bereft me of all words, lady. 3.02. 54 P
dreg espies my sweet lady in the fountain of our 3.02. 66 P
o, let my lady apprehend no fear. 3.02. 74 P
this /is the monstruosity in love, lady, that 3.02. 81 P
what offends you, lady? 3.02.144
give up to diomedes' hand | the lady cressida. 4.02. 66
troilus, | tell you the lady what she is to do, 4.03. 4
my lord, is the lady ready? 4.04. 49
here is the lady | which for antenor we deliver 4.04.109
fair lady cressid, | so please you, save the 4.04.116
lady, give me your hand, and, as we walk, | to 4.04.138
is this the lady cressid? 4.05. 17
most dearly welcome to the greeks, sweet lady. 4.05. 18
i'll take that winter from your lips, fair lady; 4.05. 24
i'll have my kiss, sir. lady, by your leave. 4.05. 35
an odd man, lady? every man is odd. 4.05. 42
may i, sweet lady, beg a kiss of you? 4.05. 47
lady, a word. i'll bring you to your father. 4.05. 53
present the fair steed to my lady cressid. 5.05. 2
madam, the lady valeria is come to visit you. COR 1.03. 26
you must go visit the good lady that lies in. 1.03. 77 P
let her alone, lady; 1.03.104 P
come, good sweet lady. 1.03.107 P
and live you yet? o my sweet lady, pardon. 2.01.180
noble lady! 3.02. 69
do you know this lady? 5.03. 63
even he, your wife, this lady, and myself, | are 5.03. 77
a goodly lady, trust me, of the hue | that i TIT 1.01.261
he and his lady both are at the lodge, | upon 2.03.254
by' lady, then i have brought up a neck to a 4.04. 48 P
she's the hopeful lady of my earth. ROM 1.02. 15
the lady widow of /vitruvio; 1.02. 66 P
a man, young lady! 1.03. 75
lady, such a man | as all the world — why, he's 1.03. 75
you call'd, my young lady ask'd for, the nurse 1.03.101 P
by'r lady, thirty years. 1.05. 33
crows, | as yonder lady o'er her fellows shows. 1.05. 49
bachelor, | her mother is the lady of the house, 1.05.113
and a good lady, and a wise and virtuous. 1.05.114
it is my lady, o, it is my love! 2.02. 10
lady, by yonder blessed moon i vow, | that tips 2.02.107
laura to his lady was a kitchen wench (marry, 2.04. 39 P
farewell, ancient lady, farewell, "lady, lady, 2.04.143 P
ancient lady, farewell, "lady, lady, lady." 2.04.144 P
ancient lady, farewell, "lady, lady, lady." 2.04.144 P
ancient lady, farewell, "lady, lady, lady." 2.04.144 P
told you, my young lady bid me inquire you out; 2.04.163 P
nurse, commend me to thy lady and mistress. 2.04.171 P
sir, my mistress is the sweetest lady — lord, 2.04.200 P
commend me to thy lady. 2.04.213 P
o god's lady dear! 2.05. 61
here comes the lady. 2.06. 16
we are undone, lady, we are undone! 3.02. 38
i come from lady juliet. 3.03. 80
says | my conceal'd lady to our cancell'd love? 3.03. 98
and slay thy lady that in thy life /lives, | by 3.03.117
commend me to thy lady, | and bid her hasten all 3.03.155
my lord, i'll tell my lady you will come. 3.03.161
your lady mother is coming to your chamber. 3.05. 39
it is my lady mother. 3.05. 65
and why, my lady wisdom? 3.05.170
go in, and tell my lady i am gone, | having 3.05.231
look, sir, here comes the lady toward my cell. 4.01. 17
happily met, my lady and my wife! 4.01. 18
why, lady! 4.05. 2
lady, lady, lady! 4.05. 13
lady, lady, lady! 4.05. 13
lady, lady, lady! 4.05. 13
my lady! 4.05. 16
i dreamt my lady came and found me dead — 5.01. 6
how doth my lady? 5.01. 14
the lady stirs. 5.03.147
i hear some noise, lady. 5.03.151
whose eyes are on this sovereign lady fix'd, TIM 1.01. 68
at mine own house, good lady. JC 2.04. 22
about the ninth hour, lady. 2.04. 23
that i have, lady, if it will please caesar | to 2.04. 28
o gentle lady, | 'tis not for you to hear what i MAC 2.03. 83
look to the lady. 2.03.119
look to the lady. 2.03.125
thine evermore, most dear lady, whilst this HAM 2.02.123 P
/sere, and the lady shall say her mind freely, 2.02.324 P
what, my young lady and mistress! 2.02.424 P
by' lady, your ladyship is nearer to heaven than 2.02.425 P
lady, shall i lie in your lap? 3.02.112 P
but, by'r lady, 'a must build churches then, or 3.02.133 P
the lady doth protest too much, methinks. 3.02.230 P
ay, lady, it was my word. 3.04. 30
how is it with you, lady? 3.04.115
one word more, good lady. 3.04.180
alas, sweet lady, what imports this song? 4.05. 27
"he is dead and gone, lady, | he is dead and 4.05. 29
how do you, pretty lady? 4.05. 41
why, e'en so, and now my lady worm's, chopless, 5.01. 88 P
and wide-skirted meads, | we make thee lady. LR 1.01. 66
my lord of burgundy, | what say you to the lady? 1.01.238
when the lady brach may stand by th' fire and 1.04.112 P
o lady, lady, shame would have it hid! 2.01. 93
o lady, lady, shame would have it hid! 2.01. 93
is your lady come? 2.04.184
thou art a lady; 2.04.267
unmerciful lady as you are, i'm none. 3.07. 33
naughty lady, | these hairs which thou dost 3.07. 37
follow me, lady. 3.07. 95
come with my lady hither. 4.02. 89
i know not, lady. 4.05. 7
my lady charg'd my duty in this business. 4.05. 18
i know your lady does not love her husband, | i 4.05. 23
i think this lady | to be my child cordelia. 4.07. 68
lady, i am not well, else i should answer | from 5.03. 73
make your loves to me, | my lady is bespoke. 5.03. 89
no tearing, lady, i perceive you know it. 5.03.158
your lady, sir, your lady; 5.03.227
your lady, sir, your lady; 5.03.227
you, | send for the lady to the sagittary, | and OTH 1.03.115
here comes the lady; 1.03.170
hail to thee, lady! 2.01. 85
o gentle lady, do not put me to't, | for i am 2.01.118
she's a most exquisite lady. 2.03. 18 P
ay, but, lady, | that policy may either last so 3.03. 13
did michael cassio, when /you woo'd my lady, 3.03. 94
note if your lady strain his entertainment 3.03.250
poor lady, she'll run mad | when she shall lack 3.03.317
well, my good lady. 3.04. 34
give me your hand. this hand is moist, my lady. 3.04. 36
lady, amen. 3.04.164
truly, /an obedient lady: 4.01.248
how do you, my good lady? 4.02. 96
he that is yours, sweet lady. 4.02.101
what is the matter, lady? 4.02.114
what name, fair lady? 4.02.118
i know a lady in venice would have walk'd 4.03. 38 P
and tell my lord and lady what hath happ'd. 5.01.127
o lady, speak again! 5.02.120
what did thy song bode, lady? 5.02.246
you shall outlive the lady whom you serve. ANT 1.02. 31
no, lady. 1.02. 80
how now, lady? 1.03. 39
i'll leave you, lady. 1.03. 86
she's a most triumphant lady, if report be 2.02.184 P
good night, dear lady. 2.03. 7
a more unhappy lady, | if this division chance, 3.04. 12
the mean time, lady, | i'll raise the 3.04. 25
welcome, lady. 3.06. 90
the white hand of a lady fever thee, | shake 3.13.138
dost thou hear, lady? 3.13.172
o, thy vild lady! 4.14. 22
o, quietness, lady! 4.15. 68
lady! 4.15. 69
this i'll report, dear lady. 5.02. 32
hold, worthy lady, hold! 5.02. 39
o, temperance, lady! 5.02. 48
that i some lady trifles have reserv'd, 5.02.165
finish, good lady, the bright day is done, | and 5.02.193
that he quit being, and his gentle lady, | big CYM 1.01. 38
o lady, weep no more, lest i give cause | to be 1.01. 93
peace, | dear lady daughter, peace! 1.01.154
that lady is not now living; 1.04. 62 P
too fair and too good for any lady in brittany. 1.04. 72 P
most precious diamond that is, nor you the lady. 1.04. 76 P
durst attempt it against any lady in the world. 1.04.112 P
what lady would you choose to assail? 1.04.125 P
commend me to the court where your lady is, with 1.04.128 P
a foolish suitor to a wedded lady | that hath 1.06. 2
thanks, fairest lady. 1.06. 31
a lady | so fair, and fasten'd to an empery 1.06.119
and | solicits here a lady that disdains | thee 1.06.147
the credit that thy lady hath of thee | deserves 1.06.157
a lady to the worthiest sir that ever | country 1.06.160
with every thing that pretty is, my lady sweet, 2.03. 25
she's my good lady, and will conceive, i hope, 2.03.153
your lady | is one of the fairest that i have 2.04. 31
not a whit, | your lady being so easy. 2.04. 47
alas, good lady! 3.04. 45
o gracious lady! 3.04. 98
good lady, | hear me with patience. 3.04.111
she's a lady | so tender of rebukes that words 3.05. 39
all courtly parts more exquisite | than lady, 3.05. 72
villain, | where is thy lady? 3.05. 82
where is thy lady? 3.05. 84
wore when he took leave of my lady and mistress. 3.05.126 P
i have belied a lady, | the princess of this 5.02. 2
he shall be lord of lady imogen, | and happier 5.04.107
mine honor'd lady! 5.05.232
lady, | the gods throw stones of sulphur on me, 5.05.239
why did you throw your wedded lady /from you? 5.05.261
here stands a lord, and there a lady weeping; PER 1.04. 47
why, wilt thou tourney for the lady? 2.01.144 P
is an armed knight that's conquered by a lady; 2.02. 26
'tis more by fortune, lady, than my merit. 2.03. 12
sir, here's a lady that wants breathing too, 2.03.100
the lady shrieks, and well-a-near | does fall in 3.ch. 51
you and your lady | take from my heart all 3.03. 3
i'll leave you, my sweet lady, for a while. 4.01. 47
to satisfy my lady. 4.01. 71
your lady seeks my life, come you between, | and 4.01. 89
o lady, | much less in blood than virtue, yet a 4.03. 6
his courses to be ordered | by lady fortune, 4.04. 48
o, here's | the lady that i sent for. 5.01. 65
she's a gallant lady. 5.01. 66
look to the lady; 5.03. 21
early in blustering morn this lady was | thrown 5.03. 22
sad lady, rise. TNK 1.01. 35
poor lady, say no more. 1.01.101
lady, lady, alack! 1.01.113
lady, lady, alack! 1.01.113
of such a virtuous greatness that this lady, 2.02.257
o my lady, | if ever thou hast felt what sorrow 2.02.275
how do you like him, lady? 2.05. 17
you | to a most noble service — to this lady, 2.05. 34
tell me, o lady fortune | (next after emily my 3.01. 15
the next, the lord of may and lady bright, | the 3.05.125
but, loving such a lady, | and justifying my 3.06. 41
duke, ask that lady | why she is fair, and why 3.06.168
you love most — wars, and this sweet lady — 3.06.203
urge it home, brave lady. 3.06.233
nor think he dies with interest in this lady. 3.06.298
oak, | and in it stuck the favor of his lady. 4.02.138
lady, you shall see men fight now. 4.02.143
to hear there a proud lady and a proud city-wife 4.03. 51 P
value's shortness, | to any lady breathing. 5.03. 89
kinsman hath confess'd the right o' th' lady 5.04.116
lead your lady off; 5.04.122
no, lady, no, my heart longs not to groan, | but VEN 785
where their dear governess and lady lies, | do LUC 443
"but, lady, if your maid may be so bold, | she 1282
ah, that i had my lady at this bay: PP 11.13
lullaby, the learned man hath got the lady gay, 15.15
unless thy lady prove unjust, | press never thou 18.21

LADYBIRD 1 FR 0.0001 REL FR 1 V 0 P

what, ladybird! ROM 1.03. 3

LADY'S 64 FR 0.0072 REL FR 48 V 16 P

to bear my lady's train, lest the base earth TGV 2.04.159
visit by night your lady's chamber-window | with 3.02. 82
go to thy lady's grave and call hers thence, 4.02.116
but think upon my grief, a lady's grief, | and 4.03. 28
and the other too like my lady's eldest son, ADO 2.01. 9 P
her to look out at her lady's chamber-window. 2.02. 17 P
the supposition of the lady's death | will 4.01.238
o, if in black my lady's brows be deck'd, | it LLL 4.03.254
but love, first learned in a lady's eyes, 4.03.324
grace, | despite of suit, to see a lady's face. 5.02.129
here, | what did you whisper in your lady's ear? 5.02.436
do not you know my lady's foot by th' squier, 5.02.474
in the sight | of thy former lady's eye; MND 3.02.457
nor the lady's, which is nice; AYL 4.01. 14 P
i heard of the good lady's death and that my AWW 4.05. 69 P
my lady's a cataian, we are politicians, TN 2.03. 75 P
do ye make an alehouse of my lady's house, that 2.03. 89 P
if you priz'd my lady's favor at any thing more 2.03.121 P
by my life, this is my lady's hand. 2.05. 86 P
now sail'd into the north of my lady's opinion, 3.02. 26 P
but that i am mad | or else the lady's mad; 4.03. 16
suit, | a gentleman, and follower of my lady's. 5.01.277
a lady's "verily" is | as potent as a lord's. WT 1.02. 50
i have seen a lady's nose | that has been blue, 2.01. 14
necklace amber, | perfume for a lady's chamber; 4.04.223
what say'st thou, boy? look in the lady's face. JN 2.01.495
which cannot hear a lady's feeble voice, | which 3.04. 41
my heart hath melted at a lady's tears, | being 5.02. 47
rascal, i could brain him with his lady's fan. 1H4 2.03. 23 P
to the welsh lady's bed. 3.01.242 P
hangs about me like an old lady's loose gown; 3.03. 3 P
terms, | such as will enter at a lady's ear, H5 5.02.100
remedy) | i mean to prove this lady's courtesy. 1H6 2.02. 58
as, liking of the lady's virtuous gifts, | her 5.01. 43
at saint albons field | this lady's husband, sir 3H6 3.02. 2
i'll make my heaven in a lady's lap, | and deck 3.02.148
he capers nimbly in a lady's chamber | to the R3 1.01. 12
what fair lady's that? H8 1.04. 91
who had | commanded nature, that my lady's womb, 2.04.189
this lady's husband here — this (do you see?) COR 4.02. 41
your lady's love against some other maid | that ROM 1.02. 97
tell | a whispering tale in a fair lady's ear, 1.05. 23
what lady's that which doth enrich the hand | of 1.05. 41
o tell me, holy friar, | where's my lady's lord? 3.03. 82
you say you do not know the lady's mind? 4.01. 4
my lady's dead! 4.05. 14
of death | is partly to behold my lady's face, 5.03. 29
he came with flowers to strew his lady's grave, 5.03.281
as rich shall romeo's by his lady's lie, | poor 5.03.303
now get you to my lady's /chamber, and tell her, HAM 5.01.193 P
since my young lady's going into france, sir, LR 1.04. 73 P
my lady's father. 1.04. 79 P
"my lady's father"? 1.04. 80 P
is he for my hand | than for your lady's. 4.05. 32
how i did thrive in this fair lady's love, | and OTH 1.03.125
out, and alas, that was my lady's voice. 5.02.119
your lady's person. is she ready? CYM 2.03. 81
you put me to forget a lady's manners | by being 2.03.105
and to fight | against my lady's kingdom. 5.01. 19
upon my lady's missing, came to me | with his 5.05.275
and with oath to violate | my lady's honor. 5.05.285
and sorts a sad look to her lady's sorrow | (for LUC 1221
forgot, | all my lady's love is lost, god wot. PP 17. 6
merit praise, | by ringing in thy lady's ear. 18.16

LADYSHIP 38 FR 0.0043 REL FR 28 V 10 P

what would your ladyship? TGV 1.02. 66
give me a note, your ladyship can set. 1.02. 78
proceed in, | but for my duty to your ladyship. 2.01.107
what means your ladyship? do you not like it? 2.01.121
please you, i'll write your ladyship another. 2.01.129
this is the gentleman i told your ladyship | had 2.04. 87
him | to be my fellow-servant to your ladyship. 2.04.105
we'll both attend upon your ladyship. 2.04.121
why then your ladyship must cut your hair. 2.07. 44
madam, good ev'n to your ladyship. 4.02. 85
i will not fail your ladyship. 4.03. 45
this is the letter to your ladyship. 4.04.124
madam, he sends your ladyship this ring. 4.04.132
god keep your ladyship still in that mind! ADO 1.01.133 P
your ladyship is ignorant what it is. LLL 2.01.101
if your ladyship would say, "thanks, pompey," i 5.02.556
i wish your ladyship all heart's content. MV 3.04. 42
how does your ladyship like it? AWW 4.05. 77 P
i marvel your ladyship takes delight in such a TN 1.05. 83 P
grace and good disposition attend your ladyship! 3.01.135
your ladyship were best to have some guard about 3.04. 12 P
and your ladyship will have it as it ought to be 5.01.295 P
benefit of my senses as well as your ladyship. 5.01.306 P
please your ladyship | to visit the next room, WT 2.02. 44
but when her humorous ladyship is by | to teach JN 3.01.119
madam, | according as your ladyship desir'd, 1H6 2.03. 12
but since your ladyship is not at leisure, 2.03. 26
i laugh to see your ladyship so fond | to think 2.03. 45
will her ladyship behold and hear our exorcisms? 2H6 1.04. 4 P
here's to your ladyship, and pledge it, madam, H8 1.04. 47
i am glad to see your ladyship. COR 1.03. 50 P
i thank your ladyship; well, good madam. 1.03. 54 P
i will most willingly attend your ladyship. TIT 4.01. 28
what are they, beseech your ladyship? ROM 3.05.106
your ladyship is nearer to heaven than when i HAM 2.02.425 P
marry, before your ladyship, i grant, | she puts OTH 2.01.105
i humbly thank your ladyship. 3.04.168

madam, good night; i humbly thank your ladyship. 4.03. 3
LADYSHIP'S 6 FR 0.0006 REL FR 2 V 4 P
borrows his wit from your ladyship's looks, and TGV 2.04. 38 P
one that attends your ladyship's command. 4.03. 5
according to your ladyship's impose, | i am thus 4.03. 8
"your ladyship's in all desired employment, LLL 4.02.135 P
if i may have your ladyship's good will to go to AWW 1.03. 18 P
he attends your ladyship's pleasure. TN 3.04. 59 P
LADYSHIPS 1 FR 0.0001 REL FR 0 V 1 P
and, if it please your ladyships, you may see AYL 1.02.114 P
LADY–SMOCKS 1 FR 0.0001 REL FR 1 V 0 P
violets blue | and lady–smocks all silver–white LLL 5.02.895
LAERTES' 1 FR 0.0001 REL FR 1 V 0 P
and wise laertes' son | did graciously plead for TIT 1.01.380
/LAERTES 1 FR 0.0001 REL FR 1 V 0 P
/that /to /laertes /i /forgot /myself, | /for HAM 5.02. 76
LAERTES 32 FR 0.0036 REL FR 27 V 5 P
and now, laertes, what's the news with you? HAM 1.02. 42
you told us of some suit, what is't, laertes? 1.02. 43
what wouldst thou beg, laertes, | that shall not 1.02. 45
what wouldst thou have, laertes? 1.02. 50
take thy fair hour, laertes, time be thine, 1.02. 62
yet here, laertes? 1.03. 55
with more impiteous haste | than young laertes, 4.05.102
/they cry, "choose we, laertes shall be king!" 4.05.107
clouds, | "laertes shall be king, laertes king!" 4.05.109
clouds, | "laertes shall be king, laertes king!" 4.05.109
calmly, good laertes. 4.05.117
what is the cause, laertes, | that thy rebellion 4.05.121
tell me, laertes, | why thou art thus incens'd. 4.05.126
good laertes, | if you desire to know the 4.05.140
laertes, i must commune with your grief, | or 4.05.203
laertes, you shall hear them. 4.07. 41
if it be so, laertes — | as how should it be so 4.07. 57
laertes, was your father dear to you? 4.07.107
but, good laertes, | will you do this, keep 4.07.128
your sister's drown'd, laertes. 4.07.164
that is laertes, a very noble youth. mark. 5.01.224
o, he is mad, laertes. 5.01.272
here is newly come to court laertes, believe me, 5.02.106 P
of laertes? 5.02.129 P
not ignorant of what excellence laertes is — 5.02.137 P
know if your pleasure hold to play with laertes, 5.02.198 P
entertainment to laertes before you fall to play 5.02.207 P
was't hamlet wrong'd laertes? 5.02.233
and when he's not himself does wrong laertes, 5.02.235
i'll be your foil, laertes; 5.02.255
come, for the third, laertes, you do but dally. 5.02.297
how is't, laertes? 5.02.305
LAFEW 5 FR 0.0005 REL FR 2 V 3 P
now, good lafew, | bring in the admiration, that AWW 2.01. 87
he was first smok'd by the old lord lafew. 3.06.104 P
what greeting will you to my lord lafew? 4.03.318 P
master lavatch, give my lord lafew this letter. 5.02. 1 P
the heavens have thought well on thee, lafew, 5.03.150
/LAG 1 FR 0.0001 REL FR 0 V 1 P
together with the common /lag of people — what TIM 3.06. 81 P
LAG 6 FR 0.0006 REL FR 6 V 0 P
content | to entertain the lag end of my life 1H4 5.01. 24
fortune in favor makes him lag behind. 1H6 3.03. 34
that came too lag to see him buried. R3 2.01. 91
the lag end of their lewdness and be laugh'd at. H8 1.03. 35
or fourteen moonshines | lag of a brother? LR 1.02. 6
that in lag hours attend | for grey approachers; TNK 5.04. 8
LAGGING 2 FR 0.0002 REL FR 2 V 0 P
four lagging winters and four wanton springs R2 1.03.214
as lagging fowls before the northern blast. LUC 1335
LAID 103 FR 0.0116 REL FR 83 V 20 P
good plots, they are laid, and our revolted WIV 3.02. 39 P
have i laid my brain in the sun and dried it, 5.05.135 P
the gold i gave to dromio is laid up | safe at ERR 2.02. 1
this drudge or diviner laid claim to me, call'd 3.02.140 P
they must be bound and laid in some dark room. 4.04. 94
the juice of it on sleeping eyelids laid | will MND 2.01.170
and laid the love–juice on some true–love's 3.02. 89
of the father are to be laid upon the children; MV 3.05. 2 P
well said — that was laid on with a trowel. AYL 1.02.106 P
then there were two cousins laid up, when the 1.03. 7 P
who laid him down and bask'd him in the sun, 2.07. 15
evils that he laid to the charge of women? 3.02.352 P
"why, thy godhead laid apart, | warr'st thou 4.03. 44
the gills fair without, the carpets laid, and SHR 4.01. 50 P
has much worthy blame laid upon him for shaking AWW 4.03. 6 P
nature's own sweet and cunning hand laid on. TN 1.05.240
death, | and in sad cypress let me be laid. 2.04. 52
stone, | and laid mine honor too unchary on't. 3.04.202
they have laid me here in hideous darkness. 4.02. 29 P
whereof being by circumstances partly laid open, WT 3.02. 18 P
nor is't directly laid to thee, the death | of 3.02.194
this is not, no, | laid to thy answer: 3.02.199
of king polixenes) it should here be laid, 3.03. 44
my lord, your sorrow was too sore laid on, 5.03. 49
i would that i were low laid in my grave, | i am JN 2.01.164
child, | the canon of the law is laid on him, 2.01.180
which gently laid my knighthood on my shoulder, R2 1.01. 79
forth thy reach he would have laid thy shame, 2.01.106
that laid the sentence of dread banishment | on 3.03.134
and, therein laid — there lies | two kinsmen 3.03.168
our plot is a good plot as ever was laid, our 1H4 2.03. 17 P
laid gifts before him, proffer'd him their oaths 4.03. 71
and laid his love and life under my foot, | yea, 2H4 3.01. 63
till his face be like a wet cloak ill laid up. 5.01. 85 P
than a joint burden laid upon us all. 5.02. 55
forget | so great indignities you laid upon me? 5.02. 69
for that i have laid by my majesty, | and H5 1.02.276
his ceremonies laid by, in his nakedness he 4.01.105 P
not all these, laid in bed majestical, | can 4.01.267
the plot is laid. 1H6 2.03. 4
as i have read, laid claim unto the crown, | and 2H6 2.02. 40
but mightier crimes are laid unto your charge, 3.01.134
causeless have laid disgraces on my head, | and 3.01.162
ay, all of you have laid your heads together — 3.01.165
have you laid fair the bed? 3.02. 11
some violent hands were laid on humphrey's life! 3.02.138
i do believe that violent hands were laid | upon 3.02.156
peep out, for all the country is laid for me; 4.10. 4 P
lenity | and harmful pity must be laid aside. 3H6 2.02. 10
down, | and with dishonor laid me on the ground, 3.03. 9
tell him, my mourning weeds are laid aside, 3.03.229
blast his harvest, /and your head were laid, 5.07. 21
plots have i laid, inductions dangerous, | by R3 1.01. 32
that laid their guilt upon my guiltless 1.02. 98
the curse my noble father laid on thee | when 1.03.173
laid open all your victories in scotland, | your 3.07. 15
and all my armor laid into my tent? 5.03. 51
or | laid any scruple in your way which might H8 2.04.151
peace, and all such emblems | laid nobly on her; 4.01. 90
fell mischiefs | our reasons laid before him, 5.01. 50
or i fall into | the trap is laid for me! 5.01.142
this is of purpose laid by some that hate me 5.02. 14
lady | heaven ever laid up to make parents happy 5.04. 7
laid falsely | i' th' plain way of his merit. COR 3.01. 60
for i had then laid wormwood to my dug, ROM 1.03. 26
till she had laid it and conjur'd it down. 2.01. 26
how if, when i am laid into the tomb, | i wake 4.03. 30
i saw her laid low in her kindred's vault, | and 5.01. 20
see what a scourge is laid upon your hate, 5.03.292
had you not fully laid my state before me, TIM 2.02.125
brought in my accompts, | laid them before you; 2.02.134
when i have laid proud athens on a heap — 4.03.102
i laid their daggers ready, | he could not miss MAC 2.02. 11
the taints and blames i laid upon myself, | for 4.03.124
it will be laid to us, whose providence | should HAM 4.01. 17
to you that 'a has laid a great wager on your 5.02.102 P
but in the imputation laid on him by them, in 5.02.142 P
the king, sir, hath laid, sir, that in a dozen 5.02.165 P
he hath laid on twelve for nine, and it would 5.02.167 P
your grace has laid the odds a' th' weaker side. 5.02.261
that hath laid knives under his pillow, and LR 3.04. 54 P
/then laid his leg | /over my thigh, and /sigh'd OTH 3.03.424
away, | and laid good 'scuses upon your ecstasy; 4.01. 79
could not have laid such terms upon his callet. 4.02.121
i have laid those sheets you bade me on the bed. 4.03. 22
for he hath laid strange courtesies and great ANT 2.02.154
chamber nothing saves | the wager you have laid. CYM 2.04. 95
and lucre in them | have laid this woe here. 4.02.325
on her and hers, | have laid most heavy hand. 5.05.465
(then weaker than your eyes) laid by his club; TNK 1.01. 67
were not spent, | rather laid out for purchase. 1.02.111
have patiently | laid up my hour to come. 2.02. 6
and marrow of my understanding laid upon ye, 3.05. 6
i laid me down | and list'ned to the words she 4.01. 62
which being laid unto | mine innocent true heart 5.01.133
lives (for this poor comfort) are laid down, 5.04. 14
this plot of death when sadly she had laid, LUC 1212
pawn'd honest looks, but laid no words to gage. 1351
honoring, | or laid great bases for eternity, SON 125. 3
bait | on purpose laid to make the taker mad: 129. 8
cupid laid by his brand and fell asleep: 153. 1
laid by his side his heart–inflaming brand, 154. 2
and down i laid to list the sad–tun'd tale, LC 4
LAIDST 1 FR 0.0001 REL FR 1 V 0 P
in that thou laidst a trap to take my life, | as 1H6 3.01. 22
LAIN *(also lien)*
LAIN 4 FR 0.0004 REL FR 3 V 1 P
thy dog that hath lain asleep in the sun. ROM 3.01. 26 P
thy wedding–day | hath death lain with thy wife. 4.05. 36
dead, | who here hath lain this two days buried. 5.03.176
or sire, | or lain in ambush to betray my life, LUC 233
L'AIR 1 FR 0.0001 REL FR 1 V 0 P
rien puis? l'air et feu? H5 4.02. 5
LAISSEZ 3 FR 0.0003 REL FR 0 V 3 P
laissez, mon seigneur, laissez, laissez! H5 5.02.253 P
laissez, mon seigneur, laissez, laissez! 5.02.253 P
laissez, mon seigneur, laissez, laissez! 5.02.253 P
LAKE 7 FR 0.0008 REL FR 5 V 2 P
that the foul lake | o'erstunk their feet. TMP 4.01.183
see her damn'd first, to pluto's damned lake, by 2H4 2.04.157 P
descend to darkness and the burning lake! 2H6 1.04. 39
i'll dive into the burning lake below, | and TIT 4.03. 44
me nero is an angler in the lake of darkness. LR 3.06. 7 P
in the great lake that lies behind the palace, TNK 4.01. 53
fair nymph | that feeds the lake with waters, or 4.01. 87
LAKES 1 FR 0.0001 REL FR 1 V 0 P
of hills, brooks, standing lakes, and groves, TMP 5.01. 33
LAKIN 2 FR 0.0002 REL FR 1 V 1 P
by'r lakin, i can go no further, sir, | my old TMP 3.03. 1
by'r lakin, a parlous fear. MND 3.01. 13 P
LAMB 39 FR 0.0044 REL FR 30 V 9 P
come you to seek the lamb here of the fox, MM 5.01.298
doing, in the figure of a lamb, the feats of a ADO 1.01. 15 P
will not hear her lamb when it baes will never 3.03. 71 P
no sheep, sweet lamb, unless we feed on your LLL 2.01.220
the nemean lion roar | 'gainst thee, thou lamb, 4.01. 89
why he hath made the ewe bleak for the lamb; MV 4.01. 74
tut, she's a lamb, a dove, a fool to him! SHR 3.02.157
i'll sacrifice the lamb that i do love, | to TN 5.01.130
men away, | and i will sit as quiet as a lamb; JN 4.01. 79
in peace was never gentle lamb more mild, | than R2 2.01.174
rising of the lark to the lodging of the lamb, H5 3.07. 32 P
the fox barks not when he would steal the lamb. 2H6 3.01. 55
as is the sucking lamb or harmless dove. 3.01. 71
is he a lamb? 3.01. 77
of the skin of an innocent lamb should be made 4.02. 79 P
the trembling lamb environed with wolves. 3H6 1.01.242
and when the lion fawns upon the lamb, | the 4.08. 49
lamb, | the lamb will never cease to follow him. 4.08. 50
as fox to lamb, or wolf to heifer's calf, | pard TRO 3.02.193
the lamb. COR 2.01. 8 P
he's a lamb indeed, that baes like a bear. 2.01. 11 P
he's a bear indeed, that lives like a lamb. 2.01. 12 P
all on a heap, like to a slaughtered lamb, | in TIT 2.03.223
when we join in league | i am a lamb, but if you 4.02.137
what, lamb! ROM 1.03. 3
but, i'll warrant him, as gentle as a lamb. 2.05. 44 P
wolvish ravening lamb! 3.02. 76
why, lamb! 4.05. 2
if thou wert the lamb, the fox would eat thee; TIM 4.03.329 P
you are yoked with a lamb | that carries anger JC 4.03.110
poor, innocent lamb | t' appease an angry god. MAC 4.03. 16
and the poor state | esteem him as a lamb, being 4.03. 54
fill'd and running — ravening first the lamb, CYM 1.06. 49
dispatch, | the lamb entreats the butcher. 3.04. 96
and never fright the silly lamb that day. VEN 1098
wolf hath seiz'd his prey, the poor lamb cries, LUC 677
she like a wearied lamb lies panting there; 737
thou sets the wolf where he the lamb may get; 878
if like a lamb he could his looks translate! SON 96.10
LAMBERT'S 1 FR 0.0001 REL FR 1 V 0 P
it, | at coventry upon saint lambert's day. R2 1.01.199
LAMBKIN 1 FR 0.0001 REL FR 1 V 0 P
sir john, thy tender lambkin now is king; 2H4 5.03.116
LAMBKINS 1 FR 0.0001 REL FR 1 V 0 P
condole the knight, for, lambkins, we will live. H5 2.01.127
LAMBS 14 FR 0.0015 REL FR 12 V 2 P
a fox to be the shepherd of thy lambs. TGV 4.04. 92
did in eaning time | fall parti–color'd lambs, MV 1.03. 88
pride is to see my ewes graze and my lambs suck. AYL 3.02. 77 P
we were as twinn'd lambs that did frisk i' th' WT 1.02. 67
lo, whilest i waited on my tender lambs, | and 1H6 1.02. 76
or else, when thou didst keep my lambs a–field, 5.04. 30
or lambs pursu'd by hunger–starved wolves. 3H6 1.04. 5
dens, | poor harmless lambs abide their enmity. 2.05. 75
wilt thou, o god, fly from such gentle lambs, R3 4.04. 22
to worry lambs and lap their gentle blood, 4.04. 50
heart | to revel in the entrails of my lambs. 4.04.229
how now, lambs? TRO 4.04. 23 P
season that they may surprise | the silly lambs: LUC 167
how many lambs might the stern wolf betray, | if SON 96. 9
LAMBSKINS 1 FR 0.0001 REL FR 0 V 1 P
and furr'd with fox and lambskins too, to MM 3.02. 8 P
LAM'D 2 FR 0.0002 REL FR 0 V 2 P
i think, when he hath lam'd me, i shall beg with ERR 4.04. 38 P
the one should be lam'd with reasons and the AYL 1.03. 8 P
LAME 18 FR 0.0020 REL FR 14 V 4 P
will not give a doit to relieve a lame beggar, TMP 2.02. 32 P
leap for joy, though they are lame with blows: LLL 5.02.291
come, lame me with reasons. AYL 1.03. 6 P
when service should in my old limbs lie lame, 2.03. 41
ay, but the feet were lame and could not bear 3.02.169 P
lame, foolish, crooked, swart, prodigious, JN 3.01. 46
what, art thou lame? 2H6 2.01. 93
true; made the lame to leap and fly away. 2.01.158
they have all new legs, and lame ones. H8 1.03. 11
unless by using means i lame the foot | of our COR 4.07. 7
o, she is lame! ROM 2.05. 4
(being not deficient, blind, or lame of sense), OTH 1.03. 63
o most lame and impotent conclusion! 2.01.161 P
time | post /on the lame feet of my rhyme, PER 4.ch. 48
the poor, lame, blind, halt, creep, cry out for LUC 902
breath is short, | youth is nimble, age is lame, PP 12. 6
so i, made lame by fortune's dearest spite, SON 37. 3
so then i am not lame, poor, nor despis'd, 37. 9
LAMELY 4 FR 0.0004 REL FR 2 V 2 P
are they not lamely writ? TGV 2.01. 91 P
verse, and therefore stood lamely in the verse. AYL 3.02.171 P
and that so lamely and unfashionable | that dogs R3 1.01. 22
limbs may halt | as lamely as their manners! TIM 4.01. 25
LAMENESS 2 FR 0.0002 REL FR 2 V 0 P
young bones, | you taking airs, with lameness! LR 2.04.164
speak of my lameness, and i straight will halt, SON 89. 3
/LAMENT 1 FR 0.0001 REL FR 1 V 0 P
/me /the /way | /how /to /lament /the /cause. R2 4.01.302
LAMENT 24 FR 0.0027 REL FR 22 V 2 P
cease to lament for that thou canst not help, TGV 3.01.243
friends no wrong, for i have none to lament me; AYL 1.02.190 P
to be found again, | lament till i am lost. WT 5.03.135
lament we may, but not revenge /thee dead. R2 1.03. 58
come mourn with me for what i do lament, | and 5.06. 47
why then lament therefore. 2H4 5.03.108
deadly, | i should lament thy miserable state. 3H6 1.04. 85
'twere childish weakness to lament or fear. 5.04. 38
whilst i awhile obsequiously lament | th' R3 1.02. 3
rest you, whiles i lament king henry's corse. 1.02. 32
i do lament the sickness of the king, | as loath 2.02. 9
if you will live, lament; 2.02. 43
of most hard temper | melt and lament for her. H8 2.03. 12
leave this faint puling, and lament as i do, COR 4.02. 52
that ever eye with sight made heart lament! TIT 2.03.205
o noble father, you lament in vain: 3.01. 27
but yet let reason govern thy lament. 3.01.218
for though /fond nature bids us all lament, ROM 4.05. 82
where joy most revels, grief doth most lament; HAM 3.02.198
change now at my end | lament nor sorrow at; ANT 4.15. 52
that matter nature must compel us to lament | our most 5.01. 29
but yet let me lament, | with tears as sovereign 5.01. 40
why lament you, pretty one? PER 4.02. 68 P
and who she finds forlorn she doth lament. LUC 1500
LAMENTABLE 16 FR 0.0018 REL FR 11 V 5 P
weep agood, | for i did play a lamentable part. TGV 4.04.166
they were all in lamentable cases! LLL 5.02.273
our play is the most lamentable comedy and most MND 1.02. 11 P
why holds thine eye that lamentable rheum, JN 3.01. 22
griefs, | tell thou the lamentable tale of me, R2 5.01. 44
tertian, that it is most lamentable to behold. H5 2.01.119 P
is not this a lamentable thing, that of the skin 2H6 4.02. 78 P
why, is not this a lamentable thing, grandsire, ROM 2.04. 31 P
o lamentable day! 4.05. 17
o lamentable day! 4.05. 30
most lamentable day, most woeful day | that ever 4.05. 50
hour | is guilty of this lamentable chance! 5.03.146
the lamentable change is from the best, | the LR 4.01. 5
that weep this lamentable divorce under her CYM 1.04. 20 P
lamentable! 1.06. 85
a thousand lamentable objects there, | in scorn LUC 1373
LAMENTABLY 2 FR 0.0002 REL FR 1 V 1 P
very pleasant thing indeed and sung lamentably. WT 4.04.190 P
is out of breath, | and sinks most lamentably. ANT 3.10. 25
LAMENTATION 10 FR 0.0011 REL FR 8 V 2 P
bestow'd her on her own lamentation, which she MM 3.01.228 P
raining the tears of lamentation | for the LLL 5.02.809
moderate lamentation is the right of the dead, AWW 1.01. 55 P
as yet the lamentation of the french | invites H5 5.pr. 36
give me no help in lamentation, | i am not R3 2.02. 66
nurse, | and i will pamper it with lamentation. 2.02. 88
aery wings | and hear your mother's lamentation! 4.04. 14
we should by this, to all our lamentation, | if COR 4.06. 34
which modern lamentation might have moved? ROM 3.02.120
joy | than thou went'st forth in lamentation. 3.03.154
LAMENTATIONS 2 FR 0.0002 REL FR 2 V 0 P
ghost | to hear the lamentations of poor anne, R3 1.02. 9
heart | in such relenting dew of lamentations, LUC 1829
LAMENTED 6 FR 0.0006 REL FR 3 V 3 P

shall be lamented, pitied, and excus'd | of ADO 4.01.216
and children are even now to be afresh lamented. WT 4.02. 25 P
to't bravely confess'd and lamented by the king) 5.02. 86 P
and it is very much lamented, brutus, | that you JC 1.02. 55
you indeed a cut, and the case to be lamented. ANT 1.02.167 P
his glory which | brought them to be lamented. 5.02.363
/LAMENTING 2 FR 0.0002 REL FR 2 V 0 P
/drown /the /lamenting /fool /in //sea–salt TIT 3.02. 20
/and /buzz /lamenting /doings /in /the /air! 3.02. 62
LAMENTING 8 FR 0.0009 REL FR 8 V 0 P
flower, | lamenting some enforced chastity. MND 3.01.200
from me | with new lamenting ancient oversights, 2H4 2.03. 47
still lamenting and mourning for suffolk's death 2H6 4.04. 22
grave, | and then return lamenting to my love. R3 1.02.261
triumphs for nothing, and lamenting toys, | is CYM 4.02.193
which gives me such lamenting | as wakes my TNK 1.01. 57
lamenting philomele had ended | the well–tun'd LUC 1079
i'll tune thy woes with my lamenting tongue, 1465
LAMENTINGS 1 FR 0.0001 REL FR 1 V 0 P
and, as they say, | lamentings heard i' th' air; MAC 2.03. 56
/LAMENTS 2 FR 0.0002 REL FR 2 V 0 P
/and /these /external /manners /of /laments R2 4.01.296
/leave /these /bitter /deep /laments, | /make TIT 3.02. 46
LAMENTS 6 FR 0.0006 REL FR 5 V 1 P
well, she laments, sir, for it, that it would WIV 3.05. 43 P
my gracious lords, to add to your laments, 1H6 1.01.103
yet he most christian–like laments his death; 2H6 3.02. 58
my heart laments that virtue cannot live | out JC 2.03. 13
each stroke laments | the place whereon it falls TNK 5.03. 4
and my laments would be drawn out too long | to LUC 1616
LAMENT'ST 1 FR 0.0001 REL FR 1 V 0 P
and study help for that which thou lament'st. TGV 3.01.244
LAMES 1 FR 0.0001 REL FR 0 V 1 P
which lames report to follow it and undoes WT 5.02. 57 P
LAMING 1 FR 0.0001 REL FR 1 V 0 P
laming | the shrine of venus or straight–pight CYM 5.05.163
LAMMAS–EVE 2 FR 0.0002 REL FR 2 V 0 P
come lammas–eve at night shall she be fourteen. ROM 1.03. 17
on lammas–eve at night shall she be fourteen, 1.03. 21
LAMMAS–TIDE 1 FR 0.0001 REL FR 1 V 0 P
how long is it now | to lammas–tide? ROM 1.03. 15
LAMORD 1 FR 0.0001 REL FR 1 V 0 P
upon my life, lamord. HAM 4.07. 92
L'AMOUR 1 FR 0.0001 REL FR 0 V 1 P
o, je vous supplie, pour l'amour de dieu, me H5 4.04. 40 P
LAMP 11 FR 0.0012 REL FR 9 V 2 P
her to but to make a lamp of her and run from ERR 3.02. 97 P
moist hesperus hath quench'd her sleepy lamp, AWW 2.01.164
my oil–dried lamp and time–bewasted light R2 1.03.221
thou art the knight of the burning lamp. 1H4 3.03. 27 P
now are they but one lamp, one light, one sun. 3H6 2.01. 31
to feed for /aye her lamp and flames of love, TRO 3.02.160
shame those stars, | as daylight doth a lamp; ROM 2.02. 20
yet dark night strangles the travelling lamp. MAC 2.04. 7
look | our lamp is spent, it's out. ANT 4.15. 85
the lamp that burns by night | dries up his oil VEN 755
from whom each lamp and shining star doth borrow 861
LAMPASS 1 FR 0.0001 REL FR 0 V 1 P
to mose in the chine, troubled with the lampass, SHR 3.02. 51 P
LAMPS 8 FR 0.0009 REL FR 8 V 0 P
take heed, | as hymen's lamps shall light you. TMP 4.01. 23
my wasting lamps some fading glimmer left, | my ERR 5.01.316
eyes, like lamps whose wasting oil is spent, 1H6 2.05. 8
and wastes | the lamps of night in revel; ANT 1.04. 5
the /e'er–remaining lamps, the belching whale PER 3.01. 62
these the bright lamps of beauty, that command TNK 4.02. 39
were never four such lamps together mix'd, | had VEN 489
where lo, two lamps burnt out in darkness lies; 1128
LANCASTER 64 FR 0.0072 REL FR 61 V 3 P
old john of gaunt, time–honored lancaster, R2 1.01. 1
for you, my noble lord of lancaster, | the 1.01.135
harry of herford, lancaster, and derby | am i, 1.03. 35
harry of herford, lancaster, and derby, 1.03.100
harry of herford, lancaster, and derby | stands 1.03.104
and to approve | henry of herford, lancaster, 1.03.113
how fares our noble uncle lancaster? 2.01. 71
words, life, and all, old lancaster hath spent. 2.01.150
well, lords, the duke of lancaster is dead. 2.01.224
my lord, my answer is to lancaster, | and i am 2.03. 70
herford, | but as i come, i come for lancaster. 2.03.114
it must be granted i am duke of lancaster. 2.03.124
great duke of lancaster, i come to thee | from 4.01.107
the devil take henry of lancaster and thee! 5.05.102
for by that name as oft as lancaster | doth 1H4 3.01. 8
with him my son, lord john of lancaster, | for 3.02.171
go bear this letter to lord john of lancaster, 3.03.195
to god | he came but to be duke of lancaster, 4.03. 61
the prince of wales, lord john of lancaster, 4.04. 29
the seat of gaunt, dukedom of lancaster. 5.01. 45
lord john of lancaster, go you with him. 5.04. 3
by god, thou hast deceiv'd me, lancaster, | i 5.04. 17
then, brother john of lancaster, to you | this 5.05. 25
under the conduct of young lancaster | and 2H4 1.01.134
with some charge to the lord john of lancaster. 1.02. 63 P
going with lord john of lancaster against the 1.02.204 P
go bear this letter to my lord of lancaster, 1.02.239 P
the duke of lancaster and westmerland; 1.03. 82
horse, | are march'd up to my lord of lancaster, 2.01.174
the prince, lord john and duke of lancaster. 4.01. 28
good my lord of lancaster, | i am not here 4.02. 30
look, look, here comes my john of lancaster. 4.05.225
strong fixed is the house of lancaster, | and 1H6 2.05.102
nor shall proud lancaster usurp my right, | nor 2H6 1.01.244
york, | to grapple with the house of lancaster; 1.01.257
whom | was john of gaunt, the duke of lancaster; 2.02. 14
till henry bullingbrook, duke of lancaster, 2.02. 21
thus got the house of lancaster the crown. 2.02. 29
with heart–blood of the house of lancaster; 2.02. 66
blood, | the honorable blood of lancaster, 4.01. 51
which now the house of lancaster usurps, | i vow 3H6 1.01. 23
best, | the proudest he that holds up lancaster, 1.01. 46
be duke of lancaster, let him be king. 1.01. 86
he is both king and duke of lancaster, | and 1.01. 87
henry of lancaster, resign thy crown. 1.01.164
now york and lancaster are reconcil'd. 1.01.204
giving the house of lancaster leave to breathe, 1.02. 13
my drift, | nor any of the house of lancaster? 1.02. 47
may make against the house of lancaster. 2.01.176
o lancaster! 2.06. 3
arm, | this arm upholds the house of lancaster. 3.03.107
oxford, oxford, for lancaster! 5.01. 59
montague, montague, for lancaster! 5.01. 67
somerset, somerset, for lancaster! 5.01. 72
the stones together, | and set up lancaster. 5.01. 85
and ne'er have stol'n the breech from lancaster. 5.05. 24
will the aspiring blood of lancaster | sink in 5.06. 61
th' untimely fall of virtuous lancaster. R3 1.02. 4
king, | pale ashes of the house of lancaster, 1.02. 6
grey | were factious for the house of lancaster; 1.03.127
times, | during the wars of york and lancaster, 1.04. 15
to fight | in quarrel of the house of lancaster. 1.04.204
thou offspring of the house of lancaster, | the 5.03.136
all this divided york and lancaster, | divided 5.05. 27
LANCE 15 FR 0.0017 REL FR 15 V 0 P
if tall, a lance ill–headed; ADO 3.01. 64
receive thy lance, and god defend the right! R2 1.03.101
go bear this lance to thomas duke of norfolk. 1.03.103
enacted wonders with his sword and lance: 1H6 1.01.122
break a lance, | and run a–tilt at death within 3.02. 50
a braver soldier never couched lance, | a 3.02.134
with the steely point of clifford's lance; 3H6 2.03. 16
and with guilty fear | let fall thy lance. R3 5.03.143
and not worth | the splinter of a lance. TRO 1.03.283
slaves, as high | as i could pick my lance. COR 1.01.200
and the strong lance of justice hurtless breaks; LR 4.06.166
which could have turn'd | a distaff to a lance, CYM 5.03. 34
practic'd more the whipstock than the lance. PER 2.02. 51
or tell of babes broach'd on the lance, or women TNK 1.03. 20
"over my altars hath he hung his lance, | his VEN 103
LANCE'S 1 FR 0.0001 REL FR 1 V 0 P
and with thy blessings steel my lance's point, R2 1.03. 74
LANCES 7 FR 0.0008 REL FR 7 V 0 P
"the armipotent mars, of lances the almighty, LLL 5.02.644
"the armipotent mars, of lances the almighty, 5.02.651
but now i see our lances are but straws, | our SHR 5.02.173
their needl's to lances, and their gentle hearts JN 5.02.157
there shall your swords and lances arbitrate R2 1.01.200
your pens to lances, and your tongue divine | to 2H4 4.01. 51
and turn our impress'd lances in our eyes LR 5.03. 50
LANCETH *(also lanch'd, launch)*
LANCETH 1 FR 0.0001 REL FR 1 V 0 P
than when he bites, but lanceth not the sore. R2 1.03.303
LANCH'D 1 FR 0.0001 REL FR 1 V 0 P
whose hand soever lanch'd their tender hearts, R3 4.04.225
/LAND 5 FR 0.0005 REL FR 5 V 0 P
/the /state /and /profit /of /this /land; R2 4.01.225
/them /he /doth /bestride /a /bleeding /land, 2H4 1.01.207
/counsell'd /thee | /to /give /away /thy /land, LR 1.04.141
/his /banners /in /our /noiseless /land, | /with 4.02. 56
/touches /us, /as /france /invades /our /land, 5.01. 25
LAND 207 FR 0.0234 REL FR 186 V 21 P
i not doubt | he came alive to land. TMP 2.01.123
bourn, bound of land, tilth, vineyard, none; 2.01.153
the sea mocks | our frustrate search on land. 3.03. 10
and on this green land | answer your summons; 4.01.130
i prophesied, if a gallows were on land, | this 5.01.217
hast thou no mouth by land? 5.01.220
this is the fairy land. ERR 2.02.189
her trim, the merry wind | blows fair from land: 4.01. 91
face of terra, the soil, the land, the earth. LLL 4.02. 7 P
whip to our tents, as roes /run o'er land. 5.02.309
when thou hast stolen away from fairy land, MND 2.01. 65
which, falling in the land, | hath every pelting 2.01. 90
the fairy land buys not the child of me. 2.01.122
and sail upon the land | to fetch me trifles, 2.01.132
sent | to bear him to my bower in fairy land. 4.01. 61
and to the other | a land itself at large, a AYL 5.04.169
you to your land, and love, and great allies; 5.04.189
thousand ducats by the year | of fruitful land, SHR 2.01.370
two thousand ducats by the year of land! 2.01.372
my land amounts not to so much in all. 2.01.373
body | to painful labor, both by sea and land; 5.02.149
he that ears my land spares my team and gives me AWW 1.03. 44 P
best haste, and go not | too far i' th' land; WT 3.03. 11
i have seen two such sights, by sea and by land! 3.03. 84 P
within a mile where my land and living lies; 4.03. 98 P
the gracious mark o' th' land, you have obscur'd 4.04. 8
heaven guard my mother's honor, and my land! JN 1.01. 70
i know not why, except to get the land; 1.01. 73
what doth move you to claim your brother's land? 1.01. 91
with half that face would he have all my land — 1.01. 93
well, sir, by this you cannot get my land; 1.01. 97
my father's land, as was my father's will. 1.01.115
your father's heir must have your father's land. 1.01.129
and like thy brother, to enjoy thy land; 1.01.135
lord of thy presence and no land beside? 1.01.137
and, to his shape, were heir to all this land, 1.01.144
bequeath thy land to him, and follow me? 1.01.149
brother, take you my land, i'll take my chance. 1.01.151
my father gave me honor, yours gave land. 1.01.164
i was, | but many a many foot of land the worse. 1.01.183
son, | i have disclaim'd sir robert and my land, 1.01.247
him time | to land his legions all as soon as i; 2.01. 59
and all th' unsettled humors of the land, | rash 2.01. 66
fresh expectation troubled not the land | with 4.02. 7
preparation | was levied in the body of a land. 4.02.112
but as i travell'd hither through the land, | i 4.02.143
nay, in the body of this fleshly land, | this 4.02.245
and heaven itself doth frown upon the land. 4.03.159
and make fair weather in your blust'ring land. 5.01. 21
shall we, upon the footing of our land, | send 5.01. 66
cause — | to grace the gentry of a land remote, 5.02. 31
acquainted me with interest to this land, | yea, 5.02. 89
after young arthur, claim this land for mine, 5.02. 94
out of the weak door of our fainting land. 5.07. 78
put on | the lineal state and glory of the land! 5.07.102
years, | complotted and contrived in this land, R2 1.01. 96
us, our state, our subjects, or our land. 1.03.190
as now our flesh is banish'd from this land; 1.03.197
as far as land will let me, by your side. 1.03.252
this land of such dear souls, this dear dear 2.01. 57
land of such dear souls, this dear dear land, 2.01. 57
thy death–bed is no lesser than thy land, 2.01. 95
the waste is no whit lesser than thy land. 2.01.103
it were a shame to let this land by lease; 2.01.110
but for thy world enjoying but this land, | is 2.01.111
moe | of noble blood in this declining land. 2.01.240
who strongly hath set footing in this land: 2.02. 48
here am i left to underprop his land, | who, 2.02. 82
comes rushing on this woeful land at once! 2.02. 99
from the most gracious regent of this land, 2.03. 77
covering your fearful land | with hard bright 3.02.110
to ear the land that hath some hope to grow, 3.02.212
the fresh green lap of fair king richard's land, 3.03. 47
that every stride he makes upon my land | is 3.03. 92
and make a dearth in this revolting land. 3.03.163
when our sea–walled garden, the whole land, | is 3.04. 43
that he had not so trimm'd and dress'd his land 3.04. 56
how blest this land would be | in this your 4.01. 18
and this land be call'd | the field of golgotha 4.01.143
speak "pardon" as 'tis current in our land, 5.03.123
the king's blood stain'd the king's own land. 5.05.110
hand | upon my head and all this famous land. 5.06. 36
i'll make a voyage to the holy land, | to wash 5.06. 49
brake off our business for the holy land. 1H4 1.01. 48
you may buy land now as cheap as stinking 2.04.359 P
known to many in our land by the name of pitch. 2.04.412 P
and all the fertile land within that bound, | to 3.01. 76
and cuts me from the best of all my land | a 3.01. 98
and on this north side win this cape of land, 3.01.112
i'll give thrice so much land | to any 3.01.135
the land is burning, percy stands on high, | and 3.03.203
teaching his duteous land | audacious cruelty. 4.03. 44
the special head of all the land together: 4.04. 28
rebellion in this land shall lose his sway, 5.05. 41
we would, dear lords, unto the holy land. 2H4 3.01.108
for him, a court, and now has he land and beefs! 3.02.327 P
he cannot so precisely weed this land | as his 4.01.203
so that this land, like an offensive wife | that 4.01.208
like lean, sterile, and bare land, manur'd, 4.03.119 P
purpose now | to lead out many to the holy land, 4.05.210
which vainly i suppos'd the holy land. 4.05.238
sir, shall we sow the hade land with wheat? 5.01. 14 P
choose what office thou wilt in the land, 'tis 5.03.124 P
"no woman shall succeed in salique land"; H5 1.02. 39
which salique land the french unjustly gloze 1.02. 40
affirm | that the land salique is in germany, 1.02. 44
female | should be inheritrix in salique land; 1.02. 51
nor did the french possess the salique land 1.02. 56
galling the gleaned land with hot assays, 1.02.151
for he is footed in this land already. 2.04.143
o, for honor of our land, | let us not hang like 3.05. 22
that sweeps through our land | with pennons 3.05. 48
so let him land, | and solemnly see him set on 5.pr. 13
your grief, the common grief of all the land. 2H6 1.01. 77
than all the princes in the land beside. 1.01.176
while they do tend the profit of the land. 1.01.204
as he loves the land | and common profit of his 1.01.205
fact | did never traitor in the land commit. 1.03.174
and thou a prince, protector of this land, 2.04. 29
wife, | and he a prince, and ruler of the land; 2.04. 43
and equity exil'd your highness' land. 3.01.146
with diamonds, | and threw it towards thy land. 3.02.108
'tis not the land i care for, wert thou thence; 3.02.359
to greet mine own land with my wishful sight. 3H6 3.01. 14
no, harry, harry, 'tis no land of thine; 3.01. 15
his land then seiz'd on by the conqueror. 3.02. 3
i'll undertake to land them on our coast, | and 3.03.205
and that the people of this blessed land | may 4.06. 21
i make you both protectors of this land, | while 4.06. 41
woe to that land that's govern'd by a child! R3 2.03. 11
for then this land was famously enrich'd | with 2.03. 19
rule, | this sickly land might solace as before. 2.03. 30
not for all this land | would i be guilty of so 3.01. 42
else wherefore breathe i in a christian land? 3.07.116
and kingly government of this your land: 3.07.132
if not to bless us and the land withal, | yet to 3.07.197
if you deny them, all the land will rue it. 3.07.222
that ever yet this land was guilty of. 4.03. 3
herself, the land, and many a christian soul, 4.04.408
thus far into the bowels of the land | have we 5.02. 3
our fathers | have in their own land beaten, 5.03.334
a hand as fruitful as the land that feeds us; H8 1.03. 56
yea, the elect o' th' land, who are assembled 2.04. 60
by all the reverend fathers of the land | and 2.04.206
from her | will fall some blessing to this land, 3.02. 51
robb'd this bewailing land | of noble buckingham 3.02.255
all the land knows that. 4.01.105
a pestilence | that does infect the land; 5.01. 46
upon this land a thousand thousand blessings, 5.04. 19
which you priz'd | richer than sea and land? TRO 2.02. 92
of tribunes, such as you, | a sea and land full. COR 5.04. 55
yet there's as little justice as at land. TIT 4.03. 9
ay, defil'd land, my lord. TIM 1.02.225
let all my land be sold. 2.02.145
to lacedaemon did my land extend. 2.02.151
and he shall wear his crown by sea and land, JC 1.03. 87
hand in hand, | posters of the sea and land, MAC 1.03. 33
what had he done, to make him fly the land? 4.02. 1
cast | the water of my land, find her disease, 5.03. 51
so nightly toils the subject of the land, | and HAM 1.01. 72
of this post–haste and romage in the land. 1.01.107
his clutch, | and hath shipped me into the land, 5.01. 73
might be in 's time a great buyer of land, with 5.01.104 P
he hath much land, and fertile; 5.02. 85 P
then, | legitimate edgar, i must have your land. LR 1.02. 16
tell him, so much the rent of his land comes to. 1.04.135 P
not in this land shall he remain uncaught; 2.01. 57
may have due note of him, and of my land, 2.01. 83
faith, he to–night hath boarded a land carract. OTH 1.02. 50
i'll sell all my land. 1.03.382 P
methinks the wind hath spoke aloud at land, | a 2.01. 5
both what by sea and land i can be able | to ANT 1.04. 78
what is his strength by land? 2.02.161
at land, thou know'st | how much we do 2.06. 25
at land indeed | thou dost o'er–count me of my 2.06. 26
and you by land. 2.06. 87 P
it cannot be denied what i have done by land. 2.06. 89 P
and you by land. 2.06. 93 P
there i deny my land service. 2.06. 94 P
we should have met you | by sea and land, 3.06. 54
refusing him at sea, | being prepar'd for land. 3.07. 40
the absolute soldiership you have by land, 3.07. 42

but if we fail, | we then can do't at land. 3.07. 53
our nineteen legions thou shalt hold by land, 3.07. 58
you keep by land | the legions and the horse 3.07. 70
but we keep whole by land. 3.07. 74
strike not by land, keep whole, provoke not 3.08. 3
hark, the land bids me tread no more upon't, 3.11. 1
our force by land | hath nobly held; 3.13.169
soldier, | by sea and land i'll fight; 4.02. 5
had once prevail'd | to make me fight at land! 4.05. 3
is to-day by sea, | we please them not by land. 4.10. 2
but being charg'd, we will be still by land, 4.11. 1
you have land enough of your own, but he added CYM 1.02. 17 P
arch and the rich crop | of sea and land, which 1.06. 34
t' enjoy thy banish'd lord and this great land! 2.01. 65
the swiftest harts have posted you by land, 2.04. 27
or stomach-qualm'd at land, a dram of this 3.04.190
with hostile forces he'll o'erspread the land, PER 1.02. 24
lop that doubt, he'll fill this land with arms, 1.02. 90
he scap'd the land to perish at the sea. 1.03. 28
such whales have i heard on a' th' land, who 2.01. 33 P
we would purge the land of these drones, that 2.01. 46 P
each took | a several land. TNK 3.01. 2
i sav'd her, | and set her safe to land; 4.01. 96
on her bare breast, the heart of all her land; LUC 439
for nimble thought can jump both sea and land SON 44. 7
LAND-DAMN 1 FR 0.0001 REL FR 1 V 0 P
i knew the villain, | i would land-damn him. WT 2.01.143
LANDED 15 FR 0.0017 REL FR 14 V 1 P
the king's son have i landed by himself, | whom TMP 1.02.221
this shore (where you were wrack'd) was landed, 5.01.161
that slender, though well landed, is an idiot; WIV 4.04. 86
well arriv'd from delphos, are both landed, WT 2.03.196
my lord, and fear | we have landed in ill time: 3.03. 3
a landless knight makes thee a landed squire. JN 1.01.177
that thou for truth giv'st out are landed here? 4.02.130
king, who lately landed | with some few private R2 3.03. 3
they are already or quickly will be landed. 3H6 4.01.132
is with a mighty power landed at milford | is R3 4.04.533
th' have left their barge and landed, | and H8 1.04. 54
the army of france is landed. LR 3.07. 3 P
i told him of the army that was landed; 4.02. 4
the legion now in gallia sooner landed | in our CYM 2.04. 18
are landed on your coast, with a supply | of 4.03. 25
LAND-FISH 1 FR 0.0001 REL FR 0 V 1 P
he's grown a very land-fish, languageless, a TRO 3.03.263 P
LANDING 2 FR 0.0002 REL FR 2 V 0 P
upon her landing, antony sent to her, | invited ANT 2.02.219
but since my landing i have understood | your PER 1.03. 33
LANDLESS 1 FR 0.0001 REL FR 1 V 0 P
a landless knight makes thee a landed squire. JN 1.01.177
LANDLORD 3 FR 0.0003 REL FR 3 V 0 P
landlord of england art thou now, not king, R2 2.01.113
under his shroud, | the universal landlord. ANT 3.13. 72
than the true gouty landlord which doth owe them LC 140
LANDMEN 1 FR 0.0001 REL FR 1 V 0 P
an absolute hope | our landmen will stand up. ANT 4.03. 11
LAND-RAKERS 1 FR 0.0001 REL FR 0 V 1 P
i am join'd with no foot land-rakers, no 1H4 2.01. 73 P
LAND-RATS 1 FR 0.0001 REL FR 0 V 1 P
there be land-rats and water-rats, water-thieves MV 1.03. 23 P
LAND'S 5 FR 0.0005 REL FR 5 V 0 P
my earnest-gaping sight of thy land's view, | i 2H6 3.02.105
let them not live to taste this land's increase R3 5.05. 38
would with treason wound this fair land's peace! 5.05. 39
of gleaning all the land's wealth into one, H8 3.02.284
his land's put to their books. TIM 1.02.200
LANDS 55 FR 0.0062 REL FR 50 V 5 P
dispose, | my goods, my lands, my reputation; TGV 2.07. 87
money buys lands, and wives are sold by fate. WIV 5.05.233
passages of alleys, creeks, and narrow lands; ERR 4.02. 38
of christian blood, thy lands and goods | are, MV 4.01.310
whose lands and revenues enrich the new duke; AYL 1.01.102 P
thy lands and all things that thou dost call 3.01. 9
make an extent upon his house and lands. 3.01. 17
you have sold your own lands to see other men's; 4.01. 23 P
and all their lands restor'd to /them again 5.04.164
to one his lands withheld, and to the other | a 5.04.168
me, | left soly heir to all his lands and goods, SHR 2.01.117
after my death the one half of my lands, | and 2.01.121
me, | in all my lands and leases whatsoever. 2.01.125
is mine only son, and heir to the lands of me, 5.01. 85 P
the world, | prizes not quantity of dirty lands; TN 2.04. 82
the lands and waters 'twixt your throne and his WT 5.01.144
he by will bequeath'd | his lands to me, and JN 1.01.110
and coops from other lands her islanders, | even 2.01. 25
house, | against the envy of less happier lands; R2 2.01. 49
his plate, his goods, his money, and his lands. 2.01.210
our lands, our lives, and all are bullingbrook's 3.02.151
and lands restor'd again be freely granted. 3.03. 41
restor'd again | to all his lands and signories. 4.01. 89
for all the temporal lands, which men devout H5 1.01. 9
lives, honors, lands, and all, hurry to loss. 1H6 4.03. 53
while his own lands are bargain'd for and sold. 2H6 1.01.231
for keeping my house, and lands, and wife and 1.03. 18 P
was better worth than all my father's lands, 1.03. 86
lands, goods, horse, armor, any thing i have 5.01. 52
so shalt thou sinow both these lands together, 3H6 2.06. 91
her suit is now to repossess those lands, 3.02. 4
then i'll warrant you all your lands, | and if 3.02. 21
pity they should lose their father's lands. 3.02. 31
then get your husband's lands, to do them good. 3.02. 40
i'll tell you how these lands are to be got. 3.02. 42
then, thy husband's lands i freely give thee. 3.02. 55
then thou shalt not have thy husband's lands. 3.02. 71
her suit is granted for her husband's lands. 3.02.117
and all his lands and goods confiscate. 4.06. 55
and of all my lands | is nothing left me but my 5.02. 25
you having lands, and blest with beauteous wives R3 5.03.321
shall these enjoy our lands? 5.03.336
to forfeit all your goods, lands, tenements, H8 3.02.342
and all the lands thou hast | lie in a pitch'd TIM 1.02.224
'tis honor with most lands to be at odds; 3.05.115
crimes, like lands, | are not inherited. 5.04. 37
i should cut off the nobles for their lands, MAC 4.03. 79
all /those his lands | which he stood seiz'd of, HAM 1.01. 88
those foresaid lands | so by his father lost; 1.01.103
importing the surrender of those lands | lost by 1.02. 23
conveyances of his lands will scarcely lie in 5.01.111 P
let me, if not by birth, have lands by wit: LR 1.02.183
of succession, as | thou refts me of my lands. CYM 3.03.103
the merchant fears, ere rich at home he lands." LUC 336
which abroad they find | of lands and mansions, LC 138
LAND-SERVICE 2 FR 0.0002 REL FR 0 V 2 P
and then for the land-service, to see how the WT 3.03. 94 P
counsel in the laws of this land-service, i did 2H4 1.02.135 P
LAND-THIEVES 1 FR 0.0001 REL FR 0 V 1 P
water-thieves and land-thieves, i mean pirates, MV 1.03. 23 P
LANE 8 FR 0.0009 REL FR 7 V 1 P
you four shall front them in the narrow lane; 1H4 2.02. 61 P
three times did richard make a lane to me, | and 3H6 1.04. 9
advantage of the ground, | the lane is guarded. CYM 5.02. 12
seen, all flying | through a strait lane; 5.03. 7
where was this lane? 5.03. 13
athwart the lane, | he, with two striplings 5.03. 18
a narrow lane, an old man, and two boys! 5.03. 52
"two boys, an old man (twice a boy), a lane, 5.03. 57
LANE'S 2 FR 0.0002 REL FR 0 V 2 P
my troth, i'll go with thee to the lane's end. MM 4.03.177 P
every lane's end, every shop, church, session, WT 4.04.685 P
LANES 3 FR 0.0003 REL FR 3 V 0 P
as stand in narrow lanes | and beat our watch R2 5.03. 8
attended him on bridges, stood in lanes, | laid 1H4 4.03. 70
with prey, | make lanes in troops aghast. TNK 1.04. 19
LANGAGE 1 FR 0.0001 REL FR 0 V 1 P
ete en angleterre, et tu bien parles le langage. H5 3.04. 2 P
LANGLEY 3 FR 0.0003 REL FR 3 V 0 P
deriv'd | from famous edmund langley, duke of 1H6 2.05. 85
the fift was edmund langley, duke of york; 2H6 2.02. 15
who was | to edmund langley, edward the third'i 2.02. 46
L'ANGLOIS 2 FR 0.0002 REL FR 0 V 2 P
dites-moi l'anglois pour le bras. H5 3.04. 21 P
il est /meilleur que l'anglois lequel je parle. 5.02.189 P
LANGTON 1 FR 0.0001 REL FR 1 V 0 P
and force perforce | keep stephen langton, JN 3.01.143
LANGUAGE 43 FR 0.0048 REL FR 34 V 9 P
you taught me language, and my profit on't | is, TMP 1.02.363
rid you | for learning me your language! 1.02.365
my language? 1.02.429
and surely | it is a sleepy language, and thou 2.01.211
where the devil should he learn our language? 2.02. 67 P
here is that which will give language to you, 2.02. 83 P
in any proportion, or in any language. MM 1.02. 22 P
let me entreat you speak the former language. 2.04.140
there is not chastity enough in language ADO 4.01. 97
if they do speak our language, 'tis our will LLL 5.02.176
they say our french lack language to deny | if AWW 2.01. 20
ay; is it not a language i speak? 2.03.189 P
upon him, speak what terrible language you will. 4.01. 3 P
choughs' language, gabble enough, and good 4.01. 19 P
and i shall lose my life for want of language. 4.01. 70
should a like language use to all degrees, | and WT 2.01. 85
you speak a language that i understand not. 3.02. 80
their dumbness, language in their very gesture; 5.02. 13 P
the language i have learnt these forty years, R2 1.03.159
any tinker in his own language during my life. 1H4 2.04. 19 P
till i have learn'd thy language, for thy tongue 3.01.205
ride, | the which in every language i pronounce, 2H4 in 7
a strange tongue, wherein, to gain the language, 4.04. 69
upbraided or abus'd in disdainful language; H5 3.06.111 P
for he is fierce and cannot brook hard language. 2H6 4.09. 45
even he escapes not | language unmannerly; H8 1.02. 27
as not to know the language i have liv'd in. 3.01. 44
that for ever mars | the honey of his language. 3.02. 22
he has strangled | his language in his tears. 5.01.157
i shall remember this bold language. 5.02.119
there's language in her eye, her cheek, her lip, TRO 4.05. 55
sword, and is ill school'd | in bolted language; COR 3.01.320
ay, if i know the letters and the language. ROM 1.02. 61
lips, let four words go by and language end! TIM 5.01.220
this is not hunters' language. CYM 3.03. 74
with language that would make me spurn the sea 5.05.294
to use one language in each several clime PER 4.04. 6
and that | i ear'd her language, liv'd in her TNK 3.01. 29
give me language such | as thou hast show'd me 3.01. 44
me and pour | this oil out of your language. 3.01.103
yet pardon me hard language. 3.01.106
names concealments in | the boldest language. 5.01.124
kissing speaks, with lustful language broken, VEN 47
LANGUAGELESS 1 FR 0.0001 REL FR 0 V 1 P
he's grown a very land-fish, languageless, a TRO 3.03.263 P
LANGUAGES 4 FR 0.0004 REL FR 0 V 4 P
they have been at a great feast of languages, LLL 5.01. 37 P
latin, and other languages, as the other in SHR 2.01. 81 P
he hath a smack of all neighboring languages; AWW 4.01. 16 P
three or four languages word for word without TN 1.03. 26 P
LANGUES 1 FR 0.0001 REL FR 0 V 1 P
les langues des hommes sont pleines de H5 5.02.115 P
LANGUISH 7 FR 0.0008 REL FR 7 V 0 P
love and languish for his sake. MND 2.02. 29
aim had ta'en a hurt, | did come to languish; AYL 2.01. 35
desperate grief cures with another's languish: ROM 1.02. 48
of death too, | that rids our dogs of languish? ANT 5.02. 42
nay, let her languish | a drop of blood a day, CYM 1.01.156
be, will 's free hours languish for | assured 1.06. 72
makes both my body pine and soul to languish, PER 1.02. 32
LANGUISH'D 2 FR 0.0002 REL FR 2 V 0 P
appetite, his sleep, | and downright languish'd. WT 2.03. 17
"i hate" | to me that languish'd for her sake; SON 145. 3
LANGUISHES 2 FR 0.0002 REL FR 1 V 1 P
is it, my good lord, the king languishes of? AWW 1.01. 32 P
a man that languishes in your displeasure. OTH 3.03. 43
LANGUISHETH 1 FR 0.0001 REL FR 1 V 0 P
even so she languisheth in her mishaps, | as VEN 603
LANGUISHING 1 FR 0.0001 REL FR 1 V 0 P
which are the movers of a languishing death, CYM 1.05. 9
LANGUISHINGS 1 FR 0.0001 REL FR 1 V 0 P
to cure the desperate languishings whereof | the AWW 1.03.229
LANGUISHMENT 3 FR 0.0003 REL FR 3 V 0 P
a speedier course /than ling'ring languishment TIT 2.01.110
as the dank earth weeps at thy languishment, LUC 1130
tune our heart-strings to true languishment. 1141
LANGUOR 1 FR 0.0001 REL FR 1 V 0 P
in the dust i write | my heart's deep languor, TIT 3.01. 13
LANK 3 FR 0.0003 REL FR 3 V 0 P
bags | are lank and lean with thy extortions. 2H6 1.03.129
about her lank and all o'er-teemed loins, | a HAM 2.02.508
and then with lank and lean discolor'd cheek, LUC 708
LANK'D 1 FR 0.0001 REL FR 1 V 0 P
soldier, that thy cheek | so much as lank'd not. ANT 1.04. 71
LANK-LEAN 1 FR 0.0001 REL FR 1 V 0 P
investing lank-lean cheeks and war-worn coats, H5 4.pr. 26
LANTERN 5 FR 0.0005 REL FR 1 V 4 P
come in with a bush of thorns and a lantern, and MND 3.01. 60 P
this man, with lantern, dog, and bush of thorn, 5.01.135
i prithee lend me thy lantern, to see my gelding 1H4 2.01. 34 P
lend me thy lantern, quoth he! 2.01. 39 P
admiral, thou bearest the lantern in the poop, 3.03. 25 P
LANTHORN 9 FR 0.0010 REL FR 4 V 5 P
therefore bear you the lanthorn. ADO 3.03. 24 P
this lanthorn doth the horned moon present — MND 5.01.239
this lanthorn doth the horned moon present; 5.01.244
the man should be put into the lanthorn. 5.01.247 P
is to tell you that the lanthorn is the moon, i 5.01.258 P
why, all these should be in the lanthorn; 5.01.260 P
though he have his own lanthorn to light him. 2H4 1.02. 48 P
my stay, my guide, and lanthorn to my feet; 2H6 2.03. 25
a lanthorn, slaught'red youth; ROM 5.03. 84
LANTHORNS 1 FR 0.0001 REL FR 1 V 0 P
and twenty glow-worms shall our lanthorns be, WIV 5.05. 78
/LAP* 1 FR 0.0001 REL FR 0 V 1 P
/i /mean, /my /head /upon /your /lap? HAM 3.02.114 P
LAP* 20 FR 0.0022 REL FR 16 V 4 P
i will live in thy heart, die in thy lap, and be ADO 5.02.102 P
fall in the fresh lap of the crimson rose, | and MND 2.01.108
the fresh green lap of fair king richard's land, R2 3.03. 47
that strew the green lap of the new-come spring? 5.02. 47
down, | and rest your gentle head upon her lap, 1H4 3.01.212
quick, quick, that i may lay my head in thy lap. 3.01.227 P
then, pistol, lay thy head in furies' lap. 2H4 5.03.106
and let her head fall into england's lap. 1H6 5.03. 26
else | but like a pleasant slumber in thy lap? 2H6 3.02.390
i'll make my heaven in a lady's lap, | and deck 3H6 3.02.148
how he did lap me | even in his /own garments, R3 2.01.116
to worry lambs and lap their gentle blood, 4.04. 50
good boy, in virgo's lap; TIT 4.03. 65
eyes, | nor ope her lap to saint-seducing gold. ROM 1.01.214
uncover, dogs, and lap! TIM 3.06. 85 P
the consecrated snow | that lies on dian's lap! 4.03.386
a sailor's wife had chestnuts in her lap, | and MAC 1.03. 4
lady, shall i lie in your lap? HAM 3.02.112 P
can from the lap of egypt's widow pluck | the ANT 2.01. 37
or from their proud lap pluck them where they SON 98. 8
LAPIS 3 FR 0.0003 REL FR 0 V 3 P
what is lapis, william? WIV 4.01. 31 P
it is lapis. 4.01. 35 P
lapis. 4.01. 37 P
LAPLAND 1 FR 0.0001 REL FR 1 V 0 P
wiles, | and lapland sorcerers inhabit here. ERR 4.03. 11
LAPP'D 3 FR 0.0003 REL FR 3 V 0 P
till that bellona's bridegroom, lapp'd in proof, MAC 1.02. 54
he, sir, was lapp'd | in a most curious mantle, CYM 5.05.360
all thy friends are lapp'd in lead; PP 20.24
LAPS* 2 FR 0.0002 REL FR 2 V 0 P
they'll take suggestion as a cat laps milk; TMP 2.01.288
and pour our treasures into foreign laps; OTH 4.03. 88
LAPS'D 1 FR 0.0001 REL FR 1 V 0 P
that, laps'd in time and passion, lets go by HAM 3.04.107
LAPSE 2 FR 0.0002 REL FR 2 V 0 P
into the staggers and the careless lapse | of AWW 2.03.163
to lapse in fullness | is sorer than to lie for CYM 3.06. 12
LAPSED 1 FR 0.0001 REL FR 1 V 0 P
out, | for which, if i be lapsed in this place, TN 3.03. 36
LAPSING 1 FR 0.0001 REL FR 1 V 0 P
size that verity | would without lapsing suffer. COR 5.02. 19
LAPWING 4 FR 0.0004 REL FR 3 V 1 P
familiar sin | with maids to seem the lapwing, MM 1.04. 32
far from her nest the lapwing cries away; ERR 4.02. 27
for look where beatrice, like a lapwing, runs ADO 3.01. 24
this lapwing runs away with the shell on his HAM 5.02.185 P
LARDED 4 FR 0.0004 REL FR 3 V 1 P
the mirth whereof so larded with my matter, WIV 4.06. 14
should wit larded with malice and malice fac'd TRO 5.01. 57 P
"larded all with sweet flowers, | which bewept HAM 4.05. 38
larded with many several sorts of reasons, 5.02. 20
LARDER 1 FR 0.0001 REL FR 0 V 1 P
good master porter, i belong to th' larder. H8 5.03. 5 P
LARDING 1 FR 0.0001 REL FR 1 V 0 P
brave soldier, doth he lie, | larding the plain; H5 4.06. 8
LARDS 3 FR 0.0003 REL FR 2 V 1 P
and lards the lean earth as he walks along. 1H4 2.02.109
it is the paster lards the brother's sides, TIM 4.03. 12
soe'er she's about, the name palamon lards it, TNK 4.03. 7 P
LARGE 75 FR 0.0084 REL FR 72 V 3 P
man) my library | was dukedom large enough: TMP 1.02.110
confer at large | of all that may concern thy TGV 3.01.255
where you with silvia may confer at large — 3.02. 61
image of the jest | i'll show you here at large. WIV 4.06. 18
are not these large enough? MM 1.04. 2
is, | i long to know the truth hereof at large. ERR 4.04.143
and hear at large discoursed all our fortunes; 5.01.396
not in him by some large jests he will make. ADO 2.03.198 P
i never tempted her with word too large, | but, 4.01. 52
so to the laws at large i write my name, | and LLL 1.01.155
and the world's large tongue | proclaims you for 5.02.842
and kiss thy fair large ears, my gentle joy. MND 4.01. 4
and lovers twain | at large discourse, while 5.01.151
withal, as large a charter as the wind, | to AYL 2.07. 48
and to the other | a land itself at large, a 5.04.169
o doricles, | your praises are too large. WT 4.04.147
my son | in the large composition of this man? JN 1.01. 88
large lengths of seas and shores | between my 1.01.105
this little abstract doth contain that large 2.01.101
here's a large mouth indeed, | that spits forth 2.01.457
give with our niece a dowry large enough, | for 2.01.469
in some large measure to thy father's death, R2 1.02. 26
shall subscribe them for large sums of gold, 1.04. 50
with letters of your love to her at large. 3.01. 41
and my large kingdom for a little grave, | a 3.03.153
appear | at large discoursed in this paper here. 5.06. 10
peace | upon such large terms and so absolute 2H4 4.01.184
this packet, please it you, contains at large. 4.04.101
which i have open'd to his grace at large, | as H5 1.01. 78
ruling in large and ample empery | o'er france 1.02.226

do not, in grant of all demands at large, 2.04.121
the circumstance i'll tell you more at large. 1H6 1.01.109
o'ercharging your free purses with large fines; 1.03. 64
but we shall meet, and break our minds at large. 1.03. 81
and large proportion of his strong–knit limbs. 2.03. 21
discover more at large what cause that was, 2.05. 59
in marriage, with a large and sumptuous dowry. 5.01. 20
i have inform'd his highness so at large, | as, 5.01. 42
whose large style | agrees not with the leanness 2H6 1.01.111
large sums of gold and dowries with their wives, 1.01.129
as more at large your grace shall understand. 2.01.173
large gifts have i bestow'd on learned clerks, 4.07. 71
and, that once gotten, doubt not of large pay. 3H6 4.07. 88
you sent a large commission | to gregory de H8 3.02.320
at this fusty stuff | the large achilles, on his TRO 1.03.162
fair leave and large security. 1.03.223
of the giant mass | of things to come at large. 1.03.346
the world's large spaces cannot parallel. 2.02.162
and fell so roundly to a large confession, | to 3.02.154
shall find him by his large and portly size. 4.05.162
there will be large cicatrices to show the COR 2.01.148 P
/throng our large temples with the shows of 3.03. 36
thou wouldst else have made thy tale large. ROM 2.04. 97 P
his large fortune, | upon his good and gracious TIM 1.01. 55
and let out | their coin upon large interest — 3.05.107
interest — i myself | rich only in large hurts. 3.05.108
to pay thy soldiers, | make large confusion; 4.03.128
not all the whips of heaven are large enough — 5.01. 61
and sell the mighty space of our large honors JC 4.03. 25
be large in mirth; MAC 3.04. 11
we shall not spend a large expense of time 5.09. 26
sure he that made us with such large discourse, HAM 4.04. 36
and all the large effects | that troop with LR 1.01.131
and your large speeches may your deeds approve, 1.01.184
he calls me to a restitution large | of gold and OTH 5.01. 15
antony, most large | in his abominations, turns ANT 3.06. 93
you have at large received | the danger of the PER 1.01. 1
let me entreat to know at large the cause | of 5.01. 62
to her marriage, | a large one, i'll assure you. TNK 4.01. 24
i have been harsh | to large confessors, and 5.01.105
to leap large lengths of miles when thou art SON 44.10
take heed, dear heart, of this large privilege, 95.13
wilt thou, whose will is large and spacious, 135. 5
one will of mine, to make thy large will more. 135.12
why so large cost, having so short a lease, 146. 5

LARGE–HANDED 1 FR 0.0001 REL FR 1 V 0 P
large–handed robbers your grave masters are, TIM 4.01. 11

LARGELY 4 FR 0.0004 REL FR 3 V 1 P
but have given largely to many to know what she WIV 2.02.199 P
i'll tell you largely of fair hero's death. ADO 5.04. 69
and our supplies live largely in the hope | of 2H4 1.03. 12
cup | and her prosperities so largely taste, PER 1.04. 53

LARGENESS 2 FR 0.0002 REL FR 2 V 0 P
earth below | fails in the promis'd largeness. TRO 1.03. 5
what largeness thinks in paradise was sawn. LC 91

LARGER 5 FR 0.0005 REL FR 5 V 0 P
a larger dare to our great enterprise, | than if 1H4 4.01. 78
and with a larger teder may he walk | than may HAM 1.03.125
to grosser issues nor to larger reach | than to OTH 3.03.219
and what may follow, | to try a larger fortune. ANT 2.06. 34
lycaonia, | with a more larger list of sceptres. 3.06. 76

LARGESS 5 FR 0.0005 REL FR 5 V 0 P
liberality, | i'll mend it with a largess. SHR 1.02.150
with too great a court | and liberal largess, R2 1.04. 44
a largess universal, like the sun, | his liberal H5 4.pr. 43
and | sent forth great largess to your offices. MAC 2.01. 14
the bounteous largess given thee to give? SON 4. 6

LARGEST 1 FR 0.0001 REL FR 1 V 0 P
that we our largest bounty may extend | where LR 1.01. 52

LARK 26 FR 0.0029 REL FR 24 V 2 P
air | more tuneable than lark to shepherd's ear MND 1.01.184
the finch, the sparrow, and the lark, | the 3.01.130
i do hear the morning lark. 4.01. 94
the crow doth sing as sweetly as the lark | when MV 5.01.102
hast hawks will soar | above the morning lark. SHR in.2. 44
what, is the jay more precious than the lark, 4.03.175
i took this lark for a bunting. AWW 2.05. 6 P
the lark, that tirra–lyra chaunts, | with heigh, WT 4.03. 9
the rising of the lark to the lodging of the H5 3.07. 32 P
stir with the lark to–morrow, gentle norfolk. R3 5.03. 56
with your theme, i could | o'ermount the lark. H8 2.03. 94
wak'd by the lark, hath rous'd the ribald crows, TRO 4.02. 9
'tis true, the raven doth not hatch a lark, TIT 2.03.149
did ever raven sing so like a lark | that gives 3.01.158
it was the nightingale, and not the lark, | that ROM 3.05. 2
it was the lark, the herald of the morn, | no 3.05. 6
nor that is not the lark whose notes do beat 3.05. 21
it is the lark that sings so out of tune, 3.05. 27
some say the lark makes sweet division; 3.05. 29
some say the lark and loathed toad change eyes; 3.05. 31
the shrill–gorg'd lark so far | cannot be seen LR 4.06. 58
hark, hark, the lark at heaven's gate sings, CYM 2.03. 20
to th' owl and morn to th' lark less welcome. 3.06. 93
lo here the gentle lark, weary of rest, | from VEN 853
and wish her lays were tuned like the lark. PP 14.18
(like to the lark at break of day arising | from SON 29.11

LARKS 3 FR 0.0003 REL FR 3 V 0 P
straws | and merry larks are ploughmen's clocks; LLL 5.02.904
shriek where mounting larks should sing. R2 3.03.183
forward, | and dare us with his cap, like larks. H8 3.02.282

LARKS'–HEELS 1 FR 0.0001 REL FR 1 V 0 P
on death–beds blowing, | larks'–heels trim; TNK 1.01. 12

LAROON 1 FR 0.0001 REL FR 0 V 1 P
laroon! WIV 1.04. 68 P

/LARTIUS 1 FR 0.0001 REL FR 1 V 0 P
titus /lartius, thou | shalt see me once more COR 1.01.239

LARTIUS 7 FR 0.0008 REL FR 5 V 2 P
and titus lartius, a most valiant roman, | these COR 1.02. 14
your lord and titus lartius are set down before 1.03. 98 P
and given to lartius and to martius battle. 1.06. 11
of warriors, | how is't with titus lartius? 1.06. 33
you, titus lartius, | must to corioles back. 1.09. 75
titus lartius writes they fought together, but 2.01.127 P
of the volsces and | to send for titus lartius, 2.02. 38

'LARUM *(also alarm, etc., alarum, etc.)*

'LARUM 2 FR 0.0002 REL FR 1 V 1 P
dwelling in a continual 'larum of jealousy, WIV 3.05. 72 P
then shall we hear their 'larum, and they ours. COR 1.04. 9

'LARUM–BELL 1 FR 0.0001 REL FR 1 V 0 P
couch | a watch–case or a common 'larum–bell? 2H4 3.01. 17

'LARUMS 2 FR 0.0002 REL FR 2 V 0 P
i not in a pitched battle heard | loud 'larums, SHR 1.02.206
and with loud 'larums welcome them to rome. TIT 1.01.147

LASCIVIOUS 15 FR 0.0017 REL FR 11 V 4 P
the loose encounters of lascivious men: TGV 2.07. 41
will find you twenty lascivious turtles ere one WIV 2.01. 81 P
count to be a dangerous and lascivious boy, who AWW 4.03.220 P
of that lascivious young boy the count, have i 4.03.300 P
lascivious metres, to whose venom sound | the R2 2.01. 19
lascivious, wanton, more than well beseems | a 1H6 3.01. 19
lascivious edward, and thou perjur'd george, 3H6 5.05. 34
chamber | to the lascivious pleasing of a lute. R3 1.01. 13
lascivious goth, and all the bitterest terms TIT 2.03.110
that's a lascivious apprehension. TIM 1.01.208 P
sound to this coward and lascivious town | our 5.04. 1
to the gross clasps of a lascivious moor — | if OTH 1.01.126
antony, | leave thy lascivious /wassails. ANT 1.04. 56
lascivious grace, in whom all ill well shows, SON 40.13
days | (making lascivious comments on thy sport) 95. 6

LASH 5 FR 0.0005 REL FR 5 V 0 P
lash hence these overweening rags of france, R3 5.03.328
her whip of cricket's bone, the lash of film, ROM 1.04. 66
how smart a lash that speech doth give my HAM 3.01. 49
why dost thou lash that whore? LR 4.06.161
to lash the rascals naked through the world OTH 4.02.143

LASH'D 1 FR 0.0001 REL FR 1 V 0 P
why, headstrong liberty is lash'd with woe: ERR 2.01. 15

/LASS 1 FR 0.0001 REL FR 1 V 0 P
farewell, sweet /lass, thy like ne'er was | for PP 17.33

LASS 9 FR 0.0010 REL FR 9 V 0 P
is it so brave a lass? TMP 3.02.103
before the legs of this sweet lass of france." LLL 5.02.555
it was a lover and his lass, | with a hey, and a AYL 5.03. 16
the house, and show you | the lass i spoke of. AWW 3.06.111
this is the prettiest low–born lass that ever WT 4.04.156
if your lass | interpretation should abuse, and 4.04.352
in thy possession lies | a lass unparallel'd. ANT 5.02.316
come, lass, let's trip it. TNK 3.05. 89
i told them — who | a lass of fourteen brided. 5.01.109

LASSES 1 FR 0.0001 REL FR 1 V 0 P
come buy, | buy, lads, or else your lasses cry: WT 4.04.229

LASS–LORN 1 FR 0.0001 REL FR 1 V 0 P
the dismissed bachelor loves, | being lass–lorn; TMP 4.01. 68

/LAST* 3 FR 0.0003 REL FR 2 V 1 P
than i have of my face when i /last saw him. MV 2.02. 98 P
/follies, | /that /was /at /last //out–fac'd /by R2 4.01.286
/when /last /i /was /at /exeter, | /the /mayor R3 4.02.103

LAST* 298 FR 0.0336 REL FR 241 V 57 P
sit still, and hear the last of our sea–sorrow: TMP 1.02.170
which i do last pronounce, is (o you wonder!) 1.02.427
although my last, no matter, since i feel | the 3.03. 50
thou and thy meaner fellows your last service 4.01. 35
at last i left them | i' th' filthy–mantled pool 4.01.181
in this last tempest. 5.01.153
since i saw you last that i fear me will never 5.01.283 P
and yet i was last chidden for being too slow. TGV 2.01. 12 P
for last morning you could not see to wipe my 2.01. 79 P
last night she enjoin'd me to write some lines 2.01. 87 P
till the last step have brought me to my love, 2.07. 36
not mine twice or thrice in that last article. 3.01.356 P
it to alice shortcake upon all–hallowmas last, a WIV 1.01.204 P
and last, as i am a gentleman, you shall, /and 2.02.253 P
carried out, the last time he search'd for him, 4.02. 32 P
him at the door with it, as they did last time. 4.02. 96 P
this will last out a night in russia | when MM 2.01.134
nine, sir; overdone by the last. 2.01.202 P
is't not drown'd i' th' last rain? 3.02. 49 P
but tuesday night last gone, in 's garden–house, 5.01.229
sixpence that i had a' we'nsday last | to pay ERR 1.02. 55
if i last in this service, you must case me in 2.01. 85
belike you thought our love would last too long 4.01. 25
to none of these, except it be the last, 5.01. 55
grief hath chang'd me since you saw me last, 5.01.298
in our last conflict four of his five wits went ADO 1.01. 65 P
as the first of may doth the last of december. 1.01.192 P
at that hour last night | talk with a ruffian at 4.01. 90
lady, were you her bedfellow last night? 4.01.147
no, truly, not, although, until last night, | i 4.01.148
him another staff, this last was broke cross. 5.01.138 P
virtues, yet at last she concluded with a sigh, 5.01.171 P
i am the last that will last keep his oath. LLL 1.01.160
i am the last that will last keep his oath. 1.01.160
that last is berowne, the merry madcap lord. 2.01.215
the last of the five vowels, if "you" repeat 5.01. 53 P
but that it bear this trial, and last love; 5.02.803
when i from thebes came last a conqueror. MND 5.01. 51
your worship was the last man in our mouths. MV 1.03. 60
"fair sir, you spet on me on wednesday last, 1.03.126
on black monday last at six a' clock i' th' 2.05. 25 P
/roof was dry | with oaths of love, at last, if 3.02.205
with oaths of love, at last, if promise last, 3.02.205
fashion of thy malice | to the last hour of act, 4.01. 19
in lieu of this last night did lie with me. 5.01.262
and i will follow thee | to the last gasp, with AYL 2.03. 70
last scene of all, | that ends this strange 2.07.163
god 'ild you for your last company. 3.03. 75 P
when last the young orlando parted from you | he 4.03. 98
when from the first to last betwixt us two 4.03.139
where left we last? SHR 3.01. 26
last night she slept not, nor to–night she shall 4.01.198
but at last i spied | an ancient angel coming 4.02. 60
and happily i have arrived at the last | unto 5.01.127
at last, though long, our jarring notes agree, 5.02. 1
inherit but the fall | of the last monarchy) see AWW 2.01. 14
in fine, made a groan of her last breath, and 4.03. 52 P
the last was the greatest, but that i have not 4.03. 91 P
he hence remov'd last night, and with more haste 5.01. 23
i had talk of you last night; 5.02. 53 P
the last that e'er i took her leave at court, 5.03. 79
thou wast in very gracious fooling last night, TN 2.03. 22 P
that old and antique song we heard last night; 2.04. 3
o fellow, come, the song we had last night. 2.04. 42
send, | after the last enchantment you did here, 3.01.112
yet, when i saw it last, it was besmear'd | as 5.01. 52
my last good deed was to entreat his stay; WT 1.02. 97
'tis far gone, | when i shall gust it last. 1.02.219
but the last — o lords, | when i have said, cry 3.02.199
be, thy mother | appear'd to me last night; 3.03. 18
how often said my dignity would last | but till 4.04.475
at the last | do as the heavens have done, 5.01. 4
grace, which never | my life may last to answer. 5.03. 8
from first to last, the onset and retire | of JN 2.01.326
and, in the last repeating, troublesome, | being 4.02. 19
o, when the last accompt 'twixt heaven and earth 4.02.216
up, | last in the field, and almost lords of it! 5.05. 8
in their throng and press to that last hold, 5.07. 19
since last i went to france to fetch his queen. R2 1.01.131
but ere i last receiv'd the sacrament | i did 1.01.139
the last leave of thee takes my weeping eye. 1.02. 74
so i regreet | the daintiest last, to make the 1.03. 68
come, that i may breathe my last | in wholesome 2.01. 1
as the last taste of sweets, is sweetest last, 2.01. 13
as the last taste of sweets, is sweetest last, 2.01. 13
his rash fierce blaze of riot cannot last, | for 2.01. 33
small show'rs last long, but sudden storms are 2.01. 35
i am the last of noble edward's sons, | of whom 2.01.171
was not so resolv'd when last we spake together. 2.03. 29
comes at the last and with a little pin | bores 3.02.169
letters came last night | to a dear friend of 3.04. 69
belong to me, | and am i last that knows it? 3.04. 94
to serve me last that i may longest keep | thy 3.04. 95
as from my death–bed, thy last living leave. 5.01. 39
'tis full three months since i did see him last. 5.03. 2
nor shall not be the last — like seely beggars 5.05. 25
soul that thou soldest him on good friday last, 1H4 1.02.115 P
it to one of his company last night at supper, a 2.01. 57 P
lips are scarce wip'd since thou drunk'st last. 2.04.154 P
he held me last night at least nine hours | in 3.01.154
i not fall'n away vilely since this last action? 3.03. 2 P
i sent | on tuesday last to listen after news. 2H4 1.01. 29
well, i cannot last ever, but it was alway yet 1.02.214 P
at last i spied his eyes, and methought he had 2.02. 81 P
'twas no longer ago than wed'sday last, i' good 2.04. 87 P
ready are to try our fortunes | to the last man. 4.02. 44
we will eat a last year's pippin of mine own 5.03. 2 P
first my fear, then my cur'sy, last my speech. ep 1 P
in th' eleventh year of the last king's reign H5 1.01. 2
a rascal that swagger'd with me last night; 4.07.126 P
the tenth of august last this dreadful lord, 1H6 1.01.110
recreants, | fight till the last gasp; 1.02.127
of which, my lord, your honor is the last. 2.05. 93
love, | and will at last break out into a flame: 3.01.190
shall we at last conclude effeminate peace? 5.04.107
ay, grief, i fear me, both at first and last. 5.05.102
and would have kept so long as breath did last! 2H6 1.01.211
be my last breathing in this mortal world! 1.02. 21
at last | hume's knavery will be the duchess' 1.02.104
so one by one we'll weed them all at last, | and 1.03. 99
last time, i danc'd attendance on his will 1.03.171
of combat shall be the last of the next month. 1.03.219 P
william of windsor was the seventh and last. 2.02. 17
think i have taken my last draught in this world 2.03. 73 P
and one shilling to the pound, the last subsidy. 4.07. 23 P
and the premised flames of the last day | knit 5.02. 41
if for the last, say ay, and to it, lords. 3H6 2.01.165
when you and i met at saint albons last, | your 2.02.103
and am i guerdon'd at the last with shame? 3.03.191
therefore, at last, i firmly am resolv'd | you 3.03.219
at last by notes of household harmony | they 4.06. 14
montague hath breath'd his last, | and to the 5.02. 40
but at last | i well might hear, delivered with 5.02. 45
last night, i /hear, they lay at stony–stratford R3 2.04. 1
i hope he is much grown since last i saw him. 2.04. 5
than when thou met'st me last where now we meet. 3.02. 99
i am in your debt for your last exercise; 3.02.110
my lord of ely, when i was last in holborn, | i 3.04. 31
and then, in speaking, not to incur the last — 3.07.152
or shall they last, and we rejoice in them? 4.02. 6
still live they, and for ever let them last! 4.02. 7
and came i not at last to comfort you? 4.04.165
last longer telling than thy kindness' date. 4.04.255
but how long shall that title "ever" last? 4.04.350
but how long fairly shall her sweet life last? 4.04.352
the last was i that felt thy tyranny. 5.03.168
how have ye done | since last we saw in france? H8 1.01. 2
master, till the last | made former wonders its. 1.01. 17
king our master | to this last costly treaty — 1.01.165
that, had the king in his last sickness fail'd, 1.02.184
the last hour | of my long weary life is come 2.01.132
for i feel | the last fit of my greatness — 3.01. 78
last, that the lady anne, | whom the king hath 3.02.402
love thyself last, cherish those hearts that 3.02.443
i have, | to the last penny, 'tis the king's. 3.02.452
at our last encounter, | the duke of buckingham 4.01. 4
at last, with easy roads, he came to leicester, 4.02. 17
which he himself | foretold should be his last, 4.02. 27
the last is for my men (they are the poorest, 4.02.148
and urge the king | to do me this last right. 4.02.158
an universal prey, | and last eat up himself. TRO 1.03.124
your last service was suff'rance, 'twas not 2.01. 95 P
i will come last; 3.03. 42
there came news from him last night. COR 1.03. 93 P
he had, before this last expedition, twenty–five 2.01.153 P
the present consul and last general | in our 2.02. 43
for this last, | before and in corioles, let me 2.02.101
power, as now at last | given hostile strokes, 3.03. 96
you had more beard when i last saw you, but your 4.03. 8 P
this last old man, | whom with a crack'd heart i 5.03. 8
but with his last attempt he wip'd it out, 5.03.146
an end, | this is the last. 5.03.172
till at the last | i seem'd his follower, not 5.06. 37
the army marvell'd at it, and, in the last, 5.06. 41
what faults he made before the last, i think 5.06. 63
his last offenses to us | shall have judicious 5.06.125
son, that was the last | that ware the imperial TIT 1.01. 5
and now at last, laden with honor's spoils, 1.01. 36
upright he held it, lords, that held it last. 1.01.200
my lord, be rul'd by me, be won at last, 1.01.442
and here display at last | what god will have 4.01. 73
face, | the last true duties of thy noble son! 5.03.155
with his yard and the tailor with his last, the ROM 1.02. 40 P
how long is't now since last yourself and i 1.05. 32
that last is true — the sweeter rest was mine. 2.03. 43
you gave us the counterfeit fairly last night. 2.04. 45 P

else, when he is found, that hour is his last. 3.01.195
and bid him come to take his last farewell. 3.02.143
eyes, look your last! 5.03.112
arms, take your last embrace! 5.03.113
look in thy last work, where thou hast feign'd TIM 1.01.222 P
he last ask'd the question. 2.02. 59 P
must i be his last refuge? 3.03. 11
of me now, | that i'll requite it last? 3.03. 19
did he bear himself | in the last conflict, and 3.05. 65
this is timon's last, | who, stuck and spangled 3.06. 90
your plague, you his, | and last so long enough! 5.01.190
they shouted thrice; what was the last cry for? JC 1.02.226
what touches us ourself shall be last serv'd. 3.01. 8
though last, not least in love, yours, good 3.01.189
be patient till the last. 3.02. 12
by the gods, this speech were else your last. 4.03. 14
the very last time we shall speak together: 5.01. 98
the last of all the romans, fare thee well! 5.03. 99
and, this last night, here in philippi fields. 5.05. 19
i dreamt last night of the three weird sisters: MAC 2.01. 20
i believe drink gave thee the lie last night. 2.03. 37 P
on tuesday last, | a falcon, tow'ring in her 2.04. 11
i made good to you | in our last conference, 3.01. 79
at first | and last, the hearty welcome. 3.04. 2
when was it she last walk'd? 5.01. 3 P
to day, | to the last syllable of recorded time; 5.05. 21
of no woman born, | yet i will try the last. 5.08. 32
last night of all, | when yond same star that's HAM 1.01. 35
our last king, | whose image even but now 1.01. 80
and at last | upon his will i seal'd my hard 1.02. 59
at last, a little shaking of mine arm, | and 2.01. 89
and to the last bended their light on me. 2.01. 97
why, thy face is valanc'd since i saw thee last; 2.02.423 P
is nearer to heaven than when i saw you last, by 2.02.426 P
of his jaw, first mouth'd, to be last swallow'd. 4.02. 19 P
last, and as much containing as all these, | her 4.05. 87
to't that day that our last king hamlet overcame 5.01.144 P
'a will last you some eight year or nine year. 5.01.167 P
a tanner will last you nine year. 5.01.168 P
been lodg'd | till the last trumpet; 5.01.230
your patience in our last night's speech, 5.01.294
although our last and least, to whose young love LR 1.01. 83
who covers faults, at last with shame derides. 1.01.281
this last surrender of his will but offend us. 1.01.305 P
/come, /come, when saw you my father last? 1.02.152 P
i' th' last night's storm i such a fellow saw, 4.01. 32
nor i know not | where i did lodge last night. 4.07. 67
know of the duke if his last purpose hold, | or 5.01. 1
and from first to last | told him our pilgrimage 5.03.196
lady, | that policy may either last so long, OTH 3.03. 14
i'll perform it | to the last article. 3.03. 22
he did, from first to last. why dost thou ask? 3.03. 96
one more, and that's the last. 5.02. 19
come, my queen, | last night you did desire it. ANT 1.01. 55
at the last, best, | see when and where she died 1.03. 61
last thing he did, dear queen, | he kiss'd — 1.05. 39
he kiss'd — the last of many doubled kisses — 1.05. 40
since i saw you last, | there's a change upon 2.06. 52
but, first | or last, your fine egyptian cookery 2.06. 63
know that to–morrow the last of many battles 4.01. 11
this last day was | a shrewd one to 's. 4.09. 4
say that the last i spoke was "antony," | and 4.13. 8
the last she spake | was "antony, most noble 4.14. 29
'tis the last service that i shall command you. 4.14.132
of many thousand kisses the poor last | i lay 4.15. 20
come then, and take the last warmth of my lips. 5.02.291
bravest at the last, | she levell'd at our 5.02.335
who was last with them? 5.02.338
what was the last | that he spake to thee? CYM 1.03. 4
much like an argument that fell out last night, 1.04. 56 P
would hazard the winning both of first and last. 1.04. 93 P
lie speechless, and his name | is at last gasp. 1.05. 53
last night 'twas on mine arm; 2.03.146
my lord, when last i went to visit her, | she 3.05. 45
last night the very gods show'd me a vision | (i 4.02.346
sharp physic is the last. PER 1.01. 72
him, and at last devour them all at a mouthful. 2.01. 31 P
bots on't, 'tis come at last, and 'tis turn'd to 2.01.118 P
and what's | the sixt and last, the which the 2.02. 40
to you | for your sweet music this last night. 2.05. 26
at last from tyre, | fame answering the most 3.ch. 21
upon thy grave | while summer days doth last. 4.01. 17
this, my last boon, give me, | for such kindness 5.02. 3
that can | from first to last resolve you. 5.03. 61
led on by heaven, and crown'd with joy at last. 5.03. 90
will long last and be more costly than | your TNK 1.01.132
of our fate, | who hath bounded our last minute. 1.02.103
been taken | when their last hurts were given, 1.04. 26
last, and greatest, | i would be thought a 2.05. 14
this blest morning | shall be the last; 3.06. 14
last let me entreat, sir. 3.06.210
i'll warrant ye he had not so few last night 4.01.137
this is my last | of vestal office; 5.01.149
be yet unbroken, | give me thy last words; 5.04. 89
i have told my last hour; 5.04. 92
had ta'en his last leave of the weeping morn, VEN 2
would they not wish the feast might ever last, 447
and as they last, their verdour still endure, 507
and yields at last to every light impression? 566
love breaks through, and picks them all at last. 576
thy violent vanities can never last. LUC 894
at last she thus begins: 1303
at last she calls to mind where hangs a piece 1366
at last she sees a wretched image bound, | that 1501
at last she smilingly with this gives o'er; 1567
at last he takes her by the bloodless hand, 1597
time, cease thou thy course and last no longer, 1765
at last it rains, and busy winds give o'er: 1790
she bade love last, and yet she fell a–turning. PP 7.16
in days long since, before these last so bad. SON 67.14
if thou wilt leave me, do not leave me last, 90. 9
though reason weep and cry, 'it is thy last.' LC 168

LASTED 2 FR 0.0002 REL FR 2 V 0 P
he lasted long, | but on us both did haggish age AWW 1.02. 28
which, whiles it lasted, gave king henry light. 3H6 2.06. 2

LASTING 17 FR 0.0019 REL FR 17 V 0 P
and set it down | with gold on lasting pillars: TMP 5.01.208
keep fresh | and lasting in her sad remembrance. TN 1.01. 31
a cup, | to give mine enemy a lasting wink; WT 1.02.317
arise forth from the couch of lasting night, JN 3.04. 27
sings | his soul and body to their lasting rest. 5.07. 24
truth | and lasting fealty to the new–made king. R2 5.02. 45
for here i hope begins our lasting joy. 3H6 5.07. 46
and showers | there had made a lasting spring. H8 3.01. 8
do this and purchase us thy lasting friends." TIT 2.03.275
time saw | in lasting labor of his pilgrimage! ROM 4.05. 45
forward, not permanent, sweet, not lasting, HAM 1.03. 8
both here and hence pursue me lasting strife, 3.02.222
died, | this world to me is a lasting storm, PER 4.01. 19
poor wasting monuments of lasting moans. LUC 798
else lasting shame | on thee and thine this 1629
live's lasting date from cancell'd destiny. 1729
my brain | full character'd with lasting memory, SON 122. 2

LASTLY 9 FR 0.0010 REL FR 6 V 3 P
and the three party is (lastly and finally) mine WIV 1.01.140 P
sixt and lastly, they have belied a lady; ADO 5.01.217 P
sixt and lastly, why they are committed; 5.01.222 P
lastly, | if i do fail in fortune of my choice, MV 2.09. 14
lastly, hurried | here to this place, i' th' WT 3.02.104
and lastly, to confirm that amity | with nuptial 3H6 3.03. 54
lastly, myself unkindly banished, | the gates TIT 5.03.104
lastly, he frets | that lepidus of the ANT 3.06. 27
honor) lastly | children of grief and ignorance. TNK 2.02. 54

LASTS 5 FR 0.0005 REL FR 3 V 2 P
pray you, sir, let him go while the humor lasts. SHR 1.02.108 P
that's a day longer than a wonder lasts. 3H6 3.02.114
and whilst this poor wealth lasts | to entertain TIM 4.03.488
the houses he makes lasts till doomsday. HAM 5.01. 59 P
flowers | whilst summer lasts and i live here, CYM 4.02.219

/LATCH 1 FR 0.0001 REL FR 1 V 0 P
bird, of flow'r, or shape, which it doth /latch, SON 113. 6

LATCH 3 FR 0.0003 REL FR 3 V 0 P
air, | where hearing should not latch them. MAC 4.03.195
which with a yielding latch, and with no more, LUC 339
this said, his guilty hand pluck'd up the latch, 358

LATCH'D 2 FR 0.0002 REL FR 2 V 0 P
but hast thou yet latch'd the athenian's eyes MND 3.02. 36
home | my unprovided body, latch'd mine arm; LR 2.01. 52

LATCHES 1 FR 0.0001 REL FR 1 V 0 P
thou | these rural latches to his entrance open, WT 4.04.438

/LATE 1 FR 0.0001 REL FR 1 V 0 P
/of /which /disease | /our /late /king /richard 2H4 4.01. 58

LATE 201 FR 0.0227 REL FR 177 V 24 P
be not too late. TMP 4.01.133
trifle to abuse me | (as late i have been), i 5.01.113
as great to me as late, and, supportable | to 5.01.145
which of you saw eglamour of late? TGV 5.02. 32
and to be up early and down late; WIV 1.04.102 P
three hours too soon than a minute too late. 2.02.313 P
stand, | in him that was of late an heretic, 4.04. 9
he's sentenc'd; 'tis too late. MM 2.02. 55
too late? 2.02. 57
you seem'd of late to make the law a tyrant, 2.04.114
of gracious order, late come from the /see, | in 3.02.219
who call'd here of late? 4.02. 74
the enmity and discord which of late | sprung ERR 1.01. 5
rather approach'd too late: 1.02. 43
come, come, antipholus, we dine too late. 2.02.219
faith, no, he comes too late, | and so tell your 3.01. 49
you have of late stood out against your brother, ADO 1.03. 21 P
our late edict shall strongly stand in force: LLL 1.01. 11
so you, to study now it is too late, | climb 1.01.108
a mess of russians left us but of late. 5.02.361
for, meeting her of late behind the wood, MND 4.01. 48
death | of learning, late deceas'd in beggary." 5.01. 53
he came too late, the ship was under sail, | but MV 2.08. 6
that have of late so huddled on his back, | enow 4.01. 28
recant | the pardon that he late pronounced here. 4.01.392
but i can tell you that of late this duke | hath AYL 1.02.277
seek, | but at fourscore it is too late a week; 2.03. 74
"where is the life that late i led? SHR 4.01.140
better once than never, for never too late. 5.01.150
i was very late more near her than i think she AWW 1.03.106 P
which late | i was in my nobler thoughts most base 2.03.170
and disgraces have of late knock'd too often at 4.01. 28 P
'tis too late to pare her nails now. 5.02. 29 P
but love that comes too late, | like a 5.03. 57
know you this ring? this ring was his of late. 5.03.227
and so is now, or was so very late; TN 1.02. 30
but i know, to be up late is to be up late. 2.03. 5 P
but i know, to be up late is to be up late. 2.03. 5 P
burn some sack, 'tis too late to go to bed now. 2.03.191 P
she did commend my yellow stockings of late, she 2.05.166 P
i saw thee late at the count orsino's. 3.01. 37 P
the vows | we made each other but so late ago. 5.01.215
she is spread of late | into a goodly bulk. WT 2.01. 19
ay, and privy | to this their late escape. 2.01. 95
tongue, who late hath beat her husband, | and 2.03. 92
he is of late much retir'd from court and is 4.02. 31 P
the feast, but they come not too late now. 4.04.236 P
it is too late, the life of all his blood | is JN 5.07. 1
here to make good the boist'rous late appeal, R2 1.01. 4
after our sentence plaining comes too late. 1.03.175
pray god we may make haste and come too late! 1.04. 64
then all too late comes counsel to be heard, 2.01. 27
that late broke from the duke of exeter, | his 2.01.281
his brother, archbishop late of canterbury, 2.01.282
after your late tossing on the breaking seas? 3.02. 3
one day too late, i fear me, noble lord, | hath 3.02. 67
to–day, to–day, unhappy day, too late, 3.02. 71
peesel, be quiet, 'tis very late, i' faith. 2H4 2.04.161 P
come, it grows late, we'll to bed. 2.04.276 P
hath wasted all his rods | on late offenders, 4.01.214
"where is the life that late i led?" 5.03.140
who are the late commissioners? H5 2.02. 61
the mercy that was quick in us but late, | by 2.02. 79
as fear may teach us out of late examples | left 2.04. 12
question your grace the late embassadors, | with 2.04. 31
late did he shine upon the english side; 1H6 1.02. 3
hath the late overthrow wrought this offense? 1.02. 49
whom henry, our late sovereign, ne'er could 1.03. 24
for treason executed in our late king's days? 2.04. 91
why didst thou say, of late thou wert despis'd? 2.05. 42
men, | forbidden late to carry any weapon, 3.01. 79
this late dissension grown betwixt the peers 3.01.188
they that of late were daring with their scoffs 3.02.113
the noble duke of bedford late deceas'd, | but 3.02.132
it is too late, i cannot send them now. 4.04. 1
too late comes rescue, he is ta'en or slain; 4.04. 42
long, sat in the council–house | early and late, 2H6 1.01. 91
thy late exploits done in the heart of france 1.01.196
this late complaint | will make but little for 1.03. 97
himself, | how insolent of late he is become, 3.01. 7
but now of late, not able to travel with her 4.02. 47 P
the fearful french, whom you late vanquished, 4.08. 42
intent | to dash our late decree in parliament 3H6 2.01.118
and hath bereft thee of thy life too late. 2.05. 93
where fame, late ent'ring at his heedful ears, 3.03. 63
from giving aid which late i promised. 3.03.148
what late misfortune is befall'n king edward? 4.04. 3
as henry's late presaging prophecy | did glad my 4.06. 92
mean | of my lord hastings' late imprisonment. R3 1.03. 90
as index to the story we late talk'd of, | to 2.02.149
too late he died that might have kept that title 3.01. 99
which since you come too late of our intent, 3.05. 69
the late request that you did sound me in. 4.02. 84
have got by the late voyage is but merely | a H8 1.03. 6
we shall be late else, which i would not be, 1.03. 65
did you not of late days hear | a buzzing of a 2.01.147
come pat betwixt too early and too late | for 2.03. 84
your late censure | both of his truth and him 3.01. 64
the late queen's gentlewoman? 3.02. 94
because all those things you have done of late 3.02.338
held a late court at dunstable — six miles off 4.01. 27
not appearance and | the king's late scruple, by 4.01. 31
and the late marriage made of none effect; 4.01. 33
o my good lord, that comfort comes too late, 4.02.120
whither so late? 5.01. 6
your friend | some touch of your late business. 5.01. 13
unwillingly, of late | heard many grievous — i 5.01. 97
i hope i am not too late, and yet the gentleman 5.02. 1
as of late days our neighbors, | the upper 5.02. 64
what, am i poor of late? TRO 3.03. 74
glorious deeds, but in these fields of late, 3.03.188
for my own part, i came in late. 4.02. 52 P
confound an hour, | and bring thy news so late? COR 1.06. 18
come i too late? 1.06. 24
come i too late? 1.06. 27
and of late, | when corn was given them gratis, 3.01. 42
martius, | whom late you have nam'd for consul. 3.01.195
the harm of unscann'd swiftness, will (too late) 3.01.311
o, he is grown most kind of late. 4.06. 11
then all too late i bring this fatal writ, | the TIT 2.03.264
supper is done, and we shall come too late. ROM 1.04.105
ah, sirrah, by my fay, it waxes late, | i'll to 1.05.126
too early seen unknown, and known too late! 1.05.139
"villain" back again | that late thou gavest me, 3.01.126
hie you, make haste, for it grows very late. 3.03.164
'tis late; 3.03.172
'tis very late, she'll not come down to–night. 3.04. 5
two, | for hark you, tybalt being slain so late, 3.04. 24
it is so very late that we | may call it early 3.04. 34
is she not down so late, or up so early? 3.05. 66
which late i noted | in tatt'red weeds, with 5.01. 38
all those which were his fellows but of late — TIM 1.01. 78
change of mood | spurns down her late beloved, 1.01. 85
and late, five thousand; 2.01. 1
though you hear now (too late), yet now's a time 2.02.143
i have but little gold of late, brave timon, 4.03. 91
doubt and suspect, alas, are plac'd too late; 4.03.512
when we may profit meet, and come too late. 5.01. 42
our late noble master! 5.01. 55
brutus, i do observe you now of late; JC 1.02. 32
i am | of late with passions of some difference, 1.02. 40
for he is superstitious grown of late, | quite 2.01.195
old, | and the late dignities heap'd up to them, MAC 1.06. 19
he hath honor'd me of late, and i have bought 1.07. 32
was it so late, friend, ere you went to bed, 2.03. 22
ere you went to bed, | that you do lie so late? 2.03. 23
and the right valiant banquo walk'd too late, 3.06. 5
men must not walk too late. 3.06. 7
or thinking by our late dear brother's death HAM 1.02. 19
he hath very oft of late | given private time to 1.03. 91
of late made many tenders | of his affection to 1.03. 99
what, have you given him any hard words of late? 2.01.104
i have of late — but wherefore i know not — 2.02.295 P
comes by the means of the late innovation. 2.02.333 P
upon that head | where late the diadem stood, 2.02.507
but woe is me, you are so sick of late, | so far 3.02.163
it is the pois'ned cup, it is too late. 5.02.292
and our affairs from england come too late. 5.02.368
these late eclipses in the sun and moon portend LR 1.02.103 P
i have perceiv'd a most faint neglect of late, 1.04. 68 P
you are too much of late i' th' frown. 1.04.190 P
by what yourself too late have spoke and done, 1.04.207
these dispositions which of late transport you 1.04.221
woe, that too late repents! 1.04.257
it pleas'd the king his master very late | to 2.02.116
being the very fellow which of late | display'd 2.04. 40
he sought my life, | but lately, very late. 3.04.168
sir, what letters had you late from france? 3.07. 42
with the traitors | late footed in the kingdom? 3.07. 45
and at her late being here | she gave strange 4.05. 24
seeing the worst, which late on hopes depended. OTH 1.03.203
it is too late. 5.02. 83
strange courtesies and great | of late upon me. ANT 2.02.155
i was of late as petty to his ends | as is the 3.12. 8
of late, when i cried "ho!" 3.13. 90
of those that serv'd mark antony but late, 4.01. 13
the truth, and i am come, | i dread, too late. 4.14.127
too late, good diomed. call my guard, i prithee. 4.14.128
sole son — a widow | that late he married), CYM 1.01. 6
she hath been reading late | the tale of tereus; 2.02. 44
i am glad i was up so late, for that's the 2.03. 33 P
not seen of late? 3.05. 52
hast any of thy late master's garments in thy 3.05.124 P
have you dream'd of late of this war's purpose? 4.02.345
these mouths who, but of late, earth, sea, and PER 1.04. 34
princes, it is too late to talk of love, | and 2.03.112
whom helicanus late | advanc'd in time to great 4.04. 15
as i late was angling | in the great lake that TNK 4.01. 52
and all amaz'd, brake off his late intent, | for VEN 469
owl (night's herald) shrieks, 'tis very late; 531
whereat th' impartial gazer late did wonder, 748

on shore | gazing upon a late embarked friend, 818
whereat she leaps, that was but late forlorn. 1026
their virtue lost, wherein they late excell'd, 1131
his eye, which late this mutiny restrains, LUC 426
that thou shalt lend me | comes all too late, 1686
which she too early and too late hath spill'd." 1801
and by chaste lucrece' soul that late complained 1839
and then too late she will repent | that thus PP 18.27
/ruin'd choirs, where late the sweet birds sang. SON 73. 4
which late her noble suit in court did shun, LC 234
LATE-BETRAYED 1 FR 0.0001 REL FR 1 V 0 P
as sure as in this late-betrayed town | great 1H6 3.02. 82
LATED 2 FR 0.0002 REL FR 2 V 0 P
now spurs the lated traveller apace | to gain MAC 3.03. 6
i am so lated in the world, that i | have lost ANT 3.11. 3
LATE-DECEASED 1 FR 0.0001 REL FR 1 V 0 P
with these our late-deceased emperor's sons. TIT 1.01.184
LATE-DESPISED 1 FR 0.0001 REL FR 1 V 0 P
your nephew, late-despised richard, comes. 1H6 2.05. 36
LATE-DISTURBED 1 FR 0.0001 REL FR 1 V 0 P
brow, | like bubbles in a late-disturbed stream, 1H4 2.03. 59
LATELY 31 FR 0.0035 REL FR 25 V 6 P
that hath lately suffer'd by a thunderbolt. TMP 2.02. 36 P
i knew not what 'twas to be beaten till lately. WIV 5.01. 26 P
for lately we were bound as you are now. ERR 5.01.294
the gentleman | that lately stole his daughter. MV 4.01.385
that did but lately foil the sinowy charles, AYL 2.02. 14
the king very lately spoke of him admiringly and AWW 1.01. 29 P
had you not lately an intent — speak truly — 1.03.218
you were lately whipt, sir, as i think. 2.02. 50 P
though lately we intended | to keep in darkness TN 5.01.152
shall these hands, so lately purg'd of blood, JN 3.01.239
king, who lately landed | with some few private R2 3.03. 3
who | lately came from the king, commands the 5.05.101
did lately meet in the intestine shock | and 1H4 1.01. 12
hear, that earl of march | hath lately married. 1.03. 85
wind | bated like eagles having lately bath'd, 4.01. 99
and fifty totter'd prodigals lately come from 4.02. 34 P
i was lately here in the end of a displeasing 2H4 ep 8 P
your highness, lately sending into france, | did H5 1.02.246
he was lately sent | from your kind aunt, 3H6 2.01.145
lately attendant on the duke of norfolk. R3 2.01.102
but lately splinter'd, knit, and join'd together 2.02.118
too, | cardinal campeius is arriv'd, and lately, H8 2.01.160
but 'tis so lately alter'd that the old name 4.01. 98
martius, 'tis true that you have lately told us, COR 1.01.227
who art thou that lately didst descend | into TIT 2.03.248
for whose dear sake thou wast but lately dead: ROM 3.03.136
ventidius lately | buried his father, by whose TIM 2.02.222
he sought my life, | but lately, very late. LR 3.04.168
i lay with cassio lately, | and, being troubled OTH 3.03.413
which, by thee, lately | is left untender'd. CYM 3.01. 9
i saw you lately | when you caught hurt in PER 4.01. 86
LATER 2 FR 0.0002 REL FR 2 V 0 P
therefore thy later vows, against thy first, JN 3.01.288
i take't, 'tis later, sir. MAC 2.01. 3
LATE-SACK'D 1 FR 0.0001 REL FR 1 V 0 P
who, like a late-sack'd island, vastly stood LUC 1740
LATEST 17 FR 0.0019 REL FR 17 V 0 P
now, at the latest minute of the hour, | grant LLL 5.02.787
the latest breath that gave the sound of words JN 3.01.230
the latest news we hear | is that the rebels R2 5.06. 1
the very latest counsel | that ever i shall 2H4 4.05.182
this is the latest parle we will admit; H5 3.03. 2
this is the latest glory of thy praise | that i, 1H6 4.02. 33
your brave father breath'd his latest gasp, 3H6 2.01.108
and to the latest gasp cried out for warwick, 5.02. 41
nestor shall apply | thy latest words. TRO 1.03. 33
their latest refuge | was to send him; COR 5.03. 11
these that i bring unto their latest home, TIT 1.01. 83
make this his latest farewell to their souls. 1.01.149
o now, sweet boy, give them their latest kiss! 5.03.169
the latest of my wealth i'll share amongst you. TIM 4.02. 23
that did the latest service to my master. JC 5.05. 67
to leave that latest which concerns him first, OTH 1.03. 28
'tis the latest thing | i shall be glad of, TNK 5.04. 29
LATE-WALKING 1 FR 0.0001 REL FR 0 V 1 P
decay of lust and late-walking through the realm WIV 5.05.144 P
LATH 5 FR 0.0005 REL FR 3 V 2 P
who, with dagger of lath, | in his rage and his TN 4.02.126
thee out of thy kingdom with a dagger of lath, 1H4 2.04.137 P
and get thee a sword, though made of a lath; 2H6 4.02. 2 P
have your lath glued within your sheath, | till TIT 2.01. 41
scarf, | bearing a tartar's painted bow of lath, ROM 1.04. 5
LATIN 12 FR 0.0013 REL FR 2 V 10 P
ay, you spake in latin then too: WIV 1.01.180 P
"hang-hog" is latin for bacon, i warrant you. 4.01. 48 P
o, that's the latin word for three farthings: LLL 3.01.137 P
o, i smell false latin, "dunghill" for unguem. 5.01. 79 P
he hath neither latin, french, nor italian, and MV 1.02. 69 P
with a priest that lacks latin, and a rich man AYL 3.02.319 P
'tis no matter, sir, what he 'leges in latin. SHR 1.02. 29 P
as cunning in greek, latin, and other languages, 2.01. 81 P
and this small packet of greek and latin books. 2.01.100
and thus in latin, praeclarissimus filius noster H5 5.02.340 P
away with him, away with him! he speaks latin. 2H6 4.07. 58 P
o, good my lord, no latin; H8 3.01. 42
LATTEN 1 FR 0.0001 REL FR 1 V 0 P
mine, | i combat challenge of this latten bilbo. WIV 1.01.162
LATTER 18 FR 0.0020 REL FR 9 V 9 P
the latter end of his commonwealth forgets the TMP 2.01.158 P
in faith, at the latter end of a sea-coal fire. WIV 1.04. 9 P
for the latter end of his name. LLL 5.02.627 P
and i will sing it in the latter end of a play, MND 4.01.217 P
both | or bring your latter hazard back again, MV 1.01.151
wonder that hath shot out in our latter times. AWW 2.03. 8 P
is something at the latter end of a dinner, but 2.05. 28 P
farewell, the latter spring! 1H4 1.02.158 P
to the latter end of a fray and the beginning of 4.02. 79
to grace this latter age with noble deeds. 5.01. 92
join together at the latter day and cry all, "we H5 4.01.137 P
your cousin, in the latter end, and she must be 5.02.314 P
neck, | and in his bosom spend my latter gasp. 1H6 2.05. 38
life, | and in devotion spend my latter days, 3H6 4.06. 43
these well express in thee thy latter spirits: TIM 5.04. 74
the foul'st best fits | my latter part of life. ANT 4.06. 38
if you, born in those latter times, | when wit's PER 1.ch. 11
heirs | may the two latter darken and expend; 3.02. 29
LATTER-BORN 1 FR 0.0001 REL FR 1 V 0 P
my wife, more careful for the latter-born, | had ERR 1.01. 78
LATTICE *(also lettice)*
LATTICE 1 FR 0.0001 REL FR 0 V 1 P
my lord, through a red lattice, and i could 2H4 2.02. 80 P
LAUD 7 FR 0.0008 REL FR 6 V 1 P
i laud them, i praise them. 1H4 3.03.191 P
laud be to god! 2H4 4.05.235
a little gilt, | more laud than gilt o'erdusted. TRO 3.03.179
laud we the gods, | and let our crooked smokes CYM 5.05.476
that to thy laud | i may advance my streamer, TNK 5.01. 58
thou back'st reproach against long-living laud, LUC 622
thou plantest scandal and displacest laud. 887
LAUDABLE 2 FR 0.0002 REL FR 1 V 1 P
do redeem it by some laudable attempt either of TN 3.02. 29 P
where to do harm | is often laudable, to do good MAC 4.02. 76
LAUDIS 1 FR 0.0001 REL FR 1 V 0 P
dii faciant laudis summa sit ista tuae! 3H6 1.03. 48
LAUDS 1 FR 0.0001 REL FR 1 V 0 P
which time she chaunted snatches of old lauds, HAM 4.07.177
LAUGH *(also loff)*
/LAUGH 1 FR 0.0001 REL FR 0 V 1 P
/shall /make /those /laugh /whose /lungs /are HAM 2.02.323 P
LAUGH 90 FR 0.0101 REL FR 56 V 34 P
lungs that they always use to laugh at nothing. TMP 2.01.175 P
so you may continue, and laugh at nothing still. 2.01.178 P
will you laugh me asleep, for i am very heavy? 2.01.188 P
i shall laugh myself to death at this 2.02.154 P
i shall never laugh but in that maid's company! WIV 1.04.152 P
be reveng'd on falstaff, and laugh at page. 2.02.311 P
we do not act that often jest and laugh; 4.02.106
where i will desire thee to laugh at my wife, 5.05.172 P
and laugh this sport o'er by a country fire — 5.05.242
spleens, | would all themselves laugh mortal. MM 2.02.123
o lord, i must laugh! ERR 3.01. 50
laugh when i am merry, and claw no man in his ADO 1.03. 17 P
did he never make you laugh? 2.01.135 P
them, and then they laugh at him and beat him. 2.01.142 P
o, she would laugh me | out of myself, press me 3.01. 75
to hear meekly, sir, and to laugh moderately; LLL 1.01.197 P
how will he triumph, leap, and laugh at it! 4.03.146
the boys, | and critic timon laugh at idle toys! 4.03.168
to make my lady laugh when she's dispos'd, 5.02.466
squier, | and laugh upon the apple of her eye? 5.02.475
and 'twere as easy | for you to laugh and leap, MV 1.01. 49
eyes, | and laugh like parrots at a bagpiper; 1.01. 53
good signiors both, when shall we laugh? 1.01. 66
if you tickle us, do we not laugh? 3.01. 65 P
at whom so oft | your grace was wont to laugh, AYL 2.02. 9
and i did laugh sans intermission | an hour by 2.07. 32
galled with my folly, | they most must laugh. 2.07. 51
i will laugh like a hyen, and that when thou art 4.01.155 P
lusty horn | is not a thing to laugh to scorn. 4.02. 18
you saw my master wink and laugh upon you? SHR 4.04. 75 P
that done, laugh well at me. AWW 2.01. 87
unless you laugh and minister occasion to him, TN 1.05. 87 P
spleen, and will laugh yourselves into stitches, 3.02. 68 P
"madam, why laugh you at such a barren rascal? 5.01.375 P
camillo and polixenes | laugh at me; WT 2.03. 24
they should not laugh if i could reach them, nor 2.03. 25
i see | i talk but idlely, and you laugh at me. R2 3.03.171
room, and lend me thy hand to laugh a little. 1H4 2.04. 2 P
to laugh at gibing boys, and stand the push | of 3.02. 66
nor a man cannot make him laugh, but that's no 2H4 4.03. 89 P
and 'a shall laugh without intervallums. 5.01. 81 P
you shall see him laugh till his face be like a 5.01. 84 P
when thousands weep more than did laugh at it. H5 1.02.296
thee in french, unless it be to laugh at me. 5.02.187 P
i laugh to see your ladyship so fond | to think 1H6 2.03. 45
it made me laugh to see the villain run. 2H6 2.01.152
and when i start, the envious people laugh, 2.04. 35
the world may laugh again, | and i may live to 2.04. 82
but i shall laugh at this a twelvemonth hence, R3 3.02. 57
i come no more to make you laugh; H8 pr 1
i cannot choose but laugh to think how she TRO 1.02.135 P
i would laugh at that miracle — yet, in a sort, 5.04. 34 P
i could weep, | and i could laugh; COR 2.01.184
inevitable strokes, | as 'tis to laugh at 'em. 4.01. 27
down, and this unnatural scene | they laugh at. 5.03.185
why dost thou laugh? it fits not with this hour. TIT 3.01.265
dost thou not laugh? ROM 1.01.183
yet i cannot choose but laugh | to think it 1.03. 50
as maids call medlars, when they laugh alone. 2.01. 36
ho, ho! i laugh to think that babe a bastard. TIM 1.02.112 P
that death in me at others' lives may laugh. 4.03.380
and for mine own part, i durst not laugh, for JC 1.02.249 P
for he will live, and laugh at this hereafter. 2.01.191
there's one did laugh in 's sleep, and one cried MAC 2.02. 20
laugh to scorn | the pow'r of man; 4.01. 79
castle's strength | will laugh a siege to scorn; 5.05. 3
but swords i smile at, weapons laugh to scorn, 5.07. 12
why did ye laugh then, when i said, "man HAM 2.02.313 P
though it makes the unskillful laugh, cannot but 3.02. 26 P
them that will themselves laugh to set on some 3.02. 41 P
some quantity of barren spectators to laugh too, 3.02. 42 P
make her laugh at that. 5.01.195 P
do not laugh at me, | for (as i am a man) i LR 4.07. 67
old tales, and laugh | at gilded butterflies, 5.03. 12
paradoxes to make fools laugh i' th' alehouse. OTH 2.01.139 P
so, so, so, so; they laugh that wins. 4.01.122 P
whom every thing becomes — to chide, to laugh, ANT 1.01. 49
pompey doth this day laugh away his fortune. 2.06.104 P
laugh at 's while we strut | to our confusion. 3.13.114
mean time | laugh at his challenge. 4.01. 6
you laugh when boys or women tell their dreams; 5.02. 74
at fools i laugh, not fear them. CYM 4.02. 96
sent hither | to make the world to laugh at me. PER 5.01.144
strong enough to laugh at misery | and bear the TNK 2.02. 2
i am wondrous merry-hearted, i could laugh now. 2.02.150
out, | we'll make thee laugh and all this rout. 3.05.147
him, but i laugh at 'em | and let 'em all alone. 4.01.126
for what we lack | we laugh, for what we have 5.04.133
nor laugh with his companions at thy state, LUC 1066
to make the weeper laugh, the laugher weep, | he LC 124
LAUGHABLE 1 FR 0.0001 REL FR 1 V 0 P
though nestor swear the jest be laughable. MV 1.01. 56
LAUGH'D 32 FR 0.0036 REL FR 18 V 14 P
'twas you we laugh'd at. TMP 2.01.176 P
you were wont, when you laugh'd, to crow like a TGV 2.01. 27 P
you'll be laugh'd at. WIV 1.01.119 P
not mark'd, or not laugh'd at, strikes him into ADO 2.01.148 P
after he hath laugh'd at such shallow follies in 2.03. 10 P
with that all laugh'd, and clapp'd him on the LLL 5.02.107
when we have laugh'd to see the sails conceive MND 2.01.128
me half a million, laugh'd at my losses, mock'd MV 3.01. 55 P
of as good as he, so he laugh'd and let me go. AYL 3.04. 37 P
creature, | whom sometime i have laugh'd with. AWW 5.03.179
duke in high despite, | laugh'd in his face; 3H6 2.01. 60
the lag end of their lewdness and be laugh'd at. H8 1.03. 35
a woman lost among ye, laugh'd at, scorn'd? 3.01.107
queen hecuba laugh'd that her eyes ran o'er. TRO 1.02.143 P
and cassandra laugh'd. 1.02.145 P
and hector laugh'd. 1.02.148 P
been a green hair, i should have laugh'd too. 1.02.153 P
they laugh'd not so much at the hair as at his 1.02.154 P
and all the rest so laugh'd, that it pass'd. 1.02.167 P
wouldst thou have laugh'd had i come coffin'd COR 2.01.176
she laugh'd, and told the moor he should not TIT 4.03. 75
and laugh'd so heartily | that both mine eyes 5.01.116
lest i be laugh'd at when i tell them so. JC 2.02. 70
did you perceive how he laugh'd at his vice? OTH 4.01.171 P
i must be laugh'd at | if, or for nothing or a ANT 2.02. 30
more laugh'd at, that i should | once name you 2.02. 33
i laugh'd him out of patience; 2.05. 19
and that night | i laugh'd him into patience; 2.05. 20
or that the negligence may well be laugh'd at, CYM 1.01. 66
slumber, | not as death's dart being laugh'd at; 4.02.211
hunting he lov'd, but love he laugh'd to scorn. VEN 4
that heavy saturn laugh'd and leapt with him. SON 98. 4
LAUGHER 1 FR 0.0001 REL FR 1 V 0 P
to make the weeper laugh, the laugher weep, | he LC 124
LAUGHEST 1 FR 0.0001 REL FR 1 V 0 P
laughest thou, wretch? 1H6 2.03. 44
LAUGHING 14 FR 0.0015 REL FR 7 V 7 P
of unhappiness and wak'd herself with laughing. ADO 2.01.346 P
why then, some be of laughing, as, ah, ha, he! 4.01. 22 P
which shallow laughing hearers give to fools. LLL 5.02.860
mislead night-wanderers, laughing at their harm? MND 2.01. 39
i am so; i do love it better than laughing. AYL 4.01. 4 P
they not quickly, i should die with laughing. SHR 3.02.241
were't not for laughing, i should pity him. 1H4 2.02.110
and let another half stand laughing by, | all H5 1.02.113
with envious looks laughing at thy shame, | that 2H6 2.04. 12
but there was such laughing! TRO 1.02.142 P
at what was all this laughing? 1.02.149 P
but there was such laughing! 1.02.165 P
strange times, that weep with laughing, not with TIM 4.03.486
worst of all follow him laughing to his grave, ANT 1.02. 67 P
LAUGHING-STOCKS 1 FR 0.0001 REL FR 0 V 1 P
you let us not be laughing-stocks to other men's WIV 3.01. 86 P
LAUGHS 9 FR 0.0010 REL FR 8 V 1 P
to laugh at my wife, that now laughs at thee. WIV 5.05.172 P
whilst man and master laughs my woes to scorn. ERR 2.02.205
from his deep chest laughs out a loud applause, TRO 1.03.163
at lovers' perjuries, | they say, jove laughs. ROM 2.02. 93
that's a maid now, and laughs at my departure, LR 1.05. 51
look how he laughs already! OTH 4.01.109
now he denies it faintly, and laughs it out. 4.01.112
(your lord, i mean) laughs from 's free lungs; CYM 1.06. 68
that laughs and weeps, and all but with a breath VEN 414
LAUGH'ST 1 FR 0.0001 REL FR 1 V 0 P
antic death, which laugh'st us here to scorn, 1H6 4.07. 18
LAUGHTER 30 FR 0.0034 REL FR 22 V 8 P
a laughter. TMP 2.01. 33 P
by virtue thou enforcest laughter — thy silly LLL 3.01. 75 P
o, i am /stabb'd with laughter! 5.02. 80
with such a zealous laughter, so profound, 5.02.116
to move wild laughter in the throat of death? 5.02.855
tears | the passion of loud laughter never shed. MND 5.01. 70
with mirth and laughter let old wrinkles come, MV 1.01. 80
how my men will stay themselves from laughter SHR in.1. 134
world's pleasure and the increase of laughter. AWW 2.04. 37 P
o, for the love of laughter, let him fetch his 3.06. 34 P
o, for the love of laughter, hinder not the 3.06. 41 P
present mirth hath present laughter; TN 2.03. 48
may rather pluck on laughter than revenge, | if 5.01.366
stopping the career | of laughter with a sigh (a WT 1.02.287
to laughter, as i take it, | if the good truth 2.01.198
making that idiot, laughter, keep men's eyes JN 3.03. 45
be argument for a week, laughter for a month, 1H4 2.02. 95 P
that intends to laughter more than i invent or 2H4 1.02. 8 P
harry in continual laughter the wearing out of 5.01. 79 P
with briers, | scars to move laughter only. COR 3.03. 52
and almost broke my heart with extreme laughter. TIT 5.01.113
so it may prove an argument of laughter | to th' TIM 3.03. 20
do never give | but thorough lust and laughter. 4.03.485
were i a common laughter, or did use | to stale JC 1.02. 72
i'll use you for my mirth, yea, for my laughter, 4.03. 49
to be but mirth and laughter to his brutus, 4.03.114
pains and benefits | to laughter and contempt, LR 1.04.287
from the best, | the worst returns to laughter. 4.01. 6
cannot restrain | from the excess of laughter. OTH 4.01. 99
ay, madam, with his eyes in flood with laughter. CYM 1.06. 74
LAUNCE 7 FR 0.0008 REL FR 1 V 6 P
launce, away, away! TGV 2.03. 33 P
launce, by mine honesty, welcome to /milan. 2.05. 1 P
but, launce, how say'st thou that my master is 2.05. 41 P
i pray thee, launce, and if thou seest my boy, 3.01.259
how now, signior launce? 3.01.280 P
i tell you what launce, his man, told me: 4.02. 75 P
where is launce? 4.02. 77 P
LAUNCELOT 27 FR 0.0030 REL FR 3 V 24 P
me, "/gobbo, launcelot /gobbo, good launcelot," MV 2.02. 4 P
launcelot /gobbo, good launcelot," or "good 2.02. 4 P
or "good /gobbo," or "good launcelot /gobbo, use 2.02. 5 P
take heed, honest launcelot, take heed, honest 2.02. 7 P
as aforesaid, "honest launcelot /gobbo, do not 2.02. 8 P
very wisely to me, "my honest friend launcelot, 2.02. 15 P
my conscience says, "launcelot, bouge not." 2.02. 19 P
can you tell me whether one launcelot, that 2.02. 46 P
talk you of young master launcelot? 2.02. 48 P
talk you of young master launcelot? 2.02. 50 P
what 'a will, we talk of young master launcelot. 2.02. 55 P
your worship's friend and launcelot, sir. 2.02. 56 P
beseech you, talk you of young master launcelot. 2.02. 58 P

of launcelot, an't please your mastership. 2.02. 59 P
ergo, master launcelot. 2.02. 60 P
talk not of master launcelot, father, for the 2.02. 61 P
i am sure you are not launcelot, my boy. 2.02. 82 P
i am launcelot, your boy that was, your son that 2.02. 84 P
but i am launcelot, the jew's man, and i am sure 2.02. 89 P
i'll be sworn, if thou be launcelot, thou art 2.02. 92 P
and, launcelot, soon at supper shalt thou see 2.03. 5
farewell, good launcelot. 2.03. 15
friend launcelot, what's the news? 2.04. 9
i'll tell my husband, launcelot, what you say. 3.05. 27 P
i shall grow jealious of you shortly, launcelot, 3.05. 29 P
not fear us, lorenzo, launcelot and i are out. 3.05. 31 P
the moor is with child by you, launcelot. 3.05. 39 P
LAUNCES 1 FR 0.0001 REL FR 0 V 1 P
all the kind of the launces have this very fault TGV 2.03. 2 P
LAUNCH *(also lanceth, lanch'd)*
LAUNCH 1 FR 0.0001 REL FR 1 V 0 P
but we do launch | diseases in our bodies. ANT 5.01. 36
LAUNCH'D 1 FR 0.0001 REL FR 1 V 0 P
whose price hath launch'd above a thousand ships
TRO 2.02. 82
LAUND 2 FR 0.0002 REL FR 2 V 0 P
for through this laund anon the deer will come, 3H6 3.01. 2
and homeward through the dark laund runs apace,
VEN 813
LAUNDRESS 2 FR 0.0002 REL FR 0 V 2 P
carry them to the laundress in datchet-mead; WIV 3.03.148 P
to the laundress, forsooth. 3.03.153 P
LAUND'RING 1 FR 0.0001 REL FR 1 V 0 P
laund'ring the silken figures in the brine LC 17
LAUNDRY 1 FR 0.0001 REL FR 0 V 1 P
or his cook — or his laundry — his washer and WIV 1.02. 4 P
LAURA 1 FR 0.0001 REL FR 0 V 1 P
laura to his lady was a kitchen wench (marry, ROM 2.04. 39 P
LAUREL 3 FR 0.0003 REL FR 3 V 0 P
adjudg'd an olive branch and laurel crown, | as 3H6 4.06. 34
cometh andronicus, bound with laurel boughs, TIT 1.01. 74
upon your sword | sit laurel victory, and smooth ANT 1.03.100
LAURELS 1 FR 0.0001 REL FR 1 V 0 P
prerogative of age, crowns, sceptres, laurels, TRO 1.03.107
LAURENCE 1 FR 0.0001 REL FR 1 V 0 P
for friar laurence met them both, | as he in TGV 5.02. 37
LAUS 1 FR 0.0001 REL FR 0 V 1 P
laus deo, /bone intelligo. LLL 5.01. 27 P
LAVATCH 1 FR 0.0001 REL FR 0 V 1 P
good master lavatch, give my lord lafew this AWW 5.02. 1 P
LAVE 3 FR 0.0003 REL FR 3 V 0 P
basins and ewers to lave her dainty hands; SHR 2.01.348
although she lave them hourly in the flood. TIT 4.02.103
must lave our honors in these flattering streams MAC 3.02. 33
LAVEE 1 FR 0.0001 REL FR 0 V 1 P
vomissement, et la /truie lavee au bourbier." H5 3.07. 65 P
LAVENDER 1 FR 0.0001 REL FR 1 V 0 P
hot lavender, mints, savory, marjorum, | the WT 4.04.104
/LAVINIA 1 FR 0.0001 REL FR 1 V 0 P
/lavinia, /go /with /me. TIT 3.02. 81
LAVINIA 38 FR 0.0043 REL FR 38 V 0 P
gracious lavinia, rome's rich ornament, | that i TIT 1.01. 52
lavinia, live, outlive thy father's days, | and 1.01.167
family, | lavinia will i make my emperess, 1.01.240
lavinia, you are not displeas'd with this? 1.01.270
thanks, sweet lavinia. 1.01.273
lavinia is surpris'd! 1.01.284
traitor, restore lavinia to the emperor. 1.01.296
that in the rescue of lavinia | with his own 1.01.417
and fear not, lords, and you, lavinia; 1.01.471
lavinia, though you left me like a churl, | i 1.01.486
you are my guest, lavinia, and your friends. 1.01.490
what, is lavinia then become so loose, | or 2.01. 65
world, | i love lavinia more than all the world. 2.01. 72
choice, | lavinia is thine elder brother's hope. 2.01. 74
won, | she is lavinia, therefore must be lov'd. 2.01. 84
lucrece was not more chaste | than this lavinia, 2.01.109
lavinia, how say you? 2.02. 16
speak, lavinia, what accursed hand | hath made 3.01. 66
'tis well, lavinia, that thou hast no hands, 3.01. 79
my soul the greatest spurn | is dear lavinia, 3.01.102
gentle lavinia, let me kiss thy lips, | or make 3.01.120
ah, my lavinia, i will wipe thy cheeks. 3.01.142
and, lavinia, thou shalt be employ'd; 3.01.281
farewell, lavinia, my noble sister, | o, would 3.01.292
but now nor lucius nor lavinia lives | but in 3.01.294
my aunt lavinia | follows me every where, i know 4.01. 1
what means my niece lavinia by these signs? 4.01. 8
how now, lavinia? 4.01. 30
lavinia, shall i read? 4.01. 46
lavinia, wert thou thus surpris'd, sweet girl? 4.01. 51
look here, lavinia. 4.01. 68
my lord, kneel down with me, lavinia, kneel, 4.01. 87
lavinia, come. 4.01.120
come, come, lavinia, look, thy foes are bound. 5.02.166
whiles that lavinia 'tween her stumps doth hold 5.02.182
lavinia, come, | receive the blood, and when 5.02.196
die, die, lavinia, and thy shame with thee, 5.03. 46
my father and lavinia shall forthwith | be 5.03.193
LAVINIA'S 3 FR 0.0003 REL FR 3 V 0 P
nest, | that died in honor and lavinia's cause. TIT 1.01.377
and plead my passions for lavinia's love. 2.01. 36
heaven's eye, | and revel in lavinia's treasury. 2.01.131
LAVISH 5 FR 0.0005 REL FR 5 V 0 P
let her have needful but not lavish means; MM 2.02. 24
had i so lavish of my presence been, | so 1H4 3.02. 39
when means and lavish manners meet together, | o
2H4 4.04. 64
among which terms he us'd his lavish tongue 1H6 2.05. 47
arm 'gainst arm, | curbing his lavish spirit; MAC 1.02. 57
LAVISHLY 1 FR 0.0001 REL FR 1 V 0 P
and some about him have too lavishly | wrested 2H4 4.02. 57
LAVOLT 1 FR 0.0001 REL FR 1 V 0 P
nor heel the high lavolt, nor sweeten talk, TRO 4.04. 86
LAVOLTAS 1 FR 0.0001 REL FR 1 V 0 P
and teach lavoltas high and swift corantos, H5 3.05. 33
LAW* *(also la*)*
/LAW* 1 FR 0.0001 REL FR 1 V 0 P
and first decree | into the /law of children. JC 3.01. 39
LAW* 218 FR 0.0246 REL FR 177 V 41 P
the law of friendship bids me to conceal, | but TGV 3.01. 5
are my mates, that make their wills their law, 5.04. 14
which have for long run by the hideous law, | as MM 1.04. 63
we must not make a scarecrow of the law, 2.01. 1
you censure him, | and pull'd the law upon you. 2.01. 16
their abuses in common houses, i know no law. 2.01. 43 P
if the law would allow it, sir. 2.01.227 P
but the law will not allow it, pompey; 2.01.228 P
if this law hold in vienna ten year, i'll rent 2.01.240 P
o just but severe law! 2.02. 41
your brother is a forfeit of the law, | and you 2.02. 71
it is the law, not i, condemn your brother. 2.02. 80
the law hath not been dead, though it hath slept 2.02. 90
that the most just law | now took your brother's 2.04. 52
i (now the voice of the recorded law) 2.04. 61
appears, | accountant to the law upon that pain. 2.04. 86
from the manacles | of the all-/binding law; 2.04. 94
you seem'd of late to make the law a tyrant, 2.04.114
bidding the law make curtsy to their will, 2.04.175
that thus can make him bite the law by th' nose, 3.01.108
my brother die by the law than my son should be 3.01.190 P
redeem your brother from the angry law; 3.01.202 P
allow'd by order of law a furr'd gown to keep 3.02. 7 P
marry, sir, he hath offended the law; 3.02. 15 P
greater forfeit to the law than angelo who hath 4.02.158 P
eminent body that enforc'd | the law against it! 4.04. 23
the very mercy of the law cries out | most 5.01.407
therefore by law thou art condemn'd to die. ERR 1.01. 25
sir, sir, i shall have law in ephesus, | to your 4.01. 83
in messina, and one that knows the law, go to, ADO 4.02. 83 P
a dangerous law against gentility. LLL 1.01.128
for charity itself fulfills the law, | and who 4.03.361
and, to begin, wench — so god help me, law! 5.02.414
according to our law | immediately provided in MND 1.01. 44
or else the law of athens yields you up | (which 1.01.119
and to that place the sharp athenian law 1.01.162
without the peril of the athenian law — 4.01.153
i beg the law, the law, upon his head. 4.01.155
i beg the law, the law, upon his head. 4.01.155
the law! MV 2.08. 17
in law, what plea so tainted and corrupt | but, 3.02. 75
if law, authority, and power deny not, | it will 3.02.289
the duke cannot deny the course of law; 3.03. 26
if you deny me, fie upon your law! 4.01.101
i stand here for law. 4.01.142
yet in such rule that the venetian law | cannot 4.01.178
i crave the law, | the penalty and forfeit of my 4.01.206
you | wrest once the law to your authority: 4.01.215
you know the law, your exposition | hath been 4.01.237
i charge you by the law, | whereof you are a 4.01.238
for the intent and purpose of the law | hath 4.01.247
the court awards it, and the law doth give it. 4.01.300
the law allows it, and the court awards it. 4.01.303
is that the law? 4.01.314
jew, | the law hath yet another hold on you. 4.01.347
fourth, or fift borough, i'll answer him by law. SHR in.1. 14 P
come, since this bar in law makes us friends, it 1.01.136 P
health, | and do as adversaries do in law, 1.02.276
and now by law, as well as reverent age, | i may 4.05. 60
fain would steal | what law does vouch mine own. AWW 2.05. 82
which are their own right by the law of nature. 4.05. 61 P
note, that keeps you from the blow of the law. TN 3.04.154 P
still you keep o' th' windy side of the law; 3.04.164 P
against him, if there be any law in illyria. 4.01. 35 P
is | by law and process of great nature thence WT 2.02. 58
awake), i tell you | 'tis rigor and not law. 3.02.114
since it is in my pow'r | to o'erthrow law, and 4.01. 8
this being done, let the law go whistle; 4.04.698 P
child, | the canon of the law is laid on him, JN 2.01.180
there's law and warrant, lady, for my curse. 3.01.184
when law can do no right, | let it be lawful 3.01.185
right, | let it be lawful that law bar no wrong; 3.01.186
law cannot give my child his kingdom here, | for 3.01.187
for he that holds his kingdom holds the law; 3.01.188
therefore, since law itself is perfect wrong, 3.01.189
how can the law forbid my tongue to curse? 3.01.190
the winking of authority | to understand a law; 4.02.212
must i rob the law? 4.03. 78
of war, | and formally, according to our law, R2 1.03. 29
thy state of law is bond-slave to the law, | and 2.01.114
thy state of law is bond-slave to the law, | and 2.01.114
i am a subject, | and i challenge law. 2.03.134
a pale | keep law and form and due proportion, 3.04. 41
with the rusty curb of old father antic the law? 1H4 1.02. 61 P
i am loath to pawn my plate, so god save me law! 2H4 2.01.155 P
you, is as red as any rose, in good truth law! 2.04. 26 P
to be eaten in thy house, contrary to the law, 2.04.345 P
i see no reason in the law of nature but i may 3.02.331 P
are brought to the correction of your law. 4.04. 85
in me, | and, in th' administration of his law, 5.02. 75
the majesty and power of law and justice, | the 5.02. 78
to trip the course of law and blunt the sword 5.02. 87
and religiously unfold | why the law salique, H5 1.02. 11
the founder of this law and female bar. 1.02. 42
of their life, | establish'd then this law: 1.02. 50
then doth it well appear the salique law | was 1.02. 54
idly suppos'd the founder of this law, | who 1.02. 59
they would hold up this salique law | to bar 1.02. 91
open, | arrest them to the answer of the law, 2.02.143
by law of nature and of nations, 'longs | to him 2.04. 80
by chrish law, 'tish ill done! 3.02. 88 P
have blowed up the town, so chrish save me law, 3.02. 92 P
there ish nothing done, so christ sa' me law! 3.02.113 P
men have defeated the law and outrun native 4.01.167 P
'tis expressly against the law of arms. 4.07. 2 P
ground and his earth, in my conscience law! 4.07.143 P
it, if there is any martial law in the world. 4.08. 44 P
cardinal, i'll be no breaker of the law; 1H6 1.03. 80
faith, i have been a truant in the law, | and 2.04. 7
it, | and therefore frame the law unto my will. 2.04. 9
but in these nice sharp quillets of the law, 2.04. 17
thou knowest the law of arms is such | that 3.04. 38
about a certain question in the law | argu'd 4.01. 95
i crave the benefit of law of arms. 4.01.100
that warranteth by law to be thy privilege. 5.04. 61
in execution | upon offenders hath exceeded law, 2H6 1.03.133
law, | and left thee to the mercy of the law. 1.03.134
prove them, and i lie open to the law; 1.03.156
let him have all the rigor of the law. 1.03.196
uncle, what shall we say to this in law? 1.03.203
this is the law, and this duke humphrey's doom. 1.03.210
and give her as a prey to law and shame, | that 2.01.194
receive the sentence of the law for /sins | such 2.03. 3
eleanor, the law, thou seest, hath judged thee; 2.03. 15
i cannot justify whom the law condemns. 2.03. 16
away, | but i in danger for the breach of law. 2.04. 66
did he not, contrary to form of law, | devise 3.01. 58
'tis meet he be condemn'd by course of law. 3.01.237
mass, 'twill be sore law then, for he was thrust 4.07. 8 P
john, it will be stinking law, for his breath 4.07. 11 P
and for this once my will shall stand for law. 3H6 4.01. 50
villain, thou know'st nor law of god nor man: R3 1.02. 70
before i be convict by course of law, | to 1.04.187
hath in the table of his law commanded | that 1.04.196
to hurl upon their heads that break his law. 1.04.200
how canst thou urge god's dreadful law to us, 1.04.209
or that we would, against the form of law, 3.05. 42
their aunt i am in law, in love their mother; 4.01. 23
that god, the law, my honor, and her love | can 4.04.341
strong arms be our conscience, swords our law! 5.03.311
if he may | find mercy in the law, 'tis his; H8 1.02.212
alleged | many sharp reasons to defeat the law. 2.01. 14
the law i bear no malice for my death; 2.01. 62
that | a woman of less place might ask by law: 2.02.111
for if the trial of the law o'ertake ye, 3.01. 96
the duke by law | found his deserts. 3.02.266
his own opinion was his law. 4.02. 37
if this law | of nature be corrupted through TRO 2.02.176
there is a law in each well-order'd nation | to 2.02.180
when what's not meet, but what must be, was law,
COR 3.01.167
he hath resisted law, | and therefore law shall 3.01.266
and therefore law shall scorn him further trial 3.01.267
traitor, if rome have law, or we have power, TIT 1.01.403
because the law hath ta'en revenge on them. 3.01.117
but even with law, against the willful sons | of 4.04. 8
that died by law for murther of our brother, 4.04. 54
let us take the law of our sides, let them begin ROM 1.01. 38 P
is the law of our side if i say ay? 1.01. 47 P
in a good quarrel, and the law on my side. 2.04.160 P
his fault concludes but what the law should end, 3.01.185
thy fault our law calls death, but the kind 3.03. 25
taking thy part, hath rush'd aside the law, 3.03. 26
the law that threat'ned death becomes thy friend 3.03.139
have, but mantua's law | is death to any he that 5.01. 66
world is not thy friend, nor the world's law, 5.01. 72
the world affords no law to make thee rich; 5.01. 73
his time, | unto the rigor of severest law. 5.03.269
right, if doing nothing be death by th' law. TIM 1.01.194 P
most true; the law shall bruise 'em. 3.05. 4
for pity is the virtue of the law, | and none 3.05. 8
who in hot blood | hath stepp'd into the law, 3.05. 12
if by this crime he owes the law his life, | why 3.05. 82
for law is strict, and war is nothing more. 3.05. 84
we are for law, he dies, urge it no more | on 3.05. 85
your grave masters are, | and pill by law. 4.01. 12
compact | well ratified by law and heraldy, HAM 1.01. 87
lost by his father, with all bands of law, | to 1.02. 24
too light, for the law of writ and the liberty: 2.02.401 P
seen the wicked prize itself | buys out the law. 3.03. 60
yet must not we put the strong law on him. 4.03. 3
but is this law? 5.01. 21 P
ay, marry, is't — crowner's quest law. 5.01. 22 P
sir, by order of law, some year elder than this, LR 1.01. 19 P
my goddess, to thy law | my services are bound. 1.02. 1
when every case in law is right; 3.02. 87
by th' law of war thou wast not bound to answer 5.03.153
upon you what restraint or grievance | the law OTH 1.02. 16
fit time | of law and course of direct session 1.02. 86
the bloody book of law | you shall yourself read 1.03. 67
for thy pains, which we | will answer as a law. ANT 3.12. 33
sooth law, i'll help. thus it must be. 4.04. 8
a voucher, | stronger than ever law could make; CYM 2.02. 40
the law | protects not us; 4.02.125
all himself, | for we do fear the law? 4.02.129
in the womb he stay'd | attending nature's law; 5.04. 38
thou art condemn'd, and must | endure our law. 5.05.299
which to prevent he made a law, | to keep her PER 1.ch. 35
life, | for that's an article within our law, 1.01. 88
in the net, like a poor man's right in the law; 2.01.117 P
believe me law, | i never kill'd a mouse, nor 4.01. 76
what says the law then? TNK 2.04. 31
thus much for law or kindred! 2.04. 32
if the law | find me, and then condemn me for't, 2.06. 13
me, | the law will have the honor of our ends. 3.06.130
better they fall by th' law than one another. 3.06.225
in her into their former law and regiment. 4.03. 96 P
have never been foul-mouth'd against thy law, 5.01. 98
than humble banks can go to law with waters 5.03. 99
and lead the majesty of law in lyam | to slip STM II.C 121
my country's head | and give the law out there. III 8
by law of nature thou art bound to breed, | that VEN 171
poor queen of love, in thine own law forlorn, 251
and dotes on what he looks, 'gainst law or duty. LUC 497
by holy human law, and common troth, | by heaven 571
'tis thou that spurn'st at right, at law, at 880
since that my case is past the help of law. 1022
grief dallied with nor law nor limit knows. 1120
forth | of wealth, of filial fear, law, kindred, LC 270
LAW-BREAKER 1 FR 0.0001 REL FR 1 V 0 P
thou art a robber, | a law-breaker, a villain. CYM 4.02. 75
LAW-DAYS 1 FR 0.0001 REL FR 1 V 0 P
keep leets and law-days and in sessions sit OTH 3.03.140
/LAWFUL 1 FR 0.0001 REL FR 1 V 0 P
/it /is /as /lawful, | /for /we /would /give TRO 5.03. 20
LAWFUL 63 FR 0.0071 REL FR 57 V 6 P
and one, | and, in the lawful name of marrying, WIV 4.06. 50
is it a lawful trade? MM 2.01.226 P
lawful mercy | is nothing kin to foul redemption 2.04.112
yet i will be content to be a lawful hangman. 4.02. 16 P
now prove | our loving lawful, and our faith not LLL 4.03.281
and that no lawful means can carry me | out of MV 4.01. 9
must be given, or the marriage is not lawful. AYL 3.03. 70 P
if this be not a lawful cause for me to leave SHR 1.02. 29 P
you see it lawful then. AWW 3.07. 30
that time and place with this deceit so lawful 3.07. 38
it speed, | is wicked meaning in a lawful deed, 3.07. 45

deed, | and lawful meaning in a lawful act, 3.07. 46
deed, | and lawful meaning in a lawful act, 3.07. 46
is't lawful, pray you, to see her women? WT 2.02. 11
shall be holy, as | you hear my spell is lawful. 5.03.105
be magic, let it be an art | lawful as eating. 5.03.111
lays most lawful claim | to this fair island and JN 1.01. 9
that thou hast under–wrought his lawful king, 2.01. 95
but on the sight of us, your lawful king, | who 2.01.222
then, by the lawful power that i have, | thou 3.01.172
lawful let it be | that i have room with rome to 3.01.179
right, | let it be lawful that law bar no wrong; 3.01.186
because we thought ourself thy lawful king; R2 3.03. 74
is it not lawful, and please your majesty, to H5 4.08.117 P
the first–begotten and the lawful heir | of 1H6 2.05. 65
thee, | doubting thy birth and lawful progeny. 3.03. 61
and therein reverenc'd for their lawful king. 5.04.140
to entertain great england's lawful king! 2H6 5.01. 4
and if he may, then am i lawful king; 3H6 1.01.137
my conscience tells me he is lawful king. 1.01.150
not took | before a true and lawful magistrate 1.02. 23
before thy sovereign and thy lawful king? 2.02. 86
seat | of england's true–anointed lawful king. 3.03. 29
am come to crave thy just and lawful aid; 3.03. 32
sister, | to england's king in lawful marriage. 3.03. 57
to link with him that were not lawful chosen. 3.03.115
war | against his brother and his lawful king? 5.01. 88
be it lawful that i invocate thy ghost | to hear R3 1.02. 8
what lawful quest have given their verdict up 1.04.184
o, make them joyful, grant their lawful suit! 3.07.203
rest thy unrest on england's lawful earth, 4.04. 29
this business, | who deem'd our marriage lawful; H8 2.04. 53
prove but our marriage lawful, by my life | and 2.04.227
him | where he shall answer, by a lawful form COR 3.01.323
to suffer lawful censure for such faults | as 3.03. 46
or more, his tribe, | to use my lawful sword! 5.06.129
wife, | that is another's lawful promis'd love. TIT 1.01.298
have all true rites and lawful ceremonies. JC 3.01.241
upon, | be it lawful i take up what's cast away. LR 1.01.253
my daughters | got 'tween the lawful sheets. 4.06.116
rip their hearts, | their papers is more lawful. 4.06.261
if it prove lawful prize, he's made for ever. OTH 1.02. 51
and in sessions sit | with meditations lawful? 3.03.141
rome, | forborne the getting of a lawful race, ANT 3.13.107
have these things set down by lawful counsel, CYM 1.04.165 P
me of my lawful pleasure she restrain'd, | and 2.05. 9
who, finger'd to make man his lawful music, PER 1.01. 82
under, | coz'ning the pillow of a lawful kiss; LUC 387
good end | for lawful policy remains enacted. 529
bred, | not spend the dowry of a lawful bed. 938
and 'gainst myself a lawful plea commence. SON 35.11
to guard the lawful reasons on thy part: 49.12
be it lawful i love thee as thou lov'st those 142. 9

LAWFULLY 4 FR 0.0004 REL FR 2 V 2 P
and lawfully by this the jew may claim | a pound MV 4.01.231
may lawfully make title to as much love as she AWW 1.03.102 P
get, he may lawfully deal for his wive's soul. PER 2.01.114 P
a wife might part us lawfully, or business, TNK 3.02. 89

LAWLESS 7 FR 0.0008 REL FR 7 V 0 P
that they may hold excus'd our lawless lives; TGV 4.01. 52
of those that lawless and incertain thought MM 3.01.126
that you should seal this lawless bloody book 2H4 4.01. 91
he needs no indirect or lawless course | to cut R3 1.04.218
enjoy, | one fit to bandy with thy lawless sons, TIT 1.01.312
there | shark'd up a list of lawless resolutes, HAM 1.01. 98
in his lawless fit, | behind the arras hearing 4.01. 8

LAWLESSLY 1 FR 0.0001 REL FR 1 V 0 P
mind, | and will not use a woman lawlessly. TGV 5.03. 14

LAWN 5 FR 0.0005 REL FR 4 V 1 P
lawn as white as driven snow, | cypress black as WT 4.04.218
for a joint–ring, nor for measures of lawn, nor OTH 4.03. 73 P
like lawn being spread upon the blushing rose, VEN 590
first red as roses that on lawn we lay, | then LUC 258
lay, | then white as lawn, the roses took away. 259

LAWNS 1 FR 0.0001 REL FR 0 V 1 P
inkles, caddises, cambrics, lawns. WT 4.04.207 P

LAWRENCE' 5 FR 0.0005 REL FR 5 V 0 P
and there she shall at friar lawrence' cell | be ROM 2.04.181
then hie you hence to friar lawrence' cell, 2.05. 68
i'll to him, he is hid at lawrence' cell. 3.02.141
having displeas'd my father, to lawrence' cell, 3.05.232
i met the youthful lord at lawrence' cell, | and 4.02. 25

LAWRENCE 3 FR 0.0003 REL FR 3 V 0 P
within the parish | saint lawrence poultney, did H8 1.02.153
what, is my daughter gone to friar lawrence? ROM 4.02. 11
by holy lawrence to fall prostrate here | and 4.02. 20

LAW'S 3 FR 0.0003 REL FR 2 V 1 P
i keep her as a vessel of thy law's fury, and LLL 1.01.274 P
the pangs of despis'd love, the law's delay, HAM 3.01. 71
in vice their law's their will; PER 1.01.103

LAWS 39 FR 0.0044 REL FR 33 V 6 P
so to enforce or qualify the laws | as to your MM 1.01. 65
we have strict statutes and most biting laws 1.03. 19
what knows the laws | that thieves do pass on 2.01. 22
laws for all faults, | but faults so 5.01.319
i am not partial to infringe our laws; ERR 1.01. 4
now trust me, were it not against our laws, 1.01.142
against the laws and statutes of this town, 5.01.126
so to the laws at large i write my name, | and LLL 1.01.155
these oaths and laws will prove an idle scorn. 1.01.309
the brain may devise laws for the blood, but a MV 1.02. 18 P
lands and goods | are, by the laws of venice, 4.01.311
it is enacted in the laws of venice, | if it be 4.01.348
for i am loath to break our country's laws. R2 2.03.169
counsel in the laws of this land–service, i did 2H4 1.02.135 P
see your most dreadful laws so loosely slighted, 5.02. 94
the laws of england are at my commandement. 5.03.136 P
sought, that to her laws | we do deliver you. H5 2.02.176
prerogatifes and laws of the wars is not kept. 4.01. 67 P
of the king's laws in now the king's quarrel. 4.01.171 P
only that the laws of england may come out of 2H6 4.07. 6 P
up, | and with the same to act controlling laws. 5.01.103
and, for i should not deal in her soft laws, 3H6 3.02.154
we must not rend our subjects from our laws, H8 1.02. 93
by all the laws of war y' are privileg'd. 1.04. 52
his faults lie open to the laws, let them, | not 3.02.334
toward the king first, then his laws, in filling 5.02. 50
is, these moral laws | of nature and of nations TRO 2.02.184
opposing laws with strokes, and here defying COR 3.03. 79
but let the laws of rome determine all, | mean TIT 1.01.407
degrees, observances, customs, and laws, TIM 4.01. 19
religious canons, civil laws are cruel; 4.03. 61
the laws, your curb and whip, in their rough 4.03.443
but shall be remedied to your public laws | at 5.04. 62
say if i do, the laws are mine, not thine; LR 5.03.159
was that mulmutius which | ordain'd our laws, CYM 3.01. 55
mulmutius made our laws, | who was the first of 3.01. 58
are you, that, 'gainst the tenor of my laws, TNK 3.06.133
pleads, in a wilderness where are no laws, | to LUC 544
to leave poor me thou hast the strength of laws, SON 49.13

LAWYER 4 FR 0.0004 REL FR 1 V 3 P
appears like a lord, sometime like a lawyer, TIM 2.02.110 P
why may not that be the skull of a lawyer? HAM 5.01. 99 P
then 'tis like the breath of an unfee'd lawyer, LR 1.04.129 P
i will make | one of her women lawyer to me, for CYM 2.03. 74

LAWYER'S 2 FR 0.0002 REL FR 1 V 1 P
nor the lawyer's, which is politic; AYL 4.01. 13 P
crack the lawyer's voice, | that he may never TIM 4.03.153

LAWYERS' 1 FR 0.0001 REL FR 1 V 0 P
o'er lawyers' fingers, who straight dream on ROM 1.04. 73

LAWYERS 4 FR 0.0004 REL FR 1 V 3 P
with lawyers in the vacation; AYL 3.02.331 P
points more than all the lawyers in bohemia can WT 4.04.205 P
first thing we do, let's kill all the lawyers. 2H6 4.02. 77 P
all scholars, lawyers, courtiers, gentlemen, 4.04. 36

/LAY* 2 FR 0.0002 REL FR 2 V 0 P
/teach /her /not /thus /to /lay | /such /violent TIT 3.02. 21
/violent /hands /can /she /lay /on /her /life? 3.02. 25

LAY* 294 FR 0.0332 REL FR 227 V 67 P
lay her a–hold, a–hold! TMP 1.01. 49 P
lay her off. 1.01. 50 P
it was a torment | to lay upon the damn'd, which 1.02.290
three inches of it, | can lay to bed for ever; 2.01.284
they will lay out ten to see a dead indian. 2.02. 32 P
but see how i lay the dust with my tears. TGV 2.03. 32 P
you must lay lime to tangle her desires | by 3.02. 68
sir, you should lay my countenance to pawn. WIV 2.02. 6 P
of them all (when the court lay at windsor) 2.02. 62 P
i must very much lay open mine own imperfection; 2.02.184 P
it, as to lay an amiable siege to the honesty of 2.02.234 P
come, lay their swords to pawn. 3.01.110 P
i will lay a plot to try that, and we will yet 3.03.190 P
and how long lay you there? 3.05. 94 P
you must lay down the treasures of your body MM 2.04. 96
lay by all nicety and prolixious blushes | that 2.04.162
imprisonment | can lay on nature is a paradise 3.01.130
of my cunning, | i will lay myself in hazard. 4.02.156 P
had he been lay, my lord, | for certain words he 5.01.128
lay bolts enough upon him. 5.01.346 P
lay hold on him. 5.01.359
lay open to my earthy, gross conceit, ERR 3.02. 34
such claim as you would lay to your horse, and 3.02. 85 P
good people, enter and lay hold on him. 5.01. 91
your goods that lay at host, sir, in the centaur 5.01.411
of the false sweet bait that we lay for it. ADO 3.01. 33
to be a thief, shall we not lay hands on him? 3.03. 55 P
carduus benedictus, and lay it to your heart; 3.04. 74 P
shape | than i can lay it down in likelihood. 4.01.236
nay, never lay thy hand upon thy sword, | i fear 5.01. 54
me | that i am forc'd to lay my reverence by, 5.01. 64
and, to conclude, what you lay to their charge. 5.01.223 P
penance your invention | can lay upon my sin; 5.01.274
i'll lay my head to any good man's hat, | these LLL 1.01.308
nor never lay his wreathed arms athwart | his 4.03.133
now to plain–dealing, lay these glozes by: 4.03.367
and lay my arms before the legs of this sweet 5.02.555
war, death, or sickness did lay siege to it, MND 1.01.142
lay breath so bitter on your bitter foe. 3.02. 44
lay them in gore, | since you have shore | with 5.01.339
match, | and on the wager lay two earthly women,
MV 3.05. 80
shall i lay perjury upon my soul? 4.01.229
therefore lay bare your bosom. 4.01.252
grecian tents, | where cressid lay that night. 5.01. 6
for, by this ring, the doctor lay with me. 5.01.259
wilt thou lay hands on me, villain? AYL 1.01. 55 P
did steal behind him as he lay along | under an 2.01. 30
there lay he, stretch'd along, like a wounded 3.02.240 P
o'ergrown with hair, | lay sleeping on his back; 4.03.107
lay couching, head on ground, with cat–like 4.03.115
for though you lay here in this goodly chamber, SHR in.2. 84
how the young folks lay their heads together! 1.02.139 P
'twas a commodity lay fretting by you; 2.01.328
lay forth the gown. 4.03. 62
if thou accountedst it shame, lay it on me, 4.03.181
lay hands on the villain. 5.01. 38 P
lay hold on him, i charge you, in the duke's 5.01. 88 P
the duke will lay upon him all the honor | that AWW 3.02. 71
hope, lay our best love and credence | upon thy 3.03. 2
for he persists | as if his life lay on't. 3.07. 43
they know his conditions and lay him in straw. 4.03.258 P
which lay nice manners by, i put you to | the 5.01. 15
lay a more noble thought upon mine honor | than 5.03.180
for your love, to lay any of them on you. TN 2.01. 7 P
lay me, o, where | sad true lover never find my 2.04. 64
i dare lay any money 'twill be nothing yet. 3.04.396 P
i dare my life lay down — and will do't, sir, WT 2.01.130
might we lay th' old proverb to your charge, 2.03. 97
the level of your dreams, | which i'll lay down. 3.02. 82
she did approach | my cabin where i lay; 3.03. 24
air'd abroad, i desire to lay my bones there. 4.02. 6 P
business, and lay aside the thoughts of sicilia. 4.02. 51 P
thou hast need of more rags to lay on thee, 4.03. 55 P
come on, lay it by; 4.04.273 P
lay it by too. another. 4.04.285 P
some hangman must put on my shroud and lay me 4.04.457
desiring thee to lay aside the sword | which JN 1.01. 12
born, | doth he lay claim to thine inheritance? 1.01. 72
of no, | that still i lay upon my mother's head, 1.01. 76
shores | between my father and my mother lay, 1.01.106
lay not my transgression to my charge | that art 1.01.256
needs must you lay your heart at his dispose, 1.01.263
upon thy cheek lay i this zealous kiss | as seal 2.01. 19
we'll lay before this town our royal bones, 2.01. 41
or lay on that shall make your shoulders crack. 2.01.146
wilt thou resign them and lay down thy arms? 2.01.154
before we will lay down our just–borne arms 2.01.345
and lay this angiers even with the ground, 2.01.399
done, | doth lay it open to urge on revenge. 4.03. 38
go i to make the french lay down their arms. 5.01. 24
he flatly says he'll not lay down his arms. 5.02.126
king, | and lay aside my high blood's royalty, R2 1.01. 71
what doth our cousin lay to mowbray's charge? 1.01. 84
foe, | once did i lay an ambush for your life, 1.01.137
let them lay by their helmets and their spears, 1.03.119
lay on our royal sword your banish'd hands; 1.03.179
to lay aside life–harming heaviness | and 2.02. 3
and therefore personally i lay my claim | to my 2.03.135
even at his feet to lay my arms and power, 3.03. 39
and lay the summer's dust with show'rs of blood 3.03. 43
i'll lay | a plot shall show us all a merry day. 4.01.333
in cradle–clothes our children where they lay, 1H4 1.01. 88
got with swearing "lay by," and spent with 1.02. 36 P
alone, i will lay him down such reasons for this 1.02.150 P
lay thine ear close to the ground, and list if 2.02. 32 P
to the king, and lay open all our proceedings. 2.03. 31 P
here i lay, and thus i bore my point. 2.04.195 P
she bids you on the wanton rushes lay you down, 3.01.211
quick, quick, that i may lay my head in thy lap. 3.01.227 P
it meet | to lay so dangerous and dear a trust 4.01. 34
lay out, lay out. 4.02. 5 P
lay out, lay out. 4.02. 5 P
rebellion lay in his way, and he found it. 5.01. 28 P
o, would the quarrel lay upon our heads, | and 5.02. 47
i lay aside that which grows to me? 2H4 1.02. 87 P
to lay down likelihoods and forms of hope. 1.03. 35
where lay the king to–night? 2.01.168
do you remember since we lay all night in the 3.02.194 P
mile–end green, when i lay at clement's inn — i 3.02.279 P
of these times | to lay a heavy and unequal hand 4.01.100
father, | the image of his power lay then in me, 5.02. 74
then, pistol, lay thy head in furies' lap. 5.03.106
i will lay odds that, ere this year expire, | we 5.05.105
but lay down our proportions to defend | against H5 1.02.137
or lay these bones in an unworthy urn, 1.02.228
so 'a bade me lay more clothes on his feet. 2.03. 22 P
and lay apart | the borrowed glories that by 2.04. 78
to lay apart their particular functions and 3.07. 38 P
indeed the french may lay twenty french crowns 4.01.225 P
our children, and our sins lay on the king! 4.01.232
comes to him where in gore he lay insteeped, 4.06. 12
i could lay on like a butcher and sit like a 5.02.141 P
or will you blame and lay the fault on me? 1H6 2.01. 57
and lay new platforms to endamage them. 2.01. 77
or aught intend'st to lay unto my charge, | do 3.01. 4
shall lay your stately and air–braving towers, 4.02. 13
come, come, and lay him in his father's arms, 4.07. 29
peace, | and lay them gently on thy tender side. 5.03. 49
lay hands upon these traitors and their trash. 2H6 1.04. 41
lay not thy hands on me; 3.02. 46
a thousand crowns, or else lay down your head. 4.01. 16
mark'd for the gallows, lay your weapons down, 4.02.123
i see them lay their heads together to surprise 4.08. 58 P
a dreadful lay! address thee instantly! 5.02. 27
race, | i lay me down a little while to breathe; 3H6 2.03. 2
why linger we? let us lay hands upon him. 3.01. 26
thee, | i lay it naked to the deadly stroke, R3 1.02.177
and lay those honors on your high desert. 1.03. 96
i lay unto the grievous charge of others. 1.03.325
some lay in dead men's skulls, and, in the holes 1.04. 29
and mock'd the dead bones that lay scatt'red by. 1.04. 33
that you depart, and lay no hands on me. 1.04.191
told me, when we both lay in the field | frozen 2.01.115
night, i /hear, they lay at stony–stratford, 2.04. 1
on him i lay that you would lay on me, | the 3.07.171
on him i lay that you would lay on me, | the 3.07.171
thus," quoth dighton, "lay the gentle babes." 4.03. 9
a book of prayers on their pillow lay, | which 4.03. 14
a charge as little honor | he meant to lay upon; H8 1.01. 78
have got a speeding trick to lay down ladies. 1.03. 40
of the sea, | hung their heads, and then lay by. 3.01. 11
else | this talking lord can lay upon my credit, 3.02.265
when the brown wench | lay kissing in your arms, 3.02.296
off | from ampthill, where the princess lay — 4.01. 28
is the goodliest woman | that ever lay by man — 4.01. 70
is come to lay his weary bones among ye; 4.02. 22
embalm me, | then lay me forth. 4.02.171
lay all the weight ye can upon my patience, | i 5.02.101
blame me for't, i'll lay ye all | by th' heels, 5.03. 78
he'll lay about him to–day, i can tell them that TRO 1.02. 56 P
peace, troyan, lay thy finger on thy lips! 1.03.240
messengers, and we lay by | our appertainings, 2.03. 79
i'll lay my life, with my disposer cressida. 3.01. 87 P
all, | lay negligent and loose regard upon him. 3.03. 41
rain, to lay this wind, or my heart will be 4.04. 53 P
lay hold upon him, priam, hold him fast, | he is 5.03. 59
would the nobility lay aside their ruth | and COR 1.01.197
come, lay aside your stitchery, i must have you 1.03. 69 P
i sometime lay here in corioles | at a poor 1.09. 82
lay | a fault on us, your tribunes, that we 2.03.226
lay the fault on us. 2.03.234
to unbuild the city, and to lay all flat. 3.01.197
that is the way to lay the city flat, | to bring 3.01.203
therefore lay hold of him; 3.01.211
lay hands upon him, | and bear him to the rock. 3.01.221
lay hands upon him. 3.01.226
masters, lay down your weapons. 3.01.329
with fire, and took | what lay before them. 4.06. 79
make way to lay them by their bretheren. TIT 1.01. 89
when he by night lay bath'd in maiden blood. 2.03.232
steel will write these words, | and lay it by. 4.01.104
hole, | where the dead corpse of bassianus lay; 5.01.105
now goes | to lay a complot to betray thy foes. 5.02.147
caius and valentine, lay hands on them. 5.02.158
in fair verona, where we lay our scene, | from ROM pr 2
i'll lay fourteen of my teeth — | and yet, to 1.03. 12
he that can lay hold of her | shall have the 1.05.116
and all my fortunes at thy foot i'll lay, | and 2.02.147
a grave, | to lay one in, another out to have. 2.03. 84
one paris, that would fain lay knife aboard; 2.04.202 P
thursday is near, lay hand on heart, advise. 3.05.190
then will i lay the serving–creature's dagger on 4.05.117 P
under yond /yew trees lay thee all along, 5.03. 3
merciful, | open the tomb, lay me with juliet. 5.03. 73
here untimely lay | the noble paris and true 5.03.258

thus honest fools lay out their wealth on TIM 1.02.235
up | my discontented troops, and lay for hearts. 3.05.114
not nature | (to whom all sores lay siege) can 4.03. 7
the world, apemantus, if it lay in thy power? 4.03.322 P
as this time | is like to lay upon us. JC 1.02.175
he was very loath to lay his fingers off it. 1.02.242 P
and look you lay it in the praetor's chair, 1.03.143
and though we lay these honors on this man | to 4.01. 19
lay it to thy heart, and farewell." MAC 1.05. 13 P
where we lay, | our chimneys were blown down, 2.03. 54
here lay duncan, | his silver skin lac'd with 2.03.111
great tyranny, lay thou thy basis sure, | for 4.03. 32
lay on, macduff, | and damn'd be him that first 5.08. 33
and lay your hands again upon my sword. HAM 1.05.158
bent, | to lay our service freely at your feet, 2.02. 31
when he lay couched in th' ominous horse, | hath 2.02.454
look you lay home to him. 3.04. 1
lay not that flattering unction to your soul, 3.04.145
to think they would lay him i' th' cold ground. 4.05. 69 P
pull'd the poor wretch from her melodious lay 4.07.182
lay her i' th' earth, | and from her fair and 5.01.238
/methought i lay | worse than the mutines in the 5.02. 5
to lay his goatish disposition on the charge of LR 1.02.127 P
lay comforts to your bosom, and bestow | your 2.01.126
but if /thy flight lay toward the roaring sea, 3.04. 10
i will lay trust upon thee; 3.05. 24 P
there is a litter ready, lay him in't, | and 3.06. 90
lay hand upon him. 4.06.188
and | to lay the blame upon her own despair, 5.03.255
lay hold upon him, if he do resist | subdue him OTH 1.02. 80
let me speak like yourself, and lay a sentence, 1.03.199
lay thy finger thus; 2.01.221 P
my fortunes against any lay worth naming, this 2.03.324 P
i lay with cassio lately, | and, being troubled 3.03.413
now, if this suit lay in bianca's /pow'r, | how 4.01.107
lay down my soul at stake. 4.02. 13
your calling back, | lay not your blame on me. 4.02. 46
to-night | lay on my bed my wedding-sheets — 4.02.105
lay by these — "— willow, willow" — | prithee 4.03. 48 P
that men must lay their murthers on your neck. 5.02.170
nay, lay thee down and roar; 5.02.198
ay, ay! o, lay me by my mistress' side. 5.02.237
if it lay in their hands to make me a cuckold, ANT 1.02. 76 P
which seem'd to tell them his remembrance lay 1.05. 57
she made great caesar lay his sword to bed; 2.02.227
therefore | to lay his gay comparisons apart, 3.13. 26
i am prompt | to lay my crown at 's feet, and 3.13. 76
give me grace to lay | my duty on your hand. 3.13. 81
kisses the poor last | i lay upon thy lips. 4.15. 21
doom, in the name lay | a moi'ty of the world. 5.01. 18
rather on nilus' mud | lay me stark-nak'd, and 5.02. 59
but if you seek | to lay on me a cruelty, by 5.02.129
i dare lay mine honor | he will remain so. CYM 1.01.174
which else an easy battery might lay flat, for 1.04. 22 P
i will lay you ten /thousand ducats to your ring 1.04.127 P
i will have it no lay. 1.04.147 P
you lay out too much pains | for purchasing but 2.03. 87
he'ld lay the future open. 3.02. 29
wilt lay the leaven on all proper men; 3.04. 62
say, where shall 's lay him? 4.02.233
nay, cadwal, we must lay his head to th' east, 4.02.255
we have done our obsequies. come lay him down. 4.02.282
lay hands on him; 5.03. 91
this tablet lay upon his breast, wherein | our 5.04.109
griefs as you yourself do lay upon yourself. PER 1.02. 66
had and have of subjects' good | on thee i lay, 1.02.119
lay the babe | upon the pillow. 3.01. 67
certain jewels | lay with you in your coffer, 3.04. 2
is dead that lay with the little baggage. 4.02. 23 P
him, if he i' th' blood-siz'd field lay swoll'n, TNK 1.01. 99
and if the lives of all my name lay on it, | i 2.02.175
now, when the credit of our town lay on it, 3.05. 56
that i lay fatting like a swine, to fight, | and 3.06. 12
lay by your anger for an hour, and dove-like, 5.01. 11
i prithee lay attention to the cry; 5.03. 91
for where they lay the shadow had forsook them, VEN 176
wood, | even so confounded in the dark she lay, 827
by this the boy that by her side lay kill'd 1165
and in his blood that on the ground lay spill'd, 1167
first red as roses that on lawn we lay, | then LUC 258
light, | and canopied in darkness sweetly lay, 398
day," quoth she, "night's scapes doth open lay, 747
"if, collatine, thine honor lay in me, | from me 834
to burn the guiltless casket where it lay! 1057
and on that pillow lay | where thou wast wont to 1620
yet neither may possess the claim they lay. 1794
let the bird of loudest lay, | on the sole PHT 1
and both for my sake lay on me this cross. SON 42.12
beauty no pencil, beauty's truth to lay; 101. 7

LAYER-UP 1 FR 0.0001 REL FR 0 V 1 P
that old age, that ill layer-up of beauty, can H5 5.02.230 P

LAYEST 3 FR 0.0003 REL FR 2 V 1 P
and, whilst thou layest in thy unhallowed dam, MV 4.01.136
thou layest the plot how. 1H4 2.01. 52 P
layest thou thy leaden mace upon my boy, | that JC 4.03.268

/LAYING 1 FR 0.0001 REL FR 1 V 0 P
water-pots, | /ay, /and /laying /autumn's /dust. LR 4.06.197

LAYING 10 FR 0.0011 REL FR 8 V 2 P
nay, i was taken up for laying them down; TGV 1.02.132
the more fool you for laying on my duty. SHR 5.02.129
i lost mine eye in laying the prize aboard, 2H6 4.01. 25
have broke their backs with laying manors on 'em H8 1.01. 84
there's laying on, take't off who will, as they TRO 1.02.207 P
by each at once her choppy finger laying | upon MAC 1.03. 44
you laying these slight sallies on my son, | as HAM 2.01. 39
that will scarce hold the laying in — 'a will 5.01.167 P
yourself | by laying defects of judgment to me; ANT 2.02. 55
them, laying by | that nothing-gift of differing CYM 3.06. 84

LAYS* 24 FR 0.0027 REL FR 18 V 6 P
he lays it on. TMP 3.02.151 P
besides these, other bars he lays before me, WIV 3.04. 7
what claim lays she to thee? ERR 3.02. 84 P
being a very beastly creature, lays claim to me. 3.02. 88 P
my love and some necessity | now lays upon you. MV 3.04. 35
is a youth here in the forest lays claim to you. AYL 5.01. 7 P
lays down his wanton siege before her beauty, AWW 3.07. 18
her mistress of the feast, and she lays it on. WT 4.03. 40 P
lays most lawful claim | to this fair island and JN 1.01. 9
john lays you plots; 3.04.146
that she will light to listen to the lays, | and 2H6 1.03. 90
that lays strong siege unto this wretch's soul, 3.03. 22
ground, | then lays his finger on his temple; H8 3.02.115
then if she that lays thee out says thou art a TRO 2.03. 31 P
on each bush | lays her full mess before you. TIM 4.03.421
his absence, sir, | lays blame upon his promise. MAC 3.04. 43
dances | as goddess-like to her admired lays. PER 5.ch. 4
his hoarse throat, | abuse young lays of love. TNK 5.01. 89
lays open all the little worms that creep; LUC 1248
and wish her lays were tuned like the lark. PP 14.18
yet nor the lays of birds, nor the sweet smell SON 98. 5
sing to the ear that doth thy lays esteem, | and 100. 7
when i was wont to greet it with my lays, | as 102. 6
wrong | that thy unkindness lays upon my heart, 139. 2

LAY'ST 2 FR 0.0002 REL FR 2 V 0 P
plantagenet, for all the claim thou lay'st, 3H6 1.01.152
thou lay'st in every gash that love hath given TRO 1.01. 62

LAY'T 2 FR 0.0002 REL FR 1 V 1 P
lay't so to his charge: WT 5.01.195
for the command, i'll lay't upon you. OTH 2.01.265 P

LAY-THOUGHTS 1 FR 0.0001 REL FR 1 V 0 P
the cardinal | but half my lay-thoughts in him, H8 1.04. 11

LAY-TO 1 FR 0.0001 REL FR 0 V 1 P
monster, lay-to your fingers. TMP 4.01.250 P

LAZAR 2 FR 0.0002 REL FR 1 V 1 P
fetch forth the lazar kite of cressid's kind, H5 2.01. 76
for i care not to be the louse of a lazar, so i TRO 5.01. 65 P

LAZAR-LIKE 1 FR 0.0001 REL FR 1 V 0 P
most lazar-like, with vile and loathsome crust, HAM 1.05. 72

LAZARS 2 FR 0.0002 REL FR 1 V 1 P
and, to relief of lazars, and weak age | of H5 1.01. 15
sworn upon't she never shrouded any but lazars. TRO 2.03. 33 P

LAZARUS 1 FR 0.0001 REL FR 0 V 1 P
slaves as ragged as lazarus in the painted cloth 1H4 4.02. 25 P

LAZY 13 FR 0.0014 REL FR 12 V 1 P
such dishonor undergo, | while i sit lazy by. TMP 3.01. 28
how shall we beguile | the lazy time, if not MND 5.01. 41
hour would detect the lazy foot of time as well AYL 3.02.304 P
o'er to executors pale | the lazy yawning drone. H5 1.02.204
our soldiers', like the night-owl's lazy flight, 3H6 2.01.130
these lazy knaves? H8 5.03. 70
y' are lazy knaves, | and here ye lie baiting of 5.03. 80
him patroclus | upon a lazy bed the livelong day TRO 1.03.147
thy brass voice through all these lazy tents, 1.03.257
worm | prick'd from the lazy finger of a /maid. ROM 1.04. 69
when he bestrides the lazy puffing clouds, | and 2.02. 31
leave 'em all behind us | like lazy clouds, TNK 2.02. 14
and now adonis, with a lazy sprite, | and with a VEN 181

/LE 1 FR 0.0001 REL FR 0 V 1 P
here comes monsieur /le beau. AYL 1.02. 91 P

LE 39 FR 0.0044 REL FR 5 V 34 P
oui, mette le au mon pocket; WIV 1.04. 54 P
say you by the french lord, monsieur le /bon? MV 1.02. 55 P
bon jour, monsieur le beau. AYL 1.02. 97 P
call him hither, good monsieur le beau. 1.02.163 P
to saint jaques le grand. AWW 3.05. 34
is a pilgrimage to saint jaques le grand; 4.03. 49 P
heard these islanders shout out | "vive le roi!" JN 5.02.104
i have from le port blanc, | a bay in britain, R2 2.01.277
ete en angleterre, et tu bien parles le langage. H5 3.04. 2 P
je pense que je suis le bon ecolier; 3.04. 13 P
dites-moi l'anglois pour le bras. 3.04. 21 P
et le coude? 3.04. 23 P
comment appelez-vous le col? 3.04. 32 P
de nick. et le menton? 3.04. 34 P
de sin. le col, de nick; le menton, de sin. 3.04. 36 P
de sin. le col, de nick; le menton, de sin. 3.04. 36 P
comment appelez-vous le pied et la robe? 3.04. 50 P
le foot, madame, et le count. 3.04. 51 P
le foot, madame, et le count. 3.04. 51 P
le foot et le count! 3.04. 52 P
le foot et le count! 3.04. 52 P
les seigneurs de france pour tout le monde. 3.04. 56 P
le foot et le count! 3.04. 56 P
le foot et le count! 3.04. 56 P
d' elbow, de nick, de sin, de foot, le count. 3.04. 59 P
le cheval volant, the pegasus, chez les narines 3.07. 14 P
"le chien est retourne a son propre vomissement, 3.07. 64 P
harry le roy. 4.01. 49 P
le roy? 4.01. 50
je pense que vous etes le gentilhomme de bonne 4.04. 2 P
monsieur le fer. 4.04. 26 P
je suis le gentilhomme de bonne maison; 4.04. 41 P
a vous donner la liberte, le franchisement. 4.04. 52 P
chevalier, je pense, le plus brave, vaillant, et 4.04. 56 P
suivez-vous le grand capitaine. 4.04. 66 P
o seigneur! le jour est perdu, tout est perdu! 4.05. 2
je quand sur le possession de france, et quand 5.02.181 P
et quand vous avez le possession de moi — let 5.02.182 P
sauf votre honneur, le francois que vous parlez, 5.02.188 P

/LEAD* 1 FR 0.0001 REL FR 1 V 0 P
/the /bedlam | /to /lead /him /where /he /would; LR 3.07.104

LEAD* 163 FR 0.0184 REL FR 138 V 25 P
lead off this ground, and let's make further TMP 2.01.323
lead away. 2.01.325
nor lead me, like a fire-brand, in the dark 2.02. 6
i prithee now lead the way without any more 2.02.173 P
o brave monster! lead the way. 2.02.188 P
lead, monster, we'll follow. 3.02.150 P
nay, pray you lead the way. WIV 1.01.305 P
suit, and lead him on with a fine-baited delay, 2.01. 95 P
whether had you rather lead mine eyes, or eye 3.02. 3 P
i hope not, i had lief as bear so much lead. 4.02.113 P
lead forth and bring you back in happiness! MM 1.01. 74
thee will i love and with thee lead my life; ERR 3.02. 67
cuts for the senior, till then, lead thou first. 5.01.423
please it your grace lead on? ADO 1.01.159 P
of the berrord, and lead his apes into hell. 2.01. 41 P
nay, if they lead to any ill, i will leave them 2.01.153 P
flow in grief, | the smallest twine may lead me. 4.01.250
as swift as lead, sir. LLL 3.01. 57 P
is not lead a metal heavy, dull, and slow? 3.01. 59
i say lead is slow. 3.01. 61
is that lead slow which is fir'd from a gun? 3.01. 62
you, and purpose now | to lead you to our court; 5.02.344
ay, and in a brooch of lead. 5.02.617 P
didst not thou lead him through the glimmering MND 2.01. 77
i'll follow you, i'll lead you about a round, 3.01.106
lead him to my bower. 3.01.197
and lead these testy rivals so astray | as one 3.02.358
and from each other look thou lead them thus, 3.02.363
up and down, | i will lead them up and down; 3.02.397
goblin, lead them up and down. 3.02.399
gold, silver, and lead, whereof who chooses his MV 1.02. 30 P
therefore i pray you lead me to the caskets | to 2.01. 23
this third, dull lead, with warning all as blunt 2.07. 8
for lead! 2.07. 17
hazard for lead? 2.07. 17
i'll then nor give nor hazard aught for lead. 2.07. 21
is't like that lead contains her? 2.07. 49
gold, silver, and base lead. 2.09. 20
but thou, thou meagre lead, | which rather 3.02.104
we'll lead you thither. AYL 4.03.161
and for your love to her lead apes in hell. SHR 2.01. 34
sirrah, lead these gentlemen | to my daughters, 2.01.108
signior baptista, shall i lead the way? 4.04. 69
and though the devil lead the measure, such are AWW 2.01. 56 P
why, he's able to lead her a coranto. 2.03. 43 P
you had my prayers to lead them on, and to keep 2.04. 17 P
now will i lead you to the house, and show you 3.06.110
art, will lead thee on | to gather from thee. 4.01. 81
i thank thee. lead me on. TN 1.02. 64
if you will lead these graces to the grave | and 1.05.242
lead me on. 3.04.372
then lead the way, good father, and heavens so 4.03. 34
so bloody, must | lead on to some foul issue. WT 2.03.153
come, and lead me | to these sorrows. 3.02.242
lead us from hence, where we may leisurely 5.03.152
hastily lead away. 5.03.155
out of the path which shall directly lead | thy JN 3.04.129
lead me to the revolts of england here. 5.04. 7
which didst lead me forth | of that sweet way i R2 3.02.204
the lives of those that he did lead to fight 1H4 1.03. 82
the boy shall lead our horses down the hill. 2.02. 78 P
bid butler lead him forth into the park. 2.03. 72
ere i lead this life long, i'll sew 2.04.116 P
i am as hot as molten lead, and as heavy too. 5.03. 33 P
god keep lead out of me! 5.03. 34 P
my lord of westmerland, lead him to his tent. 5.04. 8
come, my lord, i'll lead you to your tent. 5.04. 9
lead me, my lord? 5.04. 10
turn'd on themselves, like dull and heavy lead. 2H4 1.01.118
who is it like should lead his forces hither? 1.03. 81
sinful continents, what a life dost thou lead! 2.04.286 P
on, bardolph, lead the men away. 3.02.300 P
blunt, lead him hence, and see you guard him 4.03. 75
we will our youth lead on to higher fields, 4.04. 3
purpose now | to lead out many to the holy land, 4.05.210
make him burst his lead and rise from death. 1H6 1.01. 64
then lead me hence; 5.04. 86
go, lead the way, i long to see my prison. 2H6 2.04.110
to ireland will you lead a band of men, 3.01.312
you, | or let a /rebel lead you to your deaths? 4.08. 13
in god's name lead; 3H6 3.01. 99
land, | while i myself will lead a private life, 4.06. 42
come, lead me to the block; R3 3.04.106
and lead thy daughter to a conqueror's bed; 4.04.334
come lead me, officers, to the block of shame; 5.01. 28
let us be lead within thy bosom, richard, | and 5.03.147
i will lead forth my soldiers to the plain, 5.03.291
and who doth lead them but a paltry fellow, 5.03.323
lead in your ladies, ev'ry one. H8 1.04.103
and a measure | to lead 'em once again, and then 1.04.107
lead on a' god's name. 2.01. 78
and when old time shall lead him to his end, 2.01. 93
serve the king, and — prithee lead me in. 3.02.450
lead the way, lords, | ye must all see the queen 5.04. 72
to our pavilion shall i lead you, sir. TRO 1.03.305
i will lead the way. 3.03. 54
upon your favors swims with fins of lead, | and COR 1.01.180
lead you on. 1.01.245
these three lead on this preparation | whither 1.02. 15
gods | lead their successes as we wish our own, 1.06. 7
place | i lead espous'd my bride along with me. TIT 1.01.328
feather of lead, bright smoke, cold fire, sick ROM 1.01.180
i have a soul of lead | so stakes me to the 1.04. 15
ye, if ye should lead her in a fool's paradise, 2.04.165 P
dead, | unwieldy, slow, heavy, and pale as lead. 2.05. 17
lead, boy, which way? 5.03.168
of your woes, | and lead you even to death. 5.03.220
why dost thou lead these men about the streets? JC 1.01. 28
into what dangers would you lead me, cassius, 1.02. 63
brutus shall lead, and we will grace his heels 3.01.120
bid our commanders lead their charges off | a 4.02. 48
lead your battle softly on | upon the left hand 5.01. 16
may, | lovers in peace, lead on our days to age! 5.01. 94
why then lead on. 5.01.122
a heavy summons lies like lead upon me, | and MAC 2.01. 6
your right noble son, | lead our first battle. 5.06. 4
whither wilt thou lead me? HAM 1.05. 1
if circumstances lead me, i will find | where 2.02.157
whether love lead fortune, or else fortune love. 3.02.203
with modesty enough and likelihood to lead it: 5.01.208 P
naked soul, | which i'll entreat to lead me. LR 4.01. 45
the time's plague, when madmen lead the blind. 4.01. 46
give me thy arm; | poor tom shall lead thee. 4.01. 79
the life | that wants the means to lead it. 4.04. 20
me your hand, | i'll lead you to some biding. 4.06.224
that mine own tears | do scald like molten lead. 4.07. 47
fadom they have none | to lead their business; OTH 1.01.153
him, | lead to the sagittary the raised search; 1.01.158
pray you lead on. 1.01.180
best judgment collied, | assays to lead the way. 2.03.207
lead him off. 2.03.254
which lead directly to the door of truth | will 3.03.407
sister's view, | whither straight i'll lead you. ANT 2.02.168
lead me from hence; 2.05.109
lead me to my chamber. 2.05.119
will you lead, lords? 2.06. 81
'tis not my profit that does lead mine honor; 2.07. 76
love, i am full of lead. 3.11. 72
and will lead you | where rather i'll expect 4.02. 42
lead me. 4.04. 35
he'll lead me then in triumph? 5.02.109

lead, lead! CYM 4.04. 53
lead, lead! 4.04. 53
sir, lead 's the way. PER 5.03. 84
let him lead his line | to catch one at my heart TNK 1.01.116
pirithous, | lead on the bride. 1.01.208
lead into the city, | where, having bound things 1.04. 47
go lead the way; 2.05. 59
ira, nec ignis" — | strike up, and lead her in. 3.05. 89
i'll lead. 3.05. 90
put in a cauldron of lead and usurers' grease, 4.03. 37 P
yet is heavier | than lead itself, stings more 5.01. 97
methought alcides was | to him a sow of lead. 5.03.120
lead, courageous cousin. 5.04. 38
glory in a life | that thou art yet to lead. 5.04. 44
lead your lady off; 5.04.122
you | to lead those that the dev'l cannot rule. STM II.C 56
and lead the majesty of law in lyam | to slip II.C 121
mine eyes are turn'd to fire, my heart to lead: VEN 1072
heavy heart's lead, melt at mine eyes' red fire! 1073
all thy friends are lapp'd in lead; PP 20.24
who lead thee in their riot even there | where SON 41.11
how many gazers mightst thou lead away, | if 96.11
LEADEN 17 FR 0.0019 REL FR 16 V 1 P
in leaden contemplation have found out | such LLL 4.03.318
there's an eye | wounds like a leaden sword. 5.02.481
with leaden legs and batty wings doth creep. MND 3.02.365
what says this leaden casket? MV 2.07. 15
o you leaden messengers, | that ride upon the AWW 3.02.108
thy golden sceptre for a leaden dagger, and thy 1H4 2.04.381 P
then leaden age, | quicken'd with youthful 1H6 4.06. 12
if he be leaden, icy, cold, unwilling, | be thou R3 3.01.176
commenting | is leaden servitor to dull delay; 4.03. 52
lest leaden slumber peize me down to-morrow, 5.03.105
cushions, leaden spoons, | irons of a doit, COR 1.05. 5
will (too late) | tie leaden pounds to 's heels. 3.01.312
to you our swords have leaden points, mark JC 3.01.173
layest thou thy leaden mace upon my boy, | that 4.03.268
i have this while with leaden thoughts been OTH 3.04.177
disdain, | with leaden appetite, unapt to toy; VEN 34
now leaden slumber with live's strength doth LUC 124
LEADEN-FOOTED 1 FR 0.0001 REL FR 1 V 0 P
yet be leaden-footed | till his great rage be TNK 1.02. 84
LEADER 12 FR 0.0013 REL FR 9 V 3 P
wont to be a follower, but now you are a leader. WIV 3.02. 3 P
hence therefore, every leader to his charge, 1H4 5.01.118
gentleman, by heaven, and a most gallant leader. 2H4 3.02. 62 P
soldier that is the leader of so many thousands. 3.02.166 P
what well-appointed leader fronts us here? 4.01. 25
whilst such a worthy leader, wanting aid, | unto 1H6 1.01.143
much more a knight, a captain, and a leader. 4.01. 32
thou princely leader of our english strength, 4.03. 17
an angry hive of bees | that want their leader, 2H6 3.02.126
applaud the name of henry with your leader. 3H6 4.02. 27
limit each leader to his several charge, | and R3 5.03. 25
they have a leader, | tullus aufidius, that will COR 1.01.228
LEADER'S 2 FR 0.0002 REL FR 2 V 0 P
so our leader's /led, | and we are women's men. ANT 3.07. 69
who, flatt'red by their leader's jocund show, LUC 296
LEADERS 3 FR 0.0003 REL FR 2 V 1 P
we must follow the leaders. ADO 2.01.151 P
the leaders, having charge from you to stand, 2H4 4.02. 99
these mine eyes, true leaders to their queen, VEN 503
LEADEST 1 FR 0.0001 REL FR 1 V 0 P
that thou but leadest this fashion of thy malice MV 4.01. 18
LEADETH 2 FR 0.0002 REL FR 2 V 0 P
the path is smooth that leadeth on to danger. VEN 788
affection is my captain, and he leadeth; LUC 271
LEADING 9 FR 0.0010 REL FR 9 V 0 P
/page, | and so may i, blind fortune leading me, MV 2.01. 36
leading the men of /herfordshire to fight 1H4 1.01. 39
being men of such great leading as you are, 4.03. 17
on my knee i beg | the leading of the vaward. H5 4.03.131
shall have the leading of this foot and horse. R3 5.03.297
wilt have | the leading of thine own revenges, COR 4.05.137
from that place | i shall no leading need. LR 4.01. 78
leading him prisoner in a red rose chain; VEN 110
eye, | his eye commends the leading to his hand; LUC 436
/LEADS* 1 FR 0.0001 REL FR 1 V 0 P
delay /leads impotent and snail-pac'd beggary. R3 4.03. 53
LEADS* 31 FR 0.0035 REL FR 25 V 6 P
of the mountain foot | that leads toward mantua, TGV 5.02. 47
the sweet woman leads an ill life with him. WIV 2.02. 89 P
she leads a very frampold life with him, good 2.02. 90 P
a wife in windsor leads a better life than she 2.02.117 P
which from the vineyard to the garden leads; MM 4.01. 33
and leads me to your eyes, where i o'erlook MND 2.02.121
same knave | that leads him to these places. AWW 3.05. 83
the flow'ry way that leads to the broad gate and 4.05. 54 P
boiling | in leads or oils? WT 3.02.177
leads ancient lords and reverend bishops on | to 1H4 3.02.104
who leads his power? 4.01. 18
yes, warwick, edward dares, and leads the way. 3H6 5.01.112
go, go up to the leads, the lord mayor knocks. R3 3.07. 55
soul | leads discontented steps in foreign soil, 4.04.312
blind fear, that seeing reason leads, finds TRO 3.02. 71 P
what error leads must err; 5.02.111
are smother'd up, leads fill'd, and ridges COR 2.01.211
as if that whatsoever god who leads him | were 2.01.219
but yet a brain that leads my use of anger | to 3.02. 30
with aufidius, leads a power 'gainst rome, | and 4.06. 67
and | to melt the city leads upon your pates, 4.06. 82
he leads them like a thing | made by some other 4.06. 90
who leads towards rome a band of warlike goths, TIT 5.02.113
but it sufficeth | that brutus leads me on. JC 2.01.334
forth of doors, | yet something leads me forth. 3.03. 4
which, taken at the flood, leads on to fortune; 4.03.219
and leads the will to desperate undertakings HAM 2.01.101
'tis best to give him way, he leads himself. LR 2.04.298
what sport and revels his /addiction leads him; OTH 2.02. 6 P
for never-resting time leads summer on | to SON 5. 5
to shun the heaven that leads men to this hell. 129.14
LEAD'ST 2 FR 0.0002 REL FR 2 V 0 P
to run, | lead'st first to win some vantage. COR 1.01.160
be bold in us, we'll follow where thou lead'st, TIT 5.01. 13
LEAF 15 FR 0.0017 REL FR 13 V 2 P
an oak but with one green leaf on it would have ADO 2.01.240 P
writ a' both sides the leaf, margent and all, LLL 5.02. 8
hath now himself met with the fall of leaf. R2 3.04. 49
in very truth, do i, and 'twere an aspen leaf. 2H4 2.04.109 P
and come, i will go get a leaf of brass, | and TIT 4.01.102
your plantan leaf is excellent for that. ROM 1.02. 51
eyes, | are not within the leaf of pity writ, TIM 4.03.118
is not the leaf turn'd down | where i left JC 4.03.273
where every day i turn | the leaf to read them. MAC 1.03.152
life | is fall'n into the sear, the yellow leaf, 5.03. 23
as is the morn-dew on the myrtle leaf | to his ANT 3.12. 9
fold down the leaf where i have left. CYM 2.02. 4
nor | the leaf of eglantine, whom not to slander 4.02.223
who plucks the bud before one leaf put forth? VEN 416
flow'r was nigh, no grass, herb, leaf, or weed, 1055
LEAF'S 1 FR 0.0001 REL FR 1 V 0 P
here the leaf's turn'd down | where philomele CYM 2.02. 45
LEAFY *(see leavy)*
/LEAGU'D 1 FR 0.0001 REL FR 1 V 0 P
if partially affin'd, or /leagu'd in office, OTH 2.03.218
LEAGU'D 1 FR 0.0001 REL FR 1 V 0 P
his arms thus leagu'd. CYM 4.02.213
LEAGUE* 37 FR 0.0041 REL FR 36 V 1 P
there is such a league between my goodman and he WIV 3.02. 25 P
consecrated fount, | a league below the city; MM 4.03. 99
a league from epidamium had we sail'd | before ERR 1.01. 62
keep then fair league and truce with thy true 2.02.145
and in the wood, a league without the town MND 1.01.165
again | ere the leviathan can swim a league. 2.01.174
with league whose date till death shall never 3.02.373
i shall show you peace and fair-fac'd league; JN 2.01.417
this league that we have made | will give her 2.01.545
and our oppression hath made up this league. 3.01.106
of our inward souls | married in league, coupled 3.01.228
o, make a league with me, till i have pleas'd 4.02.126
o inglorious league! 5.01. 65
the blood of malice in a vein of league, | and 5.02. 38
and he and i | will keep a league till death. R2 5.01. 22
to make divorce of their incorporate league; H5 5.02.366
what the conditions of that league must be. 1H6 5.04.119
means | us'd intercession to obtain a league, 5.04.148
o peers of england, shameful is this league, 2H6 1.01. 98
before i would have yielded to this league. 1.01.127
kiss, | as if they vow'd some league inviolable. 3H6 2.01. 30
person, | and then to crave a league of amity, 3.03. 53
that by this league and marriage | thou draw not 3.03. 74
hand | in sign of league and amity with thee. R3 1.03.280
you peers, continue this united league. 2.01. 2
seal thou this league | with thy embracements to 2.01. 29
for france hath flaw'd the league, and hath H8 1.01. 95
for from this league | peep'd harms that menac'd 1.01.182
now he has crack'd the league | between us and 2.02. 24
a league between his highness and ferrara. 3.02.323
she's with the lion deeply still in league, TIT 4.01. 98
lords, when we join in league | i am a lamb, but 4.02.136
peace, for love, for league, and good to rome. 5.03. 23
that now he vows a league, and now invasion. LUC 287
but they must ope, this blessed league to kill, 383
this forced league doth force a further strife, 689
betwixt mine eye and heart a league is took, SON 47. 1
LEAGUER 1 FR 0.0001 REL FR 0 V 1 P
is carried into the leaguer of the adversaries, AWW 3.06. 26 P
LEAGUES* 12 FR 0.0013 REL FR 9 V 3 P
bore us some leagues to sea, where they prepared TMP 1.02.145
she that dwells | ten leagues beyond man's life; 2.01.247
the shore, five and thirty leagues off and on. 3.02. 14 P
the forest is not three leagues off; TGV 5.01. 11
ere the ships could meet by twice five leagues, ERR 1.01.100
he was not three leagues off when i left him. ADO 1.01. 4 P
from athens is her house remote seven leagues; MND 1.01.159
hang in the air a thousand leagues from hence, 1H4 3.01.224
stole a lute-case, bore it twelve leagues, and H5 3.02. 43 P
and all the peers', for surety of our leagues. 5.02.372
he lies to-night within seven leagues of rome. JC 3.01.286
thus time we waste, and long leagues make short; PER 4.04. 1
LEAH 1 FR 0.0001 REL FR 0 V 1 P
turkis, i had it of leah when i was a bachelor. MV 3.01.121 P
/LEAK 1 FR 0.0001 REL FR 1 V 0 P
"/her /boat /hath /a /leak, | /and /she /must LR 3.06. 26
LEAK 3 FR 0.0003 REL FR 2 V 1 P
a jordan, and then we leak in your chimney, and 1H4 2.01. 20 P
shall never leak, though it do work as strong 2H4 4.04. 47
there's a leak sprung, a sound one. TNK 3.04. 8
LEAK'D 1 FR 0.0001 REL FR 1 V 0 P
leak'd is our bark, | and we, poor mates, stand TIM 4.02. 19
LEAKY 2 FR 0.0002 REL FR 1 V 1 P
a nutshell and as leaky as an unstanch'd wench. TMP 1.01. 47 P
thou art so leaky | that we must leave thee to ANT 3.13. 63
/LEAN* 3 FR 0.0003 REL FR 2 V 1 P
then pharaoh's /lean kine are to be lov'd. 1H4 2.04.473 P
your loving complices | /lean on /your health, 2H4 1.01.164
sides, | the want that makes him /lean. TIM 4.03. 13
LEAN* 41 FR 0.0046 REL FR 29 V 12 P
look thee, i'll but lean, and my staff TGV 2.05. 30 P
i do lean upon justice, sir, and do bring in MM 2.01. 48 P
i have but lean luck in the match, and yet is ERR 3.02. 92 P
fat paunches have lean pates; LLL 1.01. 26
world) sometime to lean upon my poor shoulder, 5.01.102 P
lean, rent, and beggar'd by the strumpet wind! MV 2.06. 19
shifts | into the lean and slipper'd pantaloon, AYL 2.07.158
the burthen of lean and wasteful learning, the 3.02.323 P
a lean cheek, which you have not; 3.02.373 P
lean upon a rush, | the cicatrice and capable 3.05. 22
out of my lean and low ability | i'll lend you TN 3.04.344
nor lean enough to be thought a good studient; 4.02. 7 P
my saying, | howe'er you lean to th' nayward. WT 2.01. 64
you'ld be so lean, that blasts of january 4.04.111
another lean unwash'd artificer | cuts off his JN 4.02.201
whereof the hangman hath no lean wardrobe. 1H4 1.02. 73 P
and lards the lean earth as he walks along. 2.02.109
here comes lean jack, here comes bare-bone. 2.04.326 P
perceiv'd northumberland did lean to him, | the 4.03. 67
o, give me always a little, lean, old, chopp'd, 2H4 3.02.275 P
of his father, he hath, like lean, sterile, and 4.03.119 P
and something lean to cutpurse of quick hand. H5 5.01. 86
lean raw-bon'd rascals! 1H6 1.02. 35
first, lean thine aged back against mine arm, 2.05. 43
lean famine, quartering steel, and climbing fire 4.02. 11
bags | are lank and lean with thy extortions. 2H6 1.03.129
sweet duke of york, our prop to lean upon, | now 3H6 2.01. 68
lord warwick, on thy shoulder will i lean, | and 2.01.189
i'll lean upon one crutch, and fight with t' COR 1.01.242
the trees, though summer, yet forlorn and lean, TIT 2.03. 94
and that the lean abhorred monster keeps | thee ROM 5.03.104
yond cassius has a lean and hungry look, | he JC 1.02.194
as that same ague which hath made you lean. 2.02.113
fat king and your lean beggar is but variable HAM 4.03. 23 P
while i strook | the lean and wrinkled cassius, ANT 3.11. 37
fortunes you should make a staff | to lean upon; 3.13. 69
these blue-vein'd violets whereon we lean VEN 125
thick-sighted, barren, lean, and lacking juice, 136
"hard-favor'd tyrant, ugly, meagre, lean, 931
and then with lank and lean discolor'd cheek, LUC 708
lean penury within that pen doth dwell | that to SON 84. 5
LEAN'D 4 FR 0.0004 REL FR 4 V 0 P
the love that lean'd on them as slippery too, TRO 3.03. 85
you lean'd unto his sentence with what patience CYM 1.01. 78
here one man's hand lean'd on another's head, LUC 1415
forlorn, | lean'd her breast up-till a thorn, PP 20.10
LEANDER *(also limander)*
LEANDER 4 FR 0.0004 REL FR 2 V 2 P
how young leander cross'd the hellespont. TGV 1.01. 22
tow'r, | so bold leander would adventure it. 3.01.120
but in loving, leander the good swimmer, troilus ADO 5.02. 30 P
leander, he would have liv'd many a fair year AYL 4.01.100 P
LEANER 1 FR 0.0001 REL FR 1 V 0 P
great, and let not | a leaner action rend us. ANT 2.02. 19
LEAN-FAC'D 2 FR 0.0002 REL FR 2 V 0 P
brought one pinch, a hungry lean-fac'd villain, ERR 5.01.238
as lean-fac'd envy in her loathsome cave. 2H6 3.02.315
LEANING 5 FR 0.0005 REL FR 5 V 0 P
is leaning cheek to cheek? WT 1.02.285
sir," | thus, leaning on mine elbow, i begin, JN 1.01.194
breathless and faint, leaning upon my sword, 1H4 1.03. 32
thou on him leaning, and all troy on thee, TRO 5.03. 61
each leaning on their elbows and their hips. VEN 44
LEAN-LOOK'D 1 FR 0.0001 REL FR 1 V 0 P
and lean-look'd prophets whisper fearful change, R2 2.04. 11
LEANNESS 4 FR 0.0004 REL FR 3 V 1 P
watching breeds leanness, leanness is all gaunt. R2 2.01. 78
watching breeds leanness, leanness is all gaunt. 2.01. 78
agrees not with the leanness of his purse. 2H6 1.01.112
the leanness that afflicts us, the object of our COR 1.01. 20 P
LEANS 5 FR 0.0005 REL FR 3 V 2 P
she leans me out at her mistress' chamber-window ADO 3.03.146 P
see how she leans her cheek upon her hand! ROM 2.02. 23
my soul, my lord leans wondrously to discontent. TIM 3.04. 70 P
seal'd and done | that else leans on th' affair. HAM 4.03. 57
expect | to be depender on a thing that leans? CYM 1.05. 58
LEAN-WITTED 1 FR 0.0001 REL FR 1 V 0 P
a lunatic lean-witted fool, | presuming on an R2 2.01.115
LEAP 29 FR 0.0032 REL FR 25 V 4 P
cricket, to windsor chimneys shalt thou leap; WIV 5.05. 43
how will he triumph, leap, and laugh at it! LLL 4.03.146
and leap for joy, though they are lame with 5.02.291
and 'twere as easy | for you to laugh and leap, MV 1.01. 49
be clamorous and leap all civil bounds, | rather TN 1.04. 21
being ready to leap out of himself for joy of WT 5.02. 49 P
the wall is high, and yet will i leap down. JN 4.03. 1
rich men look sad, and ruffians dance and leap, R2 2.04. 12
by heaven, methinks it were an easy leap, | to 1H4 1.03.201
be it spoken, i should quickly leap into a wife. H5 5.02.139 P
leap o'er the walls for refuge in the field. 1H6 2.02. 25
whipping, leap me over this stool and run away. 2H6 2.01.140 P
whip him till he leap over that same stool. 2.01.145 P
true; made the lame to leap and fly away. 2.01.158
you take a precipit for no leap of danger, | and H8 5.01.139
leap to these arms untalk'd of and unseen! ROM 3.02. 7
o, bid me leap, rather than marry paris, | from 4.01. 77
now | leap in with me into this angry flood, JC 1.02.103
it is more worthy to leap in ourselves | than 5.05. 24
all beneath the moon | would i not leap upright. LR 4.06. 27
please, our master | will leap to be his friend; ANT 3.13. 51
chain mine arm'd neck, leap thou, attire and all 4.08. 14
take i your wish, i leap into the seas, PER 2.04. 43
and leap the garden, when i see her next, | and TNK 2.02.216
from their dark beds once more leap her eyes, VEN 1050
and bids it leap from thence, where it may find LUC 760
made, | beasts did leap and birds did sing, PP 20. 5
to leap large lengths of miles when thou art SON 44.10
do i envy those jacks that nimble leap | to kiss 128. 5
LEAP'D 2 FR 0.0002 REL FR 2 V 0 P
from me, as if ruin | leap'd from his eyes. H8 3.02.206
the lusty moor | hath leap'd into my seat; OTH 2.01.296
LEAP-FROG 1 FR 0.0001 REL FR 0 V 1 P
if i could win a lady at leap-frog, or by H5 5.02.137 P
LEAPING 2 FR 0.0002 REL FR 2 V 0 P
to outface me with leaping in her grave? HAM 5.01.278
to have turn'd my leaping time into a crutch, CYM 4.02.200
LEAPING-HOUSES 1 FR 0.0001 REL FR 0 V 1 P
and dials the signs of leaping-houses, and the 1H4 1.02. 9 P
/LEAPS 1 FR 0.0001 REL FR 1 V 0 P
/leaps /o'er /the /vaunt /and /firstlings /of TRO pr 27
LEAPS 5 FR 0.0005 REL FR 4 V 1 P
but a hot temper leaps o'er a cold decree — MV 1.02. 19 P
heart | leaps to be gone into my mother's bosom. PER 5.03. 45
imperiously he leaps, he neighs, he bounds, VEN 265
anon he rears upright, curvets, and leaps, | as 279
whereat she leaps, that was but late forlorn. 1026
LEAPT 11 FR 0.0012 REL FR 9 V 2 P
not hair), | was the first man that leapt; TMP 1.02.214
some such strange bull leapt your father's cow, ADO 5.04. 49
and all, like him that leapt into the custard; AWW 2.05. 37 P
though i swore i leapt from the window of the 4.01. 55 P
death, | and, winking, leapt into destruction. 2H4 1.03. 33
found some months asleep and leapt them over. 4.04.124
and what he is that now is leapt into it. TIT 2.03.247
he ran this way and leapt this orchard wall. ROM 2.01. 5
head, | dogs leapt the hatch, and all are fled. LR 3.06. 73
and now this lustful lord leapt from his bed, LUC 169
that heavy saturn laugh'd and leapt with him. SON 98. 4
/LEAR 2 FR 0.0002 REL FR 2 V 0 P
/sir, /i'll /bring /you /to /our /master /lear, LR 4.03. 50
/the /most /piteous /tale /of /lear /and /him 5.03.215
LEAR 13 FR 0.0014 REL FR 11 V 2 P
royal lear, | whom i have ever honor'd as my LR 1.01.139

be kent unmannerly | when lear is mad. 1.01.146
see better, lear, and let me still remain | the 1.01.158
this is not lear. 1.04.226
does lear walk thus? 1.04.227
o lear, lear, lear! 1.04.270
o lear, lear, lear! 1.04.270
o lear, lear, lear! 1.04.270
nuncle lear, nuncle lear, tarry, take the fool 1.04.315 P
nuncle lear, nuncle lear, tarry, take the fool 1.04.315 P
which he intends to lear and to cordelia, | the 5.01. 66
king lear hath lost, he and his daughter ta'en. 5.02. 6
writ | is on the life of lear and on cordelia. 5.03.247
/LEARN 3 FR 0.0003 REL FR 3 V 0 P
/complainant, /i /will /learn /thy /thought; TIT 3.02. 39
/and /by /still /practice /learn /to /know /thy 3.02. 45
/i /would /learn /that, /for /by /the /marks /of LR 1.04.232
LEARN 93 FR 0.0105 REL FR 71 V 22 P
but thy vild race | (though thou didst learn) TMP 1.02.359
where the devil should he learn our language? 2.02. 67 P
to learn his wit t' exchange the bad for better. TGV 2.06. 13
you would quickly learn to know him by his voice 4.02. 89
falstaff will learn the /humor of the age, WIV 1.03. 83
thine own confession, learn to begin thy health; MM 1.02. 38 P
away! let's go learn the truth of it. 1.02. 81 P
but we do learn | by those that know the very 1.04. 52
and let him learn to know, when maidens sue, 1.04. 80
i'll gladly learn. 2.03. 23
i do desire to learn, sir; 4.02. 56 P
ere i learn love, i'll practice to obey. ERR 2.01. 29
sir, learn to jest in good time — there's a 2.02. 64 P
i learn in this letter that don /pedro of ADO 1.01. 1 P
and thou shalt see how apt it is to learn | any 1.01.292
i will presently go learn their day of marriage. 2.02. 56 P
sweet prince, you learn me noble thankfulness. 4.01. 30
negligent student! learn her by heart. LLL 3.01. 35 P
if that she learn not of her eye to look: 4.03.248
made of, whereof it is born, | i am to learn; MV 1.01. 5
this, she is not yet so old | but she may learn; 3.02.161
she is not bred so dull but she can learn; 3.02.162
you must not learn me how to remember any AYL 1.02. 6 P
learn of the wise, and perpend: 3.02. 66 P
then learn this of me: 5.01. 40 P
she's apt to learn and thankful for good turns. SHR 2.01.165
but learn my lessons as i please myself. 3.01. 20
to learn the order of my fingering, | i must 3.01. 65
it shall do you no harm to learn. AWW 2.02. 37 P
yet, to avoid deceit, i mean to learn; JN 1.01.215
i come to learn how you have dealt for him; 5.02.121
then learn to know him now, this is the duke. R2 2.03. 40
thy very beadsmen learn to bend their bows | of 3.02.116
of him, | and learn to make a body of a limb. 3.02.187
so that by this intelligence we learn | the 3.03. 1
of holy reverence, who, i cannot learn. 3.03. 29
learn him forbearance from so foul a wrong. 4.01.120
learn, good soul, | to think our former state a 5.01. 17
you must needs learn, lord, to amend this fault; 1H4 3.01.178
learn this, thomas, | and thou shalt prove a 2H4 4.04. 41
and they will learn you by rote where services H5 3.06. 71 P
but you must learn to know such slanders of the 3.06. 79 P
have lost, or do not learn for want of time, 5.02. 57
i would have her learn, my fair cousin, how 5.02.283 P
wife, let's in, and learn to govern better, 2H6 4.09. 48
arise a knight, | and learn this lesson: 3H6 2.02. 62
must strike her sail and learn a while to serve 3.03. 5
are you yet to learn | what late misfortune is 4.04. 2
but, as i can learn, | he hearkens after R3 1.01. 53
these (as i learn) and such-like toys as these 1.01. 60
my tongue could never learn sweet smoothing word 1.02.168
makes him to send, that he may learn the ground. 1.03. 68
learn it, learn it, marquess. 1.03.260
learn it, learn it, marquess. 1.03.260
that /would /i learn of you, | as one being best 4.04.268
and wilt thou learn of me? 4.04.270
near to the town of leicester, as we learn. 5.02. 12
learn this, brother, | we live not to be grip'd H8 2.02.134
book than thou learn /a prayer without book. TRO 2.01. 18 P
toadstool! learn me the proclamation. 2.01. 21 P
i bade the vile owl go learn me the tenor of the 2.01. 90 P
o, meaning you? i will go learn more of it. 2.01.130
'sfoot, i'll learn to conjure and raise devils, 2.03. 5 P
learn how 'tis held, and what they are that must COR 1.10. 28
learn thou to make some meaner choice, | lavinia TIT 2.01. 73
o, do not learn her wrath — she taught it thee; 2.03.143
come, and learn of us | to melt in showers; 5.03.160
i neither know it, nor can learn of him. ROM 1.01.144
could we but learn from whence his sorrows grow, 1.01.154
and learn me how to lose a winning match, 3.02. 12
men must learn now with pity to dispense, | for TIM 3.02. 86
part, | i shall be glad to learn of noble men. JC 4.03. 54
we learn no other but the confident tyrant MAC 5.04. 8
and that should learn us | there's a divinity HAM 5.02. 9
than thou goest, | learn more than thou trowest, LR 1.04.122
thy fool to lie — i would fain learn to lie. 1.04.180 P
sir, i am too old to learn. 2.02.127
my life and education both do learn me | how to OTH 1.03.183
do not learn of him, emilia, though he be thy 2.01.162 P
i learn you take things ill which are not so — ANT 2.02. 29
for learn this, silius: 3.01. 13
i hourly learn | a doctrine of obedience, and 5.02. 30
one of your great knowing | should learn, being CYM 2.03. 98
and learn now, for all, | that i, which know my 2.03.106
we'll learn our freeness of a son-in-law: 5.05.421
i do beseech you | to learn of me, who stand /i' PER 4.04. 8
learn what maids have been her companions and TNK 4.03. 90 P
and learn of him, i heartily beseech thee, | to VEN 404
o, learn to love, the lesson is but plain, | and 407
where subjects' eyes do learn, do read, do look. LUC 616
wilt thou be the school where lust shall learn? 617
o, learn to read what silent love hath writ: SON 23.13
but thence i learn, and find the lesson true, 118.13
/LEARN'D 1 FR 0.0001 REL FR 1 V 0 P
/i /hardly /yet /have /learn'd | /to /insinuate, R2 4.01.164
LEARN'D 36 FR 0.0040 REL FR 26 V 10 P
first, you have learn'd, like sir proteus, to TGV 2.01. 19 P
have learn'd me how to brook this patiently. 5.03. 4
more wit than ever i learn'd before in my life; WIV 4.05. 60 P
you hear the learn'd bellario, what he writes, MV 4.01.167
where learn'd you that oath, fool? AYL 1.02. 62 P
rose at an instant, learn'd, play'd, eat 1.03. 74
that he that hath learn'd no wit by nature nor 3.02. 29 P
there is much matter to be heard and learn'd. 5.04.185
in me have i learn'd from my entertainment. TN 1.05.215 P
well divulg'd, free, learn'd, and valiant, | and 1.05.260
i learn'd it out of women's faces. WT 2.01. 12
the copy of your speed is learn'd by them; JN 4.02.113
my lord, to have learn'd his health of you. R2 2.03. 24
till i have learn'd thy language, for thy tongue 1H4 3.01.205
and further, i have learn'd, | the king himself 4.01. 90
i learn'd in worcester, as i rode along, | he 4.01.125
i am sure they never learn'd that of me. 4.02. 72 P
i have learn'd that fearful commenting | is R3 4.03. 51
the gentleman is learn'd, and a most rare H8 1.02.111
my learn'd lord cardinal, | deliver all with 1.02.142
fathers of the land | and doctors learn'd. 2.04.207
my learn'd and well-beloved servant, cranmer, 2.04.239
if you are learn'd, | be not as common fools; COR 3.01. 99
that bloody mind i think they learn'd of me, TIT 5.01.101
perhaps you have learn'd it without book. ROM 1.02. 59 P
and never learn'd | the icy precepts of respect, TIM 4.03.257
set in a note-book, learn'd, and conn'd by rote, JC 4.03. 98
and i have learn'd by the perfect'st report, MAC 1.05. 2 P
as i learn'd, | the night before there was no LR 2.04. 2
where learn'd you this, fool? 2.04. 86 P
i learn'd it in england, where indeed they are OTH 2.03. 76 P
hast thou not learn'd me how | to make perfumes? CYM 1.05. 12
learn'd indeed were that astronomer | that knew 3.02. 27
and for my sake hath learn'd to sport and dance, VEN 105
thy fault foul sin may say | he learn'd to sin, LUC 630
he learn'd but surety-like to write for me SON 134. 7
/LEARNED 1 FR 0.0001 REL FR 1 V 0 P
/sit /thou /here, /most /learned /justicer; LR 3.06. 21
LEARNED 49 FR 0.0055 REL FR 36 V 13 P
war-like, court-like, and learned preparations. WIV 2.02.228 P
i am sorry, one so learned and so wise | as you, MM 5.01.470
only get the learned writer to set down our ADO 3.05. 63 P
this learned constable is too cunning to be 5.01.228 P
ay, sir, and very learned. LLL 4.02.103 P
well learned is that tongue that well can thee 4.02.112
but love, first learned in a lady's eyes, 4.03.324
without impudency, learned without opinion, and 5.01. 5 P
illustrate, and learned gentleman, before the 5.01.122 P
and wit's own grace to grace a learned fool. 5.02. 72
that the two learned men have compiled in praise 5.02.886 P
this court, | unless bellario, a learned doctor, MV 4.01.105
a young and learned doctor to our court. 4.01.144
most learned judge! a sentence! come, prepare! 4.01.304
o upright judge! mark, jew: o learned judge! 4.01.313
o learned judge! mark, jew, a learned judge! 4.01.317
o learned judge! mark, jew, a learned judge! 4.01.317
o jew! an upright judge, a learned judge! 4.01.323
never school'd and yet learned, full of noble AYL 1.01.167 P
give me your hand. art thou learned? 5.01. 38 P
when our most learned doctors leave us, and AWW 2.01.116
faith, if the learned should speak truth of it. 2.02. 34 P
of all the learned and authentic fellows — 2.03. 12 P
then advis'd by my learned counsel in the laws 2H4 1.02.134 P
my learned lord, we pray you to proceed, | and H5 1.02. 9
seem they grave and learned? 2.02.128
with all the learned council of the realm, 2H6 1.01. 89
large gifts have i bestow'd on learned clerks, 4.07. 71
me but | by learned approbation of the judges. H8 1.02. 71
most learned reverend sir, into our kingdom, 2.02. 76
(i mean the learned ones in christian kingdoms) 2.02. 92
this just and learned priest, card'nal campeius, 2.02. 96
was he not held a learned man? 2.02.123
but he's a learned man. 3.02.395
learned and reverend fathers of his order, 4.01. 26
of all these learned men she was divorc'd, | and 4.01. 32
of th' ignorant | more learned than the ears), COR 3.02. 77
i must to the learned. ROM 1.02. 44 P
the learned pate | ducks to the golden fool. TIM 4.03. 17
i'll talk a word with this same learned theban. LR 3.04.157
and knows all /qualities, with a learned spirit, OTH 3.03.259
the worth that learned charity aye wears. PER 5.03. 94
a learned, and a poet never went | more famous TNK pr 11
and unto him i utter learned things | and many 3.05. 14
we have, as learned authors utter, wash'd a tile 3.05. 40
a learned poet says, unless by th' tail | and 3.05. 49
how | to cipher what is writ in learned books, LUC 811
well learned is that tongue that well can thee PP 5. 8
lullaby, the learned man hath got the lady gay, 15.15
LEARNEDLY 3 FR 0.0003 REL FR 1 V 2 P
and a subtle, as he most learnedly deliver'd. TMP 2.01. 45 P
all the lawyers in bohemia can learnedly handle, WT 4.04.206 P
much | he spoke, and learnedly, for life; H8 2.01. 28
LEARNED'S 1 FR 0.0001 REL FR 1 V 0 P
have added feathers to the learned's wing, | and SON 78. 7
LEARNING 35 FR 0.0039 REL FR 26 V 9 P
rid you | for learning me your language! TMP 1.02.365
place, gravity, and learning, so wide of his own WIV 3.01. 57 P
for it neither, but was paid for my learning. 4.05. 62 P
so were there a patch set on learning, to see LLL 4.02. 31
learning is but an adjunct to ourself, | and 4.03.310
and where we are, our learning likewise is. 4.03.311
do we not likewise see our learning there? 4.03.314
you hear his learning. 5.01. 51 P
muses mourning for the death | of learning, late MND 5.01. 53
three, and such branches of learning, is indeed MV 2.02. 64 P
not learning more than the fond eye doth teach, 2.09. 27
better'd with his own learning, the greatness 4.01.158 P
the burthen of lean and wasteful learning, the AYL 3.02.323 P
a course of learning and ingenious studies. SHR 1.01. 9
o this learning, what a thing it is! 1.02.159
for learning and behavior | fit for her turn, 1.02.168
the court's a learning place, and he is one — AWW 1.01.177
spirit | of teaching and of learning instantly. 1H4 5.02. 64
whose learning and good letters peace hath 2H4 4.01. 44
and learning a mere hoard of gold kept by a 4.03.115 P
for such receipt of learning is black-friars; H8 2.02.138
men | of singular integrity and learning, | yea, 2.04. 59
wit, | and to such men of gravity and learning, 3.01. 73
those twins of learning that he rais'd in you, 4.02. 58
discourse, manhood, learning, gentleness, virtue TRO 1.02.254 P
o, what learning is! ROM 3.03.160
there will little learning die then that day TIM 2.02. 82 P
and labor'd much | how to forget that learning, HAM 5.02. 35
and have my learning from some true reports ANT 2.02. 47
the sceptre, learning, physic, must | all follow CYM 4.02.268
our thing of learning /says so — | where he TNK 2.03. 51
him to th' plains, his learning makes no cry. 2.03. 54
which by a gift of learning did bear the maid PP 15.14
and of this book this learning mayst thou taste. SON 77. 4
advance | as high as learning my rude ignorance. 78.14
LEARNINGS 1 FR 0.0001 REL FR 1 V 0 P
puts to him all the learnings that his time CYM 1.01. 43
LEARNS 3 FR 0.0003 REL FR 3 V 0 P
is cupid's grandfather, and learns news of him. LLL 2.01.255
that presses them and learns them first to bear, ROM 1.04. 93
and what he learns by this | may prove his CYM 3.05.102
LEARNT 8 FR 0.0009 REL FR 7 V 1 P
marry, thus much i have learnt: LLL 2.01. 84
the language i have learnt these forty years, R2 1.03.159
brings other news | than they have learnt of me. 2H4 in 39
most immodest word | be look'd upon and learnt, 4.04. 71
my master, he hath learnt so much fence already. 2H6 2.03. 78 P
a rhyme i learnt even now | of one i danc'd ROM 1.05.142
where i have learnt me to repent the sin | of 4.02. 17
to do thus | i learnt of thee. ANT 4.14.103
/LEAR'S 1 FR 0.0001 REL FR 1 V 0 P
/the /poor /distressed /lear's /i' /th' /town, LR 4.03. 38
LEAR'S 1 FR 0.0001 REL FR 0 V 1 P
lear's shadow. LR 1.04.231 P
LEAS 3 FR 0.0003 REL FR 3 V 0 P
most bounteous lady, thy rich leas | of wheat, TMP 4.01. 60
her fallow leas | the darnel, hemlock, and rank H5 5.02. 44
dry up thy marrows, vines, and plough-torn leas, TIM 4.03.193
LEAS'D 1 FR 0.0001 REL FR 1 V 0 P
is now leas'd out — i die pronouncing it — R2 2.01. 59
LEASE 9 FR 0.0010 REL FR 7 V 2 P
that they are out by lease. TGV 5.02. 29
it were a shame to let this land by lease; R2 2.01.110
lady, a long lease for the clinking of pewter. 1H4 2.04. 45 P
that, if i might have a lease of my life for a 2H6 4.10. 5 P
macbeth | shall live the lease of nature, pay MAC 4.01. 99
so should that beauty which you hold in lease SON 13. 5
and summer's lease hath all too short a date; 18. 4
can yet the lease of my true love control, 107. 3
why so large cost, having so short a lease, 146. 5
LEASES 2 FR 0.0002 REL FR 2 V 0 P
me, | in all my lands and leases whatsoever. SHR 2.01.125
which works on leases of short-numb'red hours, SON 124.10
LEASH 3 FR 0.0003 REL FR 2 V 1 P
back, not following | my leash unwillingly. WT 4.04.466
i am sworn brother to a leash of drawers, and 1H4 2.04. 7 P
even like a fawning greyhound in the leash, | to COR 1.06. 38
LEASH'D 1 FR 0.0001 REL FR 1 V 0 P
and at his heels | (leash'd in, like hounds) H5 pr 7
LEASING 2 FR 0.0002 REL FR 1 V 1 P
now mercury indue thee with leasing, for thou TN 1.05. 97 P
his praise | have (almost) stamp'd the leasing. COR 5.02. 22
/LEAST 2 FR 0.0002 REL FR 2 V 0 P
sport best pleases that doth /least know how: LLL 5.02.516
/or /at /least /desist | /to /build /at /all? 2H4 1.03. 47
LEAST 110 FR 0.0124 REL FR 92 V 18 P
at least two glasses. TMP 1.02.240
where she, at least, is banish'd from your eye, 2.01.127
far surpasseth sycorax | as great'st does least. 3.02.103
at least bring forth a wonder, to content ye 5.01.170
o, they love least that let men know their love. TGV 1.02. 32
that is the least, lucetta, of my fear: 2.07. 68
the least whereof would quell a lover's hope, 4.02. 13
or, at the least, in hers sepulchre thine. 4.02.117
mistress page — at the least, if the love of a WIV 2.01. 11 P
and i will {at the least} keep your counsel. 4.06. 7 P
no? a dozen times at least. MM 1.02. 20 P
sin, | or of the deadly seven it is the least. 3.01.110
which is the least? 3.01.111
of despair, | when it is least expected. 4.03.111
boldly, at least. 5.01.297
him we shall stay here at the least a month, and ADO 1.01.149 P
a present remedy, at least a patient sufferance. 1.03. 8 P
and he that breaks them in the least degree LLL 1.01.156
and shall, at the least of thy sweet notice, 1.01.275 P
most power to do most harm, least knowing ill; 2.01. 58
are sweetly varied, like a scholar at the least; 4.02. 9 P
tongue-tied simplicity | in least speak most, to MND 5.01.105
so may the outward shows be least themselves — MV 3.02. 73
she moves me not, or not removes, at least, SHR 1.02. 72
at least | have leave and leisure to make love 1.02.135
horn is a foot, and so long am i at the least. 4.01. 28 P
seeming to be most which we indeed least are. 5.02.175
they that least lend it you shall lack you first AWW 1.02. 68
but unseal'd — | at least in my opinion. 4.02. 31
for i myself am best | when least in company. TN 1.04. 38
comptible, even to the least sinister usage. 1.05.176 P
that upon the least occasion more mine eyes will 2.01. 41 P
whereof the least | is not this suit of mine, WT 1.02.401
at least thus much: 2.03.165
best know | (/who least will seem to do so) my 3.02. 33
at least if you make a care | of happy holding 4.04.355
to th' fearful usage | (at least ungentle) of 5.01.154
least they desire (upon this push) to trouble 5.03.129
at least from fair five hundred pound a year. JN 1.01. 69
or if he do, let it at least be said, | they saw 5.01. 75
thus high at least, although your knee be low. R2 3.03.195
at supper, how thirty at least he fought with, 1H4 1.02.188 P
redeeming time when men think least i will. 1.02.217
sixteen at least, my lord. 2.04.175 P
he held me last night at least nine hours | in 3.01.154
the least of which haunting a nobleman | loseth 3.01.184
mine | did with the least affection of a welcome 2H4 4.05.172
at least, if thou canst, speak. 1H6 1.04. 73
there hath at least five frenchmen died to-night 2.02. 9
part | and least proportion of humanity. 2.03. 53
and not the least of these | but can do more in 2H6 1.03. 70
the least of all these signs were probable. 3.02.178
a man at least, for less i should not be; 3H6 3.01. 57
that would be ten days' wonder at the least. 3.02.113
to save, at least, the heir of edward's right; 4.04. 32
yet edward, at the least, is duke of york. 4.07. 21
i thought, at least, he would have said the king 5.01. 29
his regiment lies half a mile at least | south R3 5.03. 37
the least of you shall share his part thereof. 5.03.268

i do know | kinsmen of mine, three at the least, H8 1.01. 81
once perceive | the least rub in your fortunes, 2.01.129
spake one the least word that might | be to the 2.04.154
to meet the least occasion that may give me 3.02. 7
gone by him, or at least | strangely neglected? 3.02. 10
at least good manners — as not thus to suffer 5.02. 29
at the least, if you take it as a pleasure to COR 2.01. 31 P
with the least cause these his new honors, which 2.01.229
forget | the least of these unspeakable deserts, TIT 1.01.256
goths, | or at the least make them his enemies. 5.02. 79
i am the greatest, able to do least, | yet most ROM 5.03.223
suspect still comes where an estate is least. TIM 4.03.514
i have spoke the least. 5.02. 2
though last, not least in love, yours, good JC 3.01.189
on his head, | the least a death to nature. MAC 3.04. 27
at least we'll die with harness on our back. 5.05. 51
at least, the whisper goes so. HAM 1.01. 80
at least i am sure it may be so in denmark. 1.05.109
although our last and least, to whose young love LR 1.01. 83
thy youngest daughter does not love thee least, 1.01.152
what, in the least, | will you require in 1.01.191
if thou deni'st the least syllable of thy 2.02. 24 P
i cannot think my sister in the least | would 2.04.141
our friends at least. OTH 2.01. 57
the moor | at least into a jealousy so strong 2.01.301
or, at the least, so prove it | that the 3.03.364
stick | the small'st opinion on my least misuse? 4.02.109
suppliest me with the least advantage of hope. 4.02.177 P
cleopatra, catching but the least noise of this, ANT 1.02.140 P
the least wind i' th' world will blow them down. 2.07. 2 P
the least cause | for what you seem to fear. 3.02. 35
you shall, at least, | go see my lord aboard. CYM 1.01.177
so nigh, at least, | that though his actions 3.04.148
or at least | those which i heav'd to head! 5.05.156
some displeasure at him, at least he judg'd so; PER 1.03. 20
that's the least fear; 1.04. 71
walk half an hour, leonine, at the least. 4.01. 45
he that will fish | for my least minnow, let him TNK 1.01.116
at least to frustrate striving, and to follow 1.02. 9
and power | i' th' least of these was dreadful, 1.03. 39
so chid, or at least a sigher to be comforted. 2.01. 44 P
those are o' th' least; 3.06. 64
there is at least two hundred now with child by 4.01.129
"and not the least of all these maladies | but VEN 745
to clear this spot by death, at least, i give LUC 1053
or (at the least) this refuge let me find: 1654
or to thyself at least kind–hearted prove: SON 10.12
scope, | with what i most enjoy contented least; 29. 8
when in the least of them my life hath end; 92. 6
or, at the least, so long as brain and heart 122. 5
when most impeach'd stands least in thy control. 125.14

LEATHER 8 FR 0.0009 REL FR 4 V 4 P
in this service, you must case me in leather. ERR 2.01. 85
went, like a base–viol, in a case of leather; 4.03. 24 P
his leather skin and horns to wear. AYL 4.02. 11
bit and a head–stall of sheep's leather which, SHR 3.02. 57 P
nobility think scorn to go in leather aprons. 2H6 4.02. 12 P
his cold thin drink out of his leather bottle, 3H6 2.05. 48
wear it on both sides, like a leather jerkin. TRO 3.03.265 P
where is thy leather apron and thy rule? JC 1.01. 7

LEATHER–COATS 1 FR 0.0001 REL FR 0 V 1 P
there's a dish of leather–coats for you. 2H4 5.03. 41 P

LEATHERN 4 FR 0.0004 REL FR 3 V 1 P
their discharge did stretch his leathern coat AYL 2.01. 37
i saw her hand, she has a leathern hand, | a 4.03. 24
put on two leathern jerkins and aprons, and wait 2H4 2.02.171 P
tree, | servilely master'd with a leathern rein! VEN 392

LEATHERN–JERKIN 1 FR 0.0001 REL FR 0 V 1 P
wilt thou rob this leathern–jerkin, 1H4 2.04. 69 P

LEATHREN 1 FR 0.0001 REL FR 1 V 0 P
some war with rere–mice for their leathren wings MND 2.02. 4

LEAVE* *(also leve)*

/LEAVE* 7 FR 0.0008 REL FR 7 V 0 P
i /leave myself, my friends, and all, for love. TGV 1.01. 65
/give /sorrow /leave /a /while /to /tutor /me R2 4.01.166
/then /give /me /leave /to /go. 4.01.313
/him /did /you /leave, | /second /to /none, 2H4 2.03. 33
/leave /these /bitter /deep /laments, | /make TIT 3.02. 46
/lear, | /and /leave /you /to /attend /him. LR 4.03. 51
to the queen, | and get her /leave to part. ANT 1.02.179

LEAVE* 694 FR 0.0784 REL FR 555 V 139 P
let's take leave of him. TMP 1.01. 64
i will leave him, i have no long spoon. 2.02. 98 P
and in these fits i leave them, while i visit 3.03. 91
bids thee leave these, and with her sovereign 4.01. 72
leave your crisp channels, and on this green 4.01.130
pageant faded, | leave not a rack behind. 4.01.156
say again, where didst thou leave these varlots? 4.01.170
now let us take our leave. TGV 1.01. 56
give him leave, madam, he is a kind of chameleon 2.04. 25 P
leave off discourse of disability. 2.04.109
i'll leave you to confer of home affairs; 2.04.119
to leave my julia, shall i be forsworn; 2.06. 1
i cannot leave to love, and yet i do; 2.06. 17
but there i leave to love where i should love. 2.06. 18
all that is mine i leave at thy dispose, | my 2.07. 86
sir thurio, give us leave, i pray, a while, | we 3.01. 1
will give thee time to leave our royal court, 3.01.165
she is my essence, and i leave to be, | if i be 3.01.182
serv'd me, when i took my leave of madam silvia. 4.04. 35 P
it seems you lov'd not her, /to leave her token: 4.04. 74
leave not the mansion so long tenantless, | lest 5.04. 8
fall | and leave no memory of what it was! 5.04. 10
done, | and leave her on such slight conditions. 5.04.138
were a goot motion if we leave our pribbles and WIV 1.01. 54 P
did her grandsire leave her seven hundred pound? 1.01. 58 P
by your leave, good mistress. 1.01.193 P
i vill not for the varld i shall leave behind. 1.04. 64 P
we must give folks leave to prate; 1.04.121 P
give us leave, drawer. 2.02.159 P
by your leave, sir. i am sick till i see her. 3.02. 28 P
i'll leave you. 3.04. 53 P
by your leave; 3.05. 26 P
been into thames, ere i will leave her thus. 3.05.127 P
master slender is let the boys leave to play. 4.01. 11 P
leave your prabbles, oman. 4.01. 50 P
we'll leave a proof, by that which we will do, 4.02.104
serve got, and leave your desires, and fairies 5.05.129 P
and leave you your jealousies too, i pray you. 5.05.132 P
to th' hopeful execution do i leave you | of MM 1.01. 59
yet give leave, my lord, | that we may bring you 1.01. 60
to give me leave | to have free speech with you; 1.01. 76
i take my leave of you. 1.04. 90
but you shall come to it, by your honor's leave. 2.01.122 P
i'll take my leave, | and leave you to the 2.01.135
and leave you to the hearing of the cause, 2.01.136
from that trunk you bear, | and leave you naked. 3.01. 72
leave me a while with the maid. 3.01.177 P
can this be so? did angelo so leave her? 3.01.224 P
but leave we him to his events, with a prayer 3.02.237 P
sir, leave me your snatches, and yield me a 4.02. 6 P
give him leave to escape hence, he would not. 4.02.148 P
ho, by your leave! 4.03.111
i for a while will leave you; 5.01.257
my lord, give me leave to question, you shall 5.01.271 P
sir, by your leave. 5.01.362
friar, advise him, | i leave him to your hand. 5.01.486
i'll utter what my sorrow gives me leave. ERR 1.01. 35
to find, yet loath to leave unsought | or that, 1.01.135
so you would leave battering, i had rather have 2.02. 35 P
if not, i'll leave him to the officer. 4.01. 61
i conjure thee to leave me and be gone. 4.03. 67
i'll give thee, ere i leave thee, so much money, 4.04. 2
therefore depart, and leave him here with me. 5.01.108
i will not hence, and leave my husband here; 5.01.109
me, sorrow abides and happiness takes his leave. ADO 1.01.102 P
examine your conscience, and so i leave you. 1.01.289 P
any ill, i will leave them at the next turning. 2.01.153 P
i pray you leave me. 2.01.197 P
if it will not be, i'll leave you. 2.01.201 P
bear thee well in it, and leave us alone. 3.01. 13
i must leave you. 3.05. 44 P
father, by your leave, | will you with free and 4.01. 23
i will kiss your hand, and so i leave you. 4.01.332 P
i will leave you now to your gossip–like humor. 5.01.186 P
expect your coming, | to–night i take my leave. 5.01.297
i leave an arrant knave with your worship, which 5.01.321 P
i humbly give you leave to depart, and if a 5.01.325 P
there will i leave you too, for here comes one 5.02. 94 P
thanks to you all, and leave us. 5.03. 28
not till it leave the rider in the mire. LLL 2.01.120
then leave this chat, and, good berowne, now 4.03.280
then wish me better, i will give you leave. 5.02.342
i'll leave it by degrees. 5.02.418
ay, sweet my lord, and so i take my leave. 5.02.872
i will kiss thy royal finger, and take leave. 5.02.882 P
his power | to leave the figure or disfigure it. MND 1.01. 51
leave you your power to draw, | and i shall have 2.01.197
only give me leave, | unworthy as i am, to 2.01.206
to leave the city and commit yourself | into the 2.01.215
and leave thee to the mercy of wild beasts. 2.01.228
ere he do leave this grove, | thou shalt fly him 2.01.245
o, wilt thou darkling leave me? do not so. 2.02. 86
or as the heresies that men do leave | are hated 2.02.139
i believe we must leave the killing out, when 3.01. 14 P
why, then may you leave a casement of the great 3.01. 56 P
but why unkindly didst thou leave me so? 3.02.183
the hate i bare thee made me leave thee so? 3.02.190
a foolish heart, that i leave here behind. 3.02.319
pray you, leave your curtsy, good mounsieur. 4.01. 20 P
leave it to his discretion, and let us listen to 5.01.237 P
ye well, | we leave you now with better company. MV 1.01. 59
we two will leave you, but at dinner–time | i 1.01. 70
well, we will leave you then till dinner–time. 1.01.105
seek for you, madam, to take their leave; 1.02.124 P
be preferment | to leave a rich jew's service, 2.02.147
take leave of thy old master, and inquire | my 2.02.153
i'll take my leave of the jew in the twinkling. 2.02.167 P
i am sorry thou wilt leave my father so. 2.03. 1
by your leave, sir. 2.04. 15 P
too griev'd a heart | to take a tedious leave; 2.07. 77
choice, | immediately to leave you, and be gone. 2.09. 16
is the complexion of them all to leave the dam. 3.01. 30 P
steal both his | and leave itself unfurnish'd. 3.02.126
fair lady, by your leave, | i come by note, to 3.02.139
by your leave, | i bid my very friends and 3.02.222
with leave, bassanio, i am half yourself, | and 3.02.248
since i have your good leave to go away, | i 3.02.324
i leave him to your gracious acceptance, whose 4.01.164 P
beg that thou mayst have leave to hang thyself, 4.01.364
i pray you give me leave to go from hence, | i 4.01.395
i wish you well, and so i take my leave. 4.01.420
leave hollowing, man — here. 5.01. 43 P
upon a knife, "love me, and leave me not." 5.01.150
i dare be sworn for him he would not leave it, 5.01.172
how you do leave me to mine own protection. 5.01.235
i pray you leave me. AYL 1.01. 78 P
therefore he gives them good leave to wander. 1.01.104 P
and never leave thee till he hath ta'en thy life 1.01.151 P
ay, my liege, so please you give us leave. 1.02.157 P
in friendship counsel you | to leave this place. 1.02.262
to bear your griefs yourself, and leave me out; 1.03.103
leave me alone to woo him. 1.03.133
and did you leave him in this contemplation? 2.01. 64
something to eat, i will give thee leave to die; 2.06. 12 P
give me leave | to speak my mind, and i will 2.07. 58
a good excuse for me hereafter to leave my wife. 3.03. 94 P
o brave oliver, | leave me not behind thee; 3.03.101
these two hours, rosalind, i will leave thee. 4.01.177 P
did he leave him there, | food to the suck'd and 4.03.125
which is in the vulgar leave — the society — 5.01. 48 P
servants, leave me and her alone. SHR in.2. 116
and by my father's love and leave am arm'd 1.01. 5
leave shall you have to court her at your 1.01. 54
i knew not what to take and what to leave? 1.01.104
for a while i take my leave | to see my friends 1.02. 1
not a lawful cause for me to leave his service, 1.02. 29 P
have leave and leisure to make love to her, 1.02.136
yea, leave that labor to great hercules, | and 1.02.255
you wrong me, signior gremio, give me leave. 2.01. 46
i'll leave her houses three or four as good, 2.01.366
and so i take my leave, and thank you both. 2.01.398
then give me leave to have prerogative, | and 3.01. 6
then give me leave to read philosophy, | and 3.01. 13
you'll leave his lecture when i am in tune? 3.01. 24
you may go walk, and give me leave a while; 3.01. 59
your father prays you leave your books, | and 3.01. 82
and therefore here i mean to take my leave. 3.02.188
shall win my love, and so i take my leave, | in 4.02. 42
why, sir, i trust i may have leave to speak, 4.03. 73
sir, by your leave, having come to padua | to 4.04. 24
chance to need thee at home, therefore leave us. 5.01. 3 P
thither must i, and here i leave you, sir. 5.01. 10
to leave frivolous circumstances, i pray you 5.01. 26 P
'tis a wonder, by your leave, she will be tam'd 5.02.189
but my intents are fix'd and will not leave me. AWW 1.01.229
freely have they leave | to stand on either part 1.02. 14
my team and gives me leave to inn the crop. 1.03. 45 P
pray you leave me. 1.03.126 P
your honor | but give me leave to try success, 1.03.247
why, helen, thou shalt have my leave and love, 1.03.251
that dare leave two together, fare you well. 2.01. 98
when our most learned doctors leave us, and 2.01.116
which great love grant, and so i take my leave. 2.03. 85
give me leave to use | the help of mine own eyes 2.03.107
by thee, in what motion age will give me leave. 2.03.234 P
i leave you. 2.03.263 P
therefore away, and leave her bravely; 2.03.299
you will take your instant leave a' th' king, 2.04. 48
king, and have procur'd his leave | for present 2.05. 55
shall see you, so | i leave you to your wisdom. 2.05. 71
as't please your lordship. i'll leave you. 3.06.109
you barely leave our thorns to prick ourselves, 4.02. 19
sir, of whom he hath taken a solemn leave. 4.03. 77 P
nay, by your leave, hold your hands — though i 4.03.189 P
you, and take your leave of all your friends. 4.03.311 P
and by the leave of my good lord the king, 4.04. 13
of comfort and leave him to your lordship. 5.02. 25 P
the last that e'er i took her leave at court, 5.03. 79
he stole from florence, taking no leave, and i 5.03.144 P
go thy way, if sir toby would leave drinking, TN 1.05. 27 P
good madonna, give me leave to prove you a fool. 1.05. 58 P
to the grave | and leave the world no copy. 1.05.243
therefore i shall crave of you your leave, that 2.01. 6 P
and it would please you to take leave of her, 2.03.100 P
give me now leave to leave thee. 2.04. 72
give me now leave to leave thee. 2.04. 72
by your leave, wax. 2.05. 92 P
garden door be shut, and leave me to my hearing. 3.01. 92 P
o, by your leave, i pray you: 3.01.106
give me leave, beseech you. 3.01.111
i'll be your purse–bearer and leave you | for an 3.03. 47
give them way till he take leave, and presently 3.04.198 P
to sleep, and leave thy vain bibble babble. 4.02. 96 P
i leave my duty a little unthought of, and speak 5.01.309 P
my lord, | and leave you to your graver steps. WT 1.02.173
and mannerly distinguishment leave out | betwixt 2.01. 86
my women, come, you have leave. 2.01.124
leave me solely. 2.03. 17
you'll leave yourself | hardly one subject. 2.03.111
of our dominions, and that there thou leave it 2.03.177
leave me, | and think upon my bidding. 2.03.206
in bohemia, | there weep and leave it crying; 3.03. 32
o'er sixteen years and leave the growth untried 4.01. 6
if tinkers may have leave to live, | and bear 4.03. 19
i will even take my leave of you, and pace 4.03.112 P
i should leave grazing, were i of your flock, 4.04.109
leave your prating. 4.04.340 P
curious business that | i leave out ceremony. 4.04.515
and leave this young man in pawn till i bring it 4.04.808 P
you swear | never to marry but by my free leave? 5.01. 70
it seem'd sorrow wept to take leave of them, for 5.02. 45 P
and give me leave, | and do not say 'tis 5.03. 42
james gurney, wilt thou give us leave a while? JN 1.01.230
good leave, good philip. 1.01.231
and leave your children, wives, and you in peace 2.01.257
shall leave his native channel and o'erswell 2.01.337
leave them as naked as the vulgar air. 2.01.387
and leave those woes alone which i alone | am 3.01. 64
i leave your highness. 3.03. 14
evils that take leave, | on their departure most 3.04.114
my nobles leave me, and my state is braved, 4.02.243
give me leave to speak. 5.02.162
desires your majesty to leave the field, | and 5.03. 6
who didst thou leave to tend his majesty? 5.06. 32
with purpose presently to leave this war. 5.07. 86
i take my leave before i have begun, | for R2 1.02. 60
the last leave of thee takes my weeping eye. 1.02. 74
then let us take a ceremonious leave | and 1.03. 50
and craves to kiss your hand and take his leave. 1.03. 53
my loving lord, i take my leave of you; 1.03. 63
but you gave leave to my unwilling tongue 1.03.245
my lord, no leave take i, for i will ride, | as 1.03.251
i have too few to take my leave of you, | when 1.03.255
and yet my letters–patents give me leave. 2.03.130
give richard leave to live till richard die? 3.03.174
as from my death–bed, thy last living leave. 5.01. 39
take leave and part, for you must part forthwith 5.01. 70
where did i leave? 5.02. 4
withdraw yourselves, and leave us here alone. 5.03. 28
then give me leave that /i may turn the key, 5.03. 36
have gotten leave | to look upon my sometimes 5.05. 74
john, i prithee leave the prince and me alone, i 1H4 1.02.149 P
our vizards we will change after we leave them; 1.02.179 P
you have good leave to leave us. 1.03. 20
you have good leave to leave us. 1.03. 20
to turn true man and to leave these rogues, i am 2.02. 23 P
well, we leave that to the proof. 2.02. 69 P
i must leave you within these two hours. 2.03. 36
this evening must i leave you, gentle kate. 2.03.106
and do thou never leave calling "francis," that 2.04. 31 P
and so let me entreat you leave the house. 2.04.518
give me leave | to tell you once again that at 3.01. 35
from whom you now must steal and take no leave, 3.01. 92
here come our wives, and let us take our leave. 3.01.189
a good mouth–filling oath, and leave "in sooth," 3.01.254
lords, give us leave, the prince of wales and i 3.02. 1
hal, i prithee give me leave to breathe a while. 5.03. 44 P
i'll give you leave to powder me and eat me too 5.04.112 P
i'll grow less, for i'll purge and leave sack, 5.04.164 P
let us not leave till all our own be won. 5.05. 44
and give me leave to tell you you lie in your 2H4 1.02. 84 P
i give thee leave to tell me so? 1.02. 87 P
if thou get'st any leave of me, hang me; 1.02. 88 P

if thou tak'st leave, thou wert better be hang'd 1.02. 89 P
but, by your leave, it never yet did hurt | to 1.03. 34
me to thee, i commend thee, and i leave thee. 2.02.127 P
"i will now take my leave of these six dry, 2.04. 7 P
when wilt thou leave fighting a' days and 2.04.232 P
night, and we must hence and leave it unpick'd. 2.04.368 P
lord, i beseech you give me leave to go through 4.03. 81 P
'tis seldom when the bee doth leave her comb 4.04. 79
this from thee | will i to mine leave, as 'tis 4.05. 47
why did you leave me here alone, my lords? 4.05. 50
depart the chamber, leave us here alone. 4.05. 90
leave gormandizing, know the grave doth gape 5.05. 53
may't please your majesty to give us leave H5 1.02.237
nor leave not one behind that doth not wish 2.02. 23
and leave your england as dead midnight, still, 3.pr. 19
i must leave them, and seek some better service. 3.02. 51 P
i will not leave the half–achieved harflew 3.03. 8
and those that leave their valiant bones in 4.03. 98
which if they have as i will leave 'um them, 4.03.124
o, give us leave, great king, | to view the 4.07. 81
yet leave our cousin katherine here with us: 5.02. 95
she hath good leave. 5.02. 98
i do remember it, and here take my leave, | to 1H6 1.01.165
let's leave this town, for they are hare–brain'd 1.02. 37
back, you lords, and give us leave a while. 1.02. 70
of majesty | will'd me to leave my base vocation 1.02. 80
leave off delays, and let us raise the siege. 1.02.146
his sword did ne'er leave striking in the field. 1.04. 81
'twas time, i trow, to wake and leave our beds, 2.01. 41
you of my household, leave this peevish broil, 3.01. 92
what? will you fly, and leave lord talbot? 3.02.107
burgundy | to leave the talbot and to follow us. 3.03. 20
be patient, lords, and give them leave to speak. 4.01. 82
and leave my followers here to fight and die? 4.05. 45
then here i take my leave of thee, fair son, 4.05. 52
wilt thou yet leave the battle, boy, and fly, 4.06. 28
i prithee give me leave to curse a while. 5.03. 43
i were best to leave him, for he will not hear. 5.03. 83
o, give me leave, i have deluded you, | 'twas 5.04. 76
with whom i leave my curse: 5.04. 86
resign it then and leave thine insolence. 2H6 1.03.122
election, give me leave | to show some reason, 1.03.162
so i pray you go in god's name, and leave us. 1.04. 9 P
your grace shall give me leave, my lord of york, 1.04. 76
yet, by your leave, the wind was very high, 2.01. 3
ambitious churchman, leave to afflict my heart. 2.01.178
give me leave | in this close walk to satisfy 2.02. 2
i beseech your majesty give me leave to go; 2.03. 20
and even as willingly at thy feet i leave it 2.03. 35
come, leave your drinking, and fall to blows. 2.03. 79 P
my nell, i take my leave; 2.04. 74
but i can give the loser leave to chide. 3.01.182
and well such losers may have leave to speak. 3.01.185
what, will your highness leave the parliament? 3.01.197
and let thy suffolk take his heavy leave. 3.02.306
you bade me ban, and will you bid me leave? 3.02.333
shalt have cause to fear before i leave thee. 4.01.118
we will not leave one lord, one gentleman; 4.02.184
that you should leave me at the white hart in 4.08. 24 P
mischiefs, and makes them leave me desolate. 4.08. 58 P
for entering his fee–simple without leave. 4.10. 26 P
men, and if i do not leave you all as dead as a 4.10. 40 P
should raise so great a power without his leave, 5.01. 21
it grieves my soul to leave thee unassail'd. 5.02. 18
then leave me not, my lords, be resolute, | i 3H6 1.01. 43
peace thou! and give king henry leave to speak. 1.01.120
thou that i will leave my kingly throne, 1.01.124
thus do i leave thee. 1.01.255
brother, though i be youngest, give me leave. 1.02. 1
giving the house of lancaster leave to breathe, 1.02. 13
and thus most humbly i do take my leave. 1.02. 61
line, | and leave not one alive, i live in hell. 1.03. 33
by your leave i speak it, | you love the breeder 2.01. 41
to hold thine own and leave thine own with him. 2.02. 42
i'll leave my son my virtuous deeds behind, 2.02. 49
my gracious father, by your kingly leave, | i'll 2.02. 63
ay, good my lord, and leave us to our fortune. 2.02. 75
we'll never leave till we have hewn thee down, 2.02.168
now, lords, take leave until we meet again, 2.03. 42
and give them leave to fly that will not stay; 2.03. 50
whose soul is that which takes her heavy leave? 2.06. 42
lords, give us leave. i'll try this widow's wit. 3.02. 33
ay, good leave have you, for you will have leave 3.02. 34
for you will have leave | till youth take leave 3.02. 34
till youth take leave and leave you to the 3.02. 35
youth take leave and leave you to the crutch. 3.02. 35
i take my leave with many thousand thanks. 3.02. 56
and give my tongue–tied sorrows leave to speak. 3.03. 22
i am commanded, with your leave and favor, 3.03. 60
for shame, leave henry, and call edward king. 3.03.100
and leave your brothers to go speed elsewhere. 4.01. 58
you shall give me leave | to play the broker in 4.01. 62
and to that end i shortly mind to leave you. 4.01. 64
leave me, or tarry, edward will be king, | and 4.01. 65
leave off to wonder why i drew you hither | into 4.05. 2
i'll leave you to your fortune and be gone | to 4.07. 55
fair lords, take leave and stand not to reply. 4.08. 23
comfort, my lord! and so i take my leave. 4.08. 28
at southam i did leave him with his forces, 5.01. 9
warwick, wilt thou leave the town, and fight? 5.01.107
is't meet that he | should leave the helm and, 5.04. 7
man, | he should have leave to go away betimes, 5.04. 45
sirrah, leave us to ourselves, we must confer. 5.06. 6
and leave the world for me to bustle in! R3 1.01.152
to give me leave | by circumstance but to acquit 1.02. 76
but to give me leave | by circumstance /t' 1.02. 79
to leave this keen encounter of our wits | and 1.02.115
that it may please you leave these sad designs 1.02.210
thee to hell for shame, and leave this world, 1.03.142
and leave out thee? 1.03.215
i marvel that her grace did leave it out. 2.02.111
but leave it all to god. 2.03. 45
and in this resolution here we leave you. 3.07.218
grace, | and so most joyfully we take our leave. 3.07.245
master lieutenant, pray you, by your leave, 4.01. 13
i may not leave it so: 4.01. 26
adieu, poor soul, that tak'st thy leave of it! 4.01. 90
i humbly take my leave. 4.03. 35
head, | and leave the burthen of it all on thee. 4.04.113
pleaseth your majesty to give me leave, | i'll 4.04.487
but leave behind | your son, george stanley. 4.04.494
leave me. 5.03. 76
leave me, i say. 5.03. 78
will leave us never an understanding friend. H8 pr 22
love | not unconsidered leave your honor nor 1.02. 15
and, though we leave it with a root, thus hack'd 1.02. 97
leave those remnants | of fool and feather that 1.03. 24
by your leave, sweet ladies. 1.04. 25
but leave their flocks, and under your fair 1.04. 70
fair conduct | crave leave to view these ladies, 1.04. 71
fellows, whom to leave | is only bitter to him, 2.01. 73
so i leave him | to him that made him proud, the 2.02. 54
would it not grieve an able man to leave | so 2.02.141
o, 'tis a tender place, and i must leave her. 2.02.143
which | to leave a thousandfold more bitter than 2.03. 8
your particular fancy, | and leave me out on't. 2.03.102
and got your leave | to make this present 2.04.219
leave working. 3.01. 2
i would your grace | would leave your griefs, 3.01. 92
is stol'n away to rome, hath ta'en no leave, 3.02. 57
leave me a while. 3.02. 84
what means got, i leave to your own conscience) 3.02.327
and so we'll leave you to your meditations | how 3.02.345
o my lord, | must i then leave you? 3.02.422
to th' earth, | willing to leave their burthen. 4.02. 3
thus far, griffith, give me leave to speak him, 4.02. 32
and leave me here in wretchedness behind ye? 4.02. 84
bid the music leave, | they are harsh and heavy 4.02. 94
nay, patience, | you must not leave me yet. 4.02.166
i'll take my leave. 5.01. 9
leave me alone, | for i must think of that which 5.01. 74
you'll leave your noise anon, ye rascals; 5.03. 1 P
ye rude slaves, leave your gaping. 5.03. 3 P
so shall she leave her blessedness to one 5.04. 43
no more to me, i will leave all as i found it, TRO 1.01. 87 P
fair leave and large security. 1.03.223
is wit stirring, and leave the faction of fools. 2.01.119 P
for this time will i take my leave, my lord. 3.02.139
your leave, sweet cressid! 3.02.140
leave! 3.02.141 P
and you take leave till to–morrow morning — 3.02.141 P
that itself will leave | to be another's fool. 3.02.149
what some men do, | while some men leave to do! 3.03.133
they all rush by | and leave you /hindmost; 3.03.160
crown of falsehood, | if ever she leave troilus! 4.02.101
i'll have my kiss, sir. lady, by your leave. 4.05. 35
so to him we leave it. 4.05.226
i will rather leave to see hector than not to 5.01. 95 P
let's leave the hermit pity with our mother, 5.03. 45
but give me leave | to take that course by your 5.03. 73
hector, i take my leave. 5.03. 89
that i shall leave you one a' th's days; 5.03.103 P
the flour of all, | and leave me but the bran." COR 1.01.146
i leave your honors. 1.02. 33
beseech you give me leave to retire myself. 1.03. 27
that you might leave pricking it for pity. 1.03. 85 P
i'll leave the foe | and make my wars on you. 1.04. 39
i will be bold to take my leave of you. 2.01. 96 P
leave nothing out for length, and make us think 2.02. 49
i'll leave you. 2.03. 59
leave us to cure this cause. 3.01.234
if, by the tribunes' leave, and yours, good 3.01.280
give me leave, | i'll go to him, and undertake 3.01.321
come leave your tears: 4.01. 1
well, well, we'll leave you. 4.02. 43
leave this faint puling, and lament as i do, 4.02. 52
down before him, and leave his passage poll'd. 4.05.202 P
to leave unburnt | and still to nose th' offense 5.01. 27
but, by your leave, | i am an officer of state, 5.02. 2
therefore, fellow, | i must have leave to pass. 5.02. 23
noble mother of the world | leave unsaluted. 5.03. 50
goths have given me leave to sheathe my sword. TIT 1.01. 85
lord titus, by your leave, this maid is mine. 1.01.276
nor wish no less, and so i take my leave. 1.01.402
prince bassianus, leave to plead my deeds, 1.01.424
yew, | and leave me to this miserable death. 2.03.108
well could i leave our sport to sleep a while. 2.03.197
and so let's leave her to her silent walks. 2.04. 8
then give me leave, for losers will have leave 3.01.232
for losers will have leave | to ease their 3.01.232
and so i leave you both — like bloody villains. 4.02. 17
and leave you not a man–of–war unsearch'd. 4.03. 22
madam, depart at pleasure, leave us here. 5.02.145
do them that kindness, and take leave of them. 5.03.171
and if you leave me so, you do me wrong. ROM 1.01.196
nurse, give leave a while, | we must talk in 1.03. 7
laugh | to think it should leave crying and say, 1.03. 51
o, wilt thou leave me so unsatisfied? 2.02.125
to cease thy /suit, and leave me to my grief. 2.02.152
i am a–weary, give me leave a while. 2.05. 25
have you got leave to go to shrift to–day? 2.05. 66
i pray thee leave me to myself to–night, | for i 4.03. 2
i will die, | and leave him all; 4.05. 40
dream, that gives a dead man leave to think! 5.01. 7
since you did leave it for my office, sir. 5.01. 23
leave me, and do the thing i bid thee do. 5.01. 30
fly hence and leave me, think upon these gone, 5.03. 60
will you leave me there? TIM 2.02. 90 P
have rated my expense | as i had leave of means. 2.02.127
by your leave, sir — 3.04. 44
slink all away, leave their false vows with him, 4.02. 11
up in thee, | i'ld give thee leave to hang it. 4.03.280
so i leave you | to the protection of the 5.01.182
bring in thy ranks, but leave without thy rage; 5.04. 39
set on, and leave no ceremony out. JC 1.02. 11
he is a dreamer, let us leave him. pass. 1.02. 24
i'll leave you. 1.02. 31
for this time i will leave you; 1.02.303
let us not leave him out. 2.01.143
then leave him out. 2.01.152
we'll leave you, brutus, | and, friends, 2.01.221
of your hand | gave sign for me to leave you. 2.01.247
leave me with haste. 2.01.309
and leave us, publius, lest that the people, 3.01. 92
protest | he speaks by leave and by permission; 3.01.239
here, under leave of brutus and the rest | (for 3.02. 81
and will you give me leave? 3.02.160
you shall have leave. 3.02.163 P
that gave me public leave to speak of him. 3.02.220
think your mother chides, and leave you so. 4.03.123
rob the hybla bees, | and leave them honeyless. 5.01. 35
where did you leave him? 5.03. 55
by your leave, gods! 5.03. 89
knowledge of the broil | as thou didst leave it. MAC 1.02. 7
so humbly take my leave. 1.04. 47
leave all the rest to me. 1.05. 73
by your leave, hostess. 1.06. 31
to leave no rubs nor botches in the work — 3.01.133
you must leave this. 3.02. 35
to leave his wife, to leave his babes, | his 4.02. 6
to leave his wife, to leave his babes, | his 4.02. 6
i take my leave of you; 4.02. 22
i take my leave at once. 4.02. 30
they were well at peace when i did leave 'em. 4.03.179
is ready, | our lack is nothing but our leave. 4.03.237
your leave and favor to return to france, | from HAM 1.02. 51
and bow them to your gracious leave and pardon. 1.02. 56
have you your father's leave? 1.02. 57
lord, wrung from me my slow leave | by laborsome 1.02. 58
i do beseech you give him leave to go. 1.02. 61
grace, | occasion smiles upon a second leave. 1.03. 54
most humbly do i take my leave, my lord. 1.03. 82
leave her to heaven, | and to those thorns that 1.05. 86
where did i leave? 2.01. 51
o, give me leave, | how does my good lord hamlet 2.02.170
i will leave him, /and /suddenly /contrive /the 2.02.211 P
my lord, i will take my leave of you. 2.02.214 P
my good friends, i'll leave you /till night. 2.02.547 P
sweet gertrude, leave us two, | for we have 3.01. 28
faith, i must leave thee, love, and shortly too; 3.02.173
my operant powers their functions leave to do, 3.02.174
sweet, leave me here a while, | my spirits grow 3.02.225
murtherer, leave thy damnable faces and begin. 3.02.253 P
leave me, friends. 3.02.387
leave wringing of your hands. 3.04. 34
could you on this fair mountain leave to feed, 3.04. 66
/grained spots | as will /not leave their tinct. 3.04. 91
yea, curb and woo for leave to do him good. 3.04.155
i pray you give me leave. 4.05.114
leave us. 4.07. 42
to–morrow shall i beg leave to see your kingly 4.07. 44 P
give me leave. 5.01. 15 P
he leaves, knows what is't to leave betimes, let 5.02.224 P
standing thus unknown, shall i leave behind me! 5.02.345
with our oath, | take her, or leave her? LR 1.01.205
then leave her, sir, for, by the pow'r that made 1.01.207
leave thy drink and thy whore, | and keep in a' 1.04.124
daughters, and leave his horns without a case. 1.05. 31 P
my lord, if you/'ll give me leave, i will tread 2.02. 65 P
begins to rain, | and leave thee in the storm. 2.04. 81
when i desir'd their leave that i might pity him 3.03. 2 P
this tempest will not give me leave to ponder 3.04. 24
leave him to my displeasure. 3.07. 6 P
leave, gentle wax, and, manners, blame us not: 4.06.259
your daughter (if you have not given her leave), OTH 1.01.133
for i must leave you. 1.01.144
to leave that latest which concerns him first, 1.03. 28
othello, leave some officer behind, | and he 1.03.280
iago, | my desdemona must i leave to thee. 1.03.295
but, by your leave, not before me; 2.03.109 P
madam, i'll take my leave. 3.03. 30
me this, | to leave me but a little to myself. 3.03. 85
leave me, iago. 3.03.240
my lord, i take my leave. 3.03.241
leave it to time. 3.03.245
i once more take my leave. 3.03.257
go, leave me. 3.03.320
i will not leave him now till cassio | be call'd 3.04. 32
take it, and do't, and leave me for this time. 3.04.191
leave you? wherefore? 3.04.192
well, i must leave her company. 4.01.144 P
leave procreants alone, and shut the door; 4.02. 28
good gentlemen, let me have leave to speak. 5.02.195
would she had never given you leave to come! ANT 1.03. 21
i'll leave you, lady. 1.03. 86
antony, | leave thy lascivious /wassails. 1.04. 56
give me leave, caesar — 2.02.116
now antony | must leave her utterly. 2.02.233
let him not leave out | the color of her hair. 2.05.113
better to leave undone, than by our deed 3.01. 14
leave unexecuted | your own renowned knowledge, 3.07. 44
leave me, i pray, a little; 3.11. 22
your flying flags, | and leave his navy gazing. 3.13. 12
leaky | that we must leave thee to thy sinking, 3.13. 64
i will seek | some way to leave him. 3.13.200
i look on you | as one that takes his leave. 4.02. 29
i'll leave thee | now like a man of steel. 4.04. 32
himself to caesar | and leave his master antony; 4.06. 14
i'll take my leave. 5.02.133
i'll give thee leave | to play till doomsday. 5.02.231
avoid, and leave him. 5.02.242
should we be taking leave | as long a term as CYM 1.01.106
leave us to ourselves, and make yourself some 1.01.155
for this time leave me. 1.01.178
i did not take my leave of him, but had | most 1.03. 25
worthy he is i will leave to appear hereafter, 1.04. 33 P
let us leave here, gentlemen. 1.04. 99 P
if i come off and leave her in such honor as you 1.04.152 P
i humbly take my leave. 1.05. 45
desire my man's abode where i did leave him: 1.06. 53
twenty, for his heart, | and leave eighteen. 2.01. 56
take not away the taper, leave it burning; 2.02. 5
by your leave ho! 2.03. 65
by your leave. 2.03. 76
to leave you in your madness, 'twere my sin; 2.03. 99
so i leave /you, sir, | to th' worst of 2.03.154
or masterless leave both | to who shall find 2.04. 60
you'll give me leave to spare when you shall 2.04. 65
be pale, i beg but leave to air this jewel. 2.04. 96
good wax, thy leave. 3.02. 35
art o' th' court, | as hard to leave as keep; 3.03. 47
leave not the worthy lucius, good my lords, 3.05. 16
she should that duty leave unpaid to you | which 3.05. 48
suit he wore when he took leave of my lady and 3.05.126 P

so please you, leave me, | stick to your journal 4.02. 9
we'll leave you for this time, go in, and rest. 4.02. 43
if you will bless me, sir, and give me leave, 4.04. 44
thou'lt torture me to leave unspoken that 5.05.139
spirits | quail to remember — give me leave, i 5.05.149
have at it then, by leave. 5.05.315
then give my tongue like leave to love my head. PER 1.01.108
all leave us else; 1.02. 48
my lord, since you have given me leave to speak, 1.02.101
who never leave gaping till they swallow'd the 2.01. 33 P
funeral, | and leave us to our free election. 2.04. 33
there i'll leave it | at careful nursing. 3.01. 79
so i take my leave. 3.03. 30
his woeful queen we leave at ephesus, | unto 4.ch. 3
i'll leave you, my sweet lady, for a while. 4.01. 47
well, there's for you, leave us. 4.06. 45 P
i beseech your honor give me leave a word, and 4.06. 46 P
come, we will leave his honor and her together. 4.06. 65 P
come, let us leave her, | and the gods make her 5.01. 78
yet give me leave: 5.01.168
the king my father did in tharsus leave me, 5.01.170
so leave him all. 5.01.237
our losses fall so thick we must needs leave. TNK pr 32
leave not out a jot | o' th' sacred ceremony. 1.01.130
let us leave the city | thebes and the temptings 1.02. 3
let's leave his court, that we may nothing share 1.02. 75
leave that unreason'd. 1.02. 98
made too proud the bed, took leave o' th' moon 1.03. 52
each thing | our haste does leave imperfect. 1.04. 12
/wi' leave, they're called | arcite and palamon. 1.04. 22
go to, leave your pointing. 2.01. 51 P
leave 'em all behind us | like lazy clouds, 2.02. 13
possible our friendship | should ever leave us. 2.02.115
by your leave, gentlemen. 2.02.220
i will not leave the kingdom. 2.03. 18
he cannot | be so unmanly as to leave me here. 2.06. 19
then i'll leave you; | you are a beast now. 3.03. 46
without my leave and officers of arms? 3.06.135
i'll leave you to your prayers, and betwixt ye 5.01. 16
but first, by your leave, | i' th' way of 5.02. 19
i must ev'n leave you here. 5.02.102
and with you leave dispute | that are above our 5.04.135
had ta'en his last leave of the weeping morn, VEN 2
i pray you hence, and leave me here alone, | for 382
and leave this idle theme, this bootless chat; 422
chiefly in love, whose leave exceeds commission: 568
"where did i leave?" 715
he, | "leave me, and then the story aptly ends; 716
bids them leave quaking, bids them fear no more 899
if he had spoke, the wolf would leave his prey, 1097
so that in vent'ring ill we leave to be | the LUC 148
thyself art mighty, for thine own sake leave me; 583
leave thy peeping, | mock with thy tickling 1089
and leave the falt'ring feeble souls alive? 1768
to leave the master loveless, or kill the PP 15. 6
gone, | what acceptable audit canst thou leave? SON 4.12
were it not thy sour leisure gave sweet leave 39.10
will sourly leave her till /she have prevailed? 41. 8
to leave poor me thou hast the strength of laws, 49.13
towards thee i'll run, and give him leave to go. 51.14
gone, | save that to die, i leave my love alone. 66.14
love that well, which thou must leave ere long. 73.14
if thou wilt leave me, do not leave me last, 90. 9
if thou wilt leave me, do not leave me last, 90. 9
to leave for nothing all thy sum of good; 109.12
what labor is't to leave | the thing we have not LC 239
to leave the batt'ry that you make 'gainst mine, 277

LEAVEN 2 FR 0.0002 REL FR 1 V 1 P
speak then, thou /whinid'st leaven, speak; TRO 2.01. 14 P
wilt lay the leaven on all proper men; CYM 3.04. 62

LEAVEN'D 1 FR 0.0001 REL FR 1 V 0 P
we have with a leaven'd and prepared choice MM 1.01. 51

LEAVENING 2 FR 0.0002 REL FR 0 V 2 P
but you must tarry the leavening. TRO 1.01. 20 P
ay, to the leavening, but here's yet in the word 1.01. 23 P

LEAVES* 78 FR 0.0088 REL FR 71 V 7 P
he leaves his friends to dignify them more; TGV 1.01. 64
and leaves unquestion'd | matters of needful MM 1.01. 54
in his doublet and hose and leaves off his wit! ADO 5.01.200 P
study his bias leaves, and makes his book thine LLL 4.02.109
sweet leaves, shade folly. 4.03. 42
through the velvet leaves the wind, | all unseen 4.03.103
as he that leaves | a shallow plash to plunge SHR 1.01. 22
disguise | for such a one as leaves a gentleman 4.02. 19
when briers shall have leaves as well as thorns, AWW 4.04. 32
when the image of it leaves him he must run mad. TN 2.05.194 P
and | so leaves me to consider what is breeding WT 1.02.374
that leaves the print of blood where e'er it JN 4.03. 26
leaves them invisible, and his siege is now 5.07. 16
is hack'd down, and his summer leaves all faded, R2 1.02. 20
which his broad–spreading leaves did shelter, 3.04. 50
after a well–graced actor leaves the stage, 5.02. 24
loseth men's hearts and leaves behind a stain 1H4 3.01.185
and by his hollow whistling in the leaves 5.01. 5
o'er, and leaves his part–created cost | a naked 2H4 1.03. 60
/to french and welsh he leaves his back unarm'd, 1.03. 79
saying the sanguine color of the leaves | did 1H6 4.01. 92
the bud, | and caterpillars eat my leaves away; 2H6 3.01. 90
embrace, and kiss, and take ten thousand leaves, 3.02.354
that keeps his leaves in spite of any storm, 5.01.206
in hewing rutland when his leaves put forth, 3H6 2.06. 48
the leaves and fruit maintain'd with beauty's 3.03.126
why wither not the leaves that want their sap? R3 2.02. 42
when great leaves fall, then winter is at hand; 2.03. 33
see then, | by all your good leaves, gentlemen; H8 1.04. 85
he puts forth | the tender leaves of hopes, 3.02.353
with what a sorrow cromwell leaves his lord. 3.02.425
there, and every where, he leaves and takes, TRO 5.05. 26
carries noise, and behind him he leaves tears: COR 2.01.159 P
it him, and leaves nothing undone that may fully 2.02. 19 P
who now are here, taking their leaves of me, 4.05.133
the green leaves quiver with the cooling wind TIT 2.03. 14
upon whose leaves are drops of new–shed blood 2.03.200
hands | tremble like aspen leaves upon a lute, 2.04. 45
soft, so busily she turns the leaves! 4.01. 45
brother, see, note how she cotes the leaves. 4.01. 50
blow these sands like sibyl's leaves abroad, 4.01.105
ere he can spread his sweet leaves to the air ROM 1.01.152
for, by your leaves, you shall not stay alone 2.06. 36
nor more willingly leaves winter, such summer TIM 3.06. 31 P
that numberless upon me stuck as leaves | do on 4.03.263
in a sleep, and, giving him the lie, leaves him. MAC 2.03. 36 P
to the succeeding royalty he leaves | the 4.03.155
that shows his hoary leaves in the glassy stream HAM 4.07.167
since no man, of aught he leaves, knows what 5.02.223 P
nature | which often leaves the history unspoke LR 1.01.236
father, with wash'd eyes | cordelia leaves you. 1.01.269
let /that be left | which leaves itself. ANT 3.11. 20
hercules, whom antony lov'd, | now leaves him. 4.03. 17
and these fig leaves | have slime upon them, 5.02.351
such as th' aspic leaves | upon the caves of 5.02.352
shook down my mellow hangings, nay, my leaves, CYM 3.03. 63
the boy disdains me, | he leaves me, scorns me. 5.05.106
loath to bid farewell, we take our leaves. PER 2.05. 13
leaves tharsus and again embarks. 4.04. 27
her bud again, | and leaves him to base briers. TNK 2.02.143
by your leaves, honest friends: 2.03. 60
as caterpillars do the tender leaves. VEN 798
leaves love upon her back, deeply distress'd. 814
lust–breathed tarquin leaves the roman host, LUC 3
it, | and leaves it to be mast'red by his young, 863
his leaves will wither and his sap decay; 1168
study his bias leaves, and makes his book thine PP 5. 5
through the velvet leaves the wind | all unseen 16. 5
kirtle | embroidered all with leaves of myrtle; 19.12
check'd with frost and lusty leaves quite gone, SON 5. 7
when lofty trees i see barren of leaves, | which 12. 5
princes' favorites their fair leaves spread 25. 5
thou mayst in me behold | when yellow leaves, or 73. 2
the vacant leaves thy mind's imprint will bear, 77. 3
with so dull a cheer | that leaves look pale, 97.14
one thing expressing, leaves out difference. 105. 8
who leaves unsway'd the likeness of a man, | thy 141.11
and he takes and leaves, | in either's aptness, LC 305

LEAVEST 1 FR 0.0001 REL FR 1 V 0 P
and leavest the kingly couch | a watch–case or a 2H4 3.01. 16

LEAVE'T 1 FR 0.0001 REL FR 1 V 0 P
best conscience | is not to leave't undone, but OTH 3.03.204

LEAVE–TAKING 6 FR 0.0006 REL FR 5 V 1 P
where injury of chance | puts back leave–taking, TRO 4.04. 34
and let us not be dainty of leave–taking, | but MAC 2.03.144
strong knots of love, | without leave–taking? 4.03. 28
compliment of leave–taking between france and LR 1.01.302 P
the world | it is not worth leave–taking. ANT 5.02.298
my life be now as short | as my leave–taking. TNK 5.04. 38

/LEAVING 1 FR 0.0001 REL FR 1 V 0 P
/leaving /free /things /and /happy /shows LR 3.06.105

LEAVING 25 FR 0.0028 REL FR 21 V 4 P
leaving the fear of /god on the left hand, and WIV 2.02. 23 P
leaving his wealth and ease | a stubborn will to AYL 2.05. 52
then leaving her | in the protection of his son, TN 1.02. 37
appears in leaving his friend here in necessity 3.04.387 P
leontes leaving — | th' effects of his fond WT 4.01. 17
out the rest of thy services by leaving me now. 4.02. 11 P
leaving our rankness and irregular course, JN 5.04. 54
ras'd out my imprese, leaving me no sign, | save R2 3.01. 25
leaving his body as a paradise | t' envelop and H5 1.01. 30
coming on, leaving their wits with their wives; 3.07.148 P
leaving them but the shales and husks of men. 4.02. 18
leaving their earthly parts to choke your clime, 4.03.102
remov'd, | leaving no heir begotten of his body) 1H6 2.05. 72
leaving thy trunk for crows to feed upon. 2H6 4.10. 84
but, leaving this, what is your grace's pleasure R3 3.07.108
send it me from heaven | by leaving earth? ROM 3.05.208
bold, and forth on, | leaving no tract behind. TIM 1.01. 50
them diseases, leaving with thee their lust. 4.03. 85
in his life | became him like the leaving it. MAC 1.04. 8
leaving the fight in heighth, flies after her. ANT 3.10. 20
and leaving so his service, follow you, | so CYM 4.02.393
leaving her | the infant of your care, PER 3.03. 14
leaving his spoil perplex'd in greater pain. LUC 733
leaving no posterity, | 'twas not their PHT 59
depart, | leaving thee living in posterity? SON 6.12

LEAVY 3 FR 0.0003 REL FR 3 V 0 P
men was ever so, | since summer first was leavy. ADO 2.03. 73
your leavy screens throw down, | and show like MAC 5.06. 1
now upon | the leavy shelter that abuts against PER 5.01. 51

LECHER 4 FR 0.0004 REL FR 3 V 1 P
i will now take the lecher; WIV 3.05.144 P
you, like a lecher, out of whorish loins | are TRO 4.01. 64
the small gilded fly | does lecher in my sight. LR 4.06.113
was this a lover, or a lecher whether? PP 7.17

LECHEROUS 4 FR 0.0004 REL FR 1 V 3 P
in his house–eaves, because they are lecherous. MM 3.02.176 P
genius of famine, yet lecherous as a monkey, and 2H4 3.02.314 P
treacherous, lecherous, kindless villain! HAM 2.02.581
so that it follows, i am rough and lecherous. LR 1.02.131 P

LECHER'S 1 FR 0.0001 REL FR 0 V 1 P
in a wild field were like an old lecher's heart, LR 3.04.112 P

LECHERS 2 FR 0.0002 REL FR 2 V 0 P
the post unsanctified | of murtherous lechers; LR 4.06.275
and so did kill | the lechers in their deed. LUC 1637

/LECHERY 1 FR 0.0001 REL FR 0 V 1 P
/and /war /and /lechery /confound /all! TRO 2.03. 75 P

LECHERY 17 FR 0.0019 REL FR 2 V 15 P
against such lewdsters and their lechery | those WIV 5.03. 21
lechery? MM 1.02.139 P
is lechery so look'd after? 1.02.144
more lenity to lechery would do no harm in him. 3.02. 97 P
dangerous piece of lechery that ever was known ADO 3.03.168 P
lechery! TN 1.05.125 P
i defy lechery. 1.05.125 P
than 'a can part young limbs and lechery; 2H4 1.02.230 P
i'll after — nothing but lechery! TRO 5.01. 97 P
fry, lechery, fry! 5.02. 57 P
lechery, lechery, still wars and lechery, 5.02.194 P
lechery, lechery, still wars and lechery, 5.02.194 P
lechery, still wars and lechery, nothing else 5.02.195 P
miracle — yet, in a sort, lechery eats itself. 5.04. 35 P
lechery, sir, it provokes, and unprovokes: MAC 2.03. 29 P
may be said to be an equivocator with lechery: 2.03. 32 P
lechery, by this hand; OTH 2.01.257 P

LECON 1 FR 0.0001 REL FR 0 V 1 P
je reciterai une autre fois ma lecon ensemble: H5 3.04. 57 P

/LECTURE 1 FR 0.0001 REL FR 1 V 0 P
/a /troop | /to /read /a /lecture /of /them? R2 4.01.232

LECTURE 4 FR 0.0004 REL FR 4 V 0 P
your lecture shall have leisure for as much. SHR 3.01. 8
his lecture will be done ere you have tun'd. 3.01. 23
you'll leave his lecture when i am in tune? 3.01. 24
so by my former lecture and advice, | shall you HAM 2.01. 64

LECTURES 4 FR 0.0004 REL FR 3 V 1 P
i have heard him read many lectures against it, AYL 3.02.347 P
and see you read no other lectures to her. SHR 1.02.147
say we read lectures to you, | how youngly he COR 2.03.235
must he in thee read lectures of such shame? LUC 618

/LED 1 FR 0.0001 REL FR 1 V 0 P
so our leader's /led, | and we are women's men. ANT 3.07. 69

LED 61 FR 0.0069 REL FR 53 V 8 P
signior claudio, led by the provost to prison; MM 1.02.114 P
art thou led in triumph? 3.02. 44 P
i led them on in this distracted fear, | and MND 3.02. 31
in terms of choice i am not soly led | by nice MV 2.01. 13
/in brief, he led me to the gentle duke, | who AYL 4.03.142
love, | who led me instantly unto his cave, 4.03.145
"where is the life that late i led? SHR 4.01.140
speed her foot again, | led hither by pure love. AWW 3.04. 38
h'as led the drum before the english tragedians. 4.03.266 P
bear, yet he is oft led by the nose with gold. WT 4.04.802 P
are led so grossly by this meddling priest, JN 3.01.163
though you, and all the rest so grossly led, 3.01.168
to dismiss the powers | led by the dolphin. 5.01. 65
is not himself, but basely led | by flatterers, R2 2.01.241
i have led my ragamuffins where they are 1H4 5.03. 35 P
proper to madmen, led his powers to death, | and 2H4 1.03. 32
led on by bloody youth, guarded with rage, | and 4.01. 34
but as my betters are | that led me hither. 4.03. 66
led by th' impartial conduct of my soul; 5.02. 36
"where is the life that late i led?" 5.03.140
a black matter for the king that led them to it; H5 4.01.145 P
then broke i from the officers that led me, 1H6 1.04. 44
two mightier troops than that the dolphin led, 4.03. 7
land, | methinks i should not thus be led along, 2H6 2.04. 30
thrice i led him off, | persuaded him from any 5.03. 9
that led calm henry, though he were a king, | as 3H6 2.06. 34
led in the hand of her kind aunt of gloucester? R3 4.01. 2
armed in proof and led by shallow richmond. 5.03.219
election | is led on in the conduct of my will, TRO 2.02. 62
and will be led | at your request a little from 2.03.180
led by caius martius | associated with aufidius, COR 4.06. 75
bewray what life | we have led since thy exile. 5.03. 96
thou | must as a foreign recreant be led | with 5.03.114
and | with bloody passage led your wars even to 5.06. 75
and led my country's strength successfully, TIT 1.01.194
lords, was't not a happy star | led us to rome, 4.02. 33
led by their master to the flow'red fields, 5.01. 15
but who comes here, led by a lusty goth? 5.01. 19
but, o grief, | where hast thou led me? JC 1.03.112
either led or driven, as we point the way; 4.01. 23
battle, | you are contented to be led in triumph 5.01.108
dagger which you said | led you to duncan. MAC 3.04. 62
the english pow'r is near, led on by malcolm, 5.02. 1
charge | led by a delicate and tender prince, HAM 4.04. 48
follow their noses are led by their eyes but LR 2.04. 69 P
you should be rul'd and led | by some discretion 2.04.148
the foul fiend hath led through fire and through 3.04. 52 P
he led me to that place. 4.06. 79
your valiant strain, | and fortune led you well. 5.03. 41
he led our powers, | bore the commission of my 5.03. 63
led him, begg'd for him, sav'd him from despair; 5.03.192
and will as tenderly be led by th' nose | as OTH 1.03.401
a sin), | but partly led to diet my revenge, 2.01.294
and saw her led | between her brother and mark ANT 3.03. 9
till we perceiv'd both how you were wrong led 3.06. 80
o, whither hast thou led me, egypt? 3.11. 51
i have led you oft, carry me now, good friends, 4.14.139
led on by heaven, and crown'd with joy at last. PER 5.03. 90
and after death our spirits shall be led | to TNK 2.02.116
ev'n he that led you to this banket shall 5.04. 22
by reprobate desire thus madly led, | the roman LUC 300

LEDA 1 FR 0.0001 REL FR 0 V 1 P
were also, jupiter, a swan for the love of leda. WIV 5.05. 7 P

LEDA'S 1 FR 0.0001 REL FR 1 V 0 P
fair leda's daughter had a thousand wooers, SHR 1.02.242

LEDGER *(see leiger, liegers)*

LEDST 1 FR 0.0001 REL FR 1 V 0 P
thou not tell me, griffith, as thou ledst me, H8 4.02. 5

LEECH 1 FR 0.0001 REL FR 1 V 0 P
each | prescribe to other as each other's leech. TIM 5.04. 84

LEECHES 1 FR 0.0001 REL FR 1 V 0 P
sib to him be suck'd | from me with leeches! TNK 1.02. 73

LEEK 13 FR 0.0014 REL FR 2 V 11 P
tell him i'll knock his leek about his pate H5 4.01. 54
no scorn to wear the leek upon saint tavy's day. 4.07.103 P
but why wear you your leek to–day? 5.01. 2 P
yesterday, look you, and bid me eat my leek. 5.01. 10 P
i am qualmish at the smell of leek. 5.01. 21
and my petitions, to eat, look you, this leek; 5.01. 24 P
if you can mock a leek, you can eat a leek. 5.01. 37 P
if you can mock a leek, you can eat a leek. 5.01. 38 P
i will make him eat some part of my leek, or i 5.01. 41 P
by this leek, i will most horribly revenge — i 5.01. 47 P
will you have some more sauce to your leek? 5.01. 50 P
there is not enough leek to swear by. 5.01. 50 P
take it, or i have another leek in my pocket, 5.01. 62 P

LEEKS 5 FR 0.0005 REL FR 1 V 4 P
his eyes were green as leeks. MND 5.01.335
good service in a garden where leeks did grow, H5 4.07. 99 P
did grow, wearing leeks in their monmouth caps, 4.07. 99 P
when you take occasions to see leeks hereafter, 5.01. 56 P
ay, leeks is good. 5.01. 58 P

LEER* 5 FR 0.0005 REL FR 2 V 3 P
she carves, she gives the leer of invitation. WIV 1.03. 45 P
you leer upon me, do you? LLL 5.02.480
he hath a rosalind of a better leer than you. AYL 4.01. 67 P
i will leer upon him as 'a comes by, and do but 2H4 5.05. 6 P
here's a young lad fram'd of another leer: TIT 4.02.119

LEERS 1 FR 0.0001 REL FR 0 V 1 P
trust him when he leers than i will a serpent TRO 5.01. 90 P

LEES 3 FR 0.0003 REL FR 3 V 0 P
up | the lees and dregs of a flat tamed piece; TRO 4.01. 63
and the mere lees | is left this vault to brag MAC 2.03. 95
the very lees of such (millions of rates) TNK 1.04. 29

LEESE *(also lose)*
LEESE 1 FR 0.0001 REL FR 1 V 0 P
leese but their show, their substance still SON 5.14
LEET 1 FR 0.0001 REL FR 1 V 0 P
and say you would present her at the leet, SHR in.2. 87
LEETS 1 FR 0.0001 REL FR 1 V 0 P
keep leets and law–days and in sessions sit OTH 3.03.140
/LEFT* 5 FR 0.0005 REL FR 3 V 2 P
/so /you /left /him. 2H4 2.03. 38
/is /left /to /tyrannize /upon /my /breast, TIT 3.02. 8
/something /he /left /imperfect /in /the /state, LR 4.03. 3 P
/who /hath /he /left /behind /him /general? 4.03. 7 P
/sounded, | /and /there /i /left /him /tranc'd. 5.03.219
LEFT* 265 FR 0.0299 REL FR 225 V 40 P
stopp'd | and left me to a bootless inquisition, TMP 1.02. 35
whom i left cooling of the air with sighs, | in 1.02.222
to their suff'red labor, | i have left asleep; 1.02.232
with child, | and here was left by th' sailors. 1.02.270
and left thee there, where thou didst vent thy 1.02.280
since | they have left their viands behind; 3.03. 41
at last i left them | i' th' filthy–mantled pool 4.01.181
as you gave in charge, | just as you left them; 5.01. 9
no, this left shoe is my father; TGV 2.03. 15 P
no, no, this left shoe is my mother; 2.03. 16 P
i left them all in health. 2.04.124
for why, the fools are mad, if left alone. 3.01. 99
alas, poor lady, desolate and left! 4.04.174
thou hast no faith left now, unless thou'dst two 5.04. 50
leaving the fear of /god on the left hand, and WIV 2.02. 24 P
left her in her tears, and dried not one of them MM 3.01.225 P
and /the great care of goods at randon left, ERR 1.01. 42
and left the ship, then sinking–ripe, to us. 1.01. 77
fortune had left to both of us alike | what to 1.01.105
where have you left the money that i gave you? 1.02. 54
this fool–begg'd patience in thee will be left. 2.01. 41
i'll weep what's left away, and weeping die. 2.01.115
my neck, the great wart on my left arm, that i, 3.02.144 P
it was two ere i left him, and now the clock 4.02. 54
vault at home | there left me and my man, both 5.01.249
my wasting lamps some fading glimmer left, | my 5.01.316
and me they left with those of epidamium. 5.01.354
he was not three leagues off when i left him. ADO 1.01. 4 P
all the wealth that he hath left to be known a 1.01. 70 P
war–thoughts | have left their places vacant, in 1.01.302
with all that adam had left him before he 2.01.252 P
ever since you left it. 3.04. 69 P
thou seest that all the grace that she hath left 4.01.171
your daughter here the /princes left for dead, 4.01.202
much of my heart that none is left to protest. 4.01.287 P
him with thy bird–bolt under the left pap. LLL 4.03. 24 P
a mess of russians left us but of late. 5.02.361
fear, | and left sweet pyramus translated there; MND 3.02. 32
yet since night you left me: 3.02.275
why then you left me (o, the gods forbid!) 3.02.276
god's my life, stol'n hence, and left me asleep! 4.01.204 P
ay, that left pap, | where heart doth hop. 5.01.298
moonshine and lion are left to bury the dead. 5.01.348 P
something too prodigal | hath left me gag'd. MV 1.01.130
in belmont is a lady richly left, | and she is 1.01.161
left in the fearful guard | of an unthrifty 1.03.175
but at the next turning of all, on your left; 2.02. 42 P
state, | thou hast not left the value of a cord; 4.01.366
why, i were best to cut my left hand off, | and 5.01.177
the ring, | and how unwillingly i left the ring, 5.01.196
like argus, | if you do not, if i be left alone, 5.01.231
poor allottery my father left me by testament, AYL 1.01. 73 P
left and abandoned of his velvet /friends: 2.01. 50
left on your right hand brings you to the place. 4.03. 80
from you | he left a promise to return again 4.03. 99
i have left you commands. 5.02.121 P
for i have pisa left | and am to padua come, as SHR 1.01. 21
me, | left soly heir to all his lands and goods, 2.01.117
where left we last? 3.01. 26
how he left her with the horse upon her, how he 4.01. 76 P
curtsy with their left legs and not presume to 4.01. 93 P
but h'as left me here behind to expound the 4.04. 78 P
you know my father left me some prescriptions AWW 1.03.221
doctrine, have left off | the danger to itself? 1.03.241
his left cheek is a cheek of two pile and a half 4.05. 97 P
he left this ring behind him, | would i or not. TN 1.05.301
he left behind him myself and a sister, both 2.01. 18 P
i left no ring with her. 2.02. 17
a day–bed, where i have left olivia sleeping — 2.05. 49 P
shepherd's note since we have left our throne WT 1.02. 2
of the two fled hence | be left her to perform. 2.01.196
i'll pawn the little blood which i have left 2.03.166
and why he left your court, the gods themselves 3.02. 75
if there be any of him left, i'll bury it. 3.03.131 P
discern by that which is left of him what he is, 3.03.134 P
a footman by the garments he has left with thee. 4.03. 67 P
is there no manners left among maids? 4.04.242 P
i had not left a purse alive in the whole army. 4.04.617 P
great alexander | left his to th' worthiest; 5.01. 48
and left them | more rich for what they yielded. 5.01. 54
taking angry note, | have left me issueless; 5.01.174
man, | left to be finished by such as she, | and JN 2.01.438
'tis not an hour since i left him well. 4.03.104
i left him well. 4.03.139
and england now is left | to tug and scamble, 4.03.145
say king john, sore sick, hath left the field. 5.04. 6
i left him almost speechless, and broke out | to 5.06. 24
he is more patient | than when you left him; 5.07. 12
which he hath left so shapeless and so rude. 5.07. 27
if guilty dread have left thee so much strength R2 1.01. 73
but to the next high way, and there i left him. 1.04. 4
here am i left to underprop his land, | who, 2.02. 82
and every thing is left at six and seven. 2.02.122
why, foolish boy, the king is left behind, | and 2.03. 97
because my power is weak and all ill left; 2.03.154
only to be brief | left i his title out. 3.03. 11
and left me in reputeless banishment, | a fellow 1H4 3.02. 44
king | in deputation left behind him here, 4.03. 87
not three of my hundred and fifty left alive, 5.03. 37 P
flood | hath left a witness'd usurpation. 2H4 1.01. 63
now, have you left pursuit? 4.03. 71
and settled) left the liver white and pale, 4.03.104 P
thee | will i to mine leave, as 'tis left to me. 4.05. 47
we left the prince my brother here, my liege, 4.05. 51
when we withdrew, my liege, we left it here. 4.05. 58
his life | hath left me open to all injuries. 5.02. 8
the breath no sooner left his father's body, H5 1.01. 25
there left behind and settled certain french; 1.02. 47
whose hearts have left their bodies here in 1.02.128
if we, with thrice such powers left at home, 1.02.217
and thus thy fall hath left a kind of blot | to 2.02.138
left by the fatal and neglected english | upon 2.04. 13
some upon their wives left poor behind them, 4.01.139 P
they owe, some upon their children rawly left. 4.01.141 P
'tis certain there's not a boy left alive, and 4.07. 5 P
and of it left his son imperial lord. ep 8
and none but women left to wail the dead. 1H6 1.01. 51
i am left out; 1.01.174
fled, | but that they left me midst my enemies. 1.02. 24
i'll be so bold to take what they have left. 2.01. 78
will not this malice, somerset, be left? 4.01.108
and left us to the rage of france his sword. 4.06. 3
french, | he left me proudly, as unworthy fight. 4.07. 43
were but his picture left amongst you here, | it 4.07. 83
law, | and left thee to the mercy of the law. 2H6 1.03.134
and left behind him richard, his only son, | who 2.02. 19
for purposely therefore | left i the court, to 2.03. 53
but left that hateful office unto thee. 3.02. 93
this small inheritance my father left me 4.10. 18
north, | he slily stole away and left his men; 3H6 1.01. 3
thou wouldst have left thy dearest heart–blood 1.01.223
when we have left no protectors of the king, | with 1.02. 57
his name that valiant duke hath left with thee; 2.01. 89
his dukedom and his chair with me is left. 2.01. 90
and would my father had left me no more! 2.02. 50
ah, boy, if any life be left in thee, | throw up 2.05. 84
had left no mourning widows for our death, | and 2.06. 19
she, on his left side, craving aid for henry; 3.01. 43
you left poor henry at the bishop's palace, 5.01. 45
lands | is nothing left me but my body's length. 5.02. 26
and hast the comfort of thy children left; R3 2.02. 56
our fatherless distress was left unmoan'd, 2.02. 64
indeed, left nothing fitting for your purpose 3.07. 18
the royal tree hath left us royal fruit, | which 3.07.167
and so i left them both, | to bear this tidings 4.03. 21
about, | and left thee but a very prey to time, 4.04.106
and in record left them the heirs of shame. 5.03.335
th' have left their barge and landed, | and H8 1.04. 54
i left him private, | full of sad thoughts and 2.02. 14
i left no reverend person in this court; 2.04.221
and may be left | to some ears unrecounted. 3.02. 47
has left the cause o' th' king unhandled, and 3.02. 58
at length broke under me, and now has left me, 3.02.362
mine age | have left me naked to mine enemies. 3.02.457
and left him at primero | with the duke of 5.01. 7
store of room, no doubt, left for the ladies, 5.03. 73
soul in such a kind, | we left them all at home. TRO 1.03.286
i have abandon'd troy, left my possession, 3.03. 5
thou art left, martius — | a carbuncle entire, COR 1.04. 54
i' th' shoulder and i' th' left arm. 2.01.147 P
now you have left your voices, | i have no 2.03.172
and what is left, to lose it by his country 3.01.300
of yourself, or else | to him had left it soly. 4.07. 16
yet he hath left undone | that which shall break 4.07. 24
lavinia, though you left me like a churl, | i TIT 1.01.486
'tis not an hour since i left them there. 2.03.256
we know not where you left them all alive, | but 2.03.257
dry, | with miry slime left on them by a flood? 3.01.126
that left the camp to sin in lucrece' bed? 4.01. 64
to effect, | there's not a god left unsolicited. 4.03. 61
this one hand yet is not left to cut your throats, 5.02.181
the pretty wretch left crying and said, "ay." ROM 1.03. 44
so please you, let me now be left alone, | and 4.03. 9
and left no friendly drop | to help me after? 5.03.163
vault, | if i departed not and left him there. 5.03.277
he is gone happy, and has left me rich. TIM 1.02. 4
honest water, which ne'er left man i' th' mire. 1.02. 59
too, there would be none left to rail upon thee, 1.02.239 P
wing, | lord timon will be left a naked gull, 2.01. 31
there's not so much left to furnish out | a 3.04.114
fell from their boughs, and left me open, bare, 4.03.265
and strain what other means is left unto us | in 5.01.227
a plague consume you, wicked caitiffs left! 5.04. 71
held up his left hand, which did flame and burn JC 1.03. 16
moreover, he hath left you all his walks, | his 3.02.247
he hath left them you, | and to your heirs for 3.02.249
not the leaf turn'd down | where i left reading? 4.03.274
on | upon the left hand of the even field. 5.01. 17
upon the right hand i, keep thou the left. 5.01. 18
only i have left to say, | more is thy due than MAC 1.04. 20
why have you left the chamber? 1.07. 29
your constancy | hath left you unattended. 2.02. 66
the mere lees | is left this vault to brag of. 2.03. 96
which steals itself, when there's no mercy left. 2.03.146
why in that rawness left you wife and child, 4.03. 26
had left the flushing in her galled eyes, | she HAM 1.02.155
for 'tis a question left us yet to prove, 3.02.202
here's yet some liquor left. 5.02.342
o' both sides, and left nothing i' th' middle. LR 1.04.187 P
out went the candle, and we were left darkling. 1.04.217 P
yet have i left a daughter. 1.04.255
you have one eye left | to see some mischief on 3.07. 81
so that, dear lords, if i be left behind, | a OTH 1.03.255
captain, | left in the conduct of the bold iago, 2.01. 75
is my right hand, and this is my left /hand. 2.03.114 P
that he hath left part of his grief with me | to 3.03. 53
lik'st not that, | when cassio left my wife. 3.03.110
in your chamber, and know not who left it there! 4.01.152 P
you had then left unseen a wonderful piece of ANT 1.02.153 P
ostentation of our love, which, left unshown, 3.06. 52
which, left unshown, | is often left unlov'd. 3.06. 53
let /that be left | which leaves itself. 3.11. 19
eyes | by looking back what i have left behind 3.11. 53
spirits | to hear from me you had left antony, 3.13. 70
have i my pillow left unpress'd in rome, 3.13.106
have empty left their orbs, and shot their fires 3.13.146
the soldier | that has this morning left thee, 4.05. 5
there is left us | ourselves to end ourselves. 4.14. 21
and there is nothing left remarkable | beneath 4.15. 67
left these notes | of what commands i should be CYM 1.01.171
as a crow, or less, ere left | to after–eye him. 1.03. 15
fold down the leaf where i have left. 2.02. 4
on her left breast | a mole cinque–spotted, like 2.02. 37
a jewel that too casually | hath left mine arm. 2.03.142
outwent her, | motion and breath left out. 2.04. 85
is it that | which i left with her? 2.04.100
which, by thee, lately | is left untender'd. 3.01. 10
nay, my leaves, | and left me bare to weather. 3.03. 64
i would have left it on the board so soon | as i 3.06. 50
in this place we left them. 4.02.107
be | yet left in heaven as small a drop of pity 4.02.304
thee at the heart | and left this head on. 4.02.323
i left out one thing which the queen confess'd, 5.05.244
took a peer, | who died and left a female heir, PER 1.ch. 22
his seal'd commission, left in trust with me, 1.03. 12
have scarce strength left to give them burial. 1.04. 49
and left /me breath | nothing to think on but 2.01. 6
he should never have left till he cast bells, 2.01. 42 P
this strict charge, even as he left his life, 2.01.125
like goodly buildings left without a roof | soon 2.04. 36
here's all that is left living of your queen: 3.01. 20
behind | is left to govern it, you bear in mind, 4.04. 14
thoughts again, | where we left him, on the sea. 5.ch. 13
tyre, | i left behind an ancient substitute. 5.03. 51
when he left me, | i did not think a week could TNK 3.06. 4
you charg'd | upon the left wing of the enemy, 3.06. 75
i then left my angle | to his own skill, came 4.01. 59
that, believe me, | she left me far behind her. 4.01. 99
i left them with her | and hither came to tell 4.01.102
i wore thy picture, | palamon's on the left. 5.03. 74
can thy right hand seize love upon thy left? VEN 158
in that thy likeness still is left alive." 174
with her the horse, and left adonis there. 322
and nothing but the very smell were left me, 441
left their round turrets destitute and pale. LUC 441
she bears the load of lust he left behind, | and 734
bee, | have no perfection of my summer left, 837
himself behind | was left unseen, save to the 1426
the murd'rous knife, and, as it left the place, 1735
and blushing fled, and left her all alone. PP 9.14
then were not summer's distillation left | a SON 5. 9
that thou no form of thee hast left behind, 9. 6
care, | art left the prey of every vulgar thief. 48. 8
since i left you, mine eye is in my mind, | and 113. 1
hath left me, and i desperate now approve 147. 7
LEFTS 2 FR 0.0002 REL FR 2 V 0 P
for why thou lefts me nothing in thy will; PP 10. 8
and yet thou lefts me more than i did crave, 10. 9
LEG 39 FR 0.0044 REL FR 18 V 21 P
me to her trencher and steals her capon's leg. TGV 4.04. 9 P
see me heave up my leg and make water against a 4.04. 38 P
what? that my leg is too long? 5.02. 4
with a good leg and a good foot, uncle, and ADO 2.01. 14 P
a brow, a breast, a waist, | a leg, a limb — LLL 4.03.184
his leg is too big for hector's. 5.02.639 P
to catch the strong fellow by the leg. AYL 1.02.212 P
his leg is but so so — and yet 'tis well; 3.05.119
a linen stock on one leg and a kersey boot–hose SHR 3.02. 66 P
he that cannot make a leg, put off 's cap, kiss AWW 2.02. 10 P
hand, and say nothing, has neither leg, hands, 2.02. 11 P
by the excellent constitution of thy leg, it was TN 1.03.133 P
rather than forty shillings i had such a leg, 2.03. 21 P
by the color of his beard, the shape of his leg, 2.03.157 P
she did praise my leg being cross–garter'd, and 2.05.167 P
when your young nephew titus lost his leg. 5.01. 63
sir robert never holp to make this leg. JN 1.01.240
you make a leg, and bullingbrook says ay. R2 3.03.175
for a cup of madeira and a cold capon's leg? 1H4 1.02.116 P
well, here is my leg. 2.04.388 P
can honor set to a leg? 5.01.131 P
a white beard, a decreasing leg, an increasing 2H4 1.02.182 P
like unto the sign of the leg, and breeds no 2.04.249 P
a good leg will fall, a straight back will stoop H5 5.02.159 P
to tear the garter from thy craven's leg, 1H6 4.01. 15
thy leg a stick compared with this truncheon; 2H6 4.10. 49
the sinews of this leg | all greek, and this all TRO 4.05.126
/hanging at his /brother's leg — to what form 5.01. 56 P
our steed the leg, the tongue our trumpeter, COR 1.01.117
by her fine foot, straight leg, and quivering ROM 2.01. 19
than any man's, yet his leg excels all men's, 2.05. 41 P
sting, | lizard's leg and howlet's wing, | for a MAC 4.01. 17
/then laid his leg | /over my thigh, and /sigh'd OTH 3.03.424
my leg is cut in two. 5.01. 72
i know the shape of 's leg; CYM 4.02.309
a leg of rome shall not return to tell | what 5.03. 92
man may serve seven years for the loss of a leg, PER 4.06.172 P
arcite, | even in the wagging of a wanton leg, TNK 2.02. 15
a face, a leg, a head | stood for the whole to LUC 1427
LEGACIES 1 FR 0.0001 REL FR 1 V 0 P
how to cut off some charge in legacies. JC 4.01. 9
LEGACY 6 FR 0.0006 REL FR 4 V 2 P
it was eve's legacy, and cannot be ta'en from TGV 3.01.338 P
good receipt | shall for my legacy be sanctified AWW 1.03.245
her name, and no legacy is so rich as honesty. 3.05. 13 P
bequeathing it as a rich legacy | unto their JC 3.02.136
lost, | what legacy shall i bequeath to thee? LUC 1192
thou spend | upon thyself thy beauty's legacy? SON 4. 2
LEGATE 7 FR 0.0008 REL FR 7 V 0 P
here comes the holy legate of the pope. JN 3.01.135
and from pope innocent the legate here, | do in 3.01.139
the legate of the pope hath been with me, | and 5.01. 62
look where the holy legate comes apace, | to 5.02. 65
(not trusting to this halting legate here, 5.02.174
stay, my lord legate, you shall first receive 1H6 5.01. 51
you wrought to be a legate, by which power | you H8 3.02.311
LEGATIVE 1 FR 0.0001 REL FR 1 V 0 P
by your power legative within this kingdom H8 3.02.339
LEGE 1 FR 0.0001 REL FR 1 V 0 P
lege, domine. LLL 4.02.104
LEGERITY 1 FR 0.0001 REL FR 1 V 0 P
move | with casted slough and fresh legerity. H5 4.01. 23
'LEGES *(also allege, etc.)*
'LEGES 1 FR 0.0001 REL FR 0 V 1 P
'tis no matter, sir, what he 'leges in latin. SHR 1.02. 28 P
LEGG'D 1 FR 0.0001 REL FR 0 V 1 P
legg'd like a man! TMP 2.02. 33 P
/LEGION 1 FR 0.0001 REL FR 0 V 1 P
he hath a /legion of angels. WIV 1.03. 53 P
LEGION 3 FR 0.0003 REL FR 2 V 1 P
in little, and legion himself possess'd him, yet TN 3.04. 85 P

a legion of foul fiends | environ'd me, and R3 1.04. 58
hear | the legion now in gallia sooner landed CYM 2.04. 18
/LEGIONS 1 FR 0.0001 REL FR 1 V 0 P
to beat assailing death from his weak /legions; 1H6 4.04. 16
LEGIONS 18 FR 0.0020 REL FR 18 V 0 P
at a time, | i'll fight their legions o'er. TMP 3.03.103
him time | to land his legions all as soon as i; JN 2.01. 59
wounds | with many legions of strange fantasies, 5.07. 18
and tell the legions, "i can never win | a soul H5 2.02.124
i did send | to you for gold to pay my legions, JC 4.03. 76
our legions are brimful, our cause is ripe: 4.03.215
bills | unto the legions on the other side. 5.02. 2
power, | as cassius' legions are by antony. 5.03. 53
not in the legions | of horrid hell can come a MAC 4.03. 55
our nineteen legions thou shalt hold by land, ANT 3.07. 58
keep by land | the legions and the horse whole, 3.07. 71
caesar will i render | my legions and my horse: 3.10. 33
his coin, ships, legions, | may be a coward's, 3.13. 22
and that the legions now in gallia are | full CYM 3.07. 4
with those legions | which i have spoke of, 3.07. 12
to them the legions garrison'd in gallia, 4.02.333
the roman legions, all from gallia drawn, | are 4.03. 24
which many legions of true hearts had warm'd, SON 154. 6
LEGITIMATE 8 FR 0.0009 REL FR 7 V 1 P
i will prove it legitimate, sir, upon the oaths TN 3.02. 14 P
sirrah, your brother is legitimate, | your JN 1.01.116
whether our daughter were legitimate, H8 2.04.180
then, | legitimate edgar, i must have your land. LR 1.02. 16
is to the bastard edmund | as to th' legitimate. 1.02. 18
fine word, "legitimate"! 1.02. 18
well, my legitimate, if this letter speed | and 1.02. 19
edmund the base | shall /top th' legitimate. 1.02. 21
LEGITIMATION 1 FR 0.0001 REL FR 1 V 0 P
my land, | legitimation, name, and all is gone; JN 1.01.248
/LEGS 2 FR 0.0002 REL FR 2 V 0 P
/he /had /no /legs /that /practic'd /not /his 2H4 2.03. 23
/put /in /his /legs. LR 2.02.150
LEGS 75 FR 0.0084 REL FR 36 V 39 P
drowning to be afeard now of your four legs; TMP 2.02. 60 P
as ever went on four legs cannot make him give 2.02. 61 P
this is some monster of the isle with four legs, 2.02. 65 P
four legs and two voices; 2.02. 89 P
i'll pull thee by the lesser legs. 2.02.104 P
if any be trinculo's legs, these are they. 2.02.104 P
pinch them, arms, legs, backs, shoulders, sides, WIV 5.05. 54
and with his bad legs falls into the cinquepace ADO 2.01. 78 P
call beatrice to you, who i think hath legs. 5.02. 24 P
but your legs should do it. LLL 5.02.217
my arms before the legs of this sweet lass of 5.02.555
my legs are longer though, to run away. MND 3.02.343
with leaden legs and batty wings doth creep. 3.02.365
my legs can keep no pace with my desires. 3.02.445
or "good launcelot /gobbo, use your legs, take MV 2.02. 6 P
not for my spirits, if my legs were not weary. AYL 2.04. 2 P
no more stockings than legs, nor no more shoes SHR in.2. 10 P
scratching her legs that one shall swear she in.2. 58
with their left legs and not presume to touch a 4.01. 93 P
most fruitfully, i am there before my legs. AWW 2.02. 70 P
to see a huswife take thee between her legs, and TN 1.03.103 P
no, sir, it is legs and thighs. 1.03.140 P
taste your legs, sir, put them to motion. 3.01. 78 P
my legs do better understand me, sir, than i 3.01. 79 P
what you mean by bidding me taste my legs. 3.01. 80 P
not black in my mind, though yellow in my legs. 3.04. 27 P
if this letter move him not, his legs cannot. 3.04.171 P
him, | and if my legs were two such riding–rods, JN 1.01.140
why have those banish'd and forbidden legs R2 2.03. 90
my legs can keep no measure in delight, | when 3.04. 7
we'll walk afoot a while, and ease our legs. 1H4 2.02. 80 P
and the villains march wide betwixt the legs, as 4.02. 40 P
because their legs are both of a bigness, and 'a 2H4 2.04.244 P
acquit me, will you command me to use my legs? ep 19 P
my tongue is weary, when my legs are too, i will ep 33 P
i thought upon one pair of english legs | did H5 3.06.149
a heavy reckoning to make, when all those legs, 4.01.136 P
would fain see the man, that hath but two legs, 4.07.162 P
and i will chain these legs and arms of thine, 1H6 2.03. 39
could restore this cripple to his legs again? 2H6 2.01.131
well, sir, we must have you find your legs. 2.01.144 P
before his legs be firm to bear his body. 3.01.190
clapp'd his tail between his legs and cried; 5.01.154
your legs did better service than your hands. 3H6 2.02.104
to shape my legs of an unequal size, | to 3.02.159
i came into the world with my legs forward. 5.06. 71
with clarence, and i came hither on my legs. R3 1.04. 87 P
they have all new legs, and lame ones. H8 1.03. 11
my legs like loaden branches bow to th' earth, 4.02. 2
unless th' are drunk, sick, or have no legs. TRO 1.02. 18 P
his legs are legs for necessity, not for flexure 2.03.106 P
his legs are legs for necessity, not for flexure 2.03.106 P
are ambitious for poor knaves' caps and legs. COR 2.01. 69 P
one seven years | from these old arms and legs, 4.01. 56
can never turn the swan's black legs to white, TIT 4.02.102
in, | but every man betake him to his legs. ROM 1.04. 34
her waggon–spokes made of long spinners' legs, 1.04. 62
i doubt whether their legs be worth the sums TIM 1.02.232
false hearts should never have sound legs. 1.02.234
and we petty men | walk under his huge legs, and JC 1.02.137
though he took up my legs sometime, yet i made a
MAC 2.03. 40 P
a fair thought to lie between maids' legs. HAM 3.02.119 P
neck, monkeys by th' loins, and men by th' legs. LR 2.04. 9 P
when a /man's overlusty at legs, then he wears 2.04. 10 P
feel you your legs? 4.06. 65
those legs that brought me to a part of it. OTH 2.03.187
his legs bestrid the ocean, his rear'd arm ANT 5.02. 82
up to yond hill, | your legs are young; CYM 3.03. 11
you that your resorters stand upon sound legs. PER 4.06. 24 P
and little luce with the white legs, and TNK 3.05. 26
as ever he may go upon 's legs, for in the next 4.03. 14 P
but that | he kept him 'tween his legs, on his 5.04. 76
that arcite's legs, being higher than his head, 5.04. 78
short ears, straight legs and passing strong, VEN 297
each envious brier his weary legs do scratch, 705
LEICESTER 3 FR 0.0003 REL FR 3 V 0 P
near to the town of leicester, as we learn. R3 5.02. 12
he is, my lord, and safe in leicester town, 5.05. 10
at last, with easy roads, he came to leicester, H8 4.02. 17

LEICESTERSHIRE 1 FR 0.0001 REL FR 1 V 0 P
northampton, and in leicestershire, shalt find 3H6 4.08. 15
LEIGER *(also liegers)*
LEIGER 1 FR 0.0001 REL FR 1 V 0 P
where you shall be an everlasting leiger; MM 3.01. 58
LEISURE 65 FR 0.0073 REL FR 57 V 8 P
at pick'd leisure, | which shall be shortly, TMP 5.01.247
come to me at your convenient leisure, and you WIV 3.05.134 P
action | at our more leisure shall i render you; MM 1.03. 49
might you dispense with your leisure, i would by 3.01.153 P
i have no superfluous leisure; 3.01.157 P
which i (by my good leisure) have discredited to 3.02.247 P
i shall attend your leisure, but make haste, 4.01. 56
still pays haste, and leisure answers leisure; 5.01.410
still pays haste, and leisure answers leisure; 5.01.410
i will debate this matter at more leisure, | and ERR 4.01.100
then | i hope i shall have leisure to make good, 5.01.376
i have stomach, and wait for no man's leisure; ADO 1.03. 15 P
if your leisure serv'd, i would speak with you. 3.02. 82 P
i am sorry that your leisure serves you not. MV 4.01.405
here is a letter, read it at your leisure. 5.01.267
have leave and leisure to make love to her, SHR 1.02.136
your lecture shall have leisure for as much. 3.01. 8
who woo'd in haste, and means to wed at leisure. 3.02. 11
which at more leisure i will so excuse | as you 3.02.108
father, be quiet, he shall stay my leisure. 3.02.217
the tailor stays thy leisure, | to deck thy body 4.03. 59
when thou hast leisure, say thy prayers; AWW 1.01.212 P
and sickness | debate it at their leisure. 1.02. 75
i thank you, and will stay upon your leisure. 3.05. 45
less, | resolvedly more leisure shall express. 5.03.332
whose leisure i have stay'd, have given him time JN 2.01. 58
time | than if you had at leisure known of this. 5.06. 27
which then our leisure would not let us hear, R2 1.01. 5
ere further leisure yield them further means 1.04. 40
not, to it again, | we will stay your leisure. 1H4 1.03.258
how has he the leisure to be sick | in such a 4.01. 17
here at more leisure may your highness read, 2H4 4.04. 89
no leisure had he to enrank his men; 1H6 1.01.115
but since your ladyship is not at leisure, 2.03. 26
i will attend upon your lordship's leisure. 5.01. 55
hear ye, captain? are you not at leisure? 5.03. 97
me have | some patient leisure to excuse myself. R3 1.02. 82
had you such leisure in the time of death | to 1.04. 34
which after–hours gives leisure to repent. 4.04.293
the leisure and the fearful time | cuts off the 5.03. 97
god give us leisure for these rites of love! 5.03.101
the leisure and enforcement of the time 5.03.238
to steal from spiritual leisure a brief span H8 3.02.140
my lord, i scarce have leisure to salute you, TRO 4.02. 59
as hector's leisure and your bounties shall 4.05.273
i'll trust by leisure him that mocks me once, TIT 1.01.301
are you at leisure, holy father, now, | or shall ROM 4.01. 37
my leisure serves me, pensive daughter, now. 4.01. 39
desire you to o'er–read | (at your best leisure) JC 3.01. 5
worthy macbeth, we stay upon your leisure. MAC 1.03.148
at your kind'st leisure. 2.01. 24
i would attend his leisure | for a few words. 3.02. 3
have you so slander any moment leisure | as to HAM 1.03.133
that, on the supervise, no leisure bated, | no, 5.02. 23
here's the commission, read it at more leisure. 5.02. 26
lord, if your lordship were at leisure, i should 5.02. 89 P
and attend | the leisure of their answer, gave LR 2.04. 37
mend when thou canst, be better at thy leisure, 2.04.229
and at thy sovereign leisure read | the garboils ANT 1.03. 60
me, | and pay them at thy leisure, one by one. VEN 518
debate where leisure serves with dull debaters; LUC 1019
were it not thy sour leisure gave sweet leave SON 39.10
i must attend time's leisure with my moan, 44.12
being your vassal bound to stay your leisure. 58. 4
have no leisure taken | to weigh how once i 120. 7
LEISURELY 3 FR 0.0003 REL FR 3 V 0 P
hence, where we may leisurely | each one demand,
WT 5.03.152
so long a–growing and so leisurely | that, if R3 2.04. 19
promise more speed, but do it leisurely; LUC 1349
LEISURES 3 FR 0.0003 REL FR 3 V 0 P
we'll make our leisures to attend on yours. MV 1.01. 68
at many leisures i /propos'd. TIM 2.02.128
teen, | or any of my leisures ever charmed. LC 193
LEMAN 3 FR 0.0003 REL FR 1 V 2 P
search'd a hollow walnut for his wive's leman." WIV 4.02.164 P
i sent thee sixpence for thy leman; TN 2.03. 25 P
and fine, | and drink unto /thee, leman mine, 2H4 5.03. 47
LEMON 1 FR 0.0001 REL FR 0 V 1 P
a lemon. LLL 5.02.647 P
LENA 2 FR 0.0002 REL FR 2 V 0 P
what said popilius lena? JC 3.01. 15
popilius lena speaks not of our purposes, | for 3.01. 23
LEND 114 FR 0.0128 REL FR 93 V 21 P
lend thy hand, | and pluck my magic garment from
TMP 1.02. 23
lend me the letter; let me see what news. TGV 1.03. 55
love, lend me wings to make my purpose swift, 2.06. 42
the heaven such grace did lend her, | that she 4.02. 42
love, lend me patience to forbear a while. 5.04. 27
why, did you not lend it to alice shortcake upon WIV 1.01.203 P
i will not lend thee a penny. 2.02. 2 P
what is he, william, that does lend articles? 4.01. 39 P
lend him your kind pains | to find out this MM 5.01.246
lend me your knees, and all my life to come 5.01.431
i'll lend you all my life to do you service. 5.01.432
will you not lend a knee? 5.01.442
hard–hearted and will lend nothing for god's ADO 5.01.312 P
lend me the flourish of all gentle tongues — LLL 4.03.234
lend me your horn to make one, and i will whip 5.01. 68 P
albeit i neither lend nor borrow | by taking nor MV 1.03. 61
methoughts you said you neither lend nor borrow 1.03. 69
a cur can lend three thousand ducats?" 1.03.122
courtesies | i'll lend you thus much moneys"? 1.03.129
if thou wilt lend this money, lend it not | as 1.03.132
this money, lend it not | as to thy friends, for 1.03.132
but lend it rather to thine enemy, | who, if he 1.03.135
he was wont to lend money for a christian cur'sy 3.01. 49 P
i once did lend my body for his wealth, | which, 5.01.249
lend thine ear. SHR 4.01. 60 P
rome, | and so to tripoli, if god lend me life. 4.02. 76
they that least lend it you shall lack you first AWW 1.02. 68

lend me an arm. 1.02. 73
but lend and give where she is sure to lose; 1.03.215
i'll lend it thee, my dear; 4.02. 40
contempt his scornful perspective did lend me, 5.03. 48
good tom drum, lend me a handkercher. 5.03.321 P
your gentle hands lend us, and take our hearts. ep 6
lean and low ability | i'll lend you something. TN 3.04.345
lend me thy hand, i'll help thee. WT 4.03. 68 P
come, lend me thy hand. 4.03. 69 P
and pluck nights from me, but not lend a morrow;
R2 1.03.228
till time lend friends, and friends their 3.03.132
start away, | and lend no ear unto my purposes. 1H4 1.03.217
i prithee lend me thy lantern, to see my gelding 2.01. 34 P
i pray thee lend me thine. 2.01. 38 P
lend me thy lantern, quoth he! 2.01. 39 P
room, and lend me thy hand to laugh a little. 2.04. 2 P
lend me thy sword. 5.03. 40
i prithee lend me thy sword. 5.03. 43
i prithee lend me thy sword. 5.03. 49 P
lend to this weight such lightness with their 2H4 1.01.122
for a thousand marks, let him lend me the money, 1.02.193 P
will your lordship lend me a thousand pound to 1.02.223 P
then lend the eye a terrible aspect; H5 3.01. 9
lend me thy cloak, sir thomas. 4.01. 24
wounds will i lend the french in stead of eyes, 1H6 1.01. 87
the levied succors that should lend him aid, 4.04. 23
lend me a heart replete with thankfulness! 2H6 1.01. 20
lo here i lend thee this sharp–pointed sword, R3 1.02.174
prince, | lend favorable ear to our requests, 3.07.101
rise, and lend thine ear. 4.02. 79
i died for hope ere i could lend thee aid, | but 5.03.173
yoke together | (as i will lend you cause) my H8 3.02.151
lend me ten thousand eyes, | and i will fill TRO 2.02.101
lend you him i will | for half a hundred years. COR 1.04. 6
private friends, hereafter | will i lend ear to. 5.03. 19
lend me thy hand, and i will give thee mine. TIT 3.01.187
sound | with speedy help doth lend redress." ROM 4.05.143
that this is no time to lend money, especially TIM 3.01. 42 P
lend to each man enough, that one need not lend 3.06. 73 P
man enough, that one need not lend to another; 3.06. 74 P
stay, i will lend thee money, borrow none. 3.06.101
lend me a fool's heart and a woman's eyes, | and 5.01.157
lend me your hand. JC 3.01.297
friends, romans, countrymen, lend me your ears! 3.02. 73
but lend thy serious hearing | to what i shall HAM 1.05. 5
that lend a tyrannous and a damned light | to 2.02.460
and that shall lend a kind of easiness | to the 3.04.166
be you content to lend your patience to us, 4.05.211
than thou knowest, | lend less than thou owest, LR 1.04.120
friendship will it lend you 'gainst the tempest. 3.02. 62
lend me a looking–glass, | if that her breath 5.03.262
to my unfolding lend your prosperous ear, | and OTH 1.03.244
lend me thy handkerchief. 3.04. 52
lend me a garter. 5.01. 82
lend me a light. 5.01. 88
to lend me arms and aid when i requir'd them, ANT 2.02. 88
with the courage which the heart did lend it, 5.01. 23
i shall but lend my diamond till your return. CYM 1.04.142 P
for gold | which rottenness can lend nature; 1.06.125
if savage, | take or lend. 3.06. 24
with all my heart, | and lend my best attention. 5.05.117
dead, | my heart can lend no succor to my head. PER 1.01.169
until our stars that frown lend us a smile. 1.04.108
lend me your hands. 3.02.107
hail, sir! my lord, lend ear. 5.01. 82
sir, lend me your arm. 5.01.263
lend us a knee; TNK 1.01. 96
fee, and which i freely lend | to do these poor 1.01.198
heavens lend | a thousand differing ways to one 1.05. 13
and the charity | of one meal lend me — come 3.01. 74
sacred silver mistress, lend thine ear | (which 5.01.146
desire doth lend her force | courageously to VEN 29
her arms do lend his neck a sweet embrace; 539
dries up his oil to lend the world his light. 756
may lend thee light, as thou dost lend to other. 864
lend thee light, as thou dost lend to other." 864
o, how her eyes and tears did lend and borrow! 961
no comfortable star did lend his light, | no LUC 164
and lend it not | to darken her whose light 190
the painter was no god to lend her those, | and 1461
the help that thou shalt lend me | comes all too 1685
nature's bequest gives nothing, but doth lend, SON 4. 3
and you, but one, can every shadow lend: 53. 4
what strained touches rhetoric can lend, | thou, 82.10
dark'ning thy pow'r to lend base subjects light? 100. 4
lest sorrow lend me words, and words express 140. 3
anon their gazes lend | to every place at once, LC 26
LENDER 2 FR 0.0002 REL FR 1 V 1 P
in better plight for a lender than you are; WIV 2.02.166 P
neither a borrower nor a lender /be, | for /loan HAM 1.03. 75
LENDERS' 1 FR 0.0001 REL FR 0 V 1 P
out of plackets, thy pen from lenders' books, LR 3.04. 97 P
LENDETH 1 FR 0.0001 REL FR 1 V 0 P
thy sorrow to my sorrow lendeth | another power;
LUC 1676
/LENDING 1 FR 0.0001 REL FR 1 V 0 P
/not /grieve | /lending /me /this /acquaintance. LR 4.03. 54
LENDING 3 FR 0.0003 REL FR 3 V 0 P
the greatest grace lending grace, | ere twice AWW 2.01.160
lending him wit that to bad debtors lends: LUC 964
lending soft audience to my sweet design, | and LC 278
LENDINGS 2 FR 0.0002 REL FR 1 V 1 P
in name of lendings for your highness' soldiers, R2 1.01. 89
off, off, you lendings! LR 3.04.108 P
LENDS 17 FR 0.0019 REL FR 17 V 0 P
nor nature never lends | the smallest scruple of MM 1.01. 36
in low simplicity | he lends out money gratis, MV 1.03. 44
it lends a lustre and more great opinion, | a 1H4 4.01. 77
o, this boy | lends mettle to us all! 5.04. 24
o lord, that lends me life, | lend me a heart 2H6 1.01. 19
and see how one another lends content; ROM 1.03. 84
but passion lends them power, time means, to 2.pr. 13
yond, that vainly lends his light | to grubs and 5.03.125
how prodigal the soul | lends the tongue vows. HAM 1.03.117
that lends embracements unto every stranger. VEN 790
lending him wit that to bad debtors lends: LUC 964
lends light to all fair eyes that light will 1083

she lends them words, and she their looks doth 1498
and being frank she lends to those are free: SON 4. 4
th' offender's sorrow lends but weak relief | to 34.11
he lends thee virtue, and he stole that word 79. 9
that to his subject lends not some small glory, 84. 6
LENGTH 42 FR 0.0047 REL FR 36 V 6 P
bear it | under a cloak that is of any length. TGV 3.01.130
i'll get me one of such another length. 3.01.133
how i replied | (for this was of much length) — MM 5.01. 95
at length the sun, gazing upon the earth, ERR 1.01. 88
at length, another ship had seiz'd on us, | and, 1.01.112
bring you the length of prester john's foot, ADO 2.01.267 P
measure his woe the length and breadth of mine, 5.01. 11
me | to measure out my length on this cold bed. MND 3.02.429
time, | to eche it and to draw it out in length, MV 3.02. 23
so hard that it seems the length of seven year. AYL 3.02.316 P
sixteen businesses, a month's length a–piece, by AWW 4.03. 86 P
taking so the head, your whole head's length. R2 3.03. 14
i heard you say, "is not my arm of length, 4.01. 11
wedding it, there is such length in grief. 5.01. 94
with much ado (at length) have gotten leave | to 5.05. 74
and never shall have length of life enough | to 2H4 2.03. 58
lands | is nothing left me but my body's length. 3H6 5.02. 26
my foreward shall be drawn out all in length, R3 5.03.293
my high–blown pride | at length broke under me, H8 3.02.362
at length her grace rose, and with modest paces 4.01. 82
at length they came to th' broom–staff to me, i 5.03. 54 P
to end a tale of length, | troy in our weakness TRO 1.03.136
leave nothing out for length, and make us think COR 2.02. 49
your defenders, till at length | your ignorance 3.03.128
and at length | how goes our reck'ning? TIM 2.02.149
within my sword's length set him; MAC 4.03.234
within his truncheon's length, whilst they, HAM 1.02.204
then goes he to the length of all his arm, | and 2.01. 85
/too, than the length and breadth of a pair of 5.01.109 P
these foils have all a length? 5.02.265
if you will measure your lubber's length again, LR 1.04. 91 P
her length of sickness, with what else more ANT 1.02.120
so it must be, for now | all length is torture; 4.14. 46
if i can get him within my pistol's length, PER 1.01.166
and now at length they overflow their banks. 2.04. 24
at length | i fling my cap up; TNK 3.05. 16
for the horse | would make his length a mile, 5.04. 57
that through the length of times he stands LUC 718
at length address'd to answer his desire, | she 1606
night to–night, and length thyself to–morrow. PP 14.30
her feeble force will yield at length, | when 18.33
doth nightly make grief's length seem stronger. SON 28.14
LENGTHEN 3 FR 0.0003 REL FR 3 V 0 P
to lengthen out the worst that must be spoken: R2 3.02.199
i'll lengthen it with mine, | and, having both 2H6 1.02. 12
draw lots who first shall die to lengthen life. PER 1.04. 46
LENGTHEN'D 1 FR 0.0001 REL FR 1 V 0 P
no, no, my dream was lengthen'd after life. R3 1.04. 43
LENGTHENS 3 FR 0.0003 REL FR 3 V 0 P
which bars a thousand harms and lengthens life. SHR in.2. 136
as long as heaven and nature lengthens it. R3 4.04.353
it was. what sadness lengthens romeo's hours? ROM 1.01.163
LENGTH'NED 4 FR 0.0004 REL FR 4 V 0 P
would the word "farewell" have length'ned hours R2 1.04. 16
and, after many length'ned hours of grief, | die R3 1.03.207
cowards living | to die with length'ned shame. CYM 5.03. 13
your day is length'ned, and | the blissful dew TNK 5.04.103
LENGTH'NING 1 FR 0.0001 REL FR 1 V 0 P
shall short my word | by length'ning my return. CYM 1.06.201
LENGTHS 2 FR 0.0002 REL FR 2 V 0 P
large lengths of seas and shores | between my JN 1.01.105
to leap large lengths of miles when thou art SON 44.10
/LENITY 1 FR 0.0001 REL FR 0 V 1 P
for when /lenity and cruelty play for a kingdom, H5 3.06.112 P
LENITY 7 FR 0.0008 REL FR 6 V 1 P
a little more lenity to lechery would do no harm MM 3.02. 97 P
use lenity, sweet chuck! H5 3.02. 25
consent, | of mere compassion and of lenity, 1H6 5.04.125
this too much lenity | and harmful pity must be 3H6 2.02. 9
and what makes robbers bold but too much lenity? 2.06. 22
if none, awake | your dangerous lenity. COR 3.01. 99
away to heaven, respective lenity, | and ROM 3.01.123
LENT* 38 FR 0.0043 REL FR 32 V 6 P
as thou hast lent me wit to plot this drift. TGV 2.06. 43
lent him our terror, dress'd him with our love, MM 1.01. 19
to understand that you have lent him visitation. 3.02.240 P
my lord, he lent it me awhile, and i gave him ADO 2.01.278 P
that eye my daughter lent her, 'tis most true. 5.04. 23
withal, | and have the money by our father lent, LLL 2.01.147
this is the fool that lent out money gratis! MV 3.03. 2
madam, if god have lent a man any manners, he AWW 2.02. 8 P
who lent it you? 5.03.273
it was not lent me neither. 5.03.273
why, what a madcap hath heaven lent us here! JN 1.01. 84
and those his golden beams to you here lent R2 1.03.146
your diet and by–drinkings, and money lent you, 1H4 3.03. 73 P
whose spirit lent a fire | even to the dullest 2H4 1.01.112
what's a joint of mutton or two in a whole lent? 2.04.347 P
his skin is surely lent him, | for he's inclin'd 2H6 3.01. 77
the lent shall be as long again as it is, and 4.03. 6 P
which with a bounteous hand was kindly lent; R3 2.02. 93
for it requires the royal debt it lent you. 2.02. 95
had nature lent thee but thy mother's look, TIT 5.01. 29
he lent me counsel, and i lent him eyes. ROM 2.02. 81
he lent me counsel, and i lent him eyes. 2.02. 81
an old hare hoar, | is very good meat in lent; 2.04.136
that god had lent us but this only child, | but 3.05.165
gracious england hath | lent us good siward, and MAC 4.03.190
he vented /them, most narrow measure lent me; ANT 3.04. 8
then does he say he lent me | some shipping 3.06. 26
lucina lent not me her aid, | but took me in my CYM 5.04. 43
of face | as heaven had lent her all his grace; PER 1.ch. 24
for to the king god hath his office lent | of STM II.C 98
he hath not only lent the king his figure, | his II.C 102
cool shadow to his melting buttock lent; VEN 315
"if love have lent you twenty thousand tongues, 775
what priceless wealth the heavens had him lent LUC 17
for it was lent thee all that brood to kill. 627
but the mild glance that sly ulysses lent 1399
that piteous looks to phrygian shepherds lent; 1502
that they their passions likewise lent me | of LC 199
LENTEN 3 FR 0.0003 REL FR 0 V 3 P
a good lenten answer. TN 1.05. 9 P
sir, in a lenten pie, that is something stale ROM 2.04.132 P
man, what lenten entertainment the players shall HAM 2.02.316 P
LENTUS 2 FR 0.0002 REL FR 2 V 0 P
dominator poli, | tam lentus audis scelera? TIT 4.01. 82
tam lentus vides? 4.01. 82
L'ENVOY 16 FR 0.0018 REL FR 4 V 12 P
some riddle — come, thy l'envoy — begin. LLL 3.01. 71
no riddle, no l'envoy, no salve in the mail, sir 3.01. 72 P
no l'envoy, no l'envoy, no salve, sir, but a 3.01. 74 P
no l'envoy, no l'envoy, no salve, sir, but a 3.01. 74 P
doth the inconsiderate take salve for l'envoy, 3.01. 79 P
for l'envoy, and the word "l'envoy" for a salve? 3.01. 79 P
is not l'envoy a salve? 3.01. 80
now the l'envoy. 3.01. 86 P
i will add the l'envoy. say the moral again. 3.01. 87 P
your moral, and do you follow with my l'envoy: 3.01. 94 P
a good l'envoy, ending in the goose; 3.01. 99 P
a fat l'envoy — ay, that's a fat goose. 3.01.104
then call'd you for the l'envoy. 3.01.107 P
then the boy's fat l'envoy, the goose that you 3.01.109
i will speak that l'envoy: 3.01.115 P
i smell some l'envoy, some goose, in this. 3.01.122 P
LEONARDO 1 FR 0.0001 REL FR 1 V 0 P
i pray thee, good leonardo, think on this: MV 2.02.169
LEONATI 2 FR 0.0002 REL FR 2 V 0 P
gods, put the strength o' th' leonati in me! CYM 5.01. 31
and thrown | from leonati seat, and cast | from 5.04. 60
LEONATO 23 FR 0.0026 REL FR 9 V 14 P
good signior leonato, are you come to meet your ADO 1.01. 96 P
if signior leonato be her father, she would not 1.01.113 P
leonato — signior claudio and signior benedick 1.01.146 P
my dear friend leonato hath invited you all. 1.01.148 P
your hand, leonato, we will go together. 1.01.160 P
didst thou note the daughter of signior leonato? 1.01.163 P
hath leonato any son, my lord? 1.01.294
your brother is royally entertain'd by leonato, 1.03. 43 P
one hero, the daughter and heir of leonato. 1.03. 55 P
claudio shall marry the daughter of leonato. 2.02. 2 P
to vex claudio, to undo hero, and kill leonato. 2.02. 29 P
come hither, leonato. 2.03. 89 P
there, leonato, take her back again. 4.01. 31
no, leonato, | i never tempted her with word too 4.01. 51
leonato, stand i here? 4.01. 69
leonato, | i am sorry you must hear. 4.01. 87
signior leonato, let the friar advise you, | and 4.01.244
we have some haste, leonato. 5.01. 47
leonato and his brother. 5.01.117 P
hath reform'd signior leonato of the matter; 5.01.254 P
here, here comes master signior leonato, and the 5.01.257 P
is this the monument of leonato? 5.03. 1
signior leonato, truth it is, good signior, 5.04. 21
LEONATO'S 7 FR 0.0008 REL FR 1 V 6 P
you here, that you follow'd not to leonato's? ADO 1.01.205 P
with hero, leonato's short daughter. 1.01.214 P
good signior benedick, repair to leonato's, 1.01.276 P
even she — leonato's hero, your hero, every 3.02.106 P
i pray you watch about signior leonato's door, 3.03. 92 P
these men be bound, and brought to leonato's. 4.02. 65 P
other weeds, | and then to leonato's we will go. 5.03. 31
LEONATUS' 3 FR 0.0003 REL FR 2 V 1 P
and, 'tis thought, one of leonatus' friends. CYM 2.01. 38 P
be companion with them, | since leonatus' false. 3.06. 88
'twas leonatus' jewel, | whom thou didst banish; 5.05.143
LEO–NATUS 1 FR 0.0001 REL FR 1 V 0 P
name, | being leo–natus, doth import so much. CYM 5.05.445
LEONATUS 14 FR 0.0015 REL FR 11 V 3 P
so gain'd the sur–addition leonatus; CYM 1.01. 33
to his protection, calls him posthumus leonatus, 1.01. 41
and my leonatus | our neighbor shepherd's son! 1.01.149
the worthy leonatus is in safety | and greets 1.06. 12
as you value your trust — leonatus." 1.06. 25 P
o happy leonatus! 1.06.156
leonatus? 2.01. 39 P
leonatus! 3.02. 2
that is my lord leonatus? 3.02. 26
leonatus posthumus." 3.02. 47 P
the scriptures of the loyal leonatus, | all 3.04. 81
proof enough | to make the noble leonatus mad, 5.05.201
every villain | be call'd posthumus leonatus, 5.05.224
thou, leonatus, art the lion's whelp; 5.05.443
LEONINE 7 FR 0.0008 REL FR 7 V 0 P
does appear, | with leonine, a murtherer. PER 4.ch. 52
walk with leonine, the air is quick there, | and 4.01. 27
leonine, take her by the arm, walk with her. 4.01. 29
walk half an hour, leonine, at the least. 4.01. 45
alack that leonine was so slack, so slow! 4.02. 64
o villain leonine! 4.03. 9
dead, | nor none can know, leonine being gone. 4.03. 30
LEONTES 9 FR 0.0010 REL FR 7 V 2 P
yet, good deed, leontes, | i love thee not a jar WT 1.02. 42
have mistook, my lady, | polixenes for leontes. 2.01. 82
queen to the worthy leontes, king of sicilia, 3.02. 13 P
a true subject, leontes a jealous tyrant, his 3.02.133 P
leontes leaving — | th' effects of his fond 4.01. 17
(for so i see she must be) 'fore leontes. 4.04.545
see | leontes opening his free arms and weeping 4.04.548
and those that you'll procure from king leontes? 4.04.621
that king leontes shall not have an heir | till 5.01. 39
LEOPARD *(also libbard's, lubber's)*
LEOPARD 3 FR 0.0003 REL FR 1 V 2 P
the wolf, | or horse or oxen from the leopard, 1H6 1.05. 31
a horse, thou wouldst be seiz'd by the leopard, TIM 4.03.340 P
wert thou a leopard, thou wert germane to the 4.03.340 P
LEOPARDS 1 FR 0.0001 REL FR 1 V 0 P
lions make leopards tame. R2 1.01.174
LEPER 1 FR 0.0001 REL FR 1 V 0 P
i am no loathsome leper, look on me. 2H6 3.02. 75
LEPIDUS 24 FR 0.0027 REL FR 20 V 4 P
he and lepidus are at caesar's house. JC 3.02.264
your brother too must die; consent you, lepidus? 4.01. 2
but, lepidus, go you to caesar's house; 4.01. 7
and, in some taste, is lepidus but so: 4.01. 34
and lepidus | have put to death an hundred 4.03.174
you may see, lepidus, and henceforth know, | it ANT 1.04. 1
lepidus flatters both, | of both is flatter'd; 2.01. 14
caesar and lepidus | are in the field, a mighty 2.01. 16
no, lepidus, let him speak. 2.02. 84
let us, lepidus, | not lack your company. 2.02.168
journey, be at /the mount | before you, lepidus. 2.04. 7
i hope so, lepidus. 2.06. 57
lepidus is high/–color'd. 2.07. 4 P
ay, lepidus. 2.07. 25 P
sit — and some wine! a health to lepidus! 2.07. 29 P
this wine for lepidus! 2.07. 40
these quicksands, lepidus, | keep off them, for 2.07. 59
this health to lepidus! 2.07. 84
caesar is sad, and lepidus, | since pompey's 3.02. 4
'tis a noble lepidus. 3.02. 6
caesar and lepidus have made wars upon pompey. 3.05. 4 P
cries, "fool lepidus!" 3.05. 17
he frets | that lepidus of the triumpherate 3.06. 28
i have told him lepidus was grown too cruel, 3.06. 32
LEPROSY 4 FR 0.0004 REL FR 4 V 0 P
bosoms, and their crop | be general leprosy! TIM 4.01. 30
make the hoar leprosy ador'd, place thieves, 4.03. 36
there is no leprosy but what thou speak'st. 4.03.362
nag of egypt | (whom leprosy o'ertake!) ANT 3.10. 11
LEPROUS 2 FR 0.0002 REL FR 1 V 1 P
of my ears did pour | the leprous distillment, HAM 1.05. 64
one would marry a leprous witch to be rid on't, TNK 4.03. 47 P
LEQUEL 1 FR 0.0001 REL FR 0 V 1 P
il est /meilleur que l'anglois lequel je parle. H5 5.02.189 P
LES 23 FR 0.0026 REL FR 2 V 21 P
de hand. et les doigts? H5 3.04. 8 P
les doigts? 3.04. 9 P
ma foi, j'oublie les doigts, mais je me 3.04. 9 P
les doigts? 3.04. 10 P
les doigts, de fingres. 3.04. 12 P
comment appelez–vous les ongles? 3.04. 14 P
les ongles? /nous les appelons de nailes. 3.04. 16 P
les ongles? /nous les appelons de nailes. 3.04. 16 P
la repetition de tous les mots que vous m'avez 3.04. 26 P
vous prononcez les mots aussi droit que les 3.04. 38 P
mots aussi droit que les natifs d'angleterre. 3.04. 38 P
ils sont les mots de son mauvais, corruptible, 3.04. 53 P
et non pour les dames de honneur d'user. 3.04. 54 P
ces mots devant les seigneurs de france pour 3.04. 55 P
volant, the pegasus, chez les narines de feu! 3.07. 14 P
via! les eaux et terre. 4.02. 4
pour les ecus que vous /lui promettez, il est 4.04. 51 P
que je tombe entre les mains d'un chevalier, je 4.04. 56 P
que dit–il? que je suis semblable a les anges? 5.02.111 P
les langues des hommes sont pleines de 5.02.115 P
les dames et demoiselles pour etre baisees 5.02.258 P
is not be de fashon pour les ladies of france — 5.02.261 P
la fin couronne les /oeuvres. 2H6 5.02. 28
/LESS 3 FR 0.0003 REL FR 3 V 0 P
/and /more /and /less /do /flock /to /follow 2H4 1.01.209
/and /be't /of /less /expect | /that /matter TRO 1.03. 70
/in /no /less /working /than /are /swords /and 1.03.355
LESS 225 FR 0.0254 REL FR 180 V 45 P
we are less afraid to be drown'd than thou art. TMP 1.01. 44 P
to name the bigger light, and how the less, 1.02.335
and much less take | what i shall die to want. 3.01. 78
less than a pound shall serve me for carrying TGV 1.01.105 P
much less shall she that hath love's wings to 2.07. 11
than the wit, for the greater hides the less. 3.01.362 P
and less than this, i am sure you cannot give. 5.04. 25
as those cheek–roses | proclaim you are no less! MM 1.04. 17
i think no less. 2.01.138
heaven | with less respect than we do minister 2.02. 86
wit in them, | but in the less foul profanation. 2.02.128
more nor less to others paying | than by 3.02.265
if he be less, he's nothing, but he's more, 5.01. 58
we did believe no less. 5.01.142
less in your knowledge and your grace you show ERR 3.02. 31
his incivility confirms no less. 4.04. 46
is so indeed, he is no less than a stuff'd man. ADO 1.01. 58 P
and he that hath no beard is less than a man; 2.01. 37 P
is not for me, and he that is less than a man, i 2.01. 39 P
which shall bear no less likelihood than to see 2.02. 42 P
of men, the less you meddle or make with them, 3.03. 52 P
the plea of no less weight | than aquitaine, a LLL 2.01. 7
i am less proud to hear you tell my worth | than 2.01. 17
i think no less. 5.02. 55
i cannot give you less. 5.02.384
less than an ace, man; MND 5.01.308 P
with no less presence, but with much more love, MV 3.02. 54
make it less, | for fear i surfeit. 3.02.113
but if she be less than an honest woman, she is 3.05. 41 P
nor cut thou less nor more | but just a pound of 4.01.325
if thou tak'st more | or less than a just pound, 4.01.327
so doth the greater glory dim the less: 5.01. 93
and no less belov'd of her uncle than his own AYL 1.01.111 P
friends told me as much, and i thought no less. 4.01.184 P
with no less religion than if thou wert indeed 4.01.197 P
even daughter, welcome, in no less degree. 5.04.148
he is no less than what we say he is. SHR in.1. 71
for i will love thee ne'er the less, my girl. 1.01. 77
'tis known my father hath no less | than three 2.01.377
the longer kept, the less worth. AWW 1.01.154 P
i cannot give thee less, to be call'd grateful. 2.01.129
of that and all the progress, more and less, 5.03.331
what great ones do the less will prattle of) TN 1.02. 33
cesario, | thou know'st no less but all. 1.04. 13
very brief, and to exceeding good sense — less. 3.04.158 P
between his lord and my niece confirms no less. 3.04.187 P
i must have done no less with wit and safety. 5.01.211
which is for me less easy to commit | than you WT 1.02. 58
you never spoke what did become you less | than 1.02.282
which no less adorns | our gentry than our 1.02.392
which often hath no less prevail'd than so | on 2.01. 54
yet that dares | less appear so, in comforting 2.03. 56
and no less honest | than you are mad; 2.03. 71
wanted | less impudence to gainsay what they did 3.02. 56
easiest passage | look for no less than death. 3.02. 91
kings are no less unhappy, their issue not being 4.02. 26 P
from court and is less frequent to his princely 4.02. 32 P
pains, much less | th' adventure of her person? 5.01.155
for gnarling sorrow hath less power to bite R2 1.03.292
house, | against the envy of less happier lands; 2.01. 49
'tis nothing less: 2.02. 34
and hope to joy is little less in joy | than 2.03. 15
of much less value is my company | than your 2.03. 19
meet | with no less terror than the elements 3.03. 55

if they speak more or less than truth, they are 1H4 2.04.171 P
the more and less came in with cap and knee, 4.03. 68
i hope no less, yet needful 'tis to fear, | and, 4.04. 34
if i do grow great, i'll grow less, for i'll 5.04.164 P
buckles himself in my belt cannot live in less. 2H4 1.02.139 P
less noise, less noise! 4.05. 7
less noise, less noise! 4.05. 7
other, less fine in carat, /is more precious, 4.05.161
and not less happy, having such a son | that 5.02.110
make less thy body (hence) and more thy grace, 5.05. 52
we judge no less. H5 2.02. 39
no less for bounty bound to us | than cambridge 2.02. 92
scene flies | in motion of no less celerity 3.pr. 2
wherein thou art less happy, being fear'd, 4.01.248
and his achievements of no less account; 1H6 2.03. 8
i find thou art no less than fame hath bruited, 2.03. 68
was nothing less than bloody tyranny. 2.05.100
much less to take occasion from their mouths 4.01.130
i owe him little duty, and less love, | and take 4.04. 34
no less belov'd | than when thou wert protector 2H6 2.03. 26
and, to speak truth, thou deserv'st no less. 4.03. 10 P
to weep is to make less the depth of grief: 3H6 2.01. 85
more than i seem, and less than i was born to; 3.01. 56
a man at least, for less i should not be; 3.01. 57
it were no less, but yet i'll make a pause. 3.02. 10
she could say little less; 4.01.101
true, my good lord, i know you for no less. 4.07. 22
i thought no less; 5.04. 62
and yet brought forth less than a mother's hope, 5.06. 50
god grant that some, less noble and less loyal, R3 2.01. 92
god grant that some, less noble and less loyal, 2.01. 92
no less importing than our general good, | are 3.07. 68
yet much less spirit to curse | abides in me; 4.04.197
a grandam's name is little less in love | than 4.04.299
this night to meet here, they could do no less H8 1.04. 68
that | a woman of less place might ask by law: 2.02.111
does purpose honor to you no less flowing | than 2.03. 62
never find a heart | with less allegiance in it! 5.02. 78
less valiant than the virgin in the night, | and TRO 1.01. 11
yet ne'er the less, | my spritely brethren, i 2.02.189
not that little little less than little wit from 2.03. 13 P
as wise, no less noble, much more gentle, and 2.03.149 P
and discharging less than the tenth part of one. 3.02. 87 P
though less than yours in /past, must o'ertop 3.03.164
merits pois'd, each weighs nor less nor more, 4.01. 66
my well–fam'd lord of troy, no less to you. 4.05.173
alike, and none less dear than thine and my good COR 1.03. 23 P
no, nor a man that fears you less than he, 1.04. 14
thy friend no less | than those she placeth 1.05. 23
worse than a theft, no less than a traducement, 1.09. 22
he covets less | than misery itself would give, 2.02.126
your voices have | done many things, some less, 2.03.130
that as his worthy deeds did claim no less 2.03.186
and they are no less, | when, both your voices 3.01.102
you that will be less fearful than discreet; 3.01.150
the man you are, | with striving less to be so. 3.02. 20
how is it less or worse | that it shall hold 3.02. 48
because they then less need one another. 4.05.231 P
against us brats with no less confidence | than 4.06. 93
and is no less apparent | to th' vulgar eye, 4.07. 20
'twas to pardon | when it was less expected. 5.01. 19
very well. | could he say less? 5.01. 22
my stead, would you have heard | a mother less? 5.03.193
or granted less, aufidius? 5.03.193
that we look'd | for no less spoil than glory — 5.06. 43
made peace | with no less honor to the antiates 5.06. 79
nor wish no less, and so i take my leave. TIT 1.01.402
of a year or two | makes me less gracious, or 2.01. 32
well, more or less, or ne'er a whit at all, 4.02. 53
by having him, making yourself no less. ROM 1.03. 94
no less! nay, bigger: women grow by men. 1.03. 95
her means much less | to meet her new–beloved 2.pr. 11
'tis no less, i tell ye, for the bawdy hand of 2.04.112 P
a hair more or a hair less in his beard than 3.01. 18 P
what less than dooms–day is the prince's doom? 3.03. 9
notwithstanding, thou shalt be no less esteem'd. TIM 2.02.106 P
supper to him of purpose to have him spend less, 3.01. 25 P
milky heart, | it turns in less than two nights? 3.01. 55
we know him for no less, though we are but 3.02. 3 P
but in the mean time he wants less, my lord. 3.02. 39
steal less for this i give you, | and gold 4.03.448
their mothers, they would have done no less. JC 1.02.275 P
brutus' love to caesar was no less than his. 3.02. 19 P
not that i lov'd caesar less, but that i lov'd 3.02. 22 P
but, i assure you, | a prize no less in worth. 5.04. 27
of cawdor to me | promis'd no less to them? MAC 1.03.120
fears | are less than horrible imaginings: 1.03.138
would thou hadst less deserv'd, | that the 1.04. 18
that hast no less deserv'd, nor must be known 1.04. 30
nor must be known | no less to have done so, let 1.04. 31
whose absence is no less material to me | than 3.01.135
and delight | no less in truth than life. 4.03.130
both more and less have given him the revolt, 5.04. 12
a little more than kin, and less than kind. HAM 1.02. 65
and with no less nobility of love | than that 1.02.110
more matter, with less art. 2.02. 95
with less remorse than pyrrhus' bleeding sword 2.02.491
own honor and dignity — the less they deserve, 2.02.531 P
too, for youth no less becomes | the light and 4.07. 78
without debatement further, more or less, | he 5.02. 45
so tell him, with th' occurrents, more and less, 5.02.357
and you, our no less loving son of albany, | we LR 1.01. 42
no less than life, with grace, health, beauty, 1.01. 58
no less in space, validity, and pleasure, | than 1.01. 81
according to my bond, no more nor less. 1.01. 93
highness offer'd, | nor will you tender less. 1.01.195
i do profess to be no less than i seem, to serve 1.04. 13 P
thou showest, | speak less than thou knowest, 1.04.119
than thou knowest, | lend less than thou owest, 1.04.120
thou trowest, | set less than thou throwest; 1.04.123
"fools had ne'er less grace in a year, | for 1.04.166
hope | you less know how to value her desert 2.04.139
own disorders | deserv'd much less advancement. 2.04.200
servants, who seem no less, | which are to 3.01. 23
if i die for/'t (as no less is threat'ned me), 3.03. 17 P
no less than all. 3.03. 24
fourscore and upward, not an hour more nor less; 4.07. 60
thou art in nothing less | than i have here 5.03. 94
i am no less in blood than thou art, edmund; 5.03.168
thine hath no less reason. OTH 1.03.367 P
thou dost deliver more or less than truth, 2.03.219
prerogativ'd are they less than the base; 3.03.274
i should have known no less: ANT 1.04. 40
i could have given less matter | a better ear. 2.01. 31
'twas a shame no less | than was his loss, to 3.13. 10
less noble mind | than she which by her death 4.14. 60
keep decorum, must | no less beg than a kingdom. 5.02. 18
story is | no less in pity than his glory which 5.02.362
have made him | as little as a crow, or less, CYM 1.03. 15
of him when he was less furnish'd than now he is 1.04. 8 P
flat, for taking a beggar without less quality. 1.04. 23 P
have been often bound for no less than my life. 1.04. 27 P
and less attemptable than any the rarest of our 1.04. 60 P
or less — at first? 2.05. 15
no whit less | than in his feats deserving it), 3.01. 6
put thyself | into a havior of less fear, ere 3.04. 9
ourself | to show less sovereignty than they, 3.05. 6
then had my prize | been less, and so more equal 3.06. 77
to th' owl and morn to th' lark less welcome. 3.06. 93
no less young, more strong, not beneath him in 4.01. 10 P
great griefs, i see, med'cine the less; 4.02.243
thou mov'st no less with thy complaining than 4.02.375
so well master'd, but be sure | no less belov'd. 4.02.384
your preparation can affront no less | than what 4.03. 29
less without and more within. 5.01. 33
leonatus, and | be villainy less than 'twas! 5.05.225
my commendations great, whose merit's less. PER 2.02. 9
much less in blood than virtue, yet a princess 4.03. 7
no less than it gives a good report to a number 4.06. 39 P
shall threaten me | i fear less than my fortune. TNK 3.06.125
good by me | as by another that less loves her. 4.01. 44
and so by hoping more they have but less, | or, LUC 137
be told, | the repetition cannot make it less; 1285
scorn'd, like old men of less truth than tongue, SON 17.10
more bright than theirs, less false in rolling, 20. 5
grace and faults are lov'd of more and less: 96. 3
i love not less, though less the show appear; 102. 2
i love not less, though less the show appear; 102. 2
not that the summer is less pleasant now | than 102. 9
lie, | made more or less by thy continual haste. 123.12
and so much less of shame in me remains | by how
LC 188

LESSEN 2 FR 0.0002 REL FR 1 V 1 P
i shall lessen god's sending that way, for it is ADO 2.01. 21 P
and buckingham | shall lessen this big look. H8 1.01.119

LESSEN'D 2 FR 0.0002 REL FR 2 V 0 P
sickness much enfeebled, | my numbers lessen'd; H5 3.06.146
lessen'd herself, and in the beams o' th' sun CYM 5.05.472

LESSENS 1 FR 0.0001 REL FR 1 V 0 P
that it is place which lessens and sets off, CYM 3.03. 13

/LESSER 1 FR 0.0001 REL FR 1 V 0 P
fear | /lesser his person than an ill report; COR 1.06. 70

LESSER 31 FR 0.0035 REL FR 29 V 2 P
i'll pull thee by the lesser legs. TMP 2.02.104 P
it is the lesser blot, modesty finds, | women to TGV 5.04.108
seeming as burdened | with lesser weight, but ERR 1.01.108
with lesser weight, but not with lesser woe, 1.01.108
the more my prayer, the lesser is my grace. MND 2.02. 89
alack, for lesser knowledge! WT 2.01. 38
when the kite builds, look to lesser linen. 4.03. 24 P
and more, more strong than lesser is my fear, JN 4.02. 42
thy death–bed is no lesser than thy land, R2 2.01. 95
the waste is no whit lesser than thy land. 2.01.103
great | as is my grief, or lesser than my name! 3.03.137
set limb to limb, and thou art far the lesser; 2H6 4.10. 47
can lesser hide his love or hate than he, | for R3 3.04. 52
doth lesser blench at suff'rance than i do. TRO 1.01. 28
though no man lesser fears the greeks than i 2.02. 8
you less than he, | that's lesser than a little. COR 1.04. 15
lesser had been | the /thwartings of your 3.02. 20
watch'd ere now | all night for lesser cause, ROM 4.04. 10
fortunes, | the greater scorns the lesser. TIM 4.03. 6
lesser than macbeth, and greater. MAC 1.03. 65
others that lesser hate him | do call it valiant 5.02. 13
to whose /huge spokes ten thousand lesser things HAM 3.03. 19
malady is fix'd, | the lesser is scarce felt. LR 3.04. 9
how lesser enmities may give way to greater. ANT 2.01. 43
no lesser of her honor confident | than i did CYM 5.05.187
that caus'd a lesser villain than myself, | a 5.05.219
none that beheld him but, like lesser lights, PER 2.03. 41
this moves in him more rage and lesser pity | to LUC 468
the lesser thing should not the greater hide: 663
deep sounds make lesser noise than shallow fords 1329
'tis the lesser sin | that mine eye loves it and SON 114.13

LESS'NED 2 FR 0.0002 REL FR 2 V 0 P
and less'ned be that small, god i beseech him! R3 1.03.110
/one pain is less'ned by another's anguish; ROM 1.02. 46

LESSON 8 FR 0.0009 REL FR 8 V 0 P
to lesson me and tell me some good mean | how TGV 2.07. 5
learn | any hard lesson that may do thee good. ADO 1.01.293
arise a knight, | and learn this lesson: 3H6 2.02. 62
leaves abroad, | and where's our lesson then? TIT 4.01.106
i shall the effect of this good lesson keep | as HAM 1.03. 45
and you shall see her | take a new lesson out, TNK 2.03. 35
o, learn to love, the lesson is but plain, | and VEN 407
but thence i learn, and find the lesson true, SON 118.13

LESSON'D 3 FR 0.0003 REL FR 3 V 0 P
ay, millstones, as he lesson'd us to weep. R3 1.04.240
you not have told him | as you were lesson'd: COR 2.03.177
well hast thou lesson'd us, this shall we do. TIT 5.02.110

LESSONS 3 FR 0.0003 REL FR 3 V 0 P
but learn my lessons as i please myself. SHR 3.01. 20
my lessons make no music in three parts. 3.01. 60
he lessons his requests, and to thee sues | to ANT 3.12. 13

/LEST 2 FR 0.0002 REL FR 1 V 1 P
/lest /we /remember /still /that /we /have /none TIT 3.02. 30
in this garb, /lest /my extent to the players, HAM 2.02.373 P

LEST 157 FR 0.0177 REL FR 131 V 26 P
lest too light winning | make the prize light. TMP 1.02.452
of it, but i fear'd | lest i might anger thee. 4.01.169
lest he should take exceptions to my love, | and TGV 1.03. 81
lest the base earth | should from her vesture 2.04.159
lest it should burn above the bounds of reason. 2.07. 23
but, fearing lest my jealous aim might err, 3.01. 28
him, | lest it should ravel and be good to none, 3.02. 52
lest, growing ruinous, the building fall | and 5.04. 9
lest the lunatic knave would have search'd it; WIV 3.05.103 P
lest the devil that guides him should aid him, i 3.05.147 P
lest the oil that's in me should set hell on 5.05. 35 P
lest he transform me to a piece of cheese! 5.05. 82 P
lest i might be too rash. MM 2.02. 9
but lest you do repent | as that the sin hath 2.03. 30
lest thou a feverous life shouldst entertain, 3.01. 74
lest that your goods too soon be confiscate: ERR 1.02. 2
lest it make you choleric, and purchase me 2.02. 62 P
ay, and let none enter, lest i break your pate. 2.02.218
whence he came, lest he catch cold on 's feet. 3.01. 37
but, lest myself be guilty to self–wrong, | i'll 3.02.163
bear it with you, lest i come not time enough. 4.01. 41
but lest my liking might too sudden seem, | i ADO 1.01.314
lord, lest i should prove the mother of fools. 2.01.286 P
she knew his love, lest she'll make sport at it. 3.01. 58
yet swear not, lest ye be forsworn again. LLL 5.02.832
know, | lest, to thy peril, thou aby it dear. MND 3.02.175
for fear lest day should look their shames upon, 3.02.385
spirit, lest through thy wild behavior | i be MV 2.02.187
amen betimes, lest the devil cross my prayer, 3.01. 19 P
but lest you should not understand me well — 3.02. 7
to stop his wounds, lest he do bleed to death. 4.01.258
lest, over–eyeing of his odd behavior | (for yet SHR in.1. 95
lest you be cony–catch'd in this business. 5.01. 98 P
lest it be rather thought you affect a sorrow AWW 1.01. 52 P
too far in anger, lest thou hasten thy trial; 2.03.211 P
it were fit you knew him, lest, reposing too far 3.06. 13 P
cassocks, lest they shake themselves to pieces. 4.03.169 P
him now, lest the device take air and taint. TN 3.04.131 P
lest that it make me so unsound a man | as to 3.04.350
to kill a woodcock lest thou dispossess the soul 4.02. 59 P
lest you say | your queen and i are devils. WT 1.02. 81
dagger muzzled | lest it should bite its master, 1.02.157
lest barbarism (making me the precedent) 2.01. 84
sir, lest your justice | prove violence, in the 2.01.127
lest that the treachery of the two fled hence 2.01.195
minister of honor, | lest she should be denied. 2.02. 49
all colors | no yellow in't, lest she suspect, 2.03.107
o, cut my lace, lest my heart, cracking it, 3.02.173
on't, lest your fancy | may think anon it moves. 5.03. 60
i durst not stick a rose | lest men should say, JN 1.01.143
lest unadvis'd you stain your swords with blood. 2.01. 45
lest zeal, now melted by the windy breath | of 2.01.477
lest that their hopes prodigiously be cross'd; 3.01. 91
look to that, devil, lest that france repent, 3.01.196
lest resolution drop | out at mine eyes in 4.01. 35
lest i, by marking of your rage, forget | your 4.03. 85
lest you mistake the heavens are over our heads. R2 3.03. 17
lest, being over–proud in sap and blood, | with 3.04. 59
lest child, child's children, cry against you 4.01.149
lest you be cropp'd before you come to prime. 5.02. 51
lest thy pity prove | a serpent that will sting 5.03. 57
lest your retirement do amaze your friends. 1H4 5.04. 6
lest rest and lying still might make them look 2H4 4.05.211
peace be with us, lest we be heavier! 5.02. 26
sovereign, lest example | breed, by his H5 2.02. 45
speed, lest that our king | come here himself to 2.04.141
his prayers, lest 'a should be thought a coward; 3.02. 38 P
cap that day, lest he knock that about yours. 4.01. 57 P
him with any appearance of fear, lest he, by 4.01.111 P
lest, bleeding, you do paint the white rose red, 1H6 2.04. 50
lest it be said, "speak, sirrah, when you should 3.01. 62
lest, being suffer'd in that harmful slumber, 2H6 3.02.262
lest they consult about the giving up of some 4.07.132 P
heed, lest by your heat you burn yourselves. 5.01.160
urge it no more, lest that, in stead of words, 3H6 1.01. 98
child, | lest thou be hated both of god and man. 1.03. 9
lest in revenge thereof, sith god is just, | he 1.03. 41
lest with my sighs or tears i blast or drown 4.04. 23
lest in our need he might infect another, | and 5.04. 46
lest to thy harm thou move our patience. R3 1.03.247
lest he that is the supreme king of kings 2.01. 13
lest by a multitude | the new–heal'd wound of 2.02.124
lest thou increase the number of the dead, | and 4.01. 44
lest that the process of thy kindness | last 4.04.254
lest his son george fall | into the blind cave 5.03. 61
lest, being seen, thy brother, tender george, 5.03. 95
lest leaden slumber peize me down to–morrow, 5.03.105
great reason why — | lest i revenge. 5.03.186
in haste too, | lest he should help his father. H8 2.01. 44
lest at once | the burthen of my sorrows fall 3.01.110
lest hector or my father should perceive me, | i TRO 1.01. 36
lest perchance he think | we dare not move the 2.03. 81
lest your displeasure should enlarge itself | to 5.02. 37
lest his infection, being of catching nature, COR 3.01.308
lest parties (as he is belov'd) break out, | and 3.01.313
do't, | lest i surcease to honor mine own truth, 3.02.121
lest that thy wives with spits and boys with 4.04. 5
lest you shall chance to whip your information, 4.06. 54
lest i let forth your half–pint of blood. 5.02. 56 P
lest then the people, and patricians too, | upon TIT 1.01.445
and, lest thou shouldst detect /him, cut thy 2.04. 27
pray.— grant thou, lest faith turn to despair. ROM 1.05.104
lest that thy love prove likewise variable. 2.02.111
lest mine be about your ears ere it be out. 3.01. 81 P
lest in this marriage he should be dishonor'd 4.03. 26
lest they should spy my windpipe's dangerous TIM 1.02. 51
still to give, lest your deities be despis'd. 3.06. 72 P
then lest he may, prevent. JC 2.01. 28
lest i be laugh'd at when i tell them so. 2.02. 70
lest some friend of caesar's | should chance — 3.01. 87
and leave us, publius, lest that the people, 3.01. 92
not be in our camp, | lest it discomfort us. 5.03.106
lest occasion call us | and show us to be MAC 2.02. 67
lest our old robes sit easier than our new! 2.04. 38
lest with this piteous action you convert | my HAM 3.04.128
lest i should compare with him in excellence, 5.02.138 P
lest more mischance | on plots and errors happen 5.02.394
a little, | lest you may mar your fortunes. LR 1.01. 95
a hill, lest it break thy neck with following; 2.04. 72 P
lest it see more, prevent it. 3.07. 83
lest his ungovern'd rage dissolve the life 4.04. 19
lest my brain turn, and the deficient sight 4.06. 23
lest that th' infection of his fortune take 4.06.233
lest by his clamor (as it so fell out) | the OTH 2.03.231
lest her body and beauty unprovide my mind again 4.01.205 P
lest, being like one of heaven, the devils 4.02. 36

only, | lest my remembrance suffer ill report; ANT 2.02.156
lord, pardon — i dare not, | lest i be taken. 4.15. 23
lest, in her greatness, by some mortal stroke 5.01. 64
lest i give cause | to be suspected of more CYM 1.01. 93
upon fools, lest the reflection should hurt her. 1.02. 32 P
lest the bargain should catch cold and starve. 1.04.166 P
lest, being miss'd, i be suspected of | your 3.04.186
din | express impatience, lest you stir up mine. 5.04.112
then, lest my life be cropp'd to keep you clear, PER 1.01.141
and doubting lest he had err'd or sinn'd, | to 1.03. 21
lest this great sea of joys rushing upon me 5.01.192
lest this match between 's | be cross'd ere met. TNK 3.01. 97
let not my sense unsettle | lest i should drown, 3.02. 30
lest his race | should show i' th' world too 5.03.117
o, give it me, lest thy hard heart do steel it, VEN 375
lest jealousy, that sour unwelcome guest, 449
lest she should steal a kiss and die forsworn. 726
"lest the deceiving harmony should run | into 781
lest between them both it should be kill'd, LUC 74
lest he should hold it her own gross abuse, 1315
talk, | lest she some subtile practice smell — PP 18. 9
i fear — | lest that my mistress hear my song; 18.50
swan, | lest the requiem lack his right. PHT 16
lest my bewailed guilt should do thee shame, SON 36.10
lest the wise world should look into your moan, 71.13
lest the world should task you to recite | what 72. 1
o, lest your true love may seem false in this, 72. 9
lest i (too much profane) should do it wrong, 89.11
lest sorrow lend me words, and words express 140. 3
lest eyes well seeing thy foul faults should 148.14
lest guilty of my faults thy sweet self prove: 151. 4

LESTRAKE 2 FR 0.0002 REL FR 2 V 0 P
/foix, lestrake, bouciqualt, and charolois; H5 3.05. 45
beaumont and marle, vaudemont and lestrake. 4.08.100

/LET* 19 FR 0.0021 REL FR 14 V 5 P
/let us once lose our oaths to find ourselves, LLL 4.03.358
/let /it /command /a /mirror /hither /straight, R2 4.01.265
/before /you /said, | "/let /us /make /head." 2H4 1.01.168
/let /us /on! 1.03. 85
/let /them /alone. 2.03. 41
/well, /let /it /strike. R3 4.02.112
/why /let /it /strike? 4.02.113
i'll /let his /humors blood. TRO 2.03.212 P
/let /us /make /ready /straight. 4.04.144
/let /us /address /to /tend /on /hector's /heels 4.04.146
/the /tears /that /thy /poor /eyes /let /fall TIT 3.02. 18
/let /me /question /more /in /particular. HAM 2.02.239 P
/to /let /this /canker /of /our /nature /come 5.02. 69
/lords /and /great /men /will /not /let /me; LR 1.04.152 P
/they /will /not /let /me /have /all /the /fool 1.04.154 P
/let /us /deal /justly. 3.06. 40 P
/justicer, /why /hast /thou /let /her /scape? 3.06. 56
/to /let /these /hands /obey /my /blood, | /they 4.02. 64
/let /pity /not /be /believ'd!" 4.03. 29

LET* 2219 FR 0.2508 REL FR 1741 V 478 P
let me remember thee what thou hast promis'd, TMP 1.02.243
that made gape | the pine, and let thee out. 1.02.293
else o' th' earth | let liberty make use of; 1.02.493
keep in tunis, | and let sebastian wake." 2.01.260
then let us both be sudden. 2.01.306
i do now let loose my opinion, hold it no longer 2.02. 34 P
then to sea, boys, and let her go hang!" 2.02. 54
i prithee let me bring thee where crabs grow; 2.02.167
let me lick thy shoe. 3.02. 23 P
lo, how he mocks me! wilt thou let him, my lord? 3.02. 30 P
i am full of pleasure, | let us be jocund. 3.02.117
come on, trinculo, let us sing. 3.02.120 P
well, let him go. 3.03. 10
let it be to-night, | for, now they are 3.03. 14
no sweet aspersion shall the heavens let fall 4.01. 18
let me live here ever; 4.01.122
let it alone, thou fool, it is but trash. 4.01.224
let them be hunted soundly. 4.01.262
op'd, and let 'em forth | by my so potent art. 5.01. 49
let me embrace thine age, whose honor cannot 5.01.121
that will /not let you | believe things certain. 5.01.124
let us not burthen our remembrances with | a 5.01.199
let grief and sorrow still embrace his heart 5.01.214
the rest, and let no man take care for himself; 5.01.256 P
let me not, | since i have my dukedom got, | and ep 5
pardon'd be, | let your indulgence set me free. ep 20
now let us take our leave. TGV 1.01. 56
to milan let me hear from thee by letters | of 1.01. 57
o, they love least that let men know their love. 1.02. 32
to take a paper up that i let fall. 1.02. 71
then let it lie for those that it concerns. 1.02. 73
and let the papers lie: 1.02. 97
well, let us go. 1.02.129
you | to let him spend his time no more at home, 1.03. 14
lend me the letter; let me see what news. 1.03. 55
let me see; 2.01. 3
if not divine, | yet let her be a principality, 2.04.152
then let her alone. 2.04.167
then let me go, and hinder not my course: 2.07. 33
me, let me have | what thou think'st meet, and 2.07. 57
then let her beauty be her wedding-dow'r, | for 3.01. 78
then let me see thy cloak — | i'll get me one 3.01.132
i pray thee let me feel thy cloak upon me. 3.01.136
let me read them. 3.01.289 P
grace | let me not live to look upon your grace. 3.02. 21
let us into the city presently | to sort some 3.02. 90
then to silvia let us sing, | that silvia is 4.02. 49
to her let us garlands bring. 4.02. 53
sweet lady, let me rake it from the earth. 4.02.115
i pray thee let me look on that again. 4.04.125
let me see; 4.04.184
let go that rude uncivil touch, | thou friend of 5.04. 60
let me see. 5.04. 92
o proteus, let this habit make thee blush! 5.04.104
let me be blest to make this happy close; 5.04.117
and let them be recall'd from their exile; 5.04.155
come, let us go, we will include all jars | with 5.04.160
well, let us see honest master page. WIV 1.01. 66 P
now let us understand. 1.01.136 P
let us command to know that of your mouth, or of 1.01.227 P
let them wag; 1.03. 6 P
let him follow. 1.03. 13 P
let me see thee froth and /lime. 1.03. 14 P
why then let kibes ensue. 1.03. 32 P
let vultures gripe thy guts! 1.03. 85
nobody but has his fault — but let that pass. 1.04. 15 P
let me have thy voice in my behalf. 1.04.156 P
let me see. 2.01. 3 P
let it suffice thee, mistress page — at the 2.01. 10 P
but let thine inherit first, for i protest mine 2.01. 73 P
of her than sharp words, let it lie on my head. 2.01.184 P
let her approach. 2.02. 32 P
and let me tell you in your ear, she's as 2.02. 96 P
let them say 'tis grossly done, so it be fairly 2.02.142 P
for i must let you understand i think myself in 2.02.165 P
and i will provoke him to't, or let him wag. 2.03. 70 P
let him die; 2.03. 84 P
let us wag then. 2.03. 97 P
disarm them, and let them question. 3.01. 76 P
let them keep their limbs whole and hack our 3.01. 77 P
pray you let us not be laughing-stocks to other 3.01. 85 P
are whole, and let burnt sack be the issue. 3.01.109 P
and let us knog our prains together to be 3.01.118 P
if he take her, let him take her simply. 3.02. 76 P
why, now let me die, for i have liv'd long 3.03. 44 P
let the court of france show me such another. 3.03. 54 P
let that persuade thee there's something 3.03. 68 P
let me see't, let me see't, o, let me see't! 3.03.136 P
let me see't, let me see't, o, let me see't! 3.03.137 P
let me see't, let me see't, o, let me see't! 3.03.137 P
let me creep in here. 3.03.142 P
then make sport at me, then let me be your jest, 3.03.150 P
let me stop this way first. 3.03.164 P
let him be sent for to-morrow, eight a' clock, 3.03.197 P
good master shallow, let him woo for himself. 3.04. 50 P
let me have your good will. 3.04. 82
let me pour in some sack to the thames water; 3.05. 21 P
let her consider his frailty, and then judge of 3.05. 50 P
to make one mad, let the proverb go with me: 3.05.151 P
master slender is let the boys leave to play. 4.01. 11 P
are you not asham'd? let the clothes alone. 4.02.138 P
let me for ever be your table-sport. 4.02.162 P
let them say of me, "as jealous as ford, that 4.02.162 P
gentlemen, let him /not strike the old woman. 4.02.181 P
let me speak with the gentlemen; 4.03. 5 P
but let our plot go forward. 4.04. 12
let our wives | yet once again (to make us 4.04. 12
and let us two devise to bring him thither. 4.04. 27
well, let it not be doubted but he'll come, 4.04. 44
let them from forth a sawpit rush at once | with 4.04. 54
then let them all encircle him about, | and, 4.04. 57
let the supposed fairies pinch him sound, | and 4.04. 62
let us about it. 4.04. 80 P
let her descend, bully, let her descend; 4.05. 21 P
let her descend, bully, let her descend; 4.05. 22 P
what are they? let us know. 4.05. 42 P
sir — let me speak with you in your chamber. 4.05.121 P
let the sky rain potatoes; 5.05. 18 P
let it thunder to the tune of "green-sleeves," 5.05. 19 P
let there come a tempest of provocation, i will 5.05. 20 P
th' expressure that it bears, green let it be, 5.05. 67
oak | of herne the hunter, let us not forget. 5.05. 76
good husband, let us every one go home, | and 5.05.241
let it be so, sir john, | to master /brook you 5.05.243
as your worth is able, | and let them work. MM 1.01. 9
let there be some more test made of my mettle 1.01. 48
let us withdraw together, | and we may soon our 1.01. 81
which for this fourteen years we have let slip, 1.03. 21
let me ask, | the rather for i now must make you 1.04. 21
o, let him marry her. 1.04. 49
and let him learn to know, when maidens sue, 1.04. 80
and let it keep one shape, till custom make it 2.01. 3
ay, but yet | let us be keen, and rather cut a 2.01. 5
let but your honor know | (whom i believe to be 2.01. 8
let mine own judgment pattern out my death, 2.01. 30
bring him his confessor, let him be prepar'd, 2.01. 35
let not your worship think me the poor duke's 2.01.177 P
let him continue in his courses till thou 2.01.186 P
get you gone, and let me hear no more of you. 2.01.206 P
i advise you let me not find you before me again 2.01.245 P
no, no, let carman whip his jade, | the valiant 2.01.255
let that be mine. 2.02. 12
let her be admitted. 2.02. 22
let her have needful but not lavish means; 2.02. 24
i do beseech you let it be his fault, | and not 2.02. 35
stands in record, | and let go by the actor. 2.02. 41
let it not sound a thought upon your tongue 2.02.140
o, let her brother live! 2.02.174
do me the common right | to let me see them, and 2.03. 6
wherein (let no man hear me) i take pride, 2.04. 10
his life, if it be sin, | heaven let me bear it! 2.04. 70
let /me be ignorant, and in nothing good, | but 2.04. 76
to this supposed, or else to let him suffer — 2.04. 97
else let my brother die, | if not a fedary, but 2.04.121
faults may shake our frames), let me be bold. 2.04.133
let me entreat you speak the former language. 2.04.140
let it come on. 3.01. 43
let me know the point. 3.01. 72
sweet sister, let me live. 3.01.132
let me ask my sister pardon. 3.01.171 P
let me hear you speak farther. 3.01.205 P
in this life, that it will let this man live! 3.01.233 P
he would be drunk too, that let me inform you. 3.02.128 P
but this i can let you understand, the greater 3.02.135 P
let him be but testimonied in his own 3.02.144 P
let me desire you to make your answer before him 3.02.155 P
let him be call'd before us. 3.02.204 P
let him be furnish'd with divines, and have all 3.02.208 P
and let me desire to know how you find claudio 3.02.239 P
on angelo, | to weed my vice and let his grow! 3.02.270
let me excuse me, and believe me so, | my mirth 4.01. 12
come, let us go, | our corn's to reap, for yet 4.01. 74
by the year, and let him abide here with you; 4.02. 24 P
stay until the officer | arise to let him in; 4.02. 91
let claudio be executed by four of the clock, 4.02.120 P
let me have claudio's head sent me by five. 4.02.122 P
let this be duly perform'd, with a thought that 4.02.123 P
let this barnardine be this morning executed, 4.02.170 P
let this be done: 4.03. 86
i beseech you let it be proclaim'd betimes i' 4.04. 15 P
and let the subject see, to make them know 5.01. 14
but let your reason serve | to make the truth 5.01. 65
let this friar be found. 5.01.133
first, let her show /her face, and after speak. 5.01.168
true, | let me in safety raise me from my knees, 5.01.231
let me have way, my lord, | to find this 5.01.238
friar that set them on, | let him be sent for. 5.01.249
and let the devil | be sometime honor'd for his 5.01.292
let him speak no more. 5.01.347 P
first, provost, let me bail these gentle three. 5.01.357
but let my trial be mine own confession. 5.01.372
of my hidden pow'r | than let him so be lost. 5.01.393
since it is so, | let him not die. 5.01.448
go fetch him hither, let me look upon him. 5.01.469
one | whom he begot with child), let her appear, 5.01.511
nuptial finish'd, | let him be whipt and hang'd. 5.01.513
but ere they came — o, let me say no more! ERR 1.01. 94
good sister, let us dine, and never fret; 2.01. 6
then let your will attend on their accords. 2.01. 25
the sun shines, let foolish gnats make sport, 2.02. 30
say he dines forth, and let no creature enter. 2.02.210
ay, and let none enter, lest i break your pate. 2.02.218
go bid them let us in. 3.01. 30
let him walk from whence he came, lest he catch 3.01. 37
let my master in, luce. 3.01. 49
you'll let us in, i hope? 3.01. 54
thou baggage, let me in. 3.01. 57
let him knock till it ache. 3.01. 58
i pray thee let me in. 3.01. 78
have patience, sir, o, let it not be so! 3.01. 85
and let us to the tiger all to dinner; 3.01. 95
let not my sister read it in your eye; 3.02. 9
and let her read it in thy looks at board: 3.02. 18
let love, being light, be drowned if she sink! 3.02. 52
i pray you let me see it. 4.01. 58
let her send it. 4.01.105
avaunt, thou witch! come, dromio, let us go. 4.03. 79
give me your hand, and let me feel your pulse. 4.04. 52
there is my hand, and let it feel your ear. 4.04. 53
o, bind him, bind him! let him not come near me. 4.04.106
masters, let him go: 4.04.111
if i let him go, | the debt he owes will be 4.04.117
let us come in, that we may bind him fast, | and 5.01. 40
as roughly as my modesty would let me. 5.01. 59
then let your servants bring my husband forth. 5.01. 93
and therefore let me have him home with me. 5.01.101
for i will not let him stir | till i have us'd 5.01.102
with thy command | let him be brought forth, and 5.01.160
i, sir, am dromio, pray let me stay. 5.01.337
let him bear it for a difference between himself ADO 1.01. 68 P
let me bid you welcome, my lord, being 1.01.154 P
hits me, let him be clapp'd on the shoulder, and 1.01.258 P
in my forehead, and let me be vildly painted, 1.01.264 P
horse to hire," let them signify under my sign, 1.01.266 P
in practice let us put it presently. 1.01.328
in the mean time let me be that i am, and seek 1.03. 36 P
come, let us thither, this may prove food to my 1.03. 65 P
let us to the great supper, their cheer is the 1.03. 71 P
cousin, let him be a handsome fellow, or else 2.01. 54 P
come let us to the banquet. 2.01.171 P
let every eye negotiate for itself, | and trust 2.01.178
with a kiss, and let not him speak neither. 2.01.311 P
i pray thee sing, and let me woo no more. 2.03. 48
then sigh not so, but let them go, | and be you 2.03. 66
let her wear it out with good counsel. 2.03.201 P
of it by your daughter, let it cool the while. 2.03.206 P
let there be the same net spread for her, and 2.03.213 P
let us send her to call him in to dinner. 2.03.218 P
let it be thy part | to praise him more than 3.01. 18
and never to let beatrice know of it. 3.01. 43
therefore let benedick, like cover'd fire, 3.01. 77
let that appear hereafter, and aim better at me 3.02. 95 P
till midnight, and let the issue show itself. 3.02.130 P
let that appear when there is no need of such 3.03. 21 P
why then take no note of him, but let him go, 3.03. 28 P
why then let them alone till they are sober. 3.03. 45 P
is to let him show himself what he is and steal 3.03. 58 P
peace, and let the child wake her with crying, 3.03. 69 P
let us go sit here upon the church-bench till 3.03. 89 P
let us obey you to go with us. 3.03.175 P
let me but move one question to your daughter, 4.01. 73
come, let us go. 4.01.111
hence from her, let her die. 4.01.154
doth warrant, | let all my sins lack mercy! 4.01.180
and let my counsel sway you in this case. 4.01.201
for dead, | let her awhile be secretly kept in, 4.01.203
let this be so, and doubt not but success | will 4.01.234
signior leonato, let the friar advise you, | and 4.01.244
nay, i pray you let me go. 4.01.294 P
let them come before master constable. 4.02. 8 P
yea, marry, let them come before me. 4.02. 9 P
let the watch come forth. 4.02. 36 P
master constable, let these men be bound, and 4.02. 64 P
come let them be opinion'd. 4.02. 67 P
let them be in the hands — 4.02. 68 P
let him write down the prince's officer coxcomb. 4.02. 70 P
nor let no comforter delight mine ear, | but 5.01. 6
and let it answer every strain for strain, | as 5.01. 12
but that's no matter, let him kill one first. 5.01. 81
win me and wear me, let him answer me. 5.01. 82
do not you meddle, let me deal in this. 5.01.101
let me hear from you. 5.01.149 P
but soft you, let me be. 5.01.203 P
prince, let me go no farther to mine answer: 5.01.230 P
do you hear me, and let this count kill me. 5.01.231 P
let me see his eyes, | that when i note another 5.01.259
i beseech you let it be rememb'red in his 5.01.306 P
ere i go, let me go with that i came, which is, 5.02. 47 P
come let us hence, and put on other weeds, | and 5.03. 30
sweet, let me see your face. 5.04. 55
mean time let wonder seem familiar, | and to the 5.04. 70
familiar, | and to the chapel let us presently. 5.04. 71
let fame, that all hunt after in their lives, LLL 1.01. 1
let me say no, my liege, and if you please: 1.01. 50
what is the end of study, let me know. 1.01. 55
give me the paper, let me read the same, | and 1.01.116
let them be men of good repute and carriage. 1.02. 68 P
let me not be pent up, sir; 1.02.155 P
oath, | to let you enter his /unpeopled house. 2.01. 88

alack, let it blood. 2.01.186
let me see: 3.01.104
now you will be my purgation and let me loose. 3.01.127 P
not wounding, pity would not let me do't; 4.01. 27
let the mark have a prick in't, to mete at, if 4.01.132
let me hear a staff, a stanze, a verse; 4.02.104
let me supervise the /canzonet. 4.02.120 P
then incision | would let her out in saucers. 4.03. 96
i post from love; good lover, let me go. 4.03.186
i beseech your grace let this letter be read: 4.03.191
aside the true folk, and let the traitors stay. 4.03.209
sweet lords, sweet lovers, o, let us embrace! 4.03.210
therefore let us devise | some entertainment for 4.03.369
from the park let us conduct them thither; 4.03.371
for what is inward between us, let it pass. 5.01. 97 P
of great import indeed too — but let that pass; 5.01.101 P
but, sweet heart, let that pass. 5.01.105 P
but let that pass. 5.01.108 P
to the worthies, and let them dance the hay. 5.01.154
let me not die your debtor, | my red dominical, 5.02. 43
let it not be sweet. 5.02.236
let us complain to them what fools were here, 5.02.302
let us confess and turn it to a jest. 5.02.390
soft, let us see — | write "lord have mercy on 5.02.418
let them not approach. 5.02.511
nay, my good lord, let me o'errule you now. 5.02.515
therefore as he is, an ass, let him go. 5.02.625
i bepray you let me borrow my arms again. 5.02.696 P
master, let me take you a button-hole lower. 5.02.700 P
let not the cloud of sorrow justle it | from 5.02.748
if this thou do deny, let our hands part, 5.02.811
love, demetrius, | let me have hermia's; MND 1.01. 94
then let us teach our trial patience, | because 1.01.152
if i do it, let the audience look to their eyes. 1.02. 26 P
let not me play a woman; 1.02. 47 P
and i may hide my face, let me play thisby too. 1.02. 51 P
let me play the lion too. 1.02. 70 P
i will make the duke say, "let him roar again; 1.02. 72 P
let him roar again." 1.02. 73 P
let me go; 2.01.235
then to your offices, and let me rest. 2.02. 8
let love forbid | sleep his seat on thy eyelid. 2.02. 80
and let the prologue seem to say we will do no 3.01. 17 P
let it be written in eight and eight. 3.01. 25 P
and there indeed let him name his name, and tell 3.01. 44 P
and let him have some plaster, or some loam, or 3.01. 68 P
or let him hold his fingers thus, and through 3.01. 69 P
let her shine as gloriously | as the venus of 3.02.106
o, let me kiss | this princess of pure white, 3.02.143
lysander's love, that would not let him bide — 3.02.186
vile thing, let loose; 3.02.260
you mock me, /gentlemen, | let her not hurt me. 3.02.300
let her not strike me. 3.02.303
and now, so you will let me quiet go, | to 3.02.314
let me go. 3.02.316
let me come to her. 3.02.328
let her alone; 3.02.332
i pray you, let none of your people stir me; 4.01. 38 P
uncouple in the western valley, let them go. 4.01.107
let us hear, sweet bottom. 4.02. 33 P
in any case, let thisby have clean linen; 4.02. 39 P
and let not him that plays the lion pare his 4.02. 40 P
let him approach. 5.01.107
at the which let no man wonder. 5.01.134
let lion, moonshine, wall, and lovers twain | at 5.01.150
his discretion, and let us listen to the moon. 5.01.237 P
let your epilogue alone. 5.01.361 P
then let us say you are sad | because you are MV 1.01. 47
let me play the fool: 1.01. 79
with mirth and laughter let old wrinkles come, 1.01. 80
and let my liver rather heat with wine | than my 1.01. 81
and when i ope my lips let no dog bark!" 1.01. 94
i pray you, good bassanio, let me know it, | and 1.01.135
made him, and therefore let him pass for a man.. 1.02. 56 P
and let me see — but hear you, | methoughts you 1.03. 68
then, let me see, the rate — 1.03.104
let the forfeit | be nominated for an equal 1.03.148
and let us make incision for your love, | to 2.01. 6
well, let his father be what 'a will, we talk of 2.02. 54 P
but let it be so hasted that supper be ready at 2.02.114 P
let not the sound of shallow fopp'ry enter | my 2.05. 35
let me see, | i will survey th' inscriptions 2.07. 13
let all of his complexion choose me so. 2.07. 79
let good antonio look he keep his day, | or he 2.08. 25
of me, | let it not enter in your mind of love. 2.08. 42
i pray thee let us go and find him out | and 2.08. 51
let me see: 2.09. 23
let none presume | to wear an undeserved dignity 2.09. 39
let me say amen betimes, lest the devil cross my 3.01. 19 P
let him look to his bond. 3.01. 47 P
to call me usurer, let him look to his bond. 3.01. 48 P
a christian cur'sy, let him look to his bond. 3.01. 49 P
it so, | let fortune go to hell for it, not i. 3.02. 21
let me choose, | for as i am, i live upon the 3.02. 24
but let me to my fortune and the caskets. 3.02. 39
let music sound while he doth make his choice; 3.02. 43
let us all ring fancy's knell. 3.02. 70
away, | let it presage the ruin of your love, 3.02.173
but let me hear the letter of your friend. 3.02.314
do not persuade you to come, let not my letter." 3.02.322 P
let him alone, | i'll follow him no more with 3.03. 19
thee honest-true, | so let me find thee still. 3.04. 47
let it be as humors and conceits shall govern. 3.05. 63 P
i will anon, first let us go to dinner. 3.05. 86
nay, let me praise you while i have a stomach. 3.05. 87
no, pray thee, let it serve for table-talk; 3.05. 88
make room, and let him stand before our face. 4.01. 16
it, let the danger light | upon your charter and 4.01. 38
let me have judgment and the jew his will. 4.01. 83
shall i say to you, | "let them be free! 4.01. 94
let their beds | be made as soft as yours, and 4.01. 95
and let their palates | be season'd with such 4.01. 96
drops earliest to the ground, and so let me. 4.01.116
and for thy life let justice be accus'd. 4.01.129
i beseech you let his lack of years be no 4.01.161 P
be no impediment to let him lack a reverend 4.01.162 P
i pray you let me look upon the bond. 4.01.225
to let the wretched man outlive his wealth, | to 4.01.269
pay the bond thrice | and let the christian go. 4.01.319
give me my principal, and let me go. 4.01.336
so he will let me have | the other half in use, 4.01.382
my lord bassanio, let him have the ring. 4.01.449
let his deservings and my love withal | be 4.01.450
out, give him this deed, | and let him sign it. 4.02. 2
and ceremoniously let us prepare | some welcome 5.01. 37
and let the sounds of music | creep in our ears. 5.01. 55
let no such man be trusted. 5.01. 88
let me give light, but let me not be light, 5.01.129
let me give light, but let me not be light, 5.01.129
my honor would not let ingratitude | so much 5.01.218
let not that doctor e'er come near my house. 5.01.223
let not me take him then, | for if i do, i'll 5.01.236
let us go in, | and charge us there upon 5.01.297
let it be so. 5.01.300
let me go, i say. AYL 1.01. 65 P
and when i break that oath, let me turn monster. 1.02. 22 P
let me see — what think you of falling in love? 1.02. 25 P
let us sit and mock the good huswife fortune 1.02. 31 P
let us now stay and see it. 1.02.147 P
but let your fair eyes and gentle wishes go with 1.02.185 P
let us go thank him, and encourage him. 1.02.240
out of service, let us talk in good earnest. 1.03. 26 P
let me love him for that, and do you love him 1.03. 38 P
let me the knowledge of my fault bear with me: 1.03. 46
let it suffice thee that i trust thee not. 1.03. 55
no, let my father seek another heir. 1.03. 99
and let not search and inquisition quail | to 2.02. 20
all this i give you, let me be your servant. 2.03. 46
let me go with you, | i'll do the service of a 2.03. 53
let me see wherein | my tongue hath wrong'd him; 2.07. 83
i almost die for food, and let me have it. 2.07.104
let gentleness my strong enforcement be, | in 2.07.118
down your venerable burthen, | and let him feed. 2.07.168
hand, | and let me all your fortunes understand. 2.07.200
and let my officers of such a nature | make an 3.01. 16
let no face be kept in mind | but the fair of 3.02. 94
do lack a hind, | let him seek out rosalind. 3.02.102
but whether wisely or no, let the forest judge. 3.02.122 P
shepherd, let us make an honorable retreat, 3.02.160 P
let me stay the growth of his beard, if thou 3.02.210 P
go thou with me, and let me counsel thee. 3.03. 95 P
of as good as he, so he laugh'd and let me go. 3.04. 38 P
o, come, let us remove, | the sight of lovers 3.04. 56
if mine eyes can wound, now let them kill thee. 3.05. 16
youth, let me /be better acquainted with thee. 4.01. 1 P
occasion, let her never nurse her child herself, 4.01.175 P
examines all such offenders, and let time try. 4.01.200 P
are out, let him be judge how deep i am in love. 4.01.214 P
let your wedding be to-morrow; 5.02. 13 P
man doubt that, let him put me to my purgation. 5.04. 43 P
let me have audience for a word or two. 5.04.151
in this forest let us do those ends | that here 5.04.170
therefore paucas pallabris, let the world slide. SHR in.1. 5 P
let him come, and kindly. in.1. 14 P
let one attend him with a silver basin | full of in.1. 55
let them want nothing that my house affords. in.1. 104
such duty to the drunkard let him do, | with in.1. 113
let me entreat of you | to pardon me yet for a in.2. 118
marry, i will, let them play it. in.2. 137 P
sit by my side, and let the world slip, we shall in.2. 143 P
here let us breathe and haply institute | a 1.01. 8
and let it not displease thee, good bianca, 1.01. 76
and let me be a slave, t' achieve that maid 1.01.219
and therefore let me be thus bold with you | to 1.02.104
pray you, sir, let him go while the humor lasts. 1.02.107 P
too, | and let me have them very well perfum'd; 1.02.151
sir, let me be so bold as ask you, | did you yet 1.02.249
sir, sir, the first's for me! let her go by. 1.02.254
and let it be more than alcides' twelve. 1.02.256
let us that are poor petitioners speak too. 2.01. 72
let specialties be therefore drawn between us, 2.01.126
let him that mov'd you hither | remove you hence 2.01.195
i chafe you if i tarry. let me go. 2.01.241
o, let me see thee walk. 2.01.256
o, be thou dian, and let her be kate, | and then 2.01.260
and then let kate be chaste and dian sportful! 2.01.261
and let your father make her the assurance, 2.01.387
now let me see if i can conster it: 3.01. 41
but let it rest. 3.01. 56
which once perform'd, let all the world say no, 3.02.141
that, all amaz'd, the priest let fall the book, 3.02.161
let us entreat you stay till after dinner. 3.02.198
let me entreat you. 3.02.199
let me entreat you. 3.02.200
nay, let them go, a couple of quiet ones. 3.02.240
place, | and let bianca take her sister's room. 3.02.250
let their heads be slickly comb'd, their blue 4.01. 90 P
let them curtsy with their left legs and not 4.01. 92 P
will you let it fall? 4.01.155
better how to tame a shrew, | now let him speak; 4.01.211
take /in your love, and then let me alone. 4.02. 71
this by the way i let you understand: 4.02.116
'tis passing good, i prithee let me have it. 4.03. 18
why then the beef, and let the mustard rest. 4.03. 26
i pray you let it stand. 4.03. 44
come, tailor, let us see these ornaments; 4.03. 61
come let me have a bigger. 4.03. 68
come, tailor, let us see't. 4.03. 86
go call my men, and let us straight to him, 4.03.184
let me embrace with old vincentio, | and wander 4.05. 68
lord, let me never have a cause to sigh, | till 5.02.123
let me ask a question. AWW 1.01.112 P
let me see. 1.01.152 P
grow there and to bear — "let me not live" — 1.02. 55
when it was out — "let me not live," quoth he, 1.02. 58
let not your hate encounter with my love | for 1.03.208
let higher italy | (those bated that inherit but 2.01. 12
with vildest torture, let my life be ended. 2.01.174
property | of what i spoke, unpitied let me die, 2.01.188
let the white death sit on thy cheek for ever, 2.03. 71
let the rest go. 2.03.148
let it satisfy you, you are too old. 2.03.196 P
good, very good, let it be conceal'd awhile. 2.03.266 P
let that go. 2.05. 76
whose great decision hath much blood let forth 3.01. 3
let me see what he writes, and when he means to 3.02. 10 P
let every word weigh heavy of her worth, | that 3.04. 31
let him have his way. 3.06. 1 P
none better than to let him fetch off his drum, 3.06. 19 P
the love of laughter, let him fetch his drum; 3.06. 34 P
let him fetch off his drum in any hand. 3.06. 42 P
a pox on't, let it go, 'tis but a drum. 3.06. 46 P
and let me buy your friendly help thus far, 3.07. 15
let her in fine consent, | as we'll direct her 3.07. 19
why then to-night | let us assay our plot, which 3.07. 44
good captain, let me be th' interpreter. 4.01. 7 P
italian, or french, let him speak to me, | i'll 4.01. 72
o, let me live! 4.01. 83
but you shall let it dwell darkly with you. 4.03. 11 P
let it be forbid, sir, so should i be a great 4.03. 45 P
let me see: 4.03.161 P
nothing, but let him have thanks. 4.03.171 P
i beseech you let me answer to the particular of 4.03.182 P
let me live, sir, in a dungeon, i' th' stocks, 4.03.243 P
lord, sir, let me live, or let me see my death! 4.03.309 P
lord, sir, let me live, or let me see my death! 4.03.309 P
knows himself a braggart, | let him fear this; 4.03.335
let death and honesty | go with your impositions 4.04. 28
let his nobility remain in 's court. 4.05. 49 P
go thy ways, let my horses be well look'd to, 4.05. 58 P
let us go see your son, i pray you. 4.05.102 P
let the justices make you and fortune friends; 5.02. 33 P
let him not ask our pardon, | the nature of his 5.03. 22
let him approach | a stranger, no offender; 5.03. 25
now pray you let me see it; 5.03. 81
let your highness | lay a more noble thought 5.03.179
let thy curtsies alone, they are scurvy ones. 5.03.323 P
let us from point to point this story know, | to 5.03.325
my tongue blabs, then let mine eyes not see. TN 1.02. 63
why, let her except before excepted. 1.03. 7 P
let them hang themselves in their own straps. 1.03. 12 P
and thou let part so, sir andrew, would thou 1.03. 61 P
your hand to th' butt'ry-bar, and let it drink. 1.03. 70 P
marry, now i let go your hand, i am barren. 1.03. 79 P
let me see thee caper. 1.03.140 P
let her hang me! 1.05. 5 P
that are fools, let them use their talents. 1.05. 15 P
and for turning away, let summer bear it out. 1.05. 20 P
if he cannot, let the botcher mend him. 1.05. 46 P
let him be the devil, and he will, i care not; 1.05.128 P
and seek the crowner, and let him sit o' my coz; 1.05.134 P
let him approach. call in my gentlewoman. 1.05.163 P
good beauties, let me sustain no scorn; 1.05.175 P
good madam, let me see your face. 1.05.230 P
let him send no more — | unless, perchance, you 1.05.280
and let your fervor, like my master's, be 1.05.287
well, let it be. 1.05.298
let me yet know of you whither you are bound. 2.01. 9 P
murther me for my love, let me be your servant. 2.01. 35 P
let us therefore eat and drink. 2.03. 13 P
most certain. let our catch be "thou knave." 2.03. 63 P
for monsieur malvolio, let me alone with him. 2.03.134 P
plant you two, and let the fool make a third, 2.03.174 P
let still the woman take | an elder than herself 2.04. 29
then let thy love be younger than thyself, | or 2.04. 36
death, | and in sad cypress let me be laid. 2.04. 52
sweet, | on my black coffin let there be strown. 2.04. 60
let all the rest give place. 2.04. 79
but let concealment, like a worm i' th' bud, 2.04.111
let me be boil'd to death with melancholy. 2.05. 3 P
nay, but first, let me see, let me see, let me 2.05.111 P
but first, let me see, let me see, let me see. 2.05.111 P
but first, let me see, let me see, let me see. 2.05.111 P
hands, let thy blood and spirit embrace them, 2.05.147 P
let thy tongue tang arguments of state; 2.05.150 P
if not, let me see thee a steward still, the 2.05.156 P
not now fool myself, to let imagination jade me; 2.05.164 P
my love, let it appear in thy smiling; 2.05.175 P
let the garden door be shut, and leave me to my 3.01. 92 P
so, let me hear you speak. 3.01.122
gilt of this opportunity you let time wash off, 3.02. 25 P
let there be gall enough in thy ink, though thou 3.02. 48 P
i pray you let us satisfy our eyes | with the 3.03. 22
"if not, let me see thee a servant still." 3.04. 55 P
good maria, let this fellow be look'd to. 3.04. 61 P
let some of my people have a special care of him 3.04. 62 P
let thy tongue /tang with arguments of state; 3.04. 70 P
went away now, "let this fellow be look'd to"; 3.04. 76 P
let me enjoy my private. 3.04. 89 P
let me alone. 3.04. 96 P
let me alone with him. 3.04.109 P
nay, let me alone for swearing. 3.04.183 P
let him let the matter slip, and i'll give him 3.04.285 P
let him let the matter slip, and i'll give him 3.04.285 P
let me speak a little. 3.04.359
art a foolish fellow, | let me be clear of thee. 4.01. 4
nay, let him alone. 4.01. 33 P
let go thy hand. 4.01. 37
come, sir, i will not let you go. 4.01. 38 P
let thy fair wisdom, not thy passion, sway | in 4.01. 52
let fancy still my sense in lethe steep; 4.01. 62
if it be thus to dream, still let me sleep! 4.01. 63
now, as thou lov'st me, let me see his letter. 5.01. 1 P
this once, and let your flesh and blood obey it. 5.01. 33 P
if you will let your lady know i am here to 5.01. 42 P
sir, let your bounty take a nap, i will awake it 5.01. 48 P
get him to bed, and let his hurt be look'd to. 5.01.208 P
i should my tears let fall upon your cheek, 5.01.240
and let me see thee in thy woman's weeds. 5.01.273
and let no quarrel nor no brawl to come | taint 5.01.356
but let him say so then, and let him go; WT 1.02. 35
but let him say so then, and let him go; 1.02. 35
but let him swear so, and he shall not stay, 1.02. 36
to let him there a month behind the gest 1.02. 41
nay, let me have't; 1.02.101
let what is dear in sicily be cheap. 1.02.175
know't, | it will let in and out the enemy, 1.02.205
let that suffice. 1.02.235
me, let me know my trespass | by its own visage. 1.02.265
bears not one, | let villainy itself forswear't. 1.02.361
let us avoid. 1.02.462
and let her sport herself | with that she's big 2.01. 60
let him have knowledge who i am. 2.02. 2
if i prove honey-mouth'd, let my tongue blister; 2.02. 31

let him be, | until a time may serve. 2.03. 21
when she will take the rein i let her run, | but 2.03. 51
let him that makes but trifles of his eyes 2.03. 63
let it live. 2.03.157
let us be clear'd | of being tyrannous, since we 3.02. 4
rather | let me be punish'd, that have minded 3.02.225
let my sheep go. 3.03.126 P
let me pass | the same i am, ere ancient'st 4.01. 9
but let time's news | be known when 'tis brought 4.01. 26
let me see: 4.03. 32 P
let me see: 4.03. 36 P
the shearers prove sheep, let me be unroll'd, 4.03.121 P
bring him in, and let him approach singing. 4.04.211 P
me too; let me go thither. 4.04.302
these good men are pleas'd, let them come in; 4.04.341 P
you have let him go, | and nothing marted with 4.04.351
let me hear | what you profess. 4.04.368
let him know't. 4.04.413
prithee let him. 4.04.414
let him, my son. 4.04.415
let nature crush the sides o' th' earth together 4.04.478
let myself and fortune | tug for the time to 4.04.496
mistress (let my prophecy | come home to ye!), 4.04.648
this being done, let the law go whistle; 4.04.698 P
let us to the king. 4.04.707 P
let me pocket up my pedlar's excrement. 4.04.713 P
let me have no lying. 4.04.722 P
that shepherd be not in hand–fast, let him fly. 4.04.768 P
let him call me rogue for being so far officious 4.04.839 P
let boors and franklins say it, i'll swear it. 5.02.159 P
let him that was the cause of this have pow'r 5.03. 54
let be, let be. 5.03. 61
let be, let be. 5.03. 61
let no man mock me, | for i will kiss her. 5.03. 79
unlawful business | i am about, let them depart. 5.03. 97
be magic, let it be an art | lawful as eating. 5.03.110
if she pertain to life let her speak too. 5.03.113
an honorable conduct let him have. JN 1.01. 29
let them approach. 1.01. 47
then, good my liege, let me have what is mine, 1.01.114
then, good my mother, let me know my father; 1.01.249
let them be welcome then, we are prepar'd. 2.01. 83
let me make answer: thy usurping son. 2.01.121
let us hear them speak | whose title they admit, 2.01.199
and let us in — your king, whose labor'd 2.01.232
acknowledge then the king, and let me in. 2.01.269
and let young arthur, duke of britain, in, | who 2.01.301
unless thou let his silver water keep | a 2.01.339
then let confusion of one part confirm | the 2.01.359
by east and west let france and england mount 2.01.381
let it be so. say, where will you assault? 2.01.408
gates, | let in that amity which you have made, 2.01.537
and let belief and life encounter so | as doth 3.01. 31
state of my great grief | let kings assemble; 3.01. 71
let wives with child | pray that their burthens 3.01. 89
but on this day let seamen fear no wrack; 3.01. 92
let not the hours of this ungodly day | wear out 3.01.109
lawful let it be | that i have room with rome to 3.01.179
right, | let it be lawful that law bar no wrong; 3.01.186
a curse, | let go the hand of that arch–heretic, 3.01.192
do not let go thy hand. 3.01.195
sir, | my reverend father, let it not be so! 3.01.249
or let the church, our mother, breathe her curse 3.01.256
o, let thy vow | first made to heaven, first be 3.01.265
i had a thing to say, but let it go. 3.03. 33
let us go; 3.04.182
for heaven sake, hubert, let me not be bound! 4.01. 77
go stand within; let me alone with him. 4.01. 84
let him come back, that his compassion may 4.01. 88
let me not hold my tongue, let me not, hubert; 4.01. 99
let me not hold my tongue, let me not, hubert; 4.01. 99
let it be our suit | that you have bid us ask 4.02. 62
let it be so; 4.02. 67
then let the worst unheard fall on your head. 4.02.136
i shall yield up my crown, let him be hang'd. 4.02.157
o, let me have no subject enemies | when adverse 4.02.171
yea, without stop, didst let thy heart consent, 4.02.239
to–morrow morning let us meet him then. 4.03. 18
let hell want pains enough to torture me. 4.03.138
let not the world see fear and sad distrust 5.01. 46
o, let it not be said! 5.01. 59
let us, my liege, to arms. 5.01. 73
or if he do, let it at least be said, | they saw 5.01. 75
my lord melune, let this be copied out, | and 5.02. 1
let me wipe off this honorable dew, | that 5.02. 45
fair play of the world, | let me have audience. 5.02.119
drums, and let the tongue of war | plead for our 5.02.164
and will not let me welcome this good news. 5.03. 15
let him be brought into the orchard here. 5.07. 10
nor let my kingdom's rivers take their course 5.07. 38
straight let us seek, or straight we shall be 5.07. 79
let it be so, and you, my noble prince, | with 5.07. 96
o, let us pay the time but needful woe, | since 5.07.110
which then our leisure would not let us hear, R2 1.01. 5
let not my cold words here accuse my zeal. 1.01. 47
and let him be no kinsman to my liege, | i do 1.01. 59
mean time, let this defend my loyalty: 1.01. 67
o, let my sovereign turn away his face, | and 1.01.111
good uncle, let this end where it begun; 1.01.158
then, dear my liege, mine honor let me try; 1.01.184
let heaven revenge, for i may never lift | an 1.02. 40
let him not come there | to seek out sorrow that 1.02. 71
let me kiss my sovereign's hand | and bow my 1.03. 46
then let us take a ceremonious leave | and 1.03. 50
o, let no noble eye profane a tear | for me, if 1.03. 59
and let thy blows, doubly redoubled, | fall like 1.03. 80
let them lay by their helmets and their spears, 1.03.119
us, and let the trumpets sound | while we return 1.03.121
and blindfold death not let me see my son. 1.03.224
know, | from where you do remain let paper show. 1.03.250
as far as land will let me, by your side. 1.03.252
it were a shame to let this land by lease; 2.01.110
and let them die that age and sullens have, 2.01.139
let not to–morrow then ensue to–day; 2.01.197
and let him ne'er speak more | that speaks thy 2.01.230
nay, let us share thy thoughts, as thou dost 2.01.273
my gracious uncle, let me know my fault, | on 2.03.106
my lords of england, let me tell you this: 2.03.140
and let him never see joy that breaks that oath! 2.03.151
for god's sake fairly let her be entreated. 3.01. 37
but let thy spiders, that suck up thy venom, 3.02. 14
that they have let the dangerous enemy | measure 3.02.124
for god's sake let us sit upon the ground | and 3.02.155
and let them go | to ear the land that hath some 3.02.211
let no man speak again | to alter this, for 3.02.213
discharge my followers, let them hence away, 3.02.217
a' god's name let it go. 3.03.146
king, | and if you crown him, let me prophesy, 4.01.136
prevent it, resist it, let it not be so, | lest 4.01.148
here let us rest, if this rebellious earth 5.01. 5
good old folks and let them tell /thee tales 5.01. 41
let me unkiss the oath 'twixt thee and me; 5.01. 74
then whither he goes, thither let me go. 5.01. 85
once more, adieu, the rest let sorrow say. 5.01.102
let me see the writing. 5.02. 57
i will be satisfied, let me see the writing. 5.02. 59
boy, let me see the writing. 5.02. 69
i will be satisfied, let me see it, i say. 5.02. 71
what ho, my liege! for god's sake let me in. 5.03. 74
my dangerous cousin, let your mother in, | i 5.03. 81
this let alone will all the rest confound. 5.03. 86
his, then let them have | that mercy which true 5.03.109
say "pardon," king, let pity teach thee how. 5.03.116
this music mads me, let it sound no more, | for 5.05. 61
then let me hear | of you, my gentle cousin 1H4 1.01. 30
but let him from my thoughts. 1.01. 91
let not us that are squires of the night's body 1.02. 24 P
let us be diana's foresters, gentlemen of the 1.02. 25 P
and let men say we be men of good government, 1.02. 27 P
you, let not his report | come current for an 1.03. 67
no, on the barren mountains let him starve; 1.03. 89
then let not him be slandered with revolt. 1.03.112
let me not hear you speak of mortimer. 1.03.119
and let my soul | want mercy if i do not join 1.03.131
from the north to south, | and let them grapple. 1.03.197
o, let the hours be short, | till fields, and 1.03.301
rather let me have it as you are a false thief. 2.01. 93 P
to filthy tunes, let a cup of sack be my poison. 2.02. 46 P
my masters, let us share, and then to horse 2.02. 98 P
let me see some more. 2.03. 6 P
let him tell the king: 2.03. 34 P
let me see — about michaelmas next i shall be 2.04. 54 P
dozen more are at the door, shall i let them in? 2.04. 83 P
let them alone awhile, and then open the door. 2.04. 84 P
let them speak; 2.04.170 P
four rogues in buckrom let drive at me — 2.04.196 P
prithee let him alone, we shall have more anon. 2.04.207 P
green came at my back and let drive at me, for 2.04.223 P
shall i let them in? 2.04.490 P
deny the sheriff, so, if not, let him enter. 2.04.496 P
and so let me entreat you leave the house. 2.04.518
there let him sleep till day. 2.04.543 P
let me understand you then, | speak it in welsh. 3.01.117
but do not use it oft, let me entreat you. 3.01.174
here come our wives, and let us take our leave. 3.01.189
yet such extenuation let me beg | as, in reproof 3.02. 22
yet let me wonder, harry, | at thy affections, 3.02. 29
he had his part of it, let him pay. 3.03. 75 P
let them coin his nose, let them coin his cheeks 3.03. 78 P
them coin his nose, let them coin his cheeks. 3.03. 78 P
prithee let her alone, and list to me. 3.03. 95 P
let them come! 4.01.112
come let me taste my horse, | who is to bear me 4.01.119
forty let it be! 4.01.130
come let us take a muster speedily. 4.01.133
let it be seen to–morrow in the battle | which 4.03. 13
and let there be impawn'd | some surety for a 4.03.108
then with the losers let it sympathize, | for 5.01. 7
therefore, good cousin, let not harry know, | in 5.02. 24
there did he pause, but let me tell the world, 5.02. 65
let each man do his best, and here draw i | a 5.02. 92
of war, | and by that music let us all embrace, 5.02. 98
his willingly, let him make a carbonado of me. 5.03. 58 P
i might have let alone | the insulting hand of 5.04. 53
but let my favors hide thy mangled face, | and 5.04. 96
if not, let him kill the next percy himself. 5.04.141 P
let them that should reward valor bear the sin 5.04.149 P
brother, let us to the highest of the field, 5.04.160
let us not leave till all our own be won. 5.05. 44
let heaven kiss earth! 2H4 1.01.153
now let not nature's hand | keep the wild flood 1.01.153
let order die! 1.01.154
and let this world no longer be a stage | to 1.01.155
but let one spirit of the first–born cain 1.01.157
let him be damn'd like the glutton! 1.02. 34 P
i pray you let me speak with you. 1.02.109 P
for a thousand marks, let him lend me the money, 1.02.193 P
good master snare, let him not scape. 2.01. 25 P
the world, let him be brought in to his answer. 2.01. 31 P
let it be ten pound, if thou canst. 2.01.147 P
thee, sir john, let it be but twenty nobles. 2.01.153 P
let it alone, i'll make other shift. 2.01.156 P
faith, and let it be an excellent good thing. 2.02. 33 P
let the end try the man. 2.02. 47 P
all our loves, | first let them try themselves. 2.03. 56
let him not come hither. 2.04. 71 P
if he swagger, let him not come here. 2.04. 73 P
god let me not live, but i will murther your 2.04.134 P
with | king cerberus, and let the welkin roar. 2.04.168
no, let the fiend give fire. 2.04.182
why then let grievous, ghastly, gaping wounds 2.04.198
come let me wipe thy face. 2.04.217 P
let them play. 2.04.227 P
then let us meet them like necessities; 3.01. 93
let me see them, i beseech you. 3.02. 95 P
let me see, let me see, let me see. 3.02. 97 P
let me see, let me see, let me see. 3.02. 97 P
let me see, let me see, let me see. 3.02. 97 P
let them appear as i call; 3.02. 98 P
let them do so, let them do so. 3.02. 99 P
let them do so, let them do so. 3.02. 99 P
let me see, where is mouldy? 3.02.100 P
enough before, and you could have let me alone. 3.02.112 P
for th' other, sir john, let me see: 3.02.120 P
marry, let me have him to sit under, he's like 3.02.122 P
let that suffice, most forcible feeble. 3.02.167 P
's prince, and let it go which way it will, he 3.02.237 P
our house, let our old acquaintance be renew'd. 3.02.294 P
let time shape, and there an end. 3.02.332 P
let us sway on and face them in the field. 4.01. 24
let them have pay, and part. 4.02. 70
my lord, | and let our army be discharged too. 4.02. 92
so please you, let our trains | march by us, 4.02. 93
and, ere they be dismiss'd, let them march by. 4.02. 96
i beseech your grace let it be book'd with the 4.03. 46 P
therefore let me have right, and let desert 4.03. 54 P
let me have right, and let desert mount. 4.03. 55 P
let it shine, then. 4.03. 57 P
let it do something, my good lord, that may do 4.03. 59 P
let them go. 4.03.128 P
let there be no noise made, my gentle friends, 4.05. 1
let us withdraw into the other room. 4.05. 18
let me see him. 4.05. 53
let all the tears that should bedew my hearse 4.05.113
let me no more from this obedience rise, | which 4.05.146
feign, | o, let me in my present wildness die, 4.05.152
of it, | let god for ever keep it from my head, 4.05.174
davy, davy, davy, let me see, davy, let me see, 5.01. 9 P
let me see, davy, let me see, davy, let me see. 5.01. 10 P
let me see, davy, let me see, davy, let me see. 5.01. 10 P
let it be cast and paid. 5.01. 20 P
therefore i beseech you let him be countenanc'd. 5.01. 51 P
therefore let men take heed of their company. 5.01. 77 P
let me but bear your love, i'll bear your cares. 5.02. 58
and let us choose such limbs of noble counsel 5.02.135
"fill the cup, and let it come, | i'll pledge 5.03. 53
let him come in. 5.03. 82 P
let king cophetua know the truth thereof. 5.03.102
let us take any man's horses, the laws of 5.03.135 P
let vultures vile seize on his lungs also! 5.03.139
which i beseech you to let me have home with me. 5.05. 75 P
john, let me have five hundred of my thousand. 5.05. 83 P
and let us, ciphers to this great accompt, | on H5 pr 17
let the inheritance | descend unto the daughter. 1.02. 99
and let another half stand laughing by, | all 1.02.113
o, let their bodies follow, my dear liege, 1.02.130
let us be worried, and our nation lose | the 1.02.219
desires you let the dukedoms that you claim 1.02.256
therefore let our proportions for these wars 1.02.304
therefore let every man now task his thought, 1.02.309
let floods o'erswell, and fiends for food howl 2.01. 93
let us condole the knight, for, lambkins, we 2.01.127
let him be punish'd, sovereign, lest example 2.02. 45
o, let us yet be merciful. 2.02. 47
let us deliver | our puissance into the hand of 2.02.189
husband, let me bring thee to staines. 2.03. 1 P
let senses rule; 2.03. 49
let us to france, like horse–leeches, my boys, 2.03. 55
let huswifery appear. 2.03. 62
and let us do it with no show of fear, | no, 2.04. 23
and let us fear | the native mightiness and fate 2.04. 63
and let them know | of what a monarchy you are 2.04. 72
let it pry through the portage of the head 3.01. 10
let the brow o'erwhelm it | as fearfully as doth 3.01. 11
let us swear | that you are worth your breeding, 3.01. 27
withal, my lord, | let us not live in france; 3.05. 3
let us quit all, | and give our vineyards to a 3.05. 3
let us not hang like roping icicles | upon our 3.05. 23
let him greet england with our sharp defiance. 3.05. 37
and let him say to england that we send | to 3.05. 62
let gallows gape for dog, let man go free, | and 3.06. 42
let gallows gape for dog, let man go free, | and 3.06. 42
free, | and let not hemp his windpipe suffocate. 3.06. 43
and let not bardolph's vital thread be cut 3.06. 47
but let my horse have his due. 3.07. 3 P
but, let me see, by ten | we shall have each a 3.07.156
let him cry, "praise and glory on his head!" 4.pr. 31
he let him outlive that day to see his greatness 4.01.184 P
let it be a quarrel between us, if you live. 4.01.205 P
let us our lives, our souls, | our debts, our 4.01.230
let us but blow on them, | the vapor of our 4.02. 23
a very little little let us do, | and all is 4.02. 33
then let the trumpets sound | the tucket sonance 4.02. 34
their ragged curtains poorly are let loose, 4.02. 41
let him depart, his passport shall be made, 4.03. 36
let me speak proudly: 4.03.108
let us die! 4.05. 11
let him go hence, and with his cap in hand 4.05. 13
let us on heaps go offer up our lives. 4.05. 18
let life be short, else shame will be too long. 4.05. 23
please your majesty, let his neck answer for it, 4.08. 43 P
let there be sung non nobis and te deum, | the 4.08.123
so let him land, | and solemnly see him set on 5.pr. 13
and henceforth let a welsh correction teach you 5.01. 78 P
you have congreeted, let it not disgrace me, 5.02. 31
that i may know the let why gentle peace 5.02. 65
thing he sees there, let thine eye be thy cook. 5.02.148 P
vous avez le possession de moi — let me see, 5.02.182 P
but your request shall make me let it pass. 5.02.344
let that one article rank with the rest, | and 5.02.346
in your fair minds let this acceptance take. ep 14
let not sloth dim your honors new begot. 1H6 1.01. 79
by my consent, we'll even let them alone. 1.02. 44
question her proudly, let thy looks be stern. 1.02. 62
so, | let me thy servant and not sovereign be. 1.02.111
leave off delays, and let us raise the siege. 1.02.146
whoe'er he be, you may not be let in. 1.03. 7
that thou nor none of thine shall be let in. 1.03. 21
now beat them hence, why do you let them stay? 1.03. 54
let us look in, the sight will much delight thee 1.04. 62
glansdale, | let me have your express opinions, 1.04. 64
come in, and let us banquet royally, | after 1.06. 30
let us have knowledge at the court of guard. 2.01. 4
let them practice and converse with spirits. 2.01. 25
let us resolve to scale their flinty bulwarks. 2.01. 27
let my presumption not provoke thy wrath, | for 2.03. 70
let him that is a true–born gentleman | and 2.04. 27
let him that is no coward nor no flatterer, 2.04. 31
come, let us four to dinner. 2.04.132
age, | let dying mortimer here rest himself. 2.05. 2
breast, | and what i do imagine, let that rest. 2.05.119
do, | let me persuade you to forbear a while. 3.01.105
let richard be restored to his blood, | so shall 3.01.159
o, let no words, but deeds, revenge this treason 3.02. 49

or else let talbot perish with this shame. 3.02. 57
courageous bedford, let us now persuade you. 3.02. 93
let frantic talbot triumph for a while, | and 3.03. 5
stay, let thy humble handmaid speak to thee. 3.03. 42
now let us on, my lords, and join our powers, 3.03. 90
let him perceive how ill we brook his treason, 4.01. 74
first let me know, and then i'll answer you. 4.01. 88
let this dissension first be tried by fight, 4.01.116
betwixt ourselves let us decide it then. 4.01.119
nay, let it rest where it began at first. 4.01.121
let me persuade you take a better course. 4.01.132
and let us not forgo | that for a trifle that 4.01.149
let me be umpeer in this doubtful strife. 4.01.151
so let us still continue peace, and love. 4.01.161
and if i /wist he did — but let it rest, 4.01.180
let not your private discord keep away | the 4.04. 22
then let me stay, and, father, do you fly. 4.05. 21
during the life, let us not wrong it dead. 4.07. 50
for god's sake let him have /'em; 4.07. 89
so let them have their answers every one. 5.01. 25
let henry fret, and all the world repine. 5.02. 20
and let her head fall into england's lap. 5.03. 26
i have no power to let her pass, | my hand would 5.03. 60
first let me tell you whom you have condemn'd: 5.04. 36
maid, | spare for no faggots, let there be enow. 5.04. 56
hang up your ensigns, let your drums be still, 5.04.174
come, let us in, and with all speed provide | to 2H6 1.01. 73
let not his smoothing words | bewitch your 1.01.156
to us, | yet let us watch the haughty cardinal; 1.01.174
away from me, and let me hear no more! 1.02. 50
let me see them. 1.03. 14 P
suffolk, let them go. 1.03. 40
so let her rest; 1.03. 92
then let him be denay'd the regentship. 1.03.104
let york be regent, i will yield to him. 1.03.106
ambitious warwick, let thy betters speak. 1.03.109
let him have all the rigor of the law. 1.03.196
let somerset be regent o'er the french, 1.03.205
and let these have a day appointed them | for 1.03.207
and let us to our work. 1.04. 12 P
let him shun castles. 1.04. 35
away with them, let them be clapp'd up close, 1.04. 50
"let him shun castles; 1.04. 67
let me be blessed for the peace i make | against 2.01. 35
i pray, my lords, let me compound this strife. 2.01. 56
let never day nor night unhallowed pass, | but 2.01. 83
let me see thine eyes. 2.01.103
let them be whipt through every market town, 2.01.155
this staff of honor raught, there let it stand, 2.03. 43
lords, let him go. 2.03. 47
here let them end it, and god defend the right! 2.03. 55
let it come, i' faith, and i'll pledge you all, 2.03. 66 P
no, stir not for your lives, let her pass by. 2.04. 18
let not her penance exceed the king's commission 2.04. 75
let him die, in that he is a fox, | by nature 3.01.257
let pale–fac'd fear keep with the mean–born man, 3.01.335
let him know | we have dispatch'd the duke, as 3.02. 1
o henry, let me plead for gentle suffolk! 3.02.289
and let thy suffolk take his heavy leave. 3.02.306
where biting cold would never let grass grow, 3.02.337
o, let me entreat thee cease. 3.02.339
nor let the rain of heaven wet this place | to 3.02.341
o, let me stay, befall what may befall! 3.02.402
let me hear from thee; 3.02.405
so thou wilt let me live, and feel no pain. 3.03. 4
disturb him not, let him pass peaceably. 3.03. 25
curtain close, | and let us all to meditation. 3.03. 33
what is my ransom, master? let me know. 4.01. 15
be not so rash, take ransom, let him live. 4.01. 28
yet let not this make thee be bloody–minded; 4.01. 36
remember it, and let it make thee crestfall'n, 4.01. 59
first let my words stab him, as he hath me. 4.01. 66
no, rather let my head | stoop to the block than 4.01.124
hale him away, and let him talk no more. 4.01.131
therefore come you with us and let him go. 4.01.141
there let his head and liveless body lie, 4.01.142
to say as, let the magistrates be laboring men; 4.02. 17 P
let me alone. 4.02.102 P
break open the jails and let out the prisoners. 4.03. 16 P
thou oughtst not to let thy horse wear a cloak, 4.07. 49 P
o, let me live! 4.07.104
let them kiss one another, for they lov'd well 4.07.130 P
you, | or let a /rebel lead you to your deaths? 4.08. 13
let them break your backs with burthens, take 4.08. 28 P
let this my sword report what speech forbears. 4.10. 54
let ten thousand devils come against me, and 4.10. 60 P
let them obey that knows not how to rule; 5.01. 6
and let my sovereign, virtuous henry, | command 5.01. 48
o, let me view his visage, being dead, | that 5.01. 69
and let thy tongue be equal with thy heart. 5.01. 89
first let me ask of /these | if they can brook i 5.01.109
he is a traitor, let him to the tower, | and 5.01.134
so let it help me now against thy sword, | as i 5.02. 24
let no soldier fly. 5.02. 36
o, let the vile world end, | and the premised 5.02. 40
now let the general trumpet blow his blast, 5.02. 43
let us pursue him ere the writs go forth. 5.03. 26
by words or blows here let us win our right. 3H6 1.01. 37
parliament | let us assail the family of york. 1.01. 65
be duke of lancaster, let him be king. 1.01. 86
let me for this my life–time reign as king. 1.01.171
come, cousin, let us tell the queen these news. 1.01.182
let noble warwick, cobham, and the rest, | whom 1.02. 56
be thou reveng'd on men, and let me live. 1.03. 20
then let my father's blood open it again, | he 1.03. 23
o, let me pray before i take my death! 1.03. 35
ah, let me live in prison all my days, | and 1.03. 43
then let me die, for now thou hast no cause. 1.03. 45
boy, | and let his manly face, which promiseth 2.02. 40
to let thy tongue detect thy base–born heart? 2.02.143
let our bloody colors wave! 2.02.173
then let the earth be drunken with our blood! 2.03. 23
warwick, | let me embrace thee in my weary arms. 2.03. 45
yet let us all together to our troops, | and 2.03. 49
and let our hearts and eyes, like civil war, 2.05. 77
but let me see: 2.05. 82
wither one rose, and let the other flourish; 2.05.101
bear thee hence, and let them fight that will, 2.05.121
if friend or foe, let him be gently used. 2.06. 45
in stead whereof let this supply the room: 2.06. 54
even as thou wilt, sweet warwick, let it be; 2.06. 99
let me be duke of clarence, george of gloucester 2.06.106
let me embrace /thee, sour /adversities, | for 3.01. 24
why linger we? let us lay hands upon him. 3.01. 26
and what god will, that let your king perform; 3.01.100
yoke, but let thy dauntless mind | still ride in 3.03. 17
now, sister, let us hear your firm resolve. 3.03.129
did i let pass th' abuse done to my niece? 3.03.188
my noble queen, let former grudges pass, | and 3.03.195
let me give humble thanks for all at once. 3.03.221
let us be back'd with god, and with the seas, 4.01. 43
now therefore let us hence, and lose no hour, 4.01.148
let them go, here is | the duke. 4.03. 29
come therefore let us fly while we may fly, | if 4.04. 34
yet in this one thing let me blame your grace, 4.06. 30
let me entreat (for i command no more) | that 4.06. 59
but let us hence, my sovereign, to provide | a 4.06. 87
drummer, strike up, and let us march away. 4.07. 50
hence with him to the tower, let him not speak. 4.08. 57
the gates are open, let us enter too. 5.01. 62
that glues my lips and will not let me speak. 5.02. 38
this speak i, lords, to let you understand, | if 5.04. 33
let him depart before we need his help. 5.04. 49
bring forth the gallant, let us hear him speak. 5.05. 12
let aesop fable in a winter's night, | his 5.05. 25
let hell make crook'd my mind to answer it. 5.06. 79
come hither, bess, and let me kiss my boy. 5.07. 15
lo, in these windows that let forth thy life | i R3 1.02. 12
cursed the blood that let this blood from hence! 1.02. 16
let her be made | more miserable by the /life of 1.02. 26
my lord, stand back, and let the coffin pass. 1.02. 38
let me have | some patient leisure to excuse 1.02. 81
let him thank me that holp to send him thither; 1.02.107
and let the soul forth that adoreth thee, | i 1.02.176
let me put in your minds, if you forget, | what 1.03.130
marr'd, | that will i make before i let thee go. 1.03.165
o, let them keep it till thy sins be ripe, | and 1.03.218
o, let me make the period to my curse! 1.03.237
and would not let it forth | to find the empty, 1.04. 38
let him see our commission, and talk no more. 1.04. 89 P
so i am — to let him live. 1.04.114 P
'tis no matter, let it go. 1.04.131 P
love lord hastings, let him kiss your hand, 2.01. 21
let him be crown'd, in him your comfort lives. 2.02. 98
for god sake let not us two stay at home; 2.02.147
i hope he is, but yet let mothers doubt. 2.04. 22
how, my young york? i prithee let me hear it. 2.04. 26
or let me die, to look on /death no more! 2.04. 65
well, let them rest. 3.01.157
to–morrow are let blood at pomfret castle, | and 3.01.183
come, let us sup betimes, that afterwards | we 3.01.199
sir richard ratcliffe, let me tell thee this: 3.03. 2
come, grey, come, vaughan, let us here embrace. 3.03. 25
come, let us to our holy work again. 3.07.246
let me but meet you, ladies, /an hour hence, 4.01. 28
anointed let me be with deadly venom, | and die 4.01. 61
and, when thou wed'st, let sorrow haunt thy bed; 4.01. 73
still live they, and for ever let them last! 4.02. 7
let me have open means to come to them, | and 4.02. 76
well, let that rest. dorset is fled to richmond. 4.02. 85
o, let me think on hastings, and be gone | to 4.02.121
and let my griefs frown on the upper hand. 4.04. 37
thy womb let loose to chase us to our graves. 4.04. 54
orators of miseries, | let them have scope! 4.04.130
let not the heavens hear these tell–tale women 4.04.150
o, let me speak! 4.04.160
let me march on and not offend you, madam. 4.04.179
o, let her live! 4.04.206
there let him sink, and be the seas on him! 4.04.463
will not king richard let me speak with him? 5.01. 1
let us survey the vantage of the ground. 5.03. 15
let us consult upon to–morrow's business. 5.03. 45
soul | ere i let fall the windows of mine eyes: 5.03.116
let me sit heavy on thy soul to–morrow! 5.03.118
let me sit heavy in thy soul to–morrow, | i that 5.03.131
let me sit heavy in thy soul to–morrow, | rivers 5.03.139
think upon grey, and let thy soul despair! 5.03.141
and with guilty fear | let fall thy lance. 5.03.143
let us be lead within thy bosom, richard, | and 5.03.147
let not our babbling dreams affright our souls; 5.03.308
march on, join bravely, let us to it pell–mell; 5.03.312
if we be conquered, let men conquer us, | and 5.03.332
after the battle let george stanley die. 5.03.346
division, | o, now let richmond and elizabeth, 5.05. 29
and let their heirs (god, if thy will be so) 5.05. 32
let them not live to taste this land's increase 5.05. 38
may (if they think it well) let fall a tear; H8 pr 6
him — let some graver eye | pierce into that — 1.01. 67
and let your reason with your choler question 1.01.130
they were ratified | as he cried, "thus let be!" 1.01.171
let the king know | (as soon he shall by me) 1.01.190
let be call'd before us | that gentleman of 1.02. 4
doing, let me say | 'tis but the fate of place, 1.02. 74
let there be letters writ to every shire, | of 1.02.103
let it be nois'd | that through our intercession 1.02.105
let him on. | go forward. 1.02.176
if none, | let him not seek't of us. 1.02.213
never so ridiculous | (nay, let 'em be unmanly), 1.03. 4
for my little cure, | let me alone. 1.04. 34
let me have such a bowl may hold my thanks, 1.04. 39
let me see then, | by all your good leaves, 1.04. 84
let it go round. 1.04. 97
let the music knock it. 1.04.108
and if i have a conscience, let it sink me, 2.01. 60
yet let 'em look they glory not in mischief, 2.01. 66
nay, sir nicholas, | let it alone; 2.01.101
let me have it; | i do not talk much. 2.01.145
well, let him have them: 2.02. 10
from rome is read, | let silence be commanded. 2.04. 2
and let the foul'st contempt | shut door upon me 2.04. 42
let him in nought be trusted | for speaking 2.04.136
let me have time and counsel for my cause. 3.01. 79
have i liv'd thus long (let me speak myself, 3.01.125
now god incense him, | and let him cry "ha!" 3.02. 62
let his grace go forward, | and dare us with his 3.02.281
his faults lie open to the laws, let them, | not 3.02.334
not to let | thy hopeful service perish too. 3.02.418
let all the ends thou aim'st at be thy country's 3.02.447
as, let 'em have their rights, they are ever 4.01. 9
but this fellow | let me ne'er see again. 4.02.108
a right good husband (let him be a noble), | and 4.02.146
i will, | or let me lose the fashion of a man! 4.02.159
dead, good wench, | let me be us'd with honor; 4.02.168
and, let me tell you, it will ne'er be well — 5.01. 29
let 'em alone, and draw the curtain close; 5.02. 34
let him come in. 5.02. 42
let some o' th' guard be ready there. 5.02.130
now let me see the proudest | he, that dares 5.02.165
was it discretion, lords, to let this man, 5.02.172
like your grace | to let my tongue excuse all. 5.02.184
and let heaven | witness how dear i hold this 5.02.206
let me ne'er hope to see a chine again, | and 5.03. 26
to draw mine honor in, and let 'em win the work. 5.03. 58 P
there's a trim rabble let in. 5.03. 71
find a way out | to let the troop pass fairly; 5.03. 85
let me speak, sir, | for heaven now bids me; 5.04. 14
and the words i utter | let none think flattery, 5.04. 16
let him to field, troilus, alas, hath none. TRO 1.01. 5
i'll not meddle in it, let her be as she is; 1.01. 66 P
stay behind her father, let her to the greeks; 1.01. 81 P
let it be call'd the wild and wand'ring flood, 1.01.102
let paris bleed, 'tis but a scar to scorn; 1.01.111
let them take heed of troilus; 1.02. 57 P
so let it now, for it has been a great while 1.02.168 P
but let the ruffian boreas once enrage | the 1.03. 38
his experienc'd tongue, yet let it please both, 1.03. 68
let this be granted, and achilles' horse | makes 1.03.211
and every greek of mettle, let him know, | what 1.03.258
fair lord aeneas, let me touch your hand; 1.03.304
let us, like merchants, first show foul wares, 1.03.358
and by device let blockish ajax draw | the sort 1.03.374
let helen go; 2.02. 17
let us pay betimes | a moi'ty of that mass of 2.02.106
troy burns, or else let helen go. 2.02.112
let thy blood be thy direction till thy death; 2.03. 30 P
let it be known to him that we are here. 2.03. 78
let him be told so, lest perchance he think | we 2.03. 81
let him show us a cause. 2.03. 88 P
but let him, like an engine | not portable, lie 2.03.134
let ajax go to him. 2.03.178
o agamemnon, let it not be so! 2.03.182
let me go to him. 2.03.206
to fight, | let mars divide eternity in twain, 2.03.245
let achilles sleep: 2.03.265
let thy song be love. 3.01.110 P
let us to priam's hall | to greet the warriors. 3.01.148
o, let my lady apprehend no fear. 3.02. 74 P
let me go and try. 3.02.147
are grated | to dusty nothing, yet let memory, 3.02.189
son, | yea, let them say, to stick the heart of 3.02.195
let all pitiful goers–between be call'd to the 3.02.200 P
let all constant men be troiluses, all false 3.02.202 P
let him be sent, great princes, | and he shall 3.03. 27
let diomedes bear him, | and bring us cressid 3.03. 30
let not virtue seek | remuneration for the thing 3.03.169
his presence, let patroclus make demands to me; 3.03.271 P
let me bear another to his horse, for that's the 3.03.306 P
jove, let aeneas live, | if to my sword his fate 4.01. 26
but in mine emulous honor let him die, | with 4.01. 29
let her say what. 4.02. 27 P
would he not, a naughty man, let it sleep? 4.02. 33 P
let me embrace too. 4.04. 14 P
let us cast away nothing, for we may live to 4.04. 21 P
come kiss, and let us part. 4.04. 98
let me be privileg'd by my place and message, 4.04.130
stretch thy chest, and let thy eyes spout blood; 4.05. 10
i am not warm yet, let us fight again. 4.05.118
let me embrace thee, ajax. 4.05.135
let me confirm my princely brother's greeting: 4.05.174
o, let an old man embrace thee, | and, worthy 4.05.199
let me embrace thee, good old chronicle, | that 4.05.202
stand fair, i pray thee, let me look on thee. 4.05.235
let these threats alone | till accident or 4.05.261
i pray you let us see you in the field; 4.05.266
/loud /the /taborins, let the trumpets blow, 4.05.275
patroclus, let us feast him to the height. 5.01. 3
and let your mind be coupled with your words. 5.02. 15
you are moved, prince, let us depart, i pray, 5.02. 36
let it not be believ'd for womanhood! 5.02.129
let all untruths stand by thy stained name, 5.02.179
let grow thy sinews till their knots be strong, 5.03. 33
let me not shame respect, but give me leave | to 5.03. 73
let me read. 5.03.100
if it be so, yet bragless let it be, | great 5.09. 5
let one be sent | to pray achilles see us at our 5.09. 7
i say, at once, let your brief plagues be mercy, 5.10. 8
let him that will a scritch–owl aye be call'd 5.10. 16
plains, | let titan rise as early as he dare, 5.10. 25
let me see: 5.10. 40 P
let us kill him, and we'll have corn at our own COR 1.01. 10 P
let it be done. 1.01. 12 P
let us revenge this with our pikes, ere we 1.01. 22 P
lay aside their ruth | and let me use my sword, 1.01.198
nay, let them follow. 1.01.248
to your bands, | let us alone to guard corioles. 1.02. 27
was pleas'd to let him seek danger where he was 1.03. 12 P
and when he caught it, he let it go again, and 1.03. 61 P
let her alone, lady; 1.03.104 P
let me clip ye | in arms as sound as when i 1.06. 29
in the leash, | to let him slip at will. 1.06. 39
let him alone, | he did inform the truth. 1.06. 41
let him alone, or so many so minded, | wave thus 1.06. 73
so, let the ports be guarded; 1.07. 1
let the first budger die the other's slave, 1.08. 5
let courts and cities be | made all of 1.09. 43
let him be made an overture for th' wars! 1.09. 46
this last, | before and in corioles, let me say, 2.02.102
he's right noble. | let him be call'd for. 2.02.130
i do beseech you, | let me o'erleap that custom; 2.02.136
kindly, sir, i pray let me ha't. 2.03. 76 P
let the high office and the honor go | to one 2.03.122
therefore let him be consul. 2.03.134 P
let them assemble; 2.03.217
let them go on; 2.03.255

let me deserve so ill as you, and make me | your 3.01. 51
meiny, let them | regard me as i do not flatter, 3.01. 66
'twere well | we let the people know't. 3.01. 83
if you are not, | let them have cushions by you. 3.01.101
let deeds express | what's like to be their 3.01.132
let them not lick | the sweet which is their 3.01.156
let what is meet be said it must be meet, | and 3.01.169
the aediles ho! let him be apprehended. 3.01.172
or let us stand to our authority, | or let us 3.01.207
us stand to our authority, | or let us lose it. 3.01.208
let me desire your company. 3.01.333
let them pull all about mine ears, present me 3.02. 1
let go. 3.02. 18
let them hang! 3.02. 23
let | thy mother rather feel thy pride than fear 3.02.125
pray you let us go. 3.02.142
let them accuse me by invention; 3.02.143
death, for fine, or banishment, then let them, 3.03. 15
let them not cease, but with a din confus'd 3.03. 20
let them pronounce the steep tarpeian death, 3.03. 88
let him away! 3.03.106
let me speak. 3.03.109
let every feeble rumor shake your hearts! 3.03.125
let a guard | attend us through the city. 3.03.140
let us seem humbler after it is done | than when 4.02. 4
well, let us go together. 4.03. 52 P
let me but stand, i will not hurt your hearth. 4.05. 24 P
let me twine | mine arms about that body, where 4.05.106
let me commend thee first to those that shall 4.05.144
let me have war, say i, it exceeds peace as far 4.05.221 P
lest i let forth your half–pint of blood. 5.02. 56 P
let your general do his worst. 5.02.105 P
let it be virtuous to be obstinate. 5.03. 26
let the volsces | plough rome and harrow italy, 5.03. 33
then let the pibbles on the hungry beach 5.03. 58
then let the mutinous winds | strike the proud 5.03. 59
let us shame him with our knees. 5.03.169
come, let us go. 5.03.177
but let it come. 5.03.189
nay, let him choose | out of my files, his 5.06. 32
with what he would say, let him feel your sword, 5.06. 55
let him die for't. 5.06.119
let him be regarded | as the most noble corse 5.06.142
TIT rome, | then let my father's honors live in me, 1.01. 7
but let desert in pure election shine, | and, 1.01. 16
let us entreat by honor of his name, | whom 1.01. 39
open the gates and let me in. 1.01. 62
these that survive let rome reward with love; 1.01. 82
let it be so, and let andronicus | make this his 1.01.148
be so, and let andronicus | make this his latest 1.01.148
and let not discontent | daunt all your hopes. 1.01.267
romans, let us go; 1.01.273
but let us give him burial as becomes, | give 1.01.347
he is not with himself, let us withdraw. 1.01.368
let not young mutius then, that was thy joy, 1.01.382
but let the laws of rome determine all, | mean 1.01.407
and then let me alone, | i'll find a day to 1.01.449
and make them know what 'tis to let a queen 1.01.454
and let it be mine honor, good my lord, | that i 1.01.466
uncouple here and let us make a bay, | and wake 2.02. 3
sons, let it be your charge, as it is ours, | to 2.02. 7
come on then, horse and chariots let us have, 2.02. 18
let him that thinks of me so abjectly | know 2.03. 4
under their sweet shade, aaron, let us sit, 2.03. 16
let us sit down and mark their yellowing noise; 2.03. 20
i pray you let us hence, | and let her joy her 2.03. 82
hence, | and let her joy her raven–colored love; 2.03. 83
let not this wasp outlive, us both to sting. 2.03.132
madam, let it be your glory | to see her tears, 2.03.139
o, let me teach thee! 2.03.158
what beg'st thou then? fond woman, let me go. 2.03.172
no, let them satisfice their lust on thee. 2.03.180
ne'er let my heart know merry cheer indeed 2.03.188
and let my spleenful sons this trull deflow'r. 2.03.191
there let them bide until we have devis'd | some 2.03.284
i did, my lord, yet let me be their bail, | for 2.03.295
let them not speak a word, the guilt is plain, 2.03.301
and if thy stumps will let thee play the scribe. 2.04. 4
come let us go, and make thy father blind, | for 2.04. 52
let my tears staunch the earth's dry appetite, 3.01. 14
and let me say (that never wept before) | my 3.01. 25
ah, lucius, for thy brothers let me plead. 3.01. 30
will it consume me? let me see it then. 3.01. 62
gentle lavinia, let me kiss thy lips, | or make 3.01.120
let us that have our tongues | plot some device 3.01.133
let marcus, lucius, or thyself, old titus, | or 3.01.152
let it serve | to ransom my two nephews from 3.01.171
let me redeem my brothers both from death. 3.01.180
now let me show a brother's love to thee. 3.01.182
more hath it merited, that let it have. 3.01.196
let fools do good, and fair men call for grace, 3.01.204
but yet let reason govern thy lament. 3.01.218
now let hot aetna cool in sicily, | and be my 3.01.241
that ever death should let life bear his name, 3.01.248
come let me see what task i have to do. 3.01.275
you are a young huntsman, marcus, let alone; 4.01.101
but let her rest in her unrest a while. 4.02. 31
come let us go and pray to all the gods | for 4.02. 46
then let no man but i | do execution on my flesh 4.02. 83
then sit we down and let us all consult. 4.02.132
and let the emperor dandle him for his own. 4.02.161
then let the ladies tattle what they please. 4.02.168
sir boy, let me see your archery. 4.03. 2
and let him deliver the pigeons to the emperor 4.03. 96 P
i warrant you, sir, let me alone. 4.03.114 P
come let me see it. 4.03.115
come, marcus, let us go. publius, follow me. 4.03.121
any scath, | let him make treble satisfaction. 5.01. 8
well, let my deeds be witness of my worth: 5.01.103
"let not your sorrow die, though i am dead." 5.01.140
sirs, stop his mouth, and let him speak no more. 5.01.151
let him come near. 5.01.154
let the emperor give his pledges | unto my 5.01.163
this do thou for my love, and so let him, | as 5.02.129
nay, nay, let rape and murder stay with me, | or 5.02.134
close their mouths, let them not speak a word. 5.02.164
stop their mouths, let them not speak to me, 5.02.167
but let them hear what fearful words i utter. 5.02.168
what would you say if i should let you speak? 5.02.178
let me go grind their bones to powder small, 5.02.198
and in that paste let their vile heads be bak'd. 5.02.200
let him receive no sust'nance; 5.03. 6
o, let me teach you how to knit again | this 5.03. 70
let rome herself be bane unto herself, | and she 5.03. 73
rome's young captain, let him tell the tale, 5.03. 94
there let him stand and rave and cry for food. 5.03.180
and, being dead, let birds on her take pity. 5.03.200
ROM let us take the law of our sides, let them begin 1.01. 38 P
us take the law of our sides, let them begin. 1.01. 38 P
as i pass by, and let them take it as they list. 1.01. 40 P
thou villain capulet! — hold me not, let me go. 1.01. 79
let two more summers wither in their pride, 1.02. 10
but in that crystal scales let there be weigh'd 1.02. 96
but let them measure us by what they will, 1.04. 9
let wantons light of heart | tickle the 1.04. 35
let the porter let in susan grindstone and nell. 1.05. 8 P
let the porter let in susan grindstone and nell. 1.05. 9 P
content thee, gentle coz, let him alone, | 'a 1.05. 65
o then, dear saint, let lips do what hands do, 1.05.103
and but thou love me, let them find me here; 2.02. 76
let me stand here till thou remember it. 2.02.171
o, let us hence, i stand on sudden haste. 2.03. 93
but first let me tell ye, if ye should lead her 2.04.165 P
let me be satisfied, is't good or bad? 2.05. 37
air, and let rich /music's tongue | unfold the 2.06. 27
men's eyes were made to look, and let them gaze; 3.01. 54
this is the truth, or let benvolio die. 3.01.175
let romeo hence in haste, | else, when he is 3.01.194
let me dispute with thee of thy estate. 3.03. 63
let me come in, and you shall know my errant. 3.03. 79
a' thursday let it be — a' thursday, tell her, 3.04. 20
let me be ta'en, let me be put to death, | i am 3.05. 17
let me be ta'en, let me be put to death, | i am 3.05. 17
then, window, let day in, and let life out. 3.05. 41
then, window, let day in, and let life out. 3.05. 41
yet let me weep for such a feeling loss. 3.05. 74
let not the nurse lie with thee in thy chamber. 4.01. 92
let me see the county; 4.02. 29
let me alone, | i'll play the huswife for this 4.02. 42
so please you, let me now be left alone, | and 4.03. 9
and let the nurse this night sit up with you, 4.03. 10
ay, let the county take you in your bed, | he'll 4.05. 10
hah, let me see her. 4.05. 25
ties up my tongue and will not let me speak. 4.05. 32
let me have | a dram of poison, such 5.01. 59
seal'd up the doors and would not let us forth, 5.02. 11
think upon these gone, | let them affright thee. 5.03. 61
let me peruse this face. 5.03. 74
there rust, and let me die. 5.03.170
and let mischance be slave to patience. 5.03.221
let my old life | be sacrific'd some hour before 5.03.267
TIM on their knees and /hands, let him /slip down, 1.01. 87
pray you let us in. 1.01.255
go, | let him have a table by himself, | for he 1.02. 30
let me stay at thine apperil, timon. 1.02. 33
prithee let my meat make thee silent. 1.02. 37 P
my lord, in heart; and let the health go round. 1.02. 53
let it flow this way, my good lord. 1.02. 54
i pray let them be admitted. 1.02.121 P
welcome all, let 'em have kind admittance. 1.02.128
let the presents | be worthily entertain'd. 1.02.184
i'll hunt with him, and let them be receiv'd, 1.02.190
let all my land be sold. 2.02.145
let the request be fifty talents. 2.02.192 P
let molten coin be thy damnation, | thou disease 3.01. 52
let not that part of nature | which my lord paid 3.01. 61
but wrong to stir me up, | let me pass quietly. 3.04. 54
them all, let in the tide | of knaves once more; 3.04.116
and let the foes quietly cut their throats 3.05. 44
why, let the war receive't in valiant gore, 3.05. 83
and let out | their coin upon large interest — 3.05.106
o, sir, let it not trouble you. 3.06. 38 P
let it not cumber your better remembrance. 3.06. 46 P
to let the meat cool ere we can agree upon the 3.06. 67 P
let no assembly of twenty be without a score of 3.06. 76 P
women at the table, let a dozen of them be — as 3.06. 78 P
let me look back upon thee. 4.01. 1
let me be recorded by the righteous gods, | i am 4.02. 4
let each take some; 4.02. 27
let not thy sword skip one. 4.03.111
let not the virgin's cheek | make soft thy 4.03.115
up, | let your close fire predominate his smoke, 4.03.143
and let the unscarr'd braggarts of the war 4.03.161
do you damn others, and let this damn you, | and 4.03.165
womb, | let it no more bring out ingrateful man! 4.03.188
and let his very breath whom thou'lt observe 4.03.212
let us make the assay upon him. 4.03.403 P
let us first see peace in athens. 4.03.456 P
let me behold thy face. 4.03.493
but let the famish'd flesh slide from the bone 4.03.528
let prisons swallow 'em, | debts wither 'em to 4.03.530
o, let me stay, | and comfort you, my master. 4.03.533
ne'er see thou man, and let me ne'er see thee. 4.03.536
let it go naked, men may see't the better. 5.01. 67
countrymen, | let alcibiades know this of timon, 5.01.170
then let him know, and tell him timon speaks it, 5.01.175
and let him take't at worst — for their knives 5.01.178
to stop affliction, let him take his haste, 5.01.210
come, | and let my grave–stone be your oracle. 5.01.219
lips, let four words go by and language end! 5.01.220
let us return, | and strain what other means is 5.01.226
hazard of the spotted die | let die the spotted. 5.04. 35
let our drums strike. 5.04. 85
JC let no images | be hung with caesar's trophies. 1.01. 68
set him before me, let me see his face. 1.02. 20
he is a dreamer, let us leave him. pass. 1.02. 24
let me not hinder, cassius, your desires; 1.02. 30
but let not therefore my good friends be griev'd 1.02. 43
for let the gods so speed me as i love | the 1.02. 88
let me have men about me that are fat, 1.02.192
and after this let caesar seat him sure, | for 1.02.321
do so conjointly meet, let not men say, | "these 1.03. 29
let it be who it is; 1.03. 80
let us go, | for it is after midnight, and ere 1.03.162
let 'em enter. 2.01. 76
and let us swear our resolution. 2.01.113
so let high–sighted tyranny range on, | till 2.01.118
let us not leave him out. 2.01.143
o, let us have him, for his silver hairs | will 2.01.144
let us not break with him, | for he will never 2.01.150
prevent, | let antony and caesar fall together. 2.01.161
and let our hearts, as subtle masters do, | stir 2.01.175
let him not die, | for he will live, and laugh 2.01.190
let me work; 2.01.209
let not our looks put on our purposes, | but 2.01.225
it will not let you eat, nor talk, nor sleep; 2.01.252
let me, upon my knee, prevail in this. 2.02. 54
most mighty caesar, let me know some cause, 2.02. 69
because i love you, i will let you know. 2.02. 74
let him go | and presently prefer his suit to 3.01. 27
let me a little show it, even in this — | that 3.01. 71
do so, and let no man abide this deed, | but we 3.01. 94
and let us bathe our hands in caesar's blood 3.01.106
who else must be let blood, who else is rank; 3.01.152
let each man render me his bloody hand. 3.01.184
cry "havoc," and let slip the dogs of war, 3.01.273
we will be satisfied! let us be satisfied! 3.02. 1
that will hear me speak, let 'em stay here; 3.02. 5
let him be caesar. 3.02. 51
good countrymen, let me depart alone, | and, for 3.02. 55
stay ho, and let us hear mark antony. 3.02. 62
let him go up into the public chair, | we'll 3.02. 63
peace, let us hear what antony can say. 3.02. 71
peace ho, let us hear him. 3.02. 72
so let it be with caesar. 3.02. 77
let but the commons hear this testament — 3.02.130
and let me show you him that made the will. 3.02.159
let not a traitor live! 3.02.205 P
let me not stir you up | to such a sudden flood 3.02.210
now let it work. 3.02.260
therefore let our alliance be combin'd, | our 4.01. 43
and let us presently go sit in council, | how 4.01. 45
let us do so; 4.01. 48
let me be resolv'd. 4.02. 14
nothing but love from us) | let us not wrangle. 4.02. 45
and let no man | come to our tent till we have 4.02. 50
let /lucilius and titinius guard our door. 4.02. 52
let me tell you, cassius, you yourself | are 4.03. 9
let it appear so; 4.03. 52
let me go in to see the generals. 4.03.124
let it not, brutus. 4.03.236
let me see, let me see; 4.03.273
let me see, let me see; 4.03.273
let them set on at once; 5.02. 3
ride, ride, messala, let them all come down. 5.02. 6
and come, young cato, let us to the field. 5.03.107
according to his virtue let us use him, | with 5.05. 76
MAC let us toward the king. 1.03.152
let us speak | our free hearts each to other. 1.03.154
let me infold thee | and hold thee to my heart. 1.04. 31
let not light see my black and deep desires; 1.04. 51
yet let that be | which the eye fears, when it 1.04. 52
come, let me clutch thee. 2.01. 34
i had thought to have let in some of all 2.03. 18 P
let us meet | and question this most bloody 2.03.127
and let us not be dainty of leave–taking, | but 2.03.144
let your highness | command upon me, to the 3.01. 15
let every man be master of his time | till seven 3.01. 40
in your nature | that you can let this go? 3.01. 87
but let the frame of things disjoint, both the 3.02. 16
let your remembrance apply to banquo, | present 3.02. 30
let it come down. 3.03. 16
let the earth hide thee! 3.04. 92
and let them fight | against the churches; 4.01. 52
call 'em; let me see 'em. 4.01. 63
let me know. 4.01.105
let this pernicious hour | stand aye accursed in 4.01.133
let us seek out some desolate shade, and there 4.03. 1
let us rather | hold fast the mortal sword, and 4.03. 2
you, | let not my jealousies be your dishonors, 4.03. 29
keep it not from me, quickly let me have it. 4.03.200
let not your ears despise my tongue for ever, 4.03.201
of your sword, let grief | convert to anger; 4.03.228
bring me no more reports, let them fly all. 5.03. 1
let every soldier hew him down a bough, | and 5.04. 4
let our just censures | attend the true event, 5.04. 14
here let them lie | till famine and the ague eat 5.05. 3
let me endure your wrath, if't be not so. 5.05. 35
let us be beaten, if we cannot fight. 5.06. 8
let me find him, fortune! 5.07. 22
let fall thy blade on vulnerable crests, | i 5.08. 11
and let the angel whom thou still hast serv'd 5.08. 14
HAM and will not let belief take hold of him 1.01. 24
while, | and let us once again assail your ears, 1.01. 31
down, | and let us hear barnardo speak of this. 1.01. 34
let us impart what we have seen to–night | unto 1.01.169
farewell, and let your haste commend your duty. 1.02. 39
and let thine eye look like a friend on denmark. 1.02. 69
as of a father, for, let the world take note, 1.02.108
let not thy mother lose her prayers, hamlet, | i 1.02.118
yet, within a month — | let me not think on't! 1.02.146
for god's love let me hear! 1.02.195
writ down in our duty | to let you know of it. 1.02.223
let it be tenable in your silence still, | and 1.02.247
do not sleep, | but let me hear from you. 1.03. 4
let me not burst in ignorance, but tell | why 1.04. 46
i scent the morning air, | brief let me be. 1.05. 59
let not the royal bed of denmark be | a couch 1.05. 82
nor let thy soul contrive | against thy mother 1.05. 85
it is an honest ghost, that let me tell you. 1.05.138
let us go in together, | and still your fingers 1.05.186
and let him ply his music. 2.01. 70
but let that go. 2.02. 95
mad let us grant him then, and now remains 2.02.100
thereon, | let me be no assistant for a state, 2.02.166
let her not walk i' th' sun. 2.02.184 P
but let me conjure you, by the rights of our 2.02.283 P
let me comply with you in this garb, /lest /my 2.02.372 P
begin at this line — let me see, let me see: 2.02.449 P
begin at this line — let me see, let me see: 2.02.449 P
do you hear, let them be well us'd, for they are 2.02.523 P
let the doors be shut upon him, that he may play 3.01.131 P
let his queen–mother all alone entreat him | to 3.01.182
let her be round with him, | and i'll be plac'd 3.01.183

but let your own discretion be your tutor. 3.02. 16 P
and let those that play your clowns speak no 3.02. 38 P
no, let the candied tongue lick absurd pomp, 3.02. 60
nay then let the dev'l wear black, for i'll have 3.02.129 P
in second husband let me be accurs'd! 3.02.179
let the gall'd jade winch, our withers are 3.02.242 P
why, let the strooken deer go weep, | the hart 3.02.271
let me see one. 3.02.345 P
let not ever | the soul of nero enter this firm 3.02.393
firm bosom, | let me be cruel, not unnatural; 3.02.395
it safe with us | to let his madness range. 3.03. 2
and let me wring your heart, for so i shall, 3.04. 35
to flaming youth let virtue be as wax | and melt 3.04. 84
let the bloat king tempt you again to bed, 3.04.182
and let him, for a pair of reechy kisses, | or 3.04.184
'twere good you let him know, | for who, that's 3.04.188
let the birds fly, and like the famous ape, | to 3.04.194
let it work, | for 'tis the sport to have the 3.04.205
let it feed | even on the pith of life. 4.01. 22
and let them know both what we mean to do | and 4.01. 39
our duty in his eye, | and let him know so. 4.04. 7
and let all sleep, while to my shame i see | the 4.04. 59
let her come in. 4.05. 16
let in the maid, that out a maid | never 4.05. 54
let them guard the door. 4.05. 98
no, let 's come in. 4.05.114
let him go, gertrude, do not fear our person: 4.05.123
let him go, gertrude. 4.05.127
let him demand his fill. 4.05.130
let come what comes, only i'll be reveng'd 4.05.136
let this be so. 4.05.213
where th' offense is, let the great axe fall. 4.05.219
let them come in. 4.06. 4 P
let him bless thee too. 4.06. 8 P
your name be horatio, as i am let to know it is. 4.06. 12 P
let the king have the letters i have sent, and 4.06. 22 P
that we can let our beard be shook with danger 4.07. 32
but let him come, | it warms the very sickness 4.07. 54
soft, let me see. 4.07.154
her custom holds, | let shame say what it will; 4.07.188
and tell her, let her paint an inch thick, to 5.01.193 P
dangerous, | which let thy wisdom fear. 5.01.263
let them throw | millions of acres on us, till 5.01.280
let hercules himself do what he may, | the cat 5.01.291
kind of fighting | that would not let me sleep. 5.02. 5
let us know | our indiscretion sometime serves 5.02. 7
let a beast be lord of beasts, and his crib 5.02. 85 P
let the foils be brought, the gentleman willing, 5.02.175 P
knows what is't to leave betimes, let be. 5.02.224 P
let my disclaiming from a purpos'd evil | free 5.02.241
this is too heavy; let me see another. 5.02.264
let all the battlements their ord'nance fire. 5.02.270
cups, | and let the kettle to the trumpet speak, 5.02.275
come, let me wipe thy face. 5.02.294
ho, let the door be lock'd! 5.02.311
o, i could tell you — | but let it be. 5.02.338
let go! 5.02.343
and let me speak to /th' yet unknowing world 5.02.379
let us haste to hear it, | and call the noblest 5.02.386
but let this same be presently perform'd | even 5.02.393
let four captains | bear hamlet, like a soldier, 5.02.395
let it be so: LR 1.01.108
let pride, which she calls plainness, marry her. 1.01.129
let it fall rather, though the fork invade | the 1.01.144
and let me still remain | the true blank of 1.01.158
france, let her be thine, for we | have no such 1.01.262
let your study | be to content your lord, who 1.01.276
pray you let us /hit together; 1.01.303 P
let me, if not by birth, have lands by wit: 1.02.183
if he distaste it, let him to my sister, | whose 1.03. 14
and let his knights have colder looks among you; 1.03. 22
let me not stay a jot for dinner, go get it 1.04. 8 P
let me hire him too, here's my coxcomb. 1.04. 95 P
this, let him be whipt that first finds it so. 1.04.164 P
that let thy folly in | and thy dear judgment 1.04.271
let it stamp wrinkles in her brow of youth, 1.04.284
but let his disposition have that scope | as 1.04.292
let it be so: 1.04.305
'tis politic and safe to let him keep | at point 1.04.323
let me still take away the harms i fear, | not 1.04.329
o, let me not be mad, not mad, sweet heaven! 1.05. 46
let him fly far. 2.01. 56
let me beseech your grace not to do so. 2.02.140
let go thy hold when a great wheel runs down a 2.04. 71 P
one that goes upward, let him draw thee after. 2.04. 74 P
the fool will stay, | and let the wise man fly. 2.04. 83
let shame come when it will, i do not call it. 2.04.226
and let not women's weapons, water–drops, 2.04.277
let us withdraw, 'twill be a storm. 2.04.287
then let fall | your horrible pleasure. 3.02. 18
let the great gods, | that keep this dreadful 3.02. 49
let me alone. 3.04. 3
o, that way madness lies, let me shun that! 3.04. 21
let not the creaking of shoes nor the rustling 3.04. 94 P
let him trot by. 3.04.100 P
and let this tyrannous night take hold upon you, 3.04.151
first let me talk with this philosopher. 3.04.154
let me ask you one word in private. 3.04.160
let him take the fellow. 3.04.177
then let them anatomize regan; 3.06. 76 P
say they are persian, but let them be chang'd. 3.06. 81 P
wherefore to dover? let him answer that. 3.07. 53
at gates, and let him smell | his way to dover. 3.07. 93
let the superfluous and lust–dieted man, | that 4.01. 67
gloucester's eyes being out, | to let him live; 4.05. 10
love thee much — | let me unseal the letter. 4.05. 22
let go my hand. 4.06. 27
bid me farewell, and let me hear thee going. 4.06. 31
away, and let me die. 4.06. 48
let copulation thrive; 4.06.114
o, let me kiss that hand! 4.06.132
let me wipe it first, it smells of mortality. 4.06.133
let me have surgeons, | i am cut to th' brains. 4.06.192
let not my worser spirit tempt me again | to die 4.06.218
now let thy friendly hand | put strength enough 4.06.230
let go his arm. 4.06.234
chill not let go, zir, without vurther /cagion. 4.06.235 P
let go, slave, or thou di'st! 4.06.236
gentleman, go your gait, and let poor voke pass. 4.06.237 P
let us see. 4.06.258
"let our reciprocal vows be rememb'red. 4.06.262 P
and let this kiss | repair those violent harms 4.07. 26
he's scarce awake, let him alone a while. 4.07. 50
let the trumpet sound | for him that brought it. 5.01. 41
when time shall serve, let but the herald cry, 5.01. 48
let her who would be rid of him devise | his 5.01. 64
let the drum strike, and prove my title thine. 5.03. 81
art armed, gloucester, let the trumpet sound. 5.03. 90
let the trumpet sound, | and read out this. 5.03.107
let him appear by the third sound of the trumpet 5.03.113 P
let sorrow split my heart, if ever i | did hate 5.03.178
o, let him pass, he hates him | that would upon 5.03.314
let loose on me the justice of the state | for OTH 1.01.139
let him do his spite; 1.02. 17
and let ourselves again but understand | that, 1.03. 21
and let her speak of me before her father. 1.03.116
but let your sentence | even fall upon my life. 1.03.119
let her witness it. 1.03.170
let me speak like yourself, and lay a sentence, 1.03.199
so let the turk of cyprus us beguile, | we lose 1.03.210
and let me find a charter in your voice | t' 1.03.245
let me go with him. 1.03.259
let her have your voice. 1.03.260
let housewives make a skillet of my helm, | and 1.03.272
let it be so. 1.03.287
i prithee, let thy wife attend on her, | and 1.03.296
let us be conjunctive in our revenge against him 1.03.367 P
let me see now: 1.03.392
let the heavens | give him defense against the 2.01. 44
you men of cyprus, let her have your knees. 2.01. 84
let it not gall your patience, good iago, | that 2.01. 97
no, let me not. 2.01.116
and let the laboring bark climb hills of seas 2.01.187
let us to the castle. 2.01.201
and let thy soul be instructed. 2.01.221 P
prating — let not thy discreet heart think it. 2.01.224 P
your earliest | let me have speech with you. 2.03. 8
who let us not therefore blame. 2.03. 15 P
"and let me the canakin clink, clink; 2.03. 69
and let me the canakin clink. 2.03. 70
why then let a soldier drink." 2.03. 73
let me go, sir, or i'll knock you o'er the 2.03.153 P
no name to be known by, let us call thee devil! 2.03.282 P
the time, but let it not | exceed three days. 3.03. 62
let him come when he will; 3.03. 75
and wisdom, | to let you know my thoughts. 3.03.154
in venice they do let /god see the pranks | they 3.03.202
if more thou dost perceive, let me know more; 3.03.239
let me be thought too busy in my fears | (as 3.03.253
and let her down the wind | to prey at fortune. 3.03.262
let me but bind it hard, within this hour | it 3.03.286
let it alone. 3.03.288
she let it drop by negligence, | and, to th' 3.03.311
lodging lose this napkin, | and let him find it. 3.03.322
let him not know't, and he's not robb'd at all. 3.03.343
let us be wary, let us hide our loves"; 3.03.420
let us be wary, let us hide our loves"; 3.03.420
let him command, | and to obey shall be in me 3.03.467
within these three days let me hear thee say 3.03.472
but let her live. 3.03.475
fetch't, let me see't. 3.04. 85
pray you let cassio be receiv'd again. 3.04. 88
let that suffice you. 3.04.131
for let our finger ache, and it endues | our 3.04.146
no, let me know, | and knowing what i am, i know 4.01. 72
let the devil and his dam haunt you! 4.01.148 P
ay, let her rot, and perish, and be damn'd 4.01.181 P
and for cassio, let me be his undertaker. 4.01.211 P
let heaven requite it with the serpent's curse! 4.02. 16
let me see your eyes; | look in my face. 4.02. 25
let nobody blame him, his scorn i approve" — 4.03. 52
let husbands know | their wives have sense like 4.03. 93
then let them use us well; 4.03.102
else let them know, | the ills we do, their ills 4.03.102
let me not name it to you, you chaste stars, 5.02. 2
let him confess a truth. 5.02. 68
kill me to–morrow, let me live to–night! 5.02. 80
soft, by and by, let me the curtains draw. 5.02.104
good gentlemen, let me have leave to speak. 5.02.195
let heaven and men and devils, let them all, 5.02.221
let heaven and men and devils, let them all, 5.02.221
let him not pass, | but kill him rather. 5.02.241
let it go all. 5.02.246
the object poisons sight, | let it be hid. 5.02.365
let rome in tiber melt, and the wide arch | of ANT 1.01. 33
let me be married to three kings in a forenoon, 1.02. 26 P
let me have a child at fifty, to whom herod of 1.02. 28 P
o, let him marry a woman that cannot go, sweet 1.02. 63 P
and let her die too, and give him a worse! 1.02. 65 P
and let worse follow worse, till the worst of 1.02. 65 P
let him appear. 1.02.115
under a compelling occasion, let women die. 1.02.137 P
let our officers | have notice what we purpose. 1.02.176
let her not say 'tis i that keep you here, | i 1.03. 22
but let it be; 1.03. 72
and let it look | like perfect honor. 1.03. 79
let us go. 1.03.101
let his shames quickly | drive him to rome. 1.04. 72
shall beseech you, sir, | to let me be partaker. 1.04. 83
let witchcraft join with beauty, lust with both, 2.01. 22
but let us rear | the higher our opinion, that 2.01. 35
let antony look over caesar's head | and speak 2.02. 5
great, and let not | a leaner action rend us. 2.02. 18
let this fellow | be nothing of our strife; 2.02. 79
no, lepidus, let him speak. 2.02. 84
let me hear agrippa further speak. 2.02.123
let me have thy hand | further this act of grace 2.02.145
let her live | to join our kingdoms and our 2.02.150
let us, lepidus, | not lack your company. 2.02.168
let us go. 2.02.242
let it alone, let's to billards. come, charmian. 2.05. 3
but let ill tidings tell | themselves when they 2.05. 87
let him not leave out | the color of her hair. 2.05.113
let him for ever go — let him not, charmian — 2.05.115
let him for ever go — let him not, charmian — 2.05.115
let us know | if 'twill tie up thy discontented 2.06. 5
let me have your hand. 2.06. 48
let me shake thy hand, | i never hated thee. 2.06. 73
let me cut the cable, | and, when we are put off 2.07. 71
let me request you /off, our graver business 2.07.120
let neptune hear we bid a loud farewell | to 2.07.132
let not the piece of virtue which is set 3.02. 28
look, here i have you, thus i let you go, | and 3.02. 63
let all the number of the stars give light | to 3.02. 65
let your best love draw to that point which 3.04. 21
would not let him partake in the glory of the 3.05. 9 P
'twill be naught, | but let it be. 3.05. 23
let rome be thus | inform'd. 3.06. 19
but let determin'd things to destiny | hold 3.06. 84
let th' egyptians | and the phoenicians go 3.07. 63
let /that be left | which leaves itself. 3.11. 19
let me sit down. o juno! 3.11. 28
let him appear that's come from antony. 3.12. 1
to let him breathe between the heavens and earth 3.12. 14
let her know't. 3.13. 16
to let a fellow that will take rewards | and say 3.13.123
let him repent | thou wast not made his daughter 3.13.134
from my cold heart let heaven engender hail, 3.13.159
let the old ruffian know | i have many other 4.01. 4
let our best heads | know that to–morrow the 4.01. 10
ah, let be, let be! 4.04. 6
ah, let be, let be! 4.04. 6
let us score their backs, | and snatch 'em up, 4.07. 12
before, | and let the queen know of our /gests. 4.08. 2
but let the world rank me in register | a 4.09. 21
let us bear him | to th' court of guard; 4.09. 30
let him take thee | and hoist thee up to the 4.12. 33
and let | patient octavia plough thy visage up 4.12. 37
let me lodge lichas on the horns o' th' moon, 4.12. 45
then let it do at once | the thing why thou hast 4.14. 88
let me say, | before i strike this bloody stroke 4.14. 90
let him that loves me strike me dead. 4.14.108
give me some wine, and let me speak a little. 4.15. 42
no, let me speak, and let me rail so high, 4.15. 43
no, let me speak, and let me rail so high, 4.15. 43
but yet let me lament, | with tears as sovereign 5.01. 40
let him alone; 5.01. 71
let me report to him | your sweet dependancy, 5.02. 25
let the world see | his nobleness well acted, 5.02. 44
which your death | will never let come forth. 5.02. 46
and let the water–flies | blow me into abhorring 5.02. 59
this is my treasurer, let him speak, my lord, 5.02.142
good queen, let us entreat you. 5.02.158
let him come in. 5.02.236
nay, let her languish | a drop of blood a day, CYM 1.01.156
let him be so entertain'd amongst you as suits 1.04. 28 P
let us leave here, gentlemen. 1.04. 99 P
came in too suddenly, let it die as it was born, 1.04.121 P
let there be covenants drawn between 's. 1.04.143 P
conditions, let us have articles betwixt us. 1.04.156 P
pray let us follow 'em. 1.04.171 P
and let instructions enter | where folly now 1.05. 47
let me hear no more. 1.06.117
let me my service tender on your lips. 1.06.140
if none will do, let her remain; 2.03. 16 P
rich words to it — and then let her consider. 2.03. 19 P
if not, | let her lie still and dream. 2.03. 65
or let her beauty | look thorough a casement to 2.04. 33
let it be granted you have seen all this (and 2.04. 92
jove — | once more let me behold it. 2.04. 99
let there be no honor | where there is beauty; 2.04.108
son, let your mother end. 3.01. 39
let proof speak. 3.01. 76
service, never | let me be counted serviceable. 3.02. 15
let what is here contain'd relish of love, | of 3.02. 30
let that grieve him: 3.02. 32
who long'st | (o, let me bate!) 3.02. 54
let thine own hands take away her life. 3.04. 27 P
let it be thy first service, go. 3.05.128 P
i'll rob none but myself, and let me die, 4.02. 15
and let the stinking elder, grief, untwine | his 4.02. 59
pray you away, | let me alone with him. 4.02. 70
to let an arrogant piece of flesh threat us, 4.02.127
let ord'nance | come as the gods foresay it; 4.02.145
creek | behind our rock, and let it to the sea, 4.02.152
color | i'ld let a parish of such clotens blood, 4.02.168
those rich–left heirs that let their fathers lie 4.02.226
let us bury him, | and not protract with 4.02.231
and let us, polydore, though now our voices 4.02.235
let us | find out the prettiest daisied plot we 4.02.397
all other doubts, by time let them be clear'd, 4.03. 45
let us from it. 4.04. 1
let me make men know | more valor in me than my 5.01. 29
let us with care perform his great behest. 5.04.122
let thy effects | so follow, to be most unlike 5.04.135
our lives | may be call'd ransom, let it come. 5.05. 80
my boy, a britain born, | let him be ransom'd. 5.05. 85
let his virtue join | with my request, which 5.05. 88
is living, let the time run on | to good or bad. 5.05.128
let me end the story: | i slew him there. 5.05.286
let his arms alone, | they were not born for 5.05.305
and let it be confiscate all, so soon | as i 5.05.323
let them be joyful too, | for they shall taste 5.05.402
let him show | his skill in the construction. 5.05.432
and let our crooked smokes climb to their 5.05.477
let | a roman and a british ensign wave 5.05.479
let your breath cool yourself, telling your PER 1.01.159
let none disturb us. 1.02. 1
but let your cares o'erlook | what shipping and 1.02. 48
that kings should let their ears hear their 1.02. 62
let those cities that of plenty's cup | and her 1.04. 52
let not our ships and number of our men | be 1.04. 86
let it suffice the greatness of your powers | to 2.01. 8
i pray you let me see it. 2.01.120
and on set purpose let his armor rust | until 2.02. 54
so let it pass. 2.03. 35
but if the prince do live, let us salute him, 2.04. 27
a twelvemonth longer let me entreat you | to 2.04. 45
knights, from my daughter this i let you know, 2.05. 2
let me ask you one thing: 2.05. 32
let not conscience, | which is but cold in 4.01. 4
/lone bosom | inflame too nicely, nor let pity, 4.01. 6
let her go! 4.01. 97
let pericles believe his daughter's dead, | and 4.04. 46

household, let me be gelded like a spaniel. 4.06.124 P
yet let me obtain my wish. 5.01. 35
let us beseech you | that for our gold we may 5.01. 55
more | let me entreat to know at large the cause 5.01. 62
come, let us leave her, | and the gods make her 5.01. 78
let me rest. 5.01.235
o, let me look! 5.03. 28
if we let fall the nobleness of this, | and the TNK pr 15
let him consider. 1.01.105
let him lead his line | to catch one at my heart 1.01.116
take hands, | let us be widows to our woes; 1.01.166
let us leave the city | thebes and the temptings 1.02. 3
or let me know | why mine own barber is unblest, 1.02. 52
let | the blood of mine that's sib to him be 1.02. 71
let them break and fall | off me with that 1.02. 73
let him approach. 1.02. 93
let th' event, | that never–erring arbitrator, 1.02.113
and let us follow | the becking of our chance. 1.02.115
me, let me perish | if i think this our prison! 2.02. 61
bodies, let 'em suffer | the gall of hazard, so 2.02. 65
let me deal coldly with you: 2.02.184
and let mine honor down, and never charge? 2.02.195
let that one say so, | and use thy freedom; 2.02.197
and so fair, | let honest men ne'er love again. 2.02.231
'gainst thy window, | and let in life into thee; 2.03. 10
let the plough play to–day, i'll tickle't out 2.03. 28
that's all one, i'll go through, let her mumble. 2.03. 31
him | and the tanner's daughter to let slip now; 2.03. 44
beauty, | thus let me seal my vow'd faith. 2.05. 39
what | you want at any time, let me but know it. 2.05. 55
not, | let me find that my father ever hated — 2.05. 58
let all the dukes and all the devils roar, | he 2.06. 1
let him do | what he will with me, so he use me 2.06. 28
let not my sense unsettle | lest i should drown, 3.02. 29
let us not, | having our ancient reputation with 3.03. 10
and let me entreat you | by all the honesty and 3.03. 13
have i said, "thus let be," and "there let be," 3.05. 9
"thus let be," and "there let be," | and "then 3.05. 9
and "then let be," and no man understand me? 3.05. 10
let us alone, sir. 3.05. 31
let me have your company | till /i come to the 3.05. 65
and let him play | qui passa o' th' bells and 3.05. 85
that let fall | the birch upon the breeches of 3.05.110
and both upon our guards, then let our fury, 3.06. 29
man calls me traitor, | let me say thus much: 3.06.161
so let me be most traitor, and ye please me. 3.06.167
let 's die together, at one instant, duke. 3.06.177
only a little let him fall before me, | that i 3.06.178
last let me entreat, sir. 3.06.210
let it not fall again, sir. 3.06.272
him, but i laugh at 'em | and let 'em all alone. 4.01.127
for the tackling | let me alone. 4.01.146
make palamon a nosegay, then let him mark me — 4.03. 26 P
and let them repair to her with palamon in their 4.03. 91 P
let us put it in execution; 4.03.100 P
now let 'em enter, and before the gods | tender 5.01. 1
let the temples | burn bright with sacred fires, 5.01. 2
let no due be wanting; 5.01. 5
before i turn, let me embrace thee, cousin; 5.01. 31
why, let it be so; farewell, coz! 5.01. 33
let us go. 5.01. 68
let us rise | and bow before the goddess. 5.01.135
in't, let him | take off my wheaten garland, or 5.01.159
let her do so, | and when your fit comes, fit 5.02. 10
let it here be done. 5.03.133
let us bid farewell; 5.04. 19
and let my life be now as short | as my 5.04. 37
a day or two | let us look sadly, and give grace 5.04.125
let us be thankful | for that which is, and with 5.04.134
yet stay a while, | and let me look upon ye. ep 4
he will | against his conscience, let him hiss, ep 8
let me set up before your thoughts, good friends STM II.C 90
their sharp state, | and let this be thy maxime: III 19
make use of time, let not advantage slip, VEN 129
"for shame," he cries, "let go, and let me go, 379
"for shame," he cries, "let go, and let me go, 379
"let me excuse thy courser, gentle boy, | and 403
"you hurt my hand with wringing, let us part, 421
o, never let their crimson liveries wear! 506
"now let me say 'good night,' and so say you; 535
"fie, fie," he says, "you crush me, let me go, 611
"o, let him keep his loathsome cabin still! 637
and will not let a false sound enter there, 780
when collatine unwisely did not let | to praise LUC 10
to those two armies that would let him go, 76
let fair humanity abhor the deed | that spots 195
who with a ling'ring stay his course doth let, 328
let him return, and flatt'ring thoughts retire; 641
turns not, but swells the higher by this let. 646
"so let thy thoughts, low vassals to thy state" 666
let their exhal'd unwholesome breaths make sick 779
and let thy musty vapors march so thick | that 782
let not the jealous day behold that face, 800
"let my good name, that senseless reputation, 820
let ghastly shadows his lewd eyes affright, 971
let there bechance him pitiful mischances | to 976
and let mild women to him lose their mildness, 979
"let him have time to tear his curled hair, 981
let him have time against himself to rave, | let 982
let him have time of time's help to despair, 983
let him have time to live a loathed slave, | let 984
let him have time a beggar's orts to crave, 985
"let him have time to see his friends his foes, 988
let him have time to mark how slow time goes 990
and ever let his unrecalling crime | have time 993
at his own shadow let the thief run mad, 997
me good | is to let forth my foul defiled blood. 1029
men prove beasts, let beasts bear gentle minds." 1148
then let it not be call'd impiety, | if in this 1174
o, let it not be hild | poor women's faults that 1257
let sin, alone committed, light alone | upon his 1480
let guiltless souls be freed from guilty woe: 1482
she modestly prepares to let them know | her 1607
or (at the least) this refuge let me find: 1654
let it then suffice | to drown /one woe, one 1679
comes all too late, yet let the traitor die, 1686
interest, let no mourner say | he weeps for her, 1797
let my unsounded self, suppos'd a fool, | now 1819
strike, | let reason rule things worthy blame, PP 18. 3
let the bird of loudest lay, | on the sole PHT 1
let the priest in surplice white, | that 13
to this urn let those repair | that are either 65
then let not winter's ragged hand deface | in SON 6. 1
let those whom nature hath not made for store, 11. 9
thou shouldst print more, not let that copy die. 11.14
know | you had a father, let your son say so. 13.14
o, let me, true in love, but truly write, | and 21. 9
let them say more that like of hearsay well, | i 21.13
o, let my books be then the eloquence | and dumb 23. 9
let those who are in favor with their stars | of 25. 1
to let base clouds o'ertake me in my way, 34. 3
let me confess that we two must be twain, 36. 1
let him bring forth | eternal numbers to outlive 38.11
even for this, let us divided live, | and our 39. 5
let this sad int'rim like the ocean be | which 56. 9
o, let me suffer (being at your beck) | th' 58. 5
but let your love even with my life decay; 71.12
let him but copy what in you is writ, | not 84. 9
let not my love be call'd idolatry, | nor my 105. 1
let me not to the marriage of true minds | admit 116. 1
no, let me be obsequious in thy heart, | and 125. 9
let it then as well beseem thy heart | to mourn 132.10
then my friend's heart let my poor heart bail; 133.10
whoe'er keeps me, let my heart be his guard, 133.11
let no unkind, no fair beseechers kill; 135.13
then in the number let me pass untold, | though 136. 9
let me excuse thee: 139. 9
and let that pine to aggravate thy store; 146.10
of city, and had let go by | the swiftest hours, LC 59
hour, | let it not tell your judgment i am old, 73

LET–A 1 FR 0.0001 REL FR 0 V 1 P
i pray you let–a me speak a word with your ear. WIV 3.01. 79 P

LET–ALONE 1 FR 0.0001 REL FR 1 V 0 P
the let–alone lies not in your good will. LR 5.03. 79

LETHARGIED 1 FR 0.0001 REL FR 1 V 0 P
weakens, his discernings | are lethargied — ha! LR 1.04.229

LETHARGIES 1 FR 0.0001 REL FR 0 V 1 P
loads a' gravel in the back, lethargies, cold TRO 5.01. 19 P

LETHARGY 5 FR 0.0005 REL FR 1 V 4 P
how have you come so early by this lethargy? TN 1.05.124 P
in this time of lethargy i pick'd and cut most WT 4.04.614 P
as i take it, is a kind of lethargy, and't 2H4 1.02.112 P
peace is a very apoplexy, lethargy, mull'd, deaf COR 4.05.224 P
the lethargy must have his quiet course; OTH 4.01. 53

LETHE 6 FR 0.0006 REL FR 6 V 0 P
let fancy still my sense in lethe steep; TN 4.01. 62
may this be wash'd in lethe and forgotten? 2H4 5.02. 72
so in the lethe of thy angry soul | thou drown R3 4.04.251
sign'd in thy spoil, and crimson'd in thy lethe. JC 3.01.206
weed | that roots itself in ease on lethe wharf, HAM 1.05. 33
steep'd our sense | in soft and delicate lethe. ANT 2.07.108

LETHE'D 1 FR 0.0001 REL FR 1 V 0 P
his honor | even till a lethe'd dullness — how ANT 2.01. 27

/LET'S 4 FR 0.0004 REL FR 4 V 0 P
/ha, /let's /see. R2 4.01.294
of reason, | /let's shut our gates and sleep. TRO 2.02. 47
/come, /let's /fall /to, /and, /gentle /girl, TIT 3.02. 34
/let's /follow /the /old /earl, /and /get /the LR 3.07.103

LET'S 271 FR 0.0306 REL FR 199 V 72 P
let's assist them, | for our case is as theirs. TMP 1.01. 54
let's all sink wi' th' king. 1.01. 63
let's take leave of him. 1.01. 64
let's draw our weapons. 2.01.322
and let's make further search | for my poor son. 2.01.323
let's follow it, and after do our work. 3.02.148 P
let's see your song. how now, minion? TGV 1.02. 85
let's tune, and to it lustily a while. 4.02. 25
ay; but peace, let's hear 'em. 4.02. 38 P
let's be reveng'd on him: WIV 2.01. 93 P
let's appoint him a meeting, give him a show of 2.01. 93 P
let's consult together against this greasy 2.01.107 P
let's go in, gentlemen, but, trust me, we'll 3.03.228 P
let's go dress him like the witch of brainford. 4.02. 98 P
let's obey his humor a little further. 4.02.199 P
let's away; 5.02. 14 P
away! let's go learn the truth of it. MM 1.02. 81 P
let's withdraw. 1.02.113 P
let's write "good angel" on the devil's horn, 2.04. 16
pray you let's hear. 4.02.119 P
good friar, let's hear it. 5.01.162
this is a strange abuse. let's see thy face. 5.01.205
let's hear it. ERR 2.02. 71 P
let's call more help | to have them bound again. 4.04.145
and now let's go hand in hand, not one before 5.01.426
let's have a dance ere we are married, that we ADO 5.04.117 P
let's see the penalty. LLL 1.01.123 P
him to passion, and therefore let's hear it. 4.03.198
if you deny to dance, let's hold more chat. 5.02.228
let's part the word. 5.02.249
let's mock them still, as well known as 5.02.301
let's have the tongs and the bones. MND 4.01. 28 P
let's follow him, | and by the way let's recount 4.01.198
him, | and by the way let's recount our dreams. 4.01.199
pray you let's have no more fooling about it, MV 2.02. 83 P
let's see once more this saying grav'd in gold: 2.07. 36
sweet soul, let's in, and there expect their 5.01. 49
let's away, | and get our jewels and our wealth AYL 1.03.133
god buy you, let's meet as little as we can. 3.02.257 P
let's present him to the duke like a roman 4.02. 3 P
let's be no stoics nor no stocks, i pray, | or SHR 1.01. 31
tranio, let's go. 1.01.245
i love no chiders, sir. biondello, let's away. 1.02.226
o excellent motion! fellows, let's be gone. 1.02.278
let's hear. o fie, the treble jars. 3.01. 39
she shall, lucentio. come, gentlemen, let's go. 3.02.252
let's ha't, good grumio. 4.01. 59 P
let's see, i think 'tis now some seven a' clock, 4.03.187
kate, let's stand aside and see the end of this 5.01. 61 P
husband, let's follow, to see the end of this 5.01.142
why then let's home again. 5.01.147
come, sirrah, let's away. 5.01.147
assurance | let's each one send unto his wife, 5.02. 66
let's return again and suffice ourselves with AWW 3.05. 10 P
but let's about it. 3.07. 48
let's take the instant by the forward top; 5.03. 39
welcome, ass. now let's have a catch. TN 2.03. 18 P
let's have a song. 2.03. 31 P
and you love me, let's do't. 2.03. 60 P
let's to bed, knight. 2.03.182 P
come, let's see the event. 3.04.395 P
let's have that, good sir. WT 2.01. 26
so, let's see — it was told me i should be rich 3.03.117 P
them sprightly, | and let's be red with mirth. 4.04. 54
and let's first see moe ballads. 4.04.273 P
let's have some merry ones. 4.04.287 P
pedlar, let's have the first choice. 4.04.312 P
pray let's see these four threes of herdsmen. 4.04.335 P
let's before, as he bids us. 4.04.829 P
let's along. 5.02.112 P
let's from this place. 5.03.146
no more than he that threats. to arms let's hie! JN 3.01.347
let's purge this choler without letting blood. R2 1.01.153
come, gentlemen, let's all go visit him. 1.04. 63
let's talk of graves, of worms, and epitaphs, 3.02.145
let's choose executors and talk of wills; 3.02.148
let's march without the noise of threat'ning 3.03. 51
no, good my lord, let's fight with gentle words, 3.03.131
let's step into the shadow of these trees. 3.04. 25
come, come, in wooing sorrow let's be brief, 5.01. 93
come, let's go. 5.04. 10
come, let's hear, jack, what trick hast thou now 1H4 2.04.265 P
let's see what they be. read them. 2.04.534 P
our hands are full of business, let's away, 3.02.179
no more words, let's have her. 2H4 2.01.165 P
let's beat him before his whore. 2.04.257 P
yea, marry, let's see bullcalf. 3.02.173 P
come let's to dinner, come let's to dinner. 3.02.218 P
come let's to dinner, come let's to dinner. 3.02.218 P
let's drink together friendly and embrace, 4.02. 63
come, let's away. H5 2.03. 47
let's stab ourselves. 4.05. 7
let's to the altar. 1H6 1.01. 45
let's raise the siege; 1.02. 13
let's leave this town, for they are hare–brain'd 1.02. 37
come, let's away about it. 1.02.149
away, captains, let's get us from the walls, 3.02. 71
go, let's not forget | the noble duke of bedford 3.02.131
and, commendable prov'd, let's die in pride. 4.06. 57
then let's make haste away, and look unto the 2H6 1.01.208
my masters, let's stand close. 1.03. 1 P
come, let's be gone. 1.03. 41 P
now pray, my lord, let's see the devil's writ. 1.04. 57
come, come, let's fall in with them. 4.02. 30 P
first thing we do, let's kill all the lawyers. 4.02. 76 P
come, let's march towards london. 4.03. 17 P
come, then, let's go fight with them. 4.06. 13 P
come, let's away. 4.06. 15 P
wife, let's in, and learn to govern better, 4.09. 48
arm'd as we are, let's stay within this house. 3H6 1.01. 38
let's pluck him down. 1.01. 59
let's fight it out, and not stand cavilling thus 1.01.117
come, son, let's away. 1.01.255
let's set our men in order, | and issue forth 1.02. 69
nay, stay, let's hear the orisons he makes. 1.04.110
why then it sorts, brave warriors. let's away. 2.01.209
here comes a man, let's stay till he be past. 3.01. 12
let's seize upon him. 3.01. 23
why then, let's on our way in silent sort. 4.02. 28
come then, away, let's ha' no more ado. 4.05. 27
come therefore, let's about it speedily. 4.06.102
now, for this night, let's harbor here in york; 4.07. 79
let's levy men, and beat him back again. 4.08. 6
farewell, sweet lords, let's meet at coventry. 4.08. 32
and let's away to london | and see our gentle 5.05. 88
but come, my lord, let's away. R3 3.02. 94
and in the breath of bitter words let's smother 4.04.133
let's lack no discipline, make no delay, | for, 5.03. 17
let's whip these stragglers o'er the seas again; 5.03.327
in what kind, let's know, | is this exaction? H8 1.02. 53
let's be merry, | good my lord cardinal: 1.04.104
and then let's dream | who's best in favor. 1.04.107
let's stand close and behold him. 2.01. 55
let's think in private more. 2.01.169
let's in; 2.02. 55
let's dry our eyes; 3.02.431
let's sit down quiet | for fear we wake her; 4.02. 81
prithee let's walk. 5.01.116
draw this curtain and let's see your picture. TRO 3.02. 47 P
let's have your company, or, if you please, 4.01. 40
let's leave the hermit pity with our mother, 5.03. 45
let's hence, and hear | how the dispatch is made COR 1.01.276
let's along. 1.01.279
let's fetch him off, or make remain alike. 1.04. 62
for the love of juno, let's go. 2.01.101 P
good ladies, let's go. 2.01.133 P
let's to the capitol, | and carry with us ears 2.01.268
let's be calm. 3.01. 57
let's hear our tribune; 3.01.192
pray you let's to him. 3.01.334
come, come, let's see him out at gates, come. 3.03.142
come, let's not weep. 4.01. 54
let's not meet her. 4.02. 8
pray let's go. 4.02. 36
come, let's go. 4.02. 51
what, what, what? let's partake. 4.05.174 P
come, masters, let's home. 4.06.154 P
so did we all. but come, let's home. 4.06.156 P
let's to the capitol. 4.06.159
pray let's go. 4.06.160
come, let's away. 4.07. 56
therefore let's hence, | and with our fair 5.01. 73
let's make the best of it. 5.06.146
let's hew his limbs till they be clean consum'd. TIT 1.01.129
and so let's leave her to her silent walks. 2.04. 8
let's kiss and part, for we have much to do. 3.01.287
let's see: 4.02. 19
come, madam, let's away. ROM 1.01.159
come on, then let's to bed. 1.05.125
come let's away, the strangers all are gone. 1.05.144
i pray thee, good mercutio, let's retire. 3.01. 1
let's talk, it is not day. 3.05. 25
let's see for means. 5.01. 35
o, pray let's see't. for the lord timon, sir? TIM 1.01. 13
let's see your piece. 1.01. 28

i prithee let's be provided to show them 1.02.179
with apemantus, let's ha' some sport with 'em. 2.02. 47 P
let's make no stay. 3.06.118 P
meet, for timon's sake | let's yet be fellows. 4.02. 25
let's shake our heads, and say, | as 'twere a 4.02. 25
nay, let's seek him: 5.01. 40
name them, my lord, let's know them. 5.01.105
let's be sacrificers, but not butchers, caius. JC 2.01.166
let's kill him boldly, but not wrathfully; 2.01.172
let's carve him as a dish fit for the gods, 2.01.173
let's all cry, "peace, freedom, and liberty!" 3.01.110
let's stay and hear the will. 3.02.239
let's reason with the worst that may befall. 5.01. 96
so call the field to rest, and let's away, | to 5.05. 80
let's after him, | whose care is gone before to MAC 1.04. 56
let's away, | our tears are not yet brew'd. 2.03.123
let's briefly put on manly readiness, | and meet 2.03.133
let's not consort with them; 2.03.135
well, let's away, and say how much is done. 3.03. 22
come, let's make haste, she'll soon be back 3.05. 36
let's make us med'cines of our great revenge 4.03.214
let's do't, i pray, and i this morning know HAM 1.01.174
let's follow. 'tis not fit thus to obey him. 1.04. 88
nay, let's follow him. 1.04. 91
nay, come, let's go together. 1.05.190
pray let's have no words of this, but when they 4.05. 46 P
let's further think of this, | weigh what 4.07.148
let's follow, gertrude. 4.07.191
give it start again, | therefore let's follow. 4.07.194
let's see. LR 1.02. 34 P
let's see, let's see. 1.02. 43 P
let's see, let's see. 1.02. 43 P
come, let's in all. 3.04.175
let's see these pockets; 4.06.256
let's see, | i feel this pin prick. 4.07. 54
let's then determine | with th' ancient of war 5.01. 31
come let's away to prison: 5.03. 8
let's exchange charity. 5.03.167
let's see — | after some time, to abuse OTH 1.03.394
let's to the sea-side, ho! 2.01. 36
come, let's do so; 2.01. 40
let's meet him and receive him. 2.01.180
let's teach ourselves that honorable stop, | not 2.03. 2
let's have no more of this; 2.03.110 P
let's to our affairs. 2.03.111 P
gentlemen, let's look to our business. 2.03.112 P
platform, masters, come, let's set the watch. 2.03.120
let's think't unsafe | to come in to the cry 5.01. 43
gentlemen, let's go see poor cassio dress'd. 5.01.124
let's not confound the time with conference ANT 1.01. 45
let's grant it is not | amiss to tumble on the 1.04. 16
let it alone, let's to billiards. come, charmian. 2.05. 3
we part, and let's | draw lots who shall begin. 2.06. 60
come, let's away. 2.06.136 P
let's ha't, good soldier. 2.07.105
come, let's all take hands, | till that the 2.07.106
gentle lords, let's part, | you see we have 2.07.121
come, | let's have one other gaudy night. 3.13.182
let's mock the midnight bell. 3.13.184
let's to-night | be bounteous at our meal. 4.02. 9
let's to supper, come, | and drown consideration 4.02. 44
let's see if other watchmen | do hear what we do 4.03. 17
let's see how it will give off. 4.03. 22
let's speak to him. 4.09. 23
let's hear him, for the things he speaks | may 4.09. 24
let's do so. but he sleeps. 4.09. 25
help, friends below, let's draw him hither. 4.15. 13
let's do't after the high roman fashion, | and 4.15. 87
nay, come, let's go together. CYM 1.02. 40 P
let's follow him and pervert the present wrath 2.04.151
let's see't. 3.05.100
let's see the boy's face. 4.02.359
let's withdraw, | and meet the time as it seeks 4.03. 32
or betimes | let's reinforce, or fly. 5.02. 18
be silent; let's see further. 5.05.127
let's quit this ground, | and smoke the temple 5.05.397
set't down, let's look upon't. PER 3.02. 51
come, let's have her aboard suddenly. 4.01. 94 P
therefore let's have fresh ones, what e'er we 4.02. 10 P
let's leave his court, that we may nothing share TNK 1.02. 75
let's to the king, who, were he | a quarter 1.02.107
let's think this prison holy sanctuary | to keep 2.02. 71
the sun grows high, let's walk in. 2.02.148
let's rehearse by any means | before the ladies 2.03. 56
come, let's be gone, lads. 2.03. 73
come, lass, let's trip it. 3.05. 89
let's get her in. 4.01.149
pray bring her in | and let's see how she is. 5.02. 25
let's get her in. 5.02.107
nay, let's be offerers all. 5.04. 32
let's go off, | and bear us like the time. 5.04.136
the noble earl of shrewsbury, let's hear him. STM II.C 30 P
let's hear him. II.C 42 P
let's hear shrieve more. II.C 43 P
this' a sound fellow i tell you, let's mark him. II.C 89 P
let's us do as we may be done by. II.C 141 P
LETS* 22 FR 0.0024 REL FR 20 V 2 P
what lets but one may enter at her window? TGV 3.01.113
he can command, lets it straight feel the spur; MM 1.02.162
or else what lets it but he would be here? ERR 2.01.105
weeds the corn and still lets grow the weeding. LLL 1.01. 96
gaping wide, | every one lets forth his sprite, MND 5.01.381
wise men, | for gratiano never lets me speak. MV 1.01.107
he lets me feed with his hinds, bars me the AYL 1.01. 19 P
if nothing lets to make us happy both | but this TN 5.01.249
which lets go by some sixteen years, and makes WT 5.03. 31
lets fall his sword before your highness' feet, 1H6 3.04. 9
nurse | into a rapture lets her baby cry | while COR 2.01.207
his noble carelessness lets them plainly see't. 2.02. 14 P
yet here he lets me prate | like one i' th' 5.03.159
bird, | that lets it hop a little from his hand, ROM 2.02.178
heaven, i'll make a ghost of him that lets me! HAM 1.04. 85
that done, he lets me go, | and, with his head 2.01. 93
lets go by | th' important acting of your dread 3.04.107
who lets go by no vantages that may | prefer you CYM 2.03. 45
may they kill him without lets, | and the ladies TNK 3.05.156
"so, so," quoth he, "these lets attend the time, LUC 330
who lets so fair a house fall to decay, | which SON 13. 9
or monarch's hands that lets not bounty fall LC 41
LET'ST 3 FR 0.0003 REL FR 3 V 0 P
thou let'st thy fortune sleep — die, rather; TMP 2.01.216
frighted, thou let'st fall | from dis's waggon! WT 4.04.117
before the game is afoot thou still let'st slip. 1H4 1.03.278
LET/'T 1 FR 0.0001 REL FR 1 V 0 P
let/'t alone | and do the murther first. TMP 4.01.231
LET'T 4 FR 0.0004 REL FR 3 V 1 P
sirs, let't alone, | i will not go to-day, | SHR 4.03.193
bosom, let't not be doubted | i shall do good. WT 2.02. 51
let't alone. 5.03. 73
let't be so, good corporal nym. H5 2.01. 13 P
LETTER 207 FR 0.0234 REL FR 120 V 87 P
gav'st thou my letter to julia? TGV 1.01. 94 P
(a lost mutton) gave your letter to her (a lac'd 1.01. 96 P
a pound shall serve me for carrying your letter. 1.01.106 P
too little for carrying a letter to your lover. 1.01.109
no, you shall have it for bearing the letter. 1.01.119 P
marry, sir, the letter, very orderly, having 1.01.123 P
so much as a ducat for delivering your letter: 1.01.138 P
and yet i would i had o'erlook'd the letter; 1.02. 50
and would not force the letter to my view! 1.02. 54
pleas'd | to be so ang'red with another letter. 1.02.100
till i have found each letter in the letter, 1.02.116
till i have found each letter in the letter, 1.02.116
how now? what letter are you reading there? 1.03. 51
lend me the letter; let me see what news. 1.03. 55
i fear'd to show my father julia's letter, 1.03. 80
me, i have writ your letter | unto the secret, 2.01.104
scribe, to himself should write the letter? 2.01.140
by a letter, i should say. 2.01.150 P
why, she hath given you a letter. 2.01.159 P
that's the letter i writ to her friend. 2.01.160 P
and that letter hath she deliver'd, and there an 2.01.161 P
what say you to a letter from your friends | of 2.04. 51
what letter is this same? 3.01.137
now will he be swing'd for reading my letter — 3.01.383 P
her that ring and therewithal | this letter; 4.04. 86
madam, please you peruse this letter — | pardon 4.04.121
this is the letter to your ladyship. 4.04.124
give her this letter; WIV 1.02. 8 P
and the letter is to desire and require her to 1.02. 9 P
i have writ me here a letter to her; 1.03. 58 P
here's another letter to her. 1.03. 68 P
go, bear thou this letter to mistress page; 1.03. 73 P
you jack'nape, give-a this letter to sir hugh. 1.04.107 P
letter for letter; 2.01. 70 P
letter for letter; 2.01. 70 P
opinions, here's the twin-brother of thy letter; 2.01. 73 P
o that my husband saw this letter! 2.01.100 P
i should have borne the humor'd letter to her; 2.01.130 P
you'll not bear a letter for me, you rogue? 2.02. 19 P
coach after coach, letter after letter, gift 2.02. 65 P
coach after coach, letter after letter, gift 2.02. 66 P
she hath receiv'd your letter — for the which 2.02. 81 P
this boy will carry a letter twenty mile, as 3.02. 32 P
here is a letter will say somewhat. 4.05.123 P
i have a letter from her | of such contents as 4.06. 12
this letter then to friar peter give; MM 4.03.137
wend you with this letter. 4.03.145
every letter he hath writ hath disvouch'd other. 4.04. 1 P
i learn in this letter that don /pedro of ADO 1.01. 1 P
she tore the letter into a thousand halfpence; 2.03.140 P
for the letter that begins them all, h. 3.04. 56 P
this letter will tell you more. LLL 1.01.188 P
a letter from the magnificent armado. 1.01.191 P
will you hear this letter with attention? 1.01.215 P
i must employ him in a letter to my love. 3.01. 6 P
hither the swain, he must carry me a letter. 3.01. 50 P
i have a letter from monsieur berowne to one 4.01. 53
o, thy letter, thy letter! 4.01. 54
o, thy letter, thy letter! 4.01. 54
this letter is mistook; 4.01. 57
of feathers is he that indited this letter? 4.01. 94
who gave thee this letter? 4.01.101
thou hast mistaken his letter. 4.01.106
i will something affect the letter, for it 4.02. 55
person, be so good as read me this letter. 4.02. 91 P
will look again on the intellect of the letter, 4.02.134 P
here he hath framed a letter to a sequent of the 4.02.138 P
i beseech your grace let this letter be read: 4.03.191
o, he hath drawn my picture in his letter! 5.02. 38
debtor, | my red dominical, my golden letter: 5.02. 44
the letter is too long by half a mile. 5.02. 54
the chain were longer and the letter short? 5.02. 56
give him this letter, do it secretly, | and so MV 2.03. 7
was not that letter from fair jessica? 2.04. 28
ere i ope his letter, | i pray you tell me how 3.02.232
his letter there | will show you his estate. 3.02.235
here is a letter, lady, | the paper as the body 3.02.263
but let me hear the letter of your friend. 3.02.314
do not persuade you to come, let not my letter." 3.02.322 P
take this same letter, | and use thou all th' 3.04. 47
this letter from bellario doth commend | a young 4.01.143
time the court shall hear bellario's letter. 4.01.149
at the receipt of your letter i am very sick, 4.01.151 P
here is a letter, read it at your leisure. 5.01.267
unseal this letter soon; 5.01.275
strange accident | i chanced on this letter. 5.01.279
i'll write to him a very taunting letter, | and AYL 3.05.134
patience herself would startle at this letter, 4.03. 13
well, | this is a letter of your own device. 4.03. 20
i say she never did invent this letter, | this 4.03. 28
will you hear the letter? 4.03. 36
to show the letter that i writ to you. 5.02. 78
look on his letter, madam, here's my passport. AWW 3.02. 56
brought you this letter, gentlemen? 3.02. 62
and would you take the letter of her? 3.04. 1
do as she has done | by sending me a letter? 3.04. 3
you have not given him his mother's letter? 4.03. 2 P
i think i have his letter in my pocket. 4.03.200 P
that is not the duke's letter, sir; 4.03.212 P
master lavatch, give my lord lafew this letter. 5.02. 2 P
your ring, | and, look you, here's your letter. 5.03.311
make a third, where he shall find the letter; TN 2.03.174 P
for i know this letter will make a contemplative 2.05. 19 P
we shall have a rare letter from him; 3.02. 56 P
obey every point of the letter that i dropp'd to 3.02. 77 P
this concurs directly with the letter: 3.04. 66 P
for she incites me to that in the letter. 3.04. 68 P
if this letter move him not, his legs cannot. 3.04.171 P
now will not i deliver his letter; 3.04.184 P
therefore this letter, being so excellently 3.04.188 P
thee more than ever the bearing of letter did. 4.02.112 P
now, as thou lov'st me, let me see his letter. 5.01. 1 P
do not desire to see this letter. 5.01. 5 P
h'as here writ a letter to you; 5.01.286 P
i have your own letter that induc'd me to the 5.01.306 P
pray you peruse that letter. 5.01.330
here were presuppos'd | upon thee in the letter. 5.01.351
the letter at sir toby's great importance, | in 5.01.363
who brought that letter from the cardinal? JN 4.03. 14
go bear this letter to lord john of lancaster, 1H4 3.03.195
go bear this letter to my lord of lancaster, 2H4 1.02.238 P
there's a letter for you. 2.02.100 P
but the letter: 2.02.118 P
i'll steep this letter in sack and make him eat 2.02.135 P
a letter was deliver'd to my hands, | writ to 1H6 4.01. 11
view the letter | sent from our uncle duke of 4.01. 48
is that the worst this letter doth contain? 4.01. 66
and from the cross-row plucks the letter g, R3 1.01. 55
to love, | send her a letter of thy noble deeds: 4.04.280
my letter will resolve him of my mind. 4.05. 20
and his own letter, | the honorable board of H8 1.01. 78
the king | digest this letter of the cardinal's? 3.02. 53
the letter, as i live, with all the business | i 3.02.221
is that letter | i caus'd you write yet sent 4.02.127
come, thou shalt bear a letter to him straight. TRO 3.03.305
of idiot-worshippers, here's a letter for thee. 5.01. 7 P
here is a letter from queen hecuba, | a token 5.01. 39
here's a letter come from yond poor girl. 5.03. 99 P
the words — i think | i have the letter here; COR 1.02. 8
look, here's a letter from him; 2.01.108 P
a letter for me? 2.01.112 P
yes certain, there's a letter for you, i saw't. 2.01.113 P
a letter for me! 2.01.114 P
seest thou this letter? TIT 2.03. 46
who found this letter? 2.03.293
the moon, | your letter is with jupiter by this. 4.03. 67
i have brought you a letter and a couple of 4.04. 43 P
i wrote the letter that thy father found, | and 5.01.106
and hid the gold within that letter mentioned, 5.01.107
hath sent a letter to his father's house. ROM 2.04. 7
any man that can write may answer a letter. 2.04. 10 P
not rosemary and romeo begin both with a letter? 2.04.207 P
i know it begins with some other letter — and 2.04.211 P
or, if his mind be writ, give me his letter. 5.02. 4
who bare my letter then to romeo? 5.02. 13
the letter was not nice but full of charge, | of 5.02. 18
hold, take this letter; 5.03. 23
but he which bore my letter, friar john, | was 5.03.250
and yesternight | return'd my letter back. 5.03.252
this letter he early bid me give his father, 5.03.275
give me the letter, i will look on it. 5.03.278
this letter doth make good the friar's words, 5.03.286
your honorable letter he desires | to those have TIM 1.01. 97
there's a letter for you, sir — it came from HAM 4.06. 10 P
if this letter speed | and my invention thrive, LR 1.02. 19
why so earnestly seek you to put up that letter? 1.02. 28
it is a letter from my brother that i have not 1.02. 36 P
give me the letter, sir. 1.02. 40 P
his very opinion in the letter. 1.02. 76 P
what, have you writ that letter to my sister? 1.04.334
than comes from her demand out of the letter. 1.05. 4 P
my lord, till i have deliver'd your letter. 1.05. 7 P
would he deny his letter, said he? 2.01. 78
thou whoreson zed, thou unnecessary letter! 2.02. 64 P
comfortable beams i may | peruse this letter. 2.02.165
this approves her letter, | that she would soon 2.04.183
i have receiv'd a letter this night — 'tis 3.03. 10 P
i have lock'd the letter in my closet. 3.03. 11 P
duke | instantly know, and of that letter too. 3.03. 22
this is the letter which he spoke of, which 3.05. 10 P
to my lord your husband, show him this letter. 3.07. 2 P
i have a letter guessingly set down, | which 3.07. 47
this letter, madam, craves a speedy answer; 4.02. 82
what might import my sister's letter to him? 4.05. 6
i must needs after him, madam, with my letter. 4.05. 15
love thee much — | let me unseal the letter. 4.05. 22
before you fight the battle, ope this letter. 5.01. 40
stay till i have read the letter. 5.01. 47
preferment goes by letter and affection, | and OTH 1.01. 36
you shall yourself read in the bitter letter 1.03. 68
may be th' letter mov'd him; 4.01.235
here is a letter | found in the pocket of the 5.02.308
there is besides, in roderigo's letter, | how he 5.02.324
was a friend, to me | known but by letter; CYM 1.01. 99
the letter | that i have sent her, by her own 3.02. 17
madam, here is a letter from my lord. 3.02. 25
she hath my letter for the purpose; 3.04. 29 P
sirrah, is this letter true? 3.05.106 P
i heard no letter from my master since | i wrote 4.03. 36
accident | i had a feigned letter of my master's 5.05.279
even now, | answering the letter of the oracle, 5.05.450
now to my daughter's letter. PER 2.05. 15
a letter that she loves the knight of tyre! 2.05. 43
this letter and some certain jewels | lay with 3.04. 1
and by, to bear | a letter to my lord, my love, LUC 1293
she would not blot the letter | with words, till 1322
her letter now is seal'd, and on it writ, | "at 1331
LETTER'S 1 FR 0.0001 REL FR 0 V 1 P
he will answer the letter's master, how he dares ROM 2.04. 11 P
/LETTERS 3 FR 0.0003 REL FR 2 V 1 P
have you read o'er the /letters that i sent you? 2H4 3.01. 36
/letters, /my /lord, /from /hamlet: HAM 4.07. 36
/did /your /letters /pierce /the /queen /to /any LR 4.03. 9 P
LETTERS 119 FR 0.0134 REL FR 91 V 28 P
letters should not be known; TMP 2.01.151
to milan let me hear from thee by letters | of TGV 1.01. 57
whereof, henceforth carry your letters yourself: 1.01.146 P
that stays to bear my letters to my friends, 3.01. 53
thy letters may be here, though thou art hence, 3.01.250
hold, sirrah, bear you these letters tightly; WIV 1.03. 79
i warrant he hath a thousand of these letters, 2.01. 75 P
are these your letters, knight? 3.03.140 P
he send you both these letters at an instant? 4.04. 3 P

very day receives letters of strange tenor — MM 4.02.200 P
now will i write letters to angelo | (the 4.03. 93
these letters at fit time deliver me. 4.05. 1
at your important letters — this ill day | a ERR 5.01.138
i have already deliver'd him letters, and there ADO 1.01. 20 P
and in such great letters as they write "here is 1.01.265 P
much in the letters, nothing in the praise. LLL 5.02. 40
we have receiv'd your letters full of love; 5.02.777
our letters, madam, show'd much more than jest. 5.02.785
see these letters deliver'd, put the liveries to MV 2.02.116 P
a messenger with letters from the doctor, | new 4.01.108
bring us the letters; call the messenger. 4.01.110
which hath two letters for her name fairly set SHR 3.02. 61 P
there's letters from my mother; AWW 2.03.276
i have writ my letters, casketed my treasure, 2.05. 24
tokens and letters which she did re–send, | and 3.06.115
the stronger part of it by her own letters, 4.03. 56 P
hath offer'd him letters of commendations to the 4.03. 79 P
a file with the duke's other letters in my tent. 4.03.204 P
i have letters that my son will be here to–night 4.05. 85 P
i have letters sent me | that sets him high in 5.03. 30
shall think, by the letters that thou wilt drop, TN 2.03.164 P
for every one of these letters are in my name. 2.05.141 P
attorney'd with interchange of gifts, letters, WT 1.01. 28 P
nay, but my letters, by this means being there 4.04.619
the letters of antigonus found with it, which 5.02. 34 P
that it in golden letters should be set | among JN 3.01. 85
with letters of your love to her at large. R2 3.01. 41
letters came last night | to a dear friend of 3.04. 69
than i by letters shall direct your course. 1H4 1.03.293
have i not all their letters to meet me in arms 2.03. 27 P
what letters hast thou there? 4.01. 13
these letters come from your father. 4.01. 14
letters from him! why comes he not himself? 4.01. 15
his letters bears his mind, not i, my /lord. 4.01. 20
my lord, here are letters for you. 5.02. 79
get posts and letters, and make friends with 2H4 1.01.214
you shall have letters of me presently. 2.01.178
bid them o'er–read these letters | and well 3.01. 2
new–dated letters from northumberland, | their 4.01. 8
learning and good letters peace hath tutor'd, 4.01. 44
lords, view these letters full of bad mischance. 1H6 1.01. 89
have you perus'd the letters from the pope, 5.01. 1
with letters of commission from the king. 5.04. 95
h'as a book in his pocket with red letters in't. 2H6 4.02. 90 P
they use to write it on the top of letters; 4.02.100 P
my lord ambassador, these letters are for you, 3H6 3.03.163
and as for clarence, as my letters tell me, 3.03.208
what letters or what news | from france? 4.01. 84
my sovereign liege, no letters, and few words, 4.01. 86
what answer makes king lewis unto our letters? 4.01. 91
you shall have letters from me to my son | in R3 4.01. 49
if she convey | letters to richmond, you shall 4.02. 93
where this is question'd send our letters, with H8 1.02. 99
let there be letters writ to every shire, | of 1.02.103
the cardinal's letters to the pope miscarried, 3.02. 30
the senate has letters from the general, wherein COR 2.01.134 P
have you any letters? TIT 4.03. 79
i have received letters from great rome | which 5.01. 2
have with my knife carved in roman letters, 5.01.139
ay, if i know the letters and the language. ROM 1.02. 61
shall romeo by my letters know our drift, | and 4.01.114
speed | to mantua, with my letters to thy lord. 4.01.124
dost thou not bring me letters from the friar? 5.01. 13
hast thou no letters to me from the friar? 5.01. 31
read me the superscription of these letters, i TIM 2.02. 79 P
to timon's cave | with letters of entreaty, 5.02. 11
he did receive his letters, and is coming, | and JC 3.01.279
wherein my letters, praying on his side, 4.03. 4
i have here received letters | that young 4.03.167
myself have letters of the self–same tenure. 4.03.171
therein our letters do not well agree; 4.03.176
had you your letters from your wife, my lord? 4.03.181
nor nothing in your letters writ of her? 4.03.183
thy letters have transported me beyond | this MAC 1.05. 56
i did repel his letters, and denied | his access HAM 2.01.106
there's letters seal'd, and my two schoolfellows 3.04.202
at full, | by letters congruing to that effect, 4.03. 64
they say they have letters for you. 4.06. 3 P
means to the king, they have letters for him. 4.06. 15 P
let the king have the letters i have sent, and 4.06. 23 P
i will /give you way for these your letters, 4.06. 32
go you before to gloucester with these letters. LR 1.05. 2 P
you come with letters against the king, and take 2.02. 35 P
i did commend your highness' letters to them, 2.04. 28
deliver'd letters, spite of intermission, 2.04. 33
sir, what letters had you late from france? 3.07. 42
were all thy letters suns, i could not see. 4.06.140
and give the letters which thou find'st about me 4.06.248
the letters that he speaks of | may be my 4.06.256
my letters say a hundred and seven galleys. OTH 1.03. 3
these letters give, iago, to the pilot, | and by 3.02. 1
or did the letters work upon his blood | and 4.01.275
i pray you, in your letters, | when you shall 5.02.340
but the letters too | of many our contriving ANT 1.02.181
of this my letters | before did satisfy you. 2.02. 51
in alexandria you | did pocket up my letters; 2.02. 73
go, make thee ready, | our letters are prepar'd. 3.03. 38
accuses him of letters he had formerly wrote to 3.05. 10 P
your letters did withhold our breaking forth, 3.06. 79
have letters from me to some friends that will 3.11. 16
of rome, | comes from my lord with letters. CYM 1.06. 11
here are letters for you. 2.04. 35
damn'd pisanio | hath with his forged letters 4.02.318
the roman emperor's letters, | sent by a consul 4.02.333
and by whose letters i'll dispose myself. PER 1.02.117
court of king simonides | are letters brought, 3.ch. 24
and by cleon train'd | in music's letters, who 4.ch. 8
lord cerimon hath letters of good credit, sir, 5.03. 77
found yet moe letters sadly penn'd in blood, LC 47
LETTERS–PATENTS 3 FR 0.0003 REL FR 3 V 0 P
call in the letters–patents that he hath | by R2 2.01.202
and yet my letters–patents give me leave. 2.03.130
his goodness, | tied it by letters–patents. H8 3.02.250
LETTICE *(also lattice)*
LETTICE 2 FR 0.0002 REL FR 1 V 1 P
so, my good window of lettice, fare thee well! AWW 2.03.213 P
beauty peep'd through lettice of sear'd age. LC 14
LETTING 7 FR 0.0008 REL FR 7 V 0 P
lack advice so much | as letting her pass so. AWW 3.04. 20
let's purge this choler without letting blood. R2 1.01.153
air, | not letting it decline on the declined, TRO 4.05.189
letting it there stand | till she had laid it ROM 2.01. 25
letting "i dare not" wait upon "i would," | like MAC 1.07. 44
letting go safely by | the divine desdemona. OTH 2.01. 72
letting them thrive again | on their abatement. CYM 5.04. 20
LETT'RED 1 FR 0.0001 REL FR 0 V 1 P
monsieur, are you not lett'red? LLL 5.01. 45 P
LETTUCE 1 FR 0.0001 REL FR 0 V 1 P
so that if we will plant nettles or sow lettuce, OTH 1.03.322 P
LEUR 1 FR 0.0001 REL FR 0 V 1 P
demoiselles pour etre baisees devant leur noces, H5 5.02.259 P
LEVE *(also leave*)*
LEVE 1 FR 0.0001 REL FR 0 V 1 P
and i sall quit you with gud leve, as i may pick H5 3.02.103 P
LEVEL 27 FR 0.0030 REL FR 21 V 6 P
we steal by line and level, and't like your TMP 4.01.239 P
"steal by line and level" is an excellent pass 4.01.243 P
to my description level at my affection. MV 1.02. 38 P
his might only where qualities were level; AWW 1.03.114 P
proclaim | myself against the level of mine aim, 2.01.156
so sways she level in her husband's heart. TN 2.04. 31
arm, out of the blank | and level of my brain — WT 2.03. 6
my life stands in the level of your dreams, 3.02. 81
and hold their level with thy princely heart? 1H4 3.02. 17
you, can thrust me from a level consideration. 2H4 2.01.113 P
revolution of the times | make mountains level, 3.01. 47
may with as great aim level at the edge of a 3.02.267 P
and every thing lies level to our wish. 4.04. 7
back, | by false accuse doth level at my life. 2H6 3.01.160
ambitious york did level at thy crown, | thou 3H6 2.02. 19
and therefore level not to hit their lives. R3 4.04.203
i stood i' th' level | of a full–charg'd H8 1.02. 2
name, | shot from the deadly level of a gun, ROM 3.03.103
there's nothing level in our cursed natures TIM 4.03. 19
diameter, | as level as the cannon to his blank, HAM 4.01. 42
it shall as level to your judgment 'pear | as 4.05.152
young boys and girls | are level now with men; ANT 4.15. 66
archer hits the mark | his eye doth level at, so PER 1.01.163
love, | and that's the mark i know you level at. 2.03.113
bring me within the level of your frown, | but SON 117.11
am, and they that level | at my abuses reckon up 121. 9
"that not a heart which in his level came LC 309
LEVELL'D 5 FR 0.0005 REL FR 5 V 0 P
but if all aim but this be levell'd false, | the ADO 4.01.237
no levell'd malice | infects one comma in the TIM 1.01. 47
she levell'd at our purposes, and, being royal, ANT 5.02.336
sometimes her levell'd eyes their carriage ride, LC 22
whose sights till then were levell'd on my face, 282
LEVELS 1 FR 0.0001 REL FR 1 V 0 P
and besort | as levels with her breeding. OTH 1.03.239
'LEVEN *(also aleven, etc., eleven)*
'LEVEN 1 FR 0.0001 REL FR 0 V 1 P
every 'leven wether tods, every tod yields pound WT 4.03. 32 P
LEVERS 1 FR 0.0001 REL FR 0 V 1 P
have you any levers to lift me up again, being 1H4 2.02. 34 P
LEVIATHAN 2 FR 0.0002 REL FR 2 V 0 P
again | ere the leviathan can swim a league. MND 2.01.174
as send precepts to the leviathan | to come H5 3.03. 26
LEVIATHANS 1 FR 0.0001 REL FR 1 V 0 P
and huge leviathans | forsake unsounded deeps to TGV 3.02. 79
LEVIED 13 FR 0.0014 REL FR 13 V 0 P
a treacherous army levied, one midnight | fated TMP 1.02.128
unless a thousand marks be levied | to quit the ERR 1.01. 21
preparation | was levied in the body of a land. JN 4.02.112
what power the duke of york had levied there, R2 2.03. 34
shall — my ransom then | will soon be levied. H5 4.03.121
levied an army, weening to redeem | and have 1H6 2.05. 88
of horsemen, that were levied for this siege! 4.03. 11
the levied succors that should lend him aid, 4.04. 23
swearing that you withhold his levied host, 4.04. 31
these soldiers shall be levied, | and thou, lord 3H6 3.03.251
of his substance, to be levied | without delay; H8 1.02. 58
so levied, as before, against the polack, | with HAM 2.02. 75
all levied in my name, have in my name | took LR 5.03.104
LEVIES 3 FR 0.0003 REL FR 3 V 0 P
and give away | the benefit of our levies, COR 5.06. 66
his further gait herein, in that the levies, HAM 1.02. 31
he sent out to suppress | his nephew's levies, 2.02. 62
LEVITY 5 FR 0.0005 REL FR 5 V 0 P
that her reputation was disvalued | in levity. MM 5.01.222
ere they can hide their levity in honor. AWW 1.02. 35
else might the world convince of levity | as TRO 2.02.130
our graver business | frowns at this levity. ANT 2.07.121
he is already | traduc'd for levity, and 'tis 3.07. 13
LEVITY'S 1 FR 0.0001 REL FR 1 V 0 P
do instruct us | what levity's in youth. TIM 1.01.134
LEVY 12 FR 0.0013 REL FR 12 V 0 P
for us to levy power | proportionable to the R2 2.02.124
forthwith a power of english shall we levy, 1H4 1.01. 22
with his quality, | the which he could not levy; 2H4 4.01. 12
levy great sums of money through the realm | for 2H6 3.01. 61
you in our behalf | go levy men, and make 3H6 4.01.131
let's levy men, and beat him back again. 4.08. 6
bid him levy straight | the greatest strength R3 4.04.449
malice domestic, foreign levy, nothing, | can MAC 3.02. 25
for this immediate levy, he commands | his CYM 3.07. 9
of, whereunto your levy | must be supplyant. 3.07. 13
never did thought of mine levy offense; PER 2.05. 52
forth and levy | our worthiest instruments, TNK 1.01.162
LEVYING 2 FR 0.0002 REL FR 2 V 0 P
brutus and cassius | are levying powers; JC 4.01. 42
who now are levying | the kings o' th' earth for ANT 3.06. 67
LEWD 13 FR 0.0014 REL FR 12 V 1 P
if any woman wrong'd by this lewd fellow | (as i MM 5.01.509
how her acquaintance grew with this lewd fellow. ADO 5.01.332
that, | if thou wert near a lewd interpreter! MV 3.04. 80
fie, fie, 'tis lewd and filthy. SHR 4.03. 65
the which he hath detain'd for lewd employments, R2 1.01. 90
poor, such bare, such lewd, such mean attempts, 1H4 3.02. 13
you have been so lewd and so much engraff'd to 2H4 2.02. 62 P
thy lewd, pestiferous, and dissentious pranks, 1H6 3.01. 15
but you must trouble him with lewd complaints. R3 1.03. 61
he is not lulling on a lewd love–bed, | but on 3.07. 72
damn her, lewd minx! OTH 3.03.476
lies, | to be admir'd of lewd unhallowed eyes. LUC 392
let ghastly shadows his lewd eyes affright, 971
LEWDLY 4 FR 0.0004 REL FR 2 V 2 P
if that man should be lewdly given, he deceiveth 1H4 2.04.427 P
a sort of naughty persons, lewdly bent, | under 2H6 2.01.163
out her beauty stirs up the lewdly inclin'd. PER 4.02.144 P
and i have lied so lewdly | that women ought to TNK 4.02. 35
LEWDNESS 2 FR 0.0002 REL FR 2 V 0 P
the lag end of their lewdness and be laugh'd at. H8 1.03. 35
though lewdness court it in a shape of heaven, HAM 1.05. 54
LEWDSTERS 1 FR 0.0001 REL FR 1 V 0 P
against such lewdsters and their lechery | those WIV 5.03. 21
LEWD–TONGU'D 1 FR 0.0001 REL FR 1 V 0 P
death to thyself but to thy lewd–tongu'd wife, WT 2.03.172
LEWIS 31 FR 0.0035 REL FR 31 V 0 P
of lewis the dolphin and that lovely maid. JN 2.01.425
shall lewis have blanch, and blanch those 3.01. 3
lewis marry blanch? 3.01. 34
o lewis, stand fast! 3.01.208
o, thine honor, lewis, thine honor! 3.01.316
the purse of rich prosperity | as lewis himself; 5.02. 62
i say again, if lewis do win the day, | he is 5.04. 30
if lewis by your assistance win the day. 5.04. 39
who was the son | to lewis the emperor, and H5 1.02. 76
and lewis the son | of charles the great. 1.02. 76
also, king lewis the tenth, | who was sole heir 1.02. 77
king lewis his satisfaction, all appear | to 1.02. 88
and lewis a prince soon won with moving words. 3H6 3.01. 34
that thou shouldst stand while lewis doth sit. 3.03. 3
now therefore be it known to noble lewis, | that 3.03. 23
king lewis and lady bona, hear me speak | before 3.03. 65
look therefore, lewis, that by this league and 3.03. 74
before thy coming, lewis was henry's friend. 3.03.143
i make king lewis behold | thy sly conveyance 3.03.159
nay, mark how lewis stamps as he were nettled. 3.03.169
king lewis, i here protest in sight of heaven, 3.03.181
if king lewis vouchsafe to furnish us | with 3.03.203
that lewis of france is sending over masquers 3.03.224
as well as lewis of france or the earl of 4.01. 11
they are but lewis and warwick, i am edward, 4.01. 15
that king lewis | becomes your enemy, for 4.01. 29
what if both lewis and warwick be appeas'd | by 4.01. 34
what answer makes king lewis unto our letters? 4.01. 91
that lewis of france is sending over masquers 4.01. 94
is lewis so brave? 4.01. 96
answer | lewis and the lady bona send to him. 4.03. 56
LEZARD *(also lizard's, etc.)*
LEZARD 1 FR 0.0001 REL FR 0 V 1 P
a fitchook, a toad, a lezard, an owl, a puttock, TRO 5.01. 61 P
LIABLE 8 FR 0.0009 REL FR 7 V 1 P
day, most generous sir, is liable, congruent, LLL 5.01. 92 P
find liable to our crown and dignity, | shall JN 2.01.490
apt, liable to be employ'd in danger, | i 4.02.226
but i, | and such as to my claim are liable, 5.02.101
yet if my name were liable to fear, | i do not JC 1.02.199
and reason to my love is liable. 2.02.104
fisting of every rogue | thy ear is liable; PER 4.06.168
am not i liable to those affections, | those TNK 2.02.187
LIAR 13 FR 0.0014 REL FR 10 V 3 P
i do despise a liar as i do despise one that is WIV 1.01. 68 P
else the puck a liar call. MND 5.01.435
and sullen, | and now i find report a very liar; SHR 2.01.244
his sake, | and yet i know him a notorious liar, AWW 1.01.100
coward, an infinite and endless liar, an hourly 3.06. 10 P
how god and good men hate so foul a liar. R2 1.01.114
howsoever you have been his liar, as you say you COR 5.02. 31 P
measureless liar, thou hast made my heart | too 5.06.102
liar and slave! MAC 5.05. 34
the sun doth move, | doubt truth to be a liar, HAM 2.02.118
she's like a liar gone to burning hell: OTH 5.02.129
full sorry | that he approves the common liar, ANT 1.01. 60
of the world, | art turn'd the greatest liar. 1.03. 39
LIARS 7 FR 0.0008 REL FR 2 V 5 P
you're liars all. WT 2.03.146
promis'd you more than that, or there be liars. 4.04.238 P
lies in your sinews, or else there be liars. TRO 2.01. 99 P
die, | transparent heretics, be burnt for liars! ROM 1.02. 91
then the liars and swearers are fools; MAC 4.02. 56 P
for there are liars and swearers enow to beat 4.02. 57 P
drunkards, liars, and adulterers by an enforc'd LR 1.02.124 P
LIBBARD'S *(also leopard, etc., lubber's)*
LIBBARD'S 1 FR 0.0001 REL FR 1 V 0 P
with libbard's head on knee. LLL 5.02.548
LIBELLING 1 FR 0.0001 REL FR 1 V 0 P
what's this but libelling against the senate, TIT 4.04. 17
LIBELS 2 FR 0.0002 REL FR 2 V 0 P
by drunken prophecies, libels, and dreams, | to R3 1.01. 33
nor would the libels read | of liberal wits. TNK 5.01.101
LIBERAL 29 FR 0.0032 REL FR 26 V 3 P
and for the liberal arts | without a parallel; TMP 1.02. 73
"item, she is too liberal." TGV 3.01.348 P
who hath indeed, most like a liberal villain, ADO 4.01. 92
all liberal reason i will yield unto. LLL 2.01.167
or hide | the liberal opposition of our spirits, 5.02.733
why, there they show | something too liberal. MV 2.02.185
i see, sir, you are liberal in offers. 4.01.438
keep for me, | i will become as liberal as you, 5.01.226
kind, and liberal | to mine own children in good SHR 1.01. 98
with too great a court | and liberal largess, R2 1.04. 44
ere't be disburdened with a liberal tongue. 2.01.229
the liberal and kind offer of the king. 1H4 5.02. 2
sun, | his liberal eye doth give to every one, H5 4.pr. 44
it's sign she hath been liberal and free. 1H6 5.04. 82
beside, his wealth doth warrant a liberal dower, 5.05. 46
the people liberal, valiant, active, wealthy, 2H6 4.07. 63
witty, courteous, liberal, full of spirit. 3H6 1.02. 43
a liberal rewarder of his friends; R3 1.03.123
men of his way should be most liberal, | they H8 1.03. 61
where you are liberal of your loves and counsels 2.01.126
and this is all a liberal course allows: TIM 3.03. 40
that liberal shepherds give a grosser name, HAM 4.07.170
delicate carriages, and of very liberal conceit. 5.02.153 P
is he not a most profane and liberal counsellor? OTH 2.01.164 P
this argues fruitfulness and liberal heart; 3.04. 38
a liberal hand. 3.04. 46
no, i will speak as liberal as the north: 5.02.220
and am well studied for a liberal thanks, ANT 2.06. 47
nor would the libels read | of liberal wits. TNK 5.01.102

LIBERAL–CONCEITED 1 FR 0.0001 REL FR 0 V 1 P
assigns, and three liberal–conceited carriages; HAM 5.02.162 P
LIBERALITY 3 FR 0.0003 REL FR 2 V 1 P
over and beside | signior baptista's liberality, SHR 1.02.149
virtue, youth, liberality, and such–like, the TRO 1.02.254 P
it, | with words, fair looks, and liberality? TIT 2.01. 92
LIBERTE 1 FR 0.0001 REL FR 0 V 1 P
il est content a vous donner la liberte, le H5 4.04. 52 P
LIBERTIES 7 FR 0.0008 REL FR 7 V 0 P
and many such–like liberties of sin: ERR 1.02.102
your liberties and the charters that you bear COR 2.03.180
that will from them take | their liberties, make 2.03.215
you are at point to lose your liberties. 3.01.193
to set | upon one battle all our liberties. JC 5.01. 75
for | their liberties are now in arms, a CYM 3.01. 74
but should he wrong my liberties in my absence? PER 1.02.112
LIBERTINE 4 FR 0.0004 REL FR 4 V 0 P
for thou thyself hast been a libertine, | as AYL 2.07. 65
the air, a charter'd libertine, is still, | and H5 1.01. 48
whiles, /like a puff'd and reckless libertine, HAM 1.03. 49
tie up the libertine in a field of feasts, ANT 2.01. 23
LIBERTINES 1 FR 0.0001 REL FR 0 V 1 P
none but libertines delight in him, and the ADO 2.01.139 P
LIBERTY 83 FR 0.0093 REL FR 70 V 13 P
my liberty. TMP 1.02.245
else o' th' earth | let liberty make use of; 1.02.493
straightway, at liberty; 5.01.235
me into everlasting liberty if i tell you of it; WIV 3.03. 31 P
from too much liberty, my lucio, liberty: MM 1.02.125
from too much liberty, my lucio, liberty: 1.02.125
dead, | and liberty plucks justice by the nose; 1.03. 29
he (to give fear to use and liberty, | which 1.04. 62
deliver'd him to his liberty or executed him? 4.02.133 P
he hath evermore had the liberty of the prison; 4.02.148 P
a man is master of his liberty: ERR 2.01. 7
why should their liberty than ours be more? 2.01. 10
why, headstrong liberty is lash'd with woe: 2.01. 15
an evil angel, and bid you forsake your liberty. 4.03. 21 P
who give their eyes the liberty of gazing? 5.01. 53
his bonds, | and gain a husband by his liberty. 5.01.341
if i had my liberty, i would do my liking. ADO 1.03. 35 P
i mean setting thee at liberty, enfreedoming thy LLL 3.01.124 P
i give thee thy liberty, set thee from durance, 3.01.128 P
now go /we /in content | to liberty, and not to AYL 1.03.138
i must have liberty | withal, as large a charter 2.07. 47
thy life into death, thy liberty into bondage. 5.01. 53 P
this liberty is all that i request, | that, upon SHR 2.01. 94
you ever | the patron of my life and liberty. 4.02.114
face put on, derive a liberty | from heartiness, WT 1.02.112
abbots, imprisoned angels | set at liberty. JN 3.03. 9
as they have given these hairs their liberty!" 3.04. 72
but now i envy at their liberty, | and will 3.04. 73
our suit | that you have bid us ask his liberty, 4.02. 63
counts it your weal he have his liberty. 4.02. 66
did i hear | of any prince so wild a liberty. 1H4 5.02. 71
in liberty of bloody hand, shall range, | with H5 3.03. 12
and the liberty that follows our places stops 5.02.271 P
heir, | i lost my liberty, and they their lives. 1H6 2.05. 81
crave | i may have liberty to venge this wrong, 3.04. 42
to wall thee from the liberty of flight; 4.02. 24
charms, | and try if they can gain your liberty. 5.03. 32
hath gain'd thy daughter princely liberty. 5.03.140
now show yourselves men, 'tis for liberty. 2H6 4.02.183
is somerset at liberty? 5.01. 87
hands | he hath good usage and great liberty, 3H6 4.05. 6
seat, | and turn'd my captive state to liberty, 4.06. 3
they quite forget their loss of liberty. 4.06. 15
fear | my joy of liberty is half eclips'd. 4.06. 63
her deity | got my lord chamberlain his liberty. R3 1.01. 77
whiles kites and buzzards /prey at liberty. 1.01.133
and so doth mine. i muse why she's at liberty. 1.03.304
being pent from liberty, as i am now, | if two 1.04.258
untainted, unexamin'd, free, at liberty. 3.06. 9
to see you ta'en from liberty, to look on | the H8 1.01.205
but if it were at liberty, 'twould sure COR 2.03. 29 P
by giving liberty unto thine eyes: ROM 1.01.227
back again, | so loving–jealous of his liberty. 2.02.181
to prison, eyes, ne'er look on liberty! 3.02. 58
service, from whose help | i deriv'd liberty. TIM 1.02. 8
lust and liberty | creep in the minds and 4.01. 25
liberty! JC 3.01. 78
out, | "liberty, freedom, and enfranchisement!" 3.01. 81
let's all cry, "peace, freedom, and liberty!" 3.01.110
the men that gave their country liberty. 3.01.118
noted and most known | to youth and liberty. HAM 2.01. 24
that they may seem the taints of liberty, | the 2.01. 32
too light, for the law of writ and the liberty: 2.02.401 P
the door upon your own liberty if you deny your 3.02.339 P
his liberty is full of threats to all, | to you 4.01. 14
dearer than eyesight, space, and liberty, LR 1.01. 56
and there is full liberty of feasting from this OTH 2.02. 9 P
of yours requires | a sequester from liberty: 3.04. 40
he brings me liberty. ANT 5.02.237
for thou art a way, | i think, to liberty; CYM 5.04. 4
in their morning state | (sound and at liberty), TNK 1.04. 35
desire of liberty, a fever, madness, | 'hath set 1.04. 42
honor, | that liberty and common conversation, 2.02. 74
were we at liberty, | a wife might part us 2.02. 88
before my liberty. 2.02.159
fortune | to be one hour at liberty and grasp 2.02.208
prince pirithous | obtained his liberty; 2.02.245
were i at liberty, i would do things | of such a 2.02.256
and all the devils roar, | he is at liberty! 2.06. 2
will grow too, finely, | now he's at liberty. 5.02. 96
those pretty wrongs that liberty commits | when SON 41. 1
beck) | th' imprison'd absence of your liberty, 58. 6
and now, to tempt, all liberty /procur'd. LC 252
LIBRARY 3 FR 0.0003 REL FR 3 V 0 P
man) my library | was dukedom large enough: TMP 1.02.109
me | from mine own library with volumes that | i 1.02.167
come and take choice of all my library, | and so TIT 4.01. 34
LIBYA 4 FR 0.0004 REL FR 4 V 0 P
good my lord, | she came from libya. WT 5.01.157
to signify | not only my success in libya, sir, 5.01.166
were his brain as barren | as banks of libya TRO 1.03.328
he hath assembled | bocchus, the king of libya; ANT 3.06. 69
LICENSE 11 FR 0.0012 REL FR 8 V 3 P
i know your virtue hath a license in't, | which MM 2.04.145
that fellow is a fellow of much license; 3.02.204 P
that thou with license of free foot hast caught, AYL 2.07. 68
taunt him with the license of ink. TN 3.02. 44 P
we license your departure with your son. 1H4 1.03.123
for the fift harry from curb'd license plucks 2H4 4.05.130
hence, did give ourself | to barbarous license; H5 1.02.271
i come to thee for charitable license, | that we 4.07. 71
thou shalt have a license to kill for a hundred 2H6 4.03. 7 P
tell him that by his license fortinbras | craves HAM 4.04. 2
with such full license as both truth and malice ANT 1.02.108
LICENTIOUS 4 FR 0.0004 REL FR 4 V 0 P
shouldst thou but hear i were licentious, | and ERR 2.02.131
what rein can hold licentious wickedness | when H5 3.03. 22
fill'd the time | with all licentious measure, TIM 5.04. 4
will to my sense bend no licentious ear, | but PER 5.03. 30
LICHAS 2 FR 0.0002 REL FR 2 V 0 P
if hercules and lichas play at dice | which is MV 2.01. 32
let me lodge lichas on the horns o' th' moon, ANT 4.12. 45
LICIO *(see litio)*
/LICK 1 FR 0.0001 REL FR 1 V 0 P
/even /the //head–lugg'd /bear /would /lick, LR 4.02. 42
LICK 8 FR 0.0009 REL FR 4 V 4 P
let me lick thy shoe. TMP 3.02. 23 P
whose hand is that the forest bear doth lick? 3H6 2.02. 13
let them not lick | the sweet which is their COR 3.01.156
for i'll try if they can lick their fingers. ROM 4.02. 4 P
an ill cook that cannot lick his own fingers; 4.02. 7 P
he that cannot lick his fingers goes not with me 4.02. 7 P
and may diseases lick up their false bloods! TIM 4.03.532
no, let the candied tongue lick absurd pomp, HAM 3.02. 60
LICK'D 1 FR 0.0001 REL FR 0 V 1 P
where the glutton's dogs lick'd his sores, and 1H4 4.02. 26 P
LICKING 1 FR 0.0001 REL FR 1 V 0 P
and there another licking of his wound, VEN 915
LICTORS 1 FR 0.0001 REL FR 1 V 0 P
saucy lictors | will catch at us like strumpets, ANT 5.02.214
LID 3 FR 0.0003 REL FR 2 V 1 P
by god's lid, it does one's heart good. TRO 1.02.211 P
night nor day | hang upon his penthouse lid; MAC 1.03. 20
god's lid, his richness | and costliness of TNK 5.03. 96
LIDS 5 FR 0.0005 REL FR 4 V 1 P
item, two grey eyes, with lids to them; TN 1.05.248 P
but sweeter than the lids of juno's eyes | or WT 4.04.121
do not for ever with thy vailed lids | seek for HAM 1.02. 70
bows toward her, and would under–peep her lids, CYM 2.02. 20
save when my lids scour'd off their /brine. TNK 3.02. 28
LIE* *(also lig)*
/LIE* 4 FR 0.0004 REL FR 4 V 0 P
/and /soon /lie /richard /in /an /earthy /pit! R2 4.01.219
/lie /there /for /pavement /to /the /abject TRO 3.03.162
/the /glory /of /our /troy /doth /this /day /lie 4.04.147
/will /you /lie /down /and /rest /upon /the LR 3.06. 34
LIE* 341 FR 0.0385 REL FR 249 V 92 P
would thou mightst lie drowning | the washing of TMP 1.01. 57
so, | lie there, my art. 1.02. 25
sinner of his memory | to credit his own lie — 1.02.102
while you here do snoring lie, | open–ey'd 2.01.300
which | lie tumbling in my barefoot way, and 2.02. 11
but you'll lie like dogs, and yet say nothing 3.02. 19 P
wilt thou tell a monstrous lie, being but half a 3.02. 28 P
i do not lie. 3.02. 47
as you like this, give me the lie another time. 3.02. 77 P
i did not give the lie. 3.02. 78 P
travellers ne'er did lie, | though fools at home 3.03. 26
sounded, | and with him there lie mudded. 3.03.102
/shores | that now lie foul and muddy. 5.01. 82
there suck i, | in a cowslip's bell i lie; 5.01. 89
then let it lie for those that it concerns. TGV 1.02. 73
it will not lie where it concerns | unless it 1.02. 74
and let the papers lie: 1.02. 97
shall these papers lie like tell–tales here? 1.02.130
yet here they shall not lie, for catching cold. 1.02.133
shall i tell you a lie? WIV 1.01. 68 P
be a giantess, and lie under mount pelion. 2.01. 79 P
does he lie at the garter? 2.01.180 P
of her than sharp words, let it lie on my head. 2.01.184 P
i would have nothing lie on my head. 2.01.187 P
say, if money go before, all ways do lie open. 2.02.169 P
the peasant, and thou shalt lie with his wife. 2.02.283 P
master /brook, i will not lie to you. 3.05. 64 P
for he to–night shall lie with mistress ford. 5.05.245
yet in this life | lie hid moe thousand deaths; MM 3.01. 40
to lie in cold obstruction, and to rot; 3.01.118
with angelo to–night shall lie | his old 3.02.278
and as a /bed i'll take /them, and there lie, ERR 3.02. 49
on his face, i had rather lie in the woollen! ADO 2.01. 30 P
and now will he lie ten nights awake carving the 2.03. 17 P
would the two princes lie, and claudio lie, 4.01.152
would the two princes lie, and claudio lie, 4.01.152
if this sweet lady lie not guiltless here 4.01.169
and yet i lie not: 4.01.271 P
as valiant as hercules that only tells a lie, 4.01.322 P
with quarrelling, | some of us would lie low. 5.01. 52
that lie and cog and flout, deprave and slander, 5.01. 95
decree, | she must lie here on mere necessity. LLL 1.01.148
not, i, | but i protest i love to hear him lie, 1.01.175
by adding a tongue which i know will not lie. 2.01.253
i do nothing in the world but lie, and lie in my 4.03. 11 P
in the world but lie, and lie in my throat. 4.03. 11 P
by earth, she is not, corporal, there you lie. 4.03. 84
you lie, you are not he. 5.02.547
execute | that lie within the mercy of your wit. 5.02.846
i | upon faint primrose beds were wont to lie, MND 1.01.215
for my sake, my dear, | lie further off yet; 2.02. 44
do not lie so near. 2.02. 44
for lying so, hermia, i do not lie. 2.02. 52
for love and courtesy | lie further off, in 2.02. 57
soul, she durst not lie | near this lack–love, 2.02. 76
who would give a bird the lie, though he cry 3.01.135 P
means, | lie all unlock'd to your occasions. MV 1.01.139
take it, prince, and if my form lie there, 2.07. 61
the carcasses of many a tall ship lie buried, as 3.01. 6 P
for never shall you lie by portia's side | with 3.02.305
and that it should lie with you in your grave. 5.01.154
if i could add a lie unto a fault, | i would 5.01.186
lie not a night from home. 5.01.230
in lieu of this last night did lie with me. 5.01.262
when i am absent, then lie with my wife. 5.01.285
yonder they lie, the poor old man, their father, AYL 1.02.129 P
that is so desirous to lie with his mother earth 1.02.201 P
lie there what hidden woman's fear there will — 1.03.119
to burn the lodging where you use to lie, | and 2.03. 23
when service should in my old limbs lie lame, 2.03. 41
the greenwood tree | who loves to lie with me, 2.05. 2
here lie i down, and measure out my grave. 2.06. 2 P
women still give the lie to their consciences. 3.02.390 P
lie not, to say mine eyes are murtherers! 3.05. 19
nonino, | these pretty country folks would lie, 5.03. 24
upon a lie seven times remov'd (bear your body 5.04. 68 P
again, it was not well cut, he would say i lie: 5.04. 80 P
and so to lie circumstantial and the lie direct. 5.04. 81 P
and so to lie circumstantial and the lie direct. 5.04. 81 P
durst go no further than the lie circumstantial, 5.04. 85 P
nor he durst not give me the lie direct; 5.04. 86 P
nominate in order now the degrees of the lie? 5.04. 89 P
the sixt, the lie with circumstance; 5.04. 96 P
the seventh, the lie direct. 5.04. 96 P
all these you may avoid but the lie direct; 5.04. 97 P
you lie, in faith, for you are call'd plain kate SHR 2.01.185
there doth my father lie; 4.04. 56
nay then you lie; it is the blessed sun. 4.05. 17
our remedies oft in ourselves do lie, | which we AWW 1.01.216
i know she will lie at my house; 3.05. 31 P
therefore i'll lie with him | when i am buried. 4.02. 72
he will lie, sir, with such volubility, that you 4.03.253 P
love–thoughts lie rich when canopied with bow'rs TN 1.01. 40
sir toby, there you lie. 2.03.107
ye lie. 2.03.113 P
i have wit enough to lie straight in my bed. 2.03.136 P
lie thou there; 2.05. 21 P
as many lies as will lie in thy sheet of paper, 3.02. 46 P
in this town, | where lie my maiden weeds; 5.01.255
you lie, you lie! WT 1.02.299
you lie, you lie! 1.02.299
a day i'll visit | the chapel where they lie, 3.02.239
there lie, and there thy character; 3.03. 47
my aunts, | while we lie tumbling in the hay. 4.03. 12
no, like a bank, for love to lie and play on; 4.04.130
father died, | to lie close by his honest bones; 4.04.456
i think you know my fortunes | do all lie there. 4.04.591
a lie; 4.04.722 P
and they often give us soldiers the lie, but we 4.04.724 P
steel, therefore they do not give us the lie. 4.04.726 P
give me the lie, do; 5.02.133 P
whose sons lie scattered on the bleeding ground. JN 2.01.304
austria's head lie there, | while philip 3.02. 3
hand, | it may lie gently at the foot of peace, 5.02. 76
to lie like pawns lock'd up in chests and trunks 5.02.141
shall, | lie at the proud foot of a conqueror, 5.07.113
by all my hopes, most falsely doth he lie. R2 1.01. 68
now swallow down that lie. 1.01.132
imagine it | to lie that way thou goest, not 1.03.287
if judgment lie in them, then so do we, 2.02.133
and heavy–gaited toads lie in their way, | doing 3.02. 15
and lie full low, grav'd in the hollow ground. 3.02.140
that lie shall lie so heavy on my sword, | that 4.01. 66
that lie shall lie so heavy on my sword, | that 4.01. 66
till thou the lie–giver and that lie do lie | in 4.01. 68
till thou the lie–giver and that lie do lie | in 4.01. 68
'zounds, i lie, for they pray continually to 1H4 2.01. 79 P
peace, ye fat–guts, lie down. 2.02. 31 P
you lie, ye rogue, 'tis going to the king's 2.02. 56 P
you are a shallow, cowardly hind, and you lie. 2.03. 16 P
hal, if i tell thee a lie, spit in my face, call 2.04.194 P
lie still, ye thief, and hear the lady sing in 3.01.233 P
ye lie, hostess, bardolph was shav'd and lost 3.03. 59 P
on high, | and either we or they must lower lie. 3.03.204
that lie too heavy on the commonwealth, | cries 4.03. 80
wales, | there without ransom to lie forfeited; 4.03. 96
and by, | till then in blood by noble percy lie. 5.04.110
i lie, i am no counterfeit. 5.04.115 P
for my part, if a lie may do thee grace, | i'll 5.04.157
leave to tell you you lie in your throat if you 2H4 1.02. 85 P
me some sack, and, sweet heart, lie thou there. 2.04.183
then (happy) low, lie down! 3.01. 30
seeds | and weak beginning lie intreasured. 3.01. 85
and every third word a lie, duer paid to the 3.02.307 P
i trust, lords, we shall lie to–night together. 4.02. 97
why doth the crown lie there upon his pillow, 4.05. 21
but bear me to that chamber, there i'll lie, 4.05.239
it is much that a lie with a slight oath and a 5.01. 82 P
for in his tomb lie my affections, | and with 5.02.124
nuthook, nuthook, you lie. 5.04. 7 P
and lie pavilion'd in the fields of france. H5 1.02.129
the english lie within fifteen hundred paces of 3.07.125 P
since i may say, "now lie i like a king." 4.01. 17
their poor bodies | must lie and fester. 4.03. 88
in which array, brave soldier, doth he lie, 4.06. 7
lie drown'd and soak'd in mercenary blood; 4.07. 76
that's a lie in thy throat. 4.08. 16 P
thousand french | that in the field lie slain; 4.08. 81
there lie dead | one hundred twenty–six; 4.08. 82
the names of those their nobles that lie dead: 4.08. 91
and all her husbandry doth lie on heaps, 5.02. 39
at pleasure here we lie near orleance; 1H6 1.02. 6
for there young henry with his nobles lie. 3.02.129
shall all thy mother's hopes lie in one tomb? 4.05. 34
prove them, and i lie open to the law; 2H6 1.03.156
there let his head and liveless body lie, 4.01.142
here may his head lie on my throbbing breast; 4.04. 5
so lie thou there; 5.02. 66
to tell thee plain, i aim to lie with thee. 3H6 3.02. 69
to tell you plain, i had rather lie in prison. 3.02. 70
vow | never to lie and take his natural rest 4.03. 5
so, lie thou there. 5.02. 1
long, | i will deliver you, or else lie for you. R3 1.01.115
so will it, madam, till i lie with you. 1.02.113
a man cannot lie with his neighbor's wife, but 1.04.137 P
i to my grave, where peace and rest lie with me! 4.01. 94
here will i lie to–night — | but where 5.03. 7
yet i lie, i am not. 5.03.191
lie with our wives? 5.03.336
all men's honors | lie like one lump before him, H8 2.02. 48
cause, that she should lie i' th' bosom of | our 3.02.100
his faults lie open to the laws, let them, | not 3.02.334

so may he rest, his faults lie gently on him! 4.02. 31
one, i dare avow | (and now i should not lie), 4.02.143
and here ye lie baiting of bombards, when | ye 5.03. 81
when i do tell thee there my hopes lie drown'd, TRO 1.01. 49
in how many fadoms deep | they lie indrench'd. 1.01. 51
a woman, a man knows not at what ward you lie. 1.02.259 P
and at all these wards i lie, at a thousand 1.02.263 P
an engine | not portable, lie under this report: 2.03.135
in faith, i lie, | my thoughts were like 3.02.121
had i so good occasion to lie long | as /you, 4.01. 4
shall i not lie in publishing a truth? 5.02.119
they lie in view, but have not spoke as yet. COR 1.04. 4
how far off lie these armies? 1.04. 8
men, yet they lie deadly that tell you have good 2.01. 61 P
that dark spirit, in 's nervy arm doth lie, 2.01.160
were a malice that, giving itself the lie, would 2.02. 32 P
the dust on antique time would lie unswept, 2.03.119
to my noble heart | a lie that it must bear? 3.02.101
would half my wealth | would buy this for a lie! 4.06.160
lie in th' interpretation of the time, | and 4.07. 50
it were as virtuous to lie as to live chastely. 5.02. 27 P
my grave lords, | must give this cur the lie; 5.06.106
shall join | to thrust the lie unto him. 5.06.109
there lie thy bones, sweet mutius, with thy TIT 1.01.387
you lie. ROM 1.01. 61 P
griefs of mine own lie heavy in my breast, 1.01.186
that dreamers often lie. 1.04. 51
atomi | over men's noses as they lie asleep. 1.04. 58
this is the hag, when maids lie on their backs, 1.04. 92
good manners shall lie all in one or two men's 1.05. 3 P
now old desire doth in his death–bed lie, | and 2.pr. 1
and the demesnes that there adjacent lie, | that 2.01. 20
and where care lodges, sleep will never lie; 2.03. 36
blood for your rude brawls doth lie a–bleeding; 3.01.189
for thou wilt lie upon the wings of night, 3.02. 18
to–morrow night look that thou lie alone, | let 4.01. 91
let not the nurse lie with thee in thy chamber. 4.01. 92
where all the kindred of the capulets lie. 4.01.112
lie thou there. 4.03. 23
well, juliet, i will lie with thee to–night. 5.01. 34
death, lie thou there, by a dead man interr'd. 5.03. 87
to lie discolor'd by this place of peace? 5.03.143
we see the ground whereon these woes do lie, 5.03.179
came to this vault to die, and lie with juliet. 5.03.290
as rich shall romeo's by his lady's lie, | poor 5.03.303
then i lie not. TIM 1.01.219 P
the lands thou hast | lie in a pitch'd field. 1.02.225
it pleases time and fortune to lie heavy | upon 3.05. 10
flatterers yet wear silk, drink wine, lie soft, 4.03.206
lie where the light foam of the sea may beat 4.03.378
on special dignities, which vacant lie, | for 5.01.142
here lie i, timon, who, alive, all living men 5.04. 72
sure | it did not lie there when i went to bed. JC 2.01. 38
shall caesar send a lie? 2.02. 65
how caesar hath deserv'd to lie in death, | mark 3.01.132
dost thou lie so low? 3.01.148
strooken by many princes, | dost thou here lie! 3.01.210
i pray you, sirs, lie in my tent and sleep; 4.03.246
lie down, good sirs, | it may be i shall 4.03.250
where, where, messala, doth his body lie? 5.03. 91
within my tent his bones to–night shall lie, 5.05. 78
they must lie there. MAC 2.02. 46
ere you went to bed, | that you do lie so late? 2.03. 23
in a sleep, and, giving him the lie, leaves him. 2.03. 36 P
i believe drink gave thee the lie last night. 2.03. 37 P
but i requited him for his lie, and, i think, 2.03. 39 P
than on the torture of the mind to lie | in 3.02. 21
and must they all be hang'd that swear and lie? 4.02. 52 P
here let them lie | till famine and the ague eat 5.05. 3
my sword | i'll prove the lie thou speak'st. 5.07. 11
gives me the lie i' th' throat | as deep as to HAM 2.02.574
lady, shall i lie in your lap? 3.02.112 P
a fair thought to lie between maids' legs. 3.02.118 P
of his lands will scarcely lie in this box, and 5.01.111 P
you lie out on't, sir, and therefore 'tis not 5.01.123 P
for my part, i do not lie in't, yet it is mine. 5.01.124 P
thou dost lie in't, to be in't and say it is 5.01.125 P
'tis a quick lie, sir, 'twill away again from me 5.01.128 P
how long will a man lie i' th' earth ere he rot? 5.01.163 P
lo here i lie, | never to rise again. 5.02.318
a schoolmaster that can teach thy fool to lie — LR 1.04.180 P
thy fool to lie — i would fain learn to lie. 1.04.180 P
and you lie, sirrah, we'll have you whipt. 1.04.181 P
now, good my lord, lie here and rest awhile. 3.06. 82
'tis a lie, i am not ague–proof. 4.06.105 P
with the hell–hated lie o'erwhelm thy heart, 5.03.148
you where he lodges, is to tell you where i lie. OTH 3.04. 9 P
he lies there, were to lie in mine own throat. 3.04. 13 P
lie — 4.01. 34
lie with her? 4.01. 35 P
lie on her? 4.01. 35 P
we say lie on her, when they belie her. 4.01. 35 P
lie with her! 4.01. 36 P
alive | that nightly lie in those unproper beds 4.01. 68
she might lie by an emperor's side and command 4.01.184 P
you told a lie, an odious, damned lie; 5.02.180
you told a lie, an odious, damned lie; 5.02.180
upon my soul, a lie, a wicked lie. 5.02.181
upon my soul, a lie, a wicked lie. 5.02.181
who tells me true, though in his tale lie death, ANT 1.02. 98
forth weeds | when our quick winds lie still, 1.02.110
she did lie | in her pavilion — cloth of gold, 2.02.198
should i lie, madam? 2.05. 93
lie they upon thy hand, | and be undone by 'em! 2.05.105
lie graveless, till the flies and gnats of nile 3.13.166
torch is out, | lie down and stray no farther. 4.14. 47
you lie up to the hearing of the gods! 5.02. 95
but something given to lie, as a woman should 5.02.252 P
dost thou lie still? 5.02.296
for | his fortunes all lie speechless, and his CYM 1.05. 52
o sleep, thou ape of death, lie dull upon her, 2.02. 31
if not, | let her lie still and dream. 2.03. 65
if you will swear you have not done't, you lie, 2.04.144
to lie in watch there and to think on him? 3.04. 41
will poor folks lie, | that have afflictions on 3.06. 9
in fullness | is sorer than to lie for need; 3.06. 13
those rich–left heirs that let their fathers lie 4.02.226
are worse | than priests and fanes that lie. 4.02.242
faith, i'll lie down and sleep. 4.02.294
if i do lie and do | no harm by it, though the 4.02.377
that is my bed too, lads, and there i'll lie. 4.04. 52
kill'd thy daughter — villain–like, i lie — 5.05.218
thou scornful page, | there lie thy part. 5.05.229
that calls me traitor, i return the lie. PER 2.05. 57
and will not lie till the ship be clear'd of the 3.01. 48 P
i am the governor of this place you lie before. 5.01. 21
sweet, | lie 'fore bride and bridegroom's feet, TNK 1.01. 14
lords | lie blist'ring 'fore the visitating sun, 1.01.146
i could lie down, i am sure. 2.02.151
no, no, i lie! 3.02. 21
"traitor," | i am a villain fit to lie unburied. 3.06.171
lie there, arcite! 4.02. 43
do any thing, | lie with her, if she ask you. 5.02. 18
the right o' th' lady | did lie in you, for you 5.04.117
"witness this primrose bank whereon i lie, VEN 151
warm, | and lo i lie between that sun and thee; 194
stray lower, where the pleasant fountains lie. 234
foreknowing well, if there he came to lie, | why 245
within my bosom, whereon thou dost lie, | my 646
under whose sharp fangs on his back doth lie 663
"lie quietly, and hear a little more, | nay, do 709
as one of which doth tarquin lie revolving | the LUC 127
but they whose guilt within their bosoms lie 1342
therefore i'll lie with love, and love with me, PP 1.13
as flowers dead lie withered on the ground, | as 13. 9
all simplicity, | here enclos'd, in cinders lie. PHT 55
but things remov'd that hidden in /thee lie! SON 31. 8
my heart doth plead that thou in him dost lie 46. 5
time's best jewel from time's chest lie hid? 65.10
unless you would devise some virtuous lie, | to 72. 5
fire | that on the ashes of his youth doth lie, 73.10
when you entombed in men's eyes shall lie; 81. 8
since that my life on thy revolt doth lie; 92.10
as from my soul, which in thy breast doth lie: 109. 4
those lines that i before have writ do lie, 115. 1
for thy records and what we see doth lie, | made 123.11
therefore i lie with her, and she with me, | and 138.13
to make me give the lie to my true sight, | and 150. 3
eye, | to swear against the truth so foul a lie! 152.14

LIED 4 FR 0.0004 REL FR 2 V 2 P
didst thou not say he lied? TMP 3.02. 74 P
pride, | if hermia meant to say lysander lied. MND 2.02. 55
aside, i had lied in my throat if i had said so. 2H4 1.02. 82 P
and i have lied so lewdly | that women ought to TNK 4.02. 35

LIEF *(also lieve, live*)*

LIEF 12 FR 0.0013 REL FR 3 V 9 P
i had as lief you would tell me of a mess of WIV 3.01. 63 P
i hope not, i had lief as bear so much lead. 4.02.113 P
i had as lief be a list of an english kersey as MM 1.02. 33 P
i had as lief have the foppery of freedom as the 1.02.133 P
i had as lief thou didst break his neck as his AYL 1.01.146 P
faith, i had as lief have been myself alone. 3.02.254 P
i had as lief be woo'd of a snail. 4.01. 52 P
but i had as lief take her dowry with this SHR 1.01.131 P
i had as lief be a brownist as a politician. TN 3.02. 31 P
not, | god knows i had as lief be none as one. R2 5.02. 49
i had as lief not be as live to be | in awe of JC 1.02. 95
i had as lief trace this good action with you TNK 1.01.102

LIEFEST 1 FR 0.0001 REL FR 1 V 0 P
stirr'd up | my liefest liege to be mine enemy. 2H6 3.01.164

/LIEGE 1 FR 0.0001 REL FR 1 V 0 P
/my /gracious /liege, | you won it, wore it, 2H4 4.05.220

LIEGE 138 FR 0.0156 REL FR 131 V 7 P
sir, my liege, | do not infest your mind with TMP 5.01.245
gentle my liege — MM 5.01.415
my liege, i am advised what i say, | neither ERR 5.01.214
'tis true, my liege, this ring i had of her. 5.01.278
as sure, my liege, as i do see your grace. 5.01.280
my liege, your highness now may do me good. ADO 1.01.290
so much, dear liege, i have already sworn, LLL 1.01. 34
let me say no, my liege, and if you please: 1.01. 50
this article, my liege, yourself must break, 1.01.133
liege of all loiterers and malecontents, | dread 3.01.183
ah, good my liege, i pray thee pardon me! 4.03.150
a toy, my liege, a toy; 4.03.197
he, he, and you — and you, my liege! 4.03.204
for when would you, my liege, or you, or you, 4.03.317
ay, my liege, so please you give us leave. AYL 1.02.157 P
orlando, my liege, the youngest son of sir 1.02.222 P
then, good my liege, mistake me not so much | to 1.03. 64
pronounce that sentence then on me, my liege, 1.03. 85
my wife, my liege? AWW 2.03.106
'tis past, my liege, | and i beseech your 5.03. 4
i shall, my liege. 5.03. 27
admiringly, my liege. 5.03. 44
i'll put in bail, my liege. 5.03.285
if she, my liege, can make me know this clearly, 5.03.315
and i wish, my liege, | you had only in your WT 2.01.170
good my liege, i come; 2.03. 52
my royal liege, | he is not guilty of her coming 2.03.144
now, my liege, | tell me what blessings i have 3.02.106
now, good my liege, | sir, royal sir, forgive a 3.02.226
sir, my liege, | your eye hath too much youth 5.01.224
first, you, my liege; 5.03. 22
my liege, here is the strangest controversy JN 1.01. 44
but that i am as well begot, my liege | (fair 1.01. 77
my gracious liege, when that my father liv'd, 1.01. 95
then, good my liege, let me have what is mine, 1.01.114
philip, my liege, so is my name begun, | philip, 1.01.158
but on, my liege, for very little pains | will 3.02. 9
my liege, her ear | is stopp'd with dust: 4.02.119
with all my heart, my liege. 4.02.180
let us, my liege, to arms. 5.01. 73
my liege, my lord! 5.07. 66
i have, my liege. R2 1.01. 7
my gracious sovereign, my most loving liege! 1.01. 21
and let him be no kinsman to my liege, | i do 1.01. 59
for that my sovereign liege was in my debt, 1.01.129
then, dear my liege, mine honor let me try; 1.01.184
most mighty liege, and my companion peers, 1.03. 93
a heavy sentence, my most sovereign liege, | and 1.03.154
farewell, my liege, now no way can i stray; 1.03.206
i thank my liege that in regard of me | he 1.03.216
expedient manage must be made, my liege, | ere 1.04. 39
my liege, old gaunt commends him to your majesty 2.01.147
o my liege, | pardon me, if you please; 2.01.186
my liege, farewell! 2.01.211
comfort, my liege, why looks your grace so pale? 3.02. 75
comfort, my liege, remember who you are. 3.02. 82
more health and happiness betide my liege | than 3.02. 91
my liege, one word. 3.02.215
my liege, beware! 5.03. 39
what ho, my liege! for god's sake let me in. 5.03. 74
sweet york, be patient. hear me, gentle liege. 5.03. 91
my liege, this haste was hot in question, | and 1H4 1.01. 34
i will, my liege. 1.01.108
our house, my sovereign liege, little deserves 1.03. 10
my liege, i did deny no prisoners, | but i 1.03. 29
he never did fall off, my sovereign liege, | but 1.03. 94
hear me, my liege. 5.01. 22
we have, my liege. 2H4 3.01. 37
we left the prince my brother here, my liege, 4.05. 51
when we withdrew, my liege, we left it here. 4.05. 58
o, pardon me, my liege! 4.05.138
and dead almost, my liege, to think you were, 4.05.156
thus, my most royal liege, | accusing it, i put 4.05.164
shall we call in th' ambassador, my liege? H5 1.02. 3
and my thrice–puissant liege | is in the very 1.02.119
o, let their bodies follow, my dear liege, 1.02.130
been then more fear'd than harm'd, my liege; 1.02.155
therefore to france, my liege! 1.02.213
tennis–balls, my liege. 1.02.258
no doubt, my liege, if each man do his best. 2.02. 19
so did you me, my liege. 2.02. 64
for, my good liege, she is so idly king'd, | her 2.04. 26
self–love, my liege, is not so vile a sin | as 2.04. 74
not so, my liege, this lodging likes me better, 4.01. 16
we shall, my liege. 4.01. 28
my liege! 4.01.306
god's will, my liege, would you and i alone, 4.03. 74
here comes the herald of the french, my liege. 4.07. 66
so i will, my liege, as i live. 4.07.146 P
under captain gower, my liege. 4.07.148 P
i will, my liege. 4.07.152 P
my liege, here is a villain and a traitor, that, 4.08. 25 P
my liege, this was my glove, here is the fellow 4.08. 28 P
yes, if it please your majesty, my liege. 1H6 3.04. 15
content, my liege? 4.01. 71
pardon, my liege, that i have stay'd so long. 2H6 3.01. 94
stirr'd up | my liefest liege to be mine enemy. 3.01.164
my liege, his railing is intolerable. 3.01.172
as humphrey, prov'd by reasons, to my liege. 3.01.260
i tender so the safety of my liege. 3.01.277
that shall i do, my liege. 3.02.134
a messenger from henry, our dread liege, | to 5.01. 17
and never live but true unto his liege! 5.01. 82
my gracious liege, this too much lenity | and 3H6 2.02. 9
for shame, my liege, make them your president! 2.02. 33
my liege, the wound that bred this meeting here 2.02.121
the fruits of love i mean, my loving liege. 3.02. 59
warwick, canst thou speak against thy liege, 3.03. 95
my sovereign liege, no letters, and few words, 4.01. 86
my liege, it is young henry, earl of richmond. 4.06. 67
my liege, i'll knock once more to summon them. 4.07. 16
first, mighty liege, tell me your highness' R3 4.04.447
none good, my liege, to please you with the 4.04.457
unless for that, my liege, i cannot guess. 4.04.474
unless for that he comes to be your liege, | you 4.04.475
in kent, my liege, the guilfords are in arms, 4.04.503
'tis said, my liege, in yorkshire are in arms. 4.04.519
my liege, the duke of buckingham is taken — 4.04.531
here, most gracious liege. 5.03. 4
it is, my liege, and all things are in readiness 5.03. 52
i can, my liege. H8 1.02.188
very well, my liege. 2.04.210
most dread liege, | the good i stand on is my 5.01.121
ay, ay, my liege, | and of a lovely boy. 5.01.163
you are amaz'd, my liege, at her exclaim. TRO 5.03. 91
alas, my liege, my wife is dead to–night; ROM 5.03.210
my liege, | they are not yet come back. MAC 1.04. 2
we are men, my liege. 3.01. 90
i am one, my liege, | whom the vile blows and 3.01.107
i assure my good liege | i hold my duty as i HAM 2.02. 43
my liege, and madam, to expostulate | what 2.02. 86
fare you well, my liege, | i'll call upon you 3.03. 33
good my liege — LR 1.01.120
remember, sir, my liege, | the kings your CYM 3.01. 16
good my liege, | the day that she was missing he 4.03. 16
good my liege, | your preparation can affront no 4.03. 28
they are the issue of your loins, my liege, 5.05.330
they are, my liege, | and stay your coming to PER 2.02. 2

LIEGEMAN 2 FR 0.0002 REL FR 1 V 1 P
as thou art liegeman to us, that thou carry WT 2.03.174
the devil his true liegeman upon the cross of a 1H4 2.04.338 P

LIEGEMEN 2 FR 0.0002 REL FR 2 V 0 P
you shall become true liegemen to his crown. 1H6 5.04.128
and liegemen to the dane. HAM 1.01. 15

LIEGERS *(also leiger)*

LIEGERS 1 FR 0.0001 REL FR 1 V 0 P
quite unpeople her | of liegers for her sweet; CYM 1.05. 80

LIEGE'S 2 FR 0.0002 REL FR 2 V 0 P
and where my liege's? LLL 4.03.171
place, | my person, or my liege's sovereignty. 2H4 5.02.101

LIE–GIVER 1 FR 0.0001 REL FR 1 V 0 P
till thou the lie–giver and that lie do lie | in R2 4.01. 68

LIEN *(also lain)*

LIEN 3 FR 0.0003 REL FR 2 V 1 P
many a poor man's son would have lien still, JN 4.01. 50
a skull now hath lien you i' th' earth three and HAM 5.01.173 P
of an egyptian | that had nine hours lien dead, PER 3.02. 85

/LIEN'D 1 FR 0.0001 REL FR 1 V 0 P
of fair demesnes, youthful and nobly /lien'd, ROM 3.05.180

/LIES* 4 FR 0.0004 REL FR 4 V 0 P
/very /true, /my /grief /lies /all /within, R2 4.01.295
/there /lies /the /substance; 4.01.299
/in /troy, /there /lies /the /scene. TRO pr 1
that now on pompey's basis /lies along | no JC 3.01.115

LIES* 270 FR 0.0305 REL FR 226 V 44 P
told thee no lies, made thee no mistakings, TMP 1.02.248
full fadom five thy father lies, | of his bones 1.02.397
pockets could speak, would it not say he lies? 2.01. 67 P
where lies that? 2.01.276
here lies your brother, | no better than the 2.01.280
no better than the earth he lies upon, | if he 2.01.281

this hour | lies at my mercy all mine enemies. 4.01.263
mudded in that oozy bed | where my son lies. 5.01.152
pray you, where lies sir proteus? TGV 4.02.136 P
nay then the wanton lies; my face is black. 5.02. 10
i hope good luck lies in odd numbers. WIV 5.01. 2 P
it lies much in your holding up. MM 3.01.261 P
when it lies starkly in the traveller's bones. 4.02. 67
because their business still lies out a' door. ERR 2.01. 11
the poison of that lies in you to temper. ADO 2.02. 21 P
in my chamber–window lies a book; 2.03. 3 P
and she lies buried with her ancestors — | o, 5.01. 69
tongues | was the hero that here lies. 5.03. 4
so, ere you find where light in darkness lies, LLL 1.01. 78
if my observation (which very seldom lies), | by 2.01.228
where lies thy grief, o, tell me, good dumaine? 4.03.169
and, gentle longaville, where lies thy pain? 4.03.170
what upward lies | the street should see as she 4.03.276
they are infected, in their hearts it lies; 5.02.420
a jest's prosperity lies in the ear | of him 5.02.861
it lies in you. MND 2.01.118
happy is hermia, wheresoe'er she lies, | for she 2.02. 90
there lies your love. 4.01. 78
loud, | puts the wretch that lies in woe | in 5.01.377
here an angel in a golden bed | lies all within. MV 2.07. 59
and fancy dies | in the cradle where it lies. 3.02. 69
a fine bragging youth, and tell quaint lies, 3.04. 69
and twenty of these puny lies i'll tell, | that 3.04. 74
and the offender's life lies in the mercy | of 4.01.355
and, as much as in him lies, mines my gentility AYL 1.01. 20 P
but these are all lies: 4.01.106 P
o monstrous beast, how like a swine he lies! SHR in.1. 34
ay, if the fool could find it where it lies. 2.01.212
the door is open, sir, there lies your way; 3.02.210
the note lies in 's throat if he say i said so. 4.03.132 P
lies richer in your thoughts than on his tomb. AWW 1.02. 49
but /one that lies three thirds and uses a known 2.05. 29 P
and clap upon you two or three probable lies. 3.06. 98 P
and then to return and swear the lies he forges. 4.01. 23 P
it lies in you, my lord, to bring me in some 5.02. 46 P
grant it me, o king, in you it best lies; 5.03.145 P
prove your honor | than in my thought it lies. 5.03.184
will you hoist sail, sir? here lies your way. TN 1.05.202 P
where lies your text? 1.05.223 P
worth stooping for, there it lies in your eye; 2.02. 15 P
in delay there lies no plenty, | then come kiss 2.03. 50
so thou mayst say, the /king lies by a beggar, 3.01. 8 P
there lies your way, due west. 3.01.134
and as many lies as will lie in thy sheet of 3.02. 46 P
that lies enclosed in this trunk which you WT 1.02.435
within a mile where my land and living lies; 4.03. 98 P
why should i carry lies abroad? 4.04.271 P
lies he not bed–rid? 4.04.401
i see the play so lies | that i must bear a part 4.04.655
there lies such secrets in this farthel and box, 4.04.756 P
which fault lies on the hazards of all husbands JN 1.01.119
who says it was, he lies, i say 'twas not. 1.01.276
it lies as sightly on the back of him | as great 2.01.143
many a widow's husband grovelling lies, | coldly 2.01.305
whose fullness of perfection lies in him. 2.01.440
lady, with me, with me thy fortune lies. 3.01.337
foot of mine doth tread, | he lies before me. 3.03. 63
lies in his bed, walks up and down with me, 3.04. 94
prate | he will awake my mercy, which lies dead; 4.01. 26
and "where lies your grief?" 4.01. 48
this is the prison. what is he lies here? 4.03. 34
who speaks not truly, lies. 4.03. 92
hath troubled me so long, | lies heavy on me. 5.03. 4
how long a time lies in one little word! R2 1.03.213
where lies he? 1.04. 57
for their love | lies in their purses, and whoso 2.02.130
behind, | and in my loyal bosom lies his power. 2.03. 98
how far off lies your power? 3.02. 63
scroop, where lies our uncle with his power? 3.02.192
king richard lies | within the limits of yon 3.03. 25
there lies | two kinsmen digg'd their graves 3.03.168
and spur thee on with full as many lies | as may 4.01. 53
and spit upon him whilst i say he lies, | and 4.01. 75
him whilst i say he lies, | and lies, and lies. 4.01. 76
him whilst i say he lies, | and lies, and lies. 4.01. 76
that norfolk lies, here do i throw down this, 4.01. 84
dies, | or my sham'd life in his dishonor lies: 5.03. 71
herein all breathless lies | the mightiest of 5.06. 31
gadshill lies to–night in rochester. 1H4 1.02.129 P
be the incomprehensible lies that this same fat 1.02.187 P
but i will find him when he lies asleep, | and 1.03.221
these lies are like their father that begets 2.04.225 P
if then thou be son to me, here lies the point: 2.04.406 P
done, all's won, here breathless lies the king. 5.03. 16
many a nobleman lies stark and stiff | under the 5.03. 41
this, | where stain'd nobility lies trodden on, 5.04. 13
cousin westmerland, | our duty this way lies; 5.04. 16
and cold hand of death | lies on my tongue. 5.04. 85
father, old northumberland, | lies crafty–sick. 2H4 in 37
morton, | tell thou an earl his divination lies, 1.01. 88
uneasy lies the head that wears a crown. 3.01. 31
for lo, within a ken our army lies: 4.01.149
and every thing lies level to our wish. 4.04. 7
there lies a downy feather which stirs not. 4.05. 32
when pistol lies, do this, and fig me like | the 5.03.118
but this lies all within the will of god, | to H5 1.02.289
and silken dalliance in the wardrobe lies; 2.pr. 2
harflew | till in her ashes she lies buried. 3.03. 9
the /gimmal'd bit | lies foul with chaw'd–grass, 4.02. 50
wounds) | the noble earl of suffolk also lies. 4.06. 10
which you before so urg'd, lies in his answer. 5.02. 76
to visit her poor castle where she lies, | that 1H6 2.02. 41
york lies; 4.04. 33
see where he lies inhearsed in the arms | of the 4.07. 45
stinking and fly–blown lies here at our feet. 4.07. 76
there all is marr'd; there lies a cooling card. 5.03. 84
the envious load that lies upon his heart; 2H6 3.01.157
he lies, for i invented it myself. 4.02.155
that clifford's manhood lies upon his tongue. 3H6 2.02.125
in them, and in ourselves, our safety lies. 4.01. 46
this way, my lord, for this way lies the game. 4.05. 14
it is not his, my lord, here southam lies; 5.01. 12
with lies well steel'd with weighty arguments, R3 1.01.148
there lies the duke asleep, and there the keys. 1.04. 95

his regiment lies half a mile at least | south 5.03. 37
the penance lies on you, if these fair ladies H8 1.04. 32
therefore in him | it lies to cure me, and the 2.04.101
her bed is india, there she lies, a pearl; TRO 1.01.100
won are done, joy's soul lies in the doing. 1.02.287
by itself | lies rich in virtue and unmingled. 1.03. 30
reproof of chance | lies the true proof of men: 1.03. 34
and in his tent | lies mocking our designs. 1.03.146
whose conceit | lies in his hamstring, and doth 1.03.154
too, lies in your sinews, or else there be liars 2.01. 98 P
but it lies as coldly in him as fire in a flint, 3.03.256 P
here lies our way. 4.01. 80
honor or go or stay, | my major vow lies here; 5.01. 44
thy master now lies thinking on his bed | of 5.02. 78
here lies thy heart, thy sinews, and thy bone. 5.08. 12
you must go visit the good lady that lies in. COR 1.03. 77 P
how lies their battle? 1.06. 51
should be dieted | in praises sauc'd with lies. 1.09. 53
because that now it lies you on to speak | to 3.02. 52
for that he has | (as much as in him lies) from 3.03. 94
would unclog my heart | of what lies heavy to't. 4.02. 48
this lies glowing, i can tell you, and is almost 4.03. 25 P
if it be your will, | where great aufidius lies. 4.04. 8
of the war | destroy what lies before 'em. 4.06. 42
you had told as many lies in his behalf as you 5.02. 24 P
my remission lies | in volscian breasts. 5.02. 84
which are | as cheap as lies, he sold the blood 5.06. 46
when he lies along, | after your way his tale 5.06. 56
the /snake lies rolled in the cheerful sun, TIT 2.03. 13
lord bassianus lies /beray'd in blood, | all on 2.03.222
poor bassianus here lies murthered. 2.03.263
lies my consent and fair according voice. ROM 1.02. 19
and what obscur'd in this fair volume lies 1.03. 85
tickling a parson's nose as 'a lies asleep, 1.04. 80
there lies more peril in thine eye | than twenty 2.02. 71
else would i tear the cave where echo lies, 2.02.161
o, mickle is the powerful grace that lies | in 2.03. 15
remedies | within thy help and holy physic lies. 2.03. 52
young men's love then lies | not truly in their 2.03. 67
there lies that tybalt. 3.01.139
there lies the man, slain by young romeo, | that 3.01.144
even so lies she, | blubb'ring and weeping, 3.03. 86
bed | in that dim monument where tybalt lies. 3.05.201
lies fest'ring in his shroud, where, as they say 4.03. 43
death lies on her like an untimely frost | upon 4.05. 28
there she lies, | flower as she was, deflowered 4.05. 36
for here lies juliet, and her beauty makes 5.03. 85
thy husband in thy bosom there lies dead; 5.03.155
here lies the county slain, | and juliet 5.03.174
sovereign, here lies the county paris slain, 5.03.195
here lies my gown. TIM 3.06.117 P
the consecrated snow | that lies on dian's lap! 4.03.386
"here lies a wretched corse, of wretched soul 5.04. 70
here lies the east; doth not the day break here? JC 2.01.101
he lies to–night within seven leagues of rome. 3.01.286
now lies he there, | and none so poor to do him 3.02.119
under which | our army lies, ready to give up 5.01. 88
is not that he that lies upon the ground? 5.03. 57
he lies not like the living. o my heart! 5.03. 58
down, or else o'erleap, | for in my way it lies. MAC 1.04. 50
their drenched natures lies as in a death, 1.07. 68
a heavy summons lies like lead upon me, | and 2.01. 6
hark! who lies i' th' second chamber? 2.02. 17
there the grown serpent lies; 3.04. 28
that i may tell pale–hearted fear it lies, | and 4.01. 85
why, one that swears and lies. 4.02. 47 P
of the fiend | that lies like truth. 5.05. 43
be wary then, best safety lies in fear: HAM 1.03. 43
thus, | that, open'd, lies within our remedy. 2.02. 18
rebellious to his arm, lies where it falls, 2.02.470
there the action lies | in his true nature, and 3.03. 61
for here lies the point: 5.01. 10 P
here lies the water; 5.01. 15 P
o, that way madness lies, let me shun that! LR 3.04. 21
the let–alone lies not in your good will. 5.03. 79
that names me traitor, villain–like he lies. 5.03. 98
corrigible authority of this lies in our wills. OTH 1.03.326 P
for bragging and telling her fantastical lies. 2.01.224 P
you know, sirrah, where lieutenant cassio lies? 3.04. 2 P
i dare not say he lies any where. 3.04. 3 P
and for me to say a soldier lies, 'tis stabbing. 3.04. 5 P
for me to devise a lodging and say he lies here, 3.04. 12 P
lodging and say he lies here, or he lies there, 3.04. 12 P
minion, your dear lies dead, | and your unblest 5.01. 33
he that lies slain here, cassio, | was my dear 5.01.101
he lies to th' heart. 5.02.156
my mistress here lies murthered in her bed — 5.02.185
there lies your niece, | whose breath, indeed, 5.02.201
where lies he? ANT 2.02.159
for my peace, | i' th' east my pleasure lies. 2.03. 41
and spurns | the rush that lies before him; 3.05. 17
our fortune lies | upon this jump. 3.08. 5
wherein the worship of the whole world lies. 4.14. 86
in thy possession lies | a lass unparallel'd. 5.02.315
those springs | on chalic'd flow'rs that lies; CYM 2.03. 23
(worthy her pressing) lies a mole, right proud 2.04.135
the testimonies whereof lies bleeding in me. 3.04. 22 P
gods, what lies i have heard! 4.02. 32
a good, | that here by mountaineers lies slain. 4.02.370
here she lies, sir. PER 3.01. 55
i rage and roar | as doth the sea she lies in, 3.03. 11
"the fairest, sweetest, and best lies here, 4.04. 34
faith, my acquaintance lies little amongst them. 4.06.195 P
seem | like lies disdain'd in the reporting. 5.01.119
and there's a rock lies watching under water; TNK 3.04. 6
no, keep it, your life lies on it. 3.06. 90
in the great lake that lies behind the palace, 4.01. 53
th' wood, where palamon | lies longing for me. 4.01.145
far better, | for there the cure lies mainly. 5.02. 8
on the sinister side the heart lies; 5.03. 76
panting he lies, and breatheth in her face. VEN 62
look how a bird lies tangled in a net, | so 67
in a net, | so fast'ned in her arms adonis lies; 68
look in mine eyeballs, there thy beauty lies; 119
for on the grass she lies as she were slain, 473
love is all truth, lust full of forged lies. 804
where lo, two lamps burnt out in darkness lies; 1128
band | where her beloved collatinus lies. LUC 256

who fears sinking where such treasure lies?" 280
he takes it from the rushes where it lies, | and 318
thing, | lies at the mercy of his mortal sting. 364
her lily hand her rosy cheek lies under, 386
where like a virtuous monument she lies, | to be 391
where their dear governess and lady lies, | do 443
like to a new–kill'd bird she trembling lies; 457
so under his insulting falchion lies | harmless 509
she like a wearied lamb lies panting there; 737
cloak | immodestly lies martyr'd with disgrace. 802
which bleeding under pyrrhus' proud foot lies. 1449
here friend by friend in bloody channel lies, 1487
if in the child the father's image lies, | where 1753
i do believe her (though i know she lies) | that PP 1. 2
fuel, | making a famine where abundance lies, SON 1. 7
then being ask'd where all thy beauty lies, 2. 5
the age to come would say, "this poet lies, 17. 7
to find where your true image pictur'd lies, 24. 6
and in themselves their pride lies buried, | for 25. 7
and says in him /thy fair appearance lies. 46. 8
my grief lies onward and my joy behind. 50.14
for't lies in thee | to make him much outlive a 101.10
they know what beauty is, see where it lies, 137. 3
i do believe her, though i know she lies, | that 138. 2
me, | and in our faults by lies we flattered be. 138.14
the bath for my help lies | where cupid got new 153.13
cried, "o false blood, thou register of lies, LC 52
what a hell of witchcraft lies | in the small 288

LIEST* 42 FR 0.0047 REL FR 28 V 14 P

thou liest, malignant thing! TMP 1.02.257
thou liest, most ignorant monster, i am in case 3.02. 25 P
thou liest. 3.02. 45
thou liest, thou jesting monkey thou! 3.02. 45
thou liest, thou canst not. 3.02. 62
thou liest. 3.02. 75
thou liest; i can. TGV 3.01.292 P
froth and scum, thou liest! WIV 1.01.164
thou liest! 2.01. 51 P
varlet, thou liest! MM 2.01.167 P
thou liest, wicked varlet! 2.01.167 P
villain, thou liest, for even her very words ERR 2.02.163
yet thou liest in the bleak air. AYL 2.06. 15 P
minion, thou liest. is't not hortensio? SHR 2.01. 13
thou liest, thou thread, thou thimble, | thou 4.03.107
ergo, thou liest. 4.03.128 P
thou liest — his father is come from padua and 5.01. 30 P
but thou liest in thy throat, that is not the TN 3.04.156 P
i say thou liest, camillo, and i hate thee, WT 1.02.300
the false passage of thy throat thou liest. R2 1.01.125
land, | wherein thou liest in reputation sick, 2.01. 96
i say thou liest, | and will maintain what thou 4.01. 26
if thou deniest it twenty times, thou liest, 4.01. 38
aumerle, thou liest, his honor is as true | in 4.01. 44
surrey, thou liest. 4.01. 65
thou liest, thou art not colted, thou art 1H4 2.02. 38 P
why rather, sleep, liest thou in smoky cribs, 2H4 3.01. 9
ill rest betide the chamber where thou liest! R3 1.02.112
proud lord, thou liest! H8 3.02.252
"thou liest" unto thee with a voice as free | as COR 3.03. 73
tybalt, liest thou there in thy bloody sheet? ROM 5.03. 97
thou liest. TIM 1.01.216 P
then thou liest: 1.01.222 P
where liest a' nights, timon? 4.03.292
thou liest, abhorred tyrant, with my sword MAC 5.07. 10
i think it be thine indeed, for thou liest in't. HAM 5.01.122 P
dead, not for the quick, therefore thou liest. 5.01.127 P
shall my sister be | when thou liest howling. 5.01.242
detested kite, thou liest. LR 1.04.262
upon thy heart, whereto i speak, | thou liest. 5.03.142
filth, thou liest! OTH 5.02.231
traitor, thou liest. PER 2.05. 55

LIETH 1 FR 0.0001 REL FR 1 V 0 P

but since correction lieth in those hands R2 1.02. 4

LIEU 8 FR 0.0009 REL FR 7 V 1 P

which was, that he, in lieu o' th' premises, TMP 1.02.123
only, in lieu thereof, dispatch me hence. TGV 2.07. 88
and, in lieu thereof, impose on thee nothing but LLL 3.01.129 P
in lieu whereof | three thousand ducats, due MV 4.01.410
in lieu of this last night did lie with me. 5.01.262
yield | in lieu of all thy pains and husbandry. AYL 2.03. 65
in lieu whereof, i pray you bear me hence | from JN 5.04. 44
and, in lieu of this, | desires you let the H5 1.02.255

LIEUTENANT 43 FR 0.0048 REL FR 23 V 20 P

by this light, thou shalt be my lieutenant, TMP 3.02. 15 P
your lieutenant if you list, he's no standard. 3.02. 17 P
bid my lieutenant peto meet me at town's end. 1H4 4.02. 9 P
come, lieutenant pistol, come, bardolph. 2H4 5.05. 89 P
good morrow, lieutenant bardolph. H5 2.01. 2 P
good lieutenant! 2.01. 39 P
is an aunchient lieutenant there at the pridge, 3.06. 12 P
lieutenant, is it you whose voice i hear? 1H6 1.03. 16
master lieutenant, now that god and friends 3H6 4.06. 1
for what, lieutenant? 4.06. 9
and in good time, here the lieutenant comes. R3 4.01. 12
master lieutenant, pray you, by your leave, 4.01. 13
in personal suit to make me his lieutenant, OTH 1.01. 9
he, in good time, must his lieutenant be, | and 1.01. 32
and my lieutenant? 1.02. 34
lieutenant to the warlike moor othello, | is 2.01. 27
but, good lieutenant, is your general wiv'd? 2.01. 60
the lieutenant to–night watches on the court of 2.01.217 P
not this hour, lieutenant; 2.03. 13 P
come, lieutenant, i have a stope of wine, and 2.03. 30 P
i am for it, lieutenant; 2.03. 87 P
it's true, good lieutenant. 2.03.105 P
and so do i too, lieutenant. 2.03.108 P
the lieutenant is to be sav'd before the ancient 2.03.110 P
i pray you, after the lieutenant, go. 2.03.137
what's the matter, lieutenant? 2.03.146 P
nay, good lieutenant; 2.03.151 P
nay, good lieutenant — /god's /will, gentlemen 2.03.158
lieutenant — sir — montano — /sir — | help, 2.03.159
/god's /will, lieutenant, /hold! 2.03.162
lieutenant — sir — montano — gentlemen — 2.03.166
what, are you hurt, lieutenant? 2.03.259 P
and, good lieutenant, i think you think i love 2.03.311 P
good night, lieutenant, i must to the watch. 2.03.333 P
good morrow, good lieutenant. 3.01. 41

why, your lieutenant, cassio. 3.03. 45
now art thou my lieutenant. 3.03.479
you know, sirrah, where lieutenant cassio lies? 3.04. 1 P
how do you /now, lieutenant? 4.01.103
i thank you. how does lieutenant cassio? 4.01.222
o me, lieutenant! what villains have done this? 5.01. 56
one of my place in syria, his lieutenant, | for ANT 3.01. 18
who's his lieutenant, hear you? 3.07. 77
LIEUTENANTRY 2 FR 0.0002 REL FR 1 V 1 P
as these strip you out of your lieutenantry, it OTH 2.01.172 P
he alone | dealt on lieutenantry, and no ANT 3.11. 39
LIEUTENANT'S 1 FR 0.0001 REL FR 0 V 1 P
or under your arm, like a lieutenant's scarf? ADO 2.01.190 P
LIEUTENANTS 1 FR 0.0001 REL FR 0 V 1 P
corporals, lieutenants, gentlemen of companies 1H4 4.02. 24 P
LIEVE *(also lief, live*)*
LIEVE 3 FR 0.0003 REL FR 0 V 3 P
as had as lieve hear the devil as a drum, such 1H4 4.02. 18 P
i had as lieve helen's golden tongue had TRO 1.02.104 P
good soul, had as lieve see a toad, a very toad, ROM 2.04.203 P
LIFE *(also live*, etc.)*
/LIFE 11 FR 0.0012 REL FR 11 V 0 P
/gasping /for /life /under /great /bullingbrook, 2H4 1.01.208
/begin /to /stop | /our /very /veins /of /life. 4.01. 66
(/his /own /life /hung /upon /the /staff /he 4.01.124
more miserable by the /life of him | than i am R3 1.02. 27
/such /violent /hands /upon /her /tender /life. TIT 3.02. 22
/violent /hands /can /she /lay /on /her /life? 3.02. 25
/tears /will /quickly /melt /thy /life /away. 3.02. 51
/now, /by /my /life, | /old /fools /are /babes LR 1.03. 18
/grew /puissant /and /the /strings /of /life 5.03.217
and another /life | to pericles thy father. PER 5.01.207
call | and give them repetition to the /life. 5.01.246
LIFE 910 FR 0.1028 REL FR 789 V 121 P
thing she did | they would not take her life. TMP 1.02.267
here is every thing advantageous to life. 2.01. 50 P
she that dwells | ten leagues beyond man's life; 2.01.247
if of life you keep a care, | shake off slumber, 2.01.303
moon–calf, speak once in thy life, if thou beest 3.02. 21 P
but heart's sorrow, | and a clear life ensuing. 3.03. 82
so, with good life, | and observation strange, 3.03. 86
have given you here a third of mine own life, 4.01. 3
for quiet days, fair issue, and long life, 4.01. 24
caliban and his confederates | against my life. 4.01.141
and our little life | is rounded with a sleep. 4.01.157
of whom i have | receiv'd a second life; 5.01.195
one) had plotted with them | to take my life. 5.01.274
make it | go quick away — the story of my life, 5.01.305
i long | to hear the story of your life, which 5.01.313
sweet love, sweet lines, sweet life! TGV 1.03. 45
ay, proteus, but that life is alter'd now: 2.04.128
climb it | without apparent hazard of his life. 3.01.116
but, as thou lov'st thy life, make speed from 3.01.169
death, | but, fly i hence, i fly away from life. 3.01.187
have some malignant power upon my life; 3.01.240
besides, thy staying will abridge thy life. 3.01.247
to hazard life, and rescue you from him | that 5.04. 21
o' my life, if i were young again, the sword WIV 1.01. 40 P
it is a life that i have desir'd. i will thrive. 1.03. 19 P
the sweet woman leads an ill life with him. 2.02. 89 P
she leads a very frampold life with him, good 2.02. 90 P
in windsor leads a better life than she does: 2.02.117 P
or bid farewell to your good life for ever. 3.03.120 P
more wit than ever i learn'd before in my life; 4.05. 61 P
beam, because i know also life is a shuttle. 5.01. 23 P
upon my life then, you took the wrong. 5.05.189 P
there is a kind of character in thy life, | that MM 1.01. 27
as for the enjoying of thy life, who i would be 1.02.189 P
you | how i have ever lov'd the life removed, 1.03. 8
under whose heavy sense your brother's life 1.04. 65
doth he so seek his life? 1.04. 72
whether you had not sometime in your life 2.01. 14
deny | the jury, passing on the prisoner's life, 2.01. 19
be not a bawd's house, it is pity of her life, 2.01. 77 P
upon your tongue | against my brother's life. 2.02.141
that respites me a life whose very comfort | is 2.03. 41
falsely to take away a life true made | as to 2.04. 47
most just law | now took your brother's life, 2.04. 53
pronounce a sentence on your brother's life; 2.04. 62
a charity in sin | to save this brother's life? 2.04. 64
that i do beg his life, if it be sin, | heaven 2.04. 69
admit no other way to save his life | (as i 2.04. 88
my unsoil'd name, th' austereness of my life, 2.04.155
either death or life | shall thereby be the 3.01. 5
reason thus with life: 3.01. 6
yet in this | that bears the name of life? 3.01. 39
yet in this life | lie hid moe thousand deaths; 3.01. 39
i seek to die, | and, seeking death, find life. 3.01. 43
if you'll implore it, that will free your life, 3.01. 65
lest thou a feverous life shouldst entertain, 3.01. 74
thou art too noble to conserve a life | in base 3.01. 87
o, were it but my life, | i'd throw it down for 3.01.103
and shamed life a hateful. 3.01.116
the weariest and most loathed worldly life 3.01.128
what sin you do to save a brother's life, 3.01.133
to take life | from thine own sister's shame? 3.01.138
so out of love with life that i will sue to be 3.01.172 P
what corruption in this life, that it will let 3.01.233 P
canst thou believe thy living is a life, | so 3.02. 26
of a codpiece to take away the life of a man! 3.02.115 P
the very stream of his life, and the business he 3.02.142 P
many deceiving promises of life, which i (by my 3.02.246 P
if his own life answer the straitness of his 3.02.255 P
his life is parallel'd | even with the stroke 4.02. 79
i profess, i will plead against it with my life. 4.02.180 P
by so receiving a dishonor'd life | with ransom 4.04. 31
laboring to save his life, and would not rather 5.01.391
that life is better life, past fearing death, 5.01.397
that life is better life, past fearing death, 5.01.397
thereon dependant, for your brother's life — 5.01.406
for that he knew you, might reprouch your life, 5.01.421
and all my life to come | i'll lend you all my 5.01.431
i'll lend you all my life to do you service. 5.01.432
this world, | and squar'st thy life according. 5.01.482
that by misfortunes was my life prolong'd, | to ERR 1.01.119
but here must end the story of my life, | and 1.01.137
not being able to buy out his life | according 1.02. 5
upon my life, by some device or other | the 1.02. 95
i never spake with her in all my life. 2.02.165
thee will i love and with thee lead my life; 3.02. 67
as from a bear a man would run for life, | so 3.02.154
of pale distemperatures and foes to life? 5.01. 82
mistress, upon my life, i tell you true; 5.01.180
wars, and took | deep scars to save thy life; 5.01.193
haply i see a friend will save my life, | and 5.01.284
i never saw you in my life till now. 5.01.297
up, | yet hath my night of life some memory, 5.01.315
i never saw my father in my life. 5.01.320
i ne'er saw syracusa in my life. 5.01.326
it shall not need, thy father hath his life. 5.01.391
an account of her life to a clod of wayward marl ADO 2.01. 62 P
visor began to assume life and scold with her. 2.01.242 P
what life is in that, to be the death of this 2.02. 19 P
passion came so near the life of passion as she 2.03.105 P
for my life, to break with him about beatrice. 3.02. 74 P
rearward of reproaches, | strike at thy life. 4.01.127
nor my bad life reft me so much of friends, 4.01.196
th' idea of her life shall sweetly creep | into 4.01.224
and every lovely organ of her life | shall come 4.01.226
more moving, delicate, and full of life, | into 4.01.228
in some reclusive and religious life, | out of 4.01.242
god's my life, where's the sexton? 4.02. 70 P
so the life that died with shame | lives in 5.03. 7
and partly to save your life, for i was told you 5.04. 96 P
have cudgell'd thee out of thy single life, to 5.04.114 P
now god save thy life! LLL 2.01.191
sir, god save your life! 4.02.145 P
saith the text, is the happiness of life. 4.02.162 P
by my life, my troth, | i never swore this lady 5.02.450
dead, for my life! 5.02.720
if this austere insociable life | change not 5.02.799
mew'd, | to live a barren sister all your life, MND 1.01. 72
to protest | for aye austerity and single life. 1.01. 90
to death, or to a vow of single life. 1.01.121
thy love ne'er alter till thy sweet life end! 2.02. 61
say i — | and then end life when i end loyalty! 2.02. 63
my life for yours. 3.01. 41 P
come hither as a lion, it were pity of my life. 3.01. 43 P
my love, my life, my soul, fair helena! 3.02.246
helen, i love thee, by my life, i do! 3.02.251
ay, by my life; 3.02.277
god's my life, stol'n hence, and left me asleep! 4.01.203 P
hath he lost sixpence a day during his life; 4.02. 20 P
'tide life, 'tide death, i come without delay. 5.01.203
into this place, 'twere pity on my life. 5.01.226
go to, here's a simple line of life! MV 2.02.161 P
and to be in peril of my life with the edge of a 2.02.164 P
many a man his life hath sold | but my outside 2.07. 67
never in my life | to woo a maid in way of 2.09. 12
there may as well be amity and life | 'tween 3.02. 30
promise me life, and i'll confess the truth. 3.02. 34
from this finger, then parts life from hence; 3.02.184
he seeks my life; 3.03. 21
meet | the lord bassanio live an upright life, 3.05. 74
and for thy life let justice be accus'd. 4.01.129
a wife | which is as dear to me as life itself, 4.01.283
but life itself, my wife, and all the world, 4.01.284
are not with me esteem'd above thy life. 4.01.285
attempts | he seek the life of any citizen, 4.01.351
and the offender's life lies in the mercy | of 4.01.355
thou hast contrived against the very life | of 4.01.360
i pardon thee thy life before thou ask it. 4.01.369
nay, take my life and all, pardon not that: 4.01.374
you take my life | when you do take the means 4.01.376
even he that had held up the very life | of my 5.01.214
sweet lady, you have given me life and living, 5.01.286
he hath ta'en thy life by some indirect means or AYL 1.01.152 P
ribs, that there is little hope of life in him. 1.02.128 P
and, on my life, his malice 'gainst the lady 1.02.282
hath not old custom made this life more sweet 2.01. 2
and this our life, exempt from public haunt, 2.01. 15
yea, and of this our life, swearing that we 2.01. 60
the soil, the profit, and this kind of life, | i 2.04. 98
why, how now, monsieur, what a life is this, 2.07. 9
this life is most jolly. 2.07.183
i never lov'd my brother in my life. 3.01. 14
thy huntress' name that my full life doth sway. 3.02. 4
and how like you this shepherd's life, master 3.02. 11 P
in respect of itself, it is a good life; 3.02. 14 P
but in respect that it is a shepherd's life, it 3.02. 14 P
that it is private, it is a very vild life. 3.02. 17 P
as it is a spare life, look you, it fits my 3.02. 19 P
how brief the life of man | runs his erring 3.02.129
'od's my little life, | i think she means to 3.05. 43
by my life, she will do as i do. 4.01.158 P
make thee away, translate thy life into death, 5.01. 53 P
by my life, i do, which i tender dearly, though 5.02. 70 P
hey nonino, | how that a life was but a flower, 5.03. 28
this to be true, | i do engage my life. 5.04.166
the duke hath put on a religious life, | and 5.04.181
i ne'er drank sack in my life; SHR in.2. 6 P
upon my life, i am a lord indeed | and not a in.2. 72
which bars a thousand harms and lengthens life. in.2. 136
your fellow tranio here, to save my life, | puts 1.01.228
while i make way from hence to save my life. 1.01.234
he hath the jewel of my life in hold, | his 1.02.119
o sir, such a life, with such a wife, were 1.02.193
now, for my life, the knave doth court my love: 3.01. 49
upon my life, petruchio means but well, 3.02. 22
"where is the life that late i led? 4.01.140
rome, | and so to tripoli, if god lend me life. 4.02. 76
and come to padua, careless of your life? 4.02. 79
my life, sir? how, i pray? for that goes hard. 4.02. 80
to save your life in this extremity, | this 4.02.103
you ever | the patron of my life and liberty. 4.02.114
no, no, forsooth, i dare not for my life. 4.03. 1
villain, not for thy life! 4.03.158 P
you, for i never saw you before in all my life. 5.01. 51 P
now, for my life, hortensio fears his widow. 5.02. 16
marry, peace it bodes, and love, and quiet life, 5.02.108
thy husband is thy lord, thy life, thy keeper, 5.02.146
the well–lost life of mine on his grace's cure AWW 1.03.248
he owes the malady | that doth my life besiege. 2.01. 10
that's able to breathe life into a stone, 2.01. 73
with vildest torture, let my life be ended. 2.01.174
thy life is dear, for all that life can rate 2.01.179
for all that life can rate | worth name of life 2.01.179
rate | worth name of life in thee hath estimate: 2.01.180
i ne'er had worse luck in my life in my "o lord, 2.02. 57 P
uncertain life, and sure death. 2.03. 18 P
in this choice than throw ames–ace for my life. 2.03. 79 P
i'll beat him, by my life, if i can meet him 2.03.238 P
on my life, my lord, a bubble. 3.06. 5 P
for the promise of his life and in the highest 3.06. 29 P
for he persists | as if his life lay on't. 3.07. 43
and i shall lose my life for want of language. 4.01. 70
thou mayst inform | something to save thy life. 4.01. 83
my house, mine honor, yea, my life, be thine, 4.02. 52
the web of our life is of a mingled yarn, good 4.03. 71 P
rotten and sound, upon my life, amounts not to 4.03.167 P
my life, sir, in any case! 4.03.241 P
if your life be sav'd, will you undertake to 4.03.292 P
dear almost as his life, which gratitude 4.04. 6
son, on my life, | i have seen her wear it, and 5.03. 89
i am afeard the life of helen, lady, | was 5.03.153
great king, i am no strumpet, by my life; 5.03.292
i am sure care's an enemy to life. TN 1.03. 3 P
never in your life, i think, unless you see 1.03. 82 P
tut, there's life in't, man. 1.03.111 P
with such a suff'ring, such a deadly life, | in 1.05.265
you have a love–song, or a song of good life? 2.03. 36 P
ay, ay. i care not for good life. 2.03. 38 P
my life upon't, young though thou art, thine eye 2.04. 23
by my life, this is my lady's hand. 2.05. 86 P
m.o.a.i. doth sway my life." 2.05.107
"m.o.a.i. doth sway my life." 2.05.110 P
therefore, if you hold your life at any price, 3.04.230 P
hold, toby, on thy life i charge thee hold! 4.01. 45
his life i gave him, and did thereto add | my 5.01. 80
more than i love these eyes, more than my life, 5.01.135
above | punish my life for tainting of my love! 5.01.138
nor are you therein, by my life, deceiv'd, | you 5.01.262
was born desire yet their life to see him a man. WT 1.01. 40 P
had we pursu'd that life, | and our weak spirits 1.02. 71
were my wive's liver | infected as her life, she 1.02.305
thee as a father, if | thou bear'st my life off. 1.02.462
there is a plot against my life, my crown; 2.01. 47
no, by my life, | privy to none of this. 2.01. 95
i dare my life lay down — and will do't, sir, 2.01.130
passion more, alas, | than the queen's life? 2.03. 29
were i a tyrant, | where were her life? 2.03.123
(and by good testimony) or i'll seize thy life, 2.03.137
to save this bastard's life — for 'tis a 2.03.161
will you adventure | to save this brat's life? 2.03.163
to take away the life of our sovereign lord the 3.02. 16 P
to do so) my past life | hath been as continent, 3.02. 33
to prate and talk for life and honor 'fore | who 3.02. 41
for life, i prize it | as i weigh grief, which i 3.02. 42
my life stands in the level of your dreams, 3.02. 81
to me can life be no commodity; 3.02. 93
the crown and comfort of my life, your favor, 3.02. 94
no life | (i prize it not a straw), but for mine 3.02.109
tenderly apply to her | some remedies for life. 3.02.153
either for life or death, upon the earth | of 3.03. 45
for the life to come, i sleep out the thought of 4.03. 30 P
prig, for my life, prig! 4.03.101 P
weeds to each part of you | does give a life; 4.04. 2
you must change this purpose, | or i my life. 4.04. 40
o, hear me breathe my life | before this ancient 4.04.360
thee i can | but shorten thy life one week. 4.04.422
who, on my life, | did perish with the infant. 5.01. 43
i desire my life | once more to look on him. 5.01.137
now, had i not the dash of my former life in me, 5.02.113 P
thou wilt amend thy life? 5.02.154 P
grace, which never | my life may last to answer. 5.03. 8
to see the life as lively mock'd as ever | still 5.03. 19
even with such life of majesty (warm life, | as 5.03. 35
even with such life of majesty (warm life, | as 5.03. 35
the very life seems warm upon her lip. 5.03. 66
for from him | dear life redeems you. 5.03.103
if she pertain to life let her speak too. 5.03.113
the rather that you give his offspring life, JN 2.01. 13
my life as soon. 2.01.155
and let belief and life encounter so | as doth 3.01. 31
thou dar'st not say so, villain, for thy life. 3.01.132
away by any secret course | thy hateful life. 3.01.179
where my fortune lives, there my life dies. 3.01.338
now, by my life, this day grows wondrous hot; 3.02. 1
my life, my joy, my food, my all the world! 3.04.104
life is as tedious as a twice–told tale | vexing 3.04.108
whiles warm life plays in that infant's veins, 3.04.132
and lose it, life and all, as arthur did. 3.04.144
may be he will not touch young arthur's life, 3.04.160
that his compassion may | give life to yours. 4.01. 89
have i commandement on the pulse of life? 4.02. 92
no certain life achiev'd by others' death. 4.02.105
to break within the bloody house of life, | and 4.02.210
soul, | kneeling before this ruin of sweet life, 4.03. 65
not for my life; 4.03. 88
defend | my innocent life against an emperor. 4.03. 89
my date of life out for his sweet live's loss. 4.03.106
the life, the right, and truth of all this realm 4.03.144
where the jewel of life | by some damn'd hand 5.01. 40
my view, | retaining but a quantity of life, 5.04. 23
too late, the life of all his blood | is touch'd 5.07. 1
all the shrouds wherewith my life should sail 5.07. 53
look what i speak, my life shall prove it true: R2 1.01. 87
upon his bad life to make all this good, | that 1.01. 99
this arm shall do it, or this life be spent. 1.01.108
foe, | once did i lay an ambush for your life, 1.01.137
my life thou shalt command, but not my shame: 1.01.166
mine honor is my life, both grow in one, | take 1.01.182
one, | take honor from me, and my life is done. 1.01.183
to stir against the butchers of his life! 1.02. 3
thomas, my dear lord, my life, my gloucester, 1.02. 16
die, | who was the model of thy father's life. 1.02. 28
thou showest the naked pathway to thy life, 1.02. 31
to safeguard thine own life | the best way is to 1.02. 35
with her companion, grief, must end her life. 1.02. 55
you, cousin herford, upon pain of life, | till 1.03.140
breathe i against thee, upon pain of life. 1.03.153
my name be blotted from the book of life, | and 1.03.202
and in the sentence my own life destroyed. 1.03.242
ah, would the scandal vanish with my life, | how 2.01. 67

he loves you, on my life, and holds you dear 2.01.143
words, life, and all, old lancaster hath spent. 2.01.150
the hollow eyes of death | i spy life peering, 2.01.271
who gently would dissolve the bands of life, 2.02. 71
knowledge, | i never in my life did look on him. 2.03. 39
but if i could, by him that gave me life, | i 2.03.155
as if this flesh which walls about our life 3.02.167
now, by mine honor, by my life, by my troth, | i 5.02. 78
it is no more | than my poor life must answer. 5.02. 83
thy life answer? 5.02. 83
dies, | or my sham'd life in his dishonor lies: 5.03. 71
thou kill'st me in his life; 5.03. 72
more than thou hast, and with it joy thy life. 5.06. 26
i must give over this life, and i will give it 1H4 1.02. 95 P
i see a good amendment of life in thee, from 1.02.102 P
i smell it. upon my life, it will do well. 1.03.277
any tinker in his own language during my life. 2.04. 20 P
other english in his life than "eight shillings 2.04. 25 P
and says to his wife, "fie upon this quiet life! 2.04.105 P
ere i lead this life long, i'll sew 2.04.116 P
the better of myself, and thee, during my life; 2.04.274 P
and examine me upon the particulars of my life. 2.04.377 P
and all the courses of my life do show | i am 3.01. 41
but thou dost in thy passages of life | make me 3.02. 8
if not, the end of life cancels all bands, | and 3.02.157
do thou amend thy face, and i'll amend my life. 3.03. 25 P
by my life, | and i dare well maintain it with 4.03. 8
and i dare well maintain it with my life, | if 4.03. 9
soon after that, depriv'd him of his life, | and 4.03. 91
to entertain the lag end of my life | with quiet 5.01. 24
it will not be accepted, on my life. 5.01.115
i never in my life | did hear a challenge urg'd 5.02. 51
o gentlemen, the time of life is short! 5.02. 81
too long | if life did ride upon a dial's point, 5.02. 83
they are for the town's end, to beg during life. 5.03. 38 P
give me life, which if i can save, so; 5.03. 59 P
and show'd thou mak'st some tender of my life 5.04. 49
i better brook the loss of brittle life | than 5.04. 78
but thoughts, the slaves of life, and life, 5.04. 81
the slaves of life, and life, time's fool, | and 5.04. 81
not all this flesh | keep in a little life? 5.04.103
of a man who hath not the life of a man; 5.04.117 P
but the true and perfect image of life indeed. 5.04.119 P
in the which better part i have sav'd my life. 5.04.121 P
the horse he rode on, and, upon my life, | spoke 2H4 1.01. 58
from whence with life he never more sprung up. 1.01.111
like strengthless hinges, buckle under life, 1.01.141
that if we wrought out life 'twas ten to one, 1.01.182
there were matters against you for your life, to 1.02.133 P
and never shall have length of life enough | to 2.03. 58
sinful continents, what a life dost thou lead! 2.04.286 P
and laid his love and life under my foot, | yea, 3.01. 63
main chance of things | as yet not come to life, 3.01. 84
revives two greater in the heirs of life; 4.01.198
turning the word to sword and life to death. 4.02. 10
these tardy tricks of yours will, on my life, 4.03. 28
in | so thin that life looks through /and /will 4.04.120
thy life did manifest thou lov'dst me not, | and 4.05.104
heart | to stab at half an hour of my life. 4.05.108
give that which gave thee life unto the worms, 4.05.116
precious, | preserving life in med'cine potable; 4.05.162
even there my life must end. 4.05.235
the service that i truly did his life | hath 5.02. 7
say, | god shorten harry's happy life one day! 5.02.145
health and long life to you, master silence. 5.03. 52 P
"where is the life that late i led?" 5.03.140
for competence of life i will allow you, | that 5.05. 66
so that the art and practic part of life | must H5 1.01. 51
for some dishonest manners of their life, 1.02. 49
his sovereign's life to death and treachery. 2.02. 11
sir, | you show great mercy if you give him life 2.02. 50
captain, for his life, and i will thee requite. 3.06. 49
a lad of life, an imp of fame, | of parents good 4.01. 45
fear'd the death, they have borne life away; 4.01.172 P
to demonstrate the life of such a battle, | in 4.02. 54
in life so liveless as it shows itself. 4.02. 55
he prays you to save his life. 4.04. 44 P
let life be short, else shame will be too long. 4.05. 23
if you mark alexander's life well, harry of 4.07. 32 P
well, harry of monmouth's life is come after it 4.07. 32 P
which cannot in their huge and proper life | be 5.pr. 5
his thread of life had not so soon decay'd. 1H6 1.01. 34
if henry were recall'd to life again, | these 1.01. 66
he fighteth as one weary of his life. 1.02. 26
talbot, my life, my joy, again return'd? 1.04. 23
sir thomas gargrave, hast thou any life? 1.04. 88
and prosperous be thy life in peace and war! 2.05.114
will see his burial better than his life. 2.05.121
in that thou laidst a trap to take my life, | as 3.01. 22
touching thy spiritual function, not thy life. 3.01. 50
all the talbots in the world, to save my life. 3.02.108
sell every man his life as dear as mine, | and 4.02. 53
yield up his life unto a world of odds. 4.04. 25
never to england shall he bear his life, | but 4.04. 38
rather than life preserv'd with infamy. 4.05. 33
son, | born to eclipse thy life this afternoon. 4.05. 53
i gave thee life, and rescu'd thee from death. 4.06. 5
the life thou gav'st me first was lost and done, 4.06. 7
'tis but the short'ning of my life one day. 4.06. 37
to save a paltry life and slay bright fame, 4.06. 45
thy life to me is sweet. 4.06. 55
where is my other life? 4.07. 1
whose life was england's glory, gallia's wonder. 4.07. 48
for that which we have fled | during the life, 4.07. 50
o, that i could but call these dead to life, 4.07. 81
this argues what her kind of life hath been, 5.04. 15
o lord, that lends me life, | lend me a heart 2H6 1.01. 19
a man that ne'er saw in his life before. 2.01. 63
but that in all my life, when i was a youth. 2.01. 97
and made me climb, with danger of my life. 2.01.101
never, before this day, in all his life. 2.01.114
demanding of king henry's life and death, | and 2.01.171
born, | despoiled of your honor in your life, 2.03. 10
upon my life, began her devilish practices; 3.01. 46
i know their complot is to have my life; 3.01.147
back, | by false accuse doth level at my life. 3.01.160
and all to make away my guiltless life. 3.01.167
do seek subversion of thy harmless life? 3.01.208
the king will labor still to save his life, 3.01.239
the commons haply rise, to save his life; 3.01.240
i rather would have lost my life betimes | than 3.01.297
in life but double death, now gloucester's dead. 3.02. 55
or blood–consuming sighs recall his life, | i 3.02. 61
some violent hands were laid on humphrey's life! 3.02.138
for, seeing him, i see my life in death. 3.02.152
laid | upon the life of this thrice–famed duke. 3.02.157
as one that grasp'd | and tugg'd for life, and 3.02.173
worth, | they say is shamefully bereft of life. 3.02.269
the world shall not be ransom for thy life. 3.02.297
yet now farewell, and farewell life with thee! 3.02.356
live thou to joy thy life; 3.02.365
ah, what a sign it is of evil life, | where 3.03. 5
so bad a death argues a monstrous life. 3.03. 30
i'll give it, sir, and therefore spare my life. 4.01. 23
argo, their thread of life is spun. 4.02. 29 P
yet to recover them would lose my life. 4.07. 66
and it be but for pleading so well for his life. 4.07.107 P
and therefore yet relent, and save my life. 4.07.117
expect your highness' doom, of life or death. 4.09. 12
have a lease of my life for a thousand years, i 4.10. 5 P
but thou prefer'st thy life before thine honor; 3H6 1.01.246
your right depends not on his life or death. 1.02. 11
chaplain, away, thy priesthood saves thy life. 1.03. 3
like men born to renown by life or death. 1.04. 8
the sands are numb'red that makes up my life, 1.04. 25
here must i stay, and here my life must end. 1.04. 26
i would prolong a while the traitor's life. 1.04. 52
now in his life, against your holy oath? 1.04.105
i should not for my life but weep with him, | to 1.04.170
breasts, | for yet is hope of life and victory. 2.03. 55
methinks it were a happy life | to be no better 2.05. 21
what a life were this! 2.05. 41
yield both my life and them | to some man else, 2.05. 59
and i, who at his hands receiv'd my life, | have 2.05. 67
life, | have by my hands of life bereaved him. 2.05. 68
ah, boy, if any life be left in thee, | throw up 2.05. 84
thy father gave thee life too soon, | and hath 2.05. 92
and hath bereft thee of thy life too late. 2.05. 93
a deadly groan, like life and death's departing. 2.06. 43
dark cloudy death o'ershades his beams of life, 2.06. 62
if this right hand would buy two hours' life 2.06. 80
york | the worthy gentleman did lose his life. 3.02. 7
while life upholds this arm, | this arm upholds 3.03.106
land, | while i myself will lead a private life, 4.06. 42
shall have a high reward, and he his life? 5.05. 10
whose envious gulf did swallow up his life. 5.06. 25
is't for my life? 5.06. 29
if any spark of life be yet remaining, | down, 5.06. 66
that edward shall be fearful of his life, | and 5.06. 87
lo, in these windows that let forth thy life | i R3 1.02. 12
it is my day, my life. 1.02.130
night o'ershade thy day, and death thy life! 1.02.131
upon my life, she finds (although i cannot) 1.02.253
my charity is outrage, life my shame, | and in 1.03.276
no, no, my dream was lengthen'd after life. 1.04. 43
who shall reward you better for my life | than 1.04.230
came to you, | would not entreat for life? 1.04.260
the forfeit, sovereign, of my servant's life, 2.01.100
all | have been beholding to him in his life; 2.01.130
yet none of you would once beg for his life. 2.01.131
my husband lost his life to get the crown, | and 2.04. 57
for now he lives in fame though not in life. 3.01. 88
ay, on my life, and hopes to find you forward 3.02. 46
i hold my life as dear as /you /do yours, | and 3.02. 78
now, for my life, she's wand'ring to the tower, 4.01. 3
more miserable by the life of thee | than thou 4.01. 75
dead life, blind sight, poor mortal–living ghost 4.04. 26
world's shame, grave's due by life usurp'd, 4.04. 27
cancel his bond of life, dear god, i pray, 4.04. 77
shame serves thy life and doth thy death attend. 4.04.196
to save her life, i'll say she is not so. 4.04.213
her life is safest only in her birth. 4.04.214
if grace had blest thee with a fairer life. 4.04.221
of comfort, kingdom, kindred, freedom, life. 4.04.224
but how long fairly shall her sweet life last? 4.04.352
thy life hath it dishonor'd. 4.04.376
upon my life, my lord, i'll undertake it, | and 5.03. 42
one that never in his life | felt so much cold 5.03.325
slave, i have set my life upon a cast, | and i 5.04. 9
would by a good discourser lose some life, H8 1.01. 41
my life is spann'd already. 1.01.223
my life itself, and the best heart of it, 1.02. 1
unfit for other life, compell'd by hunger | and 1.02. 34
by my life, | this is against our pleasure. 1.02. 67
by my life, | they are a sweet society of fair 1.04. 13
much | he spoke, and learnedly, for life; 2.01. 28
for further life in this world i ne'er hope, 2.01. 69
henry the eight, life, honor, name, and all 2.01.116
hour | of my long weary life is come upon me. 2.01.133
ever | pronounce dishonor of her — by my life, 2.03. 4
by my life, | that promises moe thousands; 2.03. 96
do no more offices of life to't than | the grave 2.04.191
lawful, by my life | and kingly dignity, we are 2.04.227
set against 'em, | i know my life so even. 3.01. 37
so near mine honor | (more near my life, i fear) 3.01. 72
have my prayers | while i shall have my life. 3.01.181
it, with the place and honors, | during my life; 3.02.249
sins, the articles | collected from his life. 3.02.294
heaven had pleas'd to have given me longer life 4.02.152
all the progress | both of my life and office, i 5.02. 68
do. | remember your bold life too. 5.02.120
how much more is his life in value with him! 5.02.143
from thy endless goodness send prosperous life, 5.04. 2 P
into whose hand i give thy life. 5.04. 11
thou most reverend for /thy stretch'd–out life, TRO 1.03. 61
our project's life this shape of sense assumes: 1.03.384
none so noble | whose life were ill bestow'd, or 2.02.159
why, there you touch'd the life of our design: 2.02.194
and, by my life, you shall make it whole again 3.01. 50 P
i'll lay my life, with my disposer cressida. 3.01. 87 P
i'll play the hunter for thy life | with all my 4.01. 18
now, by anchises' life, | welcome indeed! 4.01. 22
her bawdy veins, | a grecian's life hath sunk; 4.01. 71
i shall have such a life! 4.02. 22
and thy life shall be as safe | as priam is in 4.04.115
"lo jupiter is yonder, dealing life!" 4.05.191
think'st thou to catch my life so pleasantly 4.05.249
life every man holds dear, but the dear man 5.03. 27
holds honor far more precious–dear than life. 5.03. 28
and pay thy life thou owest me for my horse. 5.06. 7
i reak not though i end my life to–day. 5.06. 26
thy goodly armor thus hath cost thy life. 5.08. 2
to close the day up, hector's life is done. 5.08. 8
shame | pursue thy life, and live aye with thy 5.10. 34
if any think brave death outweighs bad life, COR 1.06. 71
i do owe them still | my life and services. 2.02.134
that prefer | a noble life before a long, and 3.01.153
which never | i shall discharge to th' life. 3.02.106
more holy and profound, than mine own life, | my 3.03.113
(mistake me not) to save my life, for if | i had 4.05. 80
and state of bodies would bewray what life | we 5.03. 95
thou hast never in thy life | show'd thy dear 5.03.160
sir, if you'ld save your life, fly to your house 5.04. 35
behold our patroness, the life of rome! 5.05. 1
danger | which this man's life did owe you, 5.06.137
to–morrow yield up rule, resign my life, | and TIT 1.01.191
thanks, noble titus, father of my life! 1.01.253
may, | answer i must, and shall do with my life; 1.01.412
sons, | to whom i sued for my dear son's life; 1.01.453
these words, these looks, infuse new life in me. 1.01.461
ah, my sweet moor, sweeter to me than life! 2.03. 51
revenge it, as you love your mother's life, | or 2.03.114
that gave thee life when well he might have 2.03.159
for 'tis not life that i have begg'd so long, 2.03.170
kind, | have here bereft my brother of his life. 2.03.282
would not then have touch'd them for his life! 2.04. 47
and they have nurs'd this woe, in feeding life; 3.01. 74
and yet detested life not shrink thereat! 3.01.247
that ever death should let life bear his name, 3.01.248
where life hath no more interest but to breathe! 3.01.249
he loves his pledges dearer than his life. 3.01.291
of that self blood that first gave life to you, 4.02.123
jubiter, i never drank with him in all my life. 4.03. 86 P
sir, i could never say grace in all my life. 4.03.101 P
lord of my life, commander of my thoughts, 4.04. 28
let him, | as he regards his aged father's life. 5.02.130
death, | as punishment for his most wicked life. 5.03.145
if one good deed in all my life i did, | i do 5.03.189
her life was beastly and devoid of pity, | and, 5.03.199
a pair of star–cross'd lovers take their life; ROM pr 6
term | of a despised life clos'd in my breast 1.04.110
my life is my foe's debt. 1.05.118
and, on my life, hath stol'n him home to bed. 2.01. 4
my life were better ended by their hate, | than 2.02. 77
a challenge, on my life. 2.04. 8 P
buy the fee–simple of my life for an hour and a 3.01. 32 P
an envious thrust from tybalt hit the life | of 3.01.168
and all those twenty could but kill one life. 3.01.179
what the law should end, | the life of tybalt. 3.01.186
and slay thy lady that in thy life /lives, | by 3.03.117
then, window, let day in, and let life out. 3.05. 41
like death when he shuts up the day of life; 4.01.101
that almost freezes up the heat of life. 4.03. 16
o me, o me, my child, my only life! 4.05. 19
life and these lips have long been separated. 4.05. 27
life, living, all is death's. 4.05. 40
o love, o life! 4.05. 58
not life, but love in death! 4.05. 58
but heaven keeps his part in eternal life. 4.05. 70
and breath'd such life with kisses in my lips 5.01. 8
upon thy life i charge thee, | what e'er thou 5.03. 25
let my old life | be sacrific'd some hour before 5.03.267
it is a pretty mocking of the life. TIM 1.01. 35
lives in these touches, livelier than life. 1.01. 38
like madness is the glory of this life, | as 1.02.134
own part, | i never tasted timon in my life, 3.02. 77
kill, | what folly 'tis to hazard life for ill! 3.05. 37
were a sufficient briber for his life. 3.05. 61
if by this crime he owes the law his life, | why 3.05. 82
nor has he with him to | supply his life, or 4.02. 47
that the whole life of athens were in this! 4.03.281
thou shouldst hazard thy life for thy dinner; 4.03.335 P
spots of thy kindred were jurors on thy life; 4.03.342 P
and, as my lord, | still serve him with my life. 4.03.471
star–like nobleness gave life and influence | to 5.01. 63
what you and other men | think of this life; JC 1.02. 94
and those sparks of life | that should be in a 1.03. 57
but life, being weary of these worldly bars, 1.03. 96
he that cuts off twenty years of life | cuts off 3.01.101
for your life you durst not. 4.03. 62
all the voyage of their life | is bound in 4.03.220
fall, so to prevent | the time of life — arming 5.01.105
my life is run his compass. 5.03. 25
and then i swore thee, saving of thy life, 5.03. 38
my heart doth joy that yet in all my life | i 5.05. 34
thy life hath had some smatch of honor in it. 5.05. 46
his life was gentle, and the elements | so mix'd 5.05. 73
but under heavy judgment bears that life | which MAC 1.03.110
nothing in his life | became him like the 1.04. 7
/shoal of time, | we'ld jump the life to come. 1.07. 7
which thou esteem'st the ornament of life, | and 1.07. 42
the death of each day's life, sore labor's bath, 2.02. 35
and stole thence | the life o' th' building! 2.03. 69
what is't you say — the life? 2.03. 69
the wine of life is drawn, and the mere lees 2.03. 95
no man's life was to be trusted with them. 2.03.105
who wear our health but sickly in his life, 3.01.106
that i would set my life on any chance, | to 3.01.112
his being thrusts | against my near'st of life; 3.01.117
and delight | no less in truth than life. 4.03.130
her very guise, and, upon my life, fast asleep. 5.01. 20 P
my way of life | is fall'n into the sear, the 5.03. 22
treatise rouse and stir | as life were in't. 5.05. 13
i bear a charmed life, which must not yield | to 5.08. 12
by self and violent hands | took off her life; 5.09. 37
did forfeit (with his life) all /those his lands HAM 1.01. 88
or if thou hast uphoarded in thy life | extorted 1.01.136
to–night | unto young hamlet, for, upon my life, 1.01.170
it was, as i have seen it in his life, | a sable 1.02.240
i do not set my life at a pin's fee, | and for 1.04. 65
the serpent that did sting thy father's life 1.05. 39
by a brother's hand | of life, of crown, of 1.05. 75
more willingly part withal — except my life, 2.02.216 P
except my life, except my life, except my life. 2.02.217 P

except my life, except my life, except my life. 2.02.217 P
upon whose property and most dear life | a 2.02.570
respect | that makes calamity of so long life: 3.01. 68
bear, | to grunt and sweat under a weary life, 3.01. 76
man's memory may outlive his life half a year, 3.02.132 P
property | on wholesome life usurps immediately. 3.02.260
the single and peculiar life is bound | with all 3.03. 11
your bedded hair, like life in excrements, 3.04.121
and breath of life, i have no life to breathe 3.04.198
i have no life to breathe | what thou hast said 3.04.198
who was in life a foolish prating knave. 3.04.215
let it feed | even on the pith of life. 4.01. 23
should be as mortal as /an /old man's life? 4.05.161
our crown, our life, and all that we call ours, 4.05.209
hath your noble father slain | pursued my life. 4.07. 5
she is so /conjunctive to my life and soul, 4.07. 14
upon my life, lamord. 4.07. 92
of his own death shortens not his own life. 5.01. 20 P
did with desp'rate hand | foredo it own life. 5.01.221
with, ho, such bugs and goblins in my life, 5.02. 22
thrown out his angle for my proper life, | and 5.02. 66
in thee there is not half an hour's life. 5.02.315
had it th' ability of life to thank you. 5.02.373
no less than life, with grace, health, beauty, LR 1.01. 58
answer my life my judgment, | thy youngest 1.01.151
kent, on thy life, no more. 1.01.154
my life i never held but as /a pawn | to wage 1.01.155
i dare pawn down my life for him that he hath 1.02. 86 P
life and death! 1.04.296
what, did my father's godson seek your life? 2.01. 91
whose life i have spar'd at suit of his grey 2.02. 62 P
as i have life and honor, | there shall he sit 2.02.133
pension beg | to keep base life afoot. 2.04.215
nature needs, | man's life is cheap as beast's. 2.04.267
seeming | has practic'd on man's life! 3.02. 57
he sought my life, | but lately, very late. 3.04.167
if thou shouldst dally half an hour, his life, 3.06. 93
though well we may not pass upon his life 3.07. 24
us hate thee, | life would not yield to age. 4.01. 12
in my fancy pluck | upon my hateful life. 4.02. 86
lest his ungovern'd rage dissolve the life 4.04. 19
of his misery, to dispatch | his nighted life; 4.05. 13
not how conceit may rob | the treasury of life, 4.06. 43
of life, when life itself | yields to the theft. 4.06. 43
i pardon that man's life. 4.06.109
then there's life in't. 4.06.202 P
and chud ha' bin zwagger'd out of my life, 4.06.238 P
a plot upon her virtuous husband's life, | and 4.06.272
my life will be too short, | and every measure 4.07. 2
'tis wonder that thy life and wits at once | had 4.07. 40
i pant for life. 5.03.244
writ | is on the life of lear and on cordelia. 5.03.247
haste thee, for thy life. 5.03.252
resign, | during the life of this old majesty, 5.03.300
no, no, no life! 5.03.306
why should a dog, a horse, a rat, have life, 5.03.307
hath endur'd so long, | he but usurp'd his life. 5.03.318
yet, for necessity of present life, | i must OTH 1.01.155
i fetch my life and being | from men of royal 1.02. 21
but let your sentence | even fall upon my life. 1.03.120
still question'd me the story of my life | from 1.03.129
to you i am bound for life and education; 1.03.182
my life and education both do learn me | how to 1.03.183
my life upon her faith! 1.03.294
'tis the soldiers' life | to have their balmy 2.03.257
think'st thou i'ld make a life of jealousy? 3.03.177
or woe upon thy life! 3.03.366
where either i must live or bear no life; 4.02. 58
much, | and his unkindness may defeat my life, 4.02.160
with treachery and devise engines for my life. 4.02.217 P
he hath a daily beauty in his life | that makes 5.01. 19
but of life as honest | as you that thus abuse 5.01.122
no, by my life and soul! 5.02. 49
i never did | offend you in my life; 5.02. 59
the nobleness of life | is to do thus — when ANT 1.01. 36
o, excellent, i love long life better than figs. 1.02. 32 P
higher than both in blood and life, stands up 1.02.190
like the courser's hair, hath yet but life, 1.02.193
his aspect, and die | with looking on his life. 1.05. 34
she shows a body rather than a life, | a statue, 3.03. 20
all-disgraced friend, | or take his life there. 3.12. 23
as it determines, so | dissolve my life! 3.13.162
where rather i'll expect victorious life | than 4.02. 43
the foul'st best fits | my latter part of life. 4.06. 38
that life, a very rebel to my will, | may hang 4.09. 14
she rend'red life, | thy name so buried in her. 4.14. 33
and i wore my life | to spend upon his haters. 5.01. 8
if thou pleasest not, | i yield thee up my life. 5.01. 12
for her life in rome | would be eternal in our 5.01. 65
desolation does begin to make | a better life. 5.02. 2
my other elements | i give to baser life. 5.02.290
this knot intrinsicate | of life at once untie. 5.02.305
have been often bound for no less than my life. CYM 1.04. 27 P
wrought, | since the true life on't was — 2.04. 76
by my life, | i kiss'd it, and it gave me 2.04.136
this life | is nobler than attending for a check 3.03. 21
no life to ours. 3.03. 26
happ'ly this life is best, | if quiet life be 3.03. 29
this life is best, | if quiet life be best; 3.03. 30
strikes life into my speech and shows much more 3.03. 97
let thine own hands take away her life. 3.04. 28 P
no, on my life. 3.04.123
or in my life what comfort, when i am | dead to 3.04.129
of posthumus, most retir'd | hath her life been; 3.05. 37
i see a man's life is a tedious one, | i have 3.06. 1
and though you took his life, as being our foe, 4.02.250
sir, my life is yours, | i humbly set it at your 4.03. 12
sir, /find /we in life, to lock it | from action 4.04. 2
the certainty of this hard life, aye hopeless 4.04. 27
even for whom my life | is every breath a death; 5.01. 26
in hard voyages, became | the life o' th' need. 5.03. 45
for imogen's dear life take mine, and though 5.04. 22
and though | 'tis not so dear, yet 'tis a life; 5.04. 23
if you will take this audit, take this life, 5.04. 27
the action of my life is like it, which | i'll 5.04.149
by med'cine life may be prolong'd, yet death 5.05. 29
with horror, madly dying, like her life, | which 5.05. 31
was as a scorpion to her sight, whose life, 5.05. 45
should by the minute feed on life, and ling'ring 5.05. 51
i do not bid thee beg my life, good lad, | and 5.05.101
your life, good master, | must shuffle for 5.05.104
my queen, my life, my wife! 5.05.226
would cease | the present pow'r of life, but in 5.05.256
take that life, beseech you, | which i so often 5.05.414
i life would wish, and that i might | waste it PER 1.ch. 15
his wife, | his riddle told not, lost his life. 1.ch. 38
thus ready for the way of life or death, | i 1.01. 54
prince pericles, touch not, upon thy life, | for 1.01. 87
then, lest my life be cropp'd to keep you clear, 1.01.141
have after-nourishment and life by care; 1.02. 13
he flatters you, makes war upon your life. 1.02. 45
i have power | to take thy life from thee. 1.02. 57
or private treason | will take away your life. 1.02.105
or till the destinies do cut his thread of life. 1.02.108
with whom each minute threatens life or death. 1.03. 24
draw lots who first shall die to lengthen life. 1.04. 46
and give them life whom hunger starv'd half dead 1.04. 96
and have no more of life than may suffice | to 2.01. 74
this strict charge, even as he left his life, 2.01.125
he loves you well that holds his life of you. 2.02. 22
wishing it so much blood unto your life. 2.03. 77
she'll not undertake | a married life. 2.05. 4
'tis the king's subtilty to have my life. 2.05. 44
even as my life my blood that fosters it. 2.05. 89
forth, | that, as a duck for life that dives, 3.ch. 49
now, mild may be thy life! 3.01. 27
and yet the fire of life kindle again | the 3.02. 83
marina's life | /seeks to take off by treason's 4.ch. 13
my troth, | i never did her hurt in all my life. 4.01. 74
any profit, | or my life imply her any danger? 4.01. 81
your lady seeks my life, come you between, | and 4.01. 89
whilst we dispatch | this grand act of our life, TNK 1.01.164
labor through, | our gain but life and weakness. 1.02. 12
nor in a state of life; 1.04. 25
madness if i hazard thee | and take thy life, i 2.02.203
and, as i have a soul, i'll nail thy life to't! 2.02.213
and me too, | even when you please, of life. 2.02.225
for all the fortune of my life hereafter, | yon 2.02.235
upon his oath and life, must he set foot | upon 2.02.246
to discharge my life? 2.02.260
news continually, | thou art not worthy life. 2.02.267
'gainst thy window, | and let in life into thee; 2.03. 10
and to those gentle uses gave me life. 2.05. 7
the trespass thou hast done me, yea, my life, 3.01. 77
if i priz'd life so much | as to deny my act; 3.02. 23
alas, | dissolve, my life! 3.02. 29
for emily, upon my life! 3.03. 42
some country sport, upon my life, sir. 3.05. 97
no, keep it, your life lies on it. 3.06. 90
have at thy life! 3.06.131
then take my life, i'll woo thee to't. 3.06.156
as i have brought my life here to confirm it, 3.06.164
to me than begging | to take my life so basely. 3.06.267
'tis a sore life they have i' th' tother place, 4.03. 31 P
'twas thy power | to put life into dust: 5.01.110
that what was life | in him seem'd torture. 5.01.114
ev'ry blow that falls | threats a brave life, 5.03. 4
a life more worthy from him than all women, | i 5.03.143
by my short life, | i am most glad on't. 5.04. 28
and let my life be now as short | as my 5.04. 37
the gods will show their glory in a life | that 5.04. 43
i in my father's life | to take prerogative and STM III 8
saith that the world hath ending with thy life. VEN 12
me, | and were i not immortal, life were done, 197
look when a painter would surpass the life | in 289
it, | for i have heard it is a life in death, 413
till his breath breatheth life in her again. 474
do i delight to die, or life desire? 496
but now i liv'd, and life was death's annoy, 497
or butcher sire that reaves his son of life: 766
the aim of all is but to nurse the life | with LUC 141
as life for honor in fell battle's rage, | honor 145
or sire, | or lain in ambush to betray my life, 233
to their sight | must sell her joy, her life, 385
but that life liv'd in death, and death in life. 406
but that life liv'd in death, and death in life. 406
thou their fair life, and they thy fouler grave; 661
but she hath lost a dearer thing than life, 687
breaths make sick | the life of purity, the 780
or kills his life or else his quality. 875
in vain | some happy mean to end a hapless life. 1045
livery, | a dying life to living infamy. 1055
till life to death acquit my forc'd offense. 1071
when life is sham'd and death reproach's debtor. 1155
'tis honor to deprive dishonor'd life, | the one 1186
the life and feeling of her passion | she hoards 1317
wot, it was defect | of spirit, life, and bold 1346
in scorn of nature, art gave liveless life: 1374
fed, | show'd life imprison'd in a body dead. 1456
"that life was mine which thou hast here 1752
"i did give that life | which she too early and 1800
the dispers'd air, who, holding lucrece' life, 1805
that thou consum'st thyself in single life? SON 9. 2
so should the lines of life that life repair 16. 9
so should the lines of life that life repair 16. 9
it is but as a tomb | which hides your life, and 17. 4
so long lives this, and this gives life to thee. 18.14
my life, being made of four, with two alone 45. 7
my sweet love's beauty, though my lover's life: 63.12
away, | to live a second life on second head; 68. 7
but let your love even with my life decay; 71.12
away, | my life hath in this line some interest, 74. 3
so then thou hast but lost the dregs of life, 74. 9
so are you to my thoughts as food to life, | or 75. 1
your name from hence immortal life shall have, 81. 5
when others would give life and bring a tomb. 83.12
there lives more life in one of your fair eyes 83.13
away, | for term of life thou art assured mine, 92. 2
and life no longer than thy love will stay, 92. 3
when in the least of them my life hath end; 92. 6
since that my life on thy revolt doth lie; 92.10
give my love fame faster than time wastes life, 100.13
that did not better for my life provide | than 111. 3
threw, | and sav'd my life, saying "not you." 145.14
many nymphs that vow'd chaste life to keep 154. 3
his real habitude gave life and grace | to LC 114

LIFE-BLOOD 6 FR 0.0006 REL FR 6 V 0 P
word in it a gaping wound | issuing life-blood. MV 3.02.266
infect | the very life-blood of our enterprise, 1H4 4.01. 29
words of yours draw life-blood from my heart. 1H6 4.06. 43
couldst thou drain the life-blood of the child, 3H6 1.04.138
feel | my sword i' th' life-blood of thee else. H8 3.02.277
thy life-blood out, if aaron now be wise, | then TIT 4.04. 37
LIFE-HARMING 1 FR 0.0001 REL FR 1 V 0 P
to lay aside life-harming heaviness | and R2 2.02. 3
LIFELINGS 1 FR 0.0001 REL FR 0 V 1 P
'od's lifelings, here he is! TN 5.01.184 P
LIFE-POISONING 1 FR 0.0001 REL FR 1 V 0 P
life-poisoning pestilence, and frenzies wood, VEN 740
LIFE-PRESERVING 1 FR 0.0001 REL FR 1 V 0 P
and life-preserving rest | to be disturb'd, ERR 5.01. 83
LIFE-REND'RING 1 FR 0.0001 REL FR 1 V 0 P
and, like the kind life-rend'ring pelican, HAM 4.05.147
/LIFE'S 1 FR 0.0001 REL FR 1 V 0 P
/and /a /man's /life's /no /more /than /to /say HAM 5.02. 74
LIFE'S 14 FR 0.0015 REL FR 14 V 0 P
whose life's as tender to me as my soul! TGV 5.04. 37
and keep thy friend | under thy own life's key. AWW 1.01. 67
doth sustain | in life's uncertain voyage, i TIM 5.01.202
course, | chief nourisher in life's feast. MAC 2.02. 37
after life's fitful fever he sleeps well. 3.02. 23
life's but a walking shadow, a poor player, 5.05. 24
thy life's a miracle. LR 4.06. 55
o, man's life's but a span; OTH 2.03. 72
a madness, of which her life's in danger. CYM 4.03. 3
who tells us life's but breath, to trust it PER 1.01. 46
how she gins | to blow into life's flower again! 3.02. 95
showing life's triumph in the map of death, LUC 402
and death's dim look in life's mortality. 403
foul deed, my life's fair end shall free it. 1208
LIFE-TIME 1 FR 0.0001 REL FR 1 V 0 P
let me for this my life-time reign as king. 3H6 1.01.171
LIFE-WEARY 1 FR 0.0001 REL FR 1 V 0 P
veins | that the life-weary taker may fall dead, ROM 5.01. 62
/LIFT 1 FR 0.0001 REL FR 1 V 0 P
/would /lift /him /where /most /trade /of 2H4 1.01.174
LIFT 26 FR 0.0029 REL FR 23 V 3 P
you would lift the moon out of her sphere, if TMP 2.01.183 P
lift up your countenance, as it were the day WT 4.04. 49
lift up thy looks. 4.04.479
peace of heaven is theirs that lift their swords JN 2.01. 35
lift up thy brow, renowned salisbury, | and with 5.02. 54
for i may never lift | an angry arm against his R2 1.02. 40
doth with a twofold vigor lift me up | to reach 1.03. 71
to lift shrewd steel against our golden crown, 3.02. 59
that lift your vassal hands against my head, 3.03. 89
but i will lift the down-trod mortimer | as high 1H4 1.03.135
have you any levers to lift me up again, being 2.02. 34 P
can lift your blood up with persuasion. 5.02. 78
he ne'er lift up his hand but conquered. 1H6 1.01. 16
we'll both together lift our heads to heaven, 2H6 1.02. 14
sweet sacrifice, | and lift my soul to heaven. H8 2.01. 78
three pound, lift as much as his brother hector. TRO 1.02.116 P
should lift their bosoms higher than the shores, 1.03.112
at the heaven with your staves as lift them COR 1.01. 68
fury, shall lift up | their rotten privilege and 1.10. 22
o, here i lift this one hand up to heaven, | and TIT 3.01.206
hence! wilt thou lift up olympus? JC 3.01. 74
or do but lift this arm, the best of you | shall OTH 2.03.208
sweetest innocent | that e'er did lift up eye. 5.02.200
so, lift there. PER 3.02. 49
that you like rebels lift against the peace STM II.C 109
lift against the peace | lift up for peace, and II.C 110
LIFTED 3 FR 0.0003 REL FR 2 V 1 P
lifted up their noses | as they smelt music. TMP 4.01.177
she lifted the princess from the earth, and so WT 5.02. 76 P
methought | it lifted up it head and did address HAM 1.02.216
LIFTER 1 FR 0.0001 REL FR 0 V 1 P
is he so young a man and so old a lifter? TRO 1.02.117 P
LIFTING 2 FR 0.0002 REL FR 2 V 0 P
haunch of winter sings | the lifting up of day. 2H4 4.04. 93
should tear this hand | for lifting food to't? LR 3.04. 16
LIFTS 5 FR 0.0005 REL FR 5 V 0 P
of his | in aspiration lifts him from the earth. TRO 4.05. 16
why lifts she up her arms in sequence thus? TIT 4.01. 37
lifts me above the ground with cheerful thoughts ROM 5.01. 5
she lifts the coffer-lids that close his eyes, VEN 1127
the gracious light | lifts up his burning head, SON 7. 2
LIG *(also lie*)*
LIG 1 FR 0.0001 REL FR 0 V 1 P
de gud service, or i'll lig i' the grund for it; H5 3.02.115 P
LIGARIUS' 1 FR 0.0001 REL FR 0 V 1 P
some to ligarius'. JC 3.03. 38 P
LIGARIUS 6 FR 0.0006 REL FR 5 V 1 P
caius ligarius doth bear caesar hard, | who JC 2.01.215
caius ligarius, that metellus spake of. 2.01.311
caius ligarius, how? 2.01.312
such an exploit have i in hand, ligarius, | had 2.01.318
caius ligarius, | caesar was ne'er so much your 2.02.111
thou hast wrong'd caius ligarius. 2.03. 5 P
LIGGENS 1 FR 0.0001 REL FR 0 V 1 P
by god's liggens, i thank thee. 2H4 5.03. 65 P
/LIGHT* 2 FR 0.0002 REL FR 1 V 1 P
/of /so /airy /and /light /a /quality /that /it HAM 2.02.261 P
/how /light /and /portable /my /pain /seems /now LR 3.06.108
LIGHT* 315 FR 0.0356 REL FR 254 V 61 P
and teach me how | to name the bigger light, and TMP 1.02.335
of sycorax, toads, beetles, bats, light on you! 1.02.340
lest too light winning | make the prize light. 1.02.452
lest too light winning | make the prize light. 1.02.453
to whom i am subdu'd, are but light to me, 1.02.490
by this good light, this is a very shallow 2.02.144 P
by this light, a most perfidious and drunken 2.02.150 P
by this light, thou shalt be my lieutenant, 3.02. 15 P
take heed, | as hymen's lamps shall light you. 4.01. 23
best sing it to the tune of "light o' love." TGV 1.02. 80
it is too heavy for so light a tune. 1.02. 81
and that hath dazzled my reason's light; 2.04.210
know | that i had any light from thee of this. 3.01. 49
it will be light, my lord, that you may bear it 3.01.129
what light is light, if silvia be not seen? 3.01.174
what light is light, if silvia be not seen? 3.01.174
by day or night, | or any kind of light, | with WIV 2.01. 16

till we see the light of our fairies. 5.02. 2 P
is dark, light and spirits will become it well. 5.02. 11 P
torches do, | not light them for themselves; MM 1.01. 33
answer'd, he would never bring them to light. 3.02.178 P
waters from your eyes | with a light heart; 4.03.147
as there comes light from heaven, and words from 5.01.225
that's the way; for women are light at midnight. 5.01.279 P
for what obscured light the heavens did grant ERR 1.01. 66
and by the benefit of his wished light | the 1.01. 90
let love, being light, be drowned if she sink! 3.02. 52
a lamp of her and run from her by her own light. 3.02. 98 P
here she comes in the habit of a light wench; 4.03. 52 P
as much to say, "god make me a light wench." 4.03. 54 P
they appear to men like angels of light, light 4.03. 56 P
angels of light, light is an effect of fire, and 4.03. 56 P
ergo, light wenches will burn. 4.03. 57 P
and thereof comes it that his head is light. 5.01. 72
you may light on a husband that hath no beard. ADO 2.01. 32 P
otherwise 'tis light, and not heavy. 3.04. 37 P
clap 's into "light a' love"; 3.04. 44 P
ye light a' love with your heels! 3.04. 47 P
these things, come thus to light, | smother her 4.01.111
by this light, he changes more and more. 5.01.140 P
these shallow fools have brought to light, who 5.01.234 P
thee, but, by this light, i take thee for pity. 5.04. 92 P
pore upon a book | to seek the light of truth, LLL 1.01. 75
light, seeking light, doth light of light 1.01. 77
light, seeking light, doth light of light 1.01. 77
seeking light, doth light of light beguile; 1.01. 77
seeking light, doth light of light beguile; 1.01. 77
so, ere you find where light in darkness lies, 1.01. 78
your light grows dark by losing of your eyes. 1.01. 79
and give him light that it was blinded by. 1.01. 83
and that's great marvel, loving a light wench. 1.02.123 P
a woman sometimes, and you saw her in the light. 2.01.198
perchance light in the light. i desire her name. 2.01.199
perchance light in the light. i desire her name. 2.01.199
but her eye — by this light, but for her eye, i 4.03. 9 P
doth thy face through tears of mine give light. 4.03. 31
she (an attending star) scarce seen a light. 4.03.227
soonest tempt, resembling spirits of light. 4.03.253
dark needs no candles now, for dark is light. 4.03.265
light wenches may prove plagues to men forsworn; 4.03.382
had she been light, like you, | of such a merry, 5.02. 15
for a light heart lives long. 5.02. 18
your dark meaning, mouse, of this light word? 5.02. 19
a light condition in a beauty dark. 5.02. 20
we need more light to find your meaning out. 5.02. 21
you'll mar the light by taking it in snuff; 5.02. 22
so do not you, for you are a light wench. 5.02. 25
indeed i weigh not you, and therefore light. 5.02. 26
heaven's fiery eye, | by light we lose light; 5.02.376
heaven's fiery eye, | by light we lose light; 5.02.376
a light for monsieur judas! 5.02.630
and light them at the fiery glow-worm's eyes, MND 3.01.170
and both as light as tales. 3.02.133
than all yon fiery oes and eyes of light. 3.02.188
they willfully themselves exile from light, 3.02.386
for if but once thou show me thy grey light, 3.02.419
it appears, by his small light of discretion, 5.01.253 P
tongue, lose thy light, | moon, take thy flight, 5.01.304
through the house give glimmering light | by the 5.01.391
fairy sprite | hop as light as bird from brier, 5.01.394
truth will come to light; MV 2.02. 79 P
in themselves, good sooth, are too too light. 2.06. 42
it, let the danger light | upon your charter and 4.01. 38
as makes it light or heavy in the substance | or 4.01.328
that light we see is burning in my hall. 5.01. 89
let me give light, but let me not be light, 5.01.129
let me give light, but let me not be light, 5.01.129
for a light wife doth make a heavy husband, 5.01.130
we'll light upon some settled low content. AYL 2.03. 68
if i can by any means light on a fit man to SHR 1.01.110 P
in the world, and a man could light on them, 1.01.129 P
for knowing thee to be but young and light. 2.01.203
too light for such a swain as you to catch, 2.01.204
for by this light whereby i see thy beauty, 2.01.273
in his bright radiance and collateral light AWW 1.01. 88
my thoughts | in this my light deliverance, i 2.01. 82
there can be no kernel in this light nut; 2.05. 43 P
of her worth, | that he does weigh too light. 3.04. 32
if the quick fire of youth light not your mind, 4.02. 5
sallets ere we light on such another herb. 4.05. 14 P
more than light airs and recollected terms | of TN 2.04. 5
haply your eye shall light upon some toy | you 3.03. 44
good fool, help me to some light and some paper. 4.02.105 P
good fool, some ink, paper, and light; 4.02.110 P
i will fetch you light and paper and ink. 4.02.117 P
i am none, by this good light. WT 2.03. 83
if young doricles | do light upon her, she shall 4.04.179
now, by this light, were i to get again, | madam JN 1.01.259
or the light loss of england for a friend. 3.01.206
the peril of our curses light on thee | so heavy 3.01.295
we had a kind of light what would ensue. 4.03. 61
and when i mount, alive may i not light, | if i R2 1.01. 82
then thus i turn me from my country's light, 1.03.176
my oil-dried lamp and time-bewasted light 1.03.221
the man that mocks at it and sets it light. 1.03.293
and liberal largess, are grown somewhat light, 1.04. 44
light vanity, insatiate cormorant, | consuming 2.01. 38
and darts his light through every guilty hole, 3.02. 43
and some few vanities that make him light; 3.04. 86
nimble mischance, that art so light of foot, 3.04. 92
and never show thy head by day nor light. 5.06. 44
from your encounter, then they light on us. 1H4 2.02. 62 P
your whole plot too light for the counterpoise 2.03. 13 P
and wert indeed, but for the light in thy face, 3.03. 37 P
perpetual triumph, an everlasting bonfire light! 3.03. 42 P
god's light, i was never call'd so in mine own 3.03. 62 P
where you did give a fair and natural light, 5.01. 18
though he have his own lanthorn to light him. 2H4 1.02. 48 P
your ill angel is light, but i hope he that 1.02.165 P
by this light, i am well spoke on, i can hear it 2.02. 65 P
and by his light | did all the chevalry of 2.03. 19
god's light, with two points on your shoulder? 2.04.132 P
god's light, these villains will make the word 2.04.147 P
majesty, by this light flesh and corrupt blood, 2.04.295 P
that even our corn shall seem as light as chaff, 4.01.193

believe me, i am passing light in spirit. 4.02. 85
that light and weightless down | perforce must 4.05. 33
and yet that were but light payment, to dance ep 20 P
and this man | hath, for a few light crowns, H5 2.02. 89
since god so graciously hath brought to light 2.02.185
a most contagious treason come to light, look 4.08. 21 P
by this day and this light, the fellow has 4.08. 62 P
famish'd, | or with light skirmishes enfeebled. 1H6 1.04. 69
out, some light horsemen, and peruse their wings 4.02. 43
a plaguing mischief light on charles and thee! 5.03. 39
that she will light to listen to the lays, | and 2H6 1.03. 90
to believing souls | gives light in darkness, 2.01. 65
dark shall be my light, and night my day; 2.04. 40
time will bring to light in smooth duke humphrey 3.01. 65
and so god's curse light upon you all! 4.08. 32 P
now are they but one lamp, one light, one sun. 3H6 2.01. 31
when dying clouds contend with growing light, 2.05. 2
which, whiles it lasted, gave king henry light. 2.06. 2
thou /keep'st me from the light, | but i will 5.06. 84
it, | prodigious, and untimely brought to light, R3 1.02. 22
ay, gentle cousin, were it light enough. 3.01.117
then i see you will part but with light gifts! 3.01.118
day, yield me not thy light, nor, night, thy 4.04.401
how came | his practices to light? H8 3.02. 29
by this light, i'll ha' more. 5.01.171
i have (as when the sun doth light a-scorn) TRO 1.01. 37
before the sun rose he was harness'd light, 1.02. 8
fan, | puffing at all, winnows the light away, 1.03. 28
light boats sail swift, though greater hulks 2.03.266
all the contagion of the south light on you, COR 1.04. 30
i am light, and heavy. 2.01.184
were | he is enfranchised and come to light. TIT 4.02.125
come down and welcome me to this world's light; 5.02. 33
bed, | away from light steals home my heavy son, ROM 1.01.137
stars that make dark heaven light. 1.02. 25
being but heavy, i will bear the light. 1.04. 12
his shaft | to soar with his light feathers, and 1.04. 20
let wantons light of heart | tickle the 1.04. 35
more light, you knaves, and turn the tables up; 1.05. 27
go, | be quiet, or — more light, more light! 1.05. 87
go, | be quiet, or — more light, more light! 1.05. 87
soft, what light through yonder window breaks? 2.02. 2
with love's light wings did i o'erperch these 2.02. 66
therefore thou mayest think my behavior light, 2.02. 99
and not impute this yielding to light love, 2.02.105
a thousand times the worse, to want thy light. 2.02.155
the eastern clouds with streaks of light, | and 2.03. 2
o, so light a foot | will ne'er wear out the 2.06. 16
so light is vanity. 2.06. 20
a pack of blessings light upon thy back, 3.03.141
light to my chamber ho! 3.04. 33
yond light is not day-light, i know it, i; 3.05. 12
and light thee on thy way to mantua. 3.05. 15
o, now be gone, more light and light it grows. 3.05. 35
o, now be gone, more light and light it grows. 3.05. 35
more light and light, more dark and dark our 3.05. 36
more light and light, more dark and dark our 3.05. 36
my heart is wondrous light, | since this same 4.02. 46
give me the light. 5.03. 25
this vault a feasting presence full of light. 5.03. 86
yond, that vainly lends his light | to grubs and 5.03.125
anon comes one with light to ope the tomb, | and 5.03.283
as the moon does, by wanting light to give: TIM 4.03. 68
the plague of company light upon thee! 4.03.352 P
lie where the light foam of the sea may beat 4.03.378
what thou want'st by free and offer'd light. 5.01. 45
that needs must light on this ingratitude. JC 1.01. 55
give so much light that i may read by them. 2.01. 45
a curse shall light upon the limbs of men; 3.01.262
now some light. 5.03. 31
let not light see my black and deep desires; MAC 1.04. 51
entomb, | when living light should kiss it? 2.04. 10
light thickens, and the crow | makes wing to th' 3.02. 50
give us a light there, ho! 3.03. 9
a light, a light! 3.03. 14
a light, a light! 3.03. 14
who did strike out the light? 3.03. 19
how came she by that light? 5.01. 21 P
she has light by her continually, 'tis her 5.01. 22 P
giving more light than heat, extinct in both HAM 1.03.118
and to the last bended their light on me. 2.01. 97
cannot be too heavy, nor plautus too light, for 2.02.401 P
that lend a tyrannous and a damned light | to 2.02.460
nor earth to me give food, nor heaven light, 3.02.216
give me some light. away! 3.02.269 P
yet are they much too light for the /bore of the 4.06. 26 P
the light and careless livery that it wears 4.07. 79
light, ho, here! LR 2.01. 31
fated o'er men's faults light on thy daughters! 3.04. 68
false of heart, light of ear, bloody of hand; 3.04. 92 P
eyes are in a heavy case, your purse in a light, 4.06.147 P
light, i say, light! OTH 1.01.144
light, i say, light! 1.01.144
on my head if my bad blame | light on the man! 1.03.178
bring this monstrous birth to the world's light. 1.03.404
carve for his own rage | holds his soul light; 2.03.174
mince this matter, | making it light to cassio. 2.03.248
trifles light as air | are to the jealious 3.03.322
and light behaviors | quite in the wrong. 4.01.102
are his wits safe? is he not light of brain? 4.01.269
for, by this light of heaven, | i know not how i 4.02.150
no, by this heavenly light! 4.03. 65
nor i neither by this heavenly light; 4.03. 66
o, help ho! light! a surgeon! 5.01. 30
one comes in his shirt, with light and weapons. 5.01. 47
light, gentlemen! 5.01. 73
lend me a light. 5.01. 88
put out the light, and then put out the light: 5.02. 7
put out the light, and then put out the light: 5.02. 7
i can again thy former light restore, | should i 5.02. 9
but once put out thy light, | thou cunning'st 5.02. 10
promethean heat | that can thy light relume. 5.02. 13
no more light answers. ANT 1.02.176
and made the night light with drinking. 2.02.178 P
let all the number of the stars give light | to 3.02. 65
but you know strange fowl light upon neighboring CYM 1.04. 89 P
base and illustrious as the smoky light | that's 1.06.109

his pocket, we will pay him tribute for light; 3.01. 44 P
though light, take pieces for the figure's sake; 5.04. 25
the brain the heavier for being too light, the 5.04.164 P
for being too light, the purse too light, being 5.04.165 P
fair glass of light, i lov'd you, and could PER 1.01. 76
/'schew no course to keep them from the light. 1.01.136
day serves not light more faithful than i'll be. 1.02.110
he would depart, i'll give some light unto you. 1.03. 17
the which hath fire in darkness, none in light: 2.03. 44
or never more to view nor day nor light. 2.05. 17
hast thou had, my dear, | no light, no fire. 3.01. 57
you are light into my hands, where you are like 4.02. 72 P
weary of this world's light, have to themselves TNK 1.01.143
by this good light, | had i a sword, i would 2.02.264
"may you never more enjoy the light," etc. 4.01.104
"when cynthia with her borrowed light," etc. 4.01.153
to a place where the light may rather seem to 4.03. 74 P
and gallops to the /tune of "light a' love." 5.02. 54
there is but envy in that light which shows 5.03. 21
not gross to sink, but light, and will aspire. VEN 150
is love so light, sweet boy, and may it be 155
"torches are made to light, jewels to wear, 163
which through the crystal tears gave light, 491
and coal-black clouds that shadow heaven's light 533
and yields at last to every light impression? 566
dries up his oil to lend the world his light. 756
their light blown out in some mistrustful wood, 826
"o thou clear god, and patron of all light, 860
may lend thee light, as thou dost lend to other. 864
the grass stoops not, she treads on it so light, 1028
where they resign their office and their light 1039
threw unwilling light | upon the wide wound that 1051
thou being dead, the day should yet be light. 1134
in her light chariot, quickly is convey'd, 1192
more than his eyes were open'd to the light. LUC 105
no comfortable star did lend his light, | no 164
"fair torch, burn out thy light, and lend it not 190
not | to darken her whose light excelleth thine; 191
mine eyes forgo their light, my false heart 228
by the light he spies | lucretia's glove, 316
to wink, being blinded with a greater light: 375
eyes like marigolds had sheath'd their light, 397
this said, he sets his foot upon the light, 673
light, | for light and lust are deadly enemies; 674
he in his speed looks for the morning light, 745
muster thy mists to meet the eastern light, 773
that in their smoky ranks his smoth'red light 783
the light will show, character'd in my brow, 807
to unmask falsehood and bring truth to light, 940
lends light to all fair eyes that light will 1083
light to all fair eyes that light will borrow; 1083
brand not my forehead with thy piercing light, 1091
who in a salt-wav'd ocean quench their light, 1231
that through their light joy seemed to appear 1434
committed, light alone | upon his head that hath 1480
a creeping creature, with a flaming light, | and 1627
lo in the orient when the gracious light | lifts SON 7. 1
when thou thyself dost give invention light? 38. 8
to the clear day with thy much clearer light, 43. 7
nativity, once in the main of light, | crawls to 60. 5
when thou shalt be dispos'd to set me light, 88. 1
dark'ning thy pow'r to lend base subjects light? 100. 4
and every light occasion of the wind | upon his LC 86

LIGHTED* 11 FR 0.0012 REL FR 11 V 0 P
shall be paid | till hymen's torch be lighted; TMP 4.01. 97
and by good fortune i have lighted well | on SHR 1.02.167
sir walter blunt, new lighted from his horse, 1H4 1.01. 63
is lighted on poor hastings' wretched head! R3 3.04. 93
beheld them when they lighted, how they clung H8 1.01. 9
when it is lighted, come and call me here. JC 2.01. 8
shaft that's shot | hath not yet lighted, and MAC 2.03.142
and all our yesterdays have lighted fools | the 5.05. 22
mercury | new lighted on a /heaven-kissing hill, HAM 3.04. 59
kept their course, and lighted | the little o, ANT 5.02. 80
and being lighted, by the light he spies LUC 316

LIGHTEN* 3 FR 0.0003 REL FR 1 V 2 P
that we may lighten our own hearts and our ADO 5.04.118 P
now the lord lighten thee! 2H4 2.01.194 P
may proceed a gem | to lighten all this isle? H8 2.03. 79

LIGHTENS* 5 FR 0.0005 REL FR 5 V 0 P
lightens my humor with his merry jests. ERR 1.02. 21
eagle's, lightens forth | controlling majesty. R2 3.03. 69
a precious ring that lightens all this hole, TIT 2.03.227
doth cease to be | ere one can say it lightens. ROM 2.02.120
that thunders, lightens, opens graves, and roars JC 1.03. 74

LIGHTER 5 FR 0.0005 REL FR 5 V 0 P
to frown | upon sir toby and the lighter people; TN 5.01.339
my heart is ten times lighter than my looks. R3 5.03. 3
blasts my bays and my fam'd works makes lighter TNK pr 20
i have worn a lighter, | but i shall make it 3.06. 56
that day the three kings fell, but lighter. 3.06. 71

LIGHTER-HEEL'D 1 FR 0.0001 REL FR 1 V 0 P
the villain is much lighter-heel'd than i; MND 3.02.415

LIGHTEST 2 FR 0.0002 REL FR 2 V 0 P
making them lightest that wear most of it. MV 3.02. 91
i could a tale unfold whose lightest word HAM 1.05. 15

LIGHTETH 1 FR 0.0001 REL FR 1 V 0 P
whereat a waxen torch forthwith he lighteth, LUC 178

LIGHT-FOOT 1 FR 0.0001 REL FR 1 V 0 P
some light-foot friend post to the duke of R3 4.04.440

LIGHTLESS 2 FR 0.0002 REL FR 2 V 0 P
and to collatium bears the lightless fire, LUC 4
"such devils steal effects from lightless hell, 1555

LIGHTLY 12 FR 0.0013 REL FR 10 V 2 P
o, could their master come and go as lightly, TGV 3.01.142
and will not lightly trust the messenger, | that ERR 4.04. 5
your fellows, for they are but lightly rewarded. LLL 1.02.152 P
lightly conspir'd | and sworn unto the practices H5 2.02. 89
was ever feather so lightly blown to and fro as 2H6 4.08. 55 P
they love his grace but lightly | that fill his R3 1.03. 45
short summers lightly have a forward spring. 3.01. 94
i weigh it lightly, were it heavier. 3.01.121
and | believe't not lightly — though i go alone COR 4.01. 29
i beg this boon, with tears not lightly shed, TIT 2.03.289
my bosom's lord sits lightly in his throne, ROM 5.01. 3
and we punish it | seeming to bear it lightly. ANT 4.14.138

LIGHTNESS* 8 FR 0.0009 REL FR 7 V 1 P
more betray our sense | than woman's lightness? MM 2.02.169

since mine eyes are witness of her lightness, SHR 4.02. 24
to this weight such lightness with their fear 2H4 1.01.122
and the lightness of his wife shines through it; 1.02. 46 P
gust, | such is the lightness of you common men. 3H6 3.01. 89
o heavy lightness, serious vanity, | misshapen ROM 1.01.178
thence to /a lightness, and, by this declension, HAM 2.02.149
we do bear | so great weight in his lightness. ANT 1.04. 25

/LIGHTNING 1 FR 0.0001 REL FR 1 V 0 P
/nimble /stroke | /of /quick /cross /lightning? LR 4.07. 34

LIGHTNING 22 FR 0.0024 REL FR 22 V 0 P
jove's lightning, the precursors | o' th' TMP 1.02.201
i would the lightning had | burnt up those logs 3.01. 16
thy eye jove's lightning bears, thy voice his LLL 4.02.115
brief as the lightning in the collied night, MND 1.01.145
be thou as lightning in the eyes of france; JN 1.01. 24
be swift like lightning in the execution, | and R2 1.03. 79
their weapons like to lightning came and went; 3H6 2.01.129
either heav'n with lightning strike the R3 1.02. 64
secure of thunder's crack or lightning flash, TIT 2.01. 3
too like the lightning, which doth cease to be ROM 2.02.119
and to't they go like lightning, for, ere i 3.01.172
their keepers call | a lightning before death! 5.03. 90
o, how may i | call this a lightning? 5.03. 91
and when the cross blue lightning seem'd to open JC 1.03. 50
in thunder, lightning, or in rain? MAC 1.01. 2
now he'll outstare the lightning: ANT 3.13.194
fear no more the lightning flash. CYM 4.02.270
and she (like harmless lightning) throws her eye 5.05.394
hands shall never draw 'em out like lightning, TNK 2.02. 24
before that flew | the lightning of your valor. 3.06. 85
flash'd forth fire, as lightning from the sky. VEN 348
thine eye jove's lightning seems, thy voice his PP 5.11

LIGHTNINGS 1 FR 0.0001 REL FR 1 V 0 P
you nimble lightnings, dart your blinding flames LR 2.04.165

LIGHT'S 1 FR 0.0001 REL FR 1 V 0 P
feed'st thy light's flame with self-substantial SON 1. 6

LIGHTS* 32 FR 0.0036 REL FR 25 V 7 P
own eyes had the lights they were wont to have TGV 2.01. 71 P
a pit hard by herne's oak, with obscur'd lights; WIV 5.03. 14 P
break of day, | lights that do mislead the morn; MM 4.01. 4
these earthly godfathers of heaven's lights, LLL 1.01. 88
luck stirring but what lights a' my shoulders, MV 3.01. 95 P
you have given me such clear lights of favor, TN 5.01.336
behind the globe, that lights the lower world, R2 3.02. 38
and that shall be the day, when e'er it lights, 1H4 3.02.138
would have bought me lights as good cheap at the 3.03. 45 P
should notwithstanding join our lights together, 3H6 2.01. 37
the lights burn blue. R3 5.03.180
those suns of glory, those two lights of men, H8 1.01. 6
yonder 'tis, | there where we see the lights. TRO 5.01. 68
in delay | we waste our lights in vain, /like ROM 1.04. 45
waste our lights in vain, /like lights by day! 1.04. 45
all to you. lights, more lights! TIM 1.02.228
all to you. lights, more lights! 1.02.228
room | hath blaz'd with lights and bray'd with 2.02.161
o, he lights too. JC 5.03. 31
lights, lights, lights! HAM 3.02.270 P
lights, lights, lights! 3.02.270 P
lights, lights, lights! 3.02.270 P
but i do prophesy th' election lights | on 5.02.355
he that first lights on him | holla the other. LR 3.01. 54
but look, what lights come yond? OTH 1.02. 28
witness, you ever-burning lights above, | you 3.03.463
to see th' enclosed lights, now canopied | under CYM 2.02. 21
none that beheld him but, like lesser lights, PER 2.03. 41
pages and lights, to conduct | these knights 2.03.108
who, angry that the eyes fly from their lights, LUC 461
small lights are soon blown out, huge fires 647
and dying eyes gleam'd forth their ashy lights, 1378

LIGHT-WING'D 1 FR 0.0001 REL FR 1 V 0 P
when light-wing'd toys | of feather'd cupid seel OTH 1.03.268

LIK'D* 11 FR 0.0012 REL FR 7 V 4 P
several virtues | have i lik'd several women, TMP 3.01. 43
that lik'd, but had a rougher task in hand ADO 1.01.299
is, | saying i lik'd her ere i went to wars. 1.01.305
we had lik'd to have had our two noses snapp'd 5.01.115 P
that lov'd, that lik'd, that look'd with cheer. MND 5.01.294
that pleas'd me, complexions that lik'd me, and AYL ep 19 P
certain it is i lik'd her, | and boarded her i' AWW 5.03.210
his band and yours, he lik'd not the security. 2H4 1.02. 33 P
abide carnation — 'twas a color he never lik'd. H5 2.03. 34 P
'tis yours, because you lik'd it. TIM 1.02.212
what she lik'd | was then of me approv'd, what TNK 1.03. 64

/LIKE* 22 FR 0.0024 REL FR 19 V 3 P
/disguis'd /like /herne, /with /huge /horns /on WIV 4.04. 43
two of the first, /like coats in heraldry, | due MND 3.02.213
/is /this /golden /crown /like /a /deep /well R2 4.01.184
/like /to /my /followers /in /prosperity, 4.01.280
/was /this /the /face | /that, /like /the /sun, 4.01.284
/than /that /being /which /was /like /to /be? 2H4 1.01.179
/perfection /to /abuse | /to /seem /like /him; 2.03. 28
/but /rather /show /a /while /like /fearful /war 4.01. 63
/common /people /swarm /like /summer /flies, 3H6 2.06. 8
/because /that /like /a /jack /thou /keep'st R3 4.02.114
/in /like /conditions /as /our /argument, | /to TRO pr 25
/like /or /find /fault, /do /as /your /pleasures pr 30
/or, /like /a /gallant /horse /fall'n /in /first 3.03.161
/like /to /the /empress' /moor, /therefore /i TIT 3.02. 67
waste our lights in vain, /like lights by day! ROM 1.04. 45
very like, /very /like. stay'd it long? HAM 1.02.236
whiles, /like a puff'd and reckless libertine, 1.03. 49
/to /speak /to /you /like /an /honest /man, /i 2.02.268 P
/to /common /players (/as /it /is /most /like, 2.02.349 P
/on /itself, | /like /monsters /of /the /deep. LR 4.02. 50
/and /tears | /were /like /a /better /way: 4.03. 19
/the /arbiterment /is /like /to /be /bloody. 4.07. 93 P

LIKE* 1895 FR 0.2142 REL FR 1494 V 401 P
and rather like a dream than an assurance | that TMP 1.02. 45
like a good parent, did beget of him | a 1.02. 94
else exact — like one | who having into truth, 1.02. 99
with hair up-staring (then like reeds, not hair) 1.02.213
go make thyself like a nymph o' th' sea; 1.02.301
but wouldst gabble like | a thing most brutish, 1.02.356
few in millions | can speak like us. 2.01. 8
he receives comfort like cold porridge. 2.01. 10 P
if he were that which now he's like — that's 2.01.282
and when i rear my hand, do you the like, | to 2.01.295
heard a hollow burst of bellowing | like bulls, 2.01.312
nor lead me, like a fire-brand, in the dark 2.02. 6
sometime like apes that mow and chatter at me, 2.02. 9
then like hedgehogs which | lie tumbling in my 2.02. 10
looks like a foul bumbard that would shed his 2.02. 21 P
a fish, he smells like a fish; 2.02. 26 P
legg'd like a man! 2.02. 33 P
and his fins like arms! 2.02. 34 P
swom ashore, man, like a duck. 2.02.128 P
i can swim like a duck, i'll be sworn. 2.02.129 P
though thou canst swim like a duck, thou art 2.02.131 P
swim like a duck, thou art made like a goose. 2.02.131 P
says such baseness | had never like executor. 3.01. 13
form a shape, | besides yourself, to like of. 3.01. 57
if th' other two be brain'd like us, the state 3.02. 6 P
but you'll lie like dogs, and yet say nothing 3.02. 19 P
as you like this, give me the lie another time. 3.02. 77 P
dost thou like the plot, trinculo? 3.02.108 P
dew-lapp'd, like bulls, whose throats had 3.03. 45
my fellow ministers | are like invulnerable. 3.03. 66
(like poison given to work a great time after) 3.03.105
and, like the baseless fabric of this vision, 4.01.151
and, like this insubstantial pageant faded, 4.01.155
at which, like unback'd colts, they prick'd 4.01.176
now, jerkin, you are like to lose your hair, and 4.01.237 P
steal by line and level, and't like your grace. 4.01.239 P
tears runs down his beard like winter's drops 5.01. 16
for the like loss i have her sovereign aid, 5.01.143
you the like loss? 5.01.144
very like; 5.01.265
that, like a testy babe, will scratch the nurse TGV 1.02. 58
and yet methinks i do not like this tune. 1.02. 87
shall these papers lie like tell-tales here? 1.02.130
i like thy counsel; 1.03. 34
and that thou mayst perceive how well i like it, 1.03. 35
like exhibition thou shalt have from me. 1.03. 69
you have learn'd, like sir proteus, to wreathe 2.01. 19 P
to wreathe your arms, like a malecontent; 2.01. 20 P
to relish a love-song, like a robin-redbreast; 2.01. 20 P
to walk alone, like one that had the pestilence; 2.01. 21 P
to sigh, like a schoolboy that had lost his abc; 2.01. 22 P
like a young wench that had buried her grandam; 2.01. 23 P
to fast, like one that takes diet; 2.01. 24 P
to watch, like one that fears robbing; 2.01. 25 P
to speak puling, like a beggar at hallowmas. 2.01. 25 P
wont, when you laugh'd, to crow like a cock; 2.01. 27 P
when you walk'd, to walk like one of the lions; 2.01. 28 P
you, and shine through you like the water in an 2.01. 39 P
what means your ladyship? do you not like it? 2.01.121
o, be not like your mistress — be mov'd, be 2.01.175 P
receiv'd my proportion, like the prodigious son, 2.03. 3 P
o, that she could speak now like a /wood woman! 2.03. 27 P
pills, | and i must minister the like to you. 2.04.150
which, like a waxen image 'gainst a fire, 2.04.201
not like a woman, for i would prevent | the 2.07. 40
if proteus like your journey when you come, | no 2.07. 65
for love is like a child, | that longs for every 3.01.124
and i for such like petty crimes as these. 4.01. 50
i like thee well, | and will employ thee in some 4.04. 40
how like a dream is this! 5.04. 26
i'll woo you like a soldier, at arms' end, | and 5.04. 57
has brown hair, and speaks small like a woman. WIV 1.01. 48 P
yet i live like a poor gentleman born. 1.01.276 P
his filching was like an unskillful singer, he 1.03. 25 P
did seem to scorch me up like a burning-glass! 1.03. 67 P
sail like my pinnace to these golden shores. 1.03. 80
rogues, hence, avaunt, vanish like hailstones; 1.03. 81
great round beard, like a glover's paring-knife? 1.04. 21 P
i do not like des toys. 1.04. 44 P
did you ever hear the like? 2.01. 69 P
i'll entertain myself like one that i am not 2.01. 86 P
or go thou | like sir actaeon he, with ringwood 2.01.118
i like not the humor of lying. 2.01.128 P
i like it never the better for that. 2.01.179 P
have made you four tall fellows skip like rats. 2.01.229 P
through the grate, like a geminy of baboons. 2.02. 9 P
"love like a shadow flies when substance love 2.02.207
like a fair house built on another man's ground, 2.02.215 P
it shall hang like a meteor o'er the cuckold's 2.02.280 P
go before you like a man than follow him like a 3.02. 5 P
you like a man than follow him like a dwarf. 3.02. 6 P
like a many of these lisping hawthorn buds, that 3.03. 70 P
buds, that come like women in men's apparel, and 3.03. 71 P
and smell like bucklersbury in simple time — i 3.03. 72 P
he will maintain you like a gentlewoman. 3.04. 45 P
carried in a basket like a barrow of butcher's 3.05. 5 P
i like his money well. 3.05. 58 P
next, to be compass'd, like a good bilbo, in the 3.05.110 P
to be stopp'd in, like a strong distillation, 3.05.112 P
than half stew'd in grease, like a dutch dish) 3.05.119 P
glowing-hot, in that surge, like a horse-shoe; 3.05.121 P
let's go dress him like the witch of brainford. 4.02. 98 P
i like not when a oman has a great peard. 4.02.193 P
growth, we'll dress | like urchins, ouphes, and 4.04. 50
and i will be like a jack-an-apes also, to burn 4.04. 68 P
he'll speak like an anthropophaginian unto thee. 4.05. 9 P
ay, sir; like who more bold? 4.05. 54 P
set spurs and away, like three german devils, 4.05. 69 P
and i was like to be apprehended for the witch 4.05.116 P
as you see, like a poor old man, but i came from 5.01. 16 P
from her, master /brook, like a poor old woman. 5.01. 17 P
divide me like a brib'd-buck, each a haunch. 5.05. 24 P
speak i like herne the hunter? 5.05. 27 P
sing, | like to the garter's compass, in a ring. 5.05. 66
like sapphire, pearl, and rich embroidery, 5.05. 71
now, good sir john, how like you windsor wives? 5.05.106
but, like a thrifty goddess, she determines MM 1.01. 38
but do not like to stage me to their eyes; 1.01. 68
thou conclud'st like the sanctimonious pirate, 1.02. 7 P
like rats that ravin down their proper bane, | a 1.02.129
penalties | which have, like unscour'd armor, 1.02.167
as well for the encouragement of the like, which 1.02.188 P
slip, | even like an o'ergrown lion in a cave, 1.03. 22
may formally in person bear | like a true friar. 1.03. 48
to know, when maidens sue, | men give like gods; 1.04. 81
here, if it like your honor. 2.01. 33
first, and it like you, the house is a respected 2.01.162 P
you would have slipp'd like him, but he, like 2.02. 65
would have slipp'd like him, but he, like you, 2.02. 65
breathe within your lips, | like man new made. 2.02. 79
and like a prophet | looks in a glass that shows 2.02. 94
but it is tyrannous | to use it like a giant. 2.02.109
like an angry ape | plays such fantastic tricks 2.02.120
because authority, though it err like others, 2.02.134
it doth know | that's like my brother's fault. 2.02.138
is like a good thing, being often read, | grown 2.04. 8
for, like an ass whose back with ingots bows, 3.01. 26
hath (like an impediment in the current) made it 3.01.242 P
needs buy and sell men and women like beasts, we 3.02. 2 P
i do desire the like. 4.01. 51
the visage | of ragozine, more like to claudio? 4.03. 76
his actions show much like to madness, pray 4.04. 4 P
give the like notice | to valentius, rowland, 4.05. 7
that's i, and't like your grace. 5.01. 74
o that it were as like as it is true! 5.01.104
i do not like the man; 5.01.128
stand like the forfeits in a barber's shop, | as 5.01.321
when i perceive your grace, like pow'r divine, 5.01.369
like doth quit like, and measure still for 5.01.411
like doth quit like, and measure still for 5.01.411
claudio stoop'd to death, and with like haste. 5.01.415
head — | as like almost to claudio as himself. 5.01.489
if he be like your brother, for his sake | is he 5.01.490
the one so like the other | as could not be ERR 1.01. 51
whilst i had been like heedful of the other. 1.01. 82
me | that his attendant — so his case was like, 1.01.127
i to the world am like a drop of water, | that 1.02. 35
methinks your maw, like mine, should be your 1.02. 66
but were we burd'ned with like weight of pain, 2.01. 36
but, if thou live to see like right bereft, 2.01. 40
me, | that like a football you do spurn me thus? 2.01. 83
or if you like elsewhere, do it by stealth, 3.02. 7
apparel vice like virtue's harbinger; 3.02. 12
swart, like my shoe, but her face nothing like 3.02.102 P
shoe, but her face nothing like so clean kept: 3.02.103 P
she is spherical, like a globe; 3.02.114 P
but, like a shrew, you first begin to brawl. 4.01. 51
sir, like an evil angel, and bid you forsake 4.03. 20 P
he that went, like a base-viol, in a case of 4.03. 24 P
they appear to men like angels of light, light 4.03. 55 P
or rather, the prophecy like the parrot, "beware 4.04. 42 P
rings, jewels, any thing his rage did like. 5.01.144
his man with scissors nicks him like a fool; 5.01.175
these two antipholus', these two so like, | and 5.01.358
we came into the world like brother and brother; 5.01.425
o lord, he will hang upon him like a disease; ADO 1.01. 86 P
lady, for you are like an honorable father. 1.01.112 P
for all messina, as like him as she is. 1.01.115 P
being no other but as she is, i do not like her. 1.01.176 P
like the old tale, my lord: 1.01.216 P
if i do, hang me in a bottle like a cat, and 1.01.257 P
thou wilt be like a lover presently, | and tire 1.01.306
the one is too like an image and says nothing, 2.01. 8 P
and the other too like my lady's eldest son, 2.01. 9 P
the devil meet me like an old cuckold with horns 2.01. 44 P
first suit is hot and hasty, like a scotch jig, 2.01. 75 P
when i like your favor, for god defend the lute 2.01. 94 P
for god defend the lute should be like the case! 2.01. 95 P
well, i would you did like me. 2.01.100 P
about your neck, like an usurer's chain? 2.01.189 P
or under your arm, like a lieutenant's scarf? 2.01.190 P
why, that's spoken like an honest drovier; 2.01.194 P
now you strike like the blind man. 2.01.198 P
upon me that i stood like a man at a mark, with 2.01.246 P
hath your grace ne'er a brother like you? 2.01.323 P
who is thus like to be cozen'd with the 2.02. 39 P
the purpose (like an honest man and a soldier), 2.03. 19 P
faith, like enough. 2.03.103 P
doth indeed show some sparks that are like wit. 2.03.187 P
enter, like favorites | made proud by princes, 3.01. 9
for look where beatrice, like a lapwing, runs 3.01. 24
therefore let benedick, like cover'd fire, 3.01. 77
why, you speak like an ancient and most quiet 3.03. 39 P
and i will, like a true drunkard, utter all to 3.03.104 P
'a goes up and down like a gentleman. 3.03.127 P
fashioning them like pharaoh's soldiers in the 3.03.133 P
sometime like god bel's priests in the old 3.03.134 P
sometime like the shaven hercules in the 3.03.136 P
we are like to prove a goodly commodity, being 3.03.177 P
i like the new tire within excellently, if the 3.04. 13 P
behold how like a maid she blushes here! 4.01. 34
this looks not like a nuptial. 4.01. 68
who hath indeed, most like a liberal villain, 4.01. 92
i do not like thy look, i promise thee. 4.02. 44 P
whose joy of her is overwhelm'd like mine, | and 5.01. 9
moral when he shall endure | the like himself. 5.01. 31
i speak not like a dotard nor a fool, | as under 5.01. 59
runs not this speech like iron through your 5.01.245
that when i note another man like him | i may 5.01.260
your worship speaks like a most thankful and 5.01.315 P
calf in that same noble feat | much like to you, 5.04. 51
friar — | i am your husband if you like of me. 5.04. 59
but in that thou art like to be my kinsman, live 5.04.110 P
study is like the heaven's glorious sun, | that LLL 1.01. 84
berowne is like an envious sneaping frost | that 1.01.100
but like of each thing that in season grows. 1.01.107
tongue | doth ravish like enchanting harmony; 1.01.167
the town gates on his back like a porter; 1.02. 72 P
like humble/-visag'd suitors, his high will. 2.01. 34
like one that comes here to besiege his court, 2.01. 86
his heart, like an agot, with your print 2.01.236
then was venus like her mother, for her father 2.01.256
thin/-bellied doublet like a rabbit on a spit; 3.01. 19 P
hands in your pocket like a man after the old 3.01. 20 P
like the sequel, i. signior costard, adieu. 3.01.134
and wear his colors like a tumbler's hoop! 3.01.188
wife — | a woman, that is like a german /clock, 3.01.190
who now hangeth like a jewel in the ear of caelo 4.02. 4 P
and anon falleth like a crab on the face of 4.02. 6 P
are sweetly varied, like a scholar at the least; 4.02. 9 P
to me were oaks, to thee like osiers bowed. 4.02.108
why, he comes in like a perjure, wearing papers. 4.03. 46
like a demigod here sit i in the sky, | and 4.03. 77
tush, none but minstrels like of sonneting! 4.03.156
by keeping company | with men like /you, men of 4.03.178
that, like a rude and savage man of inde, | at 4.03.218
is ebony like her? 4.03.244

to look like her are chimney–sweepers black. 4.03.262
thou disputes like an infant; go whip thy gig. 5.01. 66 P
had she been light, like you, | of such a merry, 5.02. 15
any thing like? 5.02. 39
or hide your heads like cowards, and fly hence. 5.02. 86
thus, | like muscovites or russians, as i guess. 5.02.121
face, | that we (like savages) may worship it. 5.02.202
thus change i like the moon. 5.02.212
blow like sweet roses in this summer air. 5.02.293
disguis'd like muscovites, in shapeless gear; 5.02.303
nor woo in rhyme, like a blind harper's song! 5.02.405
merriment, | to dash it like a christmas comedy. 5.02.462
there's an eye | wounds like a leaden sword. 5.02.481
'a speaks not like a man of god his making. 5.02.526 P
here is like to be a good presence of worthies: 5.02.533 P
will not fight with a pole like a northren man; 5.02.694 P
and i will right myself like a soldier. 5.02.724 P
form'd by the eye and therefore, like the eye, 5.02.762
loves | in their own fashion, like a merriment. 5.02.784
our wooing doth not end like an old play: 5.02.874
like to a step–dame, or a dowager, | long MND 1.01. 5
like to a silver bow | /new bent in heaven, 1.01. 9
of color like the red rose on triumphant brier, 3.01. 94
like horse, hound, hog, bear, fire, at every 3.01.111
so, | that thou shalt like an aery spirit go. 3.01.161
we, hermia, like two artificial gods, | have 3.02.203
like to a double cherry, seeming parted, | but 3.02.209
or i will shake thee from me like a serpent! 3.02.261
like to lysander sometime frame thy tongue; 3.02.360
and sometime rail thou like demetrius; 3.02.362
and, like a forester, the groves may tread 3.02.390
was wont to swell like round and orient pearls, 4.01. 54
like tears that did their own disgrace bewail. 4.01. 56
and dewlapp'd like thessalian bulls; 4.01.122
but match'd in mouth like bells, | each under 4.01.123
but like a sickness did i loathe this food; 4.01.173
like far–off mountains turned into clouds. 4.01.188
and i have found demetrius like a jewel, | mine 4.01.191
you shall know all, that you are like to know. 5.01.117
he hath rid his prologue like a rough colt; 5.01.119 P
on this prologue like a child on a recorder — a 5.01.122 P
his speech was like a tangled chain; 5.01.125 P
and, like limander, am i trusty still. 5.01.196
and i, like helen, till the fates me kill. 5.01.197
of the sun, | following darkness like a dream, 5.01.386
like signiors and rich burghers on the flood, MV 1.01. 10
eyes, | and laugh like parrots at a bagpiper; 1.01. 53
sit like his grandsire cut in alablaster? 1.01. 84
do cream and mantle like a standing pond, | and 1.01. 89
i owe you much, and, like a willful youth, 1.01.146
hang on her temples like a golden fleece, 1.01.170
how like you the young german, the duke of 1.02. 84 P
how like a fawning publican he looks! 1.03. 41
is like a villain with a smiling cheek, | a 1.03.100
i am as like to call thee so again, | to spet on 1.03.130
i like not fair terms and a villain's mind. 1.03.179
do i look like a cudgel or a hovel–post, a staff 2.02. 68 P
like one well studied in a sad ostent | to 2.02.196
how like a younger or a prodigal | the scarfed 2.06. 14
how like the prodigal doth she return, | with 2.06. 17
and therefore, like herself, wise, fair, and 2.06. 56
is't like that lead contains her? 2.07. 49
not to th' interior, but, like the martlet, 2.09. 28
if we are like you in the rest, we will resemble 3.01. 67 P
like one of two contending in a prize, | that 3.02.141
there must be needs a like proportion | of 3.04. 14
lover of my lord, | must needs be like my lord. 3.04. 18
when we are both accoutered like young men, 3.04. 63
and speak of frays | like a fine bragging youth, 3.04. 69
garnish'd like him, that for a tricksy word 3.05. 69
how dost thou like the lord bassanio's wife? 3.05. 72
which, like your asses, and your dogs and mules, 4.01. 91
night | did pretty jessica (like a little shrow) 5.01. 21
but in his motion like an angel sings, | still 5.01. 61
was | for all the world like cutler's poetry 5.01.149
watch me like argus, | if you do not, if i be 5.01.230
this is like the mending of highways | in summer 5.01.263
you have train'd me like a peasant, obscuring AYL 1.01. 68 P
and there they live like the old robin hood of 1.01.116 P
hath no child but i, nor none is like to have; 1.02. 18 P
and wheresoe'er we went, like juno's swans, 1.03. 75
the like do you. 1.03.113
that i did suit me all points like a man? 1.03.116
which, like the toad, ugly and venomous, | wears 2.01. 13
my man's apparel and to cry like a woman; 2.04. 5 P
but if thy love were ever like to mine — | as 2.04. 28
i like this place, | and willingly could waste 2.04. 94
if you like upon report | the soil, the profit, 2.04. 97
call compliment is like th' encounter of two 2.05. 26 P
beast, | for i can no where find him like a man. 2.07. 2
time, | my lungs began to crow like chanticleer, 2.07. 30
why then my taxing like a wild goose flies, 2.07. 86
whiles, like a doe, i go to find my fawn | and 2.07.128
creeping like snail | unwillingly to school. 2.07.146
sighing like furnace, with a woeful ballad 2.07.148
of strange oaths, and bearded like the pard, 2.07.150
and how like you this shepherd's life, master 3.02. 11 P
that it is solitary, i like it very well; 3.02. 15 P
damn'd, like an ill–roasted egg all on one side. 3.02. 37 P
to western inde, | no jewel is like rosalind. 3.02. 89
though i am caparison'd like a man, i have a 3.02.195 P
i found him under a tree, like a dropp'd acorn. 3.02.235 P
lay he, stretch'd along, like a wounded knight. 3.02.240 P
he was furnish'd like a hunter. 3.02.245 P
i do not like her name. 3.02.265 P
i will speak to him like a saucy lackey, and 3.02.295 P
of the forest, like fringe upon a petticoat. 3.02.336 P
they were all like one another as halfpence are, 3.02.354 P
would now like him, now loathe him; 3.02.415 P
breeding, be married under a bush like a beggar? 3.03. 84 P
a shrunk panel, and like green timber warp, warp 3.03. 88 P
of another, for he is not like to marry me well; 3.03. 92 P
one side, breaks his staff like a noble goose. 3.04. 44 P
like foggy south, puffing with wind and rain? 3.05. 50
besides, i like you not. 3.05. 74
in a holiday humor, and like enough to consent. 4.01. 69 P
weep for nothing, like diana in the fountain, 4.01.154 P
i will laugh like a hyen, and that when thou art 4.01.156 P
herself, for she will breed it like a fool! 4.01.176 P
an unknown bottom, like the bay of portugal. 4.01.208 P
present him to the duke like a roman conqueror, 4.02. 3 P
why, she defies me, | like turk to christian. 4.03. 33
favor, and bestows himself | like a ripe sister; 4.03. 87
on so little acquaintance you should like her? 5.02. 2 P
'tis like the howling of irish wolves against 5.02.109 P
and both in a tune, like two gipsies on a horse. 5.03. 14 P
had four quarrels, and like to have fought one. 5.04. 47 P
good my lord, like this fellow. 5.04. 51 P
i like him very well. 5.04. 53 P
god 'ild you, sir, i desire you of the like. 5.04. 54 P
rich honesty dwells like a miser, sir, in a poor 5.04. 60 P
he uses his folly like a stalking–horse, and 5.04.106 P
i am not furnish'd like a beggar, therefore to ep 10 P
men, to like as much of this play as please you; ep 13 P
o monstrous beast, how like a swine he lies! SHR in.1. 34
and see him dress'd in all suits like a lady; in.1. 106
like envious floods o'errun her lovely face, in.2. 65
and paint your face, and use you like a fool. 1.01. 65
rage like an angry boar chafed with sweat? 1.02.202
with her, | or else you like not of my company. 2.01. 65
to express the like kindness, myself, that have 2.01. 77 P
gentle sir, methinks you walk like a stranger. 2.01. 86 P
me, | for i am rough, and woo not like a babe. 2.01.137
well ta'en, and like a buzzard. 2.01.206
no cock of mine, you crow too like a craven. 2.01.227
kate like the hazel–twig | is straight and 2.01.253
thy beauty that doth make me like thee well, 2.01.274
if you like me, she shall have me and mine. 2.01.383
tut, i like it not. 3.01. 79
with the glanders and like to mose in the chine, 3.02. 51 P
for all the world caparison'd like the horse; 3.02. 66 P
apparel, and not like a christian footboy or a 3.02. 70 P
'tis like you'll prove a jolly surly groom, 3.02.213
of all mad matches never was the like. 3.02.242
peter, didst ever see the like? 4.01.179 P
and here i take the like unfeigned oath, | never 4.02. 32
in gait and countenance surely like a father. 4.02. 65
fortunes | that you are like to sir vincentio. 4.02.106
i like it well, good grumio, fetch it me. 4.03. 21
love me, or love me not, i like the cap, | and 4.03. 84
'tis like /a demi–cannon. 4.03. 88
what, up and down carv'd like an apple–tart? 4.03. 89
slash, | like to a censer in a barber's shop. 4.03. 91
i see she's like to have neither cap nor gown. 4.03. 93
and if you please to like | no worse than i, 4.04. 32
that like a father you will deal with him, | and 4.04. 44
then at my lodging, and it like you. 4.04. 55
you are like to have a thin and slender pittance 4.04. 61
and how she's like to be lucentio's wife. 4.04. 66
one mess is like to be your cheer. 4.04. 70
like pleasant travellers, to break a jest | upon 4.05. 72
spoke like an officer. ha' to thee, lad! 5.02. 37
o, sir, lucentio slipp'd me like his greyhound, 5.02. 52
a woman mov'd is like a fountain troubled, 5.02.142
what was he like? AWW 1.01. 81
virginity breeds mites, much like a cheese, 1.01.141 P
marry, ill, to like him that ne'er it likes. 1.01.152 P
virginity, like an old courtier, wears her cap 1.01.156 P
just like the brooch and the toothpick, which 1.01.157 P
is like one of our french wither'd pears, it 1.01.161 P
virtue of a good wing, and i like the wear well. 1.01.204 P
in fortune nature brings | to join like likes, 1.01.223
to join like likes, and kiss like native things. 1.01.223
so like a courtier, contempt nor bitterness 1.02. 36
jowl horns together like any deer i' th' herd. 1.03. 54 P
fellows, and like to prove most sinewy swordmen. 2.01. 59 P
a traitor you do look like, but such traitors 2.01. 96
it is like a barber's chair that fits all 2.02. 17 P
i'll like a maid the better whilst i have a 2.03. 41 P
as honor's born, | and is not like the sire. 2.03.135
if thou canst like this creature as a maid, | i 2.03.142
and all, like him that leapt into the custard; 2.05. 37 P
but, like a timorous thief, most fain would 2.05. 81
but like a common and an outward man | that the 3.01. 11
country are nothing like your old ling and your 3.02. 14 P
make me but like my thoughts, and i shall prove 3.03. 10
i like him well. 3.05. 81
she says all men | have the like oaths. 4.02. 71
module, h'as deceiv'd me like a double–meaning 4.03. 99 P
he weeps like a wench that had shed her milk. 4.03.107 P
if ye pinch me like a pasty, i can say no more. 4.03.123 P
i like him well, 'tis not amiss. 4.05. 68 P
how does your ladyship like it? 4.05. 77 P
since you are like to see the king before me, 5.01. 30
the carp as you may, for he looks like a poor, 5.02. 23 P
late, | like a remorseful pardon slowly carried, 5.03. 58
sir, much like | the same upon your finger. 5.03.225
take her away, i do not like her now, | to 5.03.281
o my good lord, when i was like this maid, | i 5.03.309
it came o'er my ear like the sweet sound | that TN 1.01. 5
and my desires, like fell and cruel hounds, 1.01. 21
but like a cloistress she will veiled walk, 1.01. 27
where, like /arion on the dolphin's back, | i 1.02. 15
speech serves for authority, | the like of him. 1.02. 21
his brains turn o' th' toe like a parish–top. 1.03. 42 P
it hangs like flax on a distaff; 1.03.102 P
are they like to take dust, like mistress mall's 1.03.127 P
like to take dust, like mistress mall's picture? 1.03.127 P
you, cesario, you are like to be much advanc'd; 1.04. 2 P
what's a drunken man like, fool? 1.05.130 P
like a drown'd man, a fool, and a madman. 1.05.131 P
he'll stand at your door like a sheriff's post, 1.05.148 P
it is the more like to be feign'd. 1.05.196 P
and let your fervor, like my master's, be 1.05.287
but to gabble like tinkers at this time of night 2.03. 88 P
o, if i thought that, i'd beat him like a dog! 2.03.141 P
i can write very like my lady your niece; 2.03.159 P
how dost thou like this tune? 2.04. 20
with the innocence of love, | like the old age. 2.04. 48
but let concealment, like a worm i' th' bud, 2.04.111
she sat like patience on a monument, | smiling 2.04.114
i adore, | but silence, like a lucrece knife, 2.05.105
to inure thyself to what thou art like to be, 2.05.148 P
like aqua–vitae with a midwife. 2.05.196 P
and fools are as like husbands as pilchers are 3.01. 34 P
does walk about the orb like the sun, it shines 3.01. 38 P
and, like the haggard, check at every feather 3.01. 64
your wife is like to reap a proper man. 3.01.133
that heart, which now abhors, to like his love. 3.01.164
opinion, where you will hang like an icicle on a 3.02. 27 P
like a pedant that keeps a school i' th' church. 3.02. 75 P
i have dogg'd him like his murtherer. 3.02. 76 P
"thou kill'st me like a rogue and a villain." 3.04.162 P
at the corner of the orchard like a bum–baily. 3.04.177 P
kill one another by the look, like cockatrices. 3.04.196 P
a fiend like thee might bear my soul to hell. 3.04.217
as you are like to find him in the proof of his 3.04.265 P
in a trice, | like to the old vice, | your need 4.02.124
like a mad lad, | pare thy nails, dad. 4.02.129
like to th' egyptian thief at point of death, 5.01.118
thou never shouldst love woman like to me. 5.01.268
though, i confess, much like the character; 5.01.346
to visit bohemia on the like occasion whereon my WT 1.01. 2 P
and therefore, like a cipher | (yet standing in 1.02. 6
to keep you as a prisoner, | not like a guest: 1.02. 53
the shoots that i have, | to be full like me; 1.02.129
yet they say we are | almost as like as eggs; 1.02.130
yet were it true | to say this boy were like me. 1.02.135
how like, methought, i then was to this kernel, 1.02.159
i am like you, /they say. 1.02.208
he that wears her like her medal hanging | about 1.02.307
that should not work | maliciously, like poison; 1.02.321
make me not sighted like the basilisk. 1.02.388
should a like language use to all degrees, | and 2.01. 85
relish a truth like us, inform yourselves | we 2.01.167
and a goodly babe, | lusty and like to live. 2.02. 25
that creep like shadows by him and do sigh | at 2.03. 34
to your charge, | so like you, 'tis the worse. 2.03. 98
which hast made it | so like to him that got it, 2.03.105
aside, have done | like offices of pity. 2.03.189
forcing faults upon hermione, | i little like. 3.01. 17
a kind of love as might become | a lady like me; 3.02. 65
thy brat hath been cast out, like to itself, 3.02. 87
his presence | i am barr'd, like one infectious. 3.02. 98
'tis like to be loud weather. 3.03. 11
for ne'er was dream | so like a waking. 3.03. 19
i never saw a vessel of like sorrow, | so fill'd 3.03. 21
like very sanctity, she did approach | my cabin 3.03. 23
thou'rt like to have | a lullaby too rough. 3.03. 54
what? like a corse? 4.04.129
no, like a bank, for love to lie and play on; 4.04.130
not like a corse; 4.04.131
he looks like sooth. 4.04.171
but, my daughter, | say you the like to him? 4.04.380
we are not furnish'd like bohemia's son, | nor 4.04.588
to th' palace, and it like your worship. 4.04.716 P
your worship had like to have given us one, if 4.04.727 P
are you a courtier, and't like you, sir? 4.04.729 P
whether it like me or no, i am a courtier. 4.04.730 P
i know not, and't like you. 4.04.741 P
a son, sir, do you hear, and't like you, sir? 4.04.782 P
so his successor | was like to be the best. 5.01. 49
another, | as like hermione as is her picture, 5.01. 74
he comes not | like to his father's greatness. 5.01. 89
we are not, sir, nor are we like to be. 5.01.205
which is call'd true, is so like an old tale, 5.02. 28 P
which stands by like a weather–bitten conduit of 5.02. 55 P
like an old tale still, which will have matter 5.02. 61 P
ay, and it like your good worship. 5.02.155 P
i like your silence, it the more shows off 5.03. 21
the spirits, | standing like stone with thee. 5.03. 42
you, should be hooted at | like an old tale; 5.03.117
push) to trouble | your joys with like relation. 5.03.130
and were our father, and this son like him, | o JN 1.01. 81
i give heaven thanks i was not like to thee! 1.01. 83
because he hath a half–face like my father! 1.01. 92
and like thy brother, to enjoy thy land; 1.01.135
and i had his, sir robert's his, like him, | and 1.01.139
i like thee well. 1.01.148
and then comes answer like an absey book: 1.01.196
and fits the mounting spirit like myself; 1.01.206
in manners, being as like | as rain to water, or 2.01.127
and then our arms, like to a muzzled bear, 2.01.249
and like a jolly troop of huntsmen come | our 2.01.321
both are alike, and both alike we like. 2.01.331
do like the mutines of jerusalem, | be friends 2.01.378
how like you this wild counsel, mighty states? 2.01.395
that hangs above our heads, | i like it well. 2.01.398
if he see aught in you that makes him like, 2.01.511
yet, | like a poor beggar, raileth on the rich. 2.01.592
like a proud river peering o'er his bounds? 3.01. 23
hast thou not spoke like thunder on my side? 3.01.124
we like not this, thou dost forget thyself. 3.01.134
and like a civil war set'st oath to oath, | thy 3.01.264
or heard | of any kindred action like to this? 3.04. 14
dust, | and be a carrion monster like thyself. 3.04. 33
for then 'tis like i should forget myself. 3.04. 49
grief, | like true, inseparable, faithful loves, 3.04. 66
and like the watchful minutes to the hour, 4.01. 46
and, like a dog that is compell'd to fight, 4.01.115
o, now you look like hubert! 4.01.125
and, like a shifted wind unto a sail, | it makes 4.02. 23
like heralds 'twixt two dreadful battles set: 4.02. 78
and fly, like thought, from them to me again. 4.02.175
spoke like a sprightful noble gentleman. 4.02.177
it seem | like rivers of remorse and innocency. 4.03.110
like a kind host, the dolphin and his powers. 5.01. 32
away, and glister like the god of war | when he 5.01. 54
war, | that, like a lion fostered up at hand, 5.02. 75
to dive like buckets in concealed wells, | to 5.02.139
to lie like pawns lock'd up in chests and trunks 5.02.141
arms, | and like an eagle o'er his aery tow'rs, 5.02.149
maids | like amazons come tripping after drums, 5.02.155
flight, | and like a bated and retired flood, 5.04. 53
and the like tender of our love we make, | to 5.07.106
like a false traitor and injurious villain; R2 1.01. 91
and consequently, like a traitor coward, 1.01.102
which blood, like sacrificing abel's, cries, 1.01.104
speak like a true knight, so defend thee heaven! 1.03. 34
for mowbray and myself are like two men | that 1.03. 48
be swift like lightning in the execution, | and 1.03. 79
fall like amazing thunder on the casque |,of thy 1.03. 81
a harp, | or like a cunning instrument cas'd up, 1.03.163
you would have bid me argue like a father. 1.03.238

there is no virtue like necessity. 1.03.278
dying men | enforce attention like deep harmony. 2.01. 6
it — | like to a tenement or pelting farm. 2.01. 60
son, | that blood already, like the pelican, 2.01.126
have, | and thy unkindness be like crooked age, 2.01.133
which live like venom where no venom else | but 2.01.157
the /king's grown bankrout, like a broken man. 2.01.257
gilt, | and make high majesty look like itself, 2.01.295
which shows like grief itself, but is not so; 2.02. 15
like perspectives, which rightly gaz'd upon 2.02. 18
us, | except like curs to tear us all to pieces. 2.02.139
mind | i see thy glory like a shooting star 2.04. 19
needs must i like it well; 3.02. 4
like an unseasonable stormy day, | which makes 3.02.106
i live with bread like you, feel want, | taste 3.02.175
yet looks he like a king! 3.03. 68
down, down i come, like glist'ring phaeton, 3.03.178
makes him speak fondly like a frantic man, | yet 3.03.185
which like unruly children make their sire 3.04. 30
and like an executioner | cut off the heads of 3.04. 33
i task the earth to the like, forsworn aumerle, 4.01. 52
pomp | she came adorned hither like sweet may, 5.01. 79
sent back like hollowmas or short'st of day. 5.01. 80
or are we like to have? 5.02. 90
is he not like thee? 5.02. 94
that mind, | he is as like thee as a man may be, 5.02.108
not like to me, or any of my kin, | and yet i 5.02.109
no word like "pardon" for kings' mouths so meet. 5.03.118
in humors like the people of this world: 5.05. 10
not be the last — like seely beggars | who, 5.05. 25
back | of such as have before endur'd the like. 5.05. 30
watch, | whereto my finger, like a dial's point, 5.05. 53
a horse, | and yet i bear a burthen like an ass, 5.05. 93
which, like the meteors of a troubled heaven, 1H4 1.01. 10
the edge of war, like an ill–sheathed knife, 1.01. 17
the moon's men doth ebb and flow like the sea, 1.02. 32 P
yea, but 'tis like that they will know us by our 1.02.174 P
and like bright metal on a sullen ground, | my 1.02.212
show'd like a stubble–land at harvest–home. 1.03. 35
he was perfumed like a milliner, | and 'twixt 1.03. 36
and talk so like a waiting–gentlewoman | of guns 1.03. 55
i am stung like a tench. 2.01. 15 P
like a tench? 2.01. 16 P
and your chamber–lye breeds fleas like a loach. 2.01. 21 P
horse, and he frets like a gumm'd velvet. 2.02. 2 P
brow, | like bubbles in a late–disturbed stream, 2.03. 59
tell me flatly i am no proud jack like falstaff, 2.04. 11 P
subjects afore thee like a flock of wild geese, 2.04.138 P
and through, my sword hack'd like a hand–saw — 2.04.168 P
these lies are like their father that begets 2.04.225 P
o for breath to utter what is like thee! 2.04.246 P
done in fight, and persuaded us to do the like. 2.04.308 P
and grief, it blows a man up like a bladder. 2.04.332 P
why then, it is like, if there come a hot june 2.04.361 P
it is like we shall have good trading that way. 2.04.364 P
he doth it as like one of these harlotry players 2.04.395 P
what manner of man, and it like your majesty? 2.04.420 P
dost thou speak like a king? 2.04.433 P
behind the arras, and snorting like a horse. 2.04.529 P
foundation of the earth | shak'd like a coward. 3.01. 17
me up | with like advantage on the other side, 3.01.108
'tis like the forc'd gait of a shuffling nag. 3.01.133
heart, you swear like a comfit–maker's wife: 3.01.248 P
swear me, kate, like a lady as thou art, | a 3.01.253
not stir | but like a comet i was wond'red at, 3.02. 47
and new, | my presence, like a robe pontifical, 3.02. 56
seldom but sumptuous, show'd like a feast, | and 3.02. 58
for of no right, nor color like to right, | he 3.02.100
thou that art like enough, through vassal fear, 3.02.124
my skin hangs about me like an old lady's loose 3.03. 3 P
i am wither'd like an old apple–john. 3.03. 4 P
i would cudgel him like a dog if he would say so 3.03. 86 P
vilely of you, like a foul–mouth'd man as he is, 3.03.107 P
o, i do not like that paying back, 'tis a double 3.03.179 P
all plum'd like estridges, that with the wind 4.01. 98
wind | bated like eagles having lately bath'd, 4.01. 99
glittering in golden coats like images, | as 4.01.100
rise from the ground like feathered mercury, 4.01.106
they come like sacrifices in their trim, | and 4.01.113
who is to bear me like a thunderbolt | against 4.01.120
over the shoulders like a herald's coat without 4.02. 44 P
quality, | but stand against us like an enemy. 4.03. 37
like enough you do. 4.04. 7
eyes, | for treason is but trusted like the fox, 5.02. 9
looks, | and we shall feed like oxen at a stall, 5.02. 14
spoke your deservings like a chronicle, | making 5.02. 57
and, which became him like a prince indeed, | he 5.02. 60
semblably furnish'd like the king himself. 5.03. 21
i like not such grinning honor as sir walter 5.03. 58 P
they grow like hydra's heads. 5.04. 25
yet, in faith, thou bearest thee like a king. 5.04. 36
or thou art like | never to hold it up again! 5.04. 39
if like a christian thou hadst truly borne 5.05. 9
contention, like a horse | full of high feeding, 2H4 1.01. 9
yea, this man's brow, like to a title–leaf, 1.01. 60
turn'd on themselves, like dull and heavy lead. 1.01.118
like strengthless hinges, buckle under life, 1.01.141
breaks like a fire | out of his keeper's arms, 1.01.142
i do here walk before thee like a sow that hath 1.02. 11 P
let him be damn'd like the glutton! 1.02. 34 P
young prince up and down, like his ill angel. 1.02.164 P
prince gave you, he gave it like a rude prince, 1.02.195 P
prince, and you took it like a sensible lord. 1.02.196 P
like /one that draws the model of an house 1.03. 58
who is it like should lead his forces hither? 1.03. 81
he will foin like any devil, he will spare 2.01. 16 P
or i will ride thee a' nights like the mare. 2.01. 77 P
i think i am as like to ride the mare, if i have 2.01. 78 P
down the town that her eldest son is like you. 2.01.105 P
even like those that are kin to the king, for 2.02.111 P
times, | and be like them to percy troublesome. 2.03. 4
then join you with them, like a rib of steel, 2.03. 54
/die men like dogs! 2.04.174 P
give crowns like pins! 2.04.174 P
him down, bardolph, like a shove–groat shilling. 2.04.192 P
the rogue fled from me like quicksilver. 2.04.229 P
i' faith, and thou follow'dst him like a church. 2.04.230 P
good doll, do not speak like a death's–head, do 2.04.234 P
very smooth, like unto the sign of the leg, and 2.04.249 P
elder hath not his pole claw'd like a parrot. 2.04.259 P
like the south | borne with black vapor, doth 2.04.363
soul, | who like a brother toil'd in my affairs, 3.01. 62
then let us meet them like necessities; 3.01. 93
rumor doth double, like the voice and echo, 3.01. 97
you like well and bear your years very well. 3.02. 83 P
to sit under, he's like to be a cold soldier. 3.02.123 P
like enough, and thy father's shadow. 3.02.128 P
do you like him, sir john? 3.02.132 P
like a man made after supper of a cheese–paring. 3.02.309 P
he was for all the world like a fork'd redish, 3.02.310 P
if that rebellion | came like itself, in base 4.01. 33
like an offensive wife | that hath enrag'd him 4.01.208
so that his power, like to a fangless lion, 4.01.216
our peace will, like a broken limb united, 4.01.220
how far forth you do like their articles. 4.02. 53
i like them all, and do allow them well, | and 4.02. 54
like youthful steers unyok'd, they take their 4.02.103
west, north, south, or, like a school broke up, 4.02.104
you do not all show like gilt twopences to me, 4.03. 50 P
the element (which show like pins' heads to her) 4.03. 53 P
but thou, like a kind fellow, gavest thyself 4.03. 69 P
of his father, he hath, like lean, sterile, and 4.03.119 P
till that his passions, like a whale on ground, 4.04. 40
studies his companions | like a strange tongue, 4.04. 69
so, like gross terms, | the prince will in the 4.04. 73
sit | like a rich armor worn in heat of day, 4.05. 30
when, like the bee, tolling from every flower 4.05. 74
we bring it to the hive, and, like the bees, 4.05. 77
him, do bear themselves like foolish justices; 5.01. 67 P
together in consent, like so many wild geese. 5.01. 70 P
till his face be like a wet cloak ill laid up. 5.01. 85 P
we meet like men that had forgot to speak. 5.02. 22
that you use the same | with the like bold, just 5.02.116
thee now deliver them like a man of this world. 5.03. 97 P
this, and fig me like | the bragging spaniard. 5.03.118
i like this fair proceeding of the king's. 5.05. 97
which if like an ill venture it come unluckily ep 11 P
then should the warlike harry, like himself, H5 pr 5
heels | (leash'd in, like hounds) should famine, pr 7
year of the last king's reign | was like, and 1.01. 3
consideration like an angel came | and whipt th' 1.01. 28
grew like the summer grass, fastest by night, 1.01. 65
came pouring like the tide into a breach, | with 1.02.149
in a full and natural close, | like music. 1.02.183
where some, like magistrates, correct at home; 1.02.191
others, like merchants, venter trade abroad; 1.02.192
others, like soldiers, armed in their stings, 1.02.193
like turkish mute, shall have a tongueless mouth 1.02.232
be like a king, and show my sail of greatness 1.02.274
and plodded like a man for working–days; 1.02.277
like little body with a mighty heart, | what 2.pr. 17
thine, methinks, is like | another fall of man. 2.02.141
whereof | shall be to you as us, like glorious. 2.02.183
let us to france, like horse–leeches, my boys, 2.03. 55
doth like a miser spoil his coat with scanting 2.04. 47
in thunder and in earthquake, like a jove, 2.04.100
the portage of the head | like the brass cannon; 3.01. 11
fathers that, like so many alexanders, | have in 3.01. 19
i see you stand like greyhounds in the slips, 3.01. 31
or, like to men proud of destruction, | defy us 3.03. 4
mowing like grass | your fresh fair virgins and 3.03. 13
arrayed in flames like to the prince of fiends, 3.03. 16
let us not hang like roping icicles | upon our 3.05. 23
but one that is like to be executed for robbing 3.06.100 P
at his nose, and it is like a coal of fire, 3.06.104 P
his neigh is like the bidding of a monarch, and 3.07. 27 P
and gentle, and you rode like a kern of ireland, 3.07. 53 P
and have their heads crush'd like rotten apples! 3.07.144 P
they will eat like wolves and fight like devils. 3.07.150 P
they will eat like wolves and fight like devils. 3.07.151 P
who like a foul and ugly witch doth limp | so 4.pr. 21
like sacrifices, by their watchful fires | sit 4.pr. 23
a largess universal, like the sun, | his liberal 4.pr. 43
since i may say, "now lie i like a king." 4.01. 17
when they stoop, they stoop with the like wing. 4.01.107 P
but like a lackey, from the rise to set, 4.01.272
the horsemen sit like fixed candlesticks, | with 4.02. 45
dying like men, though buried in your dunghills, 4.03. 99
that being dead, like to the bullet's crasing, 4.03.105
hand | like a base pander hold the chamber–door 4.05. 14
our king is not like him in that; 4.07. 40 P
your majesty came not like yourself. 4.08. 50 P
which like a mighty whiffler 'fore the king 5.pr. 12
like to the senators of th' antique rome, | with 5.pr. 26
why, here he comes, swelling like a turkey–cock. 5.01. 14 P
like prisoners wildly overgrown with hair, | put 5.02. 43
but grow like savages — as soldiers will | that 5.02. 59
do you like me, kate? 5.02.107 P
pardonnez–moi, i cannot tell wat is "like me." 5.02.108 P
an angel is like you, kate, and you are like an 5.02.109 P
is like you, kate, and you are like an angel. 5.02.110 P
i could lay on like a butcher and sit like a 5.02.141 P
on like a butcher and sit like a jack–an–apes, 5.02.141 P
will hang upon my tongue like a new–married wife 5.02.179 P
warm kept, are like flies at bartholomew–tide, 5.02.308 P
like captives bound to a triumphant car. 1H6 1.01. 22
none do you like but an effeminate prince, 1.01. 35
prince, | whom like a schoolboy you may overawe. 1.01. 36
gloucester, what e'er we like, thou art 1.01. 37
the famish'd english, like pale ghosts, 1.02. 7
either they must be dieted like mules | and have 1.02. 10
or piteous they will look, like drowned mice. 1.02. 12
who ever saw the like? 1.02. 22
the other lords, like lions wanting food, | do 1.02. 27
or device | their arms are set, like clocks, 1.02. 42
glory is like a circle in the water, | which 1.02.133
now am i like that proud insulting ship | which 1.02.138
yet saint philip's daughters, were like thee. 1.02.143
plantagenet, i will, and like thee, /nero, 1.04. 95
my thoughts are whirled like a potter's wheel, 1.05. 19
a witch by fear, not force, like hannibal, 1.05. 21
dogs, | now, like to whelps, we crying run away. 1.05. 26
thy promises are like adonis' garden, | that one 1.06. 6
like to a pair of loving turtle–doves | that 2.02. 30
but now the substance shall endure the like, 2.03. 38
even like a man new haled from the rack, | so 2.05. 3
eyes, like lamps whose wasting oil is spent, 2.05. 8
arms, like to a withered vine | that droops his 2.05. 11
tongue, | else with the like i had requited him. 2.05. 50
and like a mountain, not to be remov'd. 2.05.103
and like a hermit overpass'd thy days. 2.05.117
rise, richard, like a true plantagenet, | and 3.01.171
talk like the vulgar sort of market men | that 3.02. 4
now shine it like a comet of revenge, | a 3.02. 31
do you like the taste? 3.02. 44
will ye, like soldiers, come and fight it out? 3.02. 66
like peasant footboys do they keep the walls, 3.02. 69
and dare not take up arms like gentlemen. 3.02. 70
we are like to have the overthrow again. 3.02.106
and like a peacock sweep along his tail; 3.03. 6
and have thee reverenc'd like a blessed saint. 3.03. 15
lord, | and thou be thrust out like a fugitive? 3.03. 67
have batt'red me like roaring cannon–shot, | and 3.03. 79
done like a frenchman — turn and turn again! 3.03. 85
given, | like to a trusty squire did run away; 4.01. 23
like a hedge–born swain | that doth presume to 4.01. 43
of foot, | and, like true subjects, sons of your 4.01.166
and so he did, but yet i like it not, | in that 4.01.176
stay, go, do what you will, the like do i; 4.05. 50
and like me to the peasant boys of france, | to 4.06. 48
and like a hungry lion did commence | rough 4.07. 7
ten to one | we shall not find like opportunity. 5.04.158
heart, | and like as rigor of tempestuous gusts 5.05. 5
with hope to find the like event in love, | but 5.05.105
did bear him like a noble gentleman. 2H6 1.01.184
more like a soldier than a man o' th' church, 1.01.186
all, | swear like a ruffian, and demean himself 1.01.188
still revelling like lords till all be gone; 1.01.224
like over–ripen'd corn | hanging the head at 1.02. 1
more like an empress than duke humphrey's wife. 1.03. 78
she'll hamper thee, and dandle thee like a baby. 1.03.145
no marvel, and it like your majesty, | my lord 2.01. 9
an't like your lordly lord's protectorship. 2.01. 30
his wife, and't like your worship. 2.01. 78
at berwick in the north, and't like your grace. 2.01. 81
'tis like, my lord, you will not keep your hour. 2.01.177
and convers'd with such | as, like to pitch, 2.01.192
years | should be to be protected like a child. 2.03. 29
like to a duchess, and duke humphrey's lady, 2.04. 98
like to the glorious sun's transparent beams, 3.01.353
were almost like a sharp–quill'd porpentine; 3.01.363
seen | him caper upright like a wild morisco, 3.01.365
full often, like a shag–hair'd crafty kern, 3.01.367
say that he thrive, as 'tis great like he will, 3.01.379
art thou like the adder waxen deaf? 3.02. 76
am i not witch'd like her? 3.02.119
or thou not false like him? 3.02.119
like an angry hive of bees | that want their 3.02.125
staring full ghastly, like a strangled man; 3.02.170
like to the summer's corn by tempest lodged. 3.02.176
'tis like you would not feast him like a friend, 3.02.184
'tis like you would not feast him like a friend, 3.02.184
'tis like the commons, rude unpolish'd hinds, 3.02.271
mine eyes should sparkle like the beaten flint, 3.02.317
these dread curses, like the sun 'gainst glass, 3.02.330
or like an overcharged gun, recoil, | and turns 3.02.331
else | but like a pleasant slumber in thy lap? 3.02.390
like lime–twigs set to catch my winged soul. 3.03. 16
thou grown great | and, like ambitious sylla, 4.01. 84
then is sin struck down like an ox, and 4.02. 26 P
an ox, and iniquity's throat cut like a calf. 4.02. 27 P
one livery, that they may agree like brothers, 4.02. 74 P
to thyself, like a honest plain–dealing man? 4.02.103 P
they fell before thee like sheep and oxen, and 4.03. 3 P
face | rul'd like a wandering planet over me, 4.04. 16
then we are like to have biting statutes, unless 4.07. 16 P
like to a ship that, having scap'd a tempest, 4.09. 32
but i'll make thee eat iron like an ostridge, 4.10. 28 P
and swallow my sword like a great pin, ere thou 4.10. 29 P
and like a thief to come to rob my grounds, 4.10. 34
and now, like ajax telamonius, | on sheep or 5.01. 26
more like a king, more kingly in my thoughts; 5.01. 29
i was, an't like your majesty. 5.01. 72
whose smile and frown, like to achilles' spear, 5.01.100
and, like a gallant in the brow of youth, 5.03. 4
him, | and like rich hangings in a homely house, 5.03. 12
and like an empty eagle | tire on the flesh of 3H6 1.01.268
why should i not now have the like success? 1.02. 75
turn back and fly, like ships before the wind, 1.04. 4
like men born to renown by life or death. 1.04. 8
ay, marry, sir, now looks he like a king! 1.04. 96
in thy sex | to triumph like an amazonian trull 1.04.114
trimm'd like a younker prancing to his love! 2.01. 24
wondrous strange, the like yet never heard of. 2.01. 33
their weapons like to lightning came and went; 2.01.129
our soldiers', like the night–owl's lazy flight, 2.01.130
or like /an /idle thresher with a flail, | fell 2.01.131
have wrought the easy–melting king like wax. 2.01.171
king, | and raise his issue like a loving sire; 2.02. 22
why, that is spoken like a toward prince. 2.02. 66
ay, like a dastard and a treacherous coward, 2.02.114
but thou art neither like thy sire nor dam, 2.02.135
nor dam, | but like a foul misshapen stigmatic, 2.02.136
like to a dismal clangor heard from far, 2.03. 18
why stand we like soft–hearted women here, 2.03. 25
brother | to execute the like upon thyself — 2.04. 10
this battle fares like to the morning's war, 2.05. 1
like a mighty sea | forc'd by the tide to combat 2.05. 5
like the self–same sea | forc'd to retire by 2.05. 7
and let our hearts and eyes, like civil war, 2.05. 77
fled, | and warwick rages like a chafed bull. 2.05.126
like a brace of greyhounds | having the fearful 2.05.129
they never then had sprung like summer flies; 2.06. 17
a deadly groan, like life and death's departing. 2.06. 43
like one that stands upon a promontory | and 3.02.135
to shrink mine arm up like a wither'd shrub, 3.02.156
like to a chaos, or an unlick'd bear–whelp 3.02.161
that carries no impression like the dam. 3.02.162
and i — like one lost in a thorny wood, | that 3.02.174
could, | and, like a sinon, take another troy. 3.02.190
where i must take like seat unto my fortune, 3.03. 10
what e'er it be, be thou still like thyself, 3.03. 15
it seems | as may beseem a monarch like himself. 3.03.122
i like it well that our fair queen and mistress 3.03.167

brother of clarence, how like you our choice, 4.01. 9
and meaner than myself have had like fortune. 4.01. 71
i like it better than a dangerous honor. 4.03. 17
we'll yoke together like a double shadow | to 4.06. 49
my lord, i like not of this flight of edward's; 4.06. 89
'tis like that richmond with the rest shall down 4.06.100
brother, i like not this; 4.07. 10
ay, now my sovereign speaketh like himself, 4.07. 67
like to his island, girt in with the ocean, | or 4.08. 20
spoke, | which sounded like a cannon in a vault, 5.02. 44
should leave the helm and, like a fearful lad, 5.04. 7
and make him of like spirit to himself. 5.04. 47
hope | go home to bed, and like the owl by day, 5.04. 56
speak like a subject, proud ambitious york! 5.05. 17
not like the fruit of such a goodly tree. 5.06. 52
i have no brother, i am like no brother; 5.06. 80
divine, | be resident in men like one another, 5.06. 82
what valiant foemen, like to autumn's corn, 5.07. 3
nor when thy warlike father, like a child, R3 1.02.159
their cheeks | like trees bedash'd with rain — 1.02.163
would to god my heart were flint, like edward's, 1.03.139
or edward's soft and pitiful, like mine: 1.03.140
if not, that i am queen, you bow like subjects, 1.03.160
yet that, by you depos'd, you quake like rebels? 1.03.161
die in his youth by like untimely violence! 1.03.200
outlive thy glory like my wretched self! 1.03.202
i like you, lads, about your business straight. 1.03.353
then came wand'ring by | a shadow like an angel, 1.04. 53
spoke like a tall man that respects thy 1.04.152 P
and like a traitor to the name of god | didst 1.04.205
how fain, like pilate, would i wash my hands 1.04.272
so thrive i, as i truly swear the like! 2.01. 11
or like obedient subjects follow him | to his 2.02. 45
bethink you like a careful mother | of the young 2.02. 96
i do not like the tower, of any place. 3.01. 68
thus, like the formal vice, iniquity, | i 3.01. 82
because that i am little, like an ape, | he 3.01.130
rood, | i do not like these several councils, i. 3.02. 76
nay, like enough, for i stay dinner there. 3.02.121
mine arm | is like a blasted sapling, wither'd 3.04. 69
looks | lives like a drunken sailor on a mast, 3.04. 99
looks | are at my service, like enforced smiles; 3.05. 9
to warn false traitors from the like attempts. 3.05. 49
being nothing like the noble duke my father. 3.05. 92
and his resemblance, being not like the duke. 3.07. 11
but, like dumb statues or breathing stones, 3.07. 25
i guess, | upon the like devotion as yourselves, 4.01. 9
that anne, my queen, is sick and like to die. 4.02. 57
wept like /two children in their deaths' sad 4.03. 8
woes will make them sharp and pierce like mine. 4.04.125
like a poor bark of sails and tackling reft, 4.04.234
endur'd of her, for whom you bid like sorrow. 4.04.304
your warm blood like wash and makes his trough 5.02. 9
like high-rear'd bulwarks, stand before our 5.03.242
all clinquant, all in gold, like heathen gods, H8 1.01. 19
every man that stood | show'd like a mine. 1.01. 22
like it your grace, | the state takes notice of 1.01.100
anger is like | a full hot horse, who being 1.01.132
not a man in england | can advise me like you; 1.01.135
and like a glass | did break i' th' wrenching. 1.01.166
most like a careful subject, have collected 1.02.130
which, being believ'd, | it was much like to do. 1.02.182
travel, | and understand again like honest men, 1.03. 32
dying, | go with me like good angels to my end, 2.01. 75
like a most royal prince | restor'd me to my 2.01.113
fall away | like water from ye, never found 2.01.130
blind priest, like the eldest son of fortune, 2.02. 20
a loss of her | that, like a jewel, has hung 2.02. 31
all men's honors | lie like one lump before him, 2.02. 48
i do profess | you speak not like yourself, who 2.04. 85
and like her true nobility she has | carried 2.04.143
why they are so, but, like to village curs, 2.04.160
i do not like their coming. 3.01. 21
and to deliver | (like free and honest men) our 3.01. 60
forgetting (like a good man) your late censure 3.01. 64
ye speak like honest men (pray god ye prove so!) 3.01. 69
all your studies | make me a curse like this! 3.01.124
like the lily, | that once was mistress of the 3.01.151
fall | like a bright exhalation in the evening, 3.02.226
forward, | and dare us with his cap, like larks. 3.02.282
like little wanton boys that swim on bladders, 3.02.359
and when he falls, he falls like lucifer, 3.02.371
week to go, like rams | in the old time of war, 4.01. 77
my legs like loaden branches bow to th' earth, 4.02. 2
cast thousand beams upon me, like the sun? 4.02. 89
and't like your grace — 4.02.100
too late, | 'tis like a pardon after execution. 4.02.121
although unqueen'd, yet like | a queen, and 4.02.171
'tis as like you | as cherry is to cherry. 5.01.168
said i for this, the girl was like to him? 5.01.174
and at the door too, like a post with packets. 5.02. 32
for me? | must i go like a traitor thither? 5.02.131
wait like a lousy footboy | at chamber-door? 5.02.174
may it like your grace | to let my tongue excuse 5.02.183
he stands there like a mortar-piece to blow us. 5.03. 46 P
and there they are like to dance these three 5.03. 64 P
her foes shake like a field of beaten corn, 5.04. 31
shall then be his, and like a vine grow to him. 5.04. 49
and like a mountain cedar reach his branches 5.04. 53
all the expected good w' are like to hear | for ep 8
is like that mighty fate turns to sudden sadness. TRO 1.01. 40
and, like as there were husbandry in war, 1.02. 7
the two moist elements, | like perseus' horse. 1.03. 42
when that the general is not like the hive | to 1.03. 81
and posts, like the commandment of a king, 1.03. 93
and, like a strutting player, whose conceit 1.03.153
'tis like a chime a-mending, with terms 1.03.159
of parallels, as like as vulcan and his wife; 1.03.168
keeps his tent like him, | makes factious feasts 1.03.190
a slave whose gall coins slanders like a mint, 1.03.193
or, shedding, breed a nursery of like evil, | to 1.03.319
let us, like merchants, first show foul wares, 1.03.358
among those of any wit, like a barbarian slave. 2.01. 47 P
/on /their /toes, yoke you like draught-oxen, 2.01.106 P
i will see you hang'd like clatpoles ere i come 2.01.117 P
heels | and fly like chidden mercury from jove, 2.02. 45
mercury from jove, | or like a star disorb'd? 2.02. 46
like one besotted on your sweet delights. 2.02.143
yea, like fair fruit in an unwholesome dish, 2.03.120
an unwholesome dish, | are like to rot untasted. 2.03.121
but let him, like an engine | not portable, lie 2.03.134
which, like a /bourn, a pale, a shore, confines 2.03.249
like to a strange soul upon the stygian banks 3.02. 9
like vassalage at /unawares encount'ring | the 3.02. 38
my thoughts were like unbridled children grown 3.02.122
'tis like he'll question me | why such 3.03. 42
for men, like butterflies, | show not their 3.03. 78
who, like an arch, reverb'rate | the voice again 3.03.120
or, like a gate of steel | fronting the sun, 3.03.121
like a rusty mail | in monumental mock'ry. 3.03.152
like to an ent'red tide, they all rush by | and 3.03.159
for time is like a fashionable host | that 3.03.165
place with thought and almost, like the gods, 3.03.199
and, like /a dewdrop from the lion's mane, | be 3.03.224
and danger, like an ague, subtly taints | even 3.03.232
'a stalks up and down like a peacock — a stride 3.03.251 P
ruminates like an hostess that hath no 3.03.252 P
wear it on both sides, like a leather jerkin. 3.03.265 P
my mind is troubled, like a fountain stirr'd, 3.03.308
he, like a puling cuckold, would drink up | the 4.01. 62
you, like a lecher, out of whorish loins | are 4.01. 64
the like allayment could i give my grief: 4.04. 8
'tis done like hector. 4.05. 73
and that which looks like pride is courtesy. 4.05. 82
/hemm'd thee in, | like an olympian wrastling. 4.05.194
mars, the captain of us all, | never like thee. 4.05.199
o, like a book of sport thou'lt read me o'er; 4.05.239
his mouth and promise, like brabbler the hound, 5.01. 91 P
i do not like this fooling. 5.02.101
i would croak like a raven, i would bode, i 5.02.191 P
and i myself | am like a prophet suddenly enrapt 5.03. 65
like witless antics, one another meet, | and all 5.03. 86
like scaling sculls | before the belching whale; 5.05. 22
fall down before him like a mower's swath. 5.05. 25
i like thy armor well; 5.06. 28
the troyans' trumpet sound the like, my lord. 5.08. 16
i'll haunt thee like a wicked conscience still, 5.10. 28
o' th' state, who care for you like fathers, COR 1.01. 77
that only like a gulf it did remain | i' th' 1.01. 98
never bearing | like labor with the rest, where 1.01.101
not rash like his accusers, and thus answered: 1.01.129
have, you curs, | that like nor peace nor war? 1.01.169
who's like to rise, | who thrives, and who 1.01.192
him seek danger where he was like to find fame. 1.03. 13 P
like to a harvest-man /that's task'd to mow | or 1.03. 36
mark me, and do the like. 1.04. 45
we are come off | like romans, neither foolish 1.06. 2
even like a fawning greyhound in the leash, | to 1.06. 38
if i fly, martius, | hollow me like a hare. 1.08. 7
put you | (like one that means his proper harm) 1.09. 57
he's a lamb indeed, that baes like a bear. 2.01. 11 P
he's a bear indeed, that lives like a lamb. 2.01. 12 P
with the colic, you make faces like mummers, set 2.01. 74 P
'tis most like he will. 2.01.241
i never saw the like. 2.01.268
and to remember | with honors like himself. 2.02. 48
age | man-ent'red thus, he waxed like a sea, 2.02. 99
reinforcement struck | corioles like a planet. 2.02.114
like the virtues | which our divines lose by 'em 2.03. 57
you are like to do such business. 3.01. 48
deeds express | what's like to be their words: 3.01.133
h'as spoken like a traitor, and shall answer 3.01.162
and so are like to do. 3.01.202
that seem like prudent helps, are very poisonous 3.01.220
whose rage doth rend | like interrupted waters, 3.01.248
like an unnatural dam | should now eat up her 3.01.291
say | honor and policy, like unsever'd friends, 3.02. 42
since that to both | it stands in like request? 3.02. 51
bend like his | that hath receiv'd an alms! 3.02.119
which show | like graves i' th' holy churchyard. 3.03. 51
that when he speaks not like a citizen, | you 3.03. 53
like a citizen, | you find him like a soldier; 3.03. 54
like to a lonely dragon, that his fen | makes 4.01. 30
of me aught | but what is like me formerly. 4.01. 53
smells well, but i | appear not like a guest. 4.05. 6
i'd have beaten him like a dog, but for 4.05. 51 P
ungrateful rome, | like a bold flood o'er-beat. 4.05.131
scotch'd him and notch'd him like a carbinado. 4.05.187 P
and he's as like to do't as any man i can 4.05.203 P
out of their burrows, like conies after rain, 4.05.212 P
can, | and three examples of the like hath been 4.06. 51
he leads them like a thing | made by some other 4.06. 90
his hate, | and therein show'd like enemies. 4.06.114
but like beasts | and cowardly nobles gave way 4.06.121
i do not like this news. 4.06.157
you guard like men, 'tis well. 5.02. 2
like to a bowl upon a subtle ground, | i have 5.02. 20
who like a block hath denied my access to thee. 5.02. 78 P
like a dull actor now | i have forgot my part, 5.03. 40
of full time | may show like all yourself. 5.03. 70
and stick i' th' wars | like a great sea-mark, 5.03. 74
here he lets me prate | like one i' th' stocks. 5.03.160
in corioles, and his child | like him by chance. 5.03.180
on like conditions, will have counter-seal'd. 5.03.205
when he walks, he moves like an engine, and the 5.04. 19 P
a corslet with his eye, talks like a knell, and 5.04. 21 P
your native town you enter'd like a post, | and 5.06. 49
breaking his oath and resolution like | a twist 5.06. 94
'tis there | that, like an eagle in a dove-cote, 5.06.114
whose smoke like incense doth perfume the sky. TIT 1.01.145
that like the stately /phoebe 'mongst her nymphs 1.01.316
lavinia, though you left me like a churl, | i 1.01.486
the emperor's court is like the house of fame, 2.01.126
way, and runs like swallows o'er the plain. 2.02. 24
or is it dian habited like her, | who hath 2.03. 57
all on a heap, like to a slaughtered lamb, | in 2.03.223
hole, | which, like a taper in some monument, 2.03.228
o tamora, was ever heard the like? 2.03.276
like to a bubbling fountain stirr'd with wind, 2.04. 23
sorrow concealed, like an oven stopp'd, | doth 2.04. 36
hands | tremble like aspen leaves upon a lute, 2.04. 45
rome could afford no tribunes like to these. 3.01. 44
and now like nilus it disdaineth bounds. 3.01. 71
where like a sweet melodious bird it sung 3.01. 85
how they are stain'd like meadows yet not dry, 3.01.125
or shall we cut away our hands like thine? 3.01.130
did ever raven sing so like a lark | that gives 3.01.158
aaron will have his soul black like his face. 3.01.205
woes, | but like a drunkard must i vomit them. 3.01.231
i, | even like a stony image, cold and numb. 3.01.258
beg at the gates, like tarquin and his queen. 3.01.298
will blow these sands like sibyl's leaves abroad 4.01.105
oft | for his ungrateful country done the like. 4.01.111
and so i leave you both — like bloody villains. 4.02. 17
his child is like to her, fair as you are. 4.02.154
for /then hast made it like an humble suppliant. 4.03.117
say, | when i have walked like a private man, 4.04. 75
king, be thy thoughts imperious, like thy name. 4.04. 81
like stinging bees in hottest summer's day, 5.01. 14
too like the sire for ever being good. 5.01. 50
o barbarous, beastly villains like thyself! 5.01. 97
that both mine eyes were rainy like to his; 5.01.117
ay, like a black dog, as the saying is. 5.01.122
trot like a servile footman all day long, | even 5.02. 55
good lord, how like the empress' sons they are! 5.02. 64
how like the empress and her sons you are! 5.02. 84
and when thou find'st a man that's like thyself, 5.02. 99
thy hap | to find another that is like to thee, 5.02.102
like to the earth swallow her own increase. 5.02.191
for me, most wretched, to perform the like. 5.03. 45
to, | like a forlorn and desperate castaway, 5.03. 75
and like her most whose merit most shall be; ROM 1.02. 31
speak briefly, can you like of paris' love? 1.03. 96
i'll look to like, if looking liking move; 1.03. 97
lath, | scaring the ladies like a crow-keeper, 1.04. 6
rude, too boist'rous, and it pricks like thorn. 1.04. 26
alone, | 'a bears him like a portly gentleman; 1.05. 66
my grave is like to be my wedding-bed. 1.05.135
too like the lightning, which doth cease to be 2.02.119
night, | like softest music to attending ears! 2.02.166
like a poor prisoner in his twisted gyves, | and 2.02.179
and fleckled darkness like a drunkard reels 2.03. 3
without his roe, like a dried herring: 2.04. 37 P
drivelling love is like a great natural that 2.04. 91 P
and bring thee cords made like a tackled stair, 2.04.189
your love says, like an honest gentleman, | an' 2.05. 55
"your love says, like an honest gentleman, 2.05. 60
and in their triumph die, like fire and powder, 2.06. 10
if the measure of thy joy | be heap'd like mine, 2.06. 25
thou art like one of these fellows that, when he 3.01. 5 P
am i like such a fellow? 3.01. 10 P
and to't they go like lightning, for, ere i 3.01.172
like damned guilty deeds to sinners' minds: 3.02.111
doting like me, and like me banished, | then 3.03. 67
doting like me, and like me banished, | then 3.03. 67
which, like a usurer, abound'st in all, | and 3.03.123
like powder in a skilless soldier's flask, | is 3.03.132
array, | but, like a mishaved and sullen wench, 3.03.143
do you like this haste? 3.04. 22
and yet no man like he doth grieve my heart. 3.05. 83
uneven is the course, i like it not. 4.01. 5
a thing like death to chide away this shame, 4.01. 74
like death when he shuts up the day of life; 4.01.101
stiff and stark and cold, appear like death, 4.01.103
is it not very like | the horrible conceit of 4.03. 36
resort — | alack, alack, is it not like that i, 4.03. 45
and shrikes like mandrakes' torn out of the 4.03. 47
death lies on her like an untimely frost | upon 4.05. 28
answer me like men: 4.05.125 P
provokes itself and like the current flies TIM 1.01. 24
i like your work, | and you shall find i like it 1.01.160
like your work, | and you shall find i like it. 1.01.161
things of like value differing in the owners 1.01.170
of nothing so much as that i am not like timon. 1.01.189 P
how dost thou like this jewel, apemantus? 1.01.210 P
i will fly, like a dog, the heels a' th' ass. 1.01.272 P
bleeding new, my lord, there's no meat like 'em; 1.02. 79 P
'tis to have so many like brothers commanding 1.02.104 P
joy had the like conception in our eyes, | and 1.02.110
and at that instant like a babe sprung up. 1.02.111
like madness is the glory of this life, | as 1.02.134
a fool in good clothes, and something like thee. 2.02.108 P
sometime't appears like a lord, sometime like a 2.02.109 P
appears like a lord, sometime like a lawyer, 2.02.110 P
like a lawyer, sometime like a philosopher, with 2.02.110 P
he is very often like a knight; 2.02.112 P
his friends, like physicians, | thrive, give him 3.03. 11
like those that under hot ardent zeal would set 3.03. 32 P
the like to you, kind varro. 3.04. 2
that a prodigal course | is like the sun's, but 3.04. 13
like the sun's, but not, like his, recoverable, 3.04. 13
does it now | (like all mankind) show me an iron 3.04. 83
his outsides, to wear them like his raiment, 3.05. 33
favor, pardon me | if i speak like a captain. 3.05. 41
in like manner was i in debt to my importunate 3.06. 13 P
false vows with him, | like empty purses pick'd; 4.02. 12
poverty, | walks, like contempt, alone. 4.02. 15
but only painted, like his varnish'd friends? 4.02. 36
but then renew i could not, like the moon; 4.03. 69
thine ears (like tapsters that bade welcome) 4.03.215
were i like thee, i'd throw away myself. 4.03.219
thou hast cast away thyself, being like thyself, 4.03.220
hadst thou like us from our first swath 4.03.252
ay, though it look like thee. 4.03.308 P
moe things like men! 4.03.397
like workmen, i'll example you with thievery: 4.03.435
be men like blasted woods, | and may diseases 4.03.531
that nothing but himself which looks like man 5.01.118
who, like a boar too savage, doth root up | his 5.01.165
and enter in our ears like great triumphers | in 5.01.196
i like this well, he will return again. 5.01.204
force, | and made us speak like friends. 5.02. 9
crimes, like lands, | are not inherited. 5.04. 37
like a shepherd, | approach the fold and cull 5.04. 42
bestride the narrow world | like a colossus, and JC 1.02.136
as this time | is like to lay upon us. 1.02.175
and all the rest look like a chidden train: 1.02.184
'tis very like, he hath the falling sickness. 1.02.254
the sway of earth | shakes like a thing unfirm? 1.03. 4
did flame and burn | like twenty torches join'd; 1.03. 17
to thee a man | most like this dreadful night, 1.03. 73
have thews and limbs like to their ancestors; 1.03. 81
/in favor's like the work we have in hand, 1.03.129
in us, | his countenance, like richest alchymy, 1.03.159

is | like a phantasma or a hideous dream. 2.01. 65
like to a little kingdom, suffers then | the 2.01. 68
like wrath in death and envy afterwards; 2.01.164
thou, like an exorcist, hast conjur'd up | my 2.01.323
which, like a fountain with an hundred spouts, 2.02. 77
me, | and we, like friends, will straightway go 2.02.127
that every like is not the same, o caesar, | the 2.02.128
i heard a bustling rumor, like a fray, | and the 2.04. 18
him, | i spurn thee like a cur out of my way. 3.01. 46
how like a deer, strooken by many princes, 3.01.209
i know not what may fall, i like it not. 3.01.243
(which like dumb mouths do ope their ruby lips 3.01.260
are rid like madmen through the gates of rome. 3.02.269
and turn him off | (like to the empty ass) to 4.01. 26
but hollow men, like horses hot at hand, | make 4.02. 23
and like deceitful jades | sink in the trial. 4.02. 26
/lucius, do you the like, and let no man | come 4.02. 50
was that done like cassius? 4.03. 77
i do not like your faults. 4.03. 89
check'd like a bondman, all his faults observ'd, 4.03. 97
then like a roman bear the truth i tell: 4.03.188
you show'd your /teeth like apes, and fawn'd 5.01. 41
your /teeth like apes, and fawn'd like hounds, 5.01. 41
and bow'd like bondmen, kissing caesar's feet; 5.01. 42
whilst damned casca, like a cur, behind | strook 5.01. 43
he lies not like the living. o my heart! 5.03. 58
he will be found like brutus, like himself. 5.04. 25
he will be found like brutus, like himself. 5.04. 25
lie, | most like a soldier, ordered honorably. 5.05. 79
who like a good and hardy soldier fought MAC 1.02. 4
/quarrel smiling, | show'd like a rebel's whore. 1.02. 15
(like valor's minion) carv'd out his passage 1.02. 19
thither sail, | and, like a rat without a tail, 1.03. 9
that look not like th' inhabitants o' th' earth, 1.03. 41
like our strange garments, cleave not to their 1.03.145
in his life | became him like the leaving it. 1.04. 8
but signs of nobleness, like stars, shall shine 1.04. 41
to beguile the time, | look like the time; 1.05. 64
look like th' innocent flower, | but be the 1.05. 65
that his virtues | will plead like angels, 1.07. 19
and pity, like a naked new–born babe, | striding 1.07. 21
"i would," | like the poor cat i' th' adage? 1.07. 45
a heavy summons lies like lead upon me, | and 2.01. 6
thanks, sir; the like to you! 2.01. 30
towards his design | moves like a ghost. 2.01. 56
from your graves rise up, and walk like sprites, 2.03. 79
his gash'd stabs look'd like a breach in nature 2.03.113
unnatural, | even like the deed that's done. 2.04. 11
then 'tis most like | the sovereignty will fall 2.04. 29
yet he's good that did the like for fleance. 3.04. 17
approach thou like the rugged russian bear, 3.04. 99
be, | and overcome us like a summer's cloud, 3.04.110
trouble, | like a hell–broth boil and bubble. 4.01. 19
sing, | like elves and fairies in a ring, 4.01. 42
is this | that rises like the issue of a king, 4.01. 87
come like shadows, so depart. 4.01.111
thou art too like the spirit of banquo; 4.01.112
thou other gold–bound brow, is like the first. 4.01.114
a third is like the former. 4.01.115
no boasting like a fool; 4.01.153
sword, and like good men | bestride our downfall 4.03. 3
and yell'd out | like syllable of dolor. 4.03. 8
of goodness | be like our warranted quarrel! 4.03.137
i could answer | this comfort with the like! 4.03.193
dispute it like a man. 4.03.220
like a giant's robe | upon a dwarfish thief. 5.02. 21
of the fiend | that lies like truth. 5.05. 43
throw down, | and show like those you are. 5.06. 2
where he fought, | but like a man he died. 5.09. 9
in the same figure, like the king that's dead. HAM 1.01. 41
looks 'a not like the king? mark it, horatio. 1.01. 43
most like; it /harrows me with fear and wonder. 1.01. 44
is it not like the king? 1.01. 58
so like the king | that was and is the question 1.01.110
and even the like precurse of /fear'd events, 1.01.121
and then it started like a guilty thing | upon a 1.01.148
and let thine eye look like a friend on denmark. 1.02. 69
like niobe, all tears — why, she, /even /she — 1.02.149
but no more like my father | than i to hercules. 1.02.152
in all, | i shall not look upon his like again. 1.02.188
a figure like your father, | armed at point 1.02.199
your father, | these hands are not more like. 1.02.212
itself to motion, like as it would speak; 1.02.217
very like, /very /like. stay'd it long? 1.02.236
you speak like a green girl, | unsifted in such 1.03.101
breathing like sanctified and pious bonds, | the 1.03.130
make thy two eyes, like stars, start from their 1.05. 17
end, | like quills upon the fearful porpentine. 1.05. 20
and curd, like eager droppings into milk, | the 1.05. 69
it may be, very like. 2.02.152
as i am, if like a crab you could go backward. 2.02.203 P
how like an angel in apprehension! 2.02.306 P
how like a god! 2.02.306 P
should more appear like entertainment than yours 2.02.375 P
know, "it came to pass, as most like it was" — 2.02.418
god your voice, like a piece of uncurrent gold, 2.02.427 P
we'll e'en to't like /french falc'ners — fly at 2.02.429 P
"the rugged pyrrhus, like th' hyrcanian beast — 2.02.450
with eyes like carbuncles, the hellish pyrrhus 2.02.463
/and, like a neutral to his will and matter, 2.02.481
peak | like john–a–dreams, unpregnant of my 2.02.568
must, like a whore, unpack my heart with words, 2.02.585
words, | and fall a–cursing, like a very drab, 2.02.586
play something like the murther of my father 2.02.595
most like a gentleman. 3.01. 11
like sweet bells jangled, out of time and harsh; 3.01.158
it lack'd form a little, | was not like madness. 3.01.164
madam, how like you this play? 3.02.229 P
for if the king like not the comedy, | why then 3.02.293
by th' mass and 'tis, like a camel indeed. 3.02.378 P
methinks it is like a weasel. 3.02.379 P
it is back'd like a weasel. 3.02.380 P
or like a whale? 3.02.381 P
very like a whale. 3.02.382 P
i like him not, nor stands it safe with us | to 3.03. 1
but, like a gulf, doth draw | what's near it 3.03. 16
and, like a man to double business bound, | i 3.03. 41
an eye like mars, to threaten and command, | a 3.04. 57
a station like the herald mercury | new lighted 3.04. 58
here is your husband, like a mildewed ear, 3.04. 64
these words like daggers enter in my ears. 3.04. 95
your bedded hair, like life in excrements, 3.04.121
let the birds fly, and like the famous ape, | to 3.04.194
fit, | but, like the owner of a foul disease, 4.01. 21
like some ore | among a mineral of metals base, 4.01. 25
he keeps them, like /an /ape an apple, in the 4.02. 18 P
who like not in their judgment, but their eyes, 4.03. 5
for like the hectic in my blood he rages, | and 4.03. 66
trick of fame | go to their graves like beds, 4.04. 62
like to a murd'ring–piece, in many places 4.05. 95
and, like the kind life–rend'ring pelican, 4.05.147
speak | like a good child and a true gentleman. 4.05.149
they have dealt with me like thieves of mercy, 4.06. 21 P
work like the spring that turneth wood to stone, 4.07. 20
or are you like the painting of a sorrow, | a 4.07.108
it, | and nothing is at a like goodness still, 4.07.116
then this "should" is like a spendthrift's sigh, 4.07.122
or like a creature native and indued | unto that 4.07.179
i like thy wit well, in good faith. 5.01. 45 P
makes them stand | like wonder–wounded hearers? 5.01.257
the burning zone, | make ossa like a wart! 5.01.283
as love between them like the palm might 5.02. 40
time | i do receive your offer'd love like love, 5.02.251
skill shall, like a star i' th' darkest night, 5.02.256
let four captains | bear hamlet, like a soldier, 5.02.396
sure i shall never marry like my sisters, | /to LR 1.01.103
and nothing more, may fitly like your grace, 1.01.200
and like a sister am most loath to call | your 1.01.270
starts are we like to have from him as this of 1.01.300 P
he comes like the catastrophe of the old comedy. 1.02.134 P
melancholy, with a sigh like tom o' bedlam. 1.02.135 P
nothing like the image and horror of it. 1.02.175 P
if i like thee no worse after dinner, i will not 1.04. 40 P
then 'tis like the breath of an unfee'd lawyer, 1.04.129 P
if i speak like myself in this, let him be whipt 1.04.164 P
with their manners, | shows like a riotous inn. 1.04.244
lust | makes it more like a tavern or a brothel 1.04.245
which, like an engine, wrench'd my frame of 1.04.268
for though she's as like this as a crab's like 1.05. 15 P
she's as like this as a crab's like an apple, 1.05. 15 P
she will taste as like this as a crab does to a 1.05. 18 P
like rats, oft bite the holy cords a–twain 2.02. 74
knowing nought (like dogs) but following. 2.02. 80
like the wreath of radiant fire | on /flick'ring 2.02.107
tied | sharp–tooth'd unkindness, like a vulture, 2.04.135
one minded like the weather, most unquietly. 3.01. 2
edmund, i like not this unnatural dealing. 3.03. 1 P
in a wild field were like an old lecher's heart, 3.04.112 P
only i do not like the fashion of your garments. 3.06. 79 P
we are bound to the like. 3.07. 11 P
pinion him like a thief, bring him before us. 3.07. 23
what like, offensive. 4.02. 11
ere long you are like to hear | (if you dare 4.02. 19
one way i like this well, | but being widow, and 4.02. 83
that /walk upon the beach, | appear like mice; 4.06. 18
precipitating), | thou'dst shiver'd like an egg: 4.06. 51
horns welk'd and waved like the /enridged sea. 4.06. 71
that fellow handles his bow like a crow–keeper; 4.06. 87 P
they flatter'd me like a dog, and told me i had 4.06. 97 P
and, like a scurvy politician, seem | to see the 4.06.171
i will die bravely, like a smug bridegroom. 4.06.198
of his fortune take | like hold on thee. 4.06.234
that mine own tears | do scald like molten lead. 4.07. 47
we two alone will sing like birds i' th' cage; 5.03. 9
from heaven, | and fire us hence like foxes. 5.03. 23
wears out his time, much like his master's ass, OTH 1.01. 47
do, with like timorous accent and dire yell | as 1.01. 75
let me speak like yourself, and lay a sentence, 1.03.199
i never did like molestation view | on the 2.01. 16
him, and the man commands | like a full soldier. 2.01. 36
that not another comfort like to this | succeeds 2.01.192
whereof | doth, like a poisonous mineral, gnaw 2.01.297
and in terms like bride and groom | devesting 2.03.180
here in the chase, not like a hound that hunts, 2.03.363 P
hah? i like not that. 3.03. 35
what didst not like? 3.03.110
'tis destiny unshunnable, like death. 3.03.275
upon the blood | burn like the mines of sulphur. 3.03.329
i do not like the office; 3.03.410
like to the pontic sea, | whose icy current and 3.03.453
make it a darling like your precious eye. 3.04. 66
and, like the devil, from his very arm | puff'd 3.04.136
i like the work well; 3.04.189
ere it be demanded | (as like enough it will) i 3.04.190
would you would bear your fortune like a man! 4.01. 61
lest, being like one of heaven, the devils 4.02. 36
all at one side | and sing it like poor barbary. 4.03. 33
know | their wives have sense like them; 4.03. 94
'tis like she comes to speak of cassio's death; 5.02. 92
she's like a liar gone to burning hell: 5.02.129
even like thy chastity. 5.02.276
like the base /indian, threw a pearl away 5.02.347
of the war | have glow'd like plated mars, now ANT 1.01. 4
nay, and most like. 1.01. 25
which, like the courser's hair, hath yet but 1.02.193
hold the method to enforce | the like from him. 1.03. 8
thou teachest like a fool: the way to lose him. 1.03. 10
and let it look | like perfect honor. 1.03. 80
body, | like to a vagabond flag upon the stream, 1.04. 45
yea, like the stag, when snow the pasture sheets 1.04. 65
was borne so like a soldier, that thy cheek | so 1.04. 70
like to the time o' th' year between the 1.05. 51
i shall entreat him | to answer like himself. 2.02. 4
the barge she sat in, like a burnish'd throne, 2.02.191
stood pretty dimpled boys, like smiling cupids, 2.02.202
her /gentlewomen, like the nereides, | so many 2.02.206
thou shouldst come like a fury crown'd with 2.05. 40
crown'd with snakes, | not like a formal man. 2.05. 41
i do not like "but yet," it does allay | the 2.05. 50
or i'll spurn thine eyes | like balls before me; 2.05. 64
though he be painted one way like a gorgon, 2.05.116
and well am like to do, for i perceive | four 2.06. 72
sir, like itself, and it is as broad as it hath 2.07. 42 P
that's not so good. he cannot like her long. 3.03. 14
like her? o isis! 'tis impossible. 3.03. 15
of his conquer'd kingdoms, i | demand the like. 3.06. 37
you come not | like caesar's sister. 3.06. 43
on our side like the token'd pestilence, | where 3.10. 9
when vantage like a pair of twins appear'd, 3.10. 12
the breeze upon her, like a cow in /june — 3.10. 14
on his sea–wing, and (like a doting mallard), 3.10. 19
at philippi kept | his sword e'en like a dancer, 3.11. 36
yes, like enough! 3.13. 29
like boys unto a muss, kings would start forth 3.13. 91
till like a boy you see him cringe his face, 3.13.100
and to proclaim it civilly were like | a 3.13.129
or torture, | as he shall like, to quit me. 3.13.151
like a master | married to your good service, 4.02. 30
thou look'st like him that knows a warlike 4.04. 19
like the spirit of a youth | that means to be of 4.04. 26
i'll leave thee | now like a man of steel. 4.04. 33
i had a wound here that was like a t, | but now 4.07. 7
cause, but as't had been | each man's like mine; 4.08. 7
it, were it carbuncled | like holy phoebus' car. 4.08. 29
our hack'd targets like the men that owe them. 4.08. 31
bring thee word | straight how 'tis like to go. 4.12. 3
and carouse together | like friends long lost. 4.12. 13
like a right gipsy, hath at fast and loose 4.12. 28
like the greatest spot | of all thy sex; 4.12. 35
a vapor sometime like a bear or lion, | a 4.14. 3
been laden with like frailties which before 5.02.123
saucy lictors | will catch at us like strumpets, 5.02.215
show me, my women, like a queen; 5.02.227
but she looks like sleep, | as she would catch 5.02.346
the like is on her arm. 5.02.350
the regions of the earth | for one his like, CYM 1.01. 21
and like the tyrannous breathing of the north 1.03. 36
it was much like an argument that fell out last 1.04. 56 P
i do not like her. 1.05. 33
or, like the parthian, i shall flying fight — 1.06. 20
should he make me | live, like diana's priest, 1.06.133
he sits 'mongst men like a /descended god; 1.06.169
if his wit had been like him that broke it, it 2.01. 8 P
to have smell'd like a fool. 2.01. 16 P
i must go up and down like a cock that nobody 2.01. 21 P
like the crimson drops | i' th' bottom of a 2.02. 38
so like you, sir, ambassadors from rome; 2.03. 54
(statist though i am none, nor like to be) 2.04. 16
'tis very like. 2.04. 36
like a full–acorn'd boar, a german /one, | cried 2.05. 16
like egg–shells mov'd upon their surges, crack'd 3.01. 28
pisanio, | who long'st like me to see thy lord; 3.02. 53
but not like me — yet long'st, | but in a 3.02. 54
but in a fainter kind — o, not like me, | for 3.02. 55
when you above perceive me like a crow, | that 3.03. 12
like warlike as the wolf for what we eat; 3.03. 41
cadwal, | once arviragus, in as like a figure, 3.03. 96
thou then look'dst like a villain; 3.04. 48
true honest men being heard, like false aeneas, 3.04. 58
most like, | bringing me here to kill me. 3.04.116
first, make yourself but like one. 3.04.167
she /looks us like | a thing more made of malice 3.05. 32
and if mine enemy | but fear the sword like me, 3.06. 26
the which he hearing | (as it is like him), 4.02.140
not lack | the flower that's like thy face, pale 4.02.221
nor | the azur'd harebell, like thy veins; 4.02.222
use like note and words, | save that euriphile 4.02.237
these flow'rs are like the pleasures of the 4.02.296
very eyes | are sometimes like our judgments, 4.02.302
save one that had | a rider like myself, who 4.04. 39
(lads more like to run | the country base than 5.03. 19
you that | like beasts which you shun beastly, 5.03. 27
and to grin like lions | upon the pikes o' th' 5.03. 38
like fragments in hard voyages, became | the 5.03. 44
great nature, like his ancestry, | moulded the 5.04. 48
like hardiment posthumus hath | to cymbeline 5.04. 75
the action of my life is like it, which | i'll 5.04.149
you look like romans, | and not o' th' court of 5.05. 24
with horror, madly dying, like her life, | which 5.05. 31
my heart, | that thought her like her seeming. 5.05. 65
most like a noble lord in love and one | that 5.05.171
most like i did, for i was dead. 5.05.259
hang there like fruit, my soul, | till the tree 5.05.263
covering heavens | fall on their heads like dew! 5.05.351
and she (like harmless lightning) throws her eye 5.05.394
i might | waste it for you like taper–light. PER 1.ch. 16
clothed like a bride | for embracements even of 1.01. 6
see where she comes, apparelled like the spring, 1.01. 12
her face, like heaven, enticeth thee to view 1.01. 30
yon sometimes famous princes, like thyself, 1.01. 34
objects to prepare | this body, like to them, to 1.01. 44
for death remembered should be like a mirror, 1.01. 45
like a bold champion i assume the lists, | nor 1.01. 61
for vice repeated is like the wand'ring wind, 1.01. 96
then give my tongue like leave to love my head. 1.01.108
sin, | when what is done is like an hypocrite, 1.01.122
and both like serpents are, who though they feed 1.01.132
and like an arrow shot | from a well–experienc'd 1.01.161
thou speak'st like a physician, helicanus, 1.02. 67
but like to groves, being topp'd, they higher 1.04. 9
like one another's glass to trim them by; 1.04. 27
thou speak'st like /him's untutor'd to repeat: 1.04. 74
men | be like a beacon fir'd t' amaze your eyes. 1.04. 87
are like the troyan horse was stuff'd within 1.04. 93
not to eat honey like a drone | from others' 2.ch. 18
in the net, like a poor man's right in the law; 2.01.117 P
in like necessity — | the which the gods 2.01.128
sits here like beauty's child, whom nature gat 2.02. 6
are | a model which heaven makes like to itself. 2.02. 11
to me he seems like diamond to glass. 2.03. 36
/yon king's to me like to my father's picture, 2.03. 37
had princes sit like stars about his throne, 2.03. 39
none that beheld him but, like lesser lights, 2.03. 41
where now his /son's like a glow–worm in the 2.03. 43
princes in this should live like gods above, 2.03. 59
and princes not doing so are like to gnats, 2.03. 62
like goodly buildings left without a roof | soon 2.04. 36
go search like nobles, like noble subjects, 2.04. 50
go search like nobles, like noble subjects, 2.04. 50
you shall like diamonds sit about his crown. 2.04. 53
i like that well. 2.05. 19
it had conceit, would die, as i | am like to do. 3.01. 17
'tis like a coffin, sir. 3.02. 52
our credit comes not in like the commodity, nor 4.02. 30 P

if you like her, so; 4.02. 44 P
light into my hands, where you are like to live. 4.02. 73 P
one, i like the manner of your garments well: 4.02.134 P
the heavens, the gods | do like this worst. 4.03. 21
thou art like the harpy, | which, to betray, 4.03. 46
y' are like one that superstitiously | do swear 4.03. 49
like motes and shadows see them move a while, 4.04. 21
did you ever hear the like? 4.05. 1 P
but there never came her like in meteline. 4.06. 28 P
a curse upon him, die he like a thief, | that 4.06.114
household, let me be gelded like a spaniel. 4.06.124 P
would have dealt with her like a nobleman, and 4.06.139 P
she sings like one immortal, and she dances | as 5.ch. 3
eyes, | but have been gaz'd on like a comet. 5.01. 86
you're like something that — what 5.01.102
my dearest wife was like this maid, and such a 5.01.107
seem | like lies disdain'd in the reporting. 5.01.119
for thou lookest | like one i lov'd indeed. 5.01.125
art a man, and i | have suffered like a girl. 5.01.137
look | like patience gazing on kings' graves, 5.01.138
what this maid is, or what is like to be, | that 5.01.184
like him you spake, | like him you are! 5.03. 32
like him you spake, | like him you are! 5.03. 33
no mortal officer | more like a god than you. 5.03. 63
and shake to lose his honor) is like her | that, TNK pr 5
key — like such a woman | as any of us three; 1.01. 94
like wrinkled pebbles in a /glassy stream, | you 1.01.112
into twain and doing | each side like justice, 1.03. 47
and like the elements | that know not what nor 1.03. 61
and commit it | to the like innocent cradle, 1.03. 70
comes in | like old importment's bastard) has 1.03. 80
that you shall never (like the maid flavina) 1.03. 84
like to a pair of lions smear'd with prey, 1.04. 18
then like men use 'em. 1.04. 28
of their ladies, | like tall ships under sail; 2.02. 12
leave 'em all behind us | like lazy clouds, 2.02. 14
shall we two exercise, like twins of honor, 2.02. 18
our fiery horses | like proud seas under us! 2.02. 20
/ravish'd our sides, like age, must run to rust, 2.02. 22
hands shall never draw 'em out like lightning, 2.02. 24
youths must wither | like a too-timely spring. 2.02. 28
and like young eagles teach 'em | boldly to gaze 2.02. 34
flies like a parthian quiver from our rages, 2.02. 50
the poison of pure spirits, might, like women, 2.02. 75
'tis like a beast, methinks. 2.02. 99
her, | rude and impatient, then, like chastity, 2.02.141
and like enough the duke hath taken notice 2.02.227
when he bids 'em charge, | fall on like fire. 2.02.250
how do you like him, lady? 2.05. 17
mark how his virtue, like a hidden sun, | breaks 2.05. 23
i like him better, prince, i shall not then 2.05. 47
rest, spreads like a plane | fast by a brook, 2.06. 5
by him, like a shadow, | i'll ever dwell. 2.06. 34
any gross stuff | to form me like your blazon, 3.01. 47
and then they fight like compell'd bears, would 3.01. 68
the little stars and all, that look like aglets. 3.04. 2
o for a prick now, like a nightingale, | to put 3.04. 25
i shall sleep like a top else. 3.04. 26
like true lovers, | cast yourselves in a body 3.05. 19
that i lay fatting like a swine, to fight, | and 3.06. 12
like meeting of two tides, fly strongly from us, 3.06. 30
methinks this armor's very like that, arcite, 3.06. 70
are making battle, thus like knights appointed, 3.06.134
this treachery, like a most trusty lover, | i 3.06.150
ye | now usage like to princes and to friends. 3.06.306
that methought she appear'd like the fair nymph 4.01. 86
arch'd like the great-ey'd juno's, but far 4.02. 20
him, black and shining | like ravens' wings; 4.02. 84
and curl'd, thick twin'd like ivy/-tods, | not 4.02.104
he speaks, his tongue | sounds like a trumpet. 4.02.113
gently they swell, like women new conceiv'd, 4.02.128
and there boil like a gammon of bacon that will 4.03. 38 P
whose youth, like wanton boys through bonfires, 5.01. 86
how do you like him? 5.02. 46
he turns ye like a top. 5.02. 50
but he is like his master, coy and scornful. 5.02. 63
how did you like her? 5.02.103
falls, and sounds more like | a bell than blade. 5.03. 5
i am like to know your husband 'fore yourself 5.03. 37
yet his eye | is like an engine bent, or a sharp 5.03. 42
and like him possess'd | with fire malevolent, 5.04. 62
let's go off, | and bear us like the time. 5.04.137
i would now ask ye how ye like the play, | but, ep 1
and men like ravenous fishes | would feed on STM II.C 86
that you like rebels lift against the peace II.C 109
of law in lyam | to slip him like a hound; II.C 122
spurn you like dogs, and like as if that god II.C 135
and like as if that god | owed not nor made not II.C 135
and like a bold-fac'd suitor gins to woo him. VEN 6
like a dive-dapper peering through a wave, | who 86
or like a fairy, trip upon the green, | or like 146
or like a nymph, with long dishevelled hair, 147
forceless flowers like sturdy trees support me; 152
so he were like him, and by venus' side. 180
like misty vapors when they blot the sky, 184
alone, | thing like a man, but of no woman bred! 214
sometime her arms infold him like a band: 225
hollow womb resounds like heaven's thunder; 268
his eye, which scornfully glisters like fire, 275
the hairs, who wave like feath'red wings. 306
then, like a melancholy malcontent, | he vails 313
he vails his tail that, like a falling plume, 314
sat, | and like a lowly lover down she kneels; 350
showed like two silver doves that sit a-billing. 366
"how like a jade he stood, tied to the tree, 391
fed, | his other agents aim at like delight? 400
like a red morn, that ever yet betoken'd | wrack 453
staineth, | or like the deadly bullet of a gun, 461
like the fair sun, when in his fresh array | he 483
shone like the moon in water seen by night. 492
like a wild bird being tam'd with too much 560
or like the froward infant still'd with dandling 562
affection faints not like a pale-fac'd coward, 569
like lawn being spread upon the blushing rose, 590
still, | like to a mortal butcher bent to kill. 618
his eyes like glow-worms shine when he doth fret 621
but, like an earthquake, shakes thee on my 648
on his back doth lie | an image like thyself, 664
goes | are like a labyrinth to amaze his foes. 684
your treatise makes me like you worse and worse. 774
bewitching like the wanton mermaids' songs, 777
"love comforteth like sunshine after rain, | but 799
love surfeits not, lust like a glutton dies; 803
like shrill-tongu'd tapsters answering every 849
like a milch doe, whose swelling dugs do ache, 875
whereat she starts like one that spies an adder 878
like soldiers when their captain once doth yield 893
like milk and blood being mingled both together, 902
like the proceedings of a drunken brain, | full 910
who like sluices stopp'd | the crystal tide that 956
but like a stormy day, now wind, now rain, 965
like many clouds consulting for foul weather. 972
being prison'd in her eye like pearls in glass, 980
like stars asham'd of day, themselves withdrew. 1032
who, like a king perplexed in his throne, | by 1043
sun and sharp air | lurk'd like two thieves, to 1086
"had i been tooth'd like him, i must confess, 1117
kill'd | was melted like a vapor from her sight, 1166
that what is vile shows like a virtuous deed. LUC 252
like little frosts that sometime threat the 331
where like a virtuous monument she lies, | to be 391
white | show'd like an april daisy on the grass, 395
her eyes like marigolds had sheath'd their light 397
her hair like golden threads play'd with her 400
her breasts like ivory globes circled with blue, 407
who like a foul usurper went about | from this 412
like straggling slaves for pillage fighting, 428
like to a new-kill'd bird she trembling lies; 457
first like a trumpet doth his tongue begin | to 470
which, like a falcon tow'ring in the skies, 506
like a white hind under the gripe's sharp claws, 543
thou look'st not like deceit, do not deceive me. 585
my sighs like whirlwinds labor hence to heave 586
"all which together, like a troubled ocean, 589
for kings like gods should govern every thing. 602
when they in thee the like offenses prove. 613
till, like a jade, self-will himself doth tire. 707
like to a bankrout beggar wails his case: 711
he like a thievish dog creeps sadly thence, 736
she like a wearied lamb lies panting there; 737
and grave, like water that doth eat in steel, 755
but like still-pining tantalus he sits, | and 858
but if the like the snow-white swan desire, 1011
tongue shall utter all, mine eyes like sluices, 1076
like an unpractic'd swimmer plunging still, 1098
when with like semblance it is sympathiz'd. 1113
deep woes roll forward like a gentle flood, 1118
set, | each flow'r moist'ned like a melting eye, 1227
which makes the maid weep like the dewy night. 1232
like ivory conduits coral cesterns filling: 1234
their smoothness, like a goodly champaign plain, 1247
much like a press of people at a door, | throng 1301
like dying coals burnt out in tedious nights. 1379
seemed to appear | (like bright things stain'd) 1435
woes, | for sorrow, like a heavy hanging bell, 1493
but like a constant and confirmed devil, | he 1513
whose words like wildfire burnt the shining 1523
blue circles stream'd, like rainbows in the sky. 1587
both stood like old acquaintance in a trance, 1595
who, like a late-sack'd island, vastly stood 1740
that like two spirits do suggest me still: PP 2. 2
those thoughts to me like oaks, to thee like 5. 4
to me like oaks, to thee like osiers bowed. 5. 4
like a green plum that hangs upon a tree, | and 10. 5
as if the boy should use like loving charms; 11. 8
youth like summer morn, age like winter weather, 12. 3
youth like summer morn, age like winter weather, 12. 3
youth like summer brave, age like winter bare. 12. 4
youth like summer brave, age like winter bare. 12. 4
"wander," a word for shadows like myself, | as 14.11
and wish her lays were tuned like the lark. 14.18
like a thousand vanquish'd men in bloody fight! 17.24
/lass, thy like ne'er was | for a sweet content, 17.33
words are easy, like the wind, | faithful 20.31
car, | like feeble age he reeleth from the day, SON 7.10
the world will wail thee like a makeless wife, 9. 4
scorn'd, like old men of less truth than tongue, 17.10
let them say more that like of hearsay well, | i 21.13
which, like a jewel hung in ghastly night, 27.11
wishing me like to one more rich in hope, 29. 5
hope, | featur'd like him, like him with friends 29. 6
like him, like him with friends possess'd, 29. 6
(like to the lark at break of day arising | from 29.11
like stones of worth they thinly placed are, 52. 7
but you like none, none you, for constant heart. 53.14
let this sad int'rim like the ocean be | which 56. 9
but like a sad slave stay and think of nought 57.11
like as the waves make towards the pibbled shore 60. 1
while shadows like to thee do mock my sight? 61. 4
and, like unlettered clerk, still cry "amen" 85. 6
and like enough thou know'st thy estimate; 87. 2
like a deceived husband, so love's face | may 93. 2
how like eve's apple doth thy beauty grow, | if 93.13
which, like a canker in the fragrant rose, 95. 2
if like a lamb he could his looks translate! 96.10
how like a winter hath my absence been | from 97. 1
like widowed wombs after their lords' decease: 97. 8
therefore, like her, i sometime hold my tongue, 102.13
ah, yet doth beauty, like a dial hand, | steal 104. 9
sweet boy, but yet, like prayers divine, | i 108. 5
rang'd, | like him that travels i return again, 109. 6
to what it works in, like the dyer's hand. 111. 7
whilst like a willing patient i will drink 111. 9
like as to make our appetites more keen, | with 118. 1
my mistress' eyes are nothing like the sun; 130. 1
grace, | and suit thy pity like in every part. 132.12
which like two spirits do suggest me still: 144. 2
who like a fiend | from heaven to hell is flown 145.11
like usury, applying wet to wet, | or monarch's LC 40
like unshorn velvet on that termless skin, 94
like fools that in th' imagination set | the 136
which like a cherubin above them hover'd. 319

LIKED 1 FR 0.0001 REL FR 1 V 0 P
that liked of her master as well as well might PP 15. 2

LIKEL'EST 1 FR 0.0001 REL FR 0 V 1 P
he that is likel'est to a hogshead. LLL 4.02. 86 P

LIKELIEST 1 FR 0.0001 REL FR 0 V 1 P
they are your likeliest men, and i would have 2H4 3.02.255 P

/LIKELIHOOD 1 FR 0.0001 REL FR 1 V 0 P
tell me whereon the /likelihood depends. AYL 1.03. 57

LIKELIHOOD 13 FR 0.0014 REL FR 9 V 4 P
but what likelihood is in that? MM 4.02.187 P
shall bear no less likelihood than to see me at ADO 2.02. 42 P
shape | than i can lay it down in likelihood. 4.01.236
and by all likelihood some cheer is toward. SHR 5.01. 13
and shape of likelihood the news was told; 1H4 1.01. 58
a fellow of no mark nor likelihood. 3.02. 45
as, by a lower but by loving likelihood, | were H5 5.pr. 29
what likelihood of his amendment, lords? R3 1.03. 33
be put | to no apparent likelihood of breach, 2.02.136
with modesty enough and likelihood to lead it: HAM 5.01.208 P
what likelihood? OTH 4.02.138
that would by all likelihood have confounded one CYM 1.04. 50 P
a great likelihood | of both their pardons; TNK 4.01. 6

LIKELIHOODS 4 FR 0.0004 REL FR 3 V 1 P
these likelihoods confirm her flight from hence: TGV 5.02. 43
many likelihoods inform'd me of this before, AWW 1.03.123 P
to lay down likelihoods and forms of hope. 2H4 1.03. 35
than these thin habits and poor likelihoods | of OTH 1.03.108

/LIKELY 1 FR 0.0001 REL FR 1 V 0 P
/more /likely /to /fall /in /than /to /get /o'er 2H4 1.01.171

LIKELY 29 FR 0.0032 REL FR 24 V 5 P
this is most likely! MM 5.01.103
have not seen | so likely an embassador of love. MV 2.09. 92
true, | i never thought it possible or likely. SHR 1.01.149
chok'd the respect of likely peril fear'd, | and 2H4 1.01.184
grant that our hopes (yet likely of fair birth) 1.03. 63
'fore god, a likely fellow! 3.02.175 P
in france, | not seeing what is likely to ensue. 1H6 3.01.187
conqueror, | is likely to beget more conquerors, 5.05. 74
no, my lord, nor likely to be slain; 2H6 4.05. 2 P
me, | he's very likely now to fall from him, 3H6 3.03.209
crown, | as likely to be blest in peace and war; 4.06. 35
likely in time to bless a regal throne. 4.06. 74
'tis likely, | by all conjectures: H8 2.01. 40
most likely 'tis for you; COR 1.02. 16
this is most likely! 4.06. 69
here, | that he thereby may have a likely guess, TIT 2.03.207
then is it likely thou wilt undertake | a thing ROM 4.01. 73
and is very likely to load our purposes | with TIM 5.01. 14
for he was likely, had he been put on, | to have HAM 5.02.397
have you heard of no likely wars toward, 'twixt LR 2.01. 10 P
a likely piece of work, that you should find it OTH 4.01.151 P
saw i figures | so likely to report themselves. CYM 2.04. 83
it is not likely | that when they hear their 4.04. 16
most likely, sir. PER 3.02. 78
what my thoughts | did warrant me was likely. 5.01.134
nay, most likely, for they are noble suff'rers. TNK 2.01. 31 P
'tis likely. 4.01. 51
'twas ever likely: 5.03. 68
in likely thoughts the other kills thee quickly. VEN 990

/LIKENESS 1 FR 0.0001 REL FR 1 V 0 P
/that /comes /in /likeness /of /a //coal-black TIT 3.02. 78

LIKENESS 24 FR 0.0027 REL FR 17 V 7 P
thou beest a man, show thyself in thy likeness. TMP 3.02.128 P
how may likeness made in crimes, | making MM 3.02.273
to my house in the likeness of your grace, for ADO 1.01.100 P
now, in thy likeness, one more fool appear! LLL 4.03. 44
beguile, | neighing in likeness of a filly foal; MND 2.01. 46
bowl, | in very likeness of a roasted crab, 2.01. 48
for here he comes in the likeness of a jew. MV 3.01. 20 P
so her dead likeness, i do well believe, WT 5.03. 15
here | in likeness of a new untrimmed bride. JN 3.01.209
thou old adam's likeness, set to dress this R2 3.04. 73
haunts thee in the likeness of an old fat man, a 1H4 2.04.447 P
stafford dear to-day hath bought | thy likeness, 5.03. 8
her, that he will appear in his true likeness. H5 5.02.290 P
if conjure up love in her in his true likeness, 5.02.294 P
take that, the likeness of this railer here. 3H6 5.05. 38
appear thou in the likeness of a sigh! ROM 2.01. 8
lie, | that in thy likeness thou appear to us! 2.01. 21
and in this borrowed likeness of shrunk death 4.01.104
do not assume my likeness. TIM 4.03.218
honesty can translate beauty into his likeness. HAM 3.01.113 P
that full issue | for which i raz'd my likeness. LR 1.04. 4
in that thy likeness still is left alive." VEN 174
"in tarquin's likeness i did entertain thee; LUC 596
who leaves unsway'd the likeness of a man, | thy SON 141.11

LIKER 3 FR 0.0003 REL FR 3 V 0 P
the liker you; few taller are so young. LLL 5.02.836
boy | liker in feature to his father geffrey JN 2.01.126
much liker than your painted counterfeit: SON 16. 8

LIKES* 29 FR 0.0032 REL FR 24 V 5 P
my foolish rival, that her father likes | (only TGV 2.04.174
why, ev'n what fashion thou best likes, lucetta. 2.07. 52
the music likes you not. 4.02. 55 P
you mistake; the musician likes me not. 4.02. 57 P
how likes she my discourse? 5.02. 15
it to the mood | of what it likes or loathes. MV 4.01. 52
it likes me well. SHR 4.04. 62
conceives by me! how likes hortensio that? 5.02. 23
how likes gremio these quick-witted folks? 5.02. 38
marry, ill, to like him that ne'er it likes. AWW 1.01.153 P
in fortune nature brings | to join like likes, 1.01.223
that is entertainment | my bosom likes not, nor WT 1.02.119
it likes us well, young princes; JN 2.01.533
the offer likes not; H5 3.pr. 32
not so, my liege, this lodging likes me better, 4.01. 16
which likes me better than to wish us one. 4.03. 77
the widow likes him not, she knits her brows. 3H6 3.02. 82
the widow likes it not, for she looks very sad. 3.02.110
there's some conceit or other likes him well, R3 3.04. 49
as long as hell and richard likes of it. 4.04.354
but that that likes not you pleases me best. TRO 5.02.102 P
that noble minds keep ever with their likes; JC 1.02.311
it likes us well, | and at our more considered HAM 2.02. 80
why then belike he likes it not, perdy. 3.02.294
this likes me well. 5.02.265
his countenance likes me not. LR 2.02. 90
and the general so likes your music, that he OTH 3.01. 12 P
to her | what i shall be advis'd she likes. TNK 1.03. 16
distress likes dumps when time is kept with LUC 1127

LIKEST 1 FR 0.0001 REL FR 1 V 0 P
and earthly power doth then show likest god's MV 4.01.196

LIKEWISE 27 FR 0.0030 REL FR 23 V 4 P
and i likewise will visit thee with mine. TGV 1.01. 60
i likewise hear that valentine is dead. 4.02.112
that likewise have we thought upon, and thus: WIV 4.04. 47
that he shall likewise shuffle her away, | while 4.06. 29
likewise hath | made promise to the doctor. 4.06. 33
i would require is likewise your own benefit. MM 3.01.155 P
my woes end likewise with the evening sun. ERR 1.01. 27
me up, i likewise give her most humble thanks; ADO 1.01.239 P
and where we are, our learning likewise is. LLL 4.03.311
do we not likewise see our learning there? 4.03.314
the error that love makes | is likewise yours. 5.02.772
that's likewise part of my intelligence; WT 4.02. 45 P
was likewise a snapper–up of unconsider'd 4.03. 25 P
pay, | and liquor likewise will i give to thee, H5 2.01.108
to us | than cambridge is, hath likewise sworn. 2.02. 93
most of the rest slaughter'd or took likewise. 1H6 1.01.147
i would his troubles likewise were expir'd, 2.05. 31
unmoan'd, | your widow–dolor likewise be unwept! R3 2.02. 65
lest that thy love prove likewise variable. ROM 2.02.111
for lo | my intercession likewise steads my foe. 2.03. 54
he likewise enrich'd poor straggling soldiers TIM 5.01. 6
and good | he likewise gives a frock or livery, HAM 3.04.164
this likewise is a friend. OTH 2.01. 95
which you might from relation likewise reap, CYM 2.04. 86
hast likewise blest a /place | with thy sole TNK 3.01. 10
made | may likewise be sepulcher'd in thy shade. LUC 805
that they their passions likewise lent me | of LC 199
LIKING* 32 FR 0.0036 REL FR 23 V 9 P
have an eye to make difference of men's liking: WIV 2.01. 57 P
striking | kills for faults of his own liking! MM 3.02.268
hand | than to drive liking to the name of love. ADO 1.01.300
but lest my liking might too sudden seem, | i 1.01.314
if i had my liberty, i would do my liking. 1.03. 36 P
know | how much an ill word may empoison liking. 3.01. 86
my heart is with your liking. 5.04. 32
into so strong a liking with old sir rowland's AYL 1.03. 28 P
changeable, longing and liking, proud, 3.02.411 P
i met, | upon agreement from us to his liking, SHR 1.02.182
love concerneth us to add | her father's liking, 3.02.129
might one do, sir, to lose it to her own liking? AWW 1.01.151 P
did ever in so true a flame of liking | wish 1.03.211
the king had married him | against his liking. 3.05. 54
drives me to these habits of her liking. TN 2.05.169 P
strive to qualify, | and bring him up to liking. WT 4.04.533
most sorry, you have broken from his liking, 5.01.212
that any thing he sees, which moves his liking, JN 2.01.512
and that suddenly, while i am in some liking. 1H4 3.03. 6 P
prince broke thy head for liking his father to a 2H4 2.01. 90 P
as, liking of the lady's virtuous gifts, | her 1H6 5.01. 43
as being thought to contradict your liking, 2H6 3.02.252
your anger did i | continue in my liking? H8 2.04. 33
and feebling such as stand not in their liking COR 1.01.195
i'll look to like, if looking liking move; ROM 1.03. 97
you | t' avert your liking a more worthier way LR 1.01.211
not to have it | hath lost me in your liking. 1.01.233
with whom the father liking took, | and her to PER 1.ch. 25
hope she had fix'd her liking on this gentleman, TNK 4.03. 65 P
open'd their mouths to swallow venus' liking. VEN 248
the hot charge, and bids them do their liking. LUC 434
he, | 'unless thou yoke thy liking to my will, 1633
LIKINGS 2 FR 0.0002 REL FR 1 V 1 P
another tale, if matters grow to your likings. WIV 1.01. 78 P
and needs no other suitor but his likings | /to OTH 3.01. 48
LIK'NED 1 FR 0.0001 REL FR 1 V 0 P
blood, | were lik'ned oft to kingly sepulchres; 3H6 5.02. 20
LIK'ST 4 FR 0.0004 REL FR 2 V 2 P
i pray thee tell me truly how thou lik'st her. ADO 1.01.178 P
i love thee well in that thou lik'st it not. SHR 4.03. 83
how lik'st thou this picture, apemantus? TIM 1.01.195 P
i heard thee say even now, thou lik'st not that, OTH 3.03.109
LILIES 4 FR 0.0004 REL FR 4 V 0 P
lilies of all kinds, | the flow'r–de–luce being WT 4.04.126
of nature's gifts thou mayst with lilies boast, JN 3.01. 53
this silent war of lilies and of roses, | which LUC 71
lilies that fester smell far worse than weeds. SON 94.14
LILY 17 FR 0.0019 REL FR 16 V 1 P
she is as white as a lily and as small as a wand TGV 2.03. 20 P
yet as pure | as the unsallied lily, i protest, LLL 5.02.352
these lily lips, | this cherry nose, | these MND 5.01.330
to gild refined gold, to paint the lily, | to JN 4.02. 11
like the lily, | that once was mistress of the H8 3.01.151
a most unspotted lily shall she pass | to th' 5.04. 61
had the monster seen those lily hands | tremble TIT 2.04. 44
upon a gath'red lily almost withered. 3.01.113
fresh lily, | and whiter than the sheets! CYM 2.02. 15
o sweetest, fairest lily! 4.02.201
gone, | she locks her lily fingers one in one. VEN 228
the hand, | a lily prison'd in a jail of snow, 362
whose wonted lily white | with purple tears, 1053
her lily hand her rosy cheek lies under, LUC 386
that even for anger makes the lily pale | and 478
a lily pale, with damask dye to grace her, PP 7. 5
the lily i condemned for thy hand, | and buds of SON 99. 6
LILY–BEDS 1 FR 0.0001 REL FR 1 V 0 P
where i may wallow in the lily–beds | propos'd TRO 3.02. 12
LILY–LIVER'D 2 FR 0.0002 REL FR 1 V 1 P
and over–red thy fear, | thou lily–liver'd boy. MAC 5.03. 15
a lily–liver'd, action–taking, whoreson, LR 2.02. 17 P
LILY'S 1 FR 0.0001 REL FR 1 V 0 P
nor did i wonder at the lily's white, | nor SON 98. 9
LILY–TINCTURE 1 FR 0.0001 REL FR 1 V 0 P
and pinch'd the lily–tincture of her face, TGV 4.04.155
LILY–WHITE 1 FR 0.0001 REL FR 1 V 0 P
"most radiant pyramus, most lily–white of hue, MND 3.01. 93
LIMANDER *(also leander)*
LIMANDER 1 FR 0.0001 REL FR 1 V 0 P
and, like limander, am i trusty still. MND 5.01.196
LIMB 17 FR 0.0019 REL FR 14 V 3 P
hast neither heat, affection, limb, nor beauty, MM 3.01. 37
both strength of limb, and policy of mind, ADO 4.01.198
a brow, a breast, a waist, | a leg, a limb — LLL 4.03.184
because of his great limb or joint, shall pass 5.01.128 P
without some broken limb shall acquit him well. AYL 1.01.128 P
of him, | and learn to make a body of a limb. R2 3.02.187
a perilous gash, a very limb lopp'd off — | and 1H4 4.01. 43
care i for the limb, the thews, the stature, 2H4 3.02.258 P
our peace will, like a broken limb united, 4.01.220
his lady banish'd, and a limb lopp'd off. 2H6 2.03. 42
set limb to limb, and thou art far the lesser; 4.10. 47
set limb to limb, and thou art far the lesser; 4.10. 47
as i would buy thee, view thee limb by limb. TRO 4.05.238
as i would buy thee, view thee limb by limb. 4.05.238
o, he's a limb that has but a disease: COR 3.01.294
for antony is but a limb of caesar. JC 2.01.165
face seems twain, each several limb is doubled, VEN 1067
LIMBECK 1 FR 0.0001 REL FR 1 V 0 P
and the receipt of reason | a limbeck only. MAC 1.07. 67
LIMBECKS 1 FR 0.0001 REL FR 1 V 0 P
distill'd from limbecks foul as hell within, SON 119. 2
LIMBER 1 FR 0.0001 REL FR 1 V 0 P
you put me off with limber vows; WT 1.02. 47
LIMB–MEAL 1 FR 0.0001 REL FR 1 V 0 P
o, that i had her here, to tear her limb–meal! CYM 2.04.147
LIMBO 4 FR 0.0004 REL FR 2 V 2 P
no, he's in tartar limbo, worse than hell: ERR 4.02. 32
of sathan and of limbo and of furies and i know AWW 5.03.261 P
i have some of 'em in limbo patrum, and there H8 5.03. 64 P
this, | as far from help as limbo is from bliss! TIT 3.01.149
/LIMBS 2 FR 0.0002 REL FR 2 V 0 P
/entertain'd, /limbs /are /his /instruments, TRO 1.03.354
/swords /and /bows | /directive /by /the /limbs. 1.03.356
LIMBS 45 FR 0.0050 REL FR 42 V 3 P
let them keep their limbs whole and hack our WIV 3.01. 77 P
young in limbs, in judgment old, | your answer MV 2.07. 71
when service should in my old limbs lie lame, AYL 2.03. 41
those tender limbs of thine to the event | of AWW 3.02.104
one, | to wear your gentle limbs in my affairs, 5.01. 4
thy tongue, thy face, thy limbs, actions, and TN 1.05.292
to whom am i beholding for these limbs? JN 1.01.239
and hang a calve's–skin on those recreant limbs. 3.01.129
and hang a calve's–skin on those recreant limbs. 3.01.131
and hang a calve's–skin on those recreant limbs. 3.01.133
and hang a calve's–skin on his recreant limbs. 3.01.199
if i get down, and do not break my limbs, | i'll 4.03. 6
to crush our old limbs in ungentle steel. 1H4 5.01. 13
out of his keeper's arms, even so my limbs, 2H4 1.01.143
than 'a can part young limbs and lechery; 1.02.230 P
and let us choose such limbs of noble counsel 5.02.135
whose limbs were made in england, show us here H5 3.01. 26
so do our vulgar drench their peasant limbs | in 4.07. 77
and from my weary limbs | honor is cudgell'd. 5.01. 84
and large proportion of his strong–knit limbs. 1H6 2.03. 21
rack, | so fare my limbs with long imprisonment; 2.05. 4
drops bloody sweat from his war–wearied limbs, 4.04. 18
when sapless age and weak unable limbs | should 4.05. 4
and so he comes, to rend his limbs asunder. 3H6 1.03. 15
the noble isle doth want /her proper limbs; R3 3.07.125
who set the body and the limbs | of this great H8 1.01. 46
these are the limbs o' th' plot. 1.01.220
have you limbs | to bear that load of title? 2.03. 38
of tower–hill or the limbs of limehouse, their 5.03. 62 P
he had rather venture all his limbs for honor COR 2.02. 80
that we may hew his limbs and on a pile | ad TIT 1.01. 97
let's hew his limbs till they be clean consum'd. 1.01.129
alarbus' limbs are lopp'd, | and entrails feed 1.01.143
should drive upon thy new–transformed limbs, 2.03. 64
sheaf, | these broken limbs again into one body. 5.03. 72
with unstuff'd brain | doth couch his limbs, ROM 2.03. 38
and strew this hungry churchyard with thy limbs. 5.03. 36
that their limbs may halt | as lamely as their TIM 4.01. 24
have thews and limbs like to their ancestors; JC 1.03. 81
to cut the head off and then hack the limbs — 2.01.163
a curse shall light upon the limbs of men; 3.01.262
and tediousness the limbs and outward flourishes HAM 2.02. 91
in mincing with his sword her /husband's limbs, 2.02.514
the dear repose for limbs with travel tired, SON 27. 2
lo thus by day my limbs, by night my mind, | for 27.13
LIM'D 6 FR 0.0006 REL FR 4 V 2 P
but that they are lim'd with the twigs that AWW 3.05. 24 P
i have lim'd her, but it is jove's doing, and TN 3.04. 74 P
madam, myself have lim'd a bush for her, | and 2H6 1.03. 88
have all lim'd bushes to betray thy wings, | and 2.04. 54
in my eye | where my poor young was lim'd, was 3H6 5.06. 17
birds never lim'd no secret bushes fear: LUC 88
/LIME 1 FR 0.0001 REL FR 0 V 1 P
let me see thee froth and /lime. WIV 1.03. 14 P
LIME 11 FR 0.0012 REL FR 7 V 4 P
monster, come put some lime upon your fingers, TMP 4.01.245 P
you must lay lime to tangle her desires | by TGV 3.02. 68
this man, with lime and rough–cast, doth present MND 5.01.131
would you desire lime and hair to speak better? 5.01.165 P
thy stones with lime and hair knit /up /in /thee 5.01.191
by this time from their fixed beds of lime | had JN 2.01.219
lies | within the limits of yon lime and stone, R2 3.03. 26
you rogue, here's lime in this sack too. 1H4 2.04.124 P
is worse than a cup of sack with lime in it. 2.04.126 P
who gave his blood to lime the stones together, 3H6 5.01. 84
poor bird, thou'dst never fear the net nor lime, MAC 4.02. 34
LIMED 3 FR 0.0003 REL FR 3 V 0 P
she's limed, i warrant you. ADO 3.01.104
the bird that hath been limed in a bush, | with 3H6 5.06. 13
o limed soul, that, struggling to be free, | art HAM 3.03. 68
LIME–GROVE *(see line–grove)*
LIMEHOUSE 1 FR 0.0001 REL FR 0 V 1 P
of tower–hill or the limbs of limehouse, their H8 5.03. 62 P
LIME–KILL 1 FR 0.0001 REL FR 0 V 1 P
is as hateful to me as the reek of a lime–kill. WIV 3.03. 79 P
LIME–KILLS 1 FR 0.0001 REL FR 0 V 1 P
sciaticas, lime–kills i' th' palm, incurable TRO 5.01. 21 P
LIME–TWIGS 1 FR 0.0001 REL FR 1 V 0 P
like lime–twigs set to catch my winged soul. 2H6 3.03. 16
LIMIT 20 FR 0.0022 REL FR 16 V 4 P
as my trust was, which had indeed no limit, | a TMP 1.02. 96
i, | beyond all limit of what else i' th' world, 3.01. 72
time of the contract and limit of the solemnity, MM 3.01.215 P
i'll limit thee this day | to seek thy /health ERR 1.01.150
breeds, therefore the sadness is without limit. ADO 1.03. 4 P
man, | within the limit of becoming mirth, | i LLL 2.01. 67
buried in highways out of all sanctified limit, AWW 1.01.140 P
open air, before | i have got strength of limit. WT 3.02.106
my mouth, | the farthest limit of my embassy. JN 1.01. 22
the dateless limit of thy dear exile; R2 1.03.151
so long as out of limit and true rule | you 1H4 4.03. 39
dispatch, the limit of your lives is out. R3 3.03. 8
alive, | i give a sparing limit to my tongue. 3.07.194
limit each leader to his several charge, | and 5.03. 25
is boundless and the act a slave to limit. TRO 3.02. 83 P
there is no end, no limit, measure, bound, | in ROM 3.02.125
or a debtor that not dares | to stride a limit. CYM 3.03. 35
"within this limit is relief enough, | sweet VEN 235
grief dallied with nor law nor limit knows. LUC 1120
hue, | finding thy worth a limit past my praise, SON 82. 6
LIMITATION 2 FR 0.0002 REL FR 2 V 0 P
you have stood your limitation, and the tribunes COR 2.03.138
but, as it were, in sort or limitation, | to JC 2.01.283
LIMITED 4 FR 0.0004 REL FR 3 V 1 P
how may i do it, having the hour limited, and an MM 4.02.166 P
the scope | and warrant limited unto my tongue. JN 5.02.123
is boundless theft | in limited professions. TIM 4.03.428
so bold to call, | for 'tis my limited service. MAC 2.03. 52
LIMITER 1 FR 0.0001 REL FR 1 V 0 P
port even where | the heavenly limiter pleases. TNK 5.01. 30
LIMITS 9 FR 0.0010 REL FR 8 V 1 P
yourself within the modest limits of order. TN 1.03. 9 P
so high above his limits swells the rage | of R2 3.02.109
lies | within the limits of yon lime and stone, 3.03. 26
and many limits of the charge set down | but 1H4 1.01. 35
divided it | into three limits very equally: 3.01. 72
i prithee give no limits to my tongue, | i am a 3H6 2.02.119
then into limits could i bind my woes: TIT 3.01.220
walls, | for stony limits cannot hold love out, ROM 2.02. 67
from limits far remote, where thou dost stay. SON 44. 4
LIMN'D 1 FR 0.0001 REL FR 1 V 0 P
most truly limn'd and living in your face, | be AYL 2.07.194
LIMNING 1 FR 0.0001 REL FR 1 V 0 P
life | in limning out a well–proportioned steed, VEN 290
LIMOGES *(see lymoges)*
LIMP 3 FR 0.0003 REL FR 3 V 0 P
this shadow | doth limp behind the substance. MV 3.02.129
why does the world report that kate doth limp? SHR 2.01.252
who like a foul and ugly witch doth limp | so H5 4.pr. 21
LIMP'D 1 FR 0.0001 REL FR 1 V 0 P
me hath many a weary step | limp'd in pure love; AYL 2.07.131
LIMPING 3 FR 0.0003 REL FR 3 V 0 P
april on the heel | of limping winter treads, ROM 1.02. 28
the lin'd crutch from thy old limping sire, TIM 4.01. 14
and strength by limping sway disabled, | and art SON 66. 8
LIMPS 1 FR 0.0001 REL FR 1 V 0 P
apish nation | limps after in base imitation. R2 2.01. 23
LINCOLN 2 FR 0.0002 REL FR 2 V 0 P
these lincoln washes have devoured them; JN 5.06. 41
began in private | with you, my lord of lincoln. H8 2.04.208
LINCOLNSHIRE 1 FR 0.0001 REL FR 0 V 1 P
yea, or the drone of a lincolnshire bagpipe. 1H4 1.02. 76 P
LIN'D* 8 FR 0.0009 REL FR 7 V 1 P
in fair round belly with good capon lin'd, AYL 2.07.154
all the pictures fairest lin'd | are but black 3.02. 92
wint'red garments must be lin'd, | so must 3.02.105
it was, my lord, who lin'd himself with hope, 2H4 1.03. 27
pluck the lin'd crutch from thy old limping sire TIM 4.01. 14
and when they have lin'd their coats, | do OTH 1.01. 53
out to be better lin'd than it can appear to me TNK 2.01. 5 P
his arms are brawny, | lin'd with strong sinews; 4.02.127
LINE* 44 FR 0.0049 REL FR 35 V 9 P
come, hang /them /on this line. TMP 4.01.193
mistress line, is not this my jerkin? 4.01.235 P
now is the jerkin under the line. 4.01.236 P
we steal by line and level, and't like your 4.01.239 P
"steal by line and level" is an excellent pass 4.01.243 P
lo, here in one line is his name twice writ, TGV 1.02.120
and frame some feeling line | that may discover 3.02. 75
place, | and with full line of his authority, MM 1.04. 56
with the stroke and line of his great justice. 4.02. 80
go to, here's a simple line of life! MV 2.02.160 P
of every line and trick of his sweet favor. AWW 1.01. 96
which warp'd the line of every other favor, 5.03. 49
though you perceive me not how i give line. WT 1.02.181
now doth death line his dead chaps with steel, JN 2.01.352
we will not line his thin bestained cloak | with 4.03. 24
home and discontents at home | meet in one line; 4.03.152
so low | to show the line and the predicament 1H4 1.03.168
and hath sent for you | to line his enterprise, 2.03. 83
and in that very line, harry, standest thou, 3.02. 85
hold hook and line, say i. 2H4 2.04.158 P
of the true line and stock of charles the great, H5 1.02. 71
the which marriage the line of charles the great 1.02. 84
to line and new repair our towns of war | with 2.04. 7
rak'd, | he sends you this most memorable line, 2.04. 88
being but fourth of that heroic line. 1H6 2.05. 78
clarence, from whose line | i claim the crown, 2H6 2.02. 34
such hope have all the line of john of gaunt! 3H6 1.01. 19
and till i root out their accursed line, | and 1.03. 32
all that stand about him are under the line, H8 5.03. 43 P
office, and custom, in all line of order; TRO 1.03. 88
or did line the rebel | with hidden help and MAC 1.03.112
they hail'd him father to a line of kings. 3.01. 59
will the line stretch out to th' crack of doom? 4.01.117
unfortunate souls | that trace him in his line. 4.01.153
if it live in your memory, begin at this line — HAM 2.02.449 P
when in one line two crafts directly meet. 3.04.210
all these bounds, even from this line to this, LR 1.01. 63
what | if i do line one of their hands? CYM 2.03. 67
he will line your apron with gold. PER 4.06. 58 P
let him lead his line | to catch one at my heart TNK 1.01.116
will tie the hearers to attend each line, | how LUC 818
nay, if you read this line, remember not | the SON 71. 5
away, | my life hath in this line some interest, 74. 3
but when your countenance fill'd up his line, 86.13
LINEAL 8 FR 0.0009 REL FR 8 V 0 P
our just and lineal entrance to our own; JN 2.01. 85
put on | the lineal state and glory of the land! 5.07.102
further scope | than for his lineal royalties, R2 3.03.113
it shall not force | this lineal honor from me. 2H4 4.05. 46
grandmother, | was lineal of the lady ermengare, H5 1.02. 82
from whence you spring by lineal descent. 1H6 3.01.165
birth, | the lineal glory of your royal house, R3 3.07.121
times | unto a lineal true–derived course. 3.07.200
LINEALLY 1 FR 0.0001 REL FR 1 V 0 P
from these our henry lineally descends. 3H6 3.03. 87
LINEAMENT 2 FR 0.0002 REL FR 2 V 0 P
in every lineament, branch, shape, and form; ADO 5.01. 14
examine every married lineament, | and see how ROM 1.03. 83

LINEAMENTS 7 FR 0.0008 REL FR 6 V 1 P
must be needs a like proportion | of lineaments, MV 3.04. 15
of the world, not in the lineaments of nature. AYL 1.02. 42 P
than any of her lineaments can show her. 3.05. 56
a happy gentleman in blood and lineaments, | by R2 3.01. 9
which well appeared in his lineaments, | being R3 3.05. 91
withal i did infer your lineaments, | being the 3.07. 12
all his lineaments | are as a man would wish 'em TNK 4.02.113
LINE–GROVE 1 FR 0.0001 REL FR 1 V 0 P
in the line–grove which weather–fends your cell; TMP 5.01. 10
LINEN 18 FR 0.0020 REL FR 5 V 13 P
creep in here, and throw foul linen upon him, as WIV 3.03.131 P
this 'tis to have linen and buck–baskets! 3.05.143 P
page and i will look some linen for your head. 4.02. 81 P
go up, i'll bring linen for him straight. 4.02.100 P
pluck me out all the linen. 4.02.149 P
it was enjoin'd him in rome for want of linen; LLL 5.02.713 P
in any case, let thisby have clean linen; MND 4.02. 40 P
fine linen, turkey cushions boss'd with pearl, SHR 2.01.353
with a linen stock on one leg and a kersey 3.02. 66 P
when the kite builds, look to lesser linen. WT 4.03. 24 P
one, they'll find linen enough on every hedge. 1H4 4.02. 48 P
for it is a low ebb of linen with thee when thou 2H4 2.02. 19 P
out the ruins of thy linen shall inherit his 2.02. 24 P
sir, for they have marvail's foul linen. 5.01. 35 P
those linen cheeks of thine | are counsellors to MAC 5.03. 16
senseless linen, happier therein than i! CYM 1.03. 7
get linen. PER 3.02.108
for with the nightly linen that she wears | he LUC 680
LINENS 1 FR 0.0001 REL FR 1 V 0 P
give us, with | rich garments, linens, stuffs, TMP 1.02.164
/LINES 1 FR 0.0001 REL FR 1 V 0 P
yea, watch | his /pettish /lines, his ebbs, /his TRO 2.03.130
LINES 36 FR 0.0040 REL FR 28 V 8 P
i fear my julia would not deign my lines, TGV 1.01.152
dare you presume to harbor wanton lines? 1.02. 42
sweet love, sweet lines, sweet life! 1.03. 45
me to write some lines to one she loves. 2.01. 87 P
the lines are very quaintly writ, | but (since 2.01.122
i will not look upon your master's lines; 4.04.128
woman, your husband is in his old lines again. WIV 4.02. 22 P
i fear these stubborn lines lack power to move. LLL 4.03. 53
did these rent lines show some love of thine? 4.03.216
o, then his lines would ravish savage ears | and 4.03.345
his face into more lines than is in the new map, TN 3.02. 79 P
looking on the lines | of my boy's face, WT 1.02.153
is much more general than these lines import. JN 4.03. 17
as many lines close in the dial's centre; H5 1.02.210
com'st thou with deep premeditated lines, | with 1H6 3.01. 1
them) | would make a volume of enticing lines, 5.05. 14
lines of fair comfort and encouragement. R3 5.02. 6
and sends them weapons wrapp'd about with lines
TIT 4.02. 27
do | see here in bloody lines i have set down: 5.02. 14
wretched stump, witness these crimson lines, 5.02. 22
and yon grey lines | that fret the clouds are JC 2.01.103
were no sallets in the lines to make the matter HAM 2.02.442 P
study a speech of some dozen lines, or sixteen 2.02.541 P
a speech of some dozen lines, or sixteen lines, 2.02.542 P
do, i had as live the town–crier spoke my lines. 3.02. 4 P
the lines of my body are as well drawn as his; CYM 4.01. 9 P
time hath nothing blurr'd those lines of favor 4.02.104
so should the lines of life that life repair SON 16. 9
when in eternal lines to time thou grow'st. 18.12
nor draw no lines there with thine antique pen; 19.10
these poor rude lines of thy deceased lover, 32. 4
and fill'd his brow | with lines and wrinkles, 63. 4
his beauty shall in these black lines be seen, 63.13
dulling my lines, and doing me disgrace. 103. 8
those lines that i before have writ do lie, 115. 1
this said, in top of rage the lines she rents, LC 55
/LING 1 FR 0.0001 REL FR 0 V 1 P
our old /ling and our isbels a' th' country are AWW 3.02. 13 P
LING 1 FR 0.0001 REL FR 0 V 1 P
nothing like your old ling and your isbels a' AWW 3.02. 14 P
LINGARE 1 FR 0.0001 REL FR 1 V 0 P
himself as th' heir to th' lady lingare, H5 1.02. 74
LINGER 11 FR 0.0012 REL FR 11 V 0 P
but if thou linger in my territories | longer TGV 3.01.163
fool i shall appear | by the time i linger here. MV 2.09. 74
linger your patience on, and we'll digest | th' H5 2.pr. 31
then linger not, my lord, away, take horse. 2H6 4.04. 54
come, son, away, we may not linger thus. 3H6 1.01.263
why do we linger thus? 1.02. 32
why linger we? let us lay hands upon him. 3.01. 26
and linger not our sure destructions on! TRO 5.10. 9
pent to linger | but with a grain a day, i would COR 3.03. 89
i would not have thee linger in thy pain. OTH 5.02. 88
morrow, | to linger out a purpos'd overthrow. SON 90. 8
LINGER'D 2 FR 0.0002 REL FR 1 V 1 P
we have linger'd about a match between anne page
WIV 3.02. 57 P
say that i linger'd with you at your shop | to ERR 3.01. 3
LINGERS 4 FR 0.0004 REL FR 2 V 2 P
she lingers my desires, | like to a step–dame, MND 1.01. 4
life, | which false hope lingers in extremity. R2 2.02. 72
borrowing only lingers and lingers it out, but 2H4 1.02.237 P
borrowing only lingers and lingers it out, but 1.02.237 P
LING'RED 1 FR 0.0001 REL FR 0 V 1 P
unless his abode be ling'red here by some OTH 4.02.226 P
LING'RING 13 FR 0.0014 REL FR 13 V 0 P
and do pronounce by me | ling'ring perdition TMP 3.03. 77
his death draw out | to ling'ring sufferance. MM 2.04.167
from which ling'ring penance | of such misery MV 4.01.271
but with a ling'ring dram that should not work WT 1.02.320
a stage | to feed contention in a ling'ring act; 2H4 1.01.156
one would have ling'ring wars with little cost; 1H6 1.01. 74
and, in advantage ling'ring, looks for rescue, 4.04. 19
and torture him with grievous ling'ring death. 2H6 3.02.247
a speedier course /than ling'ring languishment TIT 2.01.110
stew'd in brine, | smarting in ling'ring pickle. ANT 2.05. 66
doth think she has | strange ling'ring poisons. CYM 1.05. 34
by the minute feed on life, and ling'ring, | by 5.05. 51
who with a ling'ring stay his course doth let, LUC 328
LINGUIST 2 FR 0.0002 REL FR 1 V 1 P
and by your own report | a linguist, and a man TGV 4.01. 55
the manifold linguist and the armipotent soldier AWW 4.03.236 P
LINING 2 FR 0.0002 REL FR 2 V 0 P
as bombast and as lining to the time; LLL 5.02.781
the lining of his coffers shall make coats | to R2 1.04. 61
LINK* 5 FR 0.0005 REL FR 4 V 1 P
to link my dear friend to a common stale. ADO 4.01. 65
there was no link to color peter's hat, | and SHR 4.01.134
sir, a new link to the bucket must needs be had; 2H4 5.01. 22 P
to link with him that were not lawful chosen. 3H6 3.03.115
of more strong link asunder than can ever COR 1.01. 71
LINK'D 5 FR 0.0005 REL FR 5 V 0 P
and link'd together | with all religious JN 3.01.228
(as is fair margaret) he be link'd in love. 1H6 5.05. 76
they are so link'd in friendship | that young 3H6 4.01.116
so /lust, though to a radiant angel link'd, HAM 1.05. 55
whose love is never link'd to the deserver ANT 1.02.186
LINKS* 2 FR 0.0002 REL FR 1 V 1 P
sav'd me a thousand marks in links and torches, 1H4 3.03. 42 P
nor airless dungeon, nor strong links of iron, JC 1.03. 94
LINSEY–WOOLSEY 1 FR 0.0001 REL FR 0 V 1 P
but what linsey–woolsey hast thou to speak to us AWW 4.01. 11 P
LINSTOCK 1 FR 0.0001 REL FR 1 V 0 P
with linstock now the devilish cannon touches, H5 3.pr. 33
LINTA 1 FR 0.0001 REL FR 1 V 0 P
acordo linta. AWW 4.01. 87
/LION 2 FR 0.0002 REL FR 2 V 0 P
now the hungry /lion roars, | and the wolf MND 5.01.371
/the /lion /and /the //belly–pinched /wolf LR 3.01. 13
LION 88 FR 0.0099 REL FR 57 V 31 P
had i been seized by a hungry lion, | i would TGV 5.04. 33
slip, | even like an o'ergrown lion in a cave, MM 1.03. 22
in the figure of a lamb, the feats of a lion. ADO 1.01. 15 P
thus dost thou hear the nemean lion roar LLL 4.01. 88
your lion, that holds his poll–axe sitting on a 5.02.576 P
and thou wert a lion, we would do so. 5.02.624
let me play the lion too. MND 1.02. 70 P
then she waking looks upon | (be it on lion, 2.01.180
will not the ladies be afeard of the lion? 3.01. 27 P
a lion among ladies, is a most dreadful thing; 3.01. 30 P
a more fearful wild–fowl than your lion living; 3.01. 32 P
another prologue must tell he is not a lion. 3.01. 35 P
if you think i come hither as a lion, it were 3.01. 42 P
let not him that plays the lion pare his nails, 4.02. 41 P
this grisly beast, which lion hight by name, 5.01.139
which lion vile with bloody mouth did stain. 5.01.143
let lion, moonshine, wall, and lovers twain | at 5.01.150
i wonder if the lion be to speak. 5.01.152 P
one lion may, when many asses do. 5.01.153 P
here come two noble beasts in, a man and a lion. 5.01.218 P
when lion rough in wildest rage doth roar. 5.01.222
know that i as snug the joiner am | a lion fell, 5.01.224
if i should as lion come in strife | into this 5.01.225
this lion is a very fox for his valor. 5.01.231 P
well roar'd, lion. 5.01.265 P
well mous'd, lion. 5.01.269 P
and so the lion vanish'd. 5.01.271 P
since lion vild hath here deflow'r'd my dear; 5.01.292
moonshine and lion are left to bury the dead. 5.01.348 P
yea, mock the lion when 'a roars for prey, | to MV 2.01. 30
heart had been wounded with the claws of a lion. AYL 5.02. 23 P
the hind that would be mated by the lion | must AWW 1.01. 91
'twere | i met the ravin lion when he roar'd 3.02.117
better | to fall before the lion than the wolf! TN 3.01.129
the aweless lion could not wage the fight, | nor JN 1.01.266
richard, that robb'd the lion of his heart, 2.01. 3
robe, | that did disrobe the lion of that robe! 2.01.142
o, tremble! for you hear the lion roar. 2.01.294
by the tongue, | a cased lion by the mortal paw, 3.01.259
what, shall they seek the lion in his den, | and 5.01. 57
war, | that, like a lion fostered up at hand, 5.02. 75
in war was never lion rag'd more fierce, | in R2 2.01.173
the lion dying thrusteth forth his paw, | and 5.01. 29
which art a lion and the king of beasts? 5.01. 34
or an old lion, or a lover's lute. 1H4 1.02. 75 P
stirs | to rouse a lion than to start a hare! 1.03.198
the lion will not touch the true prince. 2.04.271 P
i for a valiant lion, and thou for a true prince 2.04.274 P
raven, | a couching lion and a ramping cat, 3.01.151
in strange concealments, valiant as a lion, 3.01.165
and why not as the lion? 3.03.148 P
the king himself is to be fear'd as the lion. 3.03.149 P
check'd him for it, and the young lion repents, 2H4 1.02.197 P
so that his power, like to a fangless lion, 4.01.216
should with his lion gait walk the whole world, H5 2.02.122
dare eat his breakfast on the lip of a lion. 3.07.146 P
and like a hungry lion did commence | rough 1H6 4.07. 7
but great men tremble when the lion roars, | and 2H6 3.01. 19
that winter lion, who in rage forgets | aged 5.03. 2
so looks the pent–up lion o'er the wretch | that 3H6 1.03. 12
troop | as doth a lion in a herd of neat, | or 2.01. 14
and when the lion fawns upon the lamb, | the 4.08. 49
under whose shade the ramping lion slept, 5.02. 13
that in their chains fetter'd the kingly lion, 5.07. 11
so looks the chafed lion | upon the daring H8 3.02.206
he is as valiant as the lion, churlish as the TRO 1.02. 21 P
and thou shalt hunt a lion that will fly | with 4.01. 20
in you, | which better fits a lion than a man. 5.03. 38
he is a lion | that i am proud to hunt. COR 1.01.235
the lion, mov'd with pity, did endure | to have TIT 2.03.151
she's with the lion deeply still in league, 4.01. 98
and the ass more captain than the lion, the TIM 3.05. 49
if thou wert the lion, the fox would beguile 4.03.328 P
thou wert the fox, the lion would suspect thee, 4.03.330 P
thou wert germane to the lion, and the spots of 4.03.341 P
my sword — | against the capitol i met a lion, JC 1.03. 20
and roars | as doth the lion in the capitol — 1.03. 75
he were no lion, were not romans hinds. 1.03.106
or the hare the lion. MAC 1.02. 35
in greediness, dog in madness, lion in prey. LR 3.04. 94 P
offenseless dog to affright an imperious lion. OTH 2.03.275 P
a vapor sometime like a bear or lion, | a ANT 4.14. 3
within him, | and as a heated lion so he looks; TNK 4.02. 82
being ireful, on the lion he will venter. VEN 628
but the blunt boar, rough bear, or lion proud, 884
"to see his face the lion walk'd along | behind 1093
as the grim lion fawneth o'er his prey, | sharp LUC 421
slaughter, | to tame the unicorn and lion wild, 956
LIONEL 4 FR 0.0004 REL FR 4 V 0 P
his grandfather was lionel duke of clarence, 1H6 2.04. 83
i derived am | from lionel duke of clarence, 2.05. 75
and the third, | lionel duke of clarence; 2H6 2.02. 13
sole daughter unto lionel duke of clarence; 2.02. 50
LIONEL'S 1 FR 0.0001 REL FR 1 V 0 P
till lionel's issue fails, his should not reign. 2H6 2.02. 56
LIONESS 7 FR 0.0008 REL FR 7 V 0 P
bush, under which bush's shade | a lioness, with AYL 4.03.114
there, | food to the suck'd and hungry lioness? 4.03.126
occasion, | made him give battle to the lioness, 4.03.130
his arm | the lioness had torn some flesh away, 4.03.147
home, | at your den, sirrah, with your lioness, JN 2.01.291
moor, | the chafed boar, the mountain lioness, TIT 4.02.138
a lioness hath whelped in the streets, | and JC 2.02. 17
LION–METTLED 1 FR 0.0001 REL FR 1 V 0 P
be lion–mettled, proud, and take no care | who MAC 4.01. 90
LION'S 21 FR 0.0023 REL FR 14 V 7 P
snug, the joiner, you the lion's part. MND 1.02. 64 P
have you the lion's part written? 1.02. 66 P
his face must be seen through the lion's neck, 3.01. 37 P
for they shall hang out for the lion's claws. 4.02. 42 P
joiner am | a lion fell, nor else no lion's dam, 5.01.224
dew, | and saw the lion's shadow ere himself, MV 5.01. 8
o, well did he become that lion's robe, | that JN 2.01.141
i would set an ox–head to your lion's hide, 2.01.292
thou wear a lion's hide! 3.01.128
turns head against the lion's armed jaws, | and, 1H4 3.02.102
thee as i fear the roaring of the lion's whelp. 3.03.147 P
hill | stood smiling to behold his lion's whelp H5 1.02.109
the man that once did sell the lion's skin 4.03. 93
and, like /a dewdrop from the lion's mane, | be TRO 3.03.224
this body | as hardy as the nemean lion's nerve. HAM 1.04. 83
'tis better playing with a lion's whelp | than ANT 3.13. 94
"when as a lion's whelp shall, to himself CYM 5.04.138 P
"when as a lion's whelp shall, to himself 5.05.435 P
thou, leonatus, art the lion's whelp; 5.05.443
save this, which is the lion's and the bear's, TNK 1.01. 53
devouring time, blunt thou the lion's paws, SON 19. 1
LIONS' 1 FR 0.0001 REL FR 1 V 0 P
renounce your soil, give sheep in lions' stead: 1H6 1.05. 29
LIONS 25 FR 0.0028 REL FR 22 V 3 P
of bellowing | like bulls, or rather lions. TMP 2.01.312
sure it was the roar | of a whole herd of lions. 2.01.316
when you walk'd, to walk like one of the lions; TGV 2.01. 28 P
law, | as mice by lions) hath pick'd out an act, MM 1.04. 64
o, wherefore, nature, didst thou lions frame? MND 5.01.291
have i not in my time heard lions roar? SHR 1.02.200
he that perforce robs lions of their hearts JN 1.01.268
whose valor plucks dead lions by the beard; 2.01.138
lions more confident, mountains and rocks | more 2.01.452
talks as familiarly of roaring lions | as maids 2.01.459
lions make leopards tame. R2 1.01.174
you are lions too, you ran away upon instinct, 1H4 2.04.299 P
as did the former lions of your blood. H5 1.02.124
the other lords, like lions wanting food, | do 1H6 1.02. 27
or tear the lions out of england's coat; 1.05. 28
to whom do lions cast their gentle looks? 3H6 2.02. 11
whiles lions war and battle for their dens, 2.05. 74
have the voice of lions and the act of hares, TRO 3.02. 88 P
where he should find you lions, finds you hares; COR 1.01.171
lions with toils, and men with flatterers; JC 2.01.206
we /are two lions litter'd in one day, | and i 2.02. 46
should have shook lions into civil streets, ANT 5.01. 16
and to grin like lions | upon the pikes o' th' CYM 5.03. 38
like to a pair of lions smear'd with prey, TNK 1.04. 18
require of him the hearts of lions and | the 5.01. 39
LION–SICK 1 FR 0.0001 REL FR 0 V 1 P
yes, lion–sick, sick of proud heart. TRO 2.03. 86 P
/LIP 1 FR 0.0001 REL FR 1 V 0 P
/on /her /ripe /lip /seem'd /not /to /know LR 4.03. 20
LIP 37 FR 0.0041 REL FR 28 V 9 P
there was a pretty redness in his lip, | a AYL 3.05.120
nor bite the lip, as angry wenches will, | nor SHR 2.01.248
nothing, has neither leg, hands, lip, nor cap; AWW 2.02. 11 P
knave, as the nun's lip to the friar's mouth, 2.02. 26 P
diana's lip | is not more smooth and rubious; TN 1.04. 31
in the contempt and anger of his lip! 3.01.146
kissing with inside lip? WT 1.02.286
contrary and falling | a lip of much contempt, 1.02.373
and copy of the father — eye, nose, lip, | the 2.03.100
you can bring | tincture or lustre in her lip, 3.02.205
the very life seems warm upon her lip. 5.03. 66
the ruddiness upon her lip is wet; 5.03. 81
and a foolish hanging of thy nether lip, that 1H4 2.04.405 P
dare eat his breakfast on the lip of a lion. H5 3.07.146 P
a cherry lip, a bonny eye, a passing pleasing R3 1.01. 94
teach not thy lip such scorn; 1.02.171
the king is angry, see, he gnaws his lip. 4.02. 27
he bites his lip, and starts, | stops on a H8 3.02.113
he hangs the lip at something. TRO 3.01.139 P
bites his lip with a politic regard, as who 3.03.254 P
there's language in her eye, her cheek, her lip, 4.05. 55
mark'd you his lip and eyes? COR 1.01.255
which time i will make a lip at the physician. 2.01.115 P
to bite his lip | and hum at good cominius much 5.01. 48
and my-true lip | hath virgin'd it e'er since. 5.03. 47
by her high forehead and her scarlet lip, | by ROM 2.01. 18
how big imagination | moves in this lip! TIM 1.01. 33
drinks | but timon's silver treads upon his lip, 3.02. 71
spur as he would to the lip of his mistress; 3.06. 66 P
arch–mock, | to lip a wanton in a secure couch, OTH 4.01. 71
to palestine for a touch of his nether lip. 4.03. 39 P
alas, why gnaw you so your nether lip? 5.02. 43
of love, | salt cleopatra, soften thy wan'd lip! ANT 2.01. 21
the juice of egypt's grape shall moist this lip. 5.02.282
haste, | i stamp this kiss upon thy currant lip. TNK 1.01.216
"the tender spring upon thy tempting lip | shows VEN 127
of hand, of foot, of lip, of eye, of brow, | i SON 106. 6
LIPP'D 1 FR 0.0001 REL FR 1 V 0 P
a hand that kings | have lipp'd, and trembled ANT 2.05. 30
LIPS' 3 FR 0.0003 REL FR 3 V 0 P
that she will draw his lips' rich treasure dry. VEN 552
entombs her outcry in her lips' sweet fold. LUC 679
coral is far more red than her lips' red; SON 130. 2
/LIPS 1 FR 0.0001 REL FR 1 V 0 P
/divide /thy /lips, /than /we /are /confident, TRO 1.03. 72
LIPS 173 FR 0.0195 REL FR 149 V 24 P
to know that of your mouth, or of your lips; WIV 1.01.229 P
hold that the lips is parcel of the mouth. 1.01.229 P
and mercy then will breathe within your lips, MM 2.02. 78

i can speak to him, i will open my lips in vain, 3.01.193 P
must be lock'd within the teeth and the lips. 3.02.135 P
take, o, take those lips away, | that so sweetly 4.01. 1
sheep, sweet lamb, unless we feed on your lips. LLL 2.01.220
my lips are no common, though several they be. 2.01.223
thy reply, i profane my lips on thy foot, my 4.01. 84 P
come, you talk greasily, your lips grow foul. 4.01.137
and when she drinks, against her lips i bob, MND 2.01. 49
o, how ripe in show | thy lips, those kissing 3.02.140
my cherry lips have often kiss'd thy stones, 5.01.190
i kiss the wall's hole, not your lips at all. 5.01.201
these lily lips, | this cherry nose, | these 5.01.330
and when i ope my lips let no dog bark!" MV 1.01. 94
here are sever'd lips, | parted with sugar 3.02.118
then open not thy lips: AYL 1.03. 82
your lips will feel them the sooner. 3.02. 60 P
he hath bought a pair of cast lips of diana. 3.04. 15 P
would open his lips when he put it into his 5.01. 34 P
that grapes were made to eat and lips to open. 5.01. 36 P
tranio, i saw her coral lips to move, | and with SHR 1.01.174
and kiss'd her lips with such a clamorous smack 3.02.178
soon hot, my very lips might freeze to my teeth, 4.01. 6 P
or i will not open my lips so wide as a bristle TN 1.05. 2 P
as, item, two lips, indifferent red; 1.05.247 P
does not toby take you a blow o' the lips then? 2.05. 68 P
lips, do not move; 2.05. 98
hands, | attested by the holy close of lips, 5.01.158
eyes, | have taken treasure from her lips — WT 5.01. 54
and your lips too, for i am well assur'd | that JN 2.01.534
him, | and kiss the lips of unacquainted change, 3.04.166
doth move the murmuring lips of discontent | to 4.02. 53
to make his bleak winds kiss my parched lips 5.07. 40
doubly portcullis'd with my teeth and lips, R2 1.03.167
with the attainder of his slanderous lips. 4.01. 24
shall daub her lips with her own children's 1H4 1.01. 6
to play with mammets and to tilt with lips. 2.03. 92
thy lips are scarce wip'd since thou drunk'st 2.04.153 P
my love, give me thy lips. H5 2.03. 47
flames a' fire, and his lips blows at his nose, 3.06.103 P
he threw his wounded arm, and kiss'd his lips, 4.06. 25
then i will kiss your lips, kate. 5.02.257 P
you have witchcraft in your lips, kate; 5.02.276 P
o, tell me when my lips do touch his cheeks, 1H6 2.05. 39
seal up your lips, and give no words but mum; 2H6 1.02. 89
fain would i go to chafe his paly lips | with 3.02.141
dying with mother's dug between its lips; 3.02.393
to have thee with thy lips to stop my mouth; 3.02.396
thy lips that kiss'd the queen shall sweep the 4.01. 75
defy them then, or else hold close thy lips. 3H6 2.02.118
and with thy lips keep in my soul a while. 5.02. 35
that glues my lips and will not let me speak. 5.02. 38
i seal upon the lips of this sweet babe. 5.07. 29
the lips of those that breathe them in the air. R3 1.03.285
their lips were four red roses on a stalk, 4.03. 12
cooling too, or ye may chance burn your lips. TRO 1.01. 26 P
peace, troyan, lay thy finger on thy lips! 1.03.240
with truant vows to her own lips he loves, | and 1.03.270
which | cold lips blow to their deities, take 4.04. 27
rudely beguiles our lips | of all rejoindure, 4.04. 35
i'll take that winter from your lips, fair lady; 4.05. 24
his insolence draws folly from my lips, | but 4.05.258
/chin he drove | the bristled lips before him. COR 2.02. 92
a beggar's tongue | make motion through my lips, 3.02.118
and to be executed ere they wipe their lips. 4.05.217 P
doth rise and fall between thy rosed lips, TIT 2.04. 24
gentle lavinia, let me kiss thy lips, | or make 3.01.120
o, take this warm kiss on thy pale cold lips, 5.03.153
kiss, | thy brother marcus tenders on thy lips. 5.03.157
how many thousand times hath these poor lips, 5.03.167
o'er ladies' lips, who straight on kisses dream, ROM 1.04. 74
my lips, two blushing pilgrims, ready stand | to 1.05. 95
have not saints lips, and holy palmers too? 1.05.101
ay, pilgrim, lips that they must use in pray'r. 1.05.102
o then, dear saint, let lips do what hands do, 1.05.103
thus from my lips, by thine, my sin is purg'd. 1.05.107
then have my lips the sin that they have took. 1.05.108
sin from my lips? 1.05.109
a gentler judgment vanish'd from his lips — 3.03. 10
and steal immortal blessing from her lips, | who 3.03. 37
the roses in thy lips and cheeks shall fade | to 4.01. 99
life and these lips have long been separated. 4.05. 27
and breath'd such life with kisses in my lips 5.01. 8
yet | is crimson in thy lips and in thy cheeks, 5.03. 95
and, lips, o you | the doors of breath, seal 5.03.113
i will kiss thy lips, | haply some poison yet 5.03.164
thy lips are warm. 5.03.167
thy lips rot off! TIM 4.03. 64
then the rot returns | to thine own lips again. 4.03. 66
words become your lips as they pass thorough 5.01.195
lips, let four words go by and language end! 5.01.220
his coward lips did from their color fly, | and JC 1.02.122
fear of opening my lips and receiving the bad 1.02.250 P
(which like dumb mouths do ope their ruby lips 3.01.260
her choppy finger laying | upon her skinny lips. MAC 1.03. 45
of our poison'd chalice | to our own lips. 1.07. 12
eclipse, | nose of turk and tartar's lips, 4.01. 29
and still your fingers on your lips, i pray. HAM 1.05.187
here hung those lips that i have kiss'd i know 5.01.188 P
who have the power | to seal th' accuser's lips. LR 4.06.170
restoration hang | thy medicine on my lips, and 4.07. 26
look her lips! 5.03.311
would she give you so much of her lips | as of OTH 2.01.100
yet again, your fingers to your lips? 2.01.176 P
met so near with their lips that their breaths 2.01.259 P
i found not cassio's kisses on her lips. 3.03.341
up kisses by the roots | that grew upon my lips; 3.03.424
noses, ears, and lips. 4.01. 42 P
head, | steep'd me in poverty to the very lips, 4.02. 50
torments will ope your lips. 5.02.305
eternity was in our lips and eyes, | bliss in ANT 1.03. 35
in) | bestow'd his lips on that unworthy place, 3.13. 84
i shall return once more | to kiss these lips, i 3.13.174
man, | commend unto his lips thy /favoring hand. 4.08. 23
it was divided | between her heart and lips. 4.14. 33
kisses the poor last | i lay upon thy lips. 4.15. 21
had my lips that power, | thus would i wear them 4.15. 39
i had rather seel my lips than to my peril 5.02.146
come then, and take the last warmth of my lips. 5.02.291
have i the aspic in my lips? 5.02.293
had i this cheek | to bathe my lips upon; CYM 1.06.100
slaver with lips as common as the stairs | that 1.06.105
let me my service tender on your lips. 1.06.140
i would not | believe her lips in opening it. 5.05. 42
i would not thy good deeds should from my lips 5.05.288
as do you love, fill to your mistress' lips — PER 2.03. 51
nay, come, your hands and lips must seal it too; 2.05. 85
that on the touching of her lips i may | melt, 5.03. 42
their sweetness fall | upon thy tasteful lips, TNK 1.01.179
i lov'd my lips the better ten days after. 2.04. 26
with cherry lips and cheeks of damask roses, 4.01. 74
his red lips, after fights, are fit for ladies. 4.02.111
"and yet not cloy thy lips with loath'd satiety, VEN 19
and gins to chide, but soon she stops his lips, 46
"if thou wilt chide, thy lips shall never open." 48
but when her lips were ready for his pay, | he 89
pay, | he winks, and turns his lips another way. 90
"touch but my lips with those fair lips of thine 115
but my lips with those fair lips of thine — 115
then why not lips on lips, since eyes in eyes? 120
then why not lips on lips, since eyes in eyes? 120
what were thy lips the worse for one poor kiss? 207
graze on my lips, and if those hills be dry, 233
he chafes her lips, a thousand ways he seeks 477
but for thy piteous lips no more had seen. 504
"pure lips, sweet seals in my soft lips 511
lips, sweet seals in my soft lips imprinted, 511
slips, | set thy seal manual on my wax-red lips. 516
whose precious taste her thirsty lips well knew, 543
their lips together glued, fall to the earth. 546
her lips are conquerors, his lips obey, | paying 549
her lips are conquerors, his lips obey, | paying 549
such nectar from his lips she had not suck'd. 572
nor thy soft hands, sweet lips, and crystal eyne 633
so do thy lips | make modest dian cloudy and 724
she looks upon his lips, and they are pale, 1123
her coral lips, her snow-white dimpled chin. LUC 420
thronging through her lips, so vanisheth | as 1041
and from his lips did fly | thin winding breath, 1406
from lips new waxen pale begins to blow | the 1663
but through his lips do throng | weak words, so 1783
her lips to mine how often hath she joined, PP 7. 7
quoth she, "he seized on my lips," | and with 11. 9
and with her lips on his did act the seizure: 11.10
though rosy lips and cheeks | within his bending SON 116. 9
whilst my poor lips, which should that harvest 128. 7
making dead wood more blest than living lips: 128.12
give them /thy fingers, me thy lips to kiss. 128.14
or, if it do, not from those lips of thine, 142. 5
those lips that love's own hand did make 145. 1
wind | upon his lips their silken parcels hurls. LC 87

LIPSBURY 1 FR 0.0001 REL FR 0 V 1 P
if i had thee in lipsbury pinfold, i would make LR 2.02. 9 P

LIQUID 9 FR 0.0010 REL FR 9 V 0 P
decking with liquid pearl the bladed grass | (a MND 1.01.211
might liquid tears or heart-offending groans 2H6 3.02. 60
the liquid drops of tears that you have shed R3 4.04.321
strong-ribb'd bark through liquid mountains cut, TRO 1.03. 40
put this in any liquid thing you will | and ROM 5.01. 77
whose liquid surge resolves | the moon into salt TIM 4.03.439
and in the morn and liquid dew of youth HAM 1.03. 41
wash me in steep-down gulfs of liquid fire! OTH 5.02.280
left | a liquid prisoner pent in walls of glass, SON 5.10

LIQUOR 18 FR 0.0020 REL FR 10 V 8 P
like a foul bumbard that would shed his liquor. TMP 2.02. 22 P
that's a brave god, and bears celestial liquor. 2.02.117
thy true subject, for the liquor is not earthly. 2.02.126 P
find this grand liquor that hath gilded 'em? 5.01.280
"item, she will often praise her liquor." TGV 3.01.345 P
if her liquor be good, she shall; 3.01.346 P
there is either liquor in his pate, or money in WIV 2.01.190 P
are welcome to me, that o'erflows such liquor. 2.02.151 P
by drop, and liquor fishermen's boots with me. 4.05. 98 P
asleep, | and drop the liquor of it in her eyes; MND 2.01.178
whose liquor hath this virtuous property, | to 3.02.367
is crack'd, and all the precious liquor spilt, R2 1.02. 19
pay, | and liquor likewise will i give to thee, H5 2.01.108
the fire that mounts the liquor till't run o'er H8 1.01.144
small, | and with this hateful liquor temper it, TIT 5.02.199
and this distilling liquor drink thou off, ROM 4.01. 94
go get thee in, and fetch me a sup of liquor. HAM 5.01. 60 P
here's yet some liquor left. 5.02.342

LIQUOR'D 1 FR 0.0001 REL FR 0 V 1 P
she will, she will, justice hath liquor'd her. 1H4 2.01. 85 P

LIQUORISH 1 FR 0.0001 REL FR 1 V 0 P
with liquorish draughts | and morsels unctious, TIM 4.03.194

LIQUORS 2 FR 0.0002 REL FR 2 V 0 P
apply | hot and rebellious liquors in my blood, AYL 2.03. 49
the cup of alteration | with divers liquors! 2H4 3.01. 53

LISBON 1 FR 0.0001 REL FR 1 V 0 P
from lisbon, barbary, and india, | and not one MV 3.02.269

/LISP 1 FR 0.0001 REL FR 0 V 1 P
you jig and amble, and you /lisp, you nickname HAM 3.01.144 P

LISP 2 FR 0.0002 REL FR 1 V 1 P
'a can carve too, and lisp; LLL 5.02.323
look you lisp and wear strange suits; AYL 4.01. 34 P

LISPING 3 FR 0.0003 REL FR 0 V 3 P
like a many of these lisping hawthorn buds, that WIV 3.03. 71 P
man, be not lisping to his /master's old tables, 2H4 2.04.266 P
the pox of such antic, lisping, affecting ROM 2.04. 28 P

LISPS 1 FR 0.0001 REL FR 1 V 0 P
he lisps in 's neighing able to entice | a TNK 5.02. 66

LI'ST* 5 FR 0.0005 REL FR 5 V 0 P
whilst thou li'st warm at home, secure and safe; SHR 5.02.151
why li'st thou with the vile | in loathsome beds 2H4 3.01. 15
in thy foul throat thou li'st! R3 1.02. 93
thou li'st, thou shag-ear'd villain! MAC 4.02. 83
hands | void of appointment, that thou li'st, TNK 3.01. 40

/LIST* 1 FR 0.0001 REL FR 1 V 0 P
i find it still, when i have /list to sleep. OTH 2.01.104

LIST* 61 FR 0.0069 REL FR 44 V 17 P
your lieutenant if you list, he's no standard. TMP 3.02. 17 P
if thou beest a devil, take't as thou list. 3.02.129 P
pay all, go to bed when she list, rise when she WIV 2.02.119 P
go to bed when she list, rise when she list, all 2.02.119 P
elves, list your names; 5.05. 42
thou art the list. MM 1.02. 30 P
i had as lief be a list of an english kersey as 1.02. 33 P
and teach your ears to list me with more heed. ERR 4.01.101
i am not such a fool to think what i list, nor i ADO 3.04. 83 P
what i list, nor i list not to think what i can, 3.04. 83 P
sir, list to me: SHR 2.01.363
eyes on every stale, | seize thee that list. 3.01. 91
on the other, gart'red with a red and blue list; 3.02. 68 P
"now take them up," quoth he, "if any list." 3.02.165
it shall be moon, or star, or what i list, | or 4.05. 7
yourself within the list of too cold an adieu. AWW 2.01. 51 P
i mean, she is the list of my voyage. TN 3.01. 77 P
what of her ensues | i list not prophesy; WT 4.01. 26
then list to me. 4.04.541
son, list to this conjunction, make this match, JN 2.01.468
and list what with our council we have done: R2 1.03.124
ground, and list if thou canst hear the tread of 1H4 2.02. 32 P
prithee let her alone, and list to me. 3.03. 95 P
the very list, the very utmost bound | of all 4.01. 51
list his discourse of war, and you shall hear H5 1.01. 43
within the weak list of a country's fashion. 5.02.270 P
but list to me, my humphrey, my sweet duke: 2H6 1.02. 35
and, madam, list to me, | for i am bold to 1.03. 92
the eldest son of fortune, | turns what he list. H8 2.02. 21
yes, 'tis the list | of those that claim their 4.01. 14
list! TRO 5.02. 17
list what work he makes | amongst your cloven COR 1.04. 20
do as thou list; 3.02.128
list to your tribunes. audience! peace, i say! 3.03. 40
and when he sleeps will she do what she list. TIT 4.01.100
as i pass by, and let them take it as they list. ROM 1.01. 41 P
come hither, good volumnius; list a word. JC 5.05. 15
rather than so, come fate into the list, | and MAC 3.01. 70
there | shark'd up a list of lawless resolutes, HAM 1.01. 98
if with too credent ear you list his songs, | or 1.03. 30
list, list, o, list! 1.05. 22
list, list, o, list! 1.05. 22
list, list, o, list! 1.05. 22
or "if we list to speak," or "there be, and if 1.05.177
the ocean, overpeering of his list, | eats not 4.05.100
that's as we list to grace him. LR 5.03. 61
list a brief tale, | and when 'tis told, o, that 5.03.182
natures more than is native to them), list me. OTH 2.01.217 P
that she may make, unmake, do what she list, 2.03.346
apart, | confine yourself but in a patient list. 4.01. 75
lycaonia, | with a more larger list of sceptres. ANT 3.06. 76
list, list! 4.03. 12
list, list! 4.03. 12
stand close, and list him. 4.09. 6
list, my marina. PER 5.01.229
list then: TNK 5.04. 48
and beef at four nobles a stone, list to me. STM II.C 3 P
morn till night, even where i list to sport me. VEN 154
but little stars may hide them when they list. LUC 1008
be where you list, your charter is so strong, SON 58. 9
and down i laid to list the sad-tun'd tale, LC 4

LISTEN 15 FR 0.0017 REL FR 14 V 1 P
will she hide her, | to listen our propose. ADO 3.01. 12
listen, ear. LLL 4.03. 43
his discretion, and let us listen to the moon. MND 5.01.237 P
listen to me, and if you speak me fair, | i'll SHR 1.02.179
king philip, listen to the cardinal. JN 3.01.198
the open ear of youth doth always listen; R2 2.01. 20
i sent | on tuesday last to listen after news. 2H4 1.01. 29
lady, vouchsafe to listen what i say. 1H6 5.03.103
that she will light to listen to the lays, | and 2H6 1.03. 90
and listen after humphrey, how he proceeds. 1.03.149
listen, fair madam, let it be your glory | to TIT 2.03.139
prithee listen well; JC 2.04. 17
and now, octavius, | listen great things. 4.01. 41
listen, but speak not to't. MAC 4.01. 89
of his gyves | might call fell things to listen, TNK 3.02. 15

LISTEN'D 1 FR 0.0001 REL FR 0 V 1 P
they listen'd to me as they would have hearken'd PER 4.02. 98 P

LISTENED 1 FR 0.0001 REL FR 1 V 0 P
he that no more must say is listened more | than R2 2.01. 9

LISTETH 1 FR 0.0001 REL FR 1 V 0 P
she takes all she can, not all she listeth. VEN 564

LIST'NED 1 FR 0.0001 REL FR 1 V 0 P
me down | and list'ned to the words she sung, TNK 4.01. 63

LIST'NING 11 FR 0.0012 REL FR 8 V 3 P
but to knock at your ear, and beseech list'ning. SHR 4.01. 66 P
do so, for it is worth the list'ning to. 1H4 2.04.211 P
it is the disease of not list'ning, the malady 2H4 1.02.121 P
almost with ravish'd list'ning, could not find H8 1.02.120
list'ning their fear, i could not say "amen," MAC 2.02. 26
that i should open to the list'ning air | how PER 1.02. 87
it nips me unto list'ning, and thick slumber 5.01.234
stands on his hinder-legs with list'ning ear, VEN 698
away he steals with open list'ning ear, | full LUC 283
all jointly list'ning, but with several graces, 1410
"look, look how list'ning priam wets his eyes, 1548

LISTS* 14 FR 0.0015 REL FR 12 V 2 P
the lists of all advice | my strength can give MM 1.01. 6
as there may between the lists and the velvet. 1.02. 29 P
and throw the rider headlong in the lists, | a R2 1.02. 52
hither | before king richard in his royal lists? 1.03. 32
in lists, on thomas mowbray, duke of norfolk, 1.03. 38
so bold | or daring-hardy as to touch the lists, 1.03. 43
back our troops and conquers as she lists: 1H6 1.05. 22
forsaketh yet the lists | by reason of his 5.05. 32
the armorer and his man, to enter the lists, 2H6 2.03. 50
a' god's name see the lists and all things fit; 2.03. 54
the lists, and full proportions are all made HAM 1.02. 32
or degree within the lists of the army will LR 5.03.111 P
like a bold champion i assume the lists, | nor PER 1.01. 61
now is she in the very lists of love, | her VEN 595

LITERATURED 1 FR 0.0001 REL FR 0 V 1 P
is good knowledge and literatured in the wars. H5 4.07.150 P

LITHER 1 FR 0.0001 REL FR 1 V 0 P
two talbots, winged through the lither sky, | in 1H6 4.07. 21

LITIGIOUS 1 FR 0.0001 REL FR 1 V 0 P
and tyrus stands | in a litigious peace. PER 3.03. 3

LITIO 7 FR 0.0008 REL FR 7 V 0 P
his name is litio, born in mantua. SHR 2.01. 60
now, litio, to you: 3.01. 56
minola, | the quaint musician, amorous litio, 3.02.147
is't possible, friend litio, that mistress 4.02. 1
i tell thee, litio, this is wonderful. 4.02. 15

mistake no more, i am not litio, | nor a 4.02. 16
then we are rid of litio. 4.02. 49

LITTER 7 FR 0.0008 REL FR 5 V 2 P

(save for the son that /she did litter here, | a TMP 1.02.282
a blind bitch's puppies, fifteen i' th' litter; WIV 3.05. 11 P
to crouch in litter of your stable planks, | to JN 5.02.140
to my litter straight, | weakness possesseth me, 5.03. 16
that hath overwhelm'd all her litter but one. 2H4 1.02. 12 P
that stout pendragon in his litter sick | came 1H6 3.02. 95
there is a litter ready, lay him in't, | and LR 3.06. 90

LITTER'D 3 FR 0.0003 REL FR 2 V 1 P

as i am, litter'd under mercury, was likewise a WT 4.03. 25 P
as they are, | though in rome litter'd; COR 3.01.238
we /are two lions litter'd in one day, | and i JC 2.02. 46

/LITTLE 5 FR 0.0005 REL FR 4 V 1 P

/little /are /we /beholding /to /your /love, R2 4.01.160
/and /little /look'd /for /at /your /helping 4.01.161
/or /get /some /little /knife /between /thy TIT 3.02. 16
/an /aery /of /children, /little /eyases, /that HAM 2.02.339 P
/strives /in /his /little /world /of /man /to LR 3.01. 10

LITTLE 524 FR 0.0592 REL FR 375 V 149 P

our cable, for our own doth little advantage. TMP 1.01. 32 P
hear a little further, | and then i'll bring 1.02.135
of that there's none, or little. 2.01. 52 P
this | who shall be of as little memory | when 2.01.233
thou dost me yet but little hurt; 2.02. 79 P
after a little time | i'll beat him too. 3.02. 85
and our little life | is rounded with a sleep. 4.01.157
has done little better than play'd the jack with 4.01.197 P
for a little | follow, and do me service. 4.01.265
'tis threefold too little for carrying a letter TGV 1.01.109
his little speaking shows his love but small. 1.02. 29
as little by such toys as may be possible: 1.02. 79
and that's the reason i love him so little. 2.04.206
a little time will melt her frozen thoughts, 3.02. 9
a little time, my lord, will kill that grief. 3.02. 15
then know that i have little wealth to lose. 4.01. 11
with you, | reaking as little what betideth me, 4.03. 40
and what says she to my little jewel? 4.04. 47 P
and yet the painter flatter'd her a little, 4.04.187
no, that it is too little. 5.02. 5
he hath but a little /whey–face, with a little WIV 1.04. 22 P
a little /whey–face, with a little yellow beard, 1.04. 23 P
sir — i pray come a little nearer this ways. 2.02. 45 P
your worship come a little nearer this ways. 2.02. 49 P
they have not so little grace, i hope. 2.02.112 P
would desire you to send her your little page, 2.02.114 P
has a marvellous infection to the little page; 2.02.115 P
to press with so little preparation upon you. 2.02.156 P
nay, keep your way, little gallant; 3.02. 1 P
here comes little robin. 3.03. 21 P
you little jack–a–lent, have you been true to us 3.03. 27 P
own part, i would little or nothing with you. 3.04. 62 P
the river with as little remorse as they would 3.05. 10 P
let's obey his humor a little further. 4.02.199 P
nan page (my daughter) and my little son, | and 4.04. 48
better a little chiding than a great deal of 5.03. 9 P
yet | let us be keen, and rather cut a little, MM 2.01. 5
stay a little while. 2.02. 26
man, | dress'd in a little brief authority, 2.02.118
in't, | which seems a little fouler than it is, 2.04.146
little honor to be much believ'd, | and most 2.04.149
a little more lenity to lechery would do no harm 3.02. 97 P
but indeed i can do you little harm; 3.02.166 P
i shall crave your forbearance a little. 4.01. 22 P
this other doth command a little door, | which 4.01. 32
little have you to say | when you depart from 4.01. 67
if it be too little for your thief, your true 4.02. 44 P
your thief, your thief thinks it little enough; 4.02. 46 P
the duke is marvellous little beholding to your 4.03.159 P
talk offend you, we'll have very little of it. 4.03.178 P
much more the better | for being a little bad; 5.01.441
'tis holy sport to be a little vain, | when the ERR 3.02. 27
left, | my dull deaf ears a little use to hear: 5.01.317
fair praise, and too little for a great praise; ADO 1.01.172 P
i were but little happy, if i could say how much 2.01.307 P
there's little of the melancholy element in her, 2.01.342 P
matter | is little cupid's crafty arrow made, 3.01. 22
and the little hangman dare not shoot at him. 3.02. 11 P
verges, sir, speaks a little /off the matter; 3.05. 9 P
and salt too little which may season give | to 4.01.142
hear me a little, | for i have only been silent 4.01.155
already that you are little better than false 4.02. 21 P
"true," said she, "a fine little one." 5.01.161 P
our court shall be a little academe, | still and LLL 1.01. 13
climb o'er the house to unlock the little gate. 1.01.109
the hearing it, but little of the marking of it. 1.01.286 P
thou pretty, because little. 1.02. 21 P
little pretty, because little. wherefore apt? 1.02. 22 P
little pretty, because little. wherefore apt? 1.02. 22 P
i thank god i have as little patience as another 1.02.165 P
and much too little of that good i saw | is my 2.01. 62
but that, it seems, he little purposeth: 2.01.141
of trotting paritors — o my little heart! 3.01.186
neglect | of his almighty dreadful little might. 3.01.203
man when king pippen of france was a little boy, 4.01.121 P
queen guinover of britain was a little wench, as 4.01.124 P
/bone /for /bene, priscian a little scratch'd, 5.01. 28 P
i made a little fault in "great." 5.02.559 P
alas, you see how 'tis — a little o'erparted. 5.02.584 P
of wrong through the little hole of discretion, 5.02.723 P
i'll speak in a monstrous little voice, "thisne! MND 1.02. 52 P
i do but beg a little changeling boy | to be my 2.01.120
it fell upon a little western flower, | before 2.01.166
note so true, | the wren with little quill — 3.01.128
you should have little reason for that. 3.01.142 P
reason and love keep little company together 3.01.144 P
and when she weeps, weeps every little flower, 3.01.199
and though she be but little, she is fierce. 3.02.325
"little" again? 3.02.326
nothing but "low" and "little"? 3.02.326
intend | never so little show of love to her, 3.02.334
my little body is a–weary of this great world. MV 1.02. 1 P
he is best, he is a little worse than a man, and 1.02. 88 P
he is worst, he is little better than a beast. 1.02. 89 P
how little is the cost i have bestowed | in 3.04. 19
to do a great right, do a little wrong, | and 4.01.216
but little; 4.01.264
your wife would give you little thanks for that 4.01.288
tarry a little, there is something else. 4.01.305
night | did pretty jessica (like a little shrow) 5.01. 21
how far that little candle throws his beams! 5.01. 90
the daylight sick, | it looks a little paler. 5.01.125
a youth, | a kind of boy, a little scrubbed boy, 5.01.162
for since the little wit that fools have was AYL 1.02. 89 P
the little foolery that wise men have makes a 1.02. 89 P
ribs, that there is little hope of life in him. 1.02.128 P
you will take little delight in it, i can tell 1.02.158 P
the little strength that i have, i would it were 1.02.194 P
and little reaks to find the way to heaven | by 2.04. 81
that little cares for buying any thing. 2.04. 90
live a little, comfort a little, cheer thyself a 2.06. 5 P
live a little, comfort a little, cheer thyself a 2.06. 5 P
comfort a little, cheer thyself a little. 2.06. 6 P
then forbear your food a little while, | whiles, 2.07.127
of every sprite | heaven would in little show. 3.02.140
shepherd, go off a little. 3.02.159 P
nay, he hath but a little beard. 3.02.208 P
god buy you, let's meet as little as we can. 3.02.257 P
dead than a great reckoning in a little room. 3.03. 15 P
go hence a little, and i shall conduct you, | if 3.04. 55
'od's my little life, | i think she means to 3.05. 43
a little riper and more lusty red | than that 3.05.121
coz, my pretty little coz, that thou didst know 4.01.205 P
love to thee | little knows this love in me; 4.03. 57
is't possible that on so little acquaintance you 5.02. 1 P
than may in some little measure draw a belief 5.02. 57 P
thou'dst thank me but a little for my counsel; SHR 1.02. 61
think scolding would do little good upon him. 1.02.109 P
and she stand him but a little, he will throw a 1.02.113 P
think you a little din can daunt mine ears? 1.02.199
we will go walk a little in the orchard, | and 2.01.111
though little fire grows great with little wind, 2.01.134
though little fire grows great with little wind, 2.01.134
now, were not i a little pot and soon hot, my 4.01. 6 P
ay, but the mustard is too hot a little. 4.03. 25
though thy little finger be arm'd in a thimble. 4.03.147 P
'a has a little gall'd me, i confess; 5.02. 60
too little payment for so great a debt. 5.02.154
i will stand for't a little, though therefore i AWW 1.01.133 P
there's little can be said in't, 'tis against 1.01.135 P
little helen, farewell. 1.01.188 P
than these boys', | and writ as little beard. 2.03. 61
title, which is within a very little of nothing. 2.04. 27 P
though little he do feel it, set down sharply. 3.04. 33
they will say, "came you off with so little?" 4.01. 39 P
and in his sleep he does little harm, save to 4.03.256 P
i have but little more to say, sir, of his 4.03.258 P
which i take to be too little for pomp to enter. 4.05. 51 P
fall, | shall /tax my fears of little vanity, 5.03.122
vanity, | having vainly fear'd too little. 5.03.123
i can say little more than i have studied, and TN 1.05.178 P
good swabber, i am to hull here a little longer. 1.05.203 P
a little, by your favor. 2.04. 25
much in our vows, but little in our love. 2.04.118
here comes the little villain. 2.05. 13 P
and yet, to crush this a little, it would bow to 2.05.140 P
if all the devils of hell be drawn in little, 3.04. 85 P
a little thing would make me tell them how much 3.04.302 P
let me speak a little. 3.04.359
hold little faith, though thou hast too much 5.01.171
i leave my duty a little unthought of, and speak 5.01.309 P
when that i was and a little tine boy, | with 5.01.389
they cannot praise us, as little accuse us. WT 1.01. 16 P
that little thinks she has been sluic'd in 's 1.02.194
if she dares trust me with her little babe, 2.02. 35
although the print be little, the whole matter 2.03. 99
i'll pawn the little blood which i have left 2.03.166
forcing faults upon hermione, | i little like. 3.01. 17
thy baby–daughter | to be or none, or little — 3.02.192
i have a little money for thee. 4.03. 77 P
have | as little skill to fear as i have purpose 4.04.152
too rough for some that know little but bowling) 4.04.330 P
not little of his care | to have them 4.04.519
consider little | what dangers, by his highness' 5.01. 26
whereupon, after a little amazedness, we were 5.02. 5 P
to be much sea–sick, and himself little better, 5.02.119 P
mark a little while. 5.03.118
something about, a little from the right, | in JN 1.01.170
this little abstract doth contain that large 2.01.101
and victory, with little loss, doth play | upon 2.01.307
made | will give her sadness very little cure. 2.01.546
thou little valiant, great in villainy! 3.01.116
for very little pains | will bring this labor to 3.02. 9
come hither, little kinsman, hark, a word. 3.03. 18
blow each dust, each straw, each little rub, 3.04.128
or as a little snow, tumbled about, | anon 3.04.176
good morrow, little prince. 4.01. 9
as little prince, having so great a title | to 4.01. 10
in sooth, i would you were a little sick, | that 4.01. 29
as patches set upon a little breach | discredit 4.02. 32
child, | his little kingdom of a forced grave. 4.02. 98
but there is little reason in your grief; 4.03. 30
thyself, | put but a little water in a spoon, 4.03.131
the little number of your doubtful friends. 5.01. 36
are turned to one thread, one little hair. 5.07. 54
face, | and bid his ears a little while be deaf, R2 1.01.112
how long a time lies in one little word! 1.03.213
but little vantage shall i reap thereby; 1.03.218
this happy breed of men, this little world, 2.01. 45
for little office | will the hateful commons 2.02.137
and hope to joy is little less in joy | than 2.03. 15
pomp, | allowing him a breath, a little scene, 3.02.164
comes at the last and with a little pin | bores 3.02.169
and my large kingdom for a little grave, | a 3.03.153
a little little grave, an obscure grave — | or 3.03.154
a little little grave, an obscure grave — | or 3.03.154
thou, thou little better thing than earth, 3.04. 78
madam, little joy have i | to breathe this news, 3.04. 81
half, | it is too little, helping him to all; 5.01. 61
being ne'er so little urg'd, another way | to 5.01. 64
that were some love, but little policy. 5.01. 84
these same thoughts people this little world, 5.05. 9
"come, little ones," and then again, | "it is as 5.05. 15
truly, little better than one of the wicked. 1H4 1.02. 94 P
little deserves | the scourge of greatness to be 1.03. 10
and 'tis no little reason bids us speed, | to 1.03.283
in faith, i'll break thy little finger, harry, 2.03. 87
room, and lend me thy hand to laugh a little. 2.04. 2 P
anon, sir. pray stay a little, my lord. 2.04. 57 P
yea, but a little charge will trench him here, 3.01.111
i'll have it so, a little charge will do it. 3.01.114
whereof a little | more than a little is by much 3.02. 72
little | more than a little is by much too much. 3.02. 73
swore little, dic'd not above seven times — a 3.03. 16 P
i hold as little counsel with weak fear | as you 4.03. 11
steps me a little higher than his vow | made to 4.03. 75
not all this flesh | keep in a little life? 5.04.103
at shrewsbury hath a little gilded over your 2H4 1.02.148 P
virtue is of so little regard in these 1.02.168 P
have of their puissance made a little taste. 2.03. 52
ah, you whoreson little valiant villain, you! 2.04.209 P
ah, you sweet little rogue, you! 2.04.216 P
thou whoreson little tidy bartholomew boar–pig, 2.04.231 P
restored | with good advice and little medicine. 3.01. 43
was i, and little john doit of staffordshire, 3.02. 19 P
o, give me always a little, lean, old, chopp'd, 3.02.275 P
show — there was a little quiver fellow, and 'a 3.02.281 P
warning to all the rest of this little kingdom, 4.03.109 P
only, we want a little personal strength; 4.04. 8
say it did so a little time before | that our 4.04.127
stay but a little, for my cloud of dignity | is 4.05. 98
of mutton, and any pretty little tiny kickshaws, 5.01. 28 P
man, i have little credit with your worship. 5.01. 49 P
and, my little soldier there, be merry. 5.03. 30 P
welcome, my little tiny thief, and welcome 5.03. 57 P
figure may | attest in little place a million, H5 pr 16
like little body with a mighty heart, | what 2.pr. 17
i say little; 2.01. 5 P
i would prick your guts a little in good terms, 2.01. 58 P
if little faults, proceeding on distemper, 2.02. 54
spoil his coat with scanting | a little cloth. 2.04. 48
a night is but small breath, and little pause, 2.04.145
the doom of death | for pax of little price. 3.06. 45
any such proverb so little kin to the purpose. 3.07. 68 P
define, | a little touch of harry in the night. 4.pr. 47
though it appear a little out of fashion, 4.01. 83
but in gross brain little wots | what watch the 4.01.282
a very little little let us do, | and all is 4.02. 33
a very little little let us do, | and all is 4.02. 33
shall yield them little, tell the constable. 4.03.125
save the phrase is a little variations. 4.07. 18 P
and also being a little intoxicates in his 4.07. 37 P
was ever known so great and little loss, | on 4.08.110
i will tell him a little piece of my desires. 5.01. 13 P
story, | in little room confining mighty men, ep 3
one would have ling'ring wars with little cost; 1H6 1.01. 74
peace, mayor, thou know'st little of my wrongs. 1.03. 59
us withal, | make us partakers of a little gain, 2.01. 52
a little herd of england's timorous deer, 4.02. 46
i owe him little duty, and less love, | and take 4.04. 34
upon my death the french can little boast; 4.05. 24
the help of one stands me in little stead. 4.06. 31
since thou dost deign to woo her little worth 5.03.151
had been a little ratsbane for thy sake! 5.04. 29
as little shall the frenchmen gain thereby. 5.04.115
will make but little for his benefit. 2H6 1.03. 98
leave | to show some reason, of no little force, 1.03.163
and humphrey is no little man in england. 3.01. 20
but little thinks we shall be of her council. 3H6 1.01. 36
and many strokes, though with a little axe, 2.01. 54
race, | i lay me down a little while to breathe; 2.03. 2
forbear awhile, we'll hear a little more. 3.01. 27
she could say little less; 4.01.101
a little fire is quickly trodden out, | which, 4.08. 7
a little gale will soon disperse that cloud, 5.03. 10
'tis sin to flatter, "good" was little better: 5.06. 3
i will maintain it with some little cost. R3 1.02.259
as little joy, my lord, as you suppose | you 1.03.150
as little joy you may suppose in me | that i 1.03.152
a little joy enjoys the queen thereof, | for i 1.03.154
nay, i prithee stay a little. 1.04.117 P
he little thought of this divided friendship. 1.04.238
me seemeth good that, with some little train, 2.02.120
why with some little train, my lord of 2.02.123
my dagger, little cousin? with all my heart. 3.01.111
what, would you have my weapon, little lord? 3.01.122
little. 3.01.125
because that i am little, like an ape, | he 3.01.130
this little prating york | was not incensed by 3.01.151
rough cradle for such little pretty ones! 4.01.100
give me some little breath, some pause, dear 4.02. 24
king, | when richmond was a little peevish boy. 4.02. 97
and little ned plantagenet, his son? 4.04.146
and there the little souls of edward's children 4.04.192
a grandam's name is little less in love | than 4.04.299
to whom as great a charge as little honor | he H8 1.01. 77
whereof | we cannot feel too little, hear too 1.02.128
if i chance to talk a little wild, forgive me; 1.04. 26
for my little cure, | let me alone. 1.04. 33
i fear, with dancing is a little heated. 1.04.100
i'll tell you in a little. 2.01. 11
the cause | he may a little grieve at. 2.01. 39
me | a little happier than my wretched father. 2.01.120
pluck off a little, | i would not be a young 2.03. 40
for little england | you'd venture an emballing 2.03. 46
i was set at work | among my maids, full little, 3.01. 75
in england | but little for my profit; 3.01. 83
she now begs | that little thought, when she set 3.01.183
tell you | you have as little honesty as honor, 3.02.271
cardinal, | you'll show a little honesty. 3.02.306
weeps to see him | so little of his great self. 3.02.336
so fare you well, my little good lord cardinal. 3.02.349
so farewell — to the little good you bear me. 3.02.350
like little wanton boys that swim on bladders, 3.02.359
some little memory of me will stir him | (i know 3.02.417
now, methinks, i feel a little ease. 4.02. 4
give him a little earth for charity!" 4.02. 23
and found the blessedness of being little; 4.02. 66
and a little | to love her for her mother's sake 4.02.136
but little, charles, | nor shall not, when my 5.01. 59
have misdemean'd yourself, and not a little: 5.02. 49
and with no little study, that my teaching | and 5.02. 69
i make as little doubt as you do conscience | in 5.02.102

my lord of winchester, y' are a little, | by 5.02.108
good my lords, | i have a little yet to say. 5.02.133
the king will suffer but the little finger | of 5.02.141
this little one shall make it holy–day. 5.04. 76
whose grossness little characters sum up; TRO 1.03.325
if ye take not that little little less than 2.03. 13 P
take not that little little less than little wit 2.03. 13 P
little less than little wit from them that they 2.03. 13 P
be led | at your request a little from himself. 2.03.181
to give me now a little benefit | out of those 3.03. 14
and /give to dust, that is a little gilt, | more 3.03.178
they think my little stomach to the war | and 3.03.220
a little proudly, and great deal misprising 4.05. 74
in the extremity of great and little, | valor 4.05. 78
with too much blood and too little brain, these 5.01. 48 P
too much brain and too little blood they do, 5.01. 50 P
stay a little while. 5.02. 54
i will venture | to /stale't a little more. COR 1.01. 92
you'll bestow a small (of what you have little) 1.01.125
how does your little son? 1.03. 53 P
you less than he, | that's lesser than a little. 1.04. 15
as if i lov'd my little should be dieted | in 1.09. 52
for a very little thief of occasion will rob you 2.01. 28 P
i know you can do very little alone, for your 2.01. 35 P
that he will give them make i as little question 2.01.230
report | a little of that worthy work perform'd 2.02. 45
no better thought of, a little help will serve; 2.03. 14 P
be in request | with those that have but little. 3.01.251
i have a heart as little apt as yours, | but yet 3.02. 29
ask'd, as free | as words to little purpose. 3.02. 89
a very little | i have yielded to. 5.03. 16
city be afire, | and then i'll speak a little. 5.03.182
it is no little thing to make | mine eyes to 5.03.195
for you to displace it with your little finger, 5.04. 5 P
mean while, sir, with the little skill i have, TIT 2.01. 43
yet there's as little justice as at land. 4.03. 9
the eagle suffers little birds to sing, | and is 4.04. 83
drawn with a team of little atomi | over men's ROM 1.04. 57
not half so big as a round little worm | prick'd 1.04. 68
stay but a little, i will come again. 2.02.138
bird, | that lets it hop a little from his hand, 2.02.178
when 'twas a little prating thing — o, there is 2.04.200 P
soul | is but a little way above our heads, 3.01.127
die, | take him and cut him out in little stars, 3.02. 22
and every cat and dog | and little mouse, every 3.03. 31
/thou fond mad man, hear me a little speak. 3.03. 52
with blood removed but little from her own? 3.03. 96
in one little body | thou counterfeits a bark, a 3.05.130
and therefore have i little /talk'd of love, 4.01. 7
up his rest | that you shall rest but little. 4.05. 7
to build his fortune i will strain a little, TIM 1.01.143
as this pomp shows to a little oil and root. 1.02.135
the little casket bring me hither. 1.02.158
there will little learning die then that day 2.02. 82 P
there was very little honor show'd in't. 3.02. 19 P
purchase the day before for a little part, and 3.02. 47 P
it shows but little love or judgment in him. 3.03. 10
one may reach deep enough and yet | find little. 3.04. 16
soldiers should brook as little wrongs as gods. 3.05.116
i have but little gold of late, brave timon, 4.03. 91
i must needs say you have a little fault; 5.01. 87
like to a little kingdom, suffers then | the JC 2.01. 68
let me a little show it, even in this — | that 3.01. 71
spoils, | shrunk to this little measure? 3.01.150
their charges off | a little from this ground. 4.02. 49
which we will niggard with a little rest. 4.03.228
a little water clears us of this deed; MAC 2.02. 64
my little spirit, see, | sits in a foggy cloud, 3.05. 34
as little is the wisdom, where the flight | so 4.02. 13
hence with your little ones. 4.02. 69
of arabia will not sweeten this little hand. 5.01. 51 P
itself professes yours, | and little is to do. 5.07. 28
rome, | a little ere the mightiest julius fell, HAM 1.01.114
a little more than kin, and less than kind. 1.02. 65
a little month, or ere those shoes were old 1.02.147
as 'twere a thing a little soil'd /wi' /th' 2.01. 40
at last, a little shaking of mine arm, | and 2.01. 89
your rest here in our court | some little time, 2.02. 14
ducats a–piece for his picture in little. 2.02.366 P
what he spake, though it lack'd form a little, 3.01.163
where little fears grow great, great love grows 3.02.172
excellent voice, in this little organ, yet 3.02.368 P
bestow this place on us a little while. 4.01. 4
we go to gain a little patch of ground | that 4.04. 18
i'll be with you straight — go a little before. 4.04. 31
to what it would, | acts little of his will. 4.05.126
them so well, | they shall go far with little. 4.05.140
or with a little shuffling, you may choose | a 4.07.137
the hand of little employment hath the daintier 5.01. 69 P
mend your speech a little, | lest you may mar LR 1.01. 94
if aught within that little seeming substance, 1.01.198
it is not little i have to say of what most 1.01.283 P
we have made of it hath /not been little. 1.01.289 P
presence until some little time hath qualified 1.02.161 P
converse with him that is wise and says little, 1.04. 16 P
thou hadst little wit in thy bald crown when 1.04.162 P
she begs, | a little to disquantity your train, 1.04.249
this house is little, the old man and 's people 2.04.288
"he that has and a little tine wit — | with 3.02. 74
o, i have ta'en | too little care of this! 3.04. 33
should have thus little mercy on their flesh? 3.04. 73
now a little fire in a wild field were like an 3.04.111 P
the little dogs and all, | trey, blanch, and 3.06. 62
cordelia, cordelia, stay a little. 5.03.272
honor | that, with the little godliness i have, OTH 1.02. 9
and little bless'd with the soft phrase of peace 1.03. 82
and little of this great world can i speak 1.03. 86
and therefore little shall i grace my cause | in 1.03. 88
she puts her tongue a little in her heart, | and 2.01.106
you have little cause to say so. 2.01.108
with as little a web as this will i ensnare as 2.01.168 P
good faith, a little one; 2.03. 66 P
though cassio did some little wrong to him, | as 2.03.242
so, with no money at all and a little more wit, 2.03.368 P
cassio entreats her a little favor of speech. 3.01. 26 P
me this, | to leave me but a little to myself. 3.03. 85
i see this hath a little dash'd your spirits. 3.03.214
your napkin is too little; 3.03.287
but with a little act upon the blood | burn like 3.03.328
to be much abus'd | than but to know't a little. 3.03.337
i pray you bring me on the way a little, | and 3.04.197
'tis but a little way that i can bring you, 3.04.199
do you withdraw yourself a little while, | he 4.01. 56
that, with this little arm and this good sword, 5.02.262
infinite book of secrecy | a little i can read. ANT 1.02. 11
if, or for nothing or a little, i | should say 2.02. 31
all little jealousies, which now seem great, 2.02.131
leave me, i pray, a little; 3.11. 22
i little thought | you would have followed. 3.11. 55
sleep a little. 4.04. 1
yet come a little — | wishers were ever fools 4.15. 36
give me some wine, and let me speak a little. 4.15. 42
course, and lighted | the little o, th' earth. 5.02. 81
nay, stay a little: CYM 1.01.109
shouldst have made him | as little as a crow, or 1.03. 15
a court | he little cares for and a daughter who 1.06.154
these boys know little they are sons to th' king 3.03. 80
thou seest him, | a little witness my obedience. 3.04. 66
be a little angry for my so rough usage; 4.01. 20 P
than themselves | for wrying but a little! 5.01. 5
you snatch some hence for little faults; 5.01. 12
'gainst whom i am too little to contend, | since PER 1.02. 17
and finding little comfort to relieve them, | i 1.02. 99
air | were all too little to content and please, 1.04. 35
to eat those little darlings whom they lov'd. 1.04. 44
the great ones eat up the little ones. 2.01. 29 P
a little daughter. 3.01. 21
look to your little mistress, on whose grace 3.03. 40
if you require a little space for prayer, | i 4.01. 67
is dead that lay with the little baggage. 4.02. 23 P
faith, my acquaintance lies little amongst them. 4.06.195 P
thou little know'st how thou dost startle me 5.01.146
o, stop there a little! 5.01.160
are almost run, | more a little, and then dumb. 5.02. 2
play do not keep | a little dull time from us, TNK pr 31
i may depart with little, while i live; 2.01. 1 P
here, with a little patience, | we shall live 2.02. 85
yon little tree, yon blooming apricock! 2.02.236
a little of all noble qualities: 2.05. 10
and out i have brought him to a little wood | a 2.06. 3
thou | so little dream'st upon my fortune that 3.01. 24
the little stars and all, that look like aglets. 3.04. 2
and little luce with the white legs, and 3.05. 26
faith, very little. love has us'd you kindly. 3.06. 67
yet a little | i did by imitation. 3.06. 80
stay a little; 3.06. 85
only a little let him fall before me, | that i 3.06.178
a little man, but of a tough soul, seeming | as 4.02.117
in a harmless distemper, sleeps little, 4.03. 4 P
note her a little further. 4.03. 28 P
rot, and consume themselves in little time. VEN 132
the heat i have from thence doth little harm, 195
"lie quietly, and hear a little more, | nay, do 709
and then my little heart were quite undone, | in 783
for every little grief to wet his eyes; 1179
devil, | little suspecteth the false worshipper: LUC 86
through little vents and crannies of the place 310
like little frosts that sometime threat the 331
a little harm done to a great good end | for 528
and waste huge stones with little water–drops. 959
but little stars may hide them when they list. 1008
the little birds that tune their morning's joy 1107
lays open all the little worms that creep; 1248
crystal walls each little mote will peep; 1251
that she her plaints a little while doth stay, 1364
gazing upon the greeks with little lust. 1384
then little strength rings out the doleful knell 1495
and little stars shot from their fixed places, 1525
grows | holds in perfection but a little moment; SON 15. 2
the little love–god, lying once asleep, | laid 154. 1
for on his visage was in little drawn | what LC 90

LITTLE–A 1 FR 0.0001 REL FR 0 V 1 P
tarry you a little–a while. WIV 1.04. 88 P

LITTLEST 1 FR 0.0001 REL FR 1 V 0 P
love is great, the littlest doubts are fear; HAM 3.02.171

/LIV'D 1 FR 0.0001 REL FR 1 V 0 P
/they /that, /when /richard /liv'd, /would /have 2H4 1.03.101

LIV'D 84 FR 0.0095 REL FR 70 V 14 P
give thanks you have liv'd so long, and make TMP 1.01. 24 P
i have liv'd fourscore years and upward; WIV 3.01. 56 P
now let me die, for i have liv'd long enough. 3.03. 44 P
have i liv'd to be carried in a basket like a 3.05. 4 P
have i liv'd to stand at the taunt of one that 5.05.142 P
of dark corners had been at home, he had liv'd. MM 4.03.158 P
he should have liv'd, | save that his riotous 4.04. 28
would yet he had liv'd! 4.04. 32
on this man condemn'd | as if my brother liv'd. 5.01.445
with her i liv'd in joy; ERR 1.01. 39
of his soul, | than when she liv'd indeed. ADO 4.01.230
that liv'd in the time of good neighbors. 5.02. 77 P
and when i liv'd, i was your other wife, | and 5.04. 60
she died, my lord, but whiles her slander liv'd. 5.04. 66
they have liv'd long on the alms–basket of words LLL 5.01. 38 P
o, you have liv'd in desolation here, | unseen, 5.02.357
"when in the world i liv'd, i was the world's 5.02.562
"when in the world i liv'd, i was the world's 5.02.568
which was the fairest dame | that liv'd, that MND 5.01.294
he would have liv'd many a fair year though hero AYL 4.01.100 P
him the most unnatural | that liv'd amongst men. 4.03.123
he was skillful enough to have liv'd still, if AWW 1.01. 30 P
to a strong mast that liv'd upon the sea; TN 1.02. 14
daughter, when my old wife liv'd, upon | this WT 4.04. 55
this hour, i have liv'd | to die when i desire. 4.04.461
as she liv'd peerless, | so her dead likeness, i 5.03. 14
sixteen years, and makes her | as she liv'd now. 5.03. 32
ay, and make it manifest where she has liv'd, 5.03.114
where liv'd? 5.03.124
my gracious liege, when that my father liv'd, JN 1.01. 95
they might have liv'd to bear and he to taste R2 3.04. 62
or four times, liv'd well and in good compass, 1H4 3.03. 19 P
upon hell–fire and dives that liv'd in purple; 3.03. 32 P
i have not liv'd all this while to have 2H4 2.04. 77 P
sell the lion's skin | while the beast liv'd, H5 4.03. 94
take her away, for she hath liv'd too long, | to 1H6 5.04. 34
thy body, | and then it liv'd in sweet elysium. 2H6 3.02.399
he durst not sit there, had your father liv'd. 3H6 1.01. 63
for who liv'd king, but i could dig his grave? 5.02. 21
thou hadst not liv'd to kill a son of mine. 5.06. 36
death, | and liv'd with looking on his images; R3 2.02. 50
again, | or die a soldier as i liv'd a king. 3.01. 93
he liv'd from all attainder of suspects. 3.05. 32
covert'st shelt'red traitor | that ever liv'd. 3.05. 34
and yet within these five hours hastings liv'd, 3.06. 8
his highness having liv'd so long with her, and H8 2.03. 2
as not to know the language i have liv'd in. 3.01. 44
have i liv'd thus long (let me speak myself, 3.01.125
whiles here he liv'd | upon this naughty earth? 5.01.137
the woefull'st man that ever liv'd in rome. TIT 3.01.289
both, | and pity 'tis you liv'd at odds so long. ROM 1.02. 5
have i once liv'd to see two honest men? TIM 5.01. 56
when caesar liv'd, he durst not thus have mov'd JC 4.03. 58
hath cassius liv'd | to be but mirth and 4.03.113
this chance, | i had liv'd a blessed time; MAC 2.03. 92
than on her feet, | died every day she liv'd. 4.03.111
i have liv'd long enough: 5.03. 22
he only liv'd but till he was a man, | the which 5.09. 6
would make mouths at him while my father liv'd, HAM 2.02.365 P
rogue, thou hast liv'd too long. ANT 2.05. 73
i have liv'd in such dishonor that the gods 4.14. 56
die when thou hast liv'd, | quicken with kissing 4.15. 38
with those my former fortunes | wherein i liv'd, 4.15. 54
his back above | the element they liv'd in. 5.02. 90
this charmian liv'd but now, she stood and spake 5.02.341
liv'd in court | (which rare it is to do) most CYM 1.01. 46
where i have liv'd at honest freedom, paid 3.03. 71
may drive us to a render | where we have liv'd, 4.04. 12
my faults, i never | had liv'd to put on this; 5.01. 9
a nobler sir ne'er liv'd | 'twixt sky and ground 5.05.145
how liv'd you? 5.05.384
that | i ear'd her language, liv'd in her eye, o TNK 3.01. 29
there such fellows liv'd when you were babes, STM II.C 63
why, there love liv'd, and there he could not VEN 246
but now i liv'd, and life was death's annoy, 497
who when he liv'd, his breath and beauty set 935
but true sweet beauty liv'd and died with him. 1080
but when adonis liv'd, sun and sharp air 1085
but that life liv'd in death, and death in life. LUC 406
devours his will, that liv'd by foul devouring. 700
when beauty liv'd and died as flowers do now, SON 68. 2
what merit liv'd in me that you should love 72. 2
"kind," and "true" have often liv'd alone, 105.13
die for goodness, who have liv'd for crime. 124.14

LIV'DST 1 FR 0.0001 REL FR 0 V 1 P
and still thou liv'dst but as a breakfast to the TIM 4.03.333 P

LIVE* *(also lief, lieve, life, etc.)*

/LIVE* 5 FR 0.0005 REL FR 5 V 0 P
/long /mayst /thou /live /in /richard's /seat R2 4.01.218
/i /should /not /live /long /after /i /saw R3 4.02.107
it, | and /live the purer with the other half. HAM 3.04.158
/if /she /live /long, | /and /in /the /end /meet LR 3.07.100
for caesar cannot /live | to be ungentle. ANT 5.01. 59

LIVE* 566 FR 0.0639 REL FR 455 V 111 P
true — save means to live. TMP 2.01. 51 P
sir, he may live. 2.01.114
long live gonzalo! 2.01.170
you 'mongst men | being most unfit to live. 3.03. 58
of mine own life, | or that for which i live; 4.01. 4
thy turfy mountains, where live nibbling sheep, 4.01. 62
let me live here ever; 4.01.122
merrily, merrily shall i live now, | under the 5.01. 93
to feed on your blood than live in your air. TGV 2.04. 28 P
bare liveries that they live by your bare words. 2.04. 46 P
which to requite, command me while i live. 3.01. 23
grace | let me not live to look upon your grace. 3.02. 21
and live as we do in this wilderness? 4.01. 61
thou shalt not live to brag what we have offer'd 4.01. 67
i take your offer, and will live with you, 4.01. 68
sure as i live, he had suffer'd for't. 4.04. 15 P
if shame live | in a disguise of love! 5.04.106
i'll ne'er be drunk whilst i live again, but in WIV 1.01.181 P
yet i live like a poor gentleman born. 1.01.275 P
mercy in vienna | live in thy tongue and heart. MM 1.01. 45
but, whilst i live, forget to drink after thee. 1.02. 38 P
truly, sir, i am a poor fellow that would live. 2.01.223 P
how would you live, pompey? 2.01.224 P
if you live to see this come to pass, say pompey 2.01.242 P
degrees, | but here they live, to end. 2.02. 99
o, let her brother live! 2.02.174
your brother cannot live. 2.04. 33
yet may he live a while; 2.04. 35
then, isabel, live chaste, and, brother, die; 2.04.184
i have hope to live, and am prepar'd to die. 3.01. 4
to sue to live, i find i seek to die, | and, 3.01. 42
yes, brother, you may live; 3.01. 63
sweet sister, let me live. 3.01.132
in this life, that it will let this man live! 3.01.233 P
causest to be done, | that is thy means to live. 3.02. 21
i drink, i eat, /array myself, and live. 3.02. 25
you better, sir, if i may live to report you. 3.02.161 P
unfit to live, or die; 4.03. 64
could all my travels warrant me they live. ERR 1.01.139
thou, or borrow, to make up the sum, | and live: 1.01.154
but, if thou live to see like right bereft, 2.01. 40
bed, | i live dis–stain'd, thou undishonored. 2.02.146
infect thy sap, and live on thy confusion. 2.02.180
i see a man here needs not live by shifts, 3.02.182
i may go the finer), i will live a bachelor. ADO 1.01.245 P
and there live we as merry as the day is long. 2.01. 49 P
is here, a man may live as quiet in hell as in a 2.01.258 P
i had as live have heard the night–raven, come 2.03. 82 P
did not think i should live till i were married. 2.03.244 P
do not live, hero, do not ope thine eyes; 4.01.123
come, lady, die to live; 4.01.253
i cannot bid you bid my daughter live — | that 5.01.279
he shall live no longer in monument than the 5.02. 79 P
i will live in thy heart, die in thy lap, and be 5.02.102 P
one hero died defil'd, but i do live, | and 5.04. 63
i do live, | and surely as i live, i am a maid. 5.04. 64
my kinsman, live unbruis'd and love my cousin. 5.04.111 P
lives, | live regist'red upon our brazen tombs, LLL 1.01. 2
sworn for three years' term to live with me, 1.01. 16
that is, to live and study here three years. 1.01. 35
crowns, | to have his title live in aquitaine; 2.01.145
a man, if i live; 3.01. 40 P

where all those pleasures live that art would 4.02.110
mew'd, | to live a barren sister all your life, MND 1.01. 72
so will i grow, so live, so die, my lord, | ere 1.01. 79
favors, | in those freckles live their savors. 2.01. 13
dote | upon the next live creature that it sees. 2.01.172
lysander, if you live, good sir, awake. 2.02.102
if i live to be as old as sibylla, i will die as MV 1.02.106 P
poor man and, god be thank'd, well to live. 2.02. 53 P
me choose, | for as i am, i live upon the rack. 3.02. 25
well then, confess and live. 3.02. 35
live thou, i live; 3.02. 61
live thou, i live; 3.02. 61
mean time | will live as maids and widows. 3.02.310
it is impossible i should live, all debts are 3.02.318 P
vow | to live in prayer and contemplation, 3.04. 28
e'en as many as could well live one by another. 3.05. 23 P
meet | the lord bassanio live an upright life, 3.05. 74
than to live still and write mine epitaph. 4.01.118
when you do take the means whereby i live. 4.01.377
he will, and if he live to be a man. 5.01.159
ay, if a woman live to be a man. 5.01.160
to do it, | unless he live until he be a man. 5.01.283
while i live i'll fear no other thing | so sore, 5.01.306
where will the old duke live? AYL 1.01.113 P
and there they live like the old robin hood of 1.01.116 P
my liege, | i cannot live out of her company. 1.03. 86
here lived i, but now live here no more. 2.03. 72
ambition shun, | and loves to live i' th' sun, 2.05. 39
live a little, comfort a little, cheer thyself a 2.06. 5 P
lack of a dinner if there live any thing in this 2.06. 17 P
as i do live by food, i met a fool, | who laid 2.07. 14
should have, | and i to live and die her slave." 3.02.154
stream of the world and to live in a nook merely 3.02.420 P
you shall tell me where in the forest you live. 3.02.432 P
we must be married, or we must live in bawdry. 3.03. 97
a scatt'red smile, and that i'll live upon. 3.05.104
upon you, and here live and die a shepherd. 5.02. 12 P
i can live no longer by thinking. 5.02. 50 P
i'll not fail, if i live. 5.02.122
master, your love must live a maid at home, SHR 1.01.182
will i live? 1.02.196
hers, | if whilst i live she will be only mine. 2.01.362
but one that scorn to live in this disguise, 4.02. 18
yourself, he shall need none so long as i live. 5.01. 24 P
grow there and to bear — "let me not live" — AWW 1.02. 55
when it was out — "let me not live," quoth he, 1.02. 58
and i | his servant live, and will his vassal 1.03.159
whether i live or die, be you the sons | of 2.01. 11
say to him i live, and observe his reports for 2.01. 45 P
as one near death to those that wish him live. 2.01.131
health shall live free, and sickness freely die. 2.01.168
i give | me and my service, ever whilst i live, 2.03.103
from courtly friends, with camping foes to live, 3.04. 14
o, let me live! 4.01. 83
for which live long to thank both heaven and me! 4.02. 67
braid, | marry that will, i live and die a maid. 4.02. 74
and truly, as i hope to live. 4.03.128 P
my reputation and credit and as i hope to live. 4.03.134 P
sir, if i were to live this present hour, i will 4.03.160 P
let me live, sir, in a dungeon, i' th' stocks, 4.03.243 P
i' th' stocks, or any where, so i may live. 4.03.245 P
lord, sir, let me live, or let me see my death! 4.03.309 P
simply the thing i am | shall make me live. 4.03.334
and, parolles, live | safest in shame! 4.03.337
flock of all affections else | that live in her; TN 1.01. 36
and thou shalt live as freely as thy lord, | to 1.04. 39
shall this fellow live? 2.05. 62 P
dost thou live by thy tabor? 3.01. 2 P
no, sir, i live by the church. 3.01. 3 P
i do live by the church; 3.01. 5 P
for i do live at my house, and my house doth 3.01. 6 P
it shall be done to-morrow morning if i live. 3.04.104 P
i will live to be thankful to thee for't. 4.02. 82 P
and too doubtful soul | may live at peace. 4.03. 28
live you the marble-breasted tyrant still. 5.01.124
no other excuse why they should desire to live. WT 1.01. 44 P
they would desire to live on crutches till he 1.01. 46 P
she would not live | the running of one glass. 1.02.305
and a goodly babe, | lusty and like to live. 2.02. 25
shall i live on to see this bastard kneel | and 2.03.155
let it live. 2.03.157
and the king shall live without an heir, if that 3.02.135 P
youth are forgiven you, you're well to live. 3.03.121 P
if tinkers may have leave to live, | and bear 4.03. 19
were i of your flock, | and only live by gazing. 4.04.110
we may live, son, to shed many more. 5.02.146 P
scarce any joy | did ever so long live; 5.03. 52
from france to england, there to live in peace. JN 2.01. 90
that faith would live again by death of need. 3.01.214
he shall not live. 3.03. 66
well, see to live; 4.01.121
doth arthur live? 4.02.260
arthur doth live, the king hath sent for you. 4.03. 75
that villain hubert told me he did live. 5.01. 42
that i must die here and live hence by truth? 5.04. 29
too good to be so, and too bad to live, | since R2 1.01. 40
in that i live, and for that will i die. 1.01.185
up thy youthful blood, be valiant and live. 1.03. 83
why, uncle, thou hast many years to live. 1.03.225
should dying men flatter with those that live? 2.01. 88
live in thy shame, but die not shame with thee! 2.01.135
love they to live that love and honor have. 2.01.138
which live like venom where no venom else | but 2.01.157
else | but only they have privilege to live. 2.01.158
and doth not herford live? 2.01.191
i live with bread like you, feel want, | taste 3.02.175
but ere the crown he looks for live in peace, 3.03. 95
for on my heart they tread now whilst i live, 3.03.158
give richard leave to live till richard die? 3.03.174
we lop away, that bearing boughs may live; 3.04. 64
thou dar'st not, coward, live to see that day. 4.01. 41
if i dare eat, or drink, or breathe, or live, 4.01. 73
as surely as i live, my lord. 4.01.102
him, | and long live henry, fourth of that name! 4.01.112
they shall not live within this world, i swear, 5.03.142
this prison where i live unto the world; 5.05. 2
that brings me food to make misfortune live? 5.05. 71
mouth | live scandaliz'd and foully spoken of. 1H4 1.03.154

what, ye knaves, young men must live! 2.02. 91 P
o, while you live, tell truth and shame the 3.01. 61
i had rather live | with cheese and garlic in a 3.01.159
in good sooth," and "as true as i live," and "as 3.01.249 P
john, you are so fretful you cannot live long. 3.03. 11 P
good compass, and now i live out of all order, 3.03. 19 P
but will/'t not live with the living? 5.01.138 P
all his offenses live upon my head | and on his 5.02. 20
and if we live, we live to tread on kings, | if 5.02. 85
and if we live, we live to tread on kings, | if 5.02. 85
sack, and live cleanly as a nobleman should do. 5.04.164 P
i had as live they would put ratsbane in my 2H4 1.02. 41 P
truth is, sir john, you live in great infamy. 1.02.136 P
buckles himself in my belt cannot live in less. 1.02.138 P
and our supplies live largely in the hope | of 1.03. 12
will i live? 2.01.161 P
no, by my faith, i must live among my neighbors; 2.04. 74 P
god let me not live, but i will murther your 2.04.134 P
very truth, sir, i had as live be hang'd, sir, 3.02.222 P
memory | shall as a pattern or a measure live, 4.04. 76
and never live to show th' incredulous world 4.05.153
and grant it may with thee in true peace live! 4.05.219
till you do live to see a son of mine | offend 5.02.105
so shall i live to speak my father's words: 5.02.107
faith, i will live so long as i may, that's the H5 2.01. 14 P
and when i cannot live any longer, i will do as 2.01. 15 P
gentlewomen that live honestly by the prick of 2.01. 34 P
i'll live by nym, and nym shall live by me. 2.01.110
i'll live by nym, and nym shall live by me. 2.01.110
condole the knight, for, lambkins, we will live. 2.01.127
withal, my lord, | let us not live in france; 3.05. 3
heart, and my duty, and my live, and my living, 3.06. 8 P
i had as live have my mistress a jade. 3.07. 59 P
if i live to see it, i will never trust his word 4.01.195 P
let it be a quarrel between us, if you live. 4.01.205 P
if ever i live to see it, i will challenge it. 4.01.217 P
and if to live, | the fewer men, the greater 4.03. 21
he that shall see this day, and live old age, 4.03. 44
shall witness live in brass of this day's work. 4.03. 97
so i will, my liege, as i live. 4.07.146 P
i will desire you to live in the mean time, and 5.01. 33 P
king henry the fift, too famous to live long! 1H6 1.01. 6
why live we idly here? 1.02. 13
and while i live, i'll ne'er fly from a man. 1.02.103
that could not live asunder day or night. 2.02. 31
york, | i will not live to be accounted warwick. 2.04.120
for live i will not if my father die. 4.05. 51
come, side by side, together live and die, | and 4.05. 54
well, go to, we'll have no bastards live, 5.04. 70
long live queen margaret, england's happiness! 2H6 1.01. 37
shall i not live to be aveng'd on her? 1.03. 82
warwick may live to be the best of all. 1.03.112
long live our sovereign richard, england's king! 2.02. 63
richard shall live to make the earl of warwick 2.02. 81
done, | live in your country here in banishment, 2.03. 12
and i may live to do you kindness if | you do it 2.04. 83
for henry weeps that thou dost live so long. 3.02.121
as surely as my soul intends to live | with that 3.02.153
live thou to joy thy life; 3.02.365
if i depart from thee, i cannot live, | and in 3.02.388
so thou wilt let me live, and feel no pain. 3.03. 4
can i make men live, whe'er they will or no? 3.03. 10
be not so rash, take ransom, let him live. 4.01. 28
will i stay | and live alone as secret as i may. 4.04. 48
that cause they have been most worthy to live. 4.07. 46 P
o, let me live! 4.07.104
and delight to live in slavery to the nobility. 4.08. 28 P
nor knows he how to live but by the spoil, 4.08. 39
were't not a shame that, whilst you live at jar, 4.08. 41
who would live turmoiled in the court | and may 4.10. 16
i'll send them all as willing as i live. 5.01. 51
may iden live to merit such a bounty, | and 5.01. 81
and never live but true unto his liege! 5.01. 82
and we will live | to see their day, and them 5.02. 88
god knows how long it is i have to live, | and 5.03. 17
for he that interrupts him shall not live. 3H6 1.01.123
or live in peace abandon'd and despis'd! 1.01.188
and whilst i live | to honor me as thy king and 1.01.197
long live king henry! plantagenet, embrace him. 1.01.202
and long live thou, and these thy forward sons! 1.01.203
be thou reveng'd on men, and let me live. 1.03. 20
line, | and leave not one alive, i live in hell. 1.03. 33
ah, let me live in prison all my days, | and 1.03. 43
ne'er may he live to see a sunshine day | that 2.01.187
year, | how many years a mortal man may live. 2.05. 29
and whiles i live, t' account this world but 3.02.169
man, | and forc'd to live in scotland a forlorn; 3.03. 26
renowned prince, how shall poor henry live, 3.03.214
long live edward the fourth! 4.07. 76
and, live we how we can, yet die we must. 5.02. 28
famous grandfather | doth live again in thee. 5.04. 53
long mayst thou live | to bear his image and 5.04. 53
why should she live, to fill the world with 5.05. 44
but i shall live, my lord, to give them thanks R3 1.01.127
he cannot live, i hope, and must not die | till 1.01.145
intent, | clarence hath not another day to live: 1.01.150
so i might live one hour in your sweet bosom. 1.02.124
but shall i live in hope? 1.02.199
all men, i hope, live so. 1.02.200
cannot a plain man live and think no harm, | but 1.03. 51
long mayst thou live to wail thy children's 1.03.203
that none of you may live his natural age, | but 1.03.212
and in that shame still live my sorrow's rage! 1.03.277
live each of you the subjects to his hate, | and 1.03.301
so i am — to let him live. 1.04.114 P
man that means to live well endeavors to trust 1.04.143 P
to trust to himself and live without it. 1.04.144 P
and said, "dear brother, live, and be a king"? 2.01.114
if you will live, lament; 2.02. 43
methinks the truth should live from age to age, 3.01. 76
so wise so young, they say do never live long. 3.01. 79
wit, | his wit set down to make his valure live. 3.01. 86
and if i live until i be a man, | i'll win our 3.01. 91
nor none that live, i hope. 3.01.147
and if they live, i hope i need not fear. 3.01.148
hate, | i live to look upon their tragedy. 3.02. 59
you live that shall cry woe for this hereafter. 3.03. 7
that by great preservation | we live to tell it, 3.05. 37

long live richard, england's worthy king! 3.07.240
and live with richmond, from the reach of hell. 4.01. 42
still live they, and for ever let them last! 4.02. 7
that edward still should live true noble prince! 4.02. 16
that i may live to say, "the dog is dead." 4.04. 78
o, let her live! 4.04.206
so she may live unscarr'd of bleeding slaughter, 4.04.210
the children live whose fathers thou hast 4.04.391
the parents live whose children thou hast 4.04.393
live and flourish! 5.03.130
live and flourish! 5.03.138
live and beget a happy race of kings! 5.03.152
let them not live to taste this land's increase 5.05. 38
that she may long live here, god say amen! 5.05. 41
their curses now | live where their prayers did; H8 1.02. 63
now, madam, may his highness live in freedom, 1.02.200
may he live | longer than i have time to tell 2.01. 90
we live not to be grip'd by meaner persons. 2.02.135
desperate to be honest), | and live a subject? 3.01. 87
they that my trust must grow to, live not here. 3.01. 89
the letter, as i live, with all the business | i 3.02.221
if we live thus tamely, | to be thus jaded by a 3.02.279
(whom, if he live, will scarce be gentlemen), 3.02.292
you to your meditations | how to live better. 3.02.346
men's evil manners live in brass, their virtues 4.02. 45
that it may find | good time, and live; 5.01. 22
mean, | which ye shall never have while i live. 5.02.182
as i live, | if the king blame me for't, i'll 5.03. 77
i could live and die in the eyes of troilus. TRO 1.02.242 P
when we vow to weep seas, live in fire, eat 3.02. 78 P
which you say live to come in my behalf. 3.03. 16
jove, let aeneas live, | if to my sword his fate 4.01. 26
for we may live to have need of such a verse. 4.04. 22 P
i'll make my match to live, | the kiss you take 4.05. 37
your fair sword, | you bid them rise and live. 5.03. 42
i do believe thee, live. 5.04. 30
pursue thy life, and live aye with thy name! 5.10. 34
general food at first | which you do live upon; COR 1.01.132
that natural competency | whereby they live. 1.01.140
and live you yet? o my sweet lady, pardon. 2.01.180
suffer't, and live with such as cannot rule, 3.01. 40
now, as i live, i will. 3.01. 64
word, i also am | longer to live most weary, and 4.05. 95
and cannot live but to thy shame, unless | it be 4.05.100
i had as live be a condemn'd man. 4.05.176 P
live, and thrive! 4.06. 23
it were as virtuous to lie as to live chastely. 5.02. 27 P
rome, | then let my father's honors live in me, TIT 1.01. 7
in peace and honor live lord titus long! 1.01.157
my noble lord and father, live in fame! 1.01.158
lavinia, live, outlive thy father's days, | and 1.01.167
long live lord titus, my beloved brother, 1.01.169
crown him and say, "long live our emperor!" 1.01.229
and say, "long live our emperor saturnine!" 1.01.233
and that he will, and shall, if lucius live. 1.01.282
but if we live we'll be as sharp with you. 1.01.410
and never whilst i live deceive men so; 3.01.189
if lucius live, he will requite your wrongs, 3.01.296
and, uncle, so will i, and if i live. 4.01.112
it shall not live. 4.02. 80
shall she live to betray this guilt of ours, | a 4.02.149
but if i live, his feigned ecstasies | shall be 4.04. 21
thy child shall live, and i will see it 5.01. 60
unless thou swear to me my child shall live. 5.01. 68
tell on thy mind, i say thy child shall live. 5.01. 69
a devil, | to live and burn in everlasting fire, 5.01.148
would i were dead, so you did live again! 5.03.173
ay, while you live, draw your neck out of collar ROM 1.01. 4 P
she hath sworn that she will still live chaste? 1.01.217
vow | do i live dead that live to tell it now. 1.01.224
vow | do i live dead that live to tell it now. 1.01.224
i warrant, and i should live a thousand years, 1.03. 46
and i might live to see thee married once, | i 1.03. 61
for nought so vile that on the earth doth live 2.03. 17
romeo slew tybalt, romeo must not live. 3.01.181
that ever i should live to see thee dead! 3.02. 63
live here in heaven and may look on her, | but 3.03. 32
where thou shalt live till we can find a time 3.03.150
i must be gone and live, or stay and die. 3.05. 11
if thou couldst, thou couldst not make him live; 3.05. 71
where that same banish'd runagate doth live, 3.05. 89
to live an unstain'd wife to my sweet love. 4.01. 88
or, if i live, is it not very like | the 4.03. 36
and you will have me live, play "heart's ease." 4.05.103 P
live and be prosperous, and farewell, good 5.03. 42
live, and hereafter say | a madman's mercy bid 5.03. 66
vouchsafe my labor, and long live your lordship! TIM 1.01.152
long may he live in fortunes! shall we in? 1.01.282
the gods keep you old enough that you may live 3.05.103
live loath'd, and long, | most smiling, smooth, 3.06. 93
and yet confusion live! 4.01. 21
or to live | but in a dream of friendship, | to 4.02. 33
whose naked natures live in all the spite | of 4.03.228
live, and love thy misery. 4.03.395
long live so, and so die. i am quit. 4.03.396
we cannot live on grass, on berries, water, | as 4.03.422
go, live rich and happy, | but thus condition'd: 4.03.525
power, and thy good name | live with authority; 5.01.163
go, live still; 5.01.188
there does not live a man." 5.03. 4
truly, sir, all that i live by is with the awl: JC 1.01. 21 P
i had as lief not be as live to be | in awe of 1.02. 95
for he will live, and laugh at this hereafter. 2.01.191
my heart laments that virtue cannot live | out 2.03. 13
if thou read this, o caesar, thou mayest live; 2.03. 15
live a thousand years, | i shall not find myself 3.01.159
than that caesar were dead, to live all freemen? 3.02. 24 P
live, brutus, live, live! 3.02. 48
live, brutus, live, live! 3.02. 48
live, brutus, live, live! 3.02. 48
let not a traitor live! 3.02.205 P
upon condition publius shall not live, | who is 4.01. 4
he shall not live; 4.01. 6
if i do live, | i will be good to thee. 4.03.265
made in caesar's heart, | crying, "long live! 5.01. 32
o, coward that i am, to live so long, | to see 5.03. 34
he shall live a man forbid; MAC 1.03. 21
live you? 1.03. 42

life, | and live a coward in thine own esteem, 1.07. 43
contend about them, | whether they live or die. 2.02. 8
then live, macduff; 4.01. 82
thou shalt not live, | that i may tell 4.01. 84
macbeth | shall live the lease of nature, pay 4.01. 99
how will you live? 4.02. 31
no, not to live. 4.03.103
and live to be the show and gaze o' th' time! 5.08. 24
long live the king! HAM 1.01. 3
as i do live, my honor'd lord, 'tis true, | and 1.02.221
and thy commandement all alone shall live 1.05.102
then you live about her waist, or in the middle 2.02.232 P
if it live in your memory, begin at this line — 2.02.448 P
epitaph than their ill report while you live. 2.02.526 P
(all but one) shall live, the rest shall keep as 3.01.148 P
do, i had as live the town–crier spoke my lines. 3.02. 3 P
and thou shalt live in this fair world behind, 3.02.175
safe | that live and feed upon your majesty. 3.03. 10
but to live | in the rank sweat of an enseamed 3.04. 91
i do not know | why yet i live to say, "this 4.04. 44
that i /shall live and tell him to his teeth, 4.07. 56
i cannot live to hear the news from england, 5.02.354
for ever, and live the belov'd of your brother. LR 1.02. 54 P
that it may live | and be a thwart disnatur'd 1.04.282
when slanders do not live in tongues; 3.02. 89
merlin shall make, for i live before his time. 3.02. 95 P
he that will think to live till he be old, 3.07. 69
might i but live to see thee in my touch, | i'ld 4.01. 23
i live | to thank thee for the love thou 4.02. 94
gloucester's eyes being out, | to let him live; 4.05. 10
if edgar live, o bless him! 4.06. 40
kent, how shall i live and work | to match thy 4.07. 1
so we'll live, | and pray, and sing, and tell 5.03. 11
shall never see so much, nor live so long. 5.03.327
that i /did love the moor to live with him, | my OTH 1.03.248
it is silliness to live, when to live is torment 1.03.308 P
is silliness to live, when to live is torment; 1.03.308 P
long live she so! and long live you to think so! 3.03.226
long live she so! and long live you to think so! 3.03.226
be a toad | and live upon the vapor of a dungeon 3.03.271
but let her live. 3.03.475
and be damn'd to–night, for she shall not live. 4.01.182 P
where either i must live or bear no life; 4.02. 58
live roderigo, | he calls me to a restitution 5.01. 14
kill me to–morrow, let me live to–night! 5.02. 80
did he live now, | this sight would make him do 5.02.206
i am not sorry neither, i'ld have thee live; 5.02.289
and indeed the tears live in an onion that ANT 1.02.169 P
let her live | to join our kingdoms and our 2.02.150
i had as live have a reed that will do me no 2.07. 12 P
thee, and | requires to live in egypt, which not 3.12. 12
if that thy father live, let him repent | thou 3.13.134
or i will live, | or bathe my dying honor in the 4.02. 5
honor in the blood | shall make it live again. 4.02. 7
'tis well th' art gone, | if it be well to live; 4.12. 40
sir, you may not live to wear | all your true 4.14.133
shot | of angry eyes, not comforted to live, CYM 1.01. 90
leave | as long a term as yet we have to live, 1.01.107
should he make me | live, like diana's priest, 1.06.133
blessed live you long, | a lady to the worthiest 1.06.159
how live? 3.04.128
our good minds | by this rude place we live in. 3.06. 65
long live caesar! 3.07. 10
flowers | whilst summer lasts and i live here, 4.02.219
i am merrier to die than thou art to live. 5.04.171 P
there are verier knaves desire to live, for all 5.04.201 P
i know not why, wherefore, | to say "live, boy." 5.05. 96
live; 5.05. 96
speak, | wilt have him live? 5.05.111
had rather thou shouldst live while nature will 5.05.151
the malice towards you to forgive you, live, 5.05.419
yet in two, | as you will live, resolve it you. PER 1.01. 71
he must not live to trumpet forth my infamy, 1.01.145
as thou | wilt live, fly after, and like an 1.01.161
but in our orbs /we'll live so round and safe, 1.02.122
master, i marvel how the fishes live in the sea. 2.01. 27 P
princes in this should live like gods above, 2.03. 59
but if the prince do live, let us salute him, 2.04. 27
if in the world he live, we'll seek him out; 2.04. 29
live, noble helicane! 2.04. 40
gentlemen, this queen will live. 3.02. 92
live, and make | us weep to hear your fate, fair 3.02.102
were as pretty a proportion to live quietly, and 4.02. 27 P
light into my hands, where you are like to live. 4.02. 73 P
ay, and you shall live in pleasure. 4.02. 76 P
to weep that you live as ye do makes pity in 4.02.119 P
several clime | where our scenes seems to live. 4.04. 7
where do you live? 5.01.113
i may depart with little, while i live; TNK 2.01. 1 P
patience, | we shall live long, and loving. 2.02. 86
what a misery | it is to live abroad, and every 2.02. 98
i shall live | to knock thy brains out with my 2.02.218
can these two live, | and have the agony of love 3.06.218
on others, on /him | live in fair dwelling. 5.03. 55
and charge me live to comfort this unfriended, 5.03.141
to live still, | have their good wishes; 5.04. 5
thou art a right good man, and while i live, 5.04. 97
not /one of you should live an aged man, | for STM II.C 83
that thine may live, when thou thyself art dead; VEN 172
base, | that it will live engraven in my face. LUC 203
to slay the tiger that doth live by slaughter, 955
let him have time to live a loathed slave, | let 984
and time to see one that by alms doth live 986
thee, | but if i live, thou liv'st in my defame. 1033
quoth she, "i live, and seek in vain | some 1044
"o, that is gone for which i sought to live, 1051
to live or die which of the twain were better, 1154
life, | the one will live, the other being dead: 1187
to those that live and think no shame of me. 1204
i should not live to speak another word; 1642
where shall i live now lucrece is unlived? 1754
then live, sweet lucrece, live again and see 1770
lucrece, live again and see | thy father die, 1770
breath, | and live to be revenged on her death. 1778
the truth i shall not know, but live in doubt, PP 2.13
all those pleasures live that art can comprehend 5. 6
crabbed age and youth cannot live together: 12. 1
poor corydon must live alone, | other help for 17.35
live with me, and be my love, | and we will all 19. 1
thee move, | then live with me, and be my love. 19.16
me move | to live with thee and be thy love. 19.20
but if thou live rememb'red not to be, | die SON 3.13
so great a sum of sums, yet canst not live? 4. 8
that beauty still may live in thine or thee. 10.14
no longer yours than you yourself here live: 13. 2
can make you live yourself in eyes of men: 16.12
and you must live drawn by your own sweet skill. 16.14
you should live twice, in it and in my rhyme. 17.14
my love shall in my verse ever live young. 19.14
which in thy breast doth live, as thine in me: 22. 7
thou art the grave where buried love doth live, 31. 9
suffic'd, | and by a part of all thy glory live. 37.12
even for this, let us divided live, | and our 39. 5
for that sweet odor which doth in it live. 54. 4
they live unwoo'd, and unrespected fade, | die 54.10
you live in this, and dwell in lovers' eyes. 55.14
and they shall live, and he in them still green. 63.14
ah, wherefore with infection should he live, 67. 1
why should he live, now nature bankrout is, 67. 9
away, | to live a second life on second head; 68. 7
is, | and live no more to shame nor me nor you. 72.12
no praise to thee but what in thee doth live. 79.12
or i shall live your epitaph to make, | or you 81. 1
you still shall live (such virtue hath my pen) 81.13
so shall i live, supposing thou art true, | like 93. 1
for there can live no hatred in thine eye, 93. 5
sweet, | though to itself it only live and die, 94.10
spite of him, i'll live in this poor rhyme, 107.11
yet this shall i ne'er know, but live in doubt, 144.13
then, soul, live thou upon thy servant's loss, 146. 9
LIVED 8 FR 0.0009 REL FR 8 V 0 P
years till now almost fourscore | here lived i, AYL 2.03. 72
but in that small most greatly lived | this star H5 ep 5
his eyeballs further out than when he lived, 2H6 3.02.169
i have lived | to see inherited my very wishes COR 2.01.198
so much differ, | and we alive that lived? TIM 3.01. 47
man | that ever lived in the tide of times. JC 3.01.257
my father,'in his habit as he lived! HAM 3.04.135
of me, | antiochus from incest lived not free; PER 2.04. 2
LIVELESS 6 FR 0.0006 REL FR 6 V 0 P
wend, | but to procrastinate his liveless end. ERR 1.01.158
up | is but a quintain, a mere liveless block. AYL 1.02.251
in life so liveless as it shows itself. H5 4.02. 55
there let his head and liveless body lie, 2H6 4.01.142
"fie, liveless picture, cold and senseless stone VEN 211
in scorn of nature, art gave liveless life: LUC 1374
LIVELIER 1 FR 0.0001 REL FR 1 V 0 P
lives in these touches, livelier than life. TIM 1.01. 38
LIVELIHOOD 3 FR 0.0003 REL FR 2 V 1 P
her sorrows takes all livelihood from her cheek. AWW 1.01. 51 P
his face | by any livelihood he show'd to–day? R3 3.04. 55
palm, | the president of pith and livelihood, VEN 26
LIVELONG 4 FR 0.0004 REL FR 4 V 0 P
upon a lazy bed the livelong day | breaks TRO 1.03.147
and there have sate | the livelong day, with JC 1.01. 41
the obscure bird | clamor'd the livelong night. MAC 2.03. 60
have heard | strange howls this livelong night; TNK 3.02. 12
LIVELY 14 FR 0.0015 REL FR 13 V 1 P
which i so lively acted with my tears | that my TGV 4.04.169
some lively touches of my daughter's favor. AYL 5.04. 27
as lively painted as the deed was done. SHR in.2. 56
o, that record is lively in my soul! TN 5.01.246
to see the life as lively mock'd as ever | still WT 5.03. 19
shall i do | now i behold thy lively body so? TIT 3.01.105
president, and lively warrant | for me, most 5.03. 44
lucio and the lively helena." ROM 1.02. 70 P
the best, | thou counterfeit'st most lively. TIM 5.01. 82
but now i died, and death was lively joy. VEN 498
her lively color kill'd with deadly cares. LUC 1593
for her griefs, so lively shown, | made me think PP 20.17
beggar'd of blood to blush through lively veins, SON 67.10
this holy fire of love | a dateless lively heat, 153. 6
LIVER* 18 FR 0.0020 REL FR 11 V 7 P
upon my heart | abates the ardor of my liver. TMP 4.01. 56
with liver burning hot. WIV 2.01.117
mourn, | if ever love had interest in his liver, ADO 4.01.231
and let my liver rather heat with wine | than my MV 1.01. 81
upon me to wash your liver as clean as a sound AYL 3.02.422 P
when liver, brain, and heart, | these sovereign TN 1.01. 36
no motion of the liver, but the palate, | that 2.04. 98
this wins him, liver and all. 2.05. 95 P
fire in your heart, and brimstone in your liver. 3.02. 21 P
so much blood in his liver as will clog the foot 3.02. 61 P
were my wive's liver | infected as her life, she WT 1.02.304
and settled) left the liver white and pale, 2H4 4.03.104 P
my knight, i will inflame thy noble liver, | and 5.05. 31
be brisk a while, and the longer liver take all. ROM 1.05. 15 P
digg'd i' th' dark, | liver of blaspheming jew, MAC 4.01. 26
i had rather heat my liver with drinking. ANT 1.02. 24 P
which i will add | to you, the liver, heart, and CYM 5.05. 14
to quench the coal which in his liver glows. LUC 47
LIVERIES 7 FR 0.0008 REL FR 3 V 4 P
by their bare liveries that they live by your TGV 2.04. 45 P
angry winter, change | their wonted liveries; MND 2.01.113
bassanio, who indeed gives rare new liveries. MV 2.02.109 P
letters deliver'd, put the liveries to making, 2.02.116 P
if i had had time to have made new liveries, i 2H4 5.05. 11 P
o, never let their crimson liveries wear! VEN 506
kept hearts in liveries, but mine own was free, LC 195
LIVERS* 10 FR 0.0011 REL FR 6 V 4 P
who, inward search'd, have livers white as milk, MV 3.02. 86
hot livers and cold purses. 1H4 2.04.323 P
the heat of our livers with the bitterness of 2H4 1.02.175 P
born, | and range with humble livers in content, H8 2.03. 20
respect | make livers pale and lustihood deject. TRO 2.02. 50
raw eyes, dirt–rotten livers, whissing lungs, 5.01. 20 P
abhorr'd | than spotted livers in the sacrifice. 5.03. 18
use thee not so hardly | as prouder livers do. CYM 3.03. 9
prithee think | there's livers out of britain. 3.04.140
we maids that have our livers perish'd, crack'd TNK 4.03. 23 P
LIVER–VEIN 1 FR 0.0001 REL FR 1 V 0 P
this is the liver–vein, which makes flesh a LLL 4.03. 72
LIVERY 28 FR 0.0031 REL FR 27 V 1 P
it now, | by putting on the destin'd livery. MM 2.04.138
o, 'tis the cunning livery of hell, | the 3.01. 94
choice, | you can endure the livery of a nun, MND 1.01. 70
the shadowed livery of the burnish'd sun, | to MV 2.01. 2
give him a livery | more guarded than his 2.02.154
by his attorneys–general to sue | his livery, R2 2.01.204
i am denied to sue my livery here, | and yet my 2.03.129
to sue his livery and beg his peace, | with 1H4 4.03. 62
and i will apparel them all in one livery, that 2H6 4.02. 74 P
to achieve | the silver livery of advised age, 5.02. 47
the king, | to be her men and wear her livery. R3 1.01. 80
her vestal livery is but sick and green, | and ROM 2.02. 8
but i'll be hang'd, sir, if he wear your livery. 3.01. 57
yet do our hearts wear timon's livery, | that TIM 4.02. 17
being nature's livery, or fortune's star, | his HAM 1.04. 32
and good | he likewise gives a frock or livery, 3.04.164
the light and careless livery that it wears 4.07. 79
in his livery | walk'd crowns and crownets; ANT 5.02. 90
a hilding for a livery, a squire's cloth, | a CYM 2.03.123
twelve moons more she'll wear diana's livery; PER 2.05. 10
see again, | a vestal livery will i take me to, 3.04. 10
whom, o goddess, | wears yet thy silver livery. 5.03. 7
face | the livery of the warlike maid appears, TNK 4.02.106
ne'er saw the beauteous livery that he wore — VEN 1107
i give | a badge of fame to slander's livery, LUC 1054
(for why her face wore sorrow's livery), | but 1222
thy youth's proud livery, so gaz'd on now, SON 2. 3
did livery falseness in a pride of truth. LC 105
LIVE'S 13 FR 0.0014 REL FR 13 V 0 P
it, and she reckon'd it | at her live's rate. AWW 5.03. 91
my date of life out for his sweet live's loss. JN 4.03.106
though richard my live's counsel would not hear, R2 2.01. 15
till then fair hope must hinder live's decay; 3H6 4.04. 16
sweetly in force unto her fair live's end. R3 4.04.351
tongue | hath almost ended his live's history. JC 5.05. 40
that will ravin up | thine own live's means! MAC 2.04. 29
to see his daughter, all his live's delight. PER 4.04. 12
leaden slumber with live's strength doth fight, LUC 124
to kill thine honor with thy live's decay; 516
my live's foul deed, my life's fair end shall 1208
live's lasting date from cancell'd destiny. 1729
until live's composition be recured | by those SON 45. 9
LIVES' 2 FR 0.0002 REL FR 2 V 0 P
which dreads not yet their lives' destruction. TIT 2.03. 50
follow'd me so near (o, our lives' sweetness! LR 5.03.185
/LIVES 3 FR 0.0003 REL FR 3 V 0 P
/lives /so /in /hope, /as /in /an /early /spring 2H4 1.03. 38
/he /down /himself /and /all /their /lives 4.01.125
and slay thy lady that in thy life /lives, | by ROM 3.03.117
LIVES 222 FR 0.0251 REL FR 202 V 20 P
we are merely cheated of our lives by drunkards. TMP 1.01. 56
but how is it | that this lives in thy mind? 1.02. 49
but that he writes | how happily he lives, how TGV 1.03. 57
my dog be the sourest–natur'd dog that lives: 2.03. 6 P
he lives not now that knows me to be in love, 3.01.265 P
that they may hold excus'd our lawless lives; 4.01. 52
for beauty lives with kindness. 4.02. 45
not so; i think she lives. 4.04. 75
one foul wrong, | lives not to act another. MM 2.02.104
reports, but the best is, he lives not in them. 4.03.160 P
fearing death, | than that which lives to fear. 5.01.398
who, wanting guilders to redeem their lives, ERR 1.01. 8
for slander lives upon succession, | for ever 3.01.105
if she lives till doomsday, she'll burn a week 3.02. 99 P
second to none that lives here in the city: 5.01. 7
no glory lives behind the back of such. ADO 3.01.110
the practice of it lives in john the bastard, 4.01.188
with shame | lives in death with glorious fame." 5.03. 8
let fame, that all hunt after in their lives, LLL 1.01. 1
eyes, | lives not alone immured in the brain, 4.03.325
for a light heart lives long. 5.02. 18
withering on the virgin thorn | grows, lives, MND 1.01. 78
by white hairs, but competency lives longer. MV 1.02. 9 P
yet it lives there uncheck'd that antonio hath a 3.01. 2 P
this roof | the enemy of all your graces lives. AYL 2.03. 18
and the other lives merrily because he feels no 3.02.321 P
than he that dies and lives by bloody drops? 3.05. 7
my father dead, my fortune lives for me, | and i SHR 1.02.191
lives my sweet son? 5.01.112
so in approof lives not his epitaph | as in your AWW 1.02. 50
but riddle–like lives sweetly where she dies! 1.03.217
does not our lives consist of the four elements? TN 2.03. 9 P
and we do not, it is pity of our lives. 2.05. 12 P
while she lives | my heart will be a burthen to WT 2.03.205
transported that | he'll think anon it lives. 5.03. 70
but it appears she lives, | though yet she speak 5.03.117
who lives and dares but say thou didst not well JN 1.01.271
to verify our title with their lives. 2.01.277
rescue those breathing lives to die in beds, 2.01.419
which only lives but by the death of faith, 3.01.212
there where my fortune lives, there my life dies 3.01.338
thy voluntary oath | lives in this bosom, dearly 3.03. 24
of a wicked heinous fault | lives in his eye; 4.02. 72
even with a treacherous fine of all your lives, 5.04. 38
despite of death that lives upon my grave, | to R2 1.01.168
be ready, as your lives shall answer it, | at 1.01.198
there lives or dies, true to king richard's 1.03. 86
are men's ends mark'd than their lives before. 2.01. 11
king severely prosecute | 'gainst us, our lives, 2.01.245
where nothing lives but crosses, cares, and 2.02. 79
with too much urging your pernicious lives, 3.01. 4
our lands, our lives, and all are bullingbrook's 3.02.151
our holy lives must win a new world's crown, 5.01. 24
mine honor lives when his dishonor dies, | or my 5.03. 70
the traitor lives, the true man's put to death. 5.03. 73
so is it in the music of men's lives. 5.05. 44
and in the reproof of this lives the jest. 1H4 1.02.190 P
the lives of those that he did lead to fight 1.03. 82
there lives not three good men unhang'd in 2.04.130 P
a comfort of retirement lives in this. 4.01. 56
you, my lord, or any scot that this day lives. 4.03. 12
supposition all our lives shall be stuck full of 5.02. 8
the lives of all your loving complices | /lean 2H4 1.01.163
it may chance cost some of us our lives, for he 2.01. 11 P
he lives upon mouldy stew'd pruins and dried 2.04.146 P
there is a history in all men's lives, 3.01. 80
she lives, master shallow. 3.02.200 P
by which his grace must mete the lives of other, 4.04. 77
nature, | and to our purposes he lives no more. 5.02. 5
but harry lives, that shall convert those tears 5.02. 60
leman mine, | and a merry heart lives long–a." 5.03. 48

that owe yourselves, your lives, and services H5 1.02. 34
for mine own part, i have not a case of lives. 3.02. 5 P
we yield our town and lives to thy soft mercy. 3.03. 48
be ransom'd, and a many poor men's lives sav'd. 4.01.123 P
let us our lives, our souls, | our debts, our 4.01.230
let us on heaps go offer up our lives. 4.05. 18
lives he, good uncle? 4.06. 4
o no, he lives, but is took prisoner, | and lord 1H6 1.01.145
his trespass yet lives guilty in thy blood, 2.04. 94
heir, | i lost my liberty, and they their lives. 2.05. 81
i, as sure as english henry lives | and as his 3.02. 80
now they meet where both their lives are done. 4.03. 38
lives, honors, lands, and all, hurry to loss. 4.03. 53
his fame lives in the world, his shame in you. 4.04. 46
to hazard all our lives in one small boat! 4.06. 33
it dies, and if it had a thousand lives. 5.04. 75
the duke yet lives that henry shall depose; 2H6 1.04. 30
"the duke yet lives that henry shall depose; 1.04. 59
no, stir not for your lives, let her pass by. 2.04. 18
the lives of those which we have lost in fight 4.01. 21
for your king, your country, and your lives, 4.05. 11
soldiers, this day have you redeem'd your lives, 4.09. 15
i'll have more lives | than drops of blood were 3H6 1.01. 96
here, their lives and thine | were not revenge 1.03. 25
desperate thieves, all hopeless of their lives, 1.04. 42
offering their own lives in their young's 2.02. 32
words will cost ten thousand lives this day. 2.02.177
if you contend, a thousand lives must wither. 2.05.102
for many lives stand between me and home; 3.02.173
henry now lives in scotland at his ease; 3.03.151
have sold their lives unto the house of york, 5.01. 74
yet lives our pilot still. 5.04. 6
still breathes, edward still lives and reigns; R3 1.01.161
or any creeping venom'd thing that lives! 1.02. 20
he lives, that loves thee better than he could. 1.02.141
let him be crown'd, in him your comfort lives. 2.02. 98
i say, without characters fame lives long. 3.01. 81
for now he lives in fame though not in life. 3.01. 88
dispatch, the limit of your lives is out. 3.03. 8
looks | lives like a drunken sailor on a mast, 3.04. 99
because, my lord, you know my mother lives. 3.05. 94
your mother lives a witness to his vow — | and 3.07.180
young edward lives: 4.02. 10
ha? am i king? 'tis so — but edward lives. 4.02. 14
richard yet lives, hell's black intelligencer, 4.04. 71
and therefore level not to hit their lives. 4.04.203
no, to their lives ill friends were contrary. 4.04.217
these famish'd beggars weary of their lives, 5.03.329
now civil wounds are stopp'd, peace lives again; 5.05. 40
after so many hours, lives, speeches spent, TRO 2.02. 1
so dying love lives still. 3.01.124
he's a bear indeed, that lives like a lamb. COR 2.01. 12 P
he did | run reeking o'er the lives of men, as 2.02.119
at antium lives he? 3.01. 17
lives not this day within the city walls. TIT 1.01. 26
he lives in fame, that died in virtue's cause. 1.01.390
to answer their suspicion with their lives. 2.03.298
therefore mine shall save my brothers' lives. 3.01.166
but now nor lucius nor lavinia lives | but in 3.01.294
but he and his shall know that justice lives 4.04. 23
cut off the proud'st conspirator that lives. 4.04. 26
your lives shall pay the forfeit of the peace. ROM 1.01. 97
love's weak childish bow she lives uncharm'd. 1.01.211
the fish lives in the sea, and 'tis much pride 1.03. 89
of cats, nothing but one of your nine lives; 3.01. 78 P
my husband lives that tybalt would have slain, 3.02.105
heaven is here | where juliet lives, and every 3.03. 30
more courtship lives | in carrion flies than 3.03. 34
as that the villain lives which slaughter'd him. 3.05. 79
that is because the traitor murderer lives. 3.05. 84
confusion's /cure lives not | in these 4.05. 65
she's not well married that lives married long, 4.05. 77
and her immortal part with angels lives. 5.01. 19
here lives a caitiff wretch would sell it him." 5.01. 52
artificial strife | lives in these touches, TIM 1.01. 38
good for their meat, and safer for their lives. 1.02. 45
who lives that's not depraved or depraves? 1.02.140
that death in me at others' lives may laugh. 4.03.380
take wealth and lives together, | do, /villains, 4.03.433
the evil that men do lives after them, | the JC 3.02. 75
the thane of cawdor lives | a prosperous MAC 1.03. 72
the thane of cawdor lives; 1.03.108
who was the thane lives yet, | but under heavy 1.03.109
whiles i threat, he lives: 2.01. 60
though our lives — 3.01.126
thou know'st that banquo and his fleance lives. 3.02. 37
feast, i hear | macduff lives in disgrace. 3.06. 23
lives in the english court, and is receiv'd | of 3.06. 26
and good men's lives | expire before the flowers 4.03.171
whiles i see lives, the gashes | do better upon 5.08. 2
know'st 'tis common, all that lives must die, HAM 1.02. 72
weal depends and rests | the lives of many. 3.03. 15
queen his mother | lives almost by his looks, 4.07. 12
there lives within the very flame of love | a 4.07.114
freedom lives hence, and banishment is here. LR 1.01.181
their pow'rs, | and hold our lives in mercy. 1.04.327
keep peace, upon your lives! 2.02. 48
then comes the time, who lives to see't, | that 3.02. 93
stands still in esperance, lives not in fear. 4.01. 4
i know when one is dead, and when one lives; 5.03.261
mist or stain the stone, | why then she lives. 5.03.264
this feather stirs, she lives! 5.03.266
if the /beam of our lives had not one scale of OTH 1.03.327 P
hold, for your lives! 2.03.165
that cuckold lives in bliss | who, certain of 3.03.167
o, that the slave had forty thousand lives! 3.03.442
lives, sir. 4.01.223
had all his hairs been lives, my great revenge 5.02. 74
make thee known, | though i lost twenty lives. 5.02.166
there's not a minute of our lives should stretch ANT 1.01. 46
our lives upon to use our strongest hands. 2.01. 51
yet, if thou say antony lives, 'tis well, | or 2.05. 43
it lives by that which nourisheth it, and the 2.07. 44 P
lucky, men did ransom lives | of me for jests; 3.13.179
lives he? | wilt thou not answer, man? 4.14.114
(whose remembrance yet | lives in men's eyes, CYM 3.01. 3
to lose, | but that he swore to take, our lives? 4.02.125
i, since of your lives you set | so slight a 4.04. 48
brain of britain, | by whom, i grant, she lives. 5.05. 15
thus, that nothing but our lives | may be call'd 5.05. 79
augustus lives to think on't; 5.05. 82
and lords and ladies in their lives | have read PER 1.ch. 7
and be resolved he lives to govern us, | or, 2.04. 31
there constant to eternity it lives. TNK pr 14
their lives concern us | much more than thebes 1.04. 32
and if the lives of all my name lay on it, | i 2.02.175
upon their lives; but with their banishments. 3.06.214
if you desire their lives, invent a way | safer 3.06.217
how their lives | might breed the ruin of my 3.06.239
for heaven's sake save their lives, and banish 3.06.251
else, never trifle, | but take our lives, duke. 3.06.261
the prisoners have their lives. 4.01. 28
be made the altar where the lives of lovers — 4.02. 61
since i know | their lives but pinch 'em. 5.03.133
whose lives (for this poor comfort) are laid 5.04. 14
hare, | or at the fox which lives by subtilty, VEN 675
there lives a son that suck'd an earthly mother, 863
adonis lives, and death is not to blame; 992
to wail his death who lives and must not die 1017
shame, | for if i die, my honor lives in thee, LUC 1032
and all my fame that lives disbursed be | to 1203
and one man's lust these many lives confounds. 1489
thee, | which used lives th' executor to be. SON 4.14
their show, their substance still lives sweet. 5.14
herein lives wisdom, beauty, and increase, 11. 5
so long lives this, and this gives life to thee. 18.14
and loathsome canker lives in sweetest bud. 35. 4
though in our lives a separable spite, | which 36. 6
his, | and, proud of many, lives upon his gains? 67.12
there lives more life in one of your fair eyes 83.13
but is profan'd, if not lives in disgrace. 127. 8

LIVEST 5 FR 0.0005 REL FR 5 V 0 P
and though thou livest and breathest, | yet art R2 1.02. 24
no warmth, no /breath shall testify thou livest; ROM 4.01. 98
horatio, i am dead, | thou livest. HAM 5.02.339
if thou livest, pericles, thou hast a heart PER 3.02. 76
or perform my bidding, or thou livest in woe; 5.01.247

LIVETH 3 FR 0.0003 REL FR 2 V 1 P
to counterfeit dying, when a man thereby liveth, 1H4 5.04.118 P
her mother liveth yet, can testify | she was the 1H6 5.04. 12
reason may suffice, | that henry liveth still; 3H6 3.03. 72

LIVIA 2 FR 0.0002 REL FR 1 V 1 P
my fair niece rosaline, /and livia; ROM 1.02. 69 P
token i have kept apart | for livia and octavia, ANT 5.02.169

LIVING 130 FR 0.0147 REL FR 104 V 26 P
(for else his project dies) to keep them living. TMP 2.01.299
and art thou living, stephano? 2.02.112 P
a living drollery. 3.03. 21
for more assurance that a living prince | does 5.01.108
but how should prospero | be living, and be here 5.01.120
o heavens, that they were living both in naples, 5.01.149
than (living dully sluggardiz'd at home) | wear TGV 1.01. 7
and why not death, rather than living torment? 3.01.170
on wheels, when she can spin for her living. 3.01.316 P
canst thou believe thy living is a life, | so MM 3.02. 26
sharp–looking wretch, | a living dead man. ERR 5.01.242
what, my dear lady disdain! are you yet living? ADO 1.01.119 P
her terminations, there were no living near her, 2.01.249 P
as honest as any man living that is an old man 3.05. 14 P
margaret, that no man living shall come over it, 5.02. 7 P
still and contemplative in living art. LLL 1.01. 14
and die, | with all these living in philosophy. 1.01. 32
and yours from long living! 2.01.192
pity you should get your living by reck'ning, 5.02.497 P
a more fearful wild–fowl than your lion living; MND 3.01. 32 P
so is the will of a living daughter curb'd by MV 1.02. 24 P
sweet lady, you have given me life and living, 5.01.286
one so young and so villainous this day living. AYL 1.01.155 P
enforce | a thievish living on the common road? 2.03. 33
most truly limn'd and living in your face, | be 2.07.194
bring him dead or living | within this 3.01. 6
no more | to seek a living in our territory. 3.01. 8
to offer to get your living by the copulation of 3.02. 80 P
mad humor of love to a living humor of madness, 3.02.419 P
would for the king's sake he were living! AWW 1.01. 22 P
dead, excessive grief the enemy to the living. 1.01. 56 P
if the living be enemy to the grief, the excess 1.01. 57 P
there is no living, none, | if bertram be away. 1.01. 84
if he were living, i would try him yet. 1.02. 72
o my dear mother, do i see you living? 5.03.319
i my brother know | yet living in my glass; TN 3.04.380
there is no lady living | so meet for this great WT 2.02. 43
within a mile where my land and living lies; 4.03. 98 P
sceptres, | and those that bear them, living. 5.01.147
that she is living, | were it but told you, 5.03.115
when living blood doth in these temples beat, JN 2.01.108
good lords, although my will to give is living, 4.02. 83
hath love in thy old blood no living fire? R2 1.02. 10
no, no, men living flatter those that die. 2.01. 89
and living too, for now his son is duke. 2.01.225
sign, | save men's opinions and my living blood, 3.01. 26
as from my death–bed, thy last living leave. 5.01. 39
i no friend will rid me of this living fear?" 5.04. 2
this dead king to the living king i'll bear; 5.05.117
but here is carlisle living, to abide | thy 5.06. 22
where is he living, clipt in with the sea | that 1H4 3.01. 43
but will/'t not live with the living? 5.01.139 P
he is indeed, and living to kill thee. 5.03. 48 P
to see what friends are living, who are dead. 5.04.161
douglas is living, and your brother yet, | but, 2H4 1.01. 82
is old double of your town living yet? 3.02. 41 P
and i had many living to upbraid | my gain of it 4.05.192
o that the living harry had the temper | of he, 5.02. 15
and therefore, living hence, did give ourself H5 1.02.270
and my live, and my living, and my uttermost 3.06. 9 P
we are enow yet living in the field | to smother 4.05. 19
myself | for living idly here in pomp and ease, 1H6 1.01.142
so will the queen, that living held him dear. 2H6 4.01.147
that living wrought me such exceeding trouble. 5.01. 70
but then aeneas bare a living load — | nothing 5.02. 64
i may conquer fortune's spite | by living low, 3H6 4.06. 20
for now they kill me with a living death. R3 1.02.152
and plant your joys in living edward's throne. 2.02.100
compare dead happiness with living woe; 4.04.119
but tell me, is young george stanley living? 5.05. 9
of our noble story | as they were living. H8 pr 27
my chaplain to no creature living but | to me 1.02.166
for living murmurers | there's places of rebuke. 2.02.130
i am the most unhappy woman living. 3.01.147
no man living | could say, "this is my wife" 4.01. 79
no other speaker of my living actions | to keep 4.02. 70
whom i most hated living, thou hast made me, 4.02. 73
nor is there living | (i speak it with a single 5.02. 72
(but few now living can behold that goodness) 5.04. 21
a pattern to all princes living with her, | and 5.04. 22
how more unfortunate than all living women | are COR 5.03. 97
this boy, to keep your name | living to time. 5.03.127
or more than any living man could bear. TIT 5.03.127
when they were living, warm'd themselves on 5.03.168
for who is living, if those two are gone? ROM 3.02. 68
he were | as living here and you no use of him. 3.05.225
that living mortals, hearing them, run mad — 4.03. 48
life, living, all is death's. 4.05. 40
poor living corse, clos'd in a dead man's tomb! 5.02. 30
they were the most needless creatures living, TIM 1.02. 97 P
for all thy living | is 'mongst the dead, and 1.02.223
when there is nothing living but thee, thou 4.03.355 P
unmatched mind, | care of your food and living; 4.03.517
of health and living now begins to mend, | and 5.01.187
nor are they living | who were the motives that 5.04. 26
i, timon, who, alive, all living men did hate; 5.04. 72
not love caesar dead | so well as brutus living; JC 3.01.134
had you rather caesar were living, and die all 3.02. 23 P
he lies not like the living. o my heart! 5.03. 58
are yet two romans living such as these? 5.03. 98
entomb, | when living light should kiss it? MAC 2.04. 10
and sure i am two men there is not living | to HAM 2.02. 20
this grave shall have a living monument. 5.01.297
if i gave them all my living, i'ld keep my LR 1.04.107 P
you, or any man living, may be drunk at a time, OTH 2.03.313 P
give me a living reason she's disloyal. 3.03.409
that lady is not now living; CYM 1.04. 62 P
and cowards living | to die with length'ned 5.03. 12
he hath been search'd among the dead and living; 5.05. 11
since she is living, let the time run on | to 5.05.128
here's all that is left living of your queen: PER 3.01. 20
word, nor did ill turn | to any living creature. 4.01. 76
sun, | and were good kings when living. TNK 1.01.147
as any palamon or any living | that is a man's 2.02.181
yet is he living, | but such a vessel 'tis that 5.04. 82
to the gods | our thanks that you are living. 5.04.101
as if the dead the living should exceed; VEN 292
i prophesy thy death, my living sorrow, | if 671
her thrall | to living death and pain perpetual; LUC 726
livery, | a dying life to living infamy. 1055
"no dame hereafter living | by my excuse shall 1714
i, | love hath forlorn me, living in thrall; PP 17.14
depart, | leaving thee living in posterity? SON 6.12
virtuous wish would bear your living flowers, 16. 7
made | by looking on thee in the living day, 43.10
shall burn | the living record of your memory. 55. 8
and steal dead seeing of his living hue? 67. 6
were born, | or durst inhabit on a living brow; 68. 4
making dead wood more blest than living lips: 128.12
remove | to spend her living in eternal love. LC 238

LIVINGS 1 FR 0.0001 REL FR 1 V 0 P
i might in virtues, beauties, livings, friends, MV 3.02.156

LIV'RY 1 FR 0.0001 REL FR 0 V 1 P
got, or a noble scar, is a good liv'ry of honor; AWW 4.05.100 P

LIV'ST 10 FR 0.0011 REL FR 8 V 2 P
but, while thou liv'st, keep a good tongue in TMP 3.02.112 P
'tis pity that thou liv'st | to walk where any ERR 5.01. 27
thou shalt think on prating whilst thou liv'st! SHR 4.03.113
so as thou liv'st in peace, die free from strife R2 5.06. 27
and while thou liv'st, dear kate, take a fellow H5 5.02.152 P
yet liv'st thou, salisbury? 1H6 1.04. 82
myself no joy in nought but that thou liv'st. 2H6 3.02.366
and thou shalt reign in quiet while thou liv'st. 3H6 1.01.173
friends suspect for traitors while thou liv'st, R3 1.03.222
thee, | but if i live, thou liv'st in my defame. LUC 1033

LIZARD'S *(also lezard)*

LIZARD'S 1 FR 0.0001 REL FR 1 V 0 P
sting, | lizard's leg and howlet's wing, | for a MAC 4.01. 17

LIZARDS' 2 FR 0.0002 REL FR 2 V 0 P
their softest touch as smart as lizards' stings! 2H6 3.02.325
as venom toads, or lizards' dreadful stings. 3H6 2.02.138

LO 90 FR 0.0101 REL FR 79 V 11 P
lo, now lo! TMP 2.02. 14
lo, now lo! 2.02. 14
lo, how he mocks me! wilt thou let him, my lord? 3.02. 30 P
lo, lo, again! bite him to death, i prithee. 3.02. 34 P
lo, lo, again! bite him to death, i prithee. 3.02. 34 P
lo, here in one line is his name twice writ, TGV 1.02.120
lo here's the chain. ERR 3.02.166
when lo, to interrupt my purpos'd rest, | toward LLL 5.02. 91
lo, he is tilting straight! 5.02.483
lo! MND 3.02.192
of sweet and bitter fancy, | lo what befell! AYL 4.03.102
and say, "lo, there is mad petruchio's wife, SHR 3.02. 19
lo, how hollow the fiend speaks within him! TN 3.04. 91 P
why, lo you now! WT 1.02.106
the love i bore your queen — lo, fool again! 3.02.228
lo upon thy wish | our messenger chatillion is JN 2.01. 50
lo in this right hand, whose protection | is 2.01.236
lo! now! now see the issue of your peace. 3.04. 21
lo, by my troth, the instrument is cold, | and 4.01.103
lo this is all — nay, yet depart not so; R2 1.02. 63
lo, as at english feasts, so i regreet | the 1.03. 67
lo here comes sir john. 2H4 2.04. 32 P
for lo, within a ken our army lies: 4.01.149
lo where it sits, | which god shall guard; 4.05. 43
lo where he comes. 4.05. 89
lo, whilest i waited on my tender lambs, | and 1H6 1.02. 76
lo, there thou stand'st, a breathing valiant man 4.02. 31
o my dear lord, lo where your son is borne! 4.07. 17
lo, i present your grace a traitor's head, | the 2H6 5.01. 66
and lo, where george of clarence sweeps along, 3H6 5.01. 76
lo, now my glory smear'd in dust and blood! 5.02. 23
it is, and lo where youthful edward comes! 5.05. 11
lo, in these windows that let forth thy life | i R3 1.02. 12
lo here i lend thee this sharp–pointed sword, 1.02.174
lo, ere i can repeat this curse again, | within 4.01. 77
lo at their birth good stars were opposite. 4.04.216
lo here this long–usurped royalty | from the 5.05. 4

lo, where comes that rock | that i advise your H8 1.01.113
lo you, my lord, | the net has fall'n upon me! 1.01.202
lo, who comes here? 2.03. 49
lo, lo, lo, lo, what modicums of wit he utters! TRO 2.01. 68 P
lo, lo, lo, lo, what modicums of wit he utters! 2.01. 68 P
lo, lo, lo, lo, what modicums of wit he utters! 2.01. 68 P
lo, lo, lo, lo, what modicums of wit he utters! 2.01. 68 P
"lo jupiter is yonder, dealing life!" 4.05.191
in faith i will lo, never trust me else. 5.02. 59
lo, citizens, he says he is content. COR 3.03. 48
lo, as the bark that hath discharg'd his fraught TIT 1.01. 71
lo at this tomb my tributary tears | i render 1.01.159
lo by thy side where rape and murder stands; 5.02. 45
shall, | lo hand in hand lucius and i will fall. 5.03.136
for lo | my intercession likewise steads my foe. ROM 2.03. 53
lo here upon thy cheek the stain doth sit | of 2.03. 75
for lo his house | is empty on the back of 5.03.203
shall they not whisper, | "lo caesar is afraid"? JC 2.02.101
lo yonder, and titinius mourning it. 5.03. 92
lo! MAC 3.04. 68
lo you, here she comes! 5.01. 19 P
lo where it comes again! HAM 1.01.126
for lo his sword, | which was declining on the 2.02.477
lo here i lie, | never to rise again. 5.02.318
lo, where he comes! OTH 2.01.181
and lo the happiness! 3.04.108
lo now, if it lay in their hands to make me a ANT 1.02. 76 P
lo thee! 4.14. 87
lo here she comes. CYM 3.02. 22
lo | the moon is down, the crickets chirp, the TNK 3.02. 34
lo, cousin, lo, our folly has undone us. 3.06.107
lo, cousin, lo, our folly has undone us. 3.06.107
lo where our sister is in expectation, | yet 5.03.105
lo he appears. 5.04. 85
warm, | and lo i lie between that sun and thee; VEN 194
but lo from forth a copse that neighbors by, | a 259
who should say, "lo thus my strength is tried; 280
when lo the unback'd breeder, full of fear, 320
lo here the gentle lark, weary of rest, | from 853
where lo, two lamps burnt out in darkness lies; 1128
"since thou art dead, lo here i prophesy, 1135
lo in this hollow cradle take thy rest, | my 1185
and lo there falls into thy boundless flood LUC 653
when lo the blushing morrow | lends light to all 1082
"lo here weeps hecuba, here priam dies, | here 1485
lo here the hopeless merchant of this loss, 1660
lo in the orient when the gracious light | lifts SON 7. 1
lo thus by day my limbs, by night my mind, | for 27.13
lo as a careful huswife runs to catch | one of 143. 1
"'and lo behold these talents of their hair, LC 204
"'lo all these trophies of affections hot, | of 218
"'lo this device was sent me from a nun, | or 232
"for lo his passion, but an art of craft, | even 295

LOA 1 FR 0.0001 REL FR 0 V 1 P
hilloa, loa! WT 3.03. 79 P

LOACH 1 FR 0.0001 REL FR 0 V 1 P
and your chamber–lye breeds fleas like a loach. 1H4 2.01. 21 P

/LOAD 1 FR 0.0001 REL FR 0 V 1 P
/my /lord — /hercules /and /his /load /too. HAM 2.02.362 P

LOAD 24 FR 0.0027 REL FR 23 V 1 P
to those that wring under the load of sorrow, ADO 5.01. 28
you do, i was wont | to load my she with knacks. WT 4.04.349
would i were able to load him with his desert! H5 3.07. 79 P
hanging the head at ceres' plenteous load? 2H6 1.02. 2
the envious load that lies upon his heart; 3.01.157
but then aeneas bare a living load — | nothing 5.02. 64
set down, set down your honorable load — | if R3 1.02. 1
come now towards chertsey with your holy load, 1.02. 29
that bear this heavy mutual load of moan, | now 2.02.113
no, | i must have patience to endure the load; 3.07.230
bear 'em, | the back is sacrifice to th' load. H8 1.02. 50
have you limbs | to bear that load of title? 2.03. 39
out of pity taken | a load would sink a navy — 3.02.383
with which the /time will load him. 5.01. 37
'tis a cruelty | to load a falling man. 5.02.112
you were us'd to load me | with precepts that COR 4.01. 9
and is very likely to load our purposes | with TIM 5.01. 14
then take we down his load, and turn him off JC 4.01. 25
desert, am bound | to load thy merit richly. CYM 1.05. 74
but to relieve them of their heavy load; PER 1.04. 91
and his full poise | becomes the rider's load. TNK 5.04. 82
i had my load before, now press'd with bearing: VEN 430
she bears the load of lust he left behind, | and LUC 734
this load of wrath that burning troy doth bear; 1474

LOADEN *(also laden)*

LOADEN 7 FR 0.0008 REL FR 7 V 0 P
came | a post from wales loaden with heavy news, 1H4 1.01. 37
sword, | for i have loaden me with many spoils, 1H6 2.01. 80
my legs like loaden branches bow to th' earth, H8 4.02. 2
the wars, and safely home | loaden with honor. COR 5.03.164
and when thy car is loaden with their heads, | i TIT 5.02. 53
fellow | loaden with irons wiser than the judge, TIM 3.05. 50
loaden with kisses, arm'd with thousand cupids, TNK 2.02. 31

LOADING 1 FR 0.0001 REL FR 1 V 0 P
look on the tragic loading of this bed; OTH 5.02.363

LOADS 3 FR 0.0003 REL FR 2 V 1 P
/catarrhs, loads a' gravel in the back, TRO 5.01. 19 P
to ease ourselves of divers sland'rous loads, JC 4.01. 20
broad wherewith | your majesty loads our house. MAC 1.06. 18

LOAF 2 FR 0.0002 REL FR 1 V 1 P
and easy it is | of a cut loaf to steal a shive, TIT 2.01. 87
by a halfpenny loaf a day, troy weight. STM II.C 7 P

LOAM 5 FR 0.0005 REL FR 2 V 3 P
and let him have some plaster, or some loam, or MND 3.01. 68 P
this loam, this rough–cast, and this stone doth 5.01.161
away, | men are but gilded loam or painted clay. R2 1.01.179
the dust is earth, of earth we make loam, and HAM 5.01.210 P
and why of that loam whereto he was converted 5.01.211 P

/LOAN 1 FR 0.0001 REL FR 1 V 0 P
for /loan oft loses both itself and friend, HAM 1.03. 76

LOAN 1 FR 0.0001 REL FR 1 V 0 P
which happies those that pay the willing loan; SON 6. 6

LOATH 32 FR 0.0036 REL FR 21 V 11 P
and that, my lord, i shall be loath to do: TGV 3.02. 39
i am very loath to be your idol, sir; 4.02.128
but i would be loath to turn them together. WIV 2.01.186 P
to speak so indirectly i am loath. MM 4.06. 1
to find, yet loath to leave unsought | or that, ERR 1.01.135
but i believe, although i seem so loath, | i am LLL 1.01.159
i would be loath to have you overflowen with a MND 4.01. 15 P
i am right loath to go; MV 2.05. 16
and for your love i would be loath to foil him, AYL 1.01.130 P
but i would be loath to fall into my dreams SHR in.2. 126 P
but loath am to produce | so bad an instrument. AWW 5.03.201
i would be loath to cast away my speech; TN 1.05.172 P
so false, i am loath to prove reason with them. 3.01. 24 P
can but stay you | where you'll be loath to be. WT 4.04.572
the sun of heaven, methought, was loath to set, JN 5.05. 1
for i am loath to break our country's laws. R2 2.03.169
yet, i would be loath to pay him before his day. 1H4 5.01.127 P
well, i am loath to gall a new–heal'd wound. 2H4 1.02.147 P
i' faith, i am loath to pawn my plate, so god 2.01.154 P
since you are tongue–tied and so loath to speak, 1H6 2.04. 25
for i were loath | to link with him that were 3H6 3.03.114
why then, though loath, yet must i be content. 4.06. 48
as loath to lose him, not your father's death; R3 2.02. 10
as loath to bear me to the slaughter–house. 3.04. 86
loath to depose the child, your brother's son; 3.07.209
the day, how loath you are to offend daylight! TRO 3.02. 48 P
he was very loath to lay his fingers off it. JC 1.02.242 P
and like a sister am most loath to call | your LR 1.01.270
i am loath to tell you what i would you knew. ANT 5.02.107
thou art some fool, | i am loath to beat thee. CYM 4.02. 86
loath to bid farewell, we take our leaves. PER 2.05. 13
honor, would be loath | to take example by her. TNK 2.02.145

LOATH'D 7 FR 0.0008 REL FR 5 V 2 P
degree | to base declension and loath'd bigamy. R3 3.07.189
is not more loath'd than an effeminate man | in TRO 3.03.218
be so lov'd and the performance so loath'd? 5.10. 39 P
live loath'd, and long, | most smiling, smooth, TIM 3.06. 93
from the loath'd warmth whereof deliver me, and LR 4.06.267 P
"and yet not cloy thy lips with loath'd satiety, VEN 19
runs, and chides his vanish'd loath'd delight. LUC 742

LOATHE 5 FR 0.0005 REL FR 4 V 1 P
o, how mine eyes do loathe his visage now! MND 4.01. 79
but like a sickness did i loathe this food; 4.01.173
would now like him, now loathe him; AYL 3.02.416 P
and began | to loathe the taste of sweetness, 1H4 3.02. 72
abus'd, and my relief | must be to loathe her. OTH 3.03.268

LOATHED 12 FR 0.0013 REL FR 12 V 0 P
the weariest and most loathed worldly life MM 3.01.128
out, loathed med'cine! MND 3.02.264
thou loathed issue of thy father's loins! R3 1.03.231
to her chance, and damn'd her loathed choice! TIT 4.02. 78
it is to me | that i must love a loathed enemy. ROM 1.05.141
some say the lark and loathed toad change eyes; 3.05. 31
my snuff and loathed part of nature should LR 4.06. 39
my father's eye | should hold her loathed, and OTH 3.04. 62
antiochus doth sin | in such a loathed manner; PER 1.01.147
thou loathed in their shame, they in thy pride. LUC 662
the sweets we wish for turn to loathed sours 867
let him have time to live a loathed slave, | let 984

LOATHER 1 FR 0.0001 REL FR 1 V 0 P
loather a hundred times to part than die. 2H6 3.02.355

LOATHES 6 FR 0.0006 REL FR 6 V 0 P
but love will not be spurr'd to what it loathes. TGV 5.02. 7
it to the mood | of what it likes or loathes. MV 4.01. 52
with what it loathes for that which is away — AWW 4.04. 25
but she, your subject, loathes such sovereignty. R3 4.04.356
hunger for that food | which nature loathes, TIM 5.04. 33
appetite, | that loathes even as it longs. TNK 1.03. 90

LOATHING 3 FR 0.0003 REL FR 3 V 0 P
the deepest loathing to the stomach brings, | or MND 2.02.138
more than a lodg'd hate and a certain loathing MV 4.01. 60
shrivell'd up | those bodies, even to loathing; PER 2.04. 10

LOATHLY 3 FR 0.0003 REL FR 3 V 0 P
the union of your bed with weeds so loathly TMP 4.01. 21
unfather'd heirs and loathly births of nature. 2H4 4.04.122
seeing how loathly opposite i stood | to his LR 2.01. 49

LOATHNESS 3 FR 0.0003 REL FR 3 V 0 P
weigh'd between loathness and obedience, at TMP 2.01.131
look not sad, | nor make replies of loathness; ANT 3.11. 18
to live, | the loathness to depart would grow. CYM 1.01.108

LOATHSOME 22 FR 0.0024 REL FR 22 V 0 P
pack | to make a loathsome abject scorn of me; ERR 4.04.103
death, how foul and loathsome is thine image! SHR in.1. 35
no better than a poor and loathsome beggar. in.1. 123
li'st thou with the vile | in loathsome beds, 2H4 3.01. 16
arms, | this loathsome sequestration have i had; 1H6 2.05. 25
my flow'ring youth | within a loathsome dungeon, 2.05. 57
i am no loathsome leper, look on me. 2H6 3.02. 75
as lean–fac'd envy in her loathsome cave. 3.02.315
lust, | and tumble me into some loathsome pit, TIT 2.03.176
straight will i bring you to the loathsome pit 2.03.193
as loathsome as a toad | amongst the fair–fac'd 4.02. 67
honey | is loathsome in his own deliciousness, ROM 2.06. 12
so early waking — what with loathsome smells, 4.03. 46
doing more murther in this loathsome world, 5.01. 81
most lazar–like, with vile and loathsome crust, HAM 1.05. 72
we prevent | the loathsome misery of age, TNK 5.04. 7
"o, let him keep his loathsome cabin still! VEN 637
the dangers of his loathsome enterprise; LUC 184
some loathsome dash the herald will contrive, 206
will cote my loathsome trespass in my looks. 812
you did fulfill | the loathsome act of lust, and 1636
and loathsome canker lives in sweetest bud. SON 35. 4

LOATHSOMENESS 2 FR 0.0002 REL FR 1 V 1 P
the loathsomeness of them offend me more than WT 4.03. 56 P
of mortal loathsomeness from the blest eye | of TNK 1.01. 45

LOATHSOMEST 1 FR 0.0001 REL FR 0 V 1 P
would make thee the loathsomest scab in greece. TRO 2.01. 29 P

LOAVES 1 FR 0.0001 REL FR 0 V 1 P
england seven halfpenny loaves sold for a penny; 2H6 4.02. 66 P

LOB 2 FR 0.0002 REL FR 2 V 0 P
farewell, thou lob of spirits; MND 2.01. 16
and their poor jades | lob down their heads, H5 4.02. 47

LOBBIES 1 FR 0.0001 REL FR 1 V 0 P
his strides, his lobbies fill with tendance, TIM 1.01. 80

LOBBY 3 FR 0.0003 REL FR 2 V 1 P
how in our voiding lobby hast thou stood | and 2H6 4.01. 61
walks four hours together | here in the lobby. HAM 2.02.161
nose him as you go up the stairs into the lobby. 4.03. 37 P

LOCAL 2 FR 0.0002 REL FR 2 V 0 P
to aery nothing | a local habitation and a name. MND 5.01. 17
that i may give the local wound a name, | and TRO 4.05.244

LOCK* 21 FR 0.0023 REL FR 18 V 3 P
pray you lock hand in hand; WIV 5.05. 77
it | to lock it in the wards of covert bosom, MM 5.01. 10
say, wherefore didst thou lock me forth to–day? ERR 4.04. 95
i did not, gentle husband, lock thee forth. 4.04. 97
i know him, 'a wears a lock. ADO 3.03.170 P
for thee i'll lock up all the gates of love, 4.01.105
wears a key in his ear and a lock hanging by it, 5.01.309 P
lock up my doors, and when you hear the drum MV 2.05. 29
to lock up honesty | and honor from th' access WT 2.02. 9
we do lock | our former scruple in our JN 2.01.369
well, i will lock his counsel in my breast, 1H6 2.05.118
i'll lock thy heaven from thee. TIM 1.02.248 P
to lock such rascal counters from his friends, JC 4.03. 80
that she should lock herself from /his resort, HAM 2.02.143
sport and repose lock from me day and night, 3.02.217
a closet lock and key of villainous secrets; OTH 4.02. 22
there lock yourself, and send him word you are ANT 4.13. 4
you the keys | that lock up your restraint. CYM 1.01. 74
force him think i have pick'd the lock and ta'en 2.02. 41
in life, to lock it | from action and adventure? 4.04. 2
able to lock jove from a synod, shall | by TNK 1.01.176

LOCK'D 29 FR 0.0032 REL FR 27 V 2 P
did hold his eyes lock'd in her crystal looks. TGV 2.04. 89
but the doors be lock'd and the keys kept safe, 3.01.111
a secret must be lock'd within the teeth and the MM 3.02.134 P
as fast lock'd up in sleep as guiltless labor 4.02. 66
but soft, my door is lock'd; ERR 3.01. 30
were not my doors lock'd up, and i shut out? 4.04. 70
perdie, your doors were lock'd, and you shut out 4.04. 71
but i confess, sir, that we were lock'd out. 4.04. 99
this woman lock'd me out this day from dinner; 5.01.218
that he din'd not at home, but was lock'd out. 5.01.256
methought all his senses were lock'd in his eye, LLL 2.01.242
i am lock'd in one of them; MV 3.02. 40
till then i'll keep him dark and safely lock'd. AWW 4.01. 94
gifts she looks from me are pack'd and lock'd WT 4.04.358
to lie like pawns lock'd up in chests and trunks JN 5.02.141
who, never so tame, so cherish'd and lock'd up, 1H4 5.02. 10
and he but naked, though lock'd up in steel, 2H6 3.02.234
lock'd into the woefull'st cask | that ever did 3.02.409
forcibly prevents | our lock'd embrasures, TRO 4.04. 37
but this thy countenance, still lock'd in steel, 4.05.195
'tis in my memory lock'd, | and you yourself HAM 1.03. 85
ho, let the door be lock'd! 5.02.311
i have lock'd the letter in my closet. LR 3.03. 11 P
are your doors lock'd? OTH 1.01. 85
lock'd in her monument. ANT 4.14.120
her chambers are all lock'd, and there's no CYM 3.05. 43
her doors lock'd? 3.05. 51
"and how her hand, in my hand being lock'd, LUC 260
thee have i not lock'd up in any chest, | save SON 48. 9

LOCK'D–UP 1 FR 0.0001 REL FR 1 V 0 P
she much amaz'd breaks ope her lock'd–up eyes, LUC 446

LOCKING 2 FR 0.0002 REL FR 2 V 0 P
for locking me out of my doors by day. ERR 4.01. 18
more than the locking up the spirits a time, CYM 1.05. 41

LOCKRAM 1 FR 0.0001 REL FR 1 V 0 P
her richest lockram 'bout her reechy neck, COR 2.01.209

LOCKS* 24 FR 0.0027 REL FR 23 V 1 P
and shivering shocks | shall break the locks MND 1.02. 33
and her sunny locks | hang on her temples like a MV 1.01.169
so are those crisped snaky golden locks, | which 3.02. 92
from the earth, and so locks her in embracing, WT 5.02. 77 P
and pluck up drowned honor by the locks, | so he 1H4 1.03.205
since we have locks to safeguard necessaries, H5 1.02.176
hand | /defile the locks of your shrill–shriking 3.03. 35
and these grey locks, the pursuivants of death, 1H6 2.05. 5
in time | break ope the locks a' th' senate, and COR 3.01.138
shuts up his windows, locks fair daylight out, ROM 1.01.139
that in gold clasps locks in the golden story; 1.03. 92
never shake | thy gory locks at me. MAC 3.04. 50
open, locks, | whoever knocks! 4.01. 46
thy knotted and combined locks to part, | and HAM 1.05. 18
be | you bees that make these locks of counsel! CYM 3.02. 36
not now be stol'n, you have locks upon you; 5.04. 1
death, who is the key | t' unbar these locks. 5.04. 8
she locks her beauties in her bud again, | and TNK 2.02.142
i'll clip my yellow locks an inch below mine e'e 3.04. 20
gone, | she locks her lily fingers one in one. VEN 228
were beauty under twenty locks kept fast, | yet 575
it off, and being gone, | play with his locks; 1090
the locks between her chamber and his will, LUC 302
"his browny locks did hang in crooked curls, LC 85

LOCUSTS 1 FR 0.0001 REL FR 0 V 1 P
food that to him now is as luscious as locusts, OTH 1.03.348 P

LODESTAR 1 FR 0.0001 REL FR 1 V 0 P
which must be lodestar to his lustful eye; LUC 179

LODESTARS 1 FR 0.0001 REL FR 1 V 0 P
your eyes are lodestars, and your tongue's sweet MND 1.01.183

LODG'D 16 FR 0.0018 REL FR 16 V 0 P
human care, and lodg'd thee | in mine own cell, TMP 1.02.346
as you shall deem yourself lodg'd in my heart, LLL 2.01.173
more than a lodg'd hate and a certain loathing MV 4.01. 60
and in my house you shall be friendly lodg'd. SHR 4.02.108
i will conduct you where you shall be lodg'd, AWW 3.05. 41
that honorable grief lodg'd here which burns WT 2.01.111
why should hard–favor'd grief be lodg'd in thee, R2 5.01. 14
if ever any grudge were lodg'd between us; R3 2.01. 66
he came to leicester, | lodg'd in the abbey; H8 4.02. 18
there are two lodg'd together. MAC 2.02. 23
though bladed corn be lodg'd, and trees blown 4.01. 55
she should in ground unsanctified been lodg'd HAM 5.01.229
out together where death's self was lodg'd; TNK 1.03. 40
so fair a form lodg'd not a mind so ill. LUC 1530
shall hate be fairer lodg'd than gentle love? SON 10.10
abide, | she was new lodg'd and newly deified. LC 84

LODGE 24 FR 0.0027 REL FR 19 V 5 P
shall lodge thee till thy wound be throughly TGV 1.02.112
i nightly lodge her in an upper tow'r, | the key 3.01. 35
himself would lodge where, senseless, they are 3.01.143
my men, kill'd my deer, and broke open my lodge. WIV 1.01.112 P
him here as melancholy as a lodge in a warren. ADO 2.01.215 P
i will visit thee at the lodge. LLL 1.02.135 P
he rather means to lodge you in the field, 2.01. 85
where do the palmers lodge, i do beseech you? AWW 3.05. 35
suburbs at the elephant | is best to lodge. TN 3.03. 40
i'll keep my stables where | i lodge my wife; WT 2.01.135

our sighs and they shall lodge the summer corn, R2 3.03.162
and by whose power i well might lodge a fear 2H4 4.05.207
for we cannot lodge and board a dozen or H5 2.01. 33 P
did he so often lodge in open field, | in 2H6 1.01. 80
and, soldiers, stay and lodge by me this night. 3H6 1.01. 32
his chief followers lodge in towns about him, 4.03. 13
he and his lady both are at the lodge, | upon TIT 2.03.254
vile part of this anatomy | doth my name lodge? ROM 3.03.107
prepare to lodge their companies to–night. JC 4.03.140
and to those thorns that in her bosom lodge | to HAM 1.05. 87
nor i know not | where i did lodge last night. LR 4.07. 67
let me lodge lichas on the horns o' th' moon, ANT 4.12. 45
i lodge in fear; CYM 2.02. 49
traveller, we should lodge them with this sign. PER 4.02.114 P
LODGED 1 FR 0.0001 REL FR 1 V 0 P
like to the summer's corn by tempest lodged. 2H6 3.02.176
LODGERS 2 FR 0.0002 REL FR 2 V 0 P
genoa, | where we were lodgers at the pegasus. SHR 4.04. 5
nor shall my nell keep lodgers. H5 2.01. 31
LODGES 5 FR 0.0005 REL FR 2 V 3 P
my brother troilus lodges there to–night. TRO 4.01. 43
and where care lodges, sleep will never lie; ROM 2.03. 36
go to! where lodges he? OTH 3.04. 7 P
to tell you where he lodges, is to tell you 3.04. 8 P
i know not where he lodges, and for me to devise 3.04. 11 P
LODGING 26 FR 0.0029 REL FR 20 V 6 P
hard lodging and thin weeds | nip not the gaudy LLL 5.02.801
and desire gratiano to come anon to my lodging. MV 2.02.118 P
of thy old master, and inquire | my lodging out. 2.02.154
disguise us at my lodging, and return | all in 2.04. 2
at gratiano's lodging some hour hence. 2.04. 26
to burn the lodging where you use to lie, | and AYL 2.03. 23
and burn sweet wood to make the lodging sweet. SHR in.1. 49
and take a lodging fit to entertain | such 1.01. 44
then at my lodging, and it like you. 4.04. 55
to–morrow, sir. best first go see your lodging. TN 3.03. 20
unto the lodging where i first did swound? 2H4 4.05.233
rising of the lark to the lodging of the lamb, H5 3.07. 32 P
not so, my liege, this lodging likes me better, 4.01. 16
fiery–footed steeds, | towards phoebus' lodging; ROM 3.02. 2
thou knowest my lodging, get me ink and paper, 5.01. 25
retire with me to my lodging, from whence i will LR 1.02.168 P
eyes, not to behold | this shameful lodging. 2.02.172
when, being not at your lodging to be found, OTH 1.02. 45
at my lodging. 1.03.374 P
i will in cassio's lodging lose this napkin, 3.03.321
for me to devise a lodging and say he lies here, 3.04. 12 P
and i was going to your lodging, cassio. 3.04.172
right proud | of that most delicate lodging. CYM 2.04.136
my lord, at my lodging, the same suit he wore 3.05.125 P
is't not mad lodging | here in the wild woods, TNK 3.03. 22
he was kept down with hard meat and ill lodging, 5.02. 97
LODGINGS 3 FR 0.0003 REL FR 3 V 0 P
see | but empty lodgings and unfurnish'd walls, R2 1.02. 68
these knights unto their several lodgings! PER 2.03.109
our lodgings, standing bleak upon the sea, 3.02. 14
LODOVICO 4 FR 0.0004 REL FR 4 V 0 P
'tis lodovico — | this comes from the duke. OTH 4.01.214
and what's the news, good cousin lodovico? 4.01.219
this lodovico is a proper man. 4.03. 35
signior lodovico? 5.01. 67
LODOWICK 5 FR 0.0005 REL FR 3 V 2 P
one that i would were here, friar lodowick. MM 5.01.125
who knows that lodowick? 5.01.126
know you that friar lodowick that she speaks of? 5.01.143
you knew that friar lodowick to be a dishonest 5.01.261 P
guiltian, cosmo, lodowick, and gratii, two AWW 4.03.163 P
LOFF *(also laugh)*
LOFF 1 FR 0.0001 REL FR 1 V 0 P
then the whole quire hold their hips and loff, MND 2.01. 55
LOFTY 17 FR 0.0019 REL FR 15 V 2 P
his humor is lofty, his discourse peremptory, LLL 5.01. 10 P
this was lofty! MND 1.02. 39 P
that look too lofty in our commonwealth: R2 3.04. 35
sound all the lofty instruments of war, | and by 1H4 5.02. 97
the furrowed sea, | breasting the lofty surge. H5 3.pr. 13
heels, | and that we are most lofty runaways. 3.05. 35
here, | it is of such a spacious lofty pitch, 1H6 2.03. 55
thus droops this lofty pine and hangs his sprays 2H6 2.03. 45
murther of a guiltless king | and lofty, proud, 4.01. 96
lofty and sour to them that lov'd him not, | but H8 4.02. 53
wept, | because they died in honor's lofty bed. TIT 3.01. 11
hence | shall this our lofty scene be acted over JC 3.01.112
doth with his lofty and shrill–sounding throat HAM 1.01.151
the lofty cedar, royal cymbeline, | personates CYM 5.05.453
ay me, the bark pill'd from the lofty pine, LUC 1167
when lofty trees i see barren of leaves, | which SON 12. 5
when sometime lofty towers i see down rased, 64. 3
LOFTY–PLUMED 1 FR 0.0001 REL FR 1 V 0 P
that france must vail her lofty–plumed crest 1H6 5.03. 25
LOG 1 FR 0.0001 REL FR 1 V 0 P
or with a log | batter his skull, or paunch him TMP 3.02. 89
LOGGATS 1 FR 0.0001 REL FR 0 V 1 P
the breeding, but to play at loggats with them? HAM 5.01. 92 P
LOGGER–HEAD 1 FR 0.0001 REL FR 1 V 0 P
thou shalt be logger–head. ROM 4.04. 21
LOGGERHEAD 1 FR 0.0001 REL FR 1 V 0 P
ah, you whoreson loggerhead! LLL 4.03.200
LOGGERHEADED 1 FR 0.0001 REL FR 1 V 0 P
you loggerheaded and unpolish'd grooms! SHR 4.01.125
LOGGERHEADS 1 FR 0.0001 REL FR 0 V 1 P
with three or four loggerheads amongst three or 1H4 2.04. 4 P
LOGIC 2 FR 0.0002 REL FR 2 V 0 P
balk logic with acquaintance that you have, SHR 1.01. 34
how how, how how, chopp'd logic! ROM 3.05.149
LOG–MAN 1 FR 0.0001 REL FR 1 V 0 P
and for your sake | am i this patient log–man. TMP 3.01. 67
LOGS 6 FR 0.0006 REL FR 6 V 0 P
i must remove | some thousands of these logs, TMP 3.01. 10
burnt up those logs that you are enjoin'd to 3.01. 17
sit down, | i'll bear your logs the while. 3.01. 24
his nail | and tom bears logs into the hall LLL 5.02.914
sirrah, fetch drier logs. ROM 4.04. 16
i have a head, sir, that will find out logs, 4.04. 18
LOINS 12 FR 0.0013 REL FR 11 V 1 P
/sire, | the mere effusion of thy proper loins, MM 3.01. 30
this shame derives itself from unknown loins"? ADO 4.01.135
that from his loins no hopeful branch may spring 3H6 3.02.126
thou loathed issue of thy father's loins! R3 1.03.231
out of whorish loins | are pleas'd to breed out TRO 4.01. 64
her womb's increase | and treasure of my loins; COR 3.03.115
from forth the fatal loins of these two foes | a ROM pr 5
brave son, deriv'd from honorable loins! JC 2.01.322
about her lank and all o'er–teemed loins, | a HAM 2.02.508
blanket my loins, elf all my hairs in knots, LR 2.03. 10
and bears by th' neck, monkeys by th' loins, and 2.04. 9 P
they are the issue of your loins, my liege, CYM 5.05.330
LOITER 1 FR 0.0001 REL FR 0 V 1 P
sir john, you loiter here too long, being you 2H4 2.01.186 P
LOITERER 1 FR 0.0001 REL FR 0 V 1 P
o illiterate loiterer! TGV 3.01.296 P
LOITERERS 1 FR 0.0001 REL FR 1 V 0 P
liege of all loiterers and malecontents, | dread LLL 3.01.183
LOITERING 1 FR 0.0001 REL FR 1 V 0 P
where have you been these two days loitering? TGV 4.04. 44
LOLLING *(also lulling)*
LOLLING 3 FR 0.0003 REL FR 2 V 1 P
the large achilles, on his press'd bed lolling, TRO 1.03.162
natural that runs lolling up and down to hide ROM 2.04. 92 P
lolling the tongue with slaught'ring — having CYM 5.03. 8
LOLLS 1 FR 0.0001 REL FR 0 V 1 P
so hangs, and lolls, and weeps upon me; OTH 4.01.139 P
LOMBARD *(see lumbert)*
LOMBARDY 1 FR 0.0001 REL FR 1 V 0 P
of arts, | i am arriv'd for fruitful lombardy, SHR 1.01. 3
/LONDON 1 FR 0.0001 REL FR 1 V 0 P
/through /proud /london /he /came /sighing /on 2H4 1.03.104
LONDON 63 FR 0.0071 REL FR 45 V 18 P
london hath receiv'd, | like a kind host, the JN 5.01. 31
set on towards london, cousin, is it so? R2 3.03.208
post you to london and you will find it so, | i 3.04. 90
meet at london london's king in woe. 3.04. 97
off, | of our two cousins coming into london. 5.02. 3
inquire at london, 'mongst the taverns there, 5.03. 5
my heart when i beheld | in london streets, that 5.05. 77
i have to london sent | the heads of salisbury, 5.06. 7
i have from oxford sent to london | the heads of 5.06. 13
and traders riding to london with fat purses. 1H4 1.02.127 P
villainous house in all london road for fleas. 2.01. 15 P
what time do you mean to come to london? 2.01. 42 P
and i rob the thieves and go merrily to london, 2.02. 95 P
though i could scape shot–free at london, i fear 5.03. 30 P
is your master here in london? 2H4 2.02.144 P
as the way between saint albons and london. 2.02.168 P
by my troth, welcome to london. 2.04.292 P
he is not there to–day, he dines in london. 4.04. 51
bardolph, and to all the cabileros about london. 5.03. 59 P
i hope to see london once ere i die. 5.03. 60 P
the king is set from london, and the scene | is H5 2.pr. 34
would i were in an alehouse in london, i would 3.02. 12 P
at his return into london under the form of a 3.06. 69 P
land, | and solemnly see him set on to london. 5.pr. 14
how london doth pour out her citizens! 5.pr. 24
now in london place him — | as yet the 5.pr. 35
as well at london bridge as at the tower. 1H6 3.01. 23
henry, | pity the city of london, pity us! 3.01. 77
means | your lady is forthcoming yet at london. 2H6 2.01.175
to–morrow toward london back again, | to look 2.01.197
at my horse heels till i do come to london, 4.03. 13 P
come, let's march towards london. 4.03. 18 P
jack cade hath gotten london bridge: 4.04. 49
and here, sitting upon london stone, i charge 4.06. 2 P
but first go and set london bridge on fire, and, 4.06. 14 P
my sword therefore broke through london gates, 4.08. 24 P
broil | i see them lording it in london streets, 4.08. 45
we shall to london get, where you are lov'd, 5.02. 81
for, as i hear, the king is fled to london, | to 5.03. 24
sound drum and trumpets, and to london all, 5.03. 32
and i'll keep london with my soldiers. 3H6 1.01.207
brother, thou shalt to london presently, | and 1.02. 36
me, | my brother montague shall post to london. 1.02. 55
i, then in london, keeper of the king, 2.01.143
and now to london all the crew are gone | to 2.01.174
to london will we march, | and once again 2.01.182
from london by the king was i press'd forth; 2.05. 64
and now to london with triumphant march, | there 2.06. 87
now to london | to see these honors in 2.06.109
to do | but march to london with our soldiers? 4.03. 61
i am inform'd that he comes towards london | to 4.04. 26
and with his troops doth march amain to london, 4.08. 4
shall rest in london till we come to him. 4.08. 22
i'll hence to london on a serious matter. 5.05. 47
to london, all in post, and, as i guess, | to 5.05. 84
and let's away to london | and see our gentle 5.05. 88
the young prince be fet | hither to london, to R3 2.02.122
sweet prince, to london, to your chamber. 3.01. 1
my lord, the mayor of london comes to greet you. 3.01. 17
lords at pomfret, when they rode from london, 3.02. 83
and towards london do they bend their power, 4.05. 17
when they were ready to set out for london, a H8 2.02. 5 P
from the king's secretary, | the other, london. 4.01.103
LONDONERS 1 FR 0.0001 REL FR 1 V 0 P
demand | what was the speech among the londoners H8 1.02.154
LONDON'S 1 FR 0.0001 REL FR 1 V 0 P
meet at london london's king in woe. R2 3.04. 97
/LONE 1 FR 0.0001 REL FR 1 V 0 P
flaming, thy /lone bosom | inflame too nicely, PER 4.01. 5
LONE 1 FR 0.0001 REL FR 0 V 1 P
is a long one for a poor lone woman to bear, and 2H4 2.01. 32 P
/LONELINESS 2 FR 0.0002 REL FR 2 V 0 P
now i see | the myst'ry of your /loneliness, and AWW 1.03.171
such an exercise may color | your /loneliness. HAM 3.01. 45
/LONELY 1 FR 0.0001 REL FR 1 V 0 P
therefore i keep it | /lonely, apart. WT 5.03. 18
LONELY 1 FR 0.0001 REL FR 1 V 0 P
like to a lonely dragon, that his fen | makes COR 4.01. 30
LONG* *(also along)*
/LONG* 6 FR 0.0006 REL FR 5 V 1 P
/long /mayst /thou /live /in /richard's /seat R2 4.01.218
/which /long /ere /this /we /offer'd /to /the 2H4 4.01. 75
/i /should /not /live /long /after /i /saw R3 4.02.107
have i thought /long to see this morning's face, ROM 4.05. 41
/how /long /have /you /been /a /sectary LR 1.02.150 P
/if /she /live /long, | /and /in /the /end /meet 3.07.100
LONG* 491 FR 0.0555 REL FR 394 V 97 P
give thanks you have liv'd so long, and make TMP 1.01. 24 P
of sea for an acre of barren ground, long heath, 1.01. 66 P
long live gonzalo! 2.01.170
i will leave him, i have no long spoon. 2.02. 99 P
and i with my long nails will dig thee pig–nuts, 2.02.168
that, if i then had wak'd after long sleep, 3.02.139
for quiet days, fair issue, and long life, 4.01. 24
long continuance, and increasing, | hourly joys 4.01.107
quickly, spirit, | thou shalt ere long be free. 5.01. 87
i long | to hear the story of your life, which 5.01.312
how long hath she been deform'd? TGV 2.01. 64 P
alas, the way is wearisome and long. 2.07. 8
in, | by longing for that food so long a time. 2.07. 17
tutor | (for long agone i have forgot to court; 3.01. 85
a cloak as long as thine will serve the turn? 3.01.131
thou hast stay'd so long that going will scarce 3.01.379 P
she shall not long continue love to him. 3.02. 48
have you long sojourn'd there? 4.01. 20
what? that my leg is too long? 5.02. 4
leave not the mansion so long tenantless, | lest 5.04. 8
pity two such friends should be long foes. 5.04.118
he will not stay long. WIV 1.04. 39 P
by my trot, i tarry too long. 1.04. 62 P
as long as i have an eye to make difference of 2.01. 56 P
there's the short and the long. 2.01.133 P
with my long sword i would have made you four 2.01.228 P
marry, this is the short and the long of it: 2.02. 59 P
and you have been a man long known to me, though 2.02.181 P
i have long lov'd her, and, i protest to you, 2.02.194 P
now let me die, for i have liv'd long enough. 3.03. 44 P
and how long lay you there? 3.05. 94 P
come, we stay too long. 4.01. 85 P
if my wind were but long enough /to /say /my 4.05.102 P
the truth is, she and i (long since contracted) 5.05.223
so long that nineteen zodiacs have gone round MM 1.02.168
which have for long run by the hideous law, | as 1.04. 63
how long have you been in this place of 2.01.258 P
and, it may be, | as long as you or i. 2.04. 36
dear sir, ere long i'll visit you again. 3.01. 46
first, that your stay with him may not be long; 3.01.247 P
they will then ere't be long. 4.02. 76
there had she not been long but she became | a ERR 1.01. 49
for with long travel i am stiff and weary. 1.02. 15
and you use these blows long, i must get a 2.02. 37 P
'tis true she rides me and i long for grass. 2.02.200
this — your long experience of /her wisdom, 3.01. 89
the chain unfinish'd made me stay thus long. 3.02.168
belike you thought our love would last too long 4.01. 25
and i, to blame, have held him here too long. 4.01. 47
do, expect spoon–meat, or bespeak a long spoon. 4.03. 61 P
he must have a long spoon that must eat with the 4.03. 63 P
you may prove it by my long ears. 4.04. 30 P
is, | i long to know the truth hereof at large. 4.04.143
i long that we were safe and sound aboard. 4.04.150
how long hath this possession held the man? 5.01. 44
long since thy husband serv'd me in my wars, 5.01.161
even for the service that long since i did thee, 5.01.191
with me — | after so long grief, such nativity! 5.01.407
and there live we as merry as the day is long. ADO 2.01. 49 P
you shake the head at so long a breathing, but i 2.01.362 P
because i have rail'd so long against marriage; 2.03.237 P
(for she has been too long a–talking of), the 3.02.103 P
me, how long have you profess'd apprehension? 3.04. 67 P
a little, | for i have only been silent so long, 4.01.156
which he hath us'd so long and never paid that 5.01.311 P
and how long is that, think you? 5.02. 81 P
'tis long of you that spur me with such LLL 2.01.118
and yours from long living! 2.01.192
and keep not too long in one tune, but a snip 3.01. 21 P
they have liv'd long on the alms–basket of words 5.01. 38 P
a word, for thou art not so long by the head as 5.01. 40 P
for a light heart lives long. 5.02. 18
the letter is too long by half a mile. 5.02. 54
o for your reason! quickly, sir — i long! 5.02.244
that which long process could not arbitrate. 5.02.743
i'll stay with patience, but the time is long. 5.02.835
that's too long for a play. 5.02.878
long withering out a young man's revenue. MND 1.01. 6
how long within this wood intend you stay? 2.01.138
you, mistress, all this coil is long of you. 3.02.339
o weary night, o long and tedious night, | abate 3.02.431
taste, | now i do wish it, love it, long for it, 4.01.175
for the short and the long is, our play is 4.02. 38 P
to wear away this long age of three hours 5.01. 33
a play there is, my lord, some ten words long, 5.01. 61
but by ten words, my lord, it is too long, 5.01. 63
she should not use a long one for such a pyramus 5.01.316 P
tongue, | we will make amends ere long; 5.01.434
murder cannot be hid long; MV 2.02. 79 P
indeed the short and the long is, i serve the 2.02.127 P
sweet friends, your patience for my long abode; 2.06. 21
for wives, | i'll watch as long for you then. 2.06. 24
too long a pause for that which you find there. 2.09. 53
for i long to see | quick cupid's post that 2.09. 99
i speak too long, but 'tis to peize the time, 3.02. 22
i will not long be troubled with you; AYL 1.01. 76 P
but it shall not be so long, this wrastler shall 1.01.171 P
now tell me how long you would have her after 4.01.143 P
you to a long and well–deserved bed; 5.04.190
i long to hear him call the drunkard husband, SHR in.1. 133
it stands so that i may hardly tarry so long. in.2. 126 P
me, | and i do hope good days and long to see. 1.02.192
scholar, that hath been long studying at rheims, 2.01. 80 P
o, how i long to have some chat with her! 2.01.162
now is the day we long have looked for. 2.01.333
why, i am past my gamouth long ago. 3.01. 71
hath all so long detain'd you from your wife, 3.02.103
i stay too long from her. 3.02.110
horn is a foot, and so long am i at the least. 4.01. 28 P
which hath as long lov'd me | as i have lov'd 4.02. 38
that teacheth tricks eleven and twenty long, 4.02. 57
i have watch'd so long | that i am dog–weary, 4.02. 59
and she to him, to stay him not too long, | i am 4.04. 30
a son of mine, which long i have not seen. 4.05. 57
yourself, he shall need none so long as i live. 5.01. 24 P
at last, though long, our jarring notes agree, 5.02. 1
he lasted long, | but on us both did haggish age AWW 1.02. 28
how long is't, count, | since the physician at 1.02. 69

i see things may serve long, but not serve ever. 2.02. 58 P
in the world, i will hold a long distance. 3.02. 24 P
for which live long to thank both heaven and me! 4.02. 67
have deserv'd it, in usurping his spurs so long. 4.03.104 P
i long to talk with the young noble soldier. 4.05.102 P
would not have knaves thrive long under /her? 5.02. 32 P
with the waves | so long as i could see. TN 1.02. 17
i'll drink to her as long as there is a passage 1.03. 39 P
yet you will be hang'd for being so long absent, 1.05. 16 P
he might have took his answer long ago. 1.05.263
i am not weary, and 'tis long to night; 3.03. 21
is it so long? 5.01.141
and since you call'd me master for so long, 5.01.324
time as long again | would be fill'd up, my WT 1.02. 3
i long. 1.02.101
so long as nature | will bear up with this 3.02.240
this exercise, so long | i daily vow to use it. 3.02.241
i'll not be long before | i call upon thee. 3.03. 8
keep | seeming and savor all the winter long. 4.04. 75
scarce any joy | did ever so long live; 5.03. 52
so long could i | stand by, a looker–on. 5.03. 84
by long and vehement suit i was seduc'd | to JN 1.01.254
i should be as merry as the day is long; 4.01. 18
out | to all our sorrows, and ere long i doubt. 4.02.102
for 'twill be | two long days' journey, lords, 4.03. 20
and he, long traded in it, makes it seem | like 4.03.109
this fever, that hath troubled me so long, 5.03. 3
and your supply, which you have wish'd so long, 5.05. 12
two men | that vow a long and weary pilgrimage. R2 1.03. 49
how long a time lies in one little word! 1.03.213
must i not serve a long apprenticehood | to 1.03.271
writ in remembrance more than things long past. 2.01. 14
small show'rs last long, but sudden storms are 2.01. 35
for sleeping england long time have i watch'd, 2.01. 77
to crop at once a too long withered flower. 2.01.134
how long shall i be patient? 2.01.163
ah, how long | shall tender duty make me suffer 2.01.163
and thus long have we stood | to watch the 3.03. 72
under whose colors he had fought so long. 4.01.100
him, | and long live henry, fourth of that name! 4.01.112
/thee tales | of woeful ages long ago betid; 5.01. 42
i'll not be long behind; 5.02.114
how long hast thou to serve, francis? 1H4 2.04. 41 P
lady, a long lease for the clinking of pewter. 2.04. 45 P
ere i lead this life long, i'll sew 2.04.116 P
my sweet creature of bumbast, how long is't ago, 2.04.327 P
john, you are so fretful you cannot live long. 3.03. 12 P
the cankers of a calm world and a long peace, 4.02. 30 P
he is, sir john. i fear we shall stay too long. 4.02. 77 P
so long as out of limit and true rule | you 4.03. 39
we find | too indirect for long continuance. 4.03.105
the king | so long in his unlucky irish wars 5.01. 53
to spend that shortness basely were too long 5.02. 82
we breathe too long. 5.04. 15
an instant and fought a long hour by shrewsbury 5.04.148 P
a hundred mark is a long one for a poor lone 2H4 2.01. 32 P
saying that ere long they should call me madam? 2.01.101 P
sir john, you loiter here too long, being you 2.01.186 P
but he did long in vain. 2.03. 14
no, no, he cannot long hold out these pangs. 4.04.117
where is he that will not stay so long | till 4.05. 80
i stay too long by thee, i weary thee. 4.05. 93
the crown immortally | long guard it yours! 4.05.144
health and long life to you, master silence. 5.03. 52 P
i have long dreamt of such a kind of man, | so 5.05. 49
i'll wait upon you, and i long to hear it. H5 1.01. 98
sacred throne, | and make you long become it! 1.02. 8
faith, i will live so long as i may, that's the 2.01. 14 P
no, by my troth, not long; 2.01. 32 P
i suerly do, that is the breff and the long. 3.02.118 P
what a long night is this! 3.07. 11 P
why do you stay so long, my lords of france? 4.02. 38
let life be short, else shame will be too long. 4.05. 23
preserve it, as long as it pleases his grace, 4.07.108 P
god, so long as your majesty is an honest man. 4.07.114 P
alas, she hath from france too long been chas'd, 5.02. 38
king henry the fift, too famous to live long! 1H6 1.01. 6
but long i will not be jack out of office. 1.01.175
my lord, methinks, is very long in talk. 1.02.118
else ne'er could he so long protract his speech. 1.02.120
thy head, | for i intend to have it ere long. 1.03. 88
pray god she prove not masculine ere long, | if 2.01. 22
long time thy shadow hath been thrall to me, 2.03. 36
rack, | so fare my limbs with long imprisonment; 2.05. 4
long after this, when henry the fift 2.05. 82
with long continuance in a settled place. 2.05.106
i trust ere long to choke thee with thine own, 3.02. 46
and there will we be too, ere it be long, | or 3.02. 75
that hath so long been resident in france? 3.04. 14
long since we were resolved of your truth, 3.04. 20
where i hope ere long | to be presented, by your 4.01.171
all long of this vile traitor somerset. 4.03. 33
won away, | long all of somerset and his delay. 4.03. 46
take her away, for she hath liv'd too long, | to 5.04. 34
long live queen margaret, england's happiness! 2H6 1.01. 37
studied so long, sat in the council–house 1.01. 90
i prophesied france will be lost ere long. 1.01.146
and would have kept so long as breath did last! 1.01.211
hast thou been long blind and now restor'd? 2.01. 74
how long hast thou been blind? 2.01. 95
o god, seest thou this, and bearest so long? 2.01.151
my lord, i long to hear it at full. 2.02. 6
long live our sovereign richard, england's king! 2.02. 63
procure me any scathe | so long as i am loyal, 2.04. 63
go, lead the way, i long to see my prison. 2.04.110
but i will remedy this gear ere long, | or sell 3.01. 91
pardon, my liege, that i have stay'd so long. 3.01. 94
he never would have stay'd in france so long. 3.01.295
by staying there so long till all were lost. 3.01.299
and fought so long, till that his thighs with 3.01.362
for henry weeps that thou dost live so long. 3.02.121
the lent shall be as long again as it is, and 4.03. 6 P
long sitting to determine poor men's causes 4.07. 88
a king | as i do long and wish to be a subject. 4.09. 6
god knows how long it is i have to live, | and 5.03. 17
long live king henry! plantagenet, embrace him. 3H6 1.01.202
and long live thou, and these thy forward sons! 1.01.203
fault, | and long hereafter say unto his child, 2.02. 36
and therefore i'll uncrown him ere't be long. 3.03.232
i long till edward fall by war's mischance, 3.03.254
thee | so long as edward is thy constant friend 4.01. 77
and therefore i'll uncrown him ere't be long." 4.01.111
and we shall have more wars before't be long. 4.06. 91
that all were well, | so 'twere not long of him; 4.07. 32
long live edward the fourth! 4.07. 76
long mayst thou live | to bear his image and 5.04. 53
well, your imprisonment shall not be long, | i R3 1.01.114
o, he hath kept an evil diet long, | and 1.01.139
i'll have her, but i will not keep her long. 1.02.229
i have too long borne | your blunt upbraidings 1.03.102
long mayst thou live to wail thy children's 1.03.203
long die thy happy days before thy death, | and, 1.03.206
i long with all my heart to see the prince. 2.04. 4
so long a–growing and so leisurely | that, if 2.04. 19
would long ere this have met us on the way. 3.01. 21
so wise so young, they say do never live long. 3.01. 79
i say, without characters fame lives long. 3.01. 81
i do, my lord, but long i cannot stay there. 3.02.119
i have been long a sleeper; 3.04. 23
the precedent was full as long a–doing, | and 3.06. 7
long live richard, england's worthy king! 3.07.240
hath he so long held out with me untir'd, | and 4.02. 44
but how long shall that title "ever" last? 4.04.350
but how long fairly shall her sweet life last? 4.04.352
as long as heaven and nature lengthens it. 4.04.353
as long as hell and richard likes of it. 4.04.354
which so long sund'red friends should dwell upon 5.03.100
long kept in britain at our mother's cost? 5.03.324
that long have frown'd upon their enmity! 5.05. 21
england hath long been mad and scarr'd herself: 5.05. 23
that she may long live here, god say amen! 5.05. 41
in a long motley coat guarded with yellow, H8 pr 16
it's long, and't may be said | it reaches far, 1.01.110
not long before your highness sped to france, 1.02.151
beaten | a long time out of play, may bring his 1.03. 45
and, as the long divorce of steel falls on me, 2.01. 76
hour | of my long weary life is come upon me. 2.01.133
that so long have slept upon | this bold bad man 2.02. 42
his highness having liv'd so long with her, and 2.03. 2
and we forgetful | in our long absence. 2.03.106
that | we are a queen (or long have dream'd so), 2.04. 71
i have spoke long, be pleas'd yourself to say 2.04.211
me his bed already, | his love, too long ago! 3.01.120
have i liv'd thus long (let me speak myself, 3.01.125
your long coat, priest, protects you, thou 3.02.276
a long farewell to all my greatness! 3.02.351
may he continue | long in his highness' favor, 3.02.396
whom the king hath in secrecy long married, 3.02.403
i have not long to trouble thee. 4.02. 77
how long her face is drawn! 4.02. 97
that so long | have follow'd both my fortunes 4.02.140
say his long trouble now is passing | out of 4.02.162
from your affairs | i hinder you too long. 5.01. 54
i long | to have this young one made a christian 5.02.212
thy endless goodness send prosperous life, long, 5.04. 2 P
his evasions have ears thus long. TRO 2.01. 69 P
i long to hear how they sped to–day. 3.01.141 P
kindred, though they be long ere they be woo'd, 3.02.110 P
had i so good occasion to lie long | as /you, 4.01. 4
bloods are now in calm, and, so long, health! 4.01. 16
we do, and long to know each other worse. 4.01. 32
doth long to see unarm'd the valiant hector. 4.05.153
that hast so long walk'd hand in hand with time. 4.05.203
y' are long about it. COR 1.01.127
how long is't since? 1.06. 14
how long continued, and what stock he springs of 2.03.237
that prefer | a noble life before a long, and 3.01.153
i shall ere long have knowledge | of my success. 5.01. 61
or of some death more long in spectatorship and 5.02. 65 P
for you, be that you are, long; 5.02.106 P
a kiss | long as my exile, sweet as my revenge! 5.03. 45
i have sate too long. 5.03.131
and all this is long of you. 5.04. 29 P
in peace and honor live lord titus long! TIT 1.01.157
long live lord titus, my beloved brother, 1.01.169
crown him and say, "long live our emperor!" 1.01.229
and say, "long live our emperor saturnine!" 1.01.233
whom thou in triumph long | hast prisoner held, 2.01. 14
ay, for these slips have made him noted long, 2.03. 86
for 'tis not life that i have begg'd so long, 2.03.170
away, for thou hast stay'd us here too long. 2.03.181
and in the fountain shall we gaze so long | till 3.01.127
it well, | i read it in the grammar long ago. 4.02. 23
trot like a servile footman all day long, | even 5.02. 55
long have i been forlorn, and all for thee. 5.02. 81
what noise is this? give me my long sword ho! ROM 1.01. 75
ay me, sad hours seem long. 1.01.161
both, | and pity 'tis you liv'd at odds so long. 1.02. 5
how long is it now | to lammas–tide? 1.03. 14
her waggon–spokes made of long spinners' legs, 1.04. 62
how long is't now since last yourself and i 1.05. 32
from nine till twelve | is /three long hours, 2.05. 11
long love doth so; 2.06. 14
for then i hope thou wilt not keep him long, 3.05. 63
be not so long to speak, i long to die, | if 4.01. 66
be not so long to speak, i long to die, | if 4.01. 66
life and these lips have long been separated. 4.05. 27
she's not well married that lives married long, 4.05. 77
how long hath he been there? 5.03.130
of breath | is not so long as is a tedious tale. 5.03.230
i have not seen you long, how goes the world? TIM 1.01. 2
this gentleman of mine hath serv'd me long; 1.01.142
vouchsafe my labor, and long live your lordship! 1.01.152
long may he live in fortunes! shall we in? 1.01.282
my father's age, | and call him to long peace. 1.02. 3
thou giv'st so long, timon (i fear me), thou 1.02.241 P
and the detention of long since due debts, 2.02. 38
that not long ago one of his men was with the 3.02. 11 P
our dinner will not recompense this long stay; 3.06. 33 P
live loath'd, and long, | most smiling, smooth, 3.06. 93
like thyself, | a madman so long, now a fool. 4.03.221
long live so, and so die. i am quit. 4.03.396
my long sickness | of health and living now 5.01.186
your plague, you his, | and last so long enough! 5.01.190
but wherefore do you hold me here so long? JC 1.02. 83
see, antony, that revels long a–nights, | is 2.02.116
i will not hold thee long. 4.03.265
made in caesar's heart, | crying, "long live! 5.01. 32
o, coward that i am, to live so long, | to see 5.03. 34
'shall not be long but i'll be here again. MAC 4.02. 23
the night is long that never finds the day. 4.03.240
i have liv'd long enough: 5.03. 22
long live the king! HAM 1.01. 3
this bird of dawning singeth all night long, 1.01.160
very like, /very /like. stay'd it long? 1.02.236
i stay too long — but here my father comes. 1.03. 52
long stay'd he so. 2.01. 88
moreover that we much did long to see you, | the 2.02. 2
o, speak of that, that do i long to hear. 2.02. 50
this is too long. 2.02.498 P
respect | that makes calamity of so long life: 3.01. 68
of yours | that i have longed long to redeliver. 3.01. 93
so long? 3.02.129 P
how long hath she been thus? 4.05. 67
and long purples | that liberal shepherds give a 4.07.169
but long it could not be | till that her 4.07.180
how long hast thou been grave–maker? 5.01.142 P
how long is that since? 5.01.145 P
how long will a man lie i' th' earth ere he rot? 5.01.163 P
long in our court have made their amorous LR 1.01. 47
"the hedge–sparrow fed the cuckoo so long, 1.04.215
shall not be a maid long, unless things be cut 1.05. 52
have been tom's food for seven long year. 3.04.139
i will not be long from you. 3.06. 3 P
the worst is not | so long as we can say, "this 4.01. 28
ere long you are like to hear | (if you dare 4.02. 19
not ha' bin zo long as 'tis by a vortnight. 4.06.239 P
he hath slept long. 4.07. 17
the wonder is, he hath endur'd so long, | he but 5.03.317
shall never see so much, nor live so long. 5.03.327
'tis not long after | but i will wear my heart OTH 1.01. 63
we lose it not, so long as we can smile. 1.03.211
it cannot be long that desdemona should continue 1.03.342 P
a just equinox, | the one as long as th' other. 2.03.125
you have known him long, and be you well assur'd 3.03. 11
lady, | that policy may either last so long, 3.03. 14
long live she so! and long live you to think so! 3.03.226
long live she so! and long live you to think so! 3.03.226
how, how oft, how long ago, and when | he hath, 4.01. 85
but now he spake | (after long seeming dead) 5.02.328
that can torment him much, and hold him long, 5.02.334
o, excellent, i love long life better than figs. ANT 1.02. 32 P
it cannot be thus long, the sides of nature 1.03. 16
in mine ears, | that long time have been barren. 2.05. 25
rogue, thou hast liv'd too long. 2.05. 73
that's not so good. he cannot like her long. 3.03. 14
is't long or round? 3.03. 29
and serving you so long! 3.03. 44
tell of her approach, | long ere she did appear; 3.06. 46
and carouse together | like friends long lost. 4.12. 13
unarm, eros, the long day's task is done, | and 4.14. 35
farewell, kind charmian, iras, long farewell. 5.02.292
how long is this ago? CYM 1.01. 61
leave | as long a term as yet we have to live, 1.01.107
you had measur'd how long a fool you were upon 1.02. 24 P
for so long | as he could make me with /this eye 1.03. 8
have i not been | thy pupil long? 1.05. 12
mine ears that have | so long attended thee. 1.06.142
blessed live you long, | a lady to the worthiest 1.06.159
how long is't since she went to milford–haven? 3.05.148 P
as i'ld give to him | (after long absence), such 3.06. 73
long live caesar! 3.07. 10
we'll not be long away. 4.02. 44
long is it since i saw him, | but time hath 4.02.103
fidele's sickness | did make my way long forth. 4.02.149
put those pow'rs in motion | that long to move. 4.03. 32
blest beams, remaining | so long a poor unknown. 4.04. 43
the time seems long, their blood thinks scorn 4.04. 53
so long a breeding as his white beard came to, 5.03. 17
overroasted rather; ready long ago. 5.04.152 P
and long of her it was | that we meet here so 5.05.271
nor place | will serve our long interrogatories. 5.05.392
did begin | was with long use account'd no sin. PER 1.ch. 30
come, gentlemen, we sit too long on trifles, 2.03. 92
weav'd the sleided silk | with fingers long, 4.ch. 22
thus time we waste, and long leagues make short; 4.04. 1
she would serve after a long voyage at sea. 4.06. 44 P
one, how long have you been at this trade? 4.06. 66 P
how long have you been of this profession? 4.06. 72 P
now do i long to hear how you were found, | how 5.03. 56
will long last and be more costly than | your TNK 1.01.132
haply so long until | the follow'd make pursuit? 1.02. 51
tied, weav'd, entangled, with so true, so long, 1.03. 42
she would long | till she had such another, and 1.03. 68
patience, | we shall live long, and loving. 2.02. 86
my rudiments | been labor'd so long with ye, 3.05. 4
the bavian, with long tail and eke long tool, 3.05.132
the bavian, with long tail and eke long tool, 3.05.132
may the stag thou hunt'st stand long, | and thy 3.05.154
in | quickly, by any means, i long to see 'em. 4.02. 65
his hair hangs long behind him, black and 4.02. 83
arm'd long and round, and on his thigh a sword 4.02. 85
now, as i have a soul, i long to see 'em. 4.02.142
ev'n thus all day long. 4.03. 18 P
do nothing all day long but pick flowers with 4.03. 25 P
and has done this long hour, to visit you. 5.02. 42
and, for a jig, come cut and long tail to him! 5.02. 49
long time upon his eye | will dwell upon his object; 5.03. 48
and ye shall have ere long, | i dare say, many a ep 15
ten kisses short as one, one long as twenty: VEN 22
which long have rain'd, making her cheeks all 83
or like a nymph, with long dishevelled hair, 147
short–jointed, fetlocks shag and long, | broad 295
"long may they kiss each other for this cure! 505
for lovers' hours are long, though seeming short 842
whereon with fearful eyes they long have gazed, 927
sit, | long after fearing to creep forth again; 1036
what canst thou boast | of things long since, or 1078
for after supper long he questioned | with LUC 122
to hold their cursed–blessed fortune long. 866
but long she thinks till he return again, | and 1359
with my tears quench troy that burns so long, 1468
and both she thinks too long with her remaining. 1572
short time seems long in sorrow's sharp 1573

with sad attention long to hear her words. 1610
and my laments would be drawn out too long | to 1616
or keep him from heart–easing words so long, 1782
hie thee, | for methinks thou stays too long. PP 12.12
long was the combat doubtful, that love with 15. 5
on th' ear, | to teach my tongue to be so long. 18.52
so long as men can breathe or eyes can see, | so SON 18.13
so long lives this, and this gives life to thee. 18.14
so long as youth and thou are of one date, | but 22. 2
and weep afresh love's long since cancell'd woe, 30. 7
forth | eternal numbers to outlive long date. 38.12
since, seldom coming, in the long year set, 52. 6
show what wealth she had | in days long since, 67.14
love that well, which thou must leave ere long. 73.14
that thou forget'st so long | to speak of that 100. 1
i teach thee how | to make him seem long hence, 101.14
so long as brain and heart | have faculty by 122. 5
tale, | ere long espied a fickle maid full pale, LC 5
"and long upon these terms i held my city, 176
LONG–A 1 FR 0.0001 REL FR 1 V 0 P
leman mine, | and a merry heart lives long–a." 2H4 5.03. 48
LONGAVILLE 11 FR 0.0012 REL FR 10 V 1 P
you three, berowne, dumaine, and longaville, LLL 1.01. 15
/lord longaville is one. 2.01. 39
solemnized | in normandy, saw i this longaville, 2.01. 43
what, longaville, and reading! 4.03. 43
o, would the king, berowne, and longaville, 4.03.121
longaville | did never sonnet for her sake 4.03.131
and, gentle longaville, where lies thy pain? 4.03.170
this, and these /pearls, to me sent longaville. 5.02. 53
lord longaville said i came o'er his heart, 5.02.278
and longaville was for my service born. 5.02.284
sweet lord longaville, rein thy tongue. 5.02.656 P
LONGBOAT'S 1 FR 0.0001 REL FR 1 V 0 P
and on our longboat's side | strike off his head 2H6 4.01. 68
LONG–CONTINUED 1 FR 0.0001 REL FR 1 V 0 P
who in /this dull and long–continued truce | is TRO 1.03.262
'LONG'D *(also belong'd, etc.)*
'LONG'D 1 FR 0.0001 REL FR 1 V 0 P
although there 'long'd | no more to th' crown H8 2.03. 48
LONG'D 4 FR 0.0004 REL FR 3 V 1 P
and how she long'd to eat adders' heads, and WT 4.04.264 P
i never long'd to hear a word till now, | say R2 5.03.115
was never subject long'd to be a king | as i do 2H6 4.09. 5
ne'er long'd my mother so | to see me first, as CYM 3.04. 2
LONG'D–FOR 1 FR 0.0001 REL FR 1 V 0 P
with any long'd–for change or better state. JN 4.02. 8
LONG–DURING 1 FR 0.0001 REL FR 1 V 0 P
as motion and long–during action tires | the LLL 4.03.303
LONGED 1 FR 0.0001 REL FR 1 V 0 P
of yours | that i have longed long to redeliver. HAM 3.01. 93
LONG–ENGRAFF'D 1 FR 0.0001 REL FR 0 V 1 P
the imperfections of long–engraff'd condition, LR 1.01.297 P
/LONGER 1 FR 0.0001 REL FR 0 V 1 P
/the /quality /no /longer /than /they /can /sing HAM 2.02.347 P
LONGER 120 FR 0.0135 REL FR 87 V 33 P
do now let loose my opinion, hold it no longer: TMP 2.02. 35 P
hope, and keep it | no longer for my flatterer. 3.03. 8
that tide will stay me longer than i should. TGV 2.02. 15
you'll lose the tide, if you tarry any longer. 2.03. 36 P
my territories | longer than swiftest expedition 3.01.164
longer than i prove loyal to your grace | let me 3.02. 20
sixteen months, and longer might have stay'd, 4.01. 21
you are not to go loose any longer, you must be WIV 4.02.123 P
no longer staying but to give the mother MM 1.04. 86
longer or shorter, he may be so fitted | that 2.04. 40
till my tale be heard, | and hold no longer out. 5.01.366
prince, | no longer session hold upon my shame, 5.01.371
but longer did we not retain much hope; ERR 1.01. 65
come, come, no longer will i be a fool, | to put 2.02.203
she'll burn a week longer than the whole world. 3.02.100 P
no longer from head to foot than from hip to hip 3.02.113 P
prays some occasion may detain us longer. ADO 1.01.150 P
i would have salv'd it with a longer treatise. 1.01.315
if we can do this, cupid is no longer an archer; 2.01.385 P
come, | or, if thou wilt hold longer argument, 2.03. 53
yea, and i will weep a while longer. 4.01.256 P
he shall live no longer in monument than the 5.02. 79 P
the chain were longer and the letter short? LLL 5.02. 56
can any face of brass hold longer out? 5.02.395
we shall chide downright, if i longer stay. MND 2.01.145
you, i, | nor longer stay in your curst company. 3.02.341
my legs are longer though, to run away. 3.02.343
by white hairs, but competency lives longer. MV 1.02. 9 P
for i am a jew if i serve the jew any longer. 2.02.113 P
i'll stay no longer question. 4.01.346
i will no longer endure it, though yet i know no AYL 1.01. 24 P
strong in me, and i will no longer endure it; 1.01. 71 P
no longer celia, but aliena. 1.03.128
i'll tarry no longer with you. 3.02.291 P
i can live no longer by thinking. 5.02. 50 P
will weary you then no longer with idle talking. 5.02. 51 P
the longer kept, the less worth. AWW 1.01.154 P
i'll stay a month longer. TN 1.03.112 P
if he mend, he is no longer dishonest; 1.05. 46 P
good swabber, i am to hull here a little longer. 1.05.204 P
will you stay no longer? 2.01. 1 P
no, faith, i'll not stay a jot longer. 3.02. 1 P
as might have drawn one to a longer voyage) 3.03. 7
if you tarry longer, | i shall give worse 4.01. 19
no longer stay. WT 1.02. 16
one sev'nnight longer. 1.02. 17
camillo, this great sir will yet stay longer. 1.02.212
most understand | bohemia stays here longer. 1.02.230
stays here longer. 1.02.230
no longer shall you gaze on't, lest your fancy 5.03. 60
no longer than we well could wash our hands | to JN 3.01.234
fellow, give place, here is no longer stay. R2 5.05. 95
third, if he fight longer than he sees reason, 1H4 1.02.185 P
i'll be no longer guilty of this sin. 2.04.241 P
i can no longer brook thy vanities. 5.04. 74
to devour the way, | staying no longer question. 2H4 1.01. 48
and let this world no longer be a stage | to 1.01.155
to me — 'twas no longer ago than wed'sday last, 2.04. 86 P
and when i cannot live any longer, i will do as H5 2.01. 15 P
us and ours, | for we no longer are defensible. 3.03. 50
now do thou watch, for i can stay no longer. 1H6 1.04. 18
no longer on saint denis will we cry, | but joan 1.06. 28
so farewell, talbot, i'll no longer trust thee. 3.03. 84
my spirit can no longer bear these harms. 4.07. 30
if i longer stay, | we shall begin our ancient 2H6 1.01.143
infection in this air | but three days longer, 3.02.288
for a thousand years, i could stay no longer. 4.10. 6 P
no longer earl of march, but duke of york; 3H6 2.01.192
stay we no longer, dreaming of renown, | but 2.01.199
defy thee, | not willing any longer conference, 2.02.171
no, wrangling woman, we'll no longer stay, 2.02.176
foreslow no longer, make we hence amain. 2.03. 56
that's a day longer than a wonder lasts. 3.02.114
i can no longer hold me patient. R3 1.03.156
last longer telling than thy kindness' date. 4.04.255
nay, we must longer kneel; i am a suitor. H8 1.02. 9
longer than i have time to tell his years; 2.01. 91
honor's train | is longer than his foreskirt. 2.03. 98
bootless | that longer you desire the court, as 2.04. 62
heaven had pleas'd to have given me longer life 4.02.152
and dreaming night will hide our joys no longer, TRO 4.02. 10
word, i also am | longer to live most weary, and COR 4.05. 95
this done, see that you take no longer days, TIT 4.02.165
be brisk a while, and the longer liver take all. ROM 1.05. 15 P
my love, | and i'll no longer be a capulet. 2.02. 36
meant indeed to occupy the argument no longer. 2.04.100 P
is longer than the tale thou dost excuse. 2.05. 34
come go, good juliet, i dare no longer stay. 5.03.159
i am so much a fool, should i stay longer, | it MAC 4.02. 28
i dare abide no longer. 4.02. 73
would have mourn'd longer — married with my HAM 1.02.151
longer, longer. 1.02.238
longer, longer. 1.02.238
theme | until my eyelids will no longer wag. 5.01.267
with laertes, or that you will take longer time. 5.02.199 P
if i could bear it longer, and not fall | to LR 4.06. 37
of this tough world | stretch him out longer. 5.03.316
i will indeed no longer endure it; OTH 4.02.178 P
you must not stay here longer, your dismission ANT 1.01. 26
i can behold no longer. 3.10. 1
rebel to my will, | may hang no longer on me. 4.09. 15
i heard of one of them no longer than yesterday, 5.02.251 P
make pastime with us a day or two, or longer. CYM 3.01. 78 P
no longer exercise | upon a valiant race thy 5.04. 82
forty days longer we do respite you; PER 1.01.116
was not best | longer for him to make his rest. 2.ch. 26
the most high gods not minding longer | to 2.04. 3
it shall no longer grieve without reproof. 2.04. 19
a twelvemonth longer let me entreat you | to 2.04. 45
choice, | and will no longer have it be delayed. 2.05. 22
but touch the ground for us no longer time TNK 1.01. 97
to delay it longer | would make the world think, 3.06. 10
she is resolv'd no longer to restrain him, VEN 579
time, cease thou thy course and last no longer, LUC 1765
no longer yours than you yourself here live: SON 13. 2
but day doth daily draw my sorrows longer, | and 28.13
this told, i joy, but then no longer glad, | i 45.13
no longer mourn for me when i am dead | than you 71. 1
and life no longer than thy love will stay, 92. 3
for that which longer nurseth the disease, 147. 2
LONGEST 5 FR 0.0005 REL FR 5 V 0 P
but it hath been the longest night | that e'er i TGV 4.02.139
night in russia | when nights are longest there. MM 2.01.135
to serve me last that i may longest keep | thy R2 3.04. 95
so longest way shall have the longest moans. 5.01. 90
so longest way shall have the longest moans. 5.01. 90
'LONGETH 2 FR 0.0002 REL FR 2 V 0 P
grace | as 'longeth to a lover's blessed case! SHR 4.02. 45
with such austerity as 'longeth to a father. 4.04. 7
LONG–EXPERIENC'D 2 FR 0.0002 REL FR 2 V 0 P
therefore, out of thy long–experienc'd time, ROM 4.01. 60
now set thy long–experienc'd wit to school. LUC 1820
LONG–GROWN 1 FR 0.0001 REL FR 1 V 0 P
the long–grown wounds of my intemperance. 1H4 3.02.156
LONG–HID 1 FR 0.0001 REL FR 1 V 0 P
and arm'd his long–hid wits advisedly, | to LUC 1816
LONG–IMPRISONED 1 FR 0.0001 REL FR 1 V 0 P
york, unloose thy long–imprisoned thoughts, 2H6 5.01. 88
'LONGING 2 FR 0.0002 REL FR 2 V 0 P
it is an honor 'longing to our house, AWW 4.02. 42
able to maintain | the many to them 'longing, H8 1.02. 32
LONGING 22 FR 0.0024 REL FR 19 V 3 P
in, | by longing for that food so long a time. TGV 2.07. 17
of, | to furnish me upon my longing journey. 2.07. 85
and longing (saving your honors' reverence) for MM 2.01. 89 P
and being great–bellied, and longing (as i said) 2.01. 99 P
as to a bed | that, longing, have been sick for, 2.04.103
changeable, longing and liking, proud, AYL 3.02.411 P
more longing, wavering, sooner lost and worn, TN 2.04. 34
for whose sight | i have a woman's longing. WT 4.04.667
but benefit no further | than vainly longing. H8 1.02. 81
i have a woman's longing, | an appetite that i TRO 3.03.237
sir, you have sav'd my longing, and i feed TIM 1.01.252
fainted, | longing for what it had not; ANT 3.06. 48
nice longing, slanders, mutability, | all faults CYM 2.05. 26
being thus quench'd | of hope, not longing, mine 5.05.196
we do our longing stay | to hear the rest untold PER 5.03. 83
joy, | which breeds a deeper longing, cure their TNK 1.01.190
how his longing | follows his friend: 1.03. 26
and all the longing maids that ever lov'd, | if 3.06.246
th' wood, where palamon | lies longing for me. 4.01.145
longing to hear the hateful foe bewray'd. LUC 1698
a longing tarriance for adonis made | under an PP 6. 4
longing still | for that which longer nurseth SON 147. 1
LONGINGS 1 FR 0.0001 REL FR 1 V 0 P
on my crown, i have | immortal longings in me. ANT 5.02.281
LONG–LANE 1 FR 0.0001 REL FR 1 V 0 P
him, | and bring our horses unto long–lane end; SHR 4.03.185
LONG–LEGG'D 1 FR 0.0001 REL FR 1 V 0 P
hence, you long–legg'd spinners, hence! MND 2.02. 21
LONG–LIV'D 1 FR 0.0001 REL FR 1 V 0 P
and burn the long–liv'd phoenix in her blood; SON 19. 4
LONG–LIVING 1 FR 0.0001 REL FR 1 V 0 P
thou back'st reproach against long–living laud, LUC 622
LONGLY 1 FR 0.0001 REL FR 1 V 0 P
master, you look'd so longly on the maid, SHR 1.01.165
LONG–PARTED 1 FR 0.0001 REL FR 1 V 0 P
as a long–parted mother with her child | plays R2 3.02. 8
'LONGS 4 FR 0.0004 REL FR 4 V 0 P
this, | no ceremony that to great ones 'longs, MM 2.02. 59
denied, which 'longs | to women of all fashion; WT 3.02.103
of nations, 'longs | to him and to his heirs, H5 2.04. 80
to his surname coriolanus 'longs more pride COR 5.03.170
LONG'S 1 FR 0.0001 REL FR 1 V 0 P
pardon old gower — this long's the text. PER 2.ch. 40
LONGS 12 FR 0.0013 REL FR 8 V 4 P
that longs for every thing that he can come by. TGV 3.01.125
but is there any else longs to see this broken AYL 1.02.141 P
to tell he longs to see his son were strong; WT 1.02. 34
yea, at all points, and longs to enter in. R2 1.03. 2
the dolphin longs for morning. H5 3.07. 90 P
he longs to eat the english. 3.07. 91 P
he longs not for the dawning as we do. 3.07.130 P
make a short shrift, he longs to see your head. R3 3.04. 95
first the lamb, | longs after for the garbage. CYM 1.06. 50
appetite, | that loathes even as it longs. TNK 1.03. 90
no, lady, no, my heart longs not to groan, | but VEN 785
looks for night, and then she longs for morrow, LUC 1571
LONG'ST 3 FR 0.0003 REL FR 3 V 0 P
pisanio, | who long'st like me to see thy lord; CYM 3.02. 53
who long'st | (o, let me bate!) 3.02. 53
but not like me — yet long'st, | but in a 3.02. 54
LONG–STAFF 1 FR 0.0001 REL FR 0 V 1 P
land–rakers, no long–staff sixpenny strikers, 1H4 2.01. 74 P
LONG–TAIL 1 FR 0.0001 REL FR 0 V 1 P
that i will, come cut and long–tail, under the WIV 3.04. 46 P
LONG–TONGU'D 2 FR 0.0002 REL FR 2 V 0 P
how now, long–tongu'd warwick, dare you speak? 3H6 2.02.102
guilt of ours, | a long–tongu'd babbling gossip? TIT 4.02.150
LONG–USURPED 1 FR 0.0001 REL FR 1 V 0 P
lo here this long–usurped royalty | from the R3 5.05. 4
LONG–VANISH'D 1 FR 0.0001 REL FR 1 V 0 P
from the worm–holes of long–vanish'd days, | nor H5 2.04. 86
LONG–WINDED 1 FR 0.0001 REL FR 0 V 1 P
of sugar–candy to make thee long–winded — if 1H4 3.03.160 P
'LOO *(also alow, hallow*, etc., holla, hollo, hollow*, etc.,loo)*
'LOO 4 FR 0.0004 REL FR 0 V 4 P
'loo, paris, 'loo! TRO 5.07. 10 P
'loo, paris, 'loo! 5.07. 10 P
'loo, paris, 'loo! 5.07. 11 P
'loo, paris, 'loo! 5.07. 11 P
LOO 2 FR 0.0002 REL FR 0 V 2 P
alow, loo, loo! LR 3.04. 77 P
alow, loo, loo! 3.04. 77 P
LOOF'D 1 FR 0.0001 REL FR 1 V 0 P
she once being loof'd, | the noble ruin of her ANT 3.10. 17
/LOOK 7 FR 0.0008 REL FR 5 V 2 P
/all /of /you /that /stand /and /look /upon /me R2 4.01.237
/to /look /upon /the /hideous /god /of /war 2H4 2.03. 35
/look /what /i /have /said, | i will avouch't in R3 1.03.113
/look /ye, /my /lord /mayor, | would you imagine 3.05. 34
/and /look /you /eat /no /more | /than /will TIT 3.02. 1
/look /where /he /stands /and /glares! LR 3.06. 23 P
/'tis /time /to /look /about, /the /powers /of 4.07. 91 P
LOOK 881 FR 0.0995 REL FR 648 V 233 P
'tis a villain, sir, | i do not love to look on. TMP 1.02.310
look, he's winding up the watch of his wit, by 2.01. 12 P
and look how well my garments sit upon me, 2.01.272
you look wearily. 3.01. 32
look thou be true; 4.01. 51
you do look, my son, in a mov'd sort, | as if 4.01.146
take a displeasure against you, look you — 4.01.202 P
look what a wardrobe here is for thee! 4.01.223 P
pray you look in. 5.01.167
look down, you gods, | and on this couple drop a 5.01.201
o, look, sir, look, sir, here is more of us. 5.01.216
o, look, sir, look, sir, here is more of us. 5.01.216
as you look | to have my pardon, trim it 5.01.293
look, here is writ "kind julia." TGV 1.02.106
look what thou want'st shall be sent after thee. 1.03. 74
that, when i look on you, i can hardly think you 2.01. 31 P
having no eyes, look you, wept herself blind at 2.03. 13 P
for, look you, she is as white as a lily and as 2.03. 20 P
to have a look of such a worthy mistress. 2.04.108
when you have done, we look to hear from you. 2.04.120
but when i look on her perfections, | there is 2.04.211
look thee, i'll but lean, and my staff 2.05. 29 P
unless i look on silvia in the day, | there is 3.01.180
the day, | there is no day for me to look upon. 3.01.181
i am but a fool, look you, and yet i have the 3.01.263 P
look you, a sweet virtue in a maid with clean 3.01.278 P
grace | let me not live to look upon your grace. 3.02. 21
servant shall play the cur with him, look you, 4.04. 2 P
i pray thee let me look on that again. 4.04.125
i will not look upon your master's lines; 4.04.128
eyes, | for i had rather wink than look on them. 5.02. 14
vouchsafe me, for my meed, but one fair look: 5.04. 23
death, | would i not undergo for one calm look? 5.04. 42
look to the boy. 5.04. 85
look up; 5.04. 87 P
the council, look you, shall desire to hear the WIV 1.01. 37 P
(i may call him my master, look you, for i keep 1.04. 95 P
you look very ill. 2.01. 36 P
why, look where he comes; 2.01.102 P
look who comes yonder. 2.01.157 P
look where my ranting host of the garter comes. 2.01.189 P
well, i will look further into't, and i have a 2.01.237 P
and, look you, he may come and go between you 2.02.124 P
will they yet look after thee? 2.02.140 P
by gar, me do look he shall clapper–de–claw me, 2.03. 68 P
desire you you will also look that way. 3.01. 9 P
as i am a christians–soul, now look you; 3.01. 94 P
look, here is a basket; 3.03.129 P
look how you drumble! 3.03.147 P
look on master fenton." 3.04. 97 P
look where his master comes; 4.01. 9 P
page and i will look some linen for your head. 4.02. 81 P
discretions of a oman as ever i did look upon. 4.04. 2 P
i tell you for good will, look you. 4.05. 79 P
the several chairs of order look you scour 5.05. 61
and nightly, meadow–fairies, look you sing, 5.05. 65
look where he comes. MM 1.01. 24
and do look to know | what doth befall you here. 1.01. 57
me | to look into the bottom of my place. 1.01. 78
and i beseech you, look into master froth here, 2.01.122 P
beseech you, sir, look in this gentleman's face. 2.01.147 P
good master froth, look upon his honor; 2.01.148 P

look you bring me in the names of some six or		2.01.272 P
look, what i will not, that i cannot do.		2.02. 52
look, here comes one;		2.03. 10
i will proclaim thee, angelo, look for't!		2.04.151
look, signior, here's your sister.		3.01. 49
but that you have a hanging look — do you call,		4.02. 34 P
look, here's the warrant, claudio, for thy death		4.02. 63
look you, sir, here is the hand and seal of the		4.02.191 P
look, th' unfolding star calls up the shepherd.		4.02.203 P
for look you, the warrant's come.		4.03. 42 P
look you, sir, here comes your ghostly father.		4.03. 48 P
you | look forward on the journey you shall go.		4.03. 58
look you speak justly.		5.01.296
look, if it please you, on this man condemn'd		5.01.444
governed his deeds, | till he did look on me.		5.01.447
go fetch him hither, let me look upon him.		5.01.469
look that you love your wife;		5.01.497
claudio, that you wrong'd, look you restore.		5.01.525
look when i serve him so, he takes it /ill.	ERR	2.01. 12
whilst i at home starve for a merry look:		2.01. 88
fair | a sunny look of his would soon repair.		2.01. 99
ay, ay, antipholus, look strange and frown,		2.02.110
look sweet, speak fair, become disloyalty;		3.02. 11
as good to wink, sweet love, as look on night.		3.02. 58
o, sir, i did not look so low.		3.02.139 P
ne'er may i look on day, nor sleep on night,		5.01.210
why look you strange on me? you know me well.		5.01.296
come go with us, we'll look to that anon.		5.01.413
look, don pedro is return'd to seek you.	ADO	1.01.202 P
shall see thee, ere i die, look pale with love.		1.01.247 P
i look for an earthquake too then.		1.01.273 P
look what will serve is fit:		1.01.318
so you walk softly, and look sweetly, and say		2.01. 88 P
look here she comes.		2.01.262 P
will you look to those things i told you of?		2.01.337 P
the night, appoint her to look out at her lady's		2.02. 17 P
look you for any other issue?		2.02. 29 P
fair, or i'll never look on her;		2.03. 32 P
for look where beatrice, like a lapwing, runs		3.01. 24
misprising what they look on, and her wit		3.01. 52
but methinks you look with your eyes as other		3.04. 91 P
dost thou look up?		4.01.119
but on this travail look for greater birth:		4.01.213
i do not like thy look, i promise thee.		4.02. 45 P
if you would know your wronger, look on me.		5.01.262
farewell, my lords, we look for you to–morrow.		5.01.329
the wolves have preyed, and look, the gentle day		5.03. 25
if my cousin do not look exceeding narrowly to		5.04.116 P
doth falsely blind the eyesight of his look.	LLL	1.01. 76
a great sign, sir, that he will look sad.		1.02. 3 P
nothing, master moth, but what they look upon.		1.02.163 P
now will i look to his remuneration.		3.01.136 P
monster ignorance, how deformed dost thou look!		4.02. 23
be a claw, look how he claws him with a talent.		4.02. 63 P
i will look again on the intellect of the letter		4.02.133 P
you may look pale, but i should blush, i know,		4.03.127
eye | dares look upon the heaven of her brow,		4.03.223
if that she learn not of her eye to look:		4.03.248
to look like her are chimney–sweepers black.		4.03.262
look, here's thy love; my foot and her face see.		4.03.273
can you still dream and pore and thereon look?		4.03.294
look you what i have from the loving king.		5.02. 4
look what you do, you do it still i' th' dark.		5.02. 24
look how you butt yourself in these sharp mocks!		5.02.251
why look you pale?		5.02.392
man, an honest man, look you, and soon dash'd.		5.02.581 P
heavenly eyes, that look into these faults,		5.02.769
mistress, look on me, | behold the window of my		5.02.837
rather your eyes must with his judgment look.	MND	1.01. 57
look you arm yourself | to fit your fancies to		1.01.117
keep promise, love. look, here comes helena.		1.01.179
o, teach me how you look, and with what art		1.01.192
if i do it, let the audience look to their eyes.		1.02. 26 P
spirit, | for i am sick when i do look on thee.		2.01.212
and i am sick when i look not on you.		2.01.213
when all the world is here to look on me?		2.01.226
and look thou meet me ere the first cock crow.		2.01.267
can, | deserve a sweet look from demetrius' eye,		2.02.127
lysander, look how i do quake with fear.		2.02.148
and we ought to look to't.		3.01. 33 P
look in the almanac!		3.01. 53 P
so should a murtherer look — so dead, so grim.		3.02. 57
so should the murthered look, and so should i,		3.02. 58
you, the murtherer, look as bright, as clear,		3.02. 60
the wind, | and helena of athens look thou find.		3.02. 95
i go, i go, look how i go, | swifter than arrow		3.02.100
look when i vow, i weep;		3.02.124
look where thy love comes;		3.02.176
and from each other look thou lead them thus,		3.02.363
for fear lest day should look their shames upon,		3.02.385
and dar'st not stand, nor look me in the face.		3.02.424
by day's approach look to be visited.		3.02.430
every man look o'er his part;		4.02. 38 P
where i have seen them shiver and look pale,		5.01. 95
friend, would go near to make a man look sad.		5.01.289 P
you look not well, signior antonio, | you have	MV	1.01. 73
why, look you how you storm!		1.03.137
i would o'erstare the sternest eyes that look,		2.01. 27
do i look like a cudgel or a hovel–post, a staff		2.02. 68 P
wear prayer–books in my pocket, look demurely,		2.02.192
jessica, my girl, | look to my house.		2.05. 16
mistress, look out at window, for all this —		2.05. 40 P
i am glad 'tis night, you do not look on me,		2.06. 34
let good antonio look he keep his day, | or he		2.08. 25
you shall look fairer ere i give or hazard.		2.09. 22
let him look to his bond.		3.01. 47 P
to call me usurer, let him look to his bond.		3.01. 48 P
a christian cur'sy, let him look to his bond.		3.01. 50 P
look on beauty, | and you shall see 'tis		3.02. 88
yet look how far | the substance of my praise		3.02.126
my eyes, my lord, can look as swift as yours:		3.02.197
jailer, look to him, tell not me of mercy.		3.03. 1
jailer, look to him.		3.03. 3
and look what notes and garments he doth give		3.04. 51
truly, for look you, the sins of the father are		3.05. 1 P
i pray you let me look upon the bond.		4.01.225
look how the floor of heaven | is thick inlaid		5.01. 58
and thou wert best look to't;	AYL	1.01.147 P
and weep, and thou must look pale and wonder.		1.01.157 P
look, here comes the duke.		1.03. 39 P
page, | and therefore look you call me ganymed.		1.03.125
wherefore do you look | upon that poor and		2.01. 56
though i look old, yet i am strong and lusty;		2.03. 47
look you, who comes here, a young man and an old		2.04. 19 P
he hath been all this day to look you.		2.05. 33 P
what, you look merrily!		2.07. 11
but look to it:		3.01. 4
as it is a spare life, look you, it fits my		3.02. 19 P
for look here what i found on a palm tree.		3.02.175 P
look but in, and you shall see him.		3.02.287 P
why do you look on me?		3.05. 41
why look you so upon me?		3.05. 69 P
shepherdess, look on him better, | and be not		3.05. 77
but do not look for further recompense | than		3.05. 97
look you lisp and wear strange suits;		4.01. 33 P
look who comes here.		4.03. 5 P
many will swoon when they do look on blood.		4.03.158
look, he recovers.		4.03.160
come, you look paler and paler.		4.03.177 P
for look you, here comes my rosalind.		5.02. 16 P
a thing it is to look into happiness through		5.02. 44 P
look, here comes a lover of mine and a lover of		5.02. 75 P
faithful shepherd — | look upon him, love him;		5.02. 82
look in the chronicles;	SHR	in.1. 4 P
but sup them well, and look unto them all,		in.1. 28
shoes, or such shoes as my toes look through the		in.2. 12 P
look how thy servants do attend on thee, | each		in.2. 33
on them to look and practice by myself.		1.01. 83
cause for me to leave his service, look you, sir		1.02. 30 P
nay, look you, sir, he tells you flatly what his		1.02. 77 P
master, master, look about you!		1.02.140 P
how now, my friend, why dost thou look so pale?		2.01.142
for fear, i promise you, if i look pale.		2.01.143
you must not look so sour.		2.01.228
here's no crab, and therefore look not sour.		2.01.230
canst not frown, thou canst not look askaunce,		2.01.247
that by degrees we mean to look into, | and		3.02.143
nay, look not big, nor stamp, nor stare, nor		3.02.228
knows not which way to stand, to look, to speak,		4.01.185
look that you take upon you as you should;		4.02.109
pluck up thy spirits, look cheerfully upon me.		4.03. 38
look what i speak, or do, or think to do, | you		4.03.192
if this be not that you look for, i have no more		4.04. 96
sun, | that every thing i look on seemeth green;		4.05. 47
look not pale, bianca, thy father will not frown		5.01.138 P
he did look far | into the service of the time,	AWW	1.02. 26
for look, thy cheeks | confess it, /t' /one to		1.03.176
a traitor you do look like, but such traitors		2.01. 96
i need not open, for i look through thee.		2.03.214 P
why, he will look upon his boot and sing, mend		3.02. 6 P
look on his letter, madam, here's my passport.		3.02. 56
look, here comes a pilgrim.		3.05. 30 P
look, he has spied us.		3.05. 89 P
and by midnight look to hear further from me.		3.06. 77 P
i must go look my twigs. he shall be caught.		3.06.107
nay, look not so upon me;		4.03.195 P
so, look about you.		4.03.312 P
look, here he comes himself.		5.02. 17 P
why do you look so strange upon your wife?		5.03.168
your ring, | and, look you, here's your letter.		5.03.311
look you now, he's out of his guard already.	TN	1.05. 86 P
go look after him.		1.05.136 P
madonna, and the fool shall look to the madman.		1.05.138 P
look you, sir, such a one i was this present.		1.05.234 P
of faith that all that look on him love him;		2.03.152 P
look how imagination blows him.		2.05. 42 P
look where the youngest wren of /nine comes.		3.02. 66 P
no worse man than sir toby to look to me!		3.04. 65 P
but my hope is better, and so look to thyself.		3.04.168 P
that they will kill one another by the look,		3.04.196 P
look then to be well edified when the fool		5.01.290 P
sir page, | look on me with your welkin eye.	WT	1.02.136
you look | as if you held a brow of much		1.02.148
you, my lords, | look on her, mark her well;		2.01. 65
i must be patient till the heavens look | with		2.01.106
look to your babe, my lord, 'tis yours.		2.03.126
easiest passage | look for no less than death.		3.02. 91
look down | and see what death is doing.		3.02.148
not move the gods | to look that way thou wert.		3.02.214
the skies look grimly | and threaten present		3.03. 3
look to thy bark, i'll not be long before | i		3.03. 8
but look thee here, boy.		3.03.112 P
look thee, a bearing–cloth for a squire's child!		3.03.115 P
look thee here, take up, take up, boy;		3.03.116 P
my service which look upon his removedness;		4.02. 36 P
when the kite builds, look to lesser linen.		4.03. 23 P
how would he look to see his work, so noble,		4.04. 21
her something | that makes her blood look on't.		4.04.160
why look you so upon me?		4.04.462
i will but look upon the hedge and follow you.		4.04.825 P
i desire my life | once more to look on him.		5.01.138
your throne and his | measur'd to look upon you;		5.01.145
dear, look up.		5.01.215
worth such gazes | than what you look on now.		5.01.227
not | that which my daughter came to look upon,		5.03. 13
you can make her do, | i am content to look on;		5.03. 92
strike all that look upon with marvel.		5.03.100
look down | and from your sacred vials pour your		5.03.121
look upon my brother.		5.03.147
pembroke, look to't.	JN	1.01. 30
should say, "look where three–farthings goes!"		1.01.143
look here upon thy brother geffrey's face:		2.01. 99
to look into the blots and stains of right.		2.01.114
sirrah, look to't, i' faith i will, i' faith.		2.01.140
look upon the years | of lewis the dolphin and		2.01.424
what say'st thou, boy? look in the lady's face.		2.01.495
why dost thou look so sadly on my son?		3.01. 20
look to that, devil, lest that france repent,		3.01.196
look to thyself, thou art in jeopardy.		3.01.346
cousin, look not sad, | thy grandame loves thee,		3.03. 2
look who comes here!		3.04. 17
cheek, | and he will look as hollow as a ghost,		3.04. 84
hot, and look thou stand | within the arras.		4.01. 1
look to't.		4.01. 7
you look pale to–day.		4.01. 28
speak a word, | nor look upon the iron angerly.		4.01. 81
he hath a stern look, but a gentle heart.		4.01. 87
though to no use but still to look on you!		4.01.102
o, now you look like hubert!		4.01.125
why look you sad?		5.01. 44
look where the holy legate comes apace, | to		5.02. 65
you look but on the outside of this work.		5.02.109
look what i speak, my life shall prove it true:	R2	1.01. 87
nor never look upon each other's face, | nor		1.03.185
look what thy soul holds dear, imagine it | to		1.03.286
gilt, | and make high majesty look like itself,		2.01.295
knowledge, | i never in my life did look on him.		2.03. 39
look on my wrongs with an indifferent eye.		2.03.116
rich men look sad, and ruffians dance and leap,		2.04. 12
have i not reason to look pale and dead?		3.02. 79
look not to the ground, | ye favorites of a king		3.02. 87
not, | to look so poorly and to speak so fair?		3.03.128
that look too lofty in our commonwealth:		3.04. 35
that my sad look | should grace the triumph of		3.04. 98
cousin, stand forth, and look upon that man.		4.01. 7
yet look up, behold, | that you in pity may		5.01. 8
look to thyself, | thou hast a traitor in thy		5.03. 39
look upon his face:		5.03.100
to look upon my sometimes royal master's face.		5.05. 75
why, look you, i am /whipt and scourg'd with	1H4	1.03.239
"look when his infant fortune came to age" | and		1.03.253
look down into the pomgarnet, ralph.		2.04. 37 P
for look you, francis, your white canvas doublet		2.04. 74 P
look to the guests within.		2.04. 81 P
give me a cup of sack to make my eyes look red,		2.04.385 P
and a corpulent, of a cheerful look, a pleasing		2.04.423 P
henceforth ne'er look on me.		2.04.446 P
look upon his face;		3.03. 77 P
love thy husband, look to thy servants, cherish		3.03.171 P
if that the devil and mischance look big | upon		4.01. 58
look how we can, or sad or merrily,		5.02. 12
with lustier maintenance than i did look for		5.04. 22
i look to be either earl or duke, i can assure		5.04.142 P
look, here comes more news.	2H4	1.01. 59
so dull, so dead in look, so woe–begone, | drew		1.01. 71
but look you pray, all you that kiss my lady		1.02.207 P
to look with forehead bold and big enough | upon		1.03. 8
and look if the fat villain have not transform'd		2.02. 71 P
he holds his place, for look you how he writes.		2.02.107 P
threw many a northward look to see his father		2.03. 13
masters, how i shake, look you, i warrant you.		2.04.105 P
therefore captains had need look to't.		2.04.150 P
look whe'er the wither'd elder hath not his pole		2.04.258 P
and look whether the fiery trigon, his man, be		2.04.265 P
look to th' door there, francis.		2.04.352 P
look, here comes good sir john.		3.02. 81 P
look to taste the due | meet for rebellion /and		4.02.116
and rotten times that you shall look upon,		4.04. 60
my gracious lord, you look beyond him quite:		4.04. 67
look here's more news.		4.04. 93
my sovereign lord, cheer up yourself, look up.		4.04.113
coming to look on you, thinking you dead, | and		4.05.155
lest rest and lying still might make them look		4.05.211
look, look, here comes my john of lancaster.		4.05.225
look, look, here comes my john of lancaster.		4.05.225
look about, davy.		5.01. 52 P
bardolph, look to our horses.		5.01. 61 P
which cannot look more hideously upon me | than		5.02. 12
you all look strangely on me, and you most.		5.02. 63
look who's at door there ho!		5.03. 70 P
look you, he must seem thus to the world.		5.05. 78 P
if you look for a good speech now, you undo me,		ep 3 P
flag, | look back into your mighty ancestors;	H5	1.02.102
yea, strike the dolphin blind to look on us.		1.02.280
look ye how they change!		2.02. 73
look to my chattels and my moveables.		2.03. 48
and, princes, look you strongly arm to meet him.		2.04. 49
for look you, the mines is not according to the		3.02. 58 P
for look you, th' athversary — you may discuss		3.02. 60 P
you may discuss unto the duke, look you — is		3.02. 61 P
in the true disciplines of the wars, look you,		3.02. 72 P
you now, will you voutsafe me, look you, a few		3.02. 95 P
in the way of argument, look you, and friendly		3.02. 98 P
and partly for the satisfaction, look you, of my		3.02.100 P
i think, look you, under your correction, there		3.02.120 P
look you, if you take the matter otherwise than		3.02.125 P
as in discretion you ought to use me, look you,		3.02.128 P
better opportunity to be required, look you, i		3.02.139 P
in a moment look to see | the blind and bloody		3.03. 33
and her foot, look you, is fixed upon a		3.06. 35 P
for if, look you, he were my brother, i would		3.06. 54 P
the french is gone off, look you, and there is		3.06. 92 P
that we should also, look you, be an ass and a		4.01. 79 P
sand, that look to be wash'd off the next tide.		4.01. 98 P
captain, if you look in the maps of the orld, i		4.07. 23 P
that the situations, look you, is both alike.		4.07. 26 P
in his ales and his angers, look you, kill his		4.07. 38 P
it is necessary, look your grace, that he keep		4.07.139 P
most contagious treason come to light, look you,		4.08. 22 P
that, look your grace, has strook the glove		4.08. 26 P
look, here is the fellow of it.		4.08. 39 P
to be no petter than a fellow, look you now, of		5.01. 8 P
prings me pread and salt yesterday, look you,		5.01. 9 P
and my petitions, to eat, look you, this leek;		5.01. 24 P
because, look you, you do not love it, nor your		5.01. 24 P
kate, i cannot look greenly, nor gasp out my		5.02.143 P
whose very shores look pale | with envy of each		5.02.350
durst not presume to look once in the face.	1H6	1.01.140
or piteous they will look, like drowned mice.		1.02. 12
mean time look gracious on thy prostrate thrall.		1.02.117
let us look in, the sight will much delight thee		1.04. 62
one eye thou hast to look to heaven for grace;		1.04. 83
speak unto talbot, nay, look up to him.		1.04. 89
did look no better to that weighty charge.		2.01. 62
for pale they look with fear, as witnessing		2.04. 63
look to it well, and say you are well warn'd.		2.04.103
why look you still so stern and tragical?		3.01.125
look on thy country, look on fertile france,		3.03. 44
look on thy country, look on fertile france,		3.03. 44
look to it, lords, let not his smoothing words	2H6	1.01.156
let's make haste away, and look unto the main.		1.01.208
look to't in time, | she'll hamper thee, and		1.03.144
and look thyself be faultless, thou wert best.		2.01.185
again, | to look into this business thoroughly,		2.01.198

look how they gaze! 2.04. 20
trowest thou that e'er i'll look upon the world, 2.04. 38
and if we did but glance a far–off look, 3.01. 10
and with dimm'd eyes | look after him, and 3.01.219
look not upon me, for thine eyes are wounding. 3.02. 51
look pale as primrose with blood–drinking sighs, 3.02. 63
i am no loathsome leper, look on me. 3.02. 75
look, on the sheets his hair, you see, is 3.02.174
i'll give a thousand pound to look upon him. 3.03. 13
look, look, it stands upright, | like lime–twigs 3.03. 15
look, look, it stands upright, | like lime–twigs 3.03. 15
look with a gentle eye upon this wretch! 3.03. 20
look on my george, i am a gentleman: 4.01. 29
but who can cease to weep and look on this? 4.04. 4
look on me well. 4.10. 38 P
nay, do not fright us with an angry look. 5.01.126
look in a glass, and call thy image so. 5.01.142
but, noble as he is, look where he comes. 5.03. 14
my lords, look where the sturdy rebel sits, 3H6 1.01. 50
ah, tutor, look where bloody clifford comes! 1.03. 2
and not with such a cruel threat'ning look. 1.03. 17
look, york, i stain'd this napkin with the blood 1.04. 79
look on the boy, | and let his manly face, which 2.02. 39
and look upon, as if the tragedy | were play'd 2.03. 27
yet look to have them buzz to offend thine ears. 2.06. 95
look, as i blow this feather from my face, | and 3.01. 84
to cross me from the golden time i look for! 3.02.127
look therefore, lewis, that by this league and 3.03. 74
look here, i throw my infamy at thee. 5.01. 82
look in his youth to have him so cut off | as, 5.05. 66
look how my ring encompasseth thy finger, | even R3 1.02.203
because i cannot flatter and look fair, | smile 1.03. 47
look when he fawns he bites; 1.03.289
why look you pale? 1.04.170
look behind you, my lord. 1.04.268
look i so pale, lord dorset, as the rest? 2.01. 84
why do you look on us, and shake your head, 2.02. 5
then, masters, look to see a troublous world. 2.03. 9
when the sun sets, who doth not look for night? 2.03. 34
or let me die, to look on /death no more! 2.04. 65
and look when i am king, claim thou of me | the 3.01.194
and look to have it yielded with all kindness. 3.01.198
hate, | i live to look upon their tragedy. 3.02. 59
when men are unprepar'd and look not for it. 3.02. 63
look how i am bewitch'd; 3.04. 68
lovel and ratcliffe, look that it be done: 3.04. 78
speak and look back, and pry on every side, 3.05. 6
look to the drawbridge there! 3.05. 15
look back, defend thee, here are enemies! 3.05. 19
look for the news that the guildhall affords. 3.05.102
and look you get a prayer–book in your hand, 3.07. 47
stay, yet look back with me unto the tower. 4.01. 97
me | that look into me with considerate eyes. 4.02. 30
look how thou dream'st! 4.02. 56
well, look unto it. 4.02. 87
stanley, look to your wife. 4.02. 92
look what is done cannot be now amended: 4.04.291
look your heart be firm, | or else his head's 4.04.495
my lord of surrey, why look you so sad? 5.03. 2
look that my staves be sound, and not too heavy. 5.03. 65
myself, | look on my forces with a gracious eye; 5.03.109
and buckingham | shall lessen this big look. H8 1.01.119
from liberty, to look on | the business present. 1.01.205
pray look to't; 1.02.101
look out there, some of ye. 1.04. 50
yet let 'em look they glory not in mischief, 2.01. 66
look into these affairs see this main end, | the 2.02. 40
look, the good man weeps! 5.01.152
look there, my lords; 5.02.133
do you look for ale and cakes here, you rude 5.03. 10 P
yesternight fairer than ever i saw her look, or TRO 1.01. 33 P
that's hector, that, that, look you, that; 1.02.199 P
look how he looks! 1.02.201 P
look you what hacks are on his helmet! 1.02.204 P
look you yonder, do you see? 1.02.205 P
look you there, there's no jesting; 1.02.206 P
look ye yonder, niece; 1.02.213 P
look well upon him, niece. 1.02.231 P
look you how his sword is bloodied, and his helm 1.02.232 P
ne'er look, ne'er look, the eagles are gone; 1.02.243 P
ne'er look, ne'er look, the eagles are gone; 1.02.243 P
and look how many grecian tents do stand 1.03. 79
what trumpet? look, menelaus. 1.03.213
nay, look upon him. 2.01. 59 P
but yet you look not well upon him, for, 2.01. 63 P
look you there. 2.01. 84 P
look you, who comes here? 2.03. 68 P
neither gave to me | good word nor look. 3.03.144
her wanton spirits look out | at every joint and 4.05. 56
stand fair, i pray thee, let me look on thee. 4.05.235
you look upon that sleeve, behold it well. 5.02. 69
look how thou diest! 5.03. 81
look how thy eye turns pale! 5.03. 81
look how thy wounds do bleed at many vents! 5.03. 82
i'll go look on. 5.04. 2 P
he is my prize, i will not look upon. 5.06. 10
look, hector, how the sun begins to set, | how 5.08. 5
for, look you, i may make the belly smile | as COR 1.01.109
of generosity | and make bold power look pale — 1.01.212
and hear a drum than look upon his schoolmaster. 1.03. 56 P
look to't; 1.04. 40
look, sir. 1.04. 61
look, here's a letter from him; 2.01.108 P
look, sir, your mother! 2.01.169
"look, sir, my wounds! 2.03. 51
look, i am going. 3.02.134
faith, look you, one cannot tell how to say that 4.05.169 P
for look you, sir, he has as many friends as 4.05.205 P
sir, as it were, durst not (look you, sir) show 4.05.207 P
and you'll look pale | before you find it other. 4.06.101
look thee, here's water to quench it. 5.02. 71 P
the gods look down, and this unnatural scene 5.03.184
to tremble under titus' threat'ning look. TIT 1.01.134
then at my suit look graciously on him; 1.01.439
sweet heart, look back. 1.01.481
why doth your highness look so pale and wan? 2.03. 90
have i not reason, think you, to look pale? 2.03. 91
heart, | aaron and thou look down into this den, 2.03.215
look for thy reward | among the nettles at the 2.03.271
look, sirs, if you can find the huntsman out, 2.03.278
yet do thy cheeks look red as titan's face 2.04. 31
faint–hearted boy, arise and look upon her. 3.01. 65
look, marcus! 3.01.110
ah, son lucius, look on her! 3.01.110
look by and by to have thy sons with thee. 3.01.201
my lord, look here; 4.01. 68
look here, lavinia. 4.01. 68
marcus, look to my house, | lucius and i'll go 4.01.120
look how the black slave smiles upon the father, 4.02.120
look ye draw home enough, and 'tis there 4.03. 3
up your pigeons, and then look for your reward. 4.03.112 P
had nature lent thee but thy mother's look, 5.01. 29
look round about the wicked streets of rome, 5.02. 98
look that you bind them fast. 5.02.165
come, come, lavinia, look, thy foes are bound. 5.02.166
turn thee, benvolio, look upon thy death. ROM 1.01. 67
at my poor house look to behold this night 1.02. 24
i'll look to like, if looking liking move; 1.03. 97
phrase, | i'll be a candle–holder and look on: 1.04. 38
remove the court–cupboard, look to the plate. 1.05. 7 P
look thou but sweet, | and i am proof against 2.02. 72
of us, look to hear nothing but discords. 3.01. 47 P
men's eyes were made to look, and let them gaze; 3.01. 54
uttered | with gentle breath, calm look, knees 3.01.156
to prison, eyes, ne'er look on liberty! 3.02. 58
for exile hath more terror in his look, | much 3.03. 13
live here in heaven and may look on her, | but 3.03. 32
but look thou stay not till the watch be set, 3.03.148
look you, she lov'd her kinsman tybalt dearly, 3.04. 3
look, love, what envious streaks | do lace the 3.05. 7
the day is broke, be wary, look about. 3.05. 40
thursday, | or never after look me in the face. 3.05.162
look to't, think on't, i do not use to jest. 3.05.189
look, sir, here comes the lady toward my cell. 4.01. 17
to–morrow night look that thou lie alone, | let 4.01. 91
see where she comes from shrift with merry look. 4.02. 15
o, look! 4.03. 55
look to the bak'd meats, good angelica, | spare 4.04. 5
look, look! o heavy day! 4.05. 18
look, look! o heavy day! 4.05. 18
revive, look up, or i will die with thee! 4.05. 20
eyes, look your last! 5.03.112
death | if i did stay to look on his intents. 5.03.134
o wife, look how our daughter bleeds! 5.03.202
look and thou shalt see. 5.03.213
give me the letter, i will look on it. 5.03.278
and rich. here is a water, look ye. TIM 1.01. 18
look, moe! 1.01. 41
look who comes here; will you be chid? 1.01.176
look in thy last work, where thou hast feign'd 1.01.222 P
healths will make thee and thy state look ill, 1.02. 57 P
look you, my good lord, | i must entreat you 1.02.168
look you, here comes my master's page. 2.02. 72 P
prithee, man, look cheerly. 2.02.214
i'll look you out a good turn, servilius. 3.02. 60
striving to make an ugly deed look fair. 3.05. 25
you cannot make gross sins look clear; 3.05. 38
live | only in bone, that none may look on you! 3.05.104
let me look back upon thee. 4.01. 1
than thy sword, | for all her cherubin look. 4.03. 64
look, so i have. 4.03.289
ay, though it look like thee. 4.03.308 P
look thee, 'tis so. 4.03.523
look you, i love you well, i'll give you gold, 5.01.100
timon, | look out and speak to friends. 5.01.128
fellow, come from the throng, look upon caesar. JC 1.02. 21
if i have veil'd my look, | i turn the trouble 1.02. 37
other, | and i will look on both indifferently; 1.02. 87
but look you, cassius, | the angry spot doth 1.02.182
and all the rest look like a chidden train: 1.02.184
yond cassius has a lean and hungry look, | he 1.02.194
you that, i'll ne'er look you i' th' face again. 1.02.281 P
you look pale, and gaze, | and put on fear, and 1.03. 59
and look you lay it in the praetor's chair, 1.03.143
look in the calendar, and bring me word. 2.01. 42
good gentlemen, look fresh and merrily; 2.01.224
and look where publius is come to fetch me. 2.02.108
if thou beest not immortal, look about you; 2.03. 7 P
yes, bring me word, boy, if thy lord look well, 2.04. 13
look how he makes to caesar; mark him. 3.01. 18
for look he smiles, and caesar doth not change. 3.01. 24
for look you, brutus, | he draws mark antony out 3.01. 25
if then thy spirit look upon us now, | shall it 3.01.195
look, in this place ran cassius' dagger through; 3.02.174
look you here, | here is himself, marr'd as you 3.02.196
look, with a spot i damn him. 4.01. 6
look, lucius, here's the book i sought for so; 4.03.252
i know young bloods look for a time of rest. 4.03.262
look, | i draw a sword against conspirators; 5.01. 50
and downward look on us | as we were sickly prey 5.01. 85
o, look, titinius, look, the villains fly! 5.03. 1
o, look, titinius, look, the villains fly! 5.03. 1
look, look, titinius, | are those my tents where 5.03. 12
look, look, titinius, | are those my tents where 5.03. 12
look whe'er he have not crown'd dead cassius! 5.03. 97
to kill him, clitus. look, he meditates. 5.05. 12
so should he look | that seems to speak things MAC 1.02. 46
look what i have. 1.03. 26
that look not like th' inhabitants o' th' earth, 1.03. 41
if you can look into the seeds of time, | and 1.03. 58
look how our partner's rapt. 1.03.142
to beguile the time, | look like the time; 1.05. 64
look like th' innocent flower, | but be the 1.05. 65
only look up clear: 1.05. 71
and wakes it now to look so green and pale | at 1.07. 37
look on't again i dare not. 2.02. 49
death's counterfeit, | and look on death itself! 2.03. 77
look to the lady. 2.03.119
look to the lady. 2.03.125
that dare look on that | which might appall the 3.04. 58
when all's done, | you look but on a stool. 3.04. 67
look! 3.04. 68
why, how now, hecat? you look angerly. 3.05. 1
brows of grace, | yet grace must still look so. 4.03. 24
did heaven look on, | and would not take their 4.03.223
look how she rubs her hands. 5.01. 26 P
hands, put on your night–gown, look not so pale. 5.01. 63 P
look after her, | remove from her the means of 5.01. 75
troops of friends, | i must not look to have; 5.03. 26
look where it comes again! HAM 1.01. 40
you tremble and look pale. 1.01. 53
but look the morn in russet mantle clad | walks 1.01.166
and let thine eye look like a friend on denmark. 1.02. 69
in all, | i shall not look upon his like again. 1.02.188
precepts in thy memory | look thou character. 1.03. 59
look to't, i charge you. 1.03.135
look, my lord, it comes! 1.04. 38
look with what courteous action | it waves you 1.04. 60
look you, sir, | inquire me first what danskers 2.01. 6
and with a look so piteous in purport | as if he 2.01. 79
but look where sadly the poor wretch comes 2.02.168
your daughter may conceive, friend, look to't. 2.02.186 P
the air, look you, this brave o'erhanging 2.02.300 P
you more, for look where my abridgment comes. 2.02.420 P
look whe'er he has not turn'd his color and has 2.02.519 P
follow that lord, and look you mock him not. 2.02.545 P
for look you how cheerfully my mother looks, and 3.02.126 P
look you, these are the stops. 3.02.360 P
why, look you now, how unworthy a thing you make 3.02.363 P
/business /as /the day | would quake to look on. 3.02.392
then i'll look up. 3.03. 50
look you lay home to him. 3.04. 1
look here upon this picture, and on this, | the 3.04. 53
look you now what follows: 3.04. 63
but look, amazement on thy mother sits, | o, 3.04.112
whereon do you look? 3.04.124
look you how pale he glares! 3.04.125
do not look upon me, | lest with this piteous 3.04.127
why, look you there! 3.04.134
look how it steals away! 3.04.134
look where he goes, even now, out at the portal! 3.04.136
alas, look here, my lord. 4.05. 37
fail, | and that our drift look through our bad 4.07.151
look to the queen there ho! 5.02.303
you that look pale, and tremble at this chance, 5.02.334
then must we look from his age to receive not LR 1.01.296 P
i will look further into't. 1.04. 71 P
look, sir, i bleed. 2.01. 41
art not asham'd to look upon this beard? 2.04.193
those wicked creatures yet do look well–favor'd 2.04.256
i will look him and privily relieve him. 3.03. 14 P
look, here comes a walking fire. 3.04.114 P
how look you? 3.07. 94
you do climb up it now. look how we labor. 4.06. 2
i'll look no more, | lest my brain turn, and the 4.06. 22
look up a–height, the shrill–gorg'd lark so far 4.06. 58
do but look up. 4.06. 59
look, look, a mouse! 4.06. 88 P
look, look, a mouse! 4.06. 88 P
look with thine ears; 4.06.151 P
o, look upon me, sir, | and hold your hand in 4.07. 56
on, | you look as you had something more to say. 5.03.202
look on her! 5.03.311
look her lips! 5.03.311
look there, look there! 5.03.312
look there, look there! 5.03.312
look up, my lord. 5.03.313
look to your house, your daughter, and your bags OTH 1.01. 80
but look, what lights come yond? 1.02. 28
to fall in love with what she fear'd to look on! 1.03. 98
look to her, moor, if thou hast eyes to see; 1.03.292
see suitors following, and not look behind: 2.01.157
delight shall she have to look on the devil? 2.01.226 P
in him that folly and green minds look after; 2.01.247 P
good michael, look you to the guard to–night. 2.03. 1
with my personal eye | will i look to't. 2.03. 6
gentlemen, let's look to our business. 2.03.112 P
look if my gentle love be not rais'd up! 2.03.250
iago, look with care about the town, | and 2.03.255
look to your wife, observe her well with cassio, 3.03.197
look to't. 3.03.200
look where she comes: 3.03.277
look, here 'tis. 3.03.313
look where he comes! 3.03.330
look here, iago, | all my fond love thus do i 3.03.444
shall nev'r look back, nev'r ebb to humble love, 3.03.458
look where he comes. 3.04. 31
most veritable, therefore look to't well. 3.04. 76
look you, cassio and my husband! 3.04.106
nor of them look for such observancy | as fits 3.04.149
look, he stirs. 4.01. 55
look how he laughs already! 4.01.109
before me! look where she comes. 4.01.145 P
let me see your eyes; | look in my face. 4.02. 26
cherubin — | ay, here, look grim as hell! 4.02. 64
look you pale? 5.01.104
look you pale, mistress? 5.01.105
i pray you look upon her. 5.01.108
look in upon me then and speak with me, | or, 5.02.257
now — how dost thou look now? 5.02.272
this look of thine will hurl my soul from heaven 5.02.274
i look down towards his feet; 5.02.286
look on the tragic loading of this bed; 5.02.363
look where they come! ANT 1.01. 10
we will not look upon him. go with us. 1.02. 87
look here, and at thy sovereign leisure read 1.03. 60
and let it look | like perfect honor. 1.03. 79
look, prithee, charmian, | how this herculean 1.03. 83
strange flesh, | which some did die to look on; 1.04. 68
let antony look over caesar's head | and speak 2.02. 5
sir, look well to my husband's house; and — 3.02. 45
look, here i have you, thus i let you go, | and 3.02. 63
herod of jewry dare not look upon you | but when 3.03. 3
o, | i follow'd that i blush to look upon. 3.11. 12
pray you look not sad, | nor make replies of 3.11. 17
of a lady fever thee, | shake thou to look on't. 3.13.139
look thou say | he makes me angry with him; 3.13.140
i look on you | as one that takes his leave. 4.02. 28
look, they weep, | and i, an ass, am onion–ey'd. 4.02. 34
may best discover, | and look on their endeavor. 4.10. 9
they know not, they cannot tell, look grimly, 4.12. 5
look out o' th' other side your monument, | his 4.15. 8
look | our lamp is spent, it's out. 4.15. 84
look you sad, friends? 5.01. 26

thee such a declining day, | or look on thine; 5.01. 39
and would gladly | look him i' th' face. 5.02. 32
you must think this, look you, that the worm 5.02.262 P
look you, the worm is not to be trusted but in 5.02.265 P
look here, love, | this diamond was my mother's. CYM 1.01.111
but | to look upon him, till the diminution | of 1.03. 18
you look on me; 1.06. 84
is it fit i went to look upon him? 2.01. 42 P
or look upon our romans, whose remembrance | is 2.04. 14
look thorough a casement to allure false hearts, 2.04. 34
basilisk unto mine eye, | kills me to look on't. 2.04.108
look | for fury not to be resisted. 3.01. 66
how look i | that i should seem to lack humanity 3.02. 15
have a fog in them | that i cannot look through. 3.02. 80
thou that paper to me with | a look untender? 3.04. 12
look | i draw the sword myself, take it, and hit 3.04. 66
go, look after. 3.05. 55
the sword like me, he'll scarcely look on't. 3.06. 26
look, here he comes, | and brings the dire 4.02.195
bid the captains look to't. 4.02.344
i am asham'd | to look upon the holy sun, to 4.04. 41
and may save | but to look back in frown. 5.03. 28
gan to look | the way that they did, and to grin 5.03. 37
look out; 5.04. 81
for, look you, sir, you know not which way you 5.04.175 P
you look like romans, | and not o' th' court of 5.05. 24
and with /th' /ostent of war will look so huge, PER 1.02. 25
how dares the plants look up to heaven, from 1.02. 55
tyre, i now look from thee then, and to tharsus 1.02.115
we do not look for reverence but for love, | and 1.04. 99
look how thou stir'st now! 2.01. 16 P
them, they ne'er come but i look to be wash'd. 2.01. 26 P
out of the calendar, and nobody look after it. 2.01. 55 P
therefore look to it. 2.05. 39
set't down, let's look upon't. 3.02. 51
to–night, | for look how fresh she looks! 3.02. 79
look to your little mistress, on whose grace 3.03. 40
none would look on her, | but cast their gazes 4.03. 32
not see thee, or else look friendly upon thee. 4.06. 89 P
yet thou dost look | like patience gazing on 5.01.137
look to the lady; 5.03. 21
look, thaisa is | recovered. 5.03. 27
o, let me look! 5.03. 28
look who kneels here! 5.03. 46
makes me look dismal will i clip to form, | and 5.03. 74
so adieu, | and heaven's good eyes look on you! TNK 1.04. 13
mean time, look tenderly to the two prisoners. 2.01. 19 P
they eat well, look merrily, discourse of many 2.01. 39 P
look yonder they are! 2.01. 48 P
it is a holiday to look on them. 2.01. 53 P
i am then | kissing the man they look for. 2.06. 37
you are going now to look upon a sun | that 3.01.120
the little stars and all, that look like aglets. 3.04. 2
with thy twinkling eyes look right and straight 3.05.117
how do i look? 3.06. 66
look to thine own well, arcite. 3.06.131
look upon 'em, | and, if you can love, end this 3.06.277
y' had best look to her, | for, if she see him 4.01.123
ask me now, sweet sister — | i may go look! 4.02. 52
look where she comes, you shall perceive her 4.03. 9 P
beheld thing maculate — look on thy virgin, 5.01.145
a day or two | let us look sadly, and give grace 5.04.125
yet stay a while, | and let me look upon ye. ep 4
look what you do offend you cry upon, | that is STM II.C 61
look how a bird lies tangled in a net, | so VEN 67
look how he can, she cannot choose but love, 79
look in mine eyeballs, there thy beauty lies; 119
look when a painter would surpass the life | in 289
look what a horse should have he did not lack, 299
for one sweet look thy help i would assure thee, 371
and at his look she flatly falleth down, | for 463
"look, the world's comforter, with weary gait, 529
bids him farewell, and look well to her heart, 580
look how a bright star shooteth from the sky, 815
look how the world's poor people are amazed | at 925
look as the fair and fiery–pointed sun, LUC 372
and death's dim look in life's mortality. 403
she dares not look, yet, winking, there appears 458
where subjects' eyes do learn, do read, do look. 616
look as the full–fed hound or gorged hawk, 694
and sorts a sad look to her lady's sorrow | (for 1221
that one might see those far–off eyes look sad. 1386
she would have said, "can lurk in such a look"; 1535
"look, look how list'ning priam wets his eyes, 1548
"look, look how list'ning priam wets his eyes, 1548
did court the lad with many a lovely look, PP 4. 3
looks as none could look but beauty's queen. 4. 4
she hotter that did look | for his approach that 6. 7
look in thy glass and tell the face thou viewest SON 3. 1
are | from his low tract and look another way: 7.12
look what an unthrift in the world doth spend 9. 9
look whom she best endow'd she gave the more; 11.11
then look i death my days should expiate. 22. 4
who plead for love and look for recompense 23.11
cries, | and look upon myself and curse my fate, 29. 4
look what is best, that best i wish in thee: 37.13
but when i sleep, in dreams they look on thee, 43. 3
when that mine eye is famish'd for a look, | or 47. 3
o, that record could with a backward look, 59. 5
they look into the beauty of thy mind, | and 69. 9
o, if (i say) you look upon this verse, | when i 71. 9
lest the wise world should look into your moan, 71.13
sight, | and by and by clean starved for a look; 75.10
look what thy memory cannot contain | commit to 77. 9
these offices, so oft as thou wilt look, | shall 77.13
i will acquaintance strangle and look strange, 89. 8
with so dull a cheer | that leaves look pale, 97.14
look in your glass, and there appears a face 103. 6
your own glass shows you when you look in it. 103.14
that every tongue says beauty should look so. 127.14
"'look here what tributes wounded fancies sent LC 197

/LOOK'D 1 FR 0.0001 REL FR 1 V 0 P
/and /little /look'd /for /at /your /helping R2 4.01.161

LOOK'D 109 FR 0.0123 REL FR 78 V 31 P
this is a strange thing as e'er i look'd on. TMP 5.01.290
when you look'd sadly, it was for want of money: TGV 2.01. 29 P
or else you had look'd through the grate, like a WIV 2.02. 9 P
she is too bright to be look'd against. 2.02.245 P
which way have you look'd for master caius, that 3.01. 3 P
is lechery so look'd after? MM 1.02.144
like pow'r divine, | hath look'd upon my passes. 5.01.370
unless i spake, or look'd, or touch'd, or carv'd ERR 2.02.118
i look'd for the chalky cliffs, but i could find 3.02.126 P
look'd he or red or pale, or sad or merrily? 4.02. 4
i noted her not, but i look'd on her. ADO 1.01.164 P
she is the sweetest lady that ever i look'd on. 1.01.188 P
i look'd upon her with a soldier's eye, | that 1.01.298
a cursing hypocrite once, you must be look'd to. 5.01.209 P
this is not so well as i look'd for, but the LLL 1.01.279 P
i would my father look'd but with my eyes. MND 1.01. 56
for ere demetrius look'd on hermia's eyne, | he 1.01.242
durst thou have look'd upon him being awake? 3.02. 69
that lov'd, that lik'd, that look'd with cheer. 5.01.294
the men that ever my foolish eyes look'd upon, MV 1.02.118 P
as any comer i have look'd on yet | for my 2.01. 21
if ever you have look'd on better days, | if AYL 2.07.113
how look'd he? 3.02.221 P
and my sister no sooner met but they look'd; 5.02. 33 P
no sooner look'd but they lov'd; 5.02. 33 P
master, you look'd so longly on the maid, SHR 1.01.165
my father is here look'd for every day, | to 4.02.117
and that you look'd for him this day in padua. 4.04. 16
let my horses be well look'd to, without any AWW 4.05. 58 P
this was look'd for at your hand, and this was TN 3.02. 24 P
good maria, let this fellow be look'd to. 3.04. 61 P
went away now, "let this fellow be look'd to"; 3.04. 76 P
get him to bed, and let his hurt be look'd to. 5.01.208 P
i have look'd on thousands, who have sped the WT 1.02.389
if you had but look'd big and spit at him, he'ld 4.03.106 P
i might have look'd upon my queen's full eyes, 5.01. 53
might i a son and daughter now have look'd on, 5.01.177
they look'd as they had heard of a world 5.02. 14 P
excels what ever yet you look'd upon | or hand 5.03. 16
and look'd upon, i hope, with cheerful eyes. JN 4.02. 2
i look'd when some of you should say | i was too R2 1.03.243
his face thou hast, for even so look'd he, 2.01.176
which, look'd on as it is, is nought but shadows 2.02. 23
it, he wishtly look'd on me | as who should say, 5.04. 7
my wive's brother, then his cheek look'd pale, 1H4 1.03.142
(if matters should be look'd into) for their own 2.01. 72 P
i look'd 'a should have sent me two and twenty 2H4 1.02. 43 P
most immodest word | be look'd upon and learnt, 4.04. 71
who look'd full gently on his warlike queen, 3H6 2.01.123
laid, | for yet i am not look'd on in the world. 5.07. 22
why, so i did, but look'd for no reply. R3 1.03.236
/thence we look'd toward england, | and cited up 1.04. 13
look'd pale when they did hear of clarence' 2.01.137
but look'd not on the poison of their hearts. 3.01. 14
and started when he look'd upon the tower, | as 3.04. 85
thee | that ever wretched age hath look'd upon. 3.04.105
i never look'd for better at his hands | after 3.05. 50
star'd each on other, and look'd deadly pale; 3.07. 26
o, when, i say, i look'd on richard's face, 4.01. 70
look'd he | o' th' inside of the paper? H8 3.02. 77
thou hast the sweetest face i ever look'd on. 4.01. 43
i look'd | you would have given me your petition 5.01.117
she look'd yesternight fairer than ever i saw TRO 1.01. 32 P
shall shake him more | than if not look'd on. 3.03. 54
look'd not lovelier | than hector's forehead COR 1.03. 41
i look'd upon him a' we'nsday half an hour 1.03. 58 P
dries, 'tis time | it should be look'd to. 1.09. 94
and look'd upon things precious as they were 2.02.125
a strange one as ever i look'd on. 4.05. 20 P
when he had carried rome and that we look'd 5.06. 42
men of heart | look'd wond'ring each at others. 5.06. 99
you are look'd for and call'd for, ask'd for and ROM 1.05. 12 P
that thou expects not, nor i look'd not for. 3.05.110
threaten'd me | ne'er look'd but on my back; JC 2.02. 11
and his gash'd stabs look'd like a breach in MAC 2.03.113
th' amazement of mine eyes | that look'd upon't. 2.04. 20
i look'd toward birnan, and anon methought | the 5.05. 33
what, look'd he frowningly? HAM 1.02.231
but, better look'd into, he truly found | it was 2.02. 64
or look'd upon this love with idle sight, | what 2.02.138
thou think alexander look'd a' this fashion i' 5.01.197 P
look'd black upon me, strook me with her tongue, LR 2.04.160
i look'd not for you yet, nor am provided | for 2.04.232
that eye that told you so look'd but a–squint. 5.03. 72
i have look'd upon the world for four times OTH 1.03.311 P
we look'd not for mark antony here. ANT 2.06.107 P
i look'd her in the face, and saw her led 3.03. 9
i could then have look'd on him without the help CYM 1.04. 4 P
is one of the fairest that i have look'd upon. 2.04. 32
but what he look'd for should oppose and she 2.05. 18
but must be look'd to speedily and strongly. 3.05. 27
did see man die, scarce ever look'd on blood, 4.04. 36
boy, | thou hast look'd thyself into my grace, 5.05. 94
now this matter must be look'd to, | for her PER 3.02.108
slaughter | the sun and moon ne'er look'd upon! 4.03. 3
no, nor look'd on us. 5.01. 80
th' moon | (which then look'd pale at parting) TNK 1.03. 53
how they would have look'd had they been victors 2.01. 32 P
it so) as ever | these eyes yet look'd on. 2.04. 11
thou most perfidious | that ever gently look'd! 3.01. 36
promises | in such a body yet i never look'd on. 4.02.119
he look'd all grace and success, and he is 5.03. 69
and costliness of spirit look'd through him, it 5.03. 97
who, being look'd on, ducks as quickly in; VEN 87
eyes, though sod in tears, look'd red and raw, LUC 1592
and some look'd black, and that false tarquin 1743
the sun look'd on the world with glorious eye, PP 6.11
and, for they look'd but with divining eyes, SON 106.11
most true it is that i have look'd on truth 110. 5

LOOK'DST 1 FR 0.0001 REL FR 1 V 0 P
thou then look'dst like a villain; CYM 3.04. 48

LOOKED 1 FR 0.0001 REL FR 1 V 0 P
now is the day we long have looked for. SHR 2.01.333

LOOKER–ON 4 FR 0.0004 REL FR 4 V 0 P
this state | made me a looker–on here in vienna, MM 5.01.317
so long could i | stand by, a looker–on. WT 5.03. 85
one that was a woeful looker–on | when as the 3H6 2.01. 45
and reverend looker–on of two fair queens. R3 4.01. 30

LOOKERS–ON 1 FR 0.0001 REL FR 1 V 0 P
his kingdom and devour | incertain lookers–on. WT 5.01. 29

LOOKEST 5 FR 0.0005 REL FR 5 V 0 P
and lookest to command the prince and realm. 1H6 1.01. 38
sweet nurse — o lord, why lookest thou sad? ROM 2.05. 21
either my eyesight fails, or thou lookest pale. 3.05. 57
from thee, for thou lookest | modest as justice, PER 5.01.120
for thou lookest | like one i lov'd indeed. 5.01.124

LOOKETH 1 FR 0.0001 REL FR 1 V 0 P
whose downward eye still looketh for a grave, VEN 1106

LOOKING 33 FR 0.0037 REL FR 28 V 5 P
wherefore this ghastly looking? TMP 2.01.309
and blowing, and looking wildly, and would needs WIV 3.03. 87 P
once thou swor'st was worth the looking on; MM 5.01.208
to feel only looking on fairest of fair: LLL 2.01.241
might shake off fifty, looking in her eye: 4.03.239
now, for not looking on a woman's face, | you 4.03.305
poke, | and, looking on it with lack–lustre eye, AYL 2.07. 21
but see, while idly i stood looking on, | i SHR 1.01.150
as on a pillory, looking through the lute, 2.01.156
from padua and here looking out at the window. 5.01. 31 P
looking on the lines | of my boy's face, WT 1.02.153
the sun looking with a southward eye upon him, 4.04.789 P
looking awry upon your lord's departure, | find R2 2.02. 21
whilst i, by looking on the praise of him, | see 1H4 1.01. 84
which before would not abide looking on. H5 5.02.311 P
looking the way her harmless young one went, 2H6 3.01.215
to shepherds looking on their silly sheep | than 3H6 2.05. 43
death, | and liv'd with looking on his images; R3 2.02. 50
looking | either for such men or such business. H8 3.01. 75
he had so, looking as it were — would i were COR 4.05.157 P
looking all downwards to behold our cheeks, TIT 3.01.124
i'll look to like, if looking liking move; ROM 1.03. 97
from the point, by looking down on caesar. JC 3.01.219
looking before and after, gave us not | that HAM 4.04. 37
his aspect, and die | with looking on his life. ANT 1.05. 34
they are in rome together, | looking for antony. 2.01. 20
eyes | by looking back what i have left behind 3.11. 53
who, looking for adventures in the world, | was PER 2.03. 83
then looking scornfully, he doth despise | his LUC 187
till looking on an englishman, the fairest that PP 15. 3
looking on darkness which the blind do see; SON 27. 8
made | by looking on thee in the living day, 43.10
be, | looking with pretty ruth upon my pain. 132. 4

//LOOKING–GLASS 1 FR 0.0001 REL FR 1 V 0 P
/some /of /you, /and /fetch /a //looking–glass. R2 4.01.268

LOOKING–GLASS 5 FR 0.0005 REL FR 5 V 0 P
but since she did neglect her looking–glass, TGV 4.04.152
practic'd smiles, | as in a looking–glass; WT 1.02.117
nor made to court an amorous looking–glass; R3 1.01. 15
i'll be at charges for a looking–glass, | and 1.02.255
lend me a looking–glass, | if that her breath LR 5.03.262

/LOOKS 2 FR 0.0002 REL FR 2 V 0 P
/whose /warp'd /looks /proclaim | /what /store LR 3.06. 53
she /looks us like | a thing more made of malice CYM 3.05. 32

LOOKS 240 FR 0.0271 REL FR 211 V 29 P
lord, how it looks about! TMP 1.02.411
how lush and lusty the grass looks! how green! 2.01. 53 P
looks like a foul bumbard that would shed his 2.02. 21 P
with your sedg'd crowns and ever–harmless looks, 4.01.129
not one of them | that yet looks on me, or would 5.01. 83
coy looks with heart–sore sighs; TGV 1.01. 30
borrows his wit from your ladyship's looks, and 2.04. 38 P
did hold his eyes lock'd in her crystal looks. 2.04. 89
know'st thou not his looks are my soul's food? 2.07. 15
i gave him gentle looks, thereby to find | that 3.01. 31
or money in his purse, when he looks so merrily. WIV 2.01.191 P
ensconce your rags, your cat–a–mountain looks, 2.02. 27 P
looks handsome in three hundred pounds a year! 3.04. 33
mercy is not itself, that oft looks so; MM 2.01.283
looks in a glass that shows what future evils, 2.02. 95
excludes all pity from our threat'ning looks: ERR 1.01. 10
aspect, | and fashion your demeanor to my looks, 2.02. 33
and let her read it in thy looks at board: 3.02. 18
alas, how fiery, and how sharp, he looks! 4.04. 50
i know it by their pale and deadly looks. 4.04. 93
ay me, poor man, how pale and wan he looks! 4.04.108
which way looks he? ADO 1.03. 53 P
how tartly that gentleman looks! 2.01. 3 P
indeed he looks younger than he did, by the loss 3.02. 48 P
this looks not like a nuptial. 4.01. 68
as i am an honest man, he looks pale. 5.01.130 P
that will not be deep search'd with saucy looks; LLL 1.01. 85
amaz'd, my lord? why looks your highness sad? 5.02.391
so did our looks. 5.02.786
the snow | and marian's nose looks red and raw; 5.02.924
love looks not with the eyes, but with the mind, MND 1.01.234
the next thing then she waking looks upon | (be 2.01.179
the moon methinks looks with a wat'ry eye; 3.01.198
persever, counterfeit sad looks, | make mouths 3.02.237
how like a fawning publican he looks! MV 1.03. 41
how much more elder art thou than thy looks! 4.01.251
the daylight sick, | it looks a little paler. 5.01.125
yet he looks successfully. AYL 1.02.153 P
that every eye which in this forest looks 3.02. 7
looks he as freshly as he did the day he 3.02.230 P
as fast as she answers thee with frowning looks, 3.05. 68 P
i'll say she looks as clear | as morning roses SHR 2.01.172
methinks he looks as though he were in love; 3.01. 88
for then she never looks upon her lure. 4.01.192
kindness in women, not their beauteous looks, 4.02. 41
sir — see where he looks out of the window. 5.01. 55 P
tribute at thy hands | but love, fair looks, and 5.02.153
steely bones | looks bleak i' th' cold wind. AWW 1.01.104
one of our french wither'd pears, it looks ill, 1.01.161 P
adore | the sun, that looks upon his worshipper, 1.03.206
sir, by /the general's looks, we shall be fain 4.03.239 P
the carp as you may, for he looks like a poor, 5.02. 23 P
he looks well on't. 5.03. 31
her business looks in her | with an importing 5.03.135
o, what a deal of scorn looks beautiful | in the TN 3.01.145
and pants and looks pale, as if a bear were at 3.04.295 P
he looks like sooth. WT 4.04.171
the gifts she looks from me are pack'd and 4.04.358
visage from our cottage, but | looks on alike. 4.04.446
lift up thy looks. 4.04.479
i thought of her, | even in these looks i made. 5.01.228
that e'er i put between your holy looks | my ill 5.03.148
i see a yielding in the looks of france; JN 2.01.474
puts on his pretty looks, repeats his words, 3.04. 95

she looks upon them with a threat'ning eye. 3.04.120
even with the fierce looks of these bloody men. 4.01. 73
my strict fast — i mean, my children's looks; R2 2.01. 80
o, full of careful business are his looks! 2.02. 75
the pale–fac'd moon looks bloody on the earth, 2.04. 10
comfort, my liege, why looks your grace so pale? 3.02. 75
to monarchize, be fear'd, and kill with looks, 3.02.165
speak sweetly, man, although thy looks be sour. 3.02.193
march on, and mark king richard how he looks. 3.03. 61
yet looks he like a king! 3.03. 68
but ere the crown he looks for live in peace, 3.03. 95
so many greedy looks of young and old | through 5.02. 13
cousin, that he stares and looks | so wildly? 5.03. 24
who then, affrighted with their bloody looks, 1H4 1.03.104
to make us strangers to his looks of love. 1.03.290
for, harry, i see virtue in his looks. 2.04.428 P
doth speak of you, his cheek looks pale, and 3.01. 9
i understand thy looks. 3.01.198
thy looks are full of speed. 3.02.162
i can tell you, looks for us all, we must away 4.02. 56 P
why say you so? looks he not for supply? 4.03. 3
the day looks pale | at his distemp'rature. 5.01. 2
it pleas'd your majesty to turn your looks | of 5.01. 30
interpretation will misquote our looks, | and we 5.02. 13
so looks the strond whereon the imperious flood 2H4 1.01. 62
but i hope he that looks upon me will take me 1.02.166 P
in | so thin that life looks through /and /will 4.04.120
on whom, as in despite, the sun looks pale, H5 3.05. 17
but freshly looks, and overbears attaint | with 4.pr. 39
beholding him, plucks comfort from his looks. 4.pr. 42
the venom of such looks we fairly hope | have 5.02. 18
to swearing and stern looks, defus'd attire, 5.02. 61
that never looks in his glass for love of any 5.02.148 P
of your heart with the looks of an empress, take 5.02.236 P
methinks your looks are sad, your cheer appal'd. 1H6 1.02. 48
question her proudly, let thy looks be stern. 1.02. 62
for talbot means no goodness by his looks. 3.02. 72
as looks the mother on her lowly babe | when 3.03. 47
if they perceive dissension in our looks, | and 4.01.139
and, in advantage ling'ring, looks for rescue, 4.04. 19
with envious looks laughing at thy shame, | that 2H6 2.04. 12
gloucester, hide thee from their hateful looks, 2.04. 23
see if thou canst outface me with thy looks. 4.10. 46
comes the queen, whose looks bewray her anger. 3H6 1.01.211
so looks the pent–up lion o'er the wretch | that 1.03. 12
ay, marry, sir, now looks he like a king! 1.04. 96
whose heavy looks foretell | some dreadful story 2.01. 43
to whom do lions cast their gentle looks? 2.02. 11
smooth the frowns of war with peaceful looks. 2.06. 32
her looks doth argue her replete with modesty, 3.02. 84
the widow likes it not, for she looks very sad. 3.02.110
and witch sweet ladies with my words and looks. 3.02.150
his looks are full of peaceful majesty, | his 4.06. 71
but the plain devil and dissembling looks? R3 1.02.236
which of you trembles not that looks on me? 1.03.159
why looks your grace so heavily to–day? 1.04. 1
thy voice is thunder, but thy looks are humble. 1.04.167
my voice is now the king's, my looks mine own. 1.04.168
my friend, i spy some pity in thy looks. 1.04.263
man | that looks not heavily and full of dread. 2.03. 40
his grace looks cheerfully and smooth this 3.04. 48
for, were he, he had shown it in his looks. 3.04. 57
who builds his hope in air of your good looks 3.04. 98
suspicion, ghastly looks | are at my service, 3.05. 8
and by that knot looks proudly on the crown, 4.03. 42
my heart is ten times lighter than my looks. 5.03. 3
heaven | that frowns on me looks sadly upon him. 5.03.287
i read in 's looks | matter against me, and his H8 1.01.125
how sad he looks! sure he is much afflicted. 2.02. 62
stops on a sudden, looks upon the ground, | then 3.02.114
so looks the chafed lion | upon the daring 3.02.206
how pale she looks, | and of an earthy cold! 4.02. 97
now by thy looks | i guess thy message. 5.01.161
look how he looks! TRO 1.02.201 P
more hack'd than hector's, and how he looks, and 1.02.234 P
a stranger to those most imperial looks | know 1.03.224
save these men's looks, who do methinks find out 3.03. 90
and that which looks like pride is courtesy. 4.05. 82
what troyan is that same that looks so heavy? 4.05. 95
who neither looks upon the heaven nor earth, 4.05.281
one eye yet looks on thee, | but with my heart 5.02.107
but, with thy grim looks and | the thunder–like COR 1.04. 58
and by his looks, methinks, | 'tis warm at 's 2.03.151
and that is there which looks | with us to break 3.03. 29
nor with sour looks afflict his gentle heart. TIT 1.01.441
these words, these looks, infuse new life in me. 1.01.461
it, | with words, fair looks, and liberality? 2.01. 92
again, | alike bewitched by the charm of looks; ROM 2.pr. 6
love from love, toward school with heavy looks. 2.02.157
so, she looks as pale as any clout in the versal 2.04.205 P
your looks are pale and wild, and do import 5.01. 28
meagre were his looks, | sharp misery had worn 5.01. 40
his looks i fear, and his intents i doubt. 5.03. 44
and with wild looks bid me devise some mean | to 5.03.240
after distasteful looks, and these hard TIM 2.02.211
man | when he looks out in an ungrateful shape! 3.02. 73
and these looks of care? 4.03.205
that nothing but himself which looks like man 5.01.118
looks with such ferret and such fiery eyes | as JC 1.02.186
and he looks | quite through the deeds of men. 1.02.202
hath chanc'd to–day | that caesar looks so sad. 1.02.218
looks in the clouds, scorning the base degrees 2.01. 26
let not our looks put on our purposes, | but 2.01.225
was, | you star'd upon me with ungentle looks. 2.01.242
what a haste looks through his eyes! MAC 1.02. 46
gentle my lord, sleek o'er your rugged looks, 3.02. 27
looks 'a not like the king? mark it, horatio. HAM 1.01. 43
brain | that looks so many fadoms to the sea 1.04. 77
and there is a kind of confession in your looks, 2.02.279 P
i'll observe his looks, | i'll tent him to the 2.02.596
for look you how cheerfully my mother looks, and 3.02.127 P
since yet thy cicatrice looks raw and red 4.03. 60
that thy rebellion looks so giant–like? 4.05.122
queen his mother | lives almost by his looks, 4.07. 12
and let his knights have colder looks among you; LR 1.03. 22
do you bandy looks with me, you rascal? 1.04. 84 P
the leisure of their answer, gave me cold looks: 2.04. 37
head | looks fearfully in the confined deep. 4.01. 74
she gave strange eliads and most speaking looks 4.05. 25
since thy outside looks so fair and warlike, 5.03.143
touching the turkish loss, yet he looks sadly, OTH 2.01. 32
appears in cassio, | and looks not on his evils. 2.03.135
honest iago, that looks dead with grieving, 2.03.177
when she seem'd to shake and fear your looks, 3.03.207
how goes it now? he looks gentler than he did. 4.03. 11
shine on those | that make their looks by his; ANT 1.05. 56
to be abus'd | by one that looks on feeders? 3.13.109
the business of this man looks out of him; 5.01. 50
but she looks like sleep, | as she would catch 5.02.346
their faces to the bent | of the king's looks, CYM 1.01. 14
a distaff to a lance, gilded pale looks; 5.03. 34
promis'd nought | but beggary and poor looks. 5.05. 10
wight did die, | as yon grim looks do testify. PER 1.ch. 40
what seest thou in our looks? 1.02. 51
waste the time, which looks for other revels. 2.03. 93
to–night, | for look how fresh she looks! 3.02. 79
and your looks foreshow | you have a gentle 4.01. 85
our dole more deadly looks than dying; TNK 1.05. 3
that's arcite looks out. 2.01. 48 P
upon a sun | that strengthens what it looks on. 3.01.121
how he looks! 4.01. 33
his face a prince | (his very looks so say him), 4.02. 78
within him, | and as a heated lion so he looks; 4.02. 82
he looks upon his love, and neighs unto her, VEN 307
looks on the dull earth with disturbed mind, 340
o, what a war of looks was then between them! 355
for looks kill love, and love by looks reviveth: 464
for looks kill love, and love by looks reviveth: 464
and never wound the heart with looks again, 1042
upon his hurt she looks so steadfastly, | that 1063
she looks upon his lips, and they are pale, 1123
could pick no meaning from their parling looks, LUC 100
that eye which looks on her confounds his wits; 290
and dotes on what he looks, 'gainst law or duty. 497
he in his speed looks for the morning light, 745
will cote my loathsome trespass in my looks. 812
men can cover crimes with bold stern looks, 1252
of the worn–out age | pawn'd honest looks, but 1351
them words, and she their looks doth borrow. 1498
that piteous looks to phrygian shepherds lent; 1502
the harmless show | an humble gait, calm looks, 1508
she looks for night, and then she longs for 1571
such looks as none could look but beauty's queen PP 4. 4
be bent, | her cloudy looks will calm yer night, 18.26
sight, | serving with looks his sacred majesty, SON 7. 4
age, | yet mortal looks adore his beauty still, 7. 7
the rose looks fair, but fairer we it deem | for 54. 3
thy looks with me, thy heart in other place. 93. 4
in many's looks the false heart's history | is 93. 7
thy looks should nothing thence but sweetness 93.12
if like a lamb he could his looks translate! 96.10
of this most balmy time | my love looks fresh, 107.10
that looks on tempests and is never shaken; 116. 6
if eyes, corrupt by over–partial looks, | be 137. 5
knows | her pretty looks have been mine enemies, 139.10
kill me outright with looks, and rid my pain. 139.14

LOOK'ST 11 FR 0.0012 REL FR 10 V 1 P
telling the bushes that thou look'st for wars, MND 3.02.408
thou look'st cheerly, and i'll be with thee AYL 2.06. 14 P
look'st thou pale, france? JN 3.01.195
yea, look'st thou pale? R2 5.02. 57
why look'st thou pale? 2H6 3.02. 27
my lovely aaron, wherefore look'st thou sad, TIT 2.03. 10
remember, | if e'er thou look'st on majesty. ANT 3.03. 18
thou look'st like him that looks a warlike 4.04. 19
this act, and look'st | so virgin–like without? CYM 3.02. 21
know'st him thou look'st on? 5.05.110
thou look'st not like deceit, do not deceive me. LUC 585

LOOK'T 1 FR 0.0001 REL FR 0 V 1 P
look't be done. OTH 4.03. 9 P

LOON *(also lown)*

LOON 1 FR 0.0001 REL FR 1 V 0 P
devil damn thee black, thou cream–fac'd loon! MAC 5.03. 11

LOOP* 2 FR 0.0002 REL FR 2 V 0 P
every loop from whence | the eye of reason may 1H4 4.01. 71
that the probation bear no hinge nor loop | to OTH 3.03.365

/LOOP'D 1 FR 0.0001 REL FR 1 V 0 P
your /loop'd and window'd raggedness, defend you LR 3.04. 31

LOOP–HOLES 1 FR 0.0001 REL FR 1 V 0 P
the very eyes of men through loop–holes thrust, LUC 1383

LOOS'D 3 FR 0.0003 REL FR 3 V 0 P
and loos'd his love–shaft smartly from his bow, MND 2.01.159
and he that loos'd them forth their brazen caves 2H6 3.02. 89
of heaven are slipp'd, dissolv'd, and loos'd, TRO 5.02.156

LOOSE 51 FR 0.0057 REL FR 40 V 11 P
daughter, | but rather loose her to an african, TMP 2.01.126
i do now let loose my opinion, hold it no longer 2.02. 35 P
the loose encounters of lascivious men: TGV 2.07. 41
you are afraid if you see the bear loose, are WIV 1.01.292 P
i have seen sackerson loose twenty times, and 1.01.295 P
toward my wife, i would turn her loose to him; 2.01.182 P
you are not to go loose any longer, you must be 4.02.123 P
that quaint in green she shall be loose enrob'd, 4.06. 41
god, for thy mercy! they are loose again. ERR 4.04.144
my master and his man are both broke loose, 5.01.169
whoever bound him, i will loose his bonds, | and 5.01.340
i will fast, being loose. LLL 1.02.156 P
no, sir, that were fast and loose; 1.02.157 P
a bargain well is as cunning as fast and loose: 3.01.103
now you will be my purgation and let me loose. 3.01.127 P
and often, at his very loose, decides | that 5.02.742
which parti–coated presence of loose love | put 5.02.766
whose influence is begot of that loose grace 5.02.859
he'll | seem to break loose — take on as you MND 3.02.258
vile thing, let loose; 3.02.260
thou wilt not only loose the forfeiture, | but, MV 4.01. 24
loose now and then | a scatt'red smile, and that AYL 3.05.103
play fast and loose with faith? JN 3.01.242
parts | against these giddy loose suggestions; 3.01.292
frequent, | with unrestrained loose companions, R2 5.03. 7
when this loose behavior i throw off | and pay 1H4 1.02.208
hangs about me like an old lady's loose gown; 3.03. 3 P
full of high feeding, madly hath broke loose, 2H4 1.01. 10
their ragged curtains poorly are let loose, H5 4.02. 41
thy womb let loose to chase us to our graves. R3 4.04. 54
loves and counsels, | be sure you be not loose; H8 2.01.127
and had their faces | been loose, this day they 4.01. 75
suddenly a file of boys behind 'em, loose shot, 5.03. 56 P
all, | lay negligent and loose regard upon him. TRO 3.03. 41
to them, | he fumbles up into a loose adieu; 4.04. 46
what, is lavinia then become so loose, | or TIT 2.01. 65
i will not loose again, | till thou art here 2.03.243
marcus, loose when i bid. 4.03. 59
being loose, unfirm, with digging up of graves, ROM 5.03. 6
does he feel his title | hang loose about him, MAC 5.02. 21
at such a time i'll loose my daughter to him. HAM 2.02.162
how dangerous is it that this man goes loose! 4.03. 2
and cast you, with the waters that you loose, LR 1.04.303
let loose on me the justice of the state | for OTH 1.01.139
of his salt and most hidden loose affection? 2.01.241 P
there are a kind of men, so loose of soul, 3.03.416
hath at fast and loose | beguil'd me to the very ANT 4.12. 28
love's tied," | "this you may loose, not me," TNK 4.01. 91
arm your prize, | i know you will not loose her. 5.03.136
her hair, nor loose nor tied in formal plat, LC 29
though slackly braided in loose negligence. 35

LOOSE–BODIED 2 FR 0.0002 REL FR 0 V 2 P
"inprimis, a loose–bodied gown" — SHR 4.03.134 P
master, if ever i said loose–bodied gown, sew me 4.03.135 P

LOOSED 2 FR 0.0002 REL FR 2 V 0 P
as many arrows loosed several ways | come to one H5 1.02.207
purport | as if he had been loosed out of hell HAM 2.01. 80

LOOSELY 2 FR 0.0002 REL FR 1 V 1 P
should not be so loosely studied as to remember 2H4 2.02. 7 P
see your most dreadful laws so loosely slighted, 5.02. 94

/LOOSEN 1 FR 0.0001 REL FR 1 V 0 P
/that /sister | /should /loosen /him /and /me. LR 5.01. 19

LOOSE–WIV'D 1 FR 0.0001 REL FR 0 V 1 P
to see a handsome man loose–wiv'd, so it is a ANT 1.02. 72 P

LOOSING 1 FR 0.0001 REL FR 1 V 0 P
both my revenge and hate | loosing upon thee, in AWW 2.03.165

LOP 4 FR 0.0004 REL FR 4 V 0 P
superfluous branches | we lop away, that bearing R2 3.04. 64
i'll lop a member off and give it you | in 1H6 5.03. 15
why, we take | from every tree, lop, bark, and H8 1.02. 96
to lop that doubt, he'll fill this land with PER 1.02. 90

LOPP'D 8 FR 0.0009 REL FR 6 V 2 P
a perilous gash, a very limb lopp'd off — | and 1H4 4.01. 43
his lady banish'd, and a limb lopp'd off. 2H6 2.03. 42
not contented that he lopp'd the branch | in 3H6 2.06. 47
alarbus' limbs are lopp'd, | and entrails feed TIT 1.01.143
stern ungentle hands | hath lopp'd and hew'd, 2.04. 17
from a stately cedar shall be lopp'd branches, CYM 5.04.141 P
from a stately cedar shall be lopp'd branches, 5.05.438 P
and thy lopp'd branches point | thy two sons 5.05.454

LOQUITUR 1 FR 0.0001 REL FR 0 V 1 P
but vir /sapit qui pauca loquitur. LLL 4.02. 80 P

/LORD 43 FR 0.0048 REL FR 33 V 10 P
/by /the /lord, thou art a tyrant to say so. WIV 3.03. 61 P
/by /the /lord, a buck–basket! 3.05. 89 P
/lord longaville is one. LLL 2.01. 39
noble /lord, | go to the rude ribs of that R2 3.03. 31
/my /lord, /dispatch, /read /o'er /these 4.01.243
/my /lord — 4.01.253
/no /lord /of /thine, /thou /haught /insulting 4.01.254
/insulting /man, | /nor /no /man's /lord. 4.01.255
/urge /it /no /more, /my /lord /northumberland. 4.01.271
his letters bears his mind, not i, my /lord. 1H4 4.01. 20
/cast /th' /event /of /war, /my /noble /lord, 2H4 1.01.166
/my /lord /your /son /had /only /but /the 1.01.192
/but, /my /most /noble /lord /of /westmerland, 4.01. 59
/o, /my /good /lord /mowbray, | /construe /the 4.01.101
/you /speak, /lord /mowbray, /now /you /know 4.01.128
/look /ye, /my /lord /mayor, | would you imagine R3 3.05. 34
/no, /by /my /troth, /my /lord. 3.07. 43
/my /lord, | he wonders to what end you have 3.07. 83
/o, /do /not /swear, /my /lord /of /buckingham. 3.07.220
/my /lord — 4.02. 99
/my /lord, /your /promise /for /the /earldom — 4.02.102
/my /lord — 4.02.108
it is, /my /lord. 5.01. 11
my /lord, farewell. H8 1.01.226
/a /word, /my /lord. TRO 2.03. 89 P
by my troth, sweet /lord, thou hast a fine 3.01.108 P
/at /that /that /i /have /kill'd, /my /lord — TIT 3.02. 53
/alas, /my /lord, /i /have /but /kill'd /a /fly. 3.02. 59
ay, by heaven, /my /lord. HAM 1.05.122
/prison, /my /lord? 2.02.242 P
/we /think /not /so, /my /lord. 2.02.248 P
/that /they /do, /my /lord — /hercules /and 2.02.361 P
/ay, /my /lord. 3.02.115 P
/hamlet! /lord /hamlet! 4.02. 2 P
/letters, /my /lord, /from /hamlet: 4.07. 36
/that /lord /that /counsell'd /thee | /to /give LR 1.04.140
/this /is /not /altogether /fool, /my /lord. 1.04.151 P
//to–night, /my /lord? OTH 1.03.278
/then /lord have mercy on me! 5.02. 57
/o /lord, /lord, /lord! 5.02. 84
/o /lord, /lord, /lord! 5.02. 84
/o /lord, /lord, /lord! 5.02. 84
/o /lord, what cry is that? 5.02.117

LORD 2705 FR 0.3057 REL FR 2147 V 558 P
my lord, it shall be done. TMP 1.02.318
lord, how it looks about! 1.02.411
as a spy, to win it | from me, the lord on't. 1.02.457
therefore, my lord — 2.01. 23
good lord, how you take it! 2.01. 81 P
my lord sebastian, | the truth you speak doth 2.01.137
had i plantation of this isle, my lord — 2.01.144
nay, good my lord, be not angry. 2.01.186 P
we two, my lord, | will guard your person while 2.01.196
although this lord of weak remembrance, this 2.01.232
prospero my lord shall know what i have done. 2.01.326
lo, how he mocks me! wilt thou let him, my lord? 3.02. 31 P
"lord," quoth he? 3.02. 32 P
i thank my noble lord. 3.02. 38 P
thou shalt be lord of it, and i'll serve thee. 3.02. 57
yea, yea, my lord. 3.02. 60
ay, lord, she will become thy bed, i warrant, 3.02.104
old lord, i cannot blame thee, | who am myself 3.03. 4
honest lord, | thou hast said well; 3.03. 34
brother, my lord the duke, | stand to, and do as 3.03. 51

good my lord, give me thy favor still. 4.01.204
on the sixt hour, at which time, my lord, | you 5.01. 4
sir, "the good old lord gonzalo," | his tears 5.01. 15
were wrack'd) was landed, | to be the lord on't. 5.01.162
sweet lord, you play me false. 5.01.172
what things are these, my lord antonio? 5.01.264
lord, lord! to see what folly reigns in us! TGV 1.02. 15
lord, lord! to see what folly reigns in us! 1.02. 15
there is no news, my lord, but that he writes 1.03. 56
my lord, i cannot be so soon provided: 1.03. 72
my lord, i will be thankful | to any happy 2.04. 52
ay, my good lord, i know the gentleman | to be 2.04. 55
ay, my good lord, a son that well deserves | the 2.04. 59
madam, my lord your father would speak with you. 2.04.116
o gentle proteus, love's a mighty lord, | and 2.04.136
that fits as well as "tell me, good my lord, 2.07. 50
my gracious lord, that which i would discover 3.01. 4
know, noble lord, they have devis'd a mean | how 3.01. 38
but, good my lord, do it so cunningly | that my 3.01. 44
adieu, my lord, sir valentine is coming. 3.01. 50
i know it well, my lord, and sure the match 3.01. 63
it will be light, my lord, that you may bear it 3.01.129
ay, my good lord. 3.01.132
why, any cloak will serve the turn, my lord. 3.01.134
they should harbor where their lord should be." 3.01.149
gone, my good lord. 3.02. 13
a little time, my lord, will kill that grief. 3.02. 15
i do, my lord. 3.02. 24
she did, my lord, when valentine was here. 3.02. 27
and that, my lord, i shall be loath to do: 3.02. 39
you have prevail'd, my lord; 3.02. 46
it is my lord the duke. 5.04.122
and fit for great employment, worthy lord. 5.04.157
what think you of this page, my lord? 5.04.164
i warrant you, my lord — more grace than boy. 5.04.166
lord, lord, your worship's a wanton! WIV 2.02. 55 P
lord, lord, your worship's a wanton! 2.02. 56 P
i'll speak it before the best lord, i would make 3.03. 51 P
my lord. MM 1.01. 2
such ample grace and honor, | it is lord angelo. 1.01. 24
now, good my lord, | let there be some more test 1.01. 47
yet give leave, my lord, | that we may bring you 1.01. 60
but from lord angelo by special charge. 1.02.119
i have deliver'd to lord angelo | (a man of 1.03. 11
gladly, my lord. 1.03. 18
would have seem'd | than in lord angelo. 1.03. 34
lord angelo is precise; 1.03. 50
governs lord angelo, a man whose blood | is very 1.04. 57
go to lord angelo, | and let him learn to know, 1.04. 79
lord angelo is severe. 2.01.282
ay, my good lord, a very virtuous maid, | and to 2.02. 20
good, good my lord, bethink you: 2.02. 87
gentle my lord, turn back. 2.02.143
good my lord, turn back. 2.02.145
o, pardon me, my lord, it oft falls out, | to 2.04.117
gentle my lord, | let me entreat you speak the 2.04.139
so then you hope of pardon from lord angelo? 3.01. 1
lord angelo, having affairs to heaven, | intends 3.01. 56
lord angelo dukes it well in his absence; 3.02. 94 P
good my lord, be good to me, your honor is 3.02.191 P
good my lord. 3.02.192 P
my lord, this is one lucio's information against 3.02.198 P
of justice | lord angelo hath to the public ear 4.02. 99
my lord hath sent you this note, and by me this 4.02.102 P
lord angelo, belike, thinking me remiss in mine 4.02.115 P
till now in the government of lord angelo, came 4.02.137 P
here is lord angelo shall give you justice; 5.01. 27
my lord, her wits, i fear me, are not firm. 5.01. 33
to try her gracious fortune with lord angelo, 5.01. 76
no, my good lord, | nor wish'd to hold my peace. 5.01. 78
my lord, i know him, 'tis a meddling friar. 5.01.127
had he been lay, my lord, | for certain words he 5.01.128
but yesternight, my lord, she and that friar, 5.01.134
i have stood by, my lord, and i have heard 5.01.138
my lord, most villainously, believe it. 5.01.149
but at this instant he is sick, my lord, | of a 5.01.151
was complaint | intended 'gainst lord angelo, 5.01.154
do you not smile at this, lord angelo? 5.01.163
pardon, my lord, i will not show my face | until 5.01.169
no, my lord. 5.01.172 P
no, my lord. 5.01.174 P
neither, my lord. 5.01.176 P
my lord, she may be a punk; 5.01.179 P
well, my lord. 5.01.183 P
my lord, i do confess i ne'er was married, | and 5.01.184
he was drunk then, my lord, it can be no better. 5.01.188 P
well, my lord. 5.01.192 P
this is no witness for lord angelo. 5.01.193
now i come to't, my lord. 5.01.194
and charges him, my lord, with such a time 5.01.197
why, just, my lord, and that is angelo, | who 5.01.202
enough, my lord. 5.01.215
my lord, i must confess i know this woman, | and 5.01.216
and, my good lord, | but tuesday night last gone 5.01.228
now, good my lord, give me the scope of justice, 5.01.234
let me have way, my lord, | to find this 5.01.238
you, lord escalus, | sit with my cousin; 5.01.245
would he were here, my lord, for he indeed 5.01.250
my lord, we'll do it throughly. 5.01.259
pray you, my lord, give me leave to question, 5.01.271 P
my lord, here comes the rascal i spoke of, here 5.01.283 P
you set these women on to slander lord angelo? 5.01.289 P
'tis he, my lord. 5.01.325
o my dread lord, | i should be guiltier than my 5.01.366
i was, my lord. 5.01.376
my lord, i am more amaz'd at his dishonor | than 5.01.380
i do, my lord. 5.01.399
o my most gracious lord, | i hope you will not 5.01.416
o my dear lord, | i crave no other, nor no 5.01.425
o my good lord! 5.01.430
merely, my lord. 5.01.454
no, my good lord; it was by private message. 5.01.460
pardon me, noble lord, | i thought it was a 5.01.462
so learned and so wise | as you, lord angelo, 5.01.471
this, my lord. 5.01.478
by this lord angelo perceives he's safe; 5.01.494
faith, my lord, i spoke it but according to the 5.01.504 P
good my lord, do not recompense me in making me 5.01.516 P
marrying a punk, my lord, is pressing to death, 5.01.522 P
i will, my lord. ERR 1.01.156
lord of the wide world and wild wat'ry seas, 2.01. 21
o lord, i must laugh! 3.01. 50
good lord! 4.01. 48
husband, | who i made lord of me and all i had, 5.01.137
no, my good lord. 5.01.207
my lord, in truth, thus far i witness with him: 5.01.255
he had, my lord, and when he ran in here, 5.01.258
i came from corinth, my most gracious lord — 5.01.366
soldier to a lady, but what is he to a lord? ADO 1.01. 55 P
a lord to a lord, a man to a man, stuff'd with 1.01. 56 P
a lord to a lord, a man to a man, stuff'd with 1.01. 56 P
o lord, he will hang upon him like a disease; 1.01. 86 P
if you swear, my lord, you shall not be forsworn 1.01.153 P
let me bid you welcome, my lord, being 1.01.155 P
like the old tale, my lord: 1.01.216 P
you speak this to fetch me in, my lord. 1.01.223 P
and in faith, my lord, i spoke mine. 1.01.225 P
and by my two faiths and troths, my lord, i 1.01.227 P
or with hunger, my lord, not with love. 1.01.250 P
hath leonato any son, my lord? 1.01.294
o my lord, | when you went onward on this ended 1.01.296
what the good–year, my lord! 1.03. 1 P
to the death, my lord. 1.03. 70 P
lord, i could not endure a husband with a beard 2.01. 29 P
troth, my lord, i have play'd the part of lady 2.01.213 P
indeed, my lord, he lent it me awhile, and i 2.01.278 P
so i would not he should do me, my lord, lest i 2.01.285 P
not sad, my lord. 2.01.290 P
neither, my lord. 2.01.292 P
yea, my lord, i thank it — poor fool, it keeps 2.01.314 P
good lord, for alliance! 2.01.318 P
no, my lord, unless i might have another for 2.01.327 P
no, sure, my lord, my mother cried, but then 2.01.334 P
of the melancholy element in her, my lord. 2.01.343 P
o lord, my lord, if they were but a week married 2.01.353 P
o lord, my lord, if they were but a week married 2.01.353 P
to–morrow, my lord. 2.01.357 P
my lord, i am for you, though it cost me ten 2.01.371 P
and i, my lord. 2.01.373 P
i will do any modest office, my lord, to help my 2.01.375 P
yea, my lord, but i can cross it. 2.02. 3 P
not honestly, my lord, but so covertly that no 2.02. 9 P
yea, my good lord. 2.03. 38
o, very well, my lord. 2.03. 41
o good my lord, tax not so bad a voice | to 2.03. 44
and an ill singer, my lord. 2.03. 76 P
the best i can, my lord. 2.03. 88 P
by my troth, my lord, i cannot tell what to 2.03. 99 P
what effects, my lord? 2.03.110 P
i would have sworn it had, my lord, especially 2.03.116 P
o my lord, wisdom and blood combating in so 2.03.163 P
never tell him, my lord. 2.03.201 P
my lord, will you walk? dinner is ready. 2.03.210 P
so says the prince and my new–trothed lord. 3.01. 38
i'll bring you thither, my lord, if you'll 3.02. 3 P
my lord and brother, god save you! 3.02. 80 P
is not your lord honorable without marriage? 3.04. 31 P
my lord, they stay for you to give your daughter 3.05. 54 P
you come hither, my lord, to marry this lady. 4.01. 4 P
none, my lord. 4.01. 16 P
what do you mean, my lord? 4.01. 43
dear my lord, if you, in your own proof, | have 4.01. 45
is my lord well, that he doth speak so wide? 4.01. 62
all this is so, but what of this, my lord? 4.01. 72
i talk'd with no man at that hour, my lord. 4.01. 86
fie, fie, they are not to be named, my lord, 4.01. 95
some haste, my lord! 5.01. 48
well, fare you well, my lord. 5.01. 48
my lord, my lord, | i'll prove it on his body, 5.01. 73
my lord, my lord, | i'll prove it on his body, 5.01. 73
my lord, my lord — 5.01.106
my lord, my lord — 5.01.106
good day, my lord. 5.01.112 P
my lord, for your many courtesies i thank you. 5.01.188 P
for my lord lack–beard there, he and i shall 5.01.192 P
hearken after their offense, my lord. 5.01.212 P
it is, my lord. 5.03. 2
she died, my lord, but whiles her slander liv'd. 5.04. 66
my lord, your brother john is ta'en in flight, 5.04.125
my loving lord, dumaine is mortified: LLL 1.01. 28
no, my good lord, i have sworn to stay with you; 1.01.111
sweet lord, and why? 1.01.126
my lord berowne, see him delivered o'er, | and 1.01.305
no, no, o lord, sir, no. 1.02. 6 P
lord, how wise you are! 1.02.138 P
good lord boyet, my beauty, though but mean, 2.01. 13
between lord perigort and the beauteous heir 2.01. 41
some merry mocking lord belike, is't so? 2.01. 52
now, what admittance, lord? 2.01. 80
our lady help my lord! he'll be forsworn. 2.01. 98
were my lord so, his ignorance were wise, 2.01.102
'tis deadly sin to keep that oath, my lord, 2.01.105
that last is berowne, the merry madcap lord. 2.01.215
regent of love–rhymes, lord of folded arms, 3.01.181
we may afford | to any lady that subdues a lord. 4.01. 40
i told you: my lord. 4.01.101
from my lord to my lady. 4.01.102
from which lord to which lady? 4.01.103
from my lord berowne, a good master of mine, 4.01.104
lord, lord, how the ladies and i have put him 4.01.141
lord, lord, how the ladies and i have put him 4.01.141
sir, i praise the lord for you, and so may my 4.02. 73 P
by the lord, this love is as mad as ajax. 4.03. 6 P
and mine too, good lord! 4.03. 91
guilty, my lord, guilty! 4.03.201
for when would you, my lord, or you, or you, 4.03.295
fair lord — | take that for your fair lady. 5.02.239
no, a fair lord calf. 5.02.248
lord longaville said i came o'er his heart, 5.02.278
i will, and so will she, i know, my lord. 5.02.314
and we that sell by gross, the lord doth know, 5.02.319
not so, my lord, it is not so, i swear; 5.02.359
ay, in truth, my lord; 5.02.362
it is not so, my lord. 5.02.364
and in that hour, my lord, | they did not bless 5.02.369
amaz'd, my lord? why looks your highness sad? 5.02.391
write "lord have mercy on us" on those three: 5.02.419
the noble lord | most honorably doth uphold his 5.02.448
and lord berowne (i thank him) is my dear. 5.02.457
o lord, sir, they would know | whether the three 5.02.485
o lord, sir, it were pity you should get your 5.02.496 P
o lord, sir, the parties themselves, the actors, 5.02.499 P
we are shame–proof, my lord; 5.02.512
nay, my good lord, let me o'errule you now. 5.02.515
a right description of our sport, my lord. 5.02.521
sweet lord longaville, rein thy tongue. 5.02.656 P
farewell, worthy lord! 5.02.736
no, no, my lord, your grace is perjur'd much, 5.02.790
not so, my lord, a twelvemonth and a day | i'll 5.02.827
oft have i heard of you, my lord berowne, 5.02.841
ay, sweet my lord, and so i take my leave. 5.02.872
my noble lord, | this man hath my consent to MND 1.01. 24
so will i grow, so live, so die, my lord, | ere 1.01. 79
i am, my lord, as well deriv'd as he, | as well 1.01. 99
tarry, rash wanton! am not i thy lord? 2.01. 63
fear not, my lord! your servant shall do so. 2.01.268
lord, what though? 2.02.109
i thought you lord of more true gentleness. 2.02.132
lord! 2.02.151
lord, what fools these mortals be! 3.02.115
my fairy lord, this must be done with haste, 3.02.378
come, my lord, and in our flight | tell me how 4.01. 99
my lord, this' my daughter here asleep, | and 4.01.128
it is, my lord. 4.01.137
pardon, my lord. 4.01.141
my lord, i shall reply amazedly, | half sleep, 4.01.146
enough, enough, my lord; 4.01.154
my lord, fair helen told me of their stealth, 4.01.160
but, my good lord, i wot not by what power 4.01.164
to her, my lord, | was i betrothed ere i /saw 4.01.171
a play there is, my lord, some ten words long, 5.01. 61
but by ten words, my lord, it is too long, 5.01. 63
and tragical, my noble lord, it is; 5.01. 66
no, my noble lord, | it is not for you. 5.01. 76
a good moral, my lord: 5.01.120 P
no wonder, my lord; 5.01.153 P
partition that ever i heard discourse, my lord. 5.01.168 P
no remedy, my lord, when walls are so willful to 5.01.208 P
the very best at a beast, my lord, that e'er i 5.01.229 P
not so, my lord; 5.01.233 P
my lord bassanio, since you have found antonio, MV 1.01. 69
how say you by the french lord, monsieur le /bon 1.02. 54 P
what think you of the scottish lord, his 1.02. 77 P
lord worshipp'd might he be! 2.02. 93 P
lord, how art thou chang'd! 2.02. 99 P
but if you fail, without more speech, my lord, 2.09. 7
here; what would my lord? 2.09. 85
before | to signify th' approaching of his lord, 2.09. 88
as this fore–spurrer comes before his lord. 2.09. 95
bassanio, lord love, if thy will it be! 2.09.101
you see me, lord bassanio, where i stand, | such 3.02.149
as from her lord, her governor, her king. 3.02.165
but now i was the lord | of this fair mansion, 3.02.167
my lord and lady, it is now our time, | that 3.02.186
good joy, my lord and lady! 3.02.188
my lord bassanio and my gentle lady, | i wish 3.02.189
my eyes, my lord, can look as swift as yours: 3.02.197
intermission | no more pertains to me, my lord, 3.02.200
yes, faith, my lord. 3.02.211
so do i, my lord, | they are entirely welcome. 3.02.224
for my part, my lord, | my purpose was not to 3.02.226
i did, my lord, | and i have reason for it. 3.02.230
not sick, my lord, unless it be in mind, | nor 3.02.234
not one, my lord. 3.02.271
and i know, my lord, | if law, authority, and 3.02.288
in bearing thus the absence of your lord. 3.04. 4
how dear a lover of my lord your husband, | i 3.04. 7
antonio, | being the bosom lover of my lord, 3.04. 17
lover of my lord, | must needs be like my lord. 3.04. 18
jessica | in place of lord bassanio and myself. 3.04. 39
goodly lord, what a wit–snapper are you! 3.05. 49 P
how dost thou like the lord bassanio's wife? 3.05. 72
meet | the lord bassanio live an upright life, 3.05. 74
he is ready at the door; he comes, my lord. 4.01. 15
my lord, here stays without | a messenger with 4.01.107
from both, my lord. bellario greets your grace. 4.01.120
i did, my lord. 4.01.170
so please my lord the duke and all the court 4.01.380
my lord bassanio, let him have the ring. 4.01.449
my lord bassanio upon more advice | hath sent 4.02. 6
you are welcome home, my lord. 5.01.132
my lord bassanio gave his ring away | unto the 5.01.179
what ring gave you, my lord? 5.01.184
that your lord | will never more break faith 5.01.252
here, lord bassanio, swear to keep this ring. 5.01.256
he cannot speak, my lord. AYL 1.02.220
treason is not inherited, my lord, | or, if we 1.03. 61
indeed, my lord, | the melancholy jaques grieves 2.01. 25
to–day my lord of amiens and myself | did steal 2.01. 29
and indeed, my lord, | the wretched animal 2.01. 35
we did, my lord, weeping and commenting | upon 2.01. 65
my lord, the roynish clown, at whom so oft 2.02. 8
my lord, he is but even now gone hence; 2.07. 3
o lord, lord, it is a hard matter for friends to 3.02.184 P
o lord, lord, it is a hard matter for friends to 3.02.184 P
your features, lord warrant us! what features? 3.03. 5 P
my lord, the first time that i ever saw him 5.04. 28
but, my good lord, this boy is forest–born, 5.04. 30
good my lord, bid him welcome. 5.04. 40 P
good my lord, like this fellow. 5.04. 51 P
is not this a rare fellow, my lord? 5.04.104 P
must accord, | or have a woman to your lord; 5.04.134
unhandsome than to see the lord the prologue. ep 3 P
why, belman is as good as he, my lord; SHR in.1. 22
i will, my lord. in.1. 30
he breathes, my lord. in.1. 32
believe me, lord, i think he cannot choose. in.1. 42
dreams, | for he is nothing but a mighty lord. in.1. 65
my lord, i warrant you we will play our part in.1. 69
there is a lord will hear you play to–night; in.1. 93
fear not, my lord, we can contain ourselves, in.1. 100
to see her noble lord restor'd to health, | who in.1. 121
o noble lord, bethink thee of thy birth, | call in.2. 30
thou art a lord, and nothing but a lord. in.2. 61

thou art a lord, and nothing but a lord. in.2. 61
am i a lord, and have i such a lady? in.2. 68
life, i am a lord indeed | and not a tinker nor in.2. 72
o yes, my lord, but very idle words, | for in.2. 83
now lord be thanked for my good amends! in.2. 97
how fares my noble lord? in.2. 100
here, noble lord, what is thy will with her? in.2. 103
my men should call me "lord"; in.2. 105
my husband and my lord, my lord and husband, | i in.2. 106
my husband and my lord, my lord and husband, | i in.2. 106
thrice–noble lord, let me entreat of you | to in.2. 118
no, my good lord, it is more pleasing stuff. in.2. 139
from all such devils, good lord deliver us! 1.01. 66
and me too, good lord! 1.01. 67
my lord, you nod, you do not mind the play. 1.01.249
my lord, 'tis but begun. 1.01.252
b mi, bianca, take him for thy lord, | c fa ut, 3.01. 75
good lord, how bright and goodly shines the moon 4.05. 2
lord, let me never have a cause to sigh, | till 5.02.123
to wound thy lord, thy king, thy governor. 5.02.138
thy husband is thy lord, thy life, thy keeper, 5.02.146
and graceless traitor to her loving lord? 5.02.160
what is it, my good lord, the king languishes of AWW 1.01. 32 P
a fistula, my lord. 1.01. 34 P
his sole child, my lord, and bequeath'd to my 1.01. 38 P
my lord, | 'tis an unseason'd courtier; 1.01. 70
good my lord, | advise him. 1.01. 71
monsieur parolles, my lord calls for you. 1.01.187 P
it is the count /rossillion, my good lord, 1.02. 18
some six months since, my lord. 1.02. 71
my master, my dear lord he is, and i | his 1.03.158
so that my lord your son were not my brother — 1.03.162
my lord your son made me to think of this; 1.03.232
o my sweet lord, that you will stay behind us! 2.01. 24
pardon, my lord, for me and for my tidings. 2.01. 61
i would you had kneel'd, my lord, to ask me 2.01. 64
but, my good lord, 'tis thus: 2.01. 68
my lord, there's one arriv'd, | if you will see 2.01. 79
ay, my good lord. 2.01.100
o lord, sir! 2.02. 41 P
o lord, sir! — thick, thick, spare not me. 2.02. 45 P
o lord, sir! — nay, put me to't, i warrant you. 2.02. 48 P
o lord, sir! — spare not me. 2.02. 51 P
do you cry, "o lord, sir!" 2.02. 52 P
indeed your "o lord, sir!" 2.02. 53 P
i ne'er had worse luck in my life in my "o lord, 2.02. 58 P
o lord, sir! — why, there't serves well again. 2.02. 62 P
yes, my good lord, | but never hope to know why 2.03.109
but follows it, my lord, to bring me down | must 2.03.112
that you are well restor'd, my lord, i'm glad. 2.03.147
pardon, my gracious lord; 2.03.167
your lord and master did well to make his 2.03.186 P
recantation? my lord? my master? 2.03.188 P
which if — lord have mercy on thee for a hen! 2.03.212 P
my lord, you give me most egregious indignity. 2.03.216 P
i have not, my lord, deserv'd it. 2.03.220 P
my lord, you do me most insupportable vexation. 2.03.230 P
off me, scurvy, old, filthy, scurvy lord! 2.03.236 P
and he were double and double a lord. 2.03.239 P
sirrah, your lord and master's married, there's 2.03.242 P
he is my good lord; 2.03.246 P
this is hard and undeserv'd measure, my lord. 2.03.257 P
madam, my lord will go away to–night, | a very 2.04. 39
yes, my lord, and of very valiant approof. 2.05. 3 P
i do assure you, my lord, he is very great in 2.05. 8 P
is there any unkindness between my lord and you, 2.05. 32 P
it may be you have mistaken him, my lord. 2.05. 40 P
fare you well, my lord, and believe this of me: 2.05. 42 P
an idle lord, i swear. 2.05. 49 P
i would not tell you what i would, my lord. 2.05. 84
i shall not break your bidding, good my lord. 2.05. 88
good my lord, | the reasons of our state i 3.01. 9
i take my young lord to be a very melancholy man 3.02. 3 P
madam, my lord is gone, for ever gone. 3.02. 46
and she deserves a lord | that twenty such rude 3.02. 81
poor lord, is't i | that chase thee from thy 3.02.102
that sings with piercing, do not touch my lord. 3.02.111
to become the wife | of a detesting lord. 3.05. 65
nay, good my lord, put him to't; 3.06. 1 P
on my life, my lord, a bubble. 3.06. 5 P
believe it, my lord, in mine own direct 3.06. 7 P
i know not what the success will be, my lord, 3.06. 80 P
is not this a strange fellow, my lord, that so 3.06. 86 P
you do not know him, my lord, as we do. 3.06. 90 P
he was first smok'd by the old lord lafew. 3.06.103 P
with all my heart, my lord. 3.06.117
no, my good lord, diana. 4.02. 2
my mother did but duty, such, my lord, | as you 4.02. 12
will you not, my lord? 4.02. 41
how now, my lord, is't not after midnight? 4.03. 84 P
y' are deceiv'd, my lord, this is monsieur 4.03.140 P
o lord, sir, let me live, or let me see my death 4.03.309 P
what greeting will you to my lord lafew? 4.03.318 P
and by the leave of my good lord the king, 4.04. 13
my lord that's gone made himself much sport out 4.05. 64 P
death and that my lord your son was upon his 4.05. 70 P
with very much content, my lord, and i wish it 4.05. 78 P
yonder's my lord your son with a patch of velvet 4.05. 94 P
lord, how we lose our pains! 5.01. 24
master lavatch, give my lord lafew this letter. 5.02. 1 P
my lord, i am a man whom fortune hath cruelly 5.02. 26 P
my name, my good lord, is parolles. 5.02. 39 P
o my good lord, you were the first that found me 5.02. 42 P
it lies in you, my lord, to bring me in some 5.02. 46 P
pardon — the young lord | did to his majesty, 5.03. 12
you remember | the daughter of this lord? 5.03. 43
you are deceiv'd, my lord, she never saw it. 5.03. 92
i am, my lord, a wretched florentine, | derived 5.03.158
my lord, i neither can nor will deny | but that 5.03.166
she's none of mine, my lord. 5.03.169
my lord, this is a fond and desp'rate creature, 5.03.178
good my lord, | ask him upon his oath, if he 5.03.184
she's impudent, my lord, | and was a common 5.03.187
he does me wrong, my lord; 5.03.189
i did, my lord, but loath am to produce | so bad 5.03.201
my lord, i do confess the ring was hers. 5.03.231
ay, my lord. 5.03.233
he's a good drum, my lord, but a naughty orator. 5.03.253 P
ay, my good lord. 5.03.270
this woman's an easy glove, my lord, she goes 5.03.277 P
but for this lord, | who hath abus'd me, as he 5.03.297
no, my good lord, | 'tis but the shadow of a 5.03.306
o my good lord, when i was like this maid, | i 5.03.309
will you go hunt, my lord? TN 1.01. 16
so please my lord, i might not be admitted, 1.01. 23
on your attendance, my lord, here. 1.04. 11
sure, my noble lord, | if she be so abandon'd to 1.04. 18
say i do speak with her, my lord, what then? 1.04. 23
i think not so, my lord. 1.04. 29
and thou shalt live as freely as thy lord, | to 1.04. 39
commission from your lord to negotiate with my 1.05.231 P
my lord and master loves you. 1.05.252
your lord does know my mind, i cannot love him, 1.05.257
get you to your lord. 1.05.279
desire him not to flatter with his lord, | nor 1.05.303
that you should put your lord into a desperate 2.02. 8 P
feste, the jester, my lord, a fool that the lady 2.04. 11 P
about your years, my lord. 2.04. 28
i think it well, my lord. 2.04. 35
a blank, my lord. 2.04.110
i would play lord pandarus of phrygia, sir, to 3.01. 51 P
you'll nothing, madam, to my lord by me? 3.01.136
o lord! 3.04.107 P
between his lord and my niece confirms no less. 3.04.187 P
to–day, my lord; 5.01. 94
what would my lord, but that he may not have, 5.01.101
what do you say, cesario? good my lord — 5.01.106
my lord would speak, my duty hushes me. 5.01.107
if it be aught to the old tune, my lord, | it is 5.01.108
still so constant, lord. 5.01.111
even what it please my lord, that shall become 5.01.116
whither, my lord? cesario, husband, stay. 5.01.143
no, my lord, not i. 5.01.145
my lord, i do protest — 5.01.170
hath been between this lady and this lord. 5.01.258
"by the lord, madam" — 5.01.291 P
"by the lord, madam, you wrong me, and the world 5.01.302 P
my lord, so please you, these things further 5.01.316
ay, my lord, this same. | how now, malvolio? 5.01.327
"by the lord, fool, i am not mad." 5.01.373 P
when at bohemia | you take my lord, i'll give WT 1.02. 40
o' th' clock behind | what lady she her lord. 1.02. 44
was not my lord | the verier wag o' th' two? 1.02. 65
he'll stay, my lord. 1.02. 87
ay, my good lord. 1.02.120
yes, if you will, my lord. 1.02.127
how? my lord? 1.02.147
are you mov'd, my lord? 1.02.150
no, my lord, i'll fight. 1.02.162
we two will walk, my lord, | and leave you to 1.02.172
ay, my good lord. 1.02.210
business, my lord? 1.02.229
be it forbid, my lord! 1.02.241
my gracious lord, | i may be negligent, foolish, 1.02.249
in your affairs, my lord, | if ever i were 1.02.254
these, my lord, | are such allow'd infirmities 1.02.262
good my lord, be cur'd | of this diseas'd 1.02.296
no, no, my lord. 1.02.299
sir, my lord, | i could do this, and that with 1.02.318
my lord, | go then; 1.02.342
i'll do't, my lord. 1.02.349
none rare, my lord. 1.02.367
i dare not know, my lord. 1.02.376
come, my gracious lord, | shall i be your 2.01. 2
why, my sweet lord? 2.01. 4
and why so, my lord? 2.01. 7
blue, my lord. 2.01. 13
you, my lord, | do but mistake. 2.01. 80
gentle my lord, | you scarce can right me 2.01. 98
adieu, my lord. 2.01.122
for her, my lord, | i dare my life lay down — 2.01.129
good my lord — 2.01.139
i had rather you did lack than i, my lord, 2.01.158
well done, my lord. 2.01.188
my lord? 2.03. 9
no noise, my lord, but needful conference 2.03. 40
i told her so, my lord, | on your displeasure's 2.03. 44
good queen, my lord, good queen, i say good 2.03. 60
a most unworthy and unnatural lord | can do no 2.03.113
look to your babe, my lord, 'tis yours. 2.03.126
any thing, my lord, | that my ability may 2.03.163
i will, my lord. 2.03.169
away the life of our sovereign lord the king, 3.02. 16 P
you, my lord, best know | (/who least will seem 3.02. 32
ay, my lord, even so | as it is here set down. 3.02.138
my lord the king! the king! 3.02.142
i'll not remember you of my own lord, | who is 3.02.230
ay, my lord, and fear | we have landed in ill 3.03. 2
put on thee by my lord, thou ne'er shalt see 3.03. 35
sir, my gracious lord, | to chide at your 4.04. 5
gracious my lord, | you know /your father's 4.04.466
even he, my lord. 4.04.473
o my lord, | i would your spirit were easier for 4.04.504
well, my lord, | if you may please to think i 4.04.520
my lord, | fear none of this. 4.04.589
true, too true, my lord. 5.01. 12
my lord should to the heavens be contrary, 5.01. 45
yet, if my lord will marry — if you will, sir, 5.01. 76
this hour, he had pair'd | well with this lord; 5.01.117
good my lord, | she came from libya. 5.01.156
that noble honor'd lord, is fear'd and lov'd? 5.01.158
my lord, | is this the daughter of a king? 5.01.207
come, good my lord. 5.01.233
my lord, your sorrow was too sore laid on, 5.03. 49
indeed, my lord, | if i had thought the sight of 5.03. 56
see, my lord, | would you not deem it breath'd? 5.03. 63
good my lord, forbear. 5.03. 80
lord of thy presence and no land beside? JN 1.01.137
my lord chatillion may from england bring | that 2.01. 46
what england says, say briefly, gentle lord, 2.01. 52
then tell us, shall your city call us lord, | in 2.01.263
lord of our presence, angiers, and of you. 2.01.367
i do, my lord, and in her eye i find | a wonder, 2.01.496
further i will not flatter you, my lord, | that 2.01.516
and this rich fair town | we make him lord of. 2.01.553
gain, be my lord, for i will worship thee. 2.01.598
my lord, i rescued her; 3.02. 7
my lord? 3.03. 66
o lord, my boy, my arthur, my fair son! 3.04.103
stay yet, lord salisbury, i'll go with thee, 4.02. 96
and, as i hear, my lord, | the lady constance in 4.02.121
the french, my lord; 4.02.161
besides, i met lord bigot and lord salisbury, 4.02.162
besides, i met lord bigot and lord salisbury, 4.02.162
my lord, they say five moons were seen to–night; 4.02.182
no had, my lord? why, did you not provoke me? 4.02.207
my lord — 4.02.230
the count melune, a noble lord of france, 4.03. 15
stand back, lord salisbury, stand back, i say; 4.03. 81
i would not have you, lord, forget yourself, 4.03. 83
lord bigot, i am none. 4.03.103
my lord melune, let this be copied out, | and 5.02. 1
my holy lord of milan, from the king | i come to 5.02.120
my lord, your valiant kinsman, faulconbridge, 5.03. 5
whoever spoke it, it is true, my lord. 5.05. 19
my liege, my lord! 5.07. 66
for you, my noble lord of lancaster, | the R2 1.01.135
my dear dear lord, | the purest treasure mortal 1.01.176
lord marshal, command our officers–at–arms | be 1.01.204
but thomas, my dear lord, my life, my gloucester 1.02. 16
my lord aumerle, is harry herford arm'd? 1.03. 1
lord marshal, let me kiss my sovereign's hand 1.03. 46
my loving lord, i take my leave of you; 1.03. 63
of you, my noble cousin, lord aumerle; 1.03. 64
farewell, my lord, securely i espy | virtue with 1.03. 97
my lord, no leave take i, for i will ride, | as 1.03.251
old john of gaunt is grievous sick, my lord, 1.04. 54
our uncle york lord governor of england; 2.01.220
that harry duke of herford, rainold lord cobham, 2.01.279
more than with parting from my lord the king. 2.02. 13
the lord northumberland, his son young harry 2.02. 53
my lord, your son was gone before i came. 2.02. 86
my lord, i had forgot to tell your lordship: 2.02. 93
how far is it, my lord, to berkeley now? 2.03. 1
believe me, noble lord, | i am a stranger here 2.03. 2
i had thought, my lord, to have learn'd his 2.03. 24
no, my good lord, he hath forsook the court, 2.03. 26
but he, my lord, is gone to ravenspurgh | to 2.03. 31
no, my good lord, for that is not forgot | which 2.03. 37
my gracious lord, i tender you my service, 2.03. 41
your presence makes us rich, most noble lord. 2.03. 63
it is my lord of berkeley, as i guess. 2.03. 68
my lord of herford, my message is to you. 2.03. 69
my lord, my answer is to lancaster, | and i am 2.03. 70
mistake me not, my lord, 'tis not my meaning 2.03. 74
to you, my lord, i come, what lord you will, 2.03. 76
to you, my lord, i come, what lord you will, 2.03. 76
were i but now lord of such hot youth | as when 2.03. 99
my lord of salisbury, we have stay'd ten days, 2.04. 1
my lord northumberland, see them dispatch'd. 3.01. 35
yea, my lord. 3.02. 2
fear not, my lord, that power that made you king 3.02. 27
he means, my lord, that we are too remiss, 3.02. 33
cannot depose | the deputy elected by the lord; 3.02. 57
welcome, my lord. 3.02. 63
nor near nor farther off, my gracious lord, 3.02. 64
one day too late, i fear me, noble lord, | hath 3.02. 67
peace have they made with him indeed, my lord. 3.02.128
my lord, wise men ne'er sit and wail their woes, 3.02.178
the news is very fair and good, my lord: 3.03. 5
it would beseem the lord northumberland | to say 3.03. 7
the castle royally is mann'd, my lord, | against 3.03. 21
yes, my good lord, | it doth contain a king. 3.03. 24
stone, | and with him are the lord aumerle, lord 3.03. 27
with him are the lord aumerle, lord salisbury, 3.03. 27
the king of heaven forbid our lord the king 3.03.101
no, good my lord, let's fight with gentle words, 3.03.131
most mighty prince, my lord northumberland, 3.03.172
my lord, in the base court he doth attend | to 3.03.176
my gracious lord — 3.03.189
my gracious lord, i come but for mine own. 3.03.196
so far be mine, my most redoubted lord, | as my 3.03.198
yea, my good lord. 3.03.209
then set before my face the lord aumerle. 4.01. 6
my lord aumerle, i know your daring tongue 4.01. 8
my lord fitzwater, i do remember well | the very 4.01. 60
as surely as i live, my lord. 4.01.102
my lord of herford here, whom you call king, 4.01.134
my lord of westminster, be it your charge | to 4.01.152
my lord, | before i freely speak my mind herein, 4.01.326
to whose flint bosom my condemned lord | is 5.01. 3
my lord, the mind of bullingbrook is chang'd, 5.01. 51
my lord, you told me you would tell the rest, 5.02. 1
at that sad stop, my lord, | where rude 5.02. 4
for aught i know, my lord, they do. 5.02. 53
my lord, 'tis nothing. 5.02. 58
what is the matter, my lord? 5.02. 73
why, what is it, my lord? 5.02. 76
my lord, some two days since i saw the prince, 5.03. 13
ah, my sour husband, my hard–hearted lord, 5.03.121
my lord, will't please you to fall to? 5.05. 98
my lord, i dare not. 5.05.100
welcome, my lord, what is the news? 5.06. 5
my lord, i have from oxford sent to london | the 5.06. 13
from your own mouth, my lord, did i this deed. 5.06. 37
this match'd with other did, my gracious lord, 1H4 1.01. 49
me sin | in envy that my lord northumberland 1.01. 79
by the lord, thou say'st true, lad. 1.02. 39 P
by the lord, i'll be a brave judge. 1.02. 64 P
an old lord of the council rated me the other 1.02. 84 P
by the lord, and i do not, i am a villain, i'll 1.02. 96 P
by the lord, i'll be a traitor then, when thou 1.02.146 P
now, my good sweet honey lord, ride with us 1.02.160 P
farewell, my lord. 1.02.194 P
my lord — 1.03. 14
yea, my good lord. 1.03. 22
came there a certain lord, neat, and trimly 1.03. 33
this bald unjointed chat of his, my lord, | i 1.03. 65
the circumstance considered, good my lord, 1.03. 70
what e'er lord harry percy then had said | to 1.03. 71
my lord northumberland: 1.03.122
you, my lord, | your son in scotland being thus 1.03.264
his brother's death at bristow, the lord scroop. 1.03.271
i'll steal to glendower and lord mortimer, 1.03.295

for mine own part, my lord, i could be well 2.03. 1 P
but i tell you, my lord fool, out of this nettle 2.03. 9 P
by the lord, our plot is a good plot as ever was 2.03. 16 P
why, my lord of york commends the plot and the 2.03. 21 P
lord edmund mortimer, my lord of york, and owen 2.03. 24 P
lord edmund mortimer, my lord of york, and owen 2.03. 25 P
o my good lord, why are you thus alone? 2.03. 37
tell me, sweet lord, what is't that takes from 2.03. 40
some heavy business hath my lord in hand, | and 2.03. 63
he is, my lord, an hour ago. 2.03. 66
one horse, my lord, he brought even now. 2.03. 68
it is, my lord. 2.03. 70
but hear you, my lord. 2.03. 73
a good boy (by the lord, so they call me!), 2.04. 13 P
my lord? 2.04. 40 P
o lord, sir, i'll be sworn upon all the books in 2.04. 49 P
anon, sir. pray stay a little, my lord. 2.04. 57 P
o lord, i would it had been two! 2.04. 60 P
my lord? 2.04. 68 P
o lord, sir, who do you mean? 2.04. 72 P
my lord, old sir john with half a dozen more are 2.04. 82 P
and ye call me coward, by the lord, i'll stab 2.04.145 P
sixteen at least, my lord. 2.04.175 P
by the lord, i knew ye as well as he that made 2.04.267 P
but, by the lord, lads, i am glad you have the 2.04.275 P
o jesu, my lord the prince! 2.04.284 P
marry, my lord, there is a nobleman of the court 2.04.287 P
my lord, do you see these meteors? 2.04.319 P
choler, my lord, if rightly taken. 2.04.324 P
my noble lord, from eastcheap. 2.04.441 P
'sblood, my lord, they are false. 2.04.443 P
my lord, the man i know. 2.04.464 P
no, my good lord, banish peto, banish bardolph, 2.04.474 P
o my lord, my lord, the sheriff with a most 2.04.482 P
o my lord, my lord, the sheriff with a most 2.04.482 P
o jesu, my lord, my lord! 2.04.486 P
o jesu, my lord, my lord! 2.04.486 P
first, pardon me, my lord. 2.04.507
one of them is well known, my gracious lord, | a 2.04.510
i will, my lord. 2.04.519
good night, my noble lord. 2.04.523
indeed, my lord, i think it be two a' clock. 2.04.525
nothing but papers, my lord. 2.04.533 P
good morrow, good my lord. 2.04.550 P
lord mortimer, and cousin glendower, | will you 3.01. 3
i | and my good lord of worcester will set forth 3.01. 83
i can speak english, lord, as well as you, | for 3.01.119
in faith, my lord, you are too willful–blame, 3.01.175
you must needs learn, lord, to amend this fault; 3.01.178
come, lord mortimer, you are as slow | as hot 3.01.263
as slow | as hot lord percy is on fire to go. 3.01.264
i shall hereafter, my thrice–gracious lord, | be 3.02. 92
percy is but my factor, good my lord, | to 3.02.147
lord mortimer of scotland hath sent word | that 3.02.164
with him my son, lord john of lancaster, | for 3.02.171
my lord, i pray you hear me. 3.03. 91 P
good my lord, hear me. 3.03. 94 P
so i told him, my lord, and i said i heard your 3.03.105 P
and, my lord, he speaks most vilely of you, like 3.03.106 P
so he doth you, my lord, and said this other day 3.03.133 P
nay, my lord, he call'd you jack, and said he 3.03.138 P
do, my lord. 3.03.185 P
my lord? 3.03.194 P
go bear this letter to lord john of lancaster, 3.03.195
this to my lord of westmerland. 3.03.196
nay, task me to my word, approve me, lord. 4.01. 9
he cannot come, my lord, he is grievous sick. 4.01. 16
he did, my lord, four days ere i set forth, 4.01. 22
pray god my news be worth a welcome, lord. 4.01. 87
my good lord of westmerland, i cry you mercy! 4.02. 51 P
do not, my lord. 4.03. 6
little counsel with weak fear | as you, my lord, 4.03. 12
brief | with winged haste to the lord marshal, 4.04. 2
my good lord, | i guess their tenor. 4.04. 6
and quick–raised power | meets with lord harry; 4.04. 13
why, my good lord, you need not fear, | there is 4.04. 21
not fear, | there is douglas and lord mortimer. 4.04. 22
but there is mordake, vernon, lord harry percy, 4.04. 24
and there is my lord of worcester, and a head 4.04. 25
the prince of wales, lord john of lancaster, 4.04. 29
doubt not, my lord, they shall be well oppos'd. 4.04. 33
for if lord percy thrive not, ere the king 4.04. 36
how now, my lord of worcester? 5.01. 9
this is not well, my lord, this is not well. 5.01. 14
house, | and yet i must remember you, my lord, 5.01. 32
return'd, | deliver up my lord of westmerland. 5.02. 28
defy him by the lord of westmerland. 5.02. 31
lord douglas, go you and tell him so. 5.02. 32
my lord, here are letters for you. 5.02. 79
my lord, prepare, the king comes on apace. 5.02. 89
the lord of stafford dear to–day hath bought 5.03. 7
king that will revenge | lord stafford's death. 5.03. 13
lord john of lancaster, go you with him. 5.04. 3
not i, my lord, unless i did bleed too. 5.04. 4
my lord of westmerland, lead him to his tent. 5.04. 8
come, my lord, i'll lead you to your tent. 5.04. 9
lead me, my lord? 5.04. 10
i did not think thee lord of such a spirit. 5.04. 18
i saw him hold lord percy at the point, | with 5.04. 21
cheerly, my lord, how fares your grace? 5.04. 44
lord, lord, how this world is given to lying! 5.04.145 P
lord, lord, how this world is given to lying! 5.04.145 P
the noble scot, lord douglas, when he saw | the 5.05. 17
that the lord bardolph doth attend him here. 2H4 1.01. 3
what news, lord bardolph? 1.01. 7
and, in the fortune of my lord your son, 1.01. 15
i spake with one, my lord, that came from thence 1.01. 25
my lord, i overrode him on the way, | and he is 1.01. 30
my lord, sir john umfrevile turn'd me back 1.01. 34
my lord, i'll tell you what: 1.01. 51
if my young lord your son have not the day, 1.01. 52
i ran from shrewsbury, my noble lord, | where 1.01. 65
your brother yet, | but, for my lord your son — 1.01. 83
i cannot think, my lord, your son is dead. 1.01.104
out | a speedy power to encounter you, my lord, 1.01.133
this strained passion doth you wrong, my lord. 1.01.161
'tis more than time, and, my most noble lord, 1.01.187
he, my lord, but he hath since done good service 1.02. 61 P
with some charge to the lord john of lancaster. 1.02. 63 P
sir, my lord would speak with you. 1.02. 91 P
my good lord! 1.02. 93 P
very well, my lord, very well. 1.02.120 P
i am as poor as job, my lord, but not so patient 1.02.126 P
my lord? 1.02.152 P
a wassail candle, my lord, all tallow; 1.02.158 P
not so, my lord. 1.02.165 P
my lord, i was born about three of the clock in 1.02.187 P
prince, and you took it like a sensible lord. 1.02.196 P
i hear you are going with lord john of lancaster 1.02.204 P
for, by the lord, i take but two shirts out with 1.02.209 P
go bear this letter to my lord of lancaster, 1.02.239 P
and first, lord marshal, what say you to it? 1.03. 4
the question then, lord hastings, standeth thus: 1.03. 15
'tis very true, lord bardolph, for indeed | it 1.03. 25
it was, my lord, who lin'd himself with hope, 1.03. 27
to us no more, nay, not so much, lord bardolph, 1.03. 69
o lord, ay! good master snare. 2.01. 6 P
good my lord, be good to me; 2.01. 63 P
o my most worshipful lord, and't please your 2.01. 69 P
it is more than for some, my lord, it is for all 2.01. 73 P
my lord, this is a poor /mad soul, and she says 2.01.104 P
yea, in truth, my lord. 2.01.117 P
my lord, i will not undergo this sneap without 2.01.122 P
no, my lord, my humble duty rememb'red, i will 2.01.125 P
the king, my lord, and harry prince of wales 2.01.134
what's the news, my lord? 2.01.167 P
at /basingstoke, my lord. 2.01.169
i hope, my lord, all's well. 2.01.170 P
what is the news, my lord? 2.01.171 P
horse, | are march'd up to my lord of lancaster, 2.01.174
comes the king back from wales, my noble lord? 2.01.177 P
my lord! 2.01.180 P
i must wait upon my good lord here, i thank you, 2.01.184 P
this is the right fencing grace, my lord, tap 2.01.193 P
now the lord lighten thee! 2.01.194 P
'a calls me /e'en /now, my lord, through a red 2.02. 79 P
marry, my lord, althaea dreamt she was deliver'd 2.02. 89 P
well, my lord. 2.02. 99 P
my lord, i'll steep this letter in sack and make 2.02.135 P
yea, my lord. 2.02.145 P
at the old place, my lord, in eastcheap. 2.02.148 P
ephesians, my lord, of the old church. 2.02.150 P
none, my lord, but old mistress quickly and 2.02.152 P
i am your shadow, my lord, i'll follow you. 2.02.159 P
o, the lord preserve thy grace! 2.04.291 P
now, the lord bless that sweet face of thine! 2.04.292 P
my lord, he will drive you out of your revenge 2.04.297 P
my lord northumberland will soon be cool'd. 3.01. 44
it cannot be, my lord. 3.01. 96
upon my soul, my lord, | the powers that you 3.01. 99
o lord, good my lord captain — 3.02.177 P
o lord, good my lord captain — 3.02.177 P
o lord, sir, i am a diseas'd man. 3.02.179 P
sir john, the lord bless you! 3.02.292 P
lord, lord, how subject we old men are to this 3.02.303 P
lord, lord, how subject we old men are to this 3.02.303 P
i think it is my lord of westmerland. 4.01. 26
the prince, lord john and duke of lancaster. 4.01. 28
say on, my lord of westmerland, in peace, | what 4.01. 29
then, my lord, | unto your grace do i in chief 4.01. 30
you, lord archbishop, | whose see is by a civil 4.01. 41
then take, my lord of westmerland, this schedule 4.01.166
my lord, we will do so. 4.01.180
no, no, my lord, note this: 4.01.195
and therefore be assur'd, my good lord marshal, 4.01.218
here is return'd my lord of westmerland. 4.01.222
my lord, we come. 4.01.226
good day to you, gentle lord archbishop, | and 4.02. 2
and so to you, lord hastings, and to all. 4.02. 3
my lord of york, it better show'd with you 4.02. 4
with you, lord bishop, | it is even so. 4.02. 15
good my lord of lancaster, | i am not here 4.02. 30
peace, | but, as i told my lord of westmerland, 4.02. 32
my lord, these griefs shall be with speed 4.02. 59
to you, my noble lord of westmerland. 4.02. 72
health to my lord, and gentle cousin, mowbray. 4.02. 78
go, my lord, | and let our army be discharged 4.02. 91
and, good my lord, so please you, let our trains 4.02. 93
go, good lord hastings, | and, ere they be 4.02. 95
my lord, our army is dispers'd already: 4.02.102
good tidings, my lord hastings! 4.02.106
and you, lord archbishop, and you, lord mowbray, 4.02.108
and you, lord archbishop, and you, lord mowbray, 4.02.108
i would be sorry, my lord, but it should be thus 4.03. 30 P
or, by the lord, i will have it in a particular 4.03. 47 P
let it do something, my good lord, that may do 4.03. 59 P
it is, my lord. 4.03. 62
i am, my lord, but as my betters are | that led 4.03. 65
my lord, i beseech you give me leave to go 4.03. 81 P
court, stand my good lord in your good report. 4.03. 83 P
i think he's gone to hunt, my lord, at windsor. 4.04. 14
i do not know, my lord. 4.04. 15
no, my good lord, he is in presence here. 4.04. 17
what would my lord and father? 4.04. 18
my gracious lord, you look beyond him quite: 4.04. 67
the earl northumberland and the lord bardolph, 4.04. 97
my sovereign lord, cheer up yourself, look up. 4.04.113
my gracious lord! 4.05. 34
find him, my lord of warwick, chide him hither. 4.05. 62
my lord, i found the prince in the next room, 4.05. 82
where is my lord of warwick? 4.05.231
my lord of warwick! 4.05.231
'tis call'd jerusalem, my noble lord. 4.05.234
how now, my lord chief justice, whither away? 5.02. 1
o, good my lord, you have lost a friend indeed, 5.02. 27
master shallow, my lord shallow — be what thou 5.03.130 P
my friends, and woe to my lord chief justice! 5.03.138 P
o the lord, that sir john were come! 5.04. 11 P
my lord chief justice, speak to that vain man. 5.05. 44
be it your charge, my lord, | to see perform'd 5.05. 70
my lord, my lord — 5.05. 93 P
my lord, my lord — 5.05. 93 P
the king hath call'd his parliament, my lord. 5.05.103
my lord, i'll tell you, that self bill is urg'd H5 1.01. 1
but how, my lord, shall we resist it now? 1.01. 6
but, my good lord, | how now for mitigation of 1.01. 69
how did this offer seem receiv'd, my lord? 1.01. 82
where is my gracious lord of canterbury? 1.02. 1
my learned lord, we pray you to proceed, | and 1.02. 9
and god forbid, my dear and faithful lord, 1.02. 13
under this conjuration speak, my lord; 1.02. 29
gracious lord, | stand for your own, unwind your 1.02.100
go, my dread lord, to your great–grandsire's 1.02.103
henry lord scroop of masham, and the third, 2.pr. 24
my lord of cambridge, and my kind lord of masham 2.02. 13
lord of cambridge, and my kind lord of masham, 2.02. 13
i one, my lord. 2.02. 62
there yours, lord scroop of masham; 2.02. 67
my lord of westmerland, and uncle exeter, | we 2.02. 70
my lord of cambridge here, | you know how apt 2.02. 85
o, | what shall i say to thee, lord scroop, thou 2.02. 94
by the name of /henry lord scroop of masham. 2.02.148 P
well, 'tis not so, my lord high constable; 2.04. 41
and bids you, in the bowels of the lord, 2.04.102
and if he be not fought withal, my lord, | let 3.05. 2
therefore, lord constable, haste on montjoy, 3.05. 61
now forth, lord constable and princes all, | and 3.05. 67
my lord of orleance, and my lord high constable, 3.07. 7 P
my lord of orleance, and my lord high constable, 3.07. 7 P
indeed, my lord, it is a most absolute and 3.07. 25 P
my lord constable, the armor that i saw in your 3.07. 69 P
stars, my lord. 3.07. 71 P
my lord high constable, the english lie within 3.07.125 P
the lord grandpre. 3.07.128 P
the lord in heaven bless thee, noble harry! 4.01. 33
my lord, your nobles, jealous of your absence, 4.01.285
i shall do't, my lord. 4.01.288
not to–day, o lord, | o, not to–day, think not 4.01.292
now, my lord constable? 4.02. 7
then, joyfully, my noble lord of bedford, | my 4.03. 8
my dear lord gloucester, and my good lord exeter 4.03. 9
dear lord gloucester, and my good lord exeter, 4.03. 9
farewell, kind lord; 4.03. 12
my sovereign lord, bestow yourself with speed. 4.03. 68
my lord, most humbly on my knee i beg | the 4.03.130
and, with a feeble gripe, says, "dear my lord, 4.06. 22
my lord of warwick, and my brother gloucester, 4.07.170
my lord of warwick, here is — praised be god 4.08. 20 P
all offenses, my lord, come from the heart. 4.08. 46 P
john duke of bourbon, and lord bouciqualt: 4.08. 77
the master of the cross–bows, lord rambures, 4.08. 94
but for thy love, by the lord, no; 5.02.152 P
it were, my lord, a hard condition for a maid to 5.02.298 P
they are then excus'd, my lord, when they see 5.02.302 P
then, good my lord, teach your cousin to consent 5.02.304 P
i will wink on her to consent, my lord, if you 5.02.306 P
as love is, my lord, before it loves. 5.02.315 P
yes, my lord, you see them perspectively: 5.02.320 P
my lord of burgundy, we'll take your oath, | and 5.02.371
and of it left his son imperial lord. ep 8
the battles of the lord of hosts he fought; 1H6 1.01. 31
betwixt the stout lord talbot and the french. 1.01.106
wherein lord talbot was o'erthrown. 1.01.108
the tenth of august last this dreadful lord, 1.01.110
and lord scales with him, and lord hungerford. 1.01.146
and lord scales with him, and lord hungerford. 1.01.146
my lord, methinks, is very long in talk. 1.02.118
my lord, where are you? 1.02.124
villains, answer you so the lord protector? 1.03. 8
the lord protect him! 1.03. 9
open the gates unto the lord protector, | or 1.03. 27
thou that contrivedst to murther our dead lord, 1.03. 34
call'd the brave lord ponton de santrailles, 1.04. 28
o lord, have mercy on us, wretched sinners! 1.04. 70
o lord, have mercy on me, woeful man! 1.04. 71
my lord, my lord, the french have gather'd head. 1.04.100
my lord, my lord, the french have gather'd head. 1.04.100
lord regent, and redoubted burgundy, | by whose 2.01. 8
and so was mine, my lord. 2.01. 66
'tis thought, lord talbot, when the fight began, 2.02. 22
by me entreats, great lord, thou wouldst 2.02. 40
you may not, my lord, despise her gentle suit. 2.02. 47
i do, my lord, and mean accordingly. 2.02. 60
by message crav'd, so is lord talbot come. 2.03. 13
stay, my lord talbot, for my lady craves | to 2.03. 29
to me, blood–thirsty lord; 2.03. 34
judge you, my lord of warwick, then between us. 2.04. 10
if i, my lord, for my opinion bleed, | opinion 2.04. 52
richard plantagenet, my lord, will come. 2.05. 18
my lord, your loving nephew now is come. 2.05. 33
of which, my lord, your honor is the last. 2.05. 93
my lord, it were your duty to forbear. 3.01. 52
methinks my lord should be religious, | and know 3.01. 54
my lord, we know your grace to be a man | just 3.01. 94
can you, my lord of winchester, behold | my 3.01.107
yield, my lord protector, yield, winchester, 3.01.112
behold, my lord of winchester, the duke | hath 3.01.122
for shame, my lord of winchester, relent! 3.01.132
well urg'd, my lord of warwick; 3.01.151
god buy, my lord, we came but to tell you | that 3.02. 73
come, my lord, | we will bestow you in some 3.02. 87
lord talbot, do not so dishonor me: 3.02. 90
what? will you fly, and leave lord talbot? 3.02.107
what wills lord talbot pleaseth burgundy. 3.02.130
ill, | who then but english henry will be lord, 3.03. 66
return, thou wandering lord! 3.03. 76
is this the lord talbot, uncle gloucester, 3.04. 13
welcome, brave captain and victorious lord! 3.04. 16
that i wear | in honor of my noble lord of york, 3.04. 30
tongue | against my lord the duke of somerset. 3.04. 34
sirrah, thy lord i honor as he is. 3.04. 35
lord bishop, set the crown upon his head. 4.01. 1
and now, lord protector, view the letter | sent 4.01. 48
he doth, my lord, and is become your foe. 4.01. 65
it is the worst, and all, my lord, he writes. 4.01. 67
why then lord talbot there shall talk with him, 4.01. 68
how say you, my lord? 4.01. 70
i go, my lord, in heart desiring still | you may 4.01. 76
and me, my lord, grant me the combat too. 4.01. 79
with him, my lord, for he hath done me wrong. 4.01. 85
and that is my petition, noble lord. 4.01.101
yet know, my lord, i was provok'd by him, | and 4.01.104
your private grudge, my lord of york, will out, 4.01.109
good lord, what madness rules in brain–sick men, 4.01.111

confirm it so, mine honorable lord. 4.01.122
and, good my lord of somerset, unite | your 4.01.164
ourself, my lord protector, and the rest, 4.01.169
my lord of york, i promise you, the king 4.01.174
they are return'd, my lord, and give it out 4.03. 3
o, send some succor to the distress'd lord! 4.03. 30
whither, my lord? 4.04. 13
from bought and sold lord talbot, | who, ring'd 4.04. 13
o my dear lord, lo where your son is borne! 4.07. 17
valiant lord talbot, earl of shrewsbury, 4.07. 61
lord talbot of goodrig and urchinfield, | lord 4.07. 64
lord strange of blackmere, lord verdon of alton, 4.07. 65
lord strange of blackmere, lord verdon of alton, 4.07. 65
lord cromwell of wingfield, lord furnival of 4.07. 66
of wingfield, lord furnival of sheffield, | the 4.07. 66
the thrice-victorious lord of falconbridge, 4.07. 67
i have, my lord, and their intent is this: 5.01. 3
well, my good lord, and as the only means | to 5.01. 8
beside, my lord, the sooner to effect | and 5.01. 15
what, is my lord of winchester install'd, | and 5.01. 28
which by my lord of winchester we mean | shall 5.01. 39
and for the proffer of my lord your master, | i 5.01. 41
and so, my lord protector, see them guarded 5.01. 48
stay, my lord legate, you shall first receive 5.01. 51
now he is gone, my lord, you need not fear. 5.02. 17
yes, there is remedy enough, my lord. 5.03.135
worth | to be the princely bride of such a lord, 5.03.152
farewell, my lord! 5.03.173
yes, my good lord, a pure unspotted heart, 5.03.182
lord regent, i do greet your excellence | with 5.04. 94
no, lord ambassador, i'll rather keep | that 5.04.144
my lord, you do not well in obstinacy | to cavil 5.04.155
tush, my good lord, this superficial tale | is 5.05. 10
intents, | to love and honor henry as her lord. 5.05. 21
therefore, my lord protector, give consent 5.05. 23
you know, my lord, your highness is betroth'd 5.05. 26
yes, my lord, her father is a king, | the king 5.05. 39
my noble lord of suffolk, or for that | my 5.05. 80
therefore shipping, post, my lord, to france, 5.05. 87
2H6 o lord, that lends me life, | lend me a heart 1.01. 19
great king of england, and my gracious lord, 1.01. 24
my lord protector, so it please your grace, 1.01. 39
pardon me, gracious lord, | some sudden qualm 1.01. 53
lord marquess, kneel down. 1.01. 63
my lord of gloucester, now ye grow too hot: 1.01.137
it was the pleasure of my lord the king. 1.01.138
my lord of winchester, i know your mind. 1.01.139
as stout and proud as he were lord of all, 1.01.187
why droops my lord, like over-ripen'd corn 1.02. 1
o nell, sweet nell, if thou dost love thy lord, 1.02. 17
what dream'd my lord? 1.02. 23
what, what, my lord? 1.02. 51
my lord protector, 'tis his highness' pleasure 1.02. 56
yes, my good lord, i'll follow presently. 1.02. 60
my lord protector will come this way by and by, 1.03. 1 P
marry, the lord protect him, for he's a good man 1.03. 4 P
the duke of suffolk and not my lord protector. 1.03. 9 P
i pray, my lord, pardon me, i took ye for my 1.03. 11 P
pardon me, i took ye for my lord protector. 1.03. 12 P
"to my lord protector"? 1.03. 13 P
against john goodman, my lord cardinal's man, 1.03. 17 P
my lord of suffolk, say, is this the guise, | is 1.03. 42
as that proud dame, the lord protector's wife: 1.03. 76
lord cardinal, i will follow eleanor, | and 1.03.148
my lord of somerset will keep me here | without 1.03.168
as we were scouring my lord of york's armor. 1.03.192 P
alas, my lord, hang me if ever i spake the words 1.03.197 P
this doom, my lord, if i may judge: 1.03.204
alas, my lord, i cannot fight; 1.03.213 P
o lord, have mercy upon me! 1.03.215 P
o lord, my heart! 1.03.216 P
my lord protector will, i doubt it not, | see 1.04. 45
lord buckingham, methinks you watch'd her well. 1.04. 55
now pray, my lord, let's see the devil's writ. 1.04. 57
a sorry breakfast for my lord protector. 1.04. 75
your grace shall give me leave, my lord of york, 1.04. 76
at your pleasure, my good lord. 1.04. 78
but what a point, my lord, your falcon made, 2.01. 5
my lord protector's hawks do tow'r so well; 2.01. 10
my lord, 'tis but a base ignoble mind | that 2.01. 13
ay, my lord cardinal, how think you by that? 2.01. 16
as who, my lord? 2.01. 29
why, as you, my lord, | an't like your lordly 2.01. 29
nothing else, my lord. 2.01. 49
that we for thee may glorify the lord. 2.01. 73
but still remember what the lord hath done. 2.01. 84
yes, my lord, if it please your grace. 2.01.135
i will, my lord. 2.01.147 P
you made in a day, my lord, whole towns to fly. 2.01.160
and so, my lord protector, by this means | your 2.01.174
'tis like, my lord, you will not keep your hour. 2.01.177
my lord, i long to hear it at full. 2.02. 6
my lord, break we off; 2.02. 77
ay, good my lord; 2.03. 52
o lord bless me, i pray god, for i am never able 2.03. 76 P
ten, my lord. 2.04. 5
come you, my lord, to see my open shame? 2.04. 19
what, gone, my lord, and bid me not farewell? 2.04. 85
i muse my lord of gloucester is not come; 3.01. 1
the reverent care i bear unto my lord | made me 3.01. 34
my lord of suffolk, buckingham, and york, 3.01. 39
take heed, my lord, the welfare of us all 3.01. 80
welcome, lord somerset. what news from france? 3.01. 83
cold news, lord somerset; 3.01. 86
all happiness unto my lord the king! 3.01. 93
'tis thought, my lord, that you took bribes of 3.01.104
it serves you well, my lord, to say so much. 3.01.119
my lord, these faults are easy, quickly answer'd 3.01.133
and here commit you to my lord cardinal | to 3.01.137
my lord of gloucester, 'tis my special hope 3.01.139
ah, gracious lord, these days are dangerous: 3.01.142
lord cardinal, he is your prisoner. 3.01.187
henry my lord is cold in great affairs, | too 3.01.224
but, my lord cardinal, and you, my lord of 3.01.246
my lord cardinal, and you, my lord of suffolk, 3.01.246
but i would have him dead, my lord of suffolk, 3.01.273
my lord of york, try what your fortune is. 3.01.309
i will, my lord, so please his majesty. 3.01.315
a charge, lord york, that i will see perform'd. 3.01.321
lord suffolk, you and i must talk of that event. 3.01.326
my lord of suffolk, within fourteen days | at 3.01.327
i'll see it truly done, my lord of york. 3.01.330
run to my lord of suffolk; 3.02. 1
here comes my lord. 3.02. 5
ay, my good lord, he's dead. 3.02. 7
'tis, my good lord. 3.02. 13
i'll call him presently, my noble lord. 3.02. 18
dead in his bed, my lord; gloucester is dead. 3.02. 29
how fares my lord? 3.02. 33
how fares my gracious lord? 3.02. 37
what, doth my lord of suffolk comfort me? 3.02. 39
why do you rate my lord of suffolk thus? 3.02. 56
what instance gives lord warwick for his vow? 3.02.159
say, if thou dar'st, proud lord of warwickshire, 3.02.201
blunt-witted lord, ignoble in demeanor! 3.02.210
if ever lady wrong'd her lord so much, | thy 3.02.211
dread lord, the commons send you word by me, 3.02.243
unless lord suffolk straight be done to death, 3.02.244
an answer from the king, my lord of salisbury! 3.02.270
but you, my lord, were glad to be employ'd, | to 3.02.273
that he was the lord embassador | sent from a 3.02.276
how fares my lord? 3.03. 1
lord card'nal, if thou think'st on heaven's 3.03. 27
lord! 4.01. 70
for daring to affy a mighty lord | unto the 4.01. 80
normans thorough thee | disdain to call us lord, 4.01. 88
my gracious lord, entreat him, speak him fair. 4.01.120
agree like brothers, and worship me their lord. 4.02. 75 P
we'll have the lord say's head for selling the 4.02.160 P
i tell you that that lord say hath gelded the 4.02.165 P
we will not leave one lord, one gentleman; 4.02.184
lord say, jack cade hath sworn to have thy head. 4.04. 19
fly, my lord! 4.04. 27
jack cade proclaims himself lord mortimer, 4.04. 28
my gracious lord, retire to killingworth, 4.04. 39
lord say, the traitors hateth thee, | therefore 4.04. 43
then linger not, my lord, away, take horse. 4.04. 54
farewell, my lord, trust not the kentish rebels. 4.04. 57
no, my lord, nor likely to be slain; 4.05. 2 P
the lord mayor craves aid of your honor from the 4.05. 4 P
now is mortimer lord of this city. 4.06. 1 P
for any that calls me other than lord mortimer. 4.06. 6 P
my lord, there's an army gather'd together in 4.06. 11 P
my lord, a prize, a prize! 4.07. 20 P
here's the lord say, which sold the towns in 4.07. 20 P
thou say, thou serge, nay, thou buckram lord! 4.07. 25 P
even the presence of lord mortimer, that i am 4.07. 30 P
my lord, when shall we go to cheapside and take 4.07.126 P
he is fled, my lord, and all his powers do yield 4.09. 10
my lord, | i'll yield myself to prison willingly 4.09. 41
i will, my lord, and doubt not so to deal | as 4.09. 46
lord, who would live turmoiled in the court 4.10. 16
here's the lord of the soil come to seize me for 4.10. 24 P
so please it you, my lord, 'twere not amiss | he 5.01. 76
health and all happiness to my lord the king! 5.01.124
if you oppose yourselves to match lord warwick. 5.01.156
my lord, i have considered with myself | the 5.01.175
proud northern lord, clifford of cumberland, 5.02. 6
how now, my noble lord? 5.02. 8
away, my lord! you are slow, for shame, away! 5.02. 72
away, my lord, away! 5.02. 90
what says lord warwick? 5.03. 27
3H6 whereat the great lord of northumberland, 1.01. 4
lord clifford, and lord stafford, all abreast, 1.01. 7
lord clifford, and lord stafford, all abreast, 1.01. 7
lord stafford's father, duke of buckingham, | is 1.01. 10
but is your grace dead, my lord of somerset? 1.01. 18
and thine, lord clifford, and you both have 1.01. 55
my gracious lord, here in the parliament | let 1.01. 64
and that the lord of westmerland shall maintain. 1.01. 88
the lord protector lost it, and not i; 1.01.111
lord clifford vows to fight in thy defense. 1.01.160
my lord of warwick, hear but one word: 1.01.170
why should you sigh, my lord? 1.01.191
not for myself, lord warwick, but my son, | whom 1.01.192
farewell, my gracious lord, i'll to my castle. 1.01.206
warwick is chancellor and the lord of callice, 1.01.238
your oath, my lord, is vain and frivolous. 1.02. 27
you, edward, shall unto my lord cobham, | with 1.02. 40
and therefore fortify your hold, my lord. 1.02. 52
and i, my lord, will bear him company. 1.03. 6
what, weeping-ripe, my lord northumberland? 1.04.172
your princely father and my loving lord! 2.01. 47
great lord of warwick, if we should recompt 2.01. 96
o valiant lord, the duke of york is slain! 2.01.100
is by the stern lord clifford done to death. 2.01.103
lord george your brother, norfolk, and myself, 2.01.138
i know it well, lord warwick, blame me not. 2.01.157
lord warwick, on thy shoulder will i lean, | and 2.01.189
welcome, my lord, to this brave town of york. 2.02. 1
doth not the object cheer your heart, my lord? 2.02. 4
my lord, cheer up your spirits, our foes are 2.02. 56
ay, good my lord, and leave us to our fortune. 2.02. 75
how now, my lord, what hap? what hope of good? 2.03. 8
mount you, my lord, towards berwick post amain. 2.05.128
to effect this marriage, so it please my lord. 2.06. 98
right gracious lord, i cannot brook delay. 3.02. 18
three, my most gracious lord. 3.02. 29
be pitiful, dread lord, and grant it then. 3.02. 32
no, gracious lord, except i cannot do it. 3.02. 47
why stops my lord? shall i not hear my task? 3.02. 52
but, mighty lord, this merry inclination 3.02. 76
then no, my lord. my suit is at an end. 3.02. 81
'tis better said than done, my gracious lord. 3.02. 90
to who, my lord? 3.02.112
my gracious lord, henry your foe is taken, | and 3.02.118
my lord and sovereign and thy vowed friend, | i 3.03. 50
doom | my elder brother, the lord aubrey vere, 3.03.102
my lord ambassador, these letters are for you, 3.03.163
and thou, lord bourbon, our high admiral, 3.03.252
for this one speech lord hastings well deserves 4.01. 47
to have the heir of the lord hungerford. 4.01. 48
to give the heir and daughter of lord scales 4.01. 52
of the lord bonville on your new wive's son, 4.01. 57
trust me, my lord, all hitherto goes well, | the 4.02. 1
fear not that, my lord. 4.02. 5
'tis the lord hastings, the king's chiefest 4.03. 11
my lord of somerset, at my request, | see that 4.03. 51
now, my lord hastings and sir william stanley, 4.05. 1
this way, my lord, for this way lies the game. 4.05. 14
brother of gloucester, lord hastings, and the 4.05. 16
to lynn, my lord — | and shipp'd from thence to 4.05. 20
my lord of somerset, what youth is that | of 4.06. 65
and the lord hastings, who attended him | in 4.06. 82
my lord, i like not of this flight of edward's; 4.06. 89
therefore, lord oxford, to prevent the worst, 4.06. 96
brother richard, lord hastings, and the rest, 4.07. 1
true, my good lord, i know you for no less. 4.07. 22
king of england and france, and lord of ireland, 4.07. 72 P
comfort, my lord! and so i take my leave. 4.08. 28
hark, hark, my lord, what shouts are these? 4.08. 51
how far hence is thy lord, mine honest fellow? 5.01. 2
it is not his, my lord, here southam lies; 5.01. 12
good day, my lord. what, at your book so hard? 5.06. 1
ay, my good lord — my lord, i should say rather 5.06. 2
my good lord — my lord, i should say rather. 5.06. 2
therefore, not "good lord." 5.06. 5
R3 alack, my lord, that fault is none of yours; 1.01. 47
that made him send lord hastings to the tower, 1.01. 68
lord hastings was /to /her /for /his delivery? 1.01. 75
her deity | got my lord chamberlain his liberty. 1.01. 77
with this, my lord, myself have nought to do. 1.01. 97
what one, my lord? 1.01.101
good time of day unto my gracious lord! 1.01.122
as much unto my good lord chamberlain! 1.01.123
with patience, noble lord, as prisoners must; 1.01.126
but i shall live, my lord, to give them thanks 1.01.127
him | than i am made by my young lord and thee! 1.02. 28
my lord, stand back, and let the coffin pass. 1.02. 38
towards chertsey, noble lord? 1.02.225
edward, her lord, whom i, some three months 1.02.240
no other harm but loss of such a lord. 1.03. 7
the loss of such a lord includes all harms. 1.03. 8
the countess richmond, good my lord of derby, 1.03. 20
be you, good lord, assur'd | i hate not you for 1.03. 23
saw you the king to-day, my lord of derby? 1.03. 30
and between them and my lord chamberlain, | and 1.03. 38
my lord, you do me shameful injury | falsely to 1.03. 87
mean | of my lord hastings' late imprisonment. 1.03. 90
she may, my lord, for — 1.03. 91
she may, lord rivers! 1.03. 92
my lord of gloucester, i have too long borne 1.03.102
and for his meed, poor lord, he is mewed up. 1.03.138
my lord of gloucester, in those busy days, 1.03.144
we follow'd then our lord, our sovereign king. 1.03.146
as little joy, my lord, as you suppose | you 1.03.150
and so wast thou, lord hastings, when my son 1.03.210
it touches you, my lord, as much as me. 1.03.261
what doth she say, my lord of buckingham? 1.03.294
nothing that i respect, my gracious lord. 1.03.295
and for your grace, and yours, my gracious lord. 1.03.320
we are, my lord, and come to have the warrant, 1.03.341
tut, tut, my lord, we will not stand to prate; 1.03.349
we will, my noble lord. 1.03.354
what was your dream, my lord? 1.04. 8
o lord, methought what pain it was to drown! 1.04. 21
no marvel, lord, though it affrighted you; 1.04. 64
i will, my lord. god give your grace good rest! 1.04. 75
you shall have wine enough, my lord, anon. 1.04.162
never, my lord, therefore prepare to die. 1.04.180
make peace with god, for you must die, my lord. 1.04.249
look behind you, my lord. 1.04.268
wife, love lord hastings, let him kiss your hand 2.01. 21
hastings, love lord marquess. 2.01. 25
a blessed labor, my most sovereign lord. 2.01. 53
of you, and you, lord rivers, and of dorset, 2.01. 67
my sovereign lord, i do beseech your highness 2.01. 76
look i so pale, lord dorset, as the rest? 2.01. 84
ay, my good lord, and no man in the presence 2.01. 85
edward, my lord, thy son, our king, is dead! 2.02. 40
ah for my husband, for my dear lord edward! 2.02. 71
ah for our father, for our dear lord clarence! 2.02. 72
with some little train, my lord of buckingham? 2.02.123
marry, my lord, lest by a multitude | the 2.02.124
my lord, whoever journeys to the prince, | for 2.02.146
such news, my lord, as grieves me to report. 2.04. 39
lord rivers and lord grey are sent to pomfret, 2.04. 42
lord rivers and lord grey are sent to pomfret, 2.04. 42
is all unknown to me, my gracious lord. 2.04. 48
my lord, the mayor of london comes to greet you. 3.01. 17
i thank you, good my lord, and thank you all. 3.01. 19
and in good time, here comes the sweating lord. 3.01. 24
welcome, my lord. what, will our mother come? 3.01. 25
lord cardinal, will your grace | persuade the 3.01. 32
if she deny, lord hastings, go with him, | and 3.01. 35
my lord of buckingham, if my weak oratory | can 3.01. 37
you are too senseless-obstinate, my lord, | too 3.01. 44
my lord, you shall overrule my mind for once. 3.01. 57
come on, lord hastings, will you go with me? 3.01. 58
i go, my lord. 3.01. 59
did julius caesar build that place, my lord? 3.01. 69
he did, my gracious lord, begin that place, 3.01. 70
upon record, my gracious lord. 3.01. 74
but say, my lord, it were not regist'red, 3.01. 75
what, my gracious lord? 3.01. 90
well, my dread lord — so must i call you now. 3.01. 97
how fares our cousin, noble lord of york? 3.01.101
o my lord, | you said that idle weeds are fast 3.01.102
he hath, my lord. 3.01.105
what, would you have my weapon, little lord? 3.01.122
my lord of york will still be cross in talk. 3.01.126
my lord, will't please you pass along? 3.01.136
what, will you go unto the tower, my lord? 3.01.140
my lord protector needs will have it so. 3.01.141
but come, my lord; 3.01.149
think you, my lord, this little prating york 3.01.151
to make william lord hastings of our mind | for 3.01.162
sound thou lord hastings | how he doth stand 3.01.170
commend me to lord william. 3.01.181
and bid my lord, for joy of this good news, 3.01.184
you shall, my lord. 3.01.189
now, my lord, what shall we do if we perceive 3.01.191
lord hastings will not yield to our complots? 3.01.192
my lord! my lord! 3.02. 1

my lord! my lord! 3.02. 1
one from the lord stanley. 3.02. 3
cannot my lord stanley sleep these tedious 3.02. 6
go, fellow, go, return unto thy lord, | bid him 3.02. 19
i'll go, my lord, and tell him what you say. 3.02. 34
many good morrows to my noble lord! 3.02. 35
it is a reeling world indeed, my lord, | and i 3.02. 38
ay, my good lord. 3.02. 42
'tis a vile thing to die, my gracious lord, 3.02. 62
my lord, good morrow, good morrow, catesby. 3.02. 74
my lord, | i hold my life as dear as /you /do 3.02. 77
wot you what, my lord? 3.02. 90
but come, my lord, let's away. 3.02. 94
well met, my lord, i am glad to see your honor. 3.02.108
what, talking with a priest, lord chamberlain? 3.02.113
i do, my lord, but long i cannot stay there. 3.02.119
who knows the lord protector's mind herein? 3.04. 7
yours, | or i of his, my lord, than you of mine. 3.04. 12
lord hastings, you and he are near in love. 3.04. 13
had you not come upon your cue, my lord, 3.04. 26
william lord hastings had pronounc'd your part 3.04. 27
than my lord hastings no man might be bolder, 3.04. 29
my lord of ely, when i was last in holborn, | i 3.04. 31
marry, and will, my lord, with all my heart. 3.04. 34
where is my lord, the duke of gloucester? 3.04. 46
the tender love i bear your grace, my lord, 3.04. 63
i say, my lord, they have deserved death. 3.04. 66
if they have done this deed, my noble lord — 3.04. 73
lord mayor — 3.05. 14
lord mayor, the reason we have sent — 3.05. 18
to murther me and my good lord of gloucester? 3.05. 39
because, my lord, i would have had you heard 3.05. 56
but, my good lord, your grace's words shall 3.05. 62
and so, my good lord mayor, we bid farewell. 3.05. 71
because, my lord, you know my mother lives. 3.05. 94
doubt not, my lord, i'll play the orator | as if 3.05. 95
were for myself — and so, my lord, adieu. 3.05. 97
is the indictment of the good lord hastings, 3.06. 1
now, by the holy mother of our lord, | the 3.07. 2
and stand between two churchmen, good my lord — 3.07. 48
go, go up to the leads, the lord mayor knocks. 3.07. 55
welcome, my lord! 3.07. 56
now, catesby, what says your lord to my request? 3.07. 58
he doth entreat your grace, my noble lord, | to 3.07. 59
ah ha, my lord, this prince is not an edward! 3.07. 71
he fears, my lord, you mean no good to him. 3.07. 87
my lord, there needs no such apology. 3.07.104
you have, my lord. 3.07.114
my lord, this argues conscience in your grace, 3.07.174
then, good my lord, take to your royal self 3.07.195
do, good my lord, your citizens entreat you. 3.07.201
refuse not, mighty lord, this proffer'd love. 3.07.202
i mean the lord protector. 4.01. 18
the lord protect him from that kingly title! 4.01. 19
say on, my loving lord. 4.02. 11
why, so you are, my thrice-renowned lord. 4.02. 13
me some little breath, some pause, dear lord, 4.02. 24
my lord? 4.02. 33
his name, my lord, is tyrrel. 4.02. 40
how now, lord stanley, what's the news? 4.02. 46
know, my loving lord, | the marquess dorset, as 4.02. 47
prove me, my gracious lord. 4.02. 68
my lord, i have consider'd in my mind | the late 4.02. 83
i hear the news, my lord. 4.02. 86
my lord, i claim the gift, my due by promise, 4.02. 88
all health, my sovereign lord! 4.03. 23
i did, my lord. 4.03. 28
my lord — 4.03. 44
bad news, my lord. 4.03. 46
her father's brother | would be her lord? 4.04.338
here, my good lord. 4.04.442
i will, my lord, with all convenient haste. 4.04.443
no, my good lord, therefore mistrust me not. 4.04.478
no, my good lord, my friends are in the north. 4.04.483
my lord, the army of great buckingham — 4.04.506
such proclamation hath been made, my lord. 4.04.517
sir thomas lovel and lord marquess dorset, 4.04.518
commend me to thy lord. 4.05. 6
well, hie thee to thy lord; 4.05. 19
no, my good lord, therefore be patient. 5.01. 2
my lord of surrey, why look you so sad? 5.03. 2
my lord of norfolk — 5.03. 4
we must both give and take, my loving lord. 5.03. 6
my lord of oxford — you, sir william brandon — 5.03. 27
where is lord stanley quarter'd, do you know? 5.03. 34
upon my life, my lord, i'll undertake it, | and 5.03. 42
it's supper-time, my lord, | it's /nine a' clock 5.03. 47
i go, my lord. 5.03. 55
i warrant you, my lord. 5.03. 57
my lord? 5.03. 59
my lord? 5.03. 67
saw'st thou the melancholy lord northumberland? 5.03. 68
it is, my lord. 5.03. 76
think on lord hastings. 5.03.156
my lord! 5.03.207
ratcliffe, my lord, 'tis i. 5.03.209
no doubt, my lord. 5.03.214
nay, good my lord, be not afraid of shadows. 5.03.215
how have you slept, my lord? 5.03.226
not i, my lord. 5.03.277
my lord? 5.03.282
arm, arm, my lord, the foe vaunts in the field. 5.03.288
call up lord stanley, bid him bring his power. 5.03.290
what says lord stanley? 5.03.342
my lord, he doth deny to come. 5.03.343
my lord, the enemy is past the marsh, | after 5.03.345
rescue, my lord of norfolk, rescue, rescue! 5.04. 1
rescue, fair lord, or else the day is lost! 5.04. 6
withdraw, my lord, i'll help you to a horse. 5.04. 8
he is, my lord, and safe in leicester town, 5.05. 10
john duke of norfolk, walter lord /ferrers, 5.05. 13
abate the edge of traitors, gracious lord, 5.05. 35
i pray you, who, my lord? H8 1.01. 49
stay, my lord, | and let your reason with your 1.01.129
my lord the duke of buckingham and earl | of 1.01.199
lo you, my lord, | the net has fall'n upon me! 1.01.202
o my lord aburga'ny, fare you well! 1.01.211
from | the king t' attach lord montacute, and 1.01.217
my good lord cardinal, they vent reproaches 1.02. 23
my lord cardinal, | you that are blam'd for it 1.02. 38
no, my lord? 1.02. 43
lord aburga'ny, to whom by oath he menac'd 1.02.137
my learn'd lord cardinal, | deliver all with 1.02.142
i told my lord the duke, by th' devil's 1.02.178
death, my lord, | their clothes are after such a 1.03. 13
faith, my lord, | i hear of none but the new 1.03. 16
now | an honest country lord, as i am, beaten 1.03. 44
well said, lord sands, | your colt's tooth is 1.03. 47
no, my lord, | nor shall not while i have a 1.03. 48
he may, my lord, h'as wherewithal: 1.03. 59
o my lord, y' are tardy; 1.04. 7
my lord sands, you are one will keep 'em waking; 1.04. 23
well said, my lord. 1.04. 30
my lord sands, | i am beholding to you; 1.04. 40
first must rise | in their fair cheeks, my lord, 1.04. 44
you are a merry gamester, | my lord sands. 1.04. 46
good lord chamberlain, | go, give 'em welcome: 1.04. 56
say, lord chamberlain, | they have done my poor 1.04. 72
my lord! 1.04. 77
i will, my lord. 1.04. 81
you do well, lord. 1.04. 87
my lord chamberlain, | prithee come hither. 1.04. 90
yes, my lord. 1.04. 99
there's fresher air, my lord, | in the next 1.04.101
let's be merry, | good my lord cardinal: 1.04.105
hither, i was lord high constable | and duke of 2.01.102
he sent command to the lord mayor straight | to 2.01.151
"my lord, the horses your lordship sent for, 2.02. 1 P
set out for london, a man of my lord cardinal's, 2.02. 5 P
well met, my lord chamberlain. 2.02. 12
my lord, you'll bear us company? 2.02. 58
thanks, my good lord chamberlain. 2.02. 61
my good lord cardinal? 2.02. 73
my good lord, have great care | i be not found a 2.02. 77
you, my lord | cardinal of york, are join'd with 2.02.104
my lord of york, was not one doctor pace | in 2.02.121
spread then, | even of yourself, lord cardinal. 2.02.125
o my lord, | would it not grieve an able man to 2.02.140
my good lord, | not your demand; 2.03. 51
my honor'd lord. 2.03. 80
lord cardinal, | to you i speak. 2.04. 68
have blown this coal betwixt my lord and me — 2.04. 79
my lord, my lord, | i am a simple woman, much 2.04.105
my lord, my lord, | i am a simple woman, much 2.04.105
now the lord help, | they vex me past my 2.04.130
my lord cardinal, | i do excuse you; 2.04.156
i speak my good lord card'nal to this point, 2.04.167
wherein he might the king his lord advertise 2.04.179
began in private | with you, my lord of lincoln. 2.04.208
my lord of canterbury, and got your leave | to 2.04.219
o, good my lord, no latin; 3.01. 42
lord cardinal, | the willing'st sin i ever yet 3.01. 48
my lord of york, out of his noble nature, | zeal 3.01. 62
my lord, i dare not make myself so guilty | to 3.01.139
may you be happy in your wish, my lord, | for i 3.02. 43
the lord forbid! 3.02. 54
but, my lord, | when returns cranmer? 3.02. 62
sharp enough, | lord, for thy justice! 3.02. 93
my lord, we have | stood here observing him. 3.02.111
good my lord, | you are full of heavenly stuff, 3.02.136
the lord increase this business! 3.02.161
to asher-house, my lord of winchester's, | till 3.02.231
proud lord, thou liest! 3.02.252
else | this talking lord can lay upon my credit, 3.02.265
if i lov'd many words, lord, i should tell you 3.02.270
my lord of norfolk, as you are truly noble, | as 3.02.289
wench | lay kissing in your arms, lord cardinal. 3.02.296
those articles, my lord, are in the king's hand: 3.02.299
o my lord, | press not a falling man too far! 3.02.332
lord cardinal, the king's further pleasure is — 3.02.337
so fare you well, my little good lord cardinal. 3.02.349
more is chosen | lord chancellor in your place. 3.02.394
install'd lord archbishop of canterbury. 3.02.401
man, unworthy now | to be thy lord and master. 3.02.414
o my lord, | must i then leave you? 3.02.421
with what a sorrow cromwell leaves his lord. 3.02.425
and that my lord of norfolk? 4.01. 42
you should be lord ambassador from the emperor, 4.02.109
o my lord, | the times and titles now are 4.02.111
o my good lord, that comfort comes too late, 4.02.120
pray you to deliver | this to my lord the king. 4.02.130
these are the whole contents, and, good my lord, 4.02.154
i thank you, honest lord. 4.02.160
farewell, | my lord. 4.02.165
came you from the king, my lord? 5.01. 6
my lord, i love you; 5.01. 16
many good-nights, my lord! i rest your servant. 5.01. 55
sir, i have brought my lord the archbishop, | as 5.01. 80
ay, my good lord. 5.01. 82
how now, my lord? 5.01. 89
my good and gracious lord of canterbury. 5.01. 92
ah, my good lord, i grieve at what i speak, 5.01. 95
late | heard many grievous — i do say, my lord, 5.01. 98
my lord, i look'd | you would have given me your 5.01.117
yes, my lord; | but yet i cannot help you. 5.02. 4
there, my lord: 5.02. 22
my lord archbishop; 5.02. 40
my good lord archbishop, i'm very sorry | to sit 5.02. 43
nay, my lord, | that cannot be; 5.02. 83
my lord, because we have business of more moment 5.02. 86
ah, my good lord of winchester — i thank you, 5.02. 93
love and meekness, lord, | become a churchman 5.02. 97
my lord, my lord, you are a sectary, | that's 5.02.105
my lord, my lord, you are a sectary, | that's 5.02.105
my lord of winchester, y' are a little, | by 5.02.108
why, my lord? 5.02.114
then thus for you, my lord, it stands agreed, 5.02.122
my lord of canterbury, | i have a suit which you 5.02.194
come, come, my lord, you'd spare your spoons. 5.02.201
once more, my lord of winchester, i charge you, 5.02.204
thus, "do my lord of canterbury | a shrewd turn, 5.02.210
thank you, good lord archbishop. 5.04. 8
stand up, lord. 5.04. 9
o lord archbishop, | thou hast made me now a man 5.04. 63
to you, my good lord mayor, | and you, good 5.04. 69
is among the greeks | a lord of troyan blood, TRO 1.02. 13
sir, my lord would instantly speak with you. 1.02.272 P
strength should be lord of imbecility, | and the 1.03.114
this shall be told our lovers, lord aeneas. 1.03.284
fair lord aeneas, let me touch your hand; 1.03.304
so shall each lord of greece, from tent to tent. 1.03.307
greece upon thee, thou mongrel beef-witted lord! 2.01. 13 P
thou sodden-witted lord! 2.01. 43 P
you scurvy lord! 2.01. 51 P
this lord, achilles, ajax, who wears his wit in 2.01. 72 P
my lord achilles! 2.03. 22 P
thersites, my lord. 2.03. 39 P
thy lord, thersites. 2.03. 46 P
commands achilles, achilles is my lord, i am 2.03. 53 P
within his tent, but ill dispos'd, my lord. 2.03. 77
dear lord, go you and greet him in his tent. 2.03.179
shall the proud lord | that bastes his arrogance 2.03.184
this thrice worthy and right valiant lord 2.03.190
this lord go to him! 2.03.198
my lord, you feed too much on this dislike. 2.03.225
thank the heavens, lord, thou art of sweet 2.03.240
be rul'd by him, lord ajax. 2.03.257
and here's a lord — come knights from east to 2.03.263
do you not follow the young lord paris? 3.01. 2 P
sir, i do depend upon the lord. 3.01. 5 P
the lord be prais'd! 3.01. 8 P
friend, know me better, i am the lord pandarus. 3.01. 11 P
at the request of paris my lord, who is there in 3.01. 31 P
fair be to you, my lord, and to all this fair 3.01. 43 P
dear lord, you are full of fair words. 3.01. 47 P
well said, my lord! well, you say so in fits. 3.01. 57 P
i have business to my lord, dear queen. 3.01. 58 P
my lord, will you vouchsafe me a word? 3.01. 59 P
but, marry, thus, my lord: 3.01. 63 P
my dear lord and most esteem'd friend, your 3.01. 63 P
my lord pandarus, honey-sweet lord — 3.01. 65 P
my lord pandarus, honey-sweet lord — 3.01. 65 P
and, my lord, he desires you, that if the king 3.01. 76 P
my lord pandarus — 3.01. 78 P
nay, but, my lord — 3.01. 83 P
ay, good my lord. 3.01. 91 P
she shall have it, my lord, if it be not my lord 3.01. 99 P
have it, my lord, if it be not my lord paris. 3.01.100 P
sweet lord, who's a-field to-day? 3.01.133 P
you know all, lord pandarus. 3.01.140 P
will you walk in, my lord? 3.02. 60 P
wish'd, my lord? the gods grant — o my lord! 3.02. 62 P
wish'd, my lord? the gods grant — o my lord! 3.02. 63 P
will you walk in, my lord? 3.02. 99 P
if my lord get a boy of you, you'll give him me. 3.02.104 P
be true to my lord; 3.02.105 P
but i was won, my lord, | with the first glance 3.02.117
my lord, i do beseech you pardon me, | 'twas not 3.02.136
for this time will i take my leave, my lord. 3.02.139
perchance, my lord, i show more craft than love, 3.02.153
so do each lord, and either greet him not, | or 3.03. 52
would you, my lord, aught with the general? 3.03. 58
nothing, my lord. 3.03. 60
proves | that no man is the lord of any thing, 3.03.115
time hath, my lord, a wallet at his back, 3.03.145
perseverance, dear my lord, | keeps honor bright 3.03.150
troy | as perfectly is ours as yours, my lord, 3.03.206
farewell, my lord; 3.03.214
ay, my lord. 3.03.290 P
it is the lord aeneas. 4.01. 2
that's my mind too. good morrow, lord aeneas. 4.01. 7
what business, lord, so early? 4.01. 35
on, lord, we'll follow you. 4.01. 50
then, sweet my lord, i'll call mine uncle down, 4.02. 2
my lord, come you again into my chamber. 4.02. 36
good morrow, lord, good morrow. 4.02. 44
my lord aeneas! 4.02. 45
come, he is here, my lord, do not deny him. 4.02. 49
my lord, i scarce have leisure to salute you, 4.02. 59
and, my lord aeneas, | we met by chance, you did 4.02. 70
good, my lord, the secrets of neighbor pandar 4.02. 72
where's my lord? 4.02. 81 P
my lord, is the lady ready? 4.04. 49
you shall be expos'd, my lord, to dangers | as 4.04. 68
nay, good my lord! 4.04. 98
my lord, will you be true? 4.04.101
at the port, lord, i'll give her to thy hand, 4.04.111
i tell thee, lord of greece, | she is as far 4.04.123
i'll answer to my lust, and know you, lord, 4.04.132
as you and lord aeneas | consent upon the order 4.05. 89
thou art, great lord, my father's sister's son, 4.05.120
my well-fam'd lord of troy, no less to you. 4.05.173
o, you, my lord? 4.05.177
i know your favor, lord ulysses, well. 4.05.213
i shall forestall thee, lord ulysses, thou! 4.05.230
my lord ulysses, tell me, i beseech you, | in 4.05.277
shall i, sweet lord, be bound to you so much, 4.05.284
will you walk on, my lord? 4.05.291
good night, my lord. 5.01. 74
good night, sweet lord menelaus. 5.01. 74
i cannot, lord, i have important business, | the 5.01. 82
now, good my lord, go off; 5.02. 40
come, my lord. 5.02. 41
how now, my lord? 5.02. 46
you shake, my lord, at something; 5.02. 50
fear me not, my lord. 5.02. 62
my lord — 5.02. 67
all's done, my lord. 5.02.115
nor mine, my lord; cressid was here but now. 5.02.128
i have been seeking you this hour, my lord. 5.02.182
my courteous lord, adieu. 5.02.185
when was my lord so much ungently temper'd | to 5.03. 1
do you hear, my lord? do you hear? 5.03. 97 P
i go, my lord. 5.05. 5
the troyans' trumpet sound the like, my lord. 5.08. 16
my lord, you do discomfort all the host. 5.10. 10
heavens bless my lord from fell aufidius! COR 1.03. 45
the threshold till my lord return from the wars. 1.03. 75 P
your lord and titus lartius are set down before 1.03. 98 P
above an hour, my lord. 1.06. 15
i shall, my lord. 1.09. 78
gifts, am bound to beg | of my lord general. 1.09. 81
you into love, | standing your friendly lord. 2.03.190
he had, my lord, and that it was which caus'd 3.01. 2

they are worn, lord consul, so | that we shall 3.01. 6
he did, my lord. 3.01. 12
of those chances | which he was lord of; 4.07. 41
my lord and husband! 5.03. 37
so he did, my lord. 5.06. 40
see, lord and father, how we have perform'd TIT 1.01.142
in peace and honor live lord titus long! 1.01.157
my noble lord and father, live in fame! 1.01.158
long live lord titus, my beloved brother, 1.01.169
lord saturnine, whose virtues will, i hope, 1.01.225
create | lord saturninus rome's great emperor, 1.01.232
it doth, my worthy lord, and in this match | i 1.01.244
presents well worthy rome's imperious lord: 1.01.250
not i, my lord, sith true nobility | warrants 1.01.271
lord titus, by your leave, this maid is mine. 1.01.276
how, sir? are you in earnest then, my lord? 1.01.277
treason, my lord! 1.01.284
follow, my lord, and i'll soon bring her back. 1.01.289
my lord, you pass not here. 1.01.290
my lord, you are unjust, and more than so, | in 1.01.292
my lord, this is impiety in you. 1.01.355
my lord, to step out of these dreary dumps, 1.01.391
and you of yours, my lord! 1.01.401
rape call you it, my lord, to seize my own, | my 1.01.405
my lord, what i have done, as best i may, 1.01.411
rome, | this noble gentleman, lord titus here, 1.01.415
my worthy lord, if ever tamora | were gracious 1.01.428
not so, my lord, the gods of rome forfend | i 1.01.434
for good lord titus' innocence in all, | whose 1.01.437
my lord, be rul'd by me, be won at last, 1.01.442
i thank your majesty, and her, my lord. 1.01.460
and let it be mine honor, good my lord, | that i 1.01.466
i have dogs, my lord, | will rouse the proudest 2.02. 20
great reason that my noble lord be rated | for 2.03. 81
lord bassianus lies /beray'd in blood, | all on 2.03.222
where is my lord the king? 2.03.259
my gracious lord, here is the bag of gold. 2.03.280
i did, my lord, yet let me be their bail, | for 2.03.295
my gracious lord, no tribune hears you speak. 3.01. 32
my lord the emperor | sends thee this word — 3.01.150
my lord, i know not, i, nor can i guess, 4.01. 16
although, my lord, i know my noble aunt | loves 4.01. 22
what roman lord it was durst do the deed; 4.01. 62
my lord, look here; 4.01. 68
o, do ye read, my lord, what she hath writ? 4.01. 77
calm thee, gentle lord, although i know | there 4.01. 83
my lord, kneel down with me, lavinia, kneel, 4.01. 87
lord junius brutus sware for lucrece' rape, 4.01. 91
i say, my lord, that if i were a man, | their 4.01.107
but me more good to see so great a lord | basely 4.02. 37
had he not reason, lord demetrius? 4.02. 39
o lord, sir, 'tis a deed of policy. 4.02.148
no, my good lord, but pluto sends you word, | if 4.03. 38
my lord, i /aim'd a mile beyond the moon, | your 4.03. 66
this was the sport, my lord. 4.03. 71
my gracious lord, my lovely saturnine, | lord of 4.04. 27
lord of my life, commander of my thoughts, 4.04. 28
my lord, there is a messenger from rome 5.01.152
lord lucius, and you princes of the goths, | the 5.01.156
good lord, how like the empress' sons they are! 5.02. 64
whiles i go tell my lord the emperor | how i 5.02.138
welcome, my lord; 5.03. 26
my lord the emperor, resolve me this: 5.03. 35
your reason, mighty lord? 5.03. 40
o lord, i cannot speak to him for weeping, | my 5.03.174
but now, my lord, what say you to my suit? ROM 1.02. 6
my lord and you were then at mantua — | nay, i 1.03. 28
and follow thee my lord throughout the world. 2.02.148
lord, lord, she will be a joyful woman. 2.04.174 P
lord, lord, she will be a joyful woman. 2.04.174 P
my mistress is the sweetest lady — lord, lord! 2.04.200 P
my mistress is the sweetest lady — lord, lord! 2.04.200 P
good sweet nurse — o lord, why lookest thou sad 2.05. 21
lord, how my head aches! 2.05. 48
my dearest cousin, and my dearer lord? 3.02. 66
ah, poor my lord, what tongue shall smooth thy 3.02. 98
o tell me, holy friar, | where's my lady's lord? 3.03. 82
o lord, i could have stay'd here all the night 3.03.159
my lord, i'll tell my lady you will come. 3.03.161
monday, my lord. 3.04. 18
my lord, i would that thursday were to–morrow. 3.04. 29
farewell, my lord. 3.04. 33
art thou gone so, love — lord, ay, husband, 3.05. 43
i pray you tell my lord and father, madam, | i 3.05.120
you are to blame, my lord, to rate her so. 3.05.169
or to dispraise my lord with that same tongue 3.05.237
my lord, we must entreat the time alone. 4.01. 40
speed | to mantua, with my letters to thy lord. 4.01.124
i met the youthful lord at lawrence' cell, | and 4.02. 25
my lord! 4.05. 16
for shame, bring juliet forth, her lord is come. 4.05. 22
my bosom's lord sits lightly in his throne, 5.01. 3
no, my good lord. 5.01. 32
see thou deliver it to my lord and father. 5.03. 24
o lord, they fight! i will go call the watch. 5.03. 71
where is my lord? 5.03.148
o, 'tis a worthy lord. TIM 1.01. 9
o, pray let's see't. for the lord timon, sir? 1.01. 13
some work, some dedication | to the great lord. 1.01. 20
how this lord is followed! 1.01. 39
tender down | their services to lord timon. 1.01. 55
one do i personate of lord timon's frame, | whom 1.01. 69
to show lord timon that mean eyes have seen 1.01. 93
ay, my good lord, five talents is his debt, 1.01. 95
lord timon, hear me speak. 1.01.110
this fellow here, lord timon, this thy creature, 1.01.116
i prithee, noble lord, | join with me to forbid 1.01.126
ay, my good lord, and she accepts of it. 1.01.135
most noble lord, | pawn me to this your honor, 1.01.146
what, my lord, dispraise? 1.01.165
my lord, 'tis rated | as those which sell would 1.01.168
believe't, dear lord, | you mend the jewel by 1.01.171
no, my good lord, he speaks the common tongue 1.01.174
heavens, that i were a lord! 1.01.227 P
hate a lord with my heart. 1.01.229 P
that i had no angry wit to be a lord. 1.01.234 P
thou art going to lord timon's feast? 1.01.260
shall we in | and taste lord timon's bounty? 1.01.274
my lord, we always have confess'd it. 1.02. 21
my lord, in heart; and let the health go round. 1.02. 53
let it flow this way, my good lord. 1.02. 54
my heart is ever at your service, my lord. 1.02. 75 P
so they were bleeding new, my lord, there's no 1.02. 78 P
might we but have that happiness, my lord, that 1.02. 85 P
i promise you, my lord, you mov'd me much. 1.02.113
please you, my lord, there are certain ladies 1.02.116 P
there comes with them a forerunner, my lord, 1.02.120 P
you see, my lord, how ample y' are belov'd. 1.02.130
my lord, you take us even at the best. 1.02.152
most thankfully, my lord. 1.02.157
my lord? 1.02.158
yes, my lord. 1.02.159
here, my lord, in readiness. 1.02.166 P
look you, my good lord, | i must entreat you 1.02.168
accept it and wear it, | kind my lord. 1.02.171
my lord, there are certain nobles of the senate 1.02.174
may it please your honor, lord lucius | (out of 1.02.181
please you, my lord, that honorable gentleman, 1.02.186 P
lord, that honorable gentleman, lord lucullus, 1.02.187 P
i bleed inwardly for my lord. 1.02.205
here, my lord, a trifle of our love. 1.02.207
and now i remember, my lord, you gave | good 1.02.210
o, i beseech you pardon me, my lord, in that. 1.02.213
you may take my word, my lord; 1.02.214
ay, defil'd land, my lord. 1.02.225
honor, and fortunes, keep with you, lord timon! 1.02.229
get on your cloak and haste you to lord timon; 2.01. 15
wing, | lord timon will be left a naked gull, 2.01. 31
here comes the lord. 2.02. 13
my lord, here is a note of certain dues. 2.02. 16
of athens here, my lord. 2.02. 17
nay, good my lord — 2.02. 26
one varro's servant, my good lord — 2.02. 27
if you did know, my lord, my master's wants — 2.02. 29
'twas due on forfeiture, my lord, six weeks 2.02. 30
your steward puts me off, my lord, | and i am 2.02. 31
this is to lord timon, this to alcibiades. 2.02. 83 P
fool, i will go with you to lord timon's. 2.02. 89 P
sometime't appears like a lord, sometime like a 2.02.109 P
aside, aside, here comes lord timon. 2.02.119 P
o my good lord, | at many times i brought in my 2.02.132
my lov'd lord, | though you hear now (too late), 2.02.142
o my good lord, the world is but a word; 2.02.152
heavens, have i said, the bounty of this lord! 2.02.164
head, sword, force, means, but is lord timon's? 2.02.167
my lord? my lord? 2.02.186 P
my lord? my lord? 2.02.186 P
you to lord lucius; 2.02.188 P
to lord lucullus you — i hunted with his honor 2.02.188 P
as you have said, my lord. 2.02.194 P
lord lucius and lucullus? humh! 2.02.195 P
i have told my lord of you, he is coming down to 3.01. 1 P
here's my lord. 3.01. 4 P
one of lord timon's men? 3.01. 5 P
athens, thy very bountiful good lord and master? 3.01. 11 P
alas, good lord! 3.01. 22 P
that part of nature | which my lord paid for, be 3.01. 62
who, the lord timon? 3.02. 1 P
but i can tell you one thing, my lord, and which 3.02. 5 P
now lord timon's happy hours are done and past, 3.02. 6 P
but believe you this, my lord, that not long ago 3.02. 10 P
his men was with the lord lucullus to borrow so 3.02. 11 P
i tell you, denied, my lord. 3.02. 16 P
see, by good hap, yonder's my lord; 3.02. 25 P
my honor'd lord — 3.02. 26 P
commend me to thy honorable virtuous lord, my 3.02. 28 P
may it please your honor, my lord hath sent — 3.02. 30 P
i am so much endear'd to that lord; 3.02. 32 P
only sent his present occasion now, my lord: 3.02. 35 P
but in the mean time he wants less, my lord. 3.02. 39
i was sending to use lord timon myself, these 3.02. 50 P
he might have tried lord lucius or lucullus; 3.03. 2
my lord, | they have all been touch'd and found 3.03. 5
how fairly this lord strives to appear foul! 3.03. 31 P
is not my lord seen yet? 3.04. 9
'tis deepest winter in lord timon's purse; 3.04. 14
your lord sends now for money. 3.04. 18
and e'en as if your lord should wear rich jewels 3.04. 23
i know my lord hath spent of timon's wealth, 3.04. 26
one of lord timon's men. 3.04. 33 P
pray is my lord ready to come forth? 3.04. 35 P
believe't, my lord and i have made an end: 3.04. 55
my soul, my lord leans wondrously to discontent. 3.04. 70 P
servilius, help! my lord, my lord! 3.04. 78
servilius, help! my lord, my lord! 3.04. 78
my lord, here is my bill. 3.04. 85 P
and mine, my lord. 3.04. 87 P
and ours, my lord. 3.04. 88 P
alas, my lord — 3.04. 91 P
five thousand crowns, my lord. 3.04. 95 P
my lord — 3.04. 97 P
my lord — 3.04. 98 P
my dear lord — 3.04.105
my lord — 3.04.107
here, my lord. 3.04.109
o my lord, | you only speak from your distracted 3.04.112
my lord, you have my voice to't; 3.05. 1
my lord — 3.05. 38
i think this honorable lord did but try us this 3.06. 3 P
my noble lord — 3.06. 39 P
my most honorable lord, i am e'en sick of shame 3.06. 41 P
know you the quality of lord timon's fury? 3.06.107 P
he's but a mad lord, and nought but humors sways 3.06.111 P
lord timon's mad. 3.06.119
poor honest lord, brought low by his own heart, 4.02. 37
my dearest lord, blest to be most accurs'd, 4.02. 42
alas, kind lord, | he's flung in rage from this 4.02. 44
raise me this beggar, and deny't that lord, 4.03. 9
is yond despis'd and ruinous man my lord? 4.03.459
and, as my lord, | still serve him with my life. 4.03.470
for his undone lord than mine eyes for you. 4.03.481
i beg of you to know me, good my lord, | t' 4.03.487
and believe it, | my most honor'd lord, | for 4.03.518
so it is said, my noble lord, but therefore 5.01. 78
so, so, my lord. 5.01. 82
most thankfully, my lord. 5.01. 91
doubt it not, worthy lord. 5.01. 92
do we, my lord? 5.01. 94
i know none such, my lord. 5.01. 99
name them, my lord, let's know them. 5.01.105
lord timon! 5.01.127
march, noble lord, | into our city with thy 5.04. 29
here, my lord. JC 1.02. 2
caesar, my lord? 1.02. 5
call'd you, my lord? 2.01. 6
i will, my lord. 2.01. 9
brutus, my lord! 2.01.233
dear my lord, | make me acquainted with your 2.01.255
withal | a woman that lord brutus took to wife. 2.01.293
my lord? 2.02. 4
i will, my lord. 2.02. 7
alas, my lord, | your wisdom is consum'd in 2.02. 48
yes, bring me word, boy, if thy lord look well, 2.04. 13
run, lucius, and commend me to my lord, | say i 2.04. 44
had you your letters from your wife, my lord? 4.03.181
no, my lord. 4.03.186
good night, my lord. 4.03.237
good night, lord brutus. 4.03.238
calls my lord? 4.03.245
ay, my lord, an't please you. 4.03.258
i have slept, my lord, already. 4.03.263
the strings, my lord, are false. 4.03.291
my lord? 4.03.294
my lord, i do not know that i did cry. 4.03.296
nothing, my lord. 4.03.298
my lord? 4.03.301
my lord? 4.03.302
did we, my lord? 4.03.304
no, my lord, i saw nothing. 4.03.305
nor i, my lord. 4.03.305
it shall be done, my lord. 4.03.308
my lord. 5.01. 69
fly further off, my lord, fly further off; 5.03. 9
mark antony is in your tents, my lord; 5.03. 10
they are, my lord. 5.03. 14
o my lord! 5.03. 26
brutus is ta'en, brutus is ta'en, my lord! 5.04. 18
statilius show'd the torchlight, but, my lord, 5.05. 2
what, i, my lord? no, not for all the world. 5.05. 6
what says my lord? 5.05. 16
not so, my lord. 5.05. 20
that's not an office for a friend, my lord. 5.05. 29
fly, fly, my lord, there is no tarrying here. 5.05. 30
fly, my lord, fly. 5.05. 43
i prithee, strato, stay thou by thy lord. 5.05. 44
give me your hand first. fare you well, my lord. 5.05. 49
but the norweyan lord, surveying vantage, | with MAC 1.02. 31
ay, my good lord. 3.01. 19
as far, my lord, as will fill up the time 3.01. 24
my lord, i will not. 3.01. 28
ay, my good lord. our time does call upon 's. 3.01. 36
they are, my lord, without the palace gate. 3.01. 46
true, my lord. 3.01.114
we shall, my lord, | perform what you command us 3.01.125
we are resolv'd, my lord. 3.01.138
how now, my lord, why do you keep alone, | of 3.02. 8
gentle my lord, sleek o'er your rugged looks, 3.02. 27
my lord, his throat is cut; 3.04. 15
ay, my good lord; 3.04. 25
my royal lord, | you do not give the cheer. 3.04. 31
here, my good lord. 3.04. 47
what, my good lord? 3.04. 48
my lord is often thus, | and hath been from his 3.04. 52
my worthy lord, | your noble friends do lack you 3.04. 82
what sights, my lord? 3.04.115
no, my lord. 4.01.136
no indeed, my lord. 4.01.137
'tis two or three, my lord, that bring you word 4.01.141
ay, my good lord. 4.01.143
fare thee well, lord, | i would not be the 4.03. 34
fie, my lord, fie, a soldier, and afeard? 5.01. 37 P
no more o' that, my lord, no more o' that; 5.01. 44 P
all is confirm'd, my lord, which was reported. 5.03. 31
not so sick, my lord, | as she is troubled with 5.03. 37
ay, my good lord; 5.03. 57
it is the cry of women, my good lord. 5.05. 8
the queen, my lord, is dead. 5.05. 16
gracious my lord, | i should report that which i 5.05. 29
this way, my lord, the castle's gently rend'red: 5.07. 24
your son, my lord, has paid a soldier's debt. 5.09. 5
my dread lord, | your leave and favor to return HAM 1.02. 50
h'ath, my lord, wrung from me my slow leave | by 1.02. 58
not so, my lord, i am too much in the sun. 1.02. 67
the same, my lord, and your poor servant ever. 1.02.162
my good lord! 1.02.166
a truant disposition, good my lord. 1.02.169
my lord, i came to see your father's funeral. 1.02.176
indeed, my lord, it followed hard upon. 1.02.179
where, my lord? 1.02.185
my lord, i think i saw him yesternight. 1.02.189
my lord, the king your father. 1.02.191
my lord, upon the platform where we watch. 1.02.213
my lord, i did, | but answer made it none. 1.02.214
as i do live, my honor'd lord, 'tis true, | and 1.02.221
we do, my lord. 1.02.225
arm'd, my lord. 1.02.227
my lord, from head to foot. 1.02.228
o yes, my lord, he wore his beaver up. 1.02.230
most humbly do i take my leave, my lord. 1.03. 82
please you, something touching the lord hamlet. 1.03. 89
he hath, my lord, of late made many tenders | of 1.03. 99
i do not know, my lord, what i should think. 1.03.104
my lord, he hath importun'd me with love | in 1.03.110
hath given countenance to his speech, my lord, 1.03.113
for lord hamlet, | believe so much in him, that 1.03.123
as to give words or talk with the lord hamlet. 1.03.134
i shall obey, my lord. 1.03.136
what does this mean, my lord? 1.04. 7
look, my lord, it comes! 1.04. 38
do not, my lord. 1.04. 64
what if it tempt you toward the flood, my lord, 1.04. 69
you shall not go, my lord. 1.04. 80
my lord, my lord! 1.05.113
my lord, my lord! 1.05.113

lord hamlet! 1.05.113
illo, ho, ho, my lord! 1.05.115
how is't, my noble lord? 1.05.117
what news, my lord? 1.05.117
good my lord, tell it. 1.05.119
not i, my lord, by heaven. 1.05.120
nor i, my lord. 1.05.120
there needs no ghost, my lord, come from the 1.05.125
these are but wild and whirling words, my lord. 1.05.133
there's no offense, my lord. 1.05.135
what is't, my lord, we will. 1.05.143
my lord, we will not. 1.05.145
in faith, | my lord, not i. 1.05.146
nor i, my lord, in faith. 1.05.146
we have sworn, my lord, already. 1.05.147
propose the oath, my lord. 1.05.152
i will, my lord. 2.01. 2
my lord, i did intend it. 2.01. 5
ay, very well, my lord. 2.01. 16
as gaming, my lord. 2.01. 24
my lord, that would dishonor him. 2.01. 27
but, my good lord — 2.01. 35
ay, my lord, | i would know that. 2.01. 36
very good, my lord. 2.01. 48
my lord, i have. 2.01. 66
good my lord. 2.01. 67
i shall, my lord. 2.01. 69
well, my lord. 2.01. 70
o, my lord, my lord, i have been so affrighted! 2.01. 72
o, my lord, my lord, i have been so affrighted! 2.01. 72
my lord, as i was sewing in my closet, | lord 2.01. 74
lord hamlet, with his doublet all unbrac'd, | no 2.01. 75
my lord, i do not know, | but truly i do fear it 2.01. 82
no, my good lord, but, as you did command, | i 2.01.105
th' embassadors from norway, my good lord, | are 2.02. 40
have i, my lord? 2.02. 43
"lord hamlet is a prince out of thy star; 2.02.141
give me leave, | how does my good lord hamlet? 2.02.171
do you know me, my lord? 2.02.173 P
not i, my lord. 2.02.175 P
honest, my lord? 2.02.177 P
that's very true, my lord. 2.02.180 P
i have, my lord. 2.02.183 P
what do you read, my lord? 2.02.191 P
what is the matter, my lord? 2.02.193 P
i mean, the matter that you read, my lord. 2.02.195 P
will you walk out of the air, my lord? 2.02.206 P
my lord, i will take my leave of you. 2.02.213 P
fare you well, my lord. 2.02.218 P
you go to seek the lord hamlet, there he is. 2.02.220 P
my honor'd lord! 2.02.222 P
my most dear lord! 2.02.223 P
neither, my lord. 2.02.231 P
none, my lord, but the world's grown honest. 2.02.237 P
to visit you, my lord, no other occasion. 2.02.271 P
what should we say, my lord? 2.02.277 P
to what end, my lord? 2.02.282 P
my lord, we were sent for. 2.02.292 P
my lord, there was no such stuff in my thoughts. 2.02.311 P
to think, my lord, if you delight not in man, 2.02.315 P
in what, my dear lord? 2.02.377 P
my lord, i have news to tell you. 2.02.389 P
my lord, i have news to tell you. 2.02.390 P
the actors are come hither, my lord. 2.02.392 P
what a treasure had he, my lord? 2.02.405 P
if you call me jephthah, my lord, i have a 2.02.411 P
what follows then, my lord? 2.02.414 P
what speech, my good lord? 2.02.433 P
'fore god, my lord, well spoken, with good 2.02.466 P
good my lord, will you see the players well 2.02.522 P
my lord, i will use them according to their 2.02.527 P
ay, my lord. 2.02.539 P
ay, my lord. 2.02.544 P
follow that lord, and look you mock him not. 2.02.545 P
good my lord! 2.02.548 P
we shall, my lord. 3.01. 28
i hear him coming. withdraw, my lord. 3.01. 54
good my lord, | how does your honor for this 3.01. 89
my lord, i have remembrances of yours | that i 3.01. 92
my honor'd lord, you know right well you did, 3.01. 96
there, my lord. 3.01.101
my lord? 3.01.103 P
could beauty, my lord, have better commerce than 3.01.108 P
indeed, my lord, you made me believe so. 3.01.115 P
at home, my lord. 3.01.130 P
you need not tell us what lord hamlet said, | we 3.01.179
my lord, do as you please, | but, if you hold it 3.01.180
how now, my lord? 3.02. 46 P
ay, my lord. 3.02. 51 P
here, sweet lord, at your service. 3.02. 53
o my dear lord — 3.02. 56
well, my lord, | if 'a steal aught the whilst 3.02. 87
my lord, you play'd once i' th' university, you 3.02. 98 P
that did i, my lord, and was accounted a good 3.02.100 P
ay, my lord, they stay upon your patience. 3.02.107 P
no, my lord. 3.02.113 P
i think nothing, my lord. 3.02.117 P
what is, my lord? 3.02.120 P
you are merry, my lord. 3.02.122 P
ay, my lord. 3.02.124 P
nay, 'tis twice two months, my lord. 3.02.128 P
what means this, my lord? 3.02.136 P
'tis brief, my lord. 3.02.153 P
discomfort you, my lord, it nothing must, | /for 3.02.166
die thy thoughts when thy first lord is dead. 3.02.215
you are as good as a chorus, my lord. 3.02.245 P
you are keen, my lord, you are keen. 3.02.248 P
how fares my lord? 3.02.267 P
very well, my lord. 3.02.288 P
good my lord, voutsafe me a word with you. 3.02.296 P
no, my lord, with choler. 3.02.303 P
good my lord, put your discourse into some frame 3.02.308 P
nay, good my lord, this courtesy is not of the 3.02.314 P
what, my lord? 3.02.320 P
my lord, you once did love me. 3.02.335 P
good my lord, what is your cause of distemper? 3.02.337 P
o my lord, if my duty be too bold, my love is 3.02.348 P
my lord, i cannot. 3.02.352 P
i know no touch of it, my lord. 3.02.356 P
my lord, the queen would speak with you, and 3.02.374 P
my lord, he's going to his mother's closet. 3.03. 27
thanks, dear my lord. 3.03. 35
part the /tithe | of your precedent lord, a vice 3.04. 98
for this same lord, | i do repent; 3.04.172
ah, mine own lord, what have i seen to–night! 4.01. 5
what have you done, my lord, with the dead body? 4.02. 5
take you me for a spunge, my lord? 4.02. 14 P
i understand you not, my lord. 4.02. 22 P
my lord, you must tell us where the body is, and 4.02. 25 P
a thing, my lord? 4.02. 29 P
where the dead body is bestow'd, my lord, | we 4.03. 12
without, my lord, guarded, to know your pleasure 4.03. 14
ho, bring in the lord. 4.03. 15
i will do't, my lord. 4.04. 7
will't please you go, my lord? 4.04. 30
alas, look here, my lord. 4.05. 37
lord, we know what we are, but know not what we 4.05. 43 P
save yourself, my lord! 4.05. 99
the rabble call him lord, | and, as the world 4.05.103
i should be greeted, if not from lord hamlet. 4.06. 6
sailors, my lord, they say, i saw them not. 4.07. 39
i am lost in it, my lord. 4.07. 54
ay, my lord, | so you will not o'errule me to a 4.07. 59
my lord, i will be rul'd, | the rather, if you 4.07. 68
what part is that, my lord? 4.07. 76
what out of this, my lord? 4.07.106
adieu, my lord, | i have a speech a' fire that 4.07.189
it might, my lord. 5.01. 81 P
which could say, "good morrow, sweet lord! 5.01. 83 P
how dost thou, sweet lord?" 5.01. 83 P
this might be my lord such–a–one, that prais'd 5.01. 84 P
that prais'd my lord such–a–one's horse, when 'a 5.01. 85 P
ay, my lord. 5.01. 87 P
not a jot more, my lord. 5.01.113 P
ay, my lord, and of calves'–skins too. 5.01.115 P
by the lord, horatio, this three years i have 5.01.138 P
what's that, my lord? 5.01.196 P
e'en so, my lord. 5.01.201 P
good my lord, be quiet. 5.01.265
remember it, my lord! 5.02. 3
ay, good my lord. 5.02. 37
no, my good lord. 5.02. 83
let a beast be lord of beasts, and his crib 5.02. 86 P
sweet lord, if your lordship were at leisure, i 5.02. 89 P
it is indifferent cold, my lord, indeed. 5.02. 97 P
exceedingly, my lord, it is very sultry — as 5.02.100 P
my lord, his majesty bade me signify to you that 5.02.101 P
nay, good my lord, for my ease, in good faith. 5.02.105 P
i mean, my lord, the opposition of your person 5.02.171 P
my lord, his majesty commended him to you by 5.02.195 P
you will lose, my lord. 5.02.209 P
nay, good my lord — 5.02.214 P
very well, my lord. 5.02.260
ay, my good lord. 5.02.266
come, my lord. 5.02.280
i will, my lord, i pray you pardon me. 5.02.291
my lord, i'll hit him now. 5.02.295
they bleed on both sides. how is it, my lord? 5.02.304
is not this your son, my lord? LR 1.01. 8 P
no, my lord. 1.01. 26 P
my lord of kent. 1.01. 27 P
i shall, my lord. 1.01. 35
nothing, my lord. 1.01. 87
good my lord, | you have begot me, bred me, 1.01. 95
that lord whose hand must take my plight shall 1.01.101
ay, my good lord. 1.01.105
so young, my lord, and true. 1.01.107
here's france and burgundy, my noble lord. 1.01.188
my lord of burgundy, | we first address toward 1.01.189
my lord of burgundy, | what say you to the lady? 1.01.237
let your study | be to content your lord, who 1.01.277
i know no news, my lord. 1.02. 29 P
nothing, my lord. 1.02. 31 P
it was not brought me, my lord; 1.02. 59 P
if the matter were good, my lord, i durst swear 1.02. 63 P
it is his hand, my lord; 1.02. 67 P
never, my lord. 1.02. 71 P
i do not well know, my lord. 1.02. 79 P
i will fitly bring you to hear my lord speak. 1.02.169 P
he says, my lord, your /daughter is not well. 1.04. 50 P
my lord, i know not what the matter is, but, to 1.04. 57 P
i beseech you pardon me, my lord, if i be 1.04. 64 P
i am none of these, my lord, i beseech your 1.04. 82 P
i'll not be strucken, my lord. 1.04. 85 P
my lord, i am guiltless as i am ignorant | of 1.04.273
it may be so, my lord. 1.04.274
no, no, my lord, | this milky gentleness and 1.04.340
i will not sleep, my lord, till i have deliver'd 1.05. 6 P
ready, my lord. 1.05. 49 P
how dost, my lord? 2.01. 89
ay, my good lord. 2.01.109
i am scarce in breath, my lord. 2.02. 52 P
my lord, if you/'ll give me leave, i will tread 2.02. 65 P
till night, my lord, and all night too. 2.02.135
come, my /good lord, away. 2.02.151
no, my lord. 2.04. 6
my lord, when at their home | i did commend your 2.04. 27
my dear lord, | you know the fiery quality of 2.04. 91
well, my good lord, i have inform'd them so. 2.04. 98
ay, my good lord. 2.04.100
why might not you, my lord, receive attendance 2.04.243
why not, my lord? 2.04.245
and speak't again, my lord, no more with me. 2.04.255
hear me, my lord: 2.04.260
where is my lord of gloucester? 2.04.294
my lord, entreat him by no means to stay. 2.04.299
shut up your doors, my lord, 'tis a wild night, 2.04.308
gracious my lord, hard by here is a hovel, 3.02. 61
here is the place, my lord; 3.04. 1
good my lord, enter, | the tyranny of the open 3.04. 1
good my lord, enter here. 3.04. 4
good my lord, enter. 3.04. 5
good my lord, enter here. 3.04. 22
our flesh and blood, my lord, is grown so vild 3.04.145
good my lord, take his offer, go into th' house. 3.04.156
importune him once more to go, my lord, | his 3.04.161
this way, my lord. 3.04.175
good my lord, soothe him; 3.04.177
how, my lord, i may be censur'd, that nature 3.05. 2 P
now, good my lord, lie here and rest awhile. 3.06. 82
post speedily to my lord your husband, show him 3.07. 1 P
dear sister, farewell, my lord of gloucester. 3.07. 12 P
my lord of gloucester hath convey'd him hence. 3.07. 15
farewell, sweet lord, and sister. 3.07. 21
hold your hand, my lord! 3.07. 72
my lord, you have one eye left | to see some 3.07. 81
how is't, my lord? 3.07. 94
o, my good lord, | i have been your tenant, and 4.01. 12
ay, my lord. 4.01. 40
welcome, my lord! 4.02. 1
madam, here comes my lord. 4.02. 28
o my good lord, the duke of cornwall's dead, 4.02. 70
both, both, my lord. 4.02. 81
no, my good lord, i met him back again. 4.02. 90
ay, my good lord; 4.02. 92
lord edmund spake not with your lord at home? 4.05. 4
lord edmund spake not with your lord at home? 4.05. 4
my lord is dead; 4.05. 30
then be't so, my good lord. how does the king? 4.07. 12
how does my royal lord? how fares your majesty? 4.07. 43
now, sweet lord, | you know the goodness i 5.01. 6
dear my lord, | be not familiar with her. 5.01. 15
i'll do't, my lord. 5.03. 34
that i create thee here | my lord and master. 5.03. 78
nor in thine, lord. 5.03. 80
'tis she is sub–contracted to this lord, | and i 5.03. 86
by nursing them, my lord. 5.03.182
to who, my lord? 5.03.249
no, my good lord, i am the very man — 5.03.287
edmund is dead, my lord. 5.03.296
he faints. my lord, my lord! 5.03.312
he faints. my lord, my lord! 5.03.312
look up, my lord. 5.03.313
you are the lord of duty; OTH 1.03.184
that i may profess | due to the moor, my lord. 1.03.189
i have done, my lord. 1.03.198
subdu'd | even to the very quality of my lord. 1.03.251
what tidings can you tell /me of my lord? 2.01. 88
well, my good lord, i'll do't. 3.02. 4
but i will have my lord and you again | as 3.03. 6
you do love my lord; 3.03. 10
my lord shall never rest, | i'll watch him tame, 3.03. 22
madam, here comes my lord. 3.03. 29
nothing, my lord; or if — i know not what. 3.03. 36
cassio, my lord? 3.03. 38
how now, my lord? 3.03. 41
good my lord, | if i have any grace or power to 3.03. 45
shall i deny you? no. farewell, my lord. 3.03. 86
my noble lord — 3.03. 93
honest, my lord? 3.03.103
my lord, for aught i know. 3.03.104
think, my lord? 3.03.105
think, my lord? 3.03.106
my lord, you know i love you. 3.03.117
good my lord, pardon me: 3.03.133
good name in man and woman, dear my lord, | is 3.03.155
o, beware, my lord, of jealousy! 3.03.165
should you do so, my lord, | my speech should 3.03.221
worthy friend — | my lord, i see y' are mov'd. 3.03.224
my lord, i take my leave. 3.03.241
my lord, i would i might entreat your honor | to 3.03.244
how now, my lord? 3.03.337
is't possible, my lord? 3.03.358
my noble lord — 3.03.367
how satisfied, my lord? 3.03.394
tell him i have mov'd my lord on his behalf, and 3.04. 19 P
how is't with you, my lord? 3.04. 33
well, my good lord. 3.04. 35
here, my lord. 3.04. 52
no, /faith, my lord. 3.04. 54
my lord is not my lord; 3.04.124
my lord is not my lord; 3.04.124
is my lord angry? 3.04.132
why then 'tis hers, my lord, and, being hers, 4.01. 12
he hath, my lord, but be you well assur'd, | no 4.01. 30
my lord! 4.01. 47
my lord, i say! 4.01. 48
my lord is fall'n into an epilepsy. 4.01. 50
there's fall'n between him and my lord | an 4.01.224
my lord? 4.01.227
is there division 'twixt my lord and cassio? 4.01.231
my lord? 4.01.234
my lord? 4.01.238
my lord, this would not be believ'd in venice, 4.01.242
my lord? 4.01.250
who, i, my lord? 4.01.251
never, my lord. 4.02. 6
never, my lord. 4.02. 10
i durst, my lord, to wager she is honest; 4.02. 12
my lord, what is your will? 4.02. 24
your wife, my lord; your true | and loyal wife. 4.02. 34
to whom, my lord? with whom? how am i false? 4.02. 40
am i the motive of these tears, my lord? 4.02. 43
i hope my noble lord esteems me honest. 4.02. 65
if to preserve this vessel for my lord | from 4.02. 83
good madam, what's the matter with my lord? 4.02. 98
why, with my lord, madam. 4.02.100
who is thy lord? 4.02.101
alas, iago, my lord hath so bewhor'd her, 4.02.115
such as she said my lord did say i was. 4.02.119
iago, | what shall i do to win my lord again? 4.02.149
my lord? 4.03. 6
i will, my lord. 4.03. 10
and tell my lord and lady what hath happ'd. 5.01.127
will you come to bed, my lord? 5.02. 24
ay, my lord. 5.02. 25
alack, my lord, what may you mean by that? 5.02. 29
what, my lord? 5.02. 69
o, banish me, my lord, but kill me not! 5.02. 78
my lord, my lord! what ho! my lord, my lord! 5.02. 85
my lord, my lord! what ho! my lord, my lord! 5.02. 85
my lord, my lord! what ho! my lord, my lord! 5.02. 85
my lord, my lord! what ho! my lord, my lord! 5.02. 85
what ho! my lord, my lord! 5.02. 89

what ho! my lord, my lord! 5.02. 89
o, good my lord, i would speak a word with you! 5.02. 90
o, good my lord! 5.02.102
o, my good lord, yonder's foul murthers done! 5.02.106
but now, my lord. 5.02.108
cassio, my lord, hath kill'd a young venetian 5.02.112
commend me to my kind lord. 5.02.125
to you, lord governor, | remains the censure of 5.02.367
news, my good lord, from rome. ANT 1.01. 18
lord alexas, sweet alexas, most any thing alexas 1.02. 1 P
/saw you my lord? 1.02. 80
here, at your service. my lord approaches. 1.02. 86
o, my lord! 1.02.104
courteous lord, one word: 1.03. 86
farewell, my lord. 1.04. 81
wilt thou be lord of all the world? 2.07. 61
wilt thou be lord of the whole world? 2.07. 62
o my good lord, | believe not all, or, if you 3.04. 10
i shall pray, "o, bless my lord and husband!" 3.04. 16
thanks to my lord. 3.04. 28
more, domitius, | my lord desires you presently; 3.05. 21
hail, caesar, and my lord! 3.06. 39
good my lord, | to come thus was i not 3.06. 55
my lord, mark antony, | hearing that you 3.06. 57
do not say so, my lord. 3.06. 62
my lord, in athens. 3.06. 64
why will my lord do so? 3.07. 29
so hath my lord dar'd him to single fight. 3.07. 30
the news is true, my lord: 3.07. 54
my lord? 3.08. 2
yes, my lord, yes; 3.11. 35
the queen, my lord, the queen. 3.11. 42
o my lord, my lord, | forgive my fearful sails! 3.11. 54
o my lord, my lord, | forgive my fearful sails! 3.11. 54
lord of his fortunes he salutes thee, and 3.12. 11
that would make his will | lord of his reason. 3.13. 4
ay, my lord. 3.13. 14
that head, my lord? 3.13. 19
to follow with allegiance a fall'n lord | does 3.13. 44
good my lord — 3.13.109
soundly, my lord. 3.13.132
that's my brave lord! 3.13.176
but since my lord | is antony again, i will be 3.13.185
call all his noble captains to my lord. 3.13.188
lord of lords! 4.08. 16
for both, my lord. 4.10. 2
why is my lord enrag'd against his love? 4.12. 31
ay, noble lord. 4.14. 1
ay, my lord. 4.14. 8
it does, my lord. 4.14. 11
what would my lord? 4.14. 55
most absolute lord, | my mistress cleopatra sent 4.14.117
now, my lord. 4.14.119
come, your lord calls! 4.14.130
dear my lord, pardon — i dare not, | lest i be 4.15. 22
how heavy weighs my lord! 4.15. 32
my lord! 4.15. 63
make your full reference freely to my lord, 5.02. 23
it thus, my master and my lord | i must obey. 5.02.116
here, my good lord. 5.02.136
this is my treasurer, let him speak, my lord, 5.02.142
my master, and my lord! 5.02.190
my lord your son drew on my master. CYM 1.01.160
you shall, at least, | go see my lord aboard. 1.01.178
well, my lord. 1.02. 41 P
of her to hold | the hand–fast to her lord. 1.05. 78
but when to my good lord i prove untrue, | i'll 1.05. 86
of rome, | comes from my lord with letters. 1.06. 11
continues well my lord? his health, beseech you? 1.06. 56
whiles the jolly britain | (your lord, i mean) 1.06. 68
will my lord say so? 1.06. 73
my lord, i fear, | has forgot britain. 1.06.112
were deeply rooted, and shall make your lord, 1.06.164
your lord, myself, and other noble friends | are 1.06.183
some dozen romans of us and your lord | (the 1.06.185
since | my lord hath interest in them, i will 1.06.195
if you please | to greet your lord with writing, 1.06.206
no, my lord; nor crop the ears of them. 2.01. 12 P
you cannot derogate, my lord. 2.01. 44 P
t' enjoy thy banish'd lord and this great land! 2.01. 65
does within, | to th' madding of her lord. 2.02. 37
day, my lord. 2.03. 10 P
i hope it be not gone to tell my lord | that i 2.03.147
madam, here is a letter from my lord. 3.02. 25
who, thy lord? 3.02. 26
that is my lord leonatus? 3.02. 26
pisanio, | who long'st like me to see thy lord; 3.02. 53
venison first shall be the lord o' th' feast, 3.03. 75
your hand, my lord. 3.05. 12
the cure whereof, my lord, | 'tis time must do. 3.05. 37
my lord, when last i went to visit her, | she 3.05. 45
o, good my lord! 3.05. 83
alas, my lord, | how can she be with him? 3.05. 89
o, my all–worthy lord! 3.05. 94
no more of "worthy lord"! 3.05. 96
i'll write to my lord she's dead. 3.05.104
well, my good lord. 3.05.116 P
i have, my lord, at my lodging, the same suit he 3.05.125 P
i shall, my lord. 3.05.129 P
ay, my noble lord. 3.05.147 P
my dear lord, | thou art one o' th' false ones. 3.06. 14
devil cloten, | hath here cut off my lord. 4.02.316
o, my lord! 4.02.332
my lord! 4.02.332
he's alive, my lord. 4.02.359
this is a lord! 5.03. 64
he shall be lord of lady imogen, | and happier 5.04.107
wilt thou hear more, my lord? 5.05.146
most like a noble lord in love and one | that 5.05.171
peace, my lord, hear, hear — 5.05.227
o my lord posthumus, | you ne'er kill'd imogen 5.05.230
i am sorry for't, my lord. 5.05.270
my lord, | now fear is from me, i'll speak troth 5.05.273
lord cloten, | upon my lady's missing, came to 5.05.274
that headless man | i thought had been my lord. 5.05.300
no, my lord; 5.05.373
ay, my good lord. 5.05.379
good my lord of rome, | call forth your 5.05.425
here, my good lord. 5.05.434
my lord, 'tis done. PER 1.01.158
my lord, prince pericles is fled. 1.01.160
my lord, | if i can get him within my pistol's 1.01.165
an angry brow, dread lord. 1.02. 52
well, my lord, since you have given me leave to 1.02.101
therefore, my lord, go travel for a while, 1.02.106
lord thaliard from antiochus is welcome. 1.03. 30
your lord has /betook himself to unknown travels 1.03. 34
o my distressed lord, even such our griefs are; 1.04. 7
here stands a lord, and there a lady weeping; 1.04. 47
where's the lord governor? 1.04. 56
i go, my lord. 1.04. 82
lord governor, for so we hear you are, | let not 1.04. 85
a better prince and benign lord, | that will 2.ch. 3
in those that practice them they are, my lord. 2.03.104
follow me then. lord helicane, a word. 2.04. 21
and since lord helicane enjoineth us, | we with 2.04. 55
may we not get access to her, my lord? 2.05. 7
the worst of all her scholars, my good lord. 2.05. 31
o, seek not to entrap me, gracious lord, | a 2.05. 45
doth my lord call? 3.02. 2
hath built lord cerimon | such strong renown as 3.02. 47
'tis so, my lord. 3.02. 56
where's my lord? 3.02.105
fear not, my lord, but think | your grace, that 3.03. 17
more dear to my respect | than yours, my lord. 3.03. 34
come, my lord. 3.03. 41
my wedded lord, i ne'er shall see again, | a 3.04. 9
lord, how your favor's chang'd | with this 4.01. 24
blame both my lord and me, that we have taken 4.01. 37
were i chief lord of all this spacious world, 4.03. 5
seas, | attended on by many a lord and knight, 4.04. 11
here comes the lord lysimachus disguis'd. 4.06. 16 P
we should have both lord and lown, if the 4.06. 18 P
my lord, she's not pac'd yet, you must take some 4.06. 63 P
here spoken holy words to the lord lysimachus. 4.06.133 P
where is lord helicanus? 5.01. 1
ho, gentlemen! my lord calls. 5.01. 7
hail, sir! my lord, lend ear. 5.01. 82
my lord, that ne'er before invited eyes, | but 5.01. 85
my lord, that, may be, hath endur'd a grief 5.01. 87
i said, my lord, if you did know my parentage, 5.01. 99
calls my lord? 5.01.181
my lord, i hear none. 5.01.227
music, my lord, i hear. 5.01.232
o my lord, | are you not pericles? 5.03. 31
lord cerimon, my lord; 5.03. 59
lord cerimon, my lord; 5.03. 59
i will, my lord. 5.03. 64
lord cerimon hath letters of good credit, sir, 5.03. 77
lord cerimon, we do our longing stay | to hear 5.03. 83
king capaneus was your lord. TNK 1.01. 59
to thy sex captive, but that this thy lord — 1.01. 81
my lord is taken | heart–deep with your distress 1.01.104
repeat my wishes | to our great lord, of whose 1.03. 2
observ'd him | since our great lord departed? 1.03. 34
lord, the diff'rence of men! 2.01. 53 P
lord arcite, you must presently to th' duke; 2.02.221
my lord, for you | i have this charge too — 2.02.259
why, my lord? 2.02.265
indeed you must, my lord. 2.02.268
and there, | lord, what a coil he keeps! 2.04. 18
and art | a very thief in love, a chaffy lord, 3.01. 41
night, | and darkness lord o' th' world! 3.02. 4
the lord steward's daughter — | do you remember 3.03. 29
the next, the lord of may and lady bright, | the 3.05.125
the same, my lord. | are they not sweet ones? 4.02.120
i wish it, | but not the cause, my lord. 4.02.144
and by thee | be styl'd the lord o' th' day. 5.01. 60
lord, how y' are grown! 5.02. 94
sir, my good lord, | your sister will no further 5.03. 10
to disseat | his lord that kept it bravely. 5.04. 73
we'll not hear my lord of surrey, no, no, no, no STM II.C 38 P
when at collatium this false lord arrived, LUC 50
and now this lustful lord leapt from his bed, 169
led, | the roman lord marcheth to lucrece' bed. 301
save of their lord no bearing yoke they knew, 409
so fares it with this fault–full lord of rome, 715
"dear lord of that dear jewel i have lost, 1191
and by, to bear | a letter to my lord, my love, 1293
"thou worthy lord | of that unworthy wife that 1303
"at ardea to my lord with more than haste." 1332
back, | brings home his lord and other company, 1584
"dear lord, thy sorrow to my sorrow lendeth 1676
each present lord began to promise aid, | as 1696
"thou wronged lord of rome," quoth he, "arise, 1818
lord, how mine eyes throw gazes to the east! PP 14.13
lord of my love, to whom in vassalage | thy SON 26. 1

LORDED 1 FR 0.0001 REL FR 1 V 0 P
he being thus lorded, | not only with what my TMP 1.02. 97

LORDING 1 FR 0.0001 REL FR 1 V 0 P
broil | i see them lording it in london streets, 2H6 4.08. 45

LORDING'S 1 FR 0.0001 REL FR 1 V 0 P
it was a lording's daughter, the fairest one of PP 15. 1

LORDINGS 2 FR 0.0002 REL FR 2 V 0 P
you were pretty lordings then? WT 1.02. 62
lordings, farewell, and say, when i am gone, | i 2H6 1.01.145

LORDLINESS 1 FR 0.0001 REL FR 1 V 0 P
doing the honor of thy lordliness | to one so ANT 5.02.161

LORDLY 7 FR 0.0008 REL FR 7 V 0 P
ay, lordly sir; 1H6 3.01. 43
but with a lordly nation | that will not trust 3.03. 62
under the lordly monarch of the north, | appear, 5.03. 6
in sight of england and her lordly peers, 2H6 1.01. 11
an't like your lordly lord's protectorship. 2.01. 30
george, profan'd, hath lost his lordly honor; R3 4.04.369
deed, | stood collatine and all his lordly crew, LUC 1731

LORD'S 32 FR 0.0036 REL FR 26 V 6 P
in our trade, and are now "for the lord's sake." MM 4.03. 19 P
free, | for the lord's tokens on you do i see. LLL 5.02.423
and this same myself | are yours — my lord's! MV 3.02.171
and manage of my house | until my lord's return. 3.04. 26
here, | until her husband and my lord's return. 3.04. 30
have deserv'd to run into my lord's displeasure. AWW 2.05. 35 P
it be to report your lord's taking of this. TN 2.02. 11 P
none of my lord's ring? 2.02. 24
a lady's "verily" is | as potent as a lord's. WT 1.02. 51
of my lord's tricks and yours when you were boys 1.02. 61
my lord's almost so far transported that | he'll 5.03. 69
looking awry upon your lord's departure, | find R2 2.02. 21
more than your lord's departure weep not — more 2.02. 25
in your lord's scale is nothing but himself, 3.04. 85
and in defense of my lord's worthiness, | i 1H6 4.01. 99
an't like your lordly lord's protectorship. 2H6 2.01. 30
thy sly conveyance and thy lord's false love, 3H6 3.03.160
than thou hast made me by my dear lord's death!" R3 4.01. 76
tell–tale women | rail on the lord's anointed. 4.04.151
which, in my lord's behalf, i come to entreat TIM 3.01. 17 P
thy lord's a bountiful gentleman, but thou art 3.01. 39 P
unto his honor has my lord's meat in him; 3.01. 57
my knowing, timon has been this lord's father, 3.02. 67
this was my lord's best hope, now all are fled, 3.03. 35
when your false masters eat of my lord's meat? 3.04. 50
second masters, | upon their first lord's neck. 4.03.506
hath broke ope | the lord's anointed temple, and MAC 2.03. 68
and a damned light | to their lord's murther. HAM 2.02.461
my lord's knave! LR 1.04. 80 P
who, with some other of the lord's dependants, 3.07. 18
of my lord's health, of his content — yet not CYM 3.02. 31
it is my lord's. PER 3.04. 4

LORDS' 1 FR 0.0001 REL FR 1 V 0 P
like widowed wombs after their lords' decease: SON 97. 8

/LORDS 4 FR 0.0004 REL FR 3 V 1 P
/may /it /please /you, /lords, /to /grant /the R2 4.01.154
/lords, /you /that /here /are /under /our 4.01.158
here /come the /lords of buckingham and derby. R3 1.03. 17
/lords /and /great /men /will /not /let /me; LR 1.04.152 P

LORDS 366 FR 0.0413 REL FR 349 V 17 P
yes, faith, and all his lords, the duke of milan TMP 1.02.438
lords that can prate | as amply and 2.01.263
but you, my brace of lords, were i so minded, 5.01.126
i perceive these lords | at this encounter do so 5.01.153
mark but the badges of these men, my lords, 5.01.267
nay, got's lords and his ladies! WIV 1.01.235 P
yet there has been knights, and lords, and 2.02. 64 P
de earl, de knight, de lords, de gentlemen, my 2.03. 92 P
are masters to their females, and their lords: ERR 2.01. 24
hear you, my lords — ADO 5.01. 47
until to–morrow morning, lords, farewell. 5.01.328
farewell, my lords, we look for you to–morrow. 5.01.329
what say you, lords? why, this was quite forgot. LLL 1.01.141
how you delight, my lords, i know not, i, | but 1.01.174
and go we, lords, to put in practice that 1.01.306
who are the votaries, my loving lords, | that 2.01. 37
well, lords, to–day we shall have our dispatch; 4.01. 5
when they strive to be | lords o'er their lords? 4.01. 38
when they strive to be | lords o'er their lords? 4.01. 38
come, lords, away. 4.01.106
berowne, one of the strange queen's lords. 4.02.130 P
sweet lords, sweet lovers, o, let us embrace! 4.03.210
and where that you have vow'd to study, lords, 4.03.292
o, we have made a vow to study, lords, | and in 4.03.315
advance your standards, and upon them, lords; 4.03.364
these lords are visited; 5.02.422
i thank you, gracious lords, | for all your fair 5.02.729
and there is two or three lords and ladies more MND 4.02. 16 P
good morrow, my good lords. MV 1.01. 65
not fear, lady, the having any of these lords. 1.02.101 P
three or four loving lords have put themselves AYL 1.01.101 P
observ'd in noble ladies | unto their lords, by SHR in.1. 112
madam, and nothing else — so lords call ladies. in.2. 111
what duty they do owe their lords and husbands. 5.02.131
i can well observe | to–day in our young lords; AWW 1.02. 33
farewell, young lords! 2.01. 1
and you, my lords, farewell! 2.01. 2
farewell, young lords! 2.01. 10
use a more spacious ceremony to the noble lords; 2.01. 51 P
go call before me all the lords in court. 2.03. 46
you are more saucy with lords and honorable 2.03.261 P
you, my lords, | look on her, mark her well; WT 2.01. 64
good my lords, | i am not prone to weeping, as 2.01.107
beseech you all, my lords, | with thoughts so 2.01.112
nay, rather, good my lords, be second to me. 2.03. 27
behold, my lords, | although the print be little 2.03. 98
these lords, my noble fellows, if they please, 2.03.143
prepare you, lords, | summon a session, that we 2.03.201
but the last — o lords, | when i have said, cry 3.02.199
then, good my lords, bear witness to his oath. 5.01. 72
good lords, although my will to give is living, JN 4.02. 83
the angry lords with all expedient haste. 4.02.268
lords, i will meet him at saint edmundsbury. 4.03. 11
for 'twill be | two long days' journey, lords, 4.03. 20
once more to–day well met, distemper'd lords! 4.03. 21
lords, i am hot with haste in seeking you. 4.03. 74
would not my lords return to me again | after 5.01. 37
return the president to these lords again, 5.02. 3
for if the french be lords of this loud day, 5.04. 14
up, | last in the field, and almost lords of it! 5.05. 8
the english lords | by his persuasion are again 5.05. 10
the lords are all come back, | and brought 5.06. 33
with whom yourself, myself, and other lords, 5.07. 93
well, lords, the duke of lancaster is dead. R2 2.01.224
but, lords, we hear this fearful tempest sing, 2.01.263
the lords of ross, beaumond, and willoughby, 2.02. 54
by this the weary lords | shall make their way 2.03. 16
and in it are the lords of york, berkeley, and 2.03. 55
here come the lords of ross and willoughby, 2.03. 57
welcome, my lords. 2.03. 59
my lords of england, let me tell you this: 2.03.140
lords, farewell! 3.01. 32
come, lords, away, | to fight with glendower and 3.01. 42
mock not my senseless conjuration, lords, | this 3.02. 23
princes and noble lords, | what answer shall i 4.01. 19
lords appellants, | your differences shall all 4.01.104
lords, be ready all. 4.01.320
i would to god, my lords, he might be found. 5.03. 4
lords, i protest my soul is full of woe | that 5.06. 45
we | will hold at windsor, so inform the lords. 1H4 1.01.104
for god's sake, lords, convey my /tristful queen 2.04.393
a shorter time shall send me to you, lords, 3.01. 90
lords, give us leave, the prince of wales and i 3.02. 1
leads ancient lords and reverend bishops on | to 3.02.104
now when the lords and barons of the realm 4.03. 66
is it good morrow, lords? 2H4 3.01. 33

why then good morrow to you all, my lords. 3.01. 35
we would, dear lords, unto the holy land. 3.01.108
here stand, my lords, and send discoverers forth 4.01. 3
and these noble lords | had not been here to 4.01. 38
please you, lords, | in sight of both our 4.01.176
i trust, lords, we shall lie to–night together. 4.02. 97
and now dispatch we toward the court, my lords, 4.03. 76
now, lords, if god doth give successful end | to 4.04. 1
not so much noise, my lords. 4.05. 16
why did you leave me here alone, my lords? 4.05. 50
therefore, my lords, omit no happy hour | that H5 1.02.300
now, lords, for france; 2.02.182
poor we call them in their native lords! 3.05. 26
great princes, barons, lords, and /knights, 3.05. 46
go with my brothers to my lords of england. 4.01. 30
the sun doth gild our armor, up, my lords! 4.02. 1
'tis positive against all exceptions, lords, 4.02. 25
why do you stay so long, my lords of france? 4.02. 38
of other lords and barons, knights and squires, 4.08. 78
the rest are princes, barons, lords, knights, 4.08. 89
where that his lords desire him to have borne 5.pr. 17
is't so, my lords of england? 5.02.331 P
my honorable lords, health to you all! 1H6 1.01. 57
lords, view these letters full of bad mischance. 1.01. 89
my gracious lords, to add to your laments, 1.01.103
four of their lords i'll change for one of ours. 1.01.151
remember, lords, your oaths to henry sworn: 1.01.162
the other lords, like lions wanting food, | do 1.02. 27
stand back, you lords, and give us leave a while 1.02. 70
fie, lords, that you, being supreme magistrates, 1.03. 57
think at the north gate, for there stands lords. 1.04. 66
how now, my lords? what, all unready so? 2.01. 39
question, my lords, no further of the case, 2.01. 72
but, lords, in all our bloody massacre, | i muse 2.02. 18
all hail, my lords! 2.02. 34
great lords and gentlemen, what means this 2.04. 1
stay, lords and gentlemen, and pluck no more, 2.04. 39
the reason mov'd these warlike lords to this 2.05. 70
lords, vouchsafe | to give me hearing what i 3.01. 27
no, my good lords, it is not that offends, | it 3.01. 35
must your bold verdict enter talk with lords?" 3.01. 63
believe me, lords, my tender years can tell, 3.01. 71
o my good lords, and virtuous henry, | pity the 3.01. 76
but join in friendship, as your lords have done. 3.01.145
therefore, my loving lords, our pleasure is 3.01.157
city, | and we be lords and rulers over roan, 3.02. 11
and, lords, accept this hearty kind embrace. 3.03. 82
now let us on, my lords, and join our powers, 3.03. 90
then judge, great lords, if i have done amiss; 4.01. 27
when first this order was ordain'd, my lords, 4.01. 33
be patient, lords, and give them leave to speak. 4.01. 82
and you, my lords, methinks you do not well | to 4.01.128
good my lords, be friends. 4.01.133
and you, my lords: 4.01.137
my lords ambassadors, your several suits | have 5.01. 34
these news, my lords, may cheer our drooping 5.02. 1
then on, my lords, and france be fortunate! 5.02. 21
my lords, and please you, 'tis not so, | i did 5.04. 10
for know, my lords, the states of christendom, 5.04. 96
since, lords of england, it is thus agreed 5.04.116
a dow'r, my lords? 5.05. 48
and therefore, lords, since he affects her most, 5.05. 59
then yield, my lords, and here conclude with me 5.05. 77
lords, with one cheerful voice welcome my love. 2H6 1.01. 36
consider, lords, he is the next of blood, | and 1.01.151
look to it, lords, let not his smoothing words 1.01.156
i fear me, lords, for all this flattering gloss, 1.01.163
still revelling like lords till all be gone; 1.01.224
not all these lords do vex me half so much | as 1.03. 75
yet must we join with him and with the lords, 1.03. 95
for my part, noble lords, i care not which, | or 1.03.101
now, lords, my choler being overblown | with 1.03.152
by these ten bones, my lords, he did speak them 1.03.190 P
come, come, my lords, these oracles | are hardly 1.04. 70
invite my lords of salisbury and warwick | to 1.04. 79
believe me, lords, for flying at the brook, | i 2.01. 1
how now, my lords? 2.01. 43
the winds grow high, so do your stomachs, lords. 2.01. 53
i pray, my lords, let me compound this strife. 2.01. 56
my lords, saint albon here hath done a miracle; 2.01.129
now, my good lords of salisbury and warwick, 2.02. 1
edward the third, my lords, had seven sons: 2.02. 10
we thank you, lords. 2.02. 64
lords, let him go. 2.03. 47
the servant of this armorer, my lords. 2.03. 58
my lords, at once: 3.01. 66
my lords, what to your wisdoms seemeth best, 3.01.195
that these great lords, and margaret our queen, 3.01.207
free lords, cold snow melts with the sun's hot 3.01.223
believe me, lords, were none more wise than i — 3.01.231
great lords, from ireland am i come amain, | to 3.01.282
send succors, lords, and stop the rage betime, 3.01.285
provide me soldiers, lords, | whiles i take 3.01.319
lords, take your places; 3.02. 19
help, lords, the king is dead. 3.02. 33
why, how now, lords? 3.02.237
well, lords, we have not got that which we have: 5.03. 20
now, by my /faith, lords, 'twas a glorious day. 5.03. 29
stay by me, my lords, | and, soldiers, stay and 3H6 1.01. 31
then leave me not, my lords, be resolute, | i 1.01. 43
my lords, look where the sturdy rebel sits, 1.01. 50
hear him, lords, | and be you silent and 1.01.121
why faint you, lords? 1.01.129
for richard, in the view of many lords, 1.01.138
suppose, my lords, he did it unconstrain'd, 1.01.143
why whisper you, my lords, and answer not? 1.01.149
what mutter you, or what conspire you, lords? 1.01.165
the northern lords that have forsworn thy colors 1.01.251
the loss of those three lords torments my heart; 1.01.270
the queen with all the northern earls and lords 1.02. 49
and, lords, bow low to him; 1.04. 94
how now, fair lords? 2.01. 95
if for the last, say ay, and to it, lords. 2.01.165
attend me, lords: 2.01.168
my royal father, cheer these noble lords, | and 2.02. 78
for god's sake, lords, give signal to the fight. 2.02.100
have done with words, my lords, and hear me 2.02.117
now, lords, take leave until we meet again, 2.03. 42
away, away! once more, sweet lords, farewell. 2.03. 48
now breathe we, lords, good fortune bids us 2.06. 31
but think you, lords, that clifford fled with 2.06. 37
lords, give us leave. i'll try this widow's wit. 3.02. 33
lords, use her /honorably. 3.02.123
my lords, forbear this talk; 4.01. 6
my lords, before it pleas'd his majesty | to 4.01. 67
speak suddenly, my lords, are we all friends? 4.02. 4
what now remains, my lords, for us to do | but 4.03. 60
make much of him, my lords, for this is he 4.06. 75
my lords, we were forewarned of your coming, 4.07. 17
what counsel, lords? 4.08. 1
fair lords, take leave and stand not to reply. 4.08. 23
farewell, sweet lords, let's meet at coventry. 4.08. 32
and, lords, towards coventry bend we our course, 4.08. 58
lords, to the field! 5.01.113
fly, lords, and save yourselves, | for warwick 5.02. 48
i mean, my lords, those powers that the queen 5.03. 7
great lords, wise men ne'er sit and wail their 5.04. 1
this speak i, lords, to let you understand, | if 5.04. 33
prepare you, lords, for edward is at hand, 5.04. 60
give signal to the fight, and to it, lords! 5.04. 72
lords, knights, and gentlemen, what i should say 5.04. 73
then in god's name, lords, | be valiant, and 5.04. 81
what likelihood of his amendment, lords? R3 1.03. 33
catesby, i come. lords, will you go with me? 1.03.321
dukes, earls, lords, gentlemen — indeed of all. 2.01. 69
come, lords, will you go | to comfort edward 2.01.139
good lords, make all the speedy haste you may. 3.01. 60
my good lords both, with all the heed i can. 3.01.187
the lords at pomfret, when they rode from london 3.02. 83
to–day the lords you /talk'd of are beheaded. 3.02. 91
but you, my honorable lords, may name the time, 3.04. 18
my noble lords and cousins all, good morrow. 3.04. 22
no delay, | for, lords, to–morrow is a busy day. 5.03. 18
good lords, conduct him to his regiment. 5.03.103
once more, good night, kind lords and gentlemen. 5.03.107
cry mercy, lords and watchful gentlemen, | that 5.03.224
have i since your departure had, my lords. 5.03.229
how far into the morning is it, lords? 5.03.234
ay, marry, | there will be woe indeed, lords; H8 1.03. 39
and a great one, | to many lords and ladies; 1.03. 53
for me, my lords, | i love him not, nor fear him 2.02. 49
what are your pleasures with me, reverent lords? 3.01. 26
my lords, i care not (so much i am happy | above 3.01. 33
my lords, i thank you both for your good wills, 3.01. 68
can you think, lords, | that any englishman dare 3.01. 83
far hence | in mine own country, lords. 3.01. 91
mend 'em for shame, my lords! 3.01.105
i am old, my lords, | and all the fellowship i 3.01.120
'tis not well, lords. 3.01.133
do what ye will, my lords; 3.01.175
my lords, you speak your pleasures. 3.02. 13
but, my lords, | she is a gallant creature, and 3.02. 48
now, my lords, | saw you the cardinal? 3.02.110
take notice, lords, he has a loyal breast, | for 3.02.200
where's your commission, lords? 3.02.233
(i mean your malice), know, officious lords, | i 3.02.237
my lords, | can ye endure to hear this arrogance 3.02.277
the rich stream | of lords and ladies, having 4.01. 63
incens'd the lords o' th' council that he is 5.01. 43
without, my noble lords? 5.02. 40
must be sudden too, | my noble lords; 5.02. 56
my good lords: 5.02. 67
(i speak it with a single heart, my lords) | a 5.02. 73
this is too much. | forbear for shame, my lords. 5.02.121
are you all agreed, lords? 5.02.126
mercy | but i must needs to th' tower, my lords? 5.02.128
stay, good my lords, | i have a little yet to 5.02.132
look there, my lords; 5.02.133
do you think, my lords, | the king will suffer 5.02.140
was it discretion, lords, to let this man, 5.02.172
well, well, my lords, respect him, | take him, 5.02.188
be friends, for shame, my lords! 5.02.194
come, lords, we trifle time away; 5.02.212
as i have made ye one, lords, one remain: 5.02.214
lead the way, lords, | ye must all see the queen 5.04. 72
kings, princes, lords! TRO 1.03.264
to see these grecian lords! 3.03.138
t' invite the troyan lords after the combat | to 3.03.236
please you walk in, my lords. 4.03. 12
are you lords a' th' field? COR 1.06. 47
like a dog, but for disturbing the lords within. 4.05. 52 P
you must report to th' volscian lords, how 5.03. 3
go tell the lords a' th' city i am here. 5.06. 1
say no more. | here come the lords. 5.06. 59
but, worthy lords, have you with heed perused 5.06. 61
hail, lords! 5.06. 70
read it not, noble lords, | but tell the traitor 5.06. 83
you lords and heads a' th' state, perfidiously 5.06. 90
pardon me, lords, 'tis the first time that ever 5.06.104
your judgments, my grave lords, | must give this 5.06.105
why, noble lords, | will you be put in mind of 5.06.116
my lords, when you shall know (as in this rage, 5.06.135
fair lords, your fortunes are alike in all, TIT 1.01.174
upright he held it, lords, that held it last. 1.01.200
proclaim our honors, lords, with trump and drum. 1.01.275
lords, accompany | your noble emperor and his 1.01.333
and fear not, lords, and you, lavinia; 1.01.471
why, how now, lords? 2.01. 45
why, lords, and think you not how dangerous | it 2.01. 63
young lords, beware! 2.01. 69
i tell you, lords, you do but plot your deaths 2.01. 78
my lords, a solemn hunting is in hand, | there 2.01.112
and you have rung it lustily, my lords — 2.02. 14
sweet lords, entreat her hear me but a word. 2.03.138
come on, my lords, the better foot before. 2.03.192
my lords, with all the humbleness i may, | i 4.02. 4
and now, young lords, was't not a happy star 4.02. 32
good morrow, lords. 4.02. 51
she is delivered, lords, she is delivered. 4.02. 61
he is your brother, lords, sensibly fed | of 4.02.122
so, brave lords, when we join in league | i am a 4.02.136
no, lords, no. 4.02.150
hark ye, lords, you see i have given her physic, 4.02.162
therefore, my lords, it highly us concerns | by 4.03. 27
why, lords, what wrongs are these! 4.04. 1
my lords, you know, /as /know the mightful gods, 4.04. 5
a goodly humor, is it not, my lords? 4.04. 19
arm, my lords! 4.04. 62
therefore, great lords, be as your titles 5.01. 5
no; i eat not lords. TIM 1.01.204 P
o, they eat lords; 1.01.206 P
nay, my lords, | ceremony was but devis'd at 1.02. 14
they say, my lords, "ira furor brevis est," 1.02. 28
i do beseech you, good my lords, keep on, | i'll 2.02. 34
rest, and 'mongst lords /i be thought a fool. 3.03. 21
my lords, then, under favor, pardon me | if i 3.05. 40
o my lords, | as you are great, be pitifully 3.05. 51
why, /i say, my lords, h'as done fair service, 3.05. 62
my lords, if not for any parts in him — 3.05. 75
my lords, | i do beseech you know me. 3.05. 88
how now, my lords? 3.06.106 P
attend the lords of france and burgundy, LR 1.01. 34
that in the natures of their lords rebel, 2.02. 76
'tis true, my lords, he did. 5.03.276
you lords and noble friends, know our intent. 5.03.297
throwing but shows of service on their lords, OTH 1.01. 52
so that, dear lords, if i be left behind, | a 1.03.255
will you lead, lords? ANT 2.06. 81
be jolly, lords. 2.07. 59
gentle lords, let's part, | you see we have 2.07.121
lord of lords! 4.08. 16
my lords, you are appointed for that office; CYM 3.05. 10
leave not the worthy lucius, good my lords, 3.05. 16
go before | this lout as he exceeds our lords, 5.02. 9
and lords and ladies in their lives | have read PER 1.ch. 7
here comes the lords of tyre. 1.03. 9 P
peace to the lords of tyre! 1.03. 29
with me? and welcome. happy day, my lords. 2.04. 22
the winds | with stench of our slain lords. TNK 1.01. 47
i have heard the fortunes | of your dead lords, 1.01. 57
our beds, | that our dear lords have none! 1.01.141
but our lords | lie blist'ring 'fore the 1.01.145
you comfort | to give your dead lords graves; 1.01.149
go and find out | the bones of your dead lords, 1.04. 7
lords and courtiers that have got maids with 4.03. 41 P
those proud lords to blame | make weak–made LUC 1259
while collatine and his consorted lords | with 1609
"but ere i name him, you fair lords," quoth she 1688
she utters this, "he, he, fair lords, 'tis he, 1721
they are the lords and owners of their faces, SON 94. 7

/LORDSHIP 2 FR 0.0002 REL FR 1 V 1 P

will't please your /lordship drink a cup of sack SHR in.2. 2
we shall hear of your /lordship anon. AWW 4.03.196 P

LORDSHIP 115 FR 0.0130 REL FR 57 V 58 P

he wond'red that your lordship | would suffer TGV 1.03. 4
i think your lordship is not ignorant | how his 1.03. 25
good, i think, your lordship sent him thither: 1.03. 29
may't please your lordship, 'tis a word or two 1.03. 52
good morrow to your lordship. MM 2.01.138
hour to–morrow | shall i attend your lordship? 2.02.160
we'll wait upon your lordship. ADO 1.03. 75 P
i think i told your lordship a year since, how 2.02. 12 P
means your lordship to be married to–morrow? 3.02. 88 P
yield my virgin patent up | unto his lordship, MND 1.01. 81
i thank your lordship, you have got me one. MV 3.02.196
"will't please your lordship cool your hands?" SHR in.1. 58
players | that offer service to your lordship. in.1. 78
so please your lordship to accept our duty. in.1. 82
sly, call not me honor nor lordship. in.2. 6 P
beseech your lordship to make some reservation AWW 2.03.244 P
but i hope your lordship thinks not him a 2.05. 1 P
if your lordship find him not a hilding, hold me 3.06. 3 P
be but your lordship present at his examination, 3.06. 28 P
when your lordship sees the bottom of /his 3.06. 36 P
as't please your lordship. i'll leave you. 3.06.109
his lordship will next morning for france. 4.03. 77 P
here's his lordship now. 4.03. 83 P
hence, it requires haste of your lordship. 4.03. 95 P
i have told your lordship already: 4.03.105 P
if your lordship be in't, as i believe you are, 4.03.114 P
i shall beseech your lordship to remain with me 4.05. 86 P
of comfort and leave him to your lordship. 5.02. 25 P
that you fly them as you swear them lordship, 5.03.156
he is not here, so please your lordship, that TN 2.04. 8 P
were i a woman, | i should your lordship. 2.04.109
my lord, i had forgot to tell your lordship: R2 2.02. 93
because your lordship was proclaimed traitor. 2.03. 30
his lordship is walk'd forth into the orchard. 2H4 1.01. 4
falstaff, and't please your lordship. 1.02. 59 P
god give your lordship good time of day. 1.02. 93 P
i am glad to see your lordship abroad. 1.02. 94 P
i heard say your lordship was sick, i hope your 1.02. 95 P
i hope your lordship goes abroad by advice. 1.02. 96 P
your lordship, though not clean past your youth, 1.02. 96 P
humbly beseech your lordship to have a reverend 1.02. 99 P
and't please your lordship, i hear his majesty 1.02.103 P
a kind of lethargy, and't please your lordship, 1.02.112 P
your lordship may minister the potion of 1.02.127 P
will your lordship lend me a thousand pound to 1.02.223 P
pleaseth your lordship | to meet his grace just 4.01.223
methinks his lordship should be humbler, | it 1H6 3.01. 56
belike your lordship takes us then for fools, 3.02. 62
are your supplications to his lordship? 2H6 1.03. 14 P
i have a suit unto your lordship. 4.07. 3 P
be it a lordship, thou shalt have it for that 4.07. 4 P
cousin of exeter, what thinks your lordship? 3H6 4.08. 34
how hath your lordship brook'd imprisonment? R3 1.01.125
then certifies your lordship that this night 3.02. 10
god keep your lordship in that gracious mind! 3.02. 56
the better that your lordship please to ask. 3.02. 97
i'll wait upon your lordship. 3.02.112
i shall return before your lordship thence. 3.02.120
i'll wait upon your lordship. 3.02.123
his lordship knows me well and loves me well. 3.04. 30
die | until your lordship came to see his end, 3.05. 53
and to that end we wish'd your lordship here, 3.05. 67
your lordship is a guest too. H8 1.03. 51
your lordship shall along. 1.03. 64
o that your lordship were but now confessor | to 1.04. 15
by my faith, | and thank your lordship. 1.04. 25
"my lord, the horses your lordship sent for, 2.02. 1 P
beseech your lordship, | vouchsafe to speak my 2.03. 70
i shall both find your lordship judge and juror, 5.02. 95
honor and lordship are my titles. TRO 3.01. 16 P

why, there it goes, god give his lordship joy! TIT 4.03. 77
your lordship ever binds him. TIM 1.01.104
humbly i thank your lordship. 1.01.149
vouchsafe my labor, and long live your lordship! 1.01.152
which i do beseech | your lordship to accept. 1.01.156
we'll bear, with your lordship. 1.01.177
please it your lordship, he hath put me off | to 2.02. 19
and i am sent expressly to your lordship. 2.02. 32
that i may make his lordship understand 2.02. 42
hath sent to your lordship to furnish him, 3.01. 19 P
please your lordship, here is the wine. 3.01. 30 P
your lordship speaks your pleasure. 3.01. 33 P
requesting your lordship to supply his instant 3.02. 35 P
i know his lordship is but merry with me; 3.02. 37
commend me bountifully to his good lordship, and 3.02. 53 P
we attend his lordship; pray signify so much. 3.04. 37 P
ever at the best, hearing well of your lordship. 3.06. 28 P
not summer more willing than we your lordship. 3.06. 30 P
unkindly with your lordship that i return'd you 3.06. 37 P
when your lordship this other day sent to me, i 3.06. 42 P
what does his lordship mean? 3.06. 86 P
i was sure your lordship did not give it me. JC 4.03.254
hail to your lordship! HAM 1.02.160
what means your lordship? 3.01.105 P
your lordship is right welcome back to denmark. 5.02. 81
sweet lord, if your lordship were at leisure, i 5.02. 89 P
i thank your lordship, it is very hot. 5.02. 94 P
your lordship speaks most infallibly of him. 5.02.121 P
if your lordship would vouchsafe the answer. 5.02.168 P
i commend my duty to your lordship. 5.02.182 P
my services to your lordship. LR 1.01. 29 P
so please your lordship, none. 1.02. 27 P
persuade me to the murther of your lordship, 2.01. 44
we'll wait upon your lordship. OTH 3.02. 6
i do beseech your lordship call her back. 4.01.249
i'll attend your lordship. CYM 1.02. 39 P
it is not fit /your lordship should undertake 2.01. 26 P
ay, it is fit for your lordship only. 2.01. 30 P
i'll attend your lordship. 2.01. 51 P
your lordship is the most patient man in loss, 2.03. 1 P
patient after the noble temper of your lordship. 2.03. 5 P
good morrow to your lordship. PER 3.02. 11
but i much marvel that your lordship, having 3.02. 21
doth your lordship call? 5.01. 8
no, but from this place to remove your lordship; TNK 2.02.261

/LORDSHIP'S 1 FR 0.0001 REL FR 1 V 0 P
this is his /lordship's man. MM 4.02.100

LORDSHIP'S 10 FR 0.0011 REL FR 6 V 4 P
as one relying on your lordship's will, | and TGV 1.03. 61
quality worthy your lordship's entertainment. AWW 3.06. 12 P
indeed he is not for your lordship's respect. 3.06.100 P
i will attend upon your lordship's leisure. 1H6 5.01. 55
he sends to know your lordship's pleasure, | if R3 3.02. 15
i am your lordship's. H8 1.03. 67
here, at your lordship's service. TIM 1.01.115
your lordship's a goodly villain. 3.03. 27 P
one of your lordship's pages. CYM 2.01. 41 P
what's your lordship's pleasure? 2.03. 80

LORDSHIPS' 1 FR 0.0001 REL FR 1 V 0 P
dance attendance on their lordships' pleasures, H8 5.02. 31

LORDSHIPS 3 FR 0.0003 REL FR 3 V 0 P
health to your lordships. H8 2.02. 61
i do beseech your lordships, | that, in this 5.02. 80
do, and with his gifts present | your lordships, TIT 4.02. 15

LORENZO 24 FR 0.0027 REL FR 21 V 3 P
most noble kinsman, | gratiano, and lorenzo. MV 1.01. 58
come, good lorenzo. 1.01.103
and i must to lorenzo and the rest, | but we 2.02.205
soon at supper shalt thou see | lorenzo, who is 2.03. 6
o lorenzo, | if thou keep promise, i shall end 2.03. 19
this is the penthouse under which lorenzo 2.06. 1
here comes lorenzo, more of this hereafter. 2.06. 20
lorenzo, and thy love. 2.06. 28
lorenzo, certain, and my love indeed, | for who 2.06. 29
and now who knows | but you, lorenzo, whether i 2.06. 31
and in their ship i am sure lorenzo is not. 2.08. 3
seen together | lorenzo and his amorous jessica. 2.08. 9
lorenzo and his infidel? 3.02.218
lorenzo and salerio, welcome hither, | if that 3.02.220
lorenzo, i commit into your hands | the 3.04. 24
you need not fear us, lorenzo, launcelot and i 3.05. 31 P
unto his son lorenzo and his daughter. 4.01.390
this deed will be well welcome to lorenzo. 4.02. 4
did young lorenzo swear he lov'd her well, 5.01. 18
did you see master lorenzo? 5.01. 41 P
master lorenzo, sola, sola! 5.01. 42 P
hence — | nor you, lorenzo — jessica, nor you. 5.01.121
lorenzo here | shall witness i set forth as soon 5.01.270
how now, lorenzo? 5.01.288

LORRAINE 2 FR 0.0002 REL FR 2 V 0 P
the crown | of charles the duke of lorraine, H5 1.02. 70
to charles, the foresaid duke of lorraine; 1.02. 83

LOSE *(also leese)*

/LOSE 1 FR 0.0001 REL FR 1 V 0 P
/i /had /rather /lose /the /battle /than /that LR 5.01. 18

LOSE 226 FR 0.0255 REL FR 190 V 36 P
ay, but to lose our bottles in the pool — TMP 4.01.208 P
now, jerkin, you are like to lose your hair, and 4.01.237 P
we shall lose our time, | and all be turn'd to 4.01.247
when did you lose your daughter? 5.01.152
the island, one dear son | shall i twice lose. 5.01.177
me, | made me neglect my studies, lose my time, TGV 1.01. 67
ass, you'll lose the tide, if you tarry any 2.03. 36 P
tut, man, i mean thou'lt lose the flood, and, in 2.03. 41 P
and, in losing the flood, lose thy voyage, and, 2.03. 42 P
and, in losing thy voyage, lose thy master, and, 2.03. 43 P
in losing thy master, lose thy service, and, in 2.03. 44 P
for fear thou shouldst lose thy tongue. 2.03. 46 P
where should i lose my tongue? 2.03. 47 P
lose the tide, and the voyage, and the master, 2.03. 50 P
julia i lose, and valentine i lose: 2.06. 19
julia i lose, and valentine i lose: 2.06. 19
if i keep them, i needs must lose myself; 2.06. 20
if i lose them, thus find i by their loss — 2.06. 21
dissolves to water, and doth lose his form. 3.02. 8
then know that i have little wealth to lose. 4.01. 11
shall i not lose my suit? WIV 1.04.143 P
if i find her honest, i lose not my labor; 2.01.239 P
shall i lose my doctor? 3.01.102 P
shall i lose my parson? 3.01.103 P
and makes us lose the good we oft might win, MM 1.04. 78
if i do lose thee, i do lose a thing | that none 3.01. 7
i do lose a thing | that none but fools would 3.01. 7
upon the act of fornication | to lose his head, 5.01. 71
you do but lose your labor. 5.01.428
i will go lose myself, | and wander up and down ERR 1.02. 30
in quest of them (unhappy), ah, lose myself. 1.02. 40
the jewel best enamelled | will lose his beauty; 2.01.110
of those but he hath the wit to lose his hair. 2.02. 85 P
choose, | for forty ducats is too much to lose. 4.03. 96
wits again, | or lose my labor in assaying it. 5.01. 97
prove that ever i lose more blood with love than ADO 1.01.250 P
that her ear lose nothing | of the false sweet 3.01. 32
so wise | to lose an oath to win a paradise?" LLL 4.03. 71
/let us once lose our oaths to find ourselves, 4.03.358
or else we lose ourselves to keep our oaths. 4.03.359
heaven's fiery eye, | by light we lose light; 5.02.376
you will lose your reputation. 5.02.702 P
of self-affairs, | my mind did lose it. MND 1.01.114
spurn me, strike me, | neglect me, lose me; 2.01.206
i swear by that which i will lose for thee, | to 3.02.252
tongue, lose thy light, | moon, take thy flight, 5.01.304
they lose it that do buy it with much care. MV 1.01. 75
in the place i go to, | and lose my hopes. 2.02.189
they have the wisdom by their wit to lose. 2.09. 81
for in choosing wrong | i lose your company; 3.02. 3
i would not lose you, and, you know yourself, 3.02. 5
then, if he lose, he makes a swan-like end, 3.02. 44
which when you part from, lose, or give away, 3.02.172
shall lose a hair through bassanio's fault. 3.02.302
ere thou shalt lose for me one drop of blood. 4.01.113
repent but you that you shall lose your friend, 4.01.278
i would lose all, ay, sacrifice them all | here 4.01.286
i should neither sell, nor give, nor lose it. 4.01.443
lose and neglect the creeping hours of time; AYL 2.07.112
i would not lose the dog for twenty pound. SHR in.1. 21
i thank thee, thou shalt not lose by it. in.2. 99
so may you lose your arms. 2.01.221
the breach yourselves made, you lose your city. AWW 1.01.125 P
keep it not, you cannot choose but lose by't. 1.01.146 P
might one do, sir, to lose it to her own liking? 1.01.150 P
'tis a commodity will lose the gloss with lying: 1.01.153 P
waters of my love | and lack not to lose still. 1.03.204
but lend and give where she is sure to lose; 1.03.215
when i lose thee again, i care not; 2.03.206 P
approach the city, we shall lose all the sight. 3.05. 2 P
lose our drum! well. 3.05. 88 P
but i shall lose the grounds i work upon. 3.07. 3
and i shall lose my life for want of language. 4.01. 70
greatest obloquy i' th' world | in me to lose. 4.02. 45
greatest obloquy i' th' world | in me to lose. 4.02. 49
lord, how we lose our pains! 5.01. 24
(since you lack virtue, i will lose a husband) 5.03.222
if i lose a scruple of this sport, let me be TN 2.05. 2 P
my lady would not lose him for more than i'll 3.04.104 P
not thou, man, thou shalt lose nothing here. WT 4.04.255 P
having no external thing to lose | but the word JN 2.01.571
and, by disjoining hands, hell lose a soul. 3.01.197
uncle, i needs must pray that thou mayst lose; 3.01.332
whoever wins, on that side shall i lose; 3.01.335
and lose it, life and all, as arthur did. 3.04.144
none, but to lose your eyes. 4.01. 90
and lose my way | among the thorns and dangers 4.03.140
since i must lose the use of all deceit? 5.04. 27
thou lack'st, and that breath wilt thou lose. R2 2.01. 30
you lose a thousand well-disposed hearts, | and 2.01.206
whilst others come to make him lose at home. 2.02. 81
leap, | the one in fear to lose what they enjoy, 2.04. 13
must he lose | the name of king? 3.03.145
what didst thou lose, jack? 1H4 3.03.100 P
rebellion in this land shall lose his sway, 5.05. 41
nor lose the good advantage of his grace | by 2H4 4.04. 28
i break, and you, my gentle creditors, lose. ep 12 P
us, | we lose the better half of our possession; H5 1.01. 8
willfulness | so soon did lose his seat (and all 1.01. 36
and our nation lose | the name of hardiness and 1.02.219
what see you in those papers that you lose | so 2.02. 72
i would not lose so great an honor | as one man 4.03. 31
win all, | and henry born at windsor lose all: 1H6 3.01.198
he dies, we lose; 4.03. 31
we lose, they daily get; 4.03. 32
thou never hadst renown, nor canst not lose it. 4.05. 40
grove | shall lose his head for his presumption. 2H6 1.02. 34
i lose indeed; 3.01.183
no, not to lose it all, as thou hast done. 3.01.296
yet to recover them would lose my life. 4.07. 66
to lose thy youth in peace, and to achieve | the 5.02. 46
are old enough now, and yet methinks you lose. 3H6 1.01.113
hath he deserv'd to lose his birthright thus? 1.01.219
should lose his birthright by his father's fault 2.02. 35
york | the worthy gentleman did lose his life. 3.02. 7
pity they should lose their father's lands. 3.02. 31
where having nothing, nothing can he lose. 3.03.152
now therefore let us hence, and lose no hour, 4.01.148
warwick may lose, that now hath won the day. 4.04. 15
judge | what 'twere to lose it and be miserable! R3 1.03.257
as loath to lose him, not your father's death; 2.02. 10
that he will lose his head ere give consent 3.04. 38
shall lose the royalty of england's throne. 3.04. 40
up to some scaffold, there to lose their heads. 4.04.243
would by a good discourser lose some life, H8 1.01. 41
that which we run at, | and lose by overrunning. 1.01.143
hear what i say, and then go home and lose me. 2.01. 57
the king loves you, | beware you lose it not. 3.01.172
knowing she will not lose her wonted greatness, 4.02.102
i will, | or let me lose the fashion of a man! 4.02.159
should lose their names, and so should justice TRO 1.03.118
for i presume brave hector would not lose | so 2.02.203
lose all the serpentine craft of thy caduceus, 2.03. 11 P
do in our eyes begin to lose their gloss, | yea, 2.03.119
that i shall lose distinction in my joys, | as 3.02. 27
and all my powers do their bestowing lose, 3.02. 37
for which we lose our heads to gild his horns! 4.05. 31
now if thou lose thy stay, | thou on him leaning 5.03. 60
i come to lose my arm, or win my sleeve. 5.03. 96
/that's task'd to mow | or all or lose his hire. COR 1.03. 37
if we lose the field, | we cannot keep the town. 1.07. 4
and end, but will | lose those he hath won. 2.01.226
to lose itself in a fog, where being three parts 2.03. 31 P
the virtues | which our divines lose by 'em. 2.03. 58
you are at point to lose your liberties. 3.01.193
us stand to our authority, | or let us lose it. 3.01.208
to lose it by his country | were to us all that 3.01.300
in peace what each of them by th' other lose 3.02. 44
yet, were there but this single plot to lose, 3.02.102
and lose advantage, which doth ever cool | i' 4.01. 43
target from thy brawn, | or lose mine arm for't. 4.05.121
into his kindness, | and cannot lose your way. 5.01. 60
alack, or we must lose | the country, our dear 5.03.109
lose not so noble a friend on vain suppose, TIT 1.01.440
his philomel must lose her tongue to-day, | thy 2.03. 43
and learn me how to lose a winning match, ROM 3.02. 12
thee at once, which thou at once wouldst lose. 3.03.121
i am sorry i shall lose a stone by thee. TIM 4.03.370
nothing can you steal | but thieves do lose it. 4.03.448
bend doth awe the world | did lose his lustre; JC 1.02.124
current when it serves, | or lose our ventures. 4.03.224
if we do lose this battle, then is this | the 5.01. 97
then, if we lose this battle, | you are 5.01.107
bears that life | which he deserves to lose. MAC 1.03.111
that thou mightst not lose the dues of rejoicing 1.05. 12 P
so i lose none | in seeking to augment it, but 2.01. 26
of reason to the dane | and lose your voice. HAM 1.02. 45
let not thy mother lose her prayers, hamlet, | i 1.02.118
or lose your heart, or your chaste treasure open 1.03. 31
turn awry, | and lose the name of action. 3.01. 87
the passion ending, doth the purpose lose. 3.02.195
o heart, lose not thy nature! 3.02.393
you will lose, my lord. 5.02.209 P
against thine enemies, ne'er /fear'd to lose it, LR 1.01.156
so lost a father | that you must lose a husband. 1.01.247
edmund, it shall lose thee nothing, do it 1.02.115 P
and woes by wrong imaginations lose | the 4.06.283
of vexation on't, | as it may lose some color. OTH 1.01. 73
we lose it not, so long as we can smile. 1.03.211
with me, both at a birth, | shall lose me. 2.03.213
i will in cassio's lodging lose this napkin, 3.03.321
where should i lose the handkerchief, emilia? 3.04. 23
i must break, | or lose myself in dotage. ANT 1.02.117
thou teachest like a fool: the way to lose him. 1.03. 10
with him at any game, | thou art sure to lose; 2.03. 27
though i lose | the praise of it by telling, you 2.06. 42
if i lose mine honor, | i lose myself; 3.04. 22
if i lose mine honor, | i lose myself; 3.04. 23
it would make any man cold to lose. CYM 2.03. 3 P
if i would lose it for a revenue | of any king's 2.03.143
i am sure | she would not lose it. 2.04.124
but to win time | to lose so bad employment, in 3.04.110
why, worthy father, what have we to lose, | but 4.02.124
and i must lose | two of the sweet'st companions 5.05.348
as jewels lose their glory if neglected, | so PER 2.02. 12
you'll lose nothing by custom. 4.02.138 P
reveal how thou at sea didst lose thy wife. 5.01.244
and shake to lose his honor) is like her | that, TNK pr 5
sensually subdu'd | we lose our human title. 1.01.233
might not a man well lose himself and love her? 2.02.155
if that will lose ye, farewell, palamon! 2.02.177
and if he lose her then, he's a cold coward. 2.02.253
to your travel, | nor shall you lose your wish. 2.05. 31
men lose when they incline to treachery, | and 3.01. 67
you'll lose all else. 3.04. 9
the other lose his head, | and all his friends; 3.06.296
that you must lose your head to-morrow morning, 4.01. 77
for i must lose my maidenhead by cocklight, 4.01.112
of mine eyes | were i to lose one — they are 5.01.155
you'll lose the noblest sight | that ev'r was 5.02. 99
we'll go with you, | i will not lose the fight. 5.02.103
will you lose this sight? 5.03. 1
i have spoke, your arcite | did not lose by't; 5.03.122
having no fair to lose, you need not fear, | the VEN 1083
and he hath won what he would lose again; LUC 688
and let mild women to him lose their mildness, 979
they that lose half with greater patience bear 1158
nor lose possession of that fair thou ow'st, SON 18.10
and our dear love lose name of single one, 39. 6
if i lose thee, my loss is my love's gain, | and 42. 9
both find each other, and i lose both twain, 42.11
but weep to have that which it fears to lose. 64.14
the hardest knife ill us'd doth lose his edge. 95.14
and sweets grown common lose their dear delight. 102.12
not seen dwellers on form and favor | lose all, 125. 6
sake, | so him i lose through my unkind abuse. 134.12

LOSEL *(see lozel)*

LOSER 4 FR 0.0004 REL FR 3 V 1 P
nobly are subdued, | and neither party loser. 2H4 4.02. 91
but i can give the loser leave to chide. 2H6 3.01.182
draw both friend and foe, | winner and loser? HAM 4.05.144
at all, unless you repute yourself such a loser. OTH 2.03.271 P

LOSERS 4 FR 0.0004 REL FR 4 V 0 P
thus losers part. MV 2.07. 77
then with the losers let it sympathize, | for 1H4 5.01. 7
and well such losers may have leave to speak. 2H6 3.01.185
for losers will have leave | to ease their TIT 3.01.232

LOSES 11 FR 0.0012 REL FR 11 V 0 P
and this deceit loses the name of craft, | of WIV 5.05.226
sword can never win | the honor that he loses. AWW 3.02. 94
of danger wins a scar, | as oft it loses all. 3.02.122
for /loan oft loses both itself and friend, HAM 1.03. 76
and must draw me | that which my father loses: LR 3.03. 24
talk with them too — | who loses and who wins; 5.03. 15
honesty's a fool | and loses that it works for. OTH 3.03.383
caesar gets money where | he loses hearts. ANT 2.01. 14
you had of her pure honor gains or loses | your CYM 2.04. 59
who loses, yet i'll weep upon his bier. TNK 3.06.308
wins | loses a noble cousin for thy sins. 4.02.156

LOSEST 3 FR 0.0003 REL FR 2 V 1 P
thou losest thy old smell. AYL 1.02.108 P
thou losest labor. MAC 5.08. 8
thou losest here, a better where to find. LR 1.01.261

LOSE'T 1 FR 0.0001 REL FR 1 V 0 P
to lose't or give't away were such perdition OTH 3.04. 67

LOSETH 3 FR 0.0003 REL FR 2 V 1 P
yet he loseth it in a kind of jollity. ERR 2.02. 89 P
loseth men's hearts and leaves behind a stain 1H4 3.01.185

loseth his pride, and never waxeth strong. VEN 420
LOSING 24 FR 0.0027 REL FR 15 V 9 P
losing his verdure, even in the prime, | and all TGV 1.01. 49
and i have play'd the sheep in losing him. 1.01. 73
and, in losing the flood, lose thy voyage, and, 2.03. 42 P
and, in losing thy voyage, lose thy master, and, 2.03. 42 P
and, in losing thy master, lose thy service, and 2.03. 43 P
and, in losing thy service — why dost thou stop 2.03. 44 P
your light grows dark by losing of your eyes. LLL 1.01. 79
"— on pain of losing her tongue." 1.01.124 P
that i follow thus | a losing suit against him. MV 4.01. 62
the process but only the losing of hope by time. AWW 1.01. 16 P
than they are in losing them when they have WT 4.02. 27 P
that she might no more be in danger of losing. 5.02. 78 P
what have you lost by losing of this day? JN 3.04.116
of unwelcome news | hath but a losing office, 2H4 1.01.101
burs, | losing both beauty and utility; H5 5.02. 53
for losing ken of albion's wished coast. 2H6 3.02.113
i shall have glory by this losing day | more JC 5.05. 36
faith, e'en with losing his wits. HAM 5.01.159 P
so find we profit | by losing of our prayers. ANT 2.01. 8
reign, | losing a mite, a mountain gain. PER 2.ch. 8
losing her woes in shows of discontent. LUC 1580
and losing her, my friend hath found that loss; SON 42.10
that thou in losing me shall win much glory. 88. 8
fears, | still losing when i saw myself to win? 119. 4
/LOSS 1 FR 0.0001 REL FR 1 V 0 P
/my /care /is /loss /of /care, /by /old /care R2 4.01.196
LOSS 132 FR 0.0149 REL FR 115 V 17 P
my father's loss, the weakness which i feel, TMP 1.02.488
for our escape | is much beyond our loss. 2.01. 3
sir, you may thank yourself for this great loss, 2.01.124
so is the dear'st o' th' loss. 2.01.136
dishonor in that, monster, but an infinite loss. 4.01.210 P
irreparable is the loss, and patience | says, it 5.01.140
for the like loss i have her sovereign aid, 5.01.143
you the like loss? 5.01.144
and, supportable | to make the dear loss, have i 5.01.146
i have consider'd well his loss of time, | and TGV 1.03. 19
if i lose them, thus find i by their loss — 2.06. 21
a hundred pound in gold more than your loss. WIV 4.06. 5
but in the loss of question), that you, his MM 2.04. 90
my habit, no loss shall touch her by my company. 3.01.178 P
will not proclaim against her maiden loss, | how 4.04. 24
to see, | i hazarded the loss of whom i lov'd. ERR 1.01.131
younger than he did, by the loss of a beard. ADO 3.02. 49 P
whether antonio have had any loss at sea or no? MV 3.01. 43 P
why, thou loss upon loss! 3.01. 92 P
why, thou loss upon loss! 3.01. 92 P
he cried upon it at the merest loss, | and twice SHR in.1. 23
loss of virginity is rational increase, and AWW 1.01.127 P
sithence, in the loss that may happen, it 1.03.120 P
that's the loss of men, though it be the getting 3.02. 41 P
some dishonor we had in the loss of that drum, 3.06. 56 P
that very envy and the tongue of loss | cried TN 5.01. 58
the loss, the gain, the ord'ring on't, is all WT 2.01.169
on thy side, | poor thing, condemn'd to loss! 2.03.192
thy mother's fault art thus expos'd | to loss, 3.03. 51
whose loss of his most precious queen and 4.02. 23 P
as if that joy were now become a loss, cries, "o 5.02. 51 P
one eye declin'd for the loss of her husband, 5.02. 74 P
and victory, with little loss, doth play | upon JN 2.01.307
gracing the scroll that tells of this war's loss 2.01.348
or the light loss of england for a friend. 3.01.206
assured loss before the match be play'd. 3.01.336
had you such a loss as i, | i could give better 3.04. 99
my date of life out for his sweet live's loss. 4.03.106
for their advantage and your highness' loss. R2 1.04. 41
the worst is worldly loss thou canst unfold. 3.02. 94
care, | and what loss is it to be rid of care? 3.02. 96
i better brook the loss of brittle life | than 1H4 5.04. 78
by travers | give then such instances of loss? 2H4 1.01. 56
so did our men, heavy in hotspur's loss, | lend 1.01.121
we all that are engaged to this loss | knew that 1.01.180
that may repeat and history his loss | to new 4.01.201
to die, we are enow | to do our country loss; H5 4.03. 21
was ever known so great and little loss, | on 4.08.110
of loss, of slaughter, and discomfiture: 1H6 1.01. 59
or the loss of those great towns | will make him 1.01. 63
that now our loss might be ten times so much? 2.01. 53
sleeping neglection doth betray to loss | the 4.03. 49
lives, honors, lands, and all, hurry to loss. 4.03. 53
your loss is great, so your regard should be; 4.05. 22
my worth unknown, no loss is known in me. 4.05. 23
the utter loss of all the realm of france. 5.04.112
and can do nought but wail her darling's loss, 2H6 3.01.216
but wherefore grieve i at an hour's poor loss, 3.02.381
the loss of those three lords torments my heart; 3H6 1.01.270
were brought me of your loss and his depart. 2.01.110
our hap is loss, our hope but sad despair, | our 2.03. 9
/e'en for the loss of thee, having no more, | as 2.05.119
for by that loss i will not purchase them. 3.02. 73
loss of some pitch'd battle against warwick? 4.04. 4
no, but the loss of his own royal person. 4.04. 5
they quite forget their loss of liberty. 4.06. 15
we are, | we might recover all our loss again. 5.02. 30
lords, wise men ne'er sit and wail their loss, 5.04. 1
no other harm but loss of such a lord. R3 1.03. 7
the loss of such a lord includes all harms. 1.03. 8
their kingdom's loss, my woeful banishment, 1.03.192
was never widow had so dear a loss. 2.02. 77
were never orphans had so dear a loss. 2.02. 78
was never mother had so dear a loss. 2.02. 79
for me to joy and weep their gain and loss; 2.04. 59
match'd not the high perfection of my loss. 4.04. 66
bett'ring thy loss makes the bad causer worse; 4.04.122
the loss you have is but a son being king, | and 4.04.307
and by that loss your daughter is made queen. 4.04.308
what a loss our ladies | will have of these trim H8 1.03. 37
truly pitying | my father's loss, like a most 2.01.113
he counsels a divorce, a loss of her | that, 2.02. 30
success or loss, what is or is not, serves | as TRO 1.03.183
as honor, loss of time, travail, expense, 2.02. 4
with such a costly loss of wealth and friends. 4.01. 61
no more my grief, in such a precious loss. 4.04. 10
and loss assume all reason | without revolt. 5.02.145
to no further harm | than so much loss of time. COR 3.01.283
present, but the loss | of what is past. 3.02. 71
and, notwithstanding all this loss of blood, TIT 2.04. 29
whose loss hath pierc'd him deep and scarr'd his 4.04. 31
that you shall all repent the loss of mine. ROM 3.01.191
yet let me weep for such a feeling loss. 3.05. 74
so shall you feel the loss, but not the friend 3.05. 75
feeling so the loss, | i cannot choose but ever 3.05. 76
that seest not thy loss in transformation! TIM 4.03.345 P
o insupportable and touching loss! JC 4.03.151
then weigh what loss your honor may sustain | if HAM 1.03. 29
offer to defend him, | stand in assured loss. LR 3.06. 95
he speak of comfort | touching the turkish loss, OTH 2.01. 32
i am most unhappy in the loss of it. 3.04.102
rather makes choice of loss | than gain which ANT 3.01. 23
'twas a shame no less | than was his loss, to 3.13. 11
loose | beguil'd me to the very heart of loss. 4.12. 29
your loss is as yourself, great; 5.02.101
to your so infinite loss, so in our trifles | i CYM 1.01.120
if in the holding or loss of that you term her 1.04. 96 P
your lordship is the most patient man in loss, 2.03. 2 P
make /not, sir, | your loss your sport. 2.04. 48
thou bid'st me to my loss; 3.05.157
out, though with the loss | of many a bold one, 5.05. 70
their dear loss, | the more of you 'twas felt, 5.05.345
to bed, | where, by the loss of maidenhead, | a PER 3.ch. 10
thy loss is more than can thy portage quit 3.01. 35
man may serve seven years for the loss of a leg, 4.06.172 P
but the main grief springs from the loss | of a 5.01. 29
nor gain | made him regard, or loss consider, TNK 1.03. 30
which do cost us | the loss of our desire! 5.04.111
could buy | dear love but loss of dear love! 5.04.112
conquer'd triumphs, | the victor has the loss; 5.04.114
as, but for loss of nestor's golden words, | it LUC 1420
lo here the hopeless merchant of this loss, 1660
my love, the loss whereof still fearing! PP 7.10
one silly cross wrought all my loss, | o 17. 9
though thou repent, yet i have still the loss: SON 34.10
a loss in love that touches me more nearly. 42. 4
if i lose thee, my loss is my love's gain, | and 42. 9
and losing her, my friend hath found that loss; 42.10
increasing store with loss, and loss with store; 64. 8
increasing store with loss, and loss with store; 64. 8
compar'd with loss of thee will not seem so. 90.14
then, soul, live thou upon thy servant's loss, 146. 9
LOSSES 16 FR 0.0018 REL FR 10 V 6 P
and a fellow that hath had losses, and one that ADO 4.02. 84 P
i would it might prove the end of his losses. MV 3.01. 18 P
me half a million, laugh'd at my losses, mock'd 3.01. 56 P
these griefs and losses have so bated me | that 3.03. 32
glancing an eye of pity on his losses, | that 4.01. 27
add | unto their losses twenty thousand crowns, SHR 5.02.113
sometimes we make us comforts of our losses! AWW 4.03. 66 P
that you shall read | in your own losses, if he H5 2.04.139
which must proportion the losses we have borne, 3.06.127 P
for our losses, his exchequer is too poor; 3.06.129 P
wailing our losses, whiles the foe doth rage, 3H6 2.03. 26
fears of hostile strokes, their aches, losses, TIM 5.01.199
even so great men great losses should endure. JC 4.03.193
seeking to give | losses their remedies." LR 2.02.170
our losses fall so thick we must needs leave. TNK pr 32
all losses are restor'd, and sorrows end. SON 30.14
/LOST 4 FR 0.0004 REL FR 4 V 0 P
/thing, /in /honor, /had /my /father /lost, 2H4 4.01.111
/him /even /o'er /the /time /he /has /lost. LR 4.07. 79
/the /friend /hath /lost /his /friend, | /and 5.03. 55
we there him /lost, | where, driven before the PER 5.ch. 13
LOST 282 FR 0.0318 REL FR 220 V 62 P
all lost! to prayers, to prayers! all lost! TMP 1.01. 51 P
all lost! to prayers, to prayers! all lost! 1.01. 52 P
he hath lost his fellows, | and strays about to 1.02.417
my son is lost and (in my rate) she too, | who 2.01.110
we have lost your son, | i fear for ever. 2.01.132
humanely taken, all, all lost, quite lost; 4.01.190
humanely taken, all, all lost, quite lost; 4.01.190
thou wert but a lost monster. 4.01.203 P
where i have lost | (how sharp the point of this 5.01.137
for i | have lost my daughter. 5.01.148
found a wife | where he himself was lost; 5.01.211
if lost, why then a grievous labor won; TGV 1.01. 33
i (a lost mutton) gave your letter to her (a 1.01. 96 P
gave me (a lost mutton) nothing for my labor. 1.01. 98 P
to sigh, like a schoolboy that had lost his abc; 2.01. 22 P
it is no matter if the tied were lost; 2.03. 37 P
when mistress bridget lost the handle of her fan WIV 2.02. 12 P
so that i have lost my edifice by mistaking the 2.02.216 P
be thus foolishly lost at a game of tick–tack. MM 1.02.190 P
there she lost a noble and renown'd brother, in 3.01.219 P
of my hidden pow'r | than let him so be lost. 5.01.393
should have died when claudio lost his head — 5.01.488
and recover the lost hair of another man. ERR 2.02. 76 P
the plainer dealer, the sooner lost; 2.02. 88 P
/e'en no time to recover hair lost by nature. 2.02.103 P
no evil lost is wail'd when it is gone. 4.02. 24
how hast thou lost thy breath? 4.02. 30
hath he not lost much wealth by wrack of sea? 5.01. 49
even for the blood | that then i lost for thee, 5.01.194
how many gentlemen have you lost in this action? ADO 1.01. 5 P
you have lost the heart of signior benedick. 2.01.276 P
your grace may well say i have lost it. 2.01.282 P
whiles we enjoy it, but being lack'd and lost, 4.01.219
'tis won as towns with fire — so won, so lost. LLL 1.01.146
from tawny spain, lost in the world's debate. 1.01.173
since to wail friends lost | is not by much so 5.02.749
the ploughman lost his sweat, and the green corn MND 2.01. 94
thus weak, lost with their fears thus strong, 3.02. 27
thus hath he lost sixpence a day during his life 4.02. 19 P
in my school–days, when i had lost one shaft, MV 1.01.140
that which i owe is lost, but if you please | to 1.01.147
i have a father, you a daughter, lost. 2.05. 57
cold indeed, and labor lost: 2.07. 74
why, the end is, he hath lost a ship. 3.01. 17 P
would you had won the fleece that he hath lost. 3.02.242
off, | and swear i lost the ring defending it. 5.01.178
most true, i have lost my teeth in your service. AYL 1.01. 83 P
fair princess, you have lost much good sport. 1.02. 99 P
wrastling, which you have lost the sight of. 1.02.110 P
the sport, monsieur, that the ladies have lost? 1.02.135 P
sir, we kept time, we lost not our time. 5.03. 38 P
i count it but time lost to hear such a foolish 5.03. 39 P
how i lost my crupper, with many things of SHR 4.01. 81 P
never virgin /got till virginity was first lost. AWW 1.01.129 P
virginity, by being once lost, may be ten times 1.01.130 P
by being ever kept, it is ever lost. 1.01.132 P
whereof | the king is render'd lost. 1.03.230
we have lost our labor, they are gone a contrary 3.05. 7 P
danger known but the modesty which is so lost. 3.05. 28 P
a drum so lost! 3.06. 47 P
and i was the first that lost thee. 5.02. 44 P
we lost a jewel of her, and our esteem | was 5.03. 1
he lost a wife | whose beauty did astonish the 5.03. 15
praising what is lost | makes the remembrance 5.03. 19
since i have lost, have lov'd, was in mine eye 5.03. 54
that methought her eyes had lost her tongue, TN 2.02. 20
more longing, wavering, sooner lost and worn, 2.04. 34
when your young nephew titus lost his leg. 5.01. 63
and tortur'd me, | since i have lost thee! 5.01.220
as he had lost some province and a region WT 1.02.369
or both yourself and me | cry lost, and so good 1.02.411
which are here | by this discovery lost. 1.02.441
i do give lost, for i do feel it gone, | but 3.02. 95
an heir, if that which is lost be not found." 3.02.135 P
remember you of my own lord, | who is lost too. 3.02.231
for the babe | is counted lost for ever, perdita 3.03. 33
i was cozen'd by the way and lost all my money? 4.04.252 P
age, thou hast lost thy labor. 4.04.760 P
not have an heir | till his lost child be found? 5.01. 40
i lost a couple, that 'twixt heaven and earth 5.01.132
and then i lost | (all mine own folly) the 5.01.134
then have you lost a sight which was to be seen, 5.02. 42 P
the child were even then lost when it was found. 5.02. 72 P
to be found again, | lament till i am lost. 5.03.135
more than we of france, | rather lost more. JN 2.01.343
is not angiers lost? 3.04. 6
wife, | young arthur is my son, and he is lost. 3.04. 47
what have you lost by losing of this day? 3.04.116
strange to think how much king john hath lost 3.04.121
grievous taxes, | and quite lost their hearts; R2 2.01.247
ancient quarrels, and quite lost their hearts. 2.01.248
say, is my kingdom lost? 3.02. 95
ay, all of them at bristow lost their heads. 3.02.142
but that is lost for being richard's friend; 5.02. 42
and therefore lost that title of respect | which 1H4 1.03. 8
when they have lost and forfeited themselves? 1.03. 88
why hast thou lost the fresh blood in thy cheeks 2.03. 44
thou hast lost much honor that thou wert not 2.04. 20 P
have in this robbery lost three hundred marks. 2.04.520
thy place in council thou hast rudely lost, 3.02. 32
for thou hast lost thy princely privilege | with 3.02. 86
of a hair was never lost in my house before. 3.03. 58 P
bardolph was shav'd and lost many a hair, and 3.03. 59 P
i have lost a seal–ring of my grandfather's 3.03. 81 P
thou hast redeem'd thy lost opinion, | and 5.04. 48
i have lost it with hallowing and singing of 2H4 1.02.189 P
there were two honors lost, yours and your son's 2.03. 16
wages, about the sack he lost at /hinckley fair? 5.01. 24 P
o, good my lord, you have lost a friend indeed, 5.02. 27
what men have you lost, fluellen? H5 3.06. 97 P
i think the duke hath lost never a man, but one 3.06.100 P
the subjects we have lost, the disgrace we have 3.06.127 P
time was blessedly lost wherein such preparation 4.01.181 P
so that, in these ten thousand they have lost, 4.08. 87
looks we fairly hope | have lost their quality, 5.02. 19
have lost, or do not learn for want of time, 5.02. 57
that they lost france, and made his england ep 12
england ne'er lost a king of so much worth. 1H6 1.01. 7
paris, guysors, poictiers, are all quite lost. 1.01. 61
is paris lost? 1.01. 65
how were they lost? what treachery was us'd? 1.01. 68
that so he might recover what was lost. 2.05. 32
my father, earl of cambridge, lost his head. 2.05. 54
heir, | i lost my liberty, and they their lives. 2.05. 81
lost, and recovered in a day again! 3.02.115
in which assault we lost twelve hundred men; 4.01. 24
themselves, and lost the realm of france! 4.01.147
in yours they will, in you all hopes are lost. 4.05. 25
the life thou gav'st me first was lost and done, 4.06. 7
have we not lost most part of all the towns, 5.04.108
i prophesied france will be lost ere long. 2H6 1.01.146
o father, maine is lost! 1.01.209
paris is lost, the state of normandy | stands on 1.01.215
till paris was besieg'd, famish'd, and lost. 1.03.172
all is lost. 3.01. 85
by means whereof his highness hath lost france. 3.01.106
i rather would have lost my life betimes | than 3.01.297
by staying there so long till all were lost. 3.01.299
and even with this i lost fair england's view, 3.02.110
the lives of those which we have lost in fight 4.01. 21
i lost mine eye in laying the prize aboard, 4.01. 25
i sold not maine, i lost not normandy, | yet to 4.07. 65
france, to france, and get what you have lost! 4.08. 49
and give me but the ten meals i have lost, and 4.10. 62 P
tell kent from me, she hath lost her best man, 4.10. 73 P
have we won one foot, | if salisbury be lost. 5.03. 7
talk not of france, sith thou hast lost it all. 3H6 1.01.110
the lord protector lost it, and not i; 1.01.111
will scare the herd, and so my shoot is lost. 3.01. 7
poor queen and son, your labor is but lost; 3.01. 32
and i — like one lost in a thorny wood, | that 3.02.174
you told not how henry the sixt hath lost | all 3.03. 89
and to repair my honor lost for him, | i here 3.03.193
the cable broke, the holding–anchor lost, | and 5.04. 4
as it is won with blood, lost be it so! R3 1.03.271
it were lost sorrow to wail one that's lost. 2.02. 11
it were lost sorrow to wail one that's lost. 2.02. 11
my husband lost his life to get the crown, | and 2.04. 57
which by his death hath lost much majesty. 3.01.100
george, profan'd, hath lost his lordly honor; 4.04.369
here, | a royal battle might be won and lost. 4.04.536
rescue, fair lord, or else the day is lost! 5.04. 6
then you lost | the view of earthly glory. H8 1.01. 13
and lost your office | on the complaint o' th' 1.02.172
about his neck, yet never lost her lustre; 2.02. 32
a woman lost among ye, laugh'd at, scorn'd? 3.01.107
in that one woman i have lost for ever. 3.02.409
faces | been loose, this day they had been lost. 4.01. 75
for since the cardinal fell that title's lost. 4.01. 96

if we have lost so many tenths of ours, | to TRO 2.02. 21
what, lost in the labyrinth of thy fury? 2.03. 1 P
ajax lack matter, if he have lost his argument. 2.03. 94 P
no sooner got but lost? 4.02. 74 P
ajax hath lost a friend, | and foams at mouth, 5.05. 35
till he hath lost his honey and his sting; 5.10. 42
killing our enemies, the blood he hath lost COR 3.01.297
consul, which he lost | by lack of stooping — 5.06. 27
fair philomela, why, she but lost her tongue, TIT 2.04. 38
tut, i have lost myself, i am not here: ROM 1.01.197
the precious treasure of his eyesight lost. 1.01.233
discords too | have lost a brace of kinsmen. 5.03.295
i have lost my gown. TIM 3.06.110 P
wits | are drown'd and lost in his calamities. 4.03. 90
rome, thou hast lost the breed of noble bloods! JC 1.02.151
beasts, | and men have lost their reason. 3.02.105
done, | when the battle's lost and won. MAC 1.01. 4
what he hath lost, noble macbeth hath won. 1.02. 67
though his bark cannot be lost, | yet it shall 1.03. 24
be not lost | so poorly in your thoughts. 2.02. 68
we have lost | best half of our affair. 3.03. 20
i have lost my hopes. 4.03. 24
those foresaid lands | so by his father lost; HAM 1.01.104
surrender of those lands | lost by his father, 1.02. 24
but you must know your father lost a father, 1.02. 89
that father lost, lost his, and the survivor 1.02. 90
that father lost, lost his, and the survivor 1.02. 90
but wherefore i know not — lost all my mirth, 2.02.296 P
their perfume lost, | take these again, for to 3.01. 98
and so have i a noble father lost, | a sister 4.07. 25
i am lost in it, my lord. 4.07. 54
not to have it | hath lost me in your liking. LR 1.01.233
i am sorry then you have so lost a father | that 1.01.246
but, o poor gloucester, | lost he his other eye? 4.02. 81
king lear hath lost, he and his daughter ta'en. 5.02. 6
know, my name is lost, | by treason's tooth 5.03.121
rings, | their precious stones new lost; 5.03.191
heart is burst, you have lost half your soul; OTH 1.01. 87
what, have you lost your wits? 1.01. 92
for i have lost him on a dangerous sea. 2.01. 46
o, but i fear — how lost you company? 2.01. 91
and would in action glorious i had lost | those 2.03.186
o, i have lost my reputation! 2.03.263 P
i have lost the immortal part of myself, and 2.03.263 P
got without merit, and lost without deserving. 2.03.269 P
you have lost no reputation at all, unless you 2.03.270 P
me, i had rather have lost my purse | full of 3.04. 25
but if she lost it, | or made a gift of it, my 3.04. 60
is't lost? 3.04. 80
it is not lost; but what and if it were? 3.04. 83
i say, it is not lost. 3.04. 85
if you have lost him, | /why, i have lost him 4.02. 46
you have lost him, | /why, i have lost him too. 4.02. 47
light of heaven, | i know not how i lost him. 4.02.151
make thee known, | though i lost twenty lives. 5.02.166
'tis a lost fear; 5.02.269
and having lost her breath, she spoke, and ANT 2.02.230
which he achiev'd by th' minute, lost his favor. 3.01. 20
mares together, | the horse were merely lost; 3.07. 8
the greater cantle of the world is lost | with 3.10. 6
the world, that i | have lost my way for ever. 3.11. 4
for indeed i have lost command, | therefore i 3.11. 23
one of them rates | all that is won and lost. 3.11. 70
all is lost! 4.12. 9
and carouse together | like friends long lost. 4.12. 13
had annex'd unto't | a million moe (now lost) — 4.14. 18
darts, | though enemy, lost aim and could not? 4.14. 71
he that hath lost her too; CYM 1.01. 11
it, 'twere a paper lost | as offer'd mercy is. 1.03. 3
th' arabian bird, and i | have lost the wager. 1.06. 18
what i have lost to–day at bowls i'll win 2.01. 49 P
'twill not be lost. 2.03.148
if i have lost it, | i should have lost the 2.04. 41
i should have lost the worth of it in gold. 2.04. 42
it may be probable she lost it; 2.04.115
for all was lost | but that the heavens fought; 5.03. 3
i lost my children; 5.05.354
o imogen, | thou hast lost by this a kingdom. 5.05.373
his wife, | his riddle told not, lost his life. PER 1.ch. 38
split, | and he, good prince, having all lost, 2.ch. 33
king pericles, have lost | this queen, worth all 3.02. 70
heavenly jewels | which pericles hath lost, 3.02. 99
we lost too much money this mart by being too 4.02. 4 P
if not, i have lost my earnest. 4.02. 44 P
how lost thou /them? 5.01.140
the duke has lost hippolyta; TNK 3.01. 1
could have restor'd | my lost strength to me, i 3.06. 6
else of after–ages | for these lost cousins. 3.06.188
she's lost | past all cure. 4.01.139
an eye as heavy | as if he had lost his mother; 4.02. 28
i am a fool, my reason is lost in me; 4.02. 34
i am sotted, | utterly lost. 4.02. 46
poor servant, thou hast lost. 5.03. 72
to buy you i have lost what's dearest to me 5.03.112
and once made perfect, never lost again." VEN 408
having lost the fair discovery of her way. 828
and, hearing him, thy power had lost his power. 944
"alas, poor world, what treasure hast thou lost! 1075
their virtue lost, wherein they late excell'd, 1131
cost | the death of all, and all together lost. LUC 147
but she hath lost a dearer thing than life, 687
a captive victor that hath lost in gain, 730
my honey lost, and i, a drone–like bee, | have 836
"dear lord of that dear jewel i have lost, 1191
lost, vaded, broken, dead within an hour. PP 13. 6
and as goods lost are seld or never found, | as 13. 7
so beauty blemish'd once, for ever lost, | in 13.11
forgot, | all my lady's love is lost, god wot. 17. 6
fled, | all our love is lost, for love is dead. 17.32
so then thou hast but lost the dregs of life, SON 74. 9
and the just pleasure lost, which is so deemed 121. 3
him have i lost, thou hast both him and me, | he 134.13
thee, | and all my honest faith in thee is lost; 152. 8
LOT 6 FR 0.0006 REL FR 5 V 1 P
however god or fortune cast my lot, | there R2 1.03. 85
hot termagant scot had paid me scot and lot too. 1H4 5.04.114 P
why — "as by lot, god wot," | and then, you HAM 2.02.416
no, antony, take the lot; ANT 2.06. 62
know best, i pray them he | be made your lot. TNK 5.03. 40
bequeath not to their lot | the shame that from LUC 534
LOTS 4 FR 0.0004 REL FR 4 V 0 P
it is lots to blanks | my name hath touch'd your COR 5.02. 10
if we draw lots, he speeds; ANT 2.03. 36
we part, and let's | draw lots who shall begin. 2.06. 61
draw lots who first shall die to lengthen life. PER 1.04. 46
LOTTERY 3 FR 0.0003 REL FR 2 V 1 P
at an earthquake, 'twould mend the lottery well; AWW 1.03. 88 P
range on, | till each man drop by lottery. JC 2.01.119
antony, octavia is | a blessed lottery to him. ANT 2.02.242
LOTT'RY 4 FR 0.0004 REL FR 3 V 1 P
therefore the lott'ry that he hath devis'd in MV 1.02. 29 P
the lott'ry of my destiny | bars me the right of 2.01. 15
no, make a lott'ry, | and by device let blockish TRO 1.03.373
i know not, 'tis put to lott'ry. 2.01.128
/LOUD 5 FR 0.0005 REL FR 5 V 0 P
/with /what /loud /applause | /didst /thou /beat 2H4 1.03. 91
/and /the /loud /trumpet /blowing /them 4.01.120
trumpet, blow /loud, | send thy brass voice TRO 1.03.256
/beat /loud /the /taborins, let the trumpets 4.05.275
too slightly timber'd for so /loud /a /wind, HAM 4.07. 22
LOUD 64 FR 0.0072 REL FR 57 V 7 P
may as well | wound the loud winds, or with TMP 3.03. 63
should have heard him so loud and so melancholy. WIV 1.04. 91 P
well | their loud applause and aves vehement; MM 1.01. 70
o, your desert speaks loud, and i should wrong 5.01. 9
speak loud and kneel before him. 5.01. 19
tears | the passion of loud laughter never shed. MND 5.01. 70
glow, | whilst the screech–owl, screeching loud, 5.01.376
thou but offend'st thy lungs to speak so loud. MV 4.01.140
mad bounds, bellowing and neighing loud, | which 5.01. 73
patience and mine to endure her loud alarums, SHR 1.01.127 P
though she chide as loud | as thunder when the 1.02. 95
i not in a pitched battle heard | loud 'larums, 1.02.206
by gogs–wouns," quoth he, and swore so loud, 3.02.160
what you seek, | that fame may cry you loud. AWW 2.01. 17
and sing them loud even in the dead of night; TN 1.05.271
i speak too loud. 3.04. 4
'tis like to be loud weather. WT 3.03. 11
shall braying trumpets and loud churlish drums, JN 3.01.303
that shall reverberate all as loud as thine. 5.02.170
and another shall | (as loud as thine) rattle 5.02.172
for if the french be lords of this loud day, 5.04. 14
as to o'erwalk a current roaring loud | on the 1H4 1.03.192
loud shouts and salutations from their mouths, 3.02. 53
the vent of hearing when loud rumor speaks? 2H4 in 2
who knocks so loud at door? 2.04.352 P
divine | to a loud trumpet and a point of war? 4.01. 52
why, the enemy is loud, you hear him all night. H5 4.01. 75 P
come, officer, as loud as e'er thou canst, | cry 1H6 1.03. 72
whose glory fills the world with loud report. 2.02. 43
within the temple hall we were too loud, | the 2.04. 3
their hands, and crying with loud voice, | "jesu 2H6 1.01.160
loyalty, and almost appears | in loud rebellion. H8 1.02. 29
a stiff tempest, | as loud and to as many tunes. 4.01. 73
speak not so loud. TRO 1.02.185 P
from his deep chest laughs out a loud applause, 1.03.163
who broils in loud applause, and make him fall 1.03.378
give with thy trumpet a loud note to troy, 4.05. 3
consort with me in loud and dear petition, 5.03. 9
peace, peace, be not so loud. COR 4.02. 12
and with loud 'larums welcome them to rome. TIT 1.01.147
who calls so loud? ROM 5.01. 57
curses, not loud but deep, mouth–honor, breath, MAC 5.03. 27
but even then the morning cock crew loud, | and HAM 1.02.218
that roars so loud and thunders in the index? 3.04. 52
he rais'd the house with loud and coward cries. LR 2.04. 43
with such loud reason to the cyprus wars OTH 1.01.150
had tongue at will, and yet was never loud, 2.01.149
either by speaking too loud, or tainting his 2.01.268 P
that drums him from his sport and speaks as loud ANT 1.04. 29
over caesar's head | and speak as loud as mars. 2.02. 6
when we debate | our trivial difference loud, we 2.02. 21
make battery to our ears with the loud music; 2.07.109
the holding every man shall /bear as loud | as 2.07.111
let neptune hear we bid a loud farewell | to 2.07.132
undo that prayer, by crying out as loud, | "o, 3.04. 17
that will be given to th' loud of noise we make. CYM 3.05. 44
whose rudeness | answer'd my steps too loud. 4.02.215
loud music is too harsh for ladies' heads, PER 2.03. 97
the sea works high, the wind is loud, and will 3.01. 48 P
knees, thank the holy gods as loud | as thunder 5.01.198
that we may nothing share | of his loud infamy; TNK 1.02. 76
keep, | to stop the loud pursuers in their yell, VEN 688
anon their loud alarums he doth hear, | and now 700
if thou turn back and my loud crying still. SON 143.14
/LOUDER 1 FR 0.0001 REL FR 1 V 0 P
/louder /the /music /there! LR 4.07. 24
LOUDER 10 FR 0.0011 REL FR 5 V 5 P
they are louder than the weather, or our office. TMP 1.01. 36 P
no, certainly. speak louder. WIV 4.02. 17 P
proclaim an enshield beauty ten times louder MM 2.04. 80
my griefs cry louder than advertisement. ADO 5.01. 32
they're busy within, you were best knock louder. SHR 5.01. 15 P
both roaring louder than the sea or weather. WT 3.03.101 P
you must speak louder, my master is deaf. 2H4 1.02. 67 P
louder! H8 3.02. 62
fetch breath that may proclaim them louder, that PER 1.04. 15
made louder by the o'erfed breast | of this most 3.ch. 3
LOUDEST 1 FR 0.0001 REL FR 1 V 0 P
let the bird of loudest lay, | on the sole PHT 1
LOUD–HOWLING 1 FR 0.0001 REL FR 1 V 0 P
and now loud–howling wolves arouse the jades 2H6 4.01. 3
LOUDLY 1 FR 0.0001 REL FR 1 V 0 P
and the rite of war | speak loudly for him. HAM 5.02.400
LOUDNESS 1 FR 0.0001 REL FR 1 V 0 P
but whisper'd, to | the loudness of his fury. TNK 1.02. 88
LOUD'ST 2 FR 0.0002 REL FR 2 V 0 P
undertake to be | her advocate to th' loud'st. WT 2.02. 37
on whose bright crest fame with her loud'st oyes TRO 4.05.143
LOUIS *(see lewis)*
LOUR *(see low'r, etc.)*
LOUSE 2 FR 0.0002 REL FR 1 V 1 P
for i care not to be the louse of a lazar, so i TRO 5.01. 65 P
the head has any, | the head and he shall louse: LR 3.02. 29
LOUSES *(also luces)*
LOUSES 1 FR 0.0001 REL FR 0 V 1 P
the dozen white louses do become an old coat WIV 1.01. 19 P
LOUSY 9 FR 0.0010 REL FR 2 V 7 P
now remembrance to–morrow on the lousy knave, WIV 3.03.240 P
a lousy knave, to have his gibes and his 3.03.242 P
upon my knowledge, he is, and lousy. AWW 4.03.194 P
arrant, rascally, beggarly, lousy knave it is. H5 4.08. 34 P
scald, beggarly, lousy, pragging knave, pistol, 5.01. 6 P
you scurvy, lousy knave, god pless you! 5.01. 18 P
heartily, scurvy, lousy knave, at my desires, 5.01. 22 P
obscure and lousy swain, king henry's blood, 2H6 4.01. 50
wait like a lousy footboy | at chamber–door? H8 5.02.174
LOUT 5 FR 0.0005 REL FR 5 V 0 P
for 'tis no trusting to yond foolish lout — TGV 4.04. 66
pronounce thee a gross lout, a mindless slave, WT 1.02.301
should be | in such a love so vile a lout as he. JN 2.01.509
nothing but a calve's–skin, most sweet lout. 3.01.220
go before | this lout as he exceeds our lords, CYM 5.02. 9
LOUTED 1 FR 0.0001 REL FR 1 V 0 P
and i am louted by a traitor villain | and 1H6 4.03. 13
LOUTS 1 FR 0.0001 REL FR 1 V 0 P
and you will rather show our general louts | how COR 3.02. 66
LOUVRE 2 FR 0.0002 REL FR 2 V 0 P
he'll make your paris louvre shake for it, H5 2.04.132
courtier may be wise | and never see the louvre. H8 1.03. 23
/LOV'D 2 FR 0.0002 REL FR 2 V 0 P
/the /king /that /lov'd /him, /as /the /state 2H4 4.01.113
she was belov'd, /she /lov'd; TRO 4.05.292
LOV'D 190 FR 0.0214 REL FR 150 V 40 P
he whom next thyself | of all the world i lov'd, TMP 1.02. 69
knowing i lov'd my books, he furnish'd me | from 1.02.166
and then i lov'd thee | and show'd thee all the 1.02.336
lov'd mall, meg, and marian, and margery, | but 2.02. 48
she lov'd not the savor of tar nor of pitch, 2.02. 52
is drown'd, | and his and mine lov'd darling. 3.03. 93
ever since you lov'd her. TGV 2.01. 65 P
i have lov'd her ever since i saw her, and still 2.01. 66 P
in breaking faith with julia whom i lov'd; 4.02. 11
he lov'd her out of all nick. 4.02. 76 P
thyself hast lov'd, and i have heard thee say 4.03. 18
she lov'd me well deliver'd it to me. 4.04. 73
it seems you lov'd not her, /to leave her token: 4.04. 74
because methinks that she lov'd you as well | as 4.04. 79
when she did think my master lov'd her well, 4.04.150
shalt be worshipp'd, kiss'd, lov'd, and ador'd; 4.04.199
i have long lov'd her, and, i protest to you, WIV 2.02.194 P
you | how i have ever lov'd the life removed, MM 1.03. 8
by my troth, isabel, i lov'd thy brother. 4.03.156 P
to see, | i hazarded the loss of whom i lov'd. ERR 1.01.131
but it is certain i am lov'd of all ladies, only ADO 1.01.125 P
how she should be lov'd nor know how she should 1.01.230 P
to claudio that he lov'd my niece your daughter 1.02. 12 P
never think that lady would have lov'd any man. 2.03. 94 P
but i persuaded them, if they lov'd benedick, 3.01. 41
but mine, and mine i lov'd, and mine i prais'd, 4.01.136
who lov'd her so, that, speaking of her foulness 4.01.153
for me to say i lov'd nothing so well as you, 4.01.270 P
happy hour, i was about to protest i lov'd you. 4.01.284 P
bring me a father that so lov'd his child, 5.01. 8
god knows i lov'd my niece, | and she is dead, 5.01. 87
in the rare semblance that i lov'd it first. 5.01.252
and when you lov'd, you were my other husband. 5.04. 61
titania wak'd, and straightway lov'd an ass. MND 3.02. 34
if e'er i lov'd her, all that love is gone. 3.02.170
since night you lov'd me; 3.02.275
was the fairest dame | that liv'd, that lov'd, 5.01.294
virgins of our clime | have lov'd it too. MV 2.01. 11
you lov'd, i lov'd; 3.02.199
you lov'd, i lov'd; 3.02.199
say how i lov'd you, speak me fair in death; 4.01.275
did young lorenzo swear he lov'd her well, 5.01. 18
daughter, and never two ladies lov'd as they do. AYL 1.01.112 P
my father lov'd sir rowland as his soul, | and 1.02.235
the duke my father lov'd his father dearly. 1.03. 29 P
i partly guess; for i have lov'd ere now. 2.04. 24
did make thee run into, | thou hast not lov'd; 2.04. 36
in thy mistress' praise, | thou hast not lov'd; 2.04. 39
my passion now makes me, | thou hast not lov'd. 2.04. 42
i am the duke | that lov'd your father. 2.07.196
i never lov'd my brother in my life. 3.01. 14
"who ever lov'd that lov'd not at first sight?" 3.05. 82
"who ever lov'd that lov'd not at first sight?" 3.05. 82
no sooner look'd but they lov'd; 5.02. 34 P
no sooner lov'd but they sigh'd; 5.02. 34 P
lov'd /none in the world so well as lucentio. SHR 4.02. 13
which hath as long lov'd me | as i have lov'd 4.02. 38
as i have lov'd this proud disdainful haggard. 4.02. 39
her matter was, she lov'd your son. AWW 1.03.110 P
for it hurts not him | that he is lov'd of me. 1.03.197
i would he lov'd his wife. 3.05. 79
by jove's great attributes | i lov'd you dearly, 4.02. 26
sir, that always lov'd a great fire, and the 4.05. 47 P
since i have lost, have lov'd, was in mine eye 5.03. 54
he lov'd her, sir, and lov'd her not. 5.03.248 P
he lov'd her, sir, and lov'd her not. 5.03.248 P
but more than that, he lov'd her, for indeed he 5.03.259 P
my father had a daughter lov'd a man, | as it TN 2.04.107
i have lov'd thee — WT 1.02.324
and a region | lov'd as he loves himself. 1.02.370
confess | i lov'd him as in honor he requir'd; 3.02. 63
not exchange flesh with one that lov'd her. 4.04.280 P
whom, it should seem, | hath sometime lov'd! 4.04.362
that noble honor'd lord, is fear'd and lov'd? 5.01.158
i do protest i never lov'd myself | till now JN 2.01.501
i honor'd him, i lov'd him, and will weep | my 4.03.105
then pharaoh's /lean kine are to be lov'd. 1H4 2.04.474 P
before, i lov'd thee as a brother, john, | but 5.04. 19
john a' gaunt lov'd him well, and betted much 2H4 3.02. 44 P
never was monarch better fear'd and lov'd | than H5 2.02. 25
how i have lov'd my king and commonweal; 2H6 2.01.187
for they lov'd well when they were alive. 4.07.131 P
even of the bonny beast he lov'd so well. 5.02. 12
we shall to london get, where you are lov'd, 5.02. 81
hadst thou but lov'd him half so well as i, | or 3H6 1.01.220
so dear i lov'd the man that i must weep. R3 3.05. 24
you few that lov'd me | and dare be bold to weep H8 2.01. 71
by our servants, by those men we lov'd most; 2.01.122

i know your majesty has always lov'd her | so 2.02.109
lov'd him next heav'n? 3.01.130
my father lov'd you, | he said he did, and with 3.02.154
if i lov'd many words, lord, i should tell you 3.02.270
lofty and sour to them that lov'd him not, | but 4.02. 53
to love her for her mother's sake that lov'd him 4.02.137
she shall be lov'd and fear'd: 5.04. 30
i have lov'd you night and day | for many weary TRO 3.02.114
but, though i lov'd you well, i woo'd you not, 3.02.126
he lov'd me — o false wench! 5.02. 70
'twas one's that lov'd me better than you will. 5.02. 89
our endeavor be so lov'd and the performance so 5.10. 39 P
agrippa, one that hath always lov'd the people. COR 1.01. 52 P
as if i lov'd my little should be dieted | in 1.09. 52
have flatter'd the people, who ne'er lov'd them; 2.02. 8 P
and there be many that they have lov'd, they 2.02. 9 P
you have not indeed lov'd the common people. 2.03. 93 P
i shall be lov'd when i am lack'd. 4.01. 15
know thou first, | i lov'd the maid i married; 4.05.114
we wish'd coriolanus | had lov'd you as we did. 4.06. 25
we lov'd him, but like beasts | and cowardly 4.06.121
rome, | lov'd me above the measure of a father, 5.03. 10
he lov'd his mother dearly. 5.04. 15 P
judge, | how i have lov'd and honored saturnine! TIT 1.01.427
won, | she is lavinia, therefore must be lov'd. 2.01. 84
the worse to her, the better lov'd of me. 2.03.167
thy grandsire lov'd thee well. 5.03.161
i aim'd so near when i suppos'd you lov'd. ROM 1.01.205
when king cophetua lov'd the beggar–maid! 2.01. 14
look you, she lov'd her kinsman tybalt dearly, 3.04. 3
my lov'd lord, | though you hear now (too late), TIM 2.02.142
thou shouldst have lov'd thyself better now. 4.03.310 P
ever young, fresh, lov'd, and delicate wooer, 4.03.384
i fear'd caesar, honor'd him, and lov'd him. JC 3.01.129
not that i lov'd caesar less, but that i lov'd 3.02. 21 P
i lov'd caesar less, but that i lov'd rome more. 3.02. 22 P
as caesar lov'd me, i weep for him; 3.02. 24 P
it is not meet you know how caesar lov'd you: 3.02.141
judge, o you gods, how dearly caesar lov'd him! 3.02.182
by his lov'd /mansionry, that the heaven's MAC 1.06. 5
you have lov'd him well; 4.03. 13
one speech in't i chiefly lov'd, 'twas aeneas' HAM 2.02.446 P
i lov'd you not. 3.01.118 P
he's lov'd of the distracted multitude, | who 4.03. 4
i lov'd your father, and we love ourself, | and 4.07. 34
i lov'd ophelia. 5.01.269
i lov'd you ever. 5.01.290
as much as child e'er lov'd, or father found; LR 1.01. 59
my lord, | you have begot me, bred me, lov'd me: 1.01. 96
i lov'd her most, and thought to set my rest 1.01.123
lov'd as my father, as my master follow'd, | as 1.01.141
most choice forsaken, and most lov'd despis'd, 1.01.251
he always lov'd our sister most, and with what 1.01.290 P
wine lov'd i /deeply, dice dearly; 3.04. 90 P
i lov'd him, friend, | no father his son dearer; 3.04.168
if fortune brag of two she lov'd and hated, 5.03.281
her father lov'd me, oft invited me; OTH 1.03.128
and bade me, if i had a friend that lov'd her, 1.03.164
she lov'd me for the dangers i had pass'd, | and 1.03.167
and i lov'd her that she did pity them. 1.03.168
me with what violence she first lov'd the moor, 2.01.222 P
bless'd, she would never have lov'd the moor. 2.01.253 P
and fear your looks, | she lov'd them most. 3.03.208
she was in love, and he she lov'd prov'd mad, 4.03. 27
that handkerchief which i so lov'd, and gave 5.02. 48
never lov'd cassio | but with such general 5.02. 59
she lov'd thee, cruel moor; 5.02.249
of one that lov'd not wisely but too well; 5.02.344
sir, you and i have lov'd, but there's not it; ANT 1.03. 88
ebb'd man, ne'er lov'd till ne'er worth love, 1.04. 43
i never lov'd you much, but i ha' prais'd ye 2.06. 76
better might we | have lov'd without this mean, 3.02. 32
'tis the god hercules, whom antony lov'd, | now 4.03. 16
my mistress lov'd thee, and her fortunes mingled 4.14. 24
rare it is to do) most prais'd, most lov'd, | a CYM 1.01. 47
it is your fault that i have lov'd posthumus: 1.01.144
cymbeline lov'd me, | and when a soldier was the 3.03. 58
be | doth miracle itself, lov'd before me. 4.02. 29
first, she confess'd she never lov'd you; 5.05. 37
and at first meeting lov'd, | continu'd so, 5.05.379
fair glass of light, i lov'd you, and could PER 1.01. 76
to eat those little darlings whom they lov'd. 1.04. 44
it kept where i kept, i so dearly lov'd it, 2.01.130
for thou lookest | like one i lov'd indeed. 5.01.125
lov'd for we did, and like the elements | that TNK 1.03. 61
is there record of any two that lov'd | better 2.02.112
then, i lov'd him, | extremely lov'd him, 2.04. 14
extremely lov'd him, infinitely lov'd him; 2.04. 15
extremely lov'd him, infinitely lov'd him; 2.04. 15
i lov'd my lips the better ten days after. 2.04. 26
she lov'd a black–hair'd man. 3.03. 31
and i could wish i had not said i lov'd her, 3.06. 40
and all the longing maids that ever lov'd, | if 3.06.246
but even now had ask'd me | whether i lov'd, i 4.02. 48
he that has | lov'd a young handsome wench then, ep 6
hunting he lov'd, but love he laugh'd to scorn. VEN 4
she's love, she loves, and yet she is not lov'd. 610
"this deed will make thee only lov'd for fear, LUC 610
their images i lov'd i view in thee, | and thou SON 31.13
and yet it may be said i lov'd her dearly; 42. 2
the wretch did know | his rider lov'd not speed, 50. 8
grace and faults are lov'd of more and less: 96. 3

LOV'DST 2 FR 0.0002 REL FR 2 V 0 P

thy life did manifest thou lov'dst me not, | and 2H4 4.05.104
mass, thou lov'dst plums well, that wouldst 2H6 2.01. 99

/LOVE 12 FR 0.0013 REL FR 11 V 1 P

/little /are /we /beholding /to /your /love, R2 4.01.160
/their //over–greedy /love /hath /surfeited. 2H4 1.03. 88
/and /all /their /prayers /and /love | /were 4.01.135
attaint | with any passion of inflaming /love, 1H6 5.05. 82
/us /from /his /soul /to /love /each /other, R3 1.04.237
now what my /love is, proof hath made you know, HAM 3.02.169
/nature /is /fine /in /love, /and /where /'tis 4.05.162
/they /did /make /love /to /this /employment, 5.02. 57
like my sisters, | /to /love /my /father /all. LR 1.01.104
/a /horse's /health, /a /boy's /love, /or /a 3.06. 19 P
fortune /love you! 5.01. 46
/a /period | /to /such /as /love /not /sorrow, 5.03.206

LOVE 2259 FR 0.2553 REL FR 1861 V 398 P

none that i more love than myself. TMP 1.01. 20 P
durst not, | so dear the love my people bore me; 1.02.141
'tis a villain, sir, | i do not love to look on. 1.02.310
thou payest, | and i the king shall love thee. 2.01.294
do you love me? 3.01. 67
else i' th' world, | do love, prize, honor you. 3.01. 73
thy vexations | were but my trials of thy love, 4.01. 6
with such love as 'tis now, the murkiest den, 4.01. 25
do you love me, master? 4.01. 48
a contract of true love to celebrate, | and some 4.01. 84
and help to celebrate | a contract of true love; 4.01.133
no, my dearest love, | i would not for the world 5.01.172
days | to the sweet glances of thy honor'd love, TGV 1.01. 4
but since thou lov'st, love still, and thrive 1.01. 9
even as i would, when i to love begin. 1.01. 10
upon some book i love i'll pray for thee. 1.01. 20
that's on some shallow story of deep love, | how 1.01. 21
that's a deep story of a deeper love, | for he 1.01. 23
love, | for he was more than over shoes in love. 1.01. 24
for you are over boots in love, | and yet you 1.01. 25
to be in love — where scorn is bought with 1.01. 29
'tis love you cavil at; i am not love. 1.01. 38
'tis love you cavil at; i am not love. 1.01. 38
love is your master, for he masters you; 1.01. 39
so eating love | inhabits in the finest wits of 1.01. 43
even so by love the young and tender wit | is 1.01. 47
from thee by letters | of thy success in love, 1.01. 58
he after honor hunts, i after love: 1.01. 63
i /leave myself, my friends, and all, for love. 1.01. 65
wouldst thou then counsel me to fall in love? 1.02. 2
me, | in thy opinion which is worthiest love? 1.02. 6
and wouldst thou have me cast my love on him? 1.02. 25
ay — if you thought your love not cast away. 1.02. 26
his little speaking shows his love but small. 1.02. 29
they do not love that do not show their love. 1.02. 31
they do not love that do not show their love. 1.02. 31
o, they love least that let men know their love. 1.02. 32
o, they love least that let men know their love. 1.02. 32
to plead for love deserves more fee than hate. 1.02. 48
fie, fie, how wayward is this foolish love, 1.02. 57
some love of yours hath writ to you in rhyme. 1.02. 76
best sing it to the tune of "light o' love." 1.02. 80
sweet love, sweet lines, sweet life! 1.03. 45
here is her oath for love, her honor's pawn: 1.03. 47
lest he should take exceptions to my love, | and 1.03. 81
excuse | hath he excepted most against my love. 1.03. 83
o, how this spring of love resembleth | the 1.03. 84
why, how know you that i am in love? 2.01. 17 P
if you love her, you cannot see her. 2.01. 68 P
because love is blind. 2.01. 70 P
for he, being in love, could not see to garter 2.01. 76 P
and you, being in love, cannot see to put on 2.01. 77 P
boy, then you are in love — for last morning 2.01. 79 P
i was in love with my bed. 2.01. 81 P
you swing'd me for my love, which makes me the 2.01. 82 P
hath taught her love himself to write unto her 2.01.168
though the chameleon love can feed on the air, i 2.01.173 P
ay, so true love should do: 2.02. 17
ay, boy, it's for love. 2.04. 4 P
he is as worthy for an empress' love | as meet 2.04. 76
why, lady, love hath twenty pair of eyes. 2.04. 95
they say that love hath not an eye at all. 2.04. 96
upon a homely object love can wink. 2.04. 98
how does your lady, and how thrives your love? 2.04.125
my tales of love were wont to weary you; 2.04.126
i have done penance for contemning love, | whose 2.04.129
sighs, | for, in revenge of my contempt of love, 2.04.133
love hath chas'd sleep from my enthralled eyes, 2.04.134
now no discourse, except it be of love; 2.04.140
and sleep, | upon the very naked name of love. 2.04.142
o, flatter me; for love delights in praises. 2.04.148
any, | except thou wilt except against my love. 2.04.155
thee, | because thou seest me dote upon my love. 2.04.173
for love, thou know'st, is full of jealousy. 2.04.177
so the remembrance of my former love | is by a 2.04.194
and so is julia that i love — | that i did love 2.04.199
that i did love, for now my love is thaw'd 2.04.200
that i did love, for now my love is thaw'd, 2.04.200
cold, | and that i love him not as i was wont: 2.04.204
o, but i love his lady too too much, | and 2.04.205
and that's the reason i love him so little. 2.04.206
that thus without advice begin to love her? 2.04.208
if i can check my erring love, i will; 2.04.213
i care not, though he burn himself in love. 2.05. 53 P
to love fair silvia, shall i be forsworn; 2.06. 2
love bade me swear, and love bids me forswear. 2.06. 6
love bade me swear, and love bids me forswear. 2.06. 6
o sweet–suggesting love, if thou hast sinn'd, 2.06. 7
i cannot leave to love, and yet i do; 2.06. 17
but there i leave to love where i should love. 2.06. 18
but there i leave to love where i should love. 2.06. 18
for love is still most precious in itself, | and 2.06. 24
rememb'ring that my love to her is dead; 2.06. 28
love, lend me wings to make my purpose swift, 2.06. 42
and ev'n in kind love i do conjure thee, | who 2.07. 2
didst thou but know the inly touch of love, 2.07. 18
as seek to quench the fire of love with words. 2.07. 20
till the last step have brought me to my love, 2.07. 36
his tears, | and instances of infinite of love, 2.07. 70
his love sincere, his thoughts immaculate, | his 2.07. 76
only deserve my love by loving him, | and 2.07. 82
this love of theirs myself have often seen, 3.01. 24
for love of you, not hate unto my friend, | hath 3.01. 46
upon advice, hath drawn my love from her, | and, 3.01. 73
of you, | but rather to beget more love in you. 3.01. 97
for love is like a child, | that longs for every 3.01.124
my wrath shall far exceed the love | i ever bore 3.01.166
here if thou stay, thou canst not see thy love; 3.01.246
even in the milk–white bosom of thy love. 3.01.252
he lives not now that knows me to be in love, 3.01.266 P
that knows me to be in love, yet i am in love, 3.01.267 P
nor who 'tis i love; 3.01.268 P
not for that neither, because i love crusts. 3.01.341 P
fear not but that she will love you | now 3.02. 1
this weak impress of love is as a figure 3.02. 6
to make the girl forget | the love of valentine, 3.02. 30
the love of valentine, and love sir thurio? 3.02. 30
she shall not long continue love to him. 3.02. 48
but say this weed her love from valentine, | it 3.02. 49
it follows not that she will love sir thurio. 3.02. 50
therefore, as you unwind her love from him, 3.02. 51
to hate young valentine and love my friend. 3.02. 65
this discipline shows thou hast been in love. 3.02. 87
thee, | love thee as our commander and our king. 4.01. 65
him, | i have access my own love to prefer — 4.02. 4
yet, spaniel–like, the more she spurns my love, 4.02. 14
for you know that love | will creep in service 4.02. 19
ay, but i hope, sir, that you love not here. 4.02. 21
love doth to her eyes repair, | to help him of 4.02. 46
return, return, and make thy love amends. 4.02. 99
i grant, sweet love, that i did love a lady; 4.02.105
i grant, sweet love, that i did love a lady; 4.02.105
/his grave | assure thyself my love is buried. 4.02.114
vouchsafe me yet your picture for my love, | the 4.02.120
and to your shadow will i make true love. 4.02.125
you as well | as you do love your lady silvia: 4.04. 80
she dreams on him that has forgot her love; 4.04. 81
you dote on her that cares not for your love. 4.04. 82
'tis pity love should be so contrary; 4.04. 83
because i love him, i must pity him. 4.04. 96
i am my master's true confirmed love; 4.04.103
since she respects my mistress' love so much. 4.04.182
alas, how love can trifle with itself! 4.04.183
if that be all the difference in his love, 4.04.190
if this fond love were not a blinded god? 4.04.196
eyes, | to make my master out of love with thee. 4.04.205
but love will not be spurr'd to what it loathes. 5.02. 7
but well, when i discourse of love and peace. 5.02. 17
eglamour | than for the love of reckless silvia. 5.02. 52
more for silvia's love | than hate of eglamour 5.02. 53
more to cross that love | than hate for silvia, 5.02. 55
than hate for silvia, that is gone for love. 5.02. 56
they love me well; 5.04. 16
that would have forc'd your honor and your love. 5.04. 22
love, lend me patience to forbear a while. 5.04. 27
o, heaven be judge how i love valentine, | whose 5.04. 36
o, 'tis the curse in love, and still approv'd, 5.04. 43
when women cannot love where they're belov'd! 5.04. 44
when proteus cannot love where he's belov'd! 5.04. 45
read over julia's heart (thy first best love), 5.04. 46
oaths | descended into perjury, to love me. 5.04. 49
in love | who respects friend? 5.04. 53
and love you 'gainst the nature of love — force 5.04. 58
and love you 'gainst the nature of love — force 5.04. 58
common friend, that's without faith or love, 5.04. 62
and, that my love may appear plain and free, 5.04. 82
if shame live | in a disguise of love! 5.04.107
i dare thee but to breathe upon my love. 5.04.131
and think thee worthy of an empress' love. 5.04.141
is a familiar beast to man, and signifies love. WIV 1.01. 21 P
cousin abraham slender, can you love her? 1.01.232 P
can you love the maid? 1.01.243 P
but if there be no great love in the beginning, 1.01.246 P
i love the sport well, but i shall as soon 1.01.290 P
i do mean to make love to ford's wife. 1.03. 44 P
i will discuss the humor of this love to /page. 1.03. 95 P
my master himself is in love with mistress anne 1.04.104 P
"ask me no reason why i love you, for though 2.01. 4 P
for though love use reason for his precisian, he 2.01. 5 P
you love sack, and so do i; 2.01. 9 P
least, if the love of a soldier can suffice — 2.01. 11 P
of a soldier can suffice — that i love thee. 2.01. 12 P
not a soldier–like phrase — but i say, love me. 2.01. 13 P
love my wife? 2.01.116 P
i love not the humor of bread and cheese /and 2.01.135 P
wife acquainted each other how they love me? 2.02.110 P
i have pursu'd her as love hath pursu'd me, 2.02.201 P
"love like a shadow flies when substance love 2.02.207
like a shadow flies when substance love pursues, 2.02.207
of what quality was your love then? 2.02.214 P
by gar, i love you; 2.03. 91 P
what made me love thee? 3.03. 68 P
but i love thee, none but thee; 3.03. 73 P
i fear you love mistress page. 3.03. 75 P
thou mightst as well say i love to walk by the 3.03. 77 P
well, heaven knows how i love you, and you shall 3.03. 80 P
i love thee. 3.03.141 P
i see i cannot get thy father's love, 3.04. 1
i should love thee but as a property. 3.04. 10
yet seek my father's love, still seek it, sir. 3.04. 19
as well as i love any woman in gloucestershire. 3.04. 43 P
love him, daughter anne. 3.04. 67
page, for that i love your daughter | in such a 3.04. 78
manners, | i must advance the colors of my love, 3.04. 81
to search his house for his wive's love. 3.05. 78 P
i see you are obsequious in your love, and i 4.02. 3 P
in the simple office of love, but in all the 4.02. 4 P
with the dear love i bear to fair anne page, 4.06. 9
a bull for thy europa, love set on thy horns. 5.05. 4 P
o powerful love, that in some respects makes a 5.05. 4 P
were also, jupiter, a swan for the love of leda. 5.05. 6 P
o omnipotent love, how near the god drew to the 5.05. 7 P
i will never take you for my love again, but i 5.05.117 P
where there was no proportion held in love. 5.05.222
in love, the heavens themselves do guide the 5.05.232
lent him our terror, dress'd him with our love, MM 1.01. 19
i love the people, | but do not like to stage me 1.01. 67
from whom we thought it meet to hide our love 1.02.152
shoulders that a milkmaid, if she be in love, 1.02.173 P
believe not that the dribbling dart of love 1.03. 2
what, do i love her, | that i desire to hear her 2.02.176
love you the man that wrong'd you? 2.03. 24
yes, as i love the woman that wrong'd him. 2.03. 25
showing we would not spare heaven as we love it, 2.03. 33
o injurious love, | that respites me a life 2.03. 40
where their untaught love | must needs appear 2.04. 29
i hate, | for his advantage that i dearly love. 2.04.120
plainly conceive, i love you. 2.04.141
my brother did love juliet, | and you tell me 2.04.142
he shall not, isabel, if you give me love. 2.04.144
i am so out of love with life that i will sue to 3.01.172 P
to the love i have in doing good a remedy 3.01.198 P
in his love toward her ever most kind and 3.01.220 P
in all reason should have quench'd her love) 3.01.242 P

sir, i know him, and i love him. 3.02.149 P
love talks with better knowledge, and knowledge 3.02.150 P
knowledge, and knowledge with /dearer love. 3.02.151 P
seals of love, but seal'd in vain, seal'd in 4.01. 6
that for the fault's love is th' offender 4.02.113
him in mine arms | with all th' effect of love. 5.01.199
i protest i love the duke as i love myself. 5.01.341 P
i protest i love the duke as i love myself. 5.01.341 P
look that you love your wife; 5.01.497
love her, angelo! 5.01.526
whom whilst i labored of a love to see, | i ERR 1.01.130
ere i learn love, i'll practice to obey. 2.01. 29
would that alone a' love he would detain, | so 2.01.107
as you love strokes, so jest with me again. 2.02. 8
you, | your sauciness will jest upon my love, 2.02. 28
for know, my love, as easy mayst thou fall | a 2.02.125
even in the spring of love, thy love–springs rot 3.02. 3
shall love, in /building, grow so /ruinous? 3.02. 4
muffle your false love with some show of 3.02. 8
(being compact of credit) that you love us; 3.02. 22
let love, being light, be drowned if she sink! 3.02. 52
as good to wink, sweet love, as look on night. 3.02. 58
why call you me love? call my sister so. 3.02. 59
thee will i love and with thee lead my life; 3.02. 67
belike you thought our love would last too long 4.01. 25
that love i begg'd for you, he begg'd of me. 4.02. 12
with what persuasion did he tempt thy love? 4.02. 13
eye | stray'd his affection in unlawful love — 5.01. 51
namely, some love that drew him oft from home. 5.01. 56
i had not a hard heart, for truly i love none. ADO 1.01.127 P
mark you this, on my allegiance, he is in love. 1.01.212 P
amen, if you love her, for the lady is very well 1.01.221 P
that i love her, i feel. 1.01.228 P
shall see thee, ere i die, look pale with love. 1.01.248 P
or with hunger, my lord, not with love. 1.01.250 P
lose more blood with love than i will get again 1.01.251 P
my love is thine to teach; 1.01.291
hand | than to drive liking to the name of love. 1.01.300
if thou dost love fair hero, cherish it, | and i 1.01.308
how sweetly you do minister to love, | that know 1.01.312
than to fashion a carriage to rob love from any. 1.03. 30 P
speak low if you speak love. 2.01. 99 P
i love you the better; the hearers may cry amen. 2.01.105 P
you are very near my brother in his love. 2.01.164 P
things | save in the office and affairs of love; 2.01.176
all hearts in love use their own tongues. 2.01.177
sir, here's a dish i love not, i cannot endure 2.01.274 P
goes on crutches till love have all his rites. 2.01.358 P
that she shall fall in love with benedick, and i 2.01.381 P
stomach, he shall fall in love with beatrice. 2.01.384 P
claudio — as in love of your brother's honor, 2.02. 37 P
a fool when he dedicates his behaviors to love, 2.03. 9 P
argument of his own scorn by falling in love — 2.03. 11 P
i will not be sworn but love may transform me to 2.03. 24 P
the prince and monsieur love! 2.03. 36 P
niece beatrice was in love with signior benedick 2.03. 91 P
him with scorn, write to him that i love him?" 2.03.129 P
writ to me, yea, though i love him, i should." 2.03.145 P
for she says she will die if he love her not, 2.03.174 P
and she will die ere she make her love known, 2.03.175 P
if she should make tender of her love, 'tis very 2.03.179 P
we go seek benedick, and tell him of her love? 2.03.200 P
i love benedick well, and i could wish he would 2.03.206 P
love me? 2.03.224 P
proudly, if i perceive the love come from her; 2.03.226 P
folly, for i will be horribly in love with her. 2.03.235 P
i do spy some marks of love in her. 2.03.246 P
if i do not love her, i am a jew. 2.03.263 P
be how benedick | is sick in love with beatrice. 3.01. 21
o god of love! 3.01. 47
she cannot love, | nor take no shape nor project 3.01. 54
certainly it were not good | she knew his love, 3.01. 58
and, benedick, love on, i will requite thee, 3.01.111
if thou dost love, my kindness shall incite thee 3.01.113
i hope he be in love. 3.02. 17 P
of blood in him to be truly touch'd with love. 3.02. 19 P
yet say i, he is in love. 3.02. 30 P
if he be not in love with some woman, there is 3.02. 40 P
as much as to say, the sweet youth's in love. 3.02. 53 P
conclude, conclude, he is in love. 3.02. 62 P
you may think i love you not; 3.02. 95 P
if you love her then, to–morrow wed her; 3.02.114 P
clap 's into "light a' love"; 3.04. 44 P
ye light a' love with your heels! 3.04. 47 P
think perchance that i think you are in love. 3.04. 81 P
my heart out of thinking, that you are in love, 3.04. 85 P
or that you will be in love, or that you can be 3.04. 86 P
you will be in love, or that you can be in love. 3.04. 86 P
show'd | bashful sincerity and comely love. 4.01. 54
for thee i'll lock up all the gates of love, 4.01.105
mourn, | if ever love had interest in his liver, 4.01.231
and though you know my inwardness and love | is 4.01.245
i do love nothing in the world so well as you — 4.01.267 P
i will swear by it that you love me, and i will 4.01.276 P
i will make him eat it that says i love not you. 4.01.277 P
i protest i love thee. 4.01.280 P
i love you with so much of my heart that none is 4.01.286 P
there is no love in you. 4.01.293 P
tarry, good beatrice. by this hand, i love thee. 4.01.324 P
use it for my love some other way than swearing 4.01.326 P
not hate him deadly, she would love him dearly. 5.01.177 P
and, i'll warrant you, for the love of beatrice. 5.01.196 P
died, and if your love | can labor aught in sad 5.01.282
"the god of love, | that sits above, | and knows 5.02. 26
turn'd over and over as my poor self in love. 5.02. 36 P
bad parts didst thou first fall in love with me? 5.02. 60 P
my good parts did you first suffer love for me? 5.02. 65 P
suffer love! 5.02. 66 P
i do suffer love indeed, for i love thee against 5.02. 67 P
love indeed, for i love thee against my will. 5.02. 67 P
for i will never love that which my friend hates 5.02. 70 P
serve god, love me, and mend. 5.02. 93 P
and i do with an eye of love requite her. 5.04. 24
when he would play the noble beast in love. 5.04. 47
do not you love me? 5.04. 74
do not you love me? 5.04. 77
'tis no such matter. then you do not love me? 5.04. 82
come, cousin, i am sure you love the gentleman. 5.04. 84

my kinsman, live unbruis'd and love my cousin. 5.04.111 P
to love, to wealth, to pomp, i pine and die, LLL 1.01. 31
not, i, | but i protest i love to hear him lie, 1.01.175
i love not to be cross'd. 1.02. 32 P
speaks the mere contrary, crosses love not him. 1.02. 34 P
i will hereupon confess i am in love; 1.02. 57 P
and as it is base for a soldier to love, so am i 1.02. 58 P
to love, so am i in love with a base wench. 1.02. 58 P
what great men have been in love? 1.02. 65 P
and he was in love. 1.02. 72 P
i am in love too. 1.02. 75 P
who was sampson's love, my dear moth? 1.02. 76 P
but to have a love of that color, methinks 1.02. 87 P
my love is most immaculate white and red. 1.02. 90 P
i do love that country girl that i took in the 1.02.117 P
and yet a better love than my master. 1.02.121 P
sing, boy, my spirit grows heavy in love. 1.02.122 P
i love thee. 1.02.141 P
is a great argument of falsehood) if i love. 1.02.171 P
and how can that be true love, which is falsely 1.02.171 P
love is a familiar; 1.02.172 P
love is a devil; 1.02.172 P
there is no evil angel but love. 1.02.173 P
be still, drum, for your manager is in love; 1.02.182 P
of all that virtue love for virtue loved; 2.01. 57
are they all in love, | that every one her own 2.01. 77
i must employ him in a letter to my love. 3.01. 7 P
will you win your love with a french brawl? 3.01. 8 P
/as if you swallow'd love with singing love, 3.01. 15 P
/as if you swallow'd love with singing love, 3.01. 15 P
as if you snuff'd up love by smelling love; 3.01. 17 P
as if you snuff'd up love by smelling love; 3.01. 17 P
call'st thou my love "hobby–horse"? 3.01. 30 P
is but a colt, and your love perhaps a hackney. 3.01. 32 P
but have you forgot your love? 3.01. 33 P
by heart you love her, because your heart cannot 3.01. 41 P
in heart you love her, because your heart is in 3.01. 42 P
her, because your heart is in love with her; 3.01. 43 P
and out of heart you love her, being out of 3.01. 44 P
o, and i, forsooth, in love! 3.01.174
i love, i sue, i seek a wife — | a woman, that 3.01.189
and, among three, to love the worst of all, | a 3.01.195
well, i will love, write, sigh, pray, sue, groan 3.01.204
some men must love my lady, and some joan. 3.01.205
shall i command thy love? 4.01. 80 P
shall i enforce thy love? 4.01. 81 P
shall i entreat thy love? 4.01. 82 P
can brook the weather that love not the wind. 4.02. 33
"if love make me forsworn, how shall i swear to 4.02.105
make me forsworn, how shall i swear to love? 4.02.105
as thou art, o, pardon love this wrong, | that 4.02.117
by the lord, this love is as mad as ajax. 4.03. 6 P
i will not love; 4.03. 8 P
light, but for her eye, i would not love her; 4.03. 10 P
by heaven, i do love, and it hath taught me to 4.03. 12 P
but do not love thyself, then thou /wilt keep 4.03. 37
in love, i hope — sweet fellowship in shame. 4.03. 47
o sweet maria, empress of my love, | these 4.03. 54
my vow was earthly, thou a heavenly love; 4.03. 64
once more i'll mark how love can vary wit. 4.03. 98
love, whose month is ever may, | spied a blossom 4.03.100
for jove, | turning mortal for thy love." 4.03.118
dumaine, thy love is far from charity, | that in 4.03.125
you do not love maria? 4.03.131
and jove for your love would infringe an oath. 4.03.142
these worms for loving, that art most in love? 4.03.152
i post from love; good lover, let me go. 4.03.186
are pick–purses in love, and we deserve to die. 4.03.205
did these rent lines show some love of thine? 4.03.216
my love (her mistress) is a gracious moon, | she 4.03.226
o, but for my love, day would turn to night! 4.03.229
by heaven, thy love is black as ebony. 4.03.243
look, here's thy love; my foot and her face see. 4.03.273
but what of this, are we not all in love? 4.03.278
but love, first learned in a lady's eyes, 4.03.324
for valor, is not love a hercules, | still 4.03.337
and when love speaks, the voice of all the gods 4.03.341
for wisdom's sake, a word that all men love, 4.03.354
the law, | and who can sever love from charity? 4.03.362
and merry hours | forerun fair love, strewing 4.03.377
as much love in rhyme | as would be cramm'd up 5.02. 6
love doth approach disguis'd, | armed in 5.02. 83
the king is my love sworn. 5.02.282
my love to thee is sound, sans crack or flaw. 5.02.415
forbid the smiling courtesy of love | the holy 5.02.745
as love is full of unbefitting strains, | all 5.02.760
which parti–coated presence of loose love | put 5.02.766
our love being yours, the error that love makes 5.02.771
the error that love makes | is likewise yours. 5.02.771
we have receiv'd your letters full of love; 5.02.777
your favors, embassadors of love; 5.02.778
if for my love (as there is no such cause) | you 5.02.792
nip not the gaudy blossoms of your love | but 5.02.802
but that it bear this trial, and last love; 5.02.803
and what to me, my love? and what to me? 5.02.817
but what to me, my love? 5.02.823
with threefold love i wish you all these three. 5.02.825
then, if i have much love, i'll give you some. 5.02.830
impose some service on me for thy love. 5.02.840
hold the plough for her sweet love three year. 5.02.884 P
sword, | and won thy love doing thee injuries; MND 1.01. 17
with faining voice verses of faining love, | and 1.01. 31
the sealing–day betwixt my love and me | for 1.01. 84
you have her father's love, demetrius, | let me 1.01. 93
scornful lysander, true, he hath my love; 1.01. 95
and what is mine my love shall render him. 1.01. 96
my love is more than his; 1.01.100
made love to nedar's daughter, helena, | and won 1.01.107
what cheer, my love? 1.01.122
how now, my love? 1.01.128
the course of true love never did run smooth; 1.01.134
o hell! to choose love by another's eyes. 1.01.140
as due to love as thoughts and dreams and sighs, 1.01.154
keep promise, love. look, here comes helena. 1.01.179
i give him curses; yet he gives me love. 1.01.196
the more i love, the more he hateth me. 1.01.199
o then, what graces in my love do dwell, | that 1.01.206
love can transpose to form and dignity. 1.01.233

love looks not with the eyes, but with the mind, 1.01.234
and therefore is love said to be a child, 1.01.238
so the boy love is perjur'd every where; 1.01.241
lover, that kills himself most gallant for love. 1.02. 24 P
it is the lady that pyramus must love. 1.02. 46 P
playing on pipes of corn and versing love | to 2.01. 67
your buskin'd mistress and your warrior love, 2.01. 71
hippolyta, | knowing i know thy love to theseus? 2.01. 76
she shall pursue it with the soul of love. 2.01.182
i love thee not; 2.01.188
tell you i do not /nor i cannot love you? 2.01.201
and even for that do i love you the more: 2.01.202
what worser place can i beg in your love | (and 2.01.208
we cannot fight for love, as men may do. 2.01.241
of hell, | to die upon the hand i love so well. 2.01.244
thou shalt fly him and he shall seek thy love. 2.01.246
a sweet athenian lady is in love | with a 2.01.260
prove | more fond on her than she upon her love; 2.01.266
love and languish for his sake. 2.02. 29
fair love, you faint with wand'ring in the wood; 2.02. 35
love takes the meaning in love's conference: 2.02. 46
friend, for love and courtesy | lie further off, 2.02. 56
thy love ne'er alter till thy sweet life end! 2.02. 61
approve | this flower's force in stirring love. 2.02. 69
let love forbid | sleep his seat on thy eyelid. 2.02. 80
what though he love your hermia? 2.02.109
not hermia but helena i love. 2.02.113
address your love and might | to honor helen and 2.02.143
on the first view to say, to swear, i love thee. 3.01.141
reason and love keep little company together 3.01.144 P
and i do love thee; 3.01.156
eyes, | to have my love to bed and to arise; 3.01.171
my mistress with a monster is in love. 3.02. 6
must perforce ensue | some true love turn'd, and 3.02. 91
she is and pale of cheer | with sighs of love, 3.02. 97
when his love he doth espy, | let her shine as 3.02.105
to what, my love, shall i compare thine eyne? 3.02.138
you both are rivals, and love hermia; 3.02.155
for you love hermia; 3.02.163
in hermia's love i yield you up my part; 3.02.165
whom i do love and will do till my death. 3.02.167
if e'er i lov'd her, all that love is gone. 3.02.170
look where thy love comes; 3.02.176
why should he stay, whom love doth press to go? 3.02.184
what love could press lysander from my side? 3.02.185
lysander's love, that would not let him bide — 3.02.186
and will you rent our ancient love asunder, | to 3.02.215
and made your other love, demetrius | (who even 3.02.224
and wherefore doth lysander | deny your love (so 3.02.229
so hung upon with love, so fortunate | (but 3.02.233
(but miserable most, to love unlov'd)? 3.02.234
my love, my life, my soul, fair helena! 3.02.246
helen, i love thee, by my life, i do! 3.02.251
to prove him false that says i love thee not. 3.02.253
i say i love thee more than he can do. 3.02.254
what change is this, | sweet love? 3.02.263
thy love? 3.02.263
o me, what news, my love! 3.02.272
no jest | that i do hate thee and love helena. 3.02.281
you thief of love! 3.02.283
i evermore did love you, hermia, | did ever keep 3.02.307
save that, in love unto demetrius, | i told him 3.02.309
for love i followed him. 3.02.311
intend | never so little show of love to her, 3.02.334
i with the morning's love have oft made sport, 3.02.389
what, wilt thou hear some music, my sweet love? 4.01. 27
or say, sweet love, what thou desirest to eat. 4.01. 30
o, how i love thee! 4.01. 45
there lies your love. 4.01. 78
my love shall hear the music of my hounds. 4.01.106
it is), my love to hermia | (melted as the snow) 4.01.165
now i do wish it, love it, long for it, | and 4.01.175
joy and fresh days of love | accompany your 5.01. 29
that have i told my love, | in glory of my 5.01. 46
scene of young pyramus | and his love thisby; 5.01. 57
i love not to see wretchedness o'ercharg'd, 5.01. 85
love, therefore, and tongue–tied simplicity | in 5.01.104
my love thou art, my love i think. 5.01.194
my love thou art, my love i think. 5.01.194
this is old ninny's tomb. where is my love? 5.01.263
asleep, my love? 5.01.324
why then you are in love. MV 1.01. 46
not in love neither? 1.01. 47
i love thee, and 'tis my love that speaks — 1.01. 87
i love thee, and 'tis my love that speaks — 1.01. 87
antonio, | i owe the most, in money and in love, 1.01.131
and from your love i have a warranty | to 1.01.132
time | to wind about my love with circumstance, 1.01.154
any rightly but one who you shall rightly love. 1.02. 33 P
would forgive him, for if he love me to madness, 1.02. 64 P
i would be friends with you, and have your love, 1.03.138
and for my love i pray you wrong me not. 1.03.170
and let us make incision for your love, | to 2.01. 6
by my love, i swear | the best–regarded virgins 2.01. 9
i am not bid for love, they flatter me, | but 2.05. 13
lorenzo, and thy love. 2.06. 28
lorenzo, certain, and my love indeed, | for who 2.06. 29
and my love indeed, | for who love i so much? 2.06. 30
but love is blind, and lovers cannot see | the 2.06. 36
why, 'tis an office of discovery, love, | and i 2.06. 43
beshrow me but i love her heartily, | for she is 2.06. 52
but more than these, in love i do deserve. 2.07. 34
of me, | let it not enter in your mind of love. 2.08. 42
and such fair ostents of love | as shall 2.08. 44
have not seen | so likely an embassador of love. 2.09. 92
bassanio, lord love, if thy will it be! 2.09.101
there's something tells me (but it is not love) 3.02. 4
what treason there is mingled with your love. 3.02. 27
which makes me fear th' enjoying of my love; 3.02. 29
'tween snow and fire, as treason and my love. 3.02. 31
confess and love | had been the very sum of my 3.02. 35
if you do love me, you will find me out. 3.02. 41
with no less presence, but with much more love, 3.02. 54
o love, be moderate, allay thy ecstasy, | in 3.02.111
away, | let it presage the ruin of your love, 3.02.173
till my very /roof was dry | with oaths of love, 3.02.205
of this fair one here | to have her love — 3.02.207
lady, | when i did first impart my love to you, 3.02.253

since you are dear bought, i will love you dear. 3.02.313
if your love do not persuade you to come, let 3.02.321 P
o love! dispatch all business, and be gone! 3.02.323
whose souls do bear an egall yoke of love, 3.04. 13
the which my love and some necessity | now lays 3.04. 34
lies, | how honorable ladies sought my love, 3.04. 70
but, touch'd with humane gentleness and love, 4.01. 25
some men there are love not a gaping pig; 4.01. 47
do all men kill the things they do not love? 4.01. 66
be judge | whether bassanio had not once a love. 4.01.277
i have a wife who i protest i love; 4.01.290
above, | in love and service to you evermore. 4.01.414
and for your love i'll take this ring from you. 4.01.427
more, | and you in love shall not deny me this! 4.01.429
let his deservings and my love withal | be 4.01.450
and waft her love | to come again to carthage. 5.01. 11
and with an unthrift love did run from venice, 5.01. 16
slander her love, and he forgave it her. 5.01. 22
since you do take it, love, so much at heart. 5.01.145
like cutler's poetry | upon a knife, "love me, 5.01.150
i gave my love a ring, and made him swear 5.01.170
and for your love i would be loath to foil him, AYL 1.01.129 P
therefore, out of my love to you, i came hither 1.01.131 P
i thank thee for thy love to me, which thou 1.01.137 P
me not with the full weight that i love thee. 1.02. 9 P
could have taught my love to take thy father for 1.02. 12 P
thou, if the truth of thy love to me were so 1.02. 13 P
let me see — what think you of falling in love? 1.02. 25 P
but love no man in good earnest, nor no further 1.02. 27 P
my father's love is enough to honor him enough. 1.02. 83 P
if you do keep your promises in love | but 1.02.243
high commendation, true applause, and love, 1.02.263
i shall desire more love and knowledge of you. 1.02.285
ensue that you should love his son dearly? 1.03. 32 P
let me love him for that, and do you love him 1.03. 38 P
him for that, and do you love him because i do. 1.03. 38 P
rosalind lacks then the love | which teacheth 1.03. 96
i love to cope him in these sullen fits, | for 2.01. 67
why do people love you? 2.03. 5
o corin, that thou knew'st how i do love her! 2.04. 23
but if thy love were ever like to mine — | as 2.04. 28
as sure i think did never man love so — | how 2.04. 29
o, thou didst then never love so heartily! 2.04. 33
folly | that ever love did make thee run into, 2.04. 35
when i was in love i broke my sword upon a stone 2.04. 47 P
so is all nature in love mortal in folly. 2.04. 56 P
if that love or gold | can in this desert place 2.04. 71
me hath many a weary step | limp'd in pure love; 2.07.131
hang there, my verse, in witness of my love, 3.02. 1
tedious homily of love have you wearied your 3.02.156 P
the worst fault you have is to be in love. 3.02.282 P
farewell, good signior love. 3.02.292 P
courtship too well, for there he fell in love. 3.02.346 P
he seems to have the quotidian of love upon him. 3.02.365 P
he taught me how to know a man in love; 3.02.370 P
youth, i would i could make thee believe i love. 3.02.386 P
may as soon make her that you love believe it, 3.02.388 P
are you so much in love as your rhymes speak? 3.02.396 P
love is merely a madness, and, i tell you, 3.02.400 P
so ordinary that the whippers are in love too. 3.02.404 P
he was to imagine me his love, his mistress; 3.02.408 P
from his mad humor of love to a living humor of 3.02.418 P
that there shall not be one spot of love in't. 3.02.424 P
now, by the faith of my love, i will. 3.02.428 P
but for his verity in love, i do think him as 3.04. 23 P
not true in love? 3.04. 26 P
after the shepherd that complain'd of love, 3.04. 48
between the pale complexion of true love | and 3.04. 53
the sight of lovers feedeth those in love. 3.04. 57
say that you love me not, but say not so | in 3.05. 2
thank heaven, fasting, for a good man's love; 3.05. 58
cry the man mercy, love him, take his offer; 3.05. 61
he's fall'n in love with your foulness, and 3.05. 66 P
foulness, and she'll fall in love with my anger. 3.05. 67 P
i pray you do not fall in love with me, | for i 3.05. 72
if you do sorrow at my grief in love, | by 3.05. 87
by giving love, your sorrow and my grief | were 3.05. 88
thou hast my love; is not that neighborly? 3.05. 90
and yet it is not that i bear thee love, | but 3.05. 93
but since that thou canst talk of love so well, 3.05. 94
so holy and so perfect is my love, | and in such 3.05. 99
think not i love him, though i ask for him; 3.05.109
would have gone near | to fall in love with him; 3.05.126
for my part, | i love him not, nor hate him not; 3.05.127
have more cause to hate him than to love him, 3.05.128
i am so; i do love it better than laughing. 4.01. 4 P
be out of love with your nativity, and almost 4.01. 35 P
break an hour's promise in love! 4.01. 44 P
part of a minute in the affairs of love, it may 4.01. 47 P
before, and he is one of the patterns of love. 4.01.100 P
and worms have eaten them, but not for love. 4.01.108 P
then love me, rosalind. 4.01.115 P
alas, dear love, i cannot lack thee two hours! 4.01.179 P
didst know how many fathom deep i am in love! 4.01.207 P
are out, let him be judge how deep i am in love. 4.01.215 P
warrant you, with pure love and troubled brain, 4.03. 3 P
and that she could not love me | were man as 4.03. 16
her love is not the hare that i do hunt; 4.03. 18
a fool, | and turn'd into the extremity of love. 4.03. 23
eyne | have power to raise such love in mine, 4.03. 51
whiles you chid me, i did love; 4.03. 54
he that brings this love to thee | little knows 4.03. 56
love to thee | little knows this love in me; 4.03. 57
that i can make, | or else by him my love deny, 4.03. 62
wilt thou love such a woman? 4.03. 67 P
her (for i see love hath made thee a tame snake) 4.03. 70 P
that if she love me, i charge her to love thee; 4.03. 71 P
that if she love me, i charge her to love thee; 4.03. 71 P
committing me unto my brother's love, | who led 4.03.144
you do love this maid? 5.01. 36 P
that but seeing, you should love her? 5.02. 3 P
but say with me, i love aliena; 5.02. 8 P
they are in the very wrath of love, and they 5.02. 40 P
if you do love rosalind so near the heart as 5.02. 62 P
faithful shepherd — | look upon him, love him; 5.02. 82
shepherd, tell this youth what 'tis to love. 5.02. 83
if this be so, why blame you me to love you? 5.02.103
if this be so, why blame you me to love you? 5.02.104
if this be so, why blame you me to love you? 5.02.105
you speak too, "why blame you me to love you?" 5.02.107 P
i would love you if i could. 5.02.111 P
as you love rosalind, meet. 5.02.119 P
as you love phebe, meet. 5.02.119 P
and as i love no woman, i'll meet. 5.02.120 P
a ding, ding, | sweet lovers love the spring. 5.03. 21
nonino, | for love is crowned with the prime, 5.03. 32
and shape be true, | why then my love adieu! 5.04.121
you to his love must accord, | or have a woman 5.04.133
you to a love, that your true faith doth merit; 5.04.188
you to your land, and love, and great allies; 5.04.189
o women, for the love you bear to men, to like ep 13 P
you, o men, for the love you bear to women (as i ep 15 P
tell him from me, as he will win my love, | he SHR in.1. 109
may show her duty and make known her love?" in.1. 117
dost thou love hawking? in.2. 43
dost thou love pictures? in.2. 49
and by my father's love and leave am arm'd 1.01. 5
if either of you both love katherina, | because 1.01. 52
because i know you well and love you well, 1.01. 53
for i will love thee ne'er the less, my girl. 1.01. 77
their love is not so great, hortensio, but we 1.01.107 P
yet, for the love i bear my sweet bianca, if i 1.01.109 P
mistress and be happy rivals in bianca's love, 1.01.117 P
that love should of a sudden take such hold? 1.01.147
on, | i found the effect of love in idleness, 1.01.151
if love have touch'd you, nought remains but so, 1.01.161
if you love the maid, | bend thoughts and wits 1.01.178
master, your love must live a maid at home, 1.01.182
be lucentio, | because so well i love lucentio. 1.01.217
be she as foul as was florentius' love, | as old 1.02. 69
more, | suitors to her and rivals in my love; 1.02.122
have leave and leisure to make love to her, 1.02.136
peace, grumio, it is the rival of my love. 1.02.141
all books of love, see that at any hand — | and 1.02.146
gremio, 'tis now no time to vent our love; 1.02.178
i love no chiders, sir. biondello, let's away. 1.02.226
that she's the choice love of signior gremio. 1.02.234
and for your love to her lead apes in hell. 2.01. 34
then tell me, if i get your daughter's love, 2.01.119
thing is well obtain'd, | that is, her love; 2.01.129
i love her ten times more than e'er i did. 2.01.161
oath, | that in a twink she won me to her love. 2.01.310
and i am one that love bianca more | than words 2.01.335
youngling, thou canst not love so dear as i. 2.01.337
greybeard, thy love doth freeze. 2.01.338
greatest dower | shall have my bianca's love. 2.01.344
disguis'd thus to get your love, "hic steterat," 3.01. 33 P
now, for my life, the knave doth court my love: 3.01. 49
methinks he looks as though he were in love; 3.01. 88
love concerneth us to add | her father's liking, 3.02.128
now, if you love me, stay. 3.02.204
and serve it thus to me that love it not? 4.01.164
i read that i profess, the art to love. 4.02. 8
o despiteful love! 4.02. 14
forswear bianca and her love for ever. 4.02. 26
shall win my love, and so i take my leave, | in 4.02. 42
nay, i have ta'en you napping, gentle love, 4.02. 46
take /in your love, and then let me alone. 4.02. 71
wants, | he does it under name of perfect love; 4.03. 12
a dish that i do love to feed upon. 4.03. 24
here, love, thou seest how diligent i am | to 4.03. 39
and now, my honey love, | will we return unto 4.03. 52
i love thee well in that thou lik'st it not. 4.03. 83
love me, or love me not, i like the cap, | and 4.03. 84
love me, or love me not, i like the cap, | and 4.03. 84
of love between your daughter and himself; 4.04. 27
and for the love he beareth to your daughter 4.04. 29
your son lucentio here | doth love my daughter, 4.04. 41
love wrought these miracles. 5.01.124
bianca's love | made me exchange my state with 5.01.124
now pray thee, love, stay. 5.01.148
marry, peace it bodes, and love, and quiet life, 5.02.108
craves no other tribute at thy hands | but love, 5.02.153
when they are bound to serve, love, and obey. 5.02.164
love all, trust a few, | do wrong to none. AWW 1.01. 64
want the best | that shall attend his love. 1.01. 73
that i should love a bright particular star 1.01. 86
th' ambition in my love thus plagues itself: 1.01. 90
would be mated by the lion | must die for love. 1.01. 92
i love him for his sake, | and yet i know him a 1.01. 99
what power is it which mounts my love so high, 1.01.220
to show her merit, that did miss her love? 1.01.227
his love and wisdom, | approv'd so to your 1.02. 9
know, madam, you love your gentlewoman entirely. 1.03. 99 P
make title to as much love as she finds. 1.03.103 P
love no god, that would not extend his might 1.03.112 P
you love my son. 1.03.173
do you love my son? 1.03.186
love you my son? 1.03.187
do not you love him, madam? 1.03.187
my love hath in't a bond | whereof the world 1.03.188
and next unto high heaven, | i love your son. 1.03.194
my friends were poor, but honest, so's my love. 1.03.195
i know i love in vain, strive against hope; 1.03.201
i still pour in the waters of my love | and lack 1.03.203
let not your hate encounter with my love | for 1.03.208
flame of liking | wish chastely and love dearly, 1.03.212
that your dian | was both herself and love, o, 1.03.213
why, helen, thou shalt have my leave and love, 1.03.251
and virtuous mistress | fall, when love please! 2.03. 58
who shuns thy love shuns all his love in me. 2.03. 73
who shuns thy love shuns all his love in me. 2.03. 73
and to imperial love, that god most high, | do 2.03. 75
love make your fortunes twenty times above | her 2.03. 82
above | her that so wishes, and her humble love! 2.03. 83
which great love grant, and so i take my leave. 2.03. 85
i cannot love her, nor will strive to do't. 2.03.145
misprision shackle up | my love and her desert; 2.03.153
the great prerogative and rite of love, | which, 2.04. 41
of my cupid's knock'd out, and i begin to love, 3.02. 16 P
hope, lay our best love and credence | upon thy 3.03. 2
prove | a lover of thy drum, hater of love. 3.03. 11
ambitious love hath so in me offended | that 3.04. 5
speed her foot again, | led hither by pure love. 3.04. 38
o, for the love of laughter, let him fetch his 3.06. 34 P
o, for the love of laughter, hinder not the 3.06. 41 P
i love not many words. 3.06. 84 P
soul, | in your fine frame hath love no quality? 4.02. 4
but i love thee | by love's own sweet constraint 4.02. 15
you believe my oaths | when i did love you ill? 4.02. 27
to swear by him whom i protest to love | that i 4.02. 28
love is holy, | and my integrity ne'er knew the 4.02. 32
thou art mine, and ever | my love, as it begins, 4.02. 37
i begin to love him for this. 4.03.262 P
more truly labor | to recompense your love. 4.04. 18
i could not have ow'd her a more rooted love. 4.05. 12 P
that thou didst love her, strikes some scores 5.03. 56
but love that comes too late, | like a 5.03. 57
our own love waking cries to see what's done, 5.03. 65
thou speak'st it falsely, as i love mine honor, 5.03.113
did he love this woman? 5.03.241 P
faith, sir, he did love her, but how? 5.03.243 P
he did love her, sir, as a gentleman loves a 5.03.245 P
i'll love her dearly, ever, ever dearly. 5.03.316
if music be the food of love, play on, | give me TN 1.01. 1
o spirit of love, how quick and fresh art thou, 1.01. 9
all this to season | a brother's dead love, 1.01. 30
to pay this debt of love but to a brother, | how 1.01. 33
how will she love when the rich golden shaft 1.01. 34
of) | that he did seek the love of fair olivia. 1.02. 34
for whose dear love, | they say, she hath 1.02. 39
call in question the continuance of his love. 1.04. 6 P
o, then unfold the passion of my love, 1.04. 24
o, such love | could be but recompens'd, though 1.05.252
how does he love me? 1.05.254
with groans that thunder love, with sighs of 1.05.256
your lord does know my mind, i cannot love him, 1.05.257
but yet i cannot love him. 1.05.262
if i did love you in my master's flame, | with 1.05.264
write loyal cantons of contemned love, | and 1.05.270
i cannot love him; 1.05.280
love make his heart of flint that you shall love 1.05.286
make his heart of flint that you shall love, 1.05.286
it were a bad recompense for your love, to lay 2.01. 7 P
if you will not murther me for my love, let me 2.01. 35 P
'tis, | poor lady, she were better love a dream. 2.02. 26
my state is desperate for my master's love; 2.02. 37
"what is love? 2.03. 47
and you love me, let's do't. 2.03. 60 P
for the love o' god, peace! 2.03. 85 P
of faith that all that look on him love him; 2.03.152 P
drop in his way some obscure epistles of love, 2.03.156 P
from my niece, and that she's in love with him. 2.03.166 P
if ever thou shalt love, | in the sweet pangs of 2.04. 15
a very echo to the seat | where love is thron'd. 2.04. 22
then let thy love be younger than thyself, | or 2.04. 36
sooth, | and dallies with the innocence of love, 2.04. 47
tell her, my love, more noble than the world, 2.04. 81
but if she cannot love you, sir? 2.04. 87
hath for your love as great a pang of heart | as 2.04. 90
you cannot love her; 2.04. 91
strong a passion | as love doth give my heart; 2.04. 95
alas, their love may be call'd appetite, | no 2.04. 97
compare | between that love a woman can bear me 2.04.102
too well what love women to men may owe; 2.04.105
she never told her love, | but let concealment, 2.04.110
was not this love indeed? 2.04.115
much in our vows, but little in our love. 2.04.118
but died thy sister of her love, my boy? 2.04.119
say | my love can give no place, bide no denay. 2.04.124
observe him, for the love of mockery; 2.05. 18 P
"jove knows i love, | but who? 2.05. 96
and in this she manifests herself to my love, 2.05.168 P
if thou entertain'st my love, let it appear in 2.05.175 P
that's a degree to love. 3.01.123
more soon | than love that would seem hid: 3.01.148
i love thee so, that, maugre all thy pride, 3.01.151
love sought is good, but given unsought is 3.01.156
that heart, which now abhors, to like his love. 3.01.164
was a great argument of love in her toward you. 3.02. 11 P
and not all love to see you (though so much | as 3.03. 6
my willing love, | the rather by these arguments 3.03. 11
but this — your true love for my master. 3.04.213
that for his love dares yet do more | than you 3.04.316
reliev'd him with such sanctity of love, | and 3.04.361
tempests are kind and salt waves fresh in love. 3.04.384
and did thereto add | my love, without retention 5.01. 81
sake | did i expose myself (pure for his love) 5.01. 83
thief at point of death, | kill what i love? 5.01.119
but this your minion, whom i know you love, 5.01.125
i'll sacrifice the lamb that i do love, | to 5.01.130
after him i love | more than i love these eyes, 5.01.134
after him i love | more than i love these eyes, 5.01.135
more, by all mores, than e'er i shall love wife. 5.01.136
above | punish my life for tainting of my love! 5.01.138
a contract of eternal bond of love, | confirm'd 5.01.156
for the love of god, a surgeon! 5.01.172 P
for the love of god, your help! 5.01.176 P
thou never shouldst love woman like to me. 5.01.268
which to hinder | were (in your love) a whip to WT 1.02. 25
i love thee not a jar o' th' clock behind | what 1.02. 43
open thy white hand | /and clap thyself my love; 1.02.104
son | (who i do think is mine and love as mine), 1.02.331
i love you better. 2.01. 6
with such a kind of love as might become | a 3.02. 64
with a love even such, | so and no other, as 3.02. 65
and toward your friend, whose love had spoke, 3.02. 69
the love i bore your queen — lo, fool again! 3.02.228
(humbling their deities to love) have taken 4.04. 26
no, like a bank, for love to lie and play on; 4.04.130
i love a ballad but even too well, if it be 4.04.188 P
if i were not in love with mopsa, thou shouldst 4.04.231 P
i love a ballet in print, a–life, for then we 4.04.260 P
thou hast sworn my love to be. 4.04.306
and handed love as you do, i was wont | to load 4.04.348
and call this | your lack of love or bounty, you 4.04.354
i would not prize them | without her love; 4.04.376
save him from danger, do him love and honor, 4.04.510
i' th' love | that i have borne your father? 4.04.516
if you may please to think i love the king | and 4.04.521
you know, | prosperity's the very bond of love, 4.04.573
man) grew so in love with the wenches' song, 4.04.606 P
women will love her, that she is a woman | more 5.01.110
made whole | with very easy arguments of love, JN 1.01. 36

dispose, | subjected tribute to commanding love, 1.01.264
embrace him, love him, give him welcome hither. 2.01. 11
hand, | but with a heart full of unstained love. 2.01. 16
kiss | as seal to this indenture of my love: 2.01. 20
strength | to make a more requital to your love! 2.01. 34
england we love, and for that england's sake 2.01. 91
and out of my dear love i'll give thee more 2.01.157
if lusty love should go in quest of beauty, 2.01.426
if zealous love should go in search of virtue, 2.01.428
if love ambitious sought a match of birth, 2.01.430
can in this book of beauty read, "i love," | her 2.01.485
should be | in such a love so vile a lout as he. 2.01.509
properly, | i will enforce it eas'ly to my love. 2.01.515
my lord, | that all i see in you is worthy love, 2.01.517
then, prince dolphin, can you love this lady? 2.01.524
nay, ask me if i can refrain from love, | for i 2.01.525
from love, | for i do love her most unfeignedly. 2.01.526
be content, | for then i should not love thee; 3.01. 49
true love | between our kingdoms and our royal 3.01.231
so newly join'd in love, so strong in both, 3.01.240
save what is opposite to england's love. 3.01.254
now shall i see thy love. 3.01.313
and with advantage means to pay thy love; 3.03. 22
yet i love thee well, | and, by my troth, i 3.03. 54
hubert, i love thee. 3.03. 67
misery's love, | o, come to me! 3.04. 35
o, what love i note | in the fair multitude of 3.04. 61
heaven | i were your son, so you would love me, 4.01. 24
i warrant i love you more than you do me. 4.01. 31
or "what good love may i perform for you?" 4.01. 49
nay, you may think my love was crafty love, 4.01. 53
nay, you may think my love was crafty love, 4.01. 53
whose private with me of the dolphin's love | is 4.03. 16
swearing allegiance and the love of soul | to 5.01. 10
swore to you | dear amity and everlasting love. 5.04. 20
the love of him, and this respect besides, | for 5.04. 41
my soul | but i do love the favor and the form 5.04. 50
and the like tender of our love we make, | to 5.07.106
speech, | in the devotion of a subject's love, R2 1.01. 31
hath love in thy old blood no living fire? 1.02. 10
god, | embrace each other's love in banishment, 1.03.184
of world | i wander from the jewels that i love. 1.03.270
love they to live that love and honor have. 2.01.138
love they to live that love and honor have. 2.01.138
as herford's love, so his, | as theirs, so mine, 2.01.145
our nearness to the king in love | is near the 2.02.127
is near the hate of those love not the king. 2.02.128
commons, for their love | lies in their purses, 2.02.129
and, as my fortune ripens with thy love, | it 2.03. 48
i wot your love pursues | a banish'd traitor. 2.03. 59
shall be your love and labor's recompense. 2.03. 62
blood, and near in love | till you did make him 3.01. 17
with letters of your love to her at large. 3.01. 41
sweet love, i see, changing his property, 3.02.135
me rather had my heart might feel your love 3.03.192
as my true service shall deserve your love. 3.03.199
tears show their love, but want their remedies. 3.03.203
the love of wicked men converts to fear, | that 5.01. 66
hand from hand, my love, and heart from heart. 5.01. 82
that were some love, but little policy. 5.01. 84
to me, or any of my kin, | and yet i love him. 5.02.110
shall i for love speak treason to thy face? 5.03. 44
fear, and not love, begets his penitence. 5.03. 56
love loving not itself, none other can. 5.03. 88
for 'tis a sign of love; 5.05. 65
and love to richard | is a strange brooch in 5.05. 65
if thou love me, 'tis time thou wert away. 5.05. 96
they love not poison that do poison need, | nor 5.06. 38
i hate the murtherer, love him murthered. 5.06. 40
betwixt my love and your high majesty. 1H4 1.03. 69
to make us strangers to his looks of love. 1.03.290
have not given me medicines to make me love him, 2.02. 19 P
in respect of the love i bear your house." 2.03. 2 P
in the respect of the love he bears our house: 2.03. 4 P
why, my horse, my love, my horse. 2.03. 76
so far afoot, i shall be weary, love. 2.03. 84
love, i love thee not, | i care not for thee, 2.03. 90
love, i love thee not, | i care not for thee, 2.03. 90
do you not love me? 2.03. 96
well, do not then, for since you love me not, 2.03. 97
since you love me not, | i will not love myself. 2.03. 98
do you not love me? 2.03. 98
i will swear | i love thee infinitely. 2.03.102
if thou love me, practice an answer. 2.04.374 P
but i will never be a truant, love, | till i 3.01.204
i love him well, he is an honest man. 3.03. 93 P
a million, thy love is worth a million; 3.03.136 P
thou owest me thy love. 3.03.137 P
love thy husband, look to thy servants, cherish 3.03.171 P
in my heart's love hath no man than yourself. 4.01. 8
some of us love you well, and even those some 4.03. 34
i would you would accept of grace and love. 4.03.112
that even our love durst not come near your 5.01. 63
we love our people well, even those we love 5.01.104
even those we love | that are misled upon your 5.01.104
of thee | if i were much in love with vanity! 5.04.106
pardon, and terms of love to all of you? 5.05. 3
make me out of love with my greatness. 2H4 2.02. 12 P
nor no cheater, but i do not love swaggering, by 2.04.103 P
i' faith, i love thee. 2.04.219 P
why does the prince love him so then? 2.04.243 P
i love thee better than i love e'er a scurvy 2.04.272 P
thee better than i love e'er a scurvy young boy 2.04.272 P
the wicked might not fall in love with thee; 2.04.320 P
and laid his love and life under my foot, | yea, 3.01. 63
offer, | and it proceeds from policy, not love. 4.01.146
that, were our royal faiths martyrs in love, 4.01.191
tokens home | of our restored love and amity. 4.02. 65
but my love to ye | shall show itself more 4.02. 75
same young sober-blooded boy doth not love me, 4.03. 88 P
therefore omit him not, blunt not his love, 4.04. 27
i shall observe him with all care and love. 4.04. 49
which nature, love, and filial tenderness 4.05. 39
thou mightst win the more thy father's love, 4.05.179
let me but bear your love, i'll bear your cares. 5.02. 58
you are, i think, assur'd i love you not. 5.02. 64
your too much love and care of me | are heavy H5 2.02. 52
you know how apt our love was to accord | to 2.02. 86
my love, give me thy lips. 2.03. 47
and a man that i love and honor with my soul, 3.06. 7 P
the duke of exeter doth love thee well. 3.06. 22
god, and i have merited some love at his hands. 3.06. 24 P
'tis good for men to love their present pains 4.01. 18
and from heart-string | i love the lovely bully. 4.01. 48
i dare say you love him not so ill to wish him 4.01.124 P
he seal'd | a testament of noble-ending love. 4.06. 27
any such, apprehend him, and thou dost me love. 4.07.159 P
because, look you, you do not love it, nor your 5.01. 25 P
shall change all griefs and quarrels into love. 5.02. 20
my duty to you both, on equal love. 5.02. 23
if you will love me soundly with your french 5.02.104 P
i know no ways to mince it in love, but directly 5.02.126 P
it in love, but directly to say "i love you"é 5.02.127 P
or if i might buffet for my love, or bound my 5.02.140 P
if thou canst love a fellow of this temper, kate 5.02.146 P
in his glass for love of any thing he sees there 5.02.148 P
if thou canst love me for this, take me! 5.02.150 P
but for thy love, by the lord, no; 5.02.151 P
yet i love thee too. 5.02.152 P
and what say'st thou then to my love? 5.02.167 P
it possible dat i sould love de enemy of france? 5.02.169 P
possible you should love the enemy of france, 5.02.171 P
loving me, you should love the friend of france; 5.02.173 P
for i love france so well that i will not part 5.02.173 P
canst thou love me? 5.02.193 P
those parts in me that you love with your heart. 5.02.201 P
gentle princess, because i love thee cruelly. 5.02.202 P
mine honor, in true english, i love thee, kate; 5.02.221 P
my fair cousin, how perfectly i love her, and 5.02.284 P
cannot so conjure up the spirit of love in her, 5.02.289 P
if conjure up love in her in his true likeness, 5.02.293 P
wink and yield, as love is blind and enforces. 5.02.300 P
as love is, my lord, before it loves. 5.02.315 P
some of you, thank love for my blindness, who 5.02.317 P
i pray you then, in love and dear alliance, 5.02.345
as man and wife, being two, are one in love, 5.02.361
i must not yield to any rites of love, | for my 1H6 1.02.113
i love no colors; 2.04. 34
mean time, in signal of my love to thee, 2.04.121
to join your hearts in love and amity. 3.01. 68
and if you love me, as you say you do, | let me 3.01.104
love for thy love and hand for hand i give. 3.01.135
love for thy love and hand for hand i give. 3.01.135
the presence of a king engenders love | amongst 3.01.180
burns under feigned ashes of forg'd love, | and 3.01.189
henceforth i charge you, as you love our favor, 4.01.135
both are my kinsmen, and i love them both. 4.01.155
so let us still continue peace, and love. 4.01.161
if you forsake the offer of their love. 4.02. 14
i owe him little duty, and less love, | and take 4.04. 34
o, if you love my mother, | dishonor not her 4.05. 13
suit, | before thou make a trial of her love? 5.03. 76
his love. 5.03.121
never yet taint with love, i send the king. 5.03.183
of his, | it was alanson that enjoy'd my love. 5.04. 73
arrive | where i may have fruition of her love. 5.05. 9
intents, | to love and honor henry as her lord. 5.05. 21
to choose for wealth and not for perfect love. 5.05. 50
(as is fair margaret) he be link'd in love. 5.05. 76
with hope to find the like event in love, | but 5.05.105
i can express no kinder sign of love | than this 2H6 1.01. 18
soul, | if sympathy of love unite our thoughts. 1.01. 23
lords, with one cheerful voice welcome my love. 1.01. 36
and make a show of love to proud duke humphrey, 1.01.241
surfeiting in joys of love | with his new bride 1.01.251
o nell, sweet nell, if thou dost love thy lord, 1.02. 17
that love to be protected | under the wings of 1.03. 37
thou ran'st a-tilt in honor of my love | and 1.03. 51
my soul | as i in duty love my king and country! 1.03.158
to tell my love unto his dumb deaf trunk, | and 3.02.144
and mere instinct of love and loyalty, | free 3.02.250
and you that love the commons, follow me. 4.02.182
i fear me, love, if that i had been dead, | thou 4.04. 23
no, my love, i should not mourn, but die for 4.04. 25
show'd how well you love your prince and country 4.09. 16
all my sons, | as pledges of my fealty and love; 5.01. 50
with thy brave bearing should i be in love, 5.02. 20
how love to me and to her son | hath made her 3H6 1.01.264
trimm'd like a younker prancing to his love! 2.01. 24
it, | you love the breeder better than the male. 2.01. 42
'tis love i bear thy glories make me speak. 2.01.158
but love to go | whither the queen intends. 2.05.138
my love and fear glu'd many friends to thee, 2.06. 5
thou didst love york, and i am son to york. 2.06. 73
from scotland am i stol'n, even of pure love, 3.01. 13
now tell me, madam, do you love your children? 3.02. 36
ay, full as dearly as i love myself. 3.02. 37
an easy task, 'tis but to love a king. 3.02. 53
but stay thee, 'tis the fruits of love i mean. 3.02. 58
the fruits of love i mean, my loving liege. 3.02. 59
what love, think'st thou, i sue so much to get? 3.02. 61
my love till death, my humble thanks, my prayers 3.02. 62
that love which virtue begs and virtue grants. 3.02. 63
no, by my troth, i did not mean such love. 3.02. 64
and she shall be my love or else my queen. 3.02. 88
and that is, to enjoy thee for my love. 3.02. 95
why, love forswore me in my mother's womb; 3.02.153
lewis, | that henry, sole possessor of my love, 3.03. 24
i come, in kindness and unfeigned love, | first, 3.03. 51
not from edward's well-meant honest love, | but 3.03. 67
tell me for truth the measure of his love | unto 3.03.120
that this his love was an /eternal plant, 3.03.124
thy sly conveyance and thy lord's false love, 3.03.160
this proveth edward's love and warwick's honesty 3.03.180
these words have turn'd my hate to love, | and i 3.03.199
my love, forbear to fawn upon their frowns. 4.01. 75
nay, whom they shall obey, and love thee too, 4.01. 79
you that love me and warwick, follow me. 4.01.123
i | stay not for the love of edward, but the 4.01.126
tell me if you love warwick more than me? 4.01.137
hath pawn'd an open hand in sign of love; 4.02. 9
for love of edward's offspring in my womb. 4.04. 18
then why should they love edward more than me? 4.08. 47
more than the nature of a brother's love! 5.01. 79
i, that have neither pity, love, nor fear. 5.06. 68
and this word "love," which greybeards call 5.06. 81
clarence and gloucester, love my lovely queen, 5.07. 26
that love the tree from whence thou sprang'st, 5.07. 31
i do love thee so | that i will shortly send thy R3 1.01.118
not all so much for love | as for another secret 1.01.157
this hand, which for thy love did kill thy love, 1.02.189
this hand, which for thy love did kill thy love, 1.02.189
shall for thy love kill a far truer love; 1.02.190
shall for thy love kill a far truer love; 1.02.190
grave, | and then return lamenting to my love. 1.02.261
that i, forsooth, am stern, and love them not? 1.03. 44
they love his grace but lightly | that fill his 1.03. 45
my brother's love, the devil, and my rage. 1.04.223
thy brother's love, our duty, and thy faults 1.04.224
/o, if you love my brother, hate not me! 1.04.226
i am his brother and i love him well. 1.04.227
dissemble not your hatred, swear your love. 2.01. 8
and with my hand i seal my true heart's love. 2.01. 10
so prosper i, as i swear perfect love! 2.01. 16
and i, as i love hastings with my heart! 2.01. 17
wife, love lord hastings, let him kiss your hand 2.01. 21
hastings, love lord marquess. 2.01. 25
this interchange of love, i here protest, | upon 2.01. 26
but with all duteous love | doth cherish you and 2.01. 33
with hate in those where i expect most love! 2.01. 35
/god, | when i am cold in love to you or yours. 2.01. 40
made peace of enmity, fair love of hate, 2.01. 51
i hate it, and desire all good men's love. 2.01. 62
why, madam, have i off'red love for this, | to 2.01. 78
who spoke of love? 2.01.109
children, peace, the king doth love you well. 2.02. 17
and he would love me dearly as a child. 2.02. 26
love, charity, obedience, and true duty! 2.02.108
now cheer each other in each other's love. 2.02.114
lord hastings, you and he are near in love. 3.04. 13
can lesser hide his love or hate than he, | for 3.04. 52
the tender love i bear your grace, my lord, 3.04. 63
the rest that love me, rise, and follow me. 3.04. 79
i bid them that did love their country's good 3.07. 21
your /wisdoms and your love to richard" — | and 3.07. 40
by heaven, we come to him in perfit love, | and 3.07. 90
so season'd with your faithful love to me, 3.07.149
your love deserves my thanks, but my desert 3.07.154
refuse not, mighty lord, this proffer'd love. 3.07.202
if you refuse it — as, in love and zeal, 3.07.208
on pure heart's love, to greet the tender prince 4.01. 4
hath he set bounds between their love and me? 4.01. 20
their aunt i am in law, in love their mother; 4.01. 23
and i will love thee and prefer thee for it. 4.02. 81
then know that from my soul i love thy daughter. 4.04.256
that thou dost love my daughter from thy soul; 4.04.259
so from thy soul's love didst thou love her 4.04.260
thy soul's love didst thou love her brothers, 4.04.260
and from my heart's love i do thank thee for it. 4.04.261
i mean that with my soul i love thy daughter, 4.04.263
if this inducement move her not to love, | send 4.04.279
say that i did all this for love of her. 4.04.288
having bought love with such a bloody spoil. 4.04.290
a grandam's name is little less in love | than 4.04.299
advantaging their love with interest | of ten 4.04.323
and her love | can make seem pleasing to her 4.04.341
say i will love her everlastingly. 4.04.349
to my proceeding, if with dear heart's love, 4.04.403
you so — | be the attorney of my love to her. 4.04.413
cuts off the ceremonious vows of love | and 5.03. 98
god give us leisure for these rites of love! 5.03.101
alack, i love myself. 5.03.187
that you would love yourself, and in that love H8 1.02. 14
and in that love | not unconsidered leave your 1.02. 14
bid him strive | to the love o' th' commonalty; 1.02.170
o, very mad, exceeding mad, in love too; 1.04. 28
with my love and duty | i would surrender it. 1.04. 80
this duke as much | they love and dote on; 2.01. 52
excellence | that angels love good men with; 2.02. 34
me, my lords, | i love him not, nor fear him; 2.02. 50
of your friends | have i not strove to love, 2.04. 30
my bond to wedlock or my love and duty, 2.04. 40
you wrong the king's love with these fears, 3.01. 81
me his bed already, | his love, too long ago! 3.01.120
princes kiss obedience, | so much they love it; 3.01.163
my heart dropp'd love, my pow'r rain'd honor, 3.02.185
surrey can be, | and all that love his follies. 3.02.275
love thyself last, cherish those hearts that 3.02.443
to love her for her mother's sake that lov'd him 4.02.137
by that you love the dearest in this world, | as 4.02.155
my lord, i love you; 5.01. 16
love and meekness, lord, | become a churchman 5.02. 97
i | am for his love and service so to him. 5.02.192
i charge you, | embrace and love this man. 5.02.205
peace, plenty, love, truth, terror, | that were 5.04. 47
i tell thee i am mad | in cressid's love; TRO 1.01. 52
as true thou tell'st me, when i say i love her, 1.01. 60
lay'st in every gash that love hath given me 1.01. 62
tell me, apollo, for thy daphne's love, | what 1.01. 98
if you love an addle egg as well as you love an 1.02.133 P
an addle egg as well as you love an idle head, 1.02.133 P
knew | love got so sweet as when desire did sue. 1.02.291
therefore this maxim out of love i teach: 1.02.292
though my heart's content firm love doth bear, 1.02.294
of which metal is not found | in fortune's love; 1.03. 23
troy, | to rouse a grecian that is true in love. 1.03.279
that means not, hath not, or is not in love! 1.03.288
hath no spark of fire | to answer for his love, 1.03.295
at mine, sir, and theirs that love music. 3.01. 24 P
niece is horribly in love with a thing you have, 3.01. 97 P
let thy song be love. 3.01.110 P
this love will undo us all. 3.01.110 P
love? ay, that it shall, i' faith. 3.01.112 P
ay, good now, love, love, nothing but love. 3.01.113 P
ay, good now, love, love, nothing but love. 3.01.113 P
ay, good now, love, love, nothing but love. 3.01.113 P
"love, love, nothing but love, still love, still 3.01.115
"love, love, nothing but love, still love, still 3.01.115
"love, love, nothing but love, still love, still 3.01.115
love, nothing but love, still love, still more! 3.01.115
so dying love lives still. 3.01.124
in love, i' faith, to the very tip of the nose. 3.01.127 P
he eats nothing but doves, love, and that breeds 3.01.128 P
thoughts beget hot deeds, and hot deeds is love. 3.01.130 P

is this the generation of love — hot blood, hot 3.01.131 P
is love a generation of vipers? 3.01.133 P
sweet, above thought i love /thee! 3.01.159
my sweet lady in the fountain of our love? 3.02. 66 P
this /is the monstruosity in love, lady, that 3.02. 81 P
i love you now, but till now not so much | but i 3.02.120
perchance, my lord, i show more craft than love, 3.02.153
but you are wise, | or else you love not; 3.02.156
for to be wise and love | exceeds man's might; 3.02.156
to feed for /aye her lamp and flames of love, 3.02.160
and weight | of such a winnowed purity in love! 3.02.167
true swains in love shall in the world to come 3.02.173
from false to false, among false maids in love, 3.02.190
the love that lean'd on them as slippery too, 3.03. 85
love, friendship, charity, are subjects all | to 3.03.173
that you are in love | with one of priam's 3.03.193
and your great love to me restrains you thus. 3.03.221
no man alive can love in such a sort | the thing 4.01. 24
the noblest hateful love, that e'er i heard of. 4.01. 34
but flies the grasps of love | with wings more 4.02. 13
no kin, no love, no blood, no soul so near me 4.02. 98
but the strong base and building of my love | is 4.02.103
i know what 'tis to love, | and would, as i 4.03. 10
my love admits no qualifying dross, | no more my 4.04. 9
i love thee in so strain'd a purity | that the 4.04. 24
hear me, love. be thou but true of heart — 4.04. 58
hear why i speak it, love. 4.04. 75
o heavens, you love me not. 4.04. 82
in love whereof, half hector stays at home; 4.05. 84
action | is more vindicative than jealous love. 4.05.107
but still sweet love is food for fortune's tooth 4.05.293
a token from her daughter, my fair love, | both 5.01. 40
the fractions of her faith, orts of her love, 5.02.158
as much /as i do cressid love, | so much by 5.02.167
for th' love of all the gods, | let's leave the 5.03. 44
you, | upon the love you bear me, get you in. 5.03. 78
my love with words and errors still she feeds, 5.03.111
i am a bastard too, i love bastards. 5.07. 16 P
and there's all the love they bear us. COR 1.01. 86 P
of his bed where he would show most love. 1.03. 5 P
had i a dozen sons, each in my love alike, and 1.03. 22 P
'tis not to save labor, nor that i want love. 1.03. 81 P
goddess fortune | fall deep in love with thee, 1.05. 21
that love this painting | wherein you see me 1.06. 68
prayer of the people, for they love not martius. 2.01. 5 P
pray you, who does the wolf love? 2.01. 7 P
for the love of juno, let's go. 2.01.101 P
so that, if they love they know not why, they 2.02. 10 P
to care whether they love or hate him manifests 2.02. 12 P
he did not care whether he had their love or no, 2.02. 16 P
he dislikes, to flatter them for their love. 2.02. 23 P
but your people, | i love them as they weigh — 2.02. 74
virtuous that i have not been common in my love. 2.03. 95 P
translate his malice towards you into love, 2.03.189
that love the fundamental part of state | more 3.01.151
when he did love his country, | it honor'd him. 3.01.303
plant love among 's! 3.03. 35
i do love | my country's good with a respect 3.03.111
hoarded plague a' th' gods | requite your love! 4.02. 12
as 'twere, in love | unseparable, shall within 4.04. 15
as hotly and as nobly with thy love | as ever in 4.05.111
the senators and patricians love him too; 4.07. 30
only make trial what your love can do | for rome 5.01. 40
and love thee no worse than thy old father 5.02. 69 P
for whose old love i have | (though i show'd 5.03. 12
no more infected with my country's love | than 5.06. 71
and so i love and honor thee and thine, | thy TIT 1.01. 49
and to the love and favor of my country | commit 1.01. 58
these that survive let rome reward with love; 1.01. 82
wife, | that is another's lawful promis'd love. 1.01.298
own, | my true betrothed love, and now my wife? 1.01.406
and plead my passions for lavinia's love. 2.01. 36
that for her love such quarrels may be broach'd, 2.01. 67
world, | i love lavinia more than all the world. 2.01. 72
they be, | and cannot brook competitors in love? 2.01. 77
would i propose to achieve her whom i love. 2.01. 80
chaste | than this lavinia, bassianus' love. 2.01.109
hence, | and let her joy her raven-colored love; 2.03. 83
revenge it, as you love your mother's life, | or 2.03.114
gain so great a happiness | as half thy love? 2.04. 21
thee this word — that, if thou love thy sons, 3.01.151
now let me show a brother's love to thee. 3.01.182
and if ye love me, as i think you do, | let's 3.01.286
for love of her that's gone, | perhaps, she 4.01. 43
a charitable wish, and full of love. 4.02. 43
'tis he the common people love so much; 4.04. 73
this do thou for my love, and so let him, | as 5.02.129
for peace, for love, for league, and good to 5.03. 23
the fearful passage of their death-mark'd love, ROM pr 9
in love? 1.01.165
of love? 1.01.167
out of her favor where i am in love. 1.01.168
alas that love, so gentle in his view, | should 1.01.169
alas that love, whose view is muffled still, 1.01.171
here's much to do with hate, but more with love. 1.01.175
why then, o brawling love! 1.01.176
this love feel i, that feel no love in this. 1.01.182
this love feel i, that feel no love in this. 1.01.182
this love that thou hast shown | doth add more 1.01.188
love is a smoke made with the fume of sighs, 1.01.190
tell me in sadness, who is that you love? 1.01.199
in sadness, cousin, i do love a woman. 1.01.204
a right good mark-man! and she's fair i love. 1.01.206
she hath forsworn to love, and in that vow | do 1.01.223
such as i love, and you, among the store | one 1.02. 22
one fairer than my love! 1.02. 92
your lady's love against some other maid | that 1.02. 97
the valiant paris seeks you for his love. 1.03. 74
can you love the gentleman? 1.03. 79
this precious book of love, this unbound lover, 1.03. 87
speak briefly, can you like of paris' love? 1.03. 96
and, to sink in it, should you burthen love — 1.04. 23
is love a tender thing? 1.04. 25
if love be rough with you, be rough with love; 1.04. 27
if love be rough with you, be rough with love; 1.04. 27
prick love for pricking, and you beat love down. 1.04. 28
prick love for pricking, and you beat love down. 1.04. 28
from the mire | /of /this /sir-reverence love, 1.04. 42
lovers' brains, and then they dream of love; 1.04. 71
did my heart love till now? 1.05. 52
my only love sprung from my only hate! 1.05.138
prodigious birth of love it is to me | that i 1.05.140
it is to me | that i must love a loathed enemy. 1.05.141
that fair for which love groan'd for and would 2.pr. 3
and she as much in love, her means much less 2.pr. 11
/pronounce but "love" and "/dove"; 2.01. 10
blind is his love and best befits the dark. 2.01. 32
if love be blind, love cannot hit the mark. 2.01. 33
if love be blind, love cannot hit the mark. 2.01. 33
it is my lady, o, it is my love! 2.02. 10
or, if thou wilt not, be but sworn my love, 2.02. 35
call me but love, and i'll be new baptiz'd; 2.02. 50
walls, | for stony limits cannot hold love out, 2.02. 67
and what love can do, that dares love attempt; 2.02. 68
and what love can do, that dares love attempt; 2.02. 68
and but thou love me, let them find me here; 2.02. 76
than death prorogued, wanting of thy love. 2.02. 78
by love, that first did prompt me to inquire; 2.02. 80
dost thou love me? 2.02. 90
if thou dost love, pronounce it faithfully; 2.02. 94
and not impute this yielding to light love, 2.02.105
lest that thy love prove likewise variable. 2.02.111
if my heart's dear love — 2.02.115
this bud of love, by summer's ripening breath, 2.02.121
for what purpose, love? 2.02.130
is as boundless as the sea, | my love as deep; 2.02.134
dear love, adieu! 2.02.136
if that thy bent of love be honorable, | thy 2.02.143
love goes toward love as schoolboys from their 2.02.156
love goes toward love as schoolboys from their 2.02.156
but love from love, toward school with heavy 2.02.157
but love from love, toward school with heavy 2.02.157
there, | rememb'ring how i love thy company. 2.02.173
then plainly know my heart's dear love is set 2.03. 57
is rosaline, that thou didst love so dear, | so 2.03. 66
young men's love then lies | not truly in their 2.03. 67
to season love, that of it doth not taste! 2.03. 72
and badst me bury love. 2.03. 83
her i love now | doth grace for grace and love 2.03. 85
doth grace for grace and love for love allow; 2.03. 86
doth grace for grace and love for love allow; 2.03. 86
thy love did read by rote that could not spell. 2.03. 88
to turn your households' rancor to pure love. 2.03. 92
(marry, she had a better love to berhyme her), 2.04. 40 P
is not this better now than groaning for love? 2.04. 89 P
for this drivelling love is like a great natural 2.04. 91 P
therefore do nimble-pinion'd doves draw love, 2.05. 7
my words would bandy her to my sweet love, | and 2.05. 14
sweet, sweet nurse, tell me, what says my love? 2.05. 54
your love says, like an honest gentleman, | an' 2.05. 55
"your love says, like an honest gentleman, 2.05. 60
by the which your love | must climb a bird's 2.05. 73
therefore love moderately: 2.06. 14
long love doth so; 2.06. 14
but my true love is grown to such excess | i 2.06. 33
the love i bear thee can afford | no better term 3.01. 60
the reason that i have to love thee | doth much 3.01. 62
but love thee better than thou canst devise, 3.01. 69
till thou shalt know the reason of my love, 3.01. 70
by their own beauties, or, if love be blind, 3.02. 9
till strange love grow bold, | think true love 3.02. 15
bold, | think true love acted simple modesty. 3.02. 16
that all the world will be in love with night, 3.02. 24
o, i have bought the mansion of a love, | but 3.02. 26
wert thou as young as i, juliet thy love, | an 3.03. 65
says | my conceal'd lady to our cancell'd love? 3.03. 98
fie, thou shamest thy shape, thy love, thy wit, 3.03.122
which should bedeck thy shape, thy love, thy wit 3.03.125
thy dear love sworn but hollow perjury, 3.03.128
killing that love which thou hast vow'd to 3.03.129
thy wit, that ornament to shape and love, 3.03.130
thou /pouts /upon thy fortune and thy love. 3.03.144
go get thee to thy love as was decreed, | ascend 3.03.146
make a desperate tender | of my child's love. 3.04. 13
bed, | acquaint her here of my son paris' love, 3.04. 16
believe me, love, it was the nightingale. 3.05. 5
look, love, what envious streaks | do lace the 3.05. 7
art thou gone so, love — lord, ay, husband, 3.05. 43
that may convey my greetings, love, to thee. 3.05. 50
and trust me, love, in my eye so do you; 3.05. 58
some grief shows much of love, | but much of 3.05. 72
come to him | to wreak the love i bore my cousin 3.05.101
but thankful even for hate that is meant love. 3.05.148
to answer, "i'll not wed, i cannot love; 3.05.185
and therefore have i little /talk'd of love, 4.01. 7
that may be must be, love, on thursday next. 4.01. 20
do not deny to him that you love me. 4.01. 24
i will confess to you that i love him. 4.01. 25
so will ye, i am sure, that you love me. 4.01. 26
to live an unstain'd wife to my sweet love. 4.01. 88
love give me strength! 4.01.125
cell, | and gave him what becomed love i might, 4.02. 26
why, love, i say! 4.05. 3
o love, o life! 4.05. 58
not life, but love in death! 4.05. 58
o, in this love, you love your child so ill 4.05. 75
you love your child so ill | that you run mad, 4.05. 75
ah me, how sweet is love itself possess'd, 5.01. 10
by heaven, i love thee better than myself, | for 5.03. 64
o my love, my wife, | death, that hath suck'd 5.03. 91
here's to my love! 5.03.119
sir, and there's my master, | one that you love. 5.03.129
their course of love, the tidings of her death; 5.03.287
heaven finds means to kill your joys with love. 5.03.293
subdues and properties to his love and tendance TIM 1.01. 57
this man of thine | attempts her love. 1.01.126
does she love him? 1.01.131
love you the maid? 1.01.134
there should be small love amongest these sweet 1.01.249
you mistake my love; 1.02. 9
honor, lord lucius | (out of his free love) hath 1.02.182
here, my lord, a trifle of our love. 1.02.207
i love and honor him, | but must not break my 2.01. 23
if i would broach the vessels of my love, | and 2.02.177
return'd to him, | so much i love his heart. 3.02. 85
it shows but little love or judgment in him. 3.03. 10
of such a nature is his politic love. 3.03. 34 P
for i know your reverend ages love | security, 3.05. 79
wert a dog, | that i might love thee something. 4.03. 56
they love thee not that use thee; 4.03. 84
i love thee better now than e'er i did. 4.03.233
world, and will love nought | but even the mere 4.03.375
live, and love thy misery. 4.03.395
love not yourselves, away, | rob one another. 4.03.444
when man was wish'd to love his enemies! 4.03.466
grant i may ever love, and rather woo | those 4.03.467
then i love thee, | because thou art a woman, 4.03.482
that which i show, heaven knows, is merely love, 4.03.515
know his gross patchery, love him, feed him, 5.01. 96
look you, i love you well, i'll give you gold, 5.01.100
the senators with one consent of love | entreat 5.01.140
even such heaps and sums of love and wealth | as 5.01.152
and write in thee the figures of their love, 5.01.154
camp | but i do prize it at my love before | the 5.01.181
but yet i love my country, and am not | one that 5.01.191
their pangs of love, with other incident throes 5.01.200
yet our old love made a particular force, | and 5.02. 8
transformed timon to our city's love | by humble 5.04. 19
and show of love as i was wont to have. JC 1.02. 34
war, | forgets the shows of love to other men. 1.02. 47
to stale with ordinary oaths my love | to every 1.02. 73
i would not, cassius, yet i love him well. 1.02. 82
for let the gods so speed me as i love | the 1.02. 88
that you do love me, i am nothing jealous; 1.02.162
i would not (so with love i might entreat you) 1.02.166
for in the ingrafted love he bears to caesar — 2.01.184
if he love caesar, all that he can do | is to 2.01.186
by all your vows of love, and that great vow 2.01.272
because i love you, i will let you know. 2.02. 74
for my dear dear love | to your proceeding bids 2.02.102
and reason to my love is liable. 2.02.104
say, i love brutus, and i honor him; 3.01.128
mark antony shall not love caesar dead | so well 3.01.133
do receive you in | with all kind love, good 3.01.176
why i, that did love caesar when i strook him, 3.01.182
though last, not least in love, yours, good 3.01.189
that i did love thee, caesar, o, 'tis true; 3.01.194
friends am i with you all, and love you all, 3.01.220
that brutus' love to caesar was no less than his 3.02. 19 P
there is tears for his love; 3.02. 27 P
is here so vile that will not love his country? 3.02. 33 P
you all did love him once, not without cause; 3.02.102
a plain blunt man | that love my friend, and 3.02.219
when love begins to sicken and decay | it useth 4.02. 20
(which should perceive nothing but love from us) 4.02. 44
do not presume too much upon my love, | i may do 4.03. 63
you love me not. 4.03. 89
have not you love enough to bear with me, | when 4.03.119
love, and be friends, as two such men should be, 4.03.131
i cannot drink too much of brutus' love. 4.03.162
not that we love words better, as you do. 5.01. 28
even for that our love of old, i prithee | hold 5.05. 27
every thing | safe toward your love and honor. MAC 1.04. 27
my dearest love, | duncan comes here to-night. 1.05. 58
the love that follows us sometime is our trouble 1.06. 11
is our trouble, | which still we thank as love. 1.06. 12
and his great love, sharp as his spur, hath holp 1.06. 23
conduct me to mine host, we love him highly, 1.06. 29
from this time | such i account thy love. 1.07. 39
how tender 'tis to love the babe that milks me; 1.07. 55
th' expedition of my violent love | outrun the 2.03.110
that had a heart to love, and in that heart 2.03.117
in that heart | courage to make 's love known? 2.03.118
off, | grapples you to the heart and love of us, 3.01.105
it is | that i to your assistance do make love, 3.01.123
so shall i, love, and so, i pray, be you. 3.02. 29
come, love and health to all, | then i'll sit 3.04. 86
all is the fear, and nothing is the love; 4.02. 12
precious motives, those strong knots of love, 4.03. 27
move only in command, | nothing in love. 5.02. 20
as honor, love, obedience, troops of friends, 5.03. 25
and with no less nobility of love | than that HAM 1.02.110
for god's love let me hear! 1.02.195
he hath importun'd me with love | in honorable 1.03.110
if thou didst ever thy dear father love — 1.05. 23
swift | as meditation or the thoughts of love, 1.05. 30
whose love was of that dignity | that it went 1.05. 48
with all my love i do commend me to you, | and 1.05.183
do, t' express his love and friending to you, 1.05.185
mad for thy love? 2.01. 82
this is the very ecstasy of love, | whose 2.01. 99
more grief to hide, than hate to utter love. 2.01.116
truth to be a liar, | but never doubt i love. 2.02.119
to reckon my groans, but that i love thee best, 2.02.121 P
but how hath she | receiv'd his love? 2.02.129
when i had seen this hot love on the wing — 2.02.132
or look'd upon this love with idle sight, | what 2.02.138
if he love her not, | and be not from his reason 2.02.164
my youth i suff'red much extremity for love — 2.02.190 P
by the obligation of our ever-preserv'd love, 2.02.286 P
if you love me, hold not off. 2.02.291 P
i have a daughter that i love passing well. 2.02.412 P
if't be th' affliction of his love or no | that 3.01. 35
the pangs of despis'd love, the law's delay, 3.01. 71
i did love you once. 3.01.114 P
love? 3.01.162
of his grief | sprung from neglected love. 3.01.178
as woman's love. 3.02.154 P
since love our hearts and hymen did our hands 3.02.159
make us again count o'er ere love be done! 3.02.162
/for women's fear and love hold quantity, | in 3.02.167
know, | and as my love is siz'd, my fear is so. 3.02.170
where love is great, the littlest doubts are 3.02.171
little fears grow great, great love grows there. 3.02.172
faith, i must leave thee, love, and shortly too; 3.02.173
such love must needs be treason in my breast. 3.02.178
are base respects of thrift, but none of love. 3.02.183
whether love lead fortune, or else fortune love. 3.02.203
whether love lead fortune, or else fortune love. 3.02.203
and hitherto doth love on fortune tend, | for 3.02.206
i could interpret between you and your love, if 3.02.246 P
the murtherer gets the love of gonzago's wife. 3.02.264 P
my lord, you once did love me. 3.02.335 P
my duty be too bold, my love is too unmannerly. 3.02.348 P

from the fair forehead of an innocent love | and 3.04. 43
you cannot call it love, for at your age | the 3.04. 68
honeying and making love | over the nasty sty! 3.04. 93
mother, for love of grace, | lay not that 3.04.144
but so much was our love, | we would not 4.01. 19
england, if my love thou hold'st at aught — 4.03. 58
pray you, love, remember. 4.05.176 P
is the great love the general gender bear him, 4.07. 18
i lov'd your father, and we love ourself, | and 4.07. 34
not that i think you did not love your father, 4.07.110
father, | but that i know love is begun by time, 4.07.111
there lives within the very flame of love | a 4.07.114
"in youth, when i did love, did love, 5.01. 61
"in youth, when i did love, did love, 5.01. 61
could not with all their quantity of love | make 5.01.270
for love of god, forbear him. 5.01.273
as love between them like the palm might 5.02. 40
time | i do receive your offer'd love like love, 5.02.251
time | i do receive your offer'd love like love, 5.02.251
i must love you, and sue to know you better. LR 1.01. 30 P
great rivals in our youngest daughter's love, 1.01. 46
which of you shall we say doth love us most, 1.01. 51
i love you more than /words can wield the matter 1.01. 55
a love that makes breath poor, and speech unable 1.01. 60
beyond all manner of so much i love you. 1.01. 61
what shall cordelia speak? love, and be silent. 1.01. 62
heart | i find she names my very deed of love; 1.01. 71
alone felicitate | in your dear highness' love. 1.01. 76
to whose young love | the vines of france and 1.01. 83
i love your majesty | according to my bond, no 1.01. 92
fit, | obey you, love you, and most honor you. 1.01. 98
husbands, if they say | they love you all? 1.01.100
my plight shall carry | half my love with him, 1.01.102
thy youngest daughter does not love thee least, 1.01.152
that good effects may spring from words of love. 1.01.185
dower with her, | or cease your quest of love? 1.01.193
i would not from your love make such a stray 1.01.209
love's not love | when it is mingled with 1.01.238
since that /respects /of /fortune are his love, 1.01.248
my love should kindle to inflam'd respect. 1.01.255
without our grace, our love, our benison. 1.01.265
love well our father; 1.01.271
our father's love is to the bastard edmund | as 1.02. 17
love cools, friendship falls off, brothers 1.02.106 P
put me in trust, to love him that is honest, to 1.04. 14 P
sir, to love a woman for singing, nor so old to 1.04. 37 P
thou serv'st me, and i'll love thee. 1.04. 88 P
i love thee." 1.04.225
drew from my heart all love, | and added to the 1.04.269
goneril, | to the great love i bear you — 1.04.312
i love thee not. 2.02. 7 P
if you do love old men, if your sweet sway 2.04.190
five and twenty, | and thou art twice her love. 2.04.260
things that love night | love not such nights as 3.02. 42
that love night | love not such nights as these. 3.02. 43
and thou shalt find a /dearer father in my love. 3.05. 25 P
i' th' way toward dover, do it for ancient love, 4.01. 43
to thank thee for the love thou show'dst the 4.02. 95
but love, dear love, and our ag'd father's right 4.04. 28
but love, dear love, and our ag'd father's right 4.04. 28
i'll love thee much — | let me unseal the 4.05. 21
i know your lady does not love her husband, | i 4.05. 23
no, do thy worst, blind cupid, i'll not love. 4.06.138 P
i know you do not love me, for your sisters 4.07. 72
speak the truth, | do you not love my sister? 5.01. 9
in honor'd love. 5.01. 9
to both these sisters have i sworn my love; 5.01. 55
in any just term am affin'd | to love the moor. OTH 1.01. 40
heaven is my judge, not i for love and duty, 1.01. 59
life, | i must show out a flag and sign of love, 1.01.156
iago, | but that i love the gentle desdemona, 1.02. 25
tale deliver | of my whole course of love — 1.03. 91
to fall in love with what she fear'd to look on! 1.03. 98
how i did thrive in this fair lady's love, | and 1.03.125
that i /did love the moor to live with him, | my 1.03.248
the rites for why i love him are bereft me, 1.03.257
i have but an hour | of love, of wordly matter 1.03.299
if thou dost, i shall never love thee after. 1.03.306 P
i never found man that knew how to love himself. 1.03.314 P
would drown myself for the love of a guinea hen, 1.03.315 P
this that you call love to be a sect or scion. 1.03.332 P
should continue her love to the moor — put 1.03.343 P
cyprus, | i have found great love amongst them. 2.01.205
say base men being in love have then a nobility 2.01.216 P
desdemona is directly in love with him. 2.01.219 P
to love him still for prating — let not thy 2.01.224 P
now i do love her too, | not out of absolute 2.01.291
make the moor thank me, love me, and reward me, 2.01.308
come, my dear love, | the purchase made, the 2.03. 8
us thus early for the love of his desdemona; 2.03. 14 P
when she speaks, is it not an alarum to love? 2.03. 27 P
whom love hath turn'd almost the wrong side out, 2.03. 52
i do love cassio well; 2.03.143
on thy love, i charge thee! 2.03.178
thy honesty and love doth mince this matter, 2.03.247
cassio, i love thee, | but never more be officer 2.03.248
look if my gentle love be not rais'd up! 2.03.250
good lieutenant, i think you think i love you. 2.03.311 P
this crack of your love shall grow stronger than 2.03.325 P
in the sincerity of love and honest kindness. 2.03.327 P
sin, | his soul is so enfetter'd to her love, 2.03.345
you do love my lord; 3.03. 10
my general will forget my love and service. 3.03. 18
good love, call him back. 3.03. 54
suit | wherein i mean to touch your love indeed, 3.03. 81
perdition catch my soul, | but i do love thee! 3.03. 91
and when i love thee not, | chaos is come again. 3.03. 91
when /you woo'd my lady, | know of your love? 3.03. 95
if thou dost love me, | show me thy thought. 3.03.115
my lord, you know i love you. 3.03.117
for i know thou'rt full of love and honesty, 3.03.118
this — | away at once with love or jealousy! 3.03.192
to show the love and duty that i bear you | with 3.03.194
consider what is spoke | comes from /my love. 3.03.217
than keep a corner in the thing i love | for 3.03.272
villain, be sure thou prove my love a whore; 3.03.359
and from hence | i'll love no friend, sith love 3.03.380
love no friend, sith love breeds such offense. 3.03.380
(prick'd to't by foolish honesty and love), | i 3.03.412
all my fond love thus do i blow to heaven. 3.03.445
yield up, o love, thy crown and hearted throne 3.03.448
shall nev'r look back, nev'r ebb to humble love, 3.03.458
i greet thy love, | not with vain thanks, but 3.03.469
and subdue my father | entirely to her love; 3.04. 60
hath founded his good fortunes on your love, 3.04. 94
exist, and be a member of his love | whom i, 3.04.112
futurity, | can ransom me into his love again, 3.04.118
indeed, sweet love, i was coming to your house. 3.04.171
not that i love you not. 3.04.196
but that you do not love me. 3.04.196
i never knew woman love man so. 4.01.110
marry her, out of her own love and flattery, not 4.01.128 P
t' atone them, for the love i bear to cassio. 4.01.233
if e'er my will did trespass 'gainst his love, 4.02.152
off | to beggarly divorcement) love him dearly, 4.02.158
may defeat my life, | but never taint my love. 4.02.161
my love doth so approve him, | that even his 4.03. 19
she was in love, and he she lov'd prov'd mad, 4.03. 27
"i call'd my love false love; 4.03. 55
"i call'd my love false love; 4.03. 55
and i will kill thee | and love thee after. 5.02. 19
heavenly, | it strikes where it doth love. 5.02. 22
general warranty of heaven | as i might love. 5.02. 61
o mistress, villainy hath made mocks with love! 5.02.151
with that recognizance and pledge of love 5.02.214
if it be love indeed, tell me how much. ANT 1.01. 14
beggary in the love that can be reckon'd. 1.01. 15
how, my love? 1.01. 24
why did he marry fulvia, and not love her? 1.01. 41
now for the love of love, and her soft hours, 1.01. 44
now for the love of love, and her soft hours, 1.01. 44
o, excellent, i love long life better than figs. 1.02. 32 P
of nothing but the finest part of pure love. 1.02.147 P
whose love is never link'd to the deserver 1.02.186
madam, methinks, if you did love him dearly, 1.03. 6
grown to strength, | are newly grown to love; 1.03. 49
o most false love! 1.03. 62
and give true evidence to his love, which stands 1.03. 74
ebb'd man, ne'er lov'd till ne'er worth love, 1.04. 43
did i, charmian, | ever love caesar so? 1.05. 67
the people love me, and the sea is mine; 2.01. 9
but all the charms of love, | salt cleopatra, 2.01. 20
you borrow one another's love for the instant, 2.02.103 P
her love to both | would each to other and all 2.02.134
you, whom no brother | did ever love so dearly. 2.02.150
music, moody food | of us that trade in love. 2.05. 2
in the marriage than the love of the parties. 2.06.119 P
his love to antony. 3.02. 18
is set | betwixt us as the cement of our love, 3.02. 29
i'll wrastle with you in my strength of love. 3.02. 62
let your best love draw to that point which 3.04. 21
can never be so equal that your love | can 3.04. 35
have prevented | the ostentation of our love, 3.06. 52
his ministers | of us and those that love you. 3.06. 89
each heart in rome does love and pity you; 3.06. 92
love, i am full of lead. 3.11. 72
that you embrace not antony | as you did love, 3.13. 57
next time i do fight, | i'll make death love me; 3.13.192
o love, | that thou couldst see my wars to–day, 4.04. 15
to business that we love we rise betime, | and 4.04. 20
why is my lord enrag'd against his love? 4.12. 31
of no more trust | than love that's hir'd! 5.02.155
command | (which my love makes religion to obey) 5.02.199
look here, love, | this diamond was my mother's. CYM 1.01.111
it is a manacle of love, i'll place it | upon 1.01.122
and that she should love this fellow, and refuse 1.02. 25 P
the love i bear him | made me to fan you thus, 1.06.176
still i swear i love you. 2.03. 90
fear'd /hopes | i barely gratify your love; 2.04. 7
love, | where there's another man. 2.04.109
upon the love and truth and vows which i | have 3.02. 12
let what is here contain'd relish of love, | of 3.02. 30
for it doth physic love — of his content, | all 3.02. 34
what your own love will out of this advise you, 3.02. 44 P
loyal to his vow, and your increasing in love. 3.02. 46 P
and hit | the innocent mansion of my love, my 3.04. 68
wing'd with fervor of her love, she's flown | to 3.05. 61
i love and hate her; 3.05. 70
i love her therefore, but | disdaining me and 3.05. 74
he is a man, i'll love him as my brother: 3.06. 71
i love thee; 4.02. 16
the weight as much, | as i do love my father. 4.02. 18
i know not why | i love this youth, and i have 4.02. 21
i love thee brotherly, but envy much | thou hast 4.02.158
these present wars shall find i love my country, 4.03. 43
that's love, | to have them fall no more: 5.01. 12
whom best i love, i cross; 5.04.101
whom she bore in hand to love | with such 5.05. 43
i love thee more and more; 5.05.109
most like a noble lord in love and one | that 5.05.171
though you did love this youth, i blame ye not, 5.05.267
you gods that made me man, and sway in love, PER 1.01. 19
but my unspotted fire of love to you. 1.01. 53
few love to hear the sins they love to act; 1.01. 92
few love to hear the sins they love to act; 1.01. 92
all love the womb that their first being bred, 1.01.107
then give my tongue like leave to love my head. 1.01.108
which love to all, of which thyself art one, 1.02. 94
we do not look for reverence but for love, | and 1.04. 99
of the world to just and tourney for her love. 2.01.110 P
honor we love, | for who hates honor hates the 2.03. 21
as do you love, fill to your mistress' lips — 2.03. 51
since they love men in arms as well as beds. 2.03. 98
princes, it is too late to talk of love, | and 2.03.112
wrong not your prince you love. 2.04. 25
if that you love prince pericles, forbear. 2.04. 42
but if i cannot win you to this love, | go 2.04. 49
then you love us, we you, and we'll clasp hands: 2.04. 57
that never aim'd so high to love your daughter, 2.05. 47
a deed might gain her love or your displeasure. 2.05. 54
to any syllable that made love to you. 2.05. 70
bestow your love and your affections | upon a 2.05. 77
yes, if you love me, sir. 2.05. 88
why do you make us love your goodly gifts | and 3.01. 23
yet for the love | of this poor infant, this 3.01. 40
i love the king your father, and yourself, 4.01. 32
now for the love of him whom jove hath mark'd TNK 1.01. 29
and his love too, who is a servant for | the 1.01. 89
dear palamon, dearer in love than blood, | and 1.02. 1
and i did love him for't. 1.03. 35
their knot of love | tied, weav'd, entangled, 1.03. 41
you talk of pirithous' and theseus' love: 1.03. 55
to water | their intertangled roots of love, but 1.03. 59
that the true love 'tween maid and maid may be 1.03. 81
the maid flavina) | love any that's call'd man. 1.03. 85
for our love, | and great apollo's mercy, all 1.04. 45
wife, ever begetting | new births of love; 2.02. 81
shall be led | to those that love eternally. 2.02.117
fair boy certain, but a fool | to love himself. 2.02.121
might not a man well lose himself and love her? 2.02.155
you love her then? 2.02.158
yes, but you must not love her. 2.02.161
i love her as a woman, to enjoy her. 2.02.164
so both may love. 2.02.165
you shall not love at all. 2.02.165
not love at all! who shall deny me? 2.02.166
yes, i love her, | and if the lives of all my 2.02.174
i love her with my soul; 2.02.176
i say again, i love, and, in loving her, 2.02.178
so unlike a noble kinsman, | to love alone? 2.02.191
i will love her, | i must, i ought to do so, and 2.02.204
and so fair, | let honest men ne'er love again. 2.02.231
and then i am sure she would love me. 2.02.243
why should i love this gentleman? 2.04. 1
what should i do to make him know i love him, 2.04. 29
and this night, or to–morrow, he shall love me. 2.04. 33
o love, | what a stout–hearted child thou art! 2.06. 8
i love him beyond love and beyond reason, | or 2.06. 11
i love him beyond love and beyond reason, | or 2.06. 11
this love of mine | will take more root within 2.06. 27
and the justice of my love, would make thee | a 3.01. 34
and art | a very thief in love, a chaffy lord, 3.01. 41
most certain | you love me not; 3.01.102
so, love and fortune for me! 3.06. 16
anger, | as you love any thing that's honorable. 3.06. 27
and justifying my love, i must not fly from't. 3.06. 42
and love | with all the justice of affection, 3.06. 50
faith, very little. love has us'd you kindly. 3.06. 67
and me my love! is there aught else to say? 3.06. 93
i love emilia, and in that i'll bury | thee and 3.06.126
that cannot love thee, he that broke thy prison 3.06.139
if in love be treason | in service of so 3.06.161
as i love most, and in that faith will perish, 3.06.163
why her eyes command me | stay here to love her; 3.06.170
by all you love most — wars, and this sweet 3.06.203
live, | and have the agony of love about 'em, 3.06.219
yours, | of more authority, i am sure more love, 3.06.231
forget i love her? 3.06.257
i must love, and will, | and for that love must 3.06.261
and for that love must and dare kill this cousin 3.06.262
and, if you can love, end this difference. 3.06.278
either this was her love to palamon, | or fear 4.01. 49
a hundred black–ey'd maids that love as i do, 4.01. 72
'tis, love! 4.01.118
young maids | of our town are in love with him, 4.01.126
here love himself sits smiling. 4.02. 14
that command | and threaten love, and what young 4.02. 40
o love, this only | from this hour is complexion 4.02. 42
my fair sister, | you must love one of them. 4.02. 68
'tis pity love should be so tyrannous. 4.02.146
and then will she be out of love with aeneas. 4.03. 16 P
crack'd to pieces with love, we shall come there 4.03. 24 P
you come to eat with her and to commune of love. 4.03. 77 P
her such green songs of love as she says palamon 4.03. 81 P
hand will honor | the very powers that love 'em. 5.01. 7
in labor | to push your name, your ancient love, 5.01. 26
our argument is love, | which if the goddess of 5.01. 70
his hoarse throat, | abuse young lays of love. 5.01. 89
him i do not love that tells close offices | the 5.01.122
come, your love palamon stays for you, child, 5.02. 41
and gallops to the /tune of "light a' love." 5.02. 54
she is horribly in love with him, poor beast, 5.02. 62
make curtsy, here your love comes. 5.02. 69
if you do, love, i'll cry. 5.02.112
plighted with | a love that grows as you decay. 5.03.111
that hath outliv'd | the love o' th' people, yea 5.04. 2
grac'd her altar, | and given you your love. 5.04.106
could buy | dear love but loss of dear love! 5.04.112
could buy | dear love but loss of dear love! 5.04.112
hunting he lov'd, but love he laugh'd to scorn. VEN 4
nimbly she fastens (o, how quick is love!); 38
look how he can, she cannot choose but love, 79
love keeps his revels where there are but twain; 123
love is a spirit all compact of fire, | not 149
is love so light, sweet boy, and may it be 155
can thy right hand seize love upon thy left? 158
his cheeks, cries, "fie, no more of love! 185
son and canst not feel | what 'tis to love? 202
how want of love tormenteth? 202
being judge in love, she cannot right her cause. 220
love made those hollows, if himself were slain, 243
why, there love liv'd, and there he could not 246
poor queen of love, in thine own law forlorn, 251
to love a cheek that smiles at thee in scorn! 252
he sees his love, and nothing else he sees, 287
he looks upon his love, and neighs unto her, 307
spurns at his love, and scorns the heat he feels 311
his love, perceiving how he was enrag'd, | grew 317
that love–sick love by pleading may be blest; 328
but when he saw his love, his youth's fair fee, 393
o, learn to love, the lesson is but plain, | and 407
"i know not love," quoth he, "nor will not know 409
my love to love is love but to disgrace it, 412
my love to love is love but to disgrace it, 412
my love to love is love but to disgrace it, 412
my ears would love | that inward beauty and 433
see, | yet should i be in love by touching thee. 438
yet would my love to thee be still as much, 442
breath perfum'd, that breedeth love by smelling. 444
for looks kill love, and love by looks reviveth: 464
for looks kill love, and love by looks reviveth: 464
but blessed bankrout that by love so thriveth! 466
her, | which cunning love did wittily prevent: 471
"fair queen," quoth he, "if any love you owe me, 523

chiefly in love, whose leave exceeds commission: 568
yet love breaks through, and picks them all at 576
now is she in the very lists of love, | her 595
she's love, she loves, and yet she is not lov'd. 610
"for where love reigns, disturbing jealousy 649
distemp'ring gentle love in his desire, | as air 653
that if i love thee, i thy death should fear. 660
so to so, | for love can comment upon every woe. 714
the earth, in love with thee, thy footing trips, 722
"if love have lent you twenty thousand tongues, 775
i hate not love, but your device in love, | that 789
i hate not love, but your device in love, | that 789
"call it not love, for love to heaven is fled, 793
"call it not love, for love to heaven is fled, 793
"love comforteth like sunshine after rain, | but 799
love surfeits not, lust like a glutton dies; 803
love is all truth, lust full of forged lies. 804
leaves love upon her back, deeply distress'd. 814
how love makes young men thrall and old men dote 837
how love is wise in folly, foolish witty. 838
and yet she hears no tidings of her love. 867
hateful divorce of love" — thus chides she 932
o hard-believing love, how strange it seems! 985
fie, fond love, thou art as full of fear | as 1021
sorrow on love hereafter shall attend; 1136
sith in his prime death doth my love destroy, 1163
they that love best their loves shall not enjoy. 1164
flames the waist | of collatine's fair love, LUC 7
i'll beg her love: 241
love thrives not in the heart that shadows 270
"then love and fortune be my gods, my guide! 351
by her untimely tears, her husband's love, | by 570
but happy monarchs still are fear'd for love; 611
yield to my love, if not, enforced hate, | in 668
for collatine's dear love be kept unspotted: 821
whose love of either to myself was nearer, 1165
my resolution, love, shall be thy boast, | by 1193
to bear | a letter to my lord, my love, my dear. 1293
(if ever, love, thy lucrece thou wilt see) 1306
sweet love, what spite hath thy fair color spent 1600
and entertain my love, else lasting shame | on 1629
when my love swears that she is made of truth, PP 1. 1
outfacing faults in love with love's ill rest. 1. 8
but wherefore says my love that she is young? 1. 9
and age in love, loves not to have years told. 1.12
therefore i'll lie with love, and love with me, 1.13
therefore i'll lie with love, and love with me, 1.13
since that our faults in love thus smother'd be. 1.14
my vow was earthly, thou a heavenly love; 3. 7
if love make me forsworn, how shall i swear to 5. 1
make me forsworn, how shall i swear to love? 5. 1
as thou art, o, do not love that wrong: 5.13
for shade, | when cytherea (all in love forlorn) 6. 3
fair is my love, but not so fair as fickle, 7. 1
each kiss her oaths of true love swearing! 7. 8
dreading my love, the loss whereof still fearing 7.10
she burnt with love, as straw with fire flameth, 7.13
she burnt out love, as soon as straw out-burneth 7.14
she fram'd the love, and yet she foil'd the 7.15
she bade love last, and yet she fell a-turning. 7.16
then must the love be great 'twixt thee and me, 8. 3
fair was the morn when the fair queen of love, 9. 1
o, my love, my love is young! 12.10
o, my love, my love is young! 12.10
combat doubtful, that love with love did fight, 15. 5
combat doubtful, that love with love did fight, 15. 5
love, whose month was ever may, | spied a 16. 2
for jove, | turning mortal for thy love." 16.18
love is dying, faith's defying, | heart's 17. 3
forgot, | all my lady's love is lost, god wot. 17. 6
where her faith was firmly fix'd in love, 17. 7
i, | love hath forlorn me, living in thrall; 17.14
fled, | all our love is lost, for love is dead. 17.32
fled, | all our love is lost, for love is dead. 17.32
live with me, and be my love, | and we will all 19. 1
thee move, | then live with me, and be my love. 19.16
if that the world and love were young, | and 19.17
me move | to live with thee and be thy love. 19.20
love and constancy is dead, | phoenix and the PHT 22
so they loved as love in twain | had the essence 25
number there in love was slain. 28
so between them love did shine, | that the 33
love hath reason, reason none, | if what parts, 47
and the dove, | co-supremes and stars of love, 51
no love toward others in that bosom sits | that SON 9.13
for shame deny that thou bear'st love to any, 10. 1
shall hate be fairer lodg'd than gentle love? 10.10
make thee another self for love of me, | that 10.13
but, love, you are | no longer yours than you 13. 1
dear my love, you know | you had a father, let 13.13
and all in war with time for love of you, | as 15.13
my love shall in my verse ever live young. 19.14
mine be thy love, and thy love's use their 20.14
o, let me, true in love, but truly write, | and 21. 9
me, my love is as fair | as any mother's child, 21.10
therefore, love, be of thyself so wary | as i, 22. 9
who plead for love and look for recompense 23.11
o, learn to read what silent love hath writ: 23.13
i, that love and am beloved | where i may not 25.13
lord of my love, to whom in vassalage | thy 26. 1
then may i dare to boast how i do love thee, 26.13
for thy sweet love rememb'red such wealth brings 29.13
and there reigns love and all love's loving 31. 3
hath dear religious love stol'n from mine eye 31. 6
thou art the grave where buried love doth live, 31. 9
reserve them for my love, not for their rhyme, 32. 7
a dearer birth than this his love had brought 32.11
for their style i'll read, his for his love." 32.14
yet him for this my love no whit disdaineth: 33.13
but those tears are pearl which thy love sheeds, 34.13
such civil war is in my love and hate, | that i 35.12
but do not so, i love thee in such sort, | as 36.13
sit, | i make my love ingrafted to this store: 37. 8
and our dear love lose name of single one, 39. 6
to entertain the time with thoughts of love, 39.11
take all my loves, my love, yea, take them all, 40. 1
no love, my love, that thou mayst true love call 40. 3
no love, my love, that thou mayst true love call 40. 3
love, my love, that thou mayst true love call, 40. 3
then if for my love thou my love receivest, | i 40. 5
then if for my love thou my love receivest, | i 40. 5
i cannot blame thee for my love thou usest, 40. 6
and yet love knows it is a greater grief | to 40.11
a loss in love that touches me more nearly. 42. 4
thou dost love her because thou know'st i love 42. 6
dost love her because thou know'st i love her, 42. 6
are gone | in tender embassy of love to thee, 45. 6
and my heart's right /thy inward love of heart. 46.14
or heart in love with sighs himself doth smother 47. 4
and in his thoughts of love doth share a part. 47. 8
so, either by thy picture or my love, | thyself 47. 9
when as thy love hath cast his utmost sum, 49. 3
eye, | when love converted from the thing it was 49. 7
laws, | since why to love i can allege no cause. 49.14
thus can my love excuse the slow offense | of my 51. 1
desire (of /perfect'st love being made) | shall 51.10
but love, for love, thus shall excuse my jade: 51.12
but love, for love, thus shall excuse my jade: 51.12
sweet love, renew thy force, be it not said 56. 1
so, love, be thou: 56. 5
the spirit of love with a perpetual dullness: 56. 8
when they see | return of love, more blest may 56.12
so true a fool is love that in your will 57.13
o no, thy love, though much, is not so great, 61. 9
it is my love that keeps mine eye awake, | mine 61.10
mine own true love that doth my rest defeat, 61.11
against my love shall be as i am now | with 63. 1
that time will come and take my love away. 64.12
that in black ink my love may still shine bright 65.14
gone, | save that to die, i leave my love alone. 66.14
for canker vice the sweetest buds doth love, 70. 7
not | the hand that writ it, for i love you so, 71. 6
but let your love even with my life decay; 71.12
what merit liv'd in me that you should love 72. 2
you should love | after my death, dear love, 72. 3
o, lest your true love may seem false in this, 72. 9
that you for love speak well of me untrue, | my 72.10
and so should you, to love things nothing worth. 72.14
perceiv'st, which makes thy love more strong, 73.13
to love that well, which thou must leave ere 73.14
o, know, sweet love, i always write of you, 76. 9
you, | and you and love are still my argument; 76.10
old, | so is my love still telling what is told. 76.14
i grant, sweet love, thy lovely argument 79. 5
my love was my decay. 80.14
and do so, love; 82. 9
but that is in my thought, whose love to you 85.11
such is my love, to thee i so belong, | that for 88.13
thou canst not, love, disgrace me half so ill, 89. 5
for i must ne'er love him whom thou dost hate. 89.14
thy love is /better than high birth to me, 91. 9
and life no longer than thy love will stay, 92. 3
stay, | for it depends upon that love of thine. 92. 4
i find, | happy to have thy love, happy to die! 92.12
so love's face | may still seem love to me, 93. 3
that in thy face sweet love should ever dwell; 93.10
but do not so, i love thee in such sort, | as 96.13
give my love fame faster than time wastes life, 100.13
both truth and beauty on my love depends; 101. 3
my love is strength'ned, though more weak in 102. 1
i love not less, though less the show appear; 102. 2
that love is merchandiz'd whose rich esteeming 102. 3
our love was new, and then but in the spring, 102. 5
let not my love be call'd idolatry, | nor my 105. 1
kind is my love to-day, to-morrow kind, | still 105. 5
can yet the lease of my true love control, 107. 3
of this most balmy time | my love looks fresh, 107.10
that may express my love, or thy dear merit? 108. 4
so that eternal love in love's fresh case 108. 9
finding the first conceit of love there bred, 108.13
that is my home of love, if i have rang'd, 109. 5
and worse essays prov'd thee my best of love. 110. 8
friend, | a god in love, to whom i am confin'd. 110.12
your love and pity doth th' impression fill 112. 1
and that your love taught it this alcumy, | to 114. 4
those that said i could not love you dearer, 115. 2
might i not then say, "now i love you best," 115.10
love is a babe, then might i not say so, | to 115.13
love is not love | which alters when it 116. 2
love is not love | which alters when it 116. 2
love alters not with his brief hours and weeks, 116.11
repay, | forgot upon your dearest love to call, 117. 3
prove | the constancy and virtue of your love. 117.14
thus policy in love, t' anticipate | the ills 118. 9
and ruin'd love, when it is built anew, | grows 119.11
nor need i tallies thy dear love to score; 122.10
if my dear love were but the child of state, 124. 1
as subject to time's love, or to time's hate, 124. 3
i love to hear her speak, yet well i know | that 130. 9
i think my love as rare | as any she belied with 130.13
thy face hath not the power to make love groan; 131. 6
thine eyes i love, and they, as pitying me, 132. 1
thus far for love my love-suit, sweet, fulfill. 136. 4
will will fulfill the treasure of thy love, | ay 136. 5
make but my name thy love, and love that still, 136.13
make but my name thy love, and love that still, 136.13
thou blind fool, love, what dost thou to mine 137. 1
when my love swears that she is made of truth, 138. 1
and age in love loves not t' have years told. 138.12
my love well knows | her pretty looks have been 139. 9
though not to love, yet, love, to tell me so, 140. 6
though not to love, yet, love, to tell me so, 140. 6
in faith, i do not love thee with mine eyes, 141. 1
love is my sin, and thy dear virtue hate, | hate 142. 1
and seal'd false bonds of love as oft as mine, 142. 7
be it lawful i love thee as thou lov'st those 142. 9
my love is as a fever, longing still | for that 147. 1
my reason, the physician to my love, | angry 147. 5
what eyes hath love put in my head, | which have 148. 1
then love doth well denote | love's eye is not 148. 7
o cunning love, with tears thou keep'st me blind 148.13
canst thou, o cruel, say i love thee not, | when 149. 1
but, love, hate on, for now i know thy mind: 149.13
who taught thee how to make me love thee more, 150. 9
o, though i love what others do abhor, | with 150.11
if thy unworthiness rais'd love in me, | more 150.13
love is too young to know what conscience is, 151. 1
yet who knows not conscience is born of love? 151. 2
doth tell my body that he may | triumph in love; 151. 8
her "love" for whose dear love i rise and fall. 151.14
her "love" for whose dear love i rise and fall. 151.14
thou art twice forsworn, to me love swearing; 152. 2
in vowing new hate after new love bearing. 152. 4
oaths of thy love, thy truth, thy constancy, 152.10
which borrow'd from this holy fire of love | a 153. 5
love's fire heats water, water cools not love. 154.14
if i had self-applied | love to myself, and to LC 77
love to myself, and to no love beside. 77
love lack'd a dwelling and made him her place; 82
for feasts of love i have been call'd unto, 181
love made them not, with acture they may be, 185
remove | to spend her living in eternal love. 238
religious love put out religion's eye. 250
as compound love to physic your cold breast. 259
o most potential love! 264

LOVE-A 1 FR 0.0001 REL FR 0 V 1 P
ay, be-gar, and de maid is love-a me. WIV 3.02. 64 P

LOVE-AFFAIRS 1 FR 0.0001 REL FR 1 V 0 P
of all that may concern thy love-affairs. TGV 3.01.256

LOVE-BED 1 FR 0.0001 REL FR 1 V 0 P
he is not lulling on a lewd love-bed, | but on R3 3.07. 72

LOVE-BOOK 1 FR 0.0001 REL FR 1 V 0 P
and on a love-book pray for my success? TGV 1.01. 19

LOVE-BROKER 1 FR 0.0001 REL FR 0 V 1 P
there is no love-broker in the world can more TN 3.02. 37 P

LOVE-CAUSE 1 FR 0.0001 REL FR 0 V 1 P
in his own person, videlicet, in a love-cause. AYL 4.01. 97 P

LOVED 12 FR 0.0013 REL FR 12 V 0 P
of all that virtue love for virtue loved; LLL 2.01. 57
but she perforce withholds the loved boy, MND 2.01. 26
since he hath got the jewel that i loved, | and MV 5.01.224
you're loved, sir; AWW 1.02. 67
for he is just and always loved us well. R2 2.01.221
who loved him | in a most dear particular. COR 5.01. 2
yet, for i loved thee, | take this along, i writ 5.02. 89
and no more, | the which he loved passing well." HAM 2.02.408
he loved me dearly, | and for his sake i wish PER 2.01.138
o loved sister, | he speaks now of as brave a TNK 5.03.114
so they loved as love in twain | had the essence PHT 25
proved, | i never writ, nor no man ever loved. SON 116.14

LOVE-DAY 1 FR 0.0001 REL FR 1 V 0 P
this day shall be a love-day, tamora. TIT 1.01.491

LOVE-DEVOURING 1 FR 0.0001 REL FR 1 V 0 P
then love-devouring death do what he dare, | it ROM 2.06. 7

LOVE-DISCOURSE 1 FR 0.0001 REL FR 1 V 0 P
i know you joy not in a love-discourse. TGV 2.04.127

LOVEDST 2 FR 0.0002 REL FR 2 V 0 P
thou lovedst him better | than ever thou lovedst JC 4.03.106
him better | than ever thou lovedst cassius. 4.03.107

LOVE-FEAT 1 FR 0.0001 REL FR 1 V 0 P
and every one his love-feat will advance | unto LLL 5.02.123

LOVE-GOD 1 FR 0.0001 REL FR 1 V 0 P
the little love-god, lying once asleep, | laid SON 154. 1

LOVE-GODS 1 FR 0.0001 REL FR 0 V 1 P
shall be ours, for we are the only love-gods. ADO 2.01.386 P

LOVE-IN-IDLENESS 1 FR 0.0001 REL FR 1 V 0 P
wound, | and maidens call it love-in-idleness. MND 2.01.168

LOVE-JUICE 2 FR 0.0002 REL FR 2 V 0 P
the athenian's eyes | with the love-juice, as i MND 3.02. 37
and laid the love-juice on some true-love's 3.02. 89

LOVE-KINDLING 1 FR 0.0001 REL FR 1 V 0 P
and his love-kindling fire did quickly steep SON 153. 3

LOVEL 4 FR 0.0004 REL FR 4 V 0 P
lovel and ratcliffe, look that it be done: R3 3.04. 78
they are friends — ratcliffe and lovel. 3.05. 21
go, lovel, with all speed to doctor shaw; 3.05.103
sir thomas lovel and lord marquess dorset, 4.04.518

LOVE-LACKING 1 FR 0.0001 REL FR 1 V 0 P
love-lacking vestals and self-loving nuns, VEN 752

LOVELESS 1 FR 0.0001 REL FR 1 V 0 P
to leave the master loveless, or kill the PP 15. 6

LOVE-LETTERS 2 FR 0.0002 REL FR 0 V 2 P
pox of your love-letters! TGV 3.01.381 P
have /i scap'd love-letters in the holiday-time WIV 2.01. 1 P

LOVELIER 2 FR 0.0002 REL FR 2 V 0 P
a sweeter and a lovelier gentleman, | fram'd in R3 1.02.242
look'd not lovelier | than hector's forehead COR 1.03. 41

LOVE-LINE 1 FR 0.0001 REL FR 1 V 0 P
a pen in 's hand | and write to her a love-line. AWW 2.01. 78

LOVELINESS 2 FR 0.0002 REL FR 1 V 1 P
satiety a fresh appetite, loveliness in favor, OTH 2.01.229 P
unthrifty loveliness, why dost thou spend | upon SON 4. 1

LOVELL 8 FR 0.0009 REL FR 8 V 0 P
what news, sir thomas lovell? H8 1.03. 16
sir thomas lovell, had the cardinal | but half 1.04. 10
sir thomas lovell, is the banket ready | i' th' 1.04. 98
sir thomas lovell, i as free forgive you | as i 2.01. 82
not yet, sir thomas lovell. 5.01. 10
'twill not, sir thomas lovell, take't of me — 5.01. 30
now, lovell, from the queen what is the news? 5.01. 61
lovell! 5.01.169

LOVELL'S 1 FR 0.0001 REL FR 1 V 0 P
the cardinal's and sir thomas lovell's heads H8 1.02.185

LOVELY 57 FR 0.0064 REL FR 54 V 3 P
i am) | should censure thus on lovely gentlemen. TGV 1.02. 19
mine | were full as lovely as is this of hers; 4.04.186
is he pardon'd, and, for your lovely sake, MM 5.01.491
why ever wast thou lovely in my eyes? ADO 4.01.130
and every lovely organ of her life | shall come 4.01.226
truth itself, that thou art lovely. LLL 4.01. 62 P
a most lovely gentleman-like man: MND 1.02. 87 P
hath | a lovely boy stolen from an indian king; 2.01. 22
spell, nor charm, | come our lovely lady nigh. 2.02. 18
most brisky juvenal and eke most lovely jew, 3.01. 95
two lovely berries moulded on one stem; 3.02.211
and thou, o wall, o sweet, o lovely wall, | that 5.01.174
thou wall, o wall, o sweet and lovely wall, 5.01.176
sweet, | even in the lovely garnish of a boy. MV 2.06. 45
like envious floods o'errun her lovely face, SHR in.2. 65
where is my lovely bride? 3.02. 92
bride | and seal the title with a lovely kiss! 3.02.123
fair lovely maid, once more good day to thee. 4.05. 33
stars | allots thee for his lovely bedfellow! 4.05. 41
of lewis the dolphin and that lovely maid. JN 2.01.425

o amiable lovely death! 3.04. 25
to put down richard, that sweet lovely rose, 1H4 1.03.175
to the harp | many an english ditty lovely well, 3.01.122
and from heart–string | i love the lovely bully. H5 4.01. 48
our fertile france, put up her lovely visage? 5.02. 37
the chief perfections of that lovely dame | (had 1H6 5.05. 12
with him the husband of this lovely lady. 2H6 1.04. 73
hath this lovely face | rul'd like a wandering 4.04. 15
how lovely! 3H6 2.05. 41
clarence and gloucester, love my lovely queen, 5.07. 26
that henry's death, my lovely edward's death, R3 1.03.191
ay, ay, my liege, | and of a lovely boy. H8 5.01.164
and therefore, lovely tamora, queen of goths, TIT 1.01.315
your noble emperor and his lovely bride, | sent 1.01.334
here, | and at my lovely tamora's entreats, | i 1.01.483
there will the lovely roman ladies troop; 2.01.113
and wake the emperor and his lovely bride, | and 2.02. 4
my lovely aaron, wherefore look'st thou sad, 2.03. 10
now will i hence to seek my lovely moor, | and 2.03.190
but, lovely niece, that mean is cut from thee. 2.04. 40
gramercy, lovely lucius. what's the news? 4.02. 7
my gracious lord, my lovely saturnine, | lord of 4.04. 27
signior placentio and his lovely nieces; ROM 1.02. 67 P
o, he's a lovely gentleman! 3.05.218
who art so lovely fair and smell'st so sweet OTH 4.02. 68
stain to all nymphs, more lovely than a man, VEN 9
these lovely caves, these round enchanting pits, 247
sitting by a brook | with young adonis, lovely, PP 4. 2
did court the lad with many a lovely look, 4. 3
thee | calls back the lovely april of her prime, SON 3.10
the lovely gaze where every eye doth dwell 5. 2
thou art more lovely and more temperate: 18. 2
and so of you, beauteous and lovely youth, 54.13
thy lovely argument | deserves the travail of a 79. 5
how sweet and lovely dost thou make the shame 95. 1
in praise of ladies dead and lovely knights, 106. 4
o thou, my lovely boy, who in thy power | dost 126. 1

LOVE–MONGER 1 FR 0.0001 REL FR 1 V 0 P
thou art an old love–monger and speakest LLL 2.01.254

LOVE–NEWS 1 FR 0.0001 REL FR 1 V 0 P
love–news, in faith. MV 2.04. 14

LOVE–PERFORMING 1 FR 0.0001 REL FR 1 V 0 P
spread thy close curtain, love–performing night, ROM 3.02. 5

LOVE–PRATE 1 FR 0.0001 REL FR 0 V 1 P
have simply misus'd our sex in your love–prate. AYL 4.01.201 P

LOVER 61 FR 0.0069 REL FR 40 V 21 P
too little for carrying a letter to your lover. TGV 1.01.109
her love himself to write unto her lover." 2.01.168
thou that my master is become a notable lover? 2.05. 42 P
i tell thee, my master is become a hot lover. 2.05. 51 P
for which the youthful lover now is gone, | and 3.01. 41
your brother and his lover have embrac'd. MM 1.04. 40
thou wilt be like a lover presently, | and tire ADO 1.01.306
that the lover, sick to death, | /wish'd himself LLL 4.03.105
i post from love; good lover, let me go. 4.03.186
some thousand verses of a faithful lover. 5.02. 50
that he would wed me, or else die my lover. 5.02.447
what is pyramus? a lover, or a tyrant? MND 1.02. 22 P
a lover, that kills himself most gallant for 1.02. 23 P
a lover is more condoling. 1.02. 40 P
ah pyramus, my lover dear! 1.02. 53 P
apply | /to your eye, | gentle lover, remedy. 3.02.452
the lunatic, the lover, and the poet | are of 5.01. 7
the lover, all as frantic, | sees helen's beauty 5.01. 10
before thisby comes back and finds her lover? 5.01.313 P
how dear a lover of my lord your husband, | i MV 3.04. 7
antonio, | being the bosom lover of my lord, 3.04. 17
though in thy youth thou wast as true a lover AYL 2.04. 26
and then the lover, | sighing like furnace, with 2.07.147
as to resolve the propositions of a lover. 3.02.233 P
then there is no true lover in the forest, else 3.02.302 P
yourself, than seeming the lover of any other. 3.02.384 P
the oath of /a lover is no stronger than the 3.04. 31 P
athwart the heart of his lover, as a puisne 3.04. 43 P
you a lover! 4.01. 40 P
break–promise, and the most hollow lover, and 4.01.193 P
if you be a true lover, hence, and not a word; 4.03. 73 P
here comes a lover of mine and a lover of hers. 5.02. 75 P
here comes a lover of mine and a lover of hers. 5.02. 75 P
it was a lover and his lass, | with a hey, and a 5.03. 16
and i shall prove | a lover of thy drum, hater AWW 3.03. 11
o, where | sad true lover never find my grave, TN 2.04. 65
and a true lover of the holy church. H5 1.01. 23
since i cannot prove a lover | to entertain R3 1.01. 28
is held no great good lover of the archbishop's, H8 4.01.104
i as your lover speak: TRO 3.03.214
had she no lover there | that wails her absence? 4.05.288
i tell thee, fellow, | thy general is my lover. COR 5.02. 14
this precious book of love, this unbound lover, ROM 1.03. 87
you are a lover, borrow cupid's wings, | and 1.04. 17
lover! 2.01. 7
a lover may bestride the gossamers | that idles 2.06. 18
i do not always follow lover, elder brother, and TIM 2.02.121 P
thy lover, artemidorus." JC 2.03. 9 P
as i slew my best lover for the good of rome, i 3.02. 45 P
and target, the lover shall not sigh gratis, the HAM 2.02.321 P
lord in love and one | that had a royal lover, CYM 5.05.172
maintain | i am as worthy and as free a lover, TNK 2.02.179
if he dare make himself a worthy lover, | yet in 2.02.251
this treachery, like a most trusty lover, | i 3.06.150
and when he smiles | he shows a lover, when he 4.02.136
and vow that lover never yet made sigh | truer 5.01.125
sat, | and like a lowly lover down she kneels; VEN 350
foul words and frowns must not repel a lover; 573
was this a lover, or a lecher whether? PP 7.17
that the lover, sick to death, | wish'd himself 16. 7
these poor rude lines of thy deceased lover, SON 32. 4

LOVER'D 1 FR 0.0001 REL FR 1 V 0 P
who, young and simple, would not be so lover'd? LC 320

LOVE–RHYMES 1 FR 0.0001 REL FR 1 V 0 P
regent of love–rhymes, lord of folded arms, LLL 3.01.181

LOVER'S 13 FR 0.0014 REL FR 11 V 2 P
hope is a lover's staff; TGV 3.01.248
the least whereof would quell a lover's hope, 4.02. 13
a lover's eyes will gaze an eagle blind. LLL 4.03.331
a lover's ear will hear the lowest sound, | when 4.03.332
tie up my lover's tongue, bring him silently. MND 3.01.201
mistook by me, | pleading for a lover's fee. 3.02.113
think what thou wilt, i am thy lover's grace; 5.01.195
nor the lover's, which is all these: AYL 4.01. 15 P
grace | as 'longeth to a lover's blessed case! SHR 4.02. 45
or an old lion, or a lover's lute. 1H4 1.02. 75 P
my death, and run into't | as to a lover's bed. ANT 4.14.101
the stroke of death is as a lover's pinch, 5.02.295
my sweet love's beauty, though my lover's life: SON 63.12

LOVERS' 9 FR 0.0010 REL FR 9 V 0 P
(a time that lovers' flights doth still conceal) MND 1.01.212
from lovers' food till morrow deep midnight. 1.01.223
being purg'd, a fire sparkling in lovers' eyes, ROM 1.01.191
gallops night by night | through lovers' brains, 1.04. 71
at lovers' perjuries, | they say, jove laughs. 2.02. 92
how silver–sweet sound lovers' tongues by night, 2.02.165
and lovers' absent hours, | more tedious than OTH 3.04.174
for lovers' hours are long, though seeming short VEN 842
you live in this, and dwell in lovers' eyes. SON 55.14

LOVERS 60 FR 0.0067 REL FR 51 V 9 P
freely to estate | on the bless'd lovers. TMP 4.01. 86
this parting strikes poor lovers dumb. TGV 2.02. 20
to see such lovers, thurio, as yourself: 2.04. 97
she will not fail, for lovers break not hours, 5.01. 4
green indeed is the color of lovers; LLL 1.02. 86 P
and send you many lovers! 2.01.125
with that which we lovers entitle "affected." 2.01.232
berowne, and longaville, | were lovers too! 4.03.122
sweet lords, sweet lovers, o, let us embrace! 4.03.210
we are wise girls to mock our lovers so. 5.02. 58
if then true lovers have been ever cross'd, | it MND 1.01.150
thou seest these lovers seek a place to fight; 3.02.354
and back to athens shall the lovers wend | with 3.02.372
there shall the pairs of faithful lovers be 4.01. 91
fair lovers, you are fortunately met; 4.01.177
strange, my theseus, that these lovers speak of. 5.01. 1
lovers and madmen have such seething brains, 5.01. 4
here come the lovers, full of joy and mirth. 5.01. 28
that vile wall, which did these lovers sunder; 5.01.132
by moonshine did these lovers think no scorn 5.01.137
wall, and lovers twain | at large discourse, 5.01.150
through which the lovers, pyramus and thisby, 5.01.159
through which the fearful lovers are to whisper. 5.01.164
lovers, make moan; 5.01.334
lovers, to bed, 'tis almost fairy time. 5.01.364
hour, | for lovers ever run before the clock. MV 2.06. 4
and lovers cannot see | the pretty follies that 2.06. 36
we that are true lovers run into strange capers; AYL 2.04. 54 P
most feigning, and lovers are given to poetry; 3.03. 20 P
in poetry may be said as lovers they do feign. 3.03. 21 P
the sight of lovers feedeth those in love. 3.04. 57
they will spit, and for lovers lacking (god warn 4.01. 76 P
a ding, ding, | sweet lovers love the spring. 5.03. 21
journeys end in lovers meeting, | every wise TN 2.03. 43
for such as i am, all true lovers are, | unstaid 2.04. 17
they are the drops of thy lovers, and they weep 2H4 4.03. 13 P
for husbands, fathers, and betrothed lovers, H5 2.04.108
this shall be told our lovers, lord aeneas. TRO 1.03.284
these lovers cry, o ho, they die! 3.01.121
they say all lovers swear more performance than 3.02. 84 P
these lovers will not keep the peace. TIT 2.01. 37
a pair of star–cross'd lovers take their life; ROM pr 6
to breathe such vows as lovers use to swear, 2.pr. 10
lovers can see to do their amorous rites | by 3.02. 8
countrymen, and lovers, hear me for my cause, JC 3.02. 13 P
may, | lovers in peace, lead on our days to age! 5.01. 94
may help these lovers | /into /your /favor. OTH 1.03.200
lovers | and men in dangerous bonds pray not CYM 3.02. 36
all lovers young, all lovers must | consign to 4.02.274
all lovers must | consign to thee and come to 4.02.274
you live as ye do makes pity in your lovers; PER 4.02.120 P
like true lovers, | cast yourselves in a body TNK 3.05. 19
and lovers yet unborn shall bless my ashes. 3.06.283
be made the altar where the lives of lovers — 4.02. 61
your two contending lovers are return'd, | and 4.02. 66
knights, kinsmen, lovers, yea, my sacrifices, 5.01. 34
and call your lovers from the stage of death, 5.04.123
for lovers say, the heart hath treble wrong VEN 329
hung with the trophies of my lovers gone, | who SON 31.10
thy lovers withering as thy sweet self grow'st; 126. 4

LOVE'S 107 FR 0.0121 REL FR 104 V 3 P
torment me for my love's forgetfulness! TGV 2.02. 12
o gentle proteus, love's a mighty lord, | and 2.04.136
less shall she that hath love's wings to fly, 2.07. 11
i do not seek to quench your love's hot fire, 2.07. 21
you are already love's firm votary | and cannot 3.02. 58
that know love's grief by his complexion! ADO 1.01.313
i, that have been love's whip, | a very beadle LLL 3.01.174
the shape of love's tyburn that hangs up 4.03. 52
that shall express my true love's fasting pain. 4.03.120
that in love's grief desir'st society: 4.03.126
love's feeling is more soft and sensible | than 4.03.334
love's tongue proves dainty bacchus gross in 4.03.336
until his ink were temp'red with love's sighs: 4.03.344
or for love's sake, a word that loves all men, 4.03.355
yet, since love's argument was first on foot, 5.02.747
nor hath love's mind of any judgment taste; MND 1.01.236
before milk–white, now purple with love's wound, 2.01.167
love takes the meaning in love's conference: 2.02. 46
love's stories written in love's richest book. 2.02.122
love's stories written in love's richest book. 2.02.122
by night | and stol'n my love's heart from him? 3.02.284
pigeons fly | to seal love's bonds new made, MV 2.06. 6
find, | must find love's prick and rosalind. AYL 3.02.112
rosalind is your love's name? 3.02.263 P
wounds invisible | that love's keen arrows make. 3.05. 31
where love's strong passion is impress'd in AWW 1.03.133
thou lov'st her, | thy love's to me religious; 2.03.183
i love thee | by love's own sweet constraint, 4.02. 16
love's night is noon. TN 3.01.148
he doth espy | himself love's traitor. JN 2.01.507
it shall be still thy true love's recompense. R2 2.03. 49
do breed love's settled passions in my heart, 1H6 5.05. 4
and want love's majesty | to strut before a R3 1.01. 16
bear her my true love's kiss; 4.04.430
as 'twere in love's particular, be more | to me, H8 3.02.189
vows, gifts, tears, and love's full sacrifice, TRO 1.02.282
heart–blood of beauty, love's invisible soul. 3.01. 33 P
for, o, love's bow | shoots buck and doe. 3.01.116
taste indeed | love's thrice–repured nectar? 3.02. 22
/hate i, and my love's upon | this enemy town. COR 4.04. 23
why, such is love's transgression. ROM 1.01.185
arm'd, | from love's weak childish bow she lives 1.01.211
under love's heavy burthen do i sink. 1.04. 22
and she steal love's sweet bait from fearful 2.pr. 8
with love's light wings did i o'erperch these 2.02. 66
th' exchange of thy love's faithful vow for mine 2.02.127
love's heralds should be thoughts, | which ten 2.05. 4
when but love's shadows are so rich in joy! 5.01. 11
to cross my obsequies and true love's rite? 5.03. 20
that murd'red my love's cousin, with which grief 5.03. 50
a cup clos'd in my true love's hand? 5.03.161
since i am sure my love's | more ponderous than LR 1.01. 77
love's not love | when it is mingled with 1.01.238
make love's quick pants in desdemona's arms, OTH 2.01. 80
that he desires you, for love's sake, to make no 3.01. 13 P
the april's in her eyes, it is love's spring, ANT 3.02. 43
(love's counsellor should fill the bores of CYM 3.02. 57
heard you say, | love's reason's without reason. 4.02. 22
love's provocations, zeal, a mistress' task, TNK 1.04. 41
prettiest posies — "thus our true love's tied," 4.01. 90
which | is true love's merit, and bless me with 5.01.128
free vent of words love's fire doth assuage, VEN 334
then love's deep groans i never shall regard, 377
to love's alarms it will not ope the gate; 424
tell me, love's master, shall we meet to–morrow? 585
to which love's eyes pays tributary gazes, | nor 632
this canker that eats up love's tender spring, 656
love's gentle spring doth always fresh remain, 801
love's golden arrow at him should have fled, 947
i rail'd on thee, fearing my love's decesse. 1002
that all love's pleasure shall not match his woe 1140
wherein i will not kiss my sweet love's flow'r." 1188
spots and stains love's modest snow–white weed. LUC 196
against love's fire fear's frost hath 355
in stead of love's coy touch, shall rudely tear 669
if thou my love's desire do contradict. 1631
outfacing faults in love with love's ill rest. PP 1. 8
o, love's best habit's in a soothing tongue, 1.11
silly queen, with more than love's good will, 9. 7
o, carve not with thy hours my love's fair brow, SON 19. 9
be thy love, and thy love's use their treasure. 20.14
to say | the perfect ceremony of love's /rite, 23. 6
and in mine own love's strength seem to decay, 23. 7
with burthen of mine own love's might. 23. 8
to hear with eyes belongs to love's fine wit. 23.14
and weep afresh love's long since cancell'd woe, 30. 7
there reigns love and all love's loving parts, 31. 3
which though it alter not love's sole effect, 36. 7
doth it steal sweet hours from love's delight. 36. 8
to bear love's wrong than hate's known injury. 40.12
if i lose thee, my loss is my love's gain, | and 42. 9
with my love's picture then my eye doth feast, 47. 5
never cut from memory | my sweet love's beauty, 63.12
so love's face | may still seem love to me, 93. 2
that smells, | if not from my love's breath? 99. 3
in my love's veins thou hast too grossly dy'd. 99. 5
rise, resty muse, my love's sweet face survey, 100. 9
so that eternal love in love's fresh case 108. 9
love's not time's fool, though rosy lips and 116. 9
o, love's best habit is in seeming trust, | and 138.11
those lips that love's own hand did make 145. 1
denote | love's eye is not so true as all men's: 148. 8
o, how can love's eye be true, | that is so 148. 9
but at my mistress' eye love's brand new fired, 153. 9
which from love's fire took heat perpetual, 154.10
love's fire heats water, water cools not love. 154.14
love's arms are peace, 'gainst rule, 'gainst LC 271

/LOVES 2 FR 0.0002 REL FR 1 V 1 P
/of /itself | /after /the /thing /it /loves. HAM 4.05.164
/that /so /tenderly /and /entirely /loves /him. LR 1.02. 97 P

LOVES 214 FR 0.0242 REL FR 167 V 47 P
whose shadow the dismissed bachelor loves, TMP 4.01. 67
yet he, of all the rest, i think best loves ye. TGV 1.02. 28
o, that our fathers would applaud our loves, 1.03. 48
she that your worship loves? 2.01. 16 P
me to write some lines to one she loves. 2.01. 88 P
but she loves you? 2.04.178
because he loves her, he despiseth me; 4.04. 95
his body for a girl that loves him not. 5.04.134
to hear | the story of your loves discovered; 5.04.171
sir, the maid loves you, and all shall be well. WIV 1.04.120 P
fenton, i'll be sworn on a book she loves you. 1.04.146 P
but anne loves him not; 1.04.163 P
he loves the gallimaufry, ford. 2.01.115
he loves your wife: 2.01.132 P
my name is nym, and falstaff loves your wife. 2.01.135 P
you to send her your little page, of all loves. 2.02.114 P
mistress anne, my cousin loves you. 3.04. 42 P
my daughter will i question how she loves you, 3.04. 90
dog bark at a crow than a man swear he loves me. ADO 1.01.132 P
how know you he loves her? 2.01.167 P
tell them that you know that hero loves me, 2.02. 35 P
yet he woos, | yet will he swear he loves. 2.03. 52
of it but that she loves him with an enrag'd 2.03.100 P
a man loves the meat in his youth that he cannot 2.03.238 P
sure | that benedick loves beatrice so entirely? 3.01. 37
thee | to bind our loves up in a holy band; 3.01.114
nay, but i know who loves him. 3.02. 63 P
and i'll be sworn upon't that he loves her, 5.04. 85
who understandeth thee not, loves thee not. LLL 4.02.100 P
one drunkard loves another of the name. 4.03. 48
or for love's sake, a word that loves all men, 4.03.355
favors too, so shall your loves | woo contrary, 5.02.134
counsels they unbosom shall | to loves mistook, 5.02.142
loves her by the foot. 5.02.668 P
and therefore met your loves | in their own 5.02.783
minute of the hour, | grant us your loves. 5.02.788
by that which knitteth souls and prospers loves, MND 1.01.172
demetrius loves your fair, o happy fair! 1.01.182
i frown upon him; yet he loves me still. 1.01.194
into the hands of one that loves you not; 2.01.216
yet hermia still loves you; 2.02.110
speak, of all loves! 2.02.154
o, why rebuke you him that loves you so? 3.02. 43
demetrius loves her; and he loves not you. 3.02.136
demetrius loves her; and he loves not you. 3.02.136

i think he only loves the world for him. MV 2.08. 50
her cousin, so loves her, being ever from their AYL 1.01.108 P
one that old frederick, your father, loves. 1.02. 82 P
whose loves | are dearer than the natural bond 1.02.275
the greenwood tree | who loves to lie with me, 2.05. 2
ambition shun, | and loves to live i' th' sun, 2.05. 39
say with her that she loves me; 5.02. 8 P
tranio, be so, because lucentio loves, | and let SHR 1.01.218
incredible to believe | how much she loves me. 2.01.307
lord, | c fa ut, that loves with all affection. 3.01. 76
there shall your master have a thousand loves, AWW 1.01.166
my flesh and blood loves my flesh and blood; 1.03. 48 P
he that loves my flesh and blood is my friend; 1.03. 48 P
sir, i am a poor friend of yours that loves you. 2.02. 43 P
and i begin to love, as an old man loves money, 3.02. 16 P
heaven delights to hear | and loves to grant, 3.04. 28
no more than a fish loves water. 3.06. 85 P
did love her, sir, as a gentleman loves a woman. 5.03.245 P
my lord and master loves you. TN 1.05.252
she loves me sure, the cunning of her passion 2.02. 22
my master loves her dearly, | and i (poor 2.02. 33
eye | hath stay'd upon some favor that it loves. 2.04. 24
reason excites to this, that my lady loves me. 2.05.165 P
"she loves another" — who calls, ha? 4.02. 79 P
we will be justified in our loves; WT 1.01. 9 P
the heavens continue their loves! 1.01. 32 P
and a region | lov'd as he loves himself. 1.02.370
he says he loves my daughter. 4.04.171
half a kiss to choose | who loves another best. 4.04.176
whom he loves | (he bade me say so) more than 5.01.145
pow'r no jot | hath she to change our loves. 5.01.218
thy grandame loves thee, and thy uncle will | as JN 3.03. 3
grief, | like true, inseparable, faithful loves, 3.04. 66
i have a way to win their loves again. 4.02.168
he loves you, on my life, and holds you dear R2 2.01.143
but that i think his father loves him not | and 1H4 1.03.231
he loves his own barn better than he loves our 2.03. 5 P
his own barn better than he loves our house. 2.03. 6 P
and i must know it, else he loves me not. 2.03. 64
but, for all our loves, | first let them try 2H4 2.03. 55
he loves thee, and thou dost neglect him, thomas 4.04. 21
indeed i think the young king loves you not. 5.02. 9
as love is, my lord, before it loves. H5 5.02.315 P
as he loves the land | and common profit of his 2H6 1.01.205
and his loves | are brazen images of canonized 1.03. 59
they know their master loves to be aloft, | and 2.01. 11
who loves the king, and will embrace his pardon, 4.08. 14
a poor esquire of kent, that loves his king. 5.01. 75
nor he that loves himself | hath not essentially 5.02. 38
neither the king, nor he that loves him best, 3H6 1.01. 45
having my country's peace and brothers' loves. 5.07. 36
he lives, that loves thee better than he could. R3 1.02.141
a man that loves not me, nor none of you. 1.03. 13
she's your wife | and loves not me, be you, good 1.03. 23
he loves me and he holds me dear. 1.04.233
he for his father's sake so loves the prince 3.01.165
i thank his grace, i know he loves me well; 3.04. 14
his lordship knows me well and loves me well. 3.04. 30
richard loves richard; 5.03.183
there is no creature loves me, | and if i die no 5.03.200
you are liberal of your loves and counsels, | be H8 2.01.126
of her that loves him with that excellence 2.02. 33
and thank the holy conclave for their loves; 2.02. 99
grace must needs deserve all strangers' loves, 2.02.101
truth loves open dealing. 3.01. 39
the king loves you, | beware you lose it not. 3.01.171
to his goodness | the model of our chaste loves, 4.02.132
you, i think helen loves him better than paris. TRO 1.02.107 P
but to prove to you that helen loves him: 1.02.118 P
but to prove to you that helen loves troilus — 1.02.128 P
that loves his mistress more than in confession 1.03.269
with truant vows to her own lips he loves, | and 1.03.270
and yet he loves himself. is't not strange? 2.03.160 P
honest fellow enough, and one that loves quails, 5.01. 52 P
young troyan ass, that loves the whore there, 5.04. 6 P
and one that loves a cup of hot wine with not a COR 2.01. 48 P
proud, and loves not the common people. 2.02. 6 P
he loves your people, | but tie him not to be 2.02. 64
we pray the gods he may deserve your loves. 2.03.157
in free contempt | when he did need your loves; 2.03.201
but your loves, | thinking upon his services, 2.03.222
for the inheritance of their loves and safeguard 3.02. 68
in asking their good loves, but thou wilt frame 3.02. 84
i'll mountebank their loves, | cog their hearts 3.02.132
whose loves i prize | as the dead carcasses of 3.03.121
he loves his pledges dearer than his life. TIT 3.01.291
she loves thee, boy, too well to do thee harm. 4.01. 6
aunt | loves me as dear as e'er my mother did, 4.01. 23
sups the fair rosaline whom thou so loves, ROM 1.02. 83
and, as thou loves me, let the porter let in 1.05. 8 P
now romeo is belov'd and loves again, | alike 2.pr. 5
nurse, that loves to hear himself talk, and will 2.04.147 P
that few things loves better | than to abhor TIM 1.01. 59
he that loves to be flatter'd is worthy o' th' 1.01.226 P
commend me to their loves; 2.02.190 P
we tender our loves to him in this suppos'd 5.01. 12
to wipe out our ingratitude with loves | above 5.04. 17
a hand | over your friend that loves you. JC 1.02. 36
he loves no plays, | as thou dost, antony; 1.02.203
caesar doth bear me hard, but he loves brutus. 1.02.313
for he loves to hear | that unicorns may be 2.01.203
he loves me well, and i have given him reasons; 2.01.219
decius brutus loves thee not; 2.03. 4 P
wherein hath caesar thus deserv'd your loves? 3.02.236
hated by one he loves, brav'd by his brother, 4.03. 96
whose loves i may not drop, but wail his fall MAC 3.01.121
do) | loves for his own ends, not for you. 3.05. 13
he loves us not, | he wants the natural touch; 4.02. 8
time | before we reckon with your several loves, 5.09. 27
it, | as needful in our loves, fitting our duty? HAM 1.01.173
i will requite your loves. 1.02.250
your loves, as mine to you, farewell. 1.02.253
perhaps he loves you now, | and now no soil nor 1.03. 14
then, if he says he loves you, | it fits your 1.03. 24
that even our loves should with our fortunes 3.02.201
if you will marry, make your loves to me, | my LR 5.03. 88
but that our loves and comforts should increase OTH 2.01.194
that cassio loves her, i do well believe't; 2.01.286
that she loves him, 'tis apt and of great credit 2.01.287
but he protests he loves you, | and needs no 3.01. 47
for if he be not one that truly loves you, 3.03. 48
who, certain of his fate, loves not his wronger; 3.03.168
suspects, yet /strongly loves! 3.03.170
say my wife is fair, feeds well, loves company, 3.03.184
but she so loves the token | (for he conjur'd 3.03.293
let us be wary, let us hide our loves"; 3.03.420
poor rogue, i think, /i' /faith, she loves me. 4.01.111
they are loves i bear to you. 5.02. 40
i am quickly ill, and well, | so antony loves. ANT 1.03. 73
but he neither loves, | nor either cares for him 2.01. 15
would each to other and all loves to both | draw 2.02.135
the heart of brothers govern in our loves, | and 2.02.147
our hearts, and never | fly off our loves again! 2.02.152
a very fine one. o, how he loves caesar! 3.02. 7
but he loves caesar best, yet he loves antony. 3.02. 15
but he loves caesar best, yet he loves antony. 3.02. 15
both he loves. 3.02. 19
let him that loves me strike me dead. 4.14.108
when thou shalt bring me word she loves my son, CYM 1.05. 49
it seems, much loves | a gallian girl at home. 1.06. 65
imperceiverant thing loves him in my despite. 4.01. 14 P
hath not deserv'd my service nor your loves, 4.04. 25
hearing us praise our loves of italy | for 5.05.161
of all the qualities that man | loves woman for, 5.05.167
why (as it were unlicens'd of your loves) | he PER 1.03. 16
he loves you well that holds his life of you. 2.02. 22
a letter that she loves the knight of tyre! 2.05. 43
each side like justice, which he loves best. TNK 1.03. 47
shall any thing that loves me perish for me? 3.06.241
good by me | as by another that less loves her. 4.01. 44
to all the under world the loves and fights | of 4.02. 24
he of the two pretenders that best loves me 5.01.158
i am palamon, | one that yet loves thee dying. 5.04. 90
a better, to prolong | your old loves to us. ep 17
being red, she loves him best, and being white, VEN 77
she's love, she loves, and yet she is not lov'd. 610
that love best their loves shall not enjoy." 1164
my restless discord loves no stops nor rests; LUC 1124
and age in love, loves not to have years told. PP 1.12
two loves i have, of comfort and despair, | that 2. 1
one knight loves both, and both in thee remain. 8.14
twain, | although our undivided loves are one: SON 36. 2
in our two loves there is but one respect, 36. 5
take all my loves, my love, yea, take them all, 40. 1
then she loves but me alone. 42.14
that mine eye loves it and doth first begin. 114.14
and age in love loves not t' have years told. 138.12
but 'tis my heart that loves what they despise, 141. 3
two loves i have of comfort and despair, | which 144. 1

LOVE–SHAFT 1 FR 0.0001 REL FR 1 V 0 P
and loos'd his love–shaft smartly from his bow, MND 2.01.159

LOVE–SHAK'D 1 FR 0.0001 REL FR 0 V 1 P
i am he that is so love–shak'd, i pray you tell AYL 3.02.367 P

LOVE–SICK 4 FR 0.0004 REL FR 4 V 0 P
to love–sick dido's sad attending ear | the TIT 5.03. 82
that | the winds were love–sick with them; ANT 2.02.194
by this the love–sick queen began to sweat, VEN 175
that love–sick love by pleading may be blest; 328

LOVE–SONG 5 FR 0.0005 REL FR 0 V 5 P
to relish a love–song, like a robin–redbreast; TGV 2.01. 20 P
would you have a love–song, or a song of good TN 2.03. 35 P
a love–song, a love–song. 2.03. 37 P
a love–song, a love–song. 2.03. 37 P
run through the ear with a love–song, the very ROM 2.04. 15 P

LOVE–SONGS 2 FR 0.0002 REL FR 0 V 2 P
trees with writing love–songs in their barks. AYL 3.02.260 P
he has the prettiest love–songs for maids, so WT 4.04.193 P

LOVE–SPRINGS 1 FR 0.0001 REL FR 1 V 0 P
in the spring of love, thy love–springs rot? ERR 3.02. 3

LOVEST 9 FR 0.0010 REL FR 5 V 4 P
'tis once, thou lovest, | and i will fit thee ADO 1.01.318
by my sword, beatrice, thou lovest me. 4.01.274 P
if thou lovest me, then | steal forth thy MND 1.01.163
eat it up all, hortensio, if thou lovest me. SHR 4.03. 50
ah, no more of that, hal, and thou lovest me! 1H4 2.04.283 P
come, i know thou lovest me; H5 5.02.197 P
by which honor i dare not swear thou lovest me, 5.02.222 P
titinius, if thou lovest me, | mount thou my JC 5.03. 14
and then thou lovest me, for my name is will. SON 136.14

LOVE–SUIT 3 FR 0.0003 REL FR 3 V 0 P
and plead his love–suit to her gentle heart? H5 5.02.101
whose love–suit hath been to me | as fearful as CYM 3.04.133
thus far for love my love–suit, sweet, fulfill. SON 136. 4

LOVETH 3 FR 0.0003 REL FR 2 V 1 P
yea, he loveth. LLL 1.02.182 P
doth love my daughter, and she loveth him, | or SHR 4.04. 41
to be reveng'd on him that loveth thee. R3 1.02.135

LOVE–THOUGHTS 1 FR 0.0001 REL FR 1 V 0 P
love–thoughts lie rich when canopied with bow'rs TN 1.01. 40

LOVE–TOKENS 1 FR 0.0001 REL FR 1 V 0 P
and interchang'd love–tokens with my child; MND 1.01. 29

LOVE–WOUNDED 1 FR 0.0001 REL FR 1 V 0 P
and here is writ "love–wounded proteus." TGV 1.02.110

/LOVING 1 FR 0.0001 REL FR 1 V 0 P
/their /loving /well /compos'd /with /gift /of TRO 4.04. 77

LOVING 126 FR 0.0142 REL FR 114 V 12 P
sighing back again, | did us but loving wrong. TMP 1.02.151
cease to persuade, my loving proteus: TGV 1.01. 1
o hateful hands, to tear such loving words! 1.02.102
may undertake | a journey to my loving proteus. 2.07. 7
only deserve my love by loving him, | and 2.07. 82
that doth goad us on | to sin in loving virtue. MM 2.02.182
the sixt of july. your loving friend, benedick. ADO 1.01.283 P
in every thing but in loving benedick. 2.03.162 P
and wise, but for loving me; 2.03.233 P
if it prove so, then loving goes by haps: 3.01.105
thee, | taming my wild heart to thy loving hand. 3.01.112
but in loving, leander the good swimmer, troilus 5.02. 30 P
my loving lord, dumaine is mortified: LLL 1.01. 28
and that's great marvel, loving a light wench. 1.02.123 P
who are the votaries, my loving lords, | that 2.01. 37
you give him for my sake but one loving kiss. 2.01.249
his loving bosom to keep down his heart. 4.03.134
thou thus to reprove | these worms for loving, 4.03.152
now prove | our loving lawful, and our faith not 4.03.281
look you what i have from the loving king. 5.02. 4
all the couples three | ever true in loving be; MND 5.01.408
become a christian and thy loving wife. MV 2.03. 21
lady is, | and claim her with a loving kiss." 3.02.138
in loving visitation was with me a young doctor 4.01.152 P
duke, and three or four loving lords have put AYL 1.01.101 P
friendship is feigning, most loving mere folly. 2.07.181
in your accoustrements, as loving yourself, than 3.02.383 P
and loving, woo? 5.02. 3 P
for thy loving voyage | is but for two months 5.04.191
age, | i may entitle thee my loving father. SHR 4.05. 61
and thou, hortensio, with thy loving widow, 5.02. 7
and graceless traitor to her loving lord? 5.02.160
with my love | for loving where you do; AWW 1.03.209
and my loving greetings | to those of mine in 1.03.252
letters, loving embassies, that they have seem'd WT 1.01. 28 P
but thou from loving england art so far | that JN 2.01. 94
you men of angiers, and my loving subjects — 2.01.203
you loving men of angiers, arthur's subjects, 2.01.204
and ne'er have spoke a loving word to you; 4.01. 51
my gracious sovereign, my most loving liege! R2 1.01. 21
and loving farewell of our several friends. 1.03. 51
my loving lord, i take my leave of you; 1.03. 63
my countrymen, my loving friends," | as were our 1.04. 34
love loving not itself, none other can. 5.03. 88
the king should keep his word in loving us. 1H4 5.02. 5
the lives of all your loving complices | /lean 2H4 1.01.163
i pray thee, loving wife, and gentle daughter, 2.03. 1
as, by a lower but by loving likelihood, | were H5 5.pr. 29
but, in loving me, you should love the friend of 5.02.172 P
like to a pair of loving turtle–doves | that 1H6 2.02. 30
my lord, your loving nephew now is come. 2.05. 33
see here, my friends and loving countrymen, 3.01.137
o loving uncle, kind duke of gloucester, | how 3.01.142
therefore, my loving lords, our pleasure is 3.01.157
you again, | no loving token to his majesty? 5.03.181
your loving uncle, twenty times his worth, 2H6 3.02.268
me, | i thank them for their tender loving care; 3.02.280
your princely father and my loving lord! 3H6 2.01. 47
amongst the loving welshmen canst procure, 2.01.180
king, | and raise his issue like a loving sire; 2.02. 22
the fruits of love i mean, my loving liege. 3.02. 59
scales | unto the brother of your loving bride. 4.01. 53
my sovereign, with the loving citizens, | like 4.08. 19
sweet oxford, and my loving montague, | and all 4.08. 30
say, somervile, what says my loving son? 5.01. 7
we are advertis'd by our loving friends | that 5.03. 18
witness the loving kiss i give the fruit. 5.07. 32
richard of york, how fares our loving brother? R3 3.01. 96
which now the loving haste of these our friends, 3.05. 54
your very worshipful and loving friends, | and 3.07.138
say on, my loving lord. 4.02. 11
know, my loving lord, | the marquess dorset, as 4.02. 47
then plainly to her tell my loving tale. 4.04.359
fellows in arms, and my most loving friends, 5.02. 1
we must both give and take, my loving lord. 5.03. 6
tell me, how fares our loving mother? 5.03. 82
more than i have said, loving countrymen, | the 5.03.237
ever belov'd and loving may his rule be; H8 2.01. 92
protection, | he's loving and most gracious. 3.01. 94
me, | and signify this loving interview | to the TRO 4.05.155
your loving motion toward the common body | to COR 2.02. 53
and, countrymen, my loving followers, | plead my TIT 1.01. 3
that i will here dismiss my loving friends; 1.01. 53
a loving nurse, a mother to his youth. 1.01.332
tear for tear, and loving kiss for kiss, | thy 5.03.156
sung thee asleep, his loving breast thy pillow; 5.03.163
some loving friends convey the emperor hence, 5.03.191
o loving hate! ROM 1.01.176
being vex'd, a sea nourish'd with loving tears. 1.01.192
she will not stay the siege of loving terms, 1.01.212
thou chidst me oft for loving rosaline. 2.03. 81
for doting, not for loving, pupil mine. 2.03. 82
gentle night, come, loving, black–brow'd night, 3.02. 20
but one, poor one, one poor and loving child, 4.05. 46
commend me to my loving countrymen — TIM 5.01.194
caesar was mighty, bold, royal, and loving. JC 3.01.127
why, 'tis a loving and a fair reply. HAM 1.02.121
so loving to my mother | that he might not 1.02.140
thy loving father, hamlet. 4.03. 50
and you, our no less loving son of albany, | we LR 1.01. 42
our very loving sister, well bemet. 5.01. 20
but he, as loving his own pride and purposes, OTH 1.01. 12
is of a constant, loving, noble nature, | and i 2.01.289
you of your pardon | for too much loving you. 3.03.213
that death's unnatural that kills for loving. 5.02. 42
death, which commits some loving act upon her, ANT 1.02.143 P
you not your child well loving, yet i find | it PER 4.03. 37
the sweet embraces of a loving wife, | loaden TNK 2.02. 30
patience, | we shall live long, and loving. 2.02. 86
had not the loving gods found this place for us, 2.02.108
and, in loving her, maintain | i am as worthy 2.02.178
dare assure you | you'll find a loving mistress. 2.05. 57
but, loving such a lady, | and justifying my 3.06. 41
the loving swine | sheath'd unaware the tusk in VEN 1115
there is no hate in loving; LUC 240
shall plead for me and tell my loving tale. 480
as if the boy should use like loving charms; PP 11. 8
and puts apparel on my tottered loving, | to SON 26.11
there reigns love and all love's loving parts, 31. 3
o, then voutsafe me but this loving thought: 32. 9
loving offenders, thus i will excuse ye: 42. 5
for, bending all my loving thoughts on thee, 88.10
even to thy pure and most most loving breast. 110.14
have put on black, and loving mourners be, 132. 3
hate of my sin, grounded on sinful loving: 142. 2
in loving thee thou know'st i am forsworn, | but 152. 1

LOVING–JEALOUS 1 FR 0.0001 REL FR 1 V 0 P
back again, | so loving–jealous of his liberty. ROM 2.02.181

LOVINGLY 1 FR 0.0001 REL FR 1 V 0 P
that hast thus lovingly reserv'd | the cordial TIT 1.01.165

LOV'ST 29 FR 0.0032 REL FR 25 V 4 P
but since thou lov'st, love still, and thrive TGV 1.01. 9
lucetta, as thou lov'st me, let me have | what 2.07. 57
now, as thou lov'st me, do him not that wrong, 2.07. 80
but, as thou lov'st thy life, make speed from 3.01.169
as thou lov'st silvia (though not for thyself) 3.01.257
sweet mistress' sake, because thou lov'st her. 4.04.177
herein i see thou lov'st me not with the full AYL 1.02. 8 P

i charge /thee tell | whom thou lov'st best; SHR 2.01. 9
nay then, thou lov'st it not; 4.03. 42
as thou lov'st her, | thy love's to me religious AWW 2.03.182
now, as thou lov'st me, let me see his letter. TN 5.01. 1 P
how thou lov'st us, show in our brother's WT 1.02.174
as thou lov'st me, camillo, wipe not out the 4.02. 10 P
and, by my troth, i think thou lov'st me well. JN 3.03. 55
name not religion, for thou lov'st the flesh, 1H6 1.01. 41
good brother, as thou lov'st and honorest arms, 3H6 1.01.116
thou lov'st me not; 5.02. 36
so may it come, thy master, whom thou lov'st, LR 1.04. 6
prithee, if thou lov'st me, tell me. 2.02. 6 P
that lov'st to make thine honesty a vice! OTH 3.03.376
if thou lov'st her, | or entertain'st a hope to TNK 2.02.169
because thou lov'st the one, and i the other. PP 8. 4
thou lov'st to hear the sweet melodious sound 8. 9
halt — | but plainly say thou lov'st her well, 18.11
why lov'st thou that which thou receiv'st not SON 8. 3
but that thou none lov'st is most evident; 10. 4
tell me thou lov'st elsewhere, but in my sight, 139. 5
be it lawful i love thee as thou lov'st those 142. 9
those that can see thou lov'st, and i am blind. 149.14
/LOW* 4 FR 0.0004 REL FR 4 V 0 P
o cross! too high to be enthrall'd to /low. MND 1.01.136
/those /that /could /speak /low /and /tardily 2H4 2.03. 26
/yet /i /think /we /are /not /brought /so /low, TIT 3.02. 76
/your /purpos'd /low /correction | /is /such /as LR 2.02.142
LOW* 98 FR 0.0110 REL FR 86 V 12 P
or to apes | with foreheads villainous low. TMP 4.01.249
too low a mistress for so high a servant. TGV 2.04.106
ay, but her forehead's low, and mine's as high. 4.04.193
and high and low beguiles the rich and poor. WIV 1.03. 86
he woos both high and low, both rich and poor, 2.01.113
when you depart from him, but, soft and low, MM 4.01. 68
o, sir, i did not look so low. ERR 3.02.139 P
faith, methinks she's too low for a high praise, ADO 1.01.171 P
speak low if you speak love. 2.01. 99 P
if low, an agot very vildly cut; 3.01. 65
with quarrelling, | some of us would lie low. 5.01. 52
bull jove, sir, had an amiable low, | and some 5.04. 48
how low soever the matter, i hope in god for LLL 1.01.192 P
a high hope for a low heaven. 1.01.194 P
esteem, | because i am so dwarfish and so low? MND 3.02.295
how low am i, thou painted maypole? 3.02.296
how low am i? 3.02.297
i am not yet so low | but that my nails can 3.02.297
nothing but "low" and "little"? 3.02.326
for that in low simplicity | he lends out money MV 1.03. 43
or | shall i bend low and in a bondman's key, 1.03.123
how much low peasantry would then be gleaned 2.09. 46
my creditors grow cruel, my estate is very low, 3.02.317 P
we'll light upon some settled low content. AYL 2.03. 68
the woman low, | and browner than her brother." 4.03. 87
and with a low submissive reverence | say, "what SHR in.1. 53
do, | with soft low tongue and lowly courtesy, in.1. 114
and bow'd his eminent top to their low ranks, AWW 1.02. 43
my low and humble name to propagate | with any 2.01.197
if there be here german, or dane, low dutch, 4.01. 71
day and night | must wear your spirits low; 5.01. 2
but falls into abatement and low price | even in TN 1.01. 13
coming, | that can sing both high and low. 2.03. 41
out of my lean and low ability | i'll lend you 3.04.344
i would that i were low laid in my grave, | i am JN 2.01.164
stoop low within those bounds we have o'erlook'd 5.04. 55
as low as to thy heart | through the false R2 1.01.124
and lie full low, grav'd in the hollow ground. 3.02.140
thus high at least, although your knee be low. 3.03.195
now in as low an ebb as the foot of the ladder, 1H4 1.02. 37 P
o, pardon me that i descend so low | to show the 1.03.167
else, | could such inordinate and low desires, 3.02. 12
in general journey–bated and brought low. 4.03. 26
sick in the world's regard, wretched and low, 4.03. 57
stoop'd his anointed head as low as death. 2H4 in 32
for it is a low ebb of linen with thee when thou 2.02. 19 P
the rest of the low countries have /made /a 2.02. 21 P
a low transformation! 2.02.174 P
then (happy) low, lie down! 3.01. 30
sweet prince, speak low, | the king your father 4.05. 16
for government, though high, and low, and lower, H5 1.02.180
upon the valleys whose low vassal seat | the 3.05. 51
will it give place to flexure and low bending? 4.01.255
i will make you to–day a squire of low degree. 5.01. 36 P
and never more abase our sight so low | as to 2H6 1.02. 15
and, lords, bow low to him; 3H6 1.04. 94
i may conquer fortune's spite | by living low, 4.06. 20
than bear so low a sail to strike to thee. 5.01. 52
and kept low shrubs from winter's pow'rful wind. 5.02. 15
so that between their titles and low name R3 1.04. 82
say i, her sovereign, am her subject low. 4.04.355
gone slightly o'er low steps and now are mounted H8 2.04.112
methinks i see thee now, thou art so low, | as ROM 3.05. 55
i saw her laid low in her kindred's vault, | and 5.01. 20
i hope it is not so low with him as he made it TIM 3.06. 5 P
to the whole race of mankind, high and low! 4.01. 40
poor honest lord, brought low by his own heart, 4.02. 37
from high to low throughout, that whoso please 5.01.209
vast neptune weep for aye | on thy low grave, on 5.04. 79
as low as to thy foot doth cassius fall, | to JC 3.01. 56
dost thou lie so low? 3.01.148
come high or low; MAC 4.01. 67
the hill of heaven | as low as to the fiends!" HAM 2.02.497
nor are those empty–hearted whose low sounds LR 1.01.153
and with this horrible object, from low farms, 2.03. 17
and dizzy 'tis, to cast one's eyes so low! 4.06. 12
gentle, and low, an excellent thing in woman. 5.03.274
and duck again as low | as hell's from heaven! OTH 2.01.188
high renown, | and thou art but of low degree. 2.03. 94
is she shrill–tongu'd or low? ANT 3.03. 12
and her forehead | as low as she would wish it. 3.03. 34
thy mind to her is now as low as were | thy CYM 3.02. 10
house with such | whose roof's as low as ours! 3.03. 2
in simple and low things to prince it much 3.03. 85
on | the low posthumus slanders so her judgment 3.05. 76
make distinction | of place 'tween high and low. 4.02.249
no more, you petty spirits of region low, 5.04. 93
and if that ever my low fortunes better, | i'll PER 2.01.142
/envied the great, nor shall the low despise. 2.03. 26

me, i was grown so low | and crestfall'n with my TNK 3.06. 6
many, | and, being low, never reliev'd by any. VEN 708
ne'er settled equally, but high or low, | that 1139
but low shrubs wither at the cedar's root. LUC 665
let thy thoughts, low vassals to thy state" — 666
the homely villain cur'sies to her low, | and, 1338
some high, some low, the painter was so nice; 1412
are | from his low tract and look another way: SON 7.12
in clamors of all size, both high and low. LC 21
LOW–BORN 1 FR 0.0001 REL FR 1 V 0 P
this is the prettiest low–born lass that ever WT 4.04.156
LOW–CROOKED 1 FR 0.0001 REL FR 1 V 0 P
low–crooked curtsies, and base spaniel fawning. JC 3.01. 43
LOW–DECLINED 1 FR 0.0001 REL FR 1 V 0 P
dispense, | my low–declined honor to advance? LUC 1705
LOWER 26 FR 0.0029 REL FR 18 V 8 P
lower, lower! TMP 1.01. 34 P
lower, lower! 1.01. 34 P
that hath to instrument this lower world | and 3.03. 54
sir, sitting (as i say) in a lower chair, sir — MM 2.01.128 P
but she herself is hit lower. LLL 4.01.118
master, let me take you a button–hole lower. 5.02.701 P
because she is something lower than myself, MND 3.02.304
"lower"? hark again. 3.02.305
vailing her high top lower than her ribs | to MV 1.01. 28
thou wert best set thy lower part where thy nose AWW 2.03.252 P
lower messes | perchance are to this business WT 1.02.227
behind the globe, that lights the lower world, R2 3.02. 38
bare–headed, lower than his proud steed's neck, 5.02. 19
ned poins and i will walk lower. 1H4 2.02. 61 P
on high, | and either we or they must lower lie. 3.03.204
speak lower, princes, for the king recovers. 2H4 4.04.129
for government, though high, and low, and lower, H5 1.02.180
i will speak lower. 4.01. 81 P
as, by a lower but by loving likelihood, | were 5.pr. 29
at lower end of the hall, hurl'd up their caps, R3 3.07. 35
patience, be near me still, and set me lower; H8 4.02. 76
a lower place, note well, | may make too great ANT 3.01. 12
of egypt, made her | of lower syria, cyprus, 3.06. 10
please, | i cannot be much lower than my knees. PER 1.02. 47
arcite is the lower of the twain; TNK 2.01. 50 P
stray lower, where the pleasant fountains lie. VEN 234
LOWEST 8 FR 0.0009 REL FR 7 V 1 P
a lover's ear will hear the lowest sound, | when LLL 4.03.332
from lowest place /when virtuous things proceed, AWW 2.03.125
for that, being one o' th' lowest, basest, COR 1.01.157
the fires i' th' lowest hell fold in the people! 3.03. 68
till the lowest stream | do kiss the most JC 1.01. 59
sound me from my lowest note to /the /top /of my HAM 3.02.367 P
the lowest and most dejected thing of fortune, LR 4.01. 3
our ground's the lowest, and we are half way PER 1.04. 78
LOWING 2 FR 0.0002 REL FR 2 V 0 P
that calf–like they my lowing follow'd through TMP 4.01.179
and as the dam runs lowing up and down, 2H6 3.01.214
LOW–LAID 1 FR 0.0001 REL FR 1 V 0 P
your low–laid son our godhead will uplift. CYM 5.04.103
LOWLINESS 5 FR 0.0005 REL FR 3 V 2 P
the beggar, for so witnesseth thy lowliness. LLL 4.01. 80 P
the night, your garments, your lowliness; H5 4.08. 52 P
but with as humble lowliness of mind | she is 1H6 5.05. 18
that lowliness is young ambition's ladder, JC 2.01. 22
bounty, perseverance, mercy, lowliness, MAC 4.03. 93
LOWLY 13 FR 0.0014 REL FR 12 V 1 P
do, | with soft low tongue and lowly courtesy, SHR in.1. 114
and banish hence these abject lowly dreams. in.2. 32
i will show myself highly fed and lowly taught. AWW 2.02. 3 P
since lowly feigning was call'd compliment. TN 3.01. 99
with a swain's wearing, and me, poor lowly maid, WT 4.04. 9
thy sun sets weeping in the lowly west, R2 2.04. 21
as looks the mother on her lowly babe | when 1H6 3.03. 47
and lowly words were ransom for their fault. 2H6 3.01.127
should die | by such a lowly vassal as thyself. 4.01.111
or lowly factor for another's gain; R3 3.07.134
verily, | i swear, 'tis better to be lowly born, H8 2.03. 19
these couchings and these lowly courtesies JC 3.01. 36
sat, | and like a lowly lover down she kneels; VEN 350
LOWN *(also loon)*
LOWN 2 FR 0.0002 REL FR 1 V 1 P
too dear, | with that he call'd the tailor lown; OTH 2.03. 92
we should have both lord and lown, if the PER 4.06. 18 P
LOWNESS 3 FR 0.0003 REL FR 3 V 0 P
to such a lowness but his unkind daughters. LR 3.04. 71
by th' height, the lowness, or the mean, if ANT 2.07. 19
dodge | and palter in the shifts of lowness, who 3.11. 63
LOW'R 3 FR 0.0003 REL FR 3 V 0 P
why at our justice seem'st thou then to low'r? R2 1.03.235
the sky doth frown and low'r upon our army. R3 5.03.283
the heavens do low'r upon you for some ill; ROM 4.05. 94
LOW–RATED 1 FR 0.0001 REL FR 1 V 0 P
french | do the low–rated english play at dice; H5 4.pr. 19
LOW'R'D 1 FR 0.0001 REL FR 1 V 0 P
and all the clouds that low'r'd upon our house R3 1.01. 3
LOW'RETH 1 FR 0.0001 REL FR 1 V 0 P
fie, how impatience low'reth in your face! ERR 2.01. 86
LOW'RING* 5 FR 0.0005 REL FR 5 V 0 P
this low'ring tempest of your home–bred hate, R2 1.03.187
what low'ring star now envies thy estate, | that 2H6 3.01.206
driving back shadows over low'ring hills; ROM 2.05. 6
by revolution low'ring, does become | the ANT 1.02.125
his low'ring brows o'erwhelming his fair sight, VEN 183
LOW'RS 1 FR 0.0001 REL FR 1 V 0 P
still is he sullen, still he low'rs and frets, VEN 75
LOW'R'ST 1 FR 0.0001 REL FR 1 V 0 P
nay, if thou low'r'st on me, do i not spend SON 149. 7
LOW'S 1 FR 0.0001 REL FR 1 V 0 P
the odds for high and low's alike. WT 5.01.207
LOW–SPIRITED 1 FR 0.0001 REL FR 0 V 1 P
there did i see that low–spirited swain, that LLL 1.01.247 P
LOW–VOIC'D 1 FR 0.0001 REL FR 1 V 0 P
madam, i heard her speak; she is low–voic'd. ANT 3.03. 13
LOYAL 34 FR 0.0038 REL FR 33 V 1 P
and a loyal sir | to him thou follow'st! TMP 5.01. 69
longer than i prove loyal to your grace | let me TGV 3.02. 20
crest, | with loyal blazon, evermore be blest! WIV 5.05. 64
write loyal cantons of contemned love, | and TN 1.05.270
who professes | myself your loyal servant, your WT 2.03. 54

proves the king, | to him will we prove loyal. JN 2.01.271
to prove myself a loyal gentleman | even in the R2 1.01.148
chest | is a bold spirit in a loyal breast. 1.01.181
throne, | a loyal, just, and upright gentleman. 1.03. 87
behind, | and in my loyal bosom lies his power. 2.03. 98
o loyal father of a treacherous son! 5.03. 60
the crown, | had still kept loyal to possession, 1H4 3.02. 43
had nobles richer and more loyal subjects, H5 1.02.127
amongst his subjects and his loyal friends, | as 1H6 3.01.181
procure me any scathe | so long as i am loyal, 2H6 2.04. 63
unless thou wert more loyal than thou art. 3.01. 96
of storm, | as every loyal subject ought to do. 3H6 4.07. 44
nor you, as we are, loyal. R3 1.04.166
god grant that some, less noble and less loyal, 2.01. 92
a loyal and obedient subject is | therein H8 3.02.180
take notice, lords, he has a loyal breast, | for 3.02.200
i'll deliver | myself your loyal servant, or COR 5.06.140
and furious, | loyal, and neutral, in a moment? MAC 2.03.109
quarrels unjust against the good and loyal, 4.03. 83
loyal and natural boy, i'll work the means | to LR 2.01. 84
and of the loyal service of his son, | when i 4.02. 7
your wife, my lord; your true | and loyal wife. OTH 4.02. 35
all happiness, that remains loyal to his vow, CYM 3.02. 46 P
the scriptures of the loyal leonatus, | all 3.04. 81
your highness, | hold me your loyal servant. 4.03. 16
forc'd it to tremble with her loyal fear! LUC 261
since thou couldst not defend thy loyal dame, 1034
but when i fear'd, i was a loyal wife: 1048
and the turtle's loyal breast | to eternity doth PHT 57
LOYALL'ST 1 FR 0.0001 REL FR 1 V 0 P
the loyall'st husband that did e'er plight troth CYM 1.01. 96
LOYALLY 1 FR 0.0001 REL FR 1 V 0 P
perform | all parts of his subjection loyally. CYM 4.03. 19
LOYALTIES 1 FR 0.0001 REL FR 1 V 0 P
hath flaw'd the heart | of all their loyalties; H8 1.02. 22
LOYALTY 25 FR 0.0028 REL FR 23 V 2 P
when i protest true loyalty to her, | she twits TGV 4.02. 7
say i — | and then end life when i end loyalty! MND 2.02. 63
thee | to the last gasp, with truth and loyalty. AYL 2.03. 70
mean time, let this defend my loyalty: R2 1.01. 67
both to defend my loyalty and truth | to god, my 1.03. 19
know not why he is away | that wisdom, loyalty, 1H4 4.01. 64
sate | crowned with faith and constant loyalty. H5 2.02. 5
and with submissive loyalty of heart | ascribes 1H6 3.04. 10
i see | the map of honor, truth, and loyalty; 2H6 3.01.203
and mere instinct of love and loyalty, | free 3.02.250
o, where is loyalty? 5.01.166
what pledge have we of thy firm loyalty? 3H6 3.03.239
this shall assure my constant loyalty, | that if 3.03.240
die | for truth, for duty, and for loyalty. R3 3.03. 4
such which breaks | the sides of loyalty, and H8 1.02. 28
my pray'rs to heaven for you, my loyalty, 3.02.177
that in the way of loyalty and truth | toward 3.02.272
chastity, | upon her nuptial vow, her loyalty, TIT 2.03.125
the service and the loyalty i owe, | in doing it MAC 1.04. 22
that nature thus gives way to loyalty, something LR 3.05. 3 P
i will persever in my course of loyalty, though 3.05. 22 P
the loyalty well held to fools does make | our ANT 3.13. 42
the feeler's soul | to th' oath of loyalty; CYM 1.06.102
beaten for loyalty | excited me to treason. 5.05.344
a figure of truth, of faith, of loyalty. PER 5.03. 92
LOZEL 1 FR 0.0001 REL FR 1 V 0 P
and, lozel, thou art worthy to be hang'd, | that WT 2.03.109
LUBBER 3 FR 0.0003 REL FR 1 V 2 P
a notable lubber — as thou reportest him to be. TGV 2.05. 45 P
i am afraid this great lubber, the world, will TN 4.01. 14 P
they clap the lubber ajax on the shoulder, | as TRO 3.03.139
LUBBERLY 1 FR 0.0001 REL FR 0 V 1 P
anne page, and she's a great lubberly boy. WIV 5.05.184 P
LUBBER'S *(also leopard, libbard's)*
LUBBER'S 2 FR 0.0002 REL FR 0 V 2 P
to dinner to the lubber's head in lumbert street 2H4 2.01. 28 P
if you will measure your lubber's length again, LR 1.04. 91 P
LUCCICOS 1 FR 0.0001 REL FR 1 V 0 P
marcus luccicos, is not he in town? OTH 1.03. 44
LUCE* 5 FR 0.0005 REL FR 4 V 1 P
the luce is the fresh fish, the salt fish is an WIV 1.01. 22 P
let my master in, luce. ERR 3.01. 49
if thy name be called luce — luce, thou hast 3.01. 53
if thy name be called luce — luce, thou hast 3.01. 53
and little luce with the white legs, and TNK 3.05. 26
LUCENTIO 37 FR 0.0041 REL FR 28 V 9 P
another sense — | i am content to be lucentio, SHR 1.01.216
be lucentio, | because so well i love lucentio. 1.01.217
tranio, be so, because lucentio loves, | and let 1.01.218
your mouth, | tranio is chang'd into lucentio. 1.01.237
that lucentio indeed had baptista's youngest 1.01.240
but in all places else /your master lucentio. 1.01.244
lucentio shall make one, | though paris came in 1.02.244
lucentio is your name, of whence, i pray? 2.01.102
i see no reason but suppos'd lucentio | must get 2.01.407
you before, "simois," i am lucentio, "hic est," 3.01. 32 P
and that lucentio that comes a–wooing, "priami," 3.01. 34 P
signior lucentio, this is the 'pointed day, 3.02. 1
what says lucentio to this shame of ours? 3.02. 7
litio, | all for my master's sake, lucentio. 3.02.148
i'll tell you, sir lucentio: 3.02.158
lucentio, you shall supply the bridegroom's 3.02.249
she shall, lucentio. come, gentlemen, let's go. 3.02.252
bianca | doth fancy any other but lucentio? 4.02. 2
lov'd /none in the world so well as lucentio. 4.02. 13
signior lucentio, | here is my hand, and here i 4.02. 27
and so farewell, signior lucentio. 4.02. 40
my son lucentio | made me acquainted with a 4.04. 25
your son lucentio here | doth love my daughter, 4.04. 40
not in my house, lucentio, for you know 4.04. 51
lucentio, gentle sir. 4.05. 58
is signior lucentio within, sir? 5.01. 18 P
you tell signior lucentio that his father is 5.01. 27 P
his name is lucentio, and he is mine only son, 5.01. 84 P
lucentio! 5.01. 87 P
tell me, thou villain, where is my son lucentio? 5.01. 90 P
then thou wert best say that i am not lucentio. 5.01.104 P
yes, i know thee to be signior lucentio. 5.01.105 P
how hast thou offended? | where is lucentio? 5.01.114
here's lucentio, | right son to the right 5.01.114
cambio is chang'd into lucentio. 5.01.123
o, sir, lucentio slipp'd me like his greyhound, 5.02. 52

'tis since the nuptial of lucentio, | come ROM 1.05. 35
LUCENTIO'S 3 FR 0.0003 REL FR 3 V 0 P
lucentio's father is arriv'd in padua, | and how SHR 4.04. 65
and how she's like to be lucentio's wife. 4.04. 66
sir, here's the door, this is lucentio's house. 5.01. 8
LUCES *(also louses)*
LUCES 1 FR 0.0001 REL FR 0 V 1 P
may give the dozen white luces in their coat. WIV 1.01. 16 P
LUCETTA 10 FR 0.0011 REL FR 10 V 0 P
but say, lucetta, now we are alone, | wouldst TGV 1.02. 1
how churlishly i chid lucetta hence, | when 1.02. 60
to call lucetta back | and ask remission for my 1.02. 64
lucetta! 1.02. 66
counsel, lucetta; 2.07. 1
gentle lucetta, fit me with such weeds | as may 2.07. 42
why, ev'n what fashion thou best likes, lucetta. 2.07. 52
out, out, lucetta, that will be ill–favor'd. 2.07. 54
lucetta, as thou lov'st me, let me have | what 2.07. 57
that is the least, lucetta, of my fear: 2.07. 68
LUCIANA 2 FR 0.0002 REL FR 2 V 0 P
sure, luciana, it is two a' clock. ERR 2.01. 3
ah, luciana, did he tempt thee so? 4.02. 1
LUCIANUS 1 FR 0.0001 REL FR 0 V 1 P
this is one lucianus, nephew to the king. HAM 3.02.244 P
LUCIFER 6 FR 0.0006 REL FR 3 V 3 P
then lucifer take all! WIV 1.03. 76
lucifer, well; 2.02.297 P
thou art more deep damn'd than prince lucifer. JN 4.03.122
bastinado and made lucifer cuckold and swore the 1H4 2.04.337 P
the devil is, as lucifer and belzebub himself, H5 4.07.138 P
and when he falls, he falls like lucifer, H8 3.02.371
LUCIFER'S 1 FR 0.0001 REL FR 0 V 1 P
and his face is lucifer's privy–kitchen, where 2H4 2.04.333 P
LUCILIUS' 1 FR 0.0001 REL FR 1 V 0 P
that thou hast prov'd lucilius' saying true. JC 5.05. 59
/LUCILIUS 1 FR 0.0001 REL FR 1 V 0 P
let /lucilius and titinius guard our door. JC 4.02. 52
LUCILIUS 9 FR 0.0010 REL FR 9 V 0 P
thou hast a servant nam'd lucilius. TIM 1.01.111
attends he here, or no? lucilius! 1.01.114
what now, lucilius, is cassius near? JC 4.02. 3
a word, lucilius, | how he receiv'd you; 4.02. 13
ever note, lucilius, | when love begins to 4.02. 19
lucilius and titinius, bid the commanders 4.03.139
ho, lucilius, hark, a word with you. 5.01. 69
even so, lucilius. 5.01. 92
lucilius, come, | and come, young cato, let us 5.03.106
LUCINA 3 FR 0.0003 REL FR 3 V 0 P
lucina lent not me her aid, | but took me in my CYM 5.04. 43
at whose conception, till lucina reigned, PER 1.01. 8
lucina, o! 3.01. 10
LUCIO 10 FR 0.0011 REL FR 6 V 4 P
from too much liberty, my lucio, liberty: MM 1.02.125
one word, good friend. lucio, a word with you. 1.02.142
i prithee, lucio, do me this kind service: 1.02.176
i thank you, good friend lucio. 1.02.192
sir, my name is lucio, well known to the duke. 3.02.159 P
one lucio | as then the messenger — 5.01. 73
signior lucio, did not you say you knew that 5.01.260 P
what can you vouch | against him, signior lucio? 5.01.324
what, resists he? help him, lucio. 5.01.350 P
lucio and the lively helena." ROM 1.02. 70 P
LUCIO'S 1 FR 0.0001 REL FR 0 V 1 P
this is one lucio's information against me. MM 3.02.198 P
LUCIUS' 1 FR 0.0001 REL FR 1 V 0 P
man, | that lucius' banishment was wrongfully, TIT 4.04. 76
/LUCIUS 1 FR 0.0001 REL FR 1 V 0 P
/lucius, do you the like, and let no man | come JC 4.02. 50
LUCIUS 78 FR 0.0088 REL FR 76 V 2 P
and that he will, and shall, if lucius live. TIT 1.01.282
help, lucius, help! 1.01.291
come, lucius, come, stay not to talk with them. 2.03.306
ah, lucius, for thy brothers let me plead. 3.01. 30
why, foolish lucius, dost thou not perceive 3.01. 53
ah, son lucius, look on her! 3.01.110
shall thy good uncle, and thy brother lucius, 3.01.122
let marcus, lucius, or thyself, old titus, | or 3.01.152
farewell, proud rome, till lucius come again; 3.01.290
but now nor lucius nor lavinia lives | but in 3.01.294
if lucius live, he will requite your wrongs, 3.01.296
stand by me, lucius, do not fear thine aunt. 4.01. 5
fear her not, lucius, somewhat doth she mean. 4.01. 9
see, lucius, see, how much she makes of thee; 4.01. 10
lucius, i will. 4.01. 29
lucius, what book is that she tosseth so? 4.01. 41
lucius, i'll fit thee, and withal my boy | shall 4.01.114
lucius and i'll go brave it at the court. 4.01.121
demetrius, here's the son of lucius, | he hath 4.02. 1
gramercy, lovely lucius. what's the news? 4.02. 7
o, well said, lucius! 4.03. 64
under conduct | of lucius, son to old andronicus 4.04. 66
is warlike lucius general of the goths? 4.04. 69
they have wish'd that lucius were their emperor. 4.04. 77
ay, but the citizens favor lucius, | and will 4.04. 79
emperor requests a parley | of warlike lucius, 4.04.102
to pluck proud lucius from the warlike goths. 4.04.110
renowmed lucius, from our troops i stray'd | to 5.01. 20
lucius, save the child | and bear it from me to 5.01. 53
why, assure thee, lucius, | 'twill vex thy soul 5.01. 61
tut, lucius, this was but a deed of charity | to 5.01. 89
lord lucius, and you princes of the goths, | the 5.01.156
i'll make him send for lucius his son; 5.02. 75
to send for lucius, thy thrice–valiant son, 5.02.112
go, gentle marcus, to thy nephew lucius; 5.02.122
again, | and cleave to no revenge but lucius. 5.02.136
welcome, lucius; 5.03. 27
shall, | lo hand in hand lucius and i will fall. 5.03.136
lucius our emperor, for well i know | the common 5.03.139
lucius, all hail, rome's royal emperor! 5.03.141
lucius, all hail, rome's gracious governor! 5.03.146
may it please your honor, lord lucius | (out of TIM 1.02.181
you to lord lucius; 2.02.188 P
lord lucius and lucullus? humh! 2.02.195 P
he might have tried lord lucius or lucullus; 3.03. 2
lucius! | what, do we meet together? 3.04. 2
lucius, lucullus, and sempronius — all. 3.04.111
what, lucius, ho! JC 2.01. 1
lucius, i say! 2.01. 3
when, lucius, when? 2.01. 5
what, lucius! 2.01. 5
get me a taper in my study, lucius. 2.01. 7
lucius! 2.01.229
lucius, who's that knocks? 2.01.309
run, lucius, and commend me to my lord, | say i 2.04. 44
you have condemn'd and noted lucius pella | for 4.03. 2
lucius, a bowl of wine! 4.03.142
fill, lucius, till the wine o'erswell the cup; 4.03.161
lucius! 4.03.231
look, lucius, here's the book i sought for so; 4.03.252
boy, lucius! 4.03.289
lucius, awake! 4.03.293
didst thou dream, lucius, that thou so criedst 4.03.295
sleep again, lucius. 4.03.299
against my brother lucius? ANT 1.02. 89
the one is caius lucius. CYM 2.03. 55
caius lucius | will do 's commission throughly. 2.04. 11
was caius lucius in the britain court | when you 2.04. 37
lucius the roman, comes to milford–haven 3.04.142
a season) 'fore noble lucius | present yourself, 3.04.172
so farewell, noble lucius. 3.05. 12
leave not the worthy lucius, good my lords, 3.05. 16
lucius hath wrote already to the emperor | how 3.05. 21
he creates | lucius proconsul; 3.07. 8
is lucius general of the forces? 3.07. 11
lucius is taken. 5.03. 84
and, caius lucius, | although the victor, we 5.05.459
the vision | which i made known to lucius, ere 5.05.468
/LUCK 1 FR 0.0001 REL FR 1 V 0 P
force and forceless care | as if that /luck, in TRO 5.05. 41
LUCK 25 FR 0.0028 REL FR 12 V 13 P
if it be my luck, so; WIV 3.04. 64 P
as good luck would have it, comes in one 3.05. 83 P
i hope good luck lies in odd numbers. 5.01. 2 P
strew good luck, ouphes, on every sacred room, 5.05. 57
sir john, we have had ill luck; 5.05.116 P
i have but lean luck in the match, and yet is ERR 3.02. 92 P
and good luck grant thee thy demetrius! MND 1.01.221
do their work, and they shall have good luck. 2.01. 41
if we have unearned luck | now to scape the 5.01.432
nor no ill luck stirring but what lights a' my MV 3.01. 94 P
yes, other men have ill luck too. 3.01. 97 P
what, what, what? ill luck, ill luck? 3.01. 99 P
what, what, what? ill luck, ill luck? 3.01. 99 P
i ne'er had worse luck in my life in my "o lord, AWW 2.02. 57 P
good luck, and't be thy will! WT 3.03. 68 P
or else 'twere hard luck, being in so 5.02.147 P
he told me that rebellion had bad luck, | and 2H4 1.01. 41
that rebellion | had met ill luck? 1.01. 51
good salisbury, and good luck go with thee! H5 4.03. 11
be opposite all planets of good luck | to my R3 4.04.402
ween you of better luck, | i mean in perjur'd H8 5.01.135
and, of that natural luck, | he beats thee ANT 2.03. 27
i hear him mock | the luck of caesar, which the 5.02.286
was there ever man had such luck? CYM 2.01. 1 P
but not to tell of good or evil luck, | of SON 14. 3
LUCKIER 1 FR 0.0001 REL FR 1 V 0 P
and hymen now with luckier issue speed 's | than ADO 5.03. 32
LUCKIEST 1 FR 0.0001 REL FR 1 V 0 P
be sanctified | by th' luckiest stars in heaven, AWW 1.03.246
LUCKILY 1 FR 0.0001 REL FR 1 V 0 P
but, seeing thou fall'st on me so luckily, | i 1H4 5.04. 33
LUCKLESS 2 FR 0.0002 REL FR 2 V 0 P
i and ten thousand in this luckless realm | had 3H6 2.06. 18
the night–crow cried, aboding luckless time; 5.06. 45
LUCKY 6 FR 0.0006 REL FR 4 V 2 P
we are lucky, boy, and to be so still requires WT 3.03.125 P
'tis a lucky day, boy, and we'll do good deeds 3.03.138 P
thee, | and tidings do i bring, and lucky joys, 2H4 5.03. 95
we doubt not of a fair and lucky war, | since H5 2.02.184
'tis meet that lucky ruler be employ'd — 2H6 3.01.291
for when mine hours | were nice and lucky, men ANT 3.13.179
LUCRE 2 FR 0.0002 REL FR 2 V 0 P
shall i, for lucre of the rest unvanquish'd, 1H6 5.04.141
malice and lucre in them | have laid this woe CYM 4.02.324
LUCRECE' 14 FR 0.0015 REL FR 14 V 0 P
that left the camp to sin in lucrece' bed? TIT 4.01. 64
lord junius brutus sware for lucrece' rape, 4.01. 91
perchance his boast of lucrece' sov'reignty LUC 36
this heraldry in lucrece' face was seen, 64
led, | the roman lord marcheth to lucrece' bed. 301
then collatine again by lucrece' side | in his 381
poor lucrece' cheeks unto her maid seem so | as 1217
till lucrece' father, that beholds her bleed, 1732
and ever since, as pitying lucrece' woes, 1747
and then in key–cold lucrece' bleeding stream 1774
the dispers'd air, who, holding lucrece' life, 1805
who pluck'd the knife from lucrece' side, 1807
burying in lucrece' wound his folly's show. 1810
and by chaste lucrece' soul that late complained 1839
LUCRECE 26 FR 0.0029 REL FR 25 V 1 P
grissel, | and roman lucrece for her chastity; SHR 2.01.296
and the impressure her lucrece, with which she TN 2.05. 92 P
i adore, | but silence, like a lucrece knife, 2.05.105
lucrece was not more chaste | than this lavinia, TIT 2.01.108
of collatine's fair love, lucrece the chaste. LUC 7
supper long he questioned | with modest lucrece, 123
fire, | so lucrece must i force to my desire." 182
and holy–thoughted lucrece to their sight | must 384
"lucrece," quoth he, "this night i must enjoy 512
but cloudy lucrece shames herself to see, | and 1084
the president whereof in lucrece view, 1261
mild patience bid fair lucrece speak | to the 1268
peace," quoth lucrece, "if it should be told, 1284
(if ever, love, thy lucrece thou wilt see) 1306
for lucrece thought he blush'd to see her shame, 1344
to this well–painted piece is lucrece come, | to 1443
on this sad shadow lucrece spends her eyes, 1457
and therefore lucrece swears he did her wrong, 1462
so lucrece, set a–work, sad tales doth tell | to 1496
who finds his lucrece clad in mourning black, 1585
me, | from that, alas, thy lucrece is not free. 1624
th' adulterate death of lucrece and her groom. 1645
for she that was thy lucrece, now attend me: 1682
where shall i live now lucrece is unlived? 1754
then live, sweet lucrece, live again and see 1770
they did conclude to bear dead lucrece thence, 1850
LUCRETIA 1 FR 0.0001 REL FR 1 V 0 P
his insulting falchion lies | harmless lucretia, LUC 510
LUCRETIA'S 2 FR 0.0002 REL FR 2 V 0 P
better part, | sad lucretia's modesty. AYL 3.02.148
by the light he spies | lucretia's glove, LUC 317
LUCRETIUS 3 FR 0.0003 REL FR 3 V 0 P
"daughter, dear daughter," old lucretius cries, LUC 1751
and bids lucretius give his sorrow place, | and 1773
"o," quoth lucretius, "i did give that life 1800
LUCULLUS 7 FR 0.0008 REL FR 3 V 4 P
lord, that honorable gentleman, lord lucullus, TIM 1.02.187 P
to lord lucullus you — i hunted with his honor 2.02.188 P
lord lucius and lucullus? humh! 2.02.195 P
men was with the lord lucullus to borrow so many 3.02. 11 P
he might have tried lord lucius or lucullus; 3.03. 2
has ventidius and lucullus denied him, | and 3.03. 8
lucius, lucullus, and sempronius — all. 3.04.111
LUCY 4 FR 0.0004 REL FR 4 V 0 P
lucy, farewell, no more my fortune can, | but 1H6 4.03. 43
here is sir william lucy, who with me | set from 4.04. 10
i did, with his contract with lady lucy, | and R3 3.07. 5
for first was he contract to lady lucy — | your 3.07.179
/LUDLOW 2 FR 0.0002 REL FR 2 V 0 P
shall be that straight shall post to /ludlow. R3 2.02.142
toward /ludlow then, for we'll not stay behind. 2.02.154
LUDLOW 1 FR 0.0001 REL FR 1 V 0 P
forthwith from ludlow the young prince be fet R3 2.02.121
LUD'S–TOWN 4 FR 0.0004 REL FR 4 V 0 P
made lud's–town with rejoicing fires bright, CYM 3.01. 32
and on the gates of lud's–town set your heads. 4.02. 99
they grow, | and set them on lud's–town. 4.02.123
so through lud's–town march, | and in the temple 5.05.481
LUFF'D *(see loof'd)*
LUG 2 FR 0.0002 REL FR 2 V 0 P
will lug your priests and servants from your TIM 4.03. 32
i'll lug the guts into the neighbor room. HAM 3.04.212
LUGGAGE 6 FR 0.0006 REL FR 4 V 2 P
what do you mean | to dote thus on such luggage? TMP 4.01.231
and bestow your luggage where you found it. 5.01.299
come bring your luggage nobly on your back. 1H4 5.04.156
with the lackeys with the luggage of our camp. H5 4.04. 75 P
kill the poys and the luggage! 4.07. 1 P
with their poor luggage | plodding to th' ports STM II.C 75
LUGG'D 1 FR 0.0001 REL FR 0 V 1 P
am as melancholy as a gib cat or a lugg'd bear. 1H4 1.02. 74 P
/LUI 1 FR 0.0001 REL FR 0 V 1 P
pour les ecus que vous /lui promettez, il est H5 4.04. 52 P
LUKE'S 3 FR 0.0003 REL FR 0 V 3 P
i will presently to saint luke's; MM 3.01.264 P
the old priest of saint luke's church is at your SHR 4.04. 88 P
me to go to saint luke's to bid the priest be 4.04.103 P
LUKEWARM 2 FR 0.0002 REL FR 2 V 0 P
even in the lukewarm blood of henry's heart. 3H6 1.02. 34
smoke and lukewarm water | is your perfection. TIM 3.06. 89
LULL 1 FR 0.0001 REL FR 1 V 0 P
or the virgin voice | that babies lull asleep! COR 3.02.115
LULLA 4 FR 0.0004 REL FR 4 V 0 P
lulla, lulla, lullaby, lulla, lulla, lullaby. MND 2.02. 15
lulla, lulla, lullaby, lulla, lulla, lullaby. 2.02. 15
lulla, lulla, lullaby, lulla, lulla, lullaby. 2.02. 15
lulla, lulla, lullaby, lulla, lulla, lullaby. 2.02. 15
LULLABY 8 FR 0.0009 REL FR 7 V 1 P
with melody | sing in our sweet lullaby, | lulla MND 2.02. 14
lulla, lulla, lullaby, lulla, lulla, lullaby. 2.02. 15
lulla, lulla, lullaby, lulla, lulla, lullaby. 2.02. 15
so good night, with lullaby. 2.02. 19
sir, lullaby to your bounty till i come again. TN 5.01. 45 P
thou'rt like to have | a lullaby too rough. WT 3.03. 55
song | of lullaby to bring her babe asleep. TIT 2.03. 29
then lullaby, the learned man hath got the lady PP 15.15
LULL'D 2 FR 0.0002 REL FR 2 V 0 P
lull'd in these flowers with dances and delight; MND 2.01.254
and lull'd with sound of sweetest melody? 2H4 3.01. 14
LULLING *(also lolling)*
LULLING 1 FR 0.0001 REL FR 1 V 0 P
he is not lulling on a lewd love–bed, | but on R3 3.07. 72
LULLS 1 FR 0.0001 REL FR 1 V 0 P
and lulls him whilst she playeth on her back, TIT 4.01. 99
LUMBERT 1 FR 0.0001 REL FR 0 V 1 P
dinner to the lubber's head in lumbert street, 2H4 2.01. 28 P
LUMP 6 FR 0.0006 REL FR 5 V 1 P
this counterfeit lump of /ore will be melted, if AWW 3.06. 37 P
is numb | (unable to support this lump of clay), 1H6 2.05. 14
hence, heap of wrath, foul indigested lump, | as 2H6 5.01.157
hope, | to wit, an indigested and deformed lump, 3H6 5.06. 51
blush, blush, thou lump of foul deformity; R3 1.02. 57
all men's honors | lie like one lump before him, H8 2.02. 48
LUMPISH 1 FR 0.0001 REL FR 1 V 0 P
for she is lumpish, heavy, melancholy, | and, TGV 3.02. 62
LUNA 1 FR 0.0001 REL FR 1 V 0 P
a title to phoebe, to luna, to the moon. LLL 4.02. 38
LUNACY 5 FR 0.0005 REL FR 4 V 1 P
that the lunacy is so ordinary that the whippers AYL 3.02.403 P
house, | as beaten hence by your strange lunacy. SHR in.2. 29
this closing with him fits his lunacy. TIT 5.02. 70
have found | the very cause of hamlet's lunacy. HAM 2.02. 49
of quiet | with turbulent and dangerous lunacy? 3.01. 4
LUNATIC 12 FR 0.0013 REL FR 8 V 4 P
lest the lunatic knave would have search'd it; WIV 3.05.103 P
house, | and tell his wife that, being lunatic, ERR 4.03. 93
to make frantic, lunatic. LLL 5.01. 26 P
the lunatic, the lover, and the poet | are of MND 5.01. 7
persuade him that he hath been lunatic, | and SHR in.1. 63
regard, | to wish me wed to one half lunatic, 2.01.287
what, is the man lunatic? 5.01. 72 P
curate, who comes to visit malvolio the lunatic. TN 4.02. 22 P
a lunatic lean–witted fool, | presuming on an R2 2.01.115
dispute not with her, she is lunatic. R3 1.03.253
sometimes with lunatic bans, sometime with LR 2.03. 19
to whose hands you have sent the lunatic king — 3.07. 46
/LUNATICS 1 FR 0.0001 REL FR 0 V 1 P
oman, art thou /lunatics? WIV 4.01. 69 P
LUNATICS 1 FR 0.0001 REL FR 0 V 1 P
why, this is lunatics! this is mad as a mad dog! WIV 4.02.124 P
LUNES 1 FR 0.0001 REL FR 1 V 0 P
these dangerous, unsafe lunes i' th' king, WT 2.02. 28

/LUNGS 1 FR 0.0001 REL FR 0 V 1 P
/those /laugh /whose /lungs /are /tickle /a' HAM 2.02.323 P
LUNGS 19 FR 0.0021 REL FR 13 V 6 P
as if it had lungs, and rotten ones. TMP 2.01. 48 P
sensible and nimble lungs that they always use 2.01.174 P
speak from thy lungs military. WIV 4.05. 17 P
the heaving of my lungs provokes me to LLL 3.01. 76 P
thou but offend'st thy lungs to speak so loud. MV 4.01.140
time, | my lungs began to crow like chanticleer, AYL 2.07. 30
i, but my lungs are wasted so | that strength of 2H4 4.05.216
let vultures vile seize on his lungs also! 5.03.139
god bless thy lungs, good knight. 5.05. 9 P
and in thy hateful lungs, yea, in thy maw, perdy H5 2.01. 49
now crack thy lungs, and split thy brazen pipe. TRO 4.05. 7
dirt–rotten livers, whissing lungs, bladders 5.01. 21 P
which ne'er came from the lungs, but even thus COR 1.01.108
so shall my lungs | coin words till their decay 3.01. 77
the lie i' th' throat | as deep as to the lungs? HAM 2.02.575
(your lord, i mean) laughs from 's free lungs; CYM 1.06. 68
as hath been belch'd on by infected lungs. PER 4.06.169
with sighs that burning lungs did raise; LC 228
o, that sad breath his spungy lungs bestowed, 326
LUPERCAL 2 FR 0.0002 REL FR 2 V 0 P
you know it is the feast of lupercal. JC 1.01. 67
you all did see that on the lupercal | i thrice 3.02. 95
LURCH 1 FR 0.0001 REL FR 0 V 1 P
am fain to shuffle, to hedge, and to lurch; WIV 2.02. 25 P
LURCH'D 1 FR 0.0001 REL FR 1 V 0 P
since | he lurch'd all swords of the garland. COR 2.02.101
LURE 3 FR 0.0003 REL FR 3 V 0 P
for then she never looks upon her lure. SHR 4.01.192
voice, | to lure this tassel–gentle back again! ROM 2.02.159
as falcons to the lure, away she flies, | the VEN 1027
/LURK 2 FR 0.0002 REL FR 2 V 0 P
/lurk, /lurk. LR 3.06.115
/lurk, /lurk. 3.06.115
LURK 8 FR 0.0009 REL FR 8 V 0 P
and sometime lurk i in a gossip's bowl, | in MND 2.01. 47
there minotaurs and ugly treasons lurk. 1H6 5.03.189
ways, or bid me lurk | where serpents are; ROM 4.01. 79
sawest thou not signs of fear lurk in mine eye? VEN 644
or tyrant folly lurk in gentle breasts? LUC 851
she would have said, "can lurk in such a look"; 1535
from her tongue "can lurk" from "cannot" took: 1537
show, | the tricks and toys that in them lurk, PP 18.39
LURK'D 3 FR 0.0003 REL FR 3 V 0 P
here in these confines slily have i lurk'd, | to R3 4.04. 3
where have you lurk'd, that you make doubt of it COR 5.04. 46
sun and sharp air | lurk'd like two thieves, to VEN 1086
LURKETH 1 FR 0.0001 REL FR 1 V 0 P
and the mute wonder lurketh in men's ears | to H5 1.01. 49
LURKING 5 FR 0.0005 REL FR 5 V 0 P
guard it, i pray thee, with a lurking adder, R2 3.02. 20
this dangerous treason lurking in our way | to H5 2.02.186
who scapes the lurking serpent's mortal sting? 3H6 2.02. 15
his soldiers lurking in the town about, | and 4.02. 15
who sees the lurking serpent steps aside; LUC 362
LURKING–PLACE 1 FR 0.0001 REL FR 1 V 0 P
there's not a hollow cave or lurking–place, | no TIT 5.02. 35
LURKS 4 FR 0.0004 REL FR 4 V 0 P
are well foretold that danger lurks within. 3H6 4.07. 12
there lurks a still and dumb–discoursive devil TRO 4.04. 90
here lurks no treason, here no envy swells, TIT 1.01.153
hid, lurks to aspire | and girdle with embracing LUC 5
LUSCIOUS 2 FR 0.0002 REL FR 1 V 1 P
quite over–canopied with luscious woodbine, MND 2.01.251
food that to him now is as luscious as locusts, OTH 1.03.348 P
LUSH 1 FR 0.0001 REL FR 0 V 1 P
how lush and lusty the grass looks! how green! TMP 2.01. 53 P
/LUST 2 FR 0.0002 REL FR 1 V 1 P
so /lust, though to a radiant angel link'd, HAM 1.05. 55
/of /lust, /as /obidicut; LR 4.01. 59 P
LUST 72 FR 0.0081 REL FR 64 V 8 P
shall never melt | mine honor into lust, to take TMP 4.01. 28
the wicked fire of lust have melted him in his WIV 2.01. 68 P
fie on lust and luxury! 5.05. 94
lust is but a bloody fire, | kindled with 5.05. 95
to be the decay of lust and late–walking through 5.05.144 P
body | to his concupiscible intemperate lust, MM 5.01. 98
thee, | by ruffian lust should be contaminate? ERR 2.02.133
my blood is mingled with the crime of lust: 2.02.141
and all these engines of lust, are not the AWW 3.05. 19 P
so lust doth play | with what it loathes for 4.04. 24
give | their bodies to the lust of english youth H5 3.05. 30
for matching more for wanton lust than honor, 3H6 3.03.210
luxury | and bestial appetite in change of lust, R3 3.05. 81
i'll answer to my lust, and know you, lord, TRO 4.04.132
there serve your lust, shadowed from heaven's TIT 2.01.130
and make his dead trunk pillow to our lust. 2.03.130
o, keep me from their worse than killing lust, 2.03.175
no, let them satisfice their lust on thee. 2.03.180
at such a bay, by turn to serve our lust. 4.02. 42
and here's the base fruit of her burning lust. 5.01. 43
lust and liberty | creep in the minds and TIM 4.01. 25
them diseases, leaving with thee their lust. 4.03. 85
down thy youth | in different beds of lust, and 4.03.257
do never give | but thorough lust and laughter. 4.03.485
could not fill up | the cestern of my lust, and MAC 4.03. 63
more pernicious root | than summer–seeming lust; 4.03. 86
won to his shameful lust | the will of my most HAM 1.05. 45
epicurism and lust | makes it more like a tavern LR 1.04.244
serv'd the lust of my mistress' heart and did 3.04. 86 P
one that slept in the contriving of lust, and 3.04. 90 P
it is merely a lust of the blood and a OTH 1.03.334 P
to the history of lust and foul thoughts. 2.01.258 P
not out of absolute lust (though peradventure 2.01.292
that she repeals him for her body's lust, | and 2.03.357
what sense had i in her stol'n hours of lust? 3.03.338
bellows and the fan | to cool a gypsy's lust. ANT 1.01. 10
let witchcraft join with beauty, lust with both, 2.01. 22
and all the unlawful issue that their lust 3.06. 7
being an abstract 'tween his lust and him. 3.06. 61
lust and rank thoughts, hers, hers; CYM 2.05. 24
on his dead body, and when my lust hath din'd 3.05.141 P
murther's as near to lust as flame to smoke; PER 1.01.138
of monstrous lust the due and just reward. 5.03. 86
lust and ignorance | the virtues of the great TNK 2.02.106
govern'd him in strength, though not in lust. VEN 42
and careless lust stirs up a desperate courage, 556
since sweating lust on earth usurp'd his name, 794
love surfeits not, lust like a glutton dies; 803
love is all truth, lust full of forged lies. 804
make, | pawning his honor to obtain his lust, LUC 156
while lust and murder wakes to stain and kill. 168
his naked armor of still–slaughtered lust, | and 188
fear | is almost chok'd by unresisted lust. 282
stuff up his lust, as minutes fill up hours; 297
stay, | his rage of lust by gazing qualified; 424
tears harden lust, though marble /wear with 560
wilt thou be the school where lust shall learn? 617
appeal, | not to seducing lust, thy rash relier. 639
falls into thy boundless flood | black lust, 654
light, | for light and lust are deadly enemies; 674
o that prone lust should stain so pure a bed! 684
and lust, the thief, far poorer than before. 693
while lust is in his pride, no exclamation | can 705
she bears the load of lust he left behind, | and 734
thought he blush'd, as knowing tarquin's lust, 1354
gazing upon the greeks with little lust. 1384
thy heat of lust, fond paris, did incur | this 1473
and one man's lust these many lives confounds. 1489
you did fulfill | the loathsome act of lust, and 1636
his scarlet lust came evidence to swear | that 1650
spirit in a waste of shame | is lust in action, SON 129. 2
and till action, lust | is perjur'd, murd'rous, 129. 2
LUST–BREATHED 1 FR 0.0001 REL FR 1 V 0 P
lust–breathed tarquin leaves the roman host, LUC 3
LUST–DIETED 1 FR 0.0001 REL FR 1 V 0 P
let the superfluous and lust–dieted man, | that LR 4.01. 67
LUSTED 1 FR 0.0001 REL FR 1 V 0 P
heart, | without control, lusted to make a prey. R3 3.05. 84
LUSTFUL 7 FR 0.0008 REL FR 7 V 0 P
softer and sweeter than the lustful bed | on SHR in.2. 38
encompass'd with thy lustful paramours! 1H6 3.02. 53
and me — | the lustful edward's title buried — 3H6 3.02.129
the lustful sons of tamora | performers of this TIT 4.01. 79
kissing speaks, with lustful language broken, VEN 47
and now this lustful lord leapt from his bed, LUC 169
which must be lodestar to his lustful eye; 179
LUSTICK 1 FR 0.0001 REL FR 0 V 1 P
lustick, as the dutchman says. AWW 2.03. 41 P
LUSTIER 3 FR 0.0003 REL FR 1 V 2 P
why, your dolphin is not lustier. AWW 2.03. 26 P
with lustier maintenance than i did look for 1H4 5.04. 22
take him down, and 'a were lustier than he is, ROM 2.04.151 P
LUSTIEST 1 FR 0.0001 REL FR 1 V 0 P
that | he would unhorse the lustiest challenger. R2 5.03. 19
LUSTIHOOD 2 FR 0.0002 REL FR 2 V 0 P
his may of youth and bloom of lustihood. ADO 5.01. 76
respect | make livers pale and lustihood deject. TRO 2.02. 50
LUSTILY 4 FR 0.0004 REL FR 3 V 1 P
let's tune, and to it lustily a while. TGV 4.02. 25
and yet i determine to fight lustily for him. H5 4.01.189 P
and you have rung it lustily, my lords — TIT 2.02. 14
anon she hears them chaunt it lustily, | and all VEN 869
LUSTRE 13 FR 0.0014 REL FR 12 V 1 P
a good lustre of conceit in a turf of earth; LLL 4.02. 87 P
you can bring | tincture or lustre in her lip, WT 3.02.205
it lends a lustre and more great opinion, | a 1H4 4.01. 77
base | that hath not noble lustre in your eyes. H5 3.01. 30
equal in lustre, were now best, now worst, | as H8 1.01. 29
about his neck, yet never lost her lustre; 2.02. 32
the lustre of the better shall exceed | by TRO 1.03.360
the lustre in your eye, heaven in your cheek, 4.04.118
you have added worth unto't and lustre, | and TIM 1.02.149
bend doth awe the world | did lose his lustre; JC 1.02.124
where is thy lustre now? LR 3.07. 84
thy lustre thickens | when he shines by. ANT 2.03. 28
no, i rather added | a lustre to it. CYM 1.01.143
LUSTROUS 2 FR 0.0002 REL FR 0 V 2 P
good sparks and lustrous, a word, good metals: AWW 2.01. 41 P
toward the south north are as lustrous as ebony; TN 4.02. 38 P
LUST'S 5 FR 0.0005 REL FR 5 V 0 P
shall with lust's blood be spotted. OTH 5.01. 36
when reason is the bawd to lust's abuse. VEN 792
rain, | but lust's effect is tempest after sun; 800
lust's winter comes ere summer half be done; 802
honest fear, bewitch'd with lust's foul charm, LUC 173
LUSTS 4 FR 0.0004 REL FR 3 V 1 P
honor, nor my lusts | burn hotter than my faith. WT 4.04. 34
but you, that are polluted with your lusts, 1H6 5.04. 43
thou hotly lusts to use her in that kind | for LR 4.06.162
motions, our carnal stings, /our unbitted lusts; OTH 1.03.331 P
LUST–STAIN'D 1 FR 0.0001 REL FR 1 V 0 P
thy bed, lust–stain'd, shall with lust's blood OTH 5.01. 36
LUSTY 39 FR 0.0044 REL FR 35 V 4 P
how lush and lusty the grass looks! how green! TMP 2.01. 53 P
himself with his good arms in lusty stroke | to 2.01.120
and young drop–heir that kill'd lusty pudding, MM 4.03. 15 P
at thee, | as once europa did at lusty jove, ADO 5.04. 46
though i look old, yet i am strong and lusty; AYL 2.03. 47
therefore my age is as a lusty winter, | frosty, 2.03. 52
a little riper and more lusty red | than that 3.05.121
the lusty horn | is not a thing to laugh to 4.02. 17
now, by the world, it is a lusty wench! SHR 2.01.160
i' faith, he'll have a lusty widow now, | that 4.02. 50
and a goodly babe, | lusty and like to live. WT 2.02. 25
when this same lusty gentleman was got. JN 1.01.108
we will bear home that lusty blood again | which 2.01.255
troop of huntsmen come | our lusty english, all 2.01.322
if lusty love should go in quest of beauty, 2.01.426
what cannoneer begot this lusty blood? 2.01.461
what lusty trumpet thus doth summon us? 5.02.117
but lusty, young, and cheerly drawing breath. R2 1.03. 66
a' gaunt, | even in the lusty havior of his son. 1.03. 77
is't a lusty yeoman? 2H4 2.01. 3 P
you were call'd lusty shallow then, cousin. 3.02. 16 P
and lusty lads roam here and there | so merrily, 5.03. 20
of lusty earls, | grandpre and roussi, H5 4.08. 98
now, | the wanton edward, and the lusty george? 3H6 1.04. 74
by him that thunders, thou hast lusty arms! TRO 4.05.136
but who comes here, led by a lusty goth? TIT 5.01. 19
such comfort as do lusty young men feel | when ROM 1.02. 26
on, lusty gentlemen! 1.04.113
and we did buffet it | with lusty sinews, JC 1.02.108
and many lusty romans | came smiling and did 2.02. 78
who, in the lusty stealth of nature, take | more LR 1.02. 11
for that i do suspect the lusty moor | hath OTH 2.01.295
shall we be lusty? TNK 2.03. 46
'tis a lusty meat. 3.03. 27
i am well and lusty, choose your arms. 3.06. 45
over one arm the lusty courser's rein, | under VEN 31
a breeding jennet, lusty, young, and proud, 260
where all the treasure of thy lusty days, | to SON 2. 6
check'd with frost and lusty leaves quite gone, 5. 7
LUTE 17 FR 0.0019 REL FR 15 V 2 P
for orpheus' lute was strung with poets' sinews, TGV 3.02. 77
for god defend the lute should be like the case! ADO 2.01. 95 P
as sweet and musical | as bright apollo's lute, LLL 4.03.340
take you the lute, and you the set of books. SHR 2.01.106
why then thou canst not break her to the lute? 2.01.147
why no, for she hath broke the lute to me. 2.01.148
as on a pillory, looking through the lute, 2.01.156
or an old lion, or a lover's lute. 1H4 1.02. 75 P
bow'r, | with ravishing division, to her lute. 3.01.208
play on the lute, beholding the towns burn: 1H6 1.04. 96
chamber | to the lascivious pleasing of a lute. R3 1.01. 13
take thy lute, wench, my soul grows sad with H8 3.01. 1
orpheus with his lute made trees, | and the 3.01. 3
hands | tremble like aspen leaves upon a lute, TIT 2.04. 45
or when to th' lute | she sung, and made the PER 4.ch. 25
touch | upon the lute doth ravish human sense; PP 8. 6
the sweet melodious sound | that phoebus' lute, 8.10
LUTE–CASE 1 FR 0.0001 REL FR 0 V 1 P
bardolph stole a lute–case, bore it twelve H5 3.02. 43 P
LUTES 1 FR 0.0001 REL FR 1 V 0 P
iron may hold with her, but never lutes. SHR 2.01.146
LUTE–STRING 1 FR 0.0001 REL FR 0 V 1 P
now crept into a lute–string and now govern'd by ADO 3.02. 60 P
LUTHERAN 1 FR 0.0001 REL FR 1 V 0 P
yet i know her for | a spleeny lutheran, and not H8 3.02. 99
LUX 1 FR 0.0001 REL FR 1 V 0 P
"lux tua vita mihi." PER 2.02. 21
LUXURIOUS 5 FR 0.0005 REL FR 4 V 1 P
she knows the heat of a luxurious bed; ADO 4.01. 41
thou damned and luxurious mountain goat, H5 4.04. 19
sleeve back to the dissembling luxurious drab, TRO 5.04. 8 P
o most insatiate and luxurious woman! TIT 5.01. 88
luxurious, avaricious, false, deceitful, MAC 4.03. 58
LUXURIOUSLY 1 FR 0.0001 REL FR 1 V 0 P
vulgar fame, you have | luxuriously pick'd out; ANT 3.13.120
LUXURY 8 FR 0.0009 REL FR 7 V 1 P
fie on lust and luxury! WIV 5.05. 94
one all of luxury, an ass, a madman, | wherein MM 5.01.501
of us, | the emptying of our fathers' luxury, H5 3.05. 6
urge his hateful luxury | and bestial appetite R3 3.05. 80
how the devil luxury, with his fat rump and TRO 5.02. 55 P
be | a couch for luxury and damned incest. HAM 1.05. 83
to't, luxury, pell–mell, for i lack soldiers. LR 4.06.117
when he most burnt in heart–wish'd luxury, | he LC 314
LYAM *(also lym)*
LYAM 1 FR 0.0001 REL FR 1 V 0 P
and lead the majesty of law in lyam | to slip STM II.C 121
LYCAONIA 1 FR 0.0001 REL FR 1 V 0 P
and amyntas, | the kings of mede and lycaonia, ANT 3.06. 75
LYCHORIDA 9 FR 0.0010 REL FR 9 V 0 P
lychorida, her nurse, she takes, | and so to sea PER 3.ch. 43
o, how, lychorida! 3.01. 6
lychorida! 3.01. 10
now, lychorida! 3.01. 14
how? how, lychorida? 3.01. 18
o lychorida, | bid nestor bring me spices, ink 3.01. 64
o, no tears, | lychorida, no tears. 3.03. 39
lychorida, our nurse, is dead, | and cursed 4.ch. 42
as my good nurse lychorida hath oft | delivered 5.01.159
LYCURGUSES 1 FR 0.0001 REL FR 0 V 1 P
as you are (i cannot call you lycurguses), if COR 2.01. 55 P
LYDIA 2 FR 0.0002 REL FR 2 V 0 P
shook, from syria | to lydia and to ionia, ANT 1.02.103
egypt, made her | of lower syria, cyprus, lydia, 3.06. 10
LYING* 26 FR 0.0029 REL FR 15 V 11 P
thou most lying slave, | whom stripes may move, TMP 1.02.344
would lodge where, senseless, they are lying! TGV 3.01.143
i like not the humor of lying. WIV 2.01.129 P
it is i | that, lying by the violet in the sun, MM 2.02.165
you bald–pated, lying rascal, you must be hooded 5.01.352 P
and, to conclude, they are lying knaves. ADO 5.01.219 P
for lying so, hermia, i do not lie. MND 2.02. 52
i would she were as lying a gossip in that as MV 3.01. 8 P
an argosy | that now is lying in marsellis road. SHR 2.01.375
'tis a commodity will lose the gloss with lying: AWW 1.01.154 P
on every grave | a lying trophy, and as oft is 2.03.139
i hate ingratitude more in a man | than lying, TN 3.04.355
let me have no lying. WT 4.04.723 P
the remnant northward lying off from trent. 1H4 3.01. 78
come, kate, thou art perfect in lying down. 3.01.226 P
lord, lord, how this world is given to lying! 5.04.146 P
subject we old men are to this vice of lying! 2H4 3.02.304 P
lest rest and lying still might make them look 4.05.211
in | thy lying tongue both numbers, i would say COR 3.03. 72
doing himself offense, whilst we, lying still, JC 4.03.201
it is as easy as lying. HAM 3.02.357 P
thou'lt have me whipt for lying; LR 1.04.184 P
but as a monument, | thus in a chapel lying! CYM 2.02. 33
be it lying, note it, | the woman's; 2.05. 22
thy corpse, | lying with simple shells. PER 3.01. 64
the little love–god, lying once asleep, | laid SON 154. 1
LYING'ST 2 FR 0.0002 REL FR 1 V 1 P
sheer ale, score me up for the lying'st knave in SHR in.2. 24 P
sit there, the lying'st knave | in christendom. 2H6 2.01.123
LYM *(also lyam)*
/LYM 1 FR 0.0001 REL FR 1 V 0 P
mongril grim, | hound or spaniel, brach or /lym, LR 3.06. 69
LYMOGES 1 FR 0.0001 REL FR 1 V 0 P
o lymoges, o austria! JN 3.01.114
LYNN 1 FR 0.0001 REL FR 1 V 0 P
to lynn, my lord — | and shipp'd from thence to 3H6 4.05. 20
LYSANDER 37 FR 0.0041 REL FR 37 V 0 P
stand forth, lysander. MND 1.01. 26
thou, lysander, thou hast given her rhymes, 1.01. 28
so is lysander. 1.01. 53
and, lysander, yield | thy crazed title to my 1.01. 91
scornful lysander, true, he hath my love; 1.01. 95
my good lysander, | i swear to thee, by cupid's 1.01.168

lysander and myself will fly this place. 1.01.203
before the time i did lysander see, | seem'd 1.01.204
there my lysander and myself shall meet; 1.01.217
keep word, lysander; 1.01.222
where is lysander and fair hermia? 2.01.189
be't so, lysander. 2.02. 39
nay, /good lysander; 2.02. 43
lysander riddles very prettily. 2.02. 53
pride, | if hermia meant to say lysander lied. 2.02. 55
lysander! 2.02.100
lysander, if you live, good sir, awake. 2.02.102
do not say so, lysander, say not so. 2.02.108
and never mayst thou come lysander near! 2.02.136
help me, lysander, help me! 2.02.145
lysander, look how i do quake with fear. 2.02.148
lysander! 2.02.151
lysander! 2.02.151
if thou hast slain lysander in his sleep, 3.02. 47
what's this to my lysander? 3.02. 62
lysander, keep thy hermia; 3.02.169
thou art not by mine eye, lysander, found; 3.02.181
what love could press lysander from my side? 3.02.185
have you not set lysander, as in scorn, | to 3.02.222
and wherefore doth lysander | deny your love (so 3.02.228
lysander, whereto tends all this? 3.02.256
are not you lysander? 3.02.273
what, with lysander? 3.02.320
like to lysander sometime frame thy tongue; 3.02.360
lysander, speak again! 3.02.404
heavens shield lysander, if they mean a fray! 3.02.447
and this lysander, this demetrius is, | this 4.01.129
LYSANDER'S 3 FR 0.0003 REL FR 3 V 0 P
i am not guilty of lysander's blood; MND 3.02. 75
lysander's love, that would not let him bide — 3.02.186
then crush this herb into lysander's eye; 3.02.366
LYSIMACHUS 4 FR 0.0004 REL FR 2 V 2 P
here comes the lord lysimachus disguis'd. PER 4.06. 16 P
here spoken holy words to the lord lysimachus. 4.06.133 P
from whence | lysimachus our tyrian ship espies, 5.ch. 18
and in it is lysimachus the governor, | who 5.01. 4
M 3 FR 0.0003 REL FR 0 V 3 P
m — malvolio; m — why, that begins my name. TN 2.05.125 P
m — malvolio; m — why, that begins my name. 2.05.125 P
m — but then there is no consonancy in the 2.05.129 P
MA 7 FR 0.0008 REL FR 2 V 5 P
ma foi, il fait fort /chaud. WIV 1.04. 51 P
ma foi, j'oublie les doigts, mais je me H5 3.04. 9 P
je reciterai une autre fois ma lecon ensemble: 3.04. 57 P
mort /dieu, ma vie! 3.05. 11
gardez ma vie, et je vous donnerai deux cents 4.04. 42 P
mort dieu, ma vie! 4.05. 3
ma foi, je ne veux point que vous abaissez votre 5.02.253 P
MAB 3 FR 0.0003 REL FR 3 V 0 P
o then i see queen mab hath been with you. ROM 1.04. 53
which oft the angry mab with blisters plagues, 1.04. 75
this is that very mab | that plats the manes of 1.04. 88
MACBETH 42 FR 0.0047 REL FR 42 V 0 P
there to meet with macbeth. MAC 1.01. 7
for brave macbeth (well he deserves that name), 1.02. 16
not this | our captains, macbeth and banquo? 1.02. 34
and with his former title greet macbeth. 1.02. 65
what he hath lost, noble macbeth hath won. 1.02. 67
a drum, a drum! | macbeth doth come. 1.03. 31
all hail, macbeth, hail to thee, thane of glamis 1.03. 48
all hail, macbeth, hail to thee, thane of cawdor 1.03. 49
all hail, macbeth, that shalt be king hereafter! 1.03. 50
lesser than macbeth, and greater. 1.03. 65
so all hail, macbeth and banquo! 1.03. 68
banquo and macbeth, all hail! 1.03. 69
the king hath happily receiv'd, macbeth, | the 1.03. 89
worthy macbeth, we stay upon your leisure. 1.03.148
macbeth does murther sleep" — the innocent 2.02. 33
sleep no more — macbeth shall sleep no more." 2.02. 40
those that macbeth hath slain. 2.04. 23
like | the sovereignty will fall upon macbeth. 2.04. 30
as upon thee, macbeth, their speeches shine — 3.01. 7
macbeth. 3.03. 1
to trade and traffic with macbeth | in riddles 3.05. 4
the gracious duncan | was pitied of macbeth; 3.06. 4
how it did grieve macbeth! 3.06. 11
macbeth! 4.01. 71
macbeth! 4.01. 71
macbeth! 4.01. 71
macbeth! macbeth! macbeth! 4.01. 77
macbeth! macbeth! macbeth! 4.01. 77
macbeth! macbeth! macbeth! 4.01. 77
for none of woman born | shall harm macbeth. 4.01. 81
macbeth shall never vanquish'd be until | great 4.01. 92
and our high–plac'd macbeth | shall live the 4.01. 98
but why | stands macbeth thus amazedly? 4.01.126
but macbeth is. 4.03. 18
black macbeth | will seem as pure as snow, and 4.03. 52
a devil more damn'd | in evils to top macbeth. 4.03. 57
better macbeth | than such an one to reign. 4.03. 65
devilish macbeth | by many of these trains hath 4.03.117
macbeth | is ripe for shaking, and the pow'rs 4.03.237
"fear not, macbeth, no man that's born of woman 5.03. 6
my name's macbeth. 5.07. 7
either thou, macbeth, | or else my sword with an 5.07. 18
MACCABAEUS *(see machabeus)*
MACDONWALD 1 FR 0.0001 REL FR 1 V 0 P
the merciless macdonwald | (worthy to be a rebel MAC 1.02. 9
MACDUFF 16 FR 0.0018 REL FR 16 V 0 P
here comes the good macduff. MAC 2.04. 20
that macduff denies his person | at our great 3.04.127
feast, i hear | macduff lives in disgrace. 3.06. 23
thither macduff | is gone to pray the holy king, 3.06. 29
sent he to macduff? 3.06. 39
beware macduff, | beware the thane of fife. 4.01. 71
then live, macduff; 4.01. 82
bring you word | macduff is fled to england. 4.01.142
the castle of macduff i will surprise, | seize 4.01.150
macduff, this noble passion, | child of 4.03.114
sinful macduff, | they were all strook for thee! 4.03.224
his uncle siward, and the good macduff. 5.02. 2
worthy macduff and we | shall take upon 's what 5.06. 4
macduff was from his mother's womb | untimely 5.08. 15
lay on, macduff, | and damn'd be him that first 5.08. 33
macduff is missing, and your noble son. 5.09. 4
MACE* 4 FR 0.0004 REL FR 2 V 2 P
more exploits with his mace than a morris–pike. ERR 4.03. 28 P
mace; WT 4.03. 46 P
the sword, the mace, the crown imperial, | the H5 4.01.261
layest thou thy leaden mace upon my boy, | that JC 4.03.268
MACEDON 6 FR 0.0006 REL FR 1 V 5 P
i think alexander the great was born in macedon. H5 4.07. 20 P
his father was called philip of macedon, as i 4.07. 20 P
i think it is in macedon where alexander is porn 4.07. 22 P
in the comparisons between macedon and monmouth, 4.07. 25 P
there is a river in macedon, and there is also 4.07. 27 P
a prince of macedon, my royal father, | and the PER 2.02. 24
MACES 1 FR 0.0001 REL FR 0 V 1 P
with these borne before us, in stead of maces, 2H6 4.07.135 P
MACHABEUS 5 FR 0.0005 REL FR 1 V 4 P
and this gallant gentleman, judas machabeus; LLL 5.01.127 P
the pedant, judas machabeus; 5.02.536 P
"judas i am, ycliped machabeus." 5.02.598
judas machabeus clipt is plain judas. 5.02.599 P
alas, poor machabeus, how hath he been baited! 5.02.631 P
MACHEVIL 1 FR 0.0001 REL FR 1 V 0 P
and set the murtherous machevil to school. 3H6 3.02.193
MACHEVILE 1 FR 0.0001 REL FR 1 V 0 P
alanson, that notorious machevile? 1H6 5.04. 74
MACHIAVEL *(see machevil, machevile, machivel)*
MACHINATION 1 FR 0.0001 REL FR 1 V 0 P
world hath so an end, | and machination ceases. LR 5.01. 46
MACHINATIONS 1 FR 0.0001 REL FR 0 V 1 P
machinations, hollowness, treachery, and all LR 1.02.112 P
MACHINE 2 FR 0.0002 REL FR 1 V 1 P
most dear lady, whilst this machine is to him, HAM 2.02.124 P
do here present this machine, or this frame. TNK 3.05.113
MACHIVEL *(also machevil, machevile)*
MACHIVEL 1 FR 0.0001 REL FR 0 V 1 P
am i a machivel? WIV 3.01.101 P
MACK'REL 1 FR 0.0001 REL FR 0 V 1 P
may buy land now as cheap as stinking mack'rel. 1H4 2.04.360 P
MACMORRIS 6 FR 0.0006 REL FR 0 V 6 P
it is captain macmorris, is it not? H5 3.02. 68 P
how now, captain macmorris, have you quit the 3.02. 86 P
captain macmorris, i beseech you now, will you 3.02. 94 P
captain macmorris, i think, look you, under your 3.02.120 P
otherwise than is meant, captain macmorris, 3.02.126 P
captain macmorris, when there is more better 3.02.138 P
MACULATE 2 FR 0.0002 REL FR 1 V 1 P
most maculate thoughts, master, are mask'd under
LLL 1.02. 92 P
which never yet | beheld thing maculate — look TNK 5.01.145
MACULATION 1 FR 0.0001 REL FR 1 V 0 P
that there is no maculation in thy heart; TRO 4.04. 64
/MAD 5 FR 0.0005 REL FR 3 V 2 P
my lord, this is a poor /mad soul, and she says 2H4 2.01.104 P
/who, /when /my /heart, /all /mad /with /misery, TIT 3.02. 9
/marcus, /no /man /should /be /mad /but /i. 3.02. 24
/he's /mad /that /trusts /in /the /tameness /of LR 3.06. 18 P
/mad in pursuit and in possession so, | had, SON 129. 9
MAD 257 FR 0.0290 REL FR 197 V 60 P
not a soul | but felt a fever of the mad, and TMP 1.02.209
i have made you mad; 3.03. 58
for why, the fools are mad, if left alone. TGV 3.01. 99
me, he'll find the young man there, and be mad! WIV 1.04. 66 P
/afore /god, a mad host. 3.01.112 P
if i have horns to make one mad, let the proverb 3.05.151 P
he is very courageous mad about his throwing 4.01. 4 P
why, this is lunatics! this is mad as a mad dog! 4.02.124 P
why, this is lunatics! this is mad as a mad dog! 4.02.124 P
hath the finest mad devil of jealousy in him, 5.01. 18 P
it was a mad fantastical trick of him to steal MM 3.02. 92 P
if she be mad — as i believe no other — | her 5.01. 60
many that are not mad | have sure more lack of 5.01. 67
not cuckold–mad — | but sure he is stark mad: ERR 2.01. 59
how many fond fools serve mad jealousy? 2.01.116
wast thou mad, | that thus so madly thou didst 2.02. 11
sleeping or waking, mad or well–advis'd? 2.02.213
it would make a man mad as a buck to be so 3.01. 72
what, are you mad, that you do reason so? 3.02. 53
not mad, but mated — how, i do not know. 3.02. 54
now, out of doubt antipholus is mad, | else 4.03. 81
the reason that i gather he is mad, | besides 4.03. 86
rage, | is a mad tale he told to–day at dinner, 4.03. 88
how say you now? is not your husband mad? 4.04. 45
peace, doting wizard, peace! i am not mad. 4.04. 58
on thee, villain, wherefore dost thou mad me? 4.04.126
be mad, good master, | cry "the devil!" 4.04.127
but for the mountain of mad flesh that claims 4.04.154 P
he is mad. 5.01. 33
and thereof came it that the man was mad. 5.01. 68
poisons more deadly than a mad dog's tooth. 5.01. 70
to be disturb'd, would mad or man or beast: 5.01. 84
with him his bondman, all as mad as he — 5.01.141
him, | and with his mad attendant and himself, 5.01.150
albeit my wrongs might make one wiser mad. 5.01.217
if he were mad, he would not plead so coldly. 5.01.273
i think you are all mated, or stark mad. 5.01.282
pestilence, and the taker runs presently mad. ADO 1.01. 88 P
you will never run mad, niece. 1.01. 93 P
a week married, they would talk themselves mad. 2.01.354 P
do you hear, my mad wenches? LLL 2.01.257
by the lord, this love is as mad as ajax. 4.03. 6 P
farewell, mad wenches, you have simple wits. 5.02.264
how now, mad spirit? MND 3.02. 4
a knavish lad, | thus to make poor females mad. 3.02.441
some that are mad if they behold a cat; MV 4.01. 48
gifts, | and if your wife be not a mad woman, 4.01.445
fetching mad bounds, bellowing and neighing loud 5.01. 73
and 'twere to me i should be mad at it. 5.01.176
with reasons and the other mad without any. AYL 1.03. 9 P
my suitor from his mad humor of love to a living 3.02.418 P
what, would you make me mad? SHR in.2. 17 P
that wench is stark mad or wonderful froward. 1.01. 69
help, /masters, help, my master is mad. 1.02. 18 P
and say, "lo, there is mad petruchio's wife, 3.02. 19
he hath some meaning in his mad attire. 3.02.124
such a mad marriage never was before. 3.02.182
be mad and merry, or go hang yourselves; 3.02.226
of all mad matches never was the like. 3.02.242
that, being mad herself, she's madly mated. 3.02.244
fie on all tir'd jades, on all mad masters, and 4.01. 1 P
and thus i'll curb her mad and headstrong humor. 4.01.209
'a will make the man mad, to make /a woman of 4.05. 35 P
why, how now, kate, i hope thou art not mad. 4.05. 42
pardon, i pray thee, for my mad mistaking. 4.05. 49
away, away, mad ass! 5.01. 84 P
carry this mad knave to the jail. 5.01. 92 P
as mad in folly, lack'd the sense to know | her AWW 5.03. 3
he lov'd her, for indeed he was mad for her, and 5.03.260 P
he is but mad yet, madonna, and the fool shall TN 1.05.137 P
if you be not mad, be gone. 1.05.199 P
my masters, are you mad? 2.03. 86 P
when the image of it leaves him he must run mad. 2.05.194 P
i am as mad as he, | if sad and merry madness 3.04. 14
why, we shall make him mad indeed. 3.04.133 P
my niece is already in the belief that he's mad. 3.04.136 P
the man grows mad, away with him! 3.04.371
are all the people mad? 4.01. 27
or i am mad, or else this is a dream. 4.01. 61
good sir topas, do not think i am mad; 4.02. 29 P
i am not mad, sir topas, i say to you this house 4.02. 40 P
i am no more mad than you are; 4.02. 47 P
then you are mad indeed, if you be no better in 4.02. 89 P
but tell me true, are you not mad indeed, or do 4.02.114 P
like a mad lad, | pare thy nails, dad. 4.02.129
to any other trust but that i am mad | or else 4.03. 15
but that i am mad | or else the lady's mad; 4.03. 16
how now, art thou mad? 5.01.293 P
me, it was she | first told me thou wast mad. 5.01.349
"by the lord, fool, i am not mad." 5.01.374 P
and no less honest | than you are mad; WT 2.03. 72
done, | and then run mad indeed — stark mad! 3.02.183
done, | and then run mad indeed — stark mad! 3.02.183
mad world, mad kings, mad composition! JN 2.01.561
mad world, mad kings, mad composition! 2.01.561
mad world, mad kings, mad composition! 2.01.561
art /not holy to belie me so, | i am not mad. 3.04. 45
i am not mad, i would to heaven i were! 3.04. 48
preach some philosophy to make me mad, | and 3.04. 51
for, being not mad, but sensible of grief, | my 3.04. 53
if i were mad, i should forget my son, | or 3.04. 57
i am not mad; 3.04. 59
thou fond mad woman, | wilt thou conceal this R2 5.02. 95
for though it have holp mad men to their wits, 5.05. 62
in me it seems it will make wise men mad. 5.05. 63
how now, how now, mad wag? 1H4 1.02. 44 P
for he made me mad | to see him shine so brisk 1.03. 53
brother, the king hath made your nephew mad. 1.03.138
none of these mad mustachio purple–hu'd 2.01. 74 P
what, art thou mad? 2.04.229 P
art thou mad? 2.04.229 P
that same mad fellow of the north, percy, and he 2.04.335 P
peace, cousin percy, you will make him mad. 3.01. 51
i am afraid my daughter will run mad, | so much 3.01.143
nay, if you melt, then will she run mad. 3.01.209
a mad fellow met me on the way and told me i had 4.02. 36 P
how now, mad wag? 4.02. 50 P
thou whoreson mad compound of majesty, by this
2H4 2.04.294 P
where i think they will talk of mad shallow yet. 3.02. 15 P
jesu, jesu, the mad days that i have spent! 3.02. 33 P
whiles the mad mothers with their howls confus'd H5 3.03. 39
mad ire and wrathful fury makes me weep, | that 1H6 4.03. 28
he talks at randon; sure the man is mad. 5.03. 85
where, from thy sight, i should be raging mad, 2H6 3.02.394
is the man grown mad? 5.01.131
thou mad misleader of thy brain–sick son! 5.01.163
thou shouldst be mad; 3H6 1.04. 89
and i, to make thee mad, do mock thee thus. 1.04. 90
as if thou were distraught and mad with terror? R3 3.05. 4
and be thy wife — if any be so mad — | more 4.01. 74
england hath long been mad and scarr'd herself: 5.05. 23
was he mad, sir? H8 1.04. 27
o, very mad, exceeding mad, in love too; 1.04. 28
o, very mad, exceeding mad, in love too; 1.04. 28
so griev'd him, | that he ran mad, and died. 2.02.129
i tell thee i am mad | in cressid's love; TRO 1.01. 51
'tis mad idolatry | to make the service greater 2.02. 56
'tis our mad sister, i do know her voice. 2.02. 98
courage of our minds, | because cassandra's mad. 2.02.122
the young prince will go mad. 4.02. 75 P
and too little brain, these two may run mad, but 5.01. 49 P
hath done to–day | mad and fantastic execution, 5.05. 38
they say she's mad. COR 4.02. 9
why, are ye mad? TIT 2.01. 75
body hearing it | should straight fall mad, or 2.03.104
if the winds rage, doth not the sea wax mad, 3.01.222
oft, | extremity of griefs would make men mad; 4.01. 19
read that hecuba of troy | ran mad for sorrow. 4.01. 21
ay, some mad message from his mad grandfather. 4.02. 3
ay, some mad message from his mad grandfather. 4.02. 3
i am not mad, i know thee well enough. 5.02. 21
but we wordly men | have miserable, mad, 5.02. 66
and, being credulous in this mad thought, | i'll 5.02. 74
i knew them all though they suppos'd me mad, 5.02.142
and calls herself revenge, and thinks me mad. 5.02.185
why, romeo, art thou mad? ROM 1.02. 53
not mad, but bound more than a madman is; 1.02. 54
torments him so, that he will sure run mad. 2.04. 5
now, these hot days, is the mad blood stirring. 3.01. 4
/thou fond mad man, hear me a little speak. 3.03. 52
fie, fie, what, are you mad? 3.05.157
god's bread, it makes me mad! 3.05.176
that living mortals, hearing them, run mad — 4.03. 48
you love your child so ill | that you run mad, 4.05. 76
or am i mad, hearing him talk of juliet, | to 5.03. 80
i'm worse than mad. TIM 3.05.105
he's but a mad lord, and nought but humors sways 3.06.111 P
lord timon's mad. 3.06.119
what, is the fellow mad? JC 3.01. 10
it will inflame you, it will make you mad. 3.02.144
thou'rt mad to say it! MAC 1.05. 31
so, it will make us mad. 2.02. 31
some say he's mad; 5.02. 13
mad for thy love? HAM 2.01. 82
that hath made him mad. 2.01.107
your noble son is mad: 2.02. 92
mad call i it, for, to define true madness, 2.02. 93

what is't but to be nothing else but mad? 2.02. 94
that he's mad, 'tis true, 'tis true 'tis pity, 2.02. 97
mad let us grant him then, and now remains 2.02.100
i am but mad north–north–west. 2.02.378 P
make mad the guilty, and appall the free, 2.02.564
go to, i'll no more on't, it hath made me mad. 3.01.147 P
alas, he's mad! 3.04.105
am not in madness, | but mad in craft. 3.04.188
mad as the sea and wind, when both contend 4.01. 7
and out of haunt | this mad young man. 4.01. 19
does he suffer this mad knave now to knock him 5.01.101 P
that young hamlet was born — he that is mad, 5.01.148 P
why, because 'a was mad. 5.01.150 P
in him there, there the men are as mad as he. 5.01.155 P
how came he mad? 5.01.156 P
a whoreson mad fellow's it was. 5.01.176 P
a pestilence on him for a mad rogue! 5.01.179 P
o, he is mad, laertes. 5.01.272
be kent unmannerly | when lear is mad. LR 1.01.146
o, let me not be mad, not mad, sweet heaven! 1.05. 46
o, let me not be mad, not mad, sweet heaven! 1.05. 46
keep me in temper, i would not be mad! 1.05. 47
what, art thou mad, old fellow? 2.02. 85
i prithee, daughter, do not make me mad. 2.04.218
o fool, i shall go mad! 2.04.286
thou sayest the king grows mad, i'll tell thee, 3.04.165
tell thee, friend, | i am almost mad myself. 3.04.166
for he's a mad yeoman that sees his son a 3.06. 13 P
'tis poor mad tom. 4.01. 26
alack, sir, he is mad. 4.01. 45
he was met even now | as mad as the vex'd sea, 4.04. 2
what, art mad? 4.06.150 P
the king is mad; 4.06.279
exasperates, makes mad her sister goneril, | and 5.01. 60
lady, she'll run mad | when she shall lack it. OTH 3.03.317
as he shall smile, othello shall go mad; 4.01.100
i am glad to see you mad. 4.01.239
she was in love, and he she lov'd prov'd mad, 4.03. 27
earth than she was wont, | and makes men mad. 5.02.111
what, are you mad? i charge you, get you home. 5.02.194
again, | though i am mad, i will not bite him. ANT 2.05. 80
i think th' art mad. the matter? 2.07. 56
and 'twas i | that the mad brutus ended. 3.11. 38
o, he's more mad | than telamon for his shield; 4.13. 1
and impatience does | become a dog that's mad. 4.15. 80
what? art thou mad? CYM 1.01.147
what, are men mad? 1.06. 32
fools are not mad folks. 2.03.101
as i am mad, i do. 2.03.102
if you'll be patient, i'll no more be mad; 2.03.103
is cadwal mad? 4.02.195
proof enough | to make the noble leonatus mad, 5.05.201
men are mad things. TNK 2.02.126
you are mad. 2.02.200
is't not mad lodging | here in the wild woods, 3.03. 22
here, my mad boys, have at ye! 3.05. 24
there's a dainty mad woman, master, | comes i' 3.05. 72
comes i' th' nick, as mad as a march hare. 3.05. 73
a mad woman? we are made, boys! 3.05. 76
and are you mad, good woman? 3.05. 77
you are not mad? 3.06.122
what ignorant and mad malicious traitors | are 3.06.132
no, sir, not well: | 'tis too true, she is mad. 4.01. 46
yet doubtless | she would run mad for this man. 4.02. 12
me | whether i lov'd, i had run mad for arcite; 4.02. 48
if one be mad, or hang or drown themselves, 4.03. 34 P
being mad before, how doth she now for wits? VEN 249
as they were mad, unto the wood they hie them, 323
the tyranny | of mad mischances and much misery: 738
her eyes are mad that they have wept till now. 1062
it shall be raging mad and silly mild, | make 1151
at his own shadow let the thief run mad, LUC 997
sometime 'tis mad and too much talk affords. 1106
make her moans mad with their sweet melody, 1108
who, mad that sorrow should his use control, 1781
bait | on purpose laid to make the taker mad: SON 129. 8
for if i should despair, i should grow mad, 140. 9
bad, | mad slanderers by mad ears believed be. 140.12
bad, | mad slanderers by mad ears believed be. 140.12
care, | and frantic mad with evermore unrest; 147.10

/MADAM 1 FR 0.0001 REL FR 0 V 1 P
/want'st /thou /eyes /at /trial, /madam? LR 3.06. 24 P

MADAM 526 FR 0.0594 REL FR 445 V 81 P
ay, madam, so you stumble not unheedfully. TGV 1.02. 3
pardon, dear madam, 'tis a passing shame | that 1.02. 17
peruse this paper, madam. 1.02. 34
madam, it will not lie where it concerns 1.02. 74
that i might sing it, madam, to a tune: 1.02. 77
no, madam, 'tis too sharp. 1.02. 88
madam, | dinner is ready, and your father stays. 1.02.127
ay, madam, you may say what sights you see; 1.02.135
madam silvia! madam silvia! 2.01. 6 P
madam silvia! madam silvia! 2.01. 6 P
go to, sir; tell me, do you know madam silvia? 2.01. 14 P
madam and mistress, a thousand good morrows. 2.01. 96 P
now trust me, madam, it came hardly off; 2.01.109
no, madam; 2.01.113
madam, they are for you. 2.01.125
if it please me, madam, what then? 2.01.132
to be a spokesman from madam silvia. 2.01.146 P
indeed, madam, i seem so. 2.04. 9 P
give him leave, madam, he is a kind of chameleon 2.04. 25 P
'tis indeed, madam, we thank the giver. 2.04. 35 P
madam, my lord your father would speak with you. 2.04.116
how did thy master part with madam julia? 2.05. 11 P
what fashion, madam, shall i make your breeches? 2.07. 49
you must needs have them with a codpiece, madam. 2.07. 53
a round hose, madam, now's not worth a pin, 2.07. 55
madam, good ev'n to your ladyship. 4.02. 85
madam, if your heart be so obdurate, | vouchsafe 4.02.119
this is the hour that madam silvia | entreated 4.03. 1
madam, madam! 4.03. 4
madam, madam! 4.03. 4
madam, i pity much your grievances, | which 4.03. 37
serv'd me, when i took my leave of madam silvia. 4.04. 36 P
ring with thee, | deliver it to madam silvia — 4.04. 72
to bring me where to speak with madam silvia. 4.04.109
from my master, sir proteus, madam. 4.04.114
ay, madam. 4.04.116
madam, please you peruse this letter — | pardon 4.04.121
pardon me, madam, i have unadvis'd | deliver'd 4.04.122
it may not be; good madam, pardon me. 4.04.126
madam, he sends your ladyship this ring. 4.04.132
i thank you, madam, that you tender her. 4.04.140
she hath been fairer, madam, than she is: 4.04.149
part, | and i was trimm'd in madam julia's gown, 4.04.161
madam, 'twas ariadne passioning | for theseus' 4.04.167
madam, this service i have done for you 5.04. 19
unhappy were you, madam, ere i came; 5.04. 29
charg'd me to deliver a ring to madam silvia, 5.04. 89 P
behold, behold, where madam mitigation comes! MM 1.02. 44 P
and it is for getting madam julietta with child. 1.02. 73 P
and there's madam juliet. 1.02.115 P
and did they bid you tell her of it, madam? ADO 3.01. 39
i pray you be not angry with me, madam, 3.01. 94
when are you married, madam? 3.01.100
we have caught her, madam. 3.01.104
madam, withdraw, the prince, the count, signior 3.04. 95 P
madam, you must come to your uncle, yonder's old 5.02. 95 P
now, madam, summon up your dearest spirits; LLL 2.01. 1
i know him, madam; 2.01. 40
you shall be welcome, madam, to my court. 2.01. 95
not for the world, fair madam, by my will. 2.01. 99
madam, i will, if suddenly i may. 2.01.111
madam, your father here doth intimate | the 2.01.128
pardon me, madam, for i meant not so. 4.01. 13
yes, madam, fair. 4.01. 16
madam, came nothing else along with that? 5.02. 5
madam, this glove. 5.02. 48
yes, madam, and moreover | some thousand verses 5.02. 49
prepare, madam, prepare! 5.02. 81
madam, and pretty mistresses, give ear: 5.02.286
good madam, if by me you'll be advis'd, | let's 5.02.300
all hail, sweet madam, and fair time of day! 5.02.339
how, madam? russians? 5.02.362
madam, speak true. 5.02.364
teach us, sweet madam, for our rude 5.02.431
madam, i was. 5.02.434
i was, fair madam. 5.02.435
madam, he swore that he did hold me dear | as 5.02.444
what mean you, madam? 5.02.450
god save you, madam! 5.02.716
i am sorry, madam, for the news i bring | is 5.02.718
madam, not so, i do beseech you stay. 5.02.728
our letters, madam, show'd much more than jest. 5.02.785
no, madam, we will bring you on your way. 5.02.873
you would be, sweet madam, if your miseries were MV 1.02. 3 P
true, madam; 1.02.117 P
the four strangers seek for you, madam, to take 1.02.123 P
madam, there is alighted at your gate | a young 2.09. 86
madam, you have bereft me of all words, | only 3.02.175
madam, it is, so you stand pleas'd withal. 3.02.209
madam, although i speak it in your presence, 3.04. 1
madam, with all my heart, | i shall obey you in 3.04. 35
madam, i go with all convenient speed. 3.04. 56
it is your music, madam, of the house. 5.01. 98
silence bestows that virtue on it, madam. 5.01.101
madam, they are not yet; 5.01.116
we are no tell–tales, madam, fear you not. 5.01.123
i thank you, madam. 5.01.133
no, by my honor, madam, by my soul, | no woman 5.01.209
what color, madam? how shall i answer you? AYL 1.02.102 P
even he, madam. 1.02.152 P
give me audience, good madam. 3.02.238 P
chamber, | and call him madam, do him obeisance. SHR in.1. 108
madam. in.2. 109
al'ce madam, or joan madam? in.2. 110
al'ce madam, or joan madam? in.2. 110
madam, and nothing else — so lords call ladies. in.2. 111
madam wife, they say that i have dream'd | and in.2. 112
madam, undress you and come now to bed. in.2. 117
come, madam wife, sit by my side, and let the in.2. 142 P
'tis a very excellent piece of work, madam lady; 1.01.253 P
here, madam: 3.01. 27
madam, my instrument's in tune. 3.01. 38
madam, 'tis now in tune. 3.01. 46
madam, before you touch the instrument, | to 3.01. 64
and in going, madam, weep o'er my father's AWW 1.01. 3 P
you shall find of the king a husband, madam; 1.01. 6 P
he hath abandon'd his physicians, madam, under 1.01. 13 P
how call'd you the man you speak of, madam? 1.01. 25 P
he was excellent indeed, madam. 1.01. 28 P
your commendations, madam, get from her tears. 1.01. 46 P
madam, i desire your holy wishes. 1.01. 59 P
madam, the care i have had to even your content, 1.03. 3 P
'tis not unknown to you, madam, i am a poor 1.03. 13 P
no, madam, 'tis not so well that i am poor, 1.03. 16 P
my poor body, madam, requires it. 1.03. 28 P
faith, madam, i have other holy reasons, such as 1.03. 32 P
i have been, madam, a wicked creature, as you 1.03. 35 P
i am out a' friends, madam, and i hope to have 1.03. 39 P
y' are shallow, madam — in great friends, for 1.03. 42 P
a prophet i, madam, and i speak the truth the 1.03. 58 P
may it please you, madam, that he bid helen come 1.03. 66 P
one good woman in ten, madam, which is a 1.03. 82 P
i know, madam, you love your gentlewoman 1.03. 99 P
madam, i was very late more near her than i 1.03.106 P
what is your pleasure, madam? 1.03.137
pardon, madam; 1.03.154
you are my mother, madam; 1.03.161
good madam, pardon me! 1.03.185
do not you love him, madam? 1.03.187
my dearest madam, | let not your hate encounter 1.03.207
madam, i had. 1.03.219
ay, madam, knowingly. 1.03.250
truly, madam, if god have lent a man any manners 2.02. 8 P
madam, my lord will go away to–night, | a very 2.04. 39
o madam, yonder is heavy news within between two 3.02. 33 P
so say i, madam, if he run away, as i hear he 3.02. 40 P
'save you, good madam. 3.02. 45
madam, my lord is gone, for ever gone. 3.02. 46
madam, he's gone to serve the duke of florence. 3.02. 52
look on his letter, madam, here's my passport. 3.02. 56
ay, madam, | and for the contents' sake are 3.02. 62
ay, madam. 3.02. 69
ay, madam, with the swiftest wing of speed. 3.02. 73
ay, madam. 3.02. 76
we serve you, madam, | in that and all your 3.02. 95
pardon me, madam, | if i had given you this at 3.04. 22
gentle madam, | you never had a servant to whose 4.04. 14
madam, i was thinking with what manners i might 4.05. 88 P
o madam, yonder's my lord your son with a patch 4.05. 94 P
true, madam, and, to comfort you with chance, TN 1.02. 8
ay, madam, well, for i was bred and born | not 1.02. 22
madam, there is at the gate a young gentleman 1.05. 99 P
i know not, madam. 1.05.102 P
sir toby, madam, your kinsman. 1.05.105 P
madam, yond young fellow swears he will speak 1.05.139 P
good madam, let me see your face. 1.05.230 P
here, madam, at your service. 1.05.299
madam, i will. 1.05.307
my duty, madam, and most humble service. 3.01. 95
your servant's servant is your servant, madam. 3.01.102
madam, i come to whet your gentle thoughts | on 3.01.105
you'll nothing, madam, to my lord by me? 3.01.136
would it be better, madam, than i am? 3.01.143
and so adieu, good madam, never more | will i my 3.01.161
he's coming, madam, but in very strange manner. 3.04. 8 P
he is sure possess'd, madam. 3.04. 9 P
no, madam, he does nothing but smile. 3.04. 11 P
madam, the young gentleman of the count orsino's 3.04. 57 P
madam — 4.01. 46 P
madam, i will. 4.01. 65
madam — 5.01.104
i am sorry, madam, i have hurt your kinsman, 5.01.209
truly, madam, he holds belzebub at the stave's 5.01.284 P
"by the lord, madam" — 5.01.292 P
no, madam, i do but read madness. 5.01.294 P
"by the lord, madam, you wrong me, and the world 5.01.302 P
ay, madam. 5.01.313 P
madam, i am most apt t' embrace your offer. 5.01.320
madam, you have done me wrong, | notorious wrong 5.01.328
good madam, hear me speak, | and let no quarrel 5.01.355
"madam, why laugh you at such a barren rascal? 5.01.374 P
no, madam. WT 1.02. 44
your guest then, madam. 1.02. 56
i may not, madam: 2.02. 7
so please you, madam, | to put apart these your 2.02. 12
and, madam, i must | be present at your 2.02. 15
most worthy madam, | your honor and your 2.02. 40
madam, if't please the queen to send the babe, 2.02. 54
madam — he hath not slept to–night, commanded 2.03. 31
good madam — 5.01. 75
pardon, madam: 5.01.103
please you to interpose, fair madam, kneel, 5.03.119
i, madam? JN 1.01. 66
madam, and if my brother had my shape | and i 1.01.138
madam, i'll follow you unto the death. 1.01.154
madam, by chance, but not by truth; 1.01.169
come, madam, and come, richard, we must speed 1.01.178
madam, i was not old sir robert's son; 1.01.233
madam, i would not wish a better father. 1.01.260
i do beseech you, madam, be content. 3.01. 42
pardon me, madam, | i may not go without you to 3.01. 65
madam, fare you well, | i'll send those powers 3.03. 69
madam, your majesty is too much sad. R2 2.02. 1
ah, madam! 2.02. 52
despair not, madam. 2.02. 67
madam, we'll play at bowls. 3.04. 3
madam, we'll dance. 3.04. 6
madam, we'll tell tales. 3.04. 10
of either, madam. 3.04. 11
madam, i'll sing. 3.04. 19
i could weep, madam, would it do you good. 3.04. 21
pardon me, madam, little joy have i | to breathe 3.04. 81
and, madam, there is order ta'en for you, | with 5.01. 53
and, madam, you must call him rutland now. 5.02. 43
madam, i know not, nor i greatly care not, | god 5.02. 48
saying that ere long they should call me madam? 2H4 2.01.101 P
madam my interpreter, what says she? H5 5.02.260 P
madam, i will. 1H6 2.03. 3
madam, | according as your ladyship desir'd, 2.03. 11
madam, it is. 2.03. 15
madam, i have been bold to trouble you; 2.03. 25
i tell you, madam, were the whole frame here, 2.03. 54
how say you, madam? 2.03. 61
madam, i have a secret to reveal. 5.03.100
sweet madam, give me hearing in a cause. 5.03.106
no, gentle madam, i unworthy am | to woo so fair 5.03.123
how say you, madam, are ye so content? 5.03.126
and, madam, at your father's castle walls 5.03.129
farewell, sweet madam! 5.03.175
but, madam, i must trouble you again, | no 5.03.180
madam, be patient. 2H6 1.03. 65
madam, myself have lim'd a bush for her, | and 1.03. 88
and, madam, list to me, | for i am bold to 1.03. 92
madam, the king is old enough himself | to give 1.03.116
madam, i am protector of the realm, | and at his 1.03.120
i cry you mercy, madam; 1.03.139
madam, sit you and fear not. 1.04. 21
what, madam, are you there? 1.04. 43
true, madam, none at all. 1.04. 49
you, madam, shall with us. 1.04. 51
madam, for myself, to heaven i do appeal, | how 2.01.186
you, madam, for you are more nobly born, 2.03. 9
why, madam, that is to the isle of man, | there 2.04. 94
it is my office, and, madam, pardon me. 2.04.102
madam, your penance done, throw off this sheet, 2.04.105
madam, 'tis true; 3.01.252
he doth revive again. madam, be patient. 3.02. 36
madam, be still — with reverence may i say — 3.02.207
how now, madam? 4.04. 21
now tell me, madam, do you love your children? 3H6 3.02. 36
and, gracious madam, in our king's behalf | i am 3.03. 59
and, madam, these for you; 3.03.166
madam, what makes you in this sudden change? 4.04. 1
yet, gracious madam, bear it as you may: 4.04. 14
but, madam, where is warwick then become? 4.04. 25
so will it, madam, till i lie with you. R3 1.02.113
have patience, madam, there's no doubt his 1.03. 1
madam, good hope, his grace speaks cheerfully. 1.03. 34
ay, madam, he desires to make atonement 1.03. 36

madam, his majesty doth call for you, | and for 1.03.319
madam, yourself is not exempt from this; 2.01. 18
first, madam, i entreat true peace of you, 2.01. 63
why, madam, have i off'red love for this, | to 2.01. 78
madam, bethink you like a careful mother | of 2.02. 96
madam, my mother, i do cry you mercy, | i did 2.02.104
madam, and you, my sister, will you go | to give 2.02.143
and so no doubt he is, my gracious madam. 2.04. 21
good madam, be not angry with the child. 2.04. 36
well, madam, and in health. 2.04. 40
madam, farewell. 2.04. 67
right well, dear madam. 4.01. 15
no, madam, no; 4.01. 26
come, madam, you must straight to westminster, 4.01. 31
full of wise care is this your counsel, madam; 4.01. 47
come, madam, come, i in all haste was sent. 4.01. 56
madam, i have a touch of your condition, | that 4.04.158
let me march on and not offend you, madam. 4.04.179
stay, madam, i must talk a word with you. 4.04.199
madam, so thrive i in my enterprise | and 4.04.236
madam, with all my heart. 4.04.270
you mock me, madam, this /is not the way | to 4.04.284
harp not on that string, madam, that is past. 4.04.364
now, madam, may his highness live in freedom, H8 1.02.200
here's to your ladyship, and pledge it, madam, 1.04. 47
therefore, madam, | it's fit this royal session 2.04. 65
your pleasure, madam? 2.04. 69
madam, you do me wrong, | i have no spleen 2.04. 88
i do beseech | you, gracious madam, to unthink 2.04.104
madam, you are call'd back. 2.04.128
they will'd me say so, madam. 3.01. 18
may it please you, noble madam, to withdraw 3.01. 27
most honor'd madam, | my lord of york, out of 3.01. 61
madam, you wrong the king's love with these 3.01. 81
madam, this is a mere distraction, | you turn 3.01.112
madam, you wander from the good we aim at. 3.01.138
madam, you'll find it so. 3.01.168
yes, madam; 4.02. 7
well, the voice goes, madam: 4.02. 11
noble madam, | men's evil manners live in brass, 4.02. 44
(which was a sin), yet in bestowing, madam, | he 4.02. 56
madam, we are here. 4.02. 85
none, madam. 4.02. 86
i am most joyful, madam, such good dreams 4.02. 93
madam, the same; your servant. 4.02.111
madam, in good health. 4.02.124
no, madam. 4.02.128
most willing, madam. 4.02.130
madam, your uncle pandarus. TRO 1.02. 38 P
but had he died in the business, madam, how then COR 1.03. 18 P
madam, the lady valeria is come to visit you. 1.03. 26
sweet madam. 1.03. 49 P
i thank your ladyship; well, good madam. 1.03. 54 P
a crack, madam. 1.03. 68 P
no, good madam, i will not out of doors. 1.03. 71 P
no, good madam, pardon me, indeed i will not 1.03. 87 P
o, good madam, there can be none yet. 1.03. 91 P
indeed, madam? 1.03. 94 P
give me excuse, good madam, i will obey you in 1.03.102 P
no, at a word, madam; 1.03.109 P
patient yourself, madam, and pardon me. TIT 1.01.121
then, madam, stand resolv'd, but hope withal 1.01.135
now, madam, are you prisoner to an emperor; 1.01.258
madam, he comforts you | can make you greater 1.01.268
what, madam, be dishonored openly, | and basely 1.01.432
madam, to you as many and as good. 2.02. 12
madam, now shall ye see | our roman hunting. 2.02. 19
madam, though venus govern your desires, 2.03. 30
no, madam, these are no venereal signs. 2.03. 37
stay, madam, here is more belongs to her: 2.03.122
i warrant you, madam, we will make that sure. 2.03.133
listen, fair madam, let it be your glory | to 2.03.139
and, madam, if my uncle marcus go, | i will most 4.01. 27
madam, depart at pleasure, leave us here. 5.02.145
madam, an hour before the worshipp'd sun ROM 1.01.118
come, madam, let's away. 1.01.159
madam, i am here, | what is your will? 1.03. 5
yes, madam, yet i cannot choose but laugh | to 1.03. 50
madam, the guests are come, supper serv'd up, 1.03.100 P
madam, your mother craves a word with you. 1.05.111
madam! 2.02.149
madam! 2.02.151
madam, good night, commend me to your daughter. 3.04. 9
madam! 3.05. 37
madam, i am not well. 3.05. 68
what villain, madam? 3.05. 80
ay, madam, from the reach of these my hands. 3.05. 85
madam, if you could find out but a man | to bear 3.05. 96
madam, in happy time, what day is that? 3.05.111
i pray you tell my lord and father, madam, | i 3.05.120
an eagle, madam, | hath not so green, so quick, 3.05.219
no, madam, we have cull'd such necessaries | as 4.03. 7
madam! 4.05. 3
madam, madam, madam! 4.05. 9
madam, madam, madam! 4.05. 9
madam, madam, madam! 4.05. 9
sir, go you in, and, madam, go with him; 4.05. 91
to know my errand, madam. JC 2.04. 3
madam, what should i do? 2.04. 10
i hear none, madam. 2.04. 17
sooth, madam, i hear nothing. 2.04. 20
madam, not yet; 2.04. 25
ay, madam, but returns again to-night. MAC 3.02. 2
madam, i will. 3.02. 4
you must have patience, madam. 4.02. 2
ay, madam, it is common. HAM 1.02. 74
seems, madam? 1.02. 76
i shall in all my best obey you, madam. 1.02.120
madam, come, | this gentle and unforc'd accord 1.02.122
my liege, and madam, to expostulate | what 2.02. 86
madam, i swear i use no art at all. 2.02. 96
good madam, stay awhile. 2.02.115
madam, it so fell out that certain players | we 3.01. 16
madam, i wish it may. 3.01. 41
madam, how like you this play? 3.02.229 P
good madam! 5.02.290
i dare not drink yet, madam; by and by. 5.02.293

ay, madam. LR 1.03. 2
he's coming, madam, i hear him. 1.03. 11
well, madam. 1.03. 21
ay, madam. 1.04.335
o madam, my old heart is crack'd, it's crack'd! 2.01. 90
i know not, madam. 'tis too bad, too bad. 2.01. 96
yes, madam, he was of that consort. 2.01. 97
i serve you, madam. 2.01.128
why, madam, if i were your father's dog, | you 2.02.136
madam, within, but never man so chang'd. 4.02. 3
madam, here comes my lord. 4.02. 28
this letter, madam, craves a speedy answer; 4.02. 82
there is means, madam. 4.04. 11
news, madam! 4.04. 20
ay, madam. 4.05. 1
madam, with much ado; 4.05. 2
no, madam. 4.05. 5
i must needs after him, madam, with my letter. 4.05. 15
i may not, madam; 4.05. 17
madam, i had rather — 4.05. 22
i, madam? 4.05. 27
would i could meet /him, madam! 4.05. 39
to be acknowledg'd, madam, is o'erpaid. 4.07. 4
pardon, dear madam, | yet to be known shortens 4.07. 8
madam, sleeps still. 4.07. 13
ay, madam; 4.07. 20
be by, good madam, when we do awake him, | i 4.07. 22
madam, do you, 'tis fittest. 4.07. 42
be comforted, good madam, the great rage, | you 4.07. 77
'tis to be doubted, madam. 5.01. 6
no, by mine honor, madam. 5.01. 14
ay, madam. OTH 2.01.121
he speaks home, madam. 2.01.165 P
good madam, do. 3.03. 3
bounteous madam, | what ever shall become of 3.03. 7
madam, here comes my lord. 3.03. 29
madam, i'll take my leave. 3.03. 30
madam, not now; 3.03. 32
i know not, madam. 3.04. 24
madam, my former suit. 3.04.110
how do you, madam? 4.02. 96
good madam, what's the matter with my lord? 4.02. 98
why, with my lord, madam. 4.02.100
what is your pleasure, madam? how is't with you? 4.02.110
madam, good night; i humbly thank your ladyship. 4.03. 3
no, madam. ANT 1.02. 81
madam? 1.02. 84
madam, methinks, if you did love him dearly, 1.03. 6
madam? 1.05. 2
why, madam? 1.05. 4
madam, i trust not so. 1.05. 7
yes, gracious madam. 1.05. 13
not in deed, madam, for i can do nothing | but 1.05. 15
ay, madam, twenty several messengers. 1.05. 62
as well as i can, madam. 2.05. 7
madam, madam — 2.05. 25
madam, madam — 2.05. 25
first, madam, he is well. 2.05. 31
good madam, hear me. 2.05. 36
madam, he's well. 2.05. 46
but yet, madam — 2.05. 49
free, madam, no; 2.05. 57
madam, he's married to octavia. 2.05. 60
good madam, patience. 2.05. 62
gracious madam, | i that do bring the news made 2.05. 66
he's married, madam. 2.05. 72
what mean you, madam? 2.05. 74
good madam, keep yourself within yourself, | the 2.05. 75
he's married, madam. 2.05. 91
should i lie, madam? 2.05. 93
many times, madam. 2.05.108
madam, in rome; 3.03. 8
she is not, madam. 3.03. 11
madam, i heard her speak; she is low-voic'd. 3.03. 13
madam, | she was a widow — 3.03. 26
brown, madam; 3.03. 33
nothing, madam. 3.03. 41
i warrant you, madam. 3.03. 48
welcome, dear madam. 3.06. 91
nay, gentle madam, to him, comfort him. 3.11. 25
madam! 3.11. 32
madam, o good empress! 3.11. 33
go to him, madam, speak to him, | he's 3.11. 43
be comforted, dear madam. 4.15. 2
madam! 4.15. 69
o madam, madam, madam! 4.15. 70
o madam, madam, madam! 4.15. 70
o madam, madam, madam! 4.15. 70
i understand not, madam. 5.02. 75
gentle madam, no. 5.02. 94
hear me, good madam: 5.02.100
madam, he will, i know't. 5.02.110
it is the emperor, madam. 5.02.113
here, madam. 5.02.141
madam, | i had rather seel my lips than to my 5.02.145
madam, i will. 5.02.196
madam, as thereto sworn by your command | (which 5.02.198
and kiss'd it, madam. CYM 1.03. 6
no, madam; 1.03. 8
madam, so i did. 1.03. 16
be assur'd, madam, | with his next vantage. 1.03. 23
the queen, madam, | desires your highness' 1.03. 37
madam, i shall. 1.03. 40
i, madam. 1.05. 2
here they are, madam. 1.05. 5
i do suspect you, madam, | but you shall do no 1.05. 31
madam, a noble gentleman of rome, | comes from 1.06. 10
change you, madam? 1.06. 11
thanks, madam, well. 1.06. 52
well, madam. 1.06. 57
ay, madam, with his eyes in flood with laughter. 1.06. 74
o, i must, madam. 1.06.204
please you, madam. 2.02. 1
almost midnight, madam. 2.02. 2
madam, here is a letter from my lord. 3.02. 25
madam, 's enough for you — and too much too. 3.02. 69
madam, you're best consider. 3.02. 77
what cheer, madam? 3.04. 39

good madam, hear me. 3.04. 57
then, madam, | i thought you would not back 3.04.115
well, madam, we must take a short farewell, 3.04.185
madam, all joy befall your grace, and you! 3.05. 9
till she be married, madam, | by bright diana, PER 3.03. 27
good madam, make me blessed in your care | in 3.03. 31
madam, my thanks and prayers. 3.03. 34
come, dearest madam. 3.03. 38
madam, this letter and some certain jewels | lay 3.04. 1
madam, if this you purpose as ye speak, 3.04. 12
i warrant you, madam. 4.01. 46
my thanks, sweet madam. 4.01. 49
hail, madam, and my queen! 5.03. 49
'tis call'd narcissus, madam. TNK 2.02.119
i think i should not, madam. 2.02.124
why, madam? 2.02.125
dainty, madam. 2.02.130
why, gentle madam? 2.02.136
yet, good madam, | sometimes her modesty will 2.02.143
that's as we bargain, madam. 2.02.152
duke your brother, | madam, i bring you news. 4.02. 56
"madam, ere i was up," replied the maid, | "the LUC 1277

MADAME 9 FR 0.0010 REL FR 0 V 9 P
un peu, madame. H5 3.04. 3 P
c'est bien dit, madame, il est fort bon anglois. 3.04. 19 P
de arma, madame. 3.04. 22 P
il est trop difficile, madame, comme je pense. 3.04. 27 P
d' elbow, madame. 3.04. 30 P
de nick, madame. 3.04. 33 P
de nailes, madame. 3.04. 46 P
le foot, madame, et le count. 3.04. 51 P
excellent, madame! 3.04. 60 P

MADAM'S 1 FR 0.0001 REL FR 1 V 0 P
and my shape as true, | as honest madam's issue? LR 1.02. 9

MADAMS 2 FR 0.0002 REL FR 2 V 0 P
our madams mock at us, and plainly say | our H5 3.05. 28
the madams too, | not us'd to toil, did almost H8 1.01. 23

MAD-BRAIN 1 FR 0.0001 REL FR 1 V 0 P
heart | unto a mad-brain rudesby full of spleen, SHR 3.02. 10

MAD-BRAIN'D 3 FR 0.0003 REL FR 3 V 0 P
this mad-brain'd bridegroom took him such a cuff SHR 3.02.163
remaineth none but mad-brain'd salisbury, | and 1H6 1.02. 15
of contumelious, beastly, mad-brain'd war, TIM 5.01.174

MAD-BRED 1 FR 0.0001 REL FR 1 V 0 P
beams, | do calm the fury of this mad-bred flaw. 2H6 3.01.354

MADCAP 7 FR 0.0008 REL FR 5 V 2 P
come on, you madcap, i'll to the alehouse with TGV 2.05. 8 P
that last is berowne, the merry madcap lord. LLL 2.01.215
lunatic, | a madcap ruffian and a swearing jack, SHR 2.01.288
why, what a madcap hath heaven lent us here! JN 1.01. 84
well then, once in my days i'll be a madcap. 1H4 1.02.142 P
'twas where the madcap duke his uncle kept — 1.03.244
son, | the nimble-footed madcap prince of wales, 4.01. 95

/MADDED 1 FR 0.0001 REL FR 1 V 0 P
/most /degenerate, /have /you /madded. LR 4.02. 43

MADDED 2 FR 0.0002 REL FR 2 V 0 P
in this plight, | it would have madded me; TIT 3.01.104
all curses madded hecuba gave the greeks, | and CYM 4.02.313

MADDING 4 FR 0.0004 REL FR 4 V 0 P
me, | madding my eagerness with her restraint, AWW 5.03.213
did | when he to madding dido would unfold | his 2H6 3.02.117
does within, | to th' madding of her lord. CYM 2.02. 37
in the distraction of this madding fever? SON 119. 8

/MADE 13 FR 0.0014 REL FR 10 V 3 P
/me /to /the /tavern /and /made /me /drunk, /and WIV 1.01.126 P
you're a /made old man; WT 3.03.120 P
/keep /all /vows /unbroke /are /made /to /thee! R2 4.01.215
/made /glory /base, /and /sovereignty /a /slave; 4.01.251
/of /mine, | /and /made /no /deeper /wounds? 4.01.279
low countries have /made /a /shift /to eat up 2H4 2.02. 22 P
/thick (/which /nature /made /his /blemish) 2.03. 24
/and /their /vow /is /made | /to /ransack /troy, TRO pr 7
/has /sorrow /made /thee /dote /already? TIT 3.02. 23
/troy /was /burnt /and /he /made /miserable? 3.02. 28
/tender /sapling, /thou /art /made /of /tears, 3.02. 50
/what /store /her /heart /is /made /an. LR 3.06. 54
/made /she /no /verbal /question? 4.03. 24

MADE 892 FR 0.1008 REL FR 722 V 170 P
made such a sinner of his memory | to credit his TMP 1.02.101
made thee more profit | than other princess' can 1.02.172
told thee no lies, made thee no mistakings, 1.02.248
and heard thee, that made gape | the pine, and 1.02.292
pinch more stinging | than bees that made 'em. 1.02.330
thou strok'st me and made much of me, wouldst 1.02.333
thy purposes | with words that made them known. 1.02.358
thy father lies, | of his bones are coral made: 1.02.398
what strange fish | hath made his meal on thee? 2.01.114
which i made of the bark of a tree with mine own 2.02.122 P
swim like a duck, thou art made like a goose. 2.02.131 P
hearken once again to the suit i made to thee? 3.02. 39 P
i have made you mad; 3.03. 58
we are such stuff | as dreams are made on; 4.01.157
the strong-bas'd promontory | have i made shake, 5.01. 47
made me neglect my studies, lose my time, | war TGV 1.01. 67
made wit with musing weak, heart sick with 1.01. 69
she, when she hath made you write to yourself? 2.01.152 P
name) | made use and fair advantage of his days; 2.04. 68
and made them watchers of mine own heart's 2.04.135
the ladder made of cords, and all the means 2.04.182
and silvia (witness heaven, that made her fair) 2.06. 25
and when the flight is made to one so dear, | of 2.07. 12
myself am one made privy to the plot. 3.01. 12
hath made me publisher of this pretense. 3.01. 47
why then a ladder, quaintly made of cords, | to 3.01.117
my youthful travel therein made me happy, | or 4.01. 34
as if the garment had been made for me; 4.04.163
and at that time i made her weep agood, | for i 4.04.165
but, by my coming, i have made you happy. 5.04. 30
the gift hath made me happy. 5.04.148
remember what i did when you made me drunk, yet WIV 1.01.172 P
kind of tender, made afar off by sir hugh here. 1.01.208 P
as sure as his guts are made of puddings. 2.01. 31 P
sword i would have made you four tall fellows 2.01.228 P
and what they made there, i know not. 2.01.236 P
that there is shrewd construction made of her. 2.02.223 P

to him, the hour is fix'd, the match is made. 2.02.290 P
he has made us his vlouting–stog. 3.01.117 P
what made me love thee? 3.03. 68 P
i ne'er made my will yet, i thank heaven. 3.04. 58 P
your father and my uncle hath made motions. 3.04. 64 P
there's a hole made in your best coat, master 3.05.141 P
likewise hath | made promise to the doctor. 4.06. 34
i do begin to perceive that i am made an ass. 5.05.119 P
see now how wit may be made a jack–a–lent, when 5.05.127 P
ever the devil could have made you our delight? 5.05.149 P
let there be some more test made of my mettle MM 1.01. 48
impiety has made a feast of thee. 1.02. 57 P
hide our love | till time had made them for us. 1.02.153
what's open made to justice, | that justice 2.01. 21
breathe within your lips, | like man new made. 2.02. 79
hath from nature stol'n | a man already made, as 2.04. 44
falsely to take away a life true made | as to 2.04. 47
(since i suppose we are made to be no stronger 2.04.132
wilt thou be made a man out of my vice? 3.01.137
only he hath made an assay of her virtue to 3.01.162 P
hath made him that gracious denial which he is 3.01.165 P
the hand that hath made you fair hath made you 3.01.181 P
hand that hath made you fair hath made you good; 3.01.181 P
the assault that angelo hath made to you, 3.01.184 P
he made trial of you only. 3.01.197 P
in the current) made it more violent and unruly. 3.01.242 P
what offense hath this man made you, sir? 3.02. 14 P
images newly made woman to be had now, for 3.02. 45 P
this angelo was not made by man and woman after 3.02.104 P
how should he be made then? 3.02.107 P
i am made to understand that you have lent him 3.02.240 P
how may likeness made in crimes, | making 3.02.273
there have i made my promise upon the heavy 4.01. 34
for i have made him know | i have a servant 4.01. 44
i have not yet made known to mariana | a word of 4.01. 48
by eight to–morrow | thou must be made immortal. 4.02. 65
you will think you have made no offense, if the 4.02.185 P
pounds, of which he made five marks ready money. 4.03. 6 P
ere twice the sun hath made his journal greeting 4.03. 88
thank thee, varrius, thou hast made good haste. 4.05. 11
we have made inquiry of you, and we hear | such 5.01. 5
this state | made me a looker–on here in vienna, 5.01.317
your highness said even now i made you a duke; 5.01.515 P
by prosperous voyages i often made | to ERR 1.01. 40
bear) | had made provision for her following me, 1.01. 47
boys, | made daily motions for our home return: 1.01. 59
my mistress made it one upon my cheek: 1.02. 46
what patch is made our porter? 3.01. 36
why at this time the doors are made against you. 3.01. 93
the day, | a vulgar comment will be made of it; 3.01.100
by this i know 'tis made. 3.01.115
if my breast had not been made of faith, and my 3.02.145
to a curtal dog, and made me turn i' th' wheel. 3.02.146
hath almost made me traitor to myself; 3.02.162
the chain unfinish'd made me stay thus long. 3.02.168
i have made it for you. 3.02.170
made it for me, sir! i bespoke it not. 3.02.171
husband, | who i made lord of me and all i had, 5.01.137
for indeed he hath made great preparation. ADO 1.01.278 P
man that were made just in the midway between 2.01. 6 P
yet it had not been amiss the rod had been made, 2.01.228 P
she would have made hercules have turn'd spit, 2.01.253 P
his grace hath made the match, and all grace say 2.01.303 P
your brother's honor, who hath made this match, 2.02. 37 P
oath on it, till he have made /an oyster of me, 2.03. 25 P
hath she made her affection known to benedick? 2.03.123 P
all other respects, and made her half myself. 2.03.170 P
like favorites | made proud by princes, that 3.01. 10
matter | is little cupid's crafty arrow made, 3.01. 22
nature, drawing of an antic, | made a foul blot; 3.01. 64
did confirm any slander that don john had made, 3.03.159 P
you'll be made bring deformed forth, i warrant 3.03.172 P
her youth, | and made defeat of her virginity — 4.01. 47
that is stronger made | which was before barr'd 4.01.150
nor fortune made such havoc of my means, | nor 4.01.195
and made a push at chance and sufferance. 5.01. 38
therefore this article is made in vain, | or LLL 1.01.139
if she be made of white and red, | her faults 1.02. 99
doth noise abroad, navarre hath made a vow, 2.01. 22
i only have made a mouth of his eye, | by adding 2.01.252
not a sore, till now made sore with shooting. 4.02. 57
o, we have made a vow to study, lords, | and in 4.03.315
he made her melancholy, sad, and heavy, | and so 5.02. 14
and ever and anon they made a doubt | presence 5.02.101
what, was your vizard made without a tongue? 5.02.242
i made a little fault in "great." 5.02.559 P
pompey hath made the challenge. 5.02.706 P
change not your offer made in heat of blood; 5.02.800
might well have made our sport a comedy. 5.02.876
i know not by what power i am made bold, | nor MND 1.01. 59
made love to nedar's daughter, helena, | and won 1.01.107
hath every pelting river made so proud | that 2.01. 91
we should be woo'd, and were not made to woo. 2.01.242
made me compare with hermia's sphery eyne! 2.02. 99
you your kindred hath made my eyes water ere now 3.01.194 P
made senseless things begin to do them wrong, 3.02. 28
the hate i bare thee made me leave thee so? 3.02.190
and made your other love, demetrius | (who even 3.02.224
now i perceive that she hath made compare 3.02.290
you minimus, of hind'ring knot–grass made; 3.02.329
i with the morning's love have oft made sport, 3.02.389
had gone forward, we had all been made men. 4.02. 18 P
i must confess, | made mine eyes water; 5.01. 69
what stuff 'tis made of, whereof it is born, | i MV 1.01. 4
i would have stay'd till i had made you merry, 1.01. 60
than if you had made waste of all i have. 1.01.157
god made him, and therefore let him pass for a 1.02. 56 P
after dinner | your hazard shall be made. 2.01. 45
we have not made good preparation. 2.04. 4
pigeons fly | to seal love's bonds new made, 2.06. 6
not i, but my affairs, have made you wait. 2.06. 22
knapp'd ginger or made her neighbors believe she 3.01. 9 P
knew the tailor that made the wings she flew 3.01. 27 P
having made one, | methinks it should have power 3.02.124
i'll not be made a soft and dull–ey'd fool | to 3.03. 14
many that have at times made moan to me; 3.03. 23
by my husband, he hath made me a christian! 3.05. 20 P
why he hath made the ewe bleak for the lamb; 4.01. 74
let their beds | be made as soft as yours, and 4.01. 96
she made me vow | that i should neither sell, 4.01.442
and made him swear | never to part with it, and 5.01.170
i am helping you to mar that which god made, a AYL 1.01. 33 P
when nature hath made a fair creature, may she 1.02. 43 P
were you made the messenger? 1.02. 59 P
be better supplied when i have made it empty. 1.02.193 P
way | to hide us from pursuit that will be made 1.03.136
hath not old custom made this life more sweet 2.01. 2
that i made yesterday in despite of my invention 2.05. 46 P
a woeful ballad | made to his mistress' eyebrow. 2.07.149
but were i not the better part made mercy, | i 3.01. 2
i think 'twas made of atalanta's heels. 3.02.276 P
truly, i would the gods had made thee poetical. 3.03. 16 P
wish then that the gods had made me poetical? 3.03. 23 P
now show the wound mine eye hath made in thee. 3.05. 20
me, | for i am falser than vows made in wine. 3.05. 73
her (for i see love hath made thee a tame snake) 4.03. 70 P
occasion, | made him give battle to the lioness, 4.03.130
that grapes were made to eat and lips to open. 5.01. 35 P
these degrees have they made a pair of stairs to 5.02. 37 P
it is to be all made of sighs and tears, | and 5.02. 84
it is to be all made of faith and service, | and 5.02. 89
it is to be all made of fantasy, | all made of 5.02. 94
all made of passion, and all made of wishes, 5.02. 95
all made of passion, and all made of wishes, 5.02. 95
when earthly things made even | atone together. 5.04.109
how silver made it good | at the hedge–corner, SHR in.1. 19
that made great jove to humble him to her hand, 1.01.169
and through the instrument my pate made way, 2.01.154
asses are made to bear, and so are you. 2.01.199
women are made to bear, and so are you. 2.01.200
i see a woman may be made a fool, | if she had 3.02.220
nathaniel's coat, sir, was not fully made, | and 4.01.132
the gown is made | just as my master had 4.03.115
but how did you desire it should be made? 4.03.119
made me acquainted with a weighty cause | of 4.04. 26
dower, | the match is made, and all is done: 4.04. 46
for our first merriment hath made thee jealous. 4.05. 76
that have by marriage made thy daughter mine, 5.01.116
love | made me exchange my state with tranio, 5.01.125
so far, would have made nature immortal, and AWW 1.01. 20 P
with the breach yourselves made, you lose your 1.01.125 P
that you were made of is metal to make virgins. 1.01.129 P
idle, made of self–love, which is the most 1.01.144 P
my lord your son made me to think of this; 1.03.232
a further use to be made than alone the recov'ry 2.03. 36 P
you have made shift to run into't, boots and 2.05. 36 P
ring, and thinks himself made in the unchaste 4.03. 18 P
in fine, made a groan of her last breath, and 4.03. 52 P
half won is match well made; 4.03.225
of your army and made such pestiferous reports 4.03.305 P
saffron would have made all the unbak'd and 4.05. 3 P
my lord that's gone made himself much sport out 4.05. 64 P
lady, of that i have made a bold charter, but i 4.05. 92 P
but since you have made the days and nights as 5.01. 3
and our esteem | was made much poorer by it; 5.03. 2
course of honor | as she had made the overture, 5.03. 99
world | till i had made mine own occasion mellow TN 1.02. 43
she made good view of me; 2.02. 19
for such as we are made /of, such we be. 2.02. 32
go to, thou art made if thou desir'st to be so; 2.05.155 P
"go to, thou art made, if thou desir'st to be 3.04. 52 P
am i made? 3.04. 54 P
bloody and so dear, | hast made thine enemies? 5.01. 72
who hath made this havoc with them? 5.01.202 P
the vows | we made each other but so late ago. 5.01.215
how have you made division of yourself? 5.01.222
that day that made my sister thirteen years. 5.01.248
and made the most notorious geck and gull | that 5.01.343
a solemn combination shall be made | of our dear 5.01.383
and royal necessities made separation of their WT 1.01. 26 P
th' offenses we have made you do we'll answer, 1.02. 83
petitions, made | his business more material. 1.02.215
his revenges must | in that be made more bitter. 1.02.457
a semicircle, | or a half–moon made with a pen. 2.01. 11
for 'tis polixenes | has made thee swell thus. 2.01. 62
all other circumstances | made up to th' deed), 2.01.179
which hast made it | so like to him that got it, 2.03.104
you have made fault | i' th' boldness of your 3.02.217
hath made thy person for the thrower–out | of my 3.03. 29
i have of thee, thine own goodness hath made. 4.02. 12 P
having made me businesses which none without 4.02. 14 P
but my father hath made her mistress of the 4.03. 40 P
she hath made me four and twenty nosegays for 4.03. 41 P
when my good falcon made her flight across | thy 4.04. 15
yet nature is made better by no mean | but 4.04. 89
that have made themselves all men of hair. 4.04.326 P
i the fairest youth | that ever made eye swerve, 4.04.374
have thy beauty scratch'd with briers and made 4.04.425
there's no disjunction to be made, but by | (as 4.04.529
yet nature might have made me as these are, 4.04.746
hang him, he'll be made an example. 4.04.817 P
so much | that heirless it hath made my kingdom, 5.01. 10
i thought of her, | even in these looks i made. 5.01.228
this is a match, | and made between 's by vows. 5.03.138
this might have been prevented and made whole JN 1.01. 35
that judge hath made me guardian to this boy, 2.01.115
i am not worth this coil that's made for me. 2.01.165
but god hath made her sin and her the plague 2.01.185
and wide havoc made | for bloody power to rush 2.01.220
who by the hand of france this day hath made 2.01.302
two such shores to two such streams made one, 2.01.443
gates, | let in that amity which you have made, 2.01.537
for this match made up | her presence would have 2.01.541
this league that we have made | will give her 2.01.545
well, | made to run even upon even ground, 2.01.576
this news hath made thee a most ugly man. 3.01. 37
and made his majesty the bawd to theirs. 3.01. 59
no bargains break that are not this day made: 3.01. 93
and our oppression hath made up this league. 3.01.106
let thy vow | first made to heaven, first be to 3.01.266
made hard with kneeling, i do pray to thee, 3.01.310
had bak'd thy blood and made it heavy, thick, 3.03. 43
thou hast made me giddy | with these ill tidings 4.02.131
accompt 'twixt heaven and earth | is to be made, 4.02.217
made it no conscience to destroy a prince. 4.02.229
hadst thou but shook thy head or made a pause 4.02.231
shame had struck me dumb, made me break off, 4.02.235
forgive the comment that my passion made | upon 4.02.263
death, made proud with pure and princely beauty! 4.03. 35
me, | and i have made a happy peace with him, 5.01. 63
and come ye now to tell me john hath made | his 5.02. 91
because that john hath made his peace with rome? 5.02. 96
but stay'd and made the western welkin blush, 5.05. 2
to be so sad to–night | as this hath made me. 5.05. 16
which made the fault that we cannot correct, R2 1.02. 5
mould, that fashioned thee | made him a man; 1.02. 24
ignorance | is made my jailer to attend on me. 1.03.169
expedient manage must be made, my liege, | ere 1.04. 39
hath made a shameful conquest of itself. 2.01. 66
and therein fasting, hast thou made me gaunt. 2.01. 81
now he that made me knows i see thee ill, | ill 2.01. 93
have ever made me sour my patient cheek, | or 2.01.169
now comes the sick hour that his surfeit made, 2.02. 84
base men by his endowments are made great. 2.03.139
made a divorce betwixt his queen and him, 3.01. 12
that power that made you king | hath power to 3.02. 27
i warrant they have made peace with bullingbrook 3.02.127
peace have they made with him indeed, my lord. 3.02.128
their souls, their peace is made | with heads, 3.02.137
and yet not so, for with a kiss 'twas made. 5.01. 75
when weeping made you break the story off, | of 5.02. 2
for now hath time made me his numb'ring clock: 5.05. 50
this hand hath made him proud with clapping him. 5.05. 86
i was not made a horse, | and yet i bear a 5.05. 92
for he made me mad | to see him shine so brisk 1H4 1.03. 53
brother, the king hath made your nephew mad. 1.03.138
i have not ballads made on you all and sung to 2.02. 45 P
match have you made with this jest of the drawer 2.04. 90 P
i made me no more ado but took all their seven 2.04.201 P
the lord, i knew ye as well as he that made ye. 2.04.268 P
the bastinado and made lucifer cuckold and swore 2.04.337 P
thou art essentially made, without seeming so. 2.04.492 P
three times hath henry bullingbrook made head 3.01. 63
once, | enlarg'd him and made a friend of him, 3.02.115
what the inside of a church is made of, i am a 3.03. 8 P
bakers' wives, they have made bolters of them. 3.03. 70 P
for thy theft hath already made thee butter. 4.02. 61 P
little higher than his vow | made to my father, 4.03. 76
and made us doff our easy robes of peace, | to 5.01. 12
indeed, | he made a blushing cital of himself, 5.02. 61
i have paid percy, i have made him sure. 5.03. 47 P
having been well, that would have made me sick, 2H4 1.01.138
being sick, have (in some measure) made me well. 1.01.139
pregnancy is made a tapster, and his quick wit 1.02.170 P
a woman should be made an ass and a beast, to 2.01. 37 P
and made her serve your uses both in purse and 2.01.115 P
eyes, and methought he had made two holes in the 2.02. 82 P
have of their puissance made a little taste. 2.03. 52
methought 'a made a shrewd thrust at your belly. 2.04.211 P
'a would have made a good pantler, 'a would 'a' 2.04.238 P
like a man made after supper of a cheese–paring. 3.02.309 P
retrait is made and execution stay'd. 4.03. 72
let there be no noise made, my gentle friends, 4.05. 1
well, peace be with him that hath made us heavy! 5.02. 25
if i had had time to have made new liveries, i 5.05. 11 P
never was such a sudden scholar made; H5 1.01. 32
you would desire the king were made a prelate; 1.01. 40
for i have made an offer to his majesty, | upon 1.01. 75
tell him he hath made a match with such a 1.02.264
days, | not measuring what use we made of them. 1.02.268
'a made a finer end, and went away and it had 2.03. 11 P
by french fathers | had twenty years been made. 2.04. 62
whose limbs were made in england, show us here 3.01. 26
fault | my father made in compassing the crown! 4.01.294
let him depart, his passport shall be made, 4.03. 36
out of my mouth, ere it is made and finished. 4.07. 43 P
you been as i took you for, i made no offense; 4.08. 55 P
to the which, as yet, | there is no answer made. 5.02. 75
fortune made his sword; ep 6
they lost france, and made his england bleed; ep 12
the church's prayers made him so prosperous. 1H6 1.01. 32
our isle be made a nourish of salt tears, | and 1.01. 50
my grisly countenance made others fly, | none 1.04. 47
but weakly guarded, where the breach was made. 2.01. 74
by him that made me, i'll maintain my words | on 2.04. 88
how joyful am i made by this contract! 3.01.143
and made me almost yield upon my knees. 3.03. 80
which join'd with him and made their march for 4.03. 8
the sword of orleance hath not made me smart; 4.06. 42
heart | suddenly made him from my side to start 4.07. 12
doubtless he would have made a noble knight. 4.07. 44
your bondage happy, to be made a queen? 5.03.111
a child, | fit to be made companion with a king. 5.03.149
have made thee fear'd and honor'd of the people; 2H6 1.01.198
style, | and must be made a subject to a duke? 1.03. 49
but what a point, my lord, your falcon made, 2.01. 5
and made me climb, with danger of my life. 2.01.101
it made me laugh to see the villain run. 2.01.152
true; made the lame to leap and fly away. 2.01.158
you made in a day, my lord, whole towns to fly. 2.01.160
resign | as ere thy father henry made it mine; 2.03. 34
was made a wonder and a pointing–stock | to 2.04. 46
made me collect these dangers in the duke. 3.01. 35
but mine is made the prologue to their play; 3.01.151
it may be judg'd i made the duke away, | so 3.02. 67
that is to see how deep my grave is made, | for 3.02.150
well–proportion'd beard made rough and rugged, 3.02.175
will suspect 'twas he that made the slaughter? 3.02.190
and get thee a sword, though made of a lath; 4.02. 1 P
of an innocent lamb should be made parchment? 4.02. 80 P
sir, he made a chimney in my father's house, and 4.02.148 P
gelded the commonwealth, and made it an eunuch; 4.02.166 P
he that made us pay one and twenty fifteens, and 4.07. 21 P
hath made me full of sickness and diseases. 4.07. 89
henry the fift, that made all france to quake, 4.08. 17
crept out of my cradle | but i was made a king, 4.09. 4
this hand was made to handle nought but gold. 5.01. 7
thy hand is made to grasp a palmer's staff | and 5.01. 97
and made a prey for carrion kites and crows 5.02. 11
hath made the wizard famous in his death. 5.02. 69
what are you made of? 5.02. 74
and where this breach now in our fortunes made 5.02. 82
hath made us by–words to our enemies. 3H6 1.01. 42

for shame, come down. he made thee duke of york. 1.01. 77
who made the dolphin and the french to stoop, 1.01.108
and made him to resign his crown perforce. 1.01.142
rather than have made that savage duke thine 1.01.224
seas, | the duke is made protector of the realm, 1.01.240
hath made her break out into terms of rage! 1.01.265
then, seeing 'twas he that made you to depose, 1.02. 26
and made an evening at the noontide prick. 1.04. 34
whose frown hath made thee faint and fly ere 1.04. 48
and made a preachment of your high descent? 1.04. 72
point | made issue from the bosom of the boy; 1.04. 81
made impudent with use of evil deeds, | i would 1.04.117
who having pinch'd a few and made them cry, 2.01. 16
by him that made us all, i am resolv'd | that 2.02.124
and tam'd the king and made the dolphin stoop; 2.02.151
but when we saw our sunshine made thy spring, 2.02.163
the match is made, she seals it with a cur'sy. 3.02. 57
when he was made a shriver, 'twas for shift. 3.02.108
hath not our brother made a worthy choice? 4.01. 3
how could he stay till warwick made return? 4.01. 5
for he hath made a solemn vow | never to lie and 4.03. 4
for that it made my imprisonment a pleasure; 4.06. 11
unsavory news! but how made he escape? 4.06. 80
the gates made fast? 4.07. 10
i am so sorry for my trespass made | that, to 5.01. 92
is proclamation made, that who finds edward 5.05. 9
and made the forest tremble when they roar'd. 5.07. 12
our seat, | and made our footstool of security. 5.07. 14
made glorious summer by this son of york; R3 1.01. 2
nor made to court an amorous looking–glass; 1.01. 15
into this breathing world, scarce half made up, 1.01. 21
that made him send lord hastings to the tower, 1.01. 68
that the queen's kindred are made gentlefolks. 1.01. 95
by the self–same hand that made these wounds! 1.02. 11
o, cursed be the hand that made these holes! 1.02. 14
let her be made | more miserable by the /life of 1.02. 26
him | than i am made by my young lord and thee! 1.02. 28
for thou hast made the happy earth thy hell, 1.02. 51
to hear the piteous moan that rutland made 1.02.157
and twenty times made pause to sob and weep, 1.02.161
beauty hath, and made them blind with weeping. 1.02.166
for it was made | for kissing, lady, not for 1.02.171
say then my peace is made. 1.02.197
prince | and made her widow to a woeful bed? 1.02.248
there's many a gentle person made a jack. 1.03. 72
hell, | such terrible impression made my dream. 1.04. 63
it made me once restore a purse of gold that (by 1.04.139 P
who made thee then a bloody minister, | when 1.04.220
since i have made my friends at peace on earth. 2.01. 6
made peace of enmity, fair love of hate, 2.01. 51
i hope the king made peace with all of us, | and 2.02.132
the weary way hath made you melancholy. 3.01. 3
our crosses on the way | have made it tedious, 3.01. 5
made him my book, wherein my soul recorded | the 3.05. 27
made prize and purchase of his wanton eye, 3.07.187
i am not made of stones, | but penetrable to 3.07.224
than thou hast made me by my dear lord's death!" 4.01. 76
made i him king for this? 4.02.120
unlawfully made drunk with innocent blood! 4.04. 30
and by that loss your daughter is made queen. 4.04.308
the unity the king my husband made | thou hadst 4.04.379
thy broken faith hath made the prey for worms. 4.04.386
such proclamation hath been made, my lord. 4.04.517
sail, and made his course again for britain. 4.04.527
the weary sun hath made a golden set, | and by 5.03. 19
one that made means to come by what he hath, 5.03.248
made precious by the foil | of england's chair, 5.03.250
master, till the last | made former wonders its. H8 1.01. 18
and, to–morrow, they | made britain india: 1.01. 21
th' ensuing night | made it a fool and beggar. 1.01. 28
but when the way was made | and pav'd with gold, 1.01.187
salisbury, | made suit to come in 's presence; 1.02.197
if granted | (as he made semblance of his duty) 1.02.198
devil monk, | hopkins, that made this mischief. 2.01. 22
and out of ruins | made my name once more noble. 2.01.115
and all | that made me happy, at one stroke has 2.01.117
as i am made without him, so i'll stand, | if 2.02. 51
so i leave him | to him that made him proud, the 2.02. 55
then you are weakly made; 2.03. 40
or made it not mine too? 2.04. 29
hind'red, oft, | the passages made toward it. 2.04.166
and made to tremble | the region of my breast, 2.04.184
her male issue | or died where they were made, 2.04.193
made to the queen to call back her appeal | she 2.04.235
orpheus with his lute made trees, | and the 3.01. 3
and showers | there had made a lasting spring. 3.01. 8
have i not made you | the prime man of the state 3.02.161
made me put this main secret in the packet | i 3.02.215
you made bold | to carry into flanders the great 3.02.318
glad your grace has made that right use of it. 3.02.386
and the late marriage made of none effect; 4.01. 33
the king has made him master | o' th' jewel 4.01.110
whom i most hated living, thou hast made me, 4.02. 73
highness' pardon, | my haste made me unmannerly. 4.02.105
the jewel house, is made master | o' th' rolls, 5.01. 34
and that her suff'rance made | almost each pang 5.01. 68
long | to have this young one made a christian. 5.02.213
as i have made ye one, lords, one remain: 5.02.214
could distribute, | i made no spare, sir. 5.03. 21
they fell on, i made good my place; 5.03. 54 P
y' have made a fine hand, fellows! 5.03. 70
lord archbishop, | thou hast made me now a man! 5.04. 64
love hath given me | the knife that made it. TRO 1.01. 63
to harbor fled, | or made a toast for neptune. 1.03. 45
they place before his hand that made the engine, 1.03.208
you must be watch'd ere you be made tame, must 3.02. 44 P
go to, a bargain made, seal it, seal it, i'll be 3.02.197 P
made tame and most familiar to my nature; 3.03. 10
which are devour'd | as fast as they are made, 3.03.149
though they are made and moulded of things past, 3.03.177
late, | made emulous missions 'mongst the gods 3.03.189
this ajax is half made of hector's blood, | in 4.05. 83
wherein my sword had not impressure made | /of 4.05.131
two months hence my will shall here be made. 5.10. 52
well, sir, what answer made the belly? COR 1.01.106
that meat was made for mouths, that the gods 1.01.207
and hear | how the dispatch is made, and in what 1.01.277
we never yet made doubt but rome was ready | to 1.02. 18
to hang by th' wall, if renown made it not stir, 1.03. 12 P
by th' vows | we have made to endure friends, 1.06. 58
corioles walls, | and made what work i pleas'd. 1.08. 9
cities be | made all of false–fac'd soothing! 1.09. 44
let him be made an overture for th' wars! 1.09. 46
to 's power he would | have made them mules, 2.01.247
and the commons made | a shower and thunder with 2.01.266
when blows have made me stay, i fled from words. 2.02. 72
when tarquin made a head for rome, he fought 2.02. 88
and by his rare example made the coward | turn 2.02.104
made you against the grain | to voice him consul 2.03.233
tullus aufidius then had made new head? 3.01. 1
which they have often made against the senate, 3.01.128
said | my praises made thee first a soldier, so, 3.02.108
is this the promise that you made your mother? 3.03. 86
and not unknit himself | the noble knot he made. 4.02. 32
city, | 'tis i that made thy widows; 4.04. 2
gave me his clothes made a false report of him. 4.05.151 P
he is so made on here within as if he were son 4.05.191 P
o, you have made good work! 4.06. 80
you have made fair work, i fear me. 4.06. 88
a thing | made by some other deity than nature, 4.06. 91
you have made good work, | you and your 4.06. 95
you have made fair work! 4.06.100
you have made fair hands, | you and your crafts! 4.06.117
you are they | that made the air unwholesome, 4.06.130
you have made | good work, you and your cry! 4.06.146
for i dare so far free him — made him fear'd, 4.07. 47
you have made good work! 5.01. 15
to infringe my vow | in the same time 'tis made? 5.03. 21
arms, | could not have made this peace. 5.03.209
in his state, as a thing made for alexander. 5.04. 22 P
made him joint–servant with me; 5.06. 31
what faults he made before the last, i think 5.06. 63
we have made peace | with no less honor to the 5.06. 78
thou hast made my heart | too great for what 5.06.102
thou com'st not to be made a scorn in rome; TIT 1.01.265
ay, for these slips have made him noted long, 2.03. 86
indeed | till all the andronici be made away. 2.03.189
that ever eye with sight made heart lament! 2.03.205
how these were they that made away his brother. 2.03.208
if fear hath made thee faint, as me it hath — 2.03.234
and made thy body bare | of her two branches, 2.04. 17
harmony | which that sweet tongue hath made, 2.04. 49
hath made thee handless in thy father's sight? 3.01. 67
and made a brine–pit with our bitter tears? 3.01.129
the vow is made. 3.01.279
that made me to fear, | although, my lord, i 4.01. 21
which made me down to throw my books, and fly — 4.01. 25
by nature made for murthers and for rapes. 4.01. 58
the midwife and the nurse well made away, | then 4.02.167
i made thee miserable | what time i threw the 4.03. 18
for /then hast made it like an humble suppliant. 4.03.117
i made unto the noise, when soon i heard | the 5.01. 25
witness these trenches made by grief and care, 5.02. 23
death, | my hand cut off and made a merry jest; 5.02.174
kill'd her for whom my tears have made me blind. 5.03. 49
and made verona's ancient citizens | cast by ROM 1.01. 92
towards him i made, but he was ware of me, | and 1.01.124
love is a smoke made with the fume of sighs, 1.01.190
younger than she are happy mothers made. 1.02. 12
and too soon marr'd are those so early made. 1.02. 13
ladies of esteem, | are made already mothers. 1.03. 71
made by the joiner squirrel or old grub, | time 1.04. 60
her waggon–spokes made of long spinners' legs, 1.04. 62
we met, we woo'd, and made exchange of vow, 2.03. 62
thou wouldst else have made thy tale large. 2.04. 97 P
i would have made it short, for i was come to 2.04. 98 P
gentlewoman, that god hath made, himself to mar. 2.04.115 P
and bring thee cords made like a tackled stair, 2.04.189
well, you have made a simple choice, you know 2.05. 38 P
men's eyes were made to look, and let them gaze; 3.01. 54
they have made worms' meat of me. 3.01.107
juliet, | thy beauty hath made me effeminate, 3.01.114
he made you for a highway to my bed, | but i, a 3.02.134
on the ground, with his own tears made drunk. 3.03. 83
that, to hear them told, have made me tremble — 4.01. 86
sirrah, what made your master in this place? 5.03.280
he wrought better that made the painter, and yet TIM 1.01.198 P
o, joy's e'en made away ere't can be born! 1.02.106 P
and that unaptness made your minister | thus to 2.02.131
the breath is gone whereof this praise is made. 2.02.170
carriage, | had his necessity made use of me, 3.02. 82
knew not what he did when he made man politic; 3.03. 28 P
believe't, my lord and i have made an end: 3.04. 55
in the last conflict, and made plenteous wounds! 3.05. 65
he has made too much plenty with /'em. 3.05. 66
so low with him as he made it seem in the trial 3.06. 6 P
great fortunes | are made thy chief afflictions. 4.02. 44
in sufferance, time | hath made thee hard in't. 4.03.269
an alteration of honor has desp'rate want made! 4.03.462
timon hath made his everlasting mansion | upon 5.01.215
yet our old love made a particular force, | and 5.02. 8
force, | and made us speak like friends. 5.02. 9
appear, | have you not made an universal shout, JC 1.01. 44
of your sounds | made in her concave shores? 1.01. 47
then i know | my answer must be made. 1.03.114
there's a bargain made. 1.03.120
i have made strong proof of my constancy, 2.01.299
as that same ague which hath made you lean. 2.02.113
made rich | with the most noble blood of all 3.01.155
ambition should be made of sterner stuff: 3.02. 92
and let me show you him that made the will. 3.02.159
see what a rent the envious casca made; 3.02.175
have, alas, i know not, | that made them do it. 3.02.214
our best friends made, our means stretch'd, 4.01. 44
mark antony | have made themselves so strong — 4.03.154
witness the hole you made in caesar's heart, 5.01. 31
if not, why then this parting was well made. 5.01.118
if not, 'tis true this parting was well made. 5.01.121
and common good to all, made one of them. 5.05. 72
question them further, they made themselves air, MAC 1.05. 4 P
hath made his pendant bed and procreant cradle. 1.06. 8
that made you break this enterprise to me? 1.07. 48
they have made themselves, and that their 1.07. 53
mine eyes are made the fools o' th' other senses 2.01. 44
that which hath made them drunk hath made me 2.02. 1
which hath made them drunk hath made me bold; 2.02. 1
legs sometime, yet i made a shift to cast him. 2.03. 41 P
confusion now hath made his masterpiece! 2.03. 66
why, by the verities on thee made good, | may 3.01. 8
this i made good to you | in our last conference 3.01. 78
you made it known to us. 3.01. 83
and shrieks that rent the air | are made, not 4.03.169
had made his course t' illume that part of HAM 1.01. 37
herein | this present object made probation. 1.01.156
and full proportions are all made | out of his 1.02. 32
form of the thing, each word made true and good, 1.02.210
my lord, i did, | but answer made it none. 1.02.215
of late made many tenders | of his affection to 1.03. 99
even with the vow | i made to her in marriage, 1.05. 50
no reck'ning made, but sent to my account | with 1.05. 78
that hath made him mad. 2.01.107
the instant burst of clamor that she made, 2.02.515
would have made milch the burning eyes of heaven 2.02.517
and most dear life | a damn'd defeat was made. 2.02.571
compos'd | as made these things more rich. 3.01. 98
indeed, my lord, you made me believe so. 3.01.115 P
go to, i'll no more on't, it hath made me mad. 3.01.147 P
some of nature's journeymen had made men, and 3.02. 34 P
journeymen had made men, and not made them well, 3.02. 34 P
now what my /love is, proof hath made you know, 3.02.169
so i shall, | if it be made of penetrable stuff, 3.04. 36
be thou assur'd, if words be made of breath, 3.04.197
replication should be made by the son of a king? 4.02. 13 P
sure he that made us with such large discourse, 4.04. 36
they say 'a made a good end — "for bonny sweet 4.05.186 P
that we are made of stuff so flat and dull 4.07. 31
he made confession of you, | and gave you such a 4.07. 95
custom hath made it in him a property of 5.01. 67 P
a pit of clay for to be made | for such a guest 5.01. 96
is not parchment made of sheep–skins? 5.01.114 P
a pit of clay for to be made | /for /such /a 5.01.120
till of this flat a mountain you have made | t' 5.01.252
in our court have made their amorous sojourn, LR 1.01. 47
i am made of that self metal as my sister, | and 1.01. 69
bear, | our potency made good, take thy reward. 1.01.172
leave her, sir, for, by the pow'r that made me, 1.01.207
observation we have made of it hath /not been 1.01.289 P
no, boy, nothing can be made out of nothing. 1.04.132 P
or whether gasted by the noise i made, | full 2.01. 55
a tailor made thee. 2.02. 55 P
or a painter could not have made him so ill, 2.02. 59 P
made you no more offense but what you speak of? 2.04. 61
made you my guardians, my depositaries, | but 2.04.251
yet fair woman but she made mouths in a glass. 3.02. 35 P
by his porridge, made him proud of heart, to 3.04. 55 P
evil disposition made him seek his death; 3.05. 6 P
or false, it hath made thee earl of gloucester. 3.05. 17 P
that made the overture of thy treasons to us, 3.07. 89
fellow saw, | which made me think a man a worm. 4.01. 33
a most poor man, made tame to fortune's blows, 4.06.221
yet to be known shortens my made intent. 4.07. 9
my two sisters | have in thy reverence made. 4.07. 28
biting falchion | i would have made /them skip. 5.03.278
leave), | i say again, hath made a gross revolt, OTH 1.01.134
if it prove lawful prize, he's made for ever. 1.02. 51
wish'd | that heaven had made her such a man. 1.03.163
hath made the flinty and steel /couch of war 1.03.230
when the blood is made dull with the act of 2.01.227 P
the wine she drinks is made of grapes. 2.01.252 P
the purchase made, the fruits are to ensue; 2.03. 9
he hath not yet made wanton the night with her; 2.03. 16 P
i have made bold, iago, | to send in to your 3.01. 33
and fools as gross | as ignorance made drunk. 3.03.405
can any thing be made of this? 3.04. 10 P
mind, and made of no such baseness | as jealious 3.04. 27
or made a gift of it, my father's eye | should 3.04. 61
made demonstrable here in cyprus to him, | hath 3.04.142
each syllable that breath made up between them. 4.02. 5
most goodly book, | made to write "whore" upon? 4.02. 72
and made you to suspect me with the moor. 4.02.147
o mistress, villainy hath made mocks with love! 5.02.151
i have made my way through more impediments 5.02.263
that he made him | brave me upon the watch, 5.02.325
and the time's state | made friends of them, ANT 1.02. 92
her passions are made of nothing but the finest 1.02.146 P
your wife and brother | made wars upon me, and 2.02. 43
made out of her impatience — which not wanted 2.02. 68
to have me out of egypt, made wars here; 2.02. 95
and made the night light with drinking. 2.02.178 P
and made | the water which they beat to follow 2.02.195
i' th' eyes, | and made their bends adornings. 2.02.208
on cleopatra too, | and made a gap in nature. 2.02.218
she made great caesar lay his sword to bed; 2.02.227
i made no such report. 2.05. 57
i that do bring the news made not the match. 2.05. 67
i have made no fault. 2.05. 74
so half my egypt were submerg'd and made | a 2.05. 94
and what | i made all–honor'd, honest, roman 2.06. 16
and that is it | hath made me rig my navy, at 2.06. 20
you have made me offer | of sicily, sardinia; 2.06. 34
pompey, would ne'er have made this treaty. 2.06. 83 P
of that purpose made more in the marriage than 2.06.118 P
they have made him drink alms–drink. 2.07. 5 P
made his will, and read it | to public ear; 3.04. 4
caesar and lepidus have made wars upon pompey. 3.05. 4 P
having made use of him in the wars 'gainst 3.05. 7 P
their lust | since then hath made between them. 3.06. 8
of egypt, made her | of lower syria, cyprus, 3.06. 9
and that | my sword, made weak by my affection, 3.11. 67
him repent | thou wast not made his daughter, 3.13.135
never anger | made good guard for itself. 4.01. 10
i wish i could be made so many men, | and all of 4.02. 16
that was like a t, | but now 'tis made an h. 4.07. 8
i made these wars for egypt, and the queen, 4.14. 15
green neptune's back | with ships made cities, 4.14. 59
enough to purchase what you have made known. 5.02.148
words you send, | though ink be made of gall. CYM 1.01.101
beggar, wouldst have made my throne | a seat for 1.01.141
of action hath made you reek as a sacrifice. 1.02. 2 P
thou shouldst have made him | as little as a 1.03. 14
and th' assault you have made to her chastity, 1.04.162 P
it is a thing i made, which hath the king | five 1.05. 62
with hands | made hard with hourly falsehood 1.06.107
the king my father shall be made acquainted | of 1.06.149

the love i bear him | made me to fan you thus, 1.06.177
made me to fan you thus, but the gods made you 1.06.177
if 'twere made | comparative for your virtues, 2.03.128
hairs above thee, | were they all made such men. 2.03.136
i hope the briefness of your answer made | the 2.04. 30
of no more bondage be to where they are made 2.04.111
if thou dost deny | thou'st made me cuckold. 2.04.146
coiner with his tools | made me a counterfeit; 2.05. 6
a kind of conquest | caesar made here, but made 3.01. 23
here, but made not here his brag | of "came, and 3.01. 23
made lud's–town with rejoicing fires bright, 3.01. 32
mulmutius made our laws, | who was the first of 3.01. 58
and vows which i | have made to thy command? 3.02. 13
tell me how wales was made so happy as | t' 3.02. 60
trims, wherein | you made great juno angry. 3.04.165
that it would be thus | hath made us forward. 3.05. 29
like | a thing more made of malice than of duty, 3.05. 33
our great court | made me to blame in memory. 3.05. 51
nights together | have made the ground my bed. 3.06. 3
it on the board so soon | as i had made my meal, 3.06. 51
fault, i should | have died had i not made it. 3.06. 57
who was made by him that made the tailor, not be 4.01. 3 P
who was made by him that made the tailor, not be 4.01. 4 P
he made those clothes, | which, as it seems, 4.02. 82
thou precious varlet, | my tailor made them not. 4.02. 84
being scarce made up, | i mean, to man, he had 4.02.109
the bird is dead | that we have made so much on. 4.02.198
jove knows what man thou mightst have made; 4.02.207
cam'st thou from where they made the stand? 5.03. 1
made good the passage, cried to those that fled, 5.03. 23
slaves, | the strides /they victors made: 5.03. 43
you are made | rather to wonder at the things 5.03. 53
for if he'll do as he is made to do, | i know 5.03. 61
great the slaughter is | here made by th' roman; 5.03. 79
and happier much by his affliction made. 5.04.108
bring'st good news, i am call'd to be made free. 5.04.194 P
you whom the gods have made | preservers of my 5.05. 1
whose kinsmen have made suit | that their good 5.05. 71
for beauty that made barren the swell'd boast 5.05.162
picture, which by his tongue being made, | and 5.05.175
made scruple of his praise, and wager'd with him 5.05.182
i had you down and might | have made you finish. 5.05.412
the vision | which i made known to lucius, ere 5.05.468
sinful dame | made many princes thither frame PER 1.ch. 32
which to prevent he made a law, | to keep her 1.ch. 35
you gods that made me man, and sway in love, 1.01. 19
what pitiful cries they made to us to help them, 2.01. 21 P
hath made the ball | for them to play upon, 2.01. 60
'twas we that made up this garment through the 2.01.149 P
or know what ground's made happy by his breath. 2.04. 28
to any syllable that made love to you. 2.05. 70
made louder by the o'erfed breast | of this most 3.ch. 3
is made with all due diligence | that horse and 3.ch. 19
surprise and fear | made me to quit the house. 3.02. 18
made familiar | to me and to my aid the blest 3.02. 34
which she made more sound | by hurting it; 4.ch. 24
lute | she sung, and made the night/–bird mute, 4.ch. 26
poop'd him, she made him roast–meat for worms. 4.02. 24 P
at the proclamation, but he made a groan at it, 4.02.108 P
on whom foul death hath made this slaughter. 4.04. 37
hath your principal made known unto you who i am 4.06. 82 P
us, | i made to it to know of whence you are. 5.01. 19
is like to be, | that thus hath made me weep. 5.01.185
and pretty din, | the regent made in metelin, 5.02. 8
she | made known herself my daughter. 5.03. 13
it to some pity, | though it were made of stone. TNK 1.01.129
where nor gain | made him regard, or loss 1.03. 30
who made too proud the bed, took leave o' th' 1.03. 52
you have made me | (i thank you, cousin arcite) 2.02. 95
night and stow her, | and all's made up again. 2.03. 33
mark how his body's made for't. 2.03. 71
what made you seek this place, sir? 2.05. 25
i have made him know it. 2.06. 12
he made such scruples of the wrong he did | to 2.06. 25
strong note of me, | hath made me near her; 3.01. 18
falsest cousin | that ever blood made kin! 3.01. 38
why may't not be | they have made prey of him? 3.02. 13
made her groan a month for't; 3.03. 35
if we can get her dance, we are made again. 3.05. 74
a mad woman? we are made, boys! 3.05. 76
if you but favor, our country pastime made is. 3.05.102
come, we are all made. 3.05.158
that oath was rashly made, and in your anger, 3.06.227
not made in passion neither, but good heed. 3.06.232
but yet perceiv'd not | who made the sound, the 4.01. 61
to bury you, | and see the house made handsome. 4.01. 79
rings she made | of rushes that grew by, and to 4.01. 88
i made in to her. 4.01. 94
away, and to the city made | with such a cry and 4.01. 97
be made the altar where the lives of lovers — 4.02. 61
and two better never yet | made mothers joy — 4.02. 63
and vow that lover never yet made sigh | truer 5.01.125
my cousin palamon | has made so fair a choice. 5.02. 92
know best, i pray them he | be made your lot. 5.03. 40
anon | th' assistants made a brave redemption, 5.03. 82
it is a cursed haste you made | if you have done 5.04. 41
as 'twere to th' music | his own hoofs made (for 5.04. 60
or what fierce sulphur else, to this end made, 5.04. 64
and 'a made my brother arthur watchins sergeant STM II.C 42 P
like as if that god | owed not nor made not you, II.C 136
nature that made thee with herself at strife, VEN 11
pure shame and aw'd resistance made him fret, 69
"torches are made to light, jewels to wear, 163
love made those hollows, if himself were slain, 243
and all this dumb play had his acts made plain 359
because adonis' heart hath made mine hard." 378
and once made perfect, never lost again." 408
"so in thyself thyself art made away, | a 763
what needeth then apology be made | to set forth LUC 31
name, | made glorious by his manly chivalry, 109
and made her thrall | to living death and pain 725
that all the faults which in thy reign are made 804
if that be made a theme for disputation, | the 822
when the one pure, the other made divine? 1164
revenge on him that made me stop my breath. 1180
of skillful painting, made for priam's troy, 1367
whose deed hath made herself herself detest. 1566
and that deep vow which brutus made before, | he 1847
when my love swears that she is made of truth, PP 1. 1
a longing tarriance for adonis made | under an 6. 4
pleasant shade, | which a grove of myrtles made, 20. 4
so lively shown, | made me think upon mine own. 20.18
whereupon it made this threne | to the phoenix PHT 49
this were to be new made when thou art old, SON 2.13
let those whom nature hath not made for store, 11. 9
so i, made lame by fortune's dearest spite, 37. 3
mine eyes be blessed made | by looking on thee 43. 9
my life, being made of four, with two alone 45. 7
his rider lov'd not speed, being made from thee. 50. 8
desire (of /perfect'st love being made) | shall 51.10
what is your substance, whereof are you made, 53. 1
of their sweet deaths are sweetest odors made: 54.12
that god forbid, that made me first your slave, 58. 1
and art made tongue–tied by authority, | and 66. 9
ere beauty's dead fleece made another gay: 68. 8
not making worse what nature made so clear, 84.10
there, | and made myself a motley to the view, 110. 2
dear, | made old offenses of affections new; 110. 4
true | that better is by evil still made better, 119.10
lie, | made more or less by thy continual haste. 123.12
when my love swears that she is made of truth, 138. 1
or made them swear against the thing they see; 152.12
love lack'd a dwelling and made him her place; LC 82
all aids, themselves made fairer by their place, 117
their own wills, and made their wills obey. 133
love made them not, with acture they may be, 185
wit well blazon'd, smil'd or made some moan. 217
whose rarest havings made the blossoms dote, 235

MADEIRA 1 FR 0.0001 REL FR 0 V 1 P
for a cup of madeira and a cold capon's leg? 1H4 1.02.116 P

MADE–UP 1 FR 0.0001 REL FR 1 V 0 P
remain assur'd | that he's a made–up villain. TIM 5.01. 98

MAD–HEADED 1 FR 0.0001 REL FR 1 V 0 P
out, you mad–headed ape! 1H4 2.03. 77

MADLY 16 FR 0.0018 REL FR 16 V 0 P
that's somewhat madly spoken. MM 5.01. 89
mad, | that thus so madly thou didst answer me? ERR 2.02. 12
us again, and madly bent on us | chas'd us away; 5.01.152
and certain stars shot madly from their spheres, MND 2.01.153
will make or man or woman madly dote | upon the 2.01.171
sever themselves and madly sweep the sky, | so, 3.02. 23
part, | and venture madly on a desperate mart. SHR 2.01.327
that, being mad herself, she's madly mated. 3.02.244
son, | or madly think a babe of clouts were he. JN 3.04. 58
full of high feeding, madly hath broke loose, 2H4 1.01. 10
so madly hot that no discourse of reason, | nor TRO 2.02.116
and madly play with my forefathers' joints, ROM 4.03. 51
with horror, madly dying, like her life, | which CYM 5.05. 31
which madly hurries her she knows not whither: VEN 904
arm, | is madly toss'd between desire and dread; LUC 171
by reprobate desire thus madly led, | the roman 300

MADLY–US'D 1 FR 0.0001 REL FR 0 V 1 P
the madly–us'd malvolio." TN 5.01.311 P

MADMAN 21 FR 0.0023 REL FR 11 V 10 P
a coward, | one all of luxury, an ass, a madman, MM 5.01.501
a madman? ERR 4.01. 93
in this the madman justly chargeth them. 5.01.213
what wert thou | till this madman show'd thee? LLL 5.02.338
that is the madman. MND 5.01. 10
here's a madman will murder me. SHR 5.01. 58 P
but your words show you a madman. 5.01. 74 P
off, i pray you, he speaks nothing but madman; TN 1.05.107 P
like a drown'd man, a fool, and a madman. 1.05.131 P
madonna, and the fool shall look to the madman. 1.05.138 P
madman, thou errest. 4.02. 42 P
nay, i'll ne'er believe a madman till i see his 4.02.116 P
well edified when the fool delivers the madman. 5.01.291 P
is this the madman? 5.01.327
not mad, but bound more than a madman is; ROM 1.02. 54
madman! 2.01. 7
be call'd desperate ones, for a madman owes 'em. TIM 3.04.102 P
like thyself, | a madman so long, now a fool. 4.03.221
shall i be frighted when a madman stares? JC 4.03. 40
tell me whether a madman be a gentleman or a LR 3.06. 9 P
madman and beggar too. 4.01. 30

MADMAN'S 4 FR 0.0004 REL FR 3 V 1 P
but as a madman's epistles are no gospels, so it TN 5.01.287 P
you put sharp weapons in a madman's hands. 2H6 3.01.347
say | a madman's mercy bid thee run away. ROM 5.03. 67
taught me to shift | into a madman's rags, t' LR 5.03.188

/MADMEN 1 FR 0.0001 REL FR 1 V 0 P
o, then i see that /madmen have no ears. ROM 3.03. 61

MADMEN 9 FR 0.0010 REL FR 5 V 4 P
lovers and madmen have such seething brains, MND 5.01. 4
as well a dark house and a whip as madmen do; AYL 3.02.401 P
the bar and crown thee for a finder of madmen. TN 3.04.141 P
with great imagination | proper to madmen, led 2H4 1.03. 32
little blood they do, i'll be a curer of madmen. TRO 5.01. 50 P
are rid like madmen through the gates of rome. JC 3.02.269
cold night will turn us all to fools and madmen. LR 3.04. 79 P
the time's plague, when madmen lead the blind. 4.01. 46
or else such stuff as madmen | tongue and brain CYM 5.04.145

MADMEN'S 1 FR 0.0001 REL FR 1 V 0 P
my thoughts and my discourse as madmen's are, SON 147.11

/MADNESS 1 FR 0.0001 REL FR 1 V 0 P
/his /roguish /madness | /allows /itself /to LR 3.07.104

MADNESS 71 FR 0.0080 REL FR 55 V 16 P
with cloven tongues | do hiss me into madness. TMP 2.02. 14
amends, with which | i fear a madness held me. 5.01.116
that any madness i ever yet beheld seem'd but WIV 4.02. 26 P
his actions show much like to madness, pray MM 4.04. 4 P
that opinion | that i am touch'd with madness. 5.01. 51
her madness hath the oddest frame of sense, 5.01. 61
of thing on thing, | as e'er i heard in madness. 5.01. 63
bred, | and what's a fever but a fit of madness? ERR 5.01. 76
day | a most outrageous fit of madness took him, 5.01.139
fetter strong madness in a silken thread, ADO 5.01. 25
cold decree — such a hare is madness the youth, MV 1.02. 19 P
him, for if he love me to madness, i shall never 1.02. 64 P
love is merely a madness, and, i tell you, AYL 3.02.400 P
mad humor of love to a living humor of madness, 3.02.419 P
conceiv'd of spleen, and born of madness, that 4.01.213 P
mad as he, | if sad and merry madness equal be. TN 3.04. 15
why, this is very midsummer madness. 3.04. 56 P
that enwraps me thus, | yet 'tis not madness. 4.03. 4
that this may be some error, but no madness, 4.03. 10
thee, fellow — fellow, thy words are madness. 5.01. 98
no, madam, i do but read madness. 5.01.294 P
if not, my senses, better pleas'd with madness, WT 4.04.484
world can match | the pleasure of that madness. 5.03. 73
lady, you utter madness, and not sorrow. JN 3.04. 43
and true obedience, of this madness cured, 2H4 4.02. 41
good lord, what madness rules in brain–sick men, 1H6 4.01.111
and were't not madness then, | to make the fox 2H6 3.01.252
o plague and madness! TRO 5.02. 35
why, my negation hath no taste of madness. 5.02.127
o madness of discourse, | that cause sets up, 5.02.142
a madness most discreet, | a choking gall, and a ROM 1.01.193
meat in one man's blood, and all the madness is, TIM 1.02. 42 P
like madness is the glory of this life, | as 1.02.134
his flight was madness. MAC 4.02. 3
of reason, | and draw you into madness? HAM 1.04. 74
mad call i it, for, to define true madness, 2.02. 93
into the madness wherein now he raves, | and all 2.02.150
though this be madness, yet there is method in't 2.02.205 P
a happiness that often madness hits on, which 2.02.210 P
but with a crafty madness keeps aloof | when we 3.01. 8
it lack'd form a little, | was not like madness. 3.01.164
madness in great ones must not /unwatch'd go. 3.01.188
it safe with us | to let his madness range. 3.03. 2
sense | is apoplex'd, for madness would not err, 3.04. 73
it is not madness | that i have utt'red. 3.04.141
will reword, which madness | would gambol from. 3.04.143
that not your trespass, but my madness speaks; 3.04.146
out, | that i essentially am not in madness, 3.04.187
o'er whom his very madness, like some ore 4.01. 25
hamlet in madness hath polonius slain, | and 4.01. 34
thy madness shall be paid with weight | /till 4.05.157
a document in madness, thoughts and remembrance 4.05.178 P
this is mere madness, | and /thus a while the 5.01.284
roughly awake, i here proclaim was madness. 5.02.232
his madness. 5.02.237
wronged, | his madness is poor hamlet's enemy. 5.02.239
o, that way madness lies, let me shun that! LR 3.04. 21
wolf in greediness, dog in madness, lion in prey 3.04. 94 P
reason in madness! 4.06.175
and now, in madness | (being full of supper and OTH 1.01. 98
upon his peace and quiet | even to madness. 2.01.311
and by and by | breaks out to savage madness. 4.01. 55
riotous madness, | to be entangled with those ANT 1.03. 29
to leave you in your madness, 'twere my sin; CYM 2.03. 99
not | absolute madness could so far have rav'd 4.02.135
a madness, of which her life's in danger. 4.03. 3
task, | desire of liberty, a fever, madness, TNK 1.04. 42
and in this madness if i hazard thee | and take 2.02.202
'tis not an engraff'd madness, but a most thick 4.03. 49 P
become the pranks and friskins of her madness. 4.03. 81 P
and in my madness might speak ill of thee; SON 140.10

MADONNA 10 FR 0.0011 REL FR 0 V 10 P
two faults, madonna, that drink and good counsel TN 1.05. 43 P
good madonna, give me leave to prove you a fool. 1.05. 57 P
dexteriously, good madonna. 1.05. 60 P
i must catechize you for it, madonna. 1.05. 62 P
good madonna, why mourn'st thou? 1.05. 66 P
i think his soul is in hell, madonna. 1.05. 68 P
the more fool, madonna, to mourn for your 1.05. 70 P
thou hast spoke for us, madonna, as if thy 1.05.112 P
he is but mad yet, madonna, and the fool shall 1.05.137 P
so i do, madonna; 5.01.298 P

MADRIGALS 3 FR 0.0003 REL FR 3 V 0 P
whose falls | melodious birds sings madrigals; WIV 3.01. 18
"melodious birds sing madrigals — | when as i 3.01. 23
by whose falls | melodious birds sing madrigals. PP 19. 8

MADS 2 FR 0.0002 REL FR 1 V 1 P
heat makes him a fool, the second mads him, and TN 1.05.133 P
this music mads me, let it sound no more, | for R2 5.05. 61

MAD'ST 7 FR 0.0008 REL FR 6 V 1 P
art the first knave that e'er mad'st a duke. MM 5.01.356
what observation mad'st thou in this case | /of ERR 4.02. 5
which this blood mad'st, revenge his death! R3 1.02. 62
tell her thou mad'st away her uncle clarence, 4.04.281
mad'st quick conveyance with her good aunt anne. 4.04.283
thou mad'st thine enemies shake, as if the world COR 1.04. 60
e'er since thou mad'st thy daughters thy mothers LR 1.04.172 P

MADWOMEN 1 FR 0.0001 REL FR 1 V 0 P
they are madwomen. TIM 1.02.133

MAECENAS 3 FR 0.0003 REL FR 2 V 1 P
i do not know, | maecenas, ask agrippa. ANT 2.02. 17
worthily spoken, maecenas. 2.02.102
half the heart of caesar, worthy maecenas! 2.02.172 P

MAGGOT 1 FR 0.0001 REL FR 1 V 0 P
have blown me full of maggot ostentation. LLL 5.02.409

MAGGOT–PIES *(also pies*)*

MAGGOT–PIES 1 FR 0.0001 REL FR 1 V 0 P
by maggot–pies and choughs and rooks brought MAC 3.04.124

MAGGOTS 2 FR 0.0002 REL FR 0 V 2 P
for if the sun breed maggots in a dead dog, HAM 2.02.181 P
to fat us, and we fat ourselves for maggots; 4.03. 23 P

MAGIC 12 FR 0.0013 REL FR 12 V 0 P
thy hand, | and pluck my magic garment from me. TMP 1.02. 24
but this rough magic | i here abjure; 5.01. 50
there's magic in thy majesty, which has | my WT 5.03. 39
if this be magic, let it be an art | lawful as 5.03.110
him, | by magic verses have contriv'd his end? 1H6 1.01. 27
see, | magic of bounty! TIM 1.01. 6
and that, distill'd by magic sleights, | shall MAC 3.05. 26
thy natural magic and dire property | on HAM 3.02.259
if she in chains of magic were not bound, OTH 1.02. 65
what conjuration, and what mighty magic | (for 1.03. 92
there's magic in the web of it. 3.04. 69
the noble ruin of her magic, antony, | claps on ANT 3.10. 18

MAGICAL 1 FR 0.0001 REL FR 1 V 0 P
that magical word of war, we have effected; ANT 3.01. 31

MAGICIAN 5 FR 0.0005 REL FR 3 V 2 P
i was three year old, convers'd with a magician, AYL 5.02. 60 P
i tender dearly, though i say i am a magician. 5.02. 71 P
uncle, | whom he reports to be a great magician, 5.04. 33
did lead to fight | against that great magician, 1H4 1.03. 83
what black magician conjures up this fiend | to R3 1.02. 34

MAGISTRATE 4 FR 0.0004 REL FR 4 V 0 P
no name of magistrate; TMP 2.01.150
before a true and lawful magistrate | that hath 3H6 1.02. 23

they choose their magistrate, | and such a one COR 3.01.104
give up yourself to form, obey the magistrate, STM II.C 146
MAGISTRATES 6 FR 0.0006 REL FR 3 V 3 P
where some, like magistrates, correct at home; H5 1.02.191
fie, lords, that you, being supreme magistrates, 1H6 1.03. 57
to say as, let the magistrates be laboring men; 2H6 4.02. 17 P
and therefore should we be magistrates. 4.02. 18 P
proud, violent, testy magistrates (alias fools) COR 2.01. 44 P
we were establish'd | the people's magistrates. 3.01.201
MAGNANIMIOUS 1 FR 0.0001 REL FR 0 V 1 P
be magnanimious in the enterprise and go on; AWW 3.06. 67 P
MAGNANIMITY 1 FR 0.0001 REL FR 1 V 0 P
words, | infuse his breast with magnanimity, 3H6 5.04. 41
MAGNANIMOUS 6 FR 0.0006 REL FR 1 V 5 P
the magnanimous and most illustrate king LLL 4.01. 64 P
as the wrathful dove or most magnanimous mouse. 2H4 3.02.160 P
duke of exeter is as magnanimous as agamemnon, H5 3.06. 6 P
or the huge, or the magnanimous, are all one 4.07. 17 P
a spur to valiant and magnanimous deeds, | whose TRO 2.02.200
for his person of the magnanimous and most 3.03.276 P
MAGNI 1 FR 0.0001 REL FR 1 V 0 P
magni dominator poli, | tam lentus audis scelera TIT 4.01. 81
MAGNIFICENCE 1 FR 0.0001 REL FR 0 V 1 P
we cannot with such magnificence — in so rare WT 1.01. 12 P
MAGNIFICENT 2 FR 0.0002 REL FR 1 V 1 P
a letter from the magnificent armado. LLL 1.01.191 P
the boy, | than whom no mortal so magnificent! 3.01.178
MAGNIFICO 1 FR 0.0001 REL FR 1 V 0 P
of this, | that the magnifico is much belov'd, OTH 1.02. 12
MAGNIFICOES 1 FR 0.0001 REL FR 1 V 0 P
himself, and the magnificoes | of greatest port, MV 3.02.280
MAGNIFI'ST 1 FR 0.0001 REL FR 1 V 0 P
him that thou magnifi'st with all these titles 1H6 4.07. 75
MAGNUS' 1 FR 0.0001 REL FR 0 V 1 P
down saint magnus' corner! 2H6 4.08. 1 P
MAGPIE *(see maggot–pies, pie*, etc.)*
MAHOMET 1 FR 0.0001 REL FR 1 V 0 P
was mahomet inspired with a dove? 1H6 1.02.140
/MAHU 1 FR 0.0001 REL FR 0 V 1 P
/mahu, /of /stealing; LR 4.01. 60 P
MAHU 1 FR 0.0001 REL FR 0 V 1 P
modo he's call'd, and mahu. LR 3.04.144 P
/MAID 1 FR 0.0001 REL FR 1 V 0 P
worm | prick'd from the lazy finger of a /maid. ROM 1.04. 69
MAID 205 FR 0.0231 REL FR 154 V 51 P
if you be maid, or no? TMP 1.02.428
no wonder, sir, | but certainly a maid. 1.02.429
through my prison once a day | behold this maid. 1.02.492
if not, i'll die your maid. 3.01. 84
done | some wanton charm upon this man and maid, 4.01. 95
what is this maid with whom thou wast at play? 5.01.185
what 'fool is she, that knows i am a maid, | and TGV 1.02. 53
stomach on your meat, | and not upon your maid. 1.02. 69
my sister crying, our maid howling, our cat 2.03. 7 P
this hat is nan, our maid. 2.03. 21 P
yet 'tis not a maid, for she hath had gossips; 3.01.270 P
yet 'tis a maid, for she is her master's maid, 3.01.271 P
for she is her master's maid, and serves for 3.01.271 P
you, a sweet virtue in a maid with clean hands. 3.01.278 P
can you carry your good will to the maid? WIV 1.01.231 P
can you love the maid? 1.01.244 P
to desire this honest gentlewoman, your maid, to 1.04. 83 P
sir, the maid loves you, and all shall be well. 1.04.120 P
i detest, an honest maid as ever broke bread. 1.04.151 P
good maid then. 2.02. 36 P
ay, be–gar, and de maid is love–a me. 3.02. 64 P
the maid hath given consent to go with him. 4.06. 45
bring you the maid, you shall not lack a priest. 4.06. 53
go you, and where you find a maid | that, ere 5.05. 49
why went you not with master doctor, maid? 5.05.219
what? is there a maid with child by him? MM 1.02. 91 P
but there's a woman with maid by him. 1.02. 92 P
ay, my good lord, a very virtuous maid, | and to 2.02. 20
be you content, fair maid, | it is the law, not 2.02. 79
but this virtuous maid | subdues me quite. 2.02.184
how now, fair maid? 2.04. 30
leave me a while with the maid. 3.01.177 P
in death to take this poor maid from the world! 3.01.232 P
this forenam'd maid hath yet in her the 3.01.239 P
shall advise this wrong'd maid to stead up your 3.01.250 P
the maid will i frame and make fit for his 3.01.255 P
i pray you be acquainted with this maid, | she 4.01. 50
a deflow'red maid! 4.04. 21
upon a wrong'd — i would fain have said a maid! 5.01. 21
are you a maid? 5.01.173 P
neither maid, widow, nor wife? 5.01.177 P
for many of them are neither maid, widow, nor 5.01.180 P
married, | and i confess besides i am no maid. 5.01.185
and now, dear maid, be you as free to us. 5.01.388
o most kind maid, | it was the swift celerity of 5.01.393
did not her kitchen maid rail, taunt, and scorn ERR 4.04. 74
husbands, if a maid could come by them. ADO 2.01.324 P
to be cozen'd with the semblance of a maid — 2.02. 39 P
a maid, and stuff'd! 3.04. 65 P
free and unconstrained soul | give me this maid, 4.01. 25
behold how like a maid she blushes here! 4.01. 34
all you that see her, that she were a maid, | by 4.01. 39
now, if you are a maid, answer to this. 4.01. 85
i do live, | and surely as i live, i am a maid. 5.04. 64
a maid of grace and complete majesty — | about LLL 1.01.136
i was taken with a maid. 1.01.297 P
this maid will not serve your turn, sir. 1.01.298 P
this maid will serve my turn, sir. 1.01.299 P
i do betray myself with blushing. maid. 1.02.133 P
this significant to the country maid jaquenetta. 3.01.131 P
be advis'd, fair maid. MND 1.01. 46
said | becomes a virtuous bachelor and a maid, 2.02. 59
my master said, | despised the athenian maid; 2.02. 73
and reason says you are the worthier maid. 2.02.116
most ungrateful maid! 3.02.195
i am a right maid for my cowardice. 3.02.302
a neat's tongue dried and a maid not vendible. MV 1.01.112
in my life | to woo a maid in way of marriage; 2.09. 13
you saw the mistress, i beheld the maid; 3.02.198
my maid nerissa and myself mean time | will live 3.02.309
none but a holy hermit and her maid. 5.01. 33
here's a young maid with travel much oppressed, AYL 2.04. 74
speak sad brow and true maid. 3.02.215 P
hard with a young maid between the contract of 3.02.313 P
you do love this maid? 5.01. 36 P
we'll show thee io as she was a maid, | and how SHR in.2. 54
ay, the woman's maid of the house. in.2. 90
why, sir, you know no house nor no such maid, in.2. 91
mates, maid, how mean you that? 1.01. 59
master, you look'd so longly on the maid, 1.01.165
if you love the maid, | bend thoughts and wits 1.01.178
master, your love must live a maid at home, 1.01.182
and undertake the teaching of the maid: 1.01.192
t' achieve that maid | whose sudden sight hath 1.01.219
a title for a maid of all titles the worst. 1.02.130
are you a suitor to the maid you talk of, yea or 1.02.228
why then the maid is mine from all the world, 2.01.384
fair lovely maid, once more good day to thee. 4.05. 33
i must not hear thee, fare thee well, kind maid! AWW 2.01.145
i'll like a maid the better whilst i have a 2.03. 42 P
fair maid, send forth thine eye. 2.03. 52
i am a simple maid, and therein wealthiest 2.03. 66
wealthiest | that i protest i simply am a maid. 2.03. 67
if thou canst like this creature as a maid, | i 2.03.142
by the misprising of a maid too virtuous | for 3.02. 31
the honor of a maid is her name, and no legacy 3.05. 12 P
many a maid hath been seduc'd by them, and the 3.05. 20 P
this young maid might do her | a shrewd turn, if 3.05. 67
a suit | corrupt the tender honor of a maid. 3.05. 72
please it this matron and this gentle maid | to 3.05. 97
braid, | marry that will, i live and die a maid. 4.02. 74
an advertisement to a proper maid in florence, 4.03.213 P
was very honest in the behalf of the maid; 4.03.219 P
a seducer flourishes, and a poor maid is undone. 5.03.146 P
he knows i am no maid, and he'll swear to't; 5.03.290
i'll swear i am a maid, and he knows not. 5.03.291
i am either maid, or else this old man's wife. 5.03.293
o my good lord, when i was like this maid, | i 5.03.309
thou kept'st a wife herself, thyself a maid. 5.03.330
a virtuous maid, the daughter of a count | that TN 1.02. 36
away, breath, | i am slain by a fair cruel maid. 2.04. 54
you would have been contracted to a maid, | nor 5.01.261
you are betroth'd both to a maid and man. 5.01.263
with a swain's wearing, and me, poor lowly maid, WT 4.04. 9
you see, sweet maid, we marry | a gentler scion 4.04. 92
into the matter, he makes the maid to answer, 4.04.198 P
there's scarce a maid westward but she sings it. 4.04.290 P
of lewis the dolphin and that lovely maid. JN 2.01.425
no external thing to lose | but the word "maid," 2.01.572
the word "maid," cheats the poor maid of that, 2.01.572
maid marian may be the deputy's wife of the ward 1H4 3.03.114 P
and to the fire–ey'd maid of smoky war | all hot 4.01.114
being a maid yet ros'd over with the virgin H5 5.02.295 P
lord, a hard condition for a maid to consign to. 5.02.298 P
for one fair french maid that stands in my way. 5.02.318 P
the cities turn'd into a maid; 5.02.321 P
so the maid that stood in the way for my wish 5.02.327 P
a holy maid hither with me i bring, | which by a 1H6 1.02. 51
fair maid, is't thou wilt do these wondrous 1.02. 64
a maid, they say. 2.01. 21
a maid? and be so martial? 2.01. 21
"thou maiden youth, be vanquish'd by a maid!" 4.07. 38
such commendations as becomes a maid, | a virgin 5.03.177
because she is a maid, | spare for no faggots, 5.04. 55
now heaven forfend, the holy maid with child? 5.04. 65
there shall not a maid be married, but she shall 2H6 4.07.121 P
would i had died a maid | and never seen thee, 3H6 1.01.216
i had rather be a country servant maid | than a R3 1.03.106
is, a fair young maid that yet wants baptism, H8 5.02.196
here, you maid! TRO 4.02. 24 P
me a kiss | when helen is a maid again and his. 4.05. 50
know thou first, | i lov'd the maid i married; COR 4.05.114
lord titus, by your leave, this maid is mine. TIT 1.01.276
ravish a maid, or plot the way to do it, 5.01.129
take the wall of any man or maid of montague's. ROM 1.01. 12 P
your lady's love against some other maid | that 1.02. 97
much upon these years | that you are now a maid. 1.03. 73
sick and pale with grief | that thou, her maid, 2.02. 6
be not her maid, since she is envious; 2.02. 7
neither, fair maid, if either thee dislike. 2.02. 61
to my bed, | but i, a maid, die maiden–widowed. 3.02.135
and yourself | had part in this fair maid, now 4.05. 67
all, | and all the better is it for the maid. 4.05. 68
the maid is fair, a' th' youngest for a bride, TIM 1.01.123
love you the maid? 1.01.134
maid, to thy master's bed, | thy mistress is o' 4.01. 12
the chariest maid is prodigal enough | if she HAM 1.03. 36
morning betime, | and i a maid at your window, 4.05. 50
let in the maid, that out a maid | never 4.05. 54
maid, that out a maid | never departed more." 4.05. 54
dear maid, kind sister, sweet ophelia! 4.05.159
thy bride–bed to have deck'd, sweet maid, | and 5.01.245
the gods to their dear shelter take thee, maid, LR 1.01.182
can buy this unpriz'd precious maid of me. 1.01.259
she that's a maid now, and laughs at my 1.05. 51
shall not be a maid long, unless things be cut 1.05. 52
whether a maid so tender, fair, and happy, | so OTH 1.02. 66
he hath achiev'd a maid | that paragons 2.01. 61
my mother had a maid call'd barbary; 4.03. 26
by such poor passion as the maid that milks ANT 4.15. 74
this maid | hight philoten, and it is said | for PER 4.ch. 17
poor maid, | born in a tempest when my mother 4.01. 17
that am a maid, though most ungentle fortune 4.06. 96
we have a maid in meteline, i durst wager, 5.01. 43
that none but i and my companion maid | be 5.01. 77
i am a maid, | my lord, that ne'er before 5.01. 84
my dearest wife was like this maid, and such a 5.01.107
what this maid is, or what is like to be, | that 5.01.184
riding, her fortunes brought the maid aboard us, 5.03. 11
more of the maid to sight than husband's pains. TNK pr 8
my precious maid, | those best affections that 1.03. 8
that the true love 'tween maid and maid may be 1.03. 81
that the true love 'tween maid and maid may be 1.03. 81
that you shall never (like the maid flavina) 1.03. 84
it is the very emblem of a maid; 2.02.137
a maid, if she have any honor, would be loath 2.02.145
"fair gentle maid, good morrow. 2.04. 24
would have trembled to deny | a blushing maid — 3.06.205
love, and what young maid dare cross 'em? 4.02. 40
face | the livery of the warlike maid appears, 4.02.106
that's a fine maid! 5.02. 70
is it a maid? 5.04. 33
with untun'd tongue she hoarsely calls her maid, LUC 1214
poor lucrece' cheeks unto her maid seem so | as 1217
even so the maid with swelling drops gan wet 1228
which makes the maid weep like the dewy night. 1232
"madam, ere i was up," replied the maid, | "the 1277
"but, lady, if your maid may be so bold, | she 1282
her maid is gone, and she prepares to write, 1296
by a gift of learning did bear the maid away: PP 15.14
a maid of dian's this advantage found, | and his SON 153. 2
tale, | ere long espied a fickle maid full pale, LC 5
'gentle maid, | have of my suffering youth some 177
he preach'd pure maid, and prais'd cold chastity 315
and new pervert a reconciled maid!" 329
MAID–CHILD 1 FR 0.0001 REL FR 1 V 0 P
but brought forth | a maid–child call'd marina, PER 5.03. 6
MAIDEN 47 FR 0.0053 REL FR 43 V 4 P
maiden, no remedy. MM 2.02. 48
will not proclaim against her maiden loss, | how 4.04. 24
contempt, farewell, and maiden pride, adieu! ADO 3.01.109
why then you are no maiden. 4.01. 87
these princes hold | against her maiden truth. 4.01.164
than that which maiden modesty doth warrant, 4.01.179
now by my maiden honor, yet as pure | as the LLL 5.02.351
and in our maiden council rated them | at 5.02.779
their blood | to undergo such maiden pilgrimage; MND 1.01. 75
passed on, | in maiden meditation, fancy–free. 2.01.164
and here the maiden, sleeping sound, | on the 2.02. 74
have you no modesty, no maiden shame, | no touch 3.02.285
and yet a maiden hath no tongue but thought — MV 3.02. 8
and not a maiden, as thou say'st he is. SHR 4.05. 44
the best brine a maiden can season her praise in AWW 1.01. 48 P
god's mercy, maiden! 1.03.149
we thank you, maiden, | but may not be so 2.01.114
your mind, | you are no maiden, but a monument. 4.02. 6
when you have conquer'd my yet maiden bed, 4.02. 57
in this town, | where lie my maiden weeds; TN 5.01.255
wherefore, gentle maiden, | do you neglect them? WT 4.04. 85
a rape | upon the maiden virtue of the crown. JN 2.01. 98
of mine | is yet a maiden and an innocent hand, 4.02.252
bravely hast thou flesh'd | thy maiden sword. 1H4 5.04.131
put off your maiden blushes, avouch the thoughts H5 5.02.235 P
are all girdled with maiden walls that war hath 5.02.322 P
so the maiden cities you talk of may wait on her 5.02.326 P
i pluck this pale and maiden blossom here, 1H6 2.04. 47
now, by this maiden blossom in my hand, | i 2.04. 75
"thou maiden youth, be vanquish'd by a maid!" 4.07. 38
whose maiden blood, thus rigorously effus'd, 5.04. 52
strew me over | with maiden flowers, that all H8 4.02.169
the bird of wonder dies, the maiden phoenix, 5.04. 40
a maiden battle then? o, i perceive you. TRO 4.05. 87
when he by night lay bath'd in maiden blood. TIT 2.03.232
else would a maiden blush bepaint my cheek | for ROM 2.02. 86
be something scanter of your maiden presence, HAM 1.03.121
her maiden strewments, and the bringing home 5.01.233
a maiden, never bold; OTH 1.03. 94
when my maiden priests are met together | before PER 5.01.242
maiden pinks, of odor faint, | daisies TNK 1.01. 4
doth quench the maiden burning of his cheeks; VEN 50
blue, | a pair of maiden worlds unconquered, LUC 408
"why should the worm intrude the maiden bud? 848
and many maiden gardens, yet unset, | with SON 16. 6
and maiden virtue rudely strumpeted, | and right 66. 6
but in her maiden hand | the fairest votary took 154. 4
MAIDENHEAD* 15 FR 0.0017 REL FR 9 V 6 P
cozen'd all the hosts of readins, of maidenhead, WIV 4.05. 78 P
carouse full measure to her maidenhead, | be mad SHR 3.02.225
and what i would, are as secret as maidenhead: TN 1.05.216 P
look big | upon the maidenhead of our affairs. 1H4 4.01. 59
such a matter to get a pottle–pot's maidenhead? 2H4 2.02. 78 P
shall pay to me her maidenhead ere they have it. 2H6 4.07.122 P
by my troth and maidenhead, | i would not be a H8 2.03. 23
and venture maidenhead for't, and so would you 2.03. 25
now, by my maidenhead at twelve year old, | i ROM 1.03. 2
and death, not romeo, take my maidenhead! 3.02.137
to bed, | where, by the loss of maidenhead, | a PER 3.ch. 10
such a maidenhead were no cheap thing, if men 4.02. 60 P
i must have your maidenhead taken off, or the 4.06.127 P
or vow'd her maidenhead | to a young handsome TNK 2.04. 13
for i must lose my maidenhead by cocklight, 4.01.112
MAIDENHEADS 5 FR 0.0005 REL FR 2 V 3 P
virgin branches yet | your maidenheads growing. WT 4.04.116
we shall buy maidenheads as they buy hobnails, 1H4 2.04.362 P
how now, how now, how go maidenheads? TRO 4.02. 23 P
the heads of the maids, or their maidenheads, ROM 1.01. 25 P
new plays and maidenheads are near akin — TNK pr 1
MAIDEN–HEARTED 1 FR 0.0001 REL FR 1 V 0 P
i am bride–habited, | but maiden–hearted. TNK 5.01.151
MAIDENHOOD 2 FR 0.0002 REL FR 1 V 1 P
so terrible shows in the wrack of maidenhood, AWW 3.05. 22 P
and had the maidenhood | of thy first fight, i 1H6 4.06. 17
MAIDENHOODS 1 FR 0.0001 REL FR 1 V 0 P
play'd for a pair of stainless maidenhoods. ROM 3.02. 13
MAIDENL'EST 1 FR 0.0001 REL FR 0 V 1 P
i am, had the maidenl'est star in the firmament LR 1.02.132 P
MAIDENLY 2 FR 0.0002 REL FR 1 V 1 P
it is not friendly, 'tis not maidenly. MND 3.02.217
what a maidenly man–at–arms are you become! 2H4 2.02. 77 P
MAIDEN'S 5 FR 0.0005 REL FR 5 V 0 P
me past the bounds | of maiden's patience. MND 3.02. 66
soly led | by nice direction of a maiden's eyes; MV 2.01. 14
turn'd, | that a maiden's heart hath burn'd?" AYL 4.03. 41
my maiden's name | sear'd otherwise; AWW 2.01.172
thy small pipe | is as the maiden's organ, TN 1.04. 33
MAIDENS' 3 FR 0.0003 REL FR 3 V 0 P
the dead men's blood, the privy maidens' groans, H5 2.04.107
the skillful | conserv'd of maidens' hearts. OTH 3.04. 75
that maidens' eyes stuck over all his face. LC 81
MAIDENS 6 FR 0.0006 REL FR 6 V 0 P
and let him learn to know, when maidens sue, MM 1.04. 80
daws, | and maidens bleach their summer smocks, LLL 5.02.906
he | that frights the maidens of the villagery, MND 2.01. 35
wound, | and maidens call it love–in–idleness. 2.01.168

if your pure maidens fall into the hand | of hot H5 3.03. 20
and cupid grant all tongue–tied maidens here TRO 3.02.210
MAIDEN–TONGU'D 1 FR 0.0001 REL FR 1 V 0 P
for maiden–tongu'd he was, and thereof free; LC 100
MAIDEN–WIDOWED 1 FR 0.0001 REL FR 1 V 0 P
to my bed, | but i, a maid, die maiden–widowed. ROM 3.02.135
MAIDHOOD 2 FR 0.0002 REL FR 2 V 0 P
by maidhood, honor, truth, and every thing, | i TN 3.01.150
by which the property of youth and maidhood OTH 1.01.172
MAID–PALE 1 FR 0.0001 REL FR 1 V 0 P
change the complexion of her maid–pale peace R2 3.03. 98
MAID'S 9 FR 0.0010 REL FR 6 V 3 P
i shall never laugh but in that maid's company! WIV 1.04.152 P
my maid's aunt, the fat woman of brainford, has 4.02. 75 P
why, it is my maid's aunt of brainford. 4.02.170 P
to conjure tears up in a poor maid's eyes | with MND 3.02.158
do i see | maid's mild behavior and sobriety. SHR 1.01. 71
me first on shore | hath my maid's garments. TN 5.01.275
play the maid's part, still answer nay, and take R3 3.07. 51
is't possible a young maid's wits | should be as HAM 4.05.160
subdue and poison this young maid's affections? OTH 1.03.112
MAIDS' 2 FR 0.0002 REL FR 1 V 1 P
one a' these maids' girdles for your waist LLL 4.01. 50
a fair thought to lie between maids' legs. HAM 3.02.118 P
MAIDS 55 FR 0.0062 REL FR 37 V 18 P
since maids, in modesty, say "no" to that TGV 1.02. 55
there pinch the maids as blue as bilberry; WIV 5.05. 45
familiar sin | with maids to seem the lapwing, MM 1.04. 32
from fasting maids whose minds are dedicate | to 2.02.154
beaten the maids a–row, and bound the doctor, ERR 5.01.170
you to heaven, here's no place for you maids." ADO 2.01. 46 P
vice, and they are dangerous weapons for maids. 5.02. 22 P
not one word more, my maids, break off, break LLL 5.02.262
widows and nine maids is a simple coming–in for MV 2.02.162 P
mean time | will live as maids and widows. 3.02.310
us, | maids as we are, to travel forth so far! AYL 1.03.109
maids are may when they are maids, but the sky 4.01.148 P
maids are may when they are maids, but the sky 4.01.148 P
and the free maids that weave their thread with TN 2.04. 45
strength (a malady | most incident to maids); WT 4.04.125
he has the prettiest love–songs for maids, so 4.04.193 P
what maids lack from head to heel. 4.04.227
is there no manners left among maids? 4.04.242 P
this ballad against the hard hearts of maids. 4.04.278 P
goes to the tune of "two maids wooing a man." 4.04.289 P
lions | as maids of thirteen do of puppy–dogs! JN 2.01.460
of kings, of beggars, old men, young men, maids, 2.01.570
for your own ladies and pale–visag'd maids 5.02.154
is not a fashion for the maids in france to kiss H5 5.02.265 P
for maids, well summer'd and warm kept, are like 5.02.307 P
i was set at work | among my maids, full little, H8 3.01. 75
from false to false, among false maids in love, TRO 3.02.190
make wells and niobes of the maids and wives, 5.10. 19
ladies and maids their scarfs and handkerchers, COR 2.01.264
from the wall, and thrust his maids to the wall. ROM 1.01. 18 P
with the men, i will be civil with the maids; 1.01. 23 P
the heads of the maids? 1.01. 24 P
ay, the heads of the maids, or their maidenheads 1.01. 25 P
this is the hag, when maids lie on their backs, 1.04. 92
were that kind of fruit | as maids call medlars, 2.01. 36
whose proof nor yells of mothers, maids, nor TIM 4.03.125
and your maids could not fill up | the cestern MAC 4.03. 62
but our cull–cold maids do dead men's fingers HAM 4.07.171
that photinus an eunuch and your maids | manage ANT 3.07. 14
maids, matrons, nay, the secrets of the grave CYM 3.04. 38
and, /with her fellow maids, /is now upon | the PER 5.01. 50
the fair–ey'd maids shall weep our banishments, TNK 2.02. 37
were there not maids enough? 2.02.121
some honest–hearted maids, will sing my dirge, 2.06. 15
do, maids will not so easily | trust men again. 2.06. 20
where be your ribands, maids? 3.05. 28
and all the longing maids that ever lov'd, | if 3.06.246
a hundred black–ey'd maids that love as i do, 4.01. 72
else, | to call the maids and pay the minstrels, 4.01.111
all the young maids | of our town are in love 4.01.125
and had in her | the coy denials of young maids, 4.02. 11
we maids that have our livers perish'd, crack'd 4.03. 23 P
and courtiers that have got maids with child, 4.03. 41 P
learn what maids have been her companions and 4.03. 90 P
the maids that kept her company | have half 5.02. 2
MAIL* 2 FR 0.0002 REL FR 1 V 1 P
riddle, no l'envoy, no salve in the mail, sir. LLL 3.01. 73 P
like a rusty mail | in monumental mock'ry. TRO 3.03.152
MAIL'D 2 FR 0.0002 REL FR 2 V 0 P
mail'd up in shame, with papers on my back, 2H6 2.04. 31
bloody brow | with his mail'd hand then wiping, COR 1.03. 35
MAILED 1 FR 0.0001 REL FR 1 V 0 P
the mailed mars shall on his /altar sit | up to 1H4 4.01.116
MAILES *(also nailes, nails)*
MAILES 1 FR 0.0001 REL FR 0 V 1 P
d' hand, de fingre, de mailes — H5 3.04. 45 P
MAIM 5 FR 0.0005 REL FR 5 V 0 P
not so deep a maim | as to be cast forth in the R2 1.03.156
your father's sickness is a maim to us. 1H4 4.01. 42
scarce himself, | that bears so shrewd a maim: 2H6 2.03. 41
think how you maim your honor | (for now i am TNK 3.06.237
and, veil'd in them, did win whom he would maim. LC 312
MAIM'D *(also main'd)*
MAIM'D 3 FR 0.0003 REL FR 3 V 0 P
'tis ten to one it maim'd you /two outright. SHR 5.02. 62
you maim'd the jurisdiction of all bishops. H8 3.02.312
i am maim'd for ever. help ho! murther, murther! OTH 5.01. 27
MAIMED 1 FR 0.0001 REL FR 1 V 0 P
and with such maimed rites? HAM 5.01.219
MAIMS 1 FR 0.0001 REL FR 1 V 0 P
and stop those maims | of shame seen through thy COR 4.05. 86
MAIN* 50 FR 0.0056 REL FR 41 V 9 P
and bid the main flood bate his usual height; MV 4.01. 72
doth an inland brook | into the main of waters. 5.01. 97
after the man | that the main harvest reaps. AYL 3.05.103
and trusty business in a main danger fail you. AWW 3.06. 15 P
and between these main parcels of dispatch 4.03. 90 P
the main consents are had, and here we'll stay 5.03. 69
even till that england, hedg'd in with the main, JN 2.01. 26
to set so rich a main | on the nice hazard of 1H4 4.01. 47
of the main chance of things | as yet not come 2H4 3.01. 83
but fear the main intendment of the scot, | who H5 1.02.144
comment appelez–vous la main en anglois? 3.04. 5 P
la main? elle est appelee de hand. 3.04. 7 P
la main, de hand; 3.04. 12 P
votre /grandeur en baisant la main d'une (notre 5.02.255 P
let's make haste away, and look unto the main. 2H6 1.01.208
unto the main? 1.01.209
that maine which by main force warwick did win, 1.01.210
main chance, father, you meant, but i meant 1.01.212
charg'd our main battle's front and, breaking in 3H6 1.01. 8
into the tumbling billows of the main. R3 1.04. 20
we will follow | in the main battle, whose 5.03.299
lord cardinal's, by commission and main power, H8 2.02. 6 P
look into these affairs see this main end, | the 2.02. 40
put your main cause into the king's protection, 3.01. 93
made me put this main secret in the packet | i 3.02.215
by the main assent | of all these learned men 4.01. 31
why then we do our main opinion crush | in taint TRO 1.03.372
we must with all our main of power stand fast; 2.03.262
as the main point of this our after–meeting, COR 2.02. 39
the main blaze of it is past, but a small thing 4.03. 20 P
quite from the main opinion he held once | of JC 2.01.196
though the main part | pertains to you alone. MAC 4.03.198
'tis his main hope; 5.04. 10
it, | is the main motive of our preparations, HAM 1.01.105
than the main voice of denmark goes withal. 1.03. 28
i doubt it is no other but the main, | his 2.02. 56
goes it against the main of poland, sir, | or 4.04. 15
or swell the curled waters 'bove the main, LR 3.01. 6
the main descry | stands on the hourly thought. 4.06.213
in the error | but the main article i do approve OTH 1.03. 11
i cannot, 'twixt the heaven and the main, 2.01. 3
even till we make the main and th' aerial blue 2.01. 39
hard at hand comes the master and main exercise, 2.01.262 P
and life, stands up | for the main soldier; ANT 1.02.191
if of my freedom 'tis the main part, take | no CYM 5.04. 16
but the main grief springs from the loss | of a PER 5.01. 29
certainly | 'tis a main goodness, cousin, that TNK 2.02. 63
nativity, once in the main of light, | crawls to SON 60. 5
and the firm soil win of the wat'ry main, 64. 7
his) | on your broad main doth willfully appear. 80. 8
MAIN–COURSE 1 FR 0.0001 REL FR 0 V 1 P
bring her to try with main–course. TMP 1.01. 35 P
MAIN'D *(also maim'd)*
MAIN'D 2 FR 0.0002 REL FR 1 V 1 P
for thereby is england main'd, and fain to go 2H6 4.02.163 P
it is a judgment main'd, and most imperfect, OTH 1.03. 99
MAINE 19 FR 0.0021 REL FR 16 V 3 P
to ireland, poictiers, anjou, touraine, maine, JN 1.01. 11
england and ireland, /anjou, touraine, maine, 2.01.152
for /anjou and fair touraine, maine, poictiers, 2.01.487
then do i give volquessen, touraine, maine, 2.01.527
maine, blois, poictiers, and tours, are won away 1H6 4.03. 45
duke of anjou and maine, yet is he poor, | and 5.03. 95
enjoy mine own, the country maine and anjou, 5.03.154
and the county of maine shall be releas'd and 2H6 1.01. 51 P
and /the /county /of maine shall be releas'd and 1.01. 59 P
hath given the duchy of anjou, and maine, | unto 1.01.110
anjou and maine? 1.01.119
o father, maine is lost! 1.01.209
that maine which by main force warwick did win, 1.01.210
chance, father, you meant, but i meant maine, 1.01.212
anjou and maine are given to the french, | paris 1.01.214
anjou and maine both given unto the french! 1.01.236
by thee anjou and maine were sold to france. 4.01. 86
say's head for selling the dukedom of maine. 4.02.161 P
i sold not maine, i lost not normandy, | yet to 4.07. 65
MAINLY 5 FR 0.0005 REL FR 4 V 1 P
four came all afront, and mainly thrust at me. 1H4 2.04.200 P
your faith in question | so mainly as my merit. TRO 4.04. 85
all things else | you mainly were stirr'd up. HAM 4.07. 9
for i am mainly ignorant | what place this is, LR 4.07. 64
far better, | for there the cure lies mainly. TNK 5.02. 8
MAINMAST 1 FR 0.0001 REL FR 0 V 1 P
now the ship boring the moon with her mainmast, WT 3.03. 92 P
MAINS 1 FR 0.0001 REL FR 0 V 1 P
que je tombe entre les mains d'un chevalier, je H5 4.04. 56 P
MAINSAIL 1 FR 0.0001 REL FR 1 V 0 P
out with the mainsail! TNK 4.01.148
MAINTAIN 44 FR 0.0049 REL FR 34 V 10 P
he will maintain you like a gentlewoman. WIV 3.04. 45 P
you have spoke, you have courage to maintain it. MM 3.02.157 P
and never could maintain his part but in the ADO 1.01.236 P
maintain a mourning ostentation, | and on your 4.01.205
thank my good father, i am able to maintain it. SHR 5.01. 76 P
maintain no words with him, good fellow. TN 4.02. 99 P
sweat in this business and maintain this war? JN 5.02.102
which to maintain i would allow him odds | and R2 1.01. 62
and further will maintain | upon his bad life to 1.01. 98
and will maintain what thou hast said is false 4.01. 27
and i dare well maintain it with my life, | if 1H4 4.03. 9
but i will maintain the word with my sword to be 2H4 3.02. 75 P
i give it you, and will maintain my word, | and 4.02. 67
'gainst all the world will rightfully maintain. 4.05.224
as much as would maintain, to the king's honor, H5 1.01. 12
he will maintain his argument as well as any 3.02. 80 P
what watch the king keeps to maintain the peace, 4.01.283
that here you maintain several factions; 1H6 1.01. 71
but dare maintain the party of the truth, 2.04. 32
ay, sharp and piercing, to maintain his truth, 2.04. 70
that shall maintain what i have said is true, 2.04. 73
i'll maintain my words | on any plot of ground 2.04. 88
and will not you maintain the thing you teach, 3.01.129
dar'st thou maintain the former words thou 3.04. 31
voice, | "jesu maintain your royal excellence!" 2H6 1.01.161
/but to maintain the king, the realm, and you? 4.07. 70
and that the lord of westmerland shall maintain. 3H6 1.01. 88
queen, | you have a father able to maintain you, 3.03.154
i will maintain it with some little cost. R3 1.02.259
not able to maintain | the many to them 'longing H8 1.02. 31
and such a one that dare | maintain — i know TRO 2.01.126
the weakest spleen | to fight for and maintain! 2.02.129
ye draw, | and maintain such a quarrel openly? TIT 2.01. 47
do you uphold and maintain in your speeches, 5.02. 72
that he will neither know how to maintain it, TIM 2.02. 2
none, but to | maintain my opinion. 4.03. 72
i have heard him oft maintain it to be fit that, LR 1.02. 72 P
go you and maintain talk with the duke, that my 3.03. 15 P
i will maintain | my truth and honor firmly. 5.03.100
the lists of the army will maintain upon edmund, 5.03.111 P
and tenantius' right | with honor to maintain. CYM 5.04. 74
maintain | i am as worthy and as free a lover, TNK 2.02.178
them, fair coz, | i'll maintain my proceedings. 3.01. 53
shown, | unless this general evil they maintain: SON 121.13
MAINTAIN'D 12 FR 0.0013 REL FR 7 V 5 P
maintain'd the change of words with any creature ADO 4.01.183
she dying, as it must be so maintain'd, | upon 4.01.214
which maintain'd so politic a state of evil that 5.02. 62 P
so far forth friendly maintain'd till by helping SHR 1.01.137 P
must be as boisterously maintain'd as gain'd; JN 3.04.136
i have maintain'd that salamander of yours with 1H4 3.03. 46 P
whose see is by a civil peace maintain'd, 2H4 4.01. 42
the fuel is gone that maintain'd that fire. H5 2.03. 43 P
should be maintain'd, assembled, and collected, 2.04. 19
exeter has very gallantly maintain'd the pridge. 3.06. 91 P
then say at once if i maintain'd the truth; 1H6 2.04. 5
leaves and fruit maintain'd with beauty's sun, 3H6 3.03.126
MAINTAINED 2 FR 0.0002 REL FR 1 V 1 P
the one maintained by the owl, th' other by the LLL 5.02.892 P
by all our country rights in rome maintained, LUC 1838
/MAINTAINS 1 FR 0.0001 REL FR 0 V 1 P
/who /maintains /'em? HAM 2.02.345 P
MAINTAINS 2 FR 0.0002 REL FR 2 V 0 P
sufficeth that i have maintains my state | and 2H6 4.10. 22
religion of mine eye | maintains such falsehood, ROM 1.02. 89
MAINTENANCE 3 FR 0.0003 REL FR 3 V 0 P
what maintenance he from his friends receives, TGV 1.03. 68
that cares for thee, | and for thy maintenance; SHR 5.02.148
with lustier maintenance than i did look for 1H4 5.04. 22
MAIN–TOP 1 FR 0.0001 REL FR 1 V 0 P
vessel of the world | strook the main–top! CYM 4.02.320
MAIS 1 FR 0.0001 REL FR 0 V 1 P
j'oublie les doigts, mais je me souviendrai. H5 3.04. 10 P
MAISON 1 FR 0.0001 REL FR 0 V 1 P
je suis le gentilhomme de bonne maison; H5 4.04. 41 P
MAJESTAS 1 FR 0.0001 REL FR 1 V 0 P
ah, sancta majestas! 2H6 5.01. 5
MAJESTEE 1 FR 0.0001 REL FR 0 V 1 P
your majestee ave fausse french enough to H5 5.02.218 P
MAJESTIC 3 FR 0.0003 REL FR 3 V 0 P
this is a most majestic vision, and | harmonious TMP 4.01.118
so get the start of the majestic world | and JC 1.02.130
to the majestic cedar join'd, whose issue CYM 5.05.457
MAJESTICAL 8 FR 0.0009 REL FR 6 V 2 P
his eye ambitious, his gait majestical, and his LLL 5.01. 11 P
a doubt | presence majestical would put him out; 5.02.102
for so appears this fleet majestical, | holding H5 3.pr. 16
not all these, laid in bed majestical, | can 4.01.267
but with a proud majestical high scorn | he 1H6 4.07. 39
the supreme seat, the throne majestical, | the R3 3.07.118
we do it wrong, being so majestical, | to offer HAM 1.01.143
this majestical roof fretted with golden fire, 2.02.301 P
MAJESTICALLY 1 FR 0.0001 REL FR 0 V 1 P
thou dost it half so gravely, so majestically, 1H4 2.04.436 P
MAJESTIES 5 FR 0.0005 REL FR 4 V 1 P
why answer not the double majesties | this JN 2.01.480
if your majesties is rememb'red of it, the H5 4.07. 97 P
to bring your most imperial majesties | unto 5.02. 26
both your majesties | might, by the sovereign HAM 2.02. 26
and he beseech'd me to entreat your majesties 3.01. 22
/MAJESTY 5 FR 0.0005 REL FR 5 V 0 P
/which /tired /majesty /did /make /thee /offer: R2 4.01.178
/all /pomp /and /majesty /i /do /forswear; 4.01.211
/proud /majesty /a /subject, /state /a /peasant. 4.01.252
/since /it /is /bankrout /of /his /majesty. 4.01.267
who, busied in his /majesty, surveys | the H5 1.02.197
MAJESTY 262 FR 0.0296 REL FR 211 V 51 P
'save his majesty! TMP 2.01.169
a maid of grace and complete majesty — | about LLL 1.01.136
and hold fair friendship with his majesty. 2.01.140
her brow, | that is not blinded by her majesty? 4.03.224
please it your majesty | command me any service 5.02.311
how fares your majesty? 5.02.726
sweet majesty, vouchsafe me — 5.02.879 P
power, | the attribute to awe and majesty, MV 4.01.191
but not /her heart, | cleopatra's majesty, AYL 3.02.146
approv'd so to your majesty, may plead | for AWW 1.02. 10
thank your majesty. 1.02. 76
health, at your bidding, serve your majesty! 2.01. 18
this is his majesty, say your mind to him. 2.01. 95
but such traitors | his majesty seldom fears. 2.01. 97
hearing your high majesty is touch'd | with that 2.01.110
please it your majesty, i have done already. 2.03. 68
in the minority of them both, his majesty, out 4.05. 73 P
and i beseech your majesty to make it | natural 5.03. 5
the young lord | did to his majesty, his mother, 5.03. 13
so please your majesty, my master hath been an 5.03.238 P
yes, so please your majesty. 5.03.258 P
to bless the bed of majesty again | with a sweet WT 5.01. 33
the majesty of the creature in resemblance of 5.02. 35 P
even with such life of majesty (warm life, | as 5.03. 35
there's magic in thy majesty, which has | my 5.03. 39
king of france | in my behavior to the majesty, JN 1.01. 3
the borrowed majesty, of england here. 1.01. 4
a strange beginning: "borrowed majesty"! 1.01. 5
ha, majesty! 2.01.350
and made his majesty the bawd to theirs. 3.01. 59
have i not pawn'd to you my majesty? 3.01. 98
me with a counterfeit | resembling majesty, 3.01.100
i muse your majesty doth seem so cold, | when 3.01.317
o fair return of banish'd majesty! 3.01.321
i am much bounden to your majesty. 3.03. 29
him so, | that he shall not offend your majesty. 3.03. 65
i'll send those powers o'er to your majesty. 3.03. 70
to know the meaning | of dangerous majesty, when 4.02.213
now for the bare–pick'd bone of majesty | doth 4.03.148
badly, i fear. how fares your majesty? 5.03. 2
desires your majesty to leave the field, | and 5.03. 6
who didst thou leave to tend his majesty? 5.06. 32
them, | and they are all about his majesty. 5.06. 36
how fares your majesty? 5.07. 34
and spleen of speed to see your majesty! 5.07. 50
hand | and bow my knee before his majesty, | for R2 1.03. 47
to entreat your majesty to visit him. 1.04. 56
this earth of majesty, this seat of mars, | this 2.01. 41

now, by my seat's right royal majesty, | wert 2.01.120
i do beseech your majesty, impute his words | to 2.01.141
liege, old gaunt commends him to your majesty. 2.01.147
gilt, | and make high majesty look like itself, 2.01.295
madam, your majesty is too much sad. 2.02. 1
so your sweet majesty, | looking awry upon your 2.02. 20
god save your majesty! 2.02. 41
no, i will to ireland to his majesty. 2.02.141
awake, thou coward majesty! 3.02. 84
thin and hairless scalps | against thy majesty; 3.02.113
eagle's, lightens forth | controlling majesty. 3.03. 70
his heart | to faithful service of your majesty. 3.03.118
will his majesty | give richard leave to live 3.03.173
what says his majesty? 3.03.184
all apart, | and show fair duty to his majesty. 3.03.188
them, | and shall the figure of god's majesty, 4.01.125
i do beseech your majesty, | to have some 5.03. 26
god save thy grace — majesty i should say, for 1H4 1.02. 17 P
and majesty might never yet endure | the moody 1.03. 18
denied | as is delivered to your majesty. 1.03. 26
betwixt my love and your high majesty. 1.03. 69
what manner of man, and it like your majesty? 2.04.421 P
so please your majesty, i would i could | quit 3.02. 18
gaze, | such as is bent on sunlike majesty, 3.02. 79
i do beseech your majesty may salve | the 3.02.155
true rule | you stand against anointed majesty. 4.03. 40
it pleas'd your majesty to turn your looks | of 5.01. 30
yet this before my father's majesty: 5.01. 96
i beseech your majesty make up, | lest your 5.04. 5
i hear his majesty is return'd with some 2H4 1.02.103 P
i talk not of his majesty. 1.02.105 P
thou whoreson mad compound of majesty, by this 2.04.294 P
many good morrows to your majesty! 3.01. 32
your majesty hath been this fortnight ill, | and 3.01.104
cured, | stoop tamely to the foot of majesty. 4.02. 42
our news shall go before us to his majesty, 4.03. 78
both which we doubt not but your majesty | shall 4.04. 11
from enemies heavens keep your majesty, | and, 4.04. 94
comfort, your majesty! 4.04.112
o majesty! 4.05. 28
what would your majesty? 4.05. 49
found no course of breath within your majesty, 4.05.150
i would his majesty had call'd me with him; 5.02. 6
good morrow, and god save your majesty! 5.02. 43
this new and gorgeous garment, majesty, | sits 5.02. 44
we hope no otherwise from your majesty. 5.02. 62
your majesty hath no just cause to hate me. 5.02. 66
the majesty and power of law and justice, | the 5.02. 78
floods, | and flow henceforth in formal majesty. 5.02.133
doth his majesty | incline to it, or no? H5 1.01. 71
for i have made an offer to his majesty, | upon 1.01. 75
with good acceptance of his majesty; 1.01. 83
may't please your majesty to give us leave 1.02.237
for that i have laid by my majesty, | and 1.02.276
better fear'd and lov'd | than is your majesty. 2.02. 26
england | do crave admittance to your majesty. 2.04. 66
from him, and thus he greets your majesty: 2.04. 76
sweeten the bitter mock you sent his majesty, 2.04.122
not so, i do beseech your majesty. 3.05. 65
god pless your majesty! 3.06. 87 P
ay, so please your majesty. 3.06. 90 P
i can tell your majesty, the duke is a prave man 3.06. 96 P
one bardolph, if your majesty know the man. 3.06.102 P
with cheerful semblance and sweet majesty; 4.pr. 40
the duke of york commends him to your majesty. 4.06. 3
here comes his majesty. 4.07. 54 P
of famous memory, an't please your majesty, and 4.07. 93 P
your majesty says very true. 4.07. 97 P
which, your majesty know, to this hour is an 4.07.100 P
i do believe your majesty takes no scorn to wear 4.07.102 P
as it pleases his grace, and his majesty too! 4.07.109 P
i need not to be ashamed of your majesty, 4.07.113 P
god, so long as your majesty is an honest man. 4.07.114 P
and't please your majesty, 'tis the gage of one 4.07.122 P
and't please your majesty, a rascal that 4.07.125 P
and a villain else, and't please your majesty, 4.07.134 P
here is his majesty. 4.08. 23 P
the glove which your majesty is take out of the 4.08. 27 P
your majesty hear now, saving your majesty's 4.08. 33 P
i hope your majesty is pear me testimony and 4.08. 35 P
glove of alanson that your majesty is give me, 4.08. 37 P
and please your majesty, let his neck answer for 4.08. 43 P
any from mine that might offend your majesty. 4.08. 48 P
your majesty came not like yourself. 4.08. 50 P
is it not lawful, and please your majesty, to 4.08.117 P
your majesty shall mock at me, i cannot speak 5.02.102 P
your majesty entendre bettre que moi. 5.02.264 P
god save your majesty! 5.02.281 P
where your majesty demands, that the king of 5.02.336 P
and in a vision full of majesty | will'd me to 1H6 1.02. 79
birth, | inferior to none but to his majesty; 3.01. 96
plantagenet | we do exhibit to your majesty. 3.01.150
occasions | at eltam place i told your majesty. 3.01.155
that grudge one thought against your majesty! 3.01.175
now will it best avail your majesty | to cross 3.01.178
yes, if it please your majesty, my liege. 3.04. 15
but i'll unto his majesty, and crave | i may 3.04. 41
beauty's princely majesty is such, | 'confounds 5.03. 70
you again, | no loving token to his majesty? 5.03.181
then swear allegiance to his majesty, | as thou 5.04.169
as by your high imperial majesty | i had in 2H6 1.01. 1
speech, | her words yclad with wisdom's majesty, 1.01. 33
methought i sat in seat of majesty | in the 1.02. 36
jesus preserve your royal majesty! 1.02. 70
what say'st thou? majesty? i am but grace. 1.02. 71
please it your majesty, this is the man | that 1.03.181
crown | and that your majesty was an usurper. 1.03.185
and't shall please your majesty, i never said 1.03.187 P
i do beseech your royal majesty, | let him have 1.03.195
therefore i beseech your majesty, do not cast 1.03.201 P
i humbly thank your royal majesty. 1.03.211
no marvel, and it like your majesty, | my lord 2.01. 9
i beseech your majesty give me leave to go; 2.03. 20
please it your majesty, | this is the day 2.03. 47
with what a majesty he bears himself, | how 3.01. 6
i will, my lord, so please his majesty. 3.01.315
murderous tyranny | sits in grim majesty, to 3.02. 50
that slily glided towards your majesty, | it 3.02.260
and therefore by his majesty i swear, | whose 3.02.285
to signify unto his majesty | that cardinal 3.02.368
and i am sent to tell his majesty | that even 3.02.377
god save your majesty! 4.02. 71 P
canst thou answer to my majesty for giving up of 4.07. 27 P
up his cap, and say, "god save his majesty!" 4.08. 15
health and glad tidings to your majesty! 4.09. 7
i was, an't like your majesty. 5.01. 72
therefore i came unto your majesty. 3H6 3.02. 41
these from our king unto your majesty. 3.03.165
i told your majesty as much before: 3.03.179
before it pleas'd his majesty | to raise my 4.01. 67
more incens'd against your majesty | than all 4.01.108
prevail, | i then crave pardon of your majesty. 4.06. 8
his looks are full of peaceful majesty, | his 4.06. 71
the duty that i owe unto your majesty | i seal 5.07. 28
and want love's majesty | to strut before a R3 1.01. 16
his majesty, | tend'ring my person's safety, 1.01. 43
belike his majesty hath some intent | that you 1.01. 49
his majesty hath straitly given in charge | that 1.01. 85
there's no doubt his majesty | will soon recover 1.03. 1
god make your majesty joyful, as you have been! 1.03. 19
and i | are come from visiting his majesty. 1.03. 32
i never did incense his majesty | against the 1.03. 84
i will acquaint his majesty | of those gross 1.03.104
madam, his majesty doth call for you, | and for 1.03.319
which by his death hath lost much majesty. 3.01.100
of time, | will well become the seat of majesty, 3.07.169
i am unfit for state and majesty. 3.07.205
pleaseth your majesty to give me leave, | i'll 4.04.487
where and what time your majesty shall please. 4.04.489
the news i have to tell your majesty | is that 4.04.509
thank your majesty. H8 1.02. 13
i know your majesty has always lov'd her | so 2.02.109
still growing in a majesty and pomp, the which 2.03. 7
the king's majesty | commends his good opinion 2.03. 60
breed | (and service to his majesty and you) 3.01. 52
pray do my service to his majesty; 3.01.179
god and your majesty | protect mine innocence, 5.01.140
at /unawares encount'ring | the eye of majesty. TRO 3.02. 39
i thank your majesty, and her, my lord. TIT 1.01.460
knees, | you shall ask pardon of his majesty. 1.01.473
and it please your majesty | to hunt the panther 1.01.492
many good morrows to your majesty; 2.02. 11
good aaron, give his majesty my hand. 3.01.193
broad wherewith | your majesty loads our house. MAC 1.06. 18
mean you his majesty? 2.03. 70
thanks to your majesty. 3.04. 2
night, and better health | attend his majesty! 3.04.120
since his majesty went into the field, i have 5.01. 4 P
form | in which the majesty of buried denmark HAM 1.01. 48
to give th' assay of arms against your majesty. 2.02. 71
to expostulate | what majesty should be, what 2.02. 87
or my dear majesty your queen here, think, | if 2.02.135
welcome — his majesty shall have tribute on me, 2.02.320 P
your majesty and we that have free souls, it 3.02.241 P
safe | that live and feed upon your majesty. 3.03. 10
the cess of majesty | dies not alone, but, like 3.03. 15
we must with all our majesty and skill | both 4.01. 31
if that his majesty would aught with us, | we 4.04. 5
where is the beauteous majesty of denmark? 4.05. 21
these to your majesty, this to the queen. 4.07. 37
i should impart a thing to you from his majesty. 5.02. 90 P
his majesty bade me signify to you that 'a has 5.02.101 P
if it please his majesty, it is the breathing 5.02.174 P
his majesty commended him to you by young osric, 5.02.195 P
i love your majesty | according to my bond, no LR 1.01. 92
all the large effects | that troop with majesty. 1.01.132
honor's bound, | when majesty falls to folly. 1.01.149
most royal majesty, | i crave no more than hath 1.01.193
i yet beseech your majesty — | if for i want 1.01.223
so please your majesty | that we may wake the 4.07. 16
how does my royal lord? how fares your majesty? 4.07. 43
resign, | during the life of this old majesty, 5.03.300
good majesty! ANT 3.03. 2
most gracious majesty! 3.03. 7
what majesty is in her gait? 3.03. 17
remember, | if e'er thou look'st on majesty. 3.03. 18
the man hath seen some majesty, and should know. 3.03. 42
hath he seen majesty? 3.03. 43
you must tell him | that majesty, to keep 5.02. 17
good morrow to your majesty, and to my gracious CYM 2.03. 36 P
his majesty bids you welcome. 3.01. 77 P
beseech your majesty, | forbear sharp speeches 3.05. 38
so please your majesty, | the roman legions, all 4.03. 23
yes, if't please your majesty. PER 2.05. 91
of what a spacious majesty, he carries, | arch'd TNK 4.02. 19
hath chid down all the majesty of england, STM II.C 73
and to add ampler majesty to this | he hath not II.C 101
and lead the majesty of law in lyam | to slip II.C 121
steps, | with gentle majesty and modest pride; VEN 278
silver breast | the sun ariseth in his majesty, 856
estate, | hiding base sin in pleats of majesty; LUC 93
grace and majesty | you might behold triumphing 1387
sight, | serving with looks his sacred majesty, SON 7. 4
wing, | and given grace a double majesty. 78. 8

MAJESTY'S 14 FR 0.0015 REL FR 7 V 7 P

but i must attend his majesty's command, to whom AWW 1.01. 4 P
what hope is there of his majesty's amendment? 1.01. 11 P
my thanks and duty are your majesty's. 1.02. 23
this man may help me to his majesty's ear, | if 5.01. 7
i am a poor man, and at your majesty's command. 5.03.251 P
stay | for nothing but his majesty's approach. R2 1.03. 6
my prisoners in your majesty's behalf. 1H4 1.03. 48
your majesty's good thoughts away from me! 3.02.131
cannot wash your majesty's welsh plood out of H5 4.07.107 P
by jeshu, i am your majesty's countryman, i care 4.07.111 P
i charge you in his majesty's name, apprehend 4.08. 17 P
majesty hear now, saving your majesty's manhood, 4.08. 33 P
i summon your grace to his majesty's parliament, 2H6 2.04. 70
i sue for exil'd majesty's repeal, | let him LUC 640

MAJOR 4 FR 0.0004 REL FR 1 V 3 P

i deny your major. 1H4 2.04.495 P
honor or go or stay, | my major vow lies here; TRO 5.01. 44
the ass in compound with the major part of your COR 2.01. 59 P
and my nativity was under ursa major, so that it LR 1.02.130 P

MAJORITY 1 FR 0.0001 REL FR 1 V 0 P

holds from all soldiers chief majority | and 1H4 3.02.109

/MAKE* 23 FR 0.0026 REL FR 20 V 3 P

which /make such wanton gambols with the wind MV 3.02. 93
/which /tired /majesty /did /make /thee /offer: R2 4.01.178
/make /me, /that /nothing /have, /with /nothing 4.01.216
/like /the /sun, /did /make /beholders /wink? 4.01.284
/before /you /said, | "/let /us /make /head." 2H4 1.01.168
/let /us /make /ready /straight. TRO 4.04.144
/not /strike /it /thus /to /make /it /still. TIT 3.02. 14
/just /against /thy /heart /make /thou /a /hole, 3.02. 17
/nor /nod, /nor /kneel, /nor /make /a /sign, 3.02. 43
/make /my /aunt /merry /with /some /pleasing 3.02. 47
/melody, | /came /here /to /make /us /merry! 3.02. 65
/bid a sick man in sadness /make his will — | a ROM 1.01.202
/the /clown /shall /make /those /laugh /whose HAM 2.02.323 P
/to /make /them /exclaim /against /their /own 2.02.350 P
/they /did /make /love /to /this /employment, 5.02. 57
/which /they /will /make /an /obedient /father. LR 1.04.235 P
/in /their /fury, /and /make /nothing /of, 3.01. 9
/so /far | /to /make /your /speed /to /dover, 3.01. 36
/one /self /mate /and /make /could /not /beget 4.03. 34
/to /make /him /even /o'er /the /time /he /has 4.07. 79
/most /just /and /heavy /causes /make /oppose. 5.01. 27
/amplify /too /much, /would /make /much /more, 5.03.207
and /make me put into contempt the suits | of CYM 3.04. 89

MAKE* 1757 FR 0.1986 REL FR 1360 V 397 P

and make yourself ready in your cabin for the TMP 1.01. 24 P
hanging, make the rope of his destiny our cable, 1.01. 31 P
to besiege, and make his bold waves tremble, 1.02.205
thy groans | did make wolves howl, and penetrate 1.02.288
go make thyself like a nymph o' th' sea; 1.02.301
he does make our fire, | fetch in our wood, and 1.02.311
took pains to make thee speak, taught thee each 1.02.354
make thee roar | that beasts shall tremble at 1.02.370
dam's god, setebos, | and make a vassal of him. 1.02.374
gone forth, i'll make you | the queen of naples. 1.02.449
but this swift business | i must uneasy make, 1.02.452
lest too light winning | make the prize light. 1.02.453
make not too rash a trial of him, for | he's 1.02.468
with this stick, | and make thy weapon drop. 1.02.474
one word more | shall make me chide thee, if not 1.02.477
else o' th' earth | let liberty make use of; 1.02.493
you make me study of that. 2.01. 82 P
what impossible matter will he make easy next? 2.01. 89 P
i myself could make | a chough of as deep chat. 2.01.265
fright a monster's ear, | to make an earthquake! 2.01.315
and let's make further search | for my poor son. 2.01.323
on prosper fall and make him | by inch–meal a 2.02. 2
there would this monster make a man; 2.02. 30 P
went on four legs cannot make him give ground"; 2.02. 61 P
monster, to make a wonder of a poor drunkard! 2.02.165 P
no more dams i'll make for fish, | nor fetch in 2.02.180
to make me slave to it, and for your sake | am i 3.01. 66
out o' doors, and make a stock–fish of thee. 3.02. 70 P
after long sleep, | will make me sleep again; 3.02.140
all praise | and make it halt behind her. 4.01. 11
heavens let fall | to make this contract grow; 4.01. 19
betrims, | to make cold nymphs chaste crowns; 4.01. 66
make holiday; 4.01.136
do that good mischief which may make this island 4.01.217
our skins with pinches, | make us strange stuff. 4.01.234
and more pinch–spotted make them | than pard or 4.01.260
by moonshine do the green sour ringlets make, 5.01. 37
whose pastime | is to make midnight mushrumps, 5.01. 39
and, supportable | to make the dear loss, have i 5.01.146
could control the moon, make flows and ebbs, 5.01.270
i not doubt, shall make it | go quick away — 5.01.304
such another proof will make me cry "baa." TGV 1.01. 93 P
like it, | the execution of it shall make known: 1.03. 36
sir, so painted to make her fair, that no man 2.01. 59 P
why then we'll make exchange: 2.02. 6
word with me, i shall make your wit bankrupt. 2.04. 42 P
beshrew me, sir, but if he make this good, | he 2.04. 75
flow'r | and make rough winter everlastingly. 2.04.163
will you make haste? 2.04.190
love, lend me wings to make my purpose swift, 2.06. 42
better forbear till proteus make return. 2.07. 14
stream, | and make a pastime of each weary step, 2.07. 35
what fashion, madam, shall i make your breeches? 2.07. 49
i fear me, it will make me scandaliz'd. 2.07. 61
as thou lov'st thy life, make speed from hence. 3.01.169
and now excess of it will make me surfeit. 3.01.222
bid him make haste and meet me at the north–gate 3.01.260
what might we do to make the girl forget | the 3.02. 29
make tigers tame, and huge leviathans | forsake 3.02. 79
if not, we'll make you sit, and rifle you. 4.01. 4
to make a virtue of necessity | and live as we 4.01. 60
return, return, and make thy love amends. 4.02. 99
and to your shadow will i make true love. 4.02.125
deceive it, | and make it but a shadow, as i am. 4.02.127
see me heave up my leg and make water against a 4.04. 38 P
in her, | but i can make respective in myself, 4.04.195
eyes, | to make my master out of love with thee. 4.04.205
i'll wear a boot, to make it somewhat rounder. 5.02. 6
are my mates, that make their wills their law, 5.04. 14
o proteus, let this habit make thee blush! 5.04.104
let me be blest to make this happy close; 5.04.117
to make such means for her as thou hast done, 5.04.137
with our discourse to make your grace to smile. 5.04.163
i will make a star chamber matter of it. WIV 1.01. 1 P
glad to do my benevolence to make atonements and 1.01. 33 P
ay, and her father is make her a petter penny. 1.01. 60 P
i will make a prief of it in my note–book, and 1.01.144 P
i will make an end of my dinner; 1.02. 12 P
i do mean to make love to ford's wife. 1.03. 44 P
dress meat and drink, make the beds, and do all 1.04. 97 P
a scurvy jack–a–nape priest to meddle or make — 1.04.110 P
as i have an eye to make difference of men's 2.01. 57 P
/god bless them and make them his servants! 2.02. 52 P
i'll make more of thy old body than i have done. 2.02.139 P
i make bold, to press with so little preparation 2.02.156 P
means as desire to make myself acquainted with 2.02.183 P
/brook, i will first make bold with your money; 2.02.252 P
i see a sword out, my finger itches to make one. 2.03. 46 P
that is, he will make thee amends. 2.03. 67 P
there will we make our peds of roses, | and a 3.01. 19
and i will one way or other make you amends. 3.01. 87 P

i'll make him dance. 3.02. 90 P
to thee and shall make thee a new doublet and 3.03. 34 P
before the best lord, i would make thee my lady. 3.03. 51 P
thou wouldst make an absolute courtier, and the 3.03. 62 P
without cause, why then make sport at me, then 3.03.150 P
heaven make you better than your thoughts! 3.03.204 P
i will hereafter make known to you why i have 3.03.225 P
there is one, i shall make two in the company. 3.03.234 P
i'll make a shaft or a bolt on't. 3.04. 24 P
he will make you a hundred and fifty pounds 3.04. 48 P
she'll make you amends, i warrant you. 3.05. 47 P
to be what i would not shall not make me tame. 3.05.150 P
if i have horns to make one mad, let the proverb 3.05.151 P
to make another experiment of his suspicion. 4.02. 35 P
but what make you here? 4.02. 54 P
shall have my horses, but i'll make them pay; 4.03. 8 P
wives | yet once again (to make us public sport) 4.04. 13
i shall make my master glad with these tidings. 4.05. 55 P
is tell–a me dat you make grand preparation for 4.05. 87 P
besides, i'll make a present recompense. 4.06. 55
crier hobgoblin, make the fairy oyes. 5.05. 41
i'll make the best in gloucestershire know on't. 5.05.180 P
make us pay down for our offense by weight | the MM 1.02.121
that she make friends | to the strict deputy; 1.02.180
the rather for i now must make you know | i am 1.04. 22
sir, make me not your story. 1.04. 30
rigor of the statute, | to make him an example. 1.04. 68
we must not make a scarecrow of the law, 2.01. 1
till custom make it | their perch and not their 2.01. 3
foully for those things | that make her good? 2.02.174
and to make me know | the nature of their crimes 2.03. 6
metal in restrained means | to make a false one. 2.04. 49
i'll make it my morn–prayer | to have it added 2.04. 71
you seem'd of late to make the law a tyrant, 2.04.114
which are as easy broke as they make forms. 2.04.126
bidding the law make curtsy to their will, 2.04.175
limb, nor beauty, | to make thy riches pleasant. 3.01. 38
therefore your best appointment make with speed, 3.01. 59
that thus can make him bite the law by th' nose, 3.01.108
go to your knees, and make ready. 3.01.170 P
i do make myself believe that you may most 3.01.199 P
maid will i frame and make fit for his attempt. 3.01.256 P
let me desire you to make your answer before him 3.02.156 P
this would make mercy swear and play the tyrant. 3.02.194 P
truth enough alive to make societies secure, but 3.02.227 P
security enough to make fellowships accurs'd. 3.02.228 P
any thing which profess'd to make him rejoice; 3.02.236 P
music oft hath such a charm | to make bad good, 4.01. 15
i shall attend your leisure, but make haste, 4.01. 56
wit | make thee the father of their idle dream 4.01. 63
to make you understand this in a manifested 4.02.159 P
i may make my case as claudio's, to cross this 4.02.167 P
make a swift return, | for i would commune with 4.03.103
i'll make all speed. 4.03.105
to make her heavenly comforts of despair, | when 4.03.110
you make my bonds still greater. 5.01. 8
see, to make them know | that outward courtesies 5.01. 14
make not impossible | that which but seems 5.01. 51
to make the truth appear where it seems hid, 5.01. 66
and all probation will make up full clear, 5.01.157
wife as strongly | as words could make up vows; 5.01.228
persons with me, ere you make that my report. 5.01.337 P
make rash remonstrance of my hidden pow'r | than 5.01.392
make it your comfort, | so happy is your brother 5.01.398
beg thou, or borrow, to make up the sum, | and ERR 1.01.153
of whom i hope to make much benefit; 1.02. 25
love, | and make a common of my serious hours. 2.02. 29
the sun shines, let foolish gnats make sport, 2.02. 30
i'll make you amends next, to give you nothing 2.02. 53 P
lest it make you choleric, and purchase me 2.02. 62 P
it would make a man mad as a buck to be so 3.01. 72
good sir, make haste. 3.01.119
make us /but believe | (being compact of credit) 3.02. 21
you, | to make it wander in an unknown field? 3.02. 38
to put her to but to make a lamp of her and run 3.02. 97 P
therefore make present satisfaction, | or i'll 4.01. 5
/sweat now, make haste! 4.02. 29
as much to say, "god make me a light wench." 4.03. 54 P
pack | to make a loathsome abject scorn of me; 4.04.103
wilt thou suffer them | to make a rescue? 4.04.111
unquiet meals make ill digestions, | thereof the 5.01. 74
prayers, | to make of him a formal man again: 5.01.105
when thou didst make him master of thy bed, | to 5.01.163
unless the fear of death doth make me dote, | i 5.01.195
albeit my wrongs might make one wiser mad. 5.01.217
i see thy age and dangers make thee dote. 5.01.330
then | i hope i shall have leisure to make good, 5.01.376
company, | and we shall make full satisfaction. 5.01.400
squarer now that will make a voyage with him to ADO 1.01. 82 P
scratching could not make it worse, and 'twere 1.01.136 P
but you must not make the full show of this till 1.03. 19 P
but by the fair weather that you make yourself. 1.03. 24 P
can you make no use of your discontent? 1.03. 38 P
i make all use of it, for i use it only. 1.03. 39 P
dress him in my apparel and make him my 2.01. 35 P
it is my cousin's duty to make cur'sy and say, 2.01. 52 P
fellow, or else make another cur'sy and say, 2.01. 55 P
not till god make men of some other mettle than 2.01. 59 P
to make an account of her life to a clod of 2.01. 62 P
revellers are ent'ring, brother, make good room. 2.01. 84 P
did he never make you laugh? 2.01.135 P
to a willow–tree, either to make him a garland, 2.01.218 P
wilt thou make a trust a transgression? 2.01.225 P
and have cleft his club to make the fire too. 2.01.254 P
what proof shall i make of that? 2.02. 27 P
of me, he shall never make me such a fool. 2.03. 26 P
he would make but a sport of it, and torment the 2.03.156 P
and she will die ere she make her love known, 2.03.175 P
if she should make tender of her love, 'tis very 2.03.178 P
not in him by some large jests he will make. 2.03.198 P
i'll make her come, i warrant you, presently. 3.01. 14
she knew his love, lest she'll make sport at it. 3.01. 58
give god thanks, and make no boast of it, and 3.03. 20 P
you shall also make no noise in the streets; 3.03. 34 P
if they make you not then the better answer, you 3.03. 46 P
men, the less you meddle or make with them, why, 3.03. 52 P
ones, poor ones may make what price they will. 3.03.114 P
i dare make his answer, none. 4.01. 18 P

to make you answer truly to your name. 4.01. 79
and i will make him eat it that says i love not 4.01.277 P
make misfortune drunk | with candle–wasters, 5.01. 17
make those that do offend you suffer too. 5.01. 40
i will make it good how you dare, with what you 5.01.146 P
thy single life, to make thee a double–dealer, 5.04.114 P
keen edge, | and make us heirs of all eternity. LLL 1.01. 7
and dainty bits | make rich the ribs, but 1.01. 27
and make a dark night too of half the day — 1.01. 45
necessity will make us all forsworn | three 1.01.149
for he hath wit to make an ill shape good, | and 2.01. 59
for you'll prove perjur'd if you make me stay. 2.01.113
your fair self should make | a yielding 'gainst 2.01.150
may | make tender of to thy true worthiness. 2.01.170
all his behaviors did make their retire | to the 2.01.234
all senses to that sense did make their repair, 2.01.240
child, make passionate my sense of hearing. 3.01. 1 P
and make them men of note — do you note? 3.01. 24 P
to make plain | some obscure precedence that 3.01. 81
a stand where you may make the fairest shoot. 4.01. 10
of one sore i an hundred make by adding but one 4.02. 61
"if love make me forsworn, how shall i swear to 4.02.105
my tears for glasses, and still make me weep. 4.03. 38
your eyes do make no /coaches; 4.03.153
three fools lack'd me fool to make up the mess. 4.03.203
where several worthies make one dignity, | where 4.03.232
and therefore is she born to make black fair. 4.03.257
the gods | make heaven drowsy with the harmony. 4.03.342
to make frantic, lunatic. 5.01. 26 P
lend me your horn to make one, and i will whip 5.01. 68 P
what a joyful father wouldest thou make me! 5.01. 77 P
that is the way to make an offense gracious, 5.01.140 P
i'll make one in a dance, or so; 5.01.153
that was the way to make his godhead wax, | for 5.02. 10
how i would make him fawn, and beg, and seek, 5.02. 62
and make him proud to make me proud that jests! 5.02. 66
and make him proud to make me proud that jests! 5.02. 66
and i make no doubt | the rest will /ne'er come 5.02.151
to make theirs ours and ours none but our own; 5.02.154
to make my lady laugh when she's dispos'd, 5.02.466
forestall our sport, to make us thus untrue? 5.02.473
with targe and shield did make my foe to sweat, 5.02.553
to make judas hang himself. 5.02.604 P
look into these faults, | suggested us to make. 5.02.770
ever to be true | to those that make us both — 5.02.774
short | to make a world–without–end bargain in. 5.02.789
or a part to tear a cat in, to make all split. MND 1.02. 30 P
far, | and make and mar | the foolish fates." 1.02. 37
i will roar, that i will make the duke say, "let 1.02. 72 P
and bootless make the breathless huswife churn, 2.01. 37
and sometime make the drink to bear no barm, 2.01. 38
i jest to oberon and make him smile | when i a 2.01. 44
and make him with fair /aegles break his faith, 2.01. 79
laid | will make or man or woman madly dote 2.01.171
herb), | i'll make her render up her page to me. 2.01.185
i'll follow thee and make a heaven of hell, | to 2.01.243
eyes, | and make her full of hateful fantasies. 2.01.258
leathren wings | to make my small elves coats, 2.02. 5
knit, | so that but one heart we can make of it; 2.02. 48
i have a device to make all well. 3.01. 16 P
make it two more; 3.01. 25 P
this is a knavery of them to make me afeard. 3.01.113 P
this is to make an ass of me, to fright me, if 3.01.120 P
honest neighbors will not make them friends. 3.01.146 P
if i cut my finger, i shall make bold with you. 3.01.183 P
pay, | if for his tender here i make some stay. 3.02. 87
the noise they make | will cause demetrius to 3.02.116
a poor soul's patience, all to make you sport. 3.02.161
could not this make thee know, | the hate i bare 3.02.189
make mouths upon me when i turn my back, | wink 3.02.238
you would not make me such an argument. 3.02.242
and make his eyeballs roll with wonted sight. 3.02.369
but, notwithstanding, haste, make no delay; 3.02.394
a knavish lad, | thus to make poor females mad. 3.02.441
peradventure, to make it the more gracious, i 4.01.218 P
make choice of which your highness will see 5.01. 43
pale, | make periods in the midst of sentences, 5.01. 96
but wonder on till truth make all things plain. 5.01.128
friend, would go near to make a man look sad. 5.01.289 P
lovers, make moan; 5.01.334
make no stay; 5.01.421
tongue, | we will make amends ere long; 5.01.434
and every object that might make me fear MV 1.01. 20
my ventures, out of doubt | would make me sad. 1.01. 22
that such a thing bechanc'd would make me sad? 1.01. 38
we'll make our leisures to attend on yours. 1.01. 68
nor do i now make moan to be abridg'd | from 1.01.126
and i no question make | to have it of my trust, 1.01.184
i hope i shall make shift to go without him. 1.02. 90 P
was this inserted to make interest good? 1.03. 94
i cannot tell, i make it breed as fast. 1.03. 96
and let us make incision for your love, | to 2.01. 6
to make me blest or cursed'st among men. 2.01. 46
under which lorenzo | desir'd us to make stand. 2.06. 2
i will make fast the doors, and gild myself 2.06. 49
now make your choice. 2.07. 3
bassanio told him he would make some speed | of 2.08. 37
of venice, i can make what merchandise i will. 3.01.128 P
me, | but if you do, you'll make me wish a sin, 3.02. 13
let music sound while he doth make his choice; 3.02. 43
make it less, | for fear i surfeit. 3.02.113
your good leave to go away, | i will make haste; 3.02.325
make room, and let him stand before our face. 4.01. 16
to wag their high tops and to make no noise 4.01. 76
therefore i do beseech you | make no moe offers, 4.01. 81
no, none that thou hast wit enough to make. 4.01.127
if she were by to hear you make the offer. 4.01.289
the wish would make else an unquiet house. 4.01.294
away, make haste. 4.01.454
which i did make him swear to keep for ever. 4.02. 14
away, make haste. 4.02. 18
kiss the trees | and they did make no noise, in 5.01. 3
you shall perceive them make a mutual stand, 5.01. 77
for a light wife doth make a heavy husband, 5.01.130
were you the clerk that is to make me cuckold? 5.01.281
now, sir, what make you here? AYL 1.01. 29 P
nothing. i am not taught to make any thing. 1.01. 30 P
marry, i prithee do, to make sport withal. 1.02. 26 P

we will make it our suit to the duke that the 1.02.181 P
yet your mistrust cannot make me a traitor. 1.03. 56
i'll make him find him. 2.02. 19
why, what make you here? 2.03. 4
that is the way to make her scorn you still. 2.04. 22
folly | that ever love did make thee run into, 2.04. 35
it will make you melancholy, monsieur jaques. 2.05. 10 P
i give heaven thanks, and make no boast of them. 2.05. 37 P
make an extent upon his house and lands. 3.01. 17
god make incision in thee! 3.02. 72 P
shepherd, let us make an honorable retreat, 3.02.160 P
youth, i would i could make thee believe i love. 3.02.385 P
you may as soon make her that you love believe 3.02.387 P
and therefore i pray the gods make me honest. 3.03. 34 P
wounds invisible | that love's keen arrows make. 3.05. 31
he'll make a proper man. 3.05.115
and faster than his tongue | did make offense, 3.05.117
i had rather have a fool to make me merry than 4.01. 28 P
make me merry than experience to make me sad — 4.01. 29 P
better jointure, i think, than you make a woman. 4.01. 56 P
make the doors upon a woman's wit, and it will 4.01.161 P
woman that cannot make her fault her husband's 4.01.174 P
how it be in tune, so it make noise enough. 4.02. 9 P
offer take | of me and all that i can make, | or 4.03. 61
what, to make thee an instrument, and play false 4.03. 67 P
i kill thee, make thee away, translate thy life 5.01. 52 P
i have promis'd to make all this matter even: 5.04. 18
from hence i go | to make these doubts all even. 5.04. 25
'tis i must make conclusion | of these most 5.04.126
for my kind offer, when i make curtsy, bid me ep 22 P
and burn sweet wood to make the lodging sweet. SHR in.1. 49
wakes, | to make a dulcet and a heavenly sound; in.1. 51
may show her duty and make known her love?" in.1. 117
what, would you make me mad? in.2. 17 P
thy hounds shall make the welkin answer them in.2. 45
to make a stale of me amongst these mates? 1.01. 58
that i may soon make good | what i have said, 1.01. 74
and make her bear the penance of her tongue? 1.01. 89
while i make way from hence to save my life. 1.01.234
execute — | to make one among these wooers. 1.01.247
have leave and leisure to make love to her, 1.02.136
lucentio shall make one, | though paris came in 1.02.244
to make a bondmaid and a slave of me — | that i 2.01. 2
to make mine eye the witness | of that report 2.01. 52
do make myself a suitor to your daughter, | unto 2.01. 90
thy beauty that doth make me like thee well, 2.01.274
never make denial; 2.01.279
a meacock wretch can make the curstest shrew. 2.01.313
and let your father make her the assurance, 2.01.387
be bride to you, if you make this assurance; 2.01.396
my lessons make no music in three parts. 3.01. 60
make friends, invite, and proclaim the banes, 3.02. 16
and make assurance here in padua | of greater 3.02.134
make it no wonder; 3.02.191
i am sent before to make a fire, and they are 4.01. 4 P
but wilt thou make a fire, or shall i complain 4.01. 29 P
to make her come and know her keeper's call, 4.01.194
my tale, | i'll make him glad to seem vincentio, 4.02. 68
then go with me to make the matter good. 4.02.115
you bid me make it orderly and well, | according 4.03. 94
hence, make your best of it. 4.03.100
belike you mean to make a puppet of me. 4.03.103
why, true, he means to make a puppet of thee. 4.03.104
says your worship means to make a puppet of her. 4.03.105 P
home, | and bid bianca make her ready straight; 4.04. 63
'a will make the man mad, to make /a woman of 4.05. 35 P
will make the man mad, to make /a woman of him. 4.05. 35 P
and withal make known | which way thou 4.05. 50
a hundred pound or two, to make merry withal? 5.01. 22 P
mother, your mistress, | and make much of her. AWW 1.01. 77
that you were made of is metal to make virgins. 1.01.130 P
within /t' /one year it will make itself two, 1.01.147 P
and would seem | to have us make denial. 1.02. 9
wound our modesty and make foul the clearness of 1.03. 6 P
ability enough to make such knaveries yours. 1.03. 12 P
may lawfully make title to as much love as she 1.03.103 P
and make you dance canary | with spritely fire 2.01. 74
of heaven, not me, make an experiment. 2.01.154
make thy demand. 2.01.191
but will you make it even? 2.01.191
so make the choice of thy own time, for i, | thy 2.01.203
why, what place make you special, when you put 2.02. 5 P
he that cannot make a leg, put off 's cap, kiss 2.02. 10 P
to make modern and familiar things supernatural 2.03. 2 P
hence is it that we make trifles of terrors, 2.03. 4 P
thy frank election make; 2.03. 55
make choice and see, | who shuns thy love shuns 2.03. 72
love make your fortunes twenty times above | her 2.03. 82
would send them to th' turk, to make eunuchs of. 2.03. 88 P
good, | to make yourself a son out of my blood. 2.03. 97
and master did well to make his recantation. 2.03.186 P
thou didst make tolerable vent of thy travel; 2.03.202 P
your lordship to make some reservation of your 2.03.245 P
dost make hose of thy sleeves? 2.03.250 P
to make the coming hour o'erflow with joy | and 2.04. 46
and make this haste as your own good proceeding, 2.04. 49
apology you think | may make it probable need. 2.04. 51
i pray you make us friends, i will pursue the 2.05. 13 P
bedded her, and sworn to make the 'not' eternal. 3.02. 22 P
make me but like my thoughts, and i shall prove 3.03. 10
i have no skill in sense | to make distinction. 3.04. 40
do you think he will make no deed at all of this 3.06. 94 P
we'll make you some sport with the fox ere we 3.06.102 P
great oaths would scarce make that be believ'd. 4.01. 60 P
i see that men make rope's in such a scarre 4.02. 38
mightily sometimes we make us comforts of our 4.03. 65 P
match, and well make it; 4.03.225
simply the thing i am | shall make me live. 4.03.334
that can such sweet use make of what they hate, 4.04. 22
but rather make you thank your pains for it. 5.01. 33
what good speed | our means will make us means. 5.01. 35
let the justices make you and fortune friends; 5.02. 33 P
and i beseech your majesty to make it | natural 5.03. 5
durst make too bold a herald of my tongue; 5.03. 46
make trivial price of serious things we have, 5.03. 61
if she, my liege, can make me know this clearly, 5.03.315
wait on me home, i'll make sport with thee. 5.03.322 P
know, | to make the even truth in pleasure flow. 5.03.326

i would not so much as make water but in a TN 1.03.130 P
bounds, | rather than make unprofited return. 1.04. 22
make that good. 1.05. 7 P
make your excuse wisely, you were best. 1.05. 30 P
make your proof. 1.05. 61 P
decays the wise, doth ever make the better fool. 1.05. 76 P
of moon with me to make one in so skipping a 1.05.201 P
make me a willow cabin at your gate, | and call 1.05.268
and make the babbling gossip of the air | cry 1.05.273
love make his heart of flint that you shall love 1.05.286
but shall we make the welkin dance indeed? 2.03. 57 P
do ye make an alehouse of my lady's house, that 2.03. 88 P
break promise with him and make a fool of him. 2.03.128 P
an ayword, and make him a common recreation, do 2.03.135 P
matter we can hardly make distinction of our 2.03.161 P
and your horse now would make him an ass. 2.03.168 P
plant you two, and let the fool make a third, 2.03.174 P
and the tailor make thy doublet of changeable 2.04. 74 P
make no compare | between that love a woman can 2.04.101
know this letter will make a contemplative idiot 2.05. 19 P
with an obedient start, make out for him. 2.05. 59 P
if i could make that resemble something in me! 2.05.119 P
o ay, make up that. he is now at a cold scent. 2.05.121 P
ay, or i'll cudgel him, and make him cry o! 2.05.133 P
i'll make one too. 2.05.207 P
nicely with words may quickly make them wanton. 3.01. 15 P
with that word might make my sister wanton. 3.01. 20 P
sir, i would it would make you invisible. 3.01. 30 P
'slight! will you make an ass o' me? 3.02. 13 P
but since you make your pleasure of your pains, 3.03. 2
i can no other answer make but thanks, | and 3.03. 14
this does make some obstruction in the blood, 3.04. 20 P
it is jove's doing, and jove make me thankful! 3.04. 75 P
why, we shall make him mad indeed. 3.04.133 P
i will make your peace with him if i can. 3.04.269 P
i'll make the motion. 3.04.288 P
stand here, make a good show on't; 3.04.288 P
a little thing would make me tell them how much 3.04.303 P
i'll make division of my present with you. 3.04.346
lest that it make me so unsound a man | as to 3.04.350
will you make me believe that i am not sent for 4.01. 1 P
make him believe thou art sir topas the curate, 4.02. 2 P
make the trial of it in any constant question. 4.02. 48 P
sir, they praise me and make an ass of me. 5.01. 17 P
your four negatives make your two affirmatives, 5.01. 21 P
sir, i would you could make it another. 5.01. 30 P
with which such scathful grapple did he make 5.01. 56
if nothing lets to make us happy both | but this 5.01.249
no sneaping winds at home, to make us say, WT 1.02. 13
of this make no conclusion, lest you say | your 1.02. 81
praise, and make 's | as fat as tame things. 1.02. 91
ere i could make thee open thy white hand | /and 1.02.103
thou dost make possible things not so held, 1.02.139
and make itself a pastime | to harder bosoms! 1.02.152
you had much ado to make his anchor hold, | when 1.02.213
make that thy question, and go rot! 1.02.324
make me not sighted like the basilisk. 1.02.388
to his eye, make known | how he hath drunk, he 2.01. 43
here's such ado to make no stain a stain | as 2.02. 17
make their pastime at my sorrow: 2.03. 24
and would by combat make her good, so were i | a 2.03. 61
savors | of tyranny, and will ignoble make you, 2.03.120
do), | i doubt not then but innocence shall make 3.02. 30
how his piety | does my deeds make the blacker! 3.02.172
all faults i make, when i shall come to know 3.02.219
make your best haste, and go not | too far i' 3.03. 10
but to make an end of the ship, to see how the 3.03. 97 P
and make stale | the glistering of this present, 4.01. 13
they cherish it to make it stay there; 4.03. 92 P
if i make not this cheat bring out another, and 4.03.120 P
for it is | a way to make us better friends, 4.04. 66
and make conceive a bark of baser kind | by bud 4.04. 94
then make /your garden rich in gillyvors, | and 4.04. 98
to make you garlands of, and my sweet friend, 4.04.128
at least if you make a care | of happy holding 4.04.355
to him, and will make | her portion equal his. 4.04.385
make for sicilia, | and there present yourself 4.04.543
we'll make an instrument of this; 4.04.624
outside of thy poverty we must make an exchange; 4.04.633 P
to go about to make me the king's brother–in–law 4.04.701 P
in this farthel will make him scratch his beard. 4.04.708 P
suffer what wit can make heavy and vengeance 4.04.772 P
i'll make it as much more, and leave this young 4.04.807 P
no fault could you make | which you have not 5.01. 2
took something good | to make a perfect woman, 5.01. 15
would make her sainted spirit | again possess 5.01. 57
make proselytes | of who she but bid follow. 5.01.108
therefore follow me | and mark what way i make. 5.01.233
i make a broken delivery of the business; 5.02. 9 P
already — | what was he that did make it? 5.03. 63
make me to think so twenty years together! 5.03. 71
i'll make the statue move indeed, descend, | and 5.03. 88
what you can make her do, | i am content to look 5.03. 91
for 'tis as easy | to make her speak as move. 5.03. 94
ay, and make it manifest where she has liv'd, 5.03.114
well, now can i make any joan a lady. JN 1.01.184
sir robert never holp to make this leg. 1.01.240
to make room for him in my husband's bed. 1.01.255
strength | to make a more requital to your love! 2.01. 34
but we will make it subject to this boy. 2.01. 43
backs, | to make a hazard of new fortunes here. 2.01. 71
let me make answer: thy usurping son. 2.01.121
or lay on that shall make your shoulders crack. 2.01.146
fire, | to make a shaking fever in your walls, 2.01.228
smoke, | to make a faithless error in your ears; 2.01.230
when i have said, make answer to us both. 2.01.235
your lion's hide, | and make a monster of you. 2.01.293
and pell–mell | make work upon ourselves, for 2.01.407
son, list to this conjunction, make this match, 2.01.468
shall gild her bridal bed and make her rich | in 2.01.491
and this rich fair town | we make him lord of. 2.01.553
teach thou this sorrow how to make me die, | and 3.01. 30
nature and fortune join'd to make thee great. 3.01. 52
good reverend father, make my person yours, 3.01.224
make such unconstant children of ourselves, | as 3.01.243
and make a riot on the gentle brow | of true 3.01.247
it is religion that doth make vows kept, | but 3.01.279
and better conquest never canst thou make | than 3.01.290
philip, make up. 3.02. 5
o, this will make my mother die with grief! 3.03. 5
thine ears, and make reply | without a tongue, 3.03. 49
preach some philosophy to make me mad, | and 3.04. 51
there's nothing in this world can make me joy: 3.04.107
may then make all the claim that arthur did. 3.04.143
you will but make it blush | and glow with shame 4.01.112
doth make the fault the worse by th' excuse: 4.02. 31
doth make a stand at what your highness will. 4.02. 39
o, make a league with me, till i have pleas'd 4.02.126
nay, but make haste; 4.02.170
of means to do ill deeds | make deeds ill done! 4.02.220
i'll make a peace between your soul and you. 4.02.250
rage, | and make them tame to their obedience! 4.02.262
and make fair weather in your blust'ring land. 5.01. 21
go i to make the french lay down their arms. 5.01. 24
and make him tremble there? 5.01. 58
send fair–play orders and make compremise, 5.01. 67
perchance the cardinal cannot make your peace; 5.01. 74
thy bosom | doth make an earthquake of nobility. 5.02. 42
to cudgel you and make you take the hatch, | to 5.02.138
what in the world should make me now deceive, 5.04. 26
to make his bleak winds kiss my parched lips 5.07. 40
and the like tender of our love we make, | to 5.07.106
nought shall make us rue, | if england to itself 5.07.117
here to make good the boist'rous late appeal, R2 1.01. 4
speak | my body shall make good upon this earth, 1.01. 37
will i make good against thee, arm to arm, 1.01. 76
upon his bad life to make all this good, | that 1.01. 99
son, | now by /my sceptre's awe i make a vow, 1.01.118
lions make leopards tame. 1.01.174
which since we cannot do to make you friends, 1.01.197
the daintiest last, to make the end most sweet: 1.03. 68
god in thy good cause make thee prosperous! 1.03. 78
and make us wade even in our kinred's blood: 1.03.138
say | i was too strict to make mine own away; 1.03.244
every tedious stride i make | will but remember 1.03.268
wants, | for we will make for ireland presently. 1.04. 52
the lining of his coffers shall make coats | to 1.04. 61
pray god we may make haste and come too late! 1.04. 64
thy frozen admonition | make pale our cheek, 2.01.118
long | shall tender duty make me suffer wrong? 2.01.164
gilt, | and make high majesty look like itself, 2.01.295
whilst others come to make him lose at home. 2.02. 81
weary lords | shall make their way seem short, 2.03. 17
tongue, | before i make reply to aught you say. 2.03. 73
and make you stoop | unto the sovereign mercy of 2.03.156
in love | till you did make him misinterpret me, 3.01. 18
would they make peace? 3.02.133
make war upon their spotted souls for this! 3.02.134
make dust our paper, and with rainy eyes | write 3.02.146
of him, | and learn to make a body of a limb. 3.02.187
we'll make foul weather with despised tears; 3.03.161
and make a dearth in this revolting land. 3.03.163
and make some pretty match with shedding tears? 3.03.165
you make a leg, and bullingbrook says ay. 3.03.175
to make the base earth proud with kissing it. 3.03.191
'twill make me think the world is full of rubs, 3.04. 4
which like unruly children make their sire 3.04. 30
thee | to make a second fall of cursed man? 3.04. 76
and some few vanities that make him light; 3.04. 86
what answer shall i make to this base man? 4.01. 20
woman, do not so, | to make my end too sudden. 5.01. 17
so two together weeping make one woe. 5.01. 86
we make woe wanton with this fond delay, | once 5.01.101
make way, unruly woman! 5.02.110
villain, i'll make thee safe. 5.03. 41
thou frantic woman, what dost thou make here? 5.03. 89
come, my old son, i pray god make thee new. 5.03.146
then treasons make me wish myself a beggar, 5.05. 33
in me it seems it will make wise men mad. 5.05. 63
that brings me food to make misfortune live? 5.05. 71
that blood should sprinkle me to make me grow. 5.06. 46
i'll make a voyage to the holy land, | to wash 5.06. 49
thou wilt, lad, i'll make one, an' i do not, 1H4 1.02.100 P
hal, wilt thou make one? 1.02.137 P
i'll so offend, to make offense a skill, 1.02.216
our own hands | have holp to make so portly. 1.03. 13
my heart, | albeit i make a hazard of my head. 1.03.128
and make the douglas' son your only mean | for 1.03.261
to make us strangers to his looks of love. 1.03.290
if i hang, i'll make a fat pair of gallows; 2.01. 67 P
into) for their own credit sake make all whole. 2.01. 73 P
up and down on her, and make her their boots. 2.01. 82 P
have not given me medicines to make me love him, 2.02. 18 P
there's enough to make us all. 2.02. 58 P
give him as much as will make him a royal man, 2.04.290 P
of england but he would make you believe it was 2.04.307 P
our noses with speargrass to make them bleed, 2.04.310 P
give me a cup of sack to make my eyes look red, 2.04.385 P
peace, cousin percy, you will make him mad. 3.01. 51
life | make me believe that thou art only mark'd 3.02. 9
do, | make blind itself with foolish tenderness. 3.02. 91
that i shall make this northren youth exchange 3.02.145
come sing me a bawdy song, make me merry. 3.03. 14 P
i make as good use of it as many a man doth of a 3.03. 29 P
what, will you make a younker of me? 3.03. 79 P
of sugar–candy to make thee long–winded — if 3.03.160 P
go make ready breakfast; 3.03.170 P
i rather of his absence make this use: 4.01. 76
if we without his help can make a head | to push 4.01. 80
take it for thy labor, and if it make twenty, 4.02. 8 P
but, sirrah, make haste, percy is already in the 4.02. 74 P
to make that worse, suff'red his kinsman march 4.03. 93
how much they do import, you would make haste. 4.04. 5
and 'tis but wisdom to make strong against him. 4.04. 39
therefore make haste. 4.04. 40
considerations infinite | do make against it. 5.01.103
his willingly, let him make a carbonado of me. 5.03. 58 P
i beseech your majesty make up, | lest your 5.04. 5
make up to clifton, i'll to sir nicholas gawsey. 5.04. 58
i'll make it greater ere i part from thee, | and 5.04. 71
i'll crop, to make a garland for my head. 5.04. 73
i should not make so dear a show of zeal; 5.04. 95
therefore i'll make him sure, yea, and i'll 5.04.125 P
i would make him eat a piece of my sword. 5.04.153 P
i, | make fearful musters and prepar'd defense, 2H4 in 12
and make thee rich for doing me such wrong. 1.01. 90
and letters, and make friends with speed — 1.01.214
the name of rebellion can tell how to make it. 1.02. 78 P
the wise may make some dram of a scruple, or 1.02.130 P
they have a good thing, to make it too common. 1.02.215 P
a good wit will make use of any thing. 1.02.247 P
wound, to marry me and make me my lady thy wife. 2.01. 92 P
if a man will make curtsy and say nothing, he is 2.01.124 P
let it alone, i'll make other shift. 2.01.156 P
humble considerations make me out of love with 2.02. 12 P
and you do not make him hang'd among you, the 2.02. 96 P
steep this letter in sack and make him eat it. 2.02.136 P
that's to make him eat twenty of his words. 2.02.137 P
a rib of steel, | to make strength stronger; 2.03. 55
you make fat rascals, mistress doll. 2.04. 41 P
i make them? 2.04. 42 P
gluttony and diseases make, i make them not. 2.04. 42 P
gluttony and diseases make, i make them not. 2.04. 43 P
if the cook help to make the gluttony, you help 2.04. 44 P
the gluttony, you help to make the diseases, 2.04. 45 P
these villains will make the word as odious as 2.04.148 P
cowardice doth not make thee wrong this virtuous 2.04.326 P
make good speed. 3.01. 3
revolution of the times | make mountains level, 3.01. 47
wilt thou make as many holes in an enemy's 3.02.153 P
thou mightst mend him and make him fit to go. 3.02.165 P
go hard but i'll make him a philosopher's two 3.02.329 P
commonwealth, | i make my quarrel in particular. 4.01. 94
i muse you make so slight a question. 4.01.165
if we can make our peace | upon such large terms 4.01.183
marshal, | if we do now make our atonement well, 4.01.219
not love me, nor a man cannot make him laugh, 4.03. 88 P
wherefore should these good news make me sick? 4.04.102
and make me as the poorest vassal is | that doth 4.05.175
/my friends, which thou must make thy friends, 4.05.204
lest rest and lying still might make them look 4.05.211
i should make four dozen of such bearded 5.01. 63 P
your royal thoughts, make the case yours: 5.02. 91
shall "do nothing but eat, and make good cheer, 5.03. 17
i would make this a bloody day to somebody. 5.04. 12 P
shallow, i will make the king do you grace. 5.05. 5 P
inflame thy noble liver, | and make thee rage. 5.05. 32
make less thy body (hence) and more thy grace, 5.05. 52
i will be the man yet that shall make you great. 5.05. 80 P
but a good conscience will make any possible ep 21 P
and make you merry with fair katherine of france ep 28 P
divide one man, | and make imaginary puissance; H5 pr 25
sacred throne, | and make you long become it! 1.02. 8
to make against your highness' claim to france 1.02. 36
make claim and title to the crown of france. 1.02. 68
may i with right and conscience make this claim? 1.02. 96
who will make road upon us | with all advantages 1.02.138
and make /her chronicle as rich with praise | as 1.02.163
make boot upon the summer's velvet buds, | which 1.02.194
and you withal shall make all gallia shake. 1.02.216
we hope to make the sender blush at it. 1.02.299
i will bestow a breakfast to make you friends, 2.01. 11 P
come, shall i make you two friends? 2.01. 90 P
of brabant and of orleance, shall make forth, 2.04. 5
he'll make your paris louvre shake for it, 2.04.132
that he would gladly make show to the world he 3.06. 83 P
i could make as true a boast as that, if i had a 3.07. 62 P
weed, | and make a moral of the devil himself. 4.01. 12
the king himself hath a heavy reckoning to make, 4.01.135 P
ay, he said so, to make us fight cheerfully; 4.01.192 P
acknowledge it, i will make it my quarrel. 4.01.210 P
mount them, and make incision in their hides, 4.02. 9
souls | may make a peaceful and a sweet retire 4.03. 86
and make them skirr away, as swift as stones 4.07. 61
how canst thou make me satisfaction? 4.08. 45
but i will make you to–day a squire of low 5.01. 36 P
i say, i will make him eat some part of my leek, 5.01. 40 P
would conjure in her, you must make a circle; 5.02.293 P
but your request shall make me let it pass. 5.02.344
to make divorce of their incorporate league; 5.02.366
a far more glorious star thy soul will make 1H6 1.01. 55
will make him burst his lead and rise from death 1.01. 64
bonfires in france forthwith i am to make, | to 1.01.153
whose bloody deeds shall make all europe quake. 1.01.156
gall — | nor men nor money hath he to make war. 1.02. 17
only this proof i'll of thy valor make, | in 1.02. 94
strife | but to make open proclamation. 1.03. 71
where is best place to make our batt'ry next? 1.04. 65
and make a quagmire of your mingled brains. 1.04.109
help salisbury to make his testament. 1.05. 17
the shame hereof will make me hide my head. 1.05. 39
dolphin, command the citizens make bonfires, 1.06. 12
that we do make our entrance several ways; 2.01. 30
and here will talbot mount, or make his grave. 2.01. 34
arm, arm! the enemy doth make assault! 2.01. 38
us withal, | make us partakers of a little gain, 2.01. 52
or make my will th' advantage of my good. 2.05.129
through which our policy must make a breach. 3.02. 2
and make thee curse the harvest of that corn. 3.02. 47
and we will make thee famous through the world. 3.03. 13
and make the cowards stand aloof at bay. 4.02. 52
name | to make a bastard and a slave of me! 4.05. 15
a phoenix that shall make all france afeard. 4.07. 93
he'll make his cap co–equal with the crown." 5.01. 33
i'll either make thee stoop and bend thy knee, 5.01. 61
suit, | before thou make a trial of her love? 5.03. 76
i'll undertake to make thee henry's queen, | to 5.03.117
news, | and make this marriage to be solemniz'd. 5.03.168
beams | upon the country where you make abode; 5.04. 88
them) | would make a volume of enticing lines, 5.05. 14
and not to seek a queen to make him rich: 5.05. 52
then let's make haste away, and look unto the 2H6 1.01.208
pirates may make cheap pennyworths of their 1.01.222
and make a show of love to proud duke humphrey, 1.01.241
force perforce i'll make him yield the crown, 1.01.258
my troublous dreams this night doth make me sad. 1.02. 22
that shall make answer to such questions | as by 1.02. 80
when from saint albons we do make return, 1.02. 83
make merry, man, | with thy confederates in this 1.02. 85
hume must make merry with the duchess' gold; 1.02. 87
will make but little for his benefit. 1.03. 98
would make thee quickly hop without thy head. 1.03.137
before we make election, give me leave | to show 1.03.162
we will make fast within a hallow'd verge. 1.04. 22

let me be blessed for the peace i make | against 2.01. 35
make up no factious numbers for the matter, | in 2.01. 39
shall one day make the duke of york a king. 2.02. 79
richard shall live to make the earl of warwick 2.02. 81
and when he please to make commotion, | 'tis to 3.01. 29
and if my death might make this island happy, 3.01.148
and all to make away my guiltless life. 3.01.167
'twill make them cool in zeal unto your grace. 3.01.177
then, | to make the fox surveyor of the fold? 3.01.253
to make commotion, as full well he can, | under 3.01.358
will make him say i mov'd him to those arms. 3.01.378
it, | and make my image but an alehouse sign. 3.02. 81
what were it but to make my sorrow greater? 3.02.148
make thee beg pardon for thy passed speech, 3.02.221
the mortal worm might make the sleep eternal. 3.02.263
there's two of you, the devil make a third, 3.02.303
and boding screech–owls make the consort full! 3.02.327
can i make men live, whe'er they will or no? 3.03. 10
see how the pangs of death do make him grin! 3.03. 24
hold up thy hand, make signal of thy hope. 3.03. 28
here shall they make their ransom on the sand, 4.01. 10
and thou that art his mate, make boot of this; 4.01. 13
yet let not this make thee be bloody–minded; 4.01. 36
remember it, and let it make thee crestfall'n, 4.01. 59
small things make base men proud. 4.01.106
skins of our enemies, to make dog's–leather of. 4.02. 24 P
and i will make it felony to drink small beer. 4.02. 67 P
nay, he can make obligations, and write 4.02. 93 P
him, i will make myself a knight presently. 4.02.119 P
o' th' ear, and that will make 'em red again. 4.07. 86 P
if when you make your pray'rs, | god should be 4.07.114
for me, i will make shift for one; 4.08. 31 P
and make the meanest of you earls and dukes? 4.08. 37
should make a start o'er seas and vanquish you? 4.08. 43
my sword make way for me, for here is no staying 4.08. 59 P
or is he but retir'd to make him strong? 4.09. 9
but i'll make thee eat iron like an ostridge, 4.10. 28 P
but i must make fair weather yet a while, | till 5.01. 30
they come, i'll warrant they'll make it good. 5.01.122
whom angry heavens do make their minister, 5.02. 34
to make a shambles of the parliament house! 3H6 1.01. 71
accurs'd be he that seeks to make them foes! 1.01.205
crown, | what is it, but to make thy sepulchre, 1.01.236
congeal'd with this, do make me wipe off both. 1.03. 52
three times did richard make a lane to me, | and 1.04. 9
come make him stand upon this molehill here 1.04. 67
i prithee grieve, to make me merry, york. 1.04. 86
and i, to make thee mad, do mock thee thus. 1.04. 90
thou wouldst be fee'd, i see, to make me sport: 1.04. 92
i would assay, proud queen, to make thee blush. 1.04.118
'tis beauty that doth oft make women proud, 1.04.128
'tis virtue that doth make them most admir'd, 1.04.130
the contrary doth make thee wond'red at. 1.04.131
to weep is to make less the depth of grief: 2.01. 85
short tale to make, we at saint albons met, 2.01.120
'tis love i bear thy glories make me speak. 2.01.158
may make against the house of lancaster. 2.01.176
shall for the fault make forfeit of his head. 2.01.197
make war with him that climb'd unto their nest, 2.02. 31
for shame, my liege, make them your president! 2.02. 33
no, nor your manhood that durst make you stay. 2.02.108
but ere sunset i'll make thee curse the deed. 2.02.116
to make this shameless callet know herself. 2.02.145
foreslow no longer, make we hence amain. 2.03. 56
nay, stay not to expostulate, make speed, | or 2.05.135
and much effuse of blood doth make me faint. 2.06. 28
and in this covert will we make our stand, 3.01. 3
her sighs will make a batt'ry in his breast, 3.01. 37
my mild entreaty shall not make you guilty. 3.01. 91
it were no less, but yet i'll make a pause. 3.02. 10
i'll make my heaven in a lady's lap, | and deck 3.02.148
shrub, | to make an envious mountain on my back, 3.02.157
i'll make my heaven to dream upon the crown, 3.02.168
to make prescription for a kingdom's worth. 3.03. 94
touching the jointure that your king must make, 3.03.136
device | by this alliance to make void my suit. 3.03.142
i make king lewis behold | thy sly conveyance 3.03.159
had he none else to make a stale but me? 3.03.260
behalf | go levy men, and make prepare for war; 4.01.131
that if about this hour he make this way, 4.05. 10
i make you both protectors of this land, | while 4.06. 41
make much of him, my lords, for this is he 4.06. 75
he'll soon find means to make the body follow. 4.07. 26
we grow stronger, then we'll make our claim; 4.07. 59
come, fellow soldier, make thou proclamation. 4.07. 70
or did he make the jest against his will? 5.01. 30
pardon me, edward, i will make amends; 5.01.100
and make him, naked, foil a man at arms. 5.04. 42
and make him of like spirit to himself. 5.04. 47
what satisfaction canst thou make | for bearing 5.05. 14
i guess, | to make a bloody supper in the tower. 5.05. 85
had i not reason, think ye, to make haste, | and 5.06. 72
let hell make crook'd my mind to answer it. 5.06. 79
the readiest way to make the wench amends | is R3 1.01.155
paul, | i'll make a corse of him that disobeys. 1.02. 37
thou canst make | no excuse current but to hang 1.02. 83
god make your majesty joyful, as you have been! 1.03. 19
he desires to make atonement | between the duke 1.03. 36
that wrens make prey where eagles dare not perch 1.03. 70
marr'd, | that will i make before i let thee go. 1.03.165
king, | as ours by murther, to make him a king! 1.03.197
o, let me make the period to my curse! 1.03.237
would insinuate with thee but to make thee sigh. 1.04.148 P
o excellent device! and make a sop of him. 1.04.157 P
make peace with god, for you must die, my lord. 1.04.249
souls | to counsel me to make my peace with god, 1.04.251
allies, | and make me happy in your unity. 2.01. 31
here | to make the blessed period of this peace. 2.01. 44
to make an act of tragic violence. 2.02. 39
and make me die a good old man! 2.02.109
sweet flow'rs are slow and weeds make haste. 2.04. 15
make war upon themselves, brother to brother, 2.04. 62
good lords, make all the speedy haste you may. 3.01. 60
wit, | his wit set down to make his valure live. 3.01. 86
to make william lord hastings of our mind | for 3.01.162
which may make you and him to rue at th' other. 3.02. 14
and make pursuit where he did mean no chase. 3.02. 30
well, catesby, ere a fortnight make me older, 3.02. 60
the princes both make high account of you — 3.02. 69
make haste, the hour of death is expiate. 3.03. 24
make a short shrift, he longs to see your head. 3.04. 95
only for saying he would make his son | heir to 3.05. 77
heart, | without control, lusted to make a prey. 3.05. 84
for on that ground i'll make a holy descant — 3.07. 49
and make (no doubt) us happy by his reign. 3.07.170
o, make them joyful, grant their lawful suit! 3.07.203
and make me die the thrall of margaret's curse, 4.01. 45
english woes shall make me smile in france. 4.04.115
thy woes will make them sharp and pierce like 4.04.125
thou cam'st on earth to make the earth my hell. 4.04.167
and do intend to make her queen of england. 4.04.264
to make amends i'll give it to your daughter; 4.04.295
i cannot make you what amends i would, 4.04.309
make bold her bashful years with your experience 4.04.326
can make seem pleasing to her tender years? 4.04.342
greatest strength and power that he can make, 4.04.450
let's lack no discipline, make no delay, | for, 5.03. 17
blunt, make some good means to speak with him, 5.03. 40
make us thy ministers of chastisement, | that we 5.03.113
wear it, enjoy it, and make much of it. 5.05. 7
and make poor england weep in streams of blood! 5.05. 37
i come no more to make you laugh; H8 pr 1
we bring | to make that only true we now intend, pr 21
of the town, | be sad, as we would make ye. pr 25
and make my vouch as strong | as shore of rock. 1.01.157
he'll carry it so | to make the sceptre his. 1.02.135
good wine, good welcome, | can make good people. 1.04. 7
yes, if i make my play. 1.04. 46
and hither make, as great embassadors | from 1.04. 55
here i'll make | my royal choice. 1.04. 85
have mercies | more than i dare make faults. 2.01. 71
me, | make of your prayers one sweet sacrifice, 2.01. 77
no black envy | shall make my grave. 2.01. 86
and with that blood will make 'em one day groan 2.01.106
for those you make friends | and give your 2.01.127
i'll make ye know your times of business. 2.02. 71
make yourself mirth with your particular fancy, 2.03.101
and make my challenge | you shall not be my 2.04. 77
upon this business my appearance make | in any 2.04.133
got your leave | to make this present summons. 2.04.220
but all hoods make not monks. 3.01. 23
but how to make ye suddenly an answer | in such 3.01. 70
all your studies | make me a curse like this! 3.01.124
i dare not make myself so guilty | to give up 3.01.139
wit | to make a seemly answer to such persons. 3.01.178
his nose | will make this sting the sooner. 3.02. 56
as thick as thought could make 'em, and | appear 3.02.195
make use now, and provide | for thine own future 3.02.420
as the shrouds make at sea in a stiff tempest, 4.01. 72
shake the press | and make 'em reel before 'em. 4.01. 79
well contented | to make your house our tow'r. 5.01.106
and your appeal to us | there make before them. 5.01.152
that i bring | will make my boldness manners. 5.01.159
the council pray'd me | to make great haste. 5.02. 3
they would shame to make me | wait else at door, 5.02. 16
pace 'em not in their hands to make 'em gentle, 5.02. 57
men that make | envy and crooked malice 5.02. 78
i make as little doubt as you do conscience | in 5.02.102
make me no more ado, but all embrace him. 5.02.193
as 'tis to make 'em sleep | on may–day morning, 5.03. 14
make way there for the princess. 5.03. 87
stand close up, or i'll make your head ache. 5.03. 88
heaven ever laid up to make parents happy | may 5.04. 7
of his name | shall be, and make new nations. 5.04. 52
this little one shall make it holy–day. 5.04. 76
my part, i'll not meddle nor make no farther. TRO 1.01. 14 P
i'll meddle nor make no more i' th' matter. 1.01. 83 P
man, that makes me smile, make hector angry? 1.02. 32 P
that's true, make no question of that. 1.02.160 P
and make a sop of all this solid globe; 1.03.113
power), | must make perforce an universal prey, 1.03.123
as stuff for these two to make paradoxes. 1.03.184
shall make it good, or do his best to do it: 1.03.274
publication, make no strain | but that achilles, 1.03.326
no, make a lott'ry, | and by device let blockish 1.03.373
and make him fall | his crest that prouder than 1.03.378
i would make thee the loathsomest scab in greece 2.01. 28 P
draught–oxen, and make you plough up the wars. 2.01.106 P
respect | make livers pale and lustihood deject. 2.02. 50
to make the service greater than the god, | and 2.02. 57
honors all engag'd | to make it gracious. 2.02.125
blood | than to make up a free determination 2.02.170
make that demand of the prover, it suffices me 2.03. 67 P
i will knead him, i'll make him supple. 2.03.221 P
i will make a complimental assault upon him, for 3.01. 39 P
by my life, you shall make it whole again — you 3.01. 51 P
and to make a sweet lady sad is a sour offense. 3.01. 72 P
for him at supper, you will make his excuse. 3.01. 77 P
well, i'll make 's excuse. 3.01. 90 P
in, after falling out, may make them three. 3.01.103 P
'twill make us proud to be his servant, paris! 3.01.155
fears make devils of cherubins, they never see 3.02. 69 P
what wouldst thou of us, troyan? make demand. 3.03. 17
cannot make boast to have that which he hath, 3.03. 98
his presence, let patroclus make demands to me; 3.03.271 P
apollo get his sinews to make catlings on. 3.03.304 P
make cressid's name the very crown of falsehood, 4.02.100
this brave shall oft make thee to hide thy head. 4.04.137
i'll make my match to live, | the kiss you take 4.05. 37
make cruel way | through ranks of greekish youth 4.05.184
and make distinct the very breach whereout 4.05.245
to make a recordation to my soul | of every 5.02.116
make wells and niobes of the maids and wives, 5.10. 19
not the patricians, make it, and | your knees to COR 1.01. 73
make edicts for usury, to support usurers; 1.01. 81 P
i may make the belly smile | as well as speak — 1.01.109
yet i can make my audit up, that all | from me 1.01.144
but make you ready your stiff bats and clubs, 1.01.161
itch of your opinion | make yourselves scabs? 1.01.166
to make him worthy whose offense subdues him, 1.01.175
i'd make a quarry | with thousands of these 1.01.198
of generosity | and make bold power look pale — 1.01.212
i'd revolt, to make | only my wars with him. 1.01.234
doubt prevailing, and to make it brief wars. 1.03.100 P
now, mars, i prithee make us quick in work, 1.04. 10
i'll leave the foe | and make my wars on you. 1.04. 40
let's fetch him off, or make remain alike. 1.04. 62
take | convenient numbers to make good the city, 1.05. 12
make you a sword of me? 1.06. 76
make good this ostentation, and you shall 1.06. 86
but cannot make my heart consent to take | a 1.09. 37
of your necks and make but an interior survey of 2.01. 40 P
palate adversely, i make a crooked face at it. 2.01. 56 P
with the colic, you make faces like mummers, set 2.01. 74 P
all the peace you make in their cause is calling 2.01. 78 P
i will make my very house reel to–night. 2.01.111 P
in which time i will make a lip at the physician 2.01.115 P
that he will give them make i as little question 2.01.230
make way, they are coming. 2.02. 36 P
and make us think | rather our state's defective 2.02. 49
are well pleas'd | to make thee consul. 2.02.133
to be ingrateful were to make a monster of the 2.03. 11 P
and to make us no better thought of, a little 2.03. 14 P
he's to make his requests by particulars, 2.03. 43 P
i will make much of your voices, and so trouble 2.03.109 P
him joy, and make him good friend to the people! 2.03.135 P
make them of no more voice | than dogs, that are 2.03.215
shall prompt them, to make road | upon 's again. 3.01. 5
ill as you, and make you | your fellow tribune. 3.01. 51
current in a ditch, | and make your channel his? 3.01. 97
the nature of our seats and make the rabble 3.01.136
that you | have holp to make this rescue? 3.01.275
sir, 'tis fit | you make strong party, or defend 3.02. 94
a beggar's tongue | make motion through my lips, 3.02.118
make them be strong, and ready for this hint 3.03. 23
with precepts that would make invincible | the 4.01. 10
what then? | he'ld make an end of thy posterity. 4.02. 26
but a small thing would make it flame again; 4.03. 21 P
straight | and make my misery serve thy turn. 4.05. 88
here do we make his friends | blush that the 4.06. 4
and defense | that rome can make against them. 4.06.128
have wrack'd for rome | to make coals cheap! 5.01. 17
more than the instant army we can make, | might 5.01. 37
only make trial what your love can do | for rome 5.01. 40
doves' eyes, | which can make gods forsworn? 5.03. 28
impossibility, to make | what cannot be, slight 5.03. 61
which should | make our eyes flow with joy, 5.03. 99
aufidius, though i cannot make true wars, | i'll 5.03.190
it is no little thing to make | mine eyes to 5.03.195
good sir, | what peace you'll make, advise me. 5.03.197
have you lurk'd, that you make doubt of it? 5.04. 46
and the shouting romans, | make the sun dance. 5.04. 51
praise the gods, | and make triumphant fires! 5.05. 3
let's make the best of it. 5.06.146
romans, make way! TIT 1.01. 64
make way to lay them by their bretheren. 1.01. 89
away with him, and make a fire straight, | and 1.01.127
make this his latest farewell to their souls. 1.01.149
tribunes, i thank you, and this suit i make, 1.01.223
family, | lavinia will i make my empress, 1.01.240
can make you greater than the queen of goths. 1.01.269
was none in rome to make a stale | but saturnine 1.01.304
and make them know what 'tis to let a queen 1.01.454
learn thou to make some meaner choice, | lavinia 2.01. 73
uncouple here and let us make a bay, | and wake 2.02. 3
when every thing doth make a gleeful boast? 2.03. 11
and make a checker'd shadow on the ground. 2.03. 15
to–day, | thy sons make pillage of her chastity, 2.03. 44
doth make your honor of his body's hue, 2.03. 73
would make such fearful and confused cries, | as 2.03.102
and make his dead trunk pillow to our lust. 2.03.130
i warrant you, madam, we will make that sure. 2.03.133
farewell, my sons, see that you make her sure. 2.03.187
and make the silken strings delight to kiss them 2.04. 46
come let us go, and make thy father blind, | for 2.04. 52
sons' sweet blood will make it shame and blush. 3.01. 15
or make some sign how i may do thee ease. 3.01.121
to make us wonder'd at in time to come. 3.01.135
ah, that this sight should make so deep a wound, 3.01.246
and make them blind with tributary tears; 3.01.269
and make proud saturnine and his emperess | beg 3.01.297
oft, | extremity of griefs would make men mad; 4.01. 19
i'll make you feed on berries and on roots, 4.02.177
sirrah, come hither, make no more ado, | but 4.03.102
frantic wretch, that holp'st to make me great, 4.04. 59
any scath, | let him make treble satisfaction. 5.01. 8
make poor men's cattle break their necks, | set 5.01.132
is it your trick to make me ope the door | that 5.02. 10
i'll make him send for lucius his son; 5.02. 75
goths, | or at the least make them his enemies. 5.02. 79
and with your blood and it i'll make a paste, 5.02.187
and make two pasties of your shameful heads, 5.02.189
be every one officious | to make this banket, 5.02.202
souls, | and make a mutual closure of our house. 5.03.134
stars that make dark heaven light. ROM 1.02. 25
and i will make thee think thy swan a crow. 1.02. 87
your consent gives strength to make /it fly. 1.03. 99
and, touching hers, make blessed my rude hand. 1.05. 51
my soul, | you'll make a mutiny among my guests! 1.05. 80
for shame, | i'll make you quiet. 1.05. 88
and make her airy tongue more hoarse than /mine, 2.02.162
the excuse that thou dost make in this delay 2.05. 33
there stays a husband to make you a wife. 2.05. 69
come, come with me, and we will make short work, 2.06. 35
it with something, make it a word and a blow. 3.01. 40 P
what, dost thou make us minstrels? 3.01. 46 P
and thou make minstrels of us, look to hear 3.01. 47 P
fiddlestick, here's that shall make you dance. 3.01. 49 P
that i mean to make bold withal, and, as you 3.01. 78 P
make haste, lest mine be about your ears ere it 3.01. 81 P
and he will make the face of heaven so fine 3.02. 23
griefs, these woes, these sorrows make me old. 3.02. 89
unless philosophy can make a juliet, | displant 3.03. 58
hie you, make haste, for it grows very late. 3.03.164
i will make a desperate tender | of my child's 3.04. 12
if thou couldst, thou couldst not make him live; 3.05. 71
shall happily make thee there a joyful bride. 3.05.115
he shall not make me there a joyful bride. 3.05.117
make the bridal bed | in that dim monument where 3.05.200
cell, | to make confession and to be absolv'd. 3.05.233
come you to make confession to this father? 4.01. 22
make haste, make haste. 4.04. 16
make haste, make haste. 4.04. 16
hie, make haste, | make haste, the bridegroom he 4.04. 26

make haste, the bridegroom he is come already, 4.04. 27
he is come already, | make haste, i say. 4.04. 28
that hath ta'en her hence to make me wail, 4.05. 31
were thinly scattered, to make up a show. 5.01. 48
the world affords no law to make thee rich; 5.01. 73
on them, | to make me die with a restorative. 5.03.166
as the time and place | doth make against me, of 5.03.225
this letter doth make good the friar's words, 5.03.286
make sacred even his stirrup, and through him TIM 1.01. 82
counterpoise, | and make him weigh with her. 1.01.146
make thy requests to thy friend. 1.01.268 P
you shall not make me welcome. 1.02. 24
prithee let my meat make thee silent. 1.02. 37 P
those healths will make thee and thy state look 1.02. 56 P
thou weep'st to make them drink, timon. 1.02.109 P
music, make their welcome! 1.02.129
we make ourselves fools to disport ourselves, 1.02.136
is, | being of no power to make his wishes good. 1.02.196
that i may make his lordship understand 2.02. 42
you make me marvel wherefore ere this time | had 2.02.124
his debts, | and make a clear way to the gods. 3.04. 76
striving to make an ugly deed look fair. 3.05. 25
can breathe, and make his wrongs | his outsides, 3.05. 32
you cannot make gross sins look clear; 3.05. 38
valor in the bearing, what make we | abroad? 3.05. 46
make not a city feast of it, to let the meat 3.06. 67 P
for your own gifts, make yourselves prais'd; 3.06. 71 P
make the meat be belov'd more than the man that 3.06. 75 P
them, you gods, make suitable for destruction. 3.06. 81 P
let's make no stay. 3.06.118 P
thus much of this will make | black white, foul 4.03. 28
make the hoar leprosy ador'd, place thieves, 4.03. 36
nations, i will make thee | do thy right nature. 4.03. 44
make use of thy salt hours, season the slaves 4.03. 86
the want whereof doth daily make revolt | in my 4.03. 92
virgin's cheek | make soft thy trenchant sword; 4.03.116
to pay thy soldiers, | make large confusion; 4.03.128
enough to make a whore forswear her trade, | and 4.03.134
her trade, | and to make whores, a bawd. 4.03.135
make curl'd-pate ruffians bald, | and let the 4.03.160
would confound thee and make thine own self the 4.03.337 P
make thine epitaph, | that death in me at 4.03.379
let us make the assay upon him. 4.03.403 P
what you are | make them best seen and known. 5.01. 69
beseech your honor | to make it known to us. 5.01. 90
you are an alcumist, make gold of that. 5.01.114
his former days, | the former man may make him. 5.01.125
and send forth us to make their sorrowed render, 5.01.149
shall make their harbor in our town till we 5.04. 53
taught thee to make vast neptune weep for aye 5.04. 78
make war breed peace, make peace stint war, make 5.04. 83
make war breed peace, make peace stint war, make 5.04. 83
make each | prescribe to other as each other's 5.04. 83
sir, we make holiday to see caesar, and to JC 1.01. 30 P
wing | will make him fly an ordinary pitch, 1.01. 73
to make them instruments of fear and warning 1.03. 70
therein, ye gods, you make the weak most strong; 1.03. 91
those that with haste will make a mighty fire 1.03.107
o rome, i make thee promise, | if the redress 2.01. 56
this shall make | our purpose necessary, and not 2.01.177
make me acquainted with your cause of grief. 2.01.256
vow | which did incorporate and make us one, 2.01.273
a piece of work that will make sick men whole. 2.01.327
but are not some whole that we must make sick? 2.01.328
antony | (by our permission) is allow'd to make. 3.02. 59
it will inflame you, it will make you mad. 3.02.144
then make a ring about the corpse of caesar, 3.02.158
we must straight make head; 4.01. 42
make gallant show and promise of their mettle; 4.02. 24
abler than yourself | to make conditions. 4.03. 32
you are, | and make your bondmen tremble. 4.03. 44
make your vaunting true, | and it shall please 4.03. 52
of your philosophy you make no use, | if you 4.03.145
them, | by them shall make a fuller number up, 4.03.208
make forth, the generals would have some words. 5.01. 25
if arguing make us sweat, | the proof of it will 5.01. 48
with horsemen, that make to him on the spur, 5.03. 29
what ill request did brutus make to thee? 5.05. 11
the conquerors can but make a fire of him; 5.05. 55
to mine, | and thrice again, to make up nine. MAC 1.03. 36
nothing afeard of what thyself didst make 1.03. 96
and make my seated heart knock at my ribs, 1.03.136
and will labor | to make thee full of growing. 1.04. 29
i'll be myself the harbinger and make joyful 1.04. 45
scarcely more | than would make up his message. 1.05. 37
make thick my blood, | stop up th' access and 1.05. 43
to make their audit at your highness' pleasure, 1.06. 27
did then adhere, and yet you would make both: 1.07. 52
as we shall make our griefs and clamor roar 1.07. 78
when 'tis, | it shall make honor for you. 2.01. 26
so, it will make us mad. 2.02. 31
i'll make so bold to call, | for 'tis my limited 2.03. 51
in that heart | courage to make 's love known? 2.03.118
as they would make | war with mankind. 2.04. 17
and with those | that would make good of bad, 2.04. 41
to make society | the sweeter welcome, we will 3.01. 41
to make them kings — the seeds of banquo kings! 3.01. 69
it is | that i to your assistance do make love, 3.01.123
and make our faces vizards to our hearts, 3.02. 34
things bad begun make strong themselves by ill. 3.02. 55
hence to th' palace gate | make it their walk. 3.03. 14
shame itself, | why do you make such faces? 3.04. 66
you make me strange | even to the disposition 3.04.111
but make amends now. 3.05. 14
come, let's make haste, she'll soon be back 3.05. 36
by a drab, | make the gruel thick and slab. 4.01. 32
but yet i'll make assurance double sure, | and 4.01. 83
what had he done, to make him fly the land? 4.02. 1
actions do not, | our fears do make us traitors. 4.02. 4
would be as a sauce | to make me hunger more, 4.03. 82
would create soldiers, make our women fight, 4.03.187
let's make us med'cines of our great revenge 4.03.214
make we our march towards birnan. 5.02. 31
host, and make discovery | err in report of us. 5.04. 6
that will with due decision make us know | what 5.04. 17
make all our trumpets speak, give them all 5.06. 9
with thy keen sword impress as make me bleed. 5.08. 10
your several loves, | and make us even with you. 5.09. 28
the rivals of my watch, bid them make haste. HAM 1.01. 13
doth make the night joint-laborer with the day: 1.01. 78
and what make you from wittenberg, horatio? 1.02.164
but what, in faith, make you from wittenberg? 1.02.168
to make it truster of your own report | against 1.02.172
heaven, i'll make a ghost of him that lets me! 1.04. 85
make thy two eyes, like stars, start from their 1.05. 17
never make known what you have seen to-night. 1.05.144
visit him, to make inquire | of his behavior. 2.01. 4
heavens make our presence and our practices 2.02. 38
and he repell'd, a short tale to make, | fell 2.02.146
way of friendship, what make you at elsinore? 2.02.270 P
and those that would make mouths at him while my 2.02.364 P
sallets in the lines to make the matter savory, 2.02.442 P
when she saw pyrrhus make malicious sport | in 2.02.513
make mad the guilty, and appall the free, 2.02.564
and lack gall | to make oppression bitter, or 2.02.578
when he himself might his quietus make | with a 3.01. 74
thus conscience does make cowards /of /us /all, 3.01. 82
know well enough what monsters you make of them. 3.01.139 P
you one face, and you make yourselves another. 3.01.143 P
god's creatures and make your wantonness /your 3.01.145 P
laugh, cannot but make the judicious grieve; 3.02. 26 P
go make you ready. 3.02. 45 P
bid the players make haste. 3.02. 49 P
make us again count o'er ere love be done! 3.02.162
shall please you to make me a wholesome answer, 3.02.315 P
make you a wholesome answer — my wit's diseas'd 3.02.321 P
such answer as i can make, you shall command, or 3.02.322 P
you now, how unworthy a thing you make of me! 3.02.364 P
this little organ, yet cannot you make it speak. 3.02.369 P
make assay, | bow, stubborn knees, and heart, 3.03. 69
preaching to stones, | would make them capable. 3.04.127
the compost on the weeds | to make them ranker. 3.04.152
make you to ravel all this matter out, | that i 3.04.186
pray you make haste. 4.03. 57
indeed would make one think there might be 4.05. 12
indeed without an oath i'll make an end on't. 4.05. 57 P
make choice of whom your wisest friends you will 4.05.205
words to speak in thine ear will make thee dumb, 4.06. 25 P
we'll make a solemn wager on your cunnings — 4.07.155
as make your bouts more violent to that end — 4.07.158
therewith fantastic garlands did she make | of 4.07.168
thee she is, therefore make her grave straight. 5.01. 3 P
make her laugh at that. 5.01.194 P
the dust is earth, of earth we make loam, and 5.01.210 P
all their quantity of love | make up my sum. 5.01.271
the burning zone, | make ossa like a wart! 5.01.283
or i could make a prologue to my brains, | they 5.02. 30
and rareness as, to make true diction of him, 5.02.118 P
i am sure you make a wanton of me. 5.02.299
heaven make thee free of it! 5.02.332
in neither can make choice of either's moi'ty. LR 1.01. 6 P
and wide-skirted meads, | we make thee lady. 1.01. 66
shall our abode | make with you by due turn. 1.01.135
the bow is bent and drawn, make from the shaft. 1.01.143
thou hast sought to make us break our /vow — 1.01.168
i would not from your love make such a stray 1.01.209
that you make known | it is no vicious blot, 1.01.226
it would make a great gap in your own honor and 1.02. 84 P
we make guilty of our disasters the sun, the 1.02.120 P
can you make no use of nothing, nuncle? 1.04.130 P
i would you would make use of your good wisdom 1.04.219
disorder'd rabble make servants of their betters 1.04.256
didst intend | to make this creature fruitful. 1.04.277
from me perforce, | should make thee worth them. 1.04.299
yes indeed, thou wouldst make a good fool. 1.05. 38 P
or worth in thee | make thy words faith'd? 2.01. 70
and thou must make a dullard of the world | if 2.01. 74
and potential spirits | to make thee seek it." 2.01. 77
boy, i'll work the means | to make thee capable. 2.01. 85
make your own purpose, | how in my strength you 2.01.111
lipsbury pinfold, i would make thee care for me. 2.02. 10 P
i'll make a sop o' th' moonshine of you, you 2.02. 32 P
thou art a strange fellow. a tailor make a man? 2.02. 56 P
that wear rags | do make their children blind, 2.04. 49
you | that to our sister you do make return. 2.04.151
if you yourselves are old, | make it your cause; 2.04.192
i prithee, daughter, do not make me mad. 2.04.218
what he his heart should make | shall of a corn 3.02. 32
of the dark, | and make them keep their caves. 3.02. 45
is strange | and can make vild things precious. 3.02. 71
must make content with his fortunes fit, 3.02. 76
this prophecy merlin shall make, for i live 3.02. 95 P
trundle-tail, | tom will make him weep and wail, 3.06. 71
any cause in nature that make these hard hearts? 3.06. 78 P
make no noise, make no noise, draw the curtains. 3.06. 83 P
make no noise, make no noise, draw the curtains. 3.06. 83 P
that thy strange mutations make us hate thee, 4.01. 11
ten masts at each make not the altitude | which 4.06. 53
who make them honors | of men's impossibilities, 4.06. 73
to wet me once, and the wind to make me chatter, 4.06.101 P
why, this would make a man a man of salt, | to 4.06.195
my boon i make it, that you know me not | till 4.07. 10
flesh and fell, | ere they shall make us weep! 5.03. 25
thou dost make thy way | to noble fortunes. 5.03. 29
if you will marry, make your loves to me, | my 5.03. 88
i'll make it on thy heart, | ere i taste bread, 5.03. 93
pleasant vices | make instruments to plague us: 5.03.172
in personal suit to make me his lieutenant, OTH 1.01. 9
rouse him, make after him, poison his delight, 1.01. 68
or else the devil will make a grandsire of you. 1.01. 91
in their power | to make this bitter to thee. 1.01.104
is dress'd in — if we make thought of this, 1.03. 26
let housewives make a skillet of my helm, | and 1.03.272
adversities | make head against my estimation! 1.03.274
make all the money thou canst. 1.03.354 P
therefore make money. 1.03.358 P
thou art sure of me — go make money. 1.03.364 P
thus do i ever make my fool my purse; 1.03.383
to be suspected — fram'd to make women false. 1.03.398
even till we make the main and th' aerial blue 2.01. 39
make love's quick pants in desdemona's arms, 2.01. 80
old fond paradoxes to make fools laugh i' th' 2.01.138 P
discords be | that e'er our hearts shall make! 2.01.199
but i'll set down the pegs that make this music, 2.01.200
make the moor thank me, love me, and reward me, 2.01.308
some to dance, some to make bonfires, each man 2.02. 4 P
i'll make thee an example. 2.03.251
me another, to make me frankly despise myself. 2.03.298 P
that she may make, unmake, do what she list, 2.03.346
and out of her own goodness make the net | that 2.03.361
pleasure and action make the hours seem short. 2.03.379
for love's sake, to make no more noise with it. 3.01. 13 P
(save that they say the wars must make example 3.03. 65
think'st thou i'ld make a life of jealousy? 3.03.177
'tis not to make me jealious | to say my wife is 3.03.183
make me to see't; 3.03.364
do deeds to make heaven weep, all earth amaz'd; 3.03.371
that lov'st to make thine honesty a vice! 3.03.376
that is, make questions, and by them answer. 3.04. 17 P
'twould make her amiable, and subdue my father 3.04. 59
make it a darling like your precious eye. 3.04. 66
what make you from home? 3.04.169
face, | for i will make him tell the tale anew: 4.01. 84
but you shall make all well. 4.01.225
'tis very much, | make her amends; 4.01.244
ay, you did wish that i would make her turn. 4.01.252
to make me | the fixed figure for the time of 4.02. 53
i should make very forges of my cheeks, | that 4.02. 74
would it not make one weep? 4.02.127
not the world's mass of vanity could make me. 4.02.164
i will make myself known to desdemona. 4.02.196 P
who would not make her husband a cuckold to make 4.03. 76 P
her husband a cuckold to make him a monarch? 4.03. 76 P
own world, and you might quickly make it right. 4.03. 82 P
i will make proof of thine. 5.01. 26
of them is hereabout, | and cannot make away. 5.01. 58
if heaven would make me such another world | of 5.02.144
i care not for thy sword, i'll make thee known, 5.02.165
this sight would make him do a desperate turn, 5.02.207
every passion fully strives | to make itself, in ANT 1.01. 51
i make not, but foresee. 1.02. 15
if it lay in their hands to make me a cuckold, 1.02. 76 P
they would make themselves whores but they'ld 1.02. 77 P
are worn out, there are members to make new. 1.02.165 P
many hot inroads | they make in italy; 1.04. 51
would stand and make his eyes grow in my brow; 1.05. 32
shine on those | that make their looks by his; 1.05. 56
dinner, and will make | no wars without-doors. 2.01. 12
and make the wars alike against my stomach, 2.02. 50
as matter whole you have to make it with, | it 2.02. 53
mine honesty | shall not make poor my greatness, 2.02. 93
to make you brothers, and to knit your hearts 2.02.125
say, "agrippa, be it so," | to make this good? 2.02.142
panted, | that she did make defect perfection, 2.02.231
make yourself my guest | whilst you abide here. 2.02.243
therefore | make space enough between you. 2.03. 24
and though i make this marriage for my peace, 2.03. 40
make thee a fortune from me. 2.05. 49
i will give thee, | and make thy fortunes proud; 2.05. 69
shall make thy peace for moving me to rage, 2.05. 70
to punish me for what you make me do | seems 2.05.100
o, that his fault should make a knave of thee, 2.05.102
she never come, | to make my heart her vassal. 2.06. 56
possess it, i'll make answer. 2.07.101
make battery to our ears with the loud music; 2.07.109
of marcus crassus' death | make me revenger. 3.01. 3
place, note well, | may make too great an act. 3.01. 13
prove such a wife | as my thoughts make thee, 3.02. 26
make me not offended | in your distrust. 3.02. 33
and make the hearts of romans serve your ends! 3.02. 37
to thee, and make | thy spirits all of comfort. 3.02. 40
three in egypt | cannot make better note. 3.03. 23
go, make thee ready, | our letters are prepar'd. 3.03. 37
make your soonest haste; 3.04. 27
the jove of power make me most weak, most weak, 3.04. 29
fly, | and make your peace with caesar. 3.11. 6
look not sad, | nor make replies of loathness; 3.11. 18
make thine own edict for thy pains, which we 3.12. 32
that would make his will | lord of his reason. 3.13. 3
the loyalty well held to fools does make | our 3.13. 42
that of his fortunes you should make a staff 3.13. 68
our clear judgments, make us | adore our errors, 3.13.113
next time i do fight, | i'll make death love me; 3.13.192
breath, but now | make boot of his distraction: 4.01. 9
honor in the blood | shall make it live again. 4.02. 7
and make as much of me | as when mine empire was 4.02. 21
to make his followers weep. 4.02. 24
the gods make this a happy day to antony! 4.05. 1
had once prevail'd | to make me fight at land! 4.05. 3
make it so known. 4.06. 3
commend thy acts, | make her thanks bless thee. 4.08. 13
through alexandria make a jolly march, | bear 4.08. 30
ear, | make mingle with our rattling taborines, 4.08. 37
with our sprightly port make the ghosts gaze. 4.14. 52
when i did make thee free, swor'st thou not then 4.14. 81
o, make an end | of what i have begun. 4.14.105
fashion, | and make death proud to take us. 4.15. 88
the breaking of so great a thing should make | a 5.01. 14
gods will give us | some faults to make us men. 5.01. 33
my desolation does begin to make | a better life 5.02. 1
make your full reference freely to my lord, 5.02. 23
rather make | my country's high pyramides my 5.02. 60
make way there! caesar! 5.02.111
mine own cause so well | to make it clear, but 5.02.122
of this seleucus does | even make me wild. 5.02.154
to make prize with you | of things that 5.02.183
cheer'd, | make not your thoughts your prisons; 5.02.185
make your best use of this. 5.02.203
for in every ten that they make, the devils mar 5.02.277 P
he'll make demand of her, and spend that kiss 5.02.302
events as these | strike those that make them; 5.02.361
that his time | could make him the receiver of, CYM 1.01. 44
and make yourself some comfort | out of your 1.01.155
if it be a sin to make a true election, she is 1.02. 27 P
long | as he could make me with /this eye or ear 1.03. 9
or i could make him swear | the shes of italy 1.03. 28
make her go back, even to the yielding, had i 1.04.104 P
but i make my wager rather against your 1.04.110 P
if you make your voyage upon her and give me 1.04.158 P
make haste. 1.05. 2
hast thou not learn'd me how | to make perfumes? 1.05. 13
from this practice but make hard your heart; 1.05. 24
not | partition make with spectacles so precious 1.06. 37
oppos'd, | should make desire vomit emptiness, 1.06. 45

my heart | with pity that doth make me sick. 1.06.119
empery | would make the great'st king double — 1.06.121
should he make me | live, like diana's priest, 1.06.132
were deeply rooted, and shall make your lord, 1.06.164
you make amends. 1.06.168
i will make bold | to send them to you, only for 1.06.197
that horrid act | of the divorce he'ld make. 2.01. 62
a voucher, | stronger than ever law could make; 2.02. 40
it would make any man cold to lose. 2.03. 3 P
make denials | increase your services; 2.03. 48
i will make | one of her women lawyer to me, for 2.03. 73
what means do you make to him? 2.04. 3
will make known | to their approvers they are 2.04. 24
kiss'd your sails, | to make your vessel nimble. 2.04. 29
i'll make a journey twice as far, t' enjoy | a 2.04. 43
make /not, sir, | your loss your sport. 2.04. 47
being so near the truth as i will make them, 2.04. 62
make pastime with us a day or two, or longer. 3.01. 77 P
be | you bees that make these locks of counsel! 3.02. 36
and for the gap | that we shall make in time, 3.02. 63
our cage | we make a choir, as doth the prison'd 3.03. 43
fear to strike and to make me certain it is done 3.04. 30 P
first, make yourself but like one. 3.04.167
which will make him know | if that his head have 3.04.174
that will be given to th' loud of noise we make. 3.05. 44
this | she wish'd me to make known; 3.05. 50
and my end | can make good use of either. 3.05. 64
our stomachs | will make what's homely savory; 3.06. 33
those clothes, | which, as it seems, make thee. 4.02. 83
i wish my brother make good time with him, | you 4.02.108
and in time | may make some stronger head, the 4.02.139
fidele's sickness | did make my way long forth. 4.02.149
mountain pine | and make him stoop to th' vale. 4.02.176
if he be gone, he'll make his grave a bed. 4.02.216
doth make distinction | of place 'tween high and 4.02.248
for nature doth abhor to make his bed | with the 4.02.357
and make him with our pikes and partisans | a 4.02.399
and make them dread it, to the doers' thrift. 5.01. 15
do your best wills, | and make me blest to obey. 5.01. 17
let me make men know | more valor in me than my 5.01. 29
to make my gift, | the more delay'd, delighted. 5.04.101
can find him, if | our grace can make him so. 5.05. 7
which i'll make bold your highness | cannot deny 5.05. 89
stand thou by our side, | make thy demand aloud. 5.05.130
proof enough | to make the noble leonatus mad, 5.05.201
with language that would make me spurn the sea 5.05.294
hardness, that i can | make no collection of it. 5.05.432
the purchase is to make men glorious, | et bonum PER 1.ch. 9
i'll make my will then, and, as sick men do 1.01. 47
who, finger'd to make man his lawful music, 1.01. 82
my pistol's length, | i'll make him sure enough; 1.01.167
since he's so great can make his will his act, 1.02. 18
and what may make him blush in being known, 1.02. 22
and make pretense of wrong that i have done him; 1.02. 91
shore, | a portly sail of ships make hitherward. 1.04. 61
already, | and make a conquest of unhappy me, 1.04. 69
are stor'd with corn to make your needy bread, 1.04. 95
does, | build his statue to make him glorious. 2.ch. 14
was not best | longer for him to make his rest. 2.ch. 26
to my desires, i could wish to make one there. 2.01.112 P
shall make the gazer joy to see him tread. 2.01.159
shalt have my best gown to make thee a pair; 2.01.163 P
to make some good, but others to exceed, | and 2.03. 16
which make a sound, but kill'd are wond'red at. 2.03. 63
therefore to make his entrance more sweet, 2.03. 64
who takes offense | at that would make me glad? 2.05. 72
either be rul'd by me, or i'll make you — | man 2.05. 83
make swift the pangs | of my queen's travails! 3.01. 13
why do you make us love your goodly gifts | and 3.01. 23
and heaven can make | to herald thee from the 3.01. 33
o, make for tharsus! 3.01. 77
make a fire within. 3.02. 80
doth appear, | to make the world twice rich. 3.02.102
live, and make | us weep to hear your fate, fair 3.02.102
the gods | make up the rest upon you! 3.03. 5
if neglection | should therein make me vile, the 3.03. 21
make me blessed in your care | in bringing up my 3.03. 31
necessity of qualities can make her be refus'd. 4.02. 49 P
thus time we waste, and long leagues make short; 4.04. 1
make raging battery upon shores of flint." 4.04. 43
that she would make a puritan of the devil, if 4.06. 9 P
our cavalleria, and make our swearers priests. 4.06. 12 P
make the judgment good | that thought you worthy 4.06. 93
of her virginity, and make the rest malleable. 4.06.142 P
therefore i will make them acquainted with your 4.06.198 P
and make a batt'ry through his /deafen'd parts, 5.01. 47
leave her, | and the gods make her prosperous! 5.01. 79
endowments which | you make more rich to owe? 5.01.117
and make /my senses credit thy relation | to 5.01.123
sent hither | to make the world to laugh at me. 5.01.144
heavens make a star of him! 5.03. 79
and make him cry from under ground, "o, fan TNK pr 18
wast near to make the male | to thy sex captive, 1.01. 80
that it shall make a counter–reflect 'gainst 1.01.127
which to do | must make some work with creon. 1.01.150
begging in our eyes | to make petition clear. 1.01.157
being able | to make mars spurn his drum. 1.01.182
sir, | as i shall here make trial of my pray'rs, 1.01.193
feast, of which i pray you | make no abatement. 1.01.225
thus dost thou still make good | the tongue o' 1.01.226
haply so long until | the follow'd make pursuit? 1.02. 52
success i dare not | make any timorous question; 1.03. 3
with prey, | make lanes in troops aghast. 1.04. 19
they have patience to make any adversity asham'd 2.01. 23 P
they would not make us their object. 2.01. 52 P
shall we make worthy uses of this place | that 2.02. 69
can be, but our imaginations | may make it ours? 2.02. 78
i would make her | so near the gods in nature, 2.02.241
if he dare make himself a worthy lover, | yet in 2.02.251
ye shall not sleep, | i'll make ye a new morris. 2.02.273
tame tempests, | and make the wild rocks wanton. 2.03. 17
another shape shall make me, | or end my 2.03. 21
what should i do to make him know i love him, 2.04. 29
my love, would make thee | a confess'd traitor! 3.01. 34
with us, | make talk for fools and cowards. 3.03. 12
then would i make | a carreck of a cockleshell, 3.04. 13
long tool, | cum multis aliis that make a dance. 3.05.133
out, | we'll make thee laugh and all this rout. 3.05.147

to delay it longer | would make the world think, 3.06. 11
all, or dost thou do it | to make me spare thee? 3.06. 47
worn a lighter, | but i shall make it serve. 3.06. 57
or i will make th' advantage of this hour | mine 3.06.123
ye make my faith reel. 3.06.212
'em never more | to make me their contention, or 3.06.253
and die for her, | make death a devil. 3.06.270
make choice then. 3.06.285
now | you make me mind her, but this very day 4.01. 37
for, and so apter | to make this cause his own. 4.02. 98
he finds 'em, | he's swift to make 'em his. 4.02.134
then will i make palamon a nosegay, then let him 4.03. 26 P
of, and thereto make an addition of some other 4.03. 84 P
but to make the number more i have great hope in 4.03. 97 P
you whose free nobleness do make my cause | your 5.01. 73
that canst make | a cripple flourish with his 5.01. 81
and make him, to the scorn of his hoarse throat, 5.01. 88
allow'st no more blood than will make a blush, 5.01.141
that's all one, if ye make a noise. 5.02. 16
make curtsy, here your love comes. 5.02. 69
three or four days | i'll make her right again. 5.02.105
nature now | shall make and act the story, the 5.03. 14
so mingled as if mirth did make him sad, | and 5.03. 52
till heavens did | make hardly one the winner. 5.03.130
the gods requite you all, and make her thankful! 5.04. 36
for the horse | would make his length a mile, 5.04. 57
heavenly charmers, | what things you make of us! 5.04.132
it is our infection will make the city shake, STM II.C 14 P
your unreverent knees, | make them your feet: II.C 111
forgiven | is safer wars than ever you can make, II.C 112
make use of time, let not advantage slip, VEN 129
i'll make a shadow for thee of my hairs; 191
for where a heart is hard they make no batt'ry." 426
what bargains may i make, still to be sealing? 512
which purchase if thou make, for fear of slips, 515
wilt thou make the match?" 586
doth make them droop with grief and hang the 666
thought of it doth make my faint heart bleed, 669
to make the cunning hounds mistake their smell, 686
to make thee hate the hunting of the boar, 711
rich preys make true men thieves; 724
thy lips | make modest dian cloudy and forlorn, 725
troubled, | make verbal repetition of her moans; 831
some twin'd about her thigh to make her stay. 873
the fear whereof doth make him shake and shudder 880
sighs dry her cheeks, tears make them wet again. 966
the strongest body shall it make most weak, 1145
make the young old, the old become a child. 1152
wit, | make something nothing by augmenting it. LUC 154
such hazard now must doting tarquin make, 155
what excuse can my invention make | when thou 225
o, how her fear did make her color rise! 257
the wind wars with his torch to make him stay, 311
on, to make his stand | on her bare breast, the 438
to make the breach and enter this sweet city. 469
both, | that to his borrowed bed he make retire, 573
"this deed will make thee only lov'd for fear, 610
make slow pursuit, or altogether balk | the prey 696
make war against proportion'd course of time; 774
let their exhal'd unwholesome breaths make sick 779
may set at noon and make perpetual night. 784
"make me not object to the tell–tale day, | the 806
to make the child a man, the man a child, | to 954
unless thou couldst return to make amends? 961
to make him curse this cursed crimeful night. 970
him pitiful mischances | to make him moan, but 977
to make more vent for passage of her breath, 1040
make her moans mad with their sweet melody, 1108
to see the salve doth make the wound ache more, 1116
make thy sad grove in my dishevell'd hair; 1129
if in this blemish'd fort i make some hole 1175
"this brief abridgment of my will i make: 1198
make weak–made women tenants to their shame. 1260
be told, | the repetition cannot make it less; 1285
she dares not thereof make discovery, | lest he 1314
deep sounds make lesser noise than shallow fords 1329
her earnest eye did make him more amazed. 1356
hold | only to flatter fools and make them bold: 1559
"o, teach me how to make mine own excuse, | or 1653
even so his sighs, his sorrows, make a saw, | to 1672
shall rotten death make conquest of the stronger 1767
held back his sorrow's tide, to make it more; 1789
if love make me forsworn, how shall i swear to PP 5. 1
't may be again, to make me wander thither: 14.10
there will i make thee a bed of roses, | with a 19. 9
shall sum my count, and make my old excuse," SON 2.11
make sweet some vial; 6. 3
be death's conquest and make worms thine heir. 6.14
make thee another self for love of me, | that 10.13
and threescore year would make the world away. 11. 8
then of thy beauty do i question make | that 12. 9
nothing 'gainst time's scythe can make defense 12.13
mightier way | make war upon this bloody tyrant, 16. 2
can make you live yourself in eyes of men: 16.12
and make the earth devour her own sweet brood; 19. 2
make glad and sorry seasons as thou fleet'st, 19. 5
which wit so poor as mine | may make seem bare, 26. 6
and night doth nightly make grief's length seem 28.14
and make me travel forth without my cloak, | to 34. 2
all men make faults, and even i in this, 35. 5
sit, | i make my love ingrafted to this store: 37. 8
and that thou teachest how to make one twain, 39.13
thou, whose shadow shadows doth make bright, 43. 5
to make some special instant special blest, | by 52.11
save where you are how happy you make those. 57.12
like as the waves make towards the pibbled shore 60. 1
if thinking on me then should make you woe. 71. 8
to make me tongue–tied, speaking of your fame. 80. 4
or i shall live your epitaph to make, | or you 81. 1
join with the spite of fortune, make me bow, 90. 3
take | all this away, and me most wretched make. 91.14
how sweet and lovely dost thou make the shame 95. 1
in hue, | could make me any summer's story tell, 98. 7
and make time's spoils despised every where. 100.12
make answer, muse: 101. 5
thee | to make him much outlive a gilded tomb, 101.11
i teach thee how | to make him seem long hence, 101.14
to make of monsters and things indigest | such 114. 5

like as to make our appetites more keen, | with 118. 1
and rather make them born to our desire | than 123. 7
bait | on purpose laid to make the taker mad: 129. 8
as those whose beauties proudly make them cruel; 131. 2
thy face hath not the power to make love groan; 131. 6
one will of mine, to make thy large will more. 135.12
make but my name thy love, and love that still, 136.13
those lips that love's own hand did make 145. 1
to make me give the lie to my true sight, | and 150. 3
who taught thee how to make me love thee more, 150. 9
to make the weeper laugh, the laugher weep, | he LC 124
by blunting us to make our wits more keen. 161
to leave the batt'ry that you make 'gainst mine, 277
and yet do question make | what i should do 321

MAKE–A 2 FR 0.0002 REL FR 0 V 2 P
have you make–a de sot of us, ha, ha? WIV 3.01.115 P
if there be one or two, i shall make–a the turd. 3.03.236 P

MAKELESS 1 FR 0.0001 REL FR 1 V 0 P
the world will wail thee like a makeless wife, SON 9. 4

MAKE–PEACE 1 FR 0.0001 REL FR 1 V 0 P
to be a make–peace shall become my age. R2 1.01.160

MAKER 4 FR 0.0004 REL FR 3 V 1 P
god, the best maker of all marriages, | combine H5 5.02.359
how can man then | (the image of his maker) hope H8 3.02.442
see what this child does, and praise my maker. 5.04. 68
denied but peace is a great maker of cuckolds. COR 4.05.229 P

MAKERS 1 FR 0.0001 REL FR 0 V 1 P
we are the makers of manners, kate; H5 5.02.271 P

/MAKES 7 FR 0.0008 REL FR 5 V 2 P
her, whose worth /makes other worthies nothing: TGV 2.04.166
and /makes milch–kine yield blood, and shakes a WIV 4.04. 33
she hath, and in that sparing /makes huge waste; ROM 1.01.218
/good /or /bad, /but /thinking /makes /it /so. HAM 2.02.250 P
/why /then /your /ambition /makes /it /one. 2.02.252 P
/when /that /which /makes /me /bend /makes /the LR 3.06.109
/which /makes /me /bend /makes /the /king /bow: 3.06.109

MAKES 395 FR 0.0446 REL FR 325 V 70 P
any strange beast there makes a man. TMP 2.02. 31 P
what's dead, | and makes my labors pleasures. 3.01. 7
your compensation makes amends, for i | have 4.01. 2
father and a wise | makes this place paradise. 4.01.124
and second father | this lady makes him to me. 5.01.196
she makes it strange, but she would be best TGV 1.02. 99
which makes me the bolder to chide you for yours 2.01. 82 P
mark the moan she makes. 2.03. 30 P
that makes me, reasonless, to reason thus? 2.04.198
he makes sweet music with th' enamell'd stones, 2.07. 28
for scorn at first makes after–love the more. 3.01. 95
that makes amends for her sour breath. 3.01.328 P
why, that word makes the faults gracious. 3.01.368 P
makes me the better to confer with thee. 3.02. 19
it makes me have a slow heart. 4.02. 64 P
to mantua, where i hear he makes abode; 4.03. 23
he makes me no more ado, but whips me out of the 4.04. 28 P
and thinking on it makes me cry "alas!" 4.04. 84
o, sir, she makes no doubt of that. 5.02. 20
makes him run through all th' sins: 5.04.112
an old cloak makes a new jerkin; WIV 1.03. 17 P
it makes me almost ready to wrangle with mine 2.01. 84 P
love, that in some respects makes a beast a man; 5.05. 5 P
a child of conscience, he makes restitution. 5.05. 29 P
the taunt of one that makes fritters of english? 5.05.143 P
and makes us lose the good we oft might win, MM 1.04. 78
before high heaven | as makes the angels weep; 2.02.122
death we fear | that makes these odds all even. 3.01. 41
that is cheap in beauty makes beauty brief in 3.01.182 P
is certain that when he makes water his urine is 3.02.110 P
that makes his opening with this bigger key. 4.01. 31
when vice makes mercy, mercy's so extended, 4.02.112
who makes that noise there? 4.03. 25 P
me quite, makes me unpregnant | and dull to all 4.04. 20
this servitude makes you to keep unwed. ERR 2.01. 26
makes me with thy strength to communicate: 2.02.176
a table full of welcome makes scarce one dainty 3.01. 23
cheer and great welcome makes a merry feast. 3.01. 26
and one that makes sport | to the prince and his LLL 4.01. 99
sore, then l to sore makes fifty sores o' sorel: 4.02. 60
his bias leaves, and makes his book thine eyes, 4.02.109
is the liver–vein, which makes flesh a deity, 4.03. 72
what makes treason here? 4.03.188
nay, it makes nothing, sir. 4.03.189
sweet, | your wits makes wise things foolish. 5.02.374
their form confounded makes most form in mirth, 5.02.519
he's a god or a painter, for he makes faces. 5.02.643 P
the error that love makes | is likewise yours. 5.02.771
it, never in the tongue | of him that makes it; 5.02.863
him with flowers, and makes him all her joy. MND 2.01. 27
mild hind | makes speed to catch the tiger — 2.01.233
that through thy bosom makes me see thy heart. 2.02.105
the ear more quick of apprehension makes; 3.02.178
two of both kinds makes up four. 3.02.438
lord, it is too long, | which makes it tedious; 5.01. 64
and such a want–wit sadness makes of me, | that MV 1.01. 6
therefore my merchandise makes me not sad. 1.01. 45
which makes her seat of belmont colchis' strond, 1.01.171
and he makes it a great appropriation to his own 1.02. 41 P
which makes me fear th' enjoying of my love; 3.02. 29
then, if he lose, he makes a swan–like end, 3.02. 44
which makes me think that this antonio, | being 3.04. 16
as makes it light or heavy in the substance | or 4.01.328
for those that she makes fair she scarce makes AYL 1.02. 37 P
that she makes fair she scarce makes honest, and 1.02. 38 P
and those that she makes honest she makes very 1.02. 38 P
she makes honest she makes very ill–favoredly. 1.02. 39 P
nature, when fortune makes nature's natural the 1.02. 49 P
foolery that wise men have makes a great show. 1.02. 90 P
company | abruptly, as my passion now makes me, 2.04. 41
that good pasture makes fat sheep; 3.02. 27 P
what makes he here? 3.02.222 P
heart th' accustom'd sight of death makes hard, 3.05. 4
you | that makes the world full of ill–favor'd 3.05. 53
and your experience makes you sad. 4.01. 27 P
o, this it is that makes your lady mourn! SHR in.2. 26
o, this is it that makes your servants droop! in.2. 27
since this bar in law makes us friends, it shall 1.01.136 P
a gentleman | and makes a god of such a cullion. 4.02. 20

for 'tis the mind that makes the body rich; 4.03.172
she inherits, which makes fair gifts fairer; AWW 1.01. 41 P
to the grief, the excess makes it soon mortal. 1.01. 58 P
your valor and fear makes in you is a virtue of 1.01.204 P
and thine ignorance makes thee away. 1.01.211 P
that makes me see, and cannot feed mine eye? 1.01.221
'tis not the many oaths that makes the truth, 4.02. 21
by her own letters, which makes her story true, 4.03. 56 P
what is lost | makes the remembrance dear. 5.03. 20
one draught above heat makes him a fool, the TN 1.05.132 P
for that's it that always makes a good voyage of 2.04. 78 P
contemplation makes a rare turkey–cock of him. 2.05. 30 P
and her t's, and thus makes she her great p's. 2.05. 87 P
my necessity | makes me to ask you for my purse? 3.04.335
fear | that makes thee strangle thy propriety. 5.01.147
physics the subject, makes old hearts fresh. WT 1.01. 39 P
he makes a july's day short as december, | and 1.02.169
let him that makes but trifles of his eyes 2.03. 63
it is an heretic that makes the fire, | not she 2.03.115
of good and bad, that makes and unfolds error, 4.01. 2
better by no mean | but nature makes that mean; 4.04. 90
adds to nature, is an art | that nature makes. 4.04. 92
her something | that makes her blood look on't. 4.04.160
into the matter, he makes the maid to answer, 4.04.198 P
that makes himself (but for our honor therein) 4.04.436
our absence makes us unthrifty to our knowledge. 5.02.111 P
sixteen years, and makes her | as she liv'd now. 5.03. 31
a landless knight makes thee a landed squire. JN 1.01.177
becomes a sun and makes your son a shadow. 2.01.500
if he see aught in you that makes him like, 2.01.511
makes it take head from all indifferency, | from 2.01.579
is | as it makes harmful all that speak of it. 3.01. 41
for grief is proud and makes his owner stoop. 3.01. 69
makes nice of no vild hold to stay him up. 3.04.138
strong reasons makes strange actions. 3.04.182
it makes the course of thoughts to fetch about, 4.02. 24
makes sound opinion sick, and truth suspected, 4.02. 26
whilst he that hears makes fearful action | with 4.02.191
it, makes it seem | like rivers of remorse and 4.03.109
and makes me more amaz'd | than had i seen the 5.02. 51
doth by the idle comments that it makes 5.07. 4
which fear, not reverence, makes thee to except. R2 1.01. 72
deep malice makes too deep incision. 1.01.155
to men in joy, but grief makes one hour ten. 1.03.261
no, misery makes sport to mock itself: 2.01. 85
makes me with heavy nothing faint and shrink. 2.02. 32
draws out our miles and makes them wearisome, 2.03. 5
my heart this covenant makes, my hand thus seals 2.03. 50
your presence makes us rich, most noble lord. 2.03. 63
which makes the silver rivers drown their shores 3.02.107
that every stride he makes upon my land | is 3.03. 92
makes him speak fondly like a frantic man, | yet 3.03.185
shrill/–voic'd suppliant makes this eager cry? 5.03. 75
not pardon twain, | but makes one pardon strong. 5.03.135
which makes him prune himself, and bristle up 1H4 1.01. 98
makes welsh as sweet as ditties highly penn'd, 3.01.206
this bottle makes an angel. 4.02. 6 P
that makes a still–stand, running neither way. 2H4 2.03. 64
vapors which environ it, makes it apprehensive, 4.03. 99 P
it, and makes it course from the inwards to the 4.03.106 P
thy sight | my worldly business makes a period. 4.05.230
that makes such waste in brief mortality. H5 1.02. 28
by this sword, he that makes the first thrust, 2.01. 99 P
for england his approaches makes as fierce | as 2.04. 9
which makes much against my manhood, if i should 3.02. 49 P
the poet makes a most excellent description of 3.06. 37 P
for our bad neighbor makes us early stirrers, 4.01. 6
"the empty vessel makes the greatest sound." 4.04. 69 P
towns, | and in a moment makes them desolate. 1H6 2.03. 66
and makes him roar these accusations forth. 3.01. 40
fortune in favor makes him lag behind. 3.03. 34
her words, | or nature makes me suddenly relent. 3.03. 59
brave duke, thy friendship makes us fresh. 3.03. 86
say, gentlemen, what makes you thus exclaim? 4.01. 83
mad ire and wrathful fury makes me weep, | that 4.03. 28
young talbot's valor makes me smile at thee. 4.07. 4
the tongue and makes the senses rough. 5.03. 71
what answer makes your grace unto my suit? 5.03.150
makes me the bolder to salute my king | with 2H6 1.01. 29
makes me from wond'ring fall to weeping joys, 1.01. 34
and that my sovereign's presence makes me mild, 3.02.219
makes them thus forward in his banishment. 3.02.253
that makes him gasp, and stare, and catch the 3.02.371
he dies, and makes no sign. 3.03. 29
the mind, | and makes it fearful and degenerate; 4.04. 2
what answer makes your grace to the rebels' 4.04. 7 P
which makes me hope you are not void of pity. 4.07. 64
mischiefs, and makes them leave me desolate. 4.08. 57 P
treasons, makes me betake me to my heels. 4.08. 64 P
makes him oppose himself against his king. 5.01.133
the hope thereof makes clifford mourn in steel. 3H6 1.01. 58
which makes thee thus presumptuous and proud, 1.01.157
or is it fear | that makes him close his eyes? 1.03. 11
the sands are numb'red that makes up my life, 1.04. 25
wrath makes him deaf; 1.04. 53
nay, stay, let's hear the orisons he makes. 1.04.110
'tis government that makes them seem divine, 1.04.132
the want thereof makes thee abominable. 1.04.133
and this soft courage makes your followers faint 2.02. 57
how many makes the hour full complete, | how 2.05. 26
and what makes robbers bold but too much lenity? 2.06. 22
what answer makes king lewis unto our letters? 4.01. 91
madam, what makes you in this sudden change? 4.04. 1
this is it that makes me bridle passion, | and 4.04. 19
are the fount that makes small brooks to flow; 4.08. 54
and yonder is the wolf that makes this spoil. 5.04. 80
that makes us wretched by the death of thee R3 1.02. 18
in that you brook it ill, it makes him worse; 1.03. 3
makes him to send, that he may learn the ground. 1.03. 68
makes the night morning and the noontide night: 1.04. 77
not meddle with it, it makes a man a coward. 1.04.134 P
untimely storms makes men expect a dearth. 2.03. 35
death makes no conquest of this conqueror, | for 3.01. 87
makes me most forward in this princely presence 3.04. 64
and makes her pew–fellow with others' moan! 4.04. 58
bett'ring thy loss makes the bad causer worse; 4.04.122
true — when avoided grace makes destiny: 4.04.219
that still use of grief makes wild grief tame, 4.04.230
even he that makes her queen. 4.04.266
he makes for england, here to claim the crown. 4.04.468
then tell me, what makes he upon the seas? 4.04.473
your warm blood like wash and makes his trough 5.02. 9
kings it makes gods, and meaner creatures kings. 5.02. 24
the force of his own merit makes his way — | a H8 1.01. 64
he makes up the file | of all the gentry; 1.01. 75
to whisper wolsey), here makes visitation — 1.01.179
is on me | which makes my whit'st part black. 1.01.209
this makes bold mouths, | tongues spit their 1.02. 60
this night he makes a supper, and a great one, 1.03. 52
two women plac'd together makes cold weather. 1.04. 22
which makes me | a little happier than my 2.01.119
a strange tongue makes my cause more strange, 3.01. 45
then makes him nothing. 3.02.208
but reverence to your calling makes me modest. 5.02.104
makes the church | the chief aim of his honor, 5.02.152
but how should this man, that makes me smile, TRO 1.02. 31 P
the ample proposition that hope makes | in all 1.03. 3
wind | makes flexible the knees of knotted oaks, 1.03. 50
makes factious feasts, rails on our state of war 1.03.191
and achilles' horse | makes many thetis' sons. 1.03.212
makes merit her election, and doth boil | (as 1.03.349
wrinkles apollo's, and makes pale the morning. 2.02. 79
not wrong, | but makes it much more heavy. 2.02.188
for request's sake only, | he makes important. 2.03.170
we'll consecrate the steps that ajax makes 2.03.183
what makes this pretty abruption? 3.02. 64 P
one touch of nature makes the whole world kin — 3.03.175
you call a virtuous sin) | makes me afeard. 4.04. 82
it is the purpose that makes strong the vow, 5.03. 23
superstitious girl | makes all these bodements. 5.03. 80
one affrights you, | the other makes you proud. COR 1.01.170
list what work he makes | amongst your cloven 1.04. 20
our thoughts, | which makes me sweat with wrath. 1.04. 27
and hark, what noise the general makes! 1.05. 9
what makes this change? 3.01. 27
by jove himself, | it makes the consuls base; 3.01.108
makes fear'd and talk'd of more than seen — 4.01. 31
our general himself makes a mistress of him, 4.05.194 P
ay, and it makes men hate one another. 4.05.230 P
delivers us thus chang'd | makes you think so. 5.03. 40
fall of either | makes the survivor heir of all. 5.06. 18
of a year or two | makes me less gracious, or TIT 2.01. 32
why makes thou it so strange? 2.01. 81
horse will follow where the game | makes way, 2.02. 24
witness the sorrow that their sister makes. 3.01.119
see, lucius, see, how much she makes of thee; 4.01. 10
revenge, which makes the foul offender quake. 5.02. 40
where civil blood makes civil hands unclean. ROM pr 4
out, | and makes himself an artificial night. 1.01.140
not having that which, having, makes them short. 1.01.164
one more, most welcome, makes my number more. 1.02. 23
she that makes dainty, | she i'll swear hath 1.05. 19
makes my flesh tremble in their different 1.05. 90
affection makes him false, he speaks not true. 3.01.177
or those eyes /shut, that makes thee answer ay, 3.02. 49
bed, | which heavy sorrow makes them apt unto. 3.03.157
some say the lark makes sweet division; 3.05. 29
god's bread, it makes me mad! 3.05.176
and her beauty makes | this vault a feasting 5.03. 85
my former sum, | which makes it five and twenty. TIM 2.01. 3
and now ingratitude makes it worse than stealth. 3.04. 27
banish usury, | that makes the senate ugly! 3.05. 99
for bounty, that makes gods, do still mar men. 4.02. 41
sides, | the want that makes him /lean. 4.03. 13
is it | that makes the wappen'd widow wed again; 4.03. 39
great sickness in his judgment | that makes it. 5.01. 30
look how he makes to caesar; mark him. JC 3.01. 18
but brutus makes mine greater than they are. 4.03. 87
which my mother gave me | makes me forgetful? 4.03.121
that my keen knife see not the wound it makes, MAC 1.05. 52
it makes him, and it mars him; 2.03. 32 P
makes him stand to, and not stand to; 2.03. 34 P
and the crow | makes wing to th' rooky wood; 3.02. 51
remove | the means that makes us strangers! 4.03.163
royal preparation | makes us hear something. 5.03. 58
makes us traduc'd and tax'd of other nations. HAM 1.04. 18
and makes each petty artere in this body | as 1.04. 82
makes vow before his uncle never more | to give 2.02. 70
respect | that makes calamity of so long life: 3.01. 68
and makes us rather bear those ills we have, 3.01. 80
tardy off, though it makes the unskillful laugh, 3.02. 25 P
the poor advanc'd makes friends of enemies. 3.02.205
since nature makes them partial, should o'erhear 3.03. 32
makes marriage vows | as false as dicers' oaths, 3.04. 44
and sweet religion makes | a rhapsody of words. 3.04. 47
keep time, | and makes as healthful music. 3.04.141
puff'd | makes mouths at the invisible event, 4.04. 50
the houses he makes lasts till doomsday. 5.01. 59 P
the wand'ring stars and makes them stand | like 5.01.256
a love that makes breath poor, and speech unable LR 1.01. 60
or he that makes his generation messes | to 1.01.117
sir, | election makes not up in such conditions. 1.01.206
and reverence of age makes the world bitter to 1.02. 47 P
what makes that frontlet on? 1.04.189 P
lust | makes it more like a tavern or a brothel 1.04.245
canst tell how an oyster makes his shell? 1.05. 25 P
spill at once | that makes ingrateful man! 3.02. 9
the man that makes his toe | what he his heart 3.02. 31
pin, /squinies the eye, and makes the hare–lip; 3.04.118 P
that i am wretched | makes thee the happier; 4.01. 66
exasperates, makes mad her sister goneril, | and 5.01. 60
judgment of the heavens, that makes us tremble, 5.03.232
ancient, what makes he here? OTH 1.02. 49
the turkish preparation makes for rhodes, | so 1.03. 14
takes, | patience her injury a mock'ry makes. 1.03.207
with a most mighty preparation makes for cyprus. 1.03.222 P
too — and behold what innovation it makes here. 2.03. 41 P
not enriches him, | and makes me poor indeed. 3.03.161
and the big wars | that makes ambition virtue! 3.03.350
it makes us, or it mars us, think on that, | and 5.01. 4
do kill the other, | every way makes my gain. 5.01. 14
a daily beauty in his life | that makes me ugly; 5.01. 20
this is the night | that either makes me, or 5.01.129
earth than she was wont, | and makes men mad. 5.02.111
be, she makes a show'r of rain as well as jove. ANT 1.02.150 P
makes his approaches to the port of rome; 1.03. 46
makes the sea serve them, which they ear and 1.04. 49
but she makes hungry | where most she satisfies; 2.02.236
rather makes choice of loss | than gain which 3.01. 23
makes his ministers | of us and those that love 3.06. 88
seize her, but | your comfort makes the rescue. 3.11. 48
look thou say | he makes me angry with him; 3.13.141
he makes me angry, | and at this time most easy 3.13.143
novice, and my heart | makes only wars on thee. 4.12. 15
and makes it indistinct | as water is in water. 4.14. 10
must be as great | as that which makes it. 4.15. 6
gone into heaviness, | that makes the weight. 4.15. 34
tell him he mocks | the pauses that he makes. 5.01. 3
command | (which my love makes religion to obey) 5.02.199
truly, she makes a very good report o' th' worm; 5.02.255 P
breeds him and makes him of his bedchamber, CYM 1.01. 42
he is with that which makes him both without and 1.04. 9 P
signior, i thank him, makes no stranger of me: 1.04.101 P
is | no danger in what show of death it makes, 1.05. 40
what makes your admiration? 1.06. 38
and makes | diana's rangers false themselves, 2.03. 68
which makes the true man kill'd and saves the 2.03. 71
such gain the cap of him that makes him fine, 3.03. 25
is in thy mind | that makes thee stare thus? 3.04. 5
ere clean it o'erthrow nature, makes it valiant. 3.06. 20
at nothing, | which the brain makes of fumes. 4.02.301
this forwardness | makes our hopes fair. 4.02.343
if this be true which makes me pale to read it? PER 1.01. 75
makes both my body pine and soul to languish, 1.02. 32
he flatters you, makes war upon your life. 1.02. 45
who by thy wisdom makes a prince thy servant, 1.02. 64
who makes the fairest show means most deceit. 1.04. 75
makes such unquiet, that the ship | should house 2.ch. 31
are | a model which heaven makes like to itself. 2.02. 11
that makes us scan | the outward habit by the 2.02. 56
his queen, with child, makes her desire — 3.ch. 40
which makes /her both th' /heart and place | of 4.ch. 10
you live as ye do makes pity in your lovers; 4.02.119 P
/she makes our profession as it were to stink 4.06.135 P
the ears she feeds, and makes them hungry, | the 5.01.112
kindness | makes my past miseries sports. 5.03. 41
makes me look dismal will i clip to form, | and 5.03. 74
blasts my bays and my fam'd works makes lighter TNK pr 20
that sharpens sundry wits, | makes me a fool. 1.01.119
which | she makes it in, from henceforth i'll 1.01.203
whose successes | makes heaven unfear'd, and 1.02. 64
him to th' plains, his learning makes no cry. 2.03. 54
any nymph, | that makes the stream seem flowers! 3.01. 9
which being glu'd together | makes morris, and 3.05.120
must be to him that makes the camp a cestron 5.01. 46
sick–thoughted venus makes amain unto him, | and VEN 5
her pale cheek, till clapping makes it red; 468
each shadow makes him stop, each murmur stay, 706
your treatise makes me like you worse and worse. 774
how love makes young men thrall and old men dote 837
the beauteous influence that makes him bright, 862
despair and hope makes thee ridiculous: 988
her sight dazzling makes the wound seem three, 1064
that makes more gashes where no breach should be 1066
yet their ambition makes them still to fight, LUC 68
thither, | he makes excuses for his being there. 114
and with good thoughts makes dispensation, 248
the sight which makes supposed terror true. 455
that even for anger makes the lily pale | and 478
eye | he rouseth up himself, and makes a pause; 541
as palmers' chat makes short their pilgrimage. 791
mightier is the thing | that makes him honor'd, 1005
mine honor be the knife's that makes my wound, 1201
which makes the maid weep like the dewy night. 1232
his bias leaves, and makes his book thine eyes, PP 5. 5
that phoebus' lute, the queen of music, makes; 8.10
makes black night beauteous and her old face new SON 27.12
makes summer's welcome thrice more wish'd, more 56.14
perceiv'st, which makes thy love more strong, 73.13
fond on praise, which makes your praises worse. 84.14
place, | but makes antiquity for aye his page, 108.12
beshrew that heart that makes my heart to groan 133. 1
that she that makes me sin awards me pain. 141.14
sets down her babe and makes all swift dispatch 143. 3
what bounds, what course, what stop he makes!' LC 109
and makes her absence valiant, not her might. 245

MAKEST 3 FR 0.0003 REL FR 3 V 0 P
thou makest the triumphery, the corner–cap of LLL 4.03. 51
makest affections bend | to godlike honors; TNK 1.01.229
"thou makest the vestal violate her oath, | thou LUC 883

MAKE'T 4 FR 0.0004 REL FR 4 V 0 P
i had rather | you felt than make't my boast. CYM 2.03.111
if you will make't an action, call witness to't. 2.03.151
if you can make't apparent | that you have 2.04. 56
i'll make't my comfort | he is a man, i'll love 3.06. 70

MAKETH 4 FR 0.0004 REL FR 4 V 0 P
o, 'tis the sun that maketh all things shine! LLL 4.03.242
rest, | yet thus far fortune maketh us amends, 3H6 4.07. 2
my woe too sensible thy passion maketh | more LUC 1678
my most true mind thus maketh mine untrue. SON 113.14

/MAKING 1 FR 0.0001 REL FR 1 V 0 P
/making /just /report | /of /how /unnatural /and LR 3.01. 37

MAKING 90 FR 0.0101 REL FR 70 V 20 P
moe widows in them of this business' making TMP 2.01.134
to my heart, | making both it unable for itself, MM 2.04. 21
made in crimes, | making practice on the times, 3.02.274
do not recompense me in making me a cuckold. 5.01.516 P
two ships from far, making amain to us, | of ERR 1.01. 92
your shop | to see the making of her carcanet, 3.01. 4
arm'd and reverted, making war against her heir. 3.02.124 P
unkind, | stigmatical in making, worse in mind. 4.02. 22
grace | as nature was in making graces dear, LLL 2.01. 10
making the bold wag by their praises bolder. 5.02.108
'a speaks not like a man of god his making. 5.02.526 P
siege to it, | making it momentany as a sound, MND 1.01.143
either i mistake your shape and making quite, 2.01. 32
more wrong | in making question of my uttermost MV 1.01.156
put the liveries to making, and desire gratiano 2.02.117 P
making them lightest that wear most of it. 3.02. 91
this making of christians will raise the price 3.05. 23 P
making such pitiful dole over them that all the AYL 1.02.130 P

is he of god's making? 3.02.205 P
almost chide god for making you that countenance 4.01. 36 P
chamber, making a sermon of continency to her, SHR 4.01.182 P
fault | i'll find about the making of the bed, 4.01.200
low ranks, | making them proud of his humility, AWW 1.02. 44
as now they are, and making practic'd smiles, WT 1.02.116
lest barbarism (making me the precedent) 2.01. 84
making that idiot, laughter, keep men's eyes JN 3.03. 45
inveterate canker of one wound | by making many. 5.02. 15
are making hither with all due expedience, | and R2 2.01.287
making the hard way sweet and delectable. 2.03. 7
making such difference 'twixt wake and sleep 1H4 3.01.216
making you ever better than his praise | by 5.02. 58
drooping west | (making the wind my post–horse),
2H4 in 4
their blood, and making many fish–meals, that 4.03. 92 P
for what i have to say is of mine own making, ep 5 P
making defeat on the full power of france, H5 1.02.107
some, making the wars their bulwark, that have 4.01.164 P
sin to think that, making god so free an offer, 4.01.183 P
you were, | making another head to fight again. 3H6 2.01.141
quoth i, "accurs'd | for making me, so young, so R3 4.01. 72
the kneading, the making of the cake, the TRO 1.01. 24 P
making their way | with those of nobler bulk! 1.03. 36
she's making her ready, she'll come straight. 3.02. 30 P
seek her, | not making any scruple of her soil, 4.01. 57
conjectural marriages, making parties strong, COR 1.01.194
feels, | making /not reservation of yourselves, 3.03.130
making the mother, wife, and child to see | the 5.03.101
and cry, "be blest | for making up this peace!" 5.03.140
making a treaty where | there was a yielding — 5.06. 67
too fair, | to merit bliss by making me despair. ROM 1.01.222
by having him, making yourself no less. 1.03. 94
to bear, | making them women of good carriage. 1.04. 94
wealth | to requite me by making rich yourself. TIM 4.03.522
making your wills | the scope of justice; 5.04. 4
thy death, | to see thy antony making his peace, JC 3.01.197
seas incarnadine, | making the green one red. MAC 2.02. 60
of sorriest fancies your companions making, 3.02. 9
making night hideous, and we fools of nature HAM 1.04. 54
honeying and making love | over the nasty sty! 3.04. 93
to mine own room again, making so bold, | my 5.02. 16
there was good sport at his making, and the LR 1.01. 23 P
had thought, by making this well known unto you, 1.04.205
and the moor are /now making the beast with two
OTH 1.01.116 P
reward me, | for making him egregiously an ass, 2.01.309
mince this matter, | making it light to cassio. 2.03.248
why, by making him uncapable of othello's place: 4.02.229 P
servant, making peace or war | as thou affects. ANT 1.03. 70
as i pleas'd, | making and marring fortunes. 3.11. 65
unseduc'd, you not making it appear otherwise, CYM 1.04.161 P
of tyre | are excellent in making ladies trip, PER 2.03.102
attends the former, | making a man a god. 3.02. 31
making, to take our imagination, | from bourn to 4.04. 3
out of bondage, making misery their mirth, and TNK 2.01. 34 P
are making battle, thus like knights appointed, 3.06.134
making them red and pale with fresh variety — VEN 21
long have rain'd, making her cheeks all wet, 83
making my arms his field, his tent my bed. 108
making it subject to the tyranny | of mad 737
fight, | making such sober action with his hand, LUC 1403
fuel, | making a famine where abundance lies, SON 1. 7
making a couplement of proud compare | with sun 21. 5
and true, | making no summer of another's green, 68.11
not making worse what nature made so clear, 84.10
his wit, | making his style admired every where. 84.12
making their tomb the womb wherein they grew? 86. 4
comes home again, on better judgment making. 87.12
halt, | against thy reasons making no defense. 89. 4
days | (making lascivious comments on thy sport) 95. 6
and beauty making beautiful old rhyme | in 106. 3
making dead wood more blest than living lips: 128.12
still, | to thy sweet will making addition thus. 135. 4
MAKINGS 1 FR 0.0001 REL FR 1 V 0 P
she had all the royal makings of a queen, | as H8 4.01. 87
/MAK'ST 1 FR 0.0001 REL FR 1 V 0 P
and /mak'st me call what i intend to do | a OTH 5.02. 64
MAK'ST 28 FR 0.0031 REL FR 27 V 1 P
who mak'st a show but dar'st not strike, thy TMP 1.02.471
thou mak'st me merry; 3.02.116
by thy approach thou mak'st me most unhappy. TGV 5.04. 31
i view the fight than thou that mak'st the fray. MV 3.02. 62
soul, harsh jew, | thou mak'st thy knife keen; 4.01.124
thou almost mak'st me waver in my faith | to 4.01.130
he, "thou mak'st a testament | as worldlings do, AYL 2.01. 47
and mak'st /conjectural fears to come into me, AWW 5.03.114
so mak'st thou faith an enemy to faith, | and JN 3.01.263
and mak'st an oath the surety for thy truth 3.01.282
yea, there thou mak'st me sad, and mak'st me sin 1H4 1.01. 78
me sad, and mak'st me sin | in envy that my lord 1.01. 78
and show'd thou mak'st some tender of my life 5.04. 49
thou mak'st use of any thing. H5 3.07. 65 P
wrinkled witch, what mak'st thou in my sight? R3 1.03.163
close impossibilities, | and mak'st them kiss! TIM 4.03.388
that mak'st my blood cold, and my hair to stare? JC 4.03.280
ha? | mak'st thou this shame thy pastime? LR 2.04. 6
and mak'st his ear | a stranger to thy thoughts. OTH 3.03.143
who is this | thou mak'st thy bloody pillow? CYM 4.02.363
what, mak'st thou me a dullard in this act? 5.05.265
as thou mak'st me, traitor! TNK 3.03. 47
that both mak'st and break'st | the stony girths 5.01. 55
what bare excuses mak'st thou to be gone! VEN 188
laud, | and mak'st fair reputation but a bawd. LUC 623
that thy sable gender mak'st | with the breath PHT 18
and, tender chorl, mak'st waste in niggarding: SON 1.12
thou mak'st faults graces that to thee resort. 96. 4
MAL 1 FR 0.0001 REL FR 1 V 0 P
and "honi soit qui mal y pense" write | in WIV 5.05. 69
MALA 1 FR 0.0001 REL FR 1 V 0 P
nothing but this; 'tis "bona terra, mala gens." 2H6 4.07. 56
MALADIES 4 FR 0.0004 REL FR 4 V 0 P
too young, | and abstinence engenders maladies. LLL 4.03.291
"and not the least of all these maladies | but VEN 745
urge, | as to prevent our maladies unseen, | we SON 118. 3
against strange maladies a sovereign cure. 153. 8
MALADY 11 FR 0.0012 REL FR 9 V 2 P
but is a physician to comment on your malady. TGV 2.01. 41 P
charg'd, | in peril to incur your former malady, SHR in.2. 122
will not confess he owes the malady | that doth AWW 2.01. 9
to prostitute our past–cure malady | to empirics 2.01.121
his strength (a malady | most incident to maids) WT 4.04.124
of not list'ning, the malady of not marking, 2H4 1.02.122 P
is dead i' th' spittle | of a malady of france, H5 5.01. 82
eyes, | see, see the pining malady of france! 1H6 3.03. 49
of man and beast the infinite malady | crust you TIM 3.06. 98
their malady convinces | the great assay of art; MAC 4.03.142
but where the greater malady is fix'd, | the LR 3.04. 8
MALAPERT 3 FR 0.0003 REL FR 2 V 1 P
an ounce or two of this malapert blood from you. TN 4.01. 44 P
untutor'd lad, thou art too malapert. 3H6 5.05. 32
peace, master marquess, you are malapert, | your R3 1.03.254
MALCHUS *(see manchus)*
MALCOLM 7 FR 0.0008 REL FR 7 V 0 P
establish our estate upon | our eldest, malcolm, MAC 1.04. 38
malcolm, awake! 2.03. 75
malcolm! 2.03. 78
malcolm and donalbain, the king's two sons, 2.04. 25
monstrous | it was for malcolm and for donalbain 3.06. 9
the english pow'r is near, led on by malcolm, 5.02. 1
what's the boy malcolm? 5.03. 3
MALCOLM'S 1 FR 0.0001 REL FR 1 V 0 P
to kiss the ground before young malcolm's feet, MAC 5.08. 28
MALCONTENT *(also malecontent, etc.)*
MALCONTENT 1 FR 0.0001 REL FR 1 V 0 P
then, like a melancholy malcontent, | he vails VEN 313
MALE 13 FR 0.0014 REL FR 7 V 6 P
sir john? art thou there, my deer? my male deer? WIV 5.05. 17 P
woman was delivered | of such a burthen male, ERR 1.01. 55
since the birth of cain, the first male child, JN 3.04. 79
the son of the female is the shadow of the male. 2H4 3.02.130 P
they fall into a kind of male green–sickness, 4.03. 93 P
sole heir male | of the true line and stock of H5 1.02. 70
it, | you love the breeder better than the male. 3H6 2.01. 42
and i, the hapless male to one sweet bird, 5.06. 15
for her male issue | or died where they were H8 2.04.192
thou art said to be achilles' male varlot. TRO 5.01. 15 P
male varlot, you rogue! what's that? 5.01. 16 P
mercy in him than there is milk in a male tiger, COR 5.04. 28 P
wast near to make the male | to thy sex captive, TNK 1.01. 80
MALE–CHILD 1 FR 0.0001 REL FR 1 V 0 P
if it conceiv'd a male–child by me, should | do H8 2.04.190
MALECONTENT *(also malcontent)*
MALECONTENT 3 FR 0.0003 REL FR 2 V 1 P
to wreathe your arms, like a malecontent; TGV 2.01. 20 P
that you stand pensive as half malecontent? 3H6 4.01. 10
is it for a wife | that thou art malecontent? 4.01. 60
MALECONTENTS 2 FR 0.0002 REL FR 1 V 1 P
thou art the mars of malecontents. WIV 1.03.104 P
liege of all loiterers and malecontents, | dread LLL 3.01.183
/MALEDICTIONS 1 FR 0.0001 REL FR 0 V 1 P
/menaces /and /maledictions /against /king /and LR 1.02.146 P
MALEFACTIONS 1 FR 0.0001 REL FR 1 V 0 P
they have proclaim'd their malefactions: HAM 2.02.592
MALEFACTOR 1 FR 0.0001 REL FR 1 V 0 P
to bring forth | some monstrous malefactor. ANT 2.05. 53
MALEFACTORS 2 FR 0.0002 REL FR 0 V 2 P
are they not malefactors? MM 2.01. 52 P
which be the malefactors? ADO 4.02. 3 P
MALES' 1 FR 0.0001 REL FR 1 V 0 P
are their males' subjects and at their controls: ERR 2.01. 19
MALES 1 FR 0.0001 REL FR 1 V 0 P
mettle should compose | nothing but males. MAC 1.07. 74
MALEVOLENCE 1 FR 0.0001 REL FR 1 V 0 P
grace | that the malevolence of fortune nothing MAC 3.06. 28
MALEVOLENT 2 FR 0.0002 REL FR 2 V 0 P
worcester, | malevolent to you in all aspects, 1H4 1.01. 97
and like him possess'd | with fire malevolent, TNK 5.04. 63
MALICE 72 FR 0.0081 REL FR 59 V 13 P
shrug'st thou, malice? TMP 1.02.367
be more, it is much dark'ned in your malice. MM 3.02.148 P
that thou but leadest this fashion of thy malice MV 4.01. 18
it must appear | that malice bears down truth. 4.01.214
his malice 'gainst the lady | will suddenly AYL 1.02.282
i rather will subject me to the malice | of a 2.03. 36
mine own direct knowledge, without any malice, AWW 3.06. 8 P
(by the very fangs of malice i swear) i am not TN 1.05.184 P
how with a sportful malice it was follow'd | may 5.01.365
in the world either malice or matter to alter it WT 1.01. 33 P
our cannons' malice vainly shall be spent JN 2.01.251
your sharpest deeds of malice on this town. 2.01.380
there is no malice in this burning coal; 4.01.108
the blood of malice in a vein of league, | and 5.02. 38
him, | if he appeal the duke on ancient malice, R2 1.01. 9
aim'd at your highness, no inveterate malice. 1.01. 14
deep malice makes too deep incision. 1.01.155
to man, as the malice of /this age shapes /them, 2H4 1.02.172 P
from envious malice of thy swelling heart. 1H6 3.01. 26
begun through malice of the bishop's men. 3.01. 75
that malice was a great and grievous sin; 3.01.128
will not this malice, somerset, be left? 4.01.108
for he hath witness of his servant's malice. 2H6 1.03.209
good uncle, hide such malice; 2.01. 25
no malice, sir, no more than well becomes | so 2.01. 27
red sparkling eyes blab his heart's malice, 3.01.154
god forbid any malice should prevail, | that 3.02. 23
though fortune's malice overthrow my state, | my 3H6 4.03. 46
by spying and avoiding fortune's malice, | for 4.06. 28
from wayward sickness and no grounded malice. R3 1.03. 29
the new–heal'd wound of malice should break out, 2.02.125
you read | the cardinal's malice and his potency H8 1.01.105
the law i bear no malice for my death; 2.01. 62
if ever any malice in your heart | were hid 2.01. 80
have out of malice | to the good queen possess'd 2.01.157
that pardons all offenses | malice ne'er meant. 2.02. 68
will or words to do it | (i mean your malice), 3.02.237
follow your envious courses, men of malice! 3.02.243
i was | from any private malice in his end, 3.02.268
oppos'd, and with a malice | of as great size. 5.01.134
this is a /piece of malice. 5.02. 8
i never sought their malice) | to quench mine 5.02. 15
that make | envy and crooked malice nourishment 5.02. 79
ye, i see, | more out of malice than integrity, 5.02.180
and fair purgation to the world than malice, 5.02.187
wit larded with malice and malice fac'd with wit TRO 5.01. 58 P
with malice and malice fac'd with wit turn him 5.01. 58 P
i utter, and spend my malice in my breath. COR 2.01. 53 P
but they | upon their ancient malice will forget 2.01.228
seem to affect the malice and displeasure of the 2.02. 21 P
to report otherwise were a malice that, giving 2.02. 32 P
translate his malice towards you into love, 2.03.189
and witness of the malice and displeasure 4.05. 72
my throat to thee and to thy ancient malice; 4.05. 96
and with the deepest malice of the war | destroy 4.06. 41
the venomous malice of my swelling heart! TIT 5.03. 13
no levell'd malice | infects one comma in the TIM 1.01. 47
'tis in the malice of mankind that he thus 4.03.452 P
our arms in strength of malice, and our hearts JC 3.01.174
pretense i fight | of treasonous malice. MAC 2.03.132
whilest our poor malice | remains in danger of 3.02. 14
malice domestic, foreign levy, nothing, | can 3.02. 25
show too bold malice | against the grace and LR 2.02.130
justly put on the vouch of very malice itself? OTH 2.01.146 P
a punishment more in policy than in malice, even 2.03.274 P
what malice was between you? 5.01.102
extenuate, | nor set down aught in malice. 5.02.343
with such full license as both truth and malice ANT 1.02.108
and will not trust one of her malice with | a CYM 1.05. 35
like | a thing more made of malice than of duty, 3.05. 33
malice and lucre in them | have laid this woe 4.02.324
the malice towards you to forgive you, live, 5.05.419
MALICIOUS 13 FR 0.0014 REL FR 12 V 1 P
approach, | commander of this hot malicious day. JN 2.01.314
pretend | malicious practices against his state. 1H6 4.01. 7
in the fear | to cope malicious censurers, which H8 1.02. 78
i hold my most malicious foe, and think not | at 2.04. 83
yes, good griffith, | i were malicious else. 4.02. 48
must | confess yourselves wondrous malicious, COR 1.01. 88
his rougher /accents for malicious sounds, | but 3.03. 55
sudden, malicious, smacking of every sin | that MAC 4.03. 59
and our vain blows malicious mockery. HAM 1.01.146
when she saw pyrrhus make malicious sport | in 2.02.513
how malicious is my fortune, that i must repent LR 3.05. 9 P
upon malicious /bravery dost thou come | to OTH 1.01.100
what ignorant and mad malicious traitors | are TNK 3.06.132
MALICIOUSLY 3 FR 0.0003 REL FR 2 V 1 P
dram that should not work | maliciously, like WT 1.02.321
nay, but speak not maliciously. COR 1.01. 35 P
hearted, breath'd, | and fight maliciously; ANT 3.13.178
MALIGN 2 FR 0.0002 REL FR 2 V 0 P
most fitly | as you malign our senators for that COR 1.01.113
though wayward fortune did malign my state, | my
PER 5.01. 89
MALIGNANCY 1 FR 0.0001 REL FR 0 V 1 P
the malignancy of my fate might perhaps TN 2.01. 4 P
MALIGNANT 7 FR 0.0008 REL FR 7 V 0 P
thou liest, malignant thing! TMP 1.02.257
have some malignant power upon my life; TGV 3.01.240
with that malignant cause wherein the honor | of AWW 2.01.111
but o malignant and ill–boding stars! 1H6 4.05. 6
are crack'd in pieces by malignant death, | and R3 2.02. 52
his will is most malignant, and it stretches H8 1.02.141
where a malignant and a turban'd turk | beat a OTH 5.02.353
MALIGNANTLY 1 FR 0.0001 REL FR 1 V 0 P
if he should still malignantly remain | fast foe COR 2.03.183
MALKIN *(also mawkin)*
MALKIN 1 FR 0.0001 REL FR 1 V 0 P
the kitchen malkin pins | her richest lockram COR 2.01.208
MALL 1 FR 0.0001 REL FR 1 V 0 P
lov'd mall, meg, and marian, and margery, | but TMP 2.02. 48
MALLARD 1 FR 0.0001 REL FR 1 V 0 P
on his sea–wing, and (like a doting mallard), ANT 3.10. 19
MALLEABLE 1 FR 0.0001 REL FR 0 V 1 P
of her virginity, and make the rest malleable. PER 4.06.143 P
MALLECHO 1 FR 0.0001 REL FR 0 V 1 P
marry, this' /miching mallecho, it means HAM 3.02.137 P
MALLET 1 FR 0.0001 REL FR 0 V 1 P
no more conceit in him than is in a mallet. 2H4 2.04.242 P
MALLICHOLY *(also allicholy, allycholly, melancholy)*
MALLICHOLY 2 FR 0.0002 REL FR 0 V 2 P
it hath taught me to rhyme and to be mallicholy; LLL 4.03. 13 P
is part of my rhyme, and here my mallicholy. 4.03. 14 P
MALLOWS 1 FR 0.0001 REL FR 1 V 0 P
or docks, or mallows. TMP 2.01.145
MALL'S 1 FR 0.0001 REL FR 0 V 1 P
like to take dust, like mistress mall's picture? TN 1.03.127 P
MALMSEY 1 FR 0.0001 REL FR 1 V 0 P
grow so nice, | metheglin, wort, and malmsey; LLL 5.02.233
MALMSEY–BUTT 2 FR 0.0002 REL FR 1 V 1 P
him into the malmsey–butt in the next room. R3 1.04.155 P
do, | i'll drown you in the malmsey–butt within. 1.04.270
MALMSEY–NOSE 1 FR 0.0001 REL FR 0 V 1 P
he comes, and that arrant malmsey–nose knave, 2H4 2.01. 39 P
MALT 1 FR 0.0001 REL FR 1 V 0 P
when brewers mar their malt with water; LR 3.02. 82
MALT–HORSE 2 FR 0.0002 REL FR 2 V 0 P
mome, malt–horse, capon, coxcomb, idiot, patch! ERR 3.01. 32
you whoreson malt–horse drudge! SHR 4.01.129
MALT–WORMS 2 FR 0.0002 REL FR 0 V 2 P
of these mad mustachio purple–hu'd malt–worms,
1H4 2.01. 75 P
where he doth nothing but roast malt–worms. 2H4 2.04.334 P
MALVOLIO 30 FR 0.0034 REL FR 9 V 21 P
what think you of this fool, malvolio? TN 1.05. 73 P
how say you to that, malvolio? 1.05. 82 P
you are sick of self–love, malvolio, and taste 1.05. 90 P
go you, malvolio; 1.05.108 P
what ho, malvolio! 1.05.299
hie thee, malvolio. 1.05.306
up her steward malvolio and bid him turn you out 2.03. 73 P
for monsieur malvolio, let me alone with him. 2.03.134 P
to be count malvolio! 2.05. 35 P
if this should be thee, malvolio? 2.05.102 P
m — malvolio; m — why, that begins my name. 2.05.125 P
yond gull malvolio is turn'd heathen, a very 3.02. 70 P
where's malvolio? 3.04. 5
where is malvolio? 3.04. 7
how now, malvolio? 3.04. 16 P
wilt thou go to bed, malvolio? 3.04. 29 P
how do you, malvolio? 3.04. 34 P
what mean'st thou by that, malvolio? 3.04. 40 P
not "malvolio," nor after my degree, but "fellow 3.04. 77 P
how do you, malvolio? 3.04. 97 P
curate, who comes to visit malvolio the lunatic. 4.02. 22 P

master malvolio? 4.02. 84 P
malvolio, malvolio, thy wits the heavens restore 4.02. 95 P
malvolio, malvolio, thy wits the heavens restore 4.02. 95 P
fetch malvolio hither. 5.01.278
the madly–us'd malvolio." 5.01.311 P
ay, my lord, this same. | how now, malvolio? 5.01.328
have i, malvolio? no. 5.01.329
alas, malvolio, this is not my writing, | though 5.01.345
toby | set this device against malvolio here, 5.01.360
MALVOLIO'S 4 FR 0.0004 REL FR 1 V 3 P
for malvolio's nose is no whipstock. TN 2.03. 26 P
we are politicians, malvolio's a peg–a–ramsey, 2.03. 76 P
malvolio's coming down this walk. 2.05. 15 P
action | is now in durance, at malvolio's suit, 5.01.276
MAMILLIUS 3 FR 0.0003 REL FR 2 V 1 P
comfort of your young prince mamillius: WT 1.01. 35 P
mamillius, | art thou my boy? 1.02.119
go play, mamillius, thou'rt an honest man. 1.02.211
MAMMET 1 FR 0.0001 REL FR 1 V 0 P
a whining mammet, in her fortune's tender, | to ROM 3.05.184
MAMMETS 1 FR 0.0001 REL FR 1 V 0 P
to play with mammets and to tilt with lips. 1H4 2.03. 92
MAMMOCK'D 1 FR 0.0001 REL FR 0 V 1 P
o, i warrant, how he mammock'd it! COR 1.03. 65 P
MAMM'RING 1 FR 0.0001 REL FR 1 V 0 P
that i should deny, | or stand so mamm'ring on. OTH 3.03. 70
/MAN* 17 FR 0.0019 REL FR 15 V 2 P
'tis true — to hurt his master, no /man else. JN 4.03. 33
/will /no /man /say /amen? R2 4.01.172
/lord /of /thine, /thou /haught /insulting /man, 4.01.254
/he /is /a /man | /who /with /a /double /surety 2H4 1.01.190
then never /was /man true. R3 1.02.195
/he /is /a /privileg'd /man. TRO 2.03. 57 P
/marcus, /no /man /should /be /mad /but /i. TIT 3.02. 24
/alas, /poor /man, /grief /has /so /wrought /on 3.02. 79
/to /speak /to /you /like /an /honest /man, /i HAM 2.02.269 P
/why, /man, /they /did /make /love /to /this 5.02. 57
/idle /old /man, | /that /still /would /manage LR 1.03. 16
/in /his /little /world /of /man /to /outscorn 3.01. 10
/thou /robed /man /of /justice, /take /thy 3.06. 36
/i /do, | /if /this /man /come /to /good. 3.07.100
/a /father, /and /a /gracious /aged /man, 4.02. 41
/a /man, /a /prince, /by /him /so /benefited! 4.02. 45
/was /big /in /clamor, /came /there /in /a /man, 5.03.209
MAN* 1861 FR 0.2103 REL FR 1122 V 739 P
me (poor man) my library | was dukedom large TMP 1.02.109
would i might | but ever see that man! 1.02.169
not hair), | was the first man that leapt; 1.02.214
this | is the third man that e'er i saw; 1.02.446
no, as i am a man. 1.02.457
i have no ambition | to see a goodlier man. 1.02.484
none, man, all idle — whores and knaves. 2.01.167 P
the man i' th' moon's too slow — till new–born 2.01.249
a man or a fish? 2.02. 25 P
there would this monster make a man; 2.02. 30 P
any strange beast there makes a man. 2.02. 31 P
legg'd like a man! 2.02. 33 P
misery acquaints a man with strange bedfellows; 2.02. 39 P
said, "as proper a man as ever went on four legs 2.02. 61 P
swom ashore, man, like a duck. 2.02.128 P
the whole butt, man. 2.02.134 P
i was the man i' th' moon, when time was. 2.02.139 P
the man i' th' moon? 2.02.146 P
sticks, but follow thee, | thou wondrous man. 2.02.164
ca–caliban | has a new master, get a new man. 2.02.185
was there ever man a coward that hath drunk so 3.02. 27 P
monster, i will kill this man. 3.02.106 P
if thou beest a man, show thyself in thy 3.02.128 P
on this island | where man doth not inhabit — 3.03. 57
done | some wanton charm upon this man and maid, 4.01. 95
holy gonzalo, honorable man, | mine eyes, ev'n 5.01. 62
all of us, ourselves, | when no man was his own. 5.01.213
every man shift for all the rest, and let no man 5.01.256 P
the rest, and let no man take care for himself; 5.01.256 P
of time, | and how he cannot be a perfect man, TGV 1.03. 20
make her fair, that no man counts of her beauty. 2.01. 60 P
why weep'st thou, man? 2.03. 35 P
it is the unkindest tied that ever any man tied. 2.03. 38 P
tut, man, i mean thou'lt lose the flood, and, in 2.03. 41 P
why, man, if the river were dry, i am able to 2.03. 51 P
come; come away, man — i was sent to call thee. 2.03. 55 P
why, man, she is mine own, | and i as rich in 2.04.168
that a man is never undone till he be hang'd, 2.05. 4 P
unworthily, disgrace the man | (a rashness that 3.01. 29
that man that hath a tongue, i say is no man, 3.01.104
that man that hath a tongue, i say is no man, 3.01.104
of men, | that no man hath access by day to her. 3.01.109
that no man hath recourse to her by night. 3.01.112
why, man? how black? 3.01.287 P
what need a man care for a stock with a wench, 3.01.309 P
he hath stay'd for a better man than thee. 3.01.376 P
by my beard, will we, for he is a proper man. 4.01. 10
a man i am cross'd with adversity; 4.01. 12
i kill'd a man, whose death i much repent, | but 4.01. 27
and a man of such perfection | as we do in our 4.01. 55
indeed because you are a banish'd man, 4.01. 57
how do you, man? 4.02. 55 P
i tell you what launce, his man, told me: 4.02. 75 P
thou subtile, perjur'd, false, disloyal man, 4.02. 95
how use doth breed a habit in a man! 5.04. 1
treacherous man, | thou hast beguil'd my hopes! 5.04. 63
were man | but constant, he were perfect; 5.04.110
your grace is welcome to a man disgrac'd, 5.04.123
it is a familiar beast to man, and signifies WIV 1.01. 21 P
where's simple, my man? can you tell, cousin? 1.01.134 P
sirrah, for all you are my man, go wait upon my 1.01.271 P
may be beholding to his friend for a man. 1.01.274 P
as soon quarrel at it as any man in england. 1.01.291 P
a softly–sprighted man, is he not? 1.04. 24 P
but he is as tall a man of his hands as any is 1.04. 25 P
run in here, good young man; 1.04. 38 P
if he had found the young man, he would have 1.04. 50 P
ay me, he'll find the young man there, and be 1.04. 65 P
the young man is an honest man. 1.04. 72 P
the young man is an honest man. 1.04. 72 P
what shall de honest man do in my closet? 1.04. 73 P
dere is no honest man dat shall come in my 1.04. 74 P
but notwithstanding, man, i'll do /you your 1.04. 92 P
twenty lascivious turtles ere one chaste man. 2.01. 81 P
and my good man too. 2.01.103 P
priest o' th' town commended him for a true man. 2.01.146 P
a man may be too confident. 2.01.186 P
i do relent. what would thou more of man? 2.02. 30
he's a very jealousy man. 2.02. 90 P
i never knew a woman so dote upon a man; 2.02.103 P
and truly master page is an honest man. 2.02.116 P
and you have been a man long known to me, though 2.02.181 P
if any man may, you may as soon as any. 2.02.236 P
would any man have thought this? 2.02.291 P
he is the wiser man, master doctor: 2.03. 38 P
been a great fighter, though now a man of peace. 2.03. 43 P
i never heard a man of his place, gravity, and 3.01. 57 P
warrant you, he's the man should fight with him. 3.01. 68 P
go before you like a man than follow him like a 3.02. 6 P
a man may hear this show'r sing in the wind. 3.02. 37 P
ford, having an honest man to your husband, to 3.03.100 P
it be not so, that you have such a man here; 3.03.113 P
if not, happy man be his dole! 3.04. 64 P
for the water swells a man; 3.05. 16 P
and bid her think what a man is: 3.05. 50 P
think of that — a man of my kidney. 3.05.114 P
a man of continual dissolution and thaw. 3.05.116 P
i'll but bring my young man here to school. 4.01. 8 P
you are utterly sham'd, and he's but a dead man. 4.02. 43 P
why, man, why? 4.02.144 P
master page, as i am a man, there was one 4.02.145 P
if you find a man there, he shall die a flea's 4.02.150 P
here's no man. 4.02.152 P
says that the very same man that beguil'd master 4.05. 36 P
as you see, like a poor old man, but i came from 5.01. 16 P
for in the shape of man, master /brook, i fear 5.01. 21 P
no man means evil but the devil, and we shall 5.02. 12 P
love, that in some respects makes a beast a man; 5.05. 5 P
in some other, a man a beast. 5.05. 5 P
no man their works must eye. 5.05. 48
but stay, i smell a man of middle–earth. 5.05. 80
a puff'd man? 5.05.152 P
nor do i think the man of safe discretion | that MM 1.01. 71
yonder man is carried to prison. 1.02. 86 P
what proclamation, man? 1.02. 94 P
(a man of stricture and firm abstinence) | my 1.03. 12
angelo, a man whose blood | is very snow–broth; 1.04. 57
before these varlets here, thou honorable man, 2.01. 87 P
master froth here, this very man, having eaten 2.01.101 P
a man of fourscore pound a year; 2.01.123 P
you, sir, ask him what this man did to my wife. 2.01.143 P
to come that she was ever respected with man, 2.01.169 P
here is the sister of the man condemn'd 2.02. 18
and neither heaven nor man grieve at the mercy. 2.02. 50
breathe within your lips, | like man new made. 2.02. 79
but man, proud man, | dress'd in a little brief 2.02.117
but man, proud man, | dress'd in a little brief 2.02.117
a young man | more fit to do another such 2.03. 13
love you the man that wrong'd you? 2.03. 24
wherein (let no man hear me) i take pride, 2.04. 10
hath from nature stol'n | a man already made, as 2.04. 44
i'll tell the world aloud | what man thou art. 2.04.154
wilt thou be made a man out of my vice? 3.01.137
in this life, that it will let this man live! 3.01.233 P
what offense hath this man made you, sir? 3.02. 14 P
is the world as it was, man? 3.02. 50 P
angelo was not made by man and woman after this 3.02.104 P
of a codpiece to take away the life of a man! 3.02.116 P
ere he would have hang'd a man for the getting a 3.02.117 P
to me, your honor is accounted a merciful man. 3.02.192 P
o, what may man within him hide, | though angel 3.02.271
here comes a man of comfort, whose advice | hath 4.01. 8
if the man be a bachelor, sir, i can; 4.02. 3 P
but if he be a married man, he's his wive's head 4.02. 4 P
your thief, your true man thinks it big enough; 4.02. 44 P
this is his /lordship's man. 4.02.100
a man that apprehends death no more dreadfully 4.02.142 P
master starve–lackey the rapier and dagger man, 4.03. 14 P
notorious pirate, | a man of claudio's years; 4.03. 72
the better, given me by so holy a man. 4.03.113
i do not like the man; 5.01.128
i know him for a man divine and holy, | not 5.01.144
on my trust, a man that never yet | did, as he 5.01.147
these women | to accuse this worthy man, but, in 5.01.307
is this the man | that you did tell us of? 5.01.324
for this new–married man approaching here, 5.01.400
lord, | i crave no other, nor no better man. 5.01.426
on this man condemn'd | as if my brother liv'd. 5.01.444
there was a friar told me of this man. 5.01.479
nay, forward, old man, do not break off so, ERR 1.01. 96
many a man would take you at your word, | and go 1.02. 17
a man is master of his liberty: 2.01. 7
man, more divine, the master of all these, 2.01. 20
here comes your man, now is your husband nigh. 2.01. 43
and no man that hath a name | by falsehood and 2.01.112
was there ever any man thus beaten out of season 2.02. 47
there's no time for a man to recover his hair 2.02. 72 P
and recover the lost hair of another man. 2.02. 76 P
but there's many a man hath more hair than wit. 2.02. 82 P
not a man of those but he hath the wit to lose 2.02. 84 P
whilst man and master laughs my woes to scorn. 2.02.205
it would make a man mad as a buck to be so 3.01. 72
a man may break a word with /you, sir, and words 3.01. 75
am i your man? 3.02. 74 P
thou art dromio, thou art my man, thou art 3.02. 75 P
i am an ass, i am a woman's man, and besides 3.02. 77 P
what woman's man, and how besides thyself? 3.02. 79 P
such a one as a man may not speak of without he 3.02. 91 P
a man may go over shoes in the grime of it. 3.02.103 P
as from a bear a man would run for life, | so 3.02.154
you are a merry man, sir, fare you well. 3.02.178
there's no man is so vain | that would refuse so 3.02.180
i see a man here needs not live by shifts, 3.02.182
a man is well holp up that trusts to you: 4.01. 22
why, man, what is the matter? 4.02. 41
there's not a man i meet but doth salute me | as 4.03. 1
the man, sir, that, when gentlemen are tir'd, 4.03. 24 P
he that brings any man to answer it that breaks 4.03. 31 P
one that thinks a man always going to bed and 4.03. 32 P
your man and you are marvellous merry, sir. 4.03. 58
fear me not, man, i will not break away; 4.04. 1
here comes my man: 4.04. 8
i charge thee, sathan, hous'd within this man, 4.04. 54
mistress, both man and master is possess'd: 4.04. 92
ay me, poor man, how pale and wan he looks! 4.04.108
go bind this man, for he is frantic too. 4.04.113
hast thou delight to see a wretched man | do 4.04.115
i know the man; what is the sum he owes? 4.04.133
how is the man esteem'd here in the city? 5.01. 4
how long hath this possession held the man? 5.01. 44
sad, | and much different from the man he was; 5.01. 46
and thereof came it that the man was mad. 5.01. 68
to be disturb'd, would mad or man or beast: 5.01. 84
prayers, | to make of him a formal man again: 5.01.105
my master and his man are both broke loose, 5.01.169
his man with scissors nicks him like a fool; 5.01.175
peace, fool, thy master and his man are here, 5.01.178
sharp–looking wretch, | a living dead man. 5.01.242
vault at home | there left me and my man, both 5.01.249
now am i dromio, and his man, unbound. 5.01.291
am sure i do not — and whatsoever a man denies, 5.01.306 P
most mighty duke, behold a man much wrong'd. 5.01.331
and so of these, which is the natural man, | and 5.01.334
if thou be'st the man | that hadst a wife once 5.01.342
from you, | and dromio my man did bring them me. 5.01.386
i see we still did meet each other's man, | and 5.01.387
a lord to a lord, a man to a man, stuff'd with ADO 1.01. 56 P
a lord to a lord, a man to a man, stuff'd with 1.01. 56 P
is so indeed, he is no less than a stuff'd man. 1.01. 59 P
off, and now is the whole man govern'd with one; 1.01. 67 P
we may guess by this what you are, being a man. 1.01.110 P
dog bark at a crow than a man swear he loves me. 1.01.132 P
do you question me, as an honest man should do, 1.01.166 P
in what key shall a man take you to go in the 1.01.186 P
hath not the world one man but he will wear his 1.01.198 P
count claudio, i can be secret as a dumb man; 1.01.210 P
"here you may see benedick the married man." 1.01.268 P
were thus much overheard by a man of mine. 1.02. 11 P
when i am merry, and claw no man in his humor. 1.03. 17 P
i cannot be said to be a flattering honest man) 1.03. 31 P
he were an excellent man that were made just in 2.01. 6 P
such a man would win any woman in the world, if 2.01. 15 P
and he that hath no beard is less than a man; 2.01. 37 P
and he that is less than a man, i am not for him 2.01. 39 P
him so ill–well, unless you were the very man. 2.01.118 P
you may do the part of an honest man in it. 2.01.166 P
now you strike like the blind man. 2.01.198 P
upon me that i stood like a man at a mark, with 2.01.246 P
is here, a man may live as quiet in hell as in a 2.01.258 P
i do much wonder that one man, seeing how much 2.03. 7 P
how much another man is a fool when he dedicates 2.03. 8 P
by falling in love — and such a man is claudio. 2.03. 12 P
the purpose (like an honest man and a soldier), 2.03. 19 P
never think that lady would have lov'd any man. 2.03. 94 P
'tis very possible he'll scorn it, for the man 2.03.180 P
he is a very proper man. 2.03.182 P
and so will he do, for the man doth fear god, 2.03.196 P
a man loves the meat in his youth that he cannot 2.03.238 P
of the brain awe a man from the career of his 2.03.241 P
to praise him more than ever man did merit. 3.01. 19
deserve | as much as may be yielded to a man; 3.01. 48
i never yet saw man, | how wise, how noble, 3.01. 59
so turns she every man the wrong side out, | and 3.01. 68
he is the only man of italy, | always excepted 3.01. 92
hath any man seen him at the barber's? 3.02. 43 P
but the barber's man hath been seen with him, 3.02. 45 P
you the most desartless man to be constable? 3.03. 10 P
to be a well–favor'd man is the gift of fortune, 3.03. 15 P
most senseless and fit man for the constable of 3.03. 23 P
you are to bid any man stand, in the prince's 3.03. 26 P
by virtue of your office, to be no true man; 3.03. 51 P
you have been always call'd a merciful man, 3.03. 62 P
much more a man who hath any honesty in him. 3.03. 64 P
one on't, with any man that knows the /statues, 3.03. 78 P
for indeed the watch ought to offend no man, and 3.03. 81 P
it is an offense to stay a man against his will. 3.03. 82 P
here, man, i am at thy elbow. 3.03. 98 P
or a hat, or a cloak, is nothing to a man. 3.03.119 P
the fashion wears out more apparel than the man. 3.03.140 P
'twill be heavier soon by the weight of a man. 3.04. 27 P
was such another, and now is he become a man. 3.04. 87 P
an old man, sir, and his wits are not so blunt 3.05. 10 P
i am as honest as any man living that is an old 3.05. 14 P
living that is an old man and no honester than i 3.05. 14 P
on your worship as of any man in the city, and 3.05. 26 P
and though i be but a poor man, i am glad to 3.05. 27 P
a good old man, sir, he will be talking; 3.05. 33 P
well, god's a good man; 3.05. 36 P
what man was he talk'd with you yesternight 4.01. 83
i talk'd with no man at that hour, my lord. 4.01. 86
lady, what man is he you are accus'd of? 4.01.176
if i know more of any man alive | than that 4.01.178
prove you that any man with me convers'd | at 4.01.181
how much might the man deserve of me that would 4.01.261 P
may a man do it? 4.01.265 P
o that i were a man! 4.01.303 P
unmitigated rancor — o god, that i were a man! 4.01.306 P
talk with a man out at a window! 4.01.309 P
o that i were a man for his sake! 4.01.317 P
i had any friend would be a man for my sake! 4.01.318 P
i cannot be a man with wishing, therefore i will 4.01.322 P
this man said, sir, that don john, the prince's 4.02. 39 P
but there is no such man, for, brother, men 5.01. 20
nay, do not quarrel with us, good old man. 5.01. 50
tush, tush, man, never fleer and jest at me; 5.01. 58
days, | do challenge thee to trial of a man. 5.01. 66
you say not right, old man. 5.01. 73
if thou kill'st me, boy, thou shalt kill a man. 5.01. 79
that dare as well answer a man indeed | as i 5.01. 89
what, man! 5.01. 92
see, see, here comes the man we went to seek. 5.01.110
as i am an honest man, he looks pale. 5.01.130 P
what, courage, man! 5.01.132 P
a sigh, thou wast the proper'st man in italy. 5.01.172 P
"here dwells benedick the married man"? 5.01.184 P
what a pretty thing man is when he goes in his 5.01.199 P
ape, but then is an ape a doctor to such a man. 5.01.202 P
me confessing to this man how don john your 5.01.235 P
that when i note another man like him | i may 5.01.260

nor i, | and yet, to satisfy this good old man, 5.01.276
this naughty man | shall face to face be brought 5.01.297
margaret, that no man living shall come over it, 5.02. 6 P
to have no man come over me? 5.02. 9 P
there's not one wise man among twenty that will 5.02. 74 P
if a man do not erect in this age his own tomb 5.02. 77 P
fear not, man, we'll tip thy horns with gold, 5.04. 44
how dost thou, benedick, the married man? 5.04. 99
no, if a man will be beaten with brains, 'a 5.04.103 P
for man is a giddy thing, and this is my 5.04.108 P
if any man be seen to talk with a woman within LLL 1.01.129 P
for every man with his affects is born, | not by 1.01.151
a man in all the world's new fashion planted, 1.01.164
a man of complements, whom right and wrong 1.01.168
a man of fire–new words, fashion's own knight. 1.01.178
it is the manner of a man to speak to a woman; 1.01.210 P
is the simplicity of man to hearken after the 1.01.217 P
— be to me, and every man that dares not fight! 1.01.227 P
anthony dull, a man of good repute, carriage, 1.01.268 P
what sign is it when a man of great spirit grows 1.02. 1 P
they are both the varnish of a complete man. 1.02. 44 P
he was a man of good carriage, great carriage, 1.02. 70 P
man. 1.02.134 P
god i have as little patience as another man, 1.02.165 P
of all perfections that a man may owe, 2.01. 6
know you the man? 2.01. 39
a man of sovereign /parts, /peerless esteem'd, 2.01. 44
berowne they call him, but a merrier man, 2.01. 66
in your pocket like a man after the old painting 3.01. 20 P
a man, if i live; 3.01. 40 P
how much carnation ribbon may a man buy for a 3.01.146 P
that was a man when king pippen of france was a 4.01.120 P
hit it, | thou canst not hit it, my good man. 4.01.126
/a' /th' /one side — o, a most dainty man! 4.01.144
ovidius naso was the man. 4.02.123 P
a true man, or a thief, that gallops so? 4.03.185
that, like a rude and savage man of inde, | at 4.03.218
i never knew man hold vile stuff so dear. 4.03.272
then homeward every man attach the hand | of his 4.03.372
offer'd by a child to an old man: 5.01. 62 P
a soldier, a man of travel, that hath seen the 5.01.107 P
and not a man of them shall have the grace, 5.02.128
that some plain man recount their purposes. 5.02.177
yet still she is the moon, and i the man. 5.02.215
say, but to parfect one man in one poor man, 5.02.502 P
but to parfect one man in one poor man, pompion 5.02.502 P
doth this man serve god? 5.02.524 P
'a speaks not like a man of god his making. 5.02.526 P
an't shall please you, a foolish mild man, an 5.02.581 P
a foolish mild man, an honest man, look you, and 5.02.581 P
a man so breathed, that certain he would fight, 5.02.653
when he breathed, he was a man. 5.02.662 P
will not fight with a pole like a northren man; 5.02.695 P
proclaims you for a man replete with mocks, 5.02.843
lord, | this man hath my consent to marry her. MND 1.01. 25
this man hath bewitch'd the bosom of my child. 1.01. 27
upon this spotted and inconstant man. 1.01.110
and ere a man hath power to say "behold!" 1.01.147
were best to call them generally, man by man, 1.02. 2 P
were best to call them generally, man by man, 1.02. 3 P
for pyramus is a sweet–fac'd man; 1.02. 86 P
a proper man as one shall see in a summer's day; 1.02. 86 P
a most lovely gentleman–like man: 1.02. 88 P
laid | will make or man or woman madly dote 2.01.171
thou shalt know the man | by the athenian 2.01.263
the will of man is by his reason sway'd; 2.02.115
is't not enough, is't not enough, young man, 2.02.125
o, that a lady, of one man refus'd, | should of 2.02.133
i am a man as other men are"; 3.01. 44 P
some man or other must present wall; 3.01. 67 P
"ninus' tomb," man. 3.01. 98 P
grey, | whose note full many a man doth mark, 3.01.132
this is the woman; but not this the man. 3.02. 42
fate o'errules, that, one man holding troth, | a 3.02. 92
you are a tame man, go! 3.02.259
did not you tell me i should know the man | by 3.02.348
known, | that every man should take his own, 3.02.459
the man shall have his mare again, and all shall 3.02.463
past the wit of man to say what dream it was. 4.01.206 P
man is but an ass, if he go about /t' expound 4.01.206 P
i was — there is no man can tell what. 4.01.208 P
i had — but man is but /a /patch'd fool, if he 4.01.209 P
the eye of man hath not heard, the ear of man 4.01.211 P
hath not heard, the ear of man hath not seen, 4.01.211 P
you have not a man in all athens able to 4.02. 7 P
the best wit of any handicraft man in athens. 4.02. 10 P
every man look o'er his part; 4.02. 38 P
this man is pyramus, if you would know; 5.01.129
this man, with lime and rough–cast, doth present 5.01.131
at the which let no man wonder. 5.01.134
this man, with lantern, dog, and bush of thorn, 5.01.135
here come two noble beasts in, a man and a lion. 5.01.217 P
myself the man i' th' moon do seem to be. 5.01.245
the man should be put into the lanthorn. 5.01.247 P
how is it else the man i' th' moon? 5.01.248 P
the lanthorn is the moon, i the man i' th' moon, 5.01.258 P
friend, would go near to make a man look sad. 5.01.289 P
beshrew my heart, but i pity the man. 5.01.290 P
less than an ace, man; 5.01.308 P
he for a man, god warr'nt us; 5.01.319 P
a stage, where every man must play a part, | and MV 1.01. 78
why should a man, whose blood is warm within, 1.01. 83
of nothing, more than any man in all venice. 1.01.115 P
made him, and therefore let him pass for a man. 1.02. 57 P
he is every man in no man. 1.02. 60 P
he is every man in no man. 1.02. 60 P
he is a little worse than a man, and when he is 1.02. 88 P
antonio is a good man. 1.03. 12 P
in saying he is a good man is to have you 1.03. 16 P
the man is notwithstanding sufficient. 1.03. 25 P
your worship was the last man in our mouths. 1.03. 60
why, fear not, man, i will not forfeit it. 1.03.156
a pound of man's flesh taken from a man | is not 1.03.165
lichas play at dice | which is the better man, 2.01. 33
master young man, you, i pray you, which is the 2.02. 33 P
is an honest exceeding poor man and, god be 2.02. 53 P
but i pray you, ergo, old man, ergo, i beseech 2.02. 57 P
well, old man, i will tell you news of your son. 2.02. 77 P
but i am launcelot, the jew's man, and i am sure 2.02. 89 P
here comes the man. 2.02.111 P
boy, sir, but the rich jew's man, that would, 2.02.123 P
i hope, an old man, shall frutify unto you — 2.02.134 P
your worship shall know by this honest old man, 2.02.139 P
though i say it, though old man, yet poor man, 2.02.139 P
say it, though old man, yet poor man, my father. 2.02.140 P
if any man in italy have a fairer table, which 2.02.158 P
nine maids is a simple coming–in for one man. 2.02.163 P
many a man his life hath sold | but my outside 2.07. 67
why, man, i saw bassanio under sail, | with him 2.08. 1
pale and common drudge | 'tween man and man; 3.02.104
pale and common drudge | 'tween man and man; 3.02.104
so much the constitution | of any constant man. 3.02.247
a creature that did bear the shape of man | so 3.02.275
of man | so keen and greedy to confound a man. 3.02.276
the dearest friend to me, the kindest man, | the 3.02.292
and use thou all th' endeavor of a man | in 3.04. 48
and speak between the change of man and boy 3.04. 66
understand a plain man in his plain meaning: 3.05. 57 P
this is no answer, thou unfeeling man, | to 4.01. 63
hates any man the thing he would not kill? 4.01. 67
what, man, courage yet! 4.01.111
there is no power in the tongue of man | to 4.01.241
o noble judge! o excellent young man! 4.01.246
to let the wretched man outlive his wealth, | to 4.01.269
but hark, i hear the footing of a man. 5.01. 24
leave hollowing, man — here. 5.01. 43 P
the man that hath no music in himself, | nor is 5.01. 83
let no such man be trusted. 5.01. 88
he knows me as the blind man knows the cuckoo, 5.01.112
this is the man, this is antonio, | to whom i am 5.01.134
he will, and if he live to be a man. 5.01.159
ay, if a woman live to be a man. 5.01.160
and neither man nor master would take aught 5.01.183
what man is there so much unreasonable, | if you 5.01.203
to do it, | unless he live until he be a man. 5.01.283
but love no man in good earnest, nor no further AYL 1.02. 27 P
there comes an old man and his three sons — 1.02.118 P
yonder they lie, the poor old man, their father, 1.02.130 P
is yonder the man? 1.02.151 P
i can tell you, there is such odds in the man. 1.02.159 P
young man, have you challeng'd charles the 1.02.168 P
now hercules be thy speed, young man! 1.02.210 P
o excellent young man! 1.02.213 P
bear him away. what is thy name, young man? 1.02.221
i would thou hadst been son to some man else: 1.02.224
had i before known this young man his son, | i 1.02.237
that i did suit me all points like a man? 1.03.116
what shall i call thee when thou art a man? 1.03.123
can it be possible that no man saw them? 2.02. 1
i'll do the service of a younger man | in all 2.03. 54
o good old man, how well in thee appears | the 2.03. 56
but, poor old man, thou prun'st a rotten tree, 2.03. 63
here, a young man and an old in solemn talk. 2.04. 20 P
as sure i think did never man love so — | how 2.04. 29
one of you question yond man | if he for gold 2.04. 64
but i am shepherd to another man, | and do not 2.04. 78
well then, if ever i thank any man, i'll thank 2.05. 25 P
and when a man thanks me heartily, methinks i 2.05. 27 P
if it do come to pass | that any man turn ass, 2.05. 51
beast, | for i can no where find him like a man. 2.07. 2
like a wild goose flies, | unclaim'd of any man. 2.07. 87
art thou thus bolden'd, man, by thy distress? 2.07. 91
there is an old poor man, | who after me hath 2.07.129
and one man in his time plays many parts, | his 2.07.142
good old man, | thou art right welcome as thy 2.07.197
of a mutton as wholesome as the sweat of a man? 3.02. 57 P
most shallow man! 3.02. 65 P
god help thee, shallow man! 3.02. 72 P
get that i wear, owe no man hate, envy no man's 3.02. 74 P
how brief the life of man | runs his erring 3.02.129
is it a man? 3.02.180 P
though i am caparison'd like a man, i have a 3.02.195 P
pour this conceal'd man out of thy mouth, as 3.02.199 P
so you may put a man in your belly. 3.02.204 P
what manner of man? 3.02.206 P
god will send more, if the man will be thankful. 3.02.209 P
latin, and a rich man that hath not the gout; 3.02.320 P
who was in his youth an inland man, one that 3.02.345 P
there is a man haunts the forest, that abuses 3.02.359 P
he taught me how to know a man in love; 3.02.370 P
but you are no such man; 3.02.382 P
am i the man yet? 3.03. 3 P
it strikes a man more dead than a great 3.03. 14 P
a man may, if he were of a fearful heart, 3.03. 48 P
is said, "many a man knows no end of his goods." 3.03. 53 P
many a man has good horns, and knows no end of 3.03. 54 P
is the single man therefore bless'd? 3.03. 58 P
forehead of a married man more honorable than 3.03. 60 P
i will not take her on gift of any man. 3.03. 68 P
the falcon her bells, so man hath his desires; 3.03. 80 P
and will you, being a man of your breeding, be 3.03. 83 P
to consider that tears do not become a man. 3.04. 3 P
of fathers, when there is such a man as orlando? 3.04. 39 P
o, that's a brave man! 3.04. 40 P
you are a thousand times a properer man | than 3.05. 51
cry the man mercy, love him, take his offer; 3.05. 61
i had rather hear you chide than this man woo. 3.05. 65
to glean the broken ears after the man | that 3.05.102
he'll make a proper man. 3.05.115
this time there was not any man died in his own 4.01. 96 P
a man that had a wife with such a wit, he might 4.01.165 P
could not love me | were man as rare as phoenix. 4.03. 17
"whiles the eye of man did woo me, | that could 4.03. 47
if you will know of me | what man i am, and how, 4.03. 96
a wretched ragged man, o'ergrown with hair, 4.03.106
watch, | when that the sleeping man should stir; 4.03.116
orlando did approach the man | and found it was 4.03.119
you a man? 4.03.163
take a good heart and counterfeit to be a man. 4.03.174 P
here comes the man you mean. 5.01. 9 P
but the wise man knows himself to be a fool." 5.01. 32 P
i will satisfy you, if ever i satisfied man, and 5.02.115 P
if any man doubt that, let him put me to my 5.04. 43 P
mine, sir, to take that that no man else will. 5.04. 59 P
where, meeting with an old religious man, 5.04.160
welcome, young man; 5.04.166
sirs, i will practice on this drunken man. SHR in.1. 36
o, that a mighty man of such descent, | of such in.2. 14
these, | which never were, nor no man ever saw. in.2. 96
any means light on a fit man to teach her that 1.01.111 P
any man is so very a fool to be married to hell? 1.01.124 P
why, man, there be good fellows in the world, 1.01.127 P
in the world, and a man could light on them, 1.01.128 P
happy man be his dole! 1.01.139 P
distinguish'd by our faces | for man or master. 1.01.201
some neapolitan, or meaner man of pisa. 1.01.205
ashore | i kill'd a man and fear i was descried. 1.01.232
is there any man has rebus'd your worship? 1.02. 7 P
fortune i have lighted well | on this young man; 1.02.168
suitors, | and will not promise her to any man, 1.02.260
sir, that you are the man | must stead us all, 1.02.263
i do present you with a man of mine, | cunning 2.01. 55
son, | a man well known throughout all italy. 2.01. 69
a mighty man of pisa; 2.01.104
well, | thou must be married to no man but me; 2.01.275
was it not to refresh the mind of man | after 3.01. 11
a–wooing, "priami," is my man tranio, "regia," 3.01. 35 P
spit in the hole, man, and tune again. 3.01. 40
and to be noted for a merry man, | he'll woo a 3.02. 14
a horse and a man | is more than one, | and yet 3.02. 84
i am to get a man — what e'er he be, | it 3.02.131
rescue thy mistress if thou be a man. 3.02.237
was ever man so beaten? 4.01. 2 P
was ever man so ray'd? 4.01. 3 P
was ever man so weary? 4.01. 3 P
the weather, a taller man than i will take cold. 4.01. 11 P
but thou know'st winter tames man, woman, and 4.01. 23 P
no man at door | to hold my stirrup nor to take 4.01.120
another way i have to man my haggard, | to make 4.01.193
'a will make the man mad, to make /a woman of 4.05. 35 P
happier the man whom favorable stars | allots 4.05. 40
this is a man, old, wrinkled, faded, withered, 4.05. 43
what if a man bring him a hundred pound or two, 5.01. 21 P
what, is the man lunatic? 5.01. 72 P
how call'd you the man you speak of, madam? AWW 1.01. 24 P
man is enemy to virginity; 1.01.112 P
man, setting down before you, will undermine you 1.01.118 P
blown down, man will quicklier be blown up. 1.01.123 P
such a man | might be a copy to these younger 1.02. 45
a man may draw his heart out ere 'a pluck one. 1.03. 88 P
that man should be at woman's command, and yet 1.03. 92 P
then here's a man stands that has brought his 2.01. 63
madam, if god have lent a man any manners, he 2.02. 8 P
right, as 'twere a man assur'd of a — 2.03. 17 P
this is the man. 2.03.104
to any count, to all counts: to what is man. 2.03.193 P
to what is count's man. 2.03.194 P
i must tell thee, sirrah, i write man; 2.03.198 P
i may say in the default, "he is a man i know." 2.03.229 P
general offense, and every man should beat thee. 2.03.255 P
a young man married is a man that's marr'd; 2.03.298
a young man married is a man that's marr'd; 2.03.298
marry, you are the wiser man; 2.04. 23 P
the soul of this man is his clothes. 2.05. 44 P
but like a common and an outward man | that the 3.01. 11
take my young lord to be a very melancholy man. 3.02. 4 P
i know a man that had this trick of melancholy 3.02. 8 P
and i begin to love, as an old man loves money, 3.02. 16 P
we must every one be a man of his own fancy, not 4.01. 17 P
reading it he chang'd almost into another man. 4.03. 5 P
i will never trust a man again for keeping his 4.03.144 P
every thing that an honest man should not have; 4.03.260 P
what an honest man should have, he has nothing. 4.03.260 P
i would do the man what honor i can, but of this 4.03.271 P
there's place and means for every man alive. 4.03.339
i would cozen the man of his wife and do his 4.05. 27 P
which bow the head, and nod at every man. 4.05.106 P
this man may help me to his majesty's ear, | if 5.01. 7
i am a man whom fortune hath cruelly scratch'd. 5.02. 26 P
i saw the man to–day, if man he be. 5.03.203
i saw the man to–day, if man he be. 5.03.203
is this the man you speak of? 5.03.233
i am a poor man, and at your majesty's command. 5.03.251 P
by jove, if ever i knew man, 'twas you. 5.03.287
he's as tall a man as any's in illyria. TN 1.03. 20 P
wit than a christian or an ordinary man has; 1.03. 84 P
tut, there's life in't, man. 1.03.111 P
as any man in illyria, whatsoever he be, under 1.03.117 P
and yet i will not compare with an old man. 1.03.119 P
simply as strong as any man in illyria. 1.03.124 P
thy happy years, | that say thou art a man. 1.04. 31
am sure i lack thee, may pass for a wise man. 1.05. 35 P
bid the dishonest man mend himself: 1.05. 45 P
nor no railing in a known discreet man, though 1.05. 96 P
'tis a fair young man, and well attended. 1.05.102 P
what's a drunken man like, fool? 1.05.130 P
like a drown'd man, a fool, and a madman. 1.05.131 P
what kind o' man is he? 1.05.150 P
what manner of man? 1.05.152 P
not yet old enough for a man, nor young enough 1.05.156 P
with him in standing water, between boy and man. 1.05.159 P
unless the master were the man. 1.05.294
same peevish messenger, | the /county's man. 1.05.301
i am the man! 2.02. 25
as i am man, | my state is desperate for my 2.02. 36
"there dwelt a man in babylon, lady, lady!" 2.03. 79 P
my father had a daughter lov'd a man, | as it 2.04.107
i would exult, man. 2.05. 7 P
no man must know." 2.05. 99
"no man must know." 2.05.100 P
"no man must know." 2.05.101 P
i will be point–devise the very man. 2.05.163 P
why, man? 3.01. 18 P
thy reason, man? 3.01. 22 P
your wife is like to reap a proper man. 3.01.133
he come, for sure the man is tainted in 's wits. 3.04. 13 P
why, how dost thou, man? 3.04. 24 P
no worse man than sir toby to look to me! 3.04. 65 P
how is't with you, man? 3.04. 88 P
what, man, defy the devil! 3.04. 97 P
what, man, 'tis not for gravity to play at 3.04.115 P
hath taken the infection of the device, man. 3.04.130 P
no man hath any quarrel to me. 3.04.226 P
clear from any image of offense done to any man. 3.04.228 P

skill, and wrath can furnish man withal. 3.04.232 P
belike this is a man of that quirk. 3.04.244 P
i beseech you, what manner of man is he? 3.04.263 P
why, man, he's a very devil, i have not seen 3.04.273 P
make me tell them how much i lack of a man. 3.04.303 P
this is the man, do thy office. 3.04.325 P
lest that it make me so unsound a man | as to 3.04.350
i hate ingratitude more in a man | than lying, 3.04.354
the man grows mad, away with him! 3.04.371
word of some great man and now applies it to a 4.01. 13 P
to be said an honest man and a good house-keeper 4.02. 8 P
as to say a careful man and a great scholar. 4.02. 9 P
how vexest thou this man! 4.02. 26 P
sir topas, never was man thus wrong'd. 4.02. 28 P
and i say there was never man thus abus'd. 4.02. 47 P
fool, there was never man so notoriously abus'd; 4.02. 87 P
i am as well in my wits as any man in illyria. 4.02.106 P
now go with me and with this holy man | into the 4.03. 23
i'll follow this good man, and go with you, 4.03. 32
here comes the man, sir, that did rescue me. 5.01. 50
you are betroth'd both to a maid and man. 5.01.263
stave's end as well as a man in his case may do. 5.01.285 P
for so you shall be while you are a man; 5.01.386
was born desire yet their life to see him a man. WT 1.01. 41 P
why, happy man be 's dole! 1.02.163
and many a man there is (even at this present, 1.02.192
go play, mamillius, thou'rt an honest man. 1.02.211
in every one of these no man is free | but that 1.02.251
resides not in that man that does not think) 1.02.272
could man so blench? 1.02.333
thee, by all the parts of man | which honor does 1.02.400
he is dishonor'd by a man which ever | profess'd 1.02.455
there was a man — 2.01. 29
good, so were i | a man, the worst about you. 2.03. 62
know of it | is that camillo was an honest man; 3.02. 74
whom i proclaim a man of truth, of mercy; 3.02.157
what ail'st thou, man? 3.03. 82 P
would i had been by, to have help'd the old man! 3.03.108 P
you're a /made old man; 3.03.120 P
from the house of a most homely shepherd, a man, 4.02. 38 P
sir, of such a man, who hath a daughter of most 4.02. 41 P
alas, poor man, a million of beating may come to 4.03. 59 P
i know this man well; 4.03. 94 P
he hath songs for man or woman, of all sizes; 4.04.191 P
do me no harm, good man" — puts him off, 4.04.199 P
him, with "whoop, do me no harm, good man." 4.04.200 P
fear not thou, man, thou shalt lose nothing here 4.04.255 P
goes to the tune of "two maids wooing a man." 4.04.289 P
know man from man? 4.04.400
know man from man? 4.04.400
sir, | you have undone a man of fourscore three, 4.04.453
that i may call thee something more than man 4.04.535
(who wants but something to be a reasonable man) 4.04.605 P
and had not the old man come in with a whoobub 4.04.615 P
fear not, man, here's no harm intended to thee. 4.04.629 P
is the time that the unjust man doth thrive. 4.04.674 P
session, hanging, yields a careful man work. 4.04.686 P
what a man you are now! 4.04.687 P
who, i may say, is no honest man, neither to his 4.04.700 P
a great man, i'll warrant; 4.04.752 P
will break the back of man, the heart of monster 4.04.770 P
has the old man e'er a son, sir, do you hear, 4.04.781 P
and if it be in man besides the king to effect 4.04.797 P
to effect your suits, here is man shall do it. 4.04.798 P
and leave this young man in pawn till i bring it 4.04.808 P
as much as this old man does when the business 4.04.821 P
we are bless'd in this man, as i may say, even 4.04.827 P
destroy'd the sweet'st companion that e'er man 5.01. 11
that she is a woman | more worth than any man; 5.01.111
to greet a man not worth her pains, much less 5.01.155
i brought the old man and his son aboard the 5.02.115 P
yet you look'd upon | or hand of man hath done; 5.03. 17
let no man mock me, | for i will kiss her. 5.03. 79
out on thee, rude man, thou dost shame thy JN 1.01. 64
my son | in the large composition of this man? 1.01. 88
and catechize | my picked man of countries. 1.01.193
colbrand the giant, that same mighty man? 1.01.225
some proper man, i hope. 1.01.250
son to the elder brother of this man, | and king 2.01.239
he is the half part of a blessed man, | left to 2.01.437
word | is but the vain breath of a common man. 3.01. 8
believe me, i do not believe thee, man, | i have 3.01. 9
this news hath made thee a most ugly man. 3.01. 37
o, that a man should speak those words to me! 3.01.130
purchase corrupted pardon of a man | who in that 3.01.166
hubert shall be your man, attend on you | with 3.03. 72
tale | vexing the dull ear of a drowsy man; 3.04.109
this is the man should do the bloody deed; 4.02. 69
mould, that fashioned thee | made him a man; R2 1.02. 24
against what man thou com'st, and what thy 1.03. 13
are to a wise man ports and happy havens. 1.03.276
the man that mocks at it and sets it light. 1.03.293
what comfort, man? how is't with aged gaunt? 2.01. 72
if it be so, out with it boldly, man, | quick is 2.01.233
the /king's grown bankrout, like a broken man. 2.01.257
thou art a banish'd man, and here art come 2.03.110
for every man that bullingbrook hath press'd 3.02. 58
dogs, easily won to fawn on any man! 3.02.130
no matter where — of comfort no man speak: 3.02.144
speak sweetly, man, although thy looks be sour. 3.02.193
let no man speak again | to alter this, for 3.02.213
on yon proud man should take it off again | with 3.03.135
makes him speak fondly like a frantic man, | yet 3.03.185
thee | to make a second fall of cursed man? 3.04. 76
cousin, stand forth, and look upon that man. 4.01. 7
what answer shall i make to this base man? 4.01. 20
no man cried "god save him!" 5.02. 28
that mind, | he is as like thee as a man may be, 5.02.108
can no man tell me of my unthrifty son? 5.03. 1
key, | that no man enter till my tale be done. 5.03. 37
o king, believe not this hard-hearted man! 5.03. 87
"i would thou wert the man | that would divorce 5.04. 8
e'er i be, | nor i, nor any man that but man is, 5.05. 39
e'er i be, | nor i, nor any man that but man is, 5.05. 39
where no man never comes, but that sad dog 5.05. 70
of that proud man that did usurp his back? 5.05. 89
thee, | since thou, created to be aw'd by man, 5.05. 91
cries out in the streets, and no man regards it. 1H4 1.02. 89 P
and now am i, if a man should speak truly, 1.02. 94 P
'tis no sin for a man to labor in his vocation. 1.02.105 P
to a true man. 1.02.110 P
for i shall never hold that man my friend 1.03. 90
the crown | upon the head of this forgetful man, 1.03.161
nicholas as truly as a man of falsehood may. 2.01. 65 P
a share in our purchase, as i am a true man. 2.01. 92 P
as drink to turn true man and to leave these 2.02. 23 P
now, my masters, happy man be his dole, say i, 2.02. 76 P
be his dole, say i, every man to his business. 2.02. 77 P
but roguery to be found in villainous man, yet a 2.04.125 P
why, you whoreson round man, what's the matter? 2.04.140 P
what, a hundred, man? 2.04.163 P
i never dealt better since i was a man; 2.04.169 P
they were bound, every man of them, or i am a 2.04.178 P
i would give no man a reason upon compulsion, i. 2.04.240 P
give him as much as will make him a royal man, 2.04.291 P
what manner of man is he? 2.04.292 P
an old man. 2.04.293 P
and grief, it blows a man up like a bladder. 2.04.332 P
there is a virtuous man whom i have often noted 2.04.417 P
what manner of man, and it like your majesty? 2.04.420 P
a goodly portly man, i' faith, and a corpulent, 2.04.422 P
if that man should be lewdly given, he deceiveth 2.04.426 P
haunts thee in the likeness of an old fat man, a 2.04.448 P
an old fat man, a tun of man is thy companion. 2.04.448 P
my lord, the man i know. 2.04.464 P
if i become not a cart as well as another man, a 2.04.497 P
well known, my gracious lord, | a gross fat man. 2.04.511
the man, i do assure you, is not here, | for i 2.04.512
send him to answer thee, or any man, | for any 2.04.516
i think there's no man speaks better welsh. 3.01. 49
why, so can i, or so can any man, | but will 3.01. 53
that man is not alive | might so have tempted 3.01.171
and the soul of every man | prophetically do 3.02. 37
use of it as many a man doth of a death's-head 3.03. 30 P
so has my husband, man by man, boy by boy, 3.03. 56 P
so has my husband, man by man, boy by boy, 3.03. 57 P
i love him well, he is an honest man. 3.03. 93 P
vilely of you, like a foul-mouth'd man as he is, 3.03.107 P
nor flesh, a man knows not where to have her. 3.03.127 P
thou art an unjust man in saying so. 3.03.129 P
thou or any man knows where to have me, thou 3.03.130 P
thou knowest, as thou art but man, i dare, but 3.03.145 P
thou seest i have more flesh than another man, 3.03.167 P
in my heart's love hath no man than yourself. 4.01. 8
no man so potent breathes upon the ground | but 4.01. 11
tush, man, mortal men, mortal men. 4.02. 67 P
yea, every man | shall be my friend again, and 5.01.107
and that no man might draw short breath to-day 5.02. 48
he gave you all the duties of a man, | trimm'd 5.02. 55
let each man do his best, and here draw i | a 5.02. 92
i could have better spar'd a better man. 5.04.104
the counterfeit of a man who hath not the life 5.04.116 P
of a man who hath not the life of a man; 5.04.117 P
to counterfeit dying, when a man thereby liveth, 5.04.118 P
did you not tell me this fat man was dead? 5.04.132
no, that's certain, i am not a double man; 5.04.138 P
if the man were alive and would deny it, 'zounds 5.04.152 P
and not a man of them brings other news | than 2H4 in 38
even such a man, so faint, so spiritless, | so 1.01. 70
me, and counsel every man | the aptest way for 1.01.212
the brain of this foolish-compounded clay, man, 1.02. 7 P
as if he had writ man ever since his father was 1.02. 26 P
and if a man is through with them in honest 1.02. 39 P
why, sir, did i say you were an honest man? 1.02. 80 P
if you say i am any other than an honest man. 1.02. 86 P
all the other gifts appertinent to man, as the 1.02.172 P
if ye will needs say i am an old man, you should 1.02.217 P
a man can no more separate age and covetousness 1.02.229 P
now possess'd | the utmost man of expectation, 1.03. 65
any devil, he will spare neither man, woman, nor 2.01. 17 P
what man of good temper would endure this 2.01. 80 P
if thou wert an honest man, thyself and the 2.01. 85 P
if a man will make curtsy and say nothing, he is 2.01.124 P
let the end try the man. 2.02. 47 P
a blessed fellow to think as every man thinks. 2.02. 57 P
every man would think me an hypocrite indeed. 2.02. 59 P
knight" — every man must know that, as oft as 2.02.110 P
i will bar no honest man my house, nor no 2.04.103 P
and look whether the fiery trigon, his man, be 2.04.266 P
may sleep when the man of action is call'd on. 2.04.376 P
but an honester and truer-hearted man — well, 2.04.384 P
since | this percy was the man nearest my soul, 3.01. 61
the which observ'd, a man may prophesy, | with a 3.01. 82
pickbone, and will squele, a cotsole man. 3.02. 21 P
i knew him a good backsword man. 3.02. 64 P
that is, when a man is, as they say, 3.02. 77 P
or when a man is being whereby 'a may be thought 3.02. 78 P
o lord, sir, i am a diseas'd man. 3.02.179 P
a man can die but once, we owe god a death. 3.02.234 P
tell me, master shallow, how to choose a man? 3.02.258 P
the stature, bulk, and big assemblance of a man? 3.02.259 P
half-fac'd fellow, shadow, give me this man. 3.02.265 P
like a man made after supper of a cheese-paring. 3.02.309 P
text | /than now to see you here an iron man, 4.02. 8
that man that sits within a monarch's heart 4.02. 11
ready are to try our fortunes | to the last man. 4.02. 44
as good a man as he, sir, whoe'er i am. 4.03. 11 P
not love me, nor a man cannot make him laugh, 4.03. 88 P
to all the rest of this little kingdom, man, to 4.03.109 P
doth the man of war stay all night, sir? 5.01. 29 P
an honest man, sir, is able to speak for himself 5.01. 46 P
quarter bear out a knave against an honest man, 5.01. 49 P
master shallow that no man could better command 5.01. 74 P
though no man be assur'd what grace to find, 5.02. 30
"happy am i, that have a man so bold, | that 5.02.108
master silence had been a man of this mettle. 5.03. 37 P
why then say an old man can do somewhat. 5.03. 78 P
not the ill wind which blows no man to good. 5.03. 86 P
thee now deliver them like a man of this world. 5.03. 97 P
harry the fift's the man. 5.03.117
there hath been a man or two kill'd about her. 5.04. 6 P
me, for the man is dead that you and pistol beat 5.04. 16 P
i'll tell you what, you thin man in a censer, i 5.04. 18 P
my lord chief justice, speak to that vain man. 5.05. 44
i know thee not, old man, fall to thy prayers. 5.05. 47
i have long dreamt of such a kind of man, | so 5.05. 49
i will be the man yet that shall make you great. 5.05. 79 P
died /a martyr, and this is not the man. ep 32 P
into a thousand parts divide one man, | and make H5 pr 24
when the man dies, let the inheritance | descend 1.02. 99
divide | the state of man in divers functions, 1.02.184
and plodded like a man for working-days; 1.02.277
therefore let every man now task his thought, 1.02.309
reigns solely in the breast of every man. 2.pr. 4
nay, but the man that was his bedfellow, | whom 2.02. 8
no doubt, my liege, if each man do his best. 2.02. 19
exeter, | enlarge the man committed yesterday, 2.02. 40
we'll yet enlarge that man, | though cambridge, 2.02. 57
and this man | hath, for a few light crowns, 2.02. 88
to /mark /the full-fraught man and best indued 2.02.139
thine, methinks, is like | another fall of man. 2.02.142
bosom, if ever man went to arthur's bosom. 2.03. 10 P
quoth i, "what, man? 2.03. 18 P
in peace there's nothing so becomes a man | as 3.01. 3
they would serve me, could not be man to me; 3.02. 30 P
indeed three such antics do not amount to a man. 3.02. 32 P
as well as any military man in the world, in the 3.02. 80 P
look you, being as good a man as yourself, both 3.02.129 P
i do not know you so good a man as myself. 3.02.132 P
and a man that i love and honor with my soul, 3.06. 7 P
he is as valiant a man as mark antony, and he is 3.06. 14 P
and he is a man of no estimation in the world, 3.06. 14 P
here is the man. 3.06. 20 P
let gallows gape for dog, let man go free, | and 3.06. 42
perceive he is not the man that he would gladly 3.06. 83 P
can tell your majesty, the duke is a prave man. 3.06. 96 P
i think the duke hath lost never a man, but one 3.06.100 P
one bardolph, if your majesty know the man. 3.06.102 P
nay, the man hath no wit that cannot, from the 3.07. 31 P
to you, i think the king is but a man, as i am. 4.01.102 P
laid by, in his nakedness he appears but a man; 4.01.105 P
no man should possess him with any appearance of 4.01.110 P
in the wars do as every sick man in his bed, 4.01.179 P
'tis certain, every man that dies ill, the ill 4.01.186 P
god's will, i pray thee wish not one man more. 4.03. 23
no, faith, my coz, wish not a man from england. 4.03. 30
as one man more methinks would share from me, 4.03. 32
this story shall the good man teach his son; 4.03. 56
perish the man whose mind is backward now! 4.03. 72
the man that once did sell the lion's skin 4.03. 93
stopp'd, | but i had not so much of man in me, 4.06. 30
and not a man of them that we shall take | shall 4.07. 64
god, so long as your majesty is an honest man. 4.07.115 P
if any man challenge this, he is a friend to 4.07.156 P
i would fain see the man, that hath but two legs 4.07.162 P
i met this man with my glove in his cap, and i 4.08. 31 P
you appear'd to me but as a common man; 4.08. 51 P
as man and wife, being two, are one in love, 5.02.361
what say'st thou, man, before dead henry's corse 1H6 1.01. 62
and while i live, i'll ne'er fly from a man. 1.02.103
but with a baser man of arms by far | once in 1.04. 30
o lord, have mercy on me, woeful man! 1.04. 71
that she may boast she hath beheld the man 2.02. 42
and he is welcome. what? is this the man? 2.03. 14
why? art not thou the man? 2.03. 48
dare no man answer in a case of truth? 2.04. 2
even like a man new haled from the rack, | so 2.05. 3
beseems | a man of thy profession and degree; 3.01. 20
lord, we know your grace to be a man | just and 3.01. 94
age, | and twit with cowardice a man half dead? 3.02. 55
what is the trust or strength of foolish man? 3.02.112
why, what is he? as good a man as york. 3.04. 36
was infamous | and ill beseeming any common man, 4.01. 31
no simple man that sees | this jarring discord 4.01.187
there thou stand'st, a breathing valiant man, 4.02. 31
sell every man his life as dear as mine, | and 4.02. 53
can, | but curse the cause i cannot aid the man. 4.03. 44
conqueror, | that ever-living man of memory, 4.03. 51
charles, | a man of great authority in france, 5.01. 18
o, charles the dolphin is a proper man, | no 5.03. 37
fond man, remember that thou hast a wife, | then 5.03. 81
he talks at randon; sure the man is mad. 5.03. 85
you have suborn'd this man | of purpose to 5.04. 21
a married man! that's most intolerable. 5.04. 79
retain but privilege of a private man? 5.04.136
more like a soldier than a man o' th' church, 2H6 1.01.186
were i a man, a duke, and next of blood, | i 1.02. 63
nay, fear not, man, | we are alone, here's none 1.02. 68
what say'st thou, man? 1.02. 74
make merry, man, | with thy confederates in this 1.02. 85
the lord protect him, for he's a good man! 1.03. 5 P
against john goodman, my lord cardinal's man, 1.03. 17 P
york is meetest man | to be your regent in the 1.03.160
force, | that york is most unmeet of any man. 1.03.164
because here is a man accused of treason. 1.03.177
this is the man | that doth accuse his master of 1.03.181
say, man, were these thy words? 1.03.186
do not cast away an honest man for a villain's 1.03.202 P
the spite of man prevaileth against me. 1.03.214 P
yea, man and birds are fain of climbing high. 2.01. 8
had not your man put up the fowl so suddenly, 2.01. 44
forsooth, a blind man at saint albon's shrine, 2.01. 61
a man that ne'er saw in his life before. 2.01. 63
to present your highness with the man. 2.01. 67
the greatest man in england but the king. 2.02. 82
with sir john stanley, in the isle of man. 2.03. 13
the armorer and his man, to enter the lists, 2.03. 50
drink, and fear not your man. 2.03. 65 P
to prove him a knave and myself an honest man; 2.03. 87 P
now | to take her with him to the isle of man. 2.04. 78
why, madam, that is to the isle of man, | there 2.04. 94
'tis not his wont to be the hindmost man, | what 3.01. 2
and humphrey is no little man in england. 3.01. 20
gloucester is a man | unsounded yet and full of 3.01. 56
hangs on the cutting short that fraudful man. 3.01. 81
thou never didst them wrong, nor no man wrong; 3.01.209
ah, york, no man alive so fain as i! 3.01.244
let pale-fac'd fear keep with the mean-born man, 3.01.335
didst ever hear a man so penitent? 3.02. 4
ah, woe is me for gloucester, wretched man! 3.02. 72
staring full ghastly, like a strangled man; 3.02.170
and charge that no man should disturb your rest 3.02.256
a cunning man did calculate my birth | and told 4.01. 34
he was an honest man, and a good bricklayer. 4.02. 40 P

being scribbled o'er, should undo a man? 4.02. 81 P
to a thing, and i was never mine own man since. 4.02. 83 P
the man is a proper man, of mine honor; 4.02. 95 P
the man is a proper man, of mine honor; 4.02. 95 P
to thyself, like a honest plain–dealing man? 4.02.104 P
be encount'red with a man as good as himself. 4.02.116 P
why dost thou quiver, man? 4.07. 92 P
kent, | took odds to combat a poor famish'd man. 4.10. 44
she hath lost her best man, and exhort all the 4.10. 73 P
me, my friend, art thou the man that slew him? 5.01. 71
/these | if they can brook i bow a knee to man. 5.01.110
is the man grown mad? 5.01.131
vow | to do a murd'rous deed, to rob a man, | to 5.01.185
ah, wretched man, would i had died a maid | and 3H6 1.01.216
child, | lest thou be hated both of god and man. 1.03. 9
he is a man, and, clifford, cope with him. 1.03. 24
why art thou patient, man? 1.04. 89
year, | how many years a mortal man may live. 2.05. 29
this man whom hand to hand i slew in fight | may 2.05. 56
yield both my life and them | to some man else, 2.05. 60
to some man else, as this dead man doth me. 2.05. 60
my father, being the earl of warwick's man, 2.05. 65
weep, wretched man; 2.05. 76
here comes a man, let's stay till he be past. 3.01. 12
no, not a man comes for redress of thee; 3.01. 20
a man at least, for less i should not be; 3.01. 57
do i not breathe a man? 3.01. 82
and go we, brothers, to the man that took him, 3.02.121
and am i then a man to be belov'd? 3.02.163
my love, | is, of a king, become a banish'd man, 3.03. 25
come on, my masters, each man take his stand, 4.03. 1
this way, man, see where the huntsmen stand. 4.05. 15
tush, man, abodements must not now affright us. 4.07. 13
the good old man would fain that all were well, 4.07. 31
what, fear not, man, but yield me up the keys, 4.07. 37
and make him, naked, foil a man at arms. 5.04. 42
for did i but suspect a fearful man, | he should 5.04. 44
he was a man; 5.05. 56
was it not she, and that good man of worship, R3 1.01. 66
i think there is no man /is secure | but the 1.01. 71
that no man shall have private conference | (of 1.01. 86
we speak no treason, man. 1.01. 90
villain, thou know'st nor law of god nor man: 1.02. 70
vouchsafe, defus'd infection of /a man, | of 1.02. 78
cannot) | myself to be a marv'llous proper man. 1.02.254
a man that loves not me, nor none of you. 1.03. 13
cannot a plain man live and think no harm, | but 1.03. 51
no man but prophesied revenge for it. 1.03.185
that, as i am a christian faithful man, | i 1.04. 4
not meddle with it, it makes a man a coward. 1.04.134 P
a man cannot steal, but it accuseth him; 1.04.135 P
a man cannot swear, but it checks him; 1.04.136 P
a man cannot lie with his neighbor's wife, but 1.04.136 P
it fills a man full of obstacles. 1.04.139 P
it beggars any man that keeps it. 1.04.141 P
and every man that means to live well endeavors 1.04.142 P
spoke like a tall man that respects thy 1.04.152 P
a man, as you are. 1.04.164
and no man in the presence | but his red color 2.01. 85
but he, poor man, by your first order died, 2.01. 88
my brother kill'd no man, his fault was thought, 2.01.105
and not a man of you | had so much grace to put 2.01.120
but for my brother not a man would speak, | nor 2.01.127
and make me die a good old man! 2.02.109
with a man | that looks not heavily and full of 2.03. 39
nor more can you distinguish of a man | than of 3.01. 9
that julius caesar was a famous man; 3.01. 84
and if i live until i be a man, 3.01. 91
come on, come on, where is your boar–spear, man? 3.02. 72
i tell thee, man, 'tis better with me now | than 3.02. 98
and when i met this holy man | the men you talk 3.02.116
than my lord hastings no man might be bolder, 3.04. 29
i think there's never a man in christendom | can 3.04. 51
marry, that with no man here he is offended; 3.04. 56
so dear i lov'd the man that i must weep. 3.05. 24
his hand — | true ornaments to know a holy man. 3.07. 99
i partly know the man; 4.02. 41
send to her by the man that slew her brothers 4.04.271
wand'red away alone, | no man knows whither. 4.04.513
go, gentlemen, every man unto his charge. 5.03.307
the king enacts more wonders than a man, 5.04. 2
i'll say | a man may weep upon his wedding–day. H8 pr 32
every man that stood | show'd like a mine. 1.01. 21
every man, | after the hideous storm that 1.01. 89
not a man in england | can advise me like you; 1.01.134
with | free pardon to each man that has denied 1.02.100
this man so complete, | who was enroll'd 'mongst 1.02.118
ah ha, | there's mischief in this man. 1.02.187
live in freedom, | and this man out of prison? 1.02.201
and see the noble ruin'd man you speak of. 2.01. 54
me, | this from a dying man receive as certain: 2.01.125
set out for london, a man of my lord cardinal's, 2.02. 5 P
so long have slept upon | this bold bad man. 2.02. 43
or this imperious man will work us all | from 2.02. 46
this good man, | this just and learned priest, 2.02. 95
have sent me such a man i would have wish'd for. 2.02.100
was he not held a learned man? 2.02.123
kept him a foreign man still, which so griev'd 2.02.128
would it not grieve an able man to leave | so 2.02.141
that man i' th' world who shall report he has 2.04.135
forgetting (like a good man) your late censure 3.01. 64
i not made you | the prime man of the state? 3.02.162
in the evening, | and no man see me more. 3.02.227
dare mate a sounder man than surrey can be, 3.02.274
how much, methinks, i could despise this man, 3.02.297
o my lord, | press not a falling man too far! 3.02.333
this is the state of man: 3.02.352
when he thinks, good easy man, full surely | his 3.02.356
is that poor man that hangs on princes' favors! 3.02.367
thy spirit wonder | a great man should decline? 3.02.375
too heavy for a man that hopes for heaven! 3.02.385
but he's a learned man. 3.02.395
i am a poor fall'n man, unworthy now | to be thy 3.02.413
how can man then | (the image of his maker) hope 3.02.441
is the goodliest woman | that ever lay by man — 4.01. 70
no man living | could say, "this is my wife" 4.01. 79
a man in much esteem with th' king, and truly 4.01.109
as a man sorely tainted, to his answer, | he 4.02. 14
alas, poor man! 4.02. 16
an old man, broken with the storms of state, 4.02. 21
he was a man | of an unbounded stomach, ever 4.02. 33
honors to his age | than man could give him, he 4.02. 68
i will, | or let me lose the fashion of a man! 4.02.159
calumnious tongues | than i myself, poor man. 5.01.113
by my holidame, | what manner of man are you? 5.01.117
look, the good man weeps! 5.01.152
as not thus to suffer | a man of his place, and 5.02. 30
a man that more detests, more stirs against, 5.02. 74
and, by that virtue, no man dare accuse you. 5.02. 85
tower, | where, being but a private man again, 5.02. 90
'tis a cruelty | to load a falling man. 5.02.112
but the little finger | of this man to be vex'd? 5.02.142
tales and informations | against this man, whose 5.02.146
good man, sit down. 5.02.165
was it discretion, lords, to let this man, 5.02.172
this good man (few of you deserve that title), 5.02.173
this honest man, wait like a lousy footboy | at 5.02.174
i charge you, | embrace and love this man. 5.02.205
good man, those joyful tears show thy true 5.02.208
in her days every man shall eat in safety 5.04. 33
lord archbishop, | thou hast made me now a man! 5.04. 64
day, no man think | h'as business at his house; 5.04. 74
they say he is a very man per se and stands TRO 1.02. 15 P
this man, lady, hath robb'd many beasts of their 1.02. 19 P
a man into whom nature hath so crowded humors 1.02. 21 P
there is no man hath a virtue that he hath not a 1.02. 24 P
nor any man an attaint but he carries some stain 1.02. 25 P
but how should this man, that makes me smile, 1.02. 31 P
hector's a gallant man. 1.02. 39 P
troilus is the better man of the two. 1.02. 60 P
do you know a man if you see him? 1.02. 64 P
no, hector is not a better man than troilus. 1.02. 79 P
is he so young a man and so old a lifter? 1.02.117 P
becomes him better than any man in all phrygia. 1.02.122 P
he will weep you an' 'twere a man born in april. 1.02.174 P
is not that a brave man? 1.02.186 P
wit, i can tell you, and he's man good enough. 1.02.191 P
in troy, whosoever, and a proper man of person. 1.02.193 P
there's a brave man, niece. 1.02.201 P
is't not a brave man? 1.02.202 P
o, a brave man! 1.02.203 P
is't not a gallant man too, is't not? 1.02.213 P
there's a man, niece! 1.02.228 P
o admirable man! 1.02.238 P
i had rather be such a man as troilus than 1.02.245 P
the greeks achilles, a better man than troilus. 1.02.248 P
do you know what a man is? 1.02.252 P
such–like, the spice and salt that season a man? 1.02.255 P
ay, a minc'd man, and then to be bak'd with no 1.02.256 P
a woman, a man knows not at what ward you lie. 1.02.258 P
one that was a man | when hector's grandsire 1.03.291
/mould | a noble man that hath no spark of fire 1.03.294
us all) a man distill'd | out of our virtues, 1.03.350
main opinion crush | in taint of our best man. 1.03.373
give him allowance for the better man, | for 1.03.376
how now, thersites, what's the matter, man? 2.01. 56
no man is beaten voluntary. 2.01. 96 P
otherwise, | he knew his man. 2.01.129
though no man lesser fears the greeks than i 2.02. 8
call it melancholy, if you will favor the man; 2.03. 87 P
think he thinks himself a better man than i am? 2.03.145 P
why should a man be proud? 2.03.151 P
i do hate a proud man, as i do hate the 2.03.158 P
here is a man — but 'tis before his face, | i 2.03.229
and yet, good faith, i wish'd myself a man, | or 3.02.127
and not a man, for being simply man, | hath any 3.03. 80
summer, | and not a man, for being simply man, 3.03. 80
a strange fellow here | writes me that man, how 3.03. 96
proves | that no man is the lord of any thing, 3.03.115
heavens, what a man is there! 3.03.126
how one man eats into another's pride, | while 3.03.136
then marvel not, thou great and complete man, 3.03.181
is not more loath'd than an effeminate man | in 3.03.218
what think you of this man that takes me for the 3.03.262 P
a man may wear it on both sides, like a leather 3.03.264 P
no man alive can love in such a sort | the thing 4.01. 24
would he not, a naughty man, let it sleep? 4.02. 32 P
you are an odd man, give even or give none. 4.05. 41
an odd man, lady? every man is odd. 4.05. 42
an odd man, lady? every man is odd. 4.05. 42
thou art too gentle and too free a man. 4.05.139
o, let an old man embrace thee, | and, worthy 4.05.199
it would discredit the blest gods, proud man, 4.05.247
she will sing any man at first sight. 5.02. 9
and any man may sing her, if he can take her 5.02. 10 P
never did young man fancy | with so eternal and 5.02.165
life every man holds dear, but the dear man 5.03. 27
dear, but the dear man | holds honor far more 5.03. 27
how now, young man, meanest thou to fight to–day 5.03. 29
in you, | which better fits a lion than a man. 5.03. 38
ache in my bones that, unless a man were curs'd, 5.03.105 P
i would have been much more a fresher man, | had 5.06. 20
strike, fellows, strike, this is the man i seek. 5.08. 10
it be, | great hector was as good a man as he. 5.09. 6
and, through the cranks and offices of man, COR 1.01.137
was ever man so proud as is this martius? 1.01.252
though he perform | to th' utmost of a man, and 1.01.268
now in first seeing he had prov'd himself a man. 1.03. 17 P
it more becomes a man | than gilt his trophy. 1.03. 39
no, nor a man that fears you less than he, 1.04. 14
there is the man of my soul's hate, aufidius, 1.05. 10
of martius' tongue | from every meaner man. 1.06. 27
as with a man busied about decrees: 1.06. 34
no more of him, he's a worthy man. 2.02. 35 P
the man i speak of cannot in the world | be 2.02. 86
he prov'd best man i' th' field, and for his 2.02. 97
worthy man! 2.02.122
to the people, there was never a worthier man. 2.03. 39 P
counterfeit the bewitchment of some popular man, 2.03.102 P
how now, my masters, have you chose this man? 2.03.155
no, no; no man saw 'em. 2.03.165
not | a man of their infirmity. 3.01. 82
this man has marr'd his fortune. 3.01.253
depopulate the city, and | be every man himself? 3.01.264
rather say, i play | the man i am. 3.02. 16
you might have been enough the man you are, 3.02. 19
send | o'er the vast world to seek a single man, 4.01. 42
was not a man my father? 4.02. 18
good man, the wounds that he does bear for rome! 4.02. 28
to hear of their readiness, and am the man, i 4.03. 47 P
speak, man: 4.05. 54
dost not | think me for the man i am, necessity 4.05. 56
never man | sigh'd truer breath; 4.05.114
he is simply the rarest man i' th' world. 4.05.161 P
i had as live be a condemn'd man. 4.05.176 P
he's as like to do't as any man i can imagine. 4.05.203 P
his crest up again and the man in blood, they 4.05.211 P
deity than nature, | that shapes man better; 4.06. 92
all undone, unless | the noble man have mercy. 4.06.108
of daily fortune ever taints | the happy man; 4.07. 39
this man, aufidius, | was my belov'd in rome; 5.02. 92
this last old man, | whom with a crack'd heart i 5.03. 8
but stand | as if a man were author of himself, 5.03. 36
"the man was noble, | but with his last attempt 5.03.145
think'st thou it honorable for a noble man 5.03.154
there's no man in the world | more bound to 's 5.03.158
short a time can alter the condition of a man? 5.04. 10 P
this martius is grown from man to dragon: 5.04. 13 P
so | as with a man by his own alms empoison'd, 5.06. 10
the man is noble and his fame folds in | this 5.06.124
a nobler man, a braver warrior, | lives not this TIT 1.01. 25
no man shed tears for noble mutius, | he lives 1.01.389
is she not then beholding to the man | that 1.01.396
take up this good old man, and cheer the heart 1.01.457
what, man, more water glideth by the mill | than 2.01. 85
the tribunes hear you not, no man is by, | and 3.01. 28
why, 'tis no matter, man: 3.01. 33
o happy man, they have befriended thee! 3.01. 52
here stands my other son, a banish'd man, | and 3.01. 99
for thou, poor man, hast drown'd it with thine 3.01.141
the woefull'st man that ever liv'd in rome. 3.01.289
i say, my lord, that if i were a man, | their 4.01.107
can you hear a good man groan | and not relent, 4.01.123
the old man hath found their guilt, | and sends 4.02. 26
then let no man but i | do execution on my flesh 4.02. 83
for the man must not be hang'd till the next 4.03. 82 P
say, | when i have walked like a private man, 4.04. 75
hither | to use as you think needful of the man. 5.01. 39
as kill a man, or else devise his death, 5.01.128
know, thou sad man, i am not tamora; 5.02. 28
and when thou find'st a man that's like thyself, 5.02. 99
tell us, old man, how shall we be employ'd? 5.02.149
or more than any living man could bear. 5.03.127
come, come, thou reverent man of rome, | and 5.03.137
no funeral rite, nor man in mourning weed, | no 5.03.196
take the wall of any man or maid of montague's. ROM 1.01. 12 P
i serve as good a man as you. 1.01. 55 P
/bid a sick man in sadness /make his will — | a 1.01.202
tut, man, one fire burns out another's burning, 1.02. 45
'a was a merry man — took up the child. 1.03. 40
a man, young lady! 1.03. 75
lady, such a man | as all the world — why, he's 1.03. 75
as all the world — why, he's a man of wax. 1.03. 76
in, | but every man betake him to his legs. 1.04. 34
what, man? 1.05. 34
you'll be the man! 1.05. 81
/nor /any /other /part | belonging to a man. 2.02. 42
what man art thou that thus bescreen'd in night 2.02. 52
encamp them still | in man as well as herbs, 2.03. 28
i bear no hatred, blessed man, for lo | my 2.03. 53
not to his father's, i spoke with his man. 2.04. 3
any man that can write may answer a letter. 2.04. 10 P
and is he a man to encounter tybalt? 2.04. 17 P
a very tall man! 2.04. 30 P
such a case as mine a man may strain courtesy. 2.04. 50 P
as yours constrains a man to bow in the hams. 2.04. 53 P
out upon you, what a man are you! 2.04.114 P
i saw no man use you at his pleasure; 2.04.157 P
i dare draw as soon as another man, if i see 2.04.159 P
within this hour my man shall be with thee, 2.04.188
is your man secret? 2.04.196
and tell her that paris is the properer man, but 2.04.204 P
send thy man away. 2.05. 19
simple choice, you know not how to choose a man. 2.05. 39 P
wilt quarrel with a man that hath a hair more or 3.01. 17 P
thou wilt quarrel with a man for cracking nuts, 3.01. 19 P
hast quarrell'd with a man for coughing in the 3.01. 25 P
any man should buy the fee–simple of my life for 3.01. 32 P
well, peace be with you, sir, here comes my man. 3.01. 56
your worship in that sense may call him man. 3.01. 59
courage, man, the hurt cannot be much. 3.01. 95
me to–morrow, and you shall find me a grave man. 3.01. 98 P
rat, a mouse, a cat, to scratch a man to death! 3.01.101 P
there lies the man, slain by young romeo, | that 3.01.144
ah, where's my man? 3.02. 88
romeo, come forth, come forth, thou fearful man: 3.03. 1
/thou fond mad man, hear me a little speak. 3.03. 52
stand up, stand up, stand, and you be a man. 3.03. 88
art thou a man? 3.03.109
unseemly woman in a seeming man, | and 3.03.112
of wax, | digressing from the valor of a man; 3.03.127
what, rouse thee, man! 3.03.135
i'll find out your man, | and he shall signify 3.03.169
and yet no man like he doth grieve my heart. 3.05. 83
if you could find out but a man | to bear a 3.05. 96
find thou the means, and i'll find such a man. 3.05.103
proportion'd as one's thought would wish a man, 3.05.182
and hide me with a dead man in his /shroud — 4.01. 85
not, | for he hath still been tried a holy man. 4.03. 29
dream, that gives a dead man leave to think! 5.01. 7
i said, | "an' if a man did need a poison now, 5.01. 50
need, | and this same needy man must sell it me. 5.01. 54
come hither, man. 5.01. 58
good gentle youth, tempt not a desp'rate man. 5.03. 59
what said my man, when my betossed soul | did 5.03. 76
death, lie thou there, by a dead man interr'd. 5.03. 87
here's romeo's man, we found him in the 5.03.182
here is a friar, and /slaughter'd romeo's man, 5.03.199
we still have known thee for a holy man. 5.03.270
where's romeo's man? 5.03.271
a most incomparable man, breath'd, as it were, TIM 1.01. 10
shap'd out a man | whom this beneath world doth 1.01. 43
with one man beckon'd from the rest below, 1.01. 74
most noble timon, call the man before thee. 1.01.113

i am a man | that from my first have been 1.01.117
this man of thine | attempts her love. 1.01.125
the man is honest. 1.01.128
the painting is almost the natural man; 1.01.157
plain–dealing, which will not cast a man a doit. 1.01.212 P
mind he carries | that ever govern'd man. 1.01.281
have got a humor there | does not become a man, 1.02. 27
furor brevis est," | but yond man is very angry. 1.02. 29
draught, is the readiest man to kill him; 1.02. 48 P
if i were a huge man, i should fear to drink at 1.02. 49 P
honest water, which ne'er left man i' th' mire. 1.02. 59
i crave no pelf, | i pray for no man but myself. 1.02. 63
so fond, | to trust man on his oath or bond; 1.02. 65
that man might ne'er be wretched for his mind. 1.02.164
no man | can justly praise but what he does 1.02.214
in all shapes that man goes up and down in from 2.02.113 P
nor thou altogether a wise man; 2.02.116 P
prithee, man, look cheerly. 2.02.214
every man has his fault, and honesty is his. 3.01. 27 P
denied that honorable man? 3.02. 19 P
see the monstrousness of man | when he looks out 3.02. 72
i was the first man | that e'er received gift 3.03. 16
knew not what he did when he made man politic; 3.03. 28 P
end, the villainies of man will set him clear. 3.03. 30 P
he is a man (setting his fate aside) | of comely 3.05. 14
wisely suffer | the worst that man can breathe, 3.05. 32
but who is man that is not angry? 3.05. 57
every man here's so. 3.06. 19 P
this is the old man still. 3.06. 61 P
each man to his stool, with that spur as he 3.06. 65 P
lend to each man enough, that one need not lend 3.06. 73 P
meat be belov'd more than the man that gives it. 3.06. 76 P
of man and beast the infinite malady | crust you 3.06. 98
hated be | of timon man and all humanity! 3.06.105
heart, | for showing me again the eyes of man! 4.03. 51
is man so hateful to thee, | that art thyself a 4.03. 52
so hateful to thee, | that art thyself a man? 4.03. 53
the gods plague thee, for thou art a man! 4.03. 75 P
dost perform, confound thee, for thou art a man! 4.03. 76 P
consumptions sow | in hollow bones of man, 4.03.152
whereof thy proud child, arrogant man, is puff'd 4.03.180
womb, | let it no more bring out ingrateful man! 4.03.188
whereof ingrateful man, with liquorish draughts 4.03.194
from it all consideration slips — | more man? 4.03.197
what man didst thou ever know unthrift that was 4.03.310 P
think thy slave man rebels, and by thy virtue 4.03.390
is no time so miserable but a man may be true. 4.03.457 P
is yond despis'd and ruinous man my lord? 4.03.459
when man was wish'd to love his enemies! 4.03.466
if thou /grant'st th' art a man, i have forgot 4.03.474
surely, this man | was born of woman. 4.03.493
i do proclaim | one honest man — mistake me not 4.03.497
thou singly honest man, | here, take; 4.03.523
ne'er see thou man, and let me ne'er see thee. 4.03.536
thou canst not paint a man | so bad as is 5.01. 31
each man apart, all single and alone, | yet an 5.01.107
that nothing but himself which looks like man 5.01.118
his former days, | the former man may make him. 5.01.125
this man was riding | from alcibiades to timon's 5.02. 9
there does not live a man." 5.03. 4
meaning, not a man | shall pass his quarter, or 5.04. 59
what man is that? JC 1.02. 18
and this man | is now become a god, and cassius 1.02.115
amaze me | a man of such a feeble temper should 1.02.129
why, man, he doth bestride the narrow world 1.02.135
but it was fam'd with more than with one man? 1.02.153
that her wide walks encompass'd but one man? 1.02.155
enough, | when there is in it but one only man. 1.02.157
i do not know the man i should avoid | so soon 1.02.200
do the players in the theatre, i am no true man. 1.02.261 P
and i had been a man of any occupation, if i 1.02.266 P
name to thee a man | most like this dreadful 1.03. 72
a man no mightier than thyself, or me, | in 1.03. 76
poor man, i know he would not be a wolf, | but 1.03.104
casca, and to such a man | that is no fleering 1.03.116
and the man entire | upon the next encounter 1.03.155
and the state of a man, | like to a little 2.01. 67
yes, every man of them; 2.01. 90
and no man here | but honors you; 2.01. 90
betimes, | and every man hence to his idle bed; 2.01.117
range on, | till each man drop by lottery. 2.01.119
shall no man else be touch'd but only caesar? 2.01.154
which sometime hath his hour with every man. 2.01.251
here is a sick man that would speak with you. 2.01.310
will crowd a feeble man almost to death. 2.04. 36
do so, and let no man abide this deed, | but we 3.01. 94
ay, every man away. 3.01.119
let each man render me his bloody hand. 3.01.184
thou art the ruins of the noblest man | that 3.01.256
i do entreat you, not a man depart, | save i 3.02. 60
and the rest | (for brutus is an honorable man, 3.02. 82
was ambitious, | and brutus is an honorable man. 3.02. 87
was ambitious, | and brutus is an honorable man. 3.02. 94
ambitious, | and sure he is an honorable man. 3.02. 99
there's not a nobler man in rome than antony. 3.02.116
me all) a plain blunt man | that love my friend, 3.02.218
to every several man, seventy–five drachmaes. 3.02.242
are you a married man or a bachelor? 3.03. 8 P
answer every man directly. 3.03. 9 P
am i a married man or a bachelor? 3.03. 14 P
then to answer every man directly and briefly, 3.03. 15 P
this is a slight unmeritable man, | meet to be 4.01. 12
and though we lay these honors on this man | to 4.01. 19
and let no man | come to our tent till we have 4.02. 50
because i knew the man, was slighted off. 4.03. 5
that struck the foremost man of all this world 4.03. 22
away, slight man! 4.03. 37
no man bears sorrow better. portia is dead. 4.03.147
young man, thou couldst not die more honorable. 5.01. 60
o that a man might know | the end of this day's 5.01.122
to this dead man than you shall see me pay. 5.03.102
keep this man safe, | give him all kindness; 5.04. 27
my life | i found no man but he was true to me. 5.05. 35
what man is that? 5.05. 52
my master's man. strato, where is thy master? 5.05. 53
and no man else hath honor by his death. 5.05. 57
up | and say to all the world, "this was a man!" 5.05. 75
what bloody man is that? MAC 1.02. 1
he shall live a man forbid; 1.03. 21
or are you aught | that man may question? 1.03. 43
shakes so my single state of man that function 1.03.140
i dare do all that may become a man; 1.07. 46
when you durst do it, then you were a man; 1.07. 49
you were, you would | be so much more the man. 1.07. 51
if a man were porter of hell gate, he should 2.03. 1 P
no man. 2.03.109
is an office | which the false man does easy. 2.03.137
let every man be master of his time | till seven 3.01. 40
jewel | given to the common enemy of man, | to 3.01. 68
to pray for this good man, and for his issue, 3.01. 88
are you a man? 3.04. 57
when the brains were out, the man would die, 3.04. 78
what man dare, i dare. 3.04. 98
being gone, | i am a man again. 3.04.107
brought forth | the secret'st man of blood. 3.04.125
laugh to scorn | the pow'r of man; 4.01. 80
what, man, ne'er pull your hat upon your brows; 4.03.208
dispute it like a man. 4.03.220
but i must also feel it as a man: 4.03.221
have thought the old man to have had so much 5.01. 39 P
and the grim alarm | excite the mortified man. 5.02. 5
no man that's born of woman | shall e'er have 5.03. 6
brandish'd by man that's of a woman born. 5.07. 13
so, | for it hath cow'd my better part of man! 5.08. 18
he only liv'd but till he was a man, | the which 5.09. 6
where he fought, | but like a man he died. 5.09. 9
for they are actions that a man might play, HAM 1.02. 84
'a was a man, take him for all in all, | i shall 1.02.187
give every man thy ear, but few thy voice, 1.03. 68
gaudy, | for the apparel oft proclaims the man, 1.03. 72
day, | thou canst not then be false to any man. 1.03. 80
pure as grace, | as infinite as man may undergo, 1.04. 34
holds such an enmity with blood of man | that 1.05. 65
say you then, would heart of man once think it? 1.05.121
you, | for every man hath business and desire, 1.05.130
and what so poor a man as hamlet is | may do, t' 1.05.184
the phrase or the addition | of man and country. 2.01. 48
it, | sith nor th' exterior nor the inward man 2.02. 6
as of a man faithful and honorable. 2.02.130
then i would you were so honest a man. 2.02.176 P
is to be one man pick'd out of ten thousand. 2.02.179 P
what /a piece of work is a man! 2.02.304 P
man delights not me — nor women neither, though 2.02.309 P
laugh then, when i said, "man delights not me"? 2.02.313 P
my lord, if you delight not in man, what lenten 2.02.315 P
the humorous man shall end his part in peace, 2.02.322 P
them, for they say an old man is twice a child. 2.02.385 P
god's bodkin, man, much better: 2.02.529 P
use every man after his desert, and who shall 2.02.530 P
pagan, nor man, have so strutted and bellow'd 3.02. 32 P
thou art e'en as just a man | as e'er my 3.02. 54
a man that fortune's buffets and rewards | hast 3.02. 67
give me that man | that is not passion's slave, 3.02. 71
what should a man do but be merry, for look you 3.02.126 P
the great man down, you mark his favorite flies, 3.02.204
and, like a man to double business bound, | i 3.03. 41
his seal | to give the world assurance of a man. 3.04. 62
this man shall set me packing; 3.04.211
apprehension kills | the unseen good old man. 4.01. 12
and out of haunt | this mad young man. 4.01. 19
how dangerous is it that this man goes loose! 4.03. 2
a man may fish with the worm that hath eat of a 4.03. 27 P
father and mother is man and wife, man and wife 4.03. 51 P
is man and wife, man and wife is one flesh — so 4.03. 52 P
and shows no cause without | why the man dies. 4.04. 29
what is a man, | if his chief good and market of 4.04. 33
speak, man. 4.05.128
here stands the man; 5.01. 16 P
if the man go to this water and drown himself, 5.01. 16 P
what man dost thou dig it for? 5.01.130 P
for no man, sir. 5.01.131 P
i have been sexton here, man and boy, thirty 5.01.162 P
how long will a man lie i' th' earth ere he rot? 5.01.163 P
but to know a man well were to know himself. 5.02.139 P
since no man, of aught he leaves, knows what 5.02.223 P
as th' art a man, | give me the cup. 5.02.342
what wouldest thou do, old man? LR 1.01.146
an admirable evasion of whoremaster man, to lay 1.02.127 P
i am no honest man if there be any good meaning 1.02.173 P
a man, sir. 1.04. 10 P
this man hath had good counsel — a hundred 1.04.322
side 's nose, that what a man cannot smell out, 1.05. 23 P
thou art a strange fellow. a tailor make a man? 2.02. 57 P
and put upon him such a deal of man | that 2.02.120
shape | that ever penury, in contempt of man, 2.03. 8
having more man than wit about me, drew. 2.04. 42
when a wise man gives thee better counsel, give 2.04. 75 P
the fool will stay, | and let the wise man fly. 2.04. 83
"inform'd" them? dost thou understand me, man? 2.04. 99
indispos'd and sickly fit | for the sound man. 2.04.112
who put my man i' th' stocks? 2.04.182
how came my man i' th' stocks? 2.04.198
you see me here, you gods, a poor old man, | as 2.04.272
the old man and 's people | cannot be well 2.04.288
followed the old man forth. he is return'd. 2.04.295
spill at once | that makes ingrateful man! 3.02. 9
a poor, infirm, weak, and despis'd old man; 3.02. 20
the man that makes his toe | what he his heart 3.02. 31
and a codpiece — that's a wise man and a fool. 3.02. 41 P
since i was man, | such sheets of fire, such 3.02. 45
i am a man | more sinn'd against than sinning. 3.02. 59
is man no more than this? 3.04.103 P
unaccommodated man is no more but such a poor, 3.04.107 P
he said it would be thus, poor banish'd man. 3.04.164
and fum, | i smell the blood of a british man.'" 3.04.184
fellow saw, | which made me think a man a worm. 4.01. 33
let the superfluous and lust–dieted man, | that 4.01. 67
should undo excess, | and each man have enough. 4.01. 71
madam, within, but never man so chang'd. 4.02. 3
o, the difference of man and man! 4.02. 26
o, the difference of man and man! 4.02. 26
milk–liver'd man, | that bear'st a cheek for 4.02. 50
that thing you speak of, | i took it for a man; 4.06. 78
a man may see how this world goes with no eyes. 4.06.150 P
why, this would make a man a man of salt, | to 4.06.195
why, this would make a man a man of salt, | to 4.06.195
a most poor man, made tame to fortune's blows, 4.06.221
nay, come not near th' old man; 4.06.240 P
i am a very foolish fond old man, | fourscore 4.07. 59
methinks i should know you, and know this man, 4.07. 63
for (as i am a man) i think this lady | to be my 4.07. 68
our sister's man is certainly miscarried. 5.01. 5
if e'er your grace had speech with man so poor, 5.01. 38
away, old man, give me thy hand, away! 5.02. 5
no further, sir, a man may rot even here. 5.02. 8
"if any man of quality or degree within the 5.03.110 P
speak, man. 5.03.223
who dead? speak, man. 5.03.226
no, my good lord, i am the very man — 5.03.287
nor no man else. 5.03.291
and, by the faith of man, | i know my price, i OTH 1.01. 10
here is the man — this moor, whom now, it seems 1.03. 71
wish'd | that heaven had made her such a man. 1.03.163
on my head if my bad blame | light on the man! 1.03.178
a man he is of honesty and trust. 1.03.284
i never found man that knew how to love himself. 1.03.314 P
come, be a man! 1.03.335 P
cassio's a proper man. 1.03.392
him, and the man commands | like a full soldier. 2.01. 35
fleet, every man put himself into triumph; 2.02. 3 P
each man to what sport and revels his /addiction 2.02. 5 P
what, man? 2.03. 43 P
a soldier's a man; 2.03. 71
to the general, nor any man of quality — i hope 2.03.107 P
as i am an honest man, i had thought you had 2.03.266 P
what, man, there are more ways to recover the 2.03.271 P
to be now a sensible man, by and by a fool, and 2.03.306 P
you, or any man living, may be drunk at a time, 2.03.313 P
or any man living, may be drunk at a time, man. 2.03.314 P
a man that languishes in your displeasure. 3.03. 43
but in a man that's just | they're close 3.03.122
why then i think cassio's an honest man. 3.03.129
good name in man and woman, dear my lord, | is 3.03.155
are you a man? 3.03.374
why, man? 3.04. 4 P
you'll never meet a more sufficient man. 3.04. 91
a man that all his time | hath founded his good 3.04. 93
is not this man jealious? 3.04. 99
'tis not a year or two shows us a man: 3.04.103
hers, | she may, i think, bestow't on any man. 4.01. 13
would you would bear your fortune like a man! 4.01. 61
good sir, be a man; 4.01. 65
grief | (a passion most /unsuiting such a man), 4.01. 77
all in all in spleen, | and nothing of a man. 4.01. 89
i never knew woman love man so. 4.01.110
chaste, and true, | there's no man happy; 4.02. 18
fie, there is no such man; it is impossible. 4.02.134
i cannot go to, man, nor 'tis not very well. 4.02.192 P
this lodovico is a proper man. 4.03. 35
a very handsome man. 4.03. 36
'tis but a man gone. 5.01. 10
some good man bear him carefully from hence, 5.01. 99
none in the world; nor do i know the man. 5.01.103
send for the man, and ask him. 5.02. 50
an honest man he is, and hates the slime | that 5.02.148
disprove this villain, if thou be'st a man. 5.02.172
man but a rush against othello's breast, | and 5.02.270
where is this rash and most unfortunate man? 5.02.283
our dungy earth alike | feeds beast as man; ANT 1.01. 36
is this the man? 1.02. 8 P
to see a handsome man loose–wiv'd, so it is a 1.02. 72 P
the man from sicyon — is there such an one? 1.02.114
deities to take the wife of a man from him, it 1.02.162 P
him, it shows to man the tailors of the earth; 1.02.163 P
there | a man who is th' /abstract of all faults 1.04. 9
and the ebb'd man, ne'er lov'd till ne'er worth 1.04. 43
him, | note him, good charmian, 'tis the man; 1.05. 54
thou with caesar paragon again | my man of men. 1.05. 72
crown'd with snakes, | not like a formal man. 2.05. 41
th' art an honest man. 2.05. 47
yourself within yourself, | the man is innocent. 2.05. 76
but that they would | have one man but a man? 2.06. 19
but that they would | have one man but a man? 2.06. 19
i came before you here a man prepar'd | to take 2.06. 40
i will praise any man that will praise me, 2.06. 88 P
here they'll be, man. 2.07. 1 P
i am the man | will give thee all the world. 2.07. 64
'a bears the third part of the world, man; 2.07. 90 P
the holding every man shall /bear as loud | as 2.07.111
so is he, being a man. 3.02. 53
a proper man. 3.03. 38
the man hath seen some majesty, and should know. 3.03. 42
what, man? 3.05. 3 P
of my kingdom, will | appear there for a man. 3.07. 18
well i know the man. 3.07. 78
i must | to the young man send humble treaties, 3.11. 62
heavens and earth, | a private man in athens: 3.12. 15
but performs | the bidding of the fullest man, 3.13. 87
i'll leave thee | now like a man of steel. 4.04. 33
behold this man, | commend unto his lips thy 4.08. 22
what man is this? 4.09. 6
his best force | is forth to man his galleys. 4.11. 3
'tis said, man, and farewell. 4.14. 92
lives he? | wilt thou not answer, man? 4.14.115
the business of this man looks out of him; 5.01. 50
sleep, that i might see | but such another man! 5.02. 78
think you there was or might be such a man | as 5.02. 93
wert thou a man, | thou wouldst have mercy on me 5.02.174
this is the man. 5.02.241
you do not meet a man but frowns. CYM 1.01. 1
(i mean, that married her, alack, good man! 1.01. 18
and such stuff within | endows a man but he. 1.01. 24
may be truly read, | what kind of man he is. 1.01. 54
of more tenderness | than doth become a man. 1.01. 95
playfellow, and he is | a man worth any woman; 1.01.146
can my sides hold, to think that man, who knows 1.06. 69
was there ever man had such luck? 2.01. 1 P
your lordship is the most patient man in loss, 2.03. 1 P
it would make any man cold to lose. 2.03. 3 P
but not every man patient after the noble temper 2.03. 4 P
winning will put any man into courage. 2.03. 7 P
which makes the true man kill'd and saves the 2.03. 71
nay, sometime hangs both thief and true man. 2.03. 72
love, | where there's another man. 2.04.110

and that most venerable man which i | did call 2.05. 3
there's no motion | that tends to vice in man, 2.05. 21
why, one that rode to 's execution, man, | could 3.02. 70
i see before me, man; 3.02. 78
man! 3.04. 3
speak, man, thy tongue | may take off some 3.04. 16
and you shall find me, wretched man, a thing 3.04. 19
see into thy end and am almost | a man already. 3.04.167
that man of hers, pisanio, her old servant, | i 3.05. 54
and truly, i would think thee an honest man. 3.05.113 P
i'll make't my comfort | he is a man, i'll love 3.06. 71
it is not vainglory for a man and his glass to 4.01. 8 P
so man and man should be, | but clay and clay 4.02. 3
so man and man should be, | but clay and clay 4.02. 3
then, and thank | the man that gave them thee. 4.02. 85
i mean, to man, he had not apprehension | of 4.02.110
jove knows what man thou mightst have made; 4.02.207
this bloody man, the care on't. 4.02.297
a headless man? 4.02.308
what thing is't that i never | did see man die, 4.04. 36
a narrow lane, an old man, and two boys! 5.03. 52
"two boys, an old man (twice a boy), a lane, 5.03. 57
'tis thought the old man and his sons were 5.03. 85
there was a fourth man, in a silly habit, | that 5.03. 86
'tween man and man they weigh not every stamp; 5.04. 24
'tween man and man they weigh not every stamp; 5.04. 24
when once he was mature for man, | in britain 5.04. 52
but a man that were to sleep your sleep, and a 5.04.173 P
that a man should have the best use of eyes to 5.04.188 P
unless a man would marry a gallows and beget 5.04.198 P
strive, man, and speak. 5.05.152
a shop of all the qualities that man | loves 5.05.166
that headless man | i thought had been my lord. 5.05.299
this man is better than the man he slew, | as 5.05.302
this man is better than the man he slew, | as 5.05.302
indeed a banish'd man, | i know not how a 5.05.319
and that to hear an old man sing | may to your PER 1.ch. 13
you gods that made me man, and sway in love, 1.01. 19
for he's no man on whom perfections wait | that, 1.01. 79
who, finger'd to make man his lawful music, 1.01. 82
for if a king bid a man be a villain, he's bound 1.03. 7 P
that man and wife | draw lots who first shall 1.04. 45
where each man | thinks all is writ he /speken 2.ch. 11
all perishen of man, of pelf, | ne aught 2.ch. 35
remember earthly man | is but a substance that 2.01. 2
why, man? 2.01. 38 P
a man whom both the waters and the wind, | in 2.01. 59
a man throng'd up with cold, my veins are chill, 2.01. 73
for that i am a man, pray you see me buried. 2.01. 77
and what a man cannot get, he may lawfully deal 2.01.114 P
till the rough seas, that spares not any man, 2.01.131
us scan | the outward habit by the inward man. 2.02. 57
not a man in private conference | or council has 2.04. 17
rul'd by me, or i'll make you — | man and wife. 2.05. 84
attends the former, | making a man a god. 3.02. 31
what else, man? 4.02. 18 P
that a man may deal withal and defy the surgeon? 4.06. 25 P
i would have you note, this is an honorable man. 4.06. 50 P
of this country, and a man whom i am bound to. 4.06. 54 P
where a man may serve seven years for the loss 4.06.171 P
this is the man that can, in aught you would, 5.01. 12
a man who for this three months hath not spoken 5.01. 24
thousand part | of my endurance, thou art a man, 5.01.136
can you remember what i call'd the man? 5.03. 52
this man, | through whom the gods have shown 5.03. 59
how will it shake the bones of that good man, TNK pr 17
yet what man | thirds his own worth (the case is 1.02. 95
the maid flavina) | love any that's call'd man. 1.03. 85
what man to man may do for our sake more: 1.04. 39
what man to man may do for our sake more: 1.04. 39
a willing man dies sleeping, and all's done. 2.02. 68
why, what's the matter, man? 2.02.133
might not a man well lose himself and love her? 2.02.155
be as that cursed man that hates his country, 2.02.199
he's a blessed man! 2.02.247
see the sports, then every man to 's tackle! 2.03. 55
i, seeing, thought he was a goodly man; 2.04. 8
vow'd her maidenhead | to a young handsome man. 2.04. 14
seen, | since hercules, a man of tougher sinews. 2.05. 2
upon my soul, a proper man! 2.05. 16
i have not seen so young a man so noble | (if he 2.05. 18
or i'll proclaim him, | and to his face, no man. 2.06. 31
i am then | kissing the man they look for. 2.06. 37
in thy rumination | that i, poor man, might 3.01. 12
have in them | a sense to know a man unarm'd, 3.02. 16
good hearty draught, it breeds good blood, man. 3.03. 17
she lov'd a black-hair'd man. 3.03. 31
and "then let be," and no man understand me? 3.05. 10
if he fail, | he's neither man nor soldier. 3.06. 4
we were not bred to talk, man. 3.06. 28
that no man but thy cousin's fit to kill thee. 3.06. 44
then as i am an honest man, and love | with all 3.06. 50
this is the man | was begg'd and banish'd, this 3.06.142
o heaven, | what more than man is this! 3.06.157
where this man calls me traitor, | let me say 3.06.160
be of good comfort, man; 4.01. 17
ye are a good man | and ever bring good news. 4.01. 24
palamon," | and "palamon was a tall young man." 4.01. 82
yes, he's a fine man. 4.01.120
heaven forbid, man! 4.01.140
come hither, you are a wise man. 4.01.141
yet doubtless | she would run mad for this man. 4.02. 12
by his seeming | should be a stout man, by his 4.02. 77
his lineaments | are as a man would wish 'em, 4.02.114
a little man, but of a tough soul, seeming | as 4.02.117
and penn'd by no worse man than giraldo, 4.03. 12 P
she ever affected any man ere she beheld palamon 4.03. 62 P
i knew a man | of eighty winters — this i told 5.01.107
there were no woman | worth so compos'd a man! 5.03. 86
there's many a man alive that hath outliv'd 5.04. 1
thou art a right good man, and while i live, 5.04. 97
no man smile? ep 4
not /one of you should live an aged man, | for STM II.C 83
stain to all nymphs, more lovely than a man, VEN 9
alone, | thing like a man, but of no woman bred! 214
thou art no man; 215
round, | would thou wert as i am, and i a man, 369
a martial man to be soft fancy's slave! LUC 200
if ever man were mov'd with woman's moans, | be 587
"the aged man that coffers up his gold | is 855
to make the child a man, the man a child, | to 954
to make the child a man, the man a child, | to 954
the mightier man, the mightier is the thing 1004
no man inveigh against the withered flow'r, 1254
that no man could distinguish what he said. 1785
my better angel is a man (right fair), | my PP 2. 3
lullaby, the learned man hath got the lady gay, 15.15
every man will be thy friend, | whilst thou hast 20.33
crowns be scant, | no man will supply thy want. 20.36
a man in hue all hues in his controlling, SON 20. 7
for no man well of such a salve can speak | that 34. 7
proved, | i never writ, nor no man ever loved. 116.14
who leaves unsway'd the likeness of a man, | thy 141.11
the better angel is a man right fair, | the 144. 3
a reverend man that graz'd his cattle nigh, LC 57
"small show of man was yet upon his chin, | his 92

MANACLE 3 FR 0.0003 REL FR 3 V 0 P
come, | i'll manacle thy neck and feet together. TMP 1.02.462
and manacle the bearard in their chains, | if 2H6 5.01.149
it is a manacle of love, i'll place it | upon CYM 1.01.122

MANACLES 4 FR 0.0004 REL FR 3 V 1 P
could fetch your brother from the manacles | of MM 2.04. 93
one that means his proper harm) in manacles, COR 1.09. 57
be led | with manacles through our streets, or 5.03.115
knock off his manacles, bring your prisoner to CYM 5.04.191 P

/MANAGE 2 FR 0.0002 REL FR 2 V 0 P
full merrily | hath this brave /manage, this LLL 5.02.482
/that /still /would /manage /those /authorities LR 1.03. 17

MANAGE 25 FR 0.0028 REL FR 18 V 7 P
and to him put | the manage of my state, as at TMP 1.02. 70
and manage it against despairing thoughts. TGV 3.01.249
hands | the husbandry and manage of my house MV 3.04. 25
they are taught their manage, and to that end AYL 1.01. 13 P
then take him up, and manage well the jest. SHR in.1. 45
which none without thee can sufficiently manage, WT 4.02. 15 P
which now the manage of two kingdoms must | with
JN 1.01. 37
expedient manage must be made, my liege, | ere R2 1.04. 39
distaff-women manage rusty bills | against thy 3.02.118
phaeton, | wanting the manage of unruly jades. 3.03.179
a jest to execute that i cannot manage alone. 1H4 1.02.162 P
speak terms of manage to thy bounding steed, 2.03. 49
come manage me your caliver. 2H4 3.02.273 P
fellow, and 'a would manage you his piece thus, 3.02.282 P
bits and spur 'em | till they obey the manage. H8 5.02. 59
wanting his manage, and they will almost | give TRO 3.03. 25
sword, | or manage it to part these men with me. ROM 1.01. 69
all | the unlucky manage of this fatal brawl: 3.01.143
ward to the son, and the son manage his revenue. LR 1.02. 74 P
fear, | to manage private and domestic quarrel? OTH 2.03.215
an eunuch and your maids | manage this war. ANT 3.07. 15
must take some pains to work her to your manage.
PER 4.06. 64 P
being therein train'd | and of kind manage; TNK 5.04. 69
he will not manage her, although he mount her, VEN 598
or he his manage by th' well-doing steed. LC 112

MANAGED 2 FR 0.0002 REL FR 2 V 0 P
shame hath a bastard fame, well managed; ERR 3.02. 19
it rest, | other affairs must now be managed. 1H6 4.01.181

MANAGER 2 FR 0.0002 REL FR 1 V 1 P
be still, drum, for your manager is in love; LLL 1.02.182 P
where is our usual manager of mirth? MND 5.01. 35

MANAGING 2 FR 0.0002 REL FR 1 V 1 P
and in the managing of quarrels you may say he ADO 2.03.190 P
whose state so many had the managing, | that H5 ep 11

MAN-AT-ARMS 1 FR 0.0001 REL FR 0 V 1 P
what a maidenly man-at-arms are you become! 2H4 2.02. 77 P

MAN-CHILD 1 FR 0.0001 REL FR 0 V 1 P
hearing he was a man-child than now in first COR 1.03. 16 P

MANCHUS 1 FR 0.0001 REL FR 1 V 0 P
king manchus of arabia; ANT 3.06. 72

MANDATE 4 FR 0.0004 REL FR 4 V 0 P
they bear the mandate — they must sweep my way,
HAM 3.04.204
your special mandate for the state affairs OTH 1.03. 72
sir, i obey the mandate, | and will return to 4.01.259
have not sent | his pow'rful mandate to you: ANT 1.01. 22

MANDRAGORA 2 FR 0.0002 REL FR 2 V 0 P
not poppy, nor mandragora, | nor all the drowsy OTH 3.03.330
ha, ha! | give me to drink mandragora. ANT 1.05. 4

MANDRAKE 2 FR 0.0002 REL FR 0 V 2 P
thou whoreson mandrake, thou art fitter to be 2H4 1.02. 14 P
as a monkey, and the whores call'd him mandrake. 3.02.315 P

MANDRAKE'S 1 FR 0.0001 REL FR 1 V 0 P
would curses kill, as doth the mandrake's groan, 2H6 3.02.310

MANDRAKES' 1 FR 0.0001 REL FR 1 V 0 P
and shrikes like mandrakes' torn out of the ROM 4.03. 47

MANE 5 FR 0.0005 REL FR 5 V 0 P
and, like /a dewdrop from the lion's mane, | be TRO 3.03.224
wind-shak'd surge, with high and monstrous mane,
OTH 2.01. 13
his braided hanging mane | upon his compass'd VEN 271
thin mane, thick tail, broad buttock, tender 298
for through his mane and tail the high wind 305

MAN-ENT'RED 1 FR 0.0001 REL FR 1 V 0 P
his pupil age | man-ent'red thus, he waxed like COR 2.02. 99

/MANES* 1 FR 0.0001 REL FR 1 V 0 P
a pile | ad /manes fratrum sacrifice his flesh TIT 1.01. 98

MANES* 2 FR 0.0002 REL FR 2 V 0 P
calm these fits, | per stygia, per manes vehor. TIT 2.01.135
that plats the manes of horses in the night, ROM 1.04. 89

MANFULLY 2 FR 0.0002 REL FR 2 V 0 P
repent, | but yet i slew him manfully in fight, TGV 4.01. 28
knighted in field, slain manfully in arms, | in TIT 1.01.196

MANGLE 2 FR 0.0002 REL FR 2 V 0 P
mangle the work of nature, and deface | the H5 2.04. 60
to mangle me with that word "banished"? ROM 3.03. 51

MANGLED 13 FR 0.0014 REL FR 13 V 0 P
the which he vents | in mangled forms. AYL 2.07. 42
but let my favors hide thy mangled face, | and 1H4 5.04. 96
or mangled shalt thou be by this my sword. H5 4.04. 39
why that the naked, poor, and mangled peace, 5.02. 34
my mangled body shows, | my blood, my want of 3H6 5.02. 7
blood, | together with his mangled myrmidons, TRO 5.05. 33
thy warlike hand, thy mangled daughter here, TIT 3.01.255
when i, thy three-hours wife, have mangled it? ROM 3.02. 99
and pluck the mangled tybalt from his shroud, 4.03. 52
take up this mangled matter at the best; OTH 1.03.173
who they should be that have thus mangled you? 5.01. 79
not see me more, or if, | a mangled shadow. ANT 4.02. 27
use the sword of caesar | hath too much mangled, CYM 3.01. 56

MANGLES 1 FR 0.0001 REL FR 1 V 0 P
your dishonor | mangles true judgment, and COR 3.01.158

MANGLING 2 FR 0.0002 REL FR 2 V 0 P
mangling by starts the full course of their H5 ep 4
and then she reprehends her mangling eye, | that VEN 1065

MANGY 1 FR 0.0001 REL FR 1 V 0 P
away, thou issue of a mangy dog! TIM 4.03.366

/MANHOOD 1 FR 0.0001 REL FR 1 V 0 P
/marry, /your /manhood /mew! LR 4.02. 68

MANHOOD 29 FR 0.0032 REL FR 21 V 8 P
but manhood is melted into cur'sies, valor into ADO 4.01.319 P
follow my voice; we'll try no manhood here. MND 3.02.412
gives manhood more approbation than ever proof
TN 3.04.181 P
there's neither honesty, manhood, nor good 1H4 1.02.139 P
if manhood, good manhood, be not forgot upon the 2.04.128 P
if manhood, good manhood, be not forgot upon the 2.04.128 P
as manhood shall compound. push home. H5 2.01. 98
which makes much against my manhood, if i should 3.02. 49 P
saving your majesty's manhood, what an arrant, 4.08. 34 P
now is it manhood, wisdom, and defense | to give 2H6 5.02. 75
no, nor your manhood that durst make you stay. 3H6 2.02.108
that clifford's manhood lies upon his tongue. 2.02.125
with sleight and manhood stole to rhesus' tents 4.02. 20
thy prime of manhood daring, bold, and venturous
R3 4.04.171
good shape, discourse, manhood, learning, TRO 1.02.253 P
manhood and honor | should have hare hearts, 2.02. 47
and manhood is call'd foolery when it stands COR 3.01.245
who dares | in purity of manhood stand upright TIM 4.03. 14
not i' th' worst rank of manhood, say't, | and i MAC 3.01.102
that even now | protest their first of manhood. 5.02. 11
that thou hast power to shake my manhood thus, LR 1.04.297
nor for my manhood, honesty, and wisdom, | to OTH 3.03.153
experience, manhood, honor, ne'er before | did ANT 3.10. 22
to some shade, | and fit you to your manhood. CYM 3.04.192
guilt within my bosom | takes off my manhood. 5.02. 2
some god hath put his mercy in your manhood, TNK 1.01. 72
blushing virgin, should take manhood to her, 2.02.258
place, which well | might justify your manhood; 3.01. 64
be sure | you tumble with audacity and manhood, 3.05. 36

MANHOODS 2 FR 0.0002 REL FR 1 V 1 P
to pie-corner (saving your manhoods) to buy a 2H4 2.01. 27 P
and hold their manhoods cheap whiles any speaks
H5 4.03. 66

MANIFEST 13 FR 0.0014 REL FR 10 V 3 P
most manifest, and not denied by himself. MM 4.02.139 P
unjust | thus to retort your manifest appeal, 5.01.301
aim better at me by that i now will manifest. ADO 3.02. 97 P
for it appears, by manifest proceeding, | that MV 4.01.358
reading | and manifest experience had collected AWW 1.03.223
ay, and make it manifest where she has liv'd, WT 5.03.114
thy life did manifest thou lov'dst me not, | and 2H4 4.05.104
stand back, thou manifest conspirator, | thou 1H6 1.03. 33
and for thy treachery, what's more manifest? 3.01. 21
you are manifest house-keepers. COR 1.03. 51 P
manifest treason! 3.01.171
prove upon thy person | thy heinous, manifest, LR 5.03. 92
and my perfect soul | shall manifest me rightly. OTH 1.02. 32

MANIFESTED 4 FR 0.0004 REL FR 3 V 1 P
that neither, singly, can be manifested, WIV 4.06. 15
make you understand this in a manifested effect, MM 4.02.160 P
you shall find | your safety manifested. 4.03. 90
then, angelo, thy fault's thus manifested; 5.01.412

MANIFESTS 2 FR 0.0002 REL FR 0 V 2 P
and in this she manifests herself to my love, TN 2.05.168 P
love or hate him manifests the true knowledge he COR 2.02. 13 P

MANIFOLD 7 FR 0.0008 REL FR 5 V 2 P
for mischiefs manifold and sorceries terrible TMP 1.02.264
the manifold linguist and the armipotent soldier AWW 4.03.236 P
forgot, | which he confesseth to be manifold, 1H4 4.03. 47
strange, | which manifold record not matches? TIM 1.01. 5
with how manifold and strong a bond | the child LR 2.01. 47
of gloucester, that he is a manifold traitor, 5.03.112 P
and the opal blend | with objects manifold: LC 216

MANIFOLDLY 1 FR 0.0001 REL FR 0 V 1 P
about thee did manifoldly dissuade me from AWW 2.03.204 P

MANIKIN 1 FR 0.0001 REL FR 0 V 1 P
this is a dear manikin to you, sir toby. TN 3.02. 53 P

MANKA 1 FR 0.0001 REL FR 0 V 1 P
o, pray, pray, pray! manka revania dulche. AWW 4.01. 78 P

MANKIND 20 FR 0.0022 REL FR 15 V 5 P
how beauteous mankind is! TMP 5.01.183
so rails against all married mankind; WIV 4.02. 23 P
why, of mankind. TN 1.05.151 P
consider, he's an enemy to mankind. 3.04. 98 P
the tenth of mankind | would hang themselves. WT 1.02.199
a mankind witch! 2.03. 68
the common curse of mankind, folly and ignorance
TRO 2.03. 28 P
are you mankind? COR 4.02. 16
does it now | (like all mankind) show me an iron TIM 3.04. 83
th' unkindest beast more kinder than mankind. 4.01. 36
hate may grow | to the whole race of mankind, 4.01. 40
destruction fang mankind! 4.03. 23
thou common whore of mankind, that puts odds 4.03. 43
i am misanthropos, and hate mankind. 4.03. 54
in the malice of mankind that he thus advises us 4.03.452 P
and disclaim'st | flinty mankind, whose eyes do 4.03.484
how fain would i have hated all mankind, | and 4.03.499
as they would make | war with mankind. MAC 2.04. 18
fought to-day | as if a god, in hate of mankind, ANT 4.08. 25
all those beauties in her | reveal'd to mankind. TNK 2.02.169

MANLIKE 1 FR 0.0001 REL FR 1 V 0 P
is not more manlike | than cleopatra; ANT 1.04. 5

MANLY 27 FR 0.0030 REL FR 25 V 2 P
a most manly wit, margaret, it will not hurt a ADO 5.02. 15 P
a trim exploit, a manly enterprise, | to conjure MND 3.02.157
drops do something drown my manly spirit. MV 2.03. 14 P
turn two mincing steps | into a manly stride; 3.04. 68
for his shrunk shank, and his big manly voice, AYL 2.07.161
home, | spending his manly marrow in her arms, AWW 2.03.281
but this effusion of such manly drops, | this JN 5.02. 49

for my manly heart doth ern. H5 2.03. 3
abate thy rage, abate thy manly rage, | abate 3.02. 23
henry hath money, you are strong and manly; 2H6 4.08. 51
bear, | so bear i thee upon my manly shoulders; 5.02. 63
boy, | and let his manly face, which promiseth 3H6 2.02. 40
time | my manly eyes did scorn an humble tear; R3 1.02.164
manly as hector, but more dangerous, | for TRO 4.05.104
here on his manly breast. ROM 3.02. 53
let's briefly put on manly readiness, | and meet MAC 2.03.133
this /tune goes manly. 4.03.235
friends, | the boy hath taught us manly duties. CYM 4.02.397
for the sake of it | be manly, and take comfort. PER 3.01. 22
that have died manly, which will seek of me TNK 3.01. 79
and yet inviting, | has this brown manly face! 4.02. 42
but such a manly color | next to an aborn; 4.02.124
mercy and manly courage | are bedfellows in his 5.03. 43
thy worthy, manly heart, be yet unbroken, | give 5.04. 88
name, | made glorious by his manly chivalry, LUC 109
here manly hector faints, here troilus sounds, 1486
till manly shame bids him possess his breath, 1777

MAN–MONSTER 1 FR 0.0001 REL FR 0 V 1 P
my man–monster hath drown'd his tongue in sack. TMP 3.02. 12 P

MANNA 1 FR 0.0001 REL FR 1 V 0 P
you drop manna in the way | of starved people. MV 5.01.294

MANN'D 5 FR 0.0005 REL FR 3 V 2 P
mann'd with three hundred men, as i have heard, R2 2.03. 54
the castle royally is mann'd, my lord, | against 3.03. 21
i was never mann'd with an agot till now, but i 2H4 1.02. 16 P
get me but a wife in the stews, i were mann'd, 1.02. 54 P
your ships are not well mann'd, | your mariners ANT 3.07. 34

MANNER* 76 FR 0.0086 REL FR 37 V 39 P
nay, i'll show you the manner of it. TGV 2.03. 14 P
with all the cunning manner of our flight, 2.04.180
quickly, which is in the manner of his nurse — WIV 1.02. 3 P
that he dares in this manner assay me? 2.01. 25 P
a chain | in a most hideous and dreadful manner. 4.04. 34
i have heard it was ever his manner to do so. MM 4.02.134 P
in most uneven and distracted manner. 4.04. 3 P
in self–same manner doth accuse my husband, 5.01.196
hero was in this manner accus'd, in this very ADO 4.02. 62 P
manner accus'd, in this very manner refus'd, and 4.02. 62 P
the grosser manner of these world's delights LLL 1.01. 29
the manner of it is, i was taken with the manner 1.01.202 P
manner of it is, i was taken with the manner. 1.01.203 P
in what manner? 1.01.204 P
in manner and form following, sir, all those 1.01.205 P
put together, is in manner and form following. 1.01.208 P
sir, for the manner — it is the manner of a man 1.01.209 P
it is the manner of a man to speak to a woman; 1.01.210 P
my lady (to the manner of the days) | in 5.02.365
you do) | in such disdainful manner me to woo. MND 2.02.130
i be obtain'd by the manner of my father's will. MV 1.02.107 P
yet tell us the manner of the wrastling. AYL 1.02.112 P
what manner of man? 3.02.205 P
yes, one, and in this manner. 3.02.407 P
stand by and mark the manner of his teaching. SHR 4.02. 5
what manner of man? TN 1.05.152 P
of very ill manner: 1.05.153 P
the shape of his leg, the manner of his gait, 2.03.157 P
he's coming, madam, but in very strange manner. 3.04. 9 P
and consequently sets down the manner how: 3.04. 72 P
i beseech you, what manner of man is he? 3.04.263 P
what manner of fellow was he that robb'd you? WT 4.03. 84 P
the manner of your bearing towards him, with 4.04.558
if you had not taken yourself with the manner. 4.04.728 P
old shepherd deliver the manner how he found it; 5.02. 4 P
so and in such manner that it seem'd sorrow wept 5.02. 44 P
death (with the manner how she came to't bravely 5.02. 85 P
nay, 'tis in a manner done already, | for many JN 5.07. 89
you have in manner with your sinful hours | made R2 3.01. 11
the manner of their taking may appear | at large 5.06. 9
what manner of man is he? 1H4 2.04.292 P
and wert taken with the manner, and ever since 2.04.315 P
what manner of man, and it like your majesty? 2.04.420 P
acquainted with your manner of wrenching the 2H4 2.01.110 P
the manner how this action hath been borne 4.04. 88
the manner and true order of the fight | this 4.04.100
the pretty and sweet manner of it forc'd | those H5 4.06. 28
all manner of men assembled here in arms this 1H6 1.03. 74 P
the treacherous manner of his mournful death, 2.02. 16
the manner of thy vile outrageous crimes, | that 3.01. 11
dare he presume to scorn us in this manner? 3H6 3.03.178
the manner and the purpose of his treasons, R3 3.05. 58
and to give order that no manner person | have 3.05.108
in desperate manner | daring th' event to th' H8 1.02. 35
in humblest manner i require your highness 2.04.145
by my holidame, | what manner of man are you? 5.01.117
'tis he, i ken the manner of his gait, | he TRO 4.05. 14
about, | in fellest manner execute your arms. 5.07. 6
showing (as the manner is) his wounds | to th' COR 2.01.235
speak to 'em, i pray you, | in wholesome manner. 2.03. 60
then, as the manner of our country is, | /in thy ROM 4.01.109
in like manner was i in debt to my importunate TIM 3.06. 13 P
tell us the manner of it, gentle casca. JC 1.02.234
can as well be hang'd as tell the manner of it: 1.02.235 P
for certain she is dead, and by strange manner. 4.03.189
to relate the manner, | were on the quarry of MAC 4.03.205
i am native here | and to the manner born, it is HAM 1.04. 15
beyond all manner of so much i love you. LR 1.01. 61
he answer'd me in the roundest manner, he would 1.04. 54 P
the matter, but | the manner of his speech; ANT 2.02.112
what manner o' thing is your crocodile? 2.07. 41 P
here's the manner of't: 3.06. 2
the manner of their deaths? 5.02.337
antiochus doth sin | in such a loathed manner; PER 1.01.147
one, i like the manner of your garments well. 4.02.134 P
express | the manner of my pity–wanting pain. SON 140. 4

MANNER'D 2 FR 0.0002 REL FR 2 V 0 P
and he is one | the truest manner'd, such a holy CYM 1.06.166
that she may be | manner'd as she is born. PER 3.03. 17

MANNERLY 6 FR 0.0006 REL FR 6 V 0 P
what thou think'st meet, and is most mannerly. TGV 2.07. 58
see | quick cupid's post that comes so mannerly. MV 2.09.100
and mannerly distinguishment leave out | betwixt WT 2.01. 86
tut, tut, here is a mannerly forbearance. 1H6 2.04. 19
much, | which mannerly devotion shows in this: ROM 1.05. 98
we'll mannerly demand thee of thy story, | so CYM 3.06. 91

MANNERLY–MODEST 1 FR 0.0001 REL FR 0 V 1 P
the wedding, mannerly–modest, as a measure, full ADO 2.01. 76 P

/MANNERS 1 FR 0.0001 REL FR 1 V 0 P
/and /these /external /manners /of /laments R2 4.01.296

MANNERS 76 FR 0.0086 REL FR 59 V 17 P
their manners are more gentle, kind, than of TMP 3.03. 32
he is as disproportion'd in his manners | as in 5.01.291
here's a million of manners. TGV 2.01. 99 P
against all checks, rebukes, and manners, | i WIV 3.04. 80
till that, i'll view the manners of the town, ERR 1.02. 12
now much beshrew my manners and my pride, | if MND 2.02. 54
if you have any pity, grace, or manners, | you 3.02.241
to his blood, | i am not to his manners. MV 2.03. 19
a like proportion | of lineaments, of manners, 3.04. 15
neither his daughter, if we judge by manners, AYL 1.02.271
or else a rude despiser of good manners, | that 2.07. 92
wast at court, thou never saw'st good manners; 3.02. 41 P
if thou never saw'st good manners, then thy 3.02. 42 P
good manners, then thy manners must be wicked, 3.02. 42 P
those that are good manners at the court are as 3.02. 46 P
she says i am not fair, that i lack manners; 4.03. 15
the book — as you have books for good manners. 5.04. 91 P
and therefore frame your manners to the time. SHR 1.01.227
you use your manners discreetly in all kind of 1.01.242
and succeed thy father | in manners, as in shape AWW 1.01. 62
if god have lent a man any manners, he may 2.02. 9 P
was thinking with what manners i might safely be 4.05. 88 P
which lay nice manners by, i put you to | the 5.01. 15
it charges me in manners the rather to express TN 2.01. 15 P
and i am yet so near the manners of my mother, 2.01. 40 P
have you no wit, manners, nor honesty, but to 2.03. 87 P
caves, | where manners ne'er were preach'd! 4.01. 49
is breeding | that changes thus his manners. WT 1.02.375
not a word, a word, we stand upon our manners. 4.04.164
is there no manners left among maids? 4.04.242 P
our country manners give our betters way. JN 1.01.156
father geffrey | than thou and john in manners, 2.01.127
our griefs, and not our manners, reason now. 4.03. 29
therefore 'twere reason you had manners now. 4.03. 31
whose manners still our tardy, apish nation R2 2.01. 22
defect of manners, want of government, | pride, 1H4 3.01.182
good manners be your speed! 3.01.188
what foolish master taught you these manners, 2H4 2.01.190 P
when means and lavish manners meet together, | o 4.04. 64
the seasons change their manners, as the year 4.04.123
for some dishonest manners of their life, H5 1.02. 49
we are the makers of manners, kate; 5.02.271 P
no, truly, 'tis more than manners will; 1H6 2.02. 54
lump, | as crooked in thy manners as thy shape! 2H6 5.01.158
this edward, whom our manners call the prince. R3 3.07.191
and i'll corrupt her manners, stain her beauty, 4.04.207
i blush, | it is to see a nobleman want manners. H8 3.02.308
men's evil manners live in brass, their virtues 4.02. 45
that i bring | will make my boldness manners. 5.01.159
at least good manners — as not thus to suffer 5.02. 29
and manners, to intrude where i am grac'd, | and TIT 2.01. 27
when good manners shall lie all in one or two ROM 1.05. 3 P
what manners is in this, | to press before thy 5.03.214
'gainst th' authority of manners, pray'd you TIM 2.02.138
instruction, manners, mysteries, and trades, 4.01. 18
limbs may halt | as lamely as their manners! 4.01. 25
men report | thou dost affect my manners, and 4.03.199
o'er–leavens | the form of plausive manners — HAM 1.04. 30
my fears forgetting manners, to /unseal | their 5.02. 17
wits to wear, | their manners are so apish." LR 1.04.169
this our court, infected with their manners, 1.04.243
leave, gentle wax, and, manners, blame us not: 4.06.259
allow the compliment | which very manners urges. 5.03.235
my manners tell me | we have your wrong rebuke. OTH 1.01.129
patience, good iago, | that i extend my manners; 2.01. 98
sympathy in years, manners, and beauties — all 2.01.230 P
these bloody accidents must excuse my manners 5.01. 94
can we, with manners, ask what was the CYM 1.04. 52 P
you put me to forget a lady's manners | by being 2.03.105
can tutor 's) to | be masters of our manners. TNK 1.02. 44
and reason has no manners | to say it is not you 1.03. 48
in manners this was false position. 3.05. 51
their face their manners most expressly told: LUC 1397
o, how thy worth with manners may i sing, | when SON 39. 1
my tongue–tied muse in manners holds her still, 85. 1
than public means which public manners breeds. 111. 4

MANNINGTREE 1 FR 0.0001 REL FR 0 V 1 P
that roasted manningtree ox with the pudding in 1H4 2.04.452 P

MANNISH 3 FR 0.0003 REL FR 3 V 0 P
as many other mannish cowards have | that do AYL 1.03.121
a woman impudent and mannish grown | is not more TRO 3.03.217
now our voices | have got the mannish crack, CYM 4.02.236

MAN–OF–WAR 1 FR 0.0001 REL FR 1 V 0 P
and leave you not a man–of–war unsearch'd. TIT 4.03. 22

MANOR 2 FR 0.0002 REL FR 0 V 2 P
to your manor of pickt–hatch! WIV 2.02. 18 P
of melancholy /sold a goodly manor for a song. AWW 3.02. 9 P

MANOR–HOUSE 1 FR 0.0001 REL FR 0 V 1 P
i was seen with her in the manor–house, sitting LLL 1.01.206 P

/MANORS 1 FR 0.0001 REL FR 1 V 0 P
/my /manors, /rents, /revenues /i /forgo; R2 4.01.212

MANORS 2 FR 0.0002 REL FR 2 V 0 P
my parks, my walks, my manors that i had, | even 3H6 5.02. 24
have broke their backs with laying manors on 'em H8 1.01. 84

MAN–QUELLER 1 FR 0.0001 REL FR 0 V 1 P
thou art a honeyseed, a man–queller, and a 2H4 2.01. 53 P

/MAN'S 5 FR 0.0005 REL FR 3 V 2 P
/insulting /man, | /nor /no /man's /lord. R2 4.01.255
it does a /man's heart good. TRO 1.02.204 P
/and /a /man's /life's /no /more /than /to /say HAM 5.02. 74
when a /man's overlusty at legs, then he wears LR 2.04. 10 P
/oats, | /if /it /be /man's /work, /i'll /do't. 5.03. 39

MAN'S 160 FR 0.0180 REL FR 96 V 64 P
nor this man's threats | to whom i am subdu'd, TMP 1.02.489
she that dwells | ten leagues beyond man's life; 2.01.247
a very scurvy tune to sing at a man's funeral. 2.02. 44 P
as a nose on a man's face, or a weathercock on a TGV 2.01.136
when a man's servant shall play the cur with him 4.04. 1 P
like a fair house built on another man's ground, WIV 2.02.215 P
inconstancy of man's disposition is able to bear 4.05.109 P
it is a man's voice. MM 1.04. 7
can you cut off a man's head? 4.02. 1 P
every true man's apparel fits your thief. 4.02. 43 P
so every true man's apparel fits your thief. 4.02. 46 P
i will not die to–day for any man's persuasion. 4.03. 59 P
i am affianc'd this man's wife as strongly | as 5.01.227
when i have cause, and smile at no man's jests; ADO 1.03. 14 P
i have stomach, and wait for no man's leisure; 1.03. 15 P
when i am drowsy, and tend on no man's business; 1.03. 16 P
leonato's hero, your hero, every man's hero. 3.02.107 P
hath no man's dagger here a point for me? 4.01.109
it is a man's office, but not yours. 4.01.266 P
but no man's virtue nor sufficiency | to be so 5.01. 29
the old man's daughter told us all. 5.01.178 P
i'll lay my head to any good man's hat, | these LLL 1.01.308
my sweet ounce of man's flesh, my incony jew! 3.01.135
if 'a have no more man's blood in his belly than 5.02.691 P
long withering out a young man's revenue. MND 1.01. 6
here is the scroll of every man's name, which is 1.02. 4 P
that i will do any man's heart good to hear me. 1.02. 71 P
hath not seen, man's hand is not able to taste, 4.01.212 P
he is a proper man's picture, but, alas, who can MV 1.02. 72 P
a pound of man's flesh taken from a man | is not 1.03.165
friend launcelot, being an honest man's son" — 2.02. 16 P
no master, sir, but a poor man's son. 2.02. 51 P
a man's son may, but in the end truth will out. 2.02. 80 P
an envious emulator of every man's good parts, a AYL 1.01.144 P
have seen cruel proof of this man's strength. 1.02.175 P
my heart to disgrace my man's apparel and to cry 2.04. 5 P
the wise man's folly is anatomiz'd | even by the 2.07. 56
church, | if ever sat at any good man's feast, 2.07.115
thou art not so unkind | as man's ingratitude; 2.07.176
owe no man hate, envy no man's happiness, glad 3.02. 74 P
that i am in this forest and in man's apparel? 3.02.230 P
when a man's verses cannot be understood, nor a 3.03. 12 P
nor a man's good wit seconded with the forward 3.03. 13 P
thank heaven, fasting, for a good man's love; 3.05. 58
this is a man's invention and his hand. 4.03. 29
you lack a man's heart. 4.03.164
look into happiness through another man's eyes! 5.02. 45 P
knavery, to take upon you another man's name. SHR 5.01. 37 P
it no more merits | the tread of a man's foot. AWW 2.03.275
for many a man's tongue shakes out his master's 2.04. 24 P
steal himself into a man's favor and for a week 3.06. 91 P
at a woman's service, and a knave at a man's. 4.05. 25 P
stop my nose, or against any man's metaphor. 5.02. 13 P
i am either maid, or else this old man's wife. 5.03.293
meeting, | every wise man's son doth know." TN 2.03. 44
good a deed as to drink when a man's a–hungry, 2.03.127 P
practice | as full of labor as a wise man's art; 3.01. 66
can more prevail in man's commendation with 3.02. 37 P
but when i came to man's estate, | with hey ho, 5.01.393
with a sense as cold | as is a dead man's nose; WT 2.01.152
force and knowledge | more than was ever man's, 4.04.375
many a poor man's son would have lien still, JN 4.01. 50
the traitor lives, the true man's put to death. R2 5.03. 73
i am an honest man's wife, and, setting thy 1H4 3.03.119 P
yea, this man's brow, like to a title–leaf, 2H4 1.01. 60
it would be every man's thought, and thou art a 2.02. 56 P
never a man's thought in the world keeps the 2.02. 58 P
than will do me good, for no man's pleasure, i. 2.04.119 P
it would have done a man's heart good to see. 3.02. 48 P
may, but if he had been a man's tailor, he'd 'a' 3.02.152 P
i would thou wert a man's tailor, that thou 3.02.164 P
no man's too good to serve 's prince, and let it 3.02.236 P
let us take any man's horses, the laws of 5.03.136 P
it will endure cold as another man's sword will; H5 2.01. 10 P
for 'a never broke any man's head but his own, 3.02. 40 P
we would not die in that man's company | that 4.03. 38
as it were, upon my man's instigation, to prove 2H6 2.03. 86 P
is not amiss to cool a man's stomach this hot 4.10. 9 P
and though man's face be fearful to their eyes, 3H6 2.02. 27
and many an old man's sigh and many a widow's, 5.06. 39
spirit that mutinies in a man's bosom. R3 1.04.138 P
then | spurn at his edict, and fulfill a man's? 1.04.198
every man's conscience is a thousand men, | to 5.02. 17
no man's pie is freed | from his ambitious H8 1.01. 52
doctor pace | in this man's place before him? 2.02.122
which went | beyond all man's endeavors. 3.02.169
easiness and childish pity | to one man's honor, 5.02. 61
date in the pie, for then the man's date is out. TRO 1.02.257 P
what propugnation is in one man's valor | to 2.02.136
for to be wise and love | exceeds man's might; 3.02.157
feed arrogance and are the proud man's fees. 3.03. 49
the man's undone for ever, for if hector break 3.03.258 P
and your affections are | a sick man's appetite, COR 1.01.178
lay here in corioles | at a poor man's house; 1.09. 83
wit will not so soon out as another man's will; 2.03. 28 P
and cannot go without any honest man's voice. 2.03.133 P
thy tears are salter than a younger man's, | and 4.01. 22
time to corrupt a man's wife is when she's 4.03. 32 P
danger | which this man's life did owe you, 5.06.137
pit, | where never man's eye may behold my body: TIT 2.03.177
doth shine upon the dead man's earthy cheeks, 2.03.229
and wonder greatly that man's face can fold | in 2.03.266
care keeps his watch in every old man's eye, ROM 2.03. 35
'warrant thee, my man's as true as steel. 2.04.198
though his face be better than any man's, yet 2.05. 40 P
i will not budge for no man's pleasure, i. 3.01. 55
poor living corse, clos'd in a dead man's tomb! 5.02. 30
for since dishonor traffics with man's nature, TIM 1.01.158
the strain of man's bred out | into baboon and 1.01.250
see so many dip their meat in one man's blood, 1.02. 41 P
when man's worst sin is, he does too much good! 4.02. 39
upright | and say, "this man's a flatterer"? 4.03. 15
with man's blood paint the ground, gules, gules. 4.03. 60
that nature being sick of man's unkindness 4.03.176
shall rome stand under one man's awe? JC 2.01. 52
i have a man's mind, but a woman's might. 2.04. 8
your voice shall be as strong as any man's | in 3.01.177
no man's life was to be trusted with them. MAC 2.03.105
seest the heavens, as troubled with man's act, 2.04. 5
if you will take a homely man's advice, | be not 4.02. 68
the dead man's knell | is there scarce ask'd for 4.03.170
take each man's censure, but reserve thy HAM 1.03. 69
oppressor's wrong, the proud man's contumely, 3.01. 70

there's hope a great man's memory may outlive 3.02.132 P
should be as mortal as /an /old man's life? 4.05.161
if a man's brains were in 's heels, were't not LR 1.05. 8 P
'tis they have put him on the old man's death, 2.01. 99
a good man's fortune may grow out at heels. 2.02.157
nature needs, | man's life is cheap as beast's. 2.04.267
weapons, water–drops, | stain my man's cheeks! 2.04.278
man's nature cannot carry | th' affliction nor 3.02. 48
seeming | has practic'd on man's life! 3.02. 57
swear not, commit not with man's sworn spouse, 3.04. 82 P
bless thee, good man's son, from the foul fiend! 4.01. 58 P
what can man's wisdom | in the restoring his 4.04. 8
and remediate | in the good man's /distress! 4.04. 18
in it a jewel | well worth a poor man's taking. 4.06. 29
i pardon that man's life. 4.06.109
that i have ta'en away this old man's daughter, OTH 1.03. 78
o, man's life's but a span; 2.03. 72
to do this is within the compass of man's wit, 3.04. 21 P
a horned man's a monster and a beast. 4.01. 62
she is cunning past man's thought. ANT 1.02.145
either thee becomes, | so does it no man's else. 1.05. 61
cause, but as't had been | each man's like mine; 4.08. 7
desire my man's abode where i did leave him: CYM 1.06. 53
and man's o'erlabor'd sense | repairs itself by 2.02. 11
i see a man's life is a tedious one, | i have 3.06. 1
gower is come, | assuming man's infirmities, PER 1.ch. 3
the earth is throng'd | by man's oppression, and 1.01.102
in the net, like a poor man's right in the law; 2.01.117 P
any palamon or any living | that is a man's son. TNK 2.02.182
i never practiced | upon man's wife, nor would 5.01.101
though of a man's complexion, | for men will VEN 215
who fears a sentence or an old man's saw | shall LUC 244
here one man's hand lean'd on another's head, 1415
and one man's lust these many lives confounds. 1489
desiring this man's art, and that man's scope, SON 29. 7
desiring this man's art, and that man's scope, 29. 7
"for further i could say, 'this man's untrue,' LC 169
MANS *(also men)*
MANS 2 FR 0.0002 REL FR 1 V 1 P
dat de tongeus of de mans is be full of deceits: H5 5.02.119 P
see how the surly warwick mans the wall! 3H6 5.01. 17
MANSION 14 FR 0.0015 REL FR 13 V 1 P
leave not the mansion so long tenantless, | lest TGV 5.04. 8
but now i was the lord | of this fair mansion, MV 3.02.168
case of a treble hoboy was a mansion for him, a 2H4 3.02.327 P
o, i have bought the mansion of a love, | but ROM 3.02. 26
tell me, that i may sack | the hateful mansion. 3.03.108
hath to the marbled mansion all above | never TIM 4.03.191
timon hath made his everlasting mansion | upon 5.01.215
his mansion and his titles, in a place | from MAC 4.02. 7
and hit | the innocent mansion of my love, my CYM 3.04. 68
peep through thy marble mansion, help, | or we 5.04. 87
it was in rome — accurs'd | the mansion where! 5.05.155
her mansion batter'd by the enemy, | her sacred LUC 1171
what a mansion have those vices got | which for SON 95. 9
dost thou upon thy fading mansion spend? 146. 6
/MANSIONRY 1 FR 0.0001 REL FR 1 V 0 P
by his lov'd /mansionry, that the heaven's MAC 1.06. 5
MANSIONS 1 FR 0.0001 REL FR 1 V 0 P
which abroad they find | of lands and mansions, LC 138
MANSLAUGHTER 1 FR 0.0001 REL FR 1 V 0 P
they labor'd | to bring manslaughter into form, TIM 3.05. 27
MANTLE 18 FR 0.0020 REL FR 16 V 2 P
begin to chase the ignorant fumes that mantle TMP 5.01. 67
and, as she fled, her mantle she did fall, MND 5.01.142
and finds his trusty thisby's mantle slain; 5.01.145
thy mantle good, | what, stain'd with blood? 5.01.282
do cream and mantle like a standing pond, | and MV 1.01. 89
the mantle of queen hermione's; WT 5.02. 32 P
whose pitchy mantle over–veil'd the earth. 1H6 2.02. 2
we, well cover'd with the night's black mantle, 3H6 4.02. 22
bating in my cheeks, | with thy black mantle; ROM 3.02. 15
you all do know this mantle. JC 3.02.170
and, in his mantle muffling up his face, | even 3.02.187
but look the morn in russet mantle clad | walks HAM 1.01.166
drinks the green mantle of the standing pool; LR 3.04.133 P
was lapp'd | in a most curious mantle, wrought CYM 5.05.361
not juno's mantle fairer than your tresses, TNK 1.01. 63
now, | by casting her black mantle over both, 5.03. 25
bed, | throwing his mantle rudely o'er his arm, LUC 170
anon he comes, and throws his mantle by, | and PP 6. 9
MANTLED 1 FR 0.0001 REL FR 1 V 0 P
the blood of others, | but mantled in your own. COR 1.06. 29
MANTLES 1 FR 0.0001 REL FR 1 V 0 P
then put my tires and mantles on him, whilst | i ANT 2.05. 22
MANTUA 19 FR 0.0021 REL FR 19 V 0 P
and i from mantua, for a gentleman, | who, in my TGV 4.01. 48
to mantua, where i hear he makes abode; 4.03. 23
of the mountain foot | that leads toward mantua, 5.02. 47
his name is litio, born in mantua. SHR 2.01. 60
of mantua. 4.02. 77
of mantua, sir? 4.02. 78
'tis death for any one in mantua | to come to 4.02. 81
my lord and you were then at mantua — | nay, i ROM 1.03. 28
set, | for then thou canst not pass to mantua, 3.03.149
sojourn in mantua. 3.03.169
and light thee on thy way to mantua. 3.05. 15
i'll send to one in mantua, | where that same 3.05. 88
night | shall romeo bear thee hence to mantua. 4.01.117
i'll send a friar with speed | to mantua, with 4.01.124
now, | whose sale is present death in mantua, 5.01. 51
welcome from mantua! 5.02. 3
so that my speed to mantua there was stay'd. 5.02. 12
but i will write again to mantua, | and keep her 5.02. 28
and then in post he came from mantua | to this 5.03.273
MANTUAN 3 FR 0.0003 REL FR 0 V 3 P
ah, good old mantuan! LLL 4.02. 95 P
old mantuan, old mantuan! 4.02. 99 P
old mantuan, old mantuan! 4.02. 99 P
MANTUA'S 1 FR 0.0001 REL FR 1 V 0 P
have, but mantua's law | is death to any he that ROM 5.01. 66
/MANU 1 FR 0.0001 REL FR 0 V 1 P
and i will whip about your infamy, /manu cita — LLL 5.01. 69 P
MANUAL 2 FR 0.0002 REL FR 2 V 0 P
there is my gage, the manual seal of death, R2 4.01. 25
slips, | set thy seal manual on my wax–red lips. VEN 516
MANUR'D 2 FR 0.0002 REL FR 0 V 2 P
sterile, and bare land, manur'd, husbanded, and 2H4 4.03.119 P
with idleness or manur'd with industry — why, OTH 1.03.324 P
MANURE 1 FR 0.0001 REL FR 1 V 0 P
the blood of english shall manure the ground, R2 4.01.137
MANUS 1 FR 0.0001 REL FR 1 V 0 P
thus did he strangle serpents in his manus. LLL 5.02.591
/MANY 7 FR 0.0008 REL FR 5 V 2 P
/and /send /him /many /years /of /sunshine /days R2 4.01.221
/that /i /have /worn /so /many /winters /out 4.01.258
/so /many /blows /upon /this /face /of /mine, 4.01.278
/the /face /which /fac'd /so /many /follies, 4.01.285
/o /thou /fond /many, /with /what /loud 2H4 1.03. 91
/in /which /there /are /many /confines, /wards, HAM 2.02.245 P
/that /many /wearing /rapiers /are /afraid /of 2.02.343 P
MANY 601 FR 0.0679 REL FR 457 V 144 P
sometime i'ld divide, | and burn in many places; TMP 1.02.199
as many vouch'd rarieties are. 2.01. 61 P
full many a lady | i have ey'd with best regard, 3.01. 39
and many a time | th' harmony of their tongues 3.01. 40
of | our human generation you shall find | many, 3.03. 34
how many goodly creatures are there here! 5.01.182
then thus: of many good i think him best. TGV 1.02. 21
and so by many winding nooks he strays | with 2.07. 31
her, | with many bitter threats of biding there. 3.01.238
"item, she hath many nameless virtues." 3.01.317 P
that hast deceiv'd so many with thy vows? 4.02. 98
as many, worthy lady, to yourself. 4.03. 7
how many masters would do this for his servant? 4.04. 29 P
how many women would do such a message? 4.04. 90
as many devils entertain; WIV 1.03. 54 P
whale (with so many tuns of oil in his belly) 2.01. 65 P
not only bought many presents to give her, but 2.02.198 P
but have given largely to many to know what she 2.02.199 P
generally allow'd for your many war–like, 2.02.228 P
like a many of these lisping hawthorn buds, that 3.03. 71 P
william, how many numbers is in nouns? 4.01. 21 P
why yet there want not many that do fear | in 4.04. 39
fenton, | heaven give you many, many merry days! 5.05.240
fenton, | heaven give you many, many merry days! 5.05.240
i have purchas'd as many diseases under her roof MM 1.02. 46 P
bore many gentlemen (myself being one) | in hand 1.04. 51
there's many have committed it. 2.02. 89
those many had not dar'd to do that evil | if 2.02. 91
for thou exists on many a thousand grains | that 3.01. 20
as many as you please. 3.01. 51 P
of his frailty) many deceiving promises of life, 3.02.246 P
drunk many times a day, if not many days 4.02.149 P
times a day, if not many days entirely drunk. 4.02.149 P
house, for here be many of her old customers. 4.03. 3 P
you have told me too many of him already, sir, 4.03.167 P
many and hearty thankings to you both. 5.01. 4
many that are not mad | have sure more lack of 5.01. 67
for many of them are neither maid, widow, nor 5.01.179 P
many a man would take you at your word, | and go ERR 1.02. 17
and many such–like liberties of sin: 1.02.102
how many fond fools serve mad jealousy? 2.01.116
but there's many a man hath more hair than wit. 2.02. 82 P
for such store, | when one is one too many? 3.01. 35
how many gentlemen have you lost in this action? ADO 1.01. 5 P
how many hath he kill'd and eaten in these wars? 1.01. 43 P
but how many hath he kill'd? 1.01. 44 P
her mother hath many times told me so. 1.01.105 P
i am not of many words, but i thank you. 1.01.157 P
your own sake, for i have many ill qualities. 2.01.102 P
banquet, just so many strange dishes. 2.03. 21 P
since many a wooer doth commence his suit | to 2.03. 50
and, with grey hairs and bruise of many days, 5.01. 65
so, though very many have been beside their wit. 5.01.127 P
my lord, for your many courtesies i thank you. 5.01.188 P
the worth of many a knight | from tawny spain, LLL 1.01.172
how many is one thrice told? 1.02. 39 P
and send you many lovers! 2.01.125
many can brook the weather that love not the 4.02. 33
say to her we have measur'd many miles, | to 5.02.184
they say that they have measur'd many a mile 5.02.186
ask them how many inches | is in one mile: 5.02.188
if they have measured many, | the measure then 5.02.189
and many miles, the princess bids you tell | how 5.02.192
tell | how many inches doth fill up one mile. 5.02.193
how many weary steps | of many weary miles you 5.02.195
steps | of many weary miles you have o'ergone 5.02.196
grey, | whose note full many a man doth mark, MND 3.01.132
ox–beef hath devour'd many a gentleman of your 3.01.193 P
eye, | or russet–pated choughs, many in sort, 3.02. 21
there is a brief how many sports are ripe. 5.01. 42
one lion may, when many asses do. 5.01.154 P
strond, | and many jasons come in quest of her. MV 1.01.172
but soft, how many months | do you desire? 1.03. 58
many a time and oft | in the rialto you have 1.03.106
chooseth me shall gain what many men desire"; 2.07. 5
chooseth me shall gain what many men desire." 2.07. 37
many a man his life hath sold | but my outside 2.07. 67
chooseth me shall gain what many men desire." 2.09. 24
what many men desire! 2.09. 25
that many may be meant | by the fool multitude, 2.09. 25
i will not choose what many men desire, 2.09. 31
how many then should cover that stand bare? 2.09. 44
how many be commanded that command? 2.09. 45
the carcasses of many a tall ship lie buried, as 3.01. 6 P
how many cowards, whose hearts are all as false 3.02. 83
many that have at times made moan to me; 3.03. 23
e'en as many as could well live one by another. 3.05. 22 P
and i do know | a many fools, that stand in 3.05. 68
you have among you many a purchas'd slave, 4.01. 90
we turn'd o'er many books together. 4.01.156 P
and many an error by the same example | will 4.01.221
that 'scuse serves many men to save their gifts, 4.01.444
stealing her soul with many vows of faith, | and 5.01. 19
how many things by season season'd are | to 5.01.107
and in the hearing of these many friends | i 5.01.241
forest of arden, and a many merry men with him; AYL 1.01.115 P
they say many young gentlemen flock to him every 1.01.117 P
as many other mannish cowards have | that do 1.03.121
at seventeen years many their fortunes seek, 2.03. 73
how many actions most ridiculous | hast thou 2.04. 30
i think of as many matters as he, but i give 2.05. 36 P
who after me hath many a weary step | limp'd in 2.07.130
and one man in his time plays many parts, | his 2.07.142
thus rosalind of many parts | by heavenly synod 3.02.149
of many faces, eyes, and hearts, | to have the 3.02.151
i have been told so of many; 3.02.343 P
i have heard him read many lectures against it, 3.02.347 P
to be touch'd with so many giddy offenses as he 3.02.349 P
is said, "many a man knows no end of his goods." 3.03. 52 P
many a man has good horns, and knows no end of 3.03. 53 P
of mine own, compounded of many simples, 4.01. 16 P
of many simples, extracted from many objects, 4.01. 17 P
he would have liv'd many a fair year though hero 4.01.101 P
thou didst know how many fathom deep i am in 4.01.206 P
many will swoon when they do look on blood. 4.03.158
of many desperate studies by his uncle, | whom 5.04. 32
woman i would kiss as many of you as had beards ep 18 P
and i am sure, as many as have good beards, or ep 21 P
though she have as many diseases as two and SHR 1.02. 80 P
a man | is more than one, | and yet not many. 3.02. 86
but after many ceremonies done, | he calls for 3.02.169
my crupper, with many things of worthy memory, 4.01. 82 P
thou hast fac'd many things. 4.03.122 P
thou hast brav'd many men, brave not me; 4.03.124 P
pitchers have ears, and i have many servants; 4.04. 52
i am poor, though many of the rich are damn'd, AWW 1.03. 17 P
many likelihoods inform'd me of this before, 1.03.123 P
on 's bed of death | many receipts he gave me; 2.01.105
for many a man's tongue shakes out his master's 2.04. 23 P
i have felt so many quirks of joy and grief 3.02. 49
many a maid hath been seduc'd by them, and the 3.05. 20 P
i love not many words. 3.06. 84 P
'tis not the many oaths that makes the truth, 4.02. 21
house, | bequeathed down from many ancestors, 4.02. 43
house, | bequeathed down from many ancestors, 4.02. 47
parcels of dispatch /effected many nicer needs. 4.03. 91 P
of him, how many horse the duke is strong." 4.03.129 P
sebastian, so many; 4.03.162 P
corambus, so many; 4.03.162 P
jaques, so many; 4.03.163 P
but that, my offenses being many, i would repent 4.03.242 P
may, but the many will be too chill and tender, 4.05. 53 P
"upon his many protestations to marry me when 5.03.139 P
sing | and speak to him in many sorts of music TN 1.02. 58
many a good hanging prevents a bad marriage; 1.05. 19 P
me, was yet of many accounted beautiful; 2.01. 26 P
i have many enemies in orsino's court, | else 2.01. 45
i knew 'twas i, for many do call me fool. 2.05. 81 P
and as many lies as will lie in thy sheet of 3.02. 46 P
and hear thou there how many fruitless pranks 4.01. 55
with one "we thank you" many thousands moe WT 1.02. 8
and many a man there is (even at this present, 1.02.192
many thousand on 's | have the disease, and 1.02.206
of pruins, and as many of raisins o' th' sun. 4.03. 48 P
and, having flown over many knavish professions, 4.03. 99 P
sir, for i have about me many parcels of charge. 4.04.257 P
and many other evidences proclaim her, with all 5.02. 37 P
a weather–bitten conduit of many kings' reigns. 5.02. 56 P
a piece many years in doing and now newly 5.02. 96 P
we may live, son, to shed many more. 5.02.146 P
without much content | in many singularities; 5.03. 12
winters cannot blow away, | so many summers dry. 5.03. 51
in vain, said many | a prayer upon her grave. 5.03.140
i was, | but many a many foot of land the worse. JN 1.01.183
i was, | but many a many foot of land the worse. 1.01.183
as many and as well–born bloods as those — 2.01.278
much work for tears in many an english mother, 2.01.303
many a widow's husband grovelling lies, | coldly 2.01.305
many a poor man's son would have lien still, 4.01. 50
with many hundreds treading on his heels; 4.02.149
told of a many thousand warlike french | that 4.02.199
inveterate canker of one wound | by making many. 5.02. 15
sworn, | and i with him, and many moe with me, 5.04. 17
wounds | with many legions of strange fantasies, 5.07. 18
for many carriages he hath dispatch'd | to the 5.07. 90
many years of happy days befall | my gracious R2 1.01. 20
why, uncle, thou hast many years to live. 1.03.225
and many moe | of noble blood in this declining 2.01.239
divides one thing entire to many objects, | like 2.02. 17
march | so many miles upon her peaceful bosom, 2.03. 93
from forth the ranks of many thousand french, 2.03.102
and spur thee on with full as many lies | as may 4.01. 53
many a time hath banish'd norfolk fought | for 4.01. 92
elect, | anointed, crowned, planted many years, 4.01.127
the time shall not be many hours of age | more 5.01. 57
so many greedy looks of young and old | through 5.02. 13
that many have and others must /sit there; 5.05. 27
thus play i in one person many people, | and 5.05. 31
and many limits of the charge set down | but 1H4 1.01. 35
call'd her to a reckoning many a time and oft. 1.02. 49 P
with many holiday and lady terms | he questioned 1.03. 46
which many a good tall fellow had destroyed | so 1.03. 62
could the noble mortimer | receive so many, and 1.03.111
how many be there of them? 2.02. 63 P
says she, "how many hast thou kill'd to–day?" 2.04.106 P
and it is known to many in our land by the name 2.04.412 P
then many an old host that i know is damn'd. 2.04.472 P
of many men | i do not bear these crossings. 3.01. 34
to the harp | many an english ditty lovely well, 3.01.122
can purge | myself of many i am charg'd withal; 3.02. 21
me beg | as, in reproof of many tales devis'd, 3.02. 23
i make as good use of it as many a man doth of a 3.03. 30 P
bardolph was shav'd and lost many a hair, and 3.03. 60 P
and many moe corrivals and dear men | of 4.04. 31
in both your armies there is many a soul | shall 5.01. 83
the king hath many marching in his coats. 5.03. 25
many a nobleman lies stark and stiff | under the 5.03. 41
at heart | so many of his shadows thou hast met 5.04. 30
though many dearer, in this bloody fray. 5.04.108
and many a creature else | had been alive this 5.05. 7
or to take note how many pair of silk stockings 2H4 2.02. 15 P
tell me how many good young princes would do so, 2.02. 29 P
threw many a northward look to see his father 2.03. 13
but many thousand reasons hold me back. 2.03. 66
strange that desire should so many years outlive 2.04.260 P
how many thousand of my poorest subjects | are 3.01. 4
many good morrows to your majesty! 3.01. 32
and to see how many of my old acquaintance are 3.02. 34 P
wilt thou make as many holes in an enemy's 3.02.153 P
soldier that is the leader of so many thousands. 3.02.167 P

silence, i will not use many words with you. 3.02.289 P
their blood, and making many fish–meals, that 4.03. 92 P
of slumber open wide | to many a watchful night, 4.05. 25
rigol hath divorc'd | so many english kings. 4.05. 37
and i had many living to upbraid | my gain of it 4.05.192
purpose now | to lead out many to the holy land, 4.05.210
it hath been prophesied to me many years, | i 4.05.236
there is many complaints, davy, against that 5.01. 40 P
together in consent, like so many wild geese. 5.01. 71 P
how many nobles then should hold their places, 5.02. 17
turning th' accomplishment of many years | into H5 pr 30
for god doth know how many now in health | shall 1.02. 18
that many things, having full reference | to one 1.02.205
as many arrows loosed several ways | come to one 1.02.207
as many ways meet in one town; 1.02.208
as many fresh streams meet in one salt sea; 1.02.209
as many lines close in the dial's centre; 1.02.210
for many a thousand widows | shall this his mock 1.02.284
fathers that, like so many alexanders, | have in 3.01. 19
correction, there is not many of your nation — 3.02.121 P
i have | almost no better than so many french; 3.06.147
that may be, for you bear a many superfluously, 3.07. 74 P
unto the gazing moon | so many horrid ghosts. 4.pr. 28
be ransom'd, and a many poor men's lives sav'd. 4.01.122 P
assail'd by robbers and die in many irreconcil'd 4.01.152 P
a many of our bodies shall no doubt | find 4.03. 95
for many of our princes (woe the while!) 4.07. 75
no, | for yet a many of your horsemen peer | and 4.07. 85
please your majesty, to tell how many is kill'd? 4.08.118 P
sword, | how many would the peaceful city quit, 5.pr. 33
who cannot see many a fair french city for one 5.02.317 P
whose state so many had the managing, | that ep 11
this day is ours, as many more shall be. 1H6 1.05. 18
sword, | for i have loaden me with many spoils, 2.01. 80
that hast by tyranny these many years | wasted 2.03. 40
which giveth many wounds when one will kill. 2.05.110
that many have their giddy brains knock'd out; 3.01. 83
goes, | for friendly counsel cuts off many foes. 3.01.184
and for thy sake have i shed many a tear. 5.04. 19
think she knows not well | (there were so many) 5.04. 81
after the slaughter of so many peers, | so many 5.04.103
so many captains, gentlemen, and soldiers, 5.04.104
and many time and oft | myself have heard a 2H6 2.01. 91
but cloaks and gowns, before this day, a many. 2.01.113
and had i twenty times so many foes, | and each 2.04. 60
many a pound of mine own proper store, | because 3.01.115
teeth, | with full as many signs of deadly hate, 3.02.314
indeed a pedlar's daughter, and sold many laces. 4.02. 46 P
for god forbid so many simple souls | should 4.04. 10
for many a time, but for a sallet, my brain–pan 4.10. 11 P
and many a time, when i have been dry and 4.10. 12 P
into as many gobbets will i cut it | as wild 5.02. 58
for richard, in the view of many lords, 3H6 1.01.138
many a battle have i won in france | when as the 1.02. 73
environed he was with many foes, | and stood 2.01. 50
and many strokes, though with a little axe, 2.01. 54
by many hands your father was subdu'd, | but 2.01. 56
and after many scorns, many foul taunts, | they 2.01. 64
and after many scorns, many foul taunts, | they 2.01. 64
and of their feather many moe proud birds, 2.01.170
proclaims him king, and many fly to him. 2.02. 71
for strokes receiv'd and many blows repaid 2.03. 3
how many makes the hour full complete, | how 2.05. 26
complete, | how many hours brings about the day, 2.05. 27
day, | how many days will finish up the year, 2.05. 28
year, | how many years a mortal man may live. 2.05. 29
so many hours must i tend my flock, | so many 2.05. 31
my flock, | so many hours must i take my rest, 2.05. 32
my rest, | so many hours must i contemplate, 2.05. 33
so many hours must i sport myself, | so many 2.05. 34
so many days my ewes have been with young, | so 2.05. 35
so many weeks ere the poor fools will ean, | so 2.05. 36
so many years ere i shall shear the fleece: 2.05. 37
my love and fear glu'd many friends to thee, 2.06. 5
how many children hast thou, widow? tell me. 3.02. 26
i take my leave with many thousand thanks. 3.02. 56
a happy thing | to be the father unto many sons. 3.02.105
for many lives stand between me and home; 3.02.173
ay, ay, for this i draw in many a tear, | and 4.04. 21
conceive, when, after many moody thoughts, | at 4.06. 13
for many men that stumble at the threshold | are 4.07. 11
the bruit thereof will bring you many friends. 4.07. 64
to london, | and many giddy people flock to him. 4.08. 5
that many a thousand | which now mistrust no 5.06. 37
and many an old man's sigh and many a widow's, 5.06. 39
and many an old man's sigh and many a widow's, 5.06. 39
and many an orphan's water–standing eye — | men 5.06. 40
there's many a gentle person made a jack. R3 1.03. 72
she may help you to many fair preferments, | and 1.03. 94
and, after many length'ned hours of grief, | die 1.03.207
that stand high have many blasts to shake them, 1.03.258
darkness, | i do beweep to many simple gulls — 1.03.327
days, | how many of you have mine eyes beheld! 2.04. 56
many good morrows to my noble lord! 3.02. 35
of spirit, | so mighty and so many my defects, 3.07.160
a care–craz'd mother to a many sons, | a 3.07.184
so many miseries have craz'd my voice | that my 4.04. 17
we have many goodly days to see: 4.04.320
for i myself have many tears to wash | hereafter 4.04.389
herself, the land, and many a christian soul, 4.04.408
throng many doubtful hollow–hearted friends, 4.04.435
what need'st thou run so many miles about, 4.04.460
with many moe confederates, are in arms. 4.04.502
crew, | and many other of great name and worth; 4.05. 16
many | have broke their backs with laying manors H8 1.01. 83
able to maintain | the many to them 'longing, 1.02. 32
it grieves many. 1.02.110
and a great one, | to many lords and ladies; 1.03. 53
alleged | many sharp reasons to defeat the law. 2.01. 14
too many curses on their heads | that were the 2.01.138
after | so many courses of the sun enthroned, 2.03. 6
and high note's | ta'en of your many virtues, 2.03. 60
and have been blest | with many children by you. 2.04. 37
the wisest prince that there had reign'd by many 2.04. 49
not to be taught | that you have many enemies, 2.04.159
that many maz'd considerings did throng | and 2.04.186
and that gave to me | many a groaning throe. 2.04.200
if i lov'd many words, lord, i should tell you 3.02.270
many more there are, | which, since they are of 3.02.330
bladders, | this many summers in a sea of glory, 3.02.360
a stiff tempest, | as loud and to as many tunes. 4.01. 73
many good–nights, my lord! i rest your servant. 5.01. 55
of late | heard many grievous — i do say, my 5.01. 98
your enemies are many, and not small; 5.01.128
i think your highness saw this many a day. 5.02. 21
you shall know many dare accuse you boldly, 5.02. 91
and what so many may do, | not being torn 5.03. 75
many days shall see her, | and yet no day 5.04. 57
reply not in how many fadoms deep | they lie TRO 1.01. 50
hath robb'd many beasts of their particular 1.02. 19 P
he is a gouty briareus, many hands and no use, 1.02. 29 P
alas, poor chin! many a wart is richer. 1.02.141 P
how many shallow bauble boats dare sail | upon 1.03. 35
and look how many grecian tents do stand 1.03. 79
hollow upon this plain, so many hollow factions. 1.03. 80
with an imperial voice — many are infect. 1.03.187
that do contrive how many hands shall strike 1.03.201
and achilles' horse | makes many thetis' sons. 1.03.212
after so many hours, lives, speeches spent, 2.02. 1
every tithe soul, 'mongst many thousand dismes, 2.02. 19
if we have lost so many tenths of ours, | to 2.02. 21
not serv'd thyself in to my table so many meals? 2.03. 42 P
lov'd you night and day | for many weary months. 3.02.115
out of those many regist'red in promise, | which 3.03. 15
she hath not given so many good words breath 4.01. 74
that with so many thousand sighs | did buy each 4.04. 39
as many farewells as be stars in heaven, | with 4.04. 44
despising many forfeits and subduements, | when 4.05.187
there's many a greek and troyan dead | since 4.05.214
when many times the captive grecian falls, 5.03. 40
and i do stand engag'd to many greeks, | even in 5.03. 68
look how thy wounds do bleed at many vents! 5.03. 82
as many as be here of pandar's hall, | your eyes 5.10. 47
which was | to take in many towns ere (almost) COR 1.02. 24
let him alone, or so many so minded, | wave thus 1.06. 73
without note, here's many else have done — 1.09. 49
do very little stand, for your helps are many, 2.01. 36 P
how many stand for consulships? 2.02. 2 P
faith, there hath been many great men that have 2.02. 7 P
and there be many that they have lov'd, they 2.02. 9 P
we have been call'd so of many, not that our 2.03. 18 P
you have receiv'd many wounds for your country. 2.03.106 P
for your voices have | done many things, some 2.03.130
fast, | we have as many friends as enemies. 3.01.231
many an ounce) he dropp'd it for his country; 3.01.299
in thy hands clutch'd as many millions, in | thy 3.03. 71
the beast | with many heads butts me away. 4.01. 2
many an heir | of these fair edifices 'fore my 4.04. 2
you, sir, he has as many friends as enemies; 4.05.206 P
it is spoke freely out of many mouths — | how 4.06. 65
as many coxcombs | as you threw caps up will he 4.06.134
and, to say the truth, so did very many of us. 4.06.143 P
if you had told as many lies in his behalf as 5.02. 24 P
city he | hath widowed and unchilded many a one, 5.06.151
pius | for many good and great deserts to rome. TIT 1.01. 24
how many sons hast thou of mine in store, | that 1.01. 94
and many unfrequented plots there are, | fitted 2.01.115
many good morrows to your majesty; 2.02. 11
madam, to you as many and as good. 2.02. 12
ten thousand swelling toads, as many urchins, 2.03.101
thine, | that hath thrown down so many enemies, 3.01.163
how many women saw this child of his? 4.02.135
but say again, how many saw the child? 4.02.140
many a time he danc'd thee on his knee, | sung 5.03.162
many a story hath he told to thee, | and bid 5.03.164
how many thousand times hath these poor lips, 5.03.167
be found, | being one too many by my weary self, ROM 1.01.128
many a morning hath he there been seen, | with 1.01.131
both by myself and many other friends, | but he, 1.01.146
feast, | whereto i have invited many a guest, 1.02. 21
which /on more view of many, mine, being one, 1.02. 32
many for many virtues excellent, | none but for 2.03. 13
many for many virtues excellent, | none but for 2.03. 13
but old folks — many feign as they were dead, 2.05. 16
the hour, | for in a minute there are many days. 3.05. 45
villain and he be many miles asunder. 3.05. 81
him with above compare | so many thousand times? 3.05.239
so many guests invite as here are writ. 4.02. 1
for i have need of many orisons | to move the 4.03. 3
where for this many hundred years the bones | of 4.03. 40
grieves me to see so many dip their meat in one TIM 1.02. 41 P
'tis to have so many like brothers commanding 1.02.104 P
at many leisures i /propos'd. 2.02.128
lord, | at many times i brought in my accompts, 2.02.133
how many prodigal bits have slaves and peasants 2.02.165
many a time and often i ha' din'd with him, and 3.01. 23 P
the lord lucullus to borrow so many talents, nay 3.02. 12 P
ne'er have denied his occasion so many talents. 3.02. 24 P
to supply his instant use with so many talents. 3.02. 36 P
with their wards | many a bounteous year, must 3.03. 38
many do keep their chambers are not sick; 3.04. 73
and slain in fight many of your enemies. 3.05. 63
which many my near occasions did urge me to put 3.06. 10 P
for many so arrive at second masters, | upon 4.03.505
many a time and oft | have you climb'd up to JC 1.01. 37
heard | where many of the best respect in rome 1.02. 59
cowards die many times before their deaths, 2.02. 32
and many lusty romans | came smiling and did 2.02. 78
your statue spouting blood in many pipes, | in 2.02. 85
pipes, | in which so many smiling romans bath'd, 2.02. 86
life | cuts off so many years of fearing death. 3.01.102
how many ages hence | shall this our lofty scene 3.01.111
how many times shall caesar bleed in sport, 3.01.114
had i as many eyes as thou hast wounds, 3.01.200
how like a deer, strooken by many princes, 3.01.209
he hath brought many captives home to rome, 3.02. 88
these many then shall die, their names are 4.01. 1
the stake, | and bay'd about with many enemies, 4.01. 49
o cassius, i am sick of many griefs. 4.03.144
should be the root and father | of many kings. MAC 3.01. 6
who bears a glass | which shows me many more; 4.01.120
of the happy throne, | and fall of many kings. 4.03. 69
that vulture in you to devour so many | as will 4.03. 74
of each several crime, | acting it many ways. 4.03. 97
by many of these trains hath sought to win me 4.03.118
a rumor | of many worthy fellows that were out, 4.03.183
and many unrough youths that even now | protest 5.02. 10
had i as many sons as i have hairs, | i would 5.09. 14
of late made many tenders | of his affection to HAM 1.03. 99
brain | that looks so many fadoms to the sea 1.04. 77
lord, | how does your honor for this many a day? 3.01. 90
but if you mouth it, as many of our players do, 3.02. 3 P
so many journeys may the sun and moon | make us 3.02.161
fear it is | to keep those many many bodies safe 3.03. 9
fear it is | to keep those many many bodies safe 3.03. 9
weal depends and rests | the lives of many. 3.03. 15
in many places | gives me superfluous death. 4.05. 95
and in his grave rain'd many a tear" — | fare 4.05.167
and hath abatements and delays as many | as 4.07.120
before 'a die — as we have many pocky corses, 5.01.166 P
larded with many several sorts of reasons, 5.02. 20
and many such–like /as's of great charge, | that 5.02. 43
and many more of the same breed that i know the 5.02.188 P
cell, | that thou so many princes at a shot | so 5.02.366
to dismantle | so many folds of favor. LR 1.01.218
thou shalt have as many dolors for thy daughters 2.04. 54 P
yea, or so many? 2.04.239
house | should many people under two commands 2.04.241
to follow in a house where twice so many | have 2.04.262
for many miles about | there's scarce a bush. 2.04.301
so beggars marry many. 3.02. 30
swore as many oaths as i spake words, and broke 3.04. 88 P
are many simples operative, whose power | will 4.04. 14
air | (so many fathom down precipitating), 4.06. 50
you have many opportunities to cut him off; 4.06.263 P
thy heinous, manifest, and many treasons, 5.03. 92
mark | many a duteous and knee–crooking knave OTH 1.01. 45
and many of the consuls, rais'd and met, | are 1.02. 43
ay, so i thought. how many, as you guess? 1.03. 36
one gender of herbs or distract it with many, 1.03.324 P
there are many events in the womb of time which 1.03.369 P
had i as many mouths as hydra, such an answer 2.03.304 P
sir, by many a wind instrument that i know. 3.01. 10 P
that came a–wooing with you, and so many a time, 3.03. 71
not to affect many proposed matches | of her own 3.03.229
and many worthy and chaste dames even thus, 4.01. 46
there's many a beast then in a populous city, 4.01. 63
in a populous city, | and many a civil monster. 4.01. 64
plague | to beguile many and be beguil'd by one) 4.01. 97
hath she forsook so many noble matches? 4.02.125
and as many to th' vantage as would store the 4.03. 84 P
prithee, how many boys and wenches must i have? ANT 1.02. 36 P
too | of many our contriving friends in rome 1.02.182
many hot inroads | they make in italy; 1.04. 50
he kiss'd — the last of many doubled kisses — 1.05. 40
so many mermaids, tended her i' th' eyes, | and 2.02.207
many times, madam. 2.05.108
kings for messengers | not many moons gone by. 3.12. 6
he needs as many, sir, as caesar has, | or needs 3.13. 49
ruffian know | i have many other ways to die; 4.01. 5
know that to–morrow the last of many battles 4.01. 11
i wish i could be made so many men, | and all of 4.02. 16
fury, for one death | might have prevented many. 4.12. 42
until | of many thousand kisses the poor last 4.15. 20
and take a queen | worth many babes and beggars! 5.02. 48
very many, men and women too. 5.02.250 P
a princess | descended of so many royal kings. 5.02.327
as many inches as you have oceans. puppies! CYM 1.02. 20 P
we had very many there could behold the sun with 1.04. 12 P
diamond of yours outlustres many i have beheld, 1.04. 73 P
i could not /but believe she excell'd many. 1.04. 75 P
there be many caesars, | ere such another julius 3.01. 11
we have yet many among us can gripe as hard as 3.01. 40 P
how many /score of miles may we well rid 3.02. 67
many times | doth ill deserve by doing well; 3.03. 53
sinon's weeping | did scandal many a holy tear, 3.04. 60
thou abus'd | so many miles with a pretense? 3.04.103
from whose so many weights of baseness cannot 3.05. 88
i saw him not these many years, and yet | i know 4.02. 66
cry out for service, | try many, all good; 4.02.373
o, i am known | of many in the army. 4.04. 22
many years, | though cloten then but young, you 4.04. 22
how many | must murther wives much better than 5.01. 3
three thousand confident, in act as many — 5.03. 29
to–day how many would have given their honors 5.03. 66
many dream not to find, neither deserve, | and 5.04.130
which, being dead many years, shall after revive 5.04.141 P
though with the loss | of many a bold one, whose 5.05. 71
which, being dead many years, shall after revive 5.05.439 P
for many years thought dead, are now reviv'd, 5.05.456
sinful dame | made many princes thither frame PER 1.ch. 32
so for her many /a wight did die, | as yon grim 1.ch. 39
air | how many worthy princes' bloods were shed 1.02. 88
here many sink, yet those which see them fall 1.04. 48
by many a dern and painful perch, | of pericles 3.ch. 15
i have been in many; 3.02. 5
death may usurp on nature many hours, | and yet 3.02. 82
seas, | attended on by many a lord and knight, 4.04. 11
this populous city will | yield many scholars. 4.06.187
did begin | as if you met decays of many kinds. TNK 1.02. 29
cabin'd | in many as dangerous as poor a corner, 1.03. 36
look merrily, discourse of many things, but 2.01. 39 P
get many more such prisoners and such daughters, 2.06. 38
they howl'd many together, | and then they /fed 3.02. 18
him i utter learned things | and many figures; 3.05. 15
we shall find | too many hours to die in, gentle 3.06.112
"this you may loose, not me," and many a one; 4.01. 91
seen it approv'd, how many times i know not, but 4.03. 97 P
we shall have many children. 5.02. 94
does stand accurs'd | of many mortal millions, 5.03. 24
name, and many a murther | set off whereto she's 5.03. 27
there's many a man alive that hath outliv'd 5.04. 1
state | stands many a father with his child. 5.04. 3
not halting under crimes | many and stale. 5.04. 11
and many will not buy | his goodness with this 5.04. 52
i dare say, many a better, to prolong | your old ep 16
the many musits through the which he goes | are VEN 683
murmur stay, | for misery is trodden on by many, 707
like many clouds consulting for foul weather. 972
alas, how many bear such shameful blows, | which LUC 832
many a dry drop seem'd a weeping tear, | shed 1375
the scalps of many, almost hid behind, | to jump 1413

stood many troyan mothers, sharing joy | to see 1431
many she sees where cares have carved some, 1445
some one | become the public plague of many moe? 1479
for one's offense why should so many fall, | to 1483
and one man's lust these many lives confounds. 1489
not speak, | till after many accents and delays, 1719
did court the lad with many a lovely look, PP 4. 3
how many tales to please me hath she coined, 7. 9
whose speechless song, being many, seeming one, SON 8.13
grant, if thou wilt, thou art belov'd of many, 10. 3
and many maiden gardens, yet unset, | with 16. 6
i sigh the lack of many a thing i sought, | and 30. 3
and moan th' expense of many a vanish'd sight; 30. 8
how many a holy and obsequious tear | hath dear 31. 5
that due of many, now is thine alone. 31.12
full many a glorious morning have i seen 33. 1
his, | and, proud of many, lives upon his gains? 67.12
how many lambs might the stern wolf betray, | if 96. 9
how many gazers mightst thou lead away, | if 96.11
whilst many nymphs that vow'd chaste life to 154. 3
which many legions of true hearts had warm'd, 154. 6
of folded schedules had she many a one, | which LC 43
crack'd many a ring of posied gold and bone, 45
you behold | the injury of many a blasting hour, 72
"many there were that did his picture get | to 134
"so many have, that never touch'd his hand, 141
experience for me many bulwarks builded | of 152
"'among the many that mine eyes have seen, | not 190
i have receiv'd from many a several fair, 206
MANY-COLOR'D 1 FR 0.0001 REL FR 1 V 0 P
wet, | the many-color'd iris, rounds thine eye? AWW 1.03.152
MANY-COLORED 1 FR 0.0001 REL FR 1 V 0 P
hail, many-colored messenger, that ne'er | dost TMP 4.01. 76
MANY-HEADED 1 FR 0.0001 REL FR 0 V 1 P
stuck not to call us the many-headed multitude. COR 2.03. 16 P
MANY'S 2 FR 0.0002 REL FR 2 V 0 P
that book in many's eyes doth share the glory, ROM 1.03. 91
in many's looks the false heart's history | is SON 93. 7
/MAP 1 FR 0.0001 REL FR 1 V 0 P
/thou /map /of /woe, /that /thus /dost /talk /in TIT 3.02. 12
MAP 12 FR 0.0013 REL FR 10 V 2 P
his face into more lines than is in the new map, TN 3.02. 79 P
thou map of honor, thou king richard's tomb, R2 5.01. 12
i have forgot the map. 1H4 3.01. 6
come, here is the map. 3.01. 69
in thy face i see | the map of honor, truth, and 2H6 3.01.203
i see (as in a map) the end of all. R3 2.04. 54
if you see this in the map of my microcosm, COR 2.01. 62 P
give me the map there. LR 1.01. 37
showing life's triumph in the map of death, LUC 402
that map which deep impression bears | of hard 1712
thus is his cheek the map of days outworn, SON 68. 1
new, | and him as for a map doth nature store, 68.13
MAPP'D 1 FR 0.0001 REL FR 0 V 1 P
should meet, if pisanio have mapp'd it truly. CYM 4.01. 2 P
MAPP'RY 1 FR 0.0001 REL FR 1 V 0 P
they call this bed-work, mapp'ry, closet-war, TRO 1.03.205
MAPS 2 FR 0.0002 REL FR 1 V 1 P
piring in maps for ports and piers and roads; MV 1.01. 19
captain, if you look in the maps of the orld, i H5 4.07. 23 P
MAR 29 FR 0.0032 REL FR 19 V 10 P
you mar our labor. TMP 1.01. 13 P
and mar the concord with too harsh a descant: TGV 1.02. 91
men their creation mar | in profiting by them. MM 2.04.127
if it mar nothing neither, | the treason and you LLL 4.03.189
you'll mar the light by taking it in snuff; 5.02. 22
far, | and make and mar | the foolish fates." MND 1.02. 37
for if i do, i'll mar the young clerk's pen. MV 5.01.237
what mar you then, sir? AYL 1.01. 31 P
i am helping you to mar that which god made, a 1.01. 32 P
i pray you mar no more trees with writing 3.02.259 P
i pray you mar no moe of my verses with reading 3.02.261 P
i did not bid you mar it to the time. SHR 4.03. 97
th' earth together, | and mar the seeds within! WT 4.04.479
you'll mar it if you kiss it; 5.03. 82
you'll mar all. COR 2.03. 58
gentlewoman, that god hath made, himself to mar.
ROM 2.04.116 P
"for himself to mar," quoth 'a! 2.04.118 P
for bounty, that makes gods, do still mar men. TIM 4.02. 41
their sharp shins, | and mar men's spurring. 4.03.153
you mar all with this starting. MAC 5.01. 44 P
a little, | lest you may mar your fortunes. LR 1.01. 95
ride, run, mar a curious tale in telling it, and 1.04. 32 P
striving to better, oft we mar what's well. 1.04.346
when brewers mar their malt with water; 3.02. 82
his part so much, | they mar my counterfeiting. 3.06. 61
every ten that they make, the devils mar five. ANT 5.02.277 P
come | give me your flowers, ere the sea mar it. PER 4.01. 26
mar not the thing that cannot be amended. LUC 578
mend, | to mar the subject that before was well? SON 103.10
MARBLE 17 FR 0.0019 REL FR 15 V 2 P
and he, a marble to her tears, is wash'd with MM 3.01.229 P
for ever be confixed here, | a marble monument! 5.01.233
unkindness blunts it more than marble hard. ERR 2.01. 93
who was most marble there chang'd color; WT 5.02. 90 P
her tears will pierce into a marble heart; 3H6 3.01. 38
plies her hard, and much rain wears the marble. 3.02. 50
and sleep in dull cold marble where no mention H8 3.02.433
milk thou suck'st from her did turn to marble, TIT 2.03.144
whole as the marble, founded as the rock, | as MAC 3.04. 21
hath op'd his ponderous and marble jaws | to HAM 1.04. 50
now, by yond marble heaven, | in the due OTH 3.03.460
peep through thy marble mansion, help, | or we CYM 5.04. 87
the marble pavement closes, he is enter'd | his 5.04.120
harden lust, though marble /wear with raining. LUC 560
for men have marble, women waxen, minds, | and 1240
and therefore are they form'd as marble will; 1241
not marble nor the gilded /monuments | of SON 55. 1
MARBLE-BREASTED 1 FR 0.0001 REL FR 1 V 0 P
live you the marble-breasted tyrant still. TN 5.01.124
MARBLE-CONSTANT 1 FR 0.0001 REL FR 1 V 0 P
now from head to foot | i am marble-constant; ANT 5.02.240
MARBLED 1 FR 0.0001 REL FR 1 V 0 P
face | hath to the marbled mansion all above TIM 4.03.191
MARBLE-HEARTED 1 FR 0.0001 REL FR 1 V 0 P
thou marble-hearted fiend, | more hideous when LR 1.04.259
MARCADE 1 FR 0.0001 REL FR 1 V 0 P
welcome, marcade, | but that thou interruptest LLL 5.02.716
MARCANTANT *(see mercantant)*
MARCELLUS 7 FR 0.0008 REL FR 6 V 1 P
if you do meet horatio and marcellus, | the HAM 1.01. 12
welcome, horatio, welcome, good marcellus. 1.01. 20
where now it burns, marcellus and myself, | the 1.01. 38
stop it, marcellus. 1.01.139
marcellus. 1.02.165
marcellus and barnardo, on their watch, | in the 1.02.197
true, sir, she was the wife of caius marcellus. ANT 2.06.110 P
/MARCH* 1 FR 0.0001 REL FR 1 V 0 P
/but, /march /away. TRO 5.10. 21
MARCH* 96 FR 0.0108 REL FR 87 V 9 P
and take | the winds of march with beauty; WT 4.04.120
who painfully with much expedient march | have JN 2.01.223
in warlike march these greens before your town, 2.01.242
of smiling peace to march a bloody host, | and 3.01.246
after a stranger, march | upon her gentle bosom, 5.02. 27
why have they dar'd to march | so many miles R2 2.03. 92
while here we march | upon the grassy carpet of 3.03. 49
let's march without the noise of threat'ning 3.03. 51
march on, and mark king richard how he looks. 3.03. 61
march sadly after, grace my mournings here, | in 5.06. 51
march all one way and be no more oppos'd 1H4 1.01. 15
hear, that earl of march | hath lately married. 1.03. 84
know his death will be a march of twelve score. 2.04.546 P
forward, | on thursday we ourselves will march. 3.02.174
you shall march | through gloucestershire; 3.02.175
must we all march? 3.03. 89 P
worse than the sun in march, | this praise doth 4.01.111
our soldiers shall march through; 4.02. 2 P
i'll not march through coventry with them, 4.02. 38 P
and the villains march wide betwixt the legs, as 4.02. 40 P
to make that worse, suff'red his kinsman march 4.03. 93
to fight with glendower and the earl of march. 5.05. 40
let our trains | march by us, that we may peruse 2H4 4.02. 94
and, ere they be dismiss'd, let them march by. 4.02. 96
which pillage they with merry march bring home H5 1.02.195
touch her soft mouth, and march. 2.03. 58
to-morrow for the march are we address'd. 3.03. 58
if they march along | unfought withal, but i 3.05. 11
his soldiers sick and famish'd in their march; 3.05. 57
but could be willing to march on to callice 3.06.141
of english legs | did march three frenchmen. 3.06.150
march to the bridge, it now draws toward night; 3.06.170
and on to-morrow bid them march away. 3.06.172
now, soldiers, march away, | and how thou 4.03.132
ay, we may march in england, or in france, | not 1H6 3.01.186
gather strength and march unto him straight. 4.01. 73
with him and made their march for burdeaux. 4.03. 8
then march to paris, royal charles of france, 5.02. 4
who married edmund mortimer, earl of march; 2H6 2.02. 36
edmund had issue, roger earl of march; 2.02. 37
she was heir | to roger earl of march, who was 2.02. 48
edmund mortimer, earl of march, | married the 4.02.136
they are all in order, and march toward us. 4.02.188 P
come, march forward. 4.02.190 P
come, let's march towards london. 4.03. 18 P
thy grandfather, roger mortimer, earl of march: 3H6 1.01.106
all the friends that thou, brave earl of march, 2.01.179
to london will we march, | and once again 2.01.182
no longer earl of march, but duke of york; 2.01.192
and in the towns, as they do march along, 2.02. 70
and now to london with triumphant march, | there 2.06. 87
to do | but march to london with our soldiers? 4.03. 61
drummer, strike up, and let us march away. 4.07. 50
and with his troops doth march amain to london, 4.08. 4
brave warriors, march amain towards coventry. 4.08. 64
and, as we hear, march on to fight with us. 5.03. 9
and, as we march, our strength will be augmented 5.03. 22
now march we hence. 5.05. 87
let me march on and not offend you, madam. R3 4.04.179
march on, march on, since we are up in arms, 4.04.528
march on, march on, since we are up in arms, 4.04.528
to salisbury, the rest march on with me. 4.04.538
from tamworth thither is but one day's march. 5.02. 13
then in god's name march! 5.02. 22
march on, join bravely, let us to it pell-mell; 5.03.312
march patiently along; TRO 5.09. 7
strike a free march. 5.10. 30
that we with smoking swords may march from hence
COR 1.04. 11
please you to march, | and four shall quickly 1.06. 83
march on, my fellows! 1.06. 85
march to assault thy country than to tread 5.03.123
they hither march amain, under conduct | of TIT 4.04. 65
march away. 5.01.165
march, noble lord, | into our city with thy TIM 5.04. 29
beware the ides of march. JC 1.02. 18
a soothsayer bids you beware the ides of march. 1.02. 19
beware the ides of march. 1.02. 23
is not to-morrow, boy, the /ides of march? 2.01. 40
sir, march is wasted fifteen days. 2.01. 59
the ides of march are come. 3.01. 1
march gently on to meet him. 4.02. 31
remember march, the ides of march remember: 4.03. 18
remember march, the ides of march remember: 4.03. 18
must end that work the ides of march begun. 5.01.113
march we on | to give obedience where 'tis truly MAC 5.02. 25
make we our march towards birnan. 5.02. 31
majesty of buried denmark | did sometimes march?
HAM 1.01. 49
and with solemn march | goes slow and stately by 1.02.201
craves the conveyance of a promis'd march | over 4.04. 3
come, march to wakes and fairs and market towns.
LR 3.06. 74 P
through alexandria make a jolly march, | bear ANT 4.08. 30
so through lud's-town march, | and in the temple CYM 5.05.481
comes i' th' nick, as mad as a march hare. TNK 3.05. 73
and in thy name | to my design march boldly. 5.01. 68
and let thy musty vapors march so thick | that LUC 782
brought | to march in ranks of better equipage; SON 32.12
MARCH-CHICK 1 FR 0.0001 REL FR 0 V 1 P
a very forward march-chick! ADO 1.03. 56 P
MARCH'D 11 FR 0.0012 REL FR 11 V 0 P
have hither march'd to your endamagement. JN 2.01.209
armors, that march'd hence so silver-bright, 2.01.315
did display them when we first march'd forth; 2.01.320
horse, | are march'd up to my lord of lancaster, 2H4 2.01.174
that he is march'd to burdeaux with his power 1H6 4.03. 4
as he march'd along, | by your espials were 4.03. 5
march'd through the city to the palace gates. 3H6 1.01. 92
march'd toward saint albons to intercept the 2.01.114
land | have we march'd on without impediment; R3 5.02. 4
smoking with pride, march'd on, to make his LUC 438
their brave hope, bold hector, march'd to field, 1430
MARCHES* 6 FR 0.0006 REL FR 5 V 1 P
his marches are expedient to this town, | his JN 2.01. 60
to stop their marches 'fore we are inflam'd. 5.01. 7
they of those marches, gracious sovereign, H5 1.02.140
charge that, in our marches through the country, 3.06.108 P
for in the marches here we heard you were, 3H6 2.01.140
our dreadful marches to delightful measures. R3 1.01. 8
MARCHETH 3 FR 0.0003 REL FR 3 V 0 P
us | that thus he marcheth with thee arm in arm? 2H6 5.01. 57
the drum your honor hears marcheth from warwick.
3H6 5.01. 13
led, | the roman lord marcheth to lucrece' bed. LUC 301
MARCHING 12 FR 0.0013 REL FR 11 V 1 P
is marching hitherwards, with him prince john. 1H4 4.01. 89
the king hath many marching in his coats. 5.03. 25
with rainy marching in the painful field; H5 4.03.111
their powers are marching unto paris-ward. 1H6 3.03. 30
for i am marching hence. 3.03. 39
kerns | is marching hitherward in proud array, 2H6 4.09. 27
when i have been dry and bravely marching, it 4.10. 13 P
by this at dunsmore, marching hitherward. 3H6 5.01. 3
you think | of marching to philippi presently? JC 4.03.197
the enemy, marching along by them, | by them 4.03.207
the british pow'rs are marching hitherward. LR 4.04. 21
pale cowards, marching on with trembling paces, LUC 1391
MARCHIONESS 3 FR 0.0003 REL FR 3 V 0 P
no less flowing | than marchioness of pembroke; H8 2.03. 63
the marchioness of pembroke? 2.03. 94
the marchioness of pembroke? 3.02. 90
MARCHPANE 1 FR 0.0001 REL FR 0 V 1 P
good thou, save me a piece of marchpane, and, as
ROM 1.05. 8 P
MARCIANS *(see martians)*
MARCIUS' *(see martius', etc.)*
/MARCUS 5 FR 0.0005 REL FR 5 V 0 P
/marcus, /unknit /that //sorrow-wreathen /knot; TIT 3.02. 4
/why, /marcus, /no /man /should /be /mad /but /i 3.02. 24
/if /marcus /did /not /name /the /word /of 3.02. 33
/hark, /marcus, /what /she /says; 3.02. 35
/what /dost /thou /strike /at, /marcus, /with 3.02. 52
MARCUS 47 FR 0.0053 REL FR 45 V 2 P
he kill'd my cousin marcus! COR 5.06.122 P
marcus andronicus, so i do affy | in thy TIT 1.01. 47
thanks, gentle tribune, noble brother marcus. 1.01.171
marcus! 1.01.364
suffer thy brother marcus to inter | his noble 1.01.375
rise, marcus, rise. 1.01.383
i know not, marcus, but i know it is | (whether 1.01.394
marcus, for thy sake and thy brother's here, 1.01.482
but who comes with our brother marcus here? 3.01. 58
why, marcus, so she is. 3.01. 63
look, marcus! 3.01.110
ah, marcus, marcus! 3.01.139
ah, marcus, marcus! 3.01.139
mark, marcus, mark! 3.01.143
let marcus, lucius, or thyself, old titus, | or 3.01.152
good uncle marcus, see how swift she comes. 4.01. 3
sweet aunt, | and, madam, if my uncle marcus go, 4.01. 27
marcus, what means this? 4.01. 30
you are a young huntsman, marcus, let alone; 4.01.101
marcus, look to my house, | lucius and i'll go 4.01.120
marcus, attend him in his ecstasy, | that hath 4.01.125
come, marcus, come; 4.03. 1
be you rememb'red, marcus, she's gone, she's 4.03. 5
marcus, we are but shrubs, no cedars we, | no 4.03. 46
but metal, marcus, steel to the very back, | yet 4.03. 48
you are a good archer, marcus; 4.03. 53
marcus, loose when i bid. 4.03. 59
marcus, the post is come. 4.03. 78
here, marcus, fold it in the oration, | for 4.03.116
come, marcus, let us go. publius, follow me. 4.03.121
pledges | unto my father and my uncle marcus, 5.01.164
marcus, my brother! 5.02.121
go, gentle marcus, to thy nephew lucius; 5.02.122
uncle marcus, since 'tis my father's mind | that 5.03. 1
marcus, we will. 5.03. 25
kiss, | thy brother marcus tenders on thy lips. 5.03.157
first, marcus brutus, will i shake with you; JC 3.01.185
when marcus brutus grows so covetous | to lock 4.03. 79
i am the son of marcus cato, ho! 5.04. 4
i am the son of marcus cato, ho! 5.04. 6
and i am brutus, marcus brutus, i, | brutus, my 5.04. 7
marcus luccicos, is not he in town? OTH 1.03. 44
but she is now the wife of marcus antonius. ANT 2.06.112 P
pleas'd fortune does of marcus crassus' death 3.01. 2
pacorus, orodes, | pays this for marcus crassus. 3.01. 5
marcus octavius, marcus justeius, | publicola, 3.07. 72
marcus octavius, marcus justeius, | publicola, 3.07. 72
MARDIAN 4 FR 0.0004 REL FR 4 V 0 P
thou, eunuch mardian! ANT 1.05. 8
my arm is sore, best play with mardian. 2.05. 4
mardian, go tell him i have slain myself; 4.13. 7
hence, mardian, | and bring me how he takes my 4.13. 9
/MARE* 1 FR 0.0001 REL FR 0 V 1 P
though patience be a tir'd /mare, yet she will H5 2.01. 23 P
MARE* 6 FR 0.0006 REL FR 4 V 2 P
the man shall have his mare again, and all shall MND 3.02.463
or i will ride thee a' nights like the mare. 2H4 2.01. 77 P
i think i am as like to ride the mare, if i have 2.01. 78 P
you know | the chestnut mare the duke has? TNK 5.02. 61
in 's neighing able to entice | a miller's mare, 5.02. 67
care, | is how to get my palfrey from the mare." VEN 384
MARE'S 1 FR 0.0001 REL FR 0 V 1 P
how now, whose mare's dead? what's the matter? 2H4 2.01. 43 P
MARES 2 FR 0.0002 REL FR 2 V 0 P
we should serve with horse and mares together, ANT 3.07. 7
the mares would bear | a soldier and his horse. 3.07. 8
MARGARELON 1 FR 0.0001 REL FR 1 V 0 P
bastard margarelon | hath doreus prisoner, | and TRO 5.05. 7
MARGARET *(also marg'ret)*

/MARGARET 3 FR 0.0003 REL FR 3 V 0 P
why then dame /margaret was ne'er thy joy. 2H6 3.02. 79
they, | might in thy palace perish /margaret. 3.02.100
die, /margaret! 3.02.120
MARGARET 67 FR 0.0075 REL FR 54 V 13 P
how much i am in the favor of margaret, the ADO 2.02. 13 P
her chamber–window, hear me call margaret hero, 2.02. 43 P
margaret hero, hear margaret term me claudio; 2.02. 44 P
good margaret, run thee to the parlor, | there 3.01. 1
hero and margaret have by this play'd their 3.02. 76 P
but know that i have to–night woo'd margaret, 3.03.145 P
and thought they margaret was hero? 3.03.153 P
but the devil my master knew she was margaret; 3.03.155 P
and saw me court margaret in hero's garments, 5.01.238 P
man | shall face to face be brought to margaret, 5.01.298
we'll talk with margaret, | how her acquaintance 5.01.331
pray thee, sweet mistress margaret, deserve well 5.02. 1 P
in so high a style, margaret, that no man living 5.02. 6 P
a most manly wit, margaret, it will not hurt a 5.02. 15 P
if you use them, margaret, you must put in the 5.02. 20 P
but margaret was in some fault for this, 5.04. 4
why then my cousin, margaret, and ursula | are 5.04. 78
margaret my name, and daughter to a king, | the 1H6 5.03. 51
a wife, | then how can margaret be thy paramour? 5.03. 82
i'll win this lady margaret. 5.03. 88
fair margaret knows | that suffolk doth not 5.03.141
prayers | shall suffolk ever have of margaret. 5.03.174
but hark you, margaret, | no princely 5.03.175
of beauteous margaret hath astonish'd me. 5.05. 2
why, what, i pray, is margaret more than that? 5.05. 36
but margaret, that is daughter to a king? 5.05. 67
lady of so high resolve | (as is fair margaret) 5.05. 76
conclude with me | that margaret shall be queen, 5.05. 78
that lady margaret do vouchsafe to come | to 5.05. 89
margaret shall now be queen, and rule the king; 5.05.107
to marry princess margaret for your grace; 2H6 1.01. 4
welcome, queen margaret, | i can express no 1.01. 17
long live queen margaret, england's happiness! 1.01. 37
the said henry shall espouse the lady margaret, 1.01. 47 P
where henry and dame margaret kneel'd to me, 1.02. 39
why, now is henry king and margaret queen, | and 2.03. 39
ay, margaret; 3.01.198
that these great lords, and margaret our queen, 3.01.207
when i have feasted with queen margaret? 4.01. 58
come, margaret, god, our hope, will succor us. 4.04. 55
can we outrun the heavens? good margaret, stay. 5.02. 73
pardon me, margaret, pardon me, sweet son, | the 3H6 1.01.228
stay, gentle margaret, and hear me speak. 1.01.257
for margaret my queen, and clifford too, | have 2.05. 16
where's captain margaret, to fence you now? 2.06. 75
by this account then, margaret may win him, 3.01. 35
o margaret, thus 'twill be, and thou, poor soul, 3.01. 53
fair queen of england, worthy margaret, | sit 3.03. 1
now margaret | must strike her sail and learn a 3.03. 4
be plain, queen margaret, and tell thy grief; 3.03. 19
this is the cause that i, poor margaret, | with 3.03. 30
injurious margaret! 3.03. 78
queen margaret, prince edward, and oxford, 3.03.109
draw near, queen margaret, and be a witness 3.03.138
and still is friend to him and margaret. 3.03.144
but say, is warwick friends with margaret? 4.01.115
that margaret your queen and my son edward | be 4.06. 60
what will your grace have done with margaret? 5.07. 37
queen margaret saw | thy murd'rous falchion R3 1.02. 93
margaret. 1.03.233
'tis done by me, and ends in "margaret." 1.03.238
and say poor margaret was a prophetess! 1.03.300
o margaret, margaret, now thy heavy curse | is 3.04. 92
o margaret, margaret, now thy heavy curse | is 3.04. 92
withdraw thee, wretched margaret; 4.04. 8
as sometimes margaret | did to thy father, 4.04.274
sorrow, | remember margaret was a prophetess." 5.01. 27
MARGARET'S 5 FR 0.0005 REL FR 5 V 0 P
and mine with hers, and thine, and margaret's. 3H6 3.03.218
in margaret's battle at saint albons slain? R3 1.03.129
now margaret's curse is fall'n upon our heads, 3.03. 15
and make me die the thrall of margaret's curse, 4.01. 45
thus margaret's curse falls heavy on my neck: 5.01. 25
MARGENT 6 FR 0.0006 REL FR 5 V 1 P
his face's own margent did cote such amazes LLL 2.01.246
writ a' both sides the leaf, margent and all, 5.02. 8
brook, | or in the beached margent of the sea, MND 2.01. 85
lies | find written in the margent of his eyes. ROM 1.03. 86
must be edified by the margent ere you had done.
HAM 5.02.155 P
threw, | upon whose weeping margent she was set,
LC 39
MARGENTS 1 FR 0.0001 REL FR 1 V 0 P
writ in the glassy margents of such books. LUC 102
MARGERY 5 FR 0.0005 REL FR 3 V 2 P
lov'd mall, meg, and marian, and margery, | but TMP 2.02. 48
and i am sure margery your wife is my mother. MV 2.02. 89 P
her name is margery indeed. 2.02. 91 P
been so tenderly officious | with lady margery, WT 2.03.160
thou as yet conferr'd | with margery jordan, the 2H6 1.02. 75
MARGIN *(see margent, etc.)*
MARG'RET *(also margaret)*
MARG'RET 1 FR 0.0001 REL FR 1 V 0 P
that marg'ret may be england's royal queen. 1H6 5.05. 24
MARIA 8 FR 0.0009 REL FR 5 V 3 P
o sweet maria, empress of my love, | these LLL 4.03. 54
you do not love maria? 4.03.131
what says maria? 5.02.833
a stope of wine, maria! TN 2.03.120 P
maria once told me she did affect me, and i have 2.05. 23 P
good maria, let this fellow be look'd to. 3.04. 60 P
maria writ | the letter at sir toby's great 5.01.362
jesu maria, what a deal of brine | hath wash'd ROM 2.03. 69
MARIAN 5 FR 0.0005 REL FR 2 V 3 P
lov'd mall, meg, and marian, and margery, | but TMP 2.02. 48
maud, bridget, marian, cic'ly, gillian, ginn! ERR 3.01. 31
ask marian hacket, the fat ale–wife of wincot, SHR in.2. 21 P
marian, i say! TN 2.03. 14 P
maid marian may be the deputy's wife of the ward
1H4 3.03.114 P
MARIANA 6 FR 0.0006 REL FR 3 V 3 P
have you not heard speak of mariana, the sister MM 3.01.209 P
honor untainted, the poor mariana advantag'd, 3.01.254 P
moated grange, resides this dejected mariana. 3.01.265 P
i have not yet made known to mariana | a word of 4.01. 48
come hither, mariana. 5.01.374
joy to you, mariana! 5.01.526
MARIANA'S 2 FR 0.0002 REL FR 2 V 0 P
his company | at mariana's house to–night. MM 4.03.140
honor, you must pardon | for mariana's sake; 5.01.403
MARIAN'S 1 FR 0.0001 REL FR 1 V 0 P
the snow | and marian's nose looks red and raw; LLL 5.02.924
MARIA'S 1 FR 0.0001 REL FR 1 V 0 P
but out of question 'tis maria's hand. TN 5.01.347
MARIGOLD 2 FR 0.0002 REL FR 2 V 0 P
the marigold, that goes to bed wi' th' sun | and WT 4.04.105
spread | but as the marigold at the sun's eye, SON 25. 6
MARIGOLDS 3 FR 0.0003 REL FR 3 V 0 P
and marigolds | shall as a carpet hang upon thy PER 4.01. 15
growing, | marigolds on death–beds blowing, TNK 1.01. 11
her eyes like marigolds had sheath'd their light LUC 397
MARINA 23 FR 0.0026 REL FR 23 V 0 P
my gentle babe marina, whom, | for she was born PER 3.03. 12
now to marina bend your mind, | whom our 4.ch. 5
in our story, she | would ever with marina be: 4.ch. 20
contends in skill | with absolute marina: 4.ch. 31
marina gets | all praises, which are paid as 4.ch. 33
present murderer does prepare | for good marina, 4.ch. 39
how now, marina, why do you keep alone? 4.01. 21
pirate valdes, | and they have seiz'd marina. 4.01. 97
please you wit | the epitaph is for marina writ 4.04. 32
marina was she call'd, and at her birth, 4.04. 38
marina thus the brothel scapes, and chances 5.ch. 1
my name is marina. 5.01.142
thou dost startle me | to call thyself marina. 5.01.147
how, a king's daughter? | and call'd marina? 5.01.150
and wherefore call'd marina? 5.01.155
call'd marina | for i was born at sea. 5.01.155
this is marina. 5.01.199
tell helicanus, my marina, tell him | o'er, 5.01.224
list, my marina. 5.01.229
come, my marina. 5.01.264
he is promis'd to be wived | to fair marina, but 5.02. 11
but brought forth | a maid–child call'd marina, 5.03. 6
and call'd marina | for she was yielded there. 5.03. 47
MARINA'S 2 FR 0.0002 REL FR 2 V 0 P
marina's life | /seeks to take off by treason's PER 4.ch. 13
on her, | but cast their gazes on marina's face; 4.03. 33
MARINER 3 FR 0.0003 REL FR 3 V 0 P
i thank thee. mariner, say, what coast is this? PER 3.01. 72
thither, gentle mariner, | alter thy course for 3.01. 74
go thy ways, good mariner, | i'll bring the body 3.01. 80
MARINERS 6 FR 0.0006 REL FR 5 V 1 P
speak to th' mariners. TMP 1.01. 3 P
all but mariners | plung'd in the foaming brine, 1.02.210
the mariners, say how thou hast dispos'd, | and 1.02.225
the mariners all under hatches stowed, | who, 1.02.230
there shalt thou find the mariners asleep 5.01. 98
your mariners are /muleters, reapers, people ANT 3.07. 35
MARITIME 1 FR 0.0001 REL FR 1 V 0 P
the borders maritime | lack blood to think on't, ANT 1.04. 51
MARJEROM 1 FR 0.0001 REL FR 1 V 0 P
and buds of marjerom had stol'n thy hair; SON 99. 7
MARJOROM 1 FR 0.0001 REL FR 0 V 1 P
sir, she was the sweet marjorom of the sallet, AWW 4.05. 16 P
MARJORUM 2 FR 0.0002 REL FR 1 V 1 P
hot lavender, mints, savory, marjorum, | the WT 4.04.104
sweet marjorum. LR 4.06. 93 P
/MARK* 5 FR 0.0005 REL FR 5 V 0 P
/now /mark /me /how /i /will /undo /myself: R2 4.01.203
/mark, /silent /king, /the /moral /of /this 4.01.290
/he /was /the /mark /and /glass, /copy /and 2H4 2.03. 31
to /mark /the full–fraught man and best indued H5 2.02.139
/mark /the /high /noises, /and /thyself /bewray LR 3.06.111
MARK* 240 FR 0.0271 REL FR 183 V 57 P
methinks he hath no drowning mark upon him, his
TMP 1.01. 29 P
i pray thee mark me — that a brother should 1.02. 67
i pray thee mark me. 1.02. 88
mark his condition, and th' event, then tell me 1.02.117
nor set | a mark so bloody on the business; 1.02.142
and — do you mark me, sir? 2.01.170
mark but the badges of these men, my lords, 5.01.267
mark the moan she makes. TGV 2.03. 30 P
he had not been there (bless the mark!) 4.04. 19 P
did not i bid thee still mark me and do as i do? 4.04. 36 P
but mark the sequel, master /brook. WIV 3.05.107 P
pray you mark; 4.01. 43 P
doth your honor mark his face? MM 2.01.149 P
nay, i beseech you mark it well. 2.01.151 P
but mark me: 2.04. 81
but mark how heavily this befell to the poor 3.01.218 P
mark what i say, which you shall find | by every 4.03.125
in a barber's shop, | as much in mark as mark. 5.01.322
as, the mark of my shoulder, the mole in my neck ERR 3.02.142 P
mark, how he trembles in his ecstasy! 4.04. 51
but on my allegiance, mark you this, on my ADO 1.01.211 P
mark how short his answer is: 1.01.213 P
upon me that i stood like a man at a mark, with 2.01.246 P
a mark marvellous well shot, for they both did LLL 4.01.130
a mark! 4.01.131
o, mark but that mark! 4.01.131
o, mark but that mark! 4.01.131
a mark, says my lady! 4.01.131
let the mark have a prick in't, to mete at, if 4.01.132
if knowledge be the mark, to know thee shall 4.02.111
once more i'll mark how love can vary wit. 4.03. 98
they do not mark me, and that brings me out. 5.02.173
i'll mark no words that smooth–fac'd wooers say. 5.02.828
grey, | whose note full many a man doth mark, MND 3.01.132
fairy king, attend and mark; 4.01. 93
and mark the musical confusion | of hounds and 4.01.110
but mark, poor knight, | what dreadful dole is 5.01.277
nor mark prodigious, such as are | despised in 5.01.412
mark what jacob did: MV 1.03. 77
mark you this, bassanio, | the devil can cite 1.03. 97
who, god bless the mark, is a kind of devil; 2.02. 24 P
mark me now, now will i raise the waters. 2.02. 49 P
some mark of virtue on his outward parts. 3.02. 82
o upright judge! mark, jew: o learned judge! 4.01.313
o learned judge! mark, jew, a learned judge! 4.01.317
mark the music. 5.01. 88
mark you but that! 5.01.243
and i shall conduct you, | if you will mark it. AYL 3.04. 56
mark how the tyrant writes. 4.03. 39
and mark what object did present itself | under 4.03.103
stand by and mark the manner of his teaching. SHR 4.02. 5
fair eyes, to be the mark | of smoky muskets? AWW 3.02.107
mark it, cesario, it is old and plain. TN 2.04. 43
sport, mark his first approach before my lady. 2.05.198 P
therefore mark my counsel, | which must be ev'n WT 1.02.408
you, my lords, | look on her, mark her well; 2.01. 65
mark and perform it — seest thou? 2.03.170
the gracious mark o' th' land, you have obscur'd 4.04. 8
come, come, he must not. | mark our contract. 4.04.417
mark your divorce, young sir, | whom son i dare 4.04.417
mark thou my words. 4.04.431
ghost that walk'd, i'ld bid you mark | her eye, 5.01. 63
therefore follow me | and mark what way i make. 5.01.233
mark a little while. 5.03.118
mark how they whisper. JN 2.01.475
and therefore mark: 3.04.130
do i turn to thee, | and mark my greeting well; R2 1.01. 36
march on, and mark king richard how he looks. 3.03. 61
didst thou not mark the king, what words he 5.04. 1
guns, and drums, and wounds, god save the mark!
1H4 1.03. 56
ay, and mark thee too, jack. 2.04.210 P
mark, jack. 2.04.252 P
mark now how a plain tale shall put you down. 2.04.254 P
but | mark how he bears his course, and runs me 3.01.107
but in the way of bargain, mark ye me, | i'll 3.01.137
a fellow of no mark nor likelihood. 3.02. 45
seal–ring of my grandfather's worth forty mark. 3.03. 82 P
a hundred mark is a long one for a poor lone 2H4 2.01. 32 P
he presents no mark to the enemy, the foeman may 3.02.266 P
by, and do but mark the countenance that he will 5.05. 7 P
arrows loosed several ways | come to one mark; H5 1.02.208
he is as valiant a man as mark antony, and he is 3.06. 14 P
mark then abounding valor in our english: 4.03.104
perpend my words, o signieur dew, and mark: 4.04. 8
'tis as arrant a piece of knavery, mark you now, 4.07. 3 P
if you mark alexander's life well, harry of 4.07. 31 P
it is not well done, mark you now, to take the 4.07. 42 P
but mark: 1H6 2.05. 79
and if your grace mark every circumstance, | you 3.01.152
call we to mind, and mark but this for proof: 3.03. 68
for that's the golden mark i seek to hit. 2H6 1.01.243
or hast thou a mark to thyself, like a honest 4.02.103 P
nay, mark how lewis stamps as he were nettled. 3H6 3.03.169
may move your hearts to pity if you mark him. R3 1.03.348
and mark how well the sequel hangs together: 3.06. 4
i think you have hit the mark; H8 2.01.165
then mark th' inducement. 2.04.170
mark but my fall, and that that ruin'd me: 3.02.439
mark her eyes! 4.02. 98
they pass by, but mark troilus above the rest. TRO 1.02.183 P
but mark troilus; 1.02.187 P
mark him, note him. 1.02.231 P
stand, thou greek, thou art a goodly mark. 5.06. 27
about me, you my myrmidons, | mark what i say. 5.07. 2
my good friends, this says the belly, mark me. COR 1.01.141
mark me, and do the like. 1.04. 45
for rome, he fought | beyond the mark of others. 2.02. 89
death's stamp, | where it did mark, it took; 2.02.108
mark you that. 2.02.146
and in the gown of humility, mark his behavior. 2.03. 40 P
mark you | his absolute "shall"? 3.01. 89
mark you this, people? 3.03. 74
and you volsces, mark, for we'll | hear nought 5.03. 92
mark what mercy his mother shall bring from him. 5.04. 26 P
let us sit down and mark their yellowing noise; TIT 2.03. 20
if they did hear, | they would not mark me; 3.01. 34
if they did mark, | they would not pity me; 3.01. 34
mark, marcus, mark! 3.01.143
mark, marcus, mark! 3.01.143
a right fair mark, fair coz, is soonest hit. ROM 1.01.207
god mark thee to his grace! 1.03. 59
if love be blind, love cannot hit the mark. 2.01. 33
thou dost not mark me. 2.04.176 P
i saw it with mine eyes — | god save the mark! 3.02. 53
son paris' love, | and bid her — mark you me? 3.04. 17
bounties over me | to mark me for his friend; TIM 3.02. 79
mark how strange it shows, | timon in this 3.04. 21
this, | whose fall the mark of his ambition is. 5.03. 10
fit was on him, i did mark | how he did shake — JC 1.02.120
tongue of his that bade the romans | mark him, 1.02.126
it was mere foolery, i did not mark it. 1.02.236 P
i saw mark antony offer him a crown — yet 'twas 1.02.236 P
i may discover them | by any mark of favor. 2.01. 76
mark antony, so well belov'd of caesar, | should 2.01.156
and for mark antony, think not of him; 2.01.181
we'll send mark antony to the senate–house, 2.02. 52
mark antony shall say i am not well, | and, for 2.02. 55
mark well metellus cimber; 2.03. 3 P
look how he makes to caesar; mark him. 3.01. 18
brutus, | he draws mark antony out of the way. 3.01. 26
thus did mark antony bid me fall down; 3.01.124
mark antony shall not love caesar dead | so well 3.01.133
but here comes antony. welcome, mark antony! 3.01.147
you our swords have leaden points, mark antony; 3.01.173
mark antony — 3.01.211
you shall, mark antony. 3.01.231
mark antony, here take you caesar's body. 3.01.244
i do, mark antony. 3.01.277
here comes his body, mourn'd by mark antony, who 3.02. 41 P
tending to caesar's glories, which mark antony 3.02. 58
stay ho, and let us hear mark antony. 3.02. 62
now mark him, he begins again to speak. 3.02.117
we'll hear the will. read it, mark antony. 3.02.138
mark how the blood of caesar followed it, | as 3.02.178
live, | who is your sister's son, mark antony. 4.01. 5
and grief that young octavius with mark antony 4.03.153
that young octavius and mark antony | come down 4.03.168
mark antony, shall we give sign of battle? 5.01. 23
mark antony is in your tents, my lord; 5.03. 10
more than octavius and mark antony | by this 5.05. 37
mark, king of scotland, mark! MAC 1.02. 28
mark, king of scotland, mark! 1.02. 28

as it is said | mark antony's was by caesar. 3.01. 56
do you mark that? 5.01. 41 P
looks 'a not like the king? mark it, horatio. HAM 1.01. 43
mark me. 1.05. 2
do you mark this, reynaldo? 2.01. 15
a little soil'd /wi' /th' working, | mark you, 2.01. 41
mine — | who in her duty and obedience, mark, 2.02.107
i behind an arras then, | mark the encounter: 2.02.164
he comes to tell me of the players, mark it. 2.02.387 P
o ho, do you mark that? 3.02.111 P
i'll mark the play. 3.02.147 P
the great man down, you mark his favorite flies, 3.02.204
nay, pray you mark. 4.05. 28 P
pray you mark. 4.05. 35 P
it is, will he, nill he, he goes, mark you that. 5.01. 17 P
couch we a while and mark. 5.01.222
that is laertes, a very noble youth. mark. 5.01.224
mark it, nuncle: LR 1.04.117 P
do you mark that? 1.04.310
do you but mark how this becomes the house! 2.04.153
mark but the penning of it. 4.06.138 P
mark. 4.06.180
mark, i say instantly, and carry it so | as i 5.03. 36
lieutenant be, | and i (/god bless the mark!) OTH 1.01. 33
you shall mark | many a duteous and 1.01. 44
mark me with what violence she first lov'd the 2.01.222 P
didst not mark that? 2.01.255 P
and given up himself to the contemplation, mark, 2.03.317 P
and mark the fleers, the gibes, and notable 4.01. 82
i say, but mark his gesture. 4.01. 87
do but go after, | and mark how he continues. 4.01.281
how much unlike art thou mark antony! ANT 1.05. 35
how goes it with my brave mark antony? 1.05. 38
mark antony | in egypt sits at dinner, and will 2.01. 11
mark antony is every hour in rome | expected. 2.01. 29
great mark antony | is now a widower. 2.02.119
when she first met mark antony, she purs'd up 2.02.186 P
sir, mark antony | will e'en but kiss octavia, 2.04. 2
sirrah, mark, we use | to say the dead are well. 2.05. 32
but mark antony | put me to some impatience. 2.06. 41
we look'd not for mark antony here. 2.06.107 P
which is mark antony. 2.06.125 P
nay, but how dearly he adores mark antony! 3.02. 8
her led | between her brother and mark antony. 3.03. 10
my lord, mark antony, | hearing that you 3.06. 57
you are abus'd | beyond the mark of thought; 3.06. 87
mark antony — 3.13.102
of those that serv'd mark antony but late, 4.01. 13
mark antony i serv'd, who best was worthy | best 5.01. 6
i am again for cydnus | to meet mark antony. 5.02.229
mark it), the eldest of them at three years old, CYM 1.01. 58
a sanguine star, | it was a mark of wonder. 5.05.365
from a well–experienc'd archer hits the mark PER 1.01.162
i know it by this mark. 2.01.138
love, | and that's the mark i know you level at. 2.03.113
mark me: 4.02.116 P
for they were a mark | worth a god's view. TNK 1.04. 20
'hath set a mark which nature could not reach to 1.04. 43
mark how his body's made for't. 2.03. 71
mark how his virtue, like a hidden sun, | breaks 2.05. 23
mark there! 3.05. 17
give me some meditation, | and mark your cue. 3.05. 94
make palamon a nosegay, then let him mark me — 4.03. 27 P
mark him. STM II.C 4 P
this' a sound fellow i tell you, let's mark him. II.C 89 P
which if you will mark | you shall perceive how II.C 91
"didst thou not mark my face? VEN 643
mark the poor wretch, to overshut his troubles, 680
thy mark is feeble age, but thy false dart 941
remain | the scornful mark of every open eye; LUC 520
let him have time to mark how slow time goes 990
with soft slow tongue, true mark of modesty, 1220
if knowledge be the mark, to know thee shall PP 5. 7
while philomela sits and sings, i sit and mark, 14.17
mark how one string, sweet husband to another, SON 8. 9
for slander's mark was ever yet the fair; 70. 2
mark how with my neglect i do dispense: 112.12
o no, it is an ever–fixed mark | that looks on 116. 5

/MARK'D 2 FR 0.0002 REL FR 2 V 0 P
/mark'd /with /a /blot, /damn'd /in /the /book R2 4.01.236
/mark'd he your music? PER 5.01. 80

MARK'D 27 FR 0.0030 REL FR 25 V 2 P
egeon, whom the fates have mark'd | to bear the ERR 1.01.140
which peradventure, not mark'd, or not laugh'd ADO 2.01.147 P
i have mark'd | a thousand blushing apparitions 4.01.158
shrouded in this bush | and mark'd you both, and LLL 4.03.136
yet mark'd i where the bolt of cupid fell. MND 2.01.165
had they mark'd him | in parcels as i did, would AYL 3.05.124
perhaps you mark'd not what's the pith of all. SHR 1.01.166
mark'd you not how her sister | began to scold 1.01.171
by, | a fellow by the hand of nature mark'd, JN 4.02.221
more are men's ends mark'd than their lives R2 2.01. 11
sir, but i mark'd him not, and yet he talk'd 1H4 1.02. 85 P
these signs have mark'd me extraordinary, | and 3.01. 40
and "well, go to," | but mark'd him not a word. 3.01.157
make me believe that thou art only mark'd | for 3.02. 9
if we are mark'd to die, we are enow | to do our H5 4.03. 20
mark'd for the gallows, lay your weapons down, 2H6 4.02.123
mark'd by the destinies to be avoided, | as 3H6 2.02.137
your brother richard mark'd him for the grave, 2.06. 40
mark'd you not | how that the guilty kindred of R3 2.01.135
mark'd you his lip and eyes? COR 1.01.255
to this your son is mark'd, and die he must, TIT 1.01.125
the news, | for villains mark'd with rape. 4.02. 9
mark'd ye his words? JC 3.02.112
when we have mark'd with blood those sleepy two MAC 1.07. 75
that rent the air | are made, not mark'd; 4.03.169
my body's mark'd | with roman swords, and my CYM 3.03. 56
now for the love of him whom jove hath mark'd TNK 1.01. 29

MARKED 2 FR 0.0002 REL FR 2 V 0 P
fool, | much marked of the melancholy jaques, AYL 2.01. 41
that by their witchcraft thus have marked me. R3 3.04. 72

MARKET 16 FR 0.0018 REL FR 9 V 7 P
that you bought, | and he ended the market. LLL 3.01.110 P
it is the right butter–women's rank to market. AYL 3.02. 98 P
talk like the vulgar sort of market men | that 1H6 3.02. 4
poor market folks that come to sell their corn. 3.02. 15
enter, go in, the market bell is rung. 3.02. 16
as market men for oxen, sheep, or horse. 5.05. 54
let them be whipt through every market town, 2H6 2.01.155
but yet i run before my horse to market: R3 1.01.160
why, i can buy me twenty at any market. MAC 4.02. 40
if his chief good and market of his time | be HAM 4.04. 34
come, march to wakes and fairs and market towns. LR 3.06. 75 P
search the market narrowly, meteline is full of PER 4.02. 3 P
but shall i search the market? 4.02. 17 P
but i'll go search the market. 4.02. 25 P
sir, hast thou cried her through the market? 4.02. 93 P
conscience, let him hiss, and kill | our market. TNK ep 9

MARKETABLE 2 FR 0.0002 REL FR 1 V 1 P
them | is a plain fish, and no doubt marketable. TMP 5.01.266
we shall be the more marketable. AYL 1.02. 96 P

MARKET–CROSSES 1 FR 0.0001 REL FR 1 V 0 P
proclaim'd at market–crosses, read in churches, 1H4 5.01. 73

MARKET–DAYS 1 FR 0.0001 REL FR 0 V 1 P
have seen him whipt three market–days together. 2H6 4.02. 58 P

MARKETH 1 FR 0.0001 REL FR 1 V 0 P
this ill presage advisedly she marketh: VEN 457

MARKET–MAID 1 FR 0.0001 REL FR 1 V 0 P
but you are come | a market–maid to rome, and ANT 3.06. 51

MARKET–PLACE 24 FR 0.0027 REL FR 21 V 3 P
me by the hangman's boys in the market–place; TGV 4.04. 56 P
i would eat his heart in the market–place. ADO 4.01.307 P
my father's bears more toward the market–place; SHR 5.01. 9
wade to the market–place in frenchmen's blood, JN 2.01. 42
in open market–place produc'd they me | to be a 1H6 1.04. 40
and here advance it in the market–place, | the 2.02. 5
go sound thy trumpet in the market–place; COR 1.05. 26
never would he | appear i' th' market–place, nor 2.01.233
of our proceedings here on th' market–place; 2.02.159
give way, he shall to th' market–place. 3.01. 31
well, on to th' market–place. 3.01.112
meet on the market–place. 3.01.330
i have been i' th' market–place; 3.02. 93
to th' market–place! 3.02.104
mother, i am going to the market–place; 3.02.131
bid them repair to th' market–place, where i, 5.06. 3
he fell down in the market–place, and foam'd at JC 1.02.252 P
sit | even at noon–day upon the market–place, 1.03. 27
then walk we forth, even to the market–place, 3.01.108
i may | produce his body to the market–place, 3.01.228
i have borne this corse | into the market–place. 3.01.292
and antony | enthron'd i' th' market–place, did ANT 2.02.215
i' th' market–place, on a tribunal silver'd, 3.06. 3
and death's the market–place, where each one TNK 1.05. 16

MARKET–PRICE 1 FR 0.0001 REL FR 1 V 0 P
inferior might | at market–price have bought. AWW 5.03.219

MARKETS 3 FR 0.0003 REL FR 3 V 0 P
at wakes and wassails, meetings, markets, fairs: LLL 5.02.318
sell when you can, you are not for all markets. AYL 3.05. 60
your store | i think is not for idle markets, TN 3.03. 46

MARKING 6 FR 0.0006 REL FR 4 V 2 P
the hearing it, but little of the marking of it. LLL 1.01.286 P
marking th' embarked traders on the flood; MND 2.01.127
lest i, by marking of your rage, forget | your JN 4.03. 85
of not list'ning, the malady of not marking, 2H4 1.02.122 P
she, marking them, begins a wailing note, | and VEN 835
marking what he tells | with trembling fear, as LUC 510

MARK–MAN 1 FR 0.0001 REL FR 1 V 0 P
a right good mark–man! and she's fair i love. ROM 1.01.206

/MARKS* 1 FR 0.0001 REL FR 1 V 0 P
/that, /for /by /the /marks /of /sovereignty, LR 1.04.232

MARKS* 40 FR 0.0045 REL FR 29 V 11 P
marry, by these special marks: TGV 2.01. 18 P
pounds, of which he made five marks ready money. MM 4.03. 7 P
unless a thousand marks be levied | to quit the ERR 1.01. 21
rate, | cannot amount unto a hundred marks, 1.01. 24
where is the thousand marks thou hadst of me? 1.02. 81
i have some marks of yours upon my pate: 1.02. 82
some of my mistress' marks upon my shoulders: 1.02. 83
but not a thousand marks between you both. 1.02. 84
thy mistress' marks? 1.02. 87
he ask'd me for a /thousand marks in gold: 2.01. 61
"where is the thousand marks i gave thee, 2.01. 65
and charg'd him with a thousand marks in gold, 3.01. 8
to her, told me what privy marks i had about me, 3.02.142 P
be talking, signior benedick, nobody marks you. ADO 1.01.117 P
i do spy some marks of love in her. 2.03.245 P
there is none of my uncle's marks upon you. AYL 3.02.369 P
what were his marks? 3.02.372 P
a hundred marks, my kate does put her down. SHR 5.02. 35
full thirty thousand marks of english coin. JN 2.01.530
patch'd with foul moles and eye–offending marks, 3.01. 47
seal of death, | that marks thee out for hell. R2 4.01. 26
brought three hundred marks with him in gold. 1H4 2.01. 56 P
have in this robbery lost three hundred marks. 2.04.520
sav'd me a thousand marks in links and torches, 3.03. 42 P
he that will caper with me for a thousand marks, 2H4 1.02.193 P
we give thee for reward a thousand marks, | and 2H6 5.01. 79
my tears shall wipe away these bloody marks; 3H6 2.05. 71
death, and hell have set their marks on him, R3 1.03.292
give her an hundred marks. i'll to the queen. H8 5.01.170
an hundred marks? 5.01.171
remains | that, in th' official marks invested, COR 2.03.140
he should have show'd us | his marks of merit, 2.03.164
can show /for rome | her enemies' marks upon me. 3.03.111
who marks the waxing tide grow wave by wave, TIT 3.01. 95
than foemen's marks upon his batt'red shield, 4.01.127
nay, some marks | of secret on her person, that CYM 5.05.205
this so darks | in philoten all graceful marks, PER 4.ch. 36
boult, take you the marks of her, the color of 4.02. 57 P
my will that marks thee for my earth's delight, LUC 487
for marks descried in men's nativity | are 538

MARL 1 FR 0.0001 REL FR 0 V 1 P
account of her life to a clod of wayward marl? ADO 2.01. 63 P

MARLE 1 FR 0.0001 REL FR 1 V 0 P
beaumont and marle, vaudemont and lestrake. H5 4.08.100

MARLET *(also martlet)*

/MARLET 1 FR 0.0001 REL FR 1 V 0 P
the temple–haunting /marlet does approve, | by MAC 1.06. 4

MARMAZET 1 FR 0.0001 REL FR 1 V 0 P
thee how | to snare the nimble marmazet. TMP 2.02.170

MARQUESS 11 FR 0.0012 REL FR 10 V 1 P
the happiest gift that ever marquess gave, | the 2H6 1.01. 15
and william de la pole, marquess of suffolk, 1.01. 44 P
lord marquess, kneel down. 1.01. 63
sent from your brother, marquess montague. 3H6 3.03.164
peace, master marquess, you are malapert, | your R3 1.03.254
learn it, learn it, marquess. 1.03.260
hastings, love lord marquess. 2.01. 25
the marquess dorset, as i hear, is fled | to 4.02. 48
sir thomas lovel and lord marquess dorset, 4.04.518
marquess dorset, | and that the earl of surrey, H8 4.01. 38
duchess of norfolk | and lady marquess dorset. 5.02.203

MARQUIS 1 FR 0.0001 REL FR 0 V 1 P
hither in company of the marquis of montferrat? MV 1.02.114 P

MARR'D 13 FR 0.0014 REL FR 12 V 1 P
hush and be mute, | or else our spell is marr'd. TMP 4.01.127
you had marr'd all else. MM 2.02.148
if voluble and sharp discourse be marr'd, ERR 2.01. 92
if he come not, then the play is marr'd. MND 4.02. 5 P
i tell thee, i, that thou hast marr'd her gown. SHR 4.03.114
a young man married is a man that's marr'd; AWW 2.03.298
there all is marr'd; there lies a cooling card. 1H6 5.03. 84
but repetition of what thou hast marr'd, | that R3 1.03.164
this man has marr'd his fortune. COR 3.01.253
and too soon marr'd are those so early made. ROM 1.02. 13
is himself, marr'd as you see with traitors. JC 3.02.197
all that is spoke is marr'd. OTH 5.02.357
to mend the hurt that his unkindness marr'd: VEN 478

MARRIAGE 118 FR 0.0133 REL FR 81 V 37 P
at the marriage of the king's fair daughter TMP 2.01. 70 P
'twas a sweet marriage, and we prosper well in 2.01. 73 P
were at tunis at the marriage of your daughter, 2.01. 98 P
when i wore it at your daughter's marriage? 2.01.106 P
nay more, our marriage hour, | with all the TGV 2.04.179
that done, our day of marriage shall be yours — 5.04.172
and desire a marriage between master abraham and WIV 1.01. 55 P
the question is concerning your marriage. 1.01.221 P
anne page for my master in the way of marriage. 1.04. 84 P
her reputation, her marriage vow, and a thousand 2.02.249 P
which forced marriage would have brought upon 5.05.230
he promis'd her marriage. MM 3.02.201 P
years since there was some speech of marriage 5.01.217
of your honor, | i thought your marriage fit; 5.01.420
match, and yet is she a wondrous fat marriage. ERR 3.02. 93 P
how dost thou mean a fat marriage? 3.02. 94 P
of mad flesh that claims marriage of me, i could 4.04.154 P
give you intelligence of an intended marriage. ADO 1.03. 44 P
name the day of marriage, and god give thee joy! 2.01.300 P
how canst thou cross this marriage? 2.02. 8 P
is in that, to be the death of this marriage? 2.02. 20 P
i will presently go learn their day of marriage. 2.02. 57 P
because i have rail'd so long against marriage; 2.03.237 P
i do but stay till your marriage be consummate, 3.02. 1 P
new gloss of your marriage as to show a child 3.02. 6 P
hath holp to effect your ensuing marriage — 3.02. 99 P
is not marriage honorable in a beggar? 3.04. 30 P
is not your lord honorable without marriage? 3.04. 31 P
only to the plain form of marriage, and you 4.01. 2 P
conjoin'd | in the state of honorable marriage, 5.04. 30
to speak to lady afterward | in way of marriage; MV 2.01. 42
in my life | to woo a maid in way of marriage; 2.09. 13
bridegroom's ear, | and summon him to marriage. 3.02. 53
feast shall be much honored in your marriage. 3.02.212
the contract of her marriage and the day it is AYL 3.02.314 P
must be given, or the marriage is not lawful. 3.03. 69 P
good priest that can tell you what marriage is. 3.03. 86 P
have they made a pair of stairs to marriage, 5.02. 38 P
or else be incontinent before marriage. 5.02. 39 P
according as marriage binds and blood breaks. 5.04. 57 P
to speak the ceremonial rites of marriage? SHR 3.02. 6
woo a thousand, 'point the day of marriage, 3.02. 15
'twere good methinks to steal our marriage, 3.02.140
such a mad marriage never was before. 3.02.182
day, | to pass assurance of a dow'r in marriage 4.02.118
that have by marriage made thy daughter mine, 5.01.116
thy marriage, sooner than thy wickedness. AWW 1.03. 38 P
are, there were no fear in marriage, for young 1.03. 51 P
your marriage comes by destiny, | your cuckoo 1.03. 62
do you know he promis'd me marriage? 5.03.255 P
and of other motions, as promising her marriage, 5.03.264 P
many a good hanging prevents a bad marriage; TN 1.05. 19 P
the rites of marriage shall be solemniz'd. JN 2.01.539
of poor bullingbrook | about his marriage, nor R2 2.01.168
you violate | a twofold marriage — 'twixt my 5.01. 72
by the which marriage the line of charles the H5 1.02. 84
which troubles oft the bed of blessed marriage, 5.02.364
prepare we for our marriage; 5.02.370
his only daughter to your grace | in marriage, 1H6 5.01. 20
marriage, uncle? 5.01. 21
news, | and make this marriage to be solemniz'd. 5.03.168
marriage is a matter of more worth | than to be 5.05. 55
fatal this marriage, cancelling your fame, 2H6 1.01. 99
had henry got an empire by his marriage, | and 1.01.153
i'll cross the sea | to effect this marriage, so 3H6 2.06. 98
sister, | to england's king in lawful marriage. 3.03. 57
that by this league and marriage | thou draw not 3.03. 74
for mocking marriage with a dame of france. 3.03.255
matter of marriage was the charge he gave me, 3.03.258
you | of this new marriage with the lady grey? 4.01. 2
yet hasty marriage seldom proveth well. 4.01. 18
him | about the marriage of the lady bona. 4.01. 31
is now dishonored by this new marriage. 4.01. 33
foreign storms than any home–bred marriage. 4.01. 38
but what said lady bona to my marriage? 4.01. 97
yet in marriage | i may not prove inferior to 4.01.121
his daughter meanly have i match'd in marriage, R3 4.03. 37
with the sweet silent hours of marriage joys; 4.04.330
it seems the marriage with his brother's wife H8 2.02. 16
and despairs, and all these for his marriage. 2.02. 28
this business, | who deem'd our marriage lawful; 2.04. 53
/a marriage 'twixt the duke of orleance and 2.04.175
respecting this our marriage with the dowager, 2.04.181
prove but our marriage lawful, by my life | and 2.04.227
his second marriage shall be publish'd, and 3.02. 68
and the late marriage made of none effect; 4.01. 33
well, think of marriage now; ROM 1.03. 69
thy purpose marriage, send me word to–morrow, 2.02.144
save what thou must combine | by holy marriage. 2.03. 61

what says he of our marriage? 2.05. 47
we can find a time | to blaze your marriage, 3.03.151
delay this marriage for a month, a week, | or, 3.05.199
and in his wisdom hastes our marriage, | to stop 4.01. 11
lest in this marriage he should be dishonor'd 4.03. 26
mean | to rid her from this second marriage, 5.03.241
know, and to the marriage | her nurse is privy; 5.03.265
if in her marriage my consent be missing, | i TIM 1.01.136
within the bond of marriage, tell me, brutus, JC 2.01.280
mirth in funeral, and with dirge in marriage, HAM 1.02. 12
did coldly furnish forth the marriage tables. 1.02.181
even with the vow | i made to her in marriage, 1.05. 50
his father's death and our /o'erhasty marriage. 2.02. 57
i say we will have no moe marriage. 3.01.147 P
the instances that second marriage move | are 3.02.182
makes marriage vows | as false as dicers' oaths, 3.04. 44
so opposite to marriage that she shunn'd | the OTH 1.02. 67
o curse of marriage! 3.03.268
by this marriage, | all little jealousies, which ANT 2.02.130
and though i make this marriage for my peace, 2.03. 40
made more in the marriage than the love of the 2.06.119 P
with marriage wherefore was he mock'd, | to be CYM 5.04. 58
a bedfellow, | in marriage pleasures playfellow; PER 1.ch. 34
by juno, that is queen of marriage, | all viands 2.03. 30
wench, | even /ripe for marriage /rite; 4.ch. 17
sir, by our tie of marriage — TNK 3.06.195
has given a sum of money to her marriage, | a 4.01. 23
this siege that hath engirt his marriage, | this LUC 221
let me not to the marriage of true minds | admit SON 116. 1
MARRIAGE-BED 3 FR 0.0003 REL FR 3 V 0 P
not this, but troubles of the marriage-bed. ERR 2.01. 27
and on the marriage-bed | of smiling peace to JN 3.01.245
i, by the honor of my marriage-bed, | after 5.02. 93
MARRIAGE-BLESSING 1 FR 0.0001 REL FR 1 V 0 P
honor, riches, marriage-blessing, | long TMP 4.01.106
MARRIAGE-DAY 4 FR 0.0004 REL FR 4 V 0 P
stay | to see our widower's second marriage-day. AWW 5.03. 70
and their stol'n marriage-day | was tybalt's ROM 5.03.233
to grace thy marriage-day, i'll beautify. PER 5.03. 76
(whose modest scenes blush on his marriage-day, TNK pr 4
MARRIAGE-DOWRY 1 FR 0.0001 REL FR 0 V 1 P
and sinew of her fortune, her marriage-dowry; MM 3.01.222 P
MARRIAGE-FEAST 2 FR 0.0002 REL FR 2 V 0 P
at a marriage-feast, | between lord perigort and LLL 2.01. 40
breast | of this most pompous marriage-feast. PER 3.ch. 4
MARRIAGES 2 FR 0.0002 REL FR 2 V 0 P
god, the best maker of all marriages, | combine H5 5.02.359
and give out | conjectural marriages, making COR 1.01.194
MARRIED 151 FR 0.0170 REL FR 96 V 55 P
would i had never | married my daughter there! TMP 2.01.109
when we are married and have more occasion to WIV 1.01.248 P
this 'tis to be married! 3.05.142 P
so rails against all married mankind; 4.02. 23 P
her master slender hath married her daughter. 5.05.173 P
if i had been married to him (for all he was in 5.05.191 P
the doctor at the dean'ry, and there married. 5.05.203 P
i ha' married oon garsoon, a boy; 5.05.205 P
you would have married her most shamefully, 5.05.221
respected with him before he married with her. MM 2.01.171 P
respected with her before i was married to her? 2.01.175 P
she should this angelo have married; 3.01.213 P
but if he be a married man, he's his wive's head 4.02. 4 P
they would else have married me to the rotten 4.03.173 P
what, are you married? 5.01.171 P
my lord, i do confess i ne'er was married, | and 5.01.184
whose weakness, married to thy /stronger state, ERR 2.02.175
what, was i married to her in my dream? 2.02.182
"here you may see benedick the married man." ADO 1.01.268 P
if they were but a week married, they would talk 2.01.354 P
did not think i should live till i were married. 2.03.244 P
when are you married, madam? 3.01.100
means your lordship to be married to-morrow? 3.02. 89 P
to be married to her. 4.01. 7 P
you come hither to be married to this count. 4.01. 9 P
not to be married, | not to knit my soul to an 4.01. 43
"here dwells benedick the married man"? 5.01.184 P
how dost thou, benedick, the married man? 5.04. 99
let's have a dance ere we are married, that we 5.04.118 P
cuckoo then on every tree | mocks married men; LLL 5.02.899
o word of fear, | unpleasing to a married ear! 5.02.902
cuckoo then on every tree | mocks married men; 5.02.908
o word of fear, | unpleasing to a married ear! 5.02.911
is two or three lords and ladies more married. MND 4.02. 16 P
i had rather be married to a death's-head with a MV 1.02. 51 P
nerissa, ere i will be married to a spunge. 1.02. 99 P
you | even at that time i may be married too. 3.02.194
i am married to a wife | which is as dear to me 4.01.282
is the forehead of a married man more honorable AYL 3.03. 60 P
will you be married, motley? 3.03. 78 P
breeding, be married under a bush like a beggar? 3.03. 84 P
but i were better to be married of him than of 3.03. 91 P
and not being well married, it will be a good 3.03. 93 P
we must be married, or we must live in bawdry. 3.03. 97
they shall be married to-morrow; 5.02. 42 P
for if you will be married to-morrow, you shall; 5.02. 73 P
i marry woman, and i'll be married to-morrow. 5.02.114 P
man, and you shall be married to-morrow. 5.02.116 P
you, and you shall be married to-morrow. 5.02.118 P
day, audrey, to-morrow will we be married. 5.03. 2 P
any man is so very a fool to be married to hell? SHR 1.01.125 P
when i shall ask the banes, and when be married. 2.01.180
well, | thou must be married to no man but me; 2.01.275
and kiss me, kate, we will be married a' sunday. 2.01.324
know | my daughter katherine is to be married. 2.01.394
that katherine and petruchio should be married, 3.02. 2
to me she's married, not unto my clothes. 3.02.117
oath, | i will be married to a wealthy widow, 4.02. 37
i knew a wench married in an afternoon as she 4.04. 99 P
gentlewoman, | thy son by this hath married. 4.05. 63
have you married my daughter without asking my 5.01.133 P
we three are married, but you two are sped. 5.02.185
your lord and master's married, there's news for AWW 2.03.242 P
o my parolles, they have married me! 2.03.272
a young man married is a man that's marr'd; 2.03.298
for the king had married him | against his 3.05. 53
already, unless thou canst say they are married. 5.03.268 P
lady of the strachy married the yeoman of the TN 2.05. 40 P
having been three months married to her, sitting 2.05. 44 P
sir, till she be married, and fools are as like 3.01. 33 P
in recompense whereof he hath married her. 5.01.364
and married a tinker's wife within a mile where WT 4.03. 97 P
that should have married a shepherd's daughter. 4.04.767 P
and would incense me | to murther her i married. 5.01. 62
you are married? 5.01.204
gone to be married? JN 3.01. 1
of our inward souls | married in league, coupled 3.01.228
against the blood that thou hast married? 3.01.301
me, | and then betwixt me and my married wife. R2 5.01. 73
hear, that earl of march | hath lately married. 1H4 1.03. 85
their spirits are so married in conjunction with 2H4 5.01. 69 P
corporal, that he is married to nell quickly, H5 2.01. 17 P
maids in france to kiss before they are married, 5.02.266 P
a married man! that's most intolerable. 1H6 5.04. 79
who married edmund mortimer, earl of march; 2H6 2.02. 36
married richard earl of cambridge, who was | to 2.02. 45
son | of edmund mortimer, who married philippe, 2.02. 49
for whilest i think i am thy married wife | and 2.04. 28
married the duke of clarence' daughter, did he 4.02.137
there shall not a maid be married, but she shall 4.07.122 P
has your king married the lady grey? 3H6 3.03.174
i must be married to my brother's daughter, | or R3 4.02. 60
single, but now married | to one above itself. H8 1.01. 15
the king already | hath married the fair lady. 3.02. 42
whom the king hath in secrecy long married, 3.02.403
the unity and married calm of states | quite TRO 1.03.100
know thou first, | i lov'd the maid i married; COR 4.05.114
and i might live to see thee married once, | i ROM 1.03. 61
how stands your dispositions to be married? 1.03. 65
examine every married lineament, | and see how 1.03. 83
if he be married, | my grave is like to be my 1.05.134
friar lawrence' cell | be shriv'd and married. 2.04.182
an hour but married, tybalt murdered, | doting 3.03. 66
her, | she shall be married to this noble earl. 3.04. 21
i would the fool were married to her grave! 3.05.140
i think it best you married with the county. 3.05.217
on thursday next be married to this county. 4.01. 49
shall i be married then to-morrow morning? 4.03. 22
because he married me before to romeo? 4.03. 27
she's not well married that lives married long, 4.05. 77
she's not well married that lives married long, 4.05. 77
but she's best married that dies married young. 4.05. 78
but she's best married that dies married young. 4.05. 78
he told me paris should have married juliet. 5.03. 78
i married them, and their stol'n marriage-day 5.03.233
betroth'd and would have married her perforce 5.03.238
are you a married man or a bachelor? JC 3.03. 8 P
am i a married man or a bachelor? 3.03. 14 P
have mourn'd longer — married with my uncle, HAM 1.02.151
the flushing in her galled eyes, | she married. 1.02.156
those that are married already (all but one) 3.01.148 P
are they married, think you? OTH 1.01.167
but i pray you, sir, | are you fast married? 1.02. 11
he's married. 1.02. 52
true i have married her; 1.03. 79
whore of venice | that married with othello. 4.02. 90
let me be married to three kings in a forenoon, ANT 1.02. 27 P
what, says the married woman you may go? 1.03. 20
i am not married, caesar; 2.02.122
madam, he's married to octavia. 2.05. 60
he's married, madam. 2.05. 72
is he married? 2.05. 89
he's married, madam. 2.05. 91
he is married? 2.05. 97
he is married? 2.05. 98
he's married to octavia. 2.05.101
pray you, is he married to cleopatra? 2.06.108 P
he married but his occasion here. 2.06.131 P
like a master | married to your good service, 4.02. 31
sole son — a widow | that late he married), CYM 1.01. 6
hath her | (i mean, that married her, alack, 1.01. 18
it must be married | to that your diamond, i'll 2.04. 97
you married ones, | if each of you should take 5.01. 2
his birth, and in | our temple was he married. 5.04.106
married your royalty, was wife to your place, 5.05. 39
she'll not undertake | a married life. PER 2.05. 4
till she be married, madam, | by bright diana, 3.03. 27
well restor'd, | and to be married shortly. TNK 5.04. 28
not their infirmity, | it was married chastity. PHT 61
by unions married, do offend thine ear, | they SON 8. 6
i grant thou wert not married to my muse, | and 82. 1
MARRIES 3 FR 0.0003 REL FR 2 V 1 P
cries it out, when your brother marries aliena, AYL 5.02. 63 P
that she which marries you must marry me, AWW 5.03.174
young prince edward marries warwick's daughter. 3H6 4.01.117
MARRING 3 FR 0.0003 REL FR 1 V 2 P
it is marring indeed, if he quarter it. WIV 1.01. 26 P
say) will (i doubt) prove mine own marring. 2H4 ep 6 P
as i pleas'd, | making and marring fortunes. ANT 3.11. 65
MARROW 6 FR 0.0006 REL FR 6 V 0 P
home, | spending his manly marrow in her arms, AWW 2.03.281
would he were wasted, marrow, bones, and all, 3H6 3.02.125
when crouching marrow in the bearer strong TIM 5.04. 9
height, | the pith and marrow of our attribute. HAM 1.04. 22
and marrow of my understanding laid upon ye, TNK 3.05. 6
my flesh is soft and plump, my marrow burning, VEN 142
MARROW-EATING 1 FR 0.0001 REL FR 1 V 0 P
the marrow-eating sickness, whose attaint VEN 741
MARROWLESS 1 FR 0.0001 REL FR 1 V 0 P
thy bones are marrowless, thy blood is cold; MAC 3.04. 93
MARROWS 2 FR 0.0002 REL FR 2 V 0 P
creep in the minds and marrows of our youth, TIM 4.01. 26
dry up thy marrows, vines, and plough-torn leas, 4.03.193
/MARRY* 1 FR 0.0001 REL FR 1 V 0 P
/marry, /your /manhood /mew! LR 4.02. 68
MARRY* 382 FR 0.0431 REL FR 164 V 218 P
i am your wife, if you will marry me; TMP 3.01. 83
marry, will i; 3.02. 40 P
marry, sir, the letter, very orderly, having TGV 1.01.123 P
marry, by these special marks: 2.01. 18 P
marry, sir, so painted to make her fair, that no 2.01. 59 P
marry, after they clos'd in earnest, they parted 2.05. 12 P
but shall she marry him? 2.05. 14 P
how then? shall he marry her? 2.05. 16 P
marry, thus: 2.05. 22 P
marry, the son of my grandfather. 3.01.295 P
marry, mine host, because i cannot be merry. 4.02. 28 P
marry, at my house. 4.02.137 P
nor how my father would enforce me marry | vain 4.03. 16
"ay, marry, do i," quoth he. 4.04. 26 P
marry, sir, i carried mistress silvia the dog 4.04. 45 P
marry, she says your dog was a cur, and tells 4.04. 48 P
marry, sir, i have matter in my head against you WIV 1.01.123 P
i will say "marry trap" with you, if you run the 1.01.167 P
marry, this, coz: 1.01.207 P
marry, is it; 1.01.223 P
i will marry her upon any reasonable demands. 1.01.225 P
will you, upon good dowry, marry her? 1.01.239 P
i will marry her, sir, at your request; 1.01.245 P
but if you say, "marry her," i will marry her; 1.01.250 P
but if you say, "marry her," i will marry her; 1.01.251 P
yes, marry, have i, what of that? 1.04.148 P
marry, were they. 2.01.178 P
ay, marry, does he. 2.01.181 P
marry, this is the short and the long of it: 2.02. 59 P
marry, she hath receiv'd your letter — for the 2.02. 81 P
marry, sir, the pittie-ward, the park-ward — 3.01. 5 P
if your husbands were dead, you two would marry. 3.02. 15 P
marry, as i told you before, john and robert, be 3.03. 9 P
marry, i thank you for it; 3.04. 52 P
good mother, do not marry me to yond fool. 3.04. 83
marry, sir, i come to your worship from mistress 3.05. 33 P
marry, this is our device: 4.04. 41
steal my nan away, | and marry her at eton. 4.04. 75
will, | and none but he, to marry with nan page. 4.04. 85
marry, sir, i come to speak with sir john 4.05. 4 P
ay, marry, was it, mussel-shell, what would you 4.05. 28 P
marry, she says that the very same man that 4.05. 36 P
and with him at eton | immediately to marry. 4.06. 25
where a priest attends, | straight marry her. 4.06. 32
marry, sir, we'll bring you to windsor, to one 5.05.165 P
came yonder at eton to marry mistress anne page, 5.05.183 P
marry, sir, that's claudio, signior claudio. MM 1.02. 64 P
o, let him marry her. 1.04. 49
marry, sir, by my wife, who, if she had been a 2.01. 79 P
marry, i thank your good worship for it. 2.01.182 P
marry, i thank your worship for it. 2.01.189 P
marry, sir, he hath offended the law; 3.02. 15 P
marry, this claudio is condemn'd for untrussing. 3.02.179 P
marry, then ginger was not much in request, for 4.03. 7 P
yes, marry, did i; 4.03.172 P
marry, sir, i think, if you handled her 5.01.275 P
go take her hence, and marry her instantly. 5.01.377
let her appear, | and he shall marry her. 5.01.512
your highness do not marry me to a whore. 5.01.514 P
upon mine honor, thou shalt marry her. 5.01.518
well, i will marry one day, but to try. ERR 2.01. 42
marry, sir, for this something that you gave me 2.02. 51 P
marry, sir, by a rule as plain as the plain bald 2.02. 69 P
marry, and did, sir: 2.02.102 P
marry, so it doth appear | by the wrongs i 3.01. 15
marry, sir, besides myself, i am due to a woman: 3.02. 81 P
marry, sir, such claim as you would lay to your 3.02. 85 P
marry, sir, she's the kitchen wench and all 3.02. 95 P
marry, sir, in her buttocks, i found it out by 3.02.117 P
marry, he must have a long spoon that must eat 4.03. 63 P
marry, it is your brother's right hand. ADO 1.03. 49 P
marry, one hero, the daughter and heir of 1.03. 54 P
i too, and he swore he would marry her to-night. 2.01.169 P
i would not marry her, though she were endow'd 2.01.251 P
marry, once before he won it of me with false 2.01.280 P
the count claudio shall marry the daughter of 2.02. 1 P
yea, marry, dost thou hear, balthasar? 2.03. 84 P
i did never think to marry. 2.03.228 P
any thing to-night why i should not marry her, 3.02.124 P
marry, not without the prince be willing, for 3.03. 79 P
he swore he would never marry, and yet now in 3.04. 88 P
marry, sir, i would have some confidence with 3.05. 2 P
marry, this it is, sir. 3.05. 6 P
marry, sir, our watch to-night, excepting your 3.05. 30 P
you come hither, my lord, to marry this lady. 4.01. 4 P
friar, you come to marry her. 4.01. 8 P
marry, that can hero, | hero itself can blot out 4.01. 81
marry, this well carried shall on her behalf 4.01.210
marry, that am i and my partner. 4.02. 4 P
yea, marry, let them come before me. 4.02. 9 P
marry, sir, we say we are none. 4.02. 24 P
yea, marry, that's the eftest way; 4.02. 36 P
marry, that he had receiv'd a thousand ducats of 4.02. 47 P
before the whole assembly, and not marry her. 4.02. 55 P
marry, thou dost wrong me, thou dissembler, thou 5.01. 53
marry, beshrew my hand, | if it should give your 5.01. 55
marry, sir, they have committed false report; 5.01.215 P
how you disgrac'd her when you should marry her. 5.01.239 P
marry, i cannot show it in rhyme; 5.02. 36 P
to-day to marry with my brother's daughter? 5.04. 37
before this friar, and swear to marry her. 5.04. 57
brief, since i do purpose to marry, i will think 5.04.105 P
marry, that did i. LLL 1.01.125
marry, thus much i have learnt: 2.01. 84
two hot sheeps, marry. 2.01.219
marry, sir, you must send the ass upon the horse 3.01. 54 P
o, marry me to one frances! 3.01.121 P
marry, sir, halfpenny farthing. 3.01.148 P
my lady goes to kill horns, but, if thou marry, 4.01.111
marry, master schoolmaster, he that is likel'est 4.02. 85 P
ay marry, there — some flattery for this evil. 4.03.282
lord, | this man hath my consent to marry her. MND 1.01. 25
your grace | consent to marry with demetrius, 1.01. 40
do you marry him. 1.01. 94
there, gentle hermia, may i marry thee; 1.01.161
marry, our play is the most lamentable comedy 1.02. 11 P
ay, marry, must you; 3.01. 90 P
marry, if he that writ it had play'd pyramus and 5.01.357 P
if i should marry him, i should marry twenty MV 1.02. 62 P
marry him, i should marry twenty husbands. 1.02. 63 P
marry, at the very next turning, turn of no hand 2.02. 43 P
marry, god forbid, the boy was the very staff of 2.02. 66 P
marry, sir, to bid my old master the jew to sup 2.04. 17 P
ay, marry, i'll be gone about it straight. 2.04. 24
marry, well rememb'red. 2.08. 26
marry, you may partly hope that your father got 3.05. 10 P
marry them to your heirs! 4.01. 94

marry, sir, i am helping you to mar that which AYL 1.01. 32 P
marry, sir, be better employ'd and be naught a 1.01. 35 P
marry, do i, sir; 1.01.122 P
marry, i prithee do, to make sport withal. 1.02. 26 P
ay, marry, now unmuzzle your wisdom. 1.02. 70 P
marry, he trots hard with a young maid between 3.02.313 P
but be it as it may be, i will marry thee; 3.03. 42 P
of another, for he is not like to marry me well; 3.03. 92 P
marry, his kisses are judas's own children. 3.04. 8 P
marry, that should you if i were your mistress, 4.01. 83 P
sister, you shall be the priest, and marry us. 4.01.125 P
pray thee marry us. 4.01.127 P
why now, as fast as she can marry us. 4.01.134 P
marry, to say she came to seek you there. 4.01.171 P
he, sir, that must marry this woman. 5.01. 46 P
brother marries aliena, shall you marry her. 5.02. 64 P
i will marry you, if ever i marry woman, and 5.02.113 P
i will marry you, if ever i marry woman, and 5.02.113 P
you say you'll marry me, if i be willing? 5.04. 11
but if you do refuse to marry me, | you'll give 5.04. 13
keep your word, phebe, that you'll marry me, 5.04. 21
that you'll marry her | if she refuse me; 5.04. 23
marry, i fare well, for here is cheer enough. SHR in.2. 101
marry, i will, let them play it. in.2. 137 P
marry, sir, to get a husband for her sister. 1.01.120 P
ay, marry, am i, sir; and now 'tis plotted. 1.01.188
and marry him to a puppet or an aglet–baby, or 1.02. 78 P
yea, and to marry her, if her dowry please. 1.02.184
marry, so i mean, sweet katherine, in thy bed; 2.01.267
and, will you, nill you, i will marry you. 2.01.271
if it would please him come and marry her!" 3.02. 20
but thus, i trust, you will not marry her. 3.02.115
hope, | and marry sweet bianca with consent. 3.02.137
ay, marry, sir, now it begins to work. 3.02.218
quick proceeders, marry! 4.02. 11
never to marry with her though she would entreat 4.02. 33
marry, god forbid! 4.02. 78
what, did he marry me to famish me? 4.03. 3
marry, and did; 4.03. 96
marry, sir, with needle and thread. 4.03.120
yes, marry, sir — see where he looks out of the 5.01. 55 P
marry, peace it bodes, and love, and quiet life, 5.02.108
marry, in blowing him down again, with the AWW 1.01.124 P
marry, ill, to like him that ne'er it likes. 1.01.152 P
ill, it eats drily, marry, 'tis a wither'd pear; 1.01.162 P
it was formerly better, marry, yet 'tis a 1.01.163 P
tell me thy reason why thou wilt marry. 1.03. 27 P
are, and indeed i do marry that i may repent. 1.03. 36 P
marry, that's a bountiful answer that fits all 2.02. 15 P
marry, to each but one! 2.03. 58
but never hope to know why i should marry her. 2.03.110
marry, you are the wiser man; 2.04. 23 P
ay, marry, is't. 3.05. 38
marry, hang you! 3.05. 91 P
to marry her, i'll add three thousand crowns 3.07. 35
he had sworn to marry me | when his wife's dead; 4.02. 71
braid, | marry that will, i live and die a maid. 4.02. 74
marry, we'll search. 4.03.202 P
marry, in coming on he has the cramp. 4.03.290 P
marry, as i take it, to rossillion, | whither i 5.01. 28
many protestations to marry me when his wife was 5.03.140 P
swear them lordship, | yet you desire to marry. 5.03.157
if you shall marry, | you give away this hand, 5.03.169
that she which marries you must marry me, 5.03.174
marry, but you shall have — and here's my hand. TN 1.03. 67 P
marry, now i let go your hand, i am barren. 1.03. 79 P
ay, marry, what is he? 1.05.127 P
marry, sir, sometimes he is a kind of puritan. 2.03.140 P
marry, hang thee, brock! 2.05.103 P
i could marry this wench for this device — 2.05.182 P
marry, i saw your niece do more favors to the 3.02. 5 P
marry, and it shall be done to–morrow morning if 3.04.103 P
marry, i'll ride your horse as well as i ride 3.04.290 P
marry, he hath better bethought him of his 3.04.297 P
marry, will i, sir; 3.04.322 P
marry, amen. 4.02.101 P
marry, sir, they praise me and make an ass of me 5.01. 17 P
marry, sir, lullaby to your bounty till i come 5.01. 45 P
marry, will i; WT 3.03.136 P
we marry | a gentler scion to the wildest stock, 4.04. 92
marry, garlic, | to mend her kissing with! 4.04.162
your ruin — marry her, | and with my best 4.04.530
you swear | never to marry but by my free leave? 5.01. 70
yet, if my lord will marry — if you will, sir, 5.01. 76
we shall not marry till thou bid'st us. 5.01. 82
the hazards of all husbands | that marry wives. JN 1.01.120
sir robert could do well — marry, to confess — 1.01.236
to these two princes, if you marry them. 2.01.445
lewis marry blanch? 3.01. 34
ay, marry, now my soul hath elbow–room; 5.07. 28
marry, would the word "farewell" have length'ned R2 1.04. 16
marry, god forbid! 4.01.114
marry then, sweet wag, when thou art king, let 1H4 1.02. 23 P
marry, i'll see thee hang'd first. 2.01. 40 P
marry and amen! 2.04.115 P
marry, my lord, there is a nobleman of the court 2.04.287 P
marry, | and i am glad of it with all my heart. 3.01.125
marry, and shall, and very willingly. 5.02. 33
and the young lion repents, marry, not in ashes 2H4 1.02.197 P
have weekly sworn to marry since i perceiv'd the 1.02.241 P
yea, marry, there's the point! 1.03. 18
marry, if thou wert an honest man, thyself and 2.01. 85 P
wound, to marry me and make me my lady thy wife. 2.01. 92 P
marry, i tell thee it is not meet that i should 2.02. 39 P
marry, my lord, althaea dreamt she was deliver'd 2.02. 89 P
marry, the immortal part needs a physician, but 2.02.104 P
he swears thou art to marry his sister nell. 2.02.129 P
must i marry your sister? 2.02.138 P
marry, there is another indictment upon thee, 2.04.343 P
marry, have we, sir. will you sit? 3.02. 94 P
yea, marry, sir. 3.02. 98 P
yea, marry, let me have him to sit under, he's 3.02.122 P
yea, marry, let's see bullcalf. 3.02.173 P
marry, then, mouldy, bullcalf, feeble, and 3.02.248 P
and then, when they marry, they get wenches. 4.03. 94 P
yea, marry, william cook, bid him come hither. 5.01. 10 P
marry, sir, thus; 5.01. 13 P
marry, good air. 5.03. 8 P
yea, marry, sir john, which i beseech you to let 5.05. 74 P
that sall i, marry. H5 3.02.104 P
marry, i wad full fain heard some question 3.02.118 P
marry, th' athversary was have possession of the 3.06. 93 P
marry, for my part, i think the duke hath lost 3.06. 99 P
marry, he told me so himself, and he said he 3.07.107 P
marry, if you would put me to verses, or to 5.02.132 P
marry, for that she's in a wrong belief, | i go 1H6 2.03. 31
ay, marry, sweeting, if we could do that, 3.03. 21
ay, marry, uncle, for i always thought | it was 5.01. 11
to marry princess margaret for your grace; 2H6 1.01. 4
marry, and shall. 1.02. 88
marry, the lord protect him, for he's a good man 1.03. 4 P
marry, when thou dar'st. 2.01. 38
marry, god forfend! 3.02. 30
marry, this: 4.02.136
ay, marry, will we; therefore get ye gone. 4.02.153
marry, thou oughtst not to let thy horse wear a 4.07. 49 P
marry, presently. 4.07.128 P
ay, marry, sir, now looks he like a king! 3H6 1.04. 96
you'ld think it strange if i should marry her. 3.02.111
marry, and shall. 5.05. 42
for then i'll marry warwick's youngest daughter. R3 1.01.153
what may she not, she may, ay, marry, may she. 1.03. 97
what, marry, may she? 1.03. 98
what, marry, may she? 1.03. 99
marry with a king, | a bachelor, and a handsome 1.03. 99
good counsel, marry! 1.03.260
marry, as for clarence, he is well repaid; 1.03.312
marry, my lord, lest by a multitude | the 2.02.124
marry, we were sent for to the justices. 2.03. 46
marry (they say) my uncle grew so fast | that he 2.04. 27
marry, my uncle clarence' angry ghost. 3.01.144
marry, and will, my lord, with all my heart. 3.04. 34
marry, that with no man here he is offended; 3.04. 56
marry, god defend his grace should say us nay! 3.07. 81
whom i will marry straight to clarence' daughter 4.02. 54
murther her brothers and then marry her — 4.02. 62
marry, is't. H8 1.01. 97
ay, marry, | there will be woe indeed, lords; 1.03. 38
marry, this is yet but young, and may be left 3.02. 47
marry, amen! 3.02. 54
he shall marry her. 3.02. 86
marry, at the white hair that helen spied on TRO 1.02.150 P
marry, this, sir, is proclaim'd through all our 2.01.121
marry, sir, at the request of paris my lord, who 3.01. 30 P
but, marry, thus, my lord: 3.01. 63 P
ay, marry, will we, sir, and we'll be waited on. TIT 4.01.122
marry, for justice, she is so employ'd, | he 4.03. 40
no, marry, i fear thee! ROM 1.01. 37 P
that shall she, marry, i remember it well. 1.03. 22
marry, that "marry" is the very theme | i came 1.03. 63
that "marry" is the very theme | i came to talk 1.03. 63
marry, 'tis time. 1.05. 85
marry, bachelor, | her mother is the lady of the 1.05.112
marry, that, i think, be young petruchio. 1.05.131
i pray, | that thou consent to marry us to–day. 2.03. 64
laura to his lady was a kitchen wench (marry, 2.04. 40 P
marry come up, i trow; 2.05. 62
marry, go before to field, he'll be your 3.01. 58
ay, a scratch, a scratch, marry, 'tis enough. 3.01. 93
marry, my child, early next thursday morn, | the 3.05.112
i will not marry yet, and when i do, i swear 3.05.121
marry, i will, and this is wisely done. 3.05.234
if, rather than to marry county paris, | thou 4.01. 71
o, bid me leap, rather than marry paris, | from 4.01. 77
home, be merry, give consent | to marry paris. 4.01. 90
marry, sir, 'tis an ill cook that cannot lick 4.02. 6 P
ay, marry, go, i say, and fetch him hither. 4.02. 30
marry and amen! 4.05. 8
marry, sir, because silver hath a sweet sound. 4.05.131 P
ay, marry, what of these? TIM 1.01. 83
marry, 'tis not monstrous in you, neither wish i 5.01. 88
ay, marry, was't, and he put it by thrice, every JC 1.02.229 P
marry, before he fell down, when he perceiv'd 1.02.263 P
as much as to say, they are fools that marry. 3.03. 18 P
marry, sir, nose–painting, sleep, and urine. MAC 2.03. 28 P
marry, he was dead. 3.06. 4
marry, well bethought. HAM 1.03. 90
marry, i will teach you: 1.03.105
ay, marry, is't, | but to my mind, though i am 1.04. 13
marry, well said, very well said. 2.01. 6
marry, none so rank | as may dishonor him, take 2.01. 20
marry, sir, here's my drift, | and i believe it 2.01. 37
at "closes in the consequence," ay, marry. 2.01. 52
if thou dost marry, i'll give thee this plague 3.01.134 P
or, if thou wilt needs marry, marry a fool, for 3.01.137 P
if thou wilt needs marry, marry a fool, for wise 3.01.137 P
marry, this' /miching mallecho, it means 3.02.137 P
marry, how? 3.02.237 P
as kill a king, and marry with his brother. 3.04. 29
ay, marry, is't — crowner's quest law. 5.01. 22 P
marry, now i can tell. 5.01. 53 P
ay, marry, why was he sent into england? 5.01.149 P
sure i shall never marry like my sisters, | /to LR 1.01.103
let pride, which she calls plainness, marry her. 1.01.129
so beggars marry many. 3.02. 30
marry, here's grace and a codpiece — that's a 3.02. 40 P
if you will marry, make your loves to me, | my 5.03. 88
all three | now marry in an instant. 5.03.230
marry, to — come, captain, will you go? OTH 1.02. 53
marry, before your ladyship, i grant, | she puts 2.01.105
marry, /god forbid! 2.03.261 P
ay, marry, are they, sir. 3.01. 7 P
marry, sir, by many a wind instrument that i 3.01. 10 P
why did i marry? 3.03.242
marry, patience, | or i shall say y' are all in 4.01. 87
she gives it out that you shall marry her. 4.01.115
i marry /her! 4.01.119 P
/faith, the cry goes that you marry her. 4.01.123 P
she is persuaded i will marry her, out of her 4.01.128 P
marry, a perfum'd one! 4.01.146 P
marry, i would not do such a thing for a 4.03. 72 P
marry, heaven forbid! 5.01. 72
why did he marry fulvia, and not love her? ANT 1.01. 41
find me to marry me with octavius caesar, and 1.02. 29 P
o, let him marry a woman that cannot go, sweet 1.02. 63 P
marry, yet | the fire of rage is in him, and CYM 1.01. 76
unless a man would marry a gallows and beget 5.04.198 P
marry, the gods forefend! 5.05.287
marry, sir, half a day's journey. PER 2.01.107 P
marry, whip the gosling, i think i shall have 4.02. 86 P
marry, hang her up for ever! 4.06.137 P
marry, hang you! 4.06.148 P
marry, come up, my dish of chastity with 4.06.150 P
your daughter, | shall marry her at pentapolis. 5.03. 72
the day | that he should marry you, at such a TNK 1.01. 60
marry, what i have (be it what it will) i will 2.01. 7 P
it may be he shall marry her; 2.02.226
yes, marry, are there; 2.03. 64
to marry him is hopeless; 2.04. 4
one would marry a leprous witch to be rid on't, 4.03. 46 P
for the purpose that will venture | to marry us, 5.02. 79
yes, marry, will we. 5.02.111
no, marry, do we not; STM II.C 18 P
marry, the removing of the strangers, which II.C 70 P
marry, god forbid that! II.C 96 P

MARRYING 11 FR 0.0012 REL FR 4 V 7 P
no marrying 'mong his subjects? TMP 2.01.166 P
you may, by marrying. WIV 1.01. 25 P
and one, | and, in the lawful name of marrying, 4.06. 50
will chafe at the doctor's marrying my daughter. 5.03. 8 P
marrying a punk, my lord, is pressing to death, MM 5.01.522 P
his honor in marrying the renown'd claudio — ADO 2.02. 23 P
bless me from marrying a usurer! WT 4.04.268 P
york, | marrying my sister that thy mother was, 1H6 2.05. 86
by marrying her which i must reach unto. R3 1.01.159
she did deceive her father, marrying you, | and OTH 3.03.206
this matter of marrying his king's daughter, CYM 1.04. 14 P

MARS* 50 FR 0.0056 REL FR 40 V 10 P
thou art the mars of malecontents. WIV 1.03.104 P
"the armipotent mars, of lances the almighty, LLL 5.02.644
"the armipotent mars, of lances the almighty, 5.02.651
the beards of hercules and frowning mars, | who, MV 3.02. 85
under mars, i. AWW 1.01.192 P
i especially think, under mars. 1.01.193 P
why under mars? 1.01.194 P
under that you must needs be born under mars. 1.01.196 P
mars dote on you for his novices! 2.01. 47 P
day, | great mars, i put myself into thy file; 3.03. 9
but my heart hath the fear of mars before it, 4.01. 29 P
this earth of majesty, this seat of mars, | this R2 2.01. 41
the black prince, that young mars of men, | from 2.03.101
hath this hotspur, mars in swathling clothes, 1H4 3.02.112
the mailed mars shall on his /altar sit | up to 4.01.116
assume the port of mars, and at his heels H5 pr 6
big mars seems bankrout in their beggar'd host, 4.02. 43
mars his true moving, even as in the heavens, 1H6 1.02. 1
cold biting winter mars our hop'd–for hay. 3H6 4.08. 61
matter against him that for ever mars | the H8 3.02. 21
mars his idiot! do, rudeness, do, camel, do, do. TRO 2.01. 53 P
to fight, | let mars divide eternity in twain, 2.03.245
themselves, | and drave great mars to faction. 3.03.190
by mars his gauntlet, thanks! 4.05.177
but, by great mars, the captain of us all, 4.05.198
but, by the forge that /stithied mars his helm, 4.05.255
well | in characters as red as mars his heart 5.02.164
nor the hand of mars | beck'ning with fiery 5.03. 52
now, mars, i prithee make us quick in work, COR 1.04. 10
why, thou mars, i tell thee, | we have a power 4.05.118
here within as if he were son and heir to mars; 4.05.192 P
hear'st thou, mars? 5.06. 99
thou valiant mars! TIM 4.03.383
it makes him, and it mars him; MAC 2.03. 32 P
an eye like mars, to threaten and command, | a HAM 3.04. 57
it makes us, or it mars us, think on that, | and OTH 5.01. 4
of the war | have glow'd like plated mars, now ANT 1.01. 4
and think | what venus did with mars. 1.05. 18
over caesar's head | and speak as loud as mars. 2.02. 6
way like a gorgon, | the other way 's a mars. 2.05.117
now all labor | mars what it does; 4.14. 48
with mars fall out, with juno chide, | that thy CYM 5.04. 32
being able | to make mars spurn his drum. TNK 1.01.182
and earn'st a deity | equal with mars. 1.01.228
by th' helm of mars, i saw them in the war, 1.04. 17
true worshippers of mars, whose spirit in you 5.01. 35
give me, great mars, | some token of thy 5.01. 60
our master mars | /hath vouch'd his oracle, and 5.04.106
she told the youngling how god mars did try her, PP 11. 3
nor mars his sword nor war's quick fire shall SON 55. 7

MARSELLIS 3 FR 0.0003 REL FR 2 V 1 P
an argosy | that now is lying in marsellis road. SHR 2.01.375
i duly am inform'd | his grace is at marsellis, AWW 4.04. 9
his highness comes post from marsellis, of as 4.05. 80 P

MARSH 1 FR 0.0001 REL FR 1 V 0 P
my lord, the enemy is past the marsh, | after R3 5.03.345

/MARSHAL 2 FR 0.0002 REL FR 1 V 1 P
/the /marshal /and /the /archbishop /are /strong 2H4 2.03. 42
/the /marshal /of /france, /monsieur /la /far. LR 4.03. 8 P

MARSHAL 15 FR 0.0017 REL FR 14 V 1 P
skill, | reason becomes the marshal to my will, MND 2.02.120
lord marshal, command our officers–at–arms | be R2 1.01.204
marshal, demand of yonder champion | the cause 1.03. 7
marshal, ask yonder knight in arms, | both who 1.03. 26
except the marshal and such officers | appointed 1.03. 44
lord marshal, let me kiss my sovereign's hand 1.03. 46
order the trial, marshal, and begin. 1.03. 99
brief | with winged haste to the lord marshal, 1H4 4.04. 2
and first, lord marshal, what say you to it? 2H4 1.03. 4
and therefore be assur'd, my good lord marshal, 4.01.218
great marshal to henry the sixt | of all his 1H6 4.07. 70
the duke of norfolk, | he to be earl marshal. H8 4.01. 19
must sweep my way, | and marshal me to knavery. HAM 3.04.205
when these /mutualities so marshal the way, hard OTH 2.01.261 P
marshal, the rest, as they deserve their grace. PER 2.03. 19

MARSHAL'S 3 FR 0.0003 REL FR 2 V 1 P
the marshal's truncheon, nor the judge's robe, MM 2.02. 61
his head for crowding among the marshal's men. 2H4 3.02.323 P
the marshal's sister | had her share too, as i TNK 3.03. 36

MARSHALSEA 1 FR 0.0001 REL FR 1 V 0 P
a marshalsea shall hold ye play these two months H8 5.03. 86

MARSHAL'ST 1 FR 0.0001 REL FR 1 V 0 P
thou marshal'st me the way that i was going, MAC 2.01. 42

MARS'S 6 FR 0.0006 REL FR 6 V 0 P

in vain, | mars's hot minion is return'd again; TMP 4.01. 98
bound and high curvet | of mars's fiery steed. AWW 2.03.283
fall | on mars's armor forg'd for proof eterne HAM 2.02.490
is with me, i met your groom | by mars's altar. TNK 1.01. 62
then shall offer | to mars's so scorn'd altar? 1.02. 20
to choke mars's drum | and turn th' alarm to 5.01. 80
MART 16 FR 0.0018 REL FR 14 V 2 P
please you, i'll meet with you upon the mart, ERR 1.02. 27
my charge was but to fetch you from the mart 1.02. 74
and from the mart he's somewhere gone to dinner. 2.01. 5
since at first | i sent him from the mart! 2.02. 6
words | didst thou deliver to me on the mart. 2.02.164
that would face me down | he met me on the mart, 3.01. 7
that you beat me at the mart, i have your hand 3.01. 12
if any bark put forth, come to the mart, | where 3.02.150
i'll to the mart and there for dromio stay: 3.02.184
him, | after you first forswore it on the mart, 5.01.262
that was us'd to come so smug upon the mart: MV 3.01. 47 P
part, | and venture madly on a desperate mart. SHR 2.01.327
to sell and mart your offices for gold | to JC 4.03. 11
and foreign mart for implements of war, | why HAM 1.01. 74
a saucy stranger in his court to mart | as in a CYM 1.06.151
too much money this mart by being too wenchless.
PER 4.02. 4 P
MARTED 1 FR 0.0001 REL FR 1 V 0 P
have let him go, | and nothing marted with him. WT 4.04.352
MARTEM 1 FR 0.0001 REL FR 1 V 0 P
"ad martem," that's for myself; TIT 4.03. 55
MARTEXT 3 FR 0.0003 REL FR 0 V 3 P
to that end i have been with sir oliver martext, AYL 3.03. 43 P
sir oliver martext, you are well met. 3.03. 64 P
wicked sir oliver, audrey, a most vile martext. 5.01. 6 P
MARTIAL 11 FR 0.0012 REL FR 9 V 2 P
we'll have a swashing and a martial outside, AYL 1.03.120
go, write it in a martial hand, be curst and TN 3.02. 42 P
their sons with arts and martial exercises; 2H4 4.05. 73
it, if there is any martial law in the world. H5 4.08. 44 P
how far'st thou, mirror of all martial men? 1H6 1.04. 74
a maid? and be so martial? 2.01. 21
warlike and martial talbot, burgundy | enshrines 3.02.118
and, with a martial scorn, with one hand beats ROM 3.01.161
with martial stalk hath he gone by our watch. HAM 1.01. 66
hand, | his foot mercurial, his martial thigh, CYM 4.02.310
a martial man to be soft fancy's slave! LUC 200
MARTIALIST 1 FR 0.0001 REL FR 1 V 0 P
and bare weeds | the gain o' th' martialist, who TNK 1.02. 16
MARTIANS 1 FR 0.0001 REL FR 1 V 0 P
springs of — | the noble house o' th' martians; COR 2.03.238
MARTINO 1 FR 0.0001 REL FR 0 V 1 P
"signior martino and his wife and daughters; ROM 1.02. 64 P
MARTIN'S 1 FR 0.0001 REL FR 1 V 0 P
expect saint martin's summer, halcyons' days, 1H6 1.02.131
MARTIUS' 2 FR 0.0002 REL FR 2 V 0 P
more than i know the sound of martius' tongue COR 1.06. 26
who, hearing of our martius' banishment, 4.06. 43
MARTIUS 79 FR 0.0089 REL FR 64 V 15 P
you know caius martius is chief enemy to the COR 1.01. 7 P
you proceed especially against caius martius? 1.01. 27 P
hail, noble martius! 1.01.163
where's caius martius? 1.01.223
martius, 'tis true that you have lately told us, 1.01.227
then, worthy martius, | attend upon cominius to 1.01.236
no, caius martius, | i'll lean upon one crutch, 1.01.241
noble martius! 1.01.247
was ever man so proud as is this martius? 1.01.252
giddy censure | will then cry out of martius, "o 1.01.269
opinion that so sticks on martius shall | of his 1.01.271
half all cominius' honors are to martius, 1.01.273
to martius, | though martius earn'd them not; 1.01.274
and all his faults | to martius shall be honors, 1.01.275
cominius, martius your old enemy | (who is of 1.02. 12
if we and caius martius chance to meet, | 'tis 1.02. 34
none less dear than thine and my good martius, i 1.03. 24 P
what is become of martius? 1.04. 48
thou art left, martius — | a carbuncle entire, 1.04. 54
o, 'tis martius! 1.04. 61
thou worthiest martius! 1.05. 25
and given to lartius and to martius battle. 1.06. 11
gods, | he has the stamp of martius, and i have 1.06. 23
martius, | we have at disadvantage fought, and 1.06. 48
as i guess, martius, | their bands i' th' vaward 1.06. 52
express his disposition, | and follow martius. 1.06. 75
if i fly, martius, | hollow me like a hare. 1.08. 6
that caius martius | wears this war's garland; 1.09. 59
clamor of the host, | martius caius coriolanus! 1.09. 65
martius caius coriolanus! 1.09. 67
martius, his name? 1.09. 90
five times, martius, | i have fought with thee; 1.10. 7
and custom 'gainst | my hate to martius. 1.10. 24
prayer of the people, for they love not martius. 2.01. 5 P
as the hungry plebeians would the noble martius. 2.01. 10 P
in what enormity is martius poor in, that you 2.01. 16 P
you blame martius for being proud? 2.01. 32 P
yet you must be saying martius is proud; 2.01. 90 P
honorable menenius, my boy martius approaches. 2.01.100 P
ha? martius coming home? 2.01.102 P
martius coming home! 2.01.106 P
martius is coming home; 2.01.145 P
these are the ushers of martius: 2.01.158 P
rome, that all alone martius did fight | within 2.01.162
hath won, | with fame, a name to martius caius; 2.01.164
my gentle martius, worthy caius, and | by 2.01.172
'tis thought | that martius shall be consul. 2.01.261
work perform'd | by martius caius coriolanus, 2.02. 46
from whence came | that ancus martius, numa's 2.03.239
martius would have all from you; 3.01.194
martius, | whom late you have nam'd for consul. 3.01.194
theirs, martius is worthy | of present death. 3.01.210
yield, martius, yield! 3.01.214
help martius, help! 3.01.226
where if you bring not martius, we'll proceed 3.01.331
this mould of martius, they to dust should grind 3.02.103
my name is caius martius, who hath done | to 4.05. 65
o martius, martius! 4.05.101
o martius, martius! 4.05.101
them more | than thee, all-noble martius. 4.05.106
worthy martius, | had we no other quarrel else 4.05.126
yet, martius, that was much. 4.05.147
was wont to thwack our general, caius martius. 4.05.179 P
caius martius was | a worthy officer i' th' war, 4.06. 29
were inshell'd when martius stood for rome, 4.06. 45
come, what talk you | of martius? 4.06. 47
how probable i do not know — that martius, 4.06. 66
weaker sort may wish | good martius home again. 4.06. 71
led by caius martius | associated with aufidius, 4.06. 75
if martius should be join'd /wi' /th' volscians 4.06. 89
your love can do | for rome, towards martius. 5.01. 41
well, and say that martius | return me, as 5.01. 41
this martius is grown from man to dragon: 5.04. 12 P
the volscians are dislodg'd, and martius gone. 5.04. 41
/unshout the noise that banish'd martius! 5.05. 4
ay, traitor, martius! 5.06. 86
"martius"? 5.06. 86
ay, martius, caius martius! 5.06. 87
ay, martius, caius martius! 5.06. 87
MARTLEMAS 1 FR 0.0001 REL FR 0 V 1 P
and how doth the martlemas, your master? 2H4 2.02.102 P
MARTLET *(also marlet)*
MARTLET 1 FR 0.0001 REL FR 1 V 0 P
not to th' interior, but, like the martlet, MV 2.09. 28
MART'RED 2 FR 0.0002 REL FR 2 V 0 P
speak, gentle sister, who hath mart'red thee? TIT 3.01. 81
nor tongue to tell me who hath mart'red thee. 3.01.107
MARTS 1 FR 0.0001 REL FR 1 V 0 P
be seen | at any syracusian marts and fairs; ERR 1.01. 17
MARTYR 4 FR 0.0004 REL FR 3 V 1 P
for oldcastle died /a martyr, and this is not 2H4 ep 32 P
o cromwell, | thou fall'st a blessed martyr! H8 3.02.449
hark, wretches, how i mean to martyr you. TIT 5.02.180
my death was noble, | dying almost a martyr. TNK 2.06. 17
/MARTYR'D 1 FR 0.0001 REL FR 1 V 0 P
/i /can /interpret /all /her /martyr'd /signs: TIT 3.02. 36
MARTYR'D 3 FR 0.0003 REL FR 2 V 1 P
despis'd, distressed, hated, martyr'd, kill'd! ROM 4.05. 59
sigh, martyr'd as 'twere i' th' deliverance, TNK 2.01. 41 P
cloak | immodestly lies martyr'd with disgrace. LUC 802
MARTYRS 2 FR 0.0002 REL FR 2 V 0 P
that, were our royal faiths martyrs in love, 2H4 4.01.191
here they stand martyrs, slain in cupid's wars; PER 1.01. 38
MARULLUS *(see murellus)*
MARVAIL'S *(also marvellous, marvell's, marv'llous, mervailous)*
MARVAIL'S 3 FR 0.0003 REL FR 0 V 3 P
and here's a marvail's convenient place for our MND 3.01. 2 P
for methinks i am marvail's hairy about the face 4.01. 24 P
sir, for they have marvail's foul linen. 2H4 5.01. 35 P
MARVEL 38 FR 0.0043 REL FR 26 V 12 P
i marvel i hear not of master /brook; WIV 3.05. 57 P
and you may marvel why i obscur'd myself, MM 5.01.390
no marvel though she pause — | they can be meek
ERR 2.01. 32
and that's great marvel, loving a light wench. LLL 1.02.123 P
i marvel thy master hath not eaten thee for a 5.01. 39 P
therefore no marvel though demetrius | do, as a MND 2.02. 96
and it is marvel he out-dwells his hour, | for MV 2.06. 3
i marvel why i answer'd not again. AYL 3.05.132
'tis marvel, but that you are but newly come, SHR 4.02. 86
i marvel cambio comes not all this while. 5.01. 7
you must not marvel, helen, at my course, AWW 2.05. 58
therefore we marvel much our cousin france 3.01. 7
i marvel your ladyship takes delight in such a TN 1.05. 83 P
and it becomes | my marvel and my message. WT 5.01.188
strike all that look upon with marvel. 5.03.100
i do not only marvel where thou spendest thy 1H4 2.04.398 P
welsh, | and 'tis no marvel he is so humorous. 3.01.230
man cannot make him laugh, but that's no marvel,
2H4 4.03. 89 P
here cometh charles, i marvel how he sped. 1H6 2.01. 48
no marvel, and it like your majesty, | my lord 2H6 2.01. 9
no marvel, lord, though it affrighted you; R3 1.04. 64
i marvel that her grace did leave it out. 2.02.111
i marvel where troilus is. TRO 1.02.219 P
i marvel where troilus is. 1.02.224 P
no marvel though you bite so sharp /at reasons, 2.02. 33
then marvel not, thou great and complete man, 3.03.181
you make me marvel wherefore ere this time | had
TIM 2.02.124
of these gentlemen, | this marvel to you. HAM 1.02.195
i marvel what kin thou and thy daughters are. LR 1.04.182 P
no marvel then, though he were ill affected: 2.01. 98
no marvel, you have so bestirr'd your valor. 2.02. 53 P
i marvel our mild husband | not met us on the 4.02. 1
and, to kill the marvel, | shall be so ever. CYM 3.01. 10
master, i marvel how the fishes live in the sea. PER 2.01. 26 P
but i much marvel that your lordship, having 3.02. 21
i marvel how they would have look'd had they TNK 2.01. 32 P
therefore no marvel though thy horse be gone. VEN 390
no marvel then though i mistake my view, | the SON 148.11
MARVELL'D 1 FR 0.0001 REL FR 1 V 0 P
the army marvell'd at it, and, in the last, COR 5.06. 41
MARVELLOUS *(also marvail's, marvell's, marv'llous, mervailous)*
MARVELLOUS 14 FR 0.0015 REL FR 5 V 9 P
marvellous sweet music! TMP 3.03. 19
her husband has a marvellous infection to the WIV 2.02.115 P
the duke is marvellous little beholding to your MM 4.03.159 P
your man and you are marvellous merry, sir. ERR 4.03. 58
a marvellous witty fellow, i assure you, but i ADO 4.02. 25 P
a mark marvellous well shot, for they both did LLL 4.01.130
marvellous well for the pen. 4.02.152 P
he is a marvellous good neighbor, faith, and a 5.02.582 P
you are marvellous forward. SHR 2.01. 73
truth's a truth, the rogues are marvellous poor. AWW 4.03.157 P
and that's a marvellous searching wine, and it 2H4 2.04. 27 P
captain jamy is a marvellous falorous gentleman, H5 3.02. 76 P
well, thou hast comforted me marvellous much. ROM 3.05.230
is in his retirement marvellous distemp'red. HAM 3.02.301 P
MARVELLOUSLY 2 FR 0.0002 REL FR 1 V 1 P
believe me, you are marvellously chang'd. MV 1.01. 76
age, or else you may be marvellously mistook. H5 3.06. 81 P
MARVELL'S 2 FR 0.0002 REL FR 1 V 1 P
indeed she has a marvell's white hand, i must TRO 1.02.136 P
you shall do marvell's wisely, good reynaldo, HAM 2.01. 3
MARVELS 1 FR 0.0001 REL FR 1 V 0 P
who marvels then, when helenus beholds | a TRO 2.02. 42
MARVEL'ST 1 FR 0.0001 REL FR 1 V 0 P
thou marvel'st at my words, but hold thee still: MAC 3.02. 54
MARV'LLOUS 2 FR 0.0002 REL FR 1 V 1 P
cannot) | myself to be a marv'llous proper man. R3 1.02.254
a marv'llous poor one. COR 4.05. 27 P
MARY 6 FR 0.0006 REL FR 2 V 4 P
my name is mary, sir. TN 1.03. 54 P
good mistress mary accost — 1.03. 55 P
where, good mistress mary? 1.05. 11 P
mistress mary, if you priz'd my lady's favor at 2.03.121 P
the duke of orleance and | our daughter mary. H8 2.04.176
by holy mary, butts, there's knavery. 5.02. 33
MARY–BUDS 1 FR 0.0001 REL FR 1 V 0 P
and winking mary-buds begin to ope their golden
CYM 2.03. 24
MARY'S 2 FR 0.0002 REL FR 2 V 0 P
for at saint mary's chapel presently | the rites JN 2.01.538
of the world's ransom, blessed mary's son; R2 2.01. 56
MASCULINE 3 FR 0.0003 REL FR 2 V 1 P
both | but this my masculine usurp'd attire, TN 5.01.250
pray god she prove not masculine ere long, | if 1H6 2.01. 22
why, his masculine whore. TRO 5.01. 17 P
MASHAM 4 FR 0.0004 REL FR 3 V 1 P
henry lord scroop of masham, and the third, H5 2.pr. 24
lord of cambridge, and my kind lord of masham, 2.02. 13
there yours, lord scroop of masham; 2.02. 67
by the name of /henry lord scroop of masham. 2.02.148 P
MASK 14 FR 0.0015 REL FR 12 V 2 P
and threw her sun-expelling mask away, | the air TGV 4.04.153
now fair befall your mask! LLL 2.01.123
you have a double tongue within your mask, | and 5.02.245
you shall play it in a mask, and you may speak MND 1.02. 49 P
blood, | and stain my favors in a bloody mask, 1H4 3.02.136
where hateful death put on his ugliest mask | to 2H4 1.01. 66
to defend mine honesty, my mask, to defend my TRO 1.02.262 P
th' unworthiest shows as fairly in the mask. 1.03. 84
and we mean well in going to this mask, | but ROM 1.04. 48
now since last yourself and i | were in a mask? 1.05. 33
thou knowest the mask of night is on my face, 2.02. 85
dark enough | to mask thy monstrous visage? JC 2.01. 81
her fan, her gloves, her mask, nor nothing? OTH 4.02. 9
to mask their brows and hide their infamy, | but LUC 794
MASK'D 11 FR 0.0012 REL FR 10 V 1 P
she, | but, being mask'd, he was not sure of it; TGV 5.02. 40
for they must all be mask'd and vizarded) | that WIV 4.06. 40
thoughts, master, are mask'd under such colors. LLL 1.02. 93 P
for, ladies, we will every one be mask'd, | and 5.02.127
the trumpet sounds, be mask'd; the maskers come. 5.02.157
fair ladies mask'd are roses in their bud; 5.02.295
not my blood | wherein thou seest me mask'd; COR 1.08. 10
some five and twenty years, and then we mask'd. ROM 1.05. 37
then give you up to the mask'd neptune and | the PER 3.03. 36
the region cloud hath mask'd him from me now. SON 33.12
if some suspect of ill mask'd not thy show, 70.13
MASKED 2 FR 0.0002 REL FR 2 V 0 P
and when i send for you, come hither masked. ADO 5.04. 12
summer's breath their masked buds discloses; SON 54. 8
MASKER 1 FR 0.0001 REL FR 1 V 0 P
honor, | join'd with a masker and a reveller! JC 5.01. 62
MASKERS 1 FR 0.0001 REL FR 1 V 0 P
the trumpet sounds, be mask'd; the maskers come.
LLL 5.02.157
MASKING 1 FR 0.0001 REL FR 1 V 0 P
masking the business from the common eye | for MAC 3.01.124
MASKS 5 FR 0.0005 REL FR 5 V 0 P
as these black masks | proclaim an enshield MM 2.04. 79
dances, masks, and merry hours | forerun fair LLL 4.03.376
damask roses, | masks for faces and for noses; WT 4.04.221
these happy masks that kiss fair ladies' brows, ROM 1.01.230
with faces fit for masks, or rather fairer CYM 5.03. 21
MASON 2 FR 0.0002 REL FR 0 V 2 P
he that builds stronger than either the mason, HAM 5.01. 42 P
who builds stronger than a mason, a shipwright, 5.01. 50 P
MASON'D 1 FR 0.0001 REL FR 1 V 0 P
from forth blue clouds | the mason'd turrets, TNK 5.01. 55
MASONRY 2 FR 0.0002 REL FR 2 V 0 P
smock, | creaking my shoes on the plain masonry, AWW 2.01. 31
and broils root out the work of masonry, | nor SON 55. 6
MASONS 1 FR 0.0001 REL FR 1 V 0 P
the singing masons building roofs of gold, | the H5 1.02.198
MASQUE 6 FR 0.0006 REL FR 5 V 1 P
what masque? MND 5.01. 40
will you prepare you for this masque to-night? MV 2.04. 22
i will not say you shall see a masque, but if 2.05. 23 P
no masque to-night, the wind is come about, 2.06. 64
this harness'd masque and unadvised revel, JN 5.02.132
now this masque | was cried incomparable; H8 1.01. 26
MASQUERS 2 FR 0.0002 REL FR 2 V 0 P
that lewis of france is sending over masquers 3H6 3.03.224
that lewis of france is sending over masquers 4.01. 94
MASQUES 3 FR 0.0003 REL FR 2 V 1 P
what masques, what dances shall we have, | to MND 5.01. 32
what, are there masques? MV 2.05. 28
i delight in masques and revels sometimes TN 1.03.113 P
MASQUING 2 FR 0.0002 REL FR 2 V 0 P
our masquing mates by this time for us stay. MV 2.06. 59
what masquing stuff is here? SHR 4.03. 87
MASS* *(also mess*)*
/MASS* 1 FR 0.0001 REL FR 1 V 0 P
/by /the /mass, 'tis morning; OTH 2.03.378
MASS* 32 FR 0.0036 REL FR 14 V 18 P
nay, by th' mass, that he did not; WIV 4.02.202 P
mass, and my elbow itch'd; ADO 3.03. 99 P
yea, by mass, that it is. 4.02. 51 P
by the mass, there is ne'er a king christen 1H4 2.01. 16 P
by the mass, lad, thou sayest true, it is like 2.04.364 P
by the mass, here comes bardolph. 2H4 2.02. 69 P
mass, thou say'st true. 2.04. 4 P
by the mass, here will be old utis, it will be 2.04. 19 P
by the mass, i was call'd any thing, and i would 3.02. 17 P
by the mass, i could anger her to th' heart. 3.02.204 P
by the mass, i have drunk too much sack at 5.03. 13 P
by the mass, you'll crack a quart together, ha, 5.03. 62 P
but, by the mass, our hearts are in the trim; H5 4.03.115
attire | have cost a mass of public treasury. 2H6 1.03.131
mass, thou lov'dst plums well, that wouldst 2.01. 99
mass, 'twill be sore law then, for he was thrust 4.07. 8 P
by th' mass, so did we all. 5.03. 16
and what hath mass or matter, by itself | lies TRO 1.03. 29
the baby figure of the giant mass | of things to 1.03.345
betimes | a moi'ty of that mass of moan to come. 2.02.107

call, | constring'd in mass by the almighty sun, 5.02.173
now, | or shall i come to you at evening mass? ROM 4.01. 38
mass, and well said, a merry whoreson, ha! 4.04. 20
it is nois'd he hath a mass of treasure. TIM 4.03.402 P
by the mass, i was about to say something. HAM 2.01. 50
by th' mass and 'tis, like a camel indeed. 3.02.378 P
glow | o'er this solidity and compound mass, 3.04. 49
witness this army of such mass and charge | led 4.04. 47
mass, i cannot tell. 5.01. 55 P
i remember a mass of things, but nothing OTH 2.03.288 P
not the world's mass of vanity could make me. 4.02.164
ay, by th' mass, will we, more. STM II.C 58 P
MASSACRE 6 FR 0.0006 REL FR 6 V 0 P
hence grew the general wrack and massacre; 1H6 1.01.135
but, lords, in all our bloody massacre, | i muse 2.02. 18
to save your subjects from such massacre | and 5.04.160
welcome destruction, blood, and massacre! R3 2.04. 53
the most arch deed of piteous massacre | that 4.03. 2
alone, | i'll find a day to massacre them all, TIT 1.01.450
MASSACRES 2 FR 0.0002 REL FR 2 V 0 P
on, | and rebels' arms triumph in massacres! 1H4 5.04. 14
i must talk of murthers, rapes, and massacres, TIT 5.01. 63
MASSES 1 FR 0.0001 REL FR 0 V 1 P
the jealous wittolly knave hath masses of money, WIV 2.02.272 P
/MASSY 1 FR 0.0001 REL FR 1 V 0 P
/with /massy /staples | /and /corresponsive /and TRO pr 17
MASSY 4 FR 0.0004 REL FR 2 V 2 P
swords are now too massy for your strengths, TMP 3.03. 67
where his codpiece seems as massy as his club? ADO 3.03.137 P
without drawing their massy irons and cutting TRO 2.03. 17 P
or it is a massy wheel, | fix'd on the summit of HAM 3.03. 17
/MAST* 1 FR 0.0001 REL FR 1 V 0 P
wilt thou upon the high and giddy /mast | seal 2H4 3.01. 18
MAST* 9 FR 0.0010 REL FR 9 V 0 P
sail, nor mast, the very rats | instinctively TMP 1.02.147
had fast'ned him unto a small spare mast, | such ERR 1.01. 79
fast'ned ourselves at either end the mast, | and 1.01. 85
to a strong mast that liv'd upon the sea; TN 1.02. 14
what though the mast be now blown overboard, 3H6 5.04. 3
and somerset another goodly mast? 5.04. 17
looks | lives like a drunken sailor on a mast, R3 3.04. 99
the oaks bear mast, the briers scarlet heps; TIM 4.03.419
and, clasping to the mast, endur'd a sea | that PER 4.01. 55
/MASTER 6 FR 0.0006 REL FR 4 V 2 P
man, | thou art right welcome as thy /master is. AYL 2.07.198
that my /master was? 2H6 1.03. 30 P
/and /the /good /king /his /master | /will LR 2.02.141
/come /help /to /bear /thy /master; 3.06.100
/so, /bless /thee, /master! 4.01. 63 P
/sir, /i'll /bring /you /to /our /master /lear, 4.03. 50
MASTER 789 FR 0.0891 REL FR 330 V 459 P
here, master; what cheer? TMP 1.01. 2 P
where's the master? 1.01. 10 P
where is the master, bos'n? 1.01. 12 P
than prospero, master of a full poor cell, | and 1.02. 20
being then appointed | master of this design, 1.02.163
all hail, great master, grave sir, hail! 1.02.189
close by, my master. 1.02.216
i thank thee, master. 1.02.293
pardon, master, | i will be correspondent to 1.02.296
that's my noble master! 1.02.299
my master through his art foresees the danger 2.01.297
"the master, the swabber, the boatswain, and i, 2.02. 46
farewell, master; farewell, farewell! 2.02.178
ca–caliban | has a new master, get a new man. 2.02.185
i would my valiant master would destroy thee. 3.02. 46
this will i tell my master. 3.02.115
what would my potent master? here i am. 4.01. 34
do you love me, master? 4.01. 48
the master and the boatswain | being awake, 5.01. 99
our master | cap'ring to eye her. 5.01.237
how fine my master is! 5.01.262
love is your master, for he masters you; TGV 1.01. 39
sir proteus! 'save you! saw you my master? 1.01. 70
you conclude that my master is a shepherd then, 1.01. 76 P
true; and thy master a shepherd. 1.01. 83 P
but i seek my master, and my master seeks not me 1.01. 87 P
i seek my master, and my master seeks not me: 1.01. 88 P
thou for wages followest thy master, thy master 1.01. 91 P
master, thy master for wages follows not thee: 1.01. 91 P
and so, sir, i'll commend you to my master. 1.01.147 P
i look on you, i can hardly think you my master. 2.01. 32 P
my master sues to her; 2.01.137
that my master, being scribe, to himself should 2.01.140
thy master is shipp'd, and thou art to post 2.03. 33 P
and, in losing thy voyage, lose thy master, and, 2.03. 43 P
and, in losing thy master, lose thy service, and 2.03. 43 P
and the voyage, and the master, and the service, 2.03. 51 P
master, sir thurio frowns on you. 2.04. 3 P
how did thy master part with madam julia? 2.05. 11 P
say'st thou that my master is become a notable 2.05. 42 P
why, fool, i meant not thee, i meant thy master. 2.05. 50 P
i tell thee, my master is become a hot lover. 2.05. 51 P
o, could their master come and go as lightly, 3.01.142
can nothing speak? master, shall i strike? 3.01.199 P
the wit to think my master is a kind of a knave; 3.01.264 P
that thy master stays for thee at the north–gate 3.01.373 P
master, be one of them; 4.01. 38
as a present to mistress silvia from my master; 4.04. 7 P
but cannot be true servant to my master, 4.04.104
from my master, sir proteus, madam. 4.04.114
go give your master this. 4.04.118
poor gentlewoman, my master wrongs her much. 4.04.141
when she did think my master lov'd her well, 4.04.150
eyes, | to make my master out of love with thee. 4.04.205
my master charg'd me to deliver a ring to madam 5.04. 88 P
and a gentleman born, master parson, who writes WIV 1.01. 9 P
which is daughter to master /george page, which 1.01. 45 P
a marriage between master abraham and mistress 1.01. 56 P
well, let us see honest master page. 1.01. 66 P
i will peat the door for master page. 1.01. 72 P
justice shallow, and here young master slender, 1.01. 76 P
i thank you for my venison, master shallow. 1.01. 80 P
master page, i am glad to see you. 1.01. 81 P
i am glad to see you, good master slender. 1.01. 88 P
he hath wrong'd me, master page. 1.01.102 P
is not that so, master page? 1.01.105 P
now, master shallow, you'll complain of me to 1.01.109 P
that is, master page (fidelicet master page) and 1.01.138 P
master page (fidelicet master page) and there is 1.01.139 P
pistol, did you pick master slender's purse? 1.01.151 P
sir john, and master mine, | i combat challenge 1.01.161
master slender, i will description the matter to 1.01.214 P
at sword and dagger with a master of fence 1.01.284 P
come, gentle master slender, come; 1.01.300 P
and see if you can see my master, master doctor 1.04. 3 P
if you can see my master, master doctor caius, 1.04. 3 P
and master slender's your master? 1.04. 18 P
and master slender's your master? 1.04. 18 P
tell master parson evans i will do what i can 1.04. 33 P
evans i will do what i can for your master. 1.04. 34 P
out alas! here comes my master. 1.04. 36 P
go, john, go inquire for my master; 1.04. 41 P
good master, be content. 1.04. 70 P
anne page for my master in the way of marriage. 1.04. 84 P
man, i'll do /you your master what good i can; 1.04. 92 P
the french doctor, my master (i may call him my 1.04. 94 P
my master (i may call him my master, look you, 1.04. 95 P
my master himself is in love with mistress anne 1.04.103 P
but notwithstanding, master fenton, i'll be 1.04.145 P
how now, master ford! 2.01.168 P
good even and twenty, good master page! 2.01.196 P
master page, will you go with us? 2.01.196 P
'tis the heart, master page, 'tis here, 'tis 2.01.227 P
i myself dwell with master doctor caius — 2.02. 46 P
master ford her husband will be from home. 2.02. 87 P
and truly master page is an honest man. 2.02.116 P
there's one master /brook below would fain speak 2.02.144 P
good master /brook, i desire more acquaintance 2.02.162 P
speak, good master /brook, i shall be glad to be 2.02.178 P
master /brook, i will first make bold with your 2.02.252 P
want no mistress ford, master /brook, you shall 2.02.260 P
master /brook, thou shalt know i will 2.02.281 P
thou, master /brook, shalt know him for knave, 2.02.284 P
/god save you, master doctor caius! 2.03. 19 P
now, good master doctor! 2.03. 20 P
he is the wiser man, master doctor: 2.03. 38 P
is it not true, master page? 2.03. 41 P
master shallow, you have yourself been a great 2.03. 42 P
bodykins, master page, though i now be old and 2.03. 44 P
justices and doctors and churchmen, master page, 2.03. 47 P
in us, we are the sons of women, master page. 2.03. 49 P
'tis true, master shallow. 2.03. 50 P
it will be found so, master page. 2.03. 51 P
master doctor caius, i am come to fetch you home 2.03. 51 P
you must go with me, master doctor. 2.03. 56 P
but first, master guest, and master page, and 2.03. 73 P
master guest, and master page, and eke cavaleiro 2.03. 74 P
adieu, good master doctor. 2.03. 81 P
pray you now, good master slender's servingman, 3.01. 1 P
which way have you look'd for master caius, that 3.01. 3 P
there comes my master, master shallow, and 3.01. 31 P
there comes my master, master shallow, and 3.01. 32 P
how now, master parson? 3.01. 36 P
do you study them both, master parson? 3.01. 45 P
come to you to do a good office, master parson. 3.01. 50 P
master doctor caius, the renown'd french 3.01. 60 P
nay, good master parson, keep in your weapon. 3.01. 73 P
so do you, good master doctor. 3.01. 75 P
well met, master ford. 3.02. 50 P
i must excuse myself, master ford. 3.02. 53 P
you have, master slender, i stand wholly for you 3.02. 61 P
but my wife, master doctor, is for you 3.02. 62 P
what say you to young master fenton? 3.02. 66 P
master doctor, you shall go, so shall you, 3.02. 81 P
shall go, so shall you, master page, and you, 3.02. 82 P
we shall have the freer wooing at master page's. 3.02. 85 P
my master, sir john, is come in at your back 3.03. 24 P
my master knows not of your being here, and has 3.03. 29 P
go tell thy master i am alone. 3.03. 36 P
help to cover your master, boy. 3.03.143 P
good master ford, be contented. 3.03.166 P
true, master page. 3.03.168 P
you use me well, master ford, do you? 3.03.202 P
you do yourself mighty wrong, master ford. 3.03.207 P
fie, fie, master ford, are you not asham'd? 3.03.214 P
'tis my fault, master page. i suffer for it. 3.03.218 P
pray you go, master page. 3.03.238 P
gentle master fenton, | yet seek my father's 3.04. 18
ye, master slender would speak a word with you. 3.04. 29 P
and how does good master fenton? 3.04. 34 P
good master shallow, let him woo for himself. 3.04. 50 P
now, master slender — 3.04. 54 P
i mean, master slender, what would you with me? 3.04. 60 P
now, master slender. 3.04. 67
what does master fenton here? 3.04. 68
nay, master page, be not impatient. 3.04. 71
good master fenton, come not to my child. 3.04. 72
no, good master fenton. 3.04. 74
come, master shallow; 3.04. 75
knowing my mind, you wrong me, master fenton. 3.04. 76
that's my master, master doctor. 3.04. 85 P
that's my master, master doctor. 3.04. 85 P
good master fenton, | i will not be your friend 3.04. 88
look on master fenton." 3.04. 97 P
but yet i would my master had mistress anne; 3.04.104 P
or i would master slender had her; 3.04.105 P
or, in sooth, i would master fenton had her. 3.04.106 P
as my word, but speciously for master fenton. 3.04.109 P
i marvel i hear not of master /brook; 3.05. 57 P
now, master /brook, you come to know what hath 3.05. 61 P
master /brook, i will not lie to you. 3.05. 64 P
very ill–favoredly, master /brook. 3.05. 67 P
no, master /brook, but the peaking cornuto her 3.05. 70 P
the peaking cornuto her husband, master /brook, 3.05. 71 P
that, master /brook, there was the rankest 3.05. 91 P
nay, you shall hear, master /brook, what i have 3.05. 95 P
met the jealous knave their master in the door, 3.05.101 P
but mark the sequel, master /brook. 3.05.107 P
hissing–hot — think of that, master /brook. 3.05.122 P
master /brook, i will be thrown into etna, as i 3.05.126 P
eight and nine is the hour, master /brook. 3.05.130 P
you shall have her, master /brook. 3.05.137 P
master /brook, you shall cuckold ford. 3.05.137 P
master ford, awake! 3.05.140 P
awake, master ford! 3.05.140 P
a hole made in your best coat, master ford. 3.05.141 P
is he at master ford's already, think'st thou? 4.01. 1 P
look where his master comes; 4.01. 9 P
master slender is let the boys leave to play. 4.01. 11 P
answer your master, be not afraid. 4.01. 20 P
three of master ford's brothers watch the door 4.02. 51 P
your master is hard at door. 4.02.109 P
but if it prove true, master page, have you any 4.02.114 P
why, this passes, master ford. 4.02.122 P
indeed, master ford, this is not well indeed. 4.02.126 P
master page, as i am a man, there was one 4.02.145 P
by my fidelity, this is not well, master ford; 4.02.153 P
master ford, you must pray, and not follow the 4.02.155 P
time | shall master slender steal my nan away, 4.04. 74
with sir john falstaff from master slender. 4.05. 5 P
my master, sir, my master slender, sent to her, 4.05. 30 P
my master, sir, my master slender, sent to her, 4.05. 30 P
man that beguil'd master slender of his chain 4.05. 37 P
i shall make my master glad with these tidings. 4.05. 56 P
here, master doctor, in perplexity and doubtful 4.05. 84 P
master fenton, talk not to me, my mind is heavy; 4.06. 1 P
i will hear you, master fenton, and i will (at 4.06. 6 P
how now, master /brook? 5.01. 9 P
master /brook, the matter will be known to–night 5.01. 9 P
i went to her, master /brook, as you see, like a 5.01. 15 P
but i came from her, master /brook, like a poor 5.01. 16 P
mad devil of jealousy in him, master /brook, 5.01. 19 P
for in the shape of man, master /brook, i fear 5.01. 21 P
along with me, i'll tell you all, master /brook. 5.01. 24 P
strange things in hand, master /brook! 5.01. 30 P
master doctor, my daughter is in green. 5.03. 1 P
master /brook, falstaff's a knave, a cuckoldly 5.05.109 P
here are his horns, master /brook; 5.05.111 P
and, master /brook, he hath enjoy'd nothing of 5.05.111 P
of money, which must be paid to master /brook. 5.05.114 P
his horses are arrested for it, master /brook. 5.05.115 P
to one master /brook that you have cozen'd of 5.05.166 P
tell her master slender hath married her 5.05.173 P
here comes master fenton. 5.05.213 P
how now, master fenton? 5.05.215 P
how chance you went not with master slender? 5.05.218 P
why went you not with master doctor, maid? 5.05.219
master fenton, | heaven give you many, many 5.05.239
to master /brook you yet shall hold your word, 5.05.244
(as i said), master froth here, this very man, MM 2.01.100 P
as you know, master froth, i could not give you 2.01.103 P
and i beseech you, look into master froth here, 2.01.122 P
was't not at hallowmas, master froth? 2.01.125 P
good master froth, look upon his honor; 2.01.148 P
how could master froth do the constable's wife 2.01.157 P
come hither to me, master froth. 2.01.203 P
master froth, i would not have you acquainted 2.01.204 P
they will draw you, master froth, and you will 2.01.205 P
no more of it, master froth. 2.01.211 P
come you hither to me, master tapster. 2.01.212 P
what's your name, master tapster? 2.01.213 P
come hither to me, master elbow; 2.01.257 P
come hither, master constable. 2.01.258 P
first, here's young master rash, he's in for a 4.03. 4 P
then is there here one master caper, at the suit 4.03. 9 P
at the suit of master three–pile the mercer, for 4.03. 10 P
we here young dizzy, and young master deep–vow, 4.03. 13 P
young master deep–vow, and master copper–spur, 4.03. 13 P
and master starve–lackey the rapier and dagger 4.03. 14 P
lusty pudding, and master forthlight the tilter, 4.03. 16 P
and brave master shoe–tie the great traveller, 4.03. 16 P
master barnardine! 4.03. 21 P
you must rise and be hang'd, master barnardine! 4.03. 22 P
pray, master barnardine, awake till you are 4.03. 32 P
that in such haste i sent to seek his master? ERR 2.01. 2
a man is master of his liberty: 2.01. 7
time is their master, and when they see time, 2.01. 8
man, more divine, the master of all these, 2.01. 20
say, is your tardy master now at hand? 2.01. 44
why, mistress, sure my master is horn–mad. 2.01. 57
quoth my master. 2.01. 70
hence, prating peasant! fetch thy master home. 2.01. 81
that's not my fault, he's master of my state. 2.01. 95
i pray you, master, tell me. 2.02. 21
i am transformed, master, am /not /i? 2.02.195
nay, master, both in mind and in my shape. 2.02.197
whilst man and master laughs my woes to scorn. 2.02.205
sirrah, if any ask you for your master, | say he 2.02.209
master, shall i be porter at the gate? 2.02.217
my master stays in the street. 3.01. 36
let my master in, luce. 3.01. 49
he comes too late, | and so tell your master. 3.01. 50
master, knock the door hard. 3.01. 58
if you went in pain, master, this knave would go 3.01. 65
they stand at the door, master, bid them welcome 3.01. 68
you would say so, master, if your garments were 3.01. 70
master, mean you so? 3.01. 81
master antipholus — 3.02.165
master, there's a bark of epidamium | that stays 4.01. 85
for nought at all | but for their owner, master, 4.01. 92
where is thy master, dromio? is he well? 4.02. 31
and bring thy master home immediately. 4.02. 64
master, here's the gold you sent me for. 4.03. 12 P
well met, well met, master antipholus. 4.03. 45
master, is this mistress sathan? 4.03. 49 P
master, if /you do, expect spoon–meat, or 4.03. 60 P
master, be wise, and if you give it her, | the 4.03. 75
might, | but surely, master, not a rag of money. 4.04. 86
mistress, both man and master is possess'd: 4.04. 92
and, gentle master, i receiv'd no gold; 4.04. 98
good master doctor, see him safe convey'd | home 4.04.122
master, i am here ent'red in bond for you. 4.04.125
be mad, good master, | cry "the devil!" 4.04.127
run, master, run! 5.01. 36
when thou didst make him master of thy bed, | to 5.01.163
my master and his man are both broke loose, 5.01.169
my master preaches patience to him, and the 5.01.174
peace, fool, thy master and his man are here, 5.01.178
o, my old master! who hath bound him here? 5.01.339
master, shall i fetch your stuff from shipboard? 5.01.409
i am your master, dromio. 5.01.412
every one /can master a grief but he that has it ADO 3.02. 28 P
both which, master constable — 3.03. 17 P

claudio, and my master, planted and plac'd and 3.03.149 P
and plac'd and possess'd by my master don john, 3.03.150 P
but the devil my master knew she was margaret; 3.03.155 P
call up the right master constable. 3.03.166 P
let them come before master constable. 4.02. 8 P
write down master gentleman conrade. 4.02. 15 P
master constable, you go not the way to examine; 4.02. 33 P
master constable — 4.02. 43 P
master constable, let these men be bound, and 4.02. 64 P
here, here comes master signior leonato, and the 5.01.257 P
speak you this in my praise, master? LLL 1.02. 24 P
hercules, master. 1.02. 66 P
sampson, master; 1.02. 70 P
a woman, master. 1.02. 77 P
most maculate thoughts, master, are mask'd under 1.02. 92 P
a dangerous rhyme, master, against the reason of 1.02.107 P
and yet a better love than my master. 1.02.121 P
nothing, master moth, but what they look upon. 1.02.162 P
master, will you win your love with a french 3.01. 8 P
no, my complete master, but to jig off a tune at 3.01. 11 P
no, master, the hobby-horse is but a colt, and 3.01. 31 P
and out of heart, master; 3.01. 37 P
minime, honest master, or rather, master, no. 3.01. 60
minime, honest master, or rather, master, no. 3.01. 60
a wonder, master! 3.01. 70
from my lord berowne, a good master of mine, 4.01.104
truly, master holofernes, the epithites are 4.02. 8 P
perge, good master holofernes, perge, so it 4.02. 53 P
god give you good morrow, master person. 4.02. 82 P
master person, quasi //pers-one. 4.02. 83 P
marry, master schoolmaster, he that is likel'est 4.02. 85 P
good master person, be so good as read me this 4.02. 90 P
so doth the hound his master, the ape his keeper 4.02.126 P
i marvel thy master hath not eaten thee for a 5.01. 39 P
is the very remuneration i had of thy master, 5.01. 73 P
master, let me take you a button-hole lower. 5.02.700 P
thrice blessed they that master so their blood MND 1.01. 74
this is he, my master said, | despised the 2.02. 72
you of more acquaintance, good master cobweb. 3.01.183 P
your mother, and to master peascod, your father. 3.01.187 P
good master peaseblossom, i shall desire you of 3.01.188 P
good master mustardseed, i know your patience 3.01.191 P
/of more acquaintance, good master mustardseed. 3.01.196 P
word the prince his master will be here to-night MV 1.02.126 P
will serve me to run from this jew my master. 2.02. 2 P
i should stay with the jew my master, who, god 2.02. 23 P
master young man, you, i pray you, which is the 2.02. 33 P
i pray you, which is the way to master jew's? 2.02. 34 P
master young gentleman, i pray you, which is the 2.02. 39 P
i pray you, which is the way to master jew's? 2.02. 40 P
talk you of young master launcelot? 2.02. 48 P
talk you of young master launcelot? 2.02. 50 P
no master, sir, but a poor man's son. 2.02. 51 P
what 'a will, we talk of young master launcelot. 2.02. 55 P
beseech you, talk you of young master launcelot. 2.02. 58 P
ergo, master launcelot. 2.02. 60 P
talk not of master launcelot, father, for the 2.02. 61 P
how dost thou and thy master agree? 2.02.100 P
give me your present to one master bassanio, who 2.02.108 P
his master and he (saving your worship's 2.02.130 P
shylock thy master spoke with me this day, | and 2.02.145
well parted between my master shylock and you, 2.02.150 P
take leave of thy old master, and inquire | my 2.02.153
where's your master? 2.02.174
to bid my old master the jew to sup to-night 2.04. 17 P
sup to-night with my new master the christian. 2.04. 18 P
my young master doth expect your reproach. 2.05. 19 P
my master antonio is at his house and desires to 3.01. 74 P
of this fair mansion, master of my servants, 3.02.168
i pray you, is my master yet return'd? 5.01. 34
did you see master lorenzo? 5.01. 41 P
master lorenzo, sola, sola! 5.01. 41 P
tell him there's a post come from my master, 5.01. 46 P
my master will be here ere morning. 5.01. 47 P
and neither man nor master would take aught 5.01.183
yonder comes my master, your brother. AYL 1.01. 26 P
god be with my old master! 1.01. 84 P
what, my young master? 2.03. 2
o my gentle master! 2.03. 2
o my sweet master! 2.03. 3
know you not, master, to /some kind of men 2.03. 10
your virtues, gentle master, | are sanctified 2.03. 12
master, go on, and i will follow thee | to the 2.03. 69
my master is of churlish disposition, | and 2.04. 80
dear master, i can go no further. 2.06. 1 P
farewell, kind master. 2.06. 3 P
you this shepherd's life, master touchstone? 3.02. 11 P
here comes young master ganymed, my new 3.02. 86 P
good even, good master what-ye-call't; 3.03. 73 P
farewell, good master oliver: 3.03. 98 P
mistress and master, you have oft inquired 3.04. 47
bounds | that the old carlot once was master of. 3.05.108
our master and mistress seeks you. 5.01. 60 P
mi perdonato, gentle master mine; SHR 1.01. 25
only, good master, while we do admire | this 1.01. 29
master, some show to welcome us to town. 1.01. 47
husht, master, here's some good pastime toward; 1.01. 68
well said, master, mum, and gaze your fill. 1.01. 73
master, it is no time to chide you now, 1.01.159
master, you look'd so longly on the maid, 1.01.165
master, your love must live a maid at home, 1.01.182
master, for my hand, | both our inventions meet 1.01.189
distinguish'd by our faces | for man or master. 1.01.201
thou shalt be master, tranio, in my stead; 1.01.202
master, has my fellow tranio stol'n your clothes 1.01.223 P
but in all places else /your master lucentio. 1.01.244
my master is grown quarrelsome. 1.02. 13
help, /masters, help, my master is mad. 1.02. 18 P
was it fit for a servant to use his master so, 1.02. 32 P
master, master, look about you! 1.02.140 P
master, master, look about you! 1.02.140 P
'tis in my head to do my master good. 2.01.406
i must believe my master, else, i promise you, 3.01. 54
good master, take it not unkindly, pray, | that 3.01. 57
master, master! 3.02. 30 P
master, master! 3.02. 30 P
fret, | i will be master of what is mine own. 3.02.229
is my master and his wife coming, grumio? 4.01. 18 P

it hath tam'd my old master and my new mistress 4.01. 24 P
for my master and mistress are almost frozen to 4.01. 37 P
is tir'd, my master and mistress fall'n out. 4.01. 54 P
hill, my master riding behind my mistress — 4.01. 67 P
you must meet my master to countenance my 4.01. 99 P
all things is ready. how near is our master? 4.01.116 P
i hear my master. 4.01.119 P
what, master, read you? first resolve me that. 4.02. 7
and may you prove, sir, master of your art! 4.02. 9
ay, mistress, and petruchio is the master, 4.02. 56
o master, master, i have watch'd so long | that 4.02. 59
o master, master, i have watch'd so long | that 4.02. 59
master, a mercantant, or a pedant, | i know not 4.02. 63
gown is made | just as my master had direction. 4.03.116
unto thee, i bid thy master cut out the gown, 4.03.126 P
master, if ever i said loose-bodied gown, sew me 4.03.135 P
away, i say, commend me to thy master. 4.03.168
you saw my master wink and laugh upon you? 4.04. 75 P
my master hath appointed me to go to saint 4.04.102 P
mine old master vincentio! 5.01. 43 P
what, my old worshipful old master? 5.01. 54 P
o, he hath murd'red his master! 5.01. 87 P
which runs himself, and catches for his master. 5.02. 53
there shall your master have a thousand loves, AWW 1.01.166
my master, my dear lord he is, and i | his 1.03.158
your lord and master did well to make his 2.03.186 P
recantation? my lord? my master? 2.03.188 P
my master? 2.03.191 P
count's master is of another style. 2.03.194 P
whom i serve above is my master. 2.03.246 P
the devil it is that's thy master. 2.03.249 P
the bloody course of war | my dearest master, 3.04. 9
where's your master? 4.03. 75 P
to suggest thee from thy master thou talk'st of; 4.05. 45 P
and the master i speak of ever keeps a good fire 4.05. 48 P
home, i mov'd the king my master to speak in the 4.05. 71 P
good master lavatch, give my lord lafew this 5.02. 1 P
not fearing the displeasure of your master, 5.03.235
my master hath been an honorable gentleman. 5.03.238 P
my lord and master loves you. TN 1.05.252
my master, not myself, lacks recompense. 1.05.285
unless the master were the man. 1.05.294
my master loves her dearly, | and i (poor 2.02. 33
be as oft with your master as with my mistress. 3.01. 40 P
but this — your true love for my master. 3.04.213
nor your name is not master cesario, nor this is 4.01. 7 P
jove bless thee, master parson. 4.02. 11 P
so i, being master parson, am master parson; 4.02. 15 P
so i, being master parson, am master parson; 4.02. 15 P
well said, master parson. 4.02. 27 P
master malvolio? 4.02. 84 P
good master fabian, grant me another request. 5.01. 2 P
your master quits you; 5.01.321
and since you call'd me master for so long, 5.01.324
dagger muzzled | lest it should bite its master, WT 1.02.157
ground to do't | is the obedience to a master; 1.02.354
fear the wolf will sooner find than the master. 3.03. 67 P
the penitent king, my master, hath sent for me, 4.02. 7 P
o master! 4.04.181 P
master, there is three carters, three shepherds, 4.04.324 P
dear sicilia | and that unhappy king, my master, 4.04.512
complaint may be to the flight of my master. 4.04.710 P
and a means to do the prince my master good; 4.04.834 P
now newly perform'd by that rare italian master, 5.02. 97 P
me your good report to the prince my master. 5.02.151 P
snatch at his master that doth tarre him on. JN 4.01.116
'tis true — to hurt his master, no /man else. 4.03. 33
yet know, my master, god omnipotent, | is R2 3.03. 85
knife, | no more shall cut his master. 1H4 1.01. 18
good morrow, master gadshill. 2.01. 53 P
now, master sheriff, what is your will with me? 2.04.506
you back again to your master for a jewel — the 2H4 1.02. 19 P
the juvenal, the prince your master, whose chin 1.02. 20 P
what said master dommelton about the satin for 1.02. 29 P
you must speak louder, my master is deaf. 1.02. 67 P
master fang, have you ent'red the action? 2.01. 1 P
o lord, ay! good master snare. 2.01. 6 P
yea, good master snare, i have ent'red him and 2.01. 9 P
good master fang, hold him sure. 2.01. 24 P
good master snare, let him not scape. 2.01. 25 P
lumbert street, to master smooth's the silk-man. 2.01. 29 P
do your offices, master fang and master snare, 2.01. 41 P
do your offices, master fang and master snare, 2.01. 41 P
now, master gower, what news? 2.01.133
come, go along with me, good master gower. 2.01.179
master gower, shall i entreat you with me to 2.01.182 P
will you sup with me, master gower? 2.01.188 P
what foolish master taught you these manners, 2.01.189 P
master gower, if they become me not, he was a 2.01.191 P
and how doth thy master, bardolph? 2.02. 98 P
and how doth the martlemas, your master? 2.02.102 P
is your master here in london? 2.02.144 P
no word to your master that i am yet come to 2.02.161 P
here will be the prince and master poins anon, 2.04. 15 P
i was before master tisick, the debuty, t' other 2.04. 85 P
quickly," says he — master dumbe, our minister, 2.04. 88 P
i am meat for your master. 2.04.126 P
bid mistress tearsheet come to my master. 2.04.388 P
to see you well, good master robert shallow. 3.02. 85 P
master /surecard, as i think? 3.02. 86 P
good master silence, it well befits you should 3.02. 89 P
well, master shallow, deep, master shallow. 3.02.161 P
well, master shallow, deep, master shallow. 3.02.161 P
am glad to see you, by my troth, master shallow. 3.02.193 P
no more of that, master shallow, /no /more /of 3.02.196 P
she lives, master shallow. 3.02.200 P
always say she could not abide master shallow. 3.02.203 P
old, old, master shallow. 3.02.206 P
heard the chimes at midnight, master shallow. 3.02.214 P
good master corporate bardolph, stand my friend, 3.02.220 P
and, good master corporal captain, for my old 3.02.229 P
will you tell me, master shallow, how to choose 3.02.257 P
give me the spirit, master shallow. 3.02.260 P
he is not his craft's master, he doth not do it 3.02.278 P
these fellows woll do well, master shallow. 3.02.287 P
god keep you, master silence, i will not use 3.02.288 P
and there will i visit master robert shallow, 4.03.129 P
you must excuse me, master robert shallow. 5.01. 3 P

give me your hand, master bardolph. 5.01. 55 P
thank thee with my heart, kind master bardolph, 5.01. 57 P
i'll follow you, good master robert shallow. 5.01. 60 P
such bearded hermits' staves as master shallow. 5.01. 64 P
if i had a suit to master shallow, i would humor 5.01. 71 P
with the imputation of being near their master; 5.01. 73 P
i would curry with master shallow that no man 5.01. 74 P
i come, master shallow, i come, master shallow. 5.01. 87 P
i come, master shallow, i come, master shallow. 5.01. 87 P
me, | i'll to the king my master that is dead, 5.02. 40
good master silence, i'll give you a health for 5.03. 23 P
give master bardolph some wine, davy. 5.03. 25 P
master page, good master page, sit. 5.03. 27 P
master page, good master page, sit. 5.03. 27 P
be merry, master bardolph, and, my little 5.03. 30 P
i did not think master silence had been a man of 5.03. 37 P
well said, master silence. 5.03. 49 P
health and long life to you, master silence. 5.03. 52 P
i'll drink to master bardolph, and to all the 5.03. 58 P
together, ha, will you not, master bardolph? 5.03. 63 P
master robert shallow, choose what office thou 5.03.122 P
carry master silence to bed. 5.03.129 P
master shallow, my lord shallow — be what thou 5.03.129 P
boot, boot, master shallow! 5.03.134 P
stand here by me, master shallow, i will make 5.05. 5 P
master shallow, i owe you a thousand pound. 5.05. 73 P
that can hardly be, master shallow. 5.05. 76 P
the prince our master | says that you savor too H5 1.02.249
you must come to my master, and your hostess. 2.01. 82 P
and the duke of exeter is master of the pridge. 3.06. 95 P
so far my king and master; 3.06.136 P
go therefore tell thy master here i am; 3.06.153
go bid thy master well advise himself. 3.06.159
so tell your master. 3.06.166
the business of the master the author of the 4.01.154 P
of his son, nor the master of his servant; 4.01.157 P
he says his name is master fer. 4.04. 27 P
master fer! 4.04. 28 P
the master of the cross-bows, lord rambures, 4.08. 94
great master of france, the brave sir guichard 4.08. 95
chief master gunner am i of this town, 1H6 1.04. 6
good master vernon, it is well objected; 2.04. 43
good master vernon, i am bound to you | that you 2.04.128
and for the proffer of my lord your master, | i 5.01. 41
against my master, thomas horner, for saying 2H6 1.03. 25 P
my master said that he was, and that the king 1.03. 31 P
in, and send for his master with a pursuivant 1.03. 34 P
in this place most master wear no breeches, 1.03.146
that doth accuse his master of high treason. 1.03.182
master hume, we are therefore provided. 1.04. 3 P
but it shall be convenient, master hume, that 1.04. 7 P
they know their master loves to be aloft, | and 2.01. 11
a plum-tree, master. 2.01. 95
o, born so, master. 2.01. 96
alas, good master, my wife desired some damsons, 2.01.100
yes, master, clear as day, i thank god and saint 2.01.105 P
red, master, red as blood. 2.01.108
alas, master, i know not. 2.01.116
no indeed, master. 2.01.120
saunder simpcox, and if it please you, master. 2.01.122
o master, that you could! 2.01.132
alas, master, i am not able to stand alone; 2.01.142
alas, master, what shall i do? 2.01.149 P
be merry, peter, and fear not thy master. 2.03. 70 P
for i am never able to deal with my master, he 2.03. 78 P
thump? then see thou thump thy master well. 2.03. 84 P
and, master sheriff, | let not her penance 2.04. 74
master, this prisoner freely give i thee, | and 4.01. 12
what is my ransom, master? let me know. 4.01. 15
to emblaze the honor that thy master got. 4.10. 71
came on the part of york, press'd by his master; 3H6 2.05. 66
master lieutenant, now that god and friends 4.06. 1
but, master mayor, if henry be your king, | yet 4.07. 20
why, master mayor, why stand you in a doubt? 4.07. 27
so, master mayor; 4.07. 35
to say the truth, so judas kiss'd his master, 5.07. 33
peace, master marquess, you are malapert, | your R3 1.03.254
go, bid thy master rise and come to me, | and we 3.02. 31
master lieutenant, pray you, by your leave, 4.01. 13
for dickon thy master is bought and sold." 5.03.305
following day | became the next day's master, H8 1.01. 17
suggests the king our master | to this last 1.01.164
and point by point the treasons of his master 1.02. 7
of these exactions, yet the king our master — 1.02. 25
his master would be serv'd before a subject, if 2.02. 7 P
that noble title | your master wed me to. 3.01.141
the king | (mine and your master) with his own 3.02.247
truth | toward the king, my ever royal master, 3.02.273
man, unworthy now | to be thy lord and master. 3.02.414
forgo | so good, so noble, and so true a master? 3.02.423
sure and safe one, though thy master miss'd it. 3.02.438
the king has made him master | o' th' jewel 4.01.110
the jewel house, is made master | o' th' rolls, 5.01. 34
i mean in perjur'd witness, than your master, 5.01.136
speak to the business, master secretary. 5.02. 36
good master secretary, | i cry your honor mercy; 5.02.112
it | to a most noble judge, the king my master. 5.02.136
good master porter, i belong to th' larder. 5.03. 4 P
do you hear, master porter? 5.03. 28 P
shall be with you presently, good master puppy. 5.03. 29 P
each troyan that is master of his heart, | let TRO 1.01. 4
the great hector's sword had lack'd a master, 1.03. 76
how now, where's thy master? 3.02. 1 P
till now not so much | but i might master it. 3.02.121
thy master now lies thinking on his bed | of 5.02. 78
the rivets all, | but i'll be master of it. 5.06. 30
where's cotus? my master calls for him. cotus! COR 4.05. 3 P
prithee call my master to him. 4.05. 21 P
prithee tell my master what a strange guest he 4.05. 35 P
no, i serve not thy master. 4.05. 45 P
how, sir? do you meddle with my master? 4.05. 46 P
who, my master? 4.05.164 P
but give them to his master for a present. TIT 4.03. 76
led by their master to the flow'red fields, 5.01. 15
my master is the great rich capulet, and if you ROM 1.02. 78 P
am i the master here, or you? 1.05. 78
he will answer the letter's master, how he dares 2.04. 11 P
it doth so, holy sir, and there's my master, 5.03.128

my master knows not but i am gone hence, | and 5.03.132
here, | i dreamt my master and another fought, 5.03.138
another fought, | and that my master slew him. 5.03.139
i brought my master news of juliet's death, 5.03.272
sirrah, what made your master in this place? 5.03.280
the tomb, | and by and by my master drew on him, 5.03.284
"commend me to your master" and the cap | plays
TIM 2.01. 18
my master is awak'd by great occasion | to call 2.02. 21
athens, thy very bountiful good lord and master? 3.01. 11 P
i see thou art a fool, and fit for thy master. 3.01. 50 P
be employ'd | now to guard sure their master. 3.03. 39
hear you, master steward, where's our master? 4.02. 1
hear you, master steward, where's our master? 4.02. 1
so noble a master fall'n, all gone, and not 4.02. 6
my dearest master! 4.03.471
no, my most worthy master, in whose breast 4.03.511
o, let me stay, | and comfort you, my master. 4.03.534
our late noble master! 5.01. 55
thus, brutus, did my master bid me kneel; JC 3.01.123
so says my master antony. 3.01.137
thy master is a wise and valiant roman, | i 3.01.138
the choice and master spirits of this age. 3.01.163
is thy master coming? 3.01.285
is come | to do you salutation from his master. 4.02. 5
your master, pindarus, | in his own change, or 4.02. 6
not doubt | but that my noble master will appear 4.02. 11
my master's man. strato, where is thy master? 5.05. 53
how died my master, strato? 5.05. 64
that did the latest service to my master. 5.05. 67
husband's to aleppo gone, master o' th' tiger; MAC 1.03. 7
to give thee from our royal master thanks, 1.03.101
is not thy master with him? 1.05. 32
is thy master stirring? 2.03. 42 P
let every man be master of his time | till seven 3.01. 40
lov'd as my father, as my master follow'd, | as LR 1.01.141
so may it come, thy master, whom thou lov'st, 1.04. 6
your countenance which i would fain call master. 1.04. 28 P
sir, more knave than fool, after your master. 1.04.314
the noble duke my master, | my worthy arch and 2.01. 58
come, i'll flesh ye, come on, young master. 2.02. 46 P
it pleas'd the king his master very late | to 2.02.116
against the grace and person of my master, 2.02.131
hail to thee, noble master! 2.04. 4
me), the king my old master must be reliev'd. 3.03. 18 P
where is the king my master? 3.06. 86
take up thy master; 3.06. 92
bless thee, master! 4.01. 39
ay, master. 4.01. 72
now, where's your master? 4.02. 2
bending his sword | to his great master, who, 4.02. 75
sense will ne'er accommodate | his master thus. 4.06. 82
that i create thee here | my lord and master. 5.03. 78
come | to bid my king and master aye good night. 5.03.236
o my good master! 5.03.268
my master calls me, i must not say no. 5.03.323
bring thou the master to the citadel; OTH 2.01.209
hard at hand comes the master and main exercise, 2.01.262 P
but by sea | he is an absolute master. ANT 2.02.163
does conquer him that did his master conquer, 3.13. 45
please, our master | will leap to be his friend; 3.13. 50
to–morrow | you'll serve another master. 4.02. 28
like a master | married to your good service, 4.02. 30
he never find more cause | to change a master. 4.05. 16
himself to caesar | and leave his master antony; 4.06. 14
and see | thy master thus with pleach'd arms, 4.14. 73
my dear master, | my captain, and my emperor: 4.14. 89
and, eros, | thy master dies thy scholar: 4.14.102
he was my master, and i wore my life | to spend 5.01. 8
if your master | would have a queen his beggar, 5.02. 15
what thou hast done thy master caesar knows, 5.02. 65
it thus, my master and my lord | i must obey. 5.02.116
my master, and my lord! 5.02.190
my lord your son drew on my master. CYM 1.01.160
but that my master rather play'd than fought 1.01.162
why came you from your master? 1.01.169
i am the master of my speeches, and would 1.04.140 P
now, master doctor, have you brought those drugs 1.05. 4
he's for his master, | and enemy to my son. 1.05. 28
thou art then | as great as is thy master — 1.05. 51
the agent for his master, | and the remembrancer 1.05. 76
to master caesar's sword, | made lud's–town with 3.01. 31
o master, what a strange infection | is fall'n 3.02. 3
o my master, | thy mind to her is now as low as 3.02. 9
thy master is not there, who was indeed | the 3.04. 70
it cannot be | but that my master is abus'd. 3.04.120
best woodman and | are master of the feast. 3.06. 29
this was my master, | a very valiant britain, 4.02.368
never | find such another master. 4.02.374
thy complaining than | thy master in bleeding. 4.02.376
i'll hide my master from the flies, as deep | as 4.02.388
and rather father thee than master thee. 4.02.395
i heard no letter from my master since | i wrote 4.03. 36
never master had | a page so kind, so duteous, 5.05. 85
ne'er thank thy master. 5.05. 96
your life, good master, | must shuffle for 5.05.104
i'll be thy master. 5.05.119
me, her master, hitting | each object with a joy 5.05.395
my good master, | i will yet do you service. 5.05.403
desire it, | commended to our master, not to us; PER 1.03. 37
what say you, master? 2.01. 15 P
faith, master, i am thinking of the poor men 2.01. 18 P
nay, master, said not i as much when i saw the 2.01. 23 P
master, i marvel how the fishes live in the sea. 2.01. 26 P
but, master, if i had been the sexton, i would 2.01. 36 P
but, master, i'll go draw up the net. 2.01. 93 P
help, master, help! 2.01.116 P
sir, you are music's master. 2.05. 30
you, | ay, so well, that you must be her master, 2.05. 38
your master will be dead ere you return, 3.02. 7
and | the master calls, and trebles their 4.01. 64
master, i have gone through for this piece you 4.02. 43 P
her reasons, her master reasons, her prayers, 4.06. 8 P
i could wish him to be my master, or rather, my 4.06.159 P
if that thy master would gain by me, | proclaim 4.06.182
but since my master and mistress hath bought you 4.06.196 P
that, if i were a woman, would be master, | but TNK 2.05. 63
and sweetly we will do it, master gerrold. 3.05. 22
freckled nell — that never fail'd her master. 3.05. 27
there's a dainty mad woman, master, | comes i' 3.05. 72
you are master of a ship? 4.01.142
where's your whistle, master? 4.01.149
bear for it, master. 4.01.151
but he is like his master, coy and scornful. 5.02. 63
our master mars | /hath vouch'd his oracle, and 5.04.106
we'll be rul'd by you, master more, if you'll STM II.C 142 P
his testy master goeth about to take him, | when VEN 319
tell me, love's master, shall we meet to–morrow? 585
and asks the weary caitiff for his master, | and 914
that liked of her master as well as well might PP 15. 2
to leave the master loveless, or kill the 15. 6
hast thou, the master mistress of my passion; SON 20. 2
even such a beauty as you master now. 106. 8
MASTER–CORD 1 FR 0.0001 REL FR 1 V 0 P
fret the string, | the master–cord on 's heart! H8 3.02.106
MASTER'D 2 FR 0.0002 REL FR 2 V 0 P
i will not say | thou shalt be so well master'd, CYM 4.02.383
tree, | servilely master'd with a leathern rein! VEN 392
MASTERDOM 1 FR 0.0001 REL FR 1 V 0 P
come | give solely sovereign sway and masterdom.
MAC 1.05. 70
MASTER–LEAVER 1 FR 0.0001 REL FR 1 V 0 P
me in register | a master–leaver and a fugitive. ANT 4.09. 22
MASTERLESS 2 FR 0.0002 REL FR 2 V 0 P
what mean these masterless and gory swords | to ROM 5.03.142
or masterless leave both | to who shall find CYM 2.04. 60
MASTERLY 4 FR 0.0004 REL FR 4 V 0 P
thou dost speak masterly. TN 2.04. 22
masterly done! WT 5.03. 65
and gave you such a masterly report | for art HAM 4.07. 96
/toged consuls can propose | as masterly as he. OTH 1.01. 26
MASTERPIECE 1 FR 0.0001 REL FR 1 V 0 P
confusion now hath made his masterpiece! MAC 2.03. 66
/MASTER'S 4 FR 0.0004 REL FR 0 V 4 P
with my /master's /ship? why, it is at sea. TGV 3.01.282 P
then come back to my /master's as soon as i can. SHR 5.01. 5 P
didst thou never see thy /master's father, 5.01. 53 P
be not lisping to his /master's old tables, his 2H4 2.04.266 P
MASTER'S 64 FR 0.0072 REL FR 42 V 22 P
tend to th' master's whistle. TMP 1.01. 7 P
yet 'tis a maid, for she is her master's maid, TGV 3.01.271 P
which to–morrow, by his master's command, he 4.02. 79 P
i am my master's true confirmed love; 4.04.103
i will not look upon your master's lines; 4.04.128
i hope my master's suit will be but cold, 4.04.181
her to solicit your master's desires to mistress WIV 1.02. 10 P
lead mine eyes, or eye your master's heels? 3.02. 4 P
know if it were my master's fortune to have her 4.05. 47 P
there is a fat friend at your master's house, ERR 5.01.415
dead upon mine and my master's false accusation;
ADO 5.01.242 P
my master's a very jew. MV 2.02.104 P
see | lorenzo, who is thy new master's guest. 2.03. 6
than to die well, and not my master's debtor. AYL 2.03. 76
not for my sake, but your master's, i advise SHR 1.01.241
litio, | all for my master's sake, lucentio. 3.02.148
touch a hair of my master's horse–tail till they 4.01. 94 P
go take it up unto thy master's use. 4.03.157
take up my mistress' gown for thy master's use! 4.03.159 P
take up my mistress' gown to his master's use! 4.03.162
sirrah, your lord and master's married, there's AWW 2.03.242 P
a man's tongue shakes out his master's undoing. 2.04. 24 P
if i did love you in my master's flame, | with TN 1.05.264
and let your fervor, like my master's, be 1.05.287
my state is desperate for my master's love; 2.02. 37
more | will i my master's tears to you deplore. 3.01.162
your passion bears | goes on my master's griefs. 3.04.207
where he sits crowned in his master's spite. 5.01.128
from this time be | your master's mistress. 5.01.326
instant of their master's death and in the view WT 5.02. 69 P
to look upon my sometimes royal master's face. R2 5.05. 75
sir, and a kinswoman of my master's. 2H4 2.02.156 P
my master's mind. H5 3.06.116
under his master's command transporting a sum of 4.01.151 P
did represent my master's blushing cheeks, 1H6 4.01. 93
bewray'd the faintness of my master's heart. 4.01.107
god, and the good wine in thy master's way. 2H6 2.03. 96 P
to bar my master's heirs in true descent — R3 3.02. 54
that they which brought me in my master's hate, 3.02. 58
his head ere give consent | his master's child, 3.04. 39
"better," here comes one of my master's kinsmen.
ROM 1.01. 58 P
my master's. 1.02. 76 P
if you did know, my lord, my master's wants — TIM 2.02. 29
look you, here comes my master's page. 2.02. 72 P
but they enter my master's house merrily, and go 2.02.101 P
i feel my master's passion. 3.01. 56
sum | your master's confidence was above mine, 3.04. 31
maid, to thy master's bed, | thy mistress is o' 4.01. 12
as 'twere a knell unto our master's fortunes, 4.02. 26
my master's man. strato, where is thy master? JC 5.05. 53
banquo, banquo, | our royal master's murther'd! MAC 2.03. 87
false steward, that stole his master's daughter. HAM 4.05.173 P
wears out his time, much like his master's ass, OTH 1.01. 47
do not abuse my master's bounty by | th' undoing ANT 5.02. 43
will not wait pinion'd at your master's court, 5.02. 53
it was thy master's. CYM 2.03.142
i know your master's pleasure and he mine: 3.01. 84
be thou honest, | do thou thy master's bidding. 3.04. 65
thy hand, thou art | no servant of thy master's. 3.04. 76
thou art too slow to do thy master's bidding 3.04. 97
sorry that i must report ye | my master's enemy. 3.05. 4
hast any of thy late master's garments in thy 3.05.124 P
i had a feigned letter of my master's | then in 5.05.279
in a frenzy, in my master's garments | (which he 5.05.282
MASTERS' 3 FR 0.0003 REL FR 3 V 0 P
for servants must their masters' minds fulfill. ERR 4.01.113
turn their own points in their masters' bosoms; R3 5.01. 24
hear it from our mouths, | or from our masters'? MAC 4.01. 63
/MASTERS 1 FR 0.0001 REL FR 0 V 1 P
help, /masters, help, my master is mad. SHR 1.02. 18 P
MASTERS 109 FR 0.0123 REL FR 63 V 46 P
the masters of some merchant, and the merchant TMP 2.01. 5
by whose aid | (weak masters though ye be) i 5.01. 41
love is your master, for he masters you; TGV 1.01. 39
how many masters would do this for his servant? 4.04. 29 P
are masters to their females, and their lords: ERR 2.01. 24
masters, let him go: 4.04.111
well, masters, good night. ADO 3.03. 84 P
well, masters, we hear our charge. 3.03. 88 P
some treason, masters; yet stand close. 3.03.106 P
masters, masters — 3.03.171 P
masters, masters — 3.03.171 P
masters — 3.03.174 P
masters, do you serve god? 4.02. 16 P
masters, it is prov'd already that you are 4.02. 20 P
masters, i charge you in the prince's name 4.02. 37 P
and this is more, masters, than you can deny. 4.02. 60 P
but, masters, remember that i am an ass; 4.02. 76 P
who have you offended, masters, that you are 5.01.226 P
and, masters, do not forget to specify, when 5.01.255 P
good morrow, masters, put your torches out. 5.03. 24
good morrow, masters — each his several way. 5.03. 29
masters, spread yourselves. MND 1.02. 15 P
but masters, here are your parts, and i am to 1.02. 98 P
masters, you ought to consider with /yourselves, 3.01. 29 P
pray, masters, fly, masters! 3.01.105 P
pray, masters, fly, masters! 3.01.105 P
masters, the duke is coming from the temple, and 4.02. 15 P
masters, i am to discourse wonders; 4.02. 29 P
finger, for the wealth | that the world masters. MV 5.01.174
sweet masters, be patient, for your father's AYL 1.01. 63 P
or charles, or something weaker, masters thee. 1.02.260
if that be all, masters, i hear no harm. SHR 1.02.188
softly, my masters! 1.02.236
farewell, sweet masters both, i must be gone. 3.01. 85
fie on all tir'd jades, on all mad masters, and 4.01. 1 P
my masters, are you mad? TN 2.03. 86 P
we'll be thy good masters. WT 5.02.174 P
now, my masters, happy man be his dole, say i, 1H4 2.02. 76 P
come, my masters, let us share, and then to 2.02. 98 P
bound them, and were masters of their wealth. 2.04.254 P
hear you, my masters, was it for me to kill the 2.04.268 P
and here i stand. judge, my masters. 2.04.439 P
now, my masters, for a true face and good 2.04.501 P
feel, masters, how i shake, look you, i warrant 2H4 2.04.105 P
as dogs upon their masters, worrying you. H5 2.02. 83
of his greener days | and these he masters now. 2.04.137
out their armed heels at their dead masters, 4.07. 80
farewell, my masters, to my task will i. 1H6 1.01.152
away, my masters, trouble us no more, | but join 3.01.144
my masters, let's stand close. 2H6 1.03. 1 P
come, my masters, the duchess, i tell you, 1.04. 1 P
well said, my masters, and welcome all. 1.04. 13 P
stand by, my masters. 2.01. 70
my masters of saint albons, have you not 2.01.133
masters, i am come hither, as it were, upon my 2.03. 85 P
come on, my masters, each man take his stand, 3H6 4.03. 1
courage, my masters! 4.03. 24
then, masters, look to see a troublous world. R3 2.03. 9
stand ho! yet are we masters of the field. TRO 5.10. 1
why, masters, my good friends, mine honest COR 1.01. 62
masters a' th' people, | we do request your 2.02. 51
masters of the people, | your multiplying spawn 2.02. 77
how now, my masters, have you chose this man? 2.03.155
masters, lay down your weapons. 3.01.329
hear me, my masters, and my common friends — 3.03.108
go, masters, get you home, be not dismay'd. 4.06.149
come, masters, let's home. 4.06.153 P
my noble masters, hear me speak. 5.06.131
masters all, be quiet, | put up your swords. 5.06.133
how now, my masters? TIT 4.03. 36
now, masters, draw. 4.03. 64
quarrel is between our masters and us their men. ROM 1.01. 19 P
in the owners | are prized by their masters. TIM 1.01.171
when men come to borrow of your masters, they 2.02.100 P
when your false masters eat of my lord's meat? 3.04. 50
i perceive our masters may throw their caps at 3.04.100 P
large–handed robbers your grave masters are, 4.01. 11
for many so arrive at second masters, | upon 4.03.505
men at some time are masters of their fates; JC 1.02.139
and let our hearts, as subtle masters do, | stir 2.01.175
has he, masters? 3.02.110
o masters! 3.02.121
you are welcome, masters, welcome all. HAM 2.02.421 P
masters, you are all welcome. 2.02.429 P
till by some elder masters of known honor | i 5.02.248
with every gale and vary of their masters, LR 2.02. 79
come, i am a king, | masters, know you that? 4.06.200
we cannot all be masters, nor all masters OTH 1.01. 43
nor all masters | cannot be truly follow'd. 1.01. 43
my very noble and approv'd good masters: 1.03. 77
to th' platform, masters, come, let's set the 2.03.120
sir — montano — /sir — | help, masters! 2.03.160
what is the matter, masters? 2.03.176
masters, play here, i will content your pains; 3.01. 1
why, masters, have your instruments been in 3.01. 3 P
but, masters, here's money for you; 3.01. 11 P
nay, stare not, masters, it is true indeed. 5.02.188
how now, masters? ANT 4.03. 18
do you hear, masters? do you hear? 4.03. 20
good masters, harm me not. CYM 3.06. 45
alas, | there is no more such masters. 4.02.371
come your ways, my masters. PER 4.02. 40 P
follow me, my masters, you shall have your money 4.02. 53 P
can tutor 's) to | be masters of our manners. TNK 1.02. 44
my masters, i'll be there, that's certain. 2.03. 24
is't now to th' end o' th' world, my masters? 5.02. 72
friends, masters, countrymen — STM II.C 27
my masters, countrymen — II.C 29
good masters, hear me speak. II.C 57
MASTERSHIP 3 FR 0.0003 REL FR 1 V 2 P
what news with your mastership? TGV 3.01.281 P
of launcelot, an't please your mastership. MV 2.02. 59 P
all boats alike | show'd mastership in floating; COR 4.01. 7
/MASTIC 1 FR 0.0001 REL FR 1 V 0 P
/when /rank /thersites /opes /his /mastic /jaws, TRO 1.03. 73
MASTIFF 1 FR 0.0001 REL FR 1 V 0 P
mastiff, greyhound, mongril grim, | hound or LR 3.06. 68
MASTIFFS 3 FR 0.0003 REL FR 1 V 2 P
their mastiffs are of unmatchable courage. H5 3.07.141 P
sympathize with the mastiffs in robustious and 3.07.148 P
pride alone | must /tarre the mastiffs on, as TRO 1.03.390
MAST'RED 3 FR 0.0003 REL FR 3 V 0 P

not by might mast'red, but by special grace. LLL 1.01.152
grace | as if he mast'red there a double spirit 1H4 5.02. 63
it, | and leaves it to be mast'red by his young, LUC 863
MAST'RING 2 FR 0.0002 REL FR 2 V 0 P
for mast'ring her that foil'd the god of fight! VEN 114
thing we have not, mast'ring what not strives, LC 240
MAST'RY 1 FR 0.0001 REL FR 1 V 0 P
some say, | groan under such a mast'ry. TNK 1.01.231
MASTS 1 FR 0.0001 REL FR 1 V 0 P
ten masts at each make not the altitude | which LR 4.06. 53
MATCH 84 FR 0.0095 REL FR 62 V 22 P
a match! TMP 2.01. 34 P
but tell me true, will't be a match? TGV 2.05. 34 P
to match my friend sir thurio to my daughter. 3.01. 62
and sure the match | were rich and honorable; 3.01. 63
and if it be a match, as nothing is impossible 3.01.369 P
the match between sir thurio and my daughter? 3.02. 23
hence, | to keep me from a most unholy match, 4.03. 30
to him, the hour is fix'd, the match is made. WIV 2.02.290 P
we have linger'd about a match between anne page 3.02. 57 P
she is no match for you. 3.04. 73
(even strong against that match | and firm for 4.06. 27
the body | that took away the match from isabel, MM 5.01.211
i have but lean luck in the match, and yet is ERR 3.02. 92 P
and truly i hold it a sin to match in my kinred. ADO 2.01. 64 P
god match me with a good dancer! 2.01.107 P
his grace hath made the match, and all grace say 2.01.303 P
i would fain have it a match, and i doubt not 2.01.368 P
your brother's honor, who hath made this match, 2.02. 38 P
lower than myself, | that i can match her. MND 3.02.305
there i have another bad match. MV 3.01. 44 P
if two gods should play some heavenly match, 3.05. 79
i could match this beginning with an old tale. AYL 1.02.120 P
old, cuckoldly ram, out of all reasonable match. 3.02. 83 P
till his fellow–fault came to match it. 3.02.356 P
'tis a match. SHR 2.01.319
was ever match clapp'd up so suddenly? 2.01.325
the gain i seek is, quiet /in the match. 2.01.330
dower, | the match is made, and all is done: 4.04. 46
a match! 'tis done. 5.02. 74
as high as word, my deed shall match thy deed. AWW 2.01.210
half won is match well made; 4.03.225
match, and well make it; 4.03.225
then shall we have a match. 5.03. 30
she'll not match above her degree, neither in TN 1.03.109 P
no settled senses of the world can match | the WT 5.03. 72
this is a match, | and made between 's by vows. 5.03.137
if love ambitious sought a match of birth, JN 2.01.430
for at this match, | with swifter spleen than 2.01.447
but without this match, | the sea enraged is not 2.01.450
son, list to this conjunction, make this match, 2.01.468
for this match made up | her presence would have 2.01.541
assured loss before the match be play'd. 3.01.336
to win this easy match play'd for a crown? 5.02.106
and make some pretty match with shedding tears?
R2 3.03.165
now shall we know if gadshill have set a match. 1H4 1.02.107 P
what cunning match have you made with this jest 2.04. 90 P
him he hath made a match with such a wrangler H5 1.02.264
poor, | and our nobility will scorn the match. 1H6 5.03. 96
whom should we match with henry, being a king, 5.05. 66
to match with her that brings no vantages. 2H6 1.01.131
if you oppose yourselves to match lord warwick. 5.01.156
but match to match i have encount'red him, | and 5.02. 10
but match to match i have encount'red him, | and 5.02. 10
the match is made, she seals it with a cur'sy. 3H6 3.02. 57
iwis your grandam had a worser match. R3 1.03.101
whose humble means match not his haughty spirit. 4.02. 37
a mint, | to match us in comparisons with dirt, TRO 1.03.194
might be affronted with the match and weight 3.02.166
i'll make my match to live, | the kiss you take 4.05. 37
it were no match, your nail against his horn. 4.05. 46
i would my arms could match thee in contention, 4.05.205
but i'll endeavor deeds to match these words, 4.05.259
thy hand upon that match. 4.05.270
art thou for hector's match? 5.04. 26
a match, sir. COR 2.03. 80 P
and in this match | i hold me highly honored of TIT 1.01.244
ne'er saw her match since first the world begun. ROM 1.02. 93
and spurs, swits and spurs, or i'll cry a match. 2.04. 70 P
and learn me how to lose a winning match, 3.02. 12
i think you are happy in this second match, 3.05.222
be a sight indeed | if one could match you. HAM 4.07.100
make such a stray | to match you where i hate; LR 1.01.210
shall i live and work | to match thy goodness? 4.07. 2
may fall to match you with her country forms, OTH 3.03.237
such perdition | as nothing else could match. 3.04. 68
thy match was mortal to him, and pure grief 5.02.205
i that do bring the news made not the match. ANT 2.05. 67
so is the queen, | that most desir'd the match. CYM 1.01. 12
i dare you to this match: 1.04.145 P
up and down like a cock that nobody can match. 2.01. 22 P
will play the cook and servant, 'tis our match. 3.06. 30
lest this match between 's | be cross'd ere met. TNK 3.01. 97
wilt thou make the match?" VEN 586
all love's pleasure shall not match his woe. 1140
/MATCH'D 1 FR 0.0001 REL FR 1 V 0 P
with tender juliet /match'd is now not fair. ROM 2.pr. 4
MATCH'D 15 FR 0.0017 REL FR 13 V 2 P
is a sharp wit match'd with too blunt a will, LLL 2.01. 49
but match'd in mouth like bells, | each under MND 4.01.123
a third cannot be match'd, unless the devil MV 3.01. 78 P
in a good father's care, | to have him match'd; SHR 4.04. 32
strength match'd with strength, and power JN 2.01.330
this match'd with other did, my gracious lord, 1H4 1.01. 49
as thou art match'd withal and grafted to, 3.02. 15
when we have match'd our rackets to these balls, H5 1.02.261
few bad words are match'd with as few good deeds 3.02. 39 P
and had he match'd according to his state, | he 3H6 2.02.152
the harder match'd, the greater victory: 5.01. 70
his daughter meanly have i match'd in marriage, R3 4.03. 37
match'd not the high perfection of my loss. 4.04. 66
still my care hath been | to have her match'd; ROM 3.05.178
unequal match'd, | pyrrhus at priam drives, in HAM 2.02.471
MATCHES 4 FR 0.0004 REL FR 4 V 0 P
of all mad matches never was the like. SHR 3.02.242
strange, | which manifold record not matches? TIM 1.01. 5
not to affect many proposed matches | of her own OTH 3.03.229
hath she forsook so many noble matches? 4.02.125
MATCHETH 1 FR 0.0001 REL FR 1 V 0 P
but why thy odor matcheth not thy show, | the SON 69.13
MATCHING 3 FR 0.0003 REL FR 3 V 0 P
that end, | as matching to his youth and vanity, H5 2.04.130
for matching more for wanton lust than honor, 3H6 3.03.210
and /blown surmises, | matching thy inference. OTH 3.03.183
MATCHLESS 3 FR 0.0003 REL FR 3 V 0 P
that a man may owe, | matchless navarre; LLL 2.01. 7
not yet mature, yet matchless, firm of word, TRO 4.05. 97
yes, a matchless beauty. TNK 2.02.154
/MATE 1 FR 0.0001 REL FR 1 V 0 P
/else /one /self /mate /and /make /could /not LR 4.03. 34
MATE 11 FR 0.0012 REL FR 10 V 1 P
the boatswain, and i, | the gunner and his mate, TMP 2.02. 47
thou, that hast no unkind mate to grieve thee, ERR 2.01. 38
me to some wither'd bough and there | my mate, WT 5.03.134
poor, base, rascally, cheating, lack–linen mate! 2H4 2.04.125 P
if thou receive me for thy warlike mate. 1H6 1.02. 92
to be disgraced by an inkhorn mate, | we and our 3.01. 99
and thou that art his mate, make boot of this; 2H6 4.01. 13
dare mate a sounder man than surrey can be, H8 3.02.274
moon, | as sun to day, as turtle to her mate, TRO 3.02.178
in top of all design, my mate in empire, ANT 5.01. 43
lent | in the possession of his beauteous mate; LUC 18
MATED* 7 FR 0.0008 REL FR 7 V 0 P
not mad, but mated — how, i do not know. ERR 3.02. 54
i think you are all mated, or stark mad. 5.01.282
that, being mad herself, she's madly mated. SHR 3.02.244
the hind that would be mated by the lion | must AWW 1.01. 91
if she be mated with an equal husband? TIM 1.01.140
my mind she has mated, and amaz'd my sight. MAC 5.01. 78
her more than haste is mated with delays, | like VEN 909
/MATER 1 FR 0.0001 REL FR 0 V 1 P
nourish'd in the womb of /pia /mater, and LLL 4.02. 69 P
MATER 2 FR 0.0002 REL FR 0 V 2 P
one of thy kin has a most weak pia mater. TN 1.05.115 P
and his pia mater is not worth the ninth part of TRO 2.01. 71 P
/MATERIAL 1 FR 0.0001 REL FR 1 V 0 P
/and /disbranch | /from /her /material /sap, LR 4.02. 35
MATERIAL 4 FR 0.0004 REL FR 3 V 1 P
a material fool! AYL 3.03. 32 P
petitions, made | his business more material. WT 1.02.216
whose absence is no less material to me | than MAC 3.01.135
which is material | to th' tender of our present CYM 1.06.207
/MATES* 1 FR 0.0001 REL FR 1 V 0 P
/when /grief /hath /mates, /and /bearing LR 3.06.107
MATES* 12 FR 0.0013 REL FR 11 V 1 P
bestow thy fawning smiles on equal mates, | and TGV 3.01.158
these are my mates, that make their wills their 5.04. 14
our masquing mates by this time for us stay. MV 2.06. 59
to make a stale of me amongst these mates? SHR 1.01. 58
mates, maid, how mean you that? 1.01. 59
no mates for you, | unless you were of gentler, 1.01. 59
aboard, carousing to his mates | after a storm, 3.02.171
which mates him first that first intends deceit. 2H6 3.01.265
we'll forward towards warwick and his mates; 3H6 4.07. 82
how now, my hardy, stout, resolved mates, | are R3 1.03.339
and we, poor mates, stand on the dying deck, TIM 4.02. 20
half–part, mates, half–part. PER 4.01. 94 P
MATHEMATICS 3 FR 0.0003 REL FR 2 V 1 P
the mathematics, and the metaphysics, | fall to SHR 1.01. 37
of mine, | cunning in music and the mathematics, 2.01. 56
as the other in music and mathematics. 2.01. 82 P
MATIN 1 FR 0.0001 REL FR 1 V 0 P
the glow–worm shows the matin to be near, | and HAM 1.05. 89
MATRON 3 FR 0.0003 REL FR 3 V 0 P
please it this matron and this gentle maid | to AWW 3.05. 97
night, | thou sober–suited matron all in black, ROM 3.02. 11
strike me the counterfeit matron, | it is her TIM 4.03.113
MATRON'S 1 FR 0.0001 REL FR 1 V 0 P
if thou canst mutine in a matron's bones, | to HAM 3.04. 83
MATRONS 4 FR 0.0004 REL FR 4 V 0 P
matrons flung gloves, | ladies and maids their COR 2.01.263
matrons, turn incontinent! TIM 4.01. 3
your matrons, and your maids could not fill up MAC 4.03. 62
maids, matrons, nay, the secrets of the grave CYM 3.04. 38
/MATTER 2 FR 0.0002 REL FR 1 V 1 P
/of /less /expect | /that /matter /needless, /of TRO 1.03. 71
/no /such /matter. HAM 2.02.267 P
MATTER 365 FR 0.0412 REL FR 199 V 166 P
what impossible matter will he make easy next? TMP 2.01. 89 P
eye and cheek proclaim | a matter from thee; 2.01.230
what's the matter? 2.01.309
what's the matter? 2.02. 57 P
no matter, since | they have left their viands 3.03. 40
although my last, no matter, since i feel | the 3.03. 50
come, come, open the matter in brief: TGV 1.01.127 P
the money and the matter may be both at once 1.01.130 P
what's the matter? 2.03. 35 P
it is no matter if the tied were lost; 2.03. 37 P
why then, how stands the matter with them? 2.05. 20 P
no matter who's displeas'd when you are gone: 2.07. 66
nay then no matter; 3.01. 58
it's no matter for that, so she sleep not in her 3.01.330 P
there's some great matter she'ld employ me in. 4.03. 3
what's the matter? 5.04. 87 P
i will make a star chamber matter of it. WIV 1.01. 2 P
what matter have you against me? 1.01.122 P
sir, i have matter in my head against you, and 1.01.123 P
ay, it is no matter. 1.01.129 P
ay, it is no matter. 1.01.131 P
there is three umpires in this matter, as i 1.01.137 P
but 'tis no matter; 1.01.181 P
i will description the matter to you, if you be 1.01.215 P
what's the matter, woman? 2.01. 43 P
grossly done, so it be fairly done, no matter. 2.02.143 P
what's the matter? 3.03. 93 P
what's the matter, good mistress page? 3.03. 97 P
why, alas, what's the matter? 3.03.105 P
what is the matter, sir? 4.05. 74 P
the mirth whereof so larded with my matter, 4.06. 14
/brook, the matter will be known to–night, or 5.01. 10 P
but 'tis no matter; 5.03. 9 P
it, that it wants matter to prevent so gross 5.05.136 P
and what's the matter? MM 2.01. 46 P
go to, go to; no matter for the dish, sir. 2.01. 95 P
now, what's the matter, provost? 2.02. 6
well; the matter? 2.02. 33
yet, as the matter now stands, he will avoid 3.01.196 P
what say'st thou to this tune, matter, and 3.02. 48 P
neither in time, matter, or other circumstance. 4.02.104 P
the matter being afoot, keep your instruction, 4.05. 3
pardon it, | the phrase is to the matter. 5.01. 90
mended again. the matter; proceed. 5.01. 91
whom it concerns to hear this matter forth, | do 5.01.255
i will debate this matter at more leisure, | and ERR 4.01.100
why, man, what is the matter? 4.02. 41
i do not know the matter, he is 'rested on the 4.02. 42
without spectacles, and i see no such matter. ADO 1.01.190 P
i have almost matter enough in me for such an 1.01.279 P
me, i was born to speak all mirth and no matter. 2.01.330 P
i will so fashion the matter that hero shall be 2.02. 47 P
opinion of another's dotage, and no such matter; 2.03.217 P
of this matter | is little cupid's crafty arrow 3.01. 21
highly that to her | all matter else seems weak. 3.01. 54
what's the matter? 3.02. 87 P
why, what's the matter? 3.02.101 P
and there be any matter of weight chances, call 3.03. 85 P
verges, sir, speaks a little /off the matter; 3.05. 10 P
but that's no matter, let him kill one first. 5.01. 81
come, 'tis no matter; 5.01.100
hath reform'd signior leonato of the matter; 5.01.255 P
why, what's the matter, | that you have such a 5.04. 40
'tis no such matter. then you do not love me? 5.04. 82
how low soever the matter, i hope in god for LLL 1.01.192 P
the matter is to me, sir, as concerning 1.01.201 P
we will talk no more of this matter. 3.01.118 P
till there be more matter in the shin. 3.01.119 P
beg a greater matter, | thou now requests but 5.02.207
that is the very defect of the matter, sir. MV 2.02.143 P
and so did mine too, as the matter falls; 3.02.202
and so now i speak my agitation of the matter; 3.05. 4 P
him, that for a tricksy word | defy the matter. 3.05. 70
and yet no matter; 5.01. 50
a quarrel ho already! what's the matter? 5.01.146
and i came to acquaint you with a matter. AYL 1.01.123 P
sullen fits, | for then he's full of matter. 2.01. 68
why, what's the matter? 2.03. 16
no matter whither, so you come not here. 2.03. 30
that's no matter; 3.02.167 P
lord, it is a hard matter for friends to meet; 3.02.184 P
'tis no matter; 3.03.106 P
and when you were gravell'd for lack of matter, 4.01. 74 P
matter, the cleanliest shift is to kiss. 4.01. 77 P
you to entreaty, and there begins new matter. 4.01. 80 P
'tis no matter how it be in tune, so it make 4.02. 8 P
has a huswive's hand — but that's no matter. 4.03. 27
though there was no great matter in the ditty, 5.03. 35 P
i have promis'd to make all this matter even: 5.04. 18
there is much matter to be heard and learn'd. 5.04.185
a good matter, surely; SHR 1.01.250 P
how now, what's the matter? 1.02. 20 P
nay, 'tis no matter, sir, what he 'leges in 1.02. 28 P
that thinks with oaths to face the matter out. 2.01.289
then go with me to make the matter good. 4.02.115
how now, what's the matter? 5.01. 71 P
that fac'd and braved me in this matter so? 5.01.121
her matter was, she lov'd your son. AWW 1.03.110 P
what's the matter, | that this distempered 1.03.150
what's the matter, sweet heart? 2.03.268 P
trust him not in matter of heavy consequence; 2.05. 44 P
what is the matter? 3.02. 35 P
you understand it not yourselves, no matter; 4.01. 4 P
no matter, his heels have deserv'd it, in 4.03.103 P
against your son, there is no fitter matter. 4.05. 76 P
my former–past proofs, howe'er the matter fall, 5.03.121
we'll sift this matter further. 5.03.124
sure you have some hideous matter to deliver, TN 1.05.206 P
my words are as full of peace as matter. 1.05.211 P
on a forgotten matter we can hardly make 2.03.160 P
no such matter, sir. 3.01. 5 P
the matter, i hope, is not great, sir — begging 3.01. 54 P
my matter hath no voice, lady, but to your own 3.01. 88 P
it is no matter how witty, so it be eloquent and 3.02. 43 P
though thou write with a goose–pen, no matter. 3.02. 50 P
why, what's the matter? does he rave? 3.04. 10
what is the matter with thee? 3.04. 25 P
more matter for a may morning. 3.04.142 P
that is not the matter i challenge thee for." 3.04.157 P
pray you, sir, do you know of this matter? 3.04.259 P
let him let the matter slip, and i'll give him 3.04.286 P
i strook him first, yet it's no matter for that. 4.01. 36 P
what's the matter? 5.01. 59
what's the matter? 5.01.174 P
the world either malice or matter to alter it. WT 1.01. 34 P
he's all my exercise, my mirth, my matter; 1.02.166
the matter, | the loss, the gain, the ord'ring 2.01.168
it is but weakness | to bear the matter thus — 2.03. 2
the whole matter | and copy of the father — eye 2.03. 99
a million of beating may come to a great matter. 4.03. 60 P
well, if it be doleful matter merrily set down, 4.04.188 P
mischief and break a foul gap into the matter, 4.04.198 P
aside, here is more matter for a hot brain. 4.04.684 P
will i present them, there may be matter in it. 4.04.842 P
tale still, which will have matter to rehearse, 5.02. 62 P
thought she had some great matter there in hand, 5.02.104 P
and pick strong matter of revolt and wrath | out JN 3.04.167
what better matter breeds for you | than i have 3.04.170
even in the matter of mine innocence; 4.01. 64
and brought in matter that should feed this fire 5.02. 85
why, uncle, what's the matter? R2 2.01.186
no matter where — of comfort no man speak: 3.02.144
no matter then who see it. 5.02. 58
it is a matter of small consequence, | which for 5.02. 61
what is the matter, my lord? 5.02. 73
what is the matter? 5.02. 79
i will not peace. what is the matter, aumerle? 5.02. 81
what is the matter with our cousin now? 5.03. 29
what is the matter, uncle? 5.03. 46
i'll read you matter deep and dangerous, | as 1H4 1.03.190
why, you whoreson round man, what's the matter? 2.04.141 P
what's the matter? 2.04.157 P
what's the matter! 2.04.158 P
instinct is a great matter; 2.04.272 P
so majestically, both in word and matter, hang 2.04.436 P

what's the matter? 2.04.488 P
a trifle, some eight-penny matter. 3.03.104 P
well, 'tis no matter, honor pricks me on. 5.01.129 P
by the stern tyrant war, | and no such matter? 2H4 in 15
'tis no matter if i do halt, i have the wars for 1.02.245 P
how now, whose mare's dead? what's the matter? 2.01. 44 P
what is the matter? keep the peace here, ho! 2.01. 61 P
what's the matter? 2.01.181 P
is't such a matter to get a pottle-pot's 2.02. 78 P
how now, what's the matter? 2.04.370 P
what's the matter? 2.04.386 P
i will devise matter enough out of this shallow 5.01. 78 P
but 'tis no matter, this poor show doth better, 5.05. 13 P
but though we think it so, it is no matter. H5 2.04. 42
if you take the matter otherwise than is meant, 3.02.125 P
it will be a black matter for the king that led 4.01.145 P
how now, how now, what's the matter? 4.08. 19 P
how now, what's the matter? 4.08. 24 P
'tis no matter for his swellings nor his 5.01. 16 P
any occasion to write for matter of grant, shall 5.02.337 P
work | to bring this matter to the wished end. 1H6 3.03. 28
approacheth, to confer about some matter. 5.04.101
and, now the matter grows to compremise, 5.04.149
marriage is a matter of more worth | than to be 5.05. 55
we'll hear more of your matter before the king. 2H6 1.03. 35 P
but to the matter that we have in hand. 1.03.159
i never said nor thought any such matter. 1.03.188 P
make up no factious numbers for the matter, | in 2.01. 39
sleeping, or waking, 'tis no matter how, | so he 3.01.263
what's the matter, suffolk? 3.02. 28
matter of marriage was the charge he gave me, 3H6 3.03.258
my thoughts aim at a further matter: 4.01.125
i'll hence to london on a serious matter. 5.05. 47
but what's the matter, clarence, may i know? R3 1.01. 51
brother of gloucester, you mistake the matter: 1.03. 62
'tis no matter, let it go. 1.04.131 P
is it not an easy matter | to make william lord 3.01.161
in deep designs, in matter of great moment, | no 3.07. 67
i read in 's looks | matter against me, and his H8 1.01.126
hour | to hear from him a matter of some moment; 1.02.163
found | matter against him that for ever mars 3.02. 21
what's the matter? 5.01. 10
i'll meddle nor make no more i' th' matter. TRO 1.01. 83 P
no matter. 1.02. 89 P
is it matter new to us | that we come short of 1.03. 10
and what hath mass or matter, by itself | lies 1.03. 29
then would come some matter from him; 2.01. 8 P
how now, thersites, what's the matter, man? 2.01. 56
ay, what's the matter? 2.01. 58 P
so i do. what's the matter? 2.01. 60 P
'tis no matter, i shall speak as much as thou 2.01.111 P
but it is no matter, thyself upon thyself! 2.03. 27 P
then will ajax lack matter, if he have lost his 2.03. 94 P
and never suffers matter of the world | enter 2.03.186
no such matter, you are wide. 3.01. 88 P
what's the matter? 4.02. 42 P
how now, what's the matter? 4.02. 43 P
how now, what's the matter? 4.02. 58
leisure to salute you, | my matter is so rash. 4.02. 60
how now? what's the matter? who was here? 4.02. 78 P
tell me, sweet uncle, what's the matter? 4.02. 81 P
o the gods! what's the matter? 4.02. 84 P
on my knees /i /beseech /you, what's the matter? 4.02. 89 P
it is no matter now i ha't again. 5.02. 72
it is no matter. 5.02. 87
words, mere words, no matter from the heart; 5.03.108
the matter? COR 1.01. 56
what's the matter, you dissentious rogues, 1.01.164
what's the matter, | that in these several 1.01.184
here. what's the matter? 1.01.223
why, 'tis no great matter; 2.01. 28 P
your worships have deliver'd the matter well, 2.01. 58 P
you are hearing a matter between party and party 2.01. 73 P
what's the matter? 2.01.259
but that's no matter, the greater part carries 2.03. 37 P
and 'twere to give again — but 'tis no matter. 2.03. 84 P
the matter? 3.01. 28
nor by th' matter which your heart prompts you, 3.02. 54
what is the matter | that being pass'd for 3.03. 58
we need not put new matter to his charge. 3.03. 76
nay, it's no matter for that. 4.05.165 P
'tis no matter; 4.06.136
what's the matter? 5.02. 59 P
why, 'tis no matter, man: TIT 3.01. 33
to take up a matter of brawl betwixt my uncle 4.03. 93 P
this is the matter. ROM 1.03. 7
conceit, more rich in matter than in words, 2.06. 30
was ever book containing such vile matter | so 3.02. 83
logs, | and never trouble peter for the matter. 4.04. 19
what is the matter? 4.05. 18
no matter, get thee gone, | and hire those 5.01. 32
no matter what, he's poor, and that's revenge TIM 3.04. 62 P
the dead — some that were hang'd, | no matter; 4.03.147
it is no matter, let no images | be hung with JC 1.01. 68
casca will tell us what the matter is. 1.02.189
it serves | for the base matter to illuminate 1.03.110
it is no matter, | enjoy the honey-heavy dew of 2.01.229
and when i ask'd you what the matter was, | you 2.01.241
if thou consider rightly of the matter, | caesar 3.02.109
that matter is answer'd directly. 3.03. 23 P
it is no matter, his name's cinna. 3.03. 33 P
what's the matter? 4.03.118
how now? what's the matter? 4.03.129
what's the matter? MAC 2.03. 65
volume of my brain, | unmix'd with baser matter. HAM 1.05.104
farewell! how now, ophelia, what's the matter? 2.01. 71
more matter, with less art. 2.02. 95
what is the matter, my lord? 2.02.193 P
i mean, the matter that you read, my lord. 2.02.195 P
sallets in the lines to make the matter savory, 2.02.442 P
nor no matter in the phrase that might indict 2.02.442 P
/and, like a neutral to his will and matter, 2.02.481
your majesties | to hear and see the matter. 3.01. 23
this something-settled matter in his heart, 3.01.173
therefore no more, but to the matter: 3.02.324 P
now, mother, what's the matter? 3.04. 8
what's the matter now? 3.04. 13
and /i the matter will reword, which madness 3.04.143
make you to ravel all this matter out, | that i 3.04.186
there's matter in these sighs, these profound 4.01. 1
death, | wherein necessity, of matter beggar'd, 4.05. 92
what is the matter? 4.05. 99
this nothing's more than matter. 4.05.174
they much too light for the /bore of the matter. 4.06. 26 P
or, if 'a do not, 'tis no great matter there. 5.01.151 P
but it is no matter. 5.01.290
we'll put the matter to the present push. 5.01.295
sir, this is the matter — 5.02.103 P
the phrase would be more germane to the matter, 5.02.159 P
here about my heart — but it is no matter. 5.02.213 P
love you more than /words can wield the matter, LR 1.01. 55
if the matter were good, my lord, i durst swear 1.02. 63 P
what grows of it, no matter. 1.03. 23
my lord, i know not what the matter is, but, to 1.04. 57 P
what's the matter, sir? 1.04.295
how now, what's the matter? part! 2.02. 44 P
weapons? arms? what's the matter here? 2.02. 47 P
what is the matter? 2.02. 49
when priests are more in word than matter; 3.02. 81
between the dukes, and a worse matter than that. 3.03. 9 P
if the matter of this paper be certain, you have 3.05. 15 P
faith, he is posted hence on serious matter. 4.05. 8
in better phrase and matter than thou didst. 4.06. 8
o, matter and impertinency mix'd! 4.06.174
come, no matter vor your foins. 4.06.244 P
if ever i did dream of such a matter, | abhor me OTH 1.01. 5
what is the matter there? 1.01. 83
what is the matter, think you? 1.02. 38
why? what's the matter? 1.03. 58
take up this mangled matter at the best; 1.03.173
hour | of love, of wordly matter and direction, 1.03.299
what's the matter, lieutenant? 2.03.146 P
what is the matter here? 2.03.164
what is the matter, masters? 2.03.176
what's the matter | that you unlace your 2.03.193
more of this matter cannot i report. 2.03.240
thy honesty and love doth mince this matter, 2.03.247
what is the matter, dear? 2.03.252
there's matter in't indeed, if he be angry. 3.04.139
what's the matter? 4.01. 49
good madam, what's the matter with my lord? 4.02. 98
what is the matter, lady? 4.02.114
what's the matter? 5.01. 50
what is the matter ho? who is't that cried? 5.01. 74
alas, what is the matter? 5.01.111
what is the matter, husband? 5.01.111
i will so. what's the matter? 5.02. 47
what's the matter with thee now? 5.02.105
what is the matter? how now, general? 5.02.168
what is the matter? 5.02.171
what is the matter? 5.02.259
though thou deny me a matter of more weight; ANT 1.02. 68 P
what's the matter? 1.03. 18
i could have given less matter | a better ear. 2.01. 31
serves for the matter that is then born in't. 2.02. 10
terms, | nor curstness grow to th' matter. 2.02. 25
as matter whole you have to make it with, | it 2.02. 53
i do not much dislike the matter, but | the 2.02.111
we had much more monstrous matter of feast, 2.02.182 P
pour out the pack of matter to mine ear, | the 2.05. 54
'tis no matter. 2.05.110
i think th' art mad. the matter? 2.07. 56
but 'tis no matter, thou shalt bring him to me 3.03. 46
yet now — no matter. 3.11. 40
no matter, sir, what i have heard or known. 5.02. 73
but what's the matter? CYM 1.01. 3
this matter of marrying his king's daughter, 1.04. 14 P
him, i doubt not, a great deal from the matter. 1.04. 17 P
what is the matter, trow? 1.06. 47
what's the matter? 3.04. 10
what's the matter, sir? 3.06. 41
the matter? 4.02.192
i am amaz'd with matter. 4.03. 28
i stand on fire: | come to the matter. 5.05.169
new matter still. 5.05.243
now this matter must be look'd to, | for her PER 3.02.108
how now, what's the matter? 4.06.131 P
wanting form, | is press'd with deeper matter. TNK 1.01.109
small winds shake him. | but what's the matter? 1.02. 89
why, what's the matter, man? 2.02.133
no matter, would it were perpetual night, | and 3.02. 3
that's no matter, | i'll argue that hereafter. 3.03. 4
what broken piece of matter soe'er she's about, 4.03. 6 P
"no matter where," quoth he, | "leave me, and VEN 715
as dry combustious matter is to fire. 1162
thy wretched wife mistook the matter so, | to LUC 1826
no matter then although my foot did stand | upon SON 44. 5
then lack'd i matter, that enfeebled mine. 86.14
in sleep a king, but waking no such matter. 87.14
"in him a plenitude of subtle matter, | applied LC 302

MATTER-A 1 FR 0.0001 REL FR 0 V 1 P
it is no matter-a ver dat. WIV 1.04.115 P

MATTER'S 2 FR 0.0002 REL FR 2 V 0 P
the matter's in my head and in my heart. AYL 3.05.137
the matter's too far driven between him | and TNK 2.03. 43

MATTERS 25 FR 0.0028 REL FR 11 V 14 P
and most poor matters | point to rich ends. TMP 3.01. 3
another tale, if matters grow to your likings. WIV 1.01. 77 P
you hear all these matters denied, gentlemen; 1.01.186 P
leaves unquestion'd | matters of needful value. MM 1.01. 55
faith, sir, few of any wit in such matters. 2.01.268 P
i think of as many matters as he, but i give AYL 2.05. 36 P
heavy matters, heavy matters! WT 3.03.112 P
heavy matters, heavy matters! 3.03.112 P
that would (if matters should be look'd into) 1H4 2.01. 72 P
when there were matters against you for your 2H4 1.02.132 P
pause, | to answer matters of this consequence. H5 2.04.146
these are no women's matters. 2H6 1.03.117
me, | i have great matters to impart to thee. 3.02.299
before them about matters they were not able to 4.07. 42 P
in charging you with matters, to commit you, H8 5.01.146
and so, intending other serious matters, | after TIM 2.02.210
i meddle with no tradesman's matters, nor JC 1.01. 22 P
no tradesman's matters, nor women's matters; 1.01. 23 P
how covert matters may be best disclos'd, | and 4.01. 46
as a book, where men | may read strange matters. MAC 1.05. 63
judgments in such matters cried in the top of HAM 2.02.438 P
do you think i meant country matters? 3.02.116 P
pray heaven it be state matters, as you think, OTH 3.04.155
but small to greater matters must give way. ANT 2.02. 11
to be glad that matters are so well disgested. 2.02.175 P

MATTHEW 1 FR 0.0001 REL FR 1 V 0 P
and thither i will send you matthew goffe. 2H6 4.05. 10

MATTOCK 3 FR 0.0003 REL FR 3 V 0 P
'tis you must dig with mattock and with spade, TIT 4.03. 11
give me that mattock and the wrenching iron. ROM 5.03. 22
we took this mattock and this spade from him, 5.03.185

MATTRESS 1 FR 0.0001 REL FR 1 V 0 P
a certain queen to caesar in a mattress. ANT 2.06. 70

MATURE 7 FR 0.0008 REL FR 5 V 2 P
since their more mature dignities and royal WT 1.01. 25 P
not yet mature, yet matchless, firm of word, TRO 4.05. 97
and is almost mature for the violent breaking COR 4.03. 25 P
and in the mature time | with this ungracious LR 4.06.275
as we rate boys who, being mature in knowledge, ANT 1.04. 31
to th' more mature | a glass that feated them, CYM 1.01. 48
when once he was mature for man, | in britain 5.04. 52

MATURELY 1 FR 0.0001 REL FR 1 V 0 P
has more ground, is more maturely season'd, TNK 1.03. 56

MATURITY 2 FR 0.0002 REL FR 2 V 0 P
pride | that hath to this maturity blown up | in TRO 1.03.317
crawls to maturity, wherewith being crown'd, SON 60. 6

MAUD 1 FR 0.0001 REL FR 1 V 0 P
maud, bridget, marian, cic'ly, gillian, ginn! ERR 3.01. 31

MAUDLIN 1 FR 0.0001 REL FR 1 V 0 P
send forth your amorous token for fair maudlin. AWW 5.03. 68

MAUDLINE 1 FR 0.0001 REL FR 1 V 0 P
here's friz and maudline. TNK 3.05. 25

MAUGRE 3 FR 0.0003 REL FR 3 V 0 P
i love thee so, that, maugre all thy pride, TN 3.01.151
this maugre all the world will i keep safe, | or TIT 4.02.110
maugre thy strength, place, youth, and eminence, LR 5.03.132

MAUL 2 FR 0.0002 REL FR 2 V 0 P
or i'll so maul you and your toasting-iron JN 4.03. 99
'tis sport to maul a runner. ANT 4.07. 14

MAUMET *(see mammet, etc.)*

MAUND 1 FR 0.0001 REL FR 1 V 0 P
a thousand favors from a maund she drew, | of LC 36

MAURI 1 FR 0.0001 REL FR 1 V 0 P
purus, | non eget mauri jaculis, nec arcu." TIT 4.02. 21

MAURITANIA 1 FR 0.0001 REL FR 0 V 1 P
he goes into mauritania and taketh away with him OTH 4.02.224 P

MAUVAIS 1 FR 0.0001 REL FR 0 V 1 P
ils sont les mots de son mauvais, corruptible, H5 3.04. 53 P

M'AVEZ 1 FR 0.0001 REL FR 0 V 1 P
les mots que vous m'avez appris des a present. H5 3.04. 26 P

MAW 7 FR 0.0008 REL FR 7 V 0 P
think | what 'tis to cram a maw or clothe a back MM 3.02. 22
methinks your maw, like mine, should be your ERR 1.02. 66
come | to thrust his icy fingers in my maw, JN 5.07. 37
in thy hateful lungs, yea, in thy maw, perdy; H5 2.01. 49
thou detestable maw, thou womb of death, ROM 5.03. 45
maw and gulf | of the ravin'd salt-sea shark, MAC 4.01. 23
do surfeit by the eye and pine the maw; VEN 602

MAWKIN *(also malkin)*

MAWKIN 1 FR 0.0001 REL FR 1 V 0 P
whilest ours was blurted at and held a mawkin PER 4.03. 34

MAWS 2 FR 0.0002 REL FR 2 V 0 P
down th' int'rest into their glutt'nous maws. TIM 3.04. 52
our monuments | shall be the maws of kites. MAC 3.04. 72

MAXIM 1 FR 0.0001 REL FR 1 V 0 P
therefore this maxim out of love i teach: TRO 1.02.292

MAXIME 1 FR 0.0001 REL FR 1 V 0 P
their sharp state, | and let this be thy maxime: STM III 19

/MAY* 9 FR 0.0010 REL FR 9 V 0 P
/may /it /please /you, /lords, /to /grant /the R2 4.01.154
/that /in /common /view | /he /may /surrender; 4.01.156
/you /may /my /glories /and /my /state /depose, 4.01.192
/may /deem /that /you /are /worthily /depos'd. 4.01.227
/that /it /may /show /me /what /a /face /i /have 4.01.266
/weigh'd | /what /wrongs /our /arms /may /do, 2H4 4.01. 68
/to /what /may /be /digested /in /a /play. TRO pr 29
/eyes /let /fall | /may /run /into /that /sink, TIT 3.02. 19
/and /i /shall, | /that /i /may /speak. LR 1.03. 25

MAY* 1792 FR 0.2025 REL FR 1371 V 421 P
for that vast of night that they may work, | all TMP 1.02.327
slave, | whom stripes may move, not kindness! 1.02.345
may know if you remain upon this island, | and 1.02.424
good instruction give | how i may bear me here. 1.02.426
sir, he may live. 2.01.114
sir, you may thank yourself for this great loss, 2.01.124
so you may continue, and laugh at nothing still. 2.01.178 P
have i seen | more that i may call men than you, 3.01. 51
to be your fellow | you may deny me, but i'll be 3.01. 85
temper'd, may as well | wound the loud winds, or 3.03. 62
what this ecstasy | may now provoke them to. 3.03.109
all sanctimonious ceremonies may | with full and 4.01. 16
bless this twain, that they may prosperous be, 4.01.104
may i be bold | to think these spirits? 4.01.119
that the blind mole may not | hear a foot fall; 4.01.194
do that good mischief which may make this island 4.01.217
much weaker | than you may call to comfort you; 5.01.147
the money and the matter may be both at once TGV 1.01.130 P
that you may ruminate. 1.02. 49
as little by such toys as may be possible: 1.02. 79
ay, madam, you may say what sights you see; 1.02.135
to-morrow, may it please you, don alphonso 1.03. 39
why then this may be yours — for this is but 2.01. 2
unheedful vows may heedfully be broken, | and he 2.06. 11
good mean | how with my honor i may undertake 2.07. 6
weeds | as may beseem some well-reputed page. 2.07. 43
to be fantastic may become a youth | of greater 2.07. 47
where, if it please you, you may intercept him. 3.01. 43
and, may i say to thee, this pride of hers, 3.01. 72
how and which way i may bestow myself | to be 3.01. 87
what lets but one may enter at her window? 3.01.113
advise me where i may have such a ladder. 3.01.122
that you may bear it | under a cloak that is of 3.01.129
thy letters may be here, though thou art hence, 3.01.250
of all that may concern thy love-affairs. 3.01.256
then may i set the world on wheels, when she can 3.01.315 P
well, that fault may be mended with a breakfast. 3.01.325 P
now, of another thing she may, and that cannot i 3.01.351 P

it may be; 3.01.359 P
where you with silvia may confer at large — 3.02. 61
where you may temper her by your persuasion | to 3.02. 64
feeling line | that may discover such integrity: 3.02. 76
that they may hold excus'd our lawless lives; 4.01. 52
that i may compass yours. 4.02. 92
to thee, | that i may venture to depart alone. 4.03. 36
it may not be; good madam, pardon me. 4.04.126
and, that my love may appear plain and free, 5.04. 82
but i may spy | more fresh in julia's with a 5.04.114
and all his ancestors (that come after him) may. WIV 1.01. 16 P
they may give the dozen white luces in their 1.01. 16 P
i may quarter, coz. 1.01. 24 P
you may, by marrying. 1.01. 25 P
yet heaven may decrease it upon better 1.01.247 P
of peace sometime may be beholding to his friend 1.01.273 P
i may not go in without your worship; 1.01.277 P
my master (i may call him my master, look you, 1.04. 94 P
priest to meddle or make — you may be gone; 1.04.110 P
that may not sully the chariness of our honesty. 2.01. 99 P
a man may be too confident. 2.01.186 P
and then you may come and see the picture, she 2.02. 86 P
look you, he may come and go between you both; 2.02.125 P
nay–word, that you may know one another's mind, 2.02.126 P
i know not how i may deserve to be your porter. 2.02.174 P
own, that i may pass with a reproof the easier, 2.02.187 P
if any man may, you may as soon as any. 2.02.236 P
if any man may, you may as soon as any. 2.02.237 P
i shall be with her (i may tell you) by her own 2.02.261 P
what they think in their hearts they may effect, 2.02.307 P
i desire you that we may be friends; 3.01.118 P
ay, and as idle as she may hang together, for 3.02. 13 P
a man may hear this show'r sing in the wind. 3.02. 37 P
he speaks holiday, he smells april and may — he 3.02. 69 P
of any reasonable stature, he may creep in here, 3.03.130 P
may be the knave bragg'd of that he could not 3.03.199 P
may be he tells you true. 3.04. 11
you may ask your father, here he comes. 3.04. 66 P
and you may know by my size that i have a kind 3.05. 12 P
may i not go out ere he come? 4.02. 49 P
do, | wives may be merry, and yet honest too: 4.02.105
why may not he be there again? 4.02.147 P
may we, with the warrant of womanhood and the 4.02.206 P
where we may take him, and disgrace him for it. 4.04. 15
the knight may be robb'd. 4.05. 15 P
i may not conceal them, sir. 4.05. 44 P
may i be bold to say so, sir? 4.05. 53 P
that it may stand till the perpetual doom | in 5.05. 58
see now how wit may be made a jack–a–lent, when 5.05.127 P
that we may bring you something on the way. MM 1.01. 61
my haste may not admit it, | nor need you, on 1.01. 62
and we may soon our satisfaction have | touching 1.01. 82
as there may between the lists and the velvet. 1.02. 29 P
believe me, this may be. 1.02. 74 P
in the seat, that it may know | he can command, 1.02.161
a milkmaid, if she be in love, may sigh it off. 1.02.173 P
i pray she may; 1.02.187 P
may your grace speak of it? 1.03. 6
who may, in th' ambush of my name, strike home, 1.03. 41
instruct me | how i may formally in person bear 1.03. 47
you may, i may not; 1.04. 9
you may, i may not; 1.04. 9
may in the sworn twelve have a thief or two 2.01. 20
you may not so extenuate his offense | for i 2.01. 27
i'll know | his pleasure, may be he will relent. 2.02. 3
i, that do speak a word, | may call it again. 2.02. 58
great men may jest with saints; 2.02.127
it be | that modesty may more betray our sense 2.02.168
that i may minister | to them accordingly. 2.03. 7
yet may he live a while; 2.04. 35
and, it may be, | as long as you or i. 2.04. 35
he may be so fitted | that his soul sicken not. 2.04. 40
no stronger | than faults may shake our frames), 2.04.133
to hear /them speak, where i may be conceal'd. 3.01. 53 P
yes, brother, you may live; 3.01. 63
believe that you may most uprighteously do a 3.01.199 P
it is a rupture that you may easily heal; 3.01.235 P
first, that your stay with him may not be long; 3.01.246 P
that the time may have all shadow and silence in 3.01.247 P
hereafter, it may compel him to her recompense; 3.01.252 P
if you think well to carry this as you may, the 3.01.257 P
dispatch with angelo, that it may be quickly. 3.01.266 P
ever the duke return (as our prayers are he may) 3.02.155 P
you better, sir, if i may live to report you. 3.02.161 P
years' continuance, may it please your honor. 3.02.196 P
events, with a prayer they may prove prosperous, 3.02.238 P
o, what may man within him hide, | though angel 3.02.271
how may likeness made in crimes, | making 3.02.273
may be i will call upon you anon for some 4.01. 23 P
"whatsoever you may hear to the contrary, let 4.02.120 P
alack, how may i do it, having the hour limited, 4.02.165 P
i may make my case as claudio's, to cross this 4.02.167 P
you, if my instructions may be your guide. 4.02.170 P
a great disguiser, and you may add to it. 4.02.174 P
morning, may sleep the sounder all the next day. 4.03. 46 P
where you may have such vantage on the duke, 4.06. 11
may seem as shy, as grave, as just, as absolute 5.01. 54
even so may angelo, | in all his dressings, 5.01. 55
it may be right, but you are i' the wrong | to 5.01. 86
he in time may come to clear himself; 5.01.150
my lord, she may be a punk; 5.01.179 P
place where he abides, | and he may fetch him. 5.01.253
this may prove worse than hanging. 5.01.360 P
and you may marvel why i obscur'd myself, 5.01.390
so may my husband. 5.01.441
if you will hang me for it, you may; 5.01.505 P
that the world may witness that my end | was ERR 1.01. 33
so, | for we may pity, though not pardon thee. 1.01. 97
which princes, would they, may not disannul, 1.01.144
and passed sentence may not be recall'd | but to 1.01.147
may he not do it by fine and recovery? 2.02. 74 P
may answer my good will and your good welcome 3.01. 20
better cheer may you have, but not with better 3.01. 29
here you must not, come again when you may. 3.01. 41
a man may break a word with /you, sir, and words 3.01. 75
that may with foul intrusion enter in, | and 3.01.103
and may it be that you have quite forgot | a 3.02. 1
we in your motion turn, and you may move us. 3.02. 24
such a one as a man may not speak of without he 3.02. 91 P
a man may go over shoes in the grime of it. 3.02.103 P
that labor may you save; see where he comes. 4.01. 14
or else you may return without your money. 4.01. 44
may we be gone? 4.03. 35 P
you may prove it by my long ears. 4.04. 29 P
it may be so, but i did never see it. 4.04.141
let us come in, that we may bind him fast, | and 5.01. 40
may it please your grace, antipholus, my husband 5.01.136
nor send him forth, that we may bear him hence. 5.01.158
ne'er may i look on day, nor sleep on night, 5.01.210
my life, | and pay the sum that may deliver me. 5.01.285
we may guess by this what you are, being a man. ADO 1.01.109 P
prays some occasion may detain us longer. 1.01.150 P
in beauty as the first of may doth the last of 1.01.192 P
the fine is (for the which i may go the finer), 1.01.245 P
the savage bull may, but if ever the sensible 1.01.262 P
"here you may see benedick the married man." 1.01.267 P
my liege, your highness now may do me good. 1.01.290
learn | any hard lesson that may do thee good. 1.01.293
that she may be the better prepar'd for an 1.02. 22 P
the full show of this till you may do it without 1.03. 20 P
thither, this may prove food to my displeasure. 1.03. 65 P
you may light on a husband that hath no beard. 2.01. 32 P
i may say so when i please. 2.01. 92 P
i love you the better; the hearers may cry amen. 2.01.105 P
you may do the part of an honest man in it. 2.01.166 P
it may be i go under that title because i am 2.01.205 P
well, i'll be reveng'd as i may. 2.01.210 P
is here, a man may live as quiet in hell as in a 2.01.258 P
therefore your grace may well say i have lost it 2.01.281 P
i may sit in a corner and cry "heigh–ho for a 2.01.319 P
may i be so converted and see with these eyes? 2.03. 22 P
not be sworn but love may transform me to an 2.03. 24 P
may be she doth but counterfeit. 2.03.102 P
the managing of quarrels you may say he is wise, 2.03.190 P
impossible, she may wear her heart out first. 2.03.203 P
i may chance have some odd quirks and remnants 2.03.235 P
yea, just so much as you may take upon a knive's 2.03.254 P
deserve | as much as may be yielded to a man; 3.01. 48
know | how much an ill word may empoison liking. 3.01. 86
if it please you — yet count claudio may hear, 3.02. 85 P
you may think i love you not; 3.02. 95 P
may this be so? 3.02.117 P
you may say they are not the men you took them 3.03. 47 P
if you meet a thief, you may suspect him, by 3.03. 50 P
by your office, you may, but i think they that 3.03. 56 P
meet the prince in the night, you may stay him. 3.03. 76 P
man that knows the /statues, he may stay him; 3.03. 79 P
ones, poor ones may make what price they will. 3.03.114 P
tush, i may as well say the fool's the fool. 3.03.123 P
you may think perchance that i think you are in 3.04. 81 P
and how you may be converted i know not, but 3.04. 90 P
now in great haste, as it may appear unto you. 3.05. 50 P
what men may do! 4.01. 19 P
may counterpoise this rich and precious gift? 4.01. 28
cover for her shame | that may be wish'd for. 4.01.117
and salt too little which may season give | to 4.01.142
and if it sort not well, you may conceal her, 4.01.240
flow in grief, | the smallest twine may lead me. 4.01.250
may a man do it? 4.01.265 P
his may of youth and bloom of lustihood. 5.01. 76
well, i will meet you, so i may have good cheer. 5.01.151 P
i note another man like him | i may avoid him. 5.01.261
and if a merry meeting may be wish'd, god 5.01.326 P
my will is your good will | may stand with ours, 5.04. 29
that we may lighten our own hearts and our 5.04.118 P
th' endeavor of this present breath may buy LLL 1.01. 5
that his own hand may strike his honor down 1.01. 20
as thus — to study where i well may dine, 1.01. 61
it may be so; 1.01.224 P
affliction may one day smile again, and till 1.01.314 P
to thy young days, which we may nominate tender. 1.02. 15 P
title to your old time, which we may name tough. 1.02. 17 P
you may do it in an hour, sir. 1.02. 37 P
that i may example my digression by some mighty 1.02.116 P
of all perfections that a man may owe, 2.01. 6
years, | no woman may approach his silent court; 2.01. 24
madam, i will, if suddenly i may. 2.01.111
may | make tender of to thy true worthiness. 2.01.169
you may not come, fair princess, within my gates 2.01.171
not unlike, sir, that may be. 2.01.208
how much carnation ribbon may a man buy for a 3.01.146 P
but being watch'd that it may still go right! 3.01.193
a stand where you may make the fairest shoot. 4.01. 10
and praise we may afford | to any lady that 4.01. 39
i may. 4.01. 81 P
so i may answer thee with one as old, that was a 4.01.122 P
have a prick in't, to mete at, if it may be. 4.01.132
the lord for you, and so may my parishioners, 4.02. 73 P
i may speak of thee as the traveller doth of 4.02. 95 P
it may concern much. 4.02.142 P
love, whose month is ever may, | spied a blossom 4.03.100
air, quoth he, thy cheeks may blow; 4.03.107
you may look pale, but i should blush, i know, 4.03.127
that i may swear beauty doth beauty lack, | if 4.03.247
that will be time, and may by us be fitted. 4.03.379
light wenches may prove plagues to men forsworn; 4.03.382
as it were, too peregrinate, as i may call it. 5.01. 14 P
if any of the audience hiss, you may cry, "well 5.01.138 P
and so may you; 5.02. 18
she says, you have it, and you may be gone. 5.02.183
that we may do it still without accompt. 5.02.200
face, | that we (like savages) may worship it. 5.02.202
take all and wean it, it may prove an ox. 5.02.250
cutting a smaller hair than may be seen; 5.02.258
conster my speeches better, if you may. 5.02.341
it grows dark, he may stumble. 5.02.630
he may not by the yard. 5.02.669 P
you may not deny it; 5.02.706 P
sweet bloods, i both may and will. 5.02.708 P
as she is mine, i may dispose of her; MND 1.01. 42
made bold, | nor how it may concern my modesty, 1.01. 60
but i beseech your grace that i may know | the 1.01. 62
the worst that may befall me in this case, | if 1.01. 63
you up | (which by no means we may extenuate) 1.01.120
there, gentle hermia, may i marry thee; 1.01.161
with helena | to do observance to a morn of may) 1.01.167
a mask, and you may speak as small as you will. 1.02. 50 P
and i may hide my face, let me play thisby too. 1.02. 51 P
you may do it extempore, for it is nothing but 1.02. 68 P
and there we may rehearse most obscenely and 1.02.107 P
we cannot fight for love, as men may do. 2.01.241
when the next thing he espies | may be the lady. 2.01.263
that he may prove | more fond on her than she 2.01.265
such separation as may well be said | becomes a 2.02. 58
why, then may you leave a casement of the great 3.01. 56 P
open, and the moon may shine in at the casement. 3.01. 58 P
if that may be, then all is well. 3.01. 72 P
believe as soon | this whole earth may be bor'd, 3.02. 53
that the moon | may through the centre creep, 3.02. 54
our sex, as well as i, may chide you for it, 3.02.218
you perhaps may think, | because she is 3.02.303
the groves may tread | even till the eastern 3.02.390
we may effect this business yet ere day. 3.02.395
east, | that i may back to athens by daylight, 3.02.433
other do, | may all to athens back again repair, 4.01. 67
they rose up early to observe | the rite of may; 4.01.133
i never may believe | these antic fables, nor 5.01. 2
one lion may, when many asses do. 5.01.153 P
of themselves, they may pass for excellent men. 5.01.216 P
may now perchance both quake and tremble here, 5.01.221
do | that in your knowledge may by me be done, MV 1.01.159
the brain may devise laws for the blood, but a 1.02. 18 P
i may neither choose who i would, nor refuse who 1.02. 23 P
unless you may be won by some other sort than 1.02.104 P
may you stead me? 1.03. 7 P
i think i may take his bond. 1.03. 27 P
be assur'd you may. 1.03. 28 P
i will be assur'd i may; 1.03. 29 P
and, that i may be assur'd, i will bethink me. 1.03. 29 P
may i speak with antonio? 1.03. 30 P
may turn by fortune from the weaker hand: 2.01. 34
and so may i, blind fortune leading me, | miss 2.01. 36
me, | miss that which one unworthier may attain, 2.01. 37
a man's son may, but in the end truth will out. 2.02. 80 P
you may tell every finger i have with my ribs. 2.02.106 P
you may do so, but let it be so hasted that 2.02.114 P
'tis vile, unless it may be quaintly ordered, 2.04. 6
enough | may not extend so far as to the lady; 2.07. 28
here do i choose, and thrive i as i may! 2.07. 60
yet do not suddenly, for it may grieve him. 2.08. 34
that many may be meant | by the fool multitude, 2.09. 25
that's certain, if the devil may be her judge. 3.01. 32 P
so will i never be, so may you miss me, | but if 3.02. 12
there may as well be amity and life | 'tween 3.02. 30
that the comparison | may stand more proper, my 3.02. 46
he may win, | and what is music then? 3.02. 47
so may the outward shows be least themselves — 3.02. 73
this, she is not yet so old | but she may learn; 3.02.161
you | even at that time i may be married too. 3.02.194
you may partly hope that your father got you not 3.05. 10 P
you may as well go stand upon the beach | and 4.01. 71
you may as well use question with the wolf | why 4.01. 73
you may as well forbid the mountain pines | to 4.01. 75
you may as well do any thing most hard, | as 4.01. 78
upon my power i may dismiss this court, | unless 4.01.104
and lawfully by this the jew may claim | a pound 4.01.231
state, | which humbleness may drive unto a fine. 4.01.372
me such exercises as may become a gentleman, or AYL 1.01. 72 P
wheel, that her gifts may henceforth be bestow'd 1.02. 32 P
may she not by fortune fall into the fire? 1.02. 44 P
that fools may not speak wisely what wise men do 1.02. 86 P
it please your ladyships, you may see the end, 1.02.114 P
thus men may grow wiser every day. 1.02.137 P
which may be better supplied when i have made it 1.02.192 P
therefore devise with me how we may fly, 1.03.100
bring us where we may rest ourselves and feed. 2.04. 73
thus we may see," quoth he, "how the world wags. 2.07. 23
have | that to your wanting may be minist'red. 2.07.126
no wit by nature nor art may complain of good 3.02. 29 P
but mountains may be remov'd with earthquakes, 3.02.185 P
out of thy mouth that i may drink thy tidings. 3.02.202 P
so you may put a man in your belly. 3.02.204 P
it may well be call'd jove's tree, when it drops 3.02.236 P
i do desire we may be better strangers. 3.02.258 P
you may as soon make her that you love believe 3.02.387 P
they swear in poetry may be said as lovers they 3.03. 21 P
sluttishness may come hereafter. 3.03. 41 P
but be it as it may be, i will marry thee; 3.03. 42 P
a man may, if he were of a fearful heart, 3.03. 48 P
dear phebe, | if ever (as that ever may be near) 3.05. 28
you | than without candle may go dark to bed — 3.05. 39
it may be said of him that cupid hath clapp'd 4.01. 47 P
maids are may when they are maids, but the sky 4.01.148 P
that may be chosen out of the gross band of the 4.01.194 P
if that an eye may profit by a tongue, | then 4.03. 83
consent with both that we may enjoy each other. 5.02. 9 P
a greater esteem than may in some little measure 5.02. 57 P
all these you may avoid but the lie direct; 5.04. 97 P
and you may avoid that too, with an if. 5.04. 98 P
that reason wonder may diminish | how thus we 5.04.139
between you and the women the play may please. ep 17 P
may show her duty and make known her love?" SHR in.1. 117
presence | may well abate the over–merry spleen, in.1. 137
it stands so that i may hardly tarry so long. in.2. 125 P
that i may soon make good | what i have said, 1.01. 74
katherina, you may stay, | for i have more to 1.01.100
why, and i trust i may go too, may i not? 1.01.102
why, and i trust i may go too, may i not? 1.01.102
you may go to the devil's dam; 1.01.105 P
hortensio, but we may blow our nails together, 1.01.107 P
that we may yet again have access to our fair 1.01.116 P
it is; may it be done? 1.01.193
con tutto /il core, ben trovato, may i say. 1.02. 24
happily to wive and thrive as best i may. 1.02. 56
she may perhaps call him half a score knaves or 1.02.110 P
that so i may, by this device, at least | have 1.02.135
if i may be bold, | tell me, i beseech you, 1.02.218
is, | she may more suitors have, and me for one. 1.02.241
then well one more may fair bianca have; 1.02.243
please ye we may contrive this afternoon | and 1.02.274
what may i call your name? 2.01. 67
may i be so bold to know the cause of your 2.01. 86 P
i may have welcome 'mongst the rest that woo, 2.01. 96

us, | that covenants may be kept on either hand. 2.01.127
iron may hold with her, but never lutes. 2.01.146
so may you lose your arms. 2.01.221
if i may have your daughter to my wife, | i'll 2.01.365
and may not young men die as well as old? 2.01.391
in time i may believe, yet i mistrust. 3.01. 51
you may go walk, and give me leave a while; 3.01. 59
is it new and old too? how may that be? 3.02. 32 P
it may not be. 3.02.199
you may be jogging whiles your boots are green. 3.02.211
i see a woman may be made a fool, | if she had 3.02.220
and may you prove, sir, master of your art! 4.02. 9
for me, that i may surely keep mine oath, | i 4.02. 36
why, sir, i trust i may have leave to speak, 4.03. 73
and well we may come there by dinner-time. 4.03.188
signior baptista may remember me | near twenty 4.04. 3
i pray the gods she may with all my heart! 4.04. 67
for parsley to stuff a rabbit, and so may you, 4.04.101 P
i may and will, if she be so contented. 4.04.105
hap what hap may, i'll roundly go about her; 4.04.107
age, | i may entitle thee my loving father. 4.05. 61
so qualified as may beseem | the spouse of any 4.05. 66
but they may chance to need thee at home, 5.01. 2 P
sir, so his mother says, if i may believe her. 5.01. 33 P
i hope i may choose, sir. 5.01. 47 P
thus strangers may be hal'd and abus'd. 5.01.108 P
please, | my hand is ready, may it do him ease. 5.02.179
that thee may furnish, and my prayers pluck down AWW 1.01. 69
how may we barricado it against him? 1.01.113 P
by being once lost, may be ten times found; 1.01.131 P
the king's disease — my project may deceive me, 1.01.228
your majesty, may plead | for amplest credence. 1.02. 10
it well may serve | a nursery to our gentry, who 1.02. 15
but they may jest | till their own scorn return 1.02. 33
if i may have your ladyship's good will to go to 1.03. 17 P
world, isbel the woman and /i will do as we may. 1.03. 19 P
may the world know them? 1.03. 34 P
are, and indeed i do marry that i may repent. 1.03. 37 P
they may jowl horns together like any deer i' 1.03. 54 P
may it please you, madam, that he bid helen come 1.03. 66 P
a man may draw his heart out ere 'a pluck one. 1.03. 88 P
may lawfully make title to as much love as she 1.03.102 P
sithence, in the loss that may happen, it 1.03.120 P
what you seek, | that fame may cry you loud. 2.01. 17
if seriously i may convey my thoughts | in this 2.01. 81
that we with thee | may spend our wonder too, or 2.01. 89
maiden, | but may not be so credulous of cure, 2.01.115
any manners, he may easily put it off at court. 2.02. 9 P
i see things may serve long, but not serve ever. 2.02. 58 P
i may truly say it is a novelty to the world. 2.03. 20 P
my knowledge, that i may say in the default, "he 2.03.229 P
profitable, and much fool may you find in you, 2.04. 36 P
apology you think | may make it probable need. 2.04. 51
it may be you have mistaken him, my lord. 2.05. 40 P
that pitiful rumor may report my flight | to 3.02.127
war | my dearest master, your dear son, may hie. 3.04. 9
gone, | he will return, and hope i may that she, 3.04. 36
you may know by their trumpets. 3.05. 8 P
may be the amorous count solicits her | in the 3.05. 69
may i be bold to acquaint his grace you are gone 3.06. 78 P
with this deceit so lawful | may prove coherent. 3.07. 39
may token to the future our past deeds. 4.02. 63
you may so in the end. 4.02. 68
i' th' stocks, or any where, so i may live. 4.03.245 P
we'll see what may be done, so you confess 4.03.246 P
that you may well perceive i have not wrong'd 4.04. 1
we may pick a thousand sallets ere we light on 4.05. 14 P
some that humble themselves may, but the many 4.05. 52 P
this man may help me to his majesty's ear, | if 5.01. 7
sir, use the carp as you may, for he looks like 5.02. 23 P
of my daughter, | that she may quickly come. 5.03. 76
and therefore know how far i may be pitied. 5.03.161
off a first so noble wife, | may justly diet me. 5.03.221
the appetite may sicken, and so die. TN 1.01. 3
o my poor brother! and so perchance may he be. 1.02. 7
an eunuch to him, | it may be worth thy pains; 1.02. 57
what else may hap, to time i will commit, | only 1.02. 60
not open my lips so wide as a bristle may enter, 1.05. 2 P
and that may you be bold to say in your foolery. 1.05. 12 P
am sure i lack thee, may pass for a wise man. 1.05. 35 P
of the house, that i may proceed in my speech. 1.05.181 P
doctrine, and much may be said of it. 1.05.222 P
even so quickly may one catch the plague? 1.05.295
you your leave, that i may bear my evils alone. 2.01. 6 P
but, come what may, i do adore thee so | that 2.01. 47
alas, their love may be call'd appetite, | no 2.04. 97
too well what love women to men may owe; 2.04.105
we men may say more, swear more, but indeed 2.04.116
"i may command where i adore, | but silence, 2.05.104
"i may command where i adore." 2.05.115 P
why, she may command me: 2.05.116 P
quickly the wrong side may be turn'd outward! 3.01. 13 P
nicely with words may quickly make them wanton. 3.01. 15 P
on purpose, that i may appear stubborn to him; 3.04. 67 P
we may carry it thus, for our pleasure and his 3.04.137 P
more matter for a may morning. 3.04.142 P
he may have mercy upon mine, but my hope is 3.04.167 P
you may have very fit occasion for't; 3.04.173 P
deny, | that honor, sav'd, may upon asking give? 3.04.212
how with mine honor may i give him that | which 3.04.214
if he may be conveniently deliver'd, i would he 4.02. 68 P
that this may be some error, but no madness, 4.03. 10
and too doubtful soul | may live at peace. 4.03. 28
that they may fairly note this act of mine! 4.03. 35
saint bennet, sir, may put you in mind — one, 5.01. 39 P
along with you, it may awake my bounty further. 5.01. 43 P
what would my lord, but that he may not have, 5.01.101
not have, | wherein olivia may seem serviceable? 5.01.102
where thou and i, henceforth, may never meet. 5.01.169
stave's end as well as a man in his case may do. 5.01.285 P
may rather pluck on laughter than revenge, | if 5.01.366
(unintelligent of our insufficience) may, though WT 1.01. 15 P
i am question'd by my fears of what may chance 1.02. 11
that may blow | no sneaping winds at home, to 1.02. 12
i may not, verily. 1.02. 45
you may ride 's | with one soft kiss a thousand 1.02. 94
this entertainment | may a free face put on, 1.02.112
't may — i grant. 1.02.114
i may be negligent, foolish, and fearful: 1.02.250
i may not answer. 1.02.397
to | a savor that may strike the dullest nostril 1.02.421
you may as well | forbid the sea for to obey the 1.02.426
there may be in the cup | a spider steep'd, and 2.01. 39
the cup | a spider steep'd, and one may drink; 2.01. 40
beseech your highness | my women may be with me, 2.01.117
i may not, madam: 2.02. 7
one so great and so forlorn | may hold together. 2.02. 21
how he may soften at the sight o' th' child: 2.02. 38
let him be, | until a time may serve. 2.03. 22
that my ability may undergo | and nobleness 2.03.164
some place | where chance may nurse or end it. 2.03.183
that we may arraign | our most disloyal lady; 2.03.202
the spirits o' th' dead | may walk again. 3.03. 17
which may, if fortune please, both breed thee, 3.03. 48
art thus expos'd | to loss, and what may follow! 3.03. 51
well may i get aboard! 3.03. 57
spectators, that i now may be | in fair bohemia, 4.01. 20
doth say, | he wishes earnestly you never may. 4.01. 32
what his happier affairs may be, are to me 4.02. 30 P
if tinkers may have leave to live, | and bear 4.03. 19
bouget, | then my account i well may give, | and 4.03. 21
a race or two of ginger, but that i may beg; 4.03. 47 P
a million of beating may come to a great matter. 4.03. 59 P
may be he has paid you more, which will shame 4.04.239 P
if i may ever know thou dost but sigh | that 4.04.427
nor the pomp that may | be thereat gleaned, for 4.04.488
this you may know, | and so deliver: 4.04.497
if you may please to think i love the king | and 4.04.521
and settled project | may suffer alteration. 4.04.525
highness, where you may | enjoy your mistress — 4.04.527
camillo, | may this (almost a miracle) be done? 4.04.534
that i may call thee something more than man 4.04.535
i think affliction may subdue the cheek, | but 4.04.576
that you may know you shall not want — one word 4.04.594
omit | nothing may give us aid. 4.04.625
the truth of your own seeming, that you may 4.04.653
at us, and we may do any thing extempore. 4.04.677 P
who, i may say, is no honest man, neither to his 4.04.700 P
this complaint may be to the flight of my master 4.04.710 P
this hour, if i may come to th' speech of him. 4.04.758 P
we are bless'd in this man, as i may say, even 4.04.827 P
which who knows how that may turn back to my 4.04.835 P
will i present them, there may be matter in it. 4.04.841 P
may drop upon his kingdom and devour | incertain 5.01. 28
will bring me to consider that which may 5.01.122
we may live, son, to shed many more. 5.02.146 P
you may say it, but not swear it. 5.02.158 P
a true gentleman may swear it in the behalf of 5.02.162 P
grace, which never | my life may last to answer. 5.03. 8
that i may say indeed | thou art hermione; 5.03. 24
on't, lest your fancy | may think anon it moves. 5.03. 61
hence, where we may leisurely | each one demand, 5.03.152
of that i doubt, as all men's children may. JN 1.01. 63
of their hearts | may easily win a woman's. 1.01.269
my lord chatillion may from england bring | that 2.01. 46
you, | and 'a may catch your hide and you alone. 2.01.136
england, how may we content | this widow lady? 2.01.547
i trust i may not trust thee, for thy word | is 3.01. 7
madam, | i may not go without you to the kings. 3.01. 66
pray that their burthens may not fall this day, 3.01. 90
dreading the curse that money may buy out, | and 3.01.164
your breeches best may carry them. 3.01.201
i may disjoin my hand, but not my faith. 3.01.262
thyself, | and may not be performed by thyself, 3.01.269
what motive may | be stronger with thee than the 3.01.313
father, i may not wish the fortune thine; 3.01.333
reason | how i may be deliver'd of these woes, 3.04. 55
that john may stand, then arthur needs must fall 3.04.139
may then make all the claim that arthur did. 3.04.143
may be he will not touch young arthur's life, 3.04.160
what may be wrought out of their discontent, 3.04.179
so great a title | to be more prince, as may be. 4.01. 11
or "what good love may i perform for you?" 4.01. 49
nay, you may think my love was crafty love, 4.01. 53
that his compassion may | give life to yours. 4.01. 88
cut out my tongue, | so i may keep mine eyes. 4.01.101
that the time's enemies may not have this | to 4.02. 61
there, tell the king, he may inquire us out. 4.03.115
i know | our party may well meet a prouder foe. 5.01. 79
may know wherefore we took the sacrament, | and 5.02. 6
hand, | it may lie gently at the foot of peace, 5.02. 76
may this be possible? may this be true? 5.04. 21
may this be possible? may this be true? 5.04. 21
where i may think the remnant of my thoughts 5.04. 46
why may not i demand | of thine affairs, as well 5.06. 4
king | yet speaks, and peradventure may recover. 5.06. 31
peace | as we with honor and respect may take, 5.07. 85
with other princes that may best be spar'd, 5.07. 97
and happily may your sweet self put on | the 5.07.101
tongue speaks, my right drawn sword may prove. R2 1.01. 46
and when i mount, alive may i not light, | if i 1.01. 82
for i may never lift | an angry arm against his 1.02. 40
where then, alas, may i complain myself? 1.02. 42
that it may enter butcher mowbray's breast! 1.02. 48
that they may break his foaming courser's back, 1.02. 51
lament we may, but not revenge /thee dead. 1.03. 58
point, | that it may enter mowbray's waxen coat, 1.03. 75
pray god we may make haste and come too late! 1.04. 64
come, that i may breathe my last | in wholesome 2.01. 1
my death's sad tale may yet undeaf his ear. 2.01. 16
may be a president and witness good | that thou 2.01.130
but by bad courses may be understood | that 2.01.213
it may be so; 2.02. 28
well, we may meet again. 2.02.149
to find out right with wrong — it may not be; 2.03.145
it may be i will go with you, but yet i'll pause 2.03.168
whose double tongue may with a mortal touch 3.02. 21
so may you by my dull and heavy eye: 3.02.196
our fair appointments may be well perus'd. 3.03. 53
comprising all that may be sworn or said, | his 3.03.111
may hourly trample on their sovereign's head; 3.03.157
speak with you, may it please you to come down. 3.03.177
we lop away, that bearing boughs may live; 3.04. 64
to serve me last that i may longest keep | thy 3.04. 95
god the plants thou graft'st may never grow. 3.04.101
and if i do not, may my hands rot off, | and 4.01. 49
lies | as may be hollowed in thy treacherous ear 4.01. 54
this, | if he may be repeal'd to try his honor. 4.01. 85
worst in this royal presence may i speak, | yet 4.01.115
that you in pity may dissolve to dew | and wash 5.01. 9
pomp | she came adorned hither like sweet may, 5.01. 79
that i may strive to kill it with a groan. 5.01.100
i do beseech you pardon me, i may not show it. 5.02. 70
that mind, | he is as like thee as a man may be, 5.02.108
which elder years | may happily bring forth. 5.03. 22
for ever may my knees grow to the earth, | my 5.03. 30
then give me leave that /i may turn the key, 5.03. 36
is danger | that we may arm us to encounter it. 5.03. 48
more sins for this forgiveness prosper may. 5.03. 84
pity may move thee "pardon" to rehearse. 5.03.128
i have been studying how i may compare | this 5.05. 1
may tear a passage thorough the flinty ribs | of 5.05. 20
the manner of their taking may appear | at large 5.06. 9
by those welshwomen done as may not be | without 1H4 1.01. 45
we may do it as secure as sleep. 1.02.130 P
what thou speakest may move and what he hears 1.02.154 P
may move and what he hears may be believ'd, that 1.02.154 P
hears may be believ'd, that the true prince may 1.02.155 P
he may be more wond'red at | by breaking through 1.02.201
may reasonably die, and never rise | to do him 1.03. 74
yet time serves wherein you may redeem | your 1.03.180
nicholas as truly as a man of falsehood may. 2.01. 65 P
that his tale to me may be nothing but "anon." 2.04. 32 P
you may buy land now as cheap as stinking 2.04.359 P
look red, that it may be thought i have wept, 2.04.385 P
if then the tree may be known by the fruit, as 2.04.428 P
it may be so. 2.04.521
(a business that this night may execute), 3.01. 81
within that space you may have drawn together 3.01. 88
the moon shines fair, you may away by night. 3.01.140
quick, quick, that i may lay my head in thy lap. 3.01.227 P
i may for some things true, wherein my youth 3.02. 26
i do beseech your majesty may salve | the 3.02.155
maid marian may be the deputy's wife of the ward 3.03.114 P
friends with my father and may do any thing. 3.03.181 P
we may boldly spend upon the hope of what | /is 4.01. 54
may turn the tide of fearful faction, | and 4.01. 67
whence | the eye of reason may pry in upon us. 4.01. 72
images, | as full of spirit as the month of may, 4.01.101
what may the king's whole battle reach unto? 4.01.129
the powers of us may serve so great a day. 4.01.132
it may not be. 4.03. 1
come, come, it may not be. 4.03. 16
and may be so we shall. 4.03.113
with some fine color that may please the eye 5.01. 75
for my part, i may speak it to my shame, | i 5.01. 93
my nephew's trespass may be well forgot, | it 5.02. 16
why may not he rise as well as i? 5.04.126 P
if i may be believ'd, so; 5.04.148 P
for my part, if a lie may do thee grace, | i'll 5.04.157
and i beseech your grace | i may dispose of him. 5.05. 24
more than he haply may retail from me. 2H4 1.01. 32
set | on bloody courses, the rude scene may end, 1.01.159
god may finish it when he will, 'tis not a hair 1.02. 23 P
he may keep it still at a face royal, for a 1.02. 24 P
he may keep his own grace, but he's almost out 1.02. 27 P
well, he may sleep in security, for he hath the 1.02. 45 P
your lordship may minister the potion of 1.02.127 P
the wise may make some dram of a scruple, or 1.02.130 P
you may thank th' unquiet time for your quiet 1.02.149 P
may hold up head without northumberland? 1.03. 17
with him, we may. 1.03. 18
it may chance cost some of us our lives, for he 2.01. 11 P
i beseech you i may have redress against them. 2.01.108 P
the one you may do with sterling money, and the 2.01.120 P
what pagan may that be? 2.02.154 P
that it may grow and sprout as high as heaven, 2.03. 60
faith, you may stroke him as gently as a puppy 2.04. 98 P
the undeserver may sleep when the man of action 2.04.376 P
which to his former strength may be restored 3.01. 42
by — | you, cousin nevil, as i may remember — 3.01. 66
the which observ'd, a man may prophesy, | with a 3.01. 82
and i may say to you, we knew where the bona 3.02. 22 P
a score of good ewes may be worth ten pounds. 3.02. 51 P
may i ask how my lady his wife doth? 3.02. 64 P
a man is being whereby 'a may be thought to be 3.02. 79 P
you may, but if he had been a man's tailor, he'd 3.02.152 P
the foeman may with as great aim level at the 3.02.266 P
in the law of nature but i may snap at him: 3.02.332 P
that your attempts may overlive the hazard | and 4.01. 15
in sight of both our battles we may meet, | /and 4.01.177
memory | that may repeat and history his loss 4.01.201
to a fangless lion, | may offer, but not hold. 4.01.217
whose dangerous eyes may well be charm'd asleep 4.02. 39
if this may please you, | discharge your powers 4.02. 60
that all their eyes may bear those tokens home 4.02. 64
us, that we may peruse the men | we should have 4.02. 94
me, and yielded, that i may justly say, with the 4.03. 40 P
my good lord, that may do me good, and call it 4.03. 59 P
here at more leisure may your highness read, 4.04. 89
may they fall | as those that i am come to tell 4.04. 95
out, | may waste the memory of the former days. 4.05.215
and grant it may with thee in true peace live! 4.05.219
may this be wash'd in lethe and forgotten? 5.02. 72
sword, | and i do wish your honors may increase, 5.02.104
that the great body of our state may go | in 5.02.136
may be | as things acquainted and familiar to us 5.02.138
or may we cram | within this wooden o the very H5 pr 12
since a crooked figure may | attest in little pr 15
may i with right and conscience make this claim? 1.02. 96
to one consent, may work contrariously, | as 1.02.206
so may a thousand actions, once afoot, | /end in 1.02.211
dolphin i am coming on | to venge me as i may, 1.02.292
that may give furth'rance to our expedition; 1.02.301
upon | that may with reasonable swiftness add 1.02.306
that this fair action may on foot be brought. 1.02.310
for, if we may, | we'll not offend one stomach 2.pr. 39
shall be smiles — but that shall be as it may. 2.01. 7 P
i will live so long as i may, that's the certain 2.01. 14 P
i cannot live any longer, i will do as i may: 2.01. 16 P
i cannot tell — things must be as they may. 2.01. 20 P
men may sleep, and they may have their throats 2.01. 21 P

and they may have their throats about them at 2.01. 21 P
it must be as it may; 2.01. 23 P
i will scour you with my rapier, as i may, in 2.01. 57 P
your gusts a little in good terms, as i may, and 2.01. 59 P
king is a good king, but it must be as it may; 2.01.126 P
so may your highness, and yet punish too. 2.02. 48
may it be possible that foreign hire | could out 2.02.100
as fear may teach us out of late examples | left 2.04. 12
that you may know | 'tis no sinister nor no 2.04. 84
and any thing that may not misbecome | the 2.04.118
th' athversary — you may discuss unto the duke, 3.02. 61 P
quit you with gud leve, as i may pick occasion; 3.02.103 P
and i'll pay't as valorously as i may, that sall 3.02.117 P
we may as bootless spend our vain command | upon 3.03. 24
age, or else you may be marvellously mistook. 3.06. 80 P
if we may pass, we will; 3.06.160
horse, and all other jades you may call beasts. 3.07. 24 P
that may be, for you bear a many superfluously, 3.07. 74 P
by her foot, that she may tread out the oath. 3.07. 95 P
you may as well say, that's a valiant flea that 3.07.145 P
gentle all | behold, as may unworthiness define, 4.pr. 46
thus may we gather honey from the weed, | and 4.01. 11
since i may say, "now lie i like a king." 4.01. 17
he may show what outward courage he will; 4.01.113 P
you may call the business of the master the 4.01.153 P
when our throats are cut, he may be ransom'd, 4.01.193 P
you may as well go about to turn the sun to ice 4.01.199 P
indeed the french may lay twenty french crowns 4.01.225 P
that their hot blood may spin in english eyes, 4.02. 10
souls | may make a peaceful and a sweet retire 4.03. 86
that every one may pare his nails with a wooden 4.04. 71 P
that we may wander o'er this bloody field | to 4.07. 72
it may be his enemy is a gentleman of great sort 4.07.135 P
favor | may haply purchase him a box a' th' ear. 4.07.173
word, | some sudden mischief may arise of it; 4.07.178
not read the story, | that i may prompt them; 5.pr. 2
even now | you may imagine him upon blackheath; 5.pr. 16
as in good time he may, from ireland coming, 5.pr. 31
that i may know the let why gentle peace 5.02. 65
happily a woman's voice may do some good, | when 5.02. 93
and you may, some of you, thank love for my 5.02.316 P
the maiden cities you talk of may wait on her; 5.02.327 P
other's happiness, | may cease their hatred; 5.02.352
that never may ill office, or fell jealousy, 5.02.363
that english may as french, french englishmen, 5.02.367
and may our oaths well kept and prosp'rous be! 5.02.374
prince, | whom like a schoolboy you may overawe. 1H6 1.01. 36
awe, | more than god or religious churchmen may. 1.01. 40
by guileful fair words peace may be obtain'd. 1.01. 77
and he may well in fretting spend his gall — 1.02. 16
more truly now may this be verified, | for none 1.02. 32
that beauty am i blest with which you may see. 1.02. 86
he may mean more than we poor men do know: 1.02.122
how may i reverently worship thee enough? 1.02.145
whoe'er he be, you may not be let in. 1.03. 7
have patience, noble duke, i may not open, | the 1.03. 18
they may vex us with shot or with assault. 1.04. 13
i'll never trouble you, if i may spy them. 1.04. 22
the other yet may rise against their force. 2.01. 32
and that hereafter ages may behold | what ruin 2.02. 10
upon the which, that every one may read, | shall 2.02. 14
that she may boast she hath beheld the man 2.02. 42
you may not, my lord, despise her gentle suit. 2.02. 47
and more than may be gathered by thy shape. 2.03. 69
that we may | taste of your wine and see what 2.03. 78
my side | that any purblind eye may find it out. 2.04. 21
direct mine arms i may embrace his neck, | and 2.05. 37
that i may kindly give one fainting kiss. 2.05. 40
and so thrive richard as thy foes may fall! 3.01.173
ay, we may march in england, or in france, | not 3.01.186
his days may finish ere that hapless time. 3.01.200
that charles the dolphin may encounter them. 3.02. 9
your grace may starve, perhaps, before that time 3.02. 48
by the sound of drum you may perceive | their 3.03. 29
powers, | and seek how we may prejudice the foe. 3.03. 91
crave | i may have liberty to venge this wrong, 3.04. 42
still | you may behold confusion of your foes. 4.01. 77
as well they may upbraid me with my crown, 4.01.156
part of thy father may be sav'd in thee. 4.05. 38
that i may bear them hence | and give them 4.07. 85
news, my lords, may cheer our drooping spirits: 5.02. 1
me this once, that france may get the field. 5.03. 12
and may ye both be suddenly surpris'd | by 5.03. 40
say, that i may honor thee. 5.03. 50
and yet a dispensation may be had. 5.03. 86
yet so my fancy may be satisfied, | and peace 5.03. 91
upon condition i may quietly | enjoy mine own, 5.03.153
stake, | that so her torture may be shortened. 5.04. 58
well | (there were so many) whom she may accuse. 5.04. 81
may never glorious sun reflex his beams | upon 5.04. 87
arrive | where i may have fruition of her love. 5.05. 9
that marg'ret may be england's royal queen. 5.05. 24
and therefore may be broke without offense. 5.05. 35
and so the earl of arminack may do, | because he 5.05. 44
company, | i may revolve and ruminate my grief. 5.05.101
england ere the thirtieth of may next ensuing. 2H6 1.01. 49 P
for suffolk's duke, may he be suffocate, | that 1.01.124
and, as we may, cherish duke humphrey's deeds 1.01.203
pirates may make cheap pennyworths of their 1.01.222
and may that thought, when i imagine ill 1.02. 19
and then we may deliver our supplications in the 1.03. 3 P
warwick may live to be the best of all. 1.03.112
this doom, my lord, if i may judge: 1.03.204
that we for thee may glorify the lord. 2.01. 73
sight may distinguish colors; 2.01.127
gone, | may honorable peace attend thy throne! 2.03. 38
uneath may she endure the flinty streets, | to 2.04. 8
the world may laugh again, | and i may live to 2.04. 82
and i may live to do you kindness if | you do it 2.04. 83
and well such losers may have leave to speak. 3.01.185
that faultless may condemn a nobleman! 3.02. 24
pray god he may acquit him of suspicion! 3.02. 25
what know i how the world may deem of me, | for 3.02. 65
it may be judg'd i made the duke away, | so 3.02. 67
nest | but may imagine how the bird was dead, 3.02.192
madam, be still — with reverence may i say — 3.02.207
that i may dew it with my mournful tears; 3.02.340
so get thee gone, that i may know my grief, 3.02.346
o, let me stay, befall what may befall! 3.02.402
can, | that this my death may never be forgot! 4.01.133
one livery, that they may agree like brothers, 4.02. 74 P
those which fly before the battle ends | may, 4.02.179
here may his head lie on my throbbing breast; 4.04. 5
will i stay | and live alone as secret as i may. 4.04. 48
the laws of england may come out of your mouth. 4.07. 6 P
for yet may england curse my wretched reign. 4.09. 49
court | and may enjoy such quiet walks as these? 4.10. 17
doornail, i pray god i may never eat grass more. 4.10. 41 P
i have | is his to use, so somerset may die. 5.01. 53
may pass into the presence of a king, | lo, i 5.01. 65
may iden live to merit such a bounty, | and 5.01. 81
they may astonish these fell–lurking curs. 5.01.146
but if we haply scape | (as well we may, if not 5.02. 80
in our fortunes made | may readily be stopp'd. 5.02. 83
tell me, may not a king adopt an heir? 3H6 1.01.135
and if he may, then am i lawful king; 1.01.137
may that ground gape, and swallow me alive, 1.01.161
but be it as it may. 1.01.194
come, son, away, we may not linger thus. 1.01.263
reveng'd may she be on that hateful duke, 1.01.266
but for a kingdom any oath may be broken: 1.02. 16
may bring forth | a bird that will revenge upon 1.04. 35
rave, and fret, that i may sing and dance. 1.04. 91
gates, | so york may overlook the town of york. 1.04.180
may make against the house of lancaster. 2.01.176
ne'er may he live to see a sunshine day | that 2.01.187
thou, | although thy husband may be menelaus; 2.02.147
yet that thy brazen gates of heaven may ope 2.03. 40
this may plant courage in their quailing breasts 2.03. 54
year, | how many years a mortal man may live. 2.05. 29
may be possessed with some store of crowns, 2.05. 57
may yet, ere night, yield both my life and them 2.05. 59
i'll bear thee hence, where i may weep my fill. 2.05.113
i'll stay above the hill, so both may shoot. 3.01. 5
by this account then, margaret may win him, 3.01. 35
and men may talk of kings, and why not i? 3.01. 58
may it please your highness to resolve me now, 3.02. 19
but now you partly may perceive my mind. 3.02. 66
from his loins no hopeful branch may spring, 3.02.126
to prove him tyrant this reason may suffice, 3.03. 71
it seems | as may beseem a monarch like himself. 3.03.122
weak, | as may appear by edward's good success, 3.03.146
marriage | i may not prove inferior to yourself. 4.01.122
vow, | that i may never have you in suspect. 4.01.142
we may surprise and take him at our pleasure? 4.02. 17
at unawares may beat down edward's guard, | and 4.02. 23
yet, gracious madam, bear it as you may: 4.04. 14
warwick may lose, that now hath won the day. 4.04. 15
come therefore let us fly while we may fly, | if 4.04. 34
and pray that i may repossess the crown. 4.05. 29
subjects may challenge nothing of their 4.06. 6
but if an humble prayer may prevail, | i then 4.06. 7
that i may conquer fortune's spite | by living 4.06. 19
may not be punish'd with my thwarting stars, 4.06. 22
and now may seem as wise as virtuous | by spying 4.06. 27
provide | a salve for any sore that may betide. 4.06. 88
in these conflicts | what may befall him, to his 4.06. 95
by what safe means the crown may be recover'd. 4.07. 52
yet, as we may, we'll meet both thee and warwick 4.07. 86
so other foes may set upon our backs. 5.01. 61
that warwick's bones may keep thine company. 5.02. 4
what's worse than murtherer, that i may name it? 5.05. 58
and i will speak, that so my heart may burst. 5.05. 60
may such purple tears be alway shed | from those 5.06. 64
but what's the matter, clarence, may i know? R3 1.01. 51
you may partake of any thing we say: 1.01. 89
if honor may be shrouded in a hearse — | whilst 1.02. 2
may fright the hopeful mother at the view, | and 1.02. 24
and if thy poor devoted servant may | but beg 1.02.206
that it may please you leave these sad designs 1.02.210
a glass, | that i may see my shadow as i pass. 1.02.263
makes him to send, that he may learn the ground. 1.03. 68
god grant we never may have need of you! 1.03. 75
you may deny that you were not the mean | of my 1.03. 89
she may, my lord, for — 1.03. 91
she may, lord rivers! 1.03. 92
she may do more, sir, than denying that: 1.03. 93
she may help you to many fair preferments, | and 1.03. 94
what may she not, she may, ay, marry, may she. 1.03. 97
what may she not, she may, ay, marry, may she. 1.03. 97
what may she not, she may, ay, marry, may she. 1.03. 97
what, marry, may she? 1.03. 98
what, marry, may she? 1.03. 99
as little joy you may suppose in me | that i 1.03.152
that none of you may live his natural age, | but 1.03.212
warrant, | that we may be admitted where he is. 1.03.342
may move your hearts to pity if you mark him. 1.03.348
you may, sir, 'tis a point of wisdom. 1.04. 98 P
our swift–winged souls may catch the king's, 2.02. 44
may send forth plenteous tears to drown the 2.02. 70
and may direct his course as please himself, 2.02.129
all may be well; 2.03. 36
good lords, make all the speedy haste you may. 3.01. 60
if i may counsel you, some day or two | your 3.01. 64
he may command me as my sovereign, | but you 3.01.108
we may digest our complots in some form. 3.01.200
and that may be determin'd at the one | which 3.02. 13
which may make you and him to rue at th' other. 3.02. 14
you may jest on, but, by the holy rood, | i do 3.02. 75
but you, my honorable lords, may name the time, 3.04. 18
who haply may | misconster us in him and wail 3.05. 60
that it may be to–day read o'er in paul's. 3.06. 3
for god doth know, and you may partly see, | how 3.07.235
to–morrow may it please you to be crown'd? 3.07.242
patience, | i may not suffer you to visit them, 4.01. 16
i may not leave it so: 4.01. 26
that my pent heart may have some scope to beat, 4.01. 34
your grace may do your pleasure. 4.02. 21
to stop all hopes whose growth may damage me. 4.02. 59
may it please you to resolve me in my suit. 4.02.117
mean time, but think how i may do thee good, 4.03. 33
that i may live to say, "the dog is dead." 4.04. 78
so she may live unscarr'd of bleeding slaughter, 4.04.210
tell her the king, that may command, entreats. 4.04.345
what, may it please you, shall i do at salisbury 4.04.453
nor none so bad but well may be reported. 4.04.458
i, as i may — that which i would i cannot — 5.03. 91
but on thy side i may not be too forward, | lest 5.03. 94
that they may crush down with a heavy fall | the 5.03.111
that we may praise thee in the victory! 5.03.114
if it please you, we may now withdraw us. 5.05. 11
that she may long live here, god say amen! 5.05. 41
can pity, here | may (if they think it well) let H8 pr 6
give | their money out of hope they may believe, pr 8
they may believe, | may here find truth too. pr 9
and so agree | the play may pass, if they be pr 11
i'll undertake may see away their shilling pr 12
i'll say | a man may weep upon his wedding–day. pr 32
it's long, and't may be said | it reaches far, 1.01.110
we may outrun | by violent swiftness that which 1.01.141
that he may furnish and instruct great teachers 1.02.113
now, madam, may his highness live in freedom, 1.02.200
if he may | find mercy in the law, 'tis his; 1.02.211
to think an english courtier may be wise | and 1.03. 22
they may, cum privilegio, "/oui" away | the lag 1.03. 34
may bring his plain–song | and have an hour of 1.03. 45
he may, my lord, h'as wherewithal: 1.03. 59
let me have such a bowl may hold my thanks, 1.04. 39
you may guess quickly what. 2.01. 7
the cause | he may a little grieve at. 2.01. 39
may he live | longer than i have time to tell 2.01. 90
ever belov'd and loving may his rule be; 2.01. 92
what may it be? 2.01.143
that you may, fair lady, | perceive i speak 2.03. 58
knows yet | but from this lady may proceed a gem 2.03. 78
you may then spare that time. 2.04. 5
till i may | be by my friends in spain advis'd, 2.04. 54
him | that i gainsay my deed, how may he wound, 2.04. 96
i may perceive | these cardinals trifle with me; 2.04.236
(i would be all) against the worst may happen. 3.01. 25
may it please you, noble madam, to withdraw 3.01. 27
ever yet committed | may be absolv'd in english. 3.01. 50
how you may hurt yourself — ay, utterly | grow 3.01.160
to meet the least occasion that may give me 3.02. 7
may you be happy in your wish, my lord, | for i 3.02. 43
and may be left | to some ears unrecounted. 3.02. 47
may be he hears the king | does whet his anger 3.02. 91
it may well be, | there is a mutiny in 's mind. 3.02.119
and ever may your highness yoke together | (as i 3.02.150
and, if you may confess it, say withal | if you 3.02.164
ye appear in every thing may bring my ruin! 3.02.242
may he continue | long in his highness' favor, 3.02.395
may have a tomb of orphants' tears wept on him! 3.02.399
that sun, i pray, may never set! 3.02.415
may i be bold to ask what that contains, | that 4.01. 13
you may read the rest. 4.01. 19
who may that be, i pray you? 4.01.108
you may command us, sir. 4.01.117
so may he rest, his faults lie gently on him! 4.02. 31
may it please your highness | to hear me speak 4.02. 46
so may he ever do, and ever flourish, | when i 4.02.125
that they may have their wages duly paid 'em, 4.02.150
that all the world may know | i was a chaste 4.02.169
pray for heartily, that it may find | good time, 5.01. 21
day, | sir (i may tell it you), i think i have 5.01. 42
your grace may enter now. 5.02. 42
and, not reform'd, may prove pernicious. 5.02. 54
pray heaven the king may never find a heart 5.02. 77
be what they will, may stand forth face to face, 5.02. 82
you may worst | of all this table say so. 5.02.113
may it please your grace — 5.02.169
may it like your grace | to let my tongue excuse 5.02.183
if a prince | may be beholding to a subject, i 5.02.191
the greatest monarch now alive may glory | in 5.02.198
how may i deserve it, | that am a poor and 5.02.199
we may as well push against powle's as stir 'em. 5.03. 16
and what so many may do, | not being torn 5.03. 75
to make parents happy | may hourly fall upon ye! 5.04. 8
cooling too, or ye may chance burn your lips. TRO 1.01. 26 P
better at home, if "would i might" were "may." 1.01.114
as may be in the world, lady. 1.02. 40 P
indeed a tapster's arithmetic may soon bring his 1.02.113 P
up in his tears an' 'twere a nettle against may. 1.02.176 P
excellent place, here we may see most bravely. 1.02.182 P
than in the glass of pandar's praise may be; 1.02.285
may one that is a herald and a prince | do a 1.03.218
how may | a stranger to those most imperial 1.03.223
and may that soldier a mere recreant prove, 1.03.287
grandam, and as chaste | as may be in the world. 1.03.300
who may you else oppose | that can from hector 1.03.333
have in mine elbows, an asinico may tutor thee. 2.01. 44 P
how may i avoid | (although my will distaste 2.02. 65
we may not think the justness of each act | such 2.02.119
well may we fight for her whom, we know well, 2.02.161
whose present courage may beat down our foes, 2.02.201
you may call it melancholy, if you will favor 2.03. 86 P
that wisdom knits not, folly may easily untie. 2.03.101 P
in, after falling out, may make them three. 3.01.103 P
ay, you may, you may. 3.01.109 P
ay, you may, you may. 3.01.109 P
fields | where i may wallow in the lily–beds 3.02. 12
prophet may you be! 3.02.183
it may do good, pride hath no other glass | to 3.03. 47
is /mirror'd there | where it may see itself. 3.03.111
and still it might, and yet it may again, | if 3.03.185
a man may wear it on both sides, like a leather 3.03.264 P
for we may live to have need of such a verse. 4.04. 22 P
how novelty may move, and parts with /person, 4.04. 79
but something may be done that we will not, 4.04. 94
air | may pierce the head of the great combatant 4.05. 5
may i, sweet lady, beg a kiss of you? 4.05. 47
you may. 4.05. 48
that i may give the local wound a name, | and 4.05.244
deeds to match these words, | or may i never — 4.05.260
you may have every day enough of hector, | if 4.05.263
that this great soldier may his welcome know. 4.05.276
and too little brain, these two may run mad, but 5.01. 49 P
stand where the torch may not discover us. 5.02. 5
and any man may sing her, if he can take her 5.02. 10 P
may worthy troilus be half attached | with that 5.02.161
you may as well | strike at the heaven with your COR 1.01. 67
it may be you have heard it, | but, since it 1.01. 90
i may make the belly smile | as well as speak — 1.01.109

that we with smoking swords may march from hence 1.04. 11
that you may be abhorr'd | farther than seen, 1.04. 32
encount'ring, | may give you thankful sacrifice. 1.06. 9
may these same instruments, which you profane, 1.09. 41
with whom we may articulate | for their own good 1.09. 77
him some way, | or wrath or craft may get him. 1.10. 16
to the pace of it | i may spur on my journey. 1.10. 33
then our office may, | during his power, go 2.01.222
nothing undone that may fully discover him their 2.02. 20 P
please you | that i may pass this doing. 2.02.139
may they perceive 's intent! 2.02.156
we may, sir, if we will. 2.03. 3 P
you may, you may. 2.03. 35 P
you may, you may. 2.03. 35 P
if it may stand with the tune of your voices 2.03. 85 P
the tune of your voices that i may be consul, i 2.03. 86 P
therefore, beseech you, i may be consul. 2.03.103 P
may i change these garments? 2.03.146
you may, sir. 2.03.146
we pray the gods he may deserve your loves. 2.03.157
he's not confirm'd, we may deny him yet. 2.03.209
confusion | may enter 'twixt the gap of both, 3.01.111
what may be sworn by, both divine and human, 3.01.141
i may be heard, i would crave a word or two, 3.01.281
you may salve so, | not what is dangerous 3.02. 70
thereto witness may | my surname, coriolanus. 4.05. 67
it | that my revengeful services may prove | as 4.05. 89
in some sort, may be said to be a ravisher, so 4.05.227 P
rais'd only that the weaker sort may wish | good 4.06. 70
you may not pass, you must return; 5.02. 5
of full time | may show like all yourself. 5.03. 70
the thing i have forsworn to grant may never 5.03. 80
the blame | may hang upon your hardness, 5.03. 91
while the volsces | may say, "this mercy we have 5.03.137
especially his mother, may prevail with him. 5.04. 6 P
that we may hew his limbs and on a pile | ad TIT 1.01. 97
thracian tyrant in his tent | may favor tamora, 1.01.139
by him that justly may | bear his betroth'd from 1.01.285
my lord, what i have done, as best i may, 1.01.411
and may, for aught thou knowest, affected be. 2.01. 28
that for her love such quarrels may be broach'd, 2.01. 67
she is a woman, therefore may be woo'd, | she is 2.01. 82
woo'd, | she is a woman, therefore may be won, 2.01. 83
ay, and as good as saturninus may. 2.01. 90
you must perforce accomplish as you may. 2.01.107
that all the court may echo with the noise. 2.02. 6
we may, each wreathed in the other's arms | (our 2.03. 25
pit, | where never man's eye may behold my body: 2.03.177
here, | that he thereby may have a likely guess, 2.03.207
reach me thy hand, that i may help thee out, 2.03.237
i may be pluck'd into the swallowing womb | of 2.03.239
me down, | that i may slumber an eternal sleep! 2.04. 15
or make some sign how i may do thee ease. 3.01.121
these miseries are more than may be borne. 3.01.243
about, | that i may turn me to each one of you, 3.01.277
inspire me, that i may this treason find! 4.01. 67
that we may know the traitors and the truth! 4.01. 76
my lords, with all the humbleness i may, | i 4.02. 4
may it please you, | my grandsire, well advis'd, 4.02. 9
need, | you may be armed and appointed well: 4.02. 16
save thou the child, so we may all be safe. 4.02.131
two may keep counsel when the third's away. 4.02.144
happily you may catch her in the sea; 4.03. 8
this wicked emperor may have shipp'd her hence, 4.03. 23
and, kinsmen, then we may go pipe for justice. 4.03. 24
and feed his humor kindly as we may, | till time 4.03. 29
may this be borne as if his traitorous sons, 4.04. 53
hang the child, that he may see it sprawl — | a 5.01. 51
that highly may advantage thee to hear. 5.01. 56
if thou wilt not, befall what may befall, | i'll 5.01. 57
the door | that so my sad decrees may fly away, 5.02. 11
which i wish may prove | more stern and bloody 5.02.202
and prompt me that my tongue may utter forth 5.03. 12
thanks, gentle romans, may i govern so, | to 5.03.147
unless good counsel may the cause remove. ROM 1.01.142
where i may read who pass'd that passing fair? 1.01.236
ere we may think her ripe to be a bride. 1.02. 11
may stand in number, though in reck'ning none. 1.02. 33
why, may one ask? 1.04. 49
this trick may chance to scath you. 1.05. 84
he may not have access | to breathe such vows as 2.pr. 9
may prove a beauteous flow'r when next we meet. 2.02.122
bondage is hoarse, and may not speak aloud, 2.02.160
women may fall, when there's no strength in men. 2.03. 80
for this alliance may so happy prove | to turn 2.03. 91
any man that can write may answer a letter. 2.04. 10 P
such a case as mine a man may strain courtesy. 2.04. 50 P
single sole of it is worn, the jest may remain, 2.04. 63 P
of you tell me where i may find the young romeo? 2.04.119 P
say, | "two may keep counsel, putting one away"? 2.04.197
he dare, | it is enough i may but call her mine. 2.06. 8
a lover may bestride the gossamers | that idles 2.06. 18
your worship in that sense may call him man. 3.01. 59
that /th' runaway's eyes may wink, and romeo 3.02. 6
that hath new robes | and may not wear them. 3.02. 31
for 'tis a throne where honor may be crown'd 3.02. 93
live here in heaven and may look on her, | but 3.03. 32
heaven and may look on her, | but romeo may not. 3.03. 33
they may seize | on the white wonder of dear 3.03. 35
but romeo may not, he is banished. 3.03. 40
flies may do this, but i from this must fly; 3.03. 41
tell me, that i may sack | the hateful mansion. 3.03.107
it may be thought we held him carelessly, 3.04. 25
very late that we | may call it early by and by. 3.04. 35
no opportunity | that may convey my greetings, 3.05. 50
for still thy eyes, which i may call the sea, 3.05.132
may not one speak? 3.05.173
herself alone, | may be put from her by society. 4.01. 14
that may be, sir, when i may be a wife. 4.01. 19
that may be, sir, when i may be a wife. 4.01. 19
that may be must be, love, on thursday next. 4.01. 20
it may be so, for it is not mine own. 4.01. 36
i hear thou must, and nothing may prorogue it, 4.01. 48
unless thou tell me how i may prevent it. 4.01. 51
well, he may chance to do some good on her. 4.02. 13
faith, we may put up our pipes and be gone. 4.05. 96 P
ay, /by my troth, the case may be amended. 4.05.100 P
if i may trust the flattering truth of sleep, 5.01. 1
veins | that the life–weary taker may fall dead, 5.01. 62
and that the trunk may be discharg'd of breath 5.01. 63
and the neglecting it | may do much danger. 5.02. 20
o, how may i | call this a lightning? 5.03. 90
else, | on whom i may confer what i have got. TIM 1.01.122
never may | that state of fortune fall into my 1.01.149
long may he live in fortunes! shall we in? 1.01.282
grant i may never prove so fond, | to trust man 1.02. 64
may it please your honor, lord lucius | (out of 1.02.181
you may take my word, my lord; 1.02.214
that i may make his lordship understand 2.02. 42
that we may account thee a whoremaster and a 2.02.104 P
a noble nature | may catch a wrench — would all 2.02.209
may these add to the number that may scald thee! 3.01. 51
may these add to the number that may scald thee! 3.01. 51
o, may diseases only work upon't! 3.01. 60
may it please your honor, my lord hath sent — 3.02. 30 P
so it may prove an argument of laughter | to th' 3.03. 20
one may reach deep enough and yet | find little. 3.04. 15
such may rail against great buildings. 3.04. 64 P
i perceive our masters may throw their caps at 3.04.100 P
these debts may well be call'd desperate ones, 3.04.101 P
the gods keep you old enough that you may live 3.05.103
live | only in bone, that none may look on you! 3.05.104
spleen and fury, | that i may strike at athens. 3.05.113
may you a better feast never behold, | you knot 3.06. 88
that their limbs may halt | as lamely as their 4.01. 24
'gainst the stream of virtue they may strive, 4.01. 27
(as their friendship) may | be merely poison! 4.01. 31
his hate may grow | to the whole race of mankind 4.01. 39
noble timon, | what friendship may i do thee? 4.03. 71
yet may your pains six months | be quite 4.03.144
paint till a horse may mire upon your face: 4.03.148
that he may never more false title plead, | nor 4.03.154
that your activity may defeat and quell | the 4.03.163
affords | to such as may the passive drugs of it 4.03.254
lie where the light foam of the sea may beat 4.03.378
that death in me at others' lives may laugh. 4.03.380
that beasts | may have the world in empire! 4.03.392
is no time so miserable but a man may be true. 4.03.457 P
grant i may ever love, and rather woo | those 4.03.467
and may diseases lick up their false bloods! 4.03.532
when we may profit meet, and come too late. 5.01. 42
let it go naked, men may see't the better. 5.01. 67
his former days, | the former man may make him. 5.01.125
bring us to him, | and /chance it as it may. 5.01.126
that i hope i may use with a safe conscience, JC 1.01. 13 P
may we do so? 1.01. 66
yet i see | thy honorable mettle may be wrought 1.02.309
but men may construe things after their fashion, 1.03. 34
praetor's chair, | where brutus may but find it; 1.03.144
in him | that at his will he may do danger with. 2.01. 17
so caesar may; 2.01. 27
then lest he may, prevent. 2.01. 28
give so much light that i may read by them. 2.01. 45
that by no means i may discover them | by any 2.01. 75
may well stretch so far | as to annoy us all; 2.01.159
it may be these apparent prodigies, | the 2.01.198
augurers | may hold him from the capitol to–day. 2.01.201
hear | that unicorns may be betray'd with trees, 2.01.204
you will not come, | their minds may change. 2.02. 96
be near me, that i may remember you. 2.02.123
i know will be, much that i fear may chance. 2.04. 32
i wish your enterprise to–day may thrive. 3.01. 13
desiring thee that publius cimber may | have an 3.01. 53
vouchsafe that antony | may safely come to him, 3.01.131
i wish we may; 3.01.144
suitor that i may | produce his body to the 3.01.227
know you how much the people may be mov'd | by 3.01.234
i know not what may fall, i like it not. 3.01.243
for my cause, and be silent, that you may hear. 3.02. 14 P
respect to mine honor, that you may believe. 3.02. 16 P
your senses, that you may the better judge. 3.02. 17 P
you may do your will; 4.01. 27
how covert matters may be best disclos'd, | and 4.01. 46
for so much trash as may be grasped thus? 4.03. 26
my love, | i may do that i shall be sorry for. 4.03. 64
it may be i shall raise you by and by | on 4.03.247
sirs, | it may be i shall otherwise bethink me. 4.03.251
the gods to–day stand friendly, that we may, 5.01. 93
let's reason with the worst that may befall. 5.01. 96
that i may rest assur'd | whether yond troops 5.03. 17
i may say "thrusting" it; 5.03. 75
or are you aught | that man may question? MAC 1.03. 43
why, chance may crown me | without my stir. 1.03.143
come what come may, | time and the hour runs 1.03.146
that i may pour my spirits in thine ear, | and 1.05. 26
as a book, where men | may read strange matters. 1.05. 63
i dare do all that may become a man; 1.07. 46
come in, tailor, here you may roast your goose. 2.03. 14 P
therefore much drink may be said to be an 2.03. 31 P
that most may claim this argument for ours? 2.03.120
hid in an auger–hole, may rush and seize us? 2.03.122
well, may you see things well done there: 2.04. 37
made good, | may they not be my oracles as well, 3.01. 9
whose loves i may not drop, but wail his fall 3.01.121
who may i rather challenge for unkindness | than 3.04. 41
which must be acted ere they may be scann'd. 3.04.139
whom you may say (if't please you) fleance 3.06. 6
work) we may again | give to our tables meat, 3.06. 33
may soon return to this our suffering country 3.06. 48
that i may tell pale–hearted fear it lies, | and 4.01. 85
that this great king may kindly say | our duties 4.01.131
what you have spoke, it may be so perchance. 4.03. 11
something | you may discern of him through me, 4.03. 15
a good and virtuous nature may recoil | in an 4.03. 19
you may be rightly just, | what ever i shall 4.03. 30
you may | convey your pleasures in a spacious 4.03. 70
and yet seem cold, the time you may so hoodwink. 4.03. 72
receive what cheer you may, | the night is long 4.03.239
you may to me, and 'tis most meet you should. 5.01. 15 P
within this three mile may you see it coming; 5.05. 36
and underwrit, | "here may you see the tyrant." 5.08. 27
come, | he may approve our eyes and speak to it. HAM 1.01. 29
well may it sort that this portentous figure 1.01.109
thing to be done | that may to thee do ease, and 1.01.131
fate, | which, happily, foreknowing may avoid, 1.01.134
while | with an attent ear, till i may deliver, 1.02.193
he may not, as unvalued persons do, | carve for 1.03. 19
act and place | may give his saying deed, which 1.03. 27
then weigh what loss your honor may sustain | if 1.03. 29
bear't that th' opposed may beware of thee. 1.03. 67
ay, fashion you may call it. go to, go to. 1.03.112
and with a larger teder may he walk | than may 1.03.125
teder may he walk | than may be given you. 1.03.126
pure as grace, | as infinite as man may undergo, 1.04. 34
what may this mean, | that thou, dead corse, 1.04. 51
the thoughts of love, | may sweep to my revenge. 1.05. 31
meet it is i set it down | that one may smile, 1.05.108
at least i am sure it may be so in denmark. 1.05.109
what is between us, | o'ermaster't as you may. 1.05.140
and what so poor a man as hamlet is | may do, t' 1.05.185
in part him — but," you may say, "not well. 2.01. 17
none so rank | as may dishonor him, take heed of 2.01. 21
quarrelling, | drabbing — you may go so far. 2.01. 26
faith, as you may season it in the charge: 2.01. 28
that they may seem the taints of liberty, | the 2.01. 32
gather | so much as from occasion you may glean, 2.02. 16
it may be, very like. 2.02.152
how may we try it further? 2.02.159
a blessing, but as your daughter may conceive, 2.02.185 P
the spirit that i have seen | may be a /dev'l, 2.02.599
'twere by accident, may here | affront ophelia. 3.01. 30
we may of their encounter frankly judge, | and 3.01. 33
and madam, i wish it may. 3.01. 41
that show of such an exercise may color | your 3.01. 44
for in that sleep of death what dreams may come, 3.01. 65
that he may play the fool no where but in 's own 3.01.131 P
and, as i may say, whirlwind of your passion, 3.02. 6 P
beget a temperance that may give it smoothness. 3.02. 8 P
for what advancement may i hope from thee | that 3.02. 57
of the knee | where thrift may follow fawning. 3.02. 62
a great man's memory may outlive his life half a 3.02.132 P
so many journeys may the sun and moon | make us 3.02.161
the terms of our estate may not endure | hazard 3.03. 5
may one be pardon'd and retain th' offense? 3.03. 56
offense's gilded hand may /shove by justice, 3.03. 58
all may be well. 3.03. 72
all his crimes broad blown, as flush as may, 3.03. 81
trip him, that his heels may kick at heaven, 3.03. 93
and that his soul may be as damn'd and black 3.03. 94
where you may see the /inmost part of you. 3.04. 20
transports his pois'ned shot, may miss our name, 4.01. 43
tell us where 'tis, that we may take it thence, 4.02. 7
a man may fish with the worm that hath eat of a 4.03. 27 P
to show you how a king may go a progress through 4.03. 30 P
as my great power thereof may give thee sense, 4.03. 59
for she may strew | dangerous conjectures in 4.05. 14
know what we are, but know not what we may be. 4.05. 44 P
o rose of may! 4.05.158
we may call it herb of grace a' sundays. 4.05.182 P
you may wear your rue with a difference. 4.05.183 P
that you may direct me | to him from whom you 4.06. 33
which may to you, perhaps, seem much unsinow'd, 4.07. 10
whose worth, if praises may go back again, 4.07. 27
shuffling, you may choose | a sword unbated, and 4.07.137
that, if i gall him slightly, | it may be death. 4.07.148
of time and means | may fit us to our shape. 4.07.150
venom'd stuck, | our purpose may hold there. 4.07.162
argal, the gallows may do well to thee. 5.01. 49 P
why may not that be the skull of a lawyer? 5.01. 98 P
to what base uses we may return, horatio! 5.01.202 P
why may not imagination trace the noble dust of 5.01.203 P
fair and unpolluted flesh | may violets spring! 5.01.240
let hercules himself do what he may, | the cat 5.01.291
that future strife | may be prevented now. LR 1.01. 45
that we our largest bounty may extend | where 1.01. 52
a little, | lest you may mar your fortunes. 1.01. 95
and your large speeches may your deeds approve, 1.01.184
that good effects may spring from words of love. 1.01.185
and nothing more, may fitly like your grace, 1.01.200
well may you prosper! 1.01.282
come to me, that of this i may speak more. 1.02. 52 P
yourself wherein you may have offended him; 1.02.159 P
may carry through itself to that full issue 1.04. 3
so may it come, thy master, whom thou lov'st, 1.04. 6
when the lady brach may stand by th' fire and 1.04.112 P
may not an ass know when the cart draws the 1.04.223 P
depend, | to be such men as may besort your age, 1.04.251
it may be so, my lord. 1.04.274
that it may live | and be a thwart disnatur'd 1.04.282
that she may feel | how sharper than a serpent's 1.04.287
he may enguard his dotage with their pow'rs, 1.04.326
well, you may fear too far. 1.04.328
reasons of your own | as may compact it more. 1.04.339
how far your eyes may pierce i cannot tell: 1.04.345
what a man cannot smell out, he may spy into. 1.05. 23 P
you may do then in time. fare you well, sir. 2.01. 13 P
that all the kingdom | may have due note of him, 2.01. 83
where may we set our horses? 2.02. 4 P
my sister may receive it much more worse | to 2.02.148
a good man's fortune may grow out at heels. 2.02.157
that by thy comfortable beams i may | peruse 2.02.164
whiles i may scape | i will preserve myself, and 2.03. 5
no, but not yet, may be he is not well: 2.04.105
and what they may incense him to, being apt | to 2.04.306
my lord, i may be censur'd, that nature thus 3.05. 2 P
is, that he may be ready for our apprehension. 3.05. 18 P
though well we may not pass upon his life 3.07. 24
wrath, which men | may blame, but not control. 3.07. 27
thee they may hurt. 4.01. 17
and worse i may be yet: 4.01. 27
our wishes on the way | may prove effects. 4.02. 15
may all the building in my fancy pluck | upon my 4.02. 85
soon may i hear and see him! 4.04. 29
i may not, madam; 4.05. 17
you may gather more. 4.05. 32
so may it be indeed. 4.06. 6
and yet i know not how conceit may rob | the 4.06. 42
a man may see how this world goes with no eyes. 4.06.150 P
letters that he speaks of | may be my friends. 4.06.257
please your majesty | that we may wake the king? 4.07. 17
pray that the right may thrive. 5.02. 2
no further, sir, a man may rot even here. 5.02. 8
merits and our safety | may equally determine. 5.03. 45
person, | the which immediacy may well stand up, 5.03. 65

a noble heart, | thy arm may do thee justice; 5.03.128
what comfort to this great decay may come 5.03.298
of vexation on't, | as it may lose some color. OTH 1.01. 73
(how ever this may gall him with some check) 1.01.148
property of youth and maidhood | may be abus'd? 1.01.173
know | where we may apprehend her and the moor? 1.01.177
every house i'll call | (i may command at most). 1.01.181
siege, and my demerits | may speak, unbonneted, 1.02. 23
something from cyprus, as i may divine; 1.02. 39
how may the duke be therewith satisfied, | whose 1.02. 88
for if such actions may have passage free, 1.02. 98
so may he with more facile question bear it, 1.03. 23
so much i challenge that i may profess | due to 1.03.188
may help these lovers | /into /your /favor. 1.03.200
storm of fortunes | may trumpet to the world. 1.03.250
she has deceiv'd her father, and may thee. 1.03.293
that he may bless this bay with his tall ship, 2.01. 79
fled from her wish, and yet said, "now i may"* 2.01.151
you may relish him more in the soldier than in 2.01.165 P
may the winds blow till they have waken'd death! 2.01.186
in choler, and happily may strike at you — 2.01.273 P
may strike at you — provoke him, that he may; 2.01.273 P
in some action | that may offend the isle. 2.03. 61
or any man living, may be drunk at a time, man. 2.03.313 P
now the general — i may say so in this respect, 2.03.315 P
that she may make, unmake, do what she list, 2.03.346
and bring him jump when he may cassio find 2.03.386
if you have any music that may not be heard, 3.01. 15 P
your converse and business | may be more free. 3.01. 39
you, | if you think fit, or that it may be done, 3.01. 51
lady, | that policy may either last so long, 3.03. 14
foh, one may smell in such, a will most rank, 3.03.232
speak of her, though i may fear | her will, 3.03.235
may fall to match you with her country forms, 3.03.237
this may do something. 3.03.324
and may; 3.03.394
and this may help to thicken other proofs | that 3.03.430
she may be honest yet. 3.03.433
patience, i say; your mind /perhaps may change. 3.03.452
you may, indeed, say so; 3.04. 44
that by your virtuous means i may again | exist, 3.04.111
hers, | she may, i think, bestow't on any man. 4.01. 13
may she give that? 4.01. 15
fellow that's but yok'd | may draw with you. 4.01. 67
/an' you'll come to supper to–night, you may; 4.01.160 P
well, i may chance to see you; 4.01.166 P
may be th' letter mov'd him; 4.01.235
i do entreat that we may sup together. 4.01.262
i may not breathe my censure | what he might be. 4.01.270
will denote him so | that i may save my speech. 4.01.280
unkindness may do much, | and his unkindness may 4.02.159
much, | and his unkindness may defeat my life, 4.02.160
and one), you may take him at your pleasure. 4.02.237 P
be near at hand, i may miscarry in't. 5.01. 6
and, besides, the moor | may unfold me to him; 5.01. 21
these may be counterfeits; 5.01. 43
what may you be? 5.01. 65
may you suspect | who they should be that have 5.01. 78
alack, my lord, what may you mean by that? 5.02. 29
i do beseech you | that i may speak with you. 5.02.102
may his pernicious soul | rot half a grain a day 5.02.155
at fifty, to whom herod of jewry may do homage. ANT 1.02. 29 P
going on, | the sides o' th' world may danger. 1.02.192
what, says the married woman you may go? 1.03. 20
you may see, lepidus, and henceforth know, | it 1.04. 1
thy freer thoughts | may not fly forth of egypt. 1.05. 12
that sleep and feeding may prorogue his honor 2.01. 26
how lesser enmities may give way to greater. 2.01. 43
how the fear of us | may cement their divisions, 2.01. 48
what's amiss, | may it be gently heard. 2.02. 20
you may be pleas'd to catch at mine intent | by 2.02. 41
which with a snaffle | you may pace easy, but 2.02. 64
as nearly as i may, | i'll play the penitent to 2.02. 91
one another's love for the instant, you may, 2.02.104 P
may i never | (to this good purpose, that so 2.02.143
come too short, | the actor may plead pardon. 2.05. 9
and what may follow, | to try a larger fortune. 2.06. 33
i crave our composition may be written | and 2.06. 58
and thus it may be. 2.06.132 P
place, note well, | may make too great an act. 3.01. 13
all may be well enough. 3.03. 47
place | we may the number of the ships behold, 3.09. 3
may be a coward's, whose ministers would prevail 3.13. 23
against the blown rose may they stop their nose 3.13. 39
dare but what it can, | no chance may shake it. 3.13. 81
whom | he may at pleasure whip, or hang, or 3.13.150
may be it is the period of your duty; 4.02. 25
that antony may seem to spend his fury | upon 4.06. 9
that heaven and earth may strike their sounds 4.08. 38
rebel to my will, | may hang no longer on me. 4.09. 15
for the things he speaks | may concern caesar. 4.09. 25
come on then, he may recover yet. 4.09. 33
where their appointment we may best discover, 4.10. 8
sir, you may not live to wear | all your true 4.14.133
that she preparedly may frame herself | to th' 5.01. 55
you see how easily she may be surpris'd. 5.02. 35
and may, through all the world; 5.02.134
what poor an instrument | may do a noble deed! 5.02.237
that i may say | the gods themselves do weep! 5.02.299
his virtue | by her election may be truly read, CYM 1.01. 53
or that the negligence may well be laugh'd at, 1.01. 66
with what patience | your wisdom may inform you. 1.01. 79
this jewel in the world | that i may see again. 1.01. 92
'twas a contention in public, which may, without 1.04. 55 P
the one may be sold or given, or if there were 1.04. 82 P
you may wear her in title yours; 1.04. 88 P
your ring may be stol'n too: 1.04. 90 P
who may this be? 1.06. 9
i may say, | the credit that thy lady hath of 1.06.156
may it please you | to take them in protection? 1.06.192
night, that dawning | may bare the raven's eye! 2.02. 49
who lets go by no vantages that may | prefer you 2.03. 45
may be she pluck'd it off | to send it me. 2.04.104
it may be probable she lost it; 2.04.115
other of them may have crook'd noses, but to owe 3.01. 37 P
if one of mean affairs | may plod it in a week, 3.02. 51
a week, why may not i | glide thither in a day? 3.02. 51
but first of all, | how we may steal from hence; 3.02. 62
how many /score of miles may we well rid 3.02. 67
are arch'd so high that giants may jet through 3.03. 5
and you may then revolve what tales i have told 3.03. 14
o boys, this story | the world may read in me: 3.03. 56
thy tongue | may take off some extremity, which 3.04. 17
thus may poor fools | believe false teachers. 3.04. 84
may the gods | direct you to the best! 3.04.192
may | this night forestall him of the coming day 3.05. 68
what he learns by this | may prove his travel, 3.05.103
spurn her home to her father, who may (happily) 4.01. 19 P
it may be heard at court that such as we | cave 4.02.137
and in time | may make some stronger head, the 4.02.139
that we the horrider may seem to those | which 4.02.331
i may wander | from east to occident, cry out 4.02.371
may drive us to a render | where we have liv'd, 4.04. 11
and may save | but to look back in frown. 5.03. 27
by med'cine life may be prolong'd, yet death 5.05. 29
that their good souls may be appeas'd with 5.05. 72
nothing but our lives | may be call'd ransom, 5.05. 80
creatures may be alike; 5.05.125
that this gentleman may render | of whom he had 5.05.135
and — which more may grieve thee, | as it doth 5.05.144
well may you, sir, | remember me at court, where 5.05.192
from your orbs, | you may reign in them now! 5.05.372
man sing | may to your wishes pleasure bring, PER 1.ch. 14
how they may be, and yet in two, | as you will 1.01. 70
honor /him, | if he suspect i may dishonor him; 1.02. 21
and what may make him blush in being known, 1.02. 22
fits kings as they are men, for they may err. 1.02. 43
when all, for mine, if i may call offense, 1.02. 92
as friends to antioch, we may feast in tyre. 1.03. 39
fetch breath that may proclaim them louder, that 1.04. 15
they may awake their helpers to comfort them. 1.04. 17
the misery of tharsus may be theirs. 1.04. 55
an heir | that may succeed as his inheritor; 1.04. 64
you happily may think | are like the troyan 1.04. 92
all that may men approve or men detect! 2.01. 51
may see the sea hath cast upon your coast — 2.01. 56
and have no more of life than may suffice | to 2.01. 74
o, sir, things must be as they may; 2.01.113 P
get, he may lawfully deal for his wive's soul. 2.01.114 P
may defend thee." 2.01.129
court, | where with it i may appear a gentleman; 2.01.141
he hopes by you his fortunes yet may flourish. 2.02. 47
he well may be a stranger, for he comes | to an 2.02. 52
he may my proffer take for an offense, | since 2.03. 68
may we not get access to her, my lord? 2.05. 7
may be (nor can i think the contrary) | as great 2.05. 79
action may | conveniently the rest convey, 3.ch. 55
we give, and therein may | use honor with you. 3.01. 25
now, mild may be thy life! 3.01. 27
heirs | may the two latter darken and expend; 3.02. 29
death may usurp on nature many hours, | and yet 3.02. 82
that she may be | manner'd as she is born. 3.03. 16
on whose grace | you may depend hereafter. 3.03. 41
where you may abide till your date expire. 3.04. 14
that she may not be raw in her entertainment. 4.02. 55 P
i may so. 4.02.132 P
see how belief may suffer by foul show! 4.04. 23
you may so, 'tis the better for you that your 4.06. 23 P
that a man may deal withal and defy the surgeon? 4.06. 25 P
to find him so, that i may worthily note him. 4.06. 51 P
where a man may serve seven years for the loss 4.06.171 P
may we not see him? 5.01. 31
you may, | but bootless is your sight; 5.01. 32
you | that for our gold we may provision have, 5.01. 56
that, may be, hath endur'd a grief | might equal 5.01. 87
from the deck | you may discern the place. 5.01.115
it may be | you think me an imposture. 5.01.176
may we see them? 5.03. 25
that on the touching of her lips i may | melt, 5.03. 42
in helicanus may you well descry | a figure of 5.03. 91
we pray our play may be so; TNK pr 9
art, may yet appear | worth two hours' travail. pr 28
pie, | may on our bridehouse perch or sing, | or 1.01. 22
as you wish your womb may thrive with fair ones, 1.01. 27
what woman i may stead that is distress'd | does 1.01. 36
of our dead kings, that we may chapel them; 1.01. 50
under the shadow of his sword may cool us; 1.01. 92
in a /glassy stream, | you may behold 'em. 1.01.113
now you may take him | drunk with his victory. 1.01.157
to school, may we perceive | walking in thebes! 1.02. 14
by mine own | i may be reasonably conceiv'd; 1.02. 48
that we may nothing share | of his loud infamy; 1.02. 75
deep a cunning, | may be outworn, never undone. 1.03. 44
the one of th' other may be said to water 1.03. 58
that the true love 'tween maid and maid may be 1.03. 81
all the good that may | be wish'd upon thy head, 1.04. 2
as may be judg'd | by their appointment. 1.04. 14
what man to man may do for our sake more: 1.04. 39
i may depart with little, while i live; 2.01. 1 P
something i may cast to you, not much. 2.01. 2 P
you may perceive a part of him. 2.01. 50 P
can be, but our imaginations | may make it ours? 2.02. 78
so both may love. 2.02.165
ye may be. 2.02.189
it may be he shall marry her; 2.02.226
how bravely may he bear himself to win her, | if 2.02.254
may i see the garden? 2.02.268
may rude wind never hurt thee! 2.02.275
do sweetly, | and god knows what may come on't. 2.03. 58
whether my brows may not be girt with garlands, 2.03. 80
place | where i may ever dwell in sight of her? 2.03. 82
may thy goodness | get thee a happy husband!" 2.04. 24
to do observance | to flow'ry may, in dian's 2.05. 51
daughters, | and shortly you may keep yourself. 2.06. 39
this is a solemn rite | they owe bloom'd may, 3.01. 3
fresher than may, sweeter | than her gold 3.01. 5
emily my sovereign), how far | i may be proud. 3.01. 17
your person | without hypocrisy i may not wish 3.01. 95
me, but enjoy't till | i may enforce my remedy. 3.01.123
we may go whistle; all the fat's i' th' fire. 3.05. 39
the next, the lord of may and lady bright, | the 3.05.125
may the stag thou hunt'st stand long, | and thy 3.05.154
may they kill him without lets, | and the ladies 3.05.156
i wish his weary soul that falls may win it. 3.06.100
that i may tell my soul he shall not have her. 3.06.179
thousand blossoms, | because they may be rotten? 3.06.244
so we may fairly carry | our swords and cause 3.06.259
what may be done? for now i feel compassion. 3.06.271
love's tied," | "this you may loose, not me," 4.01. 91
"may you never more enjoy the light," etc. 4.01.104
yet i may bind those wounds up, that must open 4.02. 1
yet these that we count errors may become him: 4.02. 31
ask me now, sweet sister — | i may go look! 4.02. 52
is a prince too, | and, if it may be, greater; 4.02. 92
too, as ever he may go upon 's legs, for in the 4.03. 14 P
they may return and settle again to execute 4.03. 71 P
a place where the light may rather seem to steal 4.03. 74 P
this may bring her to eat, to sleep, and reduce 4.03. 94 P
that to thy laud | i may advance my streamer, 5.01. 59
the file and quality i hold i may | continue in 5.01.161
she may be, | but that's all one, 'tis nothing 5.02. 31
taint mine eye | with dread sights it may shun. 5.03. 10
of many mortal millions, may even now, | by 5.03. 24
the title of a kingdom may be tried | out of 5.03. 33
arcite may win me, | and yet may palamon wound 5.03. 57
me, | and yet may palamon wound arcite to | the 5.03. 58
let's us do as we may be done by. STM II.C 141 P
doubt, but mercy may be found if you so seek it. II.C 147
and may it be | that thou should think it heavy VEN 155
that thine may live, when thou thyself art dead; 172
that love–sick love by pleading may be blest; 328
so of concealed sorrow may be said, | free vent 333
"long may they kiss each other for this cure! 505
may say, the plague is banish'd by thy breath. 510
what bargains may i make, still to be sealing? 512
the poor fool prays her that he may depart. 578
she hath assay'd as much as may be prov'd. 608
and now his grief may be compared well | to one 701
may lend thee light, as thou dost lend to other. 864
o yes, it may, thou hast no eyes to see, | but 939
what may a heavy groan advantage thee? 950
and that his beauty may the better thrive, 1011
now serves the season that they may surprise LUC 166
what following sorrow may on this arise. 186
may feel her heart (poor citizen!) 465
when pattern'd by thy fault foul sin may say 629
light, | she prays she never may behold the day: 746
where it may find | some purer chest to close so 760
may set at noon and make perpetual night. 784
made | may likewise be sepulcher'd in thy shade. 805
face, | and tarquin's eye may read the mot afar, 830
thou sets the wolf where he the lamb may get; 878
and in thy shady cell, where none may spy him, 881
and bring him where his suit may be obtained? 898
but little stars may hide them when they list. 1008
"the crow may bathe his coal–black wings in mire 1009
through which i may convey this troubled soul. 1176
that he may vow, in that sad hour of mine, 1179
"but, lady, if your maid may be so bold, | she 1282
and that deep torture may be call'd a hell, 1287
by this short schedule collatine may know | her 1312
sighs and groans and tears may grace the fashion 1319
that with my nails her beauty i may tear. 1472
and tell thy grief, that we may give redress. 1603
and what wrong else may be imagined | by foul 1622
"how may this forced stain be wip'd from me? 1701
may my pure mind with the foul act dispense, 1704
may any terms acquit me from this chance? 1706
yet neither may possess the claim they lay. 1794
fiend, | suspect i may (yet not directly tell): PP 2.10
't may be she joy'd to jest at my exile, | 't 14. 9
't may be again, to make me wander thither: 14.10
love, whose month was ever may, | spied a 16. 2
"air," quoth he, "thy cheeks may blow, | air, 16. 9
there | where thy desert may merit praise, | by 18.15
and if these pleasures may thee move, | then 19.15
it fell upon a day, | in the merry month of may, 20. 2
truth may seem, but cannot be, | beauty brag, PHT 62
when every private widow well may keep, | by SON 9. 7
change thy thought, that i may change my mind! 10. 9
that beauty still may live in thine or thee. 10.14
rough winds do shake the darling buds of may, 18. 3
love and am beloved | where i may not remove, 25.14
which wit so poor as mine | may make seem bare, 26. 6
then may i dare to boast how i do love thee, 26.13
suns of the world may stain when heaven's sun 33.14
i may not evermore acknowledge thee, | lest my 36. 9
o, how thy worth with manners may i sing, | when 39. 1
that by this separation i may give | that due to 39. 7
and yet it may be said i lov'd her dearly; 42. 2
return of love, more blest may be the view; 56.12
with my jealious thought | where you may be, or 57.10
that you yourself may privilege your time | to 58.10
in black ink my love may still shine bright. 65.14
o, lest your true love may seem false in this, 72. 9
better'd that the world may see my pleasure; 75. 8
so love's face | may still seem love to me, 93. 3
hath motion, and mine eye may be deceiv'd; 104.12
what's in the brain that ink may character 108. 1
that may express my love, or thy dear merit? 108. 4
i may be straight though they themselves be 121.11
may time disgrace and wretched /minutes kill. 126. 8
she may detain, but not still keep, her treasure 126.10
that i may not be so, nor thou belied, | bear 140.13
it grows, | thy pity may deserve to pitied be. 142.12
that my angel be turn'd fiend | suspect i may, 144.10
my soul doth tell my body that he may | triumph 151. 7
if that from him there may be aught applied LC 68
which may her suffering ecstasy assuage, | 'tis 69
a storm | as oft 'twixt may and april is to see, 102
counsel may stop a while what will not stay; 159
love made them not, with acture they may be, 185

MAY-DAY 2 FR 0.0002 REL FR 1 V 1 P
for shrove tuesday, a morris for may–day, as the AWW 2.02. 24 P
as 'tis to make 'em sleep | on may–day morning, H8 5.03. 15

MAYEST 10 FR 0.0011 REL FR 9 V 1 P
if thou mayest discern by that which is left of WT 3.03.133 P
thou mayest not wander in that labyrinth, 1H6 5.03.188
thou mayest bereave him of his wits with wonder. 5.03.195
when thou mayest tell thy tale the nearest way? R3 4.04.461
even so mayest thou the giddy men of rome. TIT 4.04. 87
if thou swear'st, | thou mayest prove false. ROM 2.02. 92
and therefore thou mayest think my behavior 2.02. 99
these poor compounds that thou mayest not sell. 5.01. 82

if thou read this, o caesar, thou mayest live; JC 2.03. 15
and therefore mayest without attaint o'erlook SON 82. 2
MAYING 1 FR 0.0001 REL FR 1 V 0 P
do we all hold against the maying? TNK 2.03. 36
MAY–MORN 1 FR 0.0001 REL FR 1 V 0 P
liege | is in the very may–morn of his youth, H5 1.02.120
/MAYOR 2 FR 0.0002 REL FR 2 V 0 P
/look /ye, /my /lord /mayor, | would you imagine R3 3.05. 34
/the /mayor /in /courtesy /show'd /me /the 4.02.104
MAYOR 20 FR 0.0022 REL FR 19 V 1 P
the mayor and all his brethren in best sort, H5 5.pr. 25
peace, mayor, thou know'st little of my wrongs. 1H6 1.03. 59
mayor, farewell; thou dost but what thou mayst. 1.03. 86
the lord mayor craves aid of your honor from the 2H6 4.05. 4 P
but, master mayor, if henry be your king, | yet 3H6 4.07. 20
why, master mayor, why stand you in a doubt? 4.07. 27
so, master mayor; 4.07. 35
my lord, the mayor of london comes to greet you.
R3 3.01. 17
he is, and see, he brings the mayor along. 3.05. 13
lord mayor — 3.05. 14
lord mayor, the reason we have sent — 3.05. 18
and so, my good lord mayor, we bid farewell. 3.05. 71
the mayor towards guildhall hies him in all post 3.05. 73
and ask'd the mayor what meant this willful 3.07. 28
will not the mayor then and his brethren come? 3.07. 44
the mayor is here at hand. 3.07. 45
go, go up to the leads, the lord mayor knocks. 3.07. 55
tell him, myself, the mayor and aldermen, | in 3.07. 66
he sent command to the lord mayor straight | to H8 2.01.151
to you, my good lord mayor, | and you, good 5.04. 69
MAYOR'S 1 FR 0.0001 REL FR 0 V 1 P
we will have the mayor's sword borne before us. 2H6 4.03. 14 P
MAYPOLE 2 FR 0.0002 REL FR 2 V 0 P
how low am i, thou painted maypole? MND 3.02.296
give us but a tree or twain | for a maypole, and TNK 3.05.145
MAY'S 1 FR 0.0001 REL FR 1 V 0 P
than wish a snow in may's new–fangled shows; LLL 1.01.106
/MAYST 1 FR 0.0001 REL FR 1 V 0 P
/long /mayst /thou /live /in /richard's /seat R2 4.01.218
MAYST 67 FR 0.0075 REL FR 61 V 6 P
cam'st here, | how thou cam'st here thou mayst. TMP 1.02. 52
where thou mayst knock a nail into his head. 3.02. 61
there thou mayst brain him, | having first 3.02. 88
and that thou mayst perceive how well i like it, TGV 1.03. 35
and, that thou mayst perceive my fear of this, 3.01. 33
as easy mayst thou fall | a drop of water in the ERR 2.02.125
and never mayst thou come lysander near! MND 2.02.136
thou mayst with better face | exact the penalty. MV 1.03.136
beg that thou mayst have leave to hang thyself, 4.01.364
thou mayst, i warrant. 4.02. 15
of a pure blush thou mayst in honor come off AYL 1.02. 29 P
hark, tranio, thou mayst hear minerva speak. SHR 1.01. 84
well mayst thou woo, and happy be thy speed! 2.01.138
it, thou mayst slide from my shoulder to my heel 4.01. 14 P
father's moral parts | mayst thou inherit too! AWW 1.02. 22
haply thou mayst inform | something to save thy 4.01. 82
for thou mayst see a sunshine and a hail | in me 5.03. 33
so thou mayst say, the /king lies by a beggar, TN 3.01. 8 P
for thou perhaps mayst move | that heart, which 3.01.163
up, that thou thereby | mayst smile at this. 4.01. 57
credent | thou mayst co–join with something, and WT 1.02.143
who mayst see | plainly as heaven sees earth and 1.02.314
shall be king | that thou mayst be a queen, and JN 2.01.123
of nature's gifts thou mayst with lilies boast, 3.01. 53
thou mayst, thou shalt, i will not go with thee. 3.01. 67
france, thou mayst hold a serpent by the tongue, 3.01.258
husband, i cannot pray that thou mayst win; 3.01.331
uncle, i needs must pray that thou mayst lose; 3.01.332
thou mayst befriend me so much as to think | i 5.06. 10
ill mayst thou thrive if thou grant any grace! R2 5.03. 99
at idle times as thou mayst and so farewell. 2H4 2.02.130 P
and noble offices thou mayst effect | of 4.04. 24
mayor, farewell; thou dost but what thou mayst. 1H6 1.03. 86
beseech /god on my knees thou mayst be turn'd to
2H6 4.10. 59 P
in dreadful war mayst thou be overcome, | or 3H6 1.01.187
long mayst thou live | to bear his image and 5.04. 53
too | thou mayst be damned for that wicked deed!
R3 1.02.103
long mayst thou live to wail thy children's 1.03.203
that thou mayst hear of us | and we of thee; COR 4.01. 39
that thou mayst prove | to shame unvulnerable, 5.03. 72
and mayst be honor'd, being cato's son. JC 5.04. 11
thou mayst revenge. MAC 3.03. 18
where such as thou mayst find him. 4.02. 82
as easy mayst thou the intrenchant air | with 5.08. 9
us — thou mayst not coldly set | our sovereign HAM 4.03. 62
that thou mayst shake the superflux to them, LR 3.04. 35
not for himself, | remain in't as thou mayst. ANT 2.06. 29
that thou mayst stand | t' enjoy thy banish'd CYM 2.01. 64
thou mayst be valiant in a better cause, | but 3.04. 72
safe mayst thou wander, safe return again! 3.05.105
that it was folly in me, thou mayst say, | and 5.05. 67
of all 'say'd yet, mayst thou prove prosperous! PER 1.01. 59
thou mayst cut a morsel off the spit. 4.02.131 P
that mayst force the king | to be his subject's TNK 5.01. 83
yet mayst thou well be tasted. VEN 128
by whose example thou reveng'd mayst be. LUC 1194
youngly thou bestow'st | thou mayst call thine, SON 11. 4
not show my head where thou mayst prove me. 26.14
love, my love, that thou mayst true love call, 40. 3
whence at pleasure thou mayst come and part, 48.12
that time of year thou mayst in me behold | when 73. 1
and of this book this learning mayst thou taste. 77. 4
thou by thy dial's shady stealth mayst know 77. 7
alone, that thou mayst take | all this away, and 91.13
thou mayst be false, and yet i know it not. 92.14
hide, | by self–example mayst thou be denied. 142.14
so will i pray that thou mayst have thy will, 143.13
MAY'T 6 FR 0.0006 REL FR 6 V 0 P
may't please your lordship, 'tis a word or two TGV 1.03. 52
may't be? WT 1.02.137
may't please your majesty to give us leave H5 1.02.237
am i given in charge, may't please your grace. 2H6 2.04. 80
may't please your highness sit. MAC 3.04. 38
why may't not be | they have made prey of him? TNK 3.02. 12
MAZARD *(see mazzard)*
MAZ'D *(also amaz'd)*
MAZ'D 2 FR 0.0002 REL FR 2 V 0 P
maz'd with a yelping kennel of french curs! 1H6 4.02. 47
that many maz'd considerings did throng | and H8 2.04.186
MAZE 4 FR 0.0004 REL FR 4 V 0 P
here's a maze trod indeed | through forth–rights TMP 3.03. 2
this is as strange a maze as e'er men trod, 5.01.242
and i have thrust myself into this maze, SHR 1.02. 55
fly, | or one encompass'd with a winding maze, LUC 1151
MAZED 1 FR 0.0001 REL FR 1 V 0 P
and the mazed world, | by their increase, now MND 2.01.113
MAZES 1 FR 0.0001 REL FR 1 V 0 P
and the quaint mazes in the wanton green | for MND 2.01. 99
/MAZZARD 1 FR 0.0001 REL FR 0 V 1 P
knock'd about the /mazzard with a sexton's spade
HAM 5.01. 89 P
MAZZARD 1 FR 0.0001 REL FR 0 V 1 P
me go, sir, or i'll knock you o'er the mazzard. OTH 2.03.154 P
/ME 63 FR 0.0071 REL FR 53 V 10 P
ME 8218 FR 0.9289 REL FR 6259 V 1959 P
MEACOCK 1 FR 0.0001 REL FR 1 V 0 P
a meacock wretch can make the curstest shrew. SHR 2.01.313
MEAD 4 FR 0.0004 REL FR 4 V 0 P
met we on hill, in dale, forest, or mead, | by MND 2.01. 83
the even mead, that erst brought sweetly forth H5 5.02. 48
th' enamell'd knacks o' th' mead or garden! TNK 3.01. 7
would root these beauties as he roots the mead. VEN 636
MEADOW–FAIRIES 1 FR 0.0001 REL FR 1 V 0 P
and nightly, meadow–fairies, look you sing, WIV 5.05. 65
MEADOWS 3 FR 0.0003 REL FR 3 V 0 P
yellow hue | do paint the meadows with delight, LLL 5.02.897
how they are stain'd like meadows yet not dry, TIT 3.01.125
kissing with golden face the meadows green, SON 33. 3
MEADS 6 FR 0.0006 REL FR 6 V 0 P
and flat meads thatch'd with stover, them to TMP 4.01. 63
blots thy beauty, as frosts do bite the meads, SHR 5.02.139
all our vineyards, fallows, meads, and hedges, H5 5.02. 54
one hour's storm will drown the fragrant meads, TIT 2.04. 54
with plenteous rivers and wide–skirted meads, LR 1.01. 65
as winter meads when sun doth melt their snow. LUC 1218
MEAGRE 7 FR 0.0008 REL FR 7 V 0 P
but thou, thou meagre lead, | which rather MV 3.02.104
the meagre cloddy earth to glittering gold. JN 3.01. 80
a ghost, | as dim and meagre as an ague's fit, 3.04. 85
of ashy semblance, meagre, pale, and bloodless, 2H6 3.02.162
meagre were his looks, | sharp misery had worn ROM 5.01. 40
he's swarth and meagre, of an eye as heavy | as TNK 4.02. 27
"hard–favor'd tyrant, ugly, meagre, lean, VEN 931
MEAL* 11 FR 0.0012 REL FR 9 V 2 P
what strange fish | hath made his meal on thee? TMP 2.01.114
one fruitful meal would set me to't. MM 4.03.154 P
no food, | and but one meal on every day beside, LLL 1.01. 40
meal and bran together | he throws without COR 3.01.320
whose meal and exercise | are still together, 4.04. 14
ere we will eat our meal in fear, and sleep | in MAC 3.02. 17
let's to–night | be bounteous at our meal. ANT 4.02. 10
it on the board so soon | as i had made my meal, CYM 3.06. 51
nature hath meal and bran, contempt and grace. 4.02. 27
and the charity | of one meal lend me — come TNK 3.01. 74
a pound, meal at nine shillings a bushel, and STM II.C 2 P
MEAL'D 1 FR 0.0001 REL FR 1 V 0 P
were he meal'd with that | which he corrects, MM 4.02. 83
MEALS 6 FR 0.0006 REL FR 2 V 4 P
unquiet meals make ill digestions, | thereof the ERR 5.01. 74
give them great meals of beef and iron and steel H5 3.07.150 P
and give me but the ten meals i have lost, and 2H6 4.10. 62 P
not serv'd thyself in to my table so many meals? TRO 2.03. 42 P
man, i should fear to drink at meals, lest they TIM 1.02. 50 P
to keep with you at meals, comfort your bed, JC 2.01.284
MEALY 1 FR 0.0001 REL FR 1 V 0 P
show not their mealy wings but to the summer, TRO 3.03. 79
/MEAN* 2 FR 0.0002 REL FR 1 V 1 P
/when /we /mean /to /build, | /we /first /survey 2H4 1.03. 41
/i /mean, /my /head /upon /your /lap? HAM 3.02.114 P
MEAN* 328 FR 0.0370 REL FR 257 V 71 P
but for the miracle | (i mean our preservation), TMP 2.01. 7
i mean, in a sort. 2.01.104 P
this my mean task | would be as heavy to me as 3.01. 4
what do you mean | to dote thus on such luggage? 4.01.230
you mistake; i mean the pound — a pinfold. TGV 1.01.107 P
there wanteth but a mean to fill your song. 1.02. 92
the mean is drown'd with /your unruly bass. 1.02. 93
hast thou observ'd that? even she, i mean. 2.01. 44 P
i mean that her beauty is exquisite, but her 2.01. 54 P
tut, man, i mean thou'lt lose the flood, and, in 2.03. 41 P
but too mean a servant | to have a look of such 2.04.107
to lesson me and tell me some good mean | how 2.07. 5
lord, they have devis'd a mean | how he her 3.01. 38
for "get you gone," she doth not mean "away!" 3.01.101
but she i mean is promis'd by her friends | unto 3.01.106
"friend," quoth i, "you mean to whip the dog?" 4.04. 25 P
i pray you be my mean | to bring me where to 4.04.108
what mean you by that saying? 5.04.167
i do mean to make love to ford's wife. WIV 1.03. 43 P
i mean, master slender, what would you with me? 3.04. 60 P
i mean it not, i seek you a better husband. 3.04. 84
no, sir, nor i mean it not. MM 2.01.120 P
does your worship mean to geld and splay all the 2.01.230 P
that there were | no earthly mean to save him, 2.04. 95
what we would have, we speak not what we mean. 2.04.118
a mean woman was delivered | of such a burthen ERR 1.01. 54
word, | and go indeed, having so good a mean. 1.02. 18
what mean you, sir? 1.02. 93
i mean not cuckold–mad — | but sure he is stark 2.01. 58
drunkard, thou, what didst thou mean by this? 3.01. 10
but though my cates be mean, take them in good 3.01. 28
master, mean you so? 3.01. 81
and in despite of mirth mean to be merry. 3.01.108
this woman that i mean, | my wife (but, i 3.01.111
how dost thou mean a fat marriage? 3.02. 94 P
what gold is this? what adam dost thou mean? 4.03. 16 P
i hope you do not mean to cheat me so? 4.03. 78
in the mean time, good signior benedick, repair ADO 1.01.275 P
in the mean time let me be that i am, and seek 1.03. 36 P
county claudio, when mean you to go to church? 2.01.355 P
for in the mean time i will so fashion the 2.02. 46 P
i mean the fashion. 3.03.121 P
what do you mean, my lord? 4.01. 43
and that count claudio did mean, upon his words, 4.02. 53 P
how pitiful i deserve" — | i mean in singing; 5.02. 30 P
mean time let wonder seem familiar, | and to the 5.04. 70
things hid and barr'd, you mean, from common LLL 1.01. 57
which, i mean, i walk'd upon: 1.01.239 P
where, i mean, i did encounter that obscene and 1.01.241 P
how mean you, sir? 1.02. 19 P
good lord boyet, my beauty, though but mean, 2.01. 13
mean time receive such welcome at my hand | as 2.01.168
my sweet soul, i mean setting thee at liberty, 3.01.123 P
can sing | a mean most meanly and in hushering 5.02.328
what mean you, madam? 5.02.450
what mean you, sir? 5.02.603 P
what mean you? 5.02.702 P
therefore if you my favor mean to get, | a 5.02.820
but herein mean i to enrich my pain, | to have MND 1.01.250
in the mean time i will draw a bill of 1.02.105 P
i mean, that my heart unto yours /is knit, | so 2.02. 47
i understand not what you mean by this. 3.02.236
heavens shield lysander, if they mean a fray! 3.02.447
it is no mean happiness, therefore, to be seated MV 1.02. 7 P
happiness, therefore, to be seated in the mean: 1.02. 8 P
water–thieves and land–thieves, i mean pirates, 1.03. 24 P
but stop my house's ears, i mean my casements; 2.05. 34
and when your honors mean to solemnize | the 3.02.192
and do you, gratiano, mean good faith? 3.02.210
my maid nerissa and myself mean time | will live 3.02.309
mean time the court shall hear bellario's letter 4.01.149
you mean to mock me after; AYL 1.02.208 P
i'll put myself in poor and mean attire, | and 1.03.111
who can come in and say that i mean her, | when 2.07. 77
thinking that i mean him, but therein suits 2.07. 81
here comes the man you mean. 5.01. 9 P
mean time, forget this new–fall'n dignity, | and 5.04.176
mates, maid, how mean you that? SHR 1.01. 59
is't he you mean? 1.02.221
hark you, sir, you mean not her to — 1.02.223
i see you do not mean to part with her, | or 2.01. 64
no such jade as you, if me you mean. 2.01.201
what, you mean my face? 2.01.234
marry, so i mean, sweet katherine, in thy bed; 2.01.267
yet oftentimes he goes but mean apparell'd. 3.02. 73
that by degrees we mean to look into, | and 3.02.143
and therefore here i mean to take my leave. 3.02.188
belike you mean to make a puppet of me. 4.03.103
even in these honest mean habiliments; 4.03.170
worse | for this poor furniture and mean array. 4.03.180
i mean hortensio is afeard of you. 5.02. 19
mistress, how mean you that? 5.02. 21
a very mean meaning. 5.02. 31
right, i mean you. 5.02. 31
and i am mean indeed, respecting you. 5.02. 32
i mean to shift my bush, | and then pursue me as 5.02. 46
for our gentlemen that mean to see | the tuscan AWW 1.02. 13
i would speak with her — helen, i mean. 1.03. 69 P
god shield you mean it not! 1.03.168
she is too mean | to have her name repeated. 3.05. 60
how do you mean? 3.05. 68
in the mean time, what hear you of these wars? 4.03. 37 P
i mean the business is not ended, as fearing to 4.03. 96 P
what dost thou mean? TN 1.03.131 P
i mean, she is the list of my voyage. 3.01. 76 P
i understand what you mean by bidding me taste 3.01. 80 P
i mean, to go, sir, to enter. 3.01. 81 P
if you mean well, | now go with me and with this 4.03. 22
mean time, sweet sister, | we will not part from 5.01.384
as swiftly followed as | i mean to utter it; WT 1.02.410
i' th' eyes of heaven and to you — i mean, | in 2.01.132
yet nature is made better by no mean | but 4.04. 89
better by no mean | but nature makes that mean; 4.04. 90
so turtles pair | that never mean to part. 4.04.155
mean mischief and break a foul gap into the 4.04.197 P
no, nor mean better. 4.04.381
see this knack (as never | i mean thou shalt), 4.04.429
in faith, i mean not | to see him any more) cast 4.04.494
what course i mean to hold | shall nothing 4.04.502
but few, | and those but mean. 5.01. 93
and in the mean time sojourn'd at my father's; JN 1.01.103
yet, to avoid deceit, i mean to learn; 1.01.215
and by whose help i mean to chastise it. 2.01.117
what dost thou mean by shaking of thy head? 3.01. 19
for even the breath of what i mean to speak 3.04.127
mean time but ask | what you would have reform'd 4.02. 43
mean time, let this defend my loyalty: R2 1.01. 67
that which in mean men we entitle patience | is 1.02. 33
fathers feed upon | is my strict fast — i mean, 2.01. 80
and shortly mean to touch our northern shore. 2.01.288
i mean the earl of wiltshire, bushy, green. 3.04. 53
which for some reasons, sir, i mean to see. 5.02. 63
i mean thou shalt have the hanging of the 1H4 1.02. 66 P
and make the douglas' son your only mean | for 1.03.261
what time do you mean to come to london? 2.01. 41 P
what a plague mean ye to colt me thus? 2.02. 37 P
o lord, sir, who do you mean? 2.04. 72 P
poor, such bare, such lewd, such mean attempts, 3.02. 13
but what mean i | to speak so true at first? 2H4 in 27
me, and i mean not to sweat extraordinarily. 1.02.209 P
sir, do you mean to stop any of william's wages, 5.01. 23 P
we do not mean the coursing snatchers only, H5 1.02.143
for there is none of you so mean and base | that 3.01. 29
cold fear, that mean and gentle all | behold, as 4.pr. 45
i will desire you to live in the mean time, and 5.01. 33 P
mean time look gracious on thy prostrate thrall. 1H6 1.02.117
shall we disturb him, since he keeps no mean? 1.02.121
he may mean more than we poor men do know: 1.02.122
i mean to tug it and to cuff you soundly. 1.03. 48
remedy) | i mean to prove this lady's courtesy. 2.02. 58
i do, my lord, and mean accordingly. 2.02. 60
mean time your cheeks do counterfeit our roses; 2.04. 62
mean time, in signal of my love to thee, 2.04.121
except you mean with obstinate repulse | to slay 3.01.113
our sacks shall be a mean to sack the city, 3.02. 10
mean and right poor, for that pure blood of mine 4.06. 23
which by my lord of winchester we mean | shall 5.01. 39
command, i mean, of virtuous chaste intents, 5.05. 20
where as the king and queen do mean to hawk. 2H6 1.02. 58
if you mean to save yourself from whipping, leap 2.01.139 P
but all in vain are these mean obsequies, | and 3.02.146

nay, that i mean to do. 4.02. 78 P
if we mean to thrive and do good, break open the 4.03. 15 P
we'll devise a mean | to reconcile you all unto 4.08. 68
if one so rude and of so mean condition | may 5.01. 64
if i mean to take possession of my right. 3H6 1.01. 44
the army of the queen mean to besiege us. 1.02. 64
i am too mean a subject for thy wrath, | be thou 1.03. 19
i mean our princely father, duke of york. 2.06. 51
in this self place where now we mean to stand. 3.01. 11
ay, but thou canst do what i mean to ask. 3.02. 48
but stay thee, 'tis the fruits of love i mean. 3.02. 58
the fruits of love i mean, my loving liege. 3.02. 59
no, by my troth, i did not mean such love. 3.02. 64
why then you mean not as i thought you did. 3.02. 65
i know i am too mean to be your queen, | and yet 3.02. 97
you cavil, widow, i did mean my queen. 3.02. 99
i mean, in bearing weight of government, | while 4.06. 51
i mean, my lords, those powers that the queen 5.03. 7
mean time, this deep disgrace in brotherhood R3 1.01.111
mean time, have patience. 1.01.116
mean time, god grants that i have need of you. 1.03. 76
you may deny that you were not the mean | of my 1.03. 89
you mean, to bear me, not to bear with me. 3.01.128
and make pursuit where he did mean no chase. 3.02. 30
how? wear the garland? dost thou mean the crown? 3.02. 41
i mean, your voice for crowning of the king. 3.04. 28
i mean, his conversation with shore's wife — 3.05. 31
he fears, my lord, you mean no good to him. 3.07. 87
should | suspect me that i mean no good to him. 3.07. 89
i mean the lord protector. 4.01. 18
inquire me out some mean poor gentleman, | whom 4.02. 53
tyrrel, i mean those bastards in the tower. 4.02. 75
mean time, but think how i may do thee good, 4.03. 33
i mean that with my soul i love thy daughter, 4.04.263
well then, who dost thou mean shall be her king? 4.04.265
to see if any mean to shrink from me. 5.03.222
i mean, who set the body and the limbs | of this H8 1.01. 46
found again | but where they mean to sink ye. 2.01.131
(i mean the learned ones in christian kingdoms) 2.02. 92
he | (i mean the bishop) did require a respite, 2.04.178
mean while must be an earnest motion | made to 2.04.234
what should this mean? 3.02.160
what should this mean? 3.02.203
will or words to do it | (i mean your malice), 3.02.237
i mean in perjur'd witness, than your master, 5.01.136
come back! what mean you? 5.01.157
would try him to the utmost had ye mean, | which 5.02.181
i mean, of ours. TRO 2.02. 20
for 'tis a cause that hath no mean dependance 2.02.192
you depend upon him, i mean. 3.01. 4 P
command, i mean, /friend. 3.01. 25 P
what mean these fellows? know they not achilles? 3.03. 70
i mean to stride your steed, and at all times COR 1.09. 71
the city, i mean of us a' th' right–hand file? 2.01. 22 P
yet i wish, sir | (i mean for your particular), 4.07. 13
mean to solicit him | for mercy to his country. 5.01. 72
i mean, thy general. 5.02. 54 P
mean while am i possess'd of that is mine. TIT 1.01.408
mean while, sir, with the little skill i have, 2.01. 43
sweet huntsman — bassianus 'tis we mean — | do 2.03.269
but, lovely niece, that mean is cut from thee. 2.04. 40
their heads, i mean. 3.01.202
alas, sweet aunt, i know not what you mean. 4.01. 4
fear her not, lucius, somewhat doth she mean. 4.01. 9
i mean she is brought a–bed. 4.02. 62
mean while here's money for thy charges. 4.03.105
and is not careful what they mean thereby, 4.04. 84
for what i mean to do | see here in bloody lines 5.02. 13
hark, wretches, how i mean to martyr you. 5.02.180
i mean, and we be in choler, we'll draw. ROM 1.01. 3 P
i mean, sir, in delay | we waste our lights in 1.04. 44
and we mean well in going to this mask, | but 1.04. 48
that i mean to make bold withal, and, as you 3.01. 78 P
no sudden mean of death, though ne'er so mean, 3.03. 45
no sudden mean of death, though ne'er so mean, 3.03. 45
in the mean time, against thou shalt awake, 4.01.113
what mean these masterless and gory swords | to 5.03.142
mean time forbear, | and let mischance be slave 5.03.220
and with wild looks bid me devise some mean | to 5.03.240
mean time i writ to romeo, | that he should 5.03.246
to show lord timon that mean eyes have seen TIM 1.01. 93
one to thyself, for i mean to give thee none. 1.01.266 P
but in the mean time he wants less, my lord. 3.02. 39
what does his lordship mean? 3.06. 86 P
i know not what you mean by that, but i am sure JC 1.02.257 P
'tis caesar that you mean; is it not, cassius? 1.03. 79
to–morrow | mean to establish caesar as a king; 1.03. 86
what mean you? 2.01.234
what mean you, caesar? 2.02. 8
that which melteth fools — i mean sweet words, 3.01. 42
no place will please me so, no mean of death, 3.01.161
so, | but what compact mean you to have with us? 3.01.215
which, pardon me, i do not mean to read — | and 3.02.131
they mean this night in sardis to be quarter'd. 4.02. 28
what do you mean? 4.03.130
they mean to warn us at philippi here, 5.01. 5
what do you mean? MAC 2.02. 37
mean you his majesty? 2.03. 70
with what i get, i mean, and so do they. 4.02. 33
it is myself i mean; 4.03. 50
what does this mean, my lord? HAM 1.04. 7
what may this mean, | that thou, dead corse, 1.04. 51
but, if't be he i mean, he's very wild, 2.01. 18
mean time, we thank you for your well–took labor 2.02. 83
i mean, the matter that you read, my lord. 2.02.195 P
though in the mean time some necessary question 3.02. 42 P
and let them know both what we mean to do | and 4.01. 39
what dost thou mean by this? 4.03. 29 P
what should this mean? 4.07. 49
i mean, sir, for /his weapon, but in the 5.02.141 P
i mean, my lord, the opposition of your person 5.02.171 P
mean time we shall express our darker purpose. LR 1.01. 36
of the news abroad, i mean the whisper'd ones, 2.01. 7 P
what do you mean? 3.07. 77
mean you to enjoy him? 5.03. 78
some good i mean to do, | despite of mine own 5.03.244
and i'll devise a mean to draw the moor | out of OTH 3.01. 37
who is't you mean? 3.03. 44

suit | wherein i mean to touch your love indeed, 3.03. 81
thou dost mean something. 3.03.108
/'zounds, what dost thou mean? 3.03.154
in the mean time, | let me be thought too busy 3.03.252
naked in bed, iago, and not mean harm? 4.01. 5
they that mean virtuously, and yet do so, | the 4.01. 7
what do you mean by this haunting of me? 4.01.147 P
what did you mean by that same handkerchief you 4.01.149 P
reason to believe now than ever (i mean purpose, 4.02.213 P
how do you mean, removing him? 4.02.228 P
alack, my lord, what may you mean by that? 5.02. 29
what you shall know mean time | of stirs abroad, ANT 1.04. 81
what mean you, madam? 2.05. 74
the lowness, or the mean, if dearth | or foison 2.07. 19
better might we | have lov'd without this mean, 3.02. 32
the mean time, lady, | i'll raise the 3.04. 25
mean time | laugh at his challenge. 4.01. 5
the last of many battles | we mean to fight. 4.01. 12
what does he mean? 4.02. 23
what mean you, sir, | to give them this 4.02. 33
peace, i say. | what should this mean? 4.03. 15
not, a swifter mean | shall outstrike thought, 4.06. 34
and he that hath her | (i mean, that married her CYM 1.01. 18
earnest of a farther good | that i mean to thee. 1.05. 66
how mean soe'er, that have their honest wills, 1.06. 8
(your lord, i mean) laughs from 's free lungs; 1.06. 68
in meaner parties | (yet who than he more mean?) 2.03.117
if one of mean affairs | may plod it in a week, 3.02. 50
such, i mean, | where they should be reliev'd. 3.06. 7
glass to confer in his own chamber — i mean, 4.01. 9 P
i mean, to man, he had not apprehension | of 4.02.110
what does he mean? 4.02.190
though mean and mighty, rotting | together, have 4.02.246
the gods do mean to strike me | to death with 5.05.234
sir, | as you did mean indeed to be our brother; 5.05.423
meaning, | for which we mean to have his head. PER 1.01.144
what mean you, sir? 2.01.135 P
he had need mean better than his outward show 2.02. 48
what mean you? 4.01. 66
i' th' mean time, look tenderly to the two TNK 2.01. 19 P
base, | my father the mean keeper of his prison, 2.04. 3
by no mean cross her, she is then distemper'd 4.01.119
too, | yea, the speed also — to go on, i mean, 5.01. 41
never can blab, nor know not what we mean. VEN 126
what dost thou mean | to stifle beauty and to 933
"thus i forestall thee, if thou mean to chide, LUC 484
and in thy dead arms do i mean to place him, 517
despitefully i mean to bear thee | unto the base 670
in vain | some happy mean to end a hapless life. 1045

MEAN–BORN 1 FR 0.0001 REL FR 1 V 0 P
let pale–fac'd fear keep with the mean–born man, 2H6 3.01.335

MEANDERS 1 FR 0.0001 REL FR 1 V 0 P
trod indeed | through forth–rights and meanders! TMP 3.03. 3

MEANER 14 FR 0.0015 REL FR 14 V 0 P
my meaner ministers | their several kinds have TMP 3.03. 87
thou and thy meaner fellows your last service 4.01. 35
some neapolitan, or meaner man of pisa. SHR 1.01.205
whom i from meaner form | have bench'd and WT 1.02.313
chok'd with ambition of the meaner sort; 1H6 2.05.123
and meaner than myself have had like fortune. 3H6 4.01. 71
kings it makes gods, and meaner creatures kings. R3 5.02. 24
we live not to be grip'd by meaner persons. H8 2.02.135
of martius' tongue | from every meaner man. COR 1.06. 27
learn thou to make some meaner choice, | lavinia TIT 2.01. 73
that they strike | a meaner than myself, since i ANT 2.05. 83
above ten thousand meaner moveables | would CYM 2.02. 29
and though it be allowed in meaner parties 2.03.116
that meaner men should vaunt | that golden hap LUC 41

MEANEST* 15 FR 0.0017 REL FR 13 V 2 P
how meanest thou? brawling in french? LLL 3.01. 10 P
what meanest thou? 5.02.674 P
clouds, | so honor peereth in the meanest habit. SHR 4.03.174
am, i yield to thee, | or to the meanest groom. 2H6 2.01.181
and make the meanest of you earls and dukes? 4.08. 37
york, if thou meanest well, i greet thee well. 5.01. 14
there's not the meanest spirit on our party TRO 2.02.156
now, young man, meanest thou to fight to–day? 5.03. 29
the capitol exceed | the meanest house in rome, COR 4.02. 40
plight | than prosecute the meanest or the best TIT 4.04. 33
but if thou meanest not well, | i do beseech ROM 2.02.150
a sight most pitiful in the meanest wretch, LR 4.06.204
maid that milks | and does the meanest chares. ANT 4.15. 75
you have abus'd me. | "his meanest garment"! CYM 2.03.150
though they did change me to the meanest bird PER 4.06.101

MEANETH 1 FR 0.0001 REL FR 1 V 0 P
this night he meaneth with a corded ladder | to TGV 2.06. 33

/MEANING 1 FR 0.0001 REL FR 1 V 0 P
/still /practice /learn /to /know /thy /meaning. TIT 3.02. 45

MEANING 62 FR 0.0070 REL FR 43 V 19 P
know thine own meaning, but wouldst gabble like TMP 1.02.356
distinctly, | there's meaning in thy snores. 2.01.218
meaning henceforth to trouble you no more. TGV 2.01.119
the ort is (according to our meaning) WIV 1.01.255 P
his meaning is good. 1.01.255 P
doubtfully, thou couldst not feel his meaning? ERR 2.01. 51 P
the folded meaning of your words' deceit. 3.02. 36
to dinner" — there's a double meaning in that. ADO 2.03.258 P
no, by my troth, i have no moral meaning; 3.04. 80 P
by my troth, there's one meaning well suited. 5.01.225 P
the meaning, pretty ingenious? LLL 3.01. 58 P
what's your dark meaning, mouse, of this light 5.02. 19
we need more light to find your meaning out. 5.02. 21
love takes the meaning in love's conference: MND 2.02. 46
whereof who chooses his meaning chooses you, MV 1.02. 31 P
my meaning in saying he is a good man is to have 1.03. 15 P
understand a plain man in his plain meaning: 3.05. 58 P
meaning me a beast. AYL 4.03. 49 P
meaning thereby that grapes were made to eat and 5.01. 35 P
he hath some meaning in his mad attire. SHR 3.02.124
to expound the meaning or moral of his signs and 4.04. 79 P
and now you know my meaning. 5.02. 30
a very mean meaning. 5.02. 31
it speed, | is wicked meaning in a lawful deed, AWW 3.07. 45
deed, | and lawful meaning in a lawful act, 3.07. 46
my meaning in't, i protest, was very honest in 4.03.218 P
dead is quick — | and now behold the meaning. 5.03.304

is that the meaning of "accost"? TN 1.03. 59 P
(not meaning to partake with me in danger) 5.01. 87
to know the meaning | of dangerous majesty, when JN 4.02.212
'tis not my meaning | to rase one title of your R2 2.03. 74
from my heart" — | meaning the king at pomfret. 5.04. 10
lavishly | wrested his meaning and authority. 2H4 4.02. 58
far off | the dolphin's meaning and our embassy? H5 1.02.240
pistol, i do partly understand your meaning. 3.06. 51 P
lord, if you will teach her to know my meaning; 5.02.307 P
once discern'd, shows that her meaning is, | no 1H6 3.02. 24
from meaning treason to our royal person | as is 2H6 3.01. 70
guess'd, believe me, for that was my meaning. 3H6 4.05. 22
till then, 'tis wisdom to conceal our meaning. 4.07. 60
come, we know your meaning, brother gloucester; R3 1.03. 73
because i will be guiltless from the meaning. 1.04. 94
heir to the crown — meaning indeed his house, 3.05. 78
be not so hasty to confound my meaning: 4.04.262
be ever double | both in his words and meaning. H8 4.02. 39
o, meaning you? i will go learn more of it. TRO 2.01.130
thou know'st our meaning. TIT 2.03.271
write down thy mind, bewray thy meaning so, 2.04. 3
take our good meaning, for our judgment sits ROM 1.04. 46
meaning to cur'sy. 2.04. 54 P
vault, | meaning to keep her closely at my cell, 5.03.255
atone your fears | with my more noble meaning, TIM 5.04. 59
open to incontinency — | that's not my meaning. HAM 2.01. 31
man if there be any good meaning toward you. LR 1.02.173 P
with best meaning have incurr'd the worst. 5.03. 4
in bed | an hour, or more, not meaning any harm? OTH 4.01. 4
read, and declare the meaning. CYM 5.05.434
he has found the meaning. PER 1.01.109
he hath found the meaning, | for which we mean 1.01.143
his meaning struck her ere his words begun. VEN 462
could pick no meaning from their parling looks, LUC 100
and would not take her meaning nor her pleasure. PP 11.12

/MEANINGS 1 FR 0.0001 REL FR 1 V 0 P
i have fair /meanings, sir. ANT 2.06. 66

MEANINGS 3 FR 0.0003 REL FR 2 V 1 P
speak'st thou in sober meanings? AYL 5.02. 69 P
iniquity, | i moralize two meanings in one word. R3 3.01. 83
something against our meanings, have prevented; 3.05. 55

MEANLY* 4 FR 0.0004 REL FR 4 V 0 P
my wife, not meanly proud of two such boys, ERR 1.01. 58
can sing | a mean most meanly and in hushering LLL 5.02.328
his daughter meanly have i match'd in marriage, R3 4.03. 37
and, though train'd up thus meanly | i' th' cave CYM 3.03. 82

MEANS* *(also moans)*

/MEANS* 3 FR 0.0003 REL FR 1 V 2 P
/contrive /the /means /of /meeting /between /him HAM 2.02.212 P
/most /like, /if /their /means /are /no /better) 2.02.349 P
/and /by /no /means | /will /yield /to /see /his LR 4.03. 40

MEANS* 278 FR 0.0314 REL FR 223 V 55 P
true — save means to live. TMP 2.01. 51 P
plot | the means that dusky dis my daughter got, 4.01. 89
have i means much weaker | than you may call to 5.01.146
how now? what means this passion at his name? TGV 1.02. 16
what means your ladyship? do you not like it? 2.01.121
and here he means to spend his time a while. 2.04. 80
and all the means | plotted and 'greed on for my 2.04.182
to make such means for her as thou hast done, 5.04.137
i had never so good means as desire to make WIV 2.02.182 P
merited, either in my mind or in my means, meed, 2.02.203 P
yes, by all means; 4.02.215 P
her father means she shall be all in white; 4.06. 35
which means she to deceive, father or mother? 4.06. 46
no man means evil but the devil, and we shall 5.02. 13 P
by the woman's means? MM 2.01. 82 P
ay, sir, by mistress overdone's means; 2.01. 83 P
let her have needful but not lavish means; 2.02. 24
as to put metal in restrained means | to make a 2.04. 48
thou'rt by no means valiant, | for thou dost 3.01. 15
causest to be done, | that is thy means to live. 3.02. 21
and this it was (for other means was none): ERR 1.01. 75
what means this jest? 2.02. 21
he gains by death that hath such means to die: 3.02. 51
till i have us'd the approved means i have, 5.01.103
my cousin means signior benedick of padua. ADO 1.01. 35 P
o, by no means, she mocks all her wooers out of 2.01.349 P
means your lordship to be married to–morrow? 3.02. 88 P
what means the fool, trow? 3.04. 59 P
nor fortune made such havoc of my means, | nor 4.01.195
ability in means, and choice of friends, | to 4.01.199
he rather means to lodge you in the field, LLL 2.01. 85
poor deer's blood, that my heart means no ill. 4.01. 35
you up | (which by no means we may extenuate) MND 1.01.120
and thus she means, videlicet — 5.01.323 P
than my faint means would grant continuance. MV 1.01.125
my purse, my person, my extremest means, | lie 1.01.138
had i but the means | to hold a rival place with 1.01.173
yet his means are in supposition: 1.03. 17 P
his wife who wins me by that means i told you, 2.01. 19
to the same diseases, heal'd by the same means, 3.01. 62 P
my friend to his mere enemy, | to feed my means. 3.02.263
and that no lawful means can carry me | out of 4.01. 9
you | make no moe offers, use no farther means, 4.01. 81
when you do take the means whereby i live. 4.01.377
ay, but the clerk that never means to do it, 5.01.282
and have by underhand means labor'd to dissuade AYL 1.01.140 P
ta'en thy life by some indirect means or other; 1.01.152 P
could give more, but that her hand lacks means. 1.02.247
and this night he means | to burn the lodging 2.03. 22
that, | he will have other means to cut you off; 2.03. 25
woo | the means of weakness and debility; 2.03. 51
sea, | till that the weary very means do ebb? 2.07. 73
and that he that wants money, means, and content 3.02. 25 P
by no means, sir. 3.02.308 P
why, what means this? 3.05. 41
life, | i think she means to tangle my eyes too! 3.05. 44
belike some noble gentleman that means SHR in.1. 75
i think 'twas soto that your honor means. in.1. 88
if i can by any means light on a fit man to 1.01.110 P
who woo'd in haste, and means to wed at leisure. 3.02. 11

yet never means to wed where he hath woo'd. 3.02. 17
upon my life, petruchio means but well, 3.02. 22
why, true, he means to make a puppet of thee. 4.03.104
she says your worship means to make a puppet of 4.03.105 P
i believe 'a means to cozen somebody in this 5.01. 38 P
means and attendants, and my loving greetings AWW 1.03.252
see what he writes, and when he means to come. 3.02. 11 P
there's place and means for every man alive. 4.03.339
though time seem so adverse and means unfit. 5.01. 26
what good speed | our means will make us means. 5.01. 35
what good speed | our means will make us means. 5.01. 35
what a plague means my niece to take the death TN 1.03. 1 P
what means this lady? 2.02. 17
you would not give means for this uncivil rule. 2.03.123 P
and by all means stir on the youth to an answer. 3.02. 58 P
there is no christian that means to be sav'd by 3.02. 71 P
the king of sicilia means to pay bohemia the WT 1.01. 6 P
what means sicilia? 1.02.146
but they are most of them means and bases; 4.03. 43 P
by which means i saw whose purse was best in 4.04.603 P
by this means being there | so soon as you 4.04.619
gold and a means to do the prince my master good 4.04.834 P
ay, by any means prove a tall fellow. 5.02.170 P
what means this scorn, thou most untoward knave?
JN 1.01.243
what means that hand upon that breast of thine? 3.01. 21
and with advantage means to pay thy love; 3.03. 22
when fortune means to men most good, | she looks 3.04.119
how oft the sight of means to do ill deeds 4.02.219
he means to recompense the pains you take | by 5.04. 15
ere further leisure yield them further means R2 1.04. 40
consuming means, soon preys upon itself. 2.01. 39
the means that heavens yield must be embrac'd, 3.02. 29
the proffered means of succors and redress. 3.02. 32
he means, my lord, that we are too remiss, 3.02. 33
what means our cousin, that he stares and looks 5.03. 24
how now, what means death in this rude assault? 5.05.105
send me your prisoners with the speediest means, 1H4 1.03.120
being the agents or base second means, | the 1.03.165
whom means your grace? 2.04.461 P
king | dismiss his power he means to visit us, 4.04. 37
whereby we stand opposed by such means | as you 5.01. 67
thee, | who never promiseth but he means to pay. 5.04. 43
your means are very slender, and your waste is 2H4 1.02.140 P
i would my means were greater and my waist 1.02.142 P
have you heard our cause and known our means, 1.03. 1
how in our means we should advance ourselves 1.03. 7
he sure means brevity in breath, short–winded. 2.02.124 P
night, | with all appliances and means to boot, 3.01. 29
when means and lavish manners meet together, | o 4.04. 64
that lack of means enforce you not to evils, 5.05. 67
and therefore we must needs admit the means H5 1.01. 68
they know your grace hath cause, and means, and 1.02.125
with men of courage and with means defendant; 2.04. 8
by the means whereof 'a faces it out, but fights 3.02. 33 P
by the means whereof 'a breaks words, and keeps 3.02. 35 P
how now, what means this, herald? 4.07. 68
by this means shall we sound what skill she hath 1H6 1.02. 63
how now, ambitious /humphrey, what means this? 1.03. 29
or by what means gots thou to be releas'd? 1.04. 25
what means he now? go ask him whither he goes. 2.03. 28
lords and gentlemen, what means this silence? 2.04. 1
for talbot means no goodness by his looks. 3.02. 72
what means his grace, that he hath chang'd his 4.01. 50
we english warriors wot not what it means. 4.07. 55
and as the only means | to stop effusion of our 5.01. 8
one, | and means to give you battle presently. 5.02. 13
hast thou by secret means | us'd intercession to 5.04.147
nephew, what means this passionate discourse, 2H6 1.01.104
what means this noise? 2.01. 57
by this means | your lady is forthcoming yet at 2.01.174
by wicked means to frame our sovereign's fall. 3.01. 52
by means whereof the towns each day revolted? 3.01. 63
who cannot steal a shape that means deceit? 3.01. 79
by means whereof his highness hath lost france. 3.01.106
by suffolk and the cardinal beauford's means. 3.02.124
mischance unto my state by suffolk's means. 3.02.284
thee, jack cade the clothier means to dress the 4.02. 4 P
belike he means, | back'd by the power of 3H6 1.01. 51
shall be the war that henry means to use. 1.01. 73
i think he means to beg a child of her. 3.02. 27
and so i chide the means that keeps me from it, 3.02.141
while we bethink a means to break it off. 3.03. 39
i have advertis'd him by secret means | that if 4.05. 9
by fair or foul means we must enter in, | for 4.07. 14
he'll soon find means to make the body follow. 4.07. 26
by what safe means the crown may be recover'd. 4.07. 52
father of warwick, know you what this means? 5.01. 81
use means for her recovery. 5.05. 45
what means this armed guard | that waits upon R3 1.01. 42
our brother is imprison'd by your means, 1.03. 77
and every man that means to live well endeavors 1.04.143 P
what means this scene of rude impatience? 2.02. 38
whose humble means match not his haughty spirit. 4.02. 37
let me have open means to come to them, | and 4.02. 76
blunt, make some good means to speak with him, 5.03. 40
one that made means to come by what he hath, 5.03.248
those that were the means to help him; 5.03.249
for want of means, poor rats, had hang'd 5.03.331
compell'd by hunger | and lack of other means, H8 1.02. 35
sent innumerable substance | (by what means got, 3.02.327
to have given me longer life | and able means, 4.02.153
what means this? 5.02. 3
what troy means fairly shall be spoke aloud. TRO 1.03.259
what means not, hath not, or is not in love! 1.03.288
if then one is, or hath, /or means to be, | that 1.03.289
in such a sort | the thing he means to kill, 4.01. 25
of envy, thou, what means thou to curse thus? 5.01. 26 P
then we shall ha' means to vent | our musty COR 1.01.225
put you | (like one that means his proper harm) 1.09. 57
seeking means | to pluck away their power, as 3.03. 95
unless by using means i lame the foot | of our 4.07. 7
good | that noble–minded titus means to thee! TIT 1.01.209
i know not what it means, away with her! 2.03.157
what means my niece lavinia by these signs? 4.01. 8
marcus, what means this? 4.01. 30
i think she means that there were more than one 4.01. 38
have by my means been butchered wrongfully? 4.04. 55
you know your mother means to feast with me, 5.02.184
i fear the emperor means no good to us. 5.03. 10
have you importun'd him by any means? ROM 1.01.145
her means much less | to meet her new–beloved 2.pr. 11
but passion lends them power, time means, to 2.pr. 13
to seek him here that means not to be found. 2.01. 42
some means to come to shrift this afternoon, 2.04.180
find thou the means, and i'll find such a man. 3.05.103
let's see for means. 5.01. 35
that heaven finds means to kill your joys with 5.03.293
his means most short, his creditors most strait. TIM 1.01. 96
o, by no means, | honest ventidius. 1.02. 8
what means that trump? how now? 1.02.115
have rated my expense | as i had leave of means. 2.02.127
head, sword, force, means, but is lord timon's? 2.02.167
when the means are gone that buy this praise, 2.02.169
know unthrift that was belov'd after his means? 4.03.312 P
who, without those means thou talk'st of, didst 4.03.313 P
thou hadst some means to keep a dog. 4.03.316 P
and strain what other means is left unto us | in 5.01.227
love | by humble message and by promis'd means. 5.04. 20
by means whereof this breast of mine hath buried JC 1.02. 49
what means this shouting? 1.02. 79
that by no means i may discover them | by any 2.01. 75
no, by no means. 2.01.143
and, you know, his means, | if he improve them, 2.01.158
he would embrace the means to come by it. 2.01.259
our best friends made, our means stretch'd, 4.01. 44
for i can raise no money by vile means. 4.03. 71
so shall he waste his means, weary his soldiers, 4.03.200
that will ravin up | thine own live's means! MAC 2.04. 29
bent to know, | by the worst means, the worst. 3.04.134
what's the disease he means? 4.03.146
remove | the means that makes us strangers! 4.03.163
remove from her the means of all annoyance, 5.01. 76
be thou familiar, but by no means vulgar: HAM 1.03. 61
no, by no means. 1.04. 62
how, and who, what means, and where they keep, 2.01. 8
as they fell out by time, by means, and place, 2.02.127
comes by the means of the late innovation. 2.02.332 P
but from what cause 'a will by no means speak. 3.01. 6
what means your lordship? 3.01.105 P
what means this, my lord? 3.02.136 P
this' /miching mallecho, it means mischief. 3.02.137 P
show, he'll not shame to tell you what it means. 3.02.146 P
not this, by no means, that i bid you do: 3.04.181
and will, and strength, and means | to do't. 4.04. 45
but when they ask you what it means, say you 4.05. 47 P
and for my means, i'll husband them so well, 4.05.139
his means of death, his obscure funeral — | no 4.05.214
give these fellows some means to the king, they 4.06. 14 P
and that he means | no more to undertake it, i 4.07. 62
weigh what convenience both of time and means 4.07.149
convey the business as i shall find means, and LR 1.02.102 P
fled this way, sir, when by no means he could — 2.01. 42
pursue him, ho! go after. by no means what? 2.01. 43
boy, i'll work the means | to make thee capable. 2.01. 84
what means your grace? 2.04.187
my lord, entreat him by no means to stay. 2.04.299
what means your graces? 3.07. 30
our means secure us, and our mere defects 4.01. 20
there is means, madam. 4.04. 11
the life | that wants the means to lead it. 4.04. 20
say thou'lt do't, | or thrive by other means. 5.03. 34
what means this bloody knife? 5.03.224
and found good means | to draw from her a prayer
OTH 1.03.151
your desires by the means i shall then have to 2.01.278 P
you shall by that perceive him and his means. 3.03.249
to furnish me with some swift means of death 3.03.478
that by your virtuous means i may again | exist, 3.04.111
babes | do it with gentle means and easy tasks. 4.02.112
i have wasted myself out of my means. 4.02.186 P
he means in flesh. ANT 1.02. 18 P
what means this? 4.02. 13
spirit of a youth | that means to be of note, 4.04. 27
know you what caesar means to do with me? 5.02.106
what means do you make to him? CYM 2.04. 3
o, for such means, | though peril to my modesty, 3.04.151
your means abroad — | you have me, rich, and i 3.04.177
neither want my means for thy relief nor my 3.05.114 P
means he not us? 4.02. 64
some falls are means the happier to arise. 4.02.403
again, | but end it by some means for imogen. 5.03. 83
who makes the fairest show means most deceit. PER 1.04. 75
known, | which from her by no means can i get. 2.05. 6
faith, by no means, she hath so strictly tied 2.05. 8
what means the /nun? she dies, help, gentlemen! 5.03. 15
by any means; TNK 2.03. 51
let's rehearse by any means | before the ladies 2.03. 56
ay, ay, by any means, dear domine. 3.05.135
by any means. 3.06. 58
discover'd how | and by whose means he escap'd, 4.01. 20
bring 'em in | quickly, by any means, i long to 4.02. 65
seeks all foul means | of boist'rous and rough 5.04. 71
where their queen | means to immure herself, and VEN 1194
these means, as frets upon an instrument, LUC 1140
pausing for means to mourn some newer way. 1365
that he finds means to burn his troy with water. 1561
with means more blessed than my barren rhyme? SON 16. 4
than public means which public manners breeds. 111. 4
what means the world to say it is not so? 148. 6

MEAN'ST* 11 FR 0.0012 REL FR 8 V 3 P
what, thou mean'st an officer? ERR 4.03. 29 P
prithee, who is't that thou mean'st? AYL 1.02. 81 P
what mean'st thou by that, malvolio? TN 3.04. 40 P
what mean'st thou, suffolk? 2H6 1.03.180
what mean'st thou, that thou help'st me not? R3 1.04.274
what mean'st thou, aaron? TIT 4.02.147
what mean'st thou by that? JC 1.01. 18
what mean'st by this? LR 2.02.108
demands | thou mean'st to have him grant thee. ANT 5.02. 11
his mean'st garment | that ever hath but clipt CYM 2.03.133
i'll be reveng'd. | "his mean'st garment"! well. 2.03.156

/MEANT 1 FR 0.0001 REL FR 0 V 1 P
such–a–one's horse, when 'a /meant to beg it, HAM 5.01. 85 P

MEANT 53 FR 0.0060 REL FR 37 V 16 P
have taken it wiselier than i meant you should. TMP 2.01. 21 P
why, fool, i meant not thee, i meant thy master. TGV 2.05. 49 P
why, fool, i meant not thee, i meant thy master. 2.05. 49 P
ay — i think my cousin meant well. WIV 1.01.257 P
i will go further than i meant, to pluck all MM 4.02.191 P
he meant he did me none: the more my spite. ERR 4.02. 8
your daughter and meant to acknowledge it this ADO 1.02. 13 P
he meant to take the present time by the top, 1.02. 14 P
i meant plain holy–thistle. 3.04. 80 P
in faith, my hand meant nothing to my sword. 5.01. 57
pardon me, madam, for i meant not so. LLL 4.01. 13
that more for praise than purpose meant to kill. 4.01. 29
pride, | if hermia meant to say lysander lied. MND 2.02. 55
that many may be meant | by the fool multitude, MV 2.09. 25
and swore | as if the vicar meant to cozen him. SHR 3.02.168
i pray you tell me what you meant by that. 5.02. 27
is it not meant damnable in us, to be trumpeters AWW 4.03. 26 P
sovereign sir, | i did not well, i meant well. WT 5.03. 3
i meant indeed to pay you with this, which if 2H4 ep 10 P
if you take the matter otherwise than is meant, H5 3.02.126 P
chance, father, you meant, but i meant maine, 2H6 1.01.212
chance, father, you meant, but i meant maine, 1.01.212
i will take my death, i never meant him any ill, 2.03. 88 P
far truer spoke than meant. 3.01.183
for things are often spoke and seldom meant; 3.01.268
when as he meant all harm. 3H6 5.07. 34
i will not reason what is meant hereby, R3 1.04. 93
ask'd the mayor what meant this willful silence. 3.07. 28
a charge as little honor | he meant to lay upon; H8 1.01. 78
play'd | the part my father meant to act upon 1.02.195
accusers, | that never knew what truth meant. 2.01.105
that pardons all offenses | malice ne'er meant. 2.02. 68
i meant to rectify my conscience — which | i 2.04.204
so deep suspicion, where all faith was meant. 3.01. 53
he was never | (but where he meant to ruin) 4.02. 40
meant for his trial | and fair purgation to the 5.02.186
you smile and mock me, as if i meant naughtily. TRO 4.02. 37
tale, and meant indeed to occupy the argument no
ROM 2.04.100 P
but thankful even for hate that is meant love. 3.05.148
except they meant to bathe in reeking wounds, MAC 1.02. 39
he did but trifle | and meant to wrack thee, but HAM 2.01.110
do you think i meant country matters? 3.02.116 P
will 'a tell us what this show meant? 3.02.143 P
roderigo meant t' have sent this damned villain; OTH 5.02.316
with which i meant | to scourge th' ingratitude ANT 2.06. 21
now the witch take me, if i meant it thus! 4.02. 37
but when he meant to quail and shake the orb, 5.02. 85
fram'd this piece, she meant thee a good turn; PER 4.02.139 P
to punish, although not done, but meant. 5.03.100
he has mistook the /brake i meant, is gone TNK 3.02. 1
as if she ever meant to /crown his valor. 4.02.109
(for to that honest purpose it was meant ye), ep 14
and meant thereby | thou shouldst print more, SON 11.13

MEANT'ST 1 FR 0.0001 REL FR 1 V 0 P
and say it was thy mother that thou meant'st, 2H6 3.02.222

MEASLES 1 FR 0.0001 REL FR 1 V 0 P
words till their decay against those measles COR 3.01. 78

MEASURABLE 1 FR 0.0001 REL FR 0 V 1 P
congruent, and measurable for the afternoon. LLL 5.01. 92 P

MEASUR'D 11 FR 0.0012 REL FR 8 V 3 P
whose honor cannot | be measur'd or confin'd. TMP 5.01.122
say to her we have measur'd many miles, | to LLL 5.02.184
they say that they have measur'd many a mile 5.02.186
if to come hither you have measur'd miles, | and 5.02.191
and so we measur'd swords and parted. AYL 5.04. 87 P
your throne and his | measur'd to look upon you; WT 5.01.145
i am assur'd, if i be measur'd rightly, | your 2H4 5.02. 65
who hath measur'd the ground? H5 3.07.127 P
of sorrow | must not be measur'd by his worth, MAC 5.09. 11
till you had measur'd how long a fool you were CYM 1.02. 23 P
far the miles are measur'd from thy friend." SON 50. 4

MEASURE 94 FR 0.0106 REL FR 67 V 27 P
shall that claribel | measure us back to naples? TMP 2.01.259
to measure kingdoms with his feeble steps; TGV 2.07. 10
come not within the measure of my wrath. 5.04.127
mine host of de jarteer to measure our weapon. WIV 1.04.118 P
be, | to guide our measure round about the tree. 5.05. 79
receiv'd no sinister measure from his judge, but MM 3.02.243 P
doth quit like, and measure still for measure. 5.01.411
doth quit like, and measure still for measure. 5.01.411
quarters, will not measure her from hip to hip. ERR 3.02.110 P
me, | and therewithal took measure of my body. 4.03. 9
in great measure. ADO 1.01. 25 P
why are you thus out of measure sad? 1.03. 2 P
there is no measure in the occasion that breeds, 1.03. 3 P
tell him there is measure in every thing, and so 2.01. 71 P
is as a scotch jig, a measure, and a cinquepace; 2.01. 74 P
mannerly–modest, as a measure, full of state and 2.01. 77 P
"i measure him," says she, "by my own spirit, 2.03.143 P
measure his woe the length and breadth of mine, 5.01. 11
and justice always whirls in equal measure: LLL 4.03.381
to tread a measure with her on this grass. 5.02.185
to tread a measure with you on this grass. 5.02.187
many, | the measure then of one is eas'ly told. 5.02.190
tell her, we measure them by weary steps. 5.02.194
then in our measure do but vouchsafe one change. 5.02.209
curtsy, sweet hearts — and so the measure ends. 5.02.221
more measure of this measure; be not nice. 5.02.222
more measure of this measure; be not nice. 5.02.222
i will condole in some measure. MND 1.02. 27 P
which now in some slight measure it will pay, 3.02. 86
me | to measure out my length on this cold bed. 3.02.429
in measure rain thy joy, scant this excess! MV 3.02.112
away, | for we must measure twenty miles to–day. 3.04. 84
here lie i down, and measure out my grave. AYL 2.06. 2 P
may in some little measure draw a belief from 5.02. 57 P
i have trod a measure, i have flatt'red a lady, 5.04. 44 P
according to the measure of their states. 5.04.175
with measure heap'd in joy, to th' measures fall 5.04.179
and shrowd and froward, so beyond all measure, SHR 1.02. 90
carouse full measure to her maidenhead, | be mad 3.02.225
and though the devil lead the measure, such are AWW 2.01. 56 P
this is hard and undeserv'd measure, my lord. 2.03.257 P
that he might take a measure of his own 4.03. 33 P
sir, is a good tripping measure, or the bells of TN 5.01. 38 P
charities | shall best instruct you, measure me; WT 2.01.114
hath not my gait in it the measure of the court? 4.04.732 P
shall, | if not fill up the measure of her will, JN 2.01.556

yet in some measure satisfy her so | that we 2.01.557
who, with his shears and measure in his hand, 4.02.196
when english measure backward their own ground 5.05. 3
in some large measure to thy father's death, R2 1.02. 26
no more | than a delightful measure or a dance, 1.03.291
measure our confines with such peaceful steps? 3.02.125
my legs can keep no measure in delight, | when 3.04. 7
when my poor heart no measure keeps in grief; 3.04. 8
being sick, have (in some measure) made me well. 2H4 1.01.139
you do measure the heat of our livers with the 1.02.175 P
memory | shall as a pattern or a measure live, 4.04. 76
for the one i have neither words nor measure; H5 5.02.134 P
and for the other i have no strength in measure, 5.02.135 P
measure, yet a reasonable measure in strength. 5.02.136 P
and now, to add more measure to your woes, | i 3H6 2.01.105
mine | or fortune given me measure of revenge. 2.03. 32
measure for measure must be answered. 2.06. 55
measure for measure must be answered. 2.06. 55
tell me for truth the measure of his love | unto 3.03.120
ladies, and a measure | to lead 'em once again, H8 1.04.106
and know by measure | of their observant toil TRO 1.03.202
fair desires, in all fair measure, fairly guide 3.01. 44 P
he cannot but with measure fit the honors COR 2.02.123
rome, after the measure | as you intended well. 5.01. 46
rome, | lov'd me above the measure of a father, 5.03. 10
but let them measure us by what they will, ROM 1.04. 9
we'll measure them a measure and be gone. 1.04. 10
we'll measure them a measure and be gone. 1.04. 10
the measure done, i'll watch her place of stand, 1.05. 50
if the measure of thy joy | be heap'd like mine, 2.06. 24
there is no end, no limit, measure, bound, | in 3.02.125
do now, | taking the measure of an unmade grave. 3.03. 70
fill'd the time | with all licentious measure, TIM 5.04. 4
spoils, | shrunk to this little measure? JC 3.01.150
anon we'll drink a measure | the table round. MAC 3.04. 11
we will perform in measure, time, and place. 5.09. 39
if you will measure your lubber's length again, LR 1.04. 90 P
will be too short, | and every measure fail me. 4.07. 3
would fain have a measure to the health of black OTH 2.03. 32 P
dotage of our general's | o'erflows the measure. ANT 1.01. 2
he vented /them, most narrow measure lent me; 3.04. 8
together rather than unfold | his measure duly. CYM 1.01. 27
o, above measure false! 2.04.113
nor measure our good minds | by this rude place 3.06. 64
o, they have shrowd measure! TNK 4.03. 34 P
measure my strangeness with my unripe years; VEN 524
and that, in guess, they measure by thy deeds, SON 69.10
but these particulars are not my measure, | all 91. 7

MEASURED 1 FR 0.0001 REL FR 1 V 0 P
if they have measured many, | the measure then LLL 5.02.189

MEASURELESS 2 FR 0.0002 REL FR 2 V 0 P
measureless liar, thou hast made my heart | too COR 5.06.102
hostess, and shut up | in measureless content. MAC 2.01. 17

MEASURES 11 FR 0.0012 REL FR 10 V 1 P
his tedious measures witn the unbated fire MV 2.06. 11
measure heap'd in joy, to th' measures fall. AYL 5.04.179
i am for other than for dancing measures. 5.04.193
measures my husband's sorrow by his woe: SHR 5.02. 29
clamors of hell, be measures to our pomp? JN 3.01.304
our dreadful marches to delightful measures. R3 1.01. 8
for a joint–ring, nor for measures of lawn, nor OTH 4.03. 73 P
then, to send | measures of wheat to rome. ANT 2.06. 37
knowing all measures, the full caesar will 3.13. 35
and that their measures are as excellent. PER 2.03.103
teaching decrepit age to tread the measures; VEN 1148

MEASURING 3 FR 0.0003 REL FR 2 V 1 P
host hath had the measuring of their weapons, WIV 2.01.207 P
days, | not measuring what use we made of them. H5 1.02.268
i, measuring his affections by my own, | which ROM 1.01.126

MEAT 70 FR 0.0079 REL FR 41 V 29 P
that you might kill your stomach on your meat, TGV 1.02. 68
by my victuals, and would fain have meat. 2.01.174 P
i cannot abide the smell of hot meat since. WIV 1.01.286 P
that's meat and drink to me, now. 1.01.294 P
scour, dress meat and drink, make the beds, and 1.04. 96 P
in the thanksgiving before meat, do relish the MM 1.02. 15 P
she is so hot, because the meat is cold: ERR 1.02. 47
the meat is cold, because you come not home: 1.02. 48
"your meat doth burn," quoth i: 2.01. 63
no, sir, i think the meat wants that i have. 2.02. 55 P
that never meat sweet–savor'd in thy taste, 2.02.117
good meat, sir, is common; 3.01. 24
thou say'st his meat was sauc'd with thy 5.01. 73
'twas the boy that stole your meat, and you'll ADO 2.01.199 P
a man loves the meat in his youth that he cannot 2.03.239 P
of his heart he eats his meat without grudging; 3.04. 89 P
bid them cover the table, serve in the meat, and MV 3.05. 59 P
for the meat, sir, it shall be cover'd; 3.05. 62 P
slut were to put good meat into an unclean dish. AYL 3.03. 36 P
it is meat and drink to me to see a clown. 5.01. 10 P
'tis burnt, and so is all the meat. SHR 4.01.161
the meat was well, if you were so contented. 4.01.169
she eat no meat to–day, nor none shall eat; 4.01.197
as with the meat, some undeserved fault | i'll 4.01.199
am starv'd for meat, giddy for lack of sleep, 4.03. 9
i fear it is too choleric a meat. 4.03. 19
that feed'st me with the very name of meat. 4.03. 32
how diligent i am | to dress thy meat myself, 4.03. 40
and so shall mine before you touch the meat. 4.03. 46
sir, you can eat none of this homely meat. AWW 2.02. 47 P
and who abstains from meat that is not gaunt? R2 2.01. 76
i am meat for your master. 2H4 2.04.125 P
what you want in meat, we'll have in drink, but 5.03. 28 P
if you be not too much cloy'd with fat meat, our ep 27 P
i have eat no meat these five days, yet, come 2H6 4.10. 39 P
porridge after meat! TRO 1.02.242 P
that meat was made for mouths, that the gods COR 1.01.207
anger's my meat; 4.02. 50
your soldiers use him as the grace 'fore meat, 4.07. 3
an old hare hoar, | is very good meat in lent; ROM 2.04.136
as full of quarrels as an egg is full of meat, 3.01. 23 P
they have made worms' meat of me. 3.01.107
ay, to see meat fill knaves, and wine heat fools TIM 1.01.261
prithee let my meat make thee silent. 1.02. 37 P
i scorn thy meat, 'twould choke me; 1.02. 38 P
see so many dip their meat in one man's blood, 1.02. 41 P
good for their meat, and safer for their lives. 1.02. 45
bleeding new, my lord, there's no meat like 'em; 1.02. 79 P
unto his honor has my lord's meat in him; 3.01. 57
when your false masters eat of my lord's meat? 3.04. 50
to let the meat cool ere we can agree upon the 3.06. 67 P
make the meat be belov'd more than the man that 3.06. 76 P
where my stomach finds meat, or, rather, where i 4.03.294 P
your greatest want is, you want much of meat. 4.03.416
kept were knaves, to serve in meat to villains. 4.03.478
upon what meat doth this our caesar feed | that JC 1.02.149
from thence, the sauce to meat is ceremony, MAC 3.04. 35
we may again | give to our tables meat, sleep to 3.06. 34
cut the egg i' th' middle and eat up the meat, LR 1.04.159 P
monster which doth mock | the meat it feeds on. OTH 3.03.167
the messengers of venice stays the meat. 4.02.170
sir, i will eat no meat, i'll not drink, sir; ANT 5.02. 49
there is cold meat i' th' cave, we'll browse on CYM 3.06. 38
here's money for my meat, | i would have left it 3.06. 49
you come in faint for want of meat, depart 5.04.161 P
i eat do seem unsavory, | wishing him my meat. PER 2.03. 32
get fire and meat for these poor men. 3.02. 3
i am gladder | i have so good meat to't. TNK 3.03. 22
'tis a lusty meat. 3.03. 27
he was kept down with hard meat and ill lodging, 5.02. 97

MEATS 2 FR 0.0002 REL FR 1 V 1 P
look to the bak'd meats, good angelica, | spare ROM 4.04. 5
a knave, a rascal, an eater of broken meats; LR 2.02. 15 P

MECHANIC 3 FR 0.0003 REL FR 3 V 0 P
the poor mechanic porters crowding in | their H5 1.02.200
it were, to stand | on more mechanic compliment. ANT 4.04. 32
mechanic slaves | with greasy aprons, rules, and 5.02.209

MECHANICAL 4 FR 0.0004 REL FR 3 V 1 P
hang him, mechanical salt–butter rogue! WIV 2.02.278 P
thither | by most mechanical and dirty hand. 2H4 5.05. 36
base dunghill villain and mechanical, | i'll 2H6 1.03.193
being mechanical, you ought not walk | upon a JC 1.01. 3

MECHANICALS 1 FR 0.0001 REL FR 1 V 0 P
hour, | a crew of patches, rude mechanicals, MND 3.02. 9

MECHANICS 1 FR 0.0001 REL FR 1 V 0 P
or capitulate | again with rome's mechanics. COR 5.03. 83

MECHANTE 1 FR 0.0001 REL FR 1 V 0 P
o mechante fortune! H5 4.05. 5

MEDAL 1 FR 0.0001 REL FR 1 V 0 P
he that wears her like her medal hanging | about WT 1.02.307

MED'CINABLE *(also medicinable)*

MED'CINABLE 3 FR 0.0003 REL FR 2 V 1 P
cross, any impediment will be med'cinable to me. ADO 2.02. 5 P
whose med'cinable eye | corrects the /ill TRO 1.03. 91
some griefs are med'cinable, that is one of them CYM 3.02. 33

MED'CINE *(also medicine, etc.)*

MED'CINE 11 FR 0.0012 REL FR 11 V 0 P
before | would give preceptial med'cine to rage, ADO 5.01. 24
out, loathed med'cine! MND 3.02.264
that knows the tinct and multiplying med'cine, AWW 5.03.102
that present med'cine must be minist'red, | or JN 5.01. 15
precious, | preserving life in med'cine potable; 2H4 4.05.162
meet we the med'cine of the sickly weal, | and MAC 5.02. 27
no med'cine in the world can do thee good; HAM 5.02.314
that great med'cine hath | with his tinct gilded ANT 1.05. 36
great griefs, i see, med'cine the less; CYM 4.02.243
by med'cine life may be prolong'd, yet death 5.05. 29
their surfeit | that craves a present med'cine, TNK 1.01.191

MED'CINES 1 FR 0.0001 REL FR 1 V 0 P
let's make us med'cines of our great revenge MAC 4.03.214

MEDDLE 20 FR 0.0022 REL FR 5 V 15 P
to know | did never meddle with my thoughts. TMP 1.02. 22
a scurvy jack–a–nape priest to meddle or make — WIV 1.04.110 P
you were best meddle with buck–washing. 3.03.155 P
true, and they are to meddle with none but the ADO 3.03. 33 P
of men, the less you meddle or make with them, 3.03. 52 P
do not you meddle, let me deal in this. 5.01.101
go ply thy needle, meddle not with her. SHR 2.01. 25
we will not meddle with him till he come; AWW 4.03. 35 P
for meddle you must, that's certain, or forswear TN 3.04.251 P
pox on't, i'll not meddle with him. 3.04.280 P
i'll not meddle with it, it makes a man a coward R3 1.04.134 P
my part, i'll not meddle nor make no farther. TRO 1.01. 14 P
faith, i'll not meddle in it, let her be as she 1.01. 66 P
i'll meddle nor make no more i' th' matter. 1.01. 83 P
(with whom relation | durst never meddle) in the 3.03.202
how, sir? do you meddle with my master? COR 4.05. 46 P
service than to meddle with thy mistress. 4.05. 47 P
no; i'll not meddle. 5.01. 38
the shoemaker should meddle with his yard and ROM 1.02. 39 P
i meddle with no tradesman's matters, nor JC 1.01. 22 P

MEDDLER 2 FR 0.0002 REL FR 2 V 0 P
and holy, | not scurvy, nor a temporary meddler, MM 5.01.145
come to the pedlar, | money's a meddler, | that WT 4.04.322

MEDDLERS 1 FR 0.0001 REL FR 0 V 1 P
and th' hadst hated meddlers sooner, thou TIM 4.03.309 P

MEDDLING 4 FR 0.0004 REL FR 4 V 0 P
my lord, i know him, 'tis a meddling friar. MM 5.01.127
on meddling monkey, or on busy ape), | she shall MND 2.01.181
are led so grossly by this meddling priest, JN 3.01.163
o, beat away the busy meddling fiend | that lays 2H6 3.03. 21

MEDE 1 FR 0.0001 REL FR 1 V 0 P
and amyntas, | the kings of mede and lycaonia, ANT 3.06. 75

MEDEA 2 FR 0.0002 REL FR 2 V 0 P
a night | medea gathered the enchanted herbs MV 5.01. 13
i cut it | as wild medea young absyrtus did; 2H6 5.02. 59

MEDIA 2 FR 0.0002 REL FR 2 V 0 P
spur through media, | mesopotamia, and the ANT 3.01. 7
great media, parthia, and armenia | he gave to 3.06. 14

MEDIATION 3 FR 0.0003 REL FR 3 V 0 P
noble offices thou mayst effect | of mediation, 2H4 4.04. 25
to induce | their mediation, must i be unfolded ANT 5.02.170
entreat their mediation to the king, | give up STM II.C 145

MEDIATORS 2 FR 0.0002 REL FR 2 V 0 P
/and, /in /conclusion, | nonsuits my mediators; OTH 1.01. 16
to trembling clients be you mediators: LUC 1020

MEDICE 1 FR 0.0001 REL FR 1 V 0 P
medice, teipsum — | protector, see to't well, 2H6 2.01. 51

MEDICINABLE *(also med'cinable)*

MEDICINABLE 2 FR 0.0002 REL FR 2 V 0 P
so, i have derision medicinable | to use between TRO 3.03. 44
as the arabian trees | their medicinable gum. OTH 5.02.351

MEDICINAL 1 FR 0.0001 REL FR 1 V 0 P
i | do come with words as medicinal as true, WT 2.03. 37

MEDICINE *(also med'cine, etc.)*

MEDICINE 16 FR 0.0018 REL FR 13 V 3 P
disease will scarce obey this medicine. WIV 3.03.192 P
others, | hath yet a kind of medicine in itself, MM 2.02.135
the miserable have no other medicine | but only 3.01. 2
about to apply a moral medicine to a mortifying ADO 1.03. 12 P
if they will patiently receive my medicine. AYL 2.07. 61
else paris, and the medicine, and the king, AWW 1.03.233
i have seen a medicine | that's able to breathe 2.01. 72
the medicine of our house, how shall we do? WT 4.04.587
restored | with good advice and little medicine. 2H4 3.01. 43
a goodly medicine for my aching bones! TRO 5.10. 35 P
poison hath residence and medicine power; ROM 2.03. 24
restoration hang | thy medicine on my lips, and LR 4.07. 26
if not, i'll ne'er trust medicine. 5.03. 96
shall ever medicine thee to that sweet sleep OTH 3.03.332
work on, | my medicine, /work! 4.01. 45
and brought to medicine a healthful state SON 118.11

MEDICINES 3 FR 0.0003 REL FR 1 V 2 P
have not given me medicines to make me love him, 1H4 2.02. 18 P
it could not be else, i have drunk medicines. 2.02. 20 P
by spells and medicines bought of mountebanks; OTH 1.03. 61

MEDITANCE 1 FR 0.0001 REL FR 1 V 0 P
is more | than others' labored meditance; TNK 1.01.136

MEDITATE 2 FR 0.0002 REL FR 1 V 1 P
i will meditate the while upon some horrid TN 3.04.199 P
will | that nothing do but meditate on blood — H5 5.02. 60

MEDITATES 1 FR 0.0001 REL FR 1 V 0 P
to kill him, clitus. look, he meditates. JC 5.05. 12

MEDITATING 5 FR 0.0005 REL FR 4 V 1 P
are you meditating on virginity? AWW 1.01.110 P
meditating that | shall dye your white rose in a 1H6 2.04. 60
but meditating with two deep divines; R3 3.07. 75
whilst i sit meditating | on that celestial H8 4.02. 79
with meditating that she must die once, | i have JC 4.03.191

/MEDITATION 1 FR 0.0001 REL FR 1 V 0 P
/betwixt /thy /begging /and /my /meditation. R3 4.02.115

MEDITATION 7 FR 0.0008 REL FR 7 V 0 P
passed on, | in maiden meditation, fancy–free. MND 2.01.164
curtain close, | and let us all to meditation. 2H6 3.03. 33
reverend fathers, | divinely bent to meditation, R3 3.07. 62
lewd love–bed, | but on his knees at meditation; 3.07. 73
swift | as meditation or the thoughts of love, HAM 1.05. 30
give me some meditation, | and mark your cue. TNK 3.05. 93
o fearful meditation! SON 65. 9

MEDITATIONS 4 FR 0.0004 REL FR 4 V 0 P
thrust yourselves | into my private meditations? H8 2.02. 65
and so we'll leave you to your meditations | how 3.02.345
continual meditations, tears, and sorrows, | he 4.02. 28
and in sessions sit | with meditations lawful? OTH 3.03.141

MEDITERRANEAN 1 FR 0.0001 REL FR 1 V 0 P
and are upon the mediterranean float | bound TMP 1.02.234

MEDITERRANEUM 1 FR 0.0001 REL FR 0 V 1 P
by the salt /wave of the mediterraneum, a sweet LLL 5.01. 58 P

MEDIUS 1 FR 0.0001 REL FR 1 V 0 P
proh deum, medius fidius, ye are all dunces! TNK 3.05. 11

MEDLAR 6 FR 0.0006 REL FR 1 V 5 P
would else have married me to the rotten medlar. MM 4.03.174 P
you, and then i shall graff it with a medlar. AYL 3.02.118 P
ripe, and that's the right virtue of the medlar. 3.02.120 P
now will he sit under a medlar tree, | and wish ROM 2.01. 34
there's a medlar for thee, eat it. TIM 4.03.304 P
dost hate a medlar? 4.03.307 P

MEDLARS 1 FR 0.0001 REL FR 1 V 0 P
were that kind of fruit | as maids call medlars, ROM 2.01. 36

MEED 19 FR 0.0021 REL FR 16 V 3 P
and duty never yet did want his meed. TGV 2.04.112
vouchsafe me, for my meed, but one fair look: 5.04. 23
either in my mind or in my means, meed, i am WIV 2.02.203 P
sent to thee, to receive the meed of punishment, LLL 1.01.266 P
when service sweat for duty, not for meed! AYL 2.03. 58
that's not my fear, my meed hath got me fame: 3H6 4.08. 38
and for his meed, poor lord, he is mewed up. R3 1.03.138
if you are hir'd for meed, go back again, | and 1.04.228
and when i have my meed, i will away, | for this 1.04.282
and for his meed | was brow–bound with the oak. COR 2.02. 97
to men | of noble minds is honorable meed. TIT 1.01.216
there's meed for meed, death for a deadly deed! 5.03. 66
there's meed for meed, death for a deadly deed! 5.03. 66
no meed but he repays | sevenfold above itself; TIM 1.01.277
on him by them, in his meed he's unfellow'd. HAM 5.02.142 P
labor be his meed. CYM 3.05.162
you are the victor's meed, the price and garland TNK 5.03. 16
for thy meed | a thousand honey secrets shalt VEN 15
and when great treasure is the meed proposed, LUC 132

MEEDS 1 FR 0.0001 REL FR 1 V 0 P
each one already blazing by our meeds, | should 3H6 2.01. 36

MEEK 8 FR 0.0009 REL FR 8 V 0 P
they can be meek that have no other cause: ERR 2.01. 33
hadst thou been meek, our title still had slept, 3H6 2.02.160
y' are meek and humble–mouth'd, | you sign your H8 2.04.107
destroyers, affable wolves, meek bears, | you TIM 3.06. 95
that i am meek and gentle with these butchers! JC 3.01.255
this duncan | hath borne his faculties so meek, MAC 1.07. 17
the honor of thy lordliness | to one so meek, ANT 5.02.162
feeble desire, all recreant, poor, and meek, LUC 710

MEEKLY 1 FR 0.0001 REL FR 0 V 1 P
to hear meekly, sir, and to laugh moderately; LLL 1.01.197 P

MEEKNESS 4 FR 0.0004 REL FR 4 V 0 P
god bless thee, and put meekness in thy breast, R3 2.02.107
in full seeming, | with meekness and humility; H8 2.04.109
thy meekness saint–like, wife–like government, 2.04.139
love and meekness, lord, | become a churchman 5.02. 97

/MEET* 2 FR 0.0002 REL FR 2 V 0 P
to be made | /for /such /a /guest /is /meet." HAM 5.01.121
/and /in /the /end /meet /the /old /course /of LR 3.07.101

MEET* 328 FR 0.0370 REL FR 262 V 66 P
would i flame distinctly, | then meet and join. TMP 1.02.201
spirit, | we must prepare to meet with caliban. 4.01.166
in thy happiness | when thou dost meet good hap; TGV 1.01. 15
he said that proteus, your son, was meet; 1.03. 12
love | as meet to be an emperor's counsellor. 2.04. 77
let me have | what thou think'st meet, and is 2.07. 58
him make haste and meet me at the north–gate. 3.01.260
where meet we? 4.02. 84
where shall i meet you? 4.03. 43
silvia at friar patrick's cell should meet me. 5.01. 3

but mount you presently and meet with me | upon 5.02. 45
it is not meet the council hear a riot; WIV 1.01. 36 P
engross'd opportunities to meet her; 2.02.196 P
the hour, sir, that sir hugh promis'd to meet. 2.03. 5 P
i would my husband would meet him in this shape. 4.02. 84 P
basket again, to meet him at the door with it, 4.02. 95 P
at court, and they are going to meet him. 4.03. 3 P
to send him word they'll meet him in the park at 4.04. 17 P
that falstaff at that oak shall meet with us, 4.04. 42
they are gone but to meet the duke, villain, do 4.05. 71 P
we could never meet. 5.05.117 P
he promis'd to meet me two hours since, and he MM 1.02. 75 P
from whom we thought it meet to hide our love 1.02.152
and most desire should meet the blow of justice; 2.02. 30
'tis meet so, daughter, but lest you do repent 2.03. 30
upon this time have i promis'd here to meet. 4.01. 18 P
if you think it meet, compound with him by the 4.02. 23 P
desire | to meet me at the consecrated fount, 4.03. 98
who do prepare to meet him at the gates, | there 4.03.131
and why meet him at the gates, and /redeliver 4.04. 5 P
to such men of sort and suit as are to meet him. 4.04. 17 P
yet behind, that/'s meet you all should know. 5.01.539
ere the ships could meet by twice five leagues, ERR 1.01.100
please you, i'll meet with you upon the mart, 1.02. 27
i'll meet you at that place some hour hence. 3.01.122
yes, if any hour meet a sergeant, 'a turns back 4.02. 56
there's not a man i meet but doth salute me | as 4.03. 1
straight after did i meet him with a chain. 4.04.140
i see we still did meet each other's man, | and 5.01.387
benedick too much, but he'll be meet with you, i ADO 1.01. 47 P
they never meet but there's a skirmish of wit 1.01. 63 P
leonato, are you come to meet your trouble? 1.01. 97 P
die while she hath such meet food to feed it as 1.01.121 P
there will the devil meet me like an old cuckold 2.01. 44 P
find me a meet hour to draw don pedro and the 2.02. 33 P
bears will not bite one another when they meet. 3.02. 79 P
if you meet a thief, you may suspect him, by 3.03. 50 P
if you meet the prince in the night, you may 3.03. 75 P
swore he would meet her as he was appointed next 3.03.160 P
our excommunication, and meet me at the jail. 3.05. 64 P
sir, i shall meet your wit in the career, and 5.01.135 P
well, i will meet you, so i may have good cheer. 5.01.151 P
my lord lack–beard there, he and i shall meet, 5.01.193 P
or study where to meet some mistress fine, LLL 1.01. 63
in oath | were all address'd to meet you, gentle 2.01. 83
complexions the cull'd sovereignty | do meet, as 4.03.231
withal | upon the next occasion that we meet, 5.02.143
therefore meet. 5.02.237
(where i did meet thee once with helena | to do MND 1.01.166
me | to–morrow truly will i meet with thee. 1.01.178
there my lysander and myself shall meet; 1.01.217
and meet me in the palace wood, a mile without 1.02.101 P
for if we meet in the city, we shall be dogg'd 1.02.103 P
we will meet, and there we may rehearse most 1.02.107 P
at the duke's oak we meet. 1.02.110 P
and now they never meet in grove or green, | by 2.01. 28
this wood, | because i cannot meet my hermia. 2.01.193
and look thou meet me ere the first cock crow. 2.01.267
for beasts that meet me run away for fear. 2.02. 95
you know, pyramus and thisby meet by moonlight. 3.01. 49 P
i'll meet thee, pyramus, at ninny's tomb." 3.01. 97
meet presently at the palace; 4.02. 37 P
lovers think no scorn | to meet at ninus' tomb, 5.01.138
wilt thou at ninny's tomb meet me straightway? 5.01.202
meet me all by break of day. 5.01.422
i pray you have in mind where we must meet. MV 1.01. 71
then meet me forthwith at the notary's; 1.03.172
meet me and gratiano | at gratiano's lodging 2.04. 25
go, tubal, and meet me at our synagogue; 3.01.129 P
so fare you well till we shall meet again. 3.04. 40
it is very meet | the lord bassanio live an 3.05. 73
padua, | and it is meet i presently set forth. 4.01.404
i pray you know me when we meet again; 4.01.419
lord, it is a hard matter for friends to meet; AYL 3.02.185 P
god buy you, let's meet as little as we can. 3.02.257 P
if i could meet that fancy–monger, i would give 3.02.363 P
who hath promis'd to meet me in this place of 3.03. 44 P
you meet in some fresh cheek the power of fancy, 3.05. 29
to–morrow meet me all together. 5.02.112 P
as you love rosalind, meet. 5.02.119 P
as you love phebe, meet. 5.02.120 P
and as i love no woman, i'll meet. 5.02.120 P
comedy, | for so your doctors hold it very meet, SHR in.2. 131
both our inventions meet and jump in one. 1.01.190
and where two raging fires meet together, | they 2.01.132
you must meet my master to countenance my 4.01. 98 P
did i not bid thee meet me in the park, | and 4.01.130
as they are, here are they come to meet you. 4.01.138
if not, elsewhere they meet with charity; 4.03. 6
fair buds, | and in no sense is meet or amiable. 5.02.141
my life, if i can meet him with any convenience, AWW 2.03.238 P
beat him, and if i could but meet him again. 2.03.241 P
to remain with me till they meet together. 4.05. 87 P
or, ere they meet, in me, o nature, cesse! 5.03. 72
all yet seems well, and if it end so meet, | the 5.03.333
where thou and i, henceforth, may never meet. TN 5.01.169
no lady living | so meet for this great errand. WT 2.02. 44
should i now meet my father, | he would not call 4.04.657
when i shall meet him in the court of heaven | i JN 3.04. 87
lords, i will meet him at saint edmundsbury. 4.03. 11
to–morrow morning let us meet him then. 4.03. 18
two long days' journey, lords, or e'er we meet. 4.03. 20
home and discontents at home | meet in one line; 4.03.152
now keep your holy word, go meet the french, 5.01. 5
to meet displeasure farther from the doors, 5.01. 60
i know | our party may well meet a prouder foe. 5.01. 79
if you think meet, this afternoon will post | to 5.07. 94
maintain i would allow him odds | and meet him, R2 1.01. 63
nor never by advised purpose meet | to plot, 1.03.188
your men, | and meet me presently at berkeley. 2.02.119
we three here part that ne'er shall meet again. 2.02.143
well, we may meet again. 2.02.149
and salisbury | is gone to meet the king, who 3.03. 3
methinks king richard and myself should meet 3.03. 54
meet at london london's king in woe. 3.04. 97
or live, | i dare meet surrey in a wilderness, 4.01. 74
no word like "pardon" for kings' mouths so meet. 5.03.118
did lately meet in the intestine shock | and 1H4 1.01. 12
therefore we meet not now. 1.01. 30
fat rogue will tell us when we meet at supper, 1.02.188 P
and meet me to–morrow night in eastcheap, there 1.02.192 P
shall happily meet | to bear our fortunes in our 1.03.297
if they meet not with saint nicholas' clerks, 2.01. 61 P
so strongly that they dare not meet each other; 2.02.106
not all their letters to meet me in arms by the 2.03. 27 P
to meet your father and the scottish power, | as 3.01. 84
and your unthought–of harry chance to meet. 3.02.141
our general forces at bridgenorth shall meet. 3.02.178
meet me to–morrow in the temple hall | at two 3.03.199
nor did he think it meet | to lay so dangerous 4.01. 33
meet and ne'er part till one drop down a corse. 4.01.123
bid my lieutenant peto meet me at town's end. 4.02. 9 P
that you and i should meet upon such terms | as 5.01. 10
i should meet upon such terms | as now we meet. 5.01. 11
posted day and night | to meet you on the way, 5.01. 36
with the best blood that i can meet withal | in 5.02. 94
piece by piece, | until i meet the king. 5.03. 28
to meet northumberland and the prelate scroop, 5.05. 37
will you have doll tearsheet meet you at supper? 2H4 2.01.163 P
i tell thee it is not meet that i should be sad, 2.02. 39 P
but i must go and meet with danger there, | or 2.03. 48
fain would i go to meet the archbishop, | but 2.03. 65
you two never meet but you fall to some discord. 2.04. 56 P
then let us meet them like necessities; 3.01. 93
in sight of both our battles we may meet, | /and 4.01.177
to meet his grace just distance 'tween our 4.01.224
meet for rebellion /and /such /acts /as /yours. 4.02.117
when means and lavish manners meet together, | o 4.04. 64
we meet like men that had forgot to speak. 5.02. 22
as many ways meet in one town; H5 1.02.208
as many fresh streams meet in one salt sea; 1.02.209
it is most meet we arm us 'gainst the foe; 2.04. 15
'tis meet we all go forth | to view the sick and 2.04. 21
and, princes, look you strongly arm to meet him. 2.04. 49
and a prating coxcomb, is it meet, think you, 4.01. 78 P
nor it is not meet he should. 4.01.100 P
if we no more meet till we meet in heaven, 4.03. 7
if we no more meet till we meet in heaven, 4.03. 7
but we shall meet, and break our minds at large. 1H6 1.03. 81
gloucester, we'll meet to thy cost, be sure: 1.03. 82
and so farewell until i meet thee next. 2.04.113
dare ye come forth and meet us in the field? 3.02. 61
when thou shalt see i'll meet thee to thy cost. 3.04. 43
and after meet you, sooner than you would. 3.04. 45
i vow'd, base knight, when i did meet thee next, 4.01. 14
and now they meet where both their lives are 4.03. 38
but meet him now, and, be it in the morn, | when 2H6 3.01. 13
'tis meet he be condemn'd by course of law. 3.01.237
'tis meet that lucky ruler be employ'd — 3.01.291
unto all they meet. 4.08. 46
i pray thee, buckingham, go and meet him, | and 4.09. 36
meet me to–morrow in saint george's field, | you 5.01. 46
meet i an infant of the house of york, | into as 5.02. 57
she shall not need, we'll meet her in the field. 3H6 1.02. 65
now, lords, take leave until we meet again, 2.03. 42
till we meet warwick with his foreign pow'r. 4.01.149
as we may, we'll meet both thee and warwick. 4.07. 86
farewell, sweet lords, let's meet at coventry. 4.08. 32
and ten to one you'll meet him in the tower. 5.01. 46
with resolution, wheresoe'er i meet thee | (as i 5.01. 95
wheresoe'er i meet thee | (as i will meet thee, 5.01. 96
bids you all farewell, to meet in heaven. 5.02. 49
away, away, to meet the queen's great power! 5.02. 50
is't meet that he | should leave the helm and, 5.04. 6
world, | to meet with joy in sweet jerusalem. 5.05. 8
that it is meet so few should fetch the prince. R3 2.02.139
would fain have come with me to meet your grace, 3.01. 29
her | to meet you at the tower and welcome you. 3.01.139
than when thou met'st me last where now we meet. 3.02. 99
farewell, until we meet again in heaven. 3.03. 26
meet me within this hour at baynard's castle. 3.05.105
let me but meet you, ladies, /an hour hence, 4.01. 28
my son | in your behalf, to meet you on the way. 4.01. 50
can make, | and meet me suddenly at salisbury. 4.04.451
i'll muster up my friends and meet your grace 4.04.488
and so fair assembly | this night to meet here, H8 1.04. 68
there ye shall meet about this weighty business. 2.02.139
to meet the least occasion that may give me 3.02. 7
why, 'tis most meet. TRO 1.03.333
therefore 'tis meet achilles meet not hector. 1.03.357
therefore 'tis meet achilles meet not hector. 1.03.357
consent | that ever hector and achilles meet, 1.03.362
it was thought meet | paris should do some 2.02. 72
but when i meet you arm'd, as black defiance 4.01. 13
/but when contention and occasion meet, | by 4.01. 17
i will go meet them; 4.02. 70
great agamemnon comes to meet us here. 4.05.159
to–morrow do i meet thee, fell as death; 4.05.269
i will not meet with you to–morrow night. 5.02. 73
would i could meet that rogue diomed! 5.02.190 P
like witless antics, one another meet, | and all 5.03. 86
i would fain see them meet, that that same young 5.04. 5 P
face, | know what it is to meet achilles angry. 5.05. 46
if we and caius martius chance to meet, | 'tis COR 1.02. 34
if e'er again i meet him beard to beard, | he's 1.10. 11
marks invested, you | anon do meet the senate. 2.03.141
do admit you and are summon'd | to meet anon, 2.03.144
when what's not meet, but what must be, was law, 3.01.167
let what is meet be said it must be meet, | and 3.01.169
let what is meet be said it must be meet, | and 3.01.169
meet on the market–place. 3.01.330
let's not meet her. 4.02. 8
could i meet 'em | but once a day, it would 4.02. 46
i will go meet the ladies. 5.04. 52
we'll meet them, | and help the joy. 5.04. 61
"and if we miss to meet him handsomely, | sweet TIT 2.03.268
herbs as these | are meet for plucking up, and 3.01.178
much less | to meet her new–beloved any where. ROM 2.pr. 12
passion lends them power, time means, to meet, 2.pr. 13
may prove a beauteous flow'r when next we meet. 2.02.122
perchance she cannot meet him — that's not so. 2.05. 3
and if we meet we shall not scape a brawl, | for 3.01. 3
and earth, all three do meet | in thee at once, 3.03.120
o, think'st thou we shall ever meet again? 3.05. 51
god knows when we shall meet again. 4.03. 14
lucius! | what, do we meet together? TIM 3.04. 3
where ever we shall meet, for timon's sake 4.02. 24
cut throats, | all that you meet are thieves. 4.03.446
how rarely does it meet with this time's guise, 4.03.465
when we may profit meet, and come too late. 5.01. 42
i'll meet you at the turn. 5.01. 47
fit i meet them. 5.01. 54
both meet to hear and answer such high things. JC 1.02.170
therefore it is meet | that noble minds keep 1.02.310
when these prodigies | do so conjointly meet, 1.03. 29
i think it is not meet, | mark antony, so well 2.01.155
caesar's wife shall meet with better dreams." 2.02. 99
it is not meet you know how caesar lov'd you: 3.02.141
unmeritable man, | meet to be sent on errands; 4.01. 13
march gently on to meet him. 4.02. 31
in such a time as this it is not meet | that 4.03. 7
'tis not meet | they be alone. 4.03.125
along ourselves, and meet them at philippi. 4.03.225
resolv'd | to meet all perils very constantly. 5.01. 91
and whether we shall meet again i know not; 5.01.114
if we do meet again, why, we shall smile; 5.01.117
if we do meet again, we'll smile indeed; 5.01.120
whilst i go to meet | the noble brutus, 5.03. 73
did i not meet thy friends? 5.03. 81
when shall we three meet again? MAC 1.01. 1
there to meet with macbeth. 1.01. 7
let us meet | and question this most bloody 2.03.127
readiness, | and meet i' th' hall together. 2.03.134
at the pit of acheron | meet me i' th' morning; 3.05. 16
you may to me, and 'tis most meet you should. 5.01. 15 P
near birnan wood | shall we well meet them; 5.02. 6
meet we the med'cine of the sickly weal, | and 5.02. 27
if you do meet horatio and marcellus, | the HAM 1.01. 12
meet it is i set it down | that one may smile, 1.05.107
as i perchance hereafter shall think meet | to 1.05.171
meet what i would have well and it destroy! 3.02.221
'tis meet that some more audience than a mother, 3.03. 31
when in one line two crafts directly meet. 3.04.210
there — a — was nothing — a — meet." 5.01. 64
clay for to be made | for such a guest is meet." 5.01. 97
if your honor judge it meet, i will place you LR 1.02. 90 P
all with me's meet that i can fashion fit. 1.02.184
we'll no more meet, no more see one another. 2.04.220
sea, | thou'dst meet the bear i' th' mouth. 3.04. 11
friend, where thou shalt meet | both welcome and 3.06. 91
would i could meet /him, madam! 4.05. 39
you know me not | till time and i think meet. 4.07. 11
it seems not meet, nor wholesome to my place, OTH 1.01.145
at nine i' th' morning here we'll meet again. 1.03.279
where shall we meet i' th' morning? 1.03.373 P
let's meet him and receive him. 2.01.180
do thou meet me presently at the harbor. 2.01.214 P
meet me by and by at the citadel. 2.01.283 P
i meet the captains at the citadel. 3.03. 59
you'll never meet a more sufficient man. 3.04. 91
i will go meet him. 3.04.138
dames even thus, | all guiltless, meet reproach. 4.01. 47
'tis meet i should be us'd so, very meet. 4.02.107
'tis meet i should be us'd so, very meet. 4.02.107
when we shall meet at compt, | this look of 5.02.273
most meet | that first we come to words, and ANT 2.06. 2
i am again for cydnus | to meet mark antony. 5.02.229
if she first meet the curled antony, | he'll 5.02.301
you do not meet a man but frowns. CYM 1.01. 1
is't not meet | that i did amplify my judgment 1.05. 16
he never can meet more mischance than come | to 2.03.132
i'll meet you in the valleys. 3.03. 78
meet thee at milford–haven! 3.05.130 P
i am near to th' place where they should meet, 4.01. 1 P
that possible strength might meet, would seek us 4.02.160
withdraw, | and meet the time as it seeks us. 4.03. 33
of her it was | that we meet here so strangely; 5.05.272
did you e'er meet? 5.05.378
as you think meet. most wretched queen! PER 3.01. 54
and at the banks of /aulis meet us with | the TNK 1.01.212
i do bleed | when such i meet, and wish great 1.02. 21
meet you no ruin but the soldier in | the cranks 1.02. 27
i meet him | and unto him i utter learned things 3.05. 13
tell me, love's master, shall we meet to–morrow? VEN 585
muster thy mists to meet the eastern light, LUC 773
thee, | but they ne'er meet with opportunity. 903
flowers distill'd, though they with winter meet, SON 5.13
but if that flow'r with base infection meet, 94.11

MEET–A 1 FR 0.0001 REL FR 0 V 1 P
vherefore vill you not meet–a me? WIV 3.01. 80 P

MEETER 2 FR 0.0002 REL FR 2 V 0 P
he therefore sends you, meeter for your spirit, H5 1.02.254
but i will tell you at some meeter season. ANT 5.01. 49

MEETEST 2 FR 0.0002 REL FR 2 V 0 P
wether of the flock, | meetest for death; MV 4.01.115
york is meetest man | to be your regent in the 2H6 1.03.160

/MEETING 1 FR 0.0001 REL FR 0 V 1 P
/the /means /of /meeting /between /him and my HAM 2.02.212 P

MEETING 39 FR 0.0044 REL FR 31 V 8 P
a breakfast, nor | befitting this first meeting. TMP 5.01.165
let's appoint him a meeting, give him a show of WIV 2.01. 94 P
receiv'd from her another ambassy of meeting. 3.05.130 P
appoint a meeting with this old fat fellow, 4.04. 14
the very instant of falstaff's and our meeting, 5.03. 15 P
to depart, and if a merry meeting may be wish'd, ADO 5.01.326 P
for, meeting her of late behind the wood, MND 4.01. 48
you here, | but meeting with salerio by the way, MV 3.02.228
i would fain see this meeting. AYL 3.03. 46 P
where, meeting with an old religious man, 5.04.160
journeys end in lovers meeting, | every wise TN 2.03. 43
is meeting noses? WT 1.02.285
is as a meeting of the petty gods, | and you the 4.04. 4
one and not | the hostess of the meeting. 4.04. 64
did you see the meeting of the two kings? 5.02. 39 P
men, | which in the very meeting fall, and die. JN 3.01. 33
fondly with her tears and smiles in meeting, R2 3.02. 9
at meeting tears the cloudy cheeks of heaven. 3.03. 57
after them and appoint them a place of meeting, 1H4 1.02.170 P
our meeting | is bridgenorth. 3.02.174
sway, | meeting the check of such another day, 5.05. 42
hazard | and fearful meeting of their opposite. 2H4 4.01. 16
peace to this meeting, wherefore we are met! H5 5.02. 1
of this good day and of this gracious meeting, 5.02. 13
the wound that bred this meeting here | cannot 3H6 2.02.121

as knots, by the conflux of meeting sap, TRO 1.03. 7
and, meeting him, /will tell him that my lady 1.03.298
meeting two such wealsmen as you are (i cannot COR 2.01. 54 P
and appoint the meeting | even at his father's TIT 4.04.102
patience perforce with willful choler meeting ROM 1.05. 89
which is now | our point of second meeting. MAC 3.01. 85
is ceremony, | meeting were bare without it. 3.04. 36
displac'd the mirth, broke the good meeting, 3.04.108
now for ourself, and for this time of meeting, HAM 1.02. 26
and meeting here the other messenger, | whose LR 2.04. 38
and at first meeting lov'd, | continu'd so, CYM 5.05.379
like meeting of two tides, fly strongly from us, TNK 3.06. 30
whose ridges with the meeting clouds contend: VEN 820
than | retire again, till meeting greater ranks, LUC 1441
MEETING–PLACE 1 FR 0.0001 REL FR 0 V 1 P
is the very description of their meeting–place, CYM 4.01. 24 P
/MEETINGS 1 FR 0.0001 REL FR 0 V 1 P
/for /missing /your /meetings /and /appointments WIV 3.01. 89 P
MEETINGS 3 FR 0.0003 REL FR 3 V 0 P
his wares | at wakes and wassails, meetings, LLL 5.02.318
our stern alarums chang'd to merry meetings, R3 1.01. 7
swains, | all our merry meetings on the plains, PP 17.30
MEETLY 1 FR 0.0001 REL FR 1 V 0 P
you can do better yet; but this is meetly. ANT 1.03. 81
MEETNESS 1 FR 0.0001 REL FR 1 V 0 P
found a kind of meetness | to be diseas'd ere SON 118. 7
/MEETS 1 FR 0.0001 REL FR 1 V 0 P
each thing /meets | in mere oppugnancy: TRO 1.03.110
MEETS 12 FR 0.0013 REL FR 12 V 0 P
when in the streets he meets such golden gifts. ERR 3.02.183
meets he on the way | the father of this seeming WT 5.01.190
and quick–raised power | meets with lord harry; 1H4 4.04. 13
and pale destruction meets thee in the face. 1H6 4.02. 27
who meets us here? R3 4.01. 1
see | how soon this mightiness meets misery; H8 pr 30
hath, /or means to be, | that one meets hector; TRO 1.03.290
he that meets hector issues from our choice, 1.03.347
his purpose meets you; 4.01. 37
the bawdy wind, that kisses all it meets, | is OTH 4.02. 78
death's the market–place, where each one meets. TNK 1.05. 16
and here she meets another sadly scowling, | to VEN 917
MEET'ST* 2 FR 0.0002 REL FR 1 V 1 P
thy vow, sirrah, when thou meet'st the fellow. H5 4.07.145 P
there, at your meet'st /advantage of the time, R3 3.05. 74
/MEG 1 FR 0.0001 REL FR 1 V 0 P
i thank thee, /meg, these words content me much.
2H6 3.02. 26
MEG 4 FR 0.0004 REL FR 1 V 3 P
lov'd mall, meg, and marian, and margery, | but TMP 2.02. 48
how now, meg? WIV 2.01.148 P
no, pray thee, good meg, i'll wear this. ADO 3.04. 8 P
to dress me, good coz, good meg, good ursula. 3.04. 98 P
MEHERCLE 1 FR 0.0001 REL FR 0 V 1 P
mehercle, if their sons be /ingenious, they LLL 4.02. 78 P
/MEILLEUR 1 FR 0.0001 REL FR 0 V 1 P
il est /meilleur que l'anglois lequel je parle. H5 5.02.189 P
MEINY 2 FR 0.0002 REL FR 2 V 0 P
for the mutable, rank–scented meiny, let them COR 3.01. 66
those contents | they summon'd up their meiny, LR 2.04. 35
MEISEN 1 FR 0.0001 REL FR 1 V 0 P
sala, | is at this day in germany call'd meisen. H5 1.02. 53
MELANCHOLIES 1 FR 0.0001 REL FR 0 V 1 P
how melancholies i am! WIV 3.01. 13 P
MELANCHOLY *(also allicholy, allycholly, mallicholy)*
MELANCHOLY 75 FR 0.0084 REL FR 40 V 35 P
for she is lumpish, heavy, melancholy, | and, TGV 3.02. 62
should have heard him so loud and so melancholy.
WIV 1.04. 91 P
how now, sweet frank, why art thou melancholy? 2.01.151 P
i melancholy? 2.01.152 P
i am not melancholy. 2.01.152 P
oft, | when i am dull with care and melancholy, ERR 1.02. 20
what doth ensue | but moody and dull melancholy, 5.01. 79
person | comes this way to the melancholy vale, 5.01.120
he is of a very melancholy disposition. ADO 2.01. 5 P
and half count john's melancholy in signior 2.01. 12 P
or not laugh'd at, strikes him into melancholy, 2.01.148 P
i found him here as melancholy as a lodge in a 2.01.214 P
there's little of the melancholy element in her, 2.01.342 P
the greatest note of it is his melancholy. 3.02. 54 P
we are high–proof melancholy and would fain have 5.01.123 P
besieged with sable–colored melancholy, i did LLL 1.01.232 P
it when a man of great spirit grows melancholy? 1.02. 2 P
how canst thou part sadness and melancholy, my 1.02. 7 P
most rude melancholy, valor gives thee place. 3.01. 68
he made her melancholy, sad, and heavy, | and so 5.02. 14
of mirth, | turn melancholy forth to funerals: MND 1.01. 14
but fish not with this melancholy bait | for MV 1.01.101
lord, | the melancholy jaques grieves at that, AYL 2.01. 26
fool, | much marked of the melancholy jaques, 2.01. 41
it will make you melancholy, monsieur jaques. 2.05. 10 P
i can suck melancholy out of a song, as a weasel 2.05. 13 P
under the shade of melancholy boughs, | lose and 2.07.111
adieu, good monsieur melancholy. 3.02.294 P
they say you are a melancholy fellow. 4.01. 3 P
i have neither the scholar's melancholy, which 4.01. 10 P
but it is a melancholy of mine own, compounded 4.01. 15 P
blood, | and melancholy is the nurse of frenzy. SHR in.2. 133
live" — | this his good melancholy oft began, AWW 1.02. 56
take my young lord to be a very melancholy man. 3.02. 4 P
that had this trick of melancholy /sold a goodly 3.02. 9 P
why is he melancholy? 3.05. 86 P
now the melancholy god protect thee, and the TN 2.04. 73 P
and with a green and yellow melancholy | she sat 2.04.113
let me be boil'd to death with melancholy. 2.05. 3 P
being addicted to a melancholy as she is, that 2.05.202 P
a new ship to purge melancholy and air himself; WT 4.04.763 P
or if that surly spirit, melancholy, | had bak'd JN 3.03. 42
with clog of conscience and sour melancholy R2 5.06. 20
i am as melancholy as a gib cat or a lugg'd bear 1H4 1.02. 73 P
thou to a hare, or the melancholy of moor–ditch? 1.02. 77 P
to thick–ey'd musing and curst melancholy? 2.03. 46
jades | that drag the tragic melancholy night; 2H6 4.01. 4
my mind was troubled with deep melancholy. 5.01. 34
the king is sickly, weak, and melancholy, | and R3 1.01.136
i pass'd, methought, the melancholy flood, 1.04. 45
the weary way hath made you melancholy. 3.01. 3
a grave | as thou canst yield a melancholy seat! 4.04. 32

saw'st thou the melancholy lord northumberland? 5.03. 68
he is melancholy without cause, and merry TRO 1.02. 26 P
you may call it melancholy, if you will favor 2.03. 87 P
if you do, our melancholy upon your head! 3.01. 69 P
eye, | my silence, an' my cloudy melancholy, TIT 2.03. 33
our instruments to melancholy bells, | our ROM 4.05. 86
a poor unmanly melancholy sprung | from change TIM 4.03.203
of his friends, drove him into this melancholy. 4.03.401 P
perhaps, | out of my weakness and my melancholy,
HAM 2.02.601
soul | o'er which his melancholy sits on brood, 3.01.165
my cue is villainous melancholy, with a sigh LR 1.02.135 P
o sovereign mistress of true melancholy, | the ANT 4.09. 12
o melancholy, | who ever yet could sound thy CYM 4.02.203
thou diedst, a most rare boy, of melancholy. 4.02.208
the sad companion, dull–ey'd melancholy, | /be PER 1.02. 2
awhile, | yon knight doth sit too melancholy, 2.03. 54
and will awake him from his melancholy. 2.03. 91
who, hearing of your melancholy state, | did 5.01.220
but a most thick and profound melancholy. TNK 4.03. 49 P
facto | the melancholy humor that infects her. 5.02. 38
melancholy | becomes him nobly. 5.03. 49
then, like a melancholy malcontent, | he vails VEN 313
sinks down to death, oppress'd with melancholy; SON 45. 8
MELANCHOLY'S 1 FR 0.0001 REL FR 1 V 0 P
o hateful error, melancholy's child, | why dost JC 5.03. 67
MELEAGER 1 FR 0.0001 REL FR 1 V 0 P
do you, | as once did meleager and the boar, TNK 3.05. 18
MELFORD 1 FR 0.0001 REL FR 0 V 1 P
suffolk, for enclosing the commons of melford." 2H6 1.03. 22 P
MELIUS 1 FR 0.0001 REL FR 1 V 0 P
glorious, | et bonum quo antiquius, eo melius. PER 1.ch. 10
MELL 1 FR 0.0001 REL FR 1 V 0 P
men are to mell with, boys are not to kiss; AWW 4.03.228
MELLIFLUOUS 1 FR 0.0001 REL FR 0 V 1 P
a mellifluous voice, as i am true knight. TN 2.03. 53 P
MELLOW 6 FR 0.0006 REL FR 6 V 0 P
till i had made mine own occasion mellow | what TN 1.02. 43
so now prosperity begins to mellow | and drop R3 4.04. 1
as hercules | did shake down mellow fruit. COR 4.06.100
tree, | but fall unshaken when they mellow be. HAM 3.02.191
shook down my mellow hangings, nay, my leaves, CYM 3.03. 63
the mellow plum doth fall, the green sticks fast VEN 527
MELLOW'D 2 FR 0.0002 REL FR 2 V 0 P
even in the downfall of his mellow'd years, 3H6 3.03.104
which, mellow'd by the stealing hours of time, R3 3.07.168
MELLOWING 1 FR 0.0001 REL FR 0 V 1 P
and delivered upon the mellowing of occasion. LLL 4.02. 70 P
MELODIOUS 10 FR 0.0011 REL FR 10 V 0 P
ay; and melodious were it, would you sing it. TGV 1.02. 83
whose falls | melodious birds sings madrigals; WIV 3.01. 18
"melodious birds sing madrigals — | when as i 3.01. 23
hounds and horns and sweet melodious birds | be TIT 2.03. 27
where like a sweet melodious bird it sung 3.01. 85
pull'd the poor wretch from her melodious lay HAM 4.07.182
bird melodious, or bird fair, | is absent hence! TNK 1.01. 17
melodious discord, heavenly tune harsh sounding,
VEN 431
thou lov'st to hear the sweet melodious sound PP 8. 9
by whose falls | melodious birds sing madrigals. 19. 8
/MELODY 1 FR 0.0001 REL FR 1 V 0 P
/that, /with /his /pretty /buzzing /melody, TIT 3.02. 64
MELODY 8 FR 0.0009 REL FR 7 V 1 P
tongue should catch your tongue's sweet melody. MND 1.01.189
with melody | sing in our sweet lullaby, | lulla 2.02. 13
philomele, with melody, etc. 2.02. 24
and lull'd with sound of sweetest melody? 2H4 3.01. 14
you shall not bob us out of our melody. TRO 3.01. 68 P
the birds chaunt melody on every bush, | the TIT 2.03. 12
wings | he can at pleasure stint their melody; 4.04. 86
make her moans mad with their sweet melody, LUC 1108
/MELT 2 FR 0.0002 REL FR 2 V 0 P
/to /melt /myself /away /in //water–drops! R2 4.01.262
/tears /will /quickly /melt /thy /life /away. TIT 3.02. 51
MELT 31 FR 0.0035 REL FR 29 V 2 P
candied be they, | and melt ere they molest! TMP 2.01.280
can, shall never melt | mine honor into lust, to 4.01. 27
a little time will melt her frozen thoughts, TGV 3.02. 9
they would melt me out of my fat drop by drop, WIV 4.05. 97 P
is the opinion that fire cannot melt out of me; ADO 1.01.232 P
so he dissolv'd, and show'rs of oaths did melt. MND 1.01.245
nay, if you melt, then will she run mad. 1H4 3.01.209
doth begin to melt | and drop upon our bare 2H4 2.04.364
of solid firmness, melt itself | into the sea, 3.01. 48
for i should melt at an offender's tears, | and 2H6 3.01.126
now melt with woe | that winter should cut off 3H6 2.03. 46
as red as fire? nay then, her wax must melt. 3.02. 51
of most hard temper | melt and lament for her. H8 2.03. 12
and | to melt the city leads upon your pates, COR 4.06. 82
i melt, and am not | of stronger earth than 5.03. 28
in winter with warm tears i'll melt the snow, TIT 3.01. 20
come, and learn of us | to melt in showers; 5.03.161
o, that this too too sallied flesh would melt, HAM 1.02.129
let virtue be as wax | and melt in her own fire. 3.04. 85
what ribs of oak, when mountains melt on them, OTH 2.01. 8
let rome in tiber melt, and the wide arch | of ANT 1.01. 33
the gold i give thee will i melt and pour | down 2.05. 34
melt egypt into nile! 2.05. 78
melt their sweets | on blossoming caesar; 4.12. 22
the crown o' th' earth doth melt. 4.15. 63
which | even women have cast off, melt thee, but PER 4.01. 7
that on the touching of her lips i may | melt, 5.03. 43
would in thy palm dissolve, or seem to melt. VEN 144
heavy heart's lead, melt at mine eyes' red fire! 1073
art, | melt at my tears and be compassionate! LUC 594
as winter meads when sun doth melt their snow. 1218
MELTED 17 FR 0.0019 REL FR 12 V 5 P
and | are melted into air, into thin air, | and, TMP 4.01.150
fire of lust have melted him in his own grease. WIV 2.01. 68 P
but manhood is melted into cur'sies, valor into ADO 4.01.319 P
my love to hermia | (melted as the snow) seems MND 4.01.166
this counterfeit lump of /ore will be melted, if AWW 3.06. 38 P
and so, with shrieks, | she melted into air. WT 3.03. 37
zeal, now melted by the windy breath | of soft JN 2.01.477
my heart hath melted at a lady's tears, | being 5.02. 47
hearts of men, they must perforce have melted, R2 5.02. 35
that melted at the sweet tale of the sun's? 1H4 2.04.121 P
as doth the melted snow | upon the valleys whose H5 3.05. 50

melted with tenderness and /kind compassion, R3 4.03. 7
being three parts melted away with rotten dews, COR 2.03. 32 P
melted down thy youth | in different beds of TIM 4.03.256
and what seem'd corporal melted, | as breath MAC 1.03. 81
nay, followed him till he had melted from | the CYM 1.03. 20
kill'd | was melted like a vapor from her sight, VEN 1166
MELTETH 2 FR 0.0002 REL FR 2 V 0 P
against whose charms faith melteth into blood. ADO 2.01.180
true quality | with that which melteth fools — JC 3.01. 42
MELTING 11 FR 0.0012 REL FR 11 V 0 P
melting the darkness, so their rising senses TMP 5.01. 66
a sea of melting pearl, which some call tears; TGV 3.01.226
and that will quickly dry thy melting tears. 3H6 1.04.174
steel thy melting heart | to hold thine own and 2.02. 41
when they do hug him in their melting bosoms. TIT 3.01.213
steel with valor | the melting spirits of women, JC 2.01.122
eyes, | albeit unused to the melting mood, OTH 5.02.349
cool shadow to his melting buttock lent; VEN 315
as is the morning's silver melting dew | against LUC 24
set, | each flow'r moist'ned like a melting eye, 1227
all melting, though our drops this diff'rence LC 300
MELTS 6 FR 0.0006 REL FR 6 V 0 P
lords, cold snow melts with the sun's hot beams: 2H6 3.01.223
and, now i fall, thy tough commixtures melts, 3H6 2.06. 6
authority melts from me. ANT 3.13. 90
by hot grief uncandied, | melts into drops; TNK 1.01.108
as mountain snow melts with the midday sun. VEN 750
which her cheek melts, as scorning it should 982
MELUNE 4 FR 0.0004 REL FR 4 V 0 P
the count melune, a noble lord of france, JN 4.03. 15
my lord melune, let this be copied out, | and 5.02. 1
it is the count melune. 5.04. 9
the count melune is slain; 5.05. 10
MEMBER 10 FR 0.0011 REL FR 8 V 2 P
but instruments of some more mightier member MM 5.01.237
here comes a member of the commonwealth. LLL 4.01. 41
you are a good member of the commonwealth. 4.02. 76 P
says you are no good member of the commonwealth,
MV 3.05. 34 P
the slave, a member of the country's peace, H5 4.01.281
and, as a branch and member of this royalty, 5.02. 5
i'll lop a member off and give it you | in 1H6 5.03. 15
count wisdom as no member of the war, TRO 1.03.198
thou shouldst not bear from me a greekish member 4.05.130
exist, and be a member of his love | whom i, OTH 3.04.112
MEMBERS 10 FR 0.0011 REL FR 6 V 4 P
sir, being members of my occupation, using MM 4.02. 37 P
all members of our cause, both here and hence, 2H4 4.01.169
as fest'red members rot but by degree, | till 1H6 3.01.191
there was a time when all the body's members COR 1.01. 96
replied | to th' discontented members, the 1.01.111
this good belly, | and you the mutinous members: 1.01.149
of the which we being members, should bring 2.03. 12 P
should bring ourselves to be monstrous members. 2.03. 13 P
our other healthful members even to a sense | of OTH 3.04.147
are worn out, there are members to make new. ANT 1.02.165 P
MEMENTO 1 FR 0.0001 REL FR 0 V 1 P
a man doth of a death's–head or a memento mori.
1H4 3.03. 30 P
MEMORABLE 4 FR 0.0004 REL FR 3 V 1 P
witness our too much memorable shame | when H5 2.04. 53
rak'd, | he sends you this most memorable line, 2.04. 88
i wear it for a memorable honor; 4.07.104
and worn as a memorable trophy of predeceas'd 5.01. 72 P
MEMORANDUMS 1 FR 0.0001 REL FR 0 V 1 P
tavern–reckonings, memorandums of bawdy–houses,
1H4 3.03.158 P
MEMORIAL 3 FR 0.0003 REL FR 2 V 1 P
statue and oblique memorial of cuckolds, a TRO 5.01. 55 P
glove, | and gives memorial dainty kisses to it, 5.02. 80
which for memorial still with thee shall stay. SON 74. 4
MEMORIALS 1 FR 0.0001 REL FR 1 V 0 P
eyes | with the memorials and the things of fame TN 3.03. 23
MEMORIES 3 FR 0.0003 REL FR 3 V 0 P
and now have toiled their unbreathed memories MND 5.01. 74
witness, | yet freshly pitied in our memories. H8 5.02. 66
these weeds are memories of those worser hours; LR 4.07. 7
MEMORIZ'D 1 FR 0.0001 REL FR 1 V 0 P
to this land, which shall | in it be memoriz'd. H8 3.02. 52
MEMORIZE 1 FR 0.0001 REL FR 1 V 0 P
reeking wounds, | or memorize another golgotha, MAC 1.02. 40
MEMORY 61 FR 0.0069 REL FR 54 V 7 P
made such a sinner of his memory | to credit his TMP 1.02.101
who shall be of as little memory | when he is 2.01.233
fall | and leave no memory of what it was! TGV 5.04. 10
he is a good sprag memory. WIV 4.01. 82 P
up, | yet hath my night of life some memory, ERR 5.01.315
else your memory is bad, going o'er it erewhile. LLL 4.01. 97
these are begot in the ventricle of memory, 4.02. 68 P
and quite divorce his memory from his part. 5.02.150
store, | and, by the near guess of my memory, MV 1.03. 54
the fool hath planted in his memory | an army of 3.05. 66
o you memory | of old sir rowland! AYL 2.03. 3
with many things of worthy memory, which now SHR 4.01. 82 P
good paulina, | who hast the memory of hermione,
WT 5.01. 50
whose memory is written on the earth | with yet 2H4 4.01. 81
and keep no tell–tale to his memory | that may 4.01.200
and their memory | shall as a pattern or a 4.04. 75
out, | may waste the memory of the former days. 4.05.215
your grandfather of famous memory, an't please H5 4.07. 92 P
in memory of her when she is dead, | her ashes, 1H6 1.06. 23
yourself, | i'll note you in my book of memory, 2.04.101
conqueror, | that ever–living man of memory, 4.03. 51
blotting your names from books of memory, 2H6 1.01.100
i thank my memory, i yet remember | some of H8 3.02.303
some little memory of me will stir him | (i know 3.02.417
are grated | to dusty nothing, yet let memory, TRO 3.02.189
i am weary, yea, my memory is tir'd. COR 1.09. 91
a good memory | and witness of the malice and 4.05. 71
a noble memory! 5.01. 17
the injury, | yet he shall have a noble memory. 5.06.153
o, it presses to my memory | like damned guilty ROM 3.02.110
noble timon, of whose memory | hereafter more. TIM 5.04. 80
yea, beg a hair of him for memory, | and, dying, JC 3.02.134
that memory, the warder of the brain, | shall be MAC 1.07. 65
pluck from the memory a rooted sorrow, | raze 5.03. 41
our dear brother's death | the memory be green, HAM 1.02. 2

and these few precepts in thy memory | look thou 1.03. 58
'tis in my memory lock'd, | and you yourself 1.03. 85
whiles memory holds a seat | in this distracted 1.05. 96
from the table of my memory | i'll wipe away all 1.05. 98
if it live in your memory, begin at this line — 2.02.448 P
hope a great man's memory may outlive his life 3.02.132 P
purpose is but the slave to memory, | of violent 3.02.188
would dozy th' arithmetic of memory, and yet but 5.02.114 P
i have some rights, of memory in this kingdom, 5.02.389
thou saidst (o, it comes o'er my memory, | as OTH 4.01. 20
/smite, | till by degrees the memory of my womb, ANT 3.13.163
shall upon record | bear hateful memory: 4.09. 9
down, that's riveted, | screw'd to my memory? CYM 2.02. 44
on, how thy memory | will then be pang'd by me. 3.04. 94
our great court | made me to blame in memory. 3.05. 51
dirge, | and tell to memory my death was noble, TNK 2.06. 16
whose twelve strong labors crown his memory, 3.06.176
ancient love, our kindred, | out of my memory; 5.01. 27
his tender heir might bear his memory: SON 1. 4
and wear their brave state out of memory: 15. 8
shall burn | the living record of your memory. 55. 8
that he shall never cut from memory | my sweet 63.11
show, | of mouthed graves will give thee memory; 77. 6
look what thy memory cannot contain | commit to 77. 9
from hence your memory death cannot take, 81. 3
my brain | full character'd with lasting memory, 122. 2

MEMPHIS 1 FR 0.0001 REL FR 1 V 0 P
i'll rear | than rhodope's /of memphis ever was. 1H6 1.06. 22

/M'EN 1 FR 0.0001 REL FR 0 V 1 P
/o, /je /m'en vois a la cour — la grande WIV 1.04. 52 P

M'EN 2 FR 0.0002 REL FR 0 V 2 P
je m'en fais la repetition de tous les mots que H5 3.04. 25 P
o seigneur dieu, je m'en oublie d' elbow. 3.04. 31 P

MEN *(also mans)*

/MEN 14 FR 0.0015 REL FR 12 V 2 P
what he hath scanted /men in hair he hath given ERR 2.02. 80 P
but wise /men, folly-fall'n, quite taint their TN 3.01. 68
/well /remember | /the /favors /of /these /men. R2 4.01.168
/the /souls /of /men | /may /deem /that /you 4.01.226
/roof | /did /keep /ten /thousand /men? 4.01.283
/but /shadows /and /the /shows /of /men, /to 2H4 1.01.193
/constrain'd | /as /men /drink /potions, /that 1.01.197
/o /thoughts /of /men /accurs'd! 1.03.107
/o /miracle /of /men! 2.03. 33
/troop /in /the /throngs /of /military /men; 4.01. 62
/even /by /those /men /that /most /have /done 4.01. 79
be copy now to /men of grosser blood, | and H5 3.01. 24
ay, you are honest /men. TIM 5.01. 71
/lords /and /great /men /will /not /let /me; LR 1.04.152 P

MEN 916 FR 0.1035 REL FR 716 V 200 P
play the men. TMP 1.01. 10 P
wench, | to th' most of men this is a caliban, 1.02.481
making | than we bring men to comfort them. 2.01.135
all men idle, all; 2.01.155
ebbing men, indeed, | most often, do so near the 2.01.226
were then my fellows, now they are my men. 2.01.274
tricks upon 's with salvages and men of inde? 2.02. 58 P
have i seen | more that i may call men than you, 3.01. 51
or that there were such men | whose heads stood 3.03. 46
you are three men of sin, whom destiny, | that 3.03. 53
you 'mongst men | being most unfit to live. 3.03. 57
and even with such-like valor men hang and drown 3.03. 59
this is as strange a maze as e'er men trod, 5.01.242
mark but the badges of these men, my lords, 5.01.267
o, they love least that let men know their love. TGV 1.02. 32
while other men, of slender reputation, | put 1.03. 6
the loose encounters of lascivious men: 2.07. 41
all these are servants to deceitful men. 2.07. 72
base men, that use them to so base effect! 2.07. 73
worth, | and kept severely from resort of men, 3.01.108
youth | thrust from the company of aweful men. 4.01. 44
black men are pearls in beauteous ladies' eyes. 5.02. 12
all men but proteus. 5.04. 54
to change their shapes than men their minds. 5.04.109
than men their minds? 5.04.110
these banish'd men, that i have kept withal, 5.04.152
withal, | are men endu'd with worthy qualities. 5.04.153
knight, you have beaten my men, kill'd my deer, WIV 1.01.111 P
i keep but three men and a boy yet, till my 1.01.274 P
in the parliament for the putting down of men. 2.01. 30 P
i shall think the worse of fat men, as long as i 2.01. 56 P
our wives are a yoke of his discarded men — 2.01.175 P
were they his men? 2.01.177 P
give your men the charge, we must be brief. 3.03. 7 P
send him by your two men to datchet-mead. 3.03.132 P
call your men, mistress ford. 3.03.144 P
she does so take on with her men; 3.05. 39 P
for i'll appoint my men to carry the basket 4.02. 95 P
i'll first direct my men what they shall do with 4.02. 99 P
we are simple men, we do not know what's brought 4.02.174 P
germans are honest men. 4.05. 72 P
gods have hot backs, what shall poor men do? 5.05. 12 P
and speechless dialect, | such as move men; MM 1.02.184
vow'd, you must not speak with men | but in the 1.04. 10
to know, when maidens sue, | men give like gods; 1.04. 81
are there not men in your ward sufficient to 2.01.267 P
could great men thunder | as jove himself does, 2.02.110
great men may jest with saints; 2.02.127
when men were fond, i smil'd and wond'red how. 2.02.186
men their creation mar | in profiting by them. 2.04.127
needs buy and sell men and women like beasts, we 3.02. 2 P
when | the steeled jailer is the friend of men. 4.02. 87
give notice to such men of sort and suit as are 4.04. 17 P
they say best men are moulded out of faults, 5.01.439
such as sea-faring men provide for storms; ERR 1.01. 80
or that, or any place that harbors men. 1.01.136
didst conclude hairy men plain dealers without 2.02. 86 P
have you not heard men say, | that time comes 4.02. 59
takes pity on decay'd men and gives them suits 4.03. 26 P
they appear to men like angels of light, light 4.03. 55 P
liv'st | to walk where any honest men resort. 5.01. 28
love — | a sin prevailing much in youthful men, 5.01. 52
one of these men is genius to the other: 5.01.333
by men of epidamium he and i, | and the twin 5.01.350
not till god make men of some other mettle than ADO 2.01. 59 P
for he both pleases men and angers them, and 2.01.141 P
ladies, sigh no more, | men were deceivers ever, 2.03. 63
the fraud of men was ever so, | since summer 2.03. 72
are you good men and true? 3.03. 1 P
you shall comprehend all vagrom men; 3.03. 25 P
may say they are not the men you took them for. 3.03. 47 P
and, for such kind of men, the less you meddle 3.03. 52 P
and two men ride of a horse, one must ride 3.05. 37 P
all men are not alike, alas, good neighbor! 3.05. 40 P
we are now to examination these men. 3.05. 59 P
o, what men dare do! 4.01. 19 P
what men may do! 4.01. 19 P
what men daily do, not knowing what they do! 4.01. 20 P
compliment, and men are only turn'd into tongue, 4.01.320 P
you in the prince's name accuse these men. 4.02. 38 P
master constable, let these men be bound, and 4.02. 64 P
men | can counsel and speak comfort to that 5.01. 20
therein do men from children nothing differ. 5.01. 33
he shall kill two of us, and men indeed; 5.01. 80
snapp'd off with two old men without teeth. 5.01.116 P
two of my brother's men bound? 5.01.210 P
officers, what offense have these men done? 5.01.213 P
here stand a pair of honorable men, | a third is 5.01.266
never paid that now men grow hard-hearted and 5.01.311 P
and brought with armed men back to messina. 5.04.126
and men sit down to that nourishment which is LLL 1.01.237 P
what great men have been in love? 1.02. 65 P
let them be men of good repute and carriage. 1.02. 69 P
be called boy, but his glory is to subdue men. 1.02.181 P
and make them men of note — do you note? 3.01. 24 P
men that most are affected to these. 3.01. 25 P
some men must love my lady, and some joan. 3.01.205
by keeping company | with men like /you, men of 4.03.178
with men like /you, men of inconstancy. 4.03.178
for wisdom's sake, a word that all men love, 4.03.354
or for love's sake, a word that loves all men, 4.03.355
or women's sake, by whom we men are men, | /let 4.03.357
or women's sake, by whom we men are men, | /let 4.03.357
light wenches may prove plagues to men forsworn; 4.03.382
men of peace, well encount'red. 5.01. 34 P
where will you find men worthy enough to present 5.01.124 P
nor god, nor i, delights in perjur'd men. 5.02.346
that the two learned men have compiled in praise 5.02.886 P
cuckoo then on every tree | mocks married men; 5.02.899
cuckoo then on every tree | mocks married men; 5.02.908
or to abjure | for ever the society of men. MND 1.01. 66
by all the vows that ever men have broke | (in 1.01.175
we cannot fight for love, as men may do. 2.01.241
or as the heresies that men do leave | are hated 2.02.139
i am a man as other men are"; 3.01. 44 P
henceforth be never numb'red among men! 3.02. 67
if you were men, as men you are in show, | you 3.02.151
if you were men, as men you are in show, | you 3.02.151
to join with men in scorning your poor friend? 3.02.216
had gone forward, we had all been made men. 4.02. 18 P
hard-handed men that work in athens here, 5.01. 72
of themselves, they may pass for excellent men. 5.01.216 P
there are a sort of men whose visages | do cream MV 1.01. 88
i must be one of these same dumb wise men, | for 1.01.106
virtuous, and holy men at their death have good 1.02. 28 P
of all the men that ever my foolish eyes look'd 1.02.117 P
but ships are but boards, sailors but men; 1.03. 22 P
and thrift is blessing, if men steal it not. 1.03. 90
to make me blest or cursed'st among men. 2.01. 46
chooseth me shall gain what many men desire"; 2.07. 5
men that hazard all | do it in hope of fair 2.07. 18
chooseth me shall gain what many men desire." 2.07. 37
chooseth me shall gain what many men desire." 2.09. 24
what many men desire! 2.09. 25
i will not choose what many men desire, 2.09. 31
yes, other men have ill luck too. 3.01. 97 P
rack, | where men enforced do speak any thing. 3.02. 33
a golden mesh t' entrap the hearts of men 3.02.122
most impenetrable cur | that ever kept with men. 3.03. 19
when we are both accoutered like young men, 3.04. 63
that men shall swear i have discontinued school 3.04. 75
why, shall we turn to men? 3.04. 78
some men there are love not a gaping pig; 4.01. 47
do all men kill the things they do not love? 4.01. 66
infuse themselves | into the trunks of men. 4.01.133
that 'scuse serves many men to save their gifts, 4.01.444
that they did give the rings away to men; 4.02. 16
forest of arden, and a many merry men with him; AYL 1.01.115 P
may not speak wisely what wise men do foolishly. 1.02. 87 P
foolery that wise men have makes a great show. 1.02. 90 P
three proper young men, of excellent growth and 1.02.121 P
"be it known unto all men by these presents." 1.02.124 P
thus men may grow wiser every day. 1.02.137 P
to /some kind of men | their graces serve them 2.03. 10
and all the men and women merely players; 2.07.140
poor men alone? 3.03. 56 P
men have died from time to time and worms have 4.01.106 P
orlando, men are april when they woo, december 4.01.147 P
him the most unnatural | that liv'd amongst men. 4.03.123
men of great worth resorted to this forest, 5.04.155
for the love you bear to men, to like as much of ep 13 P
and i charge you, o men, for the love you bear ep 14 P
and how my men will stay themselves from SHR in.1. 134
maid, | nor no such men as you have reckon'd up, in.2. 92
and twenty more such names and men as these, in.2. 95
my men should call me "lord"; in.2. 105
for to cunning men | i will be very kind, and 1.01. 97
wind as scatters young men through the world 1.02. 50
of all the men alive | i never yet beheld that 2.01. 10
to see | how tame, when men and women are alone, 2.01.312
and may not young men die as well as old? 2.01.391
thou hast brav'd many men, brave not me; 4.03.124 P
go call my men, and let us straight to him, 4.03.184
military policy how virgins might blow up men? AWW 1.01.122 P
if men could be contented to be what they are, 1.03. 50 P
will repeat, | which men full true shall find: 1.03. 61
the help of heaven we count the act of men. 2.01.152
but for me, i have an answer will serve all men. 2.02. 14 P
thou wast created for men to breathe themselves 2.03.256 P
where are my other men, monsieur? 2.05. 89
that's the loss of men, though it be the getting 3.02. 42 P
knew the crafts | that you do charge men with. 4.02. 34
i see that men make rope's in such a scarre 4.02. 38
she says all men | have the like oaths. 4.02. 70
men are to mell with, boys are not to kiss; 4.03.228
such pestiferous reports of men very nobly held, 4.03.306 P
but o, strange men, | that can such sweet use 4.04. 21
that she whom all men prais'd and whom myself, 5.03. 53
hath abjur'd the /company | and /sight of men. TN 1.02. 41
i take these wise men that crow so at these set 1.05. 88 P
a peg-a-ramsey, and "three merry men be we." 2.03. 77 P
i would have men of such constancy put to sea, 2.04. 75 P
too well what love women to men may owe; 2.04.105
we men may say more, swear more, but indeed 2.04.116
have heard of some kind of men that put quarrels 3.04.243 P
these wise men that give fools money get 4.01. 22 P
'gainst knaves and thieves men shut their gate, 5.01.395
whiles other men have gates, and those gates WT 1.02.197
never | saw i men scour so on their way. 2.01. 35
the men are not yet cold under water, nor the 3.03.105 P
i think they are given | to men of middle age. 4.04.108
abroad, therefore it behooves men to be wary. 4.04.254 P
that have made themselves all men of hair. 4.04.326 P
since these good men are pleas'd, let them come 4.04.340 P
he, and more | than he, and men — the earth, 4.04.371
how blessed are we that are not simple men! 4.04.745
(for you seem to be honest plain men) what you 4.04.794 P
men, that she is | the rarest of all women. 5.01.111
who now | has these poor men in question. 5.01.198
shall i produce the men? JN 1.01. 46
what men are you? 1.01. 49
i durst not stick a rose | lest men should say, 1.01.143
night, | and have is have, however men do catch. 1.01.173
call for our chiefest men of discipline | to 2.01. 39
hither to the walls | these men of angiers; 2.01.199
you men of angiers, and my loving subjects — 2.01.203
you loving men of angiers, arthur's subjects, 2.01.204
you men of angiers, open wide your gates, | and 2.01.300
rejoice, you men of angiers, ring your bells, 2.01.312
and now he feasts, mousing the flesh of men, 2.01.354
of kings, of beggars, old men, young men, maids, 2.01.570
of kings, of beggars, old men, young men, maids, 2.01.570
so | as doth the fury of two desperate men, 3.01. 32
shall our feast be kept with slaughtered men? 3.01.302
when fortune means to men most good, | she looks 3.04.119
even with the fierce looks of these bloody men. 4.01. 73
nay, hear me, hubert, drive these men away, 4.01. 78
thrust but these men away, and i'll forgive you, 4.01. 82
the faiths of men ne'er stained with revolt; 4.02. 6
old men and beldames in the streets | do 4.02.185
what men provided? 5.02. 98
how god and good men hate so foul a liar. R2 1.01.114
away, | men are but gilded loam or painted clay. 1.01.179
that which in mean men we entitle patience | is 1.02. 33
for mowbray and myself are like two men | that 1.03. 48
to men in joy, but grief makes one hour ten. 1.03.261
whereto, when they shall know what men are rich, 1.04. 49
but they say the tongues of dying men | enforce 2.01. 5
this happy breed of men, this little world, 2.01. 45
can sick men play so nicely with their names? 2.01. 84
should dying men flatter with those that live? 2.01. 88
no, no, men living flatter those that die. 2.01. 89
eight tall ships, three thousand men of war, 2.01.286
gentlemen, will you go muster men? 2.02.108
gentlemen, go muster up your men, | and meet me 2.02.118
keeps good old york there with his men of war? 2.03. 52
mann'd with three hundred men, as i have heard, 2.03. 54
the black prince, that young mars of men, | from 2.03.101
base men by his endowments are made great. 2.03.139
rich men look sad, and ruffians dance and leap, 2.04. 12
bring forth these men. 3.01. 1
here in the view of men | i will unfold some 3.01. 6
the breath of worldly men cannot depose | the 3.02. 56
weak men must fall, for heaven still guards the 3.02. 62
thou shalt have twelve thousand fighting men! 3.02. 70
but now the blood of twenty thousand men | did 3.02. 76
my lord, wise men ne'er sit and wail their woes, 3.02.178
men judge by the complexion of the sky | the 3.02.194
had he done so to great and growing men, | they 3.04. 61
didst send two of thy men | to execute the noble 4.01. 81
beasts, | i had been still a happy king of men. 5.01. 36
the love of wicked men converts to fear, | that 5.01. 66
bad men, you violate | a twofold marriage — 5.01. 71
as in a theatre the eyes of men, | after a 5.02. 23
steel'd | the hearts of men, they must perforce 5.02. 35
for though it have holp mad men to their wits, 5.05. 62
in me it seems it will make wise men mad. 5.05. 63
leading the men of /herfordshire to fight 1H4 1.01. 39
and let men say we be men of good government, 1.02. 27 P
and let men say we be men of good government, 1.02. 27 P
of us that are the moon's men doth ebb and flow 1.02. 31 P
o, if men were to be sav'd by merit, what hole 1.02.107 P
shall rob those men that we have already waylaid 1.02.163 P
redeeming time when men think least i will. 1.02.217
that men of your nobility and power | did gage 1.03.172
go to, homo is a common name to all men. 2.01. 95 P
what, ye knaves, young men must live! 2.02. 90 P
the thieves have bound the true men. 2.02. 93 P
such as we see when men restrain their breath 2.03. 61
lives not three good men unhang'd in england, 2.04.130 P
some six or seven fresh men set upon us — 2.04.181 P
eleven buckrom men grown out of two. 2.04.219 P
thou know these men in kendal green when it was 2.04.231 P
with it and swear it was the blood of true men. 2.04.311 P
cry | hath followed certain men unto this house. 2.04.508
what men? 2.04.509
if he have robb'd these men, | he shall be 2.04.521
of many men | i do not bear these crossings. 3.01. 34
do show | i am not in the roll of common men. 3.01. 42
been, | so common-hackney'd in the eyes of men, 3.02. 40
that men would tell their children, "this is he" 3.02. 48
aspect | as cloudy men use to their adversaries, 3.02. 83
away, | advantage feeds him fat while men delay. 3.02.180
than if the earl were here, for men must think, 4.01. 79
tush, man, mortal men, mortal men. 4.02. 67 P
tush, man, mortal men, mortal men. 4.02. 67 P
being men of such great leading as you are, 4.03. 17
wherein the fortune of ten thousand men | must 4.04. 9
and many moe corrivals and dear men | of 4.04. 31
slain, and all his men | upon the foot of fear, 5.05. 19
stuffing the ears of men with false reports. 2H4 in 8
so did our men, heavy in hotspur's loss, | lend 1.01.121
men of all sorts take a pride to gird at me. 1.02. 6 P
myself, but the cause that wit is in other men. 1.02. 10 P

to five and twenty thousand men of choice, | and 1.03. 11
using the names of men in stead of men, | like 1.03. 57
using the names of men in stead of men, | like 1.03. 57
/die men like dogs! 2.04.174 P
good wenches, how men of merit are sought after. 2.04.375 P
here come two of sir john falstaff's men, as i 3.02. 53 P
provided me here half a dozen sufficient men? 3.02. 93 P
me, there are other men fitter to go out than i. 3.02.114 P
come, sir, which men shall i have? 3.02.241 P
they are your likeliest men, and i would have 3.02.255 P
o, give me the spare men, and spare me the great 3.02.269 P
on, bardolph, lead the men away. 3.02.300 P
how subject we old men are to this vice of lying 3.02.303 P
his head for crowding among the marshal's men. 3.02.324 P
our men more perfect in the use of arms, | our 4.01.153
against ill chances men are ever merry, | but 4.02. 81
us, that we may peruse the men | we should have 4.02. 94
use his men well, davy, for they are arrant 5.01. 31 P
i would humor his men with the imputation of 5.01. 72 P
if to his men, i would curry with master shallow 5.01. 73 P
carriage is caught, as men take diseases, one of 5.01. 76 P
therefore let men take heed of their company. 5.01. 77 P
we meet like men that had forgot to speak. 5.02. 22
art now one of the greatest men in this realm. 5.03. 87 P
gape | for thee thrice wider than for other men. 5.05. 54
which men devout | by testament have given to H5 1.01. 9
that men are merriest when they are from home. 1.02.272
and three corrupted men, | one, richard earl of 2.pr. 22
men may sleep, and they may have their throats 2.01. 21 P
sweet men, come to him. 2.01.120 P
show men dutiful? 2.02.127
with men of courage and with means defendant; 2.04. 8
be merciful, great duke, to men of mould. 3.02. 22
he hath heard that men of few words are the best 3.02. 36 P
heard that men of few words are the best men, 3.02. 37 P
that piece of service the men would carry coals. 3.02. 46 P
or, like to men proud of destruction, | defy us 3.03. 4
therefore, you men of harflew, | take pity of 3.03. 27
what men have you lost, fluellen? 3.06. 97 P
and the men do sympathize with the mastiffs in 3.07.147 P
evil, | would men observingly distill it out; 4.01. 5
'tis good for men to love their present pains 4.01. 18
even as men wrack'd upon a sand, that look to be 4.01. 97 P
now, if these men do not die well, it will be a 4.01.144 P
if these men have defeated the law and outrun 4.01.166 P
though they can outstrip men, they have no wings 4.01.168 P
so that here men are punish'd for before–breach 4.01.170 P
must kings neglect, that private men enjoy! 4.01.237
and form, | creating awe and fear in other men? 4.01.247
leaving them but the shales and husks of men. 4.02. 18
of fighting men they have full threescore 4.03. 3
but one ten thousand of those men in england 4.03. 17
the fewer men, the greater share of honor. 4.03. 22
it yearns me not if men my garments wear; 4.03. 26
old men forget; 4.03. 49
why, now thou hast unwish'd five thousand men; 4.03. 76
dying like men, though buried in your dunghills, 4.03. 99
the french have reinforc'd their scatter'd men. 4.06. 36
tell you there is good men porn at monmouth. 4.07. 52 P
to sort our nobles from our common men. 4.07. 74
full fifteen hundred, besides common men. 4.08. 79
and of all other men | but five and twenty. 4.08.105
where ne'er from france arriv'd more happy men. 4.08.126
the english beach | pales in the flood with men, 5.pr. 10
that the tongues of men are full of deceits? 5.02.118 P
story, | in little room confining mighty men, ep 3
brandish'd sword did blind men with his beams; 1H6 1.01. 10
no treachery, but want of men and money. 1.01. 69
no leisure had he to enrank his men; 1.01.115
supply, | and hardly keeps his men from mutiny, 1.01.160
gall — | nor men nor money hath he to make war. 1.02. 17
what men have i! 1.02. 22
he may mean more than we poor men do know: 1.02.122
draw, men, for all this privileged place — 1.03. 46
all manner of men assembled here in arms this 1.03. 74 P
how far'st thou, mirror of all martial men? 1.04. 74
go, go, cheer up thy hungry–starved men; 1.05. 16
when they shall hear how we have play'd the men. 1.06. 16
they did amongst the troops of armed men | leap 2.02. 24
for when a world of men | could not prevail with 2.02. 48
and that i'll prove on better men than somerset, 2.04. 98
begun through malice of the bishop's men. 3.01. 75
the bishop and the duke of gloucester's men, 3.01. 78
talk like the vulgar sort of market men | that 3.02. 4
my forces and my power of men are yours. 3.03. 83
in which assault we lost twelve hundred men; 4.01. 24
good lord, what madness rules in brain–sick men, 4.01.111
as market men for oxen, sheep, or horse. 5.05. 54
but great men tremble when the lion roars, | and 2H6 3.01. 19
to ireland will you lead a band of men, 3.01.312
done, | to send me packing with an host of men: 3.01.342
'twas men i lack'd, and you will give them me; 3.01.345
i wear no knife to slaughter sleeping men, | but 3.02.197
hell, | pernicious blood–sucker of sleeping men! 3.02.226
the trait'rous warwick, with the men of bury, 3.02.240
air, | blaspheming god and cursing men on earth. 3.02.372
can i make men live, whe'er they will or no? 3.03. 10
small things make base men proud. 4.01.106
great men oft die by vild besonians: 4.01.134
to say as, let the magistrates be laboring men; 4.02. 18 P
now show yourselves men, 'tis for liberty. 4.02.183
for they are thrifty honest men, and such | as 4.02.186
o graceless men! they know not what they do. 4.04. 38
face that thou hast men about thee that usually 4.07. 38 P
to call poor men before them about matters they 4.07. 42 P
when honester men than thou go in their hose and 4.07. 50 P
you men of kent — 4.07. 54
great men have reaching hands; 4.07. 81
men shall hold of me in capite; 4.07.123 P
but now is cade driven back, his men dispers'd, 4.09. 34
yet, come thou and thy five men, and if i do not 4.10. 40 P
york not our old men spares; 5.02. 51
north, | he slily stole away and left his men; 3H6 1.01. 3
york, | or i will fill the house with armed men, 1.01.167
she is hard by with twenty thousand men; 1.02. 51
what, with five thousand men? 1.02. 66
let's set our men in order, | and issue forth 1.02. 69
five men to twenty! 1.02. 71
be thou reveng'd on men, and let me live. 1.03. 20
like men born to renown by life or death. 1.04. 8
so true men yield, with robbers so o'ermatch'd. 1.04. 64
for with a band of thirty thousand men | comes 2.02. 68
a thousand men have broke their fasts to–day 2.02.127
sad–hearted men, much overgone with care, | here 2.05.123
for wise men say it is the wisest course. 3.01. 25
and men may talk of kings, and why not i? 3.01. 58
ah, simple men, you know not what you swear! 3.01. 83
gust, | such is the lightness of you common men. 3.01. 89
thou and oxford, with five thousand men, | shall 3.03.234
you in our behalf | go levy men, and make 4.01.131
the day, | if warwick be so near as men report. 4.03. 8
what fates impose, that men must needs abide; 4.03. 58
shall here find his friends with horse and men 4.05. 12
for few men rightly temper with the stars; 4.06. 29
for many men that stumble at the threshold | are 4.07. 11
let's levy men, and beat him back again. 4.08. 6
men well inclin'd to hear what thou command'st; 4.08. 16
lords, wise men ne'er sit and wail their loss, 5.04. 1
ay, thou wast born to be a plague to men. 5.05. 28
and men ne'er spend their fury on a child. 5.05. 57
men for their sons, wives for their husbands, 5.06. 41
divine, | be resident in men like one another, 5.06. 82
two braver men | ne'er spurr'd their coursers at 5.07. 8
why, this it is, when men are rul'd by women: R3 1.01. 62
the king, | to be her men and wear her livery. 1.01. 80
all men, i hope, live so. 1.02.200
a thousand men that fishes gnaw'd upon; 1.04. 25
are you drawn forth among a world of men | to 1.04.181
clouds are seen, wise men put on their cloaks; 2.03. 32
untimely storms makes men expect a dearth. 2.03. 35
truly, the hearts of men are full of fear. 2.03. 38
oft have i heard of sanctuary men, | but 3.01. 55
when men are unprepar'd and look not for it. 3.02. 63
and so 'twill do | with some men else, that 3.02. 66
man | the men you talk of came into my mind. 3.02.117
o momentary grace of mortal men, | which we more 3.04. 96
when holy and devout religious men | are at 3.07. 92
and all good men of this ungovern'd isle. 3.07.110
cousin of buckingham, and sage grave men, 3.07.227
and die ere men can say, "god save the queen!" 4.01. 62
go muster men. 4.03. 56
men shall deal unadvisedly sometimes, | which 4.04.292
go then, and muster men; 4.04.494
what men of name resort to him? 4.05. 11
thus doth he force the swords of wicked men | to 5.01. 23
every man's conscience is a thousand men, | to 5.02. 17
call for some men of sound direction: 5.03. 16
if we be conquered, let men conquer us, | and 5.03.332
what men of name are slain on either side? 5.05. 12
those suns of glory, those two lights of men, H8 1.01. 6
men might say | till this time pomp was single, 1.01. 14
men fear the french would prove perfidious, | to 1.02.156
should juggle | men into such strange mysteries? 1.03. 2
abusing better men than they can be | out of a 1.03. 28
travel, | and understand again like honest men, 1.03. 32
men of his way should be most liberal, | they 1.03. 61
build their evils on the graves of great men, 2.01. 67
by our servants, by those men we lov'd most; 2.01.122
excellence | that angels love good men with; 2.02. 34
two equal men. 2.02.107
men | of singular integrity and learning, | yea, 2.04. 58
they should be good men, their affairs as 3.01. 22
and to deliver | (like free and honest men) our 3.01. 60
ye speak like honest men (pray god ye prove so!) 3.01. 69
wit, | and to such men of gravity and learning, 3.01. 73
looking | either for such men or such business. 3.01. 76
holy men i thought ye, | upon my soul, two 3.01.102
follow your envious courses, men of malice! 3.02.243
of all these learned men she was divorc'd, | and 4.01. 32
those men are happy, and so are all are near her 4.01. 50
but to those men that sought him, sweet as 4.02. 54
and sure those men are happy that shall have 'em 4.02.147
the last is for my men (they are the poorest, 4.02.148
but we all are men, | in our own natures frail, 5.02. 45
men that make | envy and crooked malice 5.02. 78
to men that understand you, words and weakness. 5.02.107
men so noble, | however faulty, yet should find 5.02.109
take my cause | out of the gripes of cruel men, 5.02.135
had thought i had had men of some understanding 5.02.170
was rather | (if there be faith in men) meant 5.02.186
and't please your honor, | we are but men; 5.03. 75
know within a while | all the best men are ours; ep 13
so do all men, unless th' are drunk, sick, or TRO 1.02. 17 P
men prize the thing ungain'd more than it is. 1.02.289
jove | to find persistive constancy in men? 1.03. 21
reproof of chance | lies the true proof of men: 1.03. 34
which is that god in office, guiding men? 1.03.231
or the men of troy | are ceremonious courtiers. 1.03.233
our opinion still | that we have better men. 1.03.383
not much | unlike young men, whom aristotle 2.02.166
and all men were of my mind — 2.03.215 P
at whose request do these men play? 3.01. 29 P
let all constant men be troiluses, all false 3.02.202 P
out with fortune, | must fall out with men too. 3.03. 76
for men, like butterflies, | show not their 3.03. 78
o heavens, what some men do, | while some men 3.03.132
what some men do, | while some men leave to do! 3.03.133
how some men creep in skittish fortune's hall, 3.03.134
wounds heal ill that men do give themselves. 3.03.229
prithee tarry, | you men will never tarry. 4.02. 16
but dare all imminence that gods and men 5.10. 13
soft–conscienc'd men can be content to say it COR 1.01. 37 P
the gods sent not | corn for the rich men only. 1.01.208
that bear the shapes of men, how have you run 1.04. 35
side | they have plac'd their men of trust? 1.06. 52
out my command, | which men are best inclin'd. 1.06. 85
you two are old men: 2.01. 13 P
with those that say you are reverend grave men, 2.01. 61 P
being advanc'd, declines, and then men die. 2.01.161
yet, by the faith of men, | we have some old 2.01.187
i have seen the dumb men throng to see him, and 2.01.262
hath been many great men that have flatter'd the 2.02. 7 P
sail, so men obey'd | and fell below his stem. 2.02.106
he did | run reeking o'er the lives of men, as 2.02.119
you not known | the worthiest men have done't? 2.03. 49
chairs of justice | supplied with worthy men! 3.03. 35
as the dead carcasses of unburied men | that do 3.03.122
that common chances common men could bear, 4.01. 5
of all the men i' th' world | i would have 4.05. 81
bastard children than war's a destroyer of men. 4.05.226 P
ay, and it makes men hate one another. 4.05.230 P
the second name of men, obeys his points | as if 4.06.125
you guard like men, 'tis well. 5.02. 2
whence men have read | his fame unparallel'd, 5.02. 15
to accomplish, | my best and freshest men; 5.06. 34
him, and men of heart | look'd wond'ring each at 5.06. 98
cut me to pieces, volsces, men and lads, | stain 5.06.111
and thanks to men | of noble minds is honorable TIT 1.01.215
o gentle, aged men! 3.01. 23
tribunes with their tongues doom men to death. 3.01. 47
and never whilst i live deceive men so; 3.01.189
let fools do good, and fair men call for grace, 3.01.204
oft, | extremity of griefs would make men mad; 4.01. 19
no big–bon'd men fram'd of the cyclops' size, 4.03. 47
betwixt my uncle and one of the emperal's men. 4.03. 94 P
and with a power | of high–resolved men, bent to 4.04. 64
even so mayest thou the giddy men of rome. 4.04. 87
oft have i digg'd up dead men from their graves, 5.01.135
'cause they take vengeance of such kind of men. 5.02. 63
but we wordly men | have miserable, mad, 5.02. 65
you sad–fac'd men, people and sons of rome, | by 5.03. 67
when no friends are by, men praise themselves. 5.03.118
i will push montague's men from the wall, and ROM 1.01. 17 P
quarrel is between our masters and us their men. 1.01. 20 P
when i have fought with the men, i will be civil 1.01. 22 P
draw, if you be men. 1.01. 62 P
sword, | or manage it to part these men with me. 1.01. 69
what ho, you men, you beasts! 1.01. 83
once more, on pain of death, all men depart. 1.01.103
think, | for men so old as we to keep the peace. 1.02. 3
such comfort as do lusty young men feel | when 1.02. 26
no less! nay, bigger: women grow by men. 1.03. 95
women may fall, when there's no strength in men. 2.03. 80
we talk here in the public haunt of men. 3.01. 50
no faith, no honesty in men, all perjur'd, | all 3.02. 86
they are free men, but i am banished: 3.03. 42
how should they when that wise men have no eyes? 3.03. 62
o fortune, fortune, all men call thee fickle; 3.05. 60
answer me like men: 4.05.125 P
to enter in the thoughts of desperate men! 5.01. 36
and if you had the strength | of twenty men, it 5.01. 79
how oft when men are at the point of death 5.03. 88
the senators of athens, happy men! TIM 1.01. 40
will strain a little, | for 'tis a bond in men. 1.01.144
common tongue | which all men speak with him. 1.01.175
what a number of men eats timon, and he sees 'em 1.02. 40 P
i wonder men dare trust themselves with men. 1.02. 43
i wonder men dare trust themselves with men. 1.02. 43
great men should drink with harness on their 1.02. 52
rich men sin, and i eat root. 1.02. 71
and spend our flatteries to drink those men 1.02.137
men shut their doors against a setting sun. 1.02.145
where be our men? 1.02.165
poor rogues, and usurers' men, bawds between 2.02. 60 P
are you three usurers' men? 2.02. 96 P
when men come to borrow of your masters, they 2.02. 99 P
men and men's fortunes could i frankly use | as 2.02.179
one of lord timon's men? 3.01. 5 P
not long ago one of his men was with the lord 3.02. 11 P
timon's money | has paid his men their wages. 3.02. 70
of his) | what charitable men afford to beggars. 3.02. 75
men must learn now with pity to dispense, | for 3.02. 86
one of lord timon's men. 3.04. 33 P
why do fond men expose themselves to battle, 3.05. 42
leaves winter, such summer birds are men. 3.06. 32 P
were your godheads to borrow of men, men would 3.06. 75 P
to borrow of men, men would forsake the gods. 3.06. 75 P
plagues incident to men, | your potent and 4.01. 21
for bounty, that makes gods, do still mar men. 4.02. 41
all feasts, societies, and throngs of men! 4.03. 21
men daily find it. 4.03.174
men report | thou dost affect my manners, and 4.03.198
the eyes, and hearts of men | at duty, more than 4.03.261
why shouldst thou hate men? 4.03.269
if thou hadst not been born the worst of men, 4.03.275
women nearest, but men — men are the things 4.03.320 P
but men — men are the things themselves. 4.03.320 P
give it the beasts, to be rid of the men. 4.03.323 P
thou have thyself fall in the confusion of men, 4.03.325 P
moe things like men! 4.03.397
we are not thieves, but men that much do want. 4.03.415
you must eat men. 4.03.425
i have forgot all men. 4.03.473
i never had honest men about me, i; 4.03.477
a usuring kindness, and, as rich men deal gifts, 4.03.509
thou shalt build from men; 4.03.526
give to dogs | what thou deniest to men. 4.03.530
be men like blasted woods, | and may diseases 4.03.531
wilt thou whip thine own faults in other men? 5.01. 39
have i once liv'd to see two honest men? 5.01. 56
let it go naked, men may see't the better. 5.01. 67
most honest men! 5.01. 73
y' are honest men; 5.01. 76
speak truth, y' are honest men. 5.01. 77
good honest men! 5.01. 80
at all times alike | men are not still the same; 5.01.122
and take our goodly aged men by th' beards, 5.01.172
i, timon, who, alive, all living men did hate; 5.04. 72
as proper men as ever trod upon neat's–leather JC 1.01. 25 P
why dost thou lead these men about the streets? 1.01. 28
o you hard hearts, you cruel men of rome, | knew 1.01. 36
fault | assemble all the poor men of your sort; 1.01. 57
who else would soar above the view of men, | and 1.01. 74
war, | forgets the shows of love to other men. 1.02. 47
know | that i do fawn on men and hug them hard, 1.02. 75
i cannot tell what you and other men | think of 1.02. 93
and we petty men | walk under his huge legs, and 1.02.136
men at some time are masters of their fates; 1.02.139
let me have men about me that are fat, 1.02.192
sleek–headed men and such as sleep a–nights. 1.02.193
such men are dangerous. 1.02.195
and he looks | quite through the deeds of men. 1.02.203
such men as he be never at heart's ease | whiles 1.02.208
which gives men stomach to disgest his words 1.02.301

fear, who swore they saw | men, all in fire, 1.03. 25
do so conjointly meet, let not men say, | "these 1.03. 29
but men may construe things after their fashion, 1.03. 34
a very pleasing night to honest men. 1.03. 43
it is the part of men to fear and tremble | when 1.03. 54
why old men, fools, and children calculate, 1.03. 65
know i these men that come along with you? 2.01. 89
if not the face of men, | the sufferance of our 2.01.114
swear priests and cowards, and men cautelous, 2.01.129
bad causes swear | such creatures as men doubt; 2.01.132
never follow any thing | that other men begin. 2.01.152
and in the spirit of men there is no blood; 2.01.168
lions with toils, and men with flatterers; 2.01.206
which busy care draws in the brains of men; 2.01.232
and what men to–night | have had resort to you; 2.01.275
a piece of work that will make sick men whole. 2.01.327
horses /did neigh, and dying men did groan, 2.02. 23
seems to me most strange that men should fear, 2.02. 35
and that great men shall press | for tinctures, 2.02. 88
there is but one mind in all these men, and it 2.03. 5 P
might fire the blood of ordinary men, | and turn 3.01. 37
'tis furnish'd well with men, | and men are 3.01. 66
and men are flesh and blood, and apprehensive; 3.01. 67
men, wives, and children stare, cry out, and run 3.01. 97
and drawing days out, that men stand upon. 3.01.100
the men that gave their country liberty. 3.01.118
a curse shall light upon the limbs of men; 3.01.262
shall smell above the earth | with carrion men, 3.01.275
take | the cruel issue of these bloody men, 3.01.294
the evil that men do lives after them, | the 3.02. 75
so are they all, all honorable men), | come i to 3.02. 83
beasts, | and men have lost their reason. 3.02.105
wrong, | who (you all know) are honorable men. 3.02.124
and you, | than i will wrong such honorable men. 3.02.127
you are not wood, you are not stones, but men; 3.02.142
and, being men, hearing the will of caesar, | it 3.02.143
i fear i wrong the honorable men | whose daggers 3.02.151
they were traitors; honorable men! 3.02.153
which, out of use and stal'd by other men, 4.01. 38
but hollow men, like horses hot at hand, | make 4.02. 23
part, | i shall be glad to learn of noble men. 4.03. 54
love, and be friends, as two such men should be, 4.03.131
even so great men great losses should endure. 4.03.193
there is a tide in the affairs of men | which, 4.03.218
call claudio and some other of my men, | i'll 4.03.242
since the affairs of men rests still incertain, 5.01. 95
why dost thou show to the apt thoughts of men 5.03. 68
rather have | such men my friends than enemies. 5.04. 29
with furbish'd arms and new supplies of men, MAC 1.02. 32
nor would we deign him burial of his men | till 1.02. 60
as a book, where men | may read strange matters. 1.05. 62
attend those men | our pleasure? 3.01. 44
we are men, my liege. 3.01. 90
ay, in the catalogue ye go for men, | as hounds 3.01. 91
and so of men. 3.01.100
so all men do, from hence to th' palace gate 3.03. 13
men must not walk too late. 3.06. 7
any heart alive | to hear the men deny't. 3.06. 16
why, the honest men. 4.02. 55 P
enow to beat the honest men and hang up them. 4.02. 58 P
sword, and like good men | bestride our downfall 4.03. 3
with ten thousand warlike men | already at a 4.03.134
lent us good siward, and ten thousand men; 4.03.190
of all men else i have avoided thee. 5.08. 4
so, oft it chances in particular men, | that for HAM 1.04. 23
the form of plausive manners — that these men, 1.04. 30
and sure i am two men there is not living | to 2.02. 20
rogue says here that old men have grey beards, 2.02.197 P
these are the only men. 2.02.402 P
for wise men know well enough what monsters you 3.01.138 P
some of nature's journeymen had made men, and 3.02. 34 P
and could of men distinguish her election, | sh' 3.02. 64
see | the imminent death of twenty thousand men, 4.04. 60
young men will do't, if they come to't, | by 4.05. 60
sea–faring men, sir. 4.06. 2 P
in him there, there the men are as mad as he. 5.01.155 P
that which ordinary men are fit for, i am LR 1.04. 34 P
in a year, | for wise men are grown foppish, 1.04.167
men so disorder'd, so debosh'd and bold, | that 1.04.242
depend, | to be such men as may besort your age, 1.04.251
my train are men of choice and rarest parts, 1.04.263
neck, monkeys by th' loins, and men by th' legs. 2.04. 9 P
their noses are led by their eyes but blind men, 2.04. 70 P
if you do love old men, if your sweet sway 2.04.190
and fifty men dismiss'd? 2.04.207
o sir, to willful men, | the injuries that they 2.04.302
a night pities neither wise men nor fools. 3.02. 13 P
a court'sy to our wrath, which men | may blame, 3.07. 26
go to, they are not men o' their words: 4.06.104 P
men must endure | their going hence even as 5.02. 9
know thou this, that men | are as the time is: 5.03. 30
o, /you are men of stones! 5.03.258
though in the trade of war i have slain men, OTH 1.02. 1
my life and being | from men of royal siege, and 1.02. 22
and men whose heads | /do /grow beneath their 1.03.144
men do their broken weapons rather use | than 1.03.174
that thinks men honest that but seem to be so, 1.03.400
you men of cyprus, let her have your knees. 2.01. 84
(as they say base men being in love have then a 2.01.215 P
but now | (as if some planet had unwitted men), 2.03.182
but men are men; 2.03.241
but men are men; 2.03.241
as men in rage strike those that wish them best, 2.03.243
that men should put an enemy in their mouths to 2.03.290 P
men should be what they seem, | or those that be 3.03.126
certain, men should be what they seem. 3.03.128
there are a kind of men, so loose of soul, 3.03.416
nay, we must think men are not gods, | nor of 3.04.148
i court moe women, you'll couch with moe men." 4.03. 57
o, these men, these men! 4.03. 60
o, these men, these men! 4.03. 60
desires for sport, and frailty, as men have? 4.03.101
kill men i' th' dark? 5.01. 63
yet she must die, else she'll betray more men. 5.02. 6
earth than she was wont, | and makes men mad. 5.02.111
that men must lay their murthers on your neck. 5.02.170
let heaven and men and devils, let them all, 5.02.221
/abstract of all faults | that all men follow. ANT 1.04. 10
of this earth, the arm | and burgonet of men. 1.05. 24
thou with caesar paragon again | my man of men. 1.05. 72
they shall assist | the deeds of justest men. 2.01. 2
that the men might go to wars with the women! 2.02. 65 P
no worse a husband than the best of men; 2.02.128
caesar? why, he's the jupiter of men. 3.02. 9
and that slain men | should solder up the rift. 3.04. 31
the trees by th' way | should have borne men, 3.06. 47
which might have well becom'd the best of men, 3.07. 26
so our leader's /led, | and we are women's men. 3.07. 70
lucky, men did ransom lives | of me for jests; 3.13.179
of better fortune, | he is twenty men to one. 4.02. 4
i wish i could be made so many men, | and all of 4.02. 16
o, my fortunes have | corrupted honest men! 4.05. 17
our hack'd targets like the men that owe them. 4.08. 31
when men revolted shall upon record | bear 4.09. 8
noblest of men, woo't die? 4.15. 59
young boys and girls | are level now with men; 4.15. 66
gods will give us | some faults to make us men. 5.01. 33
very many, men and women too. 5.02.250 P
which the gods give men | to excuse their after 5.02.286
what, are men mad? CYM 1.06. 32
but heavens know | some men are much to blame. 1.06. 77
he sits 'mongst men like a /descended god; 1.06.169
they are in a trunk, | attended by my men. 1.06.197
hairs above thee, | were they all made such men. 2.03.136
are men more order'd than when julius caesar 2.04. 21
is there no way for men to be, but women | must 2.05. 1
and men in dangerous bonds pray not alike; 3.02. 37
true honest men being heard, like false aeneas, 3.04. 58
wilt lay the leaven on all proper men; 3.04. 62
great men, | that had a court no bigger than 3.06. 81
that since the common men are now in action 3.07. 2
let me make men know | more valor in me than my 5.01. 29
is that we scarce are men and you are gods. 5.02. 10
pass was damm'd | with dead men hurt behind, and 5.03. 12
"our britain's harts die flying, not our men. 5.03. 24
i know you are more clement than vild men, | who 5.04. 18
then (as men report | thou orphans' father art) 5.04. 39
(in despite | of heaven and men) her purposes; 5.05. 59
he was too good to be | where ill men were, and 5.05.159
and the purchase is to make men glorious, | et bonum PER 1.ch. 9
made a law, | to keep her still and men in awe, 1.ch. 36
the king | of every virtue gives renown to men! 1.01. 14
and, as sick men do | who know the world, see 1.01. 47
a happy peace to you | and all good men, as 1.01. 51
for wisdom sees those men | blush not in actions 1.01.134
our men be vanquish'd ere they do resist, | and 1.02. 27
fits kings as they are men, for they may err. 1.02. 43
whose men and dames so jetted and adorn'd, 1.04. 26
let not our ships and number of our men | be 1.04. 86
and harborage for ourself, our ships, and men. 1.04.100
the curse of heaven and men succeed their evils! 1.04.104
be quiet then, as men should be, | till he hath 2.ch. 5
where when men been, there's seldom ease, | for 2.ch. 28
am thinking of the poor men that were cast away 2.01. 19 P
why, as men do a–land; 2.01. 28 P
sea | these fishers tell the infirmities of men, 2.01. 49
all that may men approve or men detect! 2.01. 51
all that may men approve or men detect! 2.01. 51
whom nature gat | for men to see, and seeing 2.02. 7
whereby i see that time's the king of men, 2.03. 45
since men take women's gifts for impudence. 2.03. 69
was by the rough seas reft of ships and men, 2.03. 84
of the seas | bereft of ships and men, cast on 2.03. 89
since they love men in arms as well as beds. 2.03. 98
the men of tyrus on the head | of helicanus 3.ch. 26
get fire and meat for these poor men. 3.02. 3
no cheap thing, if men were as they have been. 4.02. 61 P
if it please the gods to defend you by men, then 4.02. 90 P
to defend you by men, then men must comfort you, 4.02. 91 P
then men must comfort you, men must feed you, 4.02. 91 P
comfort you, men must feed you, men stir you up. 4.02. 91 P
as we are men | thus should we do, being TNK 1.01.231
commands men service, | and what they win in't, 1.02. 69
men of great quality, as may be judg'd | by 1.04. 14
yet they breathe | and have the name of men. 1.04. 28
then like men use 'em. 1.04. 28
they are fam'd to be a pair of absolute men. 2.01. 26 P
lord, the diff'rence of men! 2.01. 54 P
uses of this place | that all men hate so much? 2.02. 70
to keep us from corruption of worse men. 2.02. 72
us, envy of ill men | crave our acquaintance; 2.02. 90
that woo the wills of men to vanity | i see 2.02.101
we had died as they do, ill old men, unwept, 2.02.109
men are mad things. 2.02.126
and so fair, | let honest men ne'er love again. 2.02.231
and call to arms | the bold young men that, when 2.02.249
wrestled, | the best men call'd it excellent; 2.03. 76
do, maids will not so easily | trust men again. 2.06. 21
men lose when they incline to treachery, | and 3.01. 67
was a time | when young men went a–hunting, and 3.03. 40
almost all men, and yet i yielded, theseus — 3.06.207
do men proin | the straight young boughs that 3.06.242
these are men! 3.06.265
for me, a hair shall never fall of these men. 3.06.287
good ev'n, good men. 4.01.116
two such young handsome men | shall never fall 4.02. 3
and fights | of gods and such men near 'em. 4.02. 25
must these men die too? 4.02.112
lady, you shall see men fight now. 4.02.143
camp a cestron | brimm'd with the blood of men. 5.01. 47
and he is | doubtless the prim'st of men. 5.03. 70
are you men of wisdom or what are you? STM II.C 35 P
what you will have them, but not men of wisdom. II.C 37
could not have brought you to the state of men. II.C 67
and men like ravenous fishes | would feed on II.C 86
for men will kiss even by their own direction." VEN 216
rich preys make true men thieves; 724
how love makes young men thrall and old men dote 837
love makes young men thrall and old men dote, 837
persuade | the eyes of men without an orator; LUC 30
that meaner men should vaunt | that golden hap 41
since men prove beasts, let beasts bear gentle 1148
for men have marble, women waxen, minds, | and 1240
in men, as in a rough–grown grove, remain 1249
though men can cover crimes with bold stern 1252
one of my husband's men | bid thou be ready, by 1291
the very eyes of men through loop–holes thrust, 1383
inconstancy | more in women than in men remain.
PP 17.12
like a thousand vanquish'd men in bloody fight! 17.24
"had women been so strong as men, | in faith, 18.35
think women still to strive with men, | to sin 18.43
when i perceive that men as plants increase, SON 15. 5
can make you live yourself in eyes of men: 16.12
scorn'd, like old men of less truth than tongue, 17.10
so long as men can breathe or eyes can see, | so 18.13
allow | for beauty's pattern to succeeding men. 19.12
rhyme, | exceeded by the height of happier men. 32. 8
all men make faults, and even i in this, 35. 5
breath most breathes, even in the mouths of men. 81.14
all men are bad and in their badness reign. 121.14
to shun the heaven that leads men to this hell. 129.14
be anchor'd in the bay where all men ride, | why 137. 6
as testy sick men, when their deaths be near, 140. 7
so shalt thou feed on death, that feeds on men, 146.13
which yet men prove | against strange maladies a 153. 7
a bath and healthful remedy | for men diseas'd, 154.12
yet if men mov'd him, was he such a storm | as LC 101
"well could he ride, and often men would say, 106

MENAC'D 2 FR 0.0002 REL FR 2 V 0 P
this league | peep'd harms that menac'd him — H8 1.01.183
to whom by oath he menac'd | revenge upon the 1.02.137

MENACE 3 FR 0.0003 REL FR 3 V 0 P
your eyes do menace me. R3 1.04.170
and fearfully did menace me with death | if i ROM 5.03.133
who ever knew the heavens menace so? JC 1.03. 44

/MENACES 1 FR 0.0001 REL FR 0 V 1 P
/menaces /and /maledictions /against /king /and LR 1.02.146 P

MENACING 1 FR 0.0001 REL FR 1 V 0 P
palamon | has a most menacing aspect, his brow TNK 5.03. 45

MENAPHON 1 FR 0.0001 REL FR 1 V 0 P
duke menaphon, your most renowned uncle. ERR 5.01.369

MENAS 9 FR 0.0010 REL FR 8 V 1 P
i bring thee word | menecrates and menas, famous
ANT 1.04. 48
menas, i did not think | this amorous surfeiter 2.01. 32
i know not, menas, | how lesser enmities may 2.01. 42
come, menas. 2.01. 52
but give me your hand, menas; 2.06. 95 P
here's to thee, menas! 2.07. 86
there's a strong fellow, menas. 2.07. 88
menas, i'll not on shore. 2.07.130
since pompey's feast, as menas says, is troubled 3.02. 5

MEN–AT–ARMS 1 FR 0.0001 REL FR 1 V 0 P
have at you then, affection's men–at–arms. LLL 4.03.286

MEN–CHILDREN 1 FR 0.0001 REL FR 1 V 0 P
bring forth men–children only! MAC 1.07. 72

MEND 61 FR 0.0069 REL FR 40 V 21 P
go mend, go mend. MM 3.02. 27
go mend, go mend. 3.02. 27
thus i mend it: ERR 2.02.106 P
that's a fault that water will mend. 3.02.105 P
we'll mend our dinner here. 4.03. 59
serve god, love me, and mend. ADO 5.02. 93 P
where fair is not, praise cannot mend the brow. LLL 4.01. 17
most meanly and in husbering | mend him who can. 5.02.329
if you pardon, we will mend. MND 5.01.430
and we will mend thy wages. AYL 2.04. 94
mend the instance, shepherd. 3.02. 68 P
and in good earnest, and so god mend me, and by 4.01.189 P
god buy you, and god mend your voices! 5.03. 41 P
liberality, | i'll mend it with a largess. SHR 1.02.150
take that, and mend the plucking /off the other. 4.01.148
at an earthquake, 'twould mend the lottery well; AWW 1.03. 87 P
upon his boot and sing, mend the ruff and sing, 3.02. 7 P
bid the dishonest man mend himself: TN 1.05. 45 P
if he mend, he is no longer dishonest; 1.05. 46 P
if he cannot, let the botcher mend him. 1.05. 47 P
doth he not mend? 1.05. 74 P
this is an art | which does mend nature — WT 4.04. 96
marry, garlic, | to mend her kissing with! 4.04.163
i cannot mend it, i must needs confess, R2 2.03.153
that we cannot mend, | they break their faith to 3.02.100
nether–stocks, and mend them and foot them too.
1H4 2.04.117 P
"as true as i live," and "as god shall mend me," 3.01.249 P
well, god mend him! 2H4 1.02.109 P
that thou mightst mend him and make him fit to 3.02.165 P
tell you it will serve you to mend your shoes. H5 4.08. 69 P
god mend all! H8 1.02.201
you have now a broken banket, but we'll mend it. 1.04. 61
mend 'em for shame, my lords! 3.01.105
mend and charge home, | or, by the fires of COR 1.04. 38
you must return and mend it. 3.02. 26
here shall miss, our toil shall strive to mend. ROM pr 14
god shall mend my soul, | you'll make a mutiny 1.05. 79
lord, | you mend the jewel by the wearing it. TIM 1.01.172
here, i will mend thy feast. 4.03.282
first mend /my company, take away thyself. 4.03.283
so i shall mend mine own, by th' lack of thine. 4.03.284
neither wish i | you take much pains to mend. 5.01. 89
of health and living now begins to mend, | and 5.01.187
what is amiss, plague and infection mend! 5.01.221
yet if you be out, sir, i can mend you. JC 1.01. 17 P
mend me, thou saucy fellow? 1.01. 18
on any chance, | to mend it, or be rid on't. MAC 3.01.113
dull ass will not mend his pace with beating, HAM 5.01. 57 P
mend your speech a little, | lest you may mar LR 1.01. 94
mend when thou canst, be better at thy leisure, 2.04.229
since it is as it is, mend it for your own good. OTH 2.03.302 P
not to pick bad from bad, but by bad mend. 4.03.105
our worser thoughts heavens mend! ANT 1.02. 62 P
to mend the petty present, i will piece | her 1.05. 45
crown's /awry, | i'll mend it, and then play — 5.02.319
they are people such | that mend upon the world. CYM 2.04. 26
heaven mend all! 5.05. 68
to mend the hurt that his unkindness marr'd: VEN 478
nothing that the thought of hearts can mend; SON 69. 2
in others' works thou dost but mend the style, 78.11
were it not sinful then, striving to mend, | to 103. 9

MENDED 14 FR 0.0015 REL FR 8 V 6 P
well, that fault may be mended with a breakfast. TGV 3.01.325 P
mended again. the matter; proceed. MM 5.01. 91
offended, | think but this, and all is mended, MND 5.01.424

be patient, to–morrow't shall be mended, | and SHR 4.01.176
very well mended. kiss him for that, good widow. 5.02. 25
why, would that have mended my hair? TN 1.03. 97 P
any thing that's mended is but patch'd; 1.05. 47 P
show now your mended faiths, | and instantly JN 5.07. 75
of his oath–breaking, which he mended thus, | by 1H4 5.02. 37
will this gear ne'er be mended? TRO 1.01. 6 P
'tis not well mended so, it is but botch'd; TIM 4.03.285
but upon my mended judgment (if i offend /not to
CYM 1.04. 46 P
(if i offend /not to say it is mended) my 1.04. 47 P
whether we are mended, or whe'er better they, SON 59.11
MENDER 1 FR 0.0001 REL FR 0 V 1 P
which is indeed, sir, a mender of bad soles. JC 1.01. 14 P
MENDING 2 FR 0.0002 REL FR 1 V 1 P
their detractions and can put them to mending. ADO 2.03.230 P
this is like the mending of highways | in summer MV 5.01.263
MENDS 2 FR 0.0002 REL FR 1 V 1 P
she be not, she has the mends in her own hands. TRO 1.01. 68 P
still he mends. ANT 1.03. 82
MENECRATES 1 FR 0.0001 REL FR 1 V 0 P
i bring thee word | menecrates and menas, famous
ANT 1.04. 48
/MENELAUS' 1 FR 0.0001 REL FR 1 V 0 P
/the /ravish'd /helen, /menelaus' /queen, TRO pr 9
MENELAUS' 3 FR 0.0003 REL FR 3 V 0 P
paris is gor'd with menelaus' horn. TRO 1.01.112
the first was menelaus' kiss, this, mine; 4.05. 32
at menelaus' tent, most princely troilus. 4.05.279
MENELAUS 8 FR 0.0009 REL FR 6 V 2 P
thou, | although thy husband may be menelaus; 3H6 2.02.147
troilus, by menelaus. TRO 1.01.110
what trumpet? look, menelaus. 1.03.213
deserves fair helen best, | myself, or menelaus? 4.01. 55
the noble menelaus. 4.05.176
but to be menelaus, i would conspire against 5.01. 63 P
be the louse of a lazar, so i were not menelaus. 5.01. 66 P
good night, sweet lord menelaus. 5.01. 74
MENENIUS 15 FR 0.0017 REL FR 7 V 8 P
worthy menenius agrippa, one that hath always COR 1.01. 51 P
menenius, you are known well enough too. 2.01. 46 P
honorable menenius, my boy martius approaches. 2.01.100 P
ay, worthy menenius, and with most prosperous 2.01.103 P
menenius, he comes the third time home with the 2.01.124 P
menenius, ever, ever. 2.01.192
noble menenius, | be you then as the people's 3.01.327
with old menenius and those senators | that 3.03. 7
thou old and true menenius, | thy tears are 4.01. 21
we stood to't in good time. is this menenius? 4.06. 10
it is menenius. 5.02. 11
remember my name is menenius, always factionary 5.02. 29 P
thee no worse than thy old father menenius does! 5.02. 70 P
another word, menenius, | i will not hear thee 5.02. 91
now, sir, is your name menenius? 5.02. 95 P
MENON 1 FR 0.0001 REL FR 1 V 0 P
the fierce polydamas | hath beat down menon; TRO 5.05. 7
/MEN'S 1 FR 0.0001 REL FR 1 V 0 P
half all /men's hearts are his. CYM 1.06.168
MEN'S 96 FR 0.0108 REL FR 78 V 18 P
which served me as fit, by all men's judgments, TGV 4.04.162
have an eye to make difference of men's liking: WIV 2.01. 57 P
us not be laughing–stocks to other men's humors. 3.01. 86 P
that come like women in men's apparel, and smell 3.03. 72 P
guts should hale souls out of men's bodies? ADO 2.03. 60 P
commodity, being taken up of these men's bills. 3.03.178 P
no, 'tis all men's office to speak patience | to 5.01. 27
— of other men's secrets, i beseech you. LLL 1.01.230 P
or for men's sake, the /authors of these women, 4.03.356
for virtue's office never breaks men's troth. 5.02.350
the nine men's morris is fill'd up with mud, MND 2.01. 98
and poor men's cottages princes' palaces. MV 1.02. 14 P
and sat at good men's feasts, and wip'd our eyes AYL 2.07.122
no man's happiness, glad of other men's good, 3.02. 75 P
you have sold your own lands to see other men's; 4.01. 23 P
had eaten ballads and all men's ears grew to his WT 4.04.185 P
a meddler, | that doth utter all men's ware–a. 4.04.323
of that i doubt, as all men's children may. JN 1.01. 63
for new–made honor doth forget men's names; 1.01.187
keep men's eyes | and strain their cheeks to 3.03. 45
men's mouths are full of it. 4.02.161
more are men's ends mark'd than their lives R2 2.01. 11
sign, | save men's opinions and my living blood, 3.01. 26
the field of golgotha and dead men's skulls. 4.01.144
men's eyes | did scowl on gentle richard. 5.02. 27
so is it in the music of men's lives. 5.05. 44
i am, | by so much shall i falsify men's hopes, 1H4 1.02.211
loseth men's hearts and leaves behind a stain 3.01.185
that i did pluck allegiance from men's hearts, 3.02. 52
that, being daily swallowed by men's eyes, 3.02. 70
there is a history in all men's lives, 2H4 3.01. 80
coherence of his men's spirits and his. 5.01. 65 P
and the mute wonder lurketh in men's ears | to H5 1.01. 49
oaths are straws, men's faiths are wafer–cakes, 2.03. 51
the dead men's blood, the privy maidens' groans, 2.04.107
have me as familiar with men's pockets as their 3.02. 47 P
be ransom'd, and a many poor men's lives sav'd. 4.01.122 P
you speak this to feel other men's minds. 4.01.126 P
just death, kind umpire of men's miseries, 1H6 2.05. 29
men's flesh preserv'd so whole do seldom win. 2H6 3.01.301
and flagging wings | cleep dead men's graves, 4.01. 6
long sitting to determine poor men's causes 4.07. 88
and dead men's cries do fill the empty air, 5.02. 4
smile in men's faces, smooth, deceive, and cog, R3 1.03. 48
some lay in dead men's skulls, and, in the holes 1.04. 29
i hate it, and desire all good men's love. 2.01. 62
by a divine instinct men's minds mistrust 2.03. 42
all men's honors | lie like one lump before him, H8 2.02. 47
all men's! 3.02. 45
men's evil manners live in brass, their virtues 4.02. 45
men's prayers then would seek you, not their 5.02.118
man, | or that we women had men's privilege | of TRO 3.02.128
save these men's looks, who do methinks find out 3.03. 90
i do remit these young men's heinous faults. TIT 1.01.484
make poor men's cattle break their necks, | set 5.01.132
atomi | over men's noses as they lie asleep. ROM 1.04. 58
manners shall lie all in one or two men's hands, 1.05. 4 P
young men's love then lies | not truly in their 2.03. 67
yet his leg excels all men's, and for a hand and 2.05. 41 P
men's eyes were made to look, and let them gaze; 3.01. 54
quite with dead men's rattling bones, | with 4.01. 82
there is thy gold, worse poison to men's souls, 5.01. 80
upon them, fit to open | these dead men's tombs. 5.03.201
o, that men's ears should be | to counsel deaf, TIM 1.02.249
men and men's fortunes could i frankly use | as 2.02.179
pluck stout men's pillows from below their heads 4.03. 33
through the window/–bars bore at men's eyes, 4.03.117
their sharp shins, | and mar men's spurring. 4.03.153
graves only be men's works, and death their gain 5.01.222
and buy men's voices to commend our deeds. JC 2.01.146
nor the power of speech | to stir men's blood; 3.02.223
where we are, | there's daggers in men's smiles; MAC 2.03.140
and good men's lives | expire before the flowers 4.03.171
all the earth o'erwhelm them, to men's eyes. HAM 1.02.257
cull–cold maids do dead men's fingers call them. 4.07.171
perform'd | even while men's minds are wild, 5.02.394
air | hang fated o'er men's faults light on thy LR 3.04. 68
who make them honors | of men's impossibilities, 4.06. 74
men's natures wrangle with inferior things, OTH 3.04.144
and men's reports | give him much wrong'd. ANT 1.04. 39
all men's faces are true, whatsome'er their 2.06. 97 P
it is to have a name in great men's fellowship. 2.07. 12 P
i see men's judgments are | a parcel of their 3.13. 31
(whose remembrance yet | lives in men's eyes, CYM 3.01. 3
men's vows are women's traitors. 3.04. 54
gives heaven countless eyes to view men's acts, PER 1.01. 73
we expire, | and not without men's pity; TNK 5.04. 5
with cold terror doth men's minds confound. VEN 1048
for marks descried in men's nativity | are LUC 538
men's faults do seldom to themselves appear, 633
that they are so fulfill'd | with men's abuses: 1259
which steals men's eyes and women's souls SON 20. 8
when in disgrace with fortune and men's eyes, 29. 1
when you entombed in men's eyes shall lie; 81. 8
and having thee, of all men's pride i boast: 91.12
denote | love's eye is not so true as all men's: 148. 8
M'ENSEIGNEZ 1 FR 0.0001 REL FR 0 V 1 P
je te prie, m'enseignez; H5 3.04. 4 P
MENTAL 3 FR 0.0003 REL FR 3 V 0 P
the still and mental parts, | that do contrive TRO 1.03.200
that 'twixt his mental and his active parts 2.03.174
what a mental power | this eye shoots forth! TIM 1.01. 31
MENTEITH 1 FR 0.0001 REL FR 1 V 0 P
earl of athol, | of murray, angus, and menteith. 1H4 1.01. 73
MENTION 3 FR 0.0003 REL FR 3 V 0 P
and sleep in dull cold marble where no mention H8 3.02.433
and, dying, mention it within their wills, JC 3.02.135
and honor in you, | no mention of this woman. TNK 3.03. 15
MENTIONED 2 FR 0.0002 REL FR 2 V 0 P
i mentioned a son o' th' king's, which florizel WT 4.01. 22
and hid the gold within that letter mentioned, TIT 5.01.107
MENTIS 1 FR 0.0001 REL FR 0 V 1 P
tanta est erga te mentis integritas, regina H8 3.01. 40 P
MENTON 2 FR 0.0002 REL FR 0 V 2 P
de nick. et le menton? H5 3.04. 34 P
de sin. le col, de nick; le menton, de sin. 3.04. 36 P
MEPHOSTOPHILUS 1 FR 0.0001 REL FR 1 V 0 P
how now, mephostophilus? WIV 1.01.130
MERCADE *(see marcade)*
MERCANTANT 1 FR 0.0001 REL FR 1 V 0 P
master, a mercantant, or a pedant, | i know not SHR 4.02. 63
MERCATIO 1 FR 0.0001 REL FR 1 V 0 P
what think'st thou of the rich mercatio? TGV 1.02. 12
MERCENARIES 1 FR 0.0001 REL FR 1 V 0 P
there are but sixteen hundred mercenaries; H5 4.08. 88
MERCENARY 3 FR 0.0003 REL FR 3 V 0 P
my mind was never yet more mercenary. MV 4.01.418
lie drown'd and soak'd in mercenary blood; H5 4.07. 76
his countenance as if | i had been mercenary. COR 5.06. 40
MERCER 1 FR 0.0001 REL FR 0 V 1 P
at the suit of master three–pile the mercer, for MM 4.03. 10 P
MERCHANDISE 7 FR 0.0008 REL FR 5 V 2 P
as from a voyage, rich with merchandise. MND 2.01.134
antonio | is sad to think upon his merchandise. MV 1.01. 40
therefore my merchandise makes me not sad. 1.01. 45
of venice, i can make what merchandise i will. 3.01.128 P
by his father sent about merchandise do sinfully H5 4.01.148 P
sea, | i should adventure for such merchandise. ROM 2.02. 84
the merchandise which thou hast brought from ANT 2.05.104
MERCHANDIZ'D 1 FR 0.0001 REL FR 1 V 0 P
that love is merchandiz'd whose rich esteeming SON 102. 3
MERCHANT 24 FR 0.0027 REL FR 21 V 3 P
the masters of some merchant, and the merchant TMP 2.01. 5
and the merchant | have just our theme of woe; 2.01. 5
merchant of syracusa, plead no more. ERR 1.01. 3
therefore, merchant, i'll limit thee this day 1.01.150
this very day a syracusian merchant | is 1.02. 3
perhaps some merchant hath invited him, | and 2.01. 4
to see a reverent syracusian merchant, | who put 5.01.124
how doth that royal merchant, good antonio? MV 3.02.239
his back, | enow to press a royal merchant down, 4.01. 29
between the jew and antonio the merchant. 4.01.156 P
which is the merchant here? 4.01.174
needs give sentence 'gainst the merchant there. 4.01.205
you, merchant, have you any thing to say? 4.01.263
a merchant of great traffic through the world, SHR 1.01. 12
a merchant of incomparable wealth. 4.02. 98
this is a riddling merchant for the nonce: 1H6 2.03. 57
ourself the merchant, and this sailing pandar TRO 1.01.103
we turn not back the silks upon the merchant, 2.02. 69
sir, what saucy merchant was this, that was so ROM 2.04.145 P
i know the merchant. TIM 1.01. 7
art not thou a merchant? 1.01.235 P
and believe | caesar's no merchant, to make ANT 5.02.183
the merchant fears, ere rich at home he lands." LUC 336
lo here the hopeless merchant of this loss, 1660
MERCHANT–LIKE 1 FR 0.0001 REL FR 1 V 0 P
therefore, when merchant–like i sell revenge, 2H6 4.01. 41
MERCHANT–MARRING
1 FR 0.0001 REL FR 1 V 0 P
the dreadful touch | of merchant–marring rocks? MV 3.02.271
MERCHANT'S 5 FR 0.0005 REL FR 4 V 1 P
which is a pound of this poor merchant's flesh, MV 4.01. 23
by him cut off | nearest the merchant's heart. 4.01.233
a pound of that same merchant's flesh is thine, 4.01.299
faith, gentlemen, now i play a merchant's part, SHR 2.01.326
there's a whole merchant's venture of burdeaux 2H4 2.04. 63 P
MERCHANTS' 1 FR 0.0001 REL FR 1 V 0 P
attach'd | our merchants' goods at burdeaux. H8 1.01. 96
MERCHANTS 9 FR 0.0010 REL FR 8 V 1 P
rancorous outrage of your duke | to merchants, ERR 1.01. 7
i am invited, sir, to certain merchants, | of 1.02. 24
even there where merchants most do congregate, MV 1.03. 49
how now, shylock, what news among the merchants? 3.01. 22 P
twenty merchants, | the duke himself, and the 3.02.279
others, like merchants, venter trade abroad; H5 1.02.192
let us, like merchants, first show foul wares, TRO 1.03.358
ships, | and turn'd crown'd kings to merchants. 2.02. 83
prize with you | of things that merchants sold. ANT 5.02.184
MERCIES 3 FR 0.0003 REL FR 2 V 1 P
foolish boldness brought thee to their mercies TN 5.01. 70
be, and here i commit my body to your mercies. 2H4 ep 14 P
although the king have mercies | more than i H8 2.01. 70
MERCIFUL 20 FR 0.0022 REL FR 17 V 3 P
though the seas threaten, they are merciful, | i TMP 5.01.178
merciful heaven, | thou rather with thy sharp MM 2.02.114
to me, your honor is accounted a merciful man. 3.02.192 P
you have been always call'd a merciful man, ADO 3.03. 61 P
then must the jew be merciful. MV 4.01.182
be merciful, | take thrice thy money, bid me 4.01.233
you are a merciful general. AWW 4.03.126 P
though a present death | had been more merciful. WT 2.03.185
o, let us yet be merciful. H5 2.02. 47
be merciful, great duke, to men of mould. 3.02. 22
the king is merciful, if you revolt. 2H6 4.02.125
lordship judge and juror, | you are so merciful. H8 5.02. 96
in | the merciful construction of good women, ep 10
draw near them then in being merciful: TIT 1.01.118
be merciful, say "death"; ROM 3.03. 12
if thou be merciful, | open the tomb, lay me 5.03. 72
merciful powers, | restrain in me the cursed MAC 2.01. 7
merciful heaven! 4.03.207
i that am cruel am yet merciful, | i would not OTH 5.02. 87
it shall be merciful, and too severe, | and most VEN 1155
MERCIFULLY 1 FR 0.0001 REL FR 0 V 1 P
but, good kate, mock me mercifully, the rather, H5 5.02.202 P
MERCILESS 8 FR 0.0009 REL FR 8 V 0 P
not now | worthily term'd them merciless to us! ERR 1.01. 99
siege | and merciless proceeding by these french JN 2.01.214
of hinds and peasants, rude and merciless. 2H6 4.04. 33
the foe is merciless, and will not pity; 3H6 2.06. 25
and the most merciless, that e'er was heard of! R3 1.03.183
the merciless macdonwald | (worthy to be a rebel MAC 1.02. 9
so did the merciless and pitchy night | fold in VEN 821
that mother tries a merciless conclusion | who, LUC 1160
MERCURIAL 1 FR 0.0001 REL FR 1 V 0 P
his foot mercurial, his martial thigh, | the CYM 4.02.310
MERCURIES 1 FR 0.0001 REL FR 1 V 0 P
with winged heels, as english mercuries. H5 2.pr. 7
MERCURY 14 FR 0.0015 REL FR 10 V 4 P
the words of mercury are harsh after the songs LLL 5.02.930 P
now mercury indue thee with leasing, for thou TN 1.05. 97 P
as i am, litter'd under mercury, was likewise a WT 4.03. 25 P
be mercury, set feathers to thy heels, | and fly JN 4.02.174
rise from the ground like feathered mercury, 1H4 4.01.106
died, | and that a winged mercury did bear; R3 2.01. 89
wing, | jove's mercury, and herald for a king! 4.03. 55
heels | and fly like chidden mercury from jove, TRO 2.02. 45
and, mercury, lose all the serpentine craft of 2.03. 11 P
apollo, pallas, jove, or mercury, | inspire me, TIT 4.01. 66
"to mercury"; 4.03. 56
see, here's to jove, and this to mercury, | this 4.04. 14
a station like the herald mercury | new lighted HAM 3.04. 58
the strong–wing'd mercury should fetch thee up, ANT 4.15. 35
MERCUTIO 15 FR 0.0017 REL FR 12 V 3 P
mercutio and his brother valentine; ROM 1.02. 67 P
peace, peace, mercutio, peace! 1.04. 95
call, good mercutio. 2.01. 6
pardon, good mercutio, my business was great, 2.04. 49 P
i pray thee, good mercutio, let's retire. 3.01. 1
mercutio, thou consortest with romeo — 3.01. 45 P
gentle mercutio, put thy rapier up. 3.01. 84
tybalt, mercutio, the prince expressly hath 3.01. 88
good mercutio! 3.01. 90
o romeo, romeo, brave mercutio is dead! 3.01.116
he /gone in triumph, and mercutio slain! 3.01.122
which way ran he that kill'd mercutio? 3.01.137
romeo, | that slew thy kinsman, brave mercutio. 3.01.145
from tybalt hit the life | of stout mercutio, 3.01.169
romeo slew him, he slew mercutio; 3.01.182
MERCUTIO'S 4 FR 0.0004 REL FR 4 V 0 P
for mercutio's soul | is but a little way above ROM 3.01.126
with piercing steel at bold mercutio's breast, 3.01.159
not romeo, prince, he was mercutio's friend; 3.01.184
mercutio's kinsman, noble county paris! 5.03. 75
/MERCY 1 FR 0.0001 REL FR 0 V 1 P
/cry /you /mercy, /i /took /you /for /a LR 3.06. 52 P
MERCY 193 FR 0.0218 REL FR 161 V 32 P
"mercy on us!" TMP 1.01. 60
alack, for mercy! 1.02.437
mercy, mercy! 2.02. 97 P
mercy, mercy! 2.02. 97 P
by this hand, i'll turn my mercy out o' doors, 3.02. 70 P
mercy upon us! 3.02.131 P
this hour | lies at my mercy all mine enemies. 4.01.263
that it assaults | mercy itself, and frees all ep 18
o, cry you mercy, sir, i have mistook; TGV 5.04. 94
to shallow —" | mercy on me! WIV 3.01. 22 P
/god plesse you from his mercy sake, all of you! 3.01. 42 P
i cry you mercy! 3.05. 26 P
mortality and mercy in vienna | live in thy MM 1.01. 44
mercy is not itself, that oft looks so; 2.01.283
and neither heaven nor man grieve at the mercy. 2.02. 50
with one half so good a grace | as mercy does. 2.02. 63
and mercy then will breathe within your lips, 2.02. 78
lawful mercy | is nothing kin to foul redemption 2.04.112
there is a devilish mercy in the judge, | if 3.01. 64
mercy to thee would prove itself a bawd, | 'tis 3.01.149
the service, and that instructed him to mercy. 3.02.120 P
this would make mercy swear and play the tyrant. 3.02.194 P
i cry you mercy, sir, and well could wish | you 4.01. 10
when vice makes mercy, mercy's so extended, 4.02.112
the very mercy of the law cries out | most 5.01.407
should she kneel down in mercy of this fact, 5.01.434
that i crave death more willingly than mercy: 5.01.476

and pray thee take this mercy to provide | for 5.01.484
god, for thy mercy! they are loose again. ERR 4.04.144
o, i cry you mercy, friend, go you with me, and ADO 1.02. 25 P
i cry you mercy, uncle. by your grace's pardon. 2.01.339 P
doth warrant, | let all my sins lack mercy! 4.01.180
now mercy goes to kill, | and shooting well is LLL 4.01. 24
write "lord have mercy on us" on those three: 5.02.419
execute | that lie within the mercy of your wit. 5.02.846
and leave thee to the mercy of wild beasts. MND 2.01.228
i cry your worships mercy, heartily. 3.01.179 P
jailer, look to him, tell not me of mercy. MV 3.03. 1
me flatly there's no mercy for me in heaven 3.05. 32 P
pity, void and empty | from any dram of mercy. 4.01. 6
thou'lt show thy mercy and remorse more strange 4.01. 20
how shalt thou hope for mercy, rend'ring none? 4.01. 88
the quality of mercy is not strain'd, | it 4.01.184
but mercy is above this sceptred sway, | it is 4.01.193
show likest god's | when mercy seasons justice. 4.01.197
we do pray for mercy, | and that same prayer 4.01.200
teach us all to render | the deeds of mercy. 4.01.202
and the offender's life lies in the mercy | of 4.01.355
down therefore, and beg mercy of the duke. 4.01.363
what mercy can you render him, antonio? 4.01.378
cupid have mercy, not a word? AYL 1.03. 2 P
but were i not the better part made mercy, | i 3.01. 2
cry the man mercy, love him, take his offer; 3.05. 61
o mercy, god! SHR 4.03. 87
god's mercy, maiden! AWW 1.03.149
would you had kneel'd, my lord, to ask me mercy, 2.01. 64
broke thy pate, | and ask'd thee mercy for't. 2.01. 67
which if — lord have mercy on thee for a hen! 2.03.212 P
out of breath, prompt us to have mercy on him; TN 3.04.139 P
well, and god have mercy upon one of our souls! 3.04.167 P
he may have mercy upon mine, but my hope is 3.04.167 P
that mercy does, for calumny will sear | virtue WT 2.01. 73
that there thou leave it | (without more mercy) 2.03.178
whom i proclaim a man of truth, of mercy; 3.02.157
mercy on 's, a barne? 3.03. 69 P
name of mercy, when was this, boy? 3.03.103 P
mercy on me! JN 4.01. 12
his innocent prate | he will awake my mercy, 4.01. 26
that mercy which fierce fire and iron extends, 4.01.119
the infinite and boundless reach | of mercy, if 4.03.118
god for his mercy, what a tide of woes | comes R2 2.02. 98
stoop | unto the sovereign mercy of the king; 2.03.157
god for his mercy! 5.02. 75
that mercy which true prayer ought to have. 5.03.110
my soul | want mercy if i do not join with him. 1H4 1.03.132
i cry you mercy. 1.03.212
with as quick dexterity, and roar'd for mercy, 2.04.260 P
my good lord of westmerland, i cry you mercy! 4.02. 52 P
there is no seeming mercy in the king. 5.02. 34
this offer comes from mercy, not from fear. 2H4 4.01.148
and trembling, and do observance to my mercy. 4.03. 15 P
that's mercy, but too much security. H5 2.02. 44
sir, | you show great mercy if you give him life 2.02. 50
and do submit me to your highness' mercy. 2.02. 77
the mercy that was quick in us but late, | by 2.02. 79
you must not dare, for shame, to talk of mercy, 2.02. 81
god quit you in his mercy! 2.02.166
the taste whereof god of his mercy give | you 2.02.179
and to take mercy | on the poor souls for whom 2.04.103
therefore to our best mercy give yourselves, 3.03. 3
the gates of mercy shall be all shut up, | and 3.03. 10
we yield our town and lives to thy soft mercy. 3.03. 48
use mercy to them all for us, dear uncle. 3.03. 54
besides, in mercy, | the constable desires thee 4.03. 83
as i suck blood, i will some mercy show. 4.04. 64
them that we shall take | shall taste our mercy. 4.07. 65
o lord, have mercy on us, wretched sinners! 1H6 1.04. 70
o lord, have mercy on me, woeful man! 1.04. 71
alive, | if salisbury wants mercy at thy hands! 1.04. 86
then god take mercy on brave talbot's soul, 4.03. 34
i cry you mercy, 'tis but quid for quo. 5.03.109
law, | and left thee to the mercy of the law. 2H6 1.03.134
i cry you mercy, madam; 1.03.139
but god in mercy so deal with my soul | as i in 1.03.157
o lord, have mercy upon me! 1.03.215 P
and yield to mercy whilst 'tis offered you, | or 4.08. 12
than you should stoop unto a frenchman's mercy. 4.08. 48
and kneel for grace and mercy at my feet: 3H6 1.01. 75
yield to our mercy, proud plantagenet. 1.04. 30
ay, to such mercy as his ruthless arm | with 1.04. 31
open thy gate of mercy, gracious god! 1.04.177
revoke that doom of mercy, for 'tis clifford, 2.06. 46
clifford, ask mercy and obtain no grace. 2.06. 69
my mercy dried their water–flowing tears; 4.08. 43
call edward king and at his hands beg mercy? 5.01. 23
there's no hop'd–for mercy with the brothers 5.04. 35
which done, god take king edward to his mercy, R3 1.01.151
i cry thee mercy then; 1.03.234
madam, my mother, i do cry you mercy, | i did 2.02.104
i cry thee mercy; 4.04.513
have mercy, jesu! 5.03.178
cry mercy, lords and watchful gentlemen, | that 5.03.224
if he may | find mercy in the law, 'tis his; H8 1.02.212
that might have mercy on the fault thou gav'st 3.02.262
to the mercy | of a rude stream that must for 3.02.363
good master secretary, | i cry your honor mercy; 5.02.113
is there no other way of mercy | but i must 5.02.127
mercy o' me, what a multitude are here! 5.03. 67
juno have mercy! how came it cloven? TRO 1.02.120 P
if e'er thou stand at mercy of my sword, | name 4.04.114
brother, you have a vice of mercy in you, 5.03. 37
i say, at once, let your brief plagues be mercy, 5.10. 8
a treaty find | i' th' part that is at mercy? COR 1.10. 7
buy | their mercy at the price of one fair word, 3.03. 91
all undone, unless | the noble man have mercy. 4.06.108
fall down, and knee | the way into his mercy. 5.01. 6
mean to solicit him | for mercy to his country. 5.01. 73
volsces | may say, "this mercy we have show'd"; 5.03.137
i am glad thou hast set thy mercy and thy honor 5.03.200
yes, mercy, if you report him truly. 5.04. 25 P
mark what mercy his mother shall bring from him. 5.04. 27 P
there is no more mercy in him than there is milk 5.04. 28 P
sweet mercy is nobility's true badge. TIT 1.01.119
and at thy mercy shall they stoop and kneel, 5.02.118
mercy but murders, pardoning those that kill. ROM 3.01.197
this is dear mercy, and thou seest it not. 3.03. 28
'tis torture, and not mercy. 3.03. 29
o, i cry you mercy, you are the singer; 4.05.139 P
say | a madman's mercy bid thee run away. 5.03. 67
nothing emboldens sin so much as mercy. TIM 3.05. 3
but in defense, by mercy, 'tis most just. 3.05. 55
dimpled smiles from fools exhaust their mercy; 4.03.120
which steals itself, when there's no mercy left. MAC 2.03.146
bounty, perseverance, mercy, lowliness, 4.03. 93
here, as before, never, so help you mercy, | how HAM 1.05.169
so grace and mercy at your most need help you. 1.05.180
whereto serves mercy | but to confront the 3.03. 46
we cast away moan, | god 'a' mercy on his soul!" 4.05.199
they have dealt with me like thieves of mercy, 4.06. 21 P
their pow'rs, | and hold our lives in mercy. LR 1.04.327
should have thus little mercy on their flesh? 3.04. 73
o, cry you mercy, sir. 3.04.171
as for the mercy | which he intends to lear and 5.01. 65
i cry you mercy then. OTH 4.02. 88
i cry you mercy. here's cassio hurt by villains. 5.01. 69
then heaven | have mercy on me! 5.02. 34
/then /lord have mercy on me! 5.02. 57
and have you mercy too! 5.02. 58
cringe his face, | and whine aloud for mercy. ANT 3.13.101
thou a man, | thou wouldst have mercy on me. 5.02.175
it, 'twere a paper lost | as offer'd mercy is. CYM 1.03. 4
gods are more full of mercy. 5.04. 13
this mercy shows we'll joy in such a son; PER 1.01.118
some god hath put his mercy in your manhood, TNK 1.01. 72
must | with him stand to the mercy of our fate, 1.02.102
and great apollo's mercy, all our best | their 1.04. 46
'tis a benefit, | a mercy i must thank 'em for; 2.03. 2
we seek not | thy breath of mercy, theseus. 3.06.158
o theseus, | if unto neither thou show mercy. 3.06.173
for i gave him | more mercy than you found, sir, 3.06.182
shall grow to th' ground but i'll get mercy. 3.06.192
which cannot want due mercy, i beg first. 3.06.209
for mercy. 3.06.211
mercy. 3.06.211
mercy on these princes. 3.06.211
mercy and manly courage | are bedfellows in his 5.03. 43
o all you heavenly powers, where is /your mercy? 5.03.139
what say you to the mercy of the king? STM II.C 17
we accept of the king's mercy, but we will show II.C 19 P
but we will show no mercy upon the strangers. II.C 19 P
doubt, but mercy may be found if you so seek it. II.C 147
thing, | lies at the mercy of his mortal sting. LUC 364
state, | straight in her heart did mercy come, SON 145. 5

MERCY–LACKING 1 FR 0.0001 REL FR 1 V 0 P
creatures of note for mercy–lacking uses. JN 4.01.120

MERCY'S 1 FR 0.0001 REL FR 1 V 0 P
when vice makes mercy, mercy's so extended, MM 4.02.112

/MERE 1 FR 0.0001 REL FR 1 V 0 P
your pleasure was my /mere offense, my CYM 5.05.334

MERE 62 FR 0.0070 REL FR 52 V 10 P
out, alas, sir, cozenage! mere cozenage. WIV 4.05. 63 P
/sire, | the mere effusion of thy proper loins, MM 3.01. 30
upon his mere request, | being come to knowledge 5.01.152
a mere anatomy, a mountebank, | a threadbare ERR 5.01.239
decree, | she must lie here on mere necessity. LLL 1.01.148
i am forsworn "on mere necessity." 1.01.154
he speaks the mere contrary, crosses love not 1.02. 33 P
friend, | engag'd my friend to his mere enemy, MV 3.02.262
up | is but a quintain, a mere lifeless block. AYL 1.02.251
swearing that we | are mere usurpers, tyrants, 2.01. 61
is second childishness and mere oblivion, | sans 2.07.165
friendship is feigning, most loving mere folly. 2.07.181
judgments are | mere fathers of their garments; AWW 1.02. 62
the mere word's a slave | debosh'd on every tomb 2.03.137
ay, surely, mere the truth, i know his lady. 3.05. 55
my determinate voyage is mere extravagancy. TN 2.01. 12 P
to bear the matter thus — mere weakness. WT 2.03. 2
this is mere falsehood. 3.02.141
son, with mere conceit and fear | of the queen's 3.02.144
and mere dislike | of our proceedings kept the 1H4 4.01. 64
i'll none of it, honor is a mere scutcheon. 5.01.140 P
but this is mere digression from my purpose. 2H4 4.01.138
and learning a mere hoard of gold kept by a 4.03.115 P
'tis a mere french word; 1H6 4.07. 54
consent, | of mere compassion and of lenity, 5.04.125
and mere instinct of love and loyalty, | free 2H6 3.02.250
your mere enforcement shall acquittance me R3 3.07.233
madam, this is a mere distraction, | you turn H8 3.01.112
that, out of mere ambition, you have caus'd 3.02.324
to the mere undoing | of all the kingdom. 3.02.329
stifled | with the mere rankness of their joy. 4.01. 59
each thing /meets | in mere oppugnancy: TRO 1.03.111
and may that soldier a mere recreant prove, 1.03.287
i with great truth catch mere simplicity; 4.04.104
words, mere words, no matter from the heart; 5.03.108
but in mere spite, | to be full quit of those my COR 4.05. 82
a mere saciety of commendations; TIM 1.01.166
elements expos'd, | answer mere nature; 4.03.231
nought | but even the mere necessities upon't. 4.03.376
the mere want of gold, and the falling–from of 4.03.400 P
when thy first griefs were but a mere conceit, 5.04. 14
it was mere foolery, i did not mark it. JC 1.02.236 P
and the mere lees | is left this vault to brag MAC 2.03. 95
foisons to fill up your will | of your mere own. 4.03. 89
the mere despair of surgery, he cures, | hanging 4.03.152
show, | but mere /implorators of unholy suits, HAM 1.03.129
the which we are pictures, or mere beasts; 4.05. 86
this is mere madness, | and /thus a while the 5.01.284
mere fetches, | the images of revolt and flying LR 2.04. 89
and our mere defects | prove our commodities. 4.01. 20
mere prattle, without practice, | is all his OTH 1.01. 26
true, | but i, for mere suspicion in that kind, 1.03.389
in putting on the mere form of civil and humane 2.01.239 P
importing the mere perdition of the turkish 2.02. 3 P
held to fools does make | our faith mere folly; ANT 3.13. 43
nay, to thy mere confusion, thou shalt know | i CYM 4.02. 92
a good opinion, and that opinion a mere profit. PER 4.02.121 P
and | such things to be, mere monsters. TNK 1.02. 42
i see two comforts rising, two mere blessings, 2.02. 58
is but his foil, to him, a mere dull shadow; 4.02. 26
thou art a changeling to him, a mere gipsy, 4.02. 44
what a mere child is fancy, | that, having two 4.02. 52

MERED 1 FR 0.0001 REL FR 1 V 0 P
world oppos'd, he being | the mered question. ANT 3.13. 10

/MERELY 2 FR 0.0002 REL FR 1 V 1 P
/are /merely /shadows /to /the /unseen /grief R2 4.01.297
/the /ambitious /is /merely /the /shadow /of /a HAM 2.02.258 P

MERELY 27 FR 0.0030 REL FR 21 V 6 P
we are merely cheated of our lives by drunkards. TMP 1.01. 56
merely, thou art death's fool, | for him thou MM 3.01. 11
are no subjects, | intents but merely thoughts. 5.01.454
merely, my lord. 5.01.454
i would see, which will be merely a dumb show. ADO 2.03.218 P
he shall have merely justice and his bond. MV 4.01.339
and all the men and women merely players; AYL 2.07.140
love is merely a madness, and, i tell you, 3.02.400 P
the world and to live in a nook merely monastic. 3.02.421 P
merely our own traitors. AWW 4.03. 21 P
merely in hate, 'gainst any of us all, | that R2 2.01.243
have got by the late voyage is but merely | a H8 1.03. 6
and merely to revenge him on the emperor | for 2.01.162
i propose not merely to myself | the pleasures TRO 2.02.146
merely awry. COR 3.01.303
(as their friendship) may | be merely poison! TIM 4.01. 32
that which i show, heaven knows, is merely love, 4.03.515
trouble of my countenance | merely upon myself. JC 1.02. 39
rank and gross in nature | possess it merely. HAM 1.02.137
it is merely a lust of the blood and a OTH 1.03.334 P
mares together, | the horse were merely lost; ANT 3.07. 8
give up yourself merely to chance and hazard, 3.07. 47
honor was not yielded, | but conquer'd merely. 3.13. 62
some falling | merely through fear, that the CYM 5.03. 11
which is merely to the undoing of poor prentices STM II.C 8 P
thought characters and words merely but art, LC 174
"thus merely with the garment of a grace, | the 316

MEREST 1 FR 0.0001 REL FR 1 V 0 P
he cried upon it at the merest loss, | and twice SHR in.1. 23

MERIDIAN 1 FR 0.0001 REL FR 1 V 0 P
and, from that full meridian of my glory, | i H8 3.02.224

/MERIT 1 FR 0.0001 REL FR 1 V 0 P
and if on earth he do not /merit it, | in reason MV 3.05. 77

MERIT 52 FR 0.0058 REL FR 41 V 11 P
plead a new state in thy unrivall'd merit, | to TGV 5.04.144
his frailty, and then judge of my merit. WIV 3.05. 51 P
what a merit were it in death to take this poor MM 3.01.231 P
to praise him more than ever man did merit. ADO 3.01. 19
that | which simpleness and merit purchaseth. 3.01. 70
see, see, my beauty will be sav'd by merit. LLL 4.01. 21
noble respect | takes it in might, not merit. MND 5.01. 92
and be honorable | without the stamp of merit? MV 2.09. 39
were purchas'd by the merit of the wearer! 2.09. 43
you to a love, that your true faith doth merit; AYL 5.04.188
who ever strove | to show her merit, that did AWW 1.01.227
inspired merit so by breath is barr'd. 2.01.148
but that the merit of service is seldom 3.06. 60 P
judge, | that i can find should merit any hate. JN 2.01.520
and by the merit of vild gold, dross, dust, 3.01.165
a dearer merit, not so deep a maim | as to be R2 1.03.156
forgot, | right noble is thy merit, well i wot. 5.06. 18
if men were to be sav'd by merit, what hole in 1H4 1.02.107 P
good wenches, how men of merit are sought after. 2H4 2.04.375 P
sooner than quittance of desert and merit, H5 2.02. 34
may iden live to merit such a bounty, | and 2H6 5.01. 81
the force of his own merit makes his way — | a H8 1.01. 64
makes merit her election, and doth boil | (as TRO 1.03.349
without some image of th' affected merit. 2.02. 60
nor, by my will, assubjugate his merit, | as 2.03.192
our head shall go bare till merit /crown /it. 3.02. 92 P
favor — | prizes of accident as oft as merit, 3.03. 83
your faith in question | so mainly as my merit. 4.04. 85
honors, though indeed | in aught he merit not. COR 1.01.276
he should have show'd us | his marks of merit, 2.03.164
laid falsely | i' th' plain way of his merit. 3.01. 61
but he has a merit | to choke it in the 4.07. 48
too fair, | to merit bliss by making me despair. ROM 1.01.222
and like her most whose merit most shall be; 1.02. 31
they deserve, the more merit is in your bounty. HAM 2.02.532 P
that patient merit of th' unworthy takes, | when 3.01. 73
extend | where nature doth with merit challenge? LR 1.01. 53
but a provoking merit, set a–work by a 3.05. 7 P
in the authority of her merit, did justly put on OTH 2.01.146 P
oft got without merit, and lost without 2.03.269 P
sorrows, | nor purpos'd merit in futurity, | can 3.04.117
if for the sake of merit thou wilt hear me, ANT 2.07. 55
enough for the /purchase, or merit for the gift; CYM 1.04. 84 P
desert, am bound | to load thy merit richly. 1.05. 74
'tis more by fortune, lady, than my merit. PER 2.03. 12
which | is true love's merit, and bless me with TNK 5.01.128
there | where thy desert may merit praise, | by PP 18.15
thy merit hath my duty strongly knit, | to thee SON 26. 2
what merit liv'd in me that you should love 72. 2
light, | and place my merit in the eye of scorn, 88. 2
that may express my love, or thy dear merit? 108. 4
what merit do i in myself respect, | that is so 149. 9

MERITED 7 FR 0.0008 REL FR 4 V 3 P
but whatsoever i have merited, either in my mind WIV 2.02.202 P
do a poor wrong'd lady a merited benefit; MM 3.01.201 P
how i was in your grace, | how merited to be so; WT 3.02. 48
god, and i have merited some love at his hands. H5 3.06. 23 P
more hath it merited, that let it have. TIT 3.01.196
as your honors | have more than merited. LR 5.03.303
more of thee merited than a band of clotens CYM 5.05.304

MERITORIOUS 4 FR 0.0004 REL FR 3 V 1 P
it hath done meritorious service. WIV 4.02.205 P
and meritorious shall that hand be call'd, JN 3.01.176
my tongue, | seeing the deed is meritorious, 2H6 3.01.270
for 'tis a meritorious fair design | to chase LUC 1692

MERIT'S 2 FR 0.0002 REL FR 2 V 0 P
what merit's in that reason which denies | the TRO 2.02. 24
my commendations great, whose merit's less. PER 2.02. 9

MERITS 12 FR 0.0013 REL FR 11 V 1 P
sure, sweet kate, this kindness merits thanks. SHR 4.03. 41
and it no more merits | the tread of a man's AWW 2.03.274
father's bless'd | (as he from heaven merits it) WT 5.01.175
look you now, of no merits, he is come to me, H5 5.01. 8 P
he merits well to have her that doth seek her, TRO 4.01. 56
both merits pois'd, each weighs nor less nor 4.01. 66
wrong, you bate too much of your own merits. TIM 1.02.206
as we shall find their merits and our safety LR 5.03. 44
nor from mine own weak merits will i draw | the OTH 3.03.187

we fall, | we answer others' merits in our name, ANT 5.02.178
thus adjourn'd | the graces for his merits due, CYM 5.04. 79
and thou shalt find it merits not reproving, SON 142. 4
MERLIN 2 FR 0.0002 REL FR 1 V 1 P
ant, | of the dreamer merlin and his prophecies, 1H4 3.01.148
this prophecy merlin shall make, for i live LR 3.02. 95 P
MERMAID 5 FR 0.0005 REL FR 5 V 0 P
o, train me not, sweet mermaid, with thy note, ERR 3.02. 45
and heard a mermaid on a dolphin's back MND 2.01.150
i'll drown more sailors than the mermaid shall, 3H6 3.02.186
at the helm | a seeming mermaid steers; ANT 2.02.209
as if some mermaid did their ears entice, | some LUC 1411
MERMAID–LIKE 1 FR 0.0001 REL FR 1 V 0 P
and, mermaid–like, awhile they bore her up, HAM 4.07.176
MERMAID'S 2 FR 0.0002 REL FR 2 V 0 P
i'll stop mine ears against the mermaid's song. ERR 3.02.164
thy mermaid's voice hath done me double wrong: VEN 429
MERMAIDS' 1 FR 0.0001 REL FR 1 V 0 P
bewitching like the wanton mermaids' songs, VEN 777
MERMAIDS 1 FR 0.0001 REL FR 1 V 0 P
so many mermaids, tended her i' th' eyes, | and ANT 2.02.207
MERMIDONS *(also myrmidons)*
MERMIDONS 1 FR 0.0001 REL FR 0 V 1 P
and the mermidons are no bottle–ale houses. TN 2.03. 28 P
MEROPS' 1 FR 0.0001 REL FR 1 V 0 P
why, phaeton (for thou art merops' son), | wilt TGV 3.01.153
MERRIER 7 FR 0.0008 REL FR 5 V 2 P
reserve them till a merrier hour than this: ERR 1.02. 69
berowne they call him, but a merrier man, LLL 2.01. 66
swear | a merrier hour was never wasted there. MND 2.01. 57
mistress of, and would you yet /i were merrier? AYL 1.02. 4 P
indeed i have been merrier. JN 4.01. 12
a merrier day did never yet greet rome, | no, COR 5.04. 42
i am merrier to die than thou art to live. CYM 5.04.171 P
MERRIEST 3 FR 0.0003 REL FR 2 V 1 P
of two usuries, the merriest was put down, and MM 3.02. 6 P
that men are merriest when they are from home. H5 1.02.272
two girls, which hath the merriest eye — | i 1H6 2.04. 15
MERRILY 24 FR 0.0027 REL FR 17 V 7 P
the bat's back i do fly | after summer merrily. TMP 5.01. 92
merrily, merrily shall i live now, | under the 5.01. 93
merrily, merrily shall i live now, | under the 5.01. 93
or money in his purse, when he looks so merrily. WIV 2.01.191 P
look'd he or red or pale, or sad or merrily? ERR 4.02. 4
the fire, | holding a trencher, jesting merrily? LLL 5.02.477
full merrily | hath this brave /manage, this 5.02.481
what, you look merrily! AYL 2.07. 11
and the other lives merrily because he feels no 3.02.321 P
time, | to entertain it so merrily with a fool. AWW 2.02. 61
foot–path way, | and merrily hent the stile–a; WT 4.03.124
if it be doleful matter merrily set down, or a 4.04.189 P
and i rob the thieves and go merrily to london, 1H4 2.02. 94 P
now merrily to horse. 2.02.104
doomsday is near, die all, die merrily. 4.01.134
look how we can, or sad or merrily, 5.02. 12
and lusty lads roam here and there | so merrily, 2H4 5.03. 21
so merrily, | and ever among so merrily." 5.03. 22
full merrily the humble–bee doth sing, | till he TRO 5.10. 41
business, and i will merrily accompany you home. COR 4.03. 39 P
though news be sad, yet tell them merrily; ROM 2.05. 22
but they enter my master's house merrily, and go TIM 2.02.102 P
good gentlemen, look fresh and merrily; JC 2.01.224
they eat well, look merrily, discourse of many TNK 2.01. 39 P
MERRIMAN 1 FR 0.0001 REL FR 1 V 0 P
tender well my hounds | (brach merriman, the SHR in.1. 17
MERRIMENT 13 FR 0.0014 REL FR 11 V 2 P
of your brother | a merriment than a vice. MM 2.04.116
they do it but in mockery merriment, | and mock LLL 5.02.139
a consent, | knowing aforehand of our merriment, 5.02.461
but that thou interruptest our merriment. 5.02.717
loves | in their own fashion, like a merriment. 5.02.784
are bent | to set against me for your merriment. MND 3.02.146
for we have friends | that purpose merriment. MV 2.02.203
and frame your mind to mirth and merriment, SHR in.2. 135
for our first merriment hath made thee jealous. 4.05. 76
and strain their cheeks to idle merriment — | a JN 3.03. 46
out of your revenge and turn all to a merriment, 2H4 2.04.298 P
yet nature's tears are reason's merriment. ROM 4.05. 83
your songs, your flashes of merriment, that were HAM 5.01.190 P
MERRIMENTS 1 FR 0.0001 REL FR 1 V 0 P
stir up the athenian youth to merriments, MND 1.01. 12
MERRINESS 1 FR 0.0001 REL FR 0 V 1 P
shall give us cause to climb in the merriness. LLL 1.01.200 P
/MERRY 2 FR 0.0002 REL FR 2 V 0 P
/make /my /aunt /merry /with /some /pleasing TIT 3.02. 47
/melody, | /came /here /to /make /us /merry! 3.02. 65
MERRY 177 FR 0.0200 REL FR 115 V 62 P
beseech you, sir, be merry; TMP 2.01. 1
who, in this kind of merry fooling, am nothing 2.01.177 P
thou mak'st me merry; 3.02.116
come hither from the furrow and be merry. 4.01.135
marry, mine host, because i cannot be merry. TGV 4.02. 29 P
come, we'll have you merry: 4.02. 30 P
you are merry, so am i; WIV 2.01. 7 P
my merry host hath had the measuring of their 2.01.207 P
it is a merry knight. 2.01.219 P
do, | wives may be merry, and yet honest too: 4.02.105
fenton, | heaven give you many, many merry days! 5.05.240
'twas never merry world since, of two usuries, MM 3.02. 5 P
rather rejoicing to see another merry, than 3.02.235 P
than merry at any thing which profess'd to make 3.02.236 P
lightens my humor with his merry jests. ERR 1.02. 21
or i shall break that merry sconce of yours 1.02. 79
whilst i at home starve for a merry look: 2.01. 88
how now, sir, is your merry humor alter'd? 2.02. 7
i am glad to see you in this merry vein. 2.02. 20
cheer and great welcome makes a merry feast. 3.01. 26
and in despite of mirth mean to be merry. 3.01.108
you are a merry man, sir, fare you well. 3.02.178
saving your merry humor, here's the note | how 4.01. 27
her trim, the merry wind | blows fair from land: 4.01. 90
your man and you are marvellous merry, sir. 4.03. 58
there is a kind of merry war betwixt signior ADO 1.01. 62 P
laugh when i am merry, and claw no man in his 1.03. 17 P
and there live we as merry as the day is long. 2.01. 49 P
my good wit out of the "hundred merry tales" — 2.01.130 P
may be i go under that title because i am merry. 2.01.206 P
is neither sad, nor sick, nor merry, nor well; 2.01.294 P
in faith, lady, you have a merry heart. 2.01.312 P
offends me, and to be merry best becomes you, 2.01.332 P
out a' question, you were born in a merry hour. 2.01.333 P
to depart, and if a merry meeting may be wish'd, 5.01.325 P
if ever i do see the merry days of desolation LLL 1.02.159 P
some merry mocking lord belike, is't so? 2.01. 52
that last is berowne, the merry madcap lord. 2.01.215
masks, and merry hours | forerun fair love, 4.03.376
of such a merry, nimble, stirring spirit, | she 5.02. 16
my mocks come home by me, i will now be merry. 5.02.635 P
straws | and merry larks are ploughmen's clocks; 5.02.904
a merry note, | while greasy joan doth keel the 5.02.919
a merry note, | while greasy joan doth keel the 5.02.928
good piece of work, i assure you, and a merry. MND 1.02. 14 P
i am that merry wanderer of the night. 2.01. 43
merry and tragical? 5.01. 58
but more merry tears | the passion of loud 5.01. 69
us say you are sad | because you are not merry; MV 1.01. 48
and say you are merry | because you are not sad. 1.01. 49
i would have stay'd till i had made you merry, 1.01. 60
he hears merry tales and smiles not. 1.02. 48 P
and, in a merry sport, | if you repay me not on 1.03.145
give him direction for this merry bond, | and i 1.03.173
our house is hell, and thou, a merry devil, 2.03. 2
be merry, and employ your chiefest thoughts | to 2.08. 43
bid your friends welcome, show a merry cheer — 3.02.312
i am never merry when i hear sweet music. 5.01. 69
forest of arden, and a many merry men with him; AYL 1.01.115 P
i pray thee, rosalind, sweet my coz, be merry. 1.02. 2 P
my sweet rose, my dear rose, be merry. 1.02. 23 P
and turn his merry note | unto the sweet bird's 2.05. 3
here was he merry, hearing of a song. 2.07. 4
a fool to make me merry than experience to make 4.01. 28 P
will do that when you are dispos'd to be merry. 4.01.155 P
god rest you merry, sir. 5.01. 59 P
you break into some merry passion | and so SHR in.1. 97
and to be noted for a merry man, | he'll woo a 3.02. 14
though he be merry, yet withal he's honest. 3.02. 25
be mad and merry, or go hang yourselves; 3.02.226
nay, good sweet kate, be merry. 4.01.143
be merry, kate. 4.01.149
fair sir, and you my merry mistress, | that with 4.05. 53
a hundred pound or two, to make merry withal? 5.01. 22 P
she's very merry, but yet she is not well; AWW 2.04. 3 P
a peg–a–ramsey, and "three merry men be we." TN 2.03. 76 P
i warrant thou art a merry fellow and car'st for 3.01. 26 P
'twas never merry world | since lowly feigning 3.01. 98
mad as he, | if sad and merry madness equal be. 3.04. 15
merry, or sad, shall't be? WT 2.01. 23
as merry as you will. 2.01. 24
a merry heart goes all the day, | your sad tires 4.03.125
be merry, gentle! 4.04. 46
this is a merry ballad, but a very pretty one. 4.04.286 P
let's have some merry ones. 4.04.287 P
this is a passing merry one and goes to the tune 4.04.288 P
i could be merry now. JN 3.03. 67
i should be as merry as the day is long; 4.01. 18
be merry, for our time of stay is short. R2 2.01.223
i'll lay | a plot shall show us all a merry day. 4.01.334
shall we be merry? 1H4 2.04. 88 P
as merry as crickets, my lad. 2.04. 89 P
what, shall we be merry, shall we have a play 2.04.279 P
if to be old and merry be a sin, then many an 2.04.471 P
come sing me a bawdy song, make me merry. 3.03. 14 P
a merry song! 2H4 2.04.276 P
ha, 'twas a merry night. 3.02.198 P
against ill chances men are ever merry, | but 4.02. 81
therefore be merry, coz, since sudden sorrow 4.02. 83
and bid the merry bells ring to thine ear | that 4.05.111
good cheer, | and praise god for the merry year, 5.03. 18
there's a merry heart! 5.03. 23 P
be merry, master bardolph, and, my little 5.03. 30 P
and, my little soldier there, be merry. 5.03. 31 P
"be merry, be merry, my wife has all, | for 5.03. 32
"be merry, be merry, my wife has all, | for 5.03. 32
'tis merry in hall when beards wags all, | and 5.03. 34
wags all, | and welcome merry shrove–tide. 5.03. 35
be merry, be merry." 5.03. 36
be merry, be merry." 5.03. 36
i have been merry twice and once ere now. 5.03. 39 P
leman mine, | and a merry heart lives long–a." 5.03. 48
and we shall be merry, now comes in the sweet a' 5.03. 50 P
lack nothing, be merry! 5.03. 70 P
and make you merry with fair katherine of france ep 29 P
which pillage they with merry march bring home H5 1.02.195
this was a merry message. 1.02.298
her vine, the merry cheerer of the heart, 5.02. 41
make merry, man, | with thy confederates in this 2H6 1.02. 85
hume must make merry with the duchess' gold; 1.02. 87
be merry, peter, and fear not thy master. 2.03. 70 P
i say, it was never merry world in england since 4.02. 8 P
i prithee grieve, to make me merry, york. 3H6 1.04. 86
this merry inclination | accords not with the 3.02. 76
our stern alarums chang'd to merry meetings, R3 1.01. 7
and cheer his grace with quick and merry eyes. 1.03. 5
only they | that come to hear a merry, bawdy H8 pr 14
and, if you can be merry then, i'll say | a man pr 31
he would have all as merry | as, first, good 1.04. 5
or gentleman that is not freely merry | is not 1.04. 36
ladies, you are not merry. 1.04. 42
you are a merry gamester, | my lord sands. 1.04. 45
let's be merry, | good my lord cardinal: 1.04.104
the merry songs of peace to all his neighbors. 5.04. 35
without cause, and merry against the hair; TRO 1.02. 27 P
then she's a merry greek indeed. 1.02.109 P
a woeful cressid 'mongst the merry greeks! 4.04. 56
as merry as when our nuptial day was done | and COR 1.06. 31
ne'er let my heart know merry cheer indeed TIT 2.03.188
death, | my hand cut off and made a merry jest; 5.02.174
ye say honestly, rest you merry! ROM 1.02. 62 P
rest you merry! 1.02. 81 P
'a was a merry man — took up the child. 1.03. 40
go home, be merry, give consent | to marry paris 4.01. 89
see where she comes from shrift with merry look. 4.02. 15
mass, and well said, a merry whoreson, ha! 4.04. 20
o, play me some merry dump to comfort me. 4.05.107 P
at the point of death | have they been merry, 5.03. 89
masters, they approach sadly, and go away merry; TIM 2.02.101 P
i know his lordship is but merry with me; 3.02. 37
and commend me to my lord, | say i am merry. JC 2.04. 45
fortune is merry, | and in this mood will give 3.02.266
you are merry, my lord. HAM 3.02.122 P
what should a man do but be merry, for look you 3.02.126 P
then i prithee be merry, thy wit shall not go LR 1.05. 11 P
i am not merry; OTH 2.01.122
therefore be merry, cassio, | for thy solicitor 3.03. 26
next night well, fed well, was free and merry; 3.03.340
what, was he sad, or merry? ANT 1.05. 50
of hot and cold, he was nor sad nor merry. 1.05. 52
he was not merry, | which seem'd to tell them 1.05. 56
be'st thou sad or merry, | the violence of 1.05. 59
'twas merry when | you wager'd on your angling; 2.05. 15
a stranger there | so merry and so gamesome. CYM 1.06. 60
me rejoicingly, and i'll be merry in my revenge. 3.05.145 P
what, are you merry, knights? PER 2.03. 48
child of ver, | merry spring–time's harbinger, TNK 1.01. 8
we are a merry rout, or else a rable, | or 3.05.106
ladies, if we have been merry, | and have 3.05.138
if mirth did make him sad, | and sadness merry; 5.03. 53
even at this word she hears a merry horn, VEN 1025
foes, | and merry fools to mock at him resort; LUC 989
annoy, | sad souls are slain in merry company, 1110
a woeful hostess brooks not merry guests. 1125
all my merry jigs are quite forgot, | all my PP 17. 5
swains, | all our merry meetings on the plains, 17.30
it fell upon a day, | in the merry month of may, 20. 2
MERRY–HEARTED 1 FR 0.0001 REL FR 1 V 0 P
i am wondrous merry–hearted, i could laugh now. TNK 2.02.150
MERVAILOUS *(also marvail's, marvellous, marvell's, marv'llous)*
MERVAILOUS 1 FR 0.0001 REL FR 1 V 0 P
the "solus" in thy most mervailous face, | the H5 2.01. 47
ME'S 1 FR 0.0001 REL FR 1 V 0 P
all with me's meet that i can fashion fit. LR 1.02.184
MES 1 FR 0.0001 REL FR 0 V 1 P
sur mes genoux /je vous donne mille H5 4.04. 54 P
MESH 1 FR 0.0001 REL FR 1 V 0 P
a golden mesh t' entrap the hearts of men MV 3.02.122
/MESH'D 1 FR 0.0001 REL FR 1 V 0 P
/with /her /sorrow, /mesh'd /upon /her /cheeks. TIT 3.02. 38
MESHES 1 FR 0.0001 REL FR 0 V 1 P
to skip o'er the meshes of good counsel the MV 1.02. 20 P
MESOPOTAMIA 1 FR 0.0001 REL FR 1 V 0 P
mesopotamia, and the shelters whither | the ANT 3.01. 8
MESS* *(also mass*)*
MESS* 11 FR 0.0012 REL FR 7 V 4 P
as lief you would tell me of a mess of porridge. WIV 3.01. 63 P
three fools lack'd me fool to make up the mess. LLL 4.03.203
a mess of russians left us but of late. 5.02.361
one mess is like to be your cheer. SHR 4.04. 70
but that our feasts | in every mess have folly, WT 4.04. 11
he and his toothpick at my worship's mess, | and JN 1.01.190
coming in to borrow a mess of vinegar, telling 2H4 2.01. 95 P
by the mess, ere theise eyes of mine take H5 3.02.114 P
where are your mess of sons to back you now, 3H6 1.04. 73
on each bush | lays her full mess before you. TIM 4.03.421
and his crib shall stand at the king's mess. HAM 5.02. 87 P
MESSAGE 33 FR 0.0037 REL FR 28 V 5 P
your message done, hie home unto my chamber, TGV 4.04. 88
how many women would do such a message? 4.04. 90
to hear me speak the message i am sent on. 4.04.112
no, my good lord; it was by private message. MM 5.01.460
you take pleasure then in the message? ADO 2.03.253 P
a message well sympathiz'd — a horse to be LLL 3.01. 51 P
and then show you the heart of my message. TN 1.05.191 P
while upon some horrid message for a challenge. 3.04.200 P
and it becomes | my marvel and my message. WT 5.01.188
my lord of herford, my message is to you. R2 2.03. 69
this was a merry message. H5 1.02.298
is his claim, his threat'ning, and my message; 2.04.110
by message crav'd, so is lord talbot come. 1H6 2.03. 13
on what submissive message art thou sent? 4.07. 53
could send such message to their sovereign. 2H6 3.02.272
go tell this heavy message to the king. 3.02.379
i go of message from the queen to france; 4.01.114
me, but by her woman | i sent your message, who H8 5.01. 64
now by thy looks | i guess thy message. 5.01.162
a prince | do a fair message to his kingly eyes? TRO 1.03.219
let me be privileg'd by my place and message, 4.04.130
come, thou'lt do my message, wilt thou not? TIT 4.01.117
of lucius, | he hath some message to deliver us. 4.02. 2
ay, some mad message from his mad grandfather. 4.02. 3
aemilius, do this message honorably, | and if he 4.04.104
love | by humble message and by promis'd means. TIM 5.04. 20
scarcely more | than would make up his message. MAC 1.05. 37
and unfold | his message ere he come, that a 3.06. 47
he hath not fail'd to pester us with message HAM 1.02. 22
telling it, and deliver a plain message bluntly. LR 1.04. 33 P
give to a gracious message | an host of tongues, ANT 2.05. 86
i come | with message unto princely pericles, PER 1.03. 32
now message must return from whence it came. 1.03. 35
MESSAGES 2 FR 0.0002 REL FR 2 V 0 P
eyes | i did receive fair speechless messages. MV 1.01.164
henceforward do your messages yourself. ROM 2.05. 64
MESSALA 18 FR 0.0020 REL FR 18 V 0 P
and bring messala with you | immediately to us. JC 4.03.141
welcome, good messala. 4.03.163
messala, i have here received letters | that 4.03.167
no, messala. 4.03.182
nothing, messala. 4.03.184
we must die, messala. 4.03.190
farewell, good messala. 4.03.231
messala! 5.01. 70
messala, | this is my birthday; 5.01. 70
give me thy hand, messala. 5.01. 72
ride, ride, messala, ride, and give these bills 5.02. 1
ride, ride, messala, let them all come down. 5.02. 6
no, this was he, messala, | but cassius is no 5.03. 59
hie you, messala, | and i will seek for pindarus 5.03. 78
where, where, messala, doth his body lie? 5.03. 91
free from the bondage you are in, messala; 5.05. 54
ay, if messala will prefer me to you. 5.05. 62
do so, good messala. 5.05. 63
MESSALINE 2 FR 0.0002 REL FR 1 V 1 P

my father was that sebastian of messaline, whom TN 2.01. 18 P
of messaline; 5.01.232
/MESSENGER 1 FR 0.0001 REL FR 1 V 0 P
from home, | and not send back my /messenger. LR 2.04. 2
MESSENGER 56 FR 0.0063 REL FR 49 V 7 P
th' sky, | whose wat'ry arch and messenger am i, TMP 4.01. 71
hail, many-colored messenger, that ne'er | dost 4.01. 76
i must go send some better messenger: TGV 1.01.151
or fearing else some messenger, that might her 2.01.167
thankful | to any happy messenger from thence. 2.04. 53
there is a messenger | that stays to bear my 3.01. 52
and now am i, unhappy messenger, | to plead for 4.04. 99
she shall be our messenger to this paltry knight WIV 2.01.158 P
but i have another messenger to your worship. 2.02. 95 P
one lucio | as then the messenger — MM 5.01. 74
and strike you home without a messenger. ERR 1.02. 67
for god's sake send some other messenger. 2.01. 77
and will not lightly trust the messenger, | that 4.04. 5
here comes my messenger. MND 3.02. 4
a messenger with letters from the doctor, | new MV 4.01.108
bring us the letters; call the messenger. 4.01.110
but in the instant that your messenger came, in 4.01.152 P
but there is come a messenger before, | to 5.01.117
were you made the messenger? AYL 1.02. 59 P
pardon me, | i am but as a guiltless messenger. 4.03. 12
that this distempered messenger of wet, | the AWW 1.03.151
dispatch the most convenient messenger. 3.04. 34
provide this messenger. 3.04. 40
tell me your mind — i am a messenger. TN 1.05.205 P
run after that same peevish messenger, | the 1.05.300
passion | invites me in this churlish messenger. 2.02. 23
thy wish | our messenger chatillion is arriv'd! JN 2.01. 51
some speedy messenger bid her repair | to our 2.01.554
need | some messenger betwixt me and the peers, 4.02.179
thou baleful messenger, out of my sight! 2H6 3.02. 48
art thou a messenger, or come of pleasure? 5.01. 16
a messenger from henry, our dread liege, | to 5.01. 17
such a messenger | as shall revenge his death 3H6 1.01. 99
come, cousin, you shall be the messenger. 1.01.272
then, england's messenger, return in post, | and 3.03.222
now, messenger, what letters or what news | from 4.01. 84
here comes a messenger. what news? R3 2.04. 38
and beat the messenger who bids beware | of what
COR 4.06. 55
there is a messenger from rome | desires to be TIT 5.01.152
as is a winged messenger of heaven | unto the ROM 2.02. 28
again — | nor get a messenger to bring it thee, 5.02. 15
lordship that i return'd you an empty messenger. TIM 3.06. 37 P
i," | the cloudy messenger turns me his back, MAC 3.06. 41
if your messenger find him not there, seek him HAM 4.03. 34 P
person of my master, | stocking his messenger. LR 2.02.132
that he, so slightly valued in his messenger, 2.02.146
and meeting here the other messenger, | whose 2.04. 38
a messenger from the galleys. OTH 1.03. 13
no messenger but thine, and all alone, ANT 1.01. 52
'tis done already, and the messenger gone. 3.06. 31
a messenger from caesar. 3.13. 37
most kind messenger, | say to great caesar this 3.13. 73
my messenger | he hath whipt with rods, dares me 4.01. 2
the messenger | came on my guard, and at thy 4.06. 21
too slow a messenger. 5.02.321
but now the mindful messenger, come back, LUC 1583
MESSENGERS 18 FR 0.0020 REL FR 17 V 1 P
his tears pure messengers sent from his heart, TGV 2.07. 77
messengers | of strong prevailment in unhardened MND 1.01. 34
o you leaden messengers, | that ride upon the AWW 3.02.108
walls | can hide you from our messengers of war, JN 2.01.260
call in the messengers sent from the dolphin. H5 1.02.221
he /shent our messengers, and we lay by | our TRO 2.03. 79
that fret the clouds are messengers of day. JC 2.01.104
admit no messengers, receive no tokens. HAM 2.02.144
the several messengers | from hence attend LR 2.01.124
the messengers from our sister and the king. 2.02. 50 P
have sent a dozen sequent messengers | this very OTH 1.02. 41
whose messengers are here about my side, | upon 1.02. 89
the messengers of venice stays the meat. 4.02.170
call in the messengers. ANT 1.01. 29
the messengers! 1.01. 32
ay, madam, twenty several messengers. 1.05. 62
which had superfluous kings for messengers | not 3.12. 5
by those swift messengers return'd from thee, SON 45.10
MESSES 3 FR 0.0003 REL FR 2 V 1 P
lower messes | perchance are to this business WT 1.02.227
or he that makes his generation messes | to LR 1.01.117
i will chop her into messes. cuckold me! OTH 4.01.200 P
MESSINA 9 FR 0.0010 REL FR 2 V 7 P
/pedro of arragon comes this night to messina. ADO 1.01. 2 P
an uncle here in messina will be very much glad 1.01. 18 P
he set up his bills here in messina, and 1.01. 39 P
have his head on her shoulders for all messina, 1.01.114 P
a couple of as arrant knaves as any in messina. 3.05. 32 P
as pretty a piece of flesh as any is in messina, 4.02. 82 P
your brother the bastard is fled from messina. 5.01.191 P
both, | possess the people in messina here | how 5.01.281
and brought with armed men back to messina. 5.04.126
M'ESTIME 1 FR 0.0001 REL FR 0 V 1 P
et je m'estime heureux que je tombe entre les H5 4.04. 55 P
MET 141 FR 0.0159 REL FR 113 V 28 P
they all have met again | and are upon the TMP 1.02.233
breasted | the surge most swoll'n that met him. 2.01.118
i met her deity | cutting the clouds towards 4.01. 92
how thou hast met us here, whom three hours 5.01.136
for friar laurence met them both, | as he in TGV 5.02. 37
ford, by my troth, you are very well met. WIV 1.01.193 P
well met, mistress page. whither go you? 3.02. 9 P
well met, master ford. 3.02. 50 P
met the jealous knave their master in the door, 3.05.101 P
sudden, | as falstaff, she, and i are newly met, 4.04. 53
very well met, and well come. MM 4.01. 26
my very worthy cousin, fairly met! 5.01. 1
i met you at the prison, in the absence of the 5.01.328 P
that would face me down | he met me on the mart,
ERR 3.01. 7
and in the instant that i met with you | he had 4.01. 9
well met, well met, master antipholus. 4.03. 45
well met, well met, master antipholus. 4.03. 45
met us again, and madly bent on us | chas'd us 5.01.152
in the street i met him, | and in his company 5.01.225
by th' way we met | my wife, her sister, and a 5.01.235
children, | which accidentally are met together. 5.01.362
o, my good knave costard, exceedingly well met! LLL 3.01.144 P
and therefore met your loves | in their own 5.02.783
ill met by moonlight, proud titania. MND 2.01. 60
met we on hill, in dale, forest, or mead, | by 2.01. 83
are we all met? 3.01. 1 P
were met together to rehearse a play | intended 3.02. 11
fair lovers, you are fortunately met; 4.01.177
i met a fool i' th' forest, | a motley fool. AYL 2.07. 12
as i do live by food, i met a fool, | who laid 2.07. 14
sir oliver martext, you are well met. 3.03. 65 P
you are very well met. 3.03. 74 P
i met the duke yesterday, and had much question 3.04. 35 P
not very well, but i have met him oft, | and he 3.05.106
it, till you met your wive's wit going to your 4.01.168 P
and my sister no sooner met but they look'd; 5.02. 33 P
well met, honest gentleman. 5.03. 7 P
by my troth, well met. 5.03. 8 P
that i have so often met in the forest. 5.04. 42 P
faith, we met, and found the quarrel was upon 5.04. 49 P
but when the parties were met themselves, one of 5.04.100 P
reason wonder may diminish | how thus we met, 5.04.140
and you are well met, signior hortensio. SHR 1.02.163
and i have met a gentleman | hath promis'd me to 1.02.171
here is a gentleman whom by chance i met, | upon 1.02.181
signior baptista, you are happily met. 4.04. 19
happily met, the happier for thy son. 4.05. 59
we met him thitherward, for thence we came; AWW 3.02. 53
'twere | i met the ravin lion when he roar'd 3.02.117
he met the duke in the street, sir, of whom he 4.03. 76 P
now, sir, have i met you again? there's for you. TN 4.01. 24 P
even now i met him | with customary compliment,
WT 1.02.370
was he met there? his train? camillo with him? 2.01. 33
behind the tuft of pines i met them; 2.01. 34
you are well met, sir. 5.02.128 P
before angiers well met, brave austria. JN 2.01. 1
besides, i met lord bigot and lord salisbury, 4.02.162
once more to-day well met, distemper'd lords! 4.03. 21
nor met with fortune other than at feasts, 5.02. 58
and well met, gentlemen. R2 2.02. 41
hath now himself met with the fall of leaf. 3.04. 49
and approved scot, | at holmedon met, | where 1H4 1.01. 55
he durst as well have met the devil alone | as 1.03.116
and would be glad he met with some mischance, 1.03.232
that douglas and the english rebels met | the 3.02.165
a mad fellow met me on the way and told me i had 4.02. 36 P
knee, | met him in boroughs, cities, villages, 4.03. 69
so many of his shadows thou hast met | and not 5.04. 30
that rebellion | had met ill luck? 2H4 1.01. 51
along | i met and overtook a dozen captains, 2.04.358
and indirect crook'd ways | i met this crown, 4.05.185
well met, corporal nym. H5 2.01. 1 P
i met this man with my glove in his cap, and i 4.08. 31 P
peace to this meeting, wherefore we are met! 5.02. 1
face, | most worthy brother england, fairly met! 5.02. 10
against the french that met them in their bent 5.02. 16
i muse we met not with the dolphin's grace, 1H6 2.02. 19
before we met, or that a stroke was given, 4.01. 22
i met in travel toward his warlike father! 4.03. 36
still, where danger was, still there i met him, 2H6 5.03. 11
short tale to make, we at saint albons met, 3H6 2.01.120
when you and i met at saint albons last, | your 2.02.103
would long ere this have met us on the way. R3 3.01. 21
well met, my lord, i am glad to see your honor. 3.02.108
and when i met this holy man | the men you talk 3.02.116
the cause why we are met | is to determine of 3.04. 1
daughter, well met. 4.01. 5
good morrow, and well met. H8 1.01. 1
two lights of men, | met in the vale of andren. 1.01. 7
pray tell him | you met him half in heaven. 2.01. 88
well met, my lord chamberlain. 2.02. 12
all my full affections | still met the king? 3.01.130
y' are well met once again. 4.01. 1
why are we met in council? 5.02. 37
we met by chance, you did not find me here. TRO 4.02. 71
yonder comes news: a wager they have met. COR 1.04. 1
say, has our general met the enemy? 1.04. 3
whom | we met here both to thank and to remember 2.02. 47
tarquin's self he met, | and struck him on his 2.02. 94
how often he had met you, sword to sword; 3.01. 13
o, y' are well met. 4.02. 11
sir, heartily well met, and most glad of your 4.03. 48 P
a craftier tereus, cousin, hast thou met, | and TIT 2.04. 41
what, have you met with her? 4.03. 37
when and where and how | we met, we woo'd, and
ROM 2.03. 62
hast thou met with him? 2.05. 19
happily met, my lady and my wife! 4.01. 18
i met the youthful lord at lawrence' cell, | and 4.02. 25
you are kindly met, sir. TIM 3.02. 27 P
well met, good morrow, titus and hortensius. 3.04. 1
the captainship, thou shalt be met with thanks, 5.01.161
i met a courier, one mine ancient friend, | whom 5.02. 6
my sword — | against the capitol i met a lion, JC 1.03. 20
"they met me in the day of success; MAC 1.05. 1 P
we might have met them dareful, beard to beard, 5.05. 6
we have met with foes | that strike beside us. 5.07. 28
would i had met my dearest foe in heaven | or HAM 1.02.182
'old, | he met the night-mare and her nine-fold; LR 3.04.121
hot questrists after him, met him at gate, | who 3.07. 17
marvel our mild husband | not met us on the way. 4.02. 2
no, my good lord, i met him back again. 4.02. 90
he was met even now | as mad as the vex'd sea, 4.04. 1
habit | met i my father with his bleeding rings, 5.03.190
and many of the consuls, rais'd and met, | are OTH 1.02. 43
desdemona, | once more, well met at cyprus. 2.01.212
they met so near with their lips that their 2.01.259 P
when she first met mark antony, she purs'd up ANT 2.02.186 P
i did not think, sir, to have met you here. 2.06. 49
well met here. 2.06. 56
we should have met you | by sea and land, 3.06. 53
story | proud cleopatra, when she met her roman, CYM 2.04. 70
o my gentle brothers, | have we thus met? 5.05.375
how first met them? 5.05.386
when my maiden priests are met together | before PER 5.01.242
is with me, i met your groom | by mars's altar. TNK 1.01. 61
did begin | as if you met decays of many kinds. 1.02. 29
lest this match between 's | be cross'd ere met. 3.01. 98
she met him in an arbor: 3.03. 33
and there he met with brave gallants of war, 3.05. 61
i felt a kind of fear | when as i met the boar, VEN 999
met far from home, wond'ring each other's chance
LUC 1596
METAL 23 FR 0.0026 REL FR 19 V 4 P
no use of metal, corn, or wine, or oil; TMP 2.01.154
true made | as to put metal in restrained means MM 2.04. 48
as all the metal in your shop will answer. ERR 4.01. 82
is not lead a metal heavy, dull, and slow? LLL 3.01. 59
take | a breed for barren metal of his friend? MV 1.03.134
but no metal can, | no, not the hangman's axe, 4.01.124
that you were made of is metal to make virgins. AWW 1.01.130 P
and to what metal this counterfeit lump of /ore 3.06. 37 P
how now, my metal of india? TN 2.05. 14 P
that i must draw this metal from my side | to be JN 5.02. 16
and like bright metal on a sullen ground, | my 1H4 1.02.212
for from his metal was his party steeled, 2H4 1.01.116
verge | of golden metal that must round my brow R3 4.01. 59
below, | even of your metal, of your very blood; 4.04.302
th' imperial metal, circling now thy head, | had 4.04.382
i feel | of what coarse metal ye are moulded, H8 3.02.239
the fineness of which metal is not found | in TRO 1.03. 22
but metal, marcus, steel to the very back, | yet TIT 4.03. 48
they have all been touch'd and found base metal, TIM 3.03. 6
see whe'er their basest metal be not mov'd; JC 1.01. 61
no, good mother, here's metal more attractive. HAM 3.02.109 P
i am made of that self metal as my sister, | and LR 1.01. 69
hair, | with twisted metal amorously impleach'd, LC 205
METALS 3 FR 0.0003 REL FR 2 V 1 P
good sparks and lustrous, a word, good metals: AWW 2.01. 41 P
like some ore | among a mineral of metals base, HAM 4.01. 26
infusions | that dwells in vegetives, in metals, PER 3.02. 36
METAMORPHIS'D 3 FR 0.0003 REL FR 2 V 1 P
thou, julia, thou hast metamorphis'd me, | made TGV 1.01. 66
and now you are metamorphis'd with a mistress, 2.01. 30 P
were they metamorphis'd | both into one — o, TNK 5.03. 84
METAMORPHOSIS 1 FR 0.0001 REL FR 1 V 0 P
grandsire, 'tis ovid's metamorphosis, | my TIT 4.01. 42
METAPHOR 4 FR 0.0004 REL FR 0 V 4 P
i spake but by a metaphor. AWW 5.02. 11 P
sir, if your metaphor stink, i will stop my nose 5.02. 12 P
stop my nose, or against any man's metaphor. 5.02. 13 P
wherefore, sweetheart? what's your metaphor? TN 1.03. 72 P
METAPHYSICAL 1 FR 0.0001 REL FR 1 V 0 P
which fate and metaphysical aid doth seem | to MAC 1.05. 29
METAPHYSICS 1 FR 0.0001 REL FR 1 V 0 P
you, | the mathematics, and the metaphysics, SHR 1.01. 37
METE 2 FR 0.0002 REL FR 2 V 0 P
let the mark have a prick in't, to mete at, if LLL 4.01.132
by which his grace must mete the lives of other, 2H4 4.04. 77
METELIN 2 FR 0.0002 REL FR 2 V 0 P
then, | and think you now are all in metelin. PER 4.04. 51
and pretty din, | the regent made in metelin, 5.02. 8
METELINE 8 FR 0.0009 REL FR 6 V 2 P
market narrowly, meteline is full of gallants. PER 4.02. 3 P
but there never came her like in meteline. 4.06. 28 P
sir, there is a barge put off from meteline, 5.01. 3
we have a maid in meteline, i durst wager, 5.01. 43
brought me to meteline. 5.01.175
regent, sir, of meteline | speaks nobly of her. 5.01.186
sir, 'tis the governor of meteline, | who, 5.01.219
but her better stars | brought her to meteline, 5.03. 10
METELLUS 10 FR 0.0011 REL FR 9 V 1 P
to find out you. who's that? metellus cimber? JC 1.03.134
all but metellus cimber, and he's gone | to seek 1.03.149
and this, metellus cimber. 2.01. 96
now, good metellus, go along by him. 2.01.218
caius ligarius, that metellus spake of. 2.01.311
now, metellus; 2.02.120
mark well metellus cimber; 2.03. 3 P
where is metellus cimber? 3.01. 27
metellus cimber throws before thy seat | an 3.01. 34
now yours, metellus; 3.01.187
METEOR 4 FR 0.0004 REL FR 2 V 2 P
it shall hang like a meteor o'er the cuckold's WIV 2.02.280 P
light, | and be no more an exhal'd meteor, | a 1H4 5.01. 19
i miss'd the meteor once, and hit that woman, H8 5.03. 50 P
it is some meteor that the sun /exhal'd | to be ROM 3.05. 13
METEORS 6 FR 0.0006 REL FR 5 V 1 P
/of his heart's meteors tilting in his face? ERR 4.02. 6
away his natural cause | and call them meteors, JN 3.04.157
figur'd quite o'er with burning meteors. 5.02. 53
and meteors fright the fixed stars of heaven, R2 2.04. 9
which, like the meteors of a troubled heaven, 1H4 1.01. 10
my lord, do you see these meteors? 2.04.319 P
METE-YARD 1 FR 0.0001 REL FR 0 V 1 P
take thou the bill, give me thy mete-yard, and SHR 4.03.152 P
METHEGLIN 1 FR 0.0001 REL FR 1 V 0 P
grow so nice, | metheglin, wort, and malmsey; LLL 5.02.233
METHEGLINS 1 FR 0.0001 REL FR 0 V 1 P
and wine, and metheglins, and to drinkings and WIV 5.05.159 P
METHINKS 161 FR 0.0182 REL FR 126 V 35 P
methinks he hath no drowning mark upon him, his
TMP 1.01. 28 P
methinks our garments are now as fresh as when 2.01. 69 P
more — | and yet methinks i see it in thy face, 2.01.206
methinks i do. 2.01.269
methinks should not be chronicled for wise. TGV 1.01. 41
and yet methinks i do not like this tune. 1.02. 87
methinks my zeal to valentine is cold, | and 2.04.203
now, my young guest, methinks you're allycholly; 4.02. 26 P
because methinks that she lov'd you as well | as 4.04. 79
methinks you prescribe to yourself very WIV 2.02.240 P
and methinks there would be no period to the 4.02.221 P
methinks there should be terrors in him that he 4.04. 22 P
methinks his flesh is punish'd, he shall have no 4.04. 23 P
this unwonted putting-on, methinks strangely, MM 4.02.117 P
methinks i see a quick'ning in his eye. 5.01.495
methinks your maw, like mine, should be your ERR 1.02. 66
methinks they are such a gentle nation that, but 4.04.153 P
methinks you are my glass, and not my brother: 5.01.418
faith, methinks she's too low for a high praise, ADO 1.01.171 P
so say i, methinks you are sadder. 3.02. 16 P
i am out of all other tune, methinks. 3.04. 43 P
but methinks you look with your eyes as other 3.04. 91 P

methinks i should outswear cupid. LLL 1.02. 63 P
color, methinks sampson had small reason for it. 1.02. 87 P
a time methinks too short | to make a 5.02.788
but o, methinks, how slow | this old moon /wanes MND 1.01. 3
methinks, mistress, you should have little 3.01.142 P
the moon methinks looks with a wat'ry eye; 3.01.198
for methinks i am marvail's hairy about the face 4.01. 24 P
methinks i have a great desire to a bottle of 4.01. 32 P
methinks i see these things with parted eye, 4.01.189
so methinks; 4.01.190
the wall, methinks, being sensible, should curse 5.01.182 P
methinks she should not use a long one for such 5.01.316 P
methinks it should have power to steal both his MV 3.02.125
this, | and now methinks i have a mind to it. 4.01.433
and now methinks | you teach me how a beggar 4.01.439
troilus methinks mounted the troyan walls, | and 5.01. 4
methinks it sounds much sweeter than by day. 5.01.100
this night methinks is but the daylight sick, 5.01.124
methinks i have given him a penny and he renders AYL 2.05. 28 P
gentle sir, methinks you walk like a stranger. SHR 2.01. 86 P
methinks he looks as though he were in love; 3.01. 88
gentles, methinks you frown, | and wherefore 3.02. 93
'twere good methinks to steal our marriage, 3.02.140
would always say — | methinks i hear him now; AWW 1.02. 53
methinks in thee some blessed spirit doth speak 2.01.175
methinks sometimes i have no more wit than a TN 1.03. 83 P
methinks i feel this youth's perfections | with 1.05.296
why then methinks 'tis time to smile again. 3.01.126
methinks his words do from such passion fly 3.04.373
methinks | my favor here begins to warp. WT 1.02.364
habits | (methinks i so should term them) and 3.01. 5
methinks i play as i have seen them do | in 4.04.133
methinks a father | is at the nuptial of his son 4.04.394
methinks i see | leontes opening his free arms 4.04.547
would i were dead but that methinks already — 5.03. 62
still methinks | there is an air comes from her. 5.03. 77
methinks i see this hurly all on foot; JN 3.04.169
methinks nobody should be sad but i. 4.01. 13
i am amaz'd, methinks, and lose my way | among 4.03.140
and even there, methinks an angel spake. 5.02. 64
methinks i am a prophet new inspir'd, | and thus R2 2.01. 31
yet again methinks | some unborn sorrow, ripe in 2.02. 9
for methinks in you | i see old gaunt alive. 2.03.117
methinks king richard and myself should meet 3.03. 54
bullingbrook — for yon methinks he stands — 3.03. 91
by heaven, methinks it were an easy leap, | to 1H4 1.03.201
methinks my moi'ty, north from burton here, | in 3.01. 95
john, methinks they are exceeding poor and bare, 4.02. 68 P
heart, methinks now you are in an excellent good 2H4 2.04. 22 P
for this revolt of thine, methinks, is like H5 2.02.141
methinks i could not die any where so contented 4.01.126 P
as one man more methinks would share from me, 4.03. 32
methinks your looks are sad, your cheer appal'd. 1H6 1.02. 48
my lord, methinks, is very long in talk. 1.02.118
but yet, methinks, my father's execution | was 2.05. 99
methinks my lord should be religious, | and know 3.01. 54
methinks his lordship should be humbler, | it 3.01. 56
methinks i should revive the soldiers' hearts, 3.02. 97
methinks you do not well | to bear with their 4.01.128
boy, he smiles, methinks, as who should say, 4.07. 27
and yet methinks i could be well content | to be 5.03.165
methinks the realms of england, france, and 2H6 1.01.232
here 'a comes, methinks, and the queen with him. 1.03. 6 P
lord buckingham, methinks you watch'd her well. 1.04. 55
land, | methinks i should not thus be led along, 2.04. 30
but methinks he should stand in fear of fire, 4.02. 62 P
methinks already in this civil broil | i see 4.08. 44
are old enough now, and yet methinks you lose. 3H6 1.01.113
methinks we should have heard | the happy 2.01. 6
methinks 'tis prize enough to be his son. 2.01. 20
ay, now methinks i hear great warwick speak. 2.01.186
methinks it were a happy life | to be no better 2.05. 21
the other his pale cheeks, methinks, presenteth. 2.05.100
methinks these peers of france should smile at 3.03. 91
and yet methinks your grace hath not done well 4.01. 51
methinks the power that edward hath in field 4.08. 35
methinks a woman of this valiant spirit | should 5.04. 39
i am afraid, methinks, to hear you tell it. R3 1.04. 65
and since, methinks i would not grow so fast, 2.04. 14
methinks the truth should live from age to age, 3.01. 76
how much, methinks, i could despise this man, H8 3.02.297
i am able now, methinks | (out of a fortitude of 3.02.387
now, methinks, i feel a little ease. 4.02. 4
methinks i could | cry the amen, and yet my 5.01. 23
for that methinks is the curse depending on TRO 2.03. 19 P
who do methinks find out | some thing not worth 3.03. 90
methinks i hear hither your husband's drum; COR 1.03. 29
methinks i see him stamp thus, and call thus: 1.03. 32
truth, | methinks thou speak'st not well. 1.06. 14
and by his looks, methinks, | 'tis warm at 's 2.03.151
but soft, methinks i do digress too much, TIT 5.03.116
methinks i see thee now, thou art so low, | as ROM 3.05. 55
i fear it is, and yet methinks it should not, 4.03. 28
methinks i see my cousin's ghost | seeking out 4.03. 55
throne, this fortune, and this hill, methinks, TIM 1.01. 73
methinks they should invite them without knives: 1.02. 44
mine eyes cannot hold out water, methinks. 1.02.107 P
methinks, i could deal kingdoms to my friends, 1.02.220
methinks false hearts should never have sound 1.02.234
methinks he should the sooner pay his debts, 3.04. 75
methinks thou art more honest now than wise; 4.03.502
methinks there is much reason in his sayings. JC 3.02.108
that, methinks, is strange. 4.03.184
to fright you thus methinks i am too savage; MAC 4.02. 70
my father — methinks i see my father. HAM 1.02.184
but soft, methinks i scent the morning air, 1.05. 58
the lady doth protest too much, methinks. 3.02.230 P
methinks it is like a weasel. 3.02.379 P
but yet methinks it is very /sultry and hot /for 5.02. 98 P
methinks the ground is even. LR 4.06. 3
methinks thy voice is alter'd, and thou speak'st 4.06. 7
methinks y' are better spoken. 4.06. 10
methinks he seems no bigger than his head. 4.06. 16
far off methinks i hear the beaten drum. 4.06.285
methinks i should know you, and know this man, 4.07. 63
methinks our pleasure might have been demanded 5.03. 62
methinks the wind hath spoke aloud at land, | a OTH 2.01. 5
methinks it sounds a parley to provocation. 2.03. 22 P
an inviting eye; and yet methinks right modest. 2.03. 24 P
methinks it should be now a huge eclipse | of 5.02. 99
madam, methinks, if you did love him dearly, ANT 1.03. 6
why, methinks, by him, | this creature's no such 3.03. 40
methinks i hear | antony call; 5.02.283
now methinks | thy favor's good enough. CYM 3.04. 48
whereupon — | methinks i see him now — 5.05.209
'tis like a beast, methinks. TNK 2.02. 99
of all flow'rs | methinks a rose is best. 2.02.136
woman, | his face, methinks, goes that way. 2.05. 21
and that, methinks, is not so well; 2.06. 23
methinks this armor's very like that, arcite, 3.06. 70
methinks, from hence, as from a promontory 4.02. 22
methinks, of him that's first with palamon. 4.02. 90
methinks, | being so few and well dispos'd, they 4.02.121
doctor, | methinks you are i' th' wrong still. 5.02. 27
hie thee, | for methinks thou stays too long. PP 12.12
pluck, | and yet methinks i have astronomy, SON 14. 2
methinks no face so gracious is as mine, | no 62. 5
your sweet hue, which methinks still doth stand, 104.11
that all the world besides methinks are dead. 112.14

METHINK'ST 1 FR 0.0001 REL FR 0 V 1 P
methink'st thou art a general offense, and every AWW 2.03.254 P

METHOD 8 FR 0.0009 REL FR 4 V 4 P
say'st thou to this tune, matter, and method? MM 3.02. 48 P
or i will beat this method in your sconce. ERR 2.02. 34
to answer by the method, in the first of his TN 1.05.226 P
verbatim to rehearse the method of my pen. 1H6 3.01. 13
wits | and fall something into a slower method: R3 1.02.116
this be madness, yet there is method in't. HAM 2.02.206 P
but call'd it an honest method, as wholesome as 2.02.444 P
you do not hold the method to enforce | the like ANT 1.03. 7

METHODS 1 FR 0.0001 REL FR 1 V 0 P
to new-found methods and to compounds strange? SON 76. 4

/METHOUGHT 1 FR 0.0001 REL FR 1 V 0 P
/methought i lay | worse than the mutines in the HAM 5.02. 5

METHOUGHT 47 FR 0.0053 REL FR 37 V 10 P
the clouds methought would open and show riches TMP 3.02.141
methought the billows spoke, and told me of it; 3.03. 96
he beat him most unpitifully, methought. WIV 4.02.203 P
methought all his senses were lock'd in his eye, LLL 2.01.242
methought a serpent eat my heart away, | and you MND 2.02.149
methought i was enamor'd of an ass. 4.01. 77
methought i was — there is no man can tell what 4.01.207 P
methought i was, and methought i had — but man 4.01.208 P
methought i was, and methought i had — but man 4.01.209 P
if he will offer to say what methought i had. 4.01.210 P
methought he was a brother to your daughter. AYL 5.04. 29
said "a mother," | methought you saw a serpent. AWW 1.03.141
methought you said | you saw one here in court 5.03.199
methought she purg'd the air of pestilence! TN 1.01. 19
that methought her eyes had lost her tongue, 2.02. 20
methought it did relieve my passion much, | more 2.04. 4
which methought did promise | most venerable 3.04.362
how like, methought, i then was to this kernel, WT 1.02.159
only this, methought, i heard the shepherd say, 5.02. 6 P
the sun of heaven, methought, was loath to set, JN 5.05. 1
eyes, and methought he had made two holes in the 2H4 2.02. 81 P
methought 'a made a shrewd thrust at your belly. 2.04.210 P
for methought yesterday your mistress shrewdly H5 3.07. 48 P
the king | prettily, methought, did play the 1H6 4.01.175
methought this staff, mine office-badge in court 2H6 1.02. 25
methought i sat in seat of majesty | in the 1.02. 36
methought he bore him in the thickest troop | as 3H6 2.01. 13
methought that gloucester stumbled, and in R3 1.04. 18
o lord, methought what pain it was to drown! 1.04. 21
methought i had, and often did i strive | to 1.04. 36
i pass'd, methought, the melancholy flood, 1.04. 45
methought the souls of all that i had murther'd 5.03.204
methought their souls whose bodies richard 5.03.230
methought | i stood not in the smile of heaven, H8 2.04.187
a kind of face, methought — i cannot tell how COR 4.05.155 P
methought i heard a voice cry, "sleep no more! MAC 2.02. 32
and anon methought | the wood began to move. 5.05. 33
yet once methought | it lifted up it head and HAM 1.02.215
love, did love, | methought it was very sweet, 5.01. 62
o, methought there — a — was nothing — a — 5.01. 64
below, methought his eyes | were two full moons; LR 4.06. 69
methought thy very gait did prophesy | a royal 5.03.176
as i slept, methought | great jupiter, upon his CYM 5.05.426
methought i heard a dreadful clap of thunder TNK 3.06. 83
methought stood staggering whether he should 4.01. 10
that methought she appear'd like the fair nymph 4.01. 86
so charm'd me that methought alcides was | to 5.03.119

/METHOUGHTS 1 FR 0.0001 REL FR 1 V 0 P
with that, /methoughts, a legion of foul fiends R3 1.04. 58

METHOUGHTS 4 FR 0.0004 REL FR 4 V 0 P
methoughts you said you neither lend nor borrow MV 1.03. 69
methoughts i did recoil | twenty-three years, WT 1.02.154
methoughts that i had broken from the tower R3 1.04. 9
methoughts i saw a thousand fearful wracks; 1.04. 24

/METING 1 FR 0.0001 REL FR 1 V 0 P
and a hand | open as day for /meting charity; 2H4 4.04. 32

METRE 3 FR 0.0003 REL FR 2 V 1 P
what? in metre? MM 1.02. 21 P
than one of these same metre ballet-mongers. 1H4 3.01.128
rage, | and stretched metre of an antique song: SON 17.12

METRES 1 FR 0.0001 REL FR 1 V 0 P
lascivious metres, to whose venom sound | the R2 2.01. 19

METROPOLIS 1 FR 0.0001 REL FR 1 V 0 P
church, | the great metropolis and see of rome; JN 5.02. 72

MET'ST 3 FR 0.0003 REL FR 2 V 1 P
thou met'st with things dying, i with things WT 3.03.113 P
than when thou met'st me last where now we meet. R3 3.02. 99
met'st thou my posts? ANT 1.05. 61

METTE 1 FR 0.0001 REL FR 0 V 1 P
oui, mette le au mon pocket; WIV 1.04. 54 P

METTLE 30 FR 0.0034 REL FR 19 V 11 P
you are gentlemen of brave mettle; TMP 2.01.182 P
let there be some more test made of my mettle MM 1.01. 48
it not patiently, why, your mettle is the more. 3.02. 76 P
god make men of some other mettle than earth. ADO 2.01. 60 P
thou hast mettle enough in thee to kill care. 5.01.133 P
suits | his folly to the mettle of my speech? AYL 2.07. 82
i care not who knows so much of my mettle. TN 3.04.272 P
him, | so much against the mettle of your sex, 5.01.322
and if thou hast the mettle of a king, | being JN 2.01.401
that mettle, that self mould, that fashioned R2 1.02. 23
but a corinthian, a lad of mettle, a good boy 1H4 2.04. 12 P
that rascal hath good mettle in him, he will not 2.04.349 P
and now their pride and mettle is asleep, 4.03. 22
o, this boy | lends mettle to us all! 5.04. 24
master silence had been a man of this mettle. 2H4 5.03. 38 P
show us here | the mettle of your pasture; H5 3.01. 27
where have they this mettle? 3.05. 15
and plainly say | our mettle is bred out, and 3.05. 29
the fellow has mettle enough in his belly. 4.08. 63 P
and every greek of mettle, let him know, | what TRO 1.03.258
whose self-same mettle, | whereof thy proud TIM 4.03.179
he was quick mettle when he went to school. JC 1.02.296
yet i see | thy honorable mettle may be wrought 1.02.309
nor th' insuppressive mettle of our spirits, 2.01.134
make gallant show and promise of their mettle; 4.02. 24
for thy undaunted mettle should compose MAC 1.07. 73
fortinbras, | of unimproved mettle hot and full, HAM 1.01. 96
why, now i see there's mettle in thee, and even OTH 4.02.204 P
i do think there is mettle in death, which ANT 1.02.143 P
'that horse his mettle from his rider takes; LC 107

MEUS 1 FR 0.0001 REL FR 1 V 0 P
"ego et rex meus" | was still inscrib'd; H8 3.02.314

/MEW* 1 FR 0.0001 REL FR 1 V 0 P
/marry, /your /manhood /mew! LR 4.02. 68

MEW* 4 FR 0.0004 REL FR 4 V 0 P
why will you mew her up, | signior baptista, for SHR 1.01. 87
should move you to mew up | your tender kinsman, JN 4.02. 57
i had rather be a kitten and cry mew | than one 1H4 3.01.127
the cat will mew, and dog will have his day. HAM 5.01.292

MEW'D* 5 FR 0.0005 REL FR 5 V 0 P
a nun, | for aye to be in shady cloister mew'd, MND 1.01. 71
and therefore has he closely mew'd her up, SHR 1.01.183
this day should clarence closely be mew'd up R3 1.01. 38
more pity that the eagles should be mew'd, 1.01.132
thrice the brinded cat hath mew'd. MAC 4.01. 1

MEWED 2 FR 0.0002 REL FR 2 V 0 P
and for his meed, poor lord, he is mewed up. R3 1.03.138
to-night she's mewed up to her heaviness. ROM 3.04. 11

MEWLING 1 FR 0.0001 REL FR 1 V 0 P
mewling and puking in the nurse's arms. AYL 2.07.144

MEXICO 2 FR 0.0002 REL FR 1 V 1 P
upon the rialto, he hath a third at mexico, a MV 1.03. 20 P
from tripolis, from mexico, and england, | from 3.02.268

MI* 5 FR 0.0005 REL FR 3 V 2 P
ut, re, sol, la, mi, fa. LLL 4.02.100 P
mi perdonato, gentle master mine; SHR 1.01. 25
b mi, bianca, take him for thy lord, | c fa ut, 3.01. 75
e la mi, show pity, or i die." 3.01. 78
fa, sol, la, mi. LR 1.02.137 P

MICE 4 FR 0.0004 REL FR 4 V 0 P
law, | as mice by lions) hath pick'd out an act, MM 1.04. 64
or piteous they will look, like drowned mice. 1H6 1.02. 12
but mice and rats, and such small deer, | have LR 3.04.138
that /walk upon the beach, | appear like mice; 4.06. 18

MICHAEL 17 FR 0.0019 REL FR 17 V 0 P
hie, good sir michael, bear this sealed brief 1H4 4.04. 1
to-morrow, good sir michael, is a day | wherein 4.04. 8
and i fear, sir michael, | what with the 4.04. 13
and, to prevent the worst, sir michael, speed; 4.04. 35
to other friends, and so farewell, sir michael. 4.04. 41
worthy saint michael, and the golden fleece, 1H6 4.07. 69
one michael cassio, a florentine | (a fellow OTH 1.01. 20
a veronesa, michael cassio, | lieutenant to the 2.01. 26
on, | i'll have our michael cassio on the hip, 2.01.305
good michael, look you to the guard to-night. 2.03. 1
michael, good night. 2.03. 7
how comes it, michael, you are thus forgot? 2.03.188
than it should do offense to michael cassio; 2.03.222
what ever shall become of michael cassio, | he's 3.03. 8
michael cassio, | that came a-wooing with you, 3.03. 70
did michael cassio, when /you woo'd my lady, 3.03. 94
for michael cassio, | i dare be sworn i think 3.03.124

MICHAELMAS 2 FR 0.0002 REL FR 0 V 2 P
last, a fortnight afore michaelmas? WIV 1.01.205 P
me see — about michaelmas next i shall be — 1H4 2.04. 54 P

MICHER 1 FR 0.0001 REL FR 0 V 1 P
of heaven prove a micher and eat blackberries? 1H4 2.04.408 P

/MICHING 1 FR 0.0001 REL FR 0 V 1 P
marry, this' /miching mallecho, it means HAM 3.02.137 P

MICKLE 7 FR 0.0008 REL FR 7 V 0 P
one ne'er got me credit, the other mickle blame. ERR 3.01. 45
an oath of mickle might, and fury shall abate. H5 2.01. 66
rage, | to-morrow i shall die with mickle age. 1H6 4.06. 35
me | that bows unto the grave with mickle age. 2H6 5.01.174
o, mickle is the powerful grace that lies | in ROM 2.03. 15
upon this mighty morr— — of mickle weight — TNK 3.05.118
more mickle was the pain, | that nothing could PP 15. 9

MICROCOSM 1 FR 0.0001 REL FR 0 V 1 P
if you see this in the map of my microcosm, COR 2.01. 63 P

MID 2 FR 0.0002 REL FR 2 V 0 P
past the mid season. TMP 1.02.239
about the mid of night come to my tent | and R3 5.03. 77

MID-AGE 1 FR 0.0001 REL FR 1 V 0 P
virgins and boys, mid-age and wrinkled /eld, TRO 2.02.104

MIDAS 1 FR 0.0001 REL FR 1 V 0 P
hard food for midas, i will none of thee; MV 3.02.102

MIDDAY 4 FR 0.0004 REL FR 4 V 0 P
than midday sun fierce bent against their faces. 1H6 1.01. 14
have been as piercing as the midday sun | to 3H6 5.02. 17
them, | and titan, tired in the midday heat, VEN 177
as mountain snow melts with the midday sun. 750

MIDDEST *(also midst)*

MIDDEST 1 FR 0.0001 REL FR 0 V 1 P
and hell, have through the very middest of you! 2H6 4.08. 61 P

/MIDDLE 1 FR 0.0001 REL FR 1 V 0 P
/those /broils, | /beginning /in /the /middle; TRO pr 28

MIDDLE 18 FR 0.0020 REL FR 10 V 8 P
heavy | middle of the night to call upon him. MM 4.01. 35
and never, since the middle summer's spring, MND 2.01. 82
we are for you, sit i' th' middle. AYL 5.03. 10 P
at upper end o' th' table, now i' th' middle; WT 4.04. 59

these are flow'rs | of middle summer, and i 4.04.107
i think they are given | to men of middle age. 4.04.108
the middle centure of this cursed town. 1H6 2.02. 6
color, | murther thy breath in middle of a word, R3 3.05. 2
our general is cut i' th' middle, and but one COR 4.05.198 P
the middle of humanity thou never knewest, but TIM 4.03.300 P
in the dead waste and middle of the night, HAM 1.02.198
about her waist, or in the middle of her favors? 2.02.233 P
cut the egg i' th' middle and eat up the meat, LR 1.04.158 P
thy /crown i' th' middle and gav'st away both 1.04.160 P
o' both sides, and left nothing i' th' middle. 1.04.188 P
why one's nose stands i' th' middle on 's face? 1.05. 20 P
but even the very middle of my heart | is warm'd CYM 1.06. 27
resembling strong youth in his middle age, | yet SON 7. 6
MIDDLE–EARTH 1 FR 0.0001 REL FR 1 V 0 P
but stay, i smell a man of middle–earth. WIV 5.05. 80
MIDNIGHT 43 FR 0.0048 REL FR 28 V 15 P
levied, one midnight | fated to th' purpose, did TMP 1.02.128
thou call'dst me up at midnight to fetch dew 1.02.228
speak softly, | all's hush'd as midnight yet. 4.01.207
whose pastime | is to make midnight mushrumps, 5.01. 39
word they'll meet him in the park at midnight? WIV 4.04. 18 P
doth all the winter–time, at still midnight, 4.04. 30
be you in the park about midnight, at herne's 5.01. 11 P
'tis now dead midnight, and by eight to–morrow MM 4.02. 64
that's the way; for women are light at midnight. 5.01.280 P
bear it coldly but till midnight, and let the ADO 3.02.129 P
midnight, assist our moan, | help us to sigh and 5.03. 16
from lovers' food till morrow deep midnight. MND 1.01.223
and will to–morrow midnight solemnly | dance in 4.01. 88
the iron tongue of midnight hath told twelve. 5.01.363
a lover | as ever sigh'd upon a midnight pillow. AYL 2.04. 27
and by midnight look to hear further from me. AWW 3.06. 77 P
when midnight comes, knock at my chamber–window; 4.02. 54
not till after midnight; 4.03. 29 P
how now, my lord, is't not after midnight? 4.03. 84 P
to be a–bed after midnight is to be up betimes, TN 2.03. 2 P
to be up after midnight and to go to bed then, 2.03. 7 P
that to go to bed after midnight is to go to bed 2.03. 8 P
noon, midnight? WT 1.02.290
if the midnight bell | did with his iron tongue JN 3.03. 37
and with my hand at midnight held your head; 4.01. 45
age of this present twelve a' clock at midnight. 1H4 2.04. 95 P
what doth gravity out of his bed at midnight? 2.04.294 P
we have heard the chimes at midnight, master 2H4 3.02.214 P
and leave your england as dead midnight, still, H5 3.pr. 19
'tis midnight, i'll go arm myself. 3.07. 89 P
it is now dead midnight. R3 5.03.180
(as they say spirits do) at midnight, have | in H8 5.01. 14
'tis midnight, charles, | prithee to bed, and in 5.01. 72
were i as patient as the midnight sleep, | by COR 3.01. 85
for it is after midnight, and ere day | we will JC 1.03.163
how now, you secret, black, and midnight hags? MAC 4.01. 48
thou mixture rank, of midnight weeds collected, HAM 3.02.257
you shall hear more by midnight. OTH 4.01.212 P
let's mock the midnight bell. ANT 3.13.184
at the sixt hour of morn, at noon, at midnight, CYM 1.03. 31
almost midnight, madam. 2.02. 2
here's a few flow'rs, but 'bout midnight, more: 4.02.283
"for in the dreadful dead of dark midnight, LUC 1625
MIDRIFF 1 FR 0.0001 REL FR 0 V 1 P
it is all fill'd up with guts and midriff. 1H4 3.03.155 P
MIDS 1 FR 0.0001 REL FR 1 V 0 P
yet in the mids of all her pure protestings, PP 7.11
MIDST *(also middest)*
MIDST 13 FR 0.0014 REL FR 13 V 0 P
our helpful ship was splitted in the midst; ERR 1.01.103
pale, | make periods in the midst of sentences, MND 5.01. 96
what, in the midst of the street? SHR 5.01.144
fled, | but that they left me midst my enemies. 1H6 1.02. 24
but, in the midst of this bright–shining day, 3H6 5.03. 3
our archers shall be placed in the midst; R3 5.03.295
a gulf it did remain | i' th' midst a' th' body, COR 1.01. 99
our good city | cleave in the midst and perish. 3.02. 28
here i'll sit i' th' midst. MAC 3.04. 10
i' th' midst o' th' fight, | when vantage like a ANT 3.10. 11
then in the midst a tearing groan did break 4.14. 31
but in the midst of his unfruitful prayer, LUC 344
and midst the sentence so her accent breaks, 566
MIDSUMMER 3 FR 0.0003 REL FR 1 V 2 P
if it had not been for a hot midsummer night; AYL 4.01.102 P
why, this is very midsummer madness. TN 3.04. 56 P
of may, | and gorgeous as the sun at midsummer; 1H4 4.01.102
MIDWAY 5 FR 0.0005 REL FR 4 V 1 P
made just in the midway between him and benedick ADO 2.01. 7 P
midway between your tents and walls of troy, TRO 1.03.278
the crows and choughs that wing the midway air LR 4.06. 13
no midway | 'twixt these extremes at all. ANT 3.04. 19
/deafen'd parts, | which now are midway stopp'd. PER 5.01. 48
/MIDWIFE 1 FR 0.0001 REL FR 1 V 0 P
and /midwife gentle | to those that cry by night PER 3.01. 11
MIDWIFE 10 FR 0.0011 REL FR 8 V 2 P
like aqua–vitae with a midwife. TN 2.05.196 P
with lady margery, your midwife there, | to save WT 2.03.160
so, green, thou art the midwife to my woe, | and R2 2.02. 62
i knew her well, she was a midwife. 2H6 4.02. 43 P
the midwife wonder'd and the women cried, | "o, 3H6 5.06. 74
cornelia the midwife, and myself, | and no one TIT 4.02.141
the emperess, the midwife, and yourself. 4.02.143
days, | but send the midwife presently to me. 4.02.166
the midwife and the nurse well made away, | then 4.02.167
she is the fairies' midwife, and she comes | in ROM 1.04. 54
MIDWIVE'S 1 FR 0.0001 REL FR 0 V 1 P
here's the midwive's name to't, one mistress WT 4.04.269 P
MIDWIVES 1 FR 0.0001 REL FR 0 V 1 P
but the midwives say the children are not in the 2H4 2.02. 25 P
MIENNE 1 FR 0.0001 REL FR 0 V 1 P
donc votre est france et vous etes mienne. H5 5.02.184 P
MIGHT* *(also mought)*
/MIGHT* 5 FR 0.0005 REL FR 4 V 1 P
/the /dole /of /blows /your /son /might /drop. 2H4 1.01.169
//to–day /might /i, /hanging /on /hotspur's 2.03. 44
/and /might /by /no /suit /gain /our /audience. 4.01. 76
i would it /might /be hangers till then. HAM 5.02.160 P
/this /rest /might /yet /have /balm'd /thy LR 3.06. 98
MIGHT* 560 FR 0.0633 REL FR 452 V 108 P
but what my power might else exact — like one TMP 1.02. 99
then tell me | if this might be a brother. 1.02.118
would i might | but ever see that man! 1.02.168
i might call him | a thing divine, for nothing 1.02.418
me, | might i but through my prison once a day 1.02.491
what might, | worthy sebastian, o, what might — 2.01.204
might, | worthy sebastian, o, what might — ? 2.01.205
to the perpetual wink for aye might put | this 2.01.285
yet a tailor might scratch her where e'er she 2.02. 53
chiefly that i might set it in my prayers — 3.01. 35
of it, but i fear'd | lest i might anger thee. 4.01.169
that you might kill your stomach on your meat, TGV 1.02. 68
that i might sing it, madam, to a tune: 1.02. 77
some messenger, that might her mind discover, 2.01.167
but, fearing lest my jealous aim might err, 3.01. 28
what might we do to make the girl forget | the 3.02. 29
sixteen months, and longer might have stay'd, 4.01. 21
grace did lend her, | that she might admired be. 4.02. 43
and would i might be dead | if i in thought felt 4.04.171
or i would i might never come in mine own great WIV 1.01.154 P
ay, or else i would i might be hang'd, la! 1.01.258 P
with all his might | for thee to fight, | john 2.01. 17
perceive how i might be knighted. 2.01. 55 P
sir, that you might avoid him if you saw him. 2.02.276 P
otherwise you might slip away ere he came. 4.02. 53 P
how might we disguise him? 4.02. 68 P
otherwise he might put on a hat, a muffler, and 4.02. 71 P
i would all the world might be cozen'd, for i 4.05. 93 P
(so far forth as herself might be her chooser) 4.06. 11
it had been anne page, would i might never stir! 5.05.187 P
for that which, if myself might be his judge, MM 1.04. 27
and makes us lose the good we oft might win, 1.04. 78
given, might have been accus'd in fornication, 2.01. 80 P
ear, you might have your action of slander too. 2.01.180 P
lest i might be too rash. 2.02. 9
i do think that you might pardon him, | and 2.02. 49
but might you do't, and do the world no wrong, 2.02. 53
and he that might the vantage best have took 2.02. 74
that you might know it, would much better please 2.04. 32
might there not be a charity in sin | to save 2.04. 63
might but my bending down | reprieve thee from 3.01.143
might you dispense with your leisure, i would by 3.01.153 P
what, i prithee, might be the cause? 3.02.133 P
no might nor greatness in mortality | can 3.02.185
to save me from the danger that might come | if 4.03. 85
her maiden loss, | how might she tongue me! 4.04. 25
might in the times to come have ta'en revenge, 4.04. 30
for that he knew you, might reproach your life, 5.01.421
had rather it would please you i might be whipt. 5.01.506 P
might bear him company in the quest of him: ERR 1.01.129
are you there, wife? you might have come before. 3.01. 63
with words that in an honest suit might move. 4.02. 14
sir, that i might not feel your blows. 4.04. 25 P
heart and good will you might, | but surely, 4.04. 85
his word might bear my wealth at any time. 5.01. 8
albeit my wrongs might make one wiser mad. 5.01.217
but lest my liking might too sudden seem, | i ADO 1.01.314
too, for the garland he might have worn himself, 2.01.229 P
and the rod he might have bestow'd on you, who, 2.01.229 P
unless i might have another for working–days. 2.01.327 P
i might have said, "no part of it is mine; 4.01.134
how much might the man deserve of me that would 4.01.261 P
how they might hurt their enemies — if they 5.01. 98
that i might have cudgell'd thee out of thy 5.04.113 P
not by might mast'red, but by special grace. LLL 1.01.152
neglect | of his almighty dreadful little might. 3.01.203
and he it was that might rightly say, veni, vidi 4.01. 67 P
air, would i might triumph so! 4.03.108
might shake off fifty, looking in her eye: 4.03.239
she might 'a' been /a grandam ere she died. 5.02. 17
ay, or i would these hands might never part. 5.02. 57
toward that shade i might behold address'd | the 5.02. 92
and might not you | forestall our sport, to make 5.02.472
north, and south, i spread my conquering might. 5.02.563
might well have made our sport a comedy. 5.02.876
but i might see young cupid's fiery shaft MND 2.01.161
on whose eyes i might approve | this flower's 2.02. 68
address your love and might | to honor helen and 2.02.143
to take from thence all error with his might, 3.02.368
was to be gone from athens, where we might, 4.01.152
noble respect | takes it in might, not merit. 5.01. 92
with the help of a surgeon he might yet recover, 5.01.310 P
and every object that might make me fear MV 1.01. 20
what harm a wind too great might do at sea. 1.01. 24
had your eyes, you might fail of the knowing me; 2.02. 76 P
lord worshipp'd might he be! 2.02. 93 P
i would it might prove the end of his losses. 3.01. 18 P
i might in virtues, beauties, livings, friends, 3.02.156
you and i, if i might but see you at my death. 3.02.319 P
withal, that either you might stay him from his AYL 1.01.133 P
duke that the wrastling might not go forward. 1.02.182 P
the feet might bear the verses. 3.02.167 P
a poet, i might have some hope thou didst feign. 3.03. 26 P
who might be your mother, | that you insult, 3.05. 35
dead shepherd, now i find thy saw of might, 3.05. 81
lack of matter, you might take occasion to kiss. 4.01. 74 P
mind, for i protest her frown might kill me. 4.01.110 P
i might ask you for your commission, but i do 4.01.138 P
that had a wife with such a wit, he might say, 4.01.166 P
nay, you might keep that check for it, till you 4.01.167 P
how then might your prayers move? 4.03. 55
and well he might so do, | for well i know he 4.03.123
that you might excuse | his broken promise, and 4.03.153
that mortal ears might hardly endure the din? SHR 1.01.173
senis," that we might beguile the old pantaloon. 3.01. 36 P
soon hot, my very lips might freeze to my teeth, 4.01. 6 P
you might have heard it else proclaim'd about. 4.02. 87
still, | and happily we might be interrupted. 4.04. 54
military policy how virgins might blow up men? AWW 1.01.122 P
how might one do, sir, to lose it to her own 1.01.150 P
which might be felt, that we, the poorer born, 1.01.182
might with effects of them follow our friends, 1.01.184
a man | might be a copy to these younger times; 1.02. 46
i wish might be found in the calendar of my past 1.03. 4 P
and we might have a good woman born but /or 1.03. 86 P
would not extend his might only where qualities 1.03.113 P
yes, helen, you might be my daughter–in–law. 1.03.167
it might pass: 2.03.203 P
that twenty such rude boys might tend upon | and 3.02. 82
might you not know she would do as she has done 3.04. 2
at overnight, | she might have been o'erta'en; 3.04. 24
this young maid might do her | a shrewd turn, if 3.05. 67
he might at some great and trusty business in a 3.06. 14 P
it might have been recover'd. 3.06. 58 P
it might, but it is not now. 3.06. 59 P
that he might take a measure of his own 4.03. 32 P
much shame, you might begin an impudent nation. 4.03.328 P
with what manners i might safely be admitted. 4.05. 89 P
so, | he might have bought me at a common price. 5.03.190
and i had that which any inferior might | at 5.03.218
it might be yours or hers, for aught i know. 5.03.280
so please my lord, i might not be admitted, TN 1.01. 23
and might not be delivered to the world | till i 1.02. 42
i would i might never draw sword again. 1.03. 64 P
he might have took his answer long ago. 1.05.263
you might do much. | what is your parentage? 1.05.276
malignancy of my fate might perhaps distemper 2.01. 4 P
you might have sav'd me my pains, to have taken 2.02. 5 P
that their business might be every thing and 2.04. 76 P
as it might be, perhaps, were i a woman, | i 2.04.108
you might see more detraction at your heels than 2.05.137 P
dally with that word might make my sister wanton 3.01. 20 P
are out of my welkin — i might say "element," 3.01. 58 P
what might you think? 3.01.117
i wish it might, for now i am your fool. 3.01.144
as might have drawn one to a longer voyage) 3.03. 7
but jealousy what might befall your travel, 3.03. 8
might well have given us bloody argument. 3.03. 32
it might have since been answer'd in repaying 3.03. 33
a fiend like thee might bear my soul to hell. 3.04.217
which with as much safety you might answer him; 3.04.250 P
soul of our grandam might happily inhabit a bird 4.02. 52 P
his counsel now might do me golden service, 4.03. 8
your suspicion, | be blam'd for't how you might. WT 2.01.161
a moi'ty of my rest | might come to me again. 2.03. 9
might we lay th' old proverb to your charge, 2.03. 97
with such a kind of love as might become | a 3.02. 64
to whose feeling sorrows i might be some allay 4.02. 8 P
i had some flow'rs o' th' spring that might 4.04.113
sea, that you might ever do | nothing but that; 4.04.141
with wisdom i might fear, my doricles, | you 4.04.150
if i might die within this hour, i have liv'd 4.04.461
you might have pinch'd a placket, it was 4.04.609 P
yet nature might have made me as these are, 4.04.746
you might have spoken a thousand things that 5.01. 21
i might have look'd upon my queen's full eyes, 5.01. 53
might quench the zeal | of all professors else, 5.01.107
'twixt heaven and earth | might thus have stood, 5.01.133
what might i have been, | might i a son and 5.01.176
might i a son and daughter now have look'd on, 5.01.177
as beauty, | that you might well enjoy her. 5.01.215
there might you have beheld one joy crown 5.02. 43 P
that she might no more be in danger of losing. 5.02. 78 P
as now she might have done, | so much to my good 5.03. 32
this might have been prevented and made whole JN 1.01. 35
friend, your father might have kept | this calf, 1.01.123
in sooth he might; 1.01.125
my brother might not claim him, nor your father, 1.01.126
would i might never stir from off this place, 1.01.145
sir robert might have eat his part in me | upon 1.01.234
heralds, from off our tow'rs we might behold, 2.01.325
that i might sit all night and watch with you. 4.01. 30
and those thy fears might have wrought fears in 4.02.236
where these two christian armies might combine 5.02. 37
evil, that you might | the better arm you to the 5.06. 25
virtue in my tears, | that might relieve you! 5.07. 45
might from our quiet confines fright fair peace, R2 1.03.137
that he, our hope, might have retir'd his power, 2.02. 46
me rather had my heart might feel your love 3.03.192
they might have liv'd to bear and he to taste 3.04. 62
poor queen, so that thy state might be no worse, 3.04.102
i would to god, my lords, he might be found. 5.03. 4
and majesty might never yet endure | the moody 1H4 1.03. 18
so he that doth redeem her thence might wear 1.03.206
as what i think might be, but what i know | is 1.03.273
might so have tempted him as you have done, 3.01.172
and that no man might draw short breath to–day 5.02. 48
i might have let alone | the insulting hand of 5.04. 53
it, he might have moe diseases than he knew for. 2H4 1.02. 4 P
bottle, i would i might never spit white again. 1.02.211 P
how might we see falstaff bestow himself 2.02.169 P
that the wicked might not fall in love with thee 2.04.320 P
o god, that one might read the book of fate, 3.01. 45
this | king richard might create a perfect guess 3.01. 88
i would wart might have gone, sir. 3.02.163 P
name, for you might have thrust him and all his 3.02.325 P
as might hold sortance with his quality, | the 4.01. 11
off | that might so much as think you enemies. 4.01.144
what mischiefs might he set abroach | in shadow 4.02. 14
england shall give him office, honor, might; 4.05.129
welcome | give entertainment to the might of it, 4.05.173
and by whose power i well might lodge a fear 4.05.207
lest rest and lying still might make them look 4.05.211
how might a prince of my great hopes forget | so 5.02. 68
and i might see you there, davy! 5.03. 61 P
i would to god that i might die, that i might 5.04. 2 P
that i might die, that i might have thee hang'd. 5.04. 2 P
o god, that right should thus overcome might! 5.04. 25 P
your grace hath cause, and means, and might; H5 1.02.125
an oath of mickle might, and fury shall abate. 2.01. 66
one spark of evil | that might annoy my finger? 2.02.102
world, | he might return to vasty tartar back, 2.02.123
the french might have a good prey of us, if he 4.04. 75 P
throngs, | if any order might be thought upon. 4.05. 21
and please god of his grace that i might see. 4.07.164 P
any from mine that might offend your majesty. 4.08. 47 P
or if i might buffet for my love, or bound my 5.02.140 P
that now our loss might be ten times so much? 1H6 2.01. 53
that so he might recover what was lost. 2.05. 32
might but redeem the passage of your age! 2.05.108
i would prevail, if prayers might prevail, | to 3.01. 67
i should have begg'd i might have been employ'd. 4.01. 72
force | might with a sally of the very town | be 4.04. 4
talbot dead, great york might bear the name. 4.04. 9
he might have sent, and had the horse. 4.04. 33
and fly would talbot never, though he might. 4.04. 44
that talbot's name might be in thee reviv'd, 4.05. 3

that i in rage might shoot them at your faces! 4.07. 80
how france and frenchmen might be kept in awe, 2H6 1.01. 92
and if my death might make this island happy, 3.01.148
might happily have prov'd far worse than his. 3.01.306
might liquid tears or heart–offending groans 3.02. 60
they, | might in thy palace perish /margaret. 3.02.100
it, | and so i wish'd thy body might my heart. 3.02.109
the mortal worm might make the sleep eternal. 3.02.263
and so should these, if i might have my will. 4.01. 27
so might your grace's person be in danger. 4.04. 45
that, if i might have a lease of my life for a 4.10. 5 P
so wish i, i might thrust thy soul to hell. 4.10. 79
might i but know thee by thy /household badge. 5.01.201
when he might spurn him with his foot away? 3H6 1.04. 58
body | might in the ground be closed up in rest! 2.01. 76
he might have kept that glory to this day. 2.02.153
that i, in all despite, might rail at him, 2.06. 81
else might i think that clarence, edward's 4.02. 10
we are, | we might recover all our loss again. 5.02. 30
but at last | i well might hear, delivered with 5.02. 46
which industry and courage might have sav'd? 5.04. 11
lest in our need he might infect another, | and 5.04. 46
that you might still have worn the petticoat, 5.05. 23
so i might live one hour in your sweet bosom. R3 1.02.124
i would they were, that i might die at once; 1.02.151
which haply by much company might be urg'd; 2.02.137
rule, | this sickly land might solace as before. 2.03. 30
too late he died that might have kept that title 3.01. 99
i would, that i might thank you as you call me. 3.01.123
might better wear their heads | than some that 3.02. 92
which by my presence might have been concluded. 3.04. 25
than my lord hastings no man might be bolder, 3.04. 29
for i, too fond, might have prevented this. 3.04. 81
that you might well have signified the same 3.05. 59
would it might please your grace, | on our 3.07.114
you might haply think | tongue–tied ambition, 3.07.144
o, she that might have intercepted thee, | by 4.04.137
here, | a royal battle might be won and lost. 4.04.536
i wish'd might fall on me when i was found 5.01. 14
men might say | till this time pomp was single, H8 1.01. 14
england and france might through their amity 1.01.181
devil's illusions | the monk might be deceiv'd, 1.02.179
that | a woman of less place might ask by law: 2.02.111
receive | if you might please to stretch it. 2.03. 33
or | laid any scruple in your way which might 2.04.151
spake one the least word that might | be to the 2.04.154
wherein he might the king his lord advertise 2.04.179
employ'd you where high profits might come home, 3.02.158
that might have mercy on the fault thou gav'st 3.02.262
might corrupt minds procure knaves as corrupt 5.01.132
course of my authority | might go one way, and 5.02. 71
when i might see from far some forty 5.03. 51 P
better at home, if "would i might" were "may." TRO 1.01.114
ay, | i ask, that i might waken reverence, | and 1.03.227
such things as might offend the weakest spleen 2.02.128
else might the world convince of levity | as 2.02.130
till now not so much | but i might master it. 3.02.121
for to be wise and love | exceeds man's might; 3.02.157
might be affronted with the match and weight 3.02.166
and still it might, and yet it may again, | if 3.03.185
clear again, that i might water an ass at it! 3.03.311 P
i might have still held off, | and then you 4.02. 17
if i might in entreaties find success — | as 4.05.149
might send that greekish whoremasterly villain 5.04. 6 P
we might guess they reliev'd us humanely; COR 1.01. 18 P
that you might leave pricking it for pity. 1.03. 85 P
well might they fester 'gainst ingratitude, 1.09. 30
when he might act the woman in the scene, | he 2.02. 96
and might well | be taken from the people. 2.02.145
your voices might | be curses to yourselves? 2.03.184
either his gracious promise, which you might, 2.03.193
so he might | be call'd your vanquisher. 3.01. 16
that the precipitation might down stretch 3.02. 4
you might have been enough the man you are, 3.02. 19
and safeguard | of what that want might ruin. 3.02. 69
given, he might have boil'd and eaten him too. 4.05.189 P
and might have been much better, if | he could 4.06. 16
army we can make, | might stop our countryman. 5.01. 38
volsces whom you serve, you might condemn us, 5.03.134
the last, i think | might have found easy fines; 5.06. 64
that what we did was mildly as we might, TIT 1.01.475
thee life when well he might have slain thee, 2.03.159
and might not gain so great a happiness | as 2.04. 20
that i might rail at him to ease my mind! 2.04. 35
fire, | so i might have your company in hell, 5.01.149
i did | would i perform if i might have my will. 5.03.188
then most sought where most might not be found, ROM 1.01.127
and i might live to see thee married once, | i 1.03. 61
upon that hand, | that i might touch that cheek! 2.02. 25
which modern lamentation might have moved? 3.02.120
would none but i might venge my cousin's death! 3.05. 86
cell, | and gave him what becomed love i might, 4.02. 26
dumbness of the gesture | one might interpret. TIM 1.01. 34
might we but have that happiness, my lord, that 1.02. 84 P
whereby we might express some part of our zeals, 1.02. 86 P
myself poorer, that i might come nearer to you. 1.02.101 P
that man might ne'er be wretched for his mind. 1.02.164
my mouth, that i might answer thee profitably. 2.02. 76 P
that answer might have become apemantus. 2.02.118 P
that i might so have rated my expense | as i had 2.02.126
time, when i might ha' shown myself honorable! 3.02. 45 P
he might have tried lord lucius or lucullus; 3.03. 2
angry at him, | that might have known my place. 3.03. 14
but his occasions might have wooed me first; 3.03. 15
if i might beseech you, gentlemen, to repair 3.04. 68 P
he might have died in war. 3.05. 74
though his right arm might purchase his own time 3.05. 76
wert a dog, | that i might love thee something. 4.03. 56
into your eye, | that you might see your shadow. JC 1.02. 58
i would not (so with love i might entreat you) 1.02.166
i would i might go to hell among the rogues. 1.02.268 P
how that might change his nature, there's the 2.01. 13
i have a man's mind, but a woman's might. 2.04. 8
he wish'd to–day our enterprise might thrive. 3.01. 16
might fire the blood of ordinary men, | and turn 3.01. 37
but yesterday the word of caesar might | have 3.02.118
i should not urge thy duty past thy might; 4.03.261
so to–day, | if cassius might have rul'd. 5.01. 47
for fear of what might fall, so to prevent | the 5.01.104
o that a man might know | the end of this day's 5.01.122
so mix'd in him that nature might stand up | and 5.05. 74
home, | might yet enkindle you unto the crown, MAC 1.03.121
of thanks and payment | might have been mine! 1.04. 20
blow | might be the be–all and the end–all — 1.07. 5
and all things else that might | to half a soul 3.01. 81
look on that | which might appall the devil. 3.04. 59
and that well might | advise him to a caution, 3.06. 43
we might have met them dareful, beard to beard, 5.05. 6
i might not this believe | without the sensible HAM 1.01. 56
what might be toward, that this sweaty haste 1.01. 77
for they are actions that a man might play, 1.02. 84
that he might not beteem the winds of heaven 1.02.141
one with moderate haste might tell a hundreth. 1.02.237
which might deprive your sovereignty of reason, 1.04. 73
or "there be, and if they might," | or such 1.05.177
kept close, might move | more grief to hide, 2.01.115
both your majesties | might, by the sovereign 2.02. 27
that it might please you to give quiet pass 2.02. 77
but what might you think, | when i had seen this 2.02.131
before my daughter told me — what might you, 2.02.134
love with idle sight, | what might you think? 2.02.139
in the phrase that might indict the author of 2.02.443 P
when he himself might his quietus make | with a 3.01. 74
you might have rhym'd. 3.02.285 P
now might i do it /pat, now 'a is a–praying; 3.03. 73
would make one think there might be thought, 4.05. 12
motive, | why to a public count i might not go, 4.07. 17
could devise it so | that i might be the organ. 4.07. 70
that might hold | if this did blast in proof. 4.07.153
this might be the pate of a politician, which 5.01. 78 P
one that would circumvent god, might it not? 5.01. 80 P
it might, my lord. 5.01. 81 P
this might be my lord such–a–one, that prais'd 5.01. 84 P
horse, when 'a /meant to beg it, might it not? 5.01. 86 P
this fellow might be in 's time a great buyer of 5.01.103 P
whereto he was converted might they not stop a 5.01.211 P
clay, | might stop a hole to keep the wind away. 5.01.214
love between them like the palm might flourish, 5.02. 40
what i have done | that might your nature, honor 5.02.231
might in their working do you that offense, LR 1.04.212
why might not you, my lord, receive attendance 2.04.243
that things might change or cease, /tears /his 3.01. 7
i desir'd their leave that i might pity him, 3.03. 3 P
might i but live to see thee in my touch, | i'ld 4.01. 23
their punishment | might have the freer course. 4.02. 94
what might import my sister's letter to him? 4.05. 6
might not you | transport her purposes by word? 4.05. 19
thus might he pass indeed; 4.06. 47
methinks our pleasure might have been demanded 5.03. 62
what safe and nicely i might well delay | by 5.03.145
i might have sav'd her, now she's gone for ever! 5.03.271
the law (with all his might to enforce it on) OTH 1.02. 16
it so fell out) | the town might fall in fright. 2.03.232
which till to–night | i ne'er might say before. 2.03.236
wholesome wisdom | he might not but refuse you. 3.01. 47
those that be not, would they might seem none! 3.03.127
i would i might entreat your honor | to scan 3.03.244
will give you satisfaction, you might have't. 3.03.408
she might lie by an emperor's side and command 4.01.184 P
i may not breathe my censure | what he might be. 4.01.271
if what he might he is not, | i would to heaven 4.01.271
that he might stick | the small'st opinion on my 4.02.108
he might have chid me so; 4.02.113
to do the act that might the addition earn, 4.02.163
i might do't as well i' th' dark. 4.03. 67
own world, and you might quickly make it right. 4.03. 82 P
general warranty of heaven | as i might love. 5.02. 61
that i might sleep out this great gap of time ANT 1.05. 5
here at rome | might be to you in egypt; 2.02. 38
your being in egypt | might be my question. 2.02. 40
that the men might go to wars with the women! 2.02. 66 P
if it might please you, to enforce no further 2.02. 99
here they might take two thieves kissing. 2.06. 96 P
would it were all, | that it might go on wheels! 2.07. 93
for better might we | have lov'd without this 3.02. 31
is gone, | through whom i might command it? 3.03. 6
my news | i might have told hereafter. 3.05. 22
which might have well becom'd the best of men, 3.07. 26
thy beck might from the bidding of the gods 3.11. 60
submits her to thy might, and of thee craves 3.12. 17
that i might do you service | so good as you 4.02. 18
that he and caesar might | determine this great 4.04. 36
fury, for one death | might have prevented many. 4.12. 42
fearing since how it might work, hath sent | me 4.14.125
sleep, that i might see | but such another man! 5.02. 77
if it might please ye — 5.02. 78
think you there was or might be such a man | as 5.02. 93
would i might never | o'ertake pursu'd success, 5.02.102
that i might hear thee call great caesar ass 5.02.307
o blessed, that i might not! CYM 1.01.139
there might have been, | but that my master 1.01.161
a needle, that i might prick | the goer–back. 1.01.168
which else an easy battery might lay flat, for 1.04. 22 P
but yet heaven's bounty towards him might | be 1.06. 78
such boil'd stuff | as well might poison poison. 1.06.126
mine oaths of him and might not spend them at my 2.01. 5 P
that i might touch! 2.02. 16
and this you might have heard of here, by me, 2.04. 77
which you might from relation likewise reap, 2.04. 86
view on't | might well have warm'd old saturn; 2.05. 12
yet said hereafter | i might know more. 4.02. 42
might break out and swear | he'ld fetch us in; 4.02.140
that possible strength might meet, would seek us 4.02.160
pisanio might have kill'd thee at the heart 4.02.322
and might so safely, had it | been all the worth 5.05.190
i had you down and might | have made you finish. 5.05.411
wish, and that i might | waste it for you like PER 1.ch. 15
we might proceed to /cancel of your days; 1.01.113
and what was first but fear what might be done, 1.02. 14
stop the course by which it might be known. 1.02. 23
from whence an issue i might propagate, | are 1.02. 73
bethought what was past, what might succeed. 1.02. 83
how i might stop this tempest ere it came, | and 1.02. 98
king, desir'd he might know none of his secrets. 1.03. 6 P
had not a show might countervail his worth. 2.03. 56
a deed might gain her love or your displeasure. 2.05. 54
convey, | which might not what by me is told. 3.ch. 57
so | the dove of paphos might with the crow 4.ch. 32
might stand peerless by this slaughter. 4.ch. 40
wherein my death might yield her any profit, 4.01. 80
where what is done in action, more, if might, 5.ch. 23
be, hath endur'd a grief | might equal yours, if 5.01. 88
and such a one | my daughter might have been. 5.01.108
that thou thoughts' thy griefs might equal mine, 5.01.131
that peace might purge | for her repletion, and TNK 1.02. 23
excess and overflow of power, and't might be, 1.03. 4
'twas possible | they might have been recovered. 1.04. 27
the poison of pure spirits, might, like women, 2.02. 75
a wife might part us lawfully, or business, 2.02. 89
i might sicken, cousin, | where you should never 2.02. 91
might not a man well lose himself and love her? 2.02.155
that i, poor man, might eftsoons come between, 3.01. 12
two such steeds might well | be by a pair of 3.01. 20
place, which well | might justify your manhood; 3.01. 64
kinsman, you might as well | speak this, and act 3.01. 69
of his gyves | might call fell things to listen, 3.02. 15
i might; 3.03. 8
that my embraces | might thank ye, not my blows. 3.06. 23
their lives | might breed the ruin of my name, 3.06.240
yet i might perceive, | ere i departed, a great 4.01. 5
when i might well perceive | 'twas one that sung 4.01. 57
would i might end first! 4.02. 57
that hast the might, | even with an eye–glance, 5.01. 79
i think he might be brought to play at tennis. 5.02. 56
i might do hurt, for they would glance their 5.03. 61
my seat, and in that motion might | omit a ward, 5.03. 62
we, and all our might, | rest at your service. ep 17
not physick'd by respect might turn our blood STM III 13
which might accite thee to embrace and hug them, III 16
o, be not proud, nor brag not of thy might, VEN 113
slain, | he might be buried in a tomb so simple, 244
would they not wish the feast might ever last, 447
that kings might be espoused to more fame, | but LUC 20
might have excuse to work upon his wife, | as in 235
his foul thoughts might compass his fair fair, 346
in his clear bed might have reposed still! 382
lay, | till they might open to adorn the day. 399
which i to conquer sought with all my might; 488
and shame that might ensue | by that her death, 1263
that suspicion which the world might bear her. 1321
words, till action might become them better. 1323
there might you see the laboring pioner 1380
that one might see those far–off eyes look sad. 1386
you might behold triumphing in their faces; 1388
o, what art | of physiognomy might one behold! 1395
there pleading might you see grave nestor stand, 1401
by foul enforcement might be done to me, | from 1623
no rightful plea might plead for justice there. 1649
"and for my sake when i might charm thee so, 1681
that she might think me some untutor'd youth, PP 1. 3
liked of her master as well as well might be, 15. 2
may blow, | air, would i might triumph so! 16.10
worthy blame, | as well as fancy, partial might. 18. 4
these pretty pleasures might me move | to live 19.19
that thereby beauty's rose might never die, SON 1. 2
his tender heir might bear his memory: 1. 4
which husbandry in honor might uphold | against 13.10
with burthen of mine own love's might. 23. 8
that to my use it might unused stay | from hands 48. 3
to–morrow sharp'ned in his former might. 56. 4
that i might see what the old world could say 59. 9
o none, unless this miracle have might, | that 65.13
and in the praise thereof spends all his might, 80. 3
and their gross painting might be better us'd 82.13
well might show | how far a modern quill doth 83. 6
at first the very worst of fortune's might; 90.12
how many lambs might the stern wolf betray, | if 96. 9
to speak of that which gives thee all thy might? 100. 2
as easy might i from myself depart | as from my 109. 3
might i not then say, "now i love you best," 115.10
love is a babe, then might i not say so, | to 115.13
that our night of woe might have rememb'red | my 120. 9
thy pyramids built up with newer might | to me 123. 2
it might for fortune's bastard be unfather'd, 124. 2
that she might think me some untutor'd youth, 138. 3
need'st thou wound with cunning when thy might 139. 7
that they elsewhere might dart their injuries: 139.12
if i might teach thee wit, better it were, 140. 5
and in my madness might speak ill of thee; 140.10
o, from what pow'r hast thou this pow'rful might 150. 1
whereon the thought might think sometime it saw LC 10
i might as yet have been a spreading flower, 75
and makes her absence valiant, not her might. 245

MIGHTFUL 1 FR 0.0001 REL FR 1 V 0 P
my lords, you know, /as /know the mightful gods, TIT 4.04. 5

MIGHTIER 9 FR 0.0010 REL FR 9 V 0 P
but instruments of some more mightier member MM 5.01.237
and stir them up against a mightier task. JN 2.01. 55
two mightier troops than that the dolphin led, 1H6 4.03. 7
but mightier crimes are laid unto your charge, 2H6 3.01.134
a man no mightier than thyself, or me, | in JC 1.03. 76
wind, when both contend | which is the mightier. HAM 4.01. 8
the mightier man, the mightier is the thing LUC 1004
man, the mightier is the thing | that makes him 1004
but wherefore do not you a mightier way | make SON 16. 1

MIGHTIEST 7 FR 0.0008 REL FR 7 V 0 P
'tis mightiest in the mightiest, it becomes MV 4.01.188
'tis mightiest in the mightiest, it becomes 4.01.188
the mightiest space in fortune nature brings AWW 1.01.222
lies | the mightiest of thy greatest enemies, R2 5.06. 32
but kings and mightiest potentates must die, 1H6 3.02.136
provokes the mightiest hulk against the tide, 5.05. 6
rome, | a little ere the mightiest julius fell, HAM 1.01.114

MIGHTILY 16 FR 0.0018 REL FR 8 V 8 P
whose estimation do you mightily hold up — to a ADO 2.02. 24 P
the prince and claudio mightily abus'd, and don 5.02. 98 P
or if he do not mightily grace himself on thee, AYL 1.01.149 P
for her benefits are mightily misplac'd, and the 1.02. 35 P
that have so mightily persuaded him from a first 1.02.206 P
strive mightily, but eat and drink as friends. SHR 1.02.277
how mightily sometimes we make us comforts of AWW 4.03. 65 P
and how mightily some other times we drown our 4.03. 67 P

and kinreds are mightily strengthen'd. 2H4 2.02. 27 P
therein thou wrong'st thy children mightily. 3H6 3.02. 74
and his physicians fear him mightily. R3 1.01.137
long, | good king, to be so mightily abused. TIT 2.03. 87
but trusts a knave | that mightily deceives you. TIM 5.01. 94
i am mightily abus'd; LR 4.07. 52
o, never was there queen | so mightily betrayed! ANT 1.03. 25
what could he see but mightily he noted? LUC 414

MIGHTINESS 5 FR 0.0005 REL FR 5 V 0 P
will't please your mightiness to wash your hands SHR in.2. 76
us fear | the native mightiness and fate of him. H5 2.04. 64
your mightiness on both parts best can witness. 5.02. 28
see | how soon this mightiness meets misery; H8 pr 30
with that painted hope braves your mightiness; TIT 2.03.126

MIGHTST 33 FR 0.0037 REL FR 24 V 9 P
would thou mightst lie drowning | the washing of TMP 1.01. 57
thou mightst call him | a goodly person. 1.02.416
thou mightst as well say i love to walk by the WIV 3.03. 77 P
yield him my virginity, | thou mightst be freed! MM 3.01. 98
mightst thou perceive austerely in his eye ERR 4.02. 2
that thou mightst pour this conceal'd man out of AYL 3.02.199 P
that thou mightst join /her hand with his 5.04.114
would thou mightst never draw sword again. TN 1.03. 62 P
thou mightst have done this without thy beard 4.02. 64 P
how i am gall'd — mightst bespice a cup, | to WT 1.02.316
that thou mightst mend him and make him fit to 2H4 3.02.165 P
that thou mightst win the more thy father's love 4.05.179
what mightst thou do, that honor would thee do, H5 2.pr. 18
that (almost) mightst have coin'd me into gold, 2.02. 98
thou mightst as well have known all our names, 2H6 2.01.125
that thou mightst think upon these by the seal, 3.02.344
that thou mightst repossess the crown in peace, 3H6 5.07. 19
villain, thou mightst have been an emperor. TIT 5.01. 30
then mightst thou speak, then mightst thou tear ROM 3.03. 68
thou speak, then mightst thou tear thy hair, 3.03. 68
enemies then, that then thou mightst kill 'em — TIM 1.02. 82 P
to me, thou mightst have hit upon it here. 4.03.347 P
thou mightst have sooner got another service; 4.03.504
that thou mightst not lose the dues of rejoicing MAC 1.05. 11 P
modest haste which way | thou mightst deserve, LR 2.04. 26
there thou mightst behold the great image of 4.06.158 P
that mightst have had the sole son of my queen! CYM 1.01.138
sluggish /crare | mightst easil'est harbor in? 4.02.206
jove knows what man thou mightst have made; 4.02.207
arcite, thou mightst now poison me. TNK 3.03. 8
then mightst thou pause, for then i were not for VEN 137
ay me, but yet thou mightst my seat forbear, SON 41. 9
how many gazers mightst thou lead away, | if 96.11

MIGHTY 117 FR 0.0132 REL FR 107 V 10 P
of sulphurous roaring the most mighty neptune TMP 1.02.204
o gentle proteus, love's a mighty lord, | and TGV 2.04.136
your hearts are mighty, your skins are whole, WIV 3.01.108 P
you do yourself mighty wrong, master ford. 3.03.207 P
leagues, | we were encount'red by a mighty rock, ERR 1.01.101
most mighty duke, vouchsafe me speak a word: 5.01.283
most mighty duke, behold a man much wrong'd. 5.01.331
example my digression by some mighty president. LLL 1.02.116 P
here, mighty theseus. MND 5.01. 38
address'd a mighty power, which were on foot AYL 5.04.156
dreams, | for he is nothing but a mighty lord. SHR in.1. 65
o, that a mighty man of such descent, | of such in.2. 14
a mighty man of pisa; 2.01.104
yet stands off | in differences so mighty. AWW 2.03.121
mother, and his lady | offense of mighty note; 5.03. 14
and as his person's mighty, | must it be violent WT 1.02.453
in himself too mighty, | and in his parties, his 2.03. 20
receiv'd, which are mighty ones and millions. 4.03. 57 P
most certain of one mother, mighty king — JN 1.01. 59
colbrand the giant, that same mighty man? 1.01.225
how like you this wild counsel, mighty states? 2.01.395
persever not, but hear me, mighty kings. 2.01.421
ripe | the bloom that promiseth a mighty fruit. 2.01.473
i had a mighty cause | to wish him dead, but 4.02.205
withhold thine indignation, mighty heaven, | and 5.06. 37
most mighty liege, and my companion peers, R2 1.03. 93
most mighty prince, my lord northumberland, 3.03.172
he is in the mighty hold | of bullingbrook; 3.04. 83
mighty and to be fear'd, than my condition, 1H4 1.03. 6
a mighty and a fearful head they are, | if 3.02.167
speedily, | with strong and mighty preparation. 4.01. 93
the king with mighty and quick–raised power 4.04. 12
walls | are now confin'd two mighty monarchies, H5 pr 20
flag, | look back into your mighty ancestors; 1.02.102
whiles his most mighty father on a hill | stood 1.02.108
ripe for exploits and mighty enterprises. 1.02.121
will raise your highness such a mighty sum | as 1.02.133
like little body with a mighty heart, | what 2.pr. 17
to weigh | the enemy more mighty than he seems, 2.04. 44
that may not misbecome | the mighty sender, doth 2.04.119
were it the mistress court of mighty europe; 2.04.133
pig, or the great, or the mighty, or the huge, 4.07. 16 P
which like a mighty whiffler 'fore the king 5.pr. 12
story, | in little room confining mighty men, ep 3
welcome, high prince, the mighty duke of york! 1H6 3.01.176
that dogg'd the mighty army of the dolphin? 4.03. 2
do him good, | so mighty are his vowed enemies. 2H6 3.01.220
whiles i in ireland nourish a mighty band, | i 3.01.348
it is reported, mighty sovereign, | that good 3.02.122
of bury, | set all upon me, mighty sovereign. 3.02.241
for daring to affy a mighty lord | unto the 4.01. 80
and with a puissant and a mighty power | of 4.09. 25
orator, | inferring arguments of mighty force. 3H6 2.02. 44
like a mighty sea | forc'd by the tide to combat 2.05. 5
wrong, | inferreth arguments of mighty strength, 3.01. 49
but, mighty lord, this merry inclination 3.02. 76
no, mighty king of france; 3.03. 4
are mighty gossips in our monarchy. R3 1.01. 83
the mighty warwick and did fight for me? 2.01.111
the mighty dukes, | gloucester and buckingham. 2.04. 44
be not you spoke with but by mighty suit; 3.07. 46
of spirit, | so mighty and so many my defects, 3.07.160
being a bark to brook no mighty sea — | than in 3.07.162
refuse not, mighty lord, this proffer'd love. 3.07.202
say she shall be a high and mighty queen. 4.04.347
most mighty sovereign, on the western coast 4.04.433
first, mighty liege, tell me your highness' 4.04.447
i know not, mighty sovereign, but by guess. 4.04.465
they have not been commanded, mighty king. 4.04.486
most mighty sovereign, | you have no cause to 4.04.491
is with a mighty power landed at milford | is 4.04.533
least | south from the mighty power of the king. 5.03. 38
bearing a state of mighty moment in't | and H8 2.04.214
his promises were, as he then was, mighty; 4.02. 41
to the high and mighty princess of england, 5.04. 3 P
that mould up such a mighty piece as this is, 5.04. 26
the which, most mighty for thy place and sway, TRO 1.03. 60
which is the high and mighty agamemnon? 1.03.232
and mighty states characterless are grated | to 3.02.188
"achilles hath the mighty hector slain!" 5.08. 14
well | for our proud empress, mighty tamora. TIT 5.02. 26
your reason, mighty lord? 5.03. 40
a reason mighty, strong, and effectual, | a 5.03. 43
and she whom mighty kingdoms cur'sy to, | like a 5.03. 74
said he gave unto | his steward a mighty sum. TIM 5.01. 8
when the most mighty gods by tokens send | such JC 1.03. 55
those that with haste will make a mighty fire 1.03.107
whose end is purpos'd by the mighty gods? 2.02. 27
most mighty caesar, let me know some cause, 2.02. 69
to give this day a crown to mighty caesar. 2.02. 94
the mighty gods defend thee! 2.03. 8 P
most high, most mighty, and most puissant caesar 3.01. 33
caesar was mighty, bold, royal, and loving. 3.01.127
o mighty caesar! 3.01.148
then burst his mighty heart, | and, in his 3.02.186
and sell the mighty space of our large honors 4.03. 25
antony | come down upon us with a mighty power, 4.03.169
on our former ensign | two mighty eagles fell, 5.01. 80
o julius caesar, thou art mighty yet! 5.03. 94
"high and mighty, you shall know i am set naked HAM 4.07. 43 P
and fell incensed points | of mighty opposites. 5.02. 62
be certain, you have mighty business in hand. LR 3.05. 16 P
o you mighty gods! 4.06. 34
what conjuration, and what mighty magic | (for OTH 1.03. 92
the turk with a most mighty preparation makes 1.03.221 P
are in the field, a mighty strength they carry. ANT 2.01. 17
most mighty princess, that i have adventur'd CYM 1.06.172
though mean and mighty, rotting | together, have 4.02.246
mighty sir, | these two young gentlemen, that 5.05.327
here have you seen a mighty king | his child, i PER 2.ch. 1
who stood equivalent with mighty kings, | but 5.01. 91
right and straight | upon this mighty morr— — TNK 3.05.118
thou mighty one, that with thy power hast turn'd 5.01. 49
the gods are mighty, arcite. 5.04. 87
thyself art mighty, for thine own sake leave me; LUC 583
and never be forgot in mighty rome | th' 1644
"'how mighty then you are, o, hear me tell! LC 253

MIHI 1 FR 0.0001 REL FR 1 V 0 P
"lux tua vita mihi." PER 2.02. 21

/MILAN 2 FR 0.0002 REL FR 1 V 1 P
launce, by mine honesty, welcome to /milan. TGV 2.05. 2 P
if once again, | /milan shall not hold thee. 5.04.129

MILAN 26 FR 0.0029 REL FR 26 V 0 P
thy father was the duke of milan and | a prince TMP 1.02. 54
and thy father | was duke of milan, and his only 1.02. 58
it for, he needs will be | absolute milan — me 1.02.109
the dukedom yet unbow'd (alas, poor milan!) 1.02.115
and confer fair milan | with all the honors on 1.02.126
did antonio open | the gates of milan, and, i' 1.02.130
the duke of milan | and his brave son being 1.02.438
the duke of milan | and his more braver daughter 1.02.439
o thou mine heir | of naples and of milan, what 2.01.113
milan and naples have | moe widows in them of 2.01.133
that stand 'twixt me and milan, candied be they, 2.01.279
as thou got'st milan, | i'll come by naples. 2.01.291
three | from milan did supplant good prospero, 3.03. 70
and myself present | as i was sometime milan. 5.01. 86
sir king, | the wronged duke of milan, prospero. 5.01.107
very duke | which was thrust forth of milan, who 5.01.160
she | is daughter to this famous duke of milan, 5.01.192
was milan thrust from milan, that his issue 5.01.205
was milan thrust from milan, that his issue 5.01.205
and thence retire me to my milan, where | every 5.01.311
to milan let me hear from thee by letters | of TGV 1.01. 57
all happiness bechance to thee in milan. 1.01. 61
but now he parted hence to embark for milan. 1.01. 71
from milan. 4.01. 19
i pandulph, of fair milan cardinal, | and from JN 3.01.138
my holy lord of milan, from the king | i come to 5.02.120

/MILANO 1 FR 0.0001 REL FR 1 V 0 P
there is a lady in /milano here | whom i affect; TGV 3.01. 81

MILAN'S 1 FR 0.0001 REL FR 0 V 1 P
i saw the duchess of milan's gown that they ADO 3.04. 16 P

MILCH 2 FR 0.0002 REL FR 2 V 0 P
would have made milch the burning eyes of heaven HAM 2.02.517
like a milch doe, whose swelling dugs do ache, VEN 875

MILCH–KINE 2 FR 0.0002 REL FR 2 V 0 P
and /makes milch–kine yield blood, and shakes a WIV 4.04. 33
farm | i have a hundred milch–kine to the pail, SHR 2.01.357

MILD 38 FR 0.0043 REL FR 36 V 2 P
a virtuous gentlewoman, mild and beautiful! TGV 4.04.180
mild, or come not near me; ADO 2.03. 32 P
ears | and plant in tyrants mild humility. LLL 4.03.346
an't shall please you, a foolish mild man, an 5.02.581 P
the mild hind | makes speed to catch the tiger MND 2.01.232
her, | and she in mild terms begg'd my patience, 4.01. 58
strange effect | would they work in mild aspect? AYL 4.03. 53
do i see | maid's mild behavior and sobriety. SHR 1.01. 71
her wondrous qualities and mild behavior, | am 2.01. 50
smooth his fault i should have been more mild. R2 1.03.240
in peace was never gentle lamb more mild, | than 2.01.174
but be thou mild, and blush not at my shame, 2H6 2.04. 48
we know the time since he was mild and affable, 3.01. 9
the duke is virtuous, mild, and too well given 3.01. 72
and that my sovereign's presence makes me mild, 3.02.219
as mild and gentle as the cradle–babe | dying 3.02.392
women are soft, mild, pitiful, and flexible; 3H6 1.04.141
the tiger will be mild whiles she doth mourn; 3.01. 39
my mild entreaty shall not make you guilty. 3.01. 91
these were her words, utt'red with mild disdain: 4.01. 98
o, he was gentle, mild, and virtuous! R3 1.02.104
but if she be obdurate | to mild entreaties, god 3.01. 40
i will be mild and gentle in my words. 4.04.161
more mild, but yet more harmful — kind in 4.04.173
that you will be more mild and tractable. TIT 1.01.470
i marvel our mild husband | not met us on the LR 4.02. 1
testy wrath | could never be her mild companion. PER 1.01. 18
he's father, son, and husband mild; 1.01. 68
now, mild may be thy life! 3.01. 27
it shall be raging mad and silly mild, | make VEN 1151
and let mild women to him lose their mildness, LUC 979
old woes, not infant sorrows, bear them mild; 1096
mild patience bid fair lucrece speak | to the 1268
but the mild glance that sly ulysses lent 1399
so mild that patience seem'd to scorn his woes. 1505
the well–skill'd workman this mild image drew 1520
so weary, and so mild | (as if with grief or 1542
mild as a dove, but neither true nor trusty, PP 7. 2

MILDER 4 FR 0.0004 REL FR 4 V 0 P
o, sir, i find her milder than she was, | and TGV 5.02. 2
words | can no way change you to a milder form, 5.04. 56
you, | unless you were of gentler, milder mould. SHR 1.01. 60
why did you wish me milder? COR 3.02. 14

MILDEST 2 FR 0.0002 REL FR 2 V 0 P
ah, what sharp stings are in her mildest words! AWW 3.04. 18
to stir a mutiny in the mildest thoughts, | and TIT 4.01. 85

MILDEWED 1 FR 0.0001 REL FR 1 V 0 P
here is your husband, like a mildewed ear, HAM 3.04. 64

MILDEWS 1 FR 0.0001 REL FR 0 V 1 P
mildews the white wheat, and hurts the poor LR 3.04.118 P

MILDLY 9 FR 0.0010 REL FR 9 V 0 P
she never reprehended him but mildly, | when he ERR 5.01. 87
deal mildly with his youth, | for young hot R2 2.01. 69
take the correction, mildly kiss the rod, | and 5.01. 32
arm yourself | to answer mildly; COR 3.02.139
the word is "mildly." 3.02.142
ay, but mildly. 3.02.144
well, mildly be it then. mildly! 3.02.145
well, mildly be it then. mildly! 3.02.145
that what we did was mildly as we might, TIT 1.01.475

MILDNESS 8 FR 0.0009 REL FR 8 V 0 P
hearing thy mildness prais'd in every town, SHR 2.01.191
but thou with mildness entertain'st thy wooers, 2.01.250
as bold in war | as he is fam'd for mildness, 3H6 2.01.156
and bear with mildness my misfortune's cross; 4.04. 20
my mildness hath allay'd their swelling griefs, 4.08. 42
whiles, in the mildness of your sleepy thoughts, R3 3.07.123
of wisdom | than prais'd for harmful mildness. LR 1.04.344
and let mild women to him lose their mildness, LUC 979

MILE 33 FR 0.0037 REL FR 24 V 9 P
this boy will carry a letter twenty mile, as WIV 3.02. 33 P
him, he were as good go a mile on his errand. MM 3.02. 37 P
would have walk'd ten mile afoot to see a good ADO 2.03. 16 P
woman shall come within a mile of my court" — LLL 1.01.120 P
the letter is too long by half a mile. 5.02. 54
they say that they have measur'd many a mile 5.02.186
ask them how many inches | is in one mile: 5.02.189
tell | how many inches doth fill up one mile. 5.02.193
are numb'red in the travel of one mile? 5.02.197
me in the palace wood, a mile without the town, MND 1.02.102 P
kinsman not past three quarters of a mile hence, WT 4.03. 80 P
wife within a mile where my land and living lies 4.03. 98 P
asia, | which cannot go but thirty mile a day, 2H4 2.04.165
i must a dozen mile to–night. 3.02.290 P
west of this forest, scarcely off a mile, | in 4.01. 19
come, | i'll pledge you a mile to th' bottom." 5.03. 54
not to come near our person by ten mile. 5.05. 65
i will trot to–morrow a mile, and my way shall H5 3.07. 80 P
his regiment lies half a mile at least | south R3 5.03. 37
within this mile and half. COR 1.04. 8
one infect another | against the wind a mile! 1.04. 34
'tis not a mile; 1.06. 16
how couldst thou in a mile confound an hour, 1.06. 17
you that banish'd him | a mile before his tent, 5.01. 5
my lord, i /aim'd a mile beyond the moon, | your TIT 4.03. 66
within this mile break forth a hundred springs; TIM 4.03.418
almost a mile; MAC 3.03. 12
within this three mile may you see it coming; 5.05. 36
thou wilt o'ertake us hence a mile or twain | i' LR 4.01. 42
can it be six mile yet? CYM 4.02.293
brought him to a little wood | a mile hence. TNK 2.06. 4
he'll dance the morris twenty mile an hour, 5.02. 51
for the horse | would make his length a mile, 5.04. 57

MILE–A 1 FR 0.0001 REL FR 1 V 0 P
goes all the day, | your sad tires in a mile–a. WT 4.03.126

MILE–END 2 FR 0.0002 REL FR 0 V 2 P
be the officer at a place there call'd mile–end, AWW 4.03.270 P
i remember at mile–end green, when i lay at 2H4 3.02.279 P

MILES 21 FR 0.0023 REL FR 20 V 1 P
say to her we have measur'd many miles, | to LLL 5.02.184
if to come hither you have measur'd miles, | and 5.02.191
and many miles, the princess bids you tell | how 5.02.192
steps | of many weary miles you have o'ergone 5.02.196
there is a monast'ry two miles off, | and there MV 3.04. 31
away, | for we must measure twenty miles to–day. 3.04. 84
so near our public court as twenty miles, | thou AYL 1.03. 44
draws out our miles and makes them wearisome, R2 2.03. 5
march | so many miles upon her peaceful bosom, 2.03. 93
is threescore and ten miles afoot with me, and 1H4 2.02. 25 P
have thirty miles to ride yet ere dinner–time. 3.03.198
some six miles off the duke is with the soldiers 3H6 2.01.144
what need'st thou run so many miles about, R3 4.04.460
at dunstable — six miles off | from ampthill, H8 4.01. 27
was forc'd to wheel | three or four miles about, COR 1.06. 20
villain and he be many miles asunder. ROM 3.05. 81
for many miles about | there's scarce a bush. LR 2.04.301
how many /score of miles may we well rid CYM 3.02. 67
thou abus'd | so many miles with a pretense? 3.04.103
leap large lengths of miles when thou art gone, SON 44.10
"thus far the miles are measur'd from thy friend 50. 4

MILFORD 8 FR 0.0009 REL FR 7 V 1 P
is with a mighty power landed at milford | is R3 4.04.533
how far it is | to this same blessed milford. CYM 3.02. 59
accessible is none but milford way. 3.02. 82
my revenge is now at milford; 3.05.155 P
to milford go, | and find not her whom thou 3.05.159
milford, | when from the mountain top pisanio 3.06. 4
he embark'd at milford; 3.06. 61
to seek her on the mountains near to milford, 5.05.281

MILFORD–HAVEN 10 FR 0.0011 REL FR 6 V 4 P
notice that i am in cambria, at milford–haven; CYM 3.02. 44 P
he is at milford–haven. 3.02. 49
i shall give thee opportunity at milford–haven. 3.04. 28 P

the roman, comes to milford-haven | to-morrow. 3.04.142
of you | a conduct overland to milford-haven. 3.05. 8
meet thee at milford-haven! 3.05.130 P
how long is't since she went to milford-haven? 3.05.148 P
to milford-haven. 3.06. 58
yes, sir, to milford-haven, which is the way? 4.02.291
you here at milford-haven with your ships. 4.02.335

MILITARIST 1 FR 0.0001 REL FR 0 V 1 P
is monsieur parolles, the gallant militarist — AWW 4.03.141 P

/MILITARY 2 FR 0.0002 REL FR 2 V 0 P
/in /military /rules, /humors /of /blood, | /he 2H4 2.03. 30
/troop /in /the /throngs /of /military /men; 4.01. 62

MILITARY 7 FR 0.0008 REL FR 2 V 5 P
speak from thy lungs military. WIV 4.05. 17 P
most military sir, salutation. LLL 5.01. 35 P
is there no military policy how virgins might AWW 1.01.121 P
chief majority | and military title capital 1H4 3.02.110
as well as any military man in the world, in the H5 3.02. 80 P
the direction of the military discipline, that 3.02.101 P
instruct this day | with military skill, that to TNK 5.01. 58

MILK 25 FR 0.0028 REL FR 20 V 5 P
they'll take suggestion as a cat laps milk; TMP 2.01.288
"item, she can milk." TGV 3.01.278 P
"inprimis, she can milk." 3.01.301 P
honey, and milk, and sugar: there is three. LLL 5.02.231
the hall | and milk comes frozen home in pail; 5.02.915
skim milk, and sometimes labor in the quern, MND 2.01. 36
come, come to me, | with hands as pale as milk; 5.01.338
who, inward search'd, have livers white as milk, MV 3.02. 86
he weeps like a wench that had shed her milk. AWW 4.03.108 P
think his mother's milk were scarce out of him. TN 1.05.161 P
(the innocent milk in it most innocent mouth) WT 3.02.100
no inch farther, | but milk my ewes, and weep. 4.04.450
i would the milk | thy mother gave thee, when 1H6 5.04. 27
mercy in him than there is milk in a male tiger, COR 5.04. 28 P
the milk thou suck'st from her did turn to TIT 2.03.144
adversity's sweet milk, philosophy, | to comfort ROM 3.03. 55
for those milk paps, | that through the TIM 4.03.116
it is too full o' th' milk of human kindness MAC 1.05. 17
and take my milk for gall, you murth'ring 1.05. 48
pour the sweet milk of concord into hell, 4.03. 98
and curd, like eager droppings into milk, | the HAM 1.05. 69
love | the vines of france and milk of burgundy LR 1.01. 84
silk | with fingers long, small, white as milk; PER 4.ch. 22
for our milk | will relish of the pasture, and TNK 1.02. 76
like milk and blood being mingled both together, VEN 902

MILK'D 2 FR 0.0002 REL FR 1 V 1 P
dugs that her pretty chopp'd hands had milk'd; AYL 2.04. 50 P
been labor'd so long with ye, milk'd unto ye, TNK 3.05. 4

MILKING-TIME 1 FR 0.0001 REL FR 0 V 1 P
is there not milking-time? WT 4.04.244 P

MILK-LIVER'D 1 FR 0.0001 REL FR 1 V 0 P
milk-liver'd man, | that bear'st a cheek for LR 4.02. 50

MILKMAID 2 FR 0.0002 REL FR 0 V 2 P
and yet 'tis a milkmaid; TGV 3.01.269 P
so tickle on thy shoulders that a milkmaid, if MM 1.02.173 P

MILKS 2 FR 0.0002 REL FR 2 V 0 P
how tender 'tis to love the babe that milks me; MAC 1.07. 55
by such poor passion as the maid that milks ANT 4.15. 74

MILKSOP 1 FR 0.0001 REL FR 1 V 0 P
a milksop, one that never in his life | felt so R3 5.03.325

MILKSOPS 1 FR 0.0001 REL FR 1 V 0 P
boys, apes, braggarts, jacks, milksops! ADO 5.01. 91

MILK-WHITE 6 FR 0.0006 REL FR 6 V 0 P
even in the milk-white bosom of thy love. TGV 3.01.252
before milk-white, now purple with love's wound, MND 2.01.167
then will i raise aloft the milk-white rose, 2H6 1.01.254
but where the bull and cow are both milk-white, TIT 5.01. 31
hath presented to you | four milk-white horses, TIM 1.02.183
paler for sorrow than her milk-white dove, | for PP 9. 3

MILKY 3 FR 0.0003 REL FR 3 V 0 P
has friendship such a faint and milky heart, TIM 3.01. 54
which was declining on the milky head | of HAM 2.02.478
this milky gentleness and course of yours LR 1.04.341

MILL 3 FR 0.0003 REL FR 3 V 0 P
more sacks to the mill! LLL 4.03. 79
or thou goest to th' grange, or mill. WT 4.04.303
more water glideth by the mill | than wots the TIT 2.01. 85

MILLE 1 FR 0.0001 REL FR 0 V 1 P
mes genoux /je vous donne mille /remerciments; H5 4.04. 54 P

MILLER 2 FR 0.0002 REL FR 1 V 1 P
shilling and two pence a-piece of yead miller — WIV 1.01.157 P
glideth by the mill | than wots the miller of, TIT 2.01. 86

MILLER'S 1 FR 0.0001 REL FR 1 V 0 P
in 's neighing able to entice | a miller's mare, TNK 5.02. 67

MILLINER 2 FR 0.0002 REL FR 1 V 1 P
no milliner can so fit his customers with gloves WT 4.04.192 P
he was perfumed like a milliner, | and 'twixt 1H4 1.03. 36

MILLION 15 FR 0.0017 REL FR 7 V 8 P
here's a million of manners. TGV 2.01. 99 P
a million fail, confounding oath on oath. MND 3.02. 93
and hind'red me half a million, laugh'd at my MV 3.01. 55 P
i'll buckler thee against a million. SHR 3.02.239
a million of beating may come to a great matter. WT 4.03. 59 P
a million, thy love is worth a million; 1H4 3.03.136 P
a million, thy love is worth a million; 3.03.137 P
figure may | attest in little place a million, H5 pr 16
i would not for a million of gold | the cause TIT 2.01. 49
play, i remember, pleas'd not the million, 'twas HAM 2.02.436 P
a womb, | and /fertile every wish, a million. ANT 1.02. 39
it was mine had annex'd unto't | a million moe 4.14. 18
if you buy ladies' flesh at a million a dram, CYM 1.04.135 P
once, and a million! 2.04.143
grease, amongst a whole million of cutpurses, TNK 4.03. 37 P

MILLION'D 1 FR 0.0001 REL FR 1 V 0 P
whose million'd accidents | creep in 'twixt vows SON 115. 5

MILLIONS 10 FR 0.0011 REL FR 9 V 1 P
few in millions | can speak like us. TMP 2.01. 7
millions of false eyes | are stuck upon thee. MM 4.01. 59
receiv'd, which are mighty ones and millions. WT 4.03. 58 P
in thy hands clutch'd as many millions, in | thy COR 3.03. 71
their hearts, i fear, | millions of mischiefs. JC 4.01. 51
let them throw | millions of acres on us, till HAM 5.01.281
there's millions now alive | that nightly lie in OTH 4.01. 67
the very lees of such (millions of rates) TNK 1.04. 29
does stand accurs'd | of many mortal millions, 5.03. 24
that millions of strange shadows on you tend? SON 53. 2

MILLS 2 FR 0.0002 REL FR 2 V 0 P
i pray you | ('tis south the city mills) bring COR 1.10. 31
poor pelting villages, sheep-cotes, and mills, LR 2.03. 18

MILL-SIXPENCES 1 FR 0.0001 REL FR 0 V 1 P
else, of seven groats in mill-sixpences, and two WIV 1.01.155 P

MILLSTONES 3 FR 0.0003 REL FR 2 V 1 P
your eyes drop millstones, when fools' eyes fall R3 1.03.352
ay, millstones, as he lesson'd us to weep. 1.04.240
with millstones. TRO 1.02.144 P

MILL-WHEELS 1 FR 0.0001 REL FR 1 V 0 P
vent thy groans | as fast as mill-wheels strike. TMP 1.02.281

MILO 1 FR 0.0001 REL FR 1 V 0 P
bull-bearing milo his addition yield | to sinowy TRO 2.03.247

MIMIC 1 FR 0.0001 REL FR 1 V 0 P
must be answered, | and forth my mimic comes. MND 3.02. 19

MINC'D 1 FR 0.0001 REL FR 0 V 1 P
ay, a minc'd man, and then to be bak'd with no TRO 1.02.256 P

MINCE 5 FR 0.0005 REL FR 3 V 2 P
i say, time wears, hold up your head and mince. WIV 5.01. 8 P
i know no ways to mince it in love, but directly H5 5.02.126 P
throat shall cut, | and mince it sans remorse. TIM 4.03.123
thy honesty and love doth mince this matter, OTH 2.03.247
speak to me home, mince not the general tongue; ANT 1.02.105

MINCES 1 FR 0.0001 REL FR 1 V 0 P
that minces virtue, and does shake the head | to LR 4.06.120

MINCING 4 FR 0.0004 REL FR 4 V 0 P
and turn two mincing steps | into a manly stride MV 3.04. 67
an edge, | nothing so much as mincing poetry. 1H4 3.01.132
and which gifts | (saving your mincing) the H8 2.03. 31
in mincing with his sword her /husband's limbs, HAM 2.02.514

/MIND 8 FR 0.0009 REL FR 7 V 1 P
and his siege is now | against the /mind, the JN 5.07. 17
/follow'd /both /with /body /and /with /mind; 2H4 1.01.203
/am /thus /bold /to /put /your /grace /in /mind R3 4.02.110
/and /doleful /dumps /the /mind /oppress, | then ROM 4.05.127
/'tis /too /narrow /for /your /mind. HAM 2.02.253 P
/alone /suffers, /suffers /most /i' /th' /mind, LR 3.06.104
/but /then /the /mind /much /sufferance /doth 3.06.106
/things /sting | /his /mind /so /venomously, 4.03. 46

MIND 385 FR 0.0435 REL FR 313 V 72 P
have you a mind to sink? TMP 1.01. 39 P
but how is it | that this lives in thy mind? 1.02. 49
to closeness and the bettering of my mind | with 1.02. 90
for still 'tis beating in my mind, your reason 1.02.176
o, that you bore | the mind that i do! 2.01.267
i'll fall flat, | perchance he will not mind me. 2.02. 17
or two i'll walk | to still my beating mind. 4.01.163
his body uglier grows, | so his mind cankers. 4.01.192
th' affliction of my mind amends, with which | i 5.01.115
do not infest your mind with beating on | the 5.01.246
and being so hard to me that brought your mind, TGV 1.01.139 P
prove as hard to you in telling your mind. 1.01.140 P
i'll show my mind | according to my shallow 1.02. 7
i would i knew his mind. 1.02. 33
i see you have a month's mind to them. 1.02.134
some messenger, that might her mind discover, 2.01.167
that hath more mind to feed on your blood than 2.04. 27 P
he is complete in feature and in mind | with all 2.04. 73
but when i call to mind your gracious favors 3.01. 6
more than quick words do move a woman's mind. 3.01. 91
and cannot soon revolt and change your mind. 3.02. 59
silvia | entreated me to call and know her mind. 4.03. 2
he bears an honorable mind, | and will not use a 5.03. 13
so got udge me, that is a virtuous mind. WIV 1.01.185 P
but notwithstanding that, i know anne's mind — 1.04.105 P
no, i know anne's mind for that. 1.04.127 P
in windsor knows more of anne's mind than i do, 1.04.128 P
for i know anne's mind as well as another does. 1.04.164 P
faith, but you do, in my mind. 2.01. 39 P
that you may know one another's mind, and the 2.02.127 P
have merited, either in my mind or in my means, 2.02.203 P
how full of chollors i am and trempling of mind! 3.01. 12 P
keep in that mind, i'll deserve it. 3.03. 82 P
or else i could not be in that mind. 3.03. 84 P
knowing my mind, you wrong me, master fenton. 3.04. 76
send quickly to sir john, to know his mind. 4.04. 83
master fenton, talk not to me, my mind is heavy; 4.06. 1 P
and yet the guiltiness of my mind, the sudden 5.05.123 P
his natural edge | with profits of the mind — MM 1.04. 61
yet hath he in him such a mind of honor | that, 2.04.179
and fit his mind to death, for his soul's rest. 2.04.187
my mind promises with my habit, no loss shall 3.01.177 P
i have been an unlawful bawd time out of mind, 4.02. 16 P
and to transport him in the mind he is | were 4.03. 68
dark-working sorcerers that change the mind, ERR 1.02. 99
know'st thou his mind? 2.01. 47
ay, ay, he told his mind upon mine ear. 2.01. 48
i think thou art in mind, and so am i. 2.02.196
nay, master, both in mind and in my shape. 2.02.197
unkind, | stigmatical in making, worse in mind. 4.02. 22
god keep your ladyship still in that mind! ADO 1.01.133 P
would the cook were a' my mind! 1.03. 73 P
brief, too, to have all things answer my mind. 2.01.361 P
before god! and, in my mind, very wise. 2.03.185 P
would better fit your honor to change your mind. 3.02.116 P
both strength of limb, and policy of mind, 4.01.198
fare you well, boy, you know my mind. 5.01.185 P
i'll hold my mind were she an ethiope. 5.04. 38
the mind shall banquet, though the body pine; LLL 1.01. 25
whoe'er 'a was, 'a show'd a mounting mind. 4.01. 4
omne bene, say i, being of an old father's mind: 4.02. 32
henceforth my wooing mind shall be express'd 5.02.412
i wish you the peace of mind, most royal 5.02.531 P
will speak their mind in some other sort. 5.02.585 P
of self-affairs, | my mind did lose it. MND 1.01.114
love looks not with the eyes, but with the mind, 1.01.234
nor hath love's mind of any judgment taste; 1.01.236
nor none, in my mind, now you give her o'er. 3.02.135
your mind is tossing on the ocean, | there where MV 1.01. 8
i pray you have in mind where we must meet. 1.01. 71
i have a mind presages me such thrift | that i 1.01.175
i like not fair terms and a villain's mind. 1.03.179
"for the heavens, rouse up a brave mind," says 2.02. 12 P
ordered, | and better in my mind not undertook. 2.04. 7
i have no mind of feasting forth to-night; 2.05. 37
find — | a proverb never stale in thrifty mind. 2.05. 55
a golden mind stoops not to shows of dross. 2.07. 20
of me, | let it not enter in your mind of love. 2.08. 42
not sick, my lord, unless it be in mind, | nor 3.02.234
it be in mind, | nor well, unless in mind. 3.02.235
my people do already know my mind, | and will 3.04. 37
i have within my mind | a thousand raw tricks of 3.04. 76
for in my mind you are much bound to him. 4.01.407
my mind was never yet more mercenary. 4.01.418
this, | and now methinks i have a mind to it. 4.01.433
and all the world was of my father's mind. AYL 1.02.236
give me leave | to speak my mind, and i will 2.07. 59
let no face be kept in mind | but the fair of 3.02. 94
i am not in the mind; 3.03. 90 P
i would not have my right rosalind of this mind, 4.01.110 P
and by him seal up thy mind, | whether that thy 4.03. 58
was not cut well, he was in the mind it was: 5.04. 72 P
and frame your mind to mirth and merriment, SHR in.2. 135
tell me thy mind, for i have pisa left | and am 1.01. 21
my lord, you nod, you do not mind the play. 1.01.249
you, sir, he tells you flatly what his mind is. 1.02. 78 P
my mind presumes, for his own good and /ours. 1.02.213
was it not to refresh the mind of man | after 3.01. 11
your betters have endur'd me say my mind, | and 4.03. 75
for 'tis the mind that makes the body rich; 4.03.172
and the moon changes even as your mind. 4.05. 20
my mind hath been as big as one of yours, | my 5.02.170
for where an unclean mind carries virtuous AWW 1.01. 42 P
he and his physicians | are of a mind; 1.03.238
and thy mind stand to't, boy, steal away bravely 2.01. 29
this is his majesty, say your mind to him. 2.01. 95
i have no mind to isbel since i was at court. 3.02. 12 P
if the quick fire of youth light not your mind, 4.02. 5
i will believe thou hast a mind that suits TN 1.02. 50
am a fellow o' th' strangest mind i' th' world; 1.03.113 P
tell me your mind — i am a messenger. 1.05.205 P
your lord does know my mind, i cannot love him, 1.05.257
mine eye too great a flatterer for my mind. 1.05.309
she bore a mind that envy could not but call 2.01. 29 P
changeable taffata, for thy mind is a very opal. 2.04. 75 P
not black in my mind, though yellow in my legs. 3.04. 26 P
nor admire not in thy mind, why i do call thee 3.04.151 P
in nature there's no blemish but the mind; 3.04.367
saint bennet, sir, may put you in mind — one, 5.01. 39 P
it, if thou hast | the ordering of the mind too, WT 2.03.106
but that the good mind of camillo tardied | my 3.02.162
but they themselves are o' th' mind (if it be 4.04.329 P
that does take | your mind from feasting. 4.04.347
subdue the cheek, | but not take in the mind. 4.04.577
if i had a mind to be honest, i see fortune 4.04.831 P
(for him, i partly know his mind) to find thee 5.03.142
your mind is all as youthful as your blood. JN 3.04.125
shame, | this murther had not come into my mind; 4.02.223
is yet the cover of a fairer mind | than to be 4.02.258
in the physician's mind | to help him to his R2 1.04. 59
nay, speak thy mind, and let him ne'er speak 2.01.230
with the eyes of heavy mind | i see thy glory 2.04. 18
how far off from the mind of bullingbrook | it 3.03. 45
now, bagot, freely speak thy mind, | what thou 4.01. 2
my lord, | before i freely speak my mind herein, 4.01.327
what, is my richard both in shape and mind 5.01. 26
my lord, the mind of bullingbrook is chang'd, 5.01. 51
but now i know thy mind, thou dost suspect 5.02.104
sweet york, sweet husband, be not of that mind, 5.02.107
i am not yet of percy's mind, the hotspur of the 1H4 2.04.102 P
and i say the earth was not of my mind, | if you 3.01. 21
his letters bears his mind, not i, my /lord. 4.01. 20
this present grief had wip'd it from my mind. 2H4 1.01.211
'tis with my mind | as with the tide swell'd up 2.03. 62
and captains were of my mind, they would 2.04.142 P
'a has, that show a weak mind and an able body, 2.04.251 P
i'll ne'er bear a base mind. 3.02.235 P
faith, i'll bear no base mind. 3.02.240 P
th' incessant care and labor of his mind | hath 4.04.118
god put /it in thy mind to take it hence, | that 4.05.178
uncurbed plainness | tell us the dolphin's mind. H5 1.02.245
to-morrow shall you know our mind at full. 2.04.140
and eche out our performance with your mind. 3.pr. 35
for the satisfaction, look you, of my mind: 3.02.100 P
a hole in his coat, i will tell him my mind. 3.06. 85 P
my master's mind. 3.06.116
and when the mind is quick'ned, out of doubt, 4.01. 20
who, with a body fill'd and vacant mind, | gets 4.01.269
and yet i do thee wrong to mind thee of it, 4.03. 13
perish the man whose mind is backward now! 4.03. 72
the constable desires thee thou wilt mind | thy 4.03. 84
break thy mind to me in broken english — wilt 5.02.245 P
you perceive my mind? 1H6 2.02. 59
nor misconster | the mind of talbot, as you did 2.03. 74
call we to mind, and mark but this for proof: 3.03. 68
i'll call for pen and ink, and write my mind. 5.03. 66
but with as humble lowliness of mind | she is 5.05. 18
the mutual conference that my mind hath had, 2H6 1.01. 25
my lord of winchester, i know your mind. 1.01.139
gloucester bears this base and humble mind. 1.02. 62
but all his mind is bent to holiness, | to 1.03. 55
'tis but a base ignoble mind | that mounts no 2.01. 13
we know your mind at full. 2.02. 77
nell, ill can thy noble mind abrook | the abject 2.04. 10
respecting what a rancorous mind he bears | and 3.01. 24
and, had i first been put to speak my mind, | i 3.01. 43
but, in my mind, that were no policy: 3.01.238
by this i shall perceive the commons' mind, 3.01.374
stand apart, the king shall know your mind. 3.02.242
no better sign of a brave mind than a hard hand. 4.02. 20 P
oft have i heard that grief softens the mind, 4.04. 1
continue still in this so good a mind, | and 4.09. 17
my mind was troubled with deep melancholy. 5.01. 34
why, so i am — in mind, and that's enough. 3H6 3.01. 60
and come some other time to know our mind. 3.02. 17
but now you partly may perceive my mind. 3.02. 66
my mind will never grant what i perceive | your 3.02. 67
yoke, but let thy dauntless mind | still ride in 3.03. 17
i mind to tell him plainly what i think. 4.01. 8
and to that end i shortly mind to leave you. 4.01. 64
but if you mind to hold your true obedience, 4.01.140
my mind exceeds the compass of her wheel. 4.03. 47
then, for his mind, be edward england's king, 4.03. 48
my mind presageth happy gain and conquest. 5.01. 71
suspicion always haunts the guilty mind; 5.06. 11
let hell make crook'd my mind to answer it. 5.06. 79

thou wast provoked by thy bloody mind, | that R3 1.02. 99
take the devil in thy mind, and believe him not; 1.04.147 P
of you | had so much grace to put it in my mind. 2.01.121
my lord, you shall overrule my mind for once. 3.01. 57
to make william lord hastings of our mind | for 3.01.162
god keep your lordship in that gracious mind! 3.02. 56
man | the men you talk of came into my mind. 3.02.117
who knows the lord protector's mind herein? 3.04. 7
grace, we think, should soonest know his mind. 3.04. 9
both in your form and nobleness of mind; 3.07. 14
i have consider'd in my mind | the late request 4.02. 83
/once," quoth forrest, "almost chang'd my mind; 4.03. 15
and you shall understand from me her mind. 4.04.429
my mind is chang'd. stanley, what news with you? 4.04.456
my letter will resolve him of my mind. 4.05. 20
nor cheer of mind that i was wont to have. 5.03. 74
his mind and place | infecting one another, yea, H8 1.01.161
well dispos'd, the mind growing once corrupt, 1.02.116
that churchman bears a bounteous mind indeed, 1.03. 55
you bear a gentle mind, and heav'nly blessings 2.03. 57
call to mind | that i have been your wife in 2.04. 34
creature, and complete | in mind and feature. 3.02. 50
he view'd, | he did it with a serious mind; 3.02. 80
it may well be, | there is a mutiny in 's mind. 3.02.120
inventory | of your best graces in your mind; 3.02.138
myself have ventur'd | to speak my mind of him; 5.01. 41
my mind gave me, | in seeking tales and 5.02.144
your mind is the clearer, /ajax, and your TRO 2.03.153 P
and all men were of my mind — 2.03.215 P
with a mind | that doth renew swifter than blood 3.02.162
appear it to /your mind | that, through the 3.03. 3
you know my mind, i'll fight no more 'gainst 3.03. 56
my mind is troubled, like a fountain stirr'd, 3.03.308
the fountain of your mind were clear again, that 3.03.310 P
that's my mind too. good morrow, lord aeneas. 4.01. 7
and let your mind be coupled with your words. 5.02. 15
i find, | the error of our eye directs our mind. 5.02.110
unless she said, "my mind is now turn'd whore." 5.02.114
bastard instructed, bastard in mind, bastard in 5.07. 17 P
with every minute you do change a mind, | and COR 1.01.182
a' th' town, | where they shall know our mind. 1.05. 28
midnight sleep, | by jove, 'twould be my mind! 3.01. 86
it is a mind | that shall remain a poison where 3.01. 86
and by my body's action teach my mind | a most 3.02.122
and yet my mind gave me his clothes made a false 4.05.150 P
will you be put in mind of his blind fortune, 5.06.117
write down thy mind, bewray thy meaning so, TIT 2.04. 3
that i might rail at him to ease my mind! 2.04. 35
and in a tedious sampler sew'd her mind; 2.04. 39
tell on thy mind, i say thy child shall live. 5.01. 69
that bloody mind i think they learn'd of me, 5.01.101
to ease the gnawing vulture of thy mind, | by 5.02. 31
since 'tis my father's mind | that i repair to 5.03. 1
and bid thee bear his pretty tales in mind, 5.03.165
east, | a troubled mind drive me to walk abroad, ROM 1.01.120
being black, puts us in mind they hide the fair. 1.01.231
time out a' mind the fairies' coachmakers. 1.04. 61
for my mind misgives | some consequence yet 1.04.106
i will, and know her mind early to-morrow; 3.04. 10
you say you do not know the lady's mind? 4.01. 4
or, if his mind be writ, give me his letter. 5.02. 4
the noblest mind he carries | that ever govern'd TIM 1.01.280
that man might ne'er be wretched for his mind. 1.02.164
never mind | was to be so unwise, to be so kind. 2.02. 5
for his right noble mind, illustrious virtue, 3.02. 80
i'll ever serve his mind with my best will; 4.02. 49
and morsels unctious, greases his pure mind, 4.03.195
would poison were obedient and knew my mind! 4.03.297 P
love, | duty, and zeal to your unmatched mind, 4.03.516
ay, if i be alive, and your mind hold, and your JC 1.02.291 P
you have some sick offense within your mind, 2.01.268
there is but one mind in all these men, and it 2.03. 5 P
i have a man's mind, but a woman's might. 2.04. 8
but yet have i a mind | that fears him much; 3.01.144
have mind upon your health; 4.03. 36
now i change my mind, | and partly credit things 5.01. 77
he bears too great a mind. 5.01.112
or art thou but | a dagger of the mind, a false MAC 2.01. 38
and, to that dauntless temper of his mind, | he 3.01. 51
so, | for banquo's issue have i fil'd my mind, 3.01. 64
than on the torture of the mind to lie | in 3.02. 21
o, full of scorpions is my mind, dear wife! 3.02. 36
no mind that's honest | but in it shares some 4.03.197
my mind she has mated, and amaz'd my sight. 5.01. 78
the mind i sway by, and the heart i bear, 5.03. 9
canst thou not minister to a mind diseas'd, 5.03. 40
a heart unfortified, or mind impatient, | a HAM 1.02. 96
the inward service of the mind and soul | grows 1.03. 13
but to my mind, though i am native here | and to 1.04. 14
taint not thy mind, nor let thy soul contrive 1.05. 85
the flash and outbreak of a fiery mind, | a 2.01. 33
and the lady shall say her mind freely, or the 2.02.324 P
whether 'tis nobler in the mind to suffer | the 3.01. 56
for to the noble mind | rich gifts wax poor when 3.01. 99
o, what a noble mind is here o'erthrown! 3.01.150
with all the strength and armor of the mind | to 3.03. 12
if your mind dislike any thing, obey it. 5.02.217 P
my mind as generous, and my shape as true, | as LR 1.02. 8
whose mind and mine, i know, in that are one, 1.03. 15
an honest mind and plain, he must speak truth! 2.02. 99
commands the mind | to suffer with the body. 2.04.108
/this tempest in my mind | doth from my senses 3.04. 12
proud in heart and mind; 3.04. 85 P
my son | came then into my mind, and yet my mind 4.01. 34
and yet my mind | was then scarce friends with 4.01. 34
plainly, | i fear i am not in my perfect mind. 4.07. 62
i saw othello's visage in his mind, | and to his OTH 1.03.252
but to be free and bounteous to her mind. 1.03.265
that could think, and nev'r disclose her mind, 2.01.156
were well | the general were put in mind of it. 2.03.132
o now, for ever | farewell the tranquil mind! 3.03.348
patience, i say; your mind /perhaps may change. 3.03.452
but my noble moor | is true of mind, and made of 3.04. 27
fetch me the handkerchief, my mind misgives. 3.04. 89
heaven keep the monster from othello's mind! 3.04.163
her body and beauty unprovide my mind again. 4.01.206 P
that song to-night | will not go from my mind; 4.03. 31
i have a mind to strike thee ere thou speak'st; ANT 2.05. 42
bear'st thou her face in mind? 3.03. 29
and command what cost | your heart /has mind to. 3.04. 38
tricks which sorrow shoots | out of the mind. 4.02. 15
less noble mind | than she which by her death 4.14. 60
as the fits and stirs of 's mind | could best CYM 1.03. 12
she holds her virtue still, and i my mind. 1.04. 64 P
if she be furnish'd with a mind so rare, | she 1.06. 16
and to expound | his beastly mind to us, he hath 1.06.153
keep unshak'd | that temple, thy fair mind, that 2.01. 64
thy mind to her is now as low as were | thy 3.02. 10
what is in thy mind | that makes thee stare thus 3.04. 4
if you could wear a mind | dark as your fortune 3.04.143
i had no mind | to hunt this day; 4.02.147
i would we were all of one mind, and one mind 5.04.203 P
we were all of one mind, and one mind good. 5.04.204 P
and then a mind put in't, either our brags 5.05.176
and our mind partakes her private actions | to PER 1.01.152
the passions of the mind, | that have their 1.02. 11
and keep your mind, till you return to us, 1.02. 35
musings into my mind, with thousand doubts | how 1.02. 97
if the good king simonides were of my mind — 2.01. 44 P
now to marina bend your mind, | whom our 4.ch. 5
behind | is left to govern it, you bear in mind, 4.04. 14
had i brought hither a corrupted mind, | thy 4.06.104
when that his action's dregg'd with mind assur'd TNK 1.02. 97
his mind nurse equal | to these so diff'ring 1.03. 32
my mind misgives me | this fellow has a 2.03. 69
body | and fiery mind illustrate a brave father. 2.05. 22
to clear his own way with the mind and sword 3.01. 56
now | you make me mind her, but this very day 4.01. 37
i think she has a perturb'd mind, which i cannot 4.03. 59 P
her attention, for this her mind beats upon; 4.03. 78 P
are inserted 'tween her mind and eye become the 4.03. 79 P
i am of your mind, doctor. 5.02. 39
o, had thy mother borne so hard a mind, | she VEN 203
her, | she answers him, as if she knew his mind; 308
looks on the dull earth with disturbed mind, 340
for all my mind, my thought, my busy care, | is 383
was i | to be of such a weak and silly mind, 1016
and in his inward mind he doth debate | what LUC 185
behind, | and he the burthen of a guilty mind. 735
find | some purer chest to close so pure a mind. 761
at last she calls to mind where hangs a piece 1366
to jump up higher seem'd, to mock the mind. 1414
was left unseen, save to the eye of mind: 1426
so fair a form lodg'd not a mind so ill. 1530
but tarquin's shape came in her mind the while, 1536
but such a face should bear a wicked mind. 1540
abuse, | immaculate and spotless is my mind; 1656
may my pure mind with the foul act dispense, 1704
her body's stain her mind untainted clears, 1710
by children's eyes, her husband's shape in mind. SON 9. 8
change thy thought, that i may change my mind! 10. 9
begins a journey in my head | to work my mind, 27. 4
lo thus by day my limbs, by night my mind, | for 27.13
for that same groan doth put this in my mind: 50.13
since mind at first in character was done! 59. 8
they look into the beauty of thy mind, | and 69. 9
brain, | to take a new acquaintance of thy mind. 77.12
thou canst not vex me with inconstant mind, 92. 9
since i left you, mine eye is in my mind, | and 113. 1
of his quick objects hath the mind no part, 113. 7
my most true mind thus maketh mine untrue. 113.14
or whether doth my mind, being crown'd with you, 114. 1
and my great mind most kingly drinks it up: 114.10
but, love, hate on, for now i know thy mind: 149.13
that in my mind thy worst all best exceeds? 150. 8
the mind and sight distractedly commix'd. LC 28
each eye that saw him did enchant the mind, 89
to serve their eyes, and in it put their mind, 135
see | are errors of the blood, none of the mind; 184

MINDED 8 FR 0.0009 REL FR 8 V 0 P

but you, my brace of lords, were i so minded, TMP 5.01.126
that have minded you | of what you should forget WT 3.02.225
how you stand minded in the weighty difference H8 3.01. 58
let him alone, or so many so minded, | wave thus COR 1.06. 73
i minded him how royal 'twas to pardon | when it 5.01. 18
which, too much minded by herself alone, | may ROM 4.01. 13
one minded like the weather, most unquietly. LR 3.01. 2
if all were minded so, the times should cease, SON 11. 7

MINDFUL 1 FR 0.0001 REL FR 1 V 0 P

but now the mindful messenger, come back, LUC 1583

MINDING 4 FR 0.0004 REL FR 4 V 0 P

we do not come, as minding to content you, | our MND 5.01.113
minding true things by what their mock'ries be. H5 4.pr. 53
the most high gods not minding longer | to PER 2.04. 3
in't, | not minding whether i dislike or no! 2.05. 20

MINDLESS 2 FR 0.0002 REL FR 2 V 0 P

pronounce thee a gross lout, a mindless slave, WT 1.02.301
how cursed athens, mindless of thy worth, TIM 4.03. 94

MIND'S 7 FR 0.0008 REL FR 7 V 0 P

my mind's not on't, you are too hard for me. H8 5.01. 57
h'ad sent to me first, but for my mind's sake; TIM 3.03. 23
to find the mind's construction in the face: MAC 1.04. 12
a mote it is to trouble the mind's eye. HAM 1.01.112
in my mind's eye, horatio. 1.02.185
when the mind's free, | the body's delicate; LR 3.04. 11
the vacant leaves thy mind's imprint will bear, SON 77. 3

/MINDS 1 FR 0.0001 REL FR 1 V 0 P

/to /diet /rank /minds /sick /of /happiness, 2H4 4.01. 64

MINDS 61 FR 0.0069 REL FR 59 V 2 P

to change their shapes than men their minds. TGV 5.04.109
than men their minds? 5.04.110
while other sports are tasking of their minds, WIV 4.06. 30
from fasting maids whose minds are dedicate | to MM 2.02.154
did but convey unto our fearful minds | a ERR 1.01. 67
for servants must their masters' minds fulfill. 4.01.113
out of all eyes, tongues, minds, and injuries. ADO 4.01.243
know their minds, boyet. LLL 5.02.175
helen, to you our minds we will unfold: MND 1.01.208
sides, voices, and minds | had been incorporate. 3.02.207
and all their minds transfigur'd so together, 5.01. 24
which never labor'd in their minds till now; 5.01. 73
the oracle | give rest to th' minds of others — WT 2.01.191
be it thy course to busy giddy minds | with 2H4 4.05.213
grapple your minds to sternage of this navy, H5 3.pr. 18
you speak this to feel other men's minds. 4.01.126 P
all things are ready, if our minds be so. 4.03. 71
in your fair minds let this acceptance take. ep 14
cease these jars and rest your minds in peace. 1H6 1.01. 44
but we shall meet, and break our minds at large. 1.03. 81
belike she minds to play the amazon. 3H6 4.01.106
and fearless minds climb soonest unto crowns. 4.07. 62
let me put in your minds, if you forget, | what R3 1.03.130
by a divine instinct men's minds mistrust 2.03. 42
am sure have shown at full their royal minds — H8 4.01. 8
might corrupt minds procure knaves as corrupt 5.01.132
in whom the tempers and the minds of all TRO 1.03. 57
it, | nor once deject the courage of our minds, 2.02.121
and that great minds, of partial indulgence | to 2.02.178
minds sway'd by eyes are full of turpitude. 5.02.112
your own true affections, and that your minds, COR 2.03.231
to men | of noble minds is honorable meed. TIT 1.01.216
and arm the minds of infants to exclaims. 4.01. 86
like damned guilty deeds to sinners' minds: ROM 3.02.111
you see how all conditions, how all minds, | as TIM 1.01. 52
creep in the minds and marrows of our youth, 4.01. 26
who can bring noblest minds to basest ends! 4.03.464
that noble minds keep ever with their likes; JC 1.02.311
but, woe the while, our fathers' minds are dead, 1.03. 82
you will not come, | their minds may change. 2.02. 96
stir | your hearts and minds to mutiny and rage, 3.02.122
balm of hurt minds, great nature's second course MAC 2.02. 36
infected minds | to their deaf pillows will 5.01. 72
that speak my salutation in their minds; 5.09. 23
dangerous conjectures in ill-breeding minds. HAM 4.05. 15
perform'd | even while men's minds are wild, 5.02.394
to know our enemies' minds, we rip their hearts, LR 4.06.260
from hence trust not your daughters' minds | by OTH 1.01.170
in him that folly and green minds look after; 2.01.247 P
good /faith, how foolish are our minds! 4.03. 23
nor measure our good minds | by this rude place CYM 3.06. 64
uses | (the food and nourishment of noble minds) TNK 2.02. 52
wash your foul minds with tears, and those same STM II.C 108
with cold terror doth men's minds confound. VEN 1048
and cares, and troubled minds that wakes. LUC 126
men prove beasts, let beasts bear gentle minds." 1148
for men have marble, women waxen, minds, | and 1240
such childish humor from weak minds proceeds; 1825
divert strong minds to th' course of alt'ring SON 115. 8
let me not to the marriage of true minds | admit 116. 1
that i have frequent been with unknown minds, 117. 5

/MINE* 17 FR 0.0019 REL FR 16 V 1 P

lady, i will commend you to /mine /own heart. LLL 2.01.179 P
/were /they /not /mine? R2 4.01.168
/i /am, /but /still /my /griefs /are /mine. 4.01.191
/with /mine /own /tears /i /wash /away /my /balm 4.01.207
/with /mine /own /hands /i /give /away /my 4.01.208
/with /mine /own /tongue /deny /my /sacred 4.01.209
/with /mine /own /breath /release /all /duteous 4.01.210
/mine /eyes /are /full /of /tears, /i /cannot 4.01.244
/nay, /if /i /turn /mine /eyes /upon /myself, 4.01.247
/so /many /blows /upon /this /face /of /mine, 4.01.278
and when /mine oratory drew /to /an end, | i bid R3 3.07. 20
/over /your /woes /again /by /viewing /mine: 4.04. 39
/this /poor /right /hand /of /mine | /is /left TIT 3.02. 7
/mine /eyes /are /cloy'd /with /view /of 3.02. 55
/shalt /read /when /mine /begin /to /dazzle. 3.02. 85
and make her airy tongue more hoarse than /mine, ROM 2.02.162
/the /interim's /mine, | /and /a /man's /life's HAM 5.02. 73

MINE* 1247 FR 0.1409 REL FR 1047 V 200 P

i have with such provision in mine art | so TMP 1.02. 28
new created | the creatures that were mine, i 1.02. 82
should presently extirpate me and mine | out of 1.02.125
it is a hint | that wrings mine eyes to't. 1.02.135
me | from mine own library with volumes that | i 1.02.167
lady) hath mine enemies | brought to this shore; 1.02.179
it was mine art, | when i arriv'd and heard thee 1.02.291
be subject | to no sight but thine and mine, 1.02.302
this island's mine by sycorax my mother, | which 1.02.331
that you have, | which first was mine own king; 1.02.342
and lodg'd thee | in mine own cell, till thou 1.02.347
who with mine eyes (never since at ebb) beheld 1.02.436
entertainment till | mine enemy has more pow'r. 1.02.467
you cram these words into mine ears against 2.01.107
o thou mine heir | of naples and of milan, what 2.01.112
i wish mine eyes | would, with themselves, shut 2.01.191
it strook mine ear most terribly. 2.01.313
upon mine honor, sir, i heard a humming | (and 2.01.317
as mine eyes open'd, | i saw their weapons drawn 2.01.319
bark of a tree with mine own hands since i was 2.02.123 P
face remember, | save, from my glass, mine own; 3.01. 50
at mine unworthiness, that dare not offer | what 3.01. 77
and mine, with my heart in't. 3.01. 90
ay, on mine honor. 3.02.114
instruments | will hum about mine ears, and 3.02.138
and these, mine enemies, are all knit up | in 3.03. 89
is drown'd, | and his and mine lov'd darling. 3.03. 93
have given you here a third of mine own life, 4.01. 3
shall never melt | mine honor into lust, to take 4.01. 28
of this young couple | some vanity of mine art. 4.01. 41
which by mine art | i have from their confines 4.01.120
so is mine. 4.01.201 P
this hour | lies at my mercy all mine enemies. 4.01.263
mine would, sir, were i human. 5.01. 20
and mine shall. 5.01. 20
to work mine end upon their senses that | this 5.01. 53
mine eyes, ev'n sociable to the show of thine, 5.01. 63
you, brother mine, that /entertain'd ambition, 5.01. 75
but by immortal providence she's mine. 5.01.189
this thing of darkness i | acknowledge mine. 5.01.276
and what strength i have's mine own, | which is ep 2
and i likewise will visit thee with mine. TGV 1.01. 60
but, were i you, he never should be mine. 1.02. 11
letter in the letter, | except mine own name; 1.02.117
and with the vantage of mine own excuse | hath 1.03. 82
not mine: my gloves are on. 2.01. 1
ay, give it me, it's mine: 2.01. 3
o, that you had mine eyes, or your own eyes had 2.01. 71 P
to clothe mine age with angel-like perfection, 2.04. 66
made them watchers of mine own heart's sorrow. 2.04.135
have i not reason to prefer mine own? 2.04.156
why, man, she is mine own, | and i as rich in 2.04.168
/is /it mine /eye, or valentinus' praise, | her 2.04.196
launce, by mine honesty, welcome to /milan. 2.05. 1 P

all that is mine i leave at thy dispose, | my 2.07. 86
upon mine honor, he shall never know | that i 3.01. 48
where i thought the remnant of mine age | should 3.01. 74
then in dumb silence will i bury mine, | for 3.01.208
if so — i pray thee breathe it in mine ear, 3.01.241
she was mine and not mine twice or thrice in 3.01.356 P
she was mine and not mine twice or thrice in 3.01.356 P
marry, mine host, because i cannot be merry. 4.02. 28 P
and then i offer'd her mine own, who is a dog as 4.04. 57 P
mine shall not do his julia so much wrong. 4.04.137
this face of mine | were full as lovely as is 4.04.185
her hair is auburn, mine is perfect yellow: 4.04.189
her eyes are grey as glass, and so are mine; 4.04.192
nought but mine eye | could have persuaded me; 5.04. 64
free, | all that was mine in silvia i give thee. 5.04. 83
and i mine. 5.04.120
yonder is silvia; and silvia's mine. 5.04.125
is (lastly and finally) mine host of the garter. WIV 1.01.140 P
i might never come in mine own great chamber 1.01.154 P
sir john, and master mine, | i combat challenge 1.01.161
mine host of the garter! 1.03. 1 P
truly, mine host, i must turn away some of my 1.03. 4 P
do so, good mine host. 1.03. 12 P
for the revolt of mine is dangerous — that is 1.03.102 P
and i have appointed mine host of de jarteer to 1.04.118 P
inherit first, for i protest mine never shall. 2.01. 74 P
almost ready to wrangle with mine own honesty. 2.01. 85 P
pawn'd his horses to mine host of the garter. 2.01. 96 P
how now, mine host! 2.01.192 P
i follow, mine host, i follow. 2.01.195 P
good mine host o' th' garter, a word with you. 2.01.203 P
have with you, mine host. 2.01.221 P
why then the world's mine oyster, | which i with 2.02. 3
fan, i took't upon mine honor thou hadst it not. 2.02. 13 P
hand, and hiding mine honor in my necessity, am 2.02. 24 P
nobody hears — mine own people, mine own people 2.02. 50 P
hears — mine own people, mine own people. 2.02. 51 P
i must very much lay open mine own imperfection; 2.02.184 P
jack rugby — mine host de jarteer — have i not 3.01. 91 P
i'll be judgment by mine host of the garter. 3.01. 95 P
hear mine host of the garter. 3.01.100 P
whether had you rather lead mine eyes, or eye 3.02. 3 P
and i fear not mine own shame so much as his 3.03.122 P
to-morrow on the lousy knave, mine host. 3.03.240 P
truly, for mine own part, i would little or 3.04. 62 P
so did i mine, to build upon a foolish woman's 3.05. 41 P
why, none but mine own people. 4.02. 14 P
how now, mine host? 4.05. 19 P
there was, mine host, an old fat woman even now 4.05. 24 P
that there was, mine host, one that hath taught 4.05. 59 P
where is mine host? 4.05. 73 P
there is a friend of mine come to town, tells me 4.05. 76 P
vere is mine host de jarteer? 4.05. 83 P
hark, good mine host: 4.06. 18
nor need you, on mine honor, have to do | with MM 1.01. 63
your scope is as mine own, | so to enforce or 1.01. 64
let mine own judgment pattern out my death, 2.01. 30
or i'll have mine action of batt'ry on thee. 2.01.178 P
for mine own part, i never come into any room in 2.01.208 P
let that be mine. 2.02. 12
mine were the very cipher of a function, | to 2.02. 39
touch'd with that remorse | as mine is to him? 2.02. 55
is this her fault, or mine? 2.02.162
a gentlewoman of mine, | who, falling in the 2.03. 10
to have it added to the faults of mine, | and 2.04. 72
nay, but hear me, | your sense pursues not mine. 2.04. 74
believe me, on mine honor, | my words express my 2.04.147
darkness as a bride, | and hug it in mine arms. 3.01. 84
here's a gentleman, and a friend of mine. 3.02. 42 P
thinking me remiss in mine office, awakens me 4.02.116 P
by the vow of mine order i warrant you, if my 4.02.169 P
i am pale at mine heart to see thine eyes so red 4.03.151 P
by mine honesty, | if she be mad — as i believe 5.01. 59
my sisterly remorse confutes mine honor, | and i 5.01.100
when i'll depose i had him in mine arms | with 5.01.198
dare no more stretch this finger of mine than he 5.01.314
but let my trial be mine own confession. 5.01.372
give me your hand and say you will be mine, | he 5.01.492
upon mine honor, thou shalt marry her. 5.01.518
what's mine is yours, and what is yours is mine. 5.01.537
what's mine is yours, and what is yours is mine. 5.01.537
and then return and sleep within mine inn, | for ERR 1.02. 14
he that commends me to mine own content, 1.02. 33
methinks your maw, like mine, should be your 1.02. 66
ay, ay, he told his mind upon mine ear. 2.01. 48
by computation and mine host's report, | i could 2.02. 4
thou hast stol'n both mine office and my name: 3.01. 44
but to spite my wife) | upon mine hostess there. 3.01.119
since mine own doors refuse to entertain me, 3.01.120
not, | nor by what wonder you do hit of mine — 3.02. 30
i know | your weeping sister is no wife of mine, 3.02. 42
it is thyself, mine own self's better part: 3.02. 61
mine eye's clear eye, my dear heart's dearer 3.02. 62
i'll stop mine ears against the mermaid's song. 3.02.164
give me the ring of mine you had at dinner, | or 4.03. 68
a ring he hath of mine worth forty ducats, | and 4.03. 83
these ears of mine thou know'st did hear thee; 5.01. 26
i'll prove mine honor and mine honesty | against 5.01. 30
i'll prove mine honor and mine honesty | against 5.01. 30
it is a branch and parcel of mine oath, | a 5.01.106
and, gazing in mine eyes, feeling my pulse, 5.01.244
i will be sworn these ears of mine | heard you 5.01.260
though now this grained face of mine be hid | in 5.01.312
i see two husbands, or mine eyes deceive me. 5.01.332
dromio, what stuff of mine hast thou embark'd? 5.01.410
in mine eye she is the sweetest lady that ever i ADO 1.01.187 P
and in faith, my lord, i spoke mine. 1.01.225 P
my two faiths and troths, my lord, i spoke mine. 1.01.227 P
pick out mine eyes with a ballad-maker's pen and 1.01.252 P
in a thick-pleach'd alley in mine orchard, were 1.02. 10 P
were thus much overheard by a man of mine. 1.02. 11 P
lady, as you are mine, i am yours. 2.01.308 P
athwart his affection ranges evenly with mine. 2.02. 7 P
there's not a note of mine that's worth the 2.03. 55
what fire is in mine ears? 3.01.107
but truly, for mine own part, if i were as 3.05. 20 P
upon mine honor, | myself, my brother, and this 4.01. 88
i might have said, "no part of it is mine; 4.01.134
but mine, and mine i lov'd, and mine i prais'd, 4.01.136
but mine, and mine i lov'd, and mine i prais'd, 4.01.136
but mine, and mine i lov'd, and mine i prais'd, 4.01.136
and mine that i was proud on, mine so much 4.01.137
mine so much | that i myself was to myself not 4.01.137
so much | that i myself was to myself not mine, 4.01.138
time hath not yet so dried this blood of mine, 4.01.193
yet, by mine honor, i will deal in this | as 4.01.247
be friends with me than fight with mine enemy. 4.01.299 P
which falls into mine ears as profitless | as 5.01. 4
nor let no comforter delight mine ear, | but 5.01. 6
but such a one whose wrongs do suit with mine. 5.01. 7
whose joy of her is overwhelm'd like mine, | and 5.01. 9
measure his woe the length and breadth of mine, 5.01. 11
thou hast so wrong'd mine innocent child and me 5.01. 63
i say thou hast belied mine innocent child! 5.01. 67
prince, let me go no farther to mine answer: 5.01.230 P
the lady is dead upon mine and my master's false 5.01.242 P
thy breath hast kill'd | mine innocent child? 5.01.264
why then she's mine. 5.04. 55
in spending your wit in the praise of mine. LLL 2.01. 19
welcome to the wide fields too base to be mine. 2.01. 94 P
for the best ward of mine honor is rewarding my 3.01.132 P
he's a good friend of mine. 4.01. 54
from my lord berowne, a good master of mine, 4.01.104
at the father's of a certain pupil of mine, 4.02.154 P
doth thy face through tears of mine give light. 4.03. 31
if broken then, it is no fault of mine: 4.03. 69
and i had mine! 4.03. 90
and mine too, good lord! 4.03. 91
amen, so i had mine. is not that a good word? 4.03. 92
i thought to close mine eyes some half an hour; 5.02. 90
dumaine is mine, as sure as bark on tree. 5.02.285
all the fool mine? 5.02.384
upon mine honor, no. 5.02.439
despise me when i break this oath of mine. 5.02.441
for mine own part, i am, as /they say, but to 5.02.501 P
for mine own part, i know not the degree of the 5.02.506 P
for mine own part, i breathe free breath. 5.02.722 P
to flatter up these powers of mine with rest, 5.02.814
the sudden hand of death close up mine eye! 5.02.815
me, | behold the window of my heart, mine eye, 5.02.838
as she is mine, i may dispose of her; MND 1.01. 42
and what is mine my love shall render him. 1.01. 96
and she is mine, and all my right of her | i do 1.01. 97
were the world mine, demetrius being bated, 1.01.190
his folly, helena, is no fault of mine. 1.01.200
would that fault were mine! 1.01.201
he hail'd down oaths that he was only mine; 1.01.243
what wicked and dissembling glass of mine | made 2.02. 98
mine ear is much enamored of thy note; 3.01.138
so is mine eye enthralled to thy shape; 3.01.139
this wood, i have enough to serve mine owe turn. 3.01.150 P
thou art not by mine eye, lysander, found; 3.02.181
mine ear, i thank it, brought me to thy sound. 3.02.182
right, | of thine or mine, is most in helena. 3.02.337
your hands than mine are quicker for a fray; 3.02.342
eye, | steal me a while from mine own company. 3.02.436
o, how mine eyes do loathe his visage now! 4.01. 79
the object and the pleasure of mine eye, | is 4.01.170
like a jewel, | mine own, and not mine own. 4.01.192
like a jewel, | mine own, and not mine own. 4.01.192
i must confess, | made mine eyes water; 5.01. 69
stand'st between her father's ground and mine! 5.01.175
me thy chink, to blink through with mine eyne! 5.01.177
man must play a part, | and mine a sad one. MV 1.01. 79
antonio, | how much i have disabled mine estate, 1.01.123
one of the twenty to follow mine own teaching. 1.02. 17 P
and all for use of that which is mine own. 1.03.113
to prove whose blood is reddest, his or mine. 2.01. 7
this aspect of mine | hath fear'd the valiant; 2.01. 8
the fiend is at mine elbow and tempts me, saying 2.02. 2 P
be launcelot, thou art mine own flesh and blood. 2.02. 92 P
but, for mine own part, as i have set up my rest 2.02.102 P
is saying, hood mine eyes | thus with my hat, 2.02.193
and fair she is, if that mine eyes be true, 2.06. 54
cool'd my friends, heated mine enemies; 3.01. 58 P
the other half yours — | mine own, i would say; 3.02. 17
but if mine, then yours, | and so all yours. 3.02. 17
or whether, riding on the balls of mine, | seem 3.02.117
myself, and what is mine, to you and yours | is 3.02.166
and so did mine too, as the matter falls; 3.02.202
for mine own part, | i have toward heaven 3.04. 26
i demand of him | is dearly bought as mine, and 4.01.100
than to live still and write mine epitaph. 4.01.118
that took some pains in writing, he begg'd mine, 5.01.182
nor i in yours | till i again see mine! 5.01.192
now, by mine honor, which is yet mine own, 5.01.232
now, by mine honor, which is yet mine own, 5.01.232
how you do leave me to mine own protection. 5.01.235
have taught my love to take thy father for mine; AYL 1.02. 12 P
were so righteously temper'd as mine is to thee. 1.02. 14 P
by mine honor, i will, and when i break that 1.02. 21 P
no, by mine honor, but i was bid to come for you 1.02. 60 P
and mine, to eke out hers. 1.02.196 P
if i had a thunderbolt in mine eye, i can tell 1.02.214 P
but i did find him still mine enemy. 1.02.226
or have acquaintance with mine own desires; 1.03. 48
if you outstay the time, upon mine honor, | and 1.03. 88
i will give thee mine. 1.03. 91
but if thy love were ever like to mine — | as 2.04. 28
i have by hard adventure found mine own. 2.04. 45
and i mine. 2.04. 46 P
ne'er be ware of mine own wit till i break my 2.04. 58 P
and mine, but it grows something stale with me. 2.04. 62 P
and wish, for her sake more than for mine own, 2.04. 76
and as mine eye doth his effigies witness | most 2.07.193
there i shall see mine own figure. 3.02.289 P
old religious uncle of mine taught me to speak, 3.02.344 P
thou tell'st me there is murder in mine eye: 3.05. 10
and if mine eyes can wound, now let them kill 3.05. 16
lie not, to say mine eyes are murtherers! 3.05. 19
now show the wound mine eye hath made in thee. 3.05. 20
but now mine eyes, | which i have darted at thee 3.05. 24
he said mine eyes were black and my hair black, 3.05.130
but it is a melancholy of mine own, compounded 4.01. 16 P
then, in mine own person, i die. 4.01. 93 P
eyne | have power to raise such love in mine, 4.03. 51
here comes a lover of mine and a lover of hers. 5.02. 75 P
politic with my friend, smooth with mine enemy, 5.04. 46 P
sir, an ill-favor'd thing, sir, but mine own; 5.04. 58 P
a poor humor of mine, sir, to take that that no 5.04. 59 P
i will not eat my word, now thou art mine, | thy 5.04.149
mi perdonato, gentle master mine; SHR 1.01. 25
to mine own children in good bringing-up, | and 1.01. 99
pass your patience and mine to endure her loud 1.01.127 P
it is, | i would not wed her for a mine of gold. 1.02. 92
think you a little din can daunt mine ears? 1.02.199
to make mine eye the witness | of that report 2.01. 52
i do present you with a man of mine, | cunning 2.01. 55
pardon me, sir, the boldness is mine own, | that 2.01. 88
no cock of mine, you crow too like a craven. 2.01.227
hers, | if whilst i live she will be only mine. 2.01.362
if you like me, she shall have me and mine. 2.01.383
why then the maid is mine from all the world, 2.01.384
no shame but mine. 3.02. 8
go to my chamber, put on clothes of mine. 3.02.113
i'll keep mine own, despite of all the world. 3.02.142
fret, | i will be master of what is mine own. 3.02.229
i'll bring mine action on the proudest he | that 3.02.234
and since mine eyes are witness of her lightness 4.02. 24
for me, that i may surely keep mine oath, | i 4.02. 36
and so shall mine before you touch the meat. 4.03. 46
brav'd in mine own house with a skein of thread? 4.03.110
there to visit | a son of mine, which long i 4.05. 57
mine old master vincentio! 5.01. 43 P
his name is lucentio, and he is mine only son, 5.01. 85 P
that have by marriage made thy daughter mine, 5.01.116
the fouler fortune mine, and there an end. 5.02. 98
that makes me see, and cannot feed mine eye? AWW 1.01.221
in isbel's case and mine own. 1.03. 23 P
mine honorable mistress. 1.03.139
catalogue of those | that were enwombed mine. 1.03.144
religious in mine error, i adore | the sun, that 1.03.205
the well-lost life of mine on his grace's cure 1.03.248
my loving greetings | to those of mine in court. 1.03.253
eye, | safer than mine own two, more dear. 2.01.109
i will no more enforce mine office on you, 2.01.126
proclaim | myself against the level of mine aim, 2.01.156
and they were sons of mine, i'd have them whipt, 2.03. 87 P
me leave to use | the help of mine own eyes. 2.03.108
by mine honor, if i were but two hours younger, 2.03.252 P
your good will to have mine own good /fortunes. 2.04. 15 P
of the wealth i owe, | nor dare i say 'tis mine; 2.05. 80
fain would steal | what law does vouch mine own. 2.05. 82
miseries which nature owes | were mine at once. 3.02.120
my heart is heavy, and mine age is weak; 3.04. 41
my lord, in mine own direct knowledge, without 3.06. 7 P
o, ransom, ransom! do not hide mine eyes. 4.01. 67
say thou art mine, and ever | my love, as it 4.02. 36
mine honor's such a ring, | my chastity's the 4.02. 45
my house, mine honor, yea, my life, be thine, 4.02. 52
mine own company, chitopher, vaumond, bentii, 4.03.164 P
him for no other but a poor officer of mine, and 4.03.199 P
ere i can perfect mine intents, to kneel. 4.04. 4
where the impression of mine eye infixing, 5.03. 47
was in mine eye | the dust that did offend it. 5.03. 54
for mine eye, | while i was speaking, oft was 5.03. 81
this ring was mine, and, when i gave it helen, 5.03. 83
but when i had subscrib'd | to mine own fortune, 5.03. 97
'twas mine, 'twas helen's, | whoever gave it you 5.03.104
thou speak'st it falsely, as i love mine honor, 5.03.113
she's none of mine, my lord. 5.03.169
you give away this hand, and that is mine; 5.03.170
you give away heaven's vows, and those are mine; 5.03.171
you give away myself, which is known mine; 5.03.172
lay a more noble thought upon mine honor | than 5.03.180
i will return it home, | and give me mine again. 5.03.224
this ring was mine, i gave it his first wife. 5.03.279
beguiles the truer office of mine eyes? 5.03.305
will you be mine now you are doubly won? 5.03.314
mine eyes smell onions, i shall weep anon. 5.03.320
o, when mine eyes did see olivia first, TN 1.01. 18
mine own escape unfoldeth to my hope, | whereto 1.02. 19
world | till i had made mine own occasion mellow 1.02. 43
my tongue blabs, then let mine eyes not see. 1.02. 63
by mine honor, half drunk. 1.05.116 P
and subtle stealth | to creep in at mine eyes. 1.05.298
mine eye too great a flatterer for my mind. 1.05.309
least occasion more mine eyes will tell tales of 2.01. 41 P
"o mistress mine, where are you roaming? 2.03. 39
revolt, | but mine is all as hungry as the sea, 2.04.100
or o' mine either? 2.05.189 P
have you not set mine honor at the stake, | and 3.01.118
he may have mercy upon mine, but my hope is 3.04.168 P
stone, | and laid mine honor too unchary on't. 3.04.202
how with mine honor may i give him that | which 3.04.214
he started one poor heart of mine, in thee. 4.01. 59
that i am ready to distrust mine eyes | and 4.03. 13
blame not this haste of mine. 4.03. 22
that they may fairly note this act of mine! 4.03. 35
denied me mine own purse, | which i had 5.01. 90
it is as fat and fulsome to mine ear | as 5.01.109
and so had mine. 5.01.243
a most extracting frenzy of mine own | from my 5.01.281
instructs me and as mine honesty puts it to WT 1.01. 20 P
they say it is a copy out of mine. 1.02.122
one that fixes | no bourn 'twixt his and mine, 1.02.134
mine honest friend, | will you take eggs for 1.02.160
now my sworn friend and then mine enemy; 1.02.167
gates open'd, | as mine, against their will. 1.02.198
if i then deny it, | 'tis none of mine. 1.02.267
eyes | to see alike mine honor as their profits 1.02.310
a cup, | to give mine enemy a lasting wink; 1.02.317
son | (who i do think is mine and love as mine), 1.02.331
son | (who i do think is mine and love as mine), 1.02.331
me | even so as i mine own course have set down. 1.02.340
me a mirror | which shows me mine chang'd too; 1.02.382
whereof the least | is not this suit of mine, 1.02.402
me, and thy places shall | still neighbor mine. 1.02.449
it is in mine authority to command | the keys of 1.02.463
come on then, | and give't me in mine ear. 2.01. 32
by mine honor, | i'll geld 'em all; 2.01.146
upon mine honor, i | will stand betwixt you and 2.02. 63
for the harlot king | is quite beyond mine arm, 2.03. 5
lord, | on your displeasure's peril and on mine, 2.03. 45

on mine own accord i'll off, | but first i'll do 2.03. 64
this brat is none of mine, | it is the issue of 2.03. 93
mine integrity, | being counted falsehood, shall 3.02. 26
for honor, | 'tis a derivative from me to mine, 3.02. 44
(i prize it not a straw), but for mine honor, 3.02.110
i have too much believ'd mine own suspicion. 3.02.151
if the springe hold, the cock's mine. 4.03. 35 P
what will this sister of mine do with rice? 4.03. 39 P
since my desires | run not before mine honor, 4.04. 34
for i cannot be | mine own, nor any thing to any 4.04. 44
not to be buried, | but quick and in mine arms. 4.04.132
sure this robe of mine | does change my 4.04.134
by th' pattern of mine own thoughts i cut out 4.04.382
this dream of mine — | being now awake, i'll 4.04.448
on mine honor, | i'll point you where you shall 4.04.525
appointed, as if | the scene you play were mine. 4.04.593
words that follow'd | should be "remember mine." 5.01. 67
and then i lost | (all mine own folly) the 5.01.135
of such affections, | step forth mine advocate. 5.01.221
and that which angled for mine eyes (caught the 5.02. 83 P
thus have wrought you (for the stone is mine), 5.03. 58
tell me, mine own, | where hast thou been 5.03.123
thou hast found mine, | but how, is to be 5.03.138
bear mine to him, and so depart in peace. JN 1.01. 23
that is my brother's plea and none of mine, 1.01. 67
mine eye hath well examined his parts, | and 1.01. 89
then, good my liege, let me have what is mine, 1.01.114
thin | that in mine ear i durst not stick a rose 1.01.142
sir," | thus, leaning on mine elbow, i begin, 1.01.194
that holds in chase mine honor up and down? 1.01.223
for thine own gain shouldst defend mine honor? 1.01.242
sits on 's horseback at mine hostess' door, 2.01.289
my uncle's will in this respect is mine. 2.01.510
you came in arms to spill mine enemies' blood, 3.01.102
and for mine too: 3.01.185
this royal hand and mine are newly knit, | and 3.01.226
knee i beg, go not to arms | against mine uncle. 3.01.309
and wheresoe'er this foot of mine doth tread, 3.03. 62
this hair i tear is mine, | my name is constance 3.04. 45
out at mine eyes in tender womanish tears. 4.01. 36
must you with hot irons burn out both mine eyes? 4.01. 39
will you put out mine eyes, | these eyes that 4.01. 56
even in the matter of mine innocence; 4.01. 64
but for containing fire to harm mine eye. 4.01. 66
and told me hubert should put out mine eyes, | i 4.01. 69
cut out my tongue, | so i may keep mine eyes. 4.01.101
o, spare mine eyes, | though to no use but still 4.01.101
he show'd his warrant to a friend of mine. 4.02. 70
this hand of mine | is yet a maiden and an 4.02.251
startles mine eyes, and makes me more amaz'd 5.02. 51
that knit your sinews to the strength of mine. 5.02. 63
after young arthur, claim this land for mine, 5.02. 94
of thine affairs, as well as thou of mine? 5.06. 5
should scape the true acquaintance of mine ear. 5.06. 15
o cousin, thou art come to set mine eye. 5.07. 51
much strength | as to take up mine honor's pawn, R2 1.01. 74
mine honor is my life, both grow in one, | take 1.01.182
then, dear my liege, mine honor let me try; 1.01.184
and by the grace of god, and this mine arm, | to 1.03. 22
add proof unto mine armor with thy prayers, 1.03. 73
mine innocence and saint george to thrive! 1.03. 84
this feast of battle with mine adversary. 1.03. 92
norfolk, so fare as to mine enemy: 1.03.193
say | i was too strict to make mine own away; 1.03.244
his, | as theirs, so mine, and all be as it is. 2.01.146
quick is mine ear to hear of good towards him. 2.01.234
mine is not so, | for nothing hath begot my 2.02. 35
as mine hath done | by sight of what i have, 2.03. 17
o, then how quickly should this arm of mine, 2.03.103
a gentleman of mine i have dispatch'd | with 3.01. 40
yield stinging nettles to mine enemies; 3.02. 18
mine ear is open, and my heart prepar'd, | the 3.02. 93
that e'er this tongue of mine | that laid the 3.03.133
my gracious lord, i come but for mine own. 3.03.196
so far be mine, my most redoubted lord, | as my 3.03.198
as far as callice, to mine uncle's head?" 4.01. 13
or have mine honor soil'd | with the attainder 4.01. 23
and, though mine enemy, restor'd again | to all 4.01. 88
only take the sacrament | to bury mine intents, 4.01.329
go count thy way with sighs, i mine with groans. 5.01. 89
thus give i mine, and thus take i thy heart. 5.01. 96
give me mine own again, 'twere no good part | to 5.01. 97
so, now i have mine own again, be gone, | that i 5.01. 99
now, by mine honor, by my life, by my troth, | i 5.02. 78
and wilt thou pluck my fair son from mine age, 5.02. 92
an' he shall spend mine honor with his shame, 5.03. 68
mine honor lives when his dishonor dies, | or my 5.03. 70
they jar | their watches on unto mine eyes, the 5.05. 52
for though mine enemy thou hast ever been, 5.06. 28
lay, | and call'd mine percy, his plantagenet! 1H4 1.01. 89
then would i have his harry and he mine. 1.01. 90
"but, for mine own part, my lord, i could be 2.03. 1 P
i understand thy kisses, and thou mine, | and 3.01.202
not mine, in good sooth. 3.01.246 P
save mine, which hath desir'd to see thee more, 3.02. 89
i was never call'd so in mine own house before. 3.03. 63 P
shall i not take mine ease in mine inn but i 3.03. 80 P
not take mine ease in mine inn but i shall have 3.03. 80 P
mine, hal, mine. 4.02. 63 P
mine, hal, mine. 4.02. 63 P
rated mine uncle from the council-board, | in 4.03. 99
and in the morning early shall mine uncle 4.03.110
for mine own part, i could be well content | to 5.01. 23
i need no more weight than mine own bowels. 5.03. 35 P
but mine i am sure thou art, whoe'er thou be, 5.04. 37
thy name in arms were now as great as mine! 5.04. 70
upon mine honor, for a silken point | i'll give 2H4 1.01. 53
but these mine eyes saw him in bloody state, 1.01.107
but he's almost out of mine, i can assure him. 1.02. 28 P
he stabb'd me in mine own house, most beastly, 2.01. 14 P
well spoke on, i can hear it with mine own ears. 2.02. 66 P
and for mine, sir, i will govern it. 2.02.164 P
that shall be mine, for in every thing the 2.02.175 P
to rain upon remembrance with mine eyes, | that 2.03. 59
dost thou hear? it is mine ancient. 2.04. 82 P
cup of sack, do you discharge upon mine hostess. 2.04.113 P
a death's-head, do not bid me remember mine end. 2.04.235 P
no abuse, hal, a' mine honor, no abuse. 2.04.313 P
and your fairest daughter and mine, my 3.02. 6 P
as go, and yet, for mine own part, sir, i do not 3.02.223 P
and, for mine own part, have a desire to stay 3.02.225 P
sir, i did not care, for mine own part, so much. 3.02.226 P
upon mine honor, all too confident | to give 4.01.150
whereof you did complain, which, by mine honor, 4.02.114
a whole school of tongues in this belly of mine, 4.03. 19 P
else, with mine own picture on the top on't 4.03. 48 P
this from thee | will i to mine leave, as 'tis 4.05. 47
dost thou so hunger for mine empty chair | that 4.05. 94
if any rebel or vain spirit of mine | did with 4.05.171
the knave is mine honest friend, sir, therefore 5.01. 50 P
till you do live to see a son of mine | offend 5.02.105
my voice shall sound as you do prompt mine ear, 5.02.119
eat a last year's pippin of mine own graffing, 5.03. 2 P
and fine, | and drink unto /thee, leman mine, 5.03. 47
for what i have to say is of mine own making, ep 5 P
say) will (i doubt) prove mine own marring. ep 6 P
fight, but i will wink and hold out mine iron. H5 2.01. 8 P
how now, mine host pistol? 2.01. 28 P
mine host pistol, you must come to my master, 2.01. 81 P
and, for mine own part, i have not a case of 3.02. 4 P
take from another's pocket to put into mine; 3.02. 50 P
mess, ere theise eyes of mine take themselves to 3.02.114 P
mine was not bridled. 3.07. 51 P
tarry, sweet soul, for mine, then fly abreast, 4.06. 17
and all my mother came into mine eyes | and gave 4.06. 31
i have fin'd these bones of mine for ransom? 4.07. 69
never came any from mine that might offend your 4.08. 47 P
you take it for your own fault and not mine; 4.08. 54 P
i will have it all mine. 5.02.175 P
kate, when france is mine and i am yours, then 5.02.175 P
am yours, then yours is france and you are mine. 5.02.176 P
if ever thou beest mine, kate, as i have a 5.02.203 P
by mine honor, in true english, i love thee, 5.02.220 P
word thou shalt no sooner bless mine ear withal, 5.02.238 P
or whose will stands but mine? 1H6 1.03. 11
mine was secure. 2.01. 66
and so was mine, my lord. 2.01. 66
within her quarter and mine own precinct | i was 2.01. 68
fain would mine eyes be witness with mine ears 2.03. 9
fain would mine eyes be witness with mine ears 2.03. 9
poor gentleman, his wrong doth equal mine. 2.05. 22
direct mine arms i may embrace his neck, | and 2.05. 37
first, lean thine aged back against mine arm, 2.05. 43
and this is mine, sweet henry, favor him. 4.01. 81
confirm it so, mine honorable lord. 4.01.122
and mine shall ring thy dire departure out. 4.02. 41
sell every man his life as dear as mine, | and 4.02. 53
but mine it will, that no exploit have done. 4.05. 27
for that pure blood of mine | which thou didst 4.06. 23
mine own is gone. 4.07. 1
o, were mine eyeballs into bullets turn'd, 4.07. 79
so seems this gorgeous beauty to mine eyes. 5.03. 64
upon condition i may quietly | enjoy mine own, 5.03.154
content | to be mine own attorney in this case. 5.03.166
thou art no father nor friend of mine. 5.04. 9
beads, | with you, mine alder-liefest sovereign, 2H6 1.01. 28
and dimm'd mine eyes, that i can read no further 1.01. 55
or hath mine uncle beauford and myself, | with 1.01. 88
sword should shed hot blood, mine eyes no tears. 1.01.118
those provinces these arms of mine did conquer, 1.01.120
'tis known to you he is mine enemy; 1.01.148
i'll lengthen it with mine, | and, having both 1.02. 12
this staff, mine office-badge in court, | was 1.02. 25
mine is, and't please your grace, against john 1.03. 16 P
mine eyes are full of tears, my heart of grief. 2.03. 17
sorrow would solace, and mine age would ease. 2.03. 21
resign | as ere thy father henry made it mine; 2.03. 34
have i overcome mine enemies in this presence? 2.03. 98 P
and ban thine enemies, both mine and thine! 2.04. 25
many a pound of mine own proper store, | because 3.01.115
but mine is made the prologue to their play; 3.01.151
stirr'd up | my liefest liege to be mine enemy. 3.01.164
whose flood begins to flow within mine eyes; 3.01.199
and yet herein i judge mine own wit good — 3.01.232
whiles i take order for mine own affairs. 3.01.320
weaves tedious snares to trap mine enemies. 3.01.340
and bid mine eyes be packing with my heart, 3.02.111
my tongue should stumble in mine earnest words, 3.02.316
mine eyes should sparkle like the beaten flint, 3.02.317
mine hair be fix'd an end, as one distract; 3.02.318
for the earth's increase, mine for my sorrows? 3.02.385
and cry out for thee to close up mine eyes, | to 3.02.395
i lost mine eye in laying the prize aboard, 4.01. 25
this hand of mine hath writ in thy behalf, | and 4.01. 63
to a thing, and i was never mine own man since. 4.02. 83 P
the man is a proper man, of mine honor; 4.02. 96 P
the trust i have is in mine innocence, | and 4.04. 59
oppose thy steadfast-gazing eyes to mine, | see 4.10. 45
hast, | and if mine arm be heaved in the air, 4.10. 51
upon mine honor, he is prisoner. 5.01. 43
that gold must round engirt these brows of mine, 5.01. 99
in love, | but that thou art so fast mine enemy. 5.02. 21
and while 'tis mine, | it shall be stony. 5.02. 50
nothing so heavy as these woes of mine. 5.02. 65
confirm the crown to me and to mine heirs, | and 3H6 1.01.172
have forsworn thy colors | will follow mine, if 1.01.252
mine, boys? not till king henry be dead. 1.02. 10
sir john and sir hugh mortimer, mine uncles, 1.02. 62
it could not slake mine ire nor ease my heart. 1.03. 29
and in that hope i throw mine eyes to heaven, 1.04. 37
dazzle mine eyes, or do i see three suns? 2.01. 25
thou shalt know this strong right hand of mine 2.01.152
i come to pierce it, or to give thee mine. 2.01.203
till either death hath clos'd these eyes of mine 2.03. 31
i throw my hands, mine eyes, my heart to thee, 2.03. 36
ah, no, no, no, it is mine only son! 2.05. 83
upon thy wounds, that kills mine eye and heart! 2.05. 87
mine ten times so much. 2.05.112
these arms of mine shall be thy winding-sheet; 2.05.114
to greet mine own land with my wishful sight. 3.01. 14
why then mine honesty shall be my dower, | for 3.02. 72
to shrink mine arm up like a wither'd shrub, 3.02.156
from such a cause as fills mine eyes with tears 3.03. 13
thereon i pawn my credit and mine honor. 3.03.116
your grant, or your denial, shall be mine. 3.03.130
mine ear hath tempted judgment to desire. 3.03.133
that your estate requires and mine can yield. 3.03.150
mine such as fill my heart with unhop'd joys. 3.03.172
mine full of sorrow and heart's discontent. 3.03.173
and mine, fair lady bona, joins with yours. 3.03.217
and mine with hers, and thine, and margaret's. 3.03.218
i'll join mine eldest daughter, and my joy, | to 3.03.242
then this is mine opinion: 4.01. 29
leave | to play the broker in mine own behalf; 4.01. 63
but as this title honors me and mine, | so your 4.01. 72
in field | should not be able to encounter mine. 4.08. 36
i have not stopp'd mine ears to their demands, 4.08. 39
how far hence is thy lord, mine honest fellow? 5.01. 2
why then 'tis mine, if but by warwick's gift. 5.01. 35
and thou usurp'st my father's right and mine. 5.05. 37
thou hast not liv'd to kill a son of mine. 5.06. 36
in the sun | and descant on mine own deformity. R3 1.01. 27
out of my sight, thou dost infect mine eyes! 1.02.148
thine eyes, sweet lady, have infected mine. 1.02.149
eyes of thine from mine have drawn salt tears, 1.02.153
to royalize his blood i spent mine own. 1.03.124
or edward's soft and pitiful, like mine: 1.03.140
and all the pleasures you usurp are mine. 1.03.172
in thy rights as thou art stall'd in mine! 1.03.205
foul shame upon you, you have all mov'd mine. 1.03.248
and so doth mine. i muse why she's at liberty. 1.03.304
me, and howled in mine ears | such hideous cries 1.04. 59
hope this passionate humor of mine will change. 1.04.118 P
my voice is now the king's, my looks mine own. 1.04.168
our former hatred, so thrive i and mine! 2.01. 24
take hold | on me and you, and mine and yours, 2.01.133
the king mine uncle is to blame for it. 2.02. 13
all springs reduce their currents to mine eyes, 2.02. 68
alas for both, both mine, edward and clarence! 2.02. 73
their woes are parcell'd, mine is general. 2.02. 81
to touch his growth nearer than he touch'd mine. 2.04. 25
days, | how many of you have mine eyes beheld! 2.04. 56
and therefore, in mine opinion, cannot have it. 3.01. 52
have this crown of mine cut from my shoulders 3.02. 43
he knows no more of mine than i of yours, | or i 3.04. 11
yours, | or i of his, my lord, than you of mine. 3.04. 12
behold, mine arm | is like a blasted sapling, 3.04. 68
how mine enemies | to-day at pomfret bloodily 3.04. 89
when he had done, some followers of mine own, 3.07. 34
and prov'd the subject of mine own soul's curse, 4.01. 80
dar'st thou resolve to kill a friend of mine? 4.02. 69
i lurk'd, | to watch the waning of mine enemies. 4.04. 4
reverent, | give mine the benefit of seniory, 4.04. 36
and teach me how to curse mine enemies! 4.04.117
woes will make them sharp and pierce like mine. 4.04.125
honor, | canst thou demise to any child of mine? 4.04.248
mine issue of your blood upon your daughter. 4.04.298
but mine shall be a comfort to your age. 4.04.306
and when this arm of mine hath chastised | the 4.04.331
soul | ere i let fall the windows of mine eyes: 5.03.116
every man that stood | show'd like a mine. H8 1.01. 22
i do know | kinsmen of mine, three at the least, 1.01. 81
will help me nothing | to plead mine innocence; 1.01.208
lady mine, proceed. 1.02. 17
and once more in mine arms i bid him welcome, 2.02. 98
or made it not mine too? 2.04. 29
to love, although i knew | he were mine enemy? 2.04. 31
what friend of mine | that had to him deriv'd 2.04. 31
and prove it too, against mine honor aught — 2.04. 39
that | you are mine enemy, and make my challenge 2.04. 77
yea, upon mine honor, | i free you from't. 2.04.157
in such a point of weight, so near mine honor 3.01. 71
far hence | in mine own country, lords. 3.01. 91
wherein he appears | as i would wish mine enemy. 3.02. 28
mine own ends | have been mine so, that evermore 3.02.171
mine own ends | have been mine so, that evermore 3.02.172
good i ever labor'd | more than mine own; 3.02.192
wealth i have drawn together | for mine own ends 3.02.212
the king | (mine and your master) with his own 3.02.247
fairer | and spotless shall mine innocence arise 3.02.301
no sun shall ever usher forth mine honors, | or 3.02.410
to heaven, is all | i dare now call mine own. 3.02.454
he would not in mine age | have left me naked to 3.02.456
mine age | have left me naked to mine enemies. 3.02.457
actions | to keep mine honor from corruption, 4.02. 71
first, mine own service to your grace, the next, 4.02.115
mine eyes grow dim. 4.02.164
thomas, y' are a gentleman | of mine own way; 5.01. 28
if they shall fail, i, with mine enemies, | will 5.01.123
god and your majesty | protect mine innocence, 5.01.141
he's honest, on mine honor. 5.01.153
sought their malice) | to quench mine honor; 5.02. 16
that i was fain to draw mine honor in, and let 5.03. 57 P
upon my secrecy, to defend mine honesty, my mask
TRO 1.02.262 P
nothing of that shall from mine eyes appear. 1.02.295
hast no more brain than i have in mine elbows, 2.01. 44 P
will, | my will enkindled by mine eyes and ears, 2.02. 63
at mine, sir, and theirs that love music. 3.01. 24 P
sir, mine own company. 3.02.145
but in mine emulous honor let him die, | with 4.01. 29
then, sweet my lord, i'll call mine uncle down, 4.02. 2
with truth and plainness i do wear mine bare. 4.04.106
the first was menelaus' kiss, this, mine; 4.05. 32
now, hector, i have fed mine eyes on thee; 4.05.231
i prithee do not hold me to mine oath, | bid me 5.02. 26
nor mine, my lord; cressid was here but now. 5.02.128
cressid is mine, tied with the bonds of heaven. 5.02.154
that sleeve is mine that he'll bear on his helm. 5.02.169
mine honor keeps the weather of my fate. 5.03. 26
and i have a rheum in mine eyes too, and such an 5.03.104 P
masters, my good friends, mine honest neighbors, COR 1.01. 62
this is true, on mine honor, and so i pray go 1.03.101 P
so, the good horse is mine. 1.04. 5
him for a volsce, | and he shall feel mine edge. 1.04. 29
his good will | hath overta'en mine act. 1.09. 19
him beard to beard, | he's mine, or i am his. 1.10. 12
mine emulation | hath not that honor in't it had 1.10. 12
mine own desert. 2.03. 65 P
ay, /not mine own desire. 2.03. 67 P
let them pull all about mine ears, present me 3.02. 1
for the whole state, i would put mine armor on, 3.02. 34
do't, | lest i surcease to honor mine own truth, 3.02.121
thy valiantness was mine, thou suck'st it from 3.02.129

i | will answer in mine honor. 3.02.144
more holy and profound, than mine own life, | my 3.03.113
let me twine | mine arms about that body, where 4.05.107
target from thy brawn, | or lose mine arm for't. 4.05.121
for mine own part, | when i said banish him, i 4.06.139
that which shall break his neck, or hazard mine, 4.07. 25
then shortly art thou mine. 4.07. 57
mine ears against your suits are stronger than 5.02. 88
ay, and on mine, | that brought you forth this 5.03.125
thing to make | mine eyes to sweat compassion. 5.03.196
him, and i pawn'd | mine honor for his truth; 5.06. 21
serv'd his designments | in mine own person; 5.06. 35
in me, | nor wrong mine age with this indignity. TIT 1.01. 8
how many sons hast thou of mine in store, | that 1.01. 94
the cordial of mine age to glad my heart! 1.01.166
give me a staff of honor for mine age, | but not 1.01.198
owe, | mine honor's ensigns humbled at thy feet. 1.01.252
lord titus, by your leave, this maid is mine. 1.01.276
nor thou, nor he, are any sons of mine, | my 1.01.294
no son of mine, | nor thou, nor these, 1.01.343
and with these boys mine honor thou hast wounded 1.01.365
mean while am i possess'd of that is mine. 1.01.408
but on mine honor dare i undertake | for good 1.01.436
and let it be mine honor, good my lord, | that i 1.01.466
that, on mine honor, here do i protest. 1.01.477
your desires, | saturn is dominator over mine: 2.03. 31
and mine, i promise you; 2.03.196
my heart suspects more than mine eye can see. 2.03.213
heart | will not permit mine eyes once to behold 2.03.218
for pity of mine age, whose youth was spent | in 3.01. 2
and rome affords no prey | but me and mine. 3.01. 56
i wot, | thy napkin cannot drink a tear of mine, 3.01.140
and therefore mine shall save my brothers' lives 3.01.166
are meet for plucking up, and therefore mine. 3.01.178
lend me thy hand, and i will give thee mine. 3.01.187
and yet dear too, because i bought mine own. 3.01.199
come go with me into mine armory; 4.01.113
i am of age | to keep mine own, excuse it how 4.02.105
heir, | and substituted in the place of mine, 4.02.159
there to dispose this treasure in mine arms, 4.02.173
and, as i earnestly did fix mine eye | upon the 5.01. 22
that both mine eyes were rainy like to his; 5.01.117
sent to me, | to be a torment to mine enemies? 5.02. 42
death, | they have been violent to me and mine. 5.02.109
griefs of mine own lie heavy in my breast, ROM 1.01.186
doth add more grief to too much of mine own. 1.01.189
which /on more view of many, mine, being one, 1.02. 32
ay, mine own fortune in my misery. 1.02. 58
mine uncle capulet, his wife, and daughters; 1.02. 68 P
when the devout religion of mine eye | maintains 1.02. 88
shown, | but to rejoice in splendor of mine own. 1.02.101
but no more deep will i endart mine eye | than 1.03. 98
exchange of thy love's faithful vow for mine. 2.02.127
i gave thee mine before thou didst request it; 2.02.128
that last is true — the sweeter rest was mine. 2.03. 43
i have been feasting with mine enemy, | where on 2.03. 49
as mine on hers, so hers is set on mine, | and 2.03. 59
as mine on hers, so hers is set on mine, | and 2.03. 59
thy old groans yet ringing in mine ancient ears; 2.03. 74
for doting, not for loving, pupil mine. 2.03. 82
and in such a case as mine a man may strain 2.04. 50 P
he dare, | it is enough i may but call her mine. 2.06. 8
if the measure of thy joy | be heap'd like mine, 2.06. 25
which name i tender | as dearly as mine own — 3.01. 72
lest mine be about your ears ere it be out. 3.01. 81 P
that you shall all repent the loss of mine. 3.01.191
i saw the wound, i saw it with mine eyes — 3.02. 52
mine shall be spent, | when theirs are dry, for 3.02.130
and you be mine, i'll give you to my friend; 3.05.191
nor what is mine shall never do thee good. 3.05.194
thy face is mine, and thou hast sland'red it. 4.01. 35
it may be so, for it is not mine own. 4.01. 36
what further woe conspires against mine age? 5.03.212
mine heir from forth the beggars of the world, TIM 1.01.138
this gentleman of mine hath serv'd me long; 1.01.142
my hand to thee, mine honor on my promise. 1.01.148
mine eyes cannot hold out water, methinks. 1.02.106 P
and entertain'd me with mine own device. 1.02.150
i weigh my friend's affection with mine own. 1.02.216
i must serve my turn | out of mine own. 2.01. 21
mine honest friend, | i prithee but repair to me 2.02. 24
off, | and say you /found them in mine honesty. 2.02.135
to a wasteful cock | and set mine eyes at flow. 2.02.163
in some sort these wants of mine are crown'd, 2.02.181
me so far as to use mine own words to him? 3.02. 58 P
for mine own part, | i never tasted timon in my 3.02. 76
who bates mine honor shall not know my coin. 3.03. 26
for mine | is money. 3.04. 4
five thousand mine. 3.04. 29
sum | your master's confidence was above mine, 3.04. 31
here's mine. 3.04. 86 P
and mine, my lord. 3.04. 87 P
mine, fifty talents. 3.04. 93 P
fortune to lie heavy | upon a friend of mine, 3.05. 11
so i shall mend mine own, by th' lack of thine. 4.03.284
for his undone lord than mine eyes for you. 4.03.481
that mine own use invites me to cut down, | and 5.01.206
i met a courier, one mine ancient friend, | whom 5.02. 6
those enemies of timon's and mine own | whom you 5.04. 56
by means whereof this breast of mine hath buried JC 1.02. 49
and at every putting–by mine honest neighbors 1.02.231 P
and for mine own part, i durst not laugh, for 1.02.249 P
but, for mine own part, it was greek to me. 1.02.283 P
and i will set this foot of mine as far | as who 1.03.119
have i in conquest stretch'd mine arm so far, 2.02. 66
at mine own house, good lady. 2.04. 22
o caesar, read mine first; 3.01. 6
passion, i see, is catching, /for mine eyes, 3.01.283
believe me for mine honor, and have respect to 3.02. 14 P
for mine honor, and have respect to mine honor, 3.02. 15 P
wrong i mine enemies? 4.02. 38
for mine own part, | i shall be glad to learn of 4.03. 53
but brutus makes mine greater than they are. 4.03. 87
o, i could weep | my spirit from mine eyes! 4.03.100
a heart | dearer than pluto's mine, richer than 4.03.102
mine speak of seventy senators that died | by 4.03.177
i think it is the weakness of mine eyes | that 4.03.276
myself have to mine own turn'd enemy. 5.03. 2
this ensign here of mine was turning back; 5.03. 3
night hangs upon mine eyes, my bones would rest, 5.05. 41
about, | thrice to thine, and thrice to mine, MAC 1.03. 35
of thanks and payment | might have been mine! 1.04. 20
conduct me to mine host, we love him highly, 1.06. 29
mine eyes are made the fools o' th' other senses 2.01. 44
business which informs | thus to mine eyes. 2.01. 49
they pluck out mine eyes. 2.02. 56
to th' amazement of mine eyes | that look'd 2.04. 19
an unlineal hand, | no son of mine succeeding. 3.01. 63
and mine eternal jewel | given to the common 3.01. 67
so is he mine; 3.01.115
for certain friends that are both his and mine, 3.01.120
your cheeks, | when mine is blanch'd with fear. 3.04.115
for mine own good | all causes shall give way. 3.04.134
thy crown does sear mine eyeballs. 4.01.113
be your dishonors, | but mine own safeties. 4.03. 30
direction, and | unspeak mine own detraction; 4.03.123
scarcely have coveted what was mine own, | at no 4.03.127
if it be mine, | keep it not from me, quickly 4.03.199
am, | not for their own demerits, but for mine, 4.03.226
o, i could play the woman with mine eyes, | and 4.03.230
give me mine armor. 5.03. 36
come, put mine armor on; 5.03. 48
pronounce a title | more hateful to mine ear. 5.07. 9
if thou beest slain and with no stroke of mine, 5.07. 15
the roman fool, and die | on mine own sword? 5.08. 2
whose voices i desire aloud with mine: 5.09. 24
the sensible and true avouch | of mine own eyes. HAM 1.01. 58
but, in the gross and scope of mine opinion, 1.01. 68
your loves, as mine to you, farewell. 1.02.253
natural gifts were poor | to those of mine! 1.05. 52
so did it mine, | and a most instant tetter 1.05. 70
at last, a little shaking of mine arm, | and 2.01. 89
or else this brain of mine | hunts not the trail 2.02. 46
i have a daughter — have while she is mine — 2.02.106
by means, and place, | all given to mine ear. 2.02.128
in such matters cried in the top of mine — an 2.02.439 P
the murther of my father | before mine uncle. 2.02.596
note, | for i mine eyes will rivet to his face, 3.02. 85
this answer, hamlet, these words are not mine. 3.02. 97 P
no, nor mine now. 3.02. 98 P
would cost you a groaning to take off mine edge. 3.02.250 P
my crown, mine own ambition, and my queen. 3.03. 55
ah, mine own lord, what have i seen to–night! 4.01. 5
that i can keep your counsel and not mine own. 4.02. 11 P
burn out the sense and virtue of mine eye! 4.05.156
mine ache to think on't. 5.01. 92 P
mine, sir. 5.01.119 P
for my part, i do not lie in't, yet it is mine. 5.01.124 P
till i have caught her once more in mine arms. 5.01.250
and in fine withdrew | to mine own room again, 5.02. 16
if his fitness speaks, mine is ready; 5.02.201 P
in mine ignorance | your skill shall, like a 5.02.255
why, as a woodcock to mine own springe, osric: 5.02.306
i am justly kill'd with mine own treachery. 5.02.307
mine and my father's death come not upon thee, 5.02.330
this villain of mine comes under the prediction; LR 1.02.109 P
whose mind and mine, i know, in that are one, 1.03. 15
thou but rememb'rest me of mine own conception. 1.04. 67 P
have rather blam'd as mine own jealous curiosity 1.04. 69 P
there's mine, beg another of thy daughters. 1.04.108 P
home | my unprovided body, latch'd mine arm; 2.01. 52
no more, perchance, does mine, nor his, nor hers 2.02. 91
whose welcome i perceiv'd had poison'd mine — 2.04. 39
gives thee better counsel, give me mine again, i 2.04. 76 P
in my flesh, | which i must needs call mine. 2.04.223
from those that she calls servants or from mine? 2.04.244
they took from me the use of mine own house, 3.03. 3 P
i had rather break mine own. 3.04. 5
mine enemy's dog, | though he had bit me, should 4.07. 35
that mine own tears | do scald like molten lead. 4.07. 46
no, by mine honor, madam. 5.01. 14
here is mine: 5.03.128
is my privilege, | the privilege of mine honors, 5.03.130
this sword of mine shall give them instant way 5.03.150
say if i do, the laws are mine, not thine; 5.03.159
good i mean to do, | despite of mine own nature. 5.03.245
mine eyes are not o' th' best; 5.03.280
and mine, a hundred forty. OTH 1.03. 4
and mine, two hundred! 1.03. 4
since these arms of mine had seven years' pith, 1.03. 83
in this fair lady's love, | and she in mine. 1.03.126
for i mine own gain'd knowledge should profane 1.03.384
of fashion, and i dote | in mine own comforts. 2.01.207
for mine own part — no offense to the general, 2.03.106 P
love thee, | but never more be officer of mine. 2.03.249
dost thou hear, mine honest friend? 3.01. 21 P
very ill at ease, | unfit for mine own purposes. 3.03. 33
'twas mine, 'tis his, and has been slave to 3.03.158
nor from mine own weak merits will i draw | the 3.03.187
proof, | or, by the worth of mine eternal soul, 3.03.361
take mine office. 3.03.375
is now begrim'd and black | as mine own face. 3.03.388
he lies there, were to lie in mine own throat. 3.04. 13 P
was that mine? 4.01.174 P
with mine officer! 4.01.202 P
is hush'd within the hollow mine of earth | and 4.02. 79
or that mine eyes, mine ears, or any sense 4.02.154
or that mine eyes, mine ears, or any sense 4.02.154
mine eyes do itch; 4.03. 58
that thrust had been mine enemy indeed, | but 5.01. 24
mine, and most of our fortunes to–night, shall ANT 1.02. 45 P
prognostication, i cannot scratch mine ear. 1.02. 53 P
why should i think you can be mine, and true 1.03. 27
in fulvia's death, how mine receiv'd shall be. 1.03. 65
mine ear must pluck it thence. 1.05. 42
the people love me, and the sea is mine; 2.01. 9
you may be pleas'd to catch at mine intent | by 2.02. 41
those wars | which fronted mine own peace. 2.02. 61
hours had bound me up | from mine own knowledge. 2.02. 91
but mine honesty | shall not make poor my 2.02. 92
do | so far ask pardon as befits mine honor | to 2.02. 97
fortunes shall rise higher, | caesar's or mine? 2.03. 17
his cocks do win the battle still of mine, 2.03. 37
and his quails ever | beat mine, inhoop'd, at 2.03. 39
give me mine angle, we'll to th' river; 2.05. 10
ram thou thy fruitful tidings in mine ears, 2.05. 24
pour out the pack of matter to mine ear, | the 2.05. 54
your hostages i have, so have you mine; 2.06. 1
say in mine ear, what is't. 2.07. 37
'tis not my profit that does lead mine honor; 2.07. 76
mine honor, it. 2.07. 77
and mine own tongue | spleets what it speaks; 2.07.123
if i lose mine honor, | i lose myself; 3.04. 22
to see't mine eyes are blasted. 3.10. 4
mine eyes did sicken at the sight and could not 3.10. 16
mine honesty and i begin to square. 3.13. 41
mine honor was not yielded, | but conquer'd 3.13. 61
for when mine hours | were nice and lucky, men 3.13.178
of me | as when mine empire was your fellow too, 4.02. 22
mine honest friends, | i turn you not away, but, 4.02. 29
eros, mine armor, eros! 4.04. 1
eros, come, mine armor, eros! 4.04. 2
i must attend mine office, | or would have 4.06. 26
thou mine of bounty, how wouldst thou have paid 4.06. 31
cause, but as't had been | each man's like mine; 4.08. 7
chain mine arm'd neck, leap thou, attire and all 4.08. 14
mine nightingale, | we have beat them to their 4.08. 18
me, | alcides, thou mine ancestor, thy rage. 4.12. 44
whose heart i thought i had, for she had mine — 4.14. 16
which whilst it was mine had annex'd unto't | a 4.14. 17
the arm of mine own body, and the heart | where 5.01. 45
heart | where mine his thoughts did kindle — 5.01. 46
he gives me so much of mine own as i | will 5.02. 20
i cannot project mine own cause so well | to 5.02.121
mine will now be yours, | and, should we shift 5.02.151
should we shift estates, yours would be mine. 5.02.152
that mine own servant should | parcel the sum of 5.02.162
for i am sure mine nails | are stronger than 5.02.223
sure mine nails | are stronger than mine eyes. 5.02.224
now the fleeting moon | no planet is of mine. 5.02.241
and with mine eyes i'll drink the words you send CYM 1.01.100
i dare lay mine honor | he will remain so. 1.01.174
i would have broke mine eye–strings, crack'd 1.03. 17
air, and then | have turn'd mine eye and wept. 1.03. 22
should not betray | mine interest and his honor; 1.03. 30
whom i commend to you as a noble friend of mine. 1.04. 32 P
the gods to venge it, | not mine to speak on't. 1.06. 93
takes prisoner the wild motion of mine eye, 1.06.103
(as i have such a heart that both mine ears 1.06.130
away, i do condemn mine ears that have | so long 1.06.141
and pawn mine honor for their safety. 1.06.194
as if i borrow'd mine oaths of him and might not 2.01. 4 P
mine eyes are weak. 2.02. 3
would testify, t' enrich mine inventory. 2.02. 30
'tis mine, and this will witness outwardly, | as 2.02. 35
a jewel that too casually | hath left mine arm. 2.03.142
last night 'twas on mine arm; 2.03.146
sweet shortness which | was mine in britain, for 2.04. 45
pure honor gains or loses | your sword or mine, 2.04. 60
take this too, | it is a basilisk unto mine eye, 2.04.107
i know your master's pleasure and he mine: 3.01. 84
they think they are mine, and, though train'd up 3.03. 82
say, "thus mine enemy fell, | and thus i set my 3.03. 91
i'll wake mine eyeballs /out first. 3.04.101
mine action? 3.04.104
i have heard i am a strumpet, and mine ear, 3.04.113
he hath a drug of mine; 3.05. 57
gratitude, but be a diligent follower of mine. 3.05.120 P
and if mine enemy | but fear the sword like me, 3.06. 25
greeks, | and mine to boot, be darted on thee! 4.02.314
borne | as i wear mine, are titles but of scorn. 5.02. 7
i, in mine own woe charm'd, | could not find 5.03. 68
for imogen's dear life take mine, and though 5.04. 22
you rather, mine being yours; 5.04. 26
din | express impatience, lest you stir up mine. 5.04.112
mine eyes | were not in fault, for she was 5.05. 62
mine ears, that /heard her flattery, nor my 5.05. 64
thyself into my grace, | and art mine own. 5.05. 95
and win this ring | by hers and mine adultery. 5.05.186
mine italian brain | gan in your duller britain 5.05.196
o gentlemen, help | mine and your mistress! 5.05.230
mine honor'd lady! 5.05.232
not standing here | to tell this tale of mine. 5.05.297
for mine own part unfold a dangerous speech, 5.05.313
and think they are my sons, are none of mine; 5.05.329
with other spritely shows | of mine own kindred. 5.05.429
all syria — | i tell you what mine authors say. PER 1.ch. 20
here pleasures court mine eyes, and mine eyes 1.02. 6
court mine eyes, and mine eyes shun them, | and 1.02. 6
her face was to mine eye beyond all wonder; 1.02. 75
when all, for mine, if i may call offense, 1.02. 92
drew sleep out of mine eyes, blood from my 1.02. 96
and though it was mine own, part of my heritage, 2.01.123
which, to preserve mine honor, i'll perform. 2.02. 16
well, mistress, your choice agrees with mine; 2.05. 18
never did thought of mine levy offense; 2.05. 52
either frame | your will to mine — and you, sir 2.05. 82
her hither | to have blest mine eyes with her! 3.03. 9
the gods revenge it upon me and mine | to the 3.03. 24
/unscissor'd shall this hair of mine remain, 3.03. 29
a niece of mine | shall there attend you. 3.04. 15
and whispers in mine ear, "go not till he speak. 5.01. 96
parentage — good parentage — | to equal mine! 5.01. 98
that thou thoughts' thy griefs might equal mine, 5.01.131
mine own, helicanus — | she is not dead at 5.01.214
and thick slumber | hangs upon mine eyes. 5.01.235
thither, | and do upon mine altar sacrifice. 5.01.241
if he be none of mine, my sanctity | will to my 5.03. 29
blest, and mine own! 5.03. 48
when by mine own | i may be reasonably conceiv'd TNK 1.02. 47
or let me know | why mine own barber is unblest, 1.02. 53
the blood of mine that's sib to him be suck'd 1.02. 72
had mine ear | stol'n some new air, or at 1.03. 74
not | against your faith, yet i continue mine. 1.03. 97
we are an endless mine to one another; 2.02. 79
i am your heir, and you are mine; 2.02. 83
without your noble hand to close mine eyes, | or 2.02. 93
i have, | beshrew mine eyes for't! 2.02.157
first with mine eye of all those beauties in her 2.02.168
and let mine honor down, and never charge? 2.02.195
i know mine own is but a heap of ruins, | and no 2.03. 19
what e'er you are, e'r you are mine, and i shall give 2.05. 33
y' are mine, and somewhat better than your rank 2.05. 43

this love of mine | will take more root within 2.06. 27
upon my mistress, | for note you, mine she is — 3.01.118
i have not clos'd mine eyes | save when my lids 3.02. 27
clip my yellow locks an inch below mine e'e. 3.04. 20
then mine host | and his fat spouse, that 3.05.127
will be seen, | and quickly, yours or mine. 3.06. 35
that's mine then. | i'll arm you first. 3.06. 52
prithee take mine, good cousin. 3.06. 65
thou art mine aunt's son, | and that blood we 3.06. 94
is mutual — | in me, thine, and in thee, mine. 3.06. 96
will make th' advantage of this hour | mine own; 3.06.124
and, by mine honor, once again it stands, | or 3.06.289
strove to show | mine enemy in this business, 5.01. 21
then blend your spirits with mine, | you whose 5.01. 72
being laid unto | mine innocent true heart, arms 5.01.134
of mine eyes | were i to lose one — they are 5.01.154
not taint mine eye | with dread sights it may 5.03. 9
though mine be not so fair, yet are they red — VEN 116
the kiss shall be thine own as well as mine. 117
look in mine eyeballs, there thy beauty lies; 119
mine eyes are grey, and bright, and quick in 140
because adonis' heart hath made mine hard." 378
that they have murd'red this poor heart of mine, 502
and these mine eyes, true leaders to their queen 503
for my sick heart commands mine eyes to watch. 584
sawest thou not signs of fear lurk in mine eye? 644
knocks at my heart, and whispers in mine ear, 659
presenteth to mine eye | the picture of an angry 661
yet from mine ear the tempting tune is blown; 778
for know, my heart stands armed in mine ear, 779
mine ears, that to your wanton talk attended, 809
mine eyes are turn'd to fire, my heart to lead: 1072
heavy heart's lead, melt at mine eyes' red fire! 1073
mine eyes forgo their light, my false heart LUC 228
my heart shall never countermand mine eye. 276
for those thine eyes betray thee unto mine. 483
enmity, | yet strive i to embrace mine infamy." 504
that thou shalt see thy state, and pity mine." 644
cross their arms and hang their heads with mine, 793
that is as clear from this attaint of mine | as 825
night, | in vain i cavil with mine infamy, | in 1025
tongue shall utter all, mine eyes like sluices, 1076
will fix a sharp knife to affright mine eye, 1138
that he may vow, in that sad hour of mine, 1179
my shame so dead, mine honor is new born. 1190
mine honor be the knife's that makes my wound, 1201
my blood shall wash the slander of mine ill; 1207
if tears could help, mine own would do me good. 1274
"mine enemy was strong, my poor self weak | (and 1646
"o, teach me how to make mine own excuse, | or 1653
revenged on my foe, | thine, mine, his own. 1684
with swift pursuit to venge this wrong of mine, 1691
"that life was mine which thou hast here 1752
the father says, "she's mine." 1795
"o, mine she is," | replies her husband, "do not 1795
say | he weeps for her, for she was only mine, 1798
i owed her, and 'tis mine that she hath kill'd." 1803
if broken, then it is no fault of mine. PP 3.12
her lips to mine how often hath she joined, 7. 7
lord, how mine eyes throw gazes to the east! 14.13
not daring trust the office of mine eyes. 14.16
so lively shown, | made me think upon mine own. 20.18
either was the other's mine. PHT 36
"this fair child of mine | shall sum my count, SON 2.10
mine be thy love, and thy love's use their 20.14
presume not on thy heart when mine is slain, 22.13
and in mine own love's strength seem to decay, 23. 7
with burthen of mine own love's might. 23. 8
mine eye hath play'd the painter and hath 24. 1
mine eyes have drawn thy shape, and thine for me 24.10
which wit so poor as mine | may make seem bare, 26. 5
hath dear religious love stol'n from mine eye 31. 6
but out, alack, he was but one hour mine, | the 33.11
as thou being mine, mine is thy good report. 36.14
as thou being mine, mine is thy good report. 36.14
the pain be mine, but thine shall be the praise. 38.14
what can mine own praise to mine own self bring? 39. 3
what can mine own praise to mine own self bring? 39. 3
and what is't but mine own when i praise thee? 39. 4
all mine was thine, before thou hadst this more. 40. 4
when most i wink, then do mine eyes best see, 43. 1
mine eyes be blessed made | by looking on thee 43. 9
mine eye and heart are at a mortal war, | how to 46. 1
mine eye my heart /thy picture's sight would bar 46. 3
my heart mine eye the freedom of that right. 46. 4
mine eye's due is /thy outward part, | and my 46.13
betwixt mine eye and heart a league is took, 47. 1
when that mine eye is famish'd for a look, | or 47. 3
another time mine eye is my heart's guest, | and 47. 7
thou, best of dearest and mine only care, | art 48. 7
here | within the knowledge of mine own desert, 49.10
it is my love that keeps mine eye awake, | mine 61.10
mine own true love that doth my rest defeat, 61.11
sin of self–love possesseth all mine eye, | and 62. 1
methinks no face so gracious is as mine, | no 62. 5
and for myself mine own worth do define, | as i 62. 7
mine own self–love quite contrary i read; 62.11
lie, | to do more for me than mine own desert, 72. 6
then lack'd i matter, that enfeebled mine. 86.14
with mine own weakness being best acquainted, 88. 5
away, | for term of life thou art assured mine, 92. 2
as thou being mine, mine is thy good report. 96.14
as thou being mine, mine is thy good report. 96.14
hath motion, and mine eye may be deceiv'd; 104.12
not mine own fears, nor the prophetic soul | of 107. 1
counting no old thing old, thou mine, i thine, 108. 7
gor'd mine own thoughts, sold cheap what is most 110. 3
mine appetite i never more will grind | on newer 110.10
since i left you, mine eye is in my mind, | and 113. 1
my most true mind thus maketh mine untrue. 113.14
or whether shall i say mine eye saith true, 114. 3
mine eye well knows what with his gust is 114.11
that mine eye loves it and doth first begin. 114.14
how have mine eyes out of their spheres been 119. 7
mine ransoms yours, and yours must ransom me. 120.14
the wiry concord that mine ear confounds, | do i 128. 4
so that other mine | thou wilt restore to be my 134. 3
add to thy will | one will of mine, to make thy 135.12
what dost thou to mine eyes | that they behold 137. 1
or mine eyes seeing this, say this is not, | to 137.11
knows | her pretty looks have been mine enemies, 139.10
in faith, i do not love thee with mine eyes, 141. 1
nor are mine ears with thy tongue's tune 141. 5
o, but with mine compare thou thine own state, 142. 3
and seal'd false bonds of love as oft as mine, 142. 7
whom thine eyes woo as mine importune thee. 142.10
with safest distance i mine honor shielded. LC 151
"'among the many that mine eyes have seen, | not 190
kept hearts in liveries, but mine own was free, 195
my well, | and mine i pour your ocean all among: 256
"'now all these hearts that do on mine depend, 274
to leave the batt'ry that you make 'gainst mine, 277
his poison'd me, and mine did him restore. 301
MINERAL 3 FR 0.0003 REL FR 3 V 0 P
like some ore | among a mineral of metals base, HAM 4.01. 26
whereof | doth, like a poisonous mineral, gnaw OTH 2.01.297
did confess she had | for you a mortal mineral, CYM 5.05. 50
MINERALS 1 FR 0.0001 REL FR 1 V 0 P
abus'd her delicate youth with drugs or minerals OTH 1.02. 74
MINERVA 2 FR 0.0002 REL FR 2 V 0 P
hark, tranio, thou mayst hear minerva speak. SHR 1.01. 84
the shrine of venus or straight–pight minerva, CYM 5.05.164
MINE'S 5 FR 0.0005 REL FR 5 V 0 P
ay, but her forehead's low, and mine's as high. TGV 4.04.193
yes, mine's three thousand crowns; what's yours? TIM 3.04. 28
for mine's a suit | that touches caesar nearer. JC 3.01. 6
mine's not an idle cause. OTH 1.02. 95
for mine's beyond beyond — say, and speak thick
CYM 3.02. 56
MINES 9 FR 0.0010 REL FR 3 V 6 P
him lies, mines my gentility with my education. AYL 1.01. 21 P
affable, and as bountiful | as mines of india. 1H4 3.01.167
fluellen, you must come presently to the mines; H5 3.02. 55 P
to the mines? 3.02. 57 P
duke, it is not so good to come to the mines; 3.02. 58 P
the mines is not according to the disciplines of 3.02. 58 P
now, captain macmorris, have you quit the mines? 3.02. 87 P
but i will delve one yard below their mines, HAM 3.04.208
upon the blood | burn like the mines of sulphur. OTH 3.03.329
MINGLE 14 FR 0.0015 REL FR 14 V 0 P
to mingle friendship far is mingling bloods. WT 1.02.109
wouldst adventure | to mingle faith with him! 4.04.460
where it shall mingle with the state of floods, 2H4 5.02.132
where senators shall mingle tears with smiles; COR 1.09. 3
ourself will mingle with society, | and play the MAC 3.04. 3
thanes, | and mingle with the english epicures! 5.03. 8
for those that mingle reason with your passion LR 2.04.234
o heavenly mingle! ANT 1.05. 59
would you mingle eyes | with one that ties his 3.13.156
do something mingle with our younger brown, yet 4.08. 20
ear, | make mingle with our rattling taborines, 4.08. 37
in them both, | mingle their spurs together. CYM 4.02. 58
we'll mingle our bloods together in the earth, PER 1.02.113
of nature, | to mingle beauty with infirmities, VEN 735
MINGLED 16 FR 0.0018 REL FR 15 V 1 P
my blood is mingled with the crime of lust: ERR 2.02.141
what treason there is mingled with your love. MV 3.02. 27
betwixt the constant red and mingled damask. AYL 3.05.123
the web of our life is of a mingled yarn, good AWW 4.03. 71 P
and part your mingled colors once again, | turn JN 2.01.389
mingled his royalty with cap'ring fools, | had 1H4 3.02. 63
mingled with venom of suggestion | (as, force 2H4 4.04. 45
and make a quagmire of your mingled brains. 1H6 1.04.109
beauty and honor in her are so mingled | that H8 2.03. 76
when it is mingled with regards that stands LR 1.01.239
and her fortunes mingled | with thine entirely. ANT 4.14. 24
have mingled sums | to buy a present for the CYM 1.06.186
so mingled as if mirth did make him sad, | and TNK 5.03. 52
"for there his smell with others being mingled, VEN 691
like milk and blood being mingled both together, 902
but mingled so | that blushing red no guilty LUC 1510
MINGLING 3 FR 0.0003 REL FR 3 V 0 P
to mingle friendship far is mingling bloods. WT 1.02.109
by mingling them with us, the honor'd number, COR 3.01. 72
mingling my talk with tears, my grief with LUC 797
/MINIKIN 1 FR 0.0001 REL FR 1 V 0 P
/and /for /one /blast /of /thy /minikin /mouth, LR 3.06. 43
MINIM 1 FR 0.0001 REL FR 0 V 1 P
he rests his minim rests, one, two, and the ROM 2.04. 22 P
MINIME 1 FR 0.0001 REL FR 1 V 0 P
minime, honest master, or rather, master, no. LLL 3.01. 60
MINIMO 1 FR 0.0001 REL FR 1 V 0 P
but so, | "redime te captum quam queas minimo."
SHR 1.01.162
MINIMUS 1 FR 0.0001 REL FR 1 V 0 P
you minimus, of hind'ring knot–grass made; MND 3.02.329
MINING 1 FR 0.0001 REL FR 1 V 0 P
whiles rank corruption, mining all within, HAM 3.04.148
MINION 18 FR 0.0020 REL FR 18 V 0 P
in vain, | mars's hot minion is return'd again; TMP 4.01. 98
let's see your song. how now, minion? TGV 1.02. 85
you, minion, are too saucy. 1.02. 89
do you hear, you minion? ERR 3.01. 54
you'll cry for this, minion, if i beat the door 3.01. 59
you minion, you, are these your customers? 4.04. 60
minion, thou liest. is't not hortensio? SHR 2.01. 13
but this your minion, whom i know you love, TN 5.01.125
cull forth | out of one side her happy minion, JN 2.01.392
who is sweet fortune's minion and her pride, 1H4 1.01. 83
what, minion, can ye not? 2H6 1.03.138
this minion stood upon her chastity, | upon her TIT 2.03.124
and yet "not proud," mistress minion you? ROM 3.05.151
is this th' athenian minion, whom the world TIM 4.03. 81
(like valor's minion) carv'd out his passage MAC 1.02. 19
minion, your dear lies dead, | and your unblest OTH 5.01. 33
the exile of her minion is too new, | she hath CYM 2.03. 41
yet fear her, o thou minion of her pleasure, SON 126. 9
MINIONS 5 FR 0.0005 REL FR 4 V 1 P
his company must do his minions grace, | whilst ERR 2.01. 87
gentlemen of the shade, minions of the moon, and
1H4 1.02. 26 P
she vaunted 'mongst her minions t' other day, 2H6 1.03. 84
go rate thy minions, proud insulting boy! 3H6 2.02. 84
beauteous and swift, the minions of their race, MAC 2.04. 15
MINISTER 41 FR 0.0046 REL FR 32 V 9 P
and did it to minister occasion to these TMP 2.01.173 P
pills, | and i must minister the like to you. TGV 2.04.150
with less respect than we do minister | to our MM 2.02. 86
that i may minister | to them accordingly. 2.03. 7
from this to that, | as cause doth minister. 4.05. 6
how sweetly you do minister to love, | that know ADO 1.01.312
you three will but minister such assistance as i 2.01.369 P
oft does them by the weakest minister: AWW 2.01.137
and debile minister, great power, great 2.03. 34 P
unless you laugh and minister occasion to him, TN 1.05. 87 P
the minister is here. 4.02. 94 P
but durst not tempt a minister of honor, | lest WT 2.02. 48
i chose | camillo for the minister to poison 3.02.160
never lift | an angry arm against his minister. R2 1.02. 41
thee, | and minister correction to thy fault! 2.03.105
your lordship may minister the potion of 2H4 1.02.127 P
he — master dumbe, our minister, was by then — 2.04. 88 P
to ashes, | thou foul accursed minister of hell! 1H6 5.04. 93
affords | and overjoy of heart doth minister. 2H6 1.01. 31
and, for a minister of my intent, | i have 3.01.355
whom angry heavens do make their minister, 5.02. 34
avaunt, thou dreadful minister of hell! R3 1.02. 46
who made thee then a bloody minister, | when 1.04.220
did this vanity | but minister communication of H8 1.01. 86
effect wants not | a minister in his power. 1.01.108
whose minister you are, whiles here he liv'd 5.01.137
did minister | unto the appetite and affection COR 1.01.103
and that unaptness made your minister | thus to TIM 2.02.131
from the bench, | and minister in their steads! 4.01. 6
canst thou not minister to a mind diseas'd, MAC 5.03. 40
therein the patient | must minister to himself. 5.03. 46
me, | that i must be their scourge and minister. HAM 3.04.175
which the time shall more favorably minister. OTH 2.01.270 P
if i quench thee, thou flaming minister, | i can 5.02. 8
caesar, | not by a public minister of justice, ANT 5.01. 20
but fortune's knave, | a minister of her will: 5.02. 4
feast, | to him the other two shall minister, CYM 3.03. 76
and minister | what man to man may do for our TNK 1.04. 38
a perturb'd mind, which i cannot minister to. 4.03. 60 P
better never born | than minister to such harm! 5.03. 66
what me, your minister, for you obeys, | works LC 229
/MINISTERS 1 FR 0.0001 REL FR 1 V 0 P
/fraught /with /the /ministers /and /instruments TRO pr 4
MINISTERS 23 FR 0.0026 REL FR 21 V 2 P
the ministers for th' purpose hurried thence TMP 1.02.131
thee, | by help of her more potent ministers, 1.02.275
i and my fellows | are ministers of fate. 3.03. 61
my fellow ministers | are like invulnerable. 3.03. 65
my meaner ministers | their several kinds have 3.03. 87
afflicted, we two will still be the ministers. WIV 4.02.219 P
then, o you blessed ministers above, | keep me MM 5.01.115
try, | that ministers thine own death if i die. AWW 2.01.186
keep me in darkness, send ministers to me, asses TN 4.02. 92 P
on him, | and all their ministers attend on him. R3 1.03.293
make us thy ministers of chastisement, | that we 5.03.113
but on the ministers | that doth distribute it COR 3.03. 98
these are my ministers, and come with me. TIT 5.02. 60
are /they thy ministers? what are they call'd? 5.02. 61
business, | and take my ministers along with me. 5.02.133
take my milk for gall, you murth'ring ministers, MAC 1.05. 48
producing forth the cruel ministers | of this 5.09. 34
angels and ministers of grace defend us! HAM 1.04. 39
but yet i call you servile ministers, | that LR 3.02. 21
makes his ministers | of us and those that love ANT 3.06. 88
whose ministers would prevail | under the 3.13. 23
or hath moe ministers than we | that draw his CYM 5.03. 72
that ministers a potion unto me | that thou PER 1.02. 68
MINISTRATION 1 FR 0.0001 REL FR 1 V 0 P
nor does | the ministration and required office AWW 2.05. 60
MINIST'RED 6 FR 0.0006 REL FR 6 V 0 P
may | with full and holy rite be minist'red, TMP 4.01. 17
have | that to your wanting may be minist'red. AYL 2.07.126
that present med'cine must be minist'red, | or JN 5.01. 15
subtilly hath minist'red to have me dead, | lest ROM 4.03. 25
took, | as we do air, fast as 'twas minist'red, CYM 1.01. 45
there's nothing can be minist'red to nature PER 3.02. 8
MINIST'RING 1 FR 0.0001 REL FR 1 V 0 P
a minist'ring angel shall my sister be | when HAM 5.01.241
MINNOW 2 FR 0.0002 REL FR 1 V 1 P
swain, that base minnow of thy mirth" — LLL 1.01.248 P
he that will fish | for my least minnow, let him TNK 1.01.116
MINNOWS 2 FR 0.0002 REL FR 1 V 1 P
hear you this triton of the minnows? COR 3.01. 89
one salmon, you shall take a number of minnows. TNK 2.01. 5 P
MINOLA 6 FR 0.0006 REL FR 6 V 0 P
her father is baptista minola, | an affable and SHR 1.02. 97
her name is katherina minola, | renown'd in 1.02. 99
to baptista minola. 1.02.164
way | to the house of signior baptista minola? 1.02.220
gremio, | the narrow–prying father, minola, 3.02.146
and give assurance to baptista minola, | as if 4.02. 69
MINORITY 5 FR 0.0005 REL FR 3 V 2 P
he shall present hercules in minority; LLL 5.01.134 P
quoniam he seemeth in minority, | ergo i come 5.02.592
which, in the minority of them both, his majesty AWW 4.05. 72 P
and his minority | is put unto the trust of R3 1.03. 11
proving from world's minority their right: LUC 67
MINOS 1 FR 0.0001 REL FR 1 V 0 P
thy father, minos, that denied our course; 3H6 5.06. 22
MINOTAURS 1 FR 0.0001 REL FR 1 V 0 P
there minotaurs and ugly treasons lurk. 1H6 5.03.189
MINSTREL 1 FR 0.0001 REL FR 0 V 1 P
i will give you the minstrel. ROM 4.05.115 P
MINSTRELS 7 FR 0.0008 REL FR 4 V 3 P
i will bid thee draw, as we do the minstrels, ADO 5.01.129 P
tush, none but minstrels like of sonneting! LLL 4.03.156
hark, hark, i hear the minstrels play. SHR 3.02.183
what, dost thou make us minstrels? ROM 3.01. 46 P
and thou make minstrels of us, look to hear 3.01. 47 P
else, | to call the maids and pay the minstrels, TNK 4.01.111
feast–finding minstrels, tuning my defame, LUC 817
MINSTRELSY 3 FR 0.0003 REL FR 3 V 0 P
him lie, | and i will use him for my minstrelsy. LLL 1.01.176
blaz'd with lights and bray'd with minstrelsy, TIM 2.02.161
what minstrelsy, and pretty din, | the regent PER 5.02. 7
MINT* 4 FR 0.0004 REL FR 3 V 1 P
that hath a mint of phrases in his brain; LLL 1.01.165
that mint. 5.02.655
some excellent jests, fire–new from the mint, TN 3.02. 22 P

a slave whose gall coins slanders like a mint, TRO 1.03.193
MINTS 1 FR 0.0001 REL FR 1 V 0 P
hot lavender, mints, savory, marjorum, | the WT 4.04.104
MINUTE 41 FR 0.0046 REL FR 34 V 7 P
come, | the very minute bids thee ope thine ear. TMP 1.02. 37
the minute of their plot | is almost come. 4.01.141
three hours too soon than a minute too late. WIV 2.02.313 P
the minute draws on. 5.05. 2 P
now, at the latest minute of the hour, | grant LLL 5.02.787
then, for the third part of a minute, hence, MND 2.02. 2
else sighing every minute and groaning every AYL 3.02.303 P
that will divide a minute into a thousand parts, 4.01. 45 P
thousand part of a minute in the affairs of love 4.01. 46 P
promise, or come one minute behind your hour, i 4.01.191 P
knew the true minute when | exception bid him AWW 1.02. 39
into abatement and low price | even in a minute. TN 1.01. 14
one minute, nay, one quiet breath of rest. JN 3.04.134
but not a minute, king, that thou canst give. R2 1.03.226
every minute now | should be the father of some 2H4 1.01. 7
i had | that walk'd about me every minute while; 1H6 1.04. 54
and think it but a minute spent in sport. 2H6 3.02.338
could not find | his hour of speech a minute — H8 1.02.121
who fed him every minute | with words of 1.02.149
with every minute you do change a mind, | and COR 1.01.182
will speak more in a minute than he will stand ROM 2.04.148 P
that one short minute gives me in her sight. 2.06. 5
the hour, | for in a minute there are many days. 3.05. 45
some minute ere the time | of her awakening, 5.03.257
that every minute of his being thrusts | against MAC 3.01.116
each minute teems a new one. 4.03.176
the perfume and suppliance of a minute — | no HAM 1.03. 9
for every minute is expectancy | of more OTH 2.01. 41
there's not a minute of our lives should stretch ANT 1.01. 46
which he achiev'd by th' minute, lost his favor. 3.01. 20
with labor, and throes forth | each minute some. 3.07. 81
one vice but of a minute old, for one | not half CYM 2.05. 31
should by the minute feed on life, and ling'ring 5.05. 51
with whom each minute threatens life or death. PER 1.03. 24
of a king, | who died the minute i was born, 5.01.158
was my mother, who did end | the minute i began. 5.01.212
of our fate, | who hath bounded our last minute. TNK 1.02.103
there shall not be one minute in an hour VEN 1187
let, | till every minute pays the hour his debt. LUC 329
one poor retiring minute in an age | would 962
to spite me now, each minute seems /a /moon, PP 14.27
MINUTE–JACKS 1 FR 0.0001 REL FR 1 V 0 P
cap–and–knee slaves, vapors, and minute–jacks! TIM 3.06. 97
MINUTELY 1 FR 0.0001 REL FR 1 V 0 P
now minutely revolts upbraid his faith–breach; MAC 5.02. 18
MINUTE'S 7 FR 0.0008 REL FR 6 V 1 P
the good humor is to steal at a minute's rest. WIV 1.03. 27 P
joan, or spend a minute's time | in pruning me? LLL 4.03.180
before, | no int'rim, not a minute's vacancy, TN 5.01. 95
and the examples | of every minute's instance 2H4 4.01. 83
where's hourly trouble for a minute's ease. PER 2.04. 44
but in one minute's fight brings beauty under; VEN 746
who buys a minute's mirth to wail a week? LUC 213
/MINUTES 1 FR 0.0001 REL FR 1 V 0 P
may time disgrace and wretched /minutes kill. SON 126. 8
MINUTES 17 FR 0.0019 REL FR 16 V 1 P
girdle round about the earth | in forty minutes. MND 2.01.176
the tedious minutes i with her have spent. 2.02.112
hath told the thievish minutes how they pass, AWW 2.01.166
hours, minutes? WT 1.02.290
and like the watchful minutes to the hour, JN 4.01. 46
my thoughts are minutes, and with sighs they jar R2 5.05. 51
and tears, and groans | show minutes, times, and 5.05. 58
hours were cups of sack, and minutes capons, and
1H4 1.02. 7 P
thereby to see the minutes how they run: 3H6 2.05. 25
so minutes, hours, days, months, and years, 2.05. 38
with us to watch the minutes of this night, HAM 1.01. 27
what damned minutes tells he o'er | who dotes, OTH 3.03.169
stuff up his lust, as minutes fill up hours; LUC 297
soon, | but now are minutes added to the hours; PP 14.26
nor can i fortune to brief minutes tell, SON 14. 5
shore, | so do our minutes hasten to their end, 60. 2
thy dial how thy precious minutes waste; 77. 2
MINX 2 FR 0.0002 REL FR 1 V 1 P
my prayers, minx! TN 3.04.120 P
damn her, lewd minx! OTH 3.03.476
MINX'S 1 FR 0.0001 REL FR 0 V 1 P
this is some minx's token, and i must take out OTH 4.01.153 P
MIO 1 FR 0.0001 REL FR 0 V 1 P
ben venuto, molto honorato signor mio petruchio.
SHR 1.02. 26 P
MIRABLE 1 FR 0.0001 REL FR 1 V 0 P
not neoptolemus so mirable, | on whose bright TRO 4.05.142
/MIRACLE 1 FR 0.0001 REL FR 1 V 0 P
/o /miracle /of /men! 2H4 2.03. 33
MIRACLE 24 FR 0.0027 REL FR 20 V 4 P
but for the miracle | (i mean our preservation), TMP 2.01. 6
a most high miracle! 5.01.177
it was a miracle to scape suffocation. WIV 3.05.117 P
from whence, i think, you are come by miracle. ERR 5.01.265
a miracle! ADO 5.04. 91 P
which therein works a miracle in nature, MV 3.02. 90
but 'tis that miracle and queen of gems | that TN 2.04. 85
camillo, | may this (almost a miracle) be done? WT 4.04.534
eye i find | a wonder, or a wondrous miracle, JN 2.01.497
i have scap'd by miracle. 1H4 2.04.166 P
be not offended, nature's miracle, | thou art 1H6 5.03. 54
the greatest miracle that e'er ye wrought! 5.04. 66
fellow, what miracle dost thou proclaim? 2H6 2.01. 58
a miracle, a miracle! 2.01. 59
a miracle, a miracle! 2.01. 59
come to the king and tell him what miracle. 2.01. 60
my lords, saint albon here hath done a miracle; 2.01.129
duke humphrey has done a miracle to–day. 2.01.157
i would laugh at that miracle — yet, in a sort, TRO 5.04. 34 P
must be a faith that reason without miracle LR 1.01.222
thy life's a miracle. 4.06. 55
yet who this should be | doth miracle itself, CYM 4.02. 29
(besides the gods) for this great miracle. PER 5.03. 58
o none, unless this miracle have might, | that SON 65.13
MIRACLES 7 FR 0.0008 REL FR 6 V 1 P
love wrought these miracles. SHR 5.01.124
when miracles have by the great'st been denied. AWW 2.01.141
they say miracles are past, and we have our 2.03. 1 P
for miracles are ceas'd; H5 1.01. 67
grace, | to work exceeding miracles on earth. 1H6 5.04. 41
but you have done more miracles than i: 2H6 2.01.159
nothing almost sees miracles | but misery. LR 2.02.165
MIRACULOUS 3 FR 0.0003 REL FR 2 V 1 P
his word is more than the miraculous harp. TMP 2.01. 87 P
a most miraculous work in this good king, MAC 4.03.147
tongue, will speak | with most miraculous organ. HAM 2.02.594
MIRANDA 5 FR 0.0005 REL FR 5 V 0 P
and more, miranda. TMP 1.02. 48
twelve year since, miranda, twelve year since, 1.02. 53
miranda. 3.01. 36
admir'd miranda, | indeed the top of admiration! 3.01. 37
i am, in my condition, | a prince, miranda; 3.01. 60
MIR'D 1 FR 0.0001 REL FR 1 V 0 P
who smirched thus and mir'd with infamy, | i ADO 4.01.133
MIRE 10 FR 0.0011 REL FR 8 V 2 P
me with urchin–shows, pitch me i' th' mire, TMP 2.02. 5
from behind one of them, in a slough of mire; WIV 4.05. 68 P
great pails of puddled mire to quench the hair; ERR 5.01.173
not till it leave the rider in the mire. LLL 2.01.120
dun, we'll draw thee from the mire | /of /this ROM 1.04. 41
honest water, which ne'er left man i' th' mire. TIM 1.02. 59
paint till a horse may mire upon your face: 4.03.148
i' th' mire. LR 2.02. 5 P
and throw stones, cast mire upon me, set | the CYM 5.05.222
"the crow may bathe his coal–black wings in mire
LUC 1009
/MIRROR 1 FR 0.0001 REL FR 1 V 0 P
/let /it /command /a /mirror /hither /straight, R2 4.01.265
MIRROR 9 FR 0.0010 REL FR 7 V 2 P
your chang'd complexions are to me a mirror WT 1.02.381
following the mirror of all christian kings, H5 2.pr. 6
how far'st thou, mirror of all martial men? 1H6 1.04. 74
whose wisdom was a mirror to the wisest; 3H6 3.03. 84
buckingham, | the mirror of all courtesy — H8 2.01. 53
is, to hold, as 'twere, the mirror up to nature: HAM 3.02. 22 P
his semblable is his mirror, and who else would 5.02.119 P
for deeds remembered should be like a mirror, PER 1.01. 45
but now that fair fresh mirror, dim and old, LUC 1760
/MIRROR'D 1 FR 0.0001 REL FR 1 V 0 P
till it hath travell'd and is /mirror'd there TRO 3.03.110
MIRROR'S 1 FR 0.0001 REL FR 1 V 0 P
when such a spacious mirror's set before him, ANT 5.01. 34
MIRRORS 2 FR 0.0002 REL FR 2 V 0 P
but now two mirrors of his princely semblance R3 2.02. 51
that you have no such mirrors as will turn JC 1.02. 56
MIRTH 61 FR 0.0069 REL FR 48 V 13 P
one fading moment's mirth | with twenty watchful TGV 1.01. 30
we will include all jars | with triumphs, mirth, 5.04.161
i was then frugal of my mirth. WIV 2.01. 28 P
she enlargeth her mirth so far that there is 2.02.223 P
the mirth whereof so larded with my matter, 4.06. 14
my mirth it much displeas'd, but pleas'd my woe. MM 4.01. 13
and in despite of mirth mean to be merry. ERR 3.01.108
me, i was born to speak all mirth and no matter. ADO 2.01.330 P
head to the sole of his foot, he is all mirth. 3.02. 10 P
swain, that base minnow of thy mirth" — LLL 1.01.248 P
man, | within the limit of becoming mirth, | i 2.01. 67
such eruptions and sudden breaking out of mirth, 5.01.115 P
here comes boyet, and mirth is in his face. 5.02. 79
their form confounded makes most form in mirth, 5.02.519
mirth cannot move a soul in agony. 5.02.857
awake the pert and nimble spirit of mirth, MND 1.01. 13
and waxen in their mirth, and neeze, and swear 2.01. 56
here come the lovers, full of joy and mirth. 5.01. 28
where is our usual manager of mirth? 5.01. 35
very tragical mirth." 5.01. 57
with mirth and laughter let old wrinkles come, MV 1.01. 80
rather to put on | your boldest suit of mirth, 2.02.202
i show more mirth than i am mistress of, and AYL 1.02. 3 P
then is there mirth in heaven, | when earthly 5.04.108
and frame your mind to mirth and merriment, SHR in.2. 135
present mirth hath present laughter; TN 2.03. 48
he's all my exercise, my mirth, my matter; WT 1.02.166
i prithee darken not | the mirth o' th' feast. 4.04. 42
them sprightly, | and let's be red with mirth. 4.04. 54
full warm of blood, of mirth, of gossiping. JN 5.02. 59
when you perceive his blood inclin'd to mirth; 2H4 4.04. 38
free from gross passion, or of mirth or anger, H5 2.02.132
pardon the frankness of my mirth, if i answer 5.02.291 P
all france will be replete with mirth and joy, 1H6 1.06. 15
thy mirth shall turn to moan. 2.03. 44
make yourself mirth with your particular fancy, H8 2.03.101
is like that mirth fate turns to sudden sadness. TRO 1.01. 40
defects of age | must be the scene of mirth; 1.03.173
is now, she will but disease our better mirth. COR 1.03.105 P
i wish you much mirth. 1.03.110 P
i'll use you for my mirth, yea, for my laughter, JC 4.03. 49
to be but mirth and laughter to his brutus, 4.03.114
be large in mirth; MAC 3.04. 11
you have displac'd the mirth, broke the good 3.04.108
eye, | with mirth in funeral, and with dirge in HAM 1.02. 12
but wherefore i know not — lost all my mirth, 2.02.296 P
he was dispos'd to mirth, but on the sudden | a ANT 1.02. 82
if in mirth, report | that i am sudden sick. 1.03. 4
to give a kingdom for a mirth, to sit | and keep 1.04. 18
is he dispos'd to mirth? i hope he is. CYM 1.06. 58
sadness of parting, as the procuring of mirth. 5.04.160 P
how well this honest mirth becomes their labor! PER 2.01. 95
prepare for mirth, for mirth becomes a feast. 2.03. 7
prepare for mirth, for mirth becomes a feast. 2.03. 7
out of bondage, making misery their mirth, and TNK 2.01. 35 P
fool, | away with this strain'd mirth! 3.03. 43
so does arcite's mirth, | but palamon's sadness 5.03. 50
but palamon's sadness is a kind of mirth, | so 5.03. 51
so mingled as if mirth did make him sad, | and 5.03. 52
who buys a minute's mirth to wail a week? LUC 213
for mirth doth search the bottom of annoy, | sad 1109
MIRTHFUL 1 FR 0.0001 REL FR 1 V 0 P
with stately triumphs, mirthful comic shows, 3H6 5.07. 43
MIRTH–MOVING 1 FR 0.0001 REL FR 1 V 0 P
catch | the other turns to a mirth–moving jest, LLL 2.01. 71
MIRY 2 FR 0.0002 REL FR 1 V 1 P
thou shouldst have heard in how miry a place, SHR 4.01. 75 P
dry, | with miry slime left on them by a flood? TIT 3.01.126
MISADVENTUR'D 1 FR 0.0001 REL FR 1 V 0 P
whose misadventur'd piteous overthrows | doth ROM pr 7
MISADVENTURE 3 FR 0.0003 REL FR 3 V 0 P
and wild, and do import | some misadventure. ROM 5.01. 29
what misadventure is so early up, | that calls 5.03.188
the misadventure of their own eyes kill 'em; TNK 3.06.190
MISANTHROPOS 1 FR 0.0001 REL FR 1 V 0 P
i am misanthropos, and hate mankind. TIM 4.03. 54
MISAPPLIED 1 FR 0.0001 REL FR 1 V 0 P
virtue itself turns vice, being misapplied, ROM 2.03. 21
MISBECAME 1 FR 0.0001 REL FR 1 V 0 P
what i have done that misbecame my place, | my 2H4 5.02.100
MISBECOM'D 1 FR 0.0001 REL FR 1 V 0 P
eyes, | have misbecom'd our oaths and gravities, LLL 5.02.768
MISBECOME 1 FR 0.0001 REL FR 1 V 0 P
and any thing that may not misbecome | the H5 2.04.118
MISBECOMINGLY 1 FR 0.0001 REL FR 1 V 0 P
humors that | stick misbecomingly on others, on TNK 5.03. 54
MISBEGOT 1 FR 0.0001 REL FR 1 V 0 P
which indeed | is valor misbegot, and came into TIM 3.05. 29
MISBEGOTTEN 4 FR 0.0004 REL FR 3 V 1 P
that misbegotten devil faulconbridge, | in spite JN 5.04. 4
prince, | and free from other misbegotten hate, R2 1.01. 33
three misbegotten knaves in kendal green came at
1H4 2.04.221 P
base, | and misbegotten blood i spill of thine, 1H6 4.06. 22
MISBELIEVER 1 FR 0.0001 REL FR 1 V 0 P
you call me misbeliever, cut–throat dog, | and MV 1.03.111
MISBELIEVING 1 FR 0.0001 REL FR 1 V 0 P
and hither hale that misbelieving moor | to be TIT 5.03.143
MISCALL 2 FR 0.0002 REL FR 2 V 0 P
my heart will sigh when i miscall it so, | which R2 1.03.263
thou dost miscall retire. TRO 5.04. 20
MISCALL'D 1 FR 0.0001 REL FR 1 V 0 P
skill, | and simple truth miscall'd simplicity, SON 66.11
/MISCARRIED 1 FR 0.0001 REL FR 1 V 0 P
/have /since /miscarried /under /bullingbrook. 2H4 4.01.127
MISCARRIED 9 FR 0.0010 REL FR 6 V 3 P
the great soldier who miscarried at sea? MM 3.01.210 P
or by the way of progression, hath miscarried. LLL 4.02.140 P
there miscarried | a vessel of our country MV 2.08. 29
my ships have all miscarried, my creditors grow 3.02.316 P
had your husband's ring, | had quite miscarried. 5.01.251
and all that have miscarried | by underhand R3 5.01. 5
the cardinal's letters to the pope miscarried, H8 3.02. 30
and if aught in this | miscarried by my fault, ROM 5.03.267
our sister's man is certainly miscarried. LR 5.01. 5
MISCARRIES 1 FR 0.0001 REL FR 1 V 0 P
for what miscarries | shall be the general's COR 1.01.266
MISCARRY 15 FR 0.0017 REL FR 11 V 4 P
hang me by the neck if horns that year miscarry. LLL 4.01.112
i would not have him miscarry for the half of my TN 3.04. 63 P
if they miscarry, we miscarry too. JN 5.04. 3
if they miscarry, we miscarry too. 5.04. 3
if they miscarry, theirs shall second them, 2H4 4.02. 46
and the child i go with do miscarry, thou wert 5.04. 9 P
but i pray god the fruit of her womb miscarry. 5.04. 13 P
merchandise do sinfully miscarry upon the sea, H5 4.01.148 P
if he miscarry, farewell wars in france! 1H6 4.03. 16
better ten thousand base–born cades miscarry 2H6 4.08. 47
but so it must be, if the king miscarry. R3 1.03. 16
if you miscarry, | your business of the world LR 5.01. 44
be near at hand, i may miscarry in't. OTH 5.01. 6
yes, i must, sir, | else both miscarry. TNK 3.06.302
i did think | good palamon would miscarry, yet i 5.03.101
MISCARRYING 2 FR 0.0002 REL FR 2 V 0 P
distill'd | out of our virtues, who miscarrying, TRO 1.03.351
or fear of my miscarrying on his scape, | or TNK 4.01. 50
MISCHANCE 22 FR 0.0024 REL FR 21 V 1 P
in your cabin for the mischance of the hour, if TMP 1.01. 25 P
bring thee to | shall hoodwink this mischance; 4.01.206
the next ensuing hour some foul mischance TGV 2.02. 11
nimble mischance, that art so light of foot, R2 3.04. 92
and would be glad he met with some mischance, 1H4 1.03.232
if that the devil and mischance look big | upon 4.01. 58
lords, view these letters full of bad mischance. 1H6 1.01. 89
to be shame's scorn and subject of mischance! 4.06. 49
mischance unto my state by suffolk's means. 2H6 3.02.284
mischance and sorrow go along with you! 3.02.300
but now mischance hath trod my title down, | and 3H6 3.03. 8
mind | still ride in triumph over all mischance. 3.03. 18
i long till edward fall by war's mischance, 3.03.254
yet, warwick, in despite of all mischance, | of 4.03. 43
york's wife, and queen of sad mischance, | these R3 4.04.114
and let mischance be slave to patience. ROM 5.03.221
for unkindness | than pity for mischance. MAC 3.04. 42
and never come mischance between us twain! HAM 3.02.228
lest more mischance | on plots and errors happen 5.02.394
'tis some mischance, the voice is very direful. OTH 5.01. 38
he never can meet more mischance than come | to
CYM 2.03.132
with some mischance cross tarquin in his flight. LUC 968
MISCHANCES 3 FR 0.0003 REL FR 3 V 0 P
a thousand more mischances than this one | have TGV 5.03. 3
the tyranny | of mad mischances and much misery:
VEN 738
let there bechance him pitiful mischances | to LUC 976
/MISCHIEF 1 FR 0.0001 REL FR 1 V 0 P
/ere /they /have /done /their /mischief, LR 4.02. 55
MISCHIEF 43 FR 0.0048 REL FR 34 V 9 P
invert | what best is boded me to mischief! TMP 3.01. 71
do that good mischief which may make this island 4.01.217
any extremity rather than a mischief. WIV 4.02. 74 P
apply a moral medicine to a mortifying mischief. ADO 1.03. 12 P
it serve for any model to build mischief on? 1.03. 46 P
and i pray god his bad voice bode no mischief. 2.03. 81 P
o mischief strangely thwarting! 3.02.132 P
but i shall do thee mischief in the wood. MND 2.01.237
in the town, the field, | you do me mischief. 2.01.239
boy, with me, my thoughts are ripe in mischief. TN 5.01.129
mean mischief and break a foul gap into the WT 4.04.197 P
hovers in the sky | and pours down mischief. JN 3.02. 3
of broached mischief to the unborn times? 1H4 5.01. 21
'a cares not what mischief he does, if his 2H4 2.01. 15 P
and so success of mischief shall be born, | and 4.02. 47
break out into a second course of mischief, H5 4.03.106
word, | some sudden mischief may arise of it; 4.07.178
this sudden mischief never could have fall'n. 1H6 2.01. 59
you see what mischief, and what murther too, 3.01.115

hath wrought this hellish mischief unawares, 3.02. 39
a plaguing mischief light on charles and thee! 5.03. 39
till mischief and despair | drive you to break 5.04. 90
but that my heart's on future mischief set, | i 2H6 5.02. 84
and as prone to mischief | as able to perform't) H8 1.01.160
ah ha, | there's mischief in this man. 1.02.187
devil monk, | hopkins, that made this mischief. 2.01. 22
yet let 'em look they glory not in mischief, 2.01. 66
to all the volsces, | great hurt and mischief; COR 4.05. 67
complots of mischief, treason, villainies, TIT 5.01. 65
wherein i had no stroke of mischief in it? 5.01.110
o mischief, thou art swift | to enter in the ROM 5.01. 35
more whore, more mischief first; TIM 4.03.168
those that would mischief me than those that do! 4.03.468
rushing on us, should do your age some mischief. JC 3.01. 93
mischief, thou art afoot, | take thou what 3.02.260
substances | you wait on nature's mischief! MAC 1.05. 50
this' /miching mallecho, it means mischief. HAM 3.02.138 P
that with the mischief of your person it would LR 1.02.163 P
have one eye left | to see some mischief on him. 3.07. 82
to mourn a mischief that is past and gone | is OTH 1.03.204
gone | is the next way to draw new mischief on. 1.03.205
a mischief worse than civil home-bred strife, VEN 764
"why work'st thou mischief in thy pilgrimage, LUC 960
MISCHIEF'S 1 FR 0.0001 REL FR 1 V 0 P
are but felt, and seen with mischief's eyes, PER 1.04. 8
MISCHIEFS 8 FR 0.0009 REL FR 7 V 1 P
for mischiefs manifold and sorceries terrible TMP 1.02.264
what mischiefs might he set abroach | in shadow 2H4 4.02. 14
o god, what mischiefs work the wicked ones, 2H6 2.01.182
the fift hales them to an hundred mischiefs, and 4.08. 57 P
the secret mischiefs that i set abroach | i lay R3 1.03.324
princely care foreseeing those fell mischiefs H8 5.01. 49
till all these mischiefs be return'd again, TIT 3.01.273
their hearts, i fear, | millions of mischiefs. JC 4.01. 51
MISCHIEVOUS 2 FR 0.0002 REL FR 2 V 0 P
most mischievous foul sin, in chiding sin: AYL 2.07. 64
hatch'd, would as his kind grow mischievous, JC 2.01. 33
MISCONCEIVED 1 FR 0.0001 REL FR 1 V 0 P
no, misconceived! 1H6 5.04. 49
MISCONSTER *(also misconstrued)*
MISCONSTER 2 FR 0.0002 REL FR 2 V 0 P
fair lady, nor misconster | the mind of talbot, 1H6 2.03. 73
may | misconster us in him and wail his death. R3 3.05. 61
MISCONSTERS 1 FR 0.0001 REL FR 1 V 0 P
that he misconsters all that you have done. AYL 1.02.265
MISCONST'RED 1 FR 0.0001 REL FR 1 V 0 P
i be misconst'red in the place i go to, | and MV 2.02.188
MISCONSTRUCTION 1 FR 0.0001 REL FR 1 V 0 P
to strike at me, upon his misconstruction, LR 2.02.117
MISCONSTRUED *(also misconster, etc.)*
MISCONSTRUED 2 FR 0.0002 REL FR 2 V 0 P
hope, | so much misconstrued in his wantonness. 1H4 5.02. 68
alas, thou hast misconstrued every thing! JC 5.03. 84
MISCREANT 4 FR 0.0004 REL FR 4 V 0 P
thou art a traitor and a miscreant, | too good R2 1.01. 39
well, miscreant, i'll be there as soon as you, 1H6 3.04. 44
curse, miscreant, when thou com'st to the stake. 5.03. 44
o, vassal! miscreant! LR 1.01.161
MISCREATE 1 FR 0.0001 REL FR 1 V 0 P
soul | with opening titles miscreate, whose H5 1.02. 16
MISDEED 1 FR 0.0001 REL FR 1 V 0 P
that i am clear from this misdeed of edward's; 3H6 3.03.183
MISDEEDS 3 FR 0.0003 REL FR 3 V 0 P
thee, | but thou wilt be aveng'd on my misdeeds, R3 1.04. 70
then kings' misdeeds cannot be hid in clay. LUC 609
that from their own misdeeds askaunce their eyes 637
MISDEMEAN'D 1 FR 0.0001 REL FR 1 V 0 P
have misdemean'd yourself, and not a little: H8 5.02. 49
MISDEMEANORS 1 FR 0.0001 REL FR 0 V 1 P
you can separate yourself and your misdemeanors, TN 2.03. 98 P
MISDOUBT 6 FR 0.0006 REL FR 4 V 2 P
i do not misdoubt my wife; WIV 2.01.185 P
that i could neither believe nor misdoubt. AWW 1.03.125 P
if you misdoubt me that i am not she, | i know 3.07. 1
thoughts, | and change misdoubt to resolution; 2H6 3.01.332
this sudden stab of rancor i misdoubt; R3 3.02. 87
do you misdoubt | this sword, and these my ANT 3.07. 62
MISDOUBTETH 1 FR 0.0001 REL FR 1 V 0 P
with trembling wings misdoubteth every bush; 3H6 5.06. 14
MISDOUBTS 2 FR 0.0002 REL FR 2 V 0 P
our person misdoubts it; LLL 4.03.192
this land | as his misdoubts present occasion. 2H4 4.01.204
MISDREAD 1 FR 0.0001 REL FR 1 V 0 P
that have their first conception by misdread, PER 1.02. 12
MISENA 1 FR 0.0001 REL FR 1 V 0 P
about the mount misena. ANT 2.02.160
MISER 4 FR 0.0004 REL FR 3 V 1 P
rich honesty dwells like a miser, sir, in a poor AYL 5.04. 60 P
doth like a miser spoil his coat with scanting H5 2.04. 47
decrepit miser! 1H6 5.04. 7
as 'twixt a miser and his wealth is found: SON 75. 4
/MISERABLE 1 FR 0.0001 REL FR 1 V 0 P
/troy /was /burnt /and /he /made /miserable? TIT 3.02. 28
MISERABLE 35 FR 0.0039 REL FR 31 V 4 P
be not born to be hang'd, our case is miserable. TMP 1.01. 33 P
me happy, | or else i often had been miserable. TGV 4.01. 35
o miserable, unhappy that i am! 5.04. 28
the miserable have no other medicine | but only MM 3.01. 2
so fortunate | (but miserable most, to love MND 3.02.234
a miserable world! AYL 2.07. 13
hurtling | from miserable slumber i awaked. 4.03.132
o miserable lady! WT 1.02.351
hence, | poor miserable wretches, to your death; H5 2.02.178
for what's more miserable than discontent? 2H6 3.01.201
o miserable age! 4.02. 10 P
o gross and miserable ignorance! 4.02.168
deadly, | i should lament thy miserable state. 3H6 1.04. 85
o, pity, god, this miserable age! 2.05. 88
o miserable thought! 3.02.151
her be made | more miserable by the /life of him R3 1.02. 27
judge | what 'twere to lose it and be miserable! 1.03.257
o, i have pass'd a miserable night, | so full of 1.04. 2
miserable england! 3.04.103
more miserable by the life of thee | than thou 4.01. 75
yew, | and leave me to this miserable death. TIT 2.03.108
i made thee miserable | what time i threw the 4.03. 18
but we wordly men | have miserable, mad, 5.02. 66
take heed, take heed, for such die miserable. ROM 3.03.145
most miserable hour that e'er time saw | in 4.05. 44
thou shouldst desire to die, being miserable. TIM 4.03.248
not by his breath that is more miserable. 4.03.249
there is no time so miserable but a man may be 4.03.457 P
o nation miserable! MAC 4.03.103
to send the old and miserable king | to some LR 5.03. 46
what miserable praise hast thou for her that's OTH 2.01.139 P
the miserable change now at my end | lament nor ANT 4.15. 51
but most miserable | is the /desire that's CYM 1.06. 6
this miserable prince, that cuts away | a life TNK 5.03.142
o miserable end of our alliance! 5.04. 86
MISERABLY 1 FR 0.0001 REL FR 1 V 0 P
god is just, | he be as miserably slain as i. 3H6 1.03. 42
MISERICORDE 1 FR 0.0001 REL FR 0 V 1 P
o, prenez misericorde! ayez pitie de moi! H5 4.04. 12 P
/MISERIES 1 FR 0.0001 REL FR 1 V 0 P
/we /scarcely /think /our /miseries /our /foes. LR 3.06.103
MISERIES 23 FR 0.0026 REL FR 19 V 4 P
if your miseries were in the same abundance as MV 1.02. 3 P
'twere | that all the miseries which nature owes AWW 3.02.119
shores, most certain | to miseries enough; WT 4.04.568
rascals, whose miseries are to be smil'd at, 4.04.792 P
of eyes, | to weep their intermissive miseries. 1H6 1.01. 88
just death, kind umpire of men's miseries, 2.05. 29
my tear-stain'd eyes to see her miseries. 2H6 2.04. 16
so many miseries have craz'd my voice | that my R3 4.04. 17
joys, | poor breathing orators of miseries, 4.04.129
i will not wish ye half my miseries, | i have H8 3.01.108
to endure more miseries and greater far | than 3.02.389
not think to shed a tear | in all my miseries; 3.02.429
if there were reason for these miseries, | then TIT 3.01.219
these miseries are more than may be borne. 3.01.243
i have heard in some sort of thy miseries. TIM 4.03. 77
life | is bound in shallows and in miseries. JC 4.03.221
how have you known the miseries of your father? LR 5.03.181
our son is good, | take off his miseries. CYM 5.04. 86
then shall posthumus end his miseries, britain 5.04.143 P
then shall posthumus end his miseries, britain 5.05.441 P
we have heard your miseries as far as tyre, PER 1.04. 88
kindness | makes my past miseries sports. 5.03. 41
even from the bottom of these miseries, | from TNK 2.02. 56
MISERS 2 FR 0.0002 REL FR 1 V 1 P
for they pass'd by me | as misers do by beggars, TRO 3.03.143
can compare our rich misers to nothing so fitly PER 2.01. 29 P
/MISERY 1 FR 0.0001 REL FR 1 V 0 P
/who, /when /my /heart, /all /mad /with /misery, TIT 3.02. 9
MISERY 47 FR 0.0053 REL FR 41 V 6 P
misery acquaints a man with strange bedfellows; TMP 2.02. 39 P
son, | thou sham'st to acknowledge me in misery. ERR 5.01.323
penance | of such misery doth she cut me off. MV 4.01.272
"thus misery doth part | the flux of company." AYL 2.01. 51
our mistress the world, and all our misery. 3.02.279 P
pack of you | that triumph thus upon my misery! SHR 4.03. 34
hath been seduc'd by them, and the misery is, AWW 3.05. 21 P
do not tempt my misery, | lest that it make me TN 3.04.349
that he did but see | the flatness of my misery, WT 3.02.122
whom | (though bearing misery) i desire my life 5.01.137
no, misery makes sport to mock itself: R2 2.01. 85
must die, | for that's the end of human misery. 1H6 3.02.137
my body round engirt with misery — | for what's 2H6 3.01.200
not that i pity henry's misery, | but seek 3H6 3.03.264
o ill-dispersing wind of misery! R3 4.01. 52
see | how soon this mightiness meets misery; H8 pr 30
that afflicts us, the object of our misery, is COR 1.01. 21 P
he covets less | than misery itself would give, 2.02.127
straight | and make my misery serve thy turn. 4.05. 88
and your misery increase with your age! 5.02.107 P
o, could our mourning ease thy misery! TIT 2.04. 57
tongues | plot some device of further misery, 3.01.134
ay, mine own fortune in my misery. ROM 1.02. 58
looks, | sharp misery had worn him to the bones; 5.01. 41
since riches point to misery and contempt? TIM 4.02. 32
thou flatter'st misery. 4.03.234
willing misery | outlives incertain pomp, is 4.03.242
live, and love thy misery. 4.03.395
the gods out of my misery | has sent thee 4.03.524
nothing almost sees miracles | but misery. LR 2.02.166
and i'll repair the misery thou dost bear | with 4.01. 76
in pity of his misery, to dispatch | his nighted 4.05. 12
when misery could beguile the tyrant's rage, 4.06. 63
o misery! OTH 3.03.171
in our viciousness grow hard | (o misery on't!), ANT 3.13.112
being | is to exchange one misery with another, CYM 1.05. 55
o noble misery, | to be i' th' field, and ask 5.03. 64
the misery of tharsus may be theirs. PER 1.04. 55
nation, | taking advantage of our misery, 1.04. 66
out of bondage, making misery their mirth, and TNK 2.01. 34 P
strong enough to laugh at misery | and bear the 2.02. 2
what a misery | it is to live abroad, and every 2.02. 97
much, | and me as much to see his misery. 2.04. 28
we prevent | the loathsome misery of age, 5.04. 7
murmur stay, | for misery is trodden on by many, VEN 707
the tyranny | of mad mischances and much misery: 738
one that flatters thee | is no friend in misery. PP 20.30
MISERY'S 1 FR 0.0001 REL FR 1 V 0 P
misery's love, | o, come to me! JN 3.04. 35
MISFORTUNE 10 FR 0.0011 REL FR 10 V 0 P
make misfortune drunk | with candle-wasters, ADO 5.01. 17
might make me fear | misfortune to my ventures, MV 1.01. 21
and never dare misfortune cross her foot, 2.04. 35
or, if misfortune miss the first career, | be R2 1.02. 49
that brings me food to make misfortune live? 5.05. 71
what late misfortune is befall'n king edward? 3H6 4.04. 3
which, once untangled, much misfortune bodes. ROM 1.04. 91
who only by misfortune of the seas | bereft of PER 2.03. 88
now, by the gods, i pity his misfortune, | and 2.03. 90
deep impression bears | of hard misfortune, LUC 1713
MISFORTUNE'S 2 FR 0.0002 REL FR 2 V 0 P
and bear with mildness my misfortune's cross; 3H6 4.04. 20
one writ with me in sour misfortune's book! ROM 5.03. 82
MISFORTUNES 3 FR 0.0003 REL FR 3 V 0 P
that by misfortunes was my life prolong'd, | to ERR 1.01.119
bearing their own misfortunes on the back | of R2 5.05. 29
what, amaz'd | at my misfortunes? H8 3.02.374
MISGIVE 1 FR 0.0001 REL FR 1 V 0 P
so doth my heart misgive me, in these conflicts 3H6 4.06. 94
MISGIVES 4 FR 0.0004 REL FR 3 V 1 P
my heart misgives me. WIV 5.05.213 P
for my mind misgives | some consequence yet ROM 1.04.106
fetch me the handkerchief, my mind misgives. OTH 3.04. 89
my mind misgives me | this fellow has a TNK 2.03. 69
MISGIVING 1 FR 0.0001 REL FR 1 V 0 P
and my misgiving still | falls shrewdly to the JC 3.01.145
MISGOVERNED 1 FR 0.0001 REL FR 1 V 0 P
where rude misgoverned hands from windows' tops R2 5.02. 5
MISGOVERNING 1 FR 0.0001 REL FR 1 V 0 P
black lust, dishonor, shame, misgoverning, | who LUC 654
MISGOVERNMENT 1 FR 0.0001 REL FR 1 V 0 P
lady, | i am sorry for thy much misgovernment. ADO 4.01. 99
MISGRAFFED 1 FR 0.0001 REL FR 1 V 0 P
or else misgraffed in respect of years — MND 1.01.137
MISGUIDE 1 FR 0.0001 REL FR 1 V 0 P
great charms | misguide thy opposers' swords! COR 1.05. 22
MISHAP 2 FR 0.0002 REL FR 2 V 0 P
mark'd | to bear the extremity of dire mishap! ERR 1.01.141
shall we curse the planets of mishap | that 1H6 1.01. 23
MISHAPS 3 FR 0.0003 REL FR 3 V 0 P
to tell sad stories of my own mishaps. ERR 1.01.120
rest, | secure from worldly chances and mishaps! TIT 1.01.152
even so she languisheth in her mishaps, | as VEN 603
MISHAVED 1 FR 0.0001 REL FR 1 V 0 P
array, | but, like a mishaved and sullen wench, ROM 3.03.143
MISHEARD 1 FR 0.0001 REL FR 1 V 0 P
it is not so, thou hast misspoke, misheard; JN 3.01. 4
MISINTERPRET 1 FR 0.0001 REL FR 1 V 0 P
in love | till you did make him misinterpret me, R2 3.01. 18
MISINTERPRETING 1 FR 0.0001 REL FR 1 V 0 P
strict edict, | your exposition misinterpreting, PER 1.01.112
MISLEAD 2 FR 0.0002 REL FR 2 V 0 P
break of day, | lights that do mislead the morn; MM 4.01. 4
mislead night-wanderers, laughing at their harm? MND 2.01. 39
MISLEADER 2 FR 0.0002 REL FR 1 V 1 P
that villainous abominable misleader of youth, 1H4 2.04.462 P
thou mad misleader of thy brain-sick son! 2H6 5.01.163
MISLEADERS 1 FR 0.0001 REL FR 1 V 0 P
as i have done the rest of my misleaders, | not 2H4 5.05. 64
MISLEADING 1 FR 0.0001 REL FR 1 V 0 P
to plague thee for thy foul misleading me. 3H6 5.01. 97
MISLED 10 FR 0.0011 REL FR 7 V 3 P
honor, | and if their wisdoms be misled in this, ADO 4.01.187
your son was misled with a snipt-taffata fellow AWW 4.05. 1 P
you have misled a prince, a royal king, | a R2 3.01. 8
and these | herein misled by your suggestion. 1H4 4.03. 51
love | that are misled upon your cousin's part, 5.01.105
you have misled the youthful prince. 2H4 1.02.144 P
the young prince hath misled me. 1.02.145 P
king | unto the commons, whom thou hast misled, 2H6 4.08. 8
our people and our peers are both misled, | our 3H6 3.03. 35
by their high treason is his heart misled, LUC 369
MISLIKE 5 FR 0.0005 REL FR 5 V 0 P
mislike me not for my complexion, | the shadowed MV 2.01. 1
'tis not my speeches that you do mislike, | but 2H6 1.01.140
setting your scorns and your mislike aside, 3H6 4.01. 24
if he mislike | my speech and what is done, tell ANT 3.13.147
thy banishment | i not mislike, so we may fairly TNK 3.06.259
MISORD'RED 1 FR 0.0001 REL FR 1 V 0 P
the time misord'red doth, in common sense, 2H4 4.02. 33
MISPLAC'D 4 FR 0.0004 REL FR 3 V 1 P
for her benefits are mightily misplac'd, and the AYL 1.02. 35 P
the misplac'd john should entertain an hour, JN 3.04.133
before i'll see the crown so foul misplac'd. R3 3.02. 44
and gilded honor shamefully misplac'd, | and SON 66. 5
MISPLACES 1 FR 0.0001 REL FR 0 V 1 P
do you hear how he misplaces? MM 2.01. 88 P
MISPRIS'D* 3 FR 0.0003 REL FR 1 V 2 P
you spend your passion on a mispris'd mood. MND 3.02. 74
best know him, that i am altogether mispris'd. AYL 1.01.171 P
reputation shall not therefore be mispris'd. 1.02.181 P
MISPRISING 3 FR 0.0003 REL FR 3 V 0 P
misprising what they look on, and her wit ADO 3.01. 52
head | by the misprising of a maid too virtuous AWW 3.02. 31
and great deal misprising | the knight oppos'd. TRO 4.05. 74
MISPRISION* 7 FR 0.0008 REL FR 6 V 1 P
there is some strange misprision in the princes. ADO 4.01.185
sweet misprision! LLL 4.03. 96
of thy misprision must perforce ensue | some MND 3.02. 90
that dost in vile misprision shackle up | my AWW 2.03.152
misprision in the highest degree! TN 1.05. 55 P
or misprision | is guilty of this fault, and not 1H4 1.03. 27
so thy great gift, upon misprision growing, SON 87.11
MISPROUD 1 FR 0.0001 REL FR 1 V 0 P
impairing henry, strength'ning misproud york. 3H6 2.06. 7
MISQUOTE 1 FR 0.0001 REL FR 1 V 0 P
interpretation will misquote our looks, | and we 1H4 5.02. 13
MISREPORT 1 FR 0.0001 REL FR 1 V 0 P
yet | did, as he vouches, misreport your grace. MM 5.01.148
MISS 25 FR 0.0028 REL FR 22 V 3 P
but, as 'tis, | we cannot miss him. TMP 1.02.311
i shall miss thee, | but yet thou shalt have 5.01. 95
you) that will not miss you morning nor evening WIV 2.02. 98 P
well, be gone; i will not miss her. 3.05. 55 P
not the apostraphas, and so miss the accent. LLL 4.02.119 P
me, | miss that which one unworthier may attain, MV 2.01. 37
so will i never be, so may you miss me, | but if 3.02. 12
are very sensible, and yet you miss my sense: SHR 5.02. 18
to show her merit, that did miss her love? AWW 1.01.227
what i can help thee to thou shalt not miss. 1.03.256
that your free undertaking cannot miss | a WT 2.02. 42
when he shall miss me (as, in faith, i mean not 4.04.494
or, if misfortune miss the first career, | be R2 1.02. 49
i should have a heavy miss of thee | if i were 1H4 5.04.105
but, hit or miss, | our project's life this TRO 1.03.383
he would miss it rather | than carry it but by COR 2.01.237
"and if we miss to meet him handsomely, | sweet TIT 2.03.268
what here shall miss, our toil shall strive to ROM pr 14
well, in that hit you miss: 1.01.208
their daggers ready, | he could not miss 'em. MAC 2.02. 12
and to our dear friend banquo, whom we miss; 3.04. 89
i would the friends we miss were safe arriv'd. 5.09. 1
transports his pois'ned shot, may miss our name, HAM 4.01. 43
two beggars told me | i could not miss my way. CYM 3.06. 9
he saith she is immodest, blames her miss; VEN 53

MISS'D 11 FR 0.0012 REL FR 10 V 1 P
therefore a health to all that shot and miss'd. SHR 5.02. 51
at them, | howe'er unfortunate i miss'd my aim. 1H6 1.04. 4
sure and safe one, though thy master miss'd it. H8 3.02.438
i miss'd the meteor once, and hit that woman, 5.03. 49 P
is not much miss'd but with his friends; COR 4.06. 13
he that hath miss'd the princess is a thing CYM 1.01. 16
you shall be miss'd at court, | and that will 3.04.126
lest, being miss'd, i be suspected of | your 3.04.186
when was she miss'd? 3.05. 90
the moon being clouded presently is miss'd, LUC 1007
part | of thee, thy record never can be miss'd. SON 122. 8
MISSES 1 FR 0.0001 REL FR 0 V 1 P
he misses not much. TMP 2.01. 57 P
MISSHAP'D 1 FR 0.0001 REL FR 1 V 0 P
until my misshap'd trunk that bears this head 3H6 3.02.170
MISSHAPEN 7 FR 0.0008 REL FR 7 V 0 P
this misshapen knave — | his mother was a witch TMP 5.01.268
nor dam, | but like a foul misshapen stigmatic, 3H6 2.02.136
and thou misshapen dick, i tell ye all | i am 5.05. 35
on me, that halts and am misshapen thus? R3 1.02.250
misshapen chaos of well/–seeming forms, ROM 1.01.179
love, | misshapen in the conduct of them both, 3.03.131
"misshapen time, copesmate of ugly night, LUC 925
MIS–SHEATHED 1 FR 0.0001 REL FR 1 V 0 P
and it mis–sheathed in my daughter's bosom! ROM 5.03.205
/MISSING 1 FR 0.0001 REL FR 0 V 1 P
cogscomb /for /missing /your /meetings /and WIV 3.01. 89 P
MISSING 7 FR 0.0008 REL FR 7 V 0 P
there are yet missing of your company | some few TMP 5.01.254
your grace was wont to laugh, is also missing. AYL 2.02. 9
if in her marriage my consent be missing, | i TIM 1.01.136
macduff is missing, and your noble son. MAC 5.09. 4
the day that she was missing he was here; CYM 4.03. 17
upon my lady's missing, came to me | with his 5.05.275
the warm effects which she in him finds missing VEN 605
MISSINGLY 1 FR 0.0001 REL FR 0 V 1 P
but i have (missingly) noted, he is of late much WT 4.02. 31 P
MISSIONS 1 FR 0.0001 REL FR 1 V 0 P
late, | made emulous missions 'mongst the gods TRO 3.03.189
MISSIVE 1 FR 0.0001 REL FR 1 V 0 P
taunts | did gibe my missive out of audience. ANT 2.02. 74
MISSIVES 1 FR 0.0001 REL FR 0 V 1 P
the wonder of it, came missives from the king, MAC 1.05. 6 P
MISSPOKE 1 FR 0.0001 REL FR 1 V 0 P
it is not so, thou hast misspoke, misheard; JN 3.01. 4
MISS'T 1 FR 0.0001 REL FR 0 V 1 P
he could not miss't. TMP 2.01. 41 P
MIST 4 FR 0.0004 REL FR 4 V 0 P
so, | and in this mist at all adventures go. ERR 2.02.216
if that her breath will mist or stain the stone, LR 5.03.263
in his dim mist th' aspiring mountains hiding, LUC 548
and wipe the dim mist from thy doting eyne, 643
MISTA'EN 2 FR 0.0002 REL FR 2 V 0 P
unless i have mista'en his colors much | (which R3 5.03. 35
this dagger hath mista'en, for lo his house | is ROM 5.03.203
MISTAKE 43 FR 0.0048 REL FR 30 V 13 P
no; he doth but mistake the truth totally. TMP 2.01. 58 P
you mistake; i mean the pound — a pinfold. TGV 1.01.107 P
mistake the word. 3.01.284 P
you mistake; the musician likes me not. 4.02. 57 P
you must not, sir, mistake my niece. ADO 1.01. 61 P
either i mistake your shape and making quite, MND 2.01. 32
our sport shall be to take what they mistake; 5.01. 90
woman doth most mistake in her gifts to women. AYL 1.02. 36 P
mistake me not so much | to think my poverty is 1.03. 64
mistake me not, i speak but as i find. SHR 2.01. 66
mistake no more, i am not litio, | nor a 4.02. 16
you mistake, sir, you mistake, sir. 5.01. 79 P
you mistake, sir, you mistake, sir. 5.01. 79 P
you mistake, knight. TN 1.03. 56 P
you mistake, sir, i am sure; 3.04.226 P
you do mistake me, sir. 3.04.328
it has an elder sister, | or i mistake you. WT 1.02. 99
you, my lord, | do but mistake. 2.01. 81
me throughly, then, to say | you did mistake. 2.01.100
if i mistake | in those foundations which i 2.01.100
but yet hear this — mistake me not; 3.02.109
act of purposes mistook | is to mistake again; JN 3.01.275
mistake me not, my lord, 'tis not my meaning R2 2.03. 74
mistake not, uncle, further than you should. 3.03. 15
lest you mistake the heavens are over our heads. 3.03. 17
if i mistake not, thou art harry monmouth. 1H4 5.04. 59
you mistake me, sir. 2H4 1.02. 79 P
gentlemen both, you will mistake each other. H5 3.02.134 P
as you did mistake | the outward composition of 1H6 2.03. 74
this is my king, york, i do not mistake, | but 2H6 5.01.129
denier, | i do mistake my person all this while! R3 1.02.252
brother of gloucester, you mistake the matter: 1.03. 62
my pretty cousins, you mistake me both: 2.02. 8
not out of hope | (mistake me not) to save my COR 4.05. 80
you mistake my love; TIM 1.02. 9
shall perceive how you | mistake my fortunes; 2.02.184
do proclaim | one honest man — mistake me not, 4.03.497
so you mistake your husbands. HAM 3.02.252 P
you do mistake your business, my brother never ANT 2.02. 45
none in the world. you did mistake him sure. CYM 4.02.102
and yet mistake me not: TNK ep 11
to make the cunning hounds mistake their smell, VEN 686
no marvel then though i mistake my view, | the SON 148.11
MISTAKEN 9 FR 0.0010 REL FR 6 V 3 P
thou hast mistaken his letter. LLL 4.01.106
thou hast mistaken quite, | and laid the MND 3.02. 88
it may be you have mistaken him, my lord. AWW 2.05. 40 P
and she (mistaken) seems to dote on me. TN 2.02. 35
you are too much mistaken in this king. H5 2.04. 30
could wish he were | something mistaken in't. H8 1.01.195
show duty as mistaken all this while | between COR 5.03. 55
my lord, if i be mistaken, for my duty cannot be LR 1.04. 65 P
you are mistaken: CYM 1.04. 82 P
MISTAKES 6 FR 0.0006 REL FR 6 V 0 P
your grace mistakes; R2 3.03. 10
but thou mistakes me much to think i do. 2H6 5.01.130
your rage mistakes us. H8 3.01.101
'tis your passion | that thus mistakes, the TNK 3.01. 49
mistakes that aim and cleaves an infant's heart. VEN 942
for oft the eye mistakes, the brain being 1068
MISTAKETH 1 FR 0.0001 REL FR 1 V 0 P
sometime for three–foot stool mistaketh me; MND 2.01. 52
MISTAKING 10 FR 0.0011 REL FR 7 V 3 P
lost my edifice by mistaking the place where i WIV 2.02.216 P
either this is envy in you, folly, or mistaking. MM 3.02.141 P
yet sinn'd i not, | but in mistaking. ADO 5.01.275
pardon, old father, my mistaking eyes, | that SHR 4.05. 45
pardon, i pray thee, for my mad mistaking. 4.05. 49
for thy mistaking so, we pardon thee. 2H6 5.01.128
men | have miserable, mad, mistaking eyes. TIT 5.02. 66
to woe, | which you, mistaking, offer up to joy. ROM 3.02.104
proceed against him, mistaking his purpose, it LR 1.02. 83 P
or me, to whom thou gav'st it, else mistaking, SON 87.10
MISTAKINGS 1 FR 0.0001 REL FR 1 V 0 P
told thee no lies, made thee no mistakings, TMP 1.02.248
MISTAK'ST 2 FR 0.0002 REL FR 1 V 1 P
why, thou whoreson ass, thou mistak'st me. TGV 2.05. 47 P
still thou mistak'st, | or else commit'st thy MND 3.02.345
MISTEMPERED 1 FR 0.0001 REL FR 1 V 0 P
throw your mistempered weapons to the ground, ROM 1.01. 87
MISTEMP'RED 1 FR 0.0001 REL FR 1 V 0 P
this inundation of mistemp'red humor | rests by JN 5.01. 12
MISTERM'D 1 FR 0.0001 REL FR 1 V 0 P
then "banished" | is death misterm'd. ROM 3.03. 21
/MISTFUL 1 FR 0.0001 REL FR 1 V 0 P
i must perforce compound | with /mistful eyes, H5 4.06. 34
MISTHINK 1 FR 0.0001 REL FR 1 V 0 P
for these woeful chances | misthink the king, 3H6 2.05.108
MISTHOUGHT 1 FR 0.0001 REL FR 1 V 0 P
are misthought | for things that others do; ANT 5.02.176
MISTLETOE 1 FR 0.0001 REL FR 1 V 0 P
overcome with moss and baleful mistletoe; TIT 2.03. 95
MIST–LIKE 1 FR 0.0001 REL FR 1 V 0 P
mist–like infold me from the search of eyes. ROM 3.03. 73
MISTOOK 22 FR 0.0024 REL FR 16 V 6 P
you mistook, sir: TGV 1.01.113 P
your worship, sir, or else i mistook. 2.01. 10 P
o, cry you mercy, sir, i have mistook; 5.04. 94
how am i mistook in you! WIV 3.03.104 P
they mistook their erection. 3.05. 39 P
this letter is mistook; LLL 4.01. 57
counsels they unbosom shall | to loves mistook, 5.02.142
is here at hand, | and the youth, mistook by me, MND 3.02.112
believe me, king of shadows, i mistook. 3.02.347
i did but tell her she mistook her frets, | and SHR 2.01.149
so comes it, lady, you have been mistook; TN 5.01.259
you have mistook, my lady, | polixenes for WT 2.01. 81
the better act of purposes mistook | is to JN 3.01.274
for you have but mistook me all this while. R2 3.02.174
blood, | my father's purposes have been mistook, 2H4 4.02. 56
age, or else you may be marvellously mistook. H5 3.06. 81 P
yet, had he mistook him and sent to me, i should TIM 3.02. 23 P
then, brutus, i have much mistook your passion, JC 1.02. 48
purposes mistook | fall'n on th' inventors' HAM 5.02.384
what's he that hath so much thy place mistook LR 2.04. 12
he has mistook the /brake i meant, is gone TNK 3.02. 1
thy wretched wife mistook the matter so, | to LUC 1826
MISTREADINGS 1 FR 0.0001 REL FR 1 V 0 P
the rod of heaven, | to punish my mistreadings. 1H4 3.02. 11
MISTRESS' 35 FR 0.0039 REL FR 31 V 4 P
i give thee this | for thy sweet mistress' sake, TGV 4.04.177
since she respects my mistress' love so much. 4.04.182
i'll use thee kindly for thy mistress' sake 4.04.202
your mistress' name? MM 2.01.199 P
to pay the saddler for my mistress' crupper? ERR 1.02. 56
some of my mistress' marks upon my shoulders: 1.02. 83
thy mistress' marks? 1.02. 87
leans me out at her mistress' chamber–window, ADO 3.03.147 P
with sweetest touches pierce your mistress' ear, MV 5.01. 67
wearing thy hearer in thy mistress' praise, AYL 2.04. 38
a woeful ballad | made to his mistress' eyebrow. 2.07.149
and quaff carouses to our mistress' health, SHR 1.02.275
take up my mistress' gown for thy master's use! 4.03.158 P
take up my mistress' gown to his master's use! 4.03.162
our mistress' sorrows we were pitying. H8 2.03. 53
you speak truth, for their poor mistress' sake; 3.01. 47
daughter, | to be her mistress' mistress? 3.02. 95
to serve, and to deserve my mistress' grace, TIT 2.01. 34
him | to raise a spirit in his mistress' circle, ROM 2.01. 24
in his mistress' name | i conjure only but to 2.01. 28
o, he is even in my mistress' case, | just in 3.03. 84
the lust of my mistress' heart and did the act LR 3.04. 87 P
quarrel and offense | as my young mistress' dog. OTH 2.03. 51
ay, ay! o, lay me by my mistress' side. 5.02.237
he began | his mistress' picture, which by his CYM 5.05.175
as do you love, fill to your mistress' lips — PER 2.03. 51
she comes weeping for her only mistress' death. 4.01. 11
love's provocations, zeal, a mistress' task, TNK 1.04. 41
thou seest our mistress' ornaments are chaste." LUC 322
of those fair suns set in her mistress' sky, 1230
therefore my mistress' eyes are raven black, SON 127. 9
my mistress' eyes are nothing like the sun; 130. 1
but at my mistress' eye love's brand new fired, 153. 9
where cupid got new fire — my mistress' /eyes. 153.14
for men diseas'd, but i, my mistress' thrall, 154.12
/MISTRESS 2 FR 0.0002 REL FR 1 V 1 P
/mistress of passion, sways it to the mood | of MV 4.01. 51
/come /hither, /mistress. LR 3.06. 49 P
MISTRESS 397 FR 0.0448 REL FR 211 V 186 P
my mistress show'd me thee, and thy dog, and thy TMP 2.02.141
the mistress which i serve quickens what's dead, 3.01. 6
my sweet mistress | weeps when she sees me work, 3.01. 11
o most dear mistress, | the sun will set before 3.01. 21
no, noble mistress, 'tis fresh morning with me 3.01. 33
my mistress, dearest, | and i thus humble ever. 3.01. 86
mistress line, is not this my jerkin? 4.01.235 P
and now you are metamorphis'd with a mistress, TGV 2.01. 31 P
madam and mistress, a thousand good morrows. 2.01. 96 P
o, be not like your mistress — be mov'd, be 2.01.175 P
mistress? 2.04. 2 P
of my mistress then. 2.04. 6 P
but that his mistress | did hold his eyes lock'd 2.04. 88
mistress, i beseech you | confirm his welcome 2.04.100
mistress, it is: 2.04.104
too low a mistress for so high a servant. 2.04.106
to have a look of such a worthy mistress. 2.04.108
you are welcome to a worthless mistress. 2.04.113
except my mistress. 2.04.154
him as a present to mistress silvia from my 4.04. 7 P
i carried mistress silvia the dog you bade me. 4.04. 45 P
acted with my tears | that my poor mistress, 4.04.170
mistress anne page? WIV 1.01. 47 P
between master abraham and mistress anne page. 1.01. 56 P
how doth good mistress page? 1.01. 83 P
o heaven! this is mistress anne page. 1.01.190 P
how now, mistress ford? 1.01.191 P
mistress ford, by my troth, you are very well 1.01.192 P
by your leave, good mistress. 1.01.193 P
the very point of it — to mistress anne page. 1.01.224 P
here comes fair mistress anne. 1.01.259 P
would i were young for your sake, mistress anne! 1.01.260 P
i will wait on him, fair mistress anne. 1.01.263 P
mistress anne, yourself shall go first. 1.01.307 P
and there dwells one mistress quickly, which is 1.02. 2 P
acquaintance with mistress anne page; 1.02. 9 P
your master's desires to mistress anne page. 1.02. 11 P
go, bear thou this letter to mistress page; 1.03. 73 P
and thou this to mistress ford. 1.03. 73 P
a good word to mistress anne page for my master 1.04. 83 P
himself is in love with mistress anne page; 1.04.104 P
what news? how does pretty mistress anne? 1.04.137 P
let it suffice thee, mistress page — at the 2.01. 10 P
mistress page, trust me, i was going to your 2.01. 33 P
o mistress page, give me some counsel! 2.01. 41 P
will you go, mistress page? 2.01.155 P
and i pray, how does good mistress anne? 2.01.165 P
and when mistress bridget lost the handle of her 2.02. 12 P
there is one mistress ford, sir — i pray come a 2.02. 44 P
well, on. mistress ford, you say — 2.02. 47 P
well; mistress ford, what of her? 2.02. 54 P
mistress ford; come, mistress ford — 2.02. 58 P
mistress ford; come, mistress ford — 2.02. 58 P
mistress page hath her hearty commendations to 2.02. 95 P
but mistress page would desire you to send her 2.02.113 P
mistress ford and mistress page, have i 2.02.152 P
mistress ford and mistress page, have i 2.02.152 P
want no mistress ford, master /brook, you shall 2.02.260 P
i will bring thee where mistress anne page is, 2.03. 87 P
well met, mistress page. whither go you? 3.02. 9 P
of modesty from the so–seeming mistress page, 3.02. 42 P
we have appointed to dine with mistress anne, 3.02. 55 P
is come in at your back door, mistress ford, and 3.03. 25 P
mistress page, remember you your cue. 3.03. 37 P
mistress ford, i cannot cog, i cannot prate, 3.03. 48 P
i cannot cog, i cannot prate, mistress ford. 3.03. 49 P
i fear you love mistress page. 3.03. 76 P
mistress ford, mistress ford! 3.03. 85 P
mistress ford, mistress ford! 3.03. 85 P
here's mistress page at the door, sweating, and 3.03. 85 P
o mistress ford, what have you done? 3.03. 94 P
what's the matter, good mistress page? 3.03. 97 P
o well–a–day, mistress ford, having an honest 3.03. 99 P
call your men, mistress ford. 3.03.144 P
we send that foolish carrion, mistress quickly, 3.03.194 P
wife, come, mistress page, i pray you pardon me; 3.03.226 P
break their talk, mistress quickly, my kinsman 3.04. 22 P
i had a father, mistress anne; 3.04. 38 P
tell mistress anne the jest how my father stole 3.04. 40 P
mistress anne, my cousin loves you. 3.04. 42 P
now, good mistress anne — 3.04. 55 P
speak to mistress page. 3.04. 77 P
good mistress page, for that i love your 3.04. 78
farewell, gentle mistress; farewell, nan. 3.04. 94
but yet i would my master had mistress anne; 3.04.104 P
here's mistress quickly, sir, to speak with you. 3.05. 19 P
sir, i come to your worship from mistress ford. 3.05. 34 P
mistress ford? 3.05. 35 P
luck would have it, comes in one mistress page; 3.05. 84 P
forth by their mistress to carry me in the name 3.05. 99 P
mistress ford desires you to come suddenly. 4.01. 5 P
farewell, mistress page. 4.01. 83 P
mistress ford, your sorrow hath eaten up my 4.02. 1 P
not only, mistress ford, in the simple office of 4.02. 4 P
how near is he, mistress page? 4.02. 38 P
mistress page and i will look some linen for 4.02. 80 P
come hither, mistress ford, mistress ford, the 4.02.129 P
mistress ford, mistress ford, the honest woman, 4.02.129 P
i suspect without cause, mistress, do i? 4.02.132 P
what ho, mistress page! 4.02.166 P
go, mistress ford, | send quickly to sir john, 4.04. 82
they were nothing but about mistress anne page, 4.05. 47 P
mistress ford, good heart, is beaten black and 4.05.111 P
mistress page is come with me, sweet heart. 5.05. 22 P
came yonder at eton to marry mistress anne page, 5.05.183 P
vere is mistress page? 5.05.204 P
now, mistress, how chance you went not with 5.05.217 P
for he to–night shall lie with mistress ford. 5.05.245
to the ground, mistress. MM 1.02.103 P
ay, sir, by mistress overdone's means; 2.01. 83 P
as i say, this mistress elbow, being (as i say) 2.01. 97 P
and his mistress is a respected woman. 2.01.163 P
mistress overdone. 2.01.200 P
how doth my dear morsel, thy mistress? 3.02. 54 P
mistress kate keepdown was with child by him in 3.02.199 P
one would think it were mistress overdone's own 4.03. 2 P
come on, mistress. 5.01.281 P
my mistress made it one upon my cheek: ERR 1.02. 46
i from my mistress come to you in post: 1.02. 63
my mistress and her sister stays for you. 1.02. 76
what mistress, slave, hast thou? 1.02. 87
your worship's wife, my mistress at the phoenix; 1.02. 88
why, mistress, sure my master is horn–mad. 2.01. 57
"my mistress, sir," quoth i: 2.01. 67
"hang up thy mistress! 2.01. 67
i know not thy mistress, out on thy mistress!" 2.01. 68
i know not thy mistress, out on thy mistress!" 2.01. 68
quoth he, "no house, no wife, no mistress." 2.01. 71
your mistress sent to have me home to dinner? 2.02. 10
and toldst me of a mistress, and a dinner, | for 2.02. 18
some other mistress hath thy sweet aspects: 2.02.111
sweet mistress — what your name is else, i know 3.02. 29
will you send him, mistress, redemption, the 4.02. 46
master, is this mistress sathan? 4.03. 49 P
mistress, that you know. 4.03. 80
mistress, respice finem, respect your end, or 4.04. 41 P
mistress, both man and master is possess'd: 4.04. 92

o mistress, mistress, shift and save yourself! 5.01.168
o mistress, mistress, shift and save yourself! 5.01.168
mistress, upon my life, i tell you true; 5.01.180
hark, hark, i hear him, mistress; 5.01.184
i, gentle mistress. 5.01.371
pray thee, sweet mistress margaret, deserve well ADO 5.02. 1 P
or study where to meet some mistress fine, LLL 1.01. 63
and your waist, mistress, were as slender as my 4.01. 49
my love (her mistress) is a gracious moon, | she 4.03.226
man attach the hand | of his fair mistress. 4.03.373
will advance | unto his several mistress, which 5.02.124
white–handed mistress, one sweet word with thee. 5.02.230
mistress, look on me, | behold the window of my 5.02.837
and here my mistress. would that he were gone! MND 2.01. 59
your buskin'd mistress and your warrior love, 2.01. 71
methinks, mistress, you should have little 3.01.142 P
i pray you commend me to mistress squash, your 3.01.186 P
my mistress with a monster is in love. 3.02. 6
you, mistress, all this coil is long of you. 3.02.339
mistress, look out at window, for all this — MV 2.05. 40 P
his words were "farewell, mistress!" 2.05. 45
you saw the mistress, i beheld the maid; 3.02.198
that your fortune | achiev'd her mistress. 3.02.208
word | my mistress will before the break of day 5.01. 29
some welcome for the mistress of the house. 5.01. 38
within the house, your mistress is at hand, 5.01. 52
i show more mirth than i am mistress of, and AYL 1.02. 4 P
mistress, you must come away to your father. 1.02. 57 P
all promise, | your mistress shall be happy. 1.02.245
mistress, dispatch you with your safest haste, 1.03. 41
found the bed untreasur'd of their mistress. 2.02. 7
we two will rail against our mistress the world, 3.02.278 P
he was to imagine me his love, his mistress; 3.02.408 P
mistress and master, you have oft inquired 3.04. 47
disdainful shepherdess | that was his mistress. 3.04. 51
no, faith, proud mistress, hope not after it. 3.05. 45
but, mistress, know yourself, down on your knees 3.05. 57
could be out, being before his belov'd mistress? 4.01. 82 P
that should you if i were your mistress, or i 4.01. 83 P
our master and mistress seeks you. 5.01. 60 P
access to our fair mistress and be happy rivals SHR 1.01.117 P
a fine musician to instruct our mistress; 1.02.173
mistress, your father prays you leave your books 3.01. 82
faith, mistress, then i have no cause to stay. 3.01. 86
rescue thy mistress if thou be a man. 3.02.237
mistress, what's your opinion of your sister? 3.02.243
my old master and my new mistress and myself, 4.01. 25 P
or shall i complain on thee to our mistress, 4.01. 29 P
for my master and mistress are almost frozen to 4.01. 37 P
is tir'd, my master and mistress fall'n out. 4.01. 55 P
hill, my master riding behind my mistress — 4.01. 67 P
must meet my master to countenance my mistress. 4.01. 99 P
that mistress bianca | doth fancy any other but 4.02. 1
now, mistress, profit you in what you read? 4.02. 6
you, sweet dear, prove mistress of my heart! 4.02. 10
you that durst swear that your mistress bianca 4.02. 12
mistress bianca, bless you with such grace | as 4.02. 44
mistress, we have. 4.02. 49
ay, mistress, and petruchio is the master, 4.02. 56
mistress, what cheer? 4.03. 37
come, mistress kate, i'll bear you company. 4.03. 49
you are i' th' right, sir, 'tis for my mistress. 4.03.156 P
good morrow, gentle mistress, where away? 4.05. 27
fair sir, and you my merry mistress, | that with 4.05. 53
mistress, how mean you that? 5.02. 21
ay, mistress bride, hath that awakened you? 5.02. 42
go, biondello, bid your mistress come to me. 5.02. 76
my mistress sends you word | that she is busy, 5.02. 80
sirrah grumio, go to your mistress, | say i 5.02. 95
be comfortable to my mother, your mistress, AWW 1.01. 76
a mother, and a mistress, and a friend, | a 1.01.167
mine honorable mistress. 1.03.139
your pardon, noble mistress! 1.03.186
to each of you one fair and virtuous mistress 2.03. 57
you have a new mistress. 2.03.243 P
might tend upon | and call her hourly mistress. 3.02. 83
prosperous helm | as thy auspicious mistress! 3.03. 8
nor /you, mistress, | ever a friend whose 4.04. 16
that scorn'd to serve | humbly call'd mistress. 5.03. 19
good mistress accost, i desire better TN 1.03. 52 P
good mistress mary accost — 1.03. 55 P
and you part so, mistress, i would i might never 1.03. 63 P
like to take dust, like mistress mall's picture? 1.03.127 P
where, good mistress mary? 1.05. 11 P
"o mistress mine, where are you roaming? 2.03. 39
mistress mary, if you priz'd my lady's favor at 2.03.121 P
be as oft with your master as with my mistress. 3.01. 41 P
nor never none | shall mistress be of it, save i 3.01.160
how now, mistress? 3.04.106 P
from this time be | your master's mistress. 5.01.326
seen, | orsino's mistress and his fancy's queen. 5.01.388
the entreaties | of our most gracious mistress. WT 1.02.233
th' entreaties of your mistress? 1.02.234
to hear | my sovereign mistress clouded so, 1.02.280
believe this crack to be in my dread mistress 1.02.322
when you shall know your mistress | has deserv'd 2.01.119
more than mistress of | which comes to me in 3.02. 59
my father hath made her mistress of the feast, 4.03. 40 P
that which you are, mistress o' th' feast. 4.04. 68
mopsa must be your mistress; 4.04.162
midwive's name to't, one mistress tale–porter, 4.04.269 P
where you may | enjoy your mistress — from the 4.04.528
for she seems a mistress | to most that teach. 4.04.582
fortunate mistress (let my prophecy | come home 4.04.648
would he do so, i'ld beg your precious mistress, 5.01.223
by our noble and chaste mistress the moon, under 1H4 1.02. 28 P
what say'st thou, mistress quickly? 3.03. 92 P
of westmerland, and this to old mistress ursula, 2H4 1.02.240 P
i arrest you at the suit of mistress quickly. 2.01. 45 P
lord, but old mistress quickly and mistress doll 2.02.152 P
mistress quickly and mistress doll tearsheet. 2.02.153 P
mistress tearsheet would fain hear some music. 2.04. 11 P
how now, mistress doll? 2.04. 35 P
you make fat rascals, mistress doll. 2.04. 41 P
then to you, mistress dorothy, i will charge you 2.04.121 P
i know you, mistress dorothy. 2.04.127 P
hark thee hither, mistress doll. 2.04.152 P
mistress tearsheet! 2.04.385 P
bid mistress tearsheet come to my master. 2.04.387 P
of life | must be the mistress to this theoric; H5 1.01. 52
were it the mistress court of mighty europe; 2.04.133
have heard a sonnet begin so to one's mistress. 3.07. 41 P
to my courser, for my horse is my mistress. 3.07. 44 P
your mistress bears well. 3.07. 45 P
perfection of a good and particular mistress. 3.07. 47 P
yesterday your mistress shrewdly shook your back 3.07. 48 P
i had rather have my horse to my mistress. 3.07. 58 P
i had as live have my mistress a jade. 3.07. 59 P
thee, constable, my mistress wears his own hair. 3.07. 60 P
a boast as that, if i had a sow to my mistress. 3.07. 63 P
yet do i not use my horse for my mistress, or 3.07. 67 P
lie, | until the queen his mistress bury it. 2H6 4.01.143
i like it well that our fair queen and mistress 3H6 3.03.167
that trudge betwixt the king and mistress shore. R3 1.01. 73
naught to do with mistress shore? 1.01. 98
give mistress shore one gentle kiss the more. 3.01.185
after he once fell in with mistress shore. 3.05. 51
lily, | that once was mistress of the field, and H8 3.01.152
daughter, | to be her mistress' mistress? 3.02. 95
and my good mistress will | remember in my 5.01. 77
that loves his mistress more than in confession TRO 1.03.269
mistress thersites! 2.01. 36 P
so, so, rub on and kiss the mistress. 3.02. 50 P
it harder for our mistress to devise imposition 3.02. 79 P
and to diomed | you shall be mistress, and 4.04.120
service than to meddle with thy mistress. COR 4.05. 48 P
heart | than when i first my wedded mistress saw 4.05.117
our general himself makes a mistress of him, 4.05.195 P
rome's royal mistress, mistress of my heart, TIT 1.01.241
rome's royal mistress, mistress of my heart, 1.01.241
to mount aloft with thy imperial mistress, | and 2.01. 13
come, mistress, now perforce we will enjoy 2.03.134
wilt thou betray thy noble mistress thus? 4.02.106
my mistress is my mistress, this myself, | the 4.02.107
my mistress is my mistress, this myself, | the 4.02.107
show me a mistress that is passing fair, | what ROM 1.01.234
and wish his mistress were that kind of fruit 2.01. 35
nurse, commend me to thy lady and mistress. 2.04.171 P
farewell, commend me to thy mistress. 2.04.193
sir, my mistress is the sweetest lady — lord, 2.04.199 P
and yet "not proud," mistress minion you? 3.05.151
mistress! 4.05. 1
what, mistress! 4.05. 1
gramercies, good fool; how does your mistress? TIM 2.02. 68 P
my mistress is one, and i am her fool. 2.02. 99 P
spur as he would to the lip of his mistress; 3.06. 66 P
master's bed, | thy mistress is o' th' brothel! 4.01. 13
go bid thy mistress, when my drink is ready, MAC 2.01. 31
and i, the mistress of your charms, | the close 3.05. 6
and my young mistress thus i did bespeak: HAM 2.02.140
what, my young lady and mistress! 2.02.425 P
since my dear soul was mistress of her choice 3.02. 63
the moon | to stand /'s auspicious mistress. LR 2.01. 40
forth | from goneril his mistress salutations; 2.04. 32
get horses for your mistress. 3.07. 20
and when your mistress hears thus much from you, 4.05. 34
as duteous to the vices of thy mistress | as 4.06.253
come hither, gentle mistress. OTH 1.03.178
yet opinion, a sovereign mistress of effects, 1.03.225 P
welcome, mistress. 2.01. 96
my wife must move for cassio to her mistress — 2.03.383
jealious now | that this is from some mistress, 3.04.186
suit, | or voluntary dotage of some mistress, 4.01. 27
mistress! 4.01.250
some of your function, mistress; 4.02. 27
you, mistress, | that have the office opposite 4.02. 90
for you, mistress, | save you your labor. 5.01.100
look you pale, mistress? 5.01.105
come, mistress, you must tell 's another tale. 5.01.125
sweet desdemona, o sweet mistress, speak! 5.02.121
o mistress, villainy hath made mocks with love! 5.02.151
the moor hath kill'd my mistress! 5.02.167
with cassio, mistress. go to, charm your tongue. 5.02.183
my mistress here lies murthered in her bed — 5.02.185
caesar, and companion me with my mistress. ANT 1.02. 30 P
the east, | say thou, shall call her mistress." 1.05. 47
say so, villain, | thou kill'st thy mistress; 2.05. 27
o sovereign mistress of true melancholy, | the 4.09. 12
my mistress lov'd thee, and her fortunes mingled 4.14. 24
lord, | my mistress cleopatra sent me to thee. 4.14.118
the queen my mistress, | confin'd in all she has 5.01. 52
trimming up the diadem | on her dead mistress; 5.02.343
to his mistress | (for whom he now is banish'd), CYM 1.01. 50
my queen, my mistress! 1.01. 92
either your unparagon'd mistress is dead, or 1.04. 80 P
a courtier to convince the honor of my mistress, 1.04. 95 P
i should get ground of your fair mistress, 1.04.104 P
my mistress exceeds in goodness the hugeness of 1.04.144 P
the dearest bodily part of your mistress, my ten 1.04.150 P
tell thy mistress how | the case stands with her 1.05. 66
on, but think | thou hast thy mistress still; 1.05. 69
and you his mistress, only | for the most 1.06.161
you have given good morning to your mistress, 2.03. 61
brought | the knowledge of your mistress home, i 2.04. 51
"thy mistress, pisanio, hath play'd the strumpet 3.04. 21 P
my noble mistress, | here is a box, i had it 3.04.187
discover where thy mistress is, at once, | at 3.05. 95
wore when he took leave of my lady and mistress. 3.05.126 P
why should his mistress, who was made by him 4.01. 3 P
within this hour be off, thy mistress enforc'd, 4.01. 17 P
but, for my mistress, | i nothing know where she 4.03. 13
nor hear i from my mistress, who did promise 4.03. 38
that, britain, i have kill'd thy mistress; 5.01. 20
it is my mistress. 5.05.127
o gentlemen, help | mine and your mistress! 5.05.230
wake, my mistress! 5.05.233
how fares my mistress? 5.05.235
"given his mistress that confection | which i 5.05.246
'tis well, mistress, your choice agrees with PER 2.05. 18
yea, mistress, are you so peremptory? 2.05. 73
therefore hear you, mistress, either frame 2.05. 81
look to your little mistress, on whose grace 3.03. 40
and constant pen | vail to her mistress dian; 4.ch. 29
but, mistress, do you know the french knight 4.02.104 P
o, take her home, mistress, take her home. 4.02.123 P
but, mistress, if i have bargain'd for the joint 4.02.130 P
i warrant you, mistress, thunder shall not so 4.02.142 P
worse and worse, mistress, she has here spoken 4.06.132 P
come, mistress, come your /ways with me. 4.06.152 P
him to be my master, or rather, my mistress. 4.06.160 P
since my master and mistress hath bought you, 4.06.196 P
wait well, sir, | upon your mistress. TNK 2.05. 52
dare assure you | you'll find a loving mistress. 2.05. 57
to drop on such a mistress, expectation | most 3.01. 14
if | thou knew'st my mistress breath'd on me, 3.01. 28
you are going now to gaze upon my mistress, 3.01.117
and you show | more than a mistress to me; 3.06. 26
as sweet flowers as the season is mistress of, 4.03. 83 P
and, sacred silver mistress, lend thine ear 5.01.146
o mistress, | thou here dischargest me. 5.01.169
their mistress mounted through the empty skies, VEN 1191
for me, i am the mistress of my fate, | and with LUC 1069
whose swift obedience to her mistress hies; 1215
her mistress she doth give demure good morrow, 1219
i fear — | lest that my mistress hear my song; PP 18.50
hast thou, the master mistress of my passion; SON 20. 2
if nature (sovereign mistress over wrack), | as 126. 5
than in the breath that from my mistress reeks. 130. 8
my mistress when she walks treads on the ground. 130.12
sweetly suppos'd them mistress of his heart. LC 142

MISTRESSES 6 FR 0.0006 REL FR 4 V 2 P
to sir john falstaff from my two mistresses. WIV 3.04.110 P
when mistresses from common sense are hid; LLL 1.01. 64
your mistresses dare never come in rain, | for 4.03.266
madam, and pretty mistresses, give ear: 5.02.286
ah, my mistresses, which of you all | will now ROM 1.05. 18
of us fell in praise of our country mistresses; CYM 1.04. 58 P

MISTRESS'S 2 FR 0.0002 REL FR 1 V 1 P
young master ganymed, my new mistress's brother. AYL 3.02. 87 P
in your own behalf) | a mistress's command. LR 4.02. 21

MISTRISHIP 1 FR 0.0001 REL FR 0 V 1 P
yea forsooth, and your mistriship be emperial. TIT 4.04. 40 P

MISTRUST 19 FR 0.0021 REL FR 17 V 2 P
i will never mistrust my wife again, till thou WIV 5.05.133 P
i will not do them the wrong to mistrust any, i ADO 1.01.243 P
none but that ugly treason of mistrust, | which MV 3.02. 28
yet your mistrust cannot make me a traitor. AYL 1.03. 56
in time i may believe, yet i mistrust. SHR 3.01. 51
mistrust it not, for sure aeacides | was ajax, 3.01. 52
more than mistrust, that shows him worthy death. 2H6 3.01.242
when care, mistrust, and treason waits on him. 3H6 2.05. 54
which now mistrust no parcel of my fear, | and 5.06. 38
by a divine instinct men's minds mistrust R3 2.03. 42
and they indeed had no cause to mistrust; 3.02. 85
no, my good lord, therefore mistrust me not. 4.04.478
mistrust of my success hath done this deed. JC 5.03. 65
mistrust of good success hath done this deed. 5.03. 66
he needs not our mistrust, since he delivers MAC 3.03. 2
it shall not fear where it should most mistrust, VEN 1154
full of foul hope and full of fond mistrust; LUC 284
his kindled duty kindled her mistrust, | that 1352
that jealousy itself could not mistrust | false 1516

MISTRUSTED 3 FR 0.0003 REL FR 3 V 0 P
of hourly proof, | which i mistrusted not. ADO 2.01.182
all's true that is mistrusted. WT 2.01. 48
it had been vicious | to have mistrusted her; CYM 5.05. 66

MISTRUSTFUL 2 FR 0.0002 REL FR 2 V 0 P
to rest mistrustful where a noble heart | hath 3H6 4.02. 8
their light blown out in some mistrustful wood, VEN 826

MISTRUSTING 1 FR 0.0001 REL FR 1 V 0 P
he, mistrusting them, | hois'd sail, and made R3 4.04.526

MISTS 2 FR 0.0002 REL FR 2 V 0 P
by breaking through the foul and ugly mists | of 1H4 1.02.202
muster thy mists to meet the eastern light, LUC 773

MISTY 6 FR 0.0006 REL FR 6 V 0 P
graves, and from their misty jaws | breathe foul 2H6 4.01. 6
as hateful as /cocytus' misty mouth. TIT 2.03.236
no vast obscurity or misty vale, | where bloody 5.02. 36
day | stands tiptoe on the misty mountain tops. ROM 3.05. 10
like misty vapors when they blot the sky, VEN 184
and misty night | covers the shame that follows LUC 356

MISUS'D 4 FR 0.0004 REL FR 1 V 3 P
o, she misus'd me past the endurance of a block; ADO 2.01.239 P
you have simply misus'd our sex in your AYL 4.01.201 P
i have misus'd the king's press damnably. 1H4 4.02. 12 P
for that thou hast | misus'd ere us'd, by times R3 4.04.396

MISUSE 8 FR 0.0009 REL FR 6 V 2 P
we cannot misuse /him enough. WIV 4.02.103 P
proof enough to misuse the prince, to vex ADO 2.02. 28 P
terms, | as had she studied to misuse me so. SHR 2.01.159
upon whose dead corpse' there was such misuse, 1H4 1.01. 43
misuse the tenor of thy kinsman's trust? 5.05. 5
but you misuse the reverence of your place, 2H4 4.02. 23
stick | the small'st opinion on my least misuse? OTH 4.02.109
for all my vows are oaths but to misuse thee, SON 152. 7

MISUSES 1 FR 0.0001 REL FR 0 V 1 P
for he misuses thy favors so much that he swears 2H4 2.02.128 P

MITE 1 FR 0.0001 REL FR 1 V 0 P
reign, | losing a mite, a mountain gain. PER 2.ch. 8

MITES 1 FR 0.0001 REL FR 0 V 1 P
virginity breeds mites, much like a cheese, AWW 1.01.141 P

MITHRIDATES 1 FR 0.0001 REL FR 1 V 0 P
mithridates, king | of comagena; ANT 3.06. 73

MITIGATE 3 FR 0.0003 REL FR 3 V 0 P
thus much | to mitigate the justice of thy plea, MV 4.01.203
pray, uncle gloucester, mitigate this strife. 1H6 3.01. 88
to mitigate the scorn he gives his uncle, | he R3 3.01.133

MITIGATION 3 FR 0.0003 REL FR 1 V 2 P
behold, behold, where madam mitigation comes! MM 1.02. 44 P
without any mitigation or remorse of voice? TN 2.03. 90 P
how now for mitigation of this bill | urg'd by H5 1.01. 70

/MIX 1 FR 0.0001 REL FR 1 V 0 P
brothers, you /mix your sadness with some fear: 2H4 5.02. 46

MIX'D 9 FR 0.0010 REL FR 9 V 0 P
more lusty red | than that mix'd in his cheek; AYL 3.05.122
by fair persuasions, mix'd with sug'red words, 1H6 3.03. 18
this goodly summer with your winter mix'd. TIT 5.02.171
hadst thou no poison mix'd, no sharp–ground ROM 3.03. 44
so mix'd in him that nature might stand up | and JC 5.05. 74
o, matter and impertinency mix'd! LR 4.06.174
were never four such lamps together mix'd, | had VEN 489

chang'd to solace, and solace mix'd with sorrow; PP 14.23
which is not mix'd with seconds, knows no art, SON 125.11
MIXED 1 FR 0.0001 REL FR 1 V 0 P
her modest eloquence with sighs is mixed, LUC 563
MIXTURE 3 FR 0.0003 REL FR 3 V 0 P
planets | in evil mixture to disorder wander, TRO 1.03. 95
what if this mixture do not work at all? ROM 4.03. 21
thou mixture rank, of midnight weeds collected, HAM 3.02.257
MIXTURES 1 FR 0.0001 REL FR 1 V 0 P
that with some mixtures pow'rful o'er the blood, OTH 1.03.104
M.O.A.I. 4 FR 0.0004 REL FR 1 V 3 P
m.o.a.i. doth sway my life." TN 2.05.107
"m.o.a.i. doth sway my life." 2.05.110 P
m.o.a.i. — 2.05.120 P
m.o.a.i. this simulation is not as the former; 2.05.139 P
/MOAN 1 FR 0.0001 REL FR 1 V 0 P
for a sweet content, the cause of all my /moan. PP 17.34
MOAN 25 FR 0.0028 REL FR 24 V 1 P
mark the moan she makes. TGV 2.03. 30 P
midnight, assist our moan, | help us to sigh and ADO 5.03. 16
lovers, make moan; MND 5.01.334
nor do i now make moan to be abridg'd | from MV 1.01.126
many that have at times made moan to me; 3.03. 23
thy mirth shall turn to moan. 1H6 2.03. 44
whiles, in his moan, the ship splits on the rock 3H6 5.04. 10
to hear the piteous moan that rutland made R3 1.02.157
have i | (thine being but a moi'ty of my moan) 2.02. 60
that bear this heavy mutual load of moan, | now 2.02.113
and makes her pew–fellow with others' moan! 4.04. 58
betimes | a moi'ty of that mass of moan to come. TRO 2.02.107
he is gone, he is gone, | and we cast away moan, HAM 4.05.198
thou hast finish'd joy and moan. CYM 4.02.273
mute, | that still records with moan; PER 4.ch. 27
him pitiful mischances | to make him moan, but LUC 977
so woe hath wearied woe, moan tired moan, | that 1363
so woe hath wearied woe, moan tired moan, | that 1363
every thing did banish moan, | save the PP 20. 7
and moan th' expense of many a vanish'd sight; SON 30. 8
o'er | the sad account of fore–bemoaned moan, 30.11
i must attend time's leisure with my moan, 44.12
lest the wise world should look into your moan, 71.13
spend | revenge upon myself with present moan? 149. 8
so well blazon'd, smil'd or made some moan. LC 217
MOANS *(also means*)*
MOANS 9 FR 0.0010 REL FR 9 V 0 P
o wall, full often hast thou heard my moans, MND 5.01.188
so longest way shall have the longest moans. R2 5.01. 90
or, wanting that, with tears distill'd by moans. ROM 5.03. 15
streams ran by her, and murmur'd her moans, OTH 4.03. 44
troubled, | make verbal repetition of her moans; VEN 831
if ever man were mov'd with woman's moans, | be
LUC 587
poor wasting monuments of lasting moans. 798
to make him moan, but pity not his moans; 977
make her moans mad with their sweet melody, 1108
MOAT 1 FR 0.0001 REL FR 1 V 0 P
of a wall, | or as /a moat defensive to a house, R2 2.01. 48
MOATED 1 FR 0.0001 REL FR 0 V 1 P
there, at the moated grange, resides this MM 3.01.264 P
/MOBLED 1 FR 0.0001 REL FR 0 V 1 P
that's good, "/mobled /queen" /is /good. HAM 2.02.504 P
MOBLED 2 FR 0.0002 REL FR 1 V 1 P
"but who, ah woe, had seen the mobled queen" —
HAM 2.02.502
"the mobled queen"? 2.02.503 P
MOCK 90 FR 0.0101 REL FR 75 V 15 P
the purpose cherish | whiles thus you mock it! TMP 2.01.225
go in, gentlemen, but, trust me, we'll mock him. WIV 3.03.229 P
the spirit, | and mock him home to windsor. 4.04. 65
in a barber's shop, | as much in mock as mark. MM 5.01.322
i hope you will not mock me with a husband! 5.01.417
nay, mock not, mock not. ADO 1.01.285 P
nay, mock not, mock not. 1.01.285 P
if i should speak, | she would mock me into air; 3.01. 75
we are wise girls to mock our lovers so. LLL 5.02. 58
and mock for mock is only my intent. 5.02.140
and mock for mock is only my intent. 5.02.140
let's mock them still, as well known as 5.02.301
we were descried, they'll mock us now downright. 5.02.389
do, | but you must join in souls to mock me too? MND 3.02.150
and now both rivals, to mock helena. 3.02.156
i pray you, though you mock me, /gentlemen, 3.02.299
yea, mock the lion when 'a roars for prey, | to MV 2.01. 30
let us sit and mock the good huswife fortune AYL 1.02. 31 P
you mean to mock me after; 1.02.208 P
ourselves, | and mock us with our bareness. AWW 4.02. 20
nay, that's a mock. WT 2.01. 14
let no man mock me, | for i will kiss her. 5.03. 79
ear, | and mock the deep–mouth'd thunder; JN 5.02.173
no, misery makes sport to mock itself: R2 2.01. 85
i mock my name, great king, to flatter thee. 2.01. 87
mock not my senseless conjuration, lords, | this 3.02. 23
and mock not flesh and blood | with solemn 3.02.171
of the wise sit in the clouds and mock us. 2H4 2.02.143 P
for now a time is come to mock at form. 4.05.118
and mock your workings in a second body? 5.02. 90
survive, | to mock the expectation of the world, 5.02.126
and tell the pleasant prince this mock of his H5 1.02.281
shall this his mock mock out of their dear 1.02.285
shall this his mock mock out of their dear 1.02.285
mock mothers from their sons, mock castles down; 1.02.286
mock mothers from their sons, mock castles down; 1.02.286
sweeten the bitter mock you sent his majesty, 2.04.122
shall chide your trespass and return your mock 2.04.125
our madams mock at us, and plainly say | our 3.05. 28
god, why should they mock poor fellows thus? 4.03. 92
if you can mock a leek, you can eat a leek. 5.01. 37 P
to see leeks hereafter, i pray you mock at 'em, 5.01. 56 P
will you mock at an ancient tradition, /begun 5.01. 70 P
your majesty shall mock at me, i cannot speak 5.02.102 P
but, good kate, mock me mercifully, the rather, 5.02.201 P
and i, to make thee mad, do mock thee thus. 3H6 1.04. 90
they mock thee, clifford, swear as thou wast 2.06. 76
my back, | where sits deformity to mock my body; 3.02.158
you mock me, madam, this /is not the way | to R3 4.04.284
hour, | even for revenge mock my destruction! 5.01. 9
my state now will but mock me. H8 2.01.101
can say worst shall be a mock for his truth, and TRO 3.02. 97 P
you smile and mock me, as if i meant naughtily. 4.02. 37
how my achievements mock me! 4.02. 69
mock not /that /i affect th' untraded /oath, 4.05.178
as boasting show their scars | a mock is due. 4.05.291
farewell, | thou never shalt mock diomed again. 5.02. 99
the gods begin to mock me. COR 1.09. 79
no, 'tis his kind of speech, he did not mock us. 2.03.161
of him that did not ask but mock, bestow | your 2.03.207
for i mock at death | with as big heart as thou. 3.02.127
for this proud mock i'll be thy slaughter–man, TIT 4.04. 58
besides, it were a mock | apt to be render'd, JC 2.02. 96
away, and mock the time with fairest show: MAC 1.07. 81
grooms | do mock their charge with snores. 2.02. 6
i prithee do not mock me, fellow student, | i HAM 1.02.177
follow that lord, and look you mock him not. 2.02.546 P
not one now to mock your own grinning — quite 5.01.191 P
you mock me, sir. 5.02.257
one side will mock another; th' other too. LR 3.07. 71
pray do not mock me. 4.07. 58
would ever have, t' incur a general mock, | run OTH 1.02. 69
it is the green–ey'd monster which doth mock 3.03.166
dost thou mock me? 4.01. 60
i mock you not, by heaven. 4.01. 60
the good gods will mock me presently, | when i ANT 3.04. 15
let's mock the midnight bell. 3.13.184
mock not, enobarbus, | i tell you true. 4.06. 24
nod unto the world | and mock our eyes with air. 4.14. 7
i hear him mock | the luck of caesar, which the 5.02.285
to be by | and hear him mock the frenchman. CYM 1.06. 76
what an infinite mock is this, that a man should 5.04.188 P
e'er dull'd sleep | did mock sad fools withal. PER 5.01.162
to mock the subtle in themselves beguil'd, | to LUC 957
foes, | and merry fools to mock at him resort; 989
mock with thy tickling beams eyes that are 1090
to jump up higher seem'd, to mock the mind. 1414
while shadows like to thee do mock my sight? SON 61. 4
moan, | and mock you with me after i am gone. 71.14
and the sad augurs mock their own presage, 107. 6
MOCKABLE 1 FR 0.0001 REL FR 0 V 1 P
of the country is most mockable at the court. AYL 3.02. 48 P
MOCK'D 29 FR 0.0032 REL FR 21 V 8 P
i shall be rather prais'd for this than mock'd; WIV 3.02. 47 P
if he be not amaz'd, he will be mock'd; 5.03. 18 P
if he be amaz'd, he will every way be mock'd. 5.03. 19 P
time the rod | /becomes more mock'd than fear'd;
MM 1.03. 27
it is your husband mock'd you with a husband. 5.01.418
and so be mock'd withal | upon the next occasion LLL 5.02.142
and they, well mock'd, depart away with shame. 5.02.156
laugh'd at my losses, mock'd at my gains, MV 3.01. 56 P
you should not have mock'd me before. AYL 1.02.209 P
the poor souls roar'd, and the sea mock'd them; WT 3.03. 99 P
poor gentleman roar'd, and the bear mock'd him, 3.03.101 P
to see the life as lively mock'd as ever | still 5.03. 19
mock'd as ever | still sleep mock'd death. 5.03. 20
has motion in't, | as we are mock'd with art. 5.03. 68
day, | if he arise, be mock'd and wond'red at. 3H6 5.04. 57
and mock'd the dead bones that lay scatt'red by. R3 1.04. 33
a mother only mock'd with two fair babes; 4.04. 87
in fear our motion will be mock'd or carp'd at, H8 1.02. 86
he mock'd us when he begg'd our voices. COR 2.03.159
the people cry you mock'd them; 3.01. 42
who resists | are mock'd for valiant ignorance, 4.06.104
thy resolution mock'd! TIT 3.01.238
well mock'd. TIM 1.01.173
who would be so mock'd with glory, or to live 4.02. 33
they mock'd thee for too much curiosity; 4.03.302 P
smiles in such a sort | as if he mock'd himself, JC 1.02.206
those runagates, that villain | hath mock'd me. CYM 4.02. 63
with marriage wherefore was he mock'd, | to be 5.04. 58
o, i am mock'd, | and thou by some incensed god PER 5.01.142
MOCKER 4 FR 0.0004 REL FR 1 V 3 P
well said, old mocker. LLL 5.02.549
i know it is a sin to be a mocker, but he! MV 1.02. 57 P
before i come, thou art a mocker of my labor. AYL 2.06. 13 P
ah, mocker, that's the /dog's name. ROM 2.04.209 P
MOCKERIES 1 FR 0.0001 REL FR 0 V 1 P
knave, to have his gibes and his mockeries! WIV 3.03.243 P
MOCKERS 2 FR 0.0002 REL FR 1 V 1 P
never did mockers waste more idle breath. MND 3.02.168
very priests must become mockers if they shall COR 2.01. 84 P
/MOCKERY 1 FR 0.0001 REL FR 1 V 0 P
/o, /that /i /were /a /mockery /king /of /snow, R2 4.01.260
MOCKERY 9 FR 0.0010 REL FR 8 V 1 P
they do it but in mockery merriment, | and mock LLL 5.02.139
of sweet summer buds | is, as in mockery, set; MND 2.01.111
wherefore was i to this keen mockery born? 2.02.123
what mockery will it be, | to want the SHR 3.02. 4
observe him, for the love of mockery; TN 2.05. 18 P
else what a mockery should it be to swear! JN 3.01.285
misery, | but seek revenge on edward's mockery. 3H6 3.03.265
was not this mockery? COR 2.03.173
and our vain blows malicious mockery. HAM 1.01.146
MOCKING 17 FR 0.0019 REL FR 16 V 1 P
you do blaspheme the good in mocking me. MM 1.04. 38
some merry mocking lord belike, is't so? LLL 2.01. 52
they are worse fools to purchase mocking so. 5.02. 59
so shall we stay, mocking intended game, | and 5.02.155
the tongues of mocking wenches are as keen | as 5.02.256
nay, but the devil take mocking. AYL 3.02.214 P
come, come, you're mocking; SHR 5.02.132
mocking the air with colors idlely spread, | and JN 5.01. 72
everlasting shame | sits mocking in our plumes. H5 4.05. 5
for mocking marriage with a dame of france. 3H6 3.03.255
for mocking him | about the marriage of the lady 4.01. 30
and in his tent | lies mocking our designs. TRO 1.03.146
now will he be mocking. 4.02. 21
go hang yourself, you naughty mocking uncle! 4.02. 25
it is a pretty mocking of the life. TIM 1.01. 35
the smile mocking the sigh, that it would fly CYM 4.02. 54
"you mocking birds," quoth she, "your tunes LUC 1121
MOCK'RIES 1 FR 0.0001 REL FR 1 V 0 P
minding true things by what their mock'ries be. H5 4.pr. 53
MOCK'RY 5 FR 0.0005 REL FR 5 V 0 P
to trust the mock'ry of unquiet slumbers. R3 3.02. 27
like a rusty mail | in monumental mock'ry. TRO 3.03.153
unreal mock'ry, hence! MAC 3.04.106
takes, | patience her injury a mock'ry makes. OTH 1.03.207
you rhyme upon't, | and vent it for a mock'ry? CYM 5.03. 56
/MOCKS 1 FR 0.0001 REL FR 1 V 0 P
if she be false, /o, /then heaven /mocks itself! OTH 3.03.278
MOCKS 19 FR 0.0021 REL FR 15 V 4 P
lo, how he mocks me! wilt thou let him, my lord? TMP 3.02. 30 P
and the sea mocks | our frustrate search on land 3.03. 9
no means, she mocks all her wooers out of suit. ADO 2.01.349 P
it were a better death than die with mocks, 3.01. 79
look how you butt yourself in these sharp mocks! LLL 5.02.251
though my mocks come home by me, i will now be 5.02.634 P
proclaims you for a man replete with mocks, 5.02.843
cuckoo then on every tree | mocks married men; 5.02.899
cuckoo then on every tree | mocks married men; 5.02.908
afflict me with thy mocks, pity me not, | as AYL 3.05. 33
potent fault it is | that it but mocks reproof. TN 3.04.205
the man that mocks at it and sets it light. R2 1.03.293
how chance's mocks | and changes fill the cup of 2H4 3.01. 51
and knaveries, and mocks — i have forgot his H5 4.07. 49 P
uncle, my brother mocks both you and me: R3 3.01.129
i'll trust by leisure him that mocks me once, TIT 1.01.301
and whilst the babbling echo mocks the hounds, 2.03. 17
o mistress, villainy hath made mocks with love! OTH 5.02.151
tell him he mocks | the pauses that he makes. ANT 5.01. 2
MOCK'ST 1 FR 0.0001 REL FR 1 V 0 P
nay then thou mock'st me. MND 3.02.426
MOCK–VATER 2 FR 0.0002 REL FR 0 V 2 P
mock–vater? vat is dat? WIV 2.03. 59 P
then i have as much mock–vater as de englishman. 2.03. 62 P
MOCK–WATER 2 FR 0.0002 REL FR 0 V 2 P
a /word, mounseur mock–water. WIV 2.03. 58 P
mock–water, in our english tongue, is valor, 2.03. 60 P
/MODEL 3 FR 0.0003 REL FR 3 V 0 P
/survey /the /plot, /then /draw /the /model, 2H4 1.03. 42
/what /do /we /then /but /draw /anew /the /model 1.03. 46
/the /plot /of /situation /and /the /model, 1.03. 51
MODEL 11 FR 0.0012 REL FR 10 V 1 P
will it serve for any model to build mischief on ADO 1.03. 46 P
die, | who was the model of thy father's life. R2 1.02. 28
and that small model of the barren earth | which 3.02.153
showing as in a model our firm estate, | when 3.04. 42
ah, thou, the model where old troy did stand, 5.01. 11
like /one that draws the model of an house 2H4 1.03. 58
model to thy inward greatness, | like little H5 2.pr. 16
i'll draw the form and model of our battle, R3 5.03. 24
to his goodness | the model of our chaste loves, H8 4.02.132
which was the model of that danish seal; HAM 5.02. 50
are | a model which heaven makes like to itself. PER 2.02. 11
MODENA 1 FR 0.0001 REL FR 1 V 0 P
when thou once | was beaten from modena, where
ANT 1.04. 57
MODERATE 8 FR 0.0009 REL FR 4 V 4 P
o love, be moderate, allay thy ecstasy, | in MV 3.02.111
moderate lamentation is the right of the dead, AWW 1.01. 55 P
on a moderate pace i have since arriv'd but TN 2.02. 3 P
be moderate, be moderate. TRO 4.04. 1 P
be moderate, be moderate. 4.04. 1 P
how can i moderate it? 4.04. 5
so much left to furnish out | a moderate table. TIM 3.04.115
while one with moderate haste might tell a HAM 1.02.237
MODERATELY 2 FR 0.0002 REL FR 1 V 1 P
to hear meekly, sir, and to laugh moderately; LLL 1.01.197 P
therefore love moderately: ROM 2.06. 14
MODERATION 1 FR 0.0001 REL FR 1 V 0 P
why tell you me of moderation? TRO 4.04. 2
MODERN 10 FR 0.0011 REL FR 8 V 2 P
cut, | full of wise saws and modern instances; AYL 2.07.156
themselves to every modern censure worse than 4.01. 7 P
to make modern and familiar things supernatural AWW 2.03. 2 P
her /inf'nite /cunning, with her modern grace, 5.03.216
voice, | which scorns a modern invocation. JN 3.04. 42
which modern lamentation might have moved? ROM 3.02.120
where violent sorrow seems | a modern ecstasy. MAC 4.03.170
of modern seeming do prefer against him. OTH 1.03.109
dignity | as we greet modern friends withal, and ANT 5.02.167
how far a modern quill doth come too short, SON 83. 7
MODEST 50 FR 0.0056 REL FR 37 V 13 P
she's as fartuous a civil modest wife, and one WIV 2.02. 97 P
the honest woman, the modest wife, the virtuous 4.02.130 P
not show itself modest enough without a badge of
ADO 1.01. 22 P
is she not a modest young lady? 1.01.165 P
i will do any modest office, my lord, to help my 2.01.375 P
comes not that blood as modest evidence | to 4.01. 37
their savage eyes turn'd to a modest gaze, | by MV 5.01. 78
but his will hath in it a more modest working. AYL 1.02.203 P
this is call'd the quip modest. 5.04. 75 P
the second, the quip modest; 5.04. 93 P
if i achieve not this young modest girl. SHR 1.01.156
for she's not froward, but modest as the dove; 2.01.293
from your royal thoughts | a modest one, to bear AWW 2.01.128
yourself within the modest limits of order. TN 1.03. 9 P
give me modest assurance if you be the lady of 1.05.180 P
i call thee by the most modest terms, for i am 4.02. 32 P
appear more wise and modest to the world. 2H4 5.05.101
garnish'd and deck'd in modest complement, | not
H5 2.02.134
how modest in exception, and withal | how 2.04. 34
a man | as modest stillness and humility; 3.01. 4
bids them good morrow with a modest smile, | and 4.pr. 33
or modest dian, circled with her nymphs, | shall 3H6 4.08. 21
rose, and with modest paces | came to the altar, H8 4.01. 82
she is young, and of a noble modest nature, | i 4.02.135
but reverence to your calling makes me modest. 5.02.104
a blush | modest as morning when she coldly eyes TRO 1.03.229
but modest doubt is call'd | the beacon of the 2.02. 15
bemock the modest moon. COR 1.01.257
top of praises vouch'd, | would seem but modest; 1.09. 25
too modest are you; 1.09. 53
where you should but hunt | with modest warrant. 3.01.274
his power, and modest wisdom plucks me | from MAC 4.03.119
resolve me with all modest haste which way LR 2.04. 25
all my reports go with the modest truth, | nor 4.07. 5
an inviting eye; and yet methinks right modest. OTH 2.03. 25 P
with her modest eyes | and still conclusion, ANT 4.15. 27
further to boast were neither true nor modest, CYM 5.05. 18
o, sir, i can be modest. PER 4.06. 38 P
for thou lookest | modest as justice, and thou 5.01.121
(whose modest scenes blush on his marriage–day, TNK pr 4

more by virtue. | you are modest, cousin. 3.06. 82
fit for my modest suit and your free granting. 3.06.235
therefore, most modest queen, | he of the two 5.01.157
steps, | with gentle majesty and modest pride; VEN 278
thy lips | make modest dian cloudy and forlorn, 725
supper long he questioned | with modest lucrece, LUC 123
spots and stains love's modest snow-white weed. 196
play'd with her breath — | o modest wantons! 401
her modest eloquence with sighs is mixed, 563
tears | that ever modest eyes with sorrow shed. 683
MODESTIES 2 FR 0.0002 REL FR 1 V 1 P
but i am doubtful of your modesties, | lest, SHR in.1. 94
which your modesties have not craft enough to HAM 2.02.280 P
/MODESTLY 1 FR 0.0001 REL FR 1 V 0 P
words sweetly plac'd and /modestly directed. 1H6 5.03.179
MODESTLY 6 FR 0.0006 REL FR 5 V 1 P
i could wish he would modestly examine himself, ADO 2.03.207 P
life | did hear a challenge urg'd more modestly, 1H4 5.02. 52
yet, and modestly i think | the fall of every TRO 4.05.222
will modestly discover to yourself | that of JC 1.02. 69
how modestly she blows, and paints the sun TNK 2.02.139
she modestly prepares to let them know | her LUC 1607
MODESTY 54 FR 0.0061 REL FR 42 V 12 P
but, by my modesty | (the jewel in my dower), i TMP 3.01. 53
now, by my modesty, a goodly broker! TGV 1.02. 41
since maids, in modesty, say "no" to that 1.02. 55
and she, in modesty, | or else for want of idle 2.01.165
it is the lesser blot, modesty finds, | women to 5.04.108
/prais'd women's modesty; WIV 2.01. 58 P
the borrow'd veil of modesty from the so-seeming 3.02. 41 P
it be | that modesty may more betray our sense MM 2.02.168
gentleman to the extremest shore of my modesty, 3.02.252 P
wisdom, | her sober virtue, years, and modesty, ERR 3.01. 90
as roughly as my modesty would let me. 5.01. 59
her blush is guiltiness, not modesty. ADO 4.01. 42
than that which maiden modesty doth warrant, 4.01.179
made bold, | nor how it may concern my modesty,
MND 1.01. 60
you do impeach your modesty too much, | to leave 2.01.214
courtesy | lie further off, in humane modesty; 2.02. 57
have you no modesty, no maiden shame, | no touch 3.02.285
and in the modesty of fearful duty | i read as 5.01.101
to allay with some cold drops of modesty | thy MV 2.02.186
wanted the modesty | to urge the thing held as a 5.01.205
better part, | sad lucretia's modesty. AYL 3.02.148
excellent, | if it be husbanded with modesty. SHR in.1. 68
tongue, | as is the other for beauteous modesty. 1.02.253
her wit, | her affability and bashful modesty, 2.01. 49
for then we wound our modesty and make foul the
AWW 1.03. 5 P
danger known but the modesty which is so lost. 3.05. 27 P
perceive in you so excellent a touch of modesty, TN 2.01. 13 P
it then, | and tell me, in the modesty of honor, 5.01.335
and the sobriety of it, and the modesty of it, H5 4.01. 74 P
ros'd over with the virgin crimson of modesty, 5.02.296 P
of auvergne, | with modesty admiring thy renown, 1H6 2.02. 39
her looks doth argue her replete with modesty, 3H6 3.02. 84
deliver this with modesty to th' queen. H8 2.02.136
made me, | with thy religious truth and modesty, 4.02. 74
win straying souls with modesty again, | cast 5.02. 99
bold, | think true love acted simple modesty. ROM 3.02. 16
lips, | who, even in pure and vestal modesty, 3.03. 38
not stepping o'er the bounds of modesty. 4.02. 27
than you can with modesty speak in your own TIM 1.02. 93 P
then, in a friend, it is cold modesty. JC 3.01.213
set down with as much modesty as cunning. HAM 2.02.440 P
that you o'erstep not the modesty of nature: 3.02. 19 P
act | that blurs the grace and blush of modesty, 3.04. 41
him thither with modesty enough and likelihood 5.01.208 P
cheeks, | that would to cinders burn up modesty, OTH 4.02. 75
wisdom, modesty, can settle | the heart of ANT 2.02.240
with what gift beside | thy modesty can beg. 2.05. 72
though peril to my modesty, not death on't, | i CYM 3.04.152
yet still is modesty, and still retains | more TNK pr 7
sometimes her modesty will blow so far she falls 2.02.144
wanton modesty! LUC 401
with soft slow tongue, true mark of modesty, 1220
mood, | effects of terror and dear modesty, LC 202
cold modesty, hot wrath, | both fire from hence 293
MODICUMS 1 FR 0.0001 REL FR 0 V 1 P
lo, lo, lo, lo, what modicums of wit he utters! TRO 2.01. 68 P
/MODO 1 FR 0.0001 REL FR 0 V 1 P
/modo, /of /murder; LR 4.01. 61 P
MODO 1 FR 0.0001 REL FR 0 V 1 P
modo he's call'd, and mahu. LR 3.04.143 P
MODULE 2 FR 0.0002 REL FR 1 V 1 P
come, bring forth this counterfeit module, h'as AWW 4.03. 99 P
but a clod | and module of confounded royalty. JN 5.07. 58
MOE *(also more*)*
MOE 49 FR 0.0055 REL FR 41 V 8 P
moe widows in them of this business' making TMP 2.01.134
and moe diversity of sounds, all horrible, | we 5.01.234
moe reasons for this action | at our more MM 1.03. 48
yet in this life | lie hid moe thousand deaths; 3.01. 40
charges she moe than me? 5.01.200
sing no more ditties, sing no moe, | of dumps so ADO 2.03. 70
well, keep me company but two years moe, | thou MV 1.01.108
and gild myself | with some moe ducats, and be 2.06. 50
therefore i do beseech you | make no moe offers, 4.01. 81
i pray you mar no moe of my verses with reading AYL 3.02.261 P
with one "we thank you" many thousands moe WT 1.02. 8
and let's first see moe ballads. 4.04.273 P
boy, i am past moe children, but thy sons and 5.02.126 P
sworn, | and i with him, and many moe with me, JN 5.04. 17
and many moe | of noble blood in this declining R2 2.01.239
and many moe corrivals and dear men | of 1H4 4.04. 31
it, he might have moe diseases than he knew for. 2H4 1.02. 5 P
and of their feather many moe proud birds, 3H6 2.01.170
i have no moe sons of the royal blood | for thee R3 4.04.200
with many moe confederates, are in arms. 4.04.502
by my life, | that promises moe thousands; H8 2.03. 97
but that you shall sustain moe new disgraces 3.02. 5
there be moe wasps that buzz about his nose 3.02. 55
stands in the gap and trade of moe preferments, 5.01. 36
here come moe voices. COR 2.03.125
moe noble blows than ever thou wise words, | and 4.02. 21
what, hath the firmament moe suns than one? TIT 5.03. 17
this day's black fate on moe days doth depend, ROM 3.01.119
look, moe! TIM 1.01. 41
if i would sell my horse and buy twenty moe 2.01. 7
with two stones moe than 's artificial one. 2.02.111 P
moe things like men! 4.03.397
are poison, and he slays | moe than you rob. 4.03.433
no, sir, there are moe with him. JC 2.01. 72
i owe moe tears | to this dead man than you 5.03.101
send out moe horses, skirr the country round, MAC 5.03. 35
i say we will have no moe marriage. HAM 3.01.147 P
why the seven stars are no moe than seven is a LR 1.05. 35 P
get moe tapers; OTH 1.01.166
if i court moe women, you'll couch with moe men. 4.03. 57
i court moe women, you'll couch with moe men." 4.03. 57
it was mine had annex'd unto't | a million moe ANT 4.14. 18
and, as i said, there is no moe such caesars. CYM 3.01. 36 P
that hath moe kings his servants than | thyself 3.01. 63
or hath moe ministers than we | that draw his 5.03. 72
some one | become the public plague of many moe?
LUC 1479
in me moe woes than words are now depending, 1615
found yet moe letters sadly penn'd in blood, LC 47
and laboring in moe pleasures to bestow them 139
MOI *(also moy)*
MOI 4 FR 0.0004 REL FR 0 V 4 P
o, prenez misericorde! ayez pitie de moi! H5 4.04. 12 P
o, pardonnez moi! 4.04. 21 P
et quand vous avez le possession de moi — let 5.02.182 P
your majesty entendre bettre que moi. 5.02.264 P
MOIETY *(also moi'ty)*
MOIETY 1 FR 0.0001 REL FR 1 V 0 P
the clear eye's moiety and the dear heart's part SON 46.12
MOILE *(also mule)*
MOILE 1 FR 0.0001 REL FR 0 V 1 P
to be a /dog, a moile, a cat, a fitchook, a toad TRO 5.01. 61 P
MOIST 13 FR 0.0014 REL FR 12 V 1 P
and with your tears | moist it again, and frame TGV 3.02. 75
moist hesperus hath quench'd her sleepy lamp, AWW 2.01.164
have you not a moist eye, a dry hand, a yellow 2H4 1.02.180 P
tears, | the moist impediments unto my speech, 4.05.139
cut, | bounding between the two moist elements, TRO 1.03. 41
will these moist trees, | that have outliv'd the TIM 4.03.223
and the moist star | upon whose influence HAM 1.01.118
give me your hand. this hand is moist, my lady. OTH 3.04. 36
hot, hot, and moist. 3.04. 39
the juice of egypt's grape shall moist this lip. ANT 5.02.282
the huntress | all moist and cold, some say, TNK 5.01. 93
my smooth moist hand, were it with thy hand felt VEN 143
from his moist cabinet mounts up on high, | and 854
MOIST'NED 2 FR 0.0002 REL FR 2 V 0 P
at their mothers' moist'ned eyes babes shall 1H6 1.01. 49
set, | each flow'r moist'ned like a melting eye, LUC 1227
MOISTURE 4 FR 0.0004 REL FR 4 V 0 P
for all my body's moisture | scarce serves to 3H6 2.01. 79
and calls it heavenly moisture, air of grace, VEN 64
and backward drew | the heavenly moisture, that 542
"o, that infected moisture of his eye, | o, that LC 323
MOI'TY *(also moiety)*
MOI'TY 16 FR 0.0018 REL FR 12 V 4 P
and love, | forgive a moi'ty of the principal, MV 4.01. 26
griefs are thine, | thou robb'st me of a moi'ty. AWW 3.02. 66
a moi'ty of my rest | might come to me again. WT 2.03. 8
bed, which owe | a moi'ty of the throne, a great 3.02. 39
well, give me the moi'ty. 4.04.812 P
methinks my moi'ty, north from burton here, | in 1H4 3.01. 95
and for my english moi'ty, take the word of a H5 5.02.215 P
on me, whose all not equals edward's moi'ty? R3 1.02.249
have i | (thine being but a moi'ty of my moan) 2.02. 60
the other moi'ty ere you ask is given; H8 1.02. 12
betimes | a moi'ty of that mass of moan to come. TRO 2.02.107
a moi'ty competent | was gaged by our king, HAM 1.01. 90
in neither can make choice of either's moi'ty. LR 1.01. 7 P
doom, in the name lay | a moi'ty of the world. ANT 5.01. 19
thereupon pawn the moi'ty of my estate to your CYM 1.04.108 P
where we shall find | the moi'ty of a number, TNK 1.01.214
MOLDWARP 1 FR 0.0001 REL FR 1 V 0 P
with telling me of the moldwarp and the ant, 1H4 3.01.147
MOLE* 10 FR 0.0011 REL FR 9 V 1 P
that the blind mole may not | hear a foot fall; TMP 4.01.194
the mark of my shoulder, the mole in my neck, ERR 3.02.143 P
never mole, hare-lip, nor scar, | nor mark MND 5.01.411
my father had a mole upon his brow. TN 5.01.242
that for some vicious mole of nature in them, HAM 1.04. 24
well said, old mole, canst work i' th' earth so 1.05.162
on her left breast | a mole cinque-spotted, like CYM 2.02. 38
(worthy her pressing) lies a mole, right proud 2.04.135
guiderius had | upon his neck a mole, a sanguine 5.05.364
the blind mole casts | copp'd hills towards PER 1.01.100
MOLEHILL 3 FR 0.0003 REL FR 3 V 0 P
come make him stand upon this molehill here 3H6 1.04. 67
here on this molehill will i sit me down. 2.05. 14
bows, | as if olympus to a molehill should | in COR 5.03. 30
MOLES* 2 FR 0.0002 REL FR 1 V 1 P
i will bring these two moles, these blind ones, WT 4.04.836 P
patch'd with foul moles and eye-offending marks,
JN 3.01. 47
MOLEST 2 FR 0.0002 REL FR 2 V 0 P
candied be they, | and melt ere they molest! TMP 2.01.280
who doth molest my contemplation? TIT 5.02. 9
MOLESTATION 1 FR 0.0001 REL FR 1 V 0 P
i never did like molestation view | on the OTH 2.01. 16
MOLLIFICATION 1 FR 0.0001 REL FR 0 V 1 P
some mollification for your giant, sweet lady. TN 1.05.204 P
MOLLIS 2 FR 0.0002 REL FR 2 V 0 P
which we call mollis aer, and mollis aer | we CYM 5.05.447
mollis aer, and mollis aer | we term it mulier; 5.05.447
MOLTEN 3 FR 0.0003 REL FR 2 V 1 P
i am as hot as molten lead, and as heavy too. 1H4 5.03. 33 P
let molten coin be thy damnation, | thou disease TIM 3.01. 52
that mine own tears | do scald like molten lead. LR 4.07. 47
MOLTO 1 FR 0.0001 REL FR 0 V 1 P
ben venuto, molto honorato signor mio petruchio.
SHR 1.02. 25 P
MOME 1 FR 0.0001 REL FR 1 V 0 P
mome, malt-horse, capon, coxcomb, idiot, patch! ERR 3.01. 32
/MOMENT 1 FR 0.0001 REL FR 1 V 0 P
/but /in /this /extant /moment, /faith /and TRO 4.05.168
MOMENT 32 FR 0.0036 REL FR 28 V 4 P
but go to hell for an eternal moment or so, i WIV 2.01. 50 P
when in that moment (so it came to pass) MND 3.02. 33
wrastler, which charles in a moment threw him, AYL 1.02.127 P
capable impressure | thy palm some moment keeps; 3.05. 24
his incensement at this moment is so implacable, TN 3.04.238 P
then, in a moment, fortune shall cull forth JN 2.01.391
yea, at that very moment, | consideration like H5 1.01. 27
in a moment look to see | the blind and bloody 3.03. 33
what towns of any moment but we have? 1H6 1.02. 5
towns, | and in a moment makes them desolate. 2.03. 66
who in a moment even with the earth | shall lay 4.02. 12
an oath is of no moment, being not took | before 3H6 1.02. 22
in deep designs, in matter of great moment, | no R3 3.07. 67
then, in a moment, see | how soon this H8 pr 29
hour | to hear from him a matter of some moment; 1.02.163
bearing a state of mighty moment in't | and 2.04.214
lord, because we have business of more moment, 5.02. 86
his value — on the moment | follow his strides, TIM 1.01. 79
and furious, | loyal, and neutral, in a moment? MAC 2.03.109
the moment on't, for't must be done to-night, 3.01.130
from this moment | the very firstlings of my 4.01.146
have you so slander any moment leisure | as to HAM 1.03.133
and enterprises of great pitch and moment | with 3.01. 85
in our dominions, | the moment is thy death. LR 1.01.178
to th' very moment that he bade me tell it; OTH 1.03.133
something of moment then. 3.04.138
her die twenty times upon far poorer moment. ANT 1.02.142 P
and yet of moment too, for it concerns: CYM 1.06.182
which in a moment doth confound and kill | all LUC 250
even in the moment that we call them ours. 868
grows | holds in perfection but a little moment; SON 15. 2
her eye | upon the moment did her force subdue, LC 248
MOMENTANY 1 FR 0.0001 REL FR 1 V 0 P
siege to it, | making it momentany as a sound, MND 1.01.143
MOMENTARY 6 FR 0.0006 REL FR 6 V 0 P
more momentary | and sight-outrunning were not;
TMP 1.02.202
why would he for the momentary trick | be MM 3.01.113
o momentary grace of mortal men, | which we more
R3 3.04. 96
the fit is momentary, upon a thought | he will MAC 3.04. 54
whose title is as momentary | as to us death is TNK 5.04. 17
this momentary joy breeds months of pain, | this LUC 690
MOMENTARY-SWIFT 1 FR 0.0001 REL FR 1 V 0 P
with wings more momentary-swift than thought. TRO 4.02. 14
MOMENT'S 1 FR 0.0001 REL FR 1 V 0 P
one fading moment's mirth | with twenty watchful TGV 1.01. 30
MON 5 FR 0.0005 REL FR 0 V 5 P
oui, mette le au mon pocket; WIV 1.04. 54 P
du monde, mon tres cher et devin deesse? H5 5.02.217 P
dat is as it shall please de roi mon pere. 5.02.247 P
laissez, mon seigneur, laissez, laissez! 5.02.253 P
je vous supplie, mon tres puissant seigneur. 5.02.256 P
MONACHUM 2 FR 0.0002 REL FR 0 V 2 P
cucullus non facit monachum: MM 5.01.262 P
lady, "cucullus non facit monachum": TN 1.05. 56 P
MONARCH 17 FR 0.0019 REL FR 12 V 5 P
my fair, sweet, honey monarch, for, i protest, LLL 5.02.528 P
true subjects bow | to a new-crowned monarch; MV 3.02. 50
the throned monarch better than his crown. 4.01.189
and you, monarch! AWW 1.01.107 P
that, were i crown'd the most imperial monarch, WT 4.04.372
know the gallant monarch is in arms, | and like JN 5.02.148
never was monarch better fear'd and lov'd | than H5 2.02. 25
his neigh is like the bidding of a monarch, and 3.07. 28 P
a private displeasure can do against a monarch! 4.01.199 P
under the lordly monarch of the north, | appear, 1H6 5.03. 6
hath that poor monarch taught thee to insult? 3H6 1.04.124
it seems | as may beseem a monarch like himself. 3.03.122
the greatest monarch now alive may glory | in H8 5.02.198
crown'd | sole monarch of the universal earth. ROM 3.02. 94
her husband a cuckold to make him a monarch? OTH 4.03. 77 P
the ground, i was | a morsel for a monarch; ANT 1.05. 31
come, thou monarch of the vine, | plumpy bacchus 2.07.113
MONARCHIES 1 FR 0.0001 REL FR 1 V 0 P
walls | are now confin'd two mighty monarchies, H5 pr 20
MONARCHIZE 1 FR 0.0001 REL FR 1 V 0 P
to monarchize, be fear'd, and kill with looks, R2 3.02.165
MONARCHO 1 FR 0.0001 REL FR 1 V 0 P
a phantasime, a monarcho, and one that makes LLL 4.01. 99
MONARCH'S 4 FR 0.0004 REL FR 4 V 0 P
that man that sits within a monarch's heart 2H4 4.02. 11
shall in these confines with a monarch's voice JC 3.01.272
drink up the monarch's plague, this flattery? SON 114. 2
or monarch's hands that lets not bounty fall LC 41
/MONARCHS 1 FR 0.0001 REL FR 0 V 1 P
/and /our /monarchs /and /outstretch'd /heroes HAM 2.02.263 P
MONARCHS 6 FR 0.0006 REL FR 5 V 1 P
and monarchs to behold the swelling scene! H5 pr 4
your brother kings and monarchs of the earth 1.02.122
of england than a general petition of monarchs. 5.02.279 P
the gates of monarchs | are arch'd so high that CYM 3.03. 4
who has a book of all that monarchs do, | he's PER 1.01. 94
but happy monarchs still are fear'd for love; LUC 611
MONARCHY 6 FR 0.0006 REL FR 6 V 0 P
inherit but the fall | of the last monarchy) see AWW 2.01. 14
them know | of what a monarchy you are the head.
H5 2.04. 73
left me | contenteth me, and worth a monarchy. 2H6 4.10. 19
are mighty gossips in our monarchy. R3 1.01. 83
can this dark monarchy afford false clarence?" 1.04. 51
free, | and reign'd commanding in his monarchy. LC 196
MONASTERY 2 FR 0.0002 REL FR 1 V 1 P
perchance entering into some monastery, but, by MM 4.02.202 P
i stray'd | to gaze upon a ruinous monastery, TIT 5.01. 21
MONASTIC 1 FR 0.0001 REL FR 0 V 1 P
the world and to live in a nook merely monastic. AYL 3.02.421 P
MONAST'RY 2 FR 0.0002 REL FR 2 V 0 P
there is a monast'ry two miles off, | and there MV 3.04. 31
at chertsey monast'ry this noble king, | and wet R3 1.02.214
MONDAY 7 FR 0.0008 REL FR 2 V 5 P
not till monday, my dear son, which is hence a ADO 2.01.359 P
"for he swore a thing to me on monday night, 5.01.168 P
a-bleeding on black monday last at six a' clock MV 2.05. 25 P
snatch'd on monday night and most dissolutely 1H4 1.02. 34 P
monday, my lord. ROM 3.04. 18
monday! 3.04. 19
sir, a' monday morning, 'twas then indeed. HAM 2.02.388 P
MONDE 2 FR 0.0002 REL FR 0 V 2 P

les seigneurs de france pour tout le monde. H5 3.04. 56 P
la plus belle katherine du monde, mon tres cher 5.02.217 P
/MONEY 2 FR 0.0002 REL FR 0 V 2 P
/for /a /while /no /money /bid /for /argument, HAM 2.02.354 P
/put /money /enough /in /your /purse. OTH 1.03.380 P
MONEY 175 FR 0.0197 REL FR 81 V 94 P
will money buy 'em? TMP 5.01.265
that the money and the matter may be both at TGV 1.01.129 P
when you look'd sadly, it was for want of money: 2.01. 30 P
hold, there's money for thee. WIV 1.04.156 P
liquor in his pate, or money in his purse, when 2.01.190 P
after the expense of so much money, be now a 2.02.141 P
for they say, if money go before, all ways do 2.02.168 P
money is a good soldier, sir, and will on. 2.02.170 P
and i have a bag of money here troubles me. 2.02.171 P
there is money, spend it, spend it; 2.02.232 P
/brook, i will first make bold with your money; 2.02.253 P
want no money, sir john, you shall want none. 2.02.258 P
the jealous wittolly knave hath masses of money, 2.02.272 P
with her for more money than i'll speak of. 3.02. 56 P
i like his money well. 3.05. 58 P
maidenhead, of colebrook, of horses and money. 4.05. 79 P
and twenty pounds of money, which must be paid 5.05.113 P
master /brook that you have cozen'd of money, to 5.05.167 P
i think to repay that money will be a biting 5.05.169 P
money buys lands, and wives are sold by fate. 5.05.233
i do it for some piece of money, and go through MM 2.01.270 P
pounds, of which he made five marks ready money. 4.03. 7 P
there is your money that i had to keep. ERR 1.02. 8
where have you left the money that i gave you? 1.02. 54
tell me, and dally not, where is the money? 1.02. 59
in what safe place you have bestow'd my money; 1.02. 78
the villain is o'erraught of all my money. 1.02. 96
i greatly fear my money is not safe. 1.02.105
to save the money that he spends in /tiring; 2.02. 97 P
you, | and then receive my money for the chain. 3.02.175
i pray you, sir, receive the money now, | for 3.02.176
for fear you ne'er see chain nor money more. 3.02.177
clock | i shall receive the money for the same: 4.01. 11
i am not furnish'd with the present money: 4.01. 34
or else you may return without your money. 4.01. 44
why, give it to my wife, and fetch your money. 4.01. 54
the money that you owe me for the chain. 4.01. 63
mistress, redemption, the money in his desk? 4.02. 46
go, dromio, there's the money, bear it straight, 4.02. 63
some tender money to me, some invite me; 4.03. 4
i'll give thee, ere i leave thee, so much money, 4.04. 2
i think he brings the money. 4.04. 8
but where's the money? 4.04. 11
why, sir, i gave the money for the rope. 4.04. 12
alas, i sent you money to redeem you, | by 4.04. 83
money by me? 4.04. 85
might, | but surely, master, not a rag of money. 4.04. 86
i sent you money, sir, to be your bail, | by 5.01.382
uncle, and money enough in his purse, such a man ADO 2.01. 15 P
well, a horn for my money, when all's done. 2.03. 60 P
if he be sad, he wants money. 3.02. 20 P
hanging by it, and borrows money in god's name, 5.01.310 P
withal, | and have the money by our father lent, LLL 2.01.147
antonio, | i owe the most, in money and in love, MV 1.01.131
neither have i money nor commodity | to raise a 1.01.178
where money is, and i no question make | to have 1.01.184
in low simplicity | he lends out money gratis, 1.03. 44
should i not say, | "hath a dog money? 1.03.121
if thou wilt lend this money, lend it not | as 1.03.132
he was wont to lend money for a christian cur'sy 3.01. 49 P
he had | the present money to discharge the jew, 3.02.273
this is the fool that lent out money gratis! 3.03. 2
shortly have a rasher on the coals for money. 3.05. 26 P
is he not able to discharge the money? 4.01.208
shylock, there's thrice thy money off'red thee. 4.01.227
take thrice thy money, bid me tear the bond. 4.01.234
here is the money. 4.01.319
for i think you have no money in your purse. AYL 2.04. 13 P
and that he that wants money, means, and content 3.02. 25 P
take her with all faults, and money enough. SHR 1.01.130 P
why, nothing comes amiss, so money comes withal. 1.02. 82 P
for i have bills for money by exchange | from 4.02. 89
so that you had her wrinkles and i her money, i AWW 2.04. 20 P
and i begin to love, as an old man loves money, 3.02. 16 P
thou hadst need send for more money. TN 2.03.183 P
send for money, knight; 2.03.186 P
i must entreat of you some of that money. 3.04.340
what money, sir? 3.04.341
i dare lay any money 'twill be nothing yet. 3.04.396 P
there's money for thee. 4.01. 19
men that give fools money get themselves a good 4.01. 22 P
you can fool no more money out of me at this 5.01. 41 P
honest friend, | will you take eggs for money? WT 1.02.161
my money and apparel ta'en from me, and these 4.03. 61 P
dost lack any money? 4.03. 77 P
i have a little money for thee. 4.03. 77 P
i shall there have money, or any thing i want. 4.03. 82 P
offer me no money, i pray you, that kills my 4.03. 82 P
several tunes faster than you'll tell money; 4.04.184 P
thou shouldst take no money of me, but being 4.04.232 P
i was cozen'd by the way and lost all my money? 4.04.252 P
dreading the curse that money may buy out, | and JN 3.01.164
his plate, his goods, his money, and his lands. R2 2.01.210
he hath not money for these irish wars, | his 2.01.259
how shall we do for money for these wars? 2.02.104
there's money of the king's coming down the hill 1H4 2.02. 54 P
your money! 2.02.102 P
by the lord, lads, i am glad you have the money. 2.04.276 P
the money shall be paid back again with 2.04.547 P
of an hour, paid money that i borrow'd — three 3.03. 18 P
ball of wildfire, there's no purchase in money. 3.03. 40 P
know you, sir john, you owe me money, sir john, 3.03. 66 P
you owe money here besides, sir john, for your 3.03. 72 P
your diet and by-drinkings, and money lent you, 3.03. 73 P
the money is paid back again. 3.03.178 P
receive | money and order for their furniture. 3.03.202
will you give me money, captain? 4.02. 4 P
for a thousand marks, let him lend me the money, 2H4 1.02.194 P
what money is in my purse? 1.02.234 P
wert an honest man, thyself and the money too. 2.01. 86 P
the one you may do with sterling money, and the 2.01.120 P
i shall receive money a' thursday, shalt have a 2.04.275 P
for th' other, i owe her money, and whether she 2.04.339 P
him well, and betted much money on his head. 3.02. 45 P
master's command transporting a sum of money, be H5 4.01.152 P
i will none of your money. 4.08. 67 P
no treachery, but want of men and money. 1H6 1.01. 69
gall — | nor men nor money hath he to make war. 1.02. 17
men | that come to gather money for their corn. 3.02. 5
receive | the sum of money which i promised 5.01. 52
will keep me here | without discharge, money, or 2H6 1.03.169
and here, tom, take all the money that i have. 2.03. 76 P
levy great sums of money through the realm | for 3.01. 61
you, good people — there shall be no money; 4.02. 73 P
henry hath money, you are strong and manly; 4.08. 51
give | their money out of hope they may believe, H8 pr 8
the wars for my money! COR 4.05.232 P
mean while here's money for thy charges. TIT 4.03.105
how much money must i have? 4.04. 46 P
no money, on my faith, but the gleek; ROM 4.05.114 P
good even, varro. what, | you come for money? TIM 2.02. 10
found time to use 'em toward a supply of money. 2.02.192 P
that this is no time to lend money, especially 3.01. 42 P
he cannot want for money. 3.02. 9 P
some small kindnesses from him, as money, plate, 3.02. 21 P
timon's money | has paid his men their wages. 3.02. 69
for mine | is money. 3.04. 5
your lord sends now for money. 3.04. 18
of timon's gift, | for which i wait for money. 3.04. 20
wear rich jewels | and send for money for 'em. 3.04. 24
we wait for certain money here, sir. 3.04. 46
ay, | if money were as certain as your waiting, 3.04. 47
our masters may throw their caps at their money. 3.04.101 P
while they have told their money, and let out 3.05.106
not that, if money and the season can yield it. 3.06. 50 P
stay, i will lend thee money, borrow none. 3.06.101
more counsel with more money, bounteous timon. 4.03.167
for i can raise no money by vile means. JC 4.03. 71
give him this money and these notes, reynaldo. HAM 2.01. 1
there's money for thee. LR 4.06.131
eyes in your head, nor no money in your purse? 4.06.146 P
put money in thy purse; OTH 1.03.339 P
i say put money in thy purse. 1.03.341 P
love to the moor — put money in thy purse — 1.03.343 P
sequestration — put but money in thy purse. 1.03.346 P
in their wills — fill thy purse with money. 1.03.347 P
therefore put money in thy purse. 1.03.352 P
make all the money thou canst. 1.03.354 P
therefore make money. 1.03.358 P
thou art sure of me — go make money. 1.03.364 P
traverse, go, provide thy money. 1.03.371 P
my money is almost spent; 2.03.364 P
so, with no money at all and a little more wit, 2.03.368 P
but, masters, here's money for you; 3.01. 11 P
there's money for thy pains. 4.02. 93
caesar gets money where | he loses hearts. ANT 2.01. 13
of money, plate, and jewels | i am possess'd of; 5.02.138
here's money for my meat, | i would have left it CYM 3.06. 49
money, youth? 3.06. 52
fool, an empty purse, | there was no money in't. 4.02.114
we lost too much money this mart by being too PER 4.02. 4 P
my masters, you shall have your money presently. 4.02. 54 P
and have not money enough in the end to buy him 4.06.172 P
much follow'd both, for both much money gi'n, TNK pr 2
has given a sum of money to her marriage, | a 4.01. 23
MONEY-BAGS 2 FR 0.0002 REL FR 1 V 1 P
rest, | for i did dream of money-bags to-night. MV 2.05. 18
to bed of twenty money-bags at a burthen, and WT 4.04.263 P
MONEY'D 1 FR 0.0001 REL FR 1 V 0 P
the doctor is well money'd, and his friends WIV 4.04. 88
MONEY'S 2 FR 0.0002 REL FR 2 V 0 P
us, | although not valued to the money's worth. LLL 2.01.136
come to the pedlar, | money's a meddler, | that WT 4.04.322
MONEYS 7 FR 0.0008 REL FR 6 V 1 P
and seven hundred pounds of moneys, and gold, WIV 1.01. 51 P
have rated me | about my moneys and my usances. MV 1.03.108
"shylock, we would have moneys," you say so — 1.03.116
moneys is your suit. 1.03.119
courtesies | i'll lend you thus much moneys"? 1.03.129
and take no doit | of usance for my moneys, and 1.03.141
importune him for my moneys, be not ceas'd TIM 2.01. 16
'MONG *(also among, etc.)*
'MONG 4 FR 0.0004 REL FR 3 V 1 P
no marrying 'mong his subjects? TMP 2.01.166 P
'mong other things | i shall disgest it. MV 3.05. 89
councillor, | 'mong boys, grooms, and lackeys. H8 5.02. 18
that timon's fortunes 'mong his friends can sink TIM 2.02.231
MONGREL *(also mongril, mungrel, etc., mungril)*
MONGREL 1 FR 0.0001 REL FR 0 V 1 P
greece upon thee, thou mongrel beef-witted lord! TRO 2.01. 13 P
MONGRIL 2 FR 0.0002 REL FR 1 V 1 P
set me up, in policy, that mongril cur, ajax, TRO 5.04. 13 P
mastiff, greyhound, mongril grim, | hound or LR 3.06. 68
'MONGST *(also amongst)*
'MONGST 22 FR 0.0024 REL FR 22 V 0 P
you 'mongst men | being most unfit to live. TMP 3.03. 57
'mongst all foes that a friend should be the TGV 5.04. 72
i may have welcome 'mongst the rest that woo, SHR 2.01. 96
mind too, 'mongst all colors | no yellow in't, WT 2.03.106
whom fair befall in heaven 'mongst happy souls, R2 2.01.129
inquire at london, 'mongst the taverns there, 5.03. 5
great fear of my name 'mongst them were spread 1H6 1.04. 50
she vaunted 'mongst her minions t' other day, 2H6 1.03. 84
who was enroll'd 'mongst wonders, and when we, H8 1.02.119
who holds his state at door 'mongst pursuivants, 5.02. 24
every tithe soul, 'mongst many thousand dismes, TRO 2.02. 19
emulous missions 'mongst the gods themselves, 3.03.189
a woeful cressid 'mongst the merry greeks! 4.04. 56
that like the stately /phoebe 'mongst her nymphs TIT 1.01.316
for all thy living | is 'mongst the dead, and TIM 1.02.224
rest, and 'mongst lords /i be thought a fool. 3.03. 21
now 'mongst this flock of drunkards | am i to OTH 2.03. 59
he sits 'mongst men like a /descended god; CYM 1.06.169
be sprightly, for you fall 'mongst friends. 3.06. 74
'mongst friends? 3.06. 74
ripp'd, | came crying 'mongst his foes, | a 5.04. 46
tak'st, | 'mongst our mourners shalt thou go. PHT 20
MONK 6 FR 0.0006 REL FR 6 V 0 P
the king, i fear, is poison'd by a monk. JN 5.06. 23
a monk, i tell you, a resolved villain, | whose 5.06. 29
a monk o' th' chartreux. H8 1.01.221
certain words | spoke by a holy monk "that oft," 1.02.160
devil's illusions | the monk might be deceiv'd, 1.02.179
car, | confessor to him, with that devil monk, 2.01. 21
MONKEY 7 FR 0.0008 REL FR 3 V 4 P
thou liest, thou jesting monkey thou! TMP 3.02. 45
on meddling monkey, or on busy ape), | she shall MND 2.01.181
ring that he had of your daughter for a monkey. MV 3.01.119 P
an ape, more giddy in my desires than a monkey. AYL 4.01.153 P
genius of famine, yet lecherous as a monkey, and 2H4 3.02.314 P
of man's bred out | into baboon and monkey. TIM 1.01.251
now, god help thee, poor monkey! MAC 4.02. 59 P
MONKEY'S 1 FR 0.0001 REL FR 0 V 1 P
this is the monkey's own giving out. OTH 4.01.127 P
MONKEYS 5 FR 0.0005 REL FR 3 V 2 P
not have given it for a wilderness of monkeys. MV 3.01.123 P
and bears by th' neck, monkeys by th' loins, and LR 2.04. 9 P
were they as prime as goats, as hot as monkeys, OTH 3.03.403
goats and monkeys! 4.01.263
for apes and monkeys | 'twixt two such shes CYM 1.06. 39
MONKS 1 FR 0.0001 REL FR 1 V 0 P
but all hoods make not monks. H8 3.01. 23
MONMOUTH 14 FR 0.0015 REL FR 7 V 7 P
short breath to-day | but i and harry monmouth! 1H4 5.02. 49
if i mistake not, thou art harry monmouth. 5.04. 59
to noise abroad that harry monmouth fell | under 2H4 in 29
to harry monmouth, whose swift wrath beat down 1.01.109
against the welsh, himself and harry monmouth; 1.03. 83
ay, he was porn at monmouth, captain gower. H5 4.07. 11 P
in the comparisons between macedon and monmouth, 4.07. 25 P
and there is also moreover a river at monmouth. 4.07. 27 P
it is call'd wye at monmouth; 4.07. 28 P
so also harry monmouth, being in his right wits 4.07. 46 P
tell you there is good men porn at monmouth. 4.07. 53 P
wearing leeks in their monmouth caps, which, 4.07.100 P
since henry monmouth first began to reign, 1H6 2.05. 23
that henry born at monmouth should win all, 3.01.197
/MONMOUTH'S 1 FR 0.0001 REL FR 1 V 0 P
/neck, | /have /talk'd /of /monmouth's /grave. 2H4 2.03. 45
MONMOUTH'S 2 FR 0.0002 REL FR 1 V 1 P
and harry monmouth's brawn, the hulk sir john, 2H4 1.01. 19
well, harry of monmouth's life is come after it H5 4.07. 32 P
/MONOPOLY 1 FR 0.0001 REL FR 0 V 1 P
/if /i /had /a /monopoly /out, /they /would LR 1.04.153 P
MONS 1 FR 0.0001 REL FR 0 V 1 P
or mons, the hill. LLL 5.01. 84 P
MONSIEUR *(also mounseur, mounsieur)*
/MONSIEUR 1 FR 0.0001 REL FR 0 V 1 P
/the /marshal /of /france, /monsieur /la /far. LR 4.03. 8 P
MONSIEUR 39 FR 0.0044 REL FR 8 V 31 P
we'll not run, monsieur monster. TMP 3.02. 18 P
the prince and monsieur love! ADO 2.03. 36 P
a gallant lady. monsieur, fare you well. LLL 2.01.196
have a letter from monsieur berowne to one lady 4.01. 53
ay, sir, from one monsieur berowne, one of the 4.02.129 P
monsieur, are you not lett'red? 5.01. 44 P
this is the ape of form, monsieur the nice, 5.02.325
a light for monsieur judas! 5.02.630
say you by the french lord, monsieur le /bon? MV 1.02. 54 P
good monsieur charles, what's the new news at AYL 1.01. 96 P
here comes monsieur /le beau. 1.02. 91 P
bon jour, monsieur le beau. 1.02. 97 P
but what is the sport, monsieur, that the ladies 1.02.134 P
call him hither, good monsieur le beau. 1.02.163 P
monsieur the challenger, the princess calls for 1.02.165 P
it will make you melancholy, monsieur jaques. 2.05. 10 P
what you will, monsieur jaques. 2.05. 20 P
why, how now, monsieur, what a life is this, 2.07. 9
adieu, good monsieur melancholy. 3.02.294 P
farewell, monsieur traveller: 4.01. 33 P
monsieur parolles, my lord calls for you. AWW 1.01.187 P
monsieur parolles, you were born under a 1.01.190 P
sweet monsieur parolles! 2.01. 39 P
do you hear, monsieur? a word with you. 2.03.184 P
unkindness between my lord and you, monsieur? 2.05. 33 P
farewell, monsieur! 2.05. 46 P
where are my other men, monsieur? 2.05. 89
monsieur parolles. 3.05. 58
how now, monsieur? 3.06. 44 P
why, if you have a stomach, to't, monsieur: 3.06. 64 P
my lord, this is monsieur parolles, the gallant 4.03.140 P
for monsieur malvolio, let me alone with him. TN 2.03.133 P
dieu vous garde, monsieur. 3.01. 71 P
what says monsieur remorse? 1H4 1.02.113 P
monsieur le fer. H5 4.04. 26 P
que dit-il, monsieur? 4.04. 33 P
petit monsieur, que dit-il? 4.04. 49 P
one | an eminent monsieur that, it seems, much CYM 1.06. 65
who, monsieur verollus? PER 4.02.106 P
MONSIEURS 1 FR 0.0001 REL FR 1 V 0 P
now i would pray our monsieurs | to think an H8 1.03. 21
MONSTER 70 FR 0.0079 REL FR 21 V 49 P
there would this monster make a man; TMP 2.02. 30 P
this is some monster of the isle with four legs, 2.02. 65 P
a most delicate monster! 2.02. 90 P
this is a devil, and no monster. 2.02. 98 P
this good light, this is a very shallow monster! 2.02.145 P
a very weak monster! 2.02.145 P
a most poor credulous monster! 2.02.146 P
well drawn, monster, in good sooth! 2.02.147 P
light, a most perfidious and drunken monster! 2.02.151 P
myself to death at this puppy-headed monster. 2.02.155 P
a most scurvy monster! 2.02.155 P
an abominable monster! 2.02.159 P
a most ridiculous monster, to make a wonder of a 2.02.165 P
a howling monster; a drunken monster! 2.02.179 P
a howling monster; a drunken monster! 2.02.179 P
o brave monster! lead the way. 2.02.188 P
he were a brave monster indeed if they were set 3.02. 11 P
thou shalt be my lieutenant, monster, or my 3.02. 16 P
we'll not run, monsieur monster. 3.02. 18 P
thou liest, most ignorant monster, i am in case 3.02. 25 P
lie, being but half a fish and half a monster? 3.02. 29 P

that a monster should be such a natural! 3.02. 32 P
interrupt the monster one word further, and, by 3.02. 69 P
a murrain on your monster, and the devil take 3.02. 80 P
monster, i will kill this man. 3.02.106 P
at thy request, monster, i will do reason, any 3.02.119 P
no, monster, not i. 3.02.134 P
lead, monster, we'll follow. 3.02.150 P
monster, your fairy, which you say is a harmless 4.01.196 P
monster, i do smell all horse–piss, at which my 4.01.199 P
do you hear, monster? 4.01.201 P
thou wert but a lost monster. 4.01.203 P
not only disgrace and dishonor in that, monster, 4.01.210 P
yet this is your harmless fairy, monster! 4.01.212 P
o, ho, monster! 4.01.225 P
be you quiet, monster. 4.01.235 P
monster, come put some lime upon your fingers, 4.01.245 P
monster, lay–to your fingers. 4.01.250 P
i will show you a monster. WIV 3.02. 81 P
have with you to see this monster. 3.02. 92 P
o thou monster ignorance, how deformed dost thou LLL 4.02. 23
no marvel though demetrius | do, as a monster, MND 2.02. 97
my mistress with a monster is in love. 3.02. 6
and when i break that oath, let me turn monster. AYL 1.02. 22 P
a monster, a very monster in apparel, and not SHR 3.02. 69 P
a monster, a very monster in apparel, and not 3.02. 70 P
and i (poor monster) fond as much on him; TN 2.02. 34
break the back of man, the heart of monster. WT 4.04.770 P
your lion's hide, | and make a monster of you. JN 2.01.293
dust, | and be a carrion monster like thyself. 3.04. 33
that the blunt monster with uncounted heads, 2H4 in 18
the avaunt, it is a pity | would move a monster. H8 2.03. 11
cupid's pageant there is presented no monster. TRO 3.02. 75 P
a great–siz'd monster of ingratitudes. 3.03.147
grown a very land–fish, languageless, a monster. 3.03.263 P
were to make a monster of the multitude; COR 2.03. 11 P
had the monster seen those lily hands | tremble TIT 2.04. 44
and that the lean abhorred monster keeps | thee ROM 5.03.104
hang thee, monster! TIM 4.03. 88
that monster custom, who all sense doth eat, HAM 3.04.161
he cannot be such a monster — LR 1.02. 94 P
to take't again perforce! monster ingratitude! 1.05. 39 P
as if there were some monster in thy thought OTH 3.03.107
it is the green–ey'd monster which doth mock 3.03.166
it is a monster | begot upon itself, born on 3.04.161
heaven keep the monster from othello's mind! 3.04.163
a horned man's a monster and a beast. 4.01. 62
in a populous city, | and many a civil monster. 4.01. 64
being an ugly monster, | 'tis strange he hides CYM 5.03. 70
that monster envy, oft the wrack | of earned PER 4.ch. 12

MONSTER'D 1 FR 0.0001 REL FR 1 V 0 P
than idly sit | to hear my nothings monster'd. COR 2.02. 77

MONSTER–LIKE 1 FR 0.0001 REL FR 1 V 0 P
most monster–like, be shown | for poor'st ANT 4.12. 36

MONSTER'S 5 FR 0.0005 REL FR 3 V 2 P
o, 'twas a din to fright a monster's ear, | to TMP 2.01.314
but that the poor monster's in drink. 2.02.158 P
the poor monster's my subject, and he shall not 3.02. 36 P
her charmed eye release | from monster's view, MND 3.02.377
being but | the horn and noise o' th' monster's, COR 3.01. 95

/MONSTERS 2 FR 0.0002 REL FR 2 V 0 P
/of /death, | /women /will /all /turn /monsters. LR 3.07.102
/on /itself, | /like /monsters /of /the /deep. 4.02. 50

MONSTERS 11 FR 0.0012 REL FR 9 V 2 P
i wonder, sir, /sith wives are monsters to you, AWW 5.03.155
and my noble peers, | these english monsters! H5 2.02. 85
and the act of hares, are they not monsters? TRO 3.02. 89 P
teem with new monsters, whom thy upward face TIM 4.03.190
we'll have thee, as our rarer monsters are, MAC 5.08. 25
know well enough what monsters you make of them. HAM 3.01.138 P
be of such unnatural degree | that monsters it, LR 1.01.220
write you not | what monsters her accuse? CYM 3.02. 2
th' imperious seas breeds monsters; 4.02. 35
and | such things to be, mere monsters. TNK 1.02. 42
to make of monsters and things indigest | such SON 114. 5

MONSTROUS 65 FR 0.0073 REL FR 47 V 18 P
wilt thou tell a monstrous lie, being but half a TMP 3.02. 28 P
who, though they are of monstrous shape, yet, 3.03. 31
o, it is monstrous! 3.03. 95
monstrous! 3.03. 95
that's monstrous. o, that that were out! TGV 3.01.365 P
i'll speak in a monstrous little voice, "thisne! MND 1.02. 52 P
o monstrous! 3.01.104 P
the smallest monstrous mouse that creeps on 5.01.220
are, every one fault seeming monstrous till his AYL 3.02.355 P
o monstrous beast, how like a swine he lies! SHR in.1. 34
o monstrous arrogance! 4.03.107
o monstrous villain! 5.01.109 P
skill infinite or monstrous desperate. AWW 2.01.184
an answer of most monstrous size that must fit 2.02. 32 P
poor trespasses, | more monstrous standing by; WT 3.02.190
is all as monstrous to our human reason | as my 5.01. 41
thou monstrous slanderer of heaven and earth! JN 2.01.173
thou monstrous injurer of heaven and earth, 2.01.174
o monstrous! 1H4 2.04.219 P
before, i blush'd to hear his monstrous devices. 2.04.313 P
sheriff with a most monstrous watch is at the 2.04.483 P
o monstrous! 2.04.540 P
a huge half–moon, a monstrous /cantle out. 3.01. 99
curling their monstrous heads and hanging them 2H4 3.01. 23
crowd us and crush us to this monstrous form 4.02. 34
o monstrous treachery! 1H6 4.01. 61
so bad a death argues a monstrous life. 2H6 3.03. 30
o monstrous! 4.02. 87 P
o monstrous coward! what, to come behind folks? 4.07. 83 P
cade that i have slain, that monstrous traitor? 4.10. 66
and fight against that monstrous rebel cade, 5.01. 62
o monstrous traitor! 5.01.106
o monstrous fault, to harbor such a thought! 3H6 3.02.164
o monstrous, monstrous! R3 3.02. 64
o monstrous, monstrous! 3.02. 64
and this is edward's wife, that monstrous witch, 3.04. 70
hath into monstrous habits put the graces | that H8 1.02.122
nor nothing monstrous neither? TRO 3.02. 76 P
ingratitude is monstrous, and for the multitude COR 2.03. 9 P
should bring ourselves to be monstrous members. 2.03. 12 P
o monstrous! what reproachful words are these? TIT 1.01.308
shall i endure this monstrous villainy? 4.04. 51
this ingrateful seat | of monstrous friends; TIM 4.02. 46
cover | the monstrous bulk of this ingratitude 5.01. 65
marry, 'tis not monstrous in you, neither wish i 5.01. 88
to monstrous quality — why, you shall find JC 1.03. 68
of fear and warning | unto some monstrous state. 1.03. 71
dark enough | to mask thy monstrous visage? 2.01. 81
eyes | that shapes this monstrous apparition. 4.03.277
how monstrous | it was for malcolm and for MAC 3.06. 8
is it not monstrous that this player here, | but HAM 2.02.551
trice of time | commit a thing so monstrous, to LR 1.01.217
why, what a monstrous fellow art thou, thus to 2.02. 25 P
most monstrous! o! | know'st thou this paper? 5.03.160
must bring this monstrous birth to the world's OTH 1.03.404
wind–shak'd surge, with high and monstrous mane, 2.01. 13
'tis monstrous. 2.03.217
o monstrous world! 3.03.377
o monstrous! monstrous! 3.03.427
o monstrous! monstrous! 3.03.427
o monstrous act! 5.02.190
we had much more monstrous matter of feast, ANT 2.02.182 P
to bring forth | some monstrous malefactor. 2.05. 53
it's monstrous labor when i wash my brain | and 2.07. 99
of monstrous lust the due and just reward. PER 5.03. 86

MONSTROUSLY 1 FR 0.0001 REL FR 1 V 0 P
which he forswore most monstrously to have. ERR 5.01. 11

MONSTROUSNESS 1 FR 0.0001 REL FR 1 V 0 P
see the monstrousness of man | when he looks out TIM 3.02. 72

MONSTRUOSITY 1 FR 0.0001 REL FR 0 V 1 P
this /is the monstruosity in love, lady, that TRO 3.02. 81 P

MONTACUTE 1 FR 0.0001 REL FR 1 V 0 P
from | the king t' attach lord montacute, and H8 1.01.217

MONTAGUE 41 FR 0.0046 REL FR 40 V 1 P
me, | my brother montague shall post to london. 3H6 1.02. 55
out, | and therefore comes my brother montague. 2.01.167
king edward, valiant richard, montague, | stay 2.01.198
sent from your brother, marquess montague. 3.03.164
and you too, somerset and montague, | speak 4.01. 27
knows not montague that of itself | england is 4.01. 39
but, ere i go, hastings and montague, | resolve 4.01.134
so god help montague as he proves true! 4.01.143
thou, brother montague, in buckingham, 4.08. 14
sweet oxford, and my loving montague, | and all 4.08. 30
how far off is our brother montague? 5.01. 4
where is the post that came from montague? 5.01. 5
montague, montague, for lancaster! 5.01. 67
montague, montague, for lancaster! 5.01. 67
now, montague, sit fast, i seek for thee, | that 5.02. 3
ah, montague, | if thou be there, sweet brother, 5.02. 33
come quickly, montague, or i am dead. 5.02. 39
montague hath breath'd his last, | and to the 5.02. 40
and montague our topmast; 5.04. 14
them, the two brave bears, warwick and montague, 5.07. 10
a dog of the house of montague moves me. ROM 1.01. 8 P
old montague is come, | and flourishes his blade 1.01. 77
airy word, | by thee, old capulet, and montague, 1.01. 90
and, montague, come you this afternoon, | to 1.01.100
but montague is bound as well as i, | in penalty 1.02. 1
this, by his voice, should be a montague. 1.05. 54
uncle, this is a montague, our foe; 1.05. 61
his name is romeo, and a montague, | the only 1.05.136
thou art thyself, though not a montague. 2.02. 39
what's montague? 2.02. 40
art thou not romeo, and a montague? 2.02. 60
in truth, fair montague, i am too fond, | and 2.02. 98
sweet montague, be true. 2.02.137
for blood of ours, shed blood of montague. 3.01.149
he is a kinsman to the montague, | affection 3.01.176
this is that banish'd haughty montague, | that 5.03. 49
stop thy unhallowed toil, vile montague! 5.03. 54
lo his house | is empty on the back of montague, 5.03.204
come, montague, for thou art early up | to see 5.03.208
montague! 5.03.291
o brother montague, give me thy hand. 5.03.296

MONTAGUE'S 2 FR 0.0002 REL FR 0 V 2 P
take the wall of any man or maid of montague's. ROM 1.01. 12 P
i will push montague's men from the wall, and 1.01. 17 P

MONTAGUES 5 FR 0.0005 REL FR 3 V 2 P
tool, here comes /two of the house of montagues. ROM 1.01. 32 P
i hate the word | as i hate hell, all montagues, 1.01. 71
down with the montagues! 1.01. 74
and if you be not of the house of montagues, i 1.02. 80 P
run to the capulets, | raise up the montagues; 5.03.178

MONTANO 5 FR 0.0005 REL FR 5 V 0 P
signior montano, | your trusty and most valiant OTH 1.03. 39
lieutenant — sir — montano — /sir — | help, 2.03.159
lieutenant — sir — montano — gentlemen — 2.03.166
worthy montano, you were wont to be civil; 2.03.190
montano and myself being in speech, | there 2.03.225

MONTANT 1 FR 0.0001 REL FR 0 V 1 P
stock, thy reverse, thy distance, thy montant. WIV 2.03. 27 P

MONTEZ 1 FR 0.0001 REL FR 1 V 0 P
montez /a cheval! my horse, varlot lackey! ha! H5 4.02. 2

MONTFERRAT 1 FR 0.0001 REL FR 0 V 1 P
hither in company of the marquis of montferrat? MV 1.02.114 P

MONTGOMERY 3 FR 0.0003 REL FR 3 V 0 P
brother, this is sir john montgomery, | our 3H6 4.07. 40
thanks, good montgomery; 4.07. 45
thanks, brave montgomery, and thanks unto you 4.07. 77

MONTH 43 FR 0.0048 REL FR 29 V 14 P
once in a month recount what thou hast been, TMP 1.02.262
that | whereon this month i have been hammering. TGV 1.03. 18
he hath every month a new sworn brother. ADO 1.01. 72 P
him we shall stay here at the least a month, and 1.01.149 P
i had rather pray a month with mutton and LLL 1.01.302 P
your wit | what was a month old at cain's birth, 4.02. 35
the moon was a month old when adam was no more. 4.02. 39
exchange, for the moon is never but a month old; 4.02. 47 P
love, whose month is ever may, | spied a blossom 4.03.100
that's a month before | this bond expires, i do MV 1.03.157
my ships come home a month before the day. 1.03.181
i would detain you here some month or two 3.02. 9
for but a month ago i went from hence, | and TN 1.02. 31
i'll stay a month longer. 1.03.112 P
to let him there a month behind the gest WT 1.02. 41
very true, and but a month old. 4.04.267 P
we had the tune on't a month ago. 4.04.294 P
there was not full a month | between their 5.01.117
not a month | 'fore your queen died, she was 5.01.225
our doctors say this is no month to bleed. R2 1.01.157
but this our purpose now is twelve month old, 1H4 1.01. 28
be argument for a week, laughter for a month, 2.02. 96 P
meet me in arms by the ninth of the next month? 2.03. 28 P
tell me, where hast thou been this month? 2.04.432 P
met | the eleventh of this month at shrewsbury. 3.02.166
images, | as full of spirit as the month of may, 4.01.101
faintly besiege us one hour in a month. 1H6 1.02. 8
of combat shall be the last of the next month. 2H6 1.03.219 P
holden at bury the first of this next month. 2.04. 71
i'll follow thee a month, devise with thee COR 4.01. 38
in a minute than he will stand to in a month. ROM 2.04.149 P
delay this marriage for a month, a week, | or, 3.05.199
off | to the succession of new days this month. TIM 2.02. 20
by what it fed on, and yet, within a month — HAM 1.02.145
a little month, or ere those shoes were old 1.02.147
within a month, | ere yet the salt of most 1.02.153
if indeed you find him not within this month, 4.03. 36 P
next month with us. LR 1.01.287 P
if, till the expiration of your month, | you 2.04.202
made her groan a month for't; TNK 3.03. 35
and each within this month, accompanied | with 3.06.291
love, whose month was ever may, | spied a PP 16. 2
it fell upon a day, | in the merry month of may, 20. 2

MONTHLY 2 FR 0.0002 REL FR 2 V 0 P
that monthly changes in her /circled orb, | lest ROM 2.02.110
ourself, by monthly course, | with reservation LR 1.01.132

MONTH'S 2 FR 0.0002 REL FR 1 V 1 P
i see you have a month's mind to them. TGV 1.02.134
sixteen businesses, a month's length a–piece, by AWW 4.03. 86 P

MONTHS 42 FR 0.0047 REL FR 33 V 9 P
some sixteen months, and longer might have TGV 4.01. 21
from whom my absence was not six months old ERR 1.01. 44
she is two months on her way. LLL 5.02.673 P
ay, sir, for three months. MV 1.03. 2 P
for three months — well. 1.03. 3 P
three thousand ducats for three months, and 1.03. 9 P
but soft, how many months | do you desire? 1.03. 58
and for three months. 1.03. 66
i had forgot — three months — you told me so. 1.03. 67
three months from twelve; 1.03.104
within these two months, that's a month before 1.03.157
voyage | is but for two months victuall'd. AYL 5.04.192
some six months since, my lord. AWW 1.02. 71
his wife some two months since fled from his 4.03. 47 P
having been three months married to her, sitting TN 2.05. 44 P
and for three months before, | no int'rim, not a 5.01. 94
three months this youth hath tended upon me, 5.01. 99
three crabbed months had sour'd themselves to WT 1.02.102
'tis full three months since i did see him last. R2 5.03. 2
had found some months asleep and leapt them over 2H4 4.04.124
for eighteen months concluded by consent. 2H6 1.01. 42
till term of eighteen months | be full expir'd. 1.01. 67
but i was made a king, at nine months old. 4.09. 4
when i was crown'd i was but nine months old. 3H6 1.01.112
so minutes, hours, days, months, and years, 2.05. 38
i was anointed king at nine months old, | my 3.01. 76
her lord, whom i, some three months since, R3 1.02.240
was crown'd in paris but at nine months old. 2.03. 17
marshalsea shall hold ye play these two months. H8 5.03. 86
lov'd you night and day | for many weary months. TRO 3.02.115
some two months hence my will shall here be made 5.10. 52
absence did but fill /ithaca full of months. COR 1.03. 84 P
what will whole months of tears thy father's TIT 2.04. 55
yet may your pains six months | be quite TIM 4.03.144
some two months hence, up higher toward the JC 2.01.109
but two months dead! HAM 1.02.138
nay, 'tis twice two months, my lord. 3.02.128 P
o heavens, die two months ago, and not forgotten 3.02.131 P
two months since | here was a gentleman of 4.07. 81
my twelve months are expir'd, and tyrus stands PER 3.03. 2
a man who for this three months hath not spoken 5.01. 24
this momentary joy breeds months of pain, | this LUC 690

MONTJOY 5 FR 0.0005 REL FR 5 V 0 P
where is montjoy the herald? H5 3.05. 36
therefore, lord constable, haste on montjoy, 3.05. 61
montjoy. 3.06.138
there's for thy labor, montjoy. 3.06.158
and so, montjoy, fare you well. 3.06.162

MONUMENT 34 FR 0.0038 REL FR 32 V 2 P
for ever be confixed here, | a marble monument! MM 5.01.233
and on your family's old monument | hang ADO 4.01.206
live no longer in monument than the bell rings 5.02. 79 P
is this the monument of leonato? 5.03. 1
as if they saw some wondrous monument, | some SHR 3.02. 95
your mind, | you are no maiden, but a monument. AWW 4.02. 6
she sat like patience on a monument, | smiling TN 2.04.114
this monument of the victory will i bear, and 2H6 4.03. 11 P
his end, | goodness and he fill up one monument! H8 2.01. 94
this monument five hundreth years hath stood, TIT 1.01.350
hole, | which, like a taper in some monument, 2.03.228
be closed in our household's monument. 5.03.194
bed | in that dim monument where tybalt lies. ROM 3.05.201
her body sleeps in capel's monument, | and her 5.01. 18
now must i to the monument alone, | within this 5.02. 24
i discern, | it burneth in the capels' monument. 5.03.127
all run | with open outcry toward our monument. 5.03.193
to this same place, to this same monument. 5.03.274
o monument | and wonder of good deeds evilly TIM 4.03.460
this grave shall have a living monument. HAM 5.01.297
to th' monument! ANT 4.13. 3
to th' monument! 4.13. 6
to th' monument! 4.13. 10
lock'd in her monument. 4.14.120
look out o' th' other side your monument, | his 4.15. 8
confin'd in all she has, her monument, | of thy 5.01. 53
her bed, | and bear her women from the monument. 5.02.357
upon her, | and be her sense but as a monument, CYM 2.02. 32
let their fathers lie | without a monument!), 4.02.227
/ooze, | where, for a monument upon thy bones, PER 3.01. 61
her monument | is almost finished, and her 4.03. 42
where like a virtuous monument she lies, | to be LUC 391
your monument shall be my gentle verse, | which SON 81. 9

and thou in this shalt find thy monument, | when 107.13
MONUMENTAL 3 FR 0.0003 REL FR 2 V 1 P
he hath given her his monumental ring, and AWW 4.03. 17 P
like a rusty mail | in monumental mock'ry. TRO 3.03.153
snow, | and smooth as monumental alablaster. OTH 5.02. 5
/MONUMENTS 1 FR 0.0001 REL FR 1 V 0 P
not marble nor the gilded /monuments | of SON 55. 1
MONUMENTS 7 FR 0.0008 REL FR 7 V 0 P
erects | thy noble deeds as valor's monuments. 1H6 3.02.120
defacing monuments of conquer'd france, 2H6 1.01.102
this place | to wash away my woeful monuments. 3.02.342
our bruised arms hung up for monuments, | our R3 1.01. 6
our monuments | shall be the maws of kites. MAC 3.04. 71
poor wasting monuments of lasting moans. LUC 798
"to fill with worm-holes stately monuments, | to 946
MOOD* 23 FR 0.0026 REL FR 20 V 3 P
who, in my mood, i stabb'd unto the heart. TGV 4.01. 49
slave, | abetting him to thwart me in my mood! ERR 2.02.170
my wife is in a wayward mood to-day, | and will 4.04. 4
you spend your passion on a mispris'd mood. MND 3.02. 74
sways it to the mood | of what it likes or MV 4.01. 51
muddied in fortune's mood, and smell somewhat AWW 5.02. 4 P
he must observe their mood on whom he jests, TN 3.01. 62
/doth show the mood of a much troubled breast, JN 4.02. 73
fool | art thou to break into this woman's mood, 1H4 1.03.237
and now my death | changes the mood, for what in
2H4 4.05.199
since, | stabb'd in my angry mood at tewksbury? R3 1.02.241
art as hot a jack in thy mood as any in italy, ROM 3.01. 12 P
when fortune in her shift and change of mood TIM 1.01. 84
and in this mood will give us any thing. JC 3.02.267
her mood will needs be pitied. HAM 4.05. 3
will you wish on me, when the rash mood is on. LR 2.04.169
you are but now cast in his mood, a punishment OTH 2.03.273 P
eyes, | albeit unused to the melting mood, 5.02.349
fear, and in that mood | the dove will peck the ANT 3.13.195
her mood inclining that way that i spoke of, TNK 5.02. 34
who wayward once, his mood with nought agrees.
LUC 1095
know, gentle wench, it small avails my mood; 1273
in bloodless white and the encrimson'd mood, LC 201
MOODS* 5 FR 0.0005 REL FR 3 V 2 P
wraths, and his cholers, and his moods, and his H5 4.07. 36 P
one on 's father's moods. COR 1.03. 66 P
together with all forms, moods, /shapes of grief HAM 1.02. 82
being oil to fire, snow to the colder moods; LR 2.02. 77
is writ in moods and frowns and wrinkles strange SON 93. 8
MOODY 14 FR 0.0015 REL FR 12 V 2 P
how now? moody? | what is't thou canst demand? TMP 1.02.244
what doth ensue | but moody and dull melancholy,
ERR 5.01. 79
endure | the moody frontier of a servant brow. 1H4 1.03. 19
nor moody beggars, starving for a time | of 5.01. 81
but, being moody, give him time and scope, 2H4 4.04. 39
duke | hath banish'd moody discontented fury, 1H6 3.01.123
conceive, when, after many moody thoughts, | at 3H6 4.06. 13
if that your moody discontented souls | do R3 5.01. 7
observe, observe, he's moody. H8 3.02. 75
and as soon mov'd to be moody, and as soon moody
ROM 3.01. 12 P
to be moody, and as soon moody to be mov'd. 3.01. 13 P
music, moody food | of us that trade in love. ANT 2.05. 1
and moody pluto winks while orpheus plays. LUC 553
unmask, dear dear, this moody heaviness, | and 1602
MOODY-MAD 1 FR 0.0001 REL FR 1 V 0 P
fall down with a pinch, | but rather, moody-mad; 1H6 4.02. 50
/MOON 1 FR 0.0001 REL FR 1 V 0 P
to spite me now, each minute seems /a /moon, PP 14.27
MOON 134 FR 0.0151 REL FR 99 V 35 P
you would lift the moon out of her sphere, if TMP 2.01.183 P
out o' th' moon, i do assure thee. 2.02.138 P
i was the man i' th' moon, when time was. 2.02.139 P
the man i' th' moon? 2.02.146 P
and one so strong | that could control the moon, 5.01.270
shifts to strange effects, | after the moon. MM 3.01. 25
a title to phoebe, to luna, to the moon. LLL 4.02. 38
the moon was a month old when adam was no more. 4.02. 39
exchange, for the moon is never but a month old; 4.02. 47 P
nor shines the silver moon one half so bright 4.03. 29
my love (her mistress) is a gracious moon, | she 4.03.226
my face is but a moon, and clouded too. 5.02.203
vouchsafe, bright moon, and these thy stars, to 5.02.205
thus change i like the moon. 5.02.212
you took the moon at full, but now she's changed 5.02.214
yet still she is the moon, and i the man. 5.02.215
four happy days bring in | another moon; MND 1.01. 3
o, methinks, how slow | this old moon /wanes! 1.01. 4
and then the moon, like to a silver bow | /new 1.01. 9
faint hymns to the cold fruitless moon. 1.01. 73
take time to pause, and by the next new moon — 1.01. 83
therefore the moon, the governess of floods, 2.01.103
flying between the cold moon and the earth, 2.01.156
quench'd in the chaste beams of the wat'ry moon, 2.01.162
doth the moon shine that night we play our play? 3.01. 51 P
open, and the moon may shine in at the casement. 3.01. 58 P
the moon methinks looks with a wat'ry eye; 3.01.198
and that the moon | may through the centre creep 3.02. 53
compass soon, | swifter than the wand'ring moon. 4.01. 98
now is the moon used between the two neighbors. 5.01.206 P
his discretion, and let us listen to the moon. 5.01.238 P
this lanthorn doth the horned moon present — 5.01.239
this lanthorn doth the horned moon present; 5.01.244
myself the man i' th' moon do seem to be. 5.01.245
how is it else the man i' th' moon? 5.01.248 P
i am a-weary of this moon. 5.01.251 P
proceed, moon. 5.01.256 P
is to tell you that the lanthorn is the moon, i 5.01.258 P
the lanthorn is the moon, i the man i' th' moon, 5.01.258 P
for all these are in the moon. 5.01.261 P
well shone, moon. 5.01.267 P
truly, the moon shines with a good grace. 5.01.267 P
sweet moon, i thank thee for thy sunny beams; 5.01.272
i thank thee, moon, for shining now so bright; 5.01.273
moon, take thy flight, | now die, die, die, die, 5.01.305
/lion roars, | and the wolf /behowls the moon; 5.01.372
the moon shines bright. MV 5.01. 1
when the moon shone, we did not see the candle. 5.01. 92
the moon sleeps with endymion | and would not be 5.01.109
by yonder moon i swear you do me wrong; 5.01.142
the howling of irish wolves against the moon. AYL 5.02.110 P
lord, how bright and goodly shines the moon! SHR 4.05. 2
the moon! the sun — it is not moonlight now. 4.05. 3
i say it is the moon that shines so bright. 4.05. 4
it shall be moon, or star, or what i list, | or 4.05. 7
and be it moon, or sun, or what you please; 4.05. 13
i say it is the moon. 4.05. 16
i know it is the moon. 4.05. 16
and the moon changes even as your mind. 4.05. 20
'tis not that time of moon with me to make one TN 1.05.200 P
forbid the sea for to obey the moon | as or by WT 1.02.427
now the ship boring the moon with her mainmast, 3.03. 92 P
the pale moon shines by night; 4.03. 16
for never gaz'd the moon | upon the water as 4.04.172
the pale-fac'd moon looks bloody on the earth, R2 2.04. 10
take purses go by the moon and the seven stars, 1H4 1.02. 14 P
gentlemen of the shade, minions of the moon, and 1.02. 26 P
by our noble and chaste mistress the moon, under 1.02. 29 P
sea, being govern'd, as the sea is, by the moon. 1.02. 33 P
to pluck bright honor from the pale-fac'd moon, 1.03.202
the moon shines fair, you may away by night. 3.01.140
as much as the full moon doth the cinders of the 2H4 4.03. 52 P
presented them unto the gazing moon | so many H5 4.pr. 27
kate, is the sun and the moon, or rather the sun 5.02.163 P
the moon, or rather the sun and not the moon; 5.02.163 P
and dogged york, that reaches at the moon, 2H6 3.01.158
that i, being govern'd by the watery moon, | may R3 2.02. 69
and anon he casts | his eye against the moon. H8 3.02.118
i am afraid | his thinkings are below the moon, 3.02.134
as true as steel, as plantage to the moon, | as TRO 3.02.177
sun borrows of the moon when diomed keeps his 5.01. 94 P
they would hang them on the horns a' th' moon, COR 1.01.213
bemock the modest moon. 1.01.257
my as fair as noble ladies — and the moon, were 2.01. 97 P
broke, | and scarr'd the moon with splinters. 4.05.109
musty chaff, and you are smelt | above the moon. 5.01. 32
the moon of rome, chaste as the icicle | that's 5.03. 65
so pale did shine the moon on /pyramus | when he
TIT 2.03.231
my lord, i /aim'd a mile beyond the moon, | your 4.03. 66
arise, fair sun, and kill the envious moon, ROM 2.02. 4
lady, by yonder blessed moon i vow, | that tips 2.02.107
o, swear not by the moon, th' inconstant moon, 2.02.109
o, swear not by the moon, th' inconstant moon, 2.02.109
as the moon does, by wanting light to give: TIM 4.03. 68
but then renew i could not, like the moon; 4.03. 69
surge resolves | the moon into salt tears; 4.03.440
i had rather be a dog, and bay the moon, | than JC 4.03. 27
the moon is down; i have not heard the clock. MAC 2.01. 2
upon the corner of the moon | there hangs a 3.05. 23
enough | if she unmask her beauty to the moon. HAM 1.03. 37
steel | revisits thus the glimpses of the moon, 1.04. 53
so many journeys may the sun and moon | make us 3.02.161
below their mines, | and blow them at the moon. 3.04.209
all simples that have virtue | under the moon, 4.07.145
in the sun and moon portend no good to us. LR 1.02.103 P
make guilty of our disasters the sun, the moon, 1.02.121 P
conjuring the moon | to stand /'s auspicious 2.01. 39
for though it be night, yet the moon shines; 2.02. 31 P
for all beneath the moon | would i not leap 4.06. 26
of great ones, | that ebb and flow by th' moon. 5.03. 19
to follow still the changes of the moon | with OTH 3.03.178
heaven stops the nose at it, and the moon winks; 4.02. 77
should be now a huge eclipse | of sun and moon, 5.02.100
it is the very error of the moon, | she comes 5.02.109
moon and stars! ANT 3.13. 95
alack, our terrene moon | is now eclips'd, and 3.13.153
be witness to me, o thou blessed moon, | when 4.09. 7
let me lodge lichas on the horns o' th' moon, 4.12. 45
left remarkable | beneath the visiting moon. 4.15. 68
and therein stuck | a sun and moon, which kept 5.02. 80
now the fleeting moon | no planet is of mine. 5.02.240
with a blanket, or put the moon in his pocket, CYM 3.01. 44 P
and the brine and cloudy billow kiss the moon, i PER 3.01. 46 P
slaughter | the sun and moon ne'er look'd upon! 4.03. 3
showing the sun his teeth, grinning at the moon, TNK 1.01.100
made too proud the bed, took leave o' th' moon 1.03. 52
lo | the moon is down, the crickets chirp, the 3.02. 35
at some time of the moon than at other some, is 4.03. 2 P
shone like the moon in water seen by night. VEN 492
to draw the cloud that hides the silver moon. LUC 371
the moon being clouded presently is miss'd, 1007
couplement of proud compare | with sun and moon,
SON 21. 6
clouds and eclipses stain both moon and sun, 35. 3
the mortal moon hath her eclipse endur'd, | and 107. 5
MOONBEAMS 1 FR 0.0001 REL FR 1 V 0 P
to fan the moonbeams from his sleeping eyes. MND 3.01.173
MOON-CALF 4 FR 0.0004 REL FR 0 V 4 P
cam'st thou to be the siege of this moon-calf? TMP 2.02.106 P
how now, moon-calf? 2.02.135 P
moon-calf, speak once in thy life, if thou beest 3.02. 21 P
in thy life, if thou beest a good moon-calf. 3.02. 22 P
MOON-CALF'S 1 FR 0.0001 REL FR 0 V 1 P
me under the dead moon-calf's gaberdine for fear
TMP 2.02.111 P
MOONISH 1 FR 0.0001 REL FR 0 V 1 P
which time would i, being but a moonish youth, AYL 3.02.410 P
MOONLIGHT 9 FR 0.0010 REL FR 6 V 3 P
thou hast by moonlight at her window sung | with MND 1.01. 30
wood, a mile without the town, by moonlight; 1.02.102 P
ill met by moonlight, proud titania. 2.01. 60
in our round | and see our moonlight revels, go 2.01.141
that is, to bring the moonlight into a chamber; 3.01. 48 P
you know, pyramus and thisby meet by moonlight. 3.01. 50 P
how sweet the moonlight sleeps upon this bank! MV 5.01. 54
the moon! the sun — it is not moonlight now. SHR 4.05. 3
shall | by warranting moonlight corslet thee — TNK 1.01.177
MOON'S 5 FR 0.0005 REL FR 4 V 1 P
the man i' th' moon's too slow — till new-born TMP 2.01.249
every where, | swifter than the moon's sphere; MND 2.01. 7
of us that are the moon's men doth ebb and flow 1H4 1.02. 31 P
the moon's an arrant thief, | and her pale fire TIM 4.03.437
slips of yew | sliver'd in the moon's eclipse, MAC 4.01. 28
MOONS 9 FR 0.0010 REL FR 9 V 0 P
my lord, they say five moons were seen to-night; JN 4.02.182
five moons? 4.02.185
can change their moons and bring their times R2 1.03.220
and thirty dozen moons with borrowed sheen HAM 3.02.157
below, methought his eyes | were two full moons; LR 4.06. 70
till now some nine moons wasted, they have us'd OTH 1.03. 84
kings for messengers | not many moons gone by. ANT 3.12. 6
one twelve moons more she'll wear diana's livery PER 2.05. 10
pericles | come not home in twice six moons, 3.ch. 31
MOONSHINE 13 FR 0.0014 REL FR 7 V 6 P
by moonshine do the green sour ringlets make, TMP 5.01. 37
you moonshine revellers, and shades of night, WIV 5.05. 38
candles, and starlight, and moonshine be out. 5.05.102
thou now requests but moonshine in the water. LLL 5.02.208
find out moonshine, find out moonshine. MND 3.01. 54 P
find out moonshine, find out moonshine. 3.01. 54 P
or to present, the person of moonshine. 3.01. 61 P
dog, and bush of thorn, | presenteth moonshine; 5.01.136
by moonshine did these lovers think no scorn 5.01.137
let lion, moonshine, wall, and lovers twain | at 5.01.150
how chance moonshine is gone before thisby comes 5.01.312 P
moonshine and lion are left to bury the dead. 5.01.348 P
i'll make a sop o' th' moonshine of you, you LR 2.02. 32 P
MOONSHINE'S 1 FR 0.0001 REL FR 1 V 0 P
her collars of the moonshine's wat'ry beams, ROM 1.04. 65
MOONSHINES 1 FR 0.0001 REL FR 1 V 0 P
for that i am some twelve or fourteen moonshines
LR 1.02. 5
/MOOR* 3 FR 0.0003 REL FR 3 V 0 P
/like /to /the /empress' /moor, /therefore /i TIT 3.02. 67
/flattering /myself /as /if /it /were /the /moor 3.02. 72
/comes /in /likeness /of /a //coal-black /moor. 3.02. 78
MOOR* 72 FR 0.0081 REL FR 62 V 10 P
the moor is with child by you, launcelot. MV 3.05. 39 P
it is much that the moor should be more than 3.05. 40 P
ah, my sweet moor, sweeter to me than life! TIT 2.03. 51
and to be doubted that your moor and you | are 2.03. 68
plot, | accompanied but with a barbarous moor, 2.03. 78
now will i hence to seek my lovely moor, | and 2.03.190
o, tell me, did you see aaron the moor? 4.02. 52
league | i am a lamb, but if you brave the moor, 4.02.137
and told the moor he should not choose | but 4.03. 75
well are you fitted, had you but a moor. 5.02. 85
never wags | but in her company there is a moor; 5.02. 88
court | there is a queen, attended by a moor; 5.02.105
good uncle, take you in this barbarous moor, 5.03. 4
delivered, | the issue of an irreligious moor, 5.03.121
and hither hale that misbelieving moor | to be 5.03.143
leave to feed, | and batten on this moor? HAM 3.04. 67
in any just term am affin'd | to love the moor. OTH 1.01. 40
were i the moor, i would not be iago. 1.01. 57
your daughter and the moor are /now making the 1.01.116 P
to the gross clasps of a lascivious moor — | if 1.01.126
(as, if i stay, i shall) | against the moor; 1.01.147
with the moor, say'st thou? 1.01.164
know | where we may apprehend her and the moor? 1.01.177
signior, it is the moor. 1.02. 57
here comes brabantio and the valiant moor. 1.03. 47
here is the man — this moor, whom now, it seems 1.03. 71
challenge that i may profess | due to the moor, 1.03.189
come hither, moor: 1.03.192
that i /did love the moor to live with him, | my 1.03.248
adieu, brave moor, use desdemona well. 1.03.291
look to her, moor, if thou hast eyes to see; 1.03.292
should continue her love to the moor — put 1.03.343 P
i retell thee again and again, i hate the moor. 1.03.366 P
i hate the moor, | and it is thought abroad that 1.03.386
the moor is of a free and open nature, | that 1.03.399
lieutenant to the warlike moor othello, | is 2.01. 27
the moor himself at sea, | and is in full 2.01. 28
he looks sadly, | and /prays the moor be safe; 2.01. 33
/this warlike isle, | that so approve the moor! 2.01. 44
the moor! 2.01.178 P
me with what violence she first lov'd the moor, 2.01.223 P
beauties — all which the moor is defective in. 2.01.230 P
heave the gorge, disrelish and abhor the moor; 2.01.233 P
bless'd, she would never have lov'd the moor. 2.01.253 P
the moor (howbeit that i endure him not) | is of 2.01.288
for that i do suspect the lusty moor | hath 2.01.295
so, yet that i put the moor | at least into a 2.01.300
abuse him to the moor in the /rank garb | (for i 2.01.306
make the moor thank me, love me, and reward me, 2.01.308
and 'tis great pity that the noble moor | should 2.03.138
were an honest action to say | so to the moor. 2.03.142
and indeed the course | to win the moor again? 2.03.339
and then for her | to win the moor, were/'t to 2.03.343
and she for him pleads strongly to the moor, 2.03.355
good, | she shall undo her credit with the moor. 2.03.359
on — | myself a while to draw the moor apart, 2.03.385
and i'll devise a mean to draw the moor | out of 3.01. 37
the moor replies | that he you hurt is of great 3.01. 44
this was her first remembrance from the moor. 3.03.291
why, that the moor first gave to desdemona, 3.03.308
the moor already changes with my poison: 3.03.325
"cursed fate that gave thee to the moor!" 3.03.426
and, but my noble moor | is true of mind, and 3.04. 26
is this the noble moor whom our full senate 4.01.264
and made you to suspect me with the moor. 4.02.147
and, besides, the moor | may unfold me to him; 5.01. 20
the moor hath kill'd my mistress! 5.02.167
o thou dull moor, that handkerchief thou 5.02.225
which i have /here recover'd from the moor. 5.02.240
moor, she was chaste; 5.02.249
she lov'd thee, cruel moor; 5.02.249
and seize upon the fortunes of the moor, | for 5.02.366
MOOR-DITCH 1 FR 0.0001 REL FR 0 V 1 P
thou to a hare, or the melancholy of moor-ditch? 1H4 1.02. 78 P
MOORFIELDS 1 FR 0.0001 REL FR 0 V 1 P
is this moorfields to muster in? H8 5.03. 33 P
MOOR'S 1 FR 0.0001 REL FR 1 V 0 P
the moor's abus'd by some most villainous knave, OTH 4.02.139
MOORS 1 FR 0.0001 REL FR 0 V 1 P
these moors are changeable in their wills — OTH 1.03.346 P
MOORSHIP'S 1 FR 0.0001 REL FR 1 V 0 P
his moorship's ancient. OTH 1.01. 33
MOP 1 FR 0.0001 REL FR 1 V 0 P
on his toe, | will be here with mop and mow. TMP 4.01. 47
MOP'D 1 FR 0.0001 REL FR 1 V 0 P
i am mop'd: TNK 3.02. 25
MOPE 2 FR 0.0002 REL FR 1 V 1 P

to mope with his fat–brain'd followers so far H5 3.07.133 P
part of one true sense | could not so mope. HAM 3.04. 81
MOPING 1 FR 0.0001 REL FR 1 V 0 P
from them, | and were brought moping hither. TMP 5.01.240
/MOPPING 1 FR 0.0001 REL FR 0 V 1 P
/flibbertigibbet, /of /mopping /and /mowing, LR 4.01. 61 P
MOPSA 2 FR 0.0002 REL FR 1 V 1 P
mopsa must be your mistress; WT 4.04.162
if i were not in love with mopsa, thou shouldst 4.04.231 P
/MORAL 2 FR 0.0002 REL FR 2 V 0 P
/silent /king, /the /moral /of /this /sport, R2 4.01.290
/whilst /thou, /a /moral /fool, /sits /still LR 4.02. 58
MORAL 23 FR 0.0026 REL FR 11 V 12 P
about to apply a moral medicine to a mortifying ADO 1.03. 12 P
you have some moral in this benedictus. 3.04. 78 P
moral? 3.04. 79 P
no, by my troth, i have no moral meaning; 3.04. 79 P
to be so moral when he shall endure | the like 5.01. 30
there's the moral. LLL 3.01. 86 P
i will add the l'envoy. say the moral again. 3.01. 87 P
now will i begin your moral, and do you follow 3.01. 93 P
a good moral, my lord: MND 5.01.120 P
hear | the motley fool thus moral on the time, AYL 2.07. 29
admire | this virtue and this moral discipline, SHR 1.01. 30
the meaning or moral of his signs and tokens. 4.04. 79 P
thy father's moral parts | mayst thou inherit AWW 1.02. 21
to signify to you, which is the moral of it, H5 3.06. 33 P
fortune is an excellent moral. 3.06. 38 P
weed, | and make a moral of the devil himself. 4.01. 12
this moral ties me over to time and a hot summer 5.02.312 P
thought | unfit to hear moral philosophy. TRO 2.02.167
is, these moral laws | of nature and of nations 2.02.184
the moral of my wit | is "plain and true"; 4.04.107
a thousand moral paintings i can show | that TIM 1.01. 90
a pretty moral. PER 2.01. 35
a pretty moral; 2.02. 45
MORALER 1 FR 0.0001 REL FR 0 V 1 P
come, you are too severe a moraler. OTH 2.03.299 P
MORALIZE 5 FR 0.0005 REL FR 4 V 1 P
did he not moralize this spectacle? AYL 2.01. 44
i pray thee moralize them. SHR 4.04. 81 P
iniquity, | i moralize two meanings in one word. R3 3.01. 83
boar, | unlike myself thou hear'st me moralize, VEN 712
nor could she moralize his wanton sight, | more LUC 104
MORDAKE 4 FR 0.0004 REL FR 3 V 1 P
took | mordake earl of fife and eldest son | to 1H4 1.01. 71
i shall have none but mordake earl of fife. 1.01. 95
he is there too, and one mordake, and a thousand 2.04.357 P
but there is mordake, vernon, lord harry percy, 4.04. 24
MORE* *(also moe)*
/MORE* 22 FR 0.0024 REL FR 18 V 4 P
/what /more /remains? R2 4.01.222
/no /more, /but /that /you /read | /these 4.01.222
/urge /it /no /more, /my /lord /northumberland. 4.01.271
/then /be /gone /and /trouble /you /no /more. 4.01.303
/more /likely /to /fall /in /than /to /get /o'er 2H4 1.01.171
/more /than /that /being /which /was /like /to 1.01.179
/and /more /and /less /do /flock /to /follow 1.01.209
/much /more, /in /this /great /work | (/which 1.03. 48
/to /hold /your /honor /more /precise /and /nice 2.03. 40
of that, master shallow, /no /more /of /that. 3.02.196 P
/hear /me /more /plainly. 4.01. 66
/grac'd /and /did, /more /than /the /king — 4.01.137
/understand /more /clear, | /what's /past /and TRO 4.05.165
/and /look /you /eat /no /more | /than /will TIT 3.02. 1
than those that have /more coying to be strange. ROM 2.02.101
/let /me /question /more /in /particular. HAM 2.02.239 P
of my sudden /and /more /strange return. 4.07. 47 P
/a /man's /life's /no /more /than /to /say "/one 5.02. 74
/what /will /hap /more /to–night, /safe /scape LR 3.06.114
/no /more, /the /text /is /foolish. 4.02. 37
/amplify /too /much, /would /make /much /more, 5.03.207
/no /more /of /drowning, /do /you /hear? OTH 1.03.378 P
MORE* 2475 FR 0.2797 REL FR 1941 V 534 P
none that i more love than myself. TMP 1.01. 20 P
of the present, we will not hand a rope more. 1.01. 23 P
be collected, | no more amazement. 1.02. 14
i am, nor that i am more better | than prospero, 1.02. 19
more to know | did never meddle with my thoughts 1.02. 21
and more, miranda. 1.02. 48
made thee more profit | than other princess' can 1.02.172
can, that have more time | for vainer hours, and 1.02.173
here cease more questions. 1.02.184
more momentary | and sight–outrunning were not; 1.02.202
but there's more work. 1.02.238
is there more toil? 1.02.242
before the time be out? no more! 1.02.246
thee, | by help of her more potent ministers, 1.02.275
if thou more murmur'st, i will rend an oak | and 1.02.294
each pinch more stinging | than bees that made 1.02.329
rock, | who hadst deserv'd more than a prison. 1.02.362
it sounds no more; 1.02.389
and his more braver daughter could control thee, 1.02.440
soft, sir, one word more. 1.02.450
one word more: 1.02.453
entertainment till | mine enemy has more pow'r. 1.02.467
one word more | shall make me chide thee, if not 1.02.476
think'st there is no more such shapes as he, 1.02.479
his word is more than the miraculous harp. 2.01. 87 P
of it in the sea, bring forth more islands. 2.01. 94 P
prithee no more; thou dost talk nothing to me. 2.01.171
no more — | and yet methinks i see it in thy 2.01.205
i am more serious than my custom; 2.01.219
how, in stripping it, | you more invest it! 2.01.226
"i shall no more to sea, to sea, | here shall i 2.02. 42
o stephano, hast any more of this? 2.02.133 P
i'll bear him no more sticks, but follow thee, 2.02.163
now lead the way without any more talking. 2.02.173 P
no more dams i'll make for fish, | nor fetch in 2.02.180
ten times more gentle than her father's crabbed; 3.01. 8
and i should do it | with much more ease, for my 3.01. 30
have i seen | more that i may call men than you, 3.01. 51
and would no more endure | this wooden slavery 3.01. 61
and all the more it seeks to hide itself, | the 3.01. 80
but my rejoicing | at nothing can be more. 3.01. 94
if you trouble him any more in 's tale, by this 3.02. 48 P
mum then, and no more. — proceed. 3.02. 51 P
i say, to–night. no more. 3.03. 17
their manners are more gentle, kind, than of 3.03. 32
be more abstenious, | or else good night your 4.01. 53
swears he will shoot no more, but play with 4.01.100
no more! 4.01.142
that's more to me than my wetting; 4.01.211 P
and more pinch–spotted make them | than pard or 4.01.260
for more assurance that a living prince | does 5.01.108
no more yet of this, | for 'tis a chronicle of 5.01.162
o, look, sir, look, sir, here is more of us. 5.01.216
and there is in this business more than nature 5.01.243
love, | for he was more than over shoes in love. TGV 1.01. 24
once more adieu. 1.01. 53
he leaves his friends to dignify them more; 1.01. 64
or else return no more into my sight. 1.02. 47
to plead for love deserves more fee than hate. 1.02. 48
you | to let him spend his time no more at home, 1.03. 14
no more of stay: 1.03. 75
meaning henceforth to trouble you no more. 2.01.119
i would have had them writ more movingly. 2.01.128
stone, and has no more pity in him than a dog. 2.03. 11 P
that hath more mind to feed on your blood than 2.04. 27 P
no more, gentlemen, no more; 2.04. 47 P
no more, gentlemen, no more; 2.04. 47 P
once more, new servant, welcome; 2.04.118
nay more, our marriage hour, | with all the 2.04.179
how shall i dote on her with more advice, | that 2.04.207
the more thou dam'st it up, the more it burns: 2.07. 24
the more thou dam'st it up, the more it burns: 2.07. 24
more than quick words do move a woman's mind. 3.01. 91
for scorn at first makes after–love the more. 3.01. 95
of you, | but rather to beget more love in you. 3.01. 97
and think my patience, more than thy desert, 3.01.159
thank me for this more than for all the favors 3.01.161
no more; 3.01.239
she hath more qualities than a water–spaniel, 3.01.272 P
why, a horse can do no more; 3.01.276 P
"item, she hath more hair than wit, and more 3.01.353 P
more hair than wit, and more faults than hairs, 3.01.354 P
faults than hairs, and more wealth than faults." 3.01.354 P
rehearse that once more. 3.01.357 P
"item, she hath more hair than wit" — 3.01.358 P
more hair than wit? 3.01.359 P
salt, and therefore it is more than the salt; 3.01.361 P
hair that covers the wit is more than the wit, 3.01.362 P
"and more faults than hairs" — 3.01.364 P
"and more wealth than faults." 3.01.367 P
yet, spaniel–like, the more she spurns my love, 4.02. 14
the more it grows, and fawneth on her still. 4.02. 15
if i had not had more wit than he, to take a 4.04. 13 P
"you do him the more wrong," quoth i, "'twas i 4.04. 26 P
he makes me no more ado, but whips me out of the 4.04. 28 P
the more shame for him that he sends it me; 4.04.133
more to be reveng'd on eglamour | than for the 5.02. 51
more for silvia's love | than hate of eglamour 5.02. 53
more to cross that love | than hate for silvia, 5.02. 55
a thousand more mischances than this one | have 5.03. 3
and full as much (for more there cannot be) | i 5.04. 38
therefore be gone, solicit me no more. 5.04. 40
i am sorry i must never trust thee more, | but 5.04. 69
spy | more fresh in julia's with a constant eye? 5.04.115
the more degenerate and base art thou | to make 5.04.136
i warrant you, my lord — more grace than boy. 5.04.166
dog, and a fair dog — can there be more said? WIV 1.01. 97 P
are married and have more occasion to know one 1.01.248 P
i hope, upon familiarity will grow more content. 1.01.250 P
two yards, and more. 1.03. 40 P
in windsor knows more of anne's mind than i do, 1.04.128 P
than i do, nor can do more than i do with her, i 1.04.129 P
tell your worship more of the wart the next time 1.04.159 P
you are not young, no more am i; 2.01. 6 P
then there's more sympathy. 2.01. 8 P
but they do no more adhere and keep place 2.01. 62 P
blank space for different names (sure, more); 2.01. 76 P
and what he gets more of her than sharp words, 2.01.183 P
i could have told you more. 2.01.224 P
at a word, hang no more about me, i am no gibbet 2.02. 17 P
i do relent. what would thou more of man? 2.02. 30
has been earls, nay (which is more) pensioners; 2.02. 77 P
clap on more sails, pursue; 2.02.136
i'll make more of thy old body than i have done. 2.02.139 P
/brook, i desire more acquaintance of you. 2.02.162 P
spend more; 2.02.232 P
he has no more knowledge in hibocrates and galen 3.01. 65 P
break with her for more money than i'll speak of 3.02. 56 P
and we will yet have more tricks with falstaff. 3.03.191 P
therefore no more turn me to him, sweet nan. 3.04. 2
i found thee of more value | than stamps in gold 3.04. 15
she desires you once more to come to her, 3.05. 45 P
(when i was more than half stew'd in grease, 3.05.118 P
you'll undertake her no more? 3.05.125 P
truly, i thought there had been one number more, 4.01. 24 P
no, i'll come no more i' th' basket. 4.02. 49 P
satisfy me once more, once more search with me. 4.02.165 P
satisfy me once more, once more search with me. 4.02.165 P
'tis well, 'tis well, no more. 4.04. 10
and three or four more of their growth, we'll 4.04. 49
ay, sir; like who more bold? 4.05. 54 P
that hath taught me more wit than ever i learn'd 4.05. 60 P
i have suffer'd more for their sakes — more 4.05.108 P
more than the villainous inconstancy of man's 4.05.108 P
a hundred pound in gold more than your loss. 4.06. 5
prithee no more prattling. 5.01. 1 P
more fertile–fresh than all the field to see; 5.05. 68
then no more remains | but that: MM 1.01. 7
let there be some more test made of my mettle 1.01. 48
no more evasion. 1.01. 50
once more fare you well. 1.01. 72
ay, and more. 1.02. 51 P
a french crown more. 1.02. 52 P
and, which is more, within these three days his 1.02. 68 P
more grave and wrinkled than the aims and ends 1.03. 5
time the rod | /becomes more mock'd than fear'd; 1.03. 27
and it in you more dreadful would have seem'd 1.03. 33
action | at our more leisure shall i render you; 1.03. 49
that his appetite | is more to bread than stone: 1.03. 53
i speak not as desiring more, | but rather 1.04. 3
but rather wishing a more strict restraint 1.04. 4
what was done to elbow's wife, once more? 2.01.140 P
his wife is a more respected person than any of 2.01.165 P
hath she had any more than one husband? 2.01.201 P
get you gone, and let me hear no more of you. 2.01.207 P
no more of it, master froth. 2.01.211 P
be glad to give out a commission for more heads. 2.01.240 P
dispose of her | to some more fitter place; 2.02. 17
you could not with more tame a tongue desire it; 2.02. 46
thou'rt i' th' right, girl, more o' that. 2.02.129
art avis'd o' that? more on't. 2.02.132
it be | that modesty may more betray our sense 2.02.168
i would do more than that, if more were needful. 2.03. 9
i would do more than that, if more were needful. 2.03. 9
young man | more fit to do another such offense 2.03. 14
sins | stand more for number than for accompt. 2.04. 58
to be received plain, i'll speak more gross: 2.04. 82
if you be more, you're none; 2.04.135
more than our brother is our chastity. 2.04.185
grossly fear'st | thy death, which is no more. 3.01. 19
and six or seven winters more respect | than a 3.01. 75
in the current) made it more violent and unruly. 3.01.243 P
it not patiently, why, your mettle is the more. 3.02. 77 P
a little more lenity to lechery would do no harm 3.02. 97 P
if your knowledge be more, it is much dark'ned 3.02.147 P
o, you hope the duke will return no more; 3.02.164 P
but no more of this. 3.02.169 P
go to, no more words. 3.02.206 P
more nor less to others paying | than by 3.02.265
your hangman is a more penitent trade than your 4.02. 50 P
as it is, | you shall hear more ere morning. 4.02. 95
with a thought that more depends on it than we 4.02.124 P
apprehends death no more dreadfully but as a 4.02.142 P
more of him anon. 4.02.153 P
upon this, more than thanks and good fortune, by 4.02.178 P
that stabb'd pots, and i think forty more — all 4.03. 18 P
night, and i will have more time to prepare me, 4.03. 54 P
the visage | of ragozine, more like to claudio? 4.03. 76
to public thanks, | forerunning more requital. 5.01. 8
if he be less, he's nothing, but he's more, 5.01. 58
but he's more, | had i more name for badness. 5.01. 59
are not mad | have sure more lack of reason. 5.01. 68
sirrah, no more! 5.01.214
these poor informal women are no more | but 5.01.236
but instruments of some more mightier member 5.01.237
dare no more stretch this finger of mine than he 5.01.314
you indeed spoke so of him, and much more, much 5.01.338 P
let him speak no more. 5.01.347 P
i am more amaz'd at his dishonor | than at the 5.01.380
become much more the better | for being a little 5.01.440
it not, | yet did repent me, after more advice, 5.01.464
that i crave death more willingly than mercy: 5.01.476
there's more behind that is more gratulate. 5.01.529
there's more behind that is more gratulate. 5.01.529
merchant of syracusa, plead no more. ERR 1.01. 3
nay more, if any born at ephesus be seen | at 1.01. 16
my wife, more careful for the latter–born, | had 1.01. 78
but ere they came — o, let me say no more! 1.01. 94
was carried with more speed before the wind, 1.01.109
why should their liberty than ours be more? 2.01. 10
man, more divine, the master of all these, 2.01. 20
of more pre–eminence than fish and fowls, | are 2.01. 23
as much, or more, we should ourselves complain: 2.01. 37
unkindness blunts it more than marble hard. 2.01. 93
but there's many a man hath more hair than wit. 2.02. 82 P
but wrong not that wrong with a more contempt. 2.02.172
and welcome more common, for that's nothing but 3.01. 25
ay, to a niggardly host and more sparing guest: 3.01. 27
her wealth's sake use her with more kindness: 3.02. 6
than our earth's wonder, more than earth divine. 3.02. 32
far more, far more, to you do i decline. 3.02. 44
far more, far more, to you do i decline. 3.02. 44
for fear you ne'er see chain nor money more. 3.02.177
which doth amount to three odd ducats more 4.01. 30
you wrong me more, sir, in denying it. 4.01. 67
i will debate this matter at more leisure, | and 4.01.100
and teach your ears to list me with more heed. 4.01.101
he meant he did me none: the more my spite. 4.02. 8
bankrout and owes more than he's worth to season 4.02. 58
up his rest to do more exploits with his mace 4.03. 28 P
but she, more covetous, would have a chain. 4.03. 74
more company! the fiend is strong within him. 4.04.107
let's call more help | to have them bound again. 4.04.145
poisons more deadly than a mad dog's tooth. 5.01. 70
till, raising of more aid, | we came again to 5.01.153
and a rabble more | of vild confederates. 5.01.236
that ever i lose more blood with love than i ADO 1.01.250 P
too curst is more than curst. 2.01. 21 P
he that hath a beard is more than a youth, and 2.01. 36 P
and he that is more than a youth is not for me, 2.01. 38 P
no more words; the clerk is answer'd. 2.01.111 P
a voice | to slander music any more than once. 2.03. 45
i pray thee sing, and let me woo no more. 2.03. 48
sigh no more, ladies, sigh no more, | men were 2.03. 62
sigh no more, ladies, sigh no more, | men were 2.03. 62
sing no more ditties, sing no moe, | of dumps so 2.03. 70
i took no more pains for those thanks than you 2.03.250 P
"i took no more pains for those thanks than you 2.03.259 P
to praise him more than ever man did merit. 3.01. 19
and when you have seen more, and heard more, 3.02.122 P
and when you have seen more, and heard more, 3.02.122 P
with them, why, the more is for your honesty. 3.03. 53 P
much more a man who hath any honesty in him. 3.03. 64 P
one word more, honest neighbors. 3.03. 91 P
the fashion wears out more apparel than the man. 3.03.140 P
turk, there's no more sailing by the star. 3.04. 58 P
and 'twere a thousand pound more than 'tis, for 3.05. 24 P
but you are more intemperate in your blood 4.01. 59
of harm, | and never shall it more be gracious. 4.01.108
if i know more of any man alive | than that 4.01.178
shall come apparell'd in more precious habit, 4.01.227
more moving, delicate, and full of life, | into 4.01.228
and this is more, masters, than you can deny. 4.02. 60 P
a wise fellow, and, which is more, an officer, 4.02. 80 P
an officer, and, which is more, a householder, 4.02. 81 P
and, which is more, as pretty a piece of flesh 4.02. 81 P
by this light, he changes more and more. 5.01.140 P
by this light, he changes more and more. 5.01.141 P
you, she shall ne'er weigh more reasons in her 5.01.207 P
why, no, no more than reason. 5.04. 74

troth, no, no more than reason.		5.04. 77
there is no staff more reverent than one tipp'd		5.04.123 P
have no more profit of their shining nights	LLL	1.01. 90
at christmas i no more desire a rose | than wish		1.01.105
and though i have for barbarism spoke more		1.01.112
this letter will tell you more.		1.01.189 P
or, for thy more sweet understanding, a woman.		1.01.264 P
it doth amount to one more than two.		1.02. 47 P
more authority, dear boy, name more;		1.02. 67 P
more authority, dear boy, name more;		1.02. 68 P
i am more bound to you than your fellows, for		1.02.151 P
there remains unpaid | a hundred thousand more,		2.01.134
and three times as much more — and yet nothing		3.01. 47 P
would you desire more?		3.01.100 P
we will talk no more of this matter.		3.01.118 P
till there be more matter in the shin.		3.01.119 P
fair payment for foul words is more than due.		4.01. 19
that more for praise than purpose meant to kill.		4.01. 29
more fairer than fair, beautiful than beauteous,		4.01. 62 P
those parts that do fructify in us more than he.		4.02. 29
the moon was a month old when adam was no more.		4.02. 39
sore i an hundred make by adding but one more l.		4.02. 61
now, in thy likeness, one more fool appear!		4.03. 44
more sacks to the mill!		4.03. 79
once more i'll read the ode that i have writ.		4.03. 97
once more i'll mark how love can vary wit.		4.03. 98
this will i send and something else more plain		4.03.119
this audience, and i shall tell you more.		4.03.206
o, 'tis more than need.		4.03.285
love's feeling is more soft and sensible | than		4.03.334
we need more light to find your meaning out.		5.02. 21
more measure of this measure; be not nice.		5.02.222
we can afford no more at such a price.		5.02.223
if you deny to dance, let's hold more chat.		5.02.228
since you can cog, i'll play no more with you.		5.02.235
not one word more, my maids, break off, break		5.02.262
and i will wish thee never more to dance, | nor		5.02.400
dance, | nor never more in russian habit wait.		5.02.401
that more than all the world i did respect her.		5.02.437
now, to our perjury to add more terror, | we are		5.02.470
the more shame for you, judas.		5.02.602 P
more calf, certain.		5.02.640 P
more ates, more ates!		5.02.688 P
more ates, more ates!		5.02.688 P
if 'a have no more man's blood in his belly than		5.02.691 P
but more devout than this /in our respects		5.02.782
our letters, madam, show'd much more than jest.		5.02.785
if this, or more than this, i would deny, | to		5.02.813
my love is more than his;	MND	1.01.100
and (which is more than all these boasts can be)		1.01.103
broke | (in number more than ever women spoke),		1.01.176
air | more tuneable than lark to shepherd's ear		1.01.184
the more i hate, the more he follows me.		1.01.198
the more i hate, the more he follows me.		1.01.198
the more i love, the more he hateth me.		1.01.199
the more i love, the more he hateth me.		1.01.199
he no more shall see my face;		1.01.202
a lover is more condoling.		1.02. 40 P
they would have no more discretion but to hang		1.02. 80 P
hence, get thee gone, and follow me no more.		2.01.194
and even for that do i love you the more:		2.01.202
the more you beat me, i will fawn on you.		2.01.204
prove | more fond on her than she upon her love;		2.01.266
the more my prayer, the lesser is my grace.		2.02. 89
i thought you lord of more true gentleness.		2.02.132
and, for the more better assurance, tell them		3.01. 19 P
make it two more;		3.01. 25 P
for there is not a more fearful wild-fowl than		3.01. 32 P
the more the pity that some honest neighbors		3.01.145 P
i shall desire you of more acquaintance, good		3.01.182 P
i shall desire you of more acquaintance too.		3.01.188 P
i desire you /of more acquaintance, good master		3.01.195 P
a privilege never to see me more.		3.02. 79
see me no more, whether he be dead or no.		3.02. 81
you do advance your cunning more and more;		3.02.128
you do advance your cunning more and more;		3.02.128
never did mockers waste more idle breath.		3.02.168
the ear more quick of apprehension makes;		3.02.178
who more engilds the night | than all yon fiery		3.02.187
thou canst compel no more than she entreat.		3.02.249
thy threats have no more strength than her weak		3.02.250
i say i love thee more than he can do.		3.02.254
and never did desire to see thee more.		3.02.278
come one more;		3.02.437
and think no more of this night's accidents		4.01. 68
and strike more dead | than common sleep of all		4.01. 81
a cry more tuneable | was never hollow'd to, nor		4.01.124
of this discourse we more will hear anon.		4.01.178
peradventure, to make it the more gracious, i		4.01.218 P
is two or three lords and ladies more married.		4.02. 16 P
no more words.		4.02. 45 P
more strange than true.		5.01. 2
more than cool reason ever comprehends.		5.01. 6
one sees more devils than vast hell can hold;		5.01. 9
together, | more witnesseth than fancy's images,		5.01. 25
more than to us | wait in your royal walks, your		5.01. 30
but more merry tears | the passion of loud		5.01. 69
and idle theme, | no more yielding but a dream,		5.01.428
i'll tell thee more of this another time;	MV	1.01.100
of nothing, more than any man in all venice.		1.01.115 P
by something showing a more swelling port | than		1.01.124
the self-same way with more advised watch | to		1.01.142
and out of doubt you do me now more wrong | in		1.01.155
and to trouble you with no more suit, unless you		1.02.103 P
but more, for that in low simplicity | he lends		1.03. 43
the fiend gives the more friendly counsel:		2.02. 30 P
father, who, being more than sand-blind, high		2.02. 36 P
pray you let's have no more fooling about it,		2.02. 83 P
thou hast got more hair on thy chin than dobbin		2.02. 94 P
i am sure he had more hair of his tail than i		2.02. 97 P
him a livery | more guarded than his fellows';		2.02.155
nay more, while grace is saying, hood mine eyes		2.02.193
to please his grandam, never trust me more.		2.02.197
and he sleeps by day | more than the wild-cat.		2.05. 48
are, | are with more spirit chased than enjoy'd.		2.06. 13
here comes lorenzo, more of this hereafter.		2.06. 20
tell me for more certainty, | albeit i'll swear		2.06. 26
i desire no more delight | than to be under sail		2.06. 67
but more than these, in love i do deserve.		2.07. 34
let's see once more this saying grav'd in gold:		2.07. 36
but if you fail, without more speech, my lord,		2.09. 7
not learning more than the fond eye doth teach,		2.09. 27
tell me once more what title thou dost bear:		2.09. 35
did i deserve no more than a fool's head?		2.09. 59
still more fool i shall appear | by the time i		2.09. 73
no more, i pray thee.		2.09. 96
there is more difference between thy flesh and		3.01. 39 P
more between your bloods than there is between		3.01. 40 P
that the comparison | may stand more proper, my		3.02. 46
with no less presence, but with much more love,		3.02. 54
much more dismay | i view the fight than thou		3.02. 61
thy paleness moves me more than eloquence, | and		3.02.106
a thousand times more fair, ten thousand times		3.02.154
times more fair, ten thousand times more rich,		3.02.154
for intermission | no more pertains to me, my		3.02.200
the ancient roman honor more appears | than any		3.02.295
what, no more?		3.02.298
i'll have my bond, and therefore speak no more.		3.03. 13
i'll follow him no more with bootless prayers.		3.03. 20
praising of myself, | therefore no more of it.		3.04. 23
truly, the more to blame he;		3.05. 21 P
much that the moor should be more than reason;		3.05. 41 P
woman, she is indeed more than i took her for.		3.05. 42 P
yet more quarrelling with occasion!		3.05. 55 P
thou'lt show thy mercy and remorse more strange		4.01. 20
more than a lodg'd hate and a certain loathing		4.01. 60
how much more elder art thou than thy looks!		4.01.251
for herein fortune shows herself more kind		4.01.267
thou shalt have justice more than thou desir'st.		4.01.316
nor cut thou less nor more | but just a pound of		4.01.325
if thou tak'st more | or less than a just pound,		4.01.326
two things provided more, that for this favor		4.01.386
i been judge, thou shouldst have had ten more,		4.01.399
my mind was never yet more mercenary.		4.01.418
do not draw back your hand, i'll take no more,		4.01.428
there's more depends on this than on the value.		4.01.434
my lord bassanio upon more advice | hath sent		4.02. 6
no more than i am well acquitted of.		5.01.138
i never more will break an oath with thee.		5.01.248
lord | will never more break faith advisedly.		5.01.253
or, to speak more properly, stays me here at	AYL	1.01. 8 P
alone again, i'll never wrastle for prize more.		1.01.162 P
(yet i know not why) hates nothing more than he.		1.01.166 P
i show more mirth than i am mistress of, and		1.02. 3 P
no more was this knight, swearing by his honor,		1.02. 77 P
speak no more of him, you'll be whipt for		1.02. 84 P
the more pity, that fools may not speak wisely		1.02. 86 P
we shall be the more marketable.		1.02. 96 P
would counsel you to a more equal enterprise.		1.02.177 P
but his will hath in it a more modest working.		1.02.202 P
no more, no more.		1.02.216
no more, no more.		1.02.216
i am more proud to be sir rowland's son, | his		1.02.232
that could give more, but that her hand lacks		1.02.247
well, and overthrown | more than your enemies.		1.02.255
more suits you to conceive than i to speak of.		1.02.267
i shall desire more love and knowledge of you.		1.02.285
and thou wilt show more bright and seem more		1.03. 81
wilt show more bright and seem more virtuous		1.03. 81
charge thee be not thou more griev'd than i am.		1.03. 92
i have more cause.		1.03. 93
because that i am more than common tall, | that		1.03.115
hath not old custom made this life more sweet		2.01. 2
more free from peril than the envious court?		2.01. 4
and in that kind swears you do more usurp | than		2.01. 27
giving thy sum of more | to that which had too		2.01. 48
no more do yours.		2.03. 12
here lived i, but now live here no more.		2.03. 72
ay, now am i in arden, the more fool i.		2.04. 16 P
and wish, for her sake more than for mine own,		2.04. 76
my fortunes were more able to relieve her;		2.04. 77
more, more, i prithee more.		2.05. 9 P
more, more, i prithee more.		2.05. 9 P
more, more, i prithee more.		2.05. 9 P
more, i prithee more.		2.05. 12 P
more, i prithee more.		2.05. 12 P
more, i prithee more.		2.05. 14 P
more, i prithee more.		2.05. 14 P
come, more, another stanzo.		2.05. 18 P
more at your request than to please myself.		2.05. 23 P
and after one hour more 'twill be eleven, | and		2.07. 25
forbear, and eat no more.		2.07. 88
more than your force move us to gentleness.		2.07.103
presents more woeful pageants than the scene		2.07.138
or turn thou no more | to seek a living in our		3.01. 7
more villain thou.		3.01. 15
but as there is no more plenty in it, it goes		3.02. 20 P
no more but that i know the more one sickens the		3.02. 23 P
but that i know the more one sickens the worse		3.02. 23 P
a more sounder instance, come.		3.02. 61 P
o yes, i heard them all, and more, too, for some		3.02.164 P
of them had in them more feet than the verses		3.02.165 P
one inch of delay more is a south-sea of		3.02.196 P
why, god will send more, if the man will be		3.02.209 P
to these particulars is more than to answer in a		3.02.228 P
i pray you mar no more trees with writing		3.02.259 P
it strikes a man more dead than a great		3.03. 14 P
as a wall'd town is more worthier than a village		3.03. 59 P
of a married man more honorable than the bare		3.03. 60 P
by so much is a horn more precious than to want.		3.03. 63 P
winter's sisterhood kisses not more religiously,		3.04. 16 P
i see no more in you | than without candle may		3.05. 38
i see no more in you than in the ordinary | of		3.05. 42
and out of you she sees herself more proper		3.05. 55
a little riper and more lusty red | than that		3.05.121
have more cause to hate him than to love him,		3.05.128
such another trick, never come in my sight more.		4.01. 41 P
and you be so tardy, come no more in my sight.		4.01. 51 P
be your rosalind in a more coming-on disposition		4.01.112 P
i will be more jealous of thee than a barbary		4.01.150 P
hen, more clamorous than a parrot against rain,		4.01.151 P
against rain, more new-fangled than an ape, more		4.01.152 P
an ape, more giddy in my desires than a monkey.		4.01.152 P
for here comes more company.		4.03. 74 P
there is more in it. cousin ganymed!		4.03.159
by so much the more shall i to-morrow be at the		5.02. 45 P
pray you no more of this, 'tis like the howling		5.02.109 P
patience once more, whiles our compact is urg'd:		5.04. 5
times remov'd (bear your body more seeming,		5.04. 69 P
but it is no more unhandsome than to see the		ep 2 P
anon i'll give thee more instructions.	SHR	in.1. 130
wear, for i have no more doublets than backs, no		in.2. 9 P
than backs, no more stockings than legs, nor no		in.2. 9 P
than legs, nor no more shoes than feet — nay,		in.2. 10 P
nay, sometime more feet than shoes, or such		in.2. 11 P
thou hast a lady far more beautiful | than any		in.2. 62
o that once more you knew but what you are!		in.2. 78
and twenty more such names and men as these,		in.2. 95
and slept above some fifteen year or more.		in.2. 113
no, my good lord, it is more pleasing stuff.		in.2. 139
stay, | for i have more to commune with bianca.		1.01.101
saw you no more?		1.01.171
one thing more rests, that thyself execute —		1.01.246
comes there any more of it?		1.01.251 P
she shall have no more eyes to see withal than a		1.02.115 P
and her withholds from me /and other more,		1.02.121
and perhaps with more successful words | than		1.02.157
if without more words you will get you hence.		1.02.230
is, | she may more suitors have, and me for one.		1.02.241
then well one more may fair bianca have;		1.02.243
and let it be more than alcides' twelve.		1.02.256
face | which i could fancy more than any other.		2.01. 12
o then belike you fancy riches more:		2.01. 16
she is not for your turn, the more my grief.		2.01. 63
that have been more kindly beholding to you than		2.01. 78 P
i love her ten times more than e'er i did.		2.01.161
and i am one that love bianca more | than words		2.01.335
nay, i have off'red all, i have no more, | and		2.01.381
and she can have no more than all i have;		2.01.382
more pleasant, pithy, and effectual, | than hath		3.01. 68
much more a shrew of /thy impatient humor.		3.02. 29
a penny, | a horse and a man | is more than one,		3.02. 85
which at more leisure i will so excuse | as you		3.02.108
by this reck'ning he is more shrew than she.		4.01. 85 P
mistake no more, i am not litio, | nor a		4.02. 16
and here i firmly vow | never to woo her more,		4.02. 29
the more my wrong, the more his spite appears.		4.03. 2
the more my wrong, the more his spite appears.		4.03. 2
that which spites me more than all these wants,		4.03. 11
more quaint, more pleasing, nor more commendable		4.03.102
more quaint, more pleasing, nor more commendable		4.03.102
quaint, more pleasing, nor more commendable.		4.03.102
go take it hence, be gone, and say no more.		4.03.165
what, is the jay more precious than the lark,		4.03.175
lark, | because his feathers are more beautiful?		4.03.176
and therefore, if you say no more than this,		4.04. 43
be not that you look for, i have no more to say,		4.04. 96
once more toward our father's.		4.05. 1
fair lovely maid, once more good day to thee.		4.05. 33
my father's bears more toward the market-place;		5.01. 9
yet, | and show more sign of her obedience,		5.02.117
the more fool you for laying on my duty.		5.02.129
my heart as great, my reason haply more, | to		5.02.171
no more of this, helena;	AWW	1.01. 51 P
go to, no more, lest it be rather thought you		1.01. 52 P
what heaven more will, | that thee may furnish,		1.01. 68
and these great tears grace his remembrance more		1.01. 80
get you gone, sir, i'll talk with you more anon.		1.03. 64 P
there is more owing her than is paid, and more		1.03.104 P
and more shall be paid her than she'll demand.		1.03.104 P
i was very late more near her than i think she		1.03.106 P
i care no more for than i do for heaven, | so i		1.03.164
upon his worshipper, | but knows of him no more.		1.03.207
inclusive were | more than they were in note.		1.03.227
something in't | more than my father's skill,		1.03.243
use a more spacious ceremony to the noble lords;		2.01. 50 P
be more expressive to them, for they wear		2.01. 52 P
after them, and take a more dilated farewell.		2.01. 57 P
hath amaz'd me more | than i dare blame my		2.01. 84
eye, | safer than mine own two, more dear.		2.01.109
i will no more enforce mine office on you,		2.01.126
more should i question thee, and more i must —		2.01.205
more should i question thee, and more i must —		2.01.205
though more to know could not be more to trust		2.01.206
more to know could not be more to trust —		2.01.206
more, more, a hundred of them.		2.02. 42 P
more, more, a hundred of them.		2.02. 42 P
my mouth no more were broken than these boys',		2.03. 60
if not to thy estate, | a balance more replete.		2.03.176
feast | shall more attend upon the coming space,		2.03.181
i'll have no more pity of his age than i would		2.03.240 P
you are more saucy with lords and honorable		2.03.260 P
and it no more merits | the tread of a man's		2.03.274
what more commands he?		2.04. 51
come, come, no more of that.		2.05. 73
much blood let forth | and more thirsts after.		3.01. 4
here they come will tell you more;		3.02. 43 P
more i'll entreat you | written to bear along.		3.02. 94
not a hilding, hold me no more in your respect.		3.06. 4 P
no more than a fish loves water.		3.06. 85 P
it is no more | but that your daughter, ere she		3.07. 30
no more a' that.		4.02. 13
stand no more off, | but give thyself unto my		4.02. 34
they shall be no more than needful there, if		4.03. 80 P
there, if they were more than they can commend.		4.03. 81 P
if ye pinch me like a pasty, i can say no more.		4.03.123 P
therefore once more to this captain dumaine.		4.03.247 P
i have but little more to say, sir, of his		4.03.258 P
a pox upon him for me, he's more and more a cat.		4.03.264 P
a pox upon him for me, he's more and more a cat.		4.03.264 P
not, and more of his soldiership i know not,		4.03.267 P
i'll no more drumming, a plague of all drums!		4.03.298 P
captain i'll be no more, | but i will eat and		4.03.331
to whose trust | your business was more welcome.		4.04. 16
ever a friend whose thoughts more truly labor		4.04. 17
which is away — | but more of this hereafter.		4.04. 26
at home, more advanc'd by the king than by that		4.05. 5 P
i could not have ow'd her a more rooted love.		4.05. 12 P
but his fisnomy is more hotter in france than		4.05. 40 P
night, and with more haste | than is his use.		5.01. 23
to be well thank'd, | what e'er falls more.		5.01. 37
you beg a single penny more.		5.02. 37 P
you beg more than "word" then.		5.02. 40 P
whole, | not one word more of the consumed time.		5.03. 38

hath not in nature's mystery more science | than 5.03.103
win me to believe, | more than to see this ring. 5.03.120
lay a more noble thought upon mine honor | than 5.03.180
in fancy's course | are motives of more fancy, 5.03.215
faith, i know more than i'll speak. 5.03.256 P
as i said, but more than that, he lov'd her, for 5.03.259 P
of that and all the progress, more and less, 5.03.331
less, | resolvedly more leisure shall express. 5.03.332
the bitter past, more welcome is the sweet. 5.03.334
enough, no more! TN 1.01. 7
sometimes i have no more wit than a christian or 1.03. 84 P
youth | than in a nuntio's of more grave aspect. 1.04. 28
diana's lip | is not more smooth and rubious; 1.04. 32
peace, you rogue, no more o' that. 1.05. 29 P
i'll no more of you. 1.05. 41 P
the more fool, madonna, to mourn for your 1.05. 70 P
fool that has no more brain than a stone. 1.05. 85 P
we'll once more hear orsino's embassy. 1.05.166
i can say little more than i have studied, and 1.05.178 P
it is the more like to be feign'd. 1.05.196 P
have you no more to say? 1.05.229 P
let him send no more — | unless, perchance, you 1.05.280
i seem to drown her remembrance again with more. 2.01. 32 P
upon the least occasion more mine eyes will tell 2.01. 41 P
and — one thing more — that you be never so 2.02. 9 P
with a better grace, but i do it more natural. 2.03. 83 P
art any more than a steward? 2.03.114 P
virtuous, there shall be no more cakes and ale? 2.03.116 P
my lady's favor at any thing more than contempt, 2.03.122 P
thou hadst need send for more money. 2.03.183 P
more than light airs and recollected terms | of 2.04. 5
our fancies are more giddy and unfirm, | more 2.04. 33
more longing, wavering, sooner lost and worn, 2.04. 34
once more, cesario, | get thee to yond same 2.04. 79
tell her, my love, more noble than the world, 2.04. 81
we men may say more, swear more, but indeed 2.04.116
we men may say more, swear more, but indeed 2.04.116
more, but indeed | our shows are more than will; 2.04.117
she uses me with a more exalted respect than any 2.05. 26 P
you might see more detraction at your heels than 2.05.137 P
daylight and champian discovers not more. 2.05.160 P
and thou pass upon me, i'll no more with thee. 3.01. 42 P
a murd'rous guilt shows not itself more soon 3.01.147
never more | will i my master's tears to you 3.01.161
i saw your niece do more favors to the count's 3.02. 5 P
in the world can more prevail in man's 3.02. 37 P
smile his face into more lines than is in the 3.02. 79 P
more sharp than filed steel, did spur me forth, 3.03. 5
for youth is bought more oft than begg'd or 3.04. 3
lady would not lose him for more than i'll say. 3.04.105 P
you shall know more hereafter. 3.04.124 P
more matter for a may morning. 3.04.142 P
gives manhood more approbation than ever proof 3.04.181 P
but nothing of the circumstance more. 3.04.262 P
that for his love dares yet do more | than you 3.04.316
me | much more for what i cannot do for you 3.04.336
i hate ingratitude more in a man | than lying, 3.04.354
paltry boy, and more a coward than a hare. 3.04.385 P
in which thou art more puzzled than the 4.02. 43 P
i am no more mad than you are; 4.02. 47 P
shall advantage thee more than ever the bearing 4.02.111 P
you can fool no more money out of me at this 5.01. 41 P
hath tended upon me, | but more of that anon. 5.01.100
after him i love | more than i love these eyes, 5.01.135
more than i love these eyes, more than my life, 5.01.135
more, by all mores, than e'er i shall love wife. 5.01.136
comes sir toby halting — you shall hear more. 5.01.192 P
is not more twin | than these two creatures. 5.01.223
since their more mature dignities and royal WT 1.01. 25 P
two lads that thought there was no more behind 1.02. 63
petitions, made | his business more material. 1.02.216
will draw in | more than the common blocks. 1.02.225
wishing clocks more swift? 1.02.289
would do that | which should undo more doing; 1.02.312
his revenges must | in that be made more bitter. 1.02.457
in the world, | he were as much more villain: 2.01. 80
more — she's a traitor, and camillo is | a 2.01. 89
heavens look | with an aspect more favorable. 2.01.107
cease, no more. 2.01.150
and more it would content me | to have her honor 2.01.159
yourselves | we need no more of your advice. 2.01.168
judgment tried it, | without more overture. 2.01.172
though i am satisfied and need no more | than 2.01.189
my red–look'd anger be | the trumpet any more. 2.02. 33
fear you his tyrannous passion more, alas, 2.03. 28
innocent soul, | more free than he is jealous. 2.03. 30
once more, take her hence. 2.03.112
unworthy and unnatural lord | can do no more. 2.03.114
(not able to produce more accusation | than your 2.03.118
that there thou leave it | (without more mercy) 2.03.178
though a present death | had been more merciful. 2.03.185
in more than this deed does require! 2.03.190
which is more | than history can pattern, though 3.02. 35
more than mistress of | which comes to me in 3.02. 59
the gods themselves | (wotting no more than i) 3.02. 76
which to deny concerns more than avails; 3.02. 86
is indeed | more criminal in thee than it), so 3.02. 89
poor trespasses, | more monstrous standing by; 3.02.190
say no more. 3.02.216
i'll speak of her no more, nor of your children; 3.02.229
thou ne'er shalt see | thy wife paulina more." 3.03. 36
the day frowns more and more; 3.03. 54
the day frowns more and more; 3.03. 54
pray thee, good camillo, be no more importunate. 4.02. 1 P
to be more thankful to thee shall be my study, 4.02. 18 P
fatal country sicilia, prithee speak no more, 4.02. 21 P
of her is extended more than can be thought to 4.02. 43 P
thou hast need of more rags to lay on thee, 4.03. 54 P
of them offend me more than the stripes i have 4.03. 57 P
and yet it will no more but abide. 4.03. 93 P
not a more cowardly rogue in all bohemia. 4.03.105 P
a way to make us better friends, more known. 4.04. 66
no more than were i painted i would wish | this 4.04.101
points more than all the lawyers in bohemia can 4.04.205 P
that have more in them than you'ld think, sister 4.04.215 P
he hath promis'd you more than that, or there be 4.04.237 P
may be he has paid you more, which will shame 4.04.240 P
clamor your tongues, and not a word more. 4.04.248 P
it, and witnesses more than my pack will hold. 4.04.283 P
thou hast sworn it more to me: 4.04.307
o, father, you'll know more of that hereafter. 4.04.343
and he, and more | than he, and men — the earth 4.04.370
force and knowledge | more than was ever man's, 4.04.375
i shall have more than you can dream of yet, 4.04.388
pray you once more, | is not your father grown 4.04.396
briers and made | more homely than thy state. 4.04.426
sigh | that thou no more shalt see this knack 4.04.428
or /hoop his body more with thy embraces, | i 4.04.439
more straining on for plucking back, not 4.04.465
i mean not | to see him any more) cast your good 4.04.495
if your more ponderous and settled project | may 4.04.524
that i may call thee something more than man 4.04.535
a course more promising | than a wild dedication 4.04.565
i hold it the more knavery to conceal it; 4.04.681 P
aside, here is more matter for a hot brain. 4.04.684 P
he seems to be the more noble in being 4.04.751 P
to the outside of his hand, and no more ado. 4.04.804 P
i'll make it as much more, and leave this young 4.04.808 P
paid down | more penitence than done trespass. 5.01. 4
have done the time more benefit and grac'd 5.01. 22
what were more holy | than to rejoice the former 5.01. 29
and left them | more rich for what they yielded. 5.01. 55
no more such wives, therefore no wife. 5.01. 56
that she is a woman | more worth than any man; 5.01.111
prithee no more; 5.01.119
i desire my life | once more to look on him. 5.01.138
(he bade me say so) more than all the sceptres, 5.01.146
remember since you ow'd no more to time | than i 5.01.219
she was more worth such gazes | than what you 5.01.226
wisest beholder, that knew no more but seeing, 5.02. 17 P
here comes a gentleman that happily knows more. 5.02. 20 P
lady paulina's steward, he can deliver you more. 5.02. 27 P
that she might no more be in danger of losing. 5.02. 78 P
we may live, son, to shed many more. 5.02.146 P
silence, it the more shows off | your wonder; 5.03. 21
so much the more our carver's excellence, 5.03. 30
stone rebuke me | for being more stone than it? 5.03. 38
the chapel, or resolve you | for more amazement. 5.03. 87
be stone no more; 5.03. 99
strong possession much more than your right, JN 1.01. 40
of no more force to dispossess me, sir, | than 1.01.132
kneel thou down philip, but rise more great, 1.01.161
france, for france, for it is more than need. 1.01.179
anon i'll tell thee more. 1.01.232
that to my home i will no more return | till 2.01. 21
strength | to make a more requital to your love! 2.01. 34
churlish drums | cuts off more circumstance. 2.01. 77
and out of my dear love i'll give thee more 2.01.157
peace, lady, pause, or be more temperate. 2.01.195
peace, no more. 2.01.293
france, hast thou yet more blood to cast away? 2.01.334
in this hot trial more than we of france, 2.01.342
more than we of france, | rather lost more. 2.01.343
this union shall do more than battery can | to 2.01.446
lions more confident, mountains and rocks | more 2.01.452
mountains and rocks | more free from motion, no, 2.01.453
or if you will, to speak more properly, | i will 2.01.514
with her to thee, and this addition more, | full 2.01.529
from the mouth of england | add thus much more, 3.01.153
do so, king philip, hang no more in doubt. 3.01.219
what canst thou say but will perplex thee more, 3.01.222
no more than he that threats. to arms let's hie! 3.01.347
never | must i behold my pretty arthur more. 3.04. 89
having so great a title | to be more prince, as 4.01. 11
i doubt | my uncle practices more harm to me. 4.01. 20
i warrant i love you more than you do me. 4.01. 31
are you more stubborn–hard than hammer'd iron? 4.01. 67
no more. 4.01.126
silence, no more. 4.01.132
breach | discredit more in hiding of the fault 4.02. 33
and more, more strong than lesser is my fear, 4.02. 42
and more, more strong than lesser is my fear, 4.02. 42
not seek to stuff | my head with more ill news, 4.02.134
and others more, going to seek the grave | of 4.02.164
frowns | more upon humor than advis'd respect. 4.02.214
out of my sight, and never see me more! 4.02.242
presented thee more hideous than thou art. 4.02.266
run more fast. 4.02.269
is much more general than these lines import. 4.03. 17
once more to–day well met, distemper'd lords! 4.03. 21
thou art more deep damn'd than prince lucifer. 4.03.122
and makes me more amaz'd | than had i seen the 5.02. 51
he is more patient | than when you left him; 5.07. 11
since the more fair and crystal is the sky, R2 1.01. 41
once more, the more to aggravate the note, 1.01. 43
once more, the more to aggravate the note, 1.01. 43
blood | doth more solicit me than your exclaims 1.02. 2
yet one word more! 1.02. 58
i shall remember more. 1.02. 65
more than my dancing soul doth celebrate | this 1.03. 91
and now my tongue's use is to me no more | than 1.03.161
smooth his fault i should have been more mild. 1.03.240
and thy steps no more | than a delightful 1.03.290
fell sorrow's tooth doth never rankle more 1.03.302
he that no more must say is listened more | than 2.01. 9
he that no more must say is listened more | than 2.01. 9
more are men's ends mark'd than their lives 2.01. 11
writ in remembrance more than things long past. 2.01. 14
young hot colts being rag'd do rage the more. 2.01. 70
is it not more than shame to shame it so? 2.01.112
in war was never lion rag'd more fierce, | in 2.01.173
in peace was never gentle lamb more mild, | than 2.01.174
and let him ne'er speak more | that speaks thy 2.01.230
more hath he spent in peace than they in wars. 2.01.255
more than with parting from my lord the king. 2.02. 13
find shapes of grief, more than himself, to wail 2.02. 22
more than your lord's departure weep not — more 2.02. 25
lord's departure weep not — more is not seen, 2.02. 25
confirm | to more approved service and desert. 2.03. 44
which more enrich'd | shall be your love and 2.03. 61
but then more "why?" 2.03. 92
this and much more, much more than twice all 3.01. 28
and much more, much more than twice all this, 3.01. 28
more welcome is the stroke of death to me | than 3.01. 31
more health and happiness betide my liege | than 3.02. 91
that bids me be of comfort any more. 3.02.208
it doth remember me the more of sorrow; 3.04. 14
had, | it adds more sorrow to my want of joy; 3.04. 16
so, | i speak no more than every one doth know. 3.04. 91
and never brandish more revengeful steel | over 4.01. 50
not be many hours of age | more than it is, ere 5.01. 58
once more, adieu, the rest let sorrow say. 5.01.102
even so, we will adore more contempt, men's eyes 5.02. 27
it is no more | than my poor life must answer. 5.02. 82
never more come in my sight. 5.02. 86
have we more sons? 5.02. 90
as i have done, thou wouldst be more pitiful. 5.02.103
more sins for this forgiveness prosper may. 5.03. 84
shall thy old dugs once more a traitor rear? 5.03. 90
this music mads me, let it sound no more, | for 5.05. 61
more than thou hast, and with it joy thy life. 5.06. 26
no more the thirsty entrance of this soil 1H4 1.01. 5
no more shall trenching war channel her fields, 1.01. 7
march all one way and be no more oppos'd 1.01. 15
knife, | no more shall cut his master. 1.01. 18
for more uneven and unwelcome news | came from 1.01. 50
for more is to be said and to be done | than out 1.01.106
hal, i prithee trouble me no more with vanity; 1.02. 81 P
he may be more wond'red at | by breaking through 1.02.201
shall show more goodly and attract more eyes 1.02.214
shall show more goodly and attract more eyes 1.02.214
needs no more but one tongue for all those 1.03. 96
and shall it in more shame be further spoken, 1.03.177
peace, cousin, say no more. 1.03.187
the blood more stirs | to rouse a lion than to 1.03.197
then once more to your scottish prisoners: 1.03.259
for thou variest no more from picking of purses 2.01. 50 P
i think you are more beholding to the night than 2.01. 88 P
there's no more valor in that poins than in a 2.02.101 P
let me see some more. 2.03. 6 P
sir john with half a dozen more are at the door, 2.04. 82 P
geese, i'll never wear hair on my face more. 2.04.139 P
if they speak more or less than truth, they are 2.04.171 P
i made me no more ado but took all their seven 2.04.201 P
prithee let him alone, we shall have more anon. 2.04.207 P
so, two more already. 2.04.213 P
ah, no more of that, hal, and thou lovest me! 2.04.283 P
and one mordake, and a thousand blue–caps more. 2.04.357 P
though the camomile, the more it is trodden on, 2.04.400 P
/yet youth, the more it is wasted, the sooner it 2.04.401 P
but to say i know more harm in him than in 2.04.466 P
than in myself, were to say more than i know. 2.04.467 P
that he is old, the more the pity, his white 2.04.468 P
jack falstaff, and therefore more valiant, being 2.04.477 P
keep close, we'll read it at more advantage. 2.04.542 P
come, come, no more of this unprofitable chat. 3.01. 62
little | more than a little is by much too much. 3.02. 73
save mine, which hath desir'd to see thee more, 3.02. 89
my thrice–gracious lord, | be more myself. 3.02. 93
he hath more worthy interest to the state | than 3.02. 98
and, being no more in debt to years than thou, 3.02.103
there's no more faith in thee than in a stew'd 3.03.112 P
nor no more truth in thee than in a drawn fox, 3.03.113 P
thou seest i have more flesh than another man, 3.03.167 P
than another man, and therefore more frailty. 3.03.167 P
present want | seems more than we shall find it. 4.01. 45
it lends a lustre and more great opinion, | a 4.01. 77
no harm. what more? 4.01. 90
no more, no more! 4.01.111
no more, no more! 4.01.111
there is more news: 4.01.124
ten times more dishonorable ragged than an old 4.02. 30 P
sir john, 'tis more than time that i were there, 4.02. 54 P
the more and less came in with cap and knee, 4.03. 68
light, | and be no more an exhal'd meteor, | a 5.01. 19
more active, valiant, or more valiant, young, 5.01. 90
more active, valiant, or more valiant, young, 5.01. 90
more daring or more bold, is now alive | to 5.01. 91
more daring or more bold, is now alive | to 5.01. 91
life | did hear a challenge urg'd more modestly, 5.02. 52
i need no more weight than mine own bowels. 5.03. 35 P
percy, | to share with me in glory any more. 5.04. 64
more than he haply may retail from me. 2H4 1.01. 32
look, here comes more news. 1.01. 59
from whence with life he never more sprung up. 1.01.111
'tis more than time, and, my most noble lord, 1.01.187
never so few, and never yet more need. 1.01.215
intends to laughter more than i invent or is 1.02. 8 P
a man can no more separate age and covetousness 1.02.229 P
and my pension shall seem the more reasonable. 1.02.247 P
to us no more, nay, not so much, lord bardolph, 1.03. 69
it is more than for some, my lord, it is for all 2.01. 73 P
desire me to be no more so familiarity with such 2.01. 99 P
that come with such more than impudent sauciness 2.01.112 P
as i am a gentleman! come, no more words of it. 2.01.138 P
no more words, let's have her. 2.01.165 P
i have given over, i will speak no more; 2.03. 5
when you were more /endear'd to it than now, 2.03. 11
and told him there were five more sir johns, and 2.04. 6 P
i'll drink no more than will do me good, for no 2.04.119 P
no more, pistol, i would not have you go off 2.04.136 P
there's no more conceit in him than is in a 2.04.241 P
more knocking at the door! 2.04.369 P
that thou no more wilt weigh my eyelids down, 3.01. 7
to comfort you the more, i have received | a 3.01.102
'tis the more time thou wert us'd. 3.02.106 P
prick him no more. 3.02.145 P
will do my good will, sir, you can have no more. 3.02.157 P
here is two more call'd than your number, you 3.02.188 P
no more of that, master shallow, /no /more /of 3.02.196 P
our battle is more full of names than yours, 4.01.152
our men more perfect in the use of arms, | our 4.01.153
to ye | shall show itself more openly hereafter. 4.02. 76
it was more of his courtesy than your deserving. 4.03. 43 P
here at more leisure may your highness read, 4.04. 89
look here's more news. 4.04. 93
be happy, he will trouble you no more. 4.05.127
if i affect it more | than as your honor and as 4.05.144
let me no more from this obedience rise, | which 4.05.146
other, less fine in carat, /is more precious, 4.05.161
thou mightst win the more thy father's love, 4.05.179
falls upon thee in a more fairer sort; 4.05.200
though thou stand'st more sure than i could do, 4.05.202
more would i, but my lungs are wasted so | that 4.05.216

be, | which i with more than with a common pain 4.05.223
nature, | and to our purposes he lives no more. 5.02. 5
which cannot look more hideously upon me | than 5.02. 12
but entertain no more of it, good brothers, 5.02. 54
nay more, to spurn at your most royal image, 5.02. 89
pistol, utter more to me, and withal devise 5.03.133 P
more rushes, more rushes. 5.05. 1 P
more rushes, more rushes. 5.05. 1 P
make less thy body (hence) and more thy grace, 5.05. 52
appear more wise and modest to the world. 5.05.101
one word more, i beseech you. ep 26 P
or rather swaying more upon our part | than H5 1.01. 73
had nobles richer and more loyal subjects, 1.02.127
she hath been then more fear'd than harm'd, my 1.02.155
cat, | to 'tame and havoc more than she can eat. 1.02.173
dukedoms that you claim | hear no more of you. 1.02.257
when thousands weep more than did laugh at it. 1.02.296
swiftness add | more feathers to our wings; 1.02.307
him on, | and on his more advice we pardon him. 2.02. 43
breed, by his sufferance, more of such a kind. 2.02. 46
and i repent my fault more than my death, 2.02.152
never did faithful subject more rejoice | at the 2.02.161
so 'a bade me lay more clothes on his feet. 2.03. 22 P
and more than carefully it us concerns | to 2.04. 2
no, with no more than if we heard that england 2.04. 24
to weigh | the enemy more mighty than he seems, 2.04. 44
once more unto the breach, dear friends, once 3.01. 1
more unto the breach, dear friends, once more; 3.01. 1
he has no more directions in the true 3.02. 71 P
when there is more better opportunity to be 3.02.138 P
whiles a more frosty people | sweat drops of 3.05. 24
of honor edged | more sharper than your swords, 3.05. 39
horn of his hoof is more musical than the pipe 3.07. 17 P
no more, cousin. 3.07. 30 P
and 'twere more honor some were away. 3.07. 75 P
that's more than we know. 4.01.129 P
ay, or more than we should seek after; 4.01.130 P
no more is the king guilty of their damnation 4.01.174 P
of every fool whose sense no more can feel | but 4.01.235
that suffer'st more | of mortal griefs than do 4.01.241
and on it have bestowed more contrite tears, 4.01.296
more will i do; 4.01.302
if we no more meet till we meet in heaven, 4.03. 7
god's will, i pray thee wish not one man more. 4.03. 23
as one man more methinks would share from me, 4.03. 32
o, do not wish one more! 4.03. 33
thou dost not wish more help from england, coz? 4.03. 73
without more help, could fight this royal battle 4.03. 75
once more i come to know of thee, king harry, 4.03. 79
come thou no more for ransom, gentle herald, 4.03.122
thou never shalt hear herald any more. 4.03.127
i fear thou wilt once more come again for a 4.03.128 P
and nym had ten times more valor than this 4.04. 70 P
in once more! 4.05. 11
there is more good toward you peradventure than 4.08. 3 P
where ne'er from france arriv'd more happy men. 4.08.126
much more, and much more cause, | did they this 5.pr. 34
much more, and much more cause, | did they this 5.pr. 34
will you have some more sauce to your leek? 5.01. 49 P
council presently | to sit with us once more, 5.02. 80
the kingdom as to speak so much more french. 5.02.185 P
of beauty, can do no more spoil upon my face. 5.02.231 P
there is more eloquence in a sugar touch of them 5.02.276 P
more dazzled and drove back his enemies | than 1H6 1.01. 13
awe, | more than god or religious churchmen may. 1.01. 40
a far more glorious star thy soul will make 1.01. 55
news would cause him once more yield the ghost. 1.01. 67
the circumstance i'll tell you more at large. 1.01.109
more than three hours the fight continued, 1.01.120
more truly now may this be verified, | for none 1.02. 32
and hunger will enforce them to be more eager. 1.02. 38
he may mean more than we poor men do know: 1.02.122
this cardinal's more haughty than the devil. 1.03. 85
this day is ours, as many more shall be. 1.05. 18
more blessed hap did ne'er befall our state. 1.06. 10
in an urn more precious | than the rich–jewell'd 1.06. 24
more venturous or desperate than this. 2.01. 45
no, truly, 'tis more than manners will; 2.02. 54
and more than may be gathered by thy shape. 2.03. 69
too loud, | the garden here is more convenient. 2.04. 4
stay, lords and gentlemen, and pluck no more, 2.04. 39
discover more at large what cause that was, 2.05. 59
more than well beseems | a man of thy profession 3.01. 19
and for thy treachery, what's more manifest? 3.01. 21
who preferreth peace | more than i do, except i 3.01. 34
away, my masters, trouble us no more, | but join 3.01.144
and now no more ado, brave burgundy, | but 3.02.101
should grieve thee more than streams of foreign 3.03. 55
much more a knight, a captain, and a leader. 4.01. 32
no more but plain and bluntly "to the king"? 4.01. 51
i more incline to somerset than york: 4.01.154
seen decipher'd there | more rancorous spite, 4.01.185
rancorous spite, more furious raging broils, 4.01.185
but more, when envy breeds unkind division: 4.01.193
lucy, farewell, no more my fortune can, | but 4.03. 43
no more can i be severed from your side | than 4.05. 48
all these, and more, we hazard by thy stay; 4.06. 40
then talk no more of flight, it is no boot; 4.06. 52
to be a queen in bondage is more vile | than is 5.03.112
with more than half the gallian territories, 5.04.139
that which i have than, coveting for more, | be 5.04.145
and, which is more, she is not so divine, | so 5.05. 16
why, what, i pray, is margaret more than that? 5.05. 36
marriage is a matter of more worth | than to be 5.05. 55
spirit | (more than in women commonly is seen) 5.05. 71
conqueror, | is likely to beget more conquerors, 5.05. 74
nay more, an enemy unto you all, | and no great 2H6 1.01.149
his insolence is more intolerable | than all the 1.01.175
more like a soldier than a man o' th' church, 1.01.186
and never more abase our sight so low | as to 1.02. 15
away from me, and let me hear no more! 1.02. 50
we'll hear more of your matter before the king. 1.03. 35 P
but can do more in england than the king. 1.03. 71
all | cannot do more in england than the nevils: 1.03. 73
more like an empress than duke humphrey's wife. 1.03. 78
have done, for more i hardly can endure. 1.04. 38
no more than well becomes | so good a quarrel 2.01. 27
the fowl so suddenly, | we had had more sport. 2.01. 45

but you have done more miracles than i: 2.01.159
as more at large your grace shall understand. 2.01.173
what plain proceedings is more plain than this? 2.02. 53
you, madam, for you are more nobly born, 2.03. 9
or more afraid to fight, than is the appellant, 2.03. 57
peter? what more? 2.03. 82 P
what's more dangerous than this fond affiance! 3.01. 74
unless thou wert more loyal than thou art. 3.01. 96
i say no more than truth, so help me god! 3.01.120
for thousands more, that yet suspect no peril, 3.01.152
for what's more miserable than discontent? 3.01.201
believe me, lords, were none more wise than i — 3.01.231
more than mistrust, that shows him worthy death. 3.01.242
'tis york that hath more reason for his death. 3.01.245
no more, good york; 3.01.304
no more of him; 3.01.323
that henceforth he shall trouble us no more. 3.01.324
my brain, more busy than the laboring spider, 3.01.339
be woe for me, more wretched than he is. 3.02. 73
because thy flinty heart, more hard than they, 3.02. 99
ay me, i can no more! 3.02.120
no more, i say! 3.02.291
i can no more: 3.02.365
from thee to die were torture more than death. 3.02.401
o, torture me no more, i will confess. 3.03. 11
threatens more | than bargulus the strong 4.01.107
more can i bear than you dare execute. 4.01.130
hale him away, and let him talk no more. 4.01.131
they have the more need to sleep now then. 4.02. 3 P
nay more, the king's council are no good workmen 4.02. 14 P
and more than that, he can speak french, and 4.02.166 P
i desire no more. 4.03. 9 P
be wise, he'll never call ye jack cade more. 4.06. 10 P
the giving up of some more towns in france. 4.07.133 P
and could command no more content than i? 4.09. 2
doornail, i pray god i may never eat grass more. 4.10. 41 P
more like a king, more kingly in my thoughts; 5.01. 29
more like a king, more kingly in my thoughts; 5.01. 29
till henry be more weak and i more strong. 5.01. 31
till henry be more weak and i more strong. 5.01. 31
thou shalt rule no more | o'er him whom heaven 5.01.104
stigmatic, that's more than thou canst tell. 5.01.215
no more will i their babes. 5.02. 52
us | by what we can, which can no more but fly. 5.02. 77
all, | and more such days as these to us befall! 5.03. 33
i'll have more lives | than drops of blood were 3H6 1.01. 96
urge it no more, lest that, in stead of words, 1.01. 98
while you are thus employ'd, what resteth more, 1.02. 44
i dare your quenchless fury to more rage. 1.04. 28
whose tongue more poisons than the adder's tooth 1.04.112
but you are more inhuman, more inexorable, | o, 1.04.154
but you are more inhuman, more inexorable, | o, 1.04.154
o, ten times more, than tigers of hyrcania. 1.04.155
o, speak no more, for i have heard too much. 2.01. 48
again, | never, o never, shall i see more joy! 2.01. 78
the words would add more anguish than the wounds 2.01. 99
and now, to add more measure to your woes, | i 2.01.105
or more than common fear of clifford's rigor, 2.01.126
and would my father had left me no more! 2.02. 50
as brings a thousandfold more care to keep 2.02. 52
away, away! once more, sweet lords, farewell. 2.03. 48
and no more words till they have flow'd their 2.05. 72
grief more than common grief! 2.05. 94
/e'en for the loss of thee, having no more, | as 2.05.119
here sits a king more woeful than you are. 2.05.124
more than my body's parting with my soul. 2.06. 4
and his ill–boding tongue no more shall speak. 2.06. 59
forbear awhile, we'll hear a little more. 3.01. 27
she, poor wretch, for grief can speak no more; 3.01. 47
more than i seem, and less than i was born to; 3.01. 56
i speak no more than what my soul intends, | and 3.02. 94
and that is more than i will yield unto. 3.02. 96
no more than when my daughters call thee mother. 3.02.101
answer no more, for thou shalt be my queen. 3.02.106
and more unlikely | than to accomplish twenty 3.02.151
i'll drown more sailors than the mermaid shall, 3.02.186
i'll slay more gazers than the basilisk, | i'll 3.02.187
nestor, | deceive more slily than ulysses could, 3.02.189
the more we stay, the stronger grows our foe. 3.03. 40
the more i stay, the more i'll succor thee. 3.03. 41
the more i stay, the more i'll succor thee. 3.03. 41
and thou no more art prince than she is queen. 3.03. 80
and more than so, my father, | even in the 3.03.103
the more that henry was unfortunate. 3.03.118
no more my king, for he dishonors me, | but most 3.03.184
for matching more for wanton lust than honor, 3.03.210
alliance | would more have strength'ned this our 4.01. 37
i hear, yet say not much, but think the more. 4.01. 83
more incens'd against your majesty | than all 4.01.108
tell me if you love warwick more than me? 4.01.137
'tis the more honor, because more dangerous. 4.03. 15
'tis the more honor, because more dangerous. 4.03. 15
to set the crown once more on henry's head. 4.04. 27
come then, away, let's ha' no more ado. 4.05. 27
now then it is more than needful | forthwith 4.06. 53
let me entreat (for i command no more) | that 4.06. 59
he | must help you more than you are hurt by me. 4.06. 76
and we shall have more wars before't be long. 4.06. 91
and says that once more i shall interchange | my 4.07. 3
my liege, i'll knock once more to summon them. 4.07. 16
and all at once, once more a happy farewell. 4.08. 31
then why should they love edward more than me? 4.08. 47
alas, that warwick had no more forecast, | but, 5.01. 42
"wind–changing warwick now can change no more." 5.01. 57
more than the nature of a brother's love! 5.01. 79
to keep that oath were more impiety | than 5.01. 90
for i will henceforth be no more unconstant. 5.01.102
now welcome more, and ten times more belov'd, 5.01.103
now welcome more, and ten times more belov'd, 5.01.103
and more he would have said, and more he spoke, 5.02. 43
and more he would have said, and more he spoke, 5.02. 43
and give more strength to that which hath too 5.04. 9
the brothers | more than with ruthless waves, 5.04. 36
i need not add more fuel to your fire, | for 5.04. 70
therefore no more but this: 5.04. 76
thy mother felt more than a mother's pain, | and 5.06. 49
i'll hear no more; 5.06. 57
ay, and for much more slaughter after this. 5.06. 59

once more we sit in england's royal throne, 5.07. 1
more pity that the eagles should be mew'd, R3 1.01.132
to urge his hatred more to clarence | with lies 1.01.147
more direful hap betide that hated wretch | that 1.02. 17
her be made | more miserable by the /life of him 1.02. 27
more wonderful, when angels are so angry. 1.02. 74
'tis more than you deserve; 1.02.222
she may do more, sir, than denying that: 1.03. 93
but i do find more pain in banishment | than 1.03.167
ay, and much more; 1.03.262
let him see our commission, and talk no more. 1.04. 90 P
and more /in peace my soul shall part to heaven, 2.01. 5
i will never more remember | our former hatred, 2.01. 23
more than the infant that is born to–night. 2.01. 72
much more to be thus opposite with heaven, | for 2.02. 94
which would be so much the more dangerous, | by 2.02.126
it so, | 'tis more than we deserve or i expect. 2.03. 37
talk'd how i did grow | more than my brother. 2.04. 12
or let me die, to look on /death no more! 2.04. 65
i want more uncles here to welcome me. 3.01. 6
nor more can you distinguish of a man | than of 3.01. 9
then he is more beholding to you than i. 3.01.107
well then, no more but this: 3.01.169
give mistress shore one gentle kiss the more. 3.01.185
and, for more slander to thy dismal seat, | we 3.03. 13
he knows no more of mine than i of yours, | or i 3.04. 11
which we more hunt for than the grace of god! 3.04. 97
and so once more return and tell his grace. 3.07. 91
more bitterly could i expostulate, | save that, 3.07.192
/'zounds, /i'll entreat no more. 3.07.219
more miserable by the life of thee | than thou 4.01. 75
no more than with my soul i mourn for yours. 4.01. 88
no more shall be the neighbor to my counsels. 4.02. 43
there is no more but so; 4.02. 80
ely with richmond troubles me more near | than 4.03. 49
having no more but thought of what thou wast 4.04.107
of what thou wast | to torture thee the more, 4.04.108
more mild, but yet more harmful — kind in 4.04.173
more mild, but yet more harmful — kind in 4.04.173
perish | and never more behold thy face again. 4.04.187
which in the day of battle tire thee more | than 4.04.189
though far more cause, yet much less spirit to 4.04.197
as i intend more good to you and yours | than 4.04.238
once more, what news? 4.04.462
and every hour more competitors | flock to the 4.04.504
yet one thing more, good captain, do for me — 5.03. 33
once more, adieu! 5.03.102
once more, good night, kind lords and gentlemen. 5.03.107
have strook more terror to the soul of richard 5.03.217
more than i have said, loving countrymen, | the 5.03.237
why, what is that to me | more than to richmond? 5.03.286
what shall i say more than i have inferr'd? 5.03.314
the king enacts more wonders than a man, 5.04. 2
i come no more to make you laugh; H8 pr 1
well, we shall then know more, and buckingham 1.01.118
more stronger to direct you than yourself, | if 1.01.147
no more, i hope? 1.01.220
you know no more than others? 1.02. 44
most rare speaker, | to nature none more bound; 1.02.112
ten times more ugly | than ever they were fair. 1.02.117
there's something more would out of thee; 1.02.202
and once more | i show'r a welcome on ye. 1.04. 62
his person | more worthy this place than myself, 1.04. 79
so are a number more. 2.01. 9
that sought it i could wish more christians. 2.01. 64
have mercies | more than i dare make faults. 2.01. 71
and out of ruins | made my name once more noble. 2.01.115
let's think in private more. 2.01.169
whom once more i present unto your highness. 2.02. 97
and once more in mine arms i bid him welcome, 2.02. 98
to leave a thousandfold more bitter than | 'tis 2.03. 8
so much the more | must pity drop upon her. 2.03. 17
in your way | for more than blushing comes to. 2.03. 42
there 'long'd | no more to th' crown but that. 2.03. 49
more than my all is nothing: 2.03. 67
nor my wishes | more worth than empty vanities; 2.03. 69
nor no more assurance | of equal friendship and 2.04. 17
refuse you for my judge, whom, yet once more, 2.04. 82
unthink your speaking | and to say so no more. 2.04.105
you tender more your person's honor than | your 2.04.116
nor ever more | upon this business my appearance 2.04.132
but will you be more justified? 2.04.163
should | do no more offices of life to't than 2.04.191
a strange tongue makes my cause more strange, 3.01. 45
so near mine honor | (more near my life, i fear) 3.01. 72
the more shame for ye! 3.01.102
wish ye half my miseries, | i have more charity. 3.01.109
our ends are honest, | you'ld feel more comfort. 3.01.155
katherine no more | shall be call'd queen, but 3.02. 69
for him, | there's more in't than fair visage. 3.02. 88
show'r'd on me daily have been more than could 3.02.167
my pow'r rain'd honor, more | on you than any, 3.02.185
as 'twere in love's particular, be more | to me, 3.02.189
good i ever labor'd | more than mine own; 3.02.192
make 'em, and | appear in forms more horrid), 3.02.196
in the evening, | and no man see me more. 3.02.227
till i find more than will or words to do it 3.02.236
many more there are, | which, since they are of 3.02.330
more pangs and fears than wars or women have; 3.02.370
to endure more miseries and greater far | than 3.02.389
that sir thomas more is chosen | lord chancellor 3.02.393
what more? 3.02.400
where no mention | of me more must be heard of, 3.02.434
corruption wins not more than honesty. 3.02.444
and more and richer, when he strains that lady. 4.01. 46
no more of that. 4.01. 55
where a finger | could not be wedg'd in more. 4.01. 58
you must no more call it york–place, that's past 4.01. 95
he will deserve more. 4.01.113
as i walk thither, | i'll tell ye more. 4.01.117
a saucy fellow, | deserve we no more reverence? 4.02.100
i must to bed, | call in more women. 4.02.167
i can no more. 4.02.173
charles, i will play no more to–night, | my 5.01. 56
none stands under more calumnious tongues | than 5.01.112
they shall no more prevail than we give way to. 5.01.143
by this light, i'll ha' more. 5.01.171
i will have more or scold it out of him. 5.01.173

i'll have more, or else unsay't; 5.01.175
we shall hear more anon. 5.02. 35
a man that more detests, more stirs against, 5.02. 74
a man that more detests, more stirs against, 5.02. 74
lord, because we have business of more moment, 5.02. 86
more than, i fear, you are provided for. 5.02. 92
i could say more, | but reverence to your 5.02.103
how much more is his life in value with him! 5.02.143
ye, i see, | more out of malice than integrity, 5.02.180
make me no more ado, but all embrace him. 5.02.193
once more, my lord of winchester, i charge you, 5.02.204
so i grow stronger, you more honor gain. 5.02.215
never | more covetous of wisdom and fair virtue 5.04. 24
would i had known no more! 5.04. 59
there were no more comparison between the women! TRO 1.01. 42 P
i speak no more than truth. 1.01. 64 P
i'll meddle nor make no more i' th' matter. 1.01. 83 P
pray you speak no more to me, i will leave all 1.01. 87 P
he esteems her no more than i esteem an addle 1.02.131 P
but there was a more temperate fire under the 1.02.146 P
if he do, the rich shall have more. 1.02.198 P
and his helm more hack'd than hector's, and how 1.02.233 P
here comes more. 1.02.240 P
but more in troilus thousandfold i see | than in 1.02.284
men prize the thing ungain'd more than it is. 1.02.289
the herd hath more annoyance by the breeze 1.03. 48
and /seeks his praise more than he fears his 1.03.267
that loves his mistress more than in confession 1.03.269
thou hast no more brain than i have in mine 2.01. 43 P
i have bobb'd his brain more than he has beat my 2.01. 70 P
no more words, thersites, peace! 2.01.113 P
clatpoles ere i come any more to your tents. 2.01.118 P
o, meaning you? i will go learn more of it. 2.01.130
priam, | there is no lady of more softer bowels, 2.02. 11
more spungy to suck in the sense of fear, | more 2.02. 12
more ready to cry out, "who knows what follows?" 2.02. 13
i am no more touch'd than all priam's sons; 2.02.126
the reasons you allege do more conduce | to the 2.02.168
have ears more deaf than adders to the voice 2.02.172
not wrong, | but makes it much more heavy. 2.02.188
were it not glory that we more affected | than 2.02.195
of troyan blood | spent more in her defense. 2.02.198
their fraction is more our wish than their 2.03. 98 P
if any thing more than your sport and pleasure 2.03.108
what is he more than another? 2.03.142 P
no more than what he thinks he is. 2.03.143 P
no less noble, much more gentle, and altogether 2.03.149 P
much more gentle, and altogether more tractable. 2.03.150 P
of that we hold an idol more than he? 2.03.189
and add more coals to cancer when he burns 2.03.196
come, i'll hear no more of this, i'll sing you a 3.01.105 P
love, nothing but love, still love, still more! 3.01.115
shall more obey than to the edge of steel | or 3.01.152
you shall do more | than all the island kings — 3.01.153
gives us more palm in beauty than we have, | yea 3.01.157
more dregs than water, if my /fears have eyes. 3.02. 67 P
say all lovers swear more performance than they 3.02. 84 P
vowing more than the perfection of ten, and 3.02. 86 P
perchance, my lord, i show more craft than love, 3.02.153
which shall shake him more | than if not look'd 3.03. 53
know my mind, i'll fight no more 'gainst troy. 3.03. 56
a little gilt, | more laud than gilt o'erdusted. 3.03.179
the reasons are more potent and heroical. 3.03.192
which hath an operation more divine | than 3.03.203
is not more loath'd than an effeminate man | in 3.03.218
his horse, for that's the more capable creature. 3.03.307 P
the thing he means to kill, more excellently. 4.01. 25
merits pois'd, each weighs nor less nor more, 4.01. 66
with wings more momentary–swift than thought. 4.02. 14
it's more than i know, i'll be sworn. 4.02. 51 P
pandar | have not more gift in taciturnity. 4.02. 73
no more my grief, in such a precious loss. 4.04. 10
more bright in zeal than the devotion which 4.04. 26
manly as hector, but more dangerous, | for 4.05.104
action | is more vindicative than jealous love. 4.05.107
you must no more. 4.05.117
why then will i no more. 4.05.119
but there's more in me than thou understand'st. 4.05.240
i will no more trust him when he leers than i 5.01. 89 P
sweet honey greek, tempt me no more to folly. 5.02. 18
no, no, good night, i'll be your fool no more. 5.02. 32
i prithee, diomed, visit me no more. 5.02. 74
a proof of strength she could not publish more, 5.02.113
divides more wider than the sky and earth, | and 5.02.149
shall dizzy with more clamor neptune's ear | in 5.02.174
parrot will not do more for an almond than he 5.02.193 P
no more, i say. 5.03. 7
more abhorr'd | than spotted livers in the 5.03. 17
holds honor far more precious–dear than life. 5.03. 28
i would have been much more a fresher man, | had 5.06. 20
there is no more to say. 5.10. 22
no more talking on't; COR 1.01. 12 P
of more strong link asunder than can ever 1.01. 71
by calamity | thither where more attends you, 1.01. 76
and provide more piercing statutes daily to 1.01. 83 P
i will venture | to /stale't a little more. 1.01. 92
shalt see me once more strike at tullus' face. 1.01.240
better be held nor more attain'd than by | a 1.01.265
more than his singularity, he goes | upon this 1.01.278
nay more, | some parcels of their power are 1.02. 31
we shall ever strike | till one can do no more. 1.02. 36
or express yourself in a more comfortable sort. 1.03. 2 P
i sprang not more in joy at first hearing he was 1.03. 15 P
it more becomes a man | than gilt his trophy. 1.03. 39
and fight | with hearts more proof than shields. 1.04. 25
more than i know the sound of martius' tongue 1.06. 26
a serpent i abhor | more than thy fame and envy. 1.08. 4
be frighted | and, gladly quak'd, hear more; 1.09. 6
pray now, no more. 1.09. 13
which you profane, | never sound more! 1.09. 42
no more, i say! 1.09. 47
more cruel to your good report than grateful 1.09. 54
one that converses more with the buttock of the 2.01. 51 P
bleeding, the more entangled by your hearing. 2.01. 77 P
more of your conversation would infect my brain, 2.01. 94 P
he has more cause to be proud. 2.01.145 P
no more of this, it does offend my heart; 2.01.168
pray now, no more. 2.01.169
of no more soul nor fitness for the world | than 2.01.250
no more of him, he's a worthy man. 2.02. 35 P
but yet my caution was more pertinent | than the 2.02. 63
should account me the more virtuous that i have 2.03. 94 P
have | done many things, some less, some more. 2.03.130
make them of no more voice | than dogs, that are 2.03.215
him | more after our commandment than as guided 2.03.230
well, no more. 3.01. 74
no more words, we beseech you. 3.01. 75
no more? 3.01. 75
well, well, no more of that. 3.01.115
though there the people had more absolute pow'r, 3.01.116
my reasons, | more worthier than their voices. 3.01.120
no, take more! 3.01.140
of state | more than you doubt the change on't; 3.01.152
on both sides more respect. 3.01.180
(which, i dare vouch, is more than that he hath, 3.01.298
we'll hear no more. 3.01.306
one word more, one word: 3.01.309
this no more dishonors you at all | than to take 3.02. 58
of th' ignorant | more learned than the ears), 3.02. 77
it is my more dishonor | than thou of them. 3.02.124
chide me no more. 3.02.132
as i hear, more strong | than are upon you yet. 3.02.140
well, well, no more. 3.03. 57
tarpeian, never more | to enter our rome gates. 3.03.103
he's sentenc'd; no more hearing. 3.03.109
my country's good with a respect more tender, 3.03.112
more holy and profound, than mine own life, | my 3.03.113
there's no more to be said, but he is banish'd 3.03.117
makes fear'd and talk'd of more than seen — 4.01. 31
more than a wild exposture to each chance | that 4.01. 36
to banish him that strook more blows for rome 4.02. 19
you had more beard when i last saw you, but your 4.03. 8 P
and that to prove more fortunes | th' art tir'd, 4.05. 93
true," i'd not believe them more | than thee, 4.05.105
more dances my rapt heart | than when i first my 4.05.116
once more to hew thy target from thy brawn, | or 4.05.120
and more a friend than e'er an enemy; 4.05.146
but i thought there was more in him than i could 4.05.158 P
but more of thy news. 4.05.190 P
a getter of more bastard children than war's a 4.05.225 P
and so would do, | were he more angry at it. 4.06. 15
this is a happier and more comely time | than 4.06. 27
sir, | the slave's report is seconded, and more, 4.06. 63
and more, | more fearful, is deliver'd. 4.06. 64
what more fearful? 4.06. 64
can | no more atone than violent'st contrariety. 4.06. 73
he bears himself more proudlier, | even to my 4.07. 8
more than the instant army we can make, | might 5.01. 37
our general | will no more hear from thence. 5.02. 6
or of some death more long in spectatorship and 5.02. 65 P
him) once more offer'd | the first conditions, 5.03. 13
grace him only | that thought he could do more: 5.03. 16
of thy deep duty more impression show | than 5.03. 51
o, no more, no more! 5.03. 86
o, no more, no more! 5.03. 86
how more unfortunate than all living women | are 5.03. 97
perhaps thy childishness will move him more 5.03.157
no man in the world | more bound to 's mother, 5.03.159
to his surname coriolanus 'longs more pride 5.03.170
does reason our petition with more strength 5.03.176
he has wings, he's more than a creeping thing. 5.04. 14 P
and he no more remembers his mother now than an 5.04. 16 P
there is no more mercy in him than there is milk 5.04. 28 P
say no more. | here come the lords. 5.06. 58
no more infected with my country's love | than 5.06. 71
doth more than counterpoise a full third part 5.06. 77
no more. 5.06.101
with six aufidiuses, or more, his tribe, | to 5.06.128
store, | that thou wilt never render to me more! TIT 1.01. 95
my lord, you are unjust, and more than so, | in 1.01.292
one, | so trouble me no more, but get you gone. 1.01.367
speak thou no more, if all the rest will speed. 1.01.372
renowmed titus, more than half my soul — 1.01.373
i say no more, | nor wish no less, and so i take 1.01.401
that you will be more mild and tractable. 1.01.470
away, and talk not, trouble us no more. 1.01.478
makes me less gracious, or thee more fortunate; 2.01. 32
nor would your noble mother for much more | be 2.01. 51
world, | i love lavinia more than all the world. 2.01. 72
more water glideth by the mill | than wots the 2.01. 85
lucrece was not more chaste | than this lavinia, 2.01.108
i have been broad awake two hours and more. 2.02. 17
which never hopes more heaven than rests in thee 2.03. 41
now question me no more, we are espied. 2.03. 48
no more, great empress, bassianus comes. 2.03. 52
stay, madam, here is more belongs to her: 2.03.122
and one thing more | that womanhood denies my 2.03.173
my heart suspects more than mine eye can see. 2.03.213
thy hand once more; 2.03.243
o earth, i will befriend thee more with rain, 3.01. 16
grave tribunes, once more i entreat of you — 3.01. 31
is soft as wax, tribunes more hard than stones; 3.01. 45
hath hurt me more than had he kill'd me dead: 3.01. 92
sirs, strive no more: 3.01.177
more hath it merited, that let it have. 3.01.196
more than remembrance of my father's death. 3.01.240
these miseries are more than may be borne. 3.01.243
where life hath no more interest but to breathe! 3.01.249
ah, now no more will i control thy griefs. 3.01.259
cornelia never with more care | read to her sons 4.01. 12
i think she means that there were more than one 4.01. 38
ay, more there was; 4.01. 39
that hath more scars of sorrow in his heart 4.01.126
led us to rome, strangers, and more than so, 4.02. 33
but me more good to see so great a lord | basely 4.02. 37
and that would she for twenty thousand more. 4.02. 45
well, more or less, or ne'er a whit at all, 4.02. 53
yet wrung with wrongs more than our backs can 4.03. 49
sirrah, come hither, make no more ado, | but 4.03.102
rome never had more cause. 4.04. 62
the old andronicus | with words more sweet, and 4.04. 90
with words more sweet, and yet more dangerous, 4.04. 90
i'll speak no more but "vengeance rot you all!" 5.01. 58
ay, that i had not done a thousand more. 5.01.124
but that i cannot do ten thousand more. 5.01.144
sirs, stop his mouth, and let him speak no more. 5.01.151
thou hast the odds of me, therefore no more. 5.02. 19
and that more dear | than hands or tongue, her 5.02.175
more stern and bloody than the centaurs' feast. 5.02.203
and have a thousand times more cause than he 5.03. 51
or more than any living man could bear. 5.03.127
once more, on pain of death, all men depart. ROM 1.01.103
came more and more, and fought on part and part, 1.01.114
came more and more, and fought on part and part, 1.01.114
adding to clouds more clouds with his deep sighs 1.01.133
here's much to do with hate, but more with love. 1.01.175
to have it press'd | with more of thine. 1.01.188
doth add more grief to too much of mine own. 1.01.189
way | to call hers, exquisite, in question more. 1.01.229
let two more summers wither in their pride, 1.02. 10
you, among the store | one more, most welcome, 1.02. 23
one more, most welcome, makes my number more. 1.02. 23
which /on more view of many, mine, being one, 1.02. 32
not mad, but bound more than a madman is; 1.02. 54
thou wilt fall backward when thou hast more wit, 1.03. 42
but no more deep will i endart mine eye | than 1.03. 98
and more inconstant than the wind, who woos 1.04.100
more light, you knaves, and turn the tables up; 1.05. 27
'tis more, 'tis more. 1.05. 38
'tis more, 'tis more. 1.05. 38
go, | be quiet, or — more light, more light! 1.05. 87
go, | be quiet, or — more light, more light! 1.05. 87
ay, so i fear, the more is my unrest. 1.05.120
more torches here! 1.05.125
that thou, her maid, art far more fair than she. 2.02. 6
shall i hear more, or shall i speak at this? 2.02. 37
there lies more peril in thine eye | than twenty 2.02. 71
i'll prove more true | than those that have 2.02.100
i should have been more strange, i must confess, 2.02.102
the more i give to thee, | the more i have, for 2.02.134
thee, | the more i have, for both are infinite. 2.02.135
and make her airy tongue more hoarse than /mine, 2.02.162
more than prince of cats. 2.04. 19 P
for thou hast more of the wild goose in one of 2.04. 72 P
and will speak more in a minute than he will 2.04.148 P
mine, and that thy skill be more | to blazon it, 2.06. 25
conceit, more rich in matter than in words, 2.06. 30
man that hath a hair more or a hair less in his 3.01. 18 P
and that bare vowel i shall poison more | than 3.02. 46
for exile hath more terror in his look, | much 3.03. 13
more terror in his look, | much more than death. 3.03. 14
more validity, | more honorable state, more 3.03. 33
more honorable state, more courtship lives | in 3.03. 34
more courtship lives | in carrion flies than 3.03. 34
talk no more. 3.03. 60
with twenty hundred thousand times more joy 3.03.153
nay more, i doubt it not. 3.04. 14
i have more care to stay than will to go. 3.05. 23
o, now be gone, more light and light it grows. 3.05. 35
more light and light, more dark and dark our 3.05. 36
light and light, more dark and dark our woes! 3.05. 36
then weep no more. 3.05. 88
is it more sin to wish me thus forsworn, | or to 3.05.236
if i do so, it will be of more price, | being 4.01. 27
thou wrong'st it more than tears with that 4.01. 32
take these keys and fetch more spices, nurse. 4.04. 1
move them no more by crossing their high will. 4.05. 95
doing more murther in this loathsome world, 5.01. 81
more fierce and more inexorable far | than empty 5.03. 38
more fierce and more inexorable far | than empty 5.03. 38
and in despite i'll cram thee with more food. 5.03. 48
o, what more favor can i do to thee, | than with 5.03. 98
daughter's jointure, for no more | can i demand. 5.03.297
but i can give thee more, | for i will /raise 5.03.298
go hence to have more talk of these sad things; 5.03.307
for never was a story of more woe | than this of 5.03.309
blows of fortune's | more pregnantly than words. TIM 1.01. 92
and my estate deserves an heir more rais'd 1.01.119
more welcome are ye to my fortunes | than my 1.02. 19
i have told more of you to myself than you can 1.02. 93 P
more jewels yet? 1.02.159
with more than common thanks i will receive it. 1.02.208
all to you. lights, more lights! 1.02.228
pray'd you | to hold your hand more close. 2.02.139
prithee no more. 2.02.163
i am not able to do (the more beast, i say!) 3.02. 49 P
timon in this should pay more than he owes; 3.04. 22
i have no more to reckon, he to spend. 3.04. 56
i'll once more feast the rascals. 3.04.112
them all, let in the tide | of knaves once more; 3.04.117
women are more valiant | that stay at home, if 3.05. 47
and the ass more captain than the lion, the 3.05. 49
and be in debt to none — yet more to move you, 3.05. 77
for law is strict, and war is nothing more. 3.05. 84
urge it no more | on height of our displeasure. 3.05. 85
follows not summer more willing than we your 3.06. 29 P
nor more willingly leaves winter, such summer 3.06. 31 P
i'll tell you more anon. 3.06. 59 P
the meat be belov'd more than the man that gives 3.06. 76 P
th' unkindest beast more kinder than mankind. 4.01. 36
more of our fellows. 4.02. 15
not one word more: 4.02. 28
and more than that i know thee | i not desire to 4.03. 58
hath in her more destruction than thy sword, 4.03. 63
give us some gold, good timon; hast thou more? 4.03.133
well, more gold — what then? 4.03.149
that he may never more false title plead, | nor 4.03.154
there's more gold. 4.03.164
more counsel with more money, bounteous timon. 4.03.167
more counsel with more money, bounteous timon. 4.03.167
more whore, more mischief first; 4.03.168
more whore, more mischief first; 4.03.168
if i hope well, i'll never see thee more. 4.03.171
womb, | let it no more bring out ingrateful man! 4.03.188
from it all consideration slips — | more man? 4.03.197
not by his breath that is more miserable. 4.03.249
at duty, more than i could frame employment; 4.03.262
there's more gold. 4.03.445
no more, i pray — and he's a steward. 4.03.498
methinks thou art more honest now than wise; 4.03.502
together with a recompense more fruitful | than 5.01.150
the bearer strong | cries (of itself) "no more!" 5.04. 10
shall set out for reproof | fall, and no more; 5.04. 58

Line	Play	Ref.
atone your fears | with my more noble meaning,		5.04. 59
noble timon, of whose memory | hereafter more.		5.04. 81
out their shoes, to get myself into more work.	JC	1.01. 30 P
love | the name of honor more than i fear death.		1.02. 89
why should that name be sounded more than yours?		1.02.143
but it was fam'd with more than with one man?		1.02.153
i could tell you more news too.		1.02.284 P
there was more foolery yet, if i could remember		1.02.287 P
why, saw you any thing more wonderful?		1.03. 14
his affections sway'd | more than his reason.		2.01. 21
for he can do no more than caesar's arm | when		2.01.182
if it be no more, | portia is brutus' harlot,		2.01.286
well | that caesar is more dangerous than he.		2.02. 45
in one day, | and i the elder and more terrible;		2.02. 47
i'll get me to a place more void, and there		2.04. 37
is there no voice more worthy than my own, | to		3.01. 49
to sound more sweetly in great caesar's ear		3.01. 50
it shall advantage more than do us wrong.		3.01.242
be it so; | i do desire no more.		3.01.252
i lov'd caesar less, but that i lov'd rome more.		3.02. 22 P
i have done no more to caesar than you shall do		3.02. 37 P
ingratitude, more strong than traitors' arms,		3.02.185
octavius, i have seen more days than you, | and		4.01. 18
urge me no more, i shall forget myself;		4.03. 35
ay, more.		4.03. 42
for i have seen more years, i'm sure, than ye.		4.03.132
speak no more of her.		4.03.158
no more, i pray you.		4.03.166
there is no more to say?		4.03.229
no more.		4.03.229
ill spirit, i would hold more talk with thee.		4.03.288
young man, thou couldst not die more honorable.		5.01. 60
come down, behold no more.		5.03. 33
this was he, messala, | but cassius is no more.		5.03. 60
it is more worthy to leap in ourselves | than		5.05. 24
losing day | more than octavius and mark antony		5.05. 37
no more that thane of cawdor shall deceive | our	MAC	1.02. 63
stay, you imperfect speakers, tell me more:		1.03. 70
prospect of belief, | no more than to be cawdor.		1.03. 75
and at more time, | the interim having weigh'd		1.03.153
more is thy due than more than all can pay.		1.04. 21
more is thy due than more than all can pay.		1.04. 21
they have more in them than mortal knowledge.		1.05. 3 P
had scarcely more | than would make up his		1.05. 36
who dares /do more is none.		1.07. 47
and, to be more than what you were, you would		1.07. 50
you were, you would | be so much more the man.		1.07. 51
methought i heard a voice cry, "sleep no more!		2.02. 32
still it cried, "sleep no more!"		2.02. 38
and therefore cawdor | shall sleep no more —		2.02. 40
sleep no more — macbeth shall sleep no more."		2.02. 40
i'll go no more.		2.02. 47
hark, more knocking.		2.02. 66
is't known who did this more than bloody deed?		2.04. 22
but hush, no more.		3.01. 10
this is more strange | than such a murther is.		3.04. 81
more shall they speak;		3.04.133
stepp'd in so far that, should i wade no more,		3.04.136
but one word more —		4.01. 74
here's another, | more potent than the first.		4.01. 76
seek to know no more.		4.01.103
i'll see no more.		4.01.118
who bears a glass | which shows me many more;		4.01.120
but no more sights!		4.01.155
shall have more vices than it had before, | more		4.03. 47
more suffer, and more sundry ways than ever,		4.03. 48
more suffer, and more sundry ways than ever,		4.03. 48
of horrid hell can come a devil more damn'd | in		4.03. 56
would be as a sauce | to make me hunger more,		4.03. 82
deeper, grows with more pernicious root | than		4.03. 85
well, more anon.		4.03.140
to satisfy my remembrance the more strongly.		5.01. 33 P
no more o' that, my lord, no more o' that;		5.01. 44 P
no more o' that, my lord, no more o' that;		5.01. 44 P
more needs she the divine than the physician.		5.01. 74
bring me no more reports, let them fly all.		5.03. 1
what news more?		5.03. 30
both more and less have given him the revolt,		5.04. 12
upon the stage, | and then is heard no more.		5.05. 26
pronounce a title | more hateful to mine ear.		5.07. 9
no; nor more fearful.		5.07. 9
and more i beg not.		5.07. 23
and be these juggling fiends no more believ'd,		5.08. 19
he's worth more sorrow, | and that i'll spend		5.09. 16
he's worth no more;		5.09. 17
what's more to do, | which would be planted		5.09. 30
is not this something more than fantasy?	HAM	1.01. 54
more than the scope | of these delated articles		1.02. 37
the head is not more native to the heart, | the		1.02. 47
the hand more instrumental to the mouth, | than		1.02. 48
a little more than kin, and less than kind.		1.02. 65
but no more like my father | than i to hercules.		1.02.152
your father, | these hands are not more like.		1.02.212
a countenance more | in sorrow than in anger.		1.02.231
perfume and suppliance of a minute — | no more.		1.03. 10
no more but so?		1.03. 10
think it no more:		1.03. 10
tender yourself more dearly, | or (not to crack		1.03.107
giving more light than heat, extinct in both		1.03.118
more honor'd in the breach than the observance.		1.04. 16
action | it waves you to a more removed ground,		1.04. 61
without more motive, into every brain | that		1.04. 76
and so, without more circumstance at all, | i		1.05.127
once more remove, good friends.		1.05.163
there are more things in heaven and earth,		1.05.166
son, come you more nearer | than your particular		2.01. 11
might move | more grief to hide, than hate to		2.01.116
more than his father's death, that thus hath put		2.02. 8
there is not living | to whom he more adheres.		2.02. 21
us, | put your dread pleasures more into command		2.02. 28
makes vow before his uncle never more | to give		2.02. 70
and at our more considered time we'll read,		2.02. 81
more matter, with less art.		2.02. 95
and more /above, hath his solicitings, | as they		2.02.126
thing that i will not more willingly part withal		2.02.216 P
and by what more dear a better proposer can		2.02.286 P
there is something in this more than natural, if		2.02.367 P
should more appear like entertainment than yours		2.02.374 P
why — "one fair daughter, and no more, | the		2.02.407
row of the pious chanson will show you more, for		2.02.420 P
sweet, and by very much more handsome than fine.		2.02.445 P
complexion smear'd | with heraldy more dismal.		2.02.456
prithee no more.		2.02.520 P
they deserve, the more merit is in your bounty.		2.02.532 P
i'll have grounds | more relative than this —		2.02.604
is not more ugly to the thing that helps it		3.01. 51
no more, and by a sleep to say we end | the		3.01. 60
compos'd | as made these things more rich.		3.01. 98
i was the more deceiv'd.		3.01.119 P
with more offenses at my beck than i have		3.01.124 P
go to, i'll no more on't, it hath made me mad.		3.01.146 P
your clowns speak no more than is set down for		3.02. 39 P
no, good mother, here's metal more attractive.		3.02.109 P
should show itself more richer to signify this		3.02.304 P
would perhaps plunge him into more choler.		3.02.306 P
therefore no more, but to the matter:		3.02.324 P
but much more | that spirit upon whose weal		3.03. 13
'tis meet that some more audience than a mother,		3.03. 31
that, struggling to be free, | art more engag'd;		3.03. 69
up, sword, and know thou a more horrid hent:		3.03. 88
o hamlet, speak no more!		3.04. 88
o, speak to me no more!		3.04. 94
no more, sweet hamlet!		3.04. 96
no more!		3.04.101
to the next abstinence, the next more easy;		3.04.167
once more, good night, | and when you are		3.04.170
one word more, good lady.		3.04.180
a beast, no more.		4.04. 35
maid, that out a maid | never departed more."		4.05. 55
eats not the flats with more impiteous haste		4.05.101
this nothing's more than matter.		4.05.174
you shortly shall hear more.		4.07. 33
and that he means | no more to undertake it, i		4.07. 63
indeed your father's son | more than in words?		4.07.126
as make your bouts more violent to that end —		4.07.158
and the more pity that great folk should have		5.01. 26 P
hang themselves, more than their even–christen.		5.01. 28 P
cudgel thy brains no more about it, for your		5.01. 56 P
did these bones cost no more the breeding, but		5.01. 91 P
vouchers vouch him no more of his purchases, and		5.01.108 P
and must th' inheritor himself have no more, ha?		5.01.112 P
not a jot more, my lord.		5.01.113 P
why he more than another?		5.01.169 P
must there no more be done?		5.01.235
no more be done:		5.01.235
till i have caught her once more in mine arms.		5.01.250
here's the commission, read it at more leisure.		5.02. 26
without debatement further, more or less, | he		5.02. 45
thy state is the more gracious, for 'tis a vice		5.02. 84 P
else would trace him, his umbrage, nothing more.		5.02.120 P
we wrap the gentleman in our more rawer breath?		5.02.123 P
the phrase would be more germane to the matter,		5.02.158 P
and many more of the same breed that i know the		5.02.188 P
i can no more — the king, the king's to blame.		5.02.320
i am more an antique roman than a dane.		5.02.341
so tell him, with th' occurrents, more and less,		5.02.357
from his mouth whose voice will draw /on more,		5.02.392
lest more mischance | on plots and errors happen		5.02.394
i thought the king had more affected the duke of	LR	1.01. 1 P
i love you more than /words can wield the matter		1.01. 55
sure my love's | more ponderous than my tongue.		1.01. 78
draw | a third more opulent than your sisters'?		1.01. 86
according to my bond, no more nor less.		1.01. 93
kent, on thy life, no more.		1.01.154
i crave no more than hath your highness offer'd,		1.01.194
and nothing more, may fitly like your grace,		1.01.200
t' avert your liking a more worthier way | than		1.01.211
take | more composition and fierce quality		1.02. 12
come to me, that of this i may speak more.		1.02. 52 P
no more of that, i have noted it well.		1.04. 75 P
have more than thou showest, | speak less than		1.04.118
than thou owest, | ride more than thou goest,		1.04.121
than thou goest, | learn more than thou trowest,		1.04.122
and thou shalt have more | than two tens to a		1.04.126
lust | makes it more like a tavern or a brothel		1.04.245
more hideous when thou show'st thee in a child		1.04.260
never afflict yourself to know more of it, | but		1.04.291
sir, more knave than fool, after your master.		1.04.314
reasons of your own | as may compact it more.		1.04.339
/you are much more /attax'd for want of wisdom		1.04.343
beget opinion | of my more fierce endeavor.		2.01. 34
seen drunkards | do more than this in sport.		2.01. 35
he shall never more | be fear'd of doing harm.		2.01.110
no contraries hold more antipathy | than i and		2.02. 87
no more, perchance, does mine, nor his, nor hers		2.02. 91
harbor more craft and more corrupter ends | than		2.02.102
harbor more craft and more corrupter ends | than		2.02.102
my sister may receive it much more worse | to		2.02.148
smile once more, turn thy wheel!		2.02.173
having more man than wit about me, drew.		2.04. 42
made you no more offense but what you speak of?		2.04. 61
and am fallen out with my more headier will,		2.04.110
good sir, no more;		2.04.157
we'll no more meet, no more see one another.		2.04.220
we'll no more meet, no more see one another.		2.04.220
what should you need of more?		2.04.238
to no more | will i give place or notice.		2.04.248
and speak't again, my lord, no more with me.		2.04.255
look well–favor'd | when others are more wicked;		2.04.257
allow not nature more than nature needs, | man's		2.04.266
for confirmation that i am much more | than my		3.01. 44
give me your hand. have you no more to say?		3.01. 51
few words, but, to effect, more than all yet:		3.01. 52
i am a man | more sinn'd against than sinning.		3.02. 60
(more harder than the stones whereof 'tis rais'd		3.02. 64
when priests are more in word than matter;		3.02. 81
no, i will weep no more.		3.04. 17
no more of that.		3.04. 22
leave to ponder | on things would hurt me more.		3.04. 25
to them, | and show the heavens more just.		3.04. 36
is man no more than this?		3.04.103 P
unaccommodated man is no more but such a poor,		3.04.107 P
importune him once more to go, my lord, | his		3.04.161
king, it will stuff his suspicion more fully.		3.05. 21 P
lest it see more, prevent it.		3.07. 83
i have heard more since.		4.01. 35
friend, | tell me what more thou know'st.		4.02. 97
and more convenient is he for my hand | than for		4.05. 31
you may gather more.		4.05. 32
i'll look no more, | lest my brain turn, and the		4.06. 22
horse goes to't | with a more riotous appetite.		4.06.123
rip their hearts, | their papers is more lawful.		4.06.261
the modest truth, | nor more nor clipt, but so.		4.07. 6
fourscore and upward, not an hour more nor less;		4.07. 60
in, trouble him no more | till further settling.		4.07. 80
whose age had charms in it, whose title more,		5.03. 48
exalt himself, | more than in your addition.		5.03. 68
and more, much more, the time will bring it out.		5.03.164
and more, much more, the time will bring it out.		5.03.164
if more, the more th' hast wrong'd me.		5.03.169
if more, the more th' hast wrong'd me.		5.03.169
on, | you look as you had something more to say.		5.03.202
if there be more, more woeful, hold it in, | for		5.03.203
if there be more, more woeful, hold it in, | for		5.03.203
as your honors | have more than merited.		5.03.303
thou'lt come no more, | never, never, never,		5.03.308
of a battle knows | more than a spinster —	OTH	1.01. 24
you shall more command with years | than with		1.02. 60
that, as it more concerns the turk than rhodes,		1.03. 22
so may he with more facile question bear it,		1.03. 23
here is more news.		1.03. 32
of my offending | hath this extent, no more.		1.03. 81
more than pertains to feats of broils and battle		1.03. 87
without more wider and more /overt test | than		1.03.107
without more wider and more /overt test | than		1.03.107
of effects, throws a more safer voice on you.		1.03.225 P
fortunes with this more stubborn and boist'rous		1.03.227 P
your son–in–law is far more fair than black.		1.03.290
do it a more delicate way than drowning.		1.03.353 P
we will have more of this to–morrow.		1.03.371 P
every minute is expectancy | of more /arrivance.		2.01. 42
you may relish him more in the soldier than in		2.01.166 P
desdemona, | once more, well met at cyprus.		2.01.212
in their natures more than is native to them),		2.01.216 P
which the time shall more favorably minister.		2.01.269 P
and dare not task my weakness with any more.		2.03. 42 P
this is a more exquisite song than the other.		2.03. 98 P
let's have no more of this;		2.03.111 P
thou dost deliver more or less than truth,		2.03.219
more of this matter cannot i report.		2.03.240
love thee, | but never more be officer of mine.		2.03.249
there is more sense in that than in reputation.		2.03.267 P
there are more ways to recover the general again		2.03.272 P
a punishment more in policy than in malice, even		2.03.273 P
exclaim no more against it.		2.03.310 P
goodness not to do more than she is requested.		2.03.321 P
so, with no money at all and a little more wit,		2.03.368 P
away, i say, thou shalt know more hereafter.		2.03.381
for love's sake, to make no more noise with it.		3.01. 13 P
your converse and business | may be more free.		3.01. 39
i never knew a florentine more kind and honest.		3.01. 40
prithee no more;		3.03. 75
these stops of thine fright me the more;		3.03.120
nay, yet there's more in this.		3.03.130
where virtue is, these are more virtuous.		3.03.186
and on the proof, there is no more but this —		3.03.191
if more thou dost perceive, let me know more;		3.03.239
if more thou dost perceive, let me know more;		3.03.239
sees and knows more, much more, than he unfolds.		3.03.243
sees and knows more, much more, than he unfolds.		3.03.243
i once more take my leave.		3.03.257
why, how now, general? no more of that.		3.03.334
slander her and torture me, | never pray more;		3.03.369
eyes do see them bolster | more than their own.		3.03.400
you'll never meet a more sufficient man.		3.04. 91
and more i will | than for myself i dare.		3.04.130
more tedious than the dial eightscore times?		3.04.175
but i shall, in a more continuate time, | strike		3.04.178
naked with her friend in bed | an hour, or more,		4.01. 4
you well assur'd, | no more than he'll unswear.		4.01. 31
go to; say no more.		4.01.169 P
you shall hear more by midnight.		4.01.212 P
to come in to the cry without more help.		5.01. 44
nay, /an' you stare, we shall hear more anon.		5.01.107
yet she must die, else she'll betray more men.		5.02. 6
one more, one more.		5.02. 17
one more, one more.		5.02. 17
one more, and that's the last.		5.02. 19
hah, no more moving?		5.02. 93
she comes more nearer earth than she was wont,		5.02.110
o, the more angel she, | and you the blacker		5.02.130
this deed of thine is no more worthy heaven		5.02.160
and told no more | than what he found himself		5.02.176
(more than indeed belong'd to such a trifle),		5.02.228
i have made my way through more impediments		5.02.263
service, and they know't — | no more of that.		5.02.340
more fell than anguish, hunger, or the sea!		5.02.362
you shall be more beloving than beloved.	ANT	1.02. 23
though thou deny me a matter of more weight;		1.02. 69 P
with what else more serious | importeth thee to		1.02.120
ten thousand harms, more than the ills i know,		1.02.129
if there were no more women but fulvia, then had		1.02.165 P
no more light answers.		1.02.176
the death of fulvia, with more urgent touches,		1.02.180
my more particular, | and that which most with		1.03. 54
quarrel no more, but be prepar'd to know | the		1.03. 66
you'll heat my blood; no more.		1.03. 80
is not more manlike | than cleopatra;		1.04. 5
nor the queen of ptolomy | more womanly than he;		1.04. 7
of heaven, | more fiery by night's blackness;		1.04. 13
here's more news.		1.04. 33
for pompey's name strikes more | than could his		1.04. 54
with patience more | than savages could suffer.		1.04. 60
more laugh'd at, that i should | once name you		2.02. 33
no more than my residing here at rome | might be		2.02. 37
you may, when you hear no more words of pompey,		2.02.104 P
thou art a soldier only, speak no more.		2.02.107
wrong this presence, therefore speak no more.		2.02.109
we had much more monstrous matter of feast,		2.02.182 P
speak this no more.		2.03. 24
no more but when to thee.		2.03. 25
why, there's more gold.		2.05. 31
no more /of that; he did so.		2.06. 69
of that purpose made more in the marriage than		2.06.118 P

by the disposition, he cries out, "no more"; 2.07. 7 P
the higher nilus swells, | the more it promises; 2.07. 21
i'll never follow thy pall'd fortunes more. 2.07. 82
once 'tis offer'd, | shall never find it more. 2.07. 84
what would you more? 2.07.119
what needs more words? 2.07.125
ever won | more in their officer than person. 3.01. 17
who does i' th' wars more than his captain can 3.01. 21
i could do more to do antonius good, | but 3.01. 25
i have one thing more to ask him yet, good 3.03. 45
and thousands more | of semblable import — but 3.04. 2
a more unhappy lady, | if this division chance, 3.04. 12
/world, thou /hast a pair of chaps — no more, 3.05. 13
more, domitius, | my lord desires you presently; 3.05. 20
he has done all this and more | in alexandria. 3.06. 1
lycaonia, | with a more larger list of sceptres. 3.06. 76
welcome to rome, | nothing more dear to me. 3.06. 86
celerity is never more admir'd | than by the 3.07. 24
hark, the land bids me tread no more upon't, 3.11. 1
add more, | from thine invention, offers. 3.12. 28
what, no more ceremony? 3.13. 38
if from the field i shall return once more | to 3.13.173
all my sad captains, fill our bowls once more; 3.13.183
haply you shall not see me more, or if, | a 4.02. 26
tend me to–night two hours, i ask no more, | and 4.02. 32
queen's a squire | more tight at this than thou; 4.04. 15
it were, to stand | on more mechanic compliment. 4.04. 32
say that i wish he never find more cause | to 4.05. 15
myself so sorely | that i will joy no more. 4.06. 19
i have yet | room for six scotches more. 4.07. 10
o sun, thy uprise shall i see no more, | fortune 4.12. 18
o, he's more mad | than telamon for his shield; 4.13. 1
the soul and body rive not more in parting 4.13. 5
no more a soldier. 4.14. 42
now my spirit is going, | i can no more. 4.15. 59
no more but /e'en a woman, and commanded | by 4.15. 73
which sleeps, and never palates more the dung, 5.02. 7
/autumn it was | that grew the more by reaping. 5.02. 88
of no more trust | than love that's hir'd! 5.02.154
now no more | the juice of egypt's grape shall 5.02.281
no more obey the heavens than our courtiers' CYM 1.01. 2
to th' more mature | a glass that feated them, 1.01. 48
o lady, weep no more, lest i give cause | to be 1.01. 93
give cause | to be suspected of more tenderness 1.01. 94
be a pinch in death | more sharp than this is. 1.01.131
a touch more rare | subdues all pangs, all fears 1.01.135
of bloody affirmation) his to be more fair, 1.04. 59 P
more than the world enjoys. 1.04. 79 P
(as you call it) deserve more — a punishment 1.04.119 P
with no more advantage than the opportunity of a 1.04.129 P
commendation for my more free entertainment. 1.04.155 P
more than the locking up the spirits a time, 1.05. 41
spirits a time, | to be more fresh, reviving. 1.05. 42
i do not know | what is more cordial. 1.05. 64
towards him might | be us'd more thankfully. 1.06. 79
deliver with more openness your answers | to my 1.06. 88
since doubting things go ill often hurts more 1.06. 95
let me hear no more. 1.06.117
more noble than that runagate to your bed, | and 1.06.137
sets him off, | more than a mortal seeming. 1.06.171
i am not vex'd more at any thing in th' earth; 2.01. 17 P
wooer | more hateful than the foul expulsion is 2.01. 60
no more: 2.02. 42
some more time | must wear the print of his 2.03. 42
no more? 2.03. 77
that's more | than some, whose tailors are as 2.03. 78
if you'll be patient, i'll no more be mad; 2.03.103
in meaner parties | (yet who than he more mean?) 2.03.117
(on whom there is no more dependancy | but brats 2.03.118
and no more | but what thou art besides, thou 2.03.125
he never can meet more mischance than come | to 2.03.132
are men more order'd than when julius caesar 2.04. 21
more particulars | must justify my knowledge. 2.04. 78
jove — | once more let me behold it. 2.04. 99
of no more bondage be to where they are made 2.04.111
sign about her, | more evident than this; 2.04.120
as hell can hold, | were there no more but it. 2.04.141
will you hear more? 2.04.141
come, there's no more tribute to be paid. 3.01. 34 P
else, sir, no more tribute, pray you now. 3.01. 45 P
more goddess–like than wife–like, such assaults 3.02. 8
there's no more to say: 3.02. 81
paid | more pious debts to heaven than in all 3.03. 72
strikes life into my speech and shows much more 3.03. 97
you shall no more | be stomachers to my heart. 3.04. 83
no father, nor no more ado | with that harsh, 3.04.131
(the handmaids of all women, or, more truly, 3.04.156
prithee away, | there's more to be consider'd; 3.04.181
like | a thing more made of malice than of duty, 3.05. 33
that she hath all courtly parts more exquisite 3.05. 71
no more of "worthy lord"! 3.05. 96
of posthumus in more respect than my noble and 3.05.135 P
less, and so more equal ballasting | to thee, 3.06. 77
no less young, more strong, not beneath him in 4.01. 10 P
and more remarkable in single oppositions; 4.01. 13 P
yet said hereafter | i might know more. 4.02. 42
thing | more slavish did i ne'er than answering 4.02. 73
body hath a tail | more perilous than the head. 4.02.145
we'll hunt no more to–day, nor seek for danger 4.02.162
fear no more the heat o' th' sun, | nor the 4.02.258
fear no more the frown o' th' great, | thou art 4.02.264
care no more to clothe and eat, | to thee the 4.02.266
fear no more the lightning flash. 4.02.270
here's a few flow'rs, but 'bout midnight, more: 4.02.283
alas, | there is no more such masters. 4.02.371
come more, for more you're ready; 4.03. 30
come more, for more you're ready; 4.03. 30
should reserve | my crack'd one to more care. 4.04. 50
strook | me, wretch, more worth your vengeance. 5.01. 11
that's love, | to have them fall no more: 5.01. 13
men know | more valor in me than my habits show. 5.01. 30
less without and more within. 5.01. 33
work | more plentiful than tools to do't — 5.03. 9
(lads more like to run | the country base than 5.03. 19
place, more charming | with their own nobleness, 5.03. 32
no more a britain, i have resum'd again | the 5.03. 75
fight i will no more, | but yield me to the 5.03. 76
art fetter'd | more than my shanks and wrists. 5.04. 9
gods are more full of mercy. 5.04. 13
than in gyves, | desir'd more than constrain'd. 5.04. 15
i know you are more clement than vild men, | who 5.04. 18
no more, thou thunder–master, show | thy spite 5.04. 30
no more, you petty spirits of region low, 5.04. 93
to make my gift, | the more delay'd, delighted. 5.04.102
ascension is | more sweet than our blest fields. 5.04.117
you shall be call'd to no more payments, fear no 5.04.158 P
to no more payments, fear no more tavern–bills, 5.04.159 P
is there more? 5.05. 48
more, sir, and worse. 5.05. 49
i love thee more and more; 5.05.109
i love thee more and more; 5.05.109
think more and more | what's best to ask. 5.05.109
think more and more | what's best to ask. 5.05.109
no more kin to me | than i to your highness; 5.05.112
another | not more resembles that sweet rosy lad 5.05.121
and — which more may grieve thee, | as it doth 5.05.144
wilt thou hear more, my lord? 5.05.146
while nature will | than die ere i hear more. 5.05.152
dreading that her purpose | was of more danger, 5.05.254
more of thee merited than a band of clotens 5.05.304
the more of you 'twas felt, the more it shap'd 5.05.346
the more it shap'd | unto my end of stealing 5.05.346
the service that you three have done is more 5.05.353
which for more probation | i can with ease 5.05.362
ne'er mother | rejoic'd deliverance more. 5.05.370
with | i know not how much more, should be 5.05.389
when wit's more ripe, accept my rhymes, | and PER 1.ch. 12
he's more secure to keep it shut than shown; 1.01. 95
what being more known grows worse, to smother it 1.01.106
who /am no more but as the tops of trees, 1.02. 30
day serves not light more faithful than i'll be. 1.02.110
of greece gets more with begging than we can do 2.01. 64 P
and have no more of life than may suffice | to 2.01. 74
to have practic'd more the whipstock than the 2.02. 51
were more than you expect, or more than's fit, 2.03. 5
were more than you expect, or more than's fit, 2.03. 5
'tis more by fortune, lady, than my merit. 2.03. 12
some other is more fit. 2.03. 23
h'as done no more than other knights have done, 2.03. 34
therefore to make his entrance more sweet, 2.03. 64
one twelve moons more she'll wear diana's livery 2.05. 10
or never more to view nor day nor light. 2.05. 17
for a more blusterous birth had never babe. 3.01. 28
thy loss is more than can thy portage quit 3.01. 35
me | a more content in course of true delight 3.02. 39
the /vial once more. 3.02. 90
who shall not be more dear to my respect | than 3.03. 33
will i take me to, | and never more have joy. 3.04. 11
which she made more sound | by hurting it; 4.ch. 24
and yourself, | with more than foreign heart. 4.01. 33
never was waves nor wind more violent, | and 4.01. 59
three, and they can do no more than they can do; 4.02. 7 P
the more my fault | to scape his hands where i 4.02. 74
come, i am for no more bawdy–houses. 4.05. 6 P
pray you, without any more virginal fencing, 4.06. 57 P
and so stand /aloof for more serious wooing. 4.06. 87 P
how's this? how's this? some more, be sage. 4.06. 95
hold, here's more gold for thee. 4.06.113
we'll have no more gentlemen driven away. 4.06.129 P
in your supposing once more put your sight: 5.ch. 21
where what is done in action, more, if might, 5.ch. 23
yet once more | let me entreat to know at large 5.01. 61
them hungry, | the more she gives them speech. 5.01.113
endowments which | you make more rich to owe? 5.01.117
and said no more but what my thoughts | did 5.01.133
i'll hear you more, to th' bottom of your story, 5.01.164
is it no more to be your daughter than | to say 5.01.209
are almost run, | more a little, and then dumb. 5.02. 2
no more, you gods! 5.03. 40
of her lips i may | melt, and no more be seen. 5.03. 43
no mortal officer | more like a god than you. 5.03. 63
more of the maid to sight than husband's pains. TNK pr 8
more famous yet 'twixt po and silver trent. pr 12
your tresses, | nor in more bounty spread her. 1.01. 64
hast much more power on him | than ever he had 1.01. 87
poor lady, say no more. 1.01.101
will long last and be more costly than | your 1.01.132
your first thought is more | than others' 1.01.135
your premeditating | more than their actions; 1.01.137
it more imports me | than all the actions that i 1.01.172
the more proclaiming | our suit shall be 1.01.174
and | thou shalt remember nothing more than what 1.01.185
a number, for a business | more bigger–look'd. 1.01.215
once more, farewell all. 1.01.225
theirs has more ground, is more maturely 1.03. 56
has more ground, is more maturely season'd, 1.03. 56
more buckled with strong judgment, and their 1.03. 57
what not, condemn'd, | no more arraignment. 1.03. 66
and maid may be | more than in sex /dividual. 1.03. 82
i must no more believe thee in this point 1.03. 87
assurance | that we, more than his pirithous, 1.03. 95
concern us | much more than thebes is worth. 1.04. 33
what man to man may do for our sake more: 1.04. 39
our dole more deadly looks than dying; 1.05. 3
sir, i demand no more than your own offer, and i 2.01. 10 P
we will talk more of this when the solemnity is 2.01. 12 P
but no more of that now; 2.01. 17 P
to me they have no more sense of their captivity 2.01. 37 P
never more | must we behold those comforts, 2.02. 8
like lightning, | to blast whole armies, more! 2.02. 25
with their echoes, | no more now must we hallow; 2.02. 48
no more shake | our pointed javelins, whilst the 2.02. 48
here, | i am sure, a more content, and all those 2.02.100
shall i say more? 2.02.111
put but thy head out of this window more, | and, 2.02.212
no more; 2.02.218
once more | i would but see this fair one. 2.02.231
and fruit and flowers more blessed, that still 2.02.233
but never more, | upon his oath and life, must 2.02.245
are dangerous, | i'll clap more irons on you. 2.02.271
i'll see her and be near her, or no more. 2.03. 23
when he considers more, this love of mine | will 2.06. 27
love of mine | will take more root within him. 2.06. 28
get many more such prisoners and such daughters, 2.06. 38
i may not wish | more than my sword's edge on't. 3.01. 96
bequeath this plea, | and talk of it no more. 3.01.116
and, good now, | no more of these vain parleys; 3.03. 10
i'll tell you | after a draught or two more. 3.03. 19
spare it not, | the duke has more, coz. eat now. 3.03. 20
give me more wine. 3.03. 28
i'll hear no more. 3.03. 53
stop no more holes but what you should. 3.05. 83
and you show | more than a mistress to me; 3.06. 26
no more anger, | as you love any thing that's 3.06. 26
more by virtue. | you are modest, cousin. 3.06. 81
it but hold, i ask no more | for all my hopes. 3.06. 91
this only, and no more: 3.06. 94
this hand shall never more | come near thee with 3.06.102
once more farewell, my cousin. 3.06.106
i will no more be hidden, nor put off | this 3.06.118
i am, and, which is more, dares think her his. 3.06.149
o heaven, | what more than man is this! 3.06.157
to die as thee to say it, | and no more mov'd. 3.06.160
your cousin | has ten times more offended, for i 3.06.181
for i gave him | more mercy than you found, sir, 3.06.182
sir, your offenses | being no more than his. 3.06.183
of more authority, i am sure more love, | not 3.06.231
yours, | of more authority, i am sure more love, 3.06.231
swear 'em never more | to make me their 3.06.252
hear you no more? 4.01. 1
"may you never more enjoy the light," etc. 4.01.104
i can sing twenty more. 4.01.106
now if my sister — more for palamon. 4.02. 49
her distraction is more at some time of the moon 4.03. 1 P
but to make the number more i have great hope in 4.03. 98 P
your ire is more than mortal; 5.01. 14
than lead itself, stings more than nettles. 5.01. 97
allow'st no more blood than will make a blush, 5.01.141
falls, and sounds more like | a bell than blade. 5.03. 5
more exulting? 5.03. 89
could | no more be hid in him than fire in flax, 5.03. 98
a life more worthy from him than all women, | i 5.03.143
with 'em, | for we are more clear spirits. 5.04. 13
what ending could be | of more content? 5.04. 16
more to me deserving | than i can quite or speak 5.04. 34
argo they eat more in our country than they do STM II.C 5 P
shrieve more speaks. II.C 41 P
shall we hear shrieve more speak? II.C 41 P
let's hear shrieve more. II.C 44 P
shrieve more, more, more, shrieve more! II.C 45 P
shrieve more, more, more, shrieve more! II.C 45 P
shrieve more, more, more, shrieve more! II.C 45 P
shrieve more, more, more, shrieve more! II.C 45 P
more, more! II.C 49 P
more, more! II.C 49 P
ay, by th' mass, will we, more. II.C 58 P
we'll be rul'd by you, master more, if you'll II.C 142 P
but, more, the more thou hast | either of honor, III 14
but, more, the more thou hast | either of honor, III 14
the more do thou in serpents' natures think them III 17
stain to all nymphs, more lovely than a man, VEN 9
more white and red than doves or roses are: 10
what follows more, she murthers with a kiss. 54
which bred more beauty in his angry eyes: 70
her best is better'd with a more delight. 78
more thirst for drink than she for this good 92
his cheeks, cries, "fie, no more of love! 185
nay, more than flint, for stone at rain 200
words are done, her woes the more increasing; 254
and now the happy season once more fits | that 327
burneth more hotly, swelleth with more rage; 332
burneth more hotly, swelleth with more rage; 332
once more the engine of her thoughts began: 367
once more the ruby–color'd portal open'd, 451
but for thy piteous lips no more had seen. 504
he now obeys, and now no more resisteth, | while 563
for pity now she can no more detain him; 577
"and more than so, presenteth to mine eye | the 661
"lie quietly, and hear a little more, | nay, do 709
but gold that's put to use more gold begets." 768
and every tongue more moving than your own, 776
"more i could tell, but more i dare not say, 805
"more i could tell, but more i dare not say, 805
till the wild waves will have him seen no more, 819
them leave quaking, bids them fear no more — 899
her more than haste is mated with delays, | like 909
from their dark beds once more leap her eyes, 1050
that makes more gashes where no breach should be 1066
my youth with his, the more am i accurs'd." 1120
a thousand times, and now no more reflect, 1130
sweet issue of a more sweet–smelling sire — 1178
that kings might be espoused to more fame, | but LUC 20
that cloy'd with much, he pineth still for more. 98
more than his eyes were open'd to the light. 105
and so by hoping more they have but less, | or, 137
or, gaining more, the profit of excess | is but 138
that eye which him beholds, as more divine, 291
paying more slavish tribute than they owe. 299
spring, | to add a more rejoicing to the prime, 332
and give the sneaped birds more cause to sing. 333
which with a yielding latch, and with no more, 339
with more than admiration he admired | her azure 418
darkness daunts them with more dreadful sights. 462
this moves in him more rage and lesser pity | to 468
mixed, | which to her oratory adds more grace. 564
"no more," quoth he, "by heaven, i will not hear 667
to make more vent for passage of her breath, 1040
to see the salve doth make the wound ache more, 1116
ill, | no more than wax shall be accounted evil, 1245
"the more to blame my sluggard negligence. 1278
for more it is than i can well express, | and 1286
when more is felt than one hath power to tell. 1288
see sad sights moves more than hear them told, 1324
"at ardea to my lord with more than haste." 1332
speed more than speed but dull and slow she 1336
while others saucily | promise more speed, but 1349
her earnest eye did make him more amazed. 1356
the more she saw the blood his cheeks replenish, 1357
the more she thought he spied in her some 1358
thy passion maketh | more feeling–painful: 1679
but more than "he" her poor tongue could not 1718
glass, | that i no more can see what once i was! 1764
held back his sorrow's tide, to make it more; 1789
silly queen, with more than love's good will, PP 9. 7

she showed hers, he saw more wounds than one, 9.13
and yet thou lefts me more than i did crave, 10. 9
more mickle was the pain, | that nothing could 15. 9
inconstancy | more in women than in men remain. 17.12
fawn'd on him before | use his company no more. 20.48
how much more praise deserv'd thy beauty's use, SON 2. 9
look whom she best endow'd she gave the more; 11.11
and meant thereby | thou shouldst print more, 11.14
with means more blessed than my barren rhyme? 16. 4
thou art more lovely and more temperate: 18. 2
thou art more lovely and more temperate: 18. 2
an eye more bright than theirs, less false in 20. 5
let them say more that like of hearsay well, | i 21.13
more than that tongue that more hath more 23.12
than that tongue that more hath more express'd. 23.12
than that tongue that more hath more express'd. 23.12
wishing me like to one more rich in hope, 29. 5
and shalt by fortune once more re–survey | these 32. 3
no more be griev'd at that which thou hast done: 35. 1
excusing /thy sins more than /thy sins are; 35. 8
or wit, | or any of these all, or all, or more, 37. 6
ten times more in worth | than those old nine 38. 9
what hast thou then more than thou hadst before? 40. 2
all mine was thine, before thou hadst this more. 40. 4
a loss in love that touches me more nearly. 42. 4
more sharp to me than spurring to his side, 50.12
o, how much more doth beauty beauteous seem | by 54. 1
but you shall shine more bright in these 55. 3
return of love, more blest may be the view; 56.12
makes summer's welcome thrice more wish'd, more 56.14
summer's welcome thrice more wish'd, more rare. 56.14
lie, | to do more for me than mine own desert, 72. 6
and hang more praise upon deceased i | than 72. 7
is, | and live no more to shame nor me nor you. 72.12
perceiv'st, which makes thy love more strong, 73.13
there lives more life in one of your fair eyes 83.13
which can say more | than this rich praise, that 84. 1
and to the most of praise add something more, 85.10
thy sweet beloved name no more shall dwell, 89.10
cost, | of more delight than hawks or horses be; 91.11
grace and faults are lov'd of more and less: 96. 3
more flowers i noted, yet i none could see | but 99.14
is strength'ned, though more weak in seeming, 102. 1
the argument all bare is of more worth | than 103. 3
o, blame me not if i no more can write! 103. 5
and more, much more than in my verse can sit, 103.13
and more, much more than in my verse can sit, 103.13
mine appetite i never more will grind | on newer 110.10
incapable of more, replete with you, | my most 113.13
like as to make our appetites more keen, | with 118. 1
grows fairer than at first, more strong, far 119.12
and gain by ills thrice more than i have spent. 119.14
to trust those tables that receive thee more: 122.12
lie, | made more or less by thy continual haste. 123.12
which proves more short than waste or ruining? 125. 4
dwellers on form and favor | lose all, and more, 125. 6
making dead wood more blest than living lips: 128.12
coral is far more red than her lips' red; 130. 2
and in some perfumes is there more delight 130. 7
that music hath a far more pleasing sound; 130.10
more than enough am i that vex thee still, | to 135. 3
one will of mine, to make thy large will more. 135.12
is more than my o'erpress'd defense can bide? 139. 8
within be fed, without be rich no more: 146.12
and death once dead, there's no more dying then. 146.14
who taught thee how to make me love thee more, 150. 9
the more i hear and see just cause of hate? 150.10
in me, | more worthy i to be belov'd of thee. 150.14
more perjur'd eye, | to swear against the truth 152.13
ink would have seem'd more black and damned here
LC 54
yet showed his visage by that cost more dear, 96
by blunting us to make our wits more keen. 161

MORE–HAVING 1 FR 0.0001 REL FR 1 V 0 P
and my more–having would be as a sauce | to make
MAC 4.03. 81

MOREO'ER 1 FR 0.0001 REL FR 0 V 1 P
and, moreo'er, puddings and flap–jacks, and thou
PER 2.01. 82 P

MOREOVER 19 FR 0.0021 REL FR 9 V 10 P
and moreover, bully — but first, master guest, WIV 2.03. 73 P
and, moreover, god saw him when he was hid in ADO 5.01.179 P
moreover, they have spoken untruths; 5.01.216 P
moreover, sir, which indeed is not under white 5.01.304 P
and moreover i will go with thee to thy uncle's. 5.02.103 P
madam, and moreover | some thousand verses of a
LLL 5.02. 49
adding thereto, moreover, | that he would wed me 5.02.446
i understand, moreover, upon the rialto, he hath MV 1.03. 19 P
she adds, moreover, that you should put your TN 2.02. 7 P
tell me, moreover, hast thou sounded him, | if R2 1.01. 8
and i hear, moreover, his highness is fall'n 2H4 1.02.107 P
and there is also moreover a river at monmouth. H5 4.07. 27 P
moreover, thou hast put them in prison, and 2H6 4.07. 43 P
moreover, urge his hateful luxury | and bestial R3 3.05. 80
and am, moreover, suitor that i may | produce JC 3.01.227
moreover, he hath left you all his walks, | his 3.02.247
moreover that we much did long to see you, | the HAM 2.02. 2
moreover, to descry | the strength o' th' enemy. LR 4.05. 13
moreover, if you please, a niece of mine | shall PER 3.04. 15

MOREOV'R 1 FR 0.0001 REL FR 0 V 1 P
they that add, moreov'r, he's drunk nightly in TN 1.03. 36 P

MORES 1 FR 0.0001 REL FR 1 V 0 P
more, by all mores, than e'er i shall love wife. TN 5.01.136

MORGAN 3 FR 0.0003 REL FR 2 V 1 P
he hath confess'd himself to morgan, whom he AWW 4.03.108 P
myself, belarius, that am morgan call'd, | they CYM 3.03.106
i, old morgan, | am that belarius whom you 5.05.332

MORI 1 FR 0.0001 REL FR 0 V 1 P
a man doth of a death's–head or a memento mori.
1H4 3.03. 31 P

MORISCO 1 FR 0.0001 REL FR 1 V 0 P
seen | him caper upright like a wild morisco, 2H6 3.01.365

/MORN 1 FR 0.0001 REL FR 1 V 0 P
the hunt is up, the /morn is bright and grey, TIT 2.02. 1

MORN 44 FR 0.0049 REL FR 43 V 1 P
and in the morn | i'll bring you to your ship, TMP 5.01.307
o'ernight | that wait for execution in the morn. TGV 4.02.133
break of day, | lights that do mislead the morn; MM 4.01. 4
you let it be proclaim'd betimes i' th' morn. 4.04. 16 P
but the next morn betimes, | his purpose 5.01.101
from morn till night, out of his pavilion. LLL 5.02.654
with helena | to do observance to a morn of may) MND 1.01.167
i fear we shall outsleep the coming morn | as 5.01.365
she is not hot, but temperate as the morn; SHR 2.01.294
have in these parts from morn till even fought, H5 3.01. 20
the morn that i was wedded to her mother. 1H6 5.04. 24
but meet him now, and, be it in the morn, | when 2H6 3.01. 13
hath dimm'd your infant morn to aged night. R3 4.04. 16
cock | hath twice done salutation to the morn, 5.03.210
dear, trouble not yourself, the morn is cold. TRO 4.02. 1
as when the golden sun salutes the morn, | and, TIT 2.01. 5
the grey–ey'd morn smiles on the frowning night, ROM 2.03. 1
it was the lark, the herald of the morn, | no 3.05. 6
marry, my child, early next thursday morn, | the 3.05.112
each new morn | new widows howl, new orphans cry
MAC 4.03. 4
the cock, that is the trumpet to the morn, HAM 1.01.150
but look the morn in russet mantle clad | walks 1.01.166
and in the morn and liquid dew of youth 1.03. 41
why then to–morrow night, /or tuesday morn; OTH 3.03. 60
on we'nsday morn. 3.03. 61
and next morn, | ere the ninth hour, i drunk him ANT 2.05. 20
the morn is fair. good morrow, general. 4.04. 24
shall embattle | by th' second hour i' th' morn. 4.09. 4
at the sixt hour of morn, at noon, at midnight, CYM 1.03. 31
the night to th' owl and morn to th' lark less 3.06. 93
'tis the ninth hour o' th' morn. 4.02. 30
early in blustering morn this lady was | thrown PER 5.03. 22
and this beauteous morn | (the prim'st of all TNK 3.01. 18
had ta'en his last leave of the weeping morn, VEN 2
from morn till night, even where i list to sport 154
like a red morn, that ever yet betoken'd | wrack 453
when in his fresh array | he cheers the morn, 484
or morn or weary even? 495
to wake the morn and sentinel the night, | to LUC 942
scarce had the sun dried up the dewy morn, | and PP 6. 1
fair was the morn when the fair queen of love, 9. 1
youth like summer morn, age like winter weather, 12. 3
even so my sun one early morn did shine | with SON 33. 9
when his youthful morn | hath travell'd on to 63. 4

MORN–DEW 1 FR 0.0001 REL FR 1 V 0 P
his ends | as is the morn–dew on the myrtle leaf ANT 3.12. 9

MORNING 137 FR 0.0154 REL FR 93 V 44 P
'tis fresh morning with me | when you are by at TMP 3.01. 33
and as the morning steals upon the night, 5.01. 65
for last morning you could not see to wipe my TGV 2.01. 80 P
send to me in the morning, and i'll send it; 4.02.131
had myself twenty angels given me this morning, WIV 2.02. 72 P
will not miss you morning nor evening prayer, as 2.02. 99 P
i do invite you to–morrow morning to my house to 3.03.229 P
her husband goes this morning a–birding; 3.05. 45 P
her husband is this morning gone a–birding. 3.05.128 P
claudio | be executed by nine to–morrow morning.
MM 2.01. 34
to–morrow morning are to die claudio and 4.02. 7 P
as it is, | you shall hear more ere morning. 4.02. 95
let this barnardine be this morning executed, 4.02.171 P
and is hang'd betimes in the morning, may sleep 4.03. 46 P
there died this morning of a cruel fever | one 4.03. 70
good morning to you, fair and gracious daughter. 4.03.112
why, here begins his morning story right: ERR 5.01.357
at him upon my knees every morning and evening.
ADO 2.01. 29 P
as he was appointed next morning at the temple, 3.03.161 P
we would have them this morning examin'd before 3.05. 47 P
prince john is this morning secretly stol'n away 4.02. 61 P
night, which he forswore on tuesday morning. 5.01.169 P
to–morrow morning come you to my house, | and 5.01.286
until to–morrow morning, lords, farewell. 5.01.328
i will come to your worship to–morrow morning. LLL 3.01.161 P
to those fresh morning drops upon the rose, | as 4.03. 26
i do hear the morning lark. MND 4.01. 94
with ears that sweep away the morning dew; 4.01.121
and, for the morning now is something worn, 4.01.182
very vildly in the morning, when he is sober, MV 1.02. 86 P
monday last at six a' clock i' th' morning, 2.05. 25 P
he plies the duke at morning and at night, | and 3.02.277
and in the morning early will we both | fly 4.01.456
my master will be here ere morning. 5.01. 48 P
it is almost morning, | and yet i am sure you 5.01.295
and in the morning early | they found the bed AYL 2.02. 6
with his satchel | and shining morning face, 2.07.146
but why did he swear he would come this morning, 3.04. 19 P
hast hawks will soar | above the morning lark. SHR in.2. 44
to be whipt at the high cross every morning. 1.01.133 P
clear | as morning roses newly wash'd with dew; 2.01.173
the morning wears, 'tis time we were at church. 3.02.111
his lordship will next morning for france. AWW 4.03. 78 P
and this morning your departure hence, it 4.03. 94 P
it shall be done to–morrow morning if i live. TN 3.04.104 P
more matter for a may morning. 3.04.142 P
his eyes were set at eight i' th' morning. 5.01.199 P
i should have given't you to–day morning. 5.01.287 P
to–morrow morning let us meet him then. JN 4.03. 18
and most dissolutely spent on tuesday morning; 1H4 1.02. 35 P
lads, to–morrow morning by four a' clock early, 1.02.124 P
have ta'en a thousand pound this day morning. 2.04.159 P
you must to the court in the morning. 2.04.335 P
i'll to the court in the morning. 2.04.544 P
be with me betimes in the morning, and so good 2.04.548 P
and in the morning early shall mine uncle 4.03.110
will it never be morning? H5 3.07. 6 P
but i would it were morning, for i would fain be 3.07. 83 P
the dolphin longs for morning. 3.07. 90 P
and the third hour of drowsy morning /name. 4.pr. 16
is not that the morning which breaks yonder? 4.01. 85 P
bones, | ill–favoredly become the morning field. 4.02. 40
see how the morning opes her golden gates, | and 3H6 2.01. 21
and when the morning sun shall raise his car 4.07. 80
makes the night morning and the noontide night: R3 1.04. 77
grace looks cheerfully and smooth this morning; 3.04. 48
and by the second hour in the morning | desire 5.03. 31
be — | prepare thy battle early in the morning, 5.03. 88
how far into the morning is it, lords? 5.03.234
this found i on my tent this morning. 5.03.303
you he bade | attend him here this morning. H8 3.02. 82
this morning | papers of state he sent me to 3.02.120
to–morrow morning to the council–board | he be 5.01. 51
that you shall | this morning come before us, 5.01.101
and this morning see | you do appear before them 5.01.144
as 'tis to make 'em sleep | on may–day morning, 5.03. 15
this morning, uncle. TRO 1.02. 46 P
a blush | modest as morning when she coldly eyes 1.03.229
to–morrow morning call some knight to arms 2.01.124
wrinkles apollo's, and makes pale the morning. 2.02. 79
and you take leave till to–morrow morning — 3.02.142 P
it is great morning, and the hour prefix'd | for 4.03. 1
how have we spent this morning! 4.04.140
of valor, to appear | this morning to them. 5.03. 70
the night than with the forehead of the morning. COR 2.01. 53 P
and then | we pout upon the morning, are unapt 5.01. 52
this morning for ten thousand of your throats 5.04. 56
as fresh as morning dew distill'd on flowers? TIT 2.03.201
many a morning hath he there been seen, | with ROM 1.01.131
'tis almost morning, i would have thee gone — 2.02.176
when the bridegroom in the morning comes | to 4.01.107
i'll have this knot knit up to–morrow morning. 4.02. 24
shall i be married then to–morrow morning? 4.03. 22
early in the morning | see thou deliver it to my 5.03. 23
that calls our person from our morning rest? 5.03.189
a glooming peace this morning with it brings, 5.03.305
i prithee but repair to me next morning. TIM 2.02. 25
with ice, caudle thy morning taste | to cure thy 4.03.226
the morning comes upon 's. JC 2.01.221
your weak condition to the raw cold morning. 2.01.236
and suck up the humors | of the dank morning? 2.01.263
this morning are they fled away and gone, | and 5.01. 83
almost at odds with morning, which is which. MAC 3.04.126
at the pit of acheron | meet me i' th' morning; 3.05. 16
and i this morning know | where we shall find HAM 1.01.174
but even then the morning cock crew loud, | and 1.02.218
but soft, methinks i scent the morning air, 1.05. 58
sir, a' monday morning, 'twas then indeed. 2.02.388 P
valentine's day, | all in the morning betime, 4.05. 49
we'll go to supper i' th' morning. LR 3.06. 84 P
at nine i' th' morning here we'll meet again. OTH 1.03.279
where shall we meet i' th' morning? 1.03.373 P
and betimes in the morning i will beseech the 2.03.329 P
/by /the /mass, 'tis morning; 2.03.378
and did want | of what i was i' th' morning; ANT 2.02. 77
this morning, like the spirit of a youth | that 4.04. 26
the soldier | that has this morning left thee, 4.05. 5
who's gone this morning? 4.05. 6
it's almost morning, is't not? CYM 2.03. 9 P
you have given good morning to your mistress, 2.03. 61
i do think | i saw't this morning; 2.03.145
it is great morning. come away! — who's there? 4.02. 61
freed of this plight, and in their morning state TNK 1.04. 34
eyes break each morning 'gainst thy window, 2.03. 9
i come in | to bring him water in a morning, 2.04. 22
'tis now well–nigh morning; 3.02. 2
is truss'd up in a trice | to–morrow morning; 3.04. 18
therefore this blest morning | shall be the last 3.06. 13
this morning. 4.01. 34
that you must lose your head to–morrow morning, 4.01. 77
and wakes the morning, from whose silver breast VEN 855
grove, | musing the morning is so much o'erworn, 866
he in his speed looks for the morning light, LUC 745
"with rotten damps ravish the morning air; 778
the morning rise | doth cite each moving sense PP 14.14
full many a glorious morning have i seen SON 33. 1
and truly not the morning sun of heaven | better 132. 5

MORNING'S 11 FR 0.0012 REL FR 10 V 1 P
sent your worship a morning's draught of sack. WIV 2.02.146 P
i with the morning's love have oft made sport, MND 3.02.389
and inly ruminate | the morning's danger; H5 4.pr. 25
it | with sweet rehearsal of my morning's dream. 2H6 1.02. 24
this battle fares like to the morning's war, 3H6 2.05. 1
with tears augmenting the fresh morning's dew, ROM 1.01.132
i'll say yon grey is not the morning's eye, 3.05. 19
have i thought /long to see this morning's face, 4.05. 41
and bows you | to a morning's holy office. CYM 3.03. 4
as is the morning's silver melting dew | against LUC 24
the little birds that tune their morning's joy 1107

MORNINGS 2 FR 0.0002 REL FR 0 V 2 P
'a brushes his hat a' mornings; ADO 3.02. 42 P
i am advis'd to give her music a' mornings; CYM 2.03. 12 P

MORN–PRAYER 1 FR 0.0001 REL FR 1 V 0 P
i'll make it my morn–prayer | to have it added MM 2.04. 71

MOROCCO 2 FR 0.0002 REL FR 1 V 1 P
come from a fift, the prince of morocco, who MV 1.02.125 P
pause there, morocco, | and weigh thy value with 2.07. 24

MORR–– 1 FR 0.0001 REL FR 1 V 0 P
right and straight | upon this mighty morr–– — TNK 3.05.118

MORRIS* 6 FR 0.0006 REL FR 5 V 1 P
the nine men's morris is fill'd up with mud, MND 2.01. 98
for shrove tuesday, a morris for may–day, as the AWW 2.02. 24 P
ye shall not sleep, | i'll make ye a new morris. TNK 2.02.273
that 'fore thy dignity will dance a morris. 3.05.108
which being glu'd together | makes morris, and 3.05.120
he'll dance the morris twenty mile an hour, 5.02. 51

MORRIS–DANCE 1 FR 0.0001 REL FR 1 V 0 P
were busied with a whitsun morris–dance; H5 2.04. 25

MORRIS–PIKE 1 FR 0.0001 REL FR 0 V 1 P
more exploits with his mace than a morris–pike. ERR 4.03. 28 P

MORROW 124 FR 0.0140 REL FR 94 V 30 P
and so, good morrow, servant. TGV 2.01.134
sir eglamour, a thousand times good morrow. 4.03. 6
good morrow, gentle lady. 4.03. 45
good morrow, kind sir eglamour. 4.03. 46
give your worship good morrow. WIV 2.02. 33 P
good morrow, goodwife. 2.02. 34 P
give you good morrow, sir. 2.03. 21 P
good morrow, good sir hugh. 3.01. 36 P
give your worship good morrow. 3.05. 27 P
good morrow to your lordship. MM 2.01.138
good morrow; 4.02.105 P
good morrow, coz. ADO 3.04. 39 P
good morrow, sweet hero. 3.04. 40 P
good morrow, masters, put your torches out. 5.03. 24
good morrow, masters — each his several way. 5.03. 29
good morrow to this fair assembly. 5.04. 34
good morrow, prince; 5.04. 35

good morrow, claudio; 5.04. 35
good morrow, benedick. 5.04. 40
god give you good morrow, master person. LLL 4.02. 82 P
from lovers' food till morrow deep midnight. MND 1.01.223
good morrow, friends. 4.01.139
good morrow, my good lords. MV 1.01. 65
good morrow to your worship. AYL 1.01. 95 P
"good morrow, fool," quoth i. 2.07. 18
good morrow, fair ones. 4.03. 75
good morrow, neighbor baptista. SHR 2.01. 39 P
good morrow, neighbor gremio. 2.01. 40 P
good morrow, kate — for that's your name, i 2.01.182
when i should bid good morrow to my bride | and 3.02.122
good morrow, gentle mistress, where away? 4.05. 27
good morrow, noble captain. AWW 4.03.314 P
now good morrow, friends. TN 2.04. 1
good morrow, hubert. JN 4.01. 9
good morrow, little prince. 4.01. 9
and pluck nights from me, but not lend a morrow; R2 1.03.228
good morrow, ned. 1H4 1.02.111 P
good morrow, sweet hal. 1.02.112 P
good morrow, carriers, what's a' clock? 2.01. 32 P
good morrow, master gadshill. 2.01. 53 P
i think it is good morrow, is it not? 2.04.524
me betimes in the morning, and so good morrow, 2.04.549 P
good morrow, good my lord. 2.04.550 P
is it good morrow, lords? 2H4 3.01. 33
why then good morrow to you all, my lords. 3.01. 35
good morrow, good cousin shallow. 3.02. 4 P
good morrow, honest gentlemen. 3.02. 55 P
good morrow, cousin warwick, good morrow. 5.02. 20
good morrow, cousin warwick, good morrow. 5.02. 20
good morrow, cousin. 5.02. 21
good morrow, and god save your majesty! 5.02. 43
good morrow, lieutenant bardolph. H5 2.01. 2 P
bids them good morrow with a modest smile, | and 4.pr. 33
good morrow, brother bedford. 4.01. 3
good morrow, old sir thomas erpingham. 4.01. 13
do my good morrow to them, and anon | desire 4.01. 26
good morrow, gallants, want ye corn for bread? 1H6 3.02. 41
good morrow to my sovereign king and queen, R3 2.01. 47
good morrow, neighbor, whither away so fast? 2.03. 1
give you good morrow, sir. 2.03. 6
good morrow, catesby, you are early stirring. 3.02. 36
my lord, good morrow, good morrow, catesby. 3.02. 74
my lord, good morrow, good morrow, catesby. 3.02. 74
my noble lords and cousins all, good morrow. 3.04. 22
when that he bids good morrow with such spirit. 3.04. 50
good morrow, richmond! 5.03.223
good morrow, and well met. H8 1.01. 1
good morrow, ladies. 2.03. 50
good morrow, uncle pandarus. TRO 1.02. 42 P
good morrow, cousin cressid. 1.02. 43 P
good morrow, alexander. 1.02. 44 P
good morrow, ajax. 3.03. 66
good morrow. 3.03. 68
i said, "good morrow, ajax"; 3.03.260 P
that's my mind too. good morrow, lord aeneas. 4.01. 7
good morrow, all. 4.01. 51
good morrow then. 4.02. 6
good morrow, lord, good morrow. 4.02. 44
good morrow, lord, good morrow. 4.02. 44
can give, | to have't with saying "good morrow." COR 3.03. 93
good morrow, lords. TIT 4.02. 51
good morrow, cousin. ROM 1.01.160
that i shall say good night till it be morrow. 2.02.185
good morrow, father. 2.03. 31
head | so soon to bid good morrow to thy bed. 2.03. 34
good morrow to you both. 2.04. 46 P
god ye good morrow, gentlemen. 2.04.109 P
good morrow to thee, gentle apemantus! TIM 1.01.178
i be gentle, stay thou for thy good morrow — 1.01.179
well met, good morrow, titus and hortensius. 3.04. 1
good morrow, brutus, do we trouble you? JC 2.01. 87
and so good morrow to you every one. 2.01.228
vouchsafe good morrow from a feeble tongue. 2.01.313
good morrow, worthy caesar, | i come to fetch 2.02. 58
good morrow, caesar. 2.02.109
good morrow, casca. 2.02.111
good morrow, antony. 2.02.117
good morrow to you. 2.04. 33
o, never | shall sun that morrow see! MAC 1.05. 61
good morrow, noble sir. 2.03. 44
good morrow, both. 2.03. 44
which could say, "good morrow, sweet lord! HAM 5.01. 83 P
give you good morrow! LR 2.02.158
good morrow to you both. 2.04.127
and bid "good morrow, general." OTH 3.01. 2
good morrow, good lieutenant. 3.01. 41
good morrow to thee, welcome. ANT 4.04. 18
the morn is fair. good morrow, general. 4.04. 24
good morrow, general. 4.04. 25
good morrow to your majesty, and to my gracious CYM 2.03. 35 P
good morrow, fairest: sister, your sweet hand. 2.03. 86
good morrow, sir. 2.03. 87
turbands on without | good morrow to the sun. 3.03. 7
good morrow to the good simonides. PER 2.05. 1
good morrow. 3.02. 10
good morrow to your lordship. 3.02. 11
"fair gentle maid, good morrow. TNK 2.04. 24
o, good morrow. 3.06. 16
good morrow, noble kinsman. 3.06. 17
venus salutes him with this fair good morrow: VEN 859
when lo the blushing morrow | lends light to all LUC 1082
her mistress she doth give demure good morrow, 1219
looks for night, and then she longs for morrow, 1571
give not a windy night a rainy morrow, | to SON 90. 7

MORROWS 4 FR 0.0004 REL FR 3 V 1 P
madam and mistress, a thousand good morrows. TGV 2.01. 96 P
many good morrows to your majesty! 2H4 3.01. 32
many good morrows to my noble lord! R3 3.02. 35
many good morrows to your majesty; TIT 2.02. 11

MORSEL 9 FR 0.0010 REL FR 6 V 3 P
wink for aye might put | this ancient morsel, TMP 2.01.286
how doth my dear morsel, thy mistress? MM 3.02. 54 P
up | from forth this morsel of dead royalty! JN 4.03.143
now comes in the sweetest morsel of the night, 2H4 2.04.367 P
yet cam'st thou to a morsel of this feast, COR 1.09. 10
gorg'd with the dearest morsel of the earth, ROM 5.03. 46
the ground, i was | a morsel for a monarch; ANT 1.05. 31
i found you as a morsel, cold upon | dead 3.13.116
thou mayst cut a morsel off the spit. PER 4.02.131 P

MORSELS 1 FR 0.0001 REL FR 1 V 0 P
with liquorish draughts | and morsels unctious, TIM 4.03.195

MORT 5 FR 0.0005 REL FR 4 V 1 P
mort du vinaigre! is not this helen? AWW 2.03. 44 P
to sigh, as 'twere | the mort o' th' deer — o, WT 1.02.118
mort /dieu, ma vie! H5 3.05. 11
mort dieu, ma vie! 4.05. 3
mort dieu! 2H6 1.01.123

MORTAL 119 FR 0.0134 REL FR 105 V 14 P
this is no mortal business, nor no sound | that TMP 1.02.407
sir, she is mortal; 5.01.188
she excels each mortal thing | upon the dull TGV 4.02. 51
spleens, | would all themselves laugh mortal. MM 2.02.123
insensible of mortality, and desperately mortal. 4.02.145 P
for since the mortal and intestine jars | 'twixt ERR 1.01. 11
but for the stuffing — well, we are all mortal. ADO 1.01. 59 P
the boy, | than whom no mortal so magnificent! LLL 3.01.178
thought can think, nor tongue of mortal tell." 4.03. 40
by heaven, the wonder in a mortal eye! 4.03. 83
for jove, | turning mortal for thy love." 4.03.118
ever turn'd their — backs — to mortal views!" 5.02.161
"that /ever turn'd their eyes to mortal views! 5.02.163
but she, being mortal, of that boy did die, MND 2.01.135
i pray thee, gentle mortal, sing again. 3.01.137
and i will purge thy mortal grossness so, | that 3.01.160
hail, mortal! 3.01.175
kiss this shrine, this mortal breathing saint. MV 2.07. 40
but as all is mortal in nature, so is all nature AYL 2.04. 55 P
so is all nature in love mortal in folly. 2.04. 56 P
that mortal ears might hardly endure the din? SHR 1.01.173
to the grief, the excess makes it soon mortal. AWW 1.01. 58 P
put myself into my mortal preparation; 3.06. 76 P
against you, even to a mortal arbitrement, but TN 3.04.261 P
stuck in with such a mortal motion that it is 3.04.276 P
he finished indeed his mortal act | that day 5.01.247
this news is mortal to the queen. WT 3.02.148
himself | in mortal fury half so peremptory, JN 2.01.454
without th' assistance of a mortal hand. 3.01.158
by the tongue, | a cased lion by the mortal paw, 3.01.259
the purest treasure mortal times afford | is R2 1.01.177
though death be poor, it ends a mortal woe. 2.01.152
whose double tongue may with a mortal touch 3.02. 21
crown | that rounds the mortal temples of a king 3.02.161
to the extremest point | of mortal breathing. 4.01. 48
tush, man, mortal men, mortal men. 1H4 4.02. 67 P
tush, man, mortal men, mortal men. 4.02. 67 P
more | of mortal griefs than do thy worshippers? H5 4.01.242
be my last breathing in this mortal world! 2H6 1.02. 21
the mortal worm might make the sleep eternal. 3.02.263
who scapes the lurking serpent's mortal sting? 3H6 2.02. 15
head, | or bide the mortal fortune of the field? 2.02. 83
year, | how many years a mortal man may live. 2.05. 29
but i return his sworn and mortal foe. 3.03.257
hands, | i here proclaim myself thy mortal foe; 5.01. 94
alas, i blame you not, for you are mortal, | and R3 1.02. 44
and mortal eyes cannot endure the devil. 1.02. 45
thou hadst but power over his mortal body, | his 1.02. 47
would it were mortal poison for thy sake! 1.02.145
o momentary grace of mortal men, | which we more 3.04. 96
when i was mortal, my anointed body | by thee 5.03.124
to wear our mortal state to come with her, H8 2.04.229
i, her frail son, amongst my brethren mortal, 3.02.148
with him, the mortal venus, the heart–blood of TRO 3.01. 32 P
aunt, should by my mortal sword | be drained! 4.05.134
alone he ent'red | the mortal gate of th' city, COR 2.02.111
mortal, to cut it off; 3.01.295
with him prevail'd, | if not most mortal to him. 5.03.189
as any mortal body hearing it | should straight TIT 2.03.103
mortal revenge upon these traitorous goths, 4.01. 93
hath got this mortal hurt | in my behalf; ROM 3.01.110
fiend | in mortal paradise of such sweet flesh? 3.02. 82
such mortal drugs i have, but mantua's law | is 5.01. 66
the genius and the mortal instruments | are then JC 2.01. 66
they have more in them than mortal knowledge. MAC 1.05. 3 P
you spirits | that tend on mortal thoughts, 1.05. 41
with twenty mortal murthers on their crowns, 3.04. 80
pay his breath | to time and mortal custom. 4.01.100
let us rather | hold fast the mortal sword, and 4.03. 3
all mortal consequences have pronounc'd me thus: 5.03. 5
unless things mortal move them not at all, HAM 2.02.516
when we have shuffled off this mortal coil, 3.01. 66
exposing what is mortal and unsure | to all that 4.04. 51
should be as mortal as /an /old man's life? 4.05.161
so mortal that, but dip a knife in it, | where 4.07.142
do omit | their mortal natures, letting go OTH 2.01. 72
and, o you mortal engines, whose rude throats 3.03.355
if ever mortal eyes do see them bolster | more 3.03.399
if my offense be of such mortal kind | that nor 3.04.115
thy match was mortal to him, and pure grief 5.02.205
we see how mortal an unkindness is to them; ANT 1.02.134 P
by some mortal stroke | she do defeat us; 5.01. 64
this mortal house i'll ruin, | do caesar what he 5.02. 51
come, thou mortal wretch, | with thy sharp teeth 5.02.303
with so mortal a purpose as then each bore, upon CYM 1.04. 41 P
sets him off, | more than a mortal seeming. 1.06.171
which to read | would be even mortal to me. 3.04. 18
resist are grown | the mortal bugs o' th' field. 5.03. 51
show | thy spite on mortal flies: 5.04. 31
be not with mortal accidents oppress'd, | no 5.04. 99
did confess she had | for you a mortal mineral, 5.05. 50
do mean to strike me | to death with mortal joy. 5.05.235
must be look'd to, | for her relapse is mortal. PER 3.02.109
a tempest, which his mortal vessel tears, | and 4.04. 30
till the disaster that, one mortal /night, 5.01. 37
the gods can have no mortal officer | more like 5.03. 62
of mortal loathsomeness from the blest eye | of TNK 1.01. 45
for | thou, being but mortal, makest affections 1.01.229
the mounted heavens | view us their mortal herd, 1.04. 5
were here a mortal woman, and had in her | the 4.02. 10
your ire is more than mortal; 5.01. 14
the heavenly fires | did scorch his mortal son, 5.01. 92
eleven to ninety reign'st | in mortal bosoms, 5.01.131
does stand accurs'd | of many mortal millions, 5.03. 24
"o fairest mover on this mortal round, | would VEN 368
still, | like to a mortal butcher bent to kill. 618
now nature cares not for thy mortal vigor, 953
kings, | imperious supreme of all mortal things. 996
not die | till mutual overthrow of mortal kind! 1018
where mortal stars as bright as heaven's LUC 13
when heavy sleep had clos'd up mortal eyes. 163
thing, | lies at the mercy of his mortal sting. 364
and by their mortal fault brought in subjection 724
for jove, | turning mortal for thy love." PP 16.18
age, | yet mortal looks adore his beauty still, SON 7. 7
mine eye and heart are at a mortal war, | how to 46. 1
rased, | and brass eternal slave to mortal rage; 64. 4
spirits taught to write | above a mortal pitch, 86. 6
the mortal moon hath her eclipse endur'd, | and 107. 5

MORTALITY 17 FR 0.0019 REL FR 13 V 4 P
mortality and mercy in vienna | live in thy MM 1.01. 44
of freedom as the mortality of imprisonment. 1.02.134 P
no might nor greatness in mortality | can 3.02.185
insensible of mortality, and desperately mortal. 4.02.145 P
if knowledge could be set up against mortality. AWW 1.01. 31 P
it makes | foretell the ending of mortality. JN 5.07. 5
that makes such waste in brief mortality. H5 1.02. 28
of mischief, | killing in relapse of mortality. 4.03.107
here on my knee i beg mortality, | rather than 1H6 4.05. 32
sky, | in thy despite shall scape mortality. 4.07. 22
instant, | there's nothing serious in mortality: MAC 2.03. 93
let me wipe it first, it smells of mortality. LR 4.06.133
what mortality is! CYM 4.01. 15 P
hath taught | my frail mortality to know itself, PER 1.01. 42
upon me | o'erbear the shores of my mortality, 5.01.193
and death's dim look in life's mortality. LUC 403
sea, | but sad mortality o'ersways their power, SON 65. 2

MORTALITY'S 1 FR 0.0001 REL FR 1 V 0 P
we cannot hold mortality's strong hand. JN 4.02. 82

MORTAL–LIVING 1 FR 0.0001 REL FR 1 V 0 P
life, blind sight, poor mortal–living ghost, R3 4.04. 26

MORTALLY 3 FR 0.0003 REL FR 3 V 0 P
strook down | some mortally, some slightly CYM 5.03. 10
of fortune, though they haunt you mortally, PER 3.03. 6
yet i was mortally brought forth, and am | no 5.01.104

MORTALS' 1 FR 0.0001 REL FR 1 V 0 P
all know, security | is mortals' chiefest enemy. MAC 3.05. 33

MORTALS 6 FR 0.0006 REL FR 6 V 0 P
the human mortals want their winter here; MND 2.01.101
lord, what fools these mortals be! 3.02.115
was found | with these mortals on the ground. 4.01.102
looks | know them from eyes of other mortals? TRO 1.03.225
eyes | of mortals that fall back to gaze on him, ROM 2.02. 30
that living mortals, hearing them, run mad — 4.03. 48

MORTAL–STARING 1 FR 0.0001 REL FR 1 V 0 P
of bloody strokes and mortal–staring war. R3 5.03. 90

MORTAR 1 FR 0.0001 REL FR 0 V 1 P
i will tread this unbolted villain into mortar, LR 2.02. 66 P

MORTAR–PIECE 1 FR 0.0001 REL FR 0 V 1 P
he stands there like a mortar–piece to blow us. H8 5.03. 46 P

MORTGAG'D 1 FR 0.0001 REL FR 1 V 0 P
thine, | and i myself am mortgag'd to thy will, SON 134. 2

MORTIFIED 5 FR 0.0005 REL FR 5 V 0 P
my loving lord, dumaine is mortified: LLL 1.01. 28
body, | but that his wildness, mortified in him, H5 1.01. 26
hast conjur'd up | my mortified spirit. JC 2.01.324
and the grim alarm | excite the mortified man. MAC 5.02. 5
strike in their numb'd and mortified arms | pins LR 2.03. 15

MORTIFYING 2 FR 0.0002 REL FR 1 V 1 P
apply a moral medicine to a mortifying mischief. ADO 1.03. 12 P
than my heart cool with mortifying groans. MV 1.01. 82

MORTIMER 43 FR 0.0048 REL FR 35 V 8 P
news, | whose worst was that the noble mortimer, 1H4 1.01. 38
his brother–in–law, the foolish mortimer, | who, 1.03. 80
penny cost | to ransom home revolted mortimer. 1.03. 92
revolted mortimer! 1.03. 93
nor never could the noble mortimer | receive so 1.03.110
let me not hear you speak of mortimer. 1.03.119
speak of mortimer! 1.03.130
but i will lift the down–trod mortimer | as high 1.03.135
death, | trembling even at the name of mortimer. 1.03.144
proclaim my brother edmund mortimer | heir to 1.03.156
he said he would not ransom mortimer, | forbade 1.03.219
forbade my tongue to speak of mortimer, | but i 1.03.220
asleep, | and in his ear i'll hollow "mortimer!" 1.03.222
be taught to speak | nothing but "mortimer," and 1.03.225
and of york, | to join with mortimer, ha? 1.03.281
i'll steal to glendower and lord mortimer, 1.03.295
lord edmund mortimer, my lord of york, and owen 2.03. 25 P
i fear my brother mortimer doth stir | about his 2.03. 81
damn'd brawn shall play dame mortimer his wife. 2.04.110 P
and his son–in–law mortimer, and old 2.04.342 P
lord mortimer, and cousin glendower, | will you 3.01. 3
run mad, | so much she doteth on her mortimer. 3.01.144
come, lord mortimer, you are as slow | as hot 3.01.263
archbishop's grace of york, douglas, mortimer, 3.02.119
lord mortimer of scotland hath sent word | that 3.02.164
not fear, | there is douglas and lord mortimer. 4.04. 22
no, mortimer is not there. 4.04. 23
age, | let dying mortimer here rest himself. 1H6 2.05. 2
age of care, | argue the end of edmund mortimer. 2.05. 7
here dies the dusky torch of mortimer, | chok'd 2.05.122
who married edmund mortimer, earl of march; 2H6 2.02. 36
march, who was the son | of edmund mortimer, who 2.02. 49
well he can, | under the title of john mortimer. 3.01.359
for that john mortimer, which now is dead, | in 3.01.372
my father was a mortimer — 4.02. 39 P
rise up sir john mortimer. 4.02.120 P
edmund mortimer, earl of march, | married the 4.02.136
jack cade proclaims himself lord mortimer, 4.04. 28
now is mortimer lord of this city. 4.06. 1 P
for any that calls me other than lord mortimer. 4.06. 6 P
even the presence of lord mortimer, that i am 4.07. 30 P
thy grandfather, roger mortimer, earl of march: 3H6 1.01.106
sir john and sir hugh mortimer, mine uncles, 1.02. 62

MORTIMERS 1 FR 0.0001 REL FR 1 V 0 P
thus the mortimers, | in whom the title rested, 1H6 2.05. 91

MORTIS'D 1 FR 0.0001 REL FR 1 V 0 P
lesser things | are mortis'd and adjoin'd, which HAM 3.03. 20

MORTISE 1 FR 0.0001 REL FR 1 V 0 P
mountains melt on them, | can hold the mortise? OTH 2.01. 9

MORTON 4 FR 0.0004 REL FR 4 V 0 P
say, morton, didst thou come from shrewsbury? 2H4 1.01. 64
yet speak, morton, | tell thou an earl his 1.01. 87
morton is fled to richmond, | and buckingham, R3 4.03. 46
stirr'd up by dorset, buckingham, and morton, 4.04.467
MOSE 1 FR 0.0001 REL FR 0 V 1 P
with the glanders and like to mose in the chine, SHR 3.02. 51 P
MOSS 3 FR 0.0003 REL FR 3 V 0 P
is dross, | usurping ivy, brier, or idle moss, ERR 2.02.178
overcome with moss and baleful mistletoe; TIT 2.03. 95
thee all this, | yea, and furr'd moss besides. CYM 4.02.228
MOSS'D 1 FR 0.0001 REL FR 1 V 0 P
whose boughs were moss'd with age | and high top AYL 4.03.104
MOSS–GROWN 1 FR 0.0001 REL FR 1 V 0 P
topples down | steeples and moss–grown towers. 1H4 3.01. 32
/MOST 23 FR 0.0026 REL FR 17 V 6 P
/lift /him /where /most /trade /of /danger 2H4 1.01.174
/but, /my /most /noble /lord /of /westmerland, 4.01. 59
/are /enforc'd /from /our /most /quiet /there 4.01. 71
/by /those /men /that /most /have /done /us 4.01. 79
/in /england /the /most /valiant /gentleman. 4.01.130
ajax to invite the /most valorous hector to come TRO 3.03.274 P
/bids /thee, /with /most /divine /integrity, 4.05.170
where they /most breed and haunt, i have MAC 1.06. 9
/man, /i /am /most /dreadfully /attended. HAM 2.02.269 P
/and /are /most /tyrannically /clapp'd /for't. 2.02.340 P
/to /common /players (/as /it /is /most /like, 2.02.349 P
/for /pilf'rings /and /most /common /trespasses LR 2.02.144
/sit /thou /here, /most /learned /justicer; 3.06. 21
/alone /suffers, /suffers /most /i' /th' /mind, 3.06.104
/most /barbarous, /most /degenerate, /have /you 4.02. 43
/most /barbarous, /most /degenerate, /have /you 4.02. 43
/return /was /most /requir'd /and /necessary. 4.03. 6 P
/over /her /passion, /who, /most //rebel–like, 4.03. 14
/sorrow /would /be /a /rarity /most /beloved, 4.03. 23
/in /the /most /terrible /and /nimble /stroke 4.07. 33
/most /certain, /sir. 4.07. 86 P
/most /just /and /heavy /causes /make /oppose. 5.01. 27
/told /the /most /piteous /tale /of /lear /and 5.03.215
MOST 1219 FR 0.1378 REL FR 931 V 288 P
sir, most heedfully. TMP 1.02. 78
to most ignoble stooping. 1.02.116
the which this story | were most impertinent. 1.02.138
by accident most strange, bountiful fortune 1.02.178
doth depend upon | a most auspicious star, whose 1.02.182
of sulphurous roaring the most mighty neptune 1.02.204
now | must by us both be spent most preciously. 1.02.241
ministers, | and in her most unmitigable rage, 1.02.276
thou most lying slave, | whom stripes may move, 1.02.344
but wouldst gabble like | a thing most brutish, 1.02.357
most sure, the goddess | on whom these airs 1.02.422
wench, | to th' most of men this is a caliban, 1.02.481
my affections | are then most humble; 1.02.483
and a subtle, as he most learnedly deliver'd. 2.01. 45 P
the air breathes upon us here most sweetly. 2.01. 47 P
breasted | the surge most swoll'n that met him. 2.01.118
and most chirurgeonly. 2.01.141
most often, do so near the bottom run | by their 2.01.227
it strook mine ear most terribly. 2.01.313
a most delicate monster! 2.02. 89 P
a most poor credulous monster! 2.02.146 P
light, a most perfidious and drunken monster! 2.02.150 P
a most scurvy monster! 2.02.155 P
a most ridiculous monster, to make a wonder of a 2.02.165 P
and most poor matters | point to rich ends. 3.01. 3
my labors, | most /busil'est when i do it. 3.01. 15
o most dear mistress, | the sun will set before 3.01. 21
fair encounter | of two most rare affections! 3.01. 75
thou liest, most ignorant monster, i am in case 3.02. 25 P
that's most certain. 3.02. 56 P
and that most deeply to consider is | the beauty 3.02. 98
you 'mongst men | being most unfit to live. 3.03. 58
which here, in this most desolate isle, else 3.03. 80
den, | the most opportune place, the strong'st 4.01. 26
ceres, most bounteous lady, thy rich leas | of 4.01. 60
this is a most majestic vision, and | harmonious 4.01.118
most cruelly | didst thou, alonso, use me and my 5.01. 71
(whose inward pinches therefore are most strong) 5.01. 77
(and if this be at all) a most strange story. 5.01.117
for you, most wicked sir, whom to call brother 5.01.130
of milan, who most strangely | upon this shore 5.01.160
a most high miracle! 5.01.177
i have's mine own, | which is most faint. ep 3
as the most forward bud | is eaten by the canker TGV 1.01. 45
fire that's closest kept burns most of all. 1.02. 30
excuse | hath he excepted most against my love. 1.03. 83
for love is still most precious in itself, | and 2.06. 24
what thou think'st meet, and is most mannerly. 2.07. 58
since his exile she hath despis'd me most, 3.02. 3
that e'er i watch'd, and the most heaviest. 4.02.140
hence, | to keep me from a most unholy match, 4.03. 30
by thy approach thou mak'st me most unhappy. 5.04. 31
o time most accurst! 5.04. 71
examin'd my parts with most judicious iliads; WIV 1.03. 60 P
i most fehemently desire you you will also look 3.01. 8 P
yonder is a most reverend gentleman, who, belike 3.01. 52 P
person, is at most odds with his own gravity and 3.01. 54 P
but 'tis most certain your husband's coming, 3.03.113 P
trust me, he beat him most pitifully. 4.02.201 P
he beat him most unpitifully, methought. 4.02.203 P
a chain | in a most hideous and dreadful manner. 4.04. 34
you would have married her most shamefully, 5.05.221
and indeed with most painful feeling of thy MM 1.02. 36 P
of your hips has the most profound sciatica? 1.02. 59 P
but most of all agreeing with the proclamation. 1.02. 79 P
the stealth of our most mutual entertainment 1.02.154
we have strict statutes and most biting laws 1.03. 19
whom i would save, had a most noble father! 2.01. 7
(whom i believe to be most strait in virtue) 2.01. 9
or seven, the most sufficient of your parish. 2.01.273 P
there is a vice that most i do abhor, | and most 2.02. 29
and most desire should meet the blow of justice; 2.02. 30
i show it most of all when i show justice; 2.02.100
most ignorant of what he's most assur'd | (his 2.02.119
most ignorant of what he's most assur'd | (his 2.02.119
the tempter, or the tempted, who sins most, ha? 2.02.163
most dangerous | is that temptation that doth 2.02.180
i do; and bear the shame most patiently. 2.03. 20
so then it seems your most offenseful act | was 2.03. 26
that the most just law | now took your brother's 2.04. 52
thus wisdom wishes to appear most bright | when 2.04. 78
be much believ'd, | and most pernicious purpose! 2.04.150
or, by the affection that now guides me most, 2.04.168
most holy sir, i thank you. 3.01. 47
most good, most good indeed. 3.01. 55
most good, most good indeed. 3.01. 55
the sense of death is most in apprehension, 3.01. 77
the weariest and most loathed worldly life 3.01.128
denial which he is most glad to receive. 3.01.165 P
believe that you may most uprighteously do a 3.01.200 P
his love toward her ever most kind and natural; 3.01.220 P
it will grow to a most prosperous perfection. 3.01.260 P
judge, but most willingly humbles himself to the 3.02.243 P
strings | most ponderous and substantial things! 3.02.276
with whispering and most guilty diligence, | in 4.01. 38
and that i have possess'd him my most stay | can 4.01. 43
with these false and most contrarious /quests 4.01. 61
or reprieve | for the most gentle claudio. 4.02. 72
most manifest, and not denied by himself. 4.02.139 P
fever | one ragozine, a most notorious pirate, 4.03. 71
most damned angelo! 4.03.122
in most uneven and distracted manner. 4.04. 3 P
come, i have found you out a stand most fit, 4.06. 10
and she will speak most bitterly and strange. 5.01. 36
most strange! 5.01. 37
but yet most truly will i speak: 5.01. 37
this is most likely! 5.01.103
woman | most wrongfully accus'd your substitute, 5.01.140
my lord, most villainously, believe it. 5.01.149
one that hath spoke most villainous speeches of 5.01.263 P
most notedly, sir. 5.01.332 P
o most kind maid, | it was the swift celerity of 5.01.393
very mercy of the law cries out | most audible, 5.01.408
o my most gracious lord, | i hope you will not 5.01.416
and, for the most, become much more the better 5.01.440
most bounteous sir: 5.01.443
o most unhappy day! ERR 4.04.123
o most unhappy strumpet! 4.04.124
me, | though most dishonestly he doth deny it. 5.01. 3
which he forswore most monstrously to have. 5.01. 11
justice, most sacred duke, against the abbess! 5.01.133
day | a most outrageous fit of madness took him, 5.01.139
therefore, most gracious duke, with thy command 5.01.159
justice, most gracious duke, o, grant me justice 5.01.190
most mighty duke, vouchsafe me speak a word: 5.01.283
most mighty duke, behold a man much wrong'd. 5.01.331
i came from corinth, my most gracious lord — 5.01.366
to this town by that most famous warrior, | duke 5.01.368
duke menaphon, your most renowned uncle. 5.01.369
he is most in the company of the right noble ADO 1.01. 84 P
me up, i likewise give her most humble thanks; 1.01.239 P
who, the most exquisite claudio? 1.03. 50 P
your silence most offends me, and to be merry 2.01.331 P
but most wonderful that she should so dote on 2.03. 95 P
undertakes them with a most christian–like fear. 2.03.192 P
who think you the most desartless man to be 3.03. 9 P
here to be the most senseless and fit man for 3.03. 22 P
watch to babble and to talk, is most tolerable, 3.03. 36 P
speak like an ancient and most quiet watchman, 3.03. 39 P
the most peaceable way for you, if you do take a 3.03. 57 P
have here recover'd the most dangerous piece of 3.03.167 P
and your gown's a most rare fashion, i' faith. 3.04. 15 P
who hath indeed, most like a liberal villain, 4.01. 92
but fare thee well, most foul, most fair! 4.01.103
but fare thee well, most foul, most fair! 4.01.103
the which if i do not carve most curiously, say 5.01.156 P
in most profound earnest, and, i'll warrant you, 5.01.195 P
most sincerely. 5.01.198 P
worship speaks like a most thankful and reverent 5.01.315 P
it, for in most comely truth thou deservest it. 5.02. 7 P
a most manly wit, margaret, it will not hurt a 5.02. 15 P
therefore is it most expedient for the wise, if 5.02. 83 P
that eye my daughter lent her, 'tis most true. 5.04. 23
delights are vain, but that most vain | which, LLL 1.01. 72
and when it hath the thing it hunteth most, 1.01.145
armado is a most illustrious wight, | a man of 1.01.177
humor to the most wholesome physic of thy 1.01.233 P
when beasts most graze, birds best peck, and men 1.01.236 P
that obscene and most prepost'rous event that 1.01.241 P
a most fine figure! 1.02. 55 P
most sweet hercules! 1.02. 67 P
my love is most immaculate white and red. 1.02. 90 P
most maculate thoughts, master, are mask'd under 1.02. 92 P
of a child, most pretty and pathetical! 1.02. 97 P
they say so most that most his humors know. 2.01. 53
they say so most that most his humors know. 2.01. 53
most power to do most harm, least knowing ill; 2.01. 58
most power to do most harm, least knowing ill; 2.01. 58
she is a most sweet lady. 2.01.207
men that most are affected to these. 3.01. 25 P
a most acute juvenal, volable and free of grace! 3.01. 66
most rude melancholy, valor gives thee place. 3.01. 68
most sweet gardon! 3.01.171 P
heaven, that thou art fair, is most infallible; 4.01. 61 P
the magnanimous and most illustrate king 4.01. 65 P
by my troth, most pleasant. how both did fit it! 4.01.129
by my soul, a swain, a most simple clown! 4.01.140
o' my troth, most sweet jests, most incony 4.01.142
troth, most sweet jests, most incony vulgar wit! 4.01.142
/a' /th' /one side — o, a most dainty man! 4.01.144
and how most sweetly 'a will swear! 4.01.146
ah, heavens, it is /a most pathetical nit! 4.01.148
most barbarous intimation! 4.02. 13 P
hand of the most beauteous lady rosaline." 4.02.132 P
and certes the text most infallibly concludes it 4.02.163 P
o most divine kate! 4.03. 81
o most profane coxcomb! 4.03. 82
these worms for loving, that art most in love? 4.03.152
a most singular and choice epithet. 5.01. 15 P
most military sir, salutation. 5.01. 35 P
ba, most silly sheep, with a horn. 5.01. 50 P
sir, it is the king's most sweet pleasure and 5.01. 87 P
the posterior of the day, most generous sir, is 5.01. 91 P
other /importunate and most serious designs, and 5.01. 99 P
the king's command, and this most gallant, 5.01.121 P
most dull, honest dull! to our sport; away! 5.01.155
come on then, wear the favors most in sight. 5.02.136
can sing | a mean most meanly and in hushering 5.02.328
lord | most honorably doth uphold his word. 5.02.449
their form confounded makes most form in mirth, 5.02.519
you the peace of mind, most royal couplement. 5.02.531 P
"no" in /this, most tender–smelling knight. 5.02.566
most true, 'tis right; you were so, alisander. 5.02.569
most rare pompey! 5.02.683 P
most resolute pompey! 5.02.699 P
but, most esteemed greatness, will you hear the 5.02.884 P
our play is the most lamentable comedy and most MND 1.02. 11 P
most lamentable comedy and most cruel death of 1.02. 12 P
lover, that kills himself most gallant for love. 1.02. 23 P
a most lovely gentleman–like man: 1.02. 87 P
and there we may rehearse most obscenely and 1.02.108 P
are hated most of those they did deceive, | so 2.02.140
heresy, | of all be hated, but the most of me! 2.02.142
a lion among ladies, is a most dreadful thing; 3.01. 31 P
"most radiant pyramus, most lily–white of hue, 3.01. 93
"most radiant pyramus, most lily–white of hue, 3.01. 93
most brisky juvenal and eke most lovely jew, 3.01. 95
most brisky juvenal and eke most lovely jew, 3.01. 95
most ungrateful maid! 3.02.195
so fortunate | (but miserable most, to love 3.02.234
right, | of thine or mine, is most in helena. 3.02.337
my next is, "most fair pyramus." 4.01.201 P
i have had a most rare vision. 4.01.204 P
o most courageous day! 4.02. 27 P
o most happy hour! 4.02. 27 P
and, most dear actors, eat no onions nor garlic, 4.02. 42 P
tongue–tied simplicity | in least speak most, to 5.01.105
here comes bassanio, your most noble kinsman, MV 1.01. 57
i owe the most, in money and in love, | and from 1.01.131
he is sober, and most vildly in the afternoon, 1.02. 87 P
even there where merchants most do congregate, 1.03. 49
outbrave the heart most daring on the earth, 2.01. 28
well, the most courageous fiend bids me pack. 2.02. 10 P
most beautiful pagan, most sweet jew! 2.03. 10 P
most beautiful pagan, most sweet jew! 2.03. 11 P
making them lightest that wear most of it. 3.02. 91
but the guiled shore | to a most dangerous sea; 3.02. 98
it is the most impenetrable cur | that ever kept 3.03. 18
which appears most strongly | in bearing thus 3.04. 3
you may as well do any thing most hard, | as 4.01. 78
here 'tis, most reverend doctor, here it is. 4.01.226
the law, your exposition | hath been most sound. 4.01.238
most heartily i do beseech the court | to give 4.01.243
most rightful judge! 4.01.301
most learned judge! a sentence! come, prepare! 4.01.304
most worthy gentleman, i and my friend | have by 4.01.408
his ring i do accept most thankfully, | and so i 4.02. 9
most true, i have lost my teeth in your service. AYL 1.01. 82 P
thou shalt find i will most kindly requite. 1.01.138 P
blind woman doth most mistake in her gifts to 1.02. 36 P
thus most invectively he pierceth through | the 2.01. 58
how many actions most ridiculous | hast thou 2.04. 30
and in my voice most welcome shall you be. 2.04. 87
and they that are most galled with my folly, 2.07. 50
galled with my folly, | they most must laugh. 2.07. 51
most mischievous foul sin, in chiding sin: 2.07. 64
i thank you most for him. 2.07.169
most friendship is feigning, most loving mere 2.07.181
friendship is feigning, most loving mere folly. 2.07.181
this life is most jolly. 2.07.183
most truly limn'd and living in your face, | be 2.07.194
of the country is most mockable at the court. 3.02. 47 P
most shallow man! 3.02. 65 P
o most gentle jupiter, what tedious homily of 3.02.155 P
i prithee now, with most petitionary vehemence, 3.02.189 P
wonderful, and most wonderful wonderful! 3.02.191 P
but myself, against whom i know most faults. 3.02.281 P
and women are for the most part cattle of this 3.02.415 P
thee and thy goats, as the most capricious poet, 3.03. 8 P
for the truest poetry is the most feigning, and 3.03. 20 P
foul is most foul, being foul to be a scoffer. 3.05. 62
that i shall think it a most plenteous crop | to 3.05.101
rumination wraps me in a most humorous sadness. 4.01. 19 P
your hour, i will think you the most pathetical 4.01.192 P
break–promise, and the most hollow lover, and 4.01.193 P
and the most unworthy of her you call rosalind, 4.01.193 P
and he did render him the most unnatural | that 4.03.122
tears our recountments had most kindly bath'd, 4.03.140
a most wicked sir oliver, audrey, a most vile 5.01. 5 P
wicked sir oliver, audrey, a most vile martext. 5.01. 5 P
with a magician, most profound in his art, and 5.02. 61 P
give yourself to this most faithful shepherd? 5.04. 14
make conclusion | of these most strange events. 5.04.127
fingers, | a most delicious banquet by his bed, SHR in.1. 39
in brief, sir, study what you most affect. 1.01. 40
and for i know she taketh most delight | in 1.01. 92
when, with a most impatient devilish spirit, 2.01.151
me give away myself | to this most patient, 3.02.195
his wife, | and he whose wife is most obedient, 5.02. 67
that seeming to be most which we indeed least 5.02.175
mothers, which is most infallible disobedience. AWW 1.01.137 P
which is the most inhibited sin in the canon. 1.01.145 P
nay, 'tis most credible; 1.02. 4
she deliver'd in the most bitter touch of sorrow 1.03.117 P
most admirable! i have seen those wars. 2.01. 26
under the influence of the most receiv'd star, 2.01. 55 P
fellows, and like to prove most sinewy swordmen. 2.01. 59 P
when our most learned doctors leave us, and 2.01.116
and most oft there | where most it promises; 2.01.142
and most oft there | where most it promises; 2.01.143
where hope is coldest and despair most /fits. 2.01.144
but most it is presumption in us when | the help 2.01.151
but know i think, and think i know most sure, 2.01.157
it must be an answer of most monstrous size that 2.02. 32 P
most fruitfully, i am there before my legs. 2.02. 70 P
and he's of a most facinerious spirit that will 2.03. 29 P
in a most weak — 2.03. 33 P
fly, | and to imperial love, that god most high, 2.03. 75
late | was in my nobler thoughts most base, is 2.03.171
a most harsh one, and not to be understood 2.03.190 P
my lord, you give me most egregious indignity. 2.03.216 P
my lord, you do me most insupportable vexation. 2.03.230 P
i most unfeignedly beseech your lordship to make 2.03.244 P

say, | but that i am your most obedient servant. 2.05. 72
most fain would steal | what law does vouch mine 2.05. 81
dispatch the most convenient messenger. 3.04. 34
french count has done most honorable service. 3.05. 3 P
but by the ear, that hears most nobly of him. 3.05. 50
'tis a most gallant fellow. 3.05. 78
him as my kinsman, he's a most notable coward, 3.06. 9 P
this ring he holds | in most rich choice; 3.07. 26
fill the time, | herself most chastely absent. 3.07. 34
my reasons are most strong, and you shall know 4.02. 59
here in florence, of a most chaste renown, and 4.03. 15 P
holy undertaking with most austere sanctimony 4.03. 49 P
was the death of the most virtuous gentlewoman 4.05. 9 P
delicate fine hats, and most courteous feathers, 4.05.105 P
and therefore, goaded with most sharp occasions, 5.01. 14
all proportions | to a most hideous object. 5.03. 52
to reave her | of what should stead her most? 5.03. 87
he's quoted for a most perfidious slave, | with 5.03.205
most provident in peril, bind himself | (courage TN 1.02. 12
one of thy kin has a most weak pia mater. 1.05.115 P
most radiant, exquisite, and unmatchable beauty 1.05.170 P
most certain, if you are she, you do usurp 1.05.187 P
most sweet lady — 1.05.221 P
most certain. let our catch be "thou knave." 2.03. 63 P
he shall find himself most feelingly personated. 2.03.159 P
of these most brisk and giddy-paced times. 2.04. 6
of tartar, thou most excellent devil of wit! 2.05.205 P
most excellent accomplish'd lady, the heavens 3.01. 84 P
but to your own most pregnant and vouchsafed ear 3.01. 89 P
my duty, madam, and most humble service. 3.01. 95
most villainously; 3.02. 75 P
which for traffic's sake | most of our city did. 3.03. 35
it) into a most hideous opinion of his rage, 3.04.193 P
he is indeed, sir, the most skillful, bloody, 3.04.266 P
methought did promise | most venerable worth, 3.04.363
whisper o'er a couplet or two of most sage saws. 3.04.378 P
a coward, a most devout coward, religious in it. 3.04.389 P
i call thee by the most modest terms, for i am 4.02. 32 P
my most exquisite sir topas! 4.02. 62 P
that my most jealious and too doubtful soul 4.03. 27
make | with the most noble bottom of our fleet, 5.01. 57
that most ingrateful boy there by your side 5.01. 77
and i, most jocund, apt, and willingly, | to do 5.01.132
most wonderful! 5.01.225
i shall have share in this most happy wrack. 5.01.266
a most extracting frenzy of mine own | from my 5.01.281
madam, i am most apt t' embrace your offer. 5.01.320
and made the most notorious geck and gull | that 5.01.343
this practice hath most shrewdly pass'd upon 5.01.352
most freely i confess, myself and toby | set 5.01.359
he hath been most notoriously abus'd. 5.01.379
o my most sacred lady, | temptations have since WT 1.02. 76
most dear'st! 1.02.137
i think most understand | bohemia stays here 1.02.229
the entreaties | of our most gracious mistress. 1.02.233
opinion, and betimes, | for 'tis most dangerous. 1.02.298
hail, most royal sir! 1.02.366
(from him that has most cause to grieve it 2.01. 77
so, | the most replenish'd villain in the world, 2.01. 79
herself | but with her most vild principal — 2.01. 92
either thou art most ignorant by age, | or thou 2.01.173
importance 'twere | most piteous to be wild), i 2.01.182
most worthy madam, | your honor and your 2.02. 40
acquaint the queen of your most noble offer, 2.02. 46
your physician, | your most obedient counsellor; 2.03. 55
your evils, | than such as most seem yours. 2.03. 57
a most intelligencing bawd! 2.03. 69
a most unworthy and unnatural lord | can do no 2.03.113
but this most cruel usage of your queen | (not 2.03.117
that we may arraign | our most disloyal lady; 2.03.203
the climate's delicate, the air most sweet, 3.01. 1
for most it caught me, the celestial habits 3.01. 4
my third comfort | (starr'd most unluckily) is 3.02. 99
(the innocent milk in it most innocent mouth) 3.02.100
he (most humane | and fill'd with honor) to my 3.02.165
word deserves | to taste of thy most worst? 3.02.179
thou didst speak but well | when most the truth; 3.02.233
and most accurs'd am i | to be by oath enjoin'd 3.03. 52
o, the most piteous cry of the poor souls! 3.03. 90 P
though i have for the most part been air'd 4.02. 5 P
whose loss of his most precious queen and 4.02. 24 P
seldom from the house of a most homely shepherd, 4.02. 38 P
a man, who hath a daughter of most rare note. 4.02. 42 P
here and there, | i then do most go right. 4.03. 18
but they are most of them means and bases; 4.03. 43 P
poor lowly maid, | most goddess-like prank'd up. 4.04. 10
to this i am most constant, | though destiny say 4.04. 45
strength (a malady | most incident to maids); 4.04.125
that, were i crown'd the most imperial monarch, 4.04.372
thereof most worthy, were i the fairest youth 4.04.373
strength indeed | than most have of his age. 4.04.404
and most opportune to her need i have | a vessel 4.04.500
shores, most certain | to miseries enough; 4.04.567
for she seems a mistress | to most that teach. 4.04.583
i pick'd and cut most of their festival purses; 4.04.614 P
the remembrance | of his most sovereign name; 5.01. 26
the most peerless piece of earth, i think, 5.01. 94
your mother was most true to wedlock, prince, 5.01.124
most dearly welcome! 5.01.130
most royal sir, from thence; 5.01.159
most noble sir, | that which i shall report will 5.01.178
most sorry, you have broken from his liking, 5.01.212
i would most gladly know the issue of it. 5.02. 8 P
most true, if ever truth were pregnant by 5.02. 30 P
who was most marble there chang'd color; 5.02. 90 P
lays most lawful claim | to this fair island and JN 1.01. 9
most certain of one mother, mighty king — 1.01. 59
what means this scorn, thou most untoward knave? 1.01.243
is most divinely vow'd upon the right | of him 2.01.237
from love, | for i do love her most unfeignedly. 2.01.526
war | to a most base and vile-concluded peace. 2.01.586
this news hath made thee a most ugly man. 3.01. 37
nothing but a calve's-skin, most sweet lout. 3.01.220
ill, | the truth is then most done not doing it. 3.01.273
and most forsworn, to keep what thou dost swear; 3.01.287
on their departure most of all show evil. 3.04.115
when fortune means to men most good, | she looks 3.04.119
thou didst but consent | to this most cruel act, 4.03.126

favor and the form | of this most fair occasion, 5.04. 51
my gracious sovereign, my most loving liege! R2 1.01. 21
by all my hopes, most falsely doth he lie. 1.01. 68
a recreant and most degenerate traitor, | which 1.01.144
most heartily i pray | your highness to assign 1.01.150
one flourishing branch of his most royal root, 1.02. 18
the daintiest last, to make the end most sweet: 1.03. 68
most mighty liege, and my companion peers, 1.03. 93
a heavy sentence, my most sovereign liege, | and 1.03.154
his noble kinsman — most degenerate king! 2.01.262
your presence makes us rich, most noble lord. 2.03. 63
from the most gracious regent of this land, 2.03. 77
turns to the sourest and most deadly hate. 3.02.136
true faith of heart | to his most royal person; 3.03. 38
that spring from one most gracious head, | and 3.03.108
most mighty prince, my lord northumberland, 3.03.172
so far be mine, my most redoubted lord, | as my 3.03.198
thou most beauteous inn, | why should 5.01. 13
a purse of gold most resolutely snatch'd on 1H4 1.02. 33 P
on monday night and most dissolutely spent on 1.02. 34 P
not my hostess of the tavern a most sweet wench? 1.02. 40 P
not a buff jerkin a most sweet robe of durance? 1.02. 42 P
thou hast the most unsavory /similes and art 1.02. 79 P
/similes and art indeed the most comparative, 1.02. 80 P
this is the most omnipotent villain that ever 1.02.108 P
i think this be the most villainous house in all 2.01. 14 P
a pleasing eye, and a most noble carriage, and, 2.04.423 P
the sheriff with a most monstrous watch is at 2.04.482 P
my lord, he speaks most vilely of you, like a 3.03.106 P
hostess, and he slanders thee most grossly. 3.03.132 P
for indeed i had the most of them out of prison. 4.02. 41 P
'tis more than time, and, my most noble lord, 2H4 1.01.187
and i most humbly beseech your lordship to have 1.02. 99 P
and, my most noble friends, i pray you all 1.03. 2
he stabb'd me in mine own house, most beastly, 2.01. 14 P
o my most worshipful lord, and't please your 2.01. 69 P
i would think thee a most princely hypocrite. 2.02. 54 P
and what accites your most worshipful thought to 2.02. 60 P
and yours, most noble bardolph! 2.02. 74 P
troth, i kiss thee with a most constant heart. 2.04.269 P
and in the calmest and most stillest night, 3.01. 28
gentleman, by heaven, and a most gallant leader. 3.02. 62 P
most excellent, i' faith! 3.02.107 P
as the wrathful dove or most magnanimous mouse. 3.02.160 P
let that suffice, most forcible feeble. 3.02.167 P
in his true, native, and most proper shape, 4.01. 37
with grant of our most just and right desires, 4.02. 40
i will perform with a most christian care. 4.02.115
most shallowly did you these arms commence, 4.02.118
i were simply the most active fellow in europe. 4.03. 21 P
dale, a most furious knight and valorous enemy. 4.03. 38 P
most subject is the fattest soil to weeds, | and 4.04. 54
'tis needful that the most immodest word | be 4.04. 70
which my most inward true and duteous spirit 4.05.147
but thou, most fine, most honor'd, most renown'd 4.05.163
thou, most fine, most honor'd, most renown'd, 4.05.163
thou, most fine, most honor'd, most renown'd, 4.05.163
thus, my most royal liege, | accusing it, i put 4.05.164
you all look strangely on me, and you most. 5.02. 63
nay more, to spurn at your most royal image, 5.02. 89
see your most dreadful laws so loosely slighted, 5.02. 94
sit, i'll be with you anon, most sweet sir, sit. 5.03. 26 P
puff i' thy teeth, most recreant coward base! 5.03. 92
thither | by most mechanical and dirty hand. 5.05. 36
thee guard and keep, most royal imp of fame! 5.05. 42
and (as most debtors do) promise you infinitely; ep 15 P
whiles his most mighty father on a hill | stood H5 1.02.108
of this most dreadful preparation, | shake in 2.pr. 13
the "solus" in thy most mervailous face, | the 2.01. 47
thy spirits are most tall. 2.01. 68
in cash, most justly paid. 2.01.115
tertian, that it is most lamentable to behold. 2.01.119 P
at the discovery of most dangerous treason 2.02.162
my most redoubted father, | it is most meet we 2.04. 14
it is most meet we arm us 'gainst the foe; 2.04. 15
that shall first spring and be most delicate. 2.04. 40
most spend their mouths when what they seem to 2.04. 70
rak'd, | he sends you this most memorable line, 2.04. 88
from his most fam'd of famous ancestors, 2.04. 92
the plain-song is most just; 3.02. 7
and their most reverend heads dash'd to the 3.03. 37
heels, | and that we are most lofty runaways. 3.05. 35
world, but keeps the bridge most valiantly, with 3.06. 11 P
the poet makes a most excellent description of 3.06. 37 P
and there is gallant and most prave passages. 3.06. 93 P
lord, it is a most absolute and excellent horse. 3.07. 25 P
he is simply the most active gentleman of france 3.07. 97 P
a valiant and most expert gentleman. 3.07.129 P
with four or five most vile and ragged foils 4.pr. 50
fame, | of parents good, of fist most valiant. 4.01. 46
a good old commander and a most kind gentleman. 4.01. 95 P
honor, | i am the most offending soul alive. 4.03. 29
compound, | before thy most assured overthrow; 4.03. 81
most humbly on my knee i beg | the leading of 4.03.130
of one (as he thinks) the most brave, valorous, 4.04. 61 P
wherefore the king, most worthily, hath caus'd 4.07. 9 P
fought a most prave pattle here in france. 4.07. 95 P
a most contagious treason come to light, look 4.08. 21 P
and thou hast given me most bitter terms. 4.08. 42
by this leek, i will most horribly revenge — i 5.01. 47 P
to our most fair and princely cousin katherine; 5.02. 4
face, | most worthy brother england, fairly met! 5.02. 10
to bring your most imperial majesties | unto 5.02. 26
fair katherine, and most fair, | will you 5.02. 98
and i thine, most truly falsely, must needs be 5.02.191 P
enough to deceive de most sage demoiselle dat is 5.02.219 P
and therefore tell me, most fair katherine, will 5.02.234 P
but in that small most greatly lived | this star ep 5
most of the rest slaughter'd or took likewise. 1H6 1.01.147
i do, thou most usurping proditor, | and not 1.03. 31
and thence discover how with most advantage 1.04. 12
and, for myself, most part of all this night, 2.01. 67
the north, | finding his usurpation most unjust, 2.05. 68
thou art a most pernicious usurer, | froward by 3.01. 17
accept this scroll, most gracious sovereign, 3.01.148
behold the wounds, the most unnatural wounds, 3.03. 50
but always resolute in most extremes. 4.01. 38
knight, | profaning this most honorable order, 4.01. 41

arms | of the most bloody nurser of his harms! 4.07. 46
of all base passions, fear is most accurs'd. 5.02. 18
a married man! that's most intolerable. 5.04. 79
have we not lost most part of all the towns, 5.04.108
and therefore, lords, since he affects her most, 5.05. 59
most of all these reasons bindeth us | in our 5.05. 60
in the queen | to your most gracious hands, that 2H6 1.01. 13
and he of these that can do most of all | cannot 1.03. 72
though in this place most master wear no 1.03.146
force, | that york is most unmeet of any man. 1.03.164
most true, forsooth; 2.01. 91
yet he most christian-like laments his death; 3.02. 58
they say, in care of your most royal person, 3.02.254
are we in order when we are most out of order. 4.02.189 P
thou hast most traitorously corrupted the youth 4.07. 32 P
that cause they have been most worthy to live. 4.07. 46 P
wherein have i offended most? 4.07. 97
the most complete champion that ever i heard! 4.10. 55 P
and there cut off thy most ungracious head, 4.10. 82
myself | the title of this most renowned duke, 5.01.176
and thus most humbly i do take my leave. 3H6 1.02. 61
'tis virtue that doth make them most admir'd, 1.04.130
him, | which argued thee a most unloving father. 2.02. 25
three, my most gracious lord. 3.02. 29
but most himself if he could see his shame. 3.03.185
unnatural | provokes this deluge most unnatural. R3 1.02. 61
thou wast the cause, and most accurs'd effect. 1.02.120
it is a quarrel most unnatural, | to be reveng'd 1.02.134
to him that hath most cause to be a mourner, 1.02.211
and the most merciless, that e'er was heard of! 1.03.183
and seem a saint, when most i play the devil. 1.03.337
to threaten me with death is most unlawful. 1.04.188
i wash my hands | of this most grievous murther! 1.04.273
with hate in those where i expect most love! 2.01. 35
when i have most need to employ a friend, | and 2.01. 36
friend, | and most assured that he is a friend, 2.01. 37
a blessed labor, my most sovereign lord. 2.01. 53
and shall be thought most fit | for your best 3.01. 66
who is most inward with the noble duke? 3.04. 8
makes me most forward in this princely presence 3.04. 64
famous plantagenet, most gracious prince, | lend 3.07.100
grace, | and so most joyfully we take our leave. 3.07.245
james tyrrel, and your most obedient subject. 4.02. 67
the most arch deed of piteous massacre | that 4.03. 2
the most replenished sweet work of nature | that 4.03. 18
if ancient sorrow be most reverent, | give mine 4.04. 35
for happy wife, a most distressed widow; 4.04. 98
therefore take with thee my most grievous curse, 4.04.188
/god's wrong is most of all: 4.04.377
most mighty sovereign, on the western coast 4.04.433
most mighty sovereign, | you have no cause to 4.04.491
that in the sty of the most deadly boar | my son 4.05. 2
by the false faith of him whom most i trusted; 5.01. 17
fellows in arms, and my most loving friends, 5.02. 1
here, most gracious liege. 5.03. 4
and give him from me this most needful note. 5.03. 41
for the most part such | to whom as great a H8 1.01. 76
minister communication of | a most poor issue? 1.01. 87
in the name | of our most sovereign king. 1.01.202
reproaches | most bitterly on you as putter-on 1.02. 24
they are | most pestilent to th' hearing, and, 1.02. 49
gentleman is learn'd, and a most rare speaker, 1.02.111
most like a careful subject, have collected 1.02.130
his will is most malignant, and it stretches 1.02.141
men of his way should be most liberal, | they 1.03. 61
in all the rest show'd a most noble patience. 2.01. 36
like a most royal prince | restor'd me to my 2.01.113
by our servants, by those men we lov'd most; 2.01.122
a most unnatural and faithless service. 2.01.123
'tis most true | these news are every where; 2.02. 37
you'll find a most unfit time to disturb him. 2.02. 60
most learned reverend sir, into our kingdom, 2.02. 76
the most convenient place that i can think of 2.02.137
hearts of most hard temper | melt and lament for 2.03. 11
for | i am a most poor woman, and a stranger, 2.04. 15
was reputed for | a prince most prudent, of an 2.04. 46
i hold my most malicious foe, and think not | at 2.04. 83
most gracious sir, | in humblest manner i 2.04.144
most honor'd madam, | my lord of york, out of 3.01. 61
protection, | he's loving and most gracious. 3.01. 94
and to that woman (when she has done most) | yet 3.01.136
i am the most unhappy woman living. 3.01.147
most strangely. 3.02. 29
in most strange postures | we have seen him set 3.02.118
to th' good of your most sacred person and | the 3.02.173
lay upon my credit, | i answer is most false. 3.02.266
since you provoke me, shall be most notorious. 3.02.288
yet in bestowing, madam, | he was most princely: 4.02. 57
whom i most hated living, thou hast made me, 4.02. 73
i am most joyful, madam, such good dreams 4.02. 93
i most humbly pray you to deliver | this to my 4.02.129
most willing, madam. 4.02.130
speak of two | the most remark'd i' th' kingdom. 5.01. 33
a most arch-heretic, a pestilence | that does 5.01. 45
your highness | most heartily to pray for her. 5.01. 66
i have, and most unwillingly, of late | heard 5.01. 97
good occasion | most throughly to be winnowed, 5.01.110
most dread liege, | the good i stand on is my 5.01.121
and give it | to a most noble judge, the king my 5.02.136
not only good and wise but most religious; 5.02.151
let me see the proudest | he, that dares most, 5.02.166
my most dread sovereign, may it like your grace 5.02.183
in this most gracious lady | heaven ever laid up 5.04. 6
a most unspotted lily shall she pass | to th' 5.04. 61
excellent place, here we may see most bravely. TRO 1.02.182 P
the which, most mighty for thy place and sway, 1.03. 60
and thou most reverend for /thy stretch'd-out 1.03. 61
most wisely hath ulysses here discover'd | the 1.03.138
may | a stranger to those most imperial looks 1.03.224
why, 'tis most meet. 1.03.333
and buckle in a waist most fathomless | with 2.02. 30
o theft most base, | that we have stol'n what we 2.02. 92
that are | most disobedient and refractory. 2.02.182
my dear lord and most esteem'd friend, your 3.01. 63 P
commends himself most affectionately to you — 3.01. 67 P
right with right wars who shall be most right! 3.02.172
made tame and most familiar to my nature; 3.03. 10
service i have done, | in most accepted pain. 3.03. 30

that most pure spirit of sense, behold itself, 3.03.106
what things there are | most /abject in regard, 3.03.128
what things again most dear in the esteem, | and 3.03.129
person of the magnanimous and most illustrious 3.03.277 P
who most humbly desires you to invite hector to 3.03.284 P
this is the most despiteful gentle greeting, 4.01. 33
the grecians are most prompt and pregnant — 4.04. 88
devil | that tempts most cunningly, but be not 4.04. 91
most dearly welcome to the greeks, sweet lady. 4.05. 18
i thank thee, most imperious agamemnon. 4.05.172
most reverend nestor, i am glad to clasp thee. 4.05.204
most gentle and most valiant hector, welcome! 4.05.227
most gentle and most valiant hector, welcome! 4.05.227
at menelaus' tent, most princely troilus. 4.05.279
a false–hearted rogue, a most unjust knave. 5.01. 89 P
most sure she was. 5.02.126
take heed, the quarrel's most ominous to us. 5.07. 20 P
most putrefied core, so fair without, | thy 5.08. 1
most charitable care | have the patricians of COR 1.01. 65
even so most fitly | as you malign our senators 1.01.112
your most grave belly was deliberate, | not rash 1.01.128
of this most wise rebellion, thou goest foremost 1.01.158
who desires most that | which would increase his 1.01.178
you), | and titus lartius, a most valiant roman, 1.02. 14
most likely 'tis for you; 1.02. 16
of his bed where he would show most love. 1.03. 5 P
fie, you confine yourself most unreasonably. 1.03. 76 P
those are they | that most are willing. 1.06. 67
that now | refus'd most princely gifts, am bound 1.09. 80
menenius, and with most prosperous approbation. 2.01.103 P
the most sovereign prescription in galen is but 2.01.116 P
'tis most like he will. 2.01.241
most reverend and grave elders, to desire | the 2.02. 42
most willingly; 2.02. 62
chiefest virtue, and | most dignifies the haver; 2.02. 85
nod and be off to them most counterfeitly; 2.03.100 P
most sweet voices! 2.03.112
voices, thank you, | your most sweet voices. 2.03.172
which most gibingly, ungravely, he did fashion 2.03.225
upon the earth he hated | your person most; 3.01. 15
o /good but most unwise patricians! 3.01. 91
the great'st taste | most palates theirs. 3.01.104
wherein they show'd | most valor, spoke not for 3.01.127
action teach my mind | a most inherent baseness. 3.02.123
deliver you as most | abated captives to some 3.03.131
when most strook home, being gentle wounded, 4.01. 8
they are in a most warlike preparation, and hope 4.03. 17 P
i am most fortunate thus accidentally to 4.03. 37 P
supper, tell you most strange things from rome, 4.03. 40 P
a most royal one: 4.03. 43 P
well met, and most glad of your company. 4.03. 48 P
sir, i have the most cause to be glad of yours. 4.03. 51 P
word, i also am | longer to live most weary, and 4.05. 95
therefore, most absolute sir, if thou wilt have 4.05.136
most welcome! 4.05.147
o, he is grown most kind of late. 4.06. 11
this is most likely! 4.06. 69
time, | and power, unto itself most commendable, 4.07. 51
who loved him | in a most dear particular. 5.01. 3
and the most noble mother of the world | leave 5.03. 49
and to poor we | thine enmity's most capital; 5.03.104
most dangerously you have with him prevail'd, 5.03.188
with him prevail'd, | if not most mortal to him. 5.03.189
is't most certain? 5.04. 44
most welcome! 5.06. 8
most noble sir, | if you do hold the same intent 5.06. 11
you are most welcome home. 5.06. 60
as the most noble corse that ever herald | did 5.06.143
i will most thankful be, and thanks to men | of TIT 1.01.215
the cause were known to them it most concerns, 2.01. 50
brought hither in a most unlucky hour, | to find 2.03.251
the closing up of our most wretched eyes. 3.01.262
i will most willingly attend your ladyship. 4.01. 28
o most insatiate and luxurious woman! 5.01. 88
and lively warrant | for me, most wretched, to 5.03. 45
time | when it should move ye to attend me most, 5.03. 92
death, | as punishment for his most wicked life. 5.03.145
which then most sought where most might not be ROM 1.01.127
then most sought where most might not be found, 1.01.127
a madness most discreet, | a choking gall, and a 1.01.193
among the store | one more, most welcome, makes 1.02. 23
and like her most whose merit most shall be; 1.02. 31
and like her most whose merit most shall be; 1.02. 31
thou hast most kindly hit it. 2.04. 55 P
a most courteous exposition. 2.04. 56 P
very bitter sweeting, it is a most sharp sauce. 2.04. 79 P
o most wicked fiend! 3.05.235
most miserable hour that e'er time saw | in 4.05. 44
most lamentable day, most woeful day | that ever 4.05. 50
lamentable day, most woeful day | that ever, 4.05. 50
most detestable death, by thee beguil'd, | by 4.05. 56
the most you sought was her promotion, | for 4.05. 71
yet most suspected, as the time and place | doth 5.03.224
nay, that's most fit'd. TIM 1.01. 9
a most incomparable man, breath'd, as it were, 1.01. 10
and returns in peace | most rich in timon's nod. 1.01. 62
his means most short, his creditors most strait. 1.01. 96
his means most short, his creditors most strait. 1.01. 96
most noble timon, call the man before thee. 1.01.113
most noble lord, | pawn me to this your honor, 1.01.146
most welcome, sir! 1.01.247
and i feed | most hungerly on your sight. 1.01.253
the most accursed thou, that still omit'st it. 1.01.259
most honored timon, | it hath pleas'd the gods 1.02. 1
they were the most needless creatures living, 1.02. 97 P
and would most resemble sweet instruments hung 1.02. 98 P
are certain ladies most desirous of admittance. 1.02.117 P
most thankfully, my lord. 1.02.157
you gone, | put on a most importunate aspect, 2.01. 28
bold | (for that i knew it the most general way) 2.02.200
most true, he does. 3.04. 18
most true; the law shall bruise 'em. 3.05. 4
but in defense, by mercy, 'tis most just. 3.05. 55
'tis honor with most lands to be at odds; 3.05.115
my most honorable lord, i am e'en sick of shame 3.06. 41 P
most smiling, smooth, detested parasites, 3.06. 94
my dearest lord, blest to be most accurs'd, 4.02. 42
sauce his palate | with thy most operant poison! 4.03. 25

praise his most vicious strain, | and call it 4.03.213
'tis most just | that thou turn rascal; 4.03.216
hath a distracted and most wretched being, 4.03.246
no, my most worthy master, in whose breast 4.03.511
and believe it, | my most honor'd lord, | for 4.03.518
to promise is most courtly and fashionable; 5.01. 27
most honest men! 5.01. 73
the best, | thou counterfeit'st most lively. 5.01. 82
most thankfully, my lord. 5.01. 91
by two of their most reverend senate, greet thee 5.01.129
'tis most nobly spoken. 5.04. 63
stream | do kiss the most exalted shores of all. JC 1.01. 60
when the most mighty gods by tokens send | such 1.03. 55
to thee a man | most like this dreadful night, 1.03. 73
therein, ye gods, you make the weak most strong; 1.03. 91
hand, | most bloody, fiery, and most terrible. 1.03.130
hand, | most bloody, fiery, and most terrible. 1.03.130
brow by night, | when evils are most free? 2.01. 79
he says he does, being then most flattered. 2.01.208
recounts most horrid sights seen by the watch. 2.02. 16
it seems to me most strange that men should fear 2.02. 35
most mighty caesar, let me know some cause, 2.02. 69
so to most noble caesar. 2.02.118
most high, most mighty, and most puissant caesar 3.01. 33
most high, most mighty, and most puissant caesar 3.01. 33
high, most mighty, and most puissant caesar, 3.01. 33
with the most boldest and best hearts of rome. 3.01.121
with the most noble blood of all this world. 3.01.156
the bloody fingers of thy foes, | most noble! 3.01.199
room for antony, most noble antony. 3.02.166 P
this was the most unkindest cut of all; 3.02.183
o most bloody sight! 3.02.202 P
peace ho, hear antony, most noble antony! 3.02.234 P
most true. 3.02.239
most noble caesar! we'll revenge his death. 3.02.243
most noble brother, you have done me wrong. 4.02. 37
their shadows seem | a canopy most fatal, under 5.01. 87
now, most noble brutus, | the gods to–day stand 5.01. 92
lie, | most like a soldier, ordered honorably. 5.05. 79
assisted by that most disloyal traitor, | the MAC 1.02. 52
in which addition, hail, most worthy thane, 1.03.106
by the name of most kind hostess, and shut up 2.01. 16
i had most need of blessing, and "amen" | stuck 2.02. 29
most sacrilegious murther hath broke ope | the 2.03. 67
that most may claim this argument for ours? 2.03.120
and question this most bloody piece of work, 2.03.128
horses (a thing most strange and certain), 2.04. 14
then 'tis most like | the sovereignty will fall 2.04. 29
and i fear | thou play'dst most foully for't; 3.01. 3
my duties | are with a most indissoluble tie 3.01. 17
within this hour, at most, | i will advise you 3.01.127
most royal sir, fleance is scap'd. 3.04. 19
do not muse at me, my most worthy friends, | i 3.04. 84
the good meeting, | with most admir'd disorder. 3.04.109
of the most pious edward with such grace | that 3.06. 27
the most diminutive of birds, will fight, | her 4.02. 10
grows | in my most ill–compos'd affection such 4.03. 77
thy royal father | was a most sainted king; 4.03.109
a most miraculous work in this good king, 4.03.147
things were, | that were most precious to me. 4.03.223
yet all this while in a most fast sleep. 5.01. 8 P
you may to me, and 'tis most meet you should. 5.01. 15 P
you come most carefully upon your hour. HAM 1.01. 6
most like; it /harrows me with fear and wonder. 1.01. 44
why this same strict and most observant watch 1.01. 71
thereto prick'd on by a most emulate pride, 1.01. 83
in the most high and palmy state of rome, | a 1.01.113
know | where we shall find him most convenient. 1.01.175
all bands of law, | to our most valiant brother. 1.02. 25
it shows a will most incorrect to heaven, | a 1.02. 95
common | as any the most vulgar thing to sense, 1.02. 99
to reason most absurd, whose common theme | is 1.02.103
you are the most immediate to our throne, | and 1.02.109
it is most retrograde to our desire, | and we 1.02.114
ere yet the salt of most unrighteous tears | had 1.02.154
o, most wicked speed! 1.02.156
most constantly. 1.02.234
youth | contagious blastments are most imminent. 1.03. 42
/are of a most select and generous chief in that 1.03. 74
most humbly do i take my leave, my lord. 1.03. 82
of your audience been most free and bounteous. 1.03. 93
revenge his foul and most unnatural murther. 1.05. 25
murther most foul, as in the best it is, | but 1.05. 27
but this most foul, strange, and unnatural. 1.05. 28
the will of my most seeming virtuous queen. 1.05. 46
mine, | and a most instant tetter bark'd about, 1.05. 71
most lazar–like, with vile and loathsome crust, 1.05. 72
o, horrible, o, horrible, most horrible! 1.05. 80
o most pernicious woman! 1.05.105
so grace and mercy at your most need help you. 1.05.180
as are companions noted and most known | to 2.01. 23
most fair return of greetings and desires. 2.02. 60
most welcome home! 2.02. 85
my soul's idol, the most beautified ophelia" — 2.02.109 P
but that i love thee best, o most best, believe 2.02.122 P
thine evermore, most dear lady, whilst this 2.02.123 P
lack of wit, together with most weak hams; 2.02.200 P
though i most powerfully and potently believe, 2.02.201 P
my most dear lord! 2.02.223 P
o, most true, she is a strumpet. 2.02.235 P
this most excellent canopy, the air, look you, 2.02.299 P
know, "it came to pass, as most like it was" — 2.02.418
upon whose property and most dear life | a 2.02.570
this is most brave, | that i, the son of a dear 2.02.582
tongue, will speak | with most miraculous organ. 2.02.594
most like a gentleman. 3.01. 11
but of our demands | most free in his reply. 3.01. 14
'tis most true, | and he beseech'd me to entreat 3.01. 21
it | than is my deed to my most painted word. 3.01. 52
and i, of ladies most deject and wretched, 3.01.155
now see /that noble and most sovereign reason, 3.01.157
who for the most part are capable of nothing but 3.02. 11 P
and shows a most pitiful ambition in the fool 3.02. 44 P
our hands | unite comutual in most sacred bands. 3.02.160
most necessary 'tis that we forget | to pay 3.02.192
where joy most revels, grief doth most lament; 3.02.198
where joy most revels, grief doth most lament; 3.02.198
your mother, in most great affliction of spirit, 3.02.311 P

and it will discourse most eloquent music. 3.02.359 P
most holy and religious fear it is | to keep 3.03. 8
o, 'tis most sweet | when in one line two crafts 3.04.209
this counsellor | is now most still, most secret 3.04.214
counsellor | is now most still, most secret, and 3.04.214
is now most still, most secret, and most grave, 3.04.214
we would not understand what was most fit, | but 4.01. 20
and he most violent author | of his own just 4.05. 80
i'll be reveng'd | most throughly for my father. 4.05.137
death, | and am most sensibly in grief for it, 4.05.151
defense, | and for your rapier most especial, 4.07. 98
most generous, and free from all contriving, 4.07.135
of infinite jest, of most excellent fancy. 5.01.185 P
whose wicked deed thy most ingenious sense 5.01.248
that is most certain. 5.02. 11
/gentleman, full of most excellent differences, 5.02.107 P
your lordship speaks most infallibly of him. 5.02.121 P
to the hilts, most delicate carriages, and of 5.02.152 P
and through the most /profound and /winnow'd 5.02.192 P
free me so far in your most generous thoughts, 5.02.242
this case, should stir me most | to my revenge, 5.02.245
to have prov'd most royal, and, for his passage, 5.02.398
appears not which of the dukes he values most, LR 1.01. 5 P
which of you shall we say doth love us most, 1.01. 51
joys | which the most precious square of sense 1.01. 74
fit, | obey you, love you, and most honor you. 1.01. 98
i lov'd her most, and thought to set my rest 1.01.123
that justly think'st and hast most rightly said! 1.01.183
most royal majesty, | i crave no more than hath 1.01.193
this is most strange, | that she, whom even but 1.01.213
fairest cordelia, that art most rich being poor, 1.01.250
most choice forsaken, and most lov'd despis'd, 1.01.251
most choice forsaken, and most lov'd despis'd, 1.01.251
and like a sister am most loath to call | your 1.01.270
i have to say of what most nearly appertains to 1.01.284 P
that's most certain, and with you; 1.01.286 P
he always lov'd our sister most, and with what 1.01.290 P
i have perceiv'd a most faint neglect of late, 1.04. 68 P
and in the most exact regard support | the 1.04.265
o most small fault, | how ugly didst thou in 1.04.266
who hath most fortunately been inform'd | of my 2.02.167
no place | that guard and most unusual vigilance 2.03. 4
to take the basest and most poorest shape | that 2.03. 7
most serpent–like, upon the very heart. 2.04.161
one minded like the weather, most unquietly. 3.01. 2
most savage and unnatural! 3.03. 7 P
you are going, to a most /festinate preparation; 3.07. 10 P
'tis most ignobly done | to pluck me by the 3.07. 35
the lowest and most dejected thing of fortune, 4.01. 3
what most he should dislike seems pleasant to 4.02. 10
my most dear gloucester! 4.02. 25
she gave strange eliads and most speaking looks 4.05. 25
sir, | your most dear daughter — 4.06.189
a sight most pitiful in the meanest wretch, 4.06.204
most sure and vulgar; 4.06.210
a most poor man, made tame to fortune's blows, 4.06.221
most happy! 4.06.226
'tis most convenient, pray go with us. 5.01. 36
that were the most, if he should husband you. 5.03. 70
below thy foot, | a most toad–spotted traitor. 5.03.139
most monstrous! o! | know'st thou this paper? 5.03.160
the oldest hath borne most; 5.03.326
most reverend signior, do you know my voice? OTH 1.01. 93
most grave brabantio, | in simple and pure soul 1.01.106
if't be your pleasure and most wise consent 1.01.121
every house i'll call | (i may command at most). 1.01.181
'tis true, most worthy signior; 1.02. 91
your trusty and most valiant servitor, | with 1.03. 40
most potent, grave, and reverend signiors, | my 1.03. 76
away this old man's daughter, | it is most true; 1.03. 79
it is a judgment main'd, and most imperfect, 1.03. 99
wherein i spoke of most disastrous chances: 1.03.134
noble company | where most you owe obedience? 1.03.180
the turk with a most mighty preparation makes 1.03.221 P
there a substitute of most allow'd sufficiency, 1.03.224 P
the tyrant custom, most grave senators, | hath 1.03.229
most humbly therefore bending to your state, | i 1.03.235
most gracious duke, | to my unfolding lend your 1.03.243
natures would conduct us to most prepost'rous 1.03.329 P
and sufferance | on most part of their fleet. 2.01. 24
most fortunately. 2.01. 61
h'as had most favorable and happy speed: 2.01. 67
o most lame and impotent conclusion! 2.01.161 P
is he not a most profane and liberal counsellor? 2.01.163 P
now again you are most apt to play the sir in. 2.01.174 P
were now to die, | 'twere now to be most happy; 2.01.190
(as it is a most pregnant and unforc'd position) 2.01.236 P
of his salt and most hidden loose affection? 2.01.240 P
in her, she's full of most bless'd condition. 2.01.249 P
and the impediment most profitably remov'd, 2.01.279 P
he'll prove to desdemona | a most dear husband. 2.01.291
iago is most honest. 2.03. 6
she's a most exquisite lady. 2.03. 18 P
indeed she's a most fresh and delicate creature. 2.03. 20 P
where indeed they are most potent in potting; 2.03. 77 P
reputation is an idle and most false imposition; 2.03.268 P
for 'tis most easy | th' inclining desdemona to 2.03.339
and fear your looks, | she lov'd them most. 3.03.208
foh, one may smell in such, a will most rank, 3.03.232
most veritable, therefore look to't well. 3.04. 76
i am most unhappy in the loss of it. 3.04.102
how is't with you, my most fair bianca? 3.04.170
by heaven, i would most gladly have forgot it. 4.01. 19
grief | (a passion most /unsuiting such a man), 4.01. 77
i will be found most cunning in my patience; 4.01. 90
but (dost thou hear) most bloody. 4.01. 91
a most unhappy one. 4.01.232
was this fair paper, this most goodly book, 4.02. 71
the moor's abus'd by some most villainous knave, 4.02.139
you charge me most unjustly. 4.02.184 P
hast taken against me a most just exception; 4.02.207 P
protest i have dealt most directly in thy affair 4.02.208 P
your honor is most welcome. 4.03. 4
on that, | and fix most firm thy resolution. 5.01. 5
she was too fond of her most filthy bargain. 5.02.157
where is this rash and most unfortunate man? 5.02.283
most heathenish and most gross! 5.02.313
most heathenish and most gross! 5.02.313

nay, and most like. ANT 1.01. 25
sweet alexas, most any thing alexas, almost most 1.02. 1 P
any thing alexas, almost most absolute alexas, 1.02. 2 P
mine, and most of our fortunes to–night, shall 1.02. 45 P
most sweet queen — 1.03. 31
and that which most with you should safe my 1.03. 55
o most false love! 1.03. 62
most noble caesar, shalt thou have report | how 1.04. 35
now i feed myself | with most delicious poison. 1.05. 27
by your most gracious pardon, | i sing but after 1.05. 72
this is most certain that i shall deliver: 2.01. 28
that which combin'd us was most great, and let 2.02. 18
with most gladness, | and do invite you to my 2.02.166
she's a most triumphant lady, if report be 2.02.184 P
but she makes hungry | where most she satisfies; 2.02.237
the most infectious pestilence upon thee! 2.05. 61
thy face, to me | thou wouldst appear most ugly. 2.05. 97
most meet | that first we come to words, and 2.06. 2
most noble antony, | let not the piece of virtue 3.02. 27
most gracious majesty! 3.03. 7
for the most part, too, they are foolish that 3.03. 31
i find thee | most fit for business. 3.03. 37
he vented /them, most narrow measure lent me; 3.04. 8
the jove of power make me most weak, most weak, 3.04. 29
the jove of power make me most weak, most weak, 3.04. 29
hail, most dear caesar! 3.06. 39
no, my most wronged sister, cleopatra | hath 3.06. 65
ay me, most wretched, | that have my heart 3.06. 76
antony, most large | in his abominations, turns 3.06. 93
most certain. 3.06. 97
most worthy sir, you therein throw away | the 3.07. 41
which doth most consist | of war–mark'd footmen, 3.07. 43
is out of breath, | and sinks most lamentably. 3.10. 25
for our flight, | most grossly, by his own! 3.10. 28
do, most dear queen. 3.11. 26
most noble sir, arise, the queen approaches. 3.11. 46
offended reputation, | a most unnoble swerving. 3.11. 50
we scorn her most when most she offers blows. 3.11. 74
we scorn her most when most she offers blows. 3.11. 74
thus then, thou most renown'd: 3.13. 53
he is a god and knows | what is most right. 3.13. 61
most kind messenger, | say to great caesar this 3.13. 73
and at this time most easy 'tis to do't: 3.13.144
again, and fleet, threat'ning most sea–like. 3.13.171
most certain. 4.05. 11
villain of the earth, | and feel i am so most. 4.06. 30
most monster–like, be shown | for poor'st 4.12. 36
she spake | was "antony, most noble antony!" 4.14. 30
thou hast worn | most useful for thy country. 4.14. 80
most absolute lord, | my mistress cleopatra sent 4.14.117
most heavy day! 4.14.134
behold it stain'd | with his most noble blood. 5.01. 26
compel us to lament | our most persisted deeds. 5.01. 30
most noble empress, you have heard of me? 5.02. 71
most sovereign creature — 5.02. 81
which towards you are most gentle, you shall 5.02.127
nay, 'tis most certain, iras. 5.02.214
and to conquer | their most absurd intents. 5.02.226
but this is most falliable, the worm's an odd 5.02.257 P
most probable | that so she died; 5.02.353
so is the queen, | that most desir'd the match. CYM 1.01. 12
(which rare it is to do) most prais'd, most 1.01. 47
rare it is to do) most prais'd, most lov'd, | a 1.01. 47
after the slander of most stepmothers, 1.01. 71
of him, but had | most pretty things to say. 1.03. 26
i have not seen the most precious diamond that 1.04. 75 P
commanded of me these most poisonous compounds, 1.05. 8
she is fool'd | with a most false effect; 1.05. 43
but most miserable | is the /desire that's 1.06. 6
all of her that is out of door most rich! 1.06. 15
to whose kindnesses i am most infinitely tied. 1.06. 23 P
and thy most perfect goodness | her assur'd 1.06.158
his mistress, only | for the most worthiest fit. 1.06.162
most mighty princess, that i have adventur'd 1.06.172
your lordship is the most patient man in loss, 2.03. 1 P
loss, the most coldest that ever turn'd up ace. 2.03. 2 P
you are most hot and furious when you win. 2.03. 5 P
you are most bound to th' king, | who lets go by 2.03. 44
right proud | of that most delicate lodging. 2.04.136
and that most venerable man which i | did call 2.05. 3
man, a thing | the most disdain'd of fortune. 3.04. 20
tear, took pity | from most true wretchedness. 3.04. 61
most like, | bringing me here to kill me. 3.04.116
i am most glad | you think of other place. 3.04.140
he's honorable, | and doubling that, most holy. 3.04.177
of posthumus, most retir'd | hath her life been; 3.05. 36
for he believes | it is a thing most precious. 3.05. 59
i will never be | to him that is most true. 3.05.159
most welcome! 3.06. 73
thou diedst, a most rare boy, of melancholy. 4.02.208
from this most bravest vessel of the world 4.02.319
italy, most willing spirits | that promise noble 4.02.338
most welcome, bondage! 5.04. 3
so follow, to be most unlike our courtiers, | as 5.04.136
to the world, concluded | most cruel to herself. 5.05. 33
o most delicate fiend! 5.05. 47
most like a noble lord in love and one | that 5.05.171
in your duller britain operate | most vildly; 5.05.198
ay me, most credulous fool, | egregious 5.05.210
most like i did, for i was dead. 5.05.259
a most incivil one. 5.05.292
most worthy prince, as yours, is true guiderius; 5.05.358
was lapp'd | in a most curious mantle, wrought 5.05.361
mulier i divine | is this most constant wife, 5.05.449
were clipt about | with this most tender air. 5.05.452
on her and hers, | have laid most heavy hand. 5.05.465
who makes the fairest show means most deceit. PER 1.04. 75
the most high gods not minding longer | to 2.04. 3
a most virtuous princess. 2.05. 34
breast | of this most pompous marriage–feast. 3.ch. 4
tyre, | fame answering the most strange inquire, 3.ch. 22
as you think meet. most wretched queen! 3.01. 54
'tis most strange | nature should be so 3.02. 24
it smells most sweetly in my sense. 3.02. 60
o you most potent gods! 3.02. 63
most strange. 3.02. 64
most likely, sir. 3.02. 78
diamonds | of a most praised water doth appear, 3.02.101
most rare. 3.02.106
most honor'd cleon, i must needs be gone. 3.03. 1
"he that will give most shall have her first." 4.02. 59 P
despise profit where you have most gain. 4.02.118 P
though most ungentle fortune | have plac'd me in 4.06. 96
the most just god | for every graff would send a 5.01. 59
thy name, my most kind virgin? 5.01.140
most wise in general, tell me, if thou canst, 5.01.183
most heavenly music! 5.01.233
where, by her own most clear remembrance, she 5.03. 12
'tis most certain. 5.03. 20
faint, | daisies smell–less, yet most quaint, TNK 1.01. 5
most dreaded amazonian, that hast slain | the 1.01. 78
to themselves | been death's most horrid agents, 1.01.144
where e'er i find them, but such most | that, 1.02. 32
a most unbounded tyrant, whose successes | makes 1.02. 63
/wear) i followed | for my most serious decking. 1.03. 74
nay, most likely, for they are noble suff'rers. 2.01. 31 P
'tis most true, two souls | put in two noble 2.02. 64
edify the duke | most parlously in our behalfs. 2.03. 53
i shall give you | to a most noble service — to 2.05. 34
your servant | (your most unworthy creature) but 2.05. 40
a mistress, expectation | most guiltless on't. 3.01. 15
o thou most perfidious | that ever gently look'd 3.01. 35
most certain | you love me not; 3.01.101
you most coarse frieze capacities, ye /jane 3.05. 8
this treachery, like a most trusty lover, | i 3.06.150
as i love most, and in that faith will perish, 3.06.163
so let me be most traitor, and ye please me. 3.06.167
most royal brother — 3.06.195
by all you love most — wars, and this sweet 3.06.203
to crown all this, by your most noble soul, 3.06.208
but a most thick and profound melancholy. 4.03. 49 P
but they are now in a most extravagant vagary. 4.03. 73 P
o, then, most soft sweet goddess, | give me the 5.01.126
therefore, most modest queen, | he of the two 5.01.157
palamon | has a most menacing aspect, his brow 5.03. 45
by my short life, | i am most glad on't. 5.04. 29
ear | that are most /dearly sweet and bitter. 5.04. 47
in the passage | the gods have been most equal. 5.04.115
then woos best when most his choice is froward. VEN 570
the strongest body shall it make most weak, 1145
it shall not fear where it should most mistrust, 1154
and most deceiving when it seems most just; 1156
and most deceiving when it seems most just; 1156
perverse it shall be where it shows most toward, 1157
when most unseen, then most doth tyrannize. LUC 676
when most unseen, then most doth tyrannize. 676
great grief grieves most at that would do it 1117
their face their manners most expressly told: 1397
weep with equal strife | who should weep most, 1792
but that thou none lov'st is most evident; SON 10. 4
sets you most rich in youth before my sight, 15.10
if it were fill'd with your most high deserts? 17. 2
but i forbid thee one most heinous crime, | o, 19. 8
bars, | unlook'd for joy in that i honor most. 25. 4
scope, | with what i most enjoy contented least; 29. 8
when most i wink, then do mine eyes best see, 43. 1
most worthy comfort, now my greatest grief, 48. 6
yet be most proud of that which i compile, 78. 9
where breath most breathes, even in the mouths 81.14
which shall be most my glory, being dumb, | for 83.10
who is it that says most, which can say more 84. 1
and to the most of praise add something more, 85.10
take | all this away, and me most wretched make. 91.14
that do not do the thing they most do show, 94. 2
now with the drops of this most balmy time | my 107. 9
mine own thoughts, sold cheap what is most dear, 110. 3
most true it is that i have look'd on truth 110. 5
even to thy pure and most most loving breast. 110.14
even to thy pure and most most loving breast. 110.14
the most sweet favor or deformed'st creature, 113.10
my most true mind thus maketh mine untrue. 113.14
and my great mind most kingly drinks it up: 114.10
why | my most full flame should afterwards burn 115. 4
when most impeach'd stands least in thy control. 125.14
thou art the fairest and most precious jewel. 131. 4
i am perjur'd most, | for all my vows are oaths 152. 6
o most potential love! LC 264
when he most burnt in heart–wish'd luxury, | he 314

MOT 1 FR 0.0001 REL FR 1 V 0 P
face, | and tarquin's eye may read the mot afar, LUC 830

MOTE 7 FR 0.0008 REL FR 5 V 2 P
you found his mote, the king your mote did see; LLL 4.03.159
you found his mote, the king your mote did see; 4.03.159
a mote will turn the balance, which pyramus, MND 5.01.318 P
that there were but a mote in yours, | a grain, JN 4.01. 91
his bed, wash every mote out of his conscience; H5 4.01.179 P
a mote it is to trouble the mind's eye. HAM 1.01.112
crystal walls each little mote will peep; LUC 1251

MOTES 1 FR 0.0001 REL FR 1 V 0 P
like motes and shadows see them move a while, PER 4.04. 21

MOTH* 7 FR 0.0008 REL FR 3 V 4 P
who was sampson's love, my dear moth? LLL 1.02. 76 P
nothing, master moth, but what they look upon. 1.02.162 P
thou hast no feeling of it, moth. 3.01.114 P
moth, follow. 3.01.133 P
moth! MND 3.01.162
thus hath the candle sing'd the moth. MV 2.09. 79
a moth of peace, and he go to the war, | the OTH 1.03.256

/MOTHER 1 FR 0.0001 REL FR 1 V 0 P
/if /that /fly /had /a /father /and /mother? TIT 3.02. 60

MOTHER 339 FR 0.0383 REL FR 284 V 55 P
thy mother was a piece of virtue, and | she said TMP 1.02. 56
as wicked dew as e'er my mother brush'd | with 1.02.321
this island's mine by sycorax my mother, | which 1.02.331
his mother was a witch, and one so strong | that 5.01.269
my mother weeping, my father wailing, my sister TGV 2.03. 6 P
no, no, this left shoe is my mother; 2.03. 16 P
with the hole in it, is my mother, and this my 2.03. 18 P
now come i to my mother. 2.03. 27 P
three men and a boy yet, till my mother be dead. WIV 1.01.275 P
as my mother was, the first hour i was born. 2.02. 38
good mother, do not marry me to yond fool. 3.04. 83
come, mother prat, come give me your hand. 4.02.182 P
her mother (even strong against that match | and 4.06. 27
her mother hath intended | (the better to 4.06. 38
which means she to deceive, father or mother? 4.06. 46
pardon, good father! good my mother, pardon! 5.05.216
no longer staying but to give the mother MM 1.04. 86
heaven shield my mother play'd my father fair! 3.01.140
she became | a joyful mother of two goodly sons: ERR 1.01. 50
so i, to find a mother and a brother, | in quest 1.02. 39
her mother hath many times told me so. ADO 1.01.105 P
lord, lest i should prove the mother of fools. 2.01.286 P
my lord, my mother cried, but then there was a 2.01.334 P
then was venus like her mother, for her father LLL 2.01.256
robin starveling, you must play thisby's mother. MND 1.02. 61 P
his mother was a vot'ress of my order, | and, in 2.01.123
you commend me to mistress squash, your mother, 3.01.187 P
afeard my lady his mother play'd false with a MV 1.02. 43 P
was | (as his wise mother wrought in his behalf) 1.03. 73
and i am sure margery your wife is my mother. 2.02. 90 P
so the sins of my mother should be visited upon 3.05. 14 P
i fear you are damn'd both by father and mother; 3.05. 16 P
your father, i fall into charybdis, your mother. 3.05. 17 P
is so desirous to lie with his mother earth? AYL 1.02.201 P
who might be your mother, | that you insult, 3.05. 35
a witty mother! witless else her son. SHR 2.01.264
sir, so his mother says, if i may believe her. 5.01. 33 P
be comfortable to my mother, your mistress, AWW 1.01. 76
a mother, and a mistress, and a friend, | a 1.01.167
you know, helen, | i am a mother to you. 1.03.138
nay, a mother, | why not a mother? 1.03.139
nay, a mother, | why not a mother? 1.03.140
when i said "a mother," | methought you saw a 1.03.140
what's in "mother," | that you start at it? 1.03.141
i say i am your mother, | and put you in the 1.03.142
does it curd thy blood | to say i am thy mother? 1.03.150
i say i am your mother. 1.03.154
nor i your mother? 1.03.160
you are my mother, madam; 1.03.161
son were not my brother — | indeed my mother! 1.03.163
daughter and mother | so strive upon your pulse. 1.03.168
there's letters from my mother; 2.03.276
house, | acquaint my mother with my hate to her, 2.03.287
my mother greets me kindly. is she well? 2.04. 1 P
this to my mother. 2.05. 69
and now you should be as your mother was | when 4.02. 9
my mother did but duty, such, my lord, | as you 4.02. 12
i'll order take my mother shall not hear. 4.02. 55
my mother told me just how he would woo, | as if 4.02. 69
for her, writ to my lady mother i am returning, 4.03. 89 P
and cost me the dearest groans of a mother, i 4.05. 11 P
the young lord | did to his majesty, his mother, 5.03. 13
i am her mother, sir, whose age and honor | both 5.03.162
good mother, fetch my bail. 5.03.295
o my dear mother, do i see you living? 5.03.319
and i am yet so near the manners of my mother, TN 2.01. 41 P
thy mother plays, and i | play too, but so WT 1.02.187
hark ye, | the queen your mother rounds apace: 2.01. 16
conceiving the dishonor of his mother! 2.03. 13
the mother to a hopeful prince, here standing 3.02. 40
be, thy mother | appear'd to me last night; 3.03. 17
your mother was most true to wedlock, prince, 5.01.124
of the creature in resemblance of the mother; 5.02. 36 P
a loss, cries, "o, thy mother, thy mother!"; 5.02. 51 P
a loss, cries, "o, thy mother, thy mother!"; 5.02. 52 P
came to look upon, | the statue of her mother. 5.03. 14
silence, good mother, hear the embassy. JN 1.01. 6
you came not of one mother then, it seems. 1.01. 58
most certain of one mother, mighty king — 1.01. 59
i put you o'er to heaven and to my mother. 1.01. 62
on thee, rude man, thou dost shame thy mother, 1.01. 64
your tale must be how he employ'd my mother. 1.01. 98
shores | between my father and my mother lay, 1.01.106
o me, 'tis my mother. 1.01.220
therefore, good mother, | to whom am i beholding 1.01.238
"knight, knight," good mother, basilisco–like. 1.01.244
but, mother, i am not sir robert's son, | i have 1.01.246
then, good my mother, let me know my father; 1.01.249
who was it, mother? 1.01.250
ay, my mother, | with all my heart i thank thee 1.01.269
it cannot be, and if thou wert his mother. 2.01.131
there's a good mother, boy, that blots thy 2.01.132
good my mother, peace. 2.01.163
his mother shames him so, poor boy, he weeps. 2.01.166
much work for tears in many an english mother, 2.01.303
why thou against the church, our holy mother, 3.01.141
or let the church, our mother, breathe her curse 3.01.256
my mother is assailed in our tent, | and ta'en, 3.02. 6
o, this will make my mother die with grief! 3.03. 5
the first of april died | your noble mother; 4.02.121
mother dead? 4.02.127
my mother dead! 4.02.181
up the womb | of your dear mother england, blush 5.02.153
my mother, and my nurse, that bears me yet! R2 1.03.307
and i, a gasping new–deliver'd mother, | have 2.02. 65
as a long–parted mother with her child | plays 3.02. 8
good mother, be content, it is no more | than my 5.02. 82
my dangerous cousin, let your mother in, | i 5.03. 81
your mother well hath pray'd, and prove you true 5.03.145
royal man, and send him back again to my mother. 1H4 2.04.291 P
thou wert better thou hadst strook thy mother, 2H4 5.04. 10 P
and all my mother came into mine eyes | and gave H5 4.06. 31
cheeks, | god's mother deigned to appear to me, 1H6 1.02. 78
christ's mother helps me, else i were too weak. 1.02.106
helen, the mother of great constantine, | nor 1.02.142
for by my mother i derived am | from lionel duke 2.05. 74
york, | marrying my sister that thy mother was, 2.05. 86
as looks the mother on her lowly babe | when 3.03. 47
o, if you love my mother, | dishonor not her 4.05. 13
in thee thy mother dies, our household's name, 4.06. 38
her mother liveth yet, can testify | she was the 5.04. 12
the morn that i was wedded to her mother. 5.04. 24
i would the milk | thy mother gave thee, when 5.04. 28
mother jordan, be you prostrate and grovel on 2H6 1.04. 10 P
now by god's mother, priest, i'll shave your 2.01. 50
hadst thou been his mother, thou couldst have 2.01. 79
my mother, being heir unto the crown, | married 2.02. 44
thy mother took into her blameful bed | some 3.02.212
and say it was thy mother that thou meant'st, 3.02.222
my mother a plantagenet — 4.02. 42 P
whoever got thee, there thy mother stands, | for 3H6 2.02.133

how will my mother for a father's death | take 2.05.103
no more than when my daughters call thee mother. 3.02.101
and, by god's mother, i, being but a bachelor, 3.02.103
o ned, sweet ned, speak to thy mother, boy! 5.05. 51
thy mother felt more than a mother's pain, | and 5.06. 49
for i have often heard my mother say | i came 5.06. 70
may fright the hopeful mother at the view, | and R3 1.02. 24
die neither mother, wife, nor england's queen! 1.03.208
by god's holy mother, | she hath had too much 1.03.305
yet thou art a mother, | and hast the comfort of 2.02. 55
was never mother had so dear a loss. 2.02. 79
i am the mother of these griefs: 2.02. 80
comfort, dear mother, god is much displeas'd 2.02. 89
bethink you like a careful mother | of the young 2.02. 96
madam, my mother, i do cry you mercy, | i did 2.02.104
so hath this, both by his father and mother. 2.03. 22
ay, mother, but i would not have it so. 2.04. 8
i thought my mother and my brother york | would 3.01. 20
welcome, my lord. what, will our mother come? 3.01. 25
i, | the queen your mother and your brother york 3.01. 27
but by his mother was perforce withheld. 3.01. 30
can from his mother win the duke of york, | anon 3.01. 38
my good cousin buckingham | will to your mother, 3.01.138
was not incensed by his subtile mother | to 3.01.152
when that my mother went with child | of that 3.05. 86
because, my lord, you know my mother lives. 3.05. 94
now, by the holy mother of our lord, | the 3.07. 2
your mother lives a witness to his vow — | and 3.07.180
a care–craz'd mother to a many sons, | a 3.07.184
i am their mother, who shall bar me from them? 4.01. 21
i am their father's mother, i will see them. 4.01. 22
their aunt i am in law, in love their mother; 4.01. 23
and i'll salute your grace of york as mother 4.01. 29
be of good cheer. mother, how fares your grace? 4.01. 37
nor mother, wife, nor england's counted queen. 4.01. 46
a mother only mock'd with two fair babes; 4.04. 87
for joyful mother, one that wails the name; 4.04. 99
and brief, good mother, for i am in haste. 4.04.162
my daughter's mother thinks it with her soul. 4.04.257
in love | than is the doting title of a mother; 4.04.300
again shall you be mother to a king; 4.04.317
go then, my mother, to thy daughter go, | make 4.04.325
to vail the title, as her mother doth. 4.04.348
therefore, dear mother — i must call you so — 4.04.412
and be a happy mother by the deed. 4.04.427
tell me, how fares our loving mother? 5.03. 82
i, by attorney, bless thee from thy mother, 5.03. 83
god's blest mother! H8 5.01.153
grown | too headstrong for their mother. TRO 3.02.123
that any /drop thou borrow'dst from thy mother, 4.05.133
let's leave the hermit pity with our mother, 5.03. 45
wife hath dreamt, thy mother hath had visions, 5.03. 63
he did it to please his mother, and to be partly COR 1.01. 39 P
kings' entreaties a mother should not sell him 1.03. 8 P
my mother, | who has a charter to extol her 1.09. 13
look, sir, your mother! 2.01.169
know, good mother, | i had rather be their 2.01.202
i muse my mother | does not approve me further, 3.02. 7
let | thy mother rather feel thy pride than fear 3.02.126
mother, i am going to the market–place; 3.02.131
is this the promise that you made your mother? 3.03. 86
nay, mother, | where is your ancient courage? 4.01. 2
nay, mother, | resume that spirit when you were 4.01. 15
farewell, my wife, my mother, | i'll do well yet 4.01. 20
my mother, you wot well | my hazards still have 4.01. 27
come, my sweet wife, my dearest mother, and | my 4.01. 48
dismiss them home. | here comes his mother. 4.02. 8
his mother and his wife | hear nothing from him. 4.06. 18
his mother, wife, his child, | and this brave 5.01. 29
vain, | unless his noble mother and his wife — 5.01. 71
wife, mother, child i know not. 5.02. 82
my mother bows, | as if olympus to a molehill 5.03. 29
and the most noble mother of the world | leave 5.03. 49
making the mother, wife, and child to see | the 5.03.101
no man in the world | more bound to 's mother, 5.03.159
thy life | show'd thy dear mother any courtesy, 5.03.161
this fellow had a volscian to his mother; 5.03.178
o mother, mother! 5.03.182
o mother, mother! 5.03.182
o my mother, mother! 5.03.185
o my mother, mother! 5.03.185
my stead, would you have heard | a mother less? 5.03.193
o mother! 5.03.199
hope the ladies of rome, especially his mother, 5.04. 6 P
he lov'd his mother dearly. 5.04. 15 P
and he no more remembers his mother now than an 5.04. 17 P
mark what mercy his mother shall bring from him. 5.04. 27 P
repeal him with the welcome of his mother. 5.05. 5
i say "your city," to his wife and mother, 5.06. 93
a loving nurse, a mother to his youth. TIT 1.01.332
why, boy, although our mother, unadvis'd, | gave 2.01. 38
nor would your noble mother for much more | be 2.01. 51
how now, dear sovereign and our gracious mother? 2.03. 89
yet every mother breeds not sons alike — | do 2.03.146
aunt | loves me as dear as e'er my mother did, 4.01. 23
ovid's metamorphosis, | my mother gave it me. 4.01. 43
here lacks but your mother for to say amen. 4.02. 44
the gods | for our beloved mother in her pains. 4.02. 47
thou hast undone our mother. 4.02. 75
villain, i have done thy mother. 4.02. 76
aaron, it must, the mother wills it so. 4.02. 82
by this our mother is for ever sham'd. 4.02.112
go pack with him, and give the mother gold, 4.02.155
that codding spirit had they from their mother, 5.01. 99
you know your mother means to feast with me, 5.02.184
and see them ready against their mother comes. 5.02.205
whereof their mother daintily hath fed, | eating 5.03. 61
your mother. ROM 1.03. 5
i was your mother much upon these years | that 1.03. 72
madam, your mother craves a word with you. 1.05.111
what is her mother? 1.05.112
bachelor, | her mother is the lady of the house, 1.05.113
the earth that's nature's mother is her tomb; 2.03. 9
i warrant, a virtuous — where is your mother? 2.05. 57
where is my mother! 2.05. 58
an honest gentleman, | 'where is your mother?'" 2.05. 61
dead," | thy father or thy mother, nay, or both, 3.02.119
is father, mother, tybalt, romeo, juliet, | all 3.02.123
where is my father and my mother, nurse? 3.02.127
your lady mother is coming to your chamber. 3.05. 39
it is my lady mother. 3.05. 65
o sweet my mother, cast me not away! 3.05.198
common mother, thou | whose womb unmeasurable TIM 4.03.177
when that rash humor which my mother gave me JC 4.03.120
he'll think your mother chides, and leave you so 4.03.123
but kill'st the mother that engend'red thee! 5.03. 71
as birds do, mother. MAC 4.02. 32
why should i, mother? 4.02. 36
was my father a traitor, mother? 4.02. 44 P
he has kill'd me, mother: 4.02. 84
it cannot | be call'd our mother, but our grave; 4.03.166
'tis not alone my inky cloak, /good mother, HAM 1.02. 77
let not thy mother lose her prayers, hamlet, | i 1.02.118
so loving to my mother | that he might not 1.02.140
thy soul contrive | against thy mother aught. 1.05. 86
that it were better my mother had not borne me: 3.01.123 P
no, good mother, here's metal more attractive. 3.02.109 P
for look you how cheerfully my mother looks, and 3.02.127 P
the queen, your mother, in most great affliction 3.02.311 P
command, or, rather, as you say, my mother. 3.02.323 P
my mother, you say — 3.02.324 P
o wonderful son, that can so stonish a mother! 3.02.329 P
we shall obey, were she ten times our mother. 3.02.334 P
then i will come to my mother by and by. 3.02.383 P
soft, now to my mother. 3.02.392
'tis meet that some more audience than a mother, 3.03. 31
my mother stays, | this physic but prolongs thy 3.03. 95
now, mother, what's the matter? 3.04. 8
mother, you have my father much offended. 3.04. 10
and would it were not so, you are my mother. 3.04. 16
almost as bad, good mother, | as kill a king, 3.04. 28
but look, amazement on thy mother sits, | o, 3.04.112
mother, for love of grace, | lay not that 3.04.144
mother, good night indeed. 3.04.213
good night, mother. 3.04.217
farewell, dear mother. 4.03. 49 P
my mother: 4.03. 51 P
father and mother is man and wife, man and wife 4.03. 51 P
man and wife is one flesh — so, my mother. 4.03. 52 P
that have a father kill'd, a mother stain'd, 4.04. 57
the chaste unsmirched brow | of my true mother. 4.05.121
the queen his mother | lives almost by his looks 4.07. 11
but even his mother shall uncharge the practice, 4.07. 67
that hath kill'd my king and whor'd my mother, 5.02. 64
follow my mother! 5.02.327
sir, this young fellow's mother could; LR 1.01. 13 P
before he was sent for, yet was his mother fair, 1.01. 23 P
compounded with my mother under the dragon's 1.02.129 P
o, how this mother swells up toward my heart! 2.04. 56
and so much duty as my mother show'd | to you, OTH 1.03.186
did an egyptian to my mother give; 3.04. 56
my mother had a maid call'd barbary; 4.03. 26
an antique token | my father gave my mother. 5.02.217
your mother came to sicily and did find | her ANT 2.06. 45
fight with me because of the queen my mother. CYM 2.01. 20 P
that such a crafty devil as is his mother 2.01. 52
a mother hourly coining plots, a wooer | more 2.01. 59
to your majesty, and to my gracious mother! 2.03. 36 P
your mother too. 2.03.152
yet my mother seem'd | the dian of that time. 2.05. 6
son, let your mother end. 3.01. 39
they took thee for their mother, | and every day 3.03.104
ne'er long'd my mother so | to see me first, as 3.04. 2
jay of italy | (whose mother was her painting) 3.04. 50
hardness ever | of hardiness is mother. 3.06. 22
but my mother, having power of his testiness, 4.01. 20 P
down the stream | in embassy to his mother. 4.02.185
since death of my dear'st mother | it did not 4.02.190
by good euriphile, our mother. 4.02.234
sing him to th' ground, | as once to our mother; 4.02.237
thou hast created | a mother and two brothers. 5.04.125
wrought by th' hand | of his queen mother, which 5.05.362
o, what, am i | a mother to the birth of three? 5.05.369
ne'er mother | rejoic'd deliverance more. 5.05.369
i mother, wife — and yet his child. PER 1.01. 69
maid, | born in a tempest when my mother died, 4.01. 18
not o'erboard thrown me | for to seek my mother! 4.02. 67
at sea! what mother? 5.01.156
my mother was the daughter of a king, | who died 5.01.157
thaisa was my mother, who did end | the minute i 5.01.211
his mother was a wondrous handsome woman, | his TNK 2.05. 20
an eye as heavy | as if he had lost his mother; 4.02. 28
o, had thy mother borne so hard a mind, | she VEN 203
there lives a son that suck'd an earthly mother, 863
till sable night, mother of dread and fear, LUC 117
that mother tries a merciless conclusion | who, 1160
dost beguile the world, unbless some mother. SON 3. 4
resembling sire, and child, and happy mother, 8.11

MOTHER–QUEEN 1 FR 0.0001 REL FR 1 V 0 P
with him along is come the mother–queen, | an JN 2.01. 62

/MOTHER'S 2 FR 0.0002 REL FR 2 V 0 P
with gobbets of thy /mother's bleeding heart. 2H6 4.01. 85
i would divorce me from thy /mother's tomb, LR 2.04.131

MOTHER'S 78 FR 0.0088 REL FR 65 V 13 P
here's my mother's breath up and down. TGV 2.03. 29 P
to this her mother's plot | she, seemingly WIV 4.06. 32
father's wit and my mother's tongue assist me! LLL 1.02. 95 P
her mother's, i have heard. 2.01.202
that would hang us, every mother's son. MND 1.02. 78 P
sit down, every mother's son, and rehearse your 3.01. 73 P
now, by my mother's son, and that's myself, | it SHR 4.05. 6
you ne'er oppress'd me with a mother's groan, AWW 1.03.147
groan, | yet i express to you a mother's care. 1.03.148
you have not given him his mother's letter? 4.03. 1 P
one would think his mother's milk were scarce TN 1.05.161 P
that for thy mother's fault art thus expos'd WT 3.03. 50
the princess hearing of her mother's statue, 5.02. 94 P
madam, kneel, | and pray your mother's blessing. 5.03.120
heaven guard my mother's honor, and my land! JN 1.01. 70
or no, | that still i lay upon my mother's head, 1.01. 76
that this my mother's son was none of his; 1.01.111
my mother's son did get your father's heir; 1.01.128
brother by th' mother's side, give me your hand; 1.01.163
o, take his mother's thanks, a widow's thanks, 2.01. 32
grandame's wrongs, and not his mother's shames, 2.01.168
ugly, and sland'rous to thy mother's womb, 3.01. 44
curse, | a mother's curse, on her revolting son. 3.01.257
where is my mother's care, | that such an army 4.02.117
mine age, | and rob me of a happy mother's name? R2 5.02. 93
unto my mother's prayers i bend my knee. 5.03. 97
whose arms were moulded in their mother's womb, 1H4 1.01. 23
thou art my son i have partly thy mother's word, 2.04.403 P
at the same season if your mother's cat had 3.01. 18
my mother's son, sir. 2H4 3.02.127 P
thy mother's son! 3.02.128 P
shall all thy mother's hopes lie in one tomb? 1H6 4.05. 34
ay, rather than i'll shame my mother's womb. 4.05. 35
dying with mother's dug between its lips; 2H6 3.02.393
for, well i wot, thou hast thy mother's tongue. 3H6 2.02.134
why, love forswore me in my mother's womb; 3.02.153
thy mother felt more than a mother's pain, | and 5.06. 49
and yet brought forth less than a mother's hope, 5.06. 50
thou slander of thy heavy mother's womb! R3 1.03.230
that is the butt–end of a mother's blessing. 2.02.110
he is all the mother's, from the top to toe. 3.01.156
thy mother's name is ominous to children. 4.01. 40
aery wings | and hear your mother's lamentation! 4.04. 14
cur | preys on the issue of his mother's body, 4.04. 57
long kept in britain at our mother's cost? 5.03.324
to love her for her mother's sake that lov'd him H8 4.02.137
my mother's blood | runs on the dexter cheek, TRO 4.05.127
on thy mother's womb | that brought thee to this COR 5.03.124
me the duty which | to a mother's part belongs. 5.03.168
shed, | a mother's tears in passion for her son; TIT 1.01.106
revenge it, as you love your mother's life, | or 2.03.114
your mother's hand shall right your mother's 2.03.121
mother's hand shall right your mother's wrong. 2.03.121
and for our father's sake, and mother's care, 3.01.181
their mother's bedchamber should not be safe 4.01.108
had nature lent thee but thy mother's look, 5.01. 29
will hold thee dearly for thy mother's sake." 5.01. 36
thy mother's of my generation; TIM 1.01.201 P
macduff was from his mother's womb | untimely MAC 5.08. 15
i think it was to /see my mother's wedding. HAM 1.02.178
answer, i will do your mother's commandement; 3.02.316 P
sequel at the heels of this mother's admiration? 3.02.330 P
my lord, he's going to his mother's closet. 3.03. 27
and from his mother's closet hath he dragg'd him 4.01. 35
thy mother's pois'ned. 5.02.319
turn all her mother's pains and benefits | to LR 1.04.286
thou hast a sister by the mother's side, ANT 2.02.118
look here, love, | this diamond was my mother's. CYM 1.01.112
imogen, | thy mother's dead. 5.05.270
i feed | on mother's flesh which did me breed. PER 1.01. 65
and she an eater of her mother's flesh | by the 1.01.130
what was thy mother's name? 5.01.200
than | to say my mother's name was thaisa? 5.01.210
heart | leaps to be gone into my mother's bosom. 5.03. 45
for your mother's sake, | and as you wish your TNK 1.01. 26
thou art thy mother's glass, and she in thee SON 3. 9
me, my love is as fair | as any mother's child, 21.11
and play the mother's part, kiss me, be kind: 143.12

MOTHERS' 4 FR 0.0004 REL FR 4 V 0 P
ten thousand bloody crowns of mothers' sons R2 3.03. 96
when at their mothers' moist'ned eyes babes 1H6 1.01. 49
and we are govern'd with our mothers' spirits; JC 1.03. 83
children's tears nor mothers' groans respecting, LUC 431

MOTHERS 23 FR 0.0026 REL FR 20 V 3 P
the part of virginity is to accuse your mothers, AWW 1.01.137 P
or were you both our mothers, | i care no more 1.03.163
mock mothers from their sons, mock castles down; H5 1.02.286
dishonor not your mothers; 3.01. 22
whiles the mad mothers with their howls confus'd 3.03. 39
with his name the mothers still their babes? 1H6 2.03. 17
i hope he is, but yet let mothers doubt. R3 2.04. 22
think we had mothers, do not give advantage | to TRO 5.02.130
she done, prince, that can /soil our mothers? 5.02.134
in corioles wear, | and mothers that lack sons. COR 2.01.179
younger than she are happy mothers made. ROM 1.02. 12
ladies of esteem, | are made already mothers. 1.03. 71
whose proof nor yells of mothers, maids, nor TIM 4.03.125
if caesar had stabb'd their mothers, they would JC 1.02.274 P
that mothers shall but smile when they behold 3.01.267
trick'd | with blood of fathers, mothers, HAM 2.02.458
since thou mad'st thy daughters thy mothers, for LR 1.04.173 P
those mothers who, to nousle up their babes, PER 1.04. 42
the goodly mothers that have groan'd for these, TNK 3.06.245
their weeping mothers, | following the dead–cold 4.02. 4
and two better never yet | made mothers joy — 4.02. 63
and have hotly ask'd them | if they had mothers; 5.01.106
stood many troyan mothers, sharing joy | to see LUC 1431

MOTHER–WIT 1 FR 0.0001 REL FR 1 V 0 P
it is extempore, from my mother–wit. SHR 2.01.263

MOTHY 1 FR 0.0001 REL FR 0 V 1 P
with an old mothy saddle and stirrups of no SHR 3.02. 49 P

MOTION 86 FR 0.0097 REL FR 72 V 14 P
incite them to quick motion, for i must | bestow TMP 4.01. 39
o excellent motion! TGV 2.01. 94 P
it were a goot motion if we leave our pribbles WIV 1.01. 54 P
he gives her folly motion and advantage; 3.02. 35 P
would give an excellent motion to thy gait in a 3.03. 63 P
this sensible warm motion to become | a kneaded MM 3.01.119
and he is a motion generative, that's infallible 3.02.111 P
i have a motion much imports your good, 5.01.535
we in your motion turn, and you may move us. ERR 3.02. 24
as motion and long–during action tires | the LLL 4.03.303
brain, | but, with the motion of all elements, 4.03.326
the music plays, vouchsafe some motion to it. 5.02.216
nor to the motion of a schoolboy's tongue, | nor 5.02.403
art | you sway the motion of demetrius' heart. MND 1.01.193
on the balls of mine, | seem they in motion? MV 3.02.118
but in his motion like an angel sings, | still 5.01. 61
o excellent motion! fellows, let's be gone. SHR 1.02.278
dance canary | with spritely fire and motion, AWW 2.01. 75
by thee, in what motion age will give me leave. 2.03.234 P
of a council frames | by self–unable motion; 3.01. 13
no motion of the liver, but the palate, | that TN 2.04. 98
taste your legs, sir, put them to motion. 3.01. 78 P
with such a mortal motion that it is inevitable; 3.04.276 P

i'll make the motion. 3.04.288 P
then he compass'd a motion of the prodigal son, WT 4.03. 96 P
the fixure of her eye has motion in't, | as we 5.03. 67
but from the inward motion to deliver | sweet, JN 1.01.212
mountains and rocks | more free from motion, no, 2.01.453
this sway of motion, this commodity, | makes it 2.01.578
whirl about | the other four in wondrous motion. 4.02.184
the dreadful motion of a murderous thought, 4.02.255
distrust | govern the motion of a kingly eye. 5.01. 47
i am scalded with my violent motion | and spleen 5.07. 49
give it him | to keep his anger still in motion. 1H4 1.03.226
two stars keep not their motion in one sphere, 5.04. 65
to be scour'd to nothing with perpetual motion. 2H4 1.02.220 P
you with the motion of a pewterer's hammer, come 3.02.262 P
have i, in my poor and old motion, the 4.03. 33 P
setting endeavor in continual motion; H5 1.02.185
scene flies | in motion of no less celerity 3.pr. 2
how doth your grace affect their motion? 1H6 5.01. 7
yes, i agree, and thank you for your motion. 3H6 3.03.244
in fear our motion will be mock'd or carp'd at, H8 1.02. 86
mean while must be an earnest motion | made to 2.04.234
since things in motion sooner catch the eye TRO 3.03.183
hasty and tinder–like upon too trivial motion; COR 2.01. 51 P
your loving motion toward the common body | to 2.02. 53
whose every motion | was tim'd with dying cries. 2.02.109
a beggar's tongue | make motion through my lips, 3.02.118
me, andronicus, doth this motion please thee? TIT 1.01.243
she would be as swift in motion as a ball; ROM 2.05. 13
vile earth, to earth resign, end motion here, 3.02. 59
still in motion | of raging waste? TIM 2.01. 3
all in motion? 3.06.102
of a dreadful thing | and the first motion, all JC 2.01. 64
holds on his rank, | unshak'd of motion; 3.01. 70
on, | his corporal motion govern'd by my spirit; 4.01. 33
nor our strong sorrow | upon the foot of motion. MAC 2.03.125
up it head and did address | itself to motion, HAM 1.02.217
else could you not have motion, but sure that 3.04. 72
of their nation | he swore had neither motion, 4.07.101
when in your motion you are hot and dry — | as 4.07.157
to his unnatural purpose, in fell motion, | with LR 2.01. 50
with drugs or minerals | that weakens motion. OTH 1.02. 75
of spirit so still and quiet that her motion 1.03. 95
he dies upon his motion. 2.03.174
the varying tide, | to rot itself with motion. ANT 1.04. 47
i see it in my motion, have it not in my tongue; 2.03. 14
her motion and her station are as one; 3.03. 19
takes prisoner the wild motion of mine eye, CYM 1.06.103
outwent her, | motion and breath left out. 2.04. 85
for there's no motion | that tends to vice in 2.05. 20
occasion | hath cadwal now to give it motion? 4.02.188
the want is but to put those pow'rs in motion 4.03. 31
motion? PER 5.01.154
than a dove's motion when the head's pluck'd off TNK 1.01. 98
'tis in motion, | the intelligence of state came 1.02.105
my seat, and in that motion might | omit a ward, 5.03. 62
to soften it with their continual motion; LUC 591
the ear | the heavy motion that it doth behold, 1326
these present–absent with swift motion slide. SON 45. 4
wind, | in winged speed no motion shall i know. 51. 8
hath motion, and mine eye may be deceiv'd; 104.12
upon that blessed wood whose motion sounds 128. 2
defect, | commanded by the motion of thine eyes? 149.12
o, all that borrowed motion seeming owed, LC 327
MOTIONLESS 1 FR 0.0001 REL FR 1 V 0 P
foul with chaw'd–grass, still and motionless; H5 4.02. 50
MOTION'S 1 FR 0.0001 REL FR 1 V 0 P
the motion's good indeed, and be it so, SHR 1.02.279
MOTIONS 13 FR 0.0014 REL FR 7 V 6 P
give ear to his motions: WIV 1.01.214 P
no, he gives me the potions and the motions. 3.01.103 P
your father and my uncle hath made motions. 3.04. 64 P
the wanton stings and motions of the sense; MM 1.04. 59
boys, | made daily motions for our home return: ERR 1.01. 59
ideas, apprehensions, motions, revolutions. LLL 4.02. 67 P
the motions of his spirit are dull as night, MV 5.01. 86
of their going to bed, and of other motions, as AWW 5.03.263 P
are, | unstaid and skittish in all motions else, TN 2.04. 18
and in thy face strange motions have appear'd, 1H4 2.03. 60
one that still motions war and never peace, 1H6 1.03. 63
but | from sincere motions, by intelligence, H8 1.01.153
but we have reason to cool our raging motions, OTH 1.03.330 P
MOTIVE 16 FR 0.0018 REL FR 16 V 0 P
wealth | was the first motive that i woo'd thee, WIV 3.04. 14
this was your motive | for paris, was it? speak. AWW 1.03.230
as it hath fated her to be my motive | and 4.04. 20
what motive may | be stronger with thee than the JN 3.01.313
tear | the slavish motive of recanting fear, R2 1.01.193
although i did admit it as a motive | the sooner H5 2.02.156
out | at every joint and motive of her body. TRO 4.05. 57
it, | is the main motive of our preparations, HAM 1.01.105
without more motive, into every brain | that 1.04. 76
had he the motive and /the /cue for passion 2.02.561
the other motive, | why to a public count i 4.07. 16
whose motive, in this case, should stir me most 5.02.245
/fear'd to lose it, | thy safety being motive. LR 1.01.157
am i the motive of these tears, my lord? OTH 4.02. 43
for which myself, the ignorant motive, do | so ANT 2.02. 96
youth, i blame ye not, | you had a motive for't. CYM 5.05.268
MOTIVES 6 FR 0.0006 REL FR 6 V 0 P
in fancy's course | are motives of more fancy, AWW 5.03.215
who were the motives that you first went out; TIM 5.04. 27
if these be motives weak, break off betimes, JC 2.01.116
those precious motives, those strong knots of MAC 4.03. 27
and your three motives to the battle, with | i CYM 5.05.388
in brief the grounds and motives of her woe. LC 63
/MOTLEY 1 FR 0.0001 REL FR 1 V 0 P
/the /one /in /motley /here, | /the /other LR 1.04.146
MOTLEY 9 FR 0.0010 REL FR 7 V 2 P
i met a fool i' th' forest, | a motley fool. AYL 2.07. 13
in good set terms, and yet a motley fool. 2.07. 17
hear | the motley fool thus moral on the time, 2.07. 29
i am ambitious for a motley coat. 2.07. 43
invest me in my motley; 2.07. 58
will you be married, motley? 3.03. 78 P
as much to say as i wear not motley in my brain. TN 1.05. 57 P
in a long motley coat guarded with yellow, H8 pr 16
there, | and made myself a motley to the view, SON 110. 2
MOTLEY–MINDED 1 FR 0.0001 REL FR 0 V 1 P
this is the motley–minded gentleman that i have AYL 5.04. 41 P
MOTLEY'S 1 FR 0.0001 REL FR 1 V 0 P
motley's the only wear. AYL 2.07. 34
MOTS 5 FR 0.0005 REL FR 0 V 5 P
j'ai gagne deux mots d'anglois vitement. H5 3.04. 14 P
de tous les mots que vous m'avez appris des a 3.04. 26 P
vous prononcez les mots aussi droit que les 3.04. 38 P
ils sont les mots de son mauvais, corruptible, 3.04. 53 P
prononcer ces mots devant les seigneurs de 3.04. 55 P
MOTTO 3 FR 0.0003 REL FR 3 V 0 P
the motto thus, in spanish: PER 2.02. 27
the motto thus: 2.02. 38
the motto: 2.02. 44
MOUGHT *(also might*)*
MOUGHT 1 FR 0.0001 REL FR 1 V 0 P
in a vault, | that mought not be distinguish'd; 3H6 5.02. 45
/MOULD* 1 FR 0.0001 REL FR 1 V 0 P
but if there be not in our grecian /mould | a TRO 1.03.293
MOULD* 9 FR 0.0010 REL FR 9 V 0 P
you, | unless you were of gentler, milder mould. SHR 1.01. 60
the very mould and frame of hand, nail, finger. WT 2.03.103
that mettle, that self mould, that fashioned R2 1.02. 23
be merciful, great duke, to men of mould. H5 3.02. 22
that mould up such a mighty piece as this is, H8 5.04. 26
this mould of martius, they to dust should grind COR 3.02.103
then the honor'd mould | wherein this trunk was 5.03. 22
cleave not to their mould | but with the aid of MAC 1.03.145
the glass of fashion and the mould of form, HAM 3.01.153
MOULDED 9 FR 0.0010 REL FR 9 V 0 P
they say best men are moulded out of faults, MM 5.01.439
two lovely berries moulded on one stem; MND 3.02.211
why, this was moulded on a porringer — | a SHR 4.03. 64
eyes, these brows, were moulded out of his; JN 2.01.100
whose arms were moulded in their mother's womb,
1H4 1.01. 23
i feel | of what coarse metal ye are moulded, H8 3.02.239
though they are made and moulded of things past,
TRO 3.03.177
like his ancestry, | moulded the stuff so fair, CYM 5.04. 49
by the loss of maidenhead, | a babe is moulded. PER 3.ch. 11
MOULDETH 1 FR 0.0001 REL FR 1 V 0 P
that mouldeth goblins swift as frenzy's thoughts TRO 5.10. 29
MOULDS 2 FR 0.0002 REL FR 2 V 0 P
crack nature's moulds, all germains spill at LR 3.02. 8
for stealing moulds from heaven that were divine VEN 730
MOULDY 14 FR 0.0015 REL FR 0 V 14 P
away, you mouldy rogue, away! 2H4 2.04.125 P
i'll thrust my knife in your mouldy chaps, and 2.04.130 P
he lives upon mouldy stew'd pruins and dried 2.04.146 P
rafe mouldy! 3.02. 98 P
let me see, where is mouldy? 3.02.100 P
is thy name mouldy? 3.02.104 P
things that are mouldy lack use. 3.02.108 P
go to, peace, mouldy, you shall go. 3.02.116 P
mouldy, it is time you were spent. 3.02.116 P
i have three pound to free mouldy and bullcalf. 3.02.244 P
marry, then, mouldy, bullcalf, feeble, and 3.02.248 P
mouldy and bullcalf! 3.02.250 P
for you, mouldy, stay at home till you are past 3.02.250 P
whose wit was mouldy ere /your grandsires had TRO 2.01.105 P
MOULT 1 FR 0.0001 REL FR 0 V 1 P
secrecy to the king and queen moult no feather. HAM 2.02.295 P
MOULTEN 1 FR 0.0001 REL FR 1 V 0 P
a clip–wing'd griffin and a moulten raven, | a 1H4 3.01.150
MOUNCH'D *(also munch)*
MOUNCH'D 3 FR 0.0003 REL FR 3 V 0 P
lap, | and mounch'd, and mounch'd, and mounch'd.
MAC 1.03. 5
lap, | and mounch'd, and mounch'd, and mounch'd. 1.03. 5
lap, | and mounch'd, and mounch'd, and mounch'd. 1.03. 5
MOUNSEUR *(also monsieur, mounsieur)*
MOUNSEUR 1 FR 0.0001 REL FR 0 V 1 P
a /word, mounseur mock–water. WIV 2.03. 57 P
MOUNSIEUR *(also monsieur, mounseur)*
MOUNSIEUR 12 FR 0.0013 REL FR 0 V 12 P
where's mounsieur cobweb? MND 4.01. 8 P
mounsieur cobweb, good mounsieur, get you your 4.01. 10 P
mounsieur cobweb, good mounsieur, get you your 4.01. 10 P
and, good mounsieur, bring me the honey–bag. 4.01. 12 P
fret yourself too much in the action, mounsieur; 4.01. 14 P
and, good mounsieur, have a care the honey–bag 4.01. 14 P
where's mounsieur mustardseed? 4.01. 17 P
give me your neaf, mounsieur mustardseed. 4.01. 19 P
pray you, leave your curtsy, good mounsieur. 4.01. 20 P
nothing, good mounsieur, but to help cavalery 4.01. 22 P
i must to the barber's, mounsieur; 4.01. 24 P
giving up of normandy unto mounsieur basimecu, 2H6 4.07. 28 P
/MOUNT* 1 FR 0.0001 REL FR 1 V 0 P
/my /griefs, /whilst /you /mount /up /on /high. R2 4.01.189
MOUNT* 35 FR 0.0039 REL FR 32 V 3 P
way, and mount | their pricks at my footfall; TMP 2.02. 11
but mount you presently and meet with me | upon
TGV 5.02. 45
be a giantess, and lie under mount pelion. WIV 2.01. 80 P
there will we mount, and thither walk on foot. SHR 4.03.186
amen, amen! mount, chevaliers! to arms! JN 2.01.287
by east and west let france and england mount 2.01.381
and when i mount, alive may i not light, | if i R2 1.01. 82
mount thee upon his horse, | spur post, and get 5.02.111
mount, mount, my soul! 5.05.111
mount, mount, my soul! 5.05.111
let me have right, and let desert mount. 2H4 4.03. 55 P
thine's too heavy to mount. 4.03. 56 P
mount them, and make incision in their hides, H5 4.02. 9
the tucket sonance and the note to mount; 4.02. 35
and here will talbot mount, or make his grave. 1H6 2.01. 34
therefore, dear boy, mount on my swiftest horse, 4.05. 9
lays, | and never mount to trouble you again. 2H6 1.03. 91
and should you fall, he is the next will mount. 3.01. 22
mount you, my lord, towards berwick post amain.
3H6 2.05.128
when i should mount with wings of victory. R3 5.03.106
to mount aloft with thy imperial mistress, | and TIT 2.01. 13
and mount her pitch, whom thou in triumph long 2.01. 14
the base o' th' mount | is rank'd with all TIM 1.01. 64
bowing his head against the steepy mount | to 1.01. 75
mount thou my horse, and hide thy spurs in him JC 5.03. 15
fix'd on the summit of the highest mount, | to HAM 3.03. 18
stood challenger on mount of all the age | for 4.07. 28
and soberly did mount an arm–gaunt steed, | who ANT 1.05. 48
about the mount misena. 2.02.160
the journey, be at /the mount | before you, 2.04. 6
common as the stairs | that mount the capitol; CYM 1.06.106
mount, eagle, to my palace crystalline. 5.04.113
unto thy value i will mount myself | upon a PER 2.01.157
he will not manage her, although he mount her, VEN 598
whose crooked beak threats, if he mount, he dies LUC 508
MOUNTAIN 39 FR 0.0044 REL FR 33 V 6 P
thou shalt be as free | as mountain winds; TMP 1.02.500
hey, mountain, hey! 4.01.255
make them | than pard or cat o' mountain. 4.01.261
me | upon the rising of the mountain foot | that TGV 5.02. 46
i should have been a mountain of mummy. WIV 3.05. 18 P
but for the mountain of mad flesh that claims ERR 4.04.154 P
beatrice into a mountain of affection th' one ADO 2.01.367 P
at the charge–house on the top of the mountain? LLL 5.01. 83 P
at your sweet pleasure, for the mountain. 5.01. 85 P
you may as well forbid the mountain pines | to MV 4.01. 75
upon a barren mountain, and still winter | in WT 3.02.212
snow, tumbled about, | anon becomes a mountain.
JN 3.04.177
father that begets them, gross as a mountain, 1H4 2.04.226 P
whiles that his mountain sire, on mountain H5 2.04. 57
that his mountain sire, on mountain standing, 2.04. 57
thou damned and luxurious mountain goat, 4.04. 19
and like a mountain, not to be remov'd. 1H6 2.05.103
though standing naked on a mountain top, | where
2H6 3.02.336
as on a mountain top the cedar shows | that 5.01.205
shrub, | to make an envious mountain on my back,
3H6 3.02.157
made trees, | and the mountain tops that freeze, H8 3.01. 4
and like a mountain cedar reach his branches 5.04. 53
moor, | the chafed boar, the mountain lioness, TIT 4.02.138
day | stands tiptoe on the misty mountain tops. ROM 3.05. 10
set a huge mountain 'tween my heart and tongue! JC 2.04. 7
could you on this fair mountain leave to feed, HAM 3.04. 66
"white his shroud as the mountain snow" — 4.05. 36
till of this flat a mountain you have made | t' 5.01.252
a forked mountain, or blue promontory | with ANT 4.14. 5
now for our mountain sport: CYM 3.03. 10
when from the mountain top pisanio show'd thee, 3.06. 5
that by the top doth take the mountain pine 4.02.175
throws down one mountain to cast up a higher. PER 1.04. 6
reign, | losing a mite, a mountain gain. 2.ch. 8
feed where thou wilt, on mountain or in dale; VEN 232
as mountain snow melts with the midday sun. 750
as from a mountain spring that feeds a dale, LUC 1077
flatter the mountain tops with sovereign eye, SON 33. 2
the mountain or the sea, the day or night, | the 113.11
MOUNTAINEER 2 FR 0.0002 REL FR 2 V 0 P
yield, rustic mountaineer. CYM 4.02.100
who call'd me traitor, mountaineer, and swore 4.02.120
MOUNTAINEERS 2 FR 0.0002 REL FR 2 V 0 P
who would believe that there were mountaineers, TMP 3.03. 44
a good, | that here by mountaineers lies slain. CYM 4.02.370
MOUNTAINERS 1 FR 0.0001 REL FR 1 V 0 P
some villain mountainers? CYM 4.02. 71
MOUNTAIN–FOREIGNER
1 FR 0.0001 REL FR 1 V 0 P
ha, thou mountain–foreigner! WIV 1.01.161
/MOUNTAINISH 1 FR 0.0001 REL FR 1 V 0 P
case | and this your /mountainish inhumanity. STM II.C 140
MOUNTAINOUS 1 FR 0.0001 REL FR 1 V 0 P
and mountainous error be too highly heap'd | for COR 2.03.120
MOUNTAIN'S 3 FR 0.0003 REL FR 3 V 0 P
we will, fair queen, up to the mountain's top, MND 4.01.109
though we upon this mountain's basis by | took H5 4.02. 30
which labor'd after him to the mountain's top TIM 1.01. 86
MOUNTAINS 22 FR 0.0024 REL FR 21 V 1 P
thy turfy mountains, where live nibbling sheep, TMP 4.01. 62
like far–off mountains turned into clouds. MND 4.01.188
but mountains may be remov'd with earthquakes, AYL 3.02.185 P
ay, to the proof, as mountains are for winds, SHR 2.01.140
fit for the mountains and the barbarous caves, TN 4.01. 48
mountains and rocks | more free from motion, no,
JN 2.01.452
that spits forth death and mountains, rocks and 2.01.458
no, on the barren mountains let him starve; 1H4 1.03. 89
that wish'd him on the barren mountains starve. 1.03.159
the goats ran from the mountains, and the herds 3.01. 38
revolution of the times | make mountains level, 2H4 3.01. 47
peace shall stand as firm as rocky mountains. 4.01.186
that raught at mountains with outstretched arms, 3H6 1.04. 68
strong–ribb'd bark through liquid mountains cut, TRO 1.03. 40
the sun no sooner shall the mountains touch, HAM 4.01. 29
and, if thou prate of mountains, let them throw 5.01.280
what ribs of oak, when mountains melt on them, OTH 2.01. 8
but up to th' mountains! CYM 3.03. 73
we'll higher to the mountains, there secure us. 4.04. 8
to seek her on the mountains near to milford, 5.05.281
in his dim mist th' aspiring mountains hiding, LUC 548
fields, | and all the craggy mountains yield. PP 19. 4
MOUNTAIN–SQUIRE 1 FR 0.0001 REL FR 0 V 1 P
you call'd me yesterday mountain–squire, but i H5 5.01. 35 P
MOUNTANT 1 FR 0.0001 REL FR 1 V 0 P
hold up, you sluts, | your aprons mountant. TIM 4.03.136
MOUNTANTO 1 FR 0.0001 REL FR 0 V 1 P
is signior mountanto return'd from the wars or ADO 1.01. 30 P
MOUNTEBANK 3 FR 0.0003 REL FR 3 V 0 P
villain, | a mere anatomy, a mountebank, | a ERR 5.01.239
i'll mountebank their loves, | cog their hearts COR 3.02.132
i bought an unction of a mountebank, | so mortal HAM 4.07.141
MOUNTEBANKS 2 FR 0.0002 REL FR 2 V 0 P
body, | disguised cheaters, prating mountebanks, ERR 1.02.101
by spells and medicines bought of mountebanks; OTH 1.03. 61
/MOUNTED 1 FR 0.0001 REL FR 1 V 0 P
/being /mounted /and /both /roused /in /their 2H4 4.01.116
MOUNTED 18 FR 0.0020 REL FR 17 V 1 P
encounters mounted are | against your peace. LLL 5.02. 82
troilus methinks mounted the troyan walls, | and MV 5.01. 4
her worth, being mounted on the wind, | through AYL 3.02. 90
and ready mounted are they to spit forth | their JN 2.01.211
myself, well mounted, hardly have escap'd. 5.06. 42
mounted upon a hot and fiery steed, | which his R2 5.02. 8
his affections are higher mounted than ours, yet H5 4.01.106 P

sandy plains | than where castles mounted stand. 2H6 1.04. 37
plains | than where castles mounted stand." 1.04. 69
that beggars mounted run their horse to death. 3H6 1.04.127
i thought it would have mounted. 5.06. 62
gone slightly o'er low steps and now are mounted H8 2.04.112
and mounted; CYM 2.05. 17
who from the mounted heavens | view us their TNK 1.04. 4
mounted upon a steed that emily | did first 5.04. 49
her champion mounted for the hot encounter: VEN 596
their mistress mounted through the empty skies, 1191
then should i spur though mounted on the wind, SON 51. 7
MOUNTETH 1 FR 0.0001 REL FR 1 V 0 P
defense, | for courage mounteth with occasion. JN 2.01. 82
MOUNTING 7 FR 0.0008 REL FR 7 V 0 P
that the sea, mounting to th' welkin's cheek, TMP 1.02. 4
whoe'er 'a was, 'a show'd a mounting mind. LLL 4.01. 4
and fits the mounting spirit like myself; JN 1.01.206
shriek where mounting larks should sing. R2 3.03.183
the mounting bullingbrook ascends my throne, 5.01. 56
in stead of mounting barbed steeds | to fright R3 1.01. 10
another spread on 's breast, mounting his eyes, H8 1.02.205
MOUNTS 7 FR 0.0008 REL FR 5 V 2 P
all's brave that youth mounts and folly guides. AYL 3.04. 45 P
what power is it which mounts my love so high, AWW 1.01.220
o then tread down my need, and faith mounts up; JN 3.01.215
in patient stillness while his rider mounts him. H5 3.07. 23 P
that mounts no higher than a bird can soar. 2H6 2.01. 14
the fire that mounts the liquor till't run o'er H8 1.01.144
from his moist cabinet mounts up on high, | and VEN 854
MOURN 33 FR 0.0037 REL FR 32 V 1 P
then shall he mourn, | if ever love had interest ADO 4.01.230
to-night i'll mourn with hero. 5.01.330
o, this it is that makes your lady mourn! SHR in.2. 26
to mourn for your brother's soul being in heaven TN 1.05. 70 P
but shall i go mourn for that, my dear? WT 4.03. 15
and some will mourn in ashes, some coal-black, R2 5.01. 49
come mourn with me for what i do lament, | and 5.06. 47
for this i shall have time enough to mourn; 2H4 1.01.136
we mourn in black, why mourn we not in blood? 1H6 1.01. 17
we mourn in black, why mourn we not in blood? 1.01. 17
mourn not, except thou sorrow for my good, 2.05.111
we mourn, france smiles; 4.03. 32
why only, suffolk, mourn i not for thee, | and 2H6 3.02.383
my love, i should not mourn, but die for thee. 4.04. 25
the hope thereof makes clifford mourn in steel. 3H6 1.01. 58
the tiger will be mild whiles she doth mourn; 3.01. 39
no more than with my soul i mourn for yours. R3 4.01. 88
ah, who hath any cause to mourn but we? 4.04. 34
th' ground, and all the world shall mourn her. H8 5.04. 62
from hence his body, | and mourn you for him. COR 5.06.142
do not draw back, for we will mourn with thee. TIT 2.04. 56
what cause withholds you then to mourn for him? JC 3.02.103
wherein now he raves, | and all we mourn for. HAM 2.02.151
to mourn a mischief that is past and gone | is OTH 1.03.204
or, dead, give 's cause to mourn his funeral, PER 2.04. 32
we wept after her hearse, | and yet we mourn. 4.03. 42
to mourn thy crosses, with thy daughter's, call 5.01.245
king, | as he is clement if th' offender mourn, STM II.C 123
pausing for means to mourn some newer way. LUC 1365
in black mourn i, all fears scorn i, | love hath PP 17.13
no longer mourn for me when i am dead | than you SON 71. 1
yet so they mourn, becoming of their woe, | that 127.13
then as well beseem thy heart | to mourn for me, 132.11
MOURN'D 5 FR 0.0005 REL FR 3 V 2 P
that mourn'd for fashion, ignorant what to fear, ERR 1.01. 73
buried a wife, mourn'd for her, writ to my lady AWW 4.03. 88 P
thou wouldst not have mourn'd so much for me. 2H6 4.04. 24
here comes his body, mourn'd by mark antony, who JC 3.02. 41 P
would have mourn'd longer — married with my HAM 1.02.151
MOURNER 4 FR 0.0004 REL FR 4 V 0 P
to him that hath most cause to be a mourner, R3 1.02.211
indeed i am no mourner for that news, | because 3.02. 51
another flap-mouth'd mourner, black and grim, VEN 920
interest, let no mourner say | he weeps for her, LUC 1797
MOURNERS 4 FR 0.0004 REL FR 3 V 1 P
we'll in here, tarry for the mourners, and stay ROM 4.05.146 P
tak'st, | 'mongst our mourners shalt thou go. PHT 20
so suited, and they mourners seem | at such who, SON 127.10
have put on black, and loving mourners be, 132. 3
MOURNFUL 6 FR 0.0006 REL FR 6 V 0 P
family's old monument | hang mournful epitaphs, ADO 4.01.207
the treacherous manner of his mournful death, 1H6 2.02. 16
beguiles him as the mournful crocodile | with 2H6 3.01.226
that i may dew it with my mournful tears; 3.02.340
weed, | no mournful bell shall ring her burial, TIT 5.03.197
than when her mournful hymns did hush the night, SON 102.10
MOURNFULLY 1 FR 0.0001 REL FR 1 V 0 P
beat thou the drum, that it speak mournfully; COR 5.06.149
/MOURNING 1 FR 0.0001 REL FR 1 V 0 P
as those two /mourning eyes become thy face. SON 132. 9
MOURNING 21 FR 0.0023 REL FR 21 V 0 P
and the remainder mourning over them, | brimful TMP 5.01. 13
maintain a mourning ostentation, | and on your ADO 4.01.205
and though the mourning brow of progeny | forbid LLL 5.02.744
shut | my woeful self up in a mourning house, 5.02.808
"the thrice three muses mourning for the death MND 5.01. 52
and she a mourning widow of her nobles, | she H5 1.02.158
still lamenting and mourning for suffolk's death 2H6 4.04. 22
and wrap our bodies in black mourning gowns, 3H6 2.01.161
had left no mourning widows for our death, | and 2.06. 19
him, my mourning weeds are laid aside, 3.03.229
him," quoth she, "my mourning weeds are done, 4.01.104
hail, rome, victorious in thy mourning weeds! TIT 1.01. 70
o, could our mourning ease thy misery! 2.04. 57
no funeral rite, nor man in mourning weed, | no 5.03.196
here is a mourning rome, a dangerous rome, | no JC 3.01.288
lo yonder, and titinius mourning it. 5.03. 92
to give these mourning duties to your father. HAM 1.02. 88
my mourning and importun'd tears hath pitied. LR 4.04. 26
who finds his lucrece clad in mourning black, LUC 1585
about the mourning and congealed face | of that 1744
to mourn for me, since mourning doth thee grace, SON 132.11

MOURNINGLY 1 FR 0.0001 REL FR 0 V 1 P
lately spoke of him admiringly and mourningly. AWW 1.01. 29 P
MOURNINGS 1 FR 0.0001 REL FR 1 V 0 P
march sadly after, grace my mournings here, | in R2 5.06. 51
MOURNS 2 FR 0.0002 REL FR 2 V 0 P
it mourns that painting /and usurping hair LLL 4.03.255
and that his lady mourns at his disease. SHR in.1. 62
MOURN'ST 2 FR 0.0002 REL FR 1 V 1 P
good madonna, why mourn'st thou? TN 1.05. 66 P
ah, thought i, thou mourn'st in vain! PP 20.19
MOUS'D 1 FR 0.0001 REL FR 0 V 1 P
well mous'd, lion. MND 5.01.269 P
MOUSE 15 FR 0.0017 REL FR 11 V 4 P
what's your dark meaning, mouse, of this light LLL 5.02. 19
smallest monstrous mouse that creeps on floor, MND 5.01.220
not a mouse | shall disturb this hallowed house. 5.01.387
good my mouse of virtue, answer me. TN 1.05. 63 P
as the wrathful dove or most magnanimous mouse. 2H4 3.02.160 P
eggs, | playing the mouse in absence of the cat, H5 1.02.172
the mouse ne'er shunn'd the cat as they did COR 1.06. 44
tut, dun's the mouse, the constable's own word. ROM 1.04. 40
a dog, a rat, a mouse, a cat, to scratch a man 3.01.100 P
and every cat and dog | and little mouse, every 3.03. 31
not a mouse stirring. HAM 1.01. 10
pinch wanton on your cheek, call you his mouse, 3.04.183
look, look, a mouse! LR 4.06. 89 P
law, | i never kill'd a mouse, nor hurt a fly; PER 4.01. 77
in his hold-fast foot the weak mouse panteth. LUC 555
MOUSE–EATEN 1 FR 0.0001 REL FR 0 V 1 P
rascals, that stale old mouse-eaten dry cheese, TRO 5.04. 10 P
MOUSE–HUNT 1 FR 0.0001 REL FR 1 V 0 P
ay, you have been a mouse-hunt in your time, ROM 4.04. 11
MOUSE'S 1 FR 0.0001 REL FR 1 V 0 P
coal, | now couches from the mouse's hole; PER 3.ch. 6
MOUSE–TRAP 1 FR 0.0001 REL FR 0 V 1 P
"the mouse-trap." HAM 3.02.237 P
MOUSING 2 FR 0.0002 REL FR 2 V 0 P
and now he feasts, mousing the flesh of men, JN 2.01.354
was by a mousing owl hawk'd at, and kill'd. MAC 2.04. 13
/MOUTH 1 FR 0.0001 REL FR 1 V 0 P
/and /for /one /blast /of /thy /minikin /mouth, LR 3.06. 43
MOUTH 131 FR 0.0148 REL FR 90 V 41 P
open your mouth; TMP 2.02. 82 P
open your mouth; 2.02. 84 P
i will pour some in thy other mouth. 2.02. 95 P
doth thy other mouth call me? 2.02. 97 P
than to suffer | the flesh-fly blow my mouth. 3.01. 63
thou here, | this is the mouth o' th' cell. 4.01.216
to call brother | would even infect my mouth, i 5.01.131
hast thou no mouth by land? 5.01.220
thy service — why dost thou stop my mouth? TGV 2.03. 45 P
"item, she hath a sweet mouth." 3.01.327 P
let us command to know that of your mouth, or of WIV 1.01.228 P
hold that the lips is parcel of the mouth. 1.01.230 P
heaven in my mouth, | as if i did but only chew MM 2.04. 4
i say to thee) he would mouth with a beggar, 3.02.183 P
to speak, as from his mouth, what he doth know 5.01.155
and put your trial in the villain's mouth 5.01.302
to accuse this worthy man, but, in foul mouth, 5.01.307
if i had my mouth, i would bite; ADO 1.03. 35 P
signior benedick's tongue in count john's mouth, 2.01. 12 P
if you cannot, stop his mouth with a kiss, and 2.01.311 P
thy wit is as quick as the greyhound's mouth — 5.02. 12 P
peace, i will stop your mouth. 5.04. 98 P
i only have made a mouth of his eye, | by adding LLL 2.01.252
but match'd in mouth like bells, | each under MND 4.01.123
which lion vile with bloody mouth did stain. 5.01.143
with a bone in his mouth than to either of these MV 1.02. 52 P
with his mouth full of news. AYL 1.02. 92 P
bubble reputation | even in the cannon's mouth. 2.07.153
till thou canst quit thee by thy brother's mouth 3.01. 11
pour this conceal'd man out of thy mouth, as 3.02.200 P
the cork out of thy mouth that i may drink thy 3.02.202 P
you must borrow me gargantua's mouth first; 3.02.225 P
word too great for any mouth of this age's size. 3.02.226 P
threats approach'd | the opening of his mouth; 4.03.110
open his lips when he put it into his mouth, 5.01. 35 P
and not a jot of tranio in your mouth, | tranio SHR 1.01.236
my tongue to the roof of my mouth, my heart in 4.01. 7 P
as the nun's lip to the friar's mouth, nay, as AWW 2.02. 27 P
my mouth no more were broken than these boys', 2.03. 60
you into a butter-woman's mouth and buy myself 4.01. 41 P
anne, and ginger shall be hot i' th' mouth too. TN 2.03.118 P
deliver thy indignation to him by word of mouth. 2.03.130 P
i will deliver his challenge by word of mouth, 3.04.191 P
from the rude sea's enrag'd and foamy mouth 5.01. 78
than one condemn'd by the king's own mouth — WT 1.02.445
(the innocent milk in it most innocent mouth) 3.02.100
she drops booties in my mouth. 4.04.832 P
then take my king's defiance from my mouth, JN 1.01. 21
town, | turn thou the mouth of thy artillery, 2.01.403
austria and france shoot in each other's mouth. 2.01.414
the mouth of passage shall we fling wide ope, 2.01.449
here's a large mouth indeed, | that spits forth 2.01.457
and from the mouth of england | add thus much 3.01.152
not a calve's-skin stop that mouth of thine? 3.01.299
ay, alack, how new | is "husband" in my mouth! 3.01.306
bell | did with his iron tongue and brazen mouth 3.03. 38
o, that my tongue were in the thunder's mouth! 3.04. 38
with open mouth swallowing a tailor's news, 4.02.195
take from my mouth the wish of happy years. R2 1.03. 94
and all unlook'd for from your highness' mouth. 1.03.155
within my mouth you have enjail'd my tongue, 1.03.166
"grace" | in an ungracious mouth is but profane. 2.03. 89
my tongue cleave to my roof within my mouth, 5.03. 31
his words come from his mouth, ours from our 5.03.102
from your own mouth, my lord, did i this deed. 5.06. 37
and for whose death we in the world's wide mouth 1H4 1.03.153
of him, | to fill the mouth of deep defiance up, 3.02.116
put ratsbane in my mouth as offer to stop it 2H4 1.02. 42 P
either our history shall with full mouth | speak H5 1.02.230
turkish mute, shall have a tongueless mouth, 1.02.232
and, which is worse, within thy nasty mouth! 2.01. 50
touch her soft mouth, and march. 2.03. 58
run winking into the mouth of a russian bear and 3.07.143 P

familiar in his mouth as household words, 4.03. 52
to take the tales out of my mouth, ere it is 4.07. 43 P
our places stops the mouth of all find-faults, 5.02.272 P
between two dogs, which hath the deeper mouth, 1H6 2.04. 12
fift | was in the mouth of every sucking babe, 3.01.196
to have thee with thy lips to stop my mouth; 2H6 3.02.396
now will i dam up this thy yawning mouth | for 4.01. 73
the laws of england may come out of your mouth. 4.07. 7 P
for he was thrust in the mouth with a spear, and 4.07. 9 P
my mouth shall be the parliament of england. 4.07. 14 P
suppose that i am now my father's mouth: 3H6 5.05. 18
with curses in her mouth, tears in her eyes, R3 1.02.232
and drop into the rotten mouth of death. 4.04. 2
and from a mouth of honor quite cry down | this H8 1.01.137
he had a black mouth that said other of him. 1.03. 58
have your mouth fill'd up | before you open it. 2.03. 87
the king's will from his mouth expressly? 3.02.235
and odious, | i will not taint my mouth with. 3.02.332
stop my mouth. TRO 3.02.133
he will spend his mouth and promise, like 5.01. 91 P
and foams at mouth, and he is arm'd and at it, 5.05. 36
the people, | the tongues o' th' common mouth. COR 3.01. 22
his heart's his mouth; 3.01.256
nay then i'll stop your mouth. TIT 2.03.185
whose mouth is covered with rude-growing briers, 2.03.199
as hateful as /cocytus' misty mouth. 2.03.236
which overshades the mouth of that same pit 2.03.273
sirs, stop his mouth, and let him speak no more. 5.01.151
my tears will choke me if i ope my mouth. 5.03.175
to whose foul mouth no healthsome air breathes ROM 4.03. 34
seal up the mouth of outrage for a while, | till 5.03.216
would i had a rod in my mouth, that i might TIM 2.02. 76 P
and what remains will hardly stop the mouth | of 2.02.147
sound them, it doth become the mouth as well; JC 1.02.145
down in the market-place, and foam'd at mouth, 1.02.253 P
and bid me say to you by word of mouth — | o 3.01.280
the hand more instrumental to the mouth, | than HAM 1.02. 48
trippingly on the tongue, but if you mouth it, 3.02. 2 P
give it breath with your mouth, and it will 3.02.359 P
nay, and thou'lt mouth, | i'll rant as well as 5.01.283
not from his mouth, | had it th' ability of life 5.02.372
and from his mouth whose voice will draw /on 5.02.392
i am, i cannot heave | my heart into my mouth. LR 1.01. 92
sea, | thou'dst meet the bear i' th' mouth. 3.04. 11
is it not as this mouth should tear this hand 3.04. 15
be thy mouth or black or white, | tooth that 3.06. 66
shut your mouth, dame, | or with this paper 5.03.155
i had rather have this tongue cut from my mouth OTH 2.03.221
if not, he foams at mouth, and by and by 4.01. 54
no — his mouth is stopp'd; 5.02. 71
for i wear not | my dagger in my mouth. CYM 4.02. 79
me | with his sword drawn, foam'd at the mouth, 5.05.276
and /crickets sing at the oven's mouth, | are PER 3.ch. 7
there was a spaniard's mouth wat'red, and he 4.02.100 P
if i fall from that mouth, i fall with favor, TNK 3.06.282
enfranchising his mouth, his back, his breast. VEN 396
the heavenly moisture, that sweet coral mouth, 542
whose frothy mouth bepainted all with red, 901
MOUTH'D 1 FR 0.0001 REL FR 0 V 1 P
in the corner of his jaw, first mouth'd, to be HAM 4.02. 19 P
MOUTHED 2 FR 0.0002 REL FR 2 V 0 P
those mouthed wounds, which valiantly he took, 1H4 1.03. 97
show, | of mouthed graves will give thee memory; SON 77. 6
MOUTH–FILLING 1 FR 0.0001 REL FR 1 V 0 P
a good mouth-filling oath, and leave "in sooth," 1H4 3.01.254
MOUTH–FRIENDS 1 FR 0.0001 REL FR 1 V 0 P
feast never behold, | you knot of mouth-friends! TIM 3.06. 89
MOUTHFUL 1 FR 0.0001 REL FR 0 V 1 P
him, and at last devour them all at a mouthful. PER 2.01. 32 P
MOUTH–HONOR 1 FR 0.0001 REL FR 1 V 0 P
curses, not loud but deep, mouth-honor, breath, MAC 5.03. 27
MOUTH–MADE 1 FR 0.0001 REL FR 1 V 0 P
to be entangled with those mouth-made vows, ANT 1.03. 30
MOUTHS 42 FR 0.0047 REL FR 35 V 7 P
what, must our mouths be cold? TMP 1.01. 53 P
o perilous mouths, | that bear in them one and MM 2.04.172
make mouths upon me when i turn my back, | wink MND 3.02.238
your worship was the last man in our mouths. MV 1.03. 60
their battering cannon charged to the mouths, JN 2.01.382
men's mouths are full of it. 4.02.161
young arthur's death is common in their mouths, 4.02.187
one kiss shall stop our mouths, and dumbly part; R2 5.01. 95
no word like "pardon" for kings' mouths so meet. 5.03.118
loud shouts and salutations from their mouths, 1H4 3.02. 53
/thighs pack'd with wax, our mouths with honey, 2H4 4.05. 76
most spend their mouths when what they seem to H5 2.04. 70
with fatal mouths gaping on girded harflew. 3.pr. 27
and in their pale dull mouths the /gimmal'd bit 4.02. 49
and have their provender tied to their mouths, 1H6 1.02. 11
much less to take occasion from their mouths 4.01.130
open their congeal'd mouths and bleed afresh! R3 1.02. 56
this makes bold mouths, | tongues spit their H8 1.02. 60
not before the king, which stopp'd our mouths, 2.02. 9 P
but stop their mouths with stubborn bits and 5.02. 58
that meat was made for mouths, that the gods COR 1.01.207
you being their mouths, why rule you not their 3.01. 36
the noble tribunes are the people's mouths, 3.01.270
it is spoke freely out of many mouths — | how 4.06. 65
and stop their mouths if they begin to cry. TIT 5.02.161
stop close their mouths, let them not speak a 5.02.164
sirs, stop their mouths, let them not speak to 5.02.167
the mouths, the tongues, the eyes, and hearts of TIM 4.03.261
(which like dumb mouths do ope their ruby lips JC 3.01.260
sweet caesar's wounds, poor, poor, dumb mouths, 3.02.225
if th' hadst rather hear it from our mouths, MAC 4.01. 62
that would make mouths at him while my father HAM 2.02.364 P
puff'd | makes mouths at the invisible event, 4.04. 50
yet fair woman but she made mouths in a glass. LR 3.02. 36 P
name is great | in mouths of wisest censure. OTH 2.03.193
put an enemy in their mouths to steal away their 2.03.290 P
had i as many mouths as hydra, such an answer 2.03.304 P
these mouths who, but of late, earth, sea, and PER 1.04. 34
palamon in their mouths and appear with tokens, TNK 4.03. 92 P
open'd their mouths to swallow venus' liking. VEN 248
then do they spend their mouths: 695
breath most breathes, even in the mouths of men. SON 81.14

MOVABLE *(see moveable, etc.)*
/MOV'D 2 FR 0.0002 REL FR 2 V 0 P
/alas, /the /tender /boy, /in /passion /mov'd, TIT 3.02. 48
/o, /then /it /mov'd /her. LR 4.03. 15
MOV'D 72 FR 0.0081 REL FR 58 V 14 P
you do look, my son, in a mov'd sort, | as if TMP 4.01.146
as they, be kindlier mov'd than thou art? 5.01. 24
why, he, of all the rest, hath never mov'd me. TGV 1.02. 27
be not like your mistress — be mov'd, be mov'd. 2.01.175 P
be not like your mistress — be mov'd, be mov'd. 2.01.175 P
if he had been throughly mov'd, you should have WIV 1.04. 90 P
it hath not mov'd him at all. MM 4.02.152 P
pompey is mov'd. LLL 5.02.688 P
myself am mov'd to woo thee for my wife. SHR 2.01.194
mov'd! 2.01.195
let him that mov'd you hither | remove you hence 2.01.195
a woman mov'd is like a fountain troubled, 5.02.142
home, i mov'd the king my master to speak in the AWW 4.05. 71 P
are you mov'd, my lord? WT 1.02.150
the king is mov'd, and answers not to this. JN 3.01.217
in all this presence that hath mov'd me so. R2 4.01. 32
not quite out of thee, now shalt thou be mov'd. 1H4 2.04.384 P
zeal, | my father, in kind heart and pity mov'd, 4.03. 64
the reason mov'd these warlike lords to this 1H6 2.05. 70
mov'd with compassion of my country's wrack, 4.01. 56
mov'd with remorse of these outrageous broils, 5.04. 97
will make him say i mov'd him to those arms. 2H6 3.01.378
pray'rs and tears have mov'd me, gifts could 4.07. 68
hath mov'd his highness to commit me now. R3 1.01. 61
foul shame upon you, you have all mov'd mine. 1.03.248
and in no worldly suits would he be mov'd, | to 3.07. 63
now, what mov'd me to't, | i will be bold with H8 2.04.168
oppression i did reek | when i first mov'd you. 2.04.210
i then mov'd you, | my lord of canterbury, and 2.04.218
have mov'd us and our council, that you shall 5.01.100
is as a virtue fix'd, to–day was mov'd: TRO 1.02. 5
to this effect, achilles, have i mov'd you. 3.03.216
o, be not mov'd, prince troilus. 4.04.129
being mov'd, he will not spare to gird the gods. COR 1.01.256
i was hardly mov'd to come to thee; 5.02. 72 P
i was mov'd withal. 5.03.194
and highly mov'd to wrath | to be controll'd in TIT 1.01.419
the lion, mov'd with pity, did endure | to have 2.03.151
i strike quickly, being mov'd. ROM 1.01. 6 P
but thou art not quickly mov'd to strike. 1.01. 7 P
therefore, if thou art mov'd, thou run'st away. 1.01. 10 P
as any in italy, and as soon mov'd to be moody, 3.01. 12 P
to be moody, and as soon moody to be mov'd. 3.01. 13 P
i promise you, my lord, you mov'd me much. TIM 1.02.113
against your city, | in part for his sake mov'd. 5.02. 13
see whe'er their basest metal be not mov'd; JC 1.01. 61
i might entreat you) | be any further mov'd. 1.02.167
that could be mov'd to smile at any thing. 1.02.207
are not you mov'd, when all the sway of earth 1.03. 3
i have mov'd already | some certain of the 1.03.121
i could be well mov'd, if i were as you; 3.01. 58
know you how much the people may be mov'd | by 3.01.234
notice of the people, | how i had mov'd them. 3.02.271
caesar liv'd, he durst not thus have mov'd me. 4.03. 58
special cause is here, | her army is mov'd on. LR 4.06.216
this speech of yours hath mov'd me, | and shall 5.03.200
but i do see y' are mov'd. OTH 3.03.217
worthy friend — | my lord, i see y' are mov'd. 3.03.224
no, not much mov'd: 3.03.224
tell him i have mov'd my lord on his behalf, and 3.04. 19 P
may be th' letter mov'd him; 4.01.235
him, although i think | not mov'd by antony. ANT 2.01. 42
was't | that mov'd pale cassius to conspire? 2.06. 15
like egg–shells mov'd upon their surges, crack'd CYM 3.01. 28
i mov'd her to't, | having receiv'd the 5.05.342
helicanus, thou | hast mov'd us. PER 1.02. 51
but fortune, mov'd, | varies again; 3.ch. 46
why are you mov'd thus? TNK 2.02.183
to die as thee to say it, | and no more mov'd. 3.06.160
being mov'd, he strikes, what e'er is in his way VEN 623
if ever man were mov'd with woman's moans, | be LUC 587
yet if men mov'd him, was he such a storm | as LC 101
/MOVE 1 FR 0.0001 REL FR 1 V 0 P
soon as they /move, as asprays do the fish, TNK 1.01.138
MOVE 105 FR 0.0118 REL FR 92 V 13 P
slave, | whom stripes may move, not kindness! TMP 1.02.345
pity move my father | to be inclin'd my way! 1.02.447
more than quick words do move a woman's mind. TGV 3.01. 91
and speechless dialect, | such as move men; MM 1.02.184
we in your motion turn, and you may move us. ERR 3.02. 24
with words that in an honest suit might move. 4.02. 14
let me but move one question to your daughter, ADO 4.01. 73
i fear these stubborn lines lack power to move. LLL 4.03. 53
it did move him to passion, and therefore let's 4.03.198
no, to the death we will not move a foot, | nor 5.02.146
to move wild laughter in the throat of death? 5.02.855
mirth cannot move a soul in agony. 5.02.857
o that my prayers could such affection move! MND 1.01.197
i will move storms; 1.02. 27 P
doth move me | on the first view to say, to 3.01.140
move these eyes? MV 3.02.116
speak to him, ladies, see if you can move him. AYL 1.02.162 P
more than your force move us to gentleness. 2.07.103
how then might your prayers move? 4.03. 55
which seem to move and wanton with her breath, SHR in.2. 52
tranio, i saw her coral lips to move, | and with 1.01.174
that the florentine will move us | for speedy AWW 1.02. 6
speak, and move under the influence of the most 2.01. 54 P
move the still–peering air | that sings with 3.02.110
what the devil should move me to undertake the 4.01. 34 P
lips, do not move; TN 2.05. 98
for thou perhaps mayst move | that heart, which 3.01.163
do you not see you move him? 3.04.109 P
if this letter move him not, his legs cannot. 3.04.171 P
could not move the gods | to look that way thou WT 3.02.213
move still, still so, | and own no other 4.04.142
no, the bagpipe could not move you. 4.04.183 P
i'll make the statue move indeed, descend, | and 5.03. 88
for 'tis as easy | to make her speak as move. 5.03. 94
what doth move you to claim your brother's land? JN 1.01. 91
doth move the murmuring lips of discontent | to 4.02. 53
should move you to mew up | your tender kinsman, 4.02. 57
now, you stars that move in your right spheres, 5.07. 74
and wish (so please my sovereign) ere i move, R2 1.01. 45
pity may move thee "pardon" to rehearse. 5.03.128
thou speakest may move and what he hears may be 1H4 1.02.154 P
and move in that obedient orb again | where you 5.01. 17
did all the chevalry of england move | to do 2H4 2.03. 20
light and weightless down | perforce must move. 4.05. 34
and newly move | with casted slough and fresh H5 4.01. 22
i shall never move thee in french, unless it be 5.02.186 P
thy words move rage and not remorse in me. 2H6 4.01.112
lest to thy harm thou move our patience. R3 1.03.247
may move your hearts to pity if you mark him. 1.03.348
in this just cause come i to move your grace. 3.07.140
if this inducement move her not to love, | send 4.04.279
the avaunt, it is a pity | would move a monster. H8 2.03. 11
royal infant — heaven still move about her! 5.04. 17
we dare not move the question of our place, | or TRO 2.03. 82
did move your greatness and this noble state 2.03.109
how novelty may move, and parts with /person, 4.04. 79
with briers, | scars to move laughter only. COR 3.03. 52
being assur'd none but myself could move thee, i 5.02. 74 P
perhaps thy childishness will move him more 5.03.157
ere he express himself or move the people | with 5.06. 54
we will solicit heaven and move the gods | to TIT 4.03. 51
time | when it should move ye to attend me most, 5.03. 92
to move is to stir, and to be valiant is to ROM 1.01. 9 P
a dog of that house shall move me to stand! 1.01. 11 P
i'll look to like, if looking liking move; 1.03. 97
lead | so stakes me to the ground i cannot move. 1.04. 16
saints do not move, though grant for prayers' 1.05.105
then move not while my prayer's effect i take. 1.05.106
that we have had no time to move our daughter. 3.04. 2
to move the heavens to smile upon my state, 4.03. 4
move them no more by crossing their high will. 4.05. 95
and be in debt to none — yet more to move you, TIM 3.05. 77
if i could pray to move, prayers would move me; JC 3.01. 59
if i could pray to move, prayers would move me; 3.01. 59
that should move | the stones of rome to rise 3.02.229
bid them move away; 4.02. 45
have been known to move and trees to speak; MAC 3.04.122
a wild and violent sea | each way, and move. 4.02. 22
those he commands move only in command, 5.02. 19
and anon methought | the wood began to move. 5.05. 34
kept close, might move | more grief to hide, HAM 2.01.115
stars are fire, | doubt that the sun doth move, 2.02.117
unless things mortal move them not at all, 2.02.516
the instances that second marriage move | are 3.02.182
yet the unshaped use of it doth move | the 4.05. 8
persuade revenge, | it could not move thus. 4.05.170
my wife must move for cassio to her mistress — OTH 2.03.383
if i have any grace or power to move you, | his 3.03. 46
i'll move your suit | and seek to effect it to 3.04.166
if caesar move him, | let antony look over ANT 2.02. 4
and not to be seen to move in't, are the holes 2.07. 15 P
that your love | can equally move with them. 3.04. 36
yet i'll move him | to walk this way. CYM 1.01.103
i'll move the king | to any shape of thy 1.05. 70
or adder, spider, | 'twould move me sooner. 4.02. 91
put those pow'rs in motion | that long to move. 4.03. 32
how durst thy tongue move anger to our face? PER 1.02. 54
how? | do as i bid you, or you'll move me else. 2.03. 71
like motes and shadows see them move a while, 4.04. 21
i have seen you move in such a place, which well TNK 3.01. 63
thy outward parts would move | each part in me VEN 435
round clear pearls of his, that move thy pity, LUC 1553
and if these pleasures may thee move, | then PP 19.15
these pretty pleasures might me move | to live 19.19
thou /not farther than my thoughts canst move, SON 47.11
MOVEABLE 2 FR 0.0002 REL FR 2 V 0 P
i knew you at the first | you were a moveable. SHR 2.01.197
why, what's a moveable? 2.01.197
MOVEABLES 5 FR 0.0005 REL FR 5 V 0 P
us | the plate, coin, revenues, and moveables, R2 2.01.161
look to my chattels and my moveables. H5 2.03. 48
and all the moveables | whereof the king my R3 3.01.195
th' earldom of /herford, and the moveables, 4.02. 90
above ten thousand meaner moveables | would CYM 2.02. 29
MOVED 11 FR 0.0012 REL FR 11 V 0 P
that my poor mistress, moved therewithal, | wept TGV 4.04.170
if silent, why, a block moved with none. ADO 3.01. 67
nor is not moved with concord of sweet sounds, MV 5.01. 84
with which they moved | have broken with the H8 5.01. 46
you are moved, prince, let us depart, i pray, TRO 5.02. 36
then must my sea be moved with her sighs; TIT 3.01.227
and hear the sentence of your moved prince. ROM 1.01. 88
which modern lamentation might have moved? 3.02.120
but virtue, as it never will be moved, | though HAM 1.05. 53
as i am ignorant | of what hath moved you. LR 1.04.274
be moved with my tears, my sighs, my groans. LUC 588
MOVER 2 FR 0.0002 REL FR 2 V 0 P
o thou eternal mover of the heavens, | look with 2H6 3.03. 19
"o fairest mover on this mortal round, | would VEN 368
MOVERS 2 FR 0.0002 REL FR 2 V 0 P
see here these movers that do prize their hours COR 1.05. 4
which are the movers of a languishing death, CYM 1.05. 9
MOVES 25 FR 0.0028 REL FR 19 V 6 P
to me she speaks, she moves me for her theme: ERR 2.02.181
thy paleness moves me more than eloquence, | and MV 3.02.106
term, and then they perceive not how time moves. AYL 3.02.333 P
she moves me not, or not removes, at least, SHR 1.02. 72
there is no tongue that moves, none, none i' th' WT 1.02. 20
on't, lest your fancy | may think anon it moves. 5.03. 61
that any thing he sees, which moves his liking, JN 2.01.512
part needs a physician, but that moves not him; 2H4 2.02.105 P
but his passions moves me so | that hardly can i 3H6 1.04.150
for this is he that moves both wind and tide. 3.03. 48
what moves ajax thus to bay at him? TRO 2.03. 90 P
when he walks, he moves like an engine, and the COR 5.04. 19 P
a dog of the house of montague moves me. ROM 1.01. 8 P
how big imagination | moves in this lip! TIM 1.01. 33
but moves itself | in a wide sea of wax. 1.01. 46
towards his design | moves like a ghost. MAC 2.01. 56
what is't that moves your highness? 3.04. 47
that, as the star moves not but in his sphere, HAM 4.07. 15
where he arrives he moves | all hearts against LR 4.05. 10
so high as it is, and moves with it own organs. ANT 2.07. 43 P
very action speaks | in every power that moves. 3.12. 36
him hourly to your ear | as truly as he moves. CYM 3.04.151
from whence he moves | his war for britain. 3.05. 25
this moves in him more rage and lesser pity | to LUC 468
to see sad sights moves more than hear them told 1324
MOVETH 1 FR 0.0001 REL FR 1 V 0 P
he heareth not, he stirreth not, he moveth not, ROM 2.01. 15
MOVING 19 FR 0.0021 REL FR 17 V 2 P
eyes wide open — standing, speaking, moving — TMP 2.01.214
if the gentle spirit of moving words | can no TGV 5.04. 55
heaven give thee moving graces! MM 2.02. 36
more moving, delicate, and full of life, | into ADO 4.01.228
and love as mine), | without ripe moving to't? WT 1.02.332
the heavy accent of thy moving tongue, | and in R2 5.01. 47
for moving such a dish of skim–milk with so 1H4 2.03. 33 P
mars his true moving, even as in the heavens, 1H6 1.02. 1
and lewis a prince soon won with moving words. 3H6 3.01. 34
not moving | from th' casque to th' cushion, but COR 4.07. 42
i say, a moving grove. MAC 5.05. 37
how infinite in faculties, in form and moving! HAM 2.02.305 P
of moving accidents by flood and field, | of OTH 1.03.135
hah, no more moving? 5.02. 93
shall make thy peace for moving me to rage, ANT 2.05. 70
and every tongue more moving than your own, VEN 776
doth cite each moving sense from idle rest, PP 14.15
till whatsoever star that guides my moving SON 26. 9
who, moving others, are themselves as stone, 94. 3
MOVINGLY 1 FR 0.0001 REL FR 1 V 0 P
i would have had them writ more movingly. TGV 2.01.128
MOVOUSUS 1 FR 0.0001 REL FR 0 V 1 P
throca movousus, cargo, cargo, cargo. AWW 4.01. 65 P
MOV'ST 3 FR 0.0003 REL FR 3 V 0 P
horse, for wot'st thou whom thou mov'st? ANT 1.05. 22
o sun, | burn the great sphere thou mov'st in! 4.15. 10
thou mov'st no less with thy complaining than CYM 4.02.375
MOW* 7 FR 0.0008 REL FR 6 V 1 P
sometime like apes that mow and chatter at me, TMP 2.02. 9
on his toe, | will be here with mop and mow. 4.01. 47
to mow down thorns that would annoy our foot 2H6 3.01. 67
guy, nor colbrand, | to mow 'em down before me; H8 5.03. 23
like to a harvest–man /that's task'd to mow | or COR 1.03. 36
he will mow all down before him, and leave his 4.05.201 P
and nothing stands but for his scythe to mow: SON 60.12
/MOWBRAY 2 FR 0.0002 REL FR 2 V 0 P
/o, /my /good /lord /mowbray, | /construe /the 2H4 4.01.101
/you /speak, /lord /mowbray, /now /you /know 4.01.128
MOWBRAY 20 FR 0.0022 REL FR 19 V 1 P
against the duke of norfolk, thomas mowbray? R2 1.01. 6
against the duke of norfolk, thomas mowbray? 1.01. 29
now, thomas mowbray, do i turn to thee, | and 1.01. 35
that mowbray hath receiv'd eight thousand nobles 1.01. 88
fetch from false mowbray their first head and 1.01. 97
mowbray, impartial are our eyes and ears. 1.01.115
he is our subject, mowbray; 1.01.122
our cousin herford and fell mowbray fight. 1.02. 46
my name is thomas mowbray, duke of norfolk, 1.03. 16
in lists, on thomas mowbray, duke of norfolk, 1.03. 38
for mowbray and myself are like two men | that 1.03. 48
against a bird, do i with mowbray fight. 1.03. 62
to prove the duke of norfolk, thomas mowbray, 1.03.107
here standeth thomas mowbray, duke of norfolk, 1.03.110
john, a boy, and page to thomas mowbray, duke of 2H4 3.02. 26 P
mowbray, you overween to take it so; 4.01.147
are well encount'red here, my cousin mowbray, 4.02. 1
health to my lord, and gentle cousin, mowbray. 4.02. 78
and you, lord archbishop, and you, lord mowbray, 4.02.108
mowbray, the bishop scroop, hastings, and all, 4.04. 84
MOWBRAY'S 6 FR 0.0006 REL FR 6 V 0 P
what doth our cousin lay to mowbray's charge? R2 1.01. 84
where shame doth harbor, even in mowbray's face. 1.01.195
that it may enter butcher mowbray's breast! 1.02. 48
be mowbray's sins so heavy in his bosom | that 1.02. 50
for me, if i be gor'd with mowbray's spear. 1.03. 60
point, | that it may enter mowbray's waxen coat, 1.03. 75
MOW'D 1 FR 0.0001 REL FR 1 V 0 P
have we mow'd down in tops of all their pride! 3H6 5.07. 4
MOWER'S 1 FR 0.0001 REL FR 1 V 0 P
fall down before him like a mower's swath. TRO 5.05. 25
/MOWING* 1 FR 0.0001 REL FR 0 V 1 P
/flibbertigibbet, /of /mopping /and /mowing, LR 4.01. 62 P
MOWING* 1 FR 0.0001 REL FR 1 V 0 P
mowing like grass | your fresh fair virgins and H5 3.03. 13
MOWS 1 FR 0.0001 REL FR 1 V 0 P
this way, and | contemn with mows the other; CYM 1.06. 41
MOY *(also moi)*
MOY 2 FR 0.0002 REL FR 2 V 0 P
speak it in french, king, say "pardonne moy." R2 5.03.119
moy shall not serve, i will have forty moys, H5 4.04. 13
MOYS 2 FR 0.0002 REL FR 2 V 0 P
moy shall not serve, i will have forty moys, H5 4.04. 13
is that a ton of moys? 4.04. 22
MOYSES 1 FR 0.0001 REL FR 1 V 0 P
outrun us, | but moyses and valerius follow him. TGV 5.03. 8
MUCH *(also mush)*
/MUCH 13 FR 0.0014 REL FR 10 V 3 P
thy sum of more | to that which had too /much." AYL 2.01. 49
/yet /salt /water /blinds /them /not /so /much R2 4.01.245
/fruit | /hope /gives /not /so /much /warrant, 2H4 1.03. 40
/much /more, /in /this /great /work | (/which 1.03. 48
/for /we /would /give /much /to /use /violent TRO 5.03. 21
/preserve /just /so /much /strength /in /us TIT 3.02. 2
/there /has /been /much /to /do /on /both /sides HAM 2.02.352 P
/o, /there /has /been /much /throwing /about /of 2.02.358 P
/his /fault /is /much, /and /the /good /king LR 2.02.141
/but /then /the /mind /much /sufferance /doth 3.06.106
/to /the /kingdom /so /much /fear /and /danger 4.03. 5 P
/to /amplify /too /much, /would /make /much 5.03.207
/amplify /too /much, /would /make /much /more, 5.03.207
MUCH 1085 FR 0.1226 REL FR 838 V 247 P
not so much perdition as an hair | betid to any TMP 1.02. 30
of homage, and i know not how much tribute, 1.02.124
necessaries, | which since have steaded much; 1.02.165
and think'st it much to tread the ooze | of the 1.02.252
thou strok'st me and made much of me, wouldst 1.02.333

for our escape | is much beyond our loss. 2.01. 3
he misses not much. 2.01. 57 P
indeed, | which throes thee much to yield. 2.01.231
garments sit upon me, | much feater than before. 2.01.273
keep him tame, i will not take too much for him; 2.02. 77 P
and i should do it | with much more ease, for my 3.01. 30
and much less take | what i shall die to want. 3.01. 78
must i perform | much business appertaining. 3.01. 96
coward that hath drunk so much sack as i to–day? 3.02. 28 P
i cannot too much muse | such shapes, such 3.03. 36
do not give dalliance | too much the rein. 4.01. 52
have i means much weaker | than you may call to 5.01.146
at this encounter do so much admire | that they 5.01.154
to content ye | as much as me my dukedom. 5.01.171
as much to you at home; and so farewell. TGV 1.01. 62
why? couldst thou perceive so much from her? 1.01.134 P
no, not so much as a ducat for delivering your 1.01.137 P
no, not so much as "take this for thy pains." 1.01.143 P
nor need'st thou much importune me to that 1.03. 17
which i was much unwilling to proceed in, | but 2.01.106
perchance you think too much of so much pains? 2.01.112
perchance you think too much of so much pains? 2.01.112
(please you command) a thousand times as much; 2.01.114
a letter from your friends | of much good news? 2.04. 52
friends are well and have them much commended. 2.04.123
o, but i love his lady too too much, | and 2.04.205
thou hast not so much charity in thee as to go 2.05. 57 P
to wrong my friend, i shall be much forsworn. 2.06. 3
much less shall she that hath love's wings to 2.07. 11
as after much turmoil | a blessed soul doth in 2.07. 37
you, | it would be much vexation to your age. 3.01. 16
be they of much import? 3.01. 55
than for all the favors | which (all too much) i 3.01.162
so much of bad already hath possess'd them. 3.01.207
which is much in a bare christian. 3.01.273 P
that's as much as to say, "can she so?" 3.01.307 P
that's as much as to say "bastard virtues," that 3.01.318 P
which must be done by praising me as much | as 3.02. 54
as much as i can do, i will effect. 3.02. 66
ay, much is the force of heaven–bred poesy. 3.02. 71
that all the travellers do fear so much. 4.01. 6
i kill'd a man, whose death i much repent, | but 4.01. 27
as we do in our quality much want — 4.01. 56
madam, i pity much your grievances, | which 4.03. 37
me, | as much i wish all good befortune you. 4.03. 41
mine shall not do his julia so much wrong. 4.04.137
poor gentlewoman, my master wrongs her much. 4.04.141
since she respects my mistress' love so much. 4.04.182
little, | unless i flatter with myself too much. 4.04.188
time, | so much they spur their expedition. 5.01. 6
yet i have much to do | to keep them from 5.04. 16
and full as much (for more there cannot be) | i 5.04. 38
than plural faith, which is too much by one. 5.04. 52
much good do it your good heart! WIV 1.01. 81 P
i thank you as much as though i did. 1.01.280 P
she is given too much to allicholy and musing; 1.04.153 P
it is as much as i can do to keep the terms of 2.02. 21 P
never get her so much as sip on a cup with the 2.02. 75 P
after the expense of so much money, be now a 2.02.141 P
sir, i am a gentleman that have spent much. 2.02.160 P
you, wherein i must very much lay open mine own 2.02.184 P
and, i protest to you, bestow'd much on her; 2.02.195 P
only give me so much of your time in exchange of 2.02.233 P
then i have as much mock–vater as de englishman. 2.03. 62 P
he is of too high a region, he knows too much. 3.02. 74 P
i fear not mine own shame so much as his peril. 3.03.123 P
you wrong yourself too much. 3.03.167 P
i hope not, i had lief as bear so much lead. 4.02.113 P
husband will not rejoice so much at the abuse of 5.03. 7 P
from too much liberty, my lucio, liberty: MM 1.02.125
as surfeit is the father of much fast, | so 1.02.126
it, would much better please me | than to demand 2.04. 32
as much for my poor brother as myself: 2.04. 99
little honor to be much believ'd, | and most 2.04.149
o, how much is the good duke deceiv'd in angelo! 3.01.191 P
that shall not be much amiss; 3.01.195 P
and much please the absent duke, if peradventure 3.01.203 P
it lies much in your holding up. 3.01.261 P
heard the absent duke much detected for women, 3.02.121 P
be more, it is much dark'ned in your malice. 3.02.148 P
that fellow is a fellow of much license; 3.02.204 P
much upon this riddle runs the wisdom of the 3.02.228 P
my mirth it much displeas'd, but pleas'd my woe. 4.01. 13
much upon this time have i promis'd here to meet 4.01. 17 P
marry, then ginger was not much in request, for 4.03. 8 P
his actions show much like to madness, pray 4.04. 4 P
how i replied | (for this was of much length) — 5.01. 95
and, after much debatement, | my sisterly 5.01. 99
in a barber's shop, | as much in mock as mark. 5.01.322
you indeed spoke so of him, and much more, much 5.01.338 P
spoke so of him, and much more, much worse. 5.01.338 P
become much more the better | for being a little 5.01.440
good friend escalus, for thy much goodness, 5.01.528
i have a motion much imports your good, 5.01.535
but longer did we not retain much hope; ERR 1.01. 65
of whom i hope to make much benefit; 1.02. 25
as much, or more, we should ourselves complain: 2.01. 37
here's too much "out upon thee!" 3.01. 78
due, | and since i have not much importun'd you, 4.01. 2
how much your chain weighs to the utmost charect 4.01. 28
you gave me none, you wrong me much to say so. 4.01. 66
"god damn me," that's as much to say, "god make 4.03. 54 P
choose, | for forty ducats is too much to lose. 4.03. 96
i'll give thee, ere i leave thee, so much money, 4.04. 2
i wonder much | that you would put me to this 5.01. 13
sad, | and much different from the man he was; 5.01. 46
hath he not lost much wealth by wrack of sea? 5.01. 49
love — | a sin prevailing much in youthful men, 5.01. 52
him, | he shall not die, so much we tender him. 5.01.132
most mighty duke, behold a man much wrong'd. 5.01.331
take it, and much thanks for my good cheer. 5.01.393
don /pedro hath bestow'd much honor on a young ADO 1.01. 10 P
much deserv'd on his part, and equally 1.01. 12 P
here in messina will be very much glad of it. 1.01. 19 P
him letters, and there appears much joy in him, 1.01. 21 P
him, even so much that joy could not show itself 1.01. 21 P
how much better is it to weep at joy than to joy 1.01. 28 P
you tax signior benedick too much, but he'll be 1.01. 47 P
exceeds her as much in beauty as the first of 1.01.191 P
what need the bridge much broader than the flood 1.01.316
were thus much overheard by a man of mine. 1.02. 10 P
with her told her she is much wrong'd by you. 2.01.238 P
were but little happy, if i could say how much! 2.01.307 P
since, how much i am in the favor of margaret, 2.02. 13 P
i do much wonder that one man, seeing how much 2.03. 7 P
seeing how much another man is a fool when he 2.03. 8 P
the ecstasy hath so much overborne her that my 2.03.151 P
to see how much he is unworthy so good a lady. 2.03.208 P
yea, just so much as you may take upon a knive's 2.03.254 P
pains to thank me" — that's as much as to say, 2.03.260 P
deserve | as much as may be yielded to a man; 3.01. 48
know | how much an ill word may empoison liking. 3.01. 86
she cannot be so much without true judgment — 3.01. 88
stand i condemn'd for pride and scorn so much? 3.01.108
that's as much as to say, the sweet youth's in 3.02. 52 P
much more a man who hath any honesty in him. 3.03. 64 P
lady, | i am sorry for thy much misgovernment. 4.01. 99
o, one too much by thee! 4.01.129
mine so much | that i myself was to myself not 4.01.137
nor my bad life reft me so much of friends, 4.01.196
love | is very much unto the prince and claudio, 4.01.246
how much might the man deserve of me that would 4.01.261 P
i love you with so much of my heart that none is 4.01.286 P
so much for praising myself, who, i myself will 5.02. 86 P
calf in that same noble feat | much like to you, 5.04. 51
and ursula | are much deceiv'd, for they did 5.04. 79
so much, dear liege, i have already sworn, LLL 1.01. 34
too much to know is to know nought but fame; 1.01. 92
so much for the time when. 1.01.238 P
i do confess much of the hearing it, but little 1.01.285 P
i am sure you know how much the gross sum of 1.02. 45 P
thee in my rapier as much as thou didst me in 1.02. 74 P
and therefore too much odds for a spaniard's 1.02.177 P
worth | than you much willing to be counted wise 2.01. 18
haste, signify so much, while we attend, | like 2.01. 33
and much too little of that good i saw | is my 2.01. 62
marry, thus much i have learnt: 2.01. 84
which we much rather had depart withal, | and 2.01.146
you do the king my father too much wrong, | and 2.01.153
this civil war of wits were much better used 2.01.226
and three times as much more — and yet nothing 3.01. 47 P
how much carnation ribbon may a man buy for a 3.01.145 P
i am much deceived but i remember the style. 4.01. 96
i fear too much rubbing. 4.01.139
it may concern much. 4.02.142 P
we are much out a' th' way. 4.03. 74
you chide at him, offending twice as much. 4.03.130
see, | i would not have him know so much by me. 4.03.148
all three of you, to be thus much o'ershot? 4.03.158
no devil will fright thee then so much as she. 4.03.271
her feet were much too dainty for such tread! 4.03.275
as much love in rhyme | as would be cramm'd up 5.02. 6
much in the letters, nothing in the praise. 5.02. 40
you, | as much in private, and i'll bid adieu. 5.02.241
so much i hate a breaking cause to be | of 5.02.355
here, | unseen, unvisited, much to our shame. 5.02.358
much upon this 'tis; 5.02.472
how much is it? 5.02.498 P
i implore so much expense of thy royal sweet 5.02.522 P
'tis not so much worth; 5.02.558 P
speak, brave hector, we are much delighted. 5.02.665 P
lost | is not by much so wholesome–profitable 5.02.750
hath much deformed us, fashioning our humors 5.02.757
our letters, madam, show'd much more than jest. 5.02.785
no, no, my lord, your grace is perjur'd much, 5.02.790
then, if i have much love, i'll give you some. 5.02.830
i must confess that i have heard so much, | and MND 1.01.111
tempt not too much the hatred of my spirit, 2.01.211
you do impeach your modesty too much, | to leave 2.01.214
now much beshrew my manners and my pride, | if 2.02. 54
mine ear is much enamored of thy note; 3.01.138
could not a worm, an adder, do so much? 3.02. 71
you would not do me thus much injury. 3.02.148
the villain is much lighter–heel'd than i; 3.02.415
do not fret yourself too much in the action, 4.01. 13 P
i read as much as from the rattling tongue | of 5.01.102
as much as we this night have overwatch'd. 5.01.366
of me, | that i have much ado to know myself. MV 1.01. 7
you have too much respect upon the world. 1.01. 74
they lose it that do buy it with much care. 1.01. 75
antonio, | how much i have disabled mine estate, 1.01.123
i owe you much, and, like a willful youth, 1.01.146
that surfeit with too much as they that starve 1.02. 6 P
i am much afeard my lady his mother play'd false 1.02. 43 P
is he yet possess'd | how much ye would? 1.03. 65
courtesies | i'll lend you thus much moneys"? 1.03.129
and say there is much kindness in the jew. 1.03.153
play the knave and get thee, i am much deceiv'd. 2.03. 12 P
and my love indeed, | for who love i so much? 2.06. 30
on me, | for i am much asham'd of my exchange. 2.06. 35
chooseth me shall get as much as he deserves"; 2.07. 7
chooseth me shall get as much as he deserves." 2.07. 23
as much as he deserves! 2.07. 24
as much as i deserve! 2.07. 31
chooseth me shall get as much as he deserves." 2.09. 36
how much low peasantry would then be gleaned 2.09. 46
and how much honor | pick'd from the chaff and 2.09. 47
chooseth me shall get as much as he deserves." 2.09. 50
how much unlike art thou to portia! 2.09. 56
how much unlike my hopes and my deservings! 2.09. 57
chooseth me shall have as much as he deserves"! 2.09. 58
the thief gone with so much, and so much to find 3.01. 93 P
with so much, and so much to find the thief, and 3.01. 93 P
with no less presence, but with much more love, 3.02. 54
with much, much more dismay | i view the fight 3.02. 61
much more dismay | i view the fight than thou 3.02. 61
i feel too much thy blessing; 3.02.113
in my wish | to wish myself much better, yet, 3.02.152
our feast shall be much honored in your marriage 3.02.212
the world | could turn so much the constitution 3.02.246
you shall see | how much i was a braggart: 3.02.258
will much impeach the justice of the state, 3.03. 29
it is much that the moor should be more than 3.05. 40 P
i have spoke thus much | to mitigate the justice 4.01.202
how much more elder art thou than thy looks! 4.01.251
'twere good you do so much for charity. 4.01.261
be it but so much | as makes it light or heavy 4.01.327
for in my mind you are much bound to him. 4.01.407
methinks it sounds much sweeter than by day. 5.01.100
the voice, | or i am much deceiv'd, of portia. 5.01.111
you should in all sense be much bound to him, 5.01.136
for, as i hear, he was much bound for you. 5.01.137
since you do take it, love, so much at heart. 5.01.145
what man is there so much unreasonable, | if you 5.01.203
would not let ingratitude | so much besmear it. 5.01.219
on his dunghills are as much bound to him as i. AYL 1.01. 16 P
and, as much as in him lies, mines my gentility 1.01. 20 P
i have as much of my father in me as you, albeit 1.01. 49 P
and indeed so much in the heart of the world, 1.01.168 P
fair princess, you have lost much good sport. 1.02. 99 P
wherein i confess me much guilty to deny so fair 1.02.184 P
i rest much bounden to you; 1.02.286
never so much as in a thought unborn | did i 1.03. 51
mistake me not so much | to think my poverty is 1.03. 64
fool, | much marked of the melancholy jaques, 2.01. 41
your daughter and her cousin much commend | the 2.02. 12
that cannot so much as a blossom yield | in lieu 2.03. 64
shepherd's passion | is much upon my fashion. 2.04. 61
here's a young maid with travel much oppressed, 2.04. 74
plenty in it, it goes much against my stomach. 3.02. 21 P
narrow–mouth'd bottle, either too much at once, 3.02.201 P
but are you so much in love as your rhymes speak 3.02.396 P
neither rhyme nor reason can express how much. 3.02.399 P
and by how much defense is better than no skill, 3.03. 62 P
by so much is a horn more precious than to want. 3.03. 62 P
duke yesterday, and had much question with him. 3.04. 35 P
then, to have seen much, and to have nothing, is 4.01. 23 P
then, can one desire too much of a good thing? 4.01.123 P
my friends told me as much, and i thought no 4.01.184 P
and here much orlando! 4.03. 2 P
yet heard too much of phebe's cruelty. 4.03. 38
we that have good wits have much to answer for; 5.01. 11 P
by so much the more shall i to–morrow be at the 5.02. 45 P
by how much i shall think my brother happy in 5.02. 46 P
youth, you have done me much ungentleness, | to 5.02. 77
much virtue in if. 5.04.103 P
there is much matter to be heard and learn'd. 5.04.185
men, to like as much of this play as please you; ep 13 P
hand, | wherein your cunning can assist me much. SHR in.1. 92
'tis much. in.2. 116
seeing too much sadness hath congeal'd your in.2. 132
but th' art too much my friend, | and i'll not 1.02. 63
incredible to believe | how much she loves me. 2.01.307
my land amounts not to so much in all. 2.01.373
and twice as much, what e'er thou off'rest next. 2.01.380
your lecture shall have leisure for as much. 3.01. 8
much more a shrew of /thy impatient humor. 3.02. 29
it skills not much, we'll fit him to our turn — 3.02.132
and as much news as wilt thou. 4.01. 41 P
fellow, you — and thus much for greeting. 4.01.112 P
as much as an apple doth an oyster, and all one. 4.02.101 P
much good do it unto thy gentle heart! 4.03. 51
that with your strange encounter much amaz'd me, 4.05. 54
i'll venture so much of my hawk or hound, | but 5.02. 72
hound, | but twenty times so much upon my wife. 5.02. 73
mother, your mistress, | and make much of her. AWW 1.01. 77
virginity breeds mites, much like a cheese, 1.01.141 P
and the principal itself not much the worse. 1.01.149 P
you go so much backward when you fight. 1.01.200 P
it much repairs me | to talk of your good father 1.02. 30
he was much fam'd. 1.02. 71
make title to as much love as she finds. 1.03.103 P
this is not much. 2.02. 66
not much commendation to them. 2.02. 67 P
not much employment for you. you understand me? 2.02. 68 P
profitable, and much fool may you find in you, 2.04. 35 P
therefore am i found | so much unsettled. 2.05. 63
something, and scarce so much; 2.05. 83
whose great decision hath much blood let forth 3.01. 3
therefore we marvel much our cousin france 3.01. 7
lady, | the fellow has a deal of that too much, 3.02. 90
that too much, | which holds him much to have. 3.02. 91
you did never lack advice so much | as letting 3.04. 19
hearing so much, will speed her foot again, 3.04. 37
if he were honester | he were much goodlier. 3.05. 80
he has much worthy blame laid upon him for 4.03. 6 P
but women were that had receiv'd so much shame, 4.03.327 P
sir, i have not much skill in /grass. 4.05. 21 P
that's gone made himself much sport out of him. 4.05. 65 P
with very much content, my lord, and i wish it 4.05. 78 P
and our esteem | was made much poorer by it; 5.03. 2
sir, much like | the same upon your finger. 5.03.225
i would not so much as make water but in a TN 1.03.130 P
you, cesario, you are like to be much advanc'd; 1.04. 2 P
that's as much to say as i wear not motley in my 1.05. 56 P
a young gentleman much desires to speak with you 1.05.100 P
he takes on him to understand so much, and 1.05.141 P
doctrine, and much may be said of it. 1.05.222 P
you might do much. | what is your parentage? 1.05.276
though it was said she much resembled me, was 2.01. 25 P
indeed so much, | that methought her eyes had 2.02. 19
wherein the pregnant enemy does much. 2.02. 28
and i (poor monster) fond as much on him; 2.02. 34
this is much credit to you. 2.03.108 P
to–day with my lady, she is much out of quiet. 2.03.133 P
methought it did relieve my passion much, | more 2.04. 4
the lady olivia's father took much delight in. 2.04. 12 P
no woman's heart | so big, to hold so much; 2.04. 96
as hungry as the sea, | and can digest as much. 2.04.101
for still we prove | much in our vows, but 2.04.118
how much the better | to fall before the lion 3.01.128
and you find so much blood in his liver as will 3.02. 61 P
(though so much | as might have drawn one to a 3.03. 6
i have said too much unto a heart of stone, 3.04.201
that with me which with as much safety you might 3.04.249 P
i shall be much bound to you for't. 3.04.270 P
i care not who knows so much of my mettle. 3.04.272 P
make me tell them how much i lack of a man. 3.04.303 P
me | much more for what i cannot do for you 3.04.336
my having is not much; 3.04.345
i will be so much a sinner to be a double–dealer 5.01. 34 P
little faith, though thou hast too much fear. 5.01.171
they say, poor gentleman, he's much distract. 5.01.280

so it skills not much when they are deliver'd. 5.01.288 P
which i doubt not but to do myself much right, 5.01.308 P
but to do myself much right, or you much shame. 5.01.308 P
this savors not much of distraction. 5.01.314
him, | so much against the mettle of your sex, 5.01.322
though, i confess, much like the character; 5.01.346
as if you held a brow of much distraction. WT 1.02.149
there have been | (or i am much deceiv'd) 1.02.191
you had much ado to make his anchor hold, | when 1.02.213
contrary and falling | a lip of much contempt, 1.02.373
so that there be not | too much hair there, but 2.01. 10
of me, yet you | have too much blood in him. 2.01. 58
in the world, | he were as much more villain: 2.01. 80
for a worthy lady, | and one who much i honor. 2.02. 6
the queen receives | much comfort in't; 2.02. 26
at least thus much: 2.03.165
the temple much surpassing | the common praise 3.01. 2
our wife, and one | of us too much belov'd. 3.02. 4
i have too much believ'd mine own suspicion. 3.02.151
nor was't much | thou wouldst have poison'd good 3.02.187
thou canst not speak too much, i have deserv'd 3.02.215
i have show'd too much | the rashness of a woman 3.02.220
which i receive much better | than to be pitied 3.02.233
affrighted much, | i did in time collect myself 3.03. 37
from the gentleman and how much he hath eaten. 3.03.130 P
not enough consider'd (as too much i cannot), to 4.02. 18 P
he is of late much retir'd from court and is 4.02. 31 P
i have consider'd so much, camillo, and with 4.02. 34 P
sweet sir, much better than i was: 4.03.111 P
here has been too much homely foolery already. 4.04.333 P
he's simple, and tells much. 4.04.345
i was not much afeard; 4.04.442
king, my master, whom | i so much thirst to see. 4.04.513
had been the dearer by i know how much an ounce. 4.04.705 P
i'll make it as much more, and leave this young 4.04.808 P
i will give you as much as this old man does 4.04.821 P
which was so much | that heirless it hath made 5.01. 9
pains, much less | th' adventure of her person? 5.01.155
my liege, | your eye hath too much youth in't. 5.01.225
has not only his innocence (which seems much) to 5.02. 65 P
be), who began to be much sea–sick, and himself 5.02.118 P
not without much content | in many singularities 5.03. 11
hermione was not so much wrinkled, nothing | so 5.03. 28
o, not by much. 5.03. 29
so much the more our carver's excellence, 5.03. 30
so much to my good comfort as it is | now 5.03. 33
no sorrow | but kill'd itself much sooner. 5.03. 53
pow'r | to take off so much grief from you as he 5.03. 55
strong possession much more than your right, JN 1.01. 40
so much my conscience whispers in your ear, 1.01. 42
your brother did employ my father much — 1.01. 96
how much unlook'd for is this expedition! 2.01. 79
by how much unexpected, by so much | we must 2.01. 80
by so much | we must awake endeavor for defense, 2.01. 80
who painfully with much expedient march | have 2.01.223
much work for tears in many an english mother, 2.01.303
up | her presence would have interrupted much. 2.01.542
from the mouth of england | add thus much more, 3.01.153
o my gentle hubert, | we owe thee much! 3.03. 20
i am much bounden to your majesty. 3.03. 29
strange to think how much king john hath lost 3.04.121
did nor never shall | so much as frown on you? 4.01. 58
much danger do i undergo for thee. 4.01.133
face | of plain old form is much disfigured, 4.02. 22
/doth show the mood of a much troubled breast, 4.02. 73
is much more general than these lines import. 4.03. 17
return | till my attempt so much be glorified 5.02.111
thou mayst befriend me so much as to think | i 5.06. 10
i do not ask you much, | i beg cold comfort; 5.07. 41
it seems you know not then so much as we. 5.07. 81
if guilty dread have left thee so much strength R2 1.01. 73
us | so much as of a thought of ill in him. 1.01. 86
as much good stay with thee as go with me! 1.02. 57
so much for that. 2.01.155
madam, your majesty is too much sad. 2.02. 1
by so much fills their hearts with deadly hate. 2.02.131
hath very much beguil'd | the tediousness and 2.03. 11
of much less value is my company | than your 2.03. 19
the noble duke hath been too much abused. 2.03.137
with too much urging your pernicious lives, 3.01. 4
this and much more, much more than twice all 3.01. 28
and much more, much more than twice all this, 3.01. 28
and, till so much blood thither come again, 3.02. 78
go signify as much, while here we march | upon 3.03. 49
with too much riches it confound itself; 3.04. 60
amongst much other talk, that very time, | i 4.01. 14
shall i so much dishonor my fair stars | on 4.01. 21
even so, or with much more contempt, men's eyes 5.02. 27
with much ado (at length) have gotten leave | to 5.05. 74
not be | without much shame retold or spoken of. 1H4 1.01. 46
not so much as will serve to be prologue to an 1.02. 20 P
thou hast done much harm upon me, hal, god 1.02. 91 P
by how much better than my word i am, | by so 1.02.210
i am, | by so much shall i falsify men's hopes, 1.02.211
arms, | which now we hold at much uncertainty. 1.03.299
got with much ease. 2.02.104
thou hast lost much honor that thou wert not 2.04. 20 P
forsooth, five years, and as much as to — 2.04. 42 P
in barbary, sir, it cannot come to so much. 2.04. 75 P
give him as much as will make him a royal man, 2.04.290 P
play, i have much to say in the behalf of that 2.04.484 P
gelding the opposed continent as much | as on 3.01.109
an edge, | nothing so much as mincing poetry. 3.01.132
i'll give thrice so much land | to any 3.01.135
run mad, | so much she doteth on her mortimer. 3.01.144
little | more than a little is by much too much. 3.02. 73
little | more than a little is by much too much. 3.02. 73
frowns, | to show how much thou art degenerate. 3.02.128
and god forgive them that so much have sway'd 3.02.130
thence | he was much fear'd by his physicians. 4.01. 24
i wonder much, | being men of such great leading 4.03. 16
if you knew | how much they do import, you would 4.04. 5
hope, | so much misconstrued in his wantonness. 5.02. 68
harry, withdraw thyself, thou bleedest too much. 5.04. 2
they did me too much injury | that ever said i 5.04. 51
ill–weav'd ambition, how much art thou shrunk! 5.04. 88
of thee | if i were much in love with vanity! 5.04.106
it hath it original from much grief, from study, 2H4 1.02.115 P
much smaller than the smallest of his thoughts, 1.03. 30
to us no more, nay, not so much, lord bardolph, 1.03. 69
been so lewd and so much engraff'd to falstaff. 2.02. 63 P
misuses thy favors so much that he swears thou 2.02.128 P
by yea and no, which is as much as to say, as 2.02.131 P
i' faith, you have drunk too much canaries, and 2.04. 26 P
much! 2.04.133 P
i feel me much to blame | so idly to profane the 2.04.361
him well, and betted much money on his head. 3.02. 45 P
so indeed, but much of the father's substance! 3.02.130 P
sir, i did not care, for mine own part, so much. 3.02.227 P
off | that might so much as think you enemies. 4.01.144
you are too shallow, hastings, much too shallow, 4.02. 50
so much the worse, if your own rule be true. 4.02. 86
fame o'ershine you as much as the full moon doth 4.03. 52 P
come near me, now i am much ill. 4.04.111
his eye is hollow, and he changes much. 4.05. 6
he alt'red much upon the hearing it. 4.05. 13
not so much noise, my lords. 4.05. 16
it is much that a lie with a slight oath and a 5.01. 81 P
argument | is all too heavy to admit much talk. 5.02. 24
a son, | hear your own dignity so much profan'd, 5.02. 93
the mass, i have drunk too much sack at supper. 5.03. 13 P
if you be not too much cloy'd with fat meat, our ep 27 P
as much as would maintain, to the king's honor, H5 1.01. 12
did contend | without much fall of blood, whose 1.02. 25
says that you savor too much of your youth, 1.02.250
that's mercy, but too much security. 2.02. 44
him life | after the taste of much correction. 2.02. 51
your too much love and care of me | are heavy 2.02. 52
those papers that you lose | so much complexion? 2.02. 73
you are too much mistaken in this king. 2.04. 30
witness our too much memorable shame | when 2.04. 53
which makes much against my manhood, if i should 3.02. 49 P
i will verify as much in his beard. 3.02. 71 P
so much my office. 3.06.136 P
though 'tis no wisdom to confess so much | unto 3.06.143
my people are with sickness much enfeebled, | my 3.06.145
by how much "a fool's bolt is soon shot." 3.07.121 P
we shall much disgrace | with four or five most 4.pr. 49
there is much care and valor in this welshman. 4.01. 84
for our approach shall so much dare the field, 4.02. 36
stopp'd, | but i had not so much of man in me, 4.06. 30
much more, and much more cause, | did they this 5.pr. 34
much more, and much more cause, | did they this 5.pr. 34
much good do you, scald knave, heartily. 5.01. 53 P
the kingdom as to speak so much more french. 5.02.185 P
must needs be granted to be much at one. 5.02.192 P
kate, dost thou understand thus much english? 5.02.193 P
england ne'er lost a king of so much worth. 1H6 1.01. 7
us look in, the sight will much delight thee. 1.04. 62
coward of france, how much he wrongs his fame, 2.01. 16
appear | how much in duty i am bound to both. 2.01. 37
that now our loss might be ten times so much? 2.01. 53
so much applauded through the realm of france? 2.02. 36
so much fear'd abroad | that with his name the 2.03. 16
or been reguerdon'd with so much as thanks, 3.04. 23
much more a knight, a captain, and a leader. 4.01. 32
much less to take occasion from their mouths 4.01.130
'tis much, when sceptres are in children's hands 4.01.192
o, too much folly is it, well i wot, | to hazard 4.06. 32
it shall be so, disdain they ne'er so much. 5.03. 98
detract so much from that prerogative | as to be 5.04.142
not all these lords do vex me half so much | as 2H6 1.03. 75
i thought as much, he would be above the clouds. 2.01. 15
my master, he hath learnt so much fence already. 2.03. 78 P
it serves you well, my lord, to say so much. 3.01.119
not resolute, except so much were done, | for 3.01.267
i thank thee, /meg, these words content me much. 3.02. 26
if ever lady wrong'd her lord so much, | thy 3.02.211
and so much shall you give, or off goes yours. 4.01. 17
what, think you much to pay two thousand crowns, 4.01. 18
which is as much to say as, let the magistrates 4.02. 17 P
i am able to endure much. 4.02. 56 P
thou wouldst not have mourn'd so much for me. 4.04. 24
how much thou wrong'st me, heaven be my judge. 4.10. 76
that is too much presumption on thy part; 5.01. 38
but thou mistakes me much to think i do. 5.01.130
thou hast spoke too much already; get thee gone. 3H6 1.01.258
do not honor him so much | to prick thy finger, 1.04. 54
o, speak no more, for i have heard too much. 2.01. 48
this too much lenity | and harmful pity must be 2.02. 9
you said so much before, and yet you fled. 2.02.106
much is your sorrow; 2.05.112
mine ten times so much. 2.05.112
sad–hearted men, much overgone with care, | here 2.05.123
and what makes robbers bold but too much lenity? 2.06. 22
and much effuse of blood doth make me faint. 2.06. 28
win him, | for she's a woman to be pitied much. 3.01. 36
and would you not do much to do them good? 3.02. 38
plies her hard, and much rain wears the marble. 3.02. 50
what love, think'st thou, i sue so much to get? 3.02. 61
by so much is the wonder in extremes. 3.02.115
my eye's too quick, my heart o'erweens too much, 3.02.144
i told your majesty as much before: 3.03.179
so much his friend, ay, his unfeigned friend, 3.03.202
i hear, yet say not much, but think the more. 4.01. 83
make much of him, my lords, for this is he 4.06. 75
nor much oppress'd them with great subsidies, 4.08. 45
nor forward of revenge, though they much err'd. 4.08. 46
and swell so much the higher by their ebb. 4.08. 56
give more strength to that which hath too much, 5.04. 9
hold, richard, hold, for we have done too much. 5.05. 43
by heaven, i will not do thee so much ease. 5.05. 72
ay, and for much more slaughter after this. 5.06. 59
as much unto my good lord chamberlain! R3 1.01.123
his, | and have prevail'd as much on him as you. 1.01.131
not all so much for love | as for another secret 1.01.157
with all my heart, and much it joys me too, | to 1.02.219
ay, and much better blood than his or thine. 1.03.125
york's dread curse prevail so much with heaven 1.03.190
it touches you, my lord, as much as me. 1.03.261
ay, and much more; 1.03.262
she hath had too much wrong, and i repent | my 1.03.306
of you | had so much grace to put it in my mind. 2.01.121
so much interest have /i in thy sorrow | as i 2.02. 47
god is much displeas'd | that you take with 2.02. 89
much more to be thus opposite with heaven, | for 2.02. 94
which would be so much the more dangerous, | by 2.02.126
by how much the estate is green and yet 2.02.127
which haply by much company might be urg'd; 2.02.137
i hope he is much grown since last i saw him. 2.04. 5
which by his death hath lost much majesty. 3.01.100
i'll signify so much unto him straight. 3.07. 70
at their beads, 'tis much to draw them thence, 3.07. 93
of birth, | yet so much is my poverty of spirit, 3.07.159
and much i need to help you, were there need: 3.07.166
as much to you, good sister! whither away? 4.01. 7
for it stands me much upon | to stop all hopes 4.02. 58
yet much less spirit to curse | abides in me; 4.04.197
unless i have mista'en his colors much | (which 5.03. 35
much about cock–shut time, from troop to troop 5.03. 70
so much for that. 5.03. 85
life | felt so much cold as over shoes in snow? 5.03.326
wear it, enjoy it, and make much of it. 5.05. 7
th' interview | that swallowed so much treasure, H8 1.01.166
to as much end | as give a crutch to th' dead. 1.01.171
i am much too venturous | in tempting of your 1.02. 54
we cannot feel too little, hear too much. 1.02.128
which, being believ'd, | it was much like to do. 1.02.182
outgo | his father by as much as a performance 1.02.208
hold my thanks, | and save me so much talking. 1.04. 40
pray tell 'em thus much from me: 1.04. 77
i fear, too much. 1.04.101
much | he spoke, and learnedly, for life; 2.01. 27
this duke as much | they love and dote on; 2.01. 51
let me have it; | i do not talk much. 2.01.146
these sad thoughts that work too much upon him. 2.02. 57
how sad he looks! sure he is much afflicted. 2.02. 62
much joy and favor to you; 2.02.117
will, much better | she ne'er had known pomp! 2.03. 12
so much the more | must pity drop upon her. 2.03. 17
yea, as much | as you have done my truth. 2.04. 97
woman, much too weak | t' oppose your cunning. 2.04.106
i care not (so much i am happy | above a number) 3.01. 33
believe me, she has had much wrong. 3.01. 48
way to sorrow — | you have too much, good lady; 3.01. 57
'twill be much | both for your honor better and 3.01. 94
princes kiss obedience, | so much they love it; 3.01.163
now the time | gives way to us) i much fear. 3.02. 16
fellow, and hath ta'en much pain | in the king's 3.02. 72
how much, methinks, i could despise this man, 3.02.297
but, thus much, they are foul ones. 3.02.300
so much fairer | and spotless shall mine 3.02.300
a load would sink a navy — too much honor. 3.02.383
a man in much esteem with th' king, and truly 4.01.109
undoubtedly | was fashion'd to much honor. 4.02. 50
how much her grace is alter'd on the sudden? 4.02. 96
who grieves much for your weakness, and by me 4.02.117
to your ear | much weightier than this work. 5.01. 18
they had parted so much honesty among 'em — 5.02. 28
this is too much. | forbear for shame, my lords. 5.02.120
how much more is his life in value with him! 5.02.143
how much are we bound to heaven | in daily 5.02.149
i will say thus much for him, if a prince | may 5.02.190
'tis as much impossible — | unless we sweep 'em 5.03. 12
as much as one sound cudgel of four foot | (you 5.03. 19
shall this lady, | when she has so much english. 5.04. 14
and you, good brethren, i am much beholding; 5.04. 70
i have receiv'd much honor by your presence, 5.04. 71
thou dost not speak so much. TRO 1.01. 65
then troilus should have too much: 1.02.101 P
three pound, lift as much as his brother hector. 1.02.116 P
they laugh'd not so much at the hair as at his 1.02.154 P
even so much. 1.03.283
combat, | yet in the trial much opinion dwells; 1.03.336
has not so much wit — 2.01. 78 P
i shall speak as much as thou afterwards. 2.01.111 P
but superficially, not much | unlike young men, 2.02.165
not wrong, | but makes it much more heavy. 2.02.188
he is much sorry | if any thing more than your 2.03.107
much attribute he hath, and much the reason 2.03.116
and much the reason | why we ascribe it to him; 2.03.116
add, | that if he overhold his price so much, 2.03.133
is he so much? 2.03.144 P
no less noble, much more gentle, and altogether 2.03.149 P
my lord, you feed too much on this dislike. 2.03.225
i fear it much, and i do fear besides | that i 3.02. 26
if i confess much, you will play the tyrant. 3.02.119
but till now not so much | but i might master it 3.02.120
how much in having, or without or in, | i cannot 3.03. 97
though in and of him there be much consisting, 3.03.116
i was much rapt in this, | and apprehended here 3.03.123
and better would it fit achilles much | to throw 3.03.207
ay, and perhaps receive much honor by him. 3.03.226
i fear | we shall be much unwelcome. 4.01. 46
it doth import him much to speak with me. 4.02. 50
so much for nestor. 4.05. 23
shall i, sweet lord, be bound to you so much, 4.05.284
with too much blood and too little brain, these 5.01. 48 P
if with too much brain and too little blood they 5.01. 49 P
quails, but he has not so much brain as ear–wax; 5.01. 52 P
as much /as i do cressid love, | so much by 5.02.167
love, | so much by weight hate i her diomed. 5.02.168
when was my lord so much ungently temper'd | to 5.03. 1
he does, and does so much | that proof is call'd 5.05. 28
i would have been much more a fresher man, | had 5.06. 20
the volsces have much corn; COR 1.01.249
i wish you much mirth. 1.03.110 P
they do disdain us much beyond our thoughts, 1.04. 26
are too infant–like for doing much alone. 2.01. 38 P
so do i too, if it be not too much. 2.01.122 P
be silent and not confess so much were a kind of 2.02. 31 P
i will make much of your voices, and so trouble 2.03.109 P
you show too much of that | for which the people 3.01. 52
to no further harm | than so much loss of time. 3.01.283
to your fortune and | the hazard of much blood. 3.02. 61
for that he has | (as much as in him lies) from 3.03. 94
done, and sav'd | your husband so much sweat. 4.01. 19
yet, martius, that was much. 4.05.147
is not much miss'd but with his friends; 4.06. 13
and might have been much better, if | he could 4.06. 16
you that stood so much | upon the voice of 4.06. 96
lip | and hum at good cominius much unhearts me. 5.01. 49
shall poison rather | than pity note how much. 5.02. 87
'tis a spell, you see, of much power. 5.02. 96 P

only thus much i give your grace to know: TIT 1.01.413
full well shalt thou perceive how much i dare. 2.01. 44
nor would your noble mother for much more | be 2.01. 51
i had none, | to bury so much gold under a tree, 2.03. 2
or, wanting strength to do thee so much good, 2.03.238
do thou so much as dig the grave for him: 2.03.270
let's kiss and part, for we have much to do. 3.01.287
see, lucius, see, how much she makes of thee; 4.01. 10
how much money must i have? 4.04. 46 P
revenge, to do | as much as ever coriolanus did. 4.04. 68
'tis he the common people love so much; 4.04. 73
fie, publius, fie, thou art too much deceiv'd. 5.02.155
but soft, methinks i do digress too much, 5.03.116
i'll know his grievance, or be much denied. ROM 1.01.157
here's much to do with hate, but more with love. 1.01.175
doth add more grief to too much of mine own. 1.01.189
i was your mother much upon these years | that 1.03. 72
and 'tis much pride | for fair without the fair 1.03. 89
which, once untangled, much misfortune bodes. 1.04. 91
'tis not so much, 'tis not so much: 1.05. 34
'tis not so much, 'tis not so much: 1.05. 34
good pilgrim, you do wrong your hand too much, 1.05. 97
and she as much in love, her means much less 2.pr. 11
her means much less | to meet her new–beloved 2.pr. 11
yet i should kill thee with much cherishing. 2.02.183
how much salt water thrown away in waste, | to 2.03. 71
/pardon–me's, who stand so much on the new form, 2.04. 34 P
that's as much as to say, such a case as yours 2.04. 52 P
a hare that is hoar | is too much for a score, 2.04.138
heart, and, i' faith, i will tell her as much. 2.04.174 P
as much to him, else is his thanks too much. 2.06. 23
as much to him, else is his thanks too much. 2.06. 23
thee | doth much excuse the appertaining rage 3.01. 63
courage, man, the hurt cannot be much. 3.01. 95
more terror in his look, | much more than death. 3.03. 14
being our kinsman, if we revel much: 3.04. 26
by this count i shall be much in years | ere i 3.05. 46
some grief shows much of love, | but much of 3.05. 72
but much of grief shows still some want of wit. 3.05. 73
girl, thou weep'st not so much for his death, 3.05. 78
child, | but now i see this one is one too much, 3.05.166
well, thou hast comforted me marvellous much. 3.05.230
that she do give her sorrow so much sway; 4.01. 10
which, too much minded by herself alone, | may 4.01. 13
poor soul, thy face is much abus'd with tears. 4.01. 29
we shall be much unfurnish'd for this time. 4.02. 10
all our whole city is much bound to him. 4.02. 32
and the neglecting it | may do much danger. 5.02. 20
she will beshrew me much that romeo | hath had 5.02. 26
o, much i fear some ill unthrifty thing. 5.03.136
of nothing so much as that i am not like timon. TIM 1.01.189 P
does not become a man, 'tis much to blame. 1.02. 27
there's much example for't: 1.02. 46 P
much good dich thy good heart, apemantus! 1.02. 72 P
provided that i shall have much help from you: 1.02. 89 P
i promise you, my lord, you mov'd me much. 1.02.113
much! 1.02.114 P
you have done our pleasures much grace, fair 1.02.146
i must entreat you honor me so much | as to 1.02.169
you do yourselves | much wrong, you bate too 1.02.206
wrong, you bate too much of your own merits. 1.02.206
as much foolery as i have, so much wit thou 2.02.116 P
foolery as i have, so much wit thou lack'st. 2.02.117 P
you have bid me | return so much, i have shook 2.02.137
is't possible the world should so much differ, 3.01. 46
i am so much endear'd to that lord; 3.02. 31 P
return'd to him, | so much i love his heart. 3.02. 85
h'as much disgrac'd me in't, i'm angry at him, 3.03. 13
so much? 3.04. 9
'tis much deep, and it should seem by th' sum 3.04. 30
we attend his lordship; pray signify so much. 3.04. 38 P
some other hour, i should derive much from't; 3.04. 69 P
temper has forsook him, he's much out of health, 3.04. 72 P
there's not so much left to furnish out | a 3.04.114
nothing emboldens sin so much as mercy. 3.05. 3
he has made too much plenty with /'em. 3.05. 66
when man's worst sin is, he does too much good! 4.02. 39
thus much of this will make | black white, foul 4.03. 28
they mock'd thee for too much curiosity; 4.03.303 P
we are not thieves, but men that much do want. 4.03.415
your greatest want is, you want much of meat. 4.03.416
neither wish i | you take much pains to mend. 5.01. 89
we stand much hazard if they bring not timon. 5.02. 5
then, brutus, i have much mistook your passion, JC 1.02. 48
and it is very much lamented, brutus, | that you 1.02. 55
have struck but thus much show of fire from 1.02.177
a lean and hungry look, | he thinks too much; 1.02.195
he reads much, | he is a great observer, and he 1.02.201
but wherefore did you so much tempt the heavens? 1.03. 53
give so much light that i may read by them. 2.01. 45
and that were much he should, for he is given 2.01.188
to sports, to wildness, and much company. 2.01.189
impatience | which seem'd too much enkindled; 2.01.249
and could it work so much upon your shape | as 2.01.253
as it hath much prevail'd on your condition, | i 2.01.254
caesar was ne'er so much your enemy | as that 2.02.112
i know will be, much that i fear may chance. 2.04. 32
but yet have i a mind | that fears him much; 3.01.145
know you how much the people may be mov'd | by 3.01.234
methinks there is much reason in his sayings. 3.02.108
that's as much as to say, they are fools that 3.03. 17 P
are much condemn'd to have an itching palm, | to 4.03. 10
for so much trash as may be grasped thus? 4.03. 26
do not presume too much upon my love, | i may do 4.03. 63
who, much enforced, shows a hasty spark, | and 4.03.112
do you confess so much? give me your hand. 4.03.117
i cannot drink too much of brutus' love. 4.03.162
i have as much of this in art as you, | but yet 4.03.194
bear with me, good boy, i am much forgetful. 4.03.255
i trouble thee too much, but thou art willing. 4.03.259
i will not do thee so much wrong to wake thee. 4.03.270
there is so much that thou wilt kill me straight 5.04. 13
not so happy, yet much happier. MAC 1.03. 66
you were, you would | be so much more the man. 1.07. 51
therefore much drink may be said to be an 2.03. 31 P
'tis much he dares, | and, to that dauntless 3.01. 50
well, let's away, and say how much is done. 3.03. 22
if much you note him, | you shall offend him and 3.04. 55

if your art | can tell so much, shall banquo's 4.01.102
i dare not speak much further, | but cruel are 4.02. 17
i am so much a fool, should i stay longer, | it 4.02. 28
the old man to have had so much blood in him? 5.01. 40 P
or so much as it needs | to dew the sovereign 5.02. 29
sooth, | i care not if thou dost for me as much. 5.05. 40
my soul is too much charg'd | with blood of 5.08. 5
for this relief much thanks. HAM 1.01. 8
so much for him. 1.02. 25
time of meeting, | thus much the business is: 1.02. 27
not so, my lord, i am too much in the sun. 1.02. 67
nay, not so much, not two. 1.02.138
it would have much amaz'd you. 1.02.235
believe so much in him, that he is young, | and 1.03.124
habit, that too much o'er–leavens | the form of 1.04. 29
but there is, horatio, | and much offense too. 1.05.137
moreover that we much did long to see you, | the 2.02. 2
him | so much from th' understanding of himself, 2.02. 9
gather | so much as from occasion you may glean, 2.02. 16
good gentlemen, he hath much talk'd of you, 2.02. 19
you | to show us so much gentry and good will 2.02. 22
instantly to visit | my too much changed son. 2.02. 36
my youth i suff'red much extremity for love — 2.02.190 P
set down with as much modesty as cunning. 2.02.440 P
sweet, and by very much more handsome than fine. 2.02.445 P
god's bodkin, man, much better: 2.02.529 P
but with much forcing of his disposition. 3.01. 12
and it doth much content me | to hear him so 3.01. 24
'tis too much prov'd — that with devotion's 3.01. 46
nor do not saw the air too much with your hand, 3.02. 4 P
something too much of this. 3.02. 74
the lady doth protest too much, methinks. 3.02.230 P
and there is much music, excellent voice, in 3.02.368 P
but much more | that spirit upon whose weal 3.03. 13
screen'd and stood between | much heat and him. 3.04. 4
hamlet, thou hast thy father much offended. 3.04. 9
mother, you have my father much offended. 3.04. 10
but so much was our love, | we would not 4.01. 19
this is th' imposthume of much wealth and peace, 4.04. 27
she speaks much of her father, says she hears 4.05. 4
though nothing sure, yet much unhappily. 4.05. 13
last, and as much containing as all these, | her 4.05. 87
thou to me with as much speed as thou wouldest 4.06. 24 P
yet are they much too light for the /bore of the 4.06. 26 P
for england, of them i have much to tell thee. 4.06. 29 P
which may to you, perhaps, seem much unsinow'd, 4.07. 10
you have been talk'd of since your travel much, 4.07. 71
to a plurisy, | dies in his own too much. 4.07.118
too much of water hast thou, poor ophelia, | and 4.07.185
how much i had to do to calm his rage! 4.07.192
so much for this, sir, now shall you see the 5.02. 1
and labor'd much | how to forget that learning, 5.02. 34
he hath much land, and fertile; 5.02. 85 P
faith, if you did, it would not much approve me. 5.02.135 P
becomes the field, but here shows much amiss. 5.02.402
as much as child e'er lov'd, or father found; LR 1.01. 59
beyond all manner of so much i love you. 1.01. 61
and for so much as i have perus'd, i find it not 1.02. 38 P
into france, sir, the fool hath much pin'd away. 1.04. 74 P
tell him, so much the rent of his land comes to. 1.04.134 P
you are too much of late i' th' frown. 1.04.190 P
is much o' th' savor | of other your new pranks. 1.04.237
/you are much more /attax'd for want of wisdom 1.04.343
doth this instant | so much commend itself, you 2.01.114
natures of such deep trust we shall much need; 2.01.115
out of my dialect, which you discommend so much. 2.02.110 P
my sister may receive it much more worse | to 2.02.148
what's he that hath so much thy place mistook 2.04. 12
own disorders | deserv'd much less advancement. 2.04.200
father, fool me not so much | to bear it tamely; 2.04.275
for confirmation that i am much more | than my 3.01. 44
thou think'st 'tis much that this contentious 3.04. 6
my tears begin to take his part so much, | they 3.06. 60
madam, with much ado; 4.05. 2
i'll love thee much — | let me unseal the 4.05. 21
and when your mistress hears thus much from you, 4.05. 34
y' are much deceiv'd. 4.06. 9
and more, much more, the time will bring it out. 5.03.164
we that are young | shall never see so much, nor 5.03.327
i take it much unkindly | that thou, iago, who OTH 1.01. 1
wears out his time, much like his master's ass, 1.01. 47
of this, | that the magnifico is much belov'd, 1.02. 12
and so much duty as my mother show'd | to you, 1.03.186
so much i challenge that i may profess | due to 1.03.188
would she give you so much of her lips | as of 2.01.100
in faith, too much; 2.01.103
it is too much of joy. 2.01.197
his worthiness | does challenge much respect. 2.01.211
so much was his pleasure should be proclaim'd. 2.02. 7 P
and would do much | to cure him of this evil. 2.03.143
and by how much she strives to do him good, 2.03.358
i shall have so much experience for my pains; 2.03.367 P
i am much bound to you. 3.01. 55
part — to have so much to do | to bring him in! 3.03. 73
/by'r /lady, i could do much — 3.03. 74
'twas witchcraft — but i am much to blame. 3.03.211
you of your pardon | for too much loving you. 3.03.213
no, not much mov'd: 3.03.224
sees and knows more, much more, than he unfolds. 3.03.243
much will be seen in that. 3.03.252
into the vale of years (yet that's not much), 3.03.266
i swear 'tis better to be much abus'd | than but 3.03.336
much castigation, exercise devout, | for here's 3.04. 41
beshrew me much, emilia, | i was (unhandsome 3.04.150
i would do much | t' atone them, for the love i 4.01.232
'tis very much, | make her amends; 4.01.243
he is much chang'd. 4.01.268
she's a simple bawd | that cannot say as much. 4.02. 21
unkindness may do much, | and his unkindness may 4.02.159
/faith, i have heard too much; 4.02.182 P
i have much to do | but to go hang my head all 4.03. 31
there stand i in much peril. 5.01. 21
any cunning cruelty | that can torment him much, 5.02.334
if it be love indeed, tell me how much. ANT 1.01. 14
much is breeding, | which, like the courser's 1.02.192
and men's reports | give him much wrong'd. 1.04. 40
soldier, that thy cheek | so much as lank'd not. 1.04. 71
you think of him too much. 1.05. 6

how much unlike art thou mark antony! 1.05. 35
so much uncurbable her garboils, caesar, | made 2.02. 67
i grieving grant | did you too much disquiet. 2.02. 70
which was as much | as to have ask'd him pardon. 2.02. 78
i do not much dislike the matter, but | the 2.02.111
we had much more monstrous matter of feast, 2.02.182 P
is shorter, | my purposes do draw me much about. 2.04. 8
me for what you make me do | seems much unequal. 2.05.101
and carry back to sicily much tall youth | that 2.06. 7
thou know'st | how much we do o'er–count thee. 2.06. 26
you have heard much. 2.06. 65
then so much have i heard; 2.06. 67
i never lov'd you much, but i ha' prais'd ye 2.06. 76
when you have well deserv'd ten times as much 2.06. 77
thou hast serv'd me with much faith; 2.07. 58
all, four days, | than drink so much in one. 2.07.103
i repent me much | that so i harried him. 3.03. 39
you did know | how much you were my conqueror, 3.11. 66
it much would please him, | that of his fortunes 3.13. 67
and make as much of me | as when mine empire was 4.02. 21
he gives me so much of mine own as i | will 5.02. 20
our care and pity is so much upon you, | that we 5.02.188
incur i know not | how much of his displeasure. CYM 1.01.103
no, faith; not so much as his patience. 1.02. 7 P
it was much like an argument that fell out last 1.04. 56 P
with five times so much conversation, i should 1.04.103 P
nor has no friends | so much as but to prop him? 1.05. 60
it seems, much loves | a gallian girl at home. 1.06. 65
but heavens know | some men are much to blame. 1.06. 77
in himself, 'tis much; 1.06. 79
you lay out too much pains | for purchasing but 2.03. 87
i am much sorry, sir, | you put me to forget a 2.03.104
they failing, | i must die much your debtor. 2.04. 8
likewise reap, | being, as it is, much spoke of. 2.04. 87
which swell'd so much that it did almost stretch 3.01. 49
use the sword of caesar | hath too much mangled, 3.01. 56
my youth i spent | much under him; 3.01. 70
lack humanity | so much as this fact comes to? 3.02. 17
madam, 's enough for you — and too much too. 3.02. 69
in simple and low things to prince it much 3.03. 85
strikes life into my speech and shows much more 3.03. 97
how much the quantity, the weight as much, | as 4.02. 17
how much the quantity, the weight as much, | as 4.02. 17
but envy much | thou hast robb'd me of this deed 4.02.158
the bird is dead | that we have made so much on. 4.02.198
must murther wives much better than themselves 5.01. 4
and happier much by his affliction made. 5.04.108
of meat, depart reeling with too much drink; 5.04.161 P
sorry that you have paid too much, and sorry 5.04.162 P
too much, and sorry that you are paid too much; 5.04.163 P
and so much | for my peculiar care. 5.05. 82
with | i know not how much more, should be 5.05.389
name, | being leo–natus, doth import so much. 5.05.445
please, | i cannot be much lower than my knees. PER 1.02. 47
sight, | and not so much to feed on as delight; 1.04. 29
i thought as much. 1.04. 62
said not i as much when i saw the porpas how he 2.01. 23 P
we are honor'd much by good simonides. 2.03. 20
wishing it so much blood unto your life. 2.03. 77
that's as much as you would be denied | of your 2.03.105
to you as much! 2.05. 25
but i much marvel that your lordship, having 3.02. 21
world so soon | to yield thee so much profit. 4.01. 4
we lost too much money this mart by being too 4.02. 4 P
we were never so much out of creatures. 4.02. 6 P
much less in blood than virtue, yet a princess 4.03. 7
much follow'd both, for both much money gi'n, TNK pr 2
much follow'd both, for both much money gi'n, pr 2
hast much more power on him | than ever he had 1.01. 87
though much unlike | you should be so 1.01.186
as much sorry | i should be such a suitor; 1.01.187
with much labor; 1.03. 34
concern us | much more than thebes is worth. 1.04. 33
something i may cast to you, not much. 2.01. 2 P
uses of this place | that all men hate so much? 2.02. 70
he has as much to please a woman in him | (if he 2.04. 9
he grieves much, | and me as much to see his 2.04. 27
much, | and me as much to see his misery. 2.04. 28
thus much for law or kindred! 2.04. 32
sir, we are much indebted to your travel, | nor 2.05. 30
no, not so much as kiss'd me; 2.06. 22
you have been well advertis'd | how much i dare; 3.01. 59
so much for that! 3.02. 19
if i priz'd life so much | as to deny my act; 3.02. 23
not much. 3.03. 25
i have put you | to too much pains, sir. 3.06. 18
that too much, fair cousin, | is but a debt to 3.06. 18
am i fall'n much away? 3.06. 66
man calls me traitor, | let me say thus much: 3.06.161
she sung much, but no sense; 4.01. 66
o, very much! 5.02. 2
a kind gentleman, and i am much bound to him. 5.02. 44
it is much better | i am not there. 5.03. 64
he much desires | to have some speech with you. 5.04. 84
which cannot choose but much advantage the poor STM II.C 71 P
should so much come too short of your great II.C 124
might turn our blood | to much corruption. III 14
'tis much to borrow, and i will not owe it; VEN 411
yet would my love to thee be still as much, 442
a wild bird being tam'd with too much handling, 560
she hath assay'd as much as may be prov'd. 608
with much ado the cold fault cleanly out; 694
the tyranny | of mad mischances and much misery: 738
grove, | musing the morning is so much o'erworn, 866
"how much a fool was i | to be of such a weak 1015
save sometime too much wonder of his eye, LUC 95
that cloy'd with much, he pineth still for more. 98
those that much covet are with gain so fond, 134
in having much, torments us with defect | of 151
she much amaz'd breaks ope her lock'd–up eyes, 446
with too much labor drowns for want of skill. 1099
sometime 'tis mad and too much talk affords. 1106
much like a press of people at a door, | throng 1301
for much imaginary work was there, | conceit 1422
to give her so much grief, and not a tongue. 1463
cannot be," quoth she, "that so much guile" — 1534
but soft, enough — too much, i fear — | lest PP 18.49

how much more praise deserv'd thy beauty's use, SON 2. 9
for thou art much too fair | to be death's 6.13
much liker than your painted counterfeit: 16. 8
or some fierce thing replete with too much rage, 23. 3
to the clear day with thy much clearer light, 43. 7
but that, so much of earth and water wrought, 44.11
o, how much more doth beauty beauteous seem | by 54. 1
o no, thy love, though much, is not so great, 61. 9
clay, | do not so much as my poor name rehearse, 71.11
shall profit thee, and much enrich thy book. 77.14
that thou in losing me shall win much glory. 88. 8
lest i (too much profane) should do it wrong, 89.11
thee | to make him much outlive a gilded tomb, 101.11
and more, much more than in my verse can sit, 103.13
that poor retention could not so much hold, 122. 9
lose all, and more, by paying too much rent, 125. 6
my tongue–tied patience with too much disdain, 140. 2
and so much less of shame in me remains | by how LC 188
by how much of me their reproach contains. 189
not one whose flame my heart so much as warmed, 191

MUCK 1 FR 0.0001 REL FR 1 V 0 P
as they were | the common muck of the world. COR 2.02.126

MUD 10 FR 0.0011 REL FR 9 V 1 P
the nine men's morris is fill'd up with mud, MND 2.01. 98
the purest spring is not so free from mud | as i 2H6 3.01.101
that would she not, | for all the mud in egypt. H8 2.03. 92
the spring whom you have stain'd with mud, TIT 5.02.170
is bred now of your mud by the operation of your ANT 2.07. 27 P
rather on nilus' mud | lay me stark–nak'd, and 5.02. 58
mud not the fountain that gave drink to thee, LUC 577
or toads infect fair founts with venom mud? 850
roses have thorns, and silver fountains mud, SON 35. 2
bidding them find their sepulchres in mud, LC 46

MUDDED 2 FR 0.0002 REL FR 2 V 0 P
sounded, | and with him there lie mudded. TMP 3.03.102
i wish | myself were mudded in that oozy bed 5.01.151

MUDDIED 3 FR 0.0003 REL FR 1 V 2 P
now, sir, muddied in fortune's mood, and smell AWW 5.02. 4 P
displeasure, and, as he says, is muddied withal. 5.02. 22 P
the people muddied, | thick and unwholesome in HAM 4.05. 81

MUDDY 12 FR 0.0013 REL FR 8 V 4 P
/shores | that now lie foul and muddy. TMP 5.01. 82
there empty it in the muddy ditch close by the WIV 3.03. 15 P
crystal is muddy. MND 3.02.139
but whilst this muddy vesture of decay | doth MV 5.01. 64
muddy, ill–seeming, thick, bereft of beauty, SHR 5.02.143
dost think i am so muddy, so unsettled, | to WT 1.02.325
from whence this stream through muddy passages R2 5.03. 62
farewell, you muddy knave. 1H4 2.01. 97 P
a pox damn you, you muddy rascal, is that all 2H4 2.04. 39 P
hang yourself, you muddy cunger, hang yourself! 2.04. 53 P
wretch from her melodious lay | to muddy death. HAM 4.07.183
i first appear, though rude, and raw, and muddy, TNK 3.05.122

MUDDY–METTLED 1 FR 0.0001 REL FR 1 V 0 P
a dull and muddy–mettled rascal, peak | like HAM 2.02.567

MUFFLE 3 FR 0.0003 REL FR 3 V 0 P
muffle your false love with some show of ERR 3.02. 8
and pluck it o'er your brows, muffle your face, WT 4.04.651
muffle me, night, a while. ROM 5.03. 21

MUFFLED 7 FR 0.0008 REL FR 6 V 1 P
what muffled fellow's that? MM 5.01.486
and will keep him muffled | till we do hear from AWW 4.01. 90
muffled! 4.03.116 P
the duke of suffolk muffled up in rags? 2H6 4.01. 46
alas that love, whose view is muffled still, ROM 1.01.171
is not that his steward muffled so? TIM 3.04. 41
blind muffled bawd! LUC 768

MUFFLER 4 FR 0.0004 REL FR 0 V 4 P
otherwise he might put on a hat, a muffler, and WIV 4.02. 71 P
there's her thrumm'd hat and her muffler too. 4.02. 79 P
i spy a great peard under his muffler. 4.02.194 P
is painted blind, with a muffler afore his eyes, H5 3.06. 31 P

MUFFLING 1 FR 0.0001 REL FR 1 V 0 P
and, in his mantle muffling up his face, | even JC 3.02.187

MUGS 1 FR 0.0001 REL FR 0 V 1 P
come, neighbor mugs, we'll call up the gentlemen 1H4 2.01. 44 P

MULBERRIES 3 FR 0.0003 REL FR 3 V 0 P
with purple grapes, green figs, and mulberries; MND 3.01.167
is gone to th' wood to gather mulberries. TNK 4.01. 68
would bring him mulberries and ripe–red cherries VEN 1103

MULBERRY 2 FR 0.0002 REL FR 2 V 0 P
and thisby, tarrying in mulberry shade, | his MND 5.01.148
now humble as the ripest mulberry | that will COR 3.02. 79

MULE *(also moile)*

MULE 3 FR 0.0003 REL FR 2 V 1 P
mouth and buy myself another of bajazeth's mule, AWW 4.01. 42 P
bare–headed plodded by my foot–cloth mule | and 2H6 4.01. 54
and grew so ill | he could not sit his mule. H8 4.02. 16

MULES 4 FR 0.0004 REL FR 4 V 0 P
which, like your asses, and your dogs and mules, MV 4.01. 91
either they must be dieted like mules | and have 1H6 1.02. 10
to 's power he would | have made them mules, COR 2.01.247
and at thy tent is now | unloading of his mules. ANT 4.06. 23

/MULETERS 1 FR 0.0001 REL FR 1 V 0 P
your mariners are /muleters, reapers, people ANT 3.07. 35

MULETERS 1 FR 0.0001 REL FR 1 V 0 P
base muleters of france! 1H6 3.02. 68

MULIER 2 FR 0.0002 REL FR 2 V 0 P
mollis aer, and mollis aer | we term it mulier; CYM 5.05.448
which mulier i divine | is this most constant 5.05.448

MULIERES 1 FR 0.0001 REL FR 1 V 0 P
"in terram salicam mulieres ne /succedant," H5 1.02. 38

MULITEUS 1 FR 0.0001 REL FR 1 V 0 P
far, one muliteus my countryman | his wife but TIT 4.02.152

MULL'D 1 FR 0.0001 REL FR 0 V 1 P
is a very apoplexy, lethargy, mull'd, deaf, COR 4.05.224 P

MULMUTIUS 2 FR 0.0002 REL FR 2 V 0 P
our ancestor was that mulmutius which | ordain'd CYM 3.01. 54
mulmutius made our laws, | who was the first of 3.01. 58

MULTIPLIED 3 FR 0.0003 REL FR 3 V 0 P
your grace's title shall be multiplied. 2H6 1.02. 73
although by his sight his sin be multiplied. 2.01. 69
how shall this bosom multiplied digest | the COR 3.01.131

MULTIPLY 1 FR 0.0001 REL FR 1 V 0 P
i multiply | with one "we thank you" many WT 1.02. 7

MULTIPLYING 4 FR 0.0004 REL FR 4 V 0 P
that knows the tinct and multiplying med'cine, AWW 5.03.102
your multiplying spawn how can he flatter — COR 2.02. 78
take thou that too, with multiplying bans! TIM 4.01. 34
to that | the multiplying villainies of nature MAC 1.02. 11

MULTIPOTENT 1 FR 0.0001 REL FR 1 V 0 P
by jove multipotent, | thou shouldst not bear TRO 4.05.129

MULTIS 1 FR 0.0001 REL FR 1 V 0 P
long tool, | cum multis aliis that make a dance. TNK 3.05.133

MULTITUDE 18 FR 0.0020 REL FR 13 V 5 P
which the rude multitude call the afternoon. LLL 5.01. 89 P
that many may be meant | by the fool multitude, MV 2.09. 26
appear | among the buzzing pleased multitude, 3.02.180
note | in the fair multitude of those her hairs! JN 3.04. 62
the still–discordant wav'ring multitude, | can 2H4 in 19
since they, so few, watch such a multitude. 1H6 1.01.161
see how the giddy multitude do point | and nod 2H6 2.04. 21
with the rude multitude till i return. 3.02.135
his army is a ragged multitude | of hinds and 4.04. 32
so lightly blown to and fro as this multitude? 4.08. 56 P
lest by a multitude | the new–heal'd wound of R3 2.02.124
mercy o' me, what a multitude are here! H8 5.03. 67
care | withdrew me from the odds of multitude. TRO 5.04. 22
and for the multitude to be ingrateful were to COR 2.03. 10 P
were to make a monster of the multitude; 2.03. 11 P
stuck not to call us the many–headed multitude. 2.03. 17 P
patient till we have appeas'd | the multitude, JC 3.01.180
he's lov'd of the distracted multitude, | who HAM 4.03. 4

MULTITUDES 6 FR 0.0006 REL FR 6 V 0 P
and rank me with the barbarous multitudes. MV 2.09. 33
on his helm | would they were multitudes, and on 1H4 3.02.143
him | even at the heels in golden multitudes. 4.03. 73
not fit to govern and rule multitudes, | which 2H6 5.01. 94
what, multitudes, and fear? 3H6 1.04. 39
by | that nothing–gift of differing multitudes, CYM 3.06. 85

MULTITUDINOUS 2 FR 0.0002 REL FR 2 V 0 P
at once pluck out | the multitudinous tongue; COR 3.01.156
rather | the multitudinous seas incarnadine, MAC 2.02. 59

MUM 12 FR 0.0013 REL FR 6 V 6 P
mum then, and no more. — proceed. TMP 3.02. 51 P
i come to her in white, and cry "mum"; WIV 5.02. 6 P
what needs either your "mum" or her "budget"? 5.02. 9 P
i went to her in /white and cried "mum," and she 5.05.197 P
mum. MM 5.01.287 P
go to, mum, you are he. ADO 2.01.123 P
well said, master, mum, and gaze your fill. SHR 1.01. 73
grumio, mum! god save you, signior gremio. 1.02.162
seal up your lips, and give no words but mum; 2H6 1.02. 89
lord, | the citizens are mum, say not a word. R3 3.07. 3
mum, mum: LR 1.04.197
mum, mum: 1.04.197

MUMBLE 1 FR 0.0001 REL FR 1 V 0 P
that's all one, i'll go through, let her mumble. TNK 2.03. 31

MUMBLE–NEWS 1 FR 0.0001 REL FR 1 V 0 P
some mumble–news, some trencher–knight, some LLL 5.02.464

MUMBLING 2 FR 0.0002 REL FR 2 V 0 P
peace, you mumbling fool! ROM 3.05.173
mumbling of wicked charms, conjuring the moon LR 2.01. 39

MUMMERS 1 FR 0.0001 REL FR 0 V 1 P
you make faces like mummers, set up the bloody COR 2.01. 75 P

MUMMY 3 FR 0.0003 REL FR 2 V 1 P
i should have been a mountain of mummy. WIV 3.05. 18 P
witch's mummy, maw and gulf | of the ravin'd MAC 4.01. 23
and it was dy'd in mummy which the skillful OTH 3.04. 74

MUN 1 FR 0.0001 REL FR 0 V 1 P
says suum, mun, nonny. LR 3.04. 99 P

MUNCH *(also mounch'd)*

MUNCH 1 FR 0.0001 REL FR 0 V 1 P
i could munch your good dry oats. MND 4.01. 31 P

MUNDANE 1 FR 0.0001 REL FR 1 V 0 P
lost | this queen, worth all our mundane cost. PER 3.02. 71

MUNGREL *(also mongrel, mongril, mungril)*

MUNGREL 1 FR 0.0001 REL FR 0 V 1 P
where's that mungrel? LR 1.04. 49 P

MUNGRELS 1 FR 0.0001 REL FR 1 V 0 P
as hounds and greyhounds, mungrels, spaniels, MAC 3.01. 92

MUNGRIL *(also mongrel, mongril, mungrel, etc.)*

MUNGRIL 1 FR 0.0001 REL FR 0 V 1 P
pandar, and the son and heir of a mungril bitch; LR 2.02. 22 P

MUNIMENTS 1 FR 0.0001 REL FR 1 V 0 P
with other muniments and petty helps | in this COR 1.01.118

MUNITION 2 FR 0.0002 REL FR 2 V 0 P
what munition sent, | to underprop this action? JN 5.02. 98
i can, | to view th' artillery and munition, 1H6 1.01.168

MURDER *(also murther, etc.)*

/MURDER 1 FR 0.0001 REL FR 0 V 1 P
/modo, /of /murder; LR 4.01. 61 P

MURDER 25 FR 0.0028 REL FR 18 V 7 P
what, is't murder? MM 1.02.137 P
murder cannot be hid long; MV 2.02. 79 P
thou tell'st me there is murder in mine eye: AYL 3.05. 10
here's a madman will murder me. SHR 5.01. 59 P
teaching stern murder how to butcher thee. R2 1.02. 32
i'll murder all his wardrop, piece by piece, 1H4 5.03. 27
murder, murder! 2H4 2.01. 50 P
murder, murder! 2.01. 50 P
murder, i warrant now. 2.04.206 P
rob, murder, and commit | the oldest sins the 4.05.125
how easily murder is discovered! TIT 2.03.287
confer with me of murder and of death. 5.02. 34
lo by thy side where rape and murder stands; 5.02. 45
task, | so thou destroy rapine and murder there. 5.02. 59
rape and murder, therefore called so | 'cause 5.02. 62
nay, nay, let rape and murder stay with me, | or 5.02.134
the one is murder, and rape is the other's name, 5.02.156
seek, and know how this foul murder comes. ROM 5.03.198
cain's jaw–bone, that did the first murder! HAM 5.01. 77 P
o' th' conscience | to do no contriv'd murder. OTH 1.02. 3
and your reports have set the murder on. 5.02.187
bent with sin | and hid intent to murder him; PER 2.ch. 24
who at fourteen years | he sought to murder, but 5.03. 9
the gods for murder seemed so content | to 5.03. 99
while lust and murder wakes to stain and kill. LUC 168

MURDER'D 3 FR 0.0003 REL FR 3 V 0 P
and bandetto slave | murder'd sweet tully; 2H6 4.01.136
that name's cursed hand | murder'd her kinsman. ROM 3.03.105
o, falsely, falsely murder'd! OTH 5.02.117

MURDERED 4 FR 0.0004 REL FR 4 V 0 P
return | to be depos'd, and shortly murdered. 1H4 1.03.152
that had before my face murdered my father, 2H4 4.05.167
'twas her two sons that murdered bassianus; TIT 5.01. 91
love, | an hour but married, tybalt murdered, ROM 3.03. 66

/MURDERER 1 FR 0.0001 REL FR 1 V 0 P
/out /on /thee, /murderer! TIT 3.02. 54

MURDERER 4 FR 0.0004 REL FR 4 V 0 P
do this, and be a charitable murderer. TIT 2.03.178
that is because the traitor murderer lives. ROM 3.05. 84
an honorable murderer, if you will; OTH 5.02.294
a present murderer does prepare | for good PER 4.ch. 38

MURDERER'S 1 FR 0.0001 REL FR 1 V 0 P
sweaten | from the murderer's gibbet throw MAC 4.01. 66

/MURDERERS 1 FR 0.0001 REL FR 1 V 0 P
and find out /murderers in their guilty /caves; TIT 5.02. 52

MURDERERS 3 FR 0.0003 REL FR 2 V 1 P
we shall be call'd purgers, not murderers. JC 2.01.180
they were villains, murderers. 3.02.155 P
a plague upon you, murderers, traitors all! LR 5.03.270

MURDEROUS 4 FR 0.0004 REL FR 4 V 0 P
the dreadful motion of a murderous thought, JN 4.02.255
upon thy eyeballs murderous tyranny | sits in 2H6 3.02. 49
in pleasing smiles such murderous tyranny. TIT 2.03.267
bringing the murderous coward to the stake; LR 2.01. 62

MURDER'S 1 FR 0.0001 REL FR 1 V 0 P
faded, | by envy's hand and murder's bloody axe. R2 1.02. 21

MURDERS 2 FR 0.0002 REL FR 2 V 0 P
mercy but murders, pardoning those that kill. ROM 3.01.197
and smilest upon the stroke that murders me. 3.03. 23

MURD'RED 15 FR 0.0017 REL FR 13 V 2 P
it cannot be but thou hast murd'red him; MND 3.02. 56
o, he hath murd'red his master! SHR 5.01. 87 P
thy hand hath murd'red him. JN 4.02.205
pray god you have not murd'red some of them. 1H4 2.04.189 P
like the bees, | are murd'red for our pains. 2H4 4.05. 78
that good duke humphrey traitorously is murd'red 2H6 3.02.123
it cannot be but he was murd'red here, | the 3.02.177
my grandam told me he was murd'red there. R3 3.01.145
were they that murd'red our emperor's brother, TIT 5.03. 98
worser than tybalt's death, | that murd'red me; ROM 3.02.109
that murd'red my love's cousin, with which grief 3.05. 50
why, how should she be murd'red? OTH 5.02.126
of that his officer | that murd'red pompey. ANT 3.05. 19
that they have murd'red this poor heart of mine, VEN 502
which seen, her eyes /as murd'red with the view, 1031

MURD'RING 3 FR 0.0003 REL FR 3 V 0 P
their chiefest prospect murd'ring basilisks! 2H6 3.02.324
that you will war with god by murd'ring me? R3 1.04.253
murd'ring impossibility, to make | what cannot COR 5.03. 61

MURD'RING–PIECE 1 FR 0.0001 REL FR 1 V 0 P
like to a murd'ring–piece, in many places HAM 4.05. 95

/MURD'ROUS 1 FR 0.0001 REL FR 1 V 0 P
here, thou incestious /murd'rous, damned dane, HAM 5.02.325

MURD'ROUS 13 FR 0.0014 REL FR 13 V 0 P
a murd'rous guilt shows not itself more soon TN 3.01.147
i would, false murd'rous coward, on thy knee 2H6 3.02.220
by any solemn vow | to do a murd'rous deed, to 5.01.185
thy murd'rous falchion smoking in his blood; R3 1.02. 94
no doubt the murd'rous knife was dull and blunt 4.04.227
o murd'rous slumber! JC 4.03.267
o murd'rous slave! o villain! OTH 5.01. 61
o murd'rous coxcomb, what should such a fool 5.02.233
have i not found it | murd'rous to th' senses? CYM 4.02.328
fountain brutus drew | the murd'rous knife, and, LUC 1735
that on himself such murd'rous shame commits. SON 9.14
for thou art so possess'd with murd'rous hate, 10. 5
action, lust | is perjur'd, murd'rous, bloody, 129. 3

MURE 1 FR 0.0001 REL FR 1 V 0 P
hath wrought the mure that should confine it in 2H4 4.04.119

MURELLUS 1 FR 0.0001 REL FR 0 V 1 P
murellus and flavius, for pulling scarfs off JC 1.02.285 P

MURK 1 FR 0.0001 REL FR 1 V 0 P
ere twice in murk and occidental damp | moist AWW 2.01.163

MURKIEST 1 FR 0.0001 REL FR 1 V 0 P
with such love as 'tis now, the murkiest den, TMP 4.01. 25

MURKY 1 FR 0.0001 REL FR 0 V 1 P
hell is murky! MAC 5.01. 36 P

MURMUR 5 FR 0.0005 REL FR 5 V 0 P
the current that with gentle murmur glides, TGV 2.07. 25
and then 'twas fresh in murmur (as, you know, TN 1.02. 32
and heard thee murmur tales of iron wars, 1H4 2.03. 48
time | when creeping murmur and the poring dark H5 4.pr. 2
each shadow makes him stop, each murmur stay, VEN 706

MURMUR'D 1 FR 0.0001 REL FR 1 V 0 P
streams ran by her, and murmur'd her moans, OTH 4.03. 44

MURMURERS 1 FR 0.0001 REL FR 1 V 0 P
for living murmurers | there's places of rebuke. H8 2.02.130

MURMURING 4 FR 0.0004 REL FR 4 V 0 P
the rank of osiers by the murmuring stream AYL 4.03. 79
doth move the murmuring lips of discontent | to JN 4.02. 53
the murmuring surge, | that on th' unnumb'red LR 4.06. 20
or murmuring, "where's my serpent of old nile?" ANT 1.05. 25

MURMUR'ST 1 FR 0.0001 REL FR 1 V 0 P
if thou more murmur'st, i will rend an oak | and TMP 1.02.294

MURRAIN *(also murrion)*

MURRAIN 2 FR 0.0002 REL FR 0 V 2 P
a murrain on your monster, and the devil take TMP 3.02. 80 P
a murrain on't! i took this for silver. COR 1.05. 3 P

MURRAY 1 FR 0.0001 REL FR 1 V 0 P
earl of athol, | of murray, angus, and menteith. 1H4 1.01. 73

MURRION *(also murrain)*

MURRION 2 FR 0.0002 REL FR 1 V 1 P
and crows are fatted with the murrion flock; MND 2.01. 97
a red murrion a' thy jade's tricks! TRO 2.01. 19 P

MURTHER *(also murder, etc.)*

MURTHER 96 FR 0.0108 REL FR 85 V 11 P
let/'t alone | and do the murther first. TMP 4.01.232
better shame than murther. WIV 4.02. 45 P
what, will you murther me? ERR 4.04.109
he murther cries, and help from athens calls. MND 3.02. 26
if you will not murther me for my love, let me TN 2.01. 35 P
i am appointed him to murther you. WT 1.02.412
it most innocent mouth) | hal'd out to murther; 3.02.101

and would incense me | to murther her i married. 5.01. 62
shame, | this murther had not come into my mind; JN 4.02.223
4.03. 37
murther, as hating what himself hath done,
not live, but i will murther your ruff for this. 2H4 2.04.134 P
see willful adultery and murther committed. H5 2.01. 37 P
treason and murther ever kept together, | as two 2.02.105
in | wonder to wait on treason and on murther; 2.02.110
and contagious clouds | of headly murther, spoil 3.03. 32
the guilt of premeditated and contriv'd murther; 4.01.163 P
thou that contrivedst to murther our dead lord, 1H6 1.03. 34
you see what mischief, and what murther too, 3.01.115
murther not then the fruit within my womb, 5.04. 63
murther indeed, that bloody sin, i tortur'd 2H6 3.01.131
but that the guilt of murther bucklers thee, 3.02.216
crown | by shameful murther of a guiltless king 4.01. 95
spirits | you cannot but forbear to murther me. 4.07. 76
ah, clifford, murther not this innocent child, 3H6 1.03. 8
why, i can smile, and murther whiles i smile, 3.02.182
murther is thy alms–deed; 5.05. 79
king, | as ours by murther, to make him a king! R3 1.03.197
to murther me? 1.04.173
law commanded | that thou shalt do no murther. 1.04.197
for false forswearing and for murther too. 1.04.202
he sends you not to murther me for this, | for 1.04.213
i wash my hands | of this most grievous murther! 1.04.273
color, | murther thy breath in middle of a word, 3.05. 2
to murther me and my good lord of gloucester? 3.05. 39
murther her brothers and then marry her — 4.02. 62
murther, stern murther, in the direst degree; 5.03.197
murther, stern murther, in the direst degree; 5.03.197
that died by law for murther of our brother, TIT 4.04. 54
where bloody murther or detested rape | can 5.02. 37
rapine and murther, you are welcome too. 5.02. 83
good murther, stab him, he's a murtherer. 5.02.100
if they do see thee, they will murther thee. ROM 2.02. 70
did murther her, as that name's cursed hand 3.03.104
why cam'st thou now | to murther, murther our 4.05. 61
thou now | to murther, murther our solemnity? 4.05. 61
doing more murther in this loathsome world, 5.01. 81
doth make against me, of this direful murther; 5.03.225
they murther caesar!" JC 2.02. 3
thought, whose murther yet is but fantastical, MAC 1.03.139
and wither'd murther, | alarum'd by his sentinel 2.01. 52
did laugh in 's sleep, and one cried, "murther!" 2.02. 20
macbeth does murther sleep" — the innocent 2.02. 33
most sacrilegious murther hath broke ope | the 2.03. 67
murther and treason! 2.03. 74
in a woman's ear | would murther as it fell. 2.03. 86
this is more strange | than such a murther is. 3.04. 82
revenge his foul and most unnatural murther. HAM 1.05. 25
murther! 1.05. 26
murther most foul, as in the best it is, | but 1.05. 27
and a damned light | to their lord's murther. 2.02.461
can you play "the murther of gonzago"? 2.02.538 P
for murther, though it have no tongue, will 2.02.593
play something like the murther of my father 2.02.595
play is the image of a murther done in vienna. 3.02.238 P
eldest curse upon't, | a brother's murther. 3.03. 38
"forgive me my foul murther"? 3.03. 52
of those effects for which i did the murther: 3.03. 54
thou wilt not murther me? 3.04. 21
no place indeed should murther sanctuarize, 4.07.127
you make known | it is no vicious blot, murther, LR 1.01.227
persuade me to the murther of your lordship, 2.01. 44
help ho! murther, help! 2.02. 40 P
help ho! murther, murther! 2.02. 43 P
help ho! murther, murther! 2.02. 43 P
'tis worse than murther | to do upon respect 2.04. 23
how shall i murther him, iago? OTH 4.01.170 P
i am maim'd for ever. help ho! murther, murther! 5.01. 27
i am maim'd for ever. help ho! murther, murther! 5.01. 27
what ho! no watch? no passage? murther, murther! 5.01. 37
what ho! no watch? no passage? murther, murther! 5.01. 37
whose noise is this that cries on murther? 5.01. 48
ho, murther, murther! 5.01. 64
ho, murther, murther! 5.01. 64
/mak'st me call what i intend to do | a murther, 5.02. 65
murther, murther! 5.02.167
murther, murther! 5.02.167
loud, we do commit | murther in healing wounds. ANT 2.02. 22
that i should murther her, | upon the love and CYM 3.02. 11
but his jovial face — | murther in heaven? 4.02.312
must murther wives much better than themselves 5.01. 4
with his wicked wife, | did seek to murther me; PER 5.01.172
name, and many a murther | set off whereto she's TNK 5.03. 27
but back retires to rate the boar for murther. VEN 906
"guilty thou art of murther and of theft, LUC 918
for in my death i murther shameful scorn: 1189
i'll murther straight, and then i'll slaughter 1634

MURTHER'D 9 FR 0.0010 REL FR 9 V 0 P
he had thought to have murther'd wrongfully. 2H6 2.03.104
ay, to be murther'd by his enemies. 3H6 1.01.260
methought the souls of all that i had murther'd R3 5.03.204
their souls whose bodies richard murther'd 5.03.230
"glamis hath murther'd sleep, and therefore MAC 2.02. 39
banquo, banquo, | our royal master's murther'd! 2.03. 87
your royal father's murther'd. 2.03.100
for them the gracious duncan have i murther'd, 3.01. 65
were on the quarry of these murther'd deer | to 4.03.206

MURTHERED 10 FR 0.0011 REL FR 10 V 0 P
so should the murthered look, and so should i, MND 3.02. 58
all murthered — for within the hollow crown R2 3.02.160
i hate the murtherer, love him murthered. 5.06. 40
harmless richard was murthered traitorously. 2H6 2.02. 27
for i have murthered where i should not kill. 3H6 2.05.122
poor bassianus here lies murthered. TIT 2.03.263
that should have murthered bassianus here. 2.03.279
some bring the murthered body, some the 2.03.300
that i, the son of a dear /father murthered, HAM 2.02.583
my mistress here lies murthered in her bed — OTH 5.02.185

MURTHERER 25 FR 0.0028 REL FR 22 V 3 P
being a murtherer, though he were my brother. MM 4.02. 62
that angelo's a murtherer, is't not strange? 5.01. 39
that we must stand and play the murtherer in? LLL 4.01. 8
so should a murtherer look — so dead, so grim. MND 3.02. 57
yet you, the murtherer, look as bright, as clear 3.02. 60
i have dogg'd him like his murtherer. TN 3.02. 77 P
thou art a murtherer. JN 4.03. 90
second a villain and a murtherer? 4.03.102
i hate the murtherer, love him murthered. R2 5.06. 40
unless it were a bloody murtherer, | or foul 2H6 3.01.128
who being accus'd a crafty murtherer, | his 3.01.254
yet aeolus would not be a murtherer, | but left 3.02. 92
what's worse than murtherer, that i may name it? 3H6 5.05. 58
g | of edward's heirs the murtherer shall be. R3 1.01. 40
is there a murtherer here? 5.03.184
show me a murtherer, i'll deal with him. TIT 5.02. 93
good murther, stab him, he's a murtherer. 5.02.100
tybalt, that murtherer, which way ran he? ROM 3.01.138
doth not she think me an old murtherer, | now i 3.03. 94
who should against his murtherer shut the door, MAC 1.07. 15
begin, murtherer, leave thy damnable faces and HAM 3.02.253 P
see anon how the murtherer gets the love of 3.02.264 P
a murtherer and a villain! 3.04. 96
egregious murtherer, thief, any thing | that's CYM 5.05.211
does appear, | with leonine, a murtherer. PER 4.ch. 52

MURTHERER'S 2 FR 0.0002 REL FR 2 V 0 P
not till i sheathe it in a murtherer's skin. JN 4.03. 80
he's dead, and at the murtherer's horse's tail, TRO 5.10. 4

MURTHERERS 7 FR 0.0008 REL FR 7 V 0 P
should be called tyrants, butchers, murtherers! AYL 3.05. 14
lie not, to say mine eyes are murtherers! 3.05. 19
and we, i hope, sir, are no murtherers. 2H6 3.02.181
o traitors, murtherers! 3H6 5.05. 52
if two such murtherers as yourselves came to you R3 1.04.259
bring the murthered body, some the murtherers. TIT 2.03.300
there, the murtherers, | steep'd in the colors MAC 2.03.114

MURTHERING 2 FR 0.0002 REL FR 2 V 0 P
bent | the fatal balls of murthering basilisks. H5 5.02. 17
if murthering innocents be executing, | why then 3H6 5.06. 32

MURTHEROUS 6 FR 0.0006 REL FR 6 V 0 P
the detested blot | of murtherous subornation — 1H4 1.03.163
and set the murtherous machevil to school. 3H6 3.02.193
the world, | whose unavoided eye is murtherous. R3 4.01. 55
stay, murtherous villains, will you kill your TIT 4.02. 88
this murtherous shaft that's shot | hath not yet MAC 2.03.141
the post unsanctified | of murtherous lechers; LR 4.06.275

MURTHER'S 5 FR 0.0005 REL FR 5 V 0 P
or crest unto the crest, | of murther's arms. JN 4.03. 47
that slanders me with murther's crimson badge. 2H6 3.02.200
then murther's out of tune, | and sweet revenge OTH 5.02.115
murther's as near to lust as flame to smoke; PER 1.01.138
wrath, envy, treason, rape, and murther's rages, LUC 909

MURTHERS 13 FR 0.0014 REL FR 12 V 1 P
virginity murthers itself, and should be buried AWW 1.01.139 P
all murthers past do stand excus'd in this; JN 4.03. 51
in murthers and in outrage /boldly here, | but R2 3.02. 40
then murthers, treasons, and detested sins, 3.02. 44
by nature made for murthers and for rapes. TIT 4.01. 58
for i must talk of murthers, rapes, and 5.01. 63
murthers have been perform'd | too terrible for MAC 3.04. 76
with twenty mortal murthers on their crowns, 3.04. 80
his secret murthers sticking on his hands; 5.02. 17
o, my good lord, yonder's foul murthers done! OTH 5.02.106
that men must lay their murthers on your neck. 5.02.170
what follows more, she murthers with a kiss. VEN 54
black stage for tragedies and murthers fell! LUC 766

MURTH'RER 1 FR 0.0001 REL FR 1 V 0 P
heav'n with lightning strike the murth'rer dead; R3 1.02. 64

MURTH'REST 2 FR 0.0002 REL FR 2 V 0 P
thou smother'st honesty, thou murth'rest troth, LUC 885
thou nursest all and murth'rest all that are. 929

MURTH'RING 2 FR 0.0002 REL FR 2 V 0 P
but set his murth'ring knife unto the root 3H6 2.06. 49
take my milk for gall, you murth'ring ministers, MAC 1.05. 48

MURTH'ROUS 1 FR 0.0001 REL FR 1 V 0 P
a murth'rous villain, and so still thou art. R3 1.03.133

MUSCADEL 1 FR 0.0001 REL FR 1 V 0 P
mates | after a storm, quaff'd off the muscadel, SHR 3.02.172

MUSCOVITES *(also muscovits, muskos')*

MUSCOVITES 2 FR 0.0002 REL FR 2 V 0 P
thus, | like muscovites or russians, as i guess. LLL 5.02.121
disguis'd like muscovites, in shapeless gear; 5.02.303

MUSCOVITS 1 FR 0.0001 REL FR 1 V 0 P
twenty adieus, my frozen muscovits. LLL 5.02.265

MUSCOVY 1 FR 0.0001 REL FR 1 V 0 P
sea–sick, i think, coming from muscovy. LLL 5.02.393

MUS'D 1 FR 0.0001 REL FR 1 V 0 P
oft | (when he hath mus'd of taking kingdoms in) ANT 3.13. 83

MUSE* 31 FR 0.0035 REL FR 30 V 1 P
i cannot too much muse | such shapes, such TMP 3.03. 36
muse not that i thus suddenly proceed; TGV 1.03. 64
why muse you, sir? 2.01.170 P
well, i will muse no further. WIV 5.05.239
and rather muse than ask why i entreat you, AWW 2.05. 65
i muse your majesty doth seem so cold, | when JN 3.01.317
i muse you make so slight a question. 2H4 4.01.165
o for a muse of fire, that would ascend | the H5 pr 1
i muse we met not with the dolphin's grace, 1H6 2.02. 19
i muse my lord of gloucester is not come; 2H6 3.01. 1
brothers, you muse what chat we two have had. 3H6 3.02.109
and so doth mine. i muse why she's at liberty. R3 1.03.304
i muse my mother | does not approve me further, COR 3.02. 7
do not muse at me, my most worthy friends, | i MAC 3.04. 84
but my muse labors, | and thus she is deliver'd: OTH 2.01.127
so is it not with me as with that muse | stirr'd SON 21. 1
"had my friend's muse grown with this growing 32.10
how can my muse want subject to invent | while 38. 1
be thou the tenth muse, ten times more in worth 38. 9
if my slight muse do please these curious days, 38.13
so oft have i invok'd thee for my muse, | and 78. 1
and my sick muse doth give another place. 79. 4
i grant thou wert not married to my muse, | and 82. 1
my tongue–tied muse in manners holds her still, 85. 1
where art thou, muse, that thou forget'st so 100. 1
return, forgetful muse, and straight redeem | in 100. 5
rise, resty muse, my love's sweet face survey, | 100. 9
o truant muse, what shall be thy amends | for 101. 1
make answer, muse: 101. 5
then do thy office, muse; 101.13
alack, what poverty my muse brings forth, | that 103. 1

MUSES 2 FR 0.0002 REL FR 2 V 0 P
"the thrice three muses mourning for the death MND 5.01. 52
and precious phrase by all the muses fil'd. SON 85. 4

MUSET *(see musit, etc.)*

MUSH *(also much)*

MUSH 1 FR 0.0001 REL FR 0 V 1 P
my nursh–a quickly tell me so mush. WIV 3.02. 65 P

MUSHRUMPS 1 FR 0.0001 REL FR 1 V 0 P
whose pastime | is to make midnight mushrumps, TMP 5.01. 39

/MUSIC 3 FR 0.0003 REL FR 3 V 0 P
/we /shall /hear /music, /wit, /and /oracle. TRO 1.03. 74
that suck'd the honey of his /music vows, | now HAM 3.01.156
/louder /the /music /there! LR 4.07. 24

MUSIC 168 FR 0.0190 REL FR 130 V 38 P
where should this music be? TMP 1.02.388
wrack, | this music crept by me upon the waters, 1.02.392
to me, where i shall have my music for nothing. 3.02.145 P
marvellous sweet music! 3.03. 19
lifted up their noses | as they smelt music. 4.01.178
and when i have requir'd | some heavenly music 5.01. 52
he makes sweet music with th' enamell'd stones, TGV 2.07. 28
night, | there is no music in the nightingale; 3.01.179
to sort some gentlemen well skill'd in music. 3.02. 91
and give some evening music to her ear. 4.02. 17
where you shall hear music and see the gentleman 4.02. 31 P
that will be music. 4.02. 35 P
the music likes you not. 4.02. 55 P
i perceive you delight not in music. 4.02. 66 P
hark, what fine change is in the music. 4.02. 68 P
i thank you for your music, gentlemen. 4.02. 86
though music oft hath such a charm | to make bad MM 4.01. 14
vow | that never words were music to thine ear, ERR 2.02.114
hath he provided this music? ADO 1.02. 2 P
the fault will be in the music, cousin, if you 2.01. 69 P
when there was no music with him but the drum 2.03. 13 P
come, shall we hear this music? 2.03. 37
the music ended, | we'll fit the /hid–fox with a 2.03. 41
a voice | to slander music any more than once. 2.03. 45
i pray thee get us some excellent music; 2.03. 85 P
now, music, sound, and sing your solemn hymn. 5.03. 11
therefore play, music. 5.04.121 P
one who the music of his own vain tongue | doth LLL 1.01.166
not to anger bent, is music and sweet fire. 4.02.116
play, music, then! 5.02.211
the music plays, vouchsafe some motion to it. 5.02.216
their spheres, | to hear the sea–maid's music? MND 2.01.154
what, wilt thou hear some music, my sweet love? 4.01. 27
i have a reasonable good ear in music. 4.01. 28 P
titania, music call, and strike more dead | than 4.01. 81
music, ho, music, such as charmeth sleep! 4.01. 83
music, ho, music, such as charmeth sleep! 4.01. 83
sound, music! 4.01. 85
my love shall hear the music of my hounds. 4.01.106
what music? 5.01. 40
let music sound while he doth make his choice; MV 3.02. 43
he makes a swan–like end, | fading in music. 3.02. 45
he may win, | and what is music then? 3.02. 48
then music is | even as the flourish when true 3.02. 48
hand, | and bring your music forth into the air. 5.01. 53
and let the sounds of music | creep in our ears. 5.01. 55
mistress' ear, | and draw her home with music. 5.01. 68
i am never merry when i hear sweet music. 5.01. 69
sound, | or any air of music touch their ears, 5.01. 76
to a modest gaze, | by the sweet power of music; 5.01. 79
but music for the time doth change his nature. 5.01. 82
the man that hath no music in himself, | nor is 5.01. 83
mark the music. 5.01. 88
music, hark! 5.01. 97
it is your music, madam, of the house. 5.01. 98
longs to see this broken music in his sides? AYL 1.02.142 P
give us some music, and, good cousin, sing. 2.07.173
play, music! 5.04.178
procure me music ready when he wakes, | to make SHR in.1. 50
wilt thou have music? in.2. 35
talk, | music and poesy use to quicken you, 1.01. 36
for i know she taketh most delight | in music, 1.01. 93
baptista as a schoolmaster | well seen in music, 1.02.134
of mine, | cunning in music and the mathematics, 2.01. 56
as the other in music and mathematics. 2.01. 82 P
and when in music we have spent an hour, | your 3.01. 7
far | to know the cause why music was ordain'd! 3.01. 10
my lessons make no music in three parts. 3.01. 60
if music be the food of love, play on, | give me TN 1.01. 1
and speak to him in many sorts of music | that 1.02. 58
give me some music. 2.04. 1
'save thee, friend, and thy music! 3.01. 1 P
to solicit that | than music from the spheres. 3.01.110
fulsome to mine ear | as howling after music. 5.01.110
it is my father's music | to speak your deeds; WT 4.04.518
music! 5.03. 98
the setting sun, and music at the close, | as R2 2.01. 12
music do i hear? 5.05. 41
how sour sweet music is | when time is broke, 5.05. 42
so is it in the music of men's lives. 5.05. 44
this music mads me, let it sound no more; | for 5.05. 61
of war, | and by that music let us all embrace, 1H4 5.02. 98
mistress tearsheet would fain hear some music. 2H4 2.04. 12 P
the music is come, sir. 2.04.226 P
hand | will whisper music to my weary spirit. 4.05. 3
call for the music in the other room. 4.05. 4
whose music, to my thinking, pleas'd the king. 5.05.108
hear | a fearful battle rend'red you in music; H5 1.01. 44
in a full and natural close, | like music. 1.02.183
come, your answer in broken music; 5.02.243 P
for thy voice is music and thy english broken; 5.02.244 P
bell, | sings heavy music to thy timorous soul, 1H6 4.02. 40
how irksome is this music to my heart! 2H6 2.01. 54
their music frightful as the serpent's hiss, 3.02.326
thou sing'st sweet music. R3 4.02. 78
and, by'r lady, | held current music too. H8 1.03. 47
let the music knock it. 1.04.108
to his music plants and flowers | ever sprung, 3.01. 6
in sweet music is such art, | killing care and 3.01. 12
with all the choicest music of the kingdom, 4.01. 91
bid the music leave, | they are harsh and heavy 4.02. 94
what music is this? TRO 3.01. 17 P
i do but partly know, sir, it is music in parts. 3.01. 18 P
at mine, sir, and theirs that love music. 3.01. 24 P
fair prince, here is good broken music. 3.01. 49 P
and shall, albeit sweet music issues thence. 3.02.134

what music will be in him when hector has 3.03.301 P
discord's ground, the music would not please. TIT 2.01. 70
night, | like softest music to attending ears! ROM 2.02.166
good, thou shamest the music of sweet news | by 2.05. 23
the county will be here with music straight, 4.04. 22
/oppress, | then music with her silver sound" — 4.05.128
why "music with her silver sound"? 4.05.129 P
it is "music with her silver sound," because 4.05.140 P
"then music with her silver sound | with speedy 4.05.142
music, make their welcome! TIM 1.02.129
farewell, and come with better music. 1.02.246 P
feast your ears with the music awhile, if they 3.06. 34 P
i hear a tongue shriller than all the music JC 1.02. 16
he hears no music; 1.02.204
mace upon my boy, | that plays thee music? 4.03.269
and let him ply his music. HAM 2.01. 70
come, some music! 3.02.291 P
come, some music! 3.02.295 P
and it will discourse most eloquent music. 3.02.359 P
and there is much music, excellent voice, in 3.02.368 P
keep time, | and makes as healthful music. 3.04.141
the soldiers' music and the rite of war | speak 5.02.399
but i'll set down the pegs that make this music, OTH 2.01.200
and the general so likes your music, that he 3.01. 12 P
if you have any music that may not be heard, 3.01. 15 P
to hear music the general does not greatly care. 3.01. 16 P
i will play the swan, | and die in music. 5.02.248
give me some music; ANT 2.05. 1
music, moody food | of us that trade in love. 2.05. 1
the music, ho! 2.05. 2
there, | my music playing far off, i will betray 2.05. 11
make battery to our ears with the loud music; 2.07.109
music i' th' air. 4.03. 13
i would this music would come. CYM 2.03. 11 P
i am advis'd to give her music a' mornings; 2.03. 12 P
i will consider your music the better; 2.03. 28 P
him know | if that his head have ear in music; 3.04.175
who, finger'd to make man his lawful music, PER 1.01. 82
loud music is too harsh for ladies' heads, 2.03. 97
to you | for your sweet music this last night. 2.05. 26
the rough and woeful music that we have, | cause 3.02. 88
the music there! 3.02. 91
/mark'd he your music? 5.01. 80
but hark, what music? 5.01.223
but what music? 5.01.226
the music of the spheres! 5.01.229
music, my lord, i hear. 5.01.232
most heavenly music! 5.01.233
where's the rest o' th' music? TNK 3.05. 31
dancing as 'twere to th' music | his own hoofs 5.04. 59
ears' deep sweet music, and heart's deep sore VEN 432
whose tongue is music now? 1077
not to anger bent, is music and sweet fire. PP 5.12
if music and sweet poetry agree, | as they must 8. 1
sound | that phoebus' lute, the queen of music, 8.10
in surplice white, | that defunctive music can, PHT 14
music to hear, why hear'st thou music sadly? SON 8. 1
music to hear, why hear'st thou music sadly? 8. 1
but that wild music burthens every bough, | and 102.11
when thou, my music, music play'st | upon that 128. 1
music play'st | upon that blessed wood whose 128. 1
that music hath a far more pleasing sound; 130.10

MUSICAL 8 FR 0.0009 REL FR 6 V 2 P
wish | you had not found me here so musical. MM 4.01. 11
as sweet and musical | as bright apollo's lute, LLL 4.03.339
and mark the musical confusion | of hounds and MND 4.01.110
i never heard | so musical a discord, such sweet 4.01.118
if he, compact of jars, grow musical, | we shall AYL 2.07. 5
then should you be nothing but musical, for you 1H4 3.01.232 P
of his hoof is more musical than the pipe of H5 3.07. 17 P
at adventure humm'd /one | from musical coinage, TNK 1.03. 76

MUSICIAN 10 FR 0.0011 REL FR 7 V 3 P
you mistake; the musician likes me not. TGV 4.02. 57 P
of good discourse, an excellent musician, and ADO 2.03. 34 P
be thought | no better a musician than the wren. MV 5.01.106
a fine musician to instruct our mistress; SHR 1.02.173
what, will my daughter prove a good musician? 2.01.144
deceiv'd, | our fine musician groweth amorous. 3.01. 63
the quaint musician, amorous litio, | all for my 3.02.147
nor a musician, as i seem to be, | but one that 4.02. 17
by'r lady, he is a good musician. 1H4 3.01.231
an admirable musician! OTH 4.01.188 P

MUSICIAN'S 1 FR 0.0001 REL FR 0 V 1 P
nor the musician's, which is fantastical; AYL 4.01. 11 P

MUSICIANS 12 FR 0.0013 REL FR 5 V 7 P
suppose the singing birds musicians, | the grass R2 1.03.288
so, | and those musicians that shall play to you 1H4 3.01.223
pay the musicians, sirrah. 2H4 2.04.373 P
cause the musicians play me that sad note | i H8 4.02. 78
know you the musicians? TRO 3.01. 19 P
come, musicians, play. ROM 1.05. 25
musicians, o, musicians, "heart's ease, heart's 4.05.102 P
musicians, o, musicians, "heart's ease, heart's 4.05.102 P
o, musicians, because my heart itself plays "my 4.05.106 P
sound," because musicians sound for silver. 4.05.134 P
because musicians have no gold for sounding: 4.05.141 P
years old | they must be all gelt for musicians, TNK 4.01.133

/MUSIC'S 1 FR 0.0001 REL FR 1 V 0 P
air, and let rich /music's tongue | unfold the ROM 2.06. 27

MUSIC'S 3 FR 0.0003 REL FR 3 V 0 P
sir, you are music's master. PER 2.05. 30
and by cleon train'd | in music's letters, who 4.ch. 8
as they say, from iron | came music's origin), TNK 5.04. 61

MUSICS 2 FR 0.0002 REL FR 1 V 1 P
every night he comes | with musics of all sorts, AWW 3.07. 40
i have assail'd her with musics, but she CYM 2.03. 39 P

MUSING 5 FR 0.0005 REL FR 4 V 1 P
made wit with musing weak, heart sick with TGV 1.01. 69
she is given too much to allicholy and musing; WIV 1.04.154 P
to thick-ey'd musing and curst melancholy? 1H4 2.03. 46
musing and sighing, with your arms across; JC 2.01.240
grove, | musing the morning is so much o'erworn, VEN 866

MUSINGS 2 FR 0.0002 REL FR 2 V 0 P
he should still | dwell in his musings, but i am H8 3.02.133
musings into my mind, with thousand doubts | how PER 1.02. 97

/MUSIT 1 FR 0.0001 REL FR 1 V 0 P
enter your /musit, lest this match between 's TNK 3.01. 97

MUSITS 1 FR 0.0001 REL FR 1 V 0 P
the many musits through the which he goes | are VEN 683

MUSK 1 FR 0.0001 REL FR 0 V 1 P
smelling so sweetly, all musk, and so rushling, WIV 2.02. 66 P

MUSK-CAT 1 FR 0.0001 REL FR 0 V 1 P
or of fortune's cat — but not a musk-cat — AWW 5.02. 20 P

MUSKETS 1 FR 0.0001 REL FR 1 V 0 P
fair eyes, to be the mark | of smoky muskets? AWW 3.02.108

MUSKOS' *(also muscovites, muscovits)*

MUSKOS' 1 FR 0.0001 REL FR 1 V 0 P
i know you are the muskos' regiment, | and i AWW 4.01. 69

MUSK-ROSE 1 FR 0.0001 REL FR 1 V 0 P
some to kill cankers in the musk-rose buds, MND 2.02. 3

MUSK-ROSES 2 FR 0.0002 REL FR 2 V 0 P
with sweet musk-roses and with eglantine; MND 2.01.252
and stick musk-roses in thy sleek smooth head, 4.01. 3

MUSS 1 FR 0.0001 REL FR 1 V 0 P
like boys unto a muss, kings would start forth ANT 3.13. 91

MUSSELS 1 FR 0.0001 REL FR 1 V 0 P
thy food shall be | the fresh-brook mussels, TMP 1.02.464

MUSSEL-SHELL 1 FR 0.0001 REL FR 0 V 1 P
was it, mussel-shell, what would you with her? WIV 4.05. 28 P

/MUST 13 FR 0.0014 REL FR 11 V 2 P
/for /i /must /nothing /be; R2 4.01.201
/must /i /do /so? 4.01.228
/and /must /i /ravel /out | /my //weav'd-up 4.01.228
/then /must /we /rate /the /cost /of /the 2H4 1.03. 44
/fever, | /and /we /must /bleed /for /it; 4.01. 57
/it /must /be /shortly /known /to /him /from HAM 5.02. 71
/again, /and /must /be /us'd | /with /checks /as LR 1.03. 19
/and /she /must /not /speak | /why /she /dares 3.06. 27
/thou /must /not /stay /behind. 3.06.101
/her /material /sap, /perforce /must /wither, 4.02. 35
/humanity /must /perforce /prey /on /itself, 4.02. 49
/she /must /have /change, /she /must; OTH 1.03.351 P
/she /must /have /change, /she /must; 1.03.352 P

MUST 1628 FR 0.1840 REL FR 1263 V 365 P
what, must our mouths be cold? TMP 1.01. 53 P
sit down, | for thou must now know farther. 1.02. 33
now | must by us both be spent most preciously. 1.02.241
i must | once in a month recount what thou hast 1.02.261
i must eat my dinner. 1.02.330
i must obey. 1.02.372
but this swift business | i must uneasy make, 1.02.452
it must needs be of subtle, tender, and delicate 2.01. 42 P
you | must be so too, if heed me; 2.01.220
spirits hear me, | and yet i needs must curse. 2.02. 4
i must remove | some thousands of these logs, 3.01. 9
i shall discharge | what i must strive to do. 3.01. 23
for yet ere supper-time must i perform | much 3.01. 95
by your patience, | i needs must rest me. 3.03. 4
and i must use you | in such another trick. 4.01. 36
for i must | bestow upon the eyes of this young 4.01. 39
spirit, | we must prepare to meet with caliban. 4.01.166
this must crave | (and if this be at all) a most 5.01.116
which perforce, i know, | thou must restore. 5.01.134
it sound that i | must ask my child forgiveness! 5.01.198
some oracle | must rectify our knowledge. 5.01.245
two of these fellows you | must know and own, 5.01.275
your life, which must | take the ear strangely. 5.01.313
now 'tis true, | i must be here confin'd by you, ep 4
gentle breath of yours my sails | must fill, or ep 12
i perceive i must be fain to bear with you. TGV 1.01.120 P
i must go send some better messenger: 1.01.151
to-morrow thou must go. 1.03. 75
i must, where is no remedy. 2.02. 2
pills, | and i must minister the like to you. 2.04.150
is gone with her along, and i must after, | for 2.04.176
determin'd of — how i must climb her window, 2.04.181
i must unto the road, to disembark | some 2.04.187
some necessaries that i needs must use, | and 2.04.188
if i keep them, i needs must lose myself; 2.06. 20
why then your ladyship must cut your hair. 2.07. 44
you must needs have them with a codpiece, madam. 2.07. 53
that touch me near, wherein thou must be secret. 3.01. 60
but valentine, if he be ta'en, must die. 3.01.234
and must i go to him? 3.01.377 P
thou must run to him, for thou hast stay'd so 3.01.378 P
therefore it must with circumstance be spoken 3.02. 36
then you must undertake to slander him. 3.02. 38
to none, | you must provide to bottom it on me; 3.02. 53
which must be done by praising me as much | as 3.02. 54
you must lay lime to tangle her desires | by 3.02. 68
and now i must be as unjust to thurio: 4.02. 2
now must we to her window, | and give some 4.02. 16
he must carry for a present to his lady. 4.02. 79 P
because i love him, i must pity him. 4.04. 96
we must bring you to our captain. 5.03. 2
come, i must bring you to our captain's cave. 5.03. 12
i am sorry i must never trust thee more, | but 5.04. 69
i must wait on myself, must i? WIV 1.01.200 P
i must wait on myself, must i? 1.01.201 P
you must speak possitable, if you can carry her 1.01.235 P
that you must. 1.01.238 P
host, i must turn away some of my followers. 1.03. 4 P
i must cony-catch, i must shift. 1.03. 33 P
i must cony-catch, i must shift. 1.03. 34 P
young ravens must have food. 1.03. 35 P
we must give folks leave to prate; 1.04.121 P
you must send her your page, no remedy. 2.02.121 P
for i must let you understand i think myself in 2.02.165 P
you, wherein i must very much lay open mine own 2.02.184 P
you must go with me, master doctor. 2.03. 55 P
i must excuse myself, master ford. 3.02. 53 P
and so must i, sir. 3.02. 54 P
give your men the charge, we must be brief. 3.03. 7 P
nay, i must tell you, so you do; 3.03. 83 P
ay, ay; i must bear it. 3.03.209 P
why, thou must be thyself. 3.04. 3
manners, | i must advance the colors of my love, 3.04. 81
she must needs go in, | her father will be angry 3.04. 92
i must of another errand to sir john falstaff 3.04.109 P
i must carry her word quickly. 3.05. 46 P
/quae's, and your quod's, you must be preeches. 4.01. 78 P
to go loose any longer, you must be pinion'd. 4.02.123 P
master ford, you must pray, and not follow the 4.02.155 P
they must come off. 4.03. 11 P
the children must | be practic'd well to this, 4.04. 65
must my sweet nan present the fairy queen; 4.06. 20
for they must all be mask'd and vizarded) | that 4.06. 40
we two must go together. 5.03. 4 P
no man their works must eye. 5.05. 48
of money, which must be paid to master /brook. 5.05.114 P
what cannot be eschew'd must be embrac'd. 5.05.237
for you must know, we have with special soul MM 1.01. 17
in the suburbs of vienna must be pluck'd down. 1.02. 95 P
away, sir, you must go. 1.02.141
vow'd, you must not speak with men | but in the 1.04. 10
then, if you speak, you must not show your face, 1.04. 12
or, if you show your face, you must not speak. 1.04. 13
the rather for i now must make you know | i am 1.04. 22
we must not make a scarecrow of the law, 2.01. 1
sir, he must die. 2.01. 31
for which i would not plead, but that i must; 2.02. 31
for which i must not plead, but that i am | at 2.02. 32
must he needs die? 2.02. 48
he must die to-morrow. 2.02. 82
so you must be the first that gives this 2.02.106
when must he die? 2.03. 16
your partner, as i hear, must die to-morrow, 2.03. 37
must die to-morrow? 2.03. 40
their untaught love | must needs appear offense. 2.04. 30
yet he must die. 2.04. 36
you must lay down the treasures of your body 2.04. 96
then must your brother die. 2.04.104
will, | or else he must not only die the death, 2.04.165
if i must die, | i will encounter darkness as a 3.01. 82
yes, thou must die: 3.01. 86
my stay must be stolen out of other affairs; 3.01.157 P
hopes that are fallible, to-morrow you must die; 3.01.169 P
correction and instruction must both work | ere 3.02. 32
he must before the deputy, sir, he has given him 3.02. 34 P
it must be so. 3.02. 58 P
it must be so. 3.02. 60 P
too general a vice, and severity must cure it. 3.02. 99 P
'tis a secret must be lock'd within the teeth 3.02.134 P
and the business he hath helm'd, must, upon a 3.02.143 P
sparrows must not build in his house-eaves, 3.02.175 P
will not be alter'd, claudio must die to-morrow. 3.02.208 P
that the dissolution of it must cure it. 3.02.223 P
craft against vice i must apply. 3.02.277
by eight to-morrow | thou must be made immortal. 4.02. 65
there he must stay until the officer | arise to 4.02. 90
for claudio yet, | but he must die to-morrow? 4.02. 93
more depends on it than we must yet deliver. 4.02.125 P
you must rise and be hang'd, master barnardine! 4.03. 21 P
you must be so good, sir, to rise and be put to 4.03. 26 P
tell him he must awake, and that quickly too. 4.03. 30 P
o sir, you must; 4.03. 57
but barnardine must die this afternoon; 4.03. 83
thou must be patient. 4.03.152 P
you must walk by us on our other hand; 5.01. 17
for that which i must speak | must either punish 5.01. 30
that which i must speak | must either punish me, 5.01. 31
this needs must be a practice. 5.01.123
my lord, i must confess i know this woman, | and 5.01.216
you must, sir, change persons with me, ere you 5.01.336 P
lying rascal, you must be hooded, must you? 5.01.352 P
lying rascal, you must be hooded, must you? 5.01.353 P
for the friar and you must have a word anon. 5.01.359
honor, you must pardon | for mariana's sake; 5.01.402
and must be buried but as an intent | that 5.01.452
weeping before for what she saw must come, | and ERR 1.01. 71
but here must end the story of my life, | and 1.01.137
in this service, you must case me in leather. 2.01. 85
his company must do his minions grace, | whilst 2.01. 87
blows long, i must get a sconce for my head, and 2.02. 37 P
good signior angelo, you must excuse us all, 3.01. 1
nor to-day here you must not, come again when 3.01. 41
o lord, i must laugh! 3.01. 50
thither i must, although against my will, | for 4.01.112
for servants must their masters' minds fulfill. 4.01.113
he must have a long spoon that must eat with the 4.03. 63 P
have a long spoon that must eat with the devil. 4.03. 64 P
they must be bound and laid in some dark room. 4.04. 94
sir, i must have that diamond from you. 5.01.392
expectation than you must expect of me to tell ADO 1.01. 16 P
you must not, sir, mistake my niece. 1.01. 61 P
courtesy itself must convert to disdain, if you 1.01.122 P
i must be sad when i have cause, and smile at no 1.03. 13 P
but you must not make the full show of this till 1.03. 19 P
it must not be denied but i am a plain-dealing 1.03. 31 P
we must follow the leaders. 2.01.151 P
you must wear it one way, for the prince hath 2.01.191 P
he do fear god, 'a must necessarily keep peace; 2.03.193 P
and that must your daughter and her gentlewomen 2.03.214 P
why, it must be requited. 2.03.224 P
i must not seem proud; 2.03.228 P
no, the world must be peopled. 2.03.242 P
and down, | our talk must only be of benedick. 3.01. 17
my talk to thee must be how benedick | is sick 3.01. 20
you must hang it first, and draw it afterwards. 3.02. 24 P
to you, which these hobby-horses must not hear. 3.02. 73 P
you must call to the nurse and bid her still it. 3.03. 66 P
two men ride of a horse, one must ride behind. 3.05. 37 P
i must leave you. 3.05. 44 P
and we must do it wisely. 3.05. 60 P
leonato, | i am sorry you must hear. 4.01. 88
she dying, as it must be so maintain'd, | upon 4.01.214
i must say she is dead; 4.01.335 P
you must call forth the watch that are their 4.02. 34 P
i must discontinue your company. 5.01.189 P
a cursing hypocrite once, you must be look'd to. 5.01.208 P
how to pray your patience, | yet i must speak. 5.01.272
margaret, you must put in the pikes with a vice, 5.02. 20 P
but i must tell thee plainly, claudio undergoes 5.02. 56 P
and either i must shortly hear from him, or i 5.02. 58 P
madam, you must come to your uncle, yonder's old 5.02. 95 P
you must be father to your brother's daughter, 5.04. 15
friar, i must entreat your pains, i think. 5.04. 18
which is the lady i must seize upon? 5.04. 53
this article, my liege, yourself must break, LLL 1.01.133
we must of force dispense with this decree, 1.01.147
decree, | she must lie here on mere necessity. 1.01.148

and you must suffer him to take no delight nor 1.02.128 P
no penance, but 'a must fast three days a week. 1.02.129 P
for this damsel, i must keep her at the park; 1.02.130 P
where now his knowledge must prove ignorance. 2.01.103
you must not be so quick. 2.01.117
i must employ him in a letter to my love. 3.01. 6 P
hither the swain, he must carry me a letter. 3.01. 49 P
sir, you must send the ass upon the horse, for 3.01. 54 P
favor, sweet welkin, i must sigh in thy face: 3.01. 67
i must employ thee. 3.01.151 P
why, villain, thou must know first. 3.01.159 P
it must be done this afternoon. 3.01.162 P
some men must love my lady, and some joan. 3.01.205
that we must stand and play the murtherer in? 4.01. 8
indeed 'a must shoot nearer, or he'll ne'er hit 4.01.134
ay, as some days, but then no sun must shine. 4.03. 89
therefore of all hands must we be forsworn. 4.03.215
for i must tell thee it will please his grace 5.01.101 P
"thus must thou speak," and "thus thy body bear" 5.02.100
nay, you must do it soon. 5.02.211
the virtue of your eye must break my oath. 5.02.348
i must needs be friends with thee. 5.02.549
i must rather give it the rein, for it runs 5.02.657 P
you must be purged too, your sins are rack'd, 5.02.818
voice, | the other must be held the worthier. MND 1.01. 55
rather your eyes must with his judgment look. 1.01. 57
i must confess that i have heard so much, | and 1.01.111
i must employ you in some business | against our 1.01.124
we must starve our sight | from lovers' food 1.01.222
flute, you must take thisby on you. 1.02. 44 P
it is the lady that pyramus must love. 1.02. 46 P
no, no, you must play pyramus; 1.02. 55 P
robin starveling, you must play thisby's mother. 1.02. 60 P
therefore you must needs play pyramus. 1.02. 88 P
i must go seek some dewdrops here, | and hang a 2.01. 14
then i must be thy lady; 2.01. 64
to theseus must be wedded, and you come | to 2.01. 72
when i am gone, | for i must now to oberon. 2.02. 83
eye, | but you must flout my insufficiency? 2.02.128
perforce i must confess | i thought you lord of 2.02.131
pyramus must draw a sword to kill himself; 3.01. 11 P
i believe we must leave the killing out, when 3.01. 14 P
another prologue must tell he is not a lion. 3.01. 34 P
you must name his name, and half his face must 3.01. 36 P
name, and half his face must be seen through the 3.01. 37 P
lion's neck, and he himself must speak through, 3.01. 38 P
or else one must come in with a bush of thorns 3.01. 59 P
we must have a wall in the great chamber; 3.01. 62 P
some man or other must present wall; 3.01. 67 P
must i speak now? 3.01. 89 P
ay, marry, must you; 3.01. 90 P
for you must understand he goes but to see a 3.01. 90 P
why, you must not speak that yet! 3.01. 98 P
her eye, | which she must dote on in extremity. 3.02. 3
anon his thisby must be answered, | and forth my 3.02. 18
that, when he wak'd, of force she must be ey'd. 3.02. 40
of thy misprision must perforce ensue | some 3.02. 90
that must needs be sport alone. 3.02.119
do, | but you must join in souls to mock me too? 3.02.150
my fairy lord, this must be done with haste, 3.02.378
and must for aye consort with black–brow'd night 3.02.387
i must to the barber's, mounsieur; 4.01. 23 P
if my hair do but tickle me, i must scratch. 4.01. 26 P
you must say "paragon." 4.02. 13 P
which, when i saw rehears'd, i must confess, 5.01. 68
it must be your imagination then, and not theirs 5.01.213 P
courtesy, in all reason, we must stay the time. 5.01.255 P
a tomb | must cover thy sweet eyes. 5.01.329
must it be so? MV 1.01. 67
i pray you have in mind where we must meet. 1.01. 71
a stage, where every man must play a part, | and 1.01. 78
i must be one of these same dumb wise men, | for 1.01.106
you must take your chance, | and either not 2.01. 38
you must not deny me; 2.02.178 P
i must go with you to belmont. 2.02.178 P
why then you must. 2.02.180
and i must to lorenzo and the rest, | but we 2.02.205
i must needs tell thee all. 2.04. 29
descend, for you must be my torch–bearer. 2.06. 40
what, must i hold a candle to my shames? 2.06. 41
"who chooseth me must give and hazard all he 2.07. 9
"who chooseth me must give and hazard all he 2.07. 16
must give — for what? 2.07. 17
lord, | you must be gone from hence immediately. 2.09. 8
"who chooseth me must give and hazard all he 2.09. 21
and i must freely have the half of any thing 3.02.249
there must be needs a like proportion | of 3.04. 14
lover of my lord, | must needs be like my lord. 3.04. 18
away, | for we must measure twenty miles to–day. 3.04. 84
there must be something else | pawn'd with the 3.05. 81
of force | must yield to such inevitable shame 4.01. 57
then must the jew be merciful. 4.01.182
on what compulsion must i? tell me that. 4.01.183
must needs give sentence 'gainst the merchant 4.01.205
it must appear | that malice bears down truth. 4.01.213
it must not be, there is no power in venice 4.01.218
you must prepare your bosom for his knife — 4.01.245
and you must cut this flesh from off his breast, 4.01.302
therefore thou must be hang'd at the state's 4.01.367
pardon, | i must away this night toward padua, 4.01.403
dear sir, of force i must attempt you further. 4.01.421
it must appear in other ways than words, 5.01.140
you were to blame, i must be plain with you, 5.01.166
him, as i must for my own honor if he come in; AYL 1.01.130 P
him to thee as he is, i must blush and weep, and 1.01.157 P
and weep, and thou must look pale and wonder. 1.01.157 P
you must not learn me how to remember any 1.02. 6 P
mistress, you must come away to your father. 1.02. 57 P
you must if you stay here, for here is the place 1.02.144 P
thus must i from the smoke into the smother, 1.02.287
this i must do, or know not what to do; 2.03. 34
but i must comfort the weaker vessel, as doublet 2.04. 6 P
a better place, but travellers must be content. 2.04. 18 P
that your poor friends must woo your company? 2.07. 10
i must have liberty | withal, as large a charter 2.07. 47
galled with my folly, | they most must laugh. 2.07. 51
and why, sir, must they so? 2.07. 51
will not be answer'd with reason, i must die. 2.07.101 P
good manners, then thy manners must be wicked, 3.02. 42 P
wint'red garments must be lin'd, | so must 3.02.105
must be lin'd, | so must slender rosalind. 3.02.106
they that reap must sheaf and bind, | then to 3.02.107
find, | must find love's prick and rosalind. 3.02.112
you must borrow me gargantua's mouth first; 3.02.225 P
when i think, i must speak. 3.02.250 P
nay, you must call me rosalind. 3.02.434 P
truly, she must be given, or the marriage is not 3.03. 69 P
we must be married, or we must live in bawdry. 3.03. 97
we must be married, or we must live in bawdry. 3.03. 97
must you be therefore proud and pitiless? 3.05. 40
for i must tell you friendly in your ear, | sell 3.05. 59
you must begin, "will you, orlando" — 4.01.129 P
then you must say, "i take thee, rosalind, for 4.01.135 P
i must attend the duke at dinner. 4.01.180 P
we must have your doublet and hose pluck'd over 4.01.202 P
i am. what must we understand by this? 4.03. 94
for i must bear answer back | how you excuse my 4.03.179
he, sir, that must marry this woman. 5.01. 46 P
'tis i must make conclusion | of these most 5.04.126
here's eight that must take hands | to join in 5.04.128
you to his love must accord, | or have a woman 5.04.133
i must go fetch the /thirdborough. SHR in.1. 11 P
i know it well. what must i call her? in.2. 108
master, your love must live a maid at home, 1.01.182
tarry, petruchio, i must go with thee, | for in 1.02.117
that you are the man | must stead us all, and me 1.02.264
you must, as we do, gratify this gentleman, | to 1.02.271
she is your treasure, she must have a husband; 2.01. 32
i must dance barefoot on her wedding–day, | and 2.01. 33
you must not look so sour. 2.01.228
well, | thou must be married to no man but me; 2.01.275
i must and will have katherine to my wife. 2.01.280
'tis deeds must win the prize, and he of both 2.01.342
myself am strook in years, i must confess, | and 2.01.360
i must confess your offer is the best, | and let 2.01.386
she is your own, else you must pardon me; 2.01.388
but suppos'd lucentio | must get a father, 2.01.408
i must believe my master, else, i promise you, 3.01. 54
well, i must wait, | and watch withal, for, but 3.01. 61
fingering, | i must begin with rudiments of art, 3.01. 66
farewell, sweet masters both, i must be gone. 3.01. 85
i must, forsooth, be forc'd | to give my hand 3.02. 8
now must the world point at poor katherine, 3.02. 18
i must away to–day, before night come. 3.02.190
me, | for i must hence, and farewell to you all. 3.02.197
but for my bonny kate, she must with me. 3.02.227
you must meet my master to countenance my 4.01. 98 P
kate, that you must kiss, and be acquainted with 4.01.152
and till she stoop, she must not be full–gorg'd, 4.01.191
from florence, and must here deliver them. 4.02. 90
thither must i, and here i leave you, sir. 5.01. 10
nay then she must needs come. 5.02. 88
but i must attend his majesty's command, to whom AWW 1.01. 4 P
is at all times good must of necessity hold his 1.01. 8 P
lady, | you must hold the credit of your father. 1.01. 78
and collateral light | must i be comforted, not 1.01. 89
would be mated by the lion | must die for love. 1.01. 92
idolatrous fancy | must sanctify his reliques. 1.01. 98
and show what we alone must think, which never 1.01.185
you under that you must needs be born under mars 1.01.196 P
and he must needs go that the devil drives. 1.03. 29 P
he must not be my brother. 1.03.160
but, i your daughter, he must be my brother? 1.03.166
i say we must not | so stain our judgment, or 2.01.119
i must not hear thee, fare thee well, kind maid! 2.01.145
thy pains not us'd must by thyself be paid. 2.01.146
thou this to hazard needs must intimate | skill 2.01.183
more should i question thee, and more i must — 2.01.205
it must be an answer of most monstrous size that 2.02. 32 P
most monstrous size that must fit all demands. 2.02. 33 P
to bring me down | must answer for your raising? 2.03.113
which to defeat, | i must produce my power. 2.03.150
i must tell thee, sirrah, i write man; 2.03.198 P
well, i must be patient, there is no fettering 2.03.236 P
at my hand, but we must do good against evil. 2.05. 48 P
you must not marvel, helen, at my course, 2.05. 58
but you must not now slumber in it. 3.06. 73 P
i must go look my twigs. he shall be caught. 3.06.107
for we must not seem to understand him, unless 4.01. 4 P
us, whom we must produce for an interpreter. 4.01. 6 P
he must think us some band of strangers i' th' 4.01. 14 P
therefore we must every one be a man of his own 4.01. 16 P
you, interpreter, you must seem very politic. 4.01. 21 P
it must be a very plausive invention that 4.01. 26 P
i must give myself some hurts, and say i got 4.01. 37 P
i must put you into a butter–woman's mouth and 4.01. 41 P
for his presence must be the whip of the other. 4.03. 36 P
you are, you must have the patience to hear it. 4.03.115 P
there is no remedy, sir, but you must die. 4.03.303 P
therefore you must die. 4.03.307 P
you must know | i am supposed dead. 4.04. 10
under my poor instructions yet must suffer 4.04. 27
we must away: 4.04. 33
day and night | must wear your spirits low; 5.01. 2
we must to horse again. 5.01. 37
this i must say — | but first i beg my pardon 5.03. 11
son, in whom my house's name | must be digested; 5.03. 74
that she which marries you must marry me, 5.03.174
i must be patient. 5.03.219
sir toby, you must come in earlier a' nights. TN 1.03. 4 P
but you must confine yourself within the modest 1.03. 8 P
i must catechize you for it, madonna. 1.05. 62 P
what is decreed must be; 1.05.311
you must know of me then, antonio, my name is 2.01. 16 P
o time, thou must untangle this, not i, | it is 2.02. 40
sir toby, i must be round with you. 2.03. 95 P
dear heart, since i must needs be gone." 2.03.102
sooth, but you must. 2.04. 88
must she not then be answer'd? 2.04. 92
here comes the trout that must be caught with 2.05. 22 P
"you must amend your drunkenness." 2.05. 73 P
no man must know." 2.05. 99
"no man must know." 2.05.100 P
"no man must know." 2.05.101 P
when the image of it leaves him he must run mad. 2.05.194 P
he must observe their mood on whom he jests, 3.01. 62
and he is yours, and his must needs be yours: 3.01.101
under your hard construction must i sit, | to 3.01.115
you must needs yield your reason, sir andrew. 3.02. 3 P
and't be any way, it must be with valor, for 3.02. 30 P
peace, peace, we must deal gently with him. 3.04. 95 P
for meddle you must, that's certain, or forswear 3.04.251 P
i must obey. 3.04.332
i must entreat of you some of that money. 3.04.340
nay then i must have an ounce or two of this 4.01. 43 P
i must have done no less with wit and safety. 5.01.211
have it as it ought to be, you must allow vox. 5.01.295 P
you must not now deny it is your hand; 5.01.331
come, captain, | we must be neat; WT 1.02.123
or else thou must be counted | a servant grafted 1.02.245
i must believe you, sir. 1.02.333
i must be the poisoner | of good polixenes, and 1.02.352
i must | forsake the court. 1.02.361
for, to yourself, what you do know, you must, 1.02.379
for i must be | a party in this alteration, 1.02.382
i must be answer'd. 1.02.399
which must be ev'n as swiftly followed as | i 1.02.409
as she's rare, | must it be great; 1.02.453
as his person's mighty, | must it be violent; 1.02.454
his revenges must | in that be made more bitter. 1.02.456
i must be patient till the heavens look | with 2.01.106
madam, i must | be present at your conference. 2.02. 15
he must be told on't, and he shall. 2.02. 29
you must not enter. 2.03. 26
so bloody, must | lead on to some foul issue. 2.03.152
since what i am to say must be but that | which 3.02. 22
name of fault, i must not | at all acknowledge. 3.02. 60
what old or newer torture | must i receive, 3.02.178
must either stay to execute them thyself, or 4.02. 15 P
my best camillo! we must disguise ourselves. 4.02. 54 P
i must have saffron to color the warden pies; 4.03. 45 P
i must confess to you, sir, i am no fighter. 4.03.107 P
i must go buy spices for our sheep–shearing. 4.03.116 P
cannot hold when 'tis | oppos'd (as it must be) 4.04. 37
one of these two must be necessities, | which 4.04. 38
will speak, that you must change this purpose, 4.04. 39
mopsa must be your mistress; 4.04.162
but you must be tittle–tattling before all our 4.04.246 P
bear my part, you must know 'tis my occupation. 4.04.295 P
for i must go | where it fits not you to know. 4.04.297
that must be | i' th' virtue of your daughter. 4.04.386
no, he must not. 4.04.414
come, come, he must not. | mark our contract. 4.04.416
whom of force must know | the royal fool thou 4.04.423
some hangman must put on my shroud and lay me 4.04.457
i needs must think it honesty. 4.04.487
your fair princess | (for so i see she must be) 4.04.545
you forth at every sitting | what you must say; 4.04.562
outside of thy poverty we must make an exchange; 4.04.632 P
(thou must think there's a necessity in't) and 4.04.634 P
you must retire yourself | into some covert. 4.04.649
see the play so lies | that i must bear a part. 4.04.656
and box, which none must know but the king, and 4.04.757 P
thou must know the king is full of grief. 4.04.765 P
we must to the king, and show our strange sights 4.04.818 P
he must know 'tis none of your daughter nor my 4.04.819 P
so must thy grave | give way to what's seen now! 5.01. 97
in the extremity of the one, it must needs be. 5.02. 19 P
for we must be gentle, now we are gentlemen. 5.02.152 P
which now the manage of two kingdoms must | with JN 1.01. 37
or else it must go wrong with you and me; 1.01. 41
your tale must be how he employ'd my mother. 1.01. 98
your father's heir must have your father's land. 1.01.129
who dares not stir by day must walk by night, 1.01.172
richard, we must speed | for france, for france, 1.01.178
needs must you lay your heart at his dispose, 1.01.263
by so much | we must awake endeavor for defense, 2.01. 81
one must prove greatest. 2.01.332
or, if it must stand still, let wives with child 3.01. 89
well, ruffian, i must pocket up these wrongs, 3.01.200
that need must needs infer this principle, 3.01.213
which is the side that i must go withal? 3.01.327
uncle, i needs must pray that thou mayst lose; 3.01.332
of peace | must by the hungry now be fed upon. 3.03. 10
never | must i behold my pretty arthur more. 3.04. 89
must be as boisterously maintain'd as gain'd; 3.04.136
john may stand, then arthur needs must fall: 3.04.139
i must be brief, lest resolution drop | out at 4.01. 35
must you with hot irons burn out both mine eyes? 4.01. 39
young boy, i must. 4.01. 40
if heaven be pleas'd that you must use me ill, 4.01. 55
that you must use me ill, | why then you must. 4.01. 56
and with hot irons must i burn them out. 4.01. 59
your vild intent must needs seem horrible. 4.01. 95
must needs want pleading for a pair of eyes. 4.01. 98
your uncle must not know but you are dead. 4.01.127
but that your royal pleasure must be done, 4.02. 17
his passion is so ripe, it needs must break. 4.02. 79
this must be answer'd either here or hence. 4.02. 89
this must not be thus borne. 4.02.101
to safety, and return, | for i must use thee. 4.02.159
and we must embrace | this gentle offer of the 4.03. 12
must i rob the law? 4.03. 78
that present med'cine must be minist'red, | or 5.01. 15
that i must draw this metal from my side | to be 5.02. 16
i must withdraw and weep | upon the spot of this 5.02. 29
must i back | because that john hath made his 5.02. 95
since i must lose the use of all deceit? 5.04. 27
that i must die here and live hence by truth? 5.04. 29
even so must i run on, and even so stop. 5.07. 67
at worcester must his body be interr'd, | for so 5.07. 99
the blood is hot that must be cool'd for this. R2 1.01. 51
it must be great that can inherit us | so much 1.01. 85
rage must be withstood, | give me his gage. 1.01.173
with her companion, grief, must end her life. 1.02. 55
sister, farewell, i must to coventry. 1.02. 56
this must my comfort be, | that sun that warms 1.03.144
years, | my native english, now i must forgo, 1.03.160
what presence must not know, | from where you do 1.03.249
must i not serve a long apprenticehood | to 1.03.271
expedient manage must be made, my liege, | ere 1.04. 39
he that no more must say is listened more | than 2.01. 9

be york the next that must be bankrout so! 2.01.151
his time is spent, our pilgrimage must be. 2.01.154
we must supplant those rough rug–headed kerns, 2.01.156
come on, our queen, to–morrow must we part. 2.01.222
heart is great, but it must break with silence, 2.01.228
we see the very wrack that we must suffer, | and 2.01.267
well, somewhat we must do. 2.02.116
and i must find that title in your tongue, 2.03. 72
it must be granted i am duke of lancaster. 2.03.124
i cannot mend it, i must needs confess, 2.03.153
but we must win your grace to go with us | to 2.03.163
presently your souls must part your bodies — 3.01. 3
needs must i like it well; 3.02. 4
the means that heavens yield must be embrac'd, 3.02. 29
weak men must fall, for heaven still guards the 3.02. 62
to lengthen out the worst that must be spoken: 3.02.199
or not remember what i must be now! 3.03.139
what must the king do now? 3.03.143
must he submit? 3.03.143
must he be depos'd? 3.03.144
must he lose | the name of king? 3.03.145
for do we must what force will have us do. 3.03.207
then i must not say no. 3.03.209
all must be even in our government. 3.04. 36
either i must, or have mine honor soil'd | with 4.01. 23
our holy lives must win a new world's crown, 5.01. 24
you must to pomfret, not unto the tower. 5.01. 52
with all swift speed you must away to france. 5.01. 54
leave and part, for you must part forthwith. 5.01. 70
and must we be divided? must we part? 5.01. 81
and must we be divided? must we part? 5.01. 81
hearts of men, they must perforce have melted, 5.02. 35
and, madam, you must call him rutland now. 5.02. 43
it is no more | than my poor life must answer. 5.02. 83
that many have and others must /sit there; 5.05. 27
since pride must have a fall, and break the neck 5.05. 88
and for this cause a while we must neglect | our 1H4 1.01.101
i must give over this life, and i will give it 1.02. 95 P
what, ye knaves, young men must live! 2.02. 90 P
i must leave you within these two hours. 2.03. 36
and i must know it, else he loves me not. 2.03. 64
we must have bloody noses and crack'd crowns, 2.03. 93
i must not have you henceforth question me 2.03.103
whither i must, i must, and, to conclude, | this 2.03.105
whither i must, i must, and, to conclude, | this 2.03.105
this evening must i leave you, gentle kate. 2.03.106
it must of force. 2.03.117
you must to the court in the morning. 2.04.334 P
i have wept, for i must speak in passion, and i 2.04.386 P
we must all to the wars, and thy place shall be 2.04.544 P
from whom you now must steal and take no leave, 3.01. 92
not wind? it shall, it must, you see it doth. 3.01.105
you must needs learn, lord, to amend this fault; 3.01.178
wales and i | must have some private conference, 3.02. 2
which oft the ear of greatness needs must hear 3.02. 24
john, that you must needs be out of all compass, 3.03. 21 P
must we all march? 3.03. 88 P
sweet beef, i must still be good angel to thee. 3.03.177 P
on high, | and either we or they must lower lie. 3.03.204
side | must keep aloof from strict arbitrement, 4.01. 70
than if the earl were here, for men must think, 4.01. 79
you, looks for us all, we must away all night. 4.02. 57 P
of ten thousand men | must bide the touch; 4.04. 10
i must go write again | to other friends, and so 4.04. 40
and yet i must remember you, my lord, | we were 5.01. 32
o no, my nephew must not know, sir richard, 5.02. 1
survey of all the world, | must have a stop. 5.04. 83
now with joints of steel | must glove this hand; 2H4 1.01.147
o'er | to stormy passion, must perforce decay. 1.01.165
taking up, then they must stand upon security. 1.02. 41 P
you must speak louder, my master is deaf. 1.02. 67 P
pluck him by the elbow, i must speak with him. 1.02. 69 P
are in the vaward of our youth, i must confess, 1.02.177 P
perforce a third | must take up us. 1.03. 73
snare, we must arrest sir john falstaff. 2.01. 8 P
on, i must be fain to pawn both my plate and the 2.01.140 P
come, thou must not be in this humor with me, 2.01.150 P
i must wait upon my good lord here, i thank you, 2.01.184 P
ass, you bashful fool, must you be blushing? 2.02. 76 P
knight" — every man must know that, as oft as 2.02.110 P
must i marry your sister? 2.02.138 P
thing the purpose must weigh with the folly. 2.02.176 P
but i must go and meet with danger there, | or 2.03. 48
and aprons, and sir john must not know of it. 2.04. 17 P
one must bear, and that must be you, you are the 2.04. 59 P
one must bear, and that must be you, you are the 2.04. 59 P
no, by my faith, i must live among my neighbors; 2.04. 74 P
night, and we must hence and leave it unpick'd. 2.04.368 P
you must away to court, sir, presently, | a 2.04.371
and these unseasoned hours perforce must add 3.01.105
'a must then to the inns a' court shortly. 3.02. 13 P
than your number, you must have but four here, 3.02.189 P
nay, she must be old, she cannot choose but be 3.02.207 P
i must a dozen mile to–night. 3.02.290 P
i must acquaint you that i have receiv'd 4.01. 7
call the swords | which must decide it. 4.01.180
his temper therefore must be well observ'd. 4.04. 36
by which his grace must mete the lives of other, 4.04. 77
light and weightless down | perforce must move. 4.05. 34
/my friends, which thou must make thy friends, 4.05.204
then plain and right must my possession be, 4.05.222
even there my life must end. 4.05.235
you must excuse me, master robert shallow. 5.01. 3 P
sir, a new link to the bucket must needs be had; 5.01. 22 P
that must strike sail to spirits of vile sort! 5.02. 18
well, you must now speak sir john falstaff fair, 5.02. 33
we'll have in drink, but you must bear, the 5.03. 29 P
look you, he must seem thus to the world. 5.05. 78 P
'tis your thoughts that now must deck our kings, H5 pr 28
it must be thought on. 1.01. 7
of life | must be the mistress to this theoric; 1.01. 52
it must be so; 1.01. 67
and therefore we must needs admit the means 1.01. 68
we must not only arm t' invade the french, | but 1.02.136
it follows then the cat must stay at home, | yet 1.02.174
and by their hands this grace of kings must die, 2.pr. 28
there is the playhouse now, there must you sit, 2.pr. 36
i cannot tell — things must be as they may. 2.01. 20 P
it must be as it may; 2.01. 23 P
she will plod — there must be conclusions — 2.01. 24 P
mine host pistol, you must come to my master, 2.01. 81 P
we must to france together; 2.01. 91 P
is an oath, and oaths must have their course. 2.01.101
king is a good king, but it must be as it may; 2.01.125 P
you must not dare, for shame, to talk of mercy, 2.02. 81
but we our kingdom's safety must so tender, 2.02.175
he is dead, | and we must ern therefore. 2.03. 6
i must leave them, and seek some better service. 3.02. 51 P
weak stomach, and therefore i must cast it up. 3.02. 53 P
fluellen, you must come presently to the mines; 3.02. 54 P
he hath stol'n a pax, and hanged must 'a be — 3.06. 40
but you must learn to know such slanders of the 3.06. 79 P
and i must speak with him from the pridge. 3.06. 86 P
which must proportion the losses we have borne, 3.06.126 P
i must repent. 3.06.152
you must first go yourself to hazard, ere you 3.07. 87 P
and so our scene must to the battle fly; 4.pr. 48
i and my bosom must debate a while, | and then i 4.01. 31
we must bear all. 4.01.233
what infinite heart's–ease | must kings neglect, 4.01.237
speculation — | but that our honors must not. 4.02. 32
near the gulf, | thou needs must be englutted. 4.03. 83
their poor bodies | must lie and fester. 4.03. 88
i must stay with the lackeys with the luggage of 4.04. 74 P
i must perforce compound | with /mistful eyes, 4.06. 33
soldier, you must come to the king. 4.07.119 P
captain, you must needs be friends with him. 4.08. 61
there must we bring him; 5.pr. 42
must i bite? 5.01. 44 P
you must buy that peace | with full accord to 5.02. 70
katherine, and i must not blush to affirm it. 5.02.113 P
constancy, for he perforce must do thee right, 5.02.154 P
must needs be granted to be much at one. 5.02.191 P
and thou must therefore needs prove a good 5.02.205 P
would conjure in her, you must make a circle; 5.02.293 P
true likeness, he must appear naked and blind. 5.02.294 P
in the latter end, and she must be blind too. 5.02.314 P
i must inform you of a dismal fight | betwixt 1H6 1.01.105
either they must be dieted like mules | and have 1.02. 10
whoe'er helps thee, 'tis thou that must help me: 1.02.107
i must not yield to any rites of love, | for my 1.02.113
town, | something i must do to procure me grace. 1.04. 7
for aught i see, this city must be famish'd, 1.04. 68
come, come, 'tis only i that must disgrace thee. 1.05. 8
i must go victual orleance forthwith. 1.05. 14
sleeping or waking, must i still prevail, | or 2.01. 56
how i am brav'd, and must perforce endure it! 2.04.115
plantagenet, i see, must hold his tongue, | lest 3.01. 61
must your bold verdict enter talk with lords?" 3.01. 63
through which our policy must make a breach. 3.02. 2
but kings and mightiest potentates must die, 3.02.136
then thus it must be, this doth joan devise: 3.03. 17
it rest, | other affairs must now be managed. 4.01.181
that france must vail her lofty–plumed crest 5.03. 25
be so — | what ransom must i pay before i pass? 5.03. 73
why speak'st thou not? what ransom must i pay? 5.03. 77
but, madam, i must trouble you again, | no 5.03.180
out, | must i behold thy timeless cruel death? 5.04. 5
live, | especially since charles must father it. 5.04. 71
what the conditions of that league must be. 5.04.119
must he be then as shadow of himself? 5.04.133
affects, | must be companion of his nuptial bed. 5.05. 58
to you duke humphrey must unload his grief, 2H6 1.01. 76
so york must sit, and fret, and bite his tongue, 1.01.230
nay, eleanor, then must i chide outright. 1.02. 41
follow i must, i cannot go before | while 1.02. 61
hume must make merry with the duchess' gold; 1.02. 87
style, | and must be made a subject to a duke? 1.03. 49
yet must we join with him and with the lords, 1.03. 95
sirrah, or you must fight, or else be hang'd. 1.03.217
well, sir, we must have you find your legs. 2.01.144 P
i must offend before i be attainted; 2.04. 59
must you, sir john, protect my lady here? 2.04. 79
lord suffolk, you and i must talk of that event. 3.01.326
must not be shed by such a jaded groom. 4.01. 52
come, suffolk, i must waft thee to thy death. 4.01.116
'a must needs, for beggary is valiant. 4.02. 54 P
come hither, sirrah, i must examine thee. 4.02. 97 P
and so farewell, for i must hence again. 4.05. 12
i am the besom that must sweep the court clean 4.07. 31 P
now the word "sallet" must serve me to feed on. 4.10. 15 P
i must dissemble. 5.01. 13
but i must make fair weather yet a while, | till 5.01. 30
that gold must round engirt these brows of mine, 5.01. 99
for i myself must hunt this deer to death. 5.02. 15
but fly you must. 5.02. 86
it must and shall be so. content thyself. 3H6 1.01. 85
here must i stay, and here my life must end. 1.04. 26
here must i stay, and here my life must end. 1.04. 26
queen, | unless the adage must be verified, 1.04.126
but hercules himself must yield to odds; 2.01. 53
must edward fall, which peril heaven forefend! 2.01.191
lenity | and harmful pity must be laid aside. 2.02. 10
and spite of spite needs must i rest awhile. 2.03. 5
that to my foes this body must be prey, | yet 2.03. 39
so many hours must i tend my flock, | so many 2.05. 31
my flock, | so many hours must i take my rest, 2.05. 32
my rest, | so many hours must i contemplate, 2.05. 33
so many hours must i sport myself, | so many 2.05. 34
if you contend, a thousand lives must wither. 2.05.102
measure for measure must be answered. 2.06. 55
your crown content and you must be contented 3.01. 67
as red as fire? nay then, her wax must melt. 3.02. 51
must strike her sail and learn a while to serve 3.03. 5
i was, i must confess, | great albion's queen in 3.03. 6
where i must take like seat unto my fortune, 3.03. 10
touching the jointure that your king must make, 3.03.136
your king and warwick's, and must have my will. 4.01. 16
right, and you must all confess | that i was not 4.01. 69
and their true sovereign whom they must obey? 4.01. 78
nay, then i see that edward needs must down. 4.03. 42
what fates impose, that men must needs abide; 4.03. 58
these news i must confess are full of grief, 4.04. 13
till then fair hope must hinder live's decay; 4.04. 16
king edward's friends must down. 4.04. 28
why then, though loath, yet must i be content. 4.06. 48
he | must help you more than you are hurt by me. 4.06. 76
tush, man, abodements must not now affright us. 4.07. 13
by fair or foul means we must enter in, | for 4.07. 14
these gates must not be shut | but in the night 4.07. 35
away with scrupulous wit! now arms must rule. 4.07. 61
shows, | that i must yield my body to the earth, 5.02. 9
and, live we how we can, yet die we must. 5.02. 28
must by the roots be hewn up yet ere night. 5.04. 69
sirrah, leave us to ourselves, we must confer. 5.06. 6
we are the queen's abjects, and must obey. R3 1.01.106
i must perforce. farewell. 1.01.116
with patience, noble lord, as prisoners must; 1.01.126
and must not die | till george be pack'd with 1.01.145
by marrying her which i must reach unto. 1.01.159
when they are gone, then must i count my gains. 1.01.162
but so it must be, if the king miscarry. 1.03. 16
courtesy, | i must be held a rancorous enemy. 1.03. 50
but thus his simple truth must be abus'd | with 1.03. 52
but you must trouble him with lewd complaints. 1.03. 61
make peace with god, for you must die, my lord. 1.04.249
for this will out, and then i must not stay. 1.04.283
and i, unjustly too, must grant it you. 2.01.126
must gently be preserv'd, cherish'd, and kept. 2.02.119
well, my dread lord — so must i call you now. 3.01. 97
o my fair cousin, i must not say so. 3.01.106
the kindred of the queen, must die at pomfret. 3.02. 50
which, as thou know'st, unjustly must be spilt. 3.03. 23
so dear i lov'd the man that i must weep. 3.05. 24
when such ill dealing must be seen in thought. 3.06. 14
no, | i must have patience to endure the load; 3.07.230
come, madam, you must straight to westminster, 4.01. 31
of golden metal that must round my brow | were 4.01. 59
i must be married to my brother's daughter, | or 4.02. 60
we must be brief when traitors brave the field. 4.03. 57
stay, madam, i must talk a word with you. 4.04.199
and must she die for this? 4.04.206
therefore, dear mother — i must call you so — 4.04.412
is colder /tidings, yet they must be told. 4.04.534
norfolk, we must have knocks. ha, must we not? 5.03. 5
norfolk, we must have knocks. ha, must we not? 5.03. 5
we must both give and take, my loving lord. 5.03. 6
of council out, | must fetch him in he papers. H8 1.01. 80
nay, he must bear you company. 1.01.212
nay, we must longer kneel; i am a suitor. 1.02. 9
and yet must | perforce be their acquaintance. 1.02. 46
the rough brake | that virtue must go through. 1.02. 76
we must not stint | our necessary actions in the 1.02. 76
we must not rend our subjects from our laws, 1.02. 93
they must either | (for so run the conditions) 1.03. 23
nay, you must not freeze, | two women plac'd 1.04. 21
the red wine first must rise | in their fair 1.04. 43
sweet partner, | i must not yet forsake you. 1.04.104
traitor's judgment, | and by that name must die; 2.01. 59
then my guiltless blood must cry against 'em. 2.01. 68
to th' water side i must conduct your grace; 2.01. 95
had my trial, | and must needs say a noble one; 2.01.119
i must now forsake ye. 2.01.132
will have his will, and she must fall. 2.01.167
must now confess, if they have any goodness, 2.02. 90
your grace must needs deserve all strangers' 2.02.101
o, 'tis a tender place, and i must leave her. 2.02.143
so much the more | must pity drop upon her. 2.03. 18
i must tell you, | you tender more your person's 2.04.115
there must i be unloos'd, although not there 2.04.148
mean while must be an earnest motion | made to 2.04.234
they that must weigh out my afflictions, | they 3.01. 88
they that my trust must grow to, live not here. 3.01. 89
candle burns not clear, 'tis i must snuff it, 3.02. 96
my brethren mortal, | must give my tendance to. 3.02.149
i must read this paper; 3.02.208
officious lords, | i dare and must deny it. 3.02.238
it must be himself then. 3.02.251
of a rude stream that must for ever hide me. 3.02.364
o my lord, | must i then leave you? 3.02.422
must i needs forgo | so good, so noble, and so 3.02.422
where no mention | of me more must be heard of, 3.02.434
you must no more call it york–place, that's past 4.01. 95
nay, patience, | you must not leave me yet. 4.02.166
i must to bed, | call in more women. 4.02.166
i must to him too, | before he go to bed. 5.01. 8
weed, sir thomas, | and we must root him out. 5.01. 53
for i must think of that which company | would 5.01. 75
come, you and i must walk a turn together; 5.01. 93
answer, you must take | your patience to you, 5.01.104
their practices | must bear the same proportion, 5.01.129
your grace must wait till you be call'd for. 5.02. 7
but their pleasures | must be fulfill'd, and i 5.02. 19
which reformation must be sudden too, | my noble 5.02. 55
way of mercy | but i must needs to th' tower, my 5.02.128
for me? | must i go like a traitor thither? 5.02.131
i have a suit which you must not deny me: 5.02.195
you must be godfather, and answer for her. 5.02.197
you must be seeing christenings? 5.03. 9 P
but she must die, | she must, the saints must 5.04. 59
must die, | she must, the saints must have her; 5.04. 60
must die, | she must, the saints must have her; 5.04. 60
ye must all see the queen, and she must thank ye 5.04. 73
must all see the queen, and she must thank ye, 5.04. 73
a cake out of the wheat must tarry the grinding. TRO 1.01. 15 P
but you must tarry the bolting. 1.01. 17 P
but you must tarry the leavening. 1.01. 20 P
nay, you must stay the cooling too, or ye may 1.01. 25 P
fools on both sides, helen must needs be fair, 1.01. 90
the gods are above, time must friend or end. 1.02. 77 P
a brown favor (for so 'tis, i must confess) — 1.02. 94 P
a marvell's white hand, i must needs confess. 1.02.137 P
power), | must make perforce an universal prey, 1.03.123
defects of age | must be the scene of mirth; 1.03.173
up | in rank achilles must or now be cropp'd 1.03.318
pride alone | must /tarre the mastiffs on, as 1.03.390
nay, i must hold you. 2.01. 79 P
as you must needs, for you all cried "go, go" — 2.02. 85
as you must needs, for you all clapp'd your 2.02. 87
troy must not be, nor goodly ilion stand. 2.02.109
thou must tell that knowest. 2.03. 50 P
you must prepare to fight without achilles. 2.03.227
he must, he is, he cannot but be wise. 2.03.252
we must with all our main of power stand fast; 2.03.262

i must needs praise him. 3.01. 6 P
you must not know where he sups. 3.01. 86 P
i must woo you | to help unarm our hector. 3.01.149
you must be witty now: 3.02. 31 P
you must be watch'd ere you be made tame, must 3.02. 43 P
must be watch'd ere you be made tame, must you? 3.02. 44 P
that their negotiations all must slack, 3.03. 24
out with fortune, | must fall out with men too. 3.03. 76
less than yours in /past, must o'ertop yours; 3.03.164
but it must grieve young pyrrhus now at home 3.03.209
he must fight singly to–morrow with hector, and 3.03.247 P
thou must be my ambassador /to /him, thersites. 3.03.266 P
we must give up to diomedes' hand | the lady 4.02. 65
thou must be gone, wench, thou must be gone; 4.02. 90 P
thou must be gone, wench, thou must be gone; 4.02. 90 P
thou must to thy father, and be gone from 4.02. 91 P
thou must. 4.02. 95 P
and is it true that i must go from troy? 4.04. 30
must poorly sell ourselves | with the rude 4.04. 40
cries "/come" to him that instantly must die. 4.04. 51
i must then to the grecians? 4.04. 55
nay, we must use expostulation kindly, | for it 4.04. 60
the prince must think me tardy and remiss, 4.04.141
you must no more. 4.05.117
who must we answer? 4.05.176
do buss the clouds, | must kiss their own feet. 4.05.221
i must not believe you. 4.05.221
this night in banqueting must all be spent. 5.01. 46
thy better must. 5.02. 33
what error leads must err; 5.02.111
vow, | but vows to every purpose must not hold; 5.03. 24
i must not break my faith. 5.03. 71
eye, | it is decreed hector the great must die. 5.07. 8
you must in no way say he is covetous. COR 1.01. 42 P
if i must not, i need not be barren of 1.01. 44 P
and | your knees to them (not arms) must help. 1.01. 74
either you must | confess yourselves wondrous 1.01. 87
yet you must not think to fob off our disgrace 1.01. 93 P
point of battle, | the one side must have bale. 1.01.163
hunger broke stone walls, that dogs must eat, 1.01.206
we must follow you, | right worthy you priority. 1.01.246
till when | they needs must show themselves, 1.02. 21
i must have you play the idle huswife with me 1.03. 69 P
you must go visit the good lady that lies in. 1.03. 77 P
indeed i must not. 1.03.109 P
(though thanks to all) must i select from all; 1.06. 81
rome must know | the value of her own. 1.09. 20
you, titus lartius, | must to corioles back. 1.09. 76
and what they are that must | be hostages for 1.10. 28
and though i must be content to bear with those 2.01. 59 P
our very priests must become mockers if they 2.01. 84 P
yet you must be saying martius is proud; 2.01. 90 P
coriolanus must i call thee? 2.01.174
my head, | the good patricians must be visited, 2.01.196
so it must fall out | to him, or our authorities 2.01.243
we must suggest the people in what hatred | he 2.01.245
sir, the people | must have their voices; 2.02.140
we must also tell him our noble acceptance of 2.03. 8 P
what must i say? 2.03. 49
you must not speak of that. 2.03. 55
you must desire them | to think upon you. 2.03. 55
you must think, if we give you any thing, we 2.03. 71 P
but that you must | cast your election on him. 2.03.228
preoccupied with what you rather must do | than 2.03.232
must these have voices, that can yield them now, 3.01. 34
where you are bound, you must inquire your way, 3.01. 54
ignorance — it must omit | real necessities, 3.01.146
when what's not meet, but what must be, was law, 3.01.167
let what is meet be said it must be meet, | and 3.01.169
this must be patch'd | with cloth of any color. 3.01.251
his breast forges, that his tongue must vent, 3.01.257
he's a disease that must be cut away. 3.01.293
he must come, | or what is worst will follow. 3.01.333
you must return and mend it. 3.02. 26
what must i do? 3.02. 35
do it to the gods, | must i then do't to them? 3.02. 39
he must, and will. 3.02. 97
must i go show them my unbarb'd sconce? 3.02. 99
must i | with my base tongue give to my noble 3.02. 99
to my noble heart | a lie that it must bear? 3.02.101
well, i must do't. 3.02.110
must all determine here? 3.03. 43
those whose great power must try him — even 3.03. 80
and i must excuse | what cannot be amended. 4.07. 11
we must be burnt for you. 5.01. 32
good will | must have that thanks from rome, 5.01. 46
you may not pass, you must return; 5.02. 5
therefore, fellow, | i must have leave to pass. 5.02. 23
true under him, must say you cannot pass. 5.02. 33 P
you must report to th' volscian lords, how 5.03. 3
alack, or we must lose | the country, our dear 5.03.109
we must find | an evident calamity, though we 5.03.111
either thou | must as a foreign recreant be led 5.03.114
we must proceed as we do find the people. 5.06. 15
my grave lords, | must give this cur the lie; 5.06.106
him, that | must bear my beating to his grave — 5.06.108
but must my sons be slaughtered in the streets TIT 1.01.112
to this your son is mark'd, and die he must, 1.01.125
for him, | he must be buried with his bretheren. 1.01.357
may, | answer i must, and shall do with my life; 1.01.412
and must advise the emperor for his good. 1.01.464
nay, nay, sweet emperor, we must all be friends. 1.01.479
won, | she is lavinia, therefore must be lov'd. 2.01. 84
'tis policy and stratagem must do | that you 2.01.104
do | that you affect, and so must you resolve, 2.01.105
you must perforce accomplish as you may. 2.01.107
/than ling'ring languishment | must we pursue, 2.01.111
know that this gold must coin a stratagem, 2.03. 5
his philomel must lose her tongue to–day, | thy 2.03. 43
yet plead i must, | and bootless unto them. 3.01. 35
tigers must prey, and rome affords no prey | but 3.01. 55
then must my sea be moved with her sighs; 3.01.227
then must my earth with her continual tears 3.01.228
woes, | but like a drunkard must i vomit them. 3.01.231
thou art an exile, and thou must not stay. 3.01.284
aaron, it must, the mother wills it so. 4.02. 82
what, must it, nurse? 4.02. 83
physic, | and you must needs bestow her funeral; 4.02.163
no, publius and sempronius, you must do it, 4.03. 10
'tis you must dig with mattock and with spade, 4.03. 11
so that perforce you must needs stay a time. 4.03. 42
for the man must not be hang'd till the next 4.03. 82 P
at the first approach you must kneel, then kiss 4.03.110 P
how much money must i have? 4.04. 46 P
come, sirrah, you must be hang'd. 4.04. 47
"for i must bear thee to a trusty goth, | who, 5.01. 34
for i must talk of murthers, rapes, and 5.01. 63
devil, for he must not die | so sweet a death as 5.01.145
see here he comes, and i must ply my theme. 5.02. 80
parle, | these quarrels must be quietly debated. 5.03. 20
they must take it /in sense that feel it. ROM 1.01. 27 P
black and portendous must this humor prove, 1.01.141
i must to the learned. 1.02. 44 P
give leave a while, | we must talk in secret. 1.03. 8
i must hence to wait; 1.03.103 P
nay, gentle romeo, we must have you dance. 1.04. 13
you must contrary me! 1.05. 85
ay, pilgrim, lips that they must use in pray'r. 1.05.102
it is to me | that i must love a loathed enemy. 1.05.141
but to his foe suppos'd he must complain, | and 2.pr. 7
not, | the ape is dead, and i must conjure him. 2.01. 16
i should have been more strange, i must confess, 2.02.102
i must up–fill this osier cage of ours | with 2.03. 7
save what thou must combine | by holy marriage. 2.03. 60
and thou must stand by too and suffer every 2.04.155 P
my joy | must be my convoy in the secret night. 2.04.191
hie you to church, i must another way, | to 2.05. 72
must climb a bird's nest soon when it is dark. 2.05. 74
this but begins the woe others must end. 3.01.120
either thou or i, or both, must go with him. 3.01.129
beg for justice, which thou, prince, must give: 3.01.180
romeo slew tybalt, romeo must not live. 3.01.181
flies may do this, but i from this must fly; 3.03. 41
i must be gone and live, or stay and die. 3.05. 11
i must hear from thee every day in the hour, 3.05. 44
that i must wed | ere he that should be husband 3.05.118
or, if he do, it needs must be by stealth. 3.05.215
that may be must be, love, on thursday next. 4.01. 20
what must be shall be. 4.01. 21
my lord, we must entreat the time alone. 4.01. 40
i hear thou must, and nothing may prorogue it, 4.01. 48
my dismal scene i needs must act alone. 4.03. 19
i needs must wake her. 4.05. 9
i must needs wake you. 4.05. 13
need, | and this same needy man must sell it me. 5.01. 54
to juliet's grave, for there must i use thee. 5.01. 86
now must i to the monument alone, | within this 5.02. 24
a ring that i must use | in dear employment — 5.03. 31
obey and go with me, for thou must die. 5.03. 57
i must indeed, and therefore came i hither. 5.03. 58
to shake off | my friend when he must need me. TIM 1.01.101
him in itself, | it must not bear my daughter. 1.01.131
we must needs dine together. 1.01.164
you must needs dine with me; 1.01.244
that game, we must not dare | to imitate them; 1.02. 12
i must entreat you honor me so much | as to 1.02.169
i must serve my turn | out of mine own. 2.01. 20
but must not break my back to heal his finger. 2.01. 24
must not be toss'd and turn'd to me in words, 2.01. 26
i must be round with him, now he comes from 2.02. 8
for my own part, i must needs confess, i have 3.02. 20 P
men must learn now with pity to dispense, | for 3.02. 86
must he needs trouble me in't — hum! 3.03. 1
must i be his last refuge? 3.03. 11
must i take th' cure upon me? 3.03. 12
year, must be employ'd | now to guard sure their 3.03. 38
who cannot keep his wealth must keep his house. 3.03. 41
you must consider that a prodigal course | is 3.04. 12
free, and must my house | be my retentive enemy? 3.04. 80
must it be so? 3.05. 88
it must not be. 3.05. 88
me beyond them, and i must needs appear. 3.06. 12 P
we must all part | into this sea of air. 4.02. 21
must be thy subject, who in spite put stuff | to 4.03.272
you must eat men. 4.03.425
yet thanks i must you con | that you are thieves 4.03.425
but tell me true | (for i must ever doubt, 4.03.507
i must serve him so too: 5.01. 20
it must be a personating of himself; 5.01. 34
must thou needs | stand for a villain in thine 5.01. 37
i must needs say you have a little fault; 5.01. 87
me to cut down, | and shortly must i fell it. 5.01.207
which in the bluster of thy wrath must fall 5.04. 41
that needs must light on this ingratitude. JC 1.01. 55
then must i think you would not have it so. 1.02. 81
and must bend his body | if caesar carelessly 1.02.117
then i know | my answer must be made. 1.03.114
it must be by his death; 2.01. 10
thus must i piece it out: 2.01. 51
but, alas, | caesar must bleed for it! 2.01.171
but are not some whole that we must make sick? 2.01.328
that must we also. 2.01.329
as we are going, | to whom it must be done. 2.01.331
i must go in. 2.04. 39
amiss | that caesar and his senate must redress? 3.01. 32
i must prevent thee, cimber. 3.01. 35
who else must be let blood, who else is rank; 3.01.152
though now we must appear bloody and cruel, | as 3.01.165
that one of two bad ways you must conceit me, 3.01.192
and i must pause till it come back to me. 3.02.107
patience, gentle friends, i must not read it. 3.02.140
i must tell you then: 3.02.237
your brother too must die; consent you, lepidus? 4.01. 2
he must be taught, and train'd, and bid go forth 4.01. 35
we must straight make head; 4.01. 42
must i give way and room to your rash choler? 4.03. 39
o ye gods, ye gods, must i endure all this? 4.03. 41
must i bouge? 4.03. 44
must i observe you? 4.03. 45
must i stand and crouch | under your testy humor 4.03. 45
we must die, messala. 4.03.190
with meditating that she must die once, | i have 4.03.191
good reasons must of force give place to better: 4.03.203
you must note beside | that we have tried the 4.03.213
and we must take the current when it serves, 4.03.223
upon our talk, | and nature must obey necessity, 4.03.227
stand fast, titinius; we must out and talk. 5.01. 22
must end that work the ides of march begun. 5.01.113
we must not. a noble prisoner! 5.04. 15
i must report they were | as cannons overcharg'd MAC 1.02. 36
nor must be known | no less to have done so, let 1.04. 30
which honor must | not unaccompanied invest him 1.04. 39
that is a step | on which i must fall down, or 1.04. 49
that which cries, "thus thou must do," if thou 1.05. 23
he that's coming | must be provided for; 1.05. 67
false face must hide what the false heart doth 1.07. 82
these deeds must not be thought | after these 2.02. 30
they must lie there. 2.02. 46
grooms withal, | for it must seem their guilt. 2.02. 54
i must become a borrower of the night | for a 3.01. 26
and bid my will avouch it, yet i must not, | for 3.01.119
the moment on't, for't must be done to–night, 3.01.130
must embrace the fate | of that dark hour. 3.01.136
if it find heaven, must find it out to–night. 3.01.141
must lave our honors in these flattering streams 3.02. 33
you must leave this. 3.02. 35
if charnel–houses and our graves must send 3.04. 70
which must be acted ere they may be scann'd. 3.04.139
great business must be wrought ere noon: 3.05. 22
men must not walk too late. 3.06. 7
you must have patience, madam. 4.02. 2
that does so is a traitor, and must be hang'd. 4.02. 50 P
and must they all be hang'd that swear and lie? 4.02. 51 P
who must hang them? 4.02. 54 P
brows of grace, | yet grace must still look so. 4.03. 24
and i must be from thence! | my wife kill'd too? 4.03.212
but i must also feel it as a man: 4.03.221
troops of friends, | i must not look to have; 5.03. 26
therein the patient | must minister to himself. 5.03. 46
but certain issue strokes must arbitrate, 5.04. 20
fly, | but bear–like i must fight the course. 5.07. 2
which must not yield | to one of woman born. 5.08. 12
some must go off; 5.09. 2
of sorrow | must not be measur'd by his worth, 5.09. 11
yet now, i must confess, that duty done, | my HAM 1.02. 54
know'st 'tis common, all that lives must die, 1.02. 72
but you must know your father lost a father, 1.02. 89
for what we know must be, and is as common | as 1.02. 98
till he that died to–day, | "this must be so." 1.02.106
heaven and earth, | must i remember? 1.02.143
but break my heart, for i must hold my tongue. 1.02.159
the virtue of his will, but you must fear, | his 1.03. 16
and therefore must his choice be circumscrib'd 1.03. 22
and it must follow, as the night the day, | thou 1.03. 79
and that in way of caution — i must tell you, 1.03. 95
as it is a–making, | you must not take for fire. 1.03.120
and tormenting flames | must render up myself. 1.05. 4
but this eternal blazon must not be | to ears of 1.05. 21
you must not put another scandal on him, | that 2.01. 29
this must be known, which, being kept close, 2.01.115
as i perceiv'd it (i must tell you that) 2.02.133
this must not be"; 2.02.142
that you must teach me. 2.02.283 P
i tell you, must show fairly outwards, should 2.02.374 P
must, like a whore, unpack my heart with words, 2.02.585
off this mortal coil, | must give us pause. 3.01. 67
madness in great ones must not /unwatch'd go. 3.01.188
you must acquire and beget a temperance that may 3.02. 7 P
the censure of which one must, in your allowance 3.02. 27 P
i must be idle; 3.02. 90
by'r lady, 'a must build churches then, or else 3.02.133 P
discomfort you, my lord, it nothing must, | /for 3.02.166
faith, i must leave thee, love, and shortly too; 3.02.173
such love must needs be treason in my breast. 3.02.178
for some must watch, while some must sleep, 3.02.273
for some must watch, while some must sleep, 3.02.273
times | virtue itself of vice must pardon beg, 3.04.154
me, | that i must be their scourge and minister. 3.04.175
i must be cruel, only to be kind. 3.04.178
i must to england, you know that? 3.04.200
they bear the mandate — they must sweep my way, 3.04.204
you must translate, 'tis fit we understand them. 4.01. 2
deed | we must with all our majesty and skill 4.01. 31
my lord, you must tell us where the body is, and 4.02. 25 P
yet must not we put the strong law on him. 4.03. 3
even, | this sudden sending him away must seem 4.03. 8
must send thee hence | /with /fiery /quickness; 4.03. 42
in my blood he rages, | and thou must cure me. 4.03. 67
we must be patient, but i cannot choose but weep 4.05. 68 P
you must sing, "a–down, a–down," and you call 4.05.171 P
laertes, i must commune with your grief, | or 4.05.203
to earth, | that i must call't in question. 4.05.218
now must your conscience my acquittance seal, 4.07. 1
and you must put me in your heart for friend, 4.07. 2
you must not think | that we are made of stuff 4.07. 30
it must be /se /offendendo, it cannot be else. 5.01. 9 P
and must th' inheritor himself have no more, ha? 5.01.112 P
we must speak by the card, or equivocation will 5.01.137 P
an inch thick, to this favor she must come. 5.01.194 P
must there no more be done? 5.01.235
i knew you must be edified by the margent ere 5.02.155 P
and you must needs have heard, how i am punish'd 5.02.229
making, and the whoreson must be acknowledg'd. LR 1.01. 24 P
i must love you, and sue to know you better. 1.01. 30 P
that lord whose hand must take my plight shall 1.01.101
her offense | must be of such unnatural degree 1.01.219
must be a faith that reason without miracle 1.01.222
so lost a father | that you must lose a husband. 1.01.247
then must we look from his age to receive not 1.01.296 P
we must do something, and i' th' heat. 1.01.308 P
then, | legitimate edgar, i must have your land. 1.02. 16
follow him, thou must needs wear my coxcomb. 1.04.104 P
truth's a dog must to kennel, he must be whipt 1.04.111 P
a dog must to kennel, he must be whipt out, when 1.04.111 P
if she must teem, | create her child of spleen, 1.04.281
thing, of a queasy question, | which i must act. 2.01. 18
in cunning i must draw my sword upon you. 2.01. 29
and thou must make a dullard of the world | if 2.01. 74
the duke must grant me that. 2.01. 81
wherein we must have use of your advice. 2.01.121
an honest mind and plain, he must speak truth! 2.02. 99
the king must take it ill | that he, so slightly 2.02.145
good king, that must approve the common saw, 2.02.160

in my flesh, | which i must needs call mine. 2.04.223
your passion | must be content to think you old, 2.04.235
what, must i come to you | with five and twenty? 2.04.253
from rest, | and must needs taste his folly. 2.04.291
procure | must be their schoolmasters. 2.04.304
must make content with his fortunes fit, 3.02. 76
we must incline to the king. 3.03. 13 P
me), the king my old master must be reliev'd. 3.03. 18 P
and must draw me | that which my father loses: 3.03. 23
is my fortune, that i must repent to be just! 3.05. 9 P
tied to th' stake, and i must stand the course. 3.07. 54
bad is the trade that must play fool to sorrow, 4.01. 38
and yet i must. 4.01. 54
i must change names at home, and give the 4.02. 17
i must needs after him, madam, with my letter. 4.05. 15
thou must be patient; 4.06.178
the sword is out | that must destroy thee. 4.06.230
/no, /sir, you must not kneel. 4.07. 58
you must bear with me. 4.07. 82
men must endure | their going hence even as 5.02. 9
i must embrace thee. 5.03.177
my master calls me, i must not say no. 5.03.323
the weight of this sad time we must obey, 5.03.324
must be belee'd and calm'd | by debitor and OTH 1.01. 30
he, in good time, must his lieutenant be, | and 1.01. 32
but thou must needs be sure | my spirits and my 1.01.102
for i must leave you. 1.01.144
life, | i must show out a flag and sign of love, 1.01.156
i must be found. 1.02. 30
we must not think the turk is so unskillful | to 1.03. 27
we must straight employ you | against the 1.03. 48
and must be driven | to find out practices of 1.03.101
to pay grief, must of poor patience borrow. 1.03.215
you must therefore be content to slubber the 1.03.226 P
affair cries haste, | and speed must answer it. 1.03.277
you must away to–night. 1.03.277
iago, | my desdemona must i leave to thee. 1.03.295
we must obey the time. 1.03.300
she must change for youth; 1.03.349 P
must bring this monstrous birth to the world's 1.03.404
first, i must tell thee this: 2.01.218 P
her eye must be fed; 2.01.225 P
i must fetch his necessaries ashore. 2.01.284 P
welcome, iago; we must to the watch. 2.03. 12 P
and there be souls must be sav'd, and there be 2.03.103 P
be sav'd, and there be souls must not be sav'd. 2.03.103 P
you must not think then that i am drunk. 2.03.118 P
good night, lieutenant, i must to the watch. 2.03.334 P
my wife must move for cassio to her mistress — 2.03.383
(save that they say the wars must make example 3.03. 65
abus'd, and my relief | must be to loathe her. 3.03.268
'tis she must do't; 3.04.107
love again, | but to know so must be my benefit; 3.04.119
you must awhile be patient. 3.04.129
nay, we must think men are not gods, | nor of 3.04.148
'tis very good; i must be circumstanc'd. 3.04.201
them, cannot choose | but they must blab — 4.01. 29
the lethargy must have his quiet course; 4.01. 53
and his unbookish jealousy must /conster | poor 4.01.101
well, i must leave her company. 4.01.144 P
i must take out the work? 4.01.150 P
some minx's token, and i must take out the work? 4.01.153 P
/faith, i must, she'll rail in the streets else. 4.01.163 P
nay, you must forget that. 4.01.180 P
where either i must live or bear no life; 4.02. 58
we must not now displease him. 4.03. 17
"sing all a green willow must be my garland. 4.03. 51
it must not be. 5.01. 18
no, he must die. 5.01. 22
these bloody accidents must excuse my manners 5.01. 94
come, mistress, you must tell 's another tale. 5.01.125
yet she must die, else she'll betray more men. 5.02. 6
it vital growth again, | it needs must wither. 5.02. 15
i must weep, | but they are cruel tears. 5.02. 20
she said so; i must needs report the truth. 5.02.128
that men must lay their murthers on your neck. 5.02.170
uncle, i must come forth. 5.02.254
thou hast no weapon, and perforce must suffer. 5.02.256
you must forsake this room and go with us. 5.02.330
then must you speak | of one that lov'd not 5.02.343
then must thou needs find out new heaven, new ANT 1.01. 17
you must not stay here longer, your dismission 1.01. 26
you say, must change his horns with garlands! 1.02. 4 P
prithee, how many boys and wenches must i have? 1.02. 36 P
these strong egyptian fetters i must break, | or 1.02.116
i must from this enchanting queen break off; 1.02.128
i must with haste from hence. 1.02.132
i must be gone. 1.02.136
sir, you and i must part, but that's not it; 1.03. 87
i must not think there are | evils enow to 1.04. 10
(as his composure must be rare indeed | whom 1.04. 22
yet must antony | no way excuse his foils, when 1.04. 23
mine ear must pluck it thence. 1.05. 42
but small to greater matters must give way. 2.02. 11
i must be laugh'd at | if, or for nothing or a 2.02. 30
to make it with, | it must not be with this. 2.02. 54
for that you must | but say i could not help it. 2.02. 70
i must thank him only, | lest my remembrance 2.02.155
of us must pompey presently be sought, | or else 2.02.158
now antony | must leave her utterly. 2.02.233
o, come, ventidius, | you must to parthia. 2.03. 42
much tall youth | that else must perish here. 2.06. 8
and i must | rid all the sea of pirates; 2.06. 35
the praise of it by telling, you must know, 2.06. 43
thou must know, | 'tis not my profit that does 2.07. 75
afterwards well done, | but must condemn it now. 2.07. 80
the weight we must convey with 's will permit, 3.01. 36
thou must not take my former sharpness ill. 3.03. 35
believe not all, or, if you must believe, 3.04. 11
nor must not then be yielded to in this. 3.06. 38
your presence needs must puzzle antony, | take 3.07. 10
now i must | to the young man send humble 3.11. 61
leaky | that we must leave thee to thy sinking, 3.13. 64
i must stay his time. 3.13.155
caesar must think, | when one so great begins to 4.01. 6
sooth law, i'll help. thus it must be. 4.04. 8
i must attend mine office, | or would have 4.06. 26
hour, | we must return to th' court of guard. 4.09. 2

long day's task is done, | and we must sleep. 4.14. 36
so it must be, for now | all length is torture; 4.14. 45
for with a wound i must be cur'd. 4.14. 78
must be as great | as that which makes it. 4.15. 5
help me, my women — we must draw thee up. 4.15. 30
it is | that nature must compel us to lament 5.01. 29
set before him, | he needs must see himself. 5.01. 35
i must perforce | have shown to thee such a 5.01. 37
his beggar, you must tell him | that majesty, to 5.02. 16
keep decorum, must | no less beg than a kingdom. 5.02. 17
it thus, my master and my lord | i must obey. 5.02.117
must i be unfolded | with one that i have bred? 5.02.170
adieu, good queen, i must attend on caesar. 5.02.206
you must think this, look you, that the worm 5.02.262 P
you must not think i am so simple but i know the 5.02.272 P
we must forbear. CYM 1.01. 68
you must be gone, | and i shall here abide the 1.01. 88
fie, you must give way. 1.01.158
wherein he must be weigh'd rather by her value 1.04. 15 P
you must not so far prefer her 'fore ours of 1.04. 65 P
what she cannot choose | but must be, will 's 1.06. 72
that both mine ears | must not in haste abuse), 1.06.131
i must aboard to–morrow. 1.06.199
o, i must, madam. 1.06.204
then a whoreson jack–an–apes must take me up for 2.01. 4 P
and i must go up and down like a cock that 2.01. 21 P
must wear the print of his remembrance on't, 2.03. 43
we must receive him | according to the honor of 2.03. 57
forespent on us, | we must extend our notice. 2.03. 60
and must not foil | the precious note of it with 2.03.121
they failing, | i must die much your debtor. 2.04. 8
you know that we | must not continue friends. 2.04. 49
good sir, we must, | if you keep covenant. 2.04. 49
make them, | must first induce you to believe; 2.04. 63
more particulars | must justify my knowledge. 2.04. 79
so they must, | or do your honor injury. 2.04. 79
it must be married | to that your diamond, i'll 2.04. 97
for men to be, but women | must be half–workers? 2.05. 2
you must know, | till the injurious romans did 3.01. 46
what's worse, | must curtsy at the censure. 3.03. 55
pisanio, must act for me, if thy faith be not 3.04. 26 P
than to hang by th' walls, | i must be ripp'd. 3.04. 53
why, i must die; 3.04. 74
at court, | then not in britain must you bide. 3.04.135
itself, must not yet be | but by self–danger, 3.04.145
you must forget to be a woman; 3.04.154
you must | forget that rarest treasure of your 3.04.159
well, madam, we must take a short farewell, 3.04.185
my emperor hath wrote i must from hence, | and 3.05. 2
and am right sorry that i must report ye | my 3.05. 3
than they, must needs | appear unkinglike. 3.05. 6
but must be look'd to speedily and strongly. 3.05. 27
the cure whereof, my lord, | 'tis time must do. 3.05. 38
of, whereunto your levy | must be supplyant. 3.07. 14
therein i must play the workman. 4.01. 6 P
be not sick, | for you must be our huswife. 4.02. 45
all safe reason | he must have some attendants. 4.02.132
and words, | save that euriphile must be fidele. 4.02.238
nay, cadwal, we must lay his head to th' east, 4.02.255
golden lads and girls all must, | as 4.02.262
physic, must | all follow this and come to dust. 4.02.268
all lovers must | consign to thee and come to 4.02.274
who needs must know of her departure and | dost 4.03. 10
the heavens still must work. 4.03. 41
must or for britains slay us or receive us | for 4.04. 5
must murther wives much better than themselves 5.01. 4
great the answer be | britains must take. 5.03. 80
must i repent, | i cannot do it better than in 5.04. 13
you must either be directed by some that take 5.04.179 P
happiness, i must report | the queen is dead. 5.05. 26
life, good master, | must shuffle for itself. 5.05.105
confess'd, | which must approve thee honest. 5.05.245
thou art condemn'd, and must | endure our law. 5.05.298
i must | for mine own part unfold a dangerous 5.05.312
and i must lose | two of the sweet'st companions 5.05.348
her countless glory, which desert must gain; PER 1.01. 31
presumes to reach, all the whole heap must die. 1.01. 33
this body, like to them, to what i must; 1.01. 44
but i must tell you, now my thoughts revolt, 1.01. 78
he must not live to trumpet forth my infamy, 1.01.145
and therefore instantly this prince must die, 1.01.148
die, | for by his fall my honor must keep high. 1.01.149
the prince | of tyre, and thou must kill him. 1.01.156
must feel war's blow, who spares not innocence: 1.02. 93
here must i kill king pericles, and if i do it 1.03. 2 P
since he's gone, the king's seas must please: 1.03. 27
now message must return from whence it came. 1.03. 35
must have inventions to delight the taste, 1.04. 40
man | is but a substance that must yield to you; 2.01. 3
o, sir, things must be as they may; 2.01.113 P
soft, here he comes, i must dissemble it. 2.05. 23
you, | ay, so well, that you must be her master, 2.05. 38
nay, come, your hands and lips must seal it too; 2.05. 85
brief, he must hence depart to tyre: 3.ch. 39
sir, your queen must overboard. 3.01. 47 P
yield 'er, for she must overboard straight. 3.01. 53 P
but straight | must cast thee, scarcely coffin'd 3.01. 60
and humming water must o'erwhelm thy corpse, 3.01. 63
now this matter must be look'd to, | for her 3.02.108
most honor'd cleon, i must needs be gone. 3.03. 1
sea she lies in, yet the end | must be as 'tis. 3.03. 12
upon you, | must in your child be thought on. 3.03. 20
whom our fast–growing scene must find | at 4.ch. 6
what, i must have care of you. 4.01. 49
whom they have ravish'd must by me be slain. 4.01.102
sapling, and must be bow'd as i would have you. 4.02. 88 P
to defend you by men, then men must comfort you, 4.02. 91 P
then men must comfort you, men must feed you, 4.02. 91 P
you must seem to do that fearfully which you 4.02.117 P
these blushes of hers must be quench'd with some 4.02.124 P
thou sayest true, i' faith, so they must: 4.02.126 P
while our /scene must play | his daughter's woe 4.04. 48
we must either get her ravish'd or be rid of her 4.06. 4 P
faith, i must ravish her, or she'll disfurnish 4.06. 11 P
you must take some pains to work her to your 4.06. 63 P
we must take another course with you! 4.06.121 P
i must have your maidenhead taken off, or the 4.06.127 P
give me, | for such kindness must relieve me: 5.02. 4

our losses fall so thick we must needs leave. TNK pr 32
know o' th' earth | must know the centre too; 1.01.115
which to do | must make some work with creon. 1.01.150
bootless toil must recompense itself | with its 1.01.153
pasture, and we must | be vile or disobedient — 1.02. 77
therefore we must | with him stand to the mercy 1.02.101
so we must. 1.02.103
yet they | must yield their tribute there. 1.03. 8
i must no more believe thee in this point 1.03. 87
never more | must we behold those comforts, 2.02. 9
/ravish'd our sides, like age, must run to rust, 2.02. 22
and here the graces of our youths must wither 2.02. 27
here age must find us, | and which is heaviest, 2.02. 28
but dead–cold winter must inhabit here still. 2.02. 45
with their echoes, | no more now must we hallow; 2.02. 48
they must not, say they could; 2.02. 67
yes, but you must not love her. 2.02.161
lives of all my name lay on it, | i must do so; 2.02.176
i must be — | till thou art worthy, arcite, it 2.02.200
i must, i ought to do so, and i dare — | and 2.02.205
lord arcite, you must presently to th' duke; 2.02.221
i must awhile bereave you | of your fair 2.02.223
and life, must he set foot | upon this kingdom. 2.02.246
indeed you must, my lord. 2.02.268
i must | constrain you then; 2.02.269
must i go? 2.02.273
'tis a benefit, | a mercy i must thank 'em for; 2.03. 2
and she must see the duke, and she must dance 2.03. 45
she must see the duke, and she must dance too. 2.03. 45
this must be done i' th' woods. 2.03. 50
i must needs entreat you | this afternoon to 2.05. 45
sweet, you must be ready — | and you, emilia — 2.05. 48
you must guess | i have an office there. 3.01.109
sick between 's, | by bleeding must be cur'd. 3.01.114
but i must fear you first. 3.03. 9
friend, you must eat no white bread; 3.05. 80
and justifying my love, i must not fly from't. 3.06. 42
for express will, all the world must perish. 3.06.229
i must love, and will, | and for that love must 3.06.261
and for that love must and dare kill this cousin 3.06.262
if one of them were dead, as one must, are you 3.06.273
he that she refuses | must die then. 3.06.281
yes, i must, sir, | else both miscarry. 3.06.301
but you must know it, and as good by me | as by 4.01. 43
that you must lose your head to–morrow morning, 4.01. 77
and she must gather flowers to bury you, | and 4.01. 78
do, very /rearly, i must be abroad else, | to 4.01.110
for i must lose my maidenhead by cocklight, 4.01.112
you must ev'n take it patiently. 4.01.115
now with child by him — | there must be four. 4.01.130
and all these must be boys, | he has the trick 4.01.131
years old | they must be all gelt for musicians, 4.01.133
that must open | and bleed to death for my sake 4.02. 1
cannot distinguish, but must cry for both! 4.02. 54
that my unspotted youth must now be soil'd 4.02. 59
must be the sacrifice | to my unhappy beauty? 4.02. 63
my fair sister, | you must love one of them. 4.02. 68
must these men die too? 4.02.112
wench, it must be. 4.02.148
order it | fitting the persons that must use it. 4.02.151
you must bring a piece of silver on the tip of 4.03. 20 P
this you must do: 4.03. 74 P
we | the sails that must these vessels port even 5.01. 29
know my prize | must be dragg'd out of blood; 5.01. 43
force and great feat | must put my garland on, 5.01. 44
must be to him that makes the camp a cestron 5.01. 46
our stars must glister with new fire, or be 5.01. 69
a virgin flow'r, | must grow alone, unpluck'd. 5.01.168
that hostler | must rise betime that cozens him. 5.02. 60
besides, my father must be hang'd to–morrow, 5.02. 80
i must ev'n leave you here. 5.02.102
you must not from her, | but still preserve her 5.02.105
o, she must. 5.03. 11
you must be present, | you are the victor's meed 5.03. 15
you must be there; 5.03. 18
you must go. 5.03. 28
the knights must kindle | their valor at your 5.03. 29
and must needs be by | to give the service pay. 5.03. 31
but that your wills have said it must be so, 5.03.140
on one | that two must needs be blind for't! 5.03.146
to england, | why, you must needs be strangers; STM II.C 130
she bathes in water, yet her fire must burn. VEN 94
the sun doth burn my face, i must remove." 186
affection is a coal that must be cool'd, | else, 387
foul words and frowns must not repel a lover; 573
by the rights of time thou needs must have, | if 759
then, gentle shadow (truth i must confess), | i 1001
to wail his death who lives and must not die 1017
"had i been tooth'd like him, i must confess, 1117
such hazard now must doting tarquin make, LUC 155
lust, | and for himself himself he must forsake: 157
which must be lodestar to his lustful eye; 179
fire, | so lucrece must i force to my desire." 182
quoth he, "i must deflow'r: 348
but they must ope, this blessed league to kill, 383
lucrece to their sight | must sell her joy, her 385
where thou with patience must my will abide — 486
quoth he, "this night i must enjoy thee. 512
if thou deny, then force must work my way, | for 513
with foul offenders thou perforce must bear, 612
must he in thee read lectures of such shame? 618
drunken desire must vomit his receipt | ere he 703
infamy, | but i alone, alone must sit and pine, 795
so must my soul, her bark being pill'd away. 1169
how tarquin must be us'd, read it in me: 1195
mine, | and only must be wail'd by collatine." 1799
as they must needs (the sister and the brother), PP 8. 2
then must the love be great 'twixt thee and me, 8. 3
but one must be refused; 15. 9
poor corydon must live alone, | other help for 17.35
thy unus'd beauty must be tomb'd with thee, SON 4.13
that thou among the wastes of time must go, 12.10
and you must live drawn by your own sweet skill. 16.14
for through the painter must you see his skill 24. 5
that i an accessary needs must be | to that 35.13
let me confess that we two must be twain, 36. 1
kill me with spites, yet we must not be foes. 40.14
i must attend time's leisure with my moan, 44.12

lie, | as the death–bed whereon it must expire, 73.11
love that well, which thou must leave ere long. 73.14
save what is had or must from you be took. 75.12
though i (once gone) to all the world must die; 81. 6
for i must ne'er love him whom thou dost hate. 89.14
i must each day say o'er the very same, 108. 6
world, and i must strive | to know my shames and 112. 5
feel | needs must i under my transgression bow, 120. 3
mine ransoms yours, and yours must ransom me. 120.14
their rank thoughts my deeds must not be shown, 121.12
her audit (though delay'd) answer'd must be, 126.11
but slave to slavery my sweet'st friend must be? 133. 4
though in thy store's account i one must be, 136.10
the destin'd ill she must herself assay? LC 156
blood | that we must curb it upon others' proof, 163
but yield them up where i myself must render: 221
for these, of force, must your oblations be, 223
strong, | must for your victory us all congest, 258
MUSTACHIO 2 FR 0.0002 REL FR 0 V 2 P
dally with my excrement, with my mustachio; LLL 5.01.104 P
none of these mad mustachio purple–hu'd 1H4 2.01. 75 P
MUSTARD 9 FR 0.0010 REL FR 5 V 4 P
and swore by his honor the mustard was naught. AYL 1.02. 65 P
pancakes were naught and the mustard was good, 1.02. 66 P
ever he saw those pancakes or that mustard. 1.02. 80 P
what say you to a piece of beef and mustard? SHR 4.03. 23
ay, but the mustard is too hot a little. 4.03. 25
why then the beef, and let the mustard rest. 4.03. 26
nay then i will not, you shall have the mustard, 4.03. 27
why then the mustard without the beef. 4.03. 30
his wit's as thick as tewksbury mustard, there's 2H4 2.04.241 P
MUSTARDSEED 6 FR 0.0006 REL FR 2 V 4 P
and mustardseed! MND 3.01.162
mustardseed. 3.01.190
good master mustardseed, i know your patience 3.01.191 P
/of more acquaintance, good master mustardseed. 3.01.196 P
where's mounsieur mustardseed? 4.01. 17 P
give me your neaf, mounsieur mustardseed. 4.01. 19 P
MUSTER 17 FR 0.0019 REL FR 13 V 4 P
why does my blood thus muster to my heart, MM 2.04. 20
muster your wits, stand in your own defense, LLL 5.02. 85
there do muster true gait, eat, speak, and move AWW 2.01. 54 P
gentlemen, will you go muster men? R2 2.02.108
gentlemen, go muster up your men, | and meet me 2.02.118
come let us take a muster speedily. 1H4 4.01.133
and inland petty spirits muster me all to their 2H4 4.03.110 P
the muster of his kingdom too faint a number; H5 3.06.131 P
those will i muster up; 3H6 4.08. 11
in oxfordshire shalt muster up thy friends. 4.08. 18
go muster men. R3 4.03. 56
i'll muster up my friends and meet your grace 4.04.488
go then, and muster men; 4.04.494
is this moorfields to muster in? H8 5.03. 33 P
we would muster all | from twelve to seventy, COR 4.05.128
to whose weak ruins muster troops of cares, | to LUC 720
muster thy mists to meet the eastern light, 773
MUSTER–BOOK 1 FR 0.0001 REL FR 0 V 1 P
a number of shadows fill up the muster–book. 2H4 3.02.135 P
MUSTER'D 4 FR 0.0004 REL FR 4 V 0 P
an army have i muster'd in my thoughts, 1H6 1.01.101
muster'd my soldiers, gathered flocks of friends 3H6 2.01.112
command our present numbers | be muster'd; CYM 4.02.344
being not known, not muster'd | among the bands) 4.04. 10
MUSTER–FILE 1 FR 0.0001 REL FR 0 V 1 P
so that the muster–file, rotten and sound, upon AWW 4.03.166 P
MUSTERING 1 FR 0.0001 REL FR 1 V 0 P
is mustering in his clouds on our behalf R2 3.03. 86
MUSTERS 5 FR 0.0005 REL FR 5 V 0 P
i, | make fearful musters and prepar'd defense, 2H4 in 12
our present musters grow upon the file | to five 1.03. 10
but that defenses, musters, preparations, H5 2.04. 18
hasten his musters and conduct his pow'rs. LR 4.02. 16
that o'er the files and musters of the war ANT 1.01. 3
MUST'RING 1 FR 0.0001 REL FR 1 V 0 P
must'ring to the quiet cabinet | where their LUC 442
MUSTY 9 FR 0.0010 REL FR 6 V 3 P
you had musty victual, and he hath holp to eat ADO 1.01. 50 P
for a perfumer, as i was smoking a musty room, 1.03. 59 P
shall ha' means to vent | our musty superfluity. COR 1.01.226
to pick them in a pile | of noisome musty chaff. 5.01. 26
you are the musty chaff, and you are smelt 5.01. 31
green earthen pots, bladders, and musty seeds, ROM 5.01. 46
grass grows" — the proverb is something musty. HAM 3.02.344 P
and rogues forlorn | in short and musty straw? LR 4.07. 39
and let thy musty vapors march so thick | that LUC 782
MUTABILITY 2 FR 0.0002 REL FR 1 V 1 P
and inconstant, and mutability, and variation; H5 3.06. 34 P
disdain, | nice longing, slanders, mutability, CYM 2.05. 26
MUTABLE 1 FR 0.0001 REL FR 1 V 0 P
for the mutable, rank–scented meiny, let them COR 3.01. 66
MUTATION 1 FR 0.0001 REL FR 1 V 0 P
though his /humor | was nothing but mutation, ay CYM 4.02.133
MUTATIONS 1 FR 0.0001 REL FR 1 V 0 P
that thy strange mutations make us hate thee, LR 4.01. 11
MUTE 20 FR 0.0022 REL FR 19 V 1 P
hush and be mute, | or else our spell is marr'd. TMP 4.01.126
my servant straight was mute. LLL 5.02.277
say she be mute, and will not speak a word, SHR 2.01.174
thanks, sir; all the rest is mute. AWW 2.03. 77
be you his eunuch, and your mute i'll be; TN 1.02. 62
to a vision so apparent rumor | cannot be mute), WT 1.02.271
and the mute wonder lurketh in men's ears | to H5 1.01. 49
like turkish mute, shall have a tongueless mouth 1.02.232
that my woe–wearied tongue is still and mute. R3 4.04. 18
ah, why should wrath be mute and fury dumb? TIT 5.03.184
or given my heart a /winking, mute and dumb, HAM 2.02.137
that thou wilt be a voluntary mute to my design. CYM 3.05.153 P
lute | she sung, and made the night/–bird mute, PER 4.ch. 26
abandoner of revels, mute, contemplative, TNK 5.01.138
fair, but speak fair words, or else be mute. VEN 208
but when the heart's attorney once is mute, 335
will not my tongue be mute, my frail joints LUC 227
and in my hearing be you mute and dumb, | my 1123
dumb, | for i impair not beauty being mute, SON 83.11
thee, | and, thou away, the very birds are mute; 97.12
MUTES 1 FR 0.0001 REL FR 1 V 0 P
that are but mutes or audience to this act, HAM 5.02.335
MUTEST 1 FR 0.0001 REL FR 1 V 0 P
that from my mutest conscience to my tongue CYM 1.06.116
MUTINE 1 FR 0.0001 REL FR 1 V 0 P
if thou canst mutine in a matron's bones, | to HAM 3.04. 83
MUTINEER 1 FR 0.0001 REL FR 0 V 1 P
if you prove a mutineer — the next tree! TMP 3.02. 36 P
MUTINERS 1 FR 0.0001 REL FR 1 V 0 P
worshipful mutiners, | your valor puts well COR 1.01.250
MUTINES 3 FR 0.0003 REL FR 3 V 0 P
do like the mutines of jerusalem, | be friends JN 2.01.378
i lay | worse than the mutines in the /bilboes. HAM 5.02. 6
as mutines are incident, by his name | can still STM II.C 115
MUTINIES 4 FR 0.0004 REL FR 2 V 2 P
voice | was wont to cheer his dad in mutinies? 3H6 1.04. 77
spirit that mutinies in a man's bosom. R3 1.04.138 P
their mutinies and revolts, wherein they show'd COR 3.01.126
in cities, mutinies; LR 1.02.107 P
MUTINOUS 7 FR 0.0008 REL FR 7 V 0 P
noontide sun, call'd forth the mutinous winds, TMP 5.01. 42
erroneous, mutinous, and unnatural, | this 3H6 2.05. 90
not mutinous in peace, yet bold in war; 4.08. 10
the mutinous parts | that envied his receipt; COR 1.01.111
this good belly, | and you the mutinous members: 1.01.149
the dearth is great, | the people mutinous; 1.02. 11
then let the mutinous winds | strike the proud 5.03. 59
MUTINY 27 FR 0.0030 REL FR 25 V 2 P
wrong | have chose as umpeer of their mutiny. LLL 1.01.169
me, begins to mutiny against this servitude. AYL 1.01. 23 P
where will doth mutiny with wit's regard. R2 2.01. 28
fear, and mutiny | shall here inhabit, and this 4.01.142
supply, | and hardly keeps his men from mutiny, 1H6 1.01.160
mouths | to raise a mutiny betwixt yourselves. 4.01.131
thy knee, | or sack this country with a mutiny. 5.01. 62
myself have calm'd their spleenful mutiny, 2H6 3.02.128
it may well be, | there is a mutiny in 's mind. H8 3.02.120
what mutiny! TRO 1.03. 96
this mutiny were better put in hazard | than COR 2.03.256
to stir a mutiny in the mildest thoughts, | and TIT 4.01. 85
from ancient grudge break to new mutiny, | where ROM pr 3
my soul, | you'll make a mutiny among my guests! 1.05. 80
here, quite confounded with this mutiny. JC 3.01. 86
stir | your hearts and minds to mutiny and rage, 3.02.122
stir you up | to such a sudden flood of mutiny. 3.02.211
move | the stones of rome to rise and mutiny. 3.02.230
we'll mutiny. 3.02.231
of that will i cause these of cyprus to mutiny, OTH 2.01.275 P
go out and cry a mutiny. 2.03.157
my very hairs do mutiny; ANT 3.11. 13
the mutiny he there hastes t' oppress, | says to PER 3.ch. 29
gives false alarms, suggesteth mutiny, | and in VEN 651
this mutiny each part doth so surprise | that 1049
his eye, which late this mutiny restrains, LUC 426
out readily, | so with herself is she in mutiny, 1153
MUTIUS' 2 FR 0.0002 REL FR 2 V 0 P
my nephew mutius' deeds do plead for him, | he TIT 1.01.356
not i, till mutius' bones be buried. 1.01.369
MUTIUS 5 FR 0.0005 REL FR 5 V 0 P
give mutius burial with our bretheren. TIT 1.01.348
of thee | to pardon mutius and to bury him. 1.01.363
let not young mutius then, that was thy joy, 1.01.382
there lie thy bones, sweet mutius, with thy 1.01.387
no man shed tears for noble mutius, | he lives 1.01.389
MUTTER 4 FR 0.0004 REL FR 2 V 2 P
how now, wool–sack, what mutter you? 1H4 2.04.135 P
what mutter you, or what conspire you, lords? 3H6 1.01.165
how? what does his cashier'd worship mutter? TIM 3.04. 61 P
that in their sleeps will mutter their affairs; OTH 3.03.417
MUTTERED 1 FR 0.0001 REL FR 1 V 0 P
amongst the soldiers this is muttered, | that 1H6 1.01. 70
MUTTON 11 FR 0.0012 REL FR 1 V 10 P
i (a lost mutton) gave your letter to her (a TGV 1.01. 96 P
gave your letter to her (a lac'd mutton), and 1.01. 97 P
and she (a lac'd mutton) gave me (a lost mutton) 1.01. 97 P
gave me (a lost mutton) nothing for my labor. 1.01. 98 P
say to thee again) would eat mutton on fridays. MM 3.02.181 P
rather pray a month with mutton and porridge. LLL 1.01.302 P
not the grease of a mutton as wholesome as the AYL 3.02. 56 P
mutton? SHR 4.01.160
and i can cut the mutton to't. TN 1.03.122 P
what's a joint of mutton or two in a whole lent? 2H4 2.04.346 P
couple of short–legg'd hens, a joint of mutton, 5.01. 27 P
MUTTONS 2 FR 0.0002 REL FR 1 V 1 P
too small a pasture for such store of muttons. TGV 1.01.100 P
neither, | as flesh of muttons, beefs, or goats. MV 1.03.167
MUTUAL 18 FR 0.0020 REL FR 18 V 0 P
one feast, one house, one mutual happiness. TGV 5.04.173
the stealth of our most mutual entertainment MM 1.02.154
every region near | seem all one mutual cry. MND 4.01.117
you shall perceive them make a mutual stand, MV 5.01. 77
confirm'd by mutual joinder of your hands, TN 5.01.157
shall now, in mutual well–beseeming ranks, 1H4 1.01. 14
the mutual conference that my mind hath had, 2H6 1.01. 25
that bear this heavy mutual load of moan, | now R3 2.02.113
and choice (being mutual act of all our souls) TRO 1.03.348
this scattered corn into one mutual sheaf, TIT 5.03. 71
souls, | and make a mutual closure of our house. 5.03.134
the face of it is cover'd | with mutual cunning) LR 3.01. 21
when such a mutual pair | and such a twain can ANT 1.01. 37
and that blood we desire to shed is mutual — TNK 3.06. 95
not die | till mutual overthrow of mortal kind! VEN 1018
the turtle fled | in a mutual flame from hence. PHT 24
strikes each in each by mutual ordering; SON 8.10
no art, | but mutual render, only me for thee. 125.12
/MUTUALITIES 1 FR 0.0001 REL FR 0 V 1 P
when these /mutualities so marshal the way, hard OTH 2.01.261 P
MUTUALLY 5 FR 0.0005 REL FR 5 V 0 P
who mutually hath answer'd my affection | (so WIV 4.06. 10
pinch him, fairies, mutually! 5.05. 99
most offenseful act | was mutually committed? MM 2.03. 27
mutually. 2.03. 27
and, mutually participate, did minister | unto COR 1.01.103
MUZZLE 3 FR 0.0003 REL FR 2 V 1 P
i am trusted with a muzzle and enfranchis'd with ADO 1.03. 33 P
curb'd license plucks | the muzzle of restraint, 2H4 4.05.131
and i | have not the power to muzzle him, H8 1.01.121
MUZZLED 2 FR 0.0002 REL FR 2 V 0 P
my dagger muzzled | lest it should bite its WT 1.02.156
and then our arms, like to a muzzled bear, JN 2.01.249
/MY 117 FR 0.0132 REL FR 97 V 20 P
MY 13075 FR 1.4780 REL FR 10469 V 2606 P
MYRMIDON 1 FR 0.0001 REL FR 1 V 0 P
man, | for that will physic the great myrmidon, TRO 1.03.377
MYRMIDONS *(also mermidons)*
MYRMIDONS 3 FR 0.0003 REL FR 3 V 0 P
blood, | together with his mangled myrmidons, TRO 5.05. 33
come here about me, you my myrmidons, | mark 5.07. 1
on, myrmidons, and cry you all amain, 5.08. 13
MYRTLE 5 FR 0.0005 REL FR 5 V 0 P
and gnarled oak | than the soft myrtle; MM 2.02.117
as is the morn–dew on the myrtle leaf | to his ANT 3.12. 9
this said, she hasteth to a myrtle grove, VEN 865
by her, | under a myrtle shade began to woo him. PP 11. 2
kirtle | embroidered all with leaves of myrtle; 19.12
MYRTLES 1 FR 0.0001 REL FR 1 V 0 P
pleasant shade, | which a grove of myrtles made, PP 20. 4
/MYSELF 11 FR 0.0012 REL FR 9 V 2 P
/now /mark /me /how /i /will /undo /myself: R2 4.01.203
/that /my /wretchedness /doth /bait /myself, 4.01.238
/nay, /if /i /turn /mine /eyes /upon /myself, 4.01.247
/i /find /myself /a /traitor /with /the /rest; 4.01.248
/know /not /now /what /name /to /call /myself! 4.01.259
/to /melt /myself /away /in //water–drops! 4.01.262
/all /my /sins /are /writ, /and /that's /myself. 4.01.275
/flattering /myself /as /if /it /were /the /moor TIT 3.02. 72
/and /count /myself /a /king /of /infinite HAM 2.02.255 P
/that /to /laertes /i /forgot /myself, | /for 5.02. 76
/not /let /me /have /all /the /fool /to /myself, LR 1.04.155 P
MYSELF 615 FR 0.0695 REL FR 499 V 116 P
none that i more love than myself. TMP 1.01. 20 P
myself am naples, | who with mine eyes (never 1.02.435
i find not | myself dispos'd to sleep. 2.01.202
i myself could make | a chough of as deep chat. 2.01.265
i'll swear myself thy subject. 2.02.152
i shall laugh myself to death at this 2.02.154 P
who am myself attach'd with weariness | to th' 3.03. 5
of their afflictions, and shall not myself, 5.01. 22
and myself present | as i was sometime milan. 5.01. 85
her sovereign aid, | and rest myself content. 5.01.144
i wish | myself were mudded in that oozy bed 5.01.151
i /leave myself, my friends, and all, for love. TGV 1.01. 65
the dog is me, and i am myself; 2.03. 23 P
i knew him as myself: 2.04. 62
and though myself have been an idle truant, 2.04. 64
if i keep them, i needs must lose myself; 2.06. 20
find i by their loss — | for valentine, myself; 2.06. 22
i to myself am dearer than a friend, | for love 2.06. 23
i cannot now prove constant to myself, | without 2.06. 31
myself in counsel his competitor. 2.06. 35
myself am one made privy to the plot. 3.01. 12
this love of theirs myself have often seen, 3.01. 24
tow'r, | the key whereof myself have ever kept; 3.01. 36
how and which way i may bestow myself | to be 3.01. 87
because myself do want my servants' fortune. 3.01.147
i curse myself, for they are sent by me, | that 3.01.148
to die is to be banish'd from myself, | and 3.01.171
be banish'd from myself, | and silvia is myself: 3.01.172
but what woman, i will not tell myself; 3.01.269 P
myself was from verona banished | for practicing 4.01. 45
and by and by intend to chide myself | even for 4.02.103
unless i prove false traitor to myself. 4.04.105
almost as well as i do know myself. 4.04.143
i weep myself to think upon thy words. 4.04.175
little, | unless i flatter with myself too much. 4.04.188
in her, | but i can make respective in myself, 4.04.195
page (fidelicet master page) and there is myself WIV 1.01.139 P
and there is myself (fidelicet myself) and the 1.01.139 P
i must wait on myself, must i? 1.01.201 P
thrift, you rogues — myself and skirted page. 1.03. 84
and drink, make the beds, and do all myself) — 1.04. 97 P
tell–a me dat i shall have anne page for myself? 1.04.116 P
by gar, i will myself have anne page. 1.04.119 P
i'll entertain myself like one that i am not 2.01. 86 P
know some strain in me that i know not myself, 2.01. 88 P
i, i, i myself sometimes, leaving the fear of /god 2.02. 23 P
i myself dwell with master doctor caius — 2.02. 45 P
i had myself twenty angels given me this morning 2.02. 72 P
understand i think myself in better plight for a 2.02.166 P
as desire to make myself acquainted with you. 2.02.183 P
i must excuse myself, master ford. 3.02. 55 P
i would i could wash myself of the buck! 3.03.157 P
well, i will proclaim myself what i am. 3.05.144 P
prosper'd since i forswore myself at primero. 4.05.101 P
i was beaten myself into all the colors of the 4.05.115 P
i will keep my sides to myself, my shoulders for 5.05. 25 P
i think i have done myself wrong, have i not? MM 1.02. 40 P
for that which, if myself might be his judge, 1.04. 27
bore many gentlemen (myself being one) | in hand 1.04. 51
sir, i will detest myself also, as well as she, 2.01. 75 P
as much for my poor brother as myself: 2.04. 99
and strip myself to death, as to a bed | that, 2.04.102
i do make myself believe that you may most 3.01.199 P
i drink, i eat, /array myself, and live. 3.02. 25
i have kept it myself; 3.02.202 P
of my cunning, i will lay myself in hazard. 4.02.156 P
here is the head, i'll carry it myself. 4.03.102
speech of marriage | betwixt myself and her; 5.01.218
i protest i love the duke as i love myself. 5.01.341 P
and you may marvel why i obscur'd myself, 5.01.390
i find an apt remission in myself; 5.01.498
which though myself would gladly have embrac'd, ERR 1.01. 69
i will go lose myself, | and wander up and down 1.02. 30
in quest of them (unhappy), ah, lose myself. 1.02. 40
known unto these, and to myself disguis'd? 2.02.214
am i myself? 3.02. 74 P
an ass, i am a woman's man, and besides myself. 3.02. 78 P
marry, sir, besides myself, i am due to a woman: 3.02. 81 P
hath almost made me traitor to myself; 3.02.162
but, lest myself be guilty to self–wrong, | i'll 3.02.163
office, | and will have no attorney but myself, 5.01.100
myself, he, and my sister | to–day did dine 5.01.207
i would scarce trust myself, though i had sworn ADO 1.01.195 P
any, i will do myself the right to trust none; 1.01.244 P
can cross him any way, i bless myself every way. 1.03. 68 P
yea, but so i am apt to do myself wrong. 2.01.206 P
not thinking i had been myself, that i was the 2.01.243 P

i give away myself for you, and dote upon the 2.01.309 P
all other respects, and made her half myself. 2.03.170 P
they say i will bear myself proudly, if i 2.03.225 P
she would laugh me | out of myself, press me to 3.01. 76
myself, my brother, and this grieved count | did 4.01. 89
myself would, on the rearward of reproaches, 4.01.126
so much | that i myself was to myself not mine, 4.01.138
so much | that i myself was to myself not mine, 4.01.138
trumpet of his own virtues, as i am to myself. 5.02. 86 P
so much for praising myself, who, i myself will 5.02. 87 P
who, i myself will bear witness, is praiseworthy 5.02. 87 P
i myself reprehend his own person, for i am his LLL 1.01.183 P
and, as i am a gentleman, betook myself to walk: 1.01.235 P
i do betray myself with blushing. maid. 1.02.133 P
though to myself forsworn, to thee i'll faithful 4.02.107
i am coursing myself. 4.03. 2 P
myself; 5.01.126 P
i will play three myself. 5.01.143 P
and i will right myself like a soldier. 5.02.724 P
lysander and myself will fly this place. MND 1.01.203
there my lysander and myself shall meet; 1.01.217
myself, thisby's father; 1.02. 63 P
because she is something lower than myself, 3.02.304
myself the man i' th' moon do seem to be. 5.01.245
of me, | that i have much ado to know myself. MV 1.01. 7
and hedg'd me by his wit to yield myself | his 2.01. 18
the suit is impertinent to myself, as your 2.02.138 P
doors, and gild myself | with some moe ducats, 2.06. 49
deserving | were but a weak disabling of myself. 2.07. 30
though for myself alone | i would not be 3.02.150
in my wish | to wish myself much better, yet, 3.02.152
you | i would be trebled twenty times myself, 3.02.153
myself, and what is mine, to you and yours | is 3.02.166
master of my servants, | queen o'er myself; 3.02.169
servants, and this same myself | are yours — my 3.02.170
rating myself at nothing, you shall see | how 3.02.257
indeed | i have engag'd myself to a dear friend, 3.02.261
my maid nerissa and myself mean time | will live 3.02.309
this comes too near the praising of myself, 3.04. 22
jessica | in place of lord bassanio and myself. 3.04. 39
and therein do account myself well paid. 4.01.417
i will not shame myself to give you this. 4.01.431
thine own fair eyes, | wherein i see myself — 5.01.243
i had myself notice of my brother's purpose AYL 1.01.139 P
take the part of a better wrastler than myself! 1.03. 23 P
if with myself i hold intelligence, | or have 1.03. 47
i'll put myself in poor and mean attire, | and 1.03.111
to–day my lord of amiens and myself | did steal 2.01. 29
more at your request than to please myself. 2.05. 23 P
i scarce can speak to thank you for myself. 2.07.170
faith, i had as lief have been myself alone. 3.02.254 P
will chide no breather in the world but myself, 3.02.280 P
to you i give myself, for i am yours. 5.04.116
to you i give myself, for i am yours. 5.04.117
on them to look and practice by myself. SHR 1.01. 83
and i have thrust myself into this maze, 1.02. 55
unbind my hands, i'll pull them off myself, 2.01. 4
here i swear | i'll plead for you myself, but 2.01. 15
am bold to show myself a forward guest | within 2.01. 51
to express the like kindness, myself, that have 2.01. 77 P
do make myself a suitor to your daughter, | unto 2.01. 90
myself am mov'd to woo thee for my wife. 2.01.194
be patient, gentlemen, i choose her for myself. 2.01.302
myself am strook in years, i must confess, | and 2.01.360
but learn my lessons as i please myself. 3.01. 20
'twere well for kate and better for myself. 3.02.120
that have beheld me give away myself | to this 3.02.194
no, nor to–morrow — not till i please myself. 3.02.209
for me, i'll not be gone till i please myself. 3.02.212
but i with blowing the fire shall warm myself; 4.01. 10 P
my old master and my new mistress and myself, 4.01. 25 P
how diligent i am | to dress thy meat myself, 4.03. 40
now, by my mother's son, and that's myself, | it 4.05. 6
what tranio did, myself enforc'd him to; 5.01.129
i'll bear it all myself. 5.02. 79
as when thy father and myself in friendship AWW 1.02. 25
proclaim | myself against the level of mine aim, 2.01.156
i will show myself highly fed and lowly taught. 2.02. 3 P
found | myself in my incertain grounds to fail 3.01. 15
day, | great mars, i put myself into thy file; 3.03. 9
me, | whom i myself embrace to set him free." 3.04. 17
think i know your hostess | as ample as myself. 3.05. 43
my dilemmas, encourage myself in my certainty, 3.06. 75 P
put myself into my mortal preparation; 3.06. 76 P
i must give myself some hurts, and say i got 4.01. 37 P
mouth and buy myself another of bajazeth's mule, 4.01. 42 P
that she whom all men prais'd and whom myself, 5.03. 53
close | her eyes myself could win me to believe, 5.03.119
you give away myself, which is known mine; 5.03.172
i'll confine myself no finer than i am. TN 1.03. 10 P
for i myself am best | when least in company. 1.04. 37
whoe'er i woo, myself would be his wife. 1.04. 42
if i do not usurp myself, i am. 1.05.186 P
my master, not myself, lacks recompense. 1.05.285
me in manners the rather to express myself. 2.01. 15 P
he left behind him myself and a sister, both 2.01. 19 P
i do not now fool myself, to let imagination 2.05.164 P
so did i abuse | myself, my servant, and, i fear 3.01.114
only myself stood out, | for which, if i be 3.03. 35
i cannot do for you | than what befalls myself. 3.04.337
and i will dissemble myself in't, and i would i 4.02. 4 P
i profit in the knowledge of myself, and by my 5.01. 20 P
for his sake | did i expose myself (pure for his 5.01. 83
which i doubt not but to do myself much right, 5.01.308 P
myself and toby | set this device against 5.01.359
and saw myself unbreech'd | in my green velvet WT 1.02.155
to appoint myself in this vexation, sully | the 1.02.326
finding | myself thus alter'd with't. 1.02.384
for myself, i'll put | my fortunes to your 1.02.439
and i had rather glib myself than they | should 2.01.149
who professes | myself your loyal servant, your 2.03. 54
my part no other | but what comes from myself, 3.02. 25
myself on every post | proclaim'd a strumpet; 3.02.101
i did in time collect myself and thought | this 3.03. 38
sworn, i think, | to show myself a glass. 4.04. 14
let myself and fortune | tug for the time to 4.04.496
and so still think of | the wrong i did myself; 5.01. 9
being, have preserv'd | myself to see the issue. 5.03.128

and fits the mounting spirit like myself; JN 1.01.206
the shadow of myself form'd in her eye, | which, 2.01.498
i do protest i never lov'd myself | till now 2.01.501
till now infixed i beheld myself | drawn in the 2.01.502
for then 'tis like i should forget myself. 3.04. 49
woes, | and teaches me to kill or hang myself. 3.04. 56
both for myself and them — but, chief of all, 4.02. 49
for the which myself and them | bend their best 4.02. 50
between this chastis'd kingdom and myself, | and 5.02. 84
myself, well mounted, hardly have escap'd. 5.06. 42
with whom yourself, myself, and other lords, 5.07. 93
traitor, | which in myself i boldly will defend, R2 1.01.145
to prove myself a loyal gentleman | even in the 1.01.148
myself i throw, dread sovereign, at thy foot, 1.01.165
where then, alas, may i complain myself? 1.02. 42
arm, | to prove him, in defending of myself, | a 1.03. 23
for mowbray and myself are like two men | that 1.03. 48
against my will to do myself this wrong. 1.03.246
ill in myself to see, and in thee, seeing ill. 2.01. 94
so, | stay, and be secret, and myself will go. 2.01.298
king i did, to please myself | i cannot do it; 2.02. 5
who, weak with age, cannot support myself. 2.02. 83
sure | i count myself in nothing else so happy 2.03. 46
father, and myself | rescued the black prince, 2.03.100
myself, a prince by fortune of my birth, | near 3.01. 16
i had forgot myself, am i not king? 3.02. 83
and oppose not myself | against their will. 3.03. 18
methinks king richard and myself should meet 3.03. 54
and here is not a creature but myself, | i 5.05. 4
then treasons make me wish myself a beggar, 5.05. 33
sure | i will from henceforth rather be myself, 1H4 1.03. 5
he did, myself did hear it. 1.03.157
is there not my father, my uncle, and myself? 2.03. 24 P
o, i could divide myself and go to buffets, for 2.03. 32 P
since you love me not, | i will not love myself. 2.03. 98
i shall think the better of myself, and thee, 2.04.274 P
to say i know more harm in him than in myself, 2.04.467 P
for i myself at this time have employ'd him. 2.04.513
can purge | myself of many i am charg'd withal; 3.02. 21
and dress'd myself in such humility | that i did 3.02. 51
my thrice–gracious lord, | be more myself. 3.02. 93
my father and my uncle and myself | did give him 4.03. 54
looks | of favor from myself and all our house, 5.01. 31
it was myself, my brother, and his son, | that 5.01. 39
and even in thy behalf i'll thank myself | for 5.04. 97
why, percy i kill'd myself, and saw thee dead. 5.04.144
myself and you, son harry, will towards wales, 5.05. 39
i am not only witty in myself, but the cause 2H4 1.02. 10 P
prove that ever i dress myself handsome till thy 2.04.279 P
and i myself know well | how troublesome it sate 4.05.185
and do arm myself | to welcome the condition of 5.02. 10
than i do at this hour joy o'er myself, H5 2.02.163
i do not know you so good a man as myself. 3.02.132 P
'tis midnight, i'll go arm myself. 3.07. 89 P
i myself heard the king say he would not be 4.01.190 P
when alanson and myself were down together, i 4.07.154 P
i by bargain should | wear it myself. 4.07.175
and myself have play'd | the interim, by 5.pr. 42
i will slay myself | for living idly here in 1H6 1.01.141
i myself fight not once in forty year. 1.03. 91
and, for myself, most part of all this night, 2.01. 67
myself, as far as i could well discern | for 2.02. 26
no, no, i am but shadow of myself. 2.03. 50
and i myself | will see his burial better than 2.05.120
haps it i seek not to advance | or raise myself, 3.01. 32
hearts, | because i ever found them as myself. 3.02. 98
to save myself by flight. 3.02.105
myself and divers gentlemen beside | were there 4.01. 25
wife | and have no portion in the choice myself. 5.03.125
o, wert thou for myself! 5.03.187
or hath mine uncle beauford and myself, | with 2H6 1.01. 88
myself did win them both. 1.01.119
next time i'll keep my dreams unto myself, | and 1.02. 53
madam, myself have lim'd a bush for her, | and 1.03. 88
oft | myself have heard a voice to call him so. 2.01. 92
madam, for myself, to heaven i do appeal, | how 2.01.186
in this close walk to satisfy myself | in 2.02. 3
and, nevil, this i do assure myself, | richard 2.02. 80
to prove him a knave and myself an honest man; 2.03. 87 P
ah, gloucester, teach me to forget myself! 2.04. 27
myself had notice of your conventicles — | and 3.01.166
even so myself bewails good gloucester's case 3.01.217
and for myself, foe as he was to me, | might 3.02. 59
myself have calm'd their spleenful mutiny, 3.02.128
myself and beauford had him in protection, | and 3.02.180
well assur'd, | adventure to be banished myself; 3.02.350
myself no joy in nought but that thou liv'st. 3.02.366
him, i will make myself a knight presently. 4.02.119 P
he lies, for i invented it myself. 4.02.155
and i myself, | rather than bloody war shall cut 4.04. 11
but i am troubled here with them myself; 4.05. 7
and work in their shirt too, as myself, for 4.07. 52 P
i feel remorse in myself with his words; 4.07.105 P
lord, | i'll yield myself to prison willingly, 4.09. 42
fie on myself, that have a sword, and yet am 4.10. 1 P
i have considered with myself | the title of 5.01.175
for i myself must hunt this deer to death. 5.02. 15
not for myself, lord warwick, but my son, | whom 3H6 1.01.192
i here divorce myself | both from thy table, 1.01.247
lord george your brother, norfolk, and myself, 2.01.138
now, if the help of norfolk and myself, | with 2.01.178
for i myself will hunt this wolf to death. 2.04. 13
so many hours must i sport myself, | so many 2.05. 34
for how can i help them and not myself? 3.01. 21
ay, full as dearly as i love myself. 3.02. 37
why, clarence, to myself. 3.02.112
to take their rooms, ere i can place myself: 3.02.132
such | as are of better person than myself, 3.02.167
torment myself to catch the english crown; 3.02.179
and from that torment i will free myself, | or 3.02.180
fortune, | and to my humble seat conform myself. 3.03. 11
myself have often heard him say, and swear, 3.03.123
and meaner than myself have had like fortune. 4.01. 71
myself in person will straight follow you. 4.01.133
land, | while i myself will lead a private life, 4.06. 42
consent, | for on thy fortune i repose myself. 4.06. 47
hands, | i here proclaim myself thy mortal foe; 5.01. 94
i am myself alone. 5.06. 83

rest, | counting myself but bad till i be best. 5.06. 91
thine uncles and myself | have in our armors 5.07. 16
with this, my lord, myself have nought to do. R3 1.01. 97
me leave | by circumstance but to acquit myself. 1.02. 77
me have | some patient leisure to excuse myself. 1.02. 82
by such despair i should accuse myself. 1.02. 85
then bid me kill myself, and i will do it. 1.02.186
cannot) | myself to be a marv'llous proper man. 1.02.254
since i am crept in favor with myself, | i will 1.02.258
against my children, brothers, and myself, 1.03. 67
myself disgrac'd, and the nobility | held in 1.03. 78
for had i curs'd now, i had curs'd myself. 1.03.318
i, ungracious, speak unto myself | for him, poor 2.01.128
weep, | to chide my fortune, and torment myself? 2.02. 35
my soul, | and to myself become an enemy. 2.02. 37
i promise you, i scarcely know myself. 2.03. 2
myself and my good cousin buckingham | will to 3.01.137
his honor and myself are at the one, | and at 3.02. 21
for i myself am not so well provided | as else i 3.04. 44
and i myself secure, in grace and favor. 3.04. 91
fee for which i plead | were for myself — and 3.05. 97
for them | as i can say nay to thee for myself, 3.07. 53
tell him, myself, the mayor and aldermen, | in 3.07. 66
slander myself as false to edward's bed, | throw 4.04.208
even all i have — ay, and myself and all — 4.04.249
then by myself — 4.04.374
for i myself have many tears to wash | hereafter 4.04.389
myself myself confound! 4.04.399
myself myself confound! 4.04.399
without her, follows to myself and thee, 4.04.407
shall i forget myself to be myself? 4.04.420
shall i forget myself to be myself? 4.04.420
o thou whose captain i account myself, | look on 5.03.108
myself? 5.03.182
what, from myself? 5.03.185
what, myself upon myself? 5.03.186
what, myself upon myself? 5.03.186
alack, i love myself. 5.03.187
any good | that i myself have done unto myself? 5.03.188
any good | that i myself have done unto myself? 5.03.188
alas, i rather hate myself | for hateful deeds 5.03.189
myself | for hateful deeds committed by myself. 5.03.190
since that i myself | find in myself no pity to 5.03.202
i myself | find in myself no pity to myself? 5.03.203
i myself | find in myself no pity to myself? 5.03.203
his person | more worthy this place than myself, H8 1.04. 79
i myself | would for carnarvonshire, although 2.03. 47
have i liv'd thus long (let me speak myself, 3.01.125
i dare not make myself so guilty | to give up 3.01.139
if i have us'd myself unmannerly, | you know i 3.01.176
i know myself now, and i feel within me | a 3.02.378
and i myself have ventur'd | to speak my mind of 5.01. 40
under more calumnious tongues | than i myself, 5.01.113
that i shall clear myself, | lay all the weight 5.02.100
my noble partners and myself thus pray | all 5.04. 5
i propose not merely to myself | the pleasures TRO 2.02.146
and yet, good faith, i wish'd myself a man, | or 3.02.127
expos'd myself | from certain and possess'd 3.03. 6
and i myself see not the bottom of it. 3.03.309
deserves fair helen best, | myself, or menelaus? 4.01. 55
i will not be myself, nor have cognition | of 5.02. 63
and i myself | am like a prophet suddenly enrapt 5.03. 64
beseech you give me leave to retire myself. COR 1.03. 27
and, knowing myself again, | repair to th' 2.03.147
people, in whose name myself | attach thee as a 3.01.173
i could myself | take up a brace o' th' best of 3.01.242
i sup upon myself, | and so shall starve with 4.02. 50
man i am, necessity | commands me name myself. 4.05. 57
being assur'd none but myself could move thee, i 5.02. 73 P
even he, your wife, this lady, and myself, | are 5.03. 77
for myself, son, | i purpose not to wait on 5.03.118
out of that i'll work | myself a former fortune. 5.03.202
and took some pride | to do myself this wrong; 5.06. 37
i'll deliver | myself your loyal servant, or 5.06.140
love and favor of my country | commit myself, my TIT 1.01. 59
to do myself this reason and this right. 1.01.279
wouldst thou have me prove myself a bastard? 2.03.148
and 'twere my cause, i should go hang myself. 2.04. 9
my mistress is my mistress, this myself, | the 4.02.107
cornelia the midwife, and myself, | and no one 4.02.141
"ad martem," that's for myself; 4.03. 55
myself hath often heard them say, | when i have 4.04. 74
hand, | and when i had it, drew myself apart, 5.01.112
it, | accuse some innocent, and forswear myself, 5.01.130
lastly, myself unkindly banished, | the gates 5.03.104
i will show myself a tyrant: ROM 1.01. 21 P
both by myself and many other friends, | but he, 1.01.146
tut, i have lost myself, i am not here: 1.01.197
which is no part of thee, | take all myself. 2.02. 49
my name, dear saint, is hateful to myself, 2.02. 55
what she bid me say, i will keep to myself. 2.04.164 P
stratagems | upon so soft a subject as myself! 3.05.210
if all else fail, myself have power to die. 3.05.242
well, i will walk myself | to county paris, to 4.02. 44
i pray thee leave me to myself to–night, | for i 4.03. 2
noting this penury, to myself i said, | "an' if 5.01. 49
by heaven, i love thee better than myself, | for 5.03. 64
for i come hither arm'd against myself. 5.03. 65
and purge | myself condemned and myself excus'd. 5.03.227
and purge | myself condemned and myself excus'd. 5.03.227
him her resort, | myself have spoke in vain. TIM 1.01.128
i myself would have no power; 1.02. 36 P
i crave no pelf, | i pray for no man but myself. 1.02. 63
told more of you to myself than you can with 1.02. 93 P
i have often wish'd myself poorer, that i might 1.02.100 P
was i to disfurnish myself against such a good 3.02. 44 P
time, when i might ha' shown myself honorable! 3.02. 46 P
i was sending to use lord timon myself, these 3.02. 50 P
interest — i myself | rich only in large hurts. 3.05.107
were i like thee, i'd throw away myself. 4.03.219
but myself, | who had the world as my 4.03.259
myself. 4.03.315 P
he and myself | have travail'd in the great 5.01. 69
for myself, | there's not a whittle in th' 5.01.179
till now myself and such | as slept within the 5.04. 5
out their shoes, to get myself into more work. JC 1.01. 29 P
trouble of my countenance | merely upon myself. 1.02. 39
difference, | conceptions only proper to myself, 1.02. 41

that you would have me seek into myself | for 1.02. 64
you know | that i profess myself in banqueting 1.02. 77
live to be | in awe of such a thing as i myself. 1.02. 96
i did present myself | even in the aim and very 1.03. 51
giving myself a voluntary wound | here, in the 2.01.300
never shall turn back, | for i will slay myself. 3.01. 22
if i myself, there is no hour so fit | as 3.01.153
years, | i shall not find myself so apt to die; 3.01.160
pardon — | i will myself into the pulpit first, 3.01.236
i have the same dagger for myself, when it shall 3.02. 46 P
to wrong the dead, to wrong myself and you, 3.02.126
i have o'ershot myself to tell you of it. 3.02.150
urge me no more, i shall forget myself; 4.03. 35
myself have letters of the self–same tenure. 4.03.171
arming myself with patience | to stay the 5.01.105
myself have to mine own turn'd enemy. 5.03. 2
i'll rather kill myself. 5.05. 7
i myself have all the other, | and the very MAC 1.03. 14
i'll be myself the harbinger and make joyful 1.04. 45
shut the door, | not bear the knife myself. 1.07. 16
to know my deed, 'twere best not know myself. 2.02. 70
but that myself should be the root and father 3.01. 5
but wail his fall | who i myself struck down. 3.01.122
it is myself i mean; 4.03. 50
for even now | i put myself to thy direction, 4.03.122
the taints and blames i laid upon myself, | for 4.03.124
my first false speaking | was this upon myself. 4.03.131
bring thou this fiend of scotland and myself; 4.03.233
where now it burns, marcellus and myself, | the HAM 1.01. 38
horatio — or i do forget myself. 1.02.161
and tormenting flames | must render up myself. 1.05. 4
how strange or odd some'er i bear myself — | as 1.05.170
her father and myself, | we'll so bestow 3.01. 31
i am myself indifferent honest, but yet i could 3.01.121 P
behind the arras i'll convey myself | to hear 3.03. 28
lives almost by his looks, and for myself — 4.07. 12
i have seen myself, and serv'd against, the 4.07. 83
if i drown myself wittingly, it argues an act, 5.01. 10 P
i profess | myself an enemy to all other joys LR 1.01. 73
i would unstate myself to be in a due resolution 1.02. 99 P
all my living, i'ld keep my coxcombs myself. 1.04.108 P
if i speak like myself in this, let him be whipt 1.04.164 P
i heard myself proclaim'd, | and by the happy 2.03. 1
whiles i may scape | i will preserve myself, and 2.03. 6
i am cold myself. 3.02. 69
tell thee, friend, | i am almost mad myself. 3.04.166
all myself? 4.06.194
myself could else out–frown false fortune's 5.03. 6
reveal'd myself unto him, | until some half hour 5.03.193
some soul, | and such a one do i profess myself. OTH 1.01. 55
in following him, i follow but myself; 1.01. 58
shall i grace my cause | in speaking for myself. 1.03. 89
i will incontinently drown myself. 1.03.305 P
would say i would drown myself for the love of a 1.03.315 P
yet, i persuade myself, to speak the truth 2.03.223
montano and myself being in speech, | there 2.03.225
myself the crying fellow did pursue, | lest by 2.03.230
for your hurts, | myself will be your surgeon. 2.03.254
i have lost the immortal part of myself, and 2.03.264 P
me another, to make me frankly despise myself. 2.03.298 P
on — | myself a while to draw the moor apart, 2.03.385
me this, | to leave me but a little to myself. 3.03. 85
and shut myself up in some other course, | to 3.04.121
and more i will | than for myself i dare. 3.04.131
i have wasted myself out of my means. 4.02.185 P
scurvy, and begin to find myself fopp'd in it. 4.02.194 P
i will make myself known to desdemona. 4.02.196 P
i myself. 5.02.124
thought so then — i'll kill myself for grief — 5.02.192
but this, | killing myself, to die upon a kiss. 5.02.359
myself will straight aboard, and to the state 5.02.370
i must break, | or lose myself in dotage. ANT 1.02.117
now i feed myself | with most delicious poison. 1.05. 26
i | should say myself offended, and with you 2.02. 32
but next day | i told him of myself, which was 2.02. 78
for which myself, the ignorant motive, do | so 2.02. 96
that they strike | a meaner than myself, since i 2.05. 83
since i myself | have given myself the cause. 2.05. 83
since i myself | have given myself the cause. 2.05. 84
you take from me a great part of myself; 3.02. 24
if i lose mine honor, | i lose myself; 3.04. 23
i have fled myself, and have instructed cowards 3.11. 7
i have myself resolv'd upon a course | which has 3.11. 9
of which i do accuse myself so sorely | that i 4.06. 18
mine office, | or would have done't myself. 4.06. 27
mardian, go tell him i have slain myself; 4.13. 7
condemn myself to lack | the courage of a woman 4.14. 59
our caesar tells, | "i am conqueror of myself." 4.14. 62
thrice–nobler than myself! 4.14. 95
peril, that i have reserv'd | to myself nothing. 5.02.144
me, that i should not | be noble to myself. 5.02.192
myself by with a needle, that i might prick CYM 1.01.168
her nothing, though i profess myself her adorer, 1.04. 68 P
and then myself, i chiefly, | that set thee on 1.05. 72
good lord i prove untrue, | i'll choke myself. 1.05. 87
i dedicate myself to your sweet pleasure, | more 1.06.136
your lord, myself, and other noble friends | are 1.06.183
me, for | i yet not understand the case myself. 2.03. 75
lack of charity | to accuse myself i hate you; 2.03.110
i now | profess myself the winner of her honor, 2.04. 53
thus defied, | i thank thee for myself. 3.01. 68
myself, belarius, that am morgan call'd, | they 3.03.106
a fearful dream of him, | and cry myself awake? 3.04. 44
look | i draw the sword myself, take it, and hit 3.04. 67
and i grieve myself | to think, when thou shalt 3.04. 92
life is a tedious one, | i have tir'd myself; 3.06. 2
i dare speak it to myself, for it is not 4.01. 7 P
i'll rob none but myself, and let me die, 4.02. 15
clotens blood, | and praise myself for charity. 4.02.169
save one that had | a rider like myself, who 4.04. 39
of these italian weeds and suit myself | as does 5.01. 23
to the face of peril | myself i'll dedicate. 5.01. 29
that caus'd a lesser villain than myself, | a 5.05.219
which care of them, not pity of myself — | who PER 1.02. 29
i have ground the axe myself, | do but you 1.02. 58
and by whose letters i'll dispose myself. 1.02.117
i'll present myself. 1.03. 29
thou givest me somewhat to repair myself; 2.01.122
unto thy value i will mount myself | upon a 2.01.157
and i'll bring thee to the court myself. 2.01.164 P
the contrary) | as great in blood as i myself. 2.05. 80
i have one myself, | who shall not be more dear 3.03. 32
i here confess myself the king of tyre, | who, 5.03. 2
i am entreating of myself to do | that which you TNK 1.01.206
that i could wish myself a sigh to be so chid, 2.01. 43 P
myself to beg, if i priz'd life so much | as to 3.02. 23
lest i should drown, or stab, or hang myself! 3.02. 30
and i feel myself, | with this refreshing, able 3.06. 8
coz, i would, | though parcel of myself. 5.01. 24
"thrice fairer than myself," thus she began, VEN 7
to sell myself i can be well contented, | so 513
before i know myself, seek not to know me, | no 525
boar, | unlike myself thou hear'st me moralize, 712
myself a weakling, do not then ensnare me; LUC 584
"to kill myself," quoth she, "alack, what were 1156
whose love of either to myself was nearer, 1165
myself thy friend will kill myself thy foe, 1196
myself thy friend will kill myself thy foe, 1196
myself was stirring ere the break of day, | and 1280
though to myself forsworn, to thee i'll constant PP 5. 3
"wander," a word for shadows like myself, | as 14.11
be of thyself so wary | as i, not for myself, SON 22.10
mind, | for thee, and for myself, no quiet find. 27.14
cries, | and look upon myself and curse my fate, 29. 4
yet in these thoughts myself almost despising, 29. 9
myself corrupting, salving thy amiss, | excusing 35. 7
and 'gainst myself a lawful plea commence. 35.11
and this my hand against myself uprear, | to 49.11
and for myself mine own worth do define, | as i 62. 7
but when my glass shows me myself indeed, 62. 9
'tis thee (myself) that for myself i praise, 62.13
'tis thee (myself) that for myself i praise, 62.13
upon thy side against myself i'll fight, | and 88. 3
on thee, | the injuries that to myself i do, 88.11
that for thy right myself will bear all wrong. 88.14
as i'll myself disgrace, knowing thy will: 89. 7
for thee, against myself i'll vow debate, | for 89.13
as easy might i from myself depart | as from my 109. 3
so that myself bring water for my stain. 109. 8
there, | and made myself a motley to the view, 110. 2
fears, | still losing when i saw myself to win? 119. 4
so bold, | although i swear it to myself alone. 131. 8
me from myself thy cruel eye hath taken, | and 133. 5
of him, myself, and thee i am forsaken, | a 133. 7
thine, | and i myself am mortgag'd to thy will, 134. 2
myself i'll forfeit, so that other mine | thou 134. 3
not, | when i against myself with thee partake? 149. 2
not think on thee when i forgot | am of myself, 149. 4
spend | revenge upon myself with present moan? 149. 8
what merit do i in myself respect, | that is so 149. 9
fresh to myself, if i had self–applied | love to LC 76
if i had self–applied | love to myself, and to 77
finding myself in honor so forbid, | with safest 150
but yield them up where i myself must render: 221
/MYSTERIES* 1 FR 0.0001 REL FR 1 V 0 P
sun, | the /mysteries of hecat and the night; LR 1.01.110
MYSTERIES* 3 FR 0.0003 REL FR 3 V 0 P
should juggle | men into such strange mysteries? H8 1.03. 2
worth | as i can of those mysteries which heaven COR 4.02. 35
instruction, manners, mysteries, and trades, TIM 4.01. 18
MYSTERY* 18 FR 0.0020 REL FR 6 V 12 P
great comfort in this mystery of ill opinions, WIV 2.01. 72 P
fie upon him, he will discredit our mystery. MM 4.02. 29 P
do you call, sir, your occupation a mystery? 4.02. 34 P
ay, sir, a mystery. 4.02. 35 P
painting, sir, i have heard say, is a mystery; 4.02. 36 P
painting, do prove my occupation a mystery; 4.02. 38 P
but what mystery there should be in hanging, if 4.02. 39 P
sir, it is a mystery. 4.02. 41 P
if you think your mystery in stratagem can bring AWW 3.06. 65 P
hath not in nature's mystery more science | than 5.03.103
continuing, this mystery remain'd undiscover'd. WT 5.02.120 P
there is a mystery (with whom relation | durst TRO 3.03.201
us, not to have us thrive in our mystery. TIM 4.03.453 P
you would pluck out the heart of my mystery, you HAM 3.02.366 P
and take upon 's the mystery of things | as if LR 5.03. 16
your mystery, your mystery; OTH 4.02. 30
your mystery, your mystery; 4.02. 30
unclasp thy mystery. TNK 5.01.172
MYST'RY 1 FR 0.0001 REL FR 1 V 0 P
now i see | the myst'ry of your /loneliness, and AWW 1.03.171
MYTILENE *(see metelin, meteline)*
NAG 2 FR 0.0002 REL FR 2 V 0 P
'tis like the forc'd gait of a shuffling nag. 1H4 3.01.133
yon ribaudred nag of egypt | (whom leprosy ANT 3.10. 10
NAGS 1 FR 0.0001 REL FR 0 V 1 P
know we not galloway nags? 2H4 2.04.191 P
NAIADES 1 FR 0.0001 REL FR 1 V 0 P
you nymphs, call'd naiades, of the windring TMP 4.01.128
NAIL 12 FR 0.0013 REL FR 11 V 1 P
where thou mayst knock a nail into his head. TMP 3.02. 61
or as one nail by strength drives out another, TGV 2.04.193
some devils ask but the parings of one's nail, ERR 4.03. 71
and dick the shepherd blows his nail | and tom LLL 5.02.913
yard, three–quarters, half–yard, quarter, nail! SHR 4.03.108
a morris for may–day, as the nail to his hole, AWW 2.02. 24 P
the very mould and frame of hand, nail, finger. WT 2.03.103
as nail in door. the things i speak are just. 2H4 5.03.121
it were no match, your nail against his horn. TRO 4.05. 46
one nail, one nail; COR 4.07. 54
one nail, one nail; 4.07. 54
and, as i have a soul, i'll nail thy life to't! TNK 2.02.213
NAIL'D 1 FR 0.0001 REL FR 1 V 0 P
which fourteen hundred years ago were nail'd 1H4 1.01. 26
NAILES 7 FR 0.0008 REL FR 0 V 7 P
les ongles? /nous les appelons de nailes. H5 3.04. 16 P
de nailes. 3.04. 17 P
de hand, de fingres, et de nailes. 3.04. 18 P
d' hand, de fingre, de nailes, d' arma, de 3.04. 29 P
de nailes, madame. 3.04. 46 P
de nailes, de arma, de ilbow. 3.04. 47 P
d' hand, de fingre, de nailes, d' arma, d' elbow 3.04. 58 P
NAILS *(also mailes, nailes)*
NAILS 24 FR 0.0027 REL FR 19 V 5 P
and i with my long nails will dig thee pig–nuts, TMP 2.02.168
but with these nails i'll pluck out these false ERR 4.04.104
but that my nails can reach unto thine eyes. MND 3.02.298
let not him that plays the lion pare his nails, 4.02. 41 P
hortensio, but we may blow our nails together, SHR 1.01.108 P
'tis too late to pare her nails now. AWW 5.02. 29 P
like a mad lad, | pare thy nails, dad. TN 4.02.130
how these vain weak nails | may tear a passage R2 5.05. 19
one may pare his nails with a wooden dagger, and H5 4.04. 72 P
me, | and with my nails digg'd stones out of the 1H6 1.04. 45
and the very parings of our nails | shall pitch 3.01.102
could i come near your beauty with my nails, | i 2H6 1.03.141
what time the shepherd, blowing of his nails, 3H6 2.05. 3
these nails should rent that beauty from my R3 1.02.126
till that my nails were anchor'd in thine eyes; 4.04.232
ere /your grandsires had nails /on /their /toes, TRO 2.01.105 P
with her nails | she'll flea thy wolvish visage. LR 1.04.307
pins, wooden pricks, nails, sprigs of rosemary; 2.03. 16
because i would not see thy cruel nails | pluck 3.07. 56
plough thy visage up | with her prepared nails. ANT 4.12. 39
for i am sure mine nails | are stronger than 5.02.223
desperate, with her nails her flesh doth tear; LUC 739
that with my nails her beauty i may tear. 1472
she tears the senseless sinon with her nails, 1564
NAKED 55 FR 0.0062 REL FR 45 V 10 P
and sleep, | upon the very naked name of love. TGV 2.04.142
from that trunk you bear, | and leave you naked. MM 3.01. 72
and come with naked swords: ERR 4.04.145
the naked truth of it is, i have no shirt; LLL 5.02.710 P
speed | to some forlorn and naked hermitage, 5.02.795
therefore on, or strip your sword stark naked; TN 3.04.251 P
ten thousand years together, naked, fasting, WT 3.02.211
leave them as naked as the vulgar air. JN 2.01.387
thou showest the naked pathway to thy life, R2 1.02. 31
or wallow naked in december snow | by thinking 1.03.298
stand bare and naked, trembling at themselves? 3.02. 46
was poor, | upon the naked shore at ravenspurgh, 1H4 4.03. 77
cost | a naked subject to the weeping clouds 2H4 1.03. 61
alas, put up your naked weapons, put up your 2.04.207 P
your naked weapons, put up your naked weapons. 2.04.207 P
when 'a was naked, he was for all the world like 3.02.310 P
your naked infants spitted upon pikes, | whiles H5 3.03. 38
veins | to give each naked curtle–axe a stain, 4.02. 21
why that the naked, poor, and mangled peace, 5.02. 34
true likeness, he must appear naked and blind. 5.02.294 P
the appearance of a naked blind boy in her naked 5.02.297 P
of a naked blind boy in her naked seeing self? 5.02.297 P
the truth appears so naked on my side | that any 1H6 2.04. 20
and he but naked, though lock'd up in steel, 2H6 3.02.234
though standing naked on a mountain top, | where 3.02.336
and make him, naked, foil a man at arms. 3H6 5.04. 42
thee, | i lay it naked to the deadly stroke, R3 1.02.177
and thus i clothe my naked villainy | with odd 1.03.335
and did give himself | (all thin and naked) to 2.01.118
mine age | have left me naked to mine enemies. H8 3.02.457
being naked, sick, nor fane nor capitol, | the COR 1.10. 20
for i cannot | put on the gown, stand naked, and 2.02.137
my naked weapon is out. ROM 1.01. 33 P
wing, | lord timon will be left a naked gull, TIM 2.01. 31
whose naked natures live in all the spite | of 4.03.228
let it go naked, men may see't the better. 5.01. 67
there is my dagger, | and here my naked breast; JC 4.03.101
and pity, like a naked new–born babe, | striding MAC 1.07. 21
and when we have our naked frailties hid, | that 2.03.126
you shall know i am set naked on your kingdom. HAM 4.07. 44 P
"naked"! 4.07. 51
poor naked wretches, wheresoe'er you are, | that LR 3.04. 28
is that the naked fellow? 4.01. 40
and bring some covering for this naked soul, 4.01. 44
sirrah, naked fellow — 4.01. 51
or to be naked with her friend in bed | an hour, OTH 4.01. 3
naked in bed, iago, and not mean harm? 4.01. 5
to lash the rascals naked through the world 4.02.143
me, | or, naked as i am, i will assault thee. 5.02.258
whose naked breast | stepp'd before targes of CYM 5.05. 4
"who sees his true–love in her naked bed, VEN 397
his naked armor of still–slaughtered lust, | and LUC 188
and stood stark naked on the brook's green brim. PP 6.10
of thine | in thy soul's thought (all naked) SON 26. 8
the naked and concealed fiend he cover'd, | that LC 317
NAKEDNESS 4 FR 0.0004 REL FR 3 V 1 P
excuse | that which appears in proper nakedness? ADO 4.01.175
laid by, in his nakedness he appears but a man; H5 4.01.105 P
nothing i'll bear from thee | but nakedness, TIM 4.01. 33
and with presented nakedness outface | the winds LR 2.03. 11
NAM'D 19 FR 0.0021 REL FR 17 V 2 P
what you will have it nam'd, even that it is, SHR 4.05. 21
he nam'd sebastian. TN 3.04.379
my father nam'd me autolycus, who being, as i am WT 4.03. 24 P
matter breeds for you | than i have nam'd! JN 3.04.171
the friends you have nam'd uncertain, the time 1H4 2.03. 12 P
which in the time of henry nam'd the fift | was 1H6 3.01.195
'twas neither charles nor yet the duke i nam'd, 5.04. 77
and the pretense for this | is nam'd, your wars H8 1.02. 60
play me that sad note | i nam'd my knell, whilst 4.02. 79
and | by deed–achieving honor newly nam'd — COR 2.01.173
martius, | whom late you have nam'd for consul. 3.01.195
o, how my heart abhors | to hear him nam'd, and ROM 3.05.100
thou hast a servant nam'd lucilius. TIM 1.01.111
he is already nam'd, and gone to scone | to be MAC 2.04. 31
that ever scotland | in such an honor nam'd. 5.09. 30
he whom my father nam'd, your edgar? LR 2.01. 92
mischance than come | to be but nam'd of thee. CYM 2.03.133
for she was born at sea, i have nam'd so, here PER 3.03. 13
i have nam'd him oft. 5.03. 53
/NAME 13 FR 0.0014 REL FR 11 V 2 P
sir, 'a has an english /name, but his fisnomy is AWW 4.05. 39 P
/i /have /no /name, /no /title, | /no, /not R2 4.01.255
/not /that /name /was /given /me /at /the /font, 4.01.256
/know /not /now /what /name /to /call /myself! 4.01.259
/name /it, /fair /cousin. 4.01.304
/nothing /but /the /sound /of /hotspur's /name 2H4 2.03. 37
and the third hour of drowsy morning /name. H5 4.pr. 16
/it //rouge–mount, /at /which /name /i /started, R3 4.02.105
/dost /thou /urge /the /name /of /hands, | /to TIT 3.02. 26
/if /marcus /did /not /name /the /word /of 3.02. 33
/mine, | with repetition of my /romeo's /name. ROM 2.02.163

/is /your /name /goneril? LR 3.06. 49 P
/or /twice /she /heav'd /the /name /of "/father" 4.03. 25
NAME 686 FR 0.0775 REL FR 527 V 159 P
what cares these roarers for the name of king? TMP 1.01. 17 P
and teach me how | to name the bigger light, and 1.02.335
thou dost here usurp | the name thou ow'st not, 1.02.455
no name of magistrate; 2.01.150
set it in my prayers — | what is your name? 3.01. 36
i' th' name of something holy, sir, why stand 3.03. 94
organ–pipe, pronounc'd | the name of prosper; 3.03. 99
how now? what means this passion at his name? TGV 1.02. 16
being in the way, | did in your name receive it; 1.02. 40
i throw thy name against the bruising stones, 1.02.108
poor wounded name: 1.02.111
letter in the letter, | except mine own name; 1.02.117
lo, here in one line is his name twice writ, 1.02.120
and yet i will not name it — and yet i care not 2.01.117
yet hath sir proteus (for that's his name) 2.04. 67
and sleep, | upon the very naked name of love. 2.04.142
a jew, and not worth the name of a christian. 2.05. 55 P
sebastian is thy name? 4.04. 40
do not name silvia thine; 5.04.128
peter simple, you say your name is? WIV 1.04. 16 P
flemish drunkard pick'd (with the devil's name!) 2.01. 24 P
but that the name of page and ford differs! 2.01. 70 P
at thy heels — | o, odious is the name! 2.01.119
what name, sir? 2.01.120 P
my name is corporal nym; 2.01.133 P
my name is nym, and falstaff loves your wife. 2.01.134 P
to him and tell him my name is /brook — only 2.01.216 P
and thy name shall be /brook. 2.01.218 P
/brook is his name? 2.02.148 P
my name is /brook. 2.02.161 P
in this town, her husband's name is ford. 2.02.192 P
the devil himself hath not such a name. 2.02.300 P
and friend simple by your name, which way have 3.01. 2 P
what the dickens his name is my husband had him 3.02. 20 P
what do you call your knight's name, sirrah? 3.02. 21 P
he, he — i can never hit on 's name. 3.02. 24 P
to carry me in the name of foul clothes to 3.05. 99 P
never name her, child, if she be a whore. 4.01. 63 P
nay, i'll to him again in name of /brook; 4.04. 76
and one, | and, in the lawful name of marrying, 4.06. 50
and this deceit loses the name of craft, | of 5.05.226
and for a name | now puts the drowsy and MM 1.02.169
act | freshly on me — 'tis surely for a name. 1.02.171
who may, in th' ambush of my name, strike home, 1.03. 41
how now, sir, what's your name? 2.01. 45 P
the poor duke's constable, and my name is elbow. 2.01. 48 P
elbow is your name? 2.01. 59 P
your mistress' name? 2.01.199 P
what's your name, master tapster? 2.01.213 P
my mouth, | as if i did but only chew his name, 2.04. 5
my unsoil'd name, th' austereness of my life, 2.04.155
yet in this | that bears the name of life? 3.01. 39
time | that i should do what i abhor to name, 3.01.101
of the lady, and good words went with her name. 3.01.212 P
to call upon you, and i pray you your name? 3.02.158 P
sir, my name is lucio, well known to the duke. 3.02.159 P
but he's more, | had i more name for badness. 5.01. 59
his name is barnardine. 5.01.467
reft of his brother, but retain'd his name — ERR 1.01.128
and no man that hath a name | by falsehood and 2.01.112
name them. 2.02. 96 P
me, | and hurl the name of husband in my face, 2.02.135
for this time, sir, and my name is dromio. 3.01. 43
thou hast stol'n both mine office and my name: 3.01. 44
thou wouldst have chang'd thy face for a name, 3.01. 47
thy face for a name, or thy name for an ass. 3.01. 47
if thy name be called luce — luce, thou hast 3.01. 53
sweet mistress — what your name is else, i know 3.02. 29
what's her name? 3.02.108 P
but her name /and three quarters, that's an ell 3.02.109 P
ay, that's my name. 3.02.165
and charge you in the duke's name to obey me. 4.01. 70
friend, | and every one doth call me by my name: 4.03. 3
is not your name, sir, call'd antipholus? 5.01.287
but few of any sort, and none of name. ADO 1.01. 7 P
i know none of that name, lady. 1.01. 32 P
but keep your way a' god's name, i have done. 1.01.143 P
hand | than to drive liking to the name of love. 1.01.300
thus answer i in name of benedick, | but hear 2.01.172
claudio, i have woo'd in thy name, and fair hero 2.01.298 P
name the day of marriage, and god give thee joy! 2.01.300 P
when i do name him, let it be thy part | to 3.01. 18
indeed he hath an excellent good name. 3.01. 98
god hath blest you with a good name. 3.03. 14 P
are to bid any man stand, in the prince's name. 3.03. 26 P
i remember his name. 3.03.127 P
lady hero's gentlewoman, by the name of hero. 3.03.146 P
we charge you, in the prince's name, stand! 3.03.164 P
to make you answer truly to your name. 4.01. 79
who can blot that name | with any just reproach? 4.01. 80
what is your name, friend? 4.02. 10 P
i am a gentleman, sir, and my name is conrade. 4.02. 13 P
you in the prince's name accuse these men. 4.02. 38 P
and borrows money in god's name, the which he 5.01.310 P
i answer to that name. what is your will? 5.04. 73
lights, | that give a name to every fixed star, LLL 1.01. 89
and every godfather can give a name. 1.01. 93
and to the strictest decrees i'll write my name. 1.01.117
and so to the laws at large i write my name, | and 1.01.155
title to your old time, which we may name tough. 1.02. 17 P
more authority, dear boy, name more; 1.02. 68 P
wrong, | and wrong the reputation of your name, 2.01.154
the heir of alanson, /katherine her name. 2.01.195
perchance light in the light. i desire her name. 2.01.199
what's her name in the cap? 2.01.209
why, it is a fairer name than french crown! 3.01.141 P
tongues speak sweetly, then they name her name, 3.01.166
tongues speak sweetly, then they name her name, 3.01.166
one drunkard loves another of the name. 4.03. 48
it is berowne's writing, and here is his name. 4.03.199
all, | that he was fain to seal on cupid's name. 5.02. 9
name it. 5.02.239
for the latter end of his name. 5.02.627 P
here is the scroll of every man's name, which is MND 1.02. 4 P
ready. name what part i am for, and proceed. 1.02. 18 P

now name the rest of the players. 1.02. 39 P
word | is that vile name to perish on my sword! 2.02.107
you must name his name, and half his face must 3.01. 36 P
you must name his name, and half his face must 3.01. 36 P
and there indeed let him name his name, and tell 3.01. 45 P
and there indeed let him name his name, and tell 3.01. 45 P
i beseech your worship's name. 3.01.180 P
your name, honest gentleman? 3.01.184 P
your name, i beseech you, sir? 3.01.189 P
to aery nothing | a local habitation and a name. 5.01. 17
this grisly beast, which lion hight by name, 5.01.139
it doth befall | that i, one /snout by name, 5.01.156
her name is portia, nothing undervalu'd | to MV 1.01.165
her name is margery indeed. 2.02. 91 P
a title good enough to keep his name company! 3.01. 14 P
his name is balthazar. 4.01.154 P
is your name shylock? 4.01.176
shylock is my name. 4.01.176
your name, i pray you, friend? 5.01. 27
stephano is my name, and i bring word | my 5.01. 28
bear him away. what is thy name, young man? AYL 1.02.221
she robs thee of thy name, | and thou wilt show 1.03. 80
i'll have no worse a name than jove's own page, 1.03.124
what woman in the city do i name, | when that i 2.07. 74
thy huntress' name that my full life doth sway. 3.02. 4
wondering how thy name should be hang'd and 3.02.173 P
rosalind is your love's name? 3.02.263 P
i do not like her name. 3.02.265 P
all, forsooth, /deifying the name of rosalind. 3.02.363 P
a ripe age. is thy name william? 5.01. 20 P
a fair name. wast born i' the forest here? 5.01. 22 P
i will name you the degrees. 5.04. 91 P
i have forgot your name; SHR in.1. 86
tell me her father's name, and 'tis enough; 1.02. 94
her name is katherina minola, | renown'd in 1.02. 99
but if you have a stomach, to't a' god's name; 1.02.194
his name is litio, born in mantua. 2.01. 60
what may i call your name? 2.01. 67
petruchio is my name, antonio's son, | a man 2.01. 68
his name is cambio; 2.01. 82 P
lucentio is your name, of whence, i pray? 2.01.102
morrow, kate — for that's your name, i hear. 2.01.182
hath two letters for her name fairly set down in 3.02. 61 P
his name and credit shall you undertake, | and 4.02.107
wants, | he does it under name of perfect love; 4.03. 12
that feed'st me with the very name of meat. 4.03. 32
why, what a' devil's name, tailor, call'st thou 4.03. 92
come on a' god's name! 4.05. 1
my name is call'd vincentio, my dwelling pisa, 4.05. 55
what is his name? 4.05. 58
knavery, to take upon you another man's name. 5.01. 37 P
pray what do you think is his name? 5.01. 80 P
his name! 5.01. 81 P
as if i knew not his name! 5.01. 81 P
he was three years old, and his name is tranio. 5.01. 83 P
his name is lucentio, and he is mine only son, 5.01. 84 P
hold on him, i charge you, in the duke's name. 5.01. 88 P
i am from humble, he from honored name; AWW 1.03.156
my maiden's name | sear'd otherwise; 2.01.172
rate | worth name of life in thee hath estimate: 2.01.180
my low and humble name to propagate | with any 2.01.197
thou dislik'st | of virtue for the name. 2.03.124
good alone | is good, without a name; 2.03.129
loosing upon thee, in the name of justice, 2.03.165
son, | but i do wash his name out of my blood, 3.02. 67
far | his name with zealous fervor sanctify. 3.04. 11
the honor of a maid is her name, and no legacy 3.05. 12 P
his name, i pray you? 3.05. 48
what's his name? 3.05. 57
she is too mean | to have her name repeated. 3.05. 61
they told me that your name was fontibell. 4.02. 1
my name, my good lord, is parolles. 5.02. 39 P
son, in whom my house's name | must be digested; 5.03. 73
which contain'd the name | of her that threw it. 5.03. 94
of a wife you see, | the name and not the thing. 5.03.308
a noble duke, in nature as in name. TN 1.02. 25
what is his name? 1.02. 26
i have heard my father name him. 1.02. 28
my name is mary, sir. 1.03. 54 P
hallow your name to the reverberate hills, | and 1.05.272
antonio, my name is sebastian, which i call'd 2.01. 16 P
close, in the name of jesting! 2.05. 20 P
m — malvolio; m — why, that begins my name. 2.05.126 P
for every one of these letters are in my name. 2.05.141 P
i would therefore my sister had had no name, sir 3.01. 17 P
what is your name? 3.01. 96
cesario is your servant's name, fair princess. 3.01. 97
which way is he, in the name of sanctity? 3.04. 84 P
with her, nor your name is not master cesario, 4.01. 7 P
what name? 5.01.231
o, would her name were grace! WT 1.02. 99
deserves a name | as rank as any flax–wench that 1.02.276
but | i cannot name the disease, and it is 1.02.386
and my name | be yok'd with his that did betray 1.02.418
of | which comes to me in name of fault, i must 3.02. 60
bring forth, | and in apollo's name, his oracle. 3.02.118
to me for help and said his name was antigonus, 3.03. 96 P
name of mercy, when was this, boy? 3.03.103 P
error, | now take upon me, in the name of time, 4.01. 3
th' king's, which florizel | i now name to you; 4.01. 23
i' th' name of me — 4.03. 51 P
unroll'd, and my name put in the book of virtue! 4.03.122 P
o, pardon, that i name them! 4.04. 7
here's the midwive's name to't, one mistress 4.04.269 P
the remembrance | of his most sovereign name; 5.01. 26
what is thy name? JN 1.01.157
philip, my liege, so is my name begun, | philip, 1.01.158
henceforth bear his name whose form thou bearest 1.01.160
and if his name be george, i'll call him peter; 1.01.186
my land, | legitimation, name, and all is gone; 1.01.248
and this is geffrey's in the name of god. 2.01.106
with slaughter coupled to the name of kings. 2.01.349
and she again wants nothing, to name want, | if 2.01.435
do in his name religiously demand | why thou 3.01.140
this, in our foresaid holy father's name, | pope 3.01.145
what earthy name to interrogatories | can taste 3.01.147
cardinal, devise a name | so slight, unworthy, 3.01.149
even for that name, | which till this time my 3.01.306

be stronger with thee than the name of wife? 3.01.314
my name is constance, i was geffrey's wife, 3.04. 46
deed, which both our tongues held vild to name. 4.02.241
defense | cries out upon the name of salisbury! 5.02. 19
and on our actions set the name of right | with 5.02. 67
with a foul traitor's name stuff i thy throat, R2 1.01. 44
in name of lendings for your highness' soldiers, 1.01. 89
the one my duty owes, but my fair name, 1.01.167
ask him his name, and orderly proceed | to swear 1.03. 9
in god's name and the king's, say who thou art 1.03. 11
my name is thomas mowbray, duke of norfolk, 1.03. 16
what is thy name? 1.03. 31
and furbish new the name of john a' gaunt, 1.03. 76
my name be blotted from the book of life, | and 1.03.202
o, how that name befits my composition! 2.01. 73
since thou dost seek to kill my name in me, | i 2.01. 86
i mock my name, great king, to flatter thee. 2.01. 87
but what, a' god's name, doth become of this? 2.01.251
is that is not yet known what, | i cannot name; 2.02. 40
seymour, | none else of name and noble estimate. 2.03. 56
and i am come to seek that name in england, 2.03. 71
is not the king's name twenty thousand names? 3.02. 85
arm, arm, my name! 3.02. 86
great | as is my grief, or lesser than my name! 3.03.137
must he lose | the name of king? 3.03.146
a' god's name let it go. 3.03.146
him, | and long live henry, fourth of that name! 4.01.112
in god's name i'll ascend the regal throne. 4.01.113
mine age, | and rob me of a happy mother's name? 5.02. 93
i do repent me, read not my name there, | my 5.03. 52
those prisoners in your highness' name demanded, 1H4 1.03. 23
death, | trembling even at the name of mortimer. 1.03.144
go to, homo is a common name to all men. 2.01. 95 P
sweet ned — to sweeten which name of ned, i 2.04. 22 P
known to many in our land by the name of pitch. 2.04.412 P
noted in thy company, but i know not his name. 2.04.419 P
and now i remember me, his name is falstaff. 2.04.426 P
for by that name as oft as lancaster | doth 3.01. 8
how scapes he agues, in the devil's name? 3.01. 68
had his great name profaned with their scorns, 3.02. 64
and gave his countenance, against his name, | to 3.02. 65
whose hot incursions and great name in arms, 3.02.108
this in the name of god i promise here, | the 3.02.153
some | envy your great deservings and good name, 4.03. 35
he bids you name your griefs, and with all speed 4.03. 48
the odds | of his great name and estimation, 5.01. 98
of blood, | and an adopted name of privilege, 5.02. 18
with haughty arms this hateful name in us. 5.02. 40
what is thy name, that in battle thus | thou 5.03. 1
know then, my name is douglas, | and i do haunt 5.03. 3
a gallant knight he was, his name was blunt, 5.03. 20
thou speak'st as if i would deny my name. 5.04. 60
my name is harry percy. 5.04. 61
then i see | a very valiant rebel of the name. 5.04. 62
thy name in arms were now as great as mine! 5.04. 70
a gentleman well bred and of good name, | that 2H4 1.01. 26
it worse than the name of rebellion can tell how 1.02. 77 P
do you set down your name in the scroll of youth 1.02.178 P
i would to god my name were not so terrible to 1.02.218 P
a disgrace is it to me to remember thy name, or 2.02. 13 P
that, as oft as he has occasion to name himself; 2.02.111 P
i am in good name and fame with the very best. 2.04. 75 P
civil, for," said he, "you are in an ill name." 2.04. 90 P
is thy name mouldy? 3.02.104 P
is thy name wart? 3.02.139 P
and told john a' gaunt he beat his own name, for 3.02.325 P
indeed, | concurring both in name and quality. 4.01. 87
that is intended in the general's name. 4.01.164
grace of york, in god's name then set forward. 4.01.225
as a false favorite doth his prince's name, | in 4.02. 25
what's your name, sir? 4.03. 1 P
sir, and my name is colevile of the dale. 4.03. 3 P
well then, colevile is your name, a knight is 4.03. 5 P
colevile shall be still your name, a traitor 4.03. 7 P
of them all speaks any other word but my name. 4.03. 20 P
is thy name colevile? 4.03. 61
doth any name particular belong | unto the 4.05.232
we charge you, in the name of god, take heed; H5 1.02. 23
nation lose | the name of hardiness and policy. 1.02.220
and in whose name | i tell you the dolphin i am 1.02.290
doll tearsheet she by name, and her espouse. 2.01. 77
unless to dub thee with the name of traitor. 2.02.120
by the name of richard earl of cambridge. 2.02.145 P
by the name of /henry lord scroop of masham. 2.02.147 P
of high treason, by the name of thomas grey, 2.02.149 P
captiv'd by the hand | of that black name, 2.04. 56
he wills you, in the name of god almighty, 2.04. 77
a name that in my thoughts becomes me best, | if 3.03. 6
what is thy name? i know thy quality. 3.06.137
he will keep that good name still. 3.07.102 P
in brawl ridiculous) | the name of agincourt. 4.pr. 52
what is thy name? 4.01. 48
a cornish name. 4.01. 50
my name is pistol call'd. 4.01. 62
in the name of jesu christ, speak fewer. 4.01. 65 P
named, | and rouse him at the name of crispian. 4.03. 43
what is thy name? 4.04. 5 P
ask me this slave in french | what is his name. 4.04. 24
he says his name is master fer. 4.04. 27 P
call you the town's name where alexander the pig 4.07. 12 P
my prains what is the name of the other river; 4.07. 29 P
knaveries, and mocks — i have forgot his name. 4.07. 50 P
i charge you in his majesty's name, apprehend 4.08. 17 P
none else of name; 4.08.105
of grant, shall name your highness in this form, 5.02.338 P
name not religion, for thou lov'st the flesh, 1H6 1.01. 41
then come a' god's name, i fear no woman. 1.02.102
excellent pucelle, if thy name be so, | let me 1.02.110
charge and command you, in his highness' name, 1.03. 76 P
so great fear of my name 'mongst them were 1.04. 50
wretched shall france be only in my name. 1.04. 97
in whose conquering name | let us resolve to 2.01. 26
spoils, | using no other weapon but his name. 2.01. 81
that with his name the mothers still their babes 2.03. 17
god save king henry, of that name the sixt! 4.01. 2
doth but usurp the sacred name of knight, 4.01. 40
talbot dead, great york might bear the name. 4.04. 9

that talbot's name might be in thee reviv'd, 4.05. 3
is my name talbot? 4.05. 12
dishonor not her honorable name | to make a 4.05. 14
yes, your renowned name. shall flight abuse it? 4.05. 41
in thee thy mother dies, our household's name, 4.06. 38
margaret my name, and daughter to a king, | the 5.03. 51
say, earl of suffolk — if thy name be so — 5.03. 72
and i again, in henry's royal name, | as deputy 5.03.160
and so i pray you go in god's name, and leave us 2H6 1.04. 9 P
god, whose name and power | thou tremblest at, 1.04. 25
tell me, sirrah, what's my name? 2.01.115
what's his name? 2.01.117
what's thine own name? 2.01.121
as thus | to name the several colors we do wear. 2.01.126
that hath dishonored gloucester's honest name. 2.01.195
crown'd by the name of henry the fourth, 2.02. 23
a' god's name see the lists and all things fit; 2.03. 54
sirrah, what's thy name? 2.03. 80 P
death, at whose name i oft have been afeard, 2.04. 89
i do arrest you in his highness' name, | and 3.01.136
so shall my name with slander's tongue be 3.02. 68
and bear the name and port of gentlemen? 4.01. 19
my name is walter whitmore. 4.01. 31
thy name affrights me, in whose sound is death. 4.01. 33
thy name is gualtier, being rightly sounded. 4.01. 37
never yet did base dishonor blur our name | but 4.01. 39
what is thy name? 4.02. 98 P
dost thou use to write thy name? 4.02.103 P
so well brought up that i can write my name. 4.02.106 P
under his tongue, he speaks not a' god's name. 4.07.108 P
the name of henry the fift hales them to an 4.08. 56 P
alexander iden, that's my name, | a poor esquire 5.01. 74
but by circumstance | the name of valor. 5.02. 40
richard, i bear thy name, i'll venge thy death, 3H6 2.01. 87
his name that valiant duke hath left with thee; 2.01. 89
we charge you, in god's name and the king's, 3.01. 97
in god's name lead; 3.01. 99
your king's name be obey'd, | and what god will, 3.01. 99
applaud the name of henry with your leader. 4.02. 27
two of thy name, both dukes of somerset, | have 5.01. 73
then in god's name, lords, | be valiant, and 5.04. 81
what's worse than murtherer, that i may name it? 5.05. 58
because my name is george. R3 1.01. 46
and, for my name of george begins with g, | it 1.01. 58
fairer than tongue can name thee, let me have 1.02. 81
one place else, if you will hear me name it. 1.02.110
name him. 1.02.142
the self–same name, but one of better nature. 1.02.143
so that between their titles and low name 1.04. 82
in god's name, what art thou? 1.04.163
and like a traitor to the name of god | didst 1.04.205
in god's name speak, when is the royal day? 3.04. 3
but you, my honorable lords, may name the time, 3.04. 18
thy mother's name is ominous to children. 4.01. 40
what is his name? 4.02. 40
his name, my lord, is tyrrel. 4.02. 40
is thy name tyrrel? 4.02. 66
for joyful mother, one that wails the name; 4.04. 99
what comfortable hour canst thou name | that 4.04.174
my tongue should to thy ears not name my boys 4.04.231
a grandam's name is little less in love | than 4.04.299
what men of name resort to him? 4.05. 11
crew, | and many other of great name and worth; 4.05. 16
in god's name cheerly on, courageous friends, 5.02. 14
then in god's name march! 5.02. 22
besides, the king's name is a tower of strength, 5.03. 12
then, in the name of god and all these rights, 5.03.263
what men of name are slain on either side? 5.05. 12
whom from the flow of gall i name not, but H8 1.01.152
in the name | of our most sovereign king. 1.01.201
half your suit | never name to us; 1.02. 11
traitor's judgment, | and by that name must die; 2.01. 59
lead on a' god's name. 2.01. 78
and out of ruins | made my name once more noble. 2.01.115
life, honor, name, and all | that made me happy, 2.01.116
sacred person — in god's name | turn me away; 2.04. 41
if not, i' th' name of god, | your pleasure be 2.04. 56
how, i' th' name of thrift, | does he rake this 3.02.109
but 'tis so lately alter'd that the old name 4.01. 98
my royal nephew, and your name capuchius. 4.02.110
worms, and my poor name | banish'd the kingdom! 4.02.126
what is her name? 5.04. 9
his honor and the greatness of his name | shall 5.04. 51
ay, greek, that is my name. TRO 1.03.246
sends, | however it is spread in general name, 1.03.322
not ours nor worth to us | (had it our name) the 2.02. 23
we will not name desert before his birth, and, 3.02. 93 P
be call'd to the world's end after my name; 3.02.202 P
incurr'd a traitor's name, expos'd myself | from 3.03. 6
make cressid's name the very crown of falsehood, 4.02.100
name cressid, and thy life shall be as safe | as 4.04.115
if not achilles, sir, | what is your name? 4.05. 76
the worthiest of them tell me name by name; 4.05.160
the worthiest of them tell me name by name; 4.05.160
name her not now, sir, she's a deadly theme. 4.05.181
that i may give the local wound a name, | and 4.05.244
let all untruths stand by thy stained name, 5.02.179
pursue thy life, and live aye with thy name! 5.10. 34
holding corioles in the name of rome, | even COR 1.06. 37
martius, his name? 1.09. 90
he gives my son the whole name of the war. 2.01.135 P
hath won, | with fame, a name to martius caius; 2.01.164
people, in whose name myself | attach thee as a 3.01.173
forget that ever | he heard the name of death. 3.01.259
consul's worthiness, | so can i name his faults. 3.01.277
doth distribute it — in the name a' th' people, 3.03. 99
i' th' people's name, | i say it shall be so. 3.03.104
your name, i think, is adrian. 4.03. 2 P
thy name? 4.05. 53
what's thy name? 4.05. 54
man i am, necessity | commands me name myself. 4.05. 57
what is thy name? 4.05. 57
a name unmusical to the volscians' ears, | and 4.05. 58
say, what's thy name? 4.05. 59
what's thy name? 4.05. 62
i know thee not. thy name? 4.05. 64
my name is caius martius, who hath done | to 4.05. 65
only that name remains; 4.05. 73
the second name of men, obeys his points | as if 4.06.125
yet one time he did call me by my name. 5.01. 9
till he had forg'd himself a name a' th' fire 5.01. 14
lots to blanks | my name hath touch'd your ears: 5.02. 11
the virtue of your name | is not here passable. 5.02. 12
fellow, remember my name is menenius, always 5.02. 28 P
now, sir, is your name menenius? 5.02. 95 P
this boy, to keep your name | living to time. 5.03.126
which thou shalt thereby reap is such a name 5.03.143
and his name remains | to th' ensuing age 5.03.147
with that robbery, thy stol'n name | coriolanus, 5.06. 88
name not the god, thou boy of tears! 5.06.100
let us entreat by honor of his name, | whom TIT 1.01. 39
hue, | and name thee in election for the empire, 1.01.183
to advance | thy name and honorable family, 1.01.239
brother, for in that name doth nature plead — 1.01.370
father, and in that name doth nature speak — 1.01.371
for no name fits thy nature but thy own! 2.03.119
the blot and enemy to our general name! 2.03.183
when i did name her brothers, then fresh tears 3.01.111
that ever death should let life bear his name, 3.01.248
i have writ my name, | without the help of any 4.01. 70
king, be thy thoughts imperious, like thy name. 4.04. 81
whose name was once our terror, now our comfort, 5.01. 10
and in their ears tell them my dreadful name, 5.02. 39
the one is murder, and rape is the other's name, 5.02.156
go ask his name. ROM 1.05.134
his name is romeo, and a montague, | the only 1.05.136
in his mistress' name | i conjure only but to 2.01. 28
deny thy father and refuse thy name; 2.02. 34
'tis but thy name that is my enemy; 2.02. 38
o, be some other name! 2.02. 42
what's in a name? 2.02. 43
romeo, doff thy name, | and for thy name, which 2.02. 47
and for thy name, which is no part of thee, 2.02. 48
by a name | i know not how to tell thee who i am 2.02. 53
my name, dear saint, is hateful to myself, 2.02. 55
it is my soul that calls upon my name. 2.02.164
i have forgot that name, and that name's woe. 2.03. 46
i am the youngest of that name, for fault of a 2.04.122 P
ah, mocker, that's the /dog's name. 2.04.209 P
which name i tender | as dearly as mine own — 3.01. 71
i charge thee in the prince's name, obey. 3.01.140
but romeo's name speaks heavenly eloquence. 3.02. 33
poor my lord, what tongue shall smooth thy name, 3.02. 98
as if that name, | shot from the deadly level of 3.03.102
vile part of this anatomy | doth my name lodge? 3.03.107
that whiles verona by that name is known, 5.03.300
thou know'st it do, i call'd thee by thy name. TIM 1.01.187 P
way) | to them to use your signet and your name, 2.02.201
what is thy name? 4.03. 52
if i name thee. 4.03.363
name them, my lord, let's know them. 5.01.105
power, and thy good name | live with authority; 5.01.162
seek not my name: 5.04. 71
love | the name of honor more than i fear death. JC 1.02. 89
why should that name be sounded more than yours? 1.02.143
write them together, yours is as fair a name; 1.02.144
yet if my name were liable to fear, | i do not 1.02.199
the great opinion | that rome holds of his name; 1.02.319
name to thee a man | most like this dreadful 1.03. 72
o, name him not; 2.01.150
in hand | any exploit worthy the name of honor. 2.01.317
what is your name? 3.03. 5 P
what is my name? 3.03. 13 P
your name, sir, truly. 3.03. 26 P
truly, my name is cinna. 3.03. 27 P
pluck but his name out of his heart, and turn 3.03. 34 P
the name of cassius honors this corruption, 4.03. 15
i will proclaim my name about the field. 5.04. 3
for brave macbeth (well he deserves that name), MAC 1.02. 16
i' th' name of truth, | are ye fantastical, or 1.03. 52
malcolm, whom we name hereafter | the prince of 1.04. 38
by the name of most kind hostess, and shut up 2.01. 16
who's there, i' th' name of belzebub? 2.03. 4 P
who's there, in th' other devil's name? 2.03. 8 P
nor heart | cannot conceive nor name thee! 2.03. 65
when first they put the name of king upon me, 3.01. 57
demi–wolves are clipt | all by the name of dogs; 3.01. 94
a deed without a name. 4.01. 49
tyrant, whose sole name blisters our tongues, 4.03. 12
smacking of every sin | that has a name; 4.03. 60
what is thy name? 5.07. 5
though thou call'st thyself a hotter name | than 5.07. 6
frailty, thy name is woman! HAM 1.02.146
good friend — i'll change that name with you. 1.02.163
with what, i' th' name of god? 2.01. 73
turn awry, | and lose the name of action. 3.01. 87
gonzago is the duke's name, his wife, baptista. 3.02.239 P
transports his pois'ned shot, may miss our name, 4.01. 43
ground | that hath in it no profit but the name. 4.04. 19
bound for england — if your name be horatio, as 4.06. 11 P
that liberal shepherds give a grosser name, 4.07.170
president of peace | to /keep my name ungor'd. 5.02.250
o god, horatio, what a wounded name, | things 5.02.344
only we shall retain | the name, and all th' LR 1.01.136
your name, fair gentlewoman? 1.04.236
regard support | the worships of their name. 1.04.266
shake the head | to hear of pleasure's name — 4.06.121
i know thee well enough, thy name is gloucester. 4.06.177
all levied in my name, have in my name | took 5.03.104
my name, have in my name | took their discharge. 5.03.104
your name, your quality? 5.03.120
know, my name is lost, | by treason's tooth 5.03.121
in wisdom i should ask thy name, | but, since 5.03.142
thou worse than any name, read thine own evil. 5.03.157
my name is edgar, and thy father's son. 5.03.170
my name is roderigo. OTH 1.01. 95
and your name is great | in mouths of wisest 2.03.192
and spend your rich opinion for the name | of a 2.03.195
of wine, if thou hast no name to be known by, 2.03.282 P
i prithee name the time, but let it not | exceed 3.03. 62
good name in man and woman, dear my lord, | is 3.03.155
but he that filches from me my good name | robs 3.03.159
/her name, that was as fresh | as dian's visage, 3.03.386
am i that name, iago? 4.02.118
what name, fair lady? 4.02.118
let me not name it to you, you chaste stars, 5.02. 2
name cleopatra as she is call'd in rome. ANT 1.02.106
upon his son, who, high in name and power, 1.02.189
for pompey's name strikes more | than could his 1.04. 54
that i should | once name you derogately, when 2.02. 34
when to sound your name | it not concern'd me. 2.02. 34
why, this it is to have a name in great men's 2.07. 11 P
i'll humbly signify what in his name, | that 3.01. 30
promise, | and in our name, what she requires; 3.12. 28
what's your name? 3.13. 72
my name is thidias. 3.13. 73
with the hand of she here — what's her name, 3.13. 98
a tearing groan did break | the name of antony; 4.14. 32
she rend'red life, | thy name so buried in her. 4.14. 34
doom, in the name lay | a moi'ty of the world. 5.01. 18
what's thy name? 5.02. 11
my name is proculeius. 5.02. 12
we fall, | we answer others' merits in our name, 5.02.178
now to that name my courage prove my title! 5.02.288
what's his name and birth? CYM 1.01. 27
as since he hath been allow'd the name of. 1.04. 3 P
lie speechless, and his name | is at last gasp. 1.05. 52
how, my good name? 2.03. 84
she hath bought the name of whore thus dearly. 2.04.128
all faults that name, nay, that hell knows, 2.05. 27
in caesar's name pronounce i 'gainst thee; 3.01. 66
i' th' name of fame and honor which dies i' th' 3.03. 51
was the theme, my name | was not far off. 3.03. 59
sir, the event | is yet to name the winner. 3.05. 15
what's your name? 3.06. 59
thief, | hear but my name, and tremble. 4.02. 87
what's thy name? 4.02. 87
cloten, thou double villain, be thy name, | i 4.02. 89
say his name, good friend. 4.02.376
thy name? 4.02.379
thy name well fits thy faith; 4.02.381
thy faith thy name. 4.02.381
what's thy name? 5.05.117
the fit and apt construction of thy name, 5.05.444
great, | the name of help grew odious to repeat. PER 1.04. 31
gains from his subjects the name of good by his 2.01.105 P
to know of him | of whence he is, his name, and 2.03. 74
to know of you | of whence you are, your name, 2.03. 80
a gentleman of tyre, my name, pericles, | my 2.03. 81
please you to name it. 4.06. 71 P
could he speak, | would own a name too dear. 4.06.179
nothing we'll omit | that bears recovery's name. 5.01. 54
thy name, my most kind virgin? 5.01.140
my name is marina. 5.01.142
the name | was given me by one that had some 5.01.147
what was thy mother's name? 5.01.200
but tell me now | my drown'd queen's name, as in 5.01.205
than | to say my mother's name was thaisa? 5.01.210
did you not name a tempest, | a birth, and death 5.03. 33
the honor'd name | of pericles to rage the city 5.03. 96
yet they breathe | and have the name of men. TNK 1.04. 28
your friend and i have chanc'd to name you here, 2.01. 16 P
and if the lives of all my name lay on it, | i 2.02.175
to purchase name, and do my ablest service | to 2.05. 26
a chaffy lord, | nor worth the name of villain! 3.01. 42
their lives | might breed the ruin of my name, 3.06.240
i one question | of your name or his scape. 4.01. 16
soe'er she's about, the name palamon lards it, 4.03. 7 P
young sir her friend, the name of palamon, say 4.03. 76 P
i am in labor | to push your name, your ancient 5.01. 26
and in thy name | to my design march boldly. 5.01. 67
get herself | some part of a good name, and many 5.03. 27
hold, in the king's name hold! STM II.C 26
throne and sword, but given him his own name, II.C 103
are incident, by his name | can still the rout? II.C 115
when thou didst name the boar, not to dissemble, VEN 641
since sweating lust on earth usurp'd his name, 794
now she adds honors to his hateful name; 994
happ'ly that name of "chaste" unhapp'ly set LUC 8
and decks with praises collatine's high name, 108
wrong'st his honor, wound'st his princely name. 599
for blame, | to privilege dishonor in thy name? 621
and fright her crying babe with tarquin's name; 814
"let my good name, that senseless reputation, 820
fast, | thy smoothing titles to a ragged name, 892
"but ere i name him, you fair lords," quoth she 1688
would break, | she throws forth tarquin's name: 1717
but through his teeth, as if the name he tore. 1787
single nature's double name | neither two nor PHT 39
me, | unless thou take that honor from thy name. SON 36.12
and our dear love lose name of single one, 39. 6
clay, | do not so much as my poor name rehearse, 71.11
me untrue, | my name be buried where my body is, 72.11
that every word doth almost /tell my name, 76. 7
knowing a better spirit doth use your name, 80. 2
your name from hence immortal life shall have, 81. 5
thy sweet beloved name no more shall dwell, 89.10
doth spot the beauty of thy budding name! 95. 3
praise, | naming thy name blesses an ill report. 95. 8
even as when first i hallowed thy fair name. 108. 8
thence comes it that my name receives a brand, 111. 5
or if it were, it bore not beauty's name; 127. 2
sweet beauty hath no name, no holy bow'r, | but 127. 7
make but my name thy love, and love that still, 136.13
and then thou lovest me, for my name is will. 136.14
but, rising at thy name, doth point out thee 151. 9

NAMED 4 FR 0.0004 REL FR 4 V 0 P

fie, fie, they are not to be named, my lord, ADO 4.01. 95
will stand a' tiptoe when this day is named, H5 4.03. 42
and nobly named so, twice being censor, | was COR 2.03.244
loath to call | your faults as they are named. LR 1.01.271

NAMELESS 4 FR 0.0004 REL FR 3 V 1 P

unto the secret, nameless friend of yours; TGV 2.01.105
"item, she hath many nameless virtues." 3.01.317 P
'tis nameless woe, i wot. R2 2.02. 40
thy issue blurr'd with nameless bastardy; LUC 522

NAMELY 6 FR 0.0006 REL FR 5 V 1 P

namely, /e'en no time to recover hair lost by ERR 2.02.102 P
namely, some love that drew him oft from home. 5.01. 56
to him that owes it, namely this young prince, JN 2.01.248
namely, to appeal each other of high treason. R2 1.01. 27
'longs | to him and to his heirs, namely, the H5 2.04. 81
namely, to derby, hastings, buckingham — | and R3 1.03.328

NAME'S 8 FR 0.0009 REL FR 4 V 4 P

his name's parolles. AWW 5.03.202
sir, her name's a word, and to dally with that TN 3.01. 19 P
i have forgot that name, and that name's woe. ROM 2.03. 46
her, as that name's cursed hand | murder'd her 3.03.104
it is no matter, his name's cinna. JC 3.03. 33 P
my name's macbeth. MAC 5.07. 7
his name's gonzago, the story is extant, and HAM 3.02.262 P
a spirit, a spirit! he says his name's poor tom. LR 3.04. 42 P
NAMES 52 FR 0.0058 REL FR 34 V 18 P
please you repeat their names, i'll show my mind TGV 1.02. 7
he couples it to his complaining names. 1.02.124
not their fathers, and therefore have no names. 3.01.320 P
writ with blank space for different names (sure, WIV 2.01. 76 P
names! 2.02.296 P
they are devils' additions, the names of fiends; 2.02.298 P
elves, list your names; 5.05. 42
as school–maids change their names | by vain MM 1.04. 47
you bring me in the names of some six or seven, 2.01.272 P
as could not be distinguish'd but by names. ERR 1.01. 52
how can she thus then call us by our names, 2.02.166
whose names yet run smoothly in the even road of
ADO 5.02. 33 P
oaths are pass'd, and now subscribe your names, LLL 1.01. 19
then read the names of the actors; MND 1.02. 9 P
i care not for their names, they owe me nothing. AYL 2.05. 21 P
and twenty more such names and men as these, SHR in.2. 95
that i shake off these names you give me. TN 5.01. 73
our gentry than our parents' noble names, | in WT 1.02.393
your names? 4.04.719 P
for new–made honor doth forget men's names; JN 1.01.187
when we were happy we had other names. 5.04. 8
can sick men play so nicely with their names? R2 2.01. 84
is not the king's name twenty thousand names? 3.02. 85
a commodity of good names were to be bought. 1H4 1.02. 83 P
and can call them all by their christen names, 2.04. 8 P
in reckoning up the several devils' names | that 3.01.155
using the names of men in stead of men, | like 2H4 1.03. 57
out for taking their names upon you before you 2.04.143 P
our battle is more full of names than yours, 4.01.152
are perfit in the great commanders' names, and H5 3.06. 71 P
then shall our names, | familiar in his mouth as 4.03. 51
the names of those their nobles that lie dead: 4.08. 91
blotting your names from books of memory, 2H6 1.01.100
thou mightst as well have known all our names, 2.01.125
thou hadst call'd me all these bitter names. R3 1.03.235
you them all by their names as they pass by, but TRO 1.02.183 P
should lose their names, and so should justice 1.03.118
forbade all names; COR 5.01. 12
persons out | whose names are written there, and ROM 1.02. 36
find them out whose names are written here! 1.02. 38 P
to find those persons whose names are here writ, 1.02. 42 P
and can never find what names the writing person 1.02. 43 P
now in the names of all the gods at once, | upon JC 1.02.148
many then shall die, their names are prick'd. 4.01. 1
heart | i find she names my very deed of love; LR 1.01. 71
what are you there? your names? 3.04.128
i must change names at home, and give the 4.02. 17
in the world /he /is | that names me traitor, 5.03. 98
then belike my children shall have no names. ANT 1.02. 36 P
names himself pericles, | a gentleman of tyre, PER 2.03. 86
/prisoner told me | when i inquired their names? TNK 1.04. 22
nor names concealments in | the boldest language 5.01.123
NAMEST 1 FR 0.0001 REL FR 0 V 1 P
thee over–name them, and as thou namest them, i
MV 1.02. 37 P
NAME/'T 1 FR 0.0001 REL FR 0 V 1 P
why, i cannot name/'t but i shall offend. PER 4.06. 69 P
NAMING 5 FR 0.0005 REL FR 3 V 2 P
promis'd gift, | which but attends thy naming. AWW 2.03. 51
no more, whose very naming punishes me with the
WT 4.02. 21 P
why, 'tis this naming of him does him harm. TRO 2.03.228
my fortunes against any lay worth naming, this OTH 2.03.324 P
praise, | naming thy name blesses an ill report. SON 95. 8
NAN 11 FR 0.0012 REL FR 8 V 3 P
this hat is nan, our maid. TGV 2.03. 21 P
good faith, it is such another nan; WIV 1.04.150 P
therefore no more turn me to him, sweet nan. 3.04. 2
farewell, gentle mistress; farewell, nan. 3.04. 94
once to–night | give my sweet nan this ring. 3.04.100
nan page (my daughter) and my little son, | and 4.04. 48
my nan shall be the queen of all the fairies, 4.04. 71
time | shall master slender steal my nan away, 4.04. 74
will, | and none but he, to marry with nan page. 4.04. 85
must my sweet nan present the fairy queen; 4.06. 20
where is nan now, and her troop of fairies, and 5.03. 11 P
NAP* 4 FR 0.0004 REL FR 2 V 2 P
by my fay, a goodly nap, | but did i never speak SHR in.2. 81
let your bounty take a nap, i will awake it anon TN 5.01. 48 P
and turn it, and set a new nap upon it. 2H6 4.02. 6 P
strive with troubled thoughts to take a nap, R3 5.03.104
NAPES 1 FR 0.0001 REL FR 0 V 1 P
your eyes toward the napes of your necks and COR 2.01. 39 P
NAPKIN 14 FR 0.0015 REL FR 14 V 0 P
his rosalind | he sends this bloody napkin. AYL 4.03. 93
but for the bloody napkin? 4.03.138
his broken promise, and to give this napkin, 4.03.154
which in a napkin (being close convey'd) | shall SHR in.1. 127
i stain'd this napkin with the blood | that 3H6 1.04. 79
keep thou the napkin and go boast of this, | and 1.04.159
cheeks | a napkin steeped in the harmless blood 2.01. 62
i wot, | thy napkin cannot drink a tear of mine, TIT 3.01.140
his napkin, with /his true tears all bewet, 3.01.146
here, hamlet, take my napkin, rub thy brows. HAM 5.02.288
your napkin is too little; OTH 3.03.287
i am glad i have found this napkin; 3.03.290
i will in cassio's lodging lose this napkin, 3.03.321
oft did she heave her napkin to her eyne, LC 15
NAPKINS 4 FR 0.0004 REL FR 1 V 3 P
socks, foul stockings, greasy napkins, that, WIV 3.05. 91 P
half shirt is two napkins tack'd together and 1H4 4.02. 43 P
and dip their napkins in his sacred blood; JC 3.02.133
have napkins enow about you, here you'll sweat MAC 2.03. 6 P
NAPLES 30 FR 0.0034 REL FR 27 V 3 P
wi' th' king of naples | to give him annual TMP 1.02.112
this king of naples, being an enemy | to me 1.02.121
float | bound sadly home for naples, | supposing 1.02.235
wert thou, if the king of naples heard thee? 1.02.432
that wonders | to hear thee speak of naples. 1.02.434
myself am naples, | who with mine eyes (never 1.02.435
gone forth, i'll make you | the queen of naples. 1.02.450
o thou mine heir | of naples and of milan, what 2.01.113
milan and naples have | moe widows in them of 2.01.133
then tell me, | who's the next heir of naples? 2.01.245
she that from naples | can have no note, unless 2.01.247
's queen of tunis, | so is she heir of naples; 2.01.256
shall that claribel | measure us back to naples? 2.01.259
there be that can rule naples | as well as he 2.01.262
as thou got'st milan, | i'll come by naples. 2.01.292
and keep him tame, and get to naples with him, 2.02. 69 P
if in naples | i should report this now, would 3.03. 27
o heavens, that they were living both in naples, 5.01.149
that his issue | should become kings of naples? 5.01.206
i'll bring you to your ship, and so to naples, 5.01.308
be here confin'd by you, | or sent to naples. ep 5
king, | the king of naples, whosoe'er thou art. 1H6 5.03. 52
for though her father be the king of naples, 5.03. 94
but reignier, king of naples, that prevail'd. 5.04. 78
is a king, | the king of naples and jerusalem, 5.05. 40
daughter unto reignier king of naples, sicilia, 2H6 1.01. 47 P
outcast of naples, england's bloody scourge! 5.01.118
thy father bears the type of king of naples, 3H6 1.04.121
iron of naples hid with english gilt, | whose 2.02.139
have your instruments been in naples, that they OTH 3.01. 4 P
NAPLESS 1 FR 0.0001 REL FR 1 V 0 P
on him put | the napless vesture of humility, COR 2.01.234
NAPPING 2 FR 0.0002 REL FR 2 V 0 P
i know, | to be o'erheard and taken napping so. LLL 4.03.128
nay, i have ta'en you napping, gentle love, SHR 4.02. 46
NAPS 1 FR 0.0001 REL FR 1 V 0 P
as stephen sly, and old john naps of greece, SHR in.2. 93
NARBON 3 FR 0.0003 REL FR 1 V 2 P
his great right to be so — gerard de narbon. AWW 1.01. 27 P
gentlewoman the daughter of gerard de narbon? 1.01. 37 P
gerard de narbon was my father, | in what he did 2.01.101
NARCISSUS 5 FR 0.0005 REL FR 5 V 0 P
hadst thou narcissus in thy face, to me | thou ANT 2.05. 96
'tis call'd narcissus, madam. TNK 2.02.119
narcissus was a sad boy, but a heavenly. 4.02. 32
narcissus so himself himself forsook, | and died VEN 161
that had narcissus seen her as she stood, LUC 265
NARINES 1 FR 0.0001 REL FR 0 V 1 P
volant, the pegasus, chez les narines de feu! H5 3.07. 14 P
/NARROW 1 FR 0.0001 REL FR 0 V 1 P
/'tis /too /narrow /for /your /mind. HAM 2.02.253 P
NARROW 17 FR 0.0019 REL FR 13 V 4 P
passages of alleys, creeks, and narrow lands; ERR 4.02. 38
in the narrow seas that part | the french and MV 2.08. 28
ship of rich lading wrack'd on the narrow seas; 3.01. 3 P
i am for the house with the narrow gate, which i AWW 4.05. 51 P
as stand in narrow lanes | and beat our watch R2 5.03. 8
you four shall front them in the narrow lane; 1H4 2.02. 60 P
the perilous narrow ocean parts asunder. H5 pr 22
in | their heavy burthens at his narrow gate, 1.02.201
charming the narrow seas | to give you gentle 2.pr. 38
stern falconbridge commands the narrow seas, 3H6 1.01.239
hath pass'd in safety through the narrow seas, 4.08. 3
way, | for honor travels in a strait so narrow, TRO 3.03.154
stretches from an inch narrow to an ell broad! ROM 2.04. 84 P
man, he doth bestride the narrow world | like a JC 1.02.135
here the street is narrow; 2.04. 33
he vented /them, most narrow measure lent me; ANT 3.04. 8
a narrow lane, an old man, and two boys! CYM 5.03. 52
NARROWLY 3 FR 0.0003 REL FR 1 V 2 P
cousin do not look exceeding narrowly to thee. ADO 5.04.116 P
doth watch bianca's steps so narrowly, | 'twere SHR 3.02.139
search the market narrowly, meteline is full of PER 4.02. 3 P
NARROW–MOUTH'D 1 FR 0.0001 REL FR 0 V 1 P
as wine comes out of a narrow–mouth'd bottle, AYL 3.02.200 P
NARROW–PRYING 1 FR 0.0001 REL FR 1 V 0 P
the narrow–prying father, minola, | the quaint SHR 3.02.146
NASO 2 FR 0.0002 REL FR 0 V 2 P
ovidius naso was the man. LLL 4.02.123 P
and why indeed "naso," but for smelling out the 4.02.124 P
NASTY 2 FR 0.0002 REL FR 2 V 0 P
and, which is worse, within thy nasty mouth! H5 2.01. 50
honeying and making love | over the nasty sty! HAM 3.04. 94
/NATHANIEL 2 FR 0.0002 REL FR 0 V 2 P
sir /nathaniel, this berowne is one of the LLL 4.02.136 P
sir /nathaniel, as concerning some entertainment 5.01.118 P
NATHANIEL 5 FR 0.0005 REL FR 1 V 4 P
sir nathaniel, haud credo. LLL 4.02. 11 P
sir nathaniel, will you hear an extemporal 4.02. 50 P
did they please you, sir nathaniel? 4.02.151 P
call forth nathaniel, joseph, nicholas, philip, SHR 4.01. 89 P
where is nathaniel, gregory, philip? 4.01.122
NATHANIEL'S 1 FR 0.0001 REL FR 1 V 0 P
nathaniel's coat, sir, was not fully made, | and SHR 4.01.132
NATIFS 1 FR 0.0001 REL FR 0 V 1 P
mots aussi droit que les natifs d'angleterre. H5 3.04. 38 P
/NATION 1 FR 0.0001 REL FR 0 V 1 P
/and /the /nation /holds /it /no /sin /to /tarre HAM 2.02.353 P
NATION 30 FR 0.0034 REL FR 18 V 12 P
methinks they are such a gentle nation that, but ERR 4.04.153 P
he hates our sacred nation, and he rails, | even MV 1.03. 48
mock'd at my gains, scorn'd my nation, thwarted 3.01. 56 P
the curse never fell upon our nation till now, i 3.01. 85 P
much shame, you might begin an impudent nation.
AWW 4.03.328 P
and doughy youth of a nation in his color. 4.05. 4 P
o nation, that thou couldst remove! JN 5.02. 33
apish nation | limps after in base imitation. R2 2.01. 22
was alway yet the trick of our english nation, 2H4 1.02.215 P
in equal rank with the best govern'd nation, 5.02.137
and our nation lose | the name of hardiness and H5 1.02.219
correction, there is not many of your nation — 3.02.121 P
of my nation? 3.02.122 P
what ish my nation? 3.02.122 P
what ish my nation? 3.02.124 P
who talks of my nation? 3.02.124 P
nor should that nation boast it so with us, 1H6 3.03. 23
but with a lordly nation | that will not trust 3.03. 62
in france, amongst a fickle, wavering nation. 4.01.138
betwixt our nation and the aspiring french; 5.04. 99
there is a law in each well–order'd nation | to TRO 2.02.180
abated captives to some nation | that won you COR 3.03.132
hath yok'd a nation strong, train'd up in arms. TIT 1.01. 30
o nation miserable! MAC 4.03.103
the brooch indeed | and gem of all the nation. HAM 4.07. 94
the scrimers of their nation | he swore had 4.07.100
the wealthy curled /darlings of our nation, OTH 1.02. 68
and so in ours, some neighboring nation, PER 1.04. 65
well, if we had of every nation a traveller, we 4.02.113 P
to find a nation of such barbarous temper | that STM II.C 131
NATION'S 2 FR 0.0002 REL FR 2 V 0 P
even at the crying of your nation's crow, JN 5.02.144
our nation's terror and their bloody scourge! 1H6 4.02. 16
NATIONS 9 FR 0.0010 REL FR 7 V 2 P
profit of the city | consisteth of all nations. MV 3.03. 31
the courtesy of nations allows you my better, in AYL 1.01. 46 P
by law of nature and of nations, 'longs | to him H5 2.04. 80
of his name | shall be, and make new nations. H8 5.04. 52
laws | of nature and of nations speak aloud | to TRO 2.02.185
i would not be a roman, of all nations; COR 4.05.175 P
that puts odds | among the rout of nations, i TIM 4.03. 44
makes us traduc'd and tax'd of other nations. HAM 1.04. 18
permit | the curiosity of nations to deprive me, LR 1.02. 4
NATIVE 43 FR 0.0048 REL FR 38 V 5 P
why thou departedst from thy native home, | and ERR 1.01. 29
possess the same | which native she doth owe. LLL 1.02.106
for native blood is counted painting now; 4.03.259
the scarfed bark puts from her native bay, MV 2.06. 15
being native burghers of this desert city, AYL 2.01. 23
in their assign'd and native dwelling–place. 2.01. 63
are you native of this place? 3.02.338 P
to join like likes, and kiss like native things. AWW 1.01.223
breeds | a native slip to us from foreign seeds. 1.03.146
of honor again into his native quarter, be 3.06. 66 P
have sold their fortunes at their native homes, JN 2.01. 69
shall leave his native channel and o'erswell 2.01.337
and chase the native beauty from his cheek, 3.04. 83
my native english, now i must forgo, | and now R2 1.03.160
robs my tongue from breathing native breath? 1.03.173
blood | with fury from his native residence. 2.01.119
and fright our native peace with self–borne arms 2.03. 80
ere her native king | shall falter under foul 3.02. 25
commotion so /appear'd | in his true, native, 2H4 4.01. 37
we bear our civil swords and native fire | as 5.05.106
suits not in native colors with the truth; H5 1.02. 17
us fear | the native mightiness and fate of him. 2.04. 64
held | from him, the native and true challenger. 2.04. 95
poor we call them in their native lords! 3.05. 26
defeated the law and outrun native punishment, 4.01.167 P
our bodies shall no doubt | find native graves; 4.03. 96
he could not speak english in the native garb, 5.01. 76 P
bank | drove back again unto my native clime? 2H6 3.02. 84
spare england, for it is your native coast. 4.08. 50
did i put henry from his native right? 3H6 3.03.190
we fear to warrant in our native place! TRO 2.02. 96
could never be the native | of our so frank COR 3.01.129
your native town you enter'd like a post, | and 5.06. 49
back, foolish tears, back to your native spring, ROM 3.02.102
for no pulse | shall keep his native progress, 4.01. 97
contempt hereditary, | the beggar native honor. TIM 4.03. 11
for if thou path, thy native semblance on, | not JC 2.01. 83
the head is not more native to the heart, | the HAM 1.02. 47
though i am native here | and to the manner born 1.04. 14
and thus the native hue of resolution | is 3.01. 83
or like a creature native and indued | unto that 4.07.179
the native act and figure of my heart | in OTH 1.01. 62
in their natures more than is native to them), 2.01.217 P
NATIVES *(see natifs)*
NATIVITY 16 FR 0.0018 REL FR 12 V 4 P
is divinity in odd numbers, either in nativity, WIV 5.01. 4 P
from the hour of my nativity to this instant, ERR 4.04. 31 P
both, | and you the calendars of their nativity, 5.01.405
with me — | after so long grief, such nativity! 5.01.407
so born, | in their nativity all truth appears. MND 3.02.125
prodigious, such as are | despised in nativity, 5.01.413
be out of love with your nativity, and almost AYL 4.01. 36 P
at my nativity | the front of heaven was full of 1H4 3.01. 13
on fire, | and not in fear of your nativity. 3.01. 25
now cursed be the time | of thy nativity! 1H6 5.04. 27
to whom the heav'ns in thy nativity | adjudg'd 3H6 4.06. 33
thou that wast seal'd in thy nativity | the R3 1.03.228
tail, and my nativity was under ursa major, so LR 1.02.130 P
thou hast as chiding a nativity | as fire, air, PER 3.01. 32
for marks descried in men's nativity | are LUC 538
nativity, once in the main of light, | crawls to SON 60. 5
NATURAL 60 FR 0.0067 REL FR 47 V 13 P
for nothing natural | i ever saw so noble. TMP 1.02.419
that a monster should be such a natural! 3.02. 33 P
of truth, their words | are natural breath; 5.01.157
these are not natural events, they strengthen 5.01.227
but doth rebate and blunt his natural edge MM 1.04. 60
confess | a natural guiltiness such as is his, 2.02.139
his love toward her ever most kind and natural; 3.01.221 P
and so of these, which is the natural man, | and ERR 5.01.334
but, as in health, come to my natural taste, MND 4.01.174
contriver against me his natural brother; AYL 1.01.145 P
fortune makes nature's natural the cutter–off of 1.02. 49 P
who perceiveth our natural wits too dull to 1.02. 52 P
/and hath sent this natural for our whetstone; 1.02. 54 P
are dearer than the natural bond of sisters. 1.02.276
such a one is a natural philosopher. 3.02. 32 P
your majesty to make it | natural rebellion, AWW 5.03. 6
he hath indeed, almost natural; TN 1.03. 29 P
with a better grace, but i do it more natural. 2.03. 83 P
a natural perspective, that is and is not! 5.01.217
but our natural goodness | imparts this; WT 2.01.164
her natural posture! 5.03. 23
no natural exhalation in the sky, | no scope of JN 3.04.153
but they will pluck away his natural cause | and 3.04.156
and thou a natural coward, without instinct. 1H4 2.04.494 P
and curbs himself even of his natural scope 3.01.169
where you did give a fair and natural light, 5.01. 18
congreeing in a full and natural close, | like H5 1.02.182
do, | were all thy children kind and natural! 2.pr. 19
working so grossly in /a natural cause | that 2.02.107
how shall we then behold their natural tears? 4.02. 13
/and natural graces that extinguish art; 1H6 5.03.192
whom should he follow but his natural king? 3H6 1.01. 82
never to lie and take his natural rest | till 4.03. 5
that none of you may live his natural age, | but R3 1.03.212

veins | from me receive that natural competency COR 1.01.139
kind | we sucking on her natural bosom find: ROM 2.03. 12
love is like a great natural that runs lolling 2.04. 92 P
the painting is almost the natural man; TIM 1.01.157
dear divorce | 'twixt natural /son and /sire! 4.03.382
that thou art even natural in thine art. 5.01. 85
"these are their reasons, they are natural"; JC 1.03. 30
and keep the natural ruby of your cheeks, | when MAC 3.04.114
he loves us not, | he wants the natural touch; 4.02. 9
upon a wretch whose natural gifts were poor | to HAM 1.05. 51
the natural gates and alleys of the body, | and 1.05. 67
there is something in this more than natural, if 2.02.367 P
the heart–ache and the thousand natural shocks 3.01. 61
thy natural magic and dire property | on 3.02.259
loyal and natural boy, i'll work the means | to LR 2.01. 84
i am even | the natural fool of fortune. 4.06.191
i do agnize | a natural and prompt alacrity | i OTH 1.03.232
it is not caesar's natural vice to hate | /our ANT 1.04. 2
and, of that natural luck, | he beats thee 2.03. 27
ah, but some natural notes about her body, CYM 2.02. 28
with | the natural bravery of your isle, which 3.01. 18
morgan call'd, | they take for natural father. 3.03.107
more respect than my noble and natural person, 3.05.136 P
who hath upon him still that natural stamp. 5.05.366
that even her art sisters the natural roses; PER 5.ch. 7
but alas, | being a natural sister of our sex, TNK 1.01.125

NATURALIZE 1 FR 0.0001 REL FR 0 V 1 P
my instruction shall serve to naturalize thee, AWW 1.01.208 P

NATURALLY 4 FR 0.0004 REL FR 2 V 2 P
part | was aptly fitted and naturally perform'd. SHR in.1. 87
though i am not naturally honest, i am so WT 4.04.712 P
to fears, | a woman, naturally born to fears; JN 3.01. 15
the cold blood he did naturally inherit of his 2H4 4.03.118 P

/NATURE 6 FR 0.0006 REL FR 6 V 0 P
/thick (/which /nature /made /his /blemish) 2H4 2.03. 24
/loving /well /compos'd /with /gift /of /nature, TRO 4.04. 77
/nature /is /fine /in /love, /and /where /'tis HAM 4.05.162
/to /let /this /canker /of /our /nature /come 5.02. 69
/oppressed /nature /sleeps. LR 3.06. 97
/that /nature /which /contemns /it /origin 4.02. 32

NATURE 369 FR 0.0417 REL FR 318 V 51 P
in my false brother | awak'd an evil nature, and TMP 1.02. 93
my father's of a better nature, sir, | than he 1.02.497
all things in common nature should produce 2.01.160
but nature should bring forth, | of it own kind, 2.01.163
on whose nature | nurture can never stick; 4.01.188
expell'd remorse and nature, whom, with 5.01. 76
and there is in this business more than nature 5.01.243
and love you 'gainst the nature of love — force TGV 5.04. 58
if fortune thy foe were not, nature thy friend. WIV 3.03. 65 P
the nature of our people, | our city's MM 1.01. 9
nor nature never lends | the smallest scruple of 1.01. 36
but of what strength and nature | i am not yet 1.01. 79
and yet my nature never in the fight | to do in 1.03. 42
with all her double vigor, art and nature, 2.02.183
to make me know | the nature of their crimes, 2.03. 7
to pardon him that hath from nature stol'n | a 2.04. 43
but in what nature? 3.01. 69
imprisonment | can lay on nature is a paradise 3.01.130
life, | nature dispenses with the deed so far, 3.01.134
may witness that my end | was wrought by nature, ERR 1.01. 34
to recover his hair that grows bald by nature. 2.02. 73 P
/e'en no time to recover hair lost by nature. 2.02.103 P
but nature never fram'd a woman's heart | of ADO 3.01. 49
if black, why, nature, drawing of an antic, 3.01. 63
fortune, but to write and read comes by nature. 3.03. 16 P
grace | as nature was in making graces dear, LLL 2.01. 10
is of that nature that to your huge store | wise 5.02.377
transparent helena, nature shows art, | that MND 2.02.104
o, wherefore, nature, didst thou lions frame? 5.01.291
nature hath fram'd strange fellows in her time: MV 1.01. 51
which therein works a miracle in nature, 3.02. 90
of a strange nature is the suit you follow, 4.01.177
but music for the time doth change his nature. 5.01. 82
gives me, the something that nature gave me his AYL 1.01. 18 P
of the world, not in the lineaments of nature. 1.02. 42 P
when nature hath made a fair creature, may she 1.02. 43 P
though nature hath given us wit to flout at 1.02. 45 P
indeed there is fortune too hard for nature, 1.02. 48 P
but as all is mortal in nature, so is all nature 2.04. 55 P
so is all nature in love mortal in folly. 2.04. 56 P
and let my officers of such a nature | make an 3.01. 16
learn'd no wit by nature nor art may complain of 3.02. 29 P
therefore heaven nature charg'd | that one body 3.02.141
nature presently distill'd | helen's cheek, but 3.02.144
and nature, stronger than his just occasion, 4.03.129
though the nature of our quarrel yet never SHR 1.01.114 P
so far, would have made nature immortal, and AWW 1.01. 20 P
the commonwealth of nature to preserve virginity 1.01.127 P
be said in't, 'tis against the rule of nature. 1.01.136 P
limit, as a desperate offendress against nature. 1.01.141 P
the mightiest space in fortune nature brings 1.01.222
frank nature, rather curious than in haste, 1.02. 20
nature and sickness | debate it at their leisure 1.02. 74
'tis often seen | adoption strives with nature, 1.03.145
that laboring art can never ransom nature | from 2.01.118
fair, | in these to nature she's immediate heir; 2.03.132
but i am sure the younger of our nature, | that 3.01. 17
my son corrupts a well–derived nature | with his 3.02. 88
that all the miseries which nature owes | were 3.02.119
there is something in't that stings his nature; 4.03. 4 P
tenderness of her nature became as a prey to her 4.03. 51 P
no thanks for't, in the nature he delivers it. 4.03.152 P
i would repent out the remainder of nature. 4.03.243 P
that ever nature had praise for creating. 4.05. 10 P
which are their own right by the law of nature. 4.05. 62 P
the nature of his great offense is dead, | and 5.03. 23
or, ere they meet, in me, o nature, cesse! 5.03. 72
whose nature sickens but to speak a truth. 5.03.207
a noble duke, in nature as in name. TN 1.02. 25
and though that nature with a beauteous wall 1.02. 48
book, and hath all the good gifts of nature. 1.03. 28 P
for thou seest it will not /curl /by nature. 1.03. 99 P
and in dimension and the shape of nature | a 1.05.261
that nature pranks her in attracts my soul. 2.04. 86
th' offense is not of such a bloody nature, 3.03. 30
of what nature the wrongs are thou hast done him 3.04.221 P
in nature there's no blemish but the mind; 3.04.367
nor can there be that deity in my nature | of 5.01.227
but nature to her bias drew in that. 5.01.260
how sometimes nature will betray its folly! WT 1.02.151
is | by law and process of great nature thence 2.02. 58
and thou, good goddess nature, which hast made 2.03.104
so long as nature | will bear up with this 3.02.240
piedness shares | with great creating nature. 4.04. 88
yet nature is made better by no mean | but 4.04. 89
better by no mean | but nature makes that mean; 4.04. 90
over that art | which you say adds to nature, is 4.04. 91
adds to nature, is an art | that nature makes. 4.04. 92
this is an art | which does mend nature — 4.04. 96
but | the art itself is nature. 4.04. 97
let nature crush the sides o' th' earth together 4.04.478
yet nature might have made me as these are, 4.04.746
of nobleness which nature shows above her 5.02. 37 P
his work, would beguile nature of her custom, so 5.02. 99 P
which heaven shall take in nature of a fee; JN 2.01.170
nature and fortune join'd to make thee great. 3.01. 52
no scope of nature, no distemper'd day, | no 3.04.154
by, | a fellow by the hand of nature mark'd, 4.02.221
and you have slander'd nature in my form, 4.02.256
this fortress built by nature for herself R2 2.01. 43
all of one nature, of one substance bred, | did 1H4 1.01. 11
diseased nature oftentimes breaks forth | in 3.01. 26
hath sent to know | the nature of your griefs, 4.03. 42
foretells the nature of a tragic volume. 2H4 1.01. 61
no reason in the law of nature but i may snap at 3.02.331 P
a peace is of the nature of a conquest, | for 4.02. 89
unfather'd heirs and loathly births of nature. 4.04.122
which nature, love, and filial tenderness 4.05. 39
how quickly nature falls into revolt | when gold 4.05. 65
he's walk'd the way of nature, | and to our 5.02. 4
creatures that by a rule in nature teach | the H5 1.02.188
mangle the work of nature, and deface | the 2.04. 60
by law of nature and of nations, 'longs | to him 2.04. 80
disguise fair nature with hard–favor'd rage; 3.01. 8
"wonder of nature" — 3.07. 40 P
froward by nature, enemy to peace, | lascivious, 1H6 3.01. 18
her words, | or nature makes me suddenly relent. 3.03. 59
a fox, | by nature prov'd an enemy to the flock, 2H6 3.01.258
being opposites of such repairing nature. 5.03. 22
she did corrupt frail nature with some bribe, 3H6 3.02.155
when nature brought him to the door of death? 3.03.105
his head by nature fram'd to wear a crown, | his 4.06. 72
more than the nature of a brother's love! 5.01. 79
cheated of feature by dissembling nature, R3 1.01. 19
the self–same name, but one of better nature. 1.02.143
fram'd in the prodigality of nature — | young, 1.02.243
the slave of nature and the son of hell! 1.03.229
the most replenished sweet work of nature | that 4.03. 18
as long as heaven and nature lengthens it. 4.04.353
you know his nature, | that he's revengeful; H8 1.01.108
the nature of it? 1.02. 53
most rare speaker, | to nature none more bound; 1.02.112
who had | commanded nature, that my lady's womb, 2.04.189
my lord of york, out of his noble nature, | zeal 3.01. 62
and nature does require | her times of 3.02.146
of me will stir him | (i know his noble nature) 3.02.418
she is young, and of a noble modest nature, | i 4.02.135
times to repair our nature | with comforting 5.01. 3
have | in them a wilder nature than the business 5.01. 15
sure | thou hast a cruel nature and a bloody. 5.02.164
a man into whom nature hath so crowded humors TRO 1.02. 22 P
the nature of the sickness found, ulysses, 1.03.140
nature craves | all dues be rend'red to their 2.02.173
law | of nature be corrupted through affection, 2.02.177
laws | of nature and of nations speak aloud | to 2.02.185
and thy parts of nature | thrice fam'd beyond, 2.03.242
made tame and most familiar to my nature; 3.03. 10
nature, what things there are | most /abject in 3.03.127
one touch of nature makes the whole world kin — 3.03.175
thou crusty batch of nature, what's the news? 5.01. 5
with such water–flies, diminutives of nature! 5.01. 34 P
doth conduce a fight | of this strange nature, 5.02.148
what he cannot help in his nature, you account a COR 1.01. 41 P
such a nature, | tickled with good success, 1.01.259
nature teaches beasts to know their friends. 2.01. 6 P
so his gracious nature | would think upon you 2.03.187
or else it would have gall'd his surly nature, 2.03.195
if, as his nature is, he fall in rage | with 2.03.258
the nature of our seats and make the rabble 3.01.136
his nature is too noble for the world; 3.01.254
lest his infection, being of catching nature, 3.01.308
would you have me | false to my nature? 3.02. 15
i would dissemble with my nature where | my 3.02. 62
a thing | made by some other deity than nature, 4.06. 91
yet his nature | in that's no changeling, and i 4.07. 10
fish, who takes it | by sovereignty of nature. 4.07. 35
or whether nature, | not to be other than one 4.07. 41
all bond and privilege of nature, break! 5.03. 25
of intercession which | great nature cries, 5.03. 33
he bow'd his nature, never known before | but to 5.06. 24
wilt thou draw near the nature of the gods? TIT 1.01.117
brother, for in that name doth nature plead — 1.01.370
father, and in that name doth nature speak — 1.01.371
for no name fits thy nature but thy own! 2.03.119
by nature made for murthers and for rapes. 4.01. 58
o, why should nature build so foul a den, 4.01. 59
had nature lent thee but thy mother's look, 5.01. 29
a while, | for nature puts me to a heavy task. 5.03.150
of some strange nature, letting it there stand ROM 2.01. 25
by art as well as by nature, for this drivelling 2.04. 91 P
o nature, what hadst thou to do in hell | when 3.02. 80
for though /fond nature bids us all lament, 4.05. 82
i will say of it, | it tutors nature. TIM 1.01. 37
upon his good and gracious nature hanging, 1.01. 56
for since dishonor traffics with man's nature, 1.01.158
amiss — a noble nature | may catch a wrench — 2.02.208
and nature, as it grows again toward earth, | is 2.02.218
let not that part of nature | which my lord paid 3.01. 61
of such a nature is his politic love. 3.03. 34 P
not nature | (to whom all sores lay siege) can 4.03. 6
bear great fortune | but by contempt of nature. 4.03. 8
nations, i will make thee | do thy right nature. 4.03. 45
that nature being sick of man's unkindness 4.03.176
this is in thee a nature but infected, | a poor 4.03.202
elements expos'd, | answer mere nature; 4.03.231
thy nature did commence in sufferance, time 4.03.268
the bounteous huswife nature on each bush | lays 4.03.420
it almost turns my dangerous nature wild. 4.03.492
discontents are unremovably | coupled to nature. 5.01.225
hunger for that food | which nature loathes, 5.04. 33
our droplets which | from niggard nature fall, 5.04. 77
how that might change his nature, there's the JC 2.01. 13
suffers then | the nature of an insurrection. 2.01. 69
you, | but yet my nature could not bear it so. 4.03.195
upon our talk, | and nature must obey necessity, 4.03.227
so mix'd in him that nature might stand up | and 5.05. 74
the multiplying villainies of nature | do swarm MAC 1.02. 11
knock at my ribs, | against the use of nature? 1.03.137
yet do i fear thy nature, | it is too full o' 1.05. 16
that no compunctious visitings of nature | shake 1.05. 45
restrain in me the cursed thoughts that nature 2.01. 8
now o'er the one half world | nature seems dead, 2.01. 50
that death and nature do contend about them, 2.02. 7
his gash'd stabs look'd like a breach in nature 2.03.113
turn'd wild in nature, broke their stalls, flung 2.04. 16
'gainst nature still! 2.04. 27
and in his royalty of nature | reigns that which 3.01. 49
your patience so predominant in your nature 3.01. 86
according to the gift which bounteous nature 3.01. 97
on his head, | the least a death to nature. 3.04. 27
hath nature that in time will venom breed, | no 3.04. 29
macbeth | shall live the lease of nature, pay 4.01. 99
a good and virtuous nature may recoil | in an 4.03. 19
boundless intemperance | in nature is a tyranny; 4.03. 67
laid upon myself, | for strangers to my nature. 4.03.125
a great perturbation in nature, to receive at 5.01. 9 P
yet so far hath discretion fought with nature HAM 1.02. 5
must die, | passing through nature to eternity. 1.02. 73
'tis sweet and commendable in your nature, 1.02. 87
a fault against the dead, a fault to nature, 1.02.102
things rank and gross in nature | possess it 1.02.136
blood, | a violet in the youth of primy nature, 1.03. 7
for nature crescent does not grow alone | in 1.03. 11
that for some vicious mole of nature in them, 1.04. 24
guilty | (since nature cannot choose his origin) 1.04. 26
and we fools of nature | so horridly to shake 1.04. 54
till the foul crimes done in my days of nature 1.05. 12
if thou hast nature in thee, bear it not, | let 1.05. 81
that you o'erstep not the modesty of nature: 3.02. 19 P
is, to hold, as 'twere, the mirror up to nature: 3.02. 22 P
o heart, lose not thy nature! 3.02.393
since nature makes them partial, should o'erhear 3.03. 32
there the action lies | in his true nature, and 3.03. 62
for use almost can change the stamp of nature, 3.04.168
to my sick soul, as sin's true nature is, | each 4.05. 17
feats, | so criminal and so capital in nature, 4.07. 7
nature her custom holds, | let shame say what it 4.07.187
'tis dangerous when the baser nature comes 5.02. 60
sir — after what flourish your nature will. 5.02.181 P
what i have done | that might your nature, honor 5.02.231
i am satisfied in nature, | whose motive, in 5.02.244
extend | where nature doth with merit challenge? LR 1.01. 53
which nor our nature nor our place can bear, 1.01.171
than on a wretch whom nature is asham'd | almost 1.01.212
a tardiness in nature | which often leaves the 1.01.235
thou, nature, art my goddess, to thy law | my 1.02. 1
who, in the lusty stealth of nature, take | more 1.02. 11
though the wisdom of nature can reason it thus 1.02.104 P
yet nature finds itself scourg'd by the sequent 1.02.105 P
the king falls from bias of nature; 1.02.111 P
whose nature is so far from doing harms | that 1.02.180
wrench'd my frame of nature | from the fix'd 1.04.268
hear, nature, hear, dear goddess, hear! 1.04.275
i will forget my nature. 1.05. 32 P
you cowardly rascal, nature disclaims in thee: 2.02. 54 P
and constrains the garb | quite from his nature. 2.02. 98
we are not ourselves | when nature, being 2.04.108
nature in you stands on the very verge | of his 2.04.147
thy tender–hefted nature shall not give | thee 2.04.171
thou better know'st | the offices of nature, 2.04.178
allow not nature more than nature needs, | man's 2.04.266
allow not nature more than nature needs, | man's 2.04.266
nature needs not what thou gorgeous wear'st, 2.04.269
man's nature cannot carry | th' affliction nor 3.02. 48
open night's too rough | for nature to endure. 3.04. 3
nothing could have subdu'd nature | to such a 3.04. 70
censur'd, that nature thus gives way to loyalty, 3.05. 2 P
there any cause in nature that make these hard 3.06. 77 P
edmund, enkindle all the sparks of nature, | to 3.07. 86
our foster–nurse of nature is repose, | the 4.04. 12
my snuff and loathed part of nature should 4.06. 39
o ruin'd piece of nature! 4.06.134
who redeems nature from the general curse 4.06.206
cure this great breach in his abused nature, 4.07. 14
good i mean to do, | despite of mine own nature. 5.03.245
is of so flood–gate and o'erbearing nature OTH 1.03. 56
for nature so prepost'rously to err | (being not 1.03. 62
and she, in spite of nature, | of years, of 1.03. 96
so could err | against all rules of nature, and 1.03.101
the moor is of a free and open nature, | that 1.03.399
very nature will instruct her in it and compel 2.01.234 P
not) | is of a constant, loving, noble nature, 2.01.289
not, or his good nature | prizes the virtue that 2.03.133
i would not have your free and noble nature, 3.03.199
and yet how nature erring from itself — 3.03.227
whereto we see in all things nature tends — 3.03.231
nature would not invest herself in such 4.01. 39 P
is this the nature | whom passion could not 4.01.265
thou cunning'st pattern of excelling nature, | i 5.02. 11
till that the nature of your fault be known | to 5.02.336
the nature of bad news infects the teller. ANT 1.02. 95
long, the sides of nature | will not sustain it. 1.03. 16
venus where we see | the fancy outwork nature. 2.02.201
on cleopatra too, | and made a gap in nature. 2.02.218
it is | that nature must compel us to lament 5.01. 29
nature wants stuff | to vie strange forms with 5.02. 97
if thou and nature can so gently part, | the 5.02.294
importance of so slight and trivial a nature. CYM 1.04. 42 P
her malice with | a drug of such damn'd nature. 1.05. 36
hath nature given them eyes | to see this 1.06. 32
for gold | which rottenness can lend nature; 1.06.125

the cutter | was as another nature, dumb; 2.04. 84
how hard it is to hide the sparks of nature! 3.03. 79
and nature prompts them | in simple and low 3.03. 84
if sleep charge nature, | to break it with a 3.04. 42
ere clean it o'erthrow nature, makes it valiant. 3.06. 20
o worthiness of nature! 4.02. 25
nature hath meal and bran, contempt and grace. 4.02. 27
thou divine nature, thou thyself thou blazon'st 4.02.170
for nature doth abhor to make his bed | with the 4.02.357
was he | that (otherwise than noble nature did) 4.02.364
great nature, like his ancestry, | moulded the 5.04. 48
had rather thou shouldst live while nature will 5.05.151
minerva, | postures beyond brief nature; 5.05.165
short time | all offices of nature should again 5.05.257
till lucina reigned, | nature this dowry gave: PER 1.01. 9
and i (as fits my nature) do obey you. 2.01. 4
child, whom nature gat | for men to see, and 2.02. 6
there's nothing can be minist'red to nature 3.02. 8
nature should be so conversant with pain, 3.02. 25
speak of the disturbances | that nature works, 3.02. 38
death may usurp on nature many hours, | and yet 3.02. 82
nature awakes, | a warmth /breathes out of her. 3.02. 92
but if to that my nature need a spur, | the gods 3.03. 23
when nature fram'd this piece, she meant thee a 4.02.139 P
in that honor | first nature styl'd it in — TNK 1.01. 83
with that celerity and nature, which | she makes 1.01.202
yet unhard'ned in | the crimes of nature — let 1.02. 3
'hath set a mark which nature could not reach to 1.04. 43
what a wrong she has done | to youth and nature. 2.02. 40
i would make her | so near the gods in nature, 2.02.242
that nature nev'r exceeded nor nev'r shall. 2.03. 12
o state of nature, fail together in me, | since 3.02. 31
if wise nature, | with all her best endowments, 4.02. 7
they show | great and fine art in nature. 4.02.123
nature now | shall make and act the story, the 5.03. 13
what country by the nature of your error STM II.C 126
and shap'd just to that strength of nature III 4
dexter way to me | that owe it him by nature. III 12
nature that made thee with herself at strife, VEN 11
by law of nature thou art bound to breed, | that 171
till forging nature be condemn'd of treason, 729
to cross the curious workmanship of nature, | to 734
now nature cares not for thy mortal vigor, 953
balk | the prey wherein by nature they delight, LUC 697
in scorn of nature, art gave liveless life: 1374
then how when nature calls thee to be gone, SON 4.11
let those whom nature hath not made for store, 11. 9
till nature, as she wrought thee, fell a–doting, 20.10
why should he live, now nature bankrout is, 67. 9
new, | and him as for a map doth nature store, 68.13
not making worse what nature made so clear, 84.10
though in my nature reign'd | all frailties that 109. 9
and almost thence my nature is subdu'd | to what 111. 6
and heart | have faculty by nature to subsist, 122. 6
if nature (sovereign mistress over wrack), | as 126. 5
that did amplify | each stone's dear nature, LC 210
nature hath charg'd me that i hoard them not, 220
showing fair nature is both kind and tame; 311

NATURE'S 47 FR 0.0053 REL FR 41 V 6 P
chid i for that at frugal nature's frame? ADO 4.01.128
and the blots of nature's hand | shall not in MND 5.01.409
thou goest from fortune's office to nature's. AYL 1.02. 41 P
nature, when fortune makes nature's natural the 1.02. 49 P
nature's natural the cutter–off of nature's wit. 1.02. 50 P
is not fortune's work neither, but nature's, who 1.02. 52 P
than in the ordinary | of nature's sale–work. 3.05. 43
if ever we are nature's, these are ours. AWW 1.03.129
it is the show and seal of nature's truth, 1.03.132
hath not in nature's mystery more science | than 5.03.103
nature's own sweet and cunning hand laid on. TN 1.05.240
gillyvors, | which some call nature's bastards. WT 4.04. 83
of nature's gifts thou mayst with lilies boast, JN 3.01. 53
of those seven are dried by nature's course, R2 1.02. 14
now let not nature's hand | keep the wild flood 2H4 1.01.153
nature's soft nurse, how have i frighted thee, 3.01. 6
be not offended, nature's miracle, | thou art 1H6 5.03. 54
the earth that's nature's mother is her tomb; ROM 2.03. 9
yet nature's tears are reason's merriment. 4.05. 83
that nature's fragile vessel doth sustain | in TIM 5.01.201
substances | you wait on nature's mischief! MAC 1.05. 50
of hurt minds, great nature's second course, 2.02. 36
but in them nature's copy's not eterne. 3.02. 38
of nature's /germains tumble all together, 4.01. 59
being nature's livery, or fortune's star, | his HAM 1.04. 32
thought some of nature's journeymen had made men 3.02. 33 P
crack nature's moulds, all germains spill at LR 3.02. 8
nature's above art in that respect. 4.06. 86 P
(as i confess it is my nature's plague | to spy OTH 3.03.146
in nature's infinite book of secrecy | a little ANT 1.02. 10
an antony were nature's piece 'gainst fancy, 5.02. 99
a very drudge of nature's, have subdu'd me | in CYM 5.02. 5
in the womb he stay'd | attending nature's law; 5.04. 38
it was wise nature's end in the donation, | to 5.05.367
her neele composes | nature's own shape of bud, PER 5.ch. 6
all dear nature's children sweet, | lie 'fore TNK 1.01. 13
his art with nature's workmanship at strife, VEN 291
swear nature's death for framing thee so fair. 744
in men's nativity | are nature's faults, not LUC 539
single nature's double name | neither two nor PHT 39
nature's bequest gives nothing, but doth lend, SON 4. 3
by chance or nature's changing course untrimm'd: 18. 8
a woman's face with nature's own hand painted 20. 1
brow, | feeds on the rarities of nature's truth, 60.11
and husband nature's riches from expense; 94. 6
for since each hand hath put on nature's power, 127. 5
o, one by nature's outwards so commended | that LC 80

NATURES 27 FR 0.0030 REL FR 23 V 4 P
had that in't which good natures | could not TMP 1.02.359
our natures do pursue, | like rats that ravin MM 1.02.128
his judgment with the disposition of natures. 3.01.164 P
are distinct offices, | and of opposed natures. MV 2.09. 62
have kept of them tame, and know their natures. AWW 2.05. 46 P
not noted, is't, | but of the finer natures? WT 1.02.226
figuring the natures /of the times deceas'd, 2H4 3.01. 81
defective in their natures, grow to wildness. H5 5.02. 55
all, | according to their firm proposed natures. 5.02.334
in our own natures frail, and capable | of our H8 5.02. 46
all our abilities, gifts, natures, shapes, TRO 1.03.179
is rank'd with all deserts, all kind of natures, TIM 1.01. 65
there's nothing level in our cursed natures 4.03. 19
whose naked natures live in all the spite | of 4.03.228
whose thankless natures (o abhorred spirits!) 5.01. 60
their natures, and preformed faculties, | to JC 1.03. 67
their drenched natures lies as in a death, MAC 1.07. 68
you lack the season of all natures, sleep. 3.04.140
under heaven | that does afflict our natures. HAM 2.01.103
natures of such deep trust we shall much need; LR 2.01.115
that in the natures of their lords rebel, 2.02. 76
and baseness of our natures would conduct us to OTH 1.03.328 P
do omit | their mortal natures, letting go 2.01. 72
a nobility in their natures more than is native 2.01.216 P
dangerous conceits are in their natures poisons, 3.03.326
men's natures wrangle with inferior things, 3.04.144
more do thou in serpents' natures think them, STM III 17

NAUGHT 23 FR 0.0026 REL FR 15 V 8 P
not carve most curiously, say my knife's naught. ADO 5.01.156 P
a paramour is, god bless us, a thing of naught. MND 4.02. 14 P
sir, be better employ'd and be naught a while. AYL 1.01. 35 P
and swore by his honor the mustard was naught. 1.02. 65 P
it, the pancakes were naught and the mustard was 1.02. 66 P
that it is a shepherd's life, it is naught. 3.02. 15 P
though in pure truth it was corrupt and naught, H5 1.02. 73
naught to do with mistress shore? R3 1.01. 98
he that doth naught with her (excepting one) 1.01. 99
so, 'tis clear, | they'll say 'tis naught; H8 ep 5
all will be naught else. COR 3.01.230
all forsworn, all naught, all dissemblers. ROM 3.02. 87
naught that i am, | not for their own demerits, MAC 4.03.225
you are naught, you are naught. HAM 3.02.147 P
you are naught, you are naught. 3.02.147 P
beloved regan, | thy sister's naught. LR 2.04.134
'twill be naught, | but let it be. ANT 3.05. 22
naught, naught, all naught! 3.10. 1
naught, naught, all naught! 3.10. 1
naught, naught, all naught! 3.10. 1
all's but naught: 4.15. 78
o, she was naught; CYM 5.05.271
it was not she that call'd him all to naught: VEN 993

NAUGHTILY 1 FR 0.0001 REL FR 1 V 0 P
you smile and mock me, as if i meant naughtily. TRO 4.02. 37

NAUGHTY 15 FR 0.0017 REL FR 9 V 6 P
is pity of her life, for it is a naughty house. MM 2.01. 77 P
thou naughty varlet! ADO 4.02. 72 P
this naughty man | shall face to face be brought 5.01.297
o, these naughty times | puts bars between the MV 3.02. 18
thou naughty jailer, that thou art so fond | to 3.03. 9
so shines a good deed in a naughty world. 5.01. 91
he's a good drum, my lord, but a naughty orator. AWW 5.03.253 P
and tell me now, thou naughty varlet, tell me, 1H4 2.04.431 P
a sort of naughty persons, lewdly bent, | under 2H6 2.01.163
whiles here he liv'd | upon this naughty earth? H8 5.01.138
go hang yourself, you naughty mocking uncle! TRO 4.02. 25
would he not, a naughty man, let it sleep? 4.02. 32 P
thou naughty knave, what trade? JC 1.01. 15
be contented, 'tis a naughty night to swim in. LR 3.04.110 P
naughty lady, | these hairs which thou dost 3.07. 37

NAVARRE 9 FR 0.0010 REL FR 8 V 1 P
navarre shall be the wonder of the world; LLL 1.01. 12
and sole dominator of navarre, my soul's earth'i 1.01.220 P
that a man may owe, | matchless navarre; 2.01. 7
doth noise abroad, navarre hath made a vow, 2.01. 22
navarre had notice of your fair approach, | and 2.01. 81
here comes navarre. 2.01. 89
fair princess, welcome to the court of navarre. 2.01. 90
much better used | on navarre and his book–men, 2.01.227
eyes, | deceive me not now, navarre is infected. 2.01.230

NAVE* 3 FR 0.0003 REL FR 2 V 1 P
would not this nave of a wheel have his ears cut 2H4 2.04.255 P
till he unseam'd him from the nave to th' chops, MAC 1.02. 22
and bowl the round nave down the hill of heaven HAM 2.02.496

NAVEL *(also nave*, nav'l)*

NAVEL 1 FR 0.0001 REL FR 1 V 0 P
even when the navel of the state was touch'd, COR 3.01.123

N'AVEZ 1 FR 0.0001 REL FR 0 V 1 P
n'avez vous deja oublie ce que je vous ai H5 3.04. 42 P

NAVIGATION 1 FR 0.0001 REL FR 1 V 0 P
waves | confound and swallow navigation up; MAC 4.01. 54

NAV'L *(also nave*, navel)*

NAV'L 1 FR 0.0001 REL FR 0 V 1 P
they shall stand in fire up to the nav'l, and in TNK 4.03. 43 P

NAVY 9 FR 0.0010 REL FR 9 V 0 P
our navy is address'd, our power collected, 2H4 4.04. 5
grapple your minds to sternage of this navy, H5 3.pr. 18
on the western coast | rideth a puissant navy; R3 4.04.434
the britain navy is dispers'd by tempest. 4.04.521
out of pity taken | a load would sink a navy — H8 3.02.383
and that is it | hath made me rig my navy, at ANT 2.06. 20
your flying flags, | and leave his navy gazing. 3.13. 12
our sever'd navy too | have knit again, and 3.13.170
and if to–morrow | our navy thrive, i have an 4.03. 10

NAVY'S 1 FR 0.0001 REL FR 1 V 0 P
our great navy's rigg'd. ANT 3.05. 19

/NAY 5 FR 0.0005 REL FR 4 V 1 P
/nay, /all /of /you /that /stand /and /look R2 4.01.237
/nay, /if /i /turn /mine /eyes /upon /myself, 4.01.247
/nay, /their /endeavor /keeps /in /the /wonted HAM 2.02.338 P
/nay, dispatch. OTH 4.02. 30
/nay, had she been true, | if heaven would make 5.02.143

NAY 605 FR 0.0683 REL FR 376 V 229 P
nay, good, be patient. TMP 1.01. 15 P
nay, good my lord, be not angry. 2.01.186 P
our human generation you shall find | many, nay, 3.03. 34
over the boots? nay, give me not the boots. TGV 1.01. 27
nay, that i can deny by a circumstance. 1.01. 84 P
nay, in that you are astray; 1.01.103 P
nay, sir, less than a pound shall serve me for 1.01.105 P
nay, now you are too flat, | and mar the concord 1.02. 90
nay, would i were so ang'red with the same. 1.02.101
nay, i was taken up for laying them down; 1.02.132
nay, that's certain; 2.01. 36 P
nay, take them. 2.01.124
nay, i was rhyming; 2.01.143 P
the tide is now — nay, not thy tide of tears, 2.02. 14
nay, 'twill be this hour ere i have done weeping 2.03. 1 P
nay, i'll show you the manner of it. 2.03. 13 P
nay, that cannot be so neither; 2.03. 16 P
nay sure, i think she holds them prisoners still 2.04. 92
nay then he should be blind, and, being blind, 2.04. 93
nay more, our marriage hour, | with all the 2.04.179
nay, that i will not. 2.07. 63
nay then no matter; 3.01. 58
nay, a horse cannot fetch, but only carry, 3.01.276 P
nay, i'll be sworn, i have sat in the stocks for 4.04. 30 P
nay, i remember the trick you serv'd me, when i 4.04. 34 P
nay then the wanton lies; my face is black. 5.02. 10
nay, if the gentle spirit of moving words | can 5.04. 55
nay, daughter, carry the wine in, we'll drink WIV 1.01.188 P
nay, but understand me. 1.01.212 P
nay, i will do as my cousin shallow says. 1.01.217 P
nay, got's lords and his ladies! 1.01.235 P
nay, conceive me, conceive me, sweet coz; 1.01.242 P
nay, pray you lead the way. 1.01.305 P
nay, it is petter yet. 1.02. 7 P
nay, i'll ne'er believe that; 2.01. 37 P
nay, i know not; 2.01. 84 P
nay, i will consent to act any villainy against 2.01. 98 P
and yet there has been earls, nay (which is more 2.02. 77 P
nay, but do so then, and, look you, he may come 2.02.124 P
nay, good master parson, keep in your weapon. 3.01. 73 P
nay, keep your way, little gallant; 3.02. 1 P
nay, i must tell you, so you do; 3.03. 83 P
nay, follow him, gentlemen, see the issue of his 3.03.174 P
nay, master page, be not impatient. 3.04. 71
"nay," said i, "will you cast away your child on 3.04. 95 P
nay, you shall hear, master /brook, what i have 3.05. 95 P
nay, but he'll be here presently. 4.02. 97 P
nay, good, sweet husband! 4.02.180 P
nay, he will do it. 4.02.189 P
nay, by th' mass, that he did not; 4.02.202 P
nay, i'll to him again in name of /brook; 4.04. 76
nay, do not fly, i think we have watch'd you now 5.05.103
nay, not, as one would say, healthy; MM 1.02. 55 P
nay, but i know 'tis so. 1.02. 67 P
nay, i beseech you mark it well. 2.01.151 P
nay, i'll not warrant that; 2.04. 59
nay, but hear me, | your sense pursues not mine. 2.04. 73
nay, women are frail too. 2.04.124
nay, call us ten times frail, | for we are soft 2.04.128
nay, hear me, isabel. 3.01.147
nay, if there be no remedy for it but that you 3.02. 1 P
nay, if the devil have given thee proofs for sin 3.02. 30
nay, but it is not so. 4.03.117
the duke comes home to–morrow — nay, dry your 4.03.127
nay, tarry, i'll go along with thee. 4.03.165 P
nay, friar, i am a kind of bur, i shall stick. 4.03.179 P
nay, it is ten times strange. 5.01. 42
nay, it is ten times true, for truth is truth 5.01. 45
nay more, if any born at ephesus be seen | at ERR 1.01. 16
nay, forward, old man, do not break off so, 1.01. 96
nay, and you will not, sir, i'll take my heels. 1.02. 94
nay, he's at two hands with me, and that my two 2.01. 45 P
nay, he strook so plainly, i could too well feel 2.01. 52 P
nay, not sound, i pray you. 2.02. 92 P
nay, not sure, in a thing falsing. 2.02. 94 P
nay, master, both in mind and in my shape. 2.02.197
nay, come, i pray you, sir, give me the chain: 4.01. 45
a wolf, nay worse, a fellow all in buff; 4.02. 36
nay, he's a thief too: 4.02. 59
nay, she is worse, she is the devil's dam, and 4.03. 51 P
nay, 'tis for me to be patient: 4.04. 19 P
nay, rather persuade him to hold his hands. 4.04. 22 P
nay, i bear it on my shoulders, as a beggar wont 4.04. 37 P
no, i say nay to that. 5.01.372
nay then thus: 5.01.424
nay, if cupid have not spent all his quiver in ADO 1.01.271 P
nay, mock not, mock not. 1.01.285 P
nay, if they lead to any ill, i will leave them 2.01.153 P
nay, pray thee come, | or, if thou wilt hold 2.03. 52
nay, that's impossible, she may wear her heart 2.03.203 P
nay, that would be as great a soil in the new 3.02. 5 P
nay, 'a rubs himself with civet. 3.02. 50 P
nay, but his jesting spirit, which is now crept 3.02. 59 P
nay, but i know who loves him. 3.02. 63 P
nay, that were a punishment too good for them, 3.03. 4 P
nay, by'r lady, that i think 'a cannot. 3.03. 77 P
nay, by'r lady, i am not such a fool to think 3.04. 82 P
nay, i pray you let me go. 4.01.294 P
nay, but, beatrice — 4.01.311 P
nay, that's certain, we have the exhibition to 4.02. 5 P
nay, i will do so. 5.01. 41
nay, do not quarrel with us, good old man. 5.01. 50
nay, never lay thy hand upon thy sword, | i fear 5.01. 54
fence, | nay, as i am a gentleman, i will. 5.01. 85
nay then give him another staff, this last was 5.01.138 P
"nay," said i, "a good wit." 5.01.163 P
"nay," said i, "the gentleman is wise." 5.01.164 P
"nay," said i, "he hath the tongues." 5.01.166 P
nay, and you be a cursing hypocrite once, you 5.01.208 P
by yea and nay, sir, then i swore in jest. LLL 1.01. 54
nay, nothing, master moth, but what they look 1.02.162 P
nay then will i be gone. 2.01.127
nay, my choler is ended. 2.01.206
a critic, nay, a night–watch constable, | a 3.01.176
nay, to be perjur'd, which is worst of all; 3.01.194
nay, never paint me now; 4.01. 16
i do invite you too, you shall not say me nay: 4.02.165 P
nay, are you not, | all three of you, to be thus 4.03.157
nay, it makes nothing, sir. 4.03.189
nay, i have verses too, i thank berowne; 5.02. 34
nay, you must do it soon. 5.02.211
nay then two treys, and if you grow so nice, 5.02.232
nay, he can sing | a mean most meanly and in 5.02.327
nay, my good lord, let me o'errule you now. 5.02.515
nay, why dost thou stay? 5.02.626
nay, faith; MND 1.02. 47 P
nay, /good lysander; 2.02. 43
nay; 3.01. 36 P
a man doth mark, | and dares not answer nay — 3.01.133
nay, i can gleek upon occasion. 3.01.146 P
to strike me, spurn me, nay, to kill me too. 3.02.313
follow? nay; i'll go with thee, cheek by jowl. 3.02.338
nay, go not back. 3.02.340
nay then thou mock'st me. 3.02.426
nay, indeed, if you had your eyes, you might MV 2.02. 75 P

nay more, while grace is saying, hood mine eyes 2.02.193
nay, but i bar to-night, you shall not gauge me 2.02.199
nay, we will slink away in supper-time, 2.04. 1
nay, that's true, that's very true. 3.01.125 P
way, | he did entreat me, past all saying nay, 3.02.229
nay, you need not fear us, lorenzo, launcelot 3.05. 31 P
nay, but ask my opinion too of that. 3.05. 85
nay, let me praise you while i have a stomach. 3.05. 87
of the twentith part | of one poor scruple, nay, 4.01.330
nay, take my life and all, pardon not that: 4.01.374
nay, but hear me. 5.01.246
nay, now thou goest from fortune's office to AYL 1.02. 40 P
nay, if i keep not my rank — 1.02.107 P
nay, i shall ne'er be ware of mine own wit till 2.04. 58 P
nay, i care not for their names, they owe me 2.05. 21 P
nay, i hope. 3.02. 36 P
nay, but who is it? 3.02.187 P
nay, i prithee now, with most petitionary 3.02.189 P
nay, he hath but a little beard. 3.02.208 P
nay, but the devil take mocking. 3.02.214 P
nay, you must call me rosalind. 3.02.434 P
nay, pray be cover'd. 3.03. 76 P
nay certainly there is no truth in him. 3.04. 20 P
nay then god buy you, and you talk in blank 4.01. 31 P
nay, and you be so tardy, come no more in my 4.01. 51 P
nay, you were better speak first, and when you 4.01. 73 P
nay, you might keep that check for it, till you 4.01.167 P
nay, prithee be cover'd. 5.01. 17 P
nay, 'tis true. 5.02. 29 P
nor no more shoes than feet — nay, sometime SHR in.2. 11 P
nay, then 'tis time to stir him from his trance. 1.01.177
nay, how now, where are you? 1.01.222 P
nay, 'tis no matter, sir, what he 'leges in 1.02. 28 P
nay, look you, sir, he tells you flatly what his 1.02. 77 P
nay then you jest, and now i well perceive | you 2.01. 19
nay, now i see | she is your treasure, she must 2.01. 31
nay, come again, | good kate; 2.01.218
nay, come, kate, come; 2.01.228
nay, hear you, kate. in sooth you scape not so. 2.01.240
nay then good night our part! 2.01.301
nay, i have off'red all, i have no more, | and 2.01.381
nay, by saint jamy, | i hold you a penny, | a 3.02. 82
nay then, | do what thou canst, i will not go 3.02.207
nay, look not big, nor stamp, nor stare, nor 3.02.228
nay, let them go, a couple of quiet ones. 3.02.240
nay, good sweet kate, be merry. 4.01.143
nay, i have ta'en you napping, gentle love, 4.02. 46
nay then i will not, you shall have the mustard, 4.03. 27
nay then, thou lov'st it not; 4.03. 42
nay then you lie; it is the blessed sun. 4.05. 17
nay, faith, i'll see the church a' your back, 5.01. 4 P
nay, i told you your son was well belov'd in 5.01. 25 P
nay, what are you, sir? 5.01. 65 P
nay, i dare not swear it. 5.01.102 P
nay, i will give thee a kiss; 5.01.148
nay, that you shall not, since you have begun; 5.02. 44
nay then she must needs come. 5.02. 88
nay, i will win my wager better yet, | and show 5.02.116
nay, 'tis most credible; AWW 1.02. 4
nay, a mother, | why not a mother? 1.03.139
touch | is powerful to araise king pippen, nay, 2.01. 76
nay, i'll fit you, | and not be all day neither. 2.01. 90
nay, come your ways. 2.01. 93
nay, come your ways; 2.01. 94
as the nun's lip to the friar's mouth, nay, as 2.02. 27 P
o lord, sir! — nay, put me to't, i warrant you. 2.02. 48 P
nay, 'tis strange, 'tis very strange, that is 2.03. 28 P
nay, there is some comfort in the news, some 3.02. 36 P
nay, come, for if they do approach the city, we 3.05. 1 P
nay, good my lord, put him to't; 3.06. 1 P
nay, i'll speak that | which you will wonder at. 4.01. 85
nay, i assure you a peace concluded. 4.03. 40 P
a dumb innocent, that could not say him nay. 4.03.188 P
nay, by your leave, hold your hands — though i 4.03.189 P
nay, look not so upon me; 4.03.195 P
nay, i'll read it first, by your favor. 4.03.217 P
nay, you need not to stop your nose, sir; 5.02. 10 P
nay, either tell me where thou hast been, or i TN 1.05. 1 P
nay, by my troth, i know not; 2.03. 4 P
nay, good sir toby. 2.03.103 P
nay, i'll come. 2.05. 2 P
nay, patience, or we break the sinews of our 2.05. 75 P
nay, but first, let me see, let me see, let me 2.05.110 P
nay, but say true, does it work upon him? 2.05.195 P
nay, that's certain. 3.01. 14 P
nay, and thou pass upon me, i'll no more with 3.01. 42 P
nay, pursue him now, lest the device take air 3.04.131 P
nay, let me alone for swearing. 3.04.183 P
nay, if you be an undertaker, i am for you. 3.04.318 P
nay, let him alone. 4.01. 33 P
nay then i must have an ounce or two of this 4.01. 43 P
nay, come, i prithee. 4.01. 64
nay, i prithee put on this gown and this beard, 4.02. 1 P
nay, i am for all waters. 4.02. 63 P
nay, i'll ne'er believe a madman till i see his 4.02.116 P
nay, but you will? WT 1.02. 45
nay, let me have't; 1.02.101
nay, there's comfort in't, | whiles other men 1.02.196
he thinks, nay, with all confidence he swears, 1.02.414
nay, hated too, worse than the great'st 1.02.423
nay, that's a mock. 2.01. 14
nay, come sit down; then on. 2.01. 29
nay, rather, good my lords, be second to me. 2.03. 27
of 's frown, his forehead, nay, the valley, 2.03.101
nay, but my letters, by this means being there 4.04.619
nay, prithee dispatch. 4.04.640 P
nay, you shall have no hat. 4.04.658
nay, but hear me. 4.04.690 P
nay — but hear me. 4.04.691 P
nay, come away; 5.03.101
nay, present your hand. 5.03.107
nay, i would have you go before me thither. JN 1.01.155
if thou hadst said him nay, it had been sin. 1.01.275
nay, ask me if i can refrain from love, | for i 2.01.525
nay, rather turn this day out of the week, 3.01. 87
one minute, nay, one quiet breath of rest. 3.04.134
nay, you may think my love was crafty love, 4.01. 53
nay, after that, consume away in rust, | but for 4.01. 65
nay, hear me, hubert, drive these men away, 4.01. 78
nay, it perchance will sparkle in your eyes; 4.01.114
nay, but make haste; 4.02.170
nay, in the body of this fleshly land, | this 4.02.245
thou'rt damn'd as black — nay, nothing is so 4.03.121
nay, 'tis in a manner done already, | for many 5.07. 89
were he my brother, nay, my kingdom's heir, | as R2 1.01.116
lo this is all — nay, yet depart not so; 1.02. 63
nay rather, every tedious stride i make | will 1.03.268
nay, nothing, all is said. 2.01.148
nay, speak thy mind, and let him ne'er speak 2.01.230
nay, let us share thy thoughts, as thou dost 2.01.273
nay, dry your eyes — | tears show their love, 3.03.202
nay, do not say "stand up"; 5.03.111
nay, then i cannot blame his cousin king, | that 1H4 1.03.158
nay, i will; 1.03.218
nay, | i'll have a starling shall be taught to 1.03.223
nay, if you have not, to it again, | we will 1.03.257
nay, by god, soft, i know a trick worth two of 2.01. 36 P
nay, by my faith, i think you are more beholding 2.01. 88 P
nay, rather let me have it as you are a false 2.01. 93 P
nay, tell me if you speak in jest or no. 2.03. 99
nay, but hark you, francis: 2.04. 58 P
nay, that's past praying for, i have pepper'd 2.04.191 P
nay, i'll tickle ye for a young prince, i' faith 2.04.443 P
who shall say me nay? 3.01.116
nay, if you melt, then will she run mad. 3.01.209
nay, my lord, he call'd you jack, and said he 3.03.138 P
nay, and i do, i pray god my girdle break. 3.03.151 P
nay, prithee be gone. 3.03.173 P
nay, task me to my word, approve me, lord. 4.01. 9
nay, and the villains march wide betwixt the 4.02. 39 P
nay, before god, hal, if percy be alive, thou 5.03. 50 P
nay, you shall find no boy's play here, i can 5.04. 75 P
to us no more, nay, not so much, lord bardolph, 2H4 1.03. 69
nay, they will be kin to us, or they will fetch 2.02.117 P
nay, rather damn them with | king cerberus, and 2.04.167
nay, and 'a do nothing but speak nothing, 'a 2.04.193 P
nay, she must be old, she cannot choose but be 3.02.207 P
nay more, to spurn at your most royal image, 5.02. 89
nay, you shall see my orchard, where, in an 5.03. 1 P
nay, but the man that was his bedfellow, | whom H5 2.02. 8
nay sure, he's not in hell; 2.03. 9 P
nay, that 'a did not. 2.03. 30 P
nay, the man hath no wit that cannot, from the 3.07. 31 P
nay, for methought yesterday your mistress 3.07. 48 P
nay, that's right; 5.01. 1 P
nay, pray you throw none away, the skin is good 5.01. 54 P
nay, it will please him well, kate; 5.02.248 P
nay, stand thou back, i will not budge a foot: 1H6 1.03. 38
speak unto talbot, nay, look up to him. 1.04. 89
nay, then i see our wars | will turn unto a 2.02. 44
nay, if we be forbidden stones, we'll fall to it 3.01. 89 P
nay, let it rest where it began at first. 4.01.121
nay more, an enemy unto you all, | and no great 2H6 1.01.149
nay, eleanor, then must i chide outright. 1.02. 41
nay, be not angry, i am pleas'd again. 1.02. 55
nay, fear not, man, | we are alone, here's none 1.02. 68
nay, gloucester, know that thou art come too 3.01. 95
nay then, this spark will prove a raging fire, 3.01.302
nay, then a shame take all! 3.01.307
nay more, the king's council are no good workmen 4.02. 14 P
nay, that i mean to do. 4.02. 78 P
nay, then he is a conjurer. 4.02. 92 P
nay, he can make obligations, and write 4.02. 93 P
nay, 'tis too true; therefore he shall be king. 4.02.147
nay, answer if you can. 4.02.169 P
nay, john, it will be stinking law, for his 4.07. 11 P
thou say, thou serge, nay, thou buckram lord! 4.07. 25 P
nay, he nods at us, as who should say, i'll be 4.07. 94 P
nay, it shall ne'er be said, while england 4.10. 42
command my eldest son, nay, all my sons, | as 5.01. 49
nay, do not fright us with an angry look. 5.01.126
nay, we shall heat you thoroughly anon. 5.01.159
nay, before them, if we can. 5.03. 28
nay, go not from me, i will follow thee. 3H6 1.01.213
nay, stay, let's hear the orisons he makes. 1.04.110
nay, bear three daughters; 2.01. 41
nay, if thou be that princely eagle's bird, 2.01. 91
nay, warwick, single out some other chase, | for 2.04. 12
nay, stay not to expostulate, make speed, | or 2.05.135
nay, take me with thee, good sweet exeter; 2.05.137
nay, then the world goes hard | when clifford 2.06. 77
nay then whip me; he'll rather give her two. 3.02. 28
as red as fire? nay then, her wax must melt. 3.02. 51
nay, mark how lewis stamps as he were nettled. 3.03.169
nay, whom they shall obey, and love thee too, 4.01. 79
nay, then i see that edward needs must down. 4.03. 42
nay, this way, man, see where the huntsmen stand 4.05. 15
nay, be thou sure, i'll well requite thy 4.06. 10
nay, stay, sir john, a while, and we'll debate 4.07. 51
nay rather, wilt thou draw thy forces hence, 5.01. 25
nay, when? 5.01. 49
nay, take away this scolding crook-back, rather. 5.05. 30
nay, never bear me hence, dispatch me here; 5.05. 69
nay, he is dead, and slain by edward's hands. R3 1.02. 92
nay, do not pause: 1.02.179
nay, now dispatch: 1.02.181
nay, i prithee stay a little. 1.04.117 P
in weightier things you'll say a beggar nay. 3.01.119
nay, like enough, for i stay dinner there. 3.02.121
nay, for a need, thus far come near my person: 3.05. 85
play the maid's part, still answer nay, and take 3.07. 51
for them | as i can say nay to thee for myself, 3.07. 53
marry, god defend his grace should say us nay! 3.07. 81
nay then indeed she cannot choose but hate thee, 4.04.289
nay, good my lord, be not afraid of shadows. 5.03.215
nay, he must bear you company. H8 1.01.212
nay, we must longer kneel; i am a suitor. 1.02. 9
though they be never so ridiculous | (nay, let 1.03. 4
nay, you must not freeze, | two women plac'd 1.04. 21
nay, ladies, fear not; 1.04. 51
nay, sir nicholas, | let it alone; 2.01.100
nay, good troth. 2.03. 33
nay, gave notice | he was from thence discharg'd 2.04. 33
nay, before, | or god will punish me. 2.04. 74
nay forsooth, my friends, | they that must weigh 3.01. 87
nay then, farewell! 3.02.222
nay, and you weep | i am fall'n indeed. 3.02.375
nay, patience, | you must not leave me yet. 4.02.165
nay, my lord, | that cannot be; 5.02. 83
nay, you must stay the cooling too, or ye may TRO 1.01. 25 P
nay, i am sure she does. 1.02.110 P
nay, i'll watch you for that; 1.02.266 P
nay, look upon him. 2.01. 59 P
nay, but regard him well. 2.01. 61 P
nay, good ajax. 2.01. 77 P
nay, i must hold you. 2.01. 79 P
nay, if we talk of reason, | /let's shut our 2.02. 46
nay, this shall not hedge us out, we'll hear you 3.01. 60 P
nay, that shall not serve your turn, that shall 3.01. 74 P
nay, i care not for such words, no, no. 3.01. 75 P
nay, but, my lord — 3.01. 83 P
nay, you shall fight your hearts out ere i part 3.02. 51 P
nay, i'll give my word for her too. 3.02.109 P
nay then. 4.02. 54 P
nay, we must use expostulation kindly, | for it 4.04. 60
nay, good my lord! 4.04. 98
eye, her cheek, her lip, | nay, her foot speaks; 4.05. 56
nay, i have done already. 4.05.236
nay, but do then, | and let your mind be coupled 5.02. 14
nay then — 5.02. 20
nay, but you part in anger. 5.02. 45
nay, stay; 5.02. 52
nay, do not snatch it from me. 5.02. 81
nay, but speak not maliciously. COR 1.01. 35 P
nay, these are almost thoroughly persuaded; 1.01.201
nay, let them follow. 1.01.248
nay, but his taunts. 1.01.255
nay more, | some parcels of their power are 1.02. 31
nay, 'tis true. 2.01.107 P
nay, my good soldier, up; 2.01.171
nay, keep your place. 2.02. 66
nay, your wit will not so soon out as another 2.03. 27 P
nay, come away. 3.01.252
nay, temperately; your promise. 3.03. 67
nay, mother, | where is your ancient courage? 4.01. 2
nay, i prithee, woman — 4.01. 12
nay, mother, | resume that spirit when you were 4.01. 15
should hear — | nay, and you shall hear some. 4.02. 14
nay, but thou shalt stay too. 4.02. 23
nay, i knew by his face that there was something 4.05.154 P
nay, it's no matter for that. 4.05.165 P
nay, not so neither; 4.05.167 P
nay, i hear nothing; 4.06. 18
nay, if he coy'd | to hear cominius speak, i'll 5.01. 6
nay, pray be patient. 5.01. 33
nay, sometimes, | like to a bowl upon a subtle 5.02. 19
nay, but, fellow, fellow — 5.02. 58 P
measure of a father, | nay, godded me indeed. 5.03. 11
nay, go not from us thus. 5.03.131
nay, behold 's! 5.03.173
nay, let him choose | out of my files, his 5.06. 32
nay, nay, sweet emperor, we must all be friends. TIT 1.01.479
nay, nay, sweet emperor, we must all be friends. 1.01.479
ay, come, semiramis, nay, barbarous tamora, 2.03.118
nay then i'll stop your mouth. 2.03.185
nay, come, agree whose hand shall go along, 3.01.174
nay, he is your brother by the surer side, 4.02.126
nay, truly, sir, i could never say grace in all 4.03.100 P
nay, nay, let rape and murder stay with me, | or 5.02.134
nay, nay, let rape and murder stay with me, | or 5.02.134
nay, as they dare. ROM 1.01. 42 P
nay, i do bear a brain — but, as i said, | when 1.03. 29
nay, by th' rood, | she could have run and 1.03. 36
nay, he's a flower, in faith, a very flower. 1.03. 78
no less! nay, bigger: women grow by men. 1.03. 95
nay, gentle romeo, we must have you dance. 1.04. 13
nay, that's not so. 1.04. 44
nay, sit, nay, sit, good cousin capulet, | for 1.05. 30
nay, sit, nay, sit, good cousin capulet, | for 1.05. 30
nay, gentlemen, prepare not to be gone, | we 1.05.121
nay, i'll conjure too. 2.01. 6
i'll frown and be perverse, and say thee nay, 2.02. 96
nay, he will answer the letter's master, how he 2.04. 11 P
nay, i am the very pink of courtesy. 2.04. 57 P
nay, if our wits run the wild-goose chase, i am 2.04. 71 P
nay, good goose, bite not. 2.04. 78 P
nay, come, i pray thee speak, good, good nurse, 2.05. 28
nay, and there were two such, we should have 3.01. 15 P
dead," | thy father or thy mother, nay, or both, 3.02.119
nay more, i doubt it not. 3.04. 14
nay, that's most fix'd. TIM 1.01. 9
nay, sir, but hear me on: 1.01. 77
nay, my lords, | ceremony was but devis'd at 1.02. 14
nay, and you begin to rail on society once, i am 1.02.244 P
nay, good my lord — 2.02. 26
lord lucullus to borrow so many talents, nay, 3.02. 12 P
supported his estate, nay, timon's money | has 3.02. 69
nay, put out all your hands. 4.02. 28
nay, stay thou out for earnest. 4.03. 48
nay, let's seek him: 5.01. 40
nay, i beseech you, sir, be not out with me; JC 1.01. 16 P
nay, and i tell you that, i'll ne'er look you i' 1.02.281 P
nay, we will all of us be there to fetch him. 2.01.212
nay, that's certain: 3.02. 69
nay, press not so upon me, stand far off. 3.02.167
nay, i am sure it is, volumnius. 5.05. 21
nay, how will you do for a husband? MAC 4.02. 39
nay, had i pow'r, i should | pour the sweet milk 4.03. 97
nay, answer me. stand and unfold yourself. HAM 1.01. 2
nay, it is, i know not "seems." 1.02. 76
nay, not so much, not two. 1.02.138
nay, very pale. 1.02.233
nay, let's follow him. 1.04. 91
nay, but swear't. 1.05.145
nay, come, let's go together. 1.05.190
come, come — nay, speak. 2.02.276 P
nay then i have an eye of you! 2.02.290 P
nay, that follows not. 2.02.413 P
nay, do not think i flatter, | for what 3.02. 56
nay, 'tis twice two months, my lord. 3.02.128 P
nay then let the dev'l wear black, for i'll have 3.02.129 P
nay, good my lord, this courtesy is not of the 3.02.314 P
nay, then i'll set those to you that can speak. 3.04. 17
nay, i know not, is it the king? 3.04. 26

nay, but to live | in the rank sweat of an 3.04. 91
nay, pray you mark. 4.05. 28 P
nay, but, ophelia — 4.05. 34
nay, but hear you, goodman delver — 5.01. 14 P
nay, i know not. 5.01.178 P
nay, and thou'lt mouth, | i'll rant as well as 5.01.283
nay, good my lord, for my ease, in good faith. 5.02.105 P
nay, good my lord — 5.02.214 P
nay, come again. 5.02.303
nay, and thou canst not smile as the wind sits, LR 1.04.100 P
nay then — 1.04.347
nay, i know not. 2.01. 6 P
you houseless poverty, | nay, get thee in. 3.04. 27
nay, he reserv'd a blanket, else we had been all 3.04. 65 P
nay then come on, and take the chance of anger. 3.07. 79
nay, come not near th' old man; 4.06.239 P
nay, send in time. 5.03.248
nay, but he prated, | and spoke such scurvy and OTH 1.02. 6
nay, it is possible enough to judgment. 1.03. 9
nay, in all confidence, he's not for rhodes. 1.03. 31
nay, it is true, or else i am a turk: 2.01.114
nay, good lieutenant; 2.03.151 P
nay, good lieutenant — /god's /will, gentlemen 2.03.158
nay, get thee gone. 2.03.382
nay, when i have a suit | wherein i mean to 3.03. 80
nay, yet there's more in this. 3.03.130
nay, stay. thou shouldst be honest. 3.03.381
would? nay, and i will. 3.03.393
nay, this was but his dream. 3.03.427
nay, yet be wise; 3.03.432
nay, we must think men are not gods, | nor of 3.04.148
nay, you must forget that. 4.01.180 P
nay, that's not your way. 4.01.186 P
nay, that's certain. 4.01.195 P
nay, heaven doth know. 4.02.129
his scorn i approve" — | nay, that's not next. 4.03. 53 P
nay, /an' you stare, we shall hear more anon. 5.01.107
nay, guiltiness will speak, | though tongues 5.01.109
nay, /an' you strive — 5.02. 81
nay, stare not, masters, it is true indeed. 5.02.188
nay, lay thee down and roar; 5.02.198
nay, but this dotage of our general's ANT 1.01. 1
nay, hear them, antony. 1.01. 19
nay, and most like. 1.01. 25
nay, hear him. 1.02. 25 P
nay, come, tell iras hers. 1.02. 43 P
nay, if an oily palm be not a fruitful 1.02. 52 P
nay, pray you, seek no color for your going, 1.03. 32
nay then. 2.02. 28
nay then i'll run. 2.05. 73
nay certainly, i have heard the ptolomies' 2.07. 34 P
nay, but how dearly he adores mark antony! 3.02. 8
nay, nay, octavia, not only that — | that were 3.04. 1
nay, nay, octavia, not only that — | that were 3.04. 1
nay, the dust | should have ascended to the roof 3.06. 48
nay, i have done, | here comes the emperor. 3.07. 19
pray you now, | nay, do so; 3.11. 23
nay, gentle madam, to him, comfort him. 3.11. 25
nay, you were a fragment | of cneius pompey's — 3.13.117
nay, i'll help too. | what's this for? 4.04. 5
nay, weep not, gentle eros, there is left us 4.14. 21
nay, good my fellows, do not please sharp fate 4.14.135
nay, pray you, sir. 5.02.108
nay, blush not, cleopatra, i approve | your 5.02.149
nay, 'tis most certain, iras. 5.02.214
nay, that's certain. 5.02.222
nay, i will take thee too: 5.02.312
nay, stay a little: CYM 1.01.109
nay, let her languish | a drop of blood a day, 1.01.156
nay, come, let's go together. 1.02. 40 P
nay, followed him till he had melted from | the 1.03. 20
nay, i prithee take it, | it is an earnest of a 1.05. 64
nay, sometime hangs both thief and true man. 2.03. 72
'tis true — nay, keep the ring — 'tis true. 2.04.123
all faults that name, nay, that hell knows, 2.05. 27
nay, many times | doth ill deserve by doing well 3.03. 53
shook down my mellow hangings, nay, my leaves, 3.03. 63
matrons, nay, the secrets of the grave | this 3.04. 38
nay, you must | forget that rarest treasure of 3.04.159
nay, be brief: 3.04.165
point | i will conclude to hate her, nay indeed, 3.05. 78
nay, to thy mere confusion, thou shalt know | i 4.02. 92
nay, cadwal, we must lay his head to th' east, 4.02.255
nay, what hope | have we in hiding us? 4.04. 3
nay, do not wonder at it; 5.03. 53
nay, be not angry, sir. 5.03. 59
nay, nay, to th' purpose. 5.05.178
nay, nay, to th' purpose. 5.05.178
nay, some marks | of secret on her person, that 5.05.205
nay, master, said not i as much when i saw the PER 2.01. 23 P
nay then thou wilt starve sure; 2.01. 68 P
nay, how absolute she's in't, | not minding 2.05. 19
nay, come, your hands and lips must seal it too; 2.05. 85
nay, certainly to-night, | for look how fresh 3.02. 78
nay, i'll be patient. 5.01.145
nay, most likely, for they are noble suff'rers. TNK 2.01. 31 P
nay then — 3.01.118
nay, pray you — | you talk of feeding me to 3.01.118
nay, and she fail me once — you can tell, arcas 3.05. 46
one said it was an owl, | the other he said nay, 3.05. 69
nay then i'll in too. 3.06.201
nay, we'll go with you, | i will not lose the 5.02.102
nay, now the sound is "arcite." 5.03. 90
nay, let's be offerers all. 5.04. 32
nay, it has infected it with the palsy, for STM II.C 12 P
nay, this' a sound fellow i tell you, let's mark II.C 89 P
nay, certainly you are, | for to the king god II.C 97
nay, any where that not adheres to england, II.C 129
nay, more than flint, for stone at rain VEN 200
nay, do not struggle, for thou shalt not rise. 710
"nay then," quoth adon, "you will fall again 769
in love, | there a nay is plac'd without remove. PP 17. 8
strength, | and ban and brawl, and say thee nay; 18.32
full oft, | a woman's nay doth stand for nought? 18.42
nay, if you read this line, remember not | the SON 71. 5
nay, if thou lov'r'st on me, do i not spend 149. 7

NAYWARD 1 FR 0.0001 REL FR 1 V 0 P
my saying, | howe'er you lean to th' nayward. WT 2.01. 64

NAY-WORD *(also ayword)*

NAY-WORD 2 FR 0.0002 REL FR 0 V 2 P
and in any case have a nay-word, that you may WIV 2.02.126 P
and we have a nay-word how to know one another. 5.02. 5 P

NAZARITE 1 FR 0.0001 REL FR 0 V 1 P
your prophet the nazarite conjur'd the devil MV 1.03. 34 P

NE* *(also nor)*

NE* 8 FR 0.0009 REL FR 3 V 5 P
neigh abbreviated "ne." LLL 5.01. 23 P
ne intelligis, domine? 5.01. 25 P
ne, worse of worst — extended | with vildest AWW 2.01.173
"in terram salicam mulieres ne /succedant," H5 1.02. 38
je ne doute point d'apprendre, par la grace de 3.04. 40 P
je ne voudrais prononcer ces mots devant les 3.04. 55 P
ma foi, je ne veux point que vous abaissez votre 5.02.254 P
man, of pelf, | ne aught escapend but himself; PER 2.ch. 36

NEAF 2 FR 0.0002 REL FR 0 V 2 P
give me your neaf, mounsieur mustardseed. MND 4.01. 19 P
sweet knight, i kiss thy neaf. 2H4 2.04.186 P

NEANMOINS 2 FR 0.0002 REL FR 0 V 2 P
neanmoins, je reciterai une autre fois ma lecon H5 3.04. 57 P
neanmoins, pour les ecus que vous /lui promettez 4.04. 51 P

NEAPOLITAN 5 FR 0.0005 REL FR 3 V 2 P
fresh water, that | a noble neapolitan, gonzalo, TMP 1.02.161
first, there is the neapolitan prince. MV 1.02. 39 P
some neapolitan, or meaner man of pisa. SHR 1.01.205
o blood-bespotted neapolitan, | outcast of 2H6 5.01.117
or rather, the neapolitan bone-ache! TRO 2.03. 18 P

NEAPOLITAN'S 1 FR 0.0001 REL FR 0 V 1 P
he hath a horse better than the neapolitan's, a MV 1.02. 58 P

NEAPOLITANS 1 FR 0.0001 REL FR 0 V 1 P
o stephano, two neapolitans scap'd! TMP 2.02.113 P

/NEAR 2 FR 0.0002 REL FR 2 V 0 P
/an heir, and /near allied unto the duke. TGV 4.01. 47
/please /you, /draw /near. LR 4.07. 24

NEAR 230 FR 0.0260 REL FR 187 V 43 P
do so near the bottom run | by their own fear or TMP 2.01.227
wine afore, it will go near to remove his fit. 2.02. 75 P
we now are near his cell. 4.01.195
please you draw near. 5.01.319
is't near dinner-time? TGV 1.02. 67
with thee of some affairs | that touch me near, 3.01. 60
no grief did ever come so near thy heart | as 4.03. 19
come near the house, i pray you. WIV 1.04.132 P
pray you come near. 3.03.149 P
how near is he, mistress page? 4.02. 38 P
how near the god drew to the complexion of a 5.05. 7 P
it draws something near to the speech we had to MM 1.02. 78 P
she's very near her hour. 2.02. 16
as near the dawning, provost, as it is, | you 4.02. 94
shall witness to him i am near at home; 4.03. 95
and very near upon | the duke is ent'ring; 4.06. 14
a scandalous breath to fall | on him so near us? 5.01.123
come not near her. ERR 4.03. 57 P
o, bind him, bind him! let him not come near me. 4.04.106
good sir, draw near to me, i'll speak to him. 5.01. 12
he is very near by this, he was not three ADO 1.01. 3 P
you are very near my brother in his love. 2.01.163 P
there were no living near her, she would infect 2.01.249 P
mild, or come not near me; 2.03. 33 P
of passion came so near the life of passion as 2.03.105 P
then go we near her, that her ear lose nothing 3.01. 32
and it will go near to be thought so shortly. 4.02. 22 P
the spring is near when green geese are LLL 1.01. 97
we choose by the horns, yourself come not near. 4.01.115
do no wrong, | come not near our fairy queen. MND 2.02. 12
beetles black, approach not near; 2.02. 22
wake when some vile thing is near. 2.02. 34
do not lie so near. 2.02. 44
she durst not lie | near this lack-love, this 2.02. 77
and never mayst thou come lysander near! 2.02.136
here, | so near the cradle of the fairy queen? 3.01. 78
near to her close and consecrated bower, | while 3.02. 7
every region near | seem all one mutual cry. 4.01.116
pyramus draws near the wall. silence! 5.01.169 P
friend, would go near to make a man look sad. 5.01.289 P
store, | and, by the near guess of my memory, MV 1.03. 54
sun, | to whom i am a neighbor and near bred. 2.01. 3
what demigod | hath come so near creation? 3.02.116
this comes too near the praising of myself, 3.04. 22
that, | if thou wert near a lewd interpreter! 3.04. 80
let not that doctor e'er come near my house. 5.01.223
so near our public court as twenty miles, | thou AYL 1.03. 44
dear phebe, | if ever (as that ever may be near) 3.05. 28
but till that time | come not thou near me; 3.05. 32
would have gone near | to fall in love with him; 3.05.125
you do love rosalind so near the heart as your 5.02. 62 P
and brave attendants near him when he wakes, SHR in.1. 40
bid them come near. in.1. 79
all things is ready. how near is our master? 4.01.115 P
remember me | near twenty years ago in genoa, 4.04. 4
i was very late more near her than i think she AWW 1.03.106 P
as one near death to those that wish him live. 2.01.131
will you draw near? 3.02. 98
he's very near the truth in this. 4.03.151 P
and i am yet so near the manners of my mother, TN 2.01. 40 P
and i have heard herself come thus near, that, 2.05. 25 P
now is the woodcock near the gin. 2.05. 83 P
lies by a beggar, if a beggar dwells near him; 3.01. 9 P
o ho, do you come near me now? 3.04. 64 P
how far off, how near, | which way to be WT 1.02.404
art so near? 3.03. 80 P
he so near to hermione hath done hermione that 5.02.100 P
comes it not something near? 5.03. 23
near or far off, well won is still well shot, JN 1.01.174
of spain, the lady blanch, | is near to england. 2.01.424
approaching near these eyes, would drink my 4.01. 62
indeed we heard how near his death he was 4.02. 87
to souse annoyance that comes near his nest; 5.02.150
as near as i could sift him on that argument, R2 1.01. 12
draw near, | and list what with our council we 1.03.123
say | how near the tidings of our comfort is. 2.01.272
is near the hate of those love not the king. 2.02.128
we, | because we ever have been near the king. 2.02.134
near to the king in blood, and near in love 3.01. 17
blood, and near in love | till you did make him 3.01. 17
nor near nor farther off, my gracious lord, 3.02. 64
better far off than, near, be ne'er the near. 5.01. 88
better far off than, near, be ne'er the near. 5.01. 88
tell us how near is danger | that we may arm us 5.03. 47
indeed you come near me now, hal, for we that 1H4 1.02. 13 P
some private conference, but be near at hand, 3.02. 2
doomsday is near, die all, die merrily. 4.01.134
even our love durst not come near your sight 5.01. 63
and harry prince of wales | are near at hand. 2H4 2.01.135
and with what danger, near the heart of it. 3.01. 40
with a near aim, of the main chance of things 3.01. 83
upon or near the rate of thirty thousand. 4.01. 22
come near me, now i am much ill. 4.04.111
might make them look | too near unto my state. 4.05.212
with the imputation of being near their master; 5.01. 73 P
not to come near our person by ten mile. 5.05. 65
the grave doth gape, and doting death is near, H5 2.01. 61
for certainly thou art so near the gulf, | thou 4.03. 82
at pleasure here we lie near orleance; 1H6 1.02. 6
none durst come near for fear of sudden death. 1.04. 48
or soldier you perceive | near to the walls, by 2.01. 3
yes, when his holy state is touch'd so near. 3.01. 58
the earl of arminack, near knit to charles, | a 5.01. 17
have i sought every country far and near, | and, 5.04. 3
do, | because he is near kinsman unto charles. 5.05. 45
you shall go near | to call them both a pair of 2H6 1.02.102
could i come near your beauty with my nails, | i 1.03.141
bring him near the king, | his highness' 2.01. 70
first note that he is near you in descent, | and 3.01. 21
or dare to bring thy force so near the court. 5.01. 22
draw near, queen margaret, and be a witness 3H6 3.03.138
me their words as near as thou canst guess them. 4.01. 90
are near to warwick by blood and by alliance: 4.01.136
the day, | if warwick be so near as men report. 4.03. 8
now be nearest | will touch us all too near, if R3 2.03. 26
lord hastings, you and he are near in love. 3.04. 13
nay, for a need, thus far come near my person: 3.05. 85
ely with richmond troubles me more near | than 4.03. 49
near to the town of leicester, as we learn. 5.02. 12
'tis not yet near day. 5.03.220
or some about him near, have out of malice | to H8 2.01.157
wife | has crept too near his conscience. 2.02. 17
conscience | has crept too near another lady. 2.02. 18
i will have none so near else. 2.02.134
pray their graces | to come near. 3.01. 19
in such a point of weight, so near mine honor 3.01. 71
so near mine honor | (more near my life, i fear) 3.01. 72
men are happy, and so are all are near her. 4.01. 50
patience, be near me still, and set me lower; 4.02. 76
a man of his place, and so near our favor, | to 5.02. 30
there is a fellow somewhat near the door, he 5.03. 40 P
was a haberdasher's wife of small wit near him, 5.03. 47 P
as near as the extremest ends | of parallels, as TRO 1.03.167
from a tutor, and discipline come not near thee! 2.03. 30 P
no soul so near me | as the sweet troilus. 4.02. 98
of breath, | confusion's near, i cannot speak. COR 3.01.189
draw near, ye people. 3.03. 39
they are near the city? 5.04. 60
wilt thou draw near the nature of the gods? TIT 1.01.117
draw near them then in being merciful: 1.01.118
gods, | sith priest and holy water are so near, 1.01.323
so near the emperor's palace dare ye draw, | and 2.01. 46
the fields are near, and you are gallant grooms. 4.02.164
let him come near. 5.01.154
draw you near | to shed obsequious tears upon 5.03.151
i aim'd so near when i suppos'd you lov'd. ROM 1.01.205
am i come near ye now? 1.05. 20
this gentleman, the prince's near ally, | my 3.01.109
it is not yet near day. 3.05. 1
thursday is near, lay hand on heart, advise. 3.05.190
short in our provision, | 'tis now near night. 4.02. 39
i hear him near. 4.04. 23
vouchsafe me a word, it does concern you near. TIM 1.02.177
near? 1.02.178
pray draw near. 2.02. 45
pray you walk near, i'll speak with you anon. 2.02.123
which many my near occasions did urge me to put 3.06. 10 P
my worthy friends, will you draw near? 3.06. 58 P
two villains shall not be, | come not near him. 5.01.110
of the stars | give guess how near to day. JC 2.01. 3
be near me, that i may remember you. 2.02.123
and so near will i be, | that your best friends 2.02.124
come not near casca; 2.03. 2 P
he is address'd; press near and second him. 3.01. 29
what now, lucilius, is cassius near? 4.02. 3
the near in blood, | the nearer bloody. MAC 2.03.140
and near approaches | the subject of our watch. 3.03. 7
the english pow'r is near, led on by malcolm, 5.02. 1
near birnan wood | shall we well meet them; 5.02. 5
i hope the days are near at hand | that chambers 5.04. 1
now near enough; 5.06. 1
youth to itself rebels, though none else near. HAM 1.03. 44
it then draws near the season | wherein the 1.04. 5
the glow-worm shows the matin to be near, | and 1.05. 89
much extremity for love — very near this. 2.02.190 P
then is doomsday near. 2.02.238 P
one scene of it comes near the circumstance 3.02. 76
endure | hazard so near 's as doth hourly grow 3.03. 6
like a gulf, doth draw | what's near it with it. 3.03. 17
toe of the peasant comes so near the heel of the 5.01.141 P
/employment, | they are not near my conscience. 5.02. 58
his picture | i will send far and near, that all LR 2.01. 82
in contempt of man, | brought near to beast. 2.03. 9
near and on speedy foot; 4.06.213
nay, come not near th' old man; 4.06.240 P
that follow'd me so near (o, our lives' 5.03.185
they met so near with their lips that their OTH 2.01.259 P
touch me not so near; 2.03.220
for if it touch not you, it comes near nobody. 4.01.198 P
i will be near to second your attempt, and he 4.02.238 P
be near at hand, i may miscarry in't. 5.01. 6
to bear such idleness so near the heart | as ANT 1.03. 94
but, near him, thy angel | becomes a fear, as 2.03. 22
spirit | is all afraid to govern thee near him; 2.03. 30
come thou near. 3.03. 6
one ever near thee. 4.05. 7
the time of universal peace is near. 4.06. 4
and am so near the lack of charity | to accuse CYM 2.03.109
being so near the truth as i will make them, 2.04. 62
came from horse, the place | was near at hand. 3.04. 2

yea, happily, near | the residence of posthumus; 3.04.147
pray draw near. 3.06. 92
i pray draw near. 3.06. 95
i am near to th' place where they should meet, 4.01. 1 P
and my brother search | what companies are near. 4.02. 69
nothing ill come near thee! 4.02.279
to seek her on the mountains near to milford, 5.05.281
braid yourself too near for me to tell it. PER 1.01. 93
murther's as near to lust as flame to smoke; 1.01.138
we are near tharsus. 3.01. 73 P
companion maid | be suffered to come near him. 5.01. 78
new plays and maidenheads are near akin — TNK pr 1
wast near to make the male | to thy sex captive, 1.01. 80
when the north comes near her, | rude and 2.02.140
we'll see how near art can come near their 2.02.149
see how near art can come near their colors. 2.02.149
i would make her | so near the gods in nature, 2.02.242
i'll see her and be near her, or no more. 2.03. 23
strong note of me, | hath made me near her; 3.01. 18
the happier thing to be | so near emilia. 3.01. 26
i should be near the place. ho, cousin palamon! 3.03. 1
more | come near thee with such friendship. 3.06.103
left my angle | to his own skill, came near, but 4.01. 60
and fights | of gods and such men near 'em. 4.02. 25
fever's end, | to this troop come thou not near. PHT 8
from me far off, with others all too near. SON 61.14
leaves look pale, dreading the winter's near. 97.14
if thy soul check thee that i come so near, 136. 1
yet do not so, but since i am near slain, | kill 139.13
as testy sick men, when their deaths be near, 140. 7
NEARER 22 FR 0.0024 REL FR 15 V 7 P
sir — i pray come a little nearer this ways. WIV 2.02. 45 P
your worship come a little nearer this ways. 2.02. 49 P
indeed 'a must shoot nearer, or he'll ne'er hit LLL 4.01.134
coming before me is nearer to his reverence. AYL 1.01. 51 P
thy conceit is nearer death than thy powers. 2.06. 8 P
please you, come something nearer. WT 2.02. 53
the better cherish'd, still the nearer death. 1H4 5.02. 15
nearer in bloody thoughts, /but not in blood, R3 2.01. 93
to touch his growth nearer than he touch'd mine. 2.04. 25
what nearer debt in all humanity | than wife is TRO 2.02.175
myself poorer, that i might come nearer to you. TIM 1.02.101 P
draw nearer, honest flaminius. 3.01. 39 P
come nearer. 4.03.482
for mine's a suit | that touches caesar nearer. JC 3.01. 7
the near in blood, | the nearer bloody. MAC 2.03.141
son, come you more nearer | than your particular HAM 2.01. 11
your ladyship is nearer to heaven than when i 2.02.425 P
she comes more nearer earth than she was wont, OTH 5.02.110
come nearer. CYM 3.05. 91
being born your vassal, | am something nearer. 5.05.114
his complexion | nearer a brown than black; TNK 4.02. 79
whose love of either to myself was nearer, LUC 1165
NEAREST 14 FR 0.0015 REL FR 10 V 4 P
by him cut off | nearest the merchant's heart. MV 4.01.233
"nearest his heart," those are the very words. 4.01.254
with the duke, done my adieu with his nearest; AWW 4.03. 88 P
with all the nearest things to my heart, as well WT 1.02.236
king | and through him what's nearest to him, 4.04.522
foes, | which art my nearest and dearest enemy? 1H4 3.02.123
to the son of the king nearest his father, harry 2H4 2.02.120 P
since | this percy was the man nearest my soul, 3.01. 61
for emulation who shall now be nearest | will R3 2.03. 25
when thou mayest tell thy tale the nearest way? 4.04.461
in the world canst thou nearest compare to thy TIM 4.03.318 P
women nearest, but men — men are the things 4.03.320 P
and you whose places are the nearest, know | we MAC 1.04. 36
of human kindness | to catch the nearest way. 1.05. 18
NEAR–LEGG'D 1 FR 0.0001 REL FR 0 V 1 P
back and shoulder–shotten, near–legg'd before, SHR 3.02. 56 P
NEARLY 6 FR 0.0006 REL FR 4 V 2 P
confidence with you that decerns you nearly. ADO 3.05. 3 P
of something nearly that concerns yourselves. MND 1.01.126
i doubt some danger does approach you nearly. MAC 4.02. 67
to say of what most nearly appertains to us both LR 1.01.284 P
as nearly as i may, | i'll play the penitent to ANT 2.02. 91
a loss in love that touches me more nearly. SON 42. 4
NEARNESS 3 FR 0.0003 REL FR 3 V 0 P
such neighbor nearness to our sacred blood R2 1.01.119
our nearness to the king in love | is near the 2.02.127
to blow that nearness out that flames between ye TNK 5.01. 10
NEAR'S 1 FR 0.0001 REL FR 1 V 0 P
but, by your favor, | how near's the other army? LR 4.06.212
NEAR'ST 2 FR 0.0002 REL FR 2 V 0 P
and my near'st of kin | cry fie upon my grave! WT 3.02. 53
his being thrusts | against my near'st of life; MAC 3.01.117
NEAT* 11 FR 0.0012 REL FR 8 V 3 P
as of a knight well–spoken, neat, and fine; TGV 1.02. 10
companions, is all ready, and all things neat? SHR 4.01.114 P
come, captain, | we must be neat; WT 1.02.123
not neat, but cleanly, captain: 1.02.123
the heckfer, and the calf | are all call'd neat. 1.02.125
came there a certain lord, neat, and trimly 1H4 1.03. 33
wherein neat and cleanly, but to carve a capon 2.04.456 P
troop | as doth a lion in a herd of neat, | or 3H6 2.01. 14
stand, rogue, stand, you neat slave! LR 2.02. 42 P
sluttery, to such neat excellence oppos'd, CYM 1.06. 44
but his neat cookery! 4.02. 49
NEAT–HERD'S 1 FR 0.0001 REL FR 1 V 0 P
would i were | a neat–herd's daughter, and my CYM 1.01.149
NEAT–HERDS 1 FR 0.0001 REL FR 0 V 1 P
three shepherds, three neat–herds, three WT 4.04.325 P
NEATLY 1 FR 0.0001 REL FR 0 V 1 P
thing in him by wearing his apparel neatly. AWW 4.03.146 P
NEAT'S 3 FR 0.0003 REL FR 2 V 1 P
in a neat's tongue dried and a maid not vendible MV 1.01.112
what say you to a neat's foot? SHR 4.03. 17
you /eel–skin, you dried neat's tongue, you 1H4 2.04.245 P
NEAT'S–LEATHER 2 FR 0.0002 REL FR 0 V 2 P
any emperor that ever trod on neat's–leather. TMP 2.02. 70 P
ever trod upon neat's–leather have gone upon my JC 1.01. 25 P
NEB 1 FR 0.0001 REL FR 1 V 0 P
how she holds up the neb! WT 1.02.183
NEBOR *(also neighbor)*
NEBOR 1 FR 0.0001 REL FR 0 V 1 P
neighbor vocatur "nebor"; LLL 5.01. 23 P
NEBUCHADNEZZAR 1 FR 0.0001 REL FR 0 V 1 P
i am no great nebuchadnezzar, sir, i have not AWW 4.05. 20 P
NEC 3 FR 0.0003 REL FR 3 V 0 P
purus, | non eget mauri jaculis, nec arcu." TIT 4.02. 21
"et opus exegi, quod nec jovis ira, nec ignis" TNK 3.05. 88
opus exegi, quod nec jovis ira, nec ignis" — 3.05. 88
NECESSARIES 7 FR 0.0008 REL FR 6 V 1 P
rich garments, linens, stuffs, and necessaries, TMP 1.02.164
some necessaries that i needs must use, | and TGV 2.04.188
since we have locks to safeguard necessaries, H5 1.02.176
madam, we have cull'd such necessaries | as are ROM 4.03. 7
my necessaries are inbark'd. HAM 1.03. 1
i must fetch his necessaries ashore. OTH 2.01.284 P
provide him necessaries and pack my clothes up, TNK 2.06. 32
NECESSARILY 1 FR 0.0001 REL FR 0 V 1 P
he do fear god, 'a must necessarily keep peace; ADO 2.03.193 P
/NECESSARY 1 FR 0.0001 REL FR 0 V 1 P
/return /was /most /requir'd /and /necessary. LR 4.03. 6 P
NECESSARY 19 FR 0.0021 REL FR 12 V 7 P
all my others parts | of necessary fitness? MM 2.04. 23
why he, a harmless necessary cat; MV 4.01. 55
as horns are odious, they are necessary. AYL 3.03. 52 P
and a nimble hand, is necessary for a cutpurse; WT 4.04.672 P
though it be great pity, yet it is necessary. 4.04.776 P
provide us all things necessary, and meet me 1H4 1.02.192 P
and by the necessary form of this | king richard 2H4 3.01. 87
lucifer and belzebub himself, it is necessary, H5 4.07.138 P
majesty, | it were but necessary you were wak'd, 2H6 3.02.261
not stint | our necessary actions in the fear H8 1.02. 77
omission to do what is necessary | seals a TRO 3.03.230
for the table than a necessary bencher in the COR 2.01. 82 P
'tis necessary he should die. TIM 3.05. 2
this shall make | our purpose necessary, and not JC 2.01.178
fear, | seeing that death, a necessary end, 2.02. 36
in the mean time some necessary question of the HAM 3.02. 42 P
most necessary 'tis that we forget | to pay 3.02.192
if idle talk will once be necessary, | i'll not ANT 5.02. 50
of age, | nor gives to necessary wrinkles place, SON 108.11
NECESSITIED 1 FR 0.0001 REL FR 1 V 0 P
her fortunes ever stood | necessitied to help, AWW 5.03. 85
/NECESSITIES 1 FR 0.0001 REL FR 1 V 0 P
/construe /the /times /to /their /necessities, 2H4 4.01.102
NECESSITIES 11 FR 0.0012 REL FR 10 V 1 P
man | in all your business and necessities. AYL 2.03. 55
and royal necessities made separation of their WT 1.01. 25 P
one of these two must be necessities, | which 4.04. 38
are these things then necessities? 2H4 3.01. 92
then let us meet them like necessities; 3.01. 93
these should be hours for necessities, | not for H8 5.01. 2
it must omit | real necessities, and give way COR 3.01.147
nought | but even the mere necessities upon't. TIM 4.03.376
here, | and call in question our necessities. JC 4.03.165
the art of our necessities is strange | and can LR 3.02. 70
o'er your content these strong necessities, ANT 3.06. 83
NECESSITY 39 FR 0.0044 REL FR 29 V 10 P
to make a virtue of necessity | and live as we TGV 4.01. 60
a sword, and it shall bite upon my necessity. WIV 2.01.131 P
and hiding mine honor in my necessity, am fain 2.02. 24 P
the fairest grant is the necessity. ADO 1.01.317
decree, | she must lie here on mere necessity. LLL 1.01.148
necessity will make us all forsworn | three 1.01.149
i am forsworn "on mere necessity." 1.01.154
for me, | i'll rather dwell in my necessity. MV 1.03.155
the which my love and some necessity | now lays 3.04. 34
nor shalt not, till necessity be serv'd. AYL 2.07. 89
times good must of necessity hold his virtue to AWW 1.01. 8 P
now my necessity | makes me to ask you for my TN 3.04.334
his friend here in necessity and denying him; 3.04.387 P
were there necessity in your request, although WT 1.02. 22
(thou must think there's a necessity in't) and 4.04.634 P
teach thy necessity to reason thus: R2 1.03.277
there is no virtue like necessity. 1.03.278
to grim necessity, and he and i | will keep a 5.01. 21
but that necessity so bow'd the state | that i 2H4 3.01. 73
at home, | yet that is but a crush'd necessity, H5 1.02.175
god comfort him in this necessity! 1H6 4.03. 15
love, | but from deceit bred by necessity; 3H6 3.03. 68
urge the necessity and state of times, | and be R3 4.04.416
his legs are legs for necessity, not for flexure TRO 2.03.106 P
man i am, necessity | commands me name myself. COR 4.05. 56
bid him suppose some good necessity | touches TIM 2.02.227
for't, and show'd what necessity belong'd to't, 3.02. 13 P
carriage, | had his necessity made use of me, 3.02. 82
upon our talk, | and nature must obey necessity, JC 4.03.227
wherein necessity, of matter beggar'd, | will HAM 4.05. 92
as if we were villains on necessity, fools by LR 1.02.122 P
shame, that then necessity | will call discreet 1.04.213
yet, for necessity of present life, | i must OTH 1.01.155
show you such a necessity in his death that you 4.02.240 P
the strong necessity of time commands | our ANT 1.03. 42
very necessity of this thought, that i, | your 2.02. 58
men should be, | till he hath pass'd necessity. PER 2.ch. 6
in like necessity — | the which the gods 2.01.128
there's no farther necessity of qualities can 4.02. 48 P
NECESSITY'S 1 FR 0.0001 REL FR 1 V 0 P
the wolf and owl — | necessity's sharp pinch. LR 2.04.211
NECK *(also nick*)*
/NECK 2 FR 0.0002 REL FR 2 V 0 P
/might /i, /hanging /on /hotspur's /neck, 2H4 2.03. 44
/he /fastened /on /my /neck /and /bellowed /out LR 5.03.213
NECK 75 FR 0.0084 REL FR 48 V 27 P
come, | i'll manacle thy neck and feet together. TMP 1.02.462
his neck will come to your waist — a cord, sir. MM 3.02. 40 P
the mark of my shoulder, the mole in my neck, ERR 3.02.143 P
and that self chain about his neck, | which he 5.01. 10
these people saw the chain about his neck. 5.01.259
and thou wilt needs thrust thy neck into a yoke, ADO 1.01.201 P
about your neck, like an usurer's chain? 2.01.189 P
break the neck of the wax, and every one give LLL 4.01. 59
hang me by the neck if horns that year miscarry. 4.01.112
his face must be seen through the lion's neck, MND 3.01. 37 P
conscience, hanging about the neck of my heart, MV 2.02. 14 P
as lief thou didst break his neck as his finger. AYL 1.01.147 P
and a chain, that you once wore, about his neck. 3.02.182 P
falls not the axe upon the humbled neck | but 3.05. 5
about his neck | a green and gilded snake had 4.03.107
she hung about my neck, and kiss on kiss | she SHR 2.01.308
he took the bride about the neck | and kiss'd 3.02.177
with no greater a run but my head and my neck. 4.01. 16 P
item, one neck, one chin, and so forth. TN 1.05.248 P
wilt thou set thy foot o' my neck? 2.05.188 P
her like her medal hanging | about his neck, WT 1.02.308
her jewel about the neck of it; 5.02. 33 P
she hangs about his neck. 5.03.112
with signs of war about his aged neck. R2 2.02. 74
me, | have stoop'd my neck under your injuries, 3.01. 19
bare–headed, lower than his proud steed's neck, 5.02. 19
and break the neck | of that proud man that did 5.05. 88
nicholas' clerks, i'll give thee this neck. 1H4 2.01. 62 P
and in the neck of that, task'd the whole state; 4.03. 92
he could wish himself in thames up to the neck; H5 4.01.115 P
so did he turn and over suffolk's neck | he 4.06. 24
please your majesty, let his neck answer for it, 4.08. 43 P
a new–married wife about her husband's neck, 5.02.180 P
direct mine arms i may embrace his neck, | and 1H6 2.05. 37
view, | i took a costly jewel from my neck, | a 2H6 3.02.106
him with his pen and inkhorn about his neck. 4.02.110 P
yield not thy neck | to fortune's yoke, but let 3H6 3.03. 16
now thy proud neck bears half my burthen'd yoke, R3 4.04.111
thus margaret's curse falls heavy on my neck: 5.01. 25
has hung twenty years | about his neck, yet H8 2.02. 32
shall from your neck unloose his amorous fold, TRO 3.03.223
for if hector break not his neck i' th' combat, 3.03.259 P
i would they had broke 's neck! 4.02. 77 P
but a plague break thy neck — for frighting me! 5.04. 32 P
head below his knee, | and tread upon his neck. COR 1.03. 47
one i' th' neck, and two i' th' thigh — there's 2.01.151 P
her richest lockram 'bout her reechy neck, 2.01.209
there which looks | with us to break his neck. 3.03. 30
left undone | that which shall break his neck, 4.07. 25
then i have brought up a neck to a fair end. TIT 4.04. 49 P
while you live, draw your neck out of collar. ROM 1.01. 4 P
sometime she driveth o'er a soldier's neck, 1.04. 82
second masters, | upon their first lord's neck. TIM 4.03.506
like a cur, behind | strook caesar on the neck. JC 5.01. 44
or paddling in your neck with his damn'd fingers HAM 3.04.185
basket creep, | and break your own neck down. 3.04.196
dogs and bears by th' neck, monkeys by th' loins LR 2.04. 8 P
a hill, lest it break thy neck with following; 2.04. 73 P
/by /this /hand, falls me thus about my neck — OTH 4.01.136 P
that men must lay their murthers on your neck. 5.02.170
a halter'd neck which does the hangman thank ANT 3.13.130
source, and the first stone | drop in my neck; 3.13.161
chain mine arm'd neck, leap thou, attire and all 4.08. 14
bending down | his corrigible neck, his face 4.14. 74
and thus i set my foot on 's neck," even then CYM 3.03. 92
your neck, sir, is pen, book, and counters; 5.04.169 P
guiderius had | upon his neck a mole, a sanguine 5.05.364
your heart, about that neck | which is my fee, TNK 1.01.197
whose sinowy neck in battle ne'er did bow, | who VEN 99
her arms do lend his neck a sweet embrace; 539
and on his neck her yoking arms she throws. 592
she sinketh down, still hanging by his neck, 593
his short thick neck cannot be easily harmed; 627
some catch her by the neck, some kiss her face, 872
one on another's neck, do witness bear | thy SON 131.11
NECKLACE 1 FR 0.0001 REL FR 1 V 0 P
bugle–bracelet, necklace amber, | perfume for a WT 4.04.222
NECKS 11 FR 0.0012 REL FR 7 V 4 P
with bills on their necks, "be it known unto all AYL 1.02.123 P
with which he yoketh your rebellious necks, 1H6 2.03. 64
you to break your necks or hang yourselves! 5.04. 91
and smooth my way upon their headless necks; 2H6 1.02. 65
be hang'd with your pardons about your necks? 4.08. 23 P
and humbly thus, with halters on their necks, 4.09. 11
the napes of your necks and make but an interior COR 2.01. 39 P
he returning to break our necks, they respect 5.04. 33 P
make poor men's cattle break their necks, | set TIT 5.01.132
hanging a golden stamp about their necks, | put MAC 4.03.153
thousand cupids, | shall never clasp our necks; TNK 2.02. 32
NECTAR 4 FR 0.0004 REL FR 4 V 0 P
the water nectar, and the rocks pure gold. TGV 2.04.171
taste indeed | love's thrice–repured nectar? TRO 3.02. 22
sooner than such, to give us nectar with 'em, TNK 5.04. 12
such nectar from his lips she had not suck'd. VEN 572
NED 20 FR 0.0022 REL FR 6 V 14 P
good morrow, ned. 1H4 1.02.111 P
ned poins and i will walk lower. 2.02. 61 P
ned, where are our disguises? 2.02. 74 P
away, good ned. 2.02.108
ned, prithee come out of that fat room, and lend 2.04. 1 P
i tell thee, ned, thou hast lost much honor that 2.04. 20 P
but, sweet ned — to sweeten which name of ned, 2.04. 22 P
to sweeten which name of ned, i give thee this 2.04. 22 P
but, ned, to drive away the time till falstaff 2.04. 28 P
but do you use me thus, ned? 2H4 2.02.138 P
shall we steal upon them, ned, at supper? 2.02.158 P
follow me, ned. 2.02.177 P
no abuse, ned, i' th' world, honest ned, none. 2.04.318 P
no abuse, ned, i' th' world, honest ned, none. 2.04.318 P
none, ned, none; 2.04.323 P
why not ned and i | for once allow'd the 3H6 5.04. 19
o ned, sweet ned, speak to thy mother, boy! 5.05. 51
o ned, sweet ned, speak to thy mother, boy! 5.05. 51
young ned, for thee, thine uncles and myself 5.07. 16
and little ned plantagenet, his son? R3 4.04.146
NEDAR'S 2 FR 0.0002 REL FR 2 V 0 P
made love to nedar's daughter, helena, | and won MND 1.01.107
demetrius is, | this helena, old nedar's helena. 4.01.130
/NEED 2 FR 0.0002 REL FR 2 V 0 P
/being /so /great, /i /have /no /need /to /beg. R2 4.01.309
/that /need /to /be /reviv'd /and /breath'd /in 2H4 4.01.112
NEED 187 FR 0.0211 REL FR 132 V 55 P
sword, pike, knife, gun, or need of any engine, TMP 2.01.162
faith, sir, you need not fear. 3.03. 43
what need she, when she hath made you write to TGV 2.01.152 P
for valentine, i need not cite him to it. 2.04. 85
to take a note of what i stand in need of, | to 2.07. 84
what need a man care for a stock with a wench, 3.01.309 P
for then she need not be wash'd and scour'd. 3.01.312 P
partly that i have need of such a youth | that 4.04. 64
ne'er put my finger in the fire, and need not. WIV 1.04. 86 P
and the boy never need to understand any thing; 2.02.127 P
i am half afraid he will have need of washing, 3.03.182 P
when need you tell me that? 5.05.190 P
nor need you, on mine honor, have to do | with MM 1.01. 63

your place, you need not change your trade; 1.02.107 P
and the knaves, you need not to fear the bawds. 2.01.235 P
if you should need a pin, | you could not with 2.02. 45
must, upon a warranted need, give him a better 3.02.143 P
what need she be acquainted? ERR 3.02. 15
it shall not need, thy father hath his life. 5.01.391
what need the bridge much broader than the flood ADO 1.01.316
appear when there is no need of such vanity. 3.03. 21 P
for when rich villains have need of poor ones, 3.03.114 P
o, 'tis more than need. LLL 4.03.285
we need more light to find your meaning out. 5.02. 21
are all dead, there need none to be blam'd. MND 5.01.357 P
you need not fear, lady, the having any of these MV 1.02.100 P
well then, it now appears you need my help. 1.03.114
nay, you need not fear us, lorenzo, launcelot 3.05. 31 P
so had you need, | i scarce can speak to thank AYL 2.07.169
i' faith, sir, you shall never need to fear. SHR 1.01. 61
so had you need. 1.01.210
but they may chance to need thee at home, 5.01. 2 P
yourself, he shall need none so long as i live. 5.01. 24 P
thy casement i need not open, for i look through AWW 2.03.214 P
apology you think | may make it probable need. 2.04. 51
seem, | and my appointments have in them a need 2.05. 67
i hope i need not to advise you further, but i 3.05. 25 P
you shall not need to fear me. 3.05. 29 P
i need not to ask you if gold will corrupt him 4.03.277 P
you need but plead your honorable privilege. 4.05. 90 P
nay, you need not to stop your nose, sir; 5.02. 10 P
thou hadst need send for more money. TN 2.03.182 P
like to the old vice, | your need to sustain; 4.02.125
if it be so, | we need no grave to bury honesty, WT 2.01.155
why, what need we | commune with you of this, 2.01.161
yourselves | we need no more of your advice. 2.01.168
though i am satisfied and need no more | than 2.01.189
you need not fear it, sir. 2.02. 56
the need i have of thee, thine own goodness hath 4.02. 11 P
thou hast need of more rags to lay on thee, 4.03. 54 P
he shall not need to grieve | at knowing of thy 4.04.415
and most opportune to her need i have | a vessel 4.04.500
easier for advice, | or stronger for your need. 4.04.506
fram'd, but forc'd | by need and accident. 5.01. 92
france, for france, for it is more than need. JN 1.01.179
speaks not from her faith, | but from her need. 3.01.211
o, if thou grant my need, | which only lives but 3.01.211
that need must needs infer this principle, 3.01.213
that faith would live again by death of need. 3.01.214
o then tread down my need, and faith mounts up; 3.01.215
keep my need up, and faith is trodden down! 3.01.216
thou shalt not need. 3.01.320
alas, what need you be so boist'rous–rough? 4.01. 75
for he perhaps shall need | some messenger 4.02.178
whom he hath us'd rather for sport than need) 5.02.175
i shall not need transport my words by you, R2 2.03. 81
you, feel want, | taste grief, need friends: 3.02.176
for what i have i need not to repeat, | and what 3.04. 17
they love not poison that do poison need, | nor 5.06. 38
when we need | your use and counsel, we shall 1H4 1.03. 20
nor shall we need his help these fourteen days. 3.01. 87
hand, | for we shall presently have need of you. 3.02. 3
as virtuously given as a gentleman need to be, 3.03. 15 P
why, my good lord, you need not fear, | there is 4.04. 21
what need i be so forward with him that calls 5.01.128 P
i need no more weight than mine own bowels. 5.03. 34 P
i do not need your help, | and god forbid a 5.04. 10
but what need i thus | my well–known body to 2H4 in 20
never so few, and never yet more need. 1.01.215
do not the rebels need soldiers? 1.02. 74 P
us in full puissance, | you need not to be dreaded. 1.03. 78
therefore captains had need look to't. 2.04.150 P
you need not to have prick'd me, there are other 3.02.114 P
there is no need of any such redress, | or if 4.01. 95
i hop'd there was no need to trouble himself H5 2.03. 21 P
i need not to be ashamed of your majesty, 4.07.113 P
so you had need, for orleance is besieg'd; 1H6 1.01.157
now he is gone, my lord, you need not fear. 5.02. 17
and then i need not crave his courtesy. 5.03.105
"a crafty knave does need no broker," | yet am i 2H6 1.02.100
alas, sir, we did it for pure need. 2.01.154
they have the more need to sleep now then. 4.02. 3 P
so he had need, for 'tis threadbare. 4.02. 7 P
he need not fear the sword, for his coat is of 4.02. 60 P
she shall not need, we'll meet her in the field. 3H6 1.02. 65
ay, with five hundred, father, for a need. 1.02. 67
and in thy need such comfort come to thee | as 1.04.165
lest in our need he might infect another, | and 5.04. 46
let him depart before we need his help. 5.04. 49
i need not add more fuel to your fire, | for 5.04. 70
god grant we never may have need of you! R3 1.03. 75
mean time, god grants that i have need of you. 1.03. 76
when i have most need to employ a friend, | and 2.01. 36
and if they live, i hope i need not fear. 3.01.148
friends at pomfret, they do need the priest, 3.02.114
o, now i need the priest that spake to me! 3.04. 87
nay, for a need, thus far come near my person: 3.05. 85
but, god be thank'd, there is no need of me, 3.07.165
and much i need to help you, were there need: 3.07.166
and much i need to help you, were there need: 3.07.166
which in his dearest need will fly from him. 5.02. 21
we had need pray, | and heartily, for our H8 2.02. 44
what's the need? 2.04. 2
what need you note it? 2.04.129
are under the line, they need no other penance: 5.03. 43 P
he shall not need it if he have his own. TRO 1.02. 87 P
come, come, what need you blush? 3.02. 40 P
for we may live to have need of such a verse. 4.04. 22 P
i must not, i need not be barren of accusations; COR 1.01. 44 P
in free contempt | when he did need your loves; 2.03.201
we need not put new matter to his charge. 3.03. 76
because they then less need one another. 4.05.231 P
we hear not of him, neither need we fear him; 4.06. 1
your lordships, /that, when ever you have need, TIT 4.02. 15
'twas no need, i trow, | to bid me trudge. ROM 1.03. 33
table, and says, "god send me no need of thee!" 3.01. 7 P
him on the drawer, when indeed there is no need. 3.01. 9 P
o'er a gossip's bowl, | for here we need it not. 3.05.175
for i have need of many orisons | to move the 4.03. 3
what, are you busy, ho? need you my help? 4.03. 6
get thee to bed and rest, for thou hast need. 4.03. 13
i said, | "an" if a man did need a poison now, 5.01. 50
o, this same thought did but forerun my need, 5.01. 53
need and oppression starveth in thy eyes, 5.01. 70
to shake off | my friend when he must need me. TIM 1.01.101
freedom, | or my friends, if i should need 'em. 1.02. 69
think i, what need we have any friends, if we 1.02. 95 P
friends, if we should ne'er have need of 'em? 1.02. 96 P
i need not tell him that, he knows you are too 3.04. 39 P
man enough, that one need not lend to another; 3.06. 73 P
him and his worth, and our great need of him, JC 1.03.161
what need we any spur but our own cause | to 2.01.123
our cause or our performance | did need an oath; 2.01.136
i should not need, if you were gentle brutus. 2.01.279
it shall please my country to need my death. 3.02. 47 P
i had most need of blessing, and "amen" | stuck MAC 2.02. 29
what need i fear of thee? 4.01. 82
what need we fear who knows it, when none can 5.01. 37 P
so grace and mercy at your most need help you. HAM 1.05.180
the need we have to use you did provoke | our 2.02. 3
you could, for need, study a speech of some 2.02.541 P
you need not tell us what lord hamlet said, | we 3.01.179
of nothing hath not such need to hide itself. LR 1.02. 34 P
if it be nothing, i shall not need spectacles. 1.02. 35 P
when thou hadst no need to care for her frowning 1.04.192 P
natures of such deep trust we shall much need; 2.01.115
what should you need of more? 2.04.238
what need you five and twenty? 2.04.261
what need one? 2.04.263
o, reason not the need! 2.04.264
but, for true need — | you heavens, give me 2.04.270
heavens, give me that patience, patience i need! 2.04.271
from that place | i shall no leading need. 4.01. 78
were to remember that the present need | speaks ANT 2.02.101
upon a course | which has no need of you. 3.11. 10
of grace that it flows over | on all that need. 5.02. 25
we shall have need | t' employ you towards this CYM 2.03. 62
to spare when you shall find | you need it not. 2.04. 66
what shall i need to draw my sword, the paper 3.04. 32
in fullness | is sorer than to lie for need; 3.06. 13
in hard voyages, became | the life o' th' need. 5.03. 45
you shall not need, my fellow peers of tyre, PER 1.03. 10
will and what they can, | what need we /fear? 1.04. 77
what need speak i? 2.ch. 16
he had need mean better than his outward show 2.02. 48
but if to that my nature need a spur, | the gods 3.03. 23
for such provision | as our intents will need? 5.01.258
what need i | affect another's gait, which is TNK 1.02. 44
these poor slight sores | need not a plantin; 1.02. 61
having no fair to lose, you need not fear, | the VEN 1083
and therefore now i need not fear to die. LUC 1052
friend indeed, | he will help thee in thy need: PP 20.50
till i return, of posting is no need. SON 51. 4
might be better us'd | where cheeks need blood, 82.14
i never saw that you did painting need, | and 83. 1
then need i not to fear the worst of wrongs, 92. 5
nor need i tallies thy dear love to score; 122.10

NEEDED 3 FR 0.0003 REL FR 2 V 1 P
nor never needed that i should entreat, | am SHR 4.03. 8
'tis not needed yet. MAC 5.03. 33
what needed then that terrible dispatch of it LR 1.02. 32 P

NEEDER 1 FR 0.0001 REL FR 1 V 0 P
doth ever cool | i' th' absence of the needer. COR 4.01. 44

NEEDETH 1 FR 0.0001 REL FR 1 V 0 P
what needeth then apology be made | to set forth LUC 31

NEEDFUL 33 FR 0.0037 REL FR 31 V 2 P
leaves unquestion'd | matters of needful value. MM 1.01. 55
(the needful bits and curbs to headstrong weeds) 1.03. 20
it is but needful. 2.01.282
let her have needful but not lavish means; 2.02. 24
i would do more than that, if more were needful. 2.03. 9
it is needful that you frame the season for your ADO 1.03. 24 P
therefore to 's seemeth it a needful course, LLL 2.01. 25
they shall be no more than needful there, if AWW 4.03. 80 P
'fore whose throne 'tis needful, | ere i can 4.04. 3
request, although | 'twere needful i denied it. WT 1.02. 23
but needful conference | about some gossips for 2.03. 40
o, let us pay the time but needful woe, | since JN 5.07.110
i hope no less, yet needful 'tis to fear, | and, 1H4 4.04. 34
'tis needful that the most immodest word | be 2H4 4.04. 70
never so needful on the earth of france, | spur 1H6 4.03. 18
with aid of soldiers to this needful war. 3H6 2.01.147
and haste is needful in this desp'rate case. 4.01.129
now then it is more than needful | forthwith 4.06. 53
and give him from me this most needful note. R3 5.03. 41
'tis a needful fitness | that we adjourn this H8 2.04.232
to our own selves bend we our needful talk. TRO 4.04.139
hither | to use as you think needful of the man. TIT 5.01. 39
to help me sort such needful ornaments | as you ROM 4.02. 34
and what needful else | that calls upon us, by MAC 5.09. 37
it, | as needful in our loves, fitting our duty? HAM 1.01.173
yet needful too, for youth no less becomes | the 4.07. 78
bestow | your needful counsel to our businesses, LR 2.01.127
which shall be needful for your entertainment. 2.04.206
with what else needful your good grace shall OTH 1.03.286
her son gone, | so needful for this present! CYM 4.03. 8
no needful thing omitted. PER 5.03. 68
i'll bring you every needful thing. TNK 3.01. 99
there's all things needful — files and shirts 3.03. 48

NEEDING 2 FR 0.0002 REL FR 2 V 0 P
heart is bleeding, all help needing, | o cruel PP 17.15
to be diseas'd ere that there was true needing. SON 118. 8

NEEDLE *(also needl's, neele)*

NEEDLE 9 FR 0.0010 REL FR 7 V 2 P
go ply thy needle, meddle not with her. SHR 2.01. 25
marry, sir, with needle and thread. 4.03.120
as will stop the eye of helen's needle, for whom TRO 2.01. 80 P
so delicate with her needle! OTH 4.01.188 P
myself by with a needle, that i might prick CYM 1.01.168
of space had pointed him sharp as my needle; 1.03. 19
or when she would with sharp needle wound | the PER 4.ch. 23
lucretia's glove, wherein her needle sticks. LUC 317
and griping it, the needle his finger pricks, 319

NEEDLE'S 1 FR 0.0001 REL FR 1 V 0 P
to thread the postern of a small needle's eye." R2 5.05. 17

NEEDLES 2 FR 0.0002 REL FR 1 V 1 P
have with our needles created both one flower, MND 3.02.204
by the prick of their needles but it will be H5 2.01. 34 P

/NEEDLESS 2 FR 0.0002 REL FR 1 V 1 P
/of /less /expect | /that /matter /needless, /of TRO 1.03. 71
/king /and /nobles, /needless /diffidences, LR 1.02.147 P

NEEDLESS 9 FR 0.0010 REL FR 8 V 1 P
in brief, to set the needless process by — MM 5.01. 92
how needless was it then | to ask the question? LLL 2.01.116
first, for his weeping into the needless stream: AYL 2.01. 46
him and do sigh | at each his needless heavings, WT 2.03. 35
off, | when with a volley of our needless shot, JN 5.05. 5
pray god, i say, i prove a needless coward! R3 3.02. 88
that does appear, | their needless vouches? COR 2.03.117
they were the most needless creatures living, TIM 1.02. 97 P
nobler heart and brain | with needless jealousy, CYM 5.04. 66

NEEDLE–WORK 1 FR 0.0001 REL FR 1 V 0 P
pearl, | valens of venice gold in needle–work; SHR 2.01.354

NEEDL'S *(also needle, etc., neele)*

NEEDL'S 1 FR 0.0001 REL FR 1 V 0 P
their needl's to lances, and their gentle hearts JN 5.02.157

NEEDLY 1 FR 0.0001 REL FR 1 V 0 P
and needly will be rank'd with other griefs, ROM 3.02.117

NEEDS 160 FR 0.0180 REL FR 125 V 35 P
it for, he needs will be | absolute milan — me TMP 1.02.108
it must needs be of subtle, tender, and delicate 2.01. 42 P
spirits hear me, | and yet i needs must curse. 2.02. 4
by your patience, | i needs must rest me. 3.03. 4
some necessaries that i needs must use, | and TGV 2.04.188
if i keep them, i needs must lose myself; 2.06. 20
you must needs have them with a codpiece, madam. 2.07. 53
she needs not, when she knows it cowardice. 5.02. 21
and would needs speak with you presently. WIV 3.03. 87 P
she must needs go in, | her father will be angry 3.04. 92
but what needs either your "mum" or her "budget" 5.02. 8 P
must he needs die? MM 2.02. 48
their untaught love | must needs appear offense. 2.04. 30
it but that you will needs buy and sell men and 3.02. 2 P
this needs must be a practice. 5.01.123
what needs all that, and a pair of stocks in the ERR 3.01. 60
i see a man here needs not live by shifts, 3.02.182
and thou wilt needs thrust thy neck into a yoke, ADO 1.01.200 P
needs not the painted flourish of your praise: LLL 2.01. 14
your grace needs not fear it. 4.03.197
o, she needs it not. 4.03.235
dark needs no candles now, for dark is light. 4.03.265
i must needs be friends with thee. 5.02.549
therefore you must needs play pyramus. MND 1.02. 88 P
that must needs be sport alone. 3.02.119
for your play needs no excuse. 5.01.355 P
i must needs tell thee all. MV 2.04. 29
there must be needs a like proportion | of 3.04. 14
lover of my lord, | must needs be like my lord. 3.04. 18
must needs give sentence 'gainst the merchant 4.01.205
if it be true that good wine needs no bush, 'tis AYL ep 4 P
'tis true that a good play needs no epilogue. ep 4 P
nay then she must needs come. SHR 5.02. 88
under that you must needs be born under mars. AWW 1.01.196 P
wilt thou needs be a beggar? 1.03. 20 P
and he must needs go that the devil drives. 1.03. 29 P
thou this to hazard needs must intimate | skill 2.01.183
parcels of dispatch /effected many nicer needs. 4.03. 91 P
hang'd in this world needs to fear no colors. TN 1.05. 6 P
dear heart, since i must needs be gone." 2.03.102
and he is yours, and his must needs be yours: 3.01.101
you must needs yield your reason, sir andrew. 3.02. 3 P
what needs these hands? WT 2.03.127
i needs must think it honesty. 4.04.487
in the extremity of the one, it must needs be. 5.02. 19 P
needs must you lay your heart at his dispose, JN 1.01.263
that need must needs infer this principle, 3.01.213
uncle, i needs must pray that thou mayst lose; 3.01.332
john may stand, then arthur needs must fall: 3.04.139
your vild intent must needs seem horrible. 4.01. 95
must needs want pleading for a pair of eyes. 4.01. 98
his passion is so ripe, it needs must break. 4.02. 79
i cannot mend it, i must needs confess, R2 2.03.153
needs must i like it well; 3.02. 4
needs no more but one tongue for all those 1H4 1.03. 96
you must needs learn, lord, to amend this fault; 3.01.178
which oft the ear of greatness needs must hear 3.02. 24
john, that you must needs be out of all compass, 3.03. 22 P
if ye will needs say i am an old man, you should 2H4 1.02.216 P
marry, the immortal part needs a physician, but 2.02.104 P
that thou wilt needs invest thee with my honors 4.05. 95
sir, a new link to the bucket must needs be had; 5.01. 23 P
and therefore we must needs admit the means H5 1.01. 68
he needs not, it is no hidden virtue in him. 3.07.109 P
near the gulf, | thou needs must be englutted. 4.03. 83
captain, you must needs be friends with him. 4.08. 61
must needs be granted to be much at one. 5.02.192 P
and thou must therefore needs prove a good 5.02.205 P
what needs your grace | to be protector of his 2H6 1.03.118
her fume needs no spurs, | she'll gallop far 1.03.150
'a must needs, for beggary is valiant. 4.02. 54 P
will you needs be hang'd with your pardons about 4.08. 22 P
a subtle traitor needs no sophister. 5.01.191
it needs not, nor it boots thee not, proud queen 3H6 1.04.125
and spite of spite needs must i rest awhile. 2.03. 5
nay, then i see that edward needs must down. 4.03. 42
what fates impose, that men must needs abide; 4.03. 58
he needs no indirect or lawless course | to cut R3 1.04.218
my lord protector needs will have it so. 3.01.141
my lord, there needs no such apology. 3.07.104
had my trial, | and must needs say a noble one; H8 2.01.119
your grace must needs deserve all strangers' 2.02.101
was a fool — | for he would needs be virtuous. 2.02.132
must i needs forgo | so good, so noble, and so 3.02.422
way of mercy | but i must needs to th' tower, my 5.02.128
fools on both sides, helen must needs be fair, TRO 1.01. 90
a marvell's white hand, i must needs confess. 1.02.137 P
as you must needs, for you all cried "go, go" — 2.02. 85
as you must needs, for you all clapp'd your 2.02. 87
i must needs praise him. 3.01. 7 P
and what needs /these tricks? 5.01. 12 P
till when | they needs must show themselves, COR 1.02. 21
no, titus, no, the emperor needs her not, | nor TIT 1.01.299
physic, | and you must needs bestow her funeral; 4.02.163
so that perforce you must needs stay a time. 4.03. 42
or, if he do, it needs must be by stealth. ROM 3.05.215
my dismal scene i needs must act alone. 4.03. 19

i needs must wake her. 4.05. 9
i must needs wake you. 4.05. 13
we must needs dine together. TIM 1.01.164
you must needs dine with me; 1.01.244
there is true friendship, there needs none. 1.02. 18
what needs these feasts, pomps, and vainglories? 1.02.242 P
immediate are my needs, and my relief | must not 2.01. 25
for my own part, i must needs confess, i have 3.02. 20 P
must he needs trouble me in't — hum! 3.03. 1
me beyond them, and i must needs appear. 3.06. 12 P
must thou needs | stand for a villain in thine 5.01. 37
i must needs say you have a little fault; 5.01. 87
that needs must light on this ingratitude. JC 1.01. 55
he needs not our mistrust, since he delivers MAC 3.03. 2
more needs she the divine than the physician. 5.01. 74
or so much as it needs | to dew the sovereign 5.02. 29
there needs no ghost, my lord, come from the HAM 1.05.125
or, if thou wilt needs marry, marry a fool, for 3.01.137 P
such love must needs be treason in my breast. 3.02.178
for who not needs shall never lack a friend, 3.02.207
when he needs what you have glean'd, it is but 4.02. 19 P
her mood will needs be pitied. 4.05. 3
and you must needs have heard, how i am punish'd 5.02.229
follow him, thou must needs wear my coxcomb. LR 1.04.104 P
in my flesh, | which i must needs call mine. 2.04.223
allow not nature more than nature needs, | man's 2.04.266
nature needs not what thou gorgeous wear'st, 2.04.269
from rest, | and must needs taste his folly. 2.04.291
i must needs after him, madam, with my letter. 4.05. 15
but thou must needs be sure | my spirits and my OTH 1.01.102
if thou wilt needs damn thyself, do it a more 1.03.353 P
and needs no other suitor but his likings | /to 3.01. 48
it vital growth again, | it needs must wither. 5.02. 15
she said so; i must needs report the truth. 5.02.128
what needs this iterance, woman? 5.02.150
then must thou needs find out new heaven, new ANT 1.01. 17
what needs more words? 2.07.125
your presence needs must puzzle antony, | take 3.07. 10
he needs as many, sir, as caesar has, | or needs 3.13. 49
as many, sir, as caesar has, | or needs not us. 3.13. 50
set before him, | he needs must see himself. 5.01. 35
than they, must needs | appear unkinglike. CYM 3.05. 6
who needs must know of her departure and | dost 4.03. 10
most honor'd cleon, i must needs be gone. PER 3.03. 1
our losses fall so thick we must needs leave. TNK pr 32
i know | his ocean needs not my poor drops, yet 1.03. 7
and their needs | the one of th' other may be 1.03. 57
i must needs entreat you | this afternoon to 2.05. 45
your hunger needs no sauce, i see. 3.03. 25
and must needs be by | to give the service pay. 5.03. 31
on one | that two must needs be blind for't! 5.03.146
to england, | why, you must needs be strangers; STM II.C 130
dead at first, what needs a second striking? VEN 250
"but if thou needs wilt hunt, be rul'd by me, 673
by the rights of time thou needs must have, | if 759
as they must needs (the sister and the brother), PP 8. 2
as, passing all conceit, needs no defense. 8. 8
that i an accessary needs must be | to that SON 35.13
"truth needs no color with his color fix'd, 101. 6
because he needs no praise, wilt thou be dumb? 101. 9
feel | needs must i under my transgression bow, 120. 3
the boy for trial needs would touch my breast; 153.10
the one a palate hath that needs will taste, LC 167

NEED'ST 6 FR 0.0006 REL FR 5 V 1 P
nor need'st thou much importune me to that TGV 1.03. 17
when thou need'st him, there thou shalt find him 1H4 2.02. 71 P
what need'st thou run so many miles about, R3 4.04.460
therefore stay yet, thou need'st not to be gone. ROM 3.05. 16
thou need'st | but keep that count'nance still. CYM 3.04. 13
what need'st thou wound with cunning when thy SON 139. 7

NEEDY 7 FR 0.0008 REL FR 7 V 0 P
a needy, hollow–ey'd, sharp–looking wretch, | a ERR 5.01.241
because i would not tax the needy commons, 2H6 3.01.116
and joy comes well in such a needy time. ROM 3.05.105
and in his needy shop a tortoise hung, | an 5.01. 42
need, | and this same needy man must sell it me. 5.01. 54
are stor'd with corn to make your needy bread, PER 1.04. 95
born, | and needy nothing trimm'd in jollity, SON 66. 3

NEELE *(also needle, etc., needl's)*

NEELE 1 FR 0.0001 REL FR 1 V 0 P
and with her neele composes | nature's own shape PER 5.ch. 5

NE'ER *(also never, nev'r, and compounds)*

/NE'ER 3 FR 0.0003 REL FR 3 V 0 P
hour | my heavy burthen /ne'er delivered. ERR 5.01.403
i make no doubt | the rest will /ne'er come in, LLL 5.02.152
/he /ne'er /had /borne /it /out /of /coventry; 2H4 4.01.133

NE'ER 226 FR 0.0255 REL FR 182 V 44 P
italy removed | i ne'er again shall see her. TMP 2.01.112
travellers ne'er did lie, | though fools at home 3.03. 26
that ne'er | dost disobey the wife of jupiter; 4.01. 76
though ne'er so black, say they have angels' TGV 3.01.103
why, ne'er repent it, if it were done so. 4.01. 30
again, | or ne'er return again into my sight. 4.04. 60
i'll ne'er be drunk whilst i live again, but in WIV 1.01.181 P
but i'll ne'er put my finger in the fire, and 1.04. 85 P
nay, i'll ne'er believe that; 2.01. 37 P
i ne'er made my will yet, i thank heaven. 3.04. 58 P
of wilderness | ne'er issu'd from his blood. MM 3.01.142
my lord, i do confess i ne'er was married, | and 5.01.184
who thinks he knows that he ne'er knew my body, 5.01.203
the one ne'er got me credit, the other mickle ERR 3.01. 45
for fear you ne'er see chain nor money more. 3.02.177
passion | ne'er brake into extremity of rage. 5.01. 48
ne'er may i look on day, nor sleep on night, 5.01.210
i ne'er saw syracusa in my life. 5.01.326
during which time he ne'er saw syracusa: 5.01.329
hath your grace ne'er a brother like you? ADO 2.01.323 P
you, she shall ne'er weigh more reasons in her 5.01.207 P
swear me to this, and i will ne'er say no. LLL 1.01. 69
white and red, | her faults will ne'er be known, 1.02.100
must shoot nearer, or he'll ne'er hit the clout. 4.01.134
is sworn | ne'er to pluck thee from thy /thorn; 4.03.110
you'll ne'er be friends with him, 'a kill'd your 5.02. 13
thy love ne'er alter till thy sweet life end! MND 2.02. 61
i have ne'er a tongue in my head, well! MV 2.02.157 P
no, we shall ne'er win at that sport, and stake 3.02.216 P
with many vows of faith, | and ne'er a true one. 5.01. 20
the clerk will ne'er wear hair on 's face that 5.01.158
i will ne'er come in your bed | until i see the 5.01.190
i shall ne'er be ware of mine own wit till i AYL 2.04. 58 P
ne'er a fantastical knave of them all shall 3.03.106 P
nor ne'er wed woman, if you be not she. 5.04.124
i ne'er drank sack in my life; SHR in.2. 6 P
ne'er ask me what raiment i'll wear, for i have in.2. 8 P
let the world slip, we shall ne'er be younger. in.2. 143 P
for i will love thee ne'er the less, my girl. 1.01. 77
ay, sir! — ne'er a whit. 1.01.235
or an old trot with ne'er a tooth in her head, 1.02. 80 P
dost thou wrong her that did ne'er wrong thee? 2.01. 27
marry, ill, to like him that ne'er it likes. AWW 1.01.152 P
you ne'er oppress'd me with a mother's groan, 1.03.147
i ne'er had worse luck in my life in my "o lord, 2.02. 57 P
cheek for ever, | we'll ne'er come there again." 2.03. 72
to the english, the french ne'er got 'em. 2.03. 95 P
and my integrity ne'er knew the crafts | that 4.02. 33
he ne'er pays after–debts, take it before, | and 4.03.226
caves, | where manners ne'er were preach'd! TN 4.01. 49
nay, i'll ne'er believe a madman till i see his 4.02.116 P
and our weak spirits ne'er been higher rear'd WT 1.02. 72
i ne'er heard yet | that any of these bolder 3.02. 54
for ne'er was dream | so like a waking. 3.03. 18
thou ne'er shalt see | thy wife paulina more." 3.03. 35
if it be ne'er so false, a true gentleman may 5.02.162 P
me | upon good friday and ne'er broke his fast. JN 1.01.235
till this time my tongue did ne'er pronounce, 3.01.307
and creep time ne'er so slow, | yet it shall 3.03. 31
and ne'er have spoke a loving word to you; 4.01. 51
and that high royalty was ne'er pluck'd off; 4.02. 5
the faiths of men ne'er stained with revolt; 4.02. 6
and let him ne'er speak more | that speaks thy R2 2.01.230
we three here part that ne'er shall meet again. 2.02.143
that is not forgot | which ne'er i did remember. 2.03. 38
my lord, wise men ne'er sit and wail their woes, 3.02.178
being ne'er so little urg'd, another way | to 5.01. 64
better far off than, near, be ne'er the near. 5.01. 88
which the proud soul ne'er pays but to the proud 1H4 1.03. 9
there is ne'er a king christen could be better 2.01. 16 P
why, they will allow us ne'er a jordan, and then 2.01. 19 P
henceforth ne'er look on me. 2.04.446 P
ne'er seen but wond'red at, and so my state, 3.02. 57
meet and ne'er part till one drop down a corse. 4.01.123
tilly–fally, sir john, ne'er tell me; 2H4 2.04. 83 P
i'll ne'er bear a base mind. 3.02.235 P
i shall ne'er see such a fellow. 3.02.286 P
and i'll be sworn 'a ne'er saw him but once in 3.02.322 P
cut, he may be ransom'd, and we ne'er the wiser. H5 4.01.194 P
and crispin crispian shall ne'er go by, | from 4.03. 57
be he ne'er so vile, | this day shall gentle his 4.03. 62
where ne'er from france arriv'd more happy men. 4.08.126
england ne'er lost a king of so much worth. 1H6 1.01. 7
england ne'er had a king until his time: 1.01. 8
he ne'er lift up his hand but conquered. 1.01. 16
and ne'er throughout the year to church thou 1.01. 42
i would ne'er have fled, | but that they left me 1.02. 23
else ne'er could they hold out so as they do. 1.02. 43
and while i live, i'll ne'er fly from a man. 1.02.103
else ne'er could he so long protract his speech. 1.02.120
henry, our late sovereign, ne'er could brook? 1.03. 24
his sword did ne'er leave striking in the field. 1.04. 81
more blessed hap did ne'er befall our state. 1.06. 10
ne'er heard i of a warlike enterprise | more 2.01. 44
ne'er trust me then; 2.02. 48
out, | though ne'er so cunningly you smother it. 4.01.110
he that flies so will ne'er return again. 4.05. 19
it shall be so, disdain they ne'er so much. 5.03. 98
and otherwise will henry ne'er presume. 5.05. 22
a man that ne'er saw in his life before. 2H6 2.01. 63
and my consent ne'er ask'd herein before? 2.04. 72
why then dame /margaret was ne'er thy joy. 3.02. 79
with the heart there cools and ne'er returneth 3.02.166
nay, it shall ne'er be said, while england 4.10. 42
ne'er shall this blood be wiped from thy point, 4.10. 69
but ne'er till now his scandal of retire. 3H6 2.01.150
ne'er may he live to see a sunshine day | that 2.01.187
that ne'er shall dine unless thou yield the 2.02.128
and ne'er was agamemnon's brother wrong'd | by 2.02.148
death | take on with me, and ne'er be satisfied! 2.05.104
shed seas of tears, and ne'er be satisfied! 2.05.106
for from my heart thine image ne'er shall go; 2.05.116
lords, wise men ne'er sit and wail their loss, 5.04. 1
and ne'er have stol'n the breech from lancaster. 5.05. 24
and men ne'er spend their fury on a child. 5.05. 57
petitioners for blood thou ne'er put'st back. 5.05. 80
ne'er spurr'd their coursers at the trumpet's 5.07. 9
go tread the path that thou shalt ne'er return: R3 1.01.117
for further life in this world i ne'er hope, H8 2.01. 69
that pardons all offenses | malice ne'er meant. 2.02. 68
will, much better | she ne'er had known pomp! 2.03. 13
one that ne'er dream'd a joy beyond his pleasure 3.01.135
but this fellow | let me ne'er see again. 4.02.108
and, let me tell you, it will ne'er be well — 5.01. 29
let me ne'er hope to see a chine again, | and 5.03. 26
will this gear ne'er be mended? TRO 1.01. 6 P
ne'er look, ne'er look, the eagles are gone; 1.02.243 P
ne'er look, ne'er look, the eagles are gone; 1.02.243 P
paris should ne'er retract what he hath done, 2.02.141
yet ne'er the less, | my spritely brethren, i 2.02.189
come, beshrew your heart, you'll ne'er be good, 4.02. 29
would thou hadst ne'er been born! 4.02. 86 P
they ne'er car'd for us yet. COR 1.01. 79 P
which ne'er came from the lungs, but even thus 1.01.108
the mouse ne'er shunn'd the cat as they did 1.06. 44
have flatter'd the people, who ne'er lov'd them; 2.02. 8 P
say you ne'er had done't | (harp on that still) 2.03.251
well assur'd | they ne'er did service for't; 3.01.122
got on the antiates | was ne'er distributed. 3.03. 5
ne'er through an arch so hurried the blown tide, 5.04. 47
hadst thou in person ne'er offended me, | even TIT 2.03.161
ne'er let my heart know merry cheer indeed 2.03.188
is, for ne'er till now | was i a child to fear i 2.03.220
well, more or less, or ne'er a whit at all, 4.02. 53
ne'er saw her match since first the world begun. ROM 1.02. 93
the game was ne'er so fair, and i am /done. 1.04. 39
for i ne'er saw true beauty till this night. 1.05. 53
did you ne'er hear say, | "two may keep counsel, 2.04.196
will ne'er wear out the everlasting flint; 2.06. 17
to prison, eyes, ne'er look on liberty! 3.02. 58
no sudden mean of death, though ne'er so mean, 3.03. 45
for, by my soul, i'll ne'er acknowledge thee, 3.05.193
that he dares ne'er come back to challenge you; 3.05.214
all night for lesser cause, and ne'er been sick. 4.04. 10
for i should ne'er flatter thee. TIM 1.02. 39 P
honest water, which ne'er left man i' th' mire. 1.02. 59
friends, if we should ne'er have need of 'em? 1.02. 96 P
living, should we ne'er have use for 'em; 1.02. 98 P
that man might ne'er be wretched for his mind. 1.02.164
kingdoms to my friends, | and ne'er be weary. 1.02.221
told him on't, but i could ne'er get him from't. 3.01. 28 P
i should ne'er have denied his occasion so many 3.02. 23 P
he ne'er drinks | but timon's silver treads upon 3.02. 70
that were ne'er acquainted with their wards 3.03. 37
and ne'er prefer his injuries to his heart, | to 3.05. 34
(for i must ever doubt, though ne'er so sure), 4.03.507
ne'er see thou man, and let me ne'er see thee. 4.03.536
ne'er see thou man, and let me ne'er see thee. 4.03.536
you that, i'll ne'er look you i' th' face again. JC 1.02.281 P
threaten'd me | ne'er look'd but on my back; 2.02. 11
caesar was ne'er so much your enemy | as that 2.02.112
what, man, ne'er pull your hat upon your brows; MAC 4.03.208
what, will these hands ne'er be clean? 5.01. 43 P
nor sense to ecstasy was ne'er so thrall'd | but HAM 3.04. 74
how e'er my haps, my joys /were ne'er /begun. 4.03. 68
against thine enemies, ne'er /fear'd to lose it, LR 1.01.156
"fools had ne'er less grace in a year, | for 1.04.166
arrant whore, | ne'er turns the key to th' poor. 2.04. 53
the safer sense will ne'er accommodate | his 4.06. 81
if not, i'll ne'er trust medicine. 5.03. 96
a fuller blast ne'er shook our battlements. OTH 2.01. 6
which till to–night | i ne'er might say before. 2.03.236
so sweet was ne'er so fatal. 5.02. 20
perchance, iago, i will ne'er go home. 5.02.197
ebb'd man, ne'er lov'd till ne'er worth love, ANT 1.04. 43
ebb'd man, ne'er lov'd till ne'er worth love, 1.04. 43
whom ne'er the word of "no" woman heard speak, 2.02.223
pompey, would ne'er have made this treaty. 2.06. 82 P
but i'll ne'er out. 2.07. 30 P
if this division chance, ne'er stood between, 3.04. 13
honor, ne'er before | did violate so itself. 3.10. 22
ne'er long'd my mother so | to see me first, as CYM 3.04. 2
thing | more slavish did i ne'er than answering 4.02. 73
who ne'er wore rowel | nor iron on his heel! 4.04. 39
ne'er thank thy master. 5.05. 96
a nobler sir ne'er liv'd | 'twixt sky and ground 5.05.145
posthumus, | you ne'er kill'd imogen till now! 5.05.231
ne'er mother | rejoic'd deliverance more. 5.05.369
subjects punish'd that ne'er thought offense: PER 1.02. 28
time of both this truth shall ne'er convince, 1.02.123
and strangers ne'er beheld but wond'red at; 1.04. 25
when — the which i hope shall ne'er be seen — 1.04.105
them, they ne'er come but i look to be wash'd. 2.01. 26 P
such a night as this | till now i ne'er endured. 3.02. 6
my wedded lord, i ne'er shall see again, | a 3.04. 9
slaughter | the sun and moon ne'er look'd upon! 4.03. 3
twice the worth of her she had ne'er come here. 4.06. 2 P
have spoke so well, ne'er dreamt thou couldst. 4.06.103
maid, | my lord, that ne'er before invited eyes, 5.01. 85
and so fair, | let honest men ne'er love again. TNK 2.02.231
into whose port | ne'er ent'red wanton sound) to 5.01.148
twenty strike of oats, but he'll ne'er have her. 5.02. 65
whose sinowy neck in battle ne'er did bow, | who VEN 99
a nurse's song ne'er pleas'd her babe so well. 974
ne'er saw the beauteous livery that he wore — 1107
ne'er settled equally, but high or low, | that 1139
hasty spring still blasts and ne'er grows old! LUC 49
thee, | but they ne'er meet with opportunity. 903
they buy thy help, but sin ne'er gives a fee, 913
sworn | ne'er to pluck thee from thy /thorn, PP 16.12
/lass, thy like ne'er was | for a sweet content, 17.33
such heavenly touches ne'er touch'd earthly SON 17. 8
for i must ne'er love him whom thou dost hate. 89.14
yet this shall i ne'er know, but live in doubt, 144.13
till now did ne'er invite, nor never vow. LC 182
harm have i done to them, but ne'er was harmed, 194

NE'ER–CHANGING 1 FR 0.0001 REL FR 1 V 0 P
to his new kingdom of ne'er–changing night. R3 2.02. 46

NE'ER–CLOYING 1 FR 0.0001 REL FR 1 V 0 P
so, being full of your ne'er–cloying sweetness, SON 118. 5

/NE'ER–LUST–WEARIED 1 FR 0.0001 REL FR 1 V 0 P
widow pluck | the /ne'er–lust–wearied antony. ANT 2.01. 38

NE'ER–TOUCH'D 1 FR 0.0001 REL FR 1 V 0 P
want will perjure | the ne'er–touch'd vestal. ANT 3.12. 31

NE'ER–YET–BEATEN 1 FR 0.0001 REL FR 1 V 0 P
the ne'er–yet–beaten horse of parthia | we have ANT 3.01. 33

NEEZE 1 FR 0.0001 REL FR 1 V 0 P
and waxen in their mirth, and neeze, and swear MND 2.01. 56

NEFAS 1 FR 0.0001 REL FR 1 V 0 P
sit fas aut nefas, till i find the stream | to TIT 2.01.133

NEGATION 1 FR 0.0001 REL FR 1 V 0 P
why, my negation hath no taste of madness. TRO 5.02.127

NEGATIVE 1 FR 0.0001 REL FR 1 V 0 P
wilt confess, | or else be impudently negative, WT 1.02.274

NEGATIVES 1 FR 0.0001 REL FR 0 V 1 P
as kisses, if your four negatives make your two TN 5.01. 21 P

NEGLECT 24 FR 0.0027 REL FR 22 V 2 P
made me neglect my studies, lose my time, | war TGV 1.01. 67
but since she did neglect her looking–glass, 4.04.152
which, out of my neglect, was never done. 5.04. 89 P
that thou neglect me not, with that opinion MM 5.01. 50
that cupid will impose for my neglect | of his LLL 3.01.202
spurn me, strike me, | neglect me, lose me; MND 2.01.206
lose and neglect the creeping hours of time; AYL 2.07.112
and thrown into neglect the pompous court? 5.04.182
wherefore, gentle maiden, | do you neglect them? WT 4.04. 86
and for this cause a while we must neglect | our 1H4 1.01.101
he loves thee, and thou dost neglect him, thomas 2H4 4.04. 21
what infinite heart's–ease | must kings neglect, H5 4.01.237
(as well we may, if not through your neglect), 2H6 5.02. 80
trust | my absence doth neglect no great design, R3 3.04. 24
good cromwell, | neglect him not; H8 3.02.420
on your heads | clap round fines for neglect. 5.03. 80
you one), | nor construe any further my neglect, JC 1.02. 45
where i shall first begin, | and both neglect. HAM 3.03. 43

'tis strange that from their cold'st neglect LR 1.01.254
i have perceiv'd a most faint neglect of late, 1.04. 68 P
infirmity doth still neglect all office 2.04.106
so then we do neglect | the thing we have, and LUC 152
for thy neglect of truth in beauty dy'd? SON 101. 2
mark how with my neglect i do dispense: 112.12
NEGLECTED 17 FR 0.0019 REL FR 16 V 1 P
now puts the drowsy and neglected act | freshly MM 1.02.170
for your fair sakes have we neglected time, LLL 5.02.755
a beard neglected, which you have not — but i AYL 3.02.375 P
disgrace | neglected my sworn duty in that case. R2 1.01.134
yield must be embrac'd, | and not neglected; 3.02. 30
left by the fatal and neglected english | upon H5 2.04. 13
if once it be neglected, ten to one | we shall 1H6 5.04.157
gone by him, or at least | strangely neglected? H8 3.02. 11
the specialty of rule hath been neglected, | and TRO 1.03. 78
for the demand of our neglected tribute. HAM 3.01.170
of his grief | sprung from neglected love. 3.01.178
must excuse my manners | that so neglected you. OTH 5.01. 95
neglected, rather; ANT 2.02. 89
as jewels lose their glory if neglected, | so PER 2.02. 12
more proclaiming | our suit shall be neglected. TNK 1.01.175
neglected all, with swift intent he goes | to LUC 46
whilst her neglected child holds her in chase, SON 143. 5
NEGLECTING 3 FR 0.0003 REL FR 3 V 0 P
i, thus neglecting worldly ends, all dedicated TMP 1.02. 89
and the neglecting it | may do much danger. ROM 5.02. 19
neglecting an attempt of ease and gain | to wake OTH 1.03. 29
NEGLECTINGLY 1 FR 0.0001 REL FR 1 V 0 P
grief and my impatience | answer'd neglectingly, 1H4 1.03. 52
NEGLECTION 3 FR 0.0003 REL FR 3 V 0 P
sleeping neglection doth betray to loss | the 1H6 4.03. 49
and this neglection of degree it is | that by a TRO 1.03.127
if neglection | should therein make me vile, the PER 3.03. 20
NEGLECT'ST 1 FR 0.0001 REL FR 1 V 0 P
if thou neglect'st or dost unwillingly | what i TMP 1.02.368
/NEGLIGENCE 1 FR 0.0001 REL FR 1 V 0 P
/wise /in /our /negligence, /have /secret /feet LR 3.01. 32
NEGLIGENCE 14 FR 0.0015 REL FR 12 V 2 P
this is thy negligence. MND 3.02.345
you either fear his humor or my negligence, that TN 1.04. 5 P
it is something of my negligence, nothing of my 3.04.256 P
these no man is free | but that his negligence, WT 1.02.252
i play'd the fool, it was my negligence, | not 1.02.257
o negligence! H8 3.02.213
my rest and negligence befriends thee now, | but TRO 5.06. 17
that both the worlds i give to negligence, | let HAM 4.05.135
put on what weary negligence you please, | you LR 1.03. 12
dire yell | as when, by night and negligence, OTH 1.01. 76
she let it drop by negligence, | and, to th' 3.03.311
or that the negligence may well be laugh'd at, CYM 1.01. 66
"the more to blame my sluggard negligence. LUC 1278
though slackly braided in loose negligence. LC 35
NEGLIGENT 7 FR 0.0008 REL FR 6 V 1 P
negligent student! learn her by heart. LLL 3.01. 35 P
in my serious trust | and therein negligent; WT 1.02.247
i may be negligent, foolish, and fearful: 1.02.250
o, negligent and heedless discipline! 1H6 4.02. 44
all, | lay negligent and loose regard upon him. TRO 3.03. 41
you were wrong led | and we in negligent danger. ANT 3.06. 81
is never more admir'd | than by the negligent. 3.07. 25
NEGOTIATE 2 FR 0.0002 REL FR 1 V 1 P
let every eye negotiate for itself, | and trust ADO 2.01.178
from your lord to negotiate with my face? TN 1.05.232 P
NEGOTIATIONS 1 FR 0.0001 REL FR 1 V 0 P
that their negotiations all must slack, TRO 3.03. 24
NEGRO'S 1 FR 0.0001 REL FR 0 V 1 P
you can the getting up of the negro's belly; MV 3.05. 38 P
NEIGH 8 FR 0.0009 REL FR 5 V 3 P
neigh abbreviated "ne." LLL 5.01. 23 P
and neigh, and bark, and grunt, and roar, and MND 3.01.110
his neigh is like the bidding of a monarch, and H5 3.07. 27 P
hark how our steeds for present service neigh! 4.02. 8
horses /did neigh, and dying men did groan, JC 2.02. 23
horse, you'll have your nephews neigh to you; OTH 1.01.112 P
that when they hear their roman horses neigh, CYM 4.04. 17
shall neigh (no dull flesh) in his fiery race, SON 51.11
NEIGHBOR *(also nebor)*
/NEIGHBOR 1 FR 0.0001 REL FR 0 V 1 P
/neighbor, this is a gift very grateful, i am SHR 2.01. 76 P
NEIGHBOR 46 FR 0.0052 REL FR 23 V 23 P
well, give them their charge, neighbor dogberry. ADO 3.03. 7 P
come hither, neighbor seacole. 3.03. 13 P
come, neighbor. 3.03. 87 P
what would you with me, honest neighbor? 3.05. 1 P
are odorous — palabras, neighbor verges. 3.05. 16 P
well said, i' faith, neighbor verges. 3.05. 36 P
all men are not alike, alas, good neighbor! 3.05. 40 P
indeed, neighbor, he comes too short of you. 3.05. 41 P
come, neighbor. 5.01.327 P
neighbor vocatur "nebor"; LLL 5.01. 23 P
warily | i stole into a neighbor thicket by, 5.02. 94
he is a marvellous good neighbor, faith, and a 5.02.582 P
think you of the scottish lord, his neighbor? MV 1.02. 78 P
sun, | to whom i am a neighbor and near bred. 2.01. 3
when such a one as she, such is her neighbor? AYL 2.07. 78
west of this place, down in the neighbor bottom, 4.03. 78
good morrow, neighbor baptista. SHR 2.01. 39 P
good morrow, neighbor gremio. 2.01. 40 P
i am your neighbor, and was suitor first. 2.01.334
adieu, good neighbor. 2.01.399
i have told my neighbor how you have been AWW 3.05. 14 P
and his pond fish'd by his next neighbor — by WT 1.02.195
next neighbor — by | sir smile, his neighbor. 1.02.196
me, and thy places shall | still neighbor mine. 1.02.449
and this my neighbor too? 4.04.370
such neighbor nearness to our sacred blood R2 1.01.119
come, neighbor mugs, we'll call up the gentlemen 1H4 2.01. 44 P
come, neighbor, the boy shall lead our horses 2.02. 78 P
i' good faith — "neighbor quickly," says he — 2H4 2.04. 87 P
was by then — "neighbor quickly," says he, 2.04. 89 P
now, neighbor confines, purge you of your scum! 4.05.123
who hath been still a giddy neighbor to us; H5 1.02.145
though france himself and such another neighbor 3.06.157
for our bad neighbor makes us early stirrers, 4.01. 6
here, neighbor horner, i drink to you in a cup 2H6 2.03. 59 P
and fear not, neighbor, you shall do well enough 2.03. 60 P
and here, neighbor, here's a cup of charneco. 2.03. 62 P
and here's a pot of good double beer, neighbor. 2.03. 65 P
good morrow, neighbor, whither away so fast? R3 2.03. 1
no more shall be the neighbor to my counsels. 4.02. 43
the secrets of neighbor pandar | have not more TRO 4.02. 72
sweeten with thy breath | this neighbor air, and ROM 2.06. 27
forgetting thy great deeds when neighbor states, TIM 4.03. 95
i'll lug the guts into the neighbor room. HAM 3.04.212
and my leonatus | our neighbor shepherd's son! CYM 1.01.150
that all the neighbor caves, as seeming troubled VEN 830
NEIGHBOR'D 2 FR 0.0002 REL FR 2 V 0 P
best | neighbor'd by fruit of baser quality; H5 1.01. 62
shall to my bosom | be as well neighbor'd, LR 1.01.119
NEIGHBORED 1 FR 0.0001 REL FR 1 V 0 P
and sith so neighbored to his youth and havior, HAM 2.02. 12
NEIGHBORHOOD 3 FR 0.0003 REL FR 3 V 0 P
hath shook and trembled at th' ill neighborhood. H5 1.02.154
plant neighborhood and christian-like accord 5.02.353
domestic awe, night-rest, and neighborhood, TIM 4.01. 17
NEIGHBORING 5 FR 0.0005 REL FR 3 V 2 P
he hath a smack of all neighboring languages; AWW 4.01. 16 P
tenants, friends, and neighboring gentlemen. 1H4 3.01. 89
know strange fowl light upon neighboring ponds. CYM 1.04. 89 P
we have descried, upon our neighboring shore, PER 1.04. 60
and so in ours, some neighboring nation, 1.04. 65
NEIGHBORLY 2 FR 0.0002 REL FR 1 V 1 P
that he hath a neighborly charity in him, for he MV 1.02. 79 P
thou hast my love; is not that neighborly? AYL 3.05. 90
NEIGHBOR'S 4 FR 0.0004 REL FR 1 V 3 P
your wive's wit going to your neighbor's bed. AYL 4.01.168 P
a man cannot lie with his neighbor's wife, but R3 1.04.137 P
my estate and my neighbor's on th' approbation CYM 1.04.123 P
his nose being shadowed by his neighbor's ear; LUC 1416
NEIGHBORS' 1 FR 0.0001 REL FR 1 V 0 P
civil wounds plough'd up with neighbors' sword; R2 1.03.128
NEIGHBORS 23 FR 0.0026 REL FR 12 V 11 P
proceedings all my neighbors shall cry aim. WIV 3.02. 44 P
one word more, honest neighbors. ADO 3.03. 91 P
neighbors, you are tedious. 3.05. 18 P
that liv'd in the time of good neighbors. 5.02. 77 P
that some honest neighbors will not make them MND 3.01.145 P
now is the moon used between the two neighbors. 5.01.207 P
ginger or made her neighbors believe she wept MV 3.01. 9 P
neighbors and friends, though bride and SHR 3.02.246
and beyond the imagination of his neighbors, is WT 4.02. 39 P
no, by my faith, i must live among my neighbors; 2H4 2.04. 74 P
will yearly on the vigil feast his neighbors, H5 4.03. 45
can any of your neighbors tell, kate? 5.02.196 P
neighbors, god speed! R3 2.03. 6
cheer your neighbors. H8 1.04. 41
as of late days our neighbors, | the upper 5.02. 64
the merry songs of peace to all his neighbors. 5.04. 35
masters, my good friends, mine honest neighbors, COR 1.01. 62
good-en, our neighbors, 4.06. 20
farewell, kind neighbors! 4.06. 24
home to rome, | and die among our neighbors. 5.03.173
every putting-by mine honest neighbors shouted. JC 1.02.231 P
hush, my gentle neighbors! PER 3.02.106
but lo from forth a copse that neighbors by, | a VEN 259
NEIGHBOR-STAINED 1 FR 0.0001 REL FR 1 V 0 P
profaners of this neighbor-stained steel — ROM 1.01. 82
NEIGH'D 1 FR 0.0001 REL FR 1 V 0 P
who neigh'd so high that what i would have spoke ANT 1.05. 49
/NEIGHING 1 FR 0.0001 REL FR 1 V 0 P
/their /neighing /coursers /daring /of /the 2H4 4.01.117
NEIGHING 5 FR 0.0005 REL FR 5 V 0 P
beguile, | neighing in likeness of a filly foal; MND 2.01. 46
mad bounds, bellowing and neighing loud, | which MV 5.01. 73
battle heard | loud 'larums, neighing steeds, SHR 1.02.206
farewell the neighing steed and the shrill trump OTH 3.03.351
he lisps in 's neighing able to entice | a TNK 5.02. 66
NEIGHS 5 FR 0.0005 REL FR 5 V 0 P
in high and boastful neighs | piercing the H5 4.pr. 10
the neighs of horse to tell of her approach, ANT 3.06. 45
and forth she rushes, snorts, and neighs aloud. VEN 262
imperiously he leaps, he neighs, he bounds, 265
he looks upon his love, and neighs unto her, 307
NEITHER 210 FR 0.0237 REL FR 128 V 82 P
here's neither bush nor shrub to bear off any TMP 2.02. 18 P
nor go neither; 3.02. 19 P
lie like dogs, and yet say nothing neither. 3.02. 20 P
nay, that cannot be so neither; TGV 2.03. 16 P
no, neither. 2.05. 17 P
duty, | neither regarding that she is my child, 3.01. 70
neither. 3.01.196 P
but neither bended knees, pure hands held up, 3.01.231
i care not for that neither, because i love 3.01.341 P
neither. 5.02. 33
anne's mind — that's neither here nor there. WIV 1.04.106 P
become nothing else, nor that well neither. 3.03. 60 P
neither press, coffer, chest, trunk, well, vault 4.02. 61 P
and i paid nothing for it neither, but was paid 4.05. 61 P
that neither, singly, can be manifested, 4.06. 15
and neither heaven nor man grieve at the mercy. MM 2.02. 50
thou hast neither heat, affection, limb, nor 3.01. 37
the smallest article of it, neither in time, 4.02.104 P
since i see you fearful, that neither my coat, 4.02.189 P
neither, my lord. 5.01.176 P
neither maid, widow, nor wife? 5.01.177 P
for many of them are neither maid, widow, nor 5.01.180 P
neither my husband nor the slave return'd, ERR 2.01. 1
and the wherefore is neither rhyme nor reason? 2.02. 48
here is neither cheer, sir, nor welcome: 3.01. 66
which was best, we shall part with neither. 3.01. 67
but neither chain nor goldsmith came to me: 4.01. 24
neither. 5.01. 94
neither disturbed with the effect of wine, | nor 5.01.215
neither. 5.01.302
that i neither feel how she should be lov'd nor ADO 1.01.230 P
the guards are but slightly basted on neither. 1.01.287 P
neither, my lord. 2.01.292 P
the count is neither sad, nor sick, nor merry, 2.01.293 P
with a kiss, and let not him speak neither. 2.01.311 P
no, nor i neither, but most wonderful that she 2.03. 95 P
not so neither, but know that i have to-night 3.03.144 P
this was no damsel neither, sir, she was a LLL 1.01.292 P
it would neither serve for the writing nor the 1.02.113 P
but say that he, or we, as neither have, 2.01.132
be very unlearned, neither savoring of poetry, 4.02.158 P
if it mar nothing neither, | the treason and you 4.03.189
nor understood none neither, sir. 5.01.151 P
neither of either; 5.02.459
part, | neither intitled in the other's heart. 5.02.812
not so, neither; MND 3.01.149 P
not in love neither? MV 1.01. 47
neither have i money nor commodity | to raise a 1.01.178
i may neither choose who i would, nor refuse who 1.02. 23 P
he hath neither latin, french, nor italian, and 1.02. 69 P
albeit i neither lend nor borrow | by taking nor 1.03. 61
methoughts you said you neither lend nor borrow 1.03. 69
a man | is not so estimable, profitable neither, 1.03.166
and that is but a kind of bastard hope neither. 3.05. 8 P
not so, sir, neither, i know my duty. 3.05. 54 P
she made me vow | that i should neither sell, 4.01.443
sweetly as the lark | when neither is attended; 5.01.103
and neither man nor master would take aught 5.01.183
and yet give no thousand crowns neither. AYL 1.01. 87 P
nor no further in sport, neither, than with 1.02. 28 P
peradventure this is not fortune's work neither, 1.02. 52 P
neither his daughter, if we judge by manners, 1.02.271
neither rhyme nor reason can express how much. 3.02.398 P
i have neither the scholar's melancholy, which 4.01. 10 P
neither call the giddiness of it in question, 5.02. 5 P
neither do i labor for a greater esteem than may 5.02. 56 P
am i in then, that am neither a good epilogue, ep 8 P
i see she's like to have neither cap nor gown. SHR 4.03. 93
i will neither be fac'd nor brav'd. 4.03.125 P
neither art thou the worse | for this poor 4.03.179
in the balance that i could neither believe nor AWW 1.03.125 P
nay, i'll fit you, | and not be all day neither. 2.01. 91
hand, and say nothing, has neither leg, hands, 2.02. 11 P
but a trifle neither, in good faith, if the 2.02. 34 P
that the first face of neither on the start 3.02. 50
i neither can nor will deny | but that i know 5.03.166
it was not lent me neither. 5.03.273
not match above her degree, neither in estate, TN 1.03.110 P
not so, neither, but i am resolv'd on two points 1.05. 22 P
nor i neither. 2.05.186 P
master cesario, nor this is not my nose neither: 4.01. 8 P
it shall not neither. WT 2.03.158
neither. 4.04.305
what, neither? 4.04.305
neither. 4.04.305
he neither does nor shall. 4.04.393
no honest man, neither to his father nor to me, 4.04.701 P
weigh so even, | we hold our town for neither; JN 2.01.333
we will attend to neither. 5.02.163
of neither, girl; R2 3.04. 12
but neither my good word nor princely favor. 5.06. 42
there's neither honesty, manhood, nor good 1H4 1.02.139 P
neither, 'tis a woman's fault. 3.01.240 P
there's neither faith, truth, nor womanhood in 3.03.110 P
she's neither fish nor flesh, a man knows not 3.03.127 P
but i will inset you neither in gold nor silver, 2H4 1.02. 17 P
foin like any devil, he will spare neither man, 2.01. 16 P
no, nor i neither, i'll be at your elbow. 2.01. 20 P
that makes a still-stand, running neither way. 2.03. 64
nobly are subdued, | and neither party loser. 4.02. 91
and but in purged judgment trusting neither? H5 2.02.136
if they'll do neither, we will come to them, 4.07. 60
for the one i have neither words nor measure; 5.02.134 P
that, having neither the voice nor the heart of 5.02.287 P
shalt well perceive | that neither in birth, or 1H6 5.01. 59
'twas neither charles nor yet the duke i nam'd, 5.04. 77
having neither subject, wealth, nor diadem. 2H6 4.01. 82
i fear neither sword nor fire. 4.02. 59 P
neither the king, nor he that loves him best, 3H6 1.01. 45
and neither by treason nor hostility | to seek 1.01.199
but thou art neither like thy sire nor dam, 2.02.135
can neither call it perfect day nor night. 2.05. 4
breast, | yet neither conqueror nor conquered; 2.05. 12
i, that have neither pity, love, nor fear. 5.06. 68
i know it pleaseth neither of us well. R3 1.01.113
die neither mother, wife, nor england's queen! 1.03.208
urge neither charity nor shame to me. 1.03.273
this prince hath neither claim'd it nor deserv'd 3.01. 51
neither good nor bad! 4.04.459
crown, neither allied | to eminent assistants, H8 1.01. 61
which neither know | my faculties nor person, 1.02. 72
'neither the king nor 's heirs | (tell you the 1.02.168
not for that neither; 2.03. 1
which we have not done neither: ep 7
so 'tis, i must confess) — not brown neither — TRO 1.02. 94 P
nor nothing monstrous neither? 3.02. 76 P
neither gave to me | good word nor look. 3.03.143
who neither looks upon the heaven nor earth, 4.05.281
neither foolish in our stands | nor cowardly in COR 1.06. 2
you know neither me, yourselves, nor any thing. 2.01. 67 P
for coriolanus neither to care whether they love 2.02. 12 P
'twixt doing them neither good nor harm; 2.02. 18 P
neither will they bate | one jot of ceremony. 2.02.140
neither supreme, how soon confusion | may enter 3.01.110
nay, not so neither; 4.05.167 P
we hear not of him, neither need we fear him; 4.06. 1
i neither care for th' world nor your general; 5.02.102 P
i neither know it, sir, nor can learn of him. ROM 1.01.144
neither, fair maid, if either thee dislike. 2.02. 61
himself, | for he does neither affect company, TIM 1.01. 31
that he will neither know how to maintain it, 2.02. 2
neither wish i | you take much pains to mend. 5.01. 88
yet 'twas not a crown neither, 'twas one of JC 1.02.238 P
nor for yours neither. 2.01.237
for i have neither /wit, nor words, nor worth, 3.02.221
sleep shall neither night nor day | hang upon MAC 1.03. 19
who neither beg nor fear | your favors nor your 1.03. 60
neither to you nor any one, having no witness to 5.01. 17 P
neither a borrower nor a lender /be, | for /loan HAM 1.03. 75
neither, my lord. 2.02.231 P
man delights not me — nor women neither, though 2.02.309 P
be not too tame neither, but let your own 3.02. 16 P
neither having th' accent of christians nor the 3.02. 31 P
quantity, | in neither aught, or in extremity. 3.02.168
of their nation | he swore had neither motion, 4.07.101
for none, neither. 5.01.133 P
arithmetic of memory, and yet but yaw neither, 5.02.115 P

nothing, neither way. 5.02.301
that curiosity in neither can make choice of LR 1.01. 6 P
nor tripp'd neither, you base football player. 1.04. 86 P
nor i neither; 1.05. 27 P
to rail on one that is neither known of thee nor 2.02. 26 P
a night pities neither wise men nor fools. 3.02. 13 P
perpetual displeasure neither to speak of him, 3.03. 5 P
or neither? 5.01. 58
neither can be enjoy'd | if both remain alive: 5.01. 58
neither my place, nor aught i heard of business, OTH 1.03. 53
i know not, neither; 3.04.188
dart of chance | could neither graze nor pierce? 4.01.268
'tis neither here nor there. 4.03. 59
nor i neither by this heavenly light; 4.03. 66
i am not valiant neither, | but every puny 5.02.243
i am not sorry neither, i'ld have thee live; 5.02.289
but he neither loves, | nor either cares for him ANT 2.01. 15
at the full of tide, | and neither way inclines. 3.02. 50
once be necessary, | i'll not sleep neither. 5.02. 51
not so, neither; CYM 3.04.117
thou shouldst neither want my means for thy 3.05.114 P
is as good as ajax', | when neither are alive. 4.02.253
neither know i | what is betide to cloten, but 4.03. 39
which neither here i'll keep nor bear again, 5.03. 82
many dream not to find, neither deserve, | and 5.04.130
further to boast were neither true nor modest, 5.05. 18
yet neither pleasure's art can joy my spirits, PER 1.02. 9
have neither in our hearts nor outward eyes 2.03. 25
neither is our profession any trade, it's no 4.02. 38 P
neither of these are so bad as thou art, | since 4.06.161
rain, being in't, | knows neither wet nor dry. TNK 1.01.121
if he fail, | he's neither man nor soldier. 3.06. 4
o theseus, | if unto neither thou show mercy. 3.06.173
not made in passion neither, but good heed. 3.06.232
neither heard i one question | of your name or 4.01. 15
so neither for my sake should fall untimely. 4.02. 69
are equal precious — | i could doom neither; 5.01.156
that neither could find other, get herself 5.03. 26
when neither curb would crack, girth break, nor 5.04. 74
though neither eyes nor ears to hear nor see, VEN 437
and extreme fear can neither fight nor fly, LUC 230
cheeks neither red nor pale, but mingled so 1510
yet neither may possess the claim they lay. 1794
mild as a dove, but neither true nor trusty, PP 7. 2
bad in the best, though excellent in neither. 7.18
ah, neither be my share! 14. 1
wiser head, | neither too young nor yet unwed. 18. 6
double name | neither two nor one was called. PHT 40
together, | to themselves yet either neither, 43
neither in inward worth nor outward fair | can SON 16.11
no, neither he, nor his compeers by night 86. 7
be, | where neither party is nor true nor kind: LC 186
in thee hath neither sting, knot, nor confine, 265

NELL 16 FR 0.0018 REL FR 10 V 6 P
nell, sir; ERR 3.02.109 P
he swears thou art to marry his sister nell. 2H4 2.02.129 P
that he is married to nell quickly, and H5 2.01. 18 P
nor shall my nell keep lodgers. 2.01. 31
o nell, sweet nell, if thou dost love thy lord, 2H6 1.02. 17
o nell, sweet nell, if thou dost love thy lord, 1.02. 17
i go. come, nell, thou wilt ride with us? 1.02. 59
sweet nell, ill can thy noble mind abrook | the 2.04. 10
be patient, gentle nell, forget this grief. 2.04. 26
ah, nell, forbear! 2.04. 58
thy greatest help is quiet, gentle nell. 2.04. 67
my nell, i take my leave; 2.04. 74
nell, he is full of harmony. TRO 3.01. 52 P
arm'd to-day, but my nell would not have it so. 3.01.137 P
let the porter let in susan grindstone and nell. ROM 1.05. 9 P
and freckled nell — that never fail'd her TNK 3.05. 27

/NEMEAN 1 FR 0.0001 REL FR 1 V 0 P
he tumbled down upon his /nemean hide, | and TNK 1.01. 68

NEMEAN 2 FR 0.0002 REL FR 2 V 0 P
thus dost thou hear the nemean lion roar LLL 4.01. 88
this body | as hardy as the nemean lion's nerve. HAM 1.04. 83

NEMESIS 1 FR 0.0001 REL FR 1 V 0 P
your kingdom's terror and black nemesis? 1H6 4.07. 78

NEOPTOLEMUS 1 FR 0.0001 REL FR 1 V 0 P
not neoptolemus so mirable, | on whose bright TRO 4.05.142

NEPHEW 29 FR 0.0032 REL FR 27 V 2 P
'twas of his nephew proteus, your son. TGV 1.03. 3
could not be my son-in-law, | be yet my nephew. ADO 5.01.288
the young german, the duke of saxony's nephew? MV 1.02. 85 P
when your young nephew titus lost his leg. TN 5.01. 63
hand, | thy nephew and right royal sovereign. JN 1.01. 15
brother, the king hath made your nephew mad. 1H4 1.03.138
tell your nephew | the prince of wales doth join 5.01. 85
o no, my nephew must not know, sir richard, 5.02. 1
and, nephew, challeng'd you to single fight. 5.02. 46
charles duke of orleance, nephew to the king, H5 4.08. 76
but tell me, keeper, will my nephew come? 1H6 2.05. 17
my lord, your loving nephew now is come. 2.05. 33
your nephew, late-despised richard, comes. 2.05. 36
that cause, fair nephew, that imprison'd me 2.05. 55
depos'd his nephew richard, edward's son, | the 2.05. 64
with silence, nephew, be thou politic. 2.05.101
nephew, what means this passionate discourse, 2H6 1.01.104
when i imagine ill | against my king and nephew, 1.02. 20
and kiss your princely nephew, brothers both. 3H6 5.07. 27
us and the emperor (the queen's great nephew), H8 2.02. 25
my royal nephew, and your name capuchius. 4.02.110
a lord of troyan blood, nephew to hector, | they TRO 1.02. 13
my nephew mutius' deeds do plead for him, | he TIT 1.01.356
inter | his noble nephew here in virtue's nest, 1.01.376
go, gentle marcus, to thy nephew lucius; 5.02.122
rome's emperor, and nephew, break the parle, 5.03. 19
speak, nephew, were you by when it began? ROM 1.01.105
this is one lucianus, nephew to the king. HAM 3.02.244 P
the nephew to old norway, fortinbras. 4.04. 14

NEPHEW'S 3 FR 0.0003 REL FR 3 V 0 P
my nephew's trespass may be well forgot, | it 1H4 5.02. 16
scarcely hears | of this his nephew's purpose — HAM 1.02. 30
he sent out to suppress | his nephew's levies, 2.02. 62

NEPHEWS' 1 FR 0.0001 REL FR 1 V 0 P
thy nephews' souls bid thee despair and die! R3 5.03.149

NEPHEWS 5 FR 0.0005 REL FR 4 V 1 P
and welcome, nephews, from successful wars, TIT 1.01.172
the tribune and his nephews kneel for grace, | i 1.01.480
to ransom my two nephews from their death; 3.01.172
horse, you'll have your nephews neigh to you; OTH 1.01.112 P
they are sisters' children, nephews to the king. TNK 1.04. 16

NEPTUNE 12 FR 0.0013 REL FR 12 V 0 P
of sulphurous roaring the most mighty neptune TMP 1.02.204
printless foot | do chase the ebbing neptune, 5.01. 35
opening on neptune with fair blessed beams, MND 3.02.392
the green neptune | a ram and bleated; WT 4.04. 28
(at least ungentle) of the dreadful neptune, 5.01.154
back the envious siege | of wat'ry neptune, is R2 2.01. 63
to harbor fled, | or made a toast for neptune. TRO 1.03. 45
he would not flatter neptune for his trident, COR 3.01.255
taught thee to make vast neptune weep for aye TIM 5.04. 78
let neptune hear we bid a loud farewell | to ANT 2.07.132
then give you up to the mask'd neptune and | the PER 3.03. 36
power hast turn'd | green neptune into purple, TNK 5.01. 50

NEPTUNE'S 12 FR 0.0013 REL FR 12 V 0 P
and sat with me on neptune's yellow sands, MND 2.01.126
that neptune's arms, who clippeth thee about, JN 5.02. 34
of the ocean | too wide for neptune's hips; 2H4 3.01. 51
shall dizzy with more clamor neptune's ear | in TRO 5.02.174
will all great neptune's ocean wash this blood MAC 2.02. 57
upon whose influence neptune's empire stands HAM 1.01.119
neptune's salt wash and tellus' orbed ground, 3.02.156
and o'er green neptune's back | with ships made ANT 4.14. 58
which stands | as neptune's park, ribb'd and CYM 3.01. 19
their vessel shakes | on neptune's billow; PER 3.ch. 45
striv'd | god neptune's annual feast to keep, 5.ch. 17
being on shore, honoring of neptune's triumphs, 5.01. 17

NEREIDES 1 FR 0.0001 REL FR 1 V 0 P
her /gentlewomen, like the nereides, | so many ANT 2.02.206

NERISSA 17 FR 0.0019 REL FR 14 V 3 P
by my troth, nerissa, my little body is a-weary MV 1.02. 1 P
is it not hard, nerissa, that i cannot choose 1.02. 26 P
i will do any thing, nerissa, ere i will be 1.02. 99 P
come, nerissa. 1.02.132
come draw the curtain, nerissa. 2.09. 84
come, nerissa, for i long to see | quick cupid's 2.09. 99
nerissa and the rest, stand all aloof. 3.02. 42
is this true, nerissa? 3.02.208
nerissa, cheer yond stranger, bid her welcome. 3.02.237
my maid nerissa and myself mean time | will live 3.02.309
contemplation, | only attended by nerissa here, 3.04. 29
come on, nerissa, i have work in hand | that you 3.04. 57
they shall, nerissa; 3.04. 60
go in, nerissa. 5.01.118
nerissa teaches me what to believe — | i'll die 5.01.207
was the doctor, | nerissa there her clerk. 5.01.270
that my nerissa shall be sworn on is, | whether 5.01.301

NERISSA'S 1 FR 0.0001 REL FR 1 V 0 P
thing | so sore, as keeping safe nerissa's ring. MV 5.01.307

/NERO 1 FR 0.0001 REL FR 1 V 0 P
plantagenet, i will, and like thee, /nero, 1H6 1.04. 95

NERO 3 FR 0.0003 REL FR 2 V 1 P
and nero will be tainted with remorse | to hear 3H6 3.01. 40
ever | the soul of nero enter this firm bosom, HAM 3.02.394
and tells me nero is an angler in the lake of LR 3.06. 6 P

NEROES 1 FR 0.0001 REL FR 1 V 0 P
you bloody neroes, ripping up the womb | of your JN 5.02.152

NERVE 1 FR 0.0001 REL FR 1 V 0 P
this body | as hardy as the nemean lion's nerve. HAM 1.04. 83

NERVES 9 FR 0.0010 REL FR 9 V 0 P
thy nerves are in their infancy again | and have TMP 1.02.485
by those that know the very nerves of state, MM 1.04. 53
thou great commander, nerves and bone of greece, TRO 1.03. 55
the strongest nerves and small inferior veins COR 1.01.138
that, and my firm nerves | shall never tremble. MAC 3.04.101
yet ha' we | a brain that nourishes our nerves, ANT 4.08. 21
strains his young nerves, and puts himself in CYM 3.03. 94
other instruments | to his own nerves and act; TNK 1.02. 69
unless my nerves were brass or hammered steel. SON 120. 4

NERVII 1 FR 0.0001 REL FR 1 V 0 P
in his tent, | that day he overcame the nervii. JC 3.02.173

NERVY 1 FR 0.0001 REL FR 1 V 0 P
that dark spirit, in 's nervy arm doth lie, COR 2.01.160

NESSUS 2 FR 0.0002 REL FR 1 V 1 P
for rapes and ravishments he parallels nessus. AWW 4.03.251 P
the shirt of nessus is upon me; ANT 4.12. 43

N'EST 1 FR 0.0001 REL FR 0 V 1 P
leur noces, il n'est pas la coutume de france. H5 5.02.259 P

NEST 27 FR 0.0030 REL FR 22 V 5 P
show thee a jay's nest, and instruct thee how TMP 2.02.169
far from her nest the lapwing cries away; ERR 4.02. 27
who, being overjoy'd with finding a bird's nest, ADO 2.01.223 P
who, as i take it, have stol'n his bird's nest. 2.01.231 P
world what the bird hath done to her own nest. AYL 4.01.204 P
e'en a crow a' th' same nest; AWW 4.03.286 P
a nest of traitors! WT 2.03. 82
with honey, set on the head of a wasp's nest; 4.04.785 P
to souse annoyance that comes near his nest; JN 5.02.150
did oppress our nest, | grew by our feeding to 1H4 5.01. 61
to her unguarded nest the weasel (scot) | comes H5 1.02.170
a nest of hollow bosoms, which he fills | with 2.pr. 21
gloucester, see here the tainture of thy nest, 2H6 2.01.184
did seem to say, "seek not a scorpion's nest, 3.02. 86
who finds the partridge in the puttock's nest 3.02.191
make war with him that climb'd unto their nest, 3H6 2.02. 31
your aery buildeth in our aery's nest: R3 1.03.269
where in that nest of spicery they will breed 4.04.424
inter | his noble nephew here in virtue's nest, TIT 1.01.376
must climb a bird's nest soon when it is dark. ROM 2.05. 74
come from that nest | of death, contagion, and 5.03.151
her young ones in her nest, against the owl. MAC 4.02. 11
have never wing'd from view o' th' nest, nor CYM 3.03. 28
in a great pool a swan's nest. 3.04.139
the sheep are gone to fold, birds to their nest, VEN 532
and now this pale swan in her wat'ry nest LUC 1611
death is now the phoenix' nest, | and the PHT 56

NESTOR 20 FR 0.0022 REL FR 18 V 2 P
and nestor play at push-pin with the boys, | and LLL 4.03.167
though nestor swear the jest be laughable. MV 1.01. 56
i'll play the orator as well as nestor, 3H6 3.02.188
nestor shall apply | thy latest words. TRO 1.03. 32
and such again | as venerable nestor, hatch'd in 1.03. 65
now play me nestor, hem, and stroke thy beard, 1.03.165
'tis nestor right. 1.03.170
tell him of nestor, one that was a man | when 1.03.291
nestor! 1.03.310
there's ulysses and old nestor, whose wit was 2.01.104 P
thus once again says nestor from the greeks: 2.02. 2
here's nestor, | instructed by the antiquary 2.03.250
but pardon, father nestor, were your days | as 2.03.253
so much for nestor. 4.05. 23
'tis the old nestor. 4.05.201
most reverend nestor, i am glad to clasp thee. 4.05.204
old nestor tarries; 5.01. 80
that stale old mouse-eaten dry cheese, nestor, 5.04. 11 P
bid nestor bring me spices, ink and /paper, | my PER 3.01. 65
there pleading might you see grave nestor stand, LUC 1401

NESTOR-LIKE 1 FR 0.0001 REL FR 1 V 0 P
nestor-like aged, in an age of care, | argue the 1H6 2.05. 6

NESTOR'S 1 FR 0.0001 REL FR 1 V 0 P
as, but for loss of nestor's golden words, | it LUC 1420

NESTS 3 FR 0.0003 REL FR 3 V 0 P
whilst their own birds famish in their nests; TIT 2.03.154
have built | in cleopatra's sails their nests. ANT 4.12. 4
or hateful cuckoos hatch in sparrows' nests? LUC 849

NET 10 FR 0.0011 REL FR 7 V 3 P
let there be the same net spread for her, and ADO 2.03.213 P
and rather choose to hide them in a net | than H5 1.02. 93
so doth the cony struggle in the net. 3H6 1.04. 62
lo you, my lord, | the net has fall'n upon me! H8 1.01.203
poor bird, thou'dst never fear the net nor lime, MAC 4.02. 34
and out of her own goodness make the net | that OTH 2.03.361
thee to desist | for going on death's net, whom PER 1.01. 40
but, master, i'll go draw up the net. 2.01. 94 P
here's a fish hangs in the net, like a poor 2.01.117 P
look how a bird lies tangled in a net, | so VEN 67

NETHER 4 FR 0.0004 REL FR 2 V 2 P
and a foolish hanging of thy nether lip, that 1H4 2.04.405 P
that these our nether crimes | so speedily can LR 4.02. 79
to palestine for a touch of his nether lip. OTH 4.03. 39 P
alas, why gnaw you so your nether lip? 5.02. 43

NETHERLANDS 1 FR 0.0001 REL FR 0 V 1 P
where stood belgia, the netherlands? ERR 3.02.138 P

NETHER-STOCKS 2 FR 0.0002 REL FR 0 V 2 P
i lead this life long, i'll sew nether-stocks, 1H4 2.04.116 P
at legs, then he wears wooden nether-stocks. LR 2.04. 11 P

NETS 3 FR 0.0003 REL FR 1 V 2 P
shall | go sound the ocean, and cast your nets; TIT 4.03. 7
with his pencil and the painter with his nets; ROM 1.02. 41 P
ha, come and bring away the nets! PER 2.01. 13 P

NETTLE 6 FR 0.0006 REL FR 4 V 2 P
you, my lord fool, out of this nettle, danger, 1H4 2.03. 9 P
the strawberry grows underneath the nettle, H5 1.01. 60
up in his tears an' 'twere a nettle against may. TRO 1.02.176 P
we call a nettle but a nettle, and | the faults COR 2.01.190
we call a nettle but a nettle, and | the faults 2.01.190
now to be frampal, now to piss o' th' nettle! TNK 3.05. 57

NETTLED 2 FR 0.0002 REL FR 2 V 0 P
nettled and stung with pismires, when i hear 1H4 1.03.240
nay, mark how lewis stamps as he were nettled. 3H6 3.03.169

NETTLES 7 FR 0.0008 REL FR 6 V 1 P
is goads, thorns, nettles, tails of wasps), WT 1.02.329
yield stinging nettles to mine enemies; R2 3.02. 18
reward | among the nettles at the elder-tree, TIT 2.03.272
did she make | of crow-flowers, nettles, daisies HAM 4.07.169
with hardocks, hemlock, nettles, cuckoo-flow'rs, LR 4.04. 4
so that if we will plant nettles or sow lettuce, OTH 1.03.322 P
than lead itself, stings more than nettles. TNK 5.01. 97

NETTLE-SEED 1 FR 0.0001 REL FR 1 V 0 P
he'd sow't with nettle-seed. TMP 2.01.145

NEUTER 1 FR 0.0001 REL FR 1 V 0 P
be it known unto you | i do remain as neuter. R2 2.03.159

NEUTRAL 4 FR 0.0004 REL FR 4 V 0 P
and furious, | loyal, and neutral, in a moment? MAC 2.03.109
/and, like a neutral to his will and matter, HAM 2.02.481
which came from one that's of a neutral heart, LR 3.07. 48
yet to be neutral to him were dishonor; TNK 1.02.100

NEVER *(also ne'er, nev'r, and compounds)*

/NEVER 6 FR 0.0006 REL FR 5 V 1 P
/never, /o /never, /do /his /ghost /the /wrong 2H4 2.03. 39
/never, /o /never, /do /his /ghost /the /wrong 2.03. 39
with maiden walls that war hath /never ent'red. H5 5.02.322 P
/i /never /got /him. LR 2.01. 78
/i'll /never /care /what /wickedness /i /do, 3.07. 99
/be /honest, | /i /never /yet /was /valiant. 5.01. 24

NEVER 1139 FR 0.1287 REL FR 888 V 251 P
to know | did never meddle with my thoughts. TMP 1.02. 22
my slave, who never | yields us kind answer. 1.02.308
who with mine eyes (never since at ebb) beheld 1.02.436
tunis was never grac'd before with such a 2.01. 75 P
would i had never | married my daughter there! 2.01.108
if he have never drunk wine afore, it will go 2.02. 74 P
says such baseness | had never like executor. 3.01. 13
never any | with so full soul but some defect in 3.01. 43
i never saw a woman | but only sycorax my dam 3.02.100
can, shall never melt | mine honor into lust, to 4.01. 27
foison plenty, | barns and garners never empty; 4.01.111
never till this day | saw i him touch'd with 4.01.144
on whose nature | nurture can never stick; 4.01.189
i have heard renown, | but never saw before; 5.01.194
last that i fear me will never out of my bones. 5.01.283 P
love, | and yet you never swom the hellespont. TGV 1.01. 26
but, were i you, he never should be mine. 1.02. 11
why, he, of all the rest, hath never mov'd me. 1.02. 27
you never saw her since she was deform'd. 2.01. 63 P
and duty never yet did want his meed. 2.04.112
that a man is never undone till he be hang'd, 2.05. 5 P
nor never welcome to a place till some certain 2.05. 5 P
thou shalt never get such a secret from me but 2.05. 39 P
i never knew him otherwise. 2.05. 43 P
then never dream on infamy, but go. 2.07. 64
he shall never know | that i had any light from 3.01. 48
never give her o'er, | for scorn at first makes 3.01. 94
him, | your slander never can endamage him; 3.02. 43
i am sorry i must never trust thee more, | but 5.04. 69
which, out of my neglect, was never done. 5.04. 90 P
or i would i might never come in mine own great WIV 1.01.154 P
never a woman in windsor knows more of anne's 1.04.127 P
i shall never laugh but in that maid's company! 1.04.152 P
inherit first, for i protest mine never shall. 2.01. 74 P
he would never have boarded me in this fury. 2.01. 88 P
come under my hatches, i'll never to sea again. 2.01. 93 P
i never heard such a drawling, affecting rogue. 2.01.141 P

i like it never the better for that. 2.01.179 P
could never have brought her to such a canary. 2.02. 62 P
you, they could never get an eye–wink of her. 2.02. 71 P
they could never get her so much as sip on a cup 2.02. 75 P
i never knew a woman so dote upon a man; 2.02.102 P
never a wife in windsor leads a better life than 2.02.116 P
and the boy never need to understand any thing; 2.02.127 P
though i had never so good means as desire to 2.02.182 P
never. 2.02.211 P
never. 2.02.213 P
i never heard a man of his place, gravity, and 3.01. 57 P
he, he — i can never hit on 's name. 3.02. 24 P
never stand "you had rather" and "you had rather 3.03.125 P
i'll never — 3.03.142 P
for i never saw him so gross in his jealousy 3.03.188 P
never name her, child, if she be a whore. 4.01. 63 P
upon no trail, never trust me when i open again. 4.02.197 P
with fine and recovery, he will never, i think, 4.02.211 P
fie, fie, he'll never come. 4.04. 18 P
i never prosper'd since i forswore myself at 4.05.101 P
the matter will be known to–night, or never. 5.01. 10 P
he would never else cross me thus. 5.05. 36 P
we could never meet. 5.05.117 P
i will never take you for my love again, but i 5.05.117 P
i will never mistrust my wife again, till thou 5.05.133 P
it had been anne page, would i might never stir! 5.05.187 P
nor nature never lends | the smallest scruple of MM 1.01. 36
i never heard any soldier dislike it. 1.02. 17 P
for i think thou never wast where grace was said 1.02. 18 P
and yet my nature never in the fight | to do in 1.03. 42
one who never feels | the wanton stings and 1.04. 58
not see | we tread upon, and never think of it. 2.01. 26
part, i never come into any room in a tap–house, 2.01.209 P
as jove himself does, jove would never be quiet, 2.02.111
never could the strumpet, | with all her double 2.02.182
angelo had never the purpose to corrupt her; 3.01.161 P
virtue is bold, and goodness never fearful. 3.01.208 P
'twas never merry world since, of two usuries, 3.02. 5 P
and usurp the beggary he was never born to. 3.02. 93 P
i never heard the absent duke much detected for 3.02.121 P
answer'd, he would never bring them to light. 3.02.178 P
head, and i can never cut off a woman's head. 4.02. 4 P
on my trust, a man that never yet | did, as he 5.01.147
time of five years | i never spake with her, saw 5.01.223
never crave him, we are definitive. 5.01.427
good sister, let us dine, and never fret; ERR 2.01. 6
vow | that never words were music to thine ear, 2.02.114
ear, | that never object pleasing in thine eye, 2.02.115
that never touch well welcome to thy hand, 2.02.116
that never meat sweet–savor'd in thy taste, 2.02.117
i, sir? i never saw her till this time. 2.02.162
i never spake with her in all my life. 2.02.165
else it could never be | but i should know her 2.02.201
consent to pay thee that i never had! 4.01. 74
the hours come back! that did i never /hear. 4.02. 55
is mad, | else would he never so demean himself. 4.03. 82
it may be so, but i did never see it. 4.04.141
i think i had, i never did deny it. 5.01. 23
she never reprehended him but mildly, | when he 5.01. 87
and never rise until my tears and prayers | have 5.01.115
i never came within these abbey walls, | nor 5.01.266
i never saw the chain, so help me heaven; 5.01.268
i never saw you in my life till now. 5.01.297
i never saw my father in my life. 5.01.320
they never meet but there's a skirmish of wit ADO 1.01. 63 P
you will never run mad, niece. 1.01. 93 P
never came trouble to my house in the likeness 1.01. 99 P
shall i never see a bachelor of threescore again 1.01.199 P
and never could maintain his part but in the 1.01.236 P
i never can see him but i am heart–burn'd an 2.01. 3 P
niece, thou wilt never get thee a husband, if 2.01. 18 P
you could never do him so ill–well, unless you 2.01.117 P
did he never make you laugh? 2.01.135 P
she is never sad but when she sleeps, and not 2.01.343 P
of me, he shall never make me such a fool. 2.03. 26 P
virtuous, or i'll never cheapen her; 2.03. 31 P
fair, or i'll never look on her; 2.03. 32 P
and one on shore, | to one thing constant never. 2.03. 65
i did never think that lady would have lov'd any 2.03. 93 P
there was never counterfeit of passion came so 2.03.104 P
no, and swears she never will. 2.03.125 P
never tell him, my lord. 2.03.201 P
upon this, i will never trust my expectation. 2.03.212 P
i did never think to marry. 2.03.228 P
and never to let beatrice know of it. 3.01. 43
but nature never fram'd a woman's heart | of 3.01. 49
i never yet saw man, | how wise, how noble, 3.01. 59
and never gives to truth and virtue that | which 3.01. 69
when it baes will never answer a calf when he 3.03. 71 P
never speak, we charge you; 3.03.175 P
he swore he would never marry, and yet now in 3.04. 88 P
i never tempted her with word too large, | but, 4.01. 52
of harm, | and never shall it more be gracious. 4.01.108
for there was never yet philosopher | that could 5.01. 35
nay, never lay thy hand upon thy sword, | i fear 5.01. 54
tush, tush, man, never fleer and jest at me; 5.01. 58
o, in a tomb where never scandal slept, | save 5.01. 70
never any did so, though very many have been 5.01.127 P
he hath us'd so long and never paid that now men 5.01.311 P
they were never so truly turn'd over and over as 5.02. 34 P
for i will never love that which my friend hates 5.02. 70 P
her wrongs, | gives her fame which never dies. 5.03. 6
and therefore never flout at me for what i have 5.04.107 P
mirth, | i never spent an hour's talk withal. LLL 2.01. 68
i do protest i never heard of it; 2.01.157
i will never buy and sell out of this word. 3.01.142 P
and never going aright, being a watch, | but 3.01.192
nay, never paint me now; 4.01. 16
he hath never fed of the dainties that are bred 4.02. 24
exchange, for the moon is never but a month old; 4.02. 47 P
ah, never faith could hold, if not to beauty 4.02.106
did never sonnet for her sake compile, | nor 4.03.132
nor never lay his wreathed arms athwart | his 4.03.133
your mistresses dare never come in rain, | for 4.03.266
i never knew man hold vile stuff so dear. 4.03.272
never durst poet touch a pen to write | until 4.03.343
ay, or i would these hands might never part. 5.02. 57
swore | a better speech was never spoke before. 5.02.110
that can never be. 5.02.225
for it can never be | they will digest this 5.02.288
for virtue's office never breaks men's troth. 5.02.350
and i will wish thee never more to dance, | nor 5.02.400
dance, | nor never more in russian habit wait. 5.02.401
o, never will i trust to speeches penn'd, | nor 5.02.402
tongue, | nor never come in vizard to my friend, 5.02.404
troth, | i never swore this lady such an oath. 5.02.451
a twelvemonth shall you spend, and never rest, 5.02.821
it, never in the tongue | of him that makes it; 5.02.862
the course of true love never did run smooth; MND 1.01.134
she never had so sweet a changeling. 2.01. 23
and now they never meet in grove or green, | by 2.01. 28
swear | a merrier hour was never wasted there. 2.01. 57
and never, since the middle summer's spring, 2.01. 82
never harm, | nor spell, nor charm, | come our 2.02. 16
that i did never, no, nor never can, | deserve a 2.02.126
man, | that i did never, no, nor never can, 2.02.126
and never mayst thou come lysander near! 2.02.136
of pyramus and thisby that will never please. 3.01. 10 P
you can never bring in a wall. 3.01. 65 P
true as truest horse, that yet would never tire, 3.01. 96
it is, "never tire." 3.01.101 P
as truest horse, that yet would never tire." 3.01.102
a bird the lie, though he cry "cuckoo" never so? 3.01.136 P
henceforth be never numb'red among men! 3.02. 67
than thine, thou serpent, never adder stung. 3.02. 73
a privilege never to see me more. 3.02. 79
scorn and derision never come in tears. 3.02.123
never did mockers waste more idle breath. 3.02.168
and never did desire to see thee more. 3.02.278
i was never curst; 3.02.300
did ever keep your counsels, never wrong'd you; 3.02.308
intend | never so little show of love to her, 3.02.334
league whose date till death shall never end. 3.02.373
never so weary, never so in woe, | bedabbled 3.02.442
never so weary, never so in woe, | bedabbled 3.02.442
never did i hear | such gallant chiding; 4.01.114
i never heard | so musical a discord, such sweet 4.01.117
a cry more tuneable | was never hollow'd to, nor 4.01.125
i never may believe | these antic fables, nor 5.01. 2
tears | the passion of loud laughter never shed. 5.01. 70
which never labor'd in their minds till now; 5.01. 73
for never any thing can be amiss, | when 5.01. 82
never excuse; 5.01.356 P
never mole, hare–lip, nor scar, | nor mark 5.01.411
wise men, | for gratiano never lets me speak. MV 1.01.107
will no doubt never be chosen by any rightly but 1.02. 32 P
love me to madness, i shall never requite him. 1.02. 65 P
i do never use it. 1.03. 70
choose wrong | never to speak to lady afterward 2.01. 41
to please his grandam, never trust me more. 2.02.197
and never dare misfortune cross her foot, 2.04. 35
find — | a proverb never stale in thrifty mind. 2.05. 55
never so rich a gem | was set in worse than gold 2.07. 54
i never heard a passion so confus'd, | so 2.08. 12
never to unfold to any one | which casket 'twas 2.09. 10
never in my life | to woo a maid in way of 2.09. 12
that judgment is, | that did never choose amiss. 2.09. 65
a day in april never came so sweet, | to show 2.09. 93
the curse never fell upon our nation till now, i 3.01. 85 P
our nation till now, i never felt it till now. 3.01. 86 P
i shall never see my gold again. 3.01.110 P
so will i never be, so may you miss me, | but if 3.02. 12
never did i know | a creature that did bear the 3.02.274
for never shall you lie by portia's side | with 3.02.305
duke | will never grant this forfeiture to hold. 3.03. 25
i never did repent for doing good, | nor shall 3.04. 10
it, | in reason he should never come to heaven! 3.05. 78
and tartars never train'd | to offices of tender 4.01. 32
for i never knew so young a body with so old a 4.01.163 P
my mind was never yet more mercenary. 4.01.418
i am never merry when i hear sweet music. 5.01. 69
husband, | and never be bassanio so for me — 5.01.131
and made him swear | never to part with it, and 5.01.171
i never more will break an oath with thee. 5.01.248
lord | will never more break faith advisedly. 5.01.253
ay, but the clerk that never means to do it, 5.01.282
daughter, and never two ladies lov'd as they do. AYL 1.01.112 P
and never leave thee till he hath ta'en thy life 1.01.151 P
alone again, i'll never wrastle for prize more. 1.01.161 P
yet he's gentle, never school'd and yet learned, 1.01.166 P
swearing by his honor, for he never had any; 1.02. 78 P
there is but one sham'd that was never gracious; 1.02.188 P
never so much as in a thought unborn | did i 1.03. 51
shall we pass along | and never stir assailants. 1.03.114
along by him | and never stays to greet him. 2.01. 54
for in my youth i never did apply | hot and 2.03. 48
as sure i think did never man love so — | how 2.04. 29
o, thou didst then never love so heartily! 2.04. 33
i never lov'd my brother in my life. 3.01. 14
why, if thou never wast at court, thou never 3.02. 40 P
wast at court, thou never saw'st good manners; 3.02. 41 P
if thou never saw'st good manners, then thy 3.02. 41 P
your parishioners withal, and never cried, "have 3.02.157 P
i was never so berhym'd since pythagoras' time, 3.02.176 P
never talk to me, i will weep. 3.04. 1 P
such another trick, never come in my sight more. 4.01. 41 P
you shall never take her without her answer, 4.01.172 P
occasion, let her never nurse her child herself, 4.01.175 P
i say she never did invent this letter, | this 4.03. 28
so please you, for i never heard it yet; 4.03. 37
i will never have her unless thou entreat for 4.03. 72 P
there was never any thing so sudden but the 5.02. 30 P
(for yet his honor never heard a play), | you SHR in.1. 96
nap, | but did i never speak of all that time? in.2. 82
these, | which never were, nor no man ever saw. in.2. 96
i' faith, sir, you shall never need to fear. 1.01. 61
nature of our quarrel yet never brook'd parle, 1.01.114 P
true, | i never thought it possible or likely. 1.01.149
men alive | i never yet beheld that special face 2.01. 11
iron may hold with her, but never lutes. 2.01.146
never make denial; 2.01.279
that never read so far | to know the cause why 3.01. 9
that will be never, tune your instrument. 3.01. 25
yet never means to wed where he hath woo'd. 3.02. 17
would katherine had never seen him though! 3.02. 26
/old /news, and such news as you never heard of! 3.02. 31 P
such a mad marriage never was before. 3.02.182
of all mad matches never was the like. 3.02.242
swore, how she pray'd that never pray'd before; 4.01. 79 P
for then she never looks upon her lure. 4.01.192
and here i firmly vow | never to woo her more, 4.02. 29
never to marry with her though she would entreat 4.02. 33
but i, who never knew how to entreat, | nor 4.03. 7
nor never needed that i should entreat, | am 4.03. 8
i never saw a better fashion'd gown, | more 4.03.101
say as he says, or we shall never go. 4.05. 11
you, for i never saw you before in all my life. 5.01. 51 P
didst thou never see thy /master's father, 5.01. 53 P
better once than never, for never too late. 5.01.150
better once than never, for never too late. 5.01.150
then never trust me if i be afeard. 5.02. 17
for she is chang'd, as she had never been. 5.02.115
lord, let me never have a cause to sigh, | till 5.02.123
of her father never approaches her heart but the AWW 1.01. 49 P
for silence, | but never tax'd for speech. 1.01. 68
and there was never virgin /got till virginity 1.01.128 P
must think, which never | returns us thanks. 1.01.185
and i think i shall never have the blessing of 1.03. 24 P
him, | yet never know how that desert should be. 1.03.200
that laboring art can never ransom nature | from 2.01.118
i'll never do you wrong for your own sake. 2.03. 90
but never hope to know why i should marry her. 2.03.110
i'll to the tuscan wars, and never bed her. 2.03.273
where i will never come | whilst i can shake my 2.05. 90
ring upon my finger, which never shall come off, 3.02. 58 P
but in such a 'then' i write a 'never.'" 3.02. 60 P
to tell him that his sword can never win | the 3.02. 93
you did never lack advice so much | as letting 3.04. 19
upon oath, never trust my judgment in any thing. 3.06. 32 P
i will never trust a man again for keeping his 4.03.144 P
after he scores, he never pays the score. 4.03.224
you never had a servant to whose trust | your 4.04. 15
you to take it so, | the ring was never hers. 5.03. 89
you are deceiv'd, my lord, she never saw it. 5.03. 92
in heavy satisfaction and would never | receive 5.03.100
that she would never put it from her finger, 5.03.109
where you have never come, or sent it us | upon 5.03.111
she never saw it. 5.03.112
her bed in florence, | where yet she never was. 5.03.127
i never gave it him. 5.03.276
i'll never tell you. 5.03.284
though yet he never harm'd me, here i quit him. 5.03.299
would thou mightst never draw sword again. TN 1.03. 62 P
i would i might never draw sword again. 1.03. 64 P
never in your life, i think, unless you see 1.03. 82 P
as it is spoke, she never will admit me. 1.04. 20
be the lady of the house, for i never saw her. 1.05.172 P
that you be never so hardy to come again in his 2.02. 9 P
did you never see the picture of "we three"? 2.03. 16 P
i shall never begin if i hold my peace. 2.03. 70 P
bid him turn you out of doors, never trust me. 2.03. 74 P
"but i will never die." 2.03.106
if i do not, never trust me, take it how you 2.03.188 P
o, where | sad true lover never find my grave, 2.04. 65
she never told her love, | but let concealment, 2.04.110
'twas never merry world | since lowly feigning 3.01. 98
i bade you never speak again of him; 3.01.107
has, nor never none | shall mistress be of it, 3.01.159
never more | will i my master's tears to you 3.01.161
never trust me then; 3.02. 58 P
do, cuff him soundly, but never draw thy sword. 3.04.392 P
hermit of prague, that never saw pen and ink, 4.02. 13 P
sir topas, never was man thus wrong'd. 4.02. 28 P
and i say there was never man thus abus'd. 4.02. 47 P
fool, there was never man so notoriously abus'd; 4.02. 87 P
antonio never yet was thief or pirate, | though 5.01. 74
where thou and i, henceforth, may never meet. 5.01.169
i never hurt you. 5.01.187
i never had a brother; 5.01.226
thou never shouldst love woman like to me. 5.01.268
by swaggering could i never thrive, | for the 5.01.399
dearest, thou never spok'st | to better purpose. WT 1.02. 88
never? 1.02. 89
never, but once. 1.02. 89
infirmities that honesty | is never free of. 1.02.264
you never spoke what did become you less | than 1.02.282
never | saw i men scour so on their way. 2.01. 34
i never wish'd to see you sorry, now | i trust i 2.01.123
(which never tender lady hath borne greater) 2.02. 22
and never to my red–look'd anger be | the 2.02. 32
will never do him good, not one of you. 2.03.129
i never saw a vessel of like sorrow, | so fill'd 3.03. 21
i never saw | the heavens so dim by day. 3.03. 55
they are never curst but when they are hungry. 3.03.130 P
if never, yet that time himself doth say, | he 4.01. 31
doth say, | he wishes earnestly you never may. 4.01. 32
were never for a piece of beauty rarer, | nor in 4.04. 32
so turtles pair | that never mean to part. 4.04.155
for never gaz'd the moon | upon the water as 4.04.172
you would never dance again after a tabor and 4.04.182 P
he could never come better; 4.04.187 P
see this knack (as never | i mean thou shalt), 4.04.428
you swear | never to marry but by my free leave? 5.01. 70
never, paulina, so be bless'd my spirit! 5.01. 71
never till then. 5.01. 84
never saw i | wretches so quake: 5.01.198
i never heard of such another encounter, which 5.02. 56 P
grace, which never | my life may last to answer. 5.03. 7
there | my mate, that's never to be found again, 5.03.134
would i might never stir from off this place, JN 1.01.145
sir robert never holp to make this leg. 1.01.240
o'er | did never float upon the swelling tide 2.01. 74
i think | his father never was so true begot — 2.01.130
i was never so bethump'd with words | since i 2.01.466
i do protest i never lov'd myself | till now 2.01.501
day about | shall never see it but a holy day. 3.01. 82
thou fortune's champion that dost never fight 3.01.118
and better conquest never canst thou make | than 3.01.290
therefore never, never | must i behold my pretty 3.04. 88
never | must i behold my pretty arthur more. 3.04. 88
he talks to me that never had a son. 3.04. 91
it me) | and i did never ask it you again; 4.01. 44
these eyes that never did nor never shall | so 4.01. 57
these eyes that never did nor never shall | so 4.01. 57

never such a pow'r | for any foreign preparation 4.02.110
out of my sight, and never see me more! 4.02.242
within this bosom never ent'red yet | the 4.02.254
never to taste the pleasures of the world, 4.03. 68
the world, | never to be infected with delight, 4.03. 69
upon our sides it never shall be broken. 5.02. 8
eyes | that never saw the giant world enrag'd, 5.02. 57
no, no, on my soul, it never shall be said. 5.02.108
this england never did, nor never shall, | lie 5.07.112
this england never did, nor never shall, | lie 5.07.112
for i may never lift | an angry arm against his R2 1.02. 40
never did captive with a freer heart | cast off 1.03. 88
the hopeless word of "never to return" | breathe 1.03.152
you never shall, so help you truth and god, 1.03.183
nor never look upon each other's face, | nor 1.03.185
nor never write, regreet, nor reconcile | this 1.03.186
nor never by advised purpose meet | to plot, 1.03.188
fell sorrow's tooth doth never rankle more 1.03.302
in war was never lion rag'd more fierce, | in 2.01.173
in peace was never gentle lamb more mild, | than 2.01.174
grief, | or else he never would compare between. 2.01.185
that their events can never fall out good. 2.01.214
thrust into my hands, | never believe me. 2.02.111
i fear me, never. 2.02.149
knowledge, | i never in my life did look on him. 2.03. 39
and let him never see joy that breaks that oath! 2.03.151
do me good, | and never borrow any tear of thee. 3.04. 23
god the plants thou graft'st may never grow. 3.04.101
and never brandish more revengeful steel | over 4.01. 50
that honorable day shall never be seen. 4.01. 91
never more come in my sight. 5.02. 86
an' never will i rise up from the ground | till 5.02.116
a beggar begs that never begg'd before. 5.03. 78
knees, | and never see day that the happy sees, 5.03. 94
i never long'd to hear a word till now, | say 5.03.115
where no man never comes, but that sad dog 5.05. 70
and never show thy head by day nor light. 5.06. 44
i'll be damn'd for never a king's son in 1H4 1.02. 97 P
for he was never yet a breaker of proverbs. 1.02.118 P
i throw off | and pay the debt i never promised, 1.02.209
and majesty might never yet endure | the moody 1.03. 18
die, and never rise | to do him wrong or any way 1.03. 74
for i shall never hold that man my friend 1.03. 90
he never did fall off, my sovereign liege, | but 1.03. 94
never did bare and rotten policy | color her 1.03.108
nor never could the noble mortimer | receive so 1.03.110
he never did encounter with glendower. 1.03.114
where fadom–line could never touch the ground, 1.03.204
poor fellow never joy'd since the price of oats 2.01. 12 P
hast thou never an eye in thy head? 2.01. 28 P
one that never spake other english in his life 2.04. 24 P
and do thou never leave calling "francis," that 2.04. 31 P
didst thou never see titan kiss a dish of butter 2.04.120 P
geese, i'll never wear hair on my face more. 2.04.138 P
i never dealt better since i was a man; 2.04.169 P
so did he never the sparrow. 2.04.348 P
never call a true piece of gold a counterfeit. 2.04.491 P
kitten'd, though yourself had never been born. 3.01. 19
ornament, | a virtue that was never seen in you. 3.01.124
but i will never be a truant, love, | till i 3.01.204
as if thou never walk'st further than finsbury. 3.01.252
i never see thy face but i think upon hell–fire 3.03. 31 P
the /tithe of a hair was never lost in my house 3.03. 58 P
i was never call'd so in mine own house before. 3.03. 63 P
his health was never better worth than now. 4.01. 27
and such as indeed were never soldiers, but 4.02. 27 P
tut, never fear me, i am as vigilant as a cat to 4.02. 58 P
i did never see such pitiful rascals. 4.02. 64 P
i am sure they never learn'd that of me. 4.02. 72 P
and never yet did insurrection want | such 5.01. 79
who, never so tame, so cherish'd and lock'd up, 5.02. 10
i never in my life | did hear a challenge urg'd 5.02. 51
day, | england did never owe so sweet a hope, 5.02. 67
never did i hear | of any prince so wild a 5.02. 70
some of us never shall | a second time do such a 5.02. 99
thus, | i never had triumph'd upon a scot. 5.03. 15
turk gregory never did such deeds in arms as i 5.03. 45 P
or thou art like | never to hold it up again! 5.04. 40
thee, | who never promiseth but he means to pay. 5.04. 43
never talk of it. 2H4 1.01. 54
from whence with life he never more sprung up. 1.01.111
never so few, and never yet more need. 1.01.215
never so few, and never yet more need. 1.01.215
i was never mann'd with an agot till now, but i 1.02. 16 P
for a barber shall never earn sixpence out of it 1.02. 25 P
bottle, i would i might never spit white again. 1.02.212 P
it never yet did hurt | to lay down likelihoods 1.03. 34
never fear that. 1.03. 80
never a man's thought in the world keeps the 2.02. 58 P
for they never prick their finger but they say, 2.02.112 P
but i never said so. 2.02.141 P
and never shall have length of life enough | to 2.03. 58
you two never meet but you fall to some discord. 2.04. 56 P
she never could away with me. 3.02.201 P
never, never, she would always say she could not 3.02.202 P
never, never, she would always say she could not 3.02.202 P
i never knew yet but rebuke and check was the 4.03. 31 P
there's never none of these demure boys come to 4.03. 90 P
shall never leak, though it do work as strong 4.04. 47
will fortune never come with both hands full, 4.04.103
that tyranny, which never quaff'd but blood, 4.05. 85
i never thought to hear you speak again. 4.05. 91
and never live to show th' incredulous world 4.05.153
do with a fellow that never had the ache in his 5.01. 83 P
and never shall you see that i will beg | a 5.02. 37
which was never seen in such an assembly. ep 24 P
never was such a sudden scholar made; H5 1.01. 32
never came reformation in a flood | with such a 1.01. 33
nor never hydra–headed willfulness | so soon did 1.01. 35
and never noted in him any study, | any 1.01. 57
for never two such kingdoms did contend 1.02. 24
never king of england | had nobles richer and 1.02.126
mighty sum | as never did the clergy at one time 1.02.134
never went with his forces into france | but 1.02.147
we never valu'd this poor seat of england, | and 1.02.269
never was monarch better fear'd and lov'd | than 2.02. 25
"i can never win | a soul so easy as that 2.02.124
never did faithful subject more rejoice | at the 2.02.161
'a could never abide carnation — 'twas a color 2.03. 33 P
abide carnation — 'twas a color he never lik'd. 2.03. 34 P
for 'a never broke any man's head but his own, 3.02. 40 P
i think the duke hath lost never a man, but one 3.06.100 P
will it never be morning? 3.07. 6 P
elements of earth and water never appear in him, 3.07. 22 P
will it never be day? 3.07. 80 P
he never did harm, that i heard of. 3.07.100 P
never anybody saw it but his lackey. 3.07.110 P
"ill will never said well." 3.07.113 P
they could never wear such heavy head–pieces. 3.07.138 P
but i think we shall never see the end of it. 4.01. 90 P
is no king, be his cause never so spotless, if 4.01.159 P
to see it, i will never trust his word after. 4.01.195 P
you'll never trust his word after! 4.01.201 P
never sees horrid night, the child of hell; 4.01.271
thou never shalt hear herald any more. 4.03.127
i did never know so full a voice issue from so 4.04. 67 P
he never kill'd any of his friends. 4.07. 40 P
never came any from mine that might offend your 4.08. 47 P
butcher and sit like a jack–an–apes, never off. 5.02.142 P
downright oaths, which i never use till urg'd, 5.02.145 P
use till urg'd, nor never break for urging. 5.02.145 P
that never looks in his glass for love of any 5.02.147 P
for it shines bright and never changes, but 5.02.164 P
i shall never move thee in french, unless it be 5.02.186 P
that never war advance | his bleeding sword 5.02.354
that never may ill office, or fell jealousy, 5.02.363
henry is dead, and never shall revive. 1H6 1.01. 18
i know thee well, though never seen before. 1.02. 67
water, | which never ceaseth to enlarge itself, 1.02.134
one that still motions war and never peace, 1.03. 63
i'll never trouble you, if i may spy them. 1.04. 22
traitors have never other company. 2.01. 19
this sudden mischief never could have fall'n. 2.01. 59
law, | and never yet could frame my will to it, 2.04. 8
he shall submit, or i will never yield. 3.01.118
a braver soldier never couched lance, | a 3.02.134
a gentler heart did never sway in court; 3.02.135
one sudden foil shall never breed distrust. 3.03. 11
said | a stouter champion never handled sword. 3.04. 19
yet never have you tasted our reward, | or been 3.04. 22
because till now we never saw your face. 3.04. 24
never so needful on the earth of france, | spur 4.03. 18
never to england shall he bear his life, | but 4.04. 38
and fly would talbot never, though he might. 4.04. 44
thou never hadst renown, nor canst not lose it. 4.05. 40
my age was never tainted with such shame. 4.05. 46
never yet taint with love, i send the king. 5.03.183
i never had to do with wicked spirits. 5.04. 42
may never glorious sun reflex his beams | upon 5.04. 87
never to disobey | nor be rebellious to the 5.04.170
for that | my tender youth was never yet attaint 5.05. 81
france, | undoing all, as all had never been! 2H6 1.01.103
i never read but england's kings have had 1.01.128
a proper jest, and never heard before, | that 1.01.132
i never saw but humphrey duke of gloucester 1.01.183
and never more abase our sight so low | as to 1.02. 15
lays, | and never mount to trouble you again. 1.03. 91
fact | did never traitor in the land commit. 1.03.174
i never said nor thought any such matter. 1.03.187 P
i shall never be able to fight a blow. 1.03.215 P
let never day nor night unhallowed pass, | but 2.01. 83
and yet, i think, jet did he never see. 2.01.112
never, before this day, in all his life. 2.01.114
i never saw a fellow worse bestead, | or more 2.03. 56
god, for i am never able to deal with my master, 2.03. 77 P
i will take my death, i never meant him any ill, 2.03. 88 P
snar'd, | nor never seek prevention of thy foes. 2.04. 57
for soldiers' pay in france, and never sent it, 3.01. 62
i never robb'd the soldiers of their pay, | nor 3.01.108
garrisons, | and never ask'd for restitution. 3.01.118
strange tortures for offenders, never heard of, 3.01.122
i never gave them condign punishment. 3.01.130
thou never didst them wrong, nor no man wrong; 3.01.209
he never would have stay'd in france so long. 3.01.295
now, york, or never, steel thy fearful thoughts, 3.01.331
thou art | and never of the nevils' noble race. 3.02.215
where biting cold would never let grass grow, 3.02.337
never yet did base dishonor blur our name | but 4.01. 39
but jove was never slain, as thou shalt be. 4.01. 49
whose dreadful swords were never drawn in vain, 4.01. 92
can, | that this my death may never be forgot! 4.01.133
i say, it was never merry world in england since 4.02. 8 P
for his father had never a house but the cage. 4.02. 52 P
to a thing, and i was never mine own man since. 4.02. 83 P
be wise, he'll never call ye jack cade more. 4.06. 9 P
and tears have mov'd me, gifts could never. 4.07. 68
oft have i struck | those that i never saw, and 4.07. 82
i thought ye would never have given out these 4.08. 25 P
was never subject long'd to be a king | as i do 4.09. 5
assure yourselves, will never be unkind. 4.09. 19
doornail, i pray god i may never eat grass more. 4.10. 41 P
for i, that never fear'd any, am vanquish'd by 4.10. 74 P
and never live but true unto his liege! 5.01. 82
whose warlike ears could never brook retreat, 3H6 1.01. 5
i vow by heaven these eyes shall never close. 1.01. 24
would i had died a maid | and never seen thee, 1.01.217
and never seen thee, never borne thee son, 1.01.217
i never did thee harm; why wilt thou slay me? 1.03. 38
wondrous strange, the like yet never heard of. 2.01. 33
for never henceforth shall i joy again, | never, 2.01. 77
again, | never, o never, shall i see more joy! 2.01. 78
again, | never, o never, shall i see more joy! 2.01. 78
foes, | but never once again turn back and fly. 2.01.185
didst thou never hear | that things ill got had 2.02. 45
we'll never leave till we have hewn thee down, 2.02.168
i vow to god above | i'll never pause again, 2.03. 30
i'll never pause again, never stand still, 2.03. 30
i, that did never weep, now melt with woe | that 2.03. 46
hadst thou never given consent | that phaeton 2.06. 11
thy burning car never had scorch'd the earth. 2.06. 13
they never then had sprung like summer flies; 2.06. 17
and never will i undertake the thing | wherein 2.06.101
but did you never swear and break an oath? 3.01. 72
no, never such an oath, nor will not now. 3.01. 73
my mind will never grant what i perceive | your 3.02. 67
vow, | that i may never have you in suspect. 4.01.142
vow | never to lie and take his natural rest 4.03. 5
honor now or never! 4.03. 24
lamb, | the lamb will never cease to follow him. 4.08. 50
than if thou never hadst deserv'd our hate. 5.01.104
nay, never bear me hence, dispatch me here; 5.05. 69
that never dream'st on aught but butcheries. R3 1.02.100
he is in heaven, where thou shalt never come. 1.02.106
never came poison from so sweet a place. 1.02.146
never hung poison on a fouler toad. 1.02.147
these eyes, which never shed remorseful tear — 1.02.155
i never sued to friend nor enemy; 1.02.167
my tongue could never learn sweet smoothing word 1.02.168
then never /was /man true. 1.02.195
but that will never be: 1.03. 40
god grant we never may have need of you! 1.03. 75
i never did incense his majesty | against the 1.03. 84
for curses never pass | the lips of those that 1.03.284
i never did her any to my knowledge. 1.03.308
he shall never wake until the great judgment day 1.04.103 P
never, my lord, therefore prepare to die. 1.04.180
i will never more remember | our former hatred, 2.01. 23
was never widow had so dear a loss. 2.02. 77
were never orphans had so dear a loss. 2.02. 78
was never mother had so dear a loss. 2.02. 79
knows, | seldom or never jumpeth with the heart. 3.01. 11
men, | but sanctuary children never till now. 3.01. 56
so wise so young, they say do never live long. 3.01. 79
and i believe will never stand upright | till 3.02. 39
and never in my days, i do protest, | was it so 3.02. 79
i think there's never a man in christendom | can 3.04. 51
i never look'd for better at his hands | after 3.05. 50
your brother's son shall never reign our king, 3.07.215
for never yet one hour in his bed | did i enjoy 4.01. 82
for i shall never speak to thee again. 4.04.182
perish | and never more behold thy face again. 4.04.187
i never was nor never will be false. 4.04.493
i never was nor never will be false. 4.04.493
wife, | that never slept a quiet hour with thee, 5.03.160
that he was never trained up in arms. 5.03.272
one that never in his life | felt so much cold 5.03.325
will leave us never an understanding friend. H8 pr 22
that never | they shall abound as formerly. 1.01. 82
half your suit | never name to us; 1.02. 11
and never seek for aid out of himself. 1.02.114
though they be never so ridiculous | (nay, let 1.03. 3
it, | that never see 'em pace before, the spavin 1.03. 12
courtier may be wise | and never see the louvre. 1.03. 23
o beauty, | till now i never knew thee! 1.04. 76
sure he does not, | he never was so womanish. 2.01. 38
accusers, | that never knew what truth meant. 2.01.105
never found again | but where they mean to sink 2.01.130
pray god he do, he'll never know himself else. 2.02. 22
about his neck, yet never lost her lustre; 2.02. 32
she never knew harm–doing — o, now after | so 2.03. 5
this business, never desir'd | it to be stirr'd; 2.04.164
vainglory) | never yet branded with suspicion? 3.01.128
would i had never trod this english earth, | or 3.01.143
to th' king, never attempt | any thing on him; 3.02. 17
he falls like lucifer, | never to hope again. 3.02.372
never so truly happy, my good cromwell; 3.02.377
that sun, i pray, may never set! 3.02.415
never greater, | nor, i'll assure you, better 4.01. 11
such joy | i never saw before. 4.01. 76
he was never | (but where he meant to ruin) 4.02. 39
but poverty could never draw 'em from me), 4.02.149
sir, i did never win of you before. 5.01. 58
i never sought their malice) | to quench mine 5.02. 15
pray heaven the king may never find a heart 5.02. 77
mean, | which ye shall never have while i live. 5.02.182
sleep | on may–day morning, which will never be. 5.03. 15
saba was never | more covetous of wisdom and 5.04. 23
never, before | this happy child, did i get any 5.04. 64
'tis ten to one this play can never please | all ep 1
he never saw three and twenty. TRO 1.02.235 P
that she was never yet that ever knew | love got 1.02.290
rate, | and do a deed that never fortune did, 2.02. 90
and sworn upon't she never shrouded any but 2.03. 33 P
and never suffers matter of the world | enter 2.03.186
make devils of cherubins, they never see truly. 3.02. 69 P
yet reserve an ability that they never perform; 3.02. 86 P
(with whom relation | durst never meddle) in the 3.03.202
prithee tarry, | you men will never tarry. 4.02. 16
there was never a truer rhyme. 4.04. 21 P
still lock'd in steel, | i never saw till now. 4.05.196
mars, the captain of us all, | never like thee. 4.05.199
deeds to match these words, | or may i never — 4.05.260
in faith i will lo, never trust me else. 5.02. 59
farewell, | thou never shalt mock diomed again. 5.02. 99
never did young man fancy | with so eternal and 5.02.165
never go home, here starve we out the night — 5.10. 2
viand, never bearing | like labor with the rest, COR 1.01.100
we never yet made doubt but rome was ready | to 1.02. 18
to you, yet dare i never | deny your asking. 1.06. 64
which you profane, | never sound more! 1.09. 42
never would he | appear i' th' market–place, nor 2.01.232
i never saw the like. 2.01.268
never shame to hear | what you have nobly done. 2.02. 67
he never stood | to ease his breast with panting 2.02.121
you are never without your tricks; 2.03. 34 P
to the people, there was never a worthier man. 2.03. 38 P
'twas never my desire yet to trouble the poor 2.03. 69 P
spirit, | or never be so noble as a consul, 3.01. 56
could never be the native | of our so frank 3.01.129
though therein you can never be too noble, | but 3.02. 40
you have put me now to such a part which never 3.02.105
or never trust to what my tongue can do | i' th' 3.02.136
tarpeian, never more | to enter our rome gates. 3.03.103
and never of me aught | but what is like me 4.01. 52
never man | sigh'd truer breath; 4.05.114
rome, such as was never | s' incapable of help. 4.06.119
he'll never hear him. 5.01. 62
never admitted | a private whisper, no, not with 5.03. 6
i'll never | be such a gosling to obey instinct, 5.03. 34
the thing i have forsworn to grant may never 5.03. 80
thou hast never in thy life | show'd thy dear 5.03.160
a merrier day did never yet greet rome, | no, 5.04. 42
nature, never known before | but to be rough, 5.06. 24
silk, never admitting | counsel a' th' war; 5.06. 95

store, | that thou wilt never render to me more! TIT 1.01. 95
was never scythia half so barbarous. 1.01.131
of mine, | my sons would never so dishonor me. 1.01.295
thee never, nor thy traitorous haughty sons, 1.01.302
under a tree, | and never after to inherit it. 2.03. 3
which never hopes more heaven than rests in thee 2.03. 41
here never shines the sun, here nothing breeds, 2.03. 96
pit, | where never man's eye may behold my body: 2.03.177
for two and twenty sons i never wept, | because 3.01. 10
death, | and let me say (that never wept before) 3.01. 25
and never whilst i live deceive men so; 3.01.189
and threat me i shall never come to bliss | till 3.01.272
cornelia never with more care | read to her sons 4.01. 12
hunt | (o, had we never, never hunted there!), 4.01. 56
hunt | (o, had we never, never hunted there!), 4.01. 56
can never turn the swan's black legs to white, 4.02.102
jubiter, i never drank with him in all my life. 4.03. 85 P
alas, sir, i never came there. 4.03. 90 P
sir, i could never say grace in all my life. 4.03.100 P
rome never had more cause. 4.04. 62
they never do beget a coal–black calf. 5.01. 32
what, canst thou say all this and never blush? 5.01.121
for well i wot the empress never wags | but in 5.02. 87
and can never find what names the writing person ROM 1.02. 43 P
and these, who, often drown'd, could never die, 1.02. 90
and she was wean'd — i never shall forget it — 1.03. 24
a thousand years, | i never should forget it: 1.03. 47
he jests at scars that never felt a wound. 2.02. 1
henceforth i never will be romeo. 2.02. 51
and where care lodges, sleep will never lie; 2.03. 36
thou wast never with me for any thing when thou 2.04. 75 P
i do protest i never injuried thee, | but love 3.01. 68
indeed i never shall be satisfied | with romeo, 3.05. 93
proud can i never be of what i hate, | but 3.05.147
thursday, | or never after look me in the face. 3.05.162
nor what is mine shall never do thee good. 3.05.194
logs, | and never trouble peter for the matter. 4.04. 19
ready to go, but never to return. 4.05. 34
never was seen so black a day as this. 4.05. 53
thee, | and never from this /palace of dim night 5.03.107
for never was a story of more woe | than this of 5.03.309
never may | that state of fortune fall into my TIM 1.01.149
grant i may never prove so fond, | to trust man 1.02. 64
false hearts should never have sound legs. 1.02.234
never mind | was to be so unwise, to be so kind. 2.02. 5
own part, | i never tasted timon in my life, 3.02. 77
may you a better feast never behold, | you knot 3.06. 88
that he may never more false title plead, | nor 4.03.154
if i hope well, i'll never see thee more. 4.03.171
i never did thee harm. 4.03.172
the marbled mansion all above | never presented! 4.03.192
the one is filling still, never complete; 4.03.244
fortune's tender arm | with favor never clasp'd, 4.03.251
and never learn'd | the icy precepts of respect, 4.03.257
that never knew but better, is some burthen: 4.03.267
they never flatter'd thee. 4.03.270
the middle of humanity thou never knewest, but 4.03.300 P
i never had honest men about me, i; 4.03.477
whose eyes do never give | but thorough lust and 4.03.484
there's never a one of you but trusts a knave 5.01. 93
such men as he be never at heart's ease | whiles JC 1.02.208
but never till to–night, never till now, | did i 1.03. 9
but never till to–night, never till now, | did i 1.03. 9
bars, | never lacks power to dismiss itself. 1.03. 97
for he will never follow any thing | that other 2.01.151
never fear that. 2.01.202
caesar, i never stood on ceremonies, | yet now 2.02. 13
the valiant never taste of death but once. 2.02. 33
cassius or caesar never shall turn back, | for i 3.01. 21
and valiant roman, | i never thought him worse. 3.01.139
never, never! 3.02.253
never, never! 3.02.253
a friendly eye could never see such faults. 4.03. 90
never come such division 'tween our souls! 4.03.235
never, till caesar's three and thirty wounds 5.01. 53
run, | where never roman shall take note of him. 5.03. 50
thou never com'st unto a happy birth, | but 5.03. 70
o, never | shall sun that morrow see! MAC 1.05. 60
never at quiet! 2.03. 15 P
never shake | thy gory locks at me. 3.04. 49
that, and my firm nerves | shall never tremble. 3.04.102
all harms, | was never call'd to bear my part, 3.05. 8
macbeth shall never vanquish'd be until | great 4.01. 92
that will never be. 4.01. 94
dead, rise never till the wood | of birnan rise, 4.01. 97
the flighty purpose never is o'ertook | unless 4.01.145
poor bird, thou'dst never fear the net nor lime, 4.02. 34
i am yet | unknown to woman, never was forsworn, 4.03.126
the night is long that never finds the day. 4.03.240
shall never sag with doubt, nor shake with fear. 5.03. 10
but virtue, as it never will be moved, | though HAM 1.05. 53
there's never a villain dwelling in all denmark 1.05.123
never make known what you have seen to–night. 1.05.144
never to speak of this that you have seen, 1.05.153
never to speak of this that you have heard. 1.05.160
here, as before, never, so help you mercy, | how 1.05.169
that you, at such times seeing me, never shall, 1.05.173
makes vow before his uncle never more | to give 2.02. 70
truth to be a liar, | but never doubt i love. 2.02.119
speak me a speech once, but it was never acted, 2.02.435 P
and never did the cyclops' hammers fall | on 2.02.489
no, not i, | i never gave you aught. 3.01. 95
for who not needs shall never lack a friend, 3.02.207
and never come mischance between us twain! 3.02.228
to give them seals never my soul consent! 3.02.399
never alone | did the king sigh, but /with a 3.03. 22
words without thoughts never to heaven go. 3.03. 98
scourge is weigh'd, | but never the offense. 4.03. 7
why then the polack never will defend it. 4.04. 23
maid, that out a maid | never departed more." 4.05. 55
go to thy death–bed, | he never will come again. 4.05.194
into the land, | as if i had never been such." 5.01. 74
plac'd it safely, | the changeling never known. 5.02. 53
never hamlet! 5.02.233
lo here i lie, | never to rise again. 5.02.319
never believe it; 5.02.340
he never gave commandement for their death. 5.02.374
sure i shall never marry like my sisters, | /to LR 1.01.103
my life i never held but as /a pawn | to wage 1.01.155
which we durst never yet — and with strain'd 1.01.169
without miracle | should never plant in me. 1.01.223
has he never before sounded you in this business 1.02. 69 P
never, my lord. 1.02. 71 P
and from her derogate body never spring | a babe 1.04.280
never afflict yourself to know more of it, | but 1.04.291
he shall never more | be fear'd of doing harm. 2.01.110
i never gave him any. 2.02.115
never, regan: 2.04.158
no, regan, thou shalt never have my curse. 2.04.170
i never gave you kingdom, call'd you children; 3.02. 17
for there was never yet fair woman but she made 3.02. 35 P
wind and rain, i never | remember to have heard. 3.02. 47
see't shalt thou never. 3.07. 67
but better service have i never done you | than 3.07. 74
madam, within, but never man so chang'd. 4.02. 3
but have you never found my brother's way | to 5.01. 10
i never shall endure her. 5.01. 15
within our power, | shall never see his pardon; 5.01. 68
never (o fault!) 5.03.193
no more, | never, never, never, never, never! 5.03.309
no more, | never, never, never, never, never! 5.03.309
no more, | never, never, never, never, never! 5.03.309
no more, | never, never, never, never, never! 5.03.309
no more, | never, never, never, never, never! 5.03.309
we that are young | shall never see so much, nor 5.03.327
/tush, never tell me! OTH 1.01. 1
wife), | that never set a squadron in the field, 1.01. 22
a maiden, never bold; 1.03. 94
i never yet did hear | that the bruis'd heart 1.03.218
if thou dost, i shall never love thee after. 1.03.306 P
i never found man that knew how to love himself. 1.03.313 P
i could never better stead thee than now. 1.03.339 P
i never did like molestation view | on the 2.01. 16
she never yet was foolish that was fair, | for 2.01.136
she that was ever fair, and never proud, | had 2.01.148
had tongue at will, and yet was never loud, 2.01.149
never lack'd gold, and yet went never gay, 2.01.150
never lack'd gold, and yet went never gay, 2.01.150
she that in wisdom never was so frail | to 2.01.154
though true advantage never present itself; 2.01.244 P
bless'd, she would never have lov'd the moor. 2.01.253 P
knavery's plain face is never seen till us'd. 2.01.312
love thee, | but never more be officer of mine. 2.03.249
i never knew a florentine more kind and honest. 3.01. 40
he's never any thing but your true servant. 3.03. 9
my lord shall never rest, | i'll watch him tame, 3.03. 22
slander her and torture me, | never pray more; 3.03.369
never, iago. 3.03.453
then would to /god that i had never seen't! 3.04. 77
you'll never meet a more sufficient man. 3.04. 91
alas the day, i never gave him cause. 3.04.158
i never knew woman love man so. 4.01.110
what? did they never whisper? 4.02. 6
never, my lord. 4.02. 6
never. 4.02. 8
never, my lord. 4.02. 10
aches at thee, would thou hadst never been born! 4.02. 69
may defeat my life, | but never taint my love. 4.02.161
i would you had never seen him! 4.03. 18
i never did | offend you in my life; 5.02. 58
never lov'd cassio | but with such general 5.02. 59
i never gave him token. 5.02. 61
i never gave it him. 5.02. 67
a better never did itself sustain | upon a 5.02.260
dear general, i never gave you cause. 5.02.299
from this time forth i never will speak word. 5.02.304
would i had never seen her! ANT 1.02.152
whose love is never link'd to the deserver 1.02.186
would she had never given you leave to come! 1.03. 21
o, never was there queen | so mightily betrayed! 1.03. 24
my brother never | did urge me in his act. 2.02. 45
which you shall never | have tongue to charge me 2.02. 82
may i never | (to this good purpose, that so 2.02.143
our hearts, and never | fly off our loves again! 2.02.151
never, he will not: 2.02.233
would i had never come from thence, nor you 2.03. 11 P
be honest, it is never good | to bring bad news. 2.05. 85
my face, | but in my bosom shall she never come, 2.06. 55
let me shake thy hand, | i never hated thee. 2.06. 74
i never lov'd you much, but i ha' prais'd ye 2.06. 76
but there is never a fair woman has a true face. 2.06. 99 P
i'll never follow thy pall'd fortunes more. 2.07. 82
once 'tis offer'd, | shall never find it more. 2.07. 84
faults | can never be so equal that your love 3.04. 35
he'll never yield to that. 3.06. 37
celerity is never more admir'd | than by the 3.07. 24
i never saw an action of such shame; 3.10. 21
never anger | made good guard for itself. 4.01. 9
say that i wish he never find more cause | to 4.05. 15
bad a prayer as his | was never yet for sleep. 4.09. 27
the boar of thessaly | was never so emboss'd. 4.13. 3
for when she saw | (which never shall be found) 4.14.122
o charmian, i will never go from hence. 4.15. 1
a rarer spirit never | did steer humanity; 5.01. 31
which sleeps, and never palates more the dung, 5.02. 7
which your death | will never let come forth. 5.02. 46
would i might never | o'ertake pursu'd success, 5.02.102
i'll never see't! 5.02.223
that do die of it do seldom or never recover. 5.02.247 P
say, shall never be sav'd by half that they do. 5.02.256 P
and golden phoebus never be beheld | of eyes 5.02.317
i never do him wrong | but he does buy my CYM 1.01.104
i never saw him sad. 1.06. 63
but i'll never give o'er. 2.03. 16 P
of unpav'd eunuch to boot, can never amend. 2.03. 30 P
he never can meet more mischance than come | to 2.03.132
never saw i figures | so likely to report 2.04. 82
never talk on't: | she hath been colted by him. 2.04.132
spare your arithmetic, never count the turns. 2.04.142
service, never | let me be counted serviceable. 3.02. 14
to 's execution, man, | could never go so slow. 3.02. 71
have never wing'd from view o' th' nest, nor 3.03. 28
whereunto i never | purpose return. 3.04.106
and i will never fail | beginning nor supplyment 3.04.178
which i will never be | to him that is most true 3.05.158
dream often so, | and never false. 4.02.353
never | find such another master. 4.02.373
what thing is't that i never | did see man die, 4.04. 35
never bestrid a horse, save one that had | a 4.04. 38
my faults, i never | had liv'd to put on this; 5.01. 8
done aught but well, | whose face i never saw? 5.04. 36
end, i think you'll never return to tell one. 5.04.184 P
beget young gibbets, i never saw one so prone. 5.04.199 P
i never saw | such noble fury in so poor a thing 5.05. 7
first, she confess'd she never lov'd you; 5.05. 37
never master had | a page so kind, so duteous, 5.05. 85
never say hereafter | but i am truest speaker. 5.05.375
never was a war did cease | (ere bloody hands 5.05.484
testy wrath | could never be her mild companion. PER 1.01. 18
so thou never return | unless thou say prince 1.01.163
one sorrow never comes but brings an heir | that 1.04. 63
who never leave gaping till they swallow'd the 2.01. 33 P
that he should never have left till he cast 2.01. 41 P
he asks of you that never us'd to beg. 2.01. 62
i never practic'd it. 2.01. 67
or never more to view nor day nor light. 2.05. 17
protest my ears were never better fed | with 2.05. 27
that never aim'd so high to love your daughter, 2.05. 47
never did thought of mine levy offense; 2.05. 52
nor never did my actions yet commence | a deed 2.05. 53
that never relish'd of a base descent. 2.05. 60
for a more blusterous birth had never babe. 3.01. 28
such strong renown as time shall never — 3.02. 48
i never saw so huge a billow, sir, | as toss'd 3.02. 58
will i take me to, | and never more have joy. 3.04. 11
of my rhyme, | which never could i so convey, 4.ch. 49
'tis but a blow, which never shall be known. 4.01. 2
my father, as nurse says, did never fear, | but 4.01. 52
never was waves nor wind more violent, | and 4.01. 59
my troth, | i never did her hurt in all my life. 4.01. 74
i never spake bad word, nor did ill turn | to 4.01. 75
law, | i never kill'd a mouse, nor hurt a fly; 4.01. 77
we were never so much out of creatures. 4.02. 6 P
be us'd in every trade, we shall never prosper. 4.02. 12 P
he swears | never to wash his face, nor cut his 4.04. 28
she does, and swears she'll never stint, | make 4.04. 42
no, nor never shall do in such a place as this, 4.05. 2 P
but there never came her like in meteline. 4.06. 28 P
which grows to the stalk, never pluck'd yet, i 4.06. 42 P
would she had never come within my doors. 4.06.148 P
bottom of your story, | and never interrupt you. 5.01.165
she never would tell | her parentage; 5.01.187
that, | for truth can never be confirm'd enough, 5.01.201
and a poet never went | more famous yet 'twixt TNK pr 11
am going, and never yet | went i so willing way. 1.01.103
to him, | store never hurts good governors. 1.03. 6
deep a cunning, | may be outworn, never undone. 1.03. 44
pace is but to say | that you shall never (like 1.03. 84
i never saw 'em. 2.01. 45 P
never more | must we behold those comforts, 2.02. 8
never see | the hardy youths strive for the 2.02. 9
o, never | shall we two exercise, like twins of 2.02. 17
these hands shall never draw 'em out like 2.02. 24
thousand cupids, | shall never clasp our necks; 2.02. 32
the vine shall grow, but we shall never see it; 2.02. 43
so they grow together, | will never sink; 2.02. 67
where you should never know it, and so perish 2.02. 92
never till now i was in prison, arcite. 2.02.132
and let mine honor down, and never charge? 2.02.195
but never more, | upon his oath and life, must 2.02.245
may rude wind never hurt thee! 2.02.275
wicked, all my sins | could never pluck upon me. 2.03. 7
and such as you never saw. 2.03. 65
of corn, | curling the wealthy ears, never flew. 2.03. 78
'tis odds | he never will affect me. 2.04. 2
fairer spoken | was never gentleman. 2.04. 21
i'll say never a word. 3.04. 18
freckled nell — that never fail'd her master. 3.05. 27
never so pleas'd, sir. 3.05.149
and for a preface, | i never heard a better. 3.05.151
i never saw such valor. 3.06. 74
this hand shall never more | come near thee with 3.06.102
a bolder traitor never trod thy ground, | a 3.06.141
now or never, sister, | speak, not to be denied. 3.06.185
swear 'em never more | to make me their 3.06.252
else, never trifle, | but take our lives, duke. 3.06.260
no, never, duke. 3.06.266
though i think | i never shall enjoy her, yet 3.06.268
for me, a hair shall never fall of these men. 3.06.287
"may you never more enjoy the light," etc. 4.01.104
by cocklight, | 'twill never thrive else. 4.01.113
but she shall never have him, tell her so, | for 4.01.122
young handsome men | shall never fall for me; 4.02. 4
of their sons, | shall never curse my cruelty. 4.02. 6
two greater and two better never yet | made 4.02. 62
judge by the outside) | i never saw nor read of. 4.02. 75
o' my conscience, | was never soldier's friend. 4.02. 88
promises | in such a body yet i never look'd on. 4.02.119
never fainting | under the weight of arms; 4.02.129
a gammon of bacon that will never be enough. 4.03. 39 P
this i shall never do again. 5.01. 32
have never been foul–mouth'd against thy law, 5.01. 98
i never practiced | upon man's wife, nor would 5.01.100
i never at great feasts | sought to betray a 5.01.102
and vow that lover never yet made sigh | truer 5.01.125
which never yet | beheld thing maculate — look 5.01.144
you never saw him dance? 5.02. 47
better never born | than minister to such harm! 5.03. 65
i was false, | yet never treacherous. 5.04. 93
never fortune | did play a subtler game. 5.04.112
here come and sit, where never serpent hisses, VEN 17
"if thou wilt chide, thy lips shall never open." 48
forc'd to content, but never to obey, | panting 61
she swears | from his soft bosom never to remove 81
never did passenger in summer's heat | more 91
violets whereon we lean | never can blab, nor 126
being steel'd, soft sighs can never grave it. 376
then love's deep groans i never shall regard, 377
and once made perfect, never lost again." 408
loseth his pride, and never waxeth strong. 420
and she by her good will | will never rise, so 480
were never four such lamps together mix'd, | had 489
o, never let their crimson liveries wear! 506

and glutton-like she feeds, yet never filleth; 548
whose tushes never sheath'd he whetteth still, 617
many, | and, being low, never reliev'd by any. 708
end without audience and are never done. 846
and never woman yet | could rule them both 1007
and never wound the heart with looks again, 1042
and never fright the silly lamb that day. 1098
and never did he bless | my youth with his, the 1119
birds never lim'd no secret bushes fear: LUC 88
but she, that never cop'd with stranger eyes, 99
self-love had never drown'd him in the flood. 266
my heart shall never countermand mine eye. 276
take, | the blemish that will never be forgot, 536
light, | she prays she never may behold the day: 746
and my true eyes have never practic'd how | to 748
thy violent vanities can never last. 894
this bastard graff shall never come to growth. 1062
and with my trespass never will dispense, | till 1070
and never be forgot in mighty rome | th' 1644
that never was inclin'd | to accessary yieldings 1657
o, never faith could hold, if not to beauty PP 5. 2
and as goods lost are seld or never found, | as 13. 7
prove unjust, | press never thou to choose anew. 18.22
with men, | to sin and never for to saint: 18.44
that thereby beauty's rose might never die, SON 1. 2
lie | (a closet never pierc'd with crystal eyes) 46. 6
that he shall never cut from memory | my sweet 63.11
i never saw that you did painting need, | and 83. 1
but best is best, if never intermix'd"? 101. 8
to me, fair friend, you never can be old, | for 104. 1
which three till now never kept seat in one. 105.14
o, never say that i was false of heart, | though 109. 1
o, never believe, though in my nature reign'd | all 109. 9
mine appetite i never more will grind | on newer 110.10
that looks on tempests and is never shaken; 116. 6
proved, | i never writ, nor no man ever loved. 116.14
whilst it hath thought itself so blessed never? 119. 6
part | of thee, thy record never can be miss'd. 122. 8
i grant i never saw a goddess go — | my 130.11
"so many have, that never touch'd his hand, LC 141
till now did ne'er invite, nor never vow. 182
NEVER-CONQUERED 1 FR 0.0001 REL FR 1 V 0 P
am i come to scale | thy never-conquered fort; LUC 482
NEVER-DAUNTED 1 FR 0.0001 REL FR 1 V 0 P
down | the never-daunted percy to the earth, 2H4 1.01.110
NEVER-DYING 1 FR 0.0001 REL FR 1 V 0 P
what never-dying honor hath he got | against 1H4 3.02.106
NEVER-ENDING 1 FR 0.0001 REL FR 1 V 0 P
me | to endless date of never-ending woes? LUC 935
NEVER-ERRING 1 FR 0.0001 REL FR 1 V 0 P
that never-erring arbitrator, tell us | when we TNK 1.02.114
NEVER-HEARD-OF 1 FR 0.0001 REL FR 1 V 0 P
some never-heard-of tortering pain for them. TIT 2.03.285
NEVER-NEEDED 1 FR 0.0001 REL FR 1 V 0 P
refuse your aid | in this so never-needed help, COR 5.01. 34
NEVER-QUENCHING 1 FR 0.0001 REL FR 1 V 0 P
that hand shall burn in never-quenching fire R2 5.05.108
NEVER-RESTING 1 FR 0.0001 REL FR 1 V 0 P
for never-resting time leads summer on | to SON 5. 5
NEVER'S 1 FR 0.0001 REL FR 1 V 0 P
never's my day, and then a kiss of you. TRO 4.05. 52
NEVER-SURFEITED 1 FR 0.0001 REL FR 1 V 0 P
the never-surfeited sea | hath caus'd to belch TMP 3.03. 55
NEVER-WITHERING 1 FR 0.0001 REL FR 1 V 0 P
upon your never-withering banks of flow'rs. CYM 5.04. 98
NEVIL 2 FR 0.0002 REL FR 2 V 0 P
you, cousin nevil, as i may remember — | when 2H4 3.01. 66
and, nevil, this i do assure myself, | richard 2H6 2.02. 80
NEVIL'S 1 FR 0.0001 REL FR 1 V 0 P
now, by my father's badge, old nevil's crest, 2H6 5.01.202
NEVILS' 2 FR 0.0002 REL FR 2 V 0 P
and therefore i will take the nevils' parts, 2H6 1.01.240
thou art | and never of the nevils' noble race. 3.02.215
NEVILS 3 FR 0.0003 REL FR 3 V 0 P
all | i cannot do more in england than the nevils: 2H6 1.03. 73
good, | the nevils are thy subjects to command. 2.02. 8
the princely warwick, and the nevils all, 4.01. 91
NEV'R *(also ne'er, never, and compounds)*
NEV'R 20 FR 0.0022 REL FR 20 V 0 P
practic'd well to this, or they'll nev'r do't. WIV 4.04. 66
nev'r speak or think | that timon's fortunes TIM 2.02.230
nev'r did poor steward wear a truer grief | for 4.03.480
which nev'r shook hands, nor bade farewell to MAC 1.02. 21
that could think, and nev'r disclose her mind, OTH 2.01.156
compulsive course | nev'r /feels retiring ebb, 3.03.455
shall nev'r look back, nev'r ebb to humble love, 3.03.458
shall nev'r look back, nev'r ebb to humble love, 3.03.458
i nev'r saw this before. 3.04.100
(better the red-ey'd god of war nev'r /ware), TNK 2.02. 21
that nature nev'r exceeded nor nev'r shall. 2.03. 12
that nature nev'r exceeded nor nev'r shall. 2.03. 12
and three better lads nev'r danc'd | under green 2.03. 38
trod thy ground, | a falser nev'r seem'd friend. 3.06.142
that you would nev'r deny me any thing | fit for 3.06.234
they that nev'r begg'd | but they prevail'd, had 4.01. 26
nev'r reveal'd secret, for i knew none — would 5.01. 99
thine ear | (which nev'r heard scurril term, 5.01.147
nev'r cast your child away for honesty. 5.02. 21
did you nev'r see the horse he gave me? 5.02. 45
/NEW 2 FR 0.0002 REL FR 2 V 0 P
like to a silver bow | /new bent in heaven, MND 1.01. 10
/care /is /gain /of /care, /by /new /care /won; R2 4.01.197
NEW 228 FR 0.0257 REL FR 182 V 46 P
new created | the creatures that were mine, i TMP 1.02. 81
i say, or chang'd 'em, | or else new form'd 'em; 1.02. 83
being rather new dy'd than stain'd with salt 2.01. 64 P
i will furnish it anon with new contents. 2.02.143 P
ca-caliban | has a new master, get a new man. 2.02.185
ca-caliban | has a new master, get a new man. 2.02.185
o brave new world | that has such people in't! 5.01.183
'tis new to thee. 5.01.184
once more, new servant, welcome; TGV 2.04.118
plead a new state in thy unrivall'd merit, | to 5.04.144
an old cloak makes a new jerkin; WIV 1.03. 17 P
thee and shall make thee a new doublet and hose. 3.03. 35 P
with the story of the prodigal, fresh and new. 4.05. 8 P
and the new deputy now for the duke — | whether MM 1.02.157
in — but this new governor | awakes me all the 1.02.165
breathe within your lips, | like man new made. 2.02. 79
either now, or by remissness new conceiv'd, 2.02. 96
go back again, and be new beaten home? ERR 2.01. 76
would you create me new? 3.02. 39
you got the picture of old adam new apparell'd? 4.03. 13 P
he hath every month a new sworn brother. ADO 1.01. 72 P
awake carving the fashion of a new doublet; 2.03. 18 P
be as great a soil in the new gloss of your 3.02. 6 P
as to show a child his new coat and forbid him 3.02. 7 P
i like the new tire within excellently, if the 3.04. 13 P
a man in all the world's new fashion planted, LLL 1.01.164
to any french courtier for a new devis'd cur'sy. 1.02. 63 P
beauty doth varnish age, as if new born, | and 4.03.240
take time to pause, and by the next new moon — MND 1.01. 83
to seek new friends and /stranger /companies. 1.01.219
the squirrel's hoard, and fetch thee new nuts. 4.01. 36
now thou and i are new in amity, | and will 4.01. 87
to your beards, new ribands to your pumps; 4.02. 36 P
solemnity, | in nightly revels and new jollity. 5.01.370
bassanio, who indeed gives rare new liveries. MV 2.02.109 P
see | lorenzo, who is thy new master's guest. 2.03. 6
sup to-night with my new master the christian. 2.04. 18 P
pigeons fly | to seal love's bonds new made, 2.06. 6
and ruin of the times | to be new varnish'd? 2.09. 49
falls to you, | be content, and seek no new. 3.02.134
if that the youth of my new int'rest here | have 3.02.221
letters from the doctor, | new come from padua. 4.01.109
charles, what's the new news at the new court? AYL 1.01. 96 P
charles, what's the new news at the new court? 1.01. 97 P
is banish'd by his younger brother the new duke, 1.01.100 P
whose lands and revenues enrich the new duke; 1.01.103 P
what, you wrastle to-morrow before the new duke? 1.01.121 P
young master ganymed, my new mistress's brother. 3.02. 87 P
you to entreaty, and there begins new matter. 4.01. 80 P
is it new and old too? how may that be? SHR 3.02. 32 P
is coming in a new hat and an old jerkin; 3.02. 43 P
my old master and my new mistress and myself, 4.01. 24 P
the servingmen in their new fustian, /their 4.01. 47 P
speak, | and sits as one new risen from a dream. 4.01.186
senses | all but new things disdain; AWW 1.02. 61
you have a new mistress. 2.03.243 P
his face into more lines than is in the new map, TN 3.02. 79 P
present our services to a fine new prince | one WT 2.01. 17
new woo my queen, recall the good camillo, 3.02.156
he is gone aboard a new ship to purge melancholy 4.04.763 P
wink of an eye some new grace will be born. 5.02.110 P
backs, | to make a hazard of new fortunes here. JN 2.01. 71
here | in likeness of a new untrimmed bride. 3.01.209
and even before this truce, but new before, | no 3.01.233
within the scorched veins of one new burn'd. 3.01.278
ay, alack, how new | is "husband" in my mouth! 3.01.305
done, | this act is as an ancient tale new told, 4.02. 18
for putting on so new a fashion'd robe. 4.02. 27
to this effect, before you were new crown'd, 4.02. 35
new flight, | and happy newness, that intends 5.04. 60
and furbish new the name of john a' gaunt, R2 1.03. 76
so it be new, there's no respect how vile — 2.01. 25
methinks i am a prophet new inspir'd, | and thus 2.01. 31
and daily new exactions are devis'd, | as blanks 2.01.249
as i intend to thrive in this new world, 4.01. 78
our holy lives must win a new world's crown, 5.01. 24
well, bear you well in this new spring of time, 5.02. 50
come, my old son, i pray god make thee new. 5.03.146
and breathe short-winded accents of new broils 1H4 1.01. 3
sir walter blunt, new lighted from his horse, 1.01. 63
and his chin new reap'd | show'd like a 1.03. 34
charles' wain is over the new chimney, and yet 2.01. 2 P
shall run | in a new channel fair and evenly. 3.01.102
thus did i keep my person fresh and new, | my 3.02. 55
sirrah, with a new wound in your thigh, come you 5.04.128 P
and sackcloth, but in new silk and old sack. 2H4 1.02.198 P
from me | with new lamenting ancient oversights, 2.03. 47
and history his loss | to new remembrance; 4.01.202
and new happiness | added to that that i am to 4.04. 81
sir, a new link to the bucket must needs be had; 5.01. 22 P
this new and gorgeous garment, majesty, | sits 5.02. 44
if i had had time to have made new liveries, i 5.05. 11 P
to line and new repair our towns of war | with H5 2.04. 7
i richard's body have interred new, | and on it 4.01.295
the gay new coats o'er the french soldiers' 4.03.118
but hark, what new alarum is this same? 4.06. 35
let not sloth dim your honors new begot. 1H6 1.01. 79
join'd, | a holy prophetess new risen up, | is 1.04.102
and lay new platforms to endamage them. 2.01. 77
even like a man new haled from the rack, | so 2.05. 3
and doth beget new courage in our breasts. 3.03. 87
to my determin'd time thou gav'st new date. 4.06. 9
with his new bride and england's dear-bought 2H6 1.01.252
and turn it, and set a new nap upon it. 4.02. 5 P
come, thou new ruin of old clifford's house: 5.02. 61
have caus'd him, by new act of parliament, | to 3H6 2.02. 91
to revel it with him and his new bride. 3.03.225
you | of this new marriage with the lady grey? 4.01. 2
is now dishonored by this new marriage. 4.01. 33
of the lord bonville on your new wive's son, 4.01. 57
to revel it with him and his new bride." 4.01. 95
is new committed to the bishop of york, | fell 4.04. 11
shall, whiles thy head is warm and new cut off, 5.01. 55
that you should be new christ'ned in the tower. R3 1.01. 50
to his new kingdom of ne'er-changing night. 2.02. 46
before, and he begins | a new hell in himself. H8 1.01. 72
do a vessel follow | that is new trimm'd, but 1.02. 80
new customs, | though they be never so 1.03. 2
they have all new legs, and lame ones. 1.03. 11
i hear of none but the new proclamation | that's 1.03. 17
prithee call gardiner to me, my new secretary. 2.02.115
but that you shall sustain moe new disgraces 3.02. 5
no new device to beat this from his brains? 3.02.217
i feel my heart new open'd. 3.02.366
(for so we are inform'd) with new opinions, 5.02. 52
not i know you for a favorer | of this new sect? 5.02.116
her ashes new create another heir | as great in 5.04. 41
of his name | shall be, and make new nations. 5.04. 52
is it matter new to us | that we come short of TRO 1.03. 10
am become | as new into the world, strange, 3.03. 12
with the least cause these his new honors, which COR 2.01.229
tullus aufidius then had made new head? 3.01. 1
we need not put new matter to his charge. 3.03. 76
he watered his new plants with dews of flattery, 5.06. 22
life, | and set abroad new business for you all? TIT 1.01.192
these words, these looks, infuse new life in me. 1.01.461
but dawning day new comfort hath inspir'd. 2.02. 10
from ancient grudge break to new mutiny, | where ROM pr 3
who set this ancient quarrel new abroach? 1.01.104
but new strook nine. 1.01.161
take thou some new infection to thy eye, | and 1.02. 49
call me but love, and i'll be new baptiz'd; 2.02. 50
/phantasimes, these new tuners of accent! 2.04. 29 P
who stand so much on the new form, that they 2.04. 34 P
tailor for wearing his new doublet before easter 3.01. 27 P
another for tying his new shoes with old riband? 3.01. 28 P
whiter than new snow upon a raven's back. 3.02. 19
to an impatient child that hath new robes | and 3.02. 30
and juliet, dead before, | warm and new kill'd. 5.03.197
so they were bleeding new, my lord, there's no TIM 1.02. 78 P
off | to the succession of new days this month. 2.02. 20
not be, by the persuasion of his new feasting. 3.06. 8 P
teem with new monsters, whom thy upward face 4.03.190
ordinary oaths my love | to every new protester; JC 1.02. 74
for some new honors that are heap'd on caesar. 1.02.134
any man's | in the disposing of new dignities. 3.01.178
with furbish'd arms and new supplies of men, MAC 1.02. 32
new honors come upon him, | like our strange 1.03.144
events | new hatch'd to th' woeful time. 2.03. 59
and destroy your sight | with a new gorgon. 2.03. 72
lest our old robes sit easier than our new! 2.04. 38
sign that i should quickly have a new father. 4.02. 63 P
each new morn | new widows howl, new orphans cry 4.03. 4
each new morn | new widows howl, new orphans cry 4.03. 5
new morn | new widows howl, new orphans cry, new 4.03. 5
cry, new sorrows | strike heaven on the face, 4.03. 5
and each new day a gash | is added to her wounds 4.03. 40
each minute teems a new one. 4.03.176
pause, | a roused vengeance sets him new a-work, HAM 2.02.488
mercury | new lighted on a /heaven-kissing hill, 3.04. 59
down, | devis'd a new commission, wrote it fair. 5.02. 32
he'll shape his old course in a country new. LR 1.01.187
she owes, | unfriended, new adopted to our hate, 1.01.203
is much o' th' savor | of other your new pranks. 1.04.238
rings, | their precious stones new lost; 5.03.191
gone | is the next way to draw new mischief on. OTH 1.03.205
the gloss of your new fortunes with this more 1.03.227 P
but our new heraldry is hands, not hearts. 3.04. 47
and his spirits should hunt | after new fancies. 3.04. 63
then must thou needs find out new heaven, new ANT 1.01. 17
must thou needs find out new heaven, new earth. 1.01. 17
are worn out, there are members to make new. 1.02.165 P
your old smock brings forth a new petticoat, and 1.02.168 P
but he hath wag'd | new wars 'gainst pompey; 3.04. 4
who cannot be new built, nor has no friends | so CYM 1.05. 59
make your lord, | that which he is, new o'er; 1.06.165
the exile of her minion is too new, | she hath 2.03. 41
new matter still. 5.05.243
of this poor infant, this fresh new sea-farer, PER 3.01. 41
evermore attending, | new joy wait on you! 5.03.102
new plays and maidenheads are near akin — TNK pr 1
had mine ear | stol'n some new air, or at 1.03. 75
wife, ever begetting | new births of love; 2.02. 81
ye shall not sleep, | i'll make ye a new morris. 2.02.273
and you shall see her | take a new lesson out, 2.03. 35
but there be new conditions, which you'll hear 4.01. 29
gently they swell, like women new conceiv'd, 4.02.128
our stars must glister with new fire, or be 5.01. 69
these worlds in tarquin new ambition bred, | who LUC 411
my shame so dead, mine honor is new born. 1190
foretell new storms to those already spent; 1589
from lips new waxen pale begins to blow | the 1663
in thy sweet semblance my old age new born, 1759
this were to be new made when thou art old, SON 2.13
you, | as he takes from you, i ingraft you new. 15.14
black night beauteous and her old face new. 27.12
and with old woes new wail my dear time's waste; 30. 4
moan, | which i new pay as if not paid before: 30.12
blest, | by new unfolding his imprison'd pride. 52.12
set, | and you in grecian tires are painted new; 53. 8
which parts the shore where two contracted new 56.10
if there be nothing new, but that which is 59. 1
green, | robbing no old to dress his beauty new, 68.12
why is my verse so barren of new pride? 76. 1
so all my best is dressing old words new, 76.11
for as the sun is daily new and old, | so is my 76.13
brain, | to take a new acquaintance of thy mind. 77.12
may still seem love to me, though alter'd new: 93. 3
our love was new, and then but in the spring, 102. 5
what's new to speak, what now to register, 108. 3
dear, | made old offenses of affections new; 110. 4
and new faith torn | in vowing new hate after 152. 3
in vowing new hate after new love bearing. 152. 4
in vowing new hate after new love bearing. 152. 4
but at my mistress' eye love's brand new fired, 153. 9
for my help lies | where cupid got new fire — 153.14
abide, | she was new lodg'd and newly deified. LC 84
and new pervert a reconciled maid!" 329
NEW-ADDED 1 FR 0.0001 REL FR 1 V 0 P
come on refresh'd, new-added, and encourag'd; JC 4.03.209
NEW-APPEARING 2 FR 0.0002 REL FR 2 V 0 P
my /unblown flow'rs, new-appearing sweets! R3 4.04. 10
eye | doth homage to his new-appearing sight, SON 7. 3
NEW-BELOVED 1 FR 0.0001 REL FR 1 V 0 P
much less | to meet her new-beloved any where. ROM 2.pr. 12
NEW-BLEEDING 1 FR 0.0001 REL FR 1 V 0 P
many bulwarks builded | of proofs new-bleeding, LC 153
NEW-BORN 5 FR 0.0005 REL FR 4 V 1 P
till new-born chins | be rough and razorable; TMP 2.01.249
with things dying, | i with things new-born. WT 3.03.114 P
all, with one consent, praise new-born gawds, TRO 3.03.176
and pity, like a naked new-born babe, | striding MAC 1.07. 21
steel, | be soft as sinews of the new-born babe! HAM 3.03. 71
NEW-BUILT 1 FR 0.0001 REL FR 1 V 0 P
obedience, | her new-built virtue and obedience. SHR 5.02.118
NEW-COME 2 FR 0.0002 REL FR 2 V 0 P
that strew the green lap of the new-come spring? R2 5.02. 47
his new-come champion, virtuous joan of /aire, 1H6 2.02. 20

NEW-CREATE 1 FR 0.0001 REL FR 1 V 0 P
upon his blood | and new-create /this fault? OTH 4.01.276
NEW-CROWNED 1 FR 0.0001 REL FR 1 V 0 P
true subjects bow | to a new-crowned monarch; MV 3.02. 50
NEW-DATED 1 FR 0.0001 REL FR 1 V 0 P
new-dated letters from northumberland, | their 2H4 4.01. 8
NEW-DELIVER'D 1 FR 0.0001 REL FR 1 V 0 P
and i, a gasping new-deliver'd mother, | have R2 2.02. 65
NEW-DELIVERED 1 FR 0.0001 REL FR 1 V 0 P
the new-delivered hastings? R3 1.01.121
NEW-ENKINDLED 1 FR 0.0001 REL FR 1 V 0 P
with eyes as red as new-enkindled fire, | and JN 4.02.163
NEWER 7 FR 0.0008 REL FR 7 V 0 P
love | is by a newer object quite forgotten. TGV 2.04.195
what old or newer torture | must i receive, WT 3.02.177
here comes newer comfort. MAC 5.09. 19
this is some token from a newer friend; OTH 3.04.181
pausing for means to mourn some newer way. LUC 1365
i never more will grind | on newer proof, to try SON 110.11
thy pyramids built up with newer might | to me 123. 2
NEWEST 4 FR 0.0004 REL FR 4 V 0 P
the oldest sins the newest kind of ways? 2H4 4.05.126
by his plight, of the revolt | the newest state. MAC 1.02. 3
which would be worn now in their newest gloss, 1.07. 34
what's the newest grief? 4.03.174
NEW-FALL'N 3 FR 0.0003 REL FR 3 V 0 P
mean time, forget this new-fall'n dignity, | and AYL 5.04.176
nor claim no further than your new-fall'n right, 1H4 5.01. 44
as apt as new-fall'n snow takes any dint. VEN 354
NEW-FANGLED 3 FR 0.0003 REL FR 2 V 1 P
than wish a snow in may's new-fangled shows; LLL 1.01.106
against rain, more new-fangled than an ape, more
AYL 4.01.152 P
some in their garments, though new-fangled ill, SON 91. 3
NEW-FIR'D 1 FR 0.0001 REL FR 1 V 0 P
foot, | and with a heart new-fir'd i follow you, JC 2.01.332
NEW-FOUND 2 FR 0.0002 REL FR 2 V 0 P
and full of new-found oaths, which he will break TGV 4.04.130
to new-found methods and to compounds strange?
SON 76. 4
NEWGATE 1 FR 0.0001 REL FR 0 V 1 P
yea, two and two, newgate fashion. 1H4 3.03. 90 P
NEW-HATCH'D 1 FR 0.0001 REL FR 1 V 0 P
palm with entertainment | of each new-hatch'd, HAM 1.03. 65
NEW-HEAL'D 2 FR 0.0002 REL FR 1 V 1 P
well, i am loath to gall a new-heal'd wound. 2H4 1.02.147 P
the new-heal'd wound of malice should break out,
R3 2.02.125
NEW-KILL'D 1 FR 0.0001 REL FR 1 V 0 P
like to a new-kill'd bird she trembling lies; LUC 457
NEWLY 32 FR 0.0036 REL FR 27 V 5 P
sudden, | as falstaff, she, and i are newly met, WIV 4.04. 53
who, newly in the seat, that it may know | he MM 1.02.161
of pygmalion's images newly made woman to be had 3.02. 45 P
and he hath ta'en you newly into his grace, ADO 1.03. 22 P
i will have that subject newly writ o'er, that i LLL 1.02.115 P
as to rejoice at friends but newly found. 5.02.751
clear | as morning roses newly wash'd with dew; SHR 2.01.173
'tis marvel, but that you are but newly come, 4.02. 86
hath newly pass'd between this youth and me. TN 5.01.155
in doing and now newly perform'd by that rare WT 5.02. 96 P
the statue is but newly fix'd; 5.03. 47
this royal hand and mine are newly knit, | and JN 3.01.226
so newly join'd in love, so strong in both, 3.01.240
the dangers of the days but newly gone, | whose 2H4 4.01. 80
have but their stings and teeth newly ta'en out; 4.05.205
and newly move | with casted slough and fresh H5 4.01. 22
the duke of york is newly come from ireland, 2H6 4.09. 24
newly preferr'd from the king's secretary, | the H8 4.01.102
and | by deed-achieving honor newly nam'd — COR 2.01.173
you are but newly planted in your throne; TIT 1.01.444
romeo, | who had but newly entertain'd revenge, ROM 3.01.171
and juliet bleeding, warm, and newly dead, | who 5.03.175
certain nobles of the senate | newly alighted, TIM 1.02.175
world | when sects and factions were newly born. 3.05. 30
which would be planted newly with the time, | as MAC 5.09. 31
sir, here is newly come to court laertes, HAM 5.02.106 P
breath, indeed, these hands have newly stopp'd. OTH 5.02.202
grown to strength, | are newly grown to love; ANT 1.03. 49
three kings i had newly feasted, and did want 2.02. 76
or as iris | newly dropp'd down from heaven. TNK 4.01. 88
dead, | by thy bright beauty was it newly bred. LUC 490
abide, | she was new lodg'd and newly deified. LC 84
NEW-MADE 8 FR 0.0009 REL FR 8 V 0 P
for new-made honor doth forget men's names; JN 1.01.187
truth | and lasting fealty to the new-made king. R2 5.02. 45
suffolk, the new-made duke that rules the roast, 2H6 1.01.109
and from the great and new-made duke of suffolk; 1.02. 95
'tis not his new-made bride shall succor him, 3H6 3.03.207
and gold, | to wait upon this new-made empress:
TIT 2.01. 20
or bid me go into a new-made grave, | and hide ROM 4.01. 84
banish'd the new-made bridegroom from this city, 5.03.235
NEW-MARRIED 3 FR 0.0003 REL FR 2 V 1 P
for this new-married man approaching here, MM 5.01.400
upon my tongue like a new-married wife about her
H5 5.02.179 P
somewhat too early for new-married ladies. TIT 2.02. 15
NEWNESS 3 FR 0.0003 REL FR 3 V 0 P
whether it be the fault and glimpse of newness, MM 1.02.158
and happy newness, that intends old right. JN 5.04. 61
newness | of cloten's death (we being not known, CYM 4.04. 9
NEW-PLANTED 1 FR 0.0001 REL FR 1 V 0 P
his private arbors and new-planted orchards, JC 3.02.248
/NEWS 5 FR 0.0005 REL FR 4 V 1 P
news, /old /news, and such news as you never SHR 3.02. 30 P
/bushy, /what /news? R2 1.04. 53
/what /news? HAM 4.07. 36
i can call but now) i have heard /strange /news. LR 2.01. 87
/what /news? 4.02. 69
NEWS 320 FR 0.0361 REL FR 245 V 75 P
what is the news? TMP 5.01.220
the best news is, that we have safely found 5.01.221
and what news else | betideth here in absence of TGV 1.01. 58
lend me the letter; let me see what news. 1.03. 55
there is no news, my lord, but that he writes 1.03. 56
a letter from your friends | of much good news? 2.04. 52
i think 'tis no unwelcome news to you. 2.04. 81
my ears are stopp'd and cannot hear good news, 3.01.206
what is your news? 3.01.216
that thou art banish'd — o, that's the news! 3.01.219
what news with your mastership? 3.01.280 P
what news then in your paper? 3.01.285 P
the blackest news that ever thou heardst. 3.01.286 P
what news? how does pretty mistress anne? WIV 1.04.137 P
this news distracts me! 2.02.134 P
how now, my eyas-musket, what news with you? 3.03. 23 P
what's the news with you? MM 1.02. 85 P
what news abroad, friar? 3.02. 82 P
what news? 3.02. 83 P
what news, friar, of the duke? 3.02. 86 P
what news abroad i' th' world? 3.02.221 P
this news is old enough, yet it is every day's 3.02.229 P
news is old enough, yet it is every day's news. 3.02.230 P
what is the news from this good deputy? 4.01. 27
now, sir, what news? 4.02.114 P
how now, abhorson? what's the news with you? 4.03. 39 P
i can tell you strange news that you yet dreamt ADO 1.02. 4 P
what news, borachio? 1.03. 41 P
but hear these ill news with the ears of claudio 2.01.173
now, signior, what news? 5.01.111 P
will you go hear this news, signior? 5.02.101 P
is cupid's grandfather, and learns news of him. LLL 2.01.255
thy news, boyet? 5.02. 81
for the news i bring | is heavy in my tongue. 5.02.718
thanks, good egeus. what's the news with thee? MND 1.01. 21
o me, what news, my love! 3.02.272
how now, what news? MV 1.02.122 P
what news on the rialto? 1.03. 38 P
well, old man, i will tell you news of your son. 2.02. 78 P
friend launcelot, what's the news? 2.04. 9
now what news on the rialto? 3.01. 1 P
how now, shylock, what news among the merchants? 3.01. 22 P
what news from genoa? 3.01. 79 P
no news of them? 3.01. 90 P
i thank thee, good tubal, good news, good news! 3.01.106 P
i thank thee, good tubal, good news, good news! 3.01.107 P
what's the news from venice? 3.02.238
from my master, with his horn full of good news. 5.01. 47 P
and i have better news in store for you | than 5.01.274
charles, what's the new news at the new court? AYL 1.01. 97 P
there's no news at the court, sir, but the old 1.01. 98 P
no news at the court, sir, but the old news: 1.01. 99 P
with his mouth full of news. 1.02. 92 P
what's the news? 1.02. 98 P
pray what's the news? SHR 1.01.225 P
i'll tell you news indifferent good for either. 1.02.180
news, /old /news, and such news as you never 3.02. 30 P
/old /news, and such news as you never heard of! 3.02. 31 P
is it not news to /hear of petruchio's coming? 3.02. 33 P
but say, what to thine old news? 3.02. 42 P
ready, and therefore, good grumio, the news. 4.01. 40 P
and as much news as wilt thou. 4.01. 42 P
all ready; and therefore, i pray thee, news. 4.01. 53 P
what news with you, sir? 4.03. 62
how now, what news? 5.02. 80
lord and master's married, there's news for you. AWW 2.03.243 P
yonder is heavy news within between two soldiers 3.02. 33 P
there is some comfort in the news, some comfort. 3.02. 36 P
how now, what news from her? TN 1.01. 22
what is the news i' th' court? WT 1.02.367
this news is mortal to the queen. 3.02.148
but let time's news | be known when 'tis brought 4.01. 26
the news, rogero? 5.02. 21 P
this news, which is call'd true, is so like an 5.02. 27 P
this news hath made thee a most ugly man. JN 3.01. 37
not gone already, | even at that news he dies; 3.04.164
hubert, what news with you? 4.02. 68
not seek to stuff | my head with more ill news, 4.02.134
hear'st thou the news abroad, who are arriv'd? 4.02.160
with open mouth swallowing a tailor's news, 4.02.195
this news was brought to richard but even now. 5.03. 12
and will not let me welcome this good news. 5.03. 15
here: what news? 5.05. 9
ah, foul shrewd news! 5.05. 14
come, come; sans compliment, what news abroad? 5.06. 16
brief then; and what's the news? 5.06. 18
o my sweet sir, news fitting to the night, 5.06. 19
show me the very wound of this ill news; 5.06. 21
by, | which holds but till thy news be uttered, 5.07. 56
you breathe these dead news in as dead an ear. 5.07. 65
the wind sits fair for news to go for ireland, R2 2.02.123
the news is very fair and good, my lord: 3.03. 5
harsh rude tongue sound this unpleasing news? 3.04. 74
little joy have i | to breathe this news, yet 3.04. 82
gard'ner, for telling me these news of woe, 3.04.100
what news from oxford? 5.02. 52
the latest news we hear | is that the rebels 5.06. 1
welcome, my lord, what is the news? 5.06. 5
the next news is, i have to london sent | the 5.06. 7
came | a post from wales loaden with heavy news, 1H4 1.01. 37
for more uneven and unwelcome news | came from 1.01. 50
and shape of likelihood the news was told; 1.01. 58
and he hath brought us smooth and welcome news. 1.01. 66
what news? 2.02. 52 P
there's villainous news abroad. 2.04.333 P
father's beard is turn'd white with the news. 2.04.359 P
but wherefore do i tell these news to thee? 3.02.121
hal, to the news at court for the robbery, lad, 3.03.175 P
pray god my news be worth a welcome, lord. 4.01. 87
there is more news: 4.01.124
which gape and rub the elbow at the news | of 5.01. 77
uncle, what news? 5.02. 29
and not a man of them brings other news | than 2H4 in 38
what news, lord bardolph? 1.01. 7
i bring you certain news from shrewsbury. 1.01. 12
that freely rend'red me these news for true. 1.01. 27
i sent | on tuesday last to listen after news. 1.01. 29
of him | i did demand what news from shrewsbury. 1.01. 40
look, here comes more news. 1.01. 59
yet the first bringer of unwelcome news | hath 1.01.100
this is the news at full. 1.01.135
in poison there is physic, and these news, 1.01.137
now, master gower, what news? 2.01.133
i have heard better news. 2.01.166
what's the news, my lord? 2.01.167 P
what is the news, my lord? 2.01.170 P
peto, how now, what news? 2.04.354 P
now, what news? 4.01. 18
and deliver to the army | this news of peace. 4.02. 70
our news shall go before us to his majesty, 4.03. 78
look here's more news. 4.04. 93
wherefore should these good news make me sick? 4.04.102
i should rejoice now at this happy news, | and 4.04.109
heard he the good news yet? | tell it him. 4.05. 11
one pistol come from the court with news. 5.03. 81 P
and golden times, and happy news of price. 5.03. 96
o base assyrian knight, what is thy news? 5.03.101
and shall good news be baffled? 5.03.105
sir, you come with news from the court, i take 5.03.110 P
what? i do bring good news? 5.03.128
news have i that my doll is dead i' th' spittle H5 5.01. 81
these news would cause him once more yield the 1H6 1.01. 67
where's the prince dolphin? i have news for him. 1.02. 46
these news, my lords, may cheer our drooping 5.02. 1
i'll over then to england with this news, | and 5.03.167
cold news for me; 2H6 1.01.237
thither goes these news, as fast as horse can 1.04. 74
this news, i think, hath turn'd your weapon's 2.01.176
welcome, lord somerset. what news from france? 3.01. 83
cold news, lord somerset; 3.01. 86
cold news for me; 3.01. 87
whither goes vaux so fast? what news, i prithee? 3.02.367
what news are these! 3.02.380
what news? 4.04. 26
say, what news with thee? 5.01.125
come, cousin, let us tell the queen these news. 3H6 1.01.182
but stay, what news? 1.02. 48
he been ta'en, we should have heard the news; 2.01. 4
he been slain, we should have heard the news; 2.01. 5
what news abroad? 2.01. 95
if we should recompt | our baleful news, and at 2.01. 97
ten days ago i drown'd these news in tears; 2.01.104
how now? what news? 2.01.205
if this news be true, | poor queen and son, your 3.01. 31
fair queen and mistress | smiles at her news, 3.03.168
warwick, what are thy news? 3.03.171
what letters or what news | from france? 4.01. 84
these news i must confess are full of grief, 4.04. 13
what news, my friend? 4.06. 77
unsavory news! but how made he escape? 4.06. 80
that we could hear no news of his repair? 5.01. 20
even now we heard the news. 5.02. 32
ere ye come there, be sure to hear some news. 5.05. 48
what news abroad? R3 1.01.134
no news so bad abroad as this at home: 1.01.135
now, by saint john, that news is bad indeed! 1.01.138
hear you the news abroad? 2.03. 3
ill news, by'r lady — seldom comes the better. 2.03. 4
doth the news hold of good king edward's death? 2.03. 7
here comes a messenger. what news? 2.04. 38
such news, my lord, as grieves me to report. 2.04. 39
what is thy news? 2.04. 41
and bid my lord, for joy of this good news, 3.01.184
what news, what news, in this our tott'ring 3.02. 37
what news, what news, in this our tott'ring 3.02. 37
and thereupon he sends you this good news, 3.02. 48
indeed i am no mourner for that news, | because 3.02. 51
look for the news that the guildhall affords. 3.05.102
or else i swoon with this dead-killing news! 4.01. 35
despiteful tidings, o unpleasing news! 4.01. 36
how now, lord stanley, what's the news? 4.02. 46
i hear the news, my lord. 4.02. 86
kind tyrrel, am i happy in thy news? 4.03. 24
good or bad news, that thou com'st in so bluntly 4.03. 45
bad news, my lord. 4.03. 46
what news? 4.04.432
my mind is chang'd. stanley, what news with you? 4.04.456
once more, what news? 4.04.462
take thou that, till thou bring better news. 4.04.508
the news i have to tell your majesty | is that 4.04.509
buckingham is taken — | that is the best news. 4.04.532
what news, sir thomas lovell? H8 1.03. 16
'tis most true | these news are every where; 2.02. 38
i should be glad to hear such news as this 3.02. 24
what news abroad? 3.02.391
that's news indeed. 3.02.402
now, lovell, from the queen what is the news? 5.01. 61
i have news to tell you. 5.01. 94
what news, aeneas, from the field to-day? TRO 1.01.108
what news with you so early? 4.02. 46
thou crusty batch of nature, what's the news? 5.01. 5
the news is, sir, the volsces are in arms. COR 1.01.224
i'll tell you excellent news of your husband. 1.03. 90 P
there came news from him last night. 1.03. 93 P
yonder comes news: a wager they have met. 1.04. 1
thy news? 1.06. 9
confound an hour, | and bring thy news so late? 1.06. 18
augurer tells me we shall have news to-night. 2.01. 1 P
what's the news in rome? 4.03. 10 P
o slaves, i can tell you news — news, you 4.05.172 P
i can tell you news — news, you rascals! 4.05.172 P
but more of thy news. 4.05.190 P
but the bottom of the news is, our general is 4.05.197 P
some news is coming | that turns their 4.06. 59
what news? what news? 4.06. 80
what news? what news? 4.06. 80
what's the news? what's the news? 4.06. 84
what's the news? what's the news? 4.06. 84
pray now, your news? 4.06. 87
pray, your news? 4.06. 88
faith, we hear fearful news. 4.06.139
i do not like this news. 4.06.157
what's the news? 5.04. 39
good news, good news! 5.04. 40
good news, good news! 5.04. 40
this is good news. 5.04. 51
gramercy, lovely lucius. what's the news? TIT 4.02. 7
that you are both decipher'd, that's the news, 4.02. 8
news, news from heaven! 4.03. 78
news, news from heaven! 4.03. 78
what news with thee, aemilius? 4.04. 61
welcome, aemilius, what's the news from rome? 5.01.155
o honey nurse, what news? ROM 2.05. 18

though news be sad, yet tell them merrily; 2.05. 22
good, thou shamest the music of sweet news | by 2.05. 23
i would thou hadst my bones, and i thy news. 2.05. 27
is thy news good or bad? 2.05. 35
they'll be in scarlet straight at any news. 2.05. 71
o, here comes my nurse, | and she brings news; 3.02. 32
now, nurse, what news? 3.02. 34
ay me, what news? why dost thou wring thy hands? 3.02. 36
father, what news? 3.03. 4
these are news indeed! 3.05.123
my dreams presage some joyful news at hand. 5.01. 2
news from verona! 5.01. 12
o, pardon me for bringing these ill news, 5.01. 22
i brought my master news of juliet's death, 5.03.272
what news? TIM 1.02.185
how do you? what's the news? 3.06. 52 P
i could tell you more news too. JC 1.02.285 P
sirrah, what news? 5.03. 25
what news? 5.03. 27
i'll tell /the news. 5.04. 17
receiv'd, macbeth, | the news of thy success; MAC 1.03. 90
give him tending, | he brings great news. 1.05. 38
what news? 1.07. 28
what news more? 5.03. 30
and now, laertes, what's the news with you? HAM 1.02. 42
what news, my lord? 1.05.117
thou still hast been the father of good news. 2.02. 42
my news shall be the fruit to that great feast. 2.02. 52
what news? 2.02.236 P
but your news is not true. 2.02.238 P
my lord, i have news to tell you. 2.02.389 P
my lord, i have news to tell you. 2.02.390 P
i cannot live to hear the news from england, 5.02.354
what news? LR 1.02. 26
i know no news, my lord. 1.02. 29 P
you have heard of the news abroad, i mean the 2.01. 6 P
another way, | the news is not so tart. 4.02. 87
news, madam! 4.04. 20
and hear poor rogues | talk of court news; 5.03. 14
what is the news? OTH 1.02. 36
there's no composition in /these news | that 1.03. 1
here is more news. 1.03. 32
news, lads! 2.01. 20
see for the news. 2.01. 95
news, friends: 2.01.202
for, besides these beneficial news, it is the 2.02. 7 P
how now, good cassio, what's the news with you? 3.04.109
and what's the news, good cousin lodovico? 4.01.219
news, my good lord, from rome. ANT 1.01. 18
the nature of bad news infects the teller. 1.02. 95
labienus | (this is stiff news) hath with his 1.02.100
from sicyon how the news? speak there! 1.02.113
i know by that same eye there's some good news. 1.03. 19
from alexandria | this is the news: 1.04. 4
here's more news. 1.04. 33
i that do bring the news made not the match. 2.05. 67
be honest, it is never good | to bring bad news. 2.05. 86
there's strange news come, sir. 3.05. 2 P
my news | i might have told hereafter. 3.05. 21
the news is true, my lord: 3.07. 54
with news the time's with labor, and throes 3.07. 80
nothing. what news? 4.03. 4
what news? CYM 1.01.159
good news, gods! 3.02. 39
if't be summer news, | smile to't before; 3.04. 12
to be i' th' field, and ask "what news?" 5.03. 65
thou bring'st good news, i am call'd to be made 5.04.193 P
bring'st such pelting scurvy news continually, TNK 2.02.266
which will seek of me | some news from earth, 3.01. 80
tell me | news from all parts o' th' world. 3.04. 13
i bring you news, | good news. 4.01. 17
i bring you news, | good news. 4.01. 18
ye are a good man | and ever bring good news. 4.01. 25
duke your brother, | madam, i bring you news. 4.02. 56
that sometime true news, sometime false doth VEN 658
fearing some hard news from the warlike band LUC 255
no news but health from their physicians know; SON 140. 8

NEW-SAD 1 FR 0.0001 REL FR 1 V 0 P
out of a new-sad soul, that you vouchsafe | in LLL 5.02.731

NEWS-CRAMM'D 1 FR 0.0001 REL FR 0 V 1 P
then shall we be news-cramm'd. AYL 1.02. 95 P

NEW-SHED 1 FR 0.0001 REL FR 1 V 0 P
upon whose leaves are drops of new-shed blood TIT 2.03.200

NEWSMONGERS 1 FR 0.0001 REL FR 1 V 0 P
by smiling pick-thanks and base newsmongers, | i 1H4 3.02. 25

NEW-SPRUNG 1 FR 0.0001 REL FR 1 V 0 P
bows her head, the new-sprung flow'r to smell, VEN 1171

NEW'ST 1 FR 0.0001 REL FR 1 V 0 P
toys for your head | of the new'st and fin'st, WT 4.04.320

NEW-STORE 1 FR 0.0001 REL FR 1 V 0 P
to new-store france with bastard warriors. H5 3.05. 31

NEWT 2 FR 0.0002 REL FR 2 V 0 P
the gilded newt and eyeless venom'd worm, | with TIM 4.03.182
eye of newt and toe of frog, | wool of bat and MAC 4.01. 14

NEW-TA'EN 1 FR 0.0001 REL FR 0 V 1 P
her breath as short as a new-ta'en sparrow. TRO 3.02. 34 P

NEW-TRANSFORMED 1 FR 0.0001 REL FR 1 V 0 P
should drive upon thy new-transformed limbs, TIT 2.03. 64

NEW-TROTHED 1 FR 0.0001 REL FR 1 V 0 P
so says the prince and my new-trothed lord. ADO 3.01. 38

NEWTS 1 FR 0.0001 REL FR 1 V 0 P
newts and blind-worms, do no wrong, | come not MND 2.02. 11

NEW-TUN'D 1 FR 0.0001 REL FR 0 V 1 P
war, which they trick up with new-tun'd oaths; H5 3.06. 76 P

NEW-YEAR'S 1 FR 0.0001 REL FR 0 V 1 P
and give them to a dog for a new-year's gift. WIV 3.05. 8 P

NEXT 178 FR 0.0201 REL FR 129 V 49 P
he whom next thyself | of all the world i lov'd, TMP 1.02. 68
what impossible matter will he make easy next? 2.01. 90 P
then tell me, | who's the next heir of naples? 2.01.245
if you prove a mutineer — the next tree! 3.02. 36 P
the next advantage | will we take throughly. 3.03. 13
the next, our ship — | which, but three glasses 5.01.222
the next ensuing hour some foul mischance TGV 2.02. 11
unless the next word that thou speak'st | have 3.01.239
what's next? 3.01.363 P
what dangerous action, stood it next to death, 5.04. 41
worship more of the wart the next time we have WIV 1.04.159 P
next, give me your hand; 2.02.253 P
next, to be compass'd, like a good bilbo, in the 3.05.110 P
next, this is a respected fellow; MM 2.01.163 P
morning, may sleep the sounder all the next day. 4.03. 47 P
but the next morn betimes, | his purpose 5.01.101
next, it imports no reason | that with such 5.01.108
i'll make you amends next, to give you nothing ERR 2.02. 53 P
it ever changes with the next block. ADO 1.01. 77 P
any ill, i will leave them at the next turning. 2.01.154 P
even to the next willow, about your own business 2.01.187 P
as he was appointed next morning at the temple, 3.03.160 P
withal | upon the next occasion that we meet, LLL 5.02.143
and that 'a wears next his heart for a favor. 5.02.715 P
take time to pause, and by the next new moon — MND 1.01. 83
dote | upon the next live creature that it sees. 2.01.172
the next thing then she waking looks upon | (be 2.01.179
but do it when the next thing he espies | may be 2.01.262
then, what it was that next came in her eye, 3.02. 2
when they next wake, all this derision | shall 3.02.370
my next is, "most fair pyramus." 4.01.201 P
who is next? 5.01.126 P
turn up on your right hand at the next turning, MV 2.02. 41 P
next turning, but at the next turning of all, on 2.02. 42 P
marry, at the very next turning, turn of no hand 2.02. 43 P
next, if i fail | of the right casket, never in 2.09. 11
whether till the next night she had rather stay, 5.01.302
oliver martext, the vicar of the next village, AYL 3.03. 44 P
i, faith, boy, to have the next wish after, SHR 1.01.239
and twice as much, what e'er thou off'rest next. 2.01.380
on sunday next you know | my daughter katherine 2.01.393
i, madam, and i speak the truth the next way: AWW 1.03. 59 P
that before you, and next unto high heaven, | i 1.03.193
"too young" and "the next year" and "'tis too 2.01. 28
his lordship will next morning for france. 4.03. 78 P
brains are forfeit to the next tile that falls. 4.03.190 P
now jove, in his next commodity of hair, send TN 3.01. 44 P
next to thyself and my young rover, he's WT 1.02.176
and his pond fish'd by his next neighbor — by 1.02.195
please your ladyship | to visit the next room, 2.02. 45
home, home, the next way. 3.03.124 P
come, good boy, the next way home. 3.03.127 P
go you the next way with your findings; 3.03.128 P
what i do next shall be to tell the king | of 4.04.662
that, ere the next ascension-day at noon, | your JN 4.02.151
the next is this: 5.02. 69
but to the next high way, and there i left him. R2 1.04. 4
his, | and he our subjects' next degree in hope. 1.04. 36
be york the next that must be bankrout so! 2.01.151
to-morrow next | we will for ireland, and 'tis 2.01.217
on wednesday next we solemnly proclaim | our 4.01.319
stage, | are idly bent on him that enters next, 5.02. 25
the next news is, i have to london sent | the 5.06. 7
on wednesday next our council we | will hold at 1H4 1.01.103
who therewith angry, when it next came there, 1.03. 40
by richard, that dead is, the next of blood? 1.03.146
and that is the next way to give poor jades the 2.01. 9 P
meet me in arms by the ninth of the next month? 2.03. 28 P
me see — about michaelmas next i shall be — 2.04. 54 P
'tis the next way to turn tailor, or be 3.01.259 P
on wednesday next, harry, you shall set forward, 3.02.173
if not, let him kill the next percy himself. 5.04.141 P
who is next? 2H4 3.02.171 P
he that dies this year is quit for the next. 3.02.238 P
my lord, i found the prince in the next room, 4.05. 82
sand, that look to be wash'd off the next tide. H5 4.01. 98 P
next day after dawn, | doth rise and help 4.01.274
where is best place to make our batt'ry next? 1H6 1.04. 65
that one day bloom'd and fruitful were the next. 1.06. 7
and so farewell until i meet thee next. 2.04.113
shall be /wip'd out in the next parliament, 2.04.117
body) | i was the next by birth and parentage; 2.05. 73
got | first to my god and next unto your grace. 3.04. 12
i vow'd, base knight, when i did meet thee next, 4.01. 14
england ere the thirtieth of may next ensuing. 2H6 1.01. 49 P
consider, lords, he is the next of blood, | and 1.01.151
next time i'll keep my dreams unto myself, | and 1.02. 53
were i a man, a duke, and next of blood, | i 1.02. 63
next, if i be appointed for the place, | my lord 1.03.167
of combat shall be the last of the next month. 1.03.219 P
next to whom | was john of gaunt, the duke of 2.02. 13
the issue of the next son should have reign'd. 2.02. 32
holden at bury the first of this next month. 2.04. 71
and should you fall, he is the next will mount. 3.01. 22
as next the king he was successive heir, | and 3.01. 49
be, | and henry put apart, the next for me. 3.01.383
but that the next heir should succeed and reign. 3H6 1.01.146
the next degree is england's royal throne; 2.01.193
and next his throat unto the butcher's knife. 5.06. 9
clarence, thy turn is next, and then the rest, 5.06. 90
him into the malmsey-butt in the next room. R3 1.04.156 P
to-morrow, or next day, they will be here. 2.04. 3
come the next sabbath, and i will content you. 3.02.111
lord, | to visit him to-morrow or next day. 3.07. 60
following day | became the next day's master, H8 1.01. 17
for him, which buys | a place next to the king. 1.01. 66
fresher air, my lord, | in the next chamber. 1.04.102
lov'd him next heav'n? 3.01.130
i have kept you next my heart, have not alone 3.02.157
the next is, that sir thomas more is chosen 3.02.393
next, the duke of norfolk, | he to be earl 4.01. 18
first, mine own service to your grace, the next, 4.02.115
my next poor petition | is, that his noble grace 4.02.138
and so i'll tell her the next time i see her. TRO 1.01. 82 P
by him one step below, he by the next, | that 1.03.130
he by the next, | that next by him beneath; 1.03.131
ay, and good next day too. 3.03. 69
i beseech you next | to feast with me and see me 4.05.228
so, ilion, fall thou next! 5.08. 11
next, | i accept my thankfulness. COR 5.04. 58
well, bury him, and bury me the next. TIT 1.01.386
the man must not be hang'd till the next week. 4.03. 83 P
may prove a beauteous flow'r when next we meet. ROM 2.02.122
on we'nsday next — | but soft, what day is this 3.04. 17
marry, my child, early next thursday morn, | the 3.05.112
fettle your fine joints 'gainst thursday next, 3.05.153
that may be must be, love, on thursday next. 4.01. 20
on thursday next be married to this county. 4.01. 49
sleep for a week, for the next night, i warrant, 4.05. 5
the fellow that sits next him, now parts bread TIM 1.02. 46 P
i prithee but repair to me next morning. 2.02. 25
one day he gives us diamonds, next day stones. 3.06.120
upon the next encounter yields him ours. JC 1.03.156
next, caius cassius, do i take your hand; 3.01.186
upon the next tree shall thou hang alive, | till MAC 5.05. 38
a kind of easiness | to the next abstinence, the HAM 3.04.167
to the next abstinence, the next more easy; 3.04.167
next, your son gone, and he most violent author 4.05. 80
when you are ask'd this question next, say "a 5.01. 58 P
now, the next day | was our sea-fight, and what 5.02. 53
next month with us. LR 1.01.286 P
gone | is the next way to draw new mischief on. OTH 1.03.205
a vomit ere the next pottle can be fill'd. 2.03. 84 P
he that stirs next to carve for his own rage 2.03.173
i slept the next night well, fed well, was free 3.03.340
will not, come when you are next prepar'd for. 4.01.160 P
if thou the next night following enjoy not 4.02.215 P
his scorn i approve" — | nay, that's not next. 4.03. 53 P
but next day | i told him of myself, which was ANT 2.02. 77
and next morn, | ere the ninth hour, i drunk him 2.05. 20
that's the next to do. 2.06. 59
next, cleopatra does confess thy greatness, 3.12. 16
the next caesarion /smite, | till by degrees the 3.13.162
the next time i do fight, | i'll make death love 3.13.191
and drink carouses to the next day's fate, 4.08. 34
and cere up my embracements from a next | with CYM 1.01.116
be assur'd, madam, | with his next vantage. 1.03. 24
thy mistress is, at once, | at the next word. 3.05. 96
with the next benefit o' th' wind. 4.02.342
what shall be next, | pardon old gower — this PER 2.ch. 39
sir, | we have given order be next our own. 2.03.110
to the next chamber bear her. 3.02.107
next, he's the governor of this country, and a 4.06. 53 P
out, | and leap the garden, when i see her next, TNK 2.02.216
next, i pitied him; 2.04. 11
o lady fortune | (next after emily my sovereign) 3.01. 16
the best way is, the next way to a grave; 3.02. 33
the next gloves that i give her shall be dogskin 3.05. 45
the next, the lord of may and lady bright, | the 3.05.125
then the beast-eating clown, and next the fool, 3.05.131
next hear my prayers. 3.06.210
but such a manly color | next to an aborn; 4.02.125
for in the next world will dido see palamon, and 4.03. 14 P
floats but for | the surge that next approaches. 5.04. 84
thou art the next of blood, and 'tis thy right. VEN 1184
next, vouchsafe t' afford | (if ever, love, thy LUC 1305
then give me welcome, next my heaven the best, SON 110.13
and my next self thou harder hast engrossed: 133. 6

NIBBLER 1 FR 0.0001 REL FR 1 V 0 P
the tender nibbler would not touch the bait, PP 4.11

NIBBLING 3 FR 0.0003 REL FR 2 V 1 P
thy turfy mountains, where live nibbling sheep, TMP 4.01. 62
as pigeons bill, so wedlock would be nibbling. AYL 3.03. 82 P
o, sir, you would fain be nibbling. TNK 5.02. 87

NICANDER 1 FR 0.0001 REL FR 1 V 0 P
and bid nicander | bring me the satin coffin. PER 3.01. 66

NICANOR 2 FR 0.0002 REL FR 0 V 2 P
nicanor? no. COR 4.03. 6 P
will be welcome with this intelligence, nicanor. 4.03. 30 P

/NICE 1 FR 0.0001 REL FR 1 V 0 P
/to /hold /your /honor /more /precise /and /nice 2H4 2.03. 40

NICE 31 FR 0.0035 REL FR 27 V 4 P
but she is nice and coy, | and nought esteems my TGV 3.01. 82
despite his nice fence and his active practice, ADO 5.01. 75
these betray nice wenches that would be betray'd LLL 3.01. 23 P
and come here by chance, | we'll not be nice; 5.02.219
more measure of this measure; be not nice. 5.02.222
nay then two treys, and if you grow so nice, 5.02.232
this is the ape of form, monsieur the nice, 5.02.325
soly led | by nice direction of a maiden's eyes; MV 2.01. 14
nor the lady's, which is nice; AYL 4.01. 14 P
i am not so nice | to /change true rules for SHR 3.01. 80
which lay nice manners by, i put you to | the AWW 5.01. 15
makes nice of no vild hold to stay him up. JN 3.04.138
main | on the nice hazard of one doubtful hour? 1H4 4.01. 48
hence therefore, thou nice crutch! 2H4 1.01.145
yea, every idle, nice, and wanton reason, 4.01.189
o kate, nice customs cur'sy to great kings. H5 5.02.268 P
for upholding the nice fashion of your country 5.02.273 P
but in these nice sharp quillets of the law, 1H6 2.04. 17
brother, wherefore stand you on nice points? 3H6 4.07. 58
but the respects thereof are nice and trivial, R3 3.07.175
as to prenominate in nice conjecture | where TRO 4.05.250
bid him bethink | how nice the quarrel was, and ROM 3.01.154
the letter was not nice but full of charge, | of 5.02. 18
that every nice offense should bear his comment. JC 4.03. 8
o, relation! | too nice, and yet too true. MAC 4.03.174
or feed upon such nice and waterish diet, | or OTH 3.03. 15
for when mine hours | were nice and lucky, men ANT 3.13.179
nice longing, slanders, mutability, | all faults CYM 2.05. 26
to marry us, for here they are nice and foolish. TNK 5.02. 79
some high, some low, the painter was so nice; LUC 1412
and nice affections wavering stood in doubt | if LC 97

NICELY 9 FR 0.0010 REL FR 8 V 1 P
they that dally nicely with words may quickly TN 3.01. 14 P
can sick men play so nicely with their names? R2 2.01. 84
or nicely charge your understanding soul | with H5 1.02. 15
when articles too nicely urg'd be stood on. 5.02. 94
their nicely gawded cheeks to th' wanton spoil COR 2.01.217
observants | that stretch their duties nicely. LR 2.02.104
what safe and nicely i might well delay | by 5.03.145
standing, nicely | depending on their brands. CYM 2.04. 90
thy /lone bosom | inflame too nicely, nor let PER 4.01. 6

NICENESS 2 FR 0.0002 REL FR 2 V 0 P
fear and niceness | (the handmaids of all women, CYM 3.04.155
that's but a niceness. TNK 5.02. 20

NICE-PRESERVED 1 FR 0.0001 REL FR 1 V 0 P
enjoy | that nice-preserved honesty of yours. TIT 2.03.135

NICER 1 FR 0.0001 REL FR 0 V 1 P
parcels of dispatch /effected many nicer needs. AWW 4.03. 91 P

NICETY 1 FR 0.0001 REL FR 1 V 0 P
lay by all nicety and prolixious blushes | that MM 2.04.162

NICHOLAS' 1 FR 0.0001 REL FR 0 V 1 P
if they meet not with saint nicholas' clerks, 1H4 2.01. 61 P

/NICHOLAS 1 FR 0.0001 REL FR 1 V 0 P
o, /nicholas hopkins? H8 1.01.221

NICHOLAS 8 FR 0.0009 REL FR 5 V 3 P
there — and saint nicholas be thy speed! TGV 3.01.300 P
call forth nathaniel, joseph, nicholas, philip, SHR 4.01. 89 P
worshippest saint nicholas as truly as a man of 1H4 2.01. 65 P
sir nicholas gawsey hath for succor sent, | and 5.04. 45
make up to clifton, i'll to sir nicholas gawsey. 5.04. 58
to this | by a vain prophecy of nicholas henton. H8 1.02.147
then give my charge up to sir nicholas vaux, 2.01. 96
nay, sir nicholas, | let it alone; 2.01.100
NICK* *(also neck)*
/NICK* 1 FR 0.0001 REL FR 1 V 0 P
iago in the /nick | came in and satisfied him. OTH 5.02.317
NICK* 9 FR 0.0010 REL FR 1 V 8 P
he lov'd her out of all nick. TGV 4.02. 76 P
answer as i call you. nick bottom, the weaver. MND 1.02. 16 P
you, nick bottom, are set down for pyramus. 1.02. 20 P
de nick, madame. H5 3.04. 33 P
de nick. et le menton? 3.04. 34 P
de sin. le col, de nick; le menton, de sin. 3.04. 36 P
d' elbow, de nick, et de sin. 3.04. 49 P
d' arma, d' elbow, de nick, de sin, de foot, le 3.04. 59 P
comes i' th' nick, as mad as a march hare. TNK 3.05. 73
NICK'D 1 FR 0.0001 REL FR 1 V 0 P
should not then | have nick'd his captainship, ANT 3.13. 8
NICKNAME 3 FR 0.0003 REL FR 2 V 1 P
you nickname virtue; LLL 5.02.349
one nickname for her purblind son and /heir, ROM 2.01. 12
you nickname god's creatures and make your HAM 3.01.144 P
NICKS 1 FR 0.0001 REL FR 1 V 0 P
his man with scissors nicks him like a fool; ERR 5.01.175
/NIECE 1 FR 0.0001 REL FR 1 V 0 P
/thy /niece /and /i, /poor /creatures, /want TIT 3.02. 5
NIECE 59 FR 0.0066 REL FR 19 V 40 P
what is he that you ask for, niece? ADO 1.01. 34 P
faith, niece, you tax signior benedick too much, 1.01. 46 P
you must not, sir, mistake my niece. 1.01. 61 P
you will never run mad, niece. 1.01. 93 P
that he lov'd my niece your daughter and meant 1.02. 12 P
by my troth, niece, thou wilt never get thee a 2.01. 18 P
well, niece, i trust you will be rul'd by your 2.01. 50 P
well, niece, i hope to see you one day fitted 2.01. 57 P
niece, will you look to those things i told you 2.01.337 P
that your niece beatrice was in love with 2.03. 90 P
well, i am sorry for your niece. 2.03.199 P
god knows i lov'd my niece, | and she is dead, 5.01. 87
your niece regards me with an eye of favor. 5.04. 22
hath ta'en displeasure 'gainst his gentle niece, AYL 1.02.278
you, niece, provide yourself; 1.03. 87
o my dear niece, welcome thou art to me! 5.04.147
a plague means my niece to take the death of her TN 1.03. 1 P
with drinking healths to my niece. 1.03. 38 P
will not drink to my niece till his brains turn 1.03. 41 P
your niece will not be seen, or if she be, it's 1.03.106 P
i can write very like my lady your niece; 2.03.160 P
that they come from my niece, and that she's in 2.03.165 P
if i cannot recover your niece, i am a foul way 2.03.184 P
having cast me on your niece, give me this 2.05. 70 P
my niece is desirous you should enter, if your 3.01. 74 P
i am bound to your niece, sir; 3.01. 76 P
i saw your niece do more favors to the count's 3.02. 5 P
eleven places — my niece shall take note of it, 3.02. 36 P
my niece is already in the belief that he's mad. 3.04.136 P
between his lord and my niece confirms no less. 3.04.187 P
here he comes with your niece. 3.04.197 P
very wittily said to a niece of king gorboduc, 4.02. 14 P
in offense with my niece that i cannot pursue 4.02. 70 P
with her her niece, the lady blanch of spain; JN 2.01. 64
give with our niece a dowry large enough, | for 2.01.469
what say you, my niece? 2.01.521
did i let pass th' abuse done to my niece? 3H6 3.03.188
my niece plantagenet, | led in the hand of her R3 4.01. 1
you have no judgment, niece. TRO 1.02. 92 P
good niece, do, sweet niece cressida. 1.02.179 P
good niece, do, sweet niece cressida. 1.02.179 P
there's a brave man, niece. 1.02.201 P
look ye yonder, niece; 1.02.213 P
there's a man, niece! 1.02.228 P
look well upon him, niece. 1.02.232 P
fare ye well, good niece. 1.02.276 P
i will be with you, niece, by and by. 1.02.278 P
my niece is horribly in love with a thing you 3.01. 97 P
commend me to your niece. 3.01.146 P
my niece, that flies away so fast? TIT 2.04. 11
speak, gentle niece: 2.04. 16
but, lovely niece, that mean is cut from thee. 2.04. 40
patience, dear niece. 3.01.138
what means my niece lavinia by these signs? 4.01. 8
sit down, sweet niece; 4.01. 65
write thou, good niece, and here display at last 4.01. 73
my fair niece rosaline, and livia; ROM 1.02. 69 P
there lies your niece, | whose breath, indeed, OTH 5.02.201
a niece of mine | shall there attend you. PER 3.04. 15
NIECE'S 1 FR 0.0001 REL FR 0 V 1 P
my niece's chambermaid. TN 1.03. 51 P
NIECES 1 FR 0.0001 REL FR 0 V 1 P
signior placentio and his lovely nieces; ROM 1.02. 67 P
NIESSE *(also eyases)*
/NIESSE 1 FR 0.0001 REL FR 1 V 0 P
my /niesse? ROM 2.02.167
NIEVE *(see neaf)*
NIGGARD 10 FR 0.0011 REL FR 9 V 1 P
why is time such a niggard of hair, being, as it ERR 2.02. 77 P
if not from hell, the devil is a niggard, | or H8 1.01. 70
our droplets which | from niggard nature fall, TIM 5.04. 77
which we will niggard with a little rest. JC 4.03.228
be not a niggard of your speech; how goes't? MAC 4.03.180
niggard of question, but of our demands | most HAM 3.01. 13
our richest balms, | rather than niggard, waste; TNK 1.04. 32
the niggard prodigal that prais'd her so — | in LUC 79
then, beauteous niggard, why dost thou abuse SON 4. 5
i | than niggard truth would willingly impart: 72. 8
NIGGARDING 1 FR 0.0001 REL FR 1 V 0 P
and, tender chorl, mak'st waste in niggarding: SON 1.12
NIGGARDLY 4 FR 0.0004 REL FR 2 V 2 P
that could but niggardly give me sight of her; WIV 2.02.197 P
ay, to a niggardly host and more sparing guest: ERR 3.01. 27
thou not be glad to have the niggardly rascally TN 2.05. 5 P
which, of a weak and niggardly projection, H5 2.04. 46

NIGH 19 FR 0.0021 REL FR 19 V 0 P
but was not this nigh shore? TMP 1.02.216
here comes your man, now is your husband nigh. ERR 2.01. 43
spell, nor charm, | come our lovely lady nigh. MND 2.02. 18
then i well perceive you are not nigh: 2.02.155
that dost not bite so nigh | as benefits forgot; AYL 2.07.185
bear no credit, | were not the proof so nigh. WT 5.01.180
and grapple with him ere he come so nigh. JN 5.01. 61
on fire | to hear this rich reprisal is so nigh, 1H4 4.01.118
was i for this nigh wrack'd upon the sea, | and 2H6 3.02. 82
lord, cheer up your spirits, our foes are nigh, 3H6 2.02. 56
and, by thy guess, how nigh is clarence now? 5.01. 8
ah, who is nigh? 5.02. 5
you, therefore, draw nigh and take your places. TIT 5.03. 24
fell cruelty, | which is too nigh your person. MAC 4.02. 72
she that being ang'red, her revenge being nigh, OTH 2.01.152
so nigh, at least, | that though his actions CYM 3.04.148
mind, | taking no notice that she is so nigh, VEN 341
no flow'r was nigh, no grass, herb, leaf, or 1055
a reverend man that graz'd his cattle nigh, LC 57
/NIGHT 6 FR 0.0006 REL FR 6 V 0 P
shall be extinct with age and endless /night; R2 1.03.222
/this /night, /wherein /the //cub–drawn /bear LR 3.01. 12
/i' /th' /night? 4.03. 28
and raise some special officers of /night. OTH 1.01.182
/this /night. 1.03.278
till the disaster that, one mortal /night, PER 5.01. 37
NIGHT 710 FR 0.0802 REL FR 607 V 103 P
for that vast of night that they may work, | all TMP 1.02.327
and how the less, | that burn by day and night; 1.02.336
morning with me | when you are by at night. 3.01. 34
are founder'd | or night kept chain'd below. 4.01. 31
more abstenious, | or else good night your vow! 4.01. 54
and as the morning steals upon the night, 5.01. 65
you shall take your rest | for this one night; 5.01.303
last night she enjoin'd me to write some lines TGV 2.01. 87 P
this night he meaneth with a corded ladder | to 2.06. 33
this night intends to steal away your daughter; 3.01. 11
why then i would resort to her by night. 3.01.110
that no man hath recourse to her by night. 3.01.112
this very night; 3.01.124
"silvia, this night i will enfranchise thee." 3.01.151
except i be by silvia in the night, | there is 3.01.178
visit by night your lady's chamber–window | with 3.02. 82
and thy advice this night i'll put in practice: 3.02. 88
for me (by this pale queen of night i swear), 4.02.100
but it hath been the longest night | that e'er i 4.02.139
and we'll have a posset for't soon at night, in WIV 1.04. 9 P
by me, thine own true knight, | by day or night, 2.01. 15
have open eye, for thieves do foot by night. 2.01.122
come you to me at night, you shall know how i 2.02.266 P
come to me soon at night. 2.02.283 P
come to me soon at night. 2.02.286 P
in deep of night to walk by this herne's oak. 4.04. 40
the night is dark, light and spirits will become 5.02. 11 P
meeting, they will at once display to the night. 5.03. 16 P
you moonshine revellers, and shades of night, 5.05. 38
soon at night | i'll send him certain word of my MM 1.04. 88
this will last out a night in russia | when 2.01.134
if for this night he entreat you to his bed, 3.01.262 P
heavy | middle of the night to call upon him. 4.01. 35
but make haste, | the vaporous night approaches. 4.01. 57
the best and wholesom'st spirits of the night 4.02. 73
i have been drinking all night, i am not fitted 4.03. 43 P
for he that drinks all night, and is hang'd 4.03. 45 P
i have been drinking hard all night, and i will 4.03. 54 P
good night. 4.04. 19 P
but tuesday night last gone, in 's garden–house, 5.01.229
here of the fox, | good night to your redress! 5.01.299
as good to wink, sweet love, as look on night. ERR 3.02. 58
that time comes stealing on by night and day? 4.02. 60
faith, stay here this night, they will surely do 4.04.151 P
ne'er may i look on day, nor sleep on night, 5.01.210
up, | yet hath my night of life some memory, 5.01.315
/pedro of arragon comes this night to messina. ADO 1.01. 2 P
meant to acknowledge it this night in a dance; 1.02. 13 P
for the fool will eat no supper that night. 2.01.150 P
i can, at any unseasonable instant of the night, 2.02. 17 P
to see this the very night before the intended 2.02. 45 P
for to–morrow night we would have it at the lady 2.03. 86 P
for she'll be up twenty times a night, and there 2.03.132 P
ent'red, even the night before her wedding–day. 3.02.113 P
if you hear a child cry in the night, you must 3.03. 65 P
if you meet the prince in the night, you may 3.03. 76 P
well, masters, good night. 3.03. 84 P
fellows' counsels and your own, and good night. 3.03. 87 P
bids me a thousand times good night — i tell 3.03.148 P
first possess'd them, partly by the dark night, 3.03.157 P
at that hour last night | talk with a ruffian at 4.01. 90
lady, were you her bedfellow last night? 4.01.147
no, truly, not, although, until last night, | i 4.01.148
"for he swore a thing to me on monday night, 5.01.168 P
who in the night overheard me confessing to this 5.01.234 P
pardon, goddess of the night, | those that slew 5.03. 12
now, unto thy bones good night! 5.03. 22
and then, to sleep but three hours in the night, LLL 1.01. 42
when i was wont to think no harm all night, 1.01. 44
and make a dark night too of half the day — 1.01. 45
good night, my good owl. 4.01.139
the night of dew that on my cheeks down flows; 4.03. 28
o, but for my love, day would turn to night! 4.03.229
the hue of dungeons, and the school of night; 4.03.251
from morn till night, out of his pavilion. 5.02.654
days will quickly steep themselves in night; MND 1.01. 7
shall behold the night | of our solemnities. 1.01. 10
brief as the lightning in the collied night, 1.01.145
steal forth thy father's house to–morrow night; 1.01.164
to–morrow night, when phoebe doth behold | her 1.01.209
then to the wood will he to–morrow night 1.01.247
and the duchess, on his wedding–day at night. 1.02. 7 P
and desire you, to con them by to–morrow night; 1.02.101 P
i am that merry wanderer of the night. 2.01. 43
not thou lead him through the glimmering night 2.01. 77
no night is now with hymn or carol blest. 2.01.102
and, in the spiced indian air, by night, | full 2.01.124
to trust the opportunity of night | and the ill 2.01.217
that | it is not night when i do see your face, 2.01.221
face, | therefore i think i am not in the night, 2.01.222

there sleeps titania sometime of the night, 2.01.253
so good night, with lullaby. 2.02. 19
and good night, sweet friend. 2.02. 60
night and silence — who is here? 2.02. 70
doth the moon shine that night we play our play? 3.01. 51 P
yes; it doth shine that night. 3.01. 55 P
dark night, that from the eye his function takes 3.02.177
who more engilds the night | than all yon fiery 3.02.187
since night you lov'd me; 3.02.275
yet since night you left me: 3.02.275
have you come by night | and stol'n my love's 3.02.283
hie therefore, robin, overcast the night; 3.02.355
must for aye consort with black–brow'd night. 3.02.387
o weary night, o long and tedious night, | abate 3.02.431
o weary night, o long and tedious night, | abate 3.02.431
tell me how it came this night | that i sleeping 4.01.100
or in the night, imagining some fear, | how easy 5.01. 21
but all the story of the night told over, | and 5.01. 23
the trusty thisby, coming first by night, | did 5.01.140
o grim–look'd night! 5.01.170
o night with hue so black! 5.01.170
o night, which ever art when day is not! 5.01.171
o night, o night! 5.01.172
o night, o night! 5.01.172
as much as we this night have overwatch'd. 5.01.366
hath well beguil'd | the heavy gait of night. 5.01.368
now it is the time of night | that the graves, 5.01.379
so, good night unto you all. 5.01.436
i am glad 'tis night, you do not look on me, MV 2.06. 34
for the close night doth play the runaway, | and 2.06. 47
genoa, as i heard, one night fourscore ducats. 3.01.109 P
he plies the duke at morning and at night, | and 3.02.277
pardon, | i must away this night toward padua, 4.01.403
in such a night as this, | when the sweet wind 5.01. 1
in such a night | troilus methinks mounted the 5.01. 3
grecian tents, | where cressid lay that night. 5.01. 6
in such a night | did thisby fearfully o'ertrip 5.01. 6
in such a night | stood dido with a willow in 5.01. 9
in such a night | medea gathered the enchanted 5.01. 12
in such a night | did jessica steal from the 5.01. 14
in such a night | did young lorenzo swear he 5.01. 17
in such a night | did pretty jessica (like a 5.01. 20
who comes so fast in silence of the night? 5.01. 25
soft stillness and the night | become the 5.01. 56
the motions of his spirit are dull as night, 5.01. 86
this night methinks is but the daylight sick, 5.01.124
for, by these blessed candles of the night, 5.01.220
lie not a night from home. 5.01.230
in lieu of this last night did lie with me. 5.01.262
whether till the next night she had rather stay, 5.01.302
and this night he means | to burn the lodging AYL 2.03. 22
thrice–crowned queen of night, survey | with thy 3.02. 2
a great cause of the night is lack of the sun; 3.02. 28 P
if it had not been for a hot midsummer night; 4.01.102 P
of you | to pardon me yet for a night or two; SHR in.2. 119
nay then good night our part! 2.01.301
i must away to–day, before night come. 3.02.190
and for this night we'll fast for company. 4.01.177
last night she slept not, nor to–night she shall 4.01.198
and, in conclusion, she shall watch all night, 4.01.205
and there this night | we'll pass the business 4.04. 56
to watch the night in storms, the day in cold, 5.02.150
and, being a winner, god give you good night! 5.02.187
come night, end day! AWW 3.02.128
find him, which you shall see this very night. 3.06.106 P
every night he comes | with musics of all sorts, 3.07. 39
and on your finger in the night i'll put 4.02. 61
and this night he fleshes his will in the spoil 4.03. 16 P
h'as sat i' th' stocks all night, poor gallant 4.03.102 P
the cozen'd thoughts | defiles the pitchy night; 4.04. 24
but this exceeding posting day and night | must 5.01. 1
he hence remov'd last night, and with more haste 5.01. 23
i had talk of you last night; 5.02. 53 P
you brought in one night here to be her wooer. TN 1.03. 16 P
and sing them loud even in the dead of night; 1.05.271
thou wast in very gracious fooling last night, 2.03. 22 P
to gabble like tinkers at this time of night? 2.03. 88 P
for this night, to bed, and dream on the event. 2.03.175 P
good night, penthesilea. 2.03.177 P
that old and antique song we heard last night; 2.04. 3
o fellow, come, the song we had last night. 2.04. 42
love's night is noon. 3.01.148
i am not weary, and 'tis long to night; 3.03. 21
both day and night did we keep company. 5.01. 96
continent the fire | that severs day from night. 5.01.272
yourself and me | cry lost, and so good night! WT 1.02.411
nor night, nor day, no rest. 2.03. 1
for their better safety, to fly away by night." 3.02. 21 P
be, thy mother | appear'd to me last night; 3.03. 18
the pale moon shines by night; 4.03. 16
now blessed be the hour by night or day | when i JN 1.01.165
who dares not stir by day must walk by night, 1.01.172
mouth | sound on into the drowsy race of night; 3.03. 39
arise forth from the couch of lasting night, 3.04. 27
young gentlemen would be as sad as night, | only 4.01. 15
that i might sit all night and watch with you. 4.01. 30
but even this night, whose black contagious 5.04. 33
even this ill night your breathing shall expire, 5.04. 36
after such bloody toil, we bid good night, | and 5.05. 6
the stumbling night did part our weary pow'rs? 5.05. 18
thou and endless night | have done me shame. 5.06. 12
why, here walk i in the black brow of night, 5.06. 17
o my sweet sir, news fitting to the night, 5.06. 19
tell thee, hubert, half my power this night, 5.06. 39
for in a night the best part of my pow'r, | as i 5.07. 61
to dwell in solemn shades of endless night. R2 1.03.177
castle, | and there repose you for this night. 2.03.161
the cloak of night being pluck'd from off their 3.02. 45
who all this while hath revell'd in the night, 3.02. 48
from richard's night to bullingbrook's fair day. 3.02.218
letters came last night | to a dear friend of 3.04. 69
and ere thou bid good night, to quite their 5.01. 43
with cain go wander thorough shades of night, 5.06. 43
snatch'd on monday night and most dissolutely 1H4 1.02. 34 P
bespoke supper to–morrow night in eastcheap. 1.02.130 P
and meet me to–morrow night in eastcheap, there 1.02.192 P
who studies day and night | to answer all the 1.03.184
if he fall in, good night, or sink or swim. 1.03.194

it to one of his company last night at supper, a 2.01. 57 P
more beholding to the night than to fern–seed 2.01. 89 P
good night, my noble lord. 2.04.523
(a business that this night may execute), 3.01. 81
the moon shines fair, you may away by night. 3.01.140
he held me last night at least nine hours | in 3.01.154
as is the difference betwixt day and night | the 3.01.217
up gadshill in the night to catch my horse, if i 3.03. 38 P
with thee in the night betwixt tavern and tavern 3.03. 43 P
the other night i fell asleep here behind the 3.03. 97 P
you, looks for us all, we must away all night. 4.02. 57 P
and posted day and night | to meet you on the 5.01. 35
yet once ere night | i will embrace him with a 5.02. 72
drew priam's curtain in the dead of night, | and 2H4 1.01. 72
falstaff, good night. 2.04.366
now comes in the sweetest morsel of the night, 2.04.368 P
and in the calmest and most stillest night, 3.01. 28
since we lay all night in the windmill in saint 3.02.195 P
ha, 'twas a merry night. 3.02.198 P
of slumber open wide | to many a watchful night, 4.05. 25
biggen bound | snores out the watch of night. 4.05. 28
revel the night, rob, murder, and commit | the 4.05.125
doth the man of war stay all night, sir? 5.01. 29 P
be merry, now comes in the sweet a' th' night. 5.03. 51 P
we'll ride all night. 5.03.131 P
as it were, to ride day and night, and not to 5.05. 20 P
i shall be sent for soon at night. 5.05. 90 P
when my legs are too, i will bid you good night. ep 34 P
grew like the summer grass, fastest by night, H5 1.01. 65
a night is but small breath, and little pause, 2.04.145
march to the bridge, it now draws toward night; 3.06.170
what a long night is this! 3.07. 11 P
camp to camp, through the foul womb of night, 4.pr. 4
and chide the cripple tardy–gaited night, | who 4.pr. 20
of color | unto the weary and all–watched night; 4.pr. 38
define, | a little touch of harry in the night. 4.pr. 47
why, the enemy is loud, you hear him all night. 4.01. 76 P
but i believe, as cold a night as 'tis, he could 4.01.114 P
never sees horrid night, the child of hell; 4.01.271
of phoebus, and all night | sleeps in elysium; 4.01.273
and my poor soldiers tell me, yet ere night, 4.03.116
a rascal that swagger'd with me last night; 4.07.126 P
witness the night, your garments, your lowliness 4.08. 52 P
and at night, when you come into your closet, 5.02.198 P
be the heavens with black, yield day to night! 1H6 1.01. 1
this night the siege assuredly i'll raise: 1.02.130
us, | this happy night the frenchmen are secure, 2.01. 11
shall this night appear | how much in duty i am 2.01. 36
and, for myself, most part of all this night, 2.01. 67
the day begins to break, and night is fled, 2.02. 1
for smoke and dusky vapors of the night, | am 2.02. 27
that could not live asunder day or night. 2.02. 31
a thousand souls to death and deadly night. 2.04.127
by day, by night, waking and in my dreams, | in 2H6 1.01. 26
my troublous dreams this night doth make me sad. 1.02. 22
he did speak them to me in the garret one night, 1.03.191 P
deep night, dark night, the silent of the night, 1.04. 16
deep night, dark night, the silent of the night, 1.04. 16
deep night, dark night, the silent of the night, 1.04. 16
the time of night when troy was set on fire, 1.04. 17
and warwick | to sup with me to–morrow night. 1.04. 80
let never day nor night unhallowed pass, | but 2.01. 83
well, for this night we will repose us here; 2.01.196
dark shall be my light, and night my day; 2.04. 40
so help me god, as i have watch'd the night, 3.01.110
ay, night by night, in studying good for england 3.01.111
ay, night by night, in studying good for england 3.01.111
well could i curse away a winter's night, 3.02.335
jades | that drag the tragic melancholy night; 4.01. 4
defer the spoil of the city until night; 4.07.134 P
and, soldiers, stay and lodge by me this night. 3H6 1.01. 32
can neither call it perfect day nor night. 2.05. 4
may yet, ere night, yield both my life and them 2.05. 59
shut | but in the night or in the time of war. 4.07. 36
now, for this night, let's harbor here in york; 4.07. 79
must by the roots be hewn up yet ere night. 5.04. 69
let aesop fable in a winter's night, | his 5.05. 25
have in our armors watch'd the winter's night, 5.07. 17
black night o'ershade thy day, and death thy R3 1.02.131
o, i have pass'd a miserable night, | so full of 1.04. 2
i would not spend another such a night | though 1.04. 5
write of, | unto the kingdom of perpetual night. 1.04. 47
makes the night morning and the noontide night: 1.04. 77
makes the night morning and the noontide night: 1.04. 77
(all thin and naked) to the numb cold night? 2.01.118
to his new kingdom of ne'er–changing night. 2.02. 46
when the sun sets, who doth not look for night? 2.03. 34
last night, i /hear, they lay at stony–stratford 2.04. 1
grandam, one night as we did sit at supper, | my 2.04. 10
then certifies your lordship that this night 3.02. 10
and anne my wife hath bid this world good night. 4.03. 39
hath dimm'd your infant morn to aged night. 4.04. 16
save for a night of groans | endur'd of her, for 4.04.303
yield me not thy light, nor, night, thy rest! 4.04.401
good night, good captain blunt. 5.03. 44
fall | into the blind cave of eternal night. 5.03. 62
about the mid of night come to my tent | and 5.03. 77
all comfort that the dark night can afford | be 5.03. 80
once more, good night, kind lords and gentlemen. 5.03.107
and th' ensuing night | made it a fool and H8 1.01. 27
by day and night, | he's traitor to th' height. 1.02.213
this night he makes a supper, and a great one, 1.03. 52
henry guilford | this night to be comptrollers. 1.03. 67
this night he dedicates | to fair content and 1.04. 2
and so fair assembly | this night to meet here, 1.04. 68
good hour of night, sir thomas! 5.01. 5
good night, sir thomas. 5.01. 54
i wish your highness | a quiet night, and my 5.01. 77
charles, good night. | well, sir, what follows? 5.01. 78
less valiant than the virgin in the night, | and TRO 1.01. 11
patroclus, | arming to answer in a night alarm." 1.03.171
i have lov'd you night and day | for many weary 3.02.114
and dreaming night will hide our joys no longer, 4.02. 10
night hath been too brief. 4.02. 11
this night in banqueting must all be spent. 5.01. 46
so now, fair prince of troy, i bid good night. 5.01. 71
thanks and good night to the greeks' general. 5.01. 73
good night, my lord. 5.01. 74
good night, sweet lord menelaus. 5.01. 74
good night and welcome, both /at /once, to those 5.01. 77
good night. 5.01. 79
good night, great hector. 5.01. 83
and so, good night. 5.01. 87
good night. 5.02. 28
no, no, good night, i'll be your fool no more. 5.02. 32
and so, good night. 5.02. 44
i will not meet with you to–morrow night. 5.02. 73
good night. 5.02.106
and this whole night | hath nothing been but 5.03. 11
deeds worth praise, and tell you them at night. 5.03. 93
how ugly night comes breathing at his heels; 5.08. 6
the dragon wing of night o'erspreads the earth, 5.08. 17
never go home, here starve we out the night — 5.10. 2
there came news from him last night. COR 1.03. 93 P
the buttock of the night than with the forehead 2.01. 52 P
nobles of the state | at his house this night. 4.04. 10
i, it exceeds peace as far as day does night; 4.05.222 P
i have been troubled in my sleep this night, TIT 2.02. 9
they told me, here, at dead time of the night, 2.03. 99
when he by night lay bath'd in maiden blood. 2.03.232
by day and night t' attend him carefully, | and 4.03. 28
acts of black night, abominable deeds, 5.01. 64
set fire on barns and haystalks in the night, 5.01.133
care, | witness the tiring day and heavy night, 5.02. 24
ear | the story of that baleful burning night, 5.03. 83
out, | and makes himself an artificial night. ROM 1.01.140
this night i hold an old accustom'd feast, 1.02. 20
at my poor house look to behold this night 1.02. 24
among fresh fennel buds shall you this night 1.02. 29
come lammas–eve at night shall she be fourteen. 1.03. 17
on lammas–eve at night shall she be fourteen, 1.03. 21
this night you shall behold him at our feast; 1.03. 80
and in this state she gallops night by night 1.04. 70
and in this state she gallops night by night 1.04. 70
that plats the manes of horses in the night, 1.04. 89
it seems she hangs upon the cheek of night | as 1.05. 45
for i ne'er saw true beauty till this night. 1.05. 53
in spite | to scorn at our solemnity this night. 1.05. 63
i thank you, honest gentlemen, good night. 1.05.124
trees | to be consorted with the humorous night. 2.01. 31
romeo, good night, i'll to my truckle–bed, 2.01. 39
birds would sing and think it were not night. 2.02. 22
for thou art | as glorious to this night, being 2.02. 27
what man art thou that thus bescreen'd in night 2.02. 52
thou knowest the mask of night is on my face, 2.02. 85
love, | which the dark night hath so discovered. 2.02.106
sweet, good night! 2.02.120
good night, good night! 2.02.123
good night, good night! 2.02.123
o blessed, blessed night! 2.02.139
being in night, all this is but a dream, | too 2.02.140
three words, dear romeo, and good night indeed. 2.02.142
a thousand times good night! 2.02.154
how silver–sweet sound lovers' tongues by night, 2.02.165
good night, good night! 2.02.184
good night, good night! 2.02.184
that i shall say good night till it be morrow. 2.02.185
the grey–ey'd morn smiles on the frowning night, 2.03. 1
you gave us the counterfeit fairly last night. 2.04. 45 P
my joy | must be my convoy in the secret night. 2.04.191
but you shall bear the burthen soon at night. 2.05. 76
west, | and bring in cloudy night immediately. 3.02. 4
spread thy close curtain, love–performing night, 3.02. 5
if love be blind, | it best agrees with night. 3.02. 10
come, civil night, | thou sober–suited matron 3.02. 10
come, night, come, romeo, come, thou day in 3.02. 17
night, come, romeo, come, thou day in night, 3.02. 17
for thou wilt lie upon the wings of night, 3.02. 18
come, gentle night, come, loving, black–brow'd 3.02. 20
gentle night, come, loving, black–brow'd night, 3.02. 20
that all the world will be in love with night, 3.02. 24
this day | as is the night before some festival 3.02. 29
hark ye, your romeo will be here at night. 3.02.140
i could have stay'd here all the night | to hear 3.03.159
go hence, good night; 3.03.166
farewell, good night. 3.03.172
madam, good night, commend me to your daughter. 3.04. 9
good night. 3.04. 35
to be to thee this night a torch–bearer | and 3.05. 14
day, night, work, play, | alone, in company, 3.05.176
to–morrow night look that thou lie alone, | let 4.01. 91
and that very night | shall romeo bear thee 4.01.116
short in our provision, | 'tis now near night. 4.02. 39
and let the nurse this night sit up with you, 4.03. 10
good night. 4.03. 12
like | the horrible conceit of death and night, 4.03. 37
at some hours in the night spirits resort — 4.03. 44
watch'd ere now | all night for lesser cause, 4.04. 10
sleep for a week, for the next night, i warrant, 4.05. 5
the night before thy wedding–day | hath death 4.05. 35
muffle me, night, a while. 5.03. 21
thee, | and never from this /palace of dim night 5.03.107
that he should hither come as this dire night 5.03.247
thy creature, | by night frequents my house. TIM 1.01.117
have slaves and peasants | this night englutted! 2.02.166
the day serves, before black–corner'd night, 5.01. 44
i will this night, | in several hands, in at his JC 1.02.315
and yesterday the bird of night did sit | even 1.03. 26
good night then, casca; 1.03. 39
your ear is good. cassius, what night is this! 1.03. 42
a very pleasing night to honest men. 1.03. 43
submitting me unto the perilous night; 1.03. 47
to thee a man | most like this dreadful night, 1.03. 73
for now, this fearful night, | there is no stir 1.03.126
what a fearful night is this! 1.03.137
thou to show thy dang'rous brow by night, | when 2.01. 78
i have been up this hour, awake all night. 2.01. 88
themselves | betwixt your eyes and night? 2.01. 99
the unaccustom'd terror of this night, | and the 2.01.199
bed | to dare the vile contagion of the night, 2.01.265
they mean this night in sardis to be quarter'd. 4.02. 28
the deep of night is crept upon our talk, | and 4.03.226
good night. 4.03.229
good night, titinius. 4.03.232
noble cassius, | good night, and good repose. 4.03.233
this was an ill beginning of the night. 4.03.234
good night, my lord. 4.03.237
good night, good brother. 4.03.237
good night, lord brutus. 4.03.238
gentle knave, good night; 4.03.269
and, good boy, good night. 4.03.272
yet ere night | we shall try fortune in a second 5.03.109
appear'd to me | two several times by night; 5.05. 18
and, this last night, here in philippi fields. 5.05. 19
night hangs upon mine eyes, my bones would rest, 5.05. 41
sleep shall neither night nor day | hang upon MAC 1.03. 19
come, thick night, | and pall thee in the 1.05. 50
how goes the night, boy? 2.01. 1
i dreamt last night of the three weird sisters: 2.01. 20
i believe drink gave thee the lie last night. 2.03. 37 P
the night has been unruly. 2.03. 54
the obscure bird | clamor'd the livelong night. 2.03. 60
'twas a rough night. 2.03. 61
but this sore night | hath trifled former 2.04. 3
and yet dark night strangles the travelling lamp 2.04. 7
i must become a borrower of the night | for a 3.01. 26
adieu, | till you return at night. 3.01. 35
man be master of his time | till seven at night. 3.01. 41
come, seeling night, | scarf up the tender eye 3.02. 46
at once, good night. 3.04.117
good night, and better health | attend his 3.04.119
a kind good night to all! 3.04.120
what is the night? 3.04.125
this night i'll spend | unto a dismal and a 3.05. 20
the night is long that never finds the day. 4.03.240
so good night! 5.01. 77
good night, good doctor. 5.01. 79
well, good night. HAM 1.01. 11
give you good night. 1.01. 16
barnardo hath my place. | give you good night. 1.01. 18
with us to watch the minutes of this night, 1.01. 27
last night of all, | when yond same star that's 1.01. 35
what art thou that usurp'st this time of night, 1.01. 46
doth make the night joint–laborer with the day: 1.01. 78
this bird of dawning singeth all night long, 1.01.160
in the dead waste and middle of the night, 1.02.198
and i with them the third night kept the watch, 1.02.208
would the night were come! 1.02.255
and it must follow, as the night the day, | thou 1.03. 79
making night hideous, and we fools of nature 1.04. 54
doom'd for a certain term to walk the night, 1.05. 10
o day and night, but this is wondrous strange! 1.05.164
go to your rest, at night we'll feast together. 2.02. 84
why day is day, night night, and time is time, 2.02. 88
why day is day, night night, and time is time, 2.02. 88
were nothing but to waste night, day, and time; 2.02. 89
did the night resemble | when he lay couched in 2.02.453
we'll ha't to–morrow night. 2.02.540 P
my good friends, i'll leave you /till night. 2.02.547 P
already order | this night to play before him. 3.01. 21
sport and repose lock from me day and night, 3.02.217
'tis now the very witching time of night, | when 3.02.388
good night, but go not to my uncle's bed — 3.04.159
once more, good night, | and when you are 3.04.170
so, again, good night. 3.04.177
mother, good night indeed. 3.04.213
good night, mother. 3.04.217
good night, ladies, good night. 4.05. 72 P
good night, ladies, good night. 4.05. 72 P
sweet ladies, good night, good night. 4.05. 73 P
sweet ladies, good night, good night. 4.05. 73 P
skill shall, like a star i' th' darkest night, 5.02.256
good night, sweet prince, | and flights of 5.02.359
sun, | the /mysteries of hecat and the night; LR 1.01.110
the night gone by. 1.02.153 P
by day and night he wrongs me, every hour | he 1.03. 3
his duchess will be here with him this night. 2.01. 4 P
you have now the good advantage of the night. 2.01. 22
he's coming hither, now i' th' night, i' th' 2.01. 24
thus out of season, threading dark–ey'd night: 2.01.119
you rogue, for though it be night, yet the moon 2.02. 31 P
till night, my lord, and all night too. 2.02.135
till night, my lord, and all night too. 2.02.135
fortune, good night! 2.02.173
the night before there was no purpose in them 2.04. 3
they have travell'd all the night? 2.04. 89
alack, the night comes on, and the /bleak winds 2.04.300
shut up your doors, my lord, 'tis a wild night, 2.04.308
here's a night pities neither wise men nor fools 3.02. 12 P
things that love night | love not such nights as 3.02. 42
this is a brave night to cool a courtezan. 3.02. 79 P
i have receiv'd a letter this night — 'tis 3.03. 10 P
in such a night | to shut me out? 3.04. 17
in such a night as this? 3.04. 19
this cold night will turn us all to fools and 3.04. 78 P
be contented, 'tis a naughty night to swim in. 3.04.111 P
and let this tyrannous night take hold upon you, 3.04.151
as his bare head | in hell–black night endur'd, 3.07. 60
should have stood that night | against my fire, 4.07. 36
nor i know not | where i did lodge last night. 4.07. 67
come | to bid my king and master aye good night. 5.03.236
dire yell | as when, by night and negligence, OTH 1.01. 76
at this odd–even and dull watch o' th' night, 1.01.123
the goodness of the night upon you, friends! 1.02. 35
this very night at one another's heels; 1.02. 42
in this time of the night? 1.02. 94
good night to every one. 1.03.288
hell and night | must bring this monstrous birth 1.03.403
michael, good night. 2.03. 7
good night. 2.03. 11
he hath not yet made wanton the night with her; 2.03. 16 P
'tis a night of revels, the gallants desire it. 2.03. 43 P
by me that's said or done amiss this night, 2.03.201
in night, and on the court and guard of safety? 2.03.216
good night, lieutenant, i must to the watch. 2.03.333 P
good night, honest iago. 2.03.335 P
why then to–morrow night, /or tuesday morn; 3.03. 60
on tuesday noon, or night; 3.03. 61
i slept the next night well, fed well, was free 3.03.340
and say if i shall see you soon at night. 3.04.198
get me some poison, iago, this night. 4.01.204 P
this night, iago. 4.01.206 P
courage, and valor), this night show it. 4.02.214 P
if thou the next night following enjoy not 4.02.215 P

high supper–time, and the night grows to waste. 4.02.242 P
madam, good night; i humbly thank your ladyship. 4.03. 3
so get thee gone, good night. 4.03. 58
good night, good night. 4.03.104
good night, good night. 4.03.104
'tis heavy night; 5.01. 42
this is the night | that either makes me, or 5.01.128
come, my queen, | last night you did desire it. ANT 1.01. 55
and wastes | the lamps of night in revel; 1.04. 5
and made the night light with drinking. 2.02.178 P
good night, sir. 2.03. 4
good night, dear lady. 2.03. 7
good night, sir. 2.03. 8
good night. 2.03. 9
and that night | i laugh'd him into patience; 2.05. 19
pompey, good night. 2.07.119
good night. 2.07.125
why then good night indeed. 3.10. 29
come, | let's have one other gaudy night. 3.13.182
desire you | to burn this night with torches. 4.02. 41
brother, good night; to–morrow is the day. 4.03. 1
belike 'tis but a rumor. good night to you. 4.03. 5
well, sir, good night. 4.03. 6
and you. good night, good night. 4.03. 8
and you. good night, good night. 4.03. 8
the night | is shiny, and they say we shall 4.09. 2
o, bear me witness, night — 4.09. 5
the poisonous damp of night dispunge upon me, 4.09. 13
much like an argument that fell out last night, CYM 1.04. 57 P
bold | to send them to you, only for this night; 1.06.198
from fairies and the tempters of the night 2.02. 9
swift, you dragons of the night, that dawning 2.02. 48
last night 'twas on mine arm; 2.03.146
a second night of such sweet shortness which 2.04. 44
but in one night, | a storm or robbery (call it 3.03. 61
night? 3.04.136
this night forestall him of the coming day! 3.05. 69
'tis almost night, you shall have better cheer 3.06. 66
the night to th' owl and morn to th' lark less 3.06. 93
herbs that have on them cold dew o' th' night 4.02.284
i have gone all night. 4.02.294
last night the very gods show'd me a vision | (i 4.02.346
blush not in actions blacker than the night PER 1.01.135
in the day's glorious walk or peaceful night, 1.02. 4
fled, | under the covering of a careful night, 1.02. 81
now his /son's like a glow–worm in the night, 2.03. 43
to you | for your sweet music this last night. 2.05. 26
/midwife gentle | to those that cry by night, 3.01. 12
't 'as been a turbulent and stormy night. 3.02. 4
but such a night as this | till now i ne'er 3.02. 5
she died at night; 4.03. 16
o, if thou couch | but one night with her, every TNK 1.01.183
the duke himself came privately in the night, 2.01. 46 P
clap her aboard to–morrow night and stow her, 2.03. 32
and this night, or to–morrow, he shall love me. 2.04. 33
with counsel of the night, i will be here | with 3.01. 83
no matter, would it were perpetual night, | and 3.02. 3
have heard | strange howls this livelong night; 3.02. 12
good night, good night, y' are gone. 3.04. 11
good night, good night, y' are gone. 3.04. 11
by night | that seek out silent hanging. 3.05.126
i'll warrant ye he had not so few last night 4.01.137
this trial is as 'twere i' th' night, and you 5.03. 19
two emulous philomels beat the ear o' th' night 5.03.124
gentlemen, good night. ep 18
and i will wink, so shall the day seem night. VEN 122
from morn till night, even where i list to sport 154
the night of sorrow now is turn'd to day: 481
shone like the moon in water seen by night. 492
light | do summon us to part and bid good night. 534
"now let me say 'good night,' and so say you; 535
"good night," quoth she, and, ere he says "adieu 537
she says, "this night i'll waste in sorrow, 583
the night is spent." 717
"in night," quoth she, "desire sees best of all. 720
"now of this dark night i perceive the reason: 727
to shame the sun by day and her by night. 732
the lamp that burns by night | dries up his oil 755
for, by this black–fac'd night, desire's foul 773
so glides he in the night from venus' eye, 816
so did the merciless and pitchy night | fold in 821
her song was tedious and outwore the night, 841
for who hath she to spend the night withal, 847
who bids them still consort with ugly night, 1041
throbbing heart shall rock thee day and night; 1186
for he the night before, in tarquin's tent, LUC 15
till sable night, mother of dread and fear, 117
with modest lucrece, and wore out the night. 123
now stole upon the time the dead of night, 162
and misty night | covers the shame that follows 356
with pearly sweat resembling dew of night. 396
imagine her as one in dead of night | from forth 449
thy beauty hath ensnar'd thee to this night, 485
quoth he, "this night i must enjoy thee. 512
shame folded up in blind concealing night, 675
so surfeit–taking tarquin fares this night: 698
this thought through the dark night he stealeth, 729
she stays, exclaiming on the direful night, | he 741
her spite | against the unseen secrecy of night: 763
"o comfort–killing night, image of hell! 764
"o hateful, vaporous, and foggy night! 771
may set at noon and make perpetual night. 784
"were tarquin night, as he is but night's child, 785
"o night, thou furnace of foul reeking smoke! 799
"misshapen time, copesmate of ugly night, 925
to wake the morn and sentinel the night, | to 942
o, this dread night, wouldst thou one hour come 965
to make him curse this cursed crimeful night. 970
poor grooms are sightless night, kings glorious 1013
at time, at tarquin, and uncheerful night, | in 1024
and solemn night with slow sad gait descended 1081
therefore still in night would cloist'red be. 1085
for day hath nought to do what's done by night." 1092
which makes the maid weep like the dewy night. 1232
assail'd by night with circumstances strong | of 1262
she looks for night, and then she longs for 1571
on thee and thine this night i will inflict, 1630
good night, good rest. PP 14. 1
she bade good night that kept my rest away, 14. 2
ditty, | and drives away dark dreaming night. 14.20
the night so pack'd, i post unto my pretty; 14.21
were i with her, the night would post too soon, 14.25
pack night, peep day; 14.29
good day, of night now borrow: 14.29
short night to–night, and length thyself 14.30
be bent, | her cloudy looks will calm yer night, 18.26
and see the brave day sunk in hideous night; SON 12. 2
to change your day of youth to sullied night, 15.12
which, like a jewel hung in ghastly night, 27.11
makes black night beauteous and her old face new 27.12
lo thus by day my limbs, by night my mind, | for 27.13
when day's oppression is not eas'd by night, 28. 3
but day by night, and night by day, oppress'd; 28. 4
but day by night, and night by day, oppress'd; 28. 4
so flatter i the swart–complexion'd night, 28.11
and night doth nightly make grief's length seem 28.14
precious friends hid in death's dateless night, 30. 6
when in dead night /thy fair imperfect shade 43.11
keep open | my heavy eyelids to the weary night? 61. 2
morn | hath travell'd on to age's steepy night, 63. 5
which by and by black night doth take away, 73. 7
he, nor his compeers by night | giving him aid, 86. 7
give not a windy night a rainy morrow, | to 90. 7
than when her mournful hymns did hush the night, 102.10
the mountain or the sea, the day or night, | the 113.11
that our night of woe might have rememb'red | my 120. 9
follow'd it as gentle day | doth follow night, 145.11
who art as black as hell, as dark as night. 147.14

NIGHT/–BIRD 1 FR 0.0001 REL FR 1 V 0 P
lute | she sung, and made the night/–bird mute, PER 4.ch. 26

NIGHT–BRAWLER 1 FR 0.0001 REL FR 1 V 0 P
rich opinion for the name | of a night–brawler? OTH 2.03.196

NIGHT–CAP 1 FR 0.0001 REL FR 1 V 0 P
(for i fear cassio with my night–cap too), OTH 2.01.307

NIGHT–CAPS 1 FR 0.0001 REL FR 0 V 1 P
hands, and threw up their sweaty night–caps, and JC 1.02.246 P

NIGHT–CROW 1 FR 0.0001 REL FR 1 V 0 P
the night–crow cried, aboding luckless time; 3H6 5.06. 45

NIGHT–DOGS 1 FR 0.0001 REL FR 1 V 0 P
when night–dogs run, all sorts of deer are WIV 5.05.238

NIGHTED 2 FR 0.0002 REL FR 2 V 0 P
good hamlet, cast thy nighted color off, | and HAM 1.02. 68
of his misery, to dispatch | his nighted life; LR 4.05. 13

NIGHT–FLIES 1 FR 0.0001 REL FR 1 V 0 P
hush'd with buzzing night–flies to thy slumber, 2H4 3.01. 11

NIGHT–FOES 1 FR 0.0001 REL FR 1 V 0 P
tent | but to defend his person from night–foes? 3H6 4.03. 22

NIGHT–GOWN 5 FR 0.0005 REL FR 2 V 3 P
by my troth 's but a night–gown /in respect of ADO 3.04. 18 P
get on your night–gown, lest occasion call us MAC 2.02. 67
from her bed, throw her night–gown upon her, 5.01. 5 P
wash your hands, put on your night–gown, look 5.01. 62 P
shall i go fetch your night–gown? OTH 4.03. 34

/NIGHTINGALE 1 FR 0.0001 REL FR 0 V 1 P
/poor /tom /in /the /voice /of /a /nightingale. LR 3.06. 30 P

NIGHTINGALE 10 FR 0.0011 REL FR 9 V 1 P
night, | there is no music in the nightingale; TGV 3.01.179
i will roar you and 'twere any nightingale. MND 1.02. 83 P
and i think | the nightingale, if she should MV 5.01.104
plain | she sings as sweetly as a nightingale; SHR 2.01.171
it was the nightingale, and not the lark, | that ROM 3.05. 2
believe me, love, it was the nightingale. 3.05. 5
lark, the herald of the morn, | no nightingale. 3.05. 7
mine nightingale, | we have beat them to their ANT 4.08. 18
o for a prick now, like a nightingale, | to put TNK 3.04. 25
did banish moan, | save the nightingale alone. PP 20. 8

NIGHTINGALE'S 1 FR 0.0001 REL FR 1 V 0 P
and to the nightingale's complaining notes TGV 5.04. 5

NIGHTINGALES 2 FR 0.0002 REL FR 1 V 1 P
plays, | and twenty caged nightingales do sing. SHR in.2. 36
at your request! yes, nightingales answer daws. TN 3.04. 35 P

NIGHTLY 24 FR 0.0027 REL FR 23 V 1 P
with nightly tears, and daily heart–sore sighs, TGV 2.04.132
i nightly lodge her in an upper tow'r, | the key 3.01. 35
"my thoughts do harbor with my silvia nightly, 3.01.140
and nightly, meadow–fairies, look you sing, WIV 5.05. 65
be /foul, | then nightly sings the staring owl, LLL 5.02.917
the bowl, | then nightly sings the staring owl, 5.02.926
that nightly hoots and wonders | at our quaint MND 2.02. 6
solemnity, | in nightly revels and new jollity. 5.01.370
moreov'r, he's drunk nightly in your company. TN 1.03. 36 P
sentinels, | to give thee nightly visitation. TRO 4.04. 73
and i have nightly since | dreamt of encounters COR 4.05.122
breeds, | unless the nightly owl or fatal raven; TIT 2.03. 97
nightly she sings on yond pomegranate tree. ROM 3.05. 4
bears, | or hide me nightly in a charnel–house, 4.01. 81
which with sweet water nightly i will dew, | or, 5.03. 14
nightly shall be to strew thy grave and weep. 5.03. 17
these terrible dreams | that shake us nightly. MAC 3.02. 19
so nightly toils the subject of the land, | and HAM 1.01. 72
alive | that nightly lie in those unproper beds OTH 4.01. 68
emilia, | give me my nightly wearing, and adieu. 4.03. 16
for with the nightly linen that she wears | he LUC 680
the well–tun'd warble of her nightly sorrow, 1080
and night doth nightly make grief's length seem SON 28.14
which nightly gulls him with intelligence, | as 86.10

NIGHT–MARE 1 FR 0.0001 REL FR 1 V 0 P
'old, | he met the night–mare and her nine–fold; LR 3.04.121

NIGHT–OBLATIONS 1 FR 0.0001 REL FR 1 V 0 P
and will offer | night–oblations to thee. PER 5.03. 70

NIGHT–OWL 2 FR 0.0002 REL FR 1 V 1 P
shall we rouse the night–owl in a catch that TN 2.03. 58 P
dove sleeps fast that this night–owl will catch; LUC 360

NIGHT–OWL'S 1 FR 0.0001 REL FR 1 V 0 P
our soldiers', like the night–owl's lazy flight, 3H6 2.01.130

NIGHT–OWLS 1 FR 0.0001 REL FR 1 V 0 P
for night–owls shriek where mounting larks R2 3.03.183

NIGHT–RAVEN 1 FR 0.0001 REL FR 0 V 1 P
i had as live have heard the night–raven, come ADO 2.03. 82 P

NIGHT–REST 1 FR 0.0001 REL FR 1 V 0 P
domestic awe, night–rest, and neighborhood, TIM 4.01. 17

NIGHT–RULE 1 FR 0.0001 REL FR 1 V 0 P
what night–rule now about this haunted grove? MND 3.02. 5

NIGHT'S 30 FR 0.0034 REL FR 28 V 2 P
the night's dead silence | will well become such TGV 3.02. 84
this night's the time | that i should do what i MM 3.01.100
for night's swift dragons cut the clouds full MND 3.02.379
and think no more of this night's accidents 4.01. 68
in silence sad | trip we after night's shade. 4.01. 96
that are squires of the night's body be call'd 1H4 1.02. 24 P
gilded over your night's exploit on gadshill. 2H4 1.02.149 P
boastful neighs | piercing the night's dull ear; H5 4.pr. 11
and now what rests but, in night's coverture, 3H6 4.02. 13
we, well cover'd with the night's black mantle, 4.02. 22
his fearful date | with this night's revels, and ROM 1.04.109
i have night's cloak to hide me from their eyes, 2.02. 75
the day to cheer and night's dank dew to dry, 2.03. 6
night's candles are burnt out, and jocund day 3.05. 9
be sick to–morrow | for this night's watching. 4.04. 8
this night's great business into my dispatch, MAC 1.05. 68
is't night's predominance, or the day's shame, 2.04. 8
drowsy hums | hath rung night's yawning peal, 3.02. 43
whiles night's black agents to their preys do 3.02. 53
your patience in our last night's speech, HAM 5.01.294
the tyranny of the open night's too rough | for LR 3.04. 2
what a night's this! 3.04.170
i' th' last night's storm i such a fellow saw, 4.01. 32
of heaven, | more fiery by night's blackness; ANT 1.04. 13
that, after holy tie and first night's stir, TNK pr 6
the owl (night's herald) shrieks, 'tis very late VEN 531
day," quoth she, "night's scapes doth open lay, LUC 747
"were tarquin night, as he is but night's child, 785
through night's black bosom should not peep 788
to hide the truth of this false night's abuses. 1075

NIGHTS' 1 FR 0.0001 REL FR 0 V 1 P
you, though it cost me ten nights' watchings. ADO 2.01.372 P

/NIGHTS 1 FR 0.0001 REL FR 1 V 0 P
forbear to sleep the /nights, and fast the /days R3 4.04.118

NIGHTS 34 FR 0.0038 REL FR 29 V 5 P
with twenty watchful, weary, tedious nights: TGV 1.01. 31
night in russia | when nights are longest there. MM 2.01.135
and now will he lie ten nights awake carving the ADO 2.03. 17 P
have no more profit of their shining nights LLL 1.01. 90
four nights will quickly dream away the time; MND 1.01. 8
have endur'd shrewd days and nights with us, AYL 5.04.173
since you have made the days and nights as one, AWW 5.01. 3
sir toby, you must come in earlier a' nights. TN 1.03. 5 P
are wrack'd three nights ago on goodwin sands; JN 5.03. 11
and pluck nights from me, but not lend a morrow; R2 1.03.228
in winter's tedious nights sit by the fire 5.01. 40
or i will ride thee a' nights like the mare. 2H4 2.01. 77 P
leave fighting a' days and foining a' nights, 2.04.232 P
up days with toil, and nights with sleep, | had H5 4.01.279
my lord stanley sleep these tedious nights? R3 3.02. 6
pursu'd him still, and three nights after this, H8 4.02. 25
for all the frosty nights that i have watch'd, TIT 3.01. 5
go, girl, seek happy nights to happy days. ROM 1.03.105
milky heart, | it turns in less than two nights? TIM 3.01. 55
where liest a' nights, timon? 4.03.292
which shall to all our nights and days to come MAC 1.05. 69
give to our tables meat, sleep to our nights; 3.06. 34
cold stone | days and nights has thirty–one 4.01. 7
i have two nights watch'd with you, but can 5.01. 1 P
our story, | what we have two nights seen. HAM 1.01. 33
the nights are wholesome, then no planets strike 1.01.162
two nights together had these gentlemen, 1.02.196
that love night | love not such nights as these. LR 3.02. 43
seven days and nights? OTH 3.04.173
and for two nights together | have made the CYM 3.06. 2
by all the chaste nights i have ever pleas'd you TNK 3.06.200
like dying coals burnt out in tedious nights. LUC 1379
all days are nights to see till i see thee, SON 43.13
and nights bright days when dreams do show thee 43.14

NIGHT–SHRIEK 1 FR 0.0001 REL FR 1 V 0 P
would have cool'd | to hear a night–shriek, and MAC 5.05. 11

NIGHT–TAPERS 1 FR 0.0001 REL FR 1 V 0 P
and for night–tapers crop their waxen thighs MND 3.01.169

NIGHT–TRIPPING 1 FR 0.0001 REL FR 1 V 0 P
that some night–tripping fairy had exchang'd 1H4 1.01. 87

NIGHT–WAKING 1 FR 0.0001 REL FR 1 V 0 P
yet, foul night–waking cat, he doth but dally, LUC 554

NIGHT–WALKING 1 FR 0.0001 REL FR 1 V 0 P
and night–walking heralds | that trudge betwixt R3 1.01. 72

NIGHT–WANDERERS 1 FR 0.0001 REL FR 1 V 0 P
mislead night–wanderers, laughing at their harm? MND 2.01. 39

NIGHT–WAND'RERS 1 FR 0.0001 REL FR 1 V 0 P
or stonish'd as night–wand'rers often are, VEN 825

NIGHT–WAND'RING 1 FR 0.0001 REL FR 1 V 0 P
night–wand'ring weasels shriek to see him there; LUC 307

NIGHT–WATCH 1 FR 0.0001 REL FR 1 V 0 P
sigh, | a critic, nay, a night–watch constable, LLL 3.01.176

NIGHTWORK 3 FR 0.0003 REL FR 0 V 3 P
and is jane nightwork alive? 2H4 3.02.199 P
and had robin nightwork by old nightwork before 3.02.208 P
nightwork by old nightwork before i came to 3.02.209 P

NIHIL 1 FR 0.0001 REL FR 0 V 1 P
'tis "semper idem," for "obsque hoc nihil est." 2H4 5.05. 28 P

NILE 6 FR 0.0006 REL FR 6 V 0 P
or murmuring, "where's my serpent of old nile?" ANT 1.05. 25
melt egypt into nile! 2.05. 78
they take the flow o' th' nile | by certain 2.07. 17
till the flies and gnats of nile | have buried 3.13.166
as th' aspic leaves | upon the caves of nile. 5.02.353
whose tongue | outvenoms all the worms of nile, CYM 3.04. 35

NILL 4 FR 0.0004 REL FR 3 V 1 P
and, will you, nill you, i will marry you. SHR 2.01.271
it is, will he, nill he, he goes, mark you that. HAM 5.01. 17 P
i nill relate, action may | conveniently the PER 3.ch. 55
in scorn or friendship, nill i conster whether. PP 14. 8

NILUS' 2 FR 0.0002 REL FR 2 V 0 P
by the fire | that quickens nilus' slime, i go ANT 1.03. 69
rather on nilus' mud | lay me stark–nak'd, and 5.02. 58

NILUS 4 FR 0.0004 REL FR 3 V 1 P
and now like nilus it disdaineth bounds. TIT 3.01. 71
e'en as the o'erflowing nilus presageth famine. ANT 1.02. 49 P
the higher nilus swells, | the more it promises; 2.07. 20
hast thou the pretty worm of nilus there, | that 5.02.243

/NIMBLE 1 FR 0.0001 REL FR 1 V 0 P
/in /the /most /terrible /and /nimble /stroke LR 4.07. 33

NIMBLE 25 FR 0.0028 REL FR 21 V 4 P
are of such sensible and nimble lungs that they TMP 2.01.174 P
nor i, my spirits are nimble. 2.01.202
thee how | to snare the nimble marmazet. 2.02.170

as, nimble jugglers that deceive the eye, ERR 1.02. 98
poisons up | the nimble spirits in the arteries, LLL 4.03.302
of such a merry, nimble, stirring spirit, | she 5.02. 16
awake the pert and nimble spirit of mirth, MND 1.01. 13
you have a nimble wit; AYL 3.02.276 P
who with her head nimble in threats approach'd 4.03.109
a quick eye, and a nimble hand, is necessary for WT 4.04.671 P
which his nimble haste | had falsely thrust upon JN 4.02.197
nimble mischance, that art so light of foot, R2 3.04. 92
but with nimble wing | we were enforc'd, for 1H4 5.01. 64
quick, forgetive, full of nimble, fiery, and 2H4 4.03.100 P
france | that can be with a nimble galliard won; H5 1.02.252
and the nimble gunner | with linstock now the 3.pr. 32
you have dancing shoes | with nimble soles, i ROM 1.04. 15
you nimble lightnings, dart your blinding flames LR 2.04.165
kiss'd your sails, | to make your vessel nimble. CYM 2.04. 29
gently quench | thy nimble, sulphurous flashes! PER 3.01. 6
tough and nimble set, | which shows an active TNK 4.02.125
relish your nimble notes to pleasing ears, LUC 1126
youth is nimble, age is lame, | youth is hot and PP 12. 6
for nimble thought can jump both sea and land SON 44. 7
do i envy those jacks that nimble leap | to kiss 128. 5
NIMBLE–FOOTED 2 FR 0.0002 REL FR 2 V 0 P
being nimble–footed, he hath outrun us, | but TGV 5.03. 7
son, | the nimble–footed madcap prince of wales, 1H4 4.01. 95
NIMBLENESS 1 FR 0.0001 REL FR 1 V 0 P
are full of rest, defense, and nimbleness. JC 4.03.202
NIMBLE–PINION'D 1 FR 0.0001 REL FR 1 V 0 P
therefore do nimble–pinion'd doves draw love, ROM 2.05. 7
NIMBLER 2 FR 0.0002 REL FR 2 V 0 P
where horses have been nimbler than the sands CYM 3.02. 72
we shall be the nimbler. TNK 3.06. 63
/NIMBLY 1 FR 0.0001 REL FR 1 V 0 P
/that /rise /thus /nimbly /by /a /true /king's R2 4.01.318
NIMBLY 4 FR 0.0004 REL FR 3 V 1 P
you carried your guts away as nimbly, with as 1H4 2.04.259 P
he capers nimbly in a lady's chamber | to the R3 1.01. 12
the air | nimbly and sweetly recommends itself MAC 1.06. 2
bridle on a ragged bough | nimbly she fastens (o VEN 38
/NINE 3 FR 0.0003 REL FR 2 V 1 P
look where the youngest wren of /nine comes. TN 3.02. 66 P
supper–time, my lord, | it's /nine a' clock. R3 5.03. 48
/sixty /and /nine, /that /wore | /their TRO pr 5
NINE 56 FR 0.0063 REL FR 31 V 25 P
more to come to her, between eight and nine. WIV 3.05. 46 P
do so. between nine and ten, say'st thou? 3.05. 53 P
eight and nine, sir. 3.05. 54 P
'twixt eight and nine is the hour, master /brook 3.05.130 P
claudio | be executed by nine to–morrow morning. MM 2.01. 34
nine, sir; overdone by the last. 2.01.202 P
nine? 2.01.203 P
and bred, one that is a prisoner nine years old. 4.02.131 P
i have studied eight or nine wise words to speak ADO 3.02. 72 P
you shall present before her the nine worthies. LLL 5.01.117 P
say none so fit as to present the nine worthies. 5.01.123 P
and three times thrice is nine. 5.02.488
is not nine. 5.02.492 P
by jove, i always took three threes for nine. 5.02.495 P
the nine men's morris is fill'd up with mud, MND 2.01. 98
aleven widows and nine maids is a simple MV 2.02.162 P
'tis nine a' clock — our friends all stay for 2.06. 63
'tis but an hour ago since it was nine, | and AYL 2.07. 24
i was seven of the nine days out of the wonder 3.02.174 P
"among nine bad if one be good, | among nine bad AWW 1.03. 77
if one be good, | among nine bad if one be good, 1.03. 78
nine changes of the wat'ry star hath been | the WT 1.02. 1
the second and the third, nine, and some five; 2.01.145
boys, too green and idle | for girls of nine), o 3.02.182
these nine in buckram that i told thee of — 1H4 2.04.212 P
he held me last night at least nine hours | in 3.01.154
and ten times better than the nine worthies. 2H4 2.04.221 P
hath, | exceeding the nine sibyls of old rome: 1H6 1.02. 56
but i was made a king, at nine months old. 2H6 4.09. 4
when i was crown'd i was but nine months old. 3H6 1.01.112
i was anointed king at nine months old, | my 3.01. 76
was crown'd in paris but at nine months old. R3 2.03. 17
/i will buy nine sparrows for a penny, and his TRO 2.01. 71 P
two i' th' thigh — there's nine that i know. COR 2.01.152 P
but new strook nine. ROM 1.01.161
by the hour of nine. 2.02.168
the clock strook nine when i did send the nurse; 2.05. 1
and from nine till twelve | is /three long hours 2.05. 10
of cats, nothing but one of your nine lives; 3.01. 78 P
to varro and to isidore | he owes nine thousand, TIM 2.01. 2
laboring for nine. 3.04. 8
weary sev'nnights, nine times nine, | shall he MAC 1.03. 22
weary sev'nnights, nine times nine, | shall he 1.03. 22
to mine, | and thrice again, to make up nine. 1.03. 36
sow's blood, that hath eaten | her nine farrow; 4.01. 65
'a will last you some eight year or nine year. HAM 5.01.167 P
a tanner will last you nine year. 5.01.168 P
he hath laid on twelve for nine, and it would 5.02.167 P
he hath been out nine years, and away he shall LR 1.01. 32 P
nine or ten times | i had thought t' have yerk'd OTH 1.02. 4
till now some nine moons wasted, they have us'd 1.03. 84
at nine i' th' morning here we'll meet again. 1.03.279
i would have him nine years a–killing. 4.01.178 P
of an egyptian | that had nine hours lien dead, PER 3.02. 85
a pound, meal at nine shillings a bushel, and STM II.C 2 P
than those old nine which rhymers invocate, SON 38.10
NINE–FOLD 1 FR 0.0001 REL FR 1 V 0 P
'old, | he met the night–mare and her nine–fold; LR 3.04.121
NINESCORE 2 FR 0.0002 REL FR 0 V 2 P
and old ginger, ninescore and seventeen pounds, MM 4.03. 6 P
i have found'red ninescore and odd posts, and 2H4 4.03. 36 P
NINETEEN 3 FR 0.0003 REL FR 2 V 1 P
so long that nineteen zodiacs have gone round MM 1.02.168
boil'd–brains of nineteen and two–and–twenty WT 3.03. 64 P
our nineteen legions thou shalt hold by land, ANT 3.07. 58
NINETY 1 FR 0.0001 REL FR 1 V 0 P
o thou that from eleven to ninety reign'st | in TNK 5.01.130
NINNY'S'* *(also ninus')*
NINNY'S* 4 FR 0.0004 REL FR 4 V 0 P
what a pied ninny's this! TMP 3.02. 63
i'll meet thee, pyramus, at ninny's tomb." MND 3.01. 97
wilt thou at ninny's tomb meet me straightway? 5.01.202
this is old ninny's tomb. where is my love? 5.01.263
NINTH 7 FR 0.0008 REL FR 4 V 3 P
he will be the ninth worthy. LLL 5.02.578 P
meet me in arms by the ninth of the next month? 1H4 2.03. 27 P
ye me, | i'll cavil on the ninth part of a hair. 3.01.138
mater is not worth the ninth part of a sparrow. TRO 2.01. 72 P
about the ninth hour, lady. JC 2.04. 23
ere the ninth hour, i drunk him to his bed; ANT 2.05. 21
'tis the ninth hour o' th' morn. CYM 4.02. 30
NINUS' *(also ninny's*)*
NINUS' 2 FR 0.0002 REL FR 1 V 1 P
"ninus' tomb," man. MND 3.01. 98 P
lovers think no scorn | to meet at ninus' tomb, 5.01.138
NIOBE 1 FR 0.0001 REL FR 1 V 0 P
like niobe, all tears — why, she, /even /she — HAM 1.02.149
NIOBES 1 FR 0.0001 REL FR 1 V 0 P
make wells and niobes of the maids and wives, TRO 5.10. 19
NIP 3 FR 0.0003 REL FR 3 V 0 P
weeds | nip not the gaudy blossoms of your love LLL 5.02.802
here's snip and nip and cut and slish and slash, SHR 4.03. 90
these tidings nip me, and i hang the head | as TIT 4.04. 70
NIPP'D 1 FR 0.0001 REL FR 1 V 0 P
when blood is nipp'd and ways be /foul, | then LLL 5.02.916
NIPPING 2 FR 0.0002 REL FR 2 V 0 P
barren winter, with his wrathful nipping cold; 2H6 2.04. 3
it is /a nipping and an eager air. HAM 1.04. 2
NIPPLE 2 FR 0.0002 REL FR 2 V 0 P
when it did taste the wormwood on the nipple ROM 1.03. 30
have pluck'd my nipple from his boneless gums, MAC 1.07. 57
NIPS 3 FR 0.0003 REL FR 3 V 0 P
and deliberate word | nips youth i' th' head, MM 3.01. 90
his greatness is a–ripening, nips his root, H8 3.02.357
it nips me unto list'ning, and thick slumber PER 5.01.234
NIT 2 FR 0.0002 REL FR 2 V 0 P
ah, heavens, it is /a most pathetical nit! LLL 4.01.148
thou flea, thou nit, thou winter–cricket thou! SHR 4.03.109
NO *(also not)*
/NO 52 FR 0.0058 REL FR 40 V 12 P
NO 4038 FR 0.4564 REL FR 2888 V 1150 P
NOAH 1 FR 0.0001 REL FR 0 V 1 P
grand–jurymen since before noah was a sailor. TN 3.02. 17 P
NOAH'S 1 FR 0.0001 REL FR 0 V 1 P
'tis in grain, noah's flood could not do it. ERR 3.02.106 P
NOB* 2 FR 0.0002 REL FR 1 V 1 P
hob, nob, is his word; TN 3.04.240 P
it would not be sir nob in any case. JN 1.01.147
NOBILITY 36 FR 0.0040 REL FR 28 V 8 P
against his own nobility in his proper stream AWW 4.03. 24 P
let his nobility remain in 's court. 4.05. 50 P
your worth, your greatness, and nobility. JN 4.03. 86
thy bosom | doth make an earthquake of nobility. 5.02. 42
corse | betwixt the wind and his nobility. 1H4 1.03. 45
that men of your nobility and power | did gage 1.03.172
malt–worms, but with nobility and tranquility, 2.01. 75 P
and here is my speech. stand aside, nobility. 2.04.389 P
this, | where stain'd nobility lies trodden on, 5.04. 13
whelp | forage in blood of french nobility. H5 1.02.110
awake, awake, english nobility! 1H6 1.01. 78
regard, | king henry's peers and chief nobility 4.01.146
that sees | this jarring discord of nobility, 4.01.188
poor, | and our nobility will scorn the match. 5.03. 96
with such | as, like to pitch, defile nobility, 2H6 2.01.192
heir, | and such high vaunts of his nobility, 3.01. 50
true nobility is exempt from fear: 4.01.129
the nobility think scorn to go in leather aprons 4.02. 12 P
and delight to live in slavery to the nobility. 4.08. 28 P
disgrac'd, and the nobility | held in contempt, R3 1.03. 78
o that your young nobility could judge | what 1.03.256
and like her true nobility she has | carried H8 2.04.143
by a piece of scarlet, | farewell nobility! 3.02.281
the state | of our despis'd nobility, our issues 3.02.291
would the nobility lay aside their ruth | and COR 1.01.197
i sin in envying his nobility; 1.01.230
by plot, | to curb the will of the nobility. 3.01. 39
the nobility are vexed, whom we see have sided 4.02. 2
sits down, | and the nobility of rome are his. 4.07. 29
to justice, continence, and nobility; TIT 1.01. 15
of my joys, | sweet cell of virtue and nobility, 1.01. 93
sith true nobility | warrants these words in 1.01.271
and with no less nobility of love | than that HAM 1.02.110
in love have then a nobility in their natures OTH 2.01.216 P
these hands do lack nobility that they strike ANT 2.05. 82
such a constant nobility enforce a freedom out TNK 2.01. 33 P
NOBILITY'S 1 FR 0.0001 REL FR 1 V 0 P
sweet mercy is nobility's true badge. TIT 1.01.119
NOBIS 1 FR 0.0001 REL FR 1 V 0 P
let there be sung non nobis and te deum, | the H5 4.08.123
/NOBLE 3 FR 0.0003 REL FR 3 V 0 P
/cast /th' /event /of /war, /my /noble /lord, 2H4 1.01.166
/but, /my /most /noble /lord /of /westmerland, 4.01. 59
/your /noble /and /right //well–rememb'red 4.01.110
NOBLE 657 FR 0.0742 REL FR 597 V 60 P
(who had, no doubt, some noble creature in her) TMP 1.02. 7
fresh water, that | a noble neapolitan, gonzalo, 1.02.161
that's my noble master! 1.02.299
for nothing natural | i ever saw so noble. 1.02.420
noble sebastian, | thou let'st thy fortune sleep 2.01.215
no, noble mistress, 'tis fresh morning with me 3.01. 33
i thank my noble lord. 3.02. 38 P
first, noble friend, | let me embrace thine age, 5.01.120
know, noble lord, they have devis'd a mean | how TGV 3.01. 38
mettle | before so noble and so great a figure MM 1.01. 49
whom i would save, had a most noble father! 2.01. 7
thou art not noble, | for all th' accommodations 3.01. 13
thou art too noble to conserve a life | in base 3.01. 87
there she lost a noble and renown'd brother, in 3.01.219 P
how now, noble pompey? 3.02. 43 P
noble prince, | as there comes light from heaven 5.01.224
and you, my noble and well–warranted cousin, 5.01.254
pardon me, noble lord, | i thought it was a 5.01.462
most in the company of the right noble claudio. ADO 1.01. 85 P
god help the noble claudio! 1.01. 88 P
he is of a noble strain, of approv'd valor, and 2.01.379 P
noble, or not i for an angel; 2.03. 33 P
how wise, how noble, young, how rarely featur'd, 3.01. 60
sweet prince, you learn me noble thankfulness. 4.01. 30
o noble sir! 5.01.292
when he would play the noble beast in love. 5.04. 47
and got a calf in that same noble feat | much 5.04. 50
sir, the king is a noble gentleman, and my LLL 5.01. 95 P
the noble lord | most honorably doth uphold his 5.02.448
my noble lord, | this man hath my consent to MND 1.01. 24
none of noble sort | would so offend a virgin 3.02.159
and tragical, my noble lord, it is; 5.01. 66
no, my noble lord, | it is not for you. 5.01. 76
cannot do, noble respect | takes it in might, 5.01. 91
here come two noble beasts in, a man and a lion. 5.01.217 P
here comes bassanio, your most noble kinsman, MV 1.01. 57
moan to be abridg'd | from such a noble rate, 1.01.127
the several caskets to this noble prince. 2.07. 2
behold, there stand the caskets, noble prince. 2.09. 4
you have a noble and a true conceit | of godlike 3.04. 2
o noble judge! o excellent young man! 4.01.246
so says the bond, doth it not, noble judge? 4.01.253
school'd and yet learned, full of noble device, AYL 1.01.167 P
o noble fool! 2.07. 33
one side, breaks his staff like a noble goose. 3.04. 45 P
belike some noble gentleman that means SHR in.1. 75
such as he hath observ'd in noble ladies | unto in.1. 111
to see her noble lord restor'd to health, | who in.1. 121
o noble lord, bethink thee of thy birth, | call in.2. 30
how fares my noble lord? in.2. 100
here, noble lord, what is thy will with her? in.2. 103
baptista is a noble gentleman, | to whom my 1.02.238
may beseem | the spouse of any noble gentleman. 4.05. 67
no note upon my parents, his all noble. AWW 1.03.157
your pardon, noble mistress! 1.03.186
noble heroes! 2.01. 40 P
we shall, noble captain. 2.01. 46 P
use a more spacious ceremony to the noble lords; 2.01. 50 P
but you will | my noble grapes, and if my royal 2.01. 71
i play the noble huswife with the time, | to 2.02. 60
of noble bachelors stand at my bestowing, | o'er 2.03. 53
not one of those but had a noble father. 2.03. 62
italian fields | where noble fellows strike. 2.03.291
such is his noble purpose, and, believe't, | the 3.02. 70
good morrow, noble captain. 4.03.314 P
god save you, noble captain. 4.03.316 P
a scar nobly got, or a noble scar, is a good 4.05. 99 P
i long to talk with the young noble soldier. 4.05.103 P
noble she was, and thought | i stood engag'd; 5.03. 95
lay a more noble thought upon mine honor | than 5.03.180
you, that have turn'd off a first so noble wife, 5.03.220
a noble duke, in nature as in name. TN 1.02. 25
sure, my noble lord, | if she be so abandon'd to 1.04. 18
yet i suppose him virtuous, know him noble, | of 1.05.258
tell her, my love, more noble than the world, 2.04. 81
here comes my noble gull–catcher. 2.05.187 P
make | with the most noble bottom of our fleet, 5.01. 57
orsino, noble sir, | be pleas'd that i shake off 5.01. 72
i was preserv'd to serve this noble count. 5.01.256
be not amaz'd, right noble is his blood. 5.01.264
our gentry than our parents' noble names, | in WT 1.02.393
acquaint the queen of your most noble offer, 2.02. 46
these lords, my noble fellows, if they please, 2.03.143
he is touch'd | to th' noble heart. 3.02.222
how would he look to see his work, so noble, 4.04. 21
than herself, | too noble for this place. 4.04.159
seems to be the more noble in being fantastical. 4.04.751 P
that noble honor'd lord, is fear'd and lov'd? 5.01.158
most noble sir, | that which i shall report will 5.01.178
the noble combat that 'twixt joy and sorrow was 5.02. 72 P
a noble boy! who would not do thee right? JN 2.01. 18
o noble dolphin, | go with me to the king. 3.04.177
the first of april died | your noble mother; 4.02.121
spoke like a sprightful noble gentleman. 4.02.177
the count melune, a noble lord of france, 4.03. 15
and, noble dolphin, albeit we swear | a 5.02. 9
a noble temper dost thou show in this, | and 5.02. 40
what a noble combat hast /thou fought | between 5.02. 43
hail, noble prince of france! 5.02. 68
fly, noble english, you are bought and sold! 5.04. 10
let it be so, and you, my noble prince, | with 5.07. 96
for you, my noble lord of lancaster, | the R2 1.01.135
is pale cold cowardice in noble breasts. 1.02. 34
o, let no noble eye profane a tear | for me, if 1.03. 59
of you, my noble cousin, lord aumerle; 1.03. 64
how fares our noble uncle lancaster? 2.01. 71
i am the last of noble edward's sons, | of whom 2.01.171
his noble hand | did win what he did spend, and 2.01.179
moe | of noble blood in this declining land. 2.01.240
that which his noble ancestors achiev'd with 2.01.254
his noble kinsman — most degenerate king! 2.01.262
believe me, noble lord, | i am a stranger here 2.03. 2
by sight of what i have, your noble company. 2.03. 18
seymour, | none else of name and noble estimate. 2.03. 56
your presence makes us rich, most noble lord. 2.03. 63
my noble uncle! 2.03. 82
and, noble uncle, i beseech your grace | look on 2.03.115
you have a son, aumerle, my noble cousin, | had 2.03.125
the noble duke hath been too much abused. 2.03.137
the noble duke hath sworn his coming is | but 2.03.148
one day too late, i fear me, noble lord, | hath 3.02. 67
noble /lord, | go to the rude ribs of that 3.03. 31
his noble cousin is right welcome hither, | and 3.03.122
what thou dost know of noble gloucester's death, 4.01. 3
princes and noble lords, | what answer shall i 4.01. 19
thou wert cause of noble gloucester's death. 4.01. 37
thy men | to execute the noble duke at callice. 4.01. 82
would god that any in this noble presence | were 4.01.117
presence | were enough noble to be upright judge 4.01.118
noble to be upright judge | of noble richard! 4.01.119
thanks, noble peer! 5.05. 67
forgot, | right noble is thy merit, well i wot. 5.06. 18
news, | whose worst was that the noble mortimer, 1H4 1.01. 38
is, by our noble and chaste mistress the moon, 1.02. 28 P
nor never could the noble mortimer | receive so 1.03.110
those same noble scots | that are your prisoners 1.03.212
creep | of that same noble prelate well belov'd, 1.03.267
why, it cannot choose but be a noble plot. 1.03.279
a pleasing eye, and a most noble carriage, and, 2.04.423 P
my noble lord, from eastcheap. 2.04.441 P
good night, my noble lord. 2.04.523
well said, my noble scot! 4.01. 1
and witch the world with noble horsemanship. 4.01.110
a head | of gallant warriors, noble gentlemen. 4.04. 26

the noble westmerland, and warlike blunt, | and		4.04. 30
to grace this latter age with noble deeds.		5.01. 92
and by, | till then in blood by noble percy lie.		5.04.110
a noble earl, and many a creature else | had		5.05. 7
the noble scot, lord douglas, when he saw | the		5.05. 17
the noble percy slain, and all his men | upon		5.05. 19
fell | under the wrath of noble hotspur's sword,	2H4	in 30
noble earl, | i bring you certain news from		1.01. 11
i ran from shrewsbury, my noble lord, | where		1.01. 65
so fought the noble douglas" — | stopping my		1.01. 77
then was that noble worcester | so soon ta'en		1.01.125
'tis more than time, and, my most noble lord,		1.01.187
and, my most noble friends, i pray you all		1.03. 2
comes the king back from wales, my noble lord?		2.01.176 P
and yours, most noble bardolph!		2.02. 74 P
wherein the noble youth did dress themselves:		2.03. 22
heaven, | for recordation to my noble husband.		2.03. 61
and these noble lords | had not been here to		4.01. 38
to you, my noble lord of westmerland.		4.02. 72
to her), believe not the word of the noble.		4.03. 54 P
and noble offices thou mayst effect | of		4.04. 24
to weeds, | and he, the noble image of my youth,		4.04. 55
world | the noble change that i have purposed!		4.05.154
'tis call'd jerusalem, my noble lord.		4.05.234
and let us choose such limbs of noble counsel		5.02.135
my knight, i will inflame thy noble liver, | and		5.05. 31
thy doll, and helen of thy noble thoughts, | is		5.05. 33
o noble english, that could entertain | with	H5	1.02.111
help | and yours, the noble sinews of our power,		1.02.223
a noble shalt thou have, and present pay, | and		2.01.107
i shall have my noble?		2.01.114 P
see you, my princes and my noble peers, | these		2.02. 84
come they of noble family?		2.02.129
how well supplied with noble counsellors, | how		2.04. 33
base | that hath not noble lustre in your eyes.		3.01. 30
the lord in heaven bless thee, noble harry!		4.01. 33
then, joyfully, my noble lord of bedford, | my		4.03. 8
wounds) | the noble earl of suffolk also lies.		4.06. 10
it is the noble duke of gloucester.	1H6	1.03. 6
have patience, noble duke, i may not open, | the		1.03. 18
ay, noble uncle, thus ignobly us'd, | your		2.05. 35
so fell that noble earl | and was beheaded.		2.05. 90
that two such noble peers as ye should jar!		3.01. 70
see, noble charles, the beacon of our friend,		3.02. 29
erects | thy noble deeds as valor's monuments.		3.02.120
the noble duke of bedford late deceas'd, | but		3.02.132
that i wear | in honor of my noble lord of york,		3.04. 30
knights of the garter were of noble birth,		4.01. 34
this is my servant, hear him, noble prince.		4.01. 80
and that is my petition, noble lord.		4.01.101
villain | and cannot help the noble chevalier.		4.03. 14
spur to the rescue of the noble talbot, | who		4.03. 19
what joy shall noble talbot have | to bid his		4.03. 39
cries out for noble york and somerset | to beat		4.04. 15
him aid, | while he, renowned noble gentleman,		4.04. 24
that basely fled when noble talbot stood.		4.05. 17
doubtless he would have made a noble knight.		4.07. 44
knight of the noble order of saint george,		4.07. 68
this man | of purpose to obscure my noble birth.		5.04. 22
i gave a noble to the priest | the morn that i		5.04. 23
your wondrous rare description, noble earl, | of		5.05. 1
my noble lord of suffolk, or for that | my		5.05. 80
did bear him like a noble gentleman.	2H6	1.01.184
for my part, noble lords, i care not which, | or		1.03.101
noble she is;		2.01.190
here, noble henry, is my staff.		2.03. 32
nell, ill can thy noble mind abrook | the abject		2.04. 10
then, noble york, take thou this task in hand.		3.01.318
i'll call him presently, my noble lord.		3.02. 18
sighs, | and all to have the noble duke alive.		3.02. 64
and noble stock | was graft with crab–tree slip,		3.02.213
thou art | and never of the nevils' noble race.		3.02.215
ay, noble father, if our words will serve.		5.01.139
how now, my noble lord?		5.02. 8
my noble father, | three times to–day i holp him		5.03. 7
but, noble as he is, look where he comes.		5.03. 14
let noble warwick, cobham, and the rest, | whom	3H6	1.02. 56
when as the noble duke of york was slain, | your		2.01. 46
my royal father, cheer these noble lords, | and		2.02. 78
blood, | the noble gentleman gave up the ghost.		2.03. 22
now therefore be it known to noble lewis, | that		3.03. 23
my noble queen, let former grudges pass, | and		3.03.195
this noble queen | and prince shall follow with		3.03.236
to rest mistrustful where a noble heart | hath		4.02. 8
/thanks, noble clarence, worthy brother, thanks.		5.07. 30
and his noble queen | well strook in years, fair	R3	1.01. 91
forbear your conference with the noble duke.		1.01.104
with patience, noble lord, as prisoners must;		1.01.126
at chertsey monast'ry this noble king, | and wet		1.02.214
towards chertsey, noble lord?		1.02.225
scarce some two days since were worth a noble.		1.03. 81
the curse my noble father laid on thee | when		1.03.173
now fair befall thee and thy noble house!		1.03.281
we will, my noble lord.		1.03.354
the noble duke of clarence to your hands.		1.04. 92
of you, my noble cousin buckingham, | if ever		2.01. 65
god grant that some, less noble and less loyal,		2.01. 92
if that our noble father were alive?		2.02. 7
sorrow | as i had title in thy noble husband!		2.02. 48
therefore i say with noble buckingham, | that it		2.02.138
how fares our cousin, noble lord of york?		3.01.101
for the installment of this noble duke | in the		3.01.163
first, he commends him to your noble self.		3.02. 8
many good morrows to my noble lord!		3.02. 35
fatal and ominous to noble peers!		3.03. 10
now, noble peers, the cause why we are met | is		3.04. 1
who is most inward with the noble duke?		3.04. 8
my noble lords and cousins all, good morrow.		3.04. 22
if they have done this deed, my noble lord —		3.04. 73
and do not doubt, right noble princes both,		3.05. 64
child | of that insatiate edward, noble york,		3.05. 87
being nothing like the noble duke my father.		3.05. 92
he doth entreat your grace, my noble lord, | to		3.07. 59
sorry i am my noble cousin should | suspect me		3.07. 88
the noble isle doth want /her proper limbs;		3.07.125
yet to draw forth your noble ancestry | from the		3.07.198
true, noble prince.		4.02. 15
that edward still should live true noble prince!		4.02. 16

to love, | send her a letter of thy noble deeds:		4.04.280
come, noble gentlemen, | let us survey the		5.03. 14
afford | be to thy person, noble father–in–law!		5.03. 81
such noble scenes as draw the eye to flow, | we	H8	pr 4
the very persons of our noble story | as they		pr 26
heralds challeng'd | the noble spirits to arms,		1.01. 35
when these so noble benefits shall prove | not		1.02.115
you charge not in your spleen a noble person		1.02.174
no doubt he's noble;		1.03. 57
in all this noble bevy, has brought with her		1.04. 4
that noble lady | or gentleman that is not		1.04. 35
your grace is noble.		1.04. 38
a noble troop of strangers, | for so they seem.		1.04. 53
a noble company!		1.04. 64
by fame | of this so noble and so fair assembly		1.04. 67
in all the rest show'd a most noble patience.		2.01. 36
and see the noble ruin'd man you speak of.		2.01. 54
his noble friends and fellows, whom to leave		2.01. 73
my noble father, henry of buckingham, | who		2.01.107
and out of ruins | made my name once more noble.		2.01.115
had my trial, | and must needs say a noble one;		2.01.119
have any goodness, | the trial just and noble.		2.02. 91
invited by your noble self, hath sent | one		2.02. 94
all strangers' loves, | you are so noble.		2.02.102
she's noble born;		2.04.142
may it please you, noble madam, to withdraw		3.01. 27
noble lady, | i am sorry my integrity should		3.01. 50
my lord of york, out of his noble nature, | zeal		3.01. 62
to give up willingly that noble title | your		3.01.140
i know you have a gentle, noble temper, | a soul		3.01.165
a noble spirit | as yours was put into you, ever		3.01.169
this bewailing land | of noble buckingham, my		3.02.256
his noble jury and foul cause can witness.		3.02.269
my lord of norfolk, as you are truly noble, | as		3.02.289
or gild again the noble troops that waited		3.02.411
of me will stir him | (i know his noble nature)		3.02.418
must i needs forgo | so good, so noble, and so		3.02.423
carries up the train | is that old noble lady,		4.01. 52
noble madam, | men's evil manners live in brass,		4.02. 44
noble lady, | first, mine own service to your		4.02.114
she is young, and of a noble modest nature, | i		4.02.135
that his noble grace would have some pity | upon		4.02.139
a right good husband (let him be a noble), | and		4.02.146
without, my noble lords?		5.02. 40
must be sudden too, | my noble lords;		5.02. 56
men so noble, | however faulty, yet should find		5.02.109
and give it | to a most noble judge, the king my		5.02.136
you shall have | two noble partners with you,		5.02.202
my noble partners and myself thus pray | all		5.04. 5
my noble gossips, y' have been too prodigal.		5.04. 12
sol | in noble eminence enthron'd and spher'd	TRO	1.03. 90
/mould | a noble man that hath no spark of fire		1.03.294
you go, | and find the welcome of a noble foe.		1.03.309
nor none so noble | whose life were ill bestow'd		2.02.158
did move your greatness and this noble state		2.03.109
no, noble ajax, you are as strong, as valiant,		2.03.148 P
as wise, no less noble, much more gentle, and		2.03.149 P
our noble general, do not do so.		2.03.226
and tell me, noble diomed — faith, tell me true		4.01. 52
the noble menelaus.		4.05.176
hail, noble martius!	COR	1.01.163
and call him noble, that was now your hate;		1.01.183
of the city | you cry against the noble senate,		1.01.186
noble martius!		1.01.247
noble aufidius, | take your commission, hie you		1.02. 25
indeed la, 'tis a noble child.		1.03. 67 P
o noble fellow!		1.04. 52
my noble steed, known to the camp, i give him,		1.09. 61
as the hungry plebeians would the noble martius.		2.01. 10 P
how now, my as fair as noble ladies — and the		2.01. 97 P
and out of his noble carelessness lets them		2.02. 14 P
to gratify his noble service that | hath thus		2.02. 40
he's right noble. | let him be call'd for.		2.02.129
and to our noble consul | wish we all joy and		2.02.152
so, if he tell us his noble deeds, we must also		2.03. 8 P
must also tell him our noble acceptance of them.		2.03. 9 P
amen, amen. god save thee, noble consul!		2.03.136 P
springs of — | the noble house o' th' martians;		2.03.238
in authority, | against all noble sufferance.		3.01. 24
hath he not pass'd the noble and the common?		3.01. 29
spirit, | or never be so noble as a consul,		3.01. 56
that prefer | a noble life before a long, and		3.01.153
you that be noble, help him, young and old!		3.01.227
i prithee, noble friend, home to thy house;		3.01.233
his nature is too noble for the world;		3.01.254
the noble tribunes are the people's mouths,		3.01.270
noble tribunes, | it is the humane way.		3.01.324
noble menenius, | be you then as the people's		3.01.327
well said, noble woman!		3.02. 31
though therein you can never be too noble, | but		3.02. 40
noble lady!		3.02. 69
with my base tongue give to my noble heart | a		3.02.100
a noble wish.		3.03. 38
the gods preserve our noble tribunes!		3.03.143
being gentle wounded, craves | a noble cunning.		4.01. 9
dearest mother, and | my friends of noble touch;		4.01. 49
moe noble blows than ever thou wise words, | and		4.02. 21
and not unknit himself | the noble knot he made.		4.02. 32
your noble tullus aufidius /will appear well in		4.03. 33 P
tackle's torn, | thou show'st a noble vessel.		4.05. 62
thou noble thing, more dances my rapt heart		4.05.116
all undone, unless | the noble man have mercy.		4.06.108
first he was | a noble servant to them, but he		4.07. 36
a noble memory!		5.01. 17
vain, | unless his noble mother and his wife —		5.01. 71
a noble fellow, i warrant him.		5.02.109 P
and the most noble mother of the world | leave		5.03. 49
the noble sister of publicola, | the moon of		5.03. 64
rather to show a noble grace to both parts		5.03.121
"the man was noble, | but with his last attempt		5.03.145
think'st thou it honorable for a noble man		5.03.154
most noble sir, | if you do hold the same intent		5.06. 11
read it not, noble lords, | but tell the traitor		5.06. 83
why, noble lords, | will you be put in mind of		5.06.116
the man is noble and his fame folds in | this		5.06.124
my noble masters, hear me speak.		5.06.131
as the most noble corse that ever herald | did		5.06.143
the injury, | yet he shall have a noble memory.		5.06.153

noble patricians, patrons of my right, | defend	TIT	1.01. 1
thine, | thy noble brother titus and his sons,		1.01. 50
my noble lord and father, live in fame!		1.01.158
thanks, gentle tribune, noble brother marcus.		1.01.171
in right and service of their noble country.		1.01.197
to men | of noble minds is honorable meed.		1.01.216
thanks, noble titus, father of my life!		1.01.253
ay, noble titus, and resolv'd withal | to do		1.01.278
your noble emperor and his lovely bride, | sent		1.01.334
no, noble titus, but entreat of thee | to pardon		1.01.362
inter | his noble nephew here in virtue's nest,		1.01.376
no man shed tears for noble mutius, | he lives		1.01.389
this noble gentleman, lord titus here, | is in		1.01.415
lose not so noble a friend on vain suppose,		1.01.440
nor would your noble mother for much more | be		2.01. 51
great reason that my noble lord be rated | for		2.03. 81
noble tribunes, stay!		3.01. 1
o noble father, you lament in vain:		3.01. 27
weep, | or, if not so, thy noble heart to break:		3.01. 60
stay, father, for that noble hand of thine,		3.01.162
here are the heads of thy two noble sons, | and		3.01.236
farewell, andronicus, my noble father, | the		3.01.288
farewell, lavinia, my noble sister, | o, would		3.01.292
i know my noble aunt | loves me as dear as e'er		4.01. 22
wilt thou betray thy noble mistress thus?		4.02.106
case, | to see thy noble uncle thus distract?		4.03. 26
face, | the last true duties of thy noble son!		5.03.155
my noble uncle, do you know the cause?	ROM	1.01.143
o noble prince, i can discover all | the unlucky		3.01.142
thy noble shape is but a form of wax,		3.03.126
her, | she shall be married to this noble earl.		3.04. 21
morn, | the gallant, young, and noble gentleman,		3.05.113
now provided | a gentleman of noble parentage,		3.05.179
mercutio's kinsman, noble county paris!		5.03. 75
lay | the noble paris and true romeo dead.		5.03.259
noble ventidius!	TIM	1.01. 99
most noble timon, call the man before thee.		1.01.113
i prithee, noble lord, | join with me to forbid		1.01.126
most noble lord, | pawn me to this your honor,		1.01.146
a noble spirit!		1.02. 14
that with your other noble parts you'll suit		2.02. 23
noble, worthy, royal timon!		2.02.168
amiss — a noble nature | may catch a wrench —		2.02.208
a noble gentleman 'tis, if he would not keep so		3.01. 22 P
for his right noble mind, illustrious virtue,		3.02. 80
fault), | but with a noble fury and fair spirit,		3.05. 18
my noble lord —		3.06. 39 P
here's a noble feast toward.		3.06. 59 P
so noble a master fall'n, all gone, and not		4.02. 6
right, | base noble, old young, coward valiant.		4.03. 30
how came the noble timon to this change?		4.03. 67
noble timon, | what friendship may i do thee?		4.03. 70
our late noble master!		5.01. 55
so it is said, my noble lord, but therefore		5.01. 78
speak to them, noble timon.		5.01.130
noble and young — | when thy first griefs were		5.04. 13
march, noble lord, | into our city with thy		5.04. 29
atone your fears | with my more noble meaning,		5.04. 59
my noble general, timon is dead, | entomb'd upon		5.04. 65
dead | is noble timon, of whose memory		5.04. 80
have wish'd that noble brutus had his eyes.	JC	1.02. 62
rome, thou hast lost the breed of noble bloods!		1.02.151
till then, my noble friend, chew upon this:		1.02.171
he is a noble roman, and well given.		1.02.197
in execution | of any bold or noble enterprise,		1.02.298
well, brutus, thou art noble;		1.02.308
that noble minds keep ever with their likes;		1.02.311
could | but win the noble brutus to our party —		1.03.141
yourself | which every noble roman bears of you.		2.01. 93
render me worthy of this noble wife!		2.01.303
so to most noble caesar.		2.02.118
brutus is noble, wise, valiant, and honest;		3.01.126
the fortunes and affairs of noble brutus		3.01.135
with the most noble blood of all this world.		3.01.156
the bloody fingers of thy foes, | most noble!		3.01.199
the noble brutus is ascended; silence!		3.02. 11
noble antony, go up.		3.02. 64
the noble brutus | hath told you caesar was		3.02. 77
room for antony, most noble antony.		3.02.166 P
for when the noble caesar saw him stab,		3.02.184
o noble caesar!		3.02.199 P
peace there, hear the noble antony.		3.02.207 P
peace ho, hear antony, most noble antony!		3.02.234 P
most noble caesar! we'll revenge his death.		3.02.243
not doubt | but that my noble master will appear		4.02. 11
most noble brother, you have done me wrong.		4.02. 37
part, | i shall be glad to learn of noble men.		4.03. 54
my heart is thirsty for that noble pledge.		4.03.160
noble, noble cassius, | good night, and good		4.03.232
noble, noble cassius, | good night, and good		4.03.232
now, most noble brutus, | the gods to–day stand		5.01. 92
think not, thou noble roman, | that ever brutus		5.01.110
fly therefore, noble cassius, fly far off.		5.03. 11
octavius | is overthrown by noble brutus' power,		5.03. 52
whilst i go to meet | the noble brutus,		5.03. 74
o young and noble cato, art thou down?		5.04. 9
we must not. a noble prisoner!		5.04. 15
enemy | shall ever take alive the noble brutus;		5.04. 22
now is that noble vessel full of grief, | that		5.05. 13
what he hath lost, noble macbeth hath won.	MAC	1.02. 67
my noble partner | you greet with present grace,		1.03. 54
prediction | of noble having and of royal hope,		1.03. 56
noble banquo, | that hast no less deserv'd, nor		1.04. 29
fair and noble hostess, | we are your guest		1.06. 24
you do unbend your noble strength, to think | so		2.02. 42
good morrow, noble sir.		2.03. 44
worthy lord, | your noble friends do lack you.		3.04. 83
he is noble, wise, judicious, and best knows		4.02. 16
macduff, this noble passion, | child of		4.03.114
shall with my cousin, your right noble son,		5.06. 3
fight, | the noble thanes do bravely in the war,		5.07. 26
macduff is missing, and your noble son.		5.09. 4
lids | seek for thy noble father in the dust.	HAM	1.02. 71
if it assume my noble father's person, | i'll		1.02.243
/ev'l | doth all the noble substance of a doubt		1.04. 37
but know, thou noble youth, | the serpent that		1.05. 38
how is't, my noble lord?		1.05.117
your noble son is mad:		2.02. 92

how noble in reason! 2.02.304 P
for to the noble mind | rich gifts wax poor when 3.01. 99
o, what a noble mind is here o'erthrown! 3.01.150
now see /that noble and most sovereign reason, 3.01.157
bones, | no noble rite nor formal ostentation — 4.05.216
that he which hath your noble father slain 4.07. 4
and so have i a noble father lost, | a sister 4.07. 25
imagination trace the noble dust of alexander, 5.01.203 P
that is laertes, a very noble youth. mark. 5.01.224
exchange forgiveness with me, noble hamlet. 5.02.329
now cracks a noble heart. 5.02.359
do you know this noble gentleman, edmund? LR 1.01. 25 P
here's france and burgundy, my noble lord. 1.01.188
right noble burgundy, | when she was dear to us, 1.01.195
come, noble burgundy. 1.01.266
and the noble and true–hearted kent banish'd! 1.02.116 P
a credulous father and a brother noble, | whose 1.02.179
the noble duke my master, | my worthy arch and 2.01. 58
how now, my noble friend? 2.01. 86
occasions, noble gloucester, of some prize, 2.01.120
hail to thee, noble master! 2.04. 4
touch me with noble anger, | and let not women's 2.04.276
noble philosopher, your company. 3.04.172
and most speaking looks | to noble edmund. 4.05. 26
thou dost make thy way | to noble fortunes. 5.03. 30
yet am i noble as the adversary | i come to cope 5.03.123
that, if my speech offend a noble heart, | thy 5.03.127
if thou'rt noble, | i do forgive thee. 5.03.166
'tis noble kent, your friend. 5.03.269
you lords and noble friends, know our intent. 5.03.297
and your noble self | i am sure is sent for. OTH 1.02. 92
my very noble and approv'd good masters: 1.03. 77
do you perceive in all this noble company 1.03.179
my noble father, | i do perceive here a divided 1.03.180
and, noble signior, | if virtue no delighted 1.03.288
what say'st thou, noble heart? 1.03.302 P
a noble ship of venice | hath seen a grievous 2.01. 22
not) | is of a constant, loving, noble nature, 2.01.289
pleasure, our noble and valiant general, that 2.02. 1 P
isle of cyprus and our noble general othello! 2.02. 11 P
noble swelling spirits | that hold their honors 2.03. 55
and 'tis great pity that the noble moor | should 2.03.138
my noble lord — 3.03. 93
i would not have your free and noble nature, 3.03.199
my noble lord — 3.03.367
and, but my noble moor | is true of mind, and 3.04. 26
is this the noble moor whom our full senate 4.01.264
i hope my noble lord esteems me honest. 4.02. 65
hath she forsook so many noble matches? 4.02.125
that hast such noble sense of thy friend's wrong 5.01. 32
at your noble pleasure. ANT 1.02.112
most noble caesar, shalt thou have report | how 1.04. 35
here comes | the noble antony. 2.02. 14
noble friends, | that which combin'd us was most 2.02. 17
then, noble partners, | the rather for i 2.02. 22
'tis noble spoken. 2.02. 98
noble antony, | not sickness should detain me. 2.02.169
spirit which keeps thee, is | noble, courageous, 2.03. 21
but, he /away, 'tis noble. 2.03. 31
that despiteful rome | cast on my noble father. 2.06. 23
ho, noble captain, come. 2.07.135
noble ventidius, | whilst yet with parthian 3.01. 5
'tis a noble lepidus. 3.02. 6
adieu, noble agrippa. 3.02. 21
most noble antony, | let not the piece of virtue 3.02. 27
my noble brother! 3.02. 42
o noble emperor, do not fight by sea, | trust 3.07. 61
the noble ruin of her magic, antony, | claps on 3.10. 18
most noble sir, arise, the queen approaches. 3.11. 46
call all his noble captains to my lord. 3.13.188
ay, noble lord. 4.14. 1
she spake | was "antony, most noble antony!" 4.14. 30
less noble mind | than she which by her death 4.14. 60
turn from me then that noble countenance, 4.14. 85
my noble girls! 4.15. 84
and then, what's brave, what's noble, | let's 4.15. 86
behold it stain'd | with his most noble blood. 5.01. 26
most noble empress, you have heard of me? 5.02. 71
me, that i should not | be noble to myself. 5.02.192
now, noble charmian, we'll dispatch indeed, 5.02.230
what poor an instrument | may do a noble deed! 5.02.237
see him rouse himself | to praise my noble act. 5.02.285
o noble weakness! 5.02.344
whom i commend to you as a noble friend of mine. CYM 1.04. 32 P
madam, a noble gentleman of rome, | comes from 1.06. 10
more noble than that runagate to your bed, | and 1.06.137
and other noble friends | are partners in the 1.06.183
i had rather not be so noble as i am. 2.01. 18 P
every man patient after the noble temper of your 2.03. 4 P
nor no more ado | with that harsh, noble, simple 3.04.132
a season) 'fore noble lucius | present yourself, 3.04.172
my noble mistress, | here is a box, i had it 3.04.187
so farewell, noble lucius. 3.05. 12
more respect than my noble and natural person, 3.05.136 P
ay, my noble lord. 3.05.147 P
o noble strain! 4.02. 24
willing spirits | that promise noble service; 4.02.339
was he | that (otherwise than noble nature did) 4.02.364
so had you saved | the noble imogen to repent, 5.01. 10
o noble misery, | to be i' th' field, and ask 5.03. 64
never saw | such noble fury in so poor a thing; 5.05. 8
most like a noble lord in love and one | that 5.05.171
proof enough | to make the noble leonatus mad, 5.05.201
wrong not yourself then, noble helicane; PER 2.04. 26
a roof | soon fall to ruin — your noble self, 2.04. 37
live, noble helicane! 2.04. 40
go search like nobles, like noble subjects, 2.04. 50
my actions are as noble as my thoughts, | that 2.05. 59
when noble pericles shall demand his child? 4.03. 13
shame | to think of what a noble strain you are, 4.03. 24
i doubt not but thy training hath been noble. 4.06.112
that pupils lacks she none of noble race, | who 5.ch. 9
assur'd | came of a gentle kind and noble stock, 5.01. 68
thou art a grave and noble counsellor, | most 5.01.182
for it seems | you have been noble towards her. 5.01.263
noble sir, | if you have told diana's altar true 5.03. 16
i am sure | it has a noble breeder and a pure, TNK pr 10
nay, most likely, for they are noble suff'rers. 2.01. 31 P
how do you, noble cousin? 2.02. 1
where is our noble country? 2.02. 7
uses | (the food and nourishment of noble minds) 2.02. 52
two souls | put in two noble bodies, let 'em 2.02. 65
without your noble hand to close mine eyes, | or 2.02. 93
so strangely, so unlike a noble kinsman, | to 2.02.190
if that | get him a wife so noble and so fair, 2.02.230
her, | if he be noble arcite — thousand ways! 2.02.255
feed | upon the sweetness of a noble beauty, 2.03. 11
first | he bows his noble body, then salutes me 2.04. 23
a little of all noble qualities: 2.05. 10
i have not seen so young a man so noble | (if he 2.05. 18
noble theseus, | to purchase name, and do my 2.05. 25
i shall give you | to a most noble service — to 2.05. 34
sir, y' are a noble giver. 2.05. 38
dirge, | and tell to memory my death was noble, 2.06. 16
but this — | that thou art brave and noble. 3.01. 81
dares any | so noble bear a guilty business? 3.01. 90
to speak, before thy noble grace, this tenner; 3.05.123
good morrow, noble kinsman. 3.06. 17
think either, | well done, a noble recompense. 3.06. 24
give me thy noble hand. 3.06.101
scorn us, | and say we had a noble difference, 3.06.116
as thou art just, thy noble ear against us; 3.06.174
to crown all this, by your most noble soul, 3.06.208
o my noble brother, | that oath was rashly made, 3.06.226
eyes, and as noble | as ever fame yet spoke of. 3.06.276
them, | that truly noble prince pirithous, 4.01. 13
she sows into the births of noble bodies, | were 4.02. 9
to him, a mere gipsy, | and this the noble body. 4.02. 45
from the noble duke your brother, | madam, i 4.02. 55
stern, and yet noble, | which shows him hardy, 4.02. 79
wins | loses a noble cousin for thy sins. 4.02.156
they have a noble work in hand will honor | the 5.01. 6
brave a knight as e'er | did spur a noble steed. 5.03.116
noble palamon, | the gods will show their glory 5.04. 42
the noble earl of shrewsbury, let's hear him. STM II.C 30 P
submit you to these noble gentlemen, | entreat II.C 144
with noble disposition | each present lord began LUC 1695
proud of subjection, noble by the sway, | what LC 108
which late her noble suit in court did shun, 234

NOBLE–ENDING 1 FR 0.0001 REL FR 1 V 0 P
he seal'd | a testament of noble–ending love. H5 4.06. 27

NOBLEMAN 15 FR 0.0017 REL FR 7 V 8 P
this woman, | to justify this worthy nobleman, MM 5.01.159
fortune's close–stool to give to a nobleman! AWW 5.02. 17 P
and said his name was antigonus, a nobleman. WT 3.03. 97 P
out, dunghill! dar'st thou brave a nobleman? JN 4.03. 87
there is a nobleman of the court at door would 1H4 2.04.287 P
the least of which haunting a nobleman | loseth 3.01.184
many a nobleman lies stark and stiff | under the 5.03. 41
sack, and live cleanly as a nobleman should do. 5.04.165 P
sir, here comes the nobleman that committed the 2H4 1.02. 55 P
that faultless may condemn a nobleman! 2H6 3.02. 24
what nobleman is that | that with the king here 3H6 4.03. 9
i blush, | it is to see a nobleman want manners. H8 3.02.308
o, there is a nobleman in town, one paris, that ROM 2.04.201 P
the nobleman would have dealt with her like a PER 4.06.138 P
would have dealt with her like a nobleman, and 4.06.139 P

NOBLEMEN 2 FR 0.0002 REL FR 2 V 0 P
hear sweet discourse, converse with noblemen, TGV 1.03. 31
then you belike suspect these noblemen | as 2H6 3.02.186

NOBLE–MINDED 2 FR 0.0002 REL FR 2 V 0 P
hath now entrapp'd the noble–minded talbot: 1H6 4.04. 37
good | that noble–minded titus means to thee! TIT 1.01.209

NOBLENESS 19 FR 0.0021 REL FR 18 V 1 P
worthy his youth and nobleness of birth. TGV 1.03. 33
to see his nobleness, | conceiving the dishonor WT 2.03. 12
my ability may undergo | and nobleness impose; 2.03.165
the affection of nobleness which nature shows 5.02. 36 P
both in your form and nobleness of mind; R3 3.07. 14
he regard | the stamp of nobleness in any person H8 3.02. 12
time–pleasers, flatterers, foes to nobleness. COR 3.01. 45
inform | thy thoughts with nobleness, that thou 5.03. 72
you, | whose star–like nobleness gave life and TIM 5.01. 63
but signs of nobleness, like stars, shall shine MAC 1.04. 41
thy very gait did prophesy | a royal nobleness. LR 5.03.177
the nobleness of life | is to do thus — when ANT 1.01. 36
instruction got upon me | a nobleness in record; 4.14. 99
let the world see | his nobleness well acted, 5.02. 45
more charming | with their own nobleness, which CYM 5.03. 33
endowments greater | than nobleness and riches. PER 3.02. 28
if we let fall the nobleness of this, | and the TNK pr 15
you whose free nobleness do make my cause | your 5.01. 73
their nobleness peculiar to them, gives | the 5.03. 87

NOBLER 20 FR 0.0022 REL FR 19 V 1 P
yet, with my nobler reason, 'gainst my fury | do TMP 5.01. 26
but kindness, nobler ever than revenge, | and AYL 4.03.128
late | was in my nobler thoughts most base, is AWW 2.03.171
a bark of baser kind | by bud of nobler race. WT 4.04. 95
than arm thy constant and thy nobler parts JN 3.01.291
a noble person | and spoil your nobler soul; H8 1.02.175
making their way | with those of nobler bulk! TRO 1.03. 37
were she earthly, no nobler — whither do you COR 2.01. 98 P
my nobler friends, i crave their pardons. 3.01. 65
you do the nobler. 3.02. 6
a nobler man, a braver warrior, | lives not this TIT 1.01. 25
there's not a nobler man in rome than antony. JC 3.02.116
whether 'tis nobler in the mind to suffer | the HAM 3.01. 56
o antony, | nobler than my revolt is infamous, ANT 4.09. 19
and say | some nobler token i have kept apart 5.02.168
life | is nobler than attending for a check; CYM 3.03. 22
to taint his nobler heart and brain | with 5.04. 65
world, a garment | nobler than that it covers! 5.04.135
a nobler sir ne'er liv'd | 'twixt sky and ground 5.05.145
my nobler part to my gross body's treason; SON 151. 6

NOBLE'S 1 FR 0.0001 REL FR 1 V 0 P
a beggar's book | outworths a noble's blood. H8 1.01.123

/NOBLES 1 FR 0.0001 REL FR 0 V 1 P
/and /maledictions /against /king /and /nobles, LR 1.02.147 P

NOBLES 36 FR 0.0040 REL FR 32 V 4 P
my nobles leave me, and my state is braved, JN 4.02.243
your nobles will not hear you, but are gone | to 5.01. 33
so, nobles, shall you all, | that knit your 5.02. 62
that mowbray hath receiv'd eight thousand nobles R2 1.01. 88
the nobles hath he fin'd | for ancient quarrels, 2.01.247
the nobles they are fled, the commons they are 2.02. 88
thee, sir john, let it be but twenty nobles. 2H4 2.01.154 P
till that the nobles and the armed commons 2.03. 51
how many nobles then should hold their places, 5.02. 17
had nobles richer and more loyal subjects, H5 1.02.127
and she a mourning widow of her nobles, | she 1.02.158
my lord, your nobles, jealous of your absence, 4.01.285
to sort our nobles from our common men. 4.07. 74
and nobles bearing banners, there lie dead | one 4.08. 82
the names of those their nobles that lie dead: 4.08. 91
god, these nobles should such stomachs bear! 1H6 1.03. 90
for there young henry with his nobles lie. 3.02.129
thou, nor thy nobles, to the crown of england. 5.04.172
and all the peers and nobles of the realm | have 2H6 1.03.126
well, nobles, well; 3.01.341
the nobles were committed | is all unknown to me R3 2.04. 47
the dull and factious nobles of the greeks TRO 2.02.209
gentry to him | and the desire of the nobles. COR 2.01.239
the nobles bended, | as to jove's statue, and 2.01.265
your wife, your son, these senators, the nobles; 3.02. 65
against the senators, patricians, and nobles. 4.03. 15 P
for the nobles receive so to heart the 4.03. 21 P
is, and feasts the nobles of the state | at his 4.04. 9
permitted by our dastard nobles, who | have all 4.05. 75
the nobles in great earnestness are going | all 4.06. 58
and cowardly nobles gave way unto your clusters, 4.06.122
there are certain nobles of the senate | newly TIM 1.02.174
i should cut off the nobles for their lands, MAC 4.03. 79
when nobles are their tailors' tutors; LR 3.02. 83
go search like nobles, like noble subjects, PER 2.04. 50
a bushel, and beef at four nobles a stone, list STM II.C 3 P

NOBLESSE 1 FR 0.0001 REL FR 1 V 0 P
then true noblesse would | learn him forbearance R2 4.01.119

/NOBLEST 1 FR 0.0001 REL FR 1 V 0 P
on, on, you /noblest english, | whose blood is H5 3.01. 17

NOBLEST 17 FR 0.0019 REL FR 15 V 2 P
did quarrel with the noblest grace she ow'd, TMP 3.01. 45
the noblest deer hath them as huge as the rascal AYL 3.03. 57 P
why, so i do, the noblest that i have. TN 1.01. 17
the noblest hateful love, that e'er i heard of. TRO 4.01. 34
i give him you, the noblest that survives, | the TIT 1.01.102
the noblest mind he carries | that ever govern'd TIM 1.01.280
who can bring noblest minds to basest ends! 4.03.464
thou art the ruins of the noblest man | that JC 3.01.256
o, if thou wert the noblest of thy strain, 5.01. 59
this was the noblest roman of them all: 5.05. 68
hear it, | and call the noblest to the audience. HAM 5.02.387
'tis your noblest course. ANT 3.13. 78
the greatest prince o' th' world, | the noblest; 4.15. 55
noblest of men, woo't die? 4.15. 59
"he is one of the noblest note, to whose CYM 1.06. 22 P
thou do demand a prisoner, | the noblest ta'en. 5.05.100
you'll lose the noblest sight | that ev'r was TNK 5.02. 99

NOBLEST–MINDED 1 FR 0.0001 REL FR 1 V 0 P
some certain of the noblest–minded romans | to JC 1.03.122

/NOBLY 2 FR 0.0002 REL FR 2 V 0 P
/yes, /and /will /nobly /him /remunerate. TIT 1.01.398
/sir, /you /speak /nobly. LR 5.01. 28

NOBLY 37 FR 0.0041 REL FR 30 V 7 P
sin | to think but nobly of my grandmother. TMP 1.02.119
some kinds of baseness | are nobly undergone; 3.01. 3
but by the ear, that hears most nobly of him. AWW 3.05. 50
such pestiferous reports of men very nobly held, 4.03.306 P
a scar nobly got, or a noble scar, is a good 4.05. 99 P
i think nobly of the soul, and no way approve TN 4.02. 55 P
(a savage jealousy | that sometime savors nobly) 5.01.120
very nobly | have you deserv'd. WT 4.04.517
come bring your luggage nobly on your back. 1H4 5.04.156
for then both parties nobly are subdued, | and 2H4 4.02. 90
you, madam, for you are more nobly born, 2H6 2.03. 9
then nobly, york, 'tis for a crown thou fight'st 5.02. 16
and pray receive 'em nobly and conduct 'em H8 1.04. 58
'tis nobly spoken. 3.02.199
peace, and all such emblems | laid nobly on her; 4.01. 90
shall not so /stale his palm, nobly acquir'd, TRO 2.03.191
rather had eleven die nobly for their country COR 1.03. 24 P
bear | th' addition nobly ever! 1.09. 66
never shame to hear | what you have nobly done. 2.02. 68
you have deserv'd nobly of your country, and you 2.03. 88 P
your country, and you have not deserv'd nobly. 2.03. 89 P
he has done nobly, and cannot go without any 2.03.132 P
and nobly named so, twice being censor, | was 2.03.244
do contest | as hotly and as nobly with thy love 4.05.111
state, | will use you nobly and your followers. TIT 1.01.260
of fair demesnes, youthful and nobly /lien'd, ROM 3.05.180
'tis most nobly spoken. TIM 5.04. 63
blood | that every roman bears, and nobly bears, JC 2.01.137
was not that nobly done? MAC 3.06. 14
our force by land | hath nobly held; ANT 3.13.170
bruised pieces, go, | you have been nobly borne. 4.14. 43
nobly he yokes | a smiling with a sigh, as if CYM 4.02. 51
the forlorn soldier, that /so nobly fought, | he 5.05.405
nobly doom'd! 5.05.420
regent, sir, of meteline | speaks nobly of her. PER 5.01.187
melancholy | becomes him nobly. TNK 5.03. 50
thou nobly base, they basely dignified; LUC 660

NO–BODIES 1 FR 0.0001 REL FR 0 V 1 P
be–gar nor i too; there is no–bodies. WIV 3.03.213 P

NOBODY 23 FR 0.0026 REL FR 7 V 16 P
of our catch, play'd by the picture of nobody. TMP 3.02.127 P
but nobody but has his fault — but let that WIV 1.04. 14 P
i warrant thee, nobody hears — mine own people, 2.02. 50 P
truly, i am so glad you have nobody here. 4.02. 18 P
be talking, signior benedick, nobody marks you. ADO 1.01.117 P
do not wrest true speaking, i'll offend nobody. 3.04. 34 P
"just," said she, "it hurts nobody." 5.01.164 P
i would out–night you, did nobody come; MV 5.01. 23
here's nobody will steal that from thee. WT 4.04.631 P
methinks nobody should be sad but i. JN 4.01. 13
confutes me but eyes, and nobody sees me. 1H4 5.04.127 P
see thee again or no, there is nobody cares. 2H4 2.04. 68 P
she has nobody to do any thing about her when i 3.02.230 P
trust nobody, for fear you /be betray'd. 2H6 4.04. 58
ill blows the wind that profits nobody. 3H6 2.05. 55
come, patroclus, i'll speak with nobody. TRO 2.03. 69 P
why, he'll answer nobody; 3.03.268 P
for if it touch not you, it comes near nobody. OTH 4.01.199 P
let nobody blame him, his scorn i approve" — 4.03. 52

nobody come? then shall i bleed to death. 5.01. 45
nobody; 5.02.124
up and down like a cock that nobody can match. CYM 2.01. 21 P
out of the calendar, and nobody look after it. PER 2.01. 54 P
NOCES 1 FR 0.0001 REL FR 0 V 1 P
demoiselles pour etre baisees devant leur noces, H5 5.02.259 P
/NOD 1 FR 0.0001 REL FR 1 V 0 P
/nor /wink, /nor /nod, /nor /kneel, /nor /make TIT 3.02. 43
NOD 17 FR 0.0019 REL FR 11 V 6 P
i say, she did nod; TGV 1.01.113 P
and you ask me if she did nod, and i say, "ay." 1.01.114 P
nod to him, elves, and do him courtesies. MND 3.01.174
my lord, you nod, you do not mind the play. SHR 1.01.249
and if she chance to nod i'll rail and brawl, 4.01.206
which bow the head, and nod at every man. AWW 4.05.106 P
giddy multitude do point | and nod their heads, 2H6 2.04. 22
ready with every nod to tumble down | into the R3 3.04.100
if he see me, you shall see him nod at me. TRO 1.02.194 P
will he give you the nod? 1.02.196 P
the insinuating nod and be off to them most COR 2.03. 99 P
to a molehill should | in supplication nod; 5.03. 31
and returns in peace | most rich in timon's nod. TIM 1.01. 62
his body | if caesar carelessly but nod on him. JC 1.02.118
if thou dost nod, thou break'st thy instrument, 4.03.271
if thou canst nod, speak too. MAC 3.04. 69
with trees upon't that nod unto the world | and ANT 4.14. 6
NOD-AY 1 FR 0.0001 REL FR 0 V 1 P
nod-ay — why, that's "noddy." TGV 1.01.112 P
NODDED 2 FR 0.0002 REL FR 2 V 0 P
so he nodded, | and soberly did mount an ANT 1.05. 47
sister, cleopatra | hath nodded him to her. 3.06. 66
NODDING 2 FR 0.0002 REL FR 2 V 0 P
where oxlips and the nodding violet grows, MND 2.01.250
your enemies, with nodding of their plumes, COR 3.03.126
NODDLE 1 FR 0.0001 REL FR 1 V 0 P
to comb your noddle with a three-legg'd stool, SHR 1.01. 64
NODDLES 1 FR 0.0001 REL FR 0 V 1 P
well, i will smite his noddles. pray you follow. WIV 3.01.125 P
NODDY 3 FR 0.0003 REL FR 0 V 3 P
nod-ay — why, that's "noddy." TGV 1.01.112 P
and that set together is "noddy." 1.01.115 P
nothing but the word "noddy" for my pains. 1.01.124 P
NODS 6 FR 0.0006 REL FR 5 V 1 P
fearful action | with wrinkled brows, with nods, JN 4.02.192
nay, he nods at us, as who should say, i'll be 2H6 4.07. 94 P
cog, | duck with french nods and apish courtesy, R3 1.03. 49
with certain half-caps and cold-moving nods, TIM 2.02.212
as her winks and nods and gestures yield them, HAM 4.05. 11
he hears, and nods, and hums, | and then cries, TNK 3.05. 15
NOES 1 FR 0.0001 REL FR 1 V 0 P
in russet yeas and honest kersey noes. LLL 5.02.413
'NOINTED *(also anointed)*
'NOINTED 2 FR 0.0002 REL FR 1 V 1 P
that i have 'nointed an athenian's eyes; MND 3.02.351
then 'nointed over with honey, set on the head WT 4.04.784 P
NOIS'D 2 FR 0.0002 REL FR 1 V 1 P
let it be nois'd | that through our intercession H8 1.02.105
it is nois'd he hath a mass of treasure. TIM 4.03.402 P
/NOISE 1 FR 0.0001 REL FR 1 V 0 P
/alack, /what /noise /is /this? HAM 4.05. 96
NOISE 93 FR 0.0105 REL FR 78 V 15 P
there was a noise, | that's verily. TMP 2.01.320
no noise, and enter. 4.01.216
alas, what noise? WIV 5.05. 30 P
but hark, what noise? MM 4.02. 69
what noise? 4.02. 88
who makes that noise there? 4.03. 25 P
is that at the door that keeps all this noise? ERR 3.01. 61
you shall also make no noise in the streets; ADO 3.03. 35 P
all-telling fame | doth noise abroad, navarre LLL 2.01. 22
he goes but to see a noise that he heard, and is MND 3.01. 91 P
the noise they make | will cause demetrius to 3.02.116
to wag their high tops and to make no noise MV 4.01. 76
kiss the trees | and they did make no noise, in 5.01. 3
how it be in tune, so it make noise enough. AYL 4.02. 9 P
why, these balls bound, there's noise in it. AWW 2.03.297
/what noise there, ho? WT 2.03. 39
no noise, my lord, but needful conference 2.03. 40
from forth the noise and rumor of the field, JN 5.04. 45
march without the noise of threat'ning drum, R2 3.03. 51
is | to noise abroad that harry monmouth fell 2H4 in 29
and see if thou canst find out sneak's noise. 2.04. 11 P
let there be no noise made, my gentle friends, 4.05. 1
less noise, less noise! 4.05. 7
less noise, less noise! 4.05. 7
not so much noise, my lords. 4.05. 16
what noise is this? what traitors have we here? 1H6 1.03. 15
whence cometh this alarum, and the noise? 1.04. 99
if any noise or soldier you perceive | near to 2.01. 2
what means this noise? 2H6 2.01. 57
what noise is this? 3.02.236
what noise is this i hear? 4.08. 3 P
the noise of thy cross-bow | will scare the herd 3H6 3.01. 6
what dreadful noise of /waters in /my ears! R3 1.04. 22
such hideous cries that with the very noise | i, 1.04. 60
i cannot think it. hark, what noise is this? 2.02. 33
a noise of targets, or to see a fellow | in a H8 pr 15
such a noise arose | as the shrouds make at sea 4.01. 71
you'll leave your noise anon, ye rascals; 5.03. 1 P
the noise goes, this: TRO 1.02. 12
what noise? what shrike is this? 2.02. 97
their noise be our instruction. ladders ho! COR 1.04. 22
and hark, what noise the general makes! 1.05. 9
before him he carries noise, and behind him he 2.01.159 P
and ran | from th' noise of our own drums." 2.03. 54
being but | the horn and noise o' th' monster's, 3.01. 95
/unshout the noise that banish'd martius! 5.05. 4
but he returns | splitting the air with noise. 5.06. 51
no noise, but silence and eternal sleep. TIT 1.01.155
that all the court may echo with the noise. 2.02. 6
let us sit down and mark their yellowing noise; 2.03. 20
i made unto the noise, when soon i heard | the 5.01. 25
what noise is this? give me my long sword ho! ROM 1.01. 75
i hear some noise within; 2.02.136
what noise is here? 4.05. 17
i hear some noise, lady. 5.03.151
yea, noise? 5.03.169
but then a noise did scare me from the tomb, 5.03.262

bid every noise be still; peace yet again! JC 1.02. 14
what was the second noise for? 1.02.224
the noise of battle hurtled in the air; 2.02. 22
hark, boy, what noise is that? 2.04. 16
didst thou not hear a noise? MAC 2.02. 14
how is't with me, when every noise appalls me? 2.02. 55
and what noise is this? 4.01.106
what is that noise? 5.05. 7
that way the noise is. 5.07. 14
nothing but inexplicable dumb shows and noise. HAM 3.02. 12 P
wag thy tongue | in noise so rude against me? 3.04. 40
but soft, what noise? 4.02. 3 P
how now, what noise is that? 4.05.154
but stay, what noise? 4.07.162
what warlike noise is this? 5.02.349
or whether gasted by the noise i made, | full LR 2.01. 55
make no noise, make no noise, draw the curtains. 3.06. 83 P
make no noise, make no noise, draw the curtains. 3.06. 83 P
what noise? OTH 2.01. 52
but hark, what noise? 2.03.144
for love's sake, to make no more noise with it. 3.01. 13 P
whose noise is this that cries on murther? 5.01. 48
what noise is this? 5.02. 86
the noise was high. 5.02. 93
catching but the least noise of this, dies ANT 1.02.141 P
peace, what noise? 4.03. 12
follow the noise so far as we have quarter; 4.03. 21
what's the noise? 4.14.104
wherefore's this noise? 5.02.233
that will be given to th' loud of noise we make. CYM 3.05. 44
the noise is round about us. 4.04. 1
that's all one, if ye make a noise. TNK 5.02. 16
them removed and grant that this your noise STM II.C 72
when he hath ceas'd his ill-resounding noise, VEN 919
no noise but owls' and wolves' death-boding LUC 165
sounds make lesser noise than shallow fords, 1329
/NOISELESS 1 FR 0.0001 REL FR 1 V 0 P
/his /banners /in /our /noiseless /land, | /with LR 4.02. 56
NOISELESS 1 FR 0.0001 REL FR 1 V 0 P
th' inaudible and noiseless foot of time AWW 5.03. 41
NOISEMAKER 1 FR 0.0001 REL FR 0 V 1 P
hang, you whoreson, insolent noisemaker! TMP 1.01. 44 P
/NOISES 1 FR 0.0001 REL FR 1 V 0 P
/mark /the /high /noises, /and /thyself /bewray LR 3.06.111
NOISES 3 FR 0.0003 REL FR 3 V 0 P
the isle is full of noises, | sounds, and sweet TMP 3.02.135
with strange and several noises | of roaring, 5.01.232
regiment to a trull | that noises it against us. ANT 3.06. 96
NOISOME 5 FR 0.0005 REL FR 4 V 1 P
is but foul breath, and foul breath is noisome; ADO 5.02. 53 P
the noisome weeds which without profit suck R2 3.04. 38
so bees with smoke and doves with noisome stench 1H6 1.05. 23
to pick them in a pile | of noisome musty chaff. COR 5.01. 26
effects will be | both noisome and infectious. CYM 1.05. 26
NOLE 1 FR 0.0001 REL FR 1 V 0 P
take, | an ass's nole i fixed on his head. MND 3.02. 17
NOMINATE 3 FR 0.0003 REL FR 1 V 2 P
to thy young days, which we may nominate tender. LLL 1.02. 15 P
can you nominate in order now the degrees of the AYL 5.04. 88 P
but suddenly | to nominate them all, it is 2H6 2.01.128
NOMINATED 3 FR 0.0003 REL FR 2 V 1 P
king's, who is intituled, nominated, or called, LLL 5.01. 8 P
the forfeit | be nominated for an equal pound MV 1.03.149
is it so nominated in the bond? 4.01.259
NOMINATION 3 FR 0.0003 REL FR 1 V 2 P
for the nomination of the party /writing to the LLL 4.02.134 P
it is, and wants but nomination. R3 3.04. 5
what imports the nomination of this gentleman? HAM 5.02.127 P
NOMINATIVO 2 FR 0.0002 REL FR 0 V 2 P
be thus declin'd, singulariter, nominativo, hic, WIV 4.01. 41 P
nominativo, hig, hag, hog; 4.01. 42 P
/NON* 1 FR 0.0001 REL FR 1 V 0 P
/hey /non /nonny, /nonny, /hey /nonny, | and in HAM 4.05.166
NON* 8 FR 0.0009 REL FR 4 V 4 P
cucullus non facit monachum: MM 5.01.262 P
che non te /vede, che non te /prechia. LLL 4.02. 98
che non te /vede, che non te /prechia. 4.02. 98
lady, "cucullus non facit monachum": TN 1.05. 56 P
non, je reciterai a vous promptement: H5 3.04. 44 P
et non pour les dames de honneur d'user. 3.04. 54 P
let there be sung non nobis and te deum, | the 4.08.123
purus, | non eget mauri jaculis, nec arcu." TIT 4.02. 21
NONAGE 1 FR 0.0001 REL FR 1 V 0 P
which, in his nonage, council under him, | and, R3 2.03. 13
NONCE 3 FR 0.0003 REL FR 2 V 1 P
i have cases of buckrom for the nonce, to immask 1H4 1.02.180 P
this is a riddling merchant for the nonce: 1H6 2.03. 57
have preferr'd him | a chalice for the nonce, HAM 4.07.160
NON-COME 1 FR 0.0001 REL FR 0 V 1 P
that shall drive some of them to a non-come; ADO 3.05. 62 P
/NONE 7 FR 0.0008 REL FR 5 V 2 P
lov'd /none in the world so well as lucentio. SHR 4.02. 13
/i, /in /twelve /thousand, /none. R2 4.01.171
/and /none /of /this | (/though /strongly 2H4 1.01.175
/second /to /none, /unseconded /by /you, | /to 2.03. 34
/we /remember /still /that /we /have /none. TIT 3.02. 30
/why /then /'tis /none /to /you; HAM 2.02.249 P
/why, /he /had /none. 5.01. 34 P
NONE 509 FR 0.0575 REL FR 366 V 143 P
none that i more love than myself. TMP 1.01. 20 P
of that there's none, or little. 2.01. 52 P
riches, poverty, | and use of service, none; 2.01.152
bourn, bound of land, tilth, vineyard, none; 2.01.153
none, man, all idle — whores and knaves. 2.01.167 P
and margery, | but none of us car'd for kate; 2.02. 49
i will have none on't. 4.01.247
i few attendants, | and subjects none abroad. 5.01.167
without you were so simple, none else would: TGV 2.01. 37 P
sir, at my request, | but i will none of them; 2.01.127
she gave me none, except an angry word. 2.01.158 P
him, | lest it should ravel and be good to none, 3.02. 52
thou'dst two, | and that's far worse than none: 5.04. 51
better have none | than plural faith, which is 5.04. 51
none, i protest; WIV 2.01.214 P
meed, i am sure, i have receiv'd none, unless 2.02.204 P

want no money, sir john, you shall want none. 2.02.259 P
ford, master /brook, you shall want none. 2.02.261 P
but i love thee, none but thee; 3.03. 73 P
why, none but mine own people. 4.02. 14 P
of none but him, and swears he was carried out, 4.02. 31 P
door with pistols, that none shall issue out; 4.02. 52 P
will, | and none but he, to marry with nan page. 4.04. 85
he, none but he, shall have her, | though twenty 4.04. 89
will none but herne the hunter serve your turn? 5.05.104
have gone round | and none of them been worn; MM 1.02.169
none better knows than you | how i have ever 1.03. 7
some run from brakes of ice and answer none, 2.01. 39
if you be more, you're none; 2.04.135
lose a thing | that none but fools would keep. 3.01. 8
friend hast thou none, | for thine own bowels, 3.01. 28
none, but such remedy as, to save a head, | to 3.01. 61
is there none of pygmalion's images newly made 3.02. 45 P
i know none. can you tell me of any? 3.02. 87 P
none, but that there is so great a fever on 3.02.222 P
none but only a repair i' th' dark, | and that i 4.01. 42
none since the curfew rung. 4.02. 75
none, sir, none. 4.02. 93
none, sir, none. 4.02. 93
he will hear none. 4.02.147 P
if not true, none were enough. 4.03.168 P
and this it was (for other means was none): ERR 1.01. 75
there's none but asses will be bridled so. 2.01. 14
if it be, sir, i pray you eat none of it. 2.02. 60 P
ay, and let none enter, lest i break your pate. 2.02.218
if every one knows us, and we know none, | 'tis 3.02.152
there's none but witches do inhabit here, | and 3.02.156
i owe you none, till i receive the chain. 4.01. 64
you gave me none, you wrong me much to say so. 4.01. 66
he meant he did me none: the more my spite. 4.02. 8
second to none that lives here in the city: 5.01. 7
to none of these, except it be the last, 5.01. 55
he with none return'd. 5.01.232
no, none by me. 5.01.384
but few of any sort, and none of name. ADO 1.01. 7 P
i know none of that name, lady. 1.01. 32 P
there was none such in the army of any sort. 1.01. 33 P
i had not a hard heart, for truly i love none. 1.01.127 P
any, i will do myself the right to trust none; 1.01.244 P
horns" — but to a cow too curst he sends none. 2.01. 24 P
no, uncle, i'll none. 2.01. 63 P
none but libertines delight in him, and the 2.01.139 P
none, but to desire your good company. 2.01.272 P
wise, or i'll none; 2.03. 31 P
if silent, why, a block moved with none. 3.01. 67
is bidden, he is none of the prince's subjects. 3.03. 32 P
they are to meddle with none but the prince's 3.03. 33 P
i'll wear none but this. 3.04. 12 P
none, i think, and it be the right husband and 3.04. 35 P
none, my lord. 4.01. 16 P
i dare make his answer, none. 4.01. 18 P
but she is none: 4.01. 40
they know that do accuse me, i know none. 4.01.177
much of my heart that none is left to protest. 4.01.287 P
marry, sir, we say we are none. 4.02. 24 P
sir, i say to you, we are none. 4.02. 29 P
have you writ down, that they are none? 4.02. 32 P
i was taken with none, sir, i was taken with a LLL 1.01.289 P
it should none spare that come within his power. 2.01. 51
amen, so you be none. 2.01.126
it importeth none here. 4.01. 57
for none offend where all alike do dote. 4.03.124
tush, none but minstrels like of sonneting! 4.03.156
else none at all in aught proves excellent. 4.03.351
i say none so fit as to present the nine 5.01.123 P
nor understood none neither, sir. 5.01.151 P
none are so surely caught, when they are catch'd 5.02. 69
to make theirs ours and ours none but our own; 5.02.154
he wore none but a dishclout of jaquenetta's, 5.02.714 P
none, but your beauty; MND 1.01.201
forest have i gone, | but athenian found i none, 2.02. 67
nor none, in my mind, now you give her o'er. 3.02.135
none of noble sort | would so offend a virgin 3.02.159
i will none. 3.02.169
i pray you, let none of your people stir me; 4.01. 38 P
we'll none of that: 5.01. 46
are all dead, there need none to be blam'd. 5.01.357 P
that i cannot choose one, nor refuse none? MV 1.02. 26 P
let none presume | to wear an undeserved dignity 2.09. 39
you knew, none so well, none so well as you, of 3.01. 24 P
knew, none so well, none so well as you, of my 3.01. 24 P
none but that ugly treason of mistrust, | which 3.02. 28
hard food for midas, i will none of thee; 3.02.102
nor none of thee, thou pale and common drudge 3.02.103
for i am sure you can wish none from me; 3.02.191
but none can drive him from the envious plea 3.02.282
grow commendable in none only but parrots. 3.05. 46 P
how shalt thou hope for mercy, rend'ring none? 4.01. 88
no, none that thou hast wit enough to make. 4.01.127
of justice, none of us | should see salvation. 4.01.199
none but a holy hermit and her maid. 5.01. 33
hath no child but i, nor none is like to have; AYL 1.02. 18 P
friends no wrong, for i have none to lament me; 1.02.190 P
where none will sweat but for promotion, | and 2.03. 60
why, i have eat none yet. 2.07. 88
bottle, either too much at once, or none at all. 3.02.201 P
there were none principal, they were all like 3.02.353 P
there is none of my uncle's marks upon you. 3.02.369 P
dowry of his wife, 'tis none of his own getting. 3.03. 55 P
is there none here to give the woman? 3.03. 67 P
see, | none could be so abus'd in sight as he. 3.05. 79
house doth keep itself, | there's none within. 4.03. 82
by your simp'ring, none of you hates them), that ep 16 P
in the world, | and yet she is inferior to none. SHR in.2. 67
gifts are so good, here's none will hold you. 1.01.106 P
that none shall have access unto bianca | till 1.02.127
for he fears none. 1.02.210
there were none fine but adam, rafe, and gregory 4.01.136
she eat no meat to-day, nor none shall eat; 4.01.197
cap, | and it i will have, or i will have none. 4.03. 85
i'll none of it; 4.03.100
yourself, he shall need none so long as i live. 5.01. 24 P
none so dry or thirsty | will deign to sip or 5.02.144
love all, trust a few, | do wrong to none. AWW 1.01. 65

there is no living, none, | if bertram be away. 1.01. 84
there is none. 1.01.118 P
when thou hast none, remember thy friends. 1.01.213 P
were our faults, or then we thought them none. 1.03.135
sir, you can eat none of this homely meat. 2.02. 46 P
hast power to choose, and they none to forsake. 2.03. 56
boys are boys of ice, they'll none have /her. 2.03. 93 P
where great additions swell 's, and virtue none, 2.03.127
thou shalt have none, rossillion, none in france 3.02.101
shalt have none, rossillion, none in france; 3.02.101
none better than to let him fetch off his drum, 3.06. 19 P
none in the world, but return with an invention 3.06. 97 P
i'll none of him. 5.03.149 P
she's none of mine, my lord. 5.03.169
you must marry me, | either both or none. 5.03.175
if it were yours by none of all these ways, 5.03.275
if she be, it's four to one she'll none of me. TN 1.03.107 P
she'll none o' th' count. 1.03.109 P
he shall see none to fear. 1.05. 8 P
tell him i'll none of it. 1.05.302
into a desperate assurance she will none of him. 2.02. 8 P
she took the ring of me, i'll none of it. 2.02. 12 P
none of my lord's ring? 2.02. 24
why, he sent her none. 2.02. 24
sir, i can yield you none without words, and 3.01. 23 P
shameful cunning | which you knew none of yours. 3.01.117
has, nor never none | shall mistress be of it, 3.01.159
satisfaction can be none but by pangs of death 3.04.239 P
i know of none, | nor know i you by voice or any 3.04.352
none can be call'd deform'd but the unkind. 3.04.368
you can say none of this. 5.01.334
there is no tongue that moves, none, none i' th' WT 1.02. 20
no tongue that moves, none, none i' th' world, 1.02. 20
physic for't there's none. 1.02.200
if i then deny it, | 'tis none of mine. 1.02.267
i'll give no blemish to her honor, none. 1.02.341
none rare, my lord. 1.02.367
the better | by my regard, but kill'd none so. 1.02.390
no, i'll none of you. 2.01. 3
no, by my life, | privy to none of this. 2.01. 96
to-night, commanded | none should come at him. 2.03. 32
i am none, by this good light. 2.03. 83
this brat is none of mine, | it is the issue of 2.03. 93
even thou, and none but thou. 2.03.135
to crows thy baby-daughter | to be or none, or 3.02.192
made me businesses which none without thee can 4.02. 14 P
dates, none — that's out of my note; 4.03. 46 P
we'll none on't. 4.04.332 P
my lord, | fear none of this. 4.04.590
a changeling, and none of your flesh and blood. 4.04.689 P
she being none of your flesh and blood, your 4.04.693 P
it becomes none but tradesmen, and they often 4.04.723 P
say you have none. 4.04.743 P
none, sir; i have no pheasant cock, nor hen. 4.04.744 P
and box, which none must know but the king, and 4.04.757 P
he must know 'tis none of your daughter nor my 4.04.820 P
there is none worthy, | respecting her that's 5.01. 34
which none but heaven, and you, and i, shall JN 1.01. 43
that is my brother's plea and none of mine, 1.01. 67
that this my mother's son was none of his; 1.01.111
your father, | being none of his, refuse him. 1.01.127
that none so small advantage shall step forth 3.04.151
ah, none but in this iron age would do it! 4.01. 60
none, but to lose your eyes. 4.01. 90
wish him dead, but thou hadst none to kill him. 4.02.206
there's few or none do know me; 4.03. 3
yet i am none. 4.03. 91
lord bigot, i am none. 4.03.103
and none of you will bid the winter come | to 5.07. 36
faith, none for me, except the northeast wind, R2 1.04. 6
but since it would not, he had none of me. 1.04. 19
what will ensue hereof, there's none can tell; 2.01.212
for news to go for ireland, | but none returns. 2.02.124
seymour, | none else of name and noble estimate. 2.03. 56
that hath some hope to grow, | for i have none. 3.02.213
not, | god knows i had as lief be none as one. 5.02. 49
he shall be none, | we'll keep him here, then 5.02. 99
love loving not itself, none other can. 5.03. 88
in one person many people, | and none contented. 5.05. 32
i shall have none but mordake earl of fife. 1H4 1.01. 95
i should say, for grace thou wilt have none — 1.02. 18 P
what, none? 1.02. 19 P
no, i'll none of it, i pray thee keep that for 2.01. 63 P
none of these mad mustachio purple-hu'd 2.01. 74 P
these rebels, they offend none but the virtuous. 3.03.191 P
i press me none but good householders, /yeomen's 4.02. 15 P
i press'd me none but such toasts-and-butter, 4.02. 20 P
therefore i'll none of it, honor is a mere 5.01.140 P
none, my lord, but old mistress quickly and 2H4 2.02.152 P
there comes none here. 2.04. 95 P
a' my word, captain, there's none such here. 2.04.176 P
no abuse, ned, i' th' world, honest ned, none. 2.04.319 P
none, ned, none; 2.04.323 P
none, ned, none; 2.04.324 P
no, faith, boys, none. 2.04.324 P
i will none of you. 3.02.252 P
i pawn'd thee none. 4.02.112
there's never none of these demure boys come to 4.03. 90 P
how now, rain within doors, and none abroad? 4.05. 9
trust none; H5 2.03. 50
for there is none of you so mean and base | that 3.01. 29
none of the french upbraided or abus'd in 3.06.110 P
nor will do none to-morrow. 3.07.101 P
have only stomachs to eat and none to fight. 3.07.154 P
they shall have none, i swear, but these my 4.03.123
of it, for there is none to guard it but boys. 4.04. 76 P
i will none of your money. 4.08. 67 P
none else of name; 4.08.105
take it, god, | for it is none but thine! 4.08.112
nay, pray you throw none away, the skin is good 5.01. 54 P
none do you like but an effeminate prince, 1H6 1.01. 35
and none but women left to wail the dead. 1.01. 51
he sent to hell, and none durst stand him; 1.01.123
his ransom there is none but i shall pay: 1.01.148
remaineth none but mad-brain'd salisbury, | and 1.02. 15
for none but samsons and goliases | it sendeth 1.02. 33
there's none protector of the realm but i. 1.03. 12
that thou nor none of thine shall be let in. 1.03. 21
none durst come near for fear of sudden death. 1.04. 48
heaven, be thou gracious to none alive, | if 1.04. 85
for none would strike a stroke in his revenge. 1.05. 35
birth, | inferior to none but to his majesty; 3.01. 96
esteem none friends but such as are his friends, 4.01. 5
and none your foes but such as shall pretend 4.01. 6
the quarrel toucheth none but us alone, 4.01.118
alone, | tend'ring my ruin and assail'd of none, 4.07. 10
you are deceiv'd, my child is none of his, | it 5.04. 72
approves her fit for none but for a king. 5.05. 69
that margaret shall be queen, and none but she. 5.05. 78
excepting none but good duke humphrey; 2H6 1.01.193
man, | we are alone, here's none but thee and i. 1.02. 69
true, madam, none at all. 1.04. 49
comfort go with thee, | for none abides with me. 2.04. 88
say, "who's a traitor, gloucester he is none." 3.01.222
believe me, lords, were none more wise than i — 3.01.231
spare none but such as go in clouted shoon, 4.02.185
henry had none, but did usurp the place. 3H6 1.02. 25
had he none else to make a stale but me? 3.03.260
then none but i shall turn his jest to sorrow. 3.03.261
alack, my lord, that fault is none of yours; R3 1.01. 47
but i know none, and therefore am no beast. 1.02. 72
a man that loves not me, nor none of you. 1.03. 13
that none of you may live his natural age, | but 1.03.212
there's few or none will entertain it. 1.04.132 P
yet none of you would once beg for his life. 2.01.131
but none can help our harms by wailing them. 2.02.103
or by his father there were none at all; 2.03. 24
but they were none. 3.01. 16
nor none that live, i hope. 3.01.147
none are for me | that look into me with 4.02. 29
for she commanding all, obey'd of none. 4.04.104
faith, none, but humphrey hour, that call'd your 4.04.176
none good, my liege, to please you with the 4.04.457
nor none so bad but well may be reported. 4.04.458
there's none else by. 5.03.182
most rare speaker, | to nature none more bound; H8 1.02.112
if none, | let him not seek't of us. 1.02.212
i hear of none but the new proclamation | that's 1.03. 17
none here, he hopes, | in all this noble bevy, 1.04. 3
but he would bite none. 1.04. 29
i will have none so near else. 2.02.134
and the late marriage made of none effect; 4.01. 33
saw ye none enter since i slept? 4.02. 86
none, madam. 4.02. 86
know | there's none stands under more calumnious 5.01.112
and a soul | none better in my kingdom. 5.01.155
souls with modesty again, | cast none away. 5.02.100
but i find none. 5.02.171
and the words i utter | let none think flattery, 5.04. 16
let him to field, troilus, alas, hath none. TRO 1.01. 5
if none, he'll say in troy when he retires, 1.03.281
if none of them have soul in such a kind, | we 1.03.285
if none else, i am he. 1.03.290
i see none now. 2.01. 9 P
because your speech hath none that tell him so? 2.02. 36
nor none so noble | whose life were ill bestow'd 2.02.158
the elephant hath joints, but none for courtesy; 2.03.105 P
overhold his price so much, | we'll none of him; 2.03.134
he doth rely on none, | but carries on the 2.03.163
he? no! she'll none of him. they two are twain. 3.01.101 P
but i am sure none, unless the fiddler apollo 3.03.303 P
you are an odd man, give even or give none. 4.05. 41
i will none but hector. 5.05. 47
alike, and none less dear than thine and my good COR 1.03. 23 P
o, good madam, there can be none yet. 1.03. 91 P
none of you but is | able to bear against the 1.06. 78
i'll fight with none but thee, for i do hate 1.08. 1
if none, awake | your dangerous lenity. 3.01. 98
but being assur'd none but myself could move 5.02. 73 P
was none in rome to make a stale | but saturnine TIT 1.01.304
here none but soldiers and rome's servitors 1.01.352
none basely slain in brawls. 1.01.353
he that had wit would think that i had none, 2.03. 1
o, none of both but are of high desert. 3.01.170
sweet girl, for here are none but friends, 4.01. 61
may stand in number, though in reck'ning none. ROM 1.02. 33
tut, you saw her fair, none else being by, 1.02. 94
sick and green, | and none but fools do wear it; 2.02. 9
none but for some, and yet all different. 2.03. 14
scurvy knave, i am none of his flirt-gills, i am 2.04.153 P
his flirt-gills, i am none of his skains-mates. 2.04.153 P
were two such, we should have none shortly, for 3.01. 16 P
villain am i none; 3.01. 64
therefore use none. 3.01.194
and usest none in that true use indeed | which 3.03.124
would none but i might venge my cousin's death! 3.05. 86
sir, but she will none, she /gives you thanks. 3.05.139
how, will she none? 3.05.142
you shall have none ill, sir, for i'll try if 4.02. 3 P
i sell thee poison, thou hast sold me none. 5.01. 83
he'll spare none. TIM 1.01.177
one to thyself, for i mean to give thee none. 1.01.266 P
and there's none | can truly say he gives if he 1.02. 10
there is true friendship, there needs none. 1.02. 18
o, none so welcome. 1.02.217
too, there would be none left to rail upon thee, 1.02.239 P
the law, | and none but tyrants use it cruelly. 3.05. 9
his own time | and be in debt to none — yet 3.05. 77
live | only in bone, that none may look on you! 3.05.104
stay, i will lend thee money, borrow none. 3.06.101
none, but to | maintain my opinion. 4.03. 71
promise me friendship, but perform none. 4.03. 73 P
in thy rags thou know'st none, but art despis'd 4.03.303 P
hate all, curse all, show charity to none, | but 4.03.527
i know none such, my lord. 5.01. 99
of none but such as you, and you of timon. 5.01.135
seek none, conspiracy! JC 2.01. 81
i wonder none of you have thought of him. 2.01.217
i hear none, madam. 2.04. 17
none that i know will be, much that i fear may 2.04. 32
none, brutus, none. 3.02. 35
none, brutus, none. 3.02. 35
then none have i offended. 3.02. 36 P
there, | and none so poor to do him reverence. 3.02.120
thou shalt get kings, though thou be none. MAC 1.03. 67
who dares /do more is none. 1.07. 47
so i lose none | in seeking to augment it, but 2.01. 26
there is none but he | whose being i do fear; 3.01. 53
for none of woman born | shall harm macbeth. 4.01. 80
he had none; 4.02. 2
but there's no bottom, none, | in my 4.03. 60
but i have none. 4.03. 91
an older and a better soldier none | that 4.03.191
it, when none can call our pow'r to accompt? 5.01. 38 P
throw physic to the dogs, i'll none of it. 5.03. 47
and none serve with him but constrained things, 5.04. 13
such a one | am i to fear, or none. 5.07. 4
my lord, i did, | but answer made it none. HAM 1.02.215
youth to itself rebels, though none else near. 1.03. 44
marry, none so rank | as may dishonor him, take 2.01. 20
none, my lord, but the world's grown honest. 2.02.237 P
we are arrant knaves, believe none of us. 3.01.128 P
none wed the second but who kill'd the first. 3.02.180
are base respects of thrift, but none of love. 3.02.183
thoughts are ours, their ends none of our own: 3.02.213
i will speak /daggers to her, but use none. 3.02.396
none but his enemies. 4.05.145
for none, neither. 5.01.133 P
so please your lordship, none. LR 1.02. 27 P
none at all. 1.02.158 P
so far from doing harms | that he suspects none; 1.02.181
i am none of these, my lord, i beseech your 1.04. 82 P
none of these rogues and cowards | but ajax is 2.02.124
none. 2.04. 62
again, i would have none but knaves follow it, 2.04. 76 P
none but the fool, who labors to outjest | his 3.01. 16
unmerciful lady as you are, i'm none. 3.07. 33
none does offend, none, i say none, i'll able 4.06.168
none does offend, none, i say none, i'll able 4.06.168
does offend, none, i say none, i'll able 'em. 4.06.168
if none appear to prove upon thy person | thy 5.03. 91
another of his fadom they have none | to lead OTH 1.01.152
there's none so foul and foolish thereunto, 2.01.141
why, none, why, none — a slipper and subtle 2.01.241 P
none, why, none — a slipper and subtle knave, a 2.01.241 P
we have none such, sir. 3.01. 18 P
those that be not, would they might seem none! 3.03.127
touch | be not to be a strumpet, i am none. 4.02. 85
i have none. 4.02.102
nor answers have i none | but what should go by 4.02.103
i do not know; i am sure i am none such. 4.02.123
respect and acquaintance, but i find none. 4.02.190 P
wherein none can be so determinate as the 4.02.226 P
none in the world; nor do i know the man. 5.01.103
you think none but your sheets are privy to your ANT 1.02. 41 P
none our parts so poor | but was a race of 1.03. 36
graces speak | that which none else can utter. 2.02.130
to none but thee; 2.03. 25
i'll none now. 2.05. 9
i have sixty sails, caesar none better. 3.07. 49
none but friends: say boldly. 3.13. 47
from caesar's camp | say "i am none of thine." 4.05. 9
that none but antony | should conquer antony, 4.15. 16
none about caesar trust but proculeius. 4.15. 48
and my hands i'll trust, | none about caesar. 4.15. 50
none but the king? CYM 1.01. 10
there's none abroad so wholesome as that you 1.02. 3 P
your italy contains none so accomplish'd a 1.04. 94 P
we count not worth the hanging (but none human), 1.05. 20
none a stranger there | so merry and so gamesome 1.06. 59
if none will do, let her remain; 2.03. 15 P
scraps o' th' court, it is no contract, none; 2.03.115
i do believe | (statist though i am none, nor 2.04. 16
noses, but to owe such straight arms, none. 3.01. 38 P
accessible is none but milford way. 3.02. 82
the king, he rages, none | dare come about him. 3.05. 67
i'll rob none but myself, and let me die, 4.02. 15
none in the world. you did mistake him sure. 4.02.102
have knock'd out his brains, for he had none. 4.02.115
when flow'rs are none, | to winter-ground thy 4.02.228
but none of 'em can be found. 5.03. 88
there are none want eyes to direct them the way 5.04.185 P
and think they are my sons, are none of mine; 5.05.329
entice his own | to evil should be done by none. PER 1.ch. 28
for going on death's net, whom none resist. 1.01. 40
let none disturb us. 1.02. 1
king, desir'd he might know none of his secrets. 1.03. 6 P
and here, i hope, is none that envies it. 2.03. 14
none that beheld him but, like lesser lights, 2.03. 41
the which hath fire in darkness, none in light: 2.03. 44
set on | the crown of tyre, but he will none. 3.ch. 28
yet none does know but you how she came dead, 4.03. 29
dead, | nor none can know, leonine being gone. 4.03. 30
none would look on her, | but cast their gazes 4.03. 32
that pupils lacks she none of noble race, | who 5.ch. 9
provided | that none but i and my companion maid 5.01. 77
my lord, i hear none. 5.01.227
none? 5.01.228
if he be none of mine, my sanctity | will to my 5.03. 29
o, no knees, none, widow! TNK 1.01. 74
our beds, | that our dear lords have none! 1.01.141
none fit for th' dead! 1.01.141
perceive you none that do arouse your pity, 1.02. 30
or i am none | that draw i' th' sequent trace. 1.02. 59
the hand of war hurts none here, nor the seas 2.02. 87
news from earth, they shall get none but this — 3.01. 80
none | but only arcite; 3.01. 90
therefore none but arcite | in this kind is so 3.01. 91
food took i none these two days — | sipp'd some 3.02. 26
nor none so honest, arcite. 3.03. 4
for none but such dare die in these just trials. 3.06.105
none here speak for 'em, | for, ere the sun set, 3.06.183
he does no wrongs, | nor takes none. 4.02.135
nev'r reveal'd secret, for i knew none — would 5.01. 99
'tis strange if none be here — and, if he will ep 7
the sea hath bounds, but deep desire hath none, VEN 389
sorrow seemeth chief, | but none is best; 971
his all too timeless speed, if none of those. LUC 44
and in thy shady cell, where none may spy him, 881
one, | will slay the other and be nurse to none. 1162
but none where all distress and dolor dwell'd, 1446
it easeth some, though none it ever cured, | to 1581
we are their offspring, and they none of ours. 1757
such looks as none could look but beauty's queen PP 4. 4

none fairer, nor none falser to deface her. 7. 6
none fairer, nor none falser to deface her. 7. 6
other help for him i see that there is none. 17.36
none takes pity on thy pain. 20.20
but in one, | two distincts, division none: PHT 27
love hath reason, reason none, | if what parts, 47
"thou single wilt prove none." SON 8.14
but that thou none lov'st is most evident; 10. 4
o, none but unthrifts: 13.13
but you like none, none you, for constant heart. 53.14
but you like none, none you, for constant heart. 53.14
o none, unless this miracle have might, | that 65.13
in me behold | when yellow leaves, or none, or 73. 2
they that have pow'r to hurt and will do none, 94. 1
yet i none could see | but sweet or color it had 99.14
none else to me, nor i to none alive, | that my 112. 7
none else to me, nor i to none alive, | that my 112. 7
yet none knows well | to shun the heaven that 129.13
we prove | among a number one is reckon'd none: 136. 8
that's to ye sworn to none was ever said, | for LC 180
see | are errors of the blood, none of the mind; 184

NONE–SPARING 1 FR 0.0001 REL FR 1 V 0 P
of thine to the event | of the none–sparing war? AWW 3.02.105

NONINO 4 FR 0.0004 REL FR 4 V 0 P
lass, | with a hey, and a ho, and a hey nonino, AYL 5.03. 17
rye, | with a hey, and a ho, and a hey nonino, 5.03. 23
hour, | with a hey, and a ho, and a hey nonino, 5.03. 27
time, | with a hey, and a ho, and a hey nonino, 5.03. 31

/NONNY 3 FR 0.0003 REL FR 3 V 0 P
/hey /non /nonny, /nonny, /hey /nonny, | and in HAM 4.05.166
/hey /non /nonny, /nonny, /hey /nonny, | and in 4.05.166
bier, | /hey /non /nonny, /nonny, /hey /nonny, 4.05.166

NONNY 9 FR 0.0010 REL FR 8 V 1 P
all your sounds of woe | into hey nonny nonny. ADO 2.03. 69
all your sounds of woe | into hey nonny nonny. 2.03. 69
says suum, mun, nonny. LR 3.04. 99 P
hey, nonny, nonny, nonny. TNK 3.04. 21
hey, nonny, nonny, nonny. 3.04. 21
hey, nonny, nonny, nonny. 3.04. 21
hey, nonny, nonny, nonny." 3.04. 24
hey, nonny, nonny, nonny." 3.04. 24
hey, nonny, nonny, nonny." 3.04. 24

NONPAREIL 5 FR 0.0005 REL FR 5 V 0 P
he himself | calls her a nonpareil. TMP 3.02.100
you were crown'd | the nonpareil of beauty! TN 1.05.254
if thou didst it, thou art the nonpareil. MAC 3.04. 18
spake you of caesar? how, the nonpareil! ANT 3.02. 11
so doth my wife | the nonpareil of this. CYM 2.05. 8

NON–PAYMENT 1 FR 0.0001 REL FR 1 V 0 P
say for non–payment that the debt should double,
VEN 521

NON–PERFORMANCE 1 FR 0.0001 REL FR 1 V 0 P
did cry out | against the non–performance, 'twas WT 1.02.261

NON–REGARDANCE 1 FR 0.0001 REL FR 1 V 0 P
since you to non–regardance cast my faith, | and TN 5.01.121

NONSUITS 1 FR 0.0001 REL FR 1 V 0 P
/and, /in /conclusion, | nonsuits my mediators; OTH 1.01. 16

NOOK 2 FR 0.0002 REL FR 1 V 1 P
harbor | is the king's ship, in the deep nook, TMP 1.02.227
the world and to live in a nook merely monastic. AYL 3.02.420 P

NOOKS 1 FR 0.0001 REL FR 1 V 0 P
and so by many winding nooks he strays | with TGV 2.07. 31

NOOK–SHOTTEN 1 FR 0.0001 REL FR 1 V 0 P
farm | in that nook–shotten isle of albion. H5 3.05. 14

NOON 18 FR 0.0020 REL FR 15 V 3 P
at any time 'fore noon. MM 2.02.160
love's night is noon. TN 3.01.148
noon, midnight? WT 1.02.290
that, ere the next ascension–day at noon, | your JN 4.02.151
and on that day at noon, whereon he says | i 4.02.156
say that before ascension–day at noon | my crown 5.01. 26
and sleeping upon benches after noon, that thou 1H4 1.02. 4 P
the shadow | which he treads on at noon. COR 1.01.261
hand of the dial is now upon the prick of noon. ROM 2.04.113 P
great business must be wrought ere noon: MAC 3.05. 22
life and honor, | there shall he sit till noon. LR 2.02.134
till noon? 2.02.135
and i'll go to bed at noon. 3.06. 85 P
on tuesday noon, or night; OTH 3.03. 61
to reel the streets at noon, and stand the ANT 1.04. 20
at the sixt hour of morn, at noon, at midnight, CYM 1.03. 31
may set at noon and make perpetual night. LUC 784
so thou, thyself outgoing in thy noon, SON 7.13

NOON–DAY 1 FR 0.0001 REL FR 1 V 0 P
sit | even at noon–day upon the market–place, JC 1.03. 27

NOONTIDE 5 FR 0.0005 REL FR 5 V 0 P
i have bedimm'd | the noontide sun, call'd forth TMP 5.01. 42
her brother's noontide with th' antipodes. MND 3.02. 55
and made an evening at the noontide prick. 3H6 1.04. 34
makes the night morning and the noontide night: R3 1.04. 77
fair, | ere he arrive his weary noontide prick, LUC 781

NOR *(also ne*)*

/NOR 15 FR 0.0017 REL FR 14 V 1 P
tell you i do not /nor i cannot love you? MND 2.01.201
/insulting /man, | /nor /no /man's /lord. R2 4.01.255
/nor shall it, harry, for the hour is come | to 1H4 5.04. 68
/nor /do /i /as /an /enemy /to /peace | /troop 2H4 4.01. 61
/not /sigh, /nor /hold /thy /stumps /to /heaven, TIT 3.02. 42
/nor /wink, /nor /nod, /nor /kneel, /nor /make 3.02. 43
/nor /wink, /nor /nod, /nor /kneel, /nor /make 3.02. 43
/nor /nod, /nor /kneel, /nor /make /a /sign, 3.02. 43
/nor /nod, /nor /kneel, /nor /make /a /sign, 3.02. 43
/nor /no //without–book /prologue, /faintly ROM 1.04. 7
/nor /any /other /part | belonging to a man. 2.02. 41
/nor /is /not, /sure. LR 1.02. 95 P
he that keeps nor crust /nor crumb, | weary of 1.04.198
/cannot /draw /a /cart, /nor /eat /dried /oats, 5.03. 38
nor here, /nor here, | nor what ensues, but have CYM 3.02. 78

NOR 1046 FR 0.1182 REL FR 886 V 160 P
i am, nor that i am more better | than prospero, TMP 1.02. 19
nor set | a mark so bloody on the business; 1.02.141
nor tackle, sail, nor mast, the very rats 1.02.147
sail, nor mast, the very rats | instinctively 1.02.147
business, nor no sound | that the earth owes. 1.02.407
nor this man's threats | to whom i am subdu'd, 1.02.489
nor i, my spirits are nimble. 2.01.202
but they'll nor pinch, | fright me with 2.02. 4
nor lead me, like a fire–brand, in the dark 2.02. 6
here's neither bush nor shrub to bear off any 2.02. 18 P
she lov'd not the savor of tar nor of pitch, 2.02. 52
nor fetch in firing | at requiring, | nor scrape 2.02.181
nor scrape trenchering, nor wash dish. 2.02.183
nor scrape trenchering, nor wash dish. 2.02.183
nor have i seen | more that i may call men than 3.01. 50
nor can imagination form a shape, | besides 3.01. 56
nor go neither; 3.02. 19 P
nor hath not | one spirit to command: 3.02. 93
they | will not, nor cannot, use such vigilance 3.03. 16
a breakfast, nor | befitting this first meeting. 5.01.164
father | for his advice, nor thought i had one. 5.01.191
nor need'st thou much importune me to that TGV 1.03. 17
this while sheds not a tear, nor speaks a word; 2.03. 31 P
nor to his service no such joy on earth: 2.04.139
nor never welcome to a place till some certain 2.05. 5 P
child, | nor fearing me as if i were her father; 3.01. 71
nor silver–shedding tears | could penetrate her 3.01.232
nor who 'tis i love; 3.01.268 P
nor how my father would enforce me marry | vain 4.03. 16
nor i. 5.02. 33
is not satisfied | is nor of heaven nor earth, 5.04. 80
is not satisfied | is nor of heaven nor earth, 5.04. 80
i warrant you, no tell–tale nor no breed–bate. WIV 1.04. 12 P
anne's mind — that's neither here nor there. 1.04.106 P
than i do, nor can do more than i do with her, i 1.04.129 P
will not miss you morning nor evening prayer, as 2.02. 99 P
become nothing else, nor that well neither. 3.02. 60 P
be–gar nor i too; there is no–bodies. 3.03.213 P
fenton, | i will not be your friend nor enemy. 3.04. 89
into a halfpenny purse, nor into a pepper–box. 3.05.147 P
no, nor no where else but in your brain. 4.02.159 P
nor nature never lends | the smallest scruple of MM 1.01. 36
nor need you, on mine honor, have to do | with 1.01. 63
nor do i think the man of safe discretion | that 1.01. 71
no, sir, nor i mean it not. 2.01.120 P
nor it shall not be allow'd in vienna. 2.01.228 P
and neither heaven nor man grieve at the mercy. 2.02. 50
not the king's crown, nor the deputed sword, 2.02. 60
the marshal's truncheon, nor the judge's robe, 2.02. 61
nor doth she tempt; 2.02.164
life | (as i subscribe not that, nor any other, 2.04. 89
thou hast nor youth nor age, | but as it were an 3.01. 32
thou hast nor youth nor age, | but as it were an 3.01. 32
hast neither heat, affection, limb, nor beauty, 3.01. 37
then, pompey, nor now. 3.02. 82 P
no might nor greatness in mortality | can 3.02.185
more nor less to others paying | than by 3.02.265
nor, gentle daughter, fear you not at all. 4.01. 70
nor persuasion can with ease attempt you, i will 4.02.189 P
this nor hurts him, nor profits you a jot. 4.03.123
this nor hurts him, nor profits you a jot. 4.03.123
nor do not banish reason | for inequality, but 5.01. 64
no, my good lord, | nor wish'd to hold my peace. 5.01. 79
and holy, | not scurvy, nor a temporary meddler, 5.01.145
neither maid, widow, nor wife? 5.01.178 P
many of them are neither maid, widow, nor wife. 5.01.180 P
spake with her, saw her, nor heard from her, 5.01.223
his subject am i not, | nor here provincial. 5.01.316
lord, | i crave no other, nor no better man. 5.01.426
neither my husband nor the slave return'd, ERR 2.01. 1
and the wherefore is neither rhyme nor reason? 2.02. 48
i am not adriana, nor thy wife. 2.02.112
nor to–day here you must not, come again when 3.01. 41
here is neither cheer, sir, nor welcome: 3.01. 66
not, | nor by what wonder you do hit of mine — 3.02. 30
of mine, | nor to her bed no homage do i owe: 3.02. 43
thou hast no husband yet, nor i no wife. 3.02. 68
not once, nor twice, but twenty times you have. 3.02.172
for fear you ne'er see chain nor money more. 3.02.177
nor now i had not, but that i am bound | to 4.01. 3
but neither chain nor goldsmith came to me: 4.01. 24
i cannot, nor i will not, hold me still, | my 4.02. 17
nor send him forth, that we may bear him hence. 5.01.158
ne'er may i look on day, nor sleep on night, 5.01.210
nor heady–rash, provok'd with raging ire, 5.01.216
nor ever didst thou draw thy sword on me; 5.01.267
dromio, nor thou? 5.01.303
no, trust me, sir, nor i. 5.01.303
"it is not so, nor 'twas not so, but indeed, god ADO 1.01.217 P
she should be lov'd nor know how she should be 1.01.231 P
nor will you not tell me who you are? 2.01.127 P
the count is neither sad, nor sick, nor merry, 2.01.293 P
is neither sad, nor sick, nor merry, nor well; 2.01.293 P
is neither sad, nor sick, nor merry, nor well; 2.01.294 P
no, nor i neither, but most wonderful that she 2.03. 95 P
to her wit, nor no great argument of her folly, 2.03.234 P
nor take no shape nor project of affection, 3.01. 55
nor take no shape nor project of affection, 3.01. 55
what i list, nor i list not to think what i can, 3.04. 83 P
to think what i can, nor indeed i cannot think, 3.04. 83 P
trust not my reading, nor my observations, 4.01.165
my age, | my reverence, calling, nor divinity, 4.01.168
blood of mine, | nor age so eat up my invention, 4.01.194
nor fortune made such havoc of my means, | nor 4.01.195
nor my bad life reft me so much of friends, 4.01.196
i confess nothing, nor i deny nothing. 4.01.272 P
nor let no comforter delight mine ear, | but 5.01. 6
but no man's virtue nor sufficiency | to be so 5.01. 29
i speak not like a dotard nor a fool, | as under 5.01. 59
by my soul, nor i, | and yet, to satisfy this 5.01.275
nor knew not what she did when she spoke to me, 5.01.301
planet, nor i cannot woo in festival terms. 5.02. 41 P
neither serve for the writing nor the tune. LLL 1.02.114 P
suffer him to take no delight nor no penance, 1.02.129 P
neither savoring of poetry, wit, nor invention. 4.02.159 P
nor shines the silver moon one half so bright 4.03. 29
thought can think, nor tongue of mortal tell." 4.03. 40
nor never lay his wreathed arms athwart | his 4.03.133
my eyes are then no eyes, nor i berowne. 4.03.228
nor understood none neither, sir. 5.01.151 P
nor to their penn'd speech render we no grace, 5.02.147
nor god, nor i, delights in perjur'd men. 5.02.346
nor god, nor i, delights in perjur'd men. 5.02.346
dance, | nor never more in russian habit wait. 5.02.401
nor to the motion of a schoolboy's tongue, | nor 5.02.403
tongue, | nor never come in vizard to my friend, 5.02.404
nor woo in rhyme, like a blind harper's song! 5.02.405
nor shall not, if i do as i intend. 5.02.429
made bold, | nor how it may concern my modesty,
MND 1.01. 60
nor hath love's mind of any judgment taste; 1.01.236
nor doth this wood lack worlds of company, | for 2.01.223
nor spell, nor charm, | come our lovely lady 2.02. 17
never harm, | nor spell, nor charm, | come our 2.02. 17
worm nor snail, do no offense. 2.02. 23
man, | that i did never, no, nor never can, 2.02.126
nor is he dead, for aught that i can tell. 3.02. 76
nor none, in my mind, now you give her o'er. 3.02.135
you, i, | nor longer stay in your curst company. 3.02.341
and dar'st not stand, nor look me in the face. 3.02.424
was never hollow'd to, nor cheer'd with horn, 4.01.125
horn, | in crete, in sparta, nor in thessaly. 4.01.126
his tongue to conceive, nor his heart to report, 4.01.213 P
most dear actors, eat no onions nor garlic, for 4.02. 43 P
these antic fables, nor these fairy toys. 5.01. 3
joiner am | a lion fell, nor else no lion's dam, 5.01.224
never mole, hare–lip, nor scar, | nor mark 5.01.411
nor mark prodigious, such as are | despised in 5.01.412
not in one bottom trusted, | nor to one place; MV 1.01. 43
nor is my whole estate | upon the fortune of 1.01. 43
nor do i now make moan to be abridg'd | from 1.01.126
nor is the wide world ignorant of her worth, 1.01.167
neither have i money nor commodity | to raise a 1.01.178
choose who i would, nor refuse who i dislike; 1.02. 23 P
that i cannot choose one, nor refuse none? 1.02. 26 P
to him, for he understands not me, nor i him. 1.02. 69 P
french, nor italian, and you will come into the 1.02. 70 P
eat with you, drink with you, nor pray with you. 1.03. 37 P
albeit i neither lend nor borrow | by taking nor 1.03. 61
nor borrow | by taking nor by giving of excess, 1.03. 62
methoughts you said you neither lend nor borrow 1.03. 69
nor will not. come bring me unto my chance. 2.01. 43
nor thrust your head into the public street | to 2.05. 32
i'll then nor give nor hazard aught for lead. 2.07. 21
i'll then nor give nor hazard aught for lead. 2.07. 21
nor no ill luck stirring but what lights a' my 3.01. 94 P
nor none of thee, thou pale and common drudge 3.02.103
it be in mind, | nor well, unless in mind. 3.02.235
stay, | nor rest be interposer 'twixt us twain. 3.02.327
did repent for doing good, | nor shall not now: 3.04. 11
so can i give no reason, nor i will not, | more 4.01. 59
nor cut thou less nor more | but just a pound of 4.01.325
nor cut thou less nor more | but just a pound of 4.01.325
me vow | that i should neither sell, nor give, 4.01.443
i should neither sell, nor give, nor lose it. 4.01.443
he is not, nor we have not heard from him. 5.01. 35
nor is not moved with concord of sweet sounds, 5.01. 84
hence — | nor you, lorenzo — jessica, nor you. 5.01.121
hence — | nor you, lorenzo — jessica, nor you. 5.01.121
nor pluck it from his finger, for the wealth 5.01.173
and neither man nor master would take aught 5.01.183
nor i in yours | till i again see mine! 5.01.191
i have, | no, not my body nor my husband's bed. 5.01.228
hath no child but i, nor none is like to have; AYL 1.02. 18 P
no man in good earnest, nor no further in sport, 1.02. 27 P
nor did not with unbashful forehead woo | the 2.03. 50
nor shalt not, till necessity be serv'd. 2.07. 89
no wit by nature nor art may complain of good 3.02. 29 P
neither rhyme nor reason can express how much. 3.02.398 P
nor a man's good wit seconded with the forward 3.03. 13 P
he is not a pick–purse nor a horse–stealer, but 3.04. 22 P
nor i am sure there is no force in eyes | that 3.05. 26
nor your cheek of cream | that can entame my 3.05. 47
for my part, | i love him not, nor hate him not; 3.05.127
nor the musician's, which is fantastical; 4.01. 11 P
nor the courtier's, which is proud; 4.01. 12 P
nor the soldier's, which is ambitious; 4.01. 12 P
nor the lawyer's, which is politic; 4.01. 13 P
nor the lady's, which is nice; 4.01. 14 P
nor the lover's, which is all these: 4.01. 14 P
my sudden wooing, nor /her sudden consenting; 5.02. 7 P
to her that is not here, nor doth not hear. 5.02.108
nor i. 5.02.123
nor i. 5.02.124
nor he durst not give me the lie direct; 5.04. 86 P
nor ne'er wed woman, if you be not she. 5.04.124
nor cannot insinuate with you in the behalf of a ep 8 P
sly, call not me honor nor lordship. SHR in.2. 6 P
than legs, nor no more shoes than feet — nay, in.2. 10 P
indeed | and not a tinker nor christopher sly. in.2. 73
why, sir, you know no house nor no such maid, in.2. 91
maid, | nor no such men as you have reckon'd up, in.2. 92
these, | which never were, nor no man ever saw. in.2. 96
let's be no stoics nor no stocks, i pray, | or 1.01. 31
nor can we be distinguish'd by our faces | for 1.01.200
good sister, wrong me not, nor wrong yourself, 2.01. 1
nor is your firm resolve unknown to me, | in the 2.01. 92
nor bite the lip, as angry wenches will, | nor 2.01.248
nor hast thou pleasure to be cross in talk; 2.01.249
i'll not be tied to hours nor 'pointed times, 3.01. 19
no, nor to–morrow — not till i please myself. 3.02.209
nay, look not big, nor stamp, nor stare, nor 3.02.228
look not big, nor stamp, nor stare, nor fret, 3.02.228
look not big, nor stamp, nor stare, nor fret, 3.02.228
door | to hold my stirrup nor to take my horse? 4.01.121
she eat no meat to–day, nor none shall eat; 4.01.197
night she slept not, nor to–night she shall not; 4.01.198
nor a musician, as i seem to be, | but one that 4.02. 17
nor never needed that i should entreat, | am 4.03. 8
i see she's like to have neither cap nor gown. 4.03. 93
quaint, more pleasing, nor more commendable. 4.03.102
i will neither be fac'd nor brav'd. 4.03.125 P
wonder not, | nor be not grieved; 4.05. 64
contempt nor bitterness | were in his pride or AWW 1.02. 36
too, | since i nor wax nor honey can bring home, 1.02. 65
too, | since i nor wax nor honey can bring home, 1.02. 65
that i could neither believe nor misdoubt. 1.03.125 P
nor i your mother? 1.03.160
nor would i have him till i do deserve him, 1.03.199
my art is not past power, nor you past cure. 2.01.158
nothing, has neither leg, hands, lip, nor cap; 2.02. 11 P
i cannot love her, nor will strive to do't. 2.03.145
nor does | the ministration and required office 2.05. 59
of the wealth i owe, | nor dare i say 'tis mine; 2.05. 80
nor would i wish you. 3.07. 7

remain there but an hour, nor speak to me. 4.02. 58
nor believe he can have every thing in him by 4.03.145 P
nor /you, mistress, | ever a friend whose 4.04. 16
i neither can nor will deny | but that i know 5.03.166
it was not given me, nor i did not buy it. 5.03.272
her degree, neither in estate, years, nor wit; TN 1.03.110 P
nor no railing in a known discreet man, though 1.05. 95 P
enough for a man, nor young enough for a boy; 1.05.156 P
with his lord, | nor hold him up with hopes: 1.05.304
nor will you not that i go with you? 2.01. 1 P
manners, nor honesty, but to gabble like tinkers 2.03. 87 P
no respect of place, persons, nor time in you? 2.03. 91 P
nor i neither. 2.05.186 P
pride, | nor wit nor reason can my passion hide. 3.01.152
pride, | nor wit nor reason can my passion hide. 3.01.152
has, nor never none | shall mistress be of it, 3.01.159
not "malvolio," nor after my degree, but "fellow 3.04. 77 P
"wonder not, nor admire not in thy mind, why i 3.04.150 P
none, | nor know i you by voice or any feature. 3.04.353
know you, nor i am not sent to you by my lady, 4.01. 6 P
with her, nor your name is not master cesario, 4.01. 7 P
master cesario, nor this is not my nose neither: 4.01. 8 P
nor lean enough to be thought a good studient; 4.02. 7 P
nor can there be that deity in my nature | of 5.01.227
nor are you therein, by my life, deceiv'd, | you 5.01.262
and let no quarrel nor no brawl to come | taint 5.01.356
of ill–doing, nor dream'd | that any did. WT 1.02. 70
my bosom likes not, nor my brows! 1.02.119
to have nor eyes nor ears nor thought, then say 1.02.275
to have nor eyes nor ears nor thought, then say 1.02.275
to have nor eyes nor ears nor thought, then say 1.02.275
is nothing, nor nothing have these nothings, 1.02.295
nor brass nor stone nor parchment bears not one, 1.02.360
nor brass nor stone nor parchment bears not one, 1.02.360
nor brass nor stone nor parchment bears not one, 1.02.360
nor shall you be safer | than one condemn'd by 1.02.444
party to | the anger of the king, nor guilty of 2.02. 60
nor night, nor day, no rest. 2.03. 1
nor night, nor day, no rest. 2.03. 1
laugh if i could reach them, nor | shall she, 2.03. 25
nor i, nor any | but one that's here — and 2.03. 83
nor i, nor any | but one that's here — and 2.03. 83
break the holy seal | nor read the secrets in't. 3.02.130
nor was't much | thou wouldst have poison'd good 3.02.187
nor is't directly laid to thee, the death | of 3.02.194
if word nor oath | prevail not, go and see. 3.02.203
i'll speak of her no more, nor of your children; 3.02.229
water, nor the bear half din'd on the gentleman. 3.03.105 P
nor in a way so chaste, since my desires | run 4.04. 33
honor, nor my lusts | burn hotter than my faith. 4.04. 34
i cannot be | mine own, nor any thing to any, if 4.04. 44
death, nor on the birth | of trembling winter, 4.04. 80
no, nor mean better. 4.04.381
he neither does nor shall. 4.04.393
i cannot speak, nor think, | nor dare to know 4.04.451
nor think, | nor dare to know that which i know. 4.04.452
nor the pomp that may | be thereat gleaned, for 4.04.488
your knowledge, nor | concern me the reporting. 4.04.503
bohemia's son, | nor shall appear in sicilia. 4.04.589
neither to his father nor to me, to go about to 4.04.701 P
none, sir; i have no pheasant cock, nor hen. 4.04.744 P
know 'tis none of your daughter nor my sister; 4.04.820 P
nor the remembrance | of his most sovereign name 5.01. 25
nor was not to be equall'd" — thus your verse 5.01.101
we are not, sir, nor are we like to be. 5.01.205
my brother might not claim him, nor your father, JN 1.01.126
nor keep his princely heart from richard's hand. 1.01.267
nor thou | become thy great birth nor deserve a 3.01. 49
become thy great birth nor deserve a crown. 3.01. 50
these eyes that never did nor never shall | so 4.01. 57
i will not stir, nor winch, nor speak a word, 4.01. 80
i will not stir, nor winch, nor speak a word, 4.01. 80
speak a word, | nor look upon the iron angerly. 4.01. 81
nor attend the foot | that leaves the print of 4.03. 25
nor conversant with ease and idleness, | till i 4.03. 70
nor tempt the danger of my true defense, | lest 4.03. 84
nor met with fortune other than at feasts, 5.02. 58
it would not out at windows nor at doors. 5.07. 29
nor let my kingdom's rivers take their course 5.07. 38
nor entreat the north | to make his bleak winds 5.07. 39
this england never did, nor never shall, | lie 5.07.112
should nothing privilege him nor partialize R2 1.01.120
nor never look upon each other's face, | nor 1.03.185
nor never write, regreet, nor reconcile | this 1.03.186
nor reconcile | this low'ring tempest of your 1.03.186
nor never by advised purpose meet | to plot, 1.03.188
not yourself, nor strive not with your breath, 2.01. 3
gloucester's death, nor herford's banishment, 2.01.165
gaunt's rebukes, nor england's private wrongs, 2.01.166
nor the prevention of poor bullingbrook | about 2.01.167
about his marriage, nor my own disgrace, | have 2.01.168
grace me no grace, nor uncle me no uncle. 2.03. 87
nor friends, nor foes, to me welcome you are: 2.03.170
nor friends, nor foes, to me welcome you are: 2.03.170
nor with thy sweets comfort his ravenous sense, 3.02. 13
nor near nor farther off, my gracious lord, 3.02. 64
nor near nor farther off, my gracious lord, 3.02. 64
madam, i know not, nor i greatly care not, | god 5.02. 48
nor shall not be the last — like seely beggars 5.05. 25
be, | nor i, nor any man that but man is, | with 5.05. 39
e'er i be, | nor i, nor any man that but man is, 5.05. 39
not poison that do poison need, | nor do i thee. 5.06. 39
but neither my good word nor princely favor. 5.06. 42
and never show thy head by day nor light. 5.06. 44
nor bruise her flow'rets with the armed hoofs 1H4 1.01. 8
manhood, nor good fellowship in thee, nor thou 1.02.139 P
in thee, nor thou cam'st not of the blood royal, 1.02.140 P
nor never could the noble mortimer | receive so 1.03.110
me | whither i go, nor reason whereabout. 2.03.104
nor shall we need his help these fourteen days. 3.01. 87
no, nor you shall not. 3.01.116
a fellow of no mark nor likelihood. 3.02. 45
for of no right, nor color like to right, | he 3.02.100
neither faith, truth, nor womanhood in me else. 3.03.110 P
nor no more truth in thee than in a drawn fox, 3.03.113 P
she's neither fish nor flesh, a man knows not 3.03.127 P
truth, nor honesty in this bosom of thine; 3.03.154 P
nor did he think it meet | to lay so dangerous 4.01. 33

nor claim no further than your new–fall'n right, 5.01. 44
nor moody beggars, starving for a time | of 5.01. 81
nor can one england brook a double reign | of 5.04. 66
but i will inset you neither in gold nor silver, 2H4 1.02. 17 P
he will spare neither man, woman, nor child. 2.01. 17 P
no, nor i neither, i'll be at your elbow. 2.01. 20 P
nor the throng of words that come with such more 2.01.111 P
will bar no honest man my house, nor no cheater, 2.04.103 P
come, i'll drink no proofs nor no bullets. 2.04.118 P
not love me, nor a man cannot make him laugh, 4.03. 88 P
nor lose the good advantage of his grace | by 4.04. 28
no prince nor peer shall have just cause to say, 5.02.144
nor never hydra–headed willfulness | so soon did H5 1.01. 35
nor did the french possess the salique land 1.02. 56
nor shall my nell keep lodgers. 2.01. 31
nor leave not one behind that doth not wish 2.02. 23
(though war nor no known quarrel were in 2.04. 17
know | 'tis no sinister nor no awkward claim, 2.04. 85
days, | nor from the dust of old oblivion rak'd, 2.04. 87
nor, as we are, we say we will not shun it. 3.06.165
nor will do none to–morrow. 3.07.101 P
nor doth he dedicate one jot of color | unto the 4.pr. 37
there is no tiddle taddle nor pibble babble in 4.01. 71 P
nor it is not meet he should. 4.01.100 P
of his son, nor the master of his servant; 4.01.157 P
nor the tide of pomp | that beats upon the high 4.01.264
gold, | nor care i who doth feed upon my cost; 4.03. 25
matter for his swellings nor his turkey–cocks. 5.01. 16 P
you do not love it, nor your affections, and 5.01. 25 P
for the one i have neither words nor measure; 5.02.134 P
cannot look greenly, nor gasp out my eloquence, 5.02.143 P
nor i have no cunning in protestation; 5.02.143 P
use till urg'd, nor never break for urging. 5.02.145 P
neither the voice nor the heart of flattery 5.02.287 P
nor this i have not. 5.02.343
gall — | nor men nor money hath he to make war. 1H6 1.02. 17
gall — | nor men nor money hath he to make war. 1.02. 17
nor yet saint philip's daughters, were like thee 1.02.143
that thou nor none of thine shall be let in. 1.03. 21
here's beauford, that regards nor god nor king, 1.03. 60
here's beauford, that regards nor god nor king, 1.03. 60
wheel, | i know not where i am, nor what i do. 1.05. 20
of /aire, | nor any of his false confederates. 2.02. 21
fair lady, nor misconster | the mind of talbot, 2.03. 73
nor other satisfaction do i crave, | but only, 2.03. 77
let him that is no coward nor no flatterer, 2.04. 31
nor grieve that roan is so recovered: 3.03. 2
nor should that nation boast it so with us, 3.03. 23
not fearing death, nor shrinking for distress, 4.01. 37
thou never hadst renown, nor canst not lose it. 4.05. 40
cannot my body nor blood–sacrifice | entreat you 5.03. 20
o fairest beauty, do not fear nor fly, | for i 5.03. 46
thou art no father nor no friend of mine. 5.04. 9
'twas neither charles nor yet the duke i nam'd, 5.04. 77
nor be rebellious to the crown of england, 5.04.171
thou, nor thy nobles, to the crown of england. 5.04.172
nor shall proud lancaster usurp my right, | nor 2H6 1.01.244
nor hold the sceptre in his childish fist, | nor 1.01.245
fist, | nor wear the diadem upon his head, 1.01.246
i never said nor thought any such matter. 1.03.188 P
let never day nor night unhallowed pass, | but 2.01. 83
nor his? 2.01.119
i never meant him any ill, nor the king, nor the 2.03. 88 P
meant him any ill, nor the king, nor the queen; 2.03. 89 P
nor stir at nothing, till the axe of death 2.04. 49
snar'd, | nor never seek prevention of thy foes. 2.04. 57
nor change my countenance for this arrest; 3.01. 99
pay, | nor ever had one penny bribe from france. 3.01.109
me, | nor store of treasons to augment my guilt. 3.01.169
thou never didst them wrong, nor no man wrong; 3.01.209
nor set no footing on this unkind shore"? 3.02. 87
nor cease to be an arrogant controller, | though 3.02.205
nor let the rain of heaven wet this place | to 3.02.341
having neither subject, wealth, nor diadem. 4.01. 82
i fear neither sword nor fire. 4.02. 59 P
no, my lord, nor likely to be slain; 4.05. 2 P
nor knows he how to live but by the spoil, 4.08. 39
dar'st not, no, nor canst not rule a traitor. 5.01. 95
nor should thy prowess want praise and esteem, 5.02. 22
nor he that loves himself | hath not essentially 5.02. 38
you'll nor fight nor fly. 5.02. 74
you'll nor fight nor fly. 5.02. 74
day | is not itself, nor have we won one foot, 5.03. 6
neither the king, nor he that loves him best, 3H6 1.01. 45
power | of essex, norfolk, suffolk, nor of kent, 1.01.156
nor i. 1.01.181
and neither by treason nor hostility | to seek 1.01.199
my drift, | nor any of the house of lancaster? 1.02. 47
and trust not simple henry nor his oaths. 1.02. 59
it could not slake mine ire nor ease my heart. 1.03. 29
it needs not, nor it boots thee not, proud queen 1.04.125
nor can my tongue unload my heart's great 2.01. 81
nor now my scandal, richard, dost thou hear; 2.01.151
fault, | nor wittingly have i infring'd my vow. 2.02. 8
no, nor your manhood that durst make you stay. 2.02.108
but thou art neither like thy sire nor dam, 2.02.135
can neither call it perfect day nor night. 2.05. 4
breast, | yet neither conqueror nor conquered; 2.05. 12
no way to fly, nor strength to hold out flight. 2.06. 24
and he nor sees nor hears us what we say. 2.06. 63
and he nor sees nor hears us what we say. 2.06. 63
diamonds and indian stones, | nor to be seen. 3.01. 64
no, never such an oath, nor will not now. 3.01. 73
nor how to be contented with one wife, | nor how 4.03. 37
wife, | nor how to use your brothers brotherly, 4.03. 38
nor how to study for the people's welfare, | nor 4.03. 39
nor how to shroud yourself from enemies? 4.03. 40
nor posted off their suits with slow delays; 4.08. 40
nor much oppress'd them with great subsidies, 4.08. 45
nor forward of revenge, though they much err'd. 4.08. 46
nor i, but stoop with patience to my fortune. 5.05. 6
did not offend, nor were not worthy blame, | if 5.05. 54
i, that have neither pity, love, nor fear. 5.06. 68
nor made to court an amorous looking–glass; R3 1.01. 15
villain, thou know'st nor law of god nor man: 1.02. 70
villain, thou know'st nor law of god nor man: 1.02. 70
nor when thy warlike father, like a child, 1.02.159

i never sued to friend nor enemy; 1.02.167
a man that loves not me, nor none of you. 1.03. 13
to thee, that hast nor honesty nor grace: 1.03. 55
to thee, that hast nor honesty nor grace: 1.03. 55
die neither mother, wife, nor england's queen! 1.03.208
urge neither charity nor shame to me. 1.03.273
nor thou within the compass of my curse. 1.03.283
nor no one here; 1.03.284
nor you, as we are, loyal. 1.04.166
nor you, son dorset; 2.01. 19
buckingham, nor you; 2.01. 19
nor i, ungracious, speak unto myself | for him, 2.01.128
nor more can you distinguish of a man | than of 3.01. 9
prince hath neither claim'd it nor deserv'd it, 3.01. 51
you break no privilege nor charter there. 3.01. 54
nor none that live, i hope. 3.01.147
nor he deliver'd | his gracious pleasure any way 3.04. 16
amiss, | i cannot nor i will not yield to you. 3.07.207
nor mother, wife, nor england's counted queen. 4.01. 46
nor mother, wife, nor england's counted queen. 4.01. 46
thou hadst not broken, nor my brothers died. 4.04.380
day, yield me not thy light, nor, night, thy 4.04.401
nor none so bad but well may be reported. 4.04.458
neither good nor bad! 4.04.459
i never was nor never will be false. 4.04.493
nor cheer of mind that i was wont to have. 5.03. 74
nor call'd upon | for high feats done to th' H8 1.01. 60
not unconsidered leave your honor nor | the 1.02. 15
which neither know | my faculties nor person, 1.02. 73
'neither the king nor 's heirs | (tell you the 1.02.168
my lord, | nor shall not while i have a stump. 1.03. 49
nor build their evils on the graves of great men 2.01. 67
nor will i sue, although the king have mercies 2.01. 70
me, my lords, | i love him not, nor fear him; 2.02. 50
nor my prayers | are not words duly hallowed, 2.03. 67
nor my wishes | more worth than empty vanities; 2.03. 68
nor could | come pat betwixt too early and too 2.03. 83
nor no more assurance | of equal friendship and 2.04. 17
against you, nor injustice | for you or any. 2.04. 89
nor ever more | upon this business my appearance 2.04.132
nor to betray you any way to sorrow — | you 3.01. 56
nor, i'll assure you, better taken, sir. 4.01. 12
nor shall not, when my fancy's on my play. 5.01. 60
nor is there living | (i speak it with a single 5.02. 72
i am not sampson, nor sir guy, nor colbrand, 5.03. 22
i am not sampson, nor sir guy, nor colbrand, 5.03. 22
nor shall this peace sleep with her; 5.04. 39
my part, i'll not meddle nor make no farther. TRO 1.01. 14 P
i'll meddle nor make no more i' th' matter. 1.01. 83 P
nor any man an attaint but he carries some stain 1.02. 25 P
no, nor hector is not troilus in some degrees. 1.02. 69 P
nor his qualities. 1.02. 88 P
nor his beauty. 1.02. 90 P
nor, princes, is it matter new to us | that we 1.03. 10
nor i from troy come not to whisper with him. 1.03.250
to guard a thing not ours nor worth to us | (had 2.02. 22
nor the remainder viands | we do not throw in 2.02. 70
troy must not be, nor goodly ilion stand. 2.02.109
nor fear of bad success in a bad cause, | can 2.02.117
it, | nor once deject the courage of our minds, 2.02.121
what he hath done, | nor faint in the pursuit. 2.02.142
nor none so noble | whose life were ill bestow'd 2.02.158
nor, by my will, assubjugate his merit, | as 2.03.192
nor nothing monstrous neither? 3.02. 76 P
nor feels not what he owes, but by reflection; 3.03. 99
nor doth the eye itself, | that most pure spirit 3.03.105
nor doth he of himself know them for aught, 3.03.118
neither gave to me | good word nor look. 3.03.144
merits pois'd, each weighs nor less nor more, 4.01. 66
merits pois'd, each weighs nor less nor more, 4.01. 66
you'll ne'er be good, | nor suffer others. 4.02. 30
ease thy smart | by friendship nor by speaking." 4.04. 20
nor heel the high lavolt, nor sweeten talk, 4.04. 86
nor heel the high lavolt, nor sweeten talk, 4.04. 86
nor play at subtile games — fair virtues all, 4.04. 87
soon provok'd, nor being provok'd soon calm'd; 4.05. 99
nor dignifies an impare thought with breath; 4.05.103
for i'll not kill thee there, nor there, nor 4.05.254
i'll not kill thee there, nor there, nor there, 4.05.254
who neither looks upon the heaven nor earth, 4.05.281
be myself, nor have cognition | of what i feel; 5.02. 63
nor i, by pluto; 5.02.102 P
nor mine, my lord; cressid was here but now. 5.02.128
nor the hand of mars | beck'ning with fiery 5.03. 52
nor you, my brother, with your true sword drawn, 5.03. 56
have, you curs, | that like nor peace nor war? COR 1.01.169
have, you curs, | that like nor peace nor war? 1.01.169
better be held nor more attain'd than by | a 1.01.265
nor did you think it folly | to keep your great 1.02. 19
'tis not to save labor, nor that i want love. 1.03. 81 P
no, i'll nor sell nor give him; 1.04. 6
no, i'll nor sell nor give him; 1.04. 6
no, nor a man that fears you less than he, 1.04. 14
nor i. 1.04. 46
foolish in our stands | nor cowardly in retire. 1.06. 3
nor sleep nor sanctuary, | being naked, sick, 1.10. 19
nor sleep nor sanctuary, | being naked, sick, 1.10. 19
being naked, sick, nor fane nor capitol, | the 1.10. 20
being naked, sick, nor fane nor capitol, | the 1.10. 20
the prayers of priests nor times of sacrifice, 1.10. 21
you know neither me, yourselves, nor any thing. 2.01. 67 P
nor on him put | the napless vesture of humility 2.01.233
nor, showing (as the manner is) his wounds | to 2.01.235
of no more soul nor fitness for the world | than 2.01.250
'twixt doing them neither good nor harm; 2.02. 18 P
such as cannot rule, | nor ever will be ruled. 3.01. 41
as a consul, | nor yoke with him for tribune. 3.01. 57
nor has coriolanus | deserv'd this so dishonor'd 3.01. 59
no, nor power, but that | which they have given 3.01. 73
nor by th' matter which your heart prompts you, 3.02. 54
nor check my courage for what they can give, 3.03. 92
nor i. 4.06.158
i neither care for th' world nor your general; 5.02.102 P
suits, | nor from the state nor private friends, 5.03. 18
suits, | nor from the state nor private friends, 5.03. 18
requires nor child nor woman's face to see. 5.03.130
requires nor child nor woman's face to see. 5.03.130
in me, | nor wrong mine age with this indignity. TIT 1.01. 8

nor we disturb'd with prodigies on earth. 1.01.101
nor thou, nor he, are any sons of mine, | my 1.01.294
nor thou, nor he, are any sons of mine, | my 1.01.294
not, | nor her, nor thee, nor any of thy stock. 1.01.300
not, | nor her, nor thee, nor any of thy stock. 1.01.300
not, | nor her, nor thee, nor any of thy stock. 1.01.300
thee never, nor thy traitorous haughty sons, 1.01.302
nor thou, nor these, confederates in the deed 1.01.344
nor thou, nor these, confederates in the deed 1.01.344
nor wish no less, and so i take my leave. 1.01.402
nor with sour looks afflict his gentle heart. 1.01.441
nor would your noble mother for much more | be 2.01. 51
nor me, so i were one. 2.01.102
chiron, we hunt not, we, with horse nor hound, 2.02. 25
nor i no strength to climb without thy help. 2.03.242
she hath no tongue to call, nor hands to wash, 2.04. 7
nor tongue to tell me who hath mart'red thee. 3.01.107
but now nor lucius nor lavinia lives | but in 3.01.294
but now nor lucius nor lavinia lives | but in 3.01.294
my lord, i know not, i, nor can i guess, 4.01. 16
nor great alcides, nor the god of war, | shall 4.02. 95
brood, | nor great alcides, nor the god of war, 4.02. 95
and, sith there's no justice in earth nor hell, 4.03. 50
hair, | nor age nor honor shall shape privilege; 4.04. 57
hair, | nor age nor honor shall shape privilege; 4.04. 57
my heart is not compact of flint nor steel, 5.03. 88
steel, | nor can i utter all our bitter grief, 5.03. 89
no funeral rite, nor man in mourning weed, | no 5.03.196
i neither know it, nor can learn of him. ROM 1.01.144
nor bide th' encounter of assailing eyes, | nor 1.01.213
eyes, | nor ope her lap to saint–seducing gold. 1.01.214
it is nor hand nor foot, | nor arm nor face, 2.02. 40
it is nor hand nor foot, | nor arm nor face, 2.02. 40
foot, | nor arm nor face, /nor /any /other /part 2.02. 41
foot, | nor arm nor face, /nor /any /other /part 2.02. 41
nor aught so good but, strain'd from that fair 2.03. 19
so deep as a well, nor so wide as a church–door, 3.01. 96 P
nor tears nor prayers shall purchase out abuses; 3.01.193
nor tears nor prayers shall purchase out abuses; 3.01.193
nor that is not the lark whose notes do beat 3.05. 21
that thou expects not, nor i look'd not for. 3.05.110
thank me no thankings, nor proud me no prouds, 3.05.152
nor what is mine shall never do thee good. 3.05.194
if no inconstant toy, nor womanish fear, | abate 4.01.119
world is not thy friend, nor the world's law, 5.01. 72
again — | nor get a messenger to bring it thee, 5.02. 15
affect company, | nor is he fit for't indeed. TIM 1.02. 32
nor will he know his purse, or yield me this, 1.02.194
nor then silenc'd when | "commend me to your 2.01. 17
to maintain it, | nor cease his flow of riot. 2.02. 3
nor /resumes no care | of what is to continue. 2.02. 4
nor thou altogether a wise man; 2.02.116 P
i did endure | not seldom, nor no slight checks, 2.02.140
nor came any of his bounties over me | to mark 3.02. 78
nor did he soil the fact with cowardice | (/an 3.05. 16
nor more willingly leaves winter, such summer 3.06. 31 P
nor has he with him to | supply his life, or 4.02. 46
whose proof nor yells of mothers, maids, nor 4.03.125
proof nor yells of mothers, maids, nor babes, 4.03.125
nor sight of priests in holy vestments bleeding, 4.03.126
title plead, | nor sound his quillets shrilly; 4.03.155
nor on the beasts themselves, the birds and 4.03.424
lord, but therefore | came not my friend nor i. 5.01. 79
nor i. 5.01. 99
nor all deserve | the common stroke of war. 5.04. 21
nor are they such | that these great tow'rs, 5.04. 24
nor are they living | who were the motives that 5.04. 26
no tradesman's matters, nor women's matters; JC 1.01. 22 P
you one), | nor construe any further my neglect, 1.02. 45
nor stony tower, nor walls of beaten brass, 1.03. 93
nor stony tower, nor walls of beaten brass, 1.03. 93
nor airless dungeon, nor strong links of iron, 1.03. 94
nor airless dungeon, nor strong links of iron, 1.03. 94
nor th' insuppressive mettle of our spirits, 2.01.134
thou hast no figures nor no fantasies, | which 2.01.231
nor for yours neither. 2.01.237
it will not let you eat, nor talk, nor sleep; 2.01.252
it will not let you eat, nor talk, nor sleep; 2.01.252
nor heaven nor earth have been at peace to–night 2.02. 1
nor heaven nor earth have been at peace to–night 2.02. 1
wrong, nor without cause | will he be satisfied. 3.01. 47
intended to your person, | nor to no roman else. 3.01. 91
nor no instrument | of half that worth as those 3.01.154
nor his offenses enforc'd, for which he suffer'd 3.02. 39 P
for i have neither /wit, nor words, nor worth, 3.02.221
for i have neither /wit, nor words, nor worth, 3.02.221
action, nor utterance, nor the power of speech 3.02.222
nor the power of speech | to stir men's blood; 3.02.222
nor with such free and friendly conference, | as 4.02. 17
nor nothing in your letters writ of her? 4.03.183
nor i, my lord. 4.03.305
nev'r shook hands, nor bade farewell to him, MAC 1.02. 21
nor would we deign him burial of his men | till 1.02. 60
sleep shall neither night nor day | hang upon 1.03. 19
who neither beg nor fear | your favors nor your 1.03. 60
beg nor fear | your favors nor your hate. 1.03. 61
nor must be known | no less to have done so, let 1.04. 30
nor keep peace between | th' effect and /it! 1.05. 46
nor heaven peep through the blanket of the dark 1.05. 53
buttress, nor coign of vantage, but this bird 1.06. 7
nor time, nor place, | did then adhere, and yet 1.07. 51
nor time, nor place, | did then adhere, and yet 1.07. 51
tongue nor heart | cannot conceive nor name thee 2.03. 64
nor heart | cannot conceive nor name thee! 2.03. 65
nor our strong sorrow | upon the foot of motion. 2.03.124
to leave no rubs nor botches in the work — 3.01.133
nor steel, nor poison, | malice domestic, 3.02. 24
nor steel, nor poison, | malice domestic, 3.02. 24
poor bird, thou'dst never fear the net nor lime, 4.02. 34
the net nor lime, | the pitfall nor the gin. 4.02. 35
neither to you nor any one, having no witness to 5.01. 17 P
shall never sag with doubt, nor shake with fear. 5.03. 10
there is nor flying hence, nor tarrying here. 5.05. 47
there is nor flying hence, nor tarrying here. 5.05. 47
no; nor more fearful. 5.07. 9
no fairy takes, nor witch hath power to charm, HAM 1.01.163
nor have we herein barr'd | your better wisdoms, 1.02. 14
mother, | nor customary suits of solemn black, 1.02. 78
black, | nor windy suspiration of forc'd breath, 1.02. 79
breath, | no, nor the fruitful river in the eye, 1.02. 80
eye, | nor the dejected havior of the visage, 1.02. 81
it is not, nor it cannot come to good, | but 1.02.158
say so, | nor shall you do my ear that violence, 1.02.171
and now no soil nor cautel doth besmirch | the 1.03. 15
nor any unproportion'd thought his act. 1.03. 60
neither a borrower nor a lender /be, | for /loan 1.03. 75
nor let thy soul contrive | against thy mother 1.05. 85
nor i, my lord. 1.05.120
nor i, my lord, in faith. 1.05.146
it, | sith nor th' exterior nor the inward man 2.02. 6
it, | sith nor th' exterior nor the inward man 2.02. 6
nor the soles of her shoe? 2.02.230 P
man delights not me — nor women neither, though 2.02.309 P
cannot be too heavy, nor plautus too light, for 2.02.400 P
nor no matter in the phrase that might indict 2.02.442 P
nor do we find him forward to be sounded, | but 3.01. 7
nor what he spake, though it lack'd form a 3.01.163
nor do not saw the air too much with your hand, 3.02. 4 P
accent of christians nor the gait of christian, 3.02. 31 P
pagan, nor man, have so strutted and bellow'd 3.02. 32 P
no, nor mine now. 3.02. 98 P
aye, nor 'tis not strange | that even our loves 3.02.200
nor earth to me give food, nor heaven light, 3.02.216
nor earth to me give food, nor heaven light, 3.02.216
nor stands it safe with us | to let his madness 3.03. 1
nor sense to ecstasy was ne'er so thrall'd | but 3.04. 74
nor did you nothing hear? 3.04.133
nor will it yield to norway or the pole | a 4.04. 21
no trophy, sword, nor hatchment o'er his bones, 4.05.215
bones, | no noble rite nor formal ostentation — 4.05.216
he swore had neither motion, guard, nor eye, 4.07.101
death come not upon thee, | nor thine on me! 5.02.331
according to my bond, no more nor less. LR 1.01. 93
nor are those empty–hearted whose low sounds 1.01.153
which nor our nature nor our place can bear, 1.01.171
which nor our nature nor our place can bear, 1.01.171
highness offer'd, | nor will you tender less. 1.01.195
nor shall ever see | that face of hers again. 1.01.263
no displeasure in him by word nor countenance? 1.02.157 P
nor so old to dote on her for any thing. 1.04. 38 P
nor tripp'd neither, you base football player. 1.04. 86 P
he that keeps nor crust /nor crumb, | weary of 1.04.198
not scape censure, nor the redresses sleep, 1.04.210
nor i neither; 1.05. 27 P
nor i, assure thee, regan. 2.01.104
that is neither known of thee nor knows thee? 2.02. 26 P
more, perchance, does mine, nor his, nor hers. 2.02. 91
more, perchance, does mine, nor his, nor hers. 2.02. 91
well knows, | will not be rubb'd nor stopp'd. 2.02.154
nor tell tales of thee to high–judging jove. 2.04.228
you yet, nor am provided | for your fit welcome. 2.04.232
a night pities neither wise men nor fools. 3.02. 13 P
nor rain, wind, thunder, fire are my daughters. 3.02. 15
cannot carry | th' affliction nor the fear. 3.02. 49
no squire in debt, nor no poor knight; 3.02. 88
nor cutpurses come not to throngs; 3.02. 90
the creaking of shoes nor the rustling of silks 3.04. 95 P
nor thy fierce sister | in his anointed flesh 3.07. 57
the fitchew nor the soiled horse goes to't 4.06.122
eyes in your head, nor no money in your purse? 4.06.146 P
the modest truth, | nor more nor clipt, but so. 4.07. 6
the modest truth, | nor more nor clipt, but so. 4.07. 6
fourscore and upward, not an hour more nor less; 4.07. 60
nor i know not | where i did lodge last night. 4.07. 66
nor in thine, lord. 5.03. 80
nor no man else. 5.03.291
shall never see so much, nor live so long. 5.03.327
nor the division of a battle knows | more than a OTH 1.01. 23
nor all masters | cannot be truly follow'd. 1.01. 43
transported with no worse nor better guard | but 1.01.124
it seems not meet, nor wholesome to my place, 1.01.145
neither my place, nor aught i heard of business, 1.03. 53
nor doth the general care | take hold on me; 1.03. 54
nor i. 1.03.241
nor /i; 1.03.241
nor to comply with heat (the young affects | in 1.03.263
put money in thy purse — nor he his to her. 1.03.343 P
nor know i aught | but that he's well and will 2.01. 89
to the general, nor any man of quality — i hope 2.03.107 P
nor know i aught | by me that's said or done 2.03.200
nor build yourself a trouble | out of his 3.03.150
it were not for your quiet nor your good, | nor 3.03.152
nor for my manhood, honesty, and wisdom, | to 3.03.153
nor shall not, whilst 'tis in my custody. 3.03.164
nor from mine own weak merits will i draw | the 3.03.187
wear your eyes thus, not jealious nor secure. 3.03.198
speech | to grosser issues nor to larger reach 3.03.219
not poppy, nor mandragora, | nor all the drowsy 3.03.330
nor all the drowsy syrups of the world | shall 3.03.331
that the probation bear no hinge nor loop | to 3.03.365
it /yet hath felt no age nor known no sorrow. 3.04. 37
of such mortal kind | that nor my service past, 3.04.116
that nor my service past, nor present sorrows, 3.04.116
sorrows, | nor purpos'd merit in futurity, | can 3.04.117
nor should i know him | were he in favor as in 3.04.124
nor of them look for such observancy | as fits 3.04.149
think, | and no conception nor no jealious toy 3.04.156
and think it no addition, nor my wish, | to have 3.04.194
virtue | the shot of accident nor dart of chance 4.01.267
dart of chance | could neither graze nor pierce? 4.01.268
nor ever heard — nor ever did suspect. 4.02. 2
nor ever heard — nor ever did suspect. 4.02. 2
nor send you out o' th' way? 4.02. 7
her fan, her gloves, her mask, nor nothing? 4.02. 9
nor answers have i none | but what should go by 4.02.103
nor am i yet persuaded to put up in peace what 4.02.179 P
i cannot go to, man, nor 'tis not very well. 4.02.192 P
'tis neither here nor there. 4.03. 59
nor i neither by this heavenly light; 4.03. 66
for a joint–ring, nor for measures of lawn, nor 4.03. 73 P
nor for measures of lawn, nor for gowns, 4.03. 73 P
petticoats, nor caps, nor any petty exhibition; 4.03. 74 P
petticoats, nor caps, nor any petty exhibition; 4.03. 74 P
none in the world; nor do i know the man. 5.01.103
nor scar that whiter skin of hers than snow, 5.02. 4
cannot remove nor choke the strong conception 5.02. 55
extenuate, | nor set down aught in malice. 5.02.343
nor the queen of ptolomy | more womanly than he; ANT 1.04. 6
of hot and cold, he was nor sad nor merry. 1.05. 52
of hot and cold, he was nor sad nor merry. 1.05. 52
he neither loves, | nor either cares for him. 2.01. 16
terms, | nor curstness grow to th' matter. 2.02. 25
my greatness, nor my power | work without it. 2.02. 93
her, nor custom stale | her infinite variety. 2.02.234
i had never come from thence, nor you thither. 2.03. 11 P
nor what i have done by water. 2.06. 90 P
heart, nor can | her heart inform her tongue — 3.02. 47
nor must not then be yielded to in this. 3.06. 38
you have not call'd me so, nor have you cause. 3.06. 41
look not sad, | nor make replies of loathness; 3.11. 18
the queen | of audience nor desire shall fail, 3.12. 21
nor i. 4.14.109
nor any one. 4.14.110
change now at my end | lament nor sorrow at; 4.15. 52
nor by a hired knife, but that self hand | which 5.01. 21
nor once be chastis'd with the sober eye | of 5.02. 54
but if there be, nor ever were one such, | it's 5.02. 96
what you have reserv'd, nor what acknowledg'd, 5.02.180
most precious diamond that is, nor you the lady. CYM 1.04. 76 P
return he cannot, nor | continue where he is. 1.05. 53
nor has no friends | so much as but to prop him? 1.05. 59
nor i' th' judgment: 1.06. 41
nor i' th' appetite: 1.06. 43
no, my lord; nor crop the ears of them. 2.01. 12 P
nor the voice of unpav'd eunuch to boot, can 2.03. 30 P
(statist though i am none, nor like to be) 2.04. 16
nor here, /nor here, | nor what ensues, but have 3.02. 78
nor what ensues, but have a fog in them | that i 3.02. 79
th' nest, nor /know not | what air's from home. 3.03. 28
nor cymbeline dreams that they are alive. 3.03. 81
no greater wound, | nor tent to bottom that. 3.04.115
no father, nor no more ado | with that harsh, 3.04.131
i will never fail | beginning nor supplyment. 3.04.179
nor to us hath tender'd | the duty of the day. 3.05. 31
my means for thy relief nor my voice for thy 3.05.115 P
i have stol'n nought, nor would not, though i 3.06. 48
nor measure our good minds | by this rude place 3.06. 64
no, nor thy tailor, rascal, | who is thy 4.02. 81
nor seek for danger | where there's no profit. 4.02.162
pale primrose, nor | the azur'd harebell, like 4.02.221
no, nor | the leaf of eglantine, whom not to 4.02.222
o' th' sun, | nor the furious winter's rages, 4.02.259
nor th' all–dreaded thunder–stone. 4.02.271
nor no witchcraft charm thee! 4.02.277
why gone, | nor when she purposes return. 4.03. 15
nor hear i from my mistress, who did promise 4.03. 38
time nothing becoming you, | nor satisfying us. 4.04. 16
hath not deserv'd my service nor your loves, 4.04. 25
who ne'er wore rowel | nor iron on his heel! 4.04. 40
pitied nor hated, to the face of peril | myself 5.01. 28
hear him groan, | nor feel him where he strook. 5.03. 70
which neither here i'll keep nor bear again, 5.03. 82
further to boast were neither true nor modest, 5.05. 18
ears, that /heard her flattery, nor my heart, 5.05. 64
her son | is gone, we know not how, nor where. 5.05.273
but nor the time nor place | will serve our long 5.05.391
but nor the time nor place | will serve our long 5.05.391
nor ask advice of any other thought | but PER 1.01. 62
nor tell the world antiochus doth sin | in such 1.01.146
nor yet the other's distance comfort me. 1.02. 10
nor boots it me to say i honor /him, | if he 1.02. 20
nor come we to add sorrow to your tears, | but 1.04. 90
have neither in our hearts nor outward eyes 2.03. 25
/envied the great, nor shall the low despise. 2.03. 26
or never more to view nor day nor light. 2.05. 17
or never more to view nor day nor light. 2.05. 17
nor never did my actions yet commence | a deed 2.05. 53
i know, | may be (nor can i think the contrary) 2.05. 79
nor have i time | to give thee hallow'd to thy 3.01. 58
/lone bosom | inflame too nicely, nor let pity, 4.01. 6
never was waves nor wind more violent, | and 4.01. 59
word, nor did ill turn | to any living creature. 4.01. 75
law, | i never kill'd a mouse, nor hurt a fly; 4.01. 77
nor the commodity wages not with the danger; 4.02. 31 P
dead, | nor none can know, leonine being gone. 4.03. 30
never to wash his face, nor cut his hairs; 4.04. 28
no, nor never shall do in such a place as this, 4.05. 2 P
nor taken sustenance | but to prorogue his grief 5.01. 25
no, nor look'd on us. 5.01. 80
no, nor of any /shores, | yet i was mortally 5.01.103
the sland'rous cuckoo, nor | the boding raven, TNK 1.01. 19
nor | the boding raven, nor /chough /hoar, | nor 1.01. 20
raven, nor /chough /hoar, | nor chatt'ring pie, 1.01. 21
their ashes, nor to take th' offense | of mortal 1.01. 44
your tresses, | nor in more bounty spread her. 1.01. 64
wreath | was then nor thresh'd nor blasted; 1.01. 65
wreath | was then nor thresh'd nor blasted; 1.01. 65
who cannot feel nor see the rain, being in't, 1.01.120
rain, being in't, | knows neither wet nor dry. 1.01.121
thing, nor be so hardy | ever to take a husband. 1.01.204
execution, where nor gain | made him regard, or 1.03. 29
like the elements | that know not what nor why, 1.03. 62
nor in a state of life; 1.04. 25
none here, nor the seas | swallow their youth. 2.02. 87
that nature nev'r exceeded nor nev'r shall. 2.03. 12
to your travel, | nor shall you lose your wish. 2.05. 31
nor scarcely | could i persuade him to become a 2.06. 23
a chaffy lord, | nor worth the name of villain! 3.01. 42
nor none so honest, arcite. 3.03. 4
if he fail, | he's neither man nor soldier. 3.06. 4
you outwent me, | nor could my wishes reach you. 3.06. 80
nor put off | this great adventure to a second 3.06.118
sister, | i find no anger to 'em, nor no ruin: 3.06.189
nor shall he grudge to fall, | nor think he dies 3.06.297
nor think he dies with interest in this lady. 3.06.298
judge by the outside) | i never saw nor read of. 4.02. 75
he does no wrongs, | nor takes none. 4.02.135
nor would the libels read | of liberal wits. 5.01.101
nor names concealments in | the boldest language 5.01.123
nor diff'ring plunges | disroot his rider whence 5.04. 74
like as if that god | owed not nor made not you, STM II.C 136
nor that the elements | were not all appropriate II.C 136
o, be not proud, nor brag not of thy might, VEN 113

never can blab, nor know not what we mean. 126
know not love," quoth he, "nor will not know it, 409
though neither eyes nor ears to hear nor see, 437
though neither eyes nor ears to hear nor see, 437
and that i could not see, nor hear, nor touch, 440
and that i could not see, nor hear, nor touch, 440
nor thy soft hands, sweet lips, and crystal eyne 633
"bonnet nor veil henceforth no creature wear! 1081
nor sun nor wind will ever strive to kiss you: 1082
nor sun nor wind will ever strive to kiss you: 1082
but king nor peer to such a peerless dame. LUC 21
nor read the subtle shining secrecies | writ in 101
touch'd no unknown baits, nor fear'd no hooks, 103
nor could she moralize his wanton sight, | more 104
and extreme fear can neither fight nor fly, 230
the shame and fault finds no excuse nor end. 238
nor children's tears nor mothers' groans 431
nor children's tears nor mothers' groans 431
right, | nor aught obeys but his foul appetite. 546
"nor shall he smile at thee in secret thought, 1065
nor laugh with his companions at thy state, 1066
nor fold my fault in cleanly coin'd excuses; 1073
grief dallied with nor law nor limit knows. 1120
grief dallied with nor law nor limit knows. 1120
my restless discord loves no stops nor rests; 1124
that knows not parching heat nor freezing cold, 1145
nor why her fair cheeks over-wash'd with woe. 1225
cheeks neither red nor pale, but mingled so 1510
nor ashy pale the fear that false hearts have. 1512
mild as a dove, but neither true nor trusty, PP 7. 2
none fairer, nor none falser to deface her. 7. 6
and would not take her meaning nor her pleasure. 11.12
wiser head, | neither too young nor yet unwed. 18. 6
double name | neither two nor one was called. PHT 40
bereft, | nor it nor no remembrance what it was: SON 5.12
bereft, | nor it nor no remembrance what it was: 5.12
nor can i fortune to brief minutes tell, 14. 5
neither in inward worth nor outward fair | can 16.11
nor lose possession of that fair thou ow'st, 18.10
nor shall death brag thou wand'rest in his shade 18.11
nor draw no lines there with thine antique pen; 19.10
where i may not remove, nor be removed. 25.14
nor can thy shame give physic to my grief, 34. 9
shame, | nor thou with public kindness honor me, 36.11
so then i am not lame, poor, nor despis'd, 37. 9
not marble nor the gilded /monuments | of 55. 1
nor mars his sword nor war's quick fire shall 55. 7
nor mars his sword nor war's quick fire shall 55. 7
spend, | nor services to do, till you require. 57. 4
nor dare i chide the world-without-end hour, 57. 5
you, | nor think the bitterness of absence sour, 57. 7
nor dare i question with my jealious thought 57. 9
since brass, nor stone, nor earth, nor boundless 65. 1
brass, nor stone, nor earth, nor boundless sea, 65. 1
brass, nor stone, nor earth, nor boundless sea, 65. 1
nor gates of steel so strong, but time decays? 65. 8
is, | and live no more to shame nor me nor you. 72.12
is, | and live no more to shame nor me nor you. 72.12
he, nor his compeers by night | giving him aid, 86. 7
nor that affable familiar ghost | which nightly 86. 9
yet nor the lays of birds, nor the sweet smell 98. 5
nor the sweet smell | of different flowers in 98. 5
nor did i wonder at the lily's white, | nor 98. 9
nor praise the deep vermilion in the rose, 98.10
a third, nor red nor white, had stol'n of both, 99.10
a third, nor red nor white, had stol'n of both, 99.10
idolatry, | nor my beloved as an idol show, 105. 2
nor the prophetic soul | of the wide world, 107. 1
of age, | nor gives to necessary wrinkles place, 108.11
nor double penance, to correct correction. 111.12
none else to me, nor i to none alive, | that my 112. 7
nor his own vision holds what it doth catch; 113. 8
proved, | i never writ, nor no man ever loved. 116.14
nor need i tallies thy dear love to score; 122.10
not wond'ring at the present, nor the past, 123.10
pomp, nor falls | under the blow of thralled 124. 6
that it nor grows with heat nor drowns with 124.12
it nor grows with heat nor drowns with show'rs. 124.12
nor that full star that ushers in the even 132. 7
but thou wilt not, nor he will not be free, 134. 5
that i may not be so, nor thou belied, | bear 140.13
nor are mine ears with thy tongue's tune 141. 5
nor tender feeling to base touches prone, | nor 141. 6
nor taste, nor smell, desire to be invited | to 141. 7
nor taste, nor smell, desire to be invited | to 141. 7
but my five wits nor my five senses can 141. 9
nor youth all quit, but, spite of heaven's fell LC 13
her hair, nor loose nor tied in formal plat, 29
her hair, nor loose nor tied in formal plat, 29
did, | demand of him, nor being desired yielded; 149
"nor gives it satisfaction to our blood | that 162
till now did ne'er invite, nor never vow. 182
be, | where neither party is nor true nor kind: 186
be, | where neither party is nor true nor kind: 186
vow, bond, nor space, | in thee hath neither 264
in thee hath neither sting, knot, nor confine, 265

NORBERY 1 FR 0.0001 REL FR 1 V 0 P
sir john norbery, sir robert waterton, and R2 2.01.284

NORFOLK 45 FR 0.0050 REL FR 44 V 1 P
against the duke of norfolk, thomas mowbray? R2 1.01. 6
dost thou object | against the duke of norfolk, 1.01. 29
thomas of norfolk, what say'st thou to this? 1.01.110
we'll calm the duke of norfolk, you your son. 1.01.159
and, norfolk, throw down his. 1.01.162
norfolk, throw down, we bid, there is no boot. 1.01.164
the duke of norfolk, sprightfully and bold, 1.03. 3
my name is thomas mowbray, duke of norfolk, 1.03. 16
in lists, on thomas mowbray, duke of norfolk, 1.03. 38
go bear this lance to thomas duke of norfolk. 1.03.103
to prove the duke of norfolk, thomas mowbray, 1.03.107
here standeth thomas mowbray, duke of norfolk, 1.03.110
norfolk, for thee remains a heavier doom, 1.03.148
norfolk, so fare as to mine enemy: 1.03.193
i heard the banished norfolk say | that thou, 4.01. 80
that norfolk lies, here do i throw down this, 4.01. 84
all rest under gage | till norfolk be repeal'd. 4.01. 87
many a time hath banish'd norfolk fought | for 4.01. 92
why, bishop, is norfolk dead? 4.01.101
and page to thomas mowbray, duke of norfolk. 2H4 3.02. 26 P
thanks, gentle norfolk. 3H6 1.01. 31
'tis not thy southern power | of essex, norfolk, 1.01.156
and i to norfolk with my followers. 1.01.208
thou, richard, shalt to the duke of norfolk, 1.02. 38
lord george your brother, norfolk, and myself, 2.01.138
where is the duke of norfolk, gentle warwick? 2.01.142
now, if the help of norfolk and myself, | with 2.01.178
the duke of norfolk sends you word by me | the 2.01.206
shalt stir up in suffolk, norfolk, and in kent, 4.08. 12
lately attendant on the duke of norfolk. R3 2.01.102
light-foot friend post to the duke of norfolk; 4.04.440
my lord of norfolk — 5.03. 4
norfolk, we must have knocks. ha, must we not? 5.03. 5
good norfolk, hie thee to thy charge, | use 5.03. 53
stir with the lark to-morrow, gentle norfolk. 5.03. 56
john duke of norfolk, thomas earl of surrey, 5.03.296
what think'st thou, norfolk? 5.03.301
"jockey of norfolk, be not so bold, | for dickon 5.03.304
rescue, my lord of norfolk, rescue, rescue! 5.04. 1
john duke of norfolk, walter lord /ferrers, 5.05. 13
my lord of norfolk, as you are truly noble, | as H8 3.02.289
next, the duke of norfolk, | he to be earl 4.01. 18
and that my lord of norfolk? 4.01. 42
is that old noble lady, duchess of norfolk. 4.01. 52
the old duchess of norfolk | and lady marquess 5.02.202

/NORFOLK'S 1 FR 0.0001 REL FR 1 V 0 P
/to /all /the /duke /of /norfolk's /signories, 2H4 4.01.109

NORFOLK'S 1 FR 0.0001 REL FR 1 V 0 P
throw down, my son, the duke of norfolk's gage. R2 1.01.161

NORMAN 3 FR 0.0003 REL FR 3 V 0 P
normans, but bastard normans, norman bastards! H5 3.05. 10
a norman, was't? HAM 4.07. 90
a norman. 4.07. 91

NORMANDY 7 FR 0.0008 REL FR 6 V 1 P
solemnized | in normandy, saw i this longaville, LLL 2.01. 43
receiv'd deep scars in france and normandy? 2H6 1.01. 87
all, | these counties were the keys of normandy. 1.01.114
the state of normandy | stands on a tickle point 1.01.215
majesty for giving up of normandy unto mounsieur 4.07. 28 P
i sold not maine, i lost not normandy, | yet to 4.07. 65
months since | here was a gentleman of normandy: HAM 4.07. 82

NORMANS 3 FR 0.0003 REL FR 3 V 0 P
normans, but bastard normans, norman bastards! H5 3.05. 10
normans, but bastard normans, norman bastards! 3.05. 10
the false revolting normans thorough thee 2H6 4.01. 87

NORTH 38 FR 0.0043 REL FR 30 V 8 P
deep, | to run upon the sharp wind of the north, TMP 1.02.254
near her, she would infect to the north star. ADO 2.01.250 P
by east, west, north, and south, i spread my LLL 5.02.563
by the north pole, i do challenge thee. 5.02.693 P
now sail'd into the north of my lady's opinion, TN 3.02. 26 P
toward the south north are as lustrous as ebony; 4.02. 38 P
think it — | from east, west, north, and south. WT 1.02.203
i from the north. JN 2.01.411
from north to south — | austria and france 2.01.413
nor entreat the north | to make his bleak winds 5.07. 39
i towards the north, | where shivering cold and R2 5.01. 76
uneven and unwelcome news | came from the north, 1H4 1.01. 51
so honor cross it from the north to south, | and 1.03.196
yet of percy's mind, the hotspur of the north, 2.04.102 P
that same mad fellow of the north, percy, and he 2.04.336 P
methinks my moi'ty, north from burton here, | in 3.01. 95
and on this north side win this cape of land, 3.01.112
weak and wearied posts | come from the north, 2H4 2.04.357
take their courses | east, west, north, south, 4.02.104
i think at the north gate, for there stands 1H6 1.04. 66
during whose reign the percies of the north, 2.05. 67
under the lordly monarch of the north, | appear, 5.03. 6
at berwick in the north, and't like your grace. 2H6 2.01. 81
while we pursu'd the horsemen of the north, | he 3H6 1.01. 2
with all speed post with him toward the north, R3 3.02. 17
no, my good lord, my friends are in the north. 4.04.483
what do they in the north, | when they should 4.04.484
handsome, and of the best breed in the north. H8 2.02. 4 P
they would fly east, west, north, south, and COR 2.03. 22 P
upon the north side of this pleasant chase; TIT 2.03.255
woos | even now the frozen bosom of the north, ROM 1.04.101
up higher toward the north | he first presents JC 2.01.109
no, i will speak as liberal as the north: OTH 5.02.220
and like the tyrannous breathing of the north CYM 1.03. 36
the grisled north | disgorges such a tempest PER 3.ch. 47
when i was born, the wind was north. 4.01. 51
when the north comes near her, | rude and TNK 2.02.140
set it to th' north. 4.01.143

NORTHAMPTON 3 FR 0.0003 REL FR 3 V 0 P
northampton, and in leicestershire, shall find 3H6 4.08. 15
and at northampton they do rest to-night. R3 2.04. 2
stafford, and northampton, i | arrest thee of H8 1.01.200

NORTHAMPTONSHIRE 1 FR 0.0001 REL FR 1 V 0 P
born in northamptonshire, and eldest son, | as i JN 1.01. 51

NORTH-EAST 1 FR 0.0001 REL FR 1 V 0 P
by east and north-east to the king of pigmies, TNK 3.04. 15

NORTHEAST 1 FR 0.0001 REL FR 1 V 0 P
faith, none for me, except the northeast wind, R2 1.04. 6

NORTHEN *(also northern, northren)*

NORTHEN 1 FR 0.0001 REL FR 1 V 0 P
the angry northen wind | will blow these sands TIT 4.01.104

NORTHERLY 1 FR 0.0001 REL FR 0 V 1 P
me, 'tis very cold, the wind is northerly. HAM 5.02. 96 P

NORTHERN *(also northen, northren)*

NORTHERN 8 FR 0.0009 REL FR 8 V 0 P
bolted | by th' northern blasts twice o'er. WT 4.04.365
and shortly mean to touch our northern shore. R2 2.01.288
and all your northern castles yielded up, | and 3.02.201
proud northern lord, clifford of cumberland, 2H6 5.02. 6
the northern lords that have forsworn thy colors 3H6 1.01.251
the queen with all the northern earls and lords 1.02. 49
but i am constant as the northern star, | of JC 3.01. 60
as lagging fowls before the northern blast. LUC 1335

NORTH-GATE 2 FR 0.0002 REL FR 1 V 1 P
him make haste and meet me at the north-gate. TGV 3.01.260
thy master stays for thee at the north-gate. 3.01.373 P

NORTH-NORTH-EAST 1 FR 0.0001 REL FR 0 V 1 P
it standeth north-north-east and by east from LLL 1.01.245 P

NORTH-NORTH-WEST 1 FR 0.0001 REL FR 0 V 1 P
i am but mad north-north-west. HAM 2.02.378 P

NORTHREN *(also northen, northern)*

NORTHREN 2 FR 0.0002 REL FR 1 V 1 P
will not fight with a pole like a northren man; LLL 5.02.695 P
that i shall make this northren youth exchange 1H4 3.02.145

/NORTHUMBERLAND 2 FR 0.0002 REL FR 2 V 0 P
/gentle /northumberland, | /if /thy /offenses R2 4.01.229
/urge /it /no /more, /my /lord /northumberland. 4.01.271

NORTHUMBERLAND 48 FR 0.0054 REL FR 45 V 3 P
be confident to speak, northumberland: R2 2.01.274
the lord northumberland, his son young harry 2.02. 53
why have you not proclaim'd northumberland | and 2.02. 56
my lord northumberland, see them dispatch'd. 3.01. 35
it would beseem the lord northumberland | to say 3.03. 7
northumberland, say thus the king returns: 3.03.121
shall we call back northumberland, and send 3.03.129
northumberland comes back from bullingbrook. 3.03.142
most mighty prince, my lord northumberland, 3.03.172
northumberland, thou ladder wherewithal | the 5.01. 55
part us, northumberland: 5.01. 76
in envy that my lord northumberland | should be 1H4 1.01. 79
my lord northumberland: 1.03.122
his son-in-law mortimer, and old northumberland, 2.04.342 P
percy, northumberland, | the archbishop's grace 3.02.118
perceiv'd northumberland did lean to him, | the 4.03. 67
what with the sickness of northumberland, 4.04. 14
to meet northumberland and the prelate scroop, 5.05. 37
/where hotspur's father, old northumberland, 2H4 in 36
to frown upon th' enrag'd northumberland! 1.01.152
the archbishop and the earl of northumberland. 1.02.205 P
largely in the hope | of great northumberland, 1.03. 13
may hold up head without northumberland? 1.03. 17
against northumberland and the archbishop. 2.01.175
my lord northumberland will soon be cool'd. 3.01. 44
years gone | since richard and northumberland, 3.01. 58
then check'd and rated by northumberland, | did 3.01. 68
"northumberland, thou ladder by the which | my 3.01. 70
a perfect guess | that great northumberland, 3.01. 89
they say the bishop and northumberland | are 3.01. 95
new-dated letters from northumberland, | their 4.01. 8
the earl northumberland and the lord bardolph, 4.04. 97
sir thomas grey, knight, of northumberland, H5 2.pr. 25
grey of northumberland, this same is yours: 2.02. 68
name of thomas grey, knight, of northumberland. 2.02.150 P
whereat the great lord of northumberland, 3H6 1.01. 4
earl of northumberland, he slew thy father, 1.01. 54
come, bloody clifford, rough northumberland, | i 1.04. 27
speak thou, northumberland. 1.04. 53
brave warriors, clifford and northumberland, 1.04. 66
what, weeping-ripe, my lord northumberland? 1.04.172
with clifford and the haught northumberland, 2.01.169
northumberland, i hold thee reverently. 2.02.109
northumberland, then present, wept to see it. R3 1.03.186
saw'st thou the melancholy lord northumberland? 5.03. 68
what said northumberland as touching richmond? 5.03.271
for after the stout earl northumberland H8 4.02. 12
aid | to wake northumberland and warlike siward, MAC 3.06. 31

NORTHUMBERLAND'S 1 FR 0.0001 REL FR 1 V 0 P
from clifford's and northumberland's pursuit. 3H6 2.01. 3

NORTHUMBERLANDS 1 FR 0.0001 REL FR 1 V 0 P
son, | and two northumberlands — two braver men 3H6 5.07. 8

NORTHWARD 3 FR 0.0003 REL FR 3 V 0 P
bring me the fairest creature northward born, MV 2.01. 4
the remnant northward lying off from trent. 1H4 3.01. 78
threw many a northward look to see his father 2H4 2.03. 13

NORWAY 14 FR 0.0015 REL FR 14 V 0 P
norway himself, with terrible numbers, MAC 1.02. 51
whether he was combin'd | with those of norway, 1.03.112
had on | when he the ambitious norway combated. HAM 1.01. 61
us, | was, as you know, by fortinbras of norway, 1.01. 82
hath in the skirts of norway here and there 1.01. 97
we have here writ | to norway, uncle of young 1.02. 28
for bearers of this greeting to old norway, 1.02. 35
th' embassadors from norway, my good lord, | are 2.02. 40
say, voltemand, what from our brother norway? 2.02. 59
receives rebuke from norway, and, in fine, 2.02. 69
whereon old norway, overcome with joy, | gives 2.02. 72
they are of norway, sir. 4.04. 10
the nephew to old norway, fortinbras. 4.04. 14
nor will it yield to norway or the pole | a 4.04. 21

NORWAYS' 1 FR 0.0001 REL FR 1 V 0 P
that now | sweno, the norways' king, craves MAC 1.02. 59

NORWEYAN 3 FR 0.0003 REL FR 3 V 0 P
but the norweyan lord, surveying vantage, | with MAC 1.02. 31
where the norweyan banners flout the sky | and 1.02. 49
he finds thee in the stout norweyan ranks, 1.03. 95

NOSE 67 FR 0.0075 REL FR 32 V 35 P
at which my nose is in great indignation. TMP 4.01.200 P
as a nose on a man's face, or a weathercock on a TGV 2.01.136
dead, | and liberty plucks justice by the nose; MM 1.03. 29
that thus can make him bite the law by th' nose, 3.01.108
not i pluck thee by the nose for thy speeches? 5.01.340 P
o, sir, upon her nose, all o'er embellish'd with ERR 3.02.134 P
armadoes of carrects to be ballast at her nose. 3.02.137 P
sometime through /the nose, as if you snuff'd up LLL 3.01. 16 P
your nose says, no, you are not; 5.02.565
your nose smells "no" in /this, most 5.02.566
the snow | and marian's nose looks red and raw; 5.02.924
these lily lips, | this cherry nose, | these MND 5.01.331
not for nothing that my nose fell a-bleeding on MV 2.05. 24 P
and others, when the bagpipe sings i' th' nose, 4.01. 49
cours'd one another down his innocent nose | in AYL 2.01. 39
with spectacles on nose and pouch on side, | his 2.07.159
i'll slit the villain's nose, that would have SHR 5.01.131 P
best set thy lower part where thy nose stands. AWW 2.03.252 P
nay, you need not to stop your nose, sir; 5.02. 10 P
if your metaphor stink, i will stop my nose, or 5.02. 13 P
for malvolio's nose is no whipstock. TN 2.03. 27 P
to hear by the nose, it is dulcet in contagion. 2.03. 56 P
i have't in my nose too. 2.03.163 P

master cesario, nor this is not my nose neither: 4.01. 8 P
/hast smutch'd thy nose? WT 1.02.121
i have seen a lady's nose | that has been blue, 2.01. 14
with a sense as cold | as is a dead man's nose; 2.01.152
and copy of the father — eye, nose, lip, | the 2.03.100
a good nose is requisite also, to smell out work 4.04.672 P
receives not thy nose court–odor from me? 4.04.733 P
bear, yet he is oft led by the nose with gold. 4.04.802 P
anon | he gave his nose and took't away again, 1H4 1.03. 39
in the poop, but 'tis in the nose of thee. 3.03. 26 P
let them coin his nose, let them coin his cheeks 3.03. 78 P
whose zeal burns in his nose, of the wicked? 2H4 2.04.330 P
for his nose was as sharp as a pen, and 'a H5 2.03. 16 P
'a saw a flea stick upon bardolph's nose, and 'a 2.03. 41 P
and his lips blows at his nose, and it is like a 3.06.104 P
and sometimes red, but his nose is executed, and 3.06.105 P
rear up his body, wring him by the nose. 2H6 3.02. 34
but when the fox hath once got in his nose, 3H6 4.07. 25
there be moe wasps that buzz about his nose H8 3.02. 55
twenty of the dog–days now reign in 's nose; 5.03. 42 P
three times was his nose discharg'd against me; 5.03. 45 P
tongue had commended troilus for a copper nose. TRO 1.02.106 P
in love, i' faith, to the very tip of the nose. 3.01.127 P
for that i have not wash'd | my nose that bled, COR 1.09. 48
leave unburnt | and still to nose th' offense. 5.01. 28
and borne her cleanly by the keeper's nose? TIT 2.01. 94
sometime she gallops o'er a courtier's nose, ROM 1.04. 77
tickling a parson's nose as 'a lies asleep, 1.04. 80
down with the nose, | down with it flat; TIM 4.03.157
eclipse, | nose of turk and tartar's lips, MAC 4.01. 29
tweaks me by the nose, gives me the lie i' th' HAM 2.02.574
you shall nose him as you go up the stairs into 4.03. 36 P
canst tell why one's nose stands i' th' middle LR 1.05. 19 P
to keep one's eyes of either side 's nose, that 1.05. 22 P
men, and there's not a nose among twenty but can 2.04. 70 P
and will as tenderly be led by th' nose | as OTH 1.03.401
in naples, that they speak i' th' nose thus? 3.01. 4 P
o, i see that nose of yours, but not that dog i 4.01.142 P
heaven stops the nose at it, and the moon winks; 4.02. 77
not in my husband's nose. ANT 1.02. 61 P
against the blown rose may they stop their nose 3.13. 39
his nose stands high, a character of honor; TNK 4.02.110
he wrings her nose, he strikes her on the cheeks VEN 475
his nose being shadowed by his neighbor's ear; LUC 1416

NOSEGAY 1 FR 0.0001 REL FR 0 V 1 P
then will i make palamon a nosegay, then let him TNK 4.03. 26 P

NOSEGAYS 2 FR 0.0002 REL FR 1 V 1 P
knacks, trifles, nosegays, sweetmeats — MND 1.01. 34
me four and twenty nosegays for the shearers WT 4.03. 41 P

NOSE–HERBS 1 FR 0.0001 REL FR 0 V 1 P
are not herbs, you knave, they are nose–herbs. AWW 4.05. 19 P

NOSELESS 1 FR 0.0001 REL FR 1 V 0 P
that noseless, handless, hack'd and chipp'd, TRO 5.05. 34

NOSE–PAINTING 1 FR 0.0001 REL FR 0 V 1 P
marry, sir, nose–painting, sleep, and urine. MAC 2.03. 28 P

NOSES 14 FR 0.0015 REL FR 9 V 5 P
lifted up their noses | as they smelt music. TMP 4.01.177
to have had our two noses snapp'd off with two ADO 5.01.115 P
is meeting noses? WT 1.02.285
damask roses, | masks for faces and for noses; 4.04.221
we must have bloody noses and crack'd crowns, 1H4 2.03. 93
and to tickle our noses with speargrass to make 2.04.309 P
directly | their very noses had been councillors H8 1.03. 9
to see your wives dishonor'd to your noses — COR 4.06. 83
atomi | over men's noses as they lie asleep. ROM 1.04. 58
all that follow their noses are led by their LR 2.04. 69 P
he had a thousand noses, | horns welk'd and 4.06. 70
noses, ears, and lips. OTH 4.01. 42 P
we will nothing pay | for wearing our own noses. CYM 3.01. 14
other of them may have crook'd noses, but to owe 3.01. 37 P

NOSTER 1 FR 0.0001 REL FR 0 V 1 P
praeclarissimus filius noster henricus, rex H5 5.02.341 P

NOSTRA 1 FR 0.0001 REL FR 0 V 1 P
alla nostra casa ben venuto, molto honorato SHR 1.02. 25 P

NOSTRIL 5 FR 0.0005 REL FR 4 V 1 P
of villainous smell that ever offended nostril. WIV 3.05. 93 P
to | a savor that may strike the dullest nostril WT 1.02.421
now set the teeth and stretch the nostril wide, H5 3.01. 15
as ever hit my nostril. PER 3.02. 62
breast, full eye, small head, and nostril wide, VEN 296

NOSTRILS 4 FR 0.0004 REL FR 3 V 1 P
so again while stephano breathes at' nostrils. TMP 2.02. 63 P
his nostrils stretch'd with struggling; 2H6 3.02.171
let our crooked smokes climb to their nostrils CYM 5.05.477
his nostrils drink the air, and forth again | as VEN 273

NOT *(also no)*

/NOT 88 FR 0.0099 REL FR 71 V 17 P

NOT 8992 FR 1.0164 REL FR 6731 V 2261 P

NOTABLE 14 FR 0.0015 REL FR 3 V 11 P
thou that my master is become a notable lover? TGV 2.05. 42 P
a notable lubber — as thou reportest him to be. 2.05. 45 P
we shall find this friar a notable fellow. MM 5.01.267 P
this faith, thou wilt prove a notable argument. ADO 1.01.256 P
him as my kinsman, he's a most notable coward, AWW 3.06. 9 P
him will my revenge find notable cause to work. TN 2.03.153 P
rascally sheep–biter come by some notable shame? 2.05. 5 P
it cannot but turn him into a notable contempt. 2.05.203 P
set upon aguecheek a notable report of valor, 3.04.192 P
notable pirate, thou salt–water thief! 5.01. 69
a notable passion of wonder appear'd in them; WT 5.02. 15 P
you depend upon a notable gentleman; TRO 3.01. 6 P
and notable scorns | that dwell in every region OTH 4.01. 82
o notable strumpet! 5.01. 78

NOTABLY 1 FR 0.0001 REL FR 0 V 1 P
so it is, truly, and very notably discharg'd. MND 5.01.360 P

NOTARY 2 FR 0.0002 REL FR 2 V 0 P
go with me to a notary, seal me there | your MV 1.03.144
dim register and notary of shame! LUC 765

NOTARY'S 1 FR 0.0001 REL FR 1 V 0 P
then meet me forthwith at the notary's; MV 1.03.172

NOTCH'D 1 FR 0.0001 REL FR 0 V 1 P
he scotch'd him and notch'd him like a carbinado COR 4.05.187 P

NOTE 162 FR 0.0183 REL FR 126 V 36 P
she that from naples | can have no note, unless TMP 2.01.248
though they are of monstrous shape, yet, note, 3.03. 31
give me a note, your ladyship can set. TGV 1.02. 78
to take a note of what i stand in need of, | to 2.07. 84
humor on me — that is the very note of it. WIV 1.01.168 P
of such places, and goes to them by his note. 4.02. 63 P
takes note of what is done, and like a prophet MM 2.02. 94
i have ta'en a due and wary note upon't. 4.01. 37
my lord hath sent you this note, and by me this 4.02.102 P
pray you take note of it; 5.01. 80
o, train me not, sweet mermaid, with thy note, ERR 3.02. 45
here's the note | how much your chain weighs to 4.01. 27
didst thou note the daughter of signior leonato? ADO 1.01.162 P
note this before my notes: 2.03. 54
there's not a note of mine that's worth the 2.03. 55
speaks — | note notes, forsooth, and nothing. 2.03. 57
the greatest note of it is his melancholy. 3.02. 54 P
why then take no note of him, but let him go, 3.03. 28 P
that when i note another man like him | i may 5.01.260
up your eyelids, sigh a note and sing a note, LLL 3.01. 14 P
sigh a note and sing a note, sometime through 3.01. 14 P
and make them men of note — do you note? 3.01. 24 P
and make them men of note — do you note? 3.01. 25 P
would from my forehead wipe a perjur'd note: 4.03.123
folly in fools bears not so strong a note | as 5.02. 75
a merry note, | while greasy joan doth keel the 5.02.919
a merry note, | while greasy joan doth keel the 5.02.928
bill, | the throstle with his note so true, MND 3.01.127
grey, | whose note full many a man doth mark, 3.01.132
mine ear is much enamored of thy note; 3.01.138
song by rote, | to each word a warbling note. 5.01.398
but note me, signior. MV 1.03. 97
leave, | i come by note, to give and to receive. 3.02.140
for do but note a wild and wanton herd, | or 5.01. 71
no note at all of our being absent hence — 5.01.120
and turn his merry note | unto the sweet bird's AYL 2.05. 3
i'll give you a verse to this note, that i made 2.05. 46 P
'tis he. slink by, and note him. 3.02.252 P
in the ditty, yet the note was very untuneable. 5.03. 35 P
o, very well, i have perus'd the note. SHR 1.02.144
why, here is the note of the fashion to testify. 4.03.129 P
the note lies in 's throat if he say i said so. 4.03.132 P
no note upon my parents, his all noble. AWW 1.03.157
hath in't a bond | whereof the world takes note. 1.03.189
inclusive were | more than they were in note. 1.03.227
some precepts of this virgin | worthy the note. 3.05.101
answer to what i shall ask you out of a note. 4.03.127 P
mother, and his lady | offence of mighty note; 5.03. 14
eleven places — my niece shall take note of it, TN 3.02. 36 P
i did some service, of such note indeed, | that, 3.03. 27
in the habit of some sir of note, and so forth. 3.04. 73 P
a good note, that keeps you from the blow of the 3.04.153 P
whiles you are willing it shall come to note, 4.03. 29
that they may fairly note this act of mine! 4.03. 35
greatest promise that ever came into my note. WT 1.01. 36 P
the shepherd's note since we have left our 1.02. 2
didst note it? 1.02.214
a sigh (a note infallible | of breaking honesty) 1.02.287
a man, who hath a daughter of most rare note. 4.02. 42 P
dates, none — that's out of my note; 4.03. 46 P
sin, | for which the heavens, taking angry note, 5.01.173
o, what love i note | in the fair multitude of JN 3.04. 61
creatures of note for mercy–lacking uses. 4.01.120
but taking note of thy abhorr'd aspect, 4.02.224
once more, the more to aggravate the note, R2 1.01. 43
or to take note how many pair of silk stockings 2H4 2.02. 14 P
no, no, my lord, note this: 4.01.195
here is now the smith's note for shoeing and 5.01. 18 P
for we will hear, note, and believe in heart, H5 1.02. 30
the king hath note of all that they intend, | by 2.02. 6
rivets up, | give dreadful note of preparation. 4.pr. 14
upon his royal face there is no note | how dread 4.pr. 35
the tucket sonance and the note to mount; 4.02. 35
this note doth tell me of ten thousand french 4.08. 80
yourself, | i'll note you in my book of memory, 1H6 2.04.101
first note that he is near you in descent, | and 2H6 3.01. 21
came he right now to sing a raven's note, 3.02. 40
and give him from me this most needful note. R3 5.03. 41
/'a gives us note | the force of his own merit H8 1.01. 63
(whereof my sovereign would have note), they are 1.02. 48
please your highness note | this dangerous 1.02.138
what need you note it? 2.04.129
cause the musicians play me that sad note | i 4.02. 78
do you note | how much her grace is alter'd on 4.02. 95
mark him, note him. TRO 1.02.231 P
greater | than in the note of judgment; 2.03.125
rouse him and give him note of our approach, 4.01. 44
give with thy trumpet a loud note to troy, 4.05. 3
note me this, good friend: COR 1.01.127
which, without note, here's many else have done 1.09. 49
they have ta'en note of us; keep on your way. 4.02. 10
note but this fool. 4.02. 17
i have a note from the volscian state to find 4.03. 10 P
shall poison rather | than pity note how much. 5.02. 87
brother, see, note how she cotes the leaves. TIT 4.01. 50
what doth her beauty serve but as a note | where ROM 1.01.235
therefore be patient, take no note of him; 1.05. 71
do you note me? 4.05.119 P
and you re us and fa us, you note us. 4.05.120 P
my lord, here is a note of certain dues. TIM 2.02. 16
as i took note of the place, it cannot be far 5.01. 1
you | what hath proceeded worthy note to–day. JC 1.02.181
and take good note | what caesar doth, what 2.04. 14
ever note, lucilius, | when love begins to 4.02. 19
you must note beside | that we have tried the 4.03.213
run, | where never roman shall take note of him. 5.03. 50
there shall be done | a deed of dreadful note. MAC 3.02. 44
rest | that are within the note of expectation 3.03. 10
if much you note him, | you shall offend him and 3.04. 55
clatter, one of greatest note | seems bruited. 5.07. 21
as of a father, for, let the world take note, HAM 1.02.108
out, to note | that you know aught of me — this 1.05.178
give him heedful note, | for i mine eyes will 3.02. 84
i did very well note him. 3.02.290 P
sound me from my lowest note to /the /top /of my 3.02.367 P
this three years i have took note of it: 5.01.139 P
that all the kingdom | may have due note of him, LR 2.01. 83
and dare upon the warrant of my note | commend a 3.01. 18
therefore i do advise you take this note: 4.05. 29
take thou this note; 5.03. 27
note if your lady strain his entertainment OTH 3.03.250
take note, take note, o world, | to be direct 3.03.377
take note, take note, o world, | to be direct 3.03.377
take but good note, and you shall see in him ANT 1.01. 11
we'll wander through the streets and note | the 1.01. 53
note him, | note him, good charmian, 'tis the 1.05. 53
him, | note him, good charmian, 'tis the man; 1.05. 54
but note him: 1.05. 54
a lower place, note well, | may make too great 3.01. 12
three in egypt | cannot make better note. 3.03. 23
from which the world should note | something 3.13. 21
spirit of a youth | that means to be of note, 4.04. 27
he is of note. 4.09. 31
he was then of a crescent note, expected to CYM 1.04. 2 P
who has the note of them? 1.05. 2
"he is one of the noblest note, to whose 1.06. 22 P
to note the chamber, i will write all down: 2.02. 24
the precious note of it with a base slave, | a 2.03.122
be it lying, note it, | the woman's; 2.05. 22
report was once | first with the best of note. 3.03. 58
i do note | that grief and patience, rooted in 4.02. 56
use like note and words, | save that euriphile 4.02.237
even to the note o' th' king, or i'll fall in 4.03. 44
that they will waste their time upon our note, 4.04. 20
he brags his service | as if he were of note. 5.03. 94
note it not you, thaisa? PER 2.03. 57
first, i would have you note, this is an 4.06. 50 P
to find him so, that i may worthily note him. 4.06. 52 P
take some note | that for our crowned heads we TNK 1.01. 51
why, it was a note | whereon her spirits would 1.03. 76
i fix'd my note | constantly on them; 1.04. 19
she takes strong note of me, | hath made me near 3.01. 17
upon my mistress, | for note you, mine she is — 3.01.118
note her a little further. 4.03. 28 P
many will not buy | his goodness with this note; 5.04. 53
to note the fighting conflict of her hue, | how VEN 345
she, marking them, begins a wailing note, | and 835
that my posterity, sham'd with the note, | shall LUC 208
what did he note but strongly he desired? 415
who all in one, one pleasing note do sing: SON 8.12
eyes, | for they in thee a thousand errors note, 141. 2
a nun, | or sister sanctified, of holiest note, LC 233

NOTE–BOOK 3 FR 0.0003 REL FR 1 V 2 P
i will make a prief of it in my note–book, and WIV 1.01.145 P
to his /master's old tables, his note–book, his 2H4 2.04.267 P
set in a note–book, learn'd, and conn'd by rote, JC 4.03. 98

NOTED 24 FR 0.0027 REL FR 17 V 7 P
i noted her not, but i look'd on her. ADO 1.01.164 P
an amber–color'd raven was well noted. LLL 4.03. 86
sighs reek from you, noted well your passion. 4.03.138
and to be noted for a merry man, | he'll woo a SHR 3.02. 14
not noted, is't, | but of the finer natures? WT 1.02.225
(missingly) noted, he is of late much retir'd 4.02. 31 P
hand, whose worth and honesty | is richly noted; 5.03.145
the nonce, to immask our noted outward garments. 1H4 1.02.180 P
man whom i have often noted in thy company, but 2.04.418 P
and never noted in him any study, | any H5 1.01. 57
which we have noted in you to your kindred | and R3 3.07.212
this is noted, | and generally, whoever the king H8 2.01. 46
she's noted. TRO 5.02. 11 P
ay, for these slips have made him noted long, TIT 2.03. 86
which late i noted | in tatt'red weeds, with ROM 5.01. 38
flaminius, i have noted thee always wise. TIM 3.01. 31 P
you have condemn'd and noted lucius pella | for JC 4.03. 2
slips | as are companions noted and most known HAM 2.01. 23
no more of that, i have noted it well. LR 1.04. 75 P
stillness of your youth | the world hath noted, OTH 2.03.192
made of malice than of duty, | we have noted it. CYM 3.05. 34
what could he see but mightily he noted? LUC 414
the same, | and keep invention in a noted weed, SON 76. 6
more flowers i noted, yet i none could see | but 99.14

NOTEDLY 1 FR 0.0001 REL FR 0 V 1 P
most notedly, sir. MM 5.01.332 P

NOTE'S 1 FR 0.0001 REL FR 1 V 0 P
and high note's | ta'en of your many virtues, H8 2.03. 59

NOTES 22 FR 0.0024 REL FR 21 V 1 P
and to the nightingale's complaining notes TGV 5.04. 5
wilt hold longer argument, | do it in notes. ADO 2.03. 54
note this before my notes: 2.03. 54
speaks — | note notes, forsooth, and nothing. 2.03. 57
and look what notes and garments he doth give MV 3.04. 51
d sol re, one cliff, two notes have i; SHR 3.01. 77
at last, though long, our jarring notes agree, 5.02. 1
as notes whose faculties inclusive were | more AWW 1.03.226
king and camillo were very notes of admiration. WT 5.02. 11 P
both they and we, perusing o'er these notes, JN 5.02. 5
at last by notes of household harmony | they 3H6 4.06. 14
no notes of sally, for the heavens, sweet TRO 5.03. 14
sweet honey and sweet notes together fail. 5.10. 44
melodious bird it sung | sweet varied notes, TIT 3.01. 86
nor that is not the lark whose notes do beat ROM 3.05. 21
they should spy my windpipe's dangerous notes: TIM 1.02. 51
give him this money and these notes, reynaldo. HAM 2.01. 1
left these notes | of what commands i should be CYM 1.01.171
ah, but some natural notes about her body, 2.02. 28
for notes of sorrow out of tune are worse | than 4.02.241
averring notes | of chamber–hanging, pictures, 5.05.203
relish your nimble notes to pleasing ears, LUC 1126

NOTETH 1 FR 0.0001 REL FR 1 V 0 P
this solemn sympathy poor venus noteth, | over VEN 1057

NOTEWORTHY 1 FR 0.0001 REL FR 1 V 0 P
some rare noteworthy object in thy travel. TGV 1.01. 13

NOT–FEARING 1 FR 0.0001 REL FR 1 V 0 P
in our not–fearing britain than have tidings CYM 2.04. 19

/NOTHING 7 FR 0.0008 REL FR 6 V 1 P
/for /i /must /nothing /be; R2 4.01.201
/make /me, /that /nothing /have, /with /nothing 4.01.216
/that /nothing /have, /with /nothing /griev'd, 4.01.216
/where /nothing /but /the /sound /of /hotspur's 2H4 2.03. 37
/when /there /was /nothing /could /have /stay'd 4.01.121
/for /there /is /nothing /either /good /or /bad, HAM 2.02.250 P
/in /their /fury, /and /make /nothing /of, LR 3.01. 9

NOTHING 671 FR 0.0758 REL FR 444 V 227 P
i have done nothing, but in care of thee | (of TMP 1.02. 16
nothing of him that doth fade, | but doth suffer 1.02.400
for nothing natural | i ever saw so noble. 1.02.419
there's nothing ill can dwell in such a temple. 1.02.458
prithee no more; thou dost talk nothing to me. 2.01.171
lungs that they always use to laugh at nothing. 2.01.175 P

this kind of merry fooling, am nothing to you; 2.01.178 P
so you may continue, and laugh at nothing still. 2.01.179 P
i heard nothing. 2.01.313
but my rejoicing | at nothing can be more. 3.01. 94
lie like dogs, and yet say nothing neither. 3.02. 20 P
why, i said nothing. 3.02. 50 P
i did nothing. 3.02. 72 P
to me, where i shall have my music for nothing. 3.02.145 P
your heads — is nothing but heart's sorrow, 3.03. 81
of my instruction hast thou nothing bated | in 3.03. 85
gave me (a lost mutton) nothing for my labor. TGV 1.01. 98 P
having nothing but the word "noddy" for my pains 1.01.124 P
sir, i could perceive nothing at all from her; 1.01.136 P
what said she? nothing? 1.01.142 P
nothing. 1.02. 70
and is that paper nothing? 1.02. 72
nothing concerning me. 1.02. 72
my duty will i boast of, nothing else. 2.04.111
proteus, all i can is nothing | to her, whose 2.04.165
her, whose worth /makes other worthies nothing: 2.04.166
if he shake his tail and say nothing, it will. 2.05. 36 P
nothing. 3.01.198 P
can nothing speak? master, shall i strike? 3.01.199 P
nothing. 3.01.201 P
why, sir, i'll strike nothing. i pray you — 3.01.203 P
if it be a match, as nothing is impossible — 3.01.369 P
this, or else nothing, will inherit her. 3.02. 86
nothing but my fortune. 4.01. 41
i' faith, i'll eat nothing. WIV 1.01.279 P
i'll eat nothing, i thank you, sir. 1.01.302 P
i would have nothing lie on my head. 2.01.187 P
my brows become nothing else, nor that well 3.03. 60 P
own part, i would little or nothing with you. 3.04. 63 P
says my son profits nothing in the world at his 4.01. 15 P
we know nothing. 4.02.178 P
they were nothing but about mistress anne page, 4.05. 46 P
and i paid nothing for it neither, but was paid 4.05. 61 P
he hath enjoy'd nothing of ford's but his 5.05.112 P
are now so sure that nothing can dissolve us. 5.05.224
out my death, | and nothing come in partial. MM 2.01. 31
in a commonweal that do nothing but use their 2.01. 42 P
once, sir? there was nothing done to her once. 2.01.141 P
his heaven for thunder, | nothing but thunder! 2.02.114
whose minds are dedicate | to nothing temporal. 2.02.155
faults of mine, | and nothing of your answer. 2.04. 73
let /me be ignorant, and in nothing good, | but 2.04. 76
mercy | is nothing kin to foul redemption. 2.04.113
but, by chance, nothing of what is writ. 4.02.202 P
nothing goes right — we would, and we would not 4.04. 34
if he be less, he's nothing, but he's more, 5.01. 58
why, you are nothing then: 5.01.177 P
honest in nothing but in his clothes, and one 5.01.263 P
hold up your hands, say nothing; 5.01.438
there's nothing situate under heaven's eye | but ERR 2.01. 16
nothing, sir, but that i am beaten. 2.02. 41 P
for this something that you gave me for nothing. 2.02. 52 P
amends next, to give you nothing for something. 2.02. 54 P
more common, for that's nothing but words. 3.01. 25
(be it for nothing but to spite my wife) | upon 3.01.118
shoe, but her face nothing like so clean kept: 3.02.102 P
thou art sensible in nothing but blows, and so 4.04. 27 P
and have nothing at his hands for my service but 4.04. 31 P
that i was sent for nothing but a rope! 4.04. 91
will you be bound for nothing? 4.04.127
come, stand by me, fear nothing. 5.01.185
alas, he gets nothing by that. ADO 1.01. 65 P
the one is too like an image and says nothing, 2.01. 8 P
and look sweetly, and say nothing, i am yours 2.01. 89 P
speaks — | note notes, forsooth, and nothing. 2.03. 57
that her ear lose nothing | of the false sweet 3.01. 32
or a hat, or a cloak, is nothing to a man. 3.03.119 P
nothing i, but god send every one their heart's 3.04. 60 P
nothing, unless you render her again. 4.01. 29
i do love nothing in the world so well as you — 4.01.267 P
for me to say i lov'd nothing so well as you, 4.01.270 P
i confess nothing, nor i deny nothing. 4.01.272 P
i confess nothing, nor i deny nothing. 4.01.272 P
therein do men from children nothing differ. 5.01. 33
in faith, my hand meant nothing to my sword. 5.01. 57
she was charg'd with nothing | but what was true 5.01.104
i desire nothing but the reward of a villain. 5.01.243 P
and will lend nothing for god's sake. 5.01.312 P
nothing certainer: 5.04. 62
'a shall wear nothing handsome about him. 5.04.104 P
i will think nothing to any purpose that the 5.04.105 P
in reason nothing. LLL 1.01. 99
nay, nothing, master moth, but what they look 1.02.162 P
their words, and therefore i will say nothing. 1.02.164 P
nothing becomes him ill that he would well. 2.01. 46
will shall break it, will, and nothing else. 2.01.100
times as much more — and yet nothing at all. 3.01. 48 P
lieu thereof, impose on thee nothing but this: 3.01.129 P
nothing but fair is that which you inherit. 4.01. 20
imitari is nothing: 4.02.126 P
well, i do nothing in the world but lie, and lie 4.03. 11 P
nay, it makes nothing, sir. 4.03.189
if it mar nothing neither, | the treason and you 4.03.189
where nothing wants that want itself doth seek. 4.03.233
o, nothing so sure, and thereby all forsworn. 4.03.279
madam, came nothing else along with that? 5.02. 5
nothing but this? 5.02. 6
much in the letters, nothing in the praise. 5.02. 40
nothing but peace and gentle visitation. 5.02.179
nothing but peace and gentle visitation. 5.02.181
we number nothing that we spend for you; 5.02.198
do it extempore, for it is nothing but roaring. MND 1.02. 68 P
oath with oath, and you will nothing weigh. 3.02.131
nothing truer; 3.02.280
nothing but "low" and "little"? 3.02.326
nothing, good mounsieur, but to help cavalery 4.01. 22 P
sixpence a day in pyramus, or nothing. 4.02. 24 P
turns them to shapes and gives to aery nothing 5.01. 16
over, | and it is nothing, nothing in the world; 5.01. 78
over, | and it is nothing, nothing in the world; 5.01. 78
he says they can do nothing in this kind. 5.01. 88
the kinder we, to give them thanks for nothing. 5.01. 89
nothing impair'd, but all disorder'd. 5.01.126 P
for he is dead, he is nothing. 5.01.309 P

even now worth this, | and now worth nothing? MV 1.01. 36
only are reputed wise | for saying nothing; 1.01. 97
gratiano speaks an infinite deal of nothing, 1.01.114 P
nothing undervalu'd | to cato's daughter, 1.01.165
with too much as they that starve with nothing. 1.02. 7 P
for he doth nothing but talk of his horse, and 1.02. 40 P
he doth nothing but frown, as who should say, 1.02. 46 P
you know i say nothing to him, for he 1.02. 68 P
alas, fifteen wives is nothing! 2.02.162 P
to tell me i could do nothing without bidding. 2.05. 9 P
then it was not for nothing that my nose fell 2.05. 24 P
nothing else. 2.05. 45
fish withal — if it will feed nothing else, it 3.01. 53 P
turns to a wild of nothing, save of joy 3.02.182
else nothing in the world | could turn so much 3.02.245
rating myself at nothing, you shall see | how 3.02.257
when i told you | my state was nothing, i should 3.02.259
have told you | that i was worse than nothing; 3.02.260
he shall have nothing but the penalty. 4.01.322
thou shalt have nothing but the forfeiture, | to 4.01.343
a halter gratis — nothing else, for god sake. 4.01.379
i will have nothing else but only this, | and 4.01.432
nothing is good, i see, without respect; 5.01. 99
his brother, gain nothing under him but growth, AYL 1.01. 14 P
besides this nothing that he so plentifully 1.01. 16 P
nothing. i am not taught to make any thing. 1.01. 30 P
(yet i know not why) hates nothing more than he. 1.01.166 P
nothing remains but that i kindle the boy 1.01.172 P
the world no injury, for in it i have nothing. 1.02.191 P
there is nothing | that you will feed on; 2.04. 85
i care not for their names, they owe me nothing. 2.05. 22 P
and we will nothing waste till you return. 2.07.134
why, 'tis good to be sad and say nothing. 4.01. 8 P
to have seen much, and to have nothing, is to 4.01. 24 P
i will weep for nothing, like diana in the 4.01.154 P
to prey on nothing that doth seem as dead. 4.03.118
dreams, | for he is nothing but a mighty lord. SHR in.1. 65
let them want nothing that my house affords. in.1. 104
thou art a lord, and nothing but a lord. in.2. 61
madam, and nothing else — so lords call ladies. in.2. 111
why, nothing comes amiss, so money comes withal. 1.02. 81 P
why, that's nothing; 1.02.111 P
why, that is nothing; 2.01.130
why, she comes to borrow nothing of them. 4.01.105 P
faith, nothing; 4.04. 78 P
cross'd and cross'd, nothing but cross'd! 4.05. 10
now we are undone and brought to nothing. 5.01. 44 P
nothing but sit and sit, and eat and eat! 5.02. 12
padua affords nothing but what is kind. 5.02. 14
thus he his special nothing ever prologues. AWW 2.01. 92
kiss his hand, and say nothing, has neither leg, 2.02. 11 P
yet art thou good for nothing but taking up, and 2.03.207 P
she's very well, and wants nothing i' th' world; 2.04. 4 P
why, i say nothing. 2.04. 22 P
to say nothing, to do nothing, to know nothing, 2.04. 25 P
to say nothing, to do nothing, to know nothing, 2.04. 25 P
to do nothing, to know nothing, and to have 2.04. 25 P
to know nothing, and to have nothing, is to be a 2.04. 26 P
title, which is within a very little of nothing. 2.04. 27 P
sir, i can nothing say, | but that i am your 2.05. 71
nothing, indeed. 2.05. 83
a' th' country are nothing like your old ling 3.02. 13 P
"till i have no wife, i have nothing in france." 3.02. 74 P
nothing in france, until he have no wife! 3.02. 79
there's nothing here that is too good for him 3.02. 80
"till i have no wife, i have nothing in france." 3.02. 99 P
nothing in france, until he has no wife! 3.02.100
nothing acquainted with these businesses, | and 3.07. 5
it nothing steads us | to chide him from our 3.07. 41
nothing of me, has 'a? 4.03.112 P
he can say nothing of me. 4.03.117 P
nothing, but let him have thanks. 4.03.171 P
what an honest man should have, he has nothing. 4.03.261 P
grow in my requital | as nothing can unroot you. 5.01. 6
which nothing but to close | her eyes myself 5.03.118
an allow'd fool, though he do nothing but rail; TN 1.05. 95 P
discreet man, though he do nothing but reprove. 1.05. 96 P
off, i pray you, he speaks nothing but madman; 1.05.106 P
kinsman, she's nothing allied to your disorders. 2.03. 97 P
it that always makes a good voyage of nothing. 2.04. 78 P
thou art a merry fellow and car'st for nothing. 3.01. 27 P
if that be to care for nothing, sir, i would it 3.01. 30 P
you'll nothing, madam, to my lord by me? 3.01.136
no, madam, he does nothing but smile. 3.04. 11 P
nothing that can be can come between me and the 3.04. 81 P
nothing but this — your true love for my master 3.04.213
of my negligence, nothing of my purpose. 3.04.256 P
but nothing of the circumstance more. 3.04.261 P
nothing of that wonderful promise, to read him 3.04.264 P
i dare lay any money 'twill be nothing yet. 3.04.396 P
nothing that is so is so. 4.01. 8 P
talkest thou nothing but of ladies? 4.02. 26 P
you broke my head for nothing, and that that i 5.01.185 P
i think you set nothing by a bloody coxcomb. 5.01.191 P
if nothing lets to make us happy both | but this 5.01.249
thou co–active art, | and fellow'st nothing. WT 1.02.142
is whispering nothing? 1.02.284
is this nothing? 1.02.292
then the world and all that's in't is nothing, 1.02.293
the covering sky is nothing, bohemia nothing, 1.02.294
the covering sky is nothing, bohemia nothing, 1.02.294
my wife is nothing, nor nothing have these 1.02.295
is nothing, nor nothing have these nothings, 1.02.295
have these nothings, | if this be nothing. 1.02.296
theme, but nothing | of his ill–ta'en suspicion! 1.02.459
so surpris'd my sense, | that i was nothing. 3.01. 11
that thou betrayedst polixenes, 'twas nothing — 3.02.185
therefore betake thee | to nothing but despair. 3.02.210
your patience to you, | and i'll say nothing. 3.02.232
for there is nothing in the between but getting 3.03. 61 P
and to be so still requires nothing but secrecy. 3.03.126 P
they say, that from very nothing, and beyond the 4.02. 39 P
apprehend | nothing but jollity. 4.04. 25
sea, that you might ever do | nothing but that; 4.04.142
nothing she does, or seems, | but smacks of 4.04.157
not thou, man, thou shalt lose nothing here. 4.04.255 P
have let him go, | and nothing marted with him. 4.04.352
i cannot speak | so well, nothing so well; 4.04.381

and again does nothing | but what he did being 4.04.401
father (all whose joy is nothing else | but fair 4.04.408
delay'd, | but nothing alt'red. 4.04.464
to hold | shall nothing benefit your knowledge, 4.04.503
nothing so certain as your anchors, who | do 4.04.570
'twas nothing to geld a codpiece of a purse; 4.04.610 P
my sir's song, and admiring the nothing of it. 4.04.613 P
omit | nothing may give us aid. 4.04.625
they have to the king concerns him nothing, let 4.04.839 P
nothing but bonfires. 5.02. 22 P
much wrinkled, nothing | so aged as this seems. 5.03. 28
son's son, | infortunate in nothing but in thee. JN 2.01.178
and she again wants nothing, to name want, | if 2.01.435
that nothing do i see in you, | though churlish 2.01.518
hang nothing but a calve's–skin, most sweet lout 3.01.220
that nothing can allay, nothing but blood, | the 3.01.342
that nothing can allay, nothing but blood, | the 3.01.342
there's nothing in this world can make me joy: 3.04.107
damn'd as black — nay, nothing is so black — 4.03.121
nothing there holds out | but dover castle. 5.01. 30
should nothing privilege him nor partialize R2 1.01.120
stay | for nothing but his majesty's approach. 1.03. 6
boast of nothing else | but that i was a 1.03.273
nay, nothing, all is said. 2.01.148
me, and my inward soul | with nothing trembles; 2.02. 12
rightly gaz'd upon | show nothing but confusion; 2.02. 19
makes me with heavy nothing faint and shrink. 2.02. 32
'tis nothing but conceit, my gracious lady. 2.02. 33
'tis nothing less: 2.02. 34
so, | for nothing hath begot my something grief, 2.02. 36
or something hath the nothing that i grieve — 2.02. 37
where nothing lives but crosses, cares, and 2.02. 79
sure | i count myself in nothing else so happy 2.03. 46
and bids me speak of nothing but despair. 3.02. 66
and nothing can we call our own but death, | and 3.02.152
in your lord's scale is nothing but himself, 3.04. 85
and wounds the earth, if nothing else, with rage 5.01. 30
my lord, 'tis nothing. 5.02. 58
'tis nothing but some band that he is ent'red 5.02. 65
by bullingbrook, | and straight am nothing. 5.05. 38
with nothing shall be pleas'd, till he be eas'd 5.05. 40
pleas'd, till he be eas'd | with being nothing. 5.05. 41
i knew thee, hal, i knew nothing, and now am i, 1H4 1.02. 93 P
come, | and nothing pleaseth but rare accidents. 1.02.207
be taught to speak | nothing but "mortimer," and 1.03.225
that his tale to me may be nothing but "anon." 2.04. 32 P
there is nothing but roguery to be found in 2.04.125 P
wherein worthy, but in nothing? 2.04.459 P
nothing but papers, my lord. 2.04.533 P
and that would set my teeth nothing an edge, 3.01.131
an edge, | nothing so much as mincing poetry. 3.01.132
then should you be nothing but musical, for you 3.01.232 P
he? alas, he is poor, he hath nothing. 3.03. 76 P
for nothing can seem foul to those that win. 5.01. 8
account | nothing so strong and fortunate as i. 5.01. 38
that you did nothing purpose 'gainst the state, 5.01. 43
nothing but a colossus can do thee that 5.01.123 P
nothing confutes me but eyes, and nobody sees me 5.04.126 P
do now wear nothing but high shoes, and bunches 2H4 1.02. 38 P
to be scour'd to nothing with perpetual motion. 1.02.220 P
if a man will make curtsy and say nothing, he is 2.01.124 P
and, but my going, nothing can redeem it. 2.03. 8
nay, and 'a do nothing but speak nothing, 'a 2.04.193 P
and 'a do nothing but speak nothing, 'a shall be 2.04.193 P
but speak nothing, 'a shall be nothing here. 2.04.194 P
where he doth nothing but roast malt–worms. 2.04.334 P
justice hath done nothing but prate to me of the 3.02.305 P
that skill in the weapon is nothing without sack 4.03.114 P
nothing but well to thee, thomas of clarence. 4.04. 19
quoth 'a, we shall "do nothing but eat, and make 5.03. 17
lack nothing, be merry! 5.03. 69 P
desire to see him, thinking of nothing else, 5.05. 25 P
as if there were nothing else to be done but to 5.05. 27 P
offer nothing here. H5 2.01. 39 P
for i desire | nothing but odds with england. 2.04.129
in peace there's nothing so becomes a man | as 3.01. 3
breach, and we talk, and, be chrish, do nothing. 3.02.109 P
works to be done, and there ish nothing done, so 3.02.112 P
there be nothing compell'd from the villages; 3.06.109 P
nothing taken but paid for; 3.06.110 P
though all that i can do is nothing worth, 4.01.303
shame and eternal shame, nothing but shame! 4.05. 10
a woodmonger, and buy nothing of me but cudgels. 5.01. 66 P
idleness, and nothing teems | but hateful docks, 5.02. 51
will | that nothing do but meditate on blood — 5.02. 60
for me nothing remains. 1H6 1.01.174
be not amaz'd, there's nothing hid from me; 1.02. 68
was nothing less than bloody tyranny. 2.05.100
by me they nothing gain and if i stay, | 'tis 4.06. 36
will nothing turn your unrelenting hearts? 5.04. 59
this was nothing but an argument | that he that 2H6 1.02. 32
nothing else, my lord. 2.01. 49
nor stir at nothing, till the axe of death 2.04. 49
pissing–conduit run nothing but claret wine this 4.06. 4 P
nothing but this; 'tis "bona terra, mala gens." 4.07. 56
nothing so heavy as these woes of mine. 5.02. 65
that nothing sung but death to us and ours. 3H6 2.06. 57
where having nothing, nothing can he lose. 3.03.152
where having nothing, nothing can he lose. 3.03.152
may challenge nothing of their sov'reigns, | but 4.06. 6
why, and i challenge nothing but my dukedom, 4.07. 23
lands | is nothing left me but my body's length. 5.02. 26
and take his thanks that yet hath nothing else. 5.04. 59
all the world to nothing! R3 1.02.237
nothing that i respect, my gracious lord. 1.03.295
there's nothing differs but the outward fame. 1.04. 83
where nothing can proceed that toucheth us 3.02. 23
being nothing like the noble duke my father. 3.05. 92
indeed, left nothing fitting for your purpose 3.07. 18
but nothing /spake in warrant from himself. 3.07. 33
what they will impart | help nothing else, yet 4.04.131
by nothing, for this is no oath: 4.04.368
nothing but songs of death? 4.04.507
it will help me nothing | to plead mine H8 1.01.207
more than my all is nothing: 2.03. 67
there's nothing i have done yet, o' my 3.01. 30
ye turn me into nothing! 3.01.114

nothing but death | shall e'er divorce my 3.01.141
i | can nothing render but allegiant thanks, 3.02.176
then makes him nothing. 3.02.208
but his performance, as he is now, nothing. 4.02. 42
i fear nothing | what can be said against me. 5.01.125
you did nothing, sir. 5.03. 21
nothing of that shall from mine eyes appear. TRO 1.02.295
great jove's accord, | nothing so full of heart. 1.03.239
soft infancy, that nothing canst but cry, | add 2.02.105
things small as nothing, for request's sake only 2.03.169
ay, good now, love, love, nothing but love. 3.01.113 P
"love, love, nothing but love, still love, still 3.01.115
he eats nothing but doves, love, and that breeds 3.01.128 P
nor nothing monstrous neither? 3.02. 76 P
nothing but our undertakings, when we vow to 3.02. 77 P
characterless are grated | to dusty nothing, yet 3.02.189
nothing, my lord. 3.03. 60
cudgelling that he raves in saying nothing. 3.03.249 P
nothing but heavenly business | should rob my 4.01. 5
let us cast away nothing, for we may live to 4.04. 22 P
and know you, lord, | i'll nothing do on charge. 4.04.133
if not achilles, nothing. 4.05. 76
infinite as all, | the other blank as nothing. 4.05. 81
to an ass, were nothing, he is both ass and ox; 5.01. 59 P
to an ox, were nothing, /he /is both ox and ass. 5.01. 60 P
i'll after — nothing but lechery! 5.01. 97 P
nothing at all, unless that this were she. 5.02.135
wars and lechery, nothing else holds fashion. 5.02.195 P
hath nothing been but shapes and forms of 5.03. 12
they nothing doubt prevailing, and to make it COR 1.03. 99 P
it him, and leaves nothing undone that may fully 2.02. 20 P
leave nothing out for length, and make us think 2.02. 49
barr'd, it follows | nothing is done to purpose. 3.01.149
i would the gods had nothing else to do | but to 4.02. 45
throat, | and wak'd half dead with nothing. 4.05.126
this peace is nothing but to rust iron, increase 4.05.219 P
nay, i hear nothing; 4.06. 18
his mother and his wife | hear nothing from him. 4.06. 19
eyes — his raising, | nothing but his report. 4.06. 62
he was a kind of nothing, titleless, | till he 5.01. 13
for we have nothing else to ask but that | which 5.03. 88
he wants nothing of a god but eternity and a 5.04. 24 P
and with thy weapon nothing dar'st perform! TIT 2.01. 59
here never shines the sun, here nothing breeds, 2.03. 96
no, | nothing so kind, but something pitiful! 2.03.156
ay, of my pigeons, sir, nothing else. 4.03. 88 P
a fly, | and nothing grieves me heartily indeed, 5.01.143
who, nothing hurt withal, hiss'd him in scorn. ROM 1.01.112
o any thing, of nothing first /create! 1.01.177
thou talk'st of nothing. 1.04. 96
idle brain, | begot of nothing but vain fantasy, 1.04. 98
she speaks, yet she says nothing; 2.02. 12
of us, look to hear nothing but discords. 3.01. 47 P
of cats, nothing but one of your nine lives; 3.01. 77 P
is he gone and hath nothing? 3.01. 92
o, she says nothing, sir, but weeps and weeps, 3.03. 99
and all the world to nothing | that he dares 3.05.213
so, | and i am nothing slow to slack his haste. 4.01. 3
i hear thou must, and nothing may prorogue it, 4.01. 48
again, | for nothing can be ill if she be well. 5.01. 16
then she is well and nothing can be ill: 5.01. 17
of nothing so much as that i am not like timon. TIM 1.01.189 P
right, if doing nothing be death by th' law. 1.01.194 P
no, i will do nothing at thy bidding; 1.01.268 P
no, i'll nothing; 1.02.238 P
ask nothing, give it him, it foals me straight 2.01. 9
faith, nothing but an empty box, sir, which, in 3.01. 16 P
nothing doubting your present assistance therein 3.01. 20 P
"nothing doubting," says he? 3.01. 21 P
such–like trifles — nothing comparing to his — 3.02. 22 P
nothing emboldens sin so much as mercy. 3.05. 3
for law is strict, and war is nothing more. 3.05. 84
my present friends, as they are to me nothing, 3.06. 83 P
are to me nothing, so in nothing bless them, and 3.06. 83 P
bless them, and to nothing are they welcome. 3.06. 84 P
nothing i'll bear from thee | but nakedness, 4.01. 32
are we undone, cast off, nothing remaining? 4.02. 2
there's nothing level in our cursed natures 4.03. 19
when there is nothing living but thee, thou 4.03.355 P
nothing can you steal | but thieves do lose it. 4.03.447
swallow 'em, | debts wither 'em to nothing; 4.03.531
nothing else. 5.01. 9
nothing at this time but my visitation; 5.01. 18
that nothing but himself which looks like man 5.01.118
to mend, | and nothing brings me all things. 5.01.188
no talk of timon, nothing of him expect. 5.02. 14
that you do love me, i am nothing jealous; JC 1.02.162
run to the capitol, and nothing else? 2.04. 11
and so return to you, and nothing else? 2.04. 12
sooth, madam, i hear nothing. 2.04. 20
(which should perceive nothing but love from us) 4.02. 44
nothing but death shall stay me. 4.03.128
nor nothing in your letters writ of her? 4.03.183
nothing, messala. 4.03.184
nothing, my lord. 4.03.298
no, my lord, i saw nothing. 4.03.305
nothing afeard of what thyself didst make MAC 1.03. 96
in surmise, and nothing is | but what is not. 1.03.141
nothing in his life | became him like the 1.04. 7
mettle should compose | nothing but males. 1.07. 74
instant, | there's nothing serious in mortality: 2.03. 93
to be thus is nothing, | but to be safely thus. 3.01. 47
malice domestic, foreign levy, nothing, | can 3.02. 25
which is nothing | to those that know me. 3.04. 85
that the malevolence of fortune nothing | takes 3.06. 28
all is the fear, and nothing is the love; 4.02. 12
where nothing, | but who knows nothing, is once 4.03.166
but who knows nothing, is once seen to smile; 4.03.167
is ready, | our lack is nothing but our leave. 4.03.237
move only in command, | nothing in love. 5.02. 20
we doubt it nothing. 5.04. 2
full of sound and fury, | signifying nothing. 5.05. 28
i have seen nothing. HAM 1.01. 22
we doubt it nothing, heartily farewell. 1.02. 41
were nothing but to waste night, day, and time; 2.02. 89
what is't but to be nothing else but mad? 2.02. 94
why, it appeareth nothing to me but a foul and 2.02.302 P
a neutral to his will and matter, | did nothing. 2.02.482
and all for nothing! 2.02.557
unpregnant of my cause, | and can say nothing; 2.02.569
part are capable of nothing but inexplicable 3.02. 11 P
as one in suff'ring all that suffers nothing, 3.02. 66
i have nothing with this answer, hamlet, these 3.02. 96 P
i think nothing, my lord. 3.02.117 P
nothing. 3.02.121 P
discomfort you, my lord, it nothing must, | /for 3.02.166
do you see nothing there? 3.04.131
nothing at all, yet all that is i see. 3.04.132
nor did you nothing hear? 3.04.133
no, nothing but ourselves. 3.04.133
of nothing, bring me to him. 4.02. 30 P
nothing but to show you how a king may go a 4.03. 30 P
my thoughts be bloody, or be nothing worth! 4.04. 66
her speech is nothing, | yet the unshaped use of 4.05. 7
though nothing sure, yet much unhappily. 4.05. 13
will nothing stick our person to arraign | in 4.05. 93
envy | that he could nothing do but wish and beg 4.07.104
it, | and nothing is at a like goodness still, 4.07.116
methought there — a — was nothing — a — meet 5.01. 64
else would trace him, his umbrage, nothing more. 5.02.120 P
i will gain nothing but my shame and the odd 5.02.177 P
nothing, neither way. 5.02.301
nothing, my lord. LR 1.01. 87
nothing? 1.01. 88
nothing. 1.01. 89
nothing will come of nothing, speak again. 1.01. 90
nothing will come of nothing, speak again. 1.01. 90
and nothing more, may fitly like your grace, 1.01.200
nothing. i have sworn, i am firm. 1.01.245
nothing, my lord. 1.02. 31 P
the quality of nothing hath not such need to 1.02. 33 P
come, if it be nothing, i shall not need 1.02. 35 P
edmund, it shall lose thee nothing, do it 1.02.115 P
nothing like the image and horror of it. 1.02.175 P
this is nothing, fool. 1.04.128 P
of an unfee'd lawyer, you gave me nothing for't. 1.04.130 P
can you make no use of nothing, nuncle? 1.04.131 P
no, boy, nothing can be made out of nothing. 1.04.132 P
no, boy, nothing can be made out of nothing. 1.04.133 P
o' both sides, and left nothing i' th' middle. 1.04.188 P
thou art now, i am a fool, thou art nothing. 1.04.194 P
so your face bids me, though you say nothing. 1.04.196 P
have you nothing said | upon his party 'gainst 2.01. 25
and art nothing but the composition of a knave, 2.02. 21 P
away, i have nothing to do with thee. 2.02. 34 P
nothing almost sees miracles | but misery. 2.02.165
edgar i nothing am. 2.03. 21
pattern of all patience, | i will say nothing. 3.02. 38
say you nothing. 3.03. 8 P
couldst thou save nothing? 3.04. 64
nothing could have subdu'd nature | to such a 3.04. 70
unto the worst | owes nothing to thy blasts. 4.01. 9
in nothing am i chang'd | but in my garments. 4.06. 9
there is nothing done, if he return the 4.06.265 P
thou art in nothing less | than i have here 5.03. 94
nothing, but this is so. OTH 1.03. 75
he bears the sentence well that nothing bears 1.03.212
nothing at all, it is a high–wrought flood. 2.01. 2
put me to't, | for i am nothing if not critical. 2.01.119
and nothing can or shall content my soul | till 2.01.298
are nothing to your english. 2.03. 79 P
to speak the truth | shall nothing wrong him. 2.03.224
a mass of things, but nothing distinctly; 2.03.288 P
a quarrel, but nothing wherefore. 2.03.289 P
nothing, my lord; or if — i know not what. 3.03. 36
i will deny thee nothing. 3.03. 76
i will deny thee nothing; 3.03. 83
'tis something, nothing; 3.03.157
i nothing but to please his fantasy. 3.03.299
tasted her sweet body, | so i had nothing known. 3.03.347
for nothing canst thou to damnation add 3.03.372
yet we see nothing done; 3.03.432
such perdition | as nothing else could match. 3.04. 68
if they do nothing, 'tis a venial slip; 4.01. 9
all in all in spleen, | and nothing of a man. 4.01. 89
you have seen nothing then? 4.02. 1
her fan, her gloves, her mask, nor nothing? 4.02. 9
and said nothing but what i protest intendment 4.02.202 P
quick, quick, fear nothing; 5.01. 3
demand me nothing; 5.02.303
nothing extenuate, | nor set down aught in 5.02.342
a palm presages chastity, if nothing else. ANT 1.02. 47 P
it were pity to cast them away for nothing, 1.02.138 P
a great cause, they should be esteem'd nothing. 1.02.140 P
passions are made of nothing but the finest part 1.02.146 P
each thing give him way, cross him in nothing. 1.03. 9
for i can do nothing | but what indeed is honest 1.05. 15
be laugh'd at | if, or for nothing or a little, 2.02. 31
let this fellow | be nothing of our strife; 2.02. 80
to wrangle in when you have nothing else to do. 2.02.106 P
import their dangers, | would then be nothing. 2.02.133
thy plainness, | it nothing ill becomes thee. 2.06. 79
there's nothing in her yet. 3.03. 24
nothing, madam. 3.03. 41
welcome to rome, | nothing more dear to me. 3.06. 86
heard you of nothing strange about the streets? 4.03. 3
nothing. what news? 4.03. 4
and there is nothing left remarkable | beneath 4.15. 67
are fall'n into a princely hand, fear nothing. 5.02. 22
peril, that i have reserv'd | to myself nothing. 5.02.144
plac'd, and i have nothing | of woman in me; 5.02.238
give it nothing, i pray you, for it is not worth 5.02.269 P
i something fear my father's wrath, but nothing CYM 1.01. 86
as i was in france, i would abate her nothing, 1.04. 68 P
i do nothing doubt you have store of thieves; 1.04. 97 P
of what is in her chamber nothing saves | the 2.04. 94
they are to their virtues, which is nothing. 2.04.112
i'll deny nothing. 2.04.146
and we will nothing pay | for wearing our own 3.01. 13
richer than doing nothing for a /bable; 3.03. 23
we have seen nothing. 3.03. 39
my fault being nothing (as i have told you oft) 3.03. 65
ado | with that harsh, noble, simple nothing, 3.04.132
but time hath nothing blurr'd those lines of 4.02.104
though his /humor | was nothing but mutation, ay 4.02.133
triumphs for nothing, and lamenting toys, | is 4.02.193
nothing ill come near thee! 4.02.279
'twas but a bolt of nothing, shot at nothing, 4.02.300
'twas but a bolt of nothing, shot at nothing, 4.02.300
i am nothing; 4.02.367
or if not, | nothing to be were better. 4.02.368
i nothing know where she remains, why gone, 4.03. 14
a doubt | in such a time nothing becoming you, 4.04. 15
nothing routs us but | the villainy of our fears 5.02. 12
are the file when all | the rest do nothing — 5.03. 31
dream as i have done, | wake, and find nothing. 5.04.129
either both or nothing, | or senseless speaking, 5.04.146
thus, that nothing but our lives | may be call'd 5.05. 79
the wrongs he did me | were nothing prince–like; 5.05.293
where is read | nothing but curious pleasures, PER 1.01. 16
the which is good in nothing but in sight! 1.01.123
breath | nothing to think on but ensuing death. 2.01. 7
our rich misers to nothing so fitly as to a 2.01. 30 P
for here's nothing to be got now–a–days unless 2.01. 69 P
there's nothing can be minist'red to nature 3.02. 8
you'll lose nothing by custom. 4.02.138 P
yet nothing we'll omit | that bears recovery's 5.01. 53
pray you say nothing, pray you. TNK 1.01.119
and | thou shalt remember nothing more than what 1.01.185
assured | beyond its power there's nothing; 1.02. 65
that we may nothing share | of his loud infamy; 1.02. 75
nothing truer. 1.02. 79
but nothing of their own restraint and disasters 2.01. 39 P
we shall know nothing here but one another, 2.02. 41
hear nothing but the clock that tells our woes; 2.02. 42
that's nothing. 2.02.160
thing, | i care for nothing, and that's palamon. 3.02. 6
and earth, | there's nothing in thee honest. 3.03. 46
nothing, | our business is become a nullity, 3.05. 53
i would have nothing hurt thee but my sword, | a 3.06. 87
me, | till i am nothing but the scorn of women. 3.06.250
was nothing said of me | concerning the escape 4.01. 1
nothing that i heard, | for i came home before 4.01. 3
nothing but my pity. 4.01. 42
then she sung | nothing but "willow, willow, 4.01. 80
as ever you heard, but say nothing. 4.01.135
and do nothing all day long but pick flowers 4.03. 24 P
but that's all one, 'tis nothing to our purpose. 5.02. 32
alas, that's nothing. 5.02. 57
i have nothing | but this poor petticoat and two 5.02. 83
he sees his love, and nothing else he sees, VEN 287
for nothing else with his proud sight agrees. 288
though nothing but my body's bane would cure 372
they wither in their prime, prove nothing worth: 418
and nothing but the very smell were left me, 441
that nothing in him seem'd inordinate, | save LUC 94
wit, | make something nothing by augmenting it. 154
but nothing can affection's course control, | or 500
bearing away the wound that nothing healeth, 731
who nothing wants to answer her but cries, | and 1459
for why thou lefts me nothing in thy will; PP 10. 8
crave, | for why i craved nothing of thee still. 10.10
that nothing could be used to turn them both to 15.10
nature's bequest gives nothing, but doth lend, SON 4. 3
and nothing 'gainst time's scythe can make 12.13
by adding one thing to my purpose nothing. 20.12
if there be nothing new, but that which is 59. 1
and nothing stands but for his scythe to mow: 60.12
born, | and needy nothing trimm'd in jollity, 66. 3
want nothing that the thought of hearts can mend 69. 2
quite, | for you in me can nothing worthy prove; 72. 4
and so should you, to love things nothing worth. 72.14
thy looks should nothing thence but sweetness 93.12
nothing, sweet boy, but yet, like prayers divine 108. 5
to leave for nothing all thy sum of good; 109.12
for nothing this wide universe i call, | save 109.13
up with newer might | to me are nothing novel, 123. 3
to me are nothing novel, nothing strange; 123. 3
my mistress' eyes are nothing like the sun; 130. 1
in nothing art thou black save in thy deeds, 131.13
for nothing hold me, so it please thee hold 136.11
me, so it please thee hold | that nothing me, a 136.12

NOTHING–GIFT 1 FR 0.0001 REL FR 1 V 0 P
by | that nothing–gift of differing multitudes, CYM 3.06. 85

NOTHING'S 1 FR 0.0001 REL FR 1 V 0 P
this nothing's more than matter. HAM 4.05.174

NOTHINGS 3 FR 0.0003 REL FR 2 V 1 P
a known truth to pass a thousand nothings with, AWW 2.05. 30 P
is nothing, nor nothing have these nothings, WT 1.02.295
than idly sit | to hear my nothings monster'd. COR 2.02. 77

NOTICE 32 FR 0.0036 REL FR 26 V 6 P
now presently i'll give her father notice | of TGV 2.06. 36
but to give the mother | notice of my affair. MM 1.04. 87
he hath carried | notice to escalus and angelo, 4.03.130
give notice to such men of sort and suit as are 4.04. 17 P
give the like notice | to valentius, rowland, 4.05. 7
at the least of thy sweet notice, bring her to LLL 1.01.275 P
navarre had notice of your fair approach, | and 2.01. 81
i had myself notice of my brother's purpose AYL 1.01.139 P
against the french, | i have no certain notice. 2H4 1.03. 85
bring me just notice of the numbers dead | on H5 4.07.117
i'll by a sign give notice to our friends, 1H6 3.02. 8
myself had notice of your conventicles — | and 2H6 3.01.166
and given me notice of their villainies. 3.01.370
talk, | and give us notice of his inclination; R3 3.01.178
the state takes notice of the private difference H8 1.01.101
gave notice | he was from thence discharg'd? 2.04. 33
take notice, lords, he has a loyal breast, | for 3.02.200
to my poor unworthy notice, | he mock'd us when COR 2.03.158
the king my brother shall have notice of this. TIT 2.03. 85
romeo | hath had no notice of these accidents; ROM 5.02. 27
belike they had some notice of the people, | how JC 3.02.270
and given him notice that the duke of cornwall LR 2.01. 3 P
to no more | will i give place or notice. 2.04.249
would take no notice, nor build yourself a OTH 3.03.150
let our officers | have notice what we purpose. ANT 1.02.177
boot, my son, | who shall take notice of thee. CYM 1.05. 70
her with musics, but she vouchsafes no notice. 2.03. 40 P
forespent on us, | we must extend our notice. 2.03. 60
take notice that i am in cambria, at 3.02. 43 P
i'll give but notice you are dead, and send him 3.04.124
and like enough the duke hath taken notice TNK 2.02.227
mind, | taking no notice that she is so nigh, VEN 341

NOTIFY 2 FR 0.0002 REL FR 0 V 2 P

and she gives you to notify that her husband WIV 2.02. 83 P
stir hither, i shall seem to notify unto her. OTH 3.01. 29 P
NOTING 4 FR 0.0004 REL FR 3 V 1 P
not a note of mine that's worth the noting. ADO 2.03. 55
this course of fortune, | by noting of the lady. 4.01.158
noting this penury, to myself i said, | "an' if ROM 5.01. 49
matter of feast, which worthily deserv'd noting. ANT 2.02.183 P
NOTION 3 FR 0.0003 REL FR 3 V 0 P
and his own notion — | who wears my stripes COR 5.06.106
to half a soul and to a notion craz'd | say, MAC 3.01. 82
either his notion weakens, his discernings | are LR 1.04.228
NOT–OF–THE–NEWEST
1 FR 0.0001 REL FR 0 V 1 P
a kind of not–of–the–newest poor–john. TMP 2.02. 27 P
NOTORIOUS 15 FR 0.0017 REL FR 11 V 4 P
your good honor two notorious benefactors. MM 2.01. 50 P
whipping, for you have been a notorious bawd. 4.02. 14 P
fever | one ragozine, a most notorious pirate, 4.03. 71
to your notorious shame, i doubt it not. ERR 4.01. 84
what, you notorious villain, didst thou never SHR 5.01. 52 P
i would it were not notorious. AWW 1.01. 36 P
his sake, | and yet i know him a notorious liar, 1.01.100
you have done me wrong, | notorious wrong. TN 5.01.329
and made the most notorious geck and gull | that 5.01.343
alanson, that notorious machevile? 1H6 5.04. 74
since you provoke me, shall be most notorious. H8 3.02.288
curse — | wherein i did not some notorious ill: TIT 5.01.127
some base notorious knave, some scurvy fellow. OTH 4.02.140
'tis a notorious villain. 5.02.239
troth, | thou foul abettor, thou notorious bawd! LUC 886
NOTORIOUSLY 2 FR 0.0002 REL FR 1 V 1 P
fool, there was never man so notoriously abus'd; TN 4.02. 87 P
he hath been most notoriously abus'd. 5.01.379
NOT–PATED 1 FR 0.0001 REL FR 0 V 1 P
crystal–button, not–pated, agate–ring, 1H4 2.04. 70 P
NOTRE 2 FR 0.0002 REL FR 0 V 2 P
en baisant la main d'une (notre seigneur!) H5 5.02.255 P
in french, notre tres cher fils henri, roi 5.02.339 P
NOT'ST 1 FR 0.0001 REL FR 1 V 0 P
and tell me what thou not'st about the field. JC 5.03. 22
NOT–TO–BE–ENDUR'D
1 FR 0.0001 REL FR 1 V 0 P
forth | in rank and not–to–be–endur'd riots. LR 1.04.204
NOTWITHSTANDING 23 FR 0.0026 REL FR 13 V 10 P
hold notwithstanding their freshness and glosses TMP 2.01. 63 P
and, notwithstanding all her sudden quips, | the TGV 4.02. 12
but notwithstanding, man, i'll do /you your WIV 1.04. 92 P
but notwithstanding (to tell you in your ear, i 1.04.102 P
but notwithstanding that, i know anne's mind — 1.04.105 P
but notwithstanding, master fenton, i'll be 1.04.145 P
but, notwithstanding, haste, make no delay; MND 3.02.394
the man is notwithstanding sufficient. MV 1.03. 25 P
notwithstanding, use your pleasure; 3.02.320 P
grieve not you, you are welcome notwithstanding. 5.01.239
notwithstanding thy capacity | receiveth as the TN 1.01. 10
his burthenous taxations notwithstanding, | but R2 2.01.260
yet notwithstanding, being incens'd, he is flint 2H4 4.04. 33
notwithstanding the poor and untempering effect H5 5.02.223 P
yet, notwithstanding such a strait edict, | were 2H6 3.02.258
should notwithstanding join our lights together, 3H6 2.01. 37
notwithstanding she's your wife | and loves not R3 1.03. 22
should, notwithstanding that your bond of duty, H8 3.02.188
and, notwithstanding all this loss of blood, TIT 2.04. 29
whoremaster and a knave, which notwithstanding,
TIM 2.02.105 P
revels long a–nights, | is notwithstanding up. JC 2.02.117
but, notwithstanding, with my personal eye OTH 2.03. 5
notwithstanding, i fear not my ring. CYM 1.04. 97 P
/NOUGHT 1 FR 0.0001 REL FR 1 V 0 P
receiving /nought by elements so slow | but SON 44.13
NOUGHT 68 FR 0.0076 REL FR 66 V 2 P
what thou art, nought knowing | of whence i am, TMP 1.02. 18
he shall drink nought but brine, for i'll not 3.02. 66
war with good counsel, set the world at nought; TGV 1.01. 68
and coy, | and nought esteems my aged eloquence. 3.01. 83
nought but mine eye | could have persuaded me; 5.04. 64
they stay for nought at all | but for their ERR 4.01. 91
too much to know is to know nought but fame; LLL 1.01. 92
nought shall go ill; MND 3.02.462
since nought so stockish, hard, and full of rage MV 5.01. 81
when nought would be accepted but the ring, 5.01.197
if love have touch'd you, nought remains but so, SHR 1.01.161
now his important blood will nought deny | that AWW 3.07. 21
receiveth as the sea, nought enters there, | of TN 1.01. 11
only, nought for approbation | but only seeing, WT 2.01.177
that it yields nought but shame and bitterness. JN 3.04.111
nought shall make us rue, | if england to itself 5.07.117
as to be hush'd and nought at all to say. R2 1.01. 53
whose hollow womb inherits nought but bones. 2.01. 83
is, is nought but shadows | of what it is not; 2.02. 23
to have a son set your decrees at nought? 2H4 5.02. 85
pistol speaks nought but truth. 5.05. 38
there's nought in france | that can be with a H5 1.02.251
till by broad spreading it disperse to nought. 1H6 1.02.135
nought rests for me in this tumultuous strife 1.03. 70
and can do nought but wail her darling's loss, 2H6 3.01.216
what, worse than nought? 3.01.307
myself no joy in nought but that thou liv'st. 3.02.366
this hand was made to handle nought but gold. 5.01. 7
with this, my lord, myself have nought to do. R3 1.01. 97
bad is the world, and all will come to nought, 3.06. 13
to the disposing of it nought rebell'd, | order H8 1.01. 43
let him in nought be trusted | for speaking 2.04.136
she belov'd knows nought that knows not this: TRO 1.02.288
call them shames which are indeed nought else 1.03. 19
he hears nought privately that comes from troy. 1.03.249
the public power, | which he so sets at nought. COR 3.01.269
for we'll | hear nought from rome in private. 5.03. 93
remaineth nought but to inter our brethren, TIT 1.01.146
in the people's ears, there nought hath pass'd, 4.04. 7
up, | or else i will discover nought to thee. 5.01. 85
but their children's end, nought could remove, ROM pr 11
for nought so vile that on the earth doth live 2.03. 17
but a mad lord, and nought but humors sways him.
TIM 3.06.111 P
world, and will love nought | but even the mere 4.03.375
hear his speech, but say thou nought. MAC 4.01. 70
knowing nought (like dogs) but following. LR 2.02. 80
this great world | shall so wear out to nought. 4.06.135
for nought but provender, and when he's old, OTH 1.01. 48
of my despised time | is nought but bitterness. 1.01.162
with nought but truth. 4.02.185 P
for nought i did in hate, but all in honor. 5.02.295
still of mine, | when it is all to nought; ANT 2.03. 38
i have stol'n nought, nor would not, though i CYM 3.06. 48
such precious deeds in one that promis'd nought 5.05. 9
thought nought too curious, are ready now | to PER 1.04. 43
we convent nought else but woes: TNK 1.05. 9
get off your trinkets, you shall want nought. 3.03. 52
when nought serv'd, | when neither curb would 5.04. 73
that nought could buy | dear love but loss of 5.04.111
"alas, he nought esteems that face of thine, VEN 631
beauty hath nought to do with such foul fiends. 638
full of respects, yet nought at all respecting, 911
hand with all things, nought at all effecting. 912
for day hath nought to do what's done by night." LUC 1092
who wayward once, his mood with nought agrees. 1095
full oft, | a woman's nay doth stand for nought? PP 18.42
that this huge stage presenteth nought but shows SON 15. 3
but like a sad slave stay and think of nought 57.11
NOUGHT'S 1 FR 0.0001 REL FR 1 V 0 P
nought's had, all's spent, | where our desire is MAC 3.02. 4
NOUN 1 FR 0.0001 REL FR 0 V 1 P
thee that usually talk of a noun and a verb, and 2H6 4.07. 39 P
NOUNS* 2 FR 0.0002 REL FR 0 V 2 P
william, how many numbers is in nouns? WIV 4.01. 21 P
number more, because they say, "'od's nouns." 4.01. 24 P
NOURISH 7 FR 0.0008 REL FR 7 V 0 P
that show, contain, and nourish all the world, LLL 4.03.350
such as you | nourish the cause of his awaking. WT 2.03. 36
sun in march, | this praise doth nourish agues. 1H4 4.01.112
our isle be made a nourish of salt tears, | and 1H6 1.01. 50
whiles i in ireland nourish a mighty band, | i 2H6 3.01.348
in soothing them we nourish 'gainst our senate COR 3.01. 69
to save my boy, to nourish and bring him up, TIT 5.01. 84
NOURISH'D 8 FR 0.0009 REL FR 6 V 2 P
air, i am one that am nourish'd by my victuals, TGV 2.01.173 P
of memory, nourish'd in the womb of /pia /mater,
LLL 4.02. 69 P
once, | or nourish'd him as i did with my blood, 3H6 1.01.222
i say they nourish'd disobedience, fed | the COR 3.01.117
child shall live, and i will see it nourish'd. TIT 5.01. 60
being vex'd, a sea nourish'd with loving tears. ROM 1.01.192
/gum, which /oozes | from whence 'tis nourish'd. TIM 1.01. 22
consum'd with that which it was nourish'd by. SON 73.12
NOURISHED 1 FR 0.0001 REL FR 1 V 0 P
how begot, how nourished? MV 3.02. 65
NOURISHER 1 FR 0.0001 REL FR 1 V 0 P
course, | chief nourisher in life's feast. MAC 2.02. 37
NOURISHES 1 FR 0.0001 REL FR 1 V 0 P
yet ha' we | a brain that nourishes our nerves, ANT 4.08. 21
NOURISHETH 2 FR 0.0002 REL FR 1 V 1 P
'tis age that nourisheth. SHR 2.01.339
it lives by that which nourisheth it, and the ANT 2.07. 44 P
NOURISHING 1 FR 0.0001 REL FR 1 V 0 P
or feed on nourishing dishes, or keep you warm, OTH 3.03. 78
NOURISHMENT 4 FR 0.0004 REL FR 3 V 1 P
men sit down to that nourishment which is called LLL 1.01.237 P
envy and crooked malice nourishment | dare bite H8 5.02. 79
from whence | they have their nourishment? PER 1.02. 56
uses | (the food and nourishment of noble minds) TNK 2.02. 52
/NOUS 1 FR 0.0001 REL FR 0 V 1 P
les ongles? /nous les appelons de nailes. H5 3.04. 16 P
NOUSLE 1 FR 0.0001 REL FR 1 V 0 P
those mothers who, to nousle up their babes, PER 1.04. 42
NOUSLING 1 FR 0.0001 REL FR 1 V 0 P
and nousling in his flank, the loving swine VEN 1115
NOVEL 1 FR 0.0001 REL FR 1 V 0 P
up with newer might | to me are nothing novel, SON 123. 3
NOVELTY 3 FR 0.0003 REL FR 1 V 2 P
novelty is only in request, and, as it is, as MM 3.02.224 P
i may truly say it is a novelty to the world. AWW 2.03. 20 P
how novelty may move, and parts with /person, TRO 4.04. 79
NO–VERBS 1 FR 0.0001 REL FR 0 V 1 P
no, he gives me the proverbs and the no–verbs. WIV 3.01.105 P
NOVI 1 FR 0.0001 REL FR 0 V 1 P
novi /hominem tanquam te. LLL 5.01. 9 P
NOVICE 3 FR 0.0003 REL FR 3 V 0 P
a novice of this place, and the fair sister | to MM 1.04. 19
that princely novice, was struck dead by thee? R3 1.04.222
'tis thou | hast sold me to this novice, and my ANT 4.12. 14
NOVICES 2 FR 0.0002 REL FR 1 V 1 P
o, you are novices! SHR 2.01.311
mars dote on you for his novices! AWW 2.01. 47 P
NOVUM 1 FR 0.0001 REL FR 1 V 0 P
abate throw at novum, and the whole world again
LLL 5.02.544
/NOW 29 FR 0.0032 REL FR 24 V 5 P
NOW 3002 FR 0.3393 REL FR 2311 V 691 P
NOW–A–DAYS 2 FR 0.0002 REL FR 0 V 2 P
love keep little company together now–a–days. MND 3.01.144 P
nothing to be got now–a–days unless thou canst PER 2.01. 69 P
NOW–BORN 1 FR 0.0001 REL FR 1 V 0 P
shall seem expedient on the now–born brief, AWW 2.03.179
NOW'S 4 FR 0.0004 REL FR 4 V 0 P
to the present business | which now's upon 's; TMP 1.02.137
a round hose, madam, now's not worth a pin, TGV 2.07. 55
you hear now (too late), yet now's a time: TIM 2.02.143
my shipwrack now's no ill, | since i have here PER 2.01.133
NOYANCE *(also annoyance)*
NOYANCE 1 FR 0.0001 REL FR 1 V 0 P
armor of the mind | to keep itself from noyance, HAM 3.03. 13
NUBIBUS 1 FR 0.0001 REL FR 1 V 0 P
under the which is writ, "invitis nubibus." 2H6 4.01. 99
NULLITY 2 FR 0.0002 REL FR 2 V 0 P
nothing, | our business is become a nullity, TNK 3.05. 54
yea, and a woeful and a piteous nullity. 3.05. 55
NUMA'S 1 FR 0.0001 REL FR 1 V 0 P
that ancus martius, numa's daughter's son, | who COR 2.03.239
NUMB 3 FR 0.0003 REL FR 3 V 0 P
are these feet, whose strengthless stay is numb 1H6 2.05. 13
(all thin and naked) to the numb cold night? R3 2.01.118
i, | even like a stony image, cold and numb. TIT 3.01.258
NUMB'D 1 FR 0.0001 REL FR 1 V 0 P
strike in their numb'd and mortified arms | pins LR 2.03. 15
NUMBER 58 FR 0.0065 REL FR 49 V 9 P
truly, i thought there had been one number more,
WIV 4.01. 23 P
sins | stand more for number than for accompt. MM 2.04. 58
now the number is even. LLL 4.03.207
we number nothing that we spend for you; 5.02.198
broke | (in number more than ever women spoke),
MND 1.01.176
and after, every of this happy number, | that AYL 5.04.172
when you, and those poor number saved with you,
TN 1.02. 10
belike you slew great number of his people? 3.03. 29
we bear, | or add a royal number to the dead, JN 2.01.347
the little number of your doubtful friends. 5.01. 36
hath from the number of his banish'd years R2 1.03.210
accomplish'd with /the number of thy hours; 2.01.177
and all the number of his fair demands | shall 3.03.123
the number of the king exceedeth our. 1H4 4.03. 28
him, for we have a number of shadows fill up the 2H4 3.02.134 P
here is two more call'd than your number, you 3.02.188 P
i judge their number | upon or near the rate of 4.01. 21
those tears | by number into hours of happiness. 5.02. 61
the muster of his kingdom too faint a number; H5 3.06.131 P
here is the number of the slaught'red french. 4.08. 74
of princes, in this number, | and nobles bearing 4.08. 81
where is the number of our english dead? 4.08.102
holiness, | to number ave–maries on his beads; 2H6 1.03. 56
and, in the number, thee that wishest shame! 3.01.308
lest thou increase the number of the dead, | and R3 4.01. 44
who hath descried the number of the traitors? 5.03. 9
so are a number more. H8 2.01. 9
not (so much i am happy | above a number) if my 3.01. 34
a certain number | (though thanks to all) must i COR 1.06. 80
and presently, when you have drawn your number, 2.03.253
by mingling them with us, the honor'd number, 3.01. 72
sons, | half of the number that king priam had, TIT 1.01. 80
one more, most welcome, makes my number more.
ROM 1.02. 23
may stand in number, though in reck'ning none. 1.02. 33
what a number of men eats timon, and he sees 'em
TIM 1.02. 39 P
may these add to the number that may scald thee! 3.01. 51
good friends be griev'd | (among which number, JC 1.02. 44
yet in the number i do know but one | that 3.01. 68
will you be prick'd in number of our friends, 3.01.216
them, | by them shall make a fuller number up, 4.03.208
chance the king comes with so small a number? LR 2.04. 63
and danger | speak 'gainst so great a number? 2.04.240
reservation to be followed | with such a number. 2.04.253
think, speak, cast, write, sing, number, hoo! ANT 3.02. 17
let all the number of the stars give light | to 3.02. 65
place | we may the number of the ships behold, 3.09. 3
let not our ships and number of our men | be PER 1.04. 86
cried her almost to the number of her hairs, i 4.02. 94 P
it gives a good report to a number to be chaste. 4.06. 40 P
and the number | to carry such a business, forth TNK 1.01.161
where we shall find | the moi'ty of a number, 1.01.214
one salmon, you shall take a number of minnows. 2.01. 4 P
but to make the number more i have great hope in 4.03. 98 P
you that have voice and credit with the number, STM II.C 51
number there in love was slain. PHT 28
and in fresh numbers number all your graces, SON 17. 6
we prove | among a number one is reckon'd none: 136. 8
then in the number let me pass untold, | though 136. 9
NUMBER'D 2 FR 0.0002 REL FR 1 V 1 P
of as able body as when he number'd thirty. AWW 4.05. 81 P
the twinn'd stones | upon the number'd beach, CYM 1.06. 36
NUMBERLESS 2 FR 0.0002 REL FR 2 V 0 P
there cannot be those numberless offenses H8 2.01. 84
that numberless upon me stuck as leaves | do on TIM 4.03.263
/NUMBERS 1 FR 0.0001 REL FR 1 V 0 P
/sweet /harry /had /but /half /their /numbers, 2H4 2.03. 43
NUMBERS 42 FR 0.0047 REL FR 33 V 9 P
william, how many numbers is in nouns? WIV 4.01. 21 P
for thy cases and the numbers of the genders? 4.01. 70 P
i hope good luck lies in odd numbers. 5.01. 3 P
they say there is divinity in odd numbers, 5.01. 4 P
when the achiever brings home full numbers. ADO 1.01. 9 P
here are only numbers ratified, but, for the LLL 4.02.121 P
these numbers will i tear, and write in prose! 4.03. 55
out | such fiery numbers as the prompting eyes 4.03.319
the numbers true, and, were the numb'ring too, 5.02. 35
the numbers alter'd! TN 2.05.100 P
shall we go draw our numbers and set on? 2H4 1.03.109
the voice and echo, | the numbers of the feared. 3.01. 98
forth | to know the numbers of our enemies. 4.01. 4
for in the book of numbers is it writ, | when H5 1.02. 98
sorry am i his numbers are so few, | his 3.05. 56
sickness much enfeebled, | my numbers lessen'd; 3.06.146
proud of their numbers and secure in soul, | the 4.pr. 17
/if th' opposed numbers | pluck their hearts 4.01.291
bring me just notice of the numbers dead | on 4.07.117
them to admit th' excuse | of time, of numbers, 5.pr. 4
make up no factious numbers for the matter, | in 2H6 2.01. 39
the common people by numbers swarm to us. 3H6 4.02. 2
heart of our numbers, soul and only sprite | in TRO 1.03. 56
crown up the verse, | and sanctify the numbers. 3.02.183
the dreadful sagittary | appalls our numbers. 5.05. 15
take | convenient numbers to make good the city, COR 1.05. 12
in | thy lying tongue both numbers, i would say 3.03. 72
behold | dissentious numbers pest'ring streets, 4.06. 7
now is he for the numbers that petrarch flow'd ROM 2.04. 38 P
into the other street, | and part the numbers. JC 3.02. 4
norway himself, with terrible numbers, MAC 1.02. 51
shall we shadow | the numbers of our host, and 5.04. 6
o dear ophelia, i am ill at these numbers. HAM 2.02.120 P
plot | whereon the numbers cannot try the cause, 4.04. 63
upon the present state, whose numbers threaten, ANT 1.03. 52
will tie you to the numbers and the time | of CYM 3.07. 15
command our present numbers | be muster'd; 4.02.343
being so bad, such numbers seek for thee? LUC 896
and in fresh numbers number all your graces, SON 17. 6
forth | eternal numbers to outlive long date. 38.12
but now my gracious numbers are decay'd, | and 79. 3
redeem | in gentle numbers time so idly spent; 100. 6
NUMBNESS 1 FR 0.0001 REL FR 1 V 0 P
bequeath to death your numbness; WT 5.03.102
NUMB'RED 6 FR 0.0006 REL FR 6 V 0 P
are numb'red in the travel of one mile? LLL 5.02.197

henceforth be never numb'red among men! MND 3.02. 67
from her birth | had numb'red thirteen years. TN 5.01.245
now, herald, are the dead numb'red? H5 4.08. 73
the sands are numb'red that makes up my life, 3H6 1.04. 25
that had numb'red in the world | the sun to OTH 3.04. 70
NUMB'RING 4 FR 0.0004 REL FR 4 V 0 P
the numbers true, and, were the numb'ring too, LLL 5.02. 35
is numb'ring sands and drinking oceans dry; R2 2.02.146
for now hath time made me his numb'ring clock: 5.05. 50
numb'ring our ave–maries with our beads? 3H6 2.01.162
NUMBS 1 FR 0.0001 REL FR 1 V 0 P
with cold–pale weakness numbs each feeling part: VEN 892
/NUN 2 FR 0.0002 REL FR 2 V 0 P
what means the /nun? she dies, help, gentlemen! PER 5.03. 15
"'my parts had pow'r to charm a sacred /nun, LC 260
NUN 4 FR 0.0004 REL FR 2 V 2 P
choice, | you can endure the livery of a nun, MND 1.01. 70
a nun of winter's sisterhood kisses not more AYL 3.04. 16 P
many a fair year though hero had turn'd nun, if 4.01.101 P
"'lo this device was sent me from a nun, | or LC 232
NUNCIO'S *(see nuntio's)*
NUNCLE 17 FR 0.0019 REL FR 1 V 16 P
how now, nuncle? LR 1.04.105 P
mark it, nuncle: 1.04.117 P
can you make no use of nothing, nuncle? 1.04.131 P
nuncle, give me an egg, and i'll give thee two 1.04.155 P
i have us'd it, nuncle, e'er since thou mad'st 1.04.172 P
prithee, nuncle, keep a schoolmaster that can 1.04.179 P
a fool, and yet i would not be thee, nuncle: 1.04.187 P
for you know, nuncle, | "the hedge–sparrow fed 1.04.214
nuncle lear, nuncle lear, tarry, take the fool 1.04.315 P
nuncle lear, nuncle lear, tarry, take the fool 1.04.315 P
if thou wert my fool, nuncle, i'ld have thee 1.05. 41 P
cry to it, nuncle, as the cockney did to the 2.04.122 P
o nuncle, court holy–water in a dry house is 3.02. 10 P
good nuncle, in, ask thy daughters blessing. 3.02. 11 P
come not in here, nuncle, here's a spirit. 3.04. 39 P
prithee, nuncle, be contented, 'tis a naughty 3.04.110 P
prithee, nuncle, tell me whether a madman be a 3.06. 9 P
NUNN'RY 5 FR 0.0005 REL FR 0 V 5 P
get thee /to a nunn'ry, why wouldst thou be a HAM 3.01.120 P
go thy ways to a nunn'ry. 3.01.129 P
get thee to a nunn'ry, farewell! 3.01.137 P
to a nunn'ry, go, and quickly too. 3.01.139 P
to a nunn'ry, go. 3.01.149 P
NUN'S 1 FR 0.0001 REL FR 0 V 1 P
knave, as the nun's lip to the friar's mouth, AWW 2.02. 26 P
NUNS 4 FR 0.0004 REL FR 4 V 0 P
and have you nuns no farther privileges? MM 1.04. 1
they shall be praying nuns, not weeping queens; R3 4.04.202
of thee | among a sisterhood of holy nuns. ROM 5.03.157
love–lacking vestals and self–loving nuns, VEN 752
NUNTIO'S 1 FR 0.0001 REL FR 1 V 0 P
youth | than in a nuntio's of more grave aspect. TN 1.04. 28
/NUPTIAL 1 FR 0.0001 REL FR 0 V 1 P
/dissipation /of /cohorts, /nuptial /breaches, LR 1.02.148 P
NUPTIAL 20 FR 0.0022 REL FR 16 V 4 P
where i have hope to see the nuptial | of these TMP 5.01.309
to her /by oath, and the nuptial appointed; MM 3.01.214 P
the nuptial finish'd, | let him be whipt and 5.01.512
this looks not like a nuptial. ADO 4.01. 68
the catastrophe is a nuptial; LLL 4.01. 77 P
hippolyta, our nuptial hour | draws on apace. MND 1.01. 1
you in some business | against our nuptial, and 1.01.125
play | intended for great theseus' nuptial day. 3.02. 12
critical, | not sorting with a nuptial ceremony. 5.01. 55
with this same play, against your nuptial. 5.01. 75
straight shall our nuptial rites be solemniz'd; MV 2.09. 6
and i will bid the duke to the nuptial. AYL 5.02. 43 P
were the day | of celebration of that nuptial, WT 4.04. 50
a father | is at the nuptial of his son a guest 4.04.395
affects, | must be companion of his nuptial bed. 1H6 5.05. 58
to confirm that amity | with nuptial knot, if 3H6 3.03. 55
as merry as when our nuptial day was done | and COR 1.06. 31
upon her nuptial vow, her loyalty, | and with TIT 2.03.125
'tis since the nuptial of lucentio, | come ROM 1.05. 35
news, it is the celebration of his nuptial. OTH 2.02. 7 P
NUPTIALS 1 FR 0.0001 REL FR 1 V 0 P
we'll celebrate their nuptials, and ourselves PER 5.03. 80
NURS'D 7 FR 0.0008 REL FR 6 V 1 P
that thou bear'st | are nurs'd by baseness. MM 3.01. 15
but here nurs'd up and bred, one that is a 4.02.130 P
and they have nurs'd this woe, in feeding life; TIT 3.01. 74
thou wast the prettiest babe that e'er i nurs'd. ROM 1.03. 60
i nurs'd her daughter that you talk'd withal; 1.05.115
she at tharsus | was nurs'd with cleon, who at PER 5.03. 8
and thou shalt find | those children nurs'd, SON 77.11
NURSE 88 FR 0.0099 REL FR 78 V 10 P
babe, will scratch the nurse | and presently, TGV 1.02. 58
time is the nurse and breeder of all good. 3.01.245
which is in the manner of his nurse — or his WIV 1.02. 3 P
the manner of his nurse — or his dry nurse — 1.02. 4 P
the baby beats the nurse, and quite athwart MM 1.03. 30
pardon is still the nurse of second woe. 2.01.284
i will attend my husband, be his nurse, | diet ERR 5.01. 98
you must call to the nurse and bid her still it. ADO 3.03. 66 P
how if the nurse be asleep and will not hear us? 3.03. 67 P
occasion, let her never nurse her child herself, AYL 4.01.175 P
blood, | and melancholy is the nurse of frenzy. SHR in.2. 133
i am glad you did not nurse him. WT 2.01. 56
some place | where chance may nurse or end it. 2.03.183
i am too old to fawn upon a nurse, | too far in R2 1.03.170
my mother, and my nurse, that bears me yet! 1.03.307
this nurse, this teeming womb of royal kings, 2.01. 51
and if i were thy nurse, thy tongue to teach, 5.03.113
nature's soft nurse, how have i frighted thee, 2H4 3.01. 6
dear nurse of arts, plenties, and joyful births, H5 5.02. 35
the elder of them, being put to nurse, | was by 2H6 4.02.142
i am your sorrow's nurse, | and i will pamper it R3 2.02. 87
grandam, his nurse. 2.04. 32
his nurse? why, she was dead ere thou wast born. 2.04. 33
rude ragged nurse, old sullen playfellow | for 4.01.101
rome, the nurse of judgment, | invited by your H8 2.02. 93
truth shall nurse her, | holy and heavenly 5.04. 28
your prattling nurse | into a rapture lets her COR 2.01.206
or we must lose | the country, our dear nurse, 5.03.110
a loving nurse, a mother to his youth. TIT 1.01.332
what, must it, nurse? 4.02. 83
nurse, give it me, my sword shall soon dispatch 4.02. 86
the midwife and the nurse well made away, | then 4.02.167
nurse, where's my daughter? ROM 1.03. 1
nurse, give leave a while, | we must talk in 1.03. 7
nurse, come back again, | i have rememb'red me, 1.03. 8
and stint thou too, i pray thee, nurse, say i. 1.03. 58
were not i thine only nurse, | i would say thou 1.03. 67
lady ask'd for, the nurse curs'd in the pantry, 1.03.101 P
come hither, nurse. what is yond gentleman? 1.05.128
anon, good nurse! 2.02.137
a gentleman, nurse, that loves to hear himself 2.04.147 P
nurse, commend me to thy lady and mistress. 2.04.171 P
what wilt thou tell her, nurse? 2.04.175 P
and stay, good nurse — behind the abbey wall 2.04.187
what say'st thou, my dear nurse? 2.04.195
ay, nurse, what of that? both with an r. 2.04.208 P
the clock strook nine when i did send the nurse; 2.05. 1
o honey nurse, what news? 2.05. 18
now, good sweet nurse — o lord, why lookest 2.05. 21
i pray thee speak, good, good nurse, speak. 2.05. 28
sweet, sweet, sweet nurse, tell me, what says my 2.05. 54
hie to high fortune! honest nurse, farewell. 2.05. 78
o, here comes my nurse, | and she brings news; 3.02. 31
now, nurse, what news? 3.02. 34
where is my father and my mother, nurse? 3.02.127
cords, come, nurse, i'll to my wedding–bed, 3.02.136
nurse! 3.03. 91
go before, nurse; 3.03.155
nurse? 3.05. 38
o nurse, how shall this be prevented? 3.05.204
some comfort, nurse. 3.05.212
let not the nurse lie with thee in thy chamber. 4.01. 92
nurse, will you go with me into my closet | to 4.02. 33
go, nurse, go with her, we'll to church 4.02. 37
ay, those attires are best, but, gentle nurse, 4.03. 1
and let the nurse this night sit up with you, 4.03. 10
nurse! 4.03. 18
take these keys and fetch more spices, nurse. 4.04. 1
nurse! 4.04. 24
what, nurse, i say! 4.04. 24
know, and to the marriage | her nurse is privy; 5.03.266
the dung, | the beggar's nurse and caesar's. ANT 5.02. 8
at my breast, | that sucks the nurse asleep? 5.02.310
euriphile, | thou wast their nurse; CYM 3.03.104
their nurse, euriphile | (whom for the theft i 5.05.340
lychorida, her nurse, she takes, | and so to sea PER 3.ch. 43
lychorida, our nurse, is dead, | and cursed 4.ch. 42
have you | a nurse of me. 4.01. 24
my father, as nurse says, did never fear, | but 4.01. 52
as my good nurse lychorida hath oft | delivered 5.01.159
his mind nurse equal | to these so diff'ring TNK 1.03. 32
being nurse and feeder of the other four! VEN 446
by this black–fac'd night, desire's foul nurse, 773
the aim of all is but to nurse the life | with LUC 141
nurse of blame! 767
"the nurse, to still her child, will tell my 813
one, | will slay the other and be nurse to none. 1162
as tender nurse her babe from faring ill. SON 22.12
NURSE–LIKE 1 FR 0.0001 REL FR 1 V 0 P
his occasions, true, | so feat, so nurse–like. CYM 5.05. 88
NURSER 1 FR 0.0001 REL FR 1 V 0 P
arms | of the most bloody nurser of his harms! 1H6 4.07. 46
NURSERY 5 FR 0.0005 REL FR 5 V 0 P
i had | to see fair padua, nursery of arts, | i SHR 1.01. 2
it well may serve | a nursery to our gentry, who AWW 1.02. 16
or, shedding, breed a nursery of like evil, | to TRO 1.03.319
thought to set my rest | on her kind nursery. LR 1.01.124
the other, from their nursery | were stol'n, and CYM 1.01. 59
NURSE'S 4 FR 0.0004 REL FR 4 V 0 P
mewling and puking in the nurse's arms. AYL 2.07.144
but at his nurse's tears | he whin'd and roar'd COR 5.06. 96
birds | be unto us as is a nurse's song | of TIT 2.03. 28
a nurse's song ne'er pleas'd her babe so well. VEN 974
NURSES 2 FR 0.0002 REL FR 2 V 0 P
the kites and ravens | to be thy nurses! WT 2.03.187
nurses are not the fates, | to foster it, not PER 4.03. 14
NURSEST 1 FR 0.0001 REL FR 1 V 0 P
thou nursest all and murth'rest all that are. LUC 929
NURSETH 1 FR 0.0001 REL FR 1 V 0 P
for that which longer nurseth the disease, SON 147. 2
NURSH–A 1 FR 0.0001 REL FR 0 V 1 P
my nursh–a quickly tell me so mush. WIV 3.02. 65 P
NURSING 5 FR 0.0005 REL FR 4 V 1 P
he would have paid for the nursing a thousand. MM 3.02.118 P
by nursing them, my lord. LR 5.03.182
first pay me for the nursing of thy sons, | and CYM 5.05.322
nursing of my sons? 5.05.324
there i'll leave it | at careful nursing. PER 3.01. 80
NURTURE 2 FR 0.0002 REL FR 2 V 0 P
on whose nature | nurture can never stick; TMP 4.01.189
yet am i inland bred | and know some nurture. AYL 2.07. 97
NUT 6 FR 0.0006 REL FR 3 V 3 P
a drop of blood, a pin, | a nut, a cherry–stone; ERR 4.03. 73
sweetest nut hath sourest rind, | such a nut is AYL 3.02.109
nut hath sourest rind, | such a nut is rosalind. 3.02.110
concave as a cover'd goblet or a worm–eaten nut. 3.04. 25 P
there can be no kernel in this light nut; AWW 2.05. 43 P
were as good crack a fusty nut with no kernel. TRO 2.01.101 P
NUTHOOK 2 FR 0.0002 REL FR 0 V 2 P
nuthook, nuthook, you lie. 2H4 5.04. 7 P
nuthook, nuthook, you lie. 5.04. 7 P
NUTHOOK'S 1 FR 0.0001 REL FR 0 V 1 P
you, if you run the nuthook's humor on me — WIV 1.01.168 P
NUTMEG 2 FR 0.0002 REL FR 0 V 2 P
a /gilt nutmeg. LLL 5.02.646 P
he's of the color of the nutmeg. H5 3.07. 19 P
NUTMEGS 1 FR 0.0001 REL FR 0 V 1 P
nutmegs, seven; WT 4.03. 46 P
NUTRIMENT 1 FR 0.0001 REL FR 1 V 0 P
why should it thrive and turn to nutriment TIM 3.01. 58
NUTS 2 FR 0.0002 REL FR 1 V 1 P
the squirrel's hoard, and fetch thee new nuts. MND 4.01. 36
thou wilt quarrel with a man for cracking nuts, ROM 3.01. 19 P
/NUTSHELL 1 FR 0.0001 REL FR 0 V 1 P
/i /could /be /bounded /in /a /nutshell, /and HAM 2.02.254 P
NUTSHELL 1 FR 0.0001 REL FR 0 V 1 P
no stronger than a nutshell and as leaky as an TMP 1.01. 47 P
NUZZLE *(see nousle, etc.)*
NYM 17 FR 0.0019 REL FR 5 V 12 P
rascals, bardolph, nym, and pistol. WIV 1.01.125 P
away, sir corporal nym! 2.01.124
my name is corporal nym; 2.01.133 P
my name is nym, and falstaff loves your wife. 2.01.134 P
reprieves for you and your coach–fellow nym; 2.02. 8 P
to know, sir, whether one nym, sir, that 4.05. 32 P
well met, corporal nym. H5 2.01. 1 P
let't be so, good corporal nym. 2.01. 13 P
good corporal nym, show thy valor, and put up 2.01. 43 P
corporal nym, and thou wilt be friends, be 2.01.102 P
i'll live by nym, and nym shall live by me. 2.01.110
i'll live by nym, and nym shall live by me. 2.01.110
nym, thou hast spoke the right. 2.01.123
nym, rouse thy vaunting veins; 2.03. 4
for nym, he hath heard that men of few words are 3.02. 36 P
nym and bardolph are sworn brothers in filching, 3.02. 44 P
bardolph and nym had ten times more valor than 4.04. 70 P
NYMPH 11 FR 0.0012 REL FR 11 V 0 P
go make thyself like a nymph o' th' sea; TMP 1.02.301
thou gentle nymph, cherish thy forlorn swain. TGV 5.04. 12
fare thee well, nymph. MND 2.01.245
o helen, goddess, nymph, perfect, divine! 3.02.137
to call me goddess, nymph, divine and rare, 3.02.226
to strut before a wanton ambling nymph; R3 1.01. 17
this goddess, this semiramis, this nymph, | this TIT 2.01. 22
nymph, in thy orisons | be all my sins HAM 3.01. 88
yea | (we challenge too), the bank of any nymph, TNK 3.01. 8
that methought she appear'd like the fair nymph 4.01. 86
or like a nymph, with long dishevelled hair, VEN 147
NYMPHS 10 FR 0.0011 REL FR 10 V 0 P
betrims, | to make cold nymphs chaste crowns; TMP 4.01. 66
you nymphs, call'd naiades, of the windring 4.01.128
come, temperate nymphs, and help to celebrate 4.01.132
and these fresh nymphs encounter every one | in 4.01.137
what nymphs are these? MND 4.01.127
or modest dian, circled with her nymphs, | shall 3H6 4.08. 21
that like the stately /phoebe 'mongst her nymphs TIT 1.01.316
stain to all nymphs, more lovely than a man, VEN 9
all sleeping, | nymphs /back peeping fearfully. PP 17.28
whilst many nymphs that vow'd chaste life to SON 154. 3
O'* *(also a'*, of, on, one)*
/O'* 2 FR 0.0002 REL FR 1 V 1 P
/dungeons, /denmark /being /one /o' /th' /worst. HAM 2.02.246 P
/you /are /o' /th' /commission, | /sit /you /too LR 3.06. 38
O'* 282 FR 0.0318 REL FR 217 V 65 P
a pox o' your throat, you bawling, blasphemous, TMP 1.01. 40 P
to think o' th' teen that i have turn'd you to, 1.02. 64
he was indeed the duke, out o' th' substitution, 1.02.103
which was, that he, in lieu o' th' premises, 1.02.123
the precursors | o' th' dreadful thunder–claps, 1.02.202
hast dispos'd, | and all the rest o' th' fleet. 1.02.226
and for the rest o' th' fleet | (which i 1.02.232
what is the time o' th' day? 1.02.239
to do me business in the veins o' th' earth 1.02.255
go make thyself like a nymph o' th' sea; 1.02.301
and show'd thee all the qualities o' th' isle, 1.02.337
you do keep from me | the rest o' th' island. 1.02.344
and sure it waits upon | some god o' th' island. 1.02.390
all corners else o' th' earth | let liberty make 1.02.492
a pox o' that! 2.01. 78 P
at | which end o' th' beam should bow. 2.01.132
so is the dear'st o' th' loss. 2.01.136
it is the quality o' th' climate. 2.01.200
warm, o' my troth! 2.02. 34 P
out o' th' moon, i do assure thee. 2.02.138 P
i'll show thee every fertile inch o' th' island; 2.02.148
i'll turn my mercy out o' doors, and make a 3.02. 70 P
out o' your wits, and hearing too? 3.02. 78 P
a pox o' your bottle! 3.02. 79 P
thou thyself dost air — the queen o' th' sky, 4.01. 70
thou here, | this is the mouth o' th' cell. 4.01.216
make them | than pard or cat o' mountain. 4.01.261
you do yet taste | some subtleties o' th' isle, 5.01.124
you'ld be king o' the isle, sirrah? 5.01.288 P
best sing it to the tune of "light o' love." TGV 1.02. 80
o' my life, if i were young again, the sword WIV 1.01. 40 P
are you avis'd o' that? 1.04.100 P
though the priest o' th' town commended him for 2.01.145 P
good mine host o' th' garter, a word with you. 2.01.203 P
eleven o' clock the hour. 2.02.309 P
if he took you a box o' th' ear, you might have MM 2.01.180 P
thou'rt i' th' right, girl, more o' that. 2.02.129
art avis'd o' that? more on't. 2.02.132
in itself, | that skins the vice o' th' top. 2.02.136
a pox o' your throats! 4.03. 24 P
o' my troth, most sweet jests, most incony LLL 4.01.142
sore, then l to sore makes fifty sores o' sorel: 4.02. 60
you should ask me what time o' day; AYL 3.02.300 P
him that cupid hath clapp'd him o' th' shoulder, 4.01. 48 P
and once again a pot o' th' smallest ale. SHR in.2. 75
he plays o' th' viol–de–gamboys, and speaks TN 1.03. 25 P
my niece till his brains turn o' th' toe like a 1.03. 42 P
she'll none o' th' count. 1.03.109 P
i am a fellow o' th' strangest mind i' th' world 1.03.112 P
peace, you rogue, no more o' that. 1.05. 29 P
here — a plague o' these pickle–herring! 1.05.120 P
and seek the crowner, and let him sit o' my coz; 1.05.135 P
what kind o' man is he? 1.05.150 P
"o' the twelf day of december" — 2.03. 84
for the love o' god, peace! 2.03. 85 P
out o' tune, sir! 2.03.113 P
what o' that? 2.03.180 P
you know he brought me out o' favor with my lady 2.05. 8 P
does not toby take you a blow o' the lips then? 2.05. 67 P
wilt thou set thy foot o' my neck? 2.05.188 P
or o' mine either? 2.05.189 P
'slight! will you make an ass o' me? 3.02. 13 P
still you keep o' th' windy side of the law; 3.04.164 P
i love thee not a jar o' th' clock behind | what WT 1.02. 43
was not my lord | the verier wag o' th' two? 1.02. 66
to sigh, as 'twere | the mort o' th' deer — o, 1.02.118
give scandal to the blood o' th' prince my son 1.02.330
at several posterns | clear them o' th' city. 1.02.439
how he may soften at the sight o' th' child: 2.02. 38
cause were not in being — part o' th' cause, 2.03. 3
hence with her, out o' door! 2.03. 68

and the ear–deaf'ning voice o' th' oracle, | kin 3.01. 9
if th' event o' th' journey | prove as 3.01. 11
am glad at heart | to be so rid o' th' business. 3.03. 15
the spirits o' th' dead | may walk again. 3.03. 16
i mentioned a son o' th' king's, which florizel 4.01. 22
why, then comes in the sweet o' the year, | for 4.03. 3
of pruins, and as many of raisins o' th' sun. 4.03. 48 P
the gracious mark o' th' land, you have obscur'd 4.04. 8
i prithee darken not | the mirth o' th' feast. 4.04. 42
at upper end o' th' table, now i' th' middle; 4.04. 59
her face o' fire | with labor, and the thing she 4.04. 60
that which you are, mistress o' th' feast. 4.04. 68
should take on me | the hostess–ship o' th' day. 4.04. 72
the fairest flow'rs o' th' season | are our 4.04. 81
i had some flow'rs o' th' spring that might 4.04.113
i wish you | a wave o' th' sea, that you might 4.04.141
but they themselves are o' th' mind (if it be 4.04.329 P
nature crush the sides o' th' earth together, 4.04.478
peter bullcalf o' th' green! 2H4 3.02.172 P
twelve and one, ev'n at the turning o' th' tide; H5 2.03. 13 P
more like a soldier than a man o' th' church, 2H6 1.01.186
give him a box o' th' ear, and that will make 4.07. 86 P
bulk | take up the rays o' th' beneficial sun, H8 1.01. 56
he upon him | (without the privity o' th' king) 1.01. 74
cardinal | the articles o' th' combination drew 1.01.169
these are the limbs o' th' plot. 1.01.220
a monk o' th' chartreux. 1.01.221
every tree, lop, bark, and part o' th' timber; 1.02. 96
bid him strive | to the love o' th' commonalty; 1.02.170
your office | on the complaint o' th' tenants. 1.02.173
is but merely | a fit or two o' th' face — but 1.03. 7
hate him perniciously, and, o' my conscience, 2.01. 50
yea, the elect o' th' land, who are assembled 2.04. 60
(well worthy the best heir o' th' world) should 2.04.196
creature | that's paragon'd o' th' world. 2.04.231
nothing i have done yet, o' my conscience, 3.01. 30
and came to th' eye o' th' king, wherein was 3.02. 31
holiness | to stay the judgment o' th' divorce; 3.02. 33
has left the cause o' th' king unhandled, and 3.02. 58
look'd he | o' th' inside of the paper? 3.02. 78
king has made him master | o' th' jewel house, 4.01.111
is made master | o' th' rolls, and the king's 5.01. 35
incens'd the lords o' th' council that he is 5.01. 43
justice and the truth o' th' question carries 5.01.130
carries | the due o' th' verdict with it. 5.01.131
let some o' th' guard be ready there. 5.02.130
for, o' my conscience, twenty of the dog–days 5.03. 41 P
her succor, which were the hope o' th' strond, 5.03. 53 P
mercy o' me, what a multitude are here! 5.03. 67
these | your faithful friends o' th' suburbs? 5.03. 72
you i' th' chamblet, get up o' th' rail, | i'll 5.03. 89
he's one o' th' soundest judgments in troy, TRO 1.02.191 P
and you slander | the helms o' th' state, who COR 1.01. 77
the court, the heart, to th' seat o' th' brain, 1.01.136
for that, being one o' th' lowest, basest, 1.01.157
a place of potency and sway o' th' state, | if 2.03.182
springs of — | the noble house o' th' martians; 2.03.238
will be there before the stream o' th' people; 2.03.261
the people, | the tongues o' th' common mouth. 3.01. 22
being but | the horn and noise o' th' monster's, 3.01. 95
upon the part o' th' people, in whose power | we 3.01.209
though calved i' th' porch o' th' capitol! 3.01.239
myself | take up a brace o' th' best of them, 3.01.243
i cannot get him out o' th' house. 4.05. 21 P
set at upper end o' th' table; 4.05.192 P
hand, and turns up the white o' th' eye to his 4.05.196 P
clusters, | who did hoot him out o' th' city. 4.06.123
but what o' that? 5.01. 4
and his fame folds in | this orb o' th' earth. 5.06.125
the base o' th' mount | is rank'd with all TIM 1.01. 64
to be flatter'd is worthy o' th' flatterer. 1.01.227 P
bid 'em send o' th' instant | a thousand talents 2.02.198
will fare so harshly o' th' trumpet's sound; 3.06. 34 P
to general filths | convert o' th' instant, 4.01. 7
master's bed, | thy mistress is o' th' brothel! 4.01. 13
go, suck the subtle blood o' th' grape, | till 4.03.429
promising is the very air o' th' time; 5.01. 22
be as a cantherizing to the root o' th' tongue, 5.01.133
dead, | entomb'd upon the very hem o' th' sea, 5.04. 66
husband's to aleppo gone, master o' th' tiger; MAC 1.03. 7
that look not like th' inhabitants o' th' earth, 1.03. 41
in viewing o'er the rest o' th' self–same day, 1.03. 94
it is too full o' th' milk of human kindness 1.05. 17
eyes are made the fools o' th' other senses, 2.01. 44
and stole thence | the life o' th' building! 2.03. 69
acquaint you with the perfect spy o' th' time, 3.01.129
thou art the best o' th' cut–throats, | yet he's 3.04. 16
i drink to th' general joy o' th' whole table, 3.04. 88
fife, give to th' edge o' th' sword | his wife, 4.01.151
and best knows | the fits o' th' season. 4.02. 17
no more o' that, my lord, no more o' that; 5.01. 44 P
no more o' that, my lord, no more o' that; 5.01. 44 P
and wish th' estate o' th' world were now undone 5.05. 49
and live to be the show and gaze o' th' time! 5.08. 24
melancholy, with a sigh like tom o' bedlam. LR 1.02.136 P
i had rather be any kind o' thing than a fool, 1.04.186 P
thou hast par'd thy wit o' both sides, and left 1.04.187 P
here comes one o' the parings. 1.04.188 P
is much o' th' savor | of other your new pranks. 1.04.237
i'll make a sop o' th' moonshine of you, you 2.02. 32 P
though they had been but two years o' th' trade. 2.02. 60 P
she knapp'd 'em o' th' coxcombs with a stick, 2.04.124 P
thy half o' th' kingdom hast thou not forgot, 2.04.180
choose | to wage against the enmity o' th' air, 2.04.209
come out o' th' storm. 2.04.309
strike flat the thick rotundity o' th' world! 3.02. 7
is better than this rain–water out o' door. 3.02. 11 P
take heed o' th' foul fiend. 3.04. 80 P
moreover, to descry | the strength o' th' enemy. 4.05. 14
upon the crown o' th' cliff, what thing was that 4.06. 67
go to, they are not men o' their words: 4.06.104 P
you do me wrong to take me out o' th' grave: 4.07. 44
why he appears | upon this call o' th' trumpet. 5.03.119
mine eyes are not o' th' best; 5.03.280
at this odd–even and dull watch o' th' night, OTH 1.01.123
yet do i hold it very stuff o' th' conscience 1.02. 2
on the brow o' th' sea | stand ranks of people, 2.01. 53
'tis not yet ten o' th' clock. 2.03. 13 P
speak, is't out o' th' way? 3.04. 80
nor send you out o' th' way? 4.02. 7
o, bear him /out o' th' air. 5.01.104
going on, | the sides o' th' world may danger. ANT 1.02.192
like to the time o' th' year between the 1.05. 51
the third o' th' world is yours, which with a 2.02. 63
some o' their plants are ill rooted already, the 2.07. 1 P
they take the flow o' th' nile | by certain 2.07. 17
what manner o' thing is your crocodile? 2.07. 41 P
be a child o' th' time. 2.07.100
of parthia | we have jaded out o' th' field. 3.01. 34
we had not rated him | his part o' th' isle. 3.06. 26
are levying | the kings o' th' earth for war. 3.06. 68
set we our squadrons on yond side o' th' hill, 3.09. 1
i' th' midst o' th' fight, | when vantage like a 3.10. 11
with half the bulk o' th' world play'd as i 3.11. 64
o thou day o' th' world, | chain mine arm'd neck 4.08. 13
let me lodge lichas on the horns o' th' moon, 4.12. 45
look out o' th' other side your monument, | his 4.15. 8
darkling stand | the varying shore o' th' world! 4.15. 11
i liv'd, the greatest prince o' th' world, | the 4.15. 54
the crown o' th' earth doth melt. 4.15. 63
sole sir o' th' world, | i cannot project mine 5.02.120
truly, she makes a very good report o' th' worm; 5.02.255 P
yes, forsooth; i wish you joy o' th' worm. 5.02.279 P
who in the wars o' th' time | died with their CYM 1.01. 35
was in debt, it went o' th' backside the town. 1.02. 12 P
would thou grew'st unto the shores o' th' haven, 1.03. 1
and if thou canst awake by four o' th' clock, 2.02. 6
the flame o' th' taper | bows toward her, and 2.02. 19
and the contents o' th' story. 2.02. 27
up | their deer to th' stand o' th' stealer; 2.03. 70
with scraps o' th' court, it is no contract, 2.03.115
enlargement by | the consequence o' th' crown, 2.03.121
the roof o' th' chamber | with golden cherubins 2.04. 87
it did almost stretch | the sides o' th' world, 3.01. 50
have never wing'd from view o' th' nest, nor 3.03. 28
the art o' th' court, | as hard to leave as keep 3.03. 46
the toil o' th' war, | a pain that only seems to 3.03. 49
venison first shall be the lord o' th' feast, 3.03. 75
my dear lord, | thou art one o' th' false ones. 3.06. 15
'tis the ninth hour o' th' morn. 4.02. 30
know him, 'tis | cloten, the son o' th' queen. 4.02. 65
o' th' floor; 4.02.212
fear no more the heat o' th' sun, | nor the 4.02.258
fear no more the frown o' th' great, | thou art 4.02.264
herbs that have on them cold dew o' th' night 4.02.284
with the next benefit o' th' wind. 4.02.342
even to the note o' th' king, or i'll fall in 4.03. 44
gods, put the strength o' th' leonati in me! 5.01. 31
to shame the guise o' th' world, i will begin 5.01. 32
grin like lions | upon the pikes o' th' hunters. 5.03. 39
in hard voyages, became | the life o' th' need. 5.03. 45
resist are grown | the mortal bugs o' th' field. 5.03. 51
am i better | than one that's sick o' th' gout, 5.04. 5
that he deserv'd the praise o' th' world, | as 5.04. 50
the geck and scorn | o' th' other's villainy? 5.04. 68
arise my knights o' th' battle. 5.05. 20
like romans, | and not o' th' court of britain. 5.05. 25
that all th' abhorred things o' th' earth amend 5.05.216
upon me, set | the dogs o' th' street to bay me; 5.05.223
and in the beams o' th' sun | so vanish'd; 5.05.472
shall raze you out o' th' book of trespasses TNK 1.01. 33
he that will all the treasure know o' th' earth 1.01.114
leave not out a jot | o' th' sacred ceremony. 1.01.131
that your fame | knolls in the ear o' th' world. 1.01.134
thou still make good | the tongue o' th' world. 1.01.227
i' th' aid o' th' current were almost to sink, 1.02. 8
and bare weeds | the gain o' th' martialist, who 1.02. 16
what will | the fall o' th' stroke do damage? 1.02.113
made too proud the bed, took leave o' th' moon 1.03. 52
this fellow has a vengeance trick o' th' hip. 2.03. 70
and so would any young wench, o' my conscience, 2.04. 12
th' enamell'd knacks o' th' mead or garden! 3.01. 7
thou, o jewel | o' th' wood, o' th' world, hast 3.01. 10
thou, o jewel | o' th' wood, o' th' world, hast 3.01. 10
and | perfumes to kill the smell o' th' prison; 3.01. 86
night, | and darkness lord o' th' world! 3.02. 4
play o' th' virginals? 3.03. 34
tell me | news from all parts o' th' world. 3.04. 13
where's the rest o' th' music? 3.05. 31
now to be frampal, now to piss o' th' nettle! 3.05. 57
let him play | qui passa o' th' bells and bones. 3.05. 86
those are o' th' least; 3.06. 64
better, o' my conscience, | was never soldier's 4.02. 87
and by thee | be styl'd the lord o' th' day. 5.01. 60
and cur'st the world | o' th' plurisy of people! 5.01. 66
how far is't now to th' end o' th' world, my 5.02. 72
burst of clamor | is sure th' end o' th' combat. 5.03. 78
arcite's body | within an inch o' th' pyramid, 5.03. 80
two emulous philomels beat the ear o' th' night 5.03.124
that hath outliv'd | the love o' th' people, yea 5.04. 2
kinsman hath confess'd the right o' th' lady 5.04.116

/O* 30 FR 0.0034 REL FR 26 V 4 P

/o, /je /m'en vois a la cour — la grande WIV 1.04. 51 P
/o, /that /i /were /a /mockery /king /of /snow, R2 4.01.260
/o /flatt'ring /glass, | /like /to /my 4.01.279
/o, /good! 4.01.317
/o /thou /fond /many, /with /what /loud 2H4 1.03. 91
/cri'st /now, "/o /earth, /yield /us /that /king 1.03.106
/o /thoughts /of /men /accurs'd! 1.03.107
/and /him, /o /wondrous /him! 2.03. 32
/o /miracle /of /men! 2.03. 33
/never, /o /never, /do /his /ghost /the /wrong 2.03. 39
/o, /my /good /lord /mowbray, | /construe /the 4.01.101
/o, /when /the /king /did /throw /his /warder 4.01.123
/o /my /son, | god put /it in thy mind to take 4.05.177
/calen /o custure me! H5 4.04. 4 P
/o, if you love my brother, hate not me! R3 1.04.226
/o, /do /not /swear, /my /lord /of /buckingham. 3.07.220
/o, /handle /not /the /theme, /to /talk /of TIT 3.02. 29
/o, /o, /o, | /then /pardon /me /for 3.02. 68
/o, /o, /o, | /then /pardon /me /for 3.02. 68
/o, /o, /o, | /then /pardon /me /for 3.02. 68
/o /god, /i /could /be /bounded /in /a /nutshell HAM 2.02.254 P
/o, /there /has /been /much /throwing /about /of 2.02.358 P
"/o, a pit of clay for to be made | /for /such 5.01.120
/o, /sir, /are /you /come? LR 1.04.257
/o, /then /it /mov'd /her. 4.03. 15
if she be false, /o, /then heaven /mocks itself! OTH 3.03.278
no — yes, sure — /o /heaven, roderigo! 5.01. 90
/o /lord, /lord, /lord! 5.02. 84
/o /lord, what cry is that? 5.02.117
/o cleft effect! LC 293

O* 2434 FR 0.2751 REL FR 2003 V 431 P

o! TMP 1.02. 5
o, the cry did knock | against my very heart. 1.02. 8
o, woe the day! 1.02. 15
o the heavens! 1.02. 59
o, my heart bleeds | to think o' th' teen that i 1.02. 63
o, good sir, i do. 1.02. 88
o the heavens! 1.02.116
o, a cherubin | thou wast that did preserve me. 1.02.152
o, was she so? 1.02.261
o ho, o ho! 1.02.349
o ho, o ho! 1.02.349
which i do last pronounce, is (o you wonder!) 1.02.427
o, if a virgin, | and your affection not gone 1.02.448
o dear father, | make not too rash a trial of 1.02.467
o, widow dido? ay, widow dido. 2.01.102 P
o thou mine heir | of naples and of milan, what 2.01.112
might, | worthy sebastian, o, what might — ? 2.01.205
o! 2.01.223
o, out of that no hope | what great hope have 2.01.239
o, that you bore | the mind that i do! 2.01.266
o, but one word. 2.01.296
o, 'twas a din to fright a monster's ear, | to 2.01.314
do not torment me! o! 2.02. 56 P
the spirit torments me! o! 2.02. 64 P
o, defend me! 2.02. 88 P
o stephano, two neapolitans scap'd! 2.02.112 P
o stephano, hast any more of this? 2.02.133 P
o brave monster! lead the way. 2.02.188 P
o, she is | ten times more gentle than her 3.01. 7
o most dear mistress, | the sun will set before 3.01. 21
o my father, | i have broke your hest to say so! 3.01. 36
but you, o you, | so perfect and so peerless, 3.01. 46
o heaven, o earth, bear witness to this sound, 3.01. 68
o heaven, o earth, bear witness to this sound, 3.01. 68
o, forgive me my sins! 3.02.130 P
o, it is monstrous! 3.03. 95
o ferdinand, | do not smile at me that i boast 4.01. 8
o king stephano! 4.01.222 P
o peer! 4.01.222 P
o worthy stephano! 4.01.222 P
o, ho, monster! 4.01.225 P
o king stephano! 4.01.226 P
o good gonzalo, | my true preserver, and a loyal 5.01. 68
o heavens, that they were living both in naples, 5.01.149
o, wonder! 5.01.181
o brave new world | that has such people in't! 5.01.183
but o, how oddly will it sound that i | must ask 5.01.197
o, rejoice | beyond a common joy, and set it 5.01.206
o, look, sir, look, sir, here is more of us. 5.01.216
o setebos, these be brave spirits indeed! 5.01.261
o, touch me not, i am not stephano, but a cramp. 5.01.286 P
o, they love least that let men know their love. TGV 1.02. 32
o hateful hands, to tear such loving words! 1.02.102
o, that our fathers would applaud our loves, 1.03. 48
o heavenly julia! 1.03. 50
o, how this spring of love resembleth | the 1.03. 84
o, that you had mine eyes, or your own eyes had 2.01. 70 P
o excellent motion! 2.01. 94 P
o exceeding puppet! 2.01. 94 P
o, give ye good ev'n! 2.01. 98 P
o jest unseen, inscrutable; 2.01.135
o excellent device, was there ever heard a 2.01.139
o, be not like your mistress — be mov'd, be 2.01.174 P
no, the dog is himself, and i am the dog — o! 2.03. 22 P
o, that she could speak now like a /wood woman! 2.03. 27 P
o gentle proteus, love's a mighty lord, | and 2.04.136
o, flatter me; for love delights in praises. 2.04.148
o, but i love his lady too too much, | and 2.04.205
o sweet–suggesting love, if thou hast sinn'd, 2.06. 7
o, know'st thou not his looks are my soul's food 2.07. 15
o, could their master come and go as lightly, 3.01.142
that thou art banish'd — o, that's the news! 3.01.219
o, i have fed upon this woe already, | and now 3.01.221
o my dear silvia! hapless valentine! 3.01.262
o illiterate loiterer! 3.01.296 P
o villain, that set this down among her vices! 3.01.333 P
that's monstrous. o, that that were out! 3.01.365 P
o eglamour, thou art a gentleman — | think not 4.03. 11
o, 'tis a foul thing when a cur cannot keep 4.04. 9 P
o, he sends you for a picture? 4.04.115
o thou senseless form, | thou shalt be 4.04.198
o, sir, i find her milder than she was, | and 5.02. 2
o, sir, she makes no doubt of that. 5.02. 20
o, ay; and pities them. 5.02. 26
o valentine, this i endure for thee! 5.03. 15
o thou that dost inhabit in my breast, | leave 5.04. 7
o miserable, unhappy that i am! 5.04. 28
o, heaven be judge how i love valentine, | whose 5.04. 36
o, 'tis the curse in love, and still approv'd, 5.04. 43
o heaven! 5.04. 59
o time most accurst! 5.04. 71
o me unhappy! 5.04. 84
o good sir, my master charg'd me to deliver a 5.04. 88 P
o, cry you mercy, sir, i have mistook; 5.04. 94
o proteus, let this habit make thee blush! 5.04.104
o heaven! 5.04.110
o heaven! this is mistress anne page. WIV 1.01.190 P
o base hungarian wight! 1.03. 20 P
o, she did so course o'er my exteriors with such 1.03. 65 P
o, i should remember him. 1.04. 28 P
o diable, diable! 1.04. 67 P
o wicked, wicked world! 2.01. 20 P
o mistress page, give me some counsel! 2.01. 41 P
o woman — if it were not for one trifling 2.01. 44 P
o that my husband saw this letter! 2.01.100 P
at thy heels — | o, odious is the name! 2.01.119
o sir! 2.02.230 P
o, understand my drift. 2.02.242 P
o good sir! 2.02.256 P
o sweet anne page! 3.01. 70 P
o sweet anne page! 3.01.114 P

o, you are a flattering boy, now i see you'll be		3.02. 7 P
o this blessed hour!		3.03. 45 P
o sweet sir john!		3.03. 47 P
o mistress ford, what have you done?		3.03. 94 P
o well–a–day, mistress ford, having an honest		3.03. 99 P
o, how have you deceiv'd me!		3.03.128 P
let me see't, let me see't, o, let me see't!		3.03.137 P
o, what a world of vild ill–favor'd faults		3.04. 32
o boy, thou hadst a father!		3.04. 36 P
o, here he comes.		3.05. 59 P
o — vocativo, o.		4.01. 52 P
o — vocativo, o.		4.01. 52 P
o you panderly rascals, there's a knot, a /ging,		4.02.117 P
o powerful love, that in some respects makes a		5.05. 4 P
o omnipotent love, how near the god drew to the		5.05. 7 P
fault done first in the form of a beast (o jove,		5.05. 9 P
o, o, o!		5.05. 89 P
o, o, o!		5.05. 89 P
o, o, o!		5.05. 89 P
o, let him marry her.	MM	1.04. 49
o thou caitiff!		2.01.174 P
o thou varlet!		2.01.174 P
o thou wicked hannibal!		2.01.174 P
o just but severe law!		2.02. 41
o, think on that, | and mercy then will breathe		2.02. 77
o, that's sudden!		2.02. 83
o, it is excellent | to have a giant's strength;		2.02.107
o, to him, to him, wench!		2.02.124
o, fie, fie, fie!		2.02.171
o, let her brother live!		2.02.174
o cunning enemy, that, to catch a saint, | with		2.02.179
o injurious love, | that respites me a life		2.03. 40
o place, o form, | how often dost thou with thy		2.04. 12
o place, o form, | how often dost thou with thy		2.04. 12
o heavens!		2.04. 19
o, pardon me, my lord, it oft falls out, | to		2.04.117
o perilous mouths, | that bear in them one and		2.04.172
o, i do fear thee, claudio, and i quake, | lest		3.01. 73
o, 'tis the cunning livery of hell, | the		3.01. 94
o heavens, it cannot be.		3.01. 98
o, were it but my life, | i'd throw it down for		3.01.103
o isabel!		3.01.114
o you beast!		3.01.135
o faithless coward!		3.01.136
o dishonest wretch!		3.01.136
o, fie, fie, fie!		3.01.147
o hear me, isabella!		3.01.150
but, o, how much is the good duke deceiv'd in		3.01.191 P
o heavens, what stuff is here?		3.02. 4 P
o, sir, you are deceiv'd.		3.02.123 P
o, you hope the duke will return no more;		3.02.164 P
o, what may man within him hide, | though angel		3.02.271
take, o, take those lips away, | that so sweetly		4.01. 1
o place and greatness!		4.01. 59
o, death's a great disguiser, and you may add to		4.02.174 P
o, the better, sir;		4.03. 45 P
o sir, you must;		4.03. 57
o gravel heart!		4.03. 64
o, 'tis an accident that heaven provides!		4.03. 77
o, i will to him and pluck out his eyes!		4.03.119
o pretty isabella, i am pale at mine heart to		4.03.151 P
o, peace, the friar is come.		4.06. 9
o, your desert speaks loud, and i should wrong		5.01. 9
justice, o royal duke!		5.01. 20
o worthy prince, dishonor not your eye | by		5.01. 22
o worthy duke, | you bid me seek redemption of		5.01. 28
hear me, o hear me, here.		5.01. 32
o prince, i conjure thee, as thou believ'st		5.01. 48
o gracious duke, | harp not on that;		5.01. 63
o that it were as like as it is true!		5.01.104
then, o you blessed ministers above, | keep me		5.01.115
o heaven, the vanity of wretched fools!		5.01.164
but o, poor souls, | come you to seek the lamb		5.01.297
o, did you so?		5.01.330 P
o thou damnable fellow!		5.01.339 P
o my dread lord, | i should be guiltier than my		5.01.366
o, give me pardon, | that i, your vassal, have		5.01.385
o most kind maid, | it was the swift celerity of		5.01.393
o my most gracious lord, | i hope you will not		5.01.416
o my dear lord, | i crave no other, nor no		5.01.425
o my good lord!		5.01.430
o isabel!		5.01.442
but ere they came — o, let me say no more!	ERR	1.01. 94
o, had the gods done so, i had not now		1.01. 98
o — sixpence that i had a' we'nsday last | to		1.02. 55
o, know he is the bridle of your will.		2.01. 13
how comes it now, my husband, o, how comes it,		2.02.119
o, for my beads!		2.02.188
o spite of spites!		2.02.189
o, signior balthazar, either at flesh or fish,		3.01. 22
o villain, thou hast stol'n both mine office and		3.01. 44
o lord, i must laugh!		3.01. 50
have patience, sir, o, let it not be so!		3.01. 85
o, train me not, sweet mermaid, with thy note,		3.02. 45
o, soft, sir, hold you still;		3.02. 69
o, sir, upon her nose, all o'er embellish'd with		3.02.134 P
o, sir, i did not look so low.		3.02.139 P
o, yes, if any hour meet a sergeant, 'a turns		4.02. 56
o that thou wert not, poor distressed soul!		4.04. 59
o husband, god doth know you din'd at home,		4.04. 65
o, bind him, bind him! let him not come near me.		4.04.106
o most unhappy day!		4.04.123
o most unhappy strumpet!		4.04.124
o mistress, mistress, shift and save yourself!		5.01.168
most gracious duke, o, grant me justice, | even		5.01.190
o perjur'd woman!		5.01.212
o!		5.01.298
o time's extremity, | hast thou so crack'd and		5.01.308
o, my old master! who hath bound him here?		5.01.339
o, if thou be'st the same egeon, speak, | and		5.01.345
o, he's return'd, and as pleasant as ever he was	ADO	1.01. 37 P
o lord, he will hang upon him like a disease;		1.01. 86 P
o my lord, | when you went onward on this ended		1.01.296
o, i cry you mercy, friend, go you with me, and		1.02. 25 P
o, she misus'd me past the endurance of a block;		2.01.239 P
o god, sir, here's a dish i love not, i cannot		2.01.274 P
o, by no means, she mocks all her wooers out of		2.01.349 P
o lord, my lord, if they were but a week married		2.01.353 P
o, very well, my lord.		2.03. 41
o good my lord, tax not so bad a voice | to		2.03. 44
o, ay, stalk on, stalk on, the fowl sits.		2.03. 92 P
o god!		2.03.104 P
o, when she had writ it, and was reading it over		2.03.136 P
o, she tore the letter into a thousand halfpence		2.03.140 P
"o sweet benedick!		2.03.148 P
o my lord, wisdom and blood combating in so		2.03.163 P
o god of love!		3.01. 47
o, she would laugh me | out of myself, press me		3.01. 75
o, do not do your cousin such a wrong.		3.01. 87
o day untowardly turn'd!		3.02.131 P
o mischief strangely thwarting!		3.02.132 P
o plague right well prevented!		3.02.133 P
o, that exceeds, they say.		3.04. 17 P
o illegitimate construction!		3.04. 50 P
o, god help me, god help me, how long have you		3.04. 67 P
o, what men dare do!		4.01. 19 P
o, what authority and show of truth | can		4.01. 35
"true"! o god!		4.01. 68
o, god defend me, how am i beset!		4.01. 77
o hero!		4.01.100
o fate!		4.01.115
o, one too much by thee!		4.01.129
why, she, o, she is fall'n | into a pit of ink,		4.01.139
o, on my soul, my cousin is belied!		4.01.146
o, that is stronger made | which was before		4.01.150
o my father, | prove you that any man with me		4.01.180
o that i were a man!		4.01.303 P
unmitigated rancor — o god, that i were a man!		4.01.306 P
o that i were a man for his sake!		4.01.317 P
o, a stool and a cushion for the sexton.		4.02. 2 P
o villain!		4.02. 56 P
o that he were here to write me down as ass!		4.02. 75 P
o that i had been writ down an ass!		4.02. 86 P
o, in a tomb where never scandal slept, | save		5.01. 70
o noble sir!		5.01.292
o, stay but till then!		5.02. 45 P
o, these are barren tasks, too hard to keep,	LLL	1.01. 47
o! me.		1.01.257 P
which with — o, with — but with this i passion		1.01.260 P
no, no, o lord, sir, no.		1.02. 6 P
o well–knit sampson!		1.02. 73 P
o, you are welcome, sir, adieu.		2.01.213
but o — but o —		3.01. 28 P
but o — but o —		3.01. 28 P
o sir, plantan, a plain plantan:		3.01. 73 P
my lungs provokes me to ridiculous smiling — o,		3.01. 77 P
o, marry me to one frances!		3.01.121 P
o, that's the latin word for three farthings:		3.01.137 P
o, my good knave costard, exceedingly well met!		3.01.143 P
o, what is a remuneration?		3.01.147 P
o, why then three–farthing worth of silk.		3.01.149 P
o, stay, slave;		3.01.151 P
o, this afternoon.		3.01.155 P
o, thou knowest not what it is.		3.01.157 P
gardon, o sweet gardon!		3.01.170 P
o, and i, forsooth, in love!		3.01.174
of trotting paritors — o my little heart!		3.01.186
o short–liv'd pride!		4.01. 15
o heresy in fair, fit for these days!		4.01. 22
o, thy letter, thy letter!		4.01. 54
in the vulgar — o base and obscure vulgar!		4.01. 68 P
o, mark but that mark!		4.01.131
armado /a' /th' /one side — o, a most dainty		4.01.144
o thou monster ignorance, how deformed dost thou		4.02. 23
celestial as thou art, o, pardon love this wrong		4.02.117
o, but her eye — by this light, but for her eye		4.03. 9 P
o queen of queens, how far dost thou excel | no		4.03. 39
o sweet maria, empress of my love, | these		4.03. 54
o, rhymes are guards on wanton cupid's hose:		4.03. 56
o heavens, i have my wish!		4.03. 79
o most divine kate!		4.03. 81
o most profane coxcomb!		4.03. 82
o that i had my wish!		4.03. 90
o, would the king, berowne, and longaville,		4.03.121
says one, "o jove!"		4.03.139
o, what a scene of fool'ry have i seen, | of		4.03.161
o me, with what strict patience have i sat, | to		4.03.163
where lies thy grief, o, tell me, good dumaine?		4.03.169
o, dismiss this audience, and i shall tell you		4.03.206
sweet lords, sweet lovers, o, let us embrace!		4.03.210
o, but for my love, day would turn to night!		4.03.229
o, she needs it not.		4.03.235
o, 'tis the sun that maketh all things shine!		4.03.242
o /wood divine!		4.03.244
o, who can give an oath?		4.03.246
o paradox!		4.03.250
o, if in black my lady's brows be deck'd, | it		4.03.254
o, if the streets were paved with thine eyes,		4.03.274
o vile!		4.03.276
o, nothing so sure, and thereby all forsworn.		4.03.279
o, some authority how to proceed;		4.03.283
o, 'tis more than need.		4.03.285
o, we have made a vow to study, lords, | and in		4.03.315
o, then his lines would ravish savage ears | and		4.03.345
o, they have liv'd long on the alms–basket of		5.01. 38 P
o, and the heavens were so pleas'd that thou		5.01. 75 P
o, i smell false latin, "dunghill" for unguem.		5.01. 79 P
you weigh me not? o, that's you care not for me.		5.02. 27
o, he hath drawn my picture in his letter!		5.02. 38
o that your face were not so full of o's!		5.02. 45
o that i knew he were but in by th' week!		5.02. 61
o, i am /stabb'd with laughter!		5.02. 80
o vain petitioner!		5.02.207
o for your reason! quickly, sir — i long!		5.02.244
o poverty in wit, kingly–poor flout!		5.02.269
o, you have liv'd in desolation here, | unseen,		5.02.357
o, i am yours, and all that i possess!		5.02.383
o, never will i trust to speeches penn'd, | nor		5.02.402
o lord, sir, they would know | whether the three		5.02.485
o lord, sir, it were pity you should get your		5.02.496 P
o lord, sir, the parties themselves, the actors,		5.02.499 P
o, sir, you have overthrown alisander the		5.02.574 P
o, shall i say, i thank you, gentle wife?		5.02.826
cuckoo, cuckoo" — o word of fear, | unpleasing		5.02.901
cuckoo, cuckoo" — o word of fear, | unpleasing		5.02.910
but o, methinks, how slow | this old moon /wanes	MND	1.01. 3
o cross! too high to be enthrall'd to /low.		1.01.136
o spite! too old to be engag'd to young.		1.01.138
o hell! to choose love by another's eyes.		1.01.140
demetrius loves your fair, o happy fair!		1.01.182
o, were favor so, | /yours /would i catch, fair		1.01.186
o, teach me how you look, and with what art		1.01.192
o that your frowns would teach my smiles such		1.01.195
o that my prayers could such affection move!		1.01.197
o then, what graces in my love do dwell, | that		1.01.206
o, take the sense, sweet, of my innocence!		2.02. 45
o, wilt thou darkling leave me? do not so.		2.02. 86
o, i am out of breath in this fond chase!		2.02. 88
o, how fit a word | is that vile name to perish		2.02.106
o, that a lady, of one man refus'd, | should of		2.02.133
o — "as true as truest horse, that yet would		3.01.102
o monstrous!		3.01.104 P
o strange!		3.01.104 P
o bottom, thou art chang'd!		3.01.114 P
o, why rebuke you him that loves you so?		3.02. 43
o, once tell true;		3.02. 68
o brave touch!		3.02. 70
when truth kills truth, o devilish–holy fray!		3.02.129
o helen, goddess, nymph, perfect, divine!		3.02.137
o, how ripe in show | thy lips, those kissing		3.02.139
o, let me kiss | this princess of pure white,		3.02.143
o spite!		3.02.145
o hell!		3.02.145
the hasty–footed time | for parting us — o, is		3.02.201
o excellent!		3.02.247
o hated potion, hence!		3.02.264
o me, what news, my love!		3.02.272
why then you left me (o, the gods forbid!)		3.02.276
o me, you juggler!		3.02.282
o, when she is angry, she is keen and shrewd!		3.02.323
o weary night, o long and tedious night, | abate		3.02.431
o weary night, o long and tedious night, | abate		3.02.431
o, how i love thee!		4.01. 45
o, how mine eyes do loathe his visage now!		4.01. 79
o sweet bully bottom!		4.02. 19 P
o most courageous day!		4.02. 27 P
o most happy hour!		4.02. 27 P
o grim–look'd night!		5.01.170
o night with hue so black!		5.01.170
o night, which ever art when day is not!		5.01.171
o night, o night!		5.01.172
o night, o night!		5.01.172
and thou, o wall, o sweet, o lovely wall, | that		5.01.174
and thou, o wall, o sweet, o lovely wall, | that		5.01.174
and thou, o wall, o sweet, o lovely wall, | that		5.01.174
thou wall, o wall, o sweet and lovely wall,		5.01.176
thou wall, o wall, o sweet and lovely wall,		5.01.176
o wicked wall, through whom i see no bliss!		5.01.180
o wall, full often hast thou heard my moans,		5.01.188
o, kiss me through the hole of this vild wall!		5.01.200
o!		5.01.264
o spite!		5.01.276
o dainty duck!		5.01.281
o dear!		5.01.281
o fates, come, come, | cut thread and thrum,		5.01.285
o, wherefore, nature, didst thou lions frame?		5.01.291
o pyramus, arise!		5.01.326
o sisters three, | come, come to me, | with		5.01.336
o my antonio, i do know of these | that	MV	1.01. 95
o my antonio, had i but the means | to hold a		1.01.173
o me, the word choose!		1.02. 22 P
o, what a goodly outside falsehood hath!		1.03.102
o father abram, what these christians are,		1.03.160
o heavens, this is my true–begotten father, who,		2.02. 35 P
o rare fortune!		2.02.111 P
o lorenzo, | if thou keep promise, i shall end		2.03. 19
o, ten times faster venus' pigeons fly | to seal		2.06. 5
o sinful thought!		2.07. 54
o hell!		2.07. 62
o my ducats!		2.08. 15
o my daughter!		2.08. 15
o my christian ducats!		2.08. 16
o, that estates, degrees, and offices | were not		2.09. 41
o, these deliberate fools!		2.09. 80
o that i had a title good enough to keep his		3.01. 13 P
o, these naughty times | puts bars between the		3.02. 18
o happy torment, when my torturer | doth teach		3.02. 37
o love, be moderate, allay thy ecstasy, | in		3.02.111
o, then be bold to say bassanio's dead!		3.02.185
o sweet portia, | here are a few of the		3.02.250
o love! dispatch all business, and be gone!		3.02.323
o dear discretion, how his words are suited!		3.05. 65
o, be thou damn'd, inexecrable dog!		4.01.128
o wise young judge, how i do honor thee!		4.01.224
o noble judge! o excellent young man!		4.01.246
o noble judge! o excellent young man!		4.01.246
o wise and upright judge!		4.01.250
o upright judge! mark, jew: o learned judge!		4.01.313
o upright judge! mark, jew: o learned judge!		4.01.313
o learned judge! mark, jew, a learned judge!		4.01.317
o jew! an upright judge, a learned judge!		4.01.323
o, sir, very well; here in your orchard.	AYL	1.01. 41 P
o no;		1.01.107 P
o excellent young man!		1.02.213 P
o poor orlando!		1.02.259
o, how full of briers is this working–day world!		1.03. 11 P
o, they take the part of a better wrastler than		1.03. 22 P
o, a good wish upon you!		1.03. 24 P
o my poor rosalind, whither wilt thou go?		1.03. 90
o yes, into a thousand similes.		2.01. 45
o my gentle master!		2.03. 2
o my sweet master!		2.03. 3
o you memory | of old sir rowland!		2.03. 3
o, what a world is this, when what is comely		2.03. 14
o unhappy youth, | come not within these doors!		2.03. 16
o good old man, how well in thee appears | the		2.03. 56
o jupiter, how /weary are my spirits!		2.04. 1 P
o corin, that thou knew'st how i do love her!		2.04. 23
o, thou didst then never love so heartily!		2.04. 33
o phebe, phebe, phebe!		2.04. 43
o, i die for food!		2.06. 1 P
o noble fool!		2.07. 33
o worthy fool!		2.07. 36
o that i were a fool!		2.07. 42

o that your highness knew my heart in this! 3.01. 13
o rosalind, these trees shall be my books, | and 3.02. 5
o most gentle jupiter, what tedious homily of 3.02.155 P
o yes, i heard them all, and more, too, for some 3.02.164 P
o lord, lord, it is a hard matter for friends to 3.02.184 P
o wonderful, wonderful, and most wonderful 3.02.191 P
o, ominous! he comes to kill my heart. 3.02.246 P
o knowledge ill–inhabited, worse than jove in a 3.03. 10 P
not — o sweet oliver, | o brave oliver, | leave 3.03. 99
not — o sweet oliver, | o brave oliver, | leave 3.03.100
o, that's a brave man! 3.04. 40 P
o, come, let us remove, | the sight of lovers 3.04. 56
or if thou canst not, o, for shame, for shame, 3.05. 18
o dear phebe, | if ever (as that ever may be 3.05. 27
o, but she is wise. 4.01.159 P
o, that woman that cannot make her fault her 4.01.173 P
o coz, coz, coz, my pretty little coz, that thou 4.01.205 P
o, i have heard him speak of that same brother, 4.03.121
o my dear orlando, how it grieves me to see thee 5.02. 19 P
o, i know where you are. 5.02. 29 P
but o, how bitter a thing it is to look into 5.02. 43 P
keep you your word, o duke, to give your 5.04. 19
o sir, we quarrel in print, by the book — as 5.04. 90 P
juno's crown, | o blessed bond of board and bed! 5.04.142
o my dear niece, welcome thou art to me! 5.04.147
i charge you, o women, for the love you bear to ep 12 P
and i charge you, o men, for the love you bear ep 14 P
o monstrous beast, how like a swine he lies! SHR in.1. 34
o, that a mighty man of such descent, | of such in.2. 14
o, this it is that makes your lady mourn! in.2. 26
o, this is it that makes your servants droop! in.2. 27
o noble lord, bethink thee of thy birth, | call in.2. 30
o how we joy to see your wit restor'd! in.2. 77
o that once more you knew but what you are! in.2. 78
o yes, my lord, but very idle words, | for in.2. 83
o tranio, till i found it to be true, | i never 1.01.148
o yes, i saw sweet beauty in her face, | such as 1.01.167
o heavens! 1.02. 39 P
o, very well, i have perus'd the note. 1.02.144
o this learning, what a thing it is! 1.02.159
o this woodcock, what an ass it is! 1.02.160
o sir, such a life, with such a wife, were 1.02.193
o excellent motion! fellows, let's be gone. 1.02.278
o then belike you fancy riches more: 2.01. 16
o, pardon me, signior gremio, i would fain be 2.01. 74
o, how i long to have some chat with her! 2.01.162
o slow–wing'd turtle, shall a buzzard take thee? 2.01.207
a herald, kate? o, put me in thy books! 2.01.224
o sland'rous world! 2.01.253
o, let me see thee walk. 2.01.256
o, be thou dian, and let her be kate, | and then 2.01.260
o, the kindest kate! 2.01.307
o, you are novices! 2.01.311
let's hear. o fie, the treble jars. 3.01. 39
o, sir, his lackey, for all the world 3.02. 65 P
o kate, content thee, prithee be not angry. 3.02.215
o, ay, curtis, ay, and therefore fire, fire; 4.01. 19 P
o despiteful love! 4.02. 14
o master, master, i have watch'd so long | that 4.02. 59
o sir, i do, and will repute you ever | the 4.02.113
o mercy, god! 4.03. 87
o monstrous arrogance! 4.03.107
o, sir, the conceit is deeper than you think for 4.03.161
o, fie, fie, fie! 4.03.163
o no, good kate; 4.03.179
o immortal gods! 5.01. 66 P
o fine villain! 5.01. 66 P
o, i am undone! 5.01. 68 P
o villain, he is a sailmaker in bergamo. 5.01. 77 P
o, he hath murd'red his master! 5.01. 87 P
o, my son, my son! 5.01. 89 P
o monstrous villain! 5.01.108 P
o, we are spoil'd and — yonder he is. 5.01.110 P
o, sir, lucentio slipp'd me like his greyhound, 5.02. 52
o, o, petruchio, tranio hits you now. 5.02. 57
o, o, petruchio, tranio hits you now. 5.02. 57
o ho, entreat her! 5.02. 87
o vild, | intolerable, not to be endur'd! 5.02. 93
this young gentlewoman had a father — o, that AWW 1.01. 18 P
o, were that all! 1.01. 79
that your dian | was both herself and love, o, 1.03.213
o my sweet lord, that you will stay behind us! 2.01. 24
o, 'tis brave wars! 2.01. 25
o, will you eat | no grapes, my royal fox? 2.01. 69
o lord, sir! 2.02. 41 P
o lord, sir! — thick, thick, spare not me. 2.02. 45 P
o lord, sir! — nay, put me to't, i warrant you. 2.02. 48 P
o lord, sir! — spare not me. 2.02. 51 P
do you cry, "o lord, sir!" 2.02. 52 P
indeed your "o lord, sir!" 2.02. 53 P
i ne'er had worse luck in my life in my "o lord, 2.02. 57 P
o lord, sir! — why, there't serves well again. 2.02. 62 P
o my parolles, they have married me! 2.03.272
o, my knave, how does my old lady? 2.04. 18 P
o, i know him well, i, sir, he, sir, 's a good 2.05. 18 P
o madam, yonder is heavy news within between two 3.02. 33 P
o you leaden messengers, | that ride upon the 3.02.108
o, i believe with him. 3.05. 58
o, for the love of laughter, let him fetch his 3.06. 34 P
o, for the love of laughter, hinder not the 3.06. 41 P
o, ransom, ransom! do not hide mine eyes. 4.01. 67
o! 4.01. 77 P
o, pray, pray, pray! manka revania dulche. 4.01. 78 P
o, let me live! 4.01. 83
o lord, sir, let me live, or let me see my death 4.03.309 P
but o, strange men, | that can such sweet use 4.04. 21
o madam, yonder's my lord your son with a patch 4.05. 94 P
o my good lord, you were the first that found me 5.02. 42 P
which better than the first, o dear heaven, 5.03. 71
or, ere they meet, in me, o nature, cesse! 5.03. 72
grant it me, o king, in you it best lies; 5.03.145 P
o, behold this ring, | whose high respect and 5.03.191
both, both. o, pardon! 5.03.308
o my good lord, when i was like this maid, | i 5.03.309
o my dear mother, do i see you living? 5.03.319
o, it came o'er my ear like the sweet sound TN 1.01. 5
o spirit of love, how quick and fresh art thou, 1.01. 9
o, when mine eyes did see olivia first, 1.01. 18
o, she that hath a heart of that fine frame | to 1.01. 32
o my poor brother! and so perchance may he be. 1.02. 7
o that i serv'd that lady, | and might not be 1.02. 41
o knight, thou lack'st a cup of canary. 1.03. 80 P
o, had i but follow'd the arts! 1.03. 93 P
o, then unfold the passion of my love, 1.04. 24
o, you are sick of self–love, malvolio, and 1.05. 90 P
o, i have read it; 1.05.228 P
o, sir, i will not be so hard–hearted; 1.05.244 P
o, such love | could be but recompens'd, though 1.05.252
o, you should not rest | between the elements of 1.05.274
o good antonio, forgive me your trouble. 2.01. 34 P
o time, thou must untangle this, not i, | it is 2.02. 40
"o mistress mine, where are you roaming? 2.03. 39
o, stay and hear, your true–love's coming, 2.03. 40
"o no, no, no, no, you dare not." 2.03.112
o, if i thought that, i'd beat him like a dog! 2.03.141 P
o, 'twill be admirable! 2.03.171 P
o fellow, come, the song we had last night. 2.04. 42
of white, stuck all with yew, | o, prepare it! 2.04. 56
lay me, o, where | sad true lover never find my 2.04. 64
o, peace! 2.05. 30 P
o, peace! 2.05. 42 P
o, for a stone–bow, to hit him in the eye! 2.05. 46 P
o, peace, peace! 2.05. 51 P
o peace, peace, peace! now, now. 2.05. 57 P
o, peace, and the spirit of humors intimate 2.05. 84 P
o ay, make up that. he is now at a cold scent. 2.05.121 P
a should follow, but o does. 2.05.131 P
and o shall end, i hope. 2.05.132 P
ay, or i'll cudgel him, and make him cry o! 2.05.134 P
o, by your leave, i pray you: 3.01.106
o world, how apt the poor are to be proud! 3.01.127
o, what a deal of scorn looks beautiful | in the 3.01.145
o ho, do you come near me now? 3.04. 64 P
o lord! 3.04.107 P
o good sir toby, hold! here come the officers. 3.04.319 P
o heavens themselves! 3.04.357
but o, how vild an idol proves this god! 3.04.365
prove true, imagination, o, prove true, | that i 3.04.375
o, if it prove, | tempests are kind and salt 3.04.383
o, say so, and so be! 4.01. 65
o, you give me ill counsel. 5.01. 31 P
o, welcome, father! 5.01.150
o thou dissembling cub! 5.01.164
o, do not swear! 5.01.170
o, he's drunk, sir toby, an hour agone; 5.01.198 P
antonio, o my dear antonio! 5.01.218
o, that record is lively in my soul! 5.01.246
o my most sacred lady, | temptations have since WT 1.02. 76
o, would her name were grace! 1.02. 99
as 'twere | the mort o' th' deer — o, that is 1.02.118
o miserable lady! 1.02.351
o then, my best blood turn | to an infected 1.02.417
petty brands | that calumny doth use — o, i am 2.01. 72
o thou thing! 2.01. 82
o, the sacrifice! 3.01. 6
prove as successful to the queen (o be't so!) 3.01. 12
o that he were alive, and here beholding | his 3.02.120
o sir, i shall be hated to report it! 3.02.143
o, cut my lace, lest my heart, cracking it, 3.02.173
girls of nine), o, think what they have done, 3.02.182
but the last — o lords, | when i have said, cry 3.02.199
but, o thou tyrant! 3.02.207
o, the most piteous cry of the poor souls! 3.03. 90 P
with hey, the sweet birds, o, how they sing! 4.03. 6
o that ever i was born! 4.03. 50 P
o, help me, help me! 4.03. 52 P
o sir, the loathsomeness of them offend me more 4.03. 56 P
o good sir, tenderly, o! 4.03. 70 P
o good sir, tenderly, o! 4.03. 70 P
o good sir, softly, good sir! 4.03. 72 P
o, pardon, that i name them! 4.04. 7
o, the fates! 4.04. 20
o, but, sir, | your resolution cannot hold when 4.04. 35
o lady fortune, | stand you auspicious! 4.04. 51
o proserpina, | for the flow'rs now, that, 4.04.116
o, these i lack, | to make you garlands of, and 4.04.127
o doricles, | your praises are too large. 4.04.146
o master! 4.04.181 P
o, whither? 4.04.299
o, father, you'll know more of that hereafter. 4.04.343
o, hear me breathe my life | before this ancient 4.04.360
o, that must be | i' th' virtue of your daughter 4.04.386
o, my heart! 4.04.424
o sir, | you have undone a man of fourscore 4.04.452
o cursed wretch, | that knew'st this was the 4.04.458
o my lord, | i would your spirit were easier for 4.04.504
but o, the thorns we stand upon! 4.04.585
o perdita! 4.04.660
o, that's the case of the shepherd's son. 4.04.816 P
o that ever i | had squar'd me to thy counsel! 5.01. 51
o hermione, | as every present time doth boast 5.01. 95
o! 5.01.131
o my brother, | good gentleman! 5.01.147
o my poor father! 5.01.202
were now become a loss, cries, "o, thy mother, 5.02. 51 P
but o, the noble combat that 'twixt joy and 5.02. 72 P
o grave and good paulina, the great comfort 5.03. 1
o paulina, | we honor you with trouble; 5.03. 8
o, not by much. 5.03. 29
o, thus she stood, | even with such life of 5.03. 34
o royal piece, | there's magic in thy majesty, 5.03. 38
o, patience! 5.03. 46
o sweet paulina, | make me to think so twenty 5.03. 70
o, she's warm! 5.03.109
o, peace, paulina! 5.03.135
o old sir robert, father, on my knee | i give JN 1.01. 82
"o sir," says answer, "at your best command, 1.01.197
o me, 'tis my mother. 1.01.220
o, take his mother's thanks, a widow's thanks, 2.01. 32
o, well did he become that lion's robe, | that 2.01.141
o, tremble! for you hear the lion roar. 2.01.294
o, now doth death line his dead chaps with steel 2.01.352
o prudent discipline! 2.01.413
o, two such silver currents when they join | do 2.01.441
o, if thou teach me to believe this sorrow, 3.01. 29
o boy, then where art thou? 3.01. 34
but fortune, o, | she is corrupted, chang'd, and 3.01. 54
hear me, o, hear me! 3.01.112
o lymoges, o austria! 3.01.114
o lymoges, o austria! 3.01.114
o, that a man should speak those words to me! 3.01.130
o, lawful let it be | that i have room with rome 3.01.179
o lewis, stand fast! 3.01.208
o, if thou grant my need, | which only lives but 3.01.211
o then tread down my need, and faith mounts up; 3.01.215
o, be remov'd from him, and answer well! 3.01.218
o holy sir, | my reverend father, let it not be 3.01.248
o, let thy vow | first made to heaven, first be 3.01.265
o husband, hear me! 3.01.305
o, upon my knee, | made hard with kneeling, i do 3.01.309
o, thine honor, lewis, thine honor! 3.01.316
o fair return of banish'd majesty! 3.01.321
o foul revolt of french inconstancy! 3.01.322
o, this will make my mother die with grief! 3.03. 5
o my gentle hubert, | we owe thee much! 3.03. 19
o amiable lovely death! 3.04. 25
misery's love, | o, come to me! 3.04. 36
o fair affliction, peace! 3.04. 36
o, that my tongue were in the thunder's mouth! 3.04. 38
o, if i could, what grief should i forget! 3.04. 50
o, what love i note | in the fair multitude of 3.04. 61
"o that these hands could so redeem my son | as 3.04. 71
o lord, my boy, my arthur, my fair son! 3.04.103
o sir, when he shall hear of your approach, | if 3.04.162
and o, what better matter breeds for you | than 3.04.170
o noble dolphin, | go with me to the king. 3.04.177
o, save me, hubert, save me! 4.01. 72
o heaven! 4.01. 91
o, spare mine eyes, | though to no use but still 4.01.101
o, now you look like hubert! 4.01.125
o heaven! i thank you, hubert. 4.01.131
o, where hath our intelligence been drunk? 4.02.116
o, make a league with me, till i have pleas'd 4.02.126
o my gentle cousin, | hear'st thou the news 4.02.159
o, let me have no subject enemies | when adverse 4.02.171
o, when the last accompt 'twixt heaven and earth 4.02.216
o, haste thee to the peers, | throw this report 4.02.260
o, answer not! 4.02.267
o me, my uncle's spirit is in these stones. 4.03. 9
o death, made proud with pure and princely 4.03. 35
o, he is bold, and blushes not at death. 4.03. 76
o, let it not be said! 5.01. 59
o inglorious league! 5.01. 65
o, it grieves my soul, | that i must draw this 5.02. 15
o, and there | where honorable rescue and 5.02. 17
and is't not pity, o my grieved friends, | that 5.02. 24
o nation, that thou couldst remove! 5.02. 33
o, what a noble combat hast /thou fought 5.02. 43
how goes the day with us? o, tell me, hubert. 5.03. 1
o, my heart is sick! 5.03. 4
o, bravely came we off, | when with a volley of 5.05. 4
o my sweet sir, news fitting to the night, 5.06. 19
o vanity of sickness! 5.07. 13
o that there were some virtue in my tears, 5.07. 44
o, i am scalded with my violent motion | and 5.07. 49
o cousin, thou art come to set mine eye. 5.07. 51
o, let us pay the time but needful woe, | since 5.07.110
o, let my sovereign turn away his face, | and R2 1.01.111
o, god defend my soul from such deep sin! 1.01.187
o, /sit my husband's wrongs on herford's spear, 1.02. 47
o, let no noble eye profane a tear | for me, if 1.03. 59
o thou, the earthly author of my blood, | whose 1.03. 69
o, had't been a stranger, not my child, | to 1.03.239
o, to what purpose dost thou hoard thy words, 1.03.253
o, who can hold a fire in his hand | by thinking 1.03.294
o no, the apprehension of the good | gives but 1.03.300
o, but they say the tongues of dying men 2.01. 5
o, how that name befits my composition! 2.01. 73
o no, thou diest, though i the sicker be. 2.01. 91
o, had thy grandsire with a prophet's eye | seen 2.01.104
o, spare me not, my /brother edward's son, | for 2.01.124
o richard! 2.01.184
o my liege, | pardon me, if you please; 2.01.186
o, full of careful business are his looks! 2.02. 75
o, then how quickly should this arm of mine, 2.03.103
o then my father, | will you permit that i shall 2.03.118
o, call back yesterday, bid time return, | and 3.02. 69
o villains, vipers, damn'd without redemption! 3.02.129
o, belike it is the bishop of carlisle. 3.03. 30
o god, o god, that e'er this tongue of mine 3.03.133
o god, o god, that e'er this tongue of mine 3.03.133
o that i were as great | as is my grief, or 3.03.136
o, what pity is it | that he had not so trimm'd 3.04. 55
o, i am press'd to death through want of 3.04. 72
o, thou thinkest | to serve me last that i may 3.04. 94
o, forfend it, god, | that in a christian 4.01.129
o, if you raise this house against this house, 4.01.145
o heinous, strong, and bold conspiracy! 5.03. 59
o loyal father of a treacherous son! 5.03. 60
o king, believe not this hard–hearted man! 5.03. 87
o happy vantage of a kneeling knee! 5.03.132
o, how it ern'd my heart when i beheld | in 5.05. 76
o would the deed were good! 5.05.114
o that it could be prov'd | that some 1H4 1.01. 86
o rare! 1.02. 64 P
o, thou hast damnable iteration, and art indeed 1.02. 90 P
o, if men were to be sav'd by merit, what hole 1.02.107 P
o, sir, your presence is too bold and peremptory 1.03. 17
o, pardon me that i descend so low | to show the 1.03.167
o, the blood more stirs | to rouse a lion than 1.03.197
cousin" — | o, the devil take such cozeners! 1.03.255
o, let the hours be short, | till fields, and 1.03.301
o, 'tis our setter, i know his voice. 2.02. 50 P
o, we are undone, both we and ours for ever! 2.02. 86 P
o, i could divide myself and go to buffets, for 2.03. 32 P
o my good lord, why are you thus alone? 2.03. 37
o, what portents are these? 2.03. 62
o esperance! 2.03. 71
o lord, sir, i'll be sworn upon all the books in 2.04. 49 P
o lord, i would it had been two! 2.04. 60 P
o lord, sir, who do you mean? 2.04. 72 P
"o my sweet harry," says she, "how many hast 2.04.105 P
o villain, thy lips are scarce wip'd since thou 2.04.153 P
o monstrous! 2.04.219 P

o for breath to utter what is like thee! 2.04.246 P
o jesu, my lord the prince! 2.04.284 P
o villain, thou stolest a cup of sack eighteen 2.04.314 P
o, glendower. 2.04.340 P
o jesu, this is excellent sport, i' faith! 2.04.390 P
o, the father, how he holds his countenance! 2.04.392 P
o jesu, he doth it as like one of these harlotry 2.04.395 P
o my lord, my lord, the sheriff with a most 2.04.482 P
o jesu, my lord, my lord! 2.04.486 P
o monstrous! 2.04.540 P
o, then the earth shook to see the heavens on 3.01. 24
o, while you live, tell truth and shame the 3.01. 61
o, he is as tedious | as a tired horse, a 3.01.157
o, i am ignorance itself in this! 3.01.210
o, thou art a perpetual triumph, an everlasting 3.03. 40 P
o jesu, i have heard the prince tell him, i know 3.03. 83 P
o, if it should, how would thy guts fall about 3.03.152 P
o, my sweet beef, i must still be good angel to 3.03.177 P
o, i do not like that paying back, 'tis a double 3.03.179 P
o for a fine thief, of the age of two and twenty 3.03.188 P
o, i could wish this tavern were my drum! 3.03.206
o that glendower were come! 4.01.124
o no, my nephew must not know, sir richard, 5.02. 1
o, would the quarrel lay upon our heads, | and 5.02. 47
o, gentlemen, the time of life is short! 5.02. 81
o douglas, hadst thou fought at holmedon thus, 5.03. 14
o hal, i prithee give me leave to breathe a 5.03. 44 P
o, this boy | lends mettle to us all! 5.04. 23
o god, they did me too much injury | that ever 5.04. 51
o, harry, thou hast robb'd me of my youth! 5.04. 77
o, i could prophesy, | but that the earthy and 5.04. 83
o, i should have a heavy miss of thee | if i 5.04.105
o, such a day! 2H4 1.01. 20
o lord, ay! good master snare. 2.01. 6 P
o my most worshipful lord, and't please your 2.01. 69 P
o that this blossom could be kept from cankers! 2.02. 94 P
o yet, for god's sake, go not to these wars! 2.03. 9
o, fly to scotland, | till that the nobles and 2.03. 50
o, the lord preserve thy grace! 2.04.291 P
o jesu, are you come from wales? 2.04.293 P
o, run, doll, run, run, good doll. 2.04.389 P
o sleep! 3.01. 5
o gentle sleep! 3.01. 5
o thou dull god, why li'st thou with the vile 3.01. 15
canst thou, o partial sleep, give /then repose 3.01. 26
o god, that one might read the book of fate, 3.01. 45
o, if this were seen, | the happiest youth, 3.01. 53
o lord, good my lord captain — 3.02.177 P
o lord, sir, i am a diseas'd man. 3.02.179 P
o sir john, do you remember since we lay all 3.02.194 P
o, give me the spare men, and spare me the great 3.02.269 P
o, give me always a little, lean, old, chopp'd, 3.02.274 P
o, who shall believe | but you misuse the 4.02. 22
o, with what wings shall his affections fly 4.04. 65
o westmerland, thou art a summer bird, | which 4.04. 91
o me! 4.04.111
o my royal father! 4.04.112
o polish'd perturbation! 4.05. 23
o majesty! 4.05. 28
and filial tenderness | shall, o dear father, 4.05. 40
o foolish youth, | thou seek'st the greatness 4.05. 96
o my poor kingdom, sick with civil blows! 4.05.133
o, thou wilt be a wilderness again, | peopled 4.05.136
o, pardon me, my liege! 4.05.138
o, let me in my present wildness die, | and 4.05.152
how i came by the crown, o god forgive, | and 4.05.218
o, it is much that a lie with a slight oath and 5.01. 81 P
o, you shall see him laugh till his face be like 5.01. 84 P
o that the living harry had the temper | of he, 5.02. 15
o god, i fear all will be overturn'd! 5.02. 19
o, good my lord, you have lost a friend indeed, 5.02. 27
o base assyrian knight, what is thy news? 5.03.101
o joyful day! 5.03.126 P
o sweet pistol! 5.03.132 P
o the lord, that sir john were come! 5.04. 11 P
o god, that right should thus overcome might! 5.04. 24 P
o, if i had had time to have made new liveries, 5.05. 10 P
o for a muse of fire, that would ascend | the H5 pr 1
we cram | within this wooden o the very casques pr 13
o, pardon! pr 15
o noble english, that could entertain | with 1.02.111
o, let their bodies follow, my dear liege, 1.02.130
o england! 2.pr. 16
have for the gilt of france (o guilt indeed!) 2.pr. 26
o welliday, lady, if he be not hewn now, we 2.01. 36 P
o viper vile! 2.01. 46
o braggard vile and damned furious wight! 2.01. 60
o hound of crete, think'st thou my spouse to get 2.01. 73
o, let us yet be merciful. 2.02. 47
but o, | what shall i say to thee, lord scroop, 2.02. 93
o, how hast thou with jealousy infected | the 2.02.126
o, peace, prince dolphin! 2.04. 29
o, do but think | you stand upon the rivage and 3.pr. 13
o, 'tish ill done, 'tish ill done; 3.02. 92 P
o seigneur dieu, je m'en oublie d' elbow. 3.04. 31 P
o seigneur dieu! 3.04. 52 P
o dieu vivant! 3.05. 5
o, for honor of our land, | let us not hang like 3.05. 22
o then belike she was old and gentle, and you 3.07. 52 P
o now, who will behold | the royal captain of 4.pr. 28
where — o for pity! 4.pr. 49
o hard condition, | twin-born with greatness, 4.01.233
o ceremony, show me but thy worth! 4.01.244
o, be sick, great greatness, | and bid thy 4.01.251
o god of battles, steel my soldiers' hearts, 4.01.289
not to-day, o lord, | o, not to-day, think not 4.01.292
o, not to-day, think not upon the fault | my 4.01.293
o brave spirit! 4.02. 3
o that we now had here | but one ten thousand of 4.03. 16
o, do not wish one more! 4.03. 33
o seigneur dieu! 4.04. 6 P
o signieur dew should be a gentleman. 4.04. 7
perpend my words, o signieur dew, and mark: 4.04. 8
o signieur dew, thou diest on point of fox, 4.04. 9
of fox, | except, o signieur, thou do give to me 4.04. 10
o, prenez misericorde! ayez pitie de moi! 4.04. 12 P
o, pardonnez moi! 4.04. 21 P
o, je vous supplie, pour l'amour de dieu, me 4.04. 40 P
o diable! 4.05. 1
o seigneur! le jour est perdu, tout est perdu! 4.05. 2
o mechante fortune! 4.05. 5
o perdurable shame! 4.05. 7
o, 'tis a gallant king! 4.07. 10 P
o, give us leave, great king, | to view the 4.07. 81
o god, thy arm was here; 4.08.106
o fair katherine, if you will love me soundly 5.02.104 P
o bon dieu! 5.02.115 P
o kate, nice customs cur'sy to great kings. 5.02.268 P
o, whither shall we fly from this reproach? 1H6 1.01. 97
o no; 1.01.108
o no, he lives, but is took prisoner, | and lord 1.01.145
but o, the treacherous falstaff wounds my heart, 1.04. 35
o lord, have mercy on us, wretched sinners! 1.04. 70
o lord, have mercy on me, woeful man! 1.04. 71
o, would i were to die with salisbury! 1.05. 38
o, tell me when my lips do touch his cheeks, 2.05. 39
o uncle, would some part of my young years 2.05.107
o, what a scandal is it to our crown | that two 3.01. 69
o my good lords, and virtuous henry, | pity the 3.01. 76
o, how this discord doth afflict my soul! 3.01.106
o loving uncle, kind duke of gloucester, | how 3.01.142
o, let no words, but deeds, revenge this treason 3.02. 49
o, turn the edged sword another way, | strike 3.03. 52
o monstrous treachery! 4.01. 61
o, think upon the conquest of my father, | my 4.01.148
o, negligent and heedless discipline! 4.02. 44
o god, that somerset, who in proud heart | doth 4.03. 24
o, send some succor to the distress'd lord! 4.03. 30
o young john talbot, i did send for thee | to 4.05. 1
but o malignant and ill-boding stars! 4.05. 6
o, if you love my mother, | dishonor not her 4.05. 13
o, twice my father, twice am i thy son! 4.06. 6
o, too much folly is it, well i wot, | to hazard 4.06. 32
o, where's young talbot? 4.07. 2
o my dear lord, lo where your son is borne! 4.07. 17
o thou whose wounds become hard-favored death, 4.07. 23
o, no, forbear! 4.07. 49
o, were mine eyeballs into bullets turn'd, 4.07. 79
o, that i could but call these dead to life, 4.07. 81
o, hold me not with silence over-long! 5.03. 13
o, charles the dolphin is a proper man, | no 5.03. 37
o fairest beauty, do not fear nor fly, | for i 5.03. 46
o, stay! 5.03. 60
o, wert thou for myself! 5.03.187
o, burn her, burn her! 5.04. 33
o, give me leave, i have deluded you, | 'twas 5.04. 76
o warwick, warwick, i foresee with grief | the 5.04.111
o lord, that lends me life, | lend me a heart 2H6 1.01. 19
o peers of england, shameful is this league, 1.01. 98
o father, maine is lost! 1.01.209
o nell, sweet nell, if thou dost love thy lord, 1.02. 17
o lord, have mercy upon me! 1.03.215 P
o lord, my heart! 1.03.216 P
o, born so, master. 2.01. 96
o master, that you could! 2.01.132
o god, seest thou this, and bearest so long? 2.01.151
o god, what mischiefs work the wicked ones, 2.01.182
o lord bless me, i pray god, for i am never able 2.03. 76 P
o god, have i overcome mine enemies in this 2.03. 97 P
o peter, thou hast prevail'd in right! 2.03. 98 P
o that it were to do! 3.02. 3
run, go, help, help! o henry, ope thine eyes! 3.02. 35
o heavenly god! 3.02. 37
o thou that judgest all things, stay my thoughts 3.02.136
o henry, let me plead for gentle suffolk! 3.02.289
o, let me entreat thee cease. 3.02.339
o, could this kiss be printed in thy hand, 3.02.343
o, go not yet! 3.02.353
o, let me stay, befall what may befall! 3.02.402
o, torture me no more, i will confess. 3.03. 11
o thou eternal mover of the heavens, | look with 3.03. 19
o, beat away the busy meddling fiend | that lays 3.03. 21
o god, forgive him! 3.03. 29
o that i were a god, to shoot forth thunder 4.01.104
o barbarous and bloody spectacle! 4.01.144
o miserable age! 4.02. 10 P
o monstrous! 4.02. 87 P
o gross and miserable ignorance! 4.02.168
o graceless men! they know not what they do. 4.04. 38
o monstrous coward! what, to come behind folks? 4.07. 83 P
o, let me live! 4.07.104
o, brave! 4.07.129 P
o, i am slain! 4.10. 60 P
o, i could hew up rocks and fight with flint, 5.01. 24
o, let me view his visage, being dead, | that 5.01. 69
o monstrous traitor! 5.01.106
o blood-bespotted neapolitan, | outcast of 5.01.117
o, where is faith? 5.01.166
o, where is loyalty? 5.01.166
o war, thou son of hell, | whom angry heavens do 5.02. 33
o, let the vile world end, | and the premised 5.02. 40
o clifford, how thy words revive my heart! 3H6 1.01.163
o, let me pray before i take my death! 1.03. 35
o clifford, but bethink thee once again, | and 1.04. 44
o, 'tis a fault too too unpardonable! 1.04.106
o tiger's heart wrapp'd in a woman's hide! 1.04.137
o, ten times more, than tigers of hyrcania. 1.04.155
o, speak no more, for i have heard too much. 2.01. 48
o clifford, boist'rous clifford, thou hast slain 2.01. 70
again, | never, o never, shall i see more joy! 2.01. 78
o valiant lord, the duke of york is slain! 2.01.100
o warwick, warwick, that plantagenet, | which 2.01.101
are you there, butcher? o, i cannot speak! 2.02. 95
o warwick, i do bend my knee with thine, | and 2.03. 33
o god! 2.05. 21
o yes, it doth; 2.05. 46
o god! 2.05. 61
o heavy times, begetting such events! 2.05. 63
o piteous spectacle! 2.05. 73
o bloody times! 2.05. 73
o, pity, god, this miserable age! 2.05. 88
o boy! 2.05. 92
o that my death would stay these ruthful deeds! 2.05. 95
o, pity, pity, gentle heaven, pity! 2.05. 96
o lancaster! 2.06. 3
o phoebus! 2.06. 11
o, would he did! 2.06. 64
o margaret, thus 'twill be, and thou, poor soul, 3.01. 53
o miserable thought! 3.02.151
o monstrous fault, to harbor such a thought! 3.02.164
o, but impatience waiteth on true sorrow. 3.03. 42
o, is it so? 4.03. 12
o unbid spite, is sportful edward come? 5.01. 18
o cheerful colors! see where oxford comes! 5.01. 58
o, welcome, oxford, for we want thy help. 5.01. 66
o passing traitor, perjur'd and unjust! 5.01.106
with a groan, | "o, farewell, warwick!" 5.02. 47
o brave young prince! 5.04. 52
o, kill me too! 5.05. 41
o ned, sweet ned, speak to thy mother, boy! 5.05. 51
o traitors, murtherers! 5.05. 52
o, god forgive my sins, and pardon thee! 5.06. 60
o, may such purple tears be alway shed | from 5.06. 64
"o, jesus bless us, he is born with teeth!" 5.06. 75
o, belike his majesty hath some intent | that R3 1.01. 49
o, he hath kept an evil diet long, | and 1.01.139
o, cursed be the hand that made these holes! 1.02. 14
o gentlemen, see, see dead henry's wounds | open 1.02. 55
o god! 1.02. 62
o earth! 1.02. 63
o wonderful, when devils tell the /troth! 1.02. 73
o, he was gentle, mild, and virtuous! 1.02.104
o, 'twas the foulest deed to slay that babe, 1.03.182
o, let them keep it till thy sins be ripe, | and 1.03.218
o, let me make the period to my curse! 1.03.237
o, serve me well, and teach yourselves that duty 1.03.252
o that your young nobility could judge | what 1.03.256
o god that seest it, do not suffer it! 1.03.270
o princely buckingham, i'll kiss thy hand | in 1.03.279
o buckingham, take heed of yonder dog! 1.03.288
o, but remember this another day, | when he 1.03.298
o, i have pass'd a miserable night, | so full of 1.04. 2
o lord, methought what pain it was to drown! 1.04. 21
o, then began the tempest to my soul! 1.04. 44
o god! 1.04. 69
o, spare my guiltless wife and my poor children! 1.04. 72
o, in the duke of gloucester's purse. 1.04.128 P
o excellent device! and make a sop of him. 1.04.157 P
the deed, | o, know you yet he doth it publicly. 1.04.216
o no; 1.04.233
o, do not slander him, for he is kind. 1.04.241
o, sirs, consider, they that set you on | to do 1.04.254
o, if thine eye be not a flatterer, | come thou 1.04.264
o god! 2.01.132
o, they did urge it still unto the king! 2.01.138
and cry, "o clarence, my unhappy son!"? 2.02. 4
o, what cause have i | (thine being but a moi'ty 2.02. 59
o, full of danger is the duke of gloucester, 2.03. 27
o, preposterous | and frantic outrage, end thy 2.04. 63
o my lord, | you said that idle weeds are fast 3.01.102
o my fair cousin, i must not say so. 3.01.106
a greater gift? o, that's the sword to it. 3.01.116
o, then i see you will part but with light gifts 3.01.118
o, 'tis a perilous boy, | bold, quick, ingenious 3.01.154
o monstrous, monstrous! 3.02. 64
o pomfret, pomfret! 3.03. 9
o thou bloody prison! 3.03. 9
o, remember, god, | to hear her prayer for them, 3.03. 19
o, now i need the priest that spake to me! 3.04. 87
o margaret, margaret, now thy heavy curse | is 3.04. 92
o momentary grace of mortal men, | which we more 3.04. 96
o bloody richard! 3.04.103
o, make them joyful, grant their lawful suit! 3.07.203
despiteful tidings, o unpleasing news! 4.01. 36
o dorset, speak not to me, get thee gone! 4.01. 38
o ill-dispersing wind of misery! 4.01. 52
o my accursed womb, the bed of death! 4.01. 53
o, would to god that the inclusive verge | of 4.01. 58
o, when, i say, i look'd on richard's face, 4.01. 70
o bitter consequence, | that edward still should 4.02. 15
o, let me think on hastings, and be gone | to 4.02.121
"o, thus," quoth dighton, "lay the gentle babes. 4.03. 9
but o! 4.03. 16
wilt thou, o god, fly from such gentle lambs, 4.04. 22
o upright, just, and true-disposing god, | how 4.04. 55
o harry's wife, triumph not in my woes! 4.04. 59
o thou didst prophesy the time would come 4.04. 79
o thou well skill'd in curses, stay awhile, 4.04.116
my words are dull, o, quicken them with thine! 4.04.124
o, she that might have intercepted thee, | by 4.04.137
o, let me speak! 4.04.160
o, let her live! 4.04.206
o no, my reasons are too deep and dead — | too 4.04.362
o, true, good catesby. 4.04.449
o thou whose captain i account myself, | look on 5.03.108
sleeping and waking, o, defend me still! 5.03.117
o, in the battle think on buckingham, | and die 5.03.169
o coward conscience, how dost thou afflict me! 5.03.179
o no! 5.03.189
o ratcliffe, i have dream'd a fearful dream! 5.03.212
o ratcliffe, i fear, i fear! 5.03.214
o, now let richmond and elizabeth, | the true 5.05. 29
o, you go far. H8 1.01. 38
o, many | have broke their backs with laying 1.01. 83
o my lord aburga'ny, fare you well! 1.01.211
o, /nicholas hopkins? 1.01.221
o, 'tis true; 1.03. 51
o my lord, y' are tardy; 1.04. 7
o that your lordship were but now confessor | to 1.04. 15
o, very mad, exceeding mad, in love too; 1.04. 28
o beauty, | till now i never knew thee! 1.04. 75
o, god save ye! 2.01. 1
o, this is full of pity! 2.01.137
o my wolsey, | the quiet of my wounded 2.02. 73
o my lord, | would it not grieve an able man to 2.02.140
o, 'tis a tender place, and i must leave her. 2.02.143
she never knew harm-doing — o, now after | so 2.03. 5
o, god's will, much better | she ne'er had known 2.03. 12
and you, o fate! 2.03. 85
o, good my lord, no latin; 3.01. 42
o, fear him not, | his spell in that is out. 3.02. 19
o, how? how? 3.02. 29
o negligence! 3.02.213
o my lord, | press not a falling man too far! 3.02.332

o, how wretched | is that poor man that hangs on 3.02.366
o, 'tis a burden, cromwell, 'tis a burden | too 3.02.384
o, cromwell, | the king has gone beyond me! 3.02.407
o my lord, | must i then leave you? 3.02.421
then if thou fall'st, o cromwell, | thou fall'st 3.02.448
o cromwell, cromwell, | had i but serv'd my god 3.02.454
o griffith, sick to death! 4.02. 1
"o father abbot, | an old man, broken with the 4.02. 20
o my lord, | the times and titles now are 4.02.111
o my good lord, that comfort comes too late, 4.02.120
o lord archbishop, | thou hast made me now a man 5.04. 63
o pandarus, i tell thee, pandarus — | when i do TRO 1.01. 48
handlest in thy discourse, o, that her hand, 1.01. 55
but pandarus — o gods! 1.01. 94
o jupiter, there's no comparison. 1.02. 62 P
o, he smiles valiantly. 1.02.124 P
o yes, and 'twere a cloud in autumn. 1.02.126 P
o brave hector! 1.02.201 P
o, a brave man! 1.02.203 P
o brave troilus! 1.02.231 P
o admirable youth! 1.02.234 P
o admirable man! 1.02.237 P
o, when degree is shak'd, | which is the ladder 1.03.101
cries, "o, enough, patroclus, | or give me ribs 1.03.176
o thou damn'd cur! i shall — 2.01. 85 P
o, meaning you? i will go learn more of it. 2.01.130
o theft most base, | that we have stol'n what we 2.02. 92
o worthy satisfaction! 2.03. 3 P
o thou great thunder–darter of olympus, forget 2.03. 10 P
o, where? 2.03. 40 P
o, tell, tell. 2.03. 51 P
o agamemnon, let it not be so! 2.03.182
o, this is well. he rubs the vein of him. 2.03.200
o no, you shall not go. 2.03.204
o sir — 3.01. 55 P
o cupid, cupid, cupid! 3.01.111 P
for, o, love's bow | shoots buck and doe. 3.01.116
these lovers cry, o ho, they die! 3.01.121
which seems the wound to kill, | doth turn o ho! 3.01.123
o ho! 3.01.125
o ho! 3.01.126
o, here he comes! how now, how now? 3.02. 5 P
o, be thou my charon, | and give me swift 3.02. 10
o gentle pandar, | from cupid's shoulder pluck 3.02. 13
o cressid, how often have i wish'd me thus! 3.02. 61 P
wish'd, my lord? the gods grant — o my lord! 3.02. 62 P
o, let my lady apprehend no fear. 3.02. 74 P
o heavens, what have i done! 3.02.138
o that i thought it could be in a woman — | as, 3.02.158
o virtuous fight, | when right with right wars 3.02.171
o heavens, what some men do, | while some men 3.03.132
o, then beware! 3.03.228
o cressida! 4.02. 8
o foolish cressid! 4.02. 17
o the gods! what's the matter? 4.02. 84 P
o poor gentleman! 4.02. 87 P
o you immortal gods! i will not go. 4.02. 94
o you gods divine, | make cressid's name the 4.02. 99
o troilus, troilus! 4.04. 13
"o heart," as the goodly saying is, "o heart, 4.04. 15 P
as the goodly saying is, "o heart, heavy heart, 4.04. 16
o, you shall be expos'd, my lord, to dangers 4.04. 68
o heavens, "be true" again? 4.04. 74
o heavens, you love me not. 4.04. 82
o, be not mov'd, prince troilus. 4.04.129
o deadly gall, and theme of all our scorns, 4.05. 30
o, this is trim! 4.05. 33
o, these encounterers, so glib of tongue, | that 4.05. 58
a maiden battle then? o, i perceive you. 4.05. 87
o, you, my lord? 4.05.177
o, pardon, i offend. 4.05.182
o, let an old man embrace thee, | and, worthy 4.05.199
o, like a book of sport thou'lt read me o'er; 4.05.239
o, sir, to such as boasting show their scars | a 4.05.290
o plague and madness! 5.02. 35
doth that grieve thee? | o withered truth! 5.02. 46
o beauty, where is thy faith? 5.02. 67
he lov'd me — o false wench! 5.02. 70
o all you gods! 5.02. 77
o pretty, pretty pledge! 5.02. 77
ay, come — o jove! 5.02.105
o, then conclude | minds sway'd by eyes are full 5.02.111
o madness of discourse, | that cause sets up, 5.02.142
instance, o instance! 5.02.153
instance, o instance! 5.02.155
o cressid! 5.02.178
o false cressid! 5.02.178
o, contain yourself; 5.02.180
o, 'tis true. 5.03. 13
o, be persuaded! 5.03. 19
o, 'tis fair play. 5.03. 43
o priam, yield not to him! 5.03. 76
o, farewell, dear hector! 5.03. 80
o hector! 5.03. 87
o, courage, courage, princes! 5.05. 30
o traitor diomed! 5.06. 6
o, well fought, my youngest brother! 5.06. 12
o world, world, /world! 5.10. 36 P
o /traders and bawds, how earnestly are you set 5.10. 37 P
o, true–bred! COR 1.01.243
censure | will then cry out of martius, "o, if 1.01.269
o, doubt not that, | i speak from certainties. 1.02. 30
his bloody brow? o jupiter, no blood! 1.03. 38
o, i warrant, how he mammock'd it! 1.03. 64 P
o, good madam, there can be none yet. 1.03. 91 P
o, they are at it! 1.04. 21
o noble fellow! 1.04. 52
o, 'tis martius! 1.04. 61
o gods, | he has the stamp of martius, and i 1.06. 22
o! 1.06. 29
o, me alone! 1.06. 76
o general! 1.09. 11
o, well begg'd! 1.09. 87
o that you could turn your eyes toward the napes 2.01. 38 P
o that you could! 2.01. 40 P
o, no, no, no. 2.01.120 P
o, he is wounded, i thank the gods for't. 2.01.121 P
o! 2.01.169
but o, thy wife! 2.01.175
and live you yet? o my sweet lady, pardon. 2.01.180
o, welcome home; 2.01.181
o, he would miss it rather | than carry it but 2.01.237
o sir, you are not right. 2.03. 48
o me, the gods! 2.03. 54
o /good but most unwise patricians! 3.01. 91
o, he's a limb that has but a disease: 3.01.294
o, sir, sir, sir, | i would have had you put 3.02. 16
o heavens! o heavens! 4.01. 12
o heavens! o heavens! 4.01. 12
o the gods! 4.01. 37
o, y' are well met. 4.02. 11
o blessed heavens! 4.02. 20
o world, thy slippery turns! 4.04. 12
o martius, martius! 4.05.101
o, come, go in, | and take our friendly senators 4.05.131
o slaves, i can tell you news — news, you 4.05.172 P
o, he is grown most kind of late. 4.06. 11
o, you have made good work! 4.06. 80
o, ay, what else? 4.06.148
o my son, my son! 5.02. 70 P
o, a kiss | long as my exile, sweet as my 5.03. 44
o, stand up blest! 5.03. 52
o, no more, no more! 5.03. 86
o mother, mother! 5.03.182
o my mother, mother! 5.03.185
o! 5.03.185
for your son, believe it — o, believe it — 5.03.187
o mother! 5.03.199
o slave! 5.06.103
o that i had him, | with six aufidiuses, or more 5.06.127
o tullus! 5.06.131
o sacred receptacle of my joys, | sweet cell of TIT 1.01. 92
to thee, | o, think my son to be as dear to me! 1.01.108
o, if to fight for king and commonweal | were 1.01.114
o cruel, irreligious piety! 1.01.130
o, bless me here with thy victorious hand, 1.01.163
o monstrous! what reproachful words are these? 1.01.308
o titus, see! 1.01.341
o, see what thou hast done! 1.01.341
o tamora, thou bearest a woman's face — 2.03.136
o, do not learn her wrath — she taught it thee; 2.03.143
yet have i heard — o, could i find it now! 2.03.150
o, be to me, though thy hard heart say no, 2.03.155
o, let me teach thee! 2.03.158
o tamora, be call'd a gentle queen, | and with 2.03.168
o, keep me from their worse than killing lust, 2.03.175
o brother, with the dismall'st object hurt 2.03.204
o, tell me who it is, for ne'er till now | was i 2.03.220
o brother, help me with thy fainting hand — 2.03.233
o tamora, was ever heard the like? 2.03.276
o wondrous thing! 2.03.286
o, that i knew thy heart, and knew the beast, 2.04. 34
o, had the monster seen those lily hands 2.04. 44
o, could our mourning ease thy misery! 2.04. 57
o earth, i will befriend thee more with rain, 3.01. 16
o reverent tribunes! 3.01. 23
o gentle, aged men! 3.01. 23
o noble father, you lament in vain: 3.01. 27
o happy man, they have befriended thee! 3.01. 52
o, that delightful engine of her thoughts, 3.01. 82
o, say thou for her, who hath done this deed? 3.01. 87
o, thus i found her straying in the park, 3.01. 88
o, what a sympathy of woe is this, | as far from 3.01.148
o gracious emperor! 3.01.157
o gentle aaron! 3.01.157
o, none of both but are of high desert. 3.01.170
o, how this villainy | doth fat me with the very 3.01.202
o, here i lift this one hand up to heaven, | and 3.01.206
o brother, speak with possibility, | and do not 3.01.214
o, would thou wert as thou tofore hast been! 3.01.293
such a place there is where we did hunt | (o, 4.01. 56
o, why should nature build so foul a den, 4.01. 59
o, do ye read, my lord, what she hath writ? 4.01. 77
o, calm thee, gentle lord, although i know 4.01. 83
o heavens, can you hear a good man groan | and 4.01.123
o, 'tis a verse in horace, i know it well, | i 4.02. 22
o, tell me, did you see aaron the moor? 4.02. 52
o gentle aaron, we are all undone! 4.02. 55
o, that which i would hide from heaven's eye, 4.02. 59
o lord, sir, 'tis a deed of policy. 4.02.148
o publius, is not this a heavy case, | to see 4.03. 25
o, well said, lucius! 4.03. 64
o worthy goth, this is the incarnate devil 5.01. 40
o most insatiate and luxurious woman! 5.01. 88
o detestable villain, call'st thou that trimming 5.01. 94
o barbarous, beastly villains like thyself! 5.01. 97
o sweet revenge, now do i come to thee, | and, 5.02. 67
o villains, chiron and demetrius! 5.02.169
o, let me teach you how to knit again | this 5.03. 70
o, pardon me, | for when no friends are by, men 5.03.117
o, take this warm kiss on thy pale cold lips, 5.03.153
o, were the sum of these that i should pay 5.03.158
o now, sweet boy, give them their latest kiss! 5.03.169
o grandsire, grandsire, ev'n with all my heart 5.03.172
o lord, i cannot speak to him for weeping, | my 5.03.174
o, where is romeo? ROM 1.01.116
o me! 1.01.173
why then, o brawling love! 1.01.176
o loving hate! 1.01.176
o any thing, of nothing first /create! 1.01.177
o heavy lightness, serious vanity, | misshapen 1.01.178
o, she is rich in beauty, only poor | that, when 1.01.215
o, teach me how i should forget to think. 1.01.226
o then i see queen mab hath been with you. 1.04. 53
o, she doth teach the torches to burn bright! 1.05. 44
o then, dear saint, let lips do what hands do, 1.05.103
o trespass sweetly urg'd! 1.05.109
o dear account! 1.05.118
o, romeo, that she were, o that she were | an 2.01. 37
that she were, o that she were | an open/–arse, 2.01. 37
it is my lady, o, it is my love! 2.02. 10
o that she knew she were! 2.02. 11
o that i were a glove upon that hand, | that i 2.02. 24
o, speak again, bright angel, for thou art | as 2.02. 26
o romeo, romeo, wherefore art thou romeo? 2.02. 33
o, be some other name! 2.02. 42
o gentle romeo, | if thou dost love, pronounce 2.02. 93
o, swear not by the moon, th' inconstant moon, 2.02.109
o, wilt thou leave me so unsatisfied? 2.02.125
o blessed, blessed night! 2.02.139
o, for a falc'ner's voice, | to lure this 2.02.158
o, mickle is the powerful grace that lies | in 2.03. 15
o, she knew well | thy love did read by rote 2.03. 87
o, let us hence, i stand on sudden haste. 2.03. 93
o, he's the courageous captain of compliments. 2.04. 19 P
o, their bones, their bones! 2.04. 35 P
o flesh, flesh, how art thou fishified! 2.04. 37 P
o single–sol'd jest, soly singular for the 2.04. 65 P
o, here's a wit of cheverel, that stretches from 2.04. 83 P
o, thou art deceiv'd; 2.04. 98 P
when 'twas a little prating thing — o, there is 2.04.201 P
o, she is lame! 2.05. 4
o god, she comes! 2.05. 18
o honey nurse, what news? 2.05. 18
good sweet nurse — o lord, why lookest thou sad 2.05. 21
o god's lady dear! 2.05. 61
o, so light a foot | will ne'er wear out the 2.06. 16
the fee–simple! o simple! 3.01. 34 P
o calm, dishonorable, vile submission! 3.01. 73
o sweet juliet, | thy beauty hath made me 3.01.113
o romeo, romeo, brave mercutio is dead! 3.01.116
o, i am fortune's fool! 3.01.136
o noble prince, i can discover all | the unlucky 3.01.142
o my brother's child! 3.01.146
o prince! 3.01.147
o husband! 3.01.147
o, the blood is spill'd | of my dear kinsman! 3.01.147
o cousin, cousin! 3.01.150
o, i have bought the mansion of a love, | but 3.02. 26
o, here comes my nurse, | and she brings news; 3.02. 31
o romeo, romeo! 3.02. 41
o, break, my heart, poor bankrout, break at once 3.02. 57
o tybalt, tybalt, the best friend i had! 3.02. 61
o courteous tybalt, honest gentleman, | that 3.02. 62
o god, did romeo's hand shed tybalt's blood? 3.02. 71
o serpent heart, hid with a flow'ring face! 3.02. 73
o nature, what hadst thou to do in hell | when 3.02. 80
o that deceit should dwell | in such a gorgeous 3.02. 84
o, what a beast was i to chide at him! 3.02. 95
but o, it presses to my memory | like damned 3.02.110
o, find him! 3.02.142
o deadly sin! 3.03. 24
o rude unthankfulness! 3.03. 24
o friar, the damned use that word in hell; 3.03. 47
o, thou wilt speak again of banishment. 3.03. 53
o, then i see that /madmen have no ears. 3.03. 61
o holy friar, o tell me, holy friar, | where's 3.03. 81
o holy friar, o tell me, holy friar, | where's 3.03. 81
o, he is even in my mistress' case, | just in 3.03. 84
o woeful sympathy! 3.03. 85
why should you fall into so deep an o? 3.03. 90
o, she says nothing, sir, but weeps and weeps, 3.03. 99
o, tell me, friar, tell me, | in what vile part 3.03.105
o lord, i could have stay'd here all the night 3.03.159
o, what learning is! 3.03.160
o, now i would they had chang'd voices too, 3.05. 32
o, now be gone, more light and light it grows. 3.05. 35
o, by this count i shall be much in years | ere 3.05. 46
o, think'st thou we shall ever meet again? 3.05. 51
o god, i have an ill–divining soul! 3.05. 54
o fortune, fortune, all men call thee fickle; 3.05. 60
o, how my heart abhors | to hear him nam'd, and 3.05. 99
o, god–i–goden! 3.05.172
o sweet my mother, cast me not away! 3.05.198
o god! 3.05.204
o nurse, how shall this be prevented? 3.05.204
o, he's a lovely gentleman! 3.05.218
o most wicked fiend! 3.05.235
o, shut the door, and when thou hast done so, 4.01. 44
o juliet, i already know thy grief, | it strains 4.01. 46
o, bid me leap, rather than marry paris, | from 4.01. 77
give me, give me! o, tell not me of fear! 4.01.121
o, if i /wake, shall i not be distraught, 4.03. 49
o, look! 4.03. 55
o, weraday, that ever i was born! 4.05. 15
o lamentable day! 4.05. 17
look, look! o heavy day! 4.05. 18
o me, o me, my child, my only life! 4.05. 19
o me, o me, my child, my only life! 4.05. 19
o lamentable day! 4.05. 30
o woeful time! 4.05. 30
o son, the night before thy wedding–day | hath 4.05. 35
o woe! 4.05. 49
o woeful, woeful, woeful day! 4.05. 49
o day, o day, o day, o hateful day! 4.05. 52
o day, o day, o day, o hateful day! 4.05. 52
o day, o day, o day, o hateful day! 4.05. 52
o day, o day, o day, o hateful day! 4.05. 52
o woeful day, o woeful day! 4.05. 54
o woeful day, o woeful day! 4.05. 54
o love, o life! 4.05. 58
o love, o life! 4.05. 58
o child, o child! 4.05. 62
o child, o child! 4.05. 62
o, in this love, you love your child so ill 4.05. 75
musicians, o, musicians, "heart's ease, heart's 4.05.102 P
o, and you will have me live, play "heart's ease 4.05.103 P
o, musicians, because my heart itself plays "my 4.05.106 P
o, play me some merry dump to comfort me. 4.05.107 P
o, i cry you mercy, you are the singer; 4.05.139 P
o, pardon me for bringing these ill news, 5.01. 22
o mischief, thou art swift | to enter in the 5.01. 35
o, this same thought did but forerun my need, 5.01. 53
strew — | o woe, thy canopy is dust and stones! 5.03. 13
o, be gone! 5.03. 63
o lord, they fight! i will go call the watch. 5.03. 71
o, i am slain! 5.03. 72
o, give me thy hand, | one writ with me in sour 5.03. 81
o no! 5.03. 84
o, how may i | call this a lightning? 5.03. 90
o my love, my wife, | death, that hath suck'd 5.03. 91
o, what more favor can i do to thee, | than with 5.03. 98
o, here | will i set up my everlasting rest, 5.03.109
lips, o you | the doors of breath, seal with a 5.03.113

Line	Play	Ref.
o true apothecary!		5.03.119
o, much i fear some ill unthrifty thing.		5.03.136
romeo, o, pale!		5.03.144
o comfortable friar!		5.03.148
o churl, drunk all, and left no friendly drop		5.03.163
o happy dagger, | this is thy sheath;		5.03.169
o, the people in the street cry "romeo," | some		5.03.191
o heavens!		5.03.202
o wife, look how our daughter bleeds!		5.03.202
o me, this sight of death is as a bell | that		5.03.206
o thou untaught!		5.03.214
o brother montague, give me thy hand.		5.03.296
o, 'tis a worthy lord.	TIM	1.01. 9
o, pray let's see't. for the lord timon, sir?		1.01. 13
o, they eat lords;		1.01.206 P
o, by no means, | honest ventidius.		1.02. 8
o, apemantus, you are welcome.		1.02. 23
o you gods!		1.02. 39 P
o, no doubt, my good friends, but the gods		1.02. 88 P
o you gods, think i, what need we have any		1.02. 95 P
o, what a precious comfort 'tis to have so many		1.02.103 P
o, joy's e'en made away ere't can be born!		1.02.105 P
o my friends!		1.02.167
o, he's the very soul of bounty!		1.02.209
o, i beseech you pardon me, my lord, in that.		1.02.213
o, none so welcome.		1.02.217
o, that men's ears should be | to counsel deaf,		1.02.249
o my good lord, | at many times i brought in my		2.02.132
o my good lord, the world is but a word;		2.02.152
o you gods!		3.01. 55
o, may diseases only work upon't!		3.01. 60
and yet — o, see the monstrousness of man		3.02. 72
o, here's servilius;		3.04. 66 P
o my lord, | you only speak from your distracted		3.04.112
o my lords, | as you are great, be pitifully		3.05. 51
o, sir, let it not trouble you.		3.06. 38 P
the rest of your fees, o gods — the senators of		3.06. 79 P
o thou wall | that girdles in those wolves, dive		4.01. 1
o, the fierce wretchedness that glory brings us!		4.02. 30
o blessed breeding sun, draw from the earth		4.03. 1
o, a root, dear thanks!		4.03.192
o, thou shalt find —		4.03.232
o thou sweet king–killer, and dear divorce		4.03.381
o thou touch of hearts, | think thy slave man		4.03.389
o you gods!		4.03.458
o monument | and wonder of good deeds evilly		4.03.460
o, let me stay, | and comfort you, my master.		4.03.533
whose thankless natures (o abhorred spirits!)		5.01. 60
o, forget | what we are sorry for ourselves in		5.01.138
o you hard hearts, you cruel men of rome, | knew	JC	1.01. 36
o!		1.02.158
o cicero, | i have seen tempests when the		1.03. 4
but, o grief, | where hast thou led me?		1.03.111
o cassius, if you could | but win the noble		1.03.140
o, he sits high in all the people's hearts;		1.03.157
o rome, i make thee promise, | if the redress		2.01. 56
o conspiracy, | sham'st thou to show thy		2.01. 77
o then, by day | where wilt thou find a cavern		2.01. 79
o, pardon, sir, it doth;		2.01.103
o, let us have him, for his silver hairs | will		2.01.144
o, name him not;		2.01.150
o, that we then could come by caesar's spirit,		2.01.169
o ye gods!		2.01.302
o, what a time have you chose out, brave caius,		2.01.314
o caesar, these things are beyond all use, | and		2.02. 25
that every like is not the same, o caesar, | the		2.02.128
if thou read this, o caesar, thou mayest live;		2.03. 15
o constancy, be strong upon my side, | set a		2.04. 6
o brutus, | the heavens speed thee in thine		2.04. 40
o, i grow faint.		2.04. 43
o caesar, read mine first;		3.01. 6
o caesar —		3.01. 74
o mighty caesar!		3.01.148
o antony!		3.01.164
that i did love thee, caesar, o, 'tis true;		3.01.194
o world!		3.01.207
and this indeed, o world, the heart of thee.		3.01.208
o, pardon me, thou bleeding piece of earth,		3.01.254
me say to you by word of mouth — | o caesar!		3.01.281
o judgment!		3.02.104
o masters!		3.02.121
for if you should, o, what would come of it?		3.02.146
judge, o you gods, how dearly caesar lov'd him!		3.02.182
o, what a fall was there, my countrymen!		3.02.190
o, now you weep, and i perceive you feel | the		3.02.193
o piteous spectacle!		3.02.198 P
o noble caesar!		3.02.199 P
o woeful day!		3.02.200 P
o traitors, villains!		3.02.201 P
o most bloody sight!		3.02.202 P
o royal caesar!		3.02.244 P
o ye gods, ye gods, must i endure all this?		4.03. 41
o, i could weep | my spirit from mine eyes!		4.03. 99
o cassius, you are yoked with a lamb | that		4.03.110
o brutus!		4.03.118
o cassius, i am sick of many griefs.		4.03.144
o insupportable and touching loss!		4.03.151
o ye immortal gods!		4.03.157
o my dear brother!		4.03.233
o murd'rous slumber!		4.03.267
o yes, and soundless too;		5.01. 36
o you flatterers!		5.01. 44
o, if thou wert the noblest of thy strain,		5.01. 59
o that a man might know | the end of this day's		5.01.122
o, look, titinius, look, the villains fly!		5.03. 1
o cassius, brutus gave the word too early, | who		5.03. 5
o my lord!		5.03. 26
o, he lights too.		5.03. 31
o, coward that i am, to live so long, | to see		5.03. 34
o cassius, | far from this country pindarus		5.03. 48
he lies not like the living. o my heart!		5.03. 58
o setting sun, | as in thy red rays thou dost		5.03. 60
o hateful error, melancholy's child, | why dost		5.03. 67
o error, soon conceiv'd, | thou never com'st		5.03. 69
o julius caesar, thou art mighty yet!		5.03. 94
yet, countrymen! o, yet, hold up your heads!		5.04. 1
o young and noble cato, art thou down?		5.04. 9
o dardanius!		5.05. 9
o clitus!		5.05. 10
o valiant cousin, worthy gentleman!	MAC	1.02. 24
o worthiest cousin!		1.04. 14
o, never | shall sun that morrow see!		1.05. 60
o, come in, equivocator.		2.03. 11 P
o horror, horror, horror!		2.03. 64
o gentle lady, | 'tis not for you to hear what i		2.03. 83
o banquo, banquo, | our royal master's murther'd		2.03. 86
o, by whom?		2.03.100
o, yet i do repent me of my fury, | that i did		2.03.106
o, full of scorpions is my mind, dear wife!		3.02. 36
o, treachery!		3.03. 17
o slave!		3.03. 18
o proper stuff!		3.04. 59
o, these flaws and starts | (imposters to true		3.04. 62
o, well done!		4.01. 39
o scotland, scotland!		4.03.100
o nation miserable!		4.03.103
o my breast, | thy hope ends here!		4.03.113
o, relation! | too nice, and yet too true.		4.03.173
o hell–kite!		4.03.217
o, i could play the woman with mine eyes, | and		4.03.230
o, o, o!		5.01. 52 P
o, o, o!		5.01. 52 P
o, o, o!		5.01. 52 P
o, farewell, honest /soldier.	HAM	1.01. 16
happily, foreknowing may avoid, | o speak!		1.01.135
o, that this too too sallied flesh would melt,		1.02.129
o god, god, | how /weary, stale, flat, and		1.02.132
o god, a beast, that wants discourse of reason,		1.02.150
o, most wicked speed!		1.02.156
o yes, my lord, he wore his beaver up.		1.02.230
o, fear me not.		1.03. 51
o, answer me!		1.04. 45
list, list, o, list!		1.05. 22
o god!		1.05. 24
o my prophetic soul! | my uncle?		1.05. 40
o wicked wit and gifts that have the power | so		1.05. 44
o hamlet, what /a falling–off was there | from		1.05. 47
o, horrible, o, horrible, most horrible!		1.05. 80
o, horrible, o, horrible, most horrible!		1.05. 80
o all you host of heaven!		1.05. 92
o earth!		1.05. 92
o, fie, hold, hold, my heart, | and you, my		1.05. 93
o most pernicious woman!		1.05.105
o villain, villain, smiling, damned villain!		1.05.106
o, wonderful!		1.05.118
o day and night, but this is wondrous strange!		1.05.164
the time is out of joint — o cursed spite,		1.05.188
o, my lord, my lord, i have been so affrighted!		2.01. 72
o, speak of that, that do i long to hear.		2.02. 50
o dear ophelia, i am ill at these numbers.		2.02.120 P
but that i love thee best, o most best, believe		2.02.121 P
o, give me leave, | how does my good lord hamlet		2.02.170
o, most true, she is a strumpet.		2.02.235 P
o jephthah, judge of israel, what a treasure		2.02.403 P
o, old friend!		2.02.422 P
o, what a rogue and peasant slave am i!		2.02.550
o, 'tis too true!		3.01. 48
o heavy burthen!		3.01. 53
o, help him, you sweet heavens!		3.01.133 P
o, what a noble mind is here o'erthrown!		3.01.150
o, woe is me, | t' have seen what i have seen,		3.01.160
o, it offends me to the soul to hear a		3.02. 8 P
o, there be players that i have seen play — and		3.02. 28 P
o, reform it altogether.		3.02. 38 P
o my dear lord —		3.02. 56
o ho, do you mark that?		3.02.111 P
o god, your only jig–maker.		3.02.125 P
o heavens, die two months ago, and not forgotten		3.02.130 P
hobby–horse, whose epitaph is, "for o, for o,		3.02.135 P
is, "for o, for o, the hobby–horse is forgot."		3.02.135 P
o, confound the rest!		3.02.177
o, but she'll keep her word.		3.02.231 P
for thou dost know, o damon dear, | this realm		3.02.281
o good horatio, i'll take the ghost's word for a		3.02.286 P
o wonderful son, that can so stonish a mother!		3.02.328 P
o, the recorders!		3.02.345 P
o my lord, if my duty be too bold, my love is		3.02.348 P
o heart, lose not thy nature!		3.02.393
o, my offense is rank, it smells to heaven, | it		3.03. 36
but, o, what form of prayer | can serve my turn?		3.03. 51
o wretched state!		3.03. 67
o bosom black as death!		3.03. 67
o limed soul, that, struggling to be free, | art		3.03. 68
o, i am slain.		3.04. 25
o me, what hast thou done?		3.04. 25
o, what a rash and bloody deed is this!		3.04. 27
marriage vows | as false as dicers' oaths, o,		3.04. 45
o shame, where is thy blush?		3.04. 81
o hamlet, speak no more!		3.04. 88
o, speak to me no more!		3.04. 94
o, say!		3.04.109
o, step between her and her fighting soul.		3.04.113
o gentle son, | upon the heat and flame of thy		3.04.122
o hamlet, thou hast cleft my heart in twain.		3.04.156
o, throw away the worser part of it, | and /live		3.04.157
o, 'tis most sweet | when in one line two crafts		3.04.209
o heavy deed!		4.01. 12
o gertrude, come away!		4.01. 28
o, come away!		4.01. 44
o, here they come.		4.02. 4 P
o, from this time forth, | my thoughts be bloody		4.04. 65
o ho!		4.05. 33 P
o, this is the poison of deep grief, it springs		4.05. 75
o gertrude, gertrude, | when sorrows come, they		4.05. 77
o my dear gertrude, this, | like to a		4.05. 94
o, this is counter, you false danish dogs!		4.05.111
o thou vile king, | give me my father!		4.05.116
o heat, dry up my brains!		4.05.155
o rose of may!		4.05.158
o heavens, is't possible a young maid's wits		4.05.160
o, how the wheel becomes it!		4.05.172 P
do you /see this, o god?		4.05.202
o, for two special reasons, | which may to you,		4.07. 9
drown'd! o, where?		4.07.165
to contract — o — the time for — a — my		5.01. 63
o, methought there — a — was nothing — a —		5.01. 64
o, a pit of clay for to be made | for such a		5.01. 96
o, that that earth which kept the world in awe		5.01.215
o, treble woe | fall ten times /treble on that		5.01.246
o my son, what theme?		5.01.268
o, he is mad, laertes.		5.01.272
no, the drink, the drink — o my dear hamlet —		5.02.309
o villainy!		5.02.311
o, yet defend me, friends, i am but hurt.		5.02.324
is strict in his arrest — o, i could tell you		5.02.337
o god, horatio, what a wounded name, | things		5.02.344
o, i die, horatio, | the potent poison quite		5.02.352
o proud death, | what feast is toward in thine		5.02.364
o, vassal! miscreant!	LR	1.01.161
thus kent, o princes, bids you all adieu,		1.01.186
o villain, villain!		1.02. 75 P
o, these eclipses do portend these divisions!		1.02.136 P
o, you, sir, you, come you hither, sir.		1.04. 78 P
frowning, now thou art an o without a figure.		1.04.192 P
o most small fault, | how ugly didst thou in		1.04.266
o lear, lear, lear!		1.04.270
o, let me not be mad, not mad, sweet heaven!		1.05. 46
o sir, fly this place, | intelligence is given		2.01. 20
o strange and fast'ned villain!		2.01. 77
o madam, my old heart is crack'd, it's crack'd!		2.01. 90
o lady, lady, shame would have it hid!		2.01. 93
o, how this mother swells up toward my heart!		2.04. 56
o me, my heart! my rising heart! but down!		2.04.121
o, are you free?		2.04.132
o regan, she hath tied | sharp–tooth'd		2.04.134
with how deprav'd a quality — o regan!		2.04.137
o, sir, you are old, | nature in you stands on		2.04.146
o the blest gods!		2.04.168
o heavens!		2.04.189
o regan, will you take her by the hand?		2.04.194
o sides, you are too tough!		2.04.197
o, reason not the need!		2.04.264
o fool, i shall go mad!		2.04.286
o sir, to willful men, | the injuries that they		2.04.302
o nuncle, court holy–water in a dry house is		3.02. 10 P
o, ho!		3.02. 24
o regan, goneril!		3.04. 19
o, that way madness lies, let me shun that!		3.04. 21
o, i have ta'en | too little care of this!		3.04. 32
tom's a–cold — o, do de, do de, do de.		3.04. 58 P
o, cry you mercy, sir.		3.04.171
o heavens!		3.05. 12 P
o pity!		3.06. 58
hard, hard. o filthy traitor!		3.07. 32
o cruel!		3.07. 70
o you gods!		3.07. 70
o, i am slain!		3.07. 81
o!		3.07. 82
o my follies!		3.07. 91
world, world, o world!		4.01. 10
o, my good lord, | i have been your tenant, and		4.01. 12
o dear son edgar, | the food of thy abused		4.01. 21
o gods!		4.01. 25
o, the difference of man and man!		4.02. 26
o goneril, | you are not worth the dust which		4.02. 29
o vain fool!		4.02. 61
o my good lord, the duke of cornwall's dead,		4.02. 70
but, o poor gloucester, | lost he his other eye?		4.02. 80
o dear father, | it is thy business that i go		4.04. 23
o you mighty gods!		4.06. 34
if edgar live, o bless him!		4.06. 40
o thou side–piercing sight!		4.06. 85
o, well flown, bird!		4.06. 91 P
o, let me kiss that hand!		4.06.132
o ruin'd piece of nature!		4.06.134
o ho, are you there with me?		4.06.145 P
o, matter and impertinency mix'd!		4.06.174
o, here he is:		4.06.188
o untimely death!		4.06.250
o indistinguish'd space of woman's will!		4.06.271
o thou good kent, how shall i live and work | to		4.07. 1
o you kind gods!		4.07. 13
th' untun'd and jarring senses, o, wind up | of		4.07. 15
o my dear father, restoration hang | thy		4.07. 25
o, look upon me, sir, | and hold your hand in		4.07. 56
o ho, i know the riddle. — i will go.		5.01. 37
sick, o, sick!		5.03. 95
most monstrous! o! | know'st thou this paper?		5.03.160
and when 'tis told, o, that my heart would burst		5.03.183
that follow'd me so near (o, our lives'		5.03.185
never (o fault!)		5.03.193
help, help! o, help!		5.03.223
it came even from the heart of — o, she's dead!		5.03.225
o, is this he?		5.03.233
run, run, o, run!		5.03.248
o, /you are men of stones!		5.03.258
o my good master!		5.03.268
o, see, see!		5.03.305
o, let him pass, he hates him | that would upon		5.03.314
o, sir, content you;	OTH	1.01. 41
o unhappy girl!		1.01.163
o, she deceives me | past thought!		1.01.165
o heaven!		1.01.169
o treason of the blood!		1.01.169
o, would you had had her!		1.01.175
o thou foul thief, where hast thou stow'd my		1.02. 62
my daughter! o, my daughter!		1.03. 59
o villainous!		1.03.311 P
o, let the heavens | give him defense against		2.01. 44
o, behold, | the riches of the ship is come on		2.01. 82
o, but i fear — how lost you company?		2.01. 91
o, fie upon thee, slanderer!		2.01.113
o gentle lady, do not put me to't, | for i am		2.01.118
o heavy ignorance!		2.01.143 P
o most lame and impotent conclusion!		2.01.161 P
o my fair warrior!		2.01.182
o my soul's joy!		2.01.184
o, you are well tun'd now!		2.01.199
o my sweet, | i prattle out of fashion, and i		2.01.205
o, they are our friends — but one cup, i'll		2.03. 37 P
o, man's life's but a span;		2.03. 72
o sweet england!		2.03. 88 P
o, i have lost my reputation!		2.03.262 P
o thou invisible spirit of wine, if thou hast no		2.03.281 P

o /god, that men should put an enemy in their 2.03.289 P
o strange! 2.03.307 P
o, thereby hangs a tail. 3.01. 8 P
o, that's an honest fellow. 3.03. 5
o yes, and went between us very oft. 3.03.100
o, beware, my lord, of jealousy! 3.03.165
but o, what damned minutes tells he o'er | who 3.03.169
o misery! 3.03.171
o curse of marriage! 3.03.268
o, is that all? 3.03.305
o now, for ever | farewell the tranquil mind! 3.03.347
o, farewell, | farewell the neighing steed and 3.03.350
and, o you mortal engines, whose rude throats 3.03.355
o grace! 3.03.373
o heaven forgive me! 3.03.373
o wretched fool, | that lov'st to make thine 3.03.375
o monstrous world! 3.03.377
take note, take note, o world, | to be direct 3.03.377
death and damnation! o! 3.03.396
cry, "o sweet creature!" 3.03.422
o monstrous! monstrous! 3.03.427
o, that the slave had forty thousand lives! 3.03.442
yield up, o love, thy crown and hearted throne 3.03.448
o blood, blood, blood! 3.03.451
o, damn her, damn her! 3.03.476
o, hardness to dissemble! 3.04. 34
o weary reck'ning! 3.04.176
o cassio, whence came this? 3.04.180
thou saidst (o, it comes o'er my memory, | as 4.01. 20
o devil! 4.01. 43 P
o, 'tis the spite of hell, the fiend's arch–mock 4.01. 70
o, thou art wise; 'tis certain. 4.01. 74
crying, "o dear cassio!" 4.01.137 P
o, i see that nose of yours, but not that dog i 4.01.142 P
o iago! 4.01.172 P
o, the world hath not a sweeter creature! 4.01.183 P
o, she will sing the savageness out of a bear. 4.01.188 P
o, a thousand, a thousand times. 4.01.192 P
o iago, the pity of it, iago! 4.01.196 P
o, 'tis foul in her. 4.01.201 P
o devil, devil! 4.01.244
concerning this, sir — o well–painted passion! 4.01.257
o, ay, as summer flies are in the shambles, 4.02. 66
o thou weed! 4.02. 67
o thou public commoner, | i should make very 4.02. 73
o, heaven forgive us! 4.02. 88
o /heaven, that such companions thou'dst unfold, 4.02.141
o fie upon them! 4.02.145
o no; 4.02.224 P
o, pardon me; 'twill do me good to walk. 4.03. 2
will you walk, sir? | o, desdemona! 4.03. 5 P
o, these men, these men! 4.03. 60
o, i am slain. 5.01. 26
o, villain that i am! 5.01. 29
o, help ho! light! a surgeon! 5.01. 30
o brave iago, honest and just, | that hast such 5.01. 31
o, help! 5.01. 39
o wretched villain! 5.01. 41
o, i am spoil'd, undone by villains! 5.01. 54
o me, lieutenant! what villains have done this? 5.01. 56
o treacherous villains! 5.01. 58
o, help me there! 5.01. 60
o murd'rous slave! o villain! 5.01. 61
o murd'rous slave! o villain! 5.01. 61
o damn'd iago! o inhuman dog! 5.01. 62
o damn'd iago! o inhuman dog! 5.01. 62
o my dear cassio, my sweet cassio! 5.01. 76
o cassio, cassio, cassio! 5.01. 77
o notable strumpet! 5.01. 78
o, for a chair, | to bear him easily hence! 5.01. 82
alas, he faints! o, cassio, cassio, cassio! 5.01. 84
how do you, cassio? o, a chair, a chair! 5.01. 96
o, that's well said: 5.01. 98
o, bear him /out o' th' air. 5.01.104
o, did he so? i charge you go with me. 5.01.120
o, fie upon thee, strumpet! 5.01.121
o balmy breath, that dost almost persuade 5.02. 16
o perjur'd woman, thou dost stone my heart, 5.02. 63
o, my fear interprets. what, is he dead? 5.02. 73
o, banish me, my lord, but kill me not! 5.02. 78
o, good my lord, i would speak a word with you! 5.02. 90
o insupportable! 5.02. 98
o heavy hour! 5.02. 98
o, good my lord! 5.02.102
o, come in, emilia. 5.02.103
o, my good lord, yonder's foul murthers done! 5.02.106
o, falsely, falsely murder'd! 5.02.117
o lady, speak again! 5.02.120
sweet desdemona, o sweet mistress, speak! 5.02.121
o, who hath done this deed? 5.02.123
o, farewell! 5.02.125
o, the more angel she, | and you the blacker 5.02.130
o, she was heavenly true! 5.02.135
o, i were damn'd beneath all depth in hell | but 5.02.137
o mistress, villainy hath made mocks with love! 5.02.151
o gull, o dolt, | as ignorant as dirt! 5.02.163
o gull, o dolt, | as ignorant as dirt! 5.02.163
o, are you come, iago? 5.02.169
o heavens forefend! 5.02.186
o monstrous act! 5.02.190
upon't, i think — i smell't — o villainy! 5.02.191
i'll kill myself for grief — | o villainy! 5.02.193
o, o, o! 5.02.198
o, o, o! 5.02.198
o, o, o! 5.02.198
o, she was foul! 5.02.200
o /god! o heavenly /god! 5.02.218
o /god! o heavenly /god! 5.02.218
o thou dull moor, that handkerchief thou 5.02.225
o murd'rous coxcomb, what should such a fool 5.02.233
ay, ay! o, lay me by my mistress' side. 5.02.237
the ice–brook's temper — | o, here it is. 5.02.254
but (o vain boast!) 5.02.264
o ill–starr'd wench, | pale as thy smock! 5.02.272
o cursed, cursed slave! 5.02.276
o desdemon! 5.02.281
o, o! 5.02.282
o, o! 5.02.282
o thou othello, that was once so good, | fall'n 5.02.291
o villain! 5.02.313
o thou pernicious caitiff! 5.02.318
o fool, fool, fool! 5.02.323
o bloody period! 5.02.357
o spartan dog, | more fell than anguish, hunger, 5.02.361
the time, the place, the torture, o, enforce it! 5.02.369
o, that i knew this husband, which, you say, ANT 1.02. 3 P
o, excellent, i love long life better than figs. 1.02. 32 P
o, let him marry a woman that cannot go, sweet 1.02. 63 P
o, my lord! 1.02.104
o, then we bring forth weeds | when our quick 1.02.109
o, sir, you had then left unseen a wonderful 1.02.153 P
o, never was there queen | so mightily betrayed! 1.03. 24
o most false love! 1.03. 62
o, my oblivion is a very antony, | and i am all 1.03. 90
o, 'tis treason! 1.05. 7
o charmian! 1.05. 18
o happy horse, to bear the weight of antony! 1.05. 21
o well–divided disposition! 1.05. 53
o heavenly mingle! 1.05. 59
o that brave caesar! 1.05. 67
o, rare for antony! 2.02.205
therefore, o antony, stay not by his side. 2.03. 19
o, come, ventidius, | you must to parthia. 2.03. 41
o times! 2.05. 18
o, from italy! 2.05. 23
o, i would thou didst; 2.05. 93
o, that his fault should make a knave of thee, 2.05.102
i faint, o iras, charmian! 2.05.110
o antony, | you have my /father's house — but 2.07.127
o silius, silius, | i have done enough; 3.01. 11
a very fine one. o, how he loves caesar! 3.02. 7
o antony! o thou arabian bird! 3.02. 12
o antony! o thou arabian bird! 3.02. 12
like her? o isis! 'tis impossible. 3.03. 15
o my good lord, | believe not all, or, if you 3.04. 10
when i shall pray, "o, bless my lord and husband 3.04. 16
by crying out as loud, | "o, bless my brother!" 3.04. 18
o noble emperor, do not fight by sea, | trust 3.07. 61
o, /he has given example for our flight, | most 3.10. 27
o, | i follow'd that i blush to look upon. 3.11. 11
let me sit down. o juno! 3.11. 28
o fie, fie, fie! 3.11. 31
madam, o good empress! 3.11. 33
well then, sustain me. o! 3.11. 45
o, whither hast thou led me, egypt? 3.11. 51
o my lord, my lord, | forgive my fearful sails! 3.11. 54
o, my pardon! 3.11. 61
o! 3.13. 57
in our viciousness grow hard | (o misery on't!), 3.13.112
o, is't come to this? 3.13.115
o, that i were | upon the hill of basan, to 3.13.126
o love, | that thou couldst see my wars to–day, 4.04. 15
o, my fortunes have | corrupted honest men! 4.05. 16
o antony, | thou mine of bounty, how wouldst 4.06. 30
o my brave emperor, this is fought indeed! 4.07. 4
o thou day o' th' world, | chain mine arm'd neck 4.08. 13
o infinite virtue, com'st thou smiling from 4.08. 17
o, bear me witness, night — 4.09. 5
be witness to me, o thou blessed moon, | when 4.09. 7
o sovereign mistress of true melancholy, | the 4.09. 12
o antony, | nobler than my revolt is infamous, 4.09. 18
o antony! 4.09. 23
o antony! 4.09. 23
o sun, thy uprise shall i see no more, | fortune 4.12. 18
o this false soul of egypt! 4.12. 25
o, he's more mad | than telamon for his shield; 4.13. 1
o, thy vild lady! 4.14. 22
o, cleave, my sides! 4.14. 39
o, sir, pardon me! 4.14. 80
thou teachest me, o valiant eros, what | i 4.14. 96
o, dispatch me! 4.14.104
o, make an end | of what i have begun. 4.14.105
o, charmian, i will never go from hence. 4.15. 1
o sun, | burn the great sphere thou mov'st in! 4.15. 9
o antony, | antony, antony! 4.15. 11
o, quick, or i am gone. 4.15. 31
wishers were ever fools — o, come, come, come, 4.15. 37
o! 4.15. 46
o, see, my women: 4.15. 62
o, wither'd is the garland of the war, | the 4.15. 64
o, quietness, lady! 4.15. 68
o madam, madam, madam! 4.15. 70
i say, o caesar, antony is dead. 5.01. 13
o antony, | i have followed thee to this; 5.01. 35
o cleopatra! thou art taken, queen. 5.02. 38
o, temperance, lady! 5.02. 48
o, such another sleep, that i might see | but 5.02. 77
course, and lighted | the little o, th' earth. 5.02. 81
o, behold, | how pomp is followed! 5.02.150
o slave, of no more trust | than love that's 5.02.154
o rarely base! 5.02.158
o caesar, what a wounding shame is this, | that 5.02.159
o the good gods! 5.02.221
o, couldst thou speak, | that i might hear thee 5.02.306
o eastern star! 5.02.308
o, break! o, break! 5.02.310
o, break! o, break! 5.02.310
balm, as soft as air, as gentle — | o antony! 5.02.312
o, come apace, dispatch! 5.02.322
o, sir, you are too sure an augurer; 5.02.334
o caesar, | this charmian liv'd but now, she 5.02.340
o noble weakness! 5.02.344
o | dissembling courtesy! CYM 1.01. 83
o lady, weep no more, lest i give cause | to be 1.01. 93
o the gods! | when shall we see again? 1.01.123
o disloyal thing, | that shouldst repair my 1.01.131
o blessed, that i might not! 1.01.139
o thou vild one! 1.01.143
o brave sir! 1.01.166
o, content thee. 1.05. 26
o, that husband! 1.06. 3
cries "o, | can my sides hold, to think that man 1.06. 68
o dearest soul! 1.06.118
o happy leonatus! 1.06.156
o, no, no. 1.06.199
o, i must, madam. 1.06.204
o sleep, thou ape of death, lie dull upon her, 2.02. 31
o, no, no, no, 'tis true. 2.04.106
o, above measure false! 2.04.113
o, that i had her here, to tear her limb–meal! 2.04.147
o, vengeance, vengeance! 2.05. 8
o, all the devils! 2.05. 13
a full–acorn'd boar, a german /one, | cried "o!" 2.05. 17
who was once at point | (o giglet fortune!) 3.01. 31
o master, what a strange infection | is fall'n 3.02. 3
o my master, | thy mind to her is now as low as 3.02. 9
o damn'd paper, | black as the ink that's on 3.02. 19
o, learn'd indeed were that astronomer | that 3.02. 27
cruel to me as you, o, the dearest of creatures, 3.02. 42 P
o, for a horse with wings! 3.02. 48
who long'st | (o, let me bate!) 3.02. 54
but in a fainter kind — o, not like me, | for 3.02. 55
o, this life | is nobler than attending for a 3.03. 21
o boys, this story | the world may read in me: 3.03. 55
o cymbeline, heaven and my conscience knows 3.03. 99
o! 3.04. 53
by thy revolt, o husband, shall be thought | put 3.04. 55
o gracious lady! 3.04. 98
o, for such means, | though peril to my modesty, 3.04.151
cheek, | exposing it (but o, the harder heart! 3.04.161
o, good my lord! 3.05. 83
o, my all–worthy lord! 3.05. 94
o imogen, | safe mayst thou wander, safe return 3.05.104
o jove, i think | foundations fly the wretched: 3.06. 6
o noble strain! 4.02. 24
o worthiness of nature! 4.02. 25
experience, o, thou disprov'st report! 4.02. 34
o thou goddess, | thou divine nature, thou 4.02.169
o sweetest, fairest lily! 4.02.201
o melancholy, | who ever yet could sound thy 4.02.203
with charitable bill (o bill, sore shaming 4.02.225
o gods and goddesses! 4.02.295
o posthumus, alas, | where is thy head? 4.02.320
o, 'tis pregnant, pregnant! 4.02.325
o! 4.02.329
o, my lord! 4.02.332
o, i am known | of many in the army. 4.04. 21
o pisanio, | every good servant does not all 5.01. 5
so i'll die | for thee, o imogen, even for whom 5.01. 26
turn'd coward | but by example (o, a sin in war, 5.03. 36
o noble misery, | to be i' th' field, and ask 5.03. 64
o imogen, | i'll speak to thee in silence. 5.04. 28
but (o scorn!) 5.04.125
o rare one, | be not, as is our fangled world, a 5.04.133
o, of this contradiction you shall now be quit. 5.04.165 P
o, the charity of a penny cord! 5.04.166 P
o, there were desolation of jailers and 5.04.204 P
o most delicate fiend! 5.05. 47
yet, o my daughter, | that it was folly in me, 5.05. 66
'twas at a feast — o, would | our viands had 5.05.155
this her bracelet | (o cunning, how i got/'t!), 5.05.205
o, give me cord, or knife, or poison, | some 5.05.213
o imogen! 5.05.225
o imogen, | imogen, imogen! 5.05.226
o gentlemen, help | mine and your mistress! 5.05.229
o my lord posthumus, | you ne'er kill'd imogen 5.05.230
o, get thee from my sight, | thou gav'st me 5.05.236
o gods! 5.05.243
o, she was naught; 5.05.271
o, what, am i | a mother to the birth of three? 5.05.368
o imogen, | thou hast lost by this a kingdom. 5.05.372
o my gentle brothers, | have we thus met? 5.05.374
o, never say hereafter | but i am truest speaker 5.05.375
o rare instinct! 5.05.381
but, o you powers! PER 1.01. 72
o my distressed lord, even such our griefs are; 1.04. 7
o dionyza! 1.04. 10
o, 'tis too true. 1.04. 32
o, let those cities that of plenty's cup | and 1.04. 52
o, not all, my friend, not all; 2.01. 91 P
o, sir, things must be as they may; 2.01.113 P
o, attend, my daughter: 2.03. 58
o, that's as much as you would be denied | of 2.03.105
o, seek not to entrap me, gracious lord, | a 2.05. 45
o, still | thy deaf'ning, dreadful thunders, 3.01. 4
o, how, lychorida! 3.01. 6
lucina, o! 3.01. 10
o you gods! 3.01. 22
o lychorida, | bid nestor bring me spices, ink 3.01. 64
o, make for tharsus! 3.01. 77
o, you say well. 3.02. 20
o you most potent gods! 3.02. 63
o dear diana, | where am i? 3.02.104
o your sweet queen! 3.03. 7
o, no tears, | lychorida, no tears. 3.03. 38
o, our credit comes not in like the commodity, 4.02. 30 P
o, sir, we doubt it not. 4.02. 42 P
o, take her home, mistress, take her home. 4.02.123 P
o dionyza, such a piece of slaughter | the sun 4.03. 2
o lady, | much less in blood than virtue, yet a 4.03. 6
o villain leonine! 4.03. 9
o, go to. 4.03. 19
o, sir, i can be modest. 4.06. 38 P
o, you have heard something of my power, and so 4.06. 86 P
o abominable! 4.06.134 P
o, here he is. 5.01. 2
o sir, a courtesy | which if we should deny, the 5.01. 58
o, here's | the lady that i sent for. 5.01. 64
o, i am mock'd, | and thou by some incensed god 5.01.142
o, stop there a little! 5.01.160
o helicanus, strike me, honored sir, | give me a 5.01.190
o, come hither, | thou that beget'st him that 5.01.194
o helicanus, | down on thy knees, thank the holy 5.01.197
o heavens bless my girl! 5.01.223
a maid–child call'd marina, whom, o goddess, 5.03. 6
you are, you are — o royal pericles! 5.03. 14
o, she's but overjoy'd. 5.03. 21
o, let me look! 5.03. 28
o my lord, | are you not pericles? 5.03. 31
o, come, be buried | a second time within these 5.03. 43
and make him cry from under ground, "o, fan TNK pr 18
o, pity, duke! 1.01. 47
o grief and time, | fearful consumers, you will 1.01. 69
o, i hope some god, | some god hath put his 1.01. 71

o, no knees, none, widow! 1.01. 74
o, my petition was | set down in ice, which, by 1.01.106
o, woe! 1.01.110
o, pardon me! 1.01.117
o, this celebration | will long last and be more 1.01.131
but, o jove, your actions, | soon as they /move, 1.01.137
by warranting moonlight corslet thee — o, when 1.01.177
o, if thou couch | but one night with her, every 1.01.182
o, help now! | our cause cries for your knee. 1.01.199
i would pluck | and put between my breasts (o, 1.03. 67
o cousin arcite, | where is thebes now? 2.02. 6
o, never | shall we two exercise, like twins of 2.02. 17
o, that now, that now | thy false–self and thy 2.02.206
o my lady, | if ever thou hast felt what sorrow 2.02.275
o, 'twas a studied punishment, a death | beyond 2.03. 4
o, pardon me! 2.03. 50
o love, | what a stout–hearted child thou art! 2.06. 8
o queen emilia, | fresher than may, sweeter 3.01. 4
thou, o jewel | o' th' wood, o' th' world, hast 3.01. 9
tell me, o lady fortune | (next after emily my 3.01. 15
i ear'd her language, liv'd in her eye, o coz, 3.01. 29
o thou most perfidious | that ever gently look'd 3.01. 35
o you heavens, dares any | so noble bear a 3.01. 89
o state of nature, fail together in me, | since 3.02. 31
o for a prick now, like a nightingale, | to put 3.04. 25
o, let me have your company | till /i come to 3.05. 65
o, good morrow. 3.06. 16
o, retire, | for honor's sake, and safely 3.06.109
o heaven, | what more than man is this! 3.06.156
thou shalt have pity of us both, o theseus, | if 3.06.172
o my noble brother, | that oath was rashly made, 3.06.226
o duke theseus, | the goodly mothers that have 3.06.244
o all ye gods, despise me then. 3.06.258
o sir, when did you see her? 4.01. 33
o, a very fine one! 4.01.105
"o fair, o sweet," etc. 4.01.114
"o fair, o sweet," etc. 4.01.114
o, is he so? you have a sister? 4.01.121
o, who can find the bent of woman's fancy? 4.02. 33
o love, this only | from this hour is complexion 4.02. 42
o, he that's freckle–fac'd? 4.02.120
o my soft–hearted sister, what think you? 4.02.147
o, they have shrowd measure! 4.03. 33 P
one cries, "o, this smoke!" 4.03. 53 P
one cries, "o, that ever i did it behind the 4.03. 54 P
o great corrector of enormous times, | shaker of 5.01. 62
o, then, most soft sweet goddess, | give me the 5.01.126
o thou that from eleven to ninety reign'st | in 5.01.130
o sacred, shadowy, cold, and constant queen, 5.01.137
o, vouchsafe, | with that thy rare green eye — 5.01.143
o mistress, | thou here dischargest me. 5.01.169
o, very much! 5.02. 2
o, sir, you would fain be nibbling. 5.02. 87
o, she must. 5.03. 11
o, what pity | enough for such a chance! 5.03. 59
o, better never born | than minister to such 5.03. 65
were they metamorphis'd | both into one — o, 5.03. 85
o loved sister, | he speaks now of as brave a 5.03.114
o all you heavenly powers, where is /your mercy? 5.03.139
hold, hold! o, hold, hold, hold! 5.04. 40
o miserable end of our alliance! 5.04. 86
o cousin, | that we should things desire which 5.04.109
o you heavenly charmers, | what things you make 5.04.131
souls | in doing this, o desperate as you are? STM II.C 107
on a ragged bough | nimbly she fastens (o, how VEN 38
"o, pity," gan she cry, "flint–hearted boy, 95
o, be not proud, nor brag not of thy might, 113
o, had thy mother borne so hard a mind, | she 203
o, what a sight it was, wistly to view | how she 343
o, what a war of looks was then between them! 355
"o fairest mover on this mortal round, | would 368
o, give it me, lest thy hard heart do steel it, 375
o, learn to love, the lesson is but plain, | and 407
o, would thou hadst not, or i had no hearing! 428
"but o, what banquet wert thou to the taste, 445
"o, where am i?" 493
"o, thou didst kill me, kill me once again. 499
o, never let their crimson liveries wear! 506
when he did frown, o, had she then gave over, 571
o, be advis'd, thou know'st not what it is 615
"o, let him keep his loathsome cabin still! 637
"but if thou fall, o, then imagine this, | the 721
o strange excuse! 791
"o thou clear god, and patron of all light, 860
"if he be dead — o no, it cannot be, | seeing 937
o yes, it may, thou hast no eyes to see, | but 939
o, how her eyes and tears did lend and borrow! 961
o hard–believing love, how strange it seems! 985
"o jove," quoth she, "how much a fool was i | to 1015
o happiness enjoy'd but of a few, | and, if LUC 22
o rash false heat, wrapp'd in repentant cold, 48
"o shame to knighthood and to shining arms! 197
o foul dishonor to my household's grave! 198
o impious act, including all foul harms! 199
"o, what excuse can my invention make | when 225
o, how her fear did make her color rise! 257
o, had they in that darksome prison died, | then 379
play'd with her breath — | o modest wantons! 401
o, if no harder than a stone thou art, | melt at 593
o, be rememb'red, no outrageous thing | from 607
o, how are they wrapp'd in with infamies | that 636
o that prone lust should stain so pure a bed! 684
o, deeper sin than bottomless conceit | can 701
"o comfort–killing night, image of hell! 764
"o hateful, vaporous, and foggy night! 771
"o night, thou furnace of foul reeking smoke! 799
"o unseen shame, invisible disgrace! 827
o unfelt sore, crest–wounding private scar! 828
o unlook'd–for evil, | when virtue is profan'd 846
"o opportunity, thy guilt is great! 876
o, hear me then, injurious, shifting time! 930
o, this dread night, wouldst thou one hour come 965
"o time, thou tutor both to good and bad, 995
so am i now — o no, that cannot be! 1049
"o, that is gone for which i sought to live, 1051
"o eye of eyes, | why pry'st thou through my 1088
o, let it not be hild | poor women's faults that 1257
"o, peace," quoth lucrece, "if it should be told 1284
in ajax and ulysses, o, what art | of 1394
"o, teach me how to make mine own excuse, | or 1653
"o, speak," quoth she, | "how may this forced 1700
o, from thy cheeks my image thou hast torn, 1762
"o time, cease thou thy course and last no 1765
"o, mine she is," | replies her husband, "do not 1795
"o," quoth lucretius, "i did give that life 1800
o, love's best habit's in a soothing tongue, PP 1.11
o, never faith could hold, if not to beauty 5. 2
celestial as thou art, o, do not love that wrong 5.13
"o jove," quoth she, "why was not i a flood?" 6.14
o yes, dear friend, i pardon crave of thee, 10.11
o, my love, my love is young! 12.10
o, sweet shepherd, hie thee, | for methinks thou 12.11
loss, | o frowning fortune, cursed, fickle dame! 17.10
o cruel speeding, fraughted with gall. 17.16
o, change thy thought, that i may change my mind SON 10. 9
o that you were yourself! 13. 1
o, none but unthrifts: 13.13
o, carve not with thy hours my love's fair brow, 19. 9
o, let me, true in love, but truly write, | and 21. 9
o, therefore, love, be of thyself so wary | as i 22. 9
o, let my books be then the eloquence | and dumb 23. 9
o, learn to read what silent love hath writ: 23.13
o, then voutsafe me but this loving thought: 32. 9
o, give thyself the thanks if aught in me 38. 5
o, how thy worth with manners may i sing, | when 39. 1
o absence, what a torment wouldst thou prove, 39. 9
o, what excuse will my poor beast then find, 51. 5
o, how much more doth beauty beauteous seem | by 54. 1
o, let me suffer (being at your beck) | th' 58. 5
o, that record could with a backward look, 59. 5
o, sure i am the wits of former days | to 59.13
o no, thy love, though much, is not so great, 61. 9
o, how shall summer's honey breath hold out 65. 5
o fearful meditation! 65. 9
o none, unless this miracle have might, | that 65.13
o, him she stores, to show what wealth she had 67.13
o, if (i say) you look upon this verse, | when i 71. 9
o, lest the world should task you to recite 72. 1
o, lest your true love may seem false in this, 72. 9
o, know, sweet love, i always write of you, 76. 9
o, how i faint when i of you do write, | knowing 80. 1
o, what a happy title do i find, | happy to have 92.11
o, in what sweets dost thou thy sins enclose! 95. 4
o, what a mansion have those vices got | which 95. 9
o truant muse, what shall be thy amends | for 101. 1
o, blame me not if i no more can write! 103. 5
o, never say that i was false of heart, | though 109. 1
o, for my sake do you /with fortune chide, | the 111. 1
o, 'tis the first, 'tis flatt'ry in my seeing, 114. 9
o no, it is an ever–fixed mark | that looks on 116. 5
o benefit of ill! 119. 9
o, that our night of woe might have rememb'red 120. 9
o thou, my lovely boy, who in thy power | dost 126. 1
yet fear her, o thou minion of her pleasure, 126. 9
o, let it then as well beseem thy heart | to 132.10
o, love's best habit is in seeming trust, | and 138.11
o, call not me to justify the wrong | that thy 139. 1
o, but with mine compare thou thine own state, 142. 3
o me! 148. 1
o, how can love's eye be true, | that is so 148. 9
o cunning love, with tears thou keep'st me blind 148.13
canst thou, o cruel, say i love thee not, | when 149. 1
o, from what pow'r hast thou this pow'rful might 150. 1
o, though i love what others do abhor, | with 150.11
cried, "o false blood, thou register of lies, LC 52
o, one by nature's outwards so commended | that 80
o appetite, from judgment stand aloof! 166
"'o, then advance of yours that phraseless hand, 225
"'but, o my sweet, what labor is't to leave 239
"'o, pardon me, in that my boast is true: 246
"'how mighty then you are, o, hear me tell! 253
o most potential love! 264
o, how the channel to the stream gave grace! 285
"o father, what a hell of witchcraft lies | in 288
"o, that infected moisture of his eye, | o, that 323
o, that false fire which in his cheek so glowed, 324
o, that forc'd thunder from his heart did fly, 325
o, that sad breath his spungy lungs bestowed, 326
o, all that borrowed motion seeming owed, 327
OAK 27 FR 0.0030 REL FR 19 V 8 P
i will rend an oak | and peg thee in his knotty TMP 1.02.294
and rifted jove's stout oak | with his own bolt; 5.01. 45
walk round about an oak, with great ragg'd horns WIV 4.04. 31
in deep of night to walk by this herne's oak. 4.04. 40
that falstaff at that oak shall meet with us, 4.04. 42
to–night at herne's oak, just 'twixt twelve and 4.06. 19
you in the park about midnight, at herne's oak, 5.01. 11 P
are all couch'd in a pit hard by herne's oak, 5.03. 14 P
the hour draws on. to the oak, to the oak! 5.03. 23 P
the hour draws on. to the oak, to the oak! 5.03. 24 P
round about the oak | of herne the hunter, let 5.05. 75
splits the unwedgeable and gnarled oak | than MM 2.02.116
an oak but with one green leaf on it would have ADO 2.01.240 P
at the duke's oak we meet. MND 1.02.110 P
under an oak whose antique root peeps out | upon AYL 2.01. 31
object did present itself | under an old oak, 4.03.104
is rotten | as ever oak or stone was sound. WT 2.03. 91
hews down and fells the hardest–timber'd oak. 3H6 2.01. 55
whence he return'd, his brows bound with oak. COR 1.03. 15 P
and for his meed | was brow–bound with the oak. 2.02. 98
he's the rock, the oak not to be wind–shaken. 5.02.111 P
with a bolt | that should but rive an oak. 5.03.153
upon me stuck as leaves | do on the oak, have TIM 4.03.264
what ribs of oak, when mountains melt on them, OTH 2.01. 8
to seel her father's eyes up, close as oak, | he 3.03.210
and eat, | to thee the reed is as the oak. CYM 4.02.267
about his head he wears the winner's oak, | and TNK 4.02.137
OAK–CLEAVING 1 FR 0.0001 REL FR 1 V 0 P
vaunt–couriers of oak–cleaving thunderbolts, LR 3.02. 5
OAKEN 1 FR 0.0001 REL FR 0 V 1 P
the third time home with the oaken garland. COR 2.01.125 P
OAK'S 1 FR 0.0001 REL FR 1 V 0 P
to dry the old oak's sap and cherish springs, LUC 950
OAKS 7 FR 0.0008 REL FR 7 V 0 P
those thoughts to me were oaks, to thee like LLL 4.02.108
wind | makes flexible the knees of knotted oaks, TRO 1.03. 50
fins of lead, | and hews down oaks with rushes. COR 1.01.181
the oaks bear mast, the briers scarlet heps; TIM 4.03.419
the scolding winds | have riv'd the knotty oaks, JC 1.03. 6
in | with oaks unscalable and roaring waters, CYM 3.01. 20
those thoughts to me like oaks, to thee like PP 5. 4
OARED 1 FR 0.0001 REL FR 1 V 0 P
and oared | himself with his good arms in lusty TMP 2.01.119
OARS 3 FR 0.0003 REL FR 2 V 1 P
shipp'd, and thou art to post after with oars. TGV 2.03. 34 P
cut with her golden oars the silver stream, ADO 3.01. 27
the oars were silver, | which to the tune of ANT 2.02.194
OATCAKE 1 FR 0.0001 REL FR 0 V 1 P
hugh oatcake, sir, or george seacole, for they ADO 3.03. 11 P
OATEN 1 FR 0.0001 REL FR 1 V 0 P
when shepherds pipe on oaten straws | and merry LLL 5.02.903
/OATH 4 FR 0.0004 REL FR 2 V 2 P
/cracking /the /strong /warrant /of /an /oath, R2 4.01.235
mock not /that /i affect th' untraded /oath, TRO 4.05.178
/health, /a /boy's /love, /or /a /whore's /oath. LR 3.06. 19 P
/i /here /take /my /oath /before /this 3.06. 47 P
OATH 155 FR 0.0175 REL FR 138 V 17 P
swear'st grace o'erboard, not an oath on shore? TMP 5.01.219
here is her oath for love, her honor's pawn: TGV 1.03. 47
and ev'n that pow'r which gave me first my oath 2.06. 4
was affianc'd to her /by oath, and the nuptial MM 3.01.214 P
pardon me, good father, it is against my oath. 4.02.181 P
and what he with his oath | and all probation 5.01.156
against my crown, my oath, my dignity, | which ERR 1.01.143
it is a branch and parcel of mine oath, | a 5.01.106
me to an oyster, but i'll take my oath on it, ADO 2.03. 25 P
your oath is pass'd to pass away from these. LLL 1.01. 49
or, having sworn too hard–a–keeping oath, 1.01. 65
i am the last that will last keep his oath. 1.01.160
and he and his competitors in oath | were all 2.01. 82
court, | than seek a dispensation for his oath, 2.01. 87
hear me, dear lady: i have sworn an oath. 2.01. 97
'tis deadly sin to keep that oath, my lord, 2.01.105
so wise | to lose an oath to win a paradise?" 4.03. 71
and jove for your love would infringe an oath. 4.03.142
o, who can give an oath? 4.03.246
the virtue of your eye must break my oath. 5.02.348
your oath once broke, you force not to forswear. 5.02.440
despise me when i break this oath of mine. 5.02.441
troth, | i never swore this lady such an oath. 5.02.451
your oath i will not trust, but go with speed 5.02.794
two bosoms interchained with an oath, | so then MND 2.02. 49
a million fail, confounding oath on oath. 3.02. 93
a million fail, confounding oath on oath. 3.02. 93
weigh oath with oath, and you will nothing weigh 3.02.131
weigh oath with oath, and you will nothing weigh 3.02.131
the prince of arragon hath ta'en his oath, | and MV 2.09. 2
i am enjoin'd by oath to observe three things: 2.09. 9
i'll keep my oath, | patiently to bear my wroth. 2.09. 77
i have sworn an oath that i will have my bond. 3.03. 5
an oath, an oath, i have an oath in heaven! 4.01.228
an oath, an oath, i have an oath in heaven! 4.01.228
an oath, an oath, i have an oath in heaven! 4.01.228
double self, | and there's an oath of credit. 5.01.246
i never more will break an oath with thee. 5.01.248
and when i break that oath, let me turn monster. AYL 1.02. 22 P
where learn'd you that oath, fool? 1.02. 62 P
the oath of /a lover is no stronger than the 3.04. 30 P
she vied so fast, protesting oath on oath, SHR 2.01.309
she vied so fast, protesting oath on oath, 2.01.309
and here i take the like unfeigned oath, | never 4.02. 32
for me, that i may surely keep mine oath, | i 4.02. 36
with the divine forfeit of his soul upon oath, AWW 3.06. 32 P
ask him upon his oath, if he does think | he had 5.03.185
for it comes to pass oft that a terrible oath, TN 3.04.179 P
sir, he will fight with you for 's oath sake. 3.04.297 P
pray god he keep his oath! 3.04.310 P
the moon | as or by oath remove or counsel shake WT 1.02.428
if word nor oath | prevail not, go and see. 3.02.203
of my poor babe, according to thine oath, 3.03. 30
accurs'd am i | to be by oath enjoin'd to this. 3.03. 53
it becomes thy oath full well, | thou to me thy 4.04.300
will i break my oath | to this my fair belov'd. 4.04.491
then, good my lords, bear witness to his oath. 5.01. 72
man, | i have a king's oath to the contrary. JN 3.01. 10
and like a civil war set'st oath to oath, | thy 3.01.264
and like a civil war set'st oath to oath, | thy 3.01.264
and mak'st an oath the surety for thy truth 3.01.282
oath the surety for thy truth | against an oath; 3.01.283
thy voluntary oath | lives in this bosom, dearly 3.03. 23
well, | upon your oath of service to the pope, 5.01. 23
hast thou, according to thy oath and band, R2 1.01. 2
speak truly on thy knighthood and thy oath, | as 1.03. 14
who hither come engaged by my oath | (which god 1.03. 17
return again, and take an oath with thee. 1.03.178
to keep the oath that we administer: 1.03.182
whom both my oath | and duty bids defend; 2.02.112
and let him never see joy that breaks that oath! 2.03.151
let me unkiss the oath 'twixt thee and me; 5.01. 74
a good mouth–filling oath, and leave "in sooth," 1H4 3.01.254
my oath should be "by this fire, that/'s god's 3.03. 34 P
broke oath on oath, committed wrong on wrong, 4.03.101
broke oath on oath, committed wrong on wrong, 4.03.101
us, | and you did swear that oath at doncaster, 5.01. 42
hand, | forgot your oath to us at doncaster, 5.01. 58
a lie with a slight oath and a jest with a sad 2H4 5.01. 82 P
an oath of mickle might, and fury shall abate. H5 2.01. 66
sword is an oath, and oaths must have their 2.01.101
by her foot, that she may tread out the oath. 3.07. 96 P
is it fit this soldier keep his oath? 4.07.132 P
your grace, that he keep his vow and his oath. 4.07.139 P
my lord of burgundy, we'll take your oath, | and 5.02.371
now, governor of paris, take your oath: 1H6 4.01. 3
a dreadful oath, sworn with a solemn tongue! 2H6 3.02.158
against thy oath and true allegiance sworn, 5.01. 20
thou dispense with heaven for such an oath? 5.01.181
a sin, | but greater sin to keep a sinful oath. 5.01.183
wrong | but that he was bound by a solemn oath? 5.01.190
conditionally that here thou take an oath | to 3H6 1.01.196
this oath i willingly take and will perform. 1.01.201
i took an oath that he should quietly reign. 1.02. 15
but for a kingdom any oath may be broken: 1.02. 16

an oath is of no moment, being not took | before 1.02. 22
your oath, my lord, is vain and frivolous. 1.02. 27
is crown'd so soon, and broke his solemn oath? 1.04.100
now in his life, against your holy oath? 1.04.105
here's for my oath, here's for my father's death 1.04.175
touching king henry's oath and your succession. 2.01.119
his oath enrolled in the parliament; 2.01.173
to frustrate both his oath and what beside | may 2.01.175
since when, his oath is broke; 2.02. 89
what, not an oath? 2.06. 77
when clifford cannot spare his friends an oath. 2.06. 78
but did you never swear and break an oath? 3.01. 72
no, never such an oath, nor will not now. 3.01. 73
perhaps thou wilt object my holy oath: 5.01. 89
to keep that oath were more impiety | than 5.01. 90
i am bound by oath, and therefore pardon me. R3 4.01. 27
by nothing, for this is no oath: 4.04.368
if thou didst fear to break an oath with him, 4.04.378
if thou hadst fear'd to break an oath by him, 4.04.381
to whom by oath he menac'd | revenge upon the H8 1.02.137
he did discharge a horrible oath, whose tenor 1.02.206
full of protest, of oath and big compare, TRO 3.02.175
gaging me to keep | an oath that i have sworn. 5.01. 42
i prithee do not hold me to mine oath, | bid me 5.02. 26
bound with an oath to yield to his conditions; COR 5.01. 69
breaking his oath and resolution like | a twist 5.06. 94
that granted, how canst thou believe an oath? TIT 5.01. 72
careful to observe, | therefore i urge thy oath; 5.01. 78
and keeps the oath which by that god he swears, 5.01. 80
so fond, | to trust man on his oath or bond; TIM 1.02. 65
no, not an oath! JC 2.01.114
and what other oath | than honesty to honesty 2.01.126
our cause or our performance | did need an oath; 2.01.136
come now, keep thine oath; 5.03. 40
propose the oath, my lord. HAM 1.05.152
indeed without an oath i'll make an end on't. 4.05. 57 P
with our curse, and stranger'd with our oath, LR 1.01.204
of mine honors, | my oath, and my profession. 5.03.131
and fall of swords, | and cassio high in oath; OTH 2.03.235
for to deny each article with oath | cannot 5.02. 54
you have broken | the article of your oath, ANT 2.02. 82
but on, caesar, | the article of my oath. 2.02. 87
the feeler's soul | to th' oath of loyalty; CYM 1.06.102
whose strength | i will confirm with oath, which 2.04. 64
and with oath to violate | my lady's honor. 5.05.284
take thy word for faith, not ask thine oath: PER 1.02.120
bound by the indenture of his oath to be one. 1.03. 8 P
thy oath remember, thou hast sworn to do't. 4.01. 1
upon his oath and life, must he set foot | upon TNK 2.02.246
it concerns your credit | and my oath equally. 3.06.224
that oath was rashly made, and in your anger, 3.06.227
beside, i have another oath 'gainst yours, | of 3.06.230
i'll be cut a–pieces | before i take this oath. 3.06.257
whether he should follow | his rash oath, or the 4.01. 11
they knew, | and him by oath they truly honored: LUC 410
knighthood, gentry, and sweet friendship's oath, 569
"thou makest the vestal violate her oath, | thou 883
so, | to flatter thee with an infringed oath; 1061
what fool is not so wise | to break an oath, to PP 3.14
and credent soul to that strong–bonded oath LC 279
OATHABLE 1 FR 0.0001 REL FR 1 V 0 P
you are not oathable, | although i know you'll TIM 4.03.136
OATH–BREAKING 1 FR 0.0001 REL FR 1 V 0 P
of his oath–breaking, which he mended thus, | by 1H4 5.02. 37
OATHS' 1 FR 0.0001 REL FR 1 V 0 P
but why of two oaths' breach do i accuse thee, SON 152. 5
/OATHS 2 FR 0.0002 REL FR 2 V 0 P
/own /breath /release /all /duteous /oaths; R2 4.01.210
/god /pardon /all /oaths /that /are /broke /to 4.01.214
OATHS 70 FR 0.0079 REL FR 56 V 14 P
the strongest oaths are straw | to th' fire i' TMP 4.01. 52
with twenty thousand soul–confirming oaths. TGV 2.06. 16
a thousand oaths, an ocean of his tears, | and 2.07. 69
his words are bonds, his oaths are oracles, 2.07. 75
and full of new–found oaths, which he will break 4.04.130
then rend thy faith | into a thousand oaths; 5.04. 48
and all those oaths | descended into perjury, to 5.04. 48
behold her that gave aim to all thy oaths, | and 5.04.101
and your bold–beating oaths, under the shelter WIV 2.02. 28 P
with her that's gone, think'st thou thy oaths, MM 5.01.242
with circumstance and oaths so to deny | this ERR 5.01. 16
and partly by his oaths, which first possess'd ADO 3.03.156 P
your oaths are pass'd, and now subscribe your LLL 1.01. 19
subscribe to your deep oaths, and keep it too. 1.01. 23
these oaths and laws will prove an idle scorn. 1.01.309
/let us once lose our oaths to find ourselves, 4.03.358
or else we lose ourselves to keep our oaths. 4.03.359
hate a breaking cause to be | of heavenly oaths, 5.02.356
time, | play'd foul play with our oaths. 5.02.756
eyes, | have misbecom'd our oaths and gravities, 5.02.768
he hail'd down oaths that he was only mine; MND 1.01.243
so he dissolv'd, and show'rs of oaths did melt. 1.01.245
till my very /roof was dry | with oaths of love, MV 3.02.205
though not for me, yet for your vehement oaths, 5.01.155
a thing stuck on with oaths upon your finger, 5.01.168
full of strange oaths, and bearded like the pard AYL 2.07.150
speaks brave words, swears brave oaths, and 3.04. 41 P
and by all pretty oaths that are not dangerous, 4.01.189 P
that thinks with oaths to face the matter out. SHR 2.01.289
with oaths kept waking, and with brawling fed; 4.03. 10
their promises, enticements, oaths, tokens, and AWW 3.05. 19 P
three great oaths would scarce make that be 4.01. 59 P
'tis not the many oaths that makes the truth, 4.02. 21
would you believe my oaths | when i did love you 4.02. 26
therefore your oaths | are words and poor 4.02. 29
she says all men | have the like oaths. 4.02. 71
"when he swears oaths, bid him drop gold, and 4.03.223
he professes not keeping of oaths; 4.03.252 P
sir, upon the oaths of judgment and reason. TN 3.02. 14 P
you had drawn oaths from him not to stay. WT 1.02. 29
you would seek t' unsphere the stars with oaths, 1.02. 48
and given such sarcenet surety for thy oaths 1H4 3.01.251
gifts before him, proffer'd him their oaths, 4.03. 71
is an oath, and oaths must have their course. H5 2.01.101
for oaths are straws, men's faiths are 2.03. 51
war, which they trick up with new–tun'd oaths; 3.06. 76 P
only downright oaths, which i never use till 5.02.144 P
and may our oaths well kept and prosp'rous be! 5.02.374

remember, lords, your oaths to henry sworn: 1H6 1.01.162
that in alliance, amity, and oaths, | there 4.01. 62
as doth a ruler with unlawful oaths, | or one 5.05. 30
would break a thousand oaths to reign one year. 3H6 1.02. 17
and trust not simple henry nor his oaths. 1.02. 59
and tell me then, have you not broke your oaths? 3.01. 79
but do not break your oaths, for of that sin 3.01. 90
swear the oaths now to her that you have sworn TRO 3.02. 41 P
spare your oaths; TIM 4.03.139
to stale with ordinary oaths my love | to every JC 1.02. 73
makes marriage vows | as false as dicers' oaths, HAM 3.04. 45
swore as many oaths as i spake words, and broke LR 3.04. 88 P
as if i borrow'd mine oaths of him and might not CYM 2.01. 5 P
is not for any standers–by to curtal his oaths. 2.01. 11 P
whose false oaths prevail'd | before my perfect 3.03. 66
by all oaths in one, | i, and the justice of my TNK 3.01. 33
knights, by their oaths, should right poor LUC 1694
between each kiss her oaths of true love PP 7. 8
her faith, her oaths, her tears, and all were 7.12
for all my vows are oaths but to misuse thee, SON 152. 7
for i have sworn deep oaths of thy deep kindness 152. 9
oaths of thy love, thy truth, thy constancy, 152.10
/OATS 1 FR 0.0001 REL FR 1 V 0 P
/cannot /draw /a /cart, /nor /eat /dried /oats, LR 5.03. 38
OATS 5 FR 0.0005 REL FR 2 V 3 P
of wheat, rye, barley, fetches, oats, and pease; TMP 4.01. 61
i could munch your good dry oats. MND 4.01. 32 P
the oats have eaten the horses. SHR 3.02.205 P
fellow never joy'd since the price of oats rose, 1H4 2.01. 13 P
and twenty strike of oats, but he'll ne'er have TNK 5.02. 65
OB 1 FR 0.0001 REL FR 0 V 1 P
item, bread ... ob.. 1H4 2.04.539 P
OBBRAIDINGS *(also upbraidings)*
OBBRAIDINGS 1 FR 0.0001 REL FR 1 V 0 P
beauty | truly pertains (without obbraidings, TNK 3.06. 32
OBDURACY 1 FR 0.0001 REL FR 0 V 1 P
thou and falstaff, for obduracy and persistency. 2H4 2.02. 46 P
OBDURATE 9 FR 0.0010 REL FR 9 V 0 P
madam, if your heart be so obdurate, | vouchsafe TGV 4.02.119
but since he stands obdurate, | and that no MV 4.01. 8
god should be so obdurate as yourselves, | how 2H6 4.07.115
thou stern, obdurate, flinty, rough, remorseless 3H6 1.04.142
withal obdurate, do not hear him plead; R3 1.03.346
but if she be obdurate | to mild entreaties, god 3.01. 39
thee, | be not obdurate, open thy deaf ears. TIT 2.03.160
"art thou obdurate, flinty, hard as steel? VEN 199
obdurate vassals fell exploits effecting, | in LUC 429
OBEDIENCE 56 FR 0.0063 REL FR 52 V 4 P
weigh'd between loathness and obedience, at TMP 2.01.131
answer his requiring with a plausible obedience, MM 3.01.244 P
turn'd her obedience (which is due to me) | to MND 1.01. 37
and husband, | i am your wife in all obedience. SHR in.2. 107
yet, | and show more sign of her obedience, 5.02.117
obedience, | her new–built virtue and obedience. 5.02.118
but love, fair looks, and true obedience — 5.02.153
ground to do't | is the obedience to a master; WT 1.02.354
commend my best obedience to the queen. 2.02. 34
rage, | and make them tame to their obedience! JN 4.02.262
from whose obedience i forbid my soul, 4.03. 64
our people quarrel with obedience, | swearing 5.01. 9
and calmly run on in obedience | even to our 5.04. 56
obedience bids i should not bid again. R2 1.01.163
and true obedience, of this madness cured, 2H4 4.02. 41
let me no more from this obedience rise, | which 4.05.146
which is fixed, as an aim or butt, | obedience; H5 1.02.187
our obedience to the king wipes the crime of it 4.01.132 P
or bring him in obedience to your yoke. 1H6 1.01.164
thy humble servant vows obedience | and humble 3.01.166
reclaim'd | to your obedience fifty fortresses, 3.04. 6
but if you mind to hold your true obedience, 3H6 4.01.140
love, charity, obedience, and true duty! R3 2.02.108
to pass | this tractable obedience is a slave H8 1.02. 64
what kind of my obedience i should tender. 2.03. 66
vouchsafe to speak my thanks and my obedience, 2.03. 71
that i have been your wife in this obedience 2.04. 35
zeal and obedience he still bore your grace, 3.01. 63
i hold now with him | is only my obedience. 3.01.122
the hearts of princes kiss obedience, | so much 3.01.162
one that, in all obedience, makes the church 5.02.152
not fate, obedience, nor the hand of mars TRO 5.03. 52
their obedience fails | to th' greater bench. COR 3.01.165
have we not had a taste of his obedience — 3.01.316
obedience, fail in children! TIM 4.01. 4
contending 'gainst obedience, as they would make MAC 2.04. 17
we on | to give obedience where 'tis truly ow'd. 5.02. 26
as honor, love, obedience, troops of friends, 5.03. 25
who in her duty and obedience, mark, | hath HAM 2.02.107
this in obedience hath my daughter shown me, 2.02.125
you have obedience scanted, | and well are worth LR 1.01.278
and shake in pieces the heart of his obedience. 1.02. 85 P
by an enforc'd obedience of planetary influence; 1.02.125 P
whose virtue and obedience doth this instant 2.01.113
if your sweet sway | allow obedience, if you 2.04.191
noble company | where most you owe obedience? OTH 1.03.180
i hourly learn | a doctrine of obedience, and ANT 5.02. 31
past grace? obedience? CYM 1.01.136
you sin against | obedience, which you owe your 2.03.112
thou seest him, | a little witness my obedience. 3.04. 66
change | command into obedience; 3.04.155
they are o'er the bank of their obedience, STM II.C 39
forewarn us of, urging obedience to authority, II.C 94
in, in to your obedience! II.C 113
your hurly | cannot proceed but by obedience. II.C 114
whose swift obedience to her mistress hies; LUC 1215
/OBEDIENT 1 FR 0.0001 REL FR 0 V 1 P
/which /they /will /make /an /obedient /father. LR 1.04.235 P
OBEDIENT 29 FR 0.0032 REL FR 27 V 2 P
whom i with this obedient steel, three inches of TMP 2.01.283
her mother's plot | she, seemingly obedient, WIV 4.06. 33
always obedient to your grace's will, | i come MM 1.01. 25
and floating straight, obedient to the stream, ERR 1.01. 86
kisses the base ground with obedient breast? LLL 4.03.221
pleasure is, | and i am tied to be obedient — SHR 1.01.212
that bate and beat and will not be obedient. 4.01.196
his wife, | and he whose wife is most obedient, 5.02. 67
sour, | and not obedient to his honest will, 5.02.158
do thine own fortunes that obedient right AWW 2.03.160

say, | but that i am your most obedient servant. 2.05. 72
seven of my people, with an obedient start, make TN 2.05. 58 P
and, acting this in an obedient hope, | why have 5.01.340
your physician, | your most obedient counsellor; WT 2.03. 55
if my reason | will thereto be obedient, i have 4.04.483
and move in that obedient orb again | where you 1H4 5.01. 17
yours, | and do him homage as obedient subjects, 1H6 4.02. 7
or like obedient subjects follow him | to his R3 2.02. 45
james tyrrel, and your most obedient subject. 4.02. 67
a loyal and obedient subject is | therein H8 3.02.180
would poison were obedient and knew my mind! TIM 4.03.296 P
what e'er you be, i am obedient. OTH 3.03. 89
truly, /an obedient lady: 4.01.248
and she's obedient, as you say, obedient; 4.01.255
and she's obedient, as you say, obedient; 4.01.255
very obedient. 4.01.256
we'll no defense, | obedient as the scabbard. CYM 3.04. 80
whereas reproof, obedient and in order, | fits PER 1.02. 42
twice six moons, | he, obedient to their dooms, 3.ch. 32
OBEISANCE 1 FR 0.0001 REL FR 1 V 0 P
chamber, | and call him madam, do him obeisance. SHR in.1. 108
OBERON 8 FR 0.0009 REL FR 8 V 0 P
for oberon is passing fell and wrath, | because MND 2.01. 20
and jealous oberon would have the child | knight 2.01. 24
i jest to oberon and make him smile | when i a 2.01. 44
here comes oberon. 2.01. 58
what, jealous oberon? 2.01. 61
why should titania cross her oberon? 2.01.119
when i am gone, | for i must now to oberon. 2.02. 83
my oberon, what visions have i seen! 4.01. 76
/OBEY 1 FR 0.0001 REL FR 1 V 0 P
/to /let /these /hands /obey /my /blood, | /they LR 4.02. 64
OBEY 84 FR 0.0095 REL FR 71 V 13 P
obey, and be attentive. TMP 1.02. 38
i must obey. 1.02.372
come on, obey: 1.02.484
my spirits obey; 5.01. 2
disease will scarce obey this medicine. WIV 3.03.192 P
if he bid you set it down, obey him. 4.02.110 P
let's obey his humor a little further. 4.02.199 P
i shall obey him. MM 4.02.107 P
ere i learn love, i'll practice to obey. ERR 2.01. 29
if we obey them not, this will ensue: 2.02.191
and charge you in the duke's name to obey me. 4.01. 70
i do obey thee, till i give thee bail. 4.01. 80
i did obey, and sent my peasant home | for 5.01.231
let us obey you to go with us. ADO 3.03.176 P
come, we'll obey you. 3.03.180 P
young blood doth not obey an old decree. LLL 4.03.213
heart, | i shall obey you in all fair commands. MV 3.04. 36
obey the bride, you that attend on her. SHR 3.02.223
when they are bound to serve, love, and obey. 5.02.164
obey our will, which travails in thy good; AWW 2.03.158
i shall obey his will. 2.05. 57
he does obey every point of the letter that i TN 3.02. 77 P
i must obey. 3.04.332
this once, and let your flesh and blood obey it. 5.01. 33 P
forbid the sea for to obey the moon | as or by WT 1.02.427
i willingly obey your command. 4.02. 53 P
a king, woe's slave, shall kingly woe obey. R2 3.02.210
to see a son of mine | offend you and obey you, 2H4 5.02.106
let them obey that knows not how to rule; 2H6 5.01. 6
obey, audacious traitor, kneel for grace. 5.01.108
he is arrested, but will not obey. 5.01.136
command, and i'll obey. 3H6 3.01. 93
and their true sovereign whom they must obey? 4.01. 78
nay, whom they shall obey, and love thee too, 4.01. 79
we know thy charge, brakenbury, and will obey. R3 1.01.105
we are the queen's abjects, and must obey. 1.01.106
i obey. H8 1.01.210
bits and spur 'em | till they obey the manage. 5.02. 59
shall more obey than to the edge of steel | or TRO 3.01.152
he cares not, he'll obey conditions. 4.05. 72
this i'll obey. 5.01. 44
madam, i will obey you in every thing hereafter. COR 1.03.102 P
obey, i charge thee, | and follow to thine 3.01.175
i'll never | be such a gosling to obey instinct, 5.03. 35
yet should both ear and heart obey my tongue. TIT 4.04. 99
i charge thee in the prince's name, obey. ROM 3.01.140
obey and go with me, for thou must die. 5.03. 57
be crown'd with plagues, that thee alone obey! TIM 5.01. 53
upon our talk, | and nature must obey necessity, JC 4.03.227
i shall in all my best obey you, madam. HAM 1.02.120
i shall obey, my lord. 1.03.136
let's follow. 'tis not fit thus to obey him. 1.04. 88
but we both obey, | and here give up ourselves, 2.02. 29
i shall obey you. 3.01. 36
we shall obey, were she ten times our mother. 3.02.333 P
if your mind dislike any thing, obey it. 5.02.217 P
fit, | obey you, love you, and most honor you. LR 1.01. 98
obey thy parents, keep thy word's justice, swear 3.04. 80 P
t' obey in all your daughters' hard commands. 3.04.149
you are a royal one, and we obey you. 4.06.201
the weight of this sad time we must obey, 5.03.324
what if /i do obey? OTH 1.02. 87
we must obey the time. 1.03.300
command, | and to obey shall be in me remorse, 3.03.468
sir, i obey the mandate, | and will return to 4.01.259
'tis proper i obey him; 5.02.196
the very dice obey him, | and in our sports my ANT 2.03. 34
her tongue will not obey her heart, nor can 3.02. 47
by my affection, would | obey it on all cause. 3.11. 68
it thus, my master and my lord | i must obey. 5.02.117
(which my love makes religion to obey), | i tell 5.02.199
no more obey the heavens than our courtiers' CYM 1.01. 2
that you in all obey her, | save when command to 2.03. 51
do your best wills, | and make me blest to obey. 5.01. 17
and i (as fits my nature) do obey you. PER 2.01. 4
we cannot but obey | the powers above us. 3.03. 9
dian, goddess argentine, | i will obey thee. 5.01.251
hath bid him rule, and will'd you to obey; STM II.C 100
who will obey a traitor? II.C 116
give up yourself to form, obey the magistrate, II.C 146
forc'd to content, but never to obey, | panting VEN 61
her lips are conquerors, his lips obey, | paying 549
trumpet be, | to whose sound chaste wings obey. PHT 4
their own wills, and made their wills obey. LC 133

OBEY'D 9 FR 0.0010 REL FR 8 V 1 P
and at this time | his tongue obey'd his hand. AWW 1.02. 41
your king's name be obey'd, | and what god will, 3H6 3.01. 99
for she commanding all, obey'd of none. R3 4.04.104
be done, and the king's pleasure | by me obey'd! H8 1.01.216
obey'd him? 3.01.130
in some other fight, | as cause will be obey'd. COR 1.06. 83
sail, so men obey'd | and fell below his stem. 2.02.106
a dog's obey'd in office. LR 4.06.159 P
man, and worthiest | to have command obey'd. ANT 3.13. 88
OBEY'DST 1 FR 0.0001 REL FR 1 V 0 P
whom thou obey'dst thirty and six years, | and 3H6 3.03. 96
OBEYED 1 FR 0.0001 REL FR 1 V 0 P
steel his stronger strength obeyed, | yet was he VEN 111
OBEYING 3 FR 0.0003 REL FR 3 V 0 P
me again, | obeying with my wind when i do blow, 3H6 3.01. 86
obeying in commanding, and thy parts | sovereign H8 2.04.140
dexterity so obeying appetite | that what he TRO 5.05. 27
OBEYS 6 FR 0.0006 REL FR 6 V 0 P
obeys his points | as if he were his officer. COR 4.06.125
on fortinbras, which he, in brief, obeys, HAM 2.02. 68
which he frets at rather | than any jot obeys; TNK 5.04. 71
he now obeys, and now no more resisteth, | while VEN 563
right, | nor aught obeys but his foul appetite. LUC 546
what me, your minister, for you obeys, | works LC 229
/OBIDICUT 1 FR 0.0001 REL FR 0 V 1 P
/of /lust, /as /obidicut; LR 4.01. 59 P
OBJECT 45 FR 0.0050 REL FR 43 V 2 P
some rare noteworthy object in thy travel. TGV 1.01. 13
upon a homely object love can wink. 2.04. 98
love | is by a newer object quite forgotten. 2.04.195
he doth object i am too great of birth, | and WIV 3.04. 4
your eye | by throwing it on any other object, MM 5.01. 23
ear, | that never object pleasing in thine eye, ERR 2.02.115
for every object that the one doth catch | the LLL 2.01. 70
roll | to every varied object in his glance; 5.02.765
the object and the pleasure of mine eye, | is MND 4.01.170
and every object that might make me fear MV 1.01. 20
and mark what object did present itself | under AYL 4.03.103
all proportions | to a most hideous object. AWW 5.03. 52
could thought, without this object, | form such JN 4.03. 44
what dost thou object | against the duke of R2 1.01. 28
into revolt | when gold becomes her object! 2H4 4.05. 66
scaffold to bring forth | so great an object. H5 pr 11
this blot that they object against your house 1H6 2.04.116
purpose to answer what thou canst object. 3.01. 7
doth not the object cheer your heart, my lord? 3H6 2.02. 4
perhaps thou wilt object my holy oath: 5.01. 89
have now the fatal object in my eye | where my 5.06. 16
hold | in him that did object the same to thee: R3 2.04. 17
and his eye revil'd | me as his abject object; H8 1.01.127
and fix'd on spiritual object, he should still 3.02.132
and reason flies the object of all harm. TRO 2.02. 41
the present eye praises the present object. 3.03.180
that afflicts us, the object of our misery, is COR 1.01. 20 P
with the dismall'st object hurt | that ever eye TIT 2.03.204
ay me, this object kills me! 3.01. 64
herein | this present object made probation. HAM 1.01.156
she, whom even but now was your /best object, LR 1.01.214
and with this horrible object, from low farms, 2.03. 17
seest thou this object, kent? 5.03.239
things, | though great ones are their object. OTH 3.04.145
the object poisons sight, | let it be hid. 5.02.364
this object, which | takes prisoner the wild CYM 1.06.102
or fruitful object be | in eye of imogen, that 5.04. 55
her master, hitting | each object with a joy; 5.05.396
they would not make us their object. TNK 2.01. 52 P
long time his eye | will dwell upon his object; 5.03. 49
the time is spent, her object will away, | and VEN 255
fold in the object that did feed her sight. 822
"make me not object to the tell-tale day, | the LUC 806
no object but her passion's strength renews; 1103
gilding the object whereupon it gazeth; SON 20. 6
OBJECTED 1 FR 0.0001 REL FR 1 V 0 P
good master vernon, it is well objected; 1H6 2.04. 43
OBJECTIONS 3 FR 0.0003 REL FR 3 V 0 P
well | to bear with their perverse objections; 1H6 4.01.129
as for your spiteful false objections, | prove 2H6 1.03.155
speak on, sir, | i dare your worst objections. H8 3.02.307
OBJECTS 15 FR 0.0017 REL FR 12 V 3 P
figures, shapes, objects, ideas, apprehensions, LLL 4.02. 67 P
extracted from many objects, and indeed the AYL 4.01. 17 P
divides one thing entire to many objects, | like R2 2.02. 17
blaze of wrath subscribes | to tender objects, TRO 4.05.106
swear against objects, | put armor on thine ears TIM 4.03.123
so in use, | and dreadful objects so familiar, JC 3.01.266
one that feeds | on objects, arts, and 4.01. 37
different | with variable objects shall expel HAM 3.01.172
and by those fearful objects to prepare | this PER 1.01. 43
other objects that are inserted 'tween her mind TNK 4.03. 79 P
a thousand lamentable objects there, | in scorn LUC 1373
of his quick objects hath the mind no part, SON 113. 7
best | as fast as objects to his beams assemble? 114. 8
set | the goodly objects which abroad they find LC 137
and the opal blend | with objects manifold: 216
OBLATION 1 FR 0.0001 REL FR 1 V 0 P
and take thou my oblation, poor but free, SON 125.10
OBLATIONS 1 FR 0.0001 REL FR 1 V 0 P
for these, of force, must your oblations be, LC 223
OBLIGATION 6 FR 0.0006 REL FR 4 V 2 P
warrant, quittance, or obligation, armigero. WIV 1.01. 10 P
no other obligation? H8 2.03. 96
the obligation of our blood forbids | a gory TRO 4.05.122
bound | in filial obligation for some term | to HAM 1.02. 91
by the obligation of our ever-preserv'd love, 2.02.285 P
sister in the least | would fail her obligation. LR 2.04.142
OBLIGATIONS 1 FR 0.0001 REL FR 0 V 1 P
nay, he can make obligations, and write 2H6 4.02. 93 P
OBLIGED 1 FR 0.0001 REL FR 1 V 0 P
are wont | to keep obliged faith unforfeited! MV 2.06. 7
OBLIQUE 1 FR 0.0001 REL FR 0 V 1 P
the primitive statue and oblique memorial of TRO 5.01. 55 P
OBLIQUY 1 FR 0.0001 REL FR 1 V 0 P
all's obliquy; TIM 4.03. 18
/OBLIVION 1 FR 0.0001 REL FR 1 V 0 P
/husks | /and /formless /ruin /of /oblivion; TRO 4.05.167
OBLIVION 16 FR 0.0018 REL FR 14 V 2 P
the tooth of time | and razure of oblivion. MM 5.01. 13
is second childishness and mere oblivion, | sans AYL 2.07.165
which now shall die in oblivion and thou return SHR 4.01. 83 P
where dust and damn'd oblivion is the tomb | of AWW 2.03.140
and deeper than oblivion we do bury | th' 5.03. 24
putting all affairs else in oblivion, as if 2H4 5.05. 26 P
days, | nor from the dust of old oblivion rak'd, H5 2.04. 87
gulf | of dark forgetfulness and deep oblivion. R3 3.07.129
troy, | and blind oblivion swallow'd cities up, TRO 3.02.187
his back, | wherein he puts alms for oblivion, 3.03.146
lives | but in oblivion and hateful griefs. TIT 3.01.295
now whether it be | bestial oblivion, or some HAM 4.04. 40
is i would — | o, my oblivion is a very antony, ANT 1.03. 90
planting oblivion, beating reason back, VEN 557
to feed oblivion with decay of things, | to blot LUC 947
till each to raz'd oblivion yield his part | of SON 122. 7
OBLIVIOUS 1 FR 0.0001 REL FR 1 V 0 P
and with some sweet oblivious antidote | cleanse MAC 5.03. 43
OBLOQUY 4 FR 0.0004 REL FR 4 V 0 P
which were the greatest obloquy i' th' world AWW 4.02. 44
which were the greatest obloquy i' th' world 4.02. 48
which obloquy set bars before my tongue, | else 1H6 2.05. 49
and thou, the author of their obloquy, | shalt LUC 523
OBSCENE 3 FR 0.0003 REL FR 1 V 2 P
i mean, i did encounter that obscene and most LLL 1.01.241 P
should show so heinous, black, obscene a deed! R2 4.01.131
thou whoreson, obscene, greasy tallow-catch — 1H4 2.04.228 P
OBSCENELY 2 FR 0.0002 REL FR 1 V 1 P
comes so smoothly off, so obscenely as it were, LLL 4.01.143
we may rehearse most obscenely and courageously. MND 1.02.108 P
OBSCUR'D 7 FR 0.0008 REL FR 6 V 1 P
a pit hard by herne's oak, with obscur'd lights; WIV 5.03. 14 P
and you may marvel why i obscur'd myself, MM 5.01.390
of discovery, love, | and i should be obscur'd. MV 2.06. 44
you have obscur'd | with a swain's wearing, and WT 4.04. 8
and so the prince obscur'd his contemplation H5 1.01. 63
and even since then hath richard been obscur'd, 1H6 2.05. 26
and what obscur'd in this fair volume lies ROM 1.03. 85
OBSCURE 12 FR 0.0013 REL FR 9 V 3 P
some obscure precedence that hath tofore been LLL 3.01. 82
in the vulgar — o base and obscure vulgar! 4.01. 69 P
to rib her cerecloth in the obscure grave. MV 2.07. 51
drop in his way some obscure epistles of love, TN 2.03.155 P
a little little grave, an obscure grave — | or R2 3.03.154
this man | of purpose to obscure my noble birth. 1H6 5.04. 22
obscure and lousy swain, king henry's blood, 2H6 4.01. 50
steed, | and wand'red hither to an obscure plot, TIT 2.03. 77
the obscure bird | clamor'd the livelong night. MAC 2.03. 59
his means of death, his obscure funeral — | no HAM 4.05.214
an index and obscure prologue to the history of OTH 2.01.257 P
round rising hillocks, brakes obscure and rough, VEN 237
OBSCURED 3 FR 0.0003 REL FR 3 V 0 P
for what obscured light the heavens did grant ERR 1.01. 66
obscured in the circle of this forest. AYL 5.04. 34
been inform'd | of my obscured course; LR 2.02.168
OBSCURELY 2 FR 0.0002 REL FR 2 V 0 P
wherein obscurely | caesar's ambition shall be JC 1.02.319
cave-keeping evils that obscurely sleep. LUC 1250
OBSCURES 2 FR 0.0002 REL FR 2 V 0 P
a gracious voice, | obscures the show of evil? MV 3.02. 77
cynthia for shame obscures her silver shine, VEN 728
OBSCURING 1 FR 0.0001 REL FR 0 V 1 P
obscuring and hiding from me all gentleman-like AYL 1.01. 69 P
OBSCURITY 2 FR 0.0002 REL FR 2 V 0 P
no vast obscurity or misty vale, | where bloody TIT 5.02. 36
if thou destroy them not in dark obscurity? VEN 760
OBSEQUIES 7 FR 0.0008 REL FR 7 V 0 P
but all in vain are these mean obsequies, | and 2H6 3.02.146
these tears are my sweet rutland's obsequies, 3H6 1.04.147
tears | i render for my brethren's obsequies; TIT 1.01.160
the obsequies that i for thee will keep ROM 5.03. 16
to cross my obsequies and true love's rite? 5.03. 20
her obsequies have been as far enlarg'd | as we HAM 5.01.226
we have done our obsequies. come lay him down. CYM 4.02.282
OBSEQUIOUS 8 FR 0.0009 REL FR 7 V 1 P
i see you are obsequious in your love, and i WIV 4.02. 2 P
part, and in obsequious fondness | crowd to his MM 2.04. 28
and so obsequious will thy father be, | /e'en 3H6 2.05.118
near | to shed obsequious tears upon this trunk. TIT 5.03.152
for some term | to do obsequious sorrow. HAM 1.02. 92
that, doting on his own obsequious bondage, OTH 1.01. 46
how many a holy and obsequious tear | hath dear SON 31. 5
no, let me be obsequious in thy heart, | and 125. 9
OBSEQUIOUSLY 1 FR 0.0001 REL FR 1 V 0 P
whilst i awhile obsequiously lament | th' R3 1.02. 3
OBSEQUY 1 FR 0.0001 REL FR 1 V 0 P
keep the obsequy so strict. PHT 12
OBSERVANCE 18 FR 0.0020 REL FR 13 V 5 P
follow'd her with a doting observance; WIV 2.02.196 P
between you 'greed concerning her observance? MM 4.01. 41
with helena | to do observance to a morn of may) MND 1.01.167
say amen, | use all the observance of civility, MV 2.02.195
finding him, and relish it with good observance. AYL 3.02.234 P
wishes, | all adoration, duty, and observance, 5.02. 96
all purity, all trial, all observance; 5.02. 98
with true observance seek to eke out that AWW 2.05. 74
by what observance, i pray you? 3.02. 5 P
and trembling, and do observance to my mercy. 2H4 4.03. 15 P
with due observance of /thy godlike seat, TRO 1.03. 31
dispose | without observance or respect of any, 2.03.165
more honor'd in the breach than the observance. HAM 1.04. 16
with this special observance, that you o'erstep 3.02. 18 P
out of his scattering and unsure observance. OTH 3.03.151
or i have no observance. ANT 3.03. 22
by the sun, to do observance | to flow'ry may, TNK 2.05. 50
such sweet observance in this work was had, LUC 1385
OBSERVANCES 2 FR 0.0002 REL FR 2 V 0 P
but there are other strict observances: LLL 1.01. 36
degrees, observances, customs, and laws, TIM 4.01. 19
OBSERVANCY 1 FR 0.0001 REL FR 1 V 0 P
nor of them look for such observancy | as fits OTH 3.04.149
OBSERVANT 2 FR 0.0002 REL FR 2 V 0 P
of their observant toil the enemies' weight — TRO 1.03.203
why this same strict and most observant watch HAM 1.01. 71
OBSERVANTS 1 FR 0.0001 REL FR 1 V 0 P
than twenty silly-ducking observants | that LR 2.02.103
OBSERVATION 10 FR 0.0011 REL FR 8 V 2 P
and observation strange, my meaner ministers TMP 3.03. 87
what observation mad'st thou in this case | /of ERR 4.02. 5
if my observation (which very seldom lies), | by LLL 2.01.228
by my /penny of observation. 3.01. 27 P
for now our observation is perform'd, | and MND 4.01.104
hath strange places cramm'd | with observation, AYL 2.07. 41
time | that doth not /smack of observation — JN 1.01.208
tut, that's a foolish observation. 3H6 2.06.108
past | that youth and observation copied there, HAM 1.05.101
the observation we have made of it hath /not LR 1.01.289 P
OBSERVATIONS 1 FR 0.0001 REL FR 1 V 0 P
trust not my reading, nor my observations, ADO 4.01.165
OBSERV'D 15 FR 0.0017 REL FR 11 V 4 P
hast thou observ'd that? even she, i mean. TGV 2.01. 44 P
heard your guilty rhymes, observ'd your fashion, LLL 4.03.137
such as he hath observ'd in noble ladies | unto SHR in.1. 111
here is my hand, the premises observ'd, | thy AWW 2.01.201
observ'd his courtship to the common people, R2 1.04. 24
the which observ'd, a man may prophesy, | with a 2H4 3.01. 82
will, | for he is gracious if he be observ'd, 4.04. 30
his temper therefore must be well observ'd. 4.04. 36
as i am, i have observ'd these three swashers. H5 3.02. 28 P
i have observ'd thee always for a towardly TIM 3.01. 34 P
check'd like a bondman, all his faults observ'd, JC 4.03. 97
haunt, i have observ'd | the air is delicate. MAC 1.06. 9
th' observ'd of all observers, quite, quite down HAM 3.01.154
with us at sea it hath been still observ'd, and PER 3.01. 52 P
have you observ'd him | since our great lord TNK 1.03. 33
OBSERVE 34 FR 0.0038 REL FR 30 V 4 P
and wait the season, and observe the times, LLL 5.02. 63
no doubt they rose up early to observe | the MND 4.01.132
i am enjoin'd by oath to observe three things: MV 2.09. 9
he had the wit which i can well observe | to-day AWW 1.02. 32
i observe her now. 1.03.136
to him i live, and observe his reports for me. 2.01. 45 P
observe his construction of it. TN 2.03.175 P
observe him, for the love of mockery; 2.05. 18 P
he must observe their mood on whom he jests, 3.01. 62
we did observe. R2 1.04. 1
i shall observe him with all care and love. 2H4 4.04. 49
me, for they do observe | unfather'd heirs and 4.04.121
or will ye not observe | the strangeness of his 2H6 3.01. 4
observe, observe, he's moody. H8 3.02. 75
observe, observe, he's moody. 3.02. 75
and this centre | observe degree, priority, and TRO 1.03. 86
both observe and answer | the vantage of his COR 2.03.259
which i have seen thee careful to observe, TIT 5.01. 77
i come to observe, i give thee warning on't. TIM 1.02. 34
do you observe this, hostilius? 3.02. 63
i'll show you how t' observe a strange event. 3.04. 17
and let his very breath whom thou'lt observe 4.03.212
brutus, i do observe you now of late; JC 1.02. 32
must i observe you? 4.03. 45
observe her, stand close. MAC 5.01. 20 P
observe his inclination in yourself. HAM 2.01. 68
i'll observe his looks, | i'll tent him to the 2.02.596
the very comment of thy soul | observe my uncle. 3.02. 80
look to your wife, observe her well with cassio, OTH 3.03.197
set on thy wife to observe. 3.03.240
you shall observe him, | and his own courses 4.01.278
observe how antony becomes his flaw, | and what ANT 3.12. 34
pray observe her goodness. TNK 2.05. 35
you should observe her ev'ry way. 5.02. 14
OBSERVED 1 FR 0.0001 REL FR 1 V 0 P
by | the swiftest hours, observed as they flew, LC 60
OBSERVER 2 FR 0.0002 REL FR 2 V 0 P
that to th' observer doth thy history | fully MM 1.01. 28
he is a great observer, and he looks | quite JC 1.02.202
OBSERVERS 1 FR 0.0001 REL FR 1 V 0 P
th' observ'd of all observers, quite, quite down HAM 3.01.154
OBSERVING 4 FR 0.0004 REL FR 3 V 1 P
they, by observing him, do bear themselves like 2H4 5.01. 66 P
my lord, we have | stood here observing him. H8 3.02.112
and underwrite in an observing kind | his TRO 2.03.128
which i observing, | took once a pliant hour, OTH 1.03.150
OBSERVINGLY 1 FR 0.0001 REL FR 1 V 0 P
evil, | would men observingly distill it out; H5 4.01. 5
OBSQUE 1 FR 0.0001 REL FR 0 V 1 P
'tis "semper idem," for "obsque hoc nihil est." 2H4 5.05. 28 P
OBSTACLE 2 FR 0.0002 REL FR 1 V 1 P
no scruple of a scruple, no obstacle, no TN 3.04. 79 P
fie, joan, that thou wilt be so obstacle! 1H6 5.04. 17
OBSTACLES 2 FR 0.0002 REL FR 1 V 1 P
it fills a man full of obstacles. R3 1.04.139 P
first, if all obstacles were cut away, | and 3.07.156
OBSTINACY 2 FR 0.0002 REL FR 2 V 0 P
only sin | and hellish obstinacy tie thy tongue, AWW 1.03.180
you do not well in obstinacy | to cavil in the 1H6 5.04.155
OBSTINATE 5 FR 0.0005 REL FR 4 V 1 P
thou wast ever an obstinate heretic in the ADO 1.01.234 P
except you mean with obstinate repulse | to slay 1H6 3.01.113
the queen is obstinate, | stubborn to justice, H8 2.04.121
let it be virtuous to be obstinate. COR 5.03. 26
persever | in obstinate condolement is a course HAM 1.02. 93
OBSTINATELY 1 FR 0.0001 REL FR 1 V 0 P
my heart, | an esperance so obstinately strong, TRO 5.02.121
OBSTRUCTION 4 FR 0.0004 REL FR 1 V 3 P
to lie in cold obstruction, and to rot; MM 3.01.118
capacity, there is no obstruction in this. TN 2.05.118 P
this does make some obstruction in the blood, 3.04. 21 P
and yet complainest thou of obstruction? 4.02. 39 P
/OBSTRUCTIONS 1 FR 0.0001 REL FR 1 V 0 P
/and /purge /th' /obstructions /which /begin /to 2H4 4.01. 65
/OBTAIN 1 FR 0.0001 REL FR 1 V 0 P
/shall /i /obtain /it? R2 4.01.304
OBTAIN 8 FR 0.0009 REL FR 7 V 1 P
to plead for that which i would not obtain, | to TGV 4.04.100
as i woo'd for thee to obtain her, i will join ADO 3.02.126 P
means | us'd intercession to obtain a league, 1H6 5.04.148
clifford, ask mercy and obtain no grace. 3H6 2.06. 69
titus, thou shalt obtain and ask the empery. TIT 1.01.201
yet let me obtain my wish. PER 5.01. 35
yet ever to obtain his will resolving, | though LUC 129
make, | pawning his honor to obtain his lust, 156
OBTAIN'D 11 FR 0.0012 REL FR 8 V 3 P
woo hero for himself, and having obtain'd her, ADO 1.03. 63 P
with her father, and his good will obtain'd. 2.01.300 P
thanks | for my great suit so easily obtain'd. LLL 5.02.739

diana, unless i be obtain'd by the manner of my MV 1.02.107 P
i know thee well, thou hast obtain'd thy suit. 2.02.144
you have obtain'd it. 2.02.177
ay, when the special thing is well obtain'd, SHR 2.01.128
that, having this obtain'd, you presently AWW 2.04. 52
the other, when she has obtain'd your eye, WT 5.01.105
by guileful fair words peace may be obtain'd. 1H6 1.01. 77
to know who hath obtain'd the glory of the day. 4.07. 52
OBTAINED 2 FR 0.0002 REL FR 2 V 0 P
prince pirithous | obtained his liberty; TNK 2.02.245
and bring him where his suit may be obtained? LUC 898
OBTAINING 4 FR 0.0004 REL FR 2 V 2 P
at me, | that i am desperate of obtaining her. TGV 3.02. 5
for obtaining of suits? 1H4 1.02. 71 P
yea, for obtaining of suits, whereof the hangman 1.02. 72 P
the sundry dangers of his will's obtaining; LUC 128
OCCASION *(also cagion)*
/OCCASION 3 FR 0.0003 REL FR 3 V 0 P
/and /publish /the /occasion /of /our /arms. 2H4 1.03. 86
/there | /by /the /rough /torrent /of /occasion, 4.01. 72
/to /take /the /safest /occasion /by /the /front OTH 3.01. 49
OCCASION 73 FR 0.0082 REL FR 40 V 33 P
did it to minister occasion to these gentlemen, TMP 2.01.173 P
th' occasion speaks thee, and | my strong 2.01.207
and have more occasion to know one another. WIV 1.01.248 P
fee'd every slight occasion that could but 2.02.197 P
if you have occasion to use me for your own turn MM 4.02. 57 P
he heartily prays some occasion may detain us ADO 1.01.150 P
there is no measure in the occasion that breeds, 1.03. 3 P
his eye begets occasion for his wit, | for every LLL 2.01. 69
and delivered upon the mellowing of occasion. 4.02. 70 P
withal | upon the next occasion that we meet, 5.02.143
nay, i can gleek upon occasion. MND 3.01.147 P
you, | and you embrace th' occasion to depart. MV 1.01. 64
yet more quarrelling with occasion! 3.05. 55 P
lack of matter, you might take occasion to kiss. AYL 4.01. 75 P
cannot make her fault her husband's occasion, 4.01.175 P
and nature, stronger than his just occasion, 4.03.129
and weep, | till i can find occasion of revenge. SHR 2.01. 36
and tell us what occasion of import | hath all 3.02.102
till i had made mine own occasion mellow | what TN 1.02. 43
unless you laugh and minister occasion to him, 1.05. 87 P
that upon the least occasion more mine eyes will 2.01. 41 P
i sent for thee upon a sad occasion. 3.04. 19 P
you may have very fit occasion for't; 3.04.173 P
to keep in darkness what occasion now | reveals 5.01.153
bohemia on the like occasion whereon my services
WT 1.01. 2 P
i am courted now with a double occasion — gold 4.04.833 P
defense, | for courage mounteth with occasion. JN 2.01. 82
withhold thy speed, dreadful occasion! 4.02.125
favor and the form | of this most fair occasion, 5.04. 51
face | of that occasion that shall bring it on. 1H4 1.03.276
so when he had occasion to be seen, | he was but 3.02. 74
you took occasion to be quickly wooed | to gripe 5.01. 56
i well allow the occasion of our arms, | but 2H4 1.03. 5
that, as oft as he has occasion to name himself; 2.02.111 P
this land | as his misdoubts present occasion. 4.01.204
quit you with gud leve, as i may pick occasion; H5 3.02.104 P
having any occasion to write for matter of grant 5.02.337 P
much less to take occasion from their mouths 1H6 4.01.130
man, | what e'er occasion keeps him from us now. 2H6 3.01. 3
the brow of youth, | repairs him with occasion? 5.03. 5
more, | but that i seek occasion how to rise, 3H6 1.02. 45
my days, | and when i give occasion of offense, 1.03. 44
and, as occasion serves, this noble queen | and 3.03.236
for, by the way, i'll sort occasion, | as index R3 2.02.148
on what occasion, god he knows, not i, | the 3.01. 26
to meet the least occasion that may give me H8 3.02. 7
and am right glad to catch this good occasion 5.01.109
vehemency | th' occasion shall instruct you. 5.01.149
had i so good occasion to lie long | as /you, TRO 4.01. 4
/but when contention and occasion meet, | by 4.01. 17
little thief of occasion will rob you of a great COR 2.01. 29 P
man, if i see occasion in a good quarrel, and ROM 2.04.160 P
to that, sir, and you will give me occasion. 3.01. 42 P
could you not take some occasion without giving? 3.01. 43 P
my master is awak'd by great occasion | to call TIM 2.02. 21
great and instant occasion to use fifty talents, 3.01. 18 P
ne'er have denied his occasion so many talents. 3.02. 24 P
h'as only sent his present occasion now, my lord 3.02. 34 P
if his occasion were not virtuous, | i should 3.02. 40
lest occasion call us | and show us to be MAC 2.02. 67
grace, | occasion smiles upon a second leave. HAM 1.03. 54
gather | so much as from occasion you may glean, 2.02. 16
to visit you, my lord, no other occasion. 2.02.271 P
recount the occasion of my sudden /and /more 4.07. 46 P
and subtle knave, a finder/–out of occasion; OTH 2.01.242 P
do you find some occasion to anger cassio, 2.01.267 P
i would on great occasion speak with you. 4.01. 58
under a compelling occasion, let women die. ANT 1.02.137 P
he married but his occasion here. 2.06.131 P
but what occasion | hath cadwal now to give it CYM 4.02.187
and brings the dire occasion in his arms | of 4.02.196
"on what occasion break | those tears from thee, LUC 1270
and every light occasion of the wind | upon his LC 86
/OCCASIONS 1 FR 0.0001 REL FR 1 V 0 P
/i /would /breed /from /hence /occasions, /and LR 1.03. 24
OCCASIONS 15 FR 0.0017 REL FR 10 V 5 P
which hath been on the wing of all occasions. WIV 2.02.202 P
means, | lie all unlock'd to your occasions. MV 1.01.139
and therefore, goaded with most sharp occasions, AWW 5.01. 14
enemies may not have this | to grace occasions, JN 4.02. 62
there is occasions and causes why and wherefore H5 5.01. 3 P
when you take occasions to see leeks hereafter, 5.01. 55 P
especially for those occasions | at eltam place 1H6 3.01.154
and those occasions, uncle, were of force: 3.01.156
tears, | and frame my face to all occasions. 3H6 3.02.185
that my occasions have found time to use 'em TIM 2.02.191 P
but his occasions might have wooed me first; 3.03. 15
which many my near occasions did urge me to put 3.06. 10 P
how all occasions do inform against me, | and HAM 4.04. 32
occasions, noble gloucester, of some prize, LR 2.01.120
so tender over his occasions, true, | so feat, CYM 5.05. 87
OCCIDENT 2 FR 0.0002 REL FR 2 V 0 P
track | of his bright passage to the occident. R2 3.03. 67
i may wander | from east to occident, cry out CYM 4.02.372
OCCIDENTAL 1 FR 0.0001 REL FR 1 V 0 P
ere twice in murk and occidental damp | moist AWW 2.01.163
OCCULTED 1 FR 0.0001 REL FR 1 V 0 P
if his occulted guilt | do not itself unkennel HAM 3.02. 80
OCCUPAT 1 FR 0.0001 REL FR 1 V 0 P
/pene gelidus timor occupat artus: 2H6 4.01.117
OCCUPATION 9 FR 0.0010 REL FR 4 V 5 P
no occupation; TMP 2.01.155
do you call, sir, your occupation a mystery? MM 4.02. 34 P
being members of my occupation, using painting, 4.02. 37 P
painting, do prove my occupation a mystery; 4.02. 38 P
bear my part, you must know 'tis my occupation. WT 4.04.296 P
upon the voice of occupation and | the breath of COR 4.06. 97
and i had been a man of any occupation, if i JC 1.02.266 P
sir, 'tis my occupation to be plain: LR 2.02. 92
to–day, and knew'st | the royal occupation, thou ANT 4.04. 17
OCCUPATION'S 1 FR 0.0001 REL FR 1 V 0 P
othello's occupation's gone! OTH 3.03.357
OCCUPATIONS 1 FR 0.0001 REL FR 1 V 0 P
all trades in rome, | and occupations perish! COR 4.01. 14
OCCUPY 2 FR 0.0002 REL FR 0 V 2 P
make the word as odious as the word "occupy," 2H4 2.04.149 P
tale, and meant indeed to occupy the argument no
ROM 2.04.100 P
OCCURRENCE 1 FR 0.0001 REL FR 1 V 0 P
all the occurrence of my fortune since | hath TN 5.01.257
OCCURRENCES 1 FR 0.0001 REL FR 1 V 0 P
and omit | all the occurrences, what ever H5 5.pr. 40
OCCURRENTS 1 FR 0.0001 REL FR 1 V 0 P
so tell him, with th' occurrents, more and less, HAM 5.02.357
OCEAN 33 FR 0.0037 REL FR 33 V 0 P
strays | with willing sport to the wild ocean. TGV 2.07. 32
a thousand oaths, an ocean of his tears, | and 2.07. 69
she is my prize, or ocean whelm them all! WIV 2.02.137
water, | that in the ocean seeks another drop, ERR 1.02. 36
your mind is tossing on the ocean, | there where MV 1.01. 8
water keep | a peaceful progress to the ocean. JN 2.01.340
in a spoon, | and it shall be as all the ocean, 4.03.132
calmly run on in obedience | even to our ocean, 5.04. 57
the beachy girdle of the ocean | too wide for 2H4 3.01. 50
the perilous narrow ocean parts asunder. H5 pr 22
swill'd with the wild and wasteful ocean. 3.01. 14
to drain | upon his face an ocean of salt tears, 2H6 3.02.143
like to his island, girt in with the ocean, | or 3H6 4.08. 20
house | in the deep bosom of the ocean buried. R3 1.01. 4
and, having gilt the ocean with his beams, TIT 2.01. 6
for all the water in the ocean | can never turn 4.02.101
the ocean swells not so as aaron storms. 4.02.139
shall | go sound the ocean, and cast your nets; 4.03. 7
and i have seen | th' ambitious ocean swell, and JC 1.03. 7
will all great neptune's ocean wash this blood MAC 2.02. 57
the ocean, overpeering of his list, | eats not HAM 4.05.100
at whose burthen | the anger'd ocean foams, with ANT 2.06. 21
what e'er the ocean pales, or sky inclips, | is 2.07. 68
his legs bestrid the ocean, his rear'd arm 5.02. 82
i know | his ocean needs not my poor drops, yet TNK 1.03. 7
or in the ocean drench'd, or in the fire? VEN 494
"all which together, like a troubled ocean, LUC 589
who seek to stain the ocean of thy blood. 655
who in a salt–wav'd ocean quench their light, 1231
let this sad int'rim like the ocean be | which SON 56. 9
when i have seen the hungry ocean gain 64. 5
but since your worth (wide as the ocean is) 80. 5
my well, | and mine i pour your ocean all among: LC 256
OCEAN'S 1 FR 0.0001 REL FR 1 V 0 P
whose foot spurns back the ocean's roaring tides JN 2.01. 24
OCEANS 2 FR 0.0002 REL FR 1 V 1 P
is numb'ring sands and drinking oceans dry; R2 2.02.146
as many inches as you have oceans. puppies! CYM 1.02. 21 P
OCTAVIA 23 FR 0.0026 REL FR 20 V 3 P
sister by the mother's side, | admir'd octavia. ANT 2.02.119
knot, take antony | octavia to his wife; 2.02.127
power of caesar, and | his power unto octavia. 2.02.143
antony, octavia is | a blessed lottery to him. 2.02.241
my octavia, | read not my blemishes in the 2.03. 4
mark antony | will e'en but kiss octavia, and 2.04. 3
he's bound unto octavia. 2.05. 58
madam, he's married to octavia. 2.05. 60
he's married to octavia. 2.05.101
bid him | report the feature of octavia, her 2.05.112
caesar's sister is call'd octavia. 2.06.109 P
octavia is of a holy, cold, and still 2.06.122 P
shall the sighs of octavia blow the fire up in 2.06.127 P
octavia weeps | to part from rome; 3.02. 3
what, | octavia? 3.02. 46
no, sweet octavia, | you shall hear from me 3.02. 59
didst thou behold octavia? 3.03. 7
nay, nay, octavia, not only that — | that were 3.04. 1
gentle octavia, | let your best love draw to 3.04. 20
and let | patient octavia plough thy visage up 4.12. 38
your wife octavia, with her modest eyes | and 4.15. 27
chastis'd with the sober eye | of dull octavia. 5.02. 55
token i have kept apart | for livia and octavia, 5.02.169
OCTAVIO'S 1 FR 0.0001 REL FR 1 V 0 P
perceive | but cold demeanor in octavio's wing, JC 5.02. 4
OCTAVIUS' 1 FR 0.0001 REL FR 1 V 0 P
and bring us word unto octavius' tent | how JC 5.04. 31
OCTAVIUS 20 FR 0.0022 REL FR 19 V 1 P
you serve octavius caesar, do you not? JC 3.01.276
rome, | no rome of safety for octavius yet; 3.01.289
to young octavius of the state of things. 3.01.296
sir, octavius is already come to rome. 3.02.262
bring me to octavius. 3.02.271
octavius, i have seen more days than you, | and 4.01. 18
so is my horse, octavius, and for that | i do 4.01. 29
and now, octavius, | listen great things. 4.01. 40
come, antony, and young octavius, come, 4.03. 93
and grief that young octavius with mark antony 4.03.153
letters | that young octavius and mark antony 4.03.168
octavius, antony, and lepidus | have put to 4.03.174
octavius, lead your battle softly on | upon the 5.01. 16
words are better than bad strokes, octavius. 5.01. 29
early, | who, having some advantage on octavius, 5.03. 6
for octavius | is overthrown by noble brutus' 5.03. 51
losing day | more than octavius and mark antony 5.05. 37
octavius, then take him to follow thee, | that 5.05. 66
find me to marry me with octavius caesar, and ANT 1.02. 30 P
marcus octavius, marcus justeius, | publicola, 3.07. 72
OCULAR 1 FR 0.0001 REL FR 1 V 0 P
give me the ocular proof, | or, by the worth of OTH 3.03.360
/ODD 1 FR 0.0001 REL FR 1 V 0 P
to /change true rules for /odd inventions. SHR 3.01. 81
ODD 32 FR 0.0036 REL FR 21 V 11 P
in an odd angle of the isle, and sitting, | his TMP 1.02.223
company | some few odd lads you remember not. 5.01.255
i hope good luck lies in odd numbers. WIV 5.01. 2 P
they say there is divinity in odd numbers, 5.01. 3 P
which doth amount to three odd ducats more ERR 4.01. 30
i may chance have some odd quirks and remnants
ADO 2.03.236 P
no, not to be so odd and from all fashions | as 3.01. 72
spruce, too affected, too odd as it were, too LLL 5.01. 13 P
to fates and destinies, and such odd sayings, MV 2.02. 62 P
lest, over–eyeing of his odd behavior | (for yet SHR in.1. 95
'tis some odd humor pricks him to this fashion; 3.02. 72
tods, every tod yields pound and odd shilling; WT 4.03. 33 P
fifty soldiers, three hundred and odd pounds. 1H4 4.02. 14 P
i have found'ret ninescore and odd posts, and 2H4 4.03. 36 P
i think by some odd gimmors or device | their 1H6 1.02. 41
with odd old ends stol'n forth of holy writ, R3 1.03.336
eighty odd years of sorrow have i seen, | and 4.01. 95
you are an odd man, give even or give none. TRO 4.05. 41
an odd man, lady? every man is odd. 4.05. 42
an odd man, lady? every man is odd. 4.05. 42
for you know 'tis true | that you are odd, and 4.05. 44
can scarce entreat you to be odd with him. 4.05.265
but this is something odd. COR 2.03. 82 P
for your voices bear | of wounds two dozen odd; 2.03.128
a fortnight and odd days. ROM 1.03. 15
even or odd, of all days in the year, | come 1.03. 16
how strange or odd some'er i bear myself — | as HAM 1.05.170
will gain nothing but my shame and the odd hits. 5.02.178 P
him in, | on some odd time of his infirmity, OTH 2.03.127
'tis one of those odd tricks which sorrow shoots ANT 4.02. 14
this is most falliable, the worm's an odd worm. 5.02.258 P
and to their hope they such odd action yield, LUC 1433
ODD–CONCEITED 1 FR 0.0001 REL FR 1 V 0 P
with twenty odd–conceited true–love knots: TGV 2.07. 46
ODDEST 1 FR 0.0001 REL FR 1 V 0 P
her madness hath the oddest frame of sense, MM 5.01. 61
ODD–EVEN 1 FR 0.0001 REL FR 1 V 0 P
at this odd–even and dull watch o' th' night, OTH 1.01.123
ODDLY 4 FR 0.0004 REL FR 3 V 1 P
o, how oddly will it sound that i | must ask my TMP 5.01.197
how oddly he is suited! MV 1.02. 73 P
our imputation shall be oddly pois'd | in this TRO 1.03.339
how oddly thou repliest! ROM 2.05. 59
ODDS 44 FR 0.0049 REL FR 39 V 5 P
person, is at most odds with his own gravity and WIV 3.01. 54 P
death we fear | that makes these odds all even. MM 3.01. 41
therefore too much odds for a spaniard's rapier. LLL 1.02.177 P
were still at odds, being but three. 3.01. 85
were still at odds, being but three. 3.01. 90
of door, | and stayed the odds by adding four. 3.01. 92
were still at odds, being but three. 3.01. 96
out of door, | staying the odds by adding four. 3.01. 98
i can tell you, there is such odds in the man. AYL 1.02.159 P
god–a–mercy, grumio, then he shall have no odds.
SHR 4.03.154 P
the odds for high and low's alike. WT 5.01.207
which to maintain i would allow him odds | and R2 1.01. 62
and with that odds he weighs king richard down. 3.04. 89
i am content that he shall take the odds | of 1H4 5.01. 97
i will lay odds, that, ere this year expire, | we 2H4 5.05.105
for i desire | nothing but odds with england. H5 2.04.129
'tis a fearful odds. 4.03. 5
yield up his life unto a world of odds. 1H6 4.04. 25
the lists | by reason of his adversary's odds. 5.05. 33
a poor earl's daughter is unequal odds, | and 5.05. 34
kent, | took odds to combat a poor famish'd man. 2H6 4.10. 44
though the odds be great, | i doubt not, uncle, 3H6 1.02. 71
but hercules himself must yield to odds; 2.01. 53
'twas odds, belike, when valiant warwick fled: 2.01.148
with whom my soul is any jot at odds | more than R3 2.01. 71
care | withdrew me from the odds of multitude. TRO 5.04. 22
but now 'tis odds beyond arithmetic, | and COR 3.01.244
thou hast the odds of me, therefore no more. TIT 5.02. 19
both, | and pity 'tis you liv'd at odds so long. ROM 1.02. 5
this and my food are equals, there's no odds; TIM 1.02. 60
'tis honor with most lands to be at odds; 3.05.115
that puts odds | among the rout of nations, i 4.03. 43
by thy virtue | set them into confounding odds, 4.03.391
almost at odds with morning, which is which. MAC 3.04.126
i shall win at the odds. HAM 5.02.212 P
your grace has laid the odds a' th' weaker side. 5.02.261
since he is /better'd, we have therefore odds. 5.02.263
gross crime or other | that sets us all at odds. LR 1.03. 5
speak | any beginning to this peevish odds; OTH 2.03.185
natural luck, | he beats thee 'gainst the odds. ANT 2.03. 28
his quails ever | beat mine, inhoop'd, at odds. 2.03. 39
the odds is gone, | and there is nothing left 4.15. 66
the odds | is that we scarce are men and you are CYM 5.02. 9
'tis odds | he never will affect me. TNK 2.04. 1
ODE 1 FR 0.0001 REL FR 1 V 0 P
once more i'll read the ode that i have writ. LLL 4.03. 97
ODES 1 FR 0.0001 REL FR 0 V 1 P
hangs odes upon hawthorns and elegies on AYL 3.02.361 P
ODIOUS 10 FR 0.0011 REL FR 8 V 2 P
mean task | would be as heavy to me as odious, TMP 3.01. 5
at thy heels — | o, odious is the name! WIV 2.01.119
"thisby, the flowers of odious savors sweet" — MND 3.01. 82
as horns are odious, they are necessary. AYL 3.03. 52 P
a divulged shame, | traduc'd by odious ballads; AWW 2.01.172
make the word as odious as the word "occupy," 2H4 2.04.148 P
the sight of me is odious in their eyes; 2H6 4.04. 46
are, | which, since they are of you, and odious, H8 3.02.331
you told a lie, an odious, damned lie; OTH 5.02.180
great, | the name of help grew odious to repeat. PER 1.04. 31
ODOR 6 FR 0.0006 REL FR 6 V 0 P
a bank of violets, | stealing and giving odor. TN 1.01. 7
a delicate odor. PER 3.02. 61
maiden pinks, of odor faint, | daisies TNK 1.01. 4
for that sweet odor which doth in it live. SON 54. 4
but why thy odor matcheth not thy show, | the 69.13
smell | of different flowers in odor and in hue, 98. 6
ODORIFEROUS 2 FR 0.0002 REL FR 1 V 1 P
smelling out the odoriferous flowers of fancy, LLL 4.02.124 P

thou odoriferous stench! JN 3.04. 26
/ODOROUS 1 FR 0.0001 REL FR 0 V 1 P
/odorous, odorous. MND 3.01. 83 P
ODOROUS 3 FR 0.0003 REL FR 1 V 2 P
comparisons are odorous — palabras, neighbor ADO 3.05. 16 P
crown | an odorous chaplet of sweet summer buds MND 2.01.110
/odorous, odorous. 3.01. 83 P
ODORS 7 FR 0.0008 REL FR 3 V 4 P
"odors savors sweet; MND 3.01. 84
lady, the heavens rain odors on you! TN 3.01. 85 P
that youth's a rare courtier — "rain odors," 3.01. 87 P
"odors," "pregnant," and "vouchsafed"; 3.01. 90 P
urns and odors bring away, | vapors, sighs, TNK 1.05. 1
some other compounded odors which are grateful 4.03. 85 P
of their sweet deaths are sweetest odors made: SON 54.12
'OD'S* *(also god's*, got's, 'ud's)*
'OD'S* 8 FR 0.0009 REL FR 3 V 5 P
'od's plessed will! WIV 1.01.264 P
'od's me! 1.04. 62 P
'od's heartlings, that's a pretty jest indeed! 3.04. 57 P
number more, because they say, "'od's nouns." 4.01. 24 P
'od's my little life, | i think she means to AYL 3.05. 43
'od's my will! 4.03. 17
'od's lifelings, here he is! TN 5.01.184 P
'od's pittikins! CYM 4.02.293
OEILLADES *(see eliads, iliads)*
O'ER *(also over and compounds)*
/O'ER 10 FR 0.0011 REL FR 10 V 0 P
/lord, /dispatch, /read /o'er /these /articles. R2 4.01.243
/read /o'er /this /paper /while /the /glass 4.01.269
/you /knew /he /walk'd /o'er /perils, /on /an 2H4 1.01.170
/likely /to /fall /in /than /to /get /o'er; 1.01.171
/leaps /o'er /the /vaunt /and /firstlings /of TRO pr 27
/to /bid /aeneas /tell /the /tale /twice /o'er TIT 3.02. 27
/o'er courtiers' knees, that dream on cur'sies ROM 1.04. 72
"/come /o'er /the /bourn, /bessy, /to /me" — LR 3.06. 25
/sought /to /be /king /o'er /her. 4.03. 15
/to /make /him /even /o'er /the /time /he /has 4.07. 79
O'ER 209 FR 0.0236 REL FR 181 V 28 P
shall we give o'er and drown? TMP 1.01. 38 P
how i cried out then, | will cry it o'er again. 1.02.134
blow on ye, | and blister you all o'er! 1.02.324
the visitor will not give him o'er so. 2.01. 11 P
th' shore, that o'er his wave-worn basis bowed, 2.01.121
which to do, | trebles thee o'er. 2.01.221
at a time, | i'll fight their legions o'er. 3.03.103
bring the rabble | (o'er whom i give thee pow'r) 4.01. 38
my bottle, though i be o'er ears for my labor. 4.01.213 P
never give her o'er, | for scorn at first makes TGV 3.01. 94
she did so course o'er my exteriors with such a WIV 1.03. 65 P
hang like a meteor o'er the cuckold's horns. 2.02.280 P
the cudgel hallow'd and hung o'er the altar; 4.02.205 P
ignorance itself is a plummet o'er me. 5.05.163 P
and laugh this sport o'er by a country fire — 5.05.242
judgment hath | repented o'er his doom. MM 2.02. 12
give't not o'er so. 2.02. 43
of precept, he did show me | the way twice o'er. 4.01. 40
spread o'er the silver waves thy golden hairs, ERR 3.02. 48
upon her nose, all o'er embellish'd with rubies, 3.02.134 P
desk | that's cover'd o'er with turkish tapestry 4.01.104
climb o'er the house to unlock the little gate. LLL 1.01.109
my lord berowne, see him delivered o'er, | and 1.01.305
i will have that subject newly writ o'er, that i 1.02.115 P
hat penthouse-like o'er the shop of your eyes; 3.01. 18 P
constable, | a domineering pedant o'er the boy, 3.01.177
when they strive to be | lords o'er their lords? 4.01. 38
else your memory is bad, going o'er it erewhile. 4.01. 97
lord longaville said i came o'er his heart, 5.02.278
whip to our tents, as roes /run o'er land. 5.02.309
how happy some o'er other some can be! MND 1.01.226
and, at our stamp, here o'er and o'er one falls; 3.02. 25
and, at our stamp, here o'er and o'er one falls; 3.02. 25
being o'er shoes in blood, plunge in the deep, 3.02. 48
will you give her o'er? 3.02.130
nor none, in my mind, now you give her o'er. 3.02.135
till o'er their brows death-counterfeiting sleep 3.02.364
dian's bud o'er cupid's flower | hath such force 4.01. 73
every man look o'er his part; 4.02. 38 P
but a hot temper leaps o'er a cold decree — MV 1.02. 19 P
to skip o'er the meshes of good counsel the 1.02. 20 P
they come | as o'er a brook to see fair portia. 2.07. 47
alive, iwis, | silver'd o'er, and so was this. 2.09. 69
master of my servants, | queen o'er myself; 3.02.169
we turn'd o'er many books together. 4.01.156 P
i will be bound to pay it ten times o'er, | on 4.01.211
he'll go along o'er the wide world with me; AYL 1.03.132
that o'er the green corn-field did pass, | in 5.03. 18
going, madam, weep o'er my father's death anew; AWW 1.01. 3 P
o'er whom both sovereign power and father's 2.03. 54
it came o'er my ear like the sweet sound | that TN 1.01. 5
come, throw it o'er my face. 1.05.165
we'll whisper o'er a couplet or two of most sage 3.04.378 P
sir, or i'll throw your dagger o'er the house. 4.01. 28 P
knee-deep, o'er head and ears a fork'd one! WT 1.02.186
you, that are thus so tender o'er his follies, 2.03.128
that hast | a heart so tender o'er it, take it 2.03.133
o'er sixteen years and leave the growth untried 4.01. 6
my sweet friend, | to strew him o'er and o'er! 4.04.129
my sweet friend, | to strew him o'er and o'er! 4.04.129
bolted | by th' northern blasts twice o'er. 4.04.365
o'er and o'er divides him | 'twixt his 4.04.551
o'er and o'er divides him | 'twixt his 4.04.551
sweetheart's hat | and pluck it o'er your brows, 4.04.651
i put you o'er to heaven and to my mother. JN 1.01. 62
in at the window, or else o'er the hatch. 1.01.171
than now the english bottoms have waft o'er 2.01. 73
man, | and king o'er him and all that he enjoys. 2.01.240
be well advis'd, tell o'er thy tale again. 3.01. 5
like a proud river peering o'er his bounds? 3.01. 23
i'll send those powers o'er to your majesty. 3.03. 70
both they and we, perusing o'er these notes, 5.02. 5
figur'd quite o'er with burning meteors. 5.02. 53
and shall i now give o'er the yielded set? 5.02.107
arms, | and like an eagle o'er his aery tow'rs, 5.02.149
my reformation, glitt'ring o'er my fault, 1H4 1.02.213
the which, if you give o'er | to stormy passion, 2H4 1.01.164
gives o'er, and leaves his part-created cost | a 1.03. 60
have you read o'er the /letters that i sent you? 3.01. 36
which, deliver'd o'er to the voice, the tongue, 4.03.101 P
carry them here and there, jumping o'er times, H5 pr 29
delivering o'er to executors pale | the lazy 1.02.203
o'er france and all her almost kingly dukedoms, 1.02.227
how he comes o'er us with our wilder days, | not 1.02.267
than i do at this hour joy o'er myself, 2.02.163
have the pioners given o'er? 3.02. 87 P
fly o'er them all, impatient for their hour. 4.02. 52
the gay new coats o'er the french soldiers' 4.03.118
that we may wander o'er this bloody field | to 4.07. 72
your horsemen peer | and gallop o'er the field. 4.07. 86
shall we give o'er orleance, or no? 1H6 1.02.125
leap o'er the walls for refuge in the field. 2.02. 25
let somerset be regent o'er the french, 2H6 1.03.205
that parchment, being scribbled o'er, should 4.02. 81 P
should make a start o'er seas and vanquish you? 4.08. 43
and hang thee o'er my tomb when i am dead. 4.10. 68
o'er him whom heaven created for thy ruler. 5.01.105
so looks the pent-up lion o'er the wretch | that 3H6 1.03. 12
and so he walks, insulting o'er his prey, | and 1.03. 14
that it may be to-day read o'er in paul's. R3 3.06. 3
let's whip these stragglers o'er the seas again; 5.03.327
the fire that mounts the liquor till't run o'er H8 1.01.144
gone slightly o'er low steps and now are mounted 2.04.112
the which | you were now running o'er. 3.02.139
read o'er this, | and, after, this, and then to 3.02.201
will triumph o'er my person, which i weigh not, 5.01.124
now good angels | fly o'er thy royal head, and 5.01.160
th' rail, | i'll peck you o'er the pales else. 5.03. 90
queen hecuba laugh'd that her eyes ran o'er. TRO 1.02.143 P
did her eyes run o'er too? 1.02.147 P
grief hath set these jaundies o'er your cheeks? 1.03. 2
my armed fist | i'll /pash him o'er the face. 2.03.203
the fool slides o'er the ice that you should 3.03.215
/flowing and swelling o'er with arts and 4.04. 78
she is as far high-soaring o'er thy praises | as 4.04.124
o, like a book of sport thou'lt read me o'er; 4.05.239
i'll kill thee every where, yea, o'er and o'er. 4.05.256
i'll kill thee every where, yea, o'er and o'er. 4.05.256
biles and plagues | plaster you o'er, that you COR 1.04. 32
o'er them aufidius, | their very heart of hope. 1.06. 54
if i should tell thee o'er this thy day's work, 1.09. 1
he did | run reeking o'er the lives of men, as 2.02.119
send | o'er the vast world to seek a single man, 4.01. 42
way, and runs like swallows o'er the plain. TIT 2.02. 24
on him that thus doth tyrannize o'er me. 4.03. 20
but saying o'er what i have said before: ROM 1.02. 7
read o'er the volume of young paris' face, | and 1.03. 81
o'er lawyers' fingers, who straight dream on 1.04. 73
o'er ladies' lips, who straight on kisses dream, 1.04. 74
sometime she gallops o'er a courtier's nose, 1.04. 77
sometime she driveth o'er a soldier's neck, 1.04. 82
crows, | as yonder lady o'er her fellows shows. 1.05. 49
as glorious to this night, being o'er my head, 2.02. 27
utter your gravity o'er a gossip's bowl, | for 3.05.174
not stepping o'er the bounds of modesty. 4.02. 27
the infinite malady | crust you quite o'er! TIM 3.06. 99
will o'er some high-vic'd city hang his poison 4.03.110
and, waving our red weapons o'er our heads, JC 3.01.109
and kites | fly o'er our heads, and downward 5.01. 85
in viewing o'er the rest o' th' self-same day, MAC 1.03. 94
now o'er the one half world | nature seems dead, 2.01. 49
gentle my lord, sleek o'er your rugged looks, 3.02. 27
no more, | returning were as tedious as go o'er. 3.04.137
walks o'er the dew of yon high eastward hill. HAM 1.01.167
cliff | that beetles o'er his base into the sea, 1.04. 71
and, with his other hand thus o'er his brow, 2.01. 86
and pious action we do sugar o'er | the devil 3.01. 47
is sicklied o'er with the pale cast of thought, 3.01. 84
soul | o'er which his melancholy sits on brood, 3.01.165
make us again count o'er ere love be done! 3.02.162
give o'er the play. 3.02.268 P
glow | o'er this solidity and compound mass, 3.04. 49
save me, and hover o'er me with your wings, 3.04.103
o'er whom his very madness, like some ore 4.01. 25
/... | whose whisper o'er the world's diameter, 4.01. 41
no trophy, sword, nor hatchment o'er his bones, 4.05.215
beg | your sudden coming o'er to play with you. 4.07.105
in fine together, | and wager o'er your heads. 4.07.134
that i have shot my arrow o'er the house | and 5.02.243
thou bor'st thine ass on thy back o'er the dirt. LR 1.04.162 P
nature shall not give | thee o'er to harshness. 2.04.172
that keep this dreadful pudder o'er our heads, 3.02. 50
/ford and whirlpool, o'er bog and quagmire; 3.04. 53 P
air | hang fated o'er men's faults light on thy 3.04. 68
and hold your hand in benediction o'er me. 4.07. 57
that with some mixtures pow'rful o'er the blood, OTH 1.03.104
me go, sir, or i'll knock you o'er the mazzard. 2.03.153 P
what damned minutes tells he o'er | who dotes, 3.03.169
thou saidst (o, it comes o'er my memory, | as 4.01. 20
as doth the raven o'er the infectious house, 4.01. 21
now he importunes him | to tell it o'er. 4.01.114
that o'er the files and musters of the war ANT 1.01. 3
our italy | shines o'er with civil swords; 1.03. 45
being barber'd ten times o'er, goes to the feast 2.02.224
o'er your content these strong necessities, 3.06. 83
o'er my spirit | /thy full supremacy thou 3.11. 58
and o'er green neptune's back | with ships made 4.14. 58
make your lord, | that which he is, new o'er; CYM 1.06.165
but i'll never give o'er. 2.03. 16 P
(such as i can) twice o'er, i'll weep and sigh, 4.02.392
this tharsus, o'er which i have the government, PER 1.04. 21
by turning o'er authorities, i have, | together 3.02. 33
the gods will be strong with us for giving o'er. 4.02. 35 P
believe me, 'twere best i did give o'er. 5.01.166
my marina, tell him | o'er, point by point, for 5.01.225
require him he advance it o'er our heads; TNK 1.01. 93
but | playing o'er business in his hand, another 1.03. 31
hour the whoobub | will be all o'er the prison. 2.06. 36
there you have | a vantage o'er me, but enjoy't 3.01.122
o'er us the victors have | fortune, whose title 5.04. 16
and presently | backward the jade comes o'er, 5.04. 81
whiles they are o'er the bank of their obedience STM II.C 39
pursue these fearful creatures o'er the downs, VEN 677
virtue would stain that o'er with silver white. LUC 56
bed, | throwing his mantle rudely o'er his arm, 170
as the grim lion fawneth o'er his prey, | sharp 421
so o'er this sleeping soul doth tarquin stay, 423
who o'er the white sheet peers her whiter chin, 472
first hovering o'er the paper with her quill. 1297
at last she smilingly with this gives o'er: 1567
at last it rains, and busy winds give o'er: 1790
and sable curls /all silver'd o'er with white; SON 12. 4
and heavily from woe to woe tell o'er | the sad 30.10
while he insults o'er dull and speechless tribes 107.12
i must each day say o'er the very same, 108. 6
best," | when i was certain o'er incertainty, 115.11
o'er whom /thy fingers walk with gentle gait, 128.11
i strong o'er them, and you o'er me being strong LC 257
strong o'er them, and you o'er me being strong, 257
O'ERBEAR 4 FR 0.0004 REL FR 4 V 0 P
to o'erbear such | as are of better person than 3H6 3.02.166
and o'erbear | what they are us'd to bear? COR 3.01.248
all continent impediments would o'erbear | that MAC 4.03. 64
upon me | o'erbear the shores of my mortality, PER 5.01.193
O'ERBEARING 2 FR 0.0002 REL FR 2 V 0 P
o'erbearing interruption, spite of france? JN 3.04. 9
is of so flood-gate and o'erbearing nature OTH 1.03. 56
O'ERBEARS 2 FR 0.0002 REL FR 2 V 0 P
for reason's force, | o'erbears it and burns on. AWW 5.03. 8
in a riotous head, | o'erbears your officers. HAM 4.05.103
O'ER-BEAT 1 FR 0.0001 REL FR 1 V 0 P
ungrateful rome, | like a bold flood o'er-beat. COR 4.05.131
O'ERBLOWS 1 FR 0.0001 REL FR 1 V 0 P
o'erblows the filthy and contagious clouds | of H5 3.03. 31
O'ERBOARD 3 FR 0.0003 REL FR 2 V 1 P
of sack which the sailors heav'd o'erboard — by TMP 2.02.122 P
that swear'st grace o'erboard, not an oath on 5.01.219
had not o'erboard thrown me | for to seek my PER 4.02. 66
O'ERBORNE 2 FR 0.0002 REL FR 2 V 0 P
and have already | o'erborne their way, consum'd COR 4.06. 78
their friends | o'erborne i' th' former wave. CYM 5.03. 48
O'ERCAME 1 FR 0.0001 REL FR 1 V 0 P
in thirteen battles salisbury o'ercame; 1H6 1.04. 78
O'ERCAST 2 FR 0.0002 REL FR 2 V 0 P
the sun's o'ercast with blood; JN 3.01.326
but yet you see how soon the day o'ercast. R3 3.02. 86
O'ERCHARG'D 5 FR 0.0005 REL FR 5 V 0 P
i love not to see wretchedness o'ercharg'd, MND 5.01. 85
her heart is but o'ercharg'd; WT 3.02.150
with tears, and break o'ercharg'd with grief. 3H6 2.05. 78
if the sea's stomach be o'ercharg'd with gold, PER 3.02. 54
o'ercharg'd with burthen of mine own love's SON 23. 8
O'ERCHARGING 1 FR 0.0001 REL FR 1 V 0 P
o'ercharging your free purses with large fines; 1H6 1.03. 64
O'ERCLOYED 1 FR 0.0001 REL FR 1 V 0 P
whom their o'ercloyed country vomits forth | to R3 5.03.318
O'ERCOME 2 FR 0.0002 REL FR 2 V 0 P
o'ercome with pride, ambitious past all thinking COR 4.06. 31
kissing, to | o'ercome you with her show, and, CYM 5.05. 54
O'ER-COUNT 2 FR 0.0002 REL FR 2 V 0 P
thou know'st | how much we do o'er-count thee. ANT 2.06. 26
thou dost o'er-count me of my father's house; 2.06. 27
O'ERCOVER'D 1 FR 0.0001 REL FR 1 V 0 P
o'ercover'd quite with dead men's rattling bones ROM 4.01. 82
O'ER-CROWS 1 FR 0.0001 REL FR 1 V 0 P
the potent poison quite o'er-crows my spirit. HAM 5.02.353
O'ERDOING 1 FR 0.0001 REL FR 0 V 1 P
such a fellow whipt for o'erdoing termagant, it HAM 3.02. 13 P
O'ERDONE 1 FR 0.0001 REL FR 0 V 1 P
for any thing so o'erdone is from the purpose of HAM 3.02. 20 P
O'ERDUSTED 1 FR 0.0001 REL FR 1 V 0 P
a little gilt, | more laud than gilt o'erdusted. TRO 3.03.179
O'ER-DY'D 1 FR 0.0001 REL FR 1 V 0 P
but were they false | as o'er-dy'd blacks, as WT 1.02.132
O'ER-EATEN 1 FR 0.0001 REL FR 1 V 0 P
and greasy relics | of her o'er-eaten faith, are TRO 5.02.160
O'ER-EYE 1 FR 0.0001 REL FR 1 V 0 P
and wretched fools' secrets heedfully o'er-eye. LLL 4.03. 78
O'ERFED 1 FR 0.0001 REL FR 1 V 0 P
made louder by the o'erfed breast | of this most PER 3.ch. 3
O'ERFLOURISH'D 1 FR 0.0001 REL FR 1 V 0 P
are empty trunks o'erflourish'd by the devil. TN 3.04.370
O'ERFLOW 2 FR 0.0002 REL FR 2 V 0 P
to make the coming hour o'erflow with joy | and AWW 2.04. 46
heaven doth weep, doth not the earth o'erflow? TIT 3.01.221
O'ERFLOWED 1 FR 0.0001 REL FR 1 V 0 P
therefore the earth, fearing to be o'erflowed, PER 4.04. 40
O'ERFLOWING 2 FR 0.0002 REL FR 1 V 1 P
e'en as the o'erflowing nilus presageth famine. ANT 1.02. 49 P
thee into | the bound thou wast o'erflowing, at TNK 1.01. 84
O'ERFLOWS 4 FR 0.0004 REL FR 2 V 2 P
are welcome to me, that o'erflows such liquor. WIV 2.02.151 P
nobility in his proper stream o'erflows himself. AWW 4.03. 25 P
dotage of our general's | o'erflows the measure. ANT 1.01. 2
being stopp'd, the bounding banks o'erflows; LUC 1119
O'ER-FRAUGHT 1 FR 0.0001 REL FR 1 V 0 P
not speak | whispers the o'er-fraught heart, and MAC 4.03.210
O'ERGALLED 1 FR 0.0001 REL FR 1 V 0 P
their eyes o'ergalled with recourse of tears, TRO 5.03. 55
O'ERGLANC'D 1 FR 0.0001 REL FR 1 V 0 P
a /cursitory eye | o'erglanc'd the articles. H5 5.02. 78
O'ERGONE 1 FR 0.0001 REL FR 1 V 0 P
of many weary miles you have o'ergone | are LLL 5.02.196
O'ER-GREAT 1 FR 0.0001 REL FR 1 V 0 P
the o'er-great cardinal | hath show'd him gold; H8 1.01.222
O'ER-GREEN 1 FR 0.0001 REL FR 1 V 0 P
ill, | so you o'er-green my bad, my good allow? SON 112. 4
O'ERGROW 1 FR 0.0001 REL FR 1 V 0 P
them now, and they'll o'ergrow the garden, | and 2H6 3.01. 32
O'ERGROWN 4 FR 0.0004 REL FR 4 V 0 P
slip, | even like an o'ergrown lion in a cave, MM 1.03. 22
a wretched ragged man, o'ergrown with hair, AYL 4.03.106
so out of thought, and thereto so o'ergrown, CYM 4.04. 33
as corn o'ergrown by weeds, so heedful fear | is LUC 281
O'ERGROWTH 1 FR 0.0001 REL FR 1 V 0 P
by their o'ergrowth of some complexion | oft HAM 1.04. 27
O'ERHANG 1 FR 0.0001 REL FR 1 V 0 P
rock | o'erhang and jutty his confounded base, H5 3.01. 13
O'ERHANGING 1 FR 0.0001 REL FR 0 V 1 P
look you, this brave o'erhanging firmament, this HAM 2.02.300 P
/O'ERHASTY 1 FR 0.0001 REL FR 1 V 0 P
his father's death and our /o'erhasty marriage. HAM 2.02. 57
O'ERHEAR 1 FR 0.0001 REL FR 1 V 0 P

them partial, should o'erhear | the speech, of HAM 3.03. 32
O'ERHEARD 3 FR 0.0003 REL FR 3 V 0 P
i know, | to be o'erheard and taken napping so. LLL 4.03.128
confesses that she secretly o'erheard | your AYL 2.02. 81
i have o'erheard a plot of death upon him. LR 3.06. 89
O'ERJOY'D 1 FR 0.0001 REL FR 1 V 0 P
all o'erjoy'd, | save these in bonds. CYM 5.05.401
O'ERLABOR'D 1 FR 0.0001 REL FR 1 V 0 P
and man's o'erlabor'd sense | repairs itself by CYM 2.02. 11
O'ERLEAP 2 FR 0.0002 REL FR 2 V 0 P
i do beseech you, | let me o'erleap that custom; COR 2.02.136
on which i must fall down, or else o'erleap, MAC 1.04. 49
O'ERLEAPS 1 FR 0.0001 REL FR 1 V 0 P
vaulting ambition, which o'erleaps itself, | and MAC 1.07. 27
O'ER–LEAVENS 1 FR 0.0001 REL FR 1 V 0 P
habit, that too much o'er–leavens | the form of HAM 1.04. 29
O'ERLOOK 5 FR 0.0005 REL FR 5 V 0 P
where i o'erlook | love's stories written in MND 2.02.121
catesby, o'erlook the walls. R3 3.05. 17
why, fare thee well, i will o'erlook thy paper. LR 5.01. 50
but let your cares o'erlook | what shipping and PER 1.02. 48
and therefore mayest without attaint o'erlook SON 82. 2
O'ERLOOK'D 4 FR 0.0004 REL FR 4 V 0 P
and yet i would i had o'erlook'd the letter; TGV 1.02. 50
worm, thou wast o'erlook'd even in thy birth. WIV 5.05. 83
eyes, | they have o'erlook'd me and divided me: MV 3.02. 15
low within those bounds we have o'erlook'd, JN 5.04. 55
O'ERLOOKING 1 FR 0.0001 REL FR 0 V 1 P
perus'd, i find it not fit for your o'erlooking. LR 1.02. 39 P
O'ERMASTEREST 1 FR 0.0001 REL FR 1 V 0 P
which owe the crown that thou o'ermasterest? JN 2.01.109
O'ERMASTER'T 1 FR 0.0001 REL FR 1 V 0 P
what is between us, | o'ermaster't as you may. HAM 1.05.140
O'ERMATCH'D 2 FR 0.0002 REL FR 2 V 0 P
set from our o'ermatch'd forces forth for aid. 1H6 4.04. 11
so true men yield, with robbers so o'ermatch'd. 3H6 1.04. 64
O'ERMOUNT 1 FR 0.0001 REL FR 1 V 0 P
with your theme, i could | o'ermount the lark. H8 2.03. 94
O'ERNIGHT 2 FR 0.0002 REL FR 1 V 1 P
as wretches have o'ernight | that wait for TGV 4.02.132
shame her with what he saw o'ernight, and send ADO 3.03.162 P
O'ERNIGHT'S 1 FR 0.0001 REL FR 1 V 0 P
morning taste | to cure thy o'ernight's surfeit? TIM 4.03.227
O'ERPAID 1 FR 0.0001 REL FR 1 V 0 P
to be acknowledg'd, madam, is o'erpaid. LR 4.07. 4
O'ERPARTED 1 FR 0.0001 REL FR 0 V 1 P
alas, you see how 'tis — a little o'erparted. LLL 5.02.584 P
/O'ERPAST 1 FR 0.0001 REL FR 1 V 0 P
misus'd ere us'd, by times ill–us'd /o'erpast. R3 4.04.396
O'ERPAST 1 FR 0.0001 REL FR 1 V 0 P
that thou hast wronged in the time o'erpast; R3 4.04.388
O'ERPAYS 1 FR 0.0001 REL FR 1 V 0 P
and your company | o'erpays all i can do. CYM 2.04. 10
O'ERPEER 1 FR 0.0001 REL FR 1 V 0 P
be too highly heap'd | for truth to o'erpeer. COR 2.03.121
O'ERPERCH 1 FR 0.0001 REL FR 1 V 0 P
love's light wings did i o'erperch these walls, ROM 2.02. 66
O'ER–PICTURING 1 FR 0.0001 REL FR 1 V 0 P
o'er–picturing that venus where we see | the ANT 2.02.200
O'ERPOSTING 1 FR 0.0001 REL FR 0 V 1 P
time for your quiet o'erposting that action. 2H4 1.02.150 P
O'ERPOW'R'D 2 FR 0.0002 REL FR 2 V 0 P
with rage | to be o'erpow'r'd, and wilt thou, R2 5.01. 31
angel | becomes a fear, as being o'erpow'r'd: ANT 2.03. 23
O'ERPRESS'D 3 FR 0.0003 REL FR 3 V 0 P
he bestrid | an o'erpress'd roman, and i' th' COR 2.02. 93
of life kindle again | the o'erpress'd spirits. PER 3.02. 84
is more than my o'erpress'd defense can bide? SON 139. 8
O'ER–PRIZ'D 1 FR 0.0001 REL FR 1 V 0 P
o'er–priz'd all popular rate, in my false TMP 1.02. 92
O'ER–RANK 1 FR 0.0001 REL FR 1 V 0 P
shaker of o'er–rank states, thou grand decider TNK 5.01. 63
O'ERRATE 1 FR 0.0001 REL FR 0 V 1 P
sir, you o'errate my poor kindness, i was glad i CYM 1.04. 38 P
O'ERRAUGHT 2 FR 0.0002 REL FR 2 V 0 P
the villain is o'erraught of all my money. ERR 1.02. 96
that certain players | we o'erraught on the way; HAM 3.01. 17
O'ERREACH 1 FR 0.0001 REL FR 1 V 0 P
and will o'erreach them in their own devices, TIT 5.02.143
O'ERREACHED *(see o'erraught)*
O'ERREACHES 1 FR 0.0001 REL FR 0 V 1 P
which this ass now o'erreaches, one that would HAM 5.01. 79 P
O'ERREACHING 1 FR 0.0001 REL FR 0 V 1 P
matter to prevent so gross o'erreaching as this? WIV 5.05.136 P
O'ER–READ 4 FR 0.0004 REL FR 3 V 1 P
bid them o'er–read these letters | and well 2H4 3.01. 2
trebonius doth desire you to o'er–read | (at JC 3.01. 4
from my brother that i have not all o'er–read; LR 1.02. 37 P
which eyes not yet created shall o'er–read, SON 81.10
O'ERRULE 2 FR 0.0002 REL FR 2 V 0 P
nay, my good lord, let me o'errule you now. LLL 5.02.515
lord, | so you will not o'errule me to a peace. HAM 4.07. 60
O'ERRULES 1 FR 0.0001 REL FR 1 V 0 P
then fate o'errules, that, one man holding troth MND 3.02. 92
/O'ERRUN 1 FR 0.0001 REL FR 1 V 0 P
/abject /rear, | /o'errun /and /trampled /on. TRO 3.03.163
O'ERRUN 4 FR 0.0004 REL FR 3 V 1 P
boil and bubble, | till it o'errun the stew; MM 5.01.319
i will o'errun thee with /policy; AYL 5.01. 56 P
like envious floods o'errun her lovely face, SHR in.2. 65
and in thy thought o'errun my former time; 3H6 1.04. 45
O'ERRUNS 1 FR 0.0001 REL FR 1 V 0 P
a chilling sweat o'erruns my trembling joints, TIT 2.03.212
O'ERSET 1 FR 0.0001 REL FR 1 V 0 P
and since we are o'erset, venture again. 2H4 1.01.185
O'ERSHADE 1 FR 0.0001 REL FR 1 V 0 P
black night o'ershade thy day, and death thy R3 1.02.131
O'ERSHADES 2 FR 0.0002 REL FR 2 V 0 P
fear o'ershades me. WT 1.02.457
dark cloudy death o'ershades his beams of life, 3H6 2.06. 62
O'ERSHINE 1 FR 0.0001 REL FR 0 V 1 P
clear sky of fame o'ershine you as much as the 2H4 4.03. 52 P
O'ERSHOT 2 FR 0.0002 REL FR 2 V 0 P
all three of you, to be thus much o'ershot? LLL 4.03.158
i have o'ershot myself to tell you of it. JC 3.02.150
O'ERSHOW'R'D 1 FR 0.0001 REL FR 1 V 0 P
shot through and biggest tears o'ershow'r'd, PER 4.04. 26
O'ER–SIZED 1 FR 0.0001 REL FR 1 V 0 P
fire, | and thus o'er–sized with coagulate gore, HAM 2.02.462
/O'ERSKIP 1 FR 0.0001 REL FR 1 V 0 P
/the /mind /much /sufferance /doth /o'erskip, LR 3.06.106
O'ERSLIPS 1 FR 0.0001 REL FR 1 V 0 P
and when that hour o'erslips me in the day TGV 2.02. 9
O'ERSNOW'D 1 FR 0.0001 REL FR 1 V 0 P
beauty o'ersnow'd and bareness every where: SON 5. 8
O'ERSPREAD 1 FR 0.0001 REL FR 1 V 0 P
with hostile forces he'll o'erspread the land, PER 1.02. 24
O'ERSPREADS 1 FR 0.0001 REL FR 1 V 0 P
the dragon wing of night o'erspreads the earth, TRO 5.08. 17
O'ERSTARE 1 FR 0.0001 REL FR 1 V 0 P
i would o'erstare the sternest eyes that look, MV 2.01. 27
O'ERSTEP 1 FR 0.0001 REL FR 0 V 1 P
that you o'erstep not the modesty of nature: HAM 3.02. 19 P
O'ERSTRAW'D 1 FR 0.0001 REL FR 1 V 0 P
and the top o'erstraw'd | with sweets that shall VEN 1143
O'ERSTUNK 1 FR 0.0001 REL FR 1 V 0 P
that the foul lake | o'erstunk their feet. TMP 4.01.184
O'ERSWAY 2 FR 0.0002 REL FR 2 V 0 P
so pair–taunt–like would i o'ersway his state LLL 5.02. 67
if he be so resolv'd, | i can o'ersway him; JC 2.01.203
O'ERSWAYS 2 FR 0.0002 REL FR 2 V 0 P
and, but that great command o'ersways the order, HAM 5.01.228
sea, | but sad mortality o'ersways their power, SON 65. 2
O'ERSWELL 3 FR 0.0003 REL FR 3 V 0 P
shall leave his native channel and o'erswell JN 2.01.337
let floods o'erswell, and fiends for food howl H5 2.01. 93
fill, lucius, till the wine o'erswell the cup; JC 4.03.161
O'ERTA'EN 2 FR 0.0002 REL FR 2 V 0 P
fair sir, you are well o'erta'en. MV 4.02. 5
at overnight, | she might have been o'erta'en; AWW 3.04. 24
O'ERTAKE 8 FR 0.0009 REL FR 8 V 0 P
his act did not o'ertake his bad intent, | and MM 5.01.451
o'ertake me if thou canst, i scorn thy strength. 1H6 1.05. 15
for if the trial of the law o'ertake ye, H8 3.01. 96
thou wilt o'ertake us hence a mile or twain | i' LR 4.01. 42
nag of egypt | (whom leprosy o'ertake!) ANT 3.10. 11
i will o'ertake thee, cleopatra, and | weep for 4.14. 44
would i might never | o'ertake pursu'd success, 5.02.103
to let base clouds o'ertake me in my way, SON 34. 3
O'ER–TEEMED 1 FR 0.0001 REL FR 1 V 0 P
about her lank and all o'er–teemed loins, | a HAM 2.02.508
O'ERTHROW 3 FR 0.0003 REL FR 3 V 0 P
since it is in my pow'r | to o'erthrow law, and WT 4.01. 8
false allegations to o'erthrow his state? 2H6 3.01.181
ere clean it o'erthrow nature, makes it valiant. CYM 3.06. 20
O'ERTHROWN 6 FR 0.0006 REL FR 6 V 0 P
now my charms are all o'erthrown, | and what TMP ep 1
no such sport as sport by sport o'erthrown, | to LLL 5.02.153
your honor not o'erthrown by your desires, | i WT 5.01.230
wherein lord talbot was o'erthrown. 1H6 1.01.108
o, what a noble mind is here o'erthrown! HAM 3.01.150
not caesar's valor hath o'erthrown antony, | but ANT 4.15. 14
O'ERTOOK 2 FR 0.0002 REL FR 2 V 0 P
the flighty purpose never is o'ertook | unless MAC 4.01.145
there was 'a gaming, there o'ertook in 's rouse, HAM 2.01. 56
O'ERTOP 2 FR 0.0002 REL FR 2 V 0 P
less than yours in /past, must o'ertop yours; TRO 3.03.164
mountain you have made | t' o'ertop old pelion, HAM 5.01.253
O'ERTOPPING 1 FR 0.0001 REL FR 1 V 0 P
and of wisdom | o'ertopping woman's pow'r. H8 2.04. 88
O'ERTRIP 1 FR 0.0001 REL FR 1 V 0 P
a night | did thisby fearfully o'ertrip the dew, MV 5.01. 7
O'ERTURN 2 FR 0.0002 REL FR 2 V 0 P
help | we shall o'erturn it topsy–turvy down. 1H4 4.01. 82
the vapor of our valor will o'erturn them. H5 4.02. 24
O'ERVALUES 1 FR 0.0001 REL FR 0 V 1 P
which in my opinion o'ervalues it something. CYM 1.04.109 P
O'ERWALK 1 FR 0.0001 REL FR 1 V 0 P
spirit | as to o'erwalk a current roaring loud 1H4 1.03.192
O'ERWATCH'D 2 FR 0.0002 REL FR 2 V 0 P
knave, i blame thee not, thou art o'erwatch'd. JC 4.03.241
all weary and o'erwatch'd, | take vantage, heavy LR 2.02.170
O'ERWEEN 1 FR 0.0001 REL FR 0 V 1 P
might be some allay (or i o'erween to think so), WT 4.02. 8 P
O'ERWEENING 1 FR 0.0001 REL FR 1 V 0 P
oft have i seen a hot o'erweening cur | run back 2H6 5.01.151
O'ERWEENS 1 FR 0.0001 REL FR 1 V 0 P
my eye's too quick, my heart o'erweens too much, 3H6 3.02.144
O'ERWEIGH 2 FR 0.0002 REL FR 1 V 1 P
allowance, o'erweigh a whole theatre of others. HAM 3.02. 27 P
a grain of honor | they not o'erweigh us. TNK 5.04. 19
O'ERWEIGHS 1 FR 0.0001 REL FR 1 V 0 P
my false o'erweighs your true. MM 2.04.170
O'ERWHELM 6 FR 0.0006 REL FR 6 V 0 P
self–born hour | to plant and o'erwhelm custom. WT 4.01. 9
let the brow o'erwhelm it | as fearfully as doth H5 3.01. 11
thou wretch, despite o'erwhelm thee! COR 3.01.163
though all the earth o'erwhelm them, to men's HAM 1.02.257
with the hell–hated lie o'erwhelm thy heart, LR 5.03.148
and humming water must o'erwhelm thy corpse, PER 3.01. 63
O'ERWHELM'D 1 FR 0.0001 REL FR 1 V 0 P
within my view, | and wrath o'erwhelm'd my pity. COR 1.09. 86
O'ERWHELMED 1 FR 0.0001 REL FR 1 V 0 P
whilst you were here o'erwhelmed with your grief OTH 4.01. 76
O'ERWHELMING 1 FR 0.0001 REL FR 1 V 0 P
his low'ring brows o'erwhelming his fair sight, VEN 183
O'ERWORN 4 FR 0.0004 REL FR 4 V 0 P
the jealous o'erworn widow and herself, | since R3 1.01. 81
o'erworn, despised, rheumatic, and cold, VEN 135
grove, | musing the morning is so much o'erworn, 866
with time's injurious hand crush'd and o'erworn, SON 63. 2
/O'ER–WRASTLING 1 FR 0.0001 REL FR 1 V 0 P
in will | /o'er–wrastling strength in reason. TNK 1.04. 45
O'ER–WRESTED 1 FR 0.0001 REL FR 1 V 0 P
such to–be–pitied and o'er–wrested seeming | he TRO 1.03.157
O'ER–WRESTLING *(see o'er–wrastling)*
OES 1 FR 0.0001 REL FR 1 V 0 P
than all yon fiery oes and eyes of light. MND 3.02.188
/OEUVRES 1 FR 0.0001 REL FR 1 V 0 P
la fin couronne les /oeuvres. 2H6 5.02. 28
OF *(also a'*, o'*)*
/OF 197 FR 0.0222 REL FR 155 V 42 P
OF 17079 FR 1.9306 REL FR 12937 V 4142 P
/OFF 10 FR 0.0011 REL FR 7 V 3 P
do not smile at me that i boast her /off, | for TMP 4.01. 9
verges, sir, speaks a little /off the matter; ADO 3.05. 9 P
/off, coxcomb! 4.02. 69 P
and speak /off half a dozen dang'rous words, 5.01. 97
take that, and mend the plucking /off the other. SHR 4.01.148
to whistle /off these secrets, but you must be WT 4.04.245 P
/i /have /shook /off /the /regal /thoughts R2 4.01.163
/give /this /heavy /weight /from /off /my /head, 4.01.204
damned dane, | drink /off this potion! HAM 5.02.326
let me request you /off, our graver business ANT 2.07.120
OFF 474 FR 0.0535 REL FR 358 V 116 P
set her two courses off to sea again! TMP 1.01. 50 P
lay her off. 1.01. 50 P
'tis far off — | and rather like a dream than 1.02. 44
shake it off. 1.02.307
keep a care, | shake off slumber, and beware. 2.01.304
lead off this ground, and let's make further 2.01.323
bush nor shrub to bear off any weather at all. 2.02. 18 P
and their labor | delight in them /sets off; 3.01. 2
the shore, five and thirty leagues off and on. 3.02. 14 P
i'll go farther off. 3.02. 73 P
prithee stand further off. 3.02. 84 P
even here i will put off my hope, and keep it 3.03. 7
i will fetch off my bottle, though i be o'er 4.01.213 P
put off that gown, trinculo. 4.01.227 P
that shall catch | your royal fleet far off. 5.01.317
now trust me, madam, it came hardly off; TGV 2.01.109
of words, gentlemen, and quickly shot off. 2.04. 34 P
leave off discourse of disability. 2.04.109
the forest is not three leagues off; 5.01. 11
inconstancy falls off ere it begins. 5.04.113
kind of tender, made afar off by sir hugh here. WIV 1.01.208 P
yet i cannot put off my opinion so easily. 2.01.234 P
they must come off. 4.03. 11 P
eton, they threw me off from behind one of them, 4.05. 67 P
these three days his head to be chopp'd off. MM 1.02. 69 P
a milkmaid, if she be in love, may sigh it off. 1.02.174 P
this comes off well. here's a wise officer. 2.01. 57 P
break off thy song, and haste thee quick away. 4.01. 7
can you cut off a man's head? 4.02. 1 P
head, and i can never cut off a woman's head. 4.02. 5 P
executioner, and off with barnardine's head. 4.02.206 P
the world, | his head is off and sent to angelo. 4.03.116
her brother, | cut off by course of justice — 5.01. 35
brother by himself, | and not have cut him off. 5.01.112
which was broke off, | partly for that her 5.01.218
will't not off? 5.01.355 P
nay, forward, old man, do not break off so, ERR 1.01. 96
and tear the stain'd skin off my harlot brow, 2.02.136
beard they have sing'd off with brands of fire, 5.01.171
he was not three leagues off when i left him. ADO 1.01. 4 P
conflict four of his five wits went halting off, 1.01. 66 P
pluck off the bull's horns and set them in my 1.01.263 P
fetch you a hair off the great cham's beard, do 2.01.268 P
john, saw afar off in the orchard this amiable 3.03.151 P
had our two noses snapp'd off with two old men 5.01.116 P
in his doublet and hose and leaves off his wit! 5.01.200 P
but to jig off a tune at the tongue's end, LLL 3.01. 11 P
why, she that bears the bow. | finely put off! 4.01.110
when it comes so smoothly off, so obscenely as 4.01.143
might shake off fifty, looking in her eye: 4.03.239
one word more, my maids, break off, break off. 5.02.262
one word more, my maids, break off, break off. 5.02.262
we will turn it finely off, sir; 5.02.510
and ere i take this charm from off her sight MND 2.01.183
for my sake, my dear, | lie further off yet; 2.02. 44
for love and courtesy | lie further off, in 2.02. 57
hang off, thou cat, thou bur! 3.02.260
from off the head of this athenian swain, | that 4.01. 65
robin, take off this head. 4.01. 80
and in conclusion dumbly have broke off, | not 5.01. 98
is to come fairly off from the great debts MV 1.01.128
to be cut off and taken | in what part of your 1.03.150
there is a monast'ry two miles off, | and there 3.04. 31
till thou canst rail the seal from off my bond, 4.01.139
to be by him cut off | nearest the merchant's 4.01.232
penance | of such misery doth she cut me off. 4.01.272
and you must cut this flesh from off his breast, 4.01.302
therefore prepare thee to cut off the flesh. 4.01.324
why, i were best to cut my left hand off, | and 5.01.177
a pure blush thou mayst in honor come off again. AYL 1.02. 29 P
sent in this fool to cut off the argument? 1.02. 46 P
i could shake them off my coat; 1.03. 16 P
that, | he will have other means to cut you off; 2.03. 25
shepherd, go off a little. 3.02.158 P
unbind my hands, i'll pull them off myself, SHR 2.01. 4
and to cut off all strife, here sit we down: 3.01. 21
mates | after a storm, quaff'd off the muscadel, 3.02.172
she waded through the dirt to pluck him off me; 4.01. 78 P
off with my boots, you rogues! 4.01.144
off with that bable, throw it under–foot. 5.02.122
off with't while 'tis vendible; AWW 1.01.154 P
doctrine, have left off | the danger to itself? 1.03.241
too, or take off thine | by wond'ring how thou 2.01. 89
when you put off that with such contempt? 2.02. 6 P
any manners, he may easily put it off at court. 2.02. 9 P
he that cannot make a leg, put off 's cap, kiss 2.02. 10 P
there's a simple putting off. 2.02. 41 P
yet stands off | in differences so mighty. 2.03.120
thou hast a son shall take this disgrace off me, 2.03.236 P
but puts it off to a compell'd restraint; 2.04. 43
which never shall come off, and show me a child 3.02. 58 P
none better than to let him fetch off his drum, 3.06. 19 P
let him fetch off his drum in any hand. 3.06. 42 P
they will say, "came you off with so little?" 4.01. 39 P
stand no more off, | but give thyself unto my 4.02. 34
upon him for shaking off so good a wife and so 4.03. 7 P
dare not shake the snow from off their cassocks, 4.03.168 P
come, headsman, off with his head. 4.03.308 P
you, that have turn'd off a first so noble wife, 5.03.220
which on your just proceeding i'll keep off — 5.03.236
glove, my lord, she goes off and on at pleasure. 5.03.278 P
take thee between her legs, and spin it off. TN 1.03.104 P
fetch him off, i pray you, he speaks nothing but 1.05.106 P
sir toby, i will wash off gross acquaintance, i 2.05.162 P
gilt of this opportunity you let time wash off, 3.02. 26 P
are shuffled off with such uncurrent pay; 3.03. 16

go off, i discard you. 3.04. 89 P
go off. 3.04. 90 P
with a swaggering accent sharply twang'd off, 3.04.180 P
pleas'd that i shake off these names you give me 5.01. 73
you put me off with limber vows; WT 1.02. 47
i do, and will fetch off bohemia for't; 1.02.334
how far off, how near, | which way to be 1.02.404
thee as a father, if | thou bear'st my life off. 1.02.462
he who shall speak for her is afar off guilty 2.01.104
threw off his spirit, his appetite, his sleep, 2.03. 16
on mine own accord i'll off, | but first i'll do 2.03. 64
pluck but off these rags; 4.03. 52 P
rags to lay on thee, rather than have these off. 4.03. 55 P
no harm, good man" — puts him off, slights him, 4.04.199 P
no, not our kin, | farre than deucalion off. 4.04.431
you, | but as you shake off one to take another; 4.04.569
i would have fil'd keys off that hung in chains. 4.04.611 P
was the farthest off you could have been to him, 4.04.703 P
for she did print your royal father off, 5.01.125
who has | (his dignity and duty both cast off) 5.01.183
silence, the more shows off | your wonder; 5.03. 21
pow'r | to take off so much grief from you as he 5.03. 55
would i might never stir from off this place, JN 1.01.145
near or far off, well won is still well shot, 1.01.174
churlish drums | cuts off more circumstance. 2.01. 77
king, | cut off the sequence of posterity, 2.01. 96
women and fools, break off your conference. 2.01.150
heralds, from off our tow'rs we might behold, 2.01.325
so heavy as thou shalt not shake them off, | but 3.01.296
and that high royalty was ne'er pluck'd off; 4.02. 5
cuts off his tale and talks of arthur's death. 4.02.202
shame had struck me dumb, made me break off, 4.02.235
at noon | my crown i should give off? 5.01. 27
let me wipe off this honorable dew, | that 5.02. 45
the pains you take | by cutting off your heads. 5.04. 16
o, bravely came we off, | when with a volley of 5.05. 4
lords | by his persuasion are again fall'n off, 5.05. 11
dead, forsook, cast off, | and none of you will 5.07. 35
a freer heart | cast off his chains of bondage, R2 1.03. 89
off goes his bonnet to an oyster–wench, | a 1.04. 31
if then we shall shake off our slavish yoke, 2.01.291
wipe off the dust that hides our sceptre's gilt, 2.01.294
your husband, he is gone to save far off, 2.02. 80
the king had cut off my head with my brother's. 2.02.102
to wash your blood | from off my hands, here in 3.01. 6
of night being pluck'd from off their backs, 3.02. 45
can wash the balm off from an anointed king; 3.02. 55
how far off lies your power? 3.02. 63
nor near nor farther off, my gracious lord, 3.02. 64
how far off from the mind of bullingbrook | it 3.03. 45
on yon proud man should take it off again | with 3.03.135
cut off the heads of /too fast growing sprays, 3.04. 34
and if i do not, may my hands rot off, | and 4.01. 49
better far off than, near, be ne'er the near. 5.01. 88
when weeping made you break the story off, | of 5.02. 2
which with such gentle sorrow he shook off, 5.02. 31
this fest'red joint cut off, the rest rest sound 5.03. 85
to wash this blood off from my guilty hand. 5.06. 50
brake off our business for the holy land. 1H4 1.01. 48
rob them, cut this head off from my shoulders. 1.02.166 P
when this loose behavior i throw off | and pay 1.02.208
than that which hath no foil to set it off. 1.02.215
he never did fall off, my sovereign liege, | but 1.03. 94
and shook off | by him for whom these shames ye 1.03.178
and bid you play it off. 2.04. 17 P
the remnant northward lying off from trent. 3.01. 78
a perilous gash, a very limb lopp'd off — | and 4.01. 43
cut me off the heads | of all the favorites that 4.03. 85
this present enterprise set off his head, | i do 5.01. 88
but how if honor prick me off when i come on? 5.01.130 P
service for any other reason than to set me off, 2H4 1.02. 13 P
and borne, and have been fubb'd off, and fubb'd 2.01. 34 P
and have been fubb'd off, and fubb'd off, and 2.01. 34 P
and fubb'd off, and fubb'd off, from this day to 2.01. 35 P
bardolph, cut me off the villain's head, throw 2.01. 46 P
keep them off, bardolph. 2.01. 54 P
more sir johns, and, putting off his hat, said, 2.04. 6 P
for to serve bravely is to come halting off, you 2.04. 49 P
to come off the breach with his pike bent 2.04. 50 P
more, pistol, i would not have you go off here. 2.04.136 P
and drinks off candles' ends for flap–dragons, 2.04.246 P
not this nave of a wheel have his ears cut off? 2.04.256 P
come off and on swifter than he that gibbets on 3.02.263 P
will this feeble the woman's tailor run off! 3.02.269 P
as i return, i will fetch off these justices. 3.02.301 P
west of this forest, scarcely off a mile, | in 4.01. 19
every thing set off | that might so much as 4.01.143
will not go off until they hear you speak. 4.02.100
perfectness of time | cast off his followers, 4.04. 75
i cut them off, and had a purpose now | to lead 4.05.209
come, come, come, off with your boots. 5.01. 54 P
what was th' impediment that broke this off? H5 1.01. 90
or shall we sparingly show you far off | the 1.02.239
will you shog off? i would have you solus. 2.01. 45 P
if you would walk off, i would prick your guts a 2.01. 58 P
though the truth of it stands off as gross | as 2.02.103
so chrish save me, i will cut off your head. 3.02.133 P
who came off bravely, who was shot, who 3.06. 73 P
the french is gone off, look you, and there is 3.06. 92 P
we would have all such offenders so cut off; 3.06.108 P
like a kern of ireland, your french hose off, 3.07. 53 P
sand, that look to be wash'd off the next tide. 4.01. 98 P
and heads, chopp'd off in a battle, shall join 4.01.136 P
and a sweet retire | from off these fields, 4.03. 87
and there my rendezvous is quite cut off. 5.01. 83
butcher and sit like a jack–an–apes, never off. 5.02.142 P
her husband's neck, hardly to be shook off. 5.02.181 P
put off your maiden blushes, avouch the thoughts 5.02.234 P
to keep the horsemen off from breaking in. 1H6 1.01.119
leave off delays, and let us raise the siege. 1.02.146
one of thy eyes and thy cheek's side struck off! 1.04. 75
from off this brier pluck a white rose with me. 2.04. 30
pluck a red rose from off this thorn with me. 2.04. 33
prick not your finger as you pluck it off, 2.04. 49
goes, | for friendly counsel cuts off many foes. 3.01.184
keep off aloof with worthless emulation. 4.04. 21
i'll lop a member off and give it you | in 5.03. 15
a fall off of a tree. 2H6 2.01. 94
come on, sirrah, off with your doublet quickly. 2.01.147 P
my lord, break we off; 2.02. 77
his lady banish'd, and a limb lopp'd off. 2.03. 42
madam, your penance done, throw off this sheet, 2.04.105
and so break off, the day is almost spent; 3.01.325
and so much shall you give, or off goes yours. 4.01. 17
on our longboat's side | strike off his head. 4.01. 69
i say, and strike off his head presently, and 4.07.109 P
sir james cromer, and strike off his head, and 4.07.111 P
and there cut off thy most ungracious head, 4.10. 82
thrice i led him off, | persuaded him from any 5.03. 9
congeal'd with this, do make me wipe off both. 3H6 1.03. 52
off with the crown; 1.04.107
off with his head, and set it on york gates, 1.04.179
some six miles off the duke is with the soldiers 2.01.144
break off the parley, for scarce i can refrain 2.02.110
that winter should cut off our spring–time so. 2.03. 47
from off the gates of york fetch down the head, 2.06. 52
rail at him, | this hand should chop it off; 2.06. 82
off with the traitor's head, | and rear it in 2.06. 85
thy balm wash'd off wherewith thou was anointed. 3.01. 17
so do i wish the crown, being so far off, | and 3.02.140
it, | and so, i say, i'll cut the causes off, 3.02.142
tut, were it farther off, i'll pluck it down. 3.02.195
while we bethink a means to break it off. 3.03. 39
leave off to wonder why i drew you hither | into 4.05. 2
nor posted off their suits with slow delays; 4.08. 40
how far off is our brother montague? 5.01. 4
what is the body when the head is off? 5.01. 41
i had rather chop this hand off at a blow, | and 5.01. 50
shall, whiles thy head is warm and new cut off, 5.01. 55
bestride the rock, the tide will wash you off, 5.04. 31
for somerset, off with his guilty head. 5.05. 3
look in his youth to have him so cut off | as, 5.05. 66
age, | but by some unlook'd accident cut off! R3 1.03.213
to cut off those that have offended him. 1.04.219
and, as it were far off, sound thou lord 3.01.170
be thou so too, and so break off the talk, | and 3.01.177
chop off his head! 3.01.193
he dreamt the boar had rased off his helm. 3.02. 11
off with his head! 3.04. 76
yet touch this sparingly, as 'twere far off, 3.05. 93
and even here brake off, and came away. 3.07. 41
these both put off, a poor petitioner, | a 3.07.183
if i revolt, off goes young george's head; 4.05. 4
the fear of that holds off my present aid. 4.05. 5
time | cuts off the ceremonious vows of love 5.03. 98
off with his son george's head! 5.03.344
have i pluck'd off to grace thy brows withal. 5.05. 6
to them 'longing, have put off | the spinsters, H8 1.02. 32
thomas lovell's heads | should have gone off. 1.02.186
pluck off a little, | i would not be a young 2.03. 40
that thus you should proceed to put me off, 2.04. 21
no, he's settled | (not to come off) in his 3.02. 23
in spite of fortune | will bring me off again. 3.02.220
at dunstable — six miles off | from ampthill, 4.01. 27
in the choir, fell off | a distance from her; 4.01. 64
me till her pink'd porringer fell off her head, 5.03. 48 P
there's laying on, take't off who will, as they TRO 1.02.207 P
yet hold i off. 1.02.286
that can from hector bring those honors off, 1.03.334
if the dull brainless ajax come safe off, 1.03.380
of this cormorant war — | shall be strook off." 2.02. 7
and cut off | all fears attending on so dire a 2.02.133
have the soil of her fair rape | wip'd off, in 2.02.149
sirrah, walk off. 3.02. 6
shall quite strike off all service i have done, 3.03. 29
i might have still held off, | and then you 4.02. 17
now, good my lord, go off; 5.02. 40
i'll be ta'en too, | or bring him off. 5.06. 25
must not think to fob off our disgrace with a COR 1.01. 94 P
how far off lie these armies? 1.04. 8
hark you, far off! 1.04. 19
let's fetch him off, or make remain alike. 1.04. 62
we are come off | like romans, neither foolish 1.06. 1
they fought together, but aufidius got off. 2.01.128 P
that's off, that's off; 2.02. 60
that's off, that's off; 2.02. 60
aidless came off, | and with a sudden 2.02.112
the insinuating nod and be off to them most 2.03.100 P
ag'd sir, hands off. 3.01.177
mortal, to cut it off; 3.01.295
that the very hour | you take it off again? 3.03. 61
of precipitation | from off the rock tarpeian, 3.03.103
if i could shake off but one seven years | from 4.01. 55
you, you'll rejoice | that he is thus cut off. 5.06.138
and he hath cut those pretty fingers off | that TIT 2.04. 42
give me a sword, i'll chop off my hands too, 3.01. 72
chop off your hand | and send it to the king; 3.01.153
good aaron, wilt thou help to chop it off? 3.01.161
rent off thy silver hair, thy other hand 3.01.260
see, thou hast shot off one of taurus' horns. 4.03. 70
cut off the proud'st conspirator that lives. 4.04. 26
death, | my hand cut off and made a merry jest; 5.02.174
i will cut off their heads. ROM 1.01. 23 P
severity | cuts beauty off from all posterity. 1.01.220
show a fair presence and put off these frowns, 1.05. 73
cast it off. 2.02. 9
sit | of an old tear that is not wash'd off yet. 2.03. 76
thou cut'st my head off with a golden axe, | and 3.03. 22
i'll give thee armor to keep off that word: 3.03. 54
paris, | from off the battlements of any tower, 4.01. 78
and this distilling liquor drink thou off, 4.01. 94
in any liquid thing you will | and drink it off, 5.01. 78
so 'tis. this comes off well and excellent. TIM 1.01. 29
i am not of that feather to shake off | my 1.01.100
he hath put me off | to the succession of new 2.02. 19
your steward puts me off, my lord, | and i am 2.02. 31
you would throw them off, | and say you /found 2.02.134
many my near occasions did urge me to put off; 3.06. 11 P
washes it off, and sprinkles in your faces 3.06. 92
are we undone, cast off, nothing remaining? 4.02. 2
thy lips rot off! 4.03. 64
breath whom thou'lt observe | blow off thy cap; 4.03.213
i would my tongue could rot them off! 4.03.365
you were retir'd, your friends fall'n off, 5.01. 59
holy chase, | shake off their sterile curse. JC 1.02. 9
he was very loath to lay his fingers off it. 1.02.242 P
flavius, for pulling scarfs off caesar's images, 1.02.286 P
that i do bear | i can shake off at pleasure. 1.03.100
if these be motives weak, break off betimes, 2.01.116
to cut the head off and then hack the limbs — 2.01.163
than caesar's arm | when caesar's head is off. 2.01.183
he that cuts off twenty years of life | cuts off 3.01.101
life | cuts off so many years of fearing death. 3.01.102
death, | as here by caesar, and by you cut off, 3.01.162
nay, press not so upon me, stand far off. 3.02.167
how to cut off some charge in legacies. 4.01. 9
then take we down his load, and turn him off 4.01. 25
bid our commanders lead their charges off | a 4.02. 48
because i knew the man, was slighted off. 4.03. 5
from which advantage shall we cut him off | if 4.03.210
fly further off, my lord, fly further off; 5.03. 9
fly further off, my lord, fly further off; 5.03. 9
fly therefore, noble cassius, fly far off. 5.03. 11
it sets him on, and it takes him off; MAC 2.03. 33 P
shake off this downy sleep, death's counterfeit, 2.03. 76
bosoms, | whose execution takes your enemy off, 3.01.104
i should cut off the nobles for their lands, 4.03. 79
pull't off, i say. 5.03. 54
some must go off; 5.09. 2
ay, and brought off the field. 5.09. 10
by self and violent hands | took off her life; 5.09. 37
peace, break thee off! HAM 1.01. 40
good hamlet, cast thy nighted color off, | and 1.02. 68
hold off your hands. 1.04. 80
cut off even in the blossoms of my sin, 1.05. 76
if you love me, hold not off. 2.02.291 P
plucks off my beard and blows it in my face, 2.02.573
when we have shuffled off this mortal coil, 3.01. 66
now this overdone, or come tardy off, though it 3.02. 25 P
would cost you a groaning to take off mine edge. 3.02.249 P
takes off the rose | from the fair forehead of 3.04. 42
hold off the earth a while, | till i have caught 5.01.249
hold off thy hand! 5.01.263
of the axe, | my head should be strook off. 5.02. 25
i' th' darkest night, | stick fiery off indeed. 5.02.257
he hath now cast her off appears too grossly. LR 1.01.291 P
love cools, friendship falls off, brothers 1.02.107 P
that /it had it head bit off by it young." 1.04.216
thou dost think | i have cast off for ever. 1.04.310
fetches, | the images of revolt and flying off. 2.04. 90
to grudge my pleasures, to cut off my train, 2.04.174
off, off, you lendings! 3.04.108 P
off, off, you lendings! 3.04.108 P
preferment falls on him that cuts him off. 4.05. 38
go thou further off: 4.06. 30
shake patiently my great affliction off. 4.06. 36
pull off my boots; 4.06.173
you have many opportunities to cut him off; 4.06.264 P
far off methinks i hear the beaten drum. 4.06.285
i prithee put them off. 4.07. 8
be rid of him devise | his speedy taking off. 5.01. 65
lead him off. OTH 2.03.254
he shall in strangeness stand no farther off 3.03. 12
yet, if you please to /hold him off awhile, 3.03.248
i'ld whistle her off, and let her down the wind 3.03.262
time, | strike off this score of absence. 3.04.179
will (though he do shake me off | to beggarly 4.02.157
your power and your command is taken off, | and 5.02.331
i must from this enchanting queen break off; ANT 1.02.128
our hearts, and never | fly off our loves again! 2.02.152
there, | my music playing far off, i will betray 2.05. 11
i have ever held my cap off to thy fortunes. 2.07. 57
lepidus, | keep off them, for you sink. 2.07. 60
and, when we are put off, fall to their throats: 2.07. 72
most large | in his abominations, turns you off, 3.06. 94
which serve not for his vantage, he shakes off, 3.07. 33
let's see how it will give off. 4.03. 22
not more in parting | than greatness going off. 4.13. 6
off, pluck off, | the sevenfold shield of ajax 4.14. 37
off, pluck off, | the sevenfold shield of ajax 4.14. 37
die, | not cowardly put off my helmet to | my 4.15. 56
if i come off and leave her in such honor as you CYM 1.04.152 P
he hath a kind of honor sets him off, | more 1.06.170
come off, come off; 2.02. 33
come off, come off; 2.02. 33
may be she pluck'd it off | to send it me. 2.04.104
him) he was carried | from off our coast, twice 3.01. 26
which to shake off | becomes a warlike people, 3.01. 51
that it is place which lessens and sets off, 3.03. 13
was the theme, my name | was not far off. 3.03. 60
thy tongue | may take off some extremity, which 3.04. 17
shall within this hour be off, thy mistress 4.01. 17 P
cut off one cloten's head, | son to the queen 4.02.118
and put | my clouted brogues from off my feet, 4.02.214
devil cloten, | hath here cut off my lord. 4.02.316
guilt within my bosom | takes off my manhood. 5.02. 2
our son is good, | take off his miseries. 5.04. 86
knock off his manacles, bring your prisoner to 5.04.191 P
prevented it, she had | ta'en off by poison. 5.05. 47
i cut off 's head, | and am right glad he is not 5.05.295
sin, | ay, and the targets to put off the shame; PER 1.01.140
hours | shake off the golden slumber of repose. 3.02. 23
life | /seeks to take off by treason's knife, 4.ch. 14
which | even women have cast off, melt thee, but 4.01. 7
and from the ladder–tackle washes off | a 4.01. 60
thou mayst cut a morsel off the spit. 4.02.131 P
i must have your maidenhead taken off, or the 4.06.127 P
sir, there is a barge put off from meteline, 5.01. 3
a dove's motion when the head's pluck'd off; TNK 1.01. 98
break and fall | off me with that corruption! 1.02. 74
leaden–footed | till his great rage be off him. 1.02. 85
yet fate hath brought them off. 1.03. 41
this; but far off, prince. 2.05. 5
food, for yet | his iron bracelets are not off. 2.06. 8
signs | of prisonment were off me and this hand 3.01. 32
these impediments | will i file off; 3.01. 85
save when my lids scour'd off their /brine. 3.02. 28
get off your trinkets, you shall want nought. 3.03. 52
stand off then. 3.06. 89
nor put off | this great adventure to a second 3.06.118
three or four | i saw from far off cross her — 4.01.100
apprehension | which still is farther off it, go 5.01. 37
let him | take off my wheaten garland, or else 5.01.160
why do you rub my kiss off? 5.02. 88

many a murther | set off whereto she's guilty. 5.03. 28
they are coming off. 5.03.103
victor's wreath | even then fell off his head; 5.04. 80
lead your lady off; 5.04.122
let's go off, | and bear us like the time. 5.04.136
sometime he scuds far off, and there he stares, VEN 301
and all amaz'd, brake off his late intent, | for 469
"by this, poor wat, far off upon a hill, 697
by this, far off, she hears some huntsman hallow 973
the wind would blow it off, and being gone, 1089
how far i toil, still farther off from thee. SON 28. 8
from me far off, with others all too near. 61.14
from off a hill whose concave womb reworded | a LC 1
shook off my sober guards and civil fears; 298
OFFAL 3 FR 0.0003 REL FR 2 V 1 P
in a basket like a barrow of butcher's offal? WIV 3.05. 5 P
what rubbish and what offal? JC 1.03.109
all the region kites | with this slave's offal. HAM 2.02.580
OFF–CAPP'D 1 FR 0.0001 REL FR 1 V 0 P
to make me his lieutenant, | off–capp'd to him; OTH 1.01. 10
OFFEND 62 FR 0.0070 REL FR 44 V 18 P
what (but to speak of) would offend again. MM 1.02.136
me, | when i, that censure him, do so offend, 2.01. 29
and hang all that offend that way but for ten 2.01.238 P
this rank offense, | so to offend him still. 3.01.100
if bawdy talk offend you, we'll have very little 4.03.178 P
for i cannot see how sleeping should offend; ADO 3.03. 41 P
for indeed the watch ought to offend no man, and 3.03. 81 P
do not wrest true speaking, i'll offend nobody. 3.04. 34 P
make those that do offend you suffer too. 5.01. 40
for none offend where all alike do dote. LLL 4.03.124
noble sort | would so offend a virgin and extort MND 3.02.160
if we offend, it is with our good will. 5.01.108
that you should think, we come not to offend, 5.01.109
to offend and judge are distinct offices, | and MV 2.09. 61
yield to such inevitable shame | as to offend, 4.01. 58
i will no further offend you than becomes me for AYL 1.01. 79 P
a thought unborn | did i offend your highness. 1.03. 52
into some merry passion | and so offend him; SHR in.1. 98
was in mine eye | the dust that did offend it. AWW 5.03. 55
if you offend him, i for him defy you. TN 3.04.314
of them offend me more than the stripes i have WT 4.03. 56 P
him so, | that he shall not offend your majesty. JN 3.03. 65
wealth of all the world, | will not offend thee. 4.01.131
i'll so offend, to make offense a skill, 1H4 1.02.216
these rebels, they offend none but the virtuous. 3.03.191 P
you shall not hardly offend her. 2H4 2.04.117 P
to see a son of mine | offend you and obey you, 5.02.106
we'll not offend one stomach with our play. H5 2.pr. 40
they do offend our sight. 4.07. 59
any from mine that might offend your majesty. 4.08. 47 P
yet, if this servile usage once offend, | go, 1H6 5.03. 58
i must offend before i be attainted; 2H6 2.04. 59
yet look to have them buzz to offend thine ears. 3H6 2.06. 95
did not offend, nor were not worthy blame, | if 5.05. 54
let me march on and not offend you, madam. R3 4.04.179
such things as might offend the weakest spleen TRO 2.02.128
the day, how loath you are to offend daylight! 3.02. 48 P
o, pardon, i offend. 4.05.182
you train me to offend you, get you in. 5.03. 4
no more of this, it does offend my heart; COR 2.01.168
would it offend you then | that both should TIT 2.01.100
we but offend him. strike! TIM 4.03.175
or offend the stream | of regular justice in 5.04. 60
you shall offend him and extend his passion. MAC 3.04. 56
i am sorry they offend you, heartily, | yes, HAM 1.05.134
this last surrender of his will but offend us. LR 1.01.306 P
i shall offend either to detain or give it: 1.02. 41 P
none does offend, none, i say none, i'll able 4.06.168
that, if my speech offend a noble heart, | thy 5.03.127
in some action | that may offend the isle. OTH 2.03. 61
over her iniquity, give her patent to offend, 4.01.198 P
i will not stay to offend you. 4.01.247
i never did | offend you in my life; 5.02. 59
take no offense that i would not offend you; ANT 2.05. 99
to do antonius good, | but 'twould offend him; 3.01. 26
judgment (if i offend /not to say it is mended) CYM 1.04. 46 P
spirits of region low, | offend our hearing; 5.04. 94
come, other sorts offend as well as we. PER 4.02. 36 P
we offend worse. 4.02. 37 P
why, i cannot name/'t but i shall offend. 4.06. 69 P
look what you do offend you cry upon, | that is STM II.C 61
by unions married, do offend thine ear, | they SON 8. 6
OFFENDED 48 FR 0.0054 REL FR 38 V 10 P
of villainous smell that ever offended nostril. WIV 3.05. 93 P
alas, | he hath but as offended in a dream! MM 2.02. 4
marry, sir, he hath offended the law; 3.02. 15 P
if he had so offended, | he would have weigh'd 5.01.110
dispers'd those vapors that offended us, | and ERR 1.01. 89
who have you offended, masters, that you are ADO 5.01.226 P
good sir, be not offended, | she is an heir of LLL 2.01.204
if we shadows have offended, | think but this, MND 5.01.423
shame | as to offend, himself being offended; MV 4.01. 58
how hast thou offended? | where is lucentio? SHR 5.01.113
be not offended, for it hurts not him | that he AWW 1.03.196
ambitious love hath so in me offended | that 3.04. 5
be not offended, dear cesario. TN 4.01. 50
by that | i do perceive it hath offended you. 5.01.213
your flesh and blood has not offended the king, WT 4.04.694 P
what you have done hath not offended me; 1H6 2.03. 76
be not offended, nature's miracle, | thou art 5.03. 54
wherein have i offended most? 2H6 4.07. 97
yea, brother richard, are you offended too? 3H6 4.01. 19
wherein, my friends, have i offended you? R3 1.04.177
offended us you have not, but the king. 1.04.178
to cut off those that have offended him. 1.04.219
marry, that with no man here he is offended; 3.04. 56
in what have i offended you? H8 2.04. 19
andromache, i am offended with you, | upon the TRO 5.03. 77
hadst thou in person ne'er offended me, | even TIT 2.03.161
all have not offended; TIM 5.04. 35
wrath must fall | with those that have offended; 5.04. 42
if any, speak, for him have i offended. JC 3.02. 30 P
if any, speak, for him have i offended. 3.02. 32 P
if any, speak, for him have i offended. 3.02. 34 P
then none have i offended. 3.02. 36 P
this tongue had not offended so to–day, | if 5.01. 46
be not offended; MAC 4.03. 37
it is offended. HAM 1.01. 50
hamlet, thou hast thy father much offended. 3.04. 9
mother, you have my father much offended. 3.04. 10
yourself wherein you may have offended him; LR 1.02.160 P
how have i offended? 2.04.195
saints in your injuries, devils being offended, OTH 2.01.111
i | should say myself offended, and with you ANT 2.02. 32
make me not offended | in your distrust. 3.02. 33
i have offended reputation, | a most unnoble 3.11. 49
so soon as i can win th' offended king, | i will CYM 1.01. 75
how have i offended, | wherein my death might PER 4.01. 79
i cannot be offended with my trade. 4.06. 70 P
your cousin | has ten times more offended, for i TNK 3.06.181
do burn themselves for having so offended." VEN 810
/OFFENDENDO 1 FR 0.0001 REL FR 0 V 1 P
it must be /se /offendendo, it cannot be else. HAM 5.01. 9 P
OFFENDER 13 FR 0.0014 REL FR 11 V 2 P
know how easy it is to be such an offender. WIV 2.02.189 P
for the fault's love is th' offender friended. MM 4.02.113
this plaintiff here, the offender, did call me ADO 5.01.305 P
let him approach | a stranger, no offender; AWW 5.03. 26
whereon (as an offender to your father) | i gave 2H4 5.02. 81
teach, | but prove a chief offender in the same? 1H6 3.01.130
at, | and the offender granted scope of speech, 2H6 3.01.176
the cause betwixt her and this great offender. H8 5.02.156
revenge, which makes the foul offender quake. TIT 5.02. 40
comes too short | which can pursue th' offender. LR 2.01. 89
bind the offender, | and take him from our CYM 5.05.300
i would destroy th' offender, coz, i would, TNK 5.01. 23
king, | as he is clement if th' offender mourn, STM II.C 123
OFFENDER'S 4 FR 0.0004 REL FR 4 V 0 P
and the offender's life lies in the mercy | of MV 4.01.355
for i should melt at an offender's tears, | and 2H6 3.01.126
'tis so, th' offender's scourge is weigh'd, HAM 4.03. 6
th' offender's sorrow lends but weak relief | to SON 34.11
OFFENDERS' 1 FR 0.0001 REL FR 1 V 0 P
will rain hot vengeance on offenders' heads. R2 1.02. 8
OFFENDERS 12 FR 0.0013 REL FR 9 V 3 P
but which are the offenders that are to be ADO 4.02. 7 P
old justice that examines all such offenders, AYL 4.01.200 P
and on this stage | (where we offenders now) WT 5.01. 59
other offenders we will pause upon. 1H4 5.05. 15
hath wasted all his rods | on late offenders, 2H4 4.01.214
we would have all such offenders so cut off; H5 3.06.107 P
in execution | upon offenders hath exceeded law, 2H6 1.03.133
and call these foul offenders to their answers, 2.01.199
you did devise | strange tortures for offenders, 3.01.122
this princely presence | to doom th' offenders, R3 3.04. 65
with foul offenders thou perforce must bear, LUC 612
loving offenders, thus i will excuse ye: SON 42. 5
OFFENDETH 1 FR 0.0001 REL FR 1 V 0 P
a stone is silent, and offendeth not, | and TIT 3.01. 46
OFFENDING 7 FR 0.0008 REL FR 6 V 1 P
you chide at him, offending twice as much. LLL 4.03.130
to be your prisoner should import offending, WT 1.02. 57
ransacking the church, | offending charity. JN 3.04.173
came | and whipt th' offending adam out of him, H5 1.01. 29
honor, | i am the most offending soul alive. 4.03. 29
the very head and front of my offending | hath OTH 1.03. 80
th' heart, and there th' offending part burns, TNK 4.03. 44 P
OFFENDRESS 1 FR 0.0001 REL FR 0 V 1 P
limit, as a desperate offendress against nature. AWW 1.01.140 P
OFFENDS 8 FR 0.0009 REL FR 6 V 2 P
your silence most offends me, and to be merry ADO 2.01.331 P
the tongue offends not that reports his death, 2H4 1.01. 97
no, my good lords, it is not that offends, | it 1H6 3.01. 35
what offends you, lady? TRO 3.02.144
it offends me to the soul to hear a robustious HAM 3.02. 8 P
spare speech, which something now offends me — OTH 2.03.199
i have a salt and sorry rheum offends me; 3.04. 51
(your most unworthy creature) but offends you, TNK 2.05. 40
OFFEND'ST 1 FR 0.0001 REL FR 1 V 0 P
thou but offend'st thy lungs to speak so loud. MV 4.01.140
OFFENSE 119 FR 0.0134 REL FR 95 V 24 P
for what offense? TGV 4.01. 25
sorrow | be a sufficient ransom for offense, | i 5.04. 75
be not as extreme in submission as in offense; WIV 4.04. 11
th' offense is holy that she hath committed, 5.05.225
but what's his offense? MM 1.02. 89 P
make us pay down for our offense by weight | the 1.02.121
what's thy offense, claudio? 1.02.134 P
you may not so extenuate his offense | for i 2.01. 27
who is it that hath died for this offense? 2.02. 88
which a dismiss'd offense would after gall, 2.02.102
more fit to do another such offense | than die 2.03. 14
their untaught love | must needs appear offense. 2.04. 30
and his offense is so, as it appears, 2.04. 85
he would give't thee, from this rank offense, 3.01. 99
what offense hath this man made you, sir? 3.02. 13 P
hence hath offense his quick celerity, | when it 4.02.110
you will think you have made no offense, if the 4.02.185 P
for claudio's, | th' offense pardons itself. 5.01.534
was wrought by nature, not by vile offense, ERR 1.01. 34
this town, | beheaded publicly for his offense. 5.01.127
and it is an offense to stay a man against his ADO 3.03. 81 P
in language | without offense to utter them. 4.01. 98
what offense, sweet beatrice? 4.01.282 P
hearken after their offense, my lord. 5.01.212 P
officers, what offense have these men done? 5.01.213 P
thirdly, i ask thee what's their offense; 5.01.221 P
what's your offense? 5.01.229 P
that is the way to make an offense gracious, LLL 5.01.140 P
worm nor snail, do no offense. MND 2.02. 23
every offense is not a hate at first. MV 4.01. 68
and faster than his tongue | did make offense, AYL 3.05.117
and if i be, sir, is it any offense? SHR 1.02.229
methink'st thou art a general offense, and every AWW 2.03.254 P
mother, and his lady | offense of mighty note; 5.03. 14
the nature of his great offense is dead, | and 5.03. 23
to the great sender turns a sour offense, 5.03. 59
th' offense is not of such a bloody nature, TN 3.03. 30
clear from any image of offense done to any man. 3.04.228 P
to know of the knight what my offense to him is. 3.04.255 P
if this young gentleman | have done offense, i 3.04.313
i am now so far in offense with my niece that i 4.02. 69 P
charge | that art the issue of my dear offense, JN 1.01.257
tide | to do offense and scathe in christendom. 2.01. 75
save in aspect, hath all offense seal'd up; 2.01.250
now that their souls are topful of offense. 3.04.180
i'll so offend, to make offense a skill, 1H4 1.02.216
for what offense have i this fortnight been | a 2.03. 38
a time | to punish this offense in other faults. 5.02. 7
that argues but the shame of your offense: 2H4 4.01.158
some few hours | were thine without offense, and 4.05.102
you been as i took you for, i made no offense; H5 4.08. 55 P
hath the late overthrow wrought this offense? 1H6 1.02. 49
and what offense it is to flout his friends. 4.01. 75
and therefore may be broke without offense. 5.05. 35
and you, good uncle, banish all offense. 5.05. 96
my days, | and when i give occasion of offense, 3H6 1.03. 44
that they'll take no offense at our abuse. 4.01. 13
suppose they take offense without a cause; 4.01. 14
what is my offense? R3 1.04.182
for what offense? 2.04. 45
i do suspect i have done some offense | that 3.07.111
and if there be | no great offense belongs to't, H8 5.01. 12
and to make a sweet lady sad is a sour offense. TRO 3.01. 73 P
to make him worthy whose offense subdues him, COR 1.01.175
leave unburnt | and still to nose th' offense. 5.01. 28
or pities him, | for the offense he dies. TIT 5.03.182
and for that offense | immediately we do exile ROM 3.01.186
than their offense can weigh down by the dram; TIM 5.01.151
and that which would appear offense in us, | his JC 1.03.158
you have some sick offense within your mind, 2.01.268
that every nice offense should bear his comment. 4.03. 8
doing himself offense, whilst we, lying still, 4.03.201
there's no offense, my lord. HAM 1.05.135
but there is, horatio, | and much offense too. 1.05.137
is there no offense in't? 3.02.233 P
jest, poison in jest — no offense i' th' world. 3.02.235 P
o, my offense is rank, it smells to heaven, | it 3.03. 36
mercy | but to confront the visage of offense? 3.03. 47
may one be pardon'd and retain th' offense? 3.03. 56
scourge is weigh'd, | but never the offense. 4.03. 7
and where th' offense is, let the great axe fall 4.05.219
sure her offense | must be of such unnatural LR 1.01.218
his offense, honesty! 1.02.117 P
might in their working do you that offense, 1.04.212
what was th' offense you gave him? 2.02.114
made you no more offense but what you speak of? 2.04. 61
all's not offense that indiscretion finds | and 2.04.196
he'll be as full of quarrel and offense | as my OTH 2.03. 50
for mine own part — no offense to the general, 2.03.106 P
and he that is approv'd in this offense, 2.03.211
than it should do offense to michael cassio; 2.03.222
love no friend, sith love breeds such offense. 3.03.380
if my offense be of such mortal kind | that nor 3.04.115
the business of the state does him offense, 4.02.166
take no offense that i would not offend you; ANT 2.05. 99
and in his offense | should my performance 3.01. 26
break her wheel, | provok'd by my offense. 4.15. 45
and, to bar your offense herein too, i durst CYM 1.04.112 P
but i beseech your grace, without offense | (my 1.05. 6
every companion that you give offense to. 2.01. 27 P
is fit i should commit offense to my inferiors. 2.01. 29 P
with hunger, | i am fall'n in this offense. 3.06. 63
your pleasure was my /mere offense, my 5.05.334
subjects punish'd that ne'er thought offense: PER 1.02. 28
when all, for mine, if i may call offense, 1.02. 92
he may my proffer take for an offense, | since 2.03. 68
in store, | due to this heinous capital offense, 2.04. 5
never did thought of mine levy offense; 2.05. 52
who takes offense | at that would make me glad? 2.05. 71
their ashes, nor to take th' offense | of mortal TNK 1.01. 44
carry your tail without offense | or scandal to 3.05. 34
might | omit a ward, or forfeit an offense, 5.03. 63
he scowls and hates himself for his offense, LUC 738
till life to death acquit my forc'd offense. 1071
for one's offense why should so many fall, | to 1483
"what is the quality of my offense, | being 1702
and so to publish tarquin's foul offense; 1852
thus can my love excuse the slow offense | of my SON 51. 1
fault, | and i will comment upon that offense; 89. 2
OFFENSEFUL 1 FR 0.0001 REL FR 1 V 0 P
so then it seems your most offenseful act | was MM 2.03. 26
OFFENSELESS 1 FR 0.0001 REL FR 0 V 1 P
one would beat his offenseless dog to affright OTH 2.03.275 P
OFFENSE'S 2 FR 0.0002 REL FR 2 V 0 P
offense's gilded hand may /shove by justice, HAM 3.03. 58
to him that bears the strong offense's /cross. SON 34.12
/OFFENSES 3 FR 0.0003 REL FR 3 V 0 P
/if /thy /offenses /were /upon /record, | /would R2 4.01.230
/our /griefs /heavier /than /our /offenses. 2H4 4.01. 69
/quickly /down /to /tame /these /vild /offenses, LR 4.02. 47
OFFENSES 24 FR 0.0027 REL FR 16 V 8 P
he hath some offenses in him that thou wouldst MM 2.01.185 P
shalt fast for thy offenses ere thou be pardoned LLL 1.02.146 P
with so many giddy offenses as he hath generally AYL 3.02.349 P
but that, my offenses being many, i would repent AWW 4.03.242 P
th' offenses we have made you do we'll answer, WT 1.02. 83
be smil'd at, their offenses being so capital? 4.04.793 P
i could | quit all offenses with as clear excuse 1H4 3.02. 19
all his offenses live upon my head | and on his 5.02. 20
and true repentance | of all your dear offenses! H5 2.02.181
all offenses, my lord, come from the heart. 4.08. 46 P
devise strange deaths for small offenses done? 2H6 3.01. 59
there cannot be those numberless offenses H8 2.01. 84
a gracious king that pardons all offenses 2.02. 67
they are too thin and base to hide offenses. 5.02.160
there is between my will and all offenses | a TRO 5.02. 53
his last offenses to us | shall have judicious COR 5.06.125
nor his offenses enforc'd, for which he suffer'd JC 3.02. 40 P
with more offenses at my beck than i have HAM 3.01.124 P
pays dear for my offenses. CYM 1.01.106
sir, your offenses | being no more than his. TNK 3.06.182
when they in thee the like offenses prove. LUC 613
how | to cloak offenses with a cunning brow. 749
dear, | made old offenses of affections new; SON 110. 4
"'all my offenses that abroad you see | are LC 183
OFFENSIVE 2 FR 0.0002 REL FR 2 V 0 P
like an offensive wife | that hath enrag'd him 2H4 4.01.208
what like, offensive. LR 4.02. 11
/OFFER 2 FR 0.0002 REL FR 2 V 0 P
/which /tired /majesty /did /make /thee /offer: R2 4.01.178
/assurance, /offer | /this /office /to /you. LR 3.01. 41

OFFER 95 FR 0.0107 REL FR 74 V 21 P
you, sir, | do not omit the heavy offer of it. TMP 2.01.194
that dare not offer | what i desire to give; 3.01. 77
i take your offer, and will live with you, TGV 4.01. 68
what, didst thou offer her this from me? 4.04. 54 P
i do not think the knight would offer it; WIV 2.01.174 P
if by strong hand you offer to break in | now in ERR 3.01. 98
some offer me commodities to buy. 4.03. 6
offer them instances, which shall bear no less ADO 2.02. 41 P
i do embrace your offer, and dispose | for 5.01.294
change not your offer made in heat of blood; LLL 5.02.800
if he will offer to say what methought i had. MND 4.01.210 P
if he should offer to choose, and choose the MV 1.02. 92 P
this is kind i offer. 1.03.142
to offer to counsel me to stay with the jew. 2.02. 29 P
table, which doth offer to swear upon a book, i 2.02.159 P
if she were by to hear you make the offer. 4.01.289
'tis well you offer it behind her back, | the 4.01.293
i take this offer then; 4.01.318
together, and to offer to get your living by the AYL 3.02. 79 P
cry the man mercy, love him, take his offer; 3.05. 61
youth and kind | will the faithful offer take 4.03. 60
will, for my kind offer, when i make curtsy, bid ep 22 P
players | that offer service to your lordship. SHR in.1. 78
and offer me disguis'd in sober robes | to old 1.02.132
i must confess your offer is the best, | and let 2.01.386
sir, what are you that offer to beat my servant? 5.01. 63 P
to offer war where they should kneel for peace, 5.02.162
we'll take your offer kindly. AWW 3.05.101
fear, offer to betray you and deliver all the 3.06. 30 P
madam, i am most apt t' embrace your offer. TN 5.01.320
acquaint the queen of your most noble offer, WT 2.02. 46
offer me no money, i pray you, that kills my 4.03. 82 P
beard, | you offer him, if this be so, a wrong 4.04.405
to offer to have his daughter come into grace! 4.04.777 P
but if you fondly pass our proffer'd offer, JN 2.01.258
that greatness should so grossly offer it. 4.02. 94
this gentle offer of the perilous time. 4.03. 13
but are gone | to offer service to your enemy; 5.01. 34
to offer service to the duke of herford, | and R2 2.03. 32
an offer, uncle, that we will accept, | but we 2.03.162
heaven's offer we refuse, | the proffered means 3.02. 31
refuse | the offer of an hundred thousand crowns 4.01. 16
war | all hot and bleeding will we offer them. 1H4 4.01.115
and, will they take the offer of our grace, 5.01.106
we offer fair, take it advisedly. 5.01.114
the liberal and kind offer of the king. 5.02. 2
know, | in any case, the offer of the king. 5.02. 25
in my mouth as offer to stop it with security. 2H4 1.02. 42 P
but he hath forc'd us to compel this offer, 4.01.145
this offer comes from mercy, not from fear. 4.01.148
say you not then our offer is compell'd. 4.01.156
that hath enrag'd him on to offer strokes, | as 4.01.209
to a fangless lion, | may offer, but not hold. 4.01.217
for i have made an offer to his majesty, | upon H5 1.01. 75
how did this offer seem receiv'd, my lord? 1.01. 82
offer nothing here. 2.01. 39 P
back, | tells harry that the king doth offer him 3.pr. 29
the offer likes not; 3.pr. 32
fear, | and for achievement offer us his ransom. 3.05. 60
making god so free an offer, he let him outlive 4.01.184 P
let us on heaps go offer up our lives. 4.05. 18
in stead of gold, we'll offer up our arms, 1H6 1.01. 46
here, winchester, i offer thee my hand. 3.01.126
if you forsake the offer of their love. 4.02. 14
come offer at my shrine, and i will help thee." 2H6 2.01. 90
and when the king comes, offer him no violence, 3H6 1.01. 33
you turn the good we offer into envy. H8 3.01.113
if you omit | the offer of this time, i cannot 3.02. 4
far | than my weak–hearted enemies dare offer. 3.02.390
is a fool to offer to command achilles, achilles TRO 2.03. 62 P
which, as i take it, is a gentleman–like offer. ROM 2.04.178 P
to woe, | which you, mistaking, offer up to joy. 3.02.104
we are hither come to offer you our service. TIM 5.01. 72
i saw mark antony offer him a crown — yet 'twas JC 1.02.237 P
me, and wisdom | to offer up a weak, poor, MAC 4.03. 16
and here from gracious england have i offer | of 4.03. 43
majestical, | to offer it the show of violence, HAM 1.01.144
that shall not be my offer, not thy asking? 1.02. 46
and hither are they coming to offer you service. 2.02.318 P
good my lord, take his offer, go into th' house. LR 3.04.156
with thine and all that offer to defend him, 3.06. 94
you have made me offer | of sicily, sardinia; ANT 2.06. 34
that's our offer. 2.06. 39
you have heard me prepar'd | to take this offer; 2.06. 41
i will embrace | your offer. PER 3.03. 38
and will offer | night–oblations to thee. 5.03. 69
who then shall offer | to mars's so scorn'd TNK 1.02. 19
i'll offer to her | what i shall be advis'd she 1.03. 15
i demand no more than your own offer, and i will 2.01. 10 P
i do embrace you and your offer. 3.01. 93
for | your offer do't i only, sir; 3.01. 94
at whose great feet i offer up my penner. 3.05.124
take her offer. 5.02.110
offer pure incense to so pure a shrine: LUC 194
but smile and jest at every gentle offer. PP 4.12
/OFFER'D 2 FR 0.0002 REL FR 2 V 0 P
i'll entertain the /offer'd fallacy. ERR 2.02.186
/long /ere /this /we /offer'd /to /the /king, 2H4 4.01. 75
OFFER'D 25 FR 0.0028 REL FR 15 V 10 P
when every grief is entertain'd that's offer'd, TMP 2.01. 16
shalt not live to brag what we have offer'd. TGV 4.01. 67
and then i offer'd her mine own, who is a dog as 4.04. 57 P
that would refuse so fair an offer'd chain. ERR 3.02.181
offer'd by a child to an old man: LLL 5.01. 62 P
the duke hath offer'd him letters of AWW 4.03. 78 P
fairly offer'd. WT 4.04.378
which somerset hath offer'd to my house, | i 1H6 2.05.125
but that time offer'd sorrow, | this, general H8 4.01. 6
him) once more offer'd | the first conditions, COR 5.03. 13
what thou want'st by free and offer'd light. TIM 5.01. 45
why, there was a crown offer'd him; JC 1.02.221 P
and being offer'd him, he put it by with the 1.02.222 P
was the crown offer'd him thrice? 1.02.228
who offer'd him the crown? 1.02.232
then he offer'd it to him again; 1.02.240 P
and then he offer'd it the third time; 1.02.243 P
his doublet, and offer'd them his throat to cut. 1.02.265 P
time | i do receive your offer'd love like love, HAM 5.02.251
i crave no more than hath your highness offer'd, LR 1.01.194
not, time and place will be fruitfully offer'd. 4.06.265 P
seeks, and will not take when once 'tis offer'd, ANT 2.07. 83
it, 'twere a paper lost | as offer'd mercy is. CYM 1.03. 4
he offer'd to cut a caper at the proclamation, PER 4.02.107 P
this is an offer'd opportunity | i durst not TNK 2.03. 74
OFFERED 3 FR 0.0003 REL FR 3 V 0 P
and she hath offered to the doom | (which, TGV 3.01.224
and yield to mercy whilst 'tis offered you, | or 2H6 4.08. 12
i offered to awaken his regard | for 's private COR 5.01. 23
OFFERERS 1 FR 0.0001 REL FR 1 V 0 P
nay, let's be offerers all. TNK 5.04. 32
OFFERING 3 FR 0.0003 REL FR 3 V 0 P
offering their own lives in their young's 3H6 2.02. 32
offering the fortunes of his former days, | the TIM 5.01.124
plucking the entrails of an offering forth, JC 2.02. 39
OFFERINGS 1 FR 0.0001 REL FR 0 V 1 P
going to canterbury with rich offerings, and 1H4 1.02.126 P
OFFERS 12 FR 0.0013 REL FR 12 V 0 P
therefore i do beseech you | make no moe offers, MV 4.01. 81
i see, sir, you are liberal in offers. 4.01.438
and brings from him such offers of our peace JN 5.07. 84
i come with gracious offers from the king, | if 1H4 4.03. 30
and wouldst thou turn our offers contrary? 5.05. 4
offers, as i do, in a sign of peace, | his H8 3.01. 66
sacrifice, | he offers in another's enterprise, TRO 1.02.283
how you take | the offers we have sent you. ANT 2.06. 31
but these offers, | which serve not for his 3.07. 32
we scorn her most when most she offers blows. 3.11. 74
add more, | from thine invention, offers. 3.12. 29
so offers he to give what she did crave, | but VEN 88
OFFER'ST 2 FR 0.0002 REL FR 2 V 0 P
thou offer'st fairly to thy brothers' wedding: AYL 5.04.167
luxurious mountain goat, | offer'st me brass? H5 4.04. 20
OFFERT 1 FR 0.0001 REL FR 0 V 1 P
of knavery, mark you now, as can be offert; H5 4.07. 3 P
OFFIC'D 3 FR 0.0003 REL FR 3 V 0 P
did fan the house | and angels offic'd all. AWW 3.02.126
so stands this squire | offic'd with me. WT 1.02.172
my speculative and offic'd /instruments, | that OTH 1.03.270
/OFFICE 2 FR 0.0002 REL FR 2 V 0 P
/to /do /that /office /of /thine /own /good R2 4.01.177
/assurance, /offer | /this /office /to /you. LR 3.01. 42
OFFICE 137 FR 0.0154 REL FR 109 V 28 P
they are louder than the weather, or our office. TMP 1.01. 37 P
having both the key | of officer and office, set 1.02. 84
now, trust me, 'tis an office of great worth, TGV 1.02. 44
'tis an ill office for a gentleman, | especially 3.02. 40
therefore the office is indifferent, | being 3.02. 44
i would i could do a good office between you. WIV 1.01.100 P
we are come to you to do a good office, master 3.01. 49 P
mistress ford, in the simple office of love, but 4.02. 4 P
destiny, | attend your office and your quality. 5.05. 40
father, | i have on angelo impos'd the office, MM 1.03. 40
thought, by the readiness in the office, you had 2.01.261 P
do you your office, or give up your place, | and 2.02. 13
executioner, who in his office lacks a helper. 4.02. 9 P
thinking me remiss in mine office, awakens me 4.02.116 P
thus fail not to do your office, as you will 4.02.126 P
or impudence, | that yet can do thee office? 5.01.364
do you the office, friar, which consummate, 5.01.378
for which i do discharge you of your office; 5.01.461
thou hast stol'n both mine office and my name: ERR 3.01. 44
that you have quite forgot | a husband's office? 3.02. 2
nurse, | diet his sickness, for it is my office, 5.01. 99
things | save in the office and affairs of love; ADO 2.01.176
i will do any modest office, my lord, to help my 2.01.375 P
this is thy office; 3.01. 12
you may suspect him, by virtue of your office, 3.03. 51 P
truly, by your office, you may, but i think they 3.03. 56 P
it is a man's office, but not yours. 4.01.266 P
no, 'tis all men's office to speak patience | to 5.01. 27
you know your office, brother: 5.04. 14
for virtue's office never breaks men's troth. LLL 5.02.350
why, 'tis an office of discovery, love, | and i MV 2.06. 43
thou goest from fortune's office to nature's. AYL 1.02. 40 P
him, | and each one to his office when he wakes. SHR in.1. 73
on thee, | each in his office ready at thy beck. in.2. 34
cold comfort, for being slow in thy hot office? 4.01. 32 P
curtis, in every office but thine, and therefore 4.01. 35 P
that's my office. 5.02. 36
i will no more enforce mine office on you, AWW 2.01.126
the ministration and required office | on my 2.05. 60
which could not be her office to say is come, 4.03. 58 P
time was, i did him a desired office, | dear 4.04. 5
me at once both the office of god and the devil? 5.02. 49 P
beguiles the truer office of mine eyes? 5.03.305
speak your office. TN 1.05.207 P
i beseech you do me this courteous office, as to 3.04.254 P
this is the man, do thy office. 3.04.325 P
the office | becomes a woman best. WT 2.02. 29
you ha' done me a charitable office. 4.03. 76 P
who | do their best office, if they can but stay 4.04.571
give me the office | to choose you a queen. 5.01. 77
should use to do me wrong | deny their office; JN 4.01.118
whose office is this day | to feast upon whole 5.02.177
behind | to do the office for thee of revenge, 5.07. 71
when the tongue's office should be prodigal | to R2 1.03.256
sea, | which serves it in the office of a wall, 2.01. 47
for little office | will the hateful commons 2.02.137
broken his staff of office, and dispers'd | the 2.03. 27
the bloody office of his timeless end. 4.01. 5
for you my staff of office did i break | in 1H4 5.01. 34
wait on us, | and they shall do their office. 5.01.112
my office is | to noise abroad that harry 2H4 in 28
of unwelcome news | hath but a losing office, 1.01.101
england shall give him office, honor, might; 4.05.129
a foutre for thine office! 5.03.115
choose what office thou wilt in the land, 'tis 5.03.123 P
his sheets, and do the office of a warming–pan. H5 2.01. 84 P
and shall forget the office of our hand | sooner 2.02. 33
so much my office. 3.06.136 P
thou dost thy office fairly. 3.06.139
since then my office hath so far prevail'd, 5.02. 29
that never may ill office, or fell jealousy, 5.02.363
but long i will not be jack out of office. 1H6 1.01.175
and know the office that belongs to such. 3.01. 55
it is my office, and, madam, pardon me. 2H6 2.04.102
ay, ay, farewell, thy office is discharg'd. 2.04.103
but left that hateful office unto thee. 3.02. 93
that is my office, for my father's sake. 3H6 1.04.109
that taught his son the office of a fowl! 5.06. 19
the sceptred office of your ancestors, | your R3 3.07.119
and take thy office from thee on my peril. 4.01. 25
the office did | distinctly his full function. H8 1.01. 44
your office, sergeant; execute it. 1.01.198
your honor nor | the dignity of your office, is 1.02. 16
and lost your office | on the complaint o' th' 1.02.172
as't please | yourself pronounce their office. 2.04.115
since i had my office, | i have kept you next my 3.02.156
all the progress | both of my life and office, i 5.02. 68
office, and custom, in all line of order; TRO 1.03. 88
which is that god in office, guiding men? 1.03.231
general, thou shouldst have my office | ere that 5.06. 4
then our office may, | during his power, go COR 2.01.222
let the high office and the honor go | to one 2.03.122
to take | from rome all season'd office, and to 3.03. 64
a jack guardant cannot office me from my son 5.02. 62 P
turn from their office to black funeral: ROM 4.05. 85
since you did leave it for my office, sir. 5.01. 23
lord, which bears that office to signify their TIM 1.02.120 P
would i were gently put out of office | before i 1.02.201
always a villain's office, or a fool's. 4.03.237
that's not an office for a friend, my lord. JC 5.05. 29
hath been | so clear in his great office, that MAC 1.07. 18
to show an unfelt sorrow is an office | which 2.03.136
thyself and office deftly show! 4.01. 68
the insolence of office, and the spurns | that HAM 3.01. 72
have shown your father | a child–like office. LR 2.01.106
infirmity doth still neglect all office 2.04.106
a dog's obey'd in office. 4.06.159 P
who has the office? 5.03.249
the trust, the office i do hold of you, | not OTH 1.03.118
that 'twixt my sheets | /h'as done my office. 1.03.388
if partially affin'd, or /leagu'd in office, 2.03.218
take mine office. 3.03.375
i do not like the office; 3.03.410
love | whom i, with all the office of my heart, 3.04.113
that have the office opposite to saint peter, 4.02. 91
cogging, cozening slave, to get some office, 4.02.132
now turn | the office and devotion of their view ANT 1.01. 5
hands, | that yarely frame the office. 2.02.211
the world and my great office will sometimes 2.03. 1
be't so, declare thine office. 3.12. 10
i must attend mine office, | or would have 4.06. 26
but | it is an office of the gods to venge it, CYM 1.06. 92
and bows you | to a morning's holy office. 3.03. 4
my lords, you are appointed for that office; 3.05. 10
i would wish no better office than to be beadle. PER 2.01. 93 P
you must guess | i have an office there. TNK 3.01.110
and i know your office | unjustly is achiev'd. 3.01.111
this is my last | of vestal office; 5.01.150
that remain with you could wish their office 5.03. 35
for to the king god hath his office lent | of STM II.C 98
the more thou hast | either of honor, office, III 15
where they resign their office and their light VEN 1039
thy princely office how canst thou fulfill, LUC 628
time's office is to fine the hate of foes, | to 936
for who so base would such an office have | as 1000
not daring trust the office of mine eyes. PP 14.16
then do thy office, muse; SON 101.13
OFFICE–BADGE 1 FR 0.0001 REL FR 1 V 0 P
this staff, mine office–badge in court, | was 2H6 1.02. 25
OFFICER 50 FR 0.0056 REL FR 33 V 17 P
having both the key | of officer and office, set TMP 1.02. 84
worth, | and you an officer fit for the place. TGV 1.02. 45
come, officer, away! MM 1.02.193
this comes off well. here's a wise officer. 2.01. 57 P
your worship think me the poor duke's officer. 2.01.177 P
truly, officer, because he hath some offenses in 2.01.185 P
petty officer | would use his heaven for thunder 2.02.112
take him to prison, officer. 3.02. 31
there he must stay until the officer | arise to 4.02. 90
an officer! 5.01.120
or i'll attach you by this officer. ERR 4.01. 6
if not, i'll leave him to the officer. 4.01. 61
well, officer, arrest him at my suit. 4.01. 69
sum for me | or i attach you by this officer. 4.01. 73
here is thy fee, arrest him, officer. 4.01. 76
on, officer, to prison till it come. 4.01.108
what, thou mean'st an officer? 4.03. 29 P
what wilt thou do, thou peevish officer? 4.04.114
the which | he did arrest me with an officer. 5.01.230
then fairly i bespoke the officer | to go in 5.01.233
let him write down the prince's officer coxcomb. ADO 4.02. 71 P
and, which is more, an officer, and, which is 4.02. 80 P
by thy sweet grace's officer, anthony dull, a LLL 1.01.267 P
go, tubal, fee me an officer; MV 3.01.126 P
and every officer his wedding garment on? SHR 4.01. 48 P
call forth an officer. 5.01. 91 P
stay, officer, he shall not go to prison. 5.01. 95 P
spoke like an officer. ha' to thee, lad! 5.02. 37
a filthy officer he is in those suggestions for AWW 3.05. 17 P
him for no other but a poor officer of mine, and 4.03.199 P
had the honor to be the officer at a place there 4.03.269 P
each takes his fellow for an officer. 1H4 2.02.107
discuss unto me, art thou officer, | or art thou H5 4.01. 37
come, officer, as loud as e'er thou canst, | cry 1H6 1.03. 72
the thief doth fear each bush an officer. 3H6 5.06. 12
thus | given hydra here to choose an officer, COR 3.01. 93
menenius, | be you then as the people's officer. 3.01.328
caius martius was | a worthy officer i' th' war, 4.06. 30
obeys his points | as if he were his officer. 4.06.126
i am an officer of state, and come | to speak 5.02. 3
says he, | "i have already chose my officer." OTH 1.01. 17
othello, leave some officer behind, | and he 1.03.280
your officer, iago, can inform you — | while i 2.03.198
love thee, | but never more be officer of mine. 2.03.249
so drunken, and so indiscreet an officer. 2.03.279 P
with mine officer! 4.01.202 P
ever won | more in their officer than person. ANT 3.01. 17
and threats the throat of that his officer 3.05. 18
i think he would change places with his officer; CYM 5.04.175 P
the gods can have no mortal officer | more like PER 5.03. 62
OFFICERS 30 FR 0.0034 REL FR 21 V 9 P

woman, with all the officers in windsor, to WIV 3.03.107 P
to say so, but we are the poor duke's officers; ADO 3.05. 20 P
officers, what offense have these men done? 5.01.213 P
for such a sum from special officers | of LLL 2.01.161
and let my officers of such a nature | make an AYL 3.01. 16
calling my officers about me, in my branch'd TN 2.05. 47 P
o good sir toby, hold! here come the officers. 3.04.319 P
except the marshal and such officers | appointed R2 1.03. 44
wilt thou kill god's officers and the king's? 2H4 2.01. 51 P
but for these foolish officers, i beseech you i 2.01.108 P
i do desire deliverance from these officers, 2.01.127 P
pluck down my officers, break my decrees, | for 4.05.117
they have a king, and officers of sorts, | where H5 1.02.190
then broke i from the officers that led me, 1H6 1.04. 44
town, | placing therein some expert officers, 3.02.127
breathe out invectives 'gainst the officers. 3H6 1.04. 43
the king's, | to go with us unto the officers. 3.01. 98
come lead me, officers, to the block of shame; R3 5.01. 28
call thither all the officers a' th' town, COR 1.05. 27
allow their officers, and are content | to 3.03. 45
beating your officers, cursing yourselves, 3.03. 78
in his own change, or by ill officers, | hath JC 4.02. 7
what not put upon | his spungy officers, who MAC 1.07. 71
but such officers do the king best service in HAM 4.02. 16 P
in a riotous head, | o'erbears your officers. 4.05.103
some officers take them away. LR 5.03. 1
and raise some special officers of /night. OTH 1.01.182
let our officers | have notice what we purpose. ANT 1.02.176
his servants than | thyself domestic officers) CYM 3.01. 64
without my leave and officers of arms? TNK 3.06.135
OFFICERS–AT–ARMS 1 FR 0.0001 REL FR 1 V 0 P
command our officers–at–arms | be ready to R2 1.01.204
/OFFICES 1 FR 0.0001 REL FR 1 V 0 P
/draw /anew /the /model | /in /fewer /offices, 2H4 1.03. 47
OFFICES 32 FR 0.0036 REL FR 28 V 4 P
wood, and serves in offices | that profit us. TMP 1.02.312
scarce think | their eyes do offices of truth, 5.01.156
above their functions and their offices. LLL 4.03.329
then to your offices, and let me rest. MND 2.02. 8
and offices | were not deriv'd corruptly, and MV 2.09. 41
to offend and judge are distinct offices, | and 2.09. 61
never train'd | to offices of tender courtesy. 4.01. 33
aside, have done | like offices of pity. WT 2.03.189
stir | afresh within me, and these thy offices, 5.01.149
walls, | unpeopled offices, untrodden stones? R2 1.02. 69
do your offices, do your offices, master fang 2H4 2.01. 40 P
do your offices, do your offices, master fang 2.01. 41 P
master snare, do me, do me, do me your offices. 2.01. 42 P
and noble offices thou mayst effect | of 4.04. 24
thy sale of offices and towns in france, | if 2H6 1.03.135
and both are ready in their offices | at any R3 3.05. 10
should | do no more offices of life to't than H8 2.04.191
sir, | for holy offices i have a time; 3.02.144
of those that claim their offices this day | by 4.01. 15
and, through the cranks and offices of man, COR 1.01.137
what are your offices? 3.01. 35
when all our offices have been oppress'd | with TIM 2.02.158
to sell and mart your offices for gold | to JC 4.03. 11
and | sent forth great largess to your offices. MAC 2.01. 14
since he delivers | our offices, and what we 3.03. 3
thou better know'st | the offices of nature, LR 2.04.178
all offices are open, and there is full liberty OTH 2.02. 8 P
short time | all offices of nature should again CYM 5.05.257
daughter, | but bent all offices to honor her. PER 2.05. 48
all offices are done | save what i fail in. TNK 3.02. 36
him i do not love that tells close offices | the 5.01.122
these offices, so oft as thou wilt look, | shall SON 77.13
OFFICIAL 1 FR 0.0001 REL FR 1 V 0 P
remains | that, in th' official marks invested, COR 2.03.140
OFFICIOUS 6 FR 0.0006 REL FR 5 V 1 P
you are too officious | in her behalf that MND 3.02.330
you that have been so tenderly officious | with WT 2.03.159
him call me rogue for being so far officious, 4.04.839 P
(i mean your malice), know, officious lords, | i H8 3.02.237
officious, and not valiant, you have sham'd me COR 1.08. 14
be every one officious | to make this banket, TIT 5.02.201
OFF'RED 7 FR 0.0008 REL FR 5 V 2 P
and i off'red him my company to a willow–tree, ADO 2.01.217 P
shylock, there's thy money off'red thee. MV 4.01.227
nay, i have off'red all, i have no more, | and SHR 2.01.381
sue | his livery, and deny his off'red homage, R2 2.01.204
hand, | as ever off'red foul play in a state. 1H4 3.02.169
why, madam, have i off'red love for this, | to R3 2.01. 78
an ill thing to be off'red to any gentlewoman, ROM 2.04.169 P
OFF'REST 1 FR 0.0001 REL FR 1 V 0 P
and twice as much, what e'er thou off'rest next. SHR 2.01.380
OFF'RING 3 FR 0.0003 REL FR 3 V 0 P
solemn, and unearthly | it was i' th' off'ring! WT 3.01. 8
for well you know we of the off'ring side | must 1H4 4.01. 69
a priest there off'ring to it his own heart. TRO 4.03. 9
OFF'RINGS 3 FR 0.0003 REL FR 3 V 0 P
the faithfull'st off'rings have breath'd out TN 5.01.114
they are polluted off'rings, more abhorr'd TRO 5.03. 17
witchcraft celebrates | pale hecat's off'rings; MAC 2.01. 52
OFFSPRING 7 FR 0.0008 REL FR 7 V 0 P
what says that fool of hagar's offspring, ha? MV 2.05. 44
the rather that you give his offspring life, JN 2.01. 13
for love of edward's offspring in my womb. 3H6 4.04. 18
thou offspring of the house of lancaster, | the R3 5.03.136
yours, | you valiant offspring of great priamus. TRO 2.02.207
accurs'd the offspring of so foul a fiend! TIT 4.02. 79
we are their offspring, and they none of ours. LUC 1757
OF'T 2 FR 0.0002 REL FR 1 V 1 P
well, then that/'s the humor of't. H5 2.01.116 P
here's the manner of't: ANT 3.06. 2
/OFT 1 FR 0.0001 REL FR 1 V 0 P
and /oft my jealousy | shapes faults that are OTH 3.03.147
OFT 158 FR 0.0178 REL FR 140 V 18 P
if this be he you oft have wish'd to hear from. TGV 2.04.103
whose sovereignty so oft thou hast preferr'd 2.06. 15
how oft hast thou with perjury cleft the root? 5.04.103
and makes us lose the good we oft might win, MM 1.04. 78
they do you wrong to put you so oft upon't. 2.01.266 P
mercy is not itself, that oft looks so; 2.01.283
o, pardon me, my lord, it oft falls out, | to 2.04.117
and that thou oft provok'st, yet grossly fear'st 3.01. 18
though music oft hath such a charm | to make bad 4.01. 14
we have very oft awak'd him, as if to carry him 4.02.150 P
a trusty villain, sir, that very oft, | when i ERR 1.02. 19
namely, some love that drew him oft from home. 5.01. 56
"that have so oft encount'red him with scorn, ADO 2.03.128 P
that oft in field with targe and shield did make LLL 5.02.553
oft have i heard of you, my lord berowne, 5.02.841
because in choice he is so oft beguil'd. MND 1.01.239
i with the morning's love have oft made sport, 3.02.389
and by adventuring both | i oft found both. MV 1.01.144
many a time and oft | in the rialto you have 1.03.106
i oft deliver'd from his forfeitures | many that 3.03. 22
at whom so oft | your grace was wont to laugh, AYL 2.02. 8
you have oft inquired | after the shepherd that 3.04. 47
not very well, but i have met him oft, | and he 3.05.106
was't you that did so oft contrive to kill him? 4.03.134
and how oft did you say his beard was not well 5.04. 83 P
of that report which i so oft have heard. SHR 2.01. 53
withal, full oft we see | cold wisdom waiting on AWW 1.01.104
our remedies oft in ourselves do lie, | which we 1.01.216
live" — | this his good melancholy oft began, 1.02. 56
oft does them by the weakest minister: 2.01.137
oft expectation fails, and most oft there 2.01.142
and most oft there | where most it promises; 2.01.142
and oft it hits | where hope is coldest and 2.01.143
and as oft is dumb | where dust and damn'd 2.03.139
of danger wins a scar, | as oft it loses all. 3.02.122
oft our displeasures, to ourselves unjust, 5.03. 63
while i was speaking, oft was fasten'd to't. 5.03. 82
a beauteous wall | doth oft close in pollution, TN 1.02. 49
think they have thee do very oft prove fools; 1.05. 34 P
the fool should be as oft with your master as 3.01. 40 P
a vulgar proof | that very oft we pity enemies. 3.01.125
oft good turns | are shuffled off with such 3.03. 15
youth is bought more oft than begg'd or borrow'd 3.04. 3
dost thou smile so, and kiss thy hand so oft? 3.04. 33 P
for it comes to pass oft that a terrible oath, 3.04.179 P
and so prove | (as /ornament oft does) too WT 1.02.158
'twas a fear | which oft infects the wisest: 1.02.262
bear, yet he is oft led by the nose with gold. 4.04.802 P
why urgest thou so oft young arthur's death? JN 4.02.204
how oft the sight of means to do ill deeds 4.02.219
call'd her to a reckoning many a time and oft. 1H4 1.02. 50 P
for by that name as oft as lancaster | doth 3.01. 8
as oft as he hears | owen glendower spoke of. 3.01. 11
oft the teeming earth | is with a kind of colic 3.01. 27
but do not use it oft, let me entreat you. 3.01.174
which oft the ear of greatness needs must hear 3.02. 24
heard the prince tell him, i know not how oft, 3.03. 84 P
that, as oft as he has occasion to name himself; 2H4 2.02.110 P
what drink'st thou oft, in stead of homage sweet H5 4.01.250
which troubles oft the bed of blessed marriage, 5.02.364
which oft our stage hath shown; ep 13
father, i know, and oft have shot at them, 1H6 1.04. 3
oft have i seen the haughty cardinal, | more 2H6 1.01.185
and many time and oft | myself have heard a 2.01. 91
death, at whose name i oft have been afeard, 2.04. 89
oft have i seen a timely–parted ghost, | of ashy 3.02.161
great men oft die by vild besonians: 4.01.134
oft have i heard that grief softens the mind, 4.04. 1
oft have i struck | those that i never saw, and 4.07. 81
oft have i seen a hot o'erweening cur | run back 5.01.151
and beauty, that the tyrant oft reclaims, 5.02. 54
and full as oft came edward to my side | with 3H6 1.04. 11
'tis beauty that doth oft make women proud, 1.04.128
oft have i heard his praises in pursuit, | but 2.01.149
blood, | were lik'ned oft to kingly sepulchres; 5.02. 20
of those gross taunts that oft i have endur'd. R3 1.03.105
why do /you weep so oft, and beat your breast, 2.02. 3
oft have i heard of sanctuary men, | but 3.01. 55
what we oft do best, | by sick interpreters H8 1.02. 81
what worst, as oft, | hitting a grosser quality, 1.02. 83
certain words | spoke by a holy monk "that oft," 1.02.160
but oft have hind'red, oft, | the passages made 2.04.165
but oft have hind'red, oft, | the passages made 2.04.165
to fear the worst oft cures the worse. TRO 3.02. 73 P
oft have you (often have you thanks therefore) 3.03. 20
favor — | prizes of accident as oft as merit, 3.03. 83
this brave shall oft make thee to hide thy head. 4.04.137
i have, thou gallant troyan, seen thee oft, 4.05.183
yet oft, | when blows have made me stay, i fled COR 2.02. 71
and thou hast oft beheld | heart–hard'ning 4.01. 24
for i have heard my grandsire say full oft, TIT 4.01. 18
thy father hath full oft | for his ungrateful 4.01.110
oft have i digg'd up dead men from their graves, 5.01.135
oft have you heard me wish for such an hour, 5.02.159
which oft the angry mab with blisters plagues, ROM 1.04. 75
thou chidst me oft for loving rosaline. 2.03. 81
how oft when men are at the point of death 5.03. 88
how oft to–night | have my old feet stumbled at 5.03.121
and oft thou shouldst hazard thy life for thy TIM 4.03.335 P
many a time and oft | have you climb'd up to JC 1.01. 37
so oft as that shall be, | so often shall the 3.01.116
the good is oft interred with their bones; 3.02. 76
which, they say, your spirits oft walk in death, HAM 1.01.138
too oft before their buttons be disclos'd, | and 1.03. 40
gaudy, | for the apparel oft proclaims the man, 1.03. 72
for /loan oft loses both itself and friend, 1.03. 76
he hath very oft of late | given private time to 1.03. 91
so, oft it chances in particular men, | that for 1.04. 23
oft breaking down the pales and forts of reason, 1.04. 28
as oft as any passions under heaven | that does 2.01.102
we are oft to blame in this — | 'tis too much 3.01. 45
speak, | but what we do determine, oft we break. 3.02.187
and oft 'tis seen the wicked prize itself | buys 3.03. 59
lips that i have kiss'd i know not how oft. 5.01.189 P
but i have heard him oft maintain it to be fit LR 1.02. 71 P
striving to better, oft we mar what's well. 1.04.346
oft bite the holy cords a–twain | which are t' 2.02. 74
now | that you so oft have boasted to retain? 3.06. 59
full oft 'tis seen, | our means secure us, and 4.01. 19
jesters do oft prove prophets. 5.03. 71
'tis oft with difference), yet do they all OTH 1.03. 7
her father lov'd me, oft invited me; 1.03.128
lips | as of her tongue she oft bestows on me, 2.01.101
you had not kiss'd your three fingers so oft, 2.01.173 P
oft got without merit, and lost without 2.03.269 P
o yes, and went between us very oft. 3.03.100
they have it very oft that have it not. 4.01. 17
where, how, how oft, how long ago, and when | he 4.01. 85
that day appear'd, and oft before gave audience, ANT 3.06. 18
your caesar's father oft | (when he hath mus'd 3.13. 82
i have led you oft, carry me now, good friends, 4.14.139
that our great king himself doth woo me oft CYM 1.05. 14
'tis gold | which buys admittance (oft it doth), 2.03. 68
she restrain'd, | and pray'd me oft forbearance; 2.05. 10
and hath as oft a sland'rous epitaph | as record 3.03. 52
my fault being nothing (as i have told you oft) 3.03. 65
defect of judgment | is oft the cause of fear. 4.02.112
very oft importun'd me | to temper poisons for 5.05.249
monster envy, oft the wrack | of earned praise, PER 4.ch. 12
as my good nurse lychorida hath oft | delivered 5.01.159
i have nam'd him oft. 5.03. 53
are not prophets | when oft our fancies are. TNK 5.03.103
sin | which oft th' apostle did forewarn us of, STM II.C 94
out of hope are compass'd oft with vent'ring, VEN 567
for oft the eye mistakes, the brain being 1068
for by our ears our hearts oft tainted be; LUC 38
that oft they interchange each other's seat. 70
despair to gain doth traffic oft for gaining, 131
and oft that wealth doth cost | the death of all 146
charm, | doth too too oft betake him to retire, 174
have you not heard it said full oft, | a woman's PP 18.41
go well, | by oft predict that i in heaven find: SON 14. 8
these offices, so oft as thou wilt look, | shall 77.13
so oft have i invok'd thee for my muse, | and 78. 1
how oft, when thou, my music, music play'st 128. 1
and seal'd false bonds of love as oft as mine, 142. 7
oft did she heave her napkin to her eyne, LC 15
a storm | as oft 'twixt may and april is to see, 102
OFTEN 130 FR 0.0147 REL FR 107 V 23 P
you have often | begun to tell me what i am, but TMP 1.02. 33
most often, do so near the bottom run | by their 2.01.227
milan, | of whom so often i have heard renown, 5.01.193
indeed a sheep doth very often stray, | and if TGV 1.01. 74
"for often have you writ to her; 2.01.165
this love of theirs myself have often seen, 3.01. 24
dumb jewels often in their silent kind | more 3.01. 90
"item, she will often praise her liquor." 3.01.345 P
me happy, | or else i often had been miserable. 4.01. 35
we talk on | often resort unto this gentlewoman? 4.02. 74
we do not act that often jest and laugh; WIV 4.02.106
is like a good thing, being often read, | grown MM 2.04. 8
how often dost thou with thy case, thy habit, 2.04. 13
hath often still'd my brawling discontent. 4.01. 9
by prosperous voyages i often made | to ERR 1.01. 40
still | that others touch and, often touching, 2.01.111
in company i often glanced it; 5.01. 66
she hath often dreamt of unhappiness and wak'd ADO 2.01.345 P
and often, at his very loose, decides | that LLL 5.02.742
where often you and i | upon faint primrose beds MND 1.01.214
full often hath she gossip'd by my side, | and 2.01.125
and thisby, | did whisper often, very secretly. 5.01.160
o wall, full often hast thou heard my moans, 5.01.188
my cherry lips have often kiss'd thy stones, 5.01.190
is not gold, | often have you heard that told; MV 2.07. 66
i often came where i did hear of her, but cannot 3.01. 81 P
often known | to be the dowry of a second head, 3.02. 94
and they are often tarr'd over with the surgery AYL 3.02. 62 P
in which /my often rumination wraps me in a most 4.01. 19 P
that i have so often met in the forest. 5.04. 41 P
hath been often burst and now repair'd with SHR 3.02. 59 P
i have often heard | of your entire affection to 4.02. 22
ay, sir, in pisa have i often been, | pisa 4.02. 94
'tis often seen | adoption strives with nature, AWW 1.03.144
grounds to fail | as often as i guess'd. 3.01. 16
have of late knock'd too often at my door. 4.01. 28 P
often prove | rough and unhospitable. TN 3.03. 10
which often hath no less prevail'd than so | on WT 2.01. 54
the silence often of pure innocence | persuades 2.02. 39
how often have i told you 'twould be thus! 4.04.474
how often said my dignity would last | but till 4.04.475
and they often give us soldiers the lie, but we 4.04.724 P
forswear themselves as often as they speak. 5.01.200
that horse that thou so often hast bestrid, R2 5.05. 79
and start so often when thou sit'st alone? 1H4 2.03. 43
harry, which thou hast often heard of, and it is 2.04.411 P
man whom i have often noted in thy company, but 2.04.418 P
it is often so indeed, but much of the father's 2H4 3.02.130 P
guests | are often welcomest when they are gone. 1H6 2.02. 56
repeat their semblance often on the seas, | that 5.03.193
did he so often lodge in open field, | in 2H6 1.01. 80
for things are often spoke and seldom meant; 3.01.268
full often, like a shag–hair'd crafty kern, 3.01.367
how often have i tempted suffolk's tongue | (the 3.02.114
how often hast thou waited at my cup, | fed from 4.01. 56
ay, and their colors, often borne in france, 3H6 1.01.127
myself have often heard him say, and swear, 3.03.123
yet i confess that often ere this day, | when i 3.03.131
and, often but attended with weak guard, 4.05. 7
for i have often heard my mother say | i came 5.06. 70
and often did i strive | to yield the ghost; R3 1.04. 36
they often feel a world of restless cares; 1.04. 81
and often up and down my sons were toss'd | for 2.04. 58
to which | she was often cited by them, but H8 4.01. 29
o cressid, how often have i wish'd me thus! TRO 3.02. 61 P
oft have you (often have you thanks therefore) 3.03. 20
such rich beholding | as they have often given. 3.03. 92
so often hast thou beat me; COR 1.10. 8
think, should we encounter | as often as we eat. 1.10. 10
dogs, that are as often beat for barking | as 2.03.216
how often he had met you, sword to sword; 3.01. 13
which they have often made against the senate, 3.01.128
which often thus correcting thy stout heart, 3.02. 78
what, hast not thou full often strook a doe, TIT 2.01. 93
myself hath often heard them say, | when i have 4.04. 74
and these, who, often drown'd, could never die, ROM 1.02. 90
that dreamers often lie. 1.04. 51
why, i have often wish'd myself poorer, that i TIM 1.02.100 P
he is very often like a knight; 2.02.112 P
many a time and often i ha' din'd with him, and 3.01. 23 P
he has a sin that often | drowns him and takes 3.05. 67
sir, | having often of your open bounty tasted, 5.01. 58
such instigations have been often dropp'd JC 2.01. 49
so often shall the knot of us be call'd | the 3.01.117
the feast is sold | that is not often vouch'd, MAC 3.04. 33
my lord is often thus, | and hath been from his 3.04. 52
where to do harm | is often laudable, to do good 4.02. 76

which often, since my here–remain in england, 4.03.148
a happiness that often madness hits on, which HAM 2.02.210 P
but, as we often see, against some storm, | a 2.02.483
i have so often blush'd to acknowledge him, that LR 1.01. 10 P
nature | which often leaves the history unspoke 1.01.236
often the surfeits of our own behavior — we 1.02.119 P
often 'twould say, | "the fiend, the fiend!" 4.06. 78
and often did beguile her of her tears, | when i OTH 1.03.156
i have told thee often, and i retell thee again 1.03.365 P
but is he often thus? 2.03.128
that which so often you did bid me steal. 3.03.309
for often, with a solemn earnestness | (more 5.02.227
what our contempts doth often hurl from us, | we ANT 1.02.123
in time we hate that which we often fear. 1.03. 12
beg often our own harms, which the wise pow'rs 2.01. 6
which, left unshown, | is often left unlov'd. 3.06. 53
are those that often have 'gainst pompey fought; 3.07. 37
which before | have often sham'd our sex. 5.02.124
to whom i have been often bound for no less than CYM 1.04. 27 P
since doubting things go ill often hurts more 1.06. 95
and often, to our comfort, shall we find | the 3.03. 19
dream often so, | and never false. 4.02.352
who did promise | to yield me often tidings. 4.03. 39
which are often the sadness of parting, as the 5.04.159 P
that life, beseech you, | which i so often owe; 5.05.415
only i heard her | repeat this often, "palamon TNK 4.01. 67
without appetite, save often drinking, dreaming 4.03. 4 P
i have often. 5.02. 47
or stonish'd as night–wand'rers often are, VEN 825
she puts the period often from his place, | and LUC 565
their gentle sex to weep are often willing, 1237
i often did behold | in thy sweet semblance my 1758
for his approach that often there had been. PP 6. 8
her lips to mine how often hath she joined, 7. 7
and often is his gold complexion dimm'd, | and SON 18. 6
"kind," and "true" have often liv'd alone, 105.13
and often reading what contents it bears; LC 19
as often shriking undistinguish'd woe, | in 20
these often bath'd she in her fluxive eyes, 50
and often kiss'd, and often /gan to tear; 51
and often kiss'd, and often /gan to tear; 51
"well could he ride, and often men would say, 106
advice is often seen | by blunting us to make 160

OFTENTIMES 8 FR 0.0009 REL FR 8 V 0 P
and oftentimes have purpos'd to forbid | sir TGV 3.01. 26
desert) | hath oftentimes upbraided me withal: ERR 3.01.113
yet oftentimes he goes but mean apparell'd. SHR 3.02. 73
and oftentimes excusing of a fault | doth make JN 4.02. 30
diseased nature oftentimes breaks forth | in 1H4 3.01. 26
yet oftentimes it doth present harsh rage, 3.01.181
and oftentimes, to win us to our harm, | the MAC 1.03.123
their copious stories, oftentimes begun, | end VEN 845

OFT'NER 4 FR 0.0004 REL FR 3 V 1 P
your bawd — he doth oft'ner ask forgiveness. MM 4.02. 51 P
if so, my eyes are oft'ner wash'd than hers. MND 2.02. 93
being call'd | a hundred times and oft'ner, in 2H6 2.01. 88
thee, | oft'ner upon her knees than on her feet, MAC 4.03.110

OFT–SUBDUED 1 FR 0.0001 REL FR 1 V 0 P
as you fly from your oft–subdued slaves. 1H6 1.05. 32

OFT–TIMES 1 FR 0.0001 REL FR 1 V 0 P
to sadness, and oft–times | not knowing why. CYM 1.06. 62

OIL 15 FR 0.0017 REL FR 13 V 2 P
no use of metal, corn, or wine, or oil; TMP 2.01.154
whale (with so many tuns of oil in his belly) WIV 2.01. 65 P
lest the oil that's in me should set hell on 5.05. 35 P
and i have bought | the oil, the balsamum, and ERR 4.01. 89
"after my flame lacks oil, to be the snuff | of AWW 1.02. 59
when oil and fire, too strong for reason's force 5.03. 7
which hath been smooth as oil, soft as young 1H4 1.03. 7
eyes, like lamps whose wasting oil is spent, 1H6 2.05. 8
shall to my flaming wrath be oil and flax. 2H6 5.02. 55
as holy oil, edward confessor's crown, | the rod H8 4.01. 88
but, saying thus, in stead of oil and balm, TRO 1.01. 61
as this pomp shows to a little oil and root. TIM 1.02.135
being oil to fire, snow to the colder moods; LR 2.02. 77
me and pour | this oil out of your language. TNK 3.01.103
dries up his oil to lend the world his light. VEN 756

OIL–DRIED 1 FR 0.0001 REL FR 1 V 0 P
my oil–dried lamp and time–bewasted light R2 1.03.221

OILS 1 FR 0.0001 REL FR 1 V 0 P
boiling | in leads or oils? WT 3.02.177

OILY 4 FR 0.0004 REL FR 2 V 2 P
stain your own | with oily painting. WT 5.03. 83
this oily rascal is known as well as paul's. 1H4 2.04.526 P
if for i want that glib and oily art | to speak LR 1.01.224
nay, if an oily palm be not a fruitful ANT 1.02. 52 P

'OLD 1 FR 0.0001 REL FR 1 V 0 P
"swithold footed thrice the 'old, | he met the LR 3.04.120

OLD *(also auld)*

/OLD 8 FR 0.0009 REL FR 7 V 1 P
news, /old /news, and such news as you never SHR 3.02. 30 P
/care /is /loss /of /care, /by /old /care /done, R2 4.01.196
/sad /stories /chanced /in /the /times /of /old. TIT 3.02. 83
should be as mortal as /an /old man's life? HAM 4.05.161
/idle /old /man, | /that /still /would /manage LR 1.03. 16
/old /fools /are /babes /again, /and /must /be 1.03. 19
/the /end /meet /the /old /course /of /death, 3.07.101
/let's /follow /the /old /earl, /and /get /the 3.07.103

OLD 665 FR 0.0751 REL FR 417 V 248 P
for then thou wast not | out three years old. TMP 1.02. 41
what i command, i'll rack thee with old cramps, 1.02.369
the old cock. 2.01. 30 P
i can go no further, sir, | my old bones aches. 3.03. 2
old lord, i cannot blame thee, | who am myself 3.03. 4
bear with my weakness, my old brain is troubled. 4.01.159
sir, "the good old lord gonzalo," | his tears 5.01. 15
his years but young, but his experience old; TGV 2.04. 69
well, your old vice still: 3.01.284 P
and the old saying is, | black men are pearls in 5.02. 11
it is an old coat. WIV 1.01. 18 P
dozen white louses do become an old coat well; 1.01. 19 P
is the fresh fish, the salt fish is an old coat. 1.01. 23 P
she is able to overtake seventeen years old. 1.01. 54 P
an old cloak makes a new jerkin; 1.03. 17 P
here will be an old abusing of god's patience 1.04. 5 P
both young and old, one with another, ford. 2.01.114
old folks, you know, have discretion, as they 2.02.129 P
say'st thou so, old jack? 2.02.138 P
i'll make more of thy old body than i have done. 2.02.139 P
page, though i now be old and of the peace, if i 2.03. 45 P
old windsor way, and every way but the town way. 3.01. 6 P
woman, your husband is in his old lines again. 4.02. 22 P
he cannot abide the old woman of brainford. 4.02. 85 P
'tis old, but true: 4.02.107
come you and the old woman down; 4.02.167 P
old woman? what old woman's that? 4.02.169 P
old woman? what old woman's that? 4.02.169 P
a witch, a quean, an old cozening quean! 4.02.172 P
gentlemen, let him /not strike the old woman. 4.02.181 P
appoint a meeting with this old fat fellow, 4.04. 14
and has been grievously peaten as an old oman. 4.04. 21 P
there is an old tale goes, that herne the hunter 4.04. 28
there's an old woman, a fat woman, gone up into 4.05. 11 P
mine host, an old fat woman even now with me, 4.05. 24 P
i spake with the old woman about it. 4.05. 34 P
my counterfeiting the action of an old woman, 4.05.118 P
as you see, like a poor old man, but i came from 5.01. 16 P
from her, master /brook, like a poor old woman. 5.01. 17 P
old, cold, wither'd, and of intolerable entrails 5.05.153 P
old escalus, | though first in question, is thy MM 1.01. 45
and when thou art old and rich, | thou hast 3.01. 36
a year and a quarter old come philip and jacob. 3.02.201 P
this news is old enough, yet it is every day's 3.02.229 P
angelo to–night shall lie | his old betrothed 3.02.279
exacting, | and perform an old contracting. 3.02.282
and bred, one that is a prisoner nine years old. 4.02.131 P
house, for here be many of her old customers. 4.03. 3 P
for a commodity of brown paper and old ginger, 4.03. 5 P
in request, for the old women were all dead. 4.03. 8 P
if the old fantastical duke of dark corners had 4.03.156 P
our old and faithful friend, we are glad to see 5.01. 2
from whom my absence was not six months old ERR 1.01. 44
nay, forward, old man, do not break off so, 1.01. 96
in ephesus i am but two hours old, | as strange 2.02.148
he is deformed, crooked, old, and sere, 4.02. 19
you got the picture of old adam new apparell'd? 4.03. 13 P
all these old witnesses — i cannot err — 5.01.318
o, my old master! who hath bound him here? 5.01.339
speak, old egeon, if thou be'st the man | that 5.01.342
end with a jade's trick, i know you of old. ADO 1.01.145 P
like the old tale, my lord: 1.01.216 P
ere you flout old ends any further, examine your 1.01.288 P
devil meet me like an old cuckold with horns on 2.01. 44 P
some woman, there is no believing old signs. 3.02. 41 P
and the old ornament of his cheek hath already 3.02. 46 P
old signior, walk aside with me, i have studied 3.02. 71 P
like god bel's priests in the old church–window, 3.03.135 P
an old man, sir, and his wits are not so blunt 3.05. 10 P
man living that is an old man and no honester 3.05. 14 P
a good old man, sir, he will be talking; 3.05. 33 P
and on your family's old monument | hang 4.01.206
nay, do not quarrel with us, good old man. 5.01. 50
being young, or what would do | were i not old. 5.01. 62
you say not right, old man. 5.01. 73
snapp'd off with two old men without teeth. 5.01.116 P
the old man's daughter told us all. 5.01.178 P
nor i, | and yet, to satisfy this good old man, 5.01.276
an old, an old instance, beatrice, that liv'd in 5.02. 76 P
an old, an old instance, beatrice, that liv'd in 5.02. 76 P
come to your uncle, yonder's old coil at home. 5.02. 96 P
as an appertinent title to your old time, which LLL 1.02. 17 P
thou art an old love–monger and speakest 2.01.254
your pocket like a man after the old painting; 3.01. 21 P
shall i come upon thee with an old saying, that 4.01.119 P
so i may answer thee with one as old, that was a 4.01.122 P
omne bene, say i, being of an old father's mind: 4.02. 32
your wit | what was a month old at cain's birth, 4.02. 35
cain's birth, that's not five weeks old as yet? 4.02. 35
the moon was a month old when adam was no more. 4.02. 39
exchange, for the moon is never but a month old; 4.02. 47 P
ah, good old mantuan! 4.02. 94 P
old mantuan, old mantuan! 4.02. 99 P
old mantuan, old mantuan! 4.02. 99 P
"all hid, all hid," an old infant play. 4.03. 76
young blood doth not obey an old decree. 4.03.213
offer'd by a child to an old man: 5.01. 62 P
yet i have a trick | of the old rage. 5.02.417
well said, old mocker. 5.02.549
the face of an old roman coin, scarce seen. 5.02.613 P
our wooing doth not end like an old play: 5.02.874
o, methinks, how slow | this old moon /wanes! MND 1.01. 4
o spite! too old to be engag'd to young. 1.01.138
and on old hiems' /thin and icy crown | an 2.01.109
demetrius is, | this helena, old nedar's helena. 4.01.130
that is an old device; 5.01. 50
this is old ninny's tomb. where is my love? 5.01.263
with mirth and laughter let old wrinkles come, MV 1.01. 80
prove the weeping philosopher when he grows old, 1.02. 49 P
if i live to be as old as sibylla, i will die as 1.02.106 P
but i pray you, ergo, old man, ergo, i beseech 2.02. 57 P
well, old man, i will tell you news of your son. 2.02. 77 P
i hope, an old man, shall frutify unto you — 2.02.134 P
your worship shall know by this honest old man, 2.02.139 P
though i say it, though old man, yet poor man, 2.02.139 P
the old proverb is very well parted between my 2.02.149 P
take leave of thy old master, and inquire | my 2.02.153
to bid my old master the jew to sup to–night 2.04. 17 P
the difference of old shylock and bassanio. 2.05. 2
wise as bold, | young in limbs, in judgment old, 2.07. 71
out upon it, old carrion! 3.01. 35 P
this, she is not yet so old | but she may learn; 3.02.160
what, and my old venetian friend salerio? 3.02.219
i never knew so young a body with so old a head. 4.01.164 P
come you from old bellario? 4.01.169
antonio and old shylock, both stand forth. 4.01.175
i pray you show my youth old shylock's house. 4.02. 11
we shall have old swearing | that they did give 4.02. 15
the enchanted herbs | that did renew old aeson. 5.01. 14
get you with him, you old dog. AYL 1.01. 81 P
is "old dog" my reward? 1.01. 82 P
god be with my old master! 1.01. 84 P
no news at the court, sir, but the old news: 1.01. 99 P
the old duke is banish'd by his younger brother 1.01. 99 P
where will the old duke live? 1.01.113 P
they live like the old robin hood of england. 1.01.116 P
one that old frederick, your father, loves. 1.02. 82 P
thou losest thy old smell. 1.02.108 P
there comes an old man and his three sons — 1.02.118 P
i could match this beginning with an old tale. 1.02.120 P
yonder they lie, the poor old man, their father, 1.02.130 P
strong a liking with old sir rowland's youngest 1.03. 28 P
hath not old custom made this life more sweet 2.01. 2
o you memory | of old sir rowland! 2.03. 4
when service should in my old limbs lie lame, 2.03. 41
though i look old, yet i am strong and lusty; 2.03. 47
o good old man, how well in thee appears | the 2.03. 56
but, poor old man, thou prun'st a rotten tree, 2.03. 63
here, a young man and an old in solemn talk. 2.04. 20 P
no, corin, being old, thou canst not guess, 2.04. 25
there is an old poor man, | who after me hath 2.07.129
good old man, | thou art right welcome as thy 2.07.197
of a twelvemonth to a crooked–pated, old, 3.02. 82 P
but indeed an old religious uncle of mine taught 3.02.344 P
bounds | that the old carlot once was master of. 3.05.108
the poor world is almost six thousand years old, 4.01. 95 P
time is the old justice that examines all such 4.01.199 P
verily did think | that her old gloves were on, 4.03. 26
object did present itself | under an old oak, 4.03.104
good enough, for all the old gentleman's saying. 5.01. 4 P
how old are you, friend? 5.01. 17 P
the revenue that was old sir rowland's will i 5.02. 11 P
since i was three year old, convers'd with a 5.02. 60 P
i am the second son of old sir rowland, | that 5.04.152
where, meeting with an old religious man, 5.04.160
christopher sly, old sly's son of burton–heath, SHR in.2. 18 P
as stephen sly, and old john naps of greece, in.2. 93
my old friend grumio! 1.02. 20 P
gale | blows you to padua here from old verona? 1.02. 49
as old as sibyl, and as curst and shrowd | as 1.02. 70
or an old trot with ne'er a tooth in her head, 1.02. 79 P
sober robes | to old baptista as a schoolmaster 1.02.133
see, to beguile the old folks, how the young 1.02.138 P
born in verona, old /antonio's son. 1.02.190
as any one | old signior gremio has in padua, 2.01.368
that's but a cavil; he is old, i young. 2.01.390
and may not young men die as well as old? 2.01.391
an old italian fox is not so kind, my boy. 2.01.403
senis," that we might beguile the old pantaloon. 3.01. 36 P
old fashions please me best; 3.01. 80
is it new and old too? how may that be? 3.02. 32 P
but say, what to thine old news? 3.02. 42 P
is coming in a new hat and an old jerkin; 3.02. 44 P
a pair of old breeches thrice turn'd; 3.02. 44 P
an old rusty sword ta'en out of the town armory, 3.02. 46 P
with an old mothy saddle and stirrups of no 3.02. 49 P
an old hat, and the humor of forty fancies 3.02. 68 P
for it hath tam'd my old master and my new 4.01. 24 P
how now, old lad? 4.01.110 P
the rest were ragged, old, and beggarly, | yet, 4.01.137
besides, old gremio is heark'ning still, | and 4.04. 53
the old priest of saint luke's church is at your 4.04. 88 P
this is a man, old, wrinkled, faded, withered, 4.05. 43
pardon, old father, my mistaking eyes, | that 4.05. 45
do, good old grandsire, and withal make known 4.05. 50
let me embrace with old vincentio, | and wander 4.05. 68
mine old master vincentio! 5.01. 43 P
what, my old worshipful old master? 5.01. 54 P
what, my old worshipful old master? 5.01. 54 P
him up ever since he was three years old, and 5.01. 83 P
well, go thy ways, old lad, for thou shalt ha't. 5.02.181
virginity, like an old courtier, wears her cap AWW 1.01.156 P
and your virginity, your old virginity, is like 1.01.160 P
charbon the puritan and old poysam the papist, 1.03. 52 P
and of his old experience th' only darling, | he 2.01.107
you are too old, sir; 2.03.196 P
let it satisfy you, you are too old. 2.03.197 P
take this disgrace off me, scurvy, old, filthy, 2.03.236 P
o, my knave, how does my old lady? 2.04. 19 P
our old /ling and our isbels a' th' country are 3.02. 13 P
are nothing like your old ling and your isbels 3.02. 14 P
and i begin to love, as an old man loves money, 3.02. 16 P
he was first smok'd by the old lord lafew. 3.06.103 P
for we are old, and on our quick'st decrees 5.03. 40
by my old beard, | and ev'ry hair that's on't, 5.03. 76
i am either maid, or else this old man's wife. 5.03.293
and yet i will not compare with an old man. TN 1.03.119 P
how your fooling grows old, and people dislike 1.05.111 P
not yet old enough for a man, nor young enough 1.05.156 P
that old and antique song we heard last night; 2.04. 3
too old, by heaven. 2.04. 29
mark it, cesario, it is old and plain. 2.04. 43
with the innocence of love, | like the old age. 2.04. 48
did she see /thee the while, old boy? 3.02. 8 P
for, as the old hermit of prague, that never saw 4.02. 12 P
in a trice, | like to the old vice, | your need 4.02.124
is a good play, and the old saying is, the third 5.01. 37 P
if it be aught to the old tune, my lord, | it is 5.01.108
physics the subject, makes old hearts fresh. WT 1.01. 39 P
might we lay th' old proverb to your charge, 2.03. 97
what old or newer torture | must i receive, 3.02.177
would i had been by, to have help'd the old man! 3.03.107 P
you're a /made old man; 3.03.120 P
daughter, when my old wife liv'd, upon | this 4.04. 55
very true, and but a month old. 4.04.267 P
old sir, i know | she prizes not such trifles as 4.04.356
thou, old traitor, | i am sorry that by hanging 4.04.420
and had not the old man come in with a whoobub 4.04.615 P
an old sheep–whistling rogue, a ram–tender, to 4.04.776 P
has the old man e'er a son, sir, do you hear, 4.04.781 P
give you as much as this old man does when the 4.04.821 P
heard the old shepherd deliver the manner how he 5.02. 4 P
which is call'd true, is so like an old tale, 5.02. 28 P
now he thanks the old shepherd, which stands by 5.02. 54 P
like an old tale still, which will have matter 5.02. 61 P
i brought the old man and his son aboard the 5.02.115 P
you, should be hooted at | like an old tale; 5.03.117
i, an old turtle, | will wing me to some 5.03.132
if old sir robert did beget us both, | and were JN 1.01. 80
o old sir robert, father, on my knee | i give 1.01. 82
philip, good old sir robert's wive's eldest son. 1.01.159
my brother robert, old sir robert's son? 1.01.224
madam, i was not old sir robert's son; 1.01.233
that shakes the rotten carcass of old death 2.01.456

of kings, of beggars, old men, young men, maids, 2.01.570
old time the clock–setter, that bald sexton time 3.01.324
how green you are and fresh in this old world! 3.04.145
face | of plain old form is much disfigured, 4.02. 22
old men and beldames in the streets | do 4.02.185
smokes about the burning crest | of the old, 5.04. 35
and happy newness, that intends old right. 5.04. 61
old john of gaunt, time–honored lancaster, R2 1.01. 1
hath love in thy old blood no living fire? 1.02. 10
farewell, old gaunt! 1.02. 44
farewell, old gaunt! 1.02. 54
and what shall good old york there see | but 1.02. 67
i am too old to fawn upon a nurse, | too far in 1.03.170
old john of gaunt is grievous sick, my lord, 1.04. 54
old gaunt indeed, and gaunt in being old. 2.01. 74
old gaunt indeed, and gaunt in being old. 2.01. 74
liege, old gaunt commends him to your majesty. 2.01.147
words, life, and all, old lancaster hath spent. 2.01.150
keeps good old york there with his men of war? 2.03. 52
for methinks in you | i see old gaunt alive. 2.03.118
both young and old rebel, | and all goes worse 3.02.119
though you are old enough to be my heir. 3.03.205
thou old adam's likeness, set to dress this 3.04. 73
sweet soul to the bosom | of good old abraham! 4.01.104
ah, thou, the model where old troy did stand, 5.01. 11
with good old folks and let them tell /thee 5.01. 41
so many greedy looks of young and old | through 5.02. 13
though i be old, | i doubt not but to ride as 5.02.114
shall thy old dugs once more a traitor rear? 5.03. 90
come, my old son, i pray god make thee new. 5.03.146
but this our purpose now is twelve month old, 1H4 1.01. 28
art so fat–witted with drinking of old sack, and 1.02. 2 P
as the honey of hybla, my old lad of the castle. 1.02. 41 P
with the rusty curb of old father antic the law? 1.02. 61 P
or an old lion, or a lover's lute. 1.02. 75 P
an old lord of the council rated me the other 1.02. 83 P
for if i hang, old sir john hangs with me, and 2.01. 68 P
how old art thou, francis? 2.04. 53 P
old sir john with half a dozen more are at the 2.04. 82 P
humors since the old days of goodman adam to the 2.04. 93 P
go thy ways, old jack, die when thou wilt; 2.04.127 P
and one of them is fat and grows old, god help 2.04.132 P
not two or three and fifty upon poor old jack, 2.04.187 P
thou knowest my old ward: 2.04.195 P
an old man. 2.04.293 P
his son–in–law mortimer, and old northumberland, 2.04.342 P
haunts thee in the likeness of an old fat man, a 2.04.448 P
youth, falstaff, that old white–bearded sathan. 2.04.463 P
that he is old, the more the pity, his white 2.04.467 P
if to be old and merry be a sin, then many an 2.04.471 P
then many an old host that i know is damn'd. 2.04.472 P
as he is, old jack falstaff, banish not him thy 2.04.477 P
shakes the old beldame earth, and topples down 3.01. 31
for this advertisement is five days old. 3.02.172
hangs about me like an old lady's loose gown; 3.03. 3 P
i am wither'd like an old apple–john. 3.03. 4 P
dishonorable ragged than an old feaz'd ancient: 4.02. 31 P
to crush our old limbs in ungentle steel. 5.01. 13
what, old acquaintance! 5.04.102
/where hotspur's father, old northumberland, 2H4 in 36
you that are old consider not the capacities of 1.02.173 P
of youth, that are written down old with all the 1.02.179 P
is, i am only old in judgment and understanding; 1.02.192 P
and sackcloth, but in new silk and old sack. 1.02.198 P
if ye will needs say i am an old man, you should 1.02.216 P
of westmerland, and this to old mistress ursula, 1.02.240 P
doth the old boar feed in the old frank? 2.02.146 P
doth the old boar feed in the old frank? 2.02.147 P
at the old place, my lord, in eastcheap. 2.02.148 P
ephesians, my lord, of the old church. 2.02.150 P
lord, but old mistress quickly and mistress doll 2.02.152 P
of these six dry, round, old, wither'd knights." 2.04. 8 P
by the mass, here will be old utis, it will be 2.04. 19 P
by my troth, this is the old fashion, you two 2.04. 55 P
and begin to patch up thine old body for heaven? 2.04.233 P
be not lisping to his /master's old tables, his 2.04.266 P
i am old, i am old. 2.04.271 P
i am old, i am old. 2.04.271 P
to see how many of my old acquaintance are dead! 3.02. 34 P
is old double of your town living yet? 3.02. 40 P
and is old double dead? 3.02. 52 P
my old dame will be undone now for one to do her 3.02.112 P
old, old, master shallow. 3.02.206 P
old, old, master shallow. 3.02.206 P
nay, she must be old, she cannot choose but be 3.02.207 P
she cannot choose but be old, certain she's old, 3.02.208 P
she cannot choose but be old, certain she's old, 3.02.208 P
had robin nightwork by old nightwork before i 3.02.209 P
master corporal captain, for my old dame's sake, 3.02.230 P
thing about her when i am gone, and she is old, 3.02.231 P
o, give me always a little, lean, old, chopp'd, 3.02.275 P
our house, let our old acquaintance be renew'd. 3.02.294 P
how subject we old men are to this vice of lying 3.02.303 P
if the young dace be a bait for the old pike, i 3.02.331 P
have i, in my poor and old motion, the 4.03. 33 P
and the old folk (time's doting chronicles) 4.04.126
peopled with wolves, thy old inhabitants! 4.05.137
why then say an old man can do somewhat. 5.03. 78 P
what, is the old king dead? 5.03.120 P
i know thee not, old man, fall to thy prayers. 5.05. 47
so surfeit–swell'd, so old, and so profane; 5.05. 50
but there's a saying very old and true, | "if H5 1.02.166
days, | nor from the dust of old oblivion rak'd, 2.04. 87
guarded with grandsires, babies, and old women, 3.pr. 20
o then belike she was old and gentle, and you 3.07. 52 P
good morrow, old sir thomas erpingham. 4.01. 13
god–a–mercy, old heart! 4.01. 34
a good old commander and a most kind gentleman. 4.01. 95 P
good old knight, | collect them all together at 4.01.286
he that shall see this day, and live old age, 4.03. 44
old men forget; 4.03. 49
valor than this roaring devil i' th' old play, 4.04. 71 P
stones | enforced from the old assyrian slings; 4.07. 62
old i do wax, and from my weary limbs | honor is 5.01. 84
my comfort is, that old age, that ill layer–up 5.02.230 P
of old i know them; 1H6 1.02. 39
hath, | exceeding the nine sibyls of old rome: 1.02. 56
out of a great deal of old iron i chose forth. 1.02.101
bring forth the body of old salisbury, | and 2.02. 4
heavens keep old bedford safe! 3.02.100
i think her old familiar is asleep. 3.02.122
when i was young (as yet i am not old), | i do 3.04. 17
before young talbot from old talbot fly | the 4.06. 46
now my old arms are young john talbot's grave. 4.07. 32
i think this upstart is old talbot's ghost, | he 4.07. 87
the king is old enough himself | to give his 2H6 1.03.116
if he be old enough, what needs your grace | to 1.03.118
and, ten to one, old joan had not gone out. 2.01. 4
but i was made a king, at nine months old. 4.09. 4
old salisbury, shame to thy silver hair, | thou 5.01.162
why art thou old, and want'st experience? 5.01.171
now, by my father's badge, old nevil's crest, 5.01.202
york not our old men spares; 5.02. 51
come, thou new ruin of old clifford's house: 5.02. 61
as did aeneas old anchises bear, | so bear i 5.02. 62
house, | so was his will in his old feeble body. 5.03. 13
when i was crown'd i was but nine months old. 3H6 1.01.112
you are old enough now, and yet methinks you 1.01.113
ay, and old york, and yet not satisfied. 2.02. 99
i was anointed king at nine months old, | my 3.01. 76
and i forgive and quite forget old faults, | and 3.03.200
the good old man would fain that all were well, 4.07. 31
and many an old man's sigh and many a widow's, 5.06. 39
with odd old ends stol'n forth of holy writ, R3 1.03.336
and make me die a good old man! 2.02.109
was crown'd in paris but at nine months old. 2.03. 17
that he could gnaw a crust at two hours old; 2.04. 28
for making me, so young, so old a widow! 4.01. 72
old sullen playfellow | for tender princes — 4.01.101
old barren plants, to wail it with their age. 4.04.394
is a kind of puppy | to th' old dam, treason), H8 1.01.176
honest men, | or pack to their old playfellows. 1.03. 33
and when old time shall lead him to his end, 2.01. 93
bow'd would hire me, | old as i am, to queen it. 2.03. 37
there was a lady once ('tis an old story) | that 2.03. 90
i am old, my lords, | and all the fellowship i 3.01.120
weary and old with service, to the mercy | of a 3.02.363
carries up the train | is that old noble lady, 4.01. 52
like rams | in the old time of war, would shake 4.01. 78
but 'tis so lately alter'd that the old name 4.01. 98
an old man, broken with the storms of state, 4.02. 21
the old duchess of norfolk | and lady marquess 5.02.202
that had a head to hit, either young or old, 5.03. 24
is he so young a man and so old a lifter? TRO 1.02.117 P
he is old now, | but if there be not in our 1.03.292
i see them not with my old eyes, what are they? 1.03.365
there's ulysses and old nestor, whose wit was 2.01.104 P
the seas and winds, old wranglers, took a truce, 2.02. 75
and for an old aunt whom the greeks held captive 2.02. 77
when time is old /and hath forgot itself, | when 3.02.185
o, let an old man embrace thee, | and, worthy 4.05.199
'tis the old nestor. 4.05.201
let me embrace thee, good old chronicle, | that 4.05.202
and that old common arbitrator, time, | will one 4.05.225
old nestor tarries; 5.01. 80
rascals, that stale old mouse–eaten dry cheese, 5.04. 10 P
cominius, martius your old enemy | (who is of COR 1.02. 12
you two are old men: 2.01. 13 P
we have some old crab–trees here at home that 2.01.188
enforce his pride, | and his old hate unto you; 2.03.220
hence, old goat! 3.01.176
you that be noble, help him, young and old! 3.01.227
i'll try whether my old wit be in request | with 3.01.250
with old menenius and those senators | that 3.03. 7
insisting on the old prerogative | and power i' 3.03. 17
thou old and true menenius, | thy tears are 4.01. 21
one seven years | from these old arms and legs, 4.01. 56
i urg'd our old acquaintance, and the drops 5.01. 10
his revenges with the easy groans of old women, 5.02. 42 P
thee no worse than thy old father menenius does! 5.02. 70 P
this last old man, | whom with a crack'd heart i 5.03. 8
for whose old love i have | (though i show'd 5.03. 12
take up this good old man, and cheer the heart TIT 1.01.457
the unhappy sons of old andronicus, | brought 2.03.250
let marcus, lucius, or thyself, old titus, | or 3.01.152
revenge the heavens for old andronicus! 4.01.129
the old man hath found their guilt, | and sends 4.02. 26
as who should say, "old lad, i am thine own." 4.02.121
aid, | and that it comes from old andronicus, 4.03. 16
against the willful sons | of old andronicus. 4.04. 9
conduct | of lucius, son to old andronicus, 4.04. 66
i will enchant the old andronicus | with words 4.04. 89
heart | almost impregnable, his old ears deaf, 4.04. 98
even at his father's house, the old andronicus. 4.04.103
now will i to that old andronicus, | and temper 4.04.108
tell us, old man, how shall we be employ'd? 5.02.149
go, go into old titus' sorrowful house, | and 5.03.142
old montague is come, | and flourishes his blade ROM 1.01. 77
by thee, old capulet, and montague, | have 1.01. 90
beseeming ornaments | to wield old partisans, in 1.01. 94
to wield old partisans, in hands as old, 1.01. 94
to old free–town, our common judgment–place. 1.01.102
think, | for men so old as we to keep the peace. 1.02. 3
this night i hold an old accustom'd feast, 1.02. 20
eye, | and the rank poison of the old will die. 1.02. 50
now, by my maidenhead at twelve year old, | i 1.03. 2
made by the joiner squirrel or old grub, | time 1.04. 60
the son and heir of old tiberio. 1.05.129
now old desire doth in his death–bed lie, | and 2.pr. 1
care keeps his watch in every old man's eye, 2.03. 35
thy old groans yet ringing in mine ancient ears; 2.03. 74
sit | of an old tear that is not wash'd off yet. 2.03. 76
tybalt, the kinsman to old capulet, | hath sent 2.04. 6
that they cannot sit at ease on the old bench? 2.04. 35 P
an old hare hoar, | and an old hare hoar, | is 2.04.134
an old hare hoar, | and an old hare hoar, | is 2.04.135
but old folks — many feign as they were dead, 2.05. 16
another for tying his new shoes with old riband? 3.01. 29 P
griefs, these woes, these sorrows make me old. 3.02. 89
doth not she think me an old murtherer, | now i 3.03. 94
and old cakes of roses | were thinly scattered, 5.01. 47
to–night | have my old feet stumbled at graves! 5.03.122
a bell | that warns my old age to a sepulchre. 5.03.207
let my old life | be sacrific'd some hour before 5.03.267
these old fellows | have their ingratitude in TIM 2.02.214
now the gods keep you old enough that you may 3.05.103
this is the old man still. 3.06. 61 P
the lin'd crutch from thy old limping sire, 4.01. 14
right, | base noble, old young, coward valiant. 4.03. 30
yet our old love made a particular force, | and 5.02. 8
withal i am indeed, sir, a surgeon to old shoes; JC 1.01. 23 P
troy upon his shoulder | the old anchises bear, 1.02.114
why old men, fools, and children calculate, 1.03. 65
set this up with wax | upon old brutus' statue. 1.03.146
old feeble carrions, and such suffering souls 2.01.130
friendly conference, | as he hath us'd of old. 4.02. 18
old cassius still! 5.01. 63
even for that our love of old, i prithee | hold 5.05. 27
for those of old, | and the late dignities MAC 1.06. 18
hell gate, he should have old turning the key. 2.03. 2 P
lest our old robes sit easier than our new! 2.04. 38
old siward, with ten thousand warlike men 4.03.134
would have thought the old man to have had so 5.01. 39 P
leaf, | and that which should accompany old age, 5.03. 24
for bearers of this greeting to old norway, HAM 1.02. 35
or ere those shoes were old | with which she 1.02.147
and you, my sinows, grow not instant old, | but 1.05. 94
well said, old mole, canst work i' th' earth so 1.05.162
whereon old norway, overcome with joy, | gives 2.02. 72
rogue says here that old men have grey beards, 2.02.197 P
sir, shall grow old as i am, if like a crab you 2.02.203 P
these tedious old fools! 2.02.219 P
them, for they say an old man is twice a child. 2.02.385 P
am i not i' th' right, old jephthah? 2.02.410 P
o, old friend! 2.02.422 P
hellish pyrrhus | old grandsire priam seeks." 2.02.464
dost thou hear me, old friend? 2.02.537 P
so /inoculate our old stock but we shall relish 3.01.117 P
apprehension kills | the unseen good old man. 4.01. 12
the nephew to old norway, fortinbras. 4.04. 14
ere we were two days old at sea, a pirate of 4.06. 16 P
which time she chaunted snatches of old lauds, 4.07.177
mountain you have made | t' o'ertop old pelion, 5.01.253
what wouldest thou do, old man? LR 1.01.146
he'll shape his old course in a country new. 1.01.187
he comes like the catastrophe of the old comedy. 1.02.134 P
how old art thou? 1.04. 36 P
nor so old to dote on her for any thing. 1.04. 38 P
as you are old and reverend, should be wise. 1.04.240
old fond eyes, | beweep this cause again, i'll 1.04.301
have thee beaten for being old before thy time. 1.05. 42 P
shouldst not have been old till thou hadst been 1.05. 44 P
o madam, my old heart is crack'd, it's crack'd! 2.01. 90
'tis they have put him on the old man's death, 2.01. 99
our good old friend, | lay comforts to your 2.01.125
what, art thou mad, old fellow? 2.02. 85
sir, i am too old to learn. 2.02.127
o, sir, you are old, | nature in you stands on 2.04.146
"dear daughter, i confess that i am old; 2.04.154
if you do love old men, if your sweet sway 2.04.190
allow obedience, if you yourselves are old, 2.04.191
your passion | must be content to think you old, 2.04.235
you see me here, you gods, a poor old man, | as 2.04.272
the old man and 's people | cannot be well 2.04.288
followed the old man forth. he is return'd. 2.04.295
of them hath borne | against the old kind king; 3.01. 28
a poor, infirm, weak, and despis'd old man; 3.02. 20
'gainst a head | so old and white as this. 3.02. 24
me), the king my old master must be reliev'd. 3.03. 18 P
the younger rises when the old doth fall. 3.03. 25
your old kind father, whose frank heart gave all 3.04. 20
in a wild field were like an old lecher's heart, 3.04.112 P
swallows the old rat and the ditch–dog; 3.04.132 P
thy cruel nails | pluck out his poor old eyes, 3.07. 57
yet, poor old heart, he holp the heavens to rain 3.07. 62
he that will think to live till he be old, 3.07. 69
thou old unhappy traitor, | briefly thyself 4.06.228
nay, come not near th' old man; 4.06.240 P
i am a very foolish fond old man, | fourscore 4.07. 59
i am old and foolish. 4.07. 83
away, old man, give me thy hand, away! 5.02. 5
and sing, and tell old tales, and laugh | at 5.03. 12
it fit | to send the old and miserable king | to 5.03. 46
i am old now, | and these same crosses spoil me. 5.03.278
resign, | during the life of this old majesty, 5.03.300
and not by old gradation, where each second OTH 1.01. 37
for nought but provender, and when he's old, 1.01. 48
an old black ram | is tupping your white ewe. 1.01. 88
that i have ta'en away this old man's daughter, 1.03. 78
these are old fond paradoxes to make fools laugh 2.01.138 P
how does my old acquaintance of this isle? 2.01.203
the hearts of old gave hands; 3.04. 46
an old thing 'twas, but it express'd her fortune 4.03. 29
and pure grief | shore his old thread in twain. 5.02.206
no, you shall paint when you are old. ANT 1.02. 19 P
therein, that when old robes are worn out, there 1.02.164 P
your old smock brings forth a new petticoat, and 1.02.168 P
or murmuring, "where's my serpent of old nile?" 1.05. 25
this is old, what is the success? 3.05. 6 P
a lion's whelp | than with an old one dying. 3.13. 95
let the old ruffian know | i have many other 4.01. 4
then old and fond of issue, took such sorrow CYM 1.01. 37
mark it), the eldest of them at three years old, 1.01. 58
view on't | might well have warm'd old saturn; 2.05. 12
one vice but of a minute old, for one | not half 2.05. 31
a minute old, for one | not half so old as that. 2.05. 32
should we speak of | when we are old as you? 3.03. 36
at three and two years old, i stole these babes, 3.03.101
that man of hers, pisanio, her old servant, | i 3.05. 54
a narrow lane, an old man, and two boys! 5.03. 52
"two boys, an old man (twice a boy), a lane, 5.03. 57
'tis thought the old man and his sons were 5.03. 85
shall after revive, be jointed to the old stock, 5.04.142 P
why, old soldier: 5.05.306
then spare not the old father. 5.05.327
i, old morgan, | am that belarius whom you 5.05.332
shall after revive, be jointed to the old stock, 5.05.440 P
to sing a song that old was sung, | from ashes PER 1.ch. 1
and that to hear an old man sing | may to your 1.ch. 13
pardon old gower — this long's the text. 2.ch. 40
which did steal | the eyes of young and old. 4.01. 41
is it a shame to get when we are old? 4.02. 29 P
old helicanus goes along. 4.04. 13
old escanes, whom helicanus late | advanc'd in 4.04. 15

this borrowed passion stands for true old woe; 4.04. 24
empty | old receptacles, or common shores, of 4.06.175
comes in | like old importment's bastard) has TNK 1.03. 80
chanc'd to name you here, upon the old business. 2.01. 17 P
world 'tis but a gaudy shadow | that old time, 2.02.104
what had we been, old in the court of creon, 2.02.105
we had died as they do, ill old men, unwept, 2.02.109
such a vengeance | that, were i old and wicked, 2.03. 6
yet | and furnish'd with your old strength, i'll 3.06. 37
and at ten years old | they must be all gelt for 4.01.132
thou grand decider | of dusty and old titles, 5.01. 64
how old is she? 5.02. 31
cold as old saturn, and like him possess'd 5.04. 62
a better, to prolong | your old loves to us. ep 17
"were i hard–favor'd, foul, or wrinkled old, VEN 133
say, | the text is old, the orator too green, 806
love makes young men thrall and old men dote, 837
make the young old, the old become a child. 1152
make the young old, the old become a child. 1152
hasty spring still blasts and ne'er grows old! LUC 49
who fears a sentence or an old man's saw | shall 244
to blot old books and alter their contents, | to 948
to dry the old oak's sap and cherish springs, 950
old woes, not infant sorrows, bear them mild; 1096
staring on priam's wounds with her old eyes, 1448
story | the credulous old priam after slew; 1522
priam, why art thou old, and yet not wise? 1550
both stood like old acquaintance in a trance, 1595
"daughter, dear daughter," old lucretius cries, 1751
in thy sweet semblance my old age new born, 1759
but now that fair fresh mirror, dim and old, 1760
the old bees die, the young possess their hive: 1769
and wherefore say not i that i am old? PP 1.10
shall sum my count, and make my old excuse," SON 2.11
this were to be new made when thou art old, 2.13
scorn'd, like old men of less truth than tongue, 17.10
yet do thy worst, old time: 19.13
my glass shall not persuade me i am old, | so 22. 1
black night beauteous and her old face new. 27.12
and with old woes new wail my dear time's waste; 30. 4
than those old nine which rhymers invocate, 38.10
that i might see what the old world could say 59. 9
green, | robbing no old to dress his beauty new, 68.12
so all my best is dressing old words new, 76.11
for as the sun is daily new and old, | so is my 76.13
wrong, | and haply of our old acquaintance tell. 89.12
what old december's bareness every where! 97. 4
to me, fair friend, you never can be old, | for 104. 1
and beauty making beautiful old rhyme | in 106. 3
counting no old thing old, thou mine, i thine, 108. 7
counting no old thing old, thou mine, i thine, 108. 7
dear, | made old offenses of affections new; 110. 4
what thou dost foist upon us that is old, | and 123. 6
in the old age black was not counted fair, | or 127. 1
and wherefore say not i that i am old? 138.10
hour, | let it not tell your judgment i am old, LC 73
in the general bosom reign | of young, of old, 128

OLDCASTLE 1 FR 0.0001 REL FR 0 V 1 P
for oldcastle died /a martyr, and this is not 2H4 ep 32 P

OLDEN 1 FR 0.0001 REL FR 1 V 0 P
blood hath been shed ere now, i' th' olden time, MAC 3.04. 74

OLDER 5 FR 0.0005 REL FR 4 V 1 P
well, catesby, ere a fortnight make me older, R3 3.02. 60
young romeo will be older when you have found ROM 2.04.121 P
older in practice, abler than yourself | to make JC 4.03. 31
an older and a better soldier none | that MAC 4.03.191
grind | on newer proof, to try an older friend, SON 110.11

OLDEST 3 FR 0.0003 REL FR 3 V 0 P
the oldest sins the newest kind of ways? 2H4 4.05.126
as between | the young'st and oldest thing. COR 4.06. 69
the oldest hath borne most; LR 5.03.326

OLD–FAC'D 1 FR 0.0001 REL FR 1 V 0 P
'tis not the rounder of your old–fac'd walls JN 2.01.259

OLDNESS 1 FR 0.0001 REL FR 0 V 1 P
from us till our oldness cannot relish them. LR 1.02. 48 P

OLIVE 5 FR 0.0005 REL FR 4 V 1 P
i hold the olive in my hand; TN 1.05.210 P
but peace puts forth her olive every where. 2H4 4.04. 87
adjudg'd an olive branch and laurel crown, | as 3H6 4.06. 34
city, | and i will use the olive with my sword: TIM 5.04. 82
world | shall bear the olive freely. ANT 4.06. 6

OLIVER 7 FR 0.0008 REL FR 2 V 5 P
to that end i have been with sir oliver martext, AYL 3.03. 43 P
here comes sir oliver. 3.03. 64 P
sir oliver martext, you are well met. 3.03. 64 P
farewell, good master oliver: 3.03. 98 P
not — o sweet oliver, | o brave oliver, | leave 3.03. 99
not — o sweet oliver, | o brave oliver, | leave 3.03.100
a most wicked sir oliver, audrey, a most vile 5.01. 5 P

OLIVERS 1 FR 0.0001 REL FR 1 V 0 P
records | england all olivers and rolands bred 1H6 1.02. 30

OLIVES 2 FR 0.0002 REL FR 2 V 0 P
'tis at the tuft of olives here hard by. AYL 3.05. 75
and peace proclaims olives of endless age. SON 107. 8

OLIVE–TREES 1 FR 0.0001 REL FR 1 V 0 P
a sheep–cote fenc'd about with olive–trees? AYL 4.03. 77

OLIVIA 13 FR 0.0014 REL FR 8 V 5 P
o, when mine eyes did see olivia first, TN 1.01. 18
of) | that he did seek the love of fair olivia. 1.02. 34
babbling gossip of the air | cry out "olivia!" 1.05.274
were you not ev'n now with the countess olivia? 2.02. 2 P
what thriftless sighs shall poor olivia breathe? 2.02. 39
great a pang of heart | as you have for olivia. 2.04. 91
a woman can bear me | and that i owe olivia. 2.04.103
a day–bed, where i have left olivia sleeping — 2.05. 49 P
no, indeed, sir, the lady olivia has no folly. 3.01. 32 P
"thou com'st to the lady olivia, and in my sight 3.04.155 P
belong you to the lady olivia, friends? 5.01. 8 P
not have, | wherein olivia may seem serviceable? 5.01.102
gracious olivia — 5.01.105

OLIVIA'S 2 FR 0.0002 REL FR 0 V 2 P
a fool that the lady olivia's father took much TN 2.04. 12 P
art not thou the lady olivia's fool? 3.01. 31 P

OLYMPIAN 2 FR 0.0002 REL FR 2 V 0 P
rewards | as victors wear at the olympian games. 3H6 2.03. 53
/hemm'd thee in, | like an olympian wrastling. TRO 4.05.194

OLYMPUS' 1 FR 0.0001 REL FR 1 V 0 P
now climbeth tamora olympus' top, | safe out of TIT 2.01. 1

OLYMPUS 5 FR 0.0005 REL FR 4 V 1 P
o thou great thunder–darter of olympus, forget TRO 2.03. 10 P
bows, | as if olympus to a molehill should | in COR 5.03. 30
hence! wilt thou lift up olympus? JC 3.01. 74
though they do appear | as huge as high olympus. 4.03. 92
pelion, or the skyish head | of blue olympus. HAM 5.01.254

OLYMPUS–HIGH 1 FR 0.0001 REL FR 1 V 0 P
bark climb hills of seas | olympus–high, and OTH 2.01.188

OMAN *(also omans, woman)*

OMAN 11 FR 0.0012 REL FR 0 V 11 P
but can you affection the oman? WIV 1.01.227 P
for it is a oman that altogether's acquaintance 1.02. 8 P
you are a very simplicity oman; 4.01. 30 P
leave your prabbles, oman. 4.01. 50 P
oman, forbear. 4.01. 55 P
for shame, oman. 4.01. 64 P
oman, art thou /lunatics? 4.01. 69 P
yea and no, i think the oman is a witch indeed. 4.02.192 P
i like not when a oman has a great peard. 4.02.193 P
best discretions of a oman as ever i did look 4.04. 2 P
and has been grievously peaten as an old oman. 4.04. 21 P

OMANS 1 FR 0.0001 REL FR 0 V 1 P
your wife is as honest a omans as i will desires WIV 3.03.220 P

OMEN 1 FR 0.0001 REL FR 1 V 0 P
the fates | and prologue to the omen coming on, HAM 1.01.123

OMINOUS 10 FR 0.0011 REL FR 7 V 3 P
very ominous endings. ADO 5.02. 39 P
o, ominous! he comes to kill my heart. AYL 3.02.246 P
thou ominous and fearful owl of death, | our 1H6 4.02. 15
for gloucester's dukedom is too ominous. 3H6 2.06.107
fatal and ominous to noble peers! R3 3.03. 10
thy mother's name is ominous to children. 4.01. 40
my dreams will sure prove ominous to the day. TRO 5.03. 6
enrapt | to tell thee that this day is ominous: 5.03. 66
take heed, the quarrel's most ominous to us. 5.07. 20 P
when he lay couched in th' ominous horse, | hath HAM 2.02.454

OMISSION 1 FR 0.0001 REL FR 1 V 0 P
omission to do what is necessary | seals a TRO 3.03.230

OMIT 16 FR 0.0018 REL FR 16 V 0 P
whose influence | if now i court not, but omit, TMP 1.02.183
you, sir, | do not omit the heavy offer of it. 2.01.194
what if we do omit | this reprobate till he were MM 4.03. 73
omit | nothing may give us aid. WT 4.04.624
therefore omit him not, blunt not his love, 2H4 4.04. 27
omit no happy hour | that may give furth'rance H5 1.02.300
between them — and omit | all the occurrences, 5.pr. 39
if you omit | the offer of this time, i cannot H8 3.02. 3
ignorance — it must omit | real necessities, COR 3.01.146
i will omit no opportunity | that may convey my ROM 3.05. 49
sense of beauty, do omit | their mortal natures, OTH 2.01. 71
the due of honor in no point omit. CYM 3.05. 11
omit we all their dole and woe. PER 3.ch. 42
yet nothing we'll omit | that bears recovery's 5.01. 53
omit not any thing | in the pretended TNK 1.01.209
seat, and in that motion might | omit a ward, or 5.03. 63

OMIT'ST 1 FR 0.0001 REL FR 1 V 0 P
the most accursed thou, that still omit'st it. TIM 1.01.259

OMITTANCE 1 FR 0.0001 REL FR 1 V 0 P
omittance is no quittance. AYL 3.05.133

OMITTED 4 FR 0.0004 REL FR 4 V 0 P
no time shall be omitted | that will be time, LLL 4.03.378
that, his apparent open guilt omitted — | i R3 3.05. 30
omitted, all the voyage of their life | is bound JC 4.03.220
no needful thing omitted. PER 5.03. 68

OMITTING 2 FR 0.0002 REL FR 2 V 0 P
omitting the sweet benefit of time | to clothe TGV 2.04. 65
omitting suffolk's exile, my soul's treasure? 2H6 3.02.382

/OMNE 1 FR 0.0001 REL FR 0 V 1 P
gelida quando /pecus /omne sub umbra ruminat — LLL 4.02. 93 P

OMNE 1 FR 0.0001 REL FR 1 V 0 P
but omne bene, say i, being of an old father's LLL 4.02. 32

OMNES 1 FR 0.0001 REL FR 1 V 0 P
dii deaeque omnes! TNK 3.05.158

OMNIPOTENT 3 FR 0.0003 REL FR 1 V 2 P
o omnipotent love, how near the god drew to the WIV 5.05. 7 P
friends, | yet know, my master, god omnipotent, R2 3.03. 85
this is the most omnipotent villain that ever 1H4 1.02.109 P

ON *(also a'*, an*, o'*)*

/ON 56 FR 0.0063 REL FR 49 V 7 P

ON 3125 FR 0.3532 REL FR 2585 V 540 P

/ONCE 7 FR 0.0008 REL FR 6 V 1 P
/because /a /bard /of /ireland /told /me /once R3 4.02.106
which /once," quoth forrest, "almost chang'd my 4.03. 15
good night and welcome, both /at /once, to those TRO 5.01. 77
/fiends /have /been /in /poor /tom /at /once: LR 4.01. 59 P
/have /seen | /sunshine /and /rain /at /once; 4.03. 18
/once /or /twice /she /heav'd /the /name /of 4.03. 25
to be once in doubt | is /once to be resolv'd. OTH 3.03.180

ONCE 455 FR 0.0514 REL FR 385 V 70 P
not | four, or five, women once that tended me? TMP 1.02. 47
being once perfected how to grant suits, | how 1.02. 79
where once | thou call'dst me up at midnight to 1.02.227
once in a month recount what thou hast been, 1.02.262
me, | might i but through my prison once a day 1.02.491
were i in england now (as once i was) and had 2.02. 28 P
moon–calf, speak once in thy life, if thou beest 3.02. 21 P
be pleas'd to hearken once again to the suit i 3.02. 39 P
(worse than any death | can be at once) shall 3.03. 78
who once again | i tender to thy hand. 4.01. 4
once more adieu. TGV 1.01. 53
and the matter may be both at once deliver'd. 1.01.130 P
once more, new servant, welcome; 2.04.118
i'll be so bold to break the seal for once. 3.01.139
rehearse that once more. 3.01.357 P
and once again i do receive thee honest. 5.04. 78
if once again, | /milan shall not hold thee. 5.04.128
once to–night | give my sweet nan this ring. WIV 3.04. 99
she desires you once more to come to her, 3.05. 45 P
who ask'd them once or twice what they had in 3.05.102 P
satisfy me once more, once more search with me. 4.02.165 P
satisfy me once more, once more search with me. 4.02.165 P
let our wives | yet once again (to make us 4.04. 13
let them from forth a sawpit rush at once | with 4.04. 54
meeting, they will at once display to the night. 5.03. 15 P
once more fare you well. MM 1.01. 72
what was done to elbow's wife, once more? 2.01.140 P
once, sir? there was nothing done to her once. 2.01.141 P
once, sir? there was nothing done to her once. 2.01.142 P
why, all the souls that were were forfeit once, 2.02. 73
vigor, art and nature, | once stir my temper; 2.02.184
better it were a brother died at once, | than 2.04.106
i was once before him for getting a wench with 4.03.169 P
that no particular scandal once can touch | but 4.04. 27
alack, when once our grace we have forgot, 4.04. 33
which once thou swor'st was worth the looking on 5.01.208
call that same isabel here once again, i would 5.01.269 P
the time was once, when thou unurg'd wouldst vow ERR 2.02.113
once this — your long experience of /her wisdom 3.01. 89
not once, nor twice, but twenty times you have. 3.02.172
yet once again proclaim it publicly, | if any 5.01.130
once did i get him bound, and sent him home, 5.01.145
the man | that hadst a wife once call'd aemilia, 5.01.343
'tis once, thou lovest, | and i will fit thee ADO 1.01.318
once before he won it of me with false dice, 2.01.280 P
a voice | to slander music any more than once. 2.03. 45
or in the shape of two countries at once, as a 3.02. 35 P
and you be a cursing hypocrite once, you must be 5.01.208 P
at thee, | as once europa did at lusty jove, 5.04. 46
i saw him at the duke alanson's once, | and much LLL 2.01. 61
did not i dance with you in brabant once? 2.01.114
did not i dance with you in brabant once? 2.01.115
once more i'll read the ode that i have writ. 4.03. 97
once more i'll mark how love can vary wit. 4.03. 98
/let us once lose our oaths to find ourselves, 4.03.358
"once to behold," rogue. 5.02.168 P
"once to behold with your sun–beamed eyes, | — 5.02.169
twice to your visor, and half once to you. 5.02.227
your oath once broke, you force not to forswear. 5.02.440
which once disclos'd, | the ladies did change 5.02.467
by being once false for ever to be true | to 5.02.773
(where i did meet thee once with helena | to do MND 1.01.166
since once i sat upon a promontory, | and heard 2.01.149
the herb i showed thee once. 2.01.169
having once this juice, | i'll watch titania 2.01.176
you speak all your part at once, cues and all. 3.01.100 P
o, once tell true; 3.02. 68
then will two at once woo one; 3.02.118
for if but once thou show me thy grey light, 3.02.419
i was with hercules and cadmus once, | when in a 4.01.112
if i can catch him once upon the hip, | i will MV 1.03. 46
but come at once, | for the close night doth 2.06. 46
let's see once more this saying grav'd in gold: 2.07. 36
tell me once more what title thou dost bear: 2.09. 35
you | wrest once the law to your authority: 4.01.215
be judge | whether bassanio had not once a love. 4.01.277
i once did lend my body for his wealth, | which, 5.01.249
and a chain, that you once wore, about his neck. AYL 3.02.181 P
narrow–mouth'd bottle, either too much at once, 3.02.201 P
that you insult, exult, and all at once, | over 3.05. 36
bounds | that the old carlot once was master of. 3.05.108
patience once more, whiles our compact is urg'd: 5.04. 5
since once he play'd a farmer's eldest son. SHR in.1. 84
and once again a pot o' th' smallest ale. in.2. 75
o that once more you knew but what you are! in.2. 78
ashore, | we could at once put us in readiness, 1.01. 43
tranio, at once | uncase thee; 1.01.206
and he begin once, he'll rail in his rope–tricks 1.02.112 P
if once i find thee ranging, | hortensio will be 3.01. 91
which once perform'd, let all the world say no, 3.02.141
once more toward our father's. 4.05. 1
fair lovely maid, once more good day to thee. 4.05. 33
better once than never, for never too late. 5.01.150
virginity, by being once lost, may be ten times AWW 1.01.130 P
with, should be once heard and thrice beaten. 2.05. 31 P
miseries which nature owes | were mine at once. 3.02.120
i spoke with her but once | and found her 3.06.112
therefore once more to this captain dumaine. 4.03.247 P
thou put upon me at once both the office of god 5.02. 49 P
mayst see a sunshine and a hail | in me at once. 5.03. 34
and water once a day her chamber round | with TN 1.01. 28
we'll once more hear orsino's embassy. 1.05.166
fare ye well at once; 2.01. 39 P
i was ador'd once too. 2.03.181 P
whose fair flow'r | being once display'd, doth 2.04. 39
once more, cesario, | get thee to yond same 2.04. 79
maria once told me she did affect me, and i have 2.05. 23 P
once in a sea–fight 'gainst the count his 3.03. 26
sir, for this once, and let your flesh and blood 5.01. 33 P
never, but once. WT 1.02. 89
but once before i spoke to th' purpose? 1.02.100
canst with thine eyes at once see good and evil, 1.02.303
to't) once remove | the root of his opinion, 2.03. 89
once more, take her hence. 2.03.112
once a day i'll visit | the chapel where they 3.02.238
yet for this once, yea, superstitiously, | i 3.03. 40
i knew him once a servant of the prince. 4.03. 87 P
pray you once more, | is not your father grown 4.04.396
for once or twice | i was about to speak, and 4.04.442
and thus your verse | flow'd with her beauty once. 5.01.102
i desire my life | once more to look on him. 5.01.138
she is, | when once she is my wife. 5.01.209
that "once," i see, by your good father's speed, 5.01.210
but once he slander'd me with bastardy. JN 1.01. 74
and once dispatch'd him in an embassy | to 1.01. 99
and part your mingled colors once again, | turn 2.01.389
here once again we sit; 4.02. 1
once /again crown'd, | and look'd upon, i hope, 4.02. 1
this "once again" (but that your highness 4.02. 3
your highness pleas'd) | was once superfluous. 4.02. 4
once more to–day well met, distemper'd lords! 4.03. 21
up once again! 5.04. 2
once more, the more to aggravate the note, R2 1.01. 43
foe, | once did i lay an ambush for your life, 1.01.137
to crop at once a too long withered flower. 2.01.134
comes rushing on this woeful land at once! 2.02. 99
farewell at once, for once, for all, and ever. 2.02.148
farewell at once, for once, for all, and ever. 2.02.148
dar'd once to touch a dust of england's ground? 2.03. 91
for joy | to stand upon my kingdom once again. 3.02. 5
knees, | which on thy royal party granted once, 3.03.115
i live, | and buried once, why not upon my head? 3.03.159
scorns to unsay what once it hath delivered. 4.01. 9
once more, adieu, the rest let sorrow say. 5.01.102
walls | with painted imagery had said at once, 5.02. 16

shall thy old dugs once more a traitor rear? 5.03. 90
but i will have them if i once know where. 5.03.143
well then, once in my days i'll be a madcap. 1H4 1.02.142 P
and when i urg'd the ransom once again | of my 1.03.141
then once more to your scottish prisoners: 1.03.259
where you and douglas and our powers at once, 1.03.296
leave | to tell you once again that at my birth 3.01. 36
discomfited great douglas, ta'en him once, 3.02.114
to a bawdy–house not above once in a quarter — 3.03. 17 P
this encounter, | if once they join in trial. 5.01. 85
yet once ere night | i will embrace him with a 5.02. 72
being bruited once, took fire and heat away 2H4 1.01.114
which once in him abated, all the rest | turn'd 1.01.117
and i but fist him once, and 'a come but within 2.01. 21 P
and those that were thy peach–color'd once, or 2.02. 16 P
the prince once set a dish of apple–johns before 2.04. 5 P
and they be once in a calm, they are sick. 2.04. 37 P
and were these inward wars once out of hand, 3.01.107
i was once of clement's inn, where i think they 3.02. 14 P
a man can die but once, we owe god a death. 3.02.235 P
'a ne'er saw him but once in the tilt–yard, and 3.02.322 P
be look'd upon and learnt, which once attain'd, 4.04. 71
and i cannot once or twice in a quarter bear out 5.01. 48 P
or peace, or both at once, may be | as things 5.02.138
i have been merry twice and once ere now. 5.03. 39 P
i hope to see london once ere i die. 5.03. 60 P
so soon did lose his seat (and all at once) | as H5 1.01. 36
for once the eagle (england) being in prey, | to 1.02.169
so may a thousand actions, once afoot, | /end in 1.02.211
'a said once, the dev'l would have him about 2.03. 35 P
once more unto the breach, dear friends, once 3.01. 1
more unto the breach, dear friends, once more; 3.01. 1
me best, | if i begin the batt'ry once again, 3.03. 7
i once writ a sonnet in his praise and began 3.07. 39 P
once more i come to know of thee, king harry, 4.03. 79
the man that once did sell the lion's skin 4.03. 93
i fear thou wilt once more come again for a 4.03.128 P
in once more! 4.05. 11
but i would fain see it once, and please god of 4.07.164 P
to wear it in my cap till i see him once again, 5.01. 12 P
council presently | to sit with us once more, 5.02. 80
news would cause him once more yield the ghost. 1H6 1.01. 67
durst not presume to look once in the face. 1.01.140
my heart and hands thou hast at once subdu'd. 1.02.109
which caesar and his fortune bare at once. 1.02.139
i myself fight not once in forty year. 1.03. 91
once in contempt they would have barter'd me; 1.04. 31
then say at once if i maintain'd the truth; 2.04. 5
were growing time once ripened to my will. 2.04. 99
my sighs and tears, and will not once relent? 3.01.108
and once again we'll sleep secure in roan. 3.02. 19
which, once discern'd, shows that her meaning is 3.02. 24
for once i read | that stout pendragon in his 3.02. 94
when talbot hath set footing once in france 3.03. 64
once i encount'red him, and thus i said: 4.07. 37
"if once he come to be a cardinal, | he'll make 5.01. 32
help me this once, that france may get the field 5.03. 12
yet, if this servile usage once offend, | go, 5.03. 58
if once it be neglected, ten to one | we shall 5.04.157
as did the youthful paris once to greece, | with 5.05.104
with walking once about the quadrangle, | i come 2H6 1.03.153
two pulls at once — | his lady banish'd, and a 2.03. 41
my lords, at once: 3.01. 66
once by the king, and three times thrice by thee 3.02.358
for i did but seal once to a thing, and i was 4.02. 83 P
but stay, i'll read it over once again. 4.04. 14
i, | or felt that pain which i did for him once, 3H6 1.01.221
will follow mine, if once they see them spread; 1.01.252
o clifford, but bethink thee once again, | and 1.04. 44
and once again bestride our foaming steeds, 2.01.183
foaming steeds, | and once again cry "charge!" 2.01.184
foes, | but never once again turn back and fly. 2.01.185
away, away! once more, sweet lords, farewell. 2.03. 48
let me give humble thanks for all at once. 3.03.221
and for this once my will shall stand for law. 4.01. 50
to set the crown once more on henry's head. 4.04. 27
(for trust not him that hath once broken faith), 4.04. 30
and says that once more i shall interchange | my 4.07. 3
my liege, i'll knock once more to summon them. 4.07. 16
but when the fox hath once got in his nose, 4.07. 25
and, that once gotten, doubt not of large pay. 4.07. 88
and all at once, once more a happy farewell. 4.08. 31
and all at once, once more a happy farewell. 4.08. 31
and once again proclaim us king of england. 4.08. 53
for once allow'd the skillful pilot's charge? 5.04. 20
once more we sit in england's royal throne, 5.07. 1
the which thou once didst bend against her R3 1.02. 95
i would they were, that i might die at once; 1.02.151
and, in the holes | where eyes did once inhabit, 1.04. 30
it made me once restore a purse of gold that (by 1.04.139 P
then say at once what is it thou requests. 2.01. 99
yet none of you would once beg for his life. 2.01.131
my lord, you shall overrule my mind for once. 3.01. 57
after he once fell in with mistress shore. 3.05. 51
and so once more return and tell his grace. 3.07. 91
that call'd your grace | to breakfast once, 4.04.177
once more, what news? 4.04.462
once more, adieu! 5.03.102
once more, good night, kind lords and gentlemen. 5.03.107
by sick interpreters (once weak ones) is | not H8 1.02. 82
well dispos'd, the mind growing once corrupt, 1.02.116
habits put the graces | that once were his, and 1.02.123
and once more | i show'r a welcome on ye. 1.04. 62
and a measure | to lead 'em once again, and then 1.04.107
and out of ruins | made my name once more noble. 2.01.115
when they once perceive | the least rub in your 2.01.128
for when the king once heard it, out of anger 2.01.150
whom once more i present unto your highness. 2.02. 97
and once more in mine arms i bid him welcome, 2.02. 98
there was a lady once ('tis an old story) | that 2.03. 90
refuse you for my judge, whom, yet once more, 2.04. 82
not there | at once and fully satisfied), 2.04.149
lest at once | the burthen of my sorrows fall 3.01.110
lily, | that once was mistress of the field, and 3.01.152
to hear such news as this | once every hour. 3.02. 25
say wolsey, that once trod the ways of glory, 3.02.435
y' are well met once again. 4.01. 1
than but once think his place becomes thee not. 5.02.168
once more, my lord of winchester, i charge you, 5.02.204
i miss'd the meteor once, and hit that woman, 5.03. 50 P
but let the ruffian boreas once enrage | the TRO 1.03. 38
thus once again says nestor from the greeks: 2.02. 2
it, | nor once deject the courage of our minds, 2.02.121
should once set footing in your generous bosoms? 2.02.155
greatness, once fall'n out with fortune, | must 3.03. 75
the cry went once on thee, | and still it might, 3.03.184
i had good argument for kissing once. 4.05. 26
knew thy grandsire, | and once fought with him. 4.05.197
in faith, i do not. come hither once again. 5.02. 49
i say, at once, let your brief plagues be mercy, 5.10. 8
and being once subdu'd in armed tail, | sweet 5.10. 43
and though that all at once" — | you, my good COR 1.01.140
"though all at once cannot | see what i do 1.01.142
shalt see me once more strike at tullus' face. 1.01.240
once if he do require our voices, we ought not 2.03. 1 P
for once we stood up about the corn, he himself 2.03. 15 P
way should be at once to all the points a' th' 2.03. 23 P
at once pluck out | the multitudinous tongue; 3.01.155
the service of the foot | being once gangren'd, 3.01.305
being once chaf'd, he cannot | be rein'd again 3.03. 27
could i meet 'em | but once a day, it would 4.02. 47
once more to hew thy target from thy brawn, | or 4.05.120
stood for rome, | and durst not once peep out. 4.06. 46
him) once more offer'd | the first conditions, 5.03. 13
i'll trust by leisure him that mocks me once, TIT 1.01.301
horns, | as if a double hunt were heard at once, 2.03. 19
the wand'ring prince and dido once enjoyed, 2.03. 22
will not permit mine eyes once to behold | the 2.03.218
thy hand once more; 2.03.243
grave tribunes, once more i entreat of you — 3.01. 31
the dam will wake and if she wind ye once; 4.01. 97
whose name was once our terror, now our comfort, 5.01. 10
once more, on pain of death, all men depart. ROM 1.01.103
and i might live to see thee married once, | i 1.03. 61
five times in that ere once in our /five wits. 1.04. 47
which, once untangled, much misfortune bodes. 1.04. 91
break, my heart, poor bankrout, break at once! 3.02. 57
all three do meet | in thee at once, which thou 3.03.121
thee at once, which thou at once wouldst lose. 3.03.121
me alone, | i'll play the huswife for this once. 4.02. 43
now at once run on | the dashing rocks thy 5.03.117
then say at once what thou dost know in this. 5.03.228
my lord, that you would once use our hearts, TIM 1.02. 85 P
nay, and you begin to rail on society once, i am 1.02.244 P
and he that's once denied will hardly speed. 3.02. 62
good day at once. 3.04. 7
i'll once more feast the rascals. 3.04.112
them all, let in the tide | of knaves once more; 3.04.117
have i once liv'd to see two honest men? 5.01. 56
who once a day with his embossed froth | the 5.01.217
what say'st thou to me now? speak once again. JC 1.02. 22
for once, upon a raw and gusty day, | the 1.02.100
now in the names of all the gods at once, | upon 1.02.148
there was a brutus once that would have brook'd 1.02.159
and, as i told you, he put it by once; 1.02.239 P
but when he once attains the upmost round, | he 2.01. 24
quite from the main opinion he held once | of 2.01.196
i charm you, by my once commended beauty, | by 2.01.271
the valiant never taste of death but once. 2.02. 33
you all did love him once, not without cause; 3.02.102
with meditating that she must die once, | i have 4.03.191
let them set on at once; 5.02. 3
at sardis once, | and, this last night, here in 5.05. 18
so fare you well at once, for brutus' tongue 5.05. 39
by each at once her choppy finger laying | upon MAC 1.03. 44
at once, good night. 3.04.117
upon the order of your going, | but go at once. 3.04.119
thrice, and once the hedge–pig whin'd. 4.01. 2
i take my leave at once. 4.02. 30
blisters our tongues, | was once thought honest; 4.03. 13
such welcome and unwelcome things at once | 'tis 4.03.138
but who knows nothing, is once seen to smile; 4.03.167
to receive at once the benefit of sleep and do 5.01. 10 P
slaughterous thoughts, | cannot once start me. 5.05. 15
so thanks to all at once and to each one, | whom 5.09. 40
while, | and let us once again assail your ears, HAM 1.01. 31
so frown'd he once, when, in an angry parle, 1.01. 62
i saw him once, 'a was a goodly king. 1.02.186
yet once methought | it lifted up it head and 1.02.215
of life, of crown, of queen, at once dispatch'd, 1.05. 75
fare thee well at once! 1.05. 88
say you then, would heart of man once think it? 1.05.121
once more remove, good friends. 1.05.163
i heard thee speak me a speech once, but it was 2.02.434 P
was never acted, or, if it was, not above once; 2.02.435 P
i did love you once. 3.01.114 P
my lord, you play'd once i' th' university, you 3.02. 99 P
if, once i be a widow, ever i be a wife! 3.02.223
my lord, you once did love me. 3.02.335 P
once more, good night, | and when you are 3.04.170
skull had a tongue in it, and could sing once. 5.01. 76 P
'a pour'd a flagon of rhenish on my head once. 5.01.180 P
till i have caught her once more in mine arms. 5.01.250
i once did hold it, as our statists do, | a 5.02. 33
smile once more, turn thy wheel! LR 2.02.173
moulds, all germains spill at once | that makes 3.02. 8
importune him once more to go, my lord, | his 3.04.161
when the rain came to wet me once, and the wind 4.06.101 P
'tis wonder that thy life and wits at once | had 4.07. 40
would hourly die | rather than die at once!), 5.03.187
took once a pliant hour, and found good means OTH 1.03.151
desdemona, | once more, well met at cyprus. 2.01.212
to be once in doubt | is /once to be resolv'd. 3.03.179
this — | away at once with love or jealousy! 3.03.192
i once more take my leave. 3.03.257
but once put out thy light, | thou cunning'st 5.02. 10
o thou othello, that was once so good, | fall'n 5.02.291
and say besides, that in aleppo once, | where a 5.02.352
when thou once | was beaten from modena, where ANT 1.04. 56
that i should | once name you derogately, when 2.02. 34
i saw her once | hop forty paces through the 2.02.228
nourisheth it, and the elements once out of it, 2.07. 45 P
seeks, and will not take when once 'tis offer'd, 2.07. 83
she once being loof'd, | the noble ruin of her 3.10. 17
if from the field i shall return once more | to 3.13.173
all my sad captains, fill our bowls once more; 3.13.183
thou and those thy scars had once prevail'd | to 4.05. 2
reward thee | once for thy sprightly comfort, 4.07. 15
death of one person can be paid but once, | and 4.14. 27
heart, once be stronger than thy continent, 4.14. 40
do it at once, | or thy precedent services are 4.14. 82
then let it do at once | the thing why thou hast 4.14. 88
if idle talk will once be necessary, | i'll not 5.02. 50
nor once be chastis'd with the sober eye | of 5.02. 54
this knot intrinsicate | of life at once untie. 5.02.305
jove — | once more let me behold it. CYM 2.04. 99
she gave it me, and said | she priz'd it once. 2.04.104
once, and a million! 2.04.143
the fam'd cassibelan, who was once at point | (o 3.01. 30
and my report was once | first with the best of 3.03. 57
once arviragus, in as like a figure, | strikes 3.03. 96
discover where thy mistress is, at once, | at 3.05. 95
sing him to th' ground, | as once to our mother; 4.02.237
heavens, | how deeply you at once do touch me! 4.03. 4
hind that shall | once touch my shoulder. 5.03. 78
when once he was mature for man, | in britain 5.04. 52
which tells /me in that glory once he was; PER 2.03. 38
the /vial once more. 3.02. 90
walk, and be cheerful once again, reserve | that 4.01. 39
do in such a place as this, she being once gone. 4.05. 3 P
in your supposing once more put your sight: 5.ch. 21
yet once more | let me entreat to know at large 5.01. 61
at once subduing | thy force and thy affection; TNK 1.01. 84
once more, farewell all. 1.01.225
once with a time when i enjoy'd a playfellow; 1.03. 50
us, i disclaim | if thou once think upon her! 2.02.174
once more | i would but see this fair one. 2.02.231
the sports | once ended, we'll perform. 2.03. 59
driven to | when fifteen once has found us! 2.04. 7
once he kiss'd me — | i lov'd my lips the 2.04. 25
do you, | as once did meleager and the boar, 3.05. 18
nay, and she fail me once — you can tell, arcas 3.05. 46
able once again | to out–dure danger. 3.06. 9
once more farewell, my cousin. 3.06.106
it, | and, by mine honor, once again it stands, 3.06.289
for, if she see him once, she's gone — she's 4.01.124
i was once, sir, in great hope she had fix'd her 4.03. 64 P
your gentle daughter gave me freedom once; 5.04. 24
is, when the thread of hazard is once spun, | a STM III 20
and now the happy season once more fits | that VEN 327
but when the heart's attorney once is mute, 335
once more the engine of her thoughts began: 367
and once made perfect, never lost again." 408
once more the ruby–color'd portal open'd, 451
"o, thou didst kill me, kill me once again. 499
soldiers when their captain once doth yield, 893
from their dark beds once more leap her eyes, 1050
doth yet in his fair welkin once appear, | till LUC 116
which once corrupted takes the worser part; 294
that twice she doth begin ere once she speaks. 567
what dar'st thou not when once thou art a king? 606
who wayward once, his mood with nought agrees. 1095
once set on ringing, with his own weight goes; 1494
ere once she can discharge one word of woe; 1605
with this they all at once began to say, | her 1709
glass, | that i no more can see what once i was! 1764
"once," quoth she, "did i see a fair sweet youth PP 9. 9
so beauty blemish'd once, for ever lost, | in 13.11
but if fortune once do frown, | then farewell 20.45
after a thousand victories once foil'd, | is SON 25.10
and shalt by fortune once more re–survey | these 32. 3
when you have bid your servant once adieu. 57. 8
nativity, once in the main of light, | crawls to 60. 5
though i (once gone) to all the world must die; 81. 6
that you were once unkind befriends me now, 120. 1
to weigh how once i suffered in your crime. 120. 8
not once vouchsafe to hide my will in thine? 135. 6
and death once dead, there's no more dying then. 146.14
the little love–god, lying once asleep, | laid 154. 1
anon their gazes lend | to every place at once, LC 27

ONE *(also o'*)*

/ONE 35 FR 0.0039 REL FR 29 V 6 P

/one whose hard heart is button'd up with steel; ERR 4.02. 34
armado /a' /th' /one side — o, a most dainty LLL 4.01.144
within /t' /one year it will make itself two, AWW 1.01.147 P
thy cheeks | confess it, /t' /one to th' other, 1.03.177
but /one that lies three thirds and uses a known 2.05. 29 P
/in /twelve, | /found /truth /in /all /but /one; R2 4.01.171
/owes /two /buckets, /filling /one /another, 4.01.185
/shouldst /thou /find /one /heinous /article, 4.01.233
/i'll /beg /one /boon, | /and /then /be /gone 4.01.302
like /one that draws the model of an house 2H4 1.03. 58
/on /one /and /other /side, /troyan /and /greek, TRO pr 21
for honor | than /one /an /'s ears to hear it? COR 2.02. 81
where one part does disdain with cause, the 3.01.143
/one pain is less'ned by another's anguish; ROM 1.02. 46
and thou and romeo press /one heavy bier! 3.02. 60
/then /is /the /world /one. HAM 2.02.244 P
/a /goodly /one, /in /which /there /are /many 2.02.245 P
/dungeons, /denmark /being /one /o' /th' /worst. 2.02.246 P
/why /then /your /ambition /makes /it /one. 2.02.252 P
/man's /life's /no /more /than /to /say "/one." 5.02. 74
/the /one /in /motley /here, | /the /other LR 1.04.146
/and /for /one /blast /of /thy /minikin /mouth, 3.06. 43
/else /one /self /mate /and /make /could /not 4.03. 34
thou hast /one daughter | who redeems nature 4.06.205
thou hast, | they'll grind /th' /one the other. ANT 3.05. 15
but, | like a full–acorn'd boar, a german /one, CYM 2.05. 16
fair /one, all goodness that consists in beauty, PER 5.01. 70
/one | that fears not to do harm; TNK 1.02. 70
air, or at adventure humm'd /one | from musical 1.03. 75
not /one of you here present, | had there such STM II.C 62
not /one of you should live an aged man, | for II.C 83
ravenous fishes | would feed on /one another. II.C 87
/one supposition, which if you will mark | you II.C 91
let it then suffice | to drown /one woe, one LUC 1680
/one blushing shame, another white despair; SON 99. 9

ONE 1909 FR 0.2158 REL FR 1371 V 538 P

but in care of thee | (of thee my dear one, thee TMP 1.02. 17
else exact — like one | who having into truth, 1.02. 99
levied, one midnight | fated to th' purpose, did 1.02.128
for one thing she did | they would not take her 1.02.266
taught thee each hour | one thing or other. 1.02.355

soft, sir, one word more. 1.02.450
one word more: 1.02.453
one word more | shall make me chide thee, if not 1.02.476
one. tell. 2.01. 15 P
if but one of his pockets could speak, would it 2.01. 66 P
one stroke | shall free thee from the tribute 2.01.292
o, but one word. 2.01.296
i heard a humming | (and that a strange one too) 2.01.318
yond same black cloud, yond huge one, looks like 2.02. 21 P
i do not know | one of my sex; 3.01. 49
interrupt the monster one word further, and, by 3.02. 69 P
nor hath not | one spirit to command: 3.02. 94
do not, for one repulse, forgo the purpose 3.03. 12
that in arabia | there is one tree, the phoenix' 3.03. 23
one phoenix | at this hour reigning there. 3.03. 23
each putter-out of five for one will bring us 3.03. 48
as diminish | one dowle that's in my plume. 3.03. 65
but one fiend at a time, | i'll fight their 3.03.102
cry "so, so," | each one, tripping on his toe, 4.01. 46
and these fresh nymphs encounter every one | in 4.01.137
one of their kind, that relish all as sharply 5.01. 23
not one of them | that yet looks on me, or would 5.01. 82
the island, one dear son | shall i twice lose. 5.01.176
father | for his advice, nor thought i had one. 5.01.191
in one voyage | did claribel her husband find at 5.01.208
one of them | is a plain fish, and no doubt 5.01.265
and one so strong | that could control the moon, 5.01.269
and this demi-devil | (for he's a bastard one) 5.01.273
i should have been a sore one then. 5.01.289 P
you shall take your rest | for this one night; 5.01.303
one fading moment's mirth | with twenty watchful TGV 1.01. 30
twenty to one then he is shipp'd already, | and 1.01. 72
lo, here in one line is his name twice writ, 1.02.120
thus will i fold them one upon another; 1.02.125
as one relying on your lordship's will, | and 1.03. 61
then this may be yours — for this is but one. 2.01. 2
to walk alone, like one that had the pestilence; 2.01. 21 P
to fast, like one that takes diet; 2.01. 24 P
to watch, like one that fears robbing; 2.01. 25 P
when you walk'd, to walk like one of the lions; 2.01. 28 P
that's because the one is painted, and the other 2.01. 56 P
me to write some lines to one she loves. 2.01. 88 P
air, i am one that am nourish'd by my victuals, 2.01.173 P
did not this cruel-hearted cur shed one tear. 2.03. 9 P
even as one heat another heat expels, | or as 2.04.192
or as one nail by strength drives out another, 2.04.193
where, for one shot of five pence, thou shalt 2.05. 9 P
why, stand-under and under-stand is all one. 2.05. 33 P
and when the flight is made to one so dear, | of 2.07. 12
myself am one made privy to the plot. 3.01. 12
what lets but one may enter at her window? 3.01.113
and built so shelving that one cannot climb it 3.01.115
i'll get me one of such another length. 3.01.133
but that's all one, if he be but one knave. 3.01.265 P
but that's all one, if he be but one knave. 3.01.265 P
by one whom she esteemeth as his friend. 3.02. 37
master, be one of them; 4.01. 38
you would have them always play but one thing? 4.02. 71 P
i would always have one play but one thing. 4.02. 72
i would always have one play but one thing. 4.02. 72
one, lady, if you knew his pure heart's truth, 4.02. 88
one that attends your ladyship's command. 4.03. 5
one that i brought up of a puppy; 4.04. 2 P
one that i sav'd from drowning, when three or 4.04. 3 P
taught him, even as one would say precisely, 4.04. 5 P
i would have (as one should say) one that takes 4.04. 11 P
say) one that takes upon him to be a dog indeed, 4.04. 11 P
"out with the dog," says one. 4.04. 20 P
one julia, that his changing thoughts forget, 4.04.119
she says it is a fair one. 5.02. 9
a thousand more mischances than this one | have 5.03. 3
vouchsafe me, for my meed, but one fair look: 5.04. 23
death, | would i not undergo for one calm look? 5.04. 42
than plural faith, which is too much by one. 5.04. 52
now i dare not say | i have one friend alive; 5.04. 66
that one error | fills him with faults; 5.04.111
to grant one boon that i shall ask of you. 5.04.150
one feast, one house, one mutual happiness. 5.04.173
one feast, one house, one mutual happiness. 5.04.173
one feast, one house, one mutual happiness. 5.04.173
but that is all one. WIV 1.01. 30 P
a liar as i do despise one that is false, or as 1.01. 69 P
is false, or as i despise one that is not true. 1.01. 69 P
do as it shall become one that would do reason. 1.01.233 P
and have more occasion to know one another. 1.01.249 P
and there dwells one mistress quickly, which is 1.02. 2 P
a great charge to come under one body's hand. 1.04. 99 P
honest, and gentle, and one that is your friend; 1.04.140 P
one that is well-nigh worn to pieces with age to 2.01. 21 P
if it were not for one trifling respect, i could 2.01. 44 P
twenty lascivious turtles ere one chaste man. 2.01. 81 P
i'll entertain myself like one that i am not 2.01. 86 P
both young and old, one with another, ford. 2.01.114
there is one mistress ford, sir — i pray come a 2.02. 44 P
but, i warrant you, all is one with her. 2.02. 78 P
she's as fartuous a civil modest wife, and one 2.02. 98 P
if there be a kind woman in windsor, she is one. 2.02.121 P
nay-word, that you may know one another's mind, 2.02.126 P
this punk is one of cupid's carriers. 2.02.135
there's one master /brook below would fain speak 2.02.144 P
sir john, as you have one eye upon my follies, 2.02.185 P
vat be all you, one, two, tree, four, come for? 2.03. 22 P
i see a sword out, my finger itches to make one. 2.03. 46 P
and i will one way or other make you amends. 3.01. 87 P
how i love you, and you shall one day find it. 3.03. 81 P
windsor at his heels, to search for such a one. 3.03.115 P
if there is one, i shall make two in the company 3.03.234 P
if there be one or two, i shall make-a the turd. 3.03.236 P
luck would have it, comes in one mistress page; 3.05. 84 P
if i have horns to make one mad, let the proverb 3.05.151 P
truly, i thought there had been one number more, 4.01. 23 P
there was one convey'd out of my house yesterday 4.02.146 P
help to search my house this one time. 4.02.160 P
'tis one of the best discretions of a oman as 4.04. 1 P
to know, sir, whether one nym, sir, that 4.05. 32 P
one that hath taught me more wit than ever i 4.05. 59 P
they threw me off from behind one of them, in a 4.05. 68 P
the devil take one party and his dam the other! 4.05.106 P
speciously one of them. 4.05.111 P
sure, one of you does not serve heaven well, 4.05.125 P
at herne's oak, just 'twixt twelve and one, 4.06. 19
to stay for me at church, 'twixt twelve and one, 4.06. 49
and we have a nay-word how to know one another. 5.02. 5 P
and by that we know one another. 5.02. 7 P
but till 'tis one a' clock, | our dance of 5.05. 74
stand at the taunt of one that makes fritters of 5.05.143 P
and one that is as slanderous as sathan? 5.05.155 P
to one master /brook that you have cozen'd of 5.05.166 P
good husband, let us every one go home, | and 5.05.241
to one that can my part in him advertise. MM 1.01. 41
commandements, but scrap'd one out of the table. 1.02. 9 P
nay, not, as one would say, healthy; 1.02. 55 P
there's one yonder arrested and carried to 1.02. 60 P
one word, good friend. lucio, a word with you. 1.02.142
only, this one: 1.03. 50
some one with child by him? my cousin juliet? 1.04. 45
bore many gentlemen (myself being one) | in hand 1.04. 51
one who never feels | the wanton stings and 1.04. 58
and let it keep one shape, till custom make it 2.01. 3
'tis one thing to be tempted, escalus, | another 2.01. 17
one that serves a bad woman; 2.01. 63 P
that such a one and such a one were past cure of 2.01.110 P
such a one and such a one were past cure of the 2.01.110 P
hath she had any more than one husband? 2.01.201 P
become them with one half so good a grace | as 2.02. 62
and do him right that, answering one foul wrong, 2.02.103
look, here comes one; 2.03. 10
repent you, fair one, of the sin you carry? 2.03. 19
one isabel, a sister, desires access to you. 2.04. 18
play the foolish throngs with one that swounds, 2.04. 24
metal in restrained means | to make a false one. 2.04. 49
if you be one (as you are well express'd | by 2.04.136
i have no tongue but one; 2.04.139
that bear in them one and the self-same tongue, 2.04.173
in such a one as, you consenting to't, | would 3.01. 70
vouchsafe a word, young sister, but one word. 3.01.151
and dried not one of them with his comfort; 3.01.225 P
this is one lucio's information against me. 3.02.198 P
one that, above all other strifes, contended 3.02.232 P
th' one has my pity; 4.02. 61
and bred, one that is a prisoner nine years old. 4.02.131 P
one would think it were mistress overdone's own 4.03. 2 P
then is there here one master caper, at the suit 4.03. 9 P
this morning of a cruel fever | one ragozine, a 4.03. 71
one of our covent, and his confessor, | gives me 4.03.128
one fruitful meal would set me to't. 4.03.154 P
well; you'll answer this one day. fare ye well. 4.03.163 P
'tis not impossible | but one, the wicked'st 5.01. 53
i am the sister of one claudio, | condemn'd upon 5.01. 69
one lucio | as then the messenger — 5.01. 73
some one hath set you on; 5.01.112
one that i would were here, friar lodowick. 5.01.125
touch or soil with her | as she from one ungot. 5.01.142
and one that hath spoke most villainous speeches 5.01.263 P
for testimony whereof, one in the prison, | that 5.01.465
i am sorry, one so learned and so wise | as you, 5.01.470
and yet here's one in place i cannot pardon. 5.01.499
one all of luxury, an ass, a madman, | wherein 5.01.501
(as i have heard him swear himself there's one 5.01.510
the one so like the other | as could not be ERR 1.01. 51
to him one of the other twins was bound, 1.01. 81
my mistress made it one upon my cheek: 1.02. 46
well, i will marry one day, but to try. 2.01. 42
the one, to save the money that he spends in 2.02. 97 P
for if we two be one, and thou play false, | i 2.02.142
wants wit in all one word to understand. 2.02.151
full of welcome makes scarce one dainty dish. 3.01. 23
for such store, | when one is one too many? 3.01. 35
for such store, | when one is one too many? 3.01. 35
the one ne'er got me credit, the other mickle 3.01. 45
one that claims me, one that haunts me, one that 3.02. 82 P
one that claims me, one that haunts me, one that 3.02. 82 P
me, one that haunts me, one that will have me. 3.02. 82 P
such a one as a man may not speak of without he 3.02. 90 P
if every one knows us, and we know none, | 'tis 3.02.152
who would be jealous then of such a one? 4.02. 23
one that countermands | the passages of alleys, 4.02. 37
one that before the judgment carries poor souls 4.02. 40
ere i left him, and now the clock strikes one. 4.02. 54
friend, | and every one doth call me by my name: 4.03. 3
one that thinks a man always going to bed and 4.03. 31 P
both one and other he denies me now. 4.03. 85
one angelo, a goldsmith. do you know him? 4.04.132
each one with ireful passion, with drawn swords, 5.01.151
albeit my wrongs might make one wiser mad. 5.01.217
along with them | they brought one pinch, a 5.01.238
one of these men is genius to the other: 5.01.333
and these two dromios, one in semblance — 5.01.359
that by this sympathized one day's error | have 5.01.398
let's go hand in hand, not one before another. 5.01.426
off, and now is the whole man govern'd with one; ADO 1.01. 67 P
hath not the world one man but he will wear his 1.01.198 P
marry, one hero, the daughter and heir of 1.03. 54 P
the one is too like an image and says nothing, 2.01. 8 P
i hope to see you one day fitted with a husband. 2.01. 57 P
which is one? 2.01.103 P
ladies follow her, and but one visor remains. 2.01.157 P
you must wear it one way, for the prince hath 2.01.191 P
an oak but with one green leaf on it would have 2.01.240 P
use for it, a double heart for his single one. 2.01.280 P
thus goes every one to the world but i, and i am 2.01.319 P
lady beatrice, i will get you one. 2.01.321 P
i would rather have one of your father's getting 2.01.322 P
the interim undertake one of hercules' labors, 2.01.365 P
a mountain of affection th' one with th' other. 2.01.367 P
to a contaminated stale, such a one as hero. 2.02. 25 P
i do much wonder that one man, seeing how much 2.03. 7 P
one woman is fair, yet i am well; 2.03. 26 P
but till all graces be in one woman, one woman 2.03. 29 P
one woman, one woman shall not come in my grace. 2.03. 29 P
ever, | one foot in sea and one on shore, | to 2.03. 64
ever, | one foot in sea and one on shore, | to 2.03. 64
and one on shore, | to one thing constant never. 2.03. 65
so immodest to write to one that she knew would 2.03.142 P
we have ten proofs to one that blood hath the 2.03.165 P
than she will bate one breath of her accustom'd 2.03.176 P
be, when they hold one an opinion of another's 2.03.216 P
one doth not know | how much an ill word may 3.01. 85
every one /can master a grief but he that has it 3.02. 28 P
i warrant one that knows him not. 3.02. 65 P
bears will not bite one another when they meet. 3.02. 78 P
five shillings to one on't, with any man that 3.03. 78 P
one word more, honest neighbors. 3.03. 91 P
and one deformed is one of them; 3.03.169 P
and one deformed is one of them; 3.03.169 P
i, but god send every one their heart's desire! 3.04. 60 P
two men ride of a horse, one must ride behind. 3.05. 37 P
one word, sir. 3.05. 45 P
let me but move one question to your daughter, 4.01. 73
out at your window betwixt twelve and one? 4.01. 84
griev'd i, i had but one? 4.01.127
o, one too much by thee! 4.01.129
why had i one? 4.01.129
any is in messina, and one that knows the law, 4.02. 83 P
hath had losses, and one that hath two gowns, 4.02. 85 P
but such a one whose wrongs do suit with mine. 5.01. 7
if such a one will smile and stroke his beard, 5.01. 15
well, all is one. 5.01. 49
but that's no matter, let him kill one first. 5.01. 81
"true," said she, "a fine little one." 5.01.161 P
"right," says she, "a great gross one." 5.01.163 P
borachio one! 5.01.211 P
by my troth, there's one meaning well suited. 5.01.225 P
also, the watch heard them talk of one deformed. 5.01.308 P
there's not one wise man among twenty that will 5.02. 74 P
i leave you too, for here comes one in haste. 5.02. 94 P
to bind me, or undo me — one of them. 5.04. 20
one hero died defil'd, but i do live, | and 5.04. 63
staff more reverent than one tipp'd with horn. 5.04.123 P
and one day in a week to touch no food, | and LLL 1.01. 39
no food, | and but one meal on every day beside, 1.01. 40
one who the music of his own vain tongue | doth 1.01.166
affliction may one day smile again, and till 1.01.314 P
why, sadness is one and the self-same thing, 1.02. 4 P
how many is one thrice told? 1.02. 39 P
it doth amount to one more than two. 1.02. 47 P
or the three, or the two, or one of the four. 1.02. 80 P
is that one of the four complexions? 1.02. 83 P
/lord longaville is one. 2.01. 39
for every object that the one doth catch | the 2.01. 70
that every one her own hath garnished | with 2.01. 78
like one that comes here to besiege his court, 2.01. 86
being but the one half of an entire sum 2.01.130
which | one part of aquitaine is bound to us, 2.01.135
but that one half which is unsatisfied, | we 2.01.138
she hath but one for herself, to desire that 2.01.200
you give him for my sake but one loving kiss. 2.01.249
and keep not too long in one tune, but a snip 3.01. 21 P
o, marry me to one frances! 3.01.121 P
"one penny." 3.01.139 P
do one thing for me that i shall entreat. 3.01.153
one that will do the deed | though argus were 3.01.198
one a' these maids' girdles for your waist 4.01. 50
from monsieur berowne to one lady rosaline. 4.01. 53
the neck of the wax, and every one give ear. 4.01. 59
he came, one; 4.01. 70 P
no, on both in one, or one in both. 4.01. 78 P
no, on both in one, or one in both. 4.01. 78 P
one that makes sport | to the prince and his 4.01. 99
so i may answer thee with one as old, that was a 4.01.122 P
of one sore i an hundred make by adding but one 4.02. 61
sore i an hundred make by adding but one more l. 4.02. 61
and if one should be pierc'd, which is the one? 4.02. 84 P
and if one should be pierc'd, which is the one? 4.02. 84 P
ay, sir, from one monsieur berowne, one of the 4.02.129 P
berowne, one of the strange queen's lords. 4.02.129 P
this berowne is one of the votaries with the 4.02.137 P
well, she hath one a' my sonnets already: 4.03. 15 P
here comes one with a paper, god give him grace 4.03. 19 P
nor shines the silver moon one half so bright 4.03. 29
now, in thy likeness, one more fool appear! 4.03. 44
one drunkard loves another of the name. 4.03. 48
says one, "o jove!" 4.03.139
one, her hairs were gold, crystal the other's 4.03.140
where several worthies make one dignity, | where 4.03.232
lend me your horn to make one, and i will whip 5.01. 68 P
and i had but one penny in the world, thou 5.01. 71 P
i'll make one in a dance, or so; 5.01.153
one rubb'd his elbow thus, and fleer'd, and 5.02.109
and every one his love-feat will advance | unto 5.02.123
for, ladies, we will every one be mask'd, | and 5.02.127
ask them how many inches | is in one mile: 5.02.189
many, | the measure then of one is eas'ly told. 5.02.190
tell | how many inches doth fill up one mile. 5.02.193
are numb'red in the travel of one mile? 5.02.197
then in our measure do but vouchsafe one change. 5.02.209
white-handed mistress, one sweet word with thee. 5.02.230
one word in secret. 5.02.236
one word in private with you ere i die. 5.02.254
not one word more, my maids, break off, break 5.02.262
that she vouchsafe me audience for one word. 5.02.313
this is the flow'r that smiles on every one, 5.02.331
they did not bless us with one happy word. 5.02.370
it is vara fine, | for every one pursents three. 5.02.488
say, but to parfect one man in one poor man, 5.02.502 P
but to parfect one man in one poor man, pompion 5.02.502 P
art thou one of the worthies? 5.02.504 P
to have one show worse than the king's and his 5.02.513
that is all one, my fair, sweet, honey monarch, 5.02.527 P
pick out five such, take each one in his vein. 5.02.545
the one maintained by the owl, th' other by the 5.02.892 P
one that compos'd your beauties; MND 1.01. 48
and one | to whom you are but as a form in wax 1.01. 48
that's all one; 1.02. 49 P
a proper man as one shall see in a summer's day; 1.02. 86 P
the one i'll slay; 2.01.190
into the hands of one that loves you not; 2.01.216
one aloof stand sentinel. 2.02. 26
one turf shall serve as pillow for us both, 2.02. 41
one heart, one bed, two bosoms, and one troth. 2.02. 42
one heart, one bed, two bosoms, and one troth. 2.02. 42
one heart, one bed, two bosoms, and one troth. 2.02. 42
knit, | so that but one heart we can make of it; 2.02. 48
o, that a lady, of one man refus'd, | should of 2.02.133

or else one must come in with a bush of thorns 3.01. 59 P
and so every one according to his cue. 3.01. 75 P
and, at our stamp, here o'er and o'er one falls; 3.02. 25
fate o'errules, that, one man holding troth, | a 3.02. 92
then will two at once woo one; 3.02.118
she is one of this confederacy. 3.02.192
have with our needles created both one flower, 3.02.204
both on one sampler, sitting on one cushion, 3.02.205
both on one sampler, sitting on one cushion, 3.02.205
both warbling of one song, both in one key, | as 3.02.206
both warbling of one song, both in one key, | as 3.02.206
two lovely berries moulded on one stem; 3.02.211
so, with two seeming bodies but one heart, | two 3.02.212
due but to one, and crowned with one crest. 3.02.214
due but to one, and crowned with one crest. 3.02.214
astray | as one come not within another's way. 3.02.359
here comes one. 3.02.400
come one more; 3.02.437
go, one of you, find out the forester, | for now 4.01.103
every region near | seem all one mutual cry. 4.01.117
one sees more devils than vast hell can hold; 5.01. 9
for in all the play | there is not one word apt, 5.01. 65
there is not one word apt, one player fitted. 5.01. 65
one lion may, when many asses do. 5.01.153 P
it doth befall | that i, one /snout by name, 5.01.156
no die, but an ace, for him; for he is but one. 5.01.307 P
should not use a long one for such a pyramus. 5.01.316 P
gaping wide, | every one lets forth his sprite, 5.01.381
it, | my ventures are not in one bottom trusted, MV 1.01. 42
not in one bottom trusted, | nor to one place; 1.01. 43
man must play a part, | and mine a sad one. 1.01. 79
i must be one of these same dumb wise men, | for 1.01.106
in my school–days, when i had lost one shaft, 1.01.140
means | to hold a rival place with one of them, 1.01.174
than to be one of the twenty to follow mine own 1.02. 17 P
nerissa, that i cannot choose one, nor refuse 1.02. 26 P
by any rightly but one who you shall rightly 1.02. 32 P
for there is not one among them but i dote on 1.02.109 P
whiles we shut the gate upon one wooer, another 1.02.133
me, | miss that which one unworthier may attain, 2.01. 37
can you tell me whether one launcelot, that 2.02. 46 P
give me your present to one master bassanio, who 2.02.108 P
infection, sir, as one would say, to serve — 2.02.125 P
one speak for both. what would you? 2.02.141 P
nine maids is a simple coming–in for one man. 2.02.163 P
like one well studied in a sad ostent | to 2.02.196
him | to one that i would have him help to waste 2.05. 50
the one of them contains my picture, prince: 2.07. 11
one of these three contains her heavenly picture 2.07. 48
never to unfold to any one | which casket 'twas 2.09. 10
to these injunctions every one doth swear | that 2.09. 17
with one fool's head i came to woo, | but i go 2.09. 75
venetian, one that comes before | to signify th' 2.09. 87
genoa, as i heard, one night fourscore ducats. 3.01.109 P
one of them show'd me a ring that he had of your 3.01.118 P
one half of me is yours, the other half yours — 3.02. 16
i am lock'd in one of them; 3.02. 40
having made one, | methinks it should have power 3.02.124
like one of two contending in a prize, | that 3.02.141
i thank your lordship, you have got me one. 3.02.196
i got a promise of this fair one here | to have 3.02.206
what, not one hit? 3.02.267
and not one vessel scape the dreadful touch | of 3.02.270
not one, my lord. 3.02.271
and one in whom | the ancient roman honor more 3.02.294
there is but one hope in it that can do you any 3.05. 6 P
e'en as many as could well live one by another. 3.05. 23 P
and portia one, there must be something else 3.05. 81
go one, and call the jew into the court. 4.01. 14
ere thou shalt lose for me one drop of blood. 4.01.113
if thou dost shed | one drop of christian blood, 4.01.310
of the twentieth part | of one poor scruple, nay, 4.01.330
doth contrive | shall seize one half his goods; 4.01.353
to quit the fine for one half of his goods, | i 4.01.381
with many vows of faith, | and ne'er a true one. 5.01. 20
eyes he doubly sees himself, | in each eye, one. 5.01.245
there is not one so young and so villainous this AYL 1.01.154 P
one that old frederick, your father, loves. 1.02. 82 P
you'll be whipt for taxation one of these days. 1.02. 85 P
there is but one sham'd that was never gracious; 1.02.187 P
kill'd, but one dead that is willing to be so. 1.02.188 P
you shall try but one fall. 1.02.204 P
one out of suits with fortune, | that could give 1.02.246
not one to throw at a dog. 1.03. 3 P
when the one should be lam'd with reasons and 1.03. 8 P
which teacheth thee that thou and i am one. 1.03. 97
cours'd one another down his innocent nose | in 2.01. 39
one of you question yond man | if he for gold 2.04. 64
and after one hour more 'twill be eleven, | and 2.07. 25
one that hath been a courtier, | and says, if 2.07. 36
thou shalt have one. 2.07. 44
when such a one as she, such is her neighbor? 2.07. 78
and one man in his time plays many parts, | his 2.07.142
that i know the more one sickens the worse at 3.02. 23 P
such a one is a natural philosopher. 3.02. 32 P
damn'd, like an ill–roasted egg all on one side. 3.02. 38 P
nature charg'd | that one body should be fill'd 3.02.142
one inch of delay more is a south–sea of 3.02.196 P
answer me in one word. 3.02.224 P
for the one sleeps easily because he cannot 3.02.320 P
the one lacking the burthen of lean and wasteful 3.02.322 P
an inland man, one that knew courtship too well, 3.02.345 P
they were all like one another as halfpence are, 3.02.354 P
are, every one fault seeming monstrous till his 3.02.354 P
that is one of the points in the which women 3.02.389 P
yes, one, and in this manner. 3.02.407 P
that there shall not be one spot of love in't. 3.02.423 P
then one of you will prove a shrunk panel, and 3.03. 87 P
as good cause as one would desire, therefore 3.04. 5 P
that spurs his horse but on one side, breaks his 3.04. 44 P
but that's all one; 3.05.133
before, and he is one of the patterns of love. 4.01. 99 P
then, can one desire too much of a good thing? 4.01.123 P
'tis but one cast away, and so, come death! 4.01.185 P
dangerous, if you break one jot of your promise, 4.01.190 P
promise, or come one minute behind your hour, i 4.01.191 P
glass, by filling the one doth empty the other. 5.01. 42 P
sigh'd but they ask'd one another the reason; 5.02. 35 P
to have her and death were both one thing. 5.04. 17
had four quarrels, and like to have fought one. 5.04. 47 P
themselves, one of them thought but of an if, as 5.04.100 P
to one his lands withheld, and to the other | a 5.04.168
one dead, or drunk? SHR in.1. 31
let one attend him with a silver basin | full of in.1. 55
some one be ready with a costly suit, | and ask in.1. 59
him, | and each one to his office when he wakes. in.1. 73
and give them friendly welcome every one. in.1. 103
her legs that one shall swear she bleeds, | and in.2. 58
love, to labor and effect one thing specially. 1.01.118 P
both our inventions meet and jump in one. 1.01.190
one thing more rests, that thyself execute — 1.01.246
execute — | to make one among these wooers. 1.01.247
know | one rich enough to be petruchio's wife 1.02. 67
is, | she may more suitors have, and me for one. 1.02.241
then well one more may fair bianca have; 1.02.243
lucentio shall make one, | though paris came in 1.02.244
the one as famous for a scolding tongue, | as is 1.02.252
after my death the one half of my lands, | and 2.01.121
well aim'd of such a young one. 2.01.235
regard, | to wish me wed to one half lunatic, 2.01.287
and i am one that love bianca more | than words 2.01.335
as any one | old signior gremio has in padua, 2.01.367
d sol re, one cliff, two notes have i; 3.01. 77
boots that have been candle–cases, one buckled, 3.02. 45 P
one girth six times piec'd, and a woman's 3.02. 60 P
with a linen stock on one leg and a kersey 3.02. 66 P
why, that's all one. 3.02. 81 P
a penny, | a horse and a man | is more than one, 3.02. 85
both of one horse? 4.01. 69 P
one, kate, that you must kiss, and be acquainted 4.01.152
speak, | and sits as one new risen from a dream. 4.01.186
but one that scorn to live in this disguise 4.02. 18
disguise | for such a one as leaves a gentleman 4.02. 19
her | as one unworthy all the former favors 4.02. 30
'tis death for any one in mantua | to come to 4.02. 81
among them know you one vincentio? 4.02. 96
as much as an apple doth an oyster, and all one. 4.02.102 P
'twixt me and one baptista's daughter here. 4.02.119
then both or one, or any thing thou wilt. 4.03. 29
when you are gentle, you shall have one too, 4.03. 71
with one consent to have her so bestowed; 4.04. 35
one mess is like to be your cheer. 4.04. 70
'tis ten to one it maim'd you /two outright. 5.02. 62
assurance | let's each one send unto his wife, 5.02. 66
ay, and a kind one too. 5.02. 83
will deign to sip or touch one drop of it. 5.02.145
one that cares for thee, | and for thy 5.02.147
my mind hath been as big as one of yours, | my 5.02.170
'twere all one | that i should love a bright AWW 1.01. 85
one that goes with him. 1.01. 99
how might one do, sir, to lose it to her own 1.01.150 P
is like one of our french wither'd pears, it 1.01.161 P
the court's a learning place, and he is one — 1.01.177
what one, i' faith? 1.01.178 P
sever'd in religion, their heads are both one: 1.03. 54 P
"among nine bad if one be good, | among nine bad 1.03. 77
if one be good, | among nine bad if one be good, 1.03. 78
if one be good, | there's yet one good in ten." 1.03. 79
what, one good in ten? 1.03. 80 P
one good woman in ten, madam, which is a 1.03. 82 P
one in ten, quoth 'a? 1.03. 85 P
a man may draw his heart out ere 'a pluck one. 1.03. 89 P
up, and no sword worn | but one to dance with! 2.01. 33
the regiment of the spinii one captain spurio, 2.01. 42 P
my lord, there's one arriv'd, | if you will see 2.01. 79
i have spoke | with one that, in her sex, her 2.01. 83
now, fair one, does your business follow us? 2.01. 99
chiefly one, | which, as the dearest issue of 2.01.105
from your royal thoughts | a modest one, to bear 2.01.128
as one near death to those that wish him live. 2.01.131
but such a one, thy vassal, whom i know | is 2.01.199
to each of you one fair and virtuous mistress 2.03. 57
marry, to each but one! 2.03. 58
not one of those but had a noble father. 2.03. 62
fair one, i think not so. 2.03. 98
there's one grape yet; 2.03. 99 P
a most harsh one, and not to be understood 2.03.190 P
one, that she's not in heaven, whither god send 2.04. 11 P
one parolles, a filthy officer he is in those 3.05. 16 P
thither they send one another. 3.05. 31 P
the count rossillion. know you such a one? 3.05. 49
the owner of no one good quality worthy your 3.06. 11 P
to understand him, unless some one among us, 4.01. 5 P
we must every one be a man of his own fancy, not 4.01. 17 P
fancy, not to know what we speak one to another; 4.01. 18 P
you shall hear one anon. 4.01. 63 P
dead, you should be such a one | as you are now; 4.02. 7
all's one to him. 4.03.138 P
him, whether one captain dumaine be i' th' camp, 4.03.175 P
to a proper maid in florence, one diana, to take 4.03.214 P
heed of the allurement of one count rossillion, 4.03.214 P
his brother is reputed one of the best that is. 4.03.289 P
one of the greatest in the christian world 4.04. 2
since you have made the days and nights as one, 5.01. 3
i beseech your honor to hear me one single word. 5.02. 35 P
one brings thee in grace and the other brings 5.02. 49 P
whole, | not one word more of the consumed time. 5.03. 38
it to a commoner a' th' camp, | if i be one. 5.03.195
you saw one here in court could witness it. 5.03.200
though she be, she feels her young one kick. 5.03.302
one that's dead is quick — | and now behold the 5.03.303
her sweet perfections with one self king! TN 1.01. 38
that you brought in one night here to be her 1.03. 16 P
if she be, it's four to one she'll none of me. 1.03.106 P
that if one break, the other will hold; 1.05. 24 P
one of thy kin has a most weak pia mater. 1.05.115 P
there's one at the gate. 1.05.125 P
well, it's all one. 1.05.129 P
one draught above heat makes him a fool, the 1.05.132 P
one would think his mother's milk were scarce 1.05.161 P
good gentle one, give me modest assurance if you 1.05.179 P
of moon with me to make one in so skipping a 1.05.201 P
look you, sir, such a one i was this present. 1.05.234 P
item, one neck, one chin, and so forth. 1.05.248 P
item, one neck, one chin, and so forth. 1.05.248 P
even so quickly may one catch the plague? 1.05.295
and — one thing more — that you be never so 2.02. 9 P
if one knight give a — 2.03. 33 P
that will draw three souls out of one weaver? 2.03. 59 P
time i have constrain'd one to call me knave. 2.03. 68 P
a beagle, true–bred, and one that adores me. 2.03.179 P
come, but one verse. 2.04. 7
my part of death, no one so true | did share it. 2.04. 57
and pleasure will be paid, one time or another. 2.04. 70 P
she fancy, it should be one of my complexion. 2.05. 25 P
respect than any one else that follows her. 2.05. 27 P
"one sir andrew" — 2.05. 80 P
for every one of these letters are in my name. 2.05.141 P
i'll make one too. 2.05.207 P
i'll tell thee, i am almost sick for one — 3.01. 47 P
to one of your receiving | enough is shown; 3.01.120
if one should be a prey, how much the better 3.01.128
i have one heart, one bosom, and one truth, 3.01.158
i have one heart, one bosom, and one truth, 3.01.158
i have one heart, one bosom, and one truth, 3.01.158
as might have drawn one to a longer voyage) 3.03. 7
if it please the eye of one, it is with me as 3.04. 22 P
with me as the very true sonnet is, "please one, 3.04. 23 P
well, and god have mercy upon one of our souls! 3.04.167 P
that they will kill one another by the look, 3.04.196 P
i am one that had rather go with sir priest than 3.04.270 P
for his honor's sake, have one bout with you. 3.04.306 P
one, sir, that for his love dares yet do more 3.04.316
i snatch'd one half out of the jaws of death, 3.04.360
he started one poor heart of mine, in thee. 4.01. 59
for i am one of those gentle ones that will use 4.02. 32 P
though it please you to be one of my friends. 5.01. 26 P
sir, may put you in mind — one, two, three. 5.01. 39 P
years removed thing | while one would wink; 5.01. 90
send one presently to sir toby. 5.01.173 P
the count's gentleman, one cesario. 5.01.180 P
that's all one. 5.01.196 P
pardon me, sweet one, even for the vows | we 5.01.214
one face, one voice, one habit, and two persons, 5.01.216
one face, one voice, one habit, and two persons, 5.01.216
one face, one voice, one habit, and two persons, 5.01.216
one day shall crown th' alliance on't, so please 5.01.318
i was one, sir, in this enterlude — one sir 5.01.372 P
sir, in this enterlude — one sir topas, sir, 5.01.372 P
one sir topas, sir, but that's all one. 5.01.373 P
but that's all one, our play is done, | and 5.01.407
one that, indeed, physics the subject, makes old WT 1.01. 38 P
desire to live on crutches till he had one. 1.01. 46 P
with one "we thank you" many thousands moe 1.02. 8
one sev'nnight longer. 1.02. 17
your dread "verily," | one of them you shall be. 1.02. 56
i' th' sun, | and bleat the one at th' other. 1.02. 68
one good deed dying tongueless | slaughters a 1.02. 92
's | with one soft kiss a thousand furlongs ere 1.02. 95
the one for ever earn'd a royal husband; 1.02.107
as dice are to be wish'd by one that fixes | no 1.02.133
knee–deep, o'er head and ears a fork'd one! 1.02.186
in every one of these no man is free | but that 1.02.251
she would not live | the running of one glass. 1.02.306
do't, and thou hast the one half of my heart; 1.02.348
one | who, in rebellion with himself, will have 1.02.354
nor brass nor stone nor parchment bears not one, 1.02.360
than one condemn'd by the king's own mouth — 1.02.445
to a fine new prince | one of these days, and 2.01. 18
i have one | of sprites and goblins. 2.01. 25
the cup | a spider steep'd, and one may drink; 2.01. 40
but if one present | th' abhorr'd ingredient to 2.01. 42
and one that knows | what she should shame to 2.01. 90
for a worthy lady, | and one who much i honor. 2.02. 6
as well as one so great and so forlorn | may 2.02. 20
i, nor any | but one that's here — and that's 2.03. 84
you'll leave yourself | hardly one subject. 2.03.112
durst not call me so, | if she did know me one. 2.03.124
will never do him good, not one of you. 2.03.129
our wife, and one | of us too much belov'd. 3.02. 3
if one jot beyond | the bound of honor, or in 3.02. 50
his presence | i am barr'd, like one infectious. 3.02. 98
thoughts | (thoughts high for one so tender) 3.02.196
one grave shall be for both; 3.02.236
sometimes her head on one side, some another — 3.03. 20
a pretty one, a very pretty one: 3.03. 71 P
a pretty one, a very pretty one: 3.03. 71 P
law, and in one self–born hour | to plant and 4.01. 8
but one puritan amongst them, and he sings 4.03. 43 P
one of these two must be necessities, | which 4.04. 38
took to quench it | she would to each one sip. 4.04. 62
as if you were a feasted one and not | the 4.04. 63
shepherdess | (a fair one are you!), 4.04. 78
the dibble in earth to set one slip of them; 4.04.100
of all kinds, | the flow'r–de–luce being one! 4.04.127
here's one to a very doleful tune, how a 4.04.262 P
midwive's name to't, one mistress tale–porter, 4.04.269 P
not exchange flesh with one that lov'd her. 4.04.280 P
this is a merry ballad, but a very pretty one. 4.04.286 P
is a passing merry one and goes to the tune of 4.04.288 P
one three of them, by their own report, sir, 4.04.337 P
one being dead, | i shall have more than you can 4.04.387
thee i can | but shorten thy life one week. 4.04.422
th' one | he chides to hell and bids the other 4.04.552
you, | but as you shake off one to take another; 4.04.569
one of these is true: 4.04.575
you may know you shall not want — one word. 4.04.594
your worship had like to have given us one, if 4.04.727 P
and one that will either push on or pluck back 4.04.737 P
but though my case be a pitiful one, i hope i 4.04.815 P
if, one by one, you wedded all the world, | or, 5.01. 13
if, one by one, you wedded all the world, | or, 5.01. 13
you are one of those | would have him wed again. 5.01. 23
one worse, | and better us'd, would make her 5.01. 56
one that gives out himself prince florizel, 5.01. 85
the one i have almost forgot — your pardon — 5.01.104
they seem'd almost, with staring on one another, 5.02. 12 P
had heard of a world ransom'd, or one destroy'd. 5.02. 15 P
but in the extremity of the one, it must needs 5.02. 19 P
might you have beheld one joy crown another, so 5.02. 44 P
she had one eye declin'd for the loss of her 5.02. 74 P
one of the prettiest touches of all, and that 5.02. 82 P
till, from one sign of dolor to another, she did 5.02. 87 P
hermione that they say one would speak to her 5.02.101 P

but 'tis all one to me; 5.02.121 P
your exultation | partake to every one. 5.03.132
where we may leisurely | each one demand, and 5.03.153
you came not of one mother then, it seems. JN 1.01. 58
most certain of one mother, mighty king — 1.01. 59
is well known — and, as i think, one father; 1.01. 60
one that will play the devil, sir, with you, 2.01.135
one must prove greatest. 2.01.332
thou hast not sav'd one drop of blood | in this 2.01.341
then let confusion of one part confirm | the 2.01.359
cull forth | out of one side her happy minion, 2.01.392
two such shores to two such streams made one, 2.01.443
but this one word, whether thy tale be true. 3.01. 26
within the scorched veins of one new burn'd. 3.01.278
one minute, nay, one quiet breath of rest. 3.04.134
one minute, nay, one quiet breath of rest. 3.04.134
i, as one that am the tongue of these | to sound 4.02. 47
heads, | and whisper one another in the ear; 4.02.189
home and discontents at home | meet in one line; 4.03.152
and heal the inveterate canker of one wound | by 5.02. 14
commend me to one hubert with your king; 5.04. 40
to think | i come one way of the plantagenets. 5.06. 11
my life should sail | are turned to one thread, 5.07. 54
are turned to one thread, one little hair. 5.07. 54
my heart hath one poor string to stay it by, 5.07. 55
we thank you both, yet one but flatters us, | as R2 1.01. 25
the one my duty owes, but my fair name, 1.01.167
mine honor is my life, both grow in one, | take 1.01.182
edward's seven sons, whereof thyself art one, 1.02. 11
or seven fair branches springing from one root. 1.02. 13
one vial full of edward's sacred blood, | one 1.02. 17
one flourishing branch of his most royal root, 1.02. 18
yet one word more! 1.02. 58
us, | one of our souls had wand'red in the air, 1.03.195
how long a time lies in one little word! 1.03.213
to men in joy, but grief makes one hour ten. 1.03.261
or bend one wrinkle on my sovereign's face. 2.01.170
did not the one deserve to have an heir? 2.01.193
divides one thing entire to many objects, | like 2.02. 17
t' one is my sovereign, whom both my oath | and 2.02.112
where one on his side fights, thousands will fly 2.02.147
meaning | to rase one title of your honor out. 2.03. 75
leap, | the one in fear to lose what they enjoy, 2.04. 13
one day too late, i fear me, noble lord, | hath 3.02. 67
three judases, each one thrice worse than judas! 3.02.132
my liege, one word. 3.02.215
that spring from one most gracious head, | and 3.03.108
as thus to drop them still upon one place, 3.03.166
state, for every one doth so | against a change; 3.04. 27
so, | i speak no more than every one doth know. 3.04. 91
excepting one, i would he were the best | in all 4.01. 31
i have a thousand spirits in one breast, | to 4.01. 58
and hate turns one or both | to worthy danger 5.01. 67
so two together weeping make one woe. 5.01. 86
twice for one step i'll groan, the way being 5.01. 91
one kiss shall stop our mouths, and dumbly part; 5.01. 95
he, from the one side to the other turning, 5.02. 18
not, | god knows i had as lief be none as one. 5.02. 49
not pardon twain, | but makes one pardon strong. 5.03.135
thus play i in one person many people, | and 5.05. 31
all of one nature, of one substance bred, | did 1H4 1.01. 11
all of one nature, of one substance bred, | did 1.01. 11
march all one way and be no more oppos'd 1.01. 15
truly, little better than one of the wicked. 1.02. 94 P
thou wilt, lad, i'll make one, an' i do not, 1.02.100 P
hal, wilt thou make one? 1.02.137 P
whose tongue shall ask me for one penny cost 1.03. 91
needs no more but one tongue for all those 1.03. 96
i heard him tell it to one of his company last 2.01. 56 P
one that hath abundance of charge too — god 2.01. 58 P
it when thieves cannot be true one to another! 2.02. 28 P
one horse, my lord, he brought even now. 2.03. 68
so good a proficient in one quarter of an hour, 2.04. 18 P
one that never spake other english in his life 2.04. 24 P
england, and one of them is fat and grows old, 2.04.131 P
all is one for that. 2.04.155 P
he is there too, and one mordake, and a thousand 2.04.357 P
he doth it as like one of these harlotry players 2.04.395 P
one of them is well known, my gracious lord, | a 2.04.510
but one half-pennyworth of bread to this 2.04.540 P
here, | in quantity equals not one of yours. 3.01. 96
than one of these same metre ballet-mongers. 3.01.128
one that no persuasion can do good upon. 3.01.197
and one poor pennyworth of sugar-candy to make 3.03.159 P
where shall i find one that can steal well? 3.03.188 P
wealth of all our states | all at one cast? 4.01. 47
main | on the nice hazard of one doubtful hour? 4.01. 48
meet and ne'er part till one drop down a corse. 4.01.123
of death or death's hand for this one half year. 4.01.136
but that's all one, they'll find linen enough on 4.02. 47 P
two stars keep not their motion in one sphere, 5.04. 65
nor can one england brook a double reign | of 5.04. 66
for the hour is come | to end the one of us, and 5.04. 69
i spake with one, my lord, that came from thence 2H4 1.01. 25
but let one spirit of the first-born cain 1.01.157
that if we wrought out life 'twas ten to one, 1.01.182
that hath overwhelm'd all her litter but one. 1.02. 12 P
of my hand than he shall get one /of his cheek, 1.02. 22 P
though it be a shame to be on any side but one, 1.02. 75 P
but the gout galls the one, and the pox pinches 1.02.231 P
for the one or the other plays the rogue with my 1.02.244 P
one power against the french, | and one against 1.03. 71
against the french, | and one against glendower; 1.03. 72
hundred mark is a long one for a poor lone woman 2.01. 32 P
the one you may do with sterling money, and the 2.01.120 P
durst not have attach'd one of so high blood. 2.02. 3 P
as, one for superfluity, and another for use! 2.02. 17 P
shall i tell thee one thing, poins? 2.02. 32 P
i stand the push of your one thing that you will 2.02. 37 P
i could tell to thee — as to one it pleases me, 2.02. 41 P
wine, and it perfumes the blood ere one can say, 2.04. 28 P
you cannot one bear with another's confirmities. 2.04. 58 P
one must bear, and that must be you, you are the 2.04. 59 P
i am the worse when one says swagger. 2.04.104 P
for one of them, she's in hell already, and 2.04.338 P
and asking every one for sir john falstaff. 2.04.360
'tis one a' clock, and past. 3.01. 34
o god, that one might read the book of fate, 3.01. 45
same day did i fight with one samson stockfish, 3.02. 32 P
and one of the king's justices of the peace. 3.02. 58 P
will be undone now for one to do her husbandry 3.02.113 P
for he hath found to end one doubt by death 4.01.197
one time or other break some gallows' back. 4.03. 29
the world's whole strength | into one giant arm, 4.05. 45
is caught, as men take diseases, one of another; 5.01. 76 P
say, | god shorten harry's happy life one day! 5.02.145
there's one pistol come from the court with news 5.03. 80 P
thou art now one of the greatest men in this 5.03. 87 P
one word more, i beseech you. ep 26 P
into a thousand parts divide one man, | and make H5 pr 24
sum | than ever at one time the clergy yet | did 1.01. 80
whose guiltless drops | are every one a woe, a 1.02. 26
land | until four hundred one and twenty years 1.02. 57
as never did the clergy at one time | bring in 1.02.134
put into parts, doth keep in one consent, 1.02.181
having full reference | to one consent, may work 1.02.206
arrows loosed several ways | come to one mark; 1.02.208
as many ways meet in one town; 1.02.208
as many fresh streams meet in one salt sea; 1.02.209
/end in one purpose, and be all well borne 1.02.212
whereof take you one quarter into france, | and 1.02.215
one, richard earl of cambridge, and the second, 2.pr. 23
we'll not offend one stomach with our play. 2.pr. 40
it is a simple one, but what though? 2.01. 8 P
i will cut thy throat one time or other in fair 2.01. 69 P
yield the crow a pudding one of these days. 2.01. 88 P
we keep knives to cut one another's throats? 2.01. 92 P
nor leave not one behind that doth not wish 2.02. 23
i one, my lord. 2.02. 62
could out of thee extract one spark of evil 2.02.101
'a parted ev'n just between twelve and one, ev'n 2.03. 13 P
his finger's end, i knew there was but one way; 2.03. 16 P
chin is but enrich'd | with one appearing hair, 3.pr. 23
but one that is like to be executed for robbing 3.06.100 P
be executed for robbing a church, one bardolph, 3.06.101 P
i thought upon one pair of english legs | did 3.06.149
i was told that by one that knows him better 3.07.104 P
nor doth he dedicate one jot of color | unto the 4.pr. 37
sun, | his liberal eye doth give to every one, 4.pr. 44
twenty french crowns to one they will beat us, 4.01.226 P
there's five to one; 4.03. 4
but one ten thousand of those men in england 4.03. 17
god's will, i pray thee wish not one man more. 4.03. 23
as one man more methinks would share from me, 4.03. 32
o, do not wish one more! 4.03. 33
which likes me better than to wish us one. 4.03. 77
happy that he hath fall'n into the hands of one 4.04. 61 P
that every one may pare his nails with a wooden 4.04. 71 P
or the magnanimous, are all one reckonings, save 4.07. 17 P
but 'tis all one, 'tis alike as my fingers is to 4.07. 30 P
'tis the gage of one that i should fight withal, 4.07.123 P
there lie dead | one hundred twenty-six; 4.08. 83
and little loss, | on one part and on th' other? 4.08.111
there is one goat for you. 5.01. 29 P
so are you, princes english, every one. 5.02. 11
what says she, fair one? 5.02.117 P
for the one i have neither words nor measure; 5.02.134 P
if thou would have such a one, take me! 5.02.165 P
must needs be granted to be much at one. 5.02.192 P
a fair french city for one fair french maid that 5.02.318 P
let that one article rank with the rest, | and 5.02.346
combine your hearts in one, your realms in one! 5.02.360
combine your hearts in one, your realms in one! 5.02.360
as man and wife, being two, are one in love, 5.02.361
one would have ling'ring wars with little cost; 1H6 1.01. 74
arms, | of england's coat one half is cut away. 1.01. 81
cowardly fled, not having struck one stroke. 1.01.134
four of their lords i'll change for one of ours. 1.01.151
faintly besiege us one hour in a month. 1.02. 8
me, | when he sees me go back one foot or fly. 1.02. 21
he fighteth as one weary of his life. 1.02. 26
one to ten! 1.02. 34
one that still motions war and never peace, 1.03. 63
here, through this grate, i count each one, 1.04. 60
one of thy eyes and thy cheek's side struck off! 1.04. 75
one eye thou hast to look to heaven for grace; 1.04. 83
the sun with one eye vieweth all the world. 1.04. 84
the dolphin, with one joan de pucelle join'd, 1.04.101
that one day bloom'd and fruitful were the next. 1.06. 7
that, if it chance the one of us do fail, | the 2.01. 31
upon the which, that every one may read, | shall 2.02. 14
that i may kindly give one fainting kiss. 2.05. 40
which giveth many wounds when one will kill. 2.05.110
it is because no one should sway but he, | no 3.01. 37
he, | no one, but he, should be about the king; 3.01. 38
i pray, | but one imperious in another's throne? 3.01. 44
do pelt so fast at one another's pate | that 3.01. 82
that grudge one thought against your majesty! 3.01.175
one sudden foil shall never breed distrust. 3.03. 11
one drop of blood drawn from thy country's bosom 3.03. 54
and that the french were almost ten to one, 4.01. 21
that any one should therefore be suspicious | i 4.01.153
you fled for vantage, every one will swear; 4.05. 28
shall all thy mother's hopes lie in one tomb? 4.05. 34
the help of one stands me in little stead. 4.06. 31
to hazard all our lives in one small boat! 4.06. 33
'tis but the short'ning of my life one day. 4.06. 37
should reign among professors of one faith. 5.01. 14
so let them have their answers every one. 5.01. 25
was | into two parties, is now conjoin'd in one, 5.02. 12
ten to one | we shall not find like opportunity. 5.04.157
or one that at a triumph, having vow'd | to try 5.05. 31
lords, with one cheerful voice welcome my love. 2H6 1.01. 36
as to vouchsafe one glance unto the ground. 1.02. 16
so one by one we'll weed them all at last, | and 1.03. 99
so one by one we'll weed them all at last, | and 1.03. 99
which, | or somerset or york, all's one to me. 1.03.102
doth any one accuse york for a traitor? 1.03.179
he did speak them to me in the garret one night, 1.03.191 P
and, ten to one, old joan had not gone out. 2.01. 4
then send for one presently. 2.01.136
shall one day make the duke of york a king. 2.02. 79
when every one will give the time of day, | he 3.01. 14
pay, | nor ever had one penny bribe from france. 3.01.109
looking the way her harmless young one went, 3.01.215
were't not all one, an empty eagle were set | to 3.01.248
show me one scar character'd on thy skin: 3.01.300
as one that grasp'd | and tugg'd for life, and 3.02.172
mine hair be fix'd an end, as one distract; 3.02.318
by, | as one that surfeits thinking on a want. 3.02.348
set, | it is our pleasure one of them depart; 4.01.140
and i will apparel them all in one livery, that 4.02. 74 P
by her he had two children at one birth. 4.02.139
we will not leave one lord, one gentleman; 4.02.184
we will not leave one lord, one gentleman; 4.02.184
a license to kill for a hundred lacking one. 4.03. 8 P
he that made us pay one and twenty fifteens, and 4.07. 22 P
twenty fifteens, and one shilling to the pound, 4.07. 22 P
tut, when struck'st thou one blow in the field? 4.07. 79 P
let them kiss one another, for they lov'd well 4.07.130 P
for me, i will make shift for one; 4.08. 31 P
if one so rude and of so mean condition | may 5.01. 64
of one or both of us the time is come. 5.02. 13
day | is not itself, nor have we won one foot, 5.03. 6
my lord of warwick, hear but one word: 3H6 1.01.170
would break a thousand oaths to reign one year. 1.02. 17
france | when as the enemy hath been ten to one; 1.02. 74
line, | and leave not one alive, i live in hell. 1.03. 33
thou hast one son, for his sake pity me, | lest 1.03. 40
but buckler with thee blows, twice two for one. 1.04. 50
for one to thrust his hand between his teeth, 1.04. 57
and ten to one is no impeach of valor. 1.04. 60
three glorious suns, each one a perfect sun, 2.01. 26
now are they but one lamp, one light, one sun. 2.01. 31
now are they but one lamp, one light, one sun. 2.01. 31
now are they but one lamp, one light, one sun. 2.01. 31
each one already blazing by our meeds, | should 2.01. 36
one that was a woeful looker-on | when as the 2.01. 45
now one the better, then another best; 2.05. 10
the one his purple blood right well resembles, 2.05. 99
wither one rose, and let the other flourish; 2.05.101
one way or other, she is for a king, | and she 3.02. 87
like one that stands upon a promontory | and 3.02.135
and i — like one lost in a thorny wood, | that 3.02.174
my quarrel and this english queen's are one. 3.03.216
yet, ere thou go, but answer me one doubt: 3.03.238
for this one speech lord hastings well deserves 4.01. 47
nor how to be contented with one wife, | nor how 4.03. 37
yet in this one thing let me blame your grace, 4.06. 30
and ten to one you'll meet him in the tower. 5.01. 46
if case some one of you would fly from us, 5.04. 34
and i, the hapless male to one sweet bird, 5.06. 15
divine, | be resident in men like one another, 5.06. 82
king | in deadly hate the one against the other; R3 1.01. 35
he that doth naught with her (excepting one) 1.01. 99
what one, my lord? 1.01.101
yes, one place else, if you will hear me name it 1.02.110
so i might live one hour in your sweet bosom. 1.02.124
the self-same name, but one of better nature. 1.02.143
may | but beg one favor at thy gracious hand, 1.02.207
nor no one here; 1.03.284
was wont to hold me but while one tells twenty. 1.04.119 P
you have been factious one against the other. 2.01. 20
it were lost sorrow to wail one that's lost. 2.02. 11
and i for comfort have but one false glass, 2.02. 53
grandam, one night as we did sit at supper, | my 2.04. 10
iniquity, | i moralize two meanings in one word. 3.01. 83
give mistress shore one gentle kiss the more. 3.01.185
one from the lord stanley. 3.02. 3
and that may be determin'd at the one | which 3.02. 13
his honor and myself are at the one, | and at 3.02. 21
for never yet one hour in his bed | did i enjoy 4.01. 82
"girdling one another | within their alablaster 4.03. 10
one heav'd a-high, to be hurl'd down below; 4.04. 86
for joyful mother, one that wails the name; 4.04. 99
for one being sued to, one that humbly sues; 4.04.100
for one being sued to, one that humbly sues; 4.04.100
for she being feared of all, now fearing one; 4.04.103
as one being best acquainted with her humor. 4.04.269
they are as children but one step below, | even 4.04.301
of all one pain, save for a night of groans 4.04.303
some one take order buckingham be brought | to 4.04.537
from tamworth thither is but one day's march. 5.02. 13
peace | by this one bloody trial of sharp war. 5.02. 16
well, all's one for that. 5.03. 8
yet one thing more, good captain, do for me — 5.03. 33
and every one did threat | to-morrow's vengeance 5.03.205
one rais'd in blood, and one in blood 5.03.247
rais'd in blood, and one in blood established; 5.03.247
one that made means to come by what he hath, 5.03.248
one that hath ever been god's enemy. 5.03.252
they would restrain the one, distain the other. 5.03.322
one that never in his life | felt so much cold 5.03.325
ones could have weigh'd | such a compounded one? H8 1.01. 12
single, but now married | to one above itself. 1.01. 16
'twas said they saw but one, and no discerner 1.01. 32
one, certes, that promises no element | in such 1.01. 48
his mind and place | infecting one another, yea, 1.01.162
la car, | one gilbert /perk, his /chancellor — 1.01.219
stretch'd him, and, with one hand on his dagger, 1.02.204
one would take it, | that never see 'em pace 1.03. 11
this night he makes a supper, and a great one, 1.03. 52
bevy, has brought with her | one care abroad. 1.04. 5
were but now confessor | to one or two of these! 1.04. 16
my lord sands, you are one will keep 'em waking; 1.04. 23
there should be one amongst 'em, by his person 1.04. 78
such a one, they all confess, | there is indeed, 1.04. 82
viscount rochford — one of her highness' women. 1.04. 93
by heaven, she is a dainty one. 1.04. 94
lead in your ladies, ev'ry one. 1.04.103
that trick of state | was a deep envious one. 2.01. 45
me, | make of your prayers one sweet sacrifice, 2.01. 77
his end, | goodness and he fill up one monument! 2.01. 94
that blood will make 'em one day groan for't. 2.01.106
at one stroke has taken | for ever from the 2.01.117
had my trial, | and must needs say a noble one; 2.01.119
yet thus far we are one in fortunes: 2.01.121
the king will know him one day. 2.02. 21
heaven will one day open | the king's eyes, that 2.02. 41
all men's honors | lie like one lump before him, 2.02. 48
if it do, | i'll venture one; have at him! 2.02. 84
self, hath sent | one general tongue unto us: 2.02. 95
was not one doctor pace | in this man's place 2.02.121

was reckon'd one | the wisest prince that there 2.04. 48
spake one the least word that might | be to the 2.04.154
virtue finds no friends) a wife, a true one? 3.01.126
one that ne'er dream'd a joy beyond his pleasure 3.01.135
one | hath crawl'd into the favor of the king, 3.02.102
of gleaning all the land's wealth into one, 3.02.284
in that one woman i have lost for ever. 3.02.409
a sure and safe one, though thy master miss'd it 3.02.438
all were woven | so strangely in one piece. 4.01. 81
/stokesly and gardiner, the one of winchester, 4.01.101
house, | and one, already, of the privy council. 4.01.112
one that by suggestion | tied all the kingdom. 4.02. 35
he was a scholar, and a ripe and good one; 4.02. 51
one of which fell with him, | unwilling to 4.02. 59
of which there is not one, i dare avow | (and 4.02.142
it's one a' clock, boy, is't not? 5.01. 1
and who dare speak | one syllable against him? 5.01. 39
is this the honor they do one another? 5.02. 26
'tis well there's one above 'em yet. 5.02. 27
easiness and childish pity | to one man's honor, 5.02. 61
course of my authority | might go one way, and 5.02. 71
one that, in all obedience, makes the church 5.02.152
and one as great as you are? 5.02.175
long | to have this young one made a christian. 5.02.213
as i have made ye one, lords, one remain: 5.02.214
as i have made ye one, lords, one remain: 5.02.214
as much as one sound cudgel of four foot | (you 5.03. 19
this one christening will beget a thousand, here 5.03. 37 P
so shall she leave her blessedness to one 5.04. 43
this little one shall make it holy–day. 5.04. 76
'tis ten to one this play can never please | all ep 1
of good women, | for such a one we show'd 'em. ep 11
and she were a blackamoor, 'tis all one to me. TRO 1.01. 78 P
hairs on your chin — and one of them is white." 1.02.158 P
"two and fifty hairs," quoth he, "and one white. 1.02.161 P
"the fork'd one," quoth he, "pluck't out, and 1.02.164 P
he's one of the flowers of troy, i can tell you. 1.02.187 P
he's one o' th' soundest judgments in troy, 1.02.191 P
and the devil come to him, it's all one. 1.02.211 P
say one of your watches. 1.02.265 P
and that's one of the chiefest of them too. 1.02.266 P
the general's disdain'd | by him one step below, 1.03.130
may one that is a herald and a prince | do a 1.03.218
which with one voice | call agamemnon head and 1.03.221
if there be one among the fair'st of greece 1.03.265
if then one is, or hath, /or means to be, | that 1.03.289
hath, /or means to be, | that one meets hector; 1.03.290
one that was a man | when hector's grandsire 1.03.291
stomach, and such a one that dare | maintain — 2.01.125
to us | (had it our name) the value of one ten, 2.02. 23
what propugnation is in one man's valor | to 2.02.136
like one besotted on your sweet delights. 2.02.143
friend, we understand not one another; 3.01. 27 P
and discharging less than the tenth part of one. 3.02. 87 P
if ever you prove false one to another, since i 3.02.199 P
doth one pluck down another, and together | die 3.03. 86
how one man eats into another's pride, | while 3.03.136
strait so narrow, | where one but goes abreast. 3.03.155
hath a thousand sons | that one by one pursue. 3.03.157
hath a thousand sons | that one by one pursue. 3.03.157
one touch of nature makes the whole world kin — 3.03.175
that all, with one consent, praise new–born 3.03.176
you are in love | with one of priam's daughters. 3.03.194
aleven of the clock it will go one way or other. 3.03.296 P
the one and other diomed embraces. 4.01. 15
hark, there's one up. 4.02. 18
with the rude brevity and discharge of one. 4.04. 41
i'll give you boot, i'll give you three for one. 4.05. 40
in hector, | the one almost as infinite as all, 4.05. 80
one that knows the youth | even to his inches, 4.05.110
as welcome as to one | that would be rid of such 4.05.163
common arbitrator, time, | will one day end it. 4.05.226
honest fellow enough, and one that loves quails, 5.01. 52 P
i'll fetch you one. 5.02. 61
one cannot speak a word | but it straight starts 5.02.100
one eye yet looks on thee, | but with my heart 5.02.107
like witless antics, one another meet, | and all 5.03. 86
fortune of this girl, and what one thing, what 5.03.103 P
that i shall leave you one a' th's days; 5.03.104 P
now they are clapper–clawing one another; 5.04. 1 P
i think they have swallow'd one another. 5.04. 34 P
one bear will not bite another, and wherefore 5.07. 18 P
bite another, and wherefore should one bastard? 5.07. 19 P
let one be sent | to pray achilles see us at our 5.09. 7
one word, good citizens. COR 1.01. 14 P
agrippa, one that hath always lov'd the people. 1.01. 51 P
he's one honest enough; 1.01. 53 P
for that, being one o' th' lowest, basest, 1.01.157
point of battle, | the one side must have bale. 1.01.163
the one affrights you, | the other makes you 1.01.169
in awe, which else | would feed on one another? 1.01.188
and a petition granted them — a strange one, 1.01.210
i'll lean upon one crutch, and fight with t' 1.01.242
we shall ever strike | till one can do no more. 1.02. 36
for their country than one voluptuously surfeit 1.03. 25 P
one on 's father's moods. 1.03. 66 P
is gone, with one part of our roman power. 1.03. 97 P
and one infect another | against the wind a mile 1.04. 33
put you | (like one that means his proper harm) 1.09. 57
tell me one thing that i shall ask you. 2.01. 13 P
he's poor in no one fault, but stor'd with all. 2.01. 18 P
and one that loves a cup of hot wine with not a 2.01. 48 P
one that converses more with the buttock of the 2.01. 51 P
and, i think, there's one at home for you. 2.01.109 P
one i' th' neck, and two i' th' thigh — there's 2.01.151 P
only | there's one thing wanting, which i doubt 2.01.201
'tis thought of every one coriolanus will carry 2.02. 4 P
i had rather have one scratch my head i' th' sun 2.02. 75
that's thousand to one good one — when you now 2.02. 79
that's thousand to one good one — when you now 2.02. 79
neither will they bate | one jot of ceremony. 2.02.141
if all our wits were to issue out of one skull, 2.03. 22 P
and their consent of one direct way should be at 2.03. 23 P
wherein every one of us has a single honor, in 2.03. 44 P
and the honor go | to one that would do thus. 2.03.123
the one part suffered, the other will i do. 2.03.124
not one amongst us, save yourself, but says | he 2.03.162
one thus descended, | that hath beside well in 2.03.245

and such a one as he, who puts his "shall," 3.01.105
gap of both, and take | the one by th' other. 3.01.112
people give | one that speaks thus their voice? 3.01.119
hear me one word, | beseech you, tribunes, hear 3.01.214
one time will owe another. 3.01.241
to eject him hence | were but one danger, and to 3.01.286
one word more, one word: 3.01.309
one word more, one word: 3.01.309
when one but of my ordinance stood up | to speak 3.02. 12
buy | their mercy at the price of one fair word, 3.03. 91
full | of the wars' surfeits to go rove with one 4.01. 46
if i could shake off but one seven years | from 4.01. 55
we to be baited | with one that wants her wits? 4.02. 44
a most royal one: 4.03. 43 P
whose double bosoms seems to wear one heart, 4.04. 13
broke their sleep | to take the one the other, 4.04. 20
a strange one as ever i look'd on. 4.05. 20 P
a marv'llous poor one. 4.05. 27 P
take | th' one half of my commission, and set 4.05.138
finger and his thumb as one would set up a top. 4.05.153 P
but a greater soldier than he, you wot one. 4.05.163 P
look you, one cannot tell how to say that. 4.05.169 P
and but one half of what he was yesterday; 4.05.198 P
ay, and it makes men hate one another. 4.05.230 P
because they then less need one another. 4.05.231 P
and affecting one sole throne, | without 4.06. 32
if he could burn us all into one coal, | we have 4.06.137
not to be other than one thing, not moving 4.07. 42
but one of these — | as he hath spices of them 4.07. 45
one fire drives out one fire; 4.07. 54
one fire drives out one fire; 4.07. 54
one nail, one nail; 4.07. 54
one nail, one nail; 4.07. 54
yet one time he did call me by my name. 5.01. 9
of a state | to one whom they had punish'd. 5.01. 21
for one poor grain or two, to leave unburnt 5.01. 27
for one poor grain or two? 5.01. 28
i am one of those; 5.01. 29
as you say you have, i am one that, telling true 5.02. 32 P
grace to both parts | than seek the end of one, 5.03.122
here he lets me prate | like one i' th' stocks. 5.03.160
i'll be one. 5.06.148
city he | hath widowed and unchilded many a one, 5.06.151
and buried one and twenty valiant sons, TIT 1.01.195
enjoy, | one fit to bandy with thy lawless sons, 1.01.312
my foes i do repute you every one, | so trouble 1.01.366
nor me, so i were one. 2.01.102
and one thing more | that womanhood denies my 2.03.173
one hour's storm will drown the fragrant meads, 2.04. 54
is that the one will help to cut the other. 3.01. 78
for now i stand as one upon a rock, | environ'd 3.01. 93
or any one of you, chop off your hand | and send 3.01.153
o, here i lift this one hand up to heaven, | and 3.01.206
about, | that i may turn me to each one of you, 3.01.277
i think she means that there were more than one 4.01. 38
and no one else but the delivered empress. 4.02.142
far, one muliteus my countryman | his wife but 4.02.152
see, thou hast shot off one of taurus' horns. 4.03. 70
betwixt my uncle and one of the emperal's men. 4.03. 94 P
when as the one is wounded with the bait, | the 4.04. 92
things | as willingly as one would kill a fly, 5.01.142
and, if one arm's embracement will content thee, 5.02. 68
the one is murder, and rape is the other's name, 5.02.156
this one hand yet is left to cut your throats, 5.02.181
be every one officious | to make this banket, 5.02.201
what, hath the firmament moe suns than one? 5.03. 17
this scattered corn into one mutual sheaf, 5.03. 71
sheaf, | these broken limbs again into one body. 5.03. 72
if any one relieves or pities him, | for the 5.03.181
if one good deed in all my life i did, | i do 5.03.189
'tis all one; ROM 1.01. 21 P
"better," here comes one of my master's kinsmen. 1.01. 58 P
thou shalt not stir one foot to seek a foe. 1.01. 80
be found, | being one too many by my weary self, 1.01.128
a word ill urg'd to one that is so ill! 1.01.203
you, among the store | one more, most welcome, 1.02. 23
which /on more view of many, mine, being one, 1.02. 32
tut, man, one fire burns out another's burning, 1.02. 45
one desperate grief cures with another's 1.02. 48
one fairer than my love! 1.02. 92
and see how one another lends content; 1.03. 84
why, may one ask? 1.04. 49
manners shall lie all in one or two men's hands, 1.05. 3 P
i learnt even now | of one i danc'd withal. 1.05.143
speak but one rhyme, and i am satisfied; 2.01. 9
speak to my gossip venus one fair word, | one 2.01. 11
one nickname for her purblind son and /heir, 2.01. 12
doth cease to be | ere one can say it lightens. 2.02.120
by one that i'll procure to come to thee, 2.02.145
where on a sudden one hath wounded me | that's 2.03. 50
a grave, | to lay one in, another out to have. 2.03. 84
with me, | in one respect i'll thy assistant be; 2.03. 90
he rests his minim rests, one, two, and the 2.04. 22 P
more of the wild goose in one of thy wits than, 2.04. 72 P
one, gentlewoman, that god hath made, himself to 2.04.115 P
say, | "two may keep counsel, putting one away"? 2.04.197
o, there is a nobleman in town, one paris, that 2.04.201 P
that one short minute gives me in her sight. 2.06. 5
alone | till holy church incorporate two in one. 2.06. 37
thou art like one of these fellows that, when he 3.01. 5 P
have none shortly, for one would kill the other. 3.01. 16 P
gentlemen, good den, a word with one of you. 3.01. 38
and but one word with one of us? 3.01. 39 P
and but one word with one of us? 3.01. 39 P
of cats, nothing but one of your nine lives; 3.01. 77 P
scorn, with one hand beats | cold death aside, 3.01.161
and all those twenty could but kill one life. 3.01.179
that "banished," that one word "banished," 3.02.113
arise, one knocks. good romeo, hide thyself. 3.03. 71
farewell, farewell! one kiss, and i'll descend. 3.05. 42
so low, | as one dead in the bottom of a tomb. 3.05. 56
i'll send to one in mantua, | where that same 3.05. 88
one who, to put thee from thy heaviness, | hath 3.05.108
in one little body | thou counterfeits a bark, a 3.05.130
child, | but now i see this one is one too much, 3.05.166
child, | but now i see this one is one too much, 3.05.166
may not one speak? 3.05.173
but one, poor one, one poor and loving child, 4.05. 46

but one, poor one, one poor and loving child, 4.05. 46
but one, poor one, one poor and loving child, 4.05. 46
child, | but one thing to rejoice and solace in, 4.05. 47
every one prepare | to follow this fair corse 4.05. 92
one of our order, to associate me, | here in 5.02. 6
one writ with me in sour misfortune's book! 5.03. 82
here's one, a friend, and one that knows you 5.03.123
one, a friend, and one that knows you well. 5.03.123
sir, and there's my master, | one that you love. 5.03.129
anon comes one with light to ope the tomb, | and 5.03.283
dumbness of the gesture | one might interpret. TIM 1.01. 34
malice | infects one comma in the course i hold, 1.01. 48
one do i personate of lord timon's frame, | whom 1.01. 69
with one man beckon'd from the rest below, 1.01. 74
down, | not one accompanying his declining foot. 1.01. 88
more rais'd | than one which holds a trencher. 1.01.120
one only daughter have i, no kin else, | on whom 1.01.121
art not one? 1.01.217 P
shouldst have kept one to thyself, for i mean to 1.01.265 P
see so many dip their meat in one man's blood, 1.02. 41 P
like brothers commanding one another's fortunes! 1.02.105 P
dies that bears not one spurn to their graves 1.02.141
before me now | would one day stamp upon me. 1.02.144
i have one word | to say to you. 1.02.167
but rather one that smiles and still invites 2.01. 11
one varro's servant, my good lord — 2.02. 27
my mistress is one, and i am her fool. 2.02. 99 P
i could render one. 2.02.103 P
with two stones moe than 's artificial one. 2.02.111 P
one cloud of winter show'rs, | these flies are 2.02.171
one of lord timon's men? 3.01. 5 P
and one that knows what belongs to reason; 3.01. 35 P
but i can tell you one thing, my lord, and which 3.02. 4 P
that not long ago one of his men was with the 3.02. 11 P
me, i count it one of my greatest afflictions, 3.02. 55 P
and i think | one business does command us all; 3.04. 4
one may reach deep enough and yet | find little. 3.04. 15
one of lord timon's men. 3.04. 33 P
man enough, that one need not lend to another; 3.06. 73 P
one day he gives us diamonds, next day stones. 3.06.120
not | one friend to take his fortune by the arm, 4.02. 7
not one word more: 4.02. 28
twinn'd brothers of one womb, | whose 4.03. 3
if one be, | so are they all; 4.03. 15
let not thy sword skip one. 4.03.111
from forth thy plenteous bosom, one poor root! 4.03.186
the one is filling still, never complete; 4.03.244
have with one winter's brush | fell from their 4.03.264
i, that i am one now. 4.03.278
love not yourselves, away, | rob one another. 4.03.445
i do proclaim | one honest man — mistake me not 4.03.497
one honest man — mistake me not, but one; 4.03.497
gifts, | expecting in return twenty for one? 4.03.510
i'd exchange | for this one wish, that you had 4.03.521
there's never a one of you but trusts a knave 5.01. 93
wouldst not reside | but where one villain is, 5.01.111
the senators with one consent of love | entreat 5.01.140
am not | one that rejoices in the common wrack, 5.01.192
i met a courier, one mine ancient friend, | whom 5.02. 6
(among which number, cassius, be you one), | nor JC 1.02. 44
set honor in one eye and death i' th' other, 1.02. 86
but it was fam'd with more than with one man? 1.02.153
that her wide walks encompass'd but one man? 1.02.155
enough, | when there is in it but one only man. 1.02.157
a crown neither, 'twas one of these coronets — 1.02.238 P
those that understood him smil'd at one another, 1.02.283 P
close a while, for here comes one in haste. 1.03.131
it is casca, one incorporate | to our attempts. 1.03.135
shall rome stand under one man's awe? 2.01. 52
and every one doth wish | you had but that 2.01. 91
give me your hands all over, one by one. 2.01.112
give me your hands all over, one by one. 2.01.112
and so good morrow to you every one. 2.01.228
vow | which did incorporate and make us one, 2.01.273
hark, hark, one knocks. 2.01.304
there is one within, | besides the things that 2.02. 14
we /are two lions litter'd in one day, | and i 2.02. 46
mock | apt to be render'd, for some one to say, 2.02. 97
there is but one mind in all these men, and it 2.03. 5 P
they are all fire, and every one doth shine; 3.01. 64
but there's but one in all doth hold his place. 3.01. 65
yet in the number i do know but one | that 3.01. 68
that one of two bad ways you must conceit me, 3.01.192
he should stand | one of the three to share it? 4.01. 15
one that feeds | on objects, arts, and 4.01. 36
shall one of us, | that struck the foremost man 4.03. 21
hated by one he loves, brav'd by his brother, 4.03. 96
died | by their proscriptions, cicero being one. 4.03.178
cicero one? 4.03.179
farewell every one. 4.03.238
hack'd one another in the sides of caesar. 5.01. 40
to set | upon one battle all our liberties. 5.01. 75
and common good to all, made one of them. 5.05. 72
and every one did bear | thy praises in his MAC 1.03. 98
but i have spoke | with one that saw him die; 1.04. 4
as one that had been studied in his death, | to 1.04. 9
one of my fellows had the speed of him, | who, 1.05. 35
now o'er the one half world | nature seems dead, 2.01. 49
there's one did laugh in 's sleep, and one cried 2.02. 20
one did laugh in 's sleep, and one cried, 2.02. 20
one cried, "god bless us!" 2.02. 24
seas incarnadine, | making the green one red. 2.02. 60
but yet 'tis one. 2.03. 49
the house–keeper, the hunter, every one, 3.01. 96
i am one, my liege, | whom the vile blows and 3.01.107
there's but one down; the son is fled. 3.03. 20
ay, and a bold one, that dare look on that 3.04. 58
there's not a one of them but in his house | i 3.04.130
pains, | and every one shall share i' th' gains. 4.01. 40
but one word more — 4.01. 74
yet my heart | throbs to know one thing: 4.01.101
why, one that swears and lies. 4.02. 47 P
every one that does so is a traitor, and must be 4.02. 49 P
every one. 4.02. 53 P
better macbeth | than such an one to reign. 4.03. 66
if such a one be fit to govern, speak. 4.03.101
each minute teems a new one. 4.03.176
chickens, and their dam, | at one fell swoop? 4.03.219

neither to you nor any one, having no witness to 5.01. 17 P
one — two — why then 'tis time to do't. 5.01. 35 P
such a one | am i to fear, or none. 5.07. 3
clatter, one of greatest note | seems bruited. 5.07. 21
which must not yield | to one of woman born. 5.08. 13
so thanks to all at once and to each one, | whom 5.09. 40
and myself, | the bell then beating one — HAM 1.01. 39
kingdom | to be contracted in one brow of woe, 1.02. 4
while one with moderate haste might tell a 1.02.237
men, | carrying, i say, the stamp of one defect, 1.04. 31
meet it is i set it down | that one may smile, 1.05.108
and soldiers, | give me one poor request. 1.05.142
is to be one man pick'd out of ten thousand. 2.02.179 P
why — "one fair daughter, and no more, | the 2.02.407
i remember one said there were no sallets in the 2.02.441 P
one speech in't i chiefly lov'd, 'twas aeneas' 2.02.445 P
god hath given you one face, and you make 3.01.143 P
those that are married already (all but one) 3.01.148 P
the censure of which one must, in your allowance 3.02. 27 P
as one in suff'ring all that suffers nothing, 3.02. 66
one scene of it comes near the circumstance 3.02. 76
guilt | do not itself unkennel in one speech, 3.02. 81
and haply one as kind | for husband shalt thou 3.02.176
this is one lucianus, nephew to the king. 3.02.244 P
a whole one, i. 3.02.280 P
let me see one. 3.02.345 P
may one be pardon'd and retain th' offense? 3.03. 56
yet what can it, when one can not repent? 3.03. 66
or but a sickly part of one true sense | could 3.04. 80
one word more, good lady. 3.04.180
but i will delve one yard below their mines, 3.04.208
when in one line two crafts directly meet. 3.04.210
to all, | to you yourself, to us, to every one. 4.01. 15
two dishes, but to one table — that's the end. 4.03. 24 P
is man and wife, man and wife is one flesh — so 4.03. 52 P
thought which quarter'd hath but one part wisdom 4.04. 42
indeed would make one think there might be 4.05. 12
should i your true–love know | from another one? 4.05. 24
pluck such envy from him | as did that one, and 4.07. 75
be a sight indeed | if one could match you. 4.07.100
one woe doth tread upon another's heel, | so 4.07.163
lauds, | as one incapable of her own distress, 4.07.178
now o'erreaches, one that would circumvent god, 5.01. 79 P
one that was a woman, sir, but, rest her soul, 5.01.135 P
not one now to mock your own grinning — quite 5.01.191 P
prithee, horatio, tell me one thing. 5.01.195 P
come, one for me. 5.02.254
one. 5.02.280
hour | he flashes into one gross crime or other LR 1.03. 4
whose mind and mine, i know, in that are one, 1.03. 15
my boy, between a bitter fool and a sweet one? 1.04.138 P
bald crown when thou gav'st thy golden one away. 1.04.163 P
here comes one o' the parings. 1.04.188 P
a fox, when one has caught her, | and such a 1.04.317
and i have one thing, of a queasy question, 2.01. 17
one that wouldst be a bawd in way of good 2.02. 19 P
one whom i will beat into /clamorous whining, if 2.02. 23 P
thus to rail on one that is neither known of 2.02. 26 P
but the great one that goes upward, let him draw 2.04. 73 P
we'll no more meet, no more see one another. 2.04.220
how in one house | should many people under two 2.04.240
what need one? 2.04.263
i'll receive him gladly, | but not one follower. 2.04.293
one minded like the weather, most unquietly. 3.01. 2
i have one part in my heart | that's sorry yet 3.02. 72
one that slept in the contriving of lust, and 3.04. 89 P
let me ask you one word in private. 3.04.160
you, sir, i entertain for one of my hundred; 3.06. 79 P
which came from one that's of a neutral heart, 3.07. 48
of a neutral heart, | and not from one oppos'd. 3.07. 49
one side will mock another; th' other too. 3.07. 71
you have one eye left | to see some mischief on 3.07. 81
one way i like this well, | but being widow, and 4.02. 83
half way down | hangs one that gathers sampire, 4.06. 15
you are a royal one, and we obey you. 4.06.201
every one hears that, | which can distinguish 4.06.210
had speech with man so poor, | hear me one word. 5.01. 39
one? 5.01. 58
one step i have advanc'd thee, if thou dost | as 5.03. 28
the one the other poison'd for my sake, | and 5.03.241
i know when one is dead, and when one lives; 5.03.261
i know when one is dead, and when one lives; 5.03.261
she lov'd and hated, | one of them we behold. 5.03.282
one michael cassio, a florentine | (a fellow OTH 1.01. 20
some soul, | and such a one do i profess myself. 1.01. 55
you are one of those that will not serve god, if 1.01.108 P
i am one, sir, that comes to tell you your 1.01.115 P
some one way, some another. 1.01.176
this very night at one another's heels; 1.02. 42
good night to every one. 1.03.288
supply it with one gender of herbs or distract 1.03.323 P
of our lives had not one scale of reason to 1.03.327 P
one that excels the quirks of blazoning pens, 2.01. 63
'tis one iago, ancient to the general. 2.01. 66
there's one gone to the harbor? 2.01.120
bestow on a deserving woman indeed — one that, 2.01.145 P
he is a good one, and his worthiness | does 2.01.210
they are our friends — but one cup, i'll drink 2.03. 37 P
i have drunk but one cup to–night — and that 2.03. 39 P
if i can fasten but one cup upon him, | with 2.03. 48
good faith, a little one; 2.03. 66 P
a just equinox, | the one as long as th' other. 2.03.125
own second | with one of an ingraft infirmity; 2.03.140
swords out, and tilting one at other's /breast, 2.03.183
even so as one would beat his offenseless dog to 2.03.274 P
one unperfectness shows me another, to make me 2.03.297 P
hound that hunts, but one that fills up the cry. 2.03.364 P
tell her there's one cassio entreats her a 3.01. 25 P
for if he be not one that truly loves you, 3.03. 48
/then, | from one that so imperfectly /conjects, 3.03.149
foh, one may smell in such, a will most rank, 3.03.232
one of this kind is cassio. 3.03.418
i gave her such a one; 'twas my first gift. 3.03.436
one is too poor, too weak for my revenge. 3.03.443
'tis a good hand, | a frank one. 3.04. 44
he had one yesterday. 4.01. 51
plague | to beguile many and be beguil'd by one) 4.01. 97
marry, a perfum'd one! 4.01.147 P
a most unhappy one. 4.01.232
lest, being like one of heaven, the devils 4.02. 36
would it not make one weep? 4.02.127
will fashion to fall out between twelve and one) 4.02.237 P
all's one. 4.03. 23
prithee shroud me | in one of these same sheets. 4.03. 25
but to go hang my head all at one side | and 4.03. 32
here's one comes in his shirt, with light and 5.01. 47
i think that one of them is hereabout, | and 5.01. 57
that's one of them. 5.01. 61
one more, one more. 5.02. 17
one more, one more. 5.02. 17
one more, and that's the last. 5.02. 19
but while i say one prayer! 5.02. 83
world | of one entire and perfect chrysolite, 5.02.145
the one of them imports | the death of cassio to 5.02.310
of one that lov'd not wisely but too well; 5.02.344
of one not easily jealious, but, being wrought, 5.02.345
of one whose hand, | like the base /indian, 5.02.346
of one whose subdu'd eyes, | albeit unused to 5.02.348
pray then, foresee me one. ANT 1.02. 16 P
the man from sicyon — is there such an one? 1.02.114
now, play one scene | of excellent dissembling, 1.03. 78
courteous lord, one word: 1.03. 86
if you borrow one another's love for the instant 2.02.103 P
them up, | i'll think them every one an antony, 2.05. 14
though he be painted one way like a gorgon, 2.05.116
but that they would | have one man but a man? 2.06. 19
as they pinch one another by the disposition, he 2.07. 6 P
all, four days, | than drink so much in one. 2.07.103
one of my place in syria, his lieutenant, | for 3.01. 18
a very fine one. o, how he loves caesar! 3.02. 7
her motion and her station are as one; 3.03. 19
i have one thing more to ask him yet, good 3.03. 45
they say, one taurus. 3.07. 78
one of them rates | all that is won and lost. 3.11. 69
one that but performs | the bidding of the 3.13. 86
a lion's whelp | than with an old one dying. 3.13. 95
to be abus'd | by one that looks on feeders? 3.13.109
you mingle eyes | with one that ties his points? 3.13.157
come, | let's have one other gaudy night. 3.13.182
when one so great begins to rage, he's hunted 4.01. 7
of better fortune, | he is twenty men to one. 4.02. 4
'tis one of those odd tricks which sorrow shoots 4.02. 14
i look on you | as one that takes his leave. 4.02. 29
it will determine one way; 4.03. 2
one ever near thee. 4.05. 7
run one before, | and let the queen know of our 4.08. 1
this last day was | a shrewd one to 's. 4.09. 5
fury, for one death | might have prevented many. 4.12. 41
death of one person can be paid but once, | and 4.14. 27
nor any one. 4.14.110
one word, sweet queen: 4.15. 45
but if there be, nor ever were one such, | it's 5.02. 96
the honor of thy lordliness | to one so meek, 5.02.162
must i be unfolded | with one that i have bred? 5.02.171
i heard of one of them no longer than yesterday, 5.02.251 P
the regions of the earth | for one his like, CYM 1.01. 21
my residence in rome at one /philario's, | who 1.01. 97
o thou vild one! 1.01.143
by all likelihood have confounded one the other, 1.04. 51 P
the one may be sold or given, or if there were 1.04. 82 P
the one is but frail and the other casual. 1.04. 91 P
by the gods, it is one. 1.04.148 P
and will not trust one of her malice with | a 1.05. 35
being | is to exchange one misery with another, 1.05. 55
"he is one of the noblest note, to whose 1.06. 22 P
his companion, one | an eminent monsieur that, 1.06. 64
am i one, sir? 1.06. 83
that all the plagues of hell should at one time 1.06.111
and he is one | the truest manner'd, such a holy 1.06.165
would he had been one of my rank! 2.01. 15 P
and, 'tis thought, one of leonatus' friends. 2.01. 38 P
one of your lordship's pages. 2.01. 41 P
but kiss, one kiss! 2.02. 17
one, two, three: 2.02. 51
the one is caius lucius. 2.03. 55
what | if i do line one of their hands? 2.03. 67
i will make | one of her women lawyer to me, for 2.03. 74
one of your great knowing | should learn, being 2.03. 97
one bred of alms and foster'd with cold dishes, 2.03.114
is one of the fairest that i have look'd upon. 2.04. 32
cupids | of silver, each on one foot standing, 2.04. 90
or | who knows if one her women, being corrupted 2.04.116
to be believ'd | of one persuaded well of. 2.04.132
one vice but of a minute old, for one | not half 2.05. 31
a minute old, for one | not half so old as that. 2.05. 31
i do not say i am one; 3.01. 41 P
griefs are med'cinable, that is one of them, 3.02. 33
if one of mean affairs | may plod it in a week, 3.02. 50
one score 'twixt sun and sun, | madam, 's enough 3.02. 68
why, one that rode to 's execution, man, | could 3.02. 70
but in one night, | a storm or robbery (call it 3.03. 61
one but painted thus | would be interpreted a 3.04. 6
to do this business | i have not slept one wink. 3.04.100
first, make yourself but like one. 3.04.167
woman, from every one | the best she hath, and 3.05. 72
(i forgot to ask him one thing, i'll remember't 3.05.131 P
i see a man's life is a tedious one, | i have 3.06. 1
my dear lord, | thou art one o' th' false ones. 3.06. 15
society is no comfort | to one not sociable. 4.02. 13
he is but one. 4.02. 68
cut off one cloten's head, | son to the queen 4.02.118
ay, and that | from one bad thing to worse, not 4.02.134
my brother wears thee not the one half so well 4.02.202
rotting | together, have one dust, yet reverence 4.02.247
young one, | inform us of thy fortunes, for it 4.02.360
horse, save one that had | a rider like myself, 4.04. 38
should reserve | my crack'd one to more care. 4.04. 50
to an ancient soldier | (an honest one, i 5.03. 16
ten chas'd by one | are now each one the 5.03. 48
are now each one the slaughter–man of twenty. 5.03. 49
here is one: 5.03. 56
am i better | than one that's sick o' th' gout, 5.04. 5
seat, and cast | from her his dearest one, 5.04. 61
o rare one, | be not, as is our fangled world, a 5.04.133
end, i think you'll never return to tell one. 5.04.184 P
beget young gibbets, i never saw one so prone. 5.04.199 P
so should i, if i were one. 5.04.203 P
i would we were all of one mind, and one mind 5.04.203 P
we were all of one mind, and one mind good. 5.04.203 P
such precious deeds in one that promis'd nought 5.05. 9
though with the loss | of many a bold one, whose 5.05. 71
this one thing only | i will entreat: 5.05. 83
one sand another | not more resembles that sweet 5.05.120
most like a noble lord in love and one | that 5.05.171
i left out one thing which the queen confess'd, 5.05.244
a most incivil one. 5.05.292
one sin, i know, another doth provoke: PER 1.01.137
which love to all, of which thyself art one, 1.02. 94
who shuns not to break one will crack /them both 1.02.121
bound by the indenture of his oath to be one. 1.03. 9 P
throws down one mountain to cast up a higher. 1.04. 6
like one another's glass to trim them by; 1.04. 27
one sorrow never comes but brings an heir | that 1.04. 63
to my desires, i could wish to make one there. 2.01.112 P
who freely give to every one that come | to 2.03. 60
therefore each one betake him to his rest; 2.03.114
one twelve moons more she'll wear diana's livery 2.05. 10
let me ask you one thing: 2.05. 32
round, | and every one with claps can sound, 3.ch. 36
i have one myself, | who shall not be more dear 3.03. 32
our cleon hath | one daughter, and a full–grown 4.ch. 16
says one, "wolt out?" 4.01. 61
i cannot be bated one doit of a thousand pieces. 4.02. 51 P
why lament you, pretty one? 4.02. 68 P
come, young one, i like the manner of your 4.02.133 P
be one of those that thinks | the petty wrens of 4.03. 21
y' are like one that superstitiously | do swear 4.03. 49
to use one language in each several clime 4.04. 6
we have here one, sir, if she would — but there 4.06. 27 P
now, pretty one, how long have you been at this 4.06. 66 P
earlier too, sir, if now i be one. 4.06. 76 P
but i protest to thee, pretty one, my authority 4.06. 88 P
i beseech your honor one piece for me. 4.06.117 P
prithee tell me one thing first. 4.06.156 P
come now, your one thing. 4.06.157 P
money enough in the end to buy him a wooden one? 4.06.173 P
she sings like one immortal, and she dances | as 5.ch. 3
this three months hath not spoken | to any one, 5.01. 25
till the disaster that, one mortal /night, 5.01. 37
welcome, fair one! 5.01. 65
she's such a one that, were i well assur'd 5.01. 67
and such a one | my daughter might have been. 5.01.107
for thou lookest | like one i lov'd indeed. 5.01.125
name | was given me by one that had some power, 5.01.148
him lead his line | to catch one at my heart. TNK 1.01.117
o, if thou couch | but one night with her, every 1.01.183
the one of th' other may be said to water 1.03. 58
operance, our souls | did so to one another. 1.03. 64
a thousand differing ways to one sure end. 1.05. 14
death's the market–place, where each one meets. 1.05. 16
before one salmon, you shall take a number of 2.01. 4 P
i' th' deliverance, will break from one of them; 2.01. 42 P
we shall know nothing here but one another, 2.02. 41
we are an endless mine to one another; 2.02. 79
we are one another's wife, ever begetting | new 2.02. 80
we are, in one another, families: 2.02. 82
they could not be to one so fair. 2.02.123
and take one with you? 2.02.151
'tis a rare one. 2.02.153
is't but a rare one? 2.02.154
yes, if he be but one. 2.02.196
but say that one | had rather combat me? 2.02.196
let that one say so, | and use thy freedom; 2.02.197
fortune | to be one hour at liberty and grasp 2.02.208
once more | i would but see this fair one. 2.02.232
twenty to one, he'll come to speak to her, | and 2.03. 14
but that's all one, i'll go through, let her 2.03. 31
this afternoon to ride, but 'tis a rough one. 2.05. 46
by all oaths in one, | i, and the justice of my 3.01. 33
and the charity | of one meal lend me — come 3.01. 74
content and anger | in me have but one face. 3.01.108
but this one word: 3.01.116
hath grief slain fear, and, but for one thing, 3.02. 5
there's a leak sprung, a sound one. 3.04. 8
twenty to one, is truss'd up in a trice 3.04. 17
gallants of war, | by one, by two, by three–a. 3.05. 62
the one said it was an owl, | the other he said 3.05. 68
one see 'em all rewarded. 3.05.152
that was a very good one, and that day, | i well 3.06. 72
here's one, if it but hold, i ask no more | for 3.06. 91
let 's die together, at one instant, duke. 3.06.177
of love about 'em, | and not kill one another? 3.06.220
better they fall by th' law than one another. 3.06.225
shall travel, ever strangers | to one another. 3.06.256
if one of them were dead, as one must, are you 3.06.273
if one of them were dead, as one must, are you 3.06.273
neither heard i one question | of your name or 4.01. 15
to her marriage, | a large one, i'll assure you. 4.01. 24
sport, | i heard a voice, a shrill one; 4.01. 56
i might well perceive | 'twas one that sung, and 4.01. 58
"this you may loose, not me," and many a one; 4.01. 91
her — one of 'em | i knew to be your brother; 4.01.100
o, a very fine one! 4.01.105
pray did you ever hear | of one young palamon? 4.01.117
my fair sister, | you must love one of them. 4.02. 68
if one be mad, or hang or drown themselves, 4.03. 34 P
a very grievous punishment, as one would think, 4.03. 45 P
one would marry a leprous witch to be rid on't, 4.03. 46 P
one cries, "o, this smoke!" 4.03. 53 P
one cries, "o, that ever i did it behind the 4.03. 54 P
now that cannot finish | till one of us expire. 5.01. 19
this business, were't one eye | against another, 5.01. 21
one farewell! 5.01. 32
thou mighty one, that with thy power hast turn'd 5.01. 49
i had one, a woman, | and women 'twere they 5.01.106
such a one i am, | and vow that lover never yet 5.01.124
out of two i should | choose one, and pray for 5.01.153
of mine eyes | were i to lose one — they are 5.01.155
but one rose! 5.01.165
that's all one, if ye make a noise. 5.02. 16
but that's all one, 'tis nothing to our purpose. 5.02. 32
he's a very fair one. 5.02. 46
that's all one, i will have you. 5.02. 85
'tis a sweet one, | and will perfume me finely 5.02. 88

in that light which shows | the one the other. 5.03. 22
were they metamorphis'd | both into one — o, 5.03. 85
he is a good one | as ever strook at head. 5.03.108
their contentious throats, now one the higher, 5.03.125
till heavens did | make hardly one the winner. 5.03.130
i see one eye of yours conceives a tear, | the 5.03.137
that four such eyes should be so fix'd on one 5.03.145
emily | did first bestow on him — a black one, 5.04. 50
i am palamon, | one that yet loves thee dying. 5.04. 90
one kiss from fair emilia. 5.04. 94
but one hour since, i was as dearly sorry | as 5.04.129
ten kisses short as one, one long as twenty: VEN 22
ten kisses short as one, one long as twenty: 22
over one arm the lusty courser's rein, | under 31
and one sweet kiss shall pay this comptless debt 84
"thou canst not see one wrinkle in my brow, 139
what were thy lips the worse for one poor kiss? 207
give me one kiss, i'll give it thee again, | and 209
and one for int'rest, if thou wilt have twain. 210
gone, | she locks her lily fingers one in one. 228
gone, | she locks her lily fingers one in one. 228
so did this horse excel a common one, | in shape 293
with one fair hand she heaveth up his hat, | her 351
for one sweet look thy help i would assure thee, 371
who plucks the bud before one leaf put forth? 416
me, | and pay them at thy leisure, one by one. 518
me, | and pay them at thy leisure, one by one. 518
to one sore sick that hears the passing bell. 702
but in one minute's fight brings beauty under; 746
as one on shore | gazing upon a late embarked 817
whereat amaz'd as one that unaware | hath 823
whereat she starts like one that spies an adder 878
proud, | because the cry remaineth in one place, 885
here overcome, as one full of despair, | she 955
the one doth flatter thee in thoughts unlikely, 989
as full of fear | as one with treasure laden, 1022
over one shoulder doth she hang her head; 1058
"my tongue cannot express my grief for one, 1069
there shall not be one minute in an hour 1187
fight, | and every one to rest himself betakes, LUC 125
as one of which doth tarquin lie revolving | the 127
is such thwarting strife | that one for all, or 144
strife | that one for all, or all for one, we 144
th' one sweetly flatters, th' other feareth harm 172
for one sweet grape who will the vine destroy? 215
each one by him enforc'd retires his ward; 303
imagine her as one in dead of night | from forth 449
"where now i have no one to blush with me, | to 792
one poor retiring minute in an age | would 962
dread night, wouldst thou one hour come back, 965
and time to see one that by alms doth live 986
continuance tames the one, the other wild, 1097
and as one shifts, another straight ensues: 1104
fly, | or one encompass'd with a winding maze, 1151
having two sweet babes, when death takes one, 1161
when the one pure, the other made divine? 1164
life, | the one will live, the other being dead: 1187
one justly weeps, the other takes in hand | no 1235
when more is felt than one hath power to tell. 1288
one of my husband's men | bid thou be ready, by 1291
that one might see those far-off eyes look sad. 1386
that one would swear he saw them quake and 1393
o, what art | of physiognomy might one behold! 1395
here one man's hand lean'd on another's head, 1415
here one being throng'd bears back, all boll'n 1417
"why should the private pleasure of some one 1478
and one man's lust these many lives confounds. 1489
ere once she can discharge one word of woe; 1605
to tell them all with one poor tired tongue. 1617
to drown /one woe, one pair of weeping eyes. 1680
the one doth call her his, the other his, | yet 1793
friend, | i guess one angel in another's hell: PP 2.12
doubt, | till my bad angel fire my good one out. 2.14
because thou lov'st the one, and i the other. 8. 4
one god is god of both (as poets feign), | one 8.13
one knight loves both, and both in thee remain. 8.14
she showed hers, he saw more wounds than one, 9.13
a lording's daughter, the fairest one of three, 15. 1
but one must be refused; 15. 9
one silly cross wrought all my loss, | o 17. 9
the joys in bed, | one woman would another wed. 18.48
every one that flatters thee | is no friend in 20.29
if that one be prodigal, | bountiful they will 20.37
as love in twain | had the essence but in one, PHT 26
double name | neither two nor one was called. 40
"how true a twain | seemeth this concordant one! 46
thee, | or ten times happier be it ten for one; SON 6. 8
mark how one string, sweet husband to another, 8. 9
who all in one, one pleasing note do sing: 8.12
who all in one, one pleasing note do sing: 8.12
whose speechless song, being many, seeming one, 8.13
in one of thine, from that which thou departest, 11. 2
but i forbid thee one most heinous crime, | o, 19. 8
by adding one thing to my purpose nothing. 20.12
so long as youth and thou are of one date, | but 22. 2
the one by toil, the other to complain | how far 28. 7
wishing me like to one more rich in hope, 29. 5
even so my sun one early morn did shine | with 33. 9
but out, alack, he was but one hour mine, | the 33.11
twain, | although our undivided loves are one: 36. 2
in our two loves there is but one respect, 36. 5
and our dear love lose name of single one, 39. 6
and that thou teachest how to make one twain, 39.13
my friend and i are one; 42.13
since every one hath, every one, one shade, 53. 3
since every one hath, every one, one shade, 53. 3
since every one hath, every one, one shade, 53. 3
and you, but one, can every shadow lend: 53. 4
year, | the one doth shadow of your beauty show, 53.10
why write i still all one, ever the same, | and 76. 5
there lives more life in one of your fair eyes 83.13
all these i better in one general best. 91. 8
all alike my songs and praises be | to one, of 105. 4
alike my songs and praises be | to one, of one, 105. 4
one thing expressing, leaves out difference. 105. 8
three themes in one, which wondrous scope 105.12
which three till now never kept seat in one. 105.14
one on another's neck, do witness bear | thy 131.11
add to thy will | one will of mine, to make thy 135.12
think all but one, and me in that one will. 135.14
think all but one, and me in that one will. 135.14
ay, fill it full with wills, and my will one. 136. 6
we prove | among a number one is reckon'd none: 136. 8
though in thy store's account i one must be, 136.10
dissuade one foolish heart from serving thee, 141.10
one of her feathered creatures broke away, 143. 2
friend, | i guess one angel in another's hell. 144.12
doubt, | till my bad angel fire my good one out. 144.14
jet, | which one by one she in a river threw, LC 38
jet, | which one by one she in a river threw, 38
of folded schedules had she many a one, | which 43
o, one by nature's outwards so commended | that 80
the one a palate hath that needs will taste, 167
not one whose flame my heart so much as warmed, 191
lies | in the small orb of one particular tear! 289

ONE'S 15 FR 0.0017 REL FR 8 V 7 P
when one's right hand | is perjured to the bosom TGV 5.04. 67
some devils ask but the parings of one's nail, ERR 4.03. 71
boy that abuses every one's eyes because his own AYL 4.01.214 P
have heard a sonnet begin so to one's mistress. H5 3.07. 41 P
by god's lid, it does one's heart good. TRO 1.02.211 P
'twas one's that lov'd me better than you will. 5.02. 89
one's junius brutus, | sicinius velutus, and i COR 1.01.216
proportion'd as one's thought would wish a man, ROM 3.05.182
for taking one's part that's out of favor. LR 1.04. 99 P
thou canst tell why one's nose stands i' th' 1.05. 19 P
why, to keep one's eyes of either side 's nose, 1.05. 22 P
and dizzy 'tis, to cast one's eyes so low! 4.06. 12
wit, | the one's for use, the other useth it. OTH 2.01.130
and discourse fustian with one's own shadow? 2.03.281 P
for one's offense why should so many fall, | to LUC 1483

/ONES 1 FR 0.0001 REL FR 0 V 1 P
more of his purchases, and /double /ones /too, HAM 5.01.109 P

ONES 67 FR 0.0075 REL FR 41 V 26 P
as if it had lungs, and rotten ones. TMP 2.01. 48 P
this, | no ceremony that to great ones 'longs, MM 2.02. 59
for two — and sound ones too. ERR 2.02. 91 P
sure ones then. 2.02. 93 P
certain ones then. 2.02. 95 P
for when rich villains have need of poor ones, ADO 3.03.114 P
ones, poor ones may make what price they will. 3.03.114 P
are only turn'd into tongue, and trim ones too. 4.01.321 P
good morrow, fair ones. AYL 4.03. 75
read in poetry | and other books, good ones, i SHR 1.02.170
nay, let them go, a couple of quiet ones. 3.02.240
yet slight ones will not carry it. AWW 4.01. 38 P
and great ones i dare not give; 4.01. 39 P
let thy curtsies alone, they are scurvy ones. 5.03.324 P
what great ones do the less will prattle of) TN 1.02. 33
one of those gentle ones that will use the devil 4.02. 32 P
violence, in the which three great ones suffer, WT 2.01.128
(three-man song-men all, and very good ones), 4.03. 42 P
receiv'd, which are mighty ones and millions. 4.03. 58 P
let's have some merry ones. 4.04.287 P
i will bring these two moles, these blind ones, 4.04.836 P
what say these young ones? JN 2.01.521
"come, little ones," and then again, | "it is as R2 5.05. 15
me the spare men, and spare me the great ones. 2H4 3.02.270 P
o god, what mischiefs work the wicked ones, 2H6 2.01.182
eyes, | yet, in protection of their tender ones, 3H6 2.02. 28
rough cradle for such little pretty ones! R3 4.01.100
what four thron'd ones could have weigh'd | such H8 1.01. 11
by sick interpreters (once weak ones) is | not 1.02. 82
or two o' th' face — but they are shrewd ones, 1.03. 7
they have all new legs, and lame ones. 1.03. 11
but few now give so great ones. 1.03. 63
life, | they are a sweet society of fair ones. 1.04. 14
(i mean the learned ones in christian kingdoms) 2.02. 92
but, thus much, they are foul ones. 3.02.300
and sometimes falling ones. 4.01. 55
me a dozen crab-tree staves, and strong ones; 5.03. 8 P
you are a pair of strange ones. COR 2.01. 80 P
but to come by him where he stands, by ones, by 2.03. 42 P
when did the tiger's young ones teach the dam? TIT 2.03.142
these debts may well be call'd desperate ones, TIM 3.04.102 P
her young ones in her nest, against the owl. MAC 4.02. 11
hence with your little ones. 4.02. 69
all my pretty ones? 4.03.216
madness in great ones must not /unwatch'd go. HAM 3.01.188
i mean the whisper'd ones, for they are yet but LR 2.01. 7 P
hairs in my beard ere the black ones were there. 4.06. 98 P
a wall'd prison, packs and sects of great ones, 5.03. 18
three great ones of the city, | in personal suit OTH 1.01. 8
does foul pranks which fair and wise ones do. 2.01.142
yet 'tis the plague /of great ones, 3.03.273
things, | though great ones are their object. 3.04.145
no wonder, | when rich ones scarce tell true. CYM 3.06. 12
my dear lord, | thou art one o' th' false ones. 3.06. 15
you married ones, | if each of you should take 5.01. 2
no bond, but to do just ones. 5.01. 7
best of all | amongst the rar'st of good ones), 5.05.160
the great ones eat up the little ones. PER 2.01. 28 P
the great ones eat up the little ones. 2.01. 29 P
therefore let's have fresh ones, what e'er we 4.02. 10 P
as you wish your womb may thrive with fair ones, TNK 1.01. 27
though it be for great ones, yet they seldom 2.01. 3 P
and ignorance | the virtues of the great ones? 2.02.107
and yet his songs are sad ones. 2.04. 20
the birch upon the breeches of the small ones, 3.05.111
ones, | and humble with a ferula the tall ones, 3.05.112
the same, my lord. | are they not sweet ones? 4.02.121

ONE-TRUNK-INHERITING 1 FR 0.0001 REL FR 0 V 1 P
one-trunk-inheriting slave; LR 2.02. 19 P

ONEY'RS 1 FR 0.0001 REL FR 0 V 1 P
burgomasters and great oney'rs, such as can hold 1H4 2.01. 76 P

ONGLES 2 FR 0.0002 REL FR 0 V 2 P
comment appelez-vous les ongles? H5 3.04. 15 P
les ongles? /nous les appelons de nailes. 3.04. 16 P

ONION 2 FR 0.0002 REL FR 1 V 1 P
tears, | an onion will do well for such a shift, SHR in.1. 126
the tears live in an onion that should water ANT 1.02.169 P

ONION-EY'D 1 FR 0.0001 REL FR 1 V 0 P
look, they weep, | and i, an ass, am onion-ey'd. ANT 4.02. 35

ONIONS 2 FR 0.0002 REL FR 1 V 1 P
most dear actors, eat no onions nor garlic, for MND 4.02. 42 P
mine eyes smell onions, i shall weep anon. AWW 5.03.320

/ONLY 3 FR 0.0003 REL FR 3 V 0 P
/that /not /only /giv'st | /me /cause /to /wail, R2 4.01.300
/lord /your /son /had /only /but /the /corpse', 2H4 1.01.192
/that /their /weapons /only | /seem'd /on /our 1.01.197

ONLY 335 FR 0.0378 REL FR 266 V 69 P
and his only heir | and princess no worse issued TMP 1.02. 58
lorded, | not only with what my revenue yielded, 1.02. 98
of persuasion, only | professes to persuade) the 2.01.235
saw a woman | but only sycorax my dam and she; 3.02.101
there is not only disgrace and dishonor in that, 4.01.209 P
likes | (only for his possessions are so huge), TGV 2.04.175
only deserve my love by loving him, | and 2.07. 82
only, in lieu thereof, dispatch me hence. 2.07. 88
a horse cannot fetch, but only carry, therefore 3.01.277 P
to be slow in words is a woman's only virtue. 3.01.334 P
tell him my name is /brook — only for a jest. WIV 2.01.216 P
not only bought many presents to give her, but 2.02.198 P
only give me so much of your time in exchange of 2.02.233 P
at, and i shall not only receive this villainous 2.02.294 P
expense, | i seek to heal it only by his wealth. 3.04. 6
profess requital to a hair's breadth, not only, 4.02. 4 P
only for propagation of a dow'r | remaining in MM 1.02.150
only to stick it in their children's sight | for 1.03. 25
only, this one: 1.03. 50
my mouth, | as if i did but only chew his name, 2.04. 5
my brother die, | if not a fedary, but only he, 2.04.122
will, | or else he must not only die the death, 2.04.165
have no other medicine | but only hope: 3.01. 3
only he hath made an assay of her virtue to 3.01.162 P
he made trial of you only. 3.01.197 P
and the cure of it not only saves your brother, 3.01.236 P
only refer yourself to this advantage: 3.01.245 P
novelty is only in request, and, as it is, as 3.02.224 P
none but only a repair i' th' dark, | and that i 4.01. 42
that here my only son | knows not my feeble key ERR 5.01.310
i am lov'd of all ladies, only you excepted; ADO 1.01.125 P
only this commendation i can afford her, that 1.01.173 P
no child but hero, she's his only heir. 1.01.295
i make all use of it, for i use it only. 1.03. 39 P
only his gift is in devising impossible slanders 2.01.138 P
shall be ours, for we are the only love-gods. 2.01.386 P
only to despite them, i will endeavor any thing. 2.02. 31 P
and down, | our talk must only be of benedick. 3.01. 17
arrow made, | that only wounds by hearsay. 3.01. 23
he is the only man of italy, | always excepted 3.01. 92
i will only be bold with benedick for his 3.02. 7 P
only, have a care that your bills be not stol'n. 3.03. 41 P
it is the only thing for a qualm. 3.04. 74 P
only get the learned writer to set down our 3.05. 63 P
be brief — only to the plain form of marriage, 4.01. 1 P
a little, | for i have only been silent so long, 4.01.156
compliment, and men are only turn'd into tongue, 4.01.320 P
as valiant as hercules that only tells a lie, 4.01.322 P
only foul words — and thereupon i will kiss 5.02. 50 P
i only swore to study with your grace, | and LLL 1.01. 51
the only soil of his fair virtue's gloss, | if 2.01. 47
to feel only looking on fairest of fair: 2.01.241
i only have made a mouth of his eye, | by adding 2.01.252
that self-sovereignty | only for praise' sake, 4.01. 37
only for praise — and praise we may afford | to 4.01. 39
he is only an animal, only sensible in the 4.02. 26 P
an animal, only sensible in the duller parts; 4.02. 27 P
here are only numbers ratified, but, for the 4.02.121 P
and mock for mock is only my intent. 5.02.140
only to part friends. 5.02.220
your absence only. 5.02.225
and she respects me as her only son. MND 1.01.160
he hail'd down oaths that he was only mine; 1.01.243
only give me leave, | unworthy as i am, to 2.01.206
"if i were fair, thisby, i were only thine." 3.01.103
and the pleasure of mine eye, | is only helena. 4.01.171
of these | that therefore only are reputed wise MV 1.01. 96
for silence is only commendable | in a neat's 1.01.111
i think he only loves the world for him. 2.08. 50
rich, | that only to stand high in your account, 3.02.155
only my blood speaks to you in my veins, | and 3.02.176
contemplation, | only attended by nerissa here, 3.04. 29
grow commendable in none only but parrots. 3.05. 46 P
that is done too, sir, only "cover" is the word. 3.05. 51 P
thou wilt not only loose the forfeiture, | but, 4.01. 24
life lies in the mercy | of the duke only, 4.01.356
i will have nothing else but only this, | and 4.01.432
only for this, i pray you pardon me. 4.01.437
only in the world i fill up a place, which may AYL 1.02.191 P
motley's the only wear. 2.07. 34
it is my only suit — | provided that you weed 2.07. 44
your chestnut was ever the only color. 3.04. 12 P
which are the only prologues to a bad voice? 5.03. 13 P
in spring time, the only pretty /ring time, 5.03. 19
your if is the only peacemaker; 5.04.102 P
only, good master, while we do admire | this SHR 1.01. 29
her only fault, and that is faults enough, | is 1.02. 88
hers, | if whilst i live she will be only mine. 2.01.362
that "only" came well in. 2.01.363
i am my father's heir and only son. 2.01.364
his name is lucentio, and he is mine only son, 5.01. 85 P
in the process but only the losing of hope by AWW 1.01. 16 P
only doth backward pull | our slow designs when 1.01.218
not extend his might only where qualities were 1.03.113 P
only sin | and hellish obstinacy tie thy tongue, 1.03.179
and of his old experience th' only darling, | he 2.01.107
'tis only title thou disdain'st in her, the 2.03.117
only he desires | some private speech with you. 2.05. 56
for my part, i only hear your son was run away. 3.02. 43 P
here that is too good for him | but only she, 3.02. 81
a servant only, and a gentleman | which i have 3.02. 84
only in this disguise i think't no sin | to 4.02. 75
only to seem to deserve well, and to beguile the 4.03.299 P
commit, | only shape thou thy silence to my wit. TN 1.02. 61
the youth in your sight only to exasperate you, 3.02. 19 P
only myself stood out, | for which, if i be 3.03. 35
with the pin and web but theirs, theirs only, WT 1.02.291
you had only in your silent judgment tried it, 2.01.171
that lack'd sight only, nought for approbation 2.01.177
nought for approbation | but only seeing, all 2.01.178
of any point in't shall not only be | death to 2.03.171
from me to mine, | and only that i stand for. 3.02. 45

knavish professions, he settled only in rogue. 4.03. 99 P
and only therefore | desire to breed by me. 4.04.102
were i of your flock, | and only live by gazing. 4.04.110
to signify | not only my success in libya, sir, 5.01.166
only this, methought, i heard the shepherd say, 5.02. 6 P
shepherd's son, who has not only his innocence 5.02. 64 P
say, | that he is not only plagued for her sin, JN 2.01.184
which only lives but by the death of faith, 3.01.212
to swear, swears only not to be forsworn, | else 3.01.284
but thou dost swear only to be forsworn, | and 3.01.286
would be as sad as night, | only for wantonness. 4.01. 16
only you do lack | that mercy which fierce fire 4.01.118
humor | rests by you only to be qualified. 5.01. 13
else | but only they have privilege to live. R2 2.01.158
only to be brief | left i his title out. 3.03. 10
you shall not only take the sacrament | to bury 4.01.328
and make the douglas' son your only mean | for 1H4 1.03.261
and only stays but to behold the face | of that 1.03.275
why then your brown bastard is your only drink! 2.04. 73 P
i do not only marvel where thou spendest thy 2.04.398 P
not in words only, but in woes also. 2.04.416 P
make me believe that thou art only mark'd | for 3.02. 9
only this — | let each man do his best, and 5.02. 91
and who but rumor, who but only i, | make 2H4 in 11
i am not only witty in myself, but the cause 1.02. 9 P
is, i am only old in judgment and understanding; 1.02.191 P
borrowing only lingers and lingers it out, but 1.02.237 P
glasses, is the only drinking, and for thy walls 2.01.143 P
only, we want a little personal strength; 4.04. 8
only compound me with forgotten dust; 4.05.115
we must not only arm t' invade the french, | but H5 1.02.136
we do not mean the coursing snatchers only, 1.02.143
she hath herself not only well defended | but 1.02.159
hold, the quondam quickly | for the only she; 2.01. 79
and hold–fast is the only dog, my duck; 2.03. 52
saying our grace is only in our heels, | and 3.05. 34
but only in patient stillness while his rider 3.07. 22 P
to–morrow they have only stomachs to eat and 3.07.153 P
take that praise from god | which is his only. 4.08.116
only downright oaths, which i never use till 5.02.144 P
only he hath not yet subscribed this: 5.02.335
only this proof i'll of thy valor make, | in 1H6 1.02. 94
wretched shall france be only in my name. 1.04. 97
come, come, 'tis only i that must disgrace thee. 1.05. 8
but only, with your patience, that we may 2.03. 78
for my good, | only give order for my funeral. 2.05.112
is talbot slain, the frenchmen's only scourge, 4.07. 77
and as the only means | to stop effusion of our 5.01. 8
proffers his only daughter to your grace | in 5.01. 19
only reserv'd, you claim no interest | in any of 5.04.167
and left behind him richard, his only son, | who 2H6 2.02. 19
only convey me where thou art commanded. 2.04. 93
god, | for judgment only doth belong to thee. 3.02.140
why only, suffolk, mourn i not for thee, | and 3.02.383
only that the laws of england may come out of 4.07. 6 P
only for that cause they have been most worthy 4.07. 45 P
me, but only my followers' base and ignominious 4.08. 63 P
his arms are only to remove from thee | the duke 4.09. 29
thine heir, | and disinherited thine only son. 3H6 1.01.225
but only slaught'red by the ireful arm | of 2.01. 57
ah, no, no, no, it is mine only son! 2.05. 83
that only warwick's daughter shall be thine. 3.03.248
and with their helps only defend ourselves: 4.01. 45
him, | for i intend but only to surprise him. 4.02. 25
and i choose clarence only for protector. 4.06. 37
our title to the crown and only claim | our 4.07. 46
citizen | only for saying he would make his son R3 3.05. 77
only reserv'd their factor to buy souls | and 4.04. 72
a mother only mock'd with two fair babes; 4.04. 87
a queen in jest, only to fill the scene. 4.04. 91
her life is safest only in her birth. 4.04.214
and only in that safety died her brothers. 4.04.215
those that come to see | only a show or two, and H8 pr 10
only they | that come to hear a merry, bawdy pr 13
we bring | to make that only true we now intend, pr 21
that's th' appliance only | which your disease 1.01.124
only to show his pomp as well in france | as 1.01.163
here where we sit, or sit | state–statues only. 1.02. 88
whom to leave | is only bitter to him, only 2.01. 74
to leave | is only bitter to him, only dying, 2.01. 74
i hold now with him | is only my obedience. 3.01.122
the voice is now | only about her coronation. 3.02.406
the devil | and his disciples only envy at, | ye 5.02.147
not only good and wise but most religious; 5.02.151
is only in | the merciful construction of good ep 9
soul and only sprite | in whom the tempers and TRO 1.03. 56
name, | relates in purpose only to achilles. 1.03.323
small as nothing, for request's sake only, | he 2.03.169
functions, | created only to calumniate. 5.02.124
that only like a gulf it did remain | i' th' COR 1.01. 98
the gods sent not | corn for the rich men only. 1.01.208
thing but what i am, | i would wish me only he. 1.01.232
i'd revolt, to make | only my wars with him. 1.01.235
power are forth already, | and only hitherward. 1.02. 33
but tender–bodied and the only son of my womb; 1.03. 6 P
not fierce and terrible | only in strokes, but, 1.04. 58
the common distribution, at | your only choice. 1.09. 36
poison'd | with only suff'ring stain by him; 1.10. 18
from whom i have receiv'd not only greetings, 2.01.197
only | there's one thing wanting, which i doubt 2.01.200
have their provand | only for bearing burthens, 2.01.252
them for the hire | of their breath only! 2.02.150
only fair speech. 3.02. 96
with briers, | scars to move laughter only. 3.03. 52
only that name remains; 4.05. 73
rais'd only that the weaker sort may wish | good 4.06. 70
only make trial what your love can do | for rome 5.01. 40
only their ends | you have respected; 5.03. 4
to grace him only | that thought he could do 5.03. 15
only thus much i give your grace to know: TIT 1.01.413
why hast thou slain thine only daughter thus? 5.03. 55
o, she is rich in beauty, only poor | that, when ROM 1.01.215
were not i thine only nurse, | i would say thou 1.03. 67
lover, | to beautify him, only lacks a cover. 1.03. 88
a montague, | the only son of your great enemy. 1.05.137
my only love sprung from my only hate! 1.05.138
my only love sprung from my only hate! 1.05.138
name | i conjure only but to raise up him. 2.01. 29
that god had lent us but this only child, | but 3.05.165
o me, o me, my child, my only life! 4.05. 19
one only daughter have i, no kin else, | on whom TIM 1.01.121
they only now come but to feast thine eyes. 1.02.127
o, may diseases only work upon't! 3.01. 60
h'as only sent his present occasion now, my lord 3.02. 34 P
hope, now all are fled, | save only the gods. 3.03. 36
you only speak from your distracted soul; 3.04.113
you old only that you may live | only in bone, 3.05.104
interest — i myself | rich only in large hurts. 3.05.108
but only painted, like his varnish'd friends? 4.02. 36
rich only to be wretched, thy great fortunes 4.02. 43
matron, | it is her habit only that is honest, 4.03.114
only i will promise him an excellent piece. 5.01. 19
for he is set so only to himself, | that nothing 5.01.117
graves only be men's works, and death their gain 5.01.222
difference, | conceptions only proper to myself, JC 1.02. 41
enough, | when there is in it but one only man. 1.02.157
shall no man else be touch'd but only caesar? 2.01.154
only be patient till we have appeas'd | the 3.01.179
i only speak right on. 3.02.223
only i yield to die: 5.04. 12
for brutus only overcame himself, | and no man 5.05. 56
all the conspirators, save only he, | did that 5.05. 69
only in a general honest thought | and common 5.05. 71
thanks, | only to herald thee into his sight, MAC 1.03.102
only i have left to say, | more is thy due than 1.04. 20
honor must | not unaccompanied invest him only, 1.04. 40
only look up clear: 1.05. 71
of my intent, but only | vaulting ambition, 1.07. 26
and the receipt of reason | a limbeck only. 1.07. 67
bring forth men–children only! 1.07. 72
in the vessel of my peace | only for them, and 3.01. 67
only it spoils the pleasure of the time. 3.04. 97
only i say | things have been strangely borne. 3.06. 2
those he commands move only in command, 5.02. 19
he only liv'd but till he was a man, | the which 5.09. 6
these are the only men. HAM 2.02.402 P
o god, your only jig–maker. 3.02.125 P
i must be cruel, only to be kind. 3.04.178
your worm is your only emperor for diet: 4.03. 21 P
only i'll be reveng'd | most throughly for my 4.05.136
age dotes on, only got the tune of the time and, 5.02.189 P
only she comes too short, that i profess LR 1.01. 72
only we shall retain | the name, and all th' 1.01.135
not only, sir, this your all–licens'd fool, 1.04.201
remotion of the duke and her | is practice only. 2.04.115
if only to go warm were gorgeous, | why, nature 2.04.268
only i do not like the fashion of your garments. 3.06. 79 P
i am only sorry | he had no other deathsman. 4.06.257
not only take away, but let your sentence | even OTH 1.03.119
this only is the witchcraft i have us'd. 1.03.169
belov'd of those | that only have fear'd caesar; ANT 1.04. 38
it only stands | our lives upon to use our 2.01. 50
thou art a soldier only, speak no more. 2.02.107
i must thank him only, | lest my remembrance 2.02.155
pays his heart | for what his eyes eat only. 2.02.226
nay, nay, octavia, not only that — | that were 3.04. 1
only th' adulterous antony, most large | in his 3.06. 93
antony only, that would make his will | lord of 3.13. 3
novice, and my heart | makes only wars on thee. 4.12. 15
only | i here importune death awhile, until | of 4.15. 18
his only child. CYM 1.01. 56
a thing for sale, and only the gift of the gods. 1.04. 85 P
only, thus far you shall answer: 1.04.157 P
wild motion of mine eye, | firing it only here; 1.06.104
his mistress, only | for the most worthiest fit. 1.06.161
bold | to send them to you, only for this night; 1.06.198
ay, it is fit for your lordship only. 2.01. 30 P
a pain that only seems to seek out danger | i' 3.03. 50
only | affected greatness got by you, not you; 5.05. 37
this one thing only | i will entreat: 5.05. 83
the satisfaction of her knowledge only | in 5.05.251
time, | hell only danceth at so harsh a chime. PER 1.01. 85
only, my friend, i yet am unprovided | of a pair 2.01.160
a withered branch, that's only green at top; 2.02. 43
who only by misfortune of the seas | bereft of 2.03. 88
her reason to herself is only known, | which 2.05. 5
only i carried winged time | post /on the lame 4.ch. 47
she comes weeping for her only mistress' death. 4.01. 11
who only attributes | the faculties of other TNK 1.02. 67
reported in the battle to be the only doers. 2.01. 30 P
for only in thy court, of all the world, 2.05. 28
none | but only arcite; 3.01. 91
for | your offer do't i only, sir; 3.01. 94
this only, and no more: 3.06. 94
only this fears me, | the law will have the 3.06.129
only a little let him fall before me, | that i 3.06.178
only i heard her | repeat this often, "palamon 4.01. 66
thou art alone | and only beautiful, and these 4.02. 38
love, this only | from this hour is complexion. 4.02. 42
i' th' night, and you | the only star to shine. 5.03. 20
he hath not only lent the king his figure, | his STM II.C 102
venom'd sores the only sovereign plaster; VEN 916
only he hath an eye to gaze on beauty, | and LUC 496
"this deed will make thee only lov'd for fear, 610
hold | only to flatter fools and make them bold: 1559
say | he weeps for her, for she was only mine, 1798
mine, | and only must be wail'd by collatine." 1799
ornament, | and only herald to the gaudy spring, SON 1.10
thou, best of dearest and mine only care, | art 48. 7
but, for their virtue only is their show, | they 54. 9
sweet, | though to itself it only live and die, 94.10
no art, | but mutual render, only me for thee. 125.12
only my plague thus far i count my gain, | that 141.13

ONSET 5 FR 0.0005 REL FR 5 V 0 P

the turn | to give the onset to thy good advice. TGV 3.02. 93
the onset and retire | of both your armies, JN 2.01.326
and for an onset, titus, to advance | thy name TIT 1.01.238
swell in their pride, the onset still expecting. LUC 432
but in the onset come, so /shall i taste | at SON 90.11

ON'T *(also an't*)*

ON'T 125 FR 0.0141 REL FR 83 V 42 P

trunk, | and suck'd my verdure out on't. TMP 1.02. 87
you taught me language, and my profit on't | is, 1.02.363
as a spy, to win it | from me, the lord on't. 1.02.457
eye, | who hath cause to wet the grief on't. 2.01.128
and were the king on't, what would i do? 2.01.146
yet he would be king on't. 2.01.157
i will have none on't. 4.01.247
were wrack'd) was landed, | to be the lord on't. 5.01.162
mother, and this my father — a vengeance on't! TGV 2.03. 19 P
i'll make a shaft or a bolt on't. WIV 3.04. 24 P
fault in the semblance of a fowl — think on't, 5.05. 11 P
i'll make the best in gloucestershire know on't. 5.05.181 P
art avis'd o' that? more on't. MM 2.02.132
five shillings to one on't, with any man that ADO 3.03. 78 P
and excellent fashion, yours is worth ten on't. 3.04. 23 P
i am glad on't. MV 2.06. 67
her eye is sick on't; AWW 1.03.136
a pox on't, let it go, 'tis but a drum. 3.06. 46 P
for he persists | as if his life lay on't. 3.07. 43
i'll take the sacrament on't, how and which way 4.03.136 P
that has a knot on't yet. 4.03.324 P
he looks well on't. 5.03. 31
and ev'ry hair that's on't, helen, that's dead, 5.03. 77
what should i think on't? TN 2.05. 28 P
stone, | and laid mine honor too unchary on't. 3.04.202
pox on't, i'll not meddle with him. 3.04.280 P
plague on't, and i thought he had been valiant, 3.04.283 P
stand here, make a good show on't; 3.04.289 P
h'as hurt me, and there's th' end on't. 5.01.197 P
one day shall crown th' alliance on't, so please 5.01.318
the gain, the ord'ring on't, is all | properly WT 2.01.169
he must be told on't, and he shall. 2.02. 29
fasten'd and fix'd the shame on't in himself, 2.03. 15
speedy, | the time is worth the use on't. 3.01. 14
a lucky day, boy, and we'll do good deeds on't. 3.03.139 P
of the petty gods, | and you the queen on't. 4.04. 5
her something | that makes her blood look on't. 4.04.160
sleeve–hand and the work about the square on't. 4.04.210 P
we had the tune on't a month ago. 4.04.294 P
we'll none on't. 4.04.332 P
are you in earnest, sir? i smell the trick on't. 4.04.643 P
no longer shall you gaze on't, lest your fancy 5.03. 60
with mine own picture on the top on't (colevile 2H4 4.03. 49 P
i'll send some packing that yet think not on't. R3 3.02. 61
of this peace, aboded | the sudden breach on't. H8 1.01. 94
your particular fancy, | and leave me out on't. 2.03.102
which might | induce you to the question on't? 2.04.152
now i think on't, | they should be good men, 3.01. 21
my mind's not on't, you are too hard for me. 5.01. 57
would i were fairly out on't! 5.02.144
i told you a thing yesterday, think on't. TRO 1.02.171 P
were curs'd, i cannot tell what to think on't. 5.03.106 P
no more talking on't; COR 1.01. 12 P
i am glad on't, then we shall ha' means to vent 1.01.225
a murrain on't! i took this for silver. 1.05. 3 P
of state | more than you doubt the change on't; 3.01.152
he shall, sure on't. 3.01.271
directly to say the troth on't, before corioles; 4.05.186 P
the very trick on't. 4.06. 71
look to't, think on't, i do not use to jest. ROM 3.05.189
why, i am glad on't, this is well, stand up. 4.02. 28
i come to observe, i give thee warning on't. TIM 1.02. 34
often i ha' din'd with him, and told him on't, 3.01. 24 P
i ha' told him on't, but i could ne'er get him 3.01. 28 P
now, before the gods, i am asham'd on't. 3.02. 18 P
i wonder on't, he was wont to shine at seven. 3.04. 10
think not on't, sir. 3.06. 44 P
i am glad on't. JC 1.03.137
inhabitants o' th' earth, | and yet are on't? MAC 1.03. 42
look on't again i dare not. 2.02. 49
on any chance, | to mend it, or be rid on't. 3.01.113
the moment on't, for't must be done to–night, 3.01.130
what think you on't? HAM 1.01. 55
fie on't, ah fie! 1.02.135
yet, within a month — | let me not think on't! 1.02.146
go to, i'll no more on't, it hath made me mad. 3.01.146 P
what think you on't? 3.01.175
indeed without an oath i'll make an end on't. 4.05. 57 P
mine ache to think on't. 5.01. 93 P
you lie out on't, sir, and therefore 'tis not 5.01.123 P
i am sure on't, not a word. LR 2.01. 27
i have good hope | thou didst not know on't. 2.04.189
best 'parel that i have, | come on't what will. 4.01. 50
joy, | yet throw such /changes of vexation on't, OTH 1.01. 72
i am glad on't; 'tis a worthy governor. 2.01. 30
be not acknown on't; 3.03.319
and take heed on't, | make it a darling like 3.04. 65
ply desdemona well, and you are sure on't. 4.01.106
you had it, i'll take out no work on't. 4.01.155 P
/by /my /troth, i am glad on't. 4.01.238
the borders maritime | lack blood to think on't, ANT 1.04. 52
i know you could not lack, i am certain on't, 2.02. 57
shouldst have done, | and not have spoke on't! 2.07. 74
you have heard on't, sweet? 3.07. 23
his whole action grows | not in the power on't. 3.07. 69
in our viciousness grow hard | (o misery on't!), 3.13.112
of a lady fever thee, | shake thou to look on't. 3.13.139
remember'st thou any that have died on't? 5.02.249
i am very glad on't. CYM 1.01.164
the gods to venge it, | not mine to speak on't. 1.06. 93
i had a hundred pound on't; 2.01. 3 P
a pox on't! 2.01. 18 P
a stranger, and i not know on't? 2.01. 34 P
must wear the print of his remembrance on't, 2.03. 43
wrought, | since the true life on't was — 2.04. 76
basilisk unto mine eye, | kills me to look on't. 2.04.108
never talk on't: | she hath been colted by him. 2.04.132
a pudency so rosy the sweet view on't | might 2.05. 11
though peril to my modesty, not death on't, | i 3.04.152
the sword like me, he'll scarcely look on't. 3.06. 26
this bloody man, the care on't. 4.02.297
and the air on't | revengingly enfeebles me, or 5.02. 3
augustus lives to think on't; 5.05. 82
ha, bots on't, 'tis come at last, and 'tis PER 2.01.118 P
i am glad on't with all my heart. 2.05. 74
no way to be rid on't but by the way to the pox. 4.06. 15 P
keep the feast full, bate not an hour on't. TNK 1.01.220
do sweetly, | and god knows what may come on't. 2.03. 58
a mistress, expectation | most guiltless on't. 3.01. 15
i may not wish | more than my sword's edge on't. 3.01. 96
all these must be boys, | he has the trick on't; 4.01.132
the burden on't was "down–a, down–a," and penn'd 4.03. 11 P
one would marry a leprous witch to be rid on't, 4.03. 47 P

a great penn'worth on't to give half my state 4.03. 67 P
by my short life, | i am most glad on't. 5.04. 29
ONWARD 4 FR 0.0004 REL FR 4 V 0 P
when you went onward on this ended action, | i ADO 1.01.297
'tis, their own, | which we have goaded onward. COR 2.03.263
onward to troy with the blunt swains he goes, LUC 1504
my grief lies onward and my joy behind. SON 50.14
ONWARDS 1 FR 0.0001 REL FR 1 V 0 P
as thou goest onwards, still will pluck thee SON 126. 6
OON *(also un)*
OON 2 FR 0.0002 REL FR 0 V 2 P
i ha' married oon garsoon, a boy; WIV 5.05.205 P
oon pesant, by gar. 5.05.205 P
/OOZE 1 FR 0.0001 REL FR 1 V 0 P
cast thee, scarcely coffin'd, in /the /ooze, PER 3.01. 60
OOZE 5 FR 0.0005 REL FR 5 V 0 P
and think'st it much to tread the ooze | of the TMP 1.02.252
therefore my son i' th' ooze is bedded; 3.03.100
praise | as is the ooze and bottom of the sea H5 1.02.164
upon the slime and ooze scatters his grain, ANT 2.07. 22
find | the ooze, to show what coast thy sluggish CYM 4.02.205
/OOZES 1 FR 0.0001 REL FR 1 V 0 P
/gum, which /oozes | from whence 'tis nourish'd. TIM 1.01. 21
OOZY 1 FR 0.0001 REL FR 1 V 0 P
myself were mudded in that oozy bed | where my TMP 5.01.151
OPAL 2 FR 0.0002 REL FR 1 V 1 P
changeable taffata, for thy mind is a very opal. TN 2.04. 75 P
the heaven–hu'd sapphire and the opal blend LC 215
OP'D 4 FR 0.0004 REL FR 4 V 0 P
at my command | have wak'd their sleepers, op'd, TMP 5.01. 49
and op'd their arms to embrace me as a friend. TIT 5.03.108
hath op'd his ponderous and marble jaws | to HAM 1.04. 50
i op'd the coffin, | found there rich jewels, PER 5.03. 23
OPE 31 FR 0.0035 REL FR 30 V 1 P
come, | the very minute bids thee ope thine ear. TMP 1.02. 37
go fetch me something: i'll break ope the gate. ERR 3.01. 73
do not live, hero, do not ope thine eyes; ADO 4.01.123
and when i ope my lips let no dog bark!" MV 1.01. 94
ere i ope his letter, | i pray you tell me how 3.02.232
the mouth of passage shall we fling wide ope, JN 2.01.449
now, citizens of angiers, ope your gates, | let 2.01.536
run, go, help, help! o henry, ope thine eyes! 2H6 3.02. 35
set ope thy everlasting gates | to entertain my 4.09. 13
yet that thy brazen gates of heaven may ope 3H6 2.03. 40
now, warwick, wilt thou ope the city–gates, 5.01. 21
so, now the gates are ope; COR 1.04. 43
in time | break ope the locks a' th' senate, and 3.01.138
behold, the heavens do ope, | the gods look down 5.03.183
is it your trick to make me ope the door | that TIT 5.02. 10
my tears will choke me if i ope my mouth. 5.03.175
eyes, | nor ope her lap to saint–seducing gold. ROM 1.01.214
anon comes one with light to ope the tomb, | and 5.03.283
against our rampir'd gates and they shall ope, TIM 5.04. 47
the crown, he pluck'd me ope his doublet, and JC 1.02.265 P
(which like dumb mouths do ope their ruby lips 3.01.260
most sacrilegious murther hath broke ope | the MAC 2.03. 67
to his good friends thus wide i'll ope my arms, HAM 4.05.146
before you fight the battle, ope this letter. LR 5.01. 40
torments will ope your lips. OTH 5.02.305
mary–buds begin to ope their golden eyes; CYM 2.03. 24
thy crystal window ope; 5.04. 81
shed | to keep his bed of blackness unlaid ope, PER 1.02. 89
to love's alarms it will not ope the gate; VEN 424
but they must ope, this blessed league to kill, LUC 383
she much amaz'd breaks ope her lock'd–up eyes, 446
/OPEN 2 FR 0.0002 REL FR 2 V 0 P
/at /point | /to /show /their /open /banner. LR 5.01. 34
/open her before the wind! TNK 3.04. 9
OPEN 150 FR 0.0169 REL FR 116 V 34 P
purpose, did antonio open | the gates of milan, TMP 1.02.129
to be asleep | with eyes wide open — standing, 2.01.214
open your mouth; 2.02. 82 P
open your mouth; 2.02. 83 P
open your chaps again. 2.02. 86 P
the clouds methought would open and show riches 3.02.141
come, come, open the matter in brief: TGV 1.01.127 P
open your purse, that the money and the matter 1.01.129 P
my men, kill'd my deer, and broke open my lodge.
WIV 1.01.112 P
his thefts were too open; 1.03. 25 P
take heed, have open eye, for thieves do foot by 2.01.122
mine oyster, | which i with sword will open. 2.02. 4
say, if money go before, all ways do lie open. 2.02.169 P
i must very much lay open mine own imperfection; 2.02.184 P
upon no trail, never trust me when i open again. 4.02.197 P
what's open made to justice, | that justice MM 2.01. 21
because it is an open room and good for winter. 2.01.131 P
i can speak to him, i will open my lips in vain, 3.01.193 P
who talks within there? ho, open the door! ERR 3.01. 38
lay open to my earthy, gross conceit, 3.02. 34
free from these slanders and this open shame! 4.04. 67
(where we play) open, and the moon may shine in
MND 3.01. 57 P
he hath refus'd it in the open court; MV 4.01.338
then open not thy lips: AYL 1.03. 82
would open his lips when he put it into his 5.01. 34 P
that grapes were made to eat and lips to open. 5.01. 36 P
the door is open, sir, there lies your way; SHR 3.02.210
thy casement i need not open, for i look through AWW 2.03.214 P
or i will not open my lips so wide as a bristle TN 1.05. 2 P
thy fates open their hands, let thy blood and 2.05.146 P
this is open. 2.05.161 P
do not then walk too open. 3.03. 37
by my troth, thou hast an open hand. 4.01. 21 P
ere i could make thee open thy white hand | /and WT 1.02.103
how came the posterns | so easily open? 2.01. 53
so shall she have | a just and open trial. 2.03.205
whereof being by circumstances partly laid open, 3.02. 18 P
hurried | here to this place, i' th' open air, 3.02.105
thou | these rural latches to his entrance open, 4.04.438
to have an open ear, a quick eye, and a nimble 4.04.671 P
whereupon i command thee to open thy affair. 4.04.738 P
though credit be asleep and not an ear open: 5.02. 63 P
you men of angiers, open wide your gates, | and JN 2.01.300
open your gates and give the victors way. 2.01.324
with open mouth swallowing a tailor's news, 4.02.195
done, | doth lay it open to urge on revenge. 4.03. 38
belief | that, being brought into the open air, 5.07. 7
or, being open, put into his hands | that knows R2 1.03.164
the open ear of youth doth always listen; 2.01. 20
mine ear is open, and my heart prepar'd, | the 3.02. 93
he is come to open | the purple testament of 3.03. 93
open the door, secure, foolhardy king! 5.03. 43
open the door, or i will break it open. 5.03. 45
open the door, or i will break it open. 5.03. 45
speak with me, pity me, open the door! 5.03. 77
to the king, and lay open all our proceedings. 1H4 2.03. 31 P
let them alone awhile, and then open the door. 2.04. 84 P
them, gross as a mountain, open, palpable. 2.04.226 P
to hide thee from this open and apparent shame? 2.04.264 P
open your ears; 2H4 in 1
and a hand | open as day for /meting charity; 4.04. 32
that keep'st the ports of slumber open wide | to 4.05. 24
this door is open, he is gone this way. 4.05. 55
his life | hath left me open to all injuries. 5.02. 8
sequestration | from open haunts and popularity. H5 1.01. 59
their faults are open, | arrest them to the 2.02.142
open your gates. 3.03. 51
open the gates, 'tis gloucester that calls. 1H6 1.03. 4
open the gates, here's gloucester that would 1.03. 17
have patience, noble duke, i may not open, | the 1.03. 18
open the gates, or i'll shut thee out shortly. 1.03. 26
open the gates unto the lord protector, | or 1.03. 27
or we'll burst them open, if that you come not 1.03. 28
strife | but to make open proclamation. 1.03. 71
in open market–place produc'd they me | to be a 1.04. 40
and feast and banquet in the open streets, | to 1.06. 13
open your city–gates, | be humble to us, call my 4.02. 5
did he so often lodge in open field, | in 2H6 1.01. 80
prove them, and i lie open to the law; 1.03.156
now open them. 2.01.103
shall, after three days' open penance done, 2.03. 11
come you, my lord, to see my open shame? 2.04. 19
break open the jails and let out the prisoners. 4.03. 16 P
i shall be, if i claim by open war. 3H6 1.02. 19
i'll open them. 1.03. 11
then let my father's blood open it again, | he 1.03. 23
open thy gate of mercy, gracious god! 1.04.177
not knowing how to find the open air | but 3.02.177
hath pawn'd an open hand in sign of love; 4.02. 9
open the gates, we are king henry's friends. 4.07. 28
the gates are open, let us enter too. 5.01. 60
well are you welcome to /the open air. R3 1.01.124
open their congeal'd mouths and bleed afresh! 1.02. 56
or earth gape open wide and eat him quick, | as 1.02. 65
that, his apparent open guilt omitted — | i 3.05. 30
laid open all your victories in scotland, | your 3.07. 15
let me have open means to come to them, | and 4.02. 76
we are too open here to argue this; H8 2.01.168
heaven will one day open | the king's eyes, that 2.02. 41
have your mouth fill'd up | before you open it. 2.03. 88
truth loves open dealing. 3.01. 39
his faults lie open to the laws, let them, | not 3.02.334
this day was view'd in open as his queen, 3.02.404
pourest in the open ulcer of my heart | her eyes TRO 1.01. 53
what's all the doors open here? 4.02. 19 P
his heart and hand both open and both free, 4.05.100
a juggling trick — to be secretly open. 5.02. 24 P
with rushes, | they'll open of themselves. COR 1.04. 19
open the gates and let me in. TIT 1.01. 62
thee, | be not obdurate, open thy deaf ears. 2.03.160
open them, boy. 4.01. 32
earth, | thus i enforce thy rotten jaws to open, ROM 5.03. 47
merciful, | open the tomb, lay me with juliet. 5.03. 73
all run | with open outcry toward our monument. 5.03.193
upon them, fit to open | these dead men's tombs. 5.03.200
fell from their boughs, and left me open, bare, TIM 4.03.265
to athens go, | break open shops; 4.03.447
sir, | having often of your open bounty tasted, 5.01. 58
/descend, and open your uncharged ports. 5.04. 55
and when the cross blue lightning seem'd to open JC 1.03. 50
disclos'd, | and open perils surest answered. 4.01. 47
the doors are open; MAC 2.02. 5
open, locks, | whoever knocks! 4.01. 46
you see her eyes are open. 5.01. 24 P
or your chaste treasure open | to his unmast'red HAM 1.03. 31
on him, | that he is open to incontinency — 2.01. 30
open this purse and take | what it contains. LR 3.01. 45
the tyranny of the open night's too rough | for 3.04. 2
here is better than the open air, take it 3.06. 1 P
the moor is of a free and open nature, | that OTH 1.03.399
all offices are open, and there is full liberty 2.02. 8 P
he'ld lay the future open. CYM 3.02. 29
having found the back door open | of the 5.03. 45
that i should open to the list'ning air | how PER 1.02. 87
but even | your purse, still open, hath built 3.02. 47
wrench it open straight. 3.02. 53
wrench it open. 3.02. 59
will fly hence | and open this to pericles. 4.03. 23
the windows are too open. TNK 2.02.262
that must open | and bleed to death for my sake 4.02. 1
"if thou wilt chide, thy lips shall never open." VEN 48
away he steals with open list'ning ear, | full LUC 283
but as they open, they all rate his ill, | which 304
lay, | till they might open to adorn the day. 399
remain | the scornful mark of every open eye; 520
day," quoth she, "night's scapes doth open lay, 747
"thy secret pleasure turns to open shame, | thy 890
lays open all the little worms that creep; 1248
thee, | and keep my drooping eyelids open wide, SON 27. 7
is it thy will thy image should keep open | my 61. 1
OPEN/–ARSE 1 FR 0.0001 REL FR 1 V 0 P
o that she were | an open/–arse, thou a pop'rin ROM 2.01. 38
OPEN'D 13 FR 0.0014 REL FR 12 V 1 P
as mine eyes open'd, | i saw their weapons drawn TMP 2.01.319
if he were open'd and you find so much blood in TN 3.02. 61 P
other men have gates, and those gates open'd, WT 1.02.197
which i have open'd to his grace at large, | as H5 1.01. 78
that, as my hand has open'd bounty to you, | my H8 3.02.184
i feel my heart new open'd. 3.02.366
so grafted | that, when they shall be open'd, MAC 4.03. 52
thus, | that, open'd, lies within our remedy. HAM 2.02. 18
open'd (in despite | of heaven and men) her CYM 5.05. 58
open'd their mouths to swallow venus' liking. VEN 248
once more the ruby–color'd portal open'd, 451
and being open'd, threw unwilling light | upon 1051
more than his eyes were open'd to the light. LUC 105
OPENED 2 FR 0.0002 REL FR 2 V 0 P
ay, say you so? the gates shall then be opened. 3H6 4.07. 29
griefs might equal mine, | if both were opened. PER 5.01.132
OPENER 1 FR 0.0001 REL FR 1 V 0 P
the very opener and intelligencer | between the 2H4 4.02. 20
OPEN–EY'D 1 FR 0.0001 REL FR 1 V 0 P
open–ey'd conspiracy | his time doth take. TMP 2.01.301
OPENING 9 FR 0.0010 REL FR 7 V 2 P
that makes his opening with this bigger key. MM 4.01. 31
opening on neptune with fair blessed beams, MND 3.02.392
threats approach'd | the opening of his mouth; AYL 4.03.110
see | leontes opening his free arms and weeping WT 4.04.548
i was by at the opening of the farthel, heard 5.02. 3 P
soul | with opening titles miscreate, whose H5 1.02. 16
we saw him at the opening of his tent, | he is TRO 2.03. 84
for fear of opening my lips and receiving the JC 1.02.250 P
i would not | believe her lips in opening it. CYM 5.05. 42
OPENLY 8 FR 0.0009 REL FR 7 V 1 P
deny | this chain which now you wear so openly. ERR 5.01. 17
him, | hath publish'd and proclaim'd it openly. SHR 4.02. 85
since we so openly | proceed in justice, which WT 3.02. 5
and my case so openly known to the world, let 2H4 2.01. 30 P
to ye | shall show itself more openly hereafter. 4.02. 76
house, | and calls your grace usurper, openly, 2H6 4.04. 30
what, madam, be dishonored openly, | and basely TIT 1.01.432
ye draw, | and maintain such a quarrel openly? 2.01. 47
OPENNESS 1 FR 0.0001 REL FR 1 V 0 P
deliver with more openness your answers | to my CYM 1.06. 88
OPENS 6 FR 0.0006 REL FR 5 V 1 P
for whom this hungry war | opens his vasty jaws; H5 2.04.105
when he opens his purse to give us our reward, R3 1.04.129 P
it opens the eyes of expectation. TIM 5.01. 23
lightens, opens graves, and roars | as doth the JC 1.03. 74
and with his strong course opens them again. VEN 960
and with his knee the door he opens wide. LUC 359
OPEN'T 4 FR 0.0004 REL FR 1 V 3 P
open't and read it. TN 5.01.289 P
open't. WT 3.03.116 P
open't; 3.03.118 P
a loyal breast, | for you have seen him open't. H8 3.02.201
OPERANCE 1 FR 0.0001 REL FR 1 V 0 P
yet do effect | rare issues by their operance, TNK 1.03. 63
OPERANT 2 FR 0.0002 REL FR 2 V 0 P
sauce his palate | with thy most operant poison! TIM 4.03. 25
my operant powers their functions leave to do, HAM 3.02.174
OPERATE 2 FR 0.0002 REL FR 2 V 0 P
th' effect doth operate another way. TRO 5.03.109
gan in your duller britain operate | most vildly CYM 5.05.197
OPERATION 6 FR 0.0006 REL FR 3 V 3 P
sherris–sack hath a twofold operation in it. 2H4 4.03. 97 P
which hath an operation more divine | than TRO 3.03.203
and by the operation of the second cup draws him
ROM 3.01. 8 P
by all the operation of the orbs, | from whom we LR 1.01.111
now of your mud by the operation of your sun. ANT 2.07. 27 P
serpents have | edge, sting, or operation. 4.15. 26
OPERATIONS 1 FR 0.0001 REL FR 0 V 1 P
i have operations /in /my /head which be humors WIV 1.03. 89 P
OPERATIVE 1 FR 0.0001 REL FR 1 V 0 P
are many simples operative, whose power | will LR 4.04. 14
/OPES 1 FR 0.0001 REL FR 1 V 0 P
/when /rank /thersites /opes /his /mastic /jaws, TRO 1.03. 73
OPES 1 FR 0.0001 REL FR 1 V 0 P
see how the morning opes her golden gates, | and 3H6 2.01. 21
OPHELIA 20 FR 0.0022 REL FR 18 V 2 P
fear it, ophelia, fear it, my dear sister, | and HAM 1.03. 33
farewell, ophelia, and remember well | what i 1.03. 84
what is't, ophelia, he hath said to you? 1.03. 88
in few, ophelia, | do not believe his vows, for 1.03.126
farewell! how now, ophelia, what's the matter? 2.01. 71
the most beautified ophelia" — that's an ill 2.02.110 P
o dear ophelia, i am ill at these numbers. 2.02.120 P
'twere by accident, may here | affront ophelia. 3.01. 31
and for your part, ophelia, i do wish | that 3.01. 37
ophelia, walk you here. 3.01. 42
soft you now, | the fair ophelia. 3.01. 88
how now, ophelia? 3.01.178
how now, ophelia? 4.05. 22
nay, but, ophelia — 4.05. 34
pretty ophelia! 4.05. 56
poor ophelia | divided from herself and her fair 4.05. 84
dear maid, kind sister, sweet ophelia! 4.05.159
too much of water hast thou, poor ophelia, | and 4.07.185
what, the fair ophelia! 5.01.242
i lov'd ophelia. 5.01.269
/OPINION 1 FR 0.0001 REL FR 1 V 0 P
/and /thyself /bewray | /when /false /opinion, LR 3.06.112
OPINION 86 FR 0.0097 REL FR 60 V 26 P
i do now let loose my opinion, hold it no longer TMP 2.02. 35 P
me, | in thy opinion which is worthiest love? TGV 1.02. 6
wrong, | to bear a hard opinion of his truth: 2.07. 81
yet i cannot put off my opinion so easily. WIV 2.01.235 P
sir, in my poor opinion, they will to't then. MM 2.01.233 P
not, with that opinion | that i am touch'd with 5.01. 50
is the opinion that fire cannot melt out of me; ADO 1.01.232 P
they hold one an opinion of another's dotage, 2.03.216 P
without impudency, learned without opinion, and LLL 5.01. 5 P
with purpose to be dress'd in an opinion | of MV 1.01. 91
bait | for this fool gudgeon, this opinion. 1.01.102
and now, good sweet, say thy opinion, | how dost 3.05. 71
nay, but ask my opinion too of that. 3.05. 85
in my faith | to hold opinion with pythagoras, 4.01.131
he is furnish'd with my opinion, which, better'd 4.01.157 P
of all opinion that grows rank in them | that i AYL 2.07. 46
you should bear a good opinion of my knowledge, 5.02. 55 P
mistress, what's your opinion of your sister? SHR 3.02.243
but unseal'd — | at least in my opinion. AWW 4.02. 31
now sail'd into the north of my lady's opinion, TN 3.02. 27 P
into a most hideous opinion of his rage, skill, 3.04.194 P
what is the opinion of pythagoras concerning 4.02. 50 P
what think'st thou of his opinion? 4.02. 54 P
of the soul, and no way approve his opinion. 4.02. 56 P
thou shalt hold th' opinion of pythagoras ere i 4.02. 58 P
be cur'd | of this diseas'd opinion, and betimes WT 1.02.297
in my true opinion! 2.01. 37
once remove | the root of his opinion, which is 2.03. 90
makes sound opinion sick, and truth suspected, JN 4.02. 26

partly thy mother's word, partly my own opinion, 1H4 2.04.403 P
pride, haughtiness, opinion, and disdain, | the 3.01.183
opinion, that did help me to the crown, | had 3.02. 42
it lends a lustre and more great opinion, | a 4.01. 77
thou hast redeem'd thy lost opinion, | and 5.04. 48
better opinion, better confirmation, | for all 2H4 4.05.188
and to rase out | rotten opinion, who hath writ 5.02.128
partly to satisfy my opinion, and partly for the H5 3.02. 99 P
shall yield the other in the right opinion. 1H6 2.04. 42
if i, my lord, for my opinion bleed, | opinion 2.04. 52
bleed, | opinion shall be surgeon to my hurt, 2.04. 53
in my opinion yet thou seest not well. 2H6 2.01.104
myself | in craving your opinion of my title, 2.02. 4
then this is mine opinion: 3H6 4.01. 29
in my opinion, ought to be prevented. R3 2.02.131
and therefore, in mine opinion, cannot have it. 3.01. 52
our own brains and the opinion that we bring H8 pr 20
believe me, there's an ill opinion spread then, 2.02.124
commends his good opinion of you to you, and 2.03. 61
'em, | envy and base opinion set against 'em, 3.01. 36
his own opinion was his law. 4.02. 37
whom opinion crowns | the sinow and the forehand
TRO 1.03.142
says, opinion crowns | with an imperial voice — 1.03.186
combat, | yet in the trial much opinion dwells; 1.03.336
part | to steel a strong opinion to themselves? 1.03.353
why then we do our main opinion crush | in taint 1.03.372
yet go we under our opinion still | that we have 1.03.382
hector's opinion | is this in way of truth; 2.02.188
a plague of opinion! 3.03.264 P
whiles others fish with craft for great opinion, 4.04.103
barbarism, and policy grows into an ill opinion. 5.04. 17 P
that rubbing the poor itch of your opinion COR 1.01.165
opinion that so sticks on martius shall | of his 1.01.271
so, your opinion is, aufidius, | that they of 1.02. 1
here, | is in opinion and in honor wrong'd, TIT 1.01.416
none, but to | maintain my opinion. TIM 4.03. 72
all tending to the great opinion | that rome JC 1.02.318
doth wish | you had but that opinion of yourself 2.01. 92
silver hairs | will purchase us a good opinion, 2.01.145
quite from the main opinion he held once | of 2.01.196
that i held epicurus strong, | and his opinion; 5.01. 77
but, in the gross and scope of mine opinion, HAM 1.01. 68
his very opinion in the letter. LR 1.02. 75 P
some blood drawn on me would beget opinion | of 2.01. 33
of most allow'd sufficiency, yet opinion, a OTH 1.03.224 P
and spend your rich opinion for the name | of a 2.03.195
stick | the small'st opinion on my least misuse? 4.02.109
build on thee a better opinion than ever before. 4.02.206 P
but let us rear | the higher our opinion, that ANT 2.01. 36
or this gentleman's opinion by this worn out. CYM 1.04. 63 P
which in my opinion o'ervalues it something. 1.04.109 P
for your ill opinion and th' assault you have 1.04.162 P
the foul opinion | you had of her pure honor 2.04. 58
seldom but that pity begets you a good opinion, PER 4.02.120 P
a good opinion, and that opinion a mere profit. 4.02.121 P
might breed the ruin of my name, opinion! TNK 3.06.240
of foes, | to eat up errors by opinion bred, LUC 937
OPINION'D 1 FR 0.0001 REL FR 0 V 1 P
come let them be opinion'd. ADO 4.02. 67 P
OPINION'S 1 FR 0.0001 REL FR 1 V 0 P
opinion's but a fool, that makes us scan | the PER 2.02. 56
OPINIONS 14 FR 0.0015 REL FR 11 V 3 P
great comfort in this mystery of ill opinions, WIV 2.01. 72 P
sign, | save men's opinions and my living blood, R2 3.01. 26
all | speak plainly your opinions of our hopes. 2H4 1.03. 3
already 'a be kill'd with your hard opinions; ep 31 P
glansdale, | let me have your express opinions, 1H6 1.04. 64
us | in our opinions she should be preferr'd. 5.05. 61
our just opinions | and comforts to /your cause. H8 3.01. 60
he is return'd in his opinions, which | have 3.02. 64
(for so we are inform'd) with new opinions, 5.02. 52
and bring me their opinions of success. JC 2.02. 6
golden opinions from all sorts of people, MAC 1.07. 33
age | to cast beyond ourselves in our opinions, HAM 2.01.112
the most /profound and /winnow'd opinions, and 5.02.193 P
and you in ruff of your opinions cloth'd, | what STM II.C 79
OP'NING 1 FR 0.0001 REL FR 1 V 0 P
at the first op'ning of the gorgeous east, LLL 4.03.219
OPPORTUNE 2 FR 0.0002 REL FR 2 V 0 P
den, | the most opportune place, the strong'st TMP 4.01. 26
and most opportune to her need i have | a vessel WT 4.04.500
OPPORTUNITIES 3 FR 0.0003 REL FR 0 V 3 P
engross'd opportunities to meet her; WIV 2.02.196 P
when i have good opportunities for the ork. 3.01. 15 P
you have many opportunities to cut him off; LR 4.06.263 P
OPPORTUNITY 22 FR 0.0024 REL FR 16 V 6 P
if opportunity and humblest suit | cannot attain WIV 3.04. 20
to trust the opportunity of night | and the ill MND 2.01.217
gilt of this opportunity you let time wash off, TN 3.02. 25 P
there is more better opportunity to be required, H5 3.02.139 P
embrace we then this opportunity | as fitting 1H6 2.01. 13
ten to one | we shall not find like opportunity. 5.04.158
them down | for sluttish spoils of opportunity, TRO 4.05. 62
of troy | with opportunity of sharp revenge TIT 1.01.137
i will omit no opportunity | that may convey my ROM 3.05. 49
do this, if you can bring it to any opportunity. OTH 2.01.282 P
had i admittance, and opportunity to friend. CYM 1.04.106 P
more advantage than the opportunity of a second 1.04.129 P
that opportunity | which then they had to take 3.01. 14
her own command | shall give thee opportunity." 3.02. 19
i shall give thee opportunity at milford–haven. 3.04. 28 P
this is an offer'd opportunity | i durst not TNK 2.03. 74
but ill–annexed opportunity | or kills his life LUC 874
"o opportunity, thy guilt is great! 876
how comes it then, vile opportunity, | being so 895
thee, | but they ne'er meet with opportunity. 903
"why hath thy servant opportunity | betray'd the 932
"in vain i rail at opportunity, | at time, at 1023
/OPPOS'D 1 FR 0.0001 REL FR 1 V 0 P
/they /are /oppos'd /already. TRO 4.05. 94
OPPOS'D 18 FR 0.0020 REL FR 17 V 1 P
to give my hand oppos'd against my heart | unto SHR 3.02. 9
as it were, from the ends of oppos'd winds. WT 1.01. 31 P
your resolution cannot hold when 'tis | oppos'd 4.04. 37
march all one way and be no more oppos'd 1H4 1.01. 15
doubt not, my lord, they shall be well oppos'd. 4.04. 33
fly | towards fronting peril and oppos'd decay! 2H4 4.04. 66
you are potently oppos'd, and with a malice | of H8 5.01.134
and great deal misprising | the knight oppos'd. TRO 4.05. 75
oppos'd to hinder me, should stop my way, | /but 5.03. 57
what, are my doors oppos'd against my passage? TIM 3.04. 79
whom, though in general part we were oppos'd, 5.02. 7
and thou oppos'd, being of no woman born, | yet MAC 5.08. 31
motion, guard, nor eye, | if you oppos'd them. HAM 4.07.102
of a neutral heart, | and not from one oppos'd. LR 3.07. 49
oppos'd against the act, bending his sword | to 4.02. 74
face | to be oppos'd against the /warring winds? 4.07. 31
when half to half the world oppos'd, he being ANT 3.13. 9
sluttery, to such neat excellence oppos'd, CYM 1.06. 44
/OPPOSE 1 FR 0.0001 REL FR 1 V 0 P
/most /just /and /heavy /causes /make /oppose. LR 5.01. 27
OPPOSE 18 FR 0.0020 REL FR 18 V 0 P
reach, i do oppose | my patience to his fury, MV 4.01. 10
be contrary, | oppose against their wills. WT 5.01. 46
i alone, alone do me oppose | against the pope, JN 3.01.170
and oppose not myself | against their will. R2 3.03. 18
cade | oppose himself against a troop of kerns, 2H6 3.01.361
oppose thy steadfast–gazing eyes to mine, | see 4.10. 45
makes him oppose himself against his king. 5.01.133
if you oppose yourselves to match lord warwick. 5.01.156
woman, much too weak | t' oppose your cunning. H8 2.04.107
who may you else oppose | that can from hector TRO 1.03.333
to seek him there, | to oppose his hatred fully. COR 3.01. 20
oppose not scythia to ambitious rome; TIT 1.01.132
touch'd to death, | he did oppose his foe; TIM 3.05. 20
would o'erbear | that did oppose my will. MAC 4.03. 65
and in conclusion to oppose the bolt | against LR 2.04.176
in alexandria, where | i will oppose his fate. ANT 3.13.169
but what he look'd for should oppose and she CYM 2.05. 18
rebellious to oppose; TNK 1.02.101
OPPOSED 9 FR 0.0010 REL FR 9 V 0 P
humors | even to the opposed end of our intents; LLL 5.02.758
are distinct offices, | and of opposed natures. MV 2.09. 62
those opposed eyes, | which, like the meteors of 1H4 1.01. 9
gelding the opposed continent as much | as on 3.01.109
whereby we stand opposed by such means | as you 5.01. 67
/if th' opposed numbers | pluck their hearts H5 4.01.291
but eye to eye opposed | salutes each other with TRO 3.03.107
two such opposed kings encamp them still | in ROM 2.03. 27
bear't that th' opposed may beware of thee. HAM 1.03. 67
OPPOSELESS 1 FR 0.0001 REL FR 1 V 0 P
to quarrel with your great opposeless wills, LR 4.06. 38
OPPOSER 2 FR 0.0002 REL FR 1 V 1 P
black and fearful | on the opposer. AWW 3.01. 6
appear well in these wars, his great opposer, COR 4.03. 35 P
OPPOSERS' 1 FR 0.0001 REL FR 1 V 0 P
great charms | misguide thy opposers' swords! COR 1.05. 22
OPPOSERS 1 FR 0.0001 REL FR 1 V 0 P
and i' th' consul's view | slew three opposers. COR 2.02. 94
OPPOSES 1 FR 0.0001 REL FR 1 V 0 P
ignorant | how she opposes her against my will? TGV 3.02. 26
OPPOSING 4 FR 0.0004 REL FR 4 V 0 P
opposing freely | the beauty of her person to H8 4.01. 67
opposing laws with strokes, and here defying COR 3.03. 79
a sea of troubles, | and by opposing, end them. HAM 3.01. 59
by the four opposing /coigns | which the world PER 3.ch. 17
/OPPOSITE 1 FR 0.0001 REL FR 1 V 0 P
/undergo, | /to /weigh /against /his /opposite; 2H4 1.03. 55
OPPOSITE 24 FR 0.0027 REL FR 17 V 7 P
or you imagine me too unhurtful an opposite. MM 3.02.165 P
be opposite with a kinsman, surly with servants; TN 2.05.149 P
and his opposite, the youth, bears in his visage 3.02. 64 P
"be opposite with a kinsman, surly with servants 3.04. 69 P
for your opposite hath in him what youth, 3.04.231 P
and fatal opposite that you could possibly have 3.04.267 P
save what is opposite to england's love. JN 3.01.254
hazard | and fearful meeting of their opposite. 2H4 4.01. 16
loyalty, | free from a stubborn opposite intent, 2H6 3.02.251
thou art as opposite to every good | as the 3H6 1.04.134
much more to be thus opposite with heaven, | for R3 2.02. 94
lo at their birth good stars were opposite. 4.04.216
be opposite all planets of good luck | to my 4.04.402
a man, | daring an opposite to every danger. 5.04. 3
that may fully discover him their opposite. COR 2.02. 21 P
just opposite to what thou justly seem'st, | a ROM 3.02. 78
he's opposite to humanity. TIM 1.01.273
each opposite that blanks the face of joy | meet HAM 3.02.220
seeing how loathly opposite i stood | to his LR 2.01. 49
wast not bound to answer | an unknown opposite. 5.03.154
so opposite to marriage that she shunn'd | the OTH 1.02. 67
that have the office opposite to saint peter, 4.02. 91
low'ring, does become | the opposite of itself. ANT 1.02.126
so cross him with their opposite persuasion, LUC 286
OPPOSITES 3 FR 0.0003 REL FR 3 V 0 P
being opposites of such repairing nature. 2H6 5.03. 22
and fell incensed points | of mighty opposites. HAM 5.02. 62
who were the opposites of this day's strife; LR 5.03. 42
OPPOSITION 8 FR 0.0009 REL FR 6 V 2 P
or hide | the liberal opposition of our spirits, LLL 5.02.733
sedgy bank, | in single opposition hand to hand, 1H4 1.03. 99
for the counterpoise of so great an opposition." 2.03. 14 P
me to repent the sin | of disobedient opposition ROM 4.02. 18
why should we in our peevish opposition | take HAM 1.02.100
my lord, the opposition of your person in trial. 5.02.171 P
one at other's /breast, | in opposition bloody. OTH 2.03.184
found no opposition | but what he look'd for CYM 2.05. 17
OPPOSITIONS 1 FR 0.0001 REL FR 0 V 1 P
and more remarkable in single oppositions; CYM 4.01. 13 P
/OPPRESS 1 FR 0.0001 REL FR 1 V 0 P
/and /doleful /dumps /the /mind /oppress, | then ROM 4.05.127
OPPRESS 3 FR 0.0003 REL FR 3 V 0 P
did oppress our nest, | grew by our feeding to 1H4 5.01. 61
why dost thou so oppress me with thine eye? TRO 4.05.241
the mutiny he there hastes t' oppress, | says to PER 3.ch. 29
OPPRESS'D 13 FR 0.0014 REL FR 13 V 0 P
for, now they are oppress'd with travail, they TMP 3.03. 15
oppress'd with two weak evils, age and hunger, AYL 2.07.132
you ne'er oppress'd me with a mother's groan, AWW 1.03.147
oppress'd with wrongs, and therefore full of JN 3.01. 13
nor much oppress'd them with great subsidies, 3H6 4.08. 45
when all our offices have been oppress'd | with TIM 2.02.158
by their oppress'd and fear–surprised eyes, HAM 1.02.203
not ourselves | when nature, being oppress'd, LR 2.04.108
be not with mortal accidents oppress'd, | no CYM 5.04. 99
one eye | against another, arm oppress'd by arm, TNK 5.01. 22
the weak oppress'd, th' impression of strange LUC 1242
but day by night, and night by day, oppress'd; SON 28. 4
sinks down to death, oppress'd with melancholy; 45. 8
/OPPRESSED 1 FR 0.0001 REL FR 1 V 0 P
/oppressed /nature /sleeps. LR 3.06. 97
OPPRESSED 4 FR 0.0004 REL FR 4 V 0 P
here's a young maid with travel much oppressed, AYL 2.04. 74
royalties, and rights | of this oppressed boy. JN 2.01.177
zeal | in the relief of this oppressed child 2.01.245
for thee, oppressed king, i am cast down, LR 5.03. 5
OPPRESSES 1 FR 0.0001 REL FR 1 V 0 P
my dream, | belief of it oppresses me already. OTH 1.01.143
OPPRESSETH 1 FR 0.0001 REL FR 1 V 0 P
to fear the foe, since fear oppresseth strength, R2 3.02.180
OPPRESSING 2 FR 0.0002 REL FR 1 V 1 P
commend the black oppressing humor to the most
LLL 1.01.232 P
for, by oppressing and betraying me, | thou TIM 4.03.503
OPPRESSION 16 FR 0.0018 REL FR 15 V 1 P
week, | this day of shame, oppression, perjury. JN 3.01. 88
and our oppression hath made up this league. 3.01.106
craft | to counterfeit oppression of such grief R2 1.04. 14
stoop with oppression of their prodigal weight; 3.04. 31
his subjects to oppression and contempt, | and H5 2.02.172
of such as your oppression feeds upon, 1H6 4.01. 58
free from oppression or the stroke of war, | my 5.03.155
remember | how under my oppression i did reek H8 2.04.209
at thy good heart's oppression. ROM 1.01.184
too great oppression for a tender thing. 1.04. 24
need and oppression starveth in thy eyes, 5.01. 70
and lack gall | to make oppression bitter, or HAM 2.02.578
fond bondage in the oppression of aged tyranny, LR 1.02. 49 P
and our oppression | exceeds what we expected. ANT 4.07. 2
the earth is throng'd | by man's oppression, and PER 1.01.102
when day's oppression is not eas'd by night, SON 28. 3
OPPRESSOR 2 FR 0.0002 REL FR 2 V 0 P
no hard oppressor | dare take this from us; TNK 2.02. 84
the orphan pines while the oppressor feeds, LUC 905
OPPRESSOR'S 1 FR 0.0001 REL FR 1 V 0 P
th' oppressor's wrong, the proud man's contumely
HAM 3.01. 70
OPPROBRIOUSLY 1 FR 0.0001 REL FR 1 V 0 P
to taunt and scorn you thus opprobriously? R3 3.01.153
OPPUGNANCY 1 FR 0.0001 REL FR 1 V 0 P
each thing /meets | in mere oppugnancy: TRO 1.03.111
OPULENCY 1 FR 0.0001 REL FR 1 V 0 P
flatteries | that follow youth and opulency. TIM 5.01. 37
OPULENT 2 FR 0.0002 REL FR 2 V 0 P
draw | a third more opulent than your sisters'? LR 1.01. 86
i will piece | her opulent throne with kingdoms. ANT 1.05. 46
OPUS 1 FR 0.0001 REL FR 1 V 0 P
"et opus exegi, quod nec jovis ira, nec ignis" TNK 3.05. 88
/OR* 23 FR 0.0026 REL FR 20 V 3 P
just law | now took your brother's life, /or, to MM 2.04. 53
a good woman born but /or every blazing star or AWW 1.03. 86 P
/or /what /doth /this /bold /enterprise /bring 2H4 1.01.178
/or /at /least /desist | /to /build /at /all? 1.03. 47
/or /else | we fortify in paper and in figures, 1.03. 55
/from /the /king /or /in /the /present /time, 4.01.106
/or i will fetch thy rim out at thy throat | in H5 4.04. 14
hast, | i am resolv'd for death /or dignity. 2H6 5.01.194
than ever you /or yours by me were harm'd! R3 4.04.239
/of /author's /pen /or /actor's /voice, /but TRO pr 24
/like /or /find /fault, /do /as /your /pleasures pr 30
/now /good /or /bad, /'tis /but /the /chance /of pr 31
dirt, | to weaken /or discredit our exposure, 1.03.195
if then one is, or hath, /or means to be, | that 1.03.289
/or, /like /a /gallant /horse /fall'n /in /first 3.03.161
/or /get /some /little /knife /between /thy TIT 3.02. 16
/for /there /is /nothing /either /good /or /bad, HAM 2.02.250 P
/health, /a /boy's /love, /or /a /whore's /oath. LR 3.06. 19 P
"/sleepest /or /wakest /thou, /jolly /shepherd? 3.06. 41
/once /or /twice /she /heav'd /the /name /of 4.03. 25
/or /well /or /ill, /as /this /day's /battle's 4.07. 96
/or /well /or /ill, /as /this /day's /battle's 4.07. 96
why then to–morrow night, /or tuesday morn; OTH 3.03. 60
OR* 2581 FR 0.2917 REL FR 2044 V 537 P
fall to't, yarely, or we run ourselves aground. TMP 1.01. 4 P
they are louder than the weather, or our office. 1.01. 37 P
have sunk the sea within the earth or ere | it 1.02. 11
by any other house, or person? 1.02. 42
had i not | four, or five, women once that 1.02. 47
or blessed was't we did? 1.02. 61
creatures that were mine, i say, or chang'd 'em, 1.02. 82
i say, or chang'd 'em, | or else new form'd 'em; 1.02. 83
serv'd | without or grudge or grumblings. 1.02.249
serv'd | without or grudge or grumblings. 1.02.249
taught thee each hour | one thing or other. 1.02.355
if thou neglect'st or dost unwillingly | what i 1.02.368
i' th' air, or th' earth? 1.02.388
have follow'd it, | or it hath drawn me rather. 1.02.395
if you be maid, or no? 1.02.428
which, of he or adrian, for a good wager, first 2.01. 28 P
or, as 'twere perfum'd by a fen. 2.01. 49 P
of that there's none, or little. 2.01. 52 P
ay, or very falsely pocket up his report. 2.01. 68 P
or docks, or mallows. 2.01.145
or docks, or mallows. 2.01.145
no use of metal, corn, or wine, or oil; 2.01.154
no use of metal, corn, or wine, or oil; 2.01.154
should produce | without sweat or endeavor: 2.01.161
sword, pike, knife, gun, or need of any engine, 2.01.162
the bottom run | by their own fear or sloth. 2.01.228
of bellowing | like bulls, or rather lions. 2.01.312
upon our guard, | or that we quit this place. 2.01.322
a man or a fish? 2.02. 25 P
dead or alive? 2.02. 25 P
i'll be your servant, | whether you will or no. 3.01. 86
shalt be my lieutenant, monster, or my standard. 3.02. 16 P
or with a log | batter his skull, or paunch him 3.02. 89
batter his skull, or paunch him with a stake, 3.02. 90
a stake, | or cut his wezand with thy knife. 3.02. 91
or that there were such men | whose heads stood 3.03. 46
loud winds, or with bemock'd–at stabs | kill the 3.03. 63
of mine own life, | or that for which i live; 4.01. 4
when i shall think or phoebus' steeds are 4.01. 30
are founder'd | or night kept chain'd below. 4.01. 31
more abstenious, | or else good night your vow! 4.01. 54

if venus or her son, as thou dost know, | do now 4.01. 87
hush and be mute, | or else our spell is marr'd. 4.01.127
a turn or two i'll walk | to still my beating 4.01.162
or to apes | with foreheads villainous low. 4.01.248
of wine is, or i'll turn you out of my kingdom. 4.01.251 P
make them | than pard or cat o' mountain. 4.01.261
them | that yet looks on me, or would know me! 5.01. 83
me, and return | or ere your pulse twice beat. 5.01.103
whe'er thou beest he or no, | or some enchanted 5.01.111
or some enchanted trifle to abuse me | (as late 5.01.112
whose honor cannot | be measur'd or confin'd. 5.01.122
whether this be, | or be not, i'll not swear. 5.01.123
have inly wept, | or should have spoke ere this. 5.01.201
or stole it, rather. 5.01.300
be here confin'd by you, | or sent to naples. ep 5
my sails | must fill, or else my project fails, ep 12
with wit, | or else a wit by folly vanquished. TGV 1.01. 35
my horns are his horns, whether i wake or sleep. 1.01. 80 P
or else return no more into my sight. 1.02. 47
but twice, or thrice, was "proteus" written down 1.02.114
for any or for all these exercises | he said 1.03. 11
'tis a word or two | of commendations sent from 1.03. 52
please you deliberate a day or two. 1.03. 73
your worship, sir, or else i mistook. 2.01. 10 P
or your own eyes had the lights they were wont 2.01. 71 P
on a man's face, or a weathercock on a steeple! 2.01.136
or else for want of idle time, could not again 2.01.166
or fearing else some messenger, that might her 2.01.167
or as one nail by strength drives out another, 2.04.193
/is /it mine /eye, or valentinus' praise, | her 2.04.196
her true perfection, or my false transgression, 2.04.197
the love | i ever bore my daughter, or thyself. 3.01.167
mine and not mine twice or thrice in that last 3.01.356 P
this, or else nothing, will inherit her. 3.02. 86
without false vantage, or base treachery. 4.01. 29
me happy, | or else i often had been miserable. 4.01. 35
no outrages | on silly women or poor passengers. 4.01. 70
sir, but i do; or else i would be hence. 4.02. 22
or, at the least, in hers sepulchre thine. 4.02.117
when three or four of his blind brothers and 4.04. 4 P
the company of three or four gentleman-like dogs 4.04. 17 P
again, | or ne'er return again into my sight. 4.04. 60
or else, by jove i vow, | i should have 4.04.203
common friend, that's without faith or love, 5.04. 62
thurio, give back, or else embrace thy death; 5.04.126
warrant, quittance, or obligation, armigero. WIV 1.01. 10 P
is false, or as i despise one that is not true. 1.01. 69 P
or i would i might never come in mine own great 1.01.153 P
to know that of your mouth, or of your lips; 1.01.228 P
ay, or else i would i might be hang'd, la! 1.01.258 P
the manner of his nurse — or his dry nurse — 1.02. 4 P
or his dry nurse — or his cook — or his 1.02. 4 P
or his cook — or his laundry — his washer and 1.02. 4 P
with wit or steel? 1.03. 93
a scurvy jack-a-nape priest to meddle or make — 1.04.110 P
by me, thine own true knight, | by day or night, 2.01. 15
by day or night, | or any kind of light, | with 2.01. 16
but go to hell for an eternal moment or so, i 2.01. 50 P
or go thou | like sir actaeon he, with ringwood 2.01.117
heed, ere summer comes or cuckoo-birds do sing. 2.01.123
liquor in his pate, or money in his purse, when 2.01.190 P
or else you had look'd through the grate, like a 2.02. 8 P
shall i vouchsafe your worship a word or two? 2.02. 40 P
she is my prize, or ocean whelm them all! 2.02.137
take all, or half, for easing me of the carriage 2.02.173 P
have merited, either in my mind or in my means, 2.02.203 P
me, her assistant or go-between parted from me. 2.02.263 P
bottle, or a thief to walk my ambling gelding, 2.02.304 P
you bear witness that me have stay six or seven, 2.03. 36 P
and i will provoke him to't, or let him wag. 2.03. 70 P
give me my gown, or else keep it in your arms. 3.01. 34 P
and i will one way or other make you amends. 3.01. 87 P
lead mine eyes, or eye your master's heels? 3.02. 4 P
and (without any pause or staggering) take this 3.03. 12 P
or any tire of venetian admittance. 3.03. 57 P
or else i could not be in that mind. 3.03. 83 P
or bid farewell to your good life for ever. 3.03.119 P
or — it is whiting-time — send him by your two 3.03.132 P
that my husband is deceiv'd, or sir john. 3.03.179 P
if there be one or two, i shall make-a the turd. 3.03.236 P
than stamps in gold, or sums in sealed bags; 3.04. 16
i'll make a shaft or a bolt on't. 3.04. 24 P
own part, i would little or nothing with you. 3.04. 63 P
or i would master slender had her; 3.04.105 P
or, in sooth, i would master fenton had her. 3.04.105 P
who ask'd them once or twice what they had in 3.05.102 P
sure he is by this — or will be presently. 4.01. 3 P
and three or four more of their growth, we'll 4.04. 49
practic'd well to this, or they'll nev'r do't. 4.04. 66
beguil'd him of a chain, had the chain or no. 4.05. 33 P
conceal them, or thou diest. 4.05. 45 P
it were my master's fortune to have her or no. 4.05. 48 P
to have her, or no. 4.05. 51 P
which means she to deceive, father or mother? 4.06. 46
numbers, either in nativity, chance, or death. 5.01. 4 P
the matter will be known to-night, or never. 5.01. 10 P
what needs either your "mum" or her "budget"? 5.02. 9 P
jove, or who can blame me to piss my tallow? 5.05. 14 P
i was three or four times in the thought they 5.05.121 P
have swing'd him, or he should have swing'd me. 5.05.186 P
of craft, | of disobedience, or unduteous title, 5.05.227
so to enforce or qualify the laws | as to your MM 1.01. 65
in any proportion, or in any language. 1.02. 22 P
i think, or in any religion. 1.02. 23 P
whether thou art tainted or free. 1.02. 43 P
or whether that the body public be | a horse 1.02.159
place, | or in his eminence that fills it up, 1.02.164
or that his appetite | is more to bread than 1.03. 52
or, if you show your face, you must not speak. 1.04. 13
time coher'd with place, or place with wishing, 2.01. 11
or that the resolute acting of /your blood 2.01. 12
may in the sworn twelve have a thief or two 2.01. 20
was ever respected with man, woman, or child. 2.01.169 P
justice or iniquity? 2.01.172 P
ever i was respected with her, or she with me, 2.01.176 P
or i'll have mine action of batt'ry on thee. 2.01.178 P
you bring me in the names of some six or seven, 2.01.273 P
do you your office, or give up your place, | and 2.02. 13
were he my kinsman, brother, or my son, | it 2.02. 81
either now, or by remissness new conceiv'd, 2.02. 96
or stones, whose rate are either rich or poor 2.02.150
whose rate are either rich or poor | as fancy 2.02.150
is this her fault, or mine? 2.02.162
the tempter, or the tempted, who sins most, ha? 2.02.163
or what art thou, angelo? 2.02.172
penitence, if it be sound, | or hollowly put on. 2.03. 23
and, it may be, | as long as you or i. 2.04. 36
longer or shorter, he may be so fitted | that 2.04. 40
either you are ignorant, | or seem so /craftily; 2.04. 75
whose credit with the judge, or own great place, 2.04. 92
to this supposed, or else to let him suffer — 2.04. 97
or with an outstretch'd throat i'll tell the 2.04.153
will, | or else he must not only die the death, 2.04.165
or, by the affection that now guides me most, 2.04.168
tongue, | either of condemnation or approof, 2.04.174
either death or life | shall thereby be the 3.01. 5
my business is a word or two with claudio. 3.01. 48
and six or seven winters more respect | than a 3.01. 75
i abhor to name, | or else thou diest to-morrow. 3.01.102
sin, | or of the deadly seven it is the least. 3.01.110
floods, or to reside | in thrilling region of 3.01.121
or to be worse than worst | of those that 3.01.125
my lips in vain, or discover his government. 3.01.193 P
what 'tis to cram a maw or clothe a back | from 3.02. 22
or how? 3.02. 51 P
or how? 3.02. 64 P
either this is envy in you, folly, or mistaking. 3.02.141 P
or, if your knowledge be more, it is much 3.02.147 P
or you imagine me too unhurtful an opposite. 3.02.165 P
canst thou tell if claudio die to-morrow, or no? 3.02.170 P
i hope it is some pardon or reprieve | for the 4.02. 71
neither in time, matter, or other circumstance. 4.02.104 P
deliver'd him to his liberty or executed him? 4.02.133 P
fearless of what's past, present, or to come; 4.02.144 P
were you sworn to the duke, or to the deputy? 4.02.182 P
or they shall beat out my brains with billets. 4.03. 54 P
unfit to live, or die; 4.03. 64
not being believ'd, | or wring redress from you. 5.01. 32
or else thou art suborn'd against his honor | in 5.01.106
who is as free from touch or soil with her | as 5.01.141
my knees, | or else for ever be confixed here, 5.01.232
hast thou or word, or wit, or impudence, | that 5.01.363
hast thou or word, or wit, or impudence, | that 5.01.363
hast thou or word, or wit, or impudence, | that 5.01.363
yet loath to leave unsought | or that, or any ERR 1.01.136
or that, or any place that harbors men. 1.01.136
beg thou, or borrow, to make up the sum, | and 1.01.153
or i shall break that merry sconce of yours 1.02. 79
life, by some device or other | the villain is 1.02. 95
and when they see time, | they'll go or come; 2.01. 9
as much, or more, we should ourselves complain: 2.01. 37
back, slave, or i will break thy pate across. 2.01. 78
or else what lets it but he would be here? 2.01.105
or i will beat this method in your sconce. 2.02. 34
or else i shall seek my wit in my shoulders. 2.02. 38 P
unless i spake, or look'd, or touch'd, or carv'd 2.02.118
spake, or look'd, or touch'd, or carv'd to thee. 2.02.118
spake, or look'd, or touch'd, or carv'd to thee. 2.02.118
drop again, | without addition or diminishing, 2.02.128
is dross, | usurping ivy, brier, or idle moss, 2.02.178
or sleep i now and think i hear all this? 2.02.183
suck our breath, or pinch us black and blue. 2.02.192
am i in earth, in heaven, or in hell? 2.02.212
sleeping or waking, mad or well-advis'd? 2.02.213
sleeping or waking, mad or well-advis'd? 2.02.213
o, signior balthazar, either at flesh or fish, 3.01. 22
thee from the door, or sit down at the hatch: 3.01. 33
thy face for a name, or thy name for an ass. 3.01. 47
or if you like elsewhere, do it by stealth, 3.02. 7
all this my sister is, or else should be. 3.02. 65
this drudge or diviner laid claim to me, call'd 3.02.140 P
or i'll attach you by this officer. 4.01. 6
or else you may return without your money. 4.01. 44
either send the chain, or send me by some token. 4.01. 56
good sir, say whe'r you'll answer me or no: 4.01. 60
sum for me | or i attach you by this officer. 4.01. 73
yea or no? 4.02. 3
look'd he or red or pale, or sad or merrily? 4.02. 4
look'd he or red or pale, or sad or merrily? 4.02. 4
look'd he or red or pale, or sad or merrily? 4.02. 4
look'd he or red or pale, or sad or merrily? 4.02. 4
do, expect spoon-meat, or bespeak a long spoon. 4.03. 61 P
or, for my diamond, the chain you promis'd, 4.03. 69
i pray you, sir, my ring, or else the chain; 4.03. 77
respect your end, or rather, the prophecy like 4.04. 42 P
who heard me to deny it or forswear it? 5.01. 25
this is some priory, in, or we are spoil'd! 5.01. 37
to be disturb'd, would mad or man or beast: 5.01. 84
to be disturb'd, would mad or man or beast: 5.01. 84
wits again, | or lose my labor in assaying it. 5.01. 97
but had he such a chain of thee, or no? 5.01.257
i think you are all mated, or stark mad. 5.01.282
i see two husbands, or mine eyes deceive me. 5.01.332
egeon art thou not? or else his ghost? 5.01.338
signior mountanto return'd from the wars or no? ADO 1.01. 31 P
so some gentleman or other shall scape a 1.01.134 P
or would you have me speak after my custom, as 1.01.167 P
or do you play the flouting jack, to tell us 1.01.183 P
or hang my bugle in an invisible baldrick, all 1.01.241 P
anger, with sickness, or with hunger, my lord, 1.01.249 P
fellow, or else make another cur'sy and say, 2.01. 55 P
he'll but break a comparison or two on me, which 2.01.146 P
not mark'd, or not laugh'd at, strikes him into 2.01.147 P
or under your arm, like a lieutenant's scarf? 2.01.190 P
as being forsaken, or to bind him up a rod, as 2.01.219 P
speak, cousin, or, if you cannot, stop his mouth 2.01.310 P
wise, or i'll none; 2.03. 31 P
virtuous, or i'll never cheapen her; 2.03. 31 P
fair, or i'll never look on her; 2.03. 32 P
mild, or come not near me; 2.03. 32 P
noble, or not i for an angel; 2.03. 33 P
or, if thou wilt hold longer argument, | do it 2.03. 53
or undertakes them with a most christian-like 2.03.191 P
he hath twice or thrice cut cupid's bow-string, 3.02. 10 P
where is but a humor or a worm. 3.02. 27 P
or in the shape of two countries at once, as a 3.02. 34 P
yea, or to paint himself? 3.02. 57 P
i have studied eight or nine wise words to speak 3.02. 72 P
yea, or else it were pity but they should suffer 3.03. 2 P
sir, or george seacole, for they can write and 3.03. 11 P
of men, the less you meddle or make with them, 3.03. 52 P
knowest that the fashion of a doublet, or a hat, 3.03.118 P
or a hat, or a cloak, is nothing to a man. 3.03.118 P
for a hawk, a horse, or a husband? 3.04. 55 P
you are in love, or that you will be in love, or 3.04. 85 P
you will be in love, or that you can be in love. 3.04. 86 P
or those pamp'red animals | that rage in savage 4.01. 60
are these things spoken, or do i but dream? 4.01. 66
or that i yesternight | maintain'd the change of 4.01.182
or that i had any friend would be a man for my 4.01.318 P
yea, as sure as i have a thought or a soul. 4.01.330 P
being young, or what would do | were i not old. 5.01. 61
and shall, or some of us will smart for it. 5.01.109
art thou sick, or angry? 5.01.131 P
do me right, or i will protest your cowardice. 5.01.147 P
hear from him, or i will subscribe him a coward. 5.02. 58 P
to bind me, or undo me — one of them. 5.04. 20
thou think i care for a satire or an epigram? 5.04.102 P
or study where to meet some mistress fine, LLL 1.01. 63
or, having sworn too hard-a-keeping oath, 1.01. 65
or vainly comes th' admired princess hither. 1.01.140
to hear, or forbear hearing? 1.01.196 P
or to forbear both. 1.01.198 P
thou viewest, beholdest, surveyest, or seest. 1.01.244 P
or, for thy more sweet understanding, a woman. 1.01.264 P
or i apt, and my saying pretty? 1.02. 20 P
of all the four, or the three, or the two, or 1.02. 79 P
or the three, or the two, or one of the four. 1.02. 79 P
or the three, or the two, or one of the four. 1.02. 79 P
then if she fear, or be to blame, | by this you 1.02.103
or, if it were, it would neither serve for the 1.02.113 P
but say that he, or we, as neither have, 2.01.132
it, i'll repay it back, | or yield up aquitaine. 2.01.159
is she wedded or no? 2.01.211
to her will, sir, or so. 2.01.212
or your hands in your pocket like a man after 3.01. 19 P
minime, honest master, or rather, master, no. 3.01. 60
page, it is an epilogue or discourse, to make 3.01. 81
no, on both in one, or one in both. 4.01. 78 P
must shoot nearer, or he'll ne'er hit the clout. 4.01.134
were, replication, or rather ostentare, to show, 4.02. 15 P
untrained, or rather unlettered, or ratherest 4.02. 18 P
unlettered, or ratherest unconfirmed fashion, to 4.02. 18 P
become me to be vain, /indiscreet, or a fool, 4.02. 30
from thicket, | or pricket sore, or else sorel; 4.02. 59
from thicket, | or pricket sore, or else sorel; 4.02. 59
or rather, as horace says in his — what, my 4.02.101 P
accidentally, or by the way of progression, hath 4.02.139 P
with the parents of the foresaid child or pupil, 4.02.157 P
or groan for joan, or spend a minute's time | in 4.03.180
joan, or spend a minute's time | in pruning me? 4.03.180
a true man, or a thief, that gallops so? 4.03.185
i'll prove her fair, or talk till doomsday here. 4.03.270
for when would you, my lord, or you, or you, 4.03.295
for when would you, my lord, or you, or you, 4.03.295
for when would you, my liege, or you, or you, 4.03.317
for when would you, my liege, or you, or you, 4.03.317
or keeping what is sworn, you will prove fools. 4.03.353
or for love's sake, a word that loves all men, 4.03.355
or for men's sake, the /authors of these women, 4.03.356
or women's sake, by whom we men are men, | /let 4.03.357
or else we lose ourselves to keep our oaths. 4.03.359
nominated, or called, don adriano de armado. 5.01. 8 P
or the fift, if i. 5.01. 54 P
or mons, the hill. 5.01. 84 P
with some delightful ostentation, or show, or 5.01.112 P
ostentation, or show, or pageant, or antic, or 5.01.112 P
or show, or pageant, or antic, or firework. 5.01.112 P
or show, or pageant, or antic, or firework. 5.01.112 P
because of his great limb or joint, shall pass 5.01.128 P
i'll make one in a dance, or so; 5.01.153
or i will play | on the tabor to the worthies, 5.01.153
ay, or i would these hands might never part. 5.02. 57
or hide your heads like cowards, and fly hence. 5.02. 86
thus, | like muscovites or russians, as i guess. 5.02.121
or ever but in vizards show their faces? 5.02.271
are angels /vailing clouds, or roses blown. 5.02.297
my love to thee is sound, sans crack or flaw. 5.02.415
that he would wed me, or else die my lover. 5.02.447
will you have me, or your pearl again? 5.02.458
whether the three worthies shall come in or no. 5.02.486
he's a god or a painter, for he makes faces. 5.02.643 P
in your rich wisdom to excuse or hide | the 5.02.732
if this, or more than this, i would deny, | to 5.02.813
my desires, | like to a step-dame, or a dowager, MND 1.01. 5
or to her death, according to our law 1.01. 44
his power | to leave the figure or disfigure it. 1.01. 51
or to abjure | for ever the society of men. 1.01. 65
or else to wed demetrius, as he would, | or on 1.01. 88
or on diana's altar to protest | for aye 1.01. 89
or else the law of athens yields you up | (which 1.01.119
to death, or to a vow of single life. 1.01.121
ever read, | could ever hear by tale or history, 1.01.133
or else misgraffed in respect of years — 1.01.137
or else it stood upon the choice of friends — 1.01.139
or, if there were a sympathy in choice, | war, 1.01.141
war, death, or sickness did lay siege to it, 1.01.142
what is pyramus? a lover, or a tyrant? 1.02. 22 P
play ercles rarely, or a part to tear a cat in, 1.02. 29 P
beard, or your french-crown-color beard, your 1.02. 95 P
enough; hold, or cut bow-strings. 1.02.111 P
and now they never meet in grove or green, | by 2.01. 28
by fountain clear, or spangled starlight sheen, 2.01. 29
or else you are that shrewd and knavish sprite 2.01. 33
met we on hill, in dale, forest, or mead, | by 2.01. 83
or mead, | by paved fountain or by rushy brook, 2.01. 84
brook, | or in the beached margent of the sea, 2.01. 85
no night is now with hymn or carol blest. 2.01.102
laid | will make or man or woman madly dote 2.01.171
laid | will make or man or woman madly dote 2.01.171
upon | (be it on lion, bear, or wolf, or bull, 2.01.180
upon | (be it on lion, bear, or wolf, or bull, 2.01.180
on meddling monkey, or on busy ape), | she shall 2.01.181
or rather do i not in plainest truth | tell you 2.01.200

or, if thou follow me, do not believe | but i 2.01.236
be it ounce, or cat, or bear, | pard, or boar 2.02. 30
be it ounce, or cat, or bear, | pard, or boar 2.02. 30
or bear, | pard, or boar with bristled hair, 2.02. 31
dead, or asleep? 2.02.101
or as the heresies that men do leave | are hated 2.02.139
either death, or you, i'll find immediately. 2.02.156
through, saying thus, or to the same defect: 3.01. 38 P
"ladies," or "fair ladies, i would wish you," or 3.01. 39 P
i would wish you," or "i would request you," or 3.01. 40 P
"i would request you," or "i would entreat you, 3.01. 40 P
or else one must come in with a bush of thorns 3.01. 59 P
and say he comes to disfigure, or to present, 3.01. 61 P
some man or other must present wall; 3.01. 67 P
and let him have some plaster, or some loam, or 3.01. 68 P
or some loam, or some rough–cast about him, to 3.01. 68 P
or let him hold his fingers thus, and through 3.01. 69 P
thou shalt remain here, whether thou wilt or no. 3.01.153
or russet–pated choughs, many in sort, | rising 3.02. 21
see me no more, whether he be dead or no. 3.02. 81
if you have any pity, grace, or manners, | you 3.02.241
which death, or absence, soon shall remedy. 3.02.244
or i will shake thee from me like a serpent! 3.02.261
right, | of thine or mine, is most in helena. 3.02.337
or else commit'st thy knaveries willfully. 3.02.346
or say, sweet love, what thou desirest to eat. 4.01. 30
had rather have a handful or two of dried peas. 4.01. 37 P
and there is two or three lords and ladies more 4.02. 16 P
sixpence a day in pyramus, or nothing. 4.02. 24 P
or in the night, imagining some fear, | how easy 5.01. 21
night, | did scare away, or rather did affright; 5.01.141
that had in it a crannied hole or chink, 5.01.158
or to hear a bergomask dance between two of our 5.01.353 P
but how i caught it, found it, or came by it, MV 1.01. 3
or, as it were, the pageants of the sea, | do 1.01. 11
or to find both | or bring your latter hazard 1.01.150
both | or bring your latter hazard back again, 1.01.151
make | to have it of my trust, or for my sake. 1.01.185
or is your gold and silver ewes and rams? 1.03. 95
or | shall i bend low and in a bondman's key, 1.03.122
such sum or sums as are | express'd in the 1.03.147
neither, | as flesh of muttons, beefs, or goats. 1.03.167
to prove whose blood is reddest, his or mine. 2.01. 7
or swear before you choose, if you choose wrong 2.01. 40
to make me blest or cursed'st among men. 2.01. 46
good launcelot," or "good /gobbo," or "good 2.02. 4 P
or "good /gobbo," or "good launcelot /gobbo, use 2.02. 5 P
take heed, honest /gobbo," or, as aforesaid, 2.02. 8 P
man's son" — or rather an honest woman's son, 2.02. 16 P
that dwells with him, dwell with him or no? 2.02. 47 P
is indeed deceas'd, or, as you would say in 2.02. 64 P
do i look like a cudgel or a hovel–post, a staff 2.02. 68 P
a cudgel or a hovel–post, a staff, or a prop? 2.02. 69 P
me, is my boy, god rest his soul, alive or dead? 2.02. 72 P
how like a younger or a prodigal | the scarfed 2.06. 14
or shall i think in silver she's immur'd, 2.07. 52
he keep his day, | or he shall pay for this. 2.08. 26
embraced heaviness | with some delight or other. 2.08. 53
you shall look fairer ere i give or hazard. 2.09. 22
as ever knapp'd ginger or made her neighbors 3.01. 9 P
any slips of prolixity or crossing the plain 3.01. 11 P
whether antonio have had any loss at sea or no? 3.01. 43 P
tarry, pause a day or two | before you hazard, 3.02. 1
i would detain you here some month or two 3.02. 9
is fancy bred, | or in the heart or in the head? 3.02. 64
is fancy bred, | or in the heart or in the head? 3.02. 64
or whether, riding on the balls of mine, | seem 3.02.117
whether those peals of praise be his or no, | so 3.02.145
which when you part from, lose, or give away, 3.02.172
it to the mood | of what it likes or loathes. 4.01. 52
good youth, or it will fall | to cureless ruin. 4.01.141
some three or four of you | go give him 4.01.147
if thou tak'st more | or less than a just pound, 4.01.327
as makes it light or heavy in the substance | or 4.01.328
substance | or the division of the twentith part 4.01.329
that by direct or indirect attempts | he seek 4.01.350
or else i do recant | the pardon that i late 4.01.391
herd, | or race of youthful and unhandled colts, 5.01. 72
sound, | or any air of music touch their ears, 5.01. 76
the voice, | or i am much deceiv'd, of portia. 5.01.111
what talk you of the posy or the value? 5.01.151
or half her worthiness that gave the ring, | or 5.01.200
ring, | or your own honor to contain the ring, 5.01.201
or go to bed now, being two hours to day. 5.01.303
he keeps me rustically at home, or, to speak AYL 1.01. 7 P
or give me the poor allottery my father left me 1.01. 73 P
duke, and three or four loving lords have put 1.01.100 P
her exile, or have died to stay behind her. 1.01.109 P
or brook such disgrace well as he shall run into 1.01.133 P
or if he do not mightily grace himself on thee, 1.01.148 P
ta'en thy life by some indirect means or other; 1.01.152 P
or if he had, he had sworn it away before ever 1.02. 78 P
ever he saw those pancakes or that mustard. 1.02. 80 P
or as the destinies decrees. 1.02.105 P
or i, i promise thee. 1.02.140 P
your eyes, or knew yourself with your judgment, 1.02.176 P
or charles, or something weaker, masters thee. 1.02.260
or charles, or something weaker, masters thee. 1.02.260
or have acquaintance with mine own desires; 1.03. 48
if that i do not dream, or be not frantic | (as 1.03. 49
or, if we did derive it from our friends, 1.03. 62
or with a base and boist'rous sword enforce | a 2.03. 32
this i must do, or know not what to do; 2.03. 34
or if thou hast not sat as i do now, | wearing 2.04. 37
or if thou hast not broke from company 2.04. 40
if that love or gold | can in this desert place 2.04. 71
either be food for it or bring it for food to 2.06. 7 P
or what is he of basest function, | that says 2.07. 79
or else a rude despiser of good manners, | that 2.07. 92
bring him dead or living | within this 3.01. 6
or turn thou no more | to seek a living in our 3.01. 7
of good breeding or comes of a very dull kindred 3.02. 30 P
but whether wisely or no, let the forest judge. 3.02.121 P
the fairest boughs, | or at every sentence end, 3.02.136
bottle, either too much at once, or none at all. 3.02.201 P
or his chin worth a beard? 3.02.206 P
which i take to be either a fool or a cipher. 3.02.290 P
tree, or shall we go with you to your chapel? 3.03. 66 P
must be given, or the marriage is not lawful. 3.03. 69 P
we must be married, or we must live in bawdry. 3.03. 97
concave as a cover'd goblet or a worm–eaten nut. 3.04. 24 P
or if thou canst not, o, for shame, for shame, 3.05. 18
or i will scarce think you have swam in a 4.01. 37 P
or i should think my honesty ranker than my wit. 4.01. 84 P
or else she could not have the wit to do this; 4.01.160 P
promise, or come one minute behind your hour, i 4.01.190 P
or rather, bottomless — that as fast as you 4.01.209 P
that i can make, | or else by him my love deny, 4.03. 62
abandon the society of this female, or, clown, 5.01. 51 P
or, to thy better understanding, diest; 5.01. 51 P
or, to wit, i kill thee, make thee away, 5.01. 52 P
will deal in poison with thee, or in bastinado, 5.01. 54 P
poison with thee, or in bastinado, or in steel; 5.01. 55 P
or else be incontinent before marriage. 5.02. 39 P
without hawking or spitting or saying we are 5.03. 12 P
hawking or spitting or saying we are hoarse, 5.03. 12 P
or else, refusing me, to wed this shepherd; 5.04. 22
must accord, | or have a woman to your lord; 5.04.134
let me have audience for a word or two. 5.04.151
as many as have good beards, or good faces, or ep 21 P
beards, or good faces, or sweet breaths, will, ep 21 P
third, or fourth, or fift borough, i'll answer SHR in.1. 13 P
or fourth, or fift borough, i'll answer him by in.1. 13 P
one dead, or drunk? in.1. 31
even as a flatt'ring dream or worthless fancy. in.1. 44
shoes, or such shoes as my toes look through the in.2. 11 P
or wilt thou sleep? in.2. 37
or wilt thou ride? in.2. 41
or wilt thou hunt? in.2. 44
or daphne roaming through a thorny wood, in.2. 57
or do i dream? in.2. 69
or have i dream'd till now? in.2. 69
or when you wak'd, so wak'd as if you slept. in.2. 80
al'ce madam, or joan madam? in.2. 110
and slept above some fifteen year or more. in.2. 113
of you | to pardon me yet for a night or two; in.2. 119
or, if not so, until the sun be set. in.2. 120
a christmas gambold, or a tumbling–trick? in.2. 138 P
or so devote to aristotle's checks | as ovid be 1.01. 32
that wench is stark mad or wonderful froward. 1.01. 69
or, signior gremio, you, know any such, | prefer 1.01. 96
true, | i never thought it possible or likely. 1.01.149
distinguish'd by our faces | for man or master. 1.01.201
some neapolitan, or meaner man of pisa. 1.01.205
or you stol'n his? 1.01.224 P
or both? 1.01.224 P
rap me well, or i'll knock your knave's pate. 1.02. 12
sirrah, be gone, or talk not, i advise you. 1.02. 44
and shrowd | as socrates' xantippe, or a worse, 1.02. 71
she moves me not, or not removes, at least, 1.02. 72
and marry him to a puppet or an aglet–baby, or 1.02. 79 P
or an old trot with ne'er a tooth in her head, 1.02. 79 P
may perhaps call him half a score knaves or so. 1.02.111 P
will he woo her? ay — or i'll hang her. 1.02.197
you a suitor to the maid you talk of, yea or no? 1.02.228
or what you will command me will i do, | so well 2.01. 6
accept of him, or else you do me wrong. 2.01. 59
with her, | or else you like not of my company. 2.01. 65
us, | or shall i send my daughter kate to you? 2.01.167
'twill bring you gain, or perish on the seas. 2.01.329
words can witness, or your thoughts can guess. 2.01.336
things that belongs | to house or house–keeping. 2.01.356
i'll leave her houses three or four as good, 2.01.366
of man | after his studies or his usual pain? 3.01. 12
e la mi, show pity, or i die." 3.01. 78
a christian footboy or a gentleman's lackey. 3.02. 71 P
monument, | some comet or unusual prodigy? 3.02. 96
be mad and merry, or go hang yourselves; 3.02.226
or shall i complain on thee to our mistress, 4.01. 29 P
you give thanks, sweet kate, or else shall i? 4.01.159
master, a mercantant, or a pedant, | i know not 4.02. 63
travel you far on, or are you at the farthest? 4.02. 73
sir, at the farthest for a week or two, | but 4.02. 74
as who should say, if i should sleep or eat, 4.03. 13
'twere deadly sickness or else present death. 4.03. 14
mustard, | or else you get no beef of grumio. 4.03. 28
then both or one, or any thing thou wilt. 4.03. 29
then both or one, or any thing thou wilt. 4.03. 29
why, 'tis a cockle or a walnut–shell, | a knack, 4.03. 66
or else my heart concealing it will break, | and 4.03. 78
love me, or love me not, i like the cap, | and 4.03. 84
cap, | and it i will have, or i will have none. 4.03. 85
or i shall so bemete thee with thy yard | as 4.03.112
or is the adder better than the eel, | because 4.03.177
look what i speak, or do, or think to do, | you 4.03.192
look what i speak, or do, or think to do, | you 4.03.192
or both dissemble deeply their affections; 4.04. 42
to expound the meaning or moral of his signs and 4.04. 79 P
it shall be moon, or star, or what i list, | or 4.05. 7
it shall be moon, or star, or what i list, | or 4.05. 7
list, | or ere i journey to your father's house. 4.05. 8
say as he says, or we shall never go. 4.05. 11
and be it moon, or sun, or what you please; 4.05. 13
and be it moon, or sun, or what you please; 4.05. 13
sweet, | whither away, or /where is thy abode? 4.05. 38
but is this true, or is it else your pleasure, 4.05. 71
what if a man bring him a hundred pound or two, 5.01. 22 P
him, forswear him, or else we are all undone. 5.01.111 P
have at you for a /bitter jest or two! 5.02. 45
i'll venture so much of my hawk or hound, | but 5.02. 72
fair buds, | and in no sense is meet or amiable. 5.02.141
none so dry or thirsty | will deign to sip or 5.02.144
will deign to sip or touch one drop of it. 5.02.145
or seek for rule, supremacy, and sway, | when 5.02.163
nor bitterness | were in his pride or sharpness; AWW 1.02. 37
but /or every blazing star or at an earthquake, 1.03. 87 P
rescue in the first assault or ransom afterward. 1.03.116 P
were our faults, or then we thought them none. 1.03.135
or were you both our mothers, | i care no more 1.03.163
whether i live or die, be you the sons | of 2.01. 11
too, or take off thine | by wond'ring how thou 2.01. 89
so stain our judgment, or corrupt our hope, | to 2.01.120
or to dissever so | our great self and our 2.01.122
or four and twenty times the pilot's glass 2.01.165
skill infinite or monstrous desperate. 2.01.184
time, or flinch in property | of what i spoke, 2.01.187
with any branch or image of thy state; 2.01.198
the brawn–buttock, or any buttock. 2.02. 19 P
them whipt, or i would send them to th' turk, to 2.03. 87 P
or i will throw thee from my care for ever 2.03.162
acquaintance with thee, or rather my knowledge, 2.03.228 P
in yourself, sir, or were you taught to find me? 2.04. 34 P
of you than you have or will to deserve at my 2.05. 47 P
whilst i can shake my sword or hear the drum. 2.05. 91
or to the worth | of the great count himself, 3.05. 59
of enjoin'd penitents | there's four or five, to 3.05. 95
i would have that drum or another, or hic jacet. 3.06. 62 P
i would have that drum or another, or hic jacet. 3.06. 62 P
and clap upon you two or three probable lies. 3.06. 98 P
some four or five descents | since the first 3.07. 24
the turn, or the breaking of my spanish sword. 4.01. 47 P
or the baring of my beard, and to say it was in 4.01. 49 P
or to drown my clothes, and say i was stripp'd. 4.01. 52 P
if there be here german, or dane, low dutch, 4.01. 71
italian, or french, let him speak to me, | i'll 4.01. 72
he travel higher, or return again into france? 4.03. 42 P
five or six thousand, but very weak and 4.03.131 P
"five or six thousand horse," i said — i will 4.03.148 P
i will say true — "or thereabouts," set down, 4.03.149 P
or whether he thinks it were not possible with 4.03.178 P
or it is upon a file with the duke's other 4.03.204 P
i do not know if it be it or no. 4.03.208 P
i' th' stocks, or any where, so i may live. 4.03.244 P
lord, sir, let me live, or let me see my death! 4.03.309 P
of the sallet, or rather the herb of grace. 4.05. 17 P
dost thou profess thyself — a knave or a fool? 4.05. 23 P
to–morrow, or i am deceiv'd by him that in such 4.05. 82 P
whether there be a scar under't or no, the 4.05. 96 P
a scar nobly got, or a noble scar, is a good 4.05. 99 P
stop my nose, or against any man's metaphor. 5.02. 13 P
sir, or of fortune's cat — but not a musk–cat 5.02. 19 P
scorn'd a fair color, or express'd it stol'n, 5.03. 50
extended or contracted all proportions | to a 5.03. 51
or, ere they meet, in me, o nature, cesse! 5.03. 72
come, or sent it us | upon her great disaster. 5.03.111
whether i have been to blame or no, i know not. 5.03.129
who hath for four or five removes come short 5.03.131
you must marry me, | either both or none. 5.03.175
am i or that or this for what he'll utter, 5.03.208
am i or that or this for what he'll utter, 5.03.208
where did you buy it? or who gave it you? 5.03.271
it might be yours or hers, for aught i know. 5.03.280
i am either maid, or else this old man's wife. 5.03.293
and so is now, or was so very late; TN 1.02. 30
and speaks three or four languages word for word 1.03. 26 P
wit than a christian or an ordinary man has; 1.03. 84 P
do, or not do? 1.03. 91 P
your niece will not be seen, or if she be, it's 1.03.106 P
you either fear his humor or my negligence, that 1.04. 5 P
some four or five attend him — | all, if you 1.04. 36
or i will not open my lips so wide as a bristle 1.05. 1 P
being so long absent, or to be turn'd away — is 1.05. 17 P
or, if both break, your gaskins fall. 1.05. 24 P
i am sick, or not at home — what you will, to 1.05.108 P
he'll speak with you, will you or no. 1.05.154 P
peascod, or a codling when 'tis almost an apple. 1.05.158 P
he left this ring behind him, | would i or not. 1.05.302
you have a love–song, or a song of good life? 2.03. 35 P
or what are you? 2.03. 86 P
without any mitigation or remorse of voice? 2.03. 90 P
or i'll deliver thy indignation to him by word 2.03.130 P
is, or any thing constantly but a time–pleaser, 2.03.147 P
or thy affection cannot hold the bent; 2.04. 37
and pleasure will be paid, one time or another. 2.04. 71 P
perchance wind up my watch, or play with my — 2.05. 60 P
patience, or we break the sinews of our plot! 2.05. 75 P
ay, or i'll cudgel him, and make him cry o! 2.05.133 P
or o' mine either? 2.05.189 P
i' faith, or i either? 2.05.192 P
or, the church stands by thy tabor, if thy tabor 3.01. 9 P
some laudable attempt either of valor or policy. 3.02. 29 P
to him, lad, some two thousand strong, or so. 3.02. 55 P
is bought more oft than begg'd or borrow'd. 3.04. 3
no incredulous or unsafe circumstance — what 3.04. 80 P
give't or take't. 3.04.240 P
therefore on, or strip your sword stark naked; 3.04.250 P
certain, or forswear to wear iron about you. 3.04.252 P
none, | nor know i you by voice or any feature. 3.04.353
or any taint of vice whose strong corruption 3.04.356
whisper o'er a couplet or two of most sage saws. 3.04.378 P
sir, or i'll throw your dagger o'er the house. 4.01. 28 P
i must have an ounce or two of this malapert 4.01. 44 P
or i am mad, or else this is a dream. 4.01. 61
or i am mad, or else this is a dream. 4.01. 61
you not mad indeed, or do you but counterfeit? 4.02.114 P
but that i am mad | or else the lady's mad; 4.03. 16
tripping measure, or the bells of saint bennet, 5.01. 38 P
antonio never yet was thief or pirate, | though 5.01. 74
add | my love, without retention or restraint, 5.01. 81
or will not else thy craft so quickly grow, 5.01.166
but to do myself much right, or you much shame. 5.01.308 P
write from it, if you can, in hand or phrase, 5.01.332
or say 'tis not your seal, not your invention. 5.01.333
the world either malice or matter to alter it. WT 1.01. 34 P
of what may chance | or breed upon our absence, 1.02. 12
or my guest? 1.02. 55
it has an elder sister, | or i mistake you. 1.02. 99
there have been | (or i am much deceiv'd) 1.02.191
or, | if thou inclin'st that way, thou art a 1.02.242
or else thou must be counted | a servant grafted 1.02.245
or else a fool | that seest a game play'd home, 1.02.247
or your eye–glass | is thicker than a cuckold's 1.02.268
or heard | (for to a vision so apparent rumor 1.02.269
or thought (for cogitation | resides not in that 1.02.271
wilt confess, | or else be impudently negative, 1.02.274
or else a hovering temporizer, that | canst with 1.02.302
to do't, or, no, is certain | to me a break–neck. 1.02.362
or both yourself and me | cry lost, and so good 1.02.410
as he had seen't or been an instrument | to vice 1.02.415
infection | that e'er was heard or read! 1.02.424
the moon | as or by oath remove or counsel shake 1.02.428
the moon | as or by oath remove or counsel shake 1.02.428
a semicircle, | or a half–moon made with a pen. 2.01. 11
merry, or sad, shall't be? 2.01. 23

and straight | the shrug, the hum or ha (these 2.01. 71
you — or stupefied | or seeming so in skill — 2.01.165
or stupefied | or seeming so in skill — cannot, 2.01.166
or seeming so in skill — cannot, or will not, 2.01.166
ignorant by age, | or thou wert born a fool. 2.01.174
spiritual counsel had, | shall stop or spur me. 2.01.187
is rotten | as ever oak or stone was sound. 2.03. 91
(and by good testimony) or i'll seize thy life, 2.03.137
some place | where chance may nurse or end it. 2.03.183
carriage of it | will clear or end the business. 3.01. 18
course, | even to the guilt or the purgation. 3.02. 7
honor, or in act or will | that way inclining, 3.02. 51
honor, or in act or will | that way inclining, 3.02. 51
boiling | in leads or oils? 3.02.177
what old or newer torture | must i receive, 3.02.177
to crows thy baby–daughter | to be or none, or 3.02.192
thy baby–daughter | to be or none, or little — 3.02.192
you can bring | tincture or lustre in her lip, 3.02.205
heat outwardly or breath within, i'll serve you 3.02.206
either for life or death, upon the earth | of 3.03. 45
or that youth would sleep out the rest; 3.03. 60 P
a boy, or a child, i wonder? 3.03. 70 P
both roaring louder than the sea or weather. 3.03.101 P
it not a crime | to me, or my swift passage, 4.01. 5
ancient'st order was, | or what is now receiv'd. 4.01. 11
might be some allay (or i o'erween to think so), 4.02. 8 P
or take away with thee the very services thou 4.02. 16 P
a race or two of ginger, but that i may beg; 4.03. 47 P
what, by a horseman, or a footman? 4.03. 64 P
i shall there have money, or any thing i want. 4.03. 82 P
or how | should i, in these my borrowed flaunts, 4.04. 22
you must change this purpose, | or i my life. 4.04. 40
or i'll be thine, my fair, | or not my father's; 4.04. 42
or i'll be thine, my fair, | or not my father's; 4.04. 43
the lids of juno's eyes | or cytherea's breath; 4.04.122
or if — not to be buried, | but quick and in 4.04.131
nothing she does, or seems, | but smacks of 4.04.157
down, or a very pleasant thing indeed and sung 4.04.189 P
he hath songs for man or woman, of all sizes; 4.04.191 P
sings 'em over as they were gods or goddesses: 4.04.208 P
ay, good brother, or go about to think. 4.04.217 P
come buy, | buy, lads, or else your lasses cry: 4.04.229
promis'd you more than that, or there be liars. 4.04.237 P
or kill–hole? 4.04.245 P
and five or six honest wives that were present. 4.04.270 P
or thou goest to th' grange, or mill. 4.04.303
or thou goest to th' grange, or mill. 4.04.303
will you buy any tape, | or lace for your cape, 4.04.316
and call this | your lack of love or bounty, you 4.04.354
or ethiopian's tooth, or the fann'd snow that's 4.04.364
tooth, or the fann'd snow that's bolted | by th' 4.04.364
to her service, | or to their own perdition. 4.04.378
or /hoop his body more with thy embraces, | i 4.04.439
for once or twice | i was about to speak, and 4.04.442
all the sun sees, or | the close earth wombs, or 4.04.489
or the profound seas hides | in unknown fadoms, 4.04.490
easier for advice, | or stronger for your need. 4.04.506
the other grow | faster than thought or time. 4.04.554
whether it like me or no, i am a courtier. 4.04.730 P
will either push on or pluck back thy business 4.04.737 P
again with aqua–vitae or some other hot infusion 4.04.786 P
or, from the all that are, took something good 5.01. 14
had heard of a world ransom'd, or one destroy'd. 5.02. 15 P
not say if th' importance were joy or sorrow; 5.02. 18 P
for she hath privately twice or thrice a day, 5.02.105 P
or else 'twere hard luck, being in so 5.02.147 P
yet you look'd upon | or hand of man hath done; 5.03. 17
or rather, thou art she | in thy not chiding; 5.03. 25
the chapel, or resolve you | for more amazement. 5.03. 86
she has liv'd, | or how stol'n from the dead. 5.03.115
or else it must go wrong with you and me; JN 1.01. 41
but whe'er i be as true begot or no, | that 1.01. 75
or the reputed son of cordelion, | lord of thy 1.01.136
now blessed be the hour by night or day | when i 1.01.165
in at the window, or else o'er the hatch. 1.01.171
near or far off, well won is still well shot, 1.01.174
and so am i, whether i smack or no; 1.01.209
to parley or to fight, therefore prepare. 2.01. 78
as like | as rain to water, or devil to his dam. 2.01.128
or lay on that shall make your shoulders crack. 2.01.146
now shame upon you, whe'er she does or no! 2.01.167
peace, lady, pause, or be more temperate. 2.01.195
whose title they admit, arthur's or john's. 2.01.200
or shall we give the signal to our rage, | and 2.01.265
we bear, | or add a royal number to the dead, 2.01.347
make work upon ourselves, for heaven or hell. 2.01.407
win you this city without stroke or wound, 2.01.418
eye i find | a wonder, or a wondrous miracle, 2.01.497
or if you will, to speak more properly, | i will 2.01.514
envenom him with words, or get thee gone, | and 3.01. 63
or, if it must stand still, let wives with child 3.01. 89
priest | shall tithe or toll in our dominions; 3.01.154
or the light loss of england for a friend. 3.01.206
or let the church, our mother, breathe her curse 3.01.256
or if that surly spirit, melancholy, | had bak'd 3.03. 42
or if that thou couldst see me without eyes, 3.03. 48
who hath read or heard | of any kindred action 3.04. 13
woes, | and teaches me to kill or hang myself. 3.04. 56
son, | or madly think a babe of clouts were he. 3.04. 58
or as a little snow, tumbled about, | anon 3.04.176
or "what good love may i perform for you?" 4.01. 49
or, hubert, if you will, cut out my tongue, | so 4.01.100
with any long'd–for change or better state. 4.02. 8
the ice, or add another hue | unto the rainbow, 4.02. 13
or with taper–light | to seek the beauteous eye 4.02. 14
this must be answer'd either here or hence. 4.02. 89
i idly heard — if true or false i know not. 4.02.124
hadst thou but shook thy head or made a pause 4.02.231
or turn'd an eye of doubt upon my face, | as bid 4.02.233
there's few or none do know me; 4.03. 3
or rather then set forward, for 'twill be | two 4.03. 19
two long days' journey, lords, or e'er we meet. 4.03. 20
or, when he doom'd this beauty to a grave, 4.03. 39
or have you read, or heard, or could you think? 4.03. 42
or have you read, or heard, or could you think? 4.03. 42
or have you read, or heard, or could you think? 4.03. 42
or do you almost think, although you see, | that 4.03. 43
the heighth, the crest, or crest unto the crest, 4.03. 46
that ever wall–ey'd wrath or staring rage 4.03. 49
stand by, or i shall gall you, faulconbridge. 4.03. 94
if thou but frown on me, or stir thy foot, | or 4.03. 96
or teach thy hasty spleen to do me shame, | i'll 4.03. 97
or i'll so maul you and your toasting–iron 4.03. 99
or wouldst thou drown thyself, | put but a 4.03.130
or sin of thought | be guilty of the stealing 4.03.135
be minist'red, | or overthrow incurable ensues. 5.01. 16
or if he do, let it at least be said, | they saw 5.01. 75
or useful servingman and instrument | to any 5.02. 81
outside or inside, i will not return | till my 5.02.110
king john did fly an hour or two before | the 5.05. 17
speak quickly, or i shoot. 5.06. 1
i doubt he will be dead or e'er i come. 5.06. 44
let us seek, or straight we shall be sought; 5.07. 79
or worthily, as a good subject should, | on some R2 1.01. 10
earth, | or my divine soul answer it in heaven. 1.01. 38
or any other ground inhabitable | where ever 1.01. 65
what i have spoke, or thou canst worse devise. 1.01. 77
degree | or chivalrous design of knightly trial; 1.01. 81
not light, | if i be traitor or unjustly fight! 1.01. 83
or here or elsewhere to the furthest verge 1.01. 93
or here or elsewhere to the furthest verge 1.01. 93
this arm shall do it, or this life be spent. 1.01.108
away, | men are but gilded loam or painted clay. 1.01.179
or with pale beggar–fear impeach my height 1.01.189
or sound so base a parley, my teeth shall tear 1.01.192
or seven fair branches springing from one root. 1.02. 13
or, if misfortune miss the first career, | be 1.02. 49
so bold | or daring–hardy as to touch the lists, 1.03. 43
however god or fortune cast my lot, | there 1.03. 85
there lives or dies, true to king richard's 1.03. 86
me no more | than an unstringed viol or a harp, 1.03.162
a harp, | or like a cunning instrument cas'd up, 1.03.163
or, being open, put into his hands | that knows 1.03.164
contrive, or complot any ill | 'gainst us, our 1.03.189
us, our state, our subjects, or our land. 1.03.190
or suppose | devouring pestilence hangs in our 1.03.283
no more | than a delightful measure or a dance, 1.03.291
or cloy the hungry edge of appetite | by bare 1.03.296
or wallow naked in december snow | by thinking 1.03.298
of a wall, | or as /a moat defensive to a house, 2.01. 48
it — | like to a tenement or pelting farm. 2.01. 60
or bend one wrinkle on my sovereign's face. 2.01.170
grief, | or else he never would compare between. 2.01.185
or if it be, 'tis with false sorrow's eye, 2.02. 26
or something hath the nothing that i grieve — 2.02. 37
i | know how or which way to order these affairs 2.02.109
these signs forerun the death or fall of kings. 2.04. 15
unless he do profane, steal, or usurp. 3.03. 81
comprising all that may be sworn or said, | his 3.03.111
great | as is my grief, or lesser than my name! 3.03.137
or that i could forget what i have been! 3.03.138
or not remember what i must be now! 3.03.139
or i'll be buried in the king's high way, | some 3.03.155
or shall we play the wantons with our woes | and 3.03.164
of sorrow or of /joy? 3.04. 11
or if of grief, being altogether had, | it adds 3.04. 15
or have mine honor soil'd | with the attainder 4.01. 23
if i dare eat, or drink, or breathe, or live, 4.01. 73
if i dare eat, or drink, or breathe, or live, 4.01. 73
if i dare eat, or drink, or breathe, or live, 4.01. 73
but soft, but see, or rather do not see, | my 5.01. 7
and hate turns one or both | to worthy danger 5.01. 67
sent back like hollowmas or short'st of day. 5.01. 80
even so, or with much more contempt, men's eyes 5.02. 27
or are we like to have? 5.02. 90
man may be, | not like to me, or any of my kin, 5.02.109
my mouth, | unless a pardon ere i rise or speak. 5.03. 32
intended, or committed, was this fault? 5.03. 33
open the door, or i will break it open. 5.03. 45
dies, | or my sham'd life in his dishonor lies: 5.03. 71
or in thy piteous heart plant thou thine ear, 5.03.126
to oxford, or where e'er these traitors are. 5.03.141
but whether they be ta'en or slain we hear not. 5.06. 4
not be | without much shame retold or spoken of. 1H4 1.01. 46
am as melancholy as a gib cat or a lugg'd bear. 1.02. 74 P
or an old lion, or a lover's lute. 1.02. 75 P
or an old lion, or a lover's lute. 1.02. 75 P
yea, or the drone of a lincolnshire bagpipe. 1.02. 76 P
thou to a hare, or the melancholy of moor–ditch? 1.02. 77 P
will set forth before or after them and appoint 1.02.169 P
or misprision | is guilty of this fault, and not 1.03. 27
he should, or he should not — for he made me 1.03. 53
never rise | to do him wrong or any way impeach 1.03. 75
or you shall hear in such a kind from me | as 1.03.121
send us your prisoners, or you will hear of it. 1.03.124
being the agents or base second means, | the 1.03.165
the cords, the ladder, or the hangman rather? 1.03.166
days, | or fill up chronicles in time to come, 1.03.171
if he fall in, good night, or sink or swim. 1.03.194
if he fall in, good night, or sink or swim. 1.03.194
moon, | or dive into the bottom of the deep, 1.03.203
the commonwealth, or rather, not pray to her, 2.01. 80 P
some eight or ten. 2.02. 64 P
nay, tell me if you speak in jest or no. 2.03. 99
with three or four loggerheads amongst three or 2.04. 4 P
amongst three or four score hogsheads. 2.04. 5 P
a pint of bastard in the half–moon," or so. 2.04. 28 P
or, francis, a' thursday; 2.04. 66 P
or indeed, francis, when thou wilt. 2.04. 66 P
that kills me some six or seven dozen of scots 2.04.103 P
a weaver, i could sing psalms, or any thing. 2.04.133 P
if they speak more or less than truth, they are 2.04.171 P
every man of them, or i am a jew else, an ebrew 2.04.179 P
some six or seven fresh men set upon us — 2.04.180 P
if there were not two or three and fifty upon 2.04.187 P
seven, by these hilts, or i am a villain else. 2.04.206 P
at the strappado, or all the racks in the world, 2.04.237 P
as i think, his age some fifty, or, by'r lady, 2.04.424 P
heels for a rabbit–sucker or a poulter's hare. 2.04.437 P
send him to answer thee, or any man, | for any 2.04.516
which calls me pupil or hath read to me? 3.01. 45
why, so can i, or so can any man, | but will 3.01. 53
turn'd, | or a dry wheel grate on the axle–tree, 3.01.130
way to turn tailor, or be redbreast teacher. 3.01.259 P
or i will tear the reckoning from his heart. 3.02.152
money that i borrow'd — three or four times, 3.03. 18 P
a man doth of a death's–head or a memento mori. 3.03. 30 P
been an ignis fatuus or a ball of wildfire, 3.03. 39 P
hal, three or four bonds of forty pound a–piece, 3.03.101 P
thou or any man knows where to have me, thou 3.03.130 P
of the age of two and twenty or threreabouts! 3.03.189 P
on high, | and either we or they must lower lie. 3.03.204
set forth, | or hitherwards intended speedily, 4.01. 92
of death or death's hand for this one half year. 4.01.136
worse than a struck fowl or a hurt wild duck. 4.02. 20 P
albons, or the red–nose innkeeper of daventry. 4.02. 46 P
you, my lord, or any scot that this day lives. 4.03. 12
yea, or to–night. 4.03. 14
more active, valiant, or more valiant, young, 5.01. 90
more daring or more bold, is now alive | to 5.01. 91
or an arm? 5.01.132 P
or take away the grief of a wound? 5.01.132 P
look how we can, or sad or merrily, 5.02. 12
look how we can, or sad or merrily, 5.02. 12
or thou art like | never to hold it up again! 5.04. 39
or that hot termagant scot had paid me scot and 5.04.113 P
or is it fantasy that plays upon our eyesight? 5.04.135
i look to be either earl or duke, i can assure 5.04.142 P
and hold'st it fear or sin | to speak a truth. 2H4 1.01. 95
more than i invent or is invented on me: 1.02. 9 P
dram of a scruple, or indeed a scruple itself. 1.02.130 P
or, a gout of this pox! 1.02.243 P
for the one or the other plays the rogue with my 1.02.244 P
good people, bring a rescue or two. 2.01. 56 P
or i will ride thee a' nights like the mare. 2.01. 76 P
slight drollery, or the story of the prodigal, 2.01.144 P
prodigal, or the german hunting in waterwork, is 2.01.145 P
thy name, or to know thy face to–morrow, or to 2.02. 13 P
or to take note how many pair of silk stockings 2.02. 14 P
once, or to bear the inventory of thy shirts, as 2.02. 16 P
be kin to us, or they will fetch it from japhet. 2.02.117 P
there, | or it will seek me in another place, 2.03. 49
and whether i shall ever see thee again or no, 2.04. 67 P
or is thy boy of the wicked? 2.04.328 P
or honest bardolph, whose zeal burns in his nose 2.04.329 P
what's a joint of mutton or two in a whole lent? 2.04.347 P
couch | a watch–case or a common 'larum–bell? 3.01. 17
or when a man is being whereby 'a may be thought 3.02. 78 P
as the wrathful dove or most magnanimous mouse. 3.02.160 P
sware they were his fancies or his good–nights. 3.02.318 P
upon or near the rate of thirty thousand. 4.01. 22
arms, | not to break peace, or any branch of it, 4.01. 85
or if there were, it not belongs to you. 4.01. 96
or to the place of diff'rence call the swords 4.01.179
west, north, south, or, like a school broke up, 4.02.104
or shall i sweat for you? 4.03. 12 P
one time or other break some gallows' back. 4.03. 29
you think me a swallow, an arrow, or a bullet? 4.03. 33 P
be book'd with the rest of this day's deeds, or, 4.03. 47 P
grace | by seeming cold or careless of his will, 4.04. 29
work as strong | as aconitum or rash gunpowder. 4.04. 48
memory | shall as a pattern or a measure live, 4.04. 76
or else a feast | and takes away the stomach — 4.04.106
or swell my thoughts to any strain of pride, 4.05.170
if any rebel or vain spirit of mine | did with 4.05.171
and i cannot once or twice in a quarter bear out 5.01. 48 P
that either wise bearing or ignorant carriage is 5.01. 75 P
which is four terms, or two actions, and 'a 5.01. 80 P
place, | my person, or my liege's sovereignty. 5.02.101
that war, or peace, or both at once, may be | as 5.02.138
or peace, or both at once, may be | as things 5.02.138
two ways, either to utter them, or conceal them. 5.03.111 P
under which king, besonian? speak, or die. 5.03.113
harry the fourth, or fift? 5.03.114
there hath been a man or two kill'd about her. 5.04. 6 P
or may we cram | within this wooden o the very H5 pr 12
doth his majesty | incline to it, or no? 1.01. 72
or rather swaying more upon our part | than 1.01. 73
or should, or should not, bar us in our claim; 1.02. 12
or should, or should not, bar us in our claim; 1.02. 12
you should fashion, wrest, or bow your reading, 1.02. 14
or nicely charge your understanding soul | with 1.02. 15
to which is fixed, as an aim or butt, 1.02.186
bend it to our awe, | or break it all to pieces. 1.02.225
or there we'll sit, | ruling in large and ample 1.02.225
or lay these bones in an unworthy urn, 1.02.228
speak freely of our acts, or else our grave, 1.02.231
or shall we sparingly show you far off | the 1.02.239
and board a dozen or fourteen gentlewomen that 2.01. 33 P
cut thy throat one time or other in fair terms, 2.01. 69 P
or are they spare in diet, | free from gross 2.02.131
free from gross passion, or of mirth or anger, 2.02.132
free from gross passion, or of mirth or anger, 2.02.132
wheresome'er he is, either in heaven or in hell! 2.03. 8 P
three or four times. 2.03. 19 P
or else what follows? 2.04. 96
either past or not arriv'd to pith and puissance 3.pr. 21
or close the wall up with our english dead. 3.01. 2
pockets as their gloves or their handkerchers; 3.02. 48 P
as partly touching or concerning the disciplines 3.02. 96 P
de gud service, or i'll lig i' the grund for it; 3.02.115 P
ay, or go to death; 3.02.116 P
or, like to men proud of destruction, | defy us 3.03. 4
or, guilty in defense, be thus destroy'd? 3.03. 43
age, or else you may be marvellously mistook. 3.06. 80 P
of the french upbraided or abus'd in disdainful 3.06.111 P
or any such proverb so little kin to the purpose 3.07. 67 P
tent to–night, are those stars or suns upon it? 3.07. 70 P
with four or five most vile and ragged foils 4.pr. 50
or art thou base, common, and popular? 4.01. 38
ay, or more than we should seek after; 4.01.130 P
or if a servant, under his master's command 4.01.150 P
or not dying, the time was blessedly lost 4.01.181 P
or they will pluck | the gay new coats o'er the 4.03.117
or mangled shalt thou be by this my sword. 4.04. 39
with /mistful eyes, or they will issue too. 4.06. 34
the pig, or the great, or the mighty, or the 4.07. 16 P
pig, or the great, or the mighty, or the huge, 4.07. 16 P
or the mighty, or the huge, or the magnanimous, 4.07. 16 P
or the huge, or the magnanimous, are all one 4.07. 16 P
us, bid them come down, | or void the field; 4.07. 59
herald, | i know not if the day be ours or no, 4.07. 84
or if i can see my glove in his cap, which he 4.07.128 P
as any's in the universal world, or in france, 4.08. 10 P

universal world, or in france, or in england! 4.08. 10 P
silling, i warrant you, or i will change it. 4.08. 71 P
or take that praise from god | which is his only 4.08.115
of my leek, or i will peat his pate four days. 5.01. 41 P
take it, or i have another leek in my pocket, 5.01. 61 P
and galling at this gentleman twice or thrice. 5.01. 74 P
view, | what rub or what impediment there is, 5.02. 33
have lost, or do not learn for want of time, 5.02. 57
augment, or alter, as your wisdoms best | shall 5.02. 87
dignity, | any thing in or out of our demands, 5.02. 89
go with the princes, or stay here with us? 5.02. 91
put me to verses, or to dance for your sake, 5.02.132 P
or by vauting into my saddle with my armor on my 5.02.137 P
or if i might buffet for my love, or bound my 5.02.139 P
for my love, or bound my horse for her favors, i 5.02.140 P
the moon, or rather the sun and not the moon; 5.02.163 P
that never may ill office, or fell jealousy, 5.02.363
or shall we think the subtile–witted french 1H6 1.01. 25
awe, | more than god or religious churchmen may. 1.01. 40
soul will make | than julius caesar or bright — 1.01. 56
or the loss of those great towns | will make him 1.01. 63
most of the rest slaughter'd or took likewise. 1.01.147
or bring him in obedience to your yoke. 1.01.164
or piteous they will look, like drowned mice. 1.02. 12
me, | when he sees me go back one foot or fly. 1.02. 21
i think by some odd gimmors or device | their 1.02. 41
shall we give o'er orleance, or no? 1.02.125
or whose will stands but mine? 1.03. 11
thou art no friend to god or to the king. 1.03. 25
open the gates, or i'll shut thee out shortly. 1.03. 26
or we'll burst them open, if that you come not 1.03. 28
and not protector, of the king or realm. 1.03. 32
in spite of pope or dignities of church, | here 1.03. 50
not to wear, handle, or use any sword, weapon, 1.03. 78 P
use any sword, weapon, or dagger, henceforward, 1.03. 78 P
they may vex us with shot or with assault. 1.04. 13
or by what means gots thou to be releas'd? 1.04. 25
famish'd, | or with light skirmishes enfeebled. 1.04. 69
whilst any trump did sound, or drum struck up, 1.04. 80
pucelle or puzzel, dolphin or dogfish, | your 1.04.107
pucelle or puzzel, dolphin or dogfish, | your 1.04.107
devil or devil's dam, i'll conjure thee. 1.05. 5
or tear the lions out of england's coat; 1.05. 28
the wolf, | or horse or oxen from the leopard, 1.05. 31
the wolf, | or horse or oxen from the leopard, 1.05. 31
in spite of us, or aught that we could do. 1.05. 37
if any noise or soldier you perceive | near to 2.01. 2
and here will talbot mount, or make his grave. 2.01. 34
more venturous or desperate than this. 2.01. 45
sleeping or waking, must i still prevail, | or 2.01. 56
or will you blame and lay the fault on me? 2.01. 57
then how, or which way, should they first break 2.01. 71
no further of the case, | how or which way. 2.01. 73
that could not live asunder day or night. 2.02. 31
or else was wrangling somerset in th' error? 2.04. 6
or durst not for his craven heart say thus. 2.04. 87
grave, | or flourish to the height of my degree. 2.04.111
or make my will th' advantage of my good. 2.05.129
or aught intend'st to lay unto my charge, | do 3.01. 4
or thou shouldst find thou hast dishonor'd me. 3.01. 9
or am not able | verbatim to rehearse the method 3.01. 12
if i were covetous, ambitious, or perverse, | as 3.01. 29
or how haps it i seek not to advance | or raise 3.01. 31
haps it i seek not to advance | or raise myself, 3.01. 32
state holy or unhallow'd, what of that? 3.01. 59
or who should study to prefer a peace, | if holy 3.01.110
he shall submit, or i will never yield. 3.01.118
or i would see his heart out ere the priest 3.01.120
ay, we may march in england, or in france, | not 3.01.186
or else let talbot perish with this shame. 3.02. 57
fools, | to try if that our own be ours or no. 3.02. 63
or else reproach be talbot's greatest fame! 3.02. 76
france, | either to get the town again, or die: 3.02. 79
so sure i swear to get the town, or die. 3.02. 84
roan | and will be partner of your weal or woe. 3.02. 92
what is the trust or strength of foolish man? 3.02.112
her words, | or nature makes me suddenly relent. 3.03. 59
or been reguerdon'd with so much as thanks, 3.04. 23
or else this blow should broach thy dearest 3.04. 40
before we met, or that a stroke was given, 4.01. 22
or whether that such cowards ought to wear 4.01. 28
wear | this ornament of knighthood, yea or no? 4.01. 29
or doth this churlish superscription | pretend 4.01. 53
or with whom? 4.01. 84
persuade | than i am able to instruct or teach; 4.01.159
broils, | than yet can be imagin'd or suppos'd. 4.01.186
too late comes rescue, he is ta'en or slain; 4.04. 42
brave death by speaking, whether he will or no; 4.07. 25
i trow, | or be inferior to the proudest peer. 5.01. 57
that neither in birth, or for authority, | the 5.01. 59
thy knee, | or sack this country with a mutiny. 5.01. 62
wilt thou accept of ransom, yea or no? 5.03. 80
to weep | or to exclaim on fortune's fickleness. 5.03.134
that suffolk doth not flatter, face, or feign. 5.03.142
free from oppression or the stroke of war, | my 5.03.155
or else, when thou didst keep my lambs a–field, 5.04. 30
you to break your necks or hang yourselves! 5.04. 91
or we will plague thee with incessant wars. 5.04.154
or arrive | where i may have fruition of her 5.05. 8
or one that at a triumph, having vow'd | to try 5.05. 31
as market men for oxen, sheep, or horse. 5.05. 54
or for that | my tender youth was never yet 5.05. 80
my dreams, | in courtly company, or at my beads, 2H6 1.01. 27
or hath mine uncle beauford and myself, | with 1.01. 88
or thou or i, somerset, will be /protector, 1.01.178
or thou or i, somerset, will be /protector, 1.01.178
despite duke humphrey or the cardinal. 1.01.179
which i will win from france, or else be slain. 1.01.213
above the reach or compass of thy thought? 1.02. 46
which, | or somerset or york, all's one to me. 1.03.102
which, | or somerset or york, all's one to me. 1.03.102
whether your grace be worthy, yea or no, 1.03.107
here | without discharge, money, or furniture, 1.03.169
sirrah, or you must fight, or else be hang'd. 1.03.217
sirrah, or you must fight, or else be hang'd. 1.03.217
crown for this, | or all my fence shall fail. 2.01. 51
cam'st thou here by chance | or of devotion, to 2.01. 86
am, i yield to thee, | or to the meanest groom. 2.01.181
or more afraid to fight, than is the appellant, 2.03. 57
or count them happy that enjoys the sun? 2.04. 39
or will ye not observe | the strangeness of his 3.01. 4
or be admitted to your highness' council. 3.01. 27
you can, | or else conclude my words effectual. 3.01. 41
or, if he were not privy to those faults, | yet, 3.01. 47
as is the sucking lamb or harmless dove. 3.01. 71
given | to dream on evil or to work my downfall. 3.01. 73
long, | or sell my title for a glorious grave. 3.01. 92
the king, | or any groat i hoarded to my use, 3.01.113
or foul felonious thief that fleec'd poor 3.01.129
above the felon or what trespass else. 3.01.132
best, | do or undo, as if ourself were here. 3.01.196
e'er i prov'd thee false or fear'd thy faith. 3.01.205
or as the snake roll'd in a flow'ring bank, 3.01.228
sleeping, or waking, 'tis no matter how, | so he 3.01.263
now, york, or never, steel thy fearful thoughts, 3.01.331
to be, or what thou art | resign to death; 3.01.333
shall blow ten thousand souls to heaven or hell; 3.01.350
might liquid tears or heart–offending groans 3.02. 60
or blood–consuming sighs recall his life, | i 3.02. 61
shore, | or turn our stern upon a dreadful rock? 3.02. 91
or thou not false like him? 3.02.119
away even now, or i will drag thee hence. 3.02.229
death, | or banished fair england's territories, 3.02.245
in pain of your dislike, or pain of death, | yet 3.02.257
that they will guard you, whe'er you will or no, 3.02.265
answer from the king, or we will all break in! 3.02.278
or like an overcharged gun, recoil, | and turns 3.02.331
i will repeal thee, or, be well assur'd, 3.02.349
soul, | or i should breathe it so into thy body, 3.02.398
can i make men live, whe'er they will or no? 3.03. 10
or with their blood stain this discolored shore. 4.01. 11
a thousand crowns, or else lay down your head. 4.01. 16
and so much shall you give, or off goes yours. 4.01. 17
gualtier or walter, which it is, i care not. 4.01. 38
or rather, of stealing a cade of herrings. 4.02. 33 P
or hast thou a mark to thyself, like a honest 4.02.103 P
stand, villain, stand, or i'll fell thee down. 4.02.115 P
therefore yield, or die. 4.02.127
tongue of an enemy be a good counsellor, or no? 4.02.172 P
his head will stand steadier on a pole, or no. 4.07. 96 P
have i affected wealth or honor? 4.07. 98
be as free as heart can wish or tongue can tell. 4.07.125 P
bold to sound retreat or parley when i command 4.08. 4 P
you, | or let a /rebel lead you to your deaths? 4.08. 13
or is he but retir'd to make him strong? 4.09. 9
expect your highness' doom, of life or death. 4.09. 12
or unto death, to do my country good. 4.09. 43
i can eat grass, or pick a sallet another while, 4.10. 8 P
or gather wealth, i care not with what envy. 4.10. 21
or cut not out the burly–bon'd clown in chines 4.10. 56 P
words, | except a sword or sceptre balance it. 5.01. 9
art thou a messenger, or come of pleasure? 5.01. 16
or why thou, being a subject as i am, | against 5.01. 19
or dare to bring thy force so near the court. 5.01. 22
on sheep or oxen could i spend my fury. 5.01. 27
or wherefore dost abuse it if thou hast it? 5.01.172
of one or both of us the time is come. 5.02. 13
is either slain or wounded dangerous; 3H6 1.01. 11
by words or blows here let us win our right. 1.01. 37
king henry, be thy title right or wrong, | lord 1.01.159
what mutter you, or what conspire you, lords? 1.01.165
york, | or i will fill the house with armed men, 1.01.167
or live in peace abandon'd and despis'd! 1.01.188
i, | or felt that pain which i did for him once, 1.01.221
once, | or nourish'd him as i did with my blood, 1.01.222
your right depends not on his life or death. 1.02. 11
i will be king, or die. 1.02. 35
or is it fear | that makes him close his eyes? 1.03. 10
or lambs pursu'd by hunger–starved wolves. 1.04. 5
like men born to renown by life or death. 1.04. 8
and cried, "a crown, or else a glorious tomb! 1.04. 16
a sceptre, or an earthly sepulchre!" 1.04. 17
or, with the rest, where is your darling, 1.04. 78
unto us, | or as the south to the septentrion. 1.04.136
or whether he be scap'd away or no | from 2.01. 2
or whether he be scap'd away or no | from 2.01. 2
or had he scap'd, methinks we should have heard 2.01. 6
or as a bear, encompass'd round with dogs, | who 2.01. 15
dazzle mine eyes, or do i see three suns? 2.01. 25
thy death, | or die renowned by attempting it. 2.01. 88
either that is thine, or else thou wert not his. 2.01. 94
or whether 'twas report of her success, | or 2.01.125
or more than common fear of clifford's rigor, 2.01.126
or like /an /idle thresher with a flail, | fell 2.01.131
or shall we on the helmets of our foes | tell 2.01.163
i come to pierce it, or to give thee mine. 2.01.203
head, | or bide the mortal fortune of the field? 2.02. 83
thee, | or any he the proudest of thy sort. 2.02. 97
defy them then, or else hold close thy lips. 2.02.118
say, henry, shall i have my right, or no? 2.02.126
as venom toads, or lizards' dreadful stings. 2.02.138
or bath'd thy growing with our heated bloods. 2.02.169
and either victory, or else a grave. 2.02.174
or strike, ungentle death! 2.03. 6
mine | or fortune given me measure of revenge. 2.03. 32
where e'er it be, in heaven or in earth. 2.03. 43
expostulate, make speed, | or else come after. 2.05.136
do, | or as thy father and his father did, 2.06. 15
if friend or foe, let him be gently used. 2.06. 45
fight closer or, good faith, you'll catch a blow 3.02. 23
please you dismiss me, either with ay or no. 3.02. 78
one way or other, she is for a king, | and she 3.02. 87
and she shall be my love or else my queen. 3.02. 88
or an unlick'd bear–whelp | that carries no 3.02.161
myself, | or hew my way out with a bloody axe. 3.02.181
your grant, or your denial, shall be mine. 3.03.130
warwick, this is some post to us or thee. 3.03.162
or than for strength and safety of our country. 3.03.211
well as lewis of france or the earl of warwick, 4.01. 11
she better would have fitted me or clarence; 4.01. 54
or else you would not have bestow'd the heir 4.01. 56
leave me, or tarry, edward will be king, | and 4.01. 65
what danger or what sorrow can befall thee | so 4.01. 76
what letters or what news | from france? 4.01. 84
they are already or quickly will be landed. 4.01.132
till warwick or himself be quite suppress'd. 4.03. 6
honor now or never! 4.03. 24
stay, or thou diest! 4.03. 27
his guard | or by his foe surpris'd at unawares; 4.04. 9
lest with my sighs or tears i blast or drown 4.04. 23
lest with my sighs or tears i blast or drown 4.04. 23
by fair or foul means we must enter in, | for 4.07. 14
shut | but in the night or in the time of war. 4.07. 36
or modest dian, circled with her nymphs, | shall 4.08. 21
where slept our scouts, or how are they seduc'd, 5.01. 19
or did he make the jest against his will? 5.01. 30
strike now, or else the iron cools. 5.01. 49
or shall we beat the stones about thine ears? 5.01.108
come to me, friend or foe, | and tell me who is 5.02. 5
and tell me who is victor, york or warwick? 5.02. 6
come quickly, montague, or i am dead. 5.02. 39
or else you famish — that's a threefold death. 5.04. 32
'twere childish weakness to lament or fear. 5.04. 38
peace, willful boy, or i will charm your tongue. 5.05. 31
heave it shall some weight, or break my back: 5.07. 24
long, | i will deliver you, or else lie for you. R3 1.01.115
or any creeping venom'd thing that lives! 1.02. 20
villains, set down the corse, or, by saint paul, 1.02. 36
or, by saint paul, i'll strike thee to my foot, 1.02. 41
or earth gape open wide and eat him quick, | as 1.02. 65
take up the sword again, or take up me. 1.02.183
and entertain a score or two of tailors | to 1.02.256
or, if she be accus'd on true report, | bear 1.03. 27
or thee? 1.03. 57
or thee? 1.03. 57
or any of your faction? 1.03. 57
ere you were queen, ay, or your husband king, 1.03.120
ay, and much better blood than his or thine. 1.03.125
or edward's soft and pitiful, like mine: 1.03.140
there's few or none will entertain it. 1.04.131 P
or who pronounc'd | the bitter sentence of poor 1.04.185
he needs no indirect or lawless course | to cut 1.04.218
/god, | when i am cold in love to you or yours. 2.01. 40
by false intelligence or wrong surmise | hold me 2.01. 55
me a foe — | if i /unwittingly, or in my rage, 2.01. 57
but when your carters or your waiting vassals 2.01.122
or like obedient subjects follow him | to his 2.02. 45
or by his father there were none at all; 2.03. 24
it so, | 'tis more than we deserve or i expect. 2.03. 37
to–morrow, or next day, they will be here. 2.04. 3
why, or for what, the nobles were committed | is 2.04. 47
or let me die, to look on /death no more! 2.04. 65
knows, | seldom or never jumpeth with the heart. 3.01. 11
not | to tell us whether they will come or no! 3.01. 23
some day or two | your highness shall repose you 3.01. 64
or else reported | successively from age to age, 3.01. 72
again, | or die a soldier as i liv'd a king. 3.01. 93
yours, | or i of his, my lord, than you of mine. 3.04. 12
there's some conceit or other likes him well, 3.04. 49
can lesser hide his love or hate than he, | for 3.04. 52
/mayor, | would you imagine, or almost believe, 3.05. 35
think you we are turks or infidels? 3.05. 41
or that we would, against the form of law, 3.05. 42
even where his raging eye or savage heart, 3.05. 83
and towards three or four a' clock | look for 3.05.101
untouch'd or slightly handled in discourse. 3.07. 19
but, like dumb statues or breathing stones, 3.07. 25
lord, | to visit him to–morrow or next day. 3.07. 60
or lowly factor for another's gain; 3.07.134
silence, | or bitterly to speak in your reproof, 3.07.142
best fitteth my degree or your condition. 3.07.143
yet know, whe'er you accept our suit or no, 3.07.214
back, | to bear her burthen whe'er i will or no, 3.07.229
but if black scandal or foul–fac'd reproach 3.07.231
or else i swoon with this dead–killing news! 4.01. 35
or shall they last, and we rejoice in them? 4.02. 6
or else my kingdom stands on brittle glass. 4.02. 61
good or bad news, that thou com'st in so bluntly 4.03. 45
or with the clamorous report of war | thus will 4.04.153
or i with grief and extreme age shall perish 4.04.186
or shall i say her uncle? 4.04.338
or he that slew her brothers and her uncles? 4.04.339
ratcliffe, thyself — or catesby — where is he? 4.04.441
or else his head's assurance is but frail. 4.04.496
banks | if they were his assistants, yea or no; 4.04.524
at pembroke or at /ha'rford–west in wales. 4.05. 10
six or seven thousand is their utmost power. 5.03. 10
rescue, fair lord, or else the day is lost! 5.04. 6
those that come to see | only a show or two, and H8 pr 10
or to see a fellow | in a long motley coat pr 15
or has given all before, and he begins | a new 1.01. 71
or proclaim | there's difference in no persons. 1.01.138
quench, | or but allay, the fire of passion. 1.01.149
or wolf, or both (for he is equal rav'nous | as 1.01.159
or wolf, or both (for he is equal rav'nous | as 1.01.159
or else you suffer | too hard an exclamation. 1.02. 51
(once weak ones) is | not ours, or not allow'd; 1.02. 83
in fear our motion will be mock'd or carp'd at, 1.02. 86
here where we sit, or sit | state–statues only. 1.02. 87
is but merely | a fit or two o' th' face — but 1.03. 7
had been councillors | to pepin or clotharius, 1.03. 10
honest men, | or pack to their old playfellows. 1.03. 33
were but now confessor | to one or two of these! 1.04. 16
lady | or gentleman that is not freely merry 1.04. 36
you are a churchman, or, i'll tell you, cardinal 1.04. 88
but all | was either pitied in him or forgotten. 2.01. 29
or some about him near, have out of malice | to 2.01.157
or this imperious man will work us all | from 2.02. 46
glad, or sorry | as i saw it inclin'd. 2.04. 26
or made it not mine too? 2.04. 29
or which of your friends | have i not strove to 2.04. 29
my bond to wedlock or my love and duty, 2.04. 40
that | we are a queen (or long have dream'd so), 2.04. 71
nay, before, | or god will punish me. 2.04. 75
against you, nor injustice | for you or any. 2.04. 90
or how far further shall, is warranted | by a 2.04. 91
or | laid any scruple in your way which might 2.04.150
or ever | have to you, but with thanks to god 2.04.152
present state, | or touch of her good person? 2.04.156
her male issue | or died where they were made, 2.04.193
or shortly after | this world had air'd them. 2.04.193
and grief of heart | fall asleep, or hearing, 3.01. 14
looking | either for such men or such business. 3.01. 76
or be a known friend, 'gainst his highness' 3.01. 85

or felt the flatteries that grow upon it! 3.01.144
gone by him, or at least | strangely neglected? 3.02. 10
it, say withal | if you are bound to us, or no. 3.02.165
till i find more than will or words to do it 3.02.236
that, without the king's assent or knowledge, 3.02.310
you writ to rome, or else | to foreign princes, 3.02.313
the knowledge | either of king or council, when 3.02.317
the king's will or the state's allowance, | a 3.02.322
more pangs and fears than wars or women have; 3.02.370
or gild again the noble troops that waited 3.02.411
down | to rest a while, some half an hour or so, 4.01. 66
i will, | or let me lose the fashion of a man! 4.02.159
or else no witness | would come against you. 5.01.107
or i fall into | the trap is laid for me! 5.01.141
i will have more or scold it out of him. 5.01.173
i'll have more, or else unsay't; 5.01.175
that had a head to hit, either young or old, 5.03. 24
he or she, cuckold or cuckold–maker, | let me 5.03. 25
or old, | he or she, cuckold or cuckold–maker, 5.03. 25
or have we some strange indian with the great 5.03. 33 P
of tower–hill or the limbs of limehouse, their 5.03. 62 P
or i'll find | a marshalsea shall hold ye play 5.03. 85
stand close up, or i'll make your head ache. 5.03. 88
to take their ease, | and sleep an act or two; ep 3
TRO cooling too, or ye may chance burn your lips. 1.01. 26 P
than ever i saw her look, or any woman else. 1.01. 33 P
lest hector or my father should perceive me, | i 1.01. 36
i do not care whether you do or no. 1.01. 80 P
unless th' are drunk, sick, or have no legs. 1.02. 17 P
many hands and no use, or purblind argus, all 1.02. 29 P
the gods are above, time must friend or end. 1.02. 78 P
he has not past three or four hairs on his chin 1.02.112 P
a sister were a grace, or a daughter a goddess, 1.02.236 P
and what hath mass or matter, by itself | lies 1.03. 29
to harbor fled, | or made a toast for neptune. 1.03. 45
force should be right, or rather, right and 1.03.116
enough, patroclus, | or give me ribs of steel! 1.03.177
excitements to the field, or speech for truce, 1.03.182
success or loss, what is or is not, serves | as 1.03.183
success or loss, what is or is not, serves | as 1.03.183
or those that with the fineness of their souls 1.03.209
or the men of troy | are ceremonious courtiers. 1.03.233
shall make it good, or do his best to do it: 1.03.274
that means not, hath not, or is not in love! 1.03.288
if then one is, or hath, /or means to be, | that 1.03.289
in rank achilles must or now be cropp'd | or, 1.03.318
in rank achilles must or now be cropp'd | or, 1.03.319
a scantling | of good or bad unto the general, 1.03.342
but, hit or miss, | our project's life this 1.03.383
lies in your sinews, or else there be liars. 2.01. 99 P
mercury from jove, | or like a star disorb'd? 2.02. 46
troy burns, or else let helen go. 2.02.112
or is your blood | so madly hot that no 2.02.115
without a heart to dare, or sword to draw, 2.02.157
whose life were ill bestow'd, or death unfam'd, 2.02.159
or rather, the neapolitan bone–ache! 2.03. 18 P
of our place, | or know not what we are. 2.03. 83
dispose | without observance or respect of any, 2.03.165
or covetous of praise — 2.03.237
ay, or surly borne — 2.03.238
or strange, or self–affected! 2.03.239
or strange, or self–affected! 2.03.239
the edge of steel | or force of greekish sinews. 3.01.153
sounding destruction, or some joy too fine, 3.02. 23
man, | or that we women had men's privilege | of 3.02.128
but you are wise, | or else you love not; 3.02.156
or that persuasion could but thus convince me 3.02.164
if i be false, or swerve a hair from truth, 3.02.184
false | as air, as water, wind, or sandy earth, 3.02.192
as fox to lamb, or wolf to heifer's calf, | pard 3.02.193
pard to the hind, or step–dame to her son, | yea 3.02.194
or else disdainfully, which shall shake him more 3.03. 53
parted, | how much in having, or without or in, 3.03. 97
parted, | how much in having, or without or in, 3.03. 97
reverb'rate | the voice again, or, like a gate 3.03.121
or /hedge aside from the direct forthright, 3.03.158
than breath or pen can give expressure to. 3.03.204
aleven of the clock it will go one way or other. 3.03.296 P
as heart can think or courage execute. 4.01. 14
let's have your company, or, if you please, 4.01. 40
(or rather call my thought a certain knowledge) 4.01. 42
deserves fair helen best, | myself, or menelaus? 4.01. 55
or brew it to a weak and colder palate, | the 4.04. 7
or my heart will be blown up by /th' /root. 4.04. 54 P
in kissing, do you render or receive? 4.05. 36
you are an odd man, give even or give none. 4.05. 41
or do you purpose | a victor shall be known? 4.05. 66
or shall they be divided | by any voice or order 4.05. 69
be divided | by any voice or order of the field? 4.05. 70
it, either to the uttermost, | or else a breath. 4.05. 92
him — whether there, or there, or there? 4.05.243
him — whether there, or there, or there? 4.05.243
deeds to match these words, | or may i never — 4.05.260
alone | till accident or purpose bring you to't. 4.05.262
the surgeon's box, or the patient's wound. 5.01. 11 P
fall greeks, fail fame, honor or go or stay, 5.01. 43
fall greeks, fail fame, honor or go or stay, 5.01. 43
a puttock, or a herring without a roe, i would 5.01. 62 P
both /at /once, to those | that go or tarry. 5.01. 78
diomed, | keep hector company an hour or two. 5.01. 81
i come to lose my arm, or win my sleeve. 5.03. 96
patroclus ta'en or slain, and palamedes | sore 5.05. 13
diomed, | to reinforcement, or we perish all. 5.05. 16
and there they fly or die, like scaling sculls 5.05. 22
i'll be ta'en too, | or bring him off. 5.06. 25
who shall tell priam so, or hecuba? 5.10. 15
or if you cannot weep, yet give some groans, 5.10. 49
COR wondrous malicious, | or be accus'd of folly. 1.01. 89
but it proceeds or comes from them to you, | and 1.01.153
of fire upon the ice, | or hailstone in the sun. 1.01.174
but it is not known | whether for east or west. 1.02. 10
or express yourself in a more comfortable sort. 1.03. 1 P
/that's task'd to mow | or all or lose his hire. 1.03. 37
/that's task'd to mow | or all or lose his hire. 1.03. 37
or whether his fall enrag'd him, or how 'twas, 1.03. 63 P
or whether his fall enrag'd him, or how 'twas, 1.03. 63 P
or, by the fires of heaven, i'll leave the foe 1.04. 39
let's fetch him off, or make remain alike. 1.04. 62

was forc'd to wheel | three or four miles about, 1.06. 20
ransoming him, or pitying, threat'ning th' other 1.06. 36
let him alone, or so many so minded, | wave thus 1.06. 73
nose that bled, or foil'd some debile wretch — 1.09. 48
you shall perceive | whether i blush or no; 1.09. 70
him beard to beard, | he's mine, or i am his. 1.10. 12
him some way, | or wrath or craft may get him. 1.10. 16
him some way, | or wrath or craft may get him. 1.10. 16
good or bad? 2.01. 3 P
or else your actions would grow wondrous single; 2.01. 36 P
or to be entomb'd in an ass's pack–saddle. 2.01. 89 P
it must fall out | to him, or our authorities, 2.01.244
care whether they love or hate him manifests the 2.02. 12 P
he did not care whether he had their love or no, 2.02. 17 P
or, seeing it, of such childish friendliness 2.03.175
or else it would have gall'd his surly nature, 2.03.195
or had you tongues to cry | against the 2.03.204
stop, | or all will fall in broil. 3.01. 33
spirit, | or never be so noble as a consul, 3.01. 56
or i shall shake thy bones | out of thy garments 3.01.178
or let us stand to our authority, | or let us 3.01.207
us stand to our authority, | or let us lose it. 3.01.208
his trident, | or jove for 's power to thunder. 3.01.256
i may be heard, i would crave a word or two, 3.01.281
he must come, | or what is worst will follow. 3.01.334
death on the wheel, or at wild horses' heels, 3.02. 2
heels, | or pile ten hills on the tarpeian rock, 3.02. 3
ordinance stood up | to speak of peace or war. 3.02. 13
how is it less or worse | that it shall hold 3.02. 48
or say to them, | thou art their soldier, and, 3.02. 80
or defend yourself | by calmness or by absence. 3.02. 94
or defend yourself | by calmness or by absence. 3.02. 95
or the virgin voice | that babies lull asleep! 3.02.114
or never trust to what my tongue can do | i' th' 3.02.136
death, for fine, or banishment, then let them, 3.03. 15
son | will or exceed the common or be caught 4.01. 32
will or exceed the common or be caught | with 4.01. 32
target from thy brawn, | or lose mine arm for't. 4.05.121
of rome, | or rudely visit them in parts remote, 4.05.142
summer butterflies, | or butchers killing flies. 4.06. 95
of yourself, or else | to him had left it soly. 4.07. 15
that which shall break his neck, or hazard mine, 4.07. 25
or whether nature, | not to be other than one 4.07. 41
for one poor grain or two, to leave unburnt 5.01. 27
for one poor grain or two? 5.01. 28
the morning, are unapt | to give or to forgive; 5.01. 53
or with the palsied intercession of such a 5.02. 43 P
or of some death more long in spectatorship and 5.02. 65 P
or those doves' eyes, | which can make gods 5.03. 27
or, if you'ld ask, remember this before: 5.03. 79
or capitulate | again with rome's mechanics. 5.03. 82
alack, or we must lose | the country, our dear 5.03.109
the country, our dear nurse, or else thy person, 5.03.110
or else | triumphantly tread on thy country's 5.03.115
or granted less, aufidius? 5.03.193
ere he express himself or move the people | with 5.06. 54
with six aufidiuses, or more, his tribe, | to 5.06.128
servant, or endure | your heaviest censure. 5.06.140
TIT or climb my palace, till from forth this place 1.01.327
and shall, or him we will accompany. 1.01.358
but i know it is | (whether by device or no, the 1.01.395
traitor, if rome have law, or we have power, 1.01.403
secure of thunder's crack or lightning flash, 2.01. 3
'tis not the difference of a year or two | makes 2.01. 31
makes me less gracious, or thee more fortunate; 2.01. 32
become so loose, | or bassianus so degenerate, 2.01. 66
without controlment, justice, or revenge? 2.01. 68
or know ye not, in rome | how furious and 2.01. 75
why then it seems some certain snatch or so 2.01. 95
this way, or not at all, stand you in hope. 2.01.119
or is it dian habited like her, | who hath 2.03. 57
breeds, | unless the nightly owl or fatal raven; 2.03. 97
should straight fall mad, or else die suddenly. 2.03.104
or be ye not henceforth call'd my children. 2.03.115
or, wanting strength to do thee so much good, 2.03.238
again, | till thou art here aloft or i below. 2.03.244
or, had he heard the heavenly harmony | which 2.04. 48
weep, | or, if not so, thy noble heart to break: 3.01. 60
or brought a faggot to bright–burning troy? 3.01. 69
or make some sign how i may do thee ease. 3.01.121
or shall we cut away our hands like thine? 3.01.130
or shall we bite our tongues, and in dumb shows 3.01.131
let marcus, lucius, or thyself, old titus, | or 3.01.152
or any one of you, chop off your hand | and send 3.01.153
or with our sighs we'll breathe the welkin dim, 3.01.211
unless some fit or frenzy do possess her; 4.01. 17
or else to heaven she heaves them for revenge. 4.01. 40
or slunk not saturnine, as tarquin erst, | that 4.01. 63
apollo, pallas, jove, or mercury, | inspire me, 4.01. 66
and see their blood or die with this reproach. 4.01. 94
groan | and not relent, or not compassion him? 4.01.124
well, more or less, or ne'er a whit at all, 4.02. 53
well, more or less, or ne'er a whit at all, 4.02. 53
now help, or woe betide thee evermore! 4.02. 56
or some of you shall smoke for it in rome. 4.02.111
thinks, with jove in heaven, or some where else, 4.03. 41
than prosecute the meanest or the best | for 4.04. 33
with frost, or grass beat down with storms. 4.04. 71
than baits to fish, or honey–stalks to sheep, 4.04. 91
up, | or else i will discover nought to thee. 5.01. 85
as kill a man, or else devise his death, 5.01.128
ravish a maid, or plot the way to do it, 5.01.129
there's not a hollow cave or lurking–place, | no 5.02. 35
no vast obscurity or misty vale, | where bloody 5.02. 36
where bloody murther or detested rape | can 5.02. 37
stab them, or tear them on thy chariot–wheels, 5.02. 47
goths, | or at the least make them his enemies. 5.02. 79
me, | or else i'll call my brother back again, 5.02.135
and that more dear | than hands or tongue, her 5.02.176
or who hath brought the fatal engine in | that 5.03. 86
or more than any living man could bear. 5.03.127
if any one relieves or pities him, | for the 5.03.181
ROM take the wall of any man or maid of montague's. 1.01. 12 P
the heads of the maids, or their maidenheads, 1.01. 25 P
sword, | or manage it to part these men with me. 1.01. 69
to the air | or dedicate his beauty to the /sun. 1.01.153
i'll know his grievance, or be much denied. 1.01.157
i'll pay that doctrine, or else die in debt. 1.01.238

even or odd, of all days in the year, | come 1.03. 16
or shall we on without apology? 1.04. 2
made by the joiner squirrel or old grub, | time 1.04. 60
being thus frighted, swears a prayer or two, 1.04. 87
manners shall lie all in one or two men's hands, 1.05. 3 P
am i the master here, or you? 1.05. 78
go, | be quiet, or — more light, more light! 1.05. 87
or, if thou wilt not, be but sworn my love, 2.02. 35
shall i hear more, or shall i speak at this? 2.02. 37
or if thou thinkest i am too quickly won, | i'll 2.02. 95
or, if thou wilt, swear by thy gracious self, 2.02.113
or if not so, then here i hit it right — | our 2.03. 41
hildings and harlots, thisby a grey eye or so, 2.04. 43 P
and spurs, swits and spurs, or i'll cry a match. 2.04. 69 P
is thy news good or bad? 2.05. 35
let me be satisfied, is't good or bad? 2.05. 37
man that hath a hair more or a hair less in his 3.01. 18 P
place, | or reason coldly of your grievances, 3.01. 52
coldly of your grievances, | or else depart; 3.01. 53
into some house, benvolio, | or i shall faint. 3.01.106
either thou or i, or both, must go with him. 3.01.129
either thou or i, or both, must go with him. 3.01.129
this is the truth, or let benvolio die. 3.01.175
their amorous rites | by their own beauties, or, 3.02. 9
or those eyes /shut, that makes thee answer ay, 3.02. 49
ay, | if he be slain, say ay, or if not, no. 3.02. 50
brief sounds determine my weal or woe. 3.02. 51
or, if sour woe delights in fellowship | and 3.02.116
dead," | thy father or thy mother, nay, or both, 3.02.119
dead," | thy father or thy mother, nay, or both, 3.02.119
or by the break of day /disguis'd from hence. 3.03.168
we'll keep no great ado — a friend or two, 3.04. 23
i must be gone and live, or stay and die. 3.05. 11
either my eyesight fails, or thou lookest pale. 3.05. 57
is she not down so late, or up so early? 3.05. 66
or i will drag thee on a hurdle thither. 3.05.155
thursday, | or never after look me in the face. 3.05.162
or, if you do not, make the bridal bed | in that 3.05.200
or, if he do, it needs must be by stealth. 3.05.215
or if it did not, | your first is dead, or 3.05.223
or 'twere as good he were | as living here and 3.05.224
or to dispraise my lord with that same tongue 3.05.237
now, | or shall i come to you at evening mass? 4.01. 38
or my true heart with treacherous revolt | turn 4.01. 58
give me some present counsel, or, behold, 4.01. 61
or walk in thievish ways, or bid me lurk | where 4.01. 79
ways, or bid me lurk | where serpents are; 4.01. 79
bears, | or hide me nightly in a charnel–house, 4.01. 81
or bid me go into a new–made grave, | and hide 4.01. 84
and i will do it without fear or doubt, | to 4.01. 87
or, if i live, is it not very like | the 4.03. 36
revive, look up, or i will die with thee! 4.05. 20
or, if his mind be writ, give me his letter. 5.02. 4
or, wanting that, with tears distill'd by moans. 5.03. 15
what e'er thou hearest or seest, stand all aloof 5.03. 26
far | than empty tigers or the roaring sea. 5.03. 39
or did i dream it so? 5.03. 79
or am i mad, hearing him talk of juliet, | to 5.03. 80
or in my cell there would she kill herself. 5.03.242
TIM attends he here, or no? lucilius! 1.01.114
away, unpeaceable dog, or i'll spurn thee hence! 1.01.270 P
so fond, | to trust man on his oath or bond; 1.02. 65
or a harlot for her weeping, | or a dog that 1.02. 66
her weeping, | or a dog that seems a–sleeping, 1.02. 67
seems a–sleeping, | or a keeper with my freedom, 1.02. 68
freedom, | or my friends, if i should need 'em. 1.02. 69
and what better or properer can we call our own 1.02.102 P
who lives that's not depraved or depraves? 1.02.140
nor will he know his purse, or yield me this, 1.02.194
if you suspect my husbandry or falsehood, | call 2.02.155
nev'r speak or think | that timon's fortunes 2.02.230
he might have tried lord lucius or lucullus; 3.03. 2
it shows but little love or judgment in him. 3.03. 10
friend, or brother, | he forfeits his own blood 3.05. 86
or to live | but in a dream of friendship, | to 4.02. 33
supply his life, or that which can command it. 4.02. 47
dost thou, or dost thou not, heaven's curse upon 4.03.132
always a villain's office, or a fool's. 4.03.237
where my stomach finds meat, or, rather, where i 4.03.294 P
either in hope or present, i'd exchange | for 4.03.520
performance is a kind of will or testament 5.01. 28
hang them, or stab them, drown them in a draught 5.01.102
ere thou hadst power or we had cause of fear, 5.04. 15
thy glove, | or any token of thine honor else, 5.04. 50
or offend the stream | of regular justice in 5.04. 60
JC or did use | to stale with ordinary oaths my 1.02. 72
or if you know | that i profess myself in 1.02. 76
caesar cried, "help me, cassius, or i sink!" 1.02.111
he said, if he had done or said any thing amiss, 1.02.270 P
three or four wenches, where i stood, cried, 1.02.271 P
in execution | of any bold or noble enterprise, 1.02.298
or, if you will, | come home to me, and i will 1.02.305
for we will shake him, or worse days endure. 1.02.322
or else the world, too saucy with the gods, 1.03. 12
in a roman you do want, | or else you use not. 1.03. 59
a man no mightier than thyself, or me, | in 1.03. 76
there is no stir or walking in the streets; 1.03.127
there's two or three of us have seen strange 1.03.138
is | like a phantasma or a hideous dream. 2.01. 65
that this shall be, or we will fall for it? 2.01.128
to think that or our cause or our performance 2.01.135
to think that or our cause or our performance 2.01.135
whether caesar will come forth to–day or no; 2.01.194
for here have been | some six or seven, who did 2.01.277
but, as it were, in sort or limitation, | to 2.01.283
cassius or caesar never shall turn back, | for i 3.01. 21
conceit me, | either a coward or a flatterer. 3.01.193
or shall we on, and not depend on you? 3.01.217
or else were this a savage spectacle. 3.01.223
resolv'd | if brutus so unkindly knock'd or no; 3.02.180
are you a married man or a bachelor? 3.03. 8 P
am i a married man or a bachelor? 3.03. 14 P
as a friend or an enemy? 3.03. 21 P
or here or at the capitol. 4.01. 11
or here or at the capitol. 4.01. 11
either led or driven, as we point the way; 4.01. 23
in his own change, or by ill officers, | hath 4.02. 7
or, by the gods, this speech were else your last 4.03. 14

current when it serves, | or lose our ventures. 4.03.224
and touch thy instrument a strain or two? 4.03.257
art thou some god, some angel, or some devil, 4.03.279
or till another caesar | have added slaughter to 5.01. 54
whether yond troops are friend or enemy. 5.03. 18
yield, or thou diest. 5.04. 12
when you do find him, or alive or dead, | he 5.04. 24
when you do find him, or alive or dead, | he 5.04. 24
go on, | and see whe'er brutus be alive or dead, 5.04. 30
he is or ta'en or slain. 5.05. 3
he is or ta'en or slain. 5.05. 3
in thunder, lightning, or in rain? MAC 1.01. 2
or the hare the lion. 1.02. 35
reeking wounds, | or memorize another golgotha, 1.02. 40
or are you aught | that man may question? 1.03. 42
or that indeed | which outwardly ye show? 1.03. 53
or why | upon this blasted heath you stop our 1.03. 76
or have we eaten on the insane root | that takes 1.03. 84
do contend | which should be thine or his. 1.03. 93
or did line the rebel | with hidden help and 1.03.112
or that with both | he labor'd in his country's 1.03.113
on which i must fall down, or else o'erleap, 1.04. 49
striding the blast, or heaven's cherubin, hors'd 1.07. 22
or art thou but | a dagger of the mind, a false 2.01. 37
th' other senses, | or else worth all the rest. 2.01. 45
knell, | that summons thee to heaven or to hell. 2.01. 64
contend about them, | whether they live or die. 2.02. 8
is't night's predominance, or the day's shame, 2.04. 8
of the night | for a dark hour or twain. 3.01. 27
on any chance, | to mend it, or be rid on't. 3.01.113
the arm'd rhinoceros, or th' hyrcan tiger, 3.04.100
or be alive again, | and dare me to the desert 3.04.102
to bear my part, | or show the glory of our art? 3.05. 9
hear it from our mouths, | or from our masters'? 4.01. 63
come high or low; 4.01. 67
who chafes, who frets, or where conspirers are: 4.01. 91
'tis two or three, my lord, that bring you word 4.01.141
not | whether it was his wisdom or his fear. 4.02. 5
or else climb upward | to what they were before. 4.02. 24
or wear it on my sword, yet my poor country 4.03. 46
in their caps, | dying or e'er they sicken. 4.03.173
or is it a fee–grief | due to some single breast 4.03.196
or so much as it needs | to dew the sovereign 5.02. 29
push | will cheer me ever, or /disseat me now. 5.03. 21
what rhubarb, cyme, or what purgative drug, 5.03. 55
such a one | am i to fear, or none. 5.07. 4
or else my sword with an unbattered edge | i 5.07. 19
if thou hast any sound, or use of voice, | speak HAM 1.01.128
or if thou hast uphoarded in thy life | extorted 1.01.136
whether in sea or fire, in earth or air, | th' 1.01.153
whether in sea or fire, in earth or air, | th' 1.01.153
or thinking by our late dear brother's death 1.02. 19
a heart unfortified, or mind impatient, | an 1.02. 96
or that the everlasting had not fix'd | his 1.02.131
or ere those shoes were old | with which she 1.02.147
horatio — or i do forget myself. 1.02.161
foe in heaven | or ever i had seen that day, 1.02.183
pale, or red? 1.02.232
or lose your heart, or your chaste treasure open 1.03. 31
or your chaste treasure open | to his unmast'red 1.03. 31
or (not to crack the wind of the poor phrase, 1.03.108
as to give words or talk with the lord hamlet. 1.03.134
or by some habit, that too much o'er–leavens 1.04. 29
being nature's livery, or fortune's star, | his 1.04. 32
be thou a spirit of health, or goblin damn'd, 1.04. 40
with thee airs from heaven, or blasts from hell, 1.04. 41
hell, | be thy intents wicked, or charitable, 1.04. 42
or to the dreadful summit of the cliff | that 1.04. 70
swift | as meditation or the thoughts of love, 1.05. 30
how strange or odd some'er i bear myself — | as 1.05.170
with arms encumb'red thus, or this headshake, 1.05.174
or by pronouncing of some doubtful phrase, | as 1.05.175
well, we know," or "we could, and if we would," 1.05.176
or "if we list to speak," or "there be, and if 1.05.177
or "if we list to speak," or "there be, and if 1.05.177
or such ambiguous giving out, to note | that you 1.05.178
ay, or drinking, fencing, swearing, quarrelling, 2.01. 25
"good sir," or so, or "friend," or "gentleman," 2.01. 46
"good sir," or so, or "friend," or "gentleman," 2.01. 46
or "friend," or "gentleman," | according to the 2.01. 46
according to the phrase or the addition | of man 2.01. 47
i saw him yesterday, or th' other day, | or then 2.01. 54
or then, or then, with such or such, and, as you 2.01. 55
or then, or then, with such or such, and, as you 2.01. 55
or then, or then, with such or such, and, as you 2.01. 55
or, perchance, | "i saw him enter such a house 2.01. 57
of sale," | videlicet, a brothel, or so forth. 2.01. 59
or else this brain of mine | hunts not the trail 2.02. 46
or rather say, the cause of this defect, | for 2.02.102
or my dear majesty your queen here, think, | if 2.02.135
think, | if i had play'd the desk or table–book, 2.02.136
or given my heart a /winking, mute and dumb, 2.02.137
or look'd upon this love with idle sight, | what 2.02.138
about her waist, or in the middle of her favors? 2.02.232 P
direct with me, whether you were sent for or no! 2.02.288 P
freely, or the /blank verse shall halt for't. 2.02.325 P
scene individable, or poem unlimited; 2.02.399 P
once, but it was never acted, or, if it was, not 2.02.435 P
say on, he's for a jig or a tale of bawdry, or 2.02.500 P
for a jig or a tale of bawdry, or he sleeps. 2.02.500 P
a speech of some dozen lines, or sixteen lines, 2.02.541 P
what's hecuba to him, or he to /hecuba, | that 2.02.559
or ere this | i should 'a' fatted all the region 2.02.578
if't be th' affliction of his love or no | that 3.01. 35
to be, or not to be, that is the question: 3.01. 55
or to take arms against a sea of troubles, | and 3.01. 58
to give them shape, or time to act them in. 3.01.126 P
or, if thou wilt needs marry, marry a fool, for 3.01.137 P
or confine him where | your wisdom best shall 3.01.186
now this overdone, or come tardy off, though it 3.02. 25 P
then, or else shall 'a suffer not thinking on, 3.02.133 P
ay, or any show that you will show him. 3.02.144 P
is this a prologue, or the posy of a ring? 3.02.152 P
quantity, | in neither aught, or in extremity. 3.02.168
the violence of either grief or joy | their own 3.02.196
whether love lead fortune, or else fortune love. 3.02.203
as i can make, you shall command, or, rather, as 3.02.323 P
or like a whale? 3.02.381 P
or it is a massy wheel, | fix'd on the summit of 3.03. 17
ere we come to fall, | or /pardon'd being down? 3.03. 50
when he is drunk asleep, or in his rage, | or in 3.03. 89
or in th' incestious pleasure of his bed, | at 3.03. 90
or about some act | that has no relish of 3.03. 91
ears without hands or eyes, smelling sans all, 3.04. 79
or but a sickly part of one true sense | could 3.04. 80
and good | he likewise gives a frock or livery, 3.04.164
and either /... the devil or throw him out, 3.04.169
or paddling in your neck with his damn'd fingers 3.04.185
appliance are reliev'd, | or not at all. 4.03. 11
the main of poland, sir, | or for some frontier? 4.04. 16
nor will it yield to norway or the pole | a 4.04. 21
or some craven scruple | of thinking too 4.04. 40
my thoughts be bloody, or be nothing worth! 4.04. 66
the which we are pictures, or mere beasts; 4.05. 86
commune with your grief, | or you deny me right. 4.05.204
if by direct or by collateral hand | they find 4.05.207
my virtue or my plague, be it either which — 4.07. 13
or is it some abuse, and no such thing? 4.07. 50
or are you like the painting of a sorrow, | a 4.07.108
a kind of week or snuff that will abate it, 4.07.115
or with a little shuffling, you may choose | a 4.07.137
this project | should have a back or second, 4.07.153
or like a creature native and indued | unto that 4.07.179
in this world to drown or hang themselves, more 5.01. 28 P
the mason, the shipwright, or the carpenter? 5.01. 42 P
than a mason, a shipwright, or a carpenter? 5.01. 51 P
or of a courtier, which could say, "good morrow, 5.01. 82 P
speak by the card, or equivocation will undo us. 5.01.138 P
'a shall recover his wits there, or, if 'a do 5.01.151 P
'a will last you some eight year or nine year. 5.01.167 P
pelion, or the skyish head | of blue olympus. 5.01.253
or i could make a prologue to my brains, | they 5.02. 30
without debatement further, more or less, | he 5.02. 45
of him, he is the card or calendar of gentry; 5.02.109 P
with laertes, or that you will take longer time. 5.02.198 P
now or whensoever, provided i be so able as now. 5.02.202 P
if hamlet give the first or second hit, | or 5.02.268
hit, | or quit in answer of the third exchange, 5.02.269
that are but mutes or audience to this act, 5.02.335
if aught of woe or wonder, cease your search. 5.02.363
beyond what can be valued, rich or rare, | no LR 1.01. 57
as much as child e'er lov'd, or father found; 1.01. 59
or he that makes his generation messes | to 1.01.117
or, whilst i can vent clamor from my throat, 1.01.165
dower with her, | or cease your quest of love? 1.01.193
or all of it, with our displeasure piec'd, | and 1.01.199
with our oath, | take her, or leave her? 1.01.205
or your fore–vouch'd affection | fall into taint 1.01.220
it is no vicious blot, murther, or foulness, 1.01.227
no unchaste action, or dishonored step, | that 1.01.228
for that i am some twelve or fourteen moonshines 1.02. 5
i shall offend either to detain or give it: 1.02. 41 P
this but as an essay or taste of my virtue. 1.02. 45 P
he flashes into one gross crime or other | that 1.03. 4
makes it more like a tavern or a brothel | than 1.04.245
or whether gasted by the noise i made, | full 2.01. 55
or worth in thee | make thy words faith'd? 2.01. 69
you rogue, or i'll so carbonado your shanks! 2.02. 37 P
a stone–cutter or a painter could not have made 2.02. 58 P
way | thou mightst deserve, or they impose, this 2.04. 26
or at their chamber–door i'll beat the drum 2.04.118
or rather a disease that's in my flesh, | which 2.04.222
a bile, | a plague–sore, or embossed carbuncle, 2.04.224
yea, or so many? 2.04.239
from those that she calls servants or from mine? 2.04.244
to no more | will i give place or notice. 2.04.249
or five? 2.04.261
a hundred thousand flaws | or ere i'll weep. 2.04.286
or swell the curled waters 'bove the main, 3.01. 6
that things might change or cease, /tears /his 3.01. 7
or the hard rein which both of them hath borne 3.01. 27
or something deeper, | whereof, perchance, these 3.01. 28
of him, entreat for him, or any way sustain him. 3.03. 5 P
this treason were not — or not i the detector! 3.05. 13 P
true or false, it hath made thee earl of 3.05. 17 P
me whether a madman be a gentleman or a yeoman? 3.06. 10 P
be thy mouth or black or white, | tooth that 3.06. 66
be thy mouth or black or white, | tooth that 3.06. 66
hound or spaniel, brach or /lym, | or bobtail 3.06. 69
mongril grim, | hound or spaniel, brach or /lym, 3.06. 69
or /lym, | or bobtail /tike or trundle–tail, 3.06. 70
or /lym, | or bobtail /tike or trundle–tail, 3.06. 70
some five or six and thirty of his knights, 3.07. 16
thou wilt o'ertake us hence a mile or twain | i' 4.01. 42
do as i bid thee, or rather do thy pleasure; 4.01. 47
alive or dead? 4.06. 45
but have i fall'n, or no? 4.06. 56
lark so far | cannot be seen or heard. 4.06. 59
let go, slave, or thou di'st! 4.06.236
or ice try whither your costard or my ballow be 4.06.241 P
whither your costard or my ballow be the harder. 4.06.241 P
or whether since he is advis'd by aught | to 5.01. 2
or neither? 5.01. 58
say thou'lt do't, | or thrive by other means. 5.03. 34
they are ready | to–morrow, or at further space, 5.03. 53
"if any man of quality or degree within the 5.03.110 P
dame, | or with this paper shall i /stopple it. 5.03.156
heart, if ever i | did hate thee or thy father. 5.03.179
produce the bodies, be they alive or dead. 5.03.231
if that her breath will mist or stain the stone, 5.03.263
or image of that horror? 5.03.265
or else the devil will make a grandsire of you. OTH 1.01. 91
if she be in her chamber or your house, | let 1.01.138
nine or ten times | i had thought t' have yerk'd 1.02. 4
or put upon you what restraint or grievance 1.02. 15
or put upon you what restraint or grievance 1.02. 15
abus'd her delicate youth with drugs or minerals 1.02. 74
himself, | or any of my brothers of the state, 1.02. 96
(being not deficient, blind, or lame of sense), 1.03. 63
or with some dram, conjur'd to this effect, | he 1.03.105
or came it by request, and such fair question 1.03.113
which, as a grise or step, may help these lovers 1.03.200
these sentences, to sugar or to gall, | being 1.03.216
determine, | either for her stay or going; 1.03.276
'tis in ourselves that we are thus or thus. 1.03.320 P
so that if we will plant nettles or sow lettuce, 1.03.322 P
one gender of herbs or distract it with many, 1.03.323 P
sterile with idleness or manur'd with industry 1.03.324 P
this that you call love to be a sect or scion. 1.03.332 P
nay, it is true, or else i am a turk: 2.01.114
speaking too loud, or tainting his discipline, 2.01.268 P
or from what other course you please, which the 2.01.268 P
and nothing can or shall content my soul | till 2.01.298
or failing so, yet that i put the moor | at 2.01.300
not, or his good nature | prizes the virtue that 2.03.133
me go, sir, or i'll knock you o'er the mazzard. 2.03.153 P
by me that's said or done amiss this night, 2.03.201
or do but lift this arm, the best of you | shall 2.03.208
if partially affin'd, or /leagu'd in office, 2.03.218
thou dost deliver more or less than truth, 2.03.219
you, or any man living, may be drunk at a time, 2.03.313 P
you, | if you think fit, or that it may be done, 3.01. 51
or feed upon such nice and waterish diet, | or 3.03. 15
diet, | or breed itself so out of circumstances, 3.03. 16
nothing, my lord; or if — i know not what. 3.03. 36
if i have any grace or power to move you, | his 3.03. 46
on tuesday noon, or night; 3.03. 61
that i should deny, | or stand so mamm'ring on. 3.03. 70
or feed on nourishing dishes, or keep you warm, 3.03. 78
or feed on nourishing dishes, or keep you warm, 3.03. 78
or sue to you to do a peculiar profit | to your 3.03. 79
or those that be not, would they might seem none 3.03.127
draw | the smallest fear or doubt of her revolt, 3.03.188
this — | away at once with love or jealousy! 3.03.192
with any strong or vehement importunity; 3.03.251
or for i am declin'd | into the vale of years 3.03.265
or, by the worth of mine eternal soul, | thou 3.03.361
or, at the least, so prove it | that the 3.03.364
or woe upon thy life! 3.03.366
or sense? 3.03.374
if there be cords, or knives, | poison, or fire, 3.03.388
poison, or fire, or suffocating streams, | i'll 3.03.389
poison, or fire, or suffocating streams, | i'll 3.03.389
if it be that, or any /that was hers, | it 3.03.440
lodging and say he lies here, or he lies there, 3.04. 12 P
or made a gift of it, my father's eye | should 3.04. 61
to lose't or give't away were such perdition 3.04. 67
'tis not a year or two shows us a man: 3.04.103
or some unhatch'd practice | made demonstrable 3.04.141
or to be naked with her friend in bed | an hour, 4.01. 3
naked with her friend in bed | an hour, or more, 4.01. 4
or heard him say — as knaves be such abroad, 4.01. 25
suit, | or voluntary dotage of some mistress, 4.01. 27
convinced or supplied them, cannot choose | but 4.01. 28
or i shall say y' are all in all in spleen, 4.01. 88
or did the letters work upon his blood | and 4.01.275
cough, or cry "hem," if anybody come. 4.02. 29
where either i must live or bear no life; 4.02. 58
the which my current runs | or else dries up: 4.02. 60
or keep it as a cestern for foul toads | to knot 4.02. 61
either in discourse of thought or actual deed, 4.02.153
or that mine eyes, mine ears, or any sense 4.02.154
or any sense | delighted them /in any other form 4.02.154
or that i do not yet, and ever did, | and ever 4.02.156
or else break out in peevish jealousies, 4.03. 89
or say they strike us, | or scant our former 4.03. 90
us, | or scant our former having in despite: 4.03. 91
it makes us, or it mars us, think on that, | and 5.01. 4
or cassio him, or each do kill the other, 5.01. 13
or cassio him, or each do kill the other, 5.01. 13
two or three groan. 5.01. 42
are you of good or evil? 5.01. 65
know we this face or no? 5.01. 88
that either makes me, or foredoes me quite. 5.01.129
me, | or, naked as i am, i will assault thee. 5.02.258
a word or two before you go. 5.02.338
more fell than anguish, hunger, or the sea! 5.02.362
or who knows | if the scarce–bearded caesar have ANT 1.01. 20
"do this, or this; 1.01. 22
perform't, or else we damn thee." 1.01. 24
when it concerns the fool or coward. 1.02. 96
i must break, | or lose myself in dotage. 1.02.117
or thou, the greatest soldier of the world, 1.03. 38
which are, or cease, | as you shall give th' 1.03. 67
servant, making peace or war | as thou affects. 1.03. 70
or | /vouchsaf'd to think he had partners. 1.04. 7
stands he, or sits he? 1.05. 19
or does he walk? 1.05. 20
or is he on his horse? 1.05. 20
or murmuring, "where's my serpent of old nile?" 1.05. 25
what, was he sad, or merry? 1.05. 50
be'st thou sad or merry, | the violence of 1.05. 59
a several greeting, | or i'll unpeople egypt. 1.05. 78
which are not so — | or being, concern you not. 2.02. 30
be laugh'd at | if, or for nothing or a little, 2.02. 31
be laugh'd at | if, or for nothing or a little, 2.02. 31
or, if you borrow one another's love for the 2.02.103 P
presently be sought, | or else he seeks out us. 2.02.159
or my reporter devis'd well for her. 2.02.188 P
fortunes shall rise higher, | caesar's or mine? 2.03. 17
be it art or hap, | he hath spoken true. 2.03. 33
or friends with caesar, or not captive to him, 2.05. 44
or friends with caesar, or not captive to him, 2.05. 44
or i'll spurn thine eyes | like balls before me; 2.05. 63
but, first | or last, your fine egyptian cookery 2.06. 63
the lowness, or the mean, if dearth | or foison 2.07. 19
or the mean, if dearth | or foison follow. 2.07. 20
what e'er the ocean pales, or sky inclips, | is 2.07. 68
is she shrill–tongu'd or low? 3.03. 12
or i have no observance. 3.03. 22
is't long or round? 3.03. 29
him, he not /took't, | or did it from his teeth. 3.04. 10
believe not all, or, if you must believe, 3.04. 11
both as the same, or rather ours the elder — 3.10. 13
all–disgraced friend, | or take his life there. 3.12. 23
is antony or we in fault for this? 3.13. 2
as many, sir, as caesar has, | or needs not us. 3.13. 50
whom | he may at pleasure whip, or hang, or 3.13.150
he may at pleasure whip, or hang, or torture, 3.13.150
or i will live, | or bathe my dying honor in the 4.02. 5
or bathe my dying honor in the blood | shall 4.02. 6
haply you shall not see me more, or if, | a 4.02. 26
or from caesar's camp | say "i am none of thine. 4.05. 8
mine office, | or would have done't myself. 4.06. 27

i would they'ld fight i' th' fire or i' th' air; 4.10. 3
vanish, or i shall give thee thy deserving, 4.12. 32
a vapor sometime like a bear or lion, | a 4.14. 3
or blue promontory | with trees upon't that nod 4.14. 5
once, | or thy precedent services are all | but 4.14. 83
serpents have | edge, sting, or operation. 4.15. 26
o, quick, or i am gone. 4.15. 31
thee such a declining day, | or look on thine; 5.01. 39
no matter, sir, what i have heard or known. 5.02. 73
you laugh when boys or women tell their dreams; 5.02. 74
think you there was or might be such a man | as 5.02. 93
or i shall show the cinders of my spirits 5.02.173
that do die of it do seldom or never recover. 5.02.247 P
or that the negligence may well be laugh'd at, CYM 1.01. 66
long | as he could make me with /this eye or ear 1.03. 9
with glove or hat or handkerchief | still waving 1.03. 11
with glove or hat or handkerchief | still waving 1.03. 11
have made him | as little as a crow, or less, 1.03. 15
or i could make him swear | the shes of italy 1.03. 28
or have charg'd him, | at the sixt hour of morn, 1.03. 30
or ere i could | give him that parting kiss 1.03. 33
confounded one the other, or have fall'n both. 1.04. 51 P
or this gentleman's opinion by this worn out. 1.04. 62 P
is dead, or she's outpriz'd by a trifle. 1.04. 80 P
the one may be sold or given, or if there were 1.04. 82 P
or if there were wealth enough for the /purchase 1.04. 83 P
enough for the /purchase, or merit for the gift; 1.04. 84 P
a cunning thief, or a (that way) accomplish'd 1.04. 92 P
if in the holding or loss of that you term her 1.04. 96 P
or, like the parthian, i shall flying fight — 1.06. 20
knows | by history, report, or his own proof, 1.06. 70
to know | something of me, or what concerns me: 1.06. 94
for certainties | either are past remedies, or, 1.06. 97
or she that bore you was no queen, and you 1.06.127
or i shall short my word | by length'ning my 1.06.200
or to report of you | what i shall think is good 2.03. 84
or look upon our romans, whose remembrance | is 2.04. 14
or let her beauty | look thorough a casement to 2.04. 33
or is't not | too dull for your good wearing? 2.04. 40
and not the wronger | of her or you, having 2.04. 55
you had of her pure honor gains or loses | your 2.04. 59
pure honor gains or loses | your sword or mine, 2.04. 60
or masterless leave both | to who shall find 2.04. 60
the banks, or for | the press of boats or pride. 2.04. 71
the banks, or for | the press of boats or pride. 2.04. 72
have heard of here, by me, | or by some other. 2.04. 78
so they must, | or do your honor injury. 2.04. 80
or | who knows if one her women, being corrupted 2.04.115
or less — at first? 2.05. 15
that hell knows, | why, hers, in part or all; 2.05. 28
with a blanket, or put the moon in his pocket, 3.01. 43 P
make pastime with us a day or two, or longer. 3.01. 78 P
make pastime with us a day or two, or longer. 3.01. 78 P
why should excuse be born or e'er begot? 3.02. 65
or a debtor that not dares | to stride a limit. 3.03. 34
or so slipp'ry that | the fear's as bad as 3.03. 48
a storm or robbery (call it what you will) 3.03. 62
or in my life what comfort, when i am | dead to 3.04.129
(the handmaids of all women, or, more truly, 3.04.156
or stomach–qualm'd at land, a dram of this 3.04.190
or, wing'd with fervor of her love, she's flown 3.05. 61
gone she is | to death or to dishonor, and my 3.05. 63
or else | thou art straightway with the fiends. 3.05. 82
or, by jupiter, | i will not ask again. 3.05. 84
from thy heart, or rip | thy heart to find it. 3.05. 86
speak, or thy silence on the instant is | thy 3.05. 97
or this, or perish. 3.05.101
or this, or perish. 3.05.101
on them, knowing 'tis | a punishment or trial? 3.06. 11
if savage, | take or lend. 3.06. 24
or, if not, | an earthly paragon! 3.06. 42
to have begg'd or bought what i have took. 3.06. 47
or i, what e'er it be, | what pain it cost, what 3.06. 79
well or ill, | i am bound to you. 4.02. 45
were it toad, or adder, spider, | 'twould move 4.02. 90
he so undertaking, | or they so suffering. 4.02.143
us portends, | or what his death will bring us. 4.02.183
or dead, or sleeping on him? 4.02.356
or dead, or sleeping on him? 4.02.356
bed | with the defunct, or sleep upon the dead. 4.02.358
or who was he | that (otherwise than noble 4.02.363
or if not, | nothing to be were better. 4.02.367
to the note o' th' king, or i'll fall in them. 4.03. 44
must or for britains slay us or receive us | for 4.04. 5
must or for britains slay us or receive us | for 4.04. 5
revengingly enfeebles me, or could this carl, 5.02. 4
or betimes | let's reinforce, or fly. 5.02. 17
or betimes | let's reinforce, or fly. 5.02. 18
or rather fairer | than those for preservation 5.03. 21
than those for preservation cas'd, or shame), 5.03. 22
or we are romans and will give you that | like 5.03. 26
those that would die or e'er resist are grown 5.03. 50
or hath moe ministers than we | that draw his 5.03. 72
ay, or a stomach. 5.04. 2
or fruitful object be | in eye of imogen, that 5.04. 55
or we poor ghosts will cry | to th' shining 5.04. 88
help, jupiter, or we appeal, | and from thy 5.04. 91
or else such stuff as madmen | tongue and brain 5.04.145
either both or nothing, | or senseless speaking, 5.04.146
or senseless speaking, or a speaking such | as 5.04.147
or a speaking such | as sense cannot untie. 5.04.147
or to take upon yourself that which i am sure 5.04.180 P
or jump the after–inquiry on your own peril; 5.04.182 P
is living, let the time run on | to good or bad. 5.05.129
or, by our greatness and the grace of it 5.05.132
or at least | those which i heav'd to head! 5.05.156
the shrine of venus or straight–pight minerva, 5.05.164
or his description | prov'd us unspeaking sots. 5.05.177
o, give me cord, or knife, or poison, | some 5.05.213
o, give me cord, or knife, or poison, | some 5.05.213
yon celestial tree | (or die in th' adventure), PER 1.01. 22
thus ready for the way of life or death, | i 1.01. 54
either expound now, or receive your sentence. 1.01. 90
in the day's glorious walk or peaceful night, 1.02. 4
prince, pardon me, or strike me, if you please, 1.02. 46
who either by public war or private treason 1.02.104
or till the destinies do cut his thread of life. 1.02.108
and doubting lest he had err'd or sinn'd, | to 1.03. 21
with whom each minute threatens life or death. 1.03. 24
it, | or can conceal his hunger till he famish? 1.04. 12
or pay you with unthankfulness in thought, | be 1.04.102
be it our wives, our children, or ourselves, 1.04.103
come away, or i'll fetch th' with a wanton. 2.01. 17 P
all that may men approve or men detect! 2.01. 51
this day i'll rise, or else add ill to ill. 2.01.166
were more than you expect, or more than's fit, 2.03. 5
knights have done, | h'as broken a staff or so; 2.03. 35
how? | do as i bid you, or you'll move me else. 2.03. 71
or council has respect with him but he. 2.04. 18
or know what ground's made happy by his breath. 2.04. 28
or, dead, give 's cause to mourn his funeral, 2.04. 32
or never more to view nor day nor light. 2.05. 17
in't, | not minding whether i dislike or no! 2.05. 20
a deed might gain her love or your displeasure. 2.05. 54
or my hand subscribe | to any syllable that made 2.05. 69
either be rul'd by me, or i'll make you — | man 2.05. 83
honor, | or tie my pleasure up in silken bags, 3.02. 41
or when she would with sharp needle wound | the 4.ch. 23
or when to th' lute | she sung, and made the 4.ch. 25
or when | she would with rich and constant pen 4.ch. 27
any profit, | or my life imply her any danger? 4.01. 81
three or four thousand chequins were as pretty a 4.02. 26 P
or that these pirates, |·not enough barbarous, 4.02. 65
an honest woman, or not a woman. 4.02. 85
if fires be hot, knives sharp, or waters deep, 4.02.146
must either get her ravish'd or be rid of her. 4.06. 5 P
or she'll disfurnish us of all our cavalleria, 4.06. 11 P
were you a gamester at five, or at seven? 4.06. 75 P
not see thee, or else look friendly upon thee. 4.06. 89 P
off, or the common hangman shall execute it. 4.06.127 P
i could wish him to be my master, or rather, my 4.06.159 P
empty | old receptacles, or common shores, of 4.06.175
own shape of bud, bird, branch, or berry, | that 5.ch. 6
patience, good sir! | or here i'll cease. 5.01.145
what this maid is, or what is like to be, | that 5.01.184
or perform my bidding, or thou livest in woe; 5.01.247
or perform my bidding, or thou livest in woe; 5.01.247
of the air, | bird melodious, or bird fair, | is TNK 1.01. 17
pie, | may on our bridehouse perch or sing, | or 1.01. 22
perch or sing, | or with them any discord bring, 1.01. 23
that i have foregone | or futurely can cope. 1.01.174
think | of rotten kings or blubber'd queens? 1.01.180
force, | or sentencing for aye their vigor dumb, 1.01.195
us to an eddy | where we should turn or drown; 1.02. 11
hard, and harsher | than strife or war could be. 1.02. 26
or to be fond upon | another's way of speech, 1.02. 46
or let me know | why mine own barber is unblest, 1.02. 52
or to go tiptoe | before the street be foul? 1.02. 57
or i am none | that draw i' th' sequent trace. 1.02. 59
and we must | be vile or disobedient — not his 1.02. 78
or it shall be, | on fail of some condition? 1.02.104
when our friends don their helms, or put to sea, 1.03. 19
or tell of babes broach'd on the lance, or women 1.03. 20
lance, or women | that have sod their infants in 1.03. 20
nor gain | made him regard, or loss consider, 1.03. 30
air, or at adventure humm'd /one | from musical 1.03. 75
so chid, or at least a sigher to be comforted. 2.01. 44 P
a wife might part us lawfully, or business, 2.02. 89
to close mine eyes, | or prayers to the gods. 2.02. 94
or were they all hard–hearted? 2.02.122
or entertain'st a hope to blast my wishes, 2.02.170
as any palamon or any living | that is a man'i 2.02.181
shape shall make me, | or end my fortunes. 2.03. 22
i'll see her and be near her, or no more. 2.03. 23
or vow'd her maidenhead | to a young handsome 2.04. 13
thus much for law or kindred! 2.04. 32
and this night, or to–morrow, he shall love me. 2.04. 33
love and beyond reason, | or wit, or safety. 2.06. 12
love and beyond reason, | or wit, or safety. 2.06. 12
for use me so he shall, or i'll proclaim him, 2.06. 30
or all | th' enamell'd knacks o' th' mead or 3.01. 6
th' enamell'd knacks o' th' mead or garden! 3.01. 7
sense unsettle | lest i should drown, or stab, 3.02. 30
lest i should drown, or stab, or hang myself! 3.02. 30
i'll tell you | after a draught or two more. 3.03. 19
or two, or three, or ten. 3.03. 36
or two, or three, or ten. 3.03. 36
or two, or three, or ten. 3.03. 36
up with a course or two, and tack about, boys! 3.04. 10
tail without offense | or scandal to the ladies; 3.05. 35
or a conjurer. 3.05. 84
fable, | we are a merry rout, or else a rable, 3.05.106
or company, or by a figure, choris, | that 'fore 3.05.107
or company, or by a figure, choris, | that 'fore 3.05.107
do here present this machine, or this frame. 3.05.113
give us but a tree or twain | for a maypole, and 3.05.144
will be seen, | and quickly, yours or mine. 3.06. 35
or, if you feel yourself not fitting yet | and 3.06. 36
all, or dost thou do it | to make me spare thee? 3.06. 46
or i will make th' advantage of this hour | mine 3.06.123
i dare as well | die as discourse or sleep. 3.06.129
now or never, sister, | speak, not to be denied. 3.06.185
to make me their contention, or to know me, | to 3.06.253
once again it stands, | or both shall die: 3.06.290
or the sweet compassion | of those two ladies; 4.01. 11
i one question | of your name or his scape. 4.01. 16
or fear of my miscarrying on his scape, | or 4.01. 50
fear of my miscarrying on his scape, | or both. 4.01. 51
and, by the smallness of it, | a boy or woman. 4.01. 59
or as iris | newly dropp'd down from heaven. 4.01. 87
three or four | i saw from far off cross her — 4.01. 99
silver on the tip of your tongue, or no ferry. 4.03. 21 P
if one be mad, or hang or drown themselves, 4.03. 34 P
if one be mad, or hang or drown themselves, 4.03. 35 P
glister with new fire, or be | to–day extinct. 5.01. 69
or else grant | the file and quality i hold i 5.01.160
i'll warrant you within these three or four days 5.02.104
bent, or a sharp weapon | in a soft sheath; 5.03. 42
might | omit a ward, or forfeit an offense, 5.03. 63
to me deserving | than i can quite or speak of. 5.04. 35
or what fierce sulphur else, to this end made, 5.04. 64
a day or two | let us look sadly, and give grace 5.04.124
are you men of wisdom or what are you? STM II.C 35 P
or how can well that proclamation sound | when II.C 117
go you to france or flanders, | to any german II.C 127
to any german province, spain or portigal, | nay II.C 128
more white and red than doves or roses are: VEN 10
till either gorge be stuff'd, or prey be gone; 58
"were i hard–favor'd, foul, or wrinkled old, 133
would in thy palm dissolve, or seem to melt. 144
or like a fairy, trip upon the green, | or like 146
or like a nymph, with long dishevelled hair, 147
or what great danger dwells upon my suit? 206
fair, but speak fair words, or else be mute. 208
feed where thou wilt, on mountain or in dale; 232
his flattering "holla," or his "stand, i say"? 284
what cares he now for curb or pricking spur, 285
spur, | for rich caparisons or trappings gay? 286
and whe'er he run or fly they know not whether; 304
an oven that is stopp'd, or river stay'd, 331
jail of snow, | or ivory in an alablaster band, 363
o, would thou hadst not, or i had no hearing! 428
or were i deaf, thy outward parts would move 435
or as the wolf doth grin before he barketh, | or 459
or as the berry breaks before it staineth, | or 460
staineth, | or like the deadly bullet of a gun, 461
quoth she, "in earth or heaven, | or in the 493
or in the ocean drench'd, or in the fire? 494
or in the ocean drench'd, or in the fire? 494
or morn or weary even? 495
or morn or weary even? 495
do i delight to die, or life desire? 496
fast, | or being early pluck'd is sour to taste. 528
or as the fleet–foot roe that's tir'd with 561
or like the froward infant still'd with dandling 562
hare, | or at the fox which lives by subtilty, 675
or at the roe which no encounter dare; 676
or theirs whose desperate hands themselves do 765
or butcher sire that reaves his son of life: 766
or stonish'd as night–wand'rers often are, 825
but the blunt boar, rough bear, or lion proud, 884
trifles, unwitnessed with eye or ear, | thy 1023
or as the snail, whose tender horns being hit, 1033
flow'r was nigh, no grass, herb, leaf, or weed, 1055
of things long since, or any thing ensuing? 1078
ne'er settled equally, but high or low, | that 1139
or why is collatine the publisher | of that rich LUC 33
or, gaining more, the profit of excess | is but 138
strife | that one for all, or all for one, we 144
or sells eternity to get a toy? 214
or what fond beggar, but to touch the crown, 216
"had collatinus kill'd my son or sire, | or lain 232
or sire, | or lain in ambush to betray my life, 233
or were he not my dear friend, this desire 234
wife, | as in revenge or quittal of such strife; 236
who fears a sentence or an old man's saw | shall 244
"why hunt i then for color or excuses? 267
or as those bars which stop the hourly dial, 327
that dazzleth them, or else some shame supposed, 377
and dotes on what he looks, 'gainst law or duty. 497
or stop the headlong fury of his speed. 501
worse than a slavish wipe or birth–hour's blot; 537
look as the full–fed hound or gorged hawk, 694
unapt for tender smell, or speedy flight, | make 695
or altogether balk | the prey wherein by nature 696
can curb his heat, or rein his rash desire, 706
or if thou wilt permit the sun to climb | his 775
or hateful cuckoos hatch in sparrows' nests? 849
or toads infect fair founts with venom mud? 850
or tyrant folly lurk in gentle breasts? 851
or kings be breakers of their own behests? 852
or kills his life or else his quality. 875
or kills his life or else his quality. 875
or free that soul which wretchedness hath 900
that makes him honor'd, or begets him hate; 1005
or that which from discharged cannon fumes. 1043
fly, | or one encompass'd with a winding maze, 1151
to live or die which of the twain were better, 1154
"my body or my soul, which was the dearer, 1163
they drown their eyes or break their hearts. 1239
is form'd in them by force, by fraud, or skill. 1243
eye | receives the scroll without or yea or no, 1340
eye | receives the scroll without or yea or no, 1340
or blot with hell–born sin such saint–like forms 1519
(as if with grief or travail he had fainted), 1543
or (at the least) this refuge let me find: 1654
or keep him from heart–easing words so long, 1782
who should weep most, for daughter or for wife. 1792
help wounds, or grief help grievous deeds? 1822
or he refus'd to take /her figured proffer, PP 4.10
was this a lover, or a lecher whether? 7.17
and as goods lost are seld or never found, | as 13. 7
in scorn or friendship, nill i conster whether. 14. 8
the master loveless, or kill the gallant knight: 15. 6
let those repair | that are either true or fair; PHT 66
pity the world, or else this glutton be, | to SON 1.13
or who is he so fond will be the tomb, | of his 3. 7
thee, | or ten times happier be it ten for one; 6. 8
or else receiv'st with pleasure thine annoy? 8. 4
or to thyself at least kind–hearted prove: 10.12
that beauty still may live in thine or thee. 10.14
but not to tell of good or evil luck, | of 14. 3
of plagues, of dearths, or seasons' quality; 14. 4
wind, | or say with princes if it shall go well, 14. 7
or else of thee this i prognosticate: 14.13
which this time's pencil, or my pupil pen, 16.10
by chance or nature's changing course untrimm'd: 18. 8
so long as men can breathe or eyes can see, | so 18.13
or some fierce thing replete with too much rage, 23. 3
for whether beauty, birth, or wealth, or wit, 37. 5
for whether beauty, birth, or wealth, or wit, 37. 5
or any of these all, or all, or more, | entitled 37. 6
or any of these all, or all, or more, | entitled 37. 6
or wit, | or any of these all, or all, or more, 37. 6
or heart in love with sighs himself doth smother 47. 4
so, either by thy picture or my love, | thyself 47. 9
or, if they sleep, thy picture in my sight 47.13
placed are, | or captain jewels in the carcanet. 52. 8
or as the wardrobe which the robe doth hide, 52.10
where you may be, or your affairs suppose, | but 57.10
or at your hand th' account of hours to crave, 58. 3
not blame your pleasure, be it ill or well. 58.14
whether we are mended, or whe'er better they, 59.11
they, | or whether revolution be the same. 59.12

king | are vanishing, or vanish'd out of sight, 63. 7
of state, | or state itself confounded to decay, 64.10
or what strong hand can hold his swift foot back 65.11
or who his spoil /of beauty can forbid? 65.12
were born, | or durst inhabit on a living brow; 68. 4
either not assail'd, or victor being charg'd, 70.10
in me behold | when yellow leaves, or none, or 73. 2
or none, or few, do hang | upon those boughs 73. 2
or as sweet–season'd showers are to the ground; 75. 2
possessing or pursuing no delight | save what is 75.11
save what is had or must from you be took. 75.12
day by day, | or gluttoning on all, or all away. 75.14
day by day, | or gluttoning on all, or all away. 75.14
so far from variation or quick change? 76. 2
or (being wrack'd) i am a worthless boat, | he 80.11
or i shall live your epitaph to make, | or you 81. 1
or you survive when i in earth am rotten, | from 81. 2
i found (or thought i found) you did exceed 83. 3
or me, to whom thou gav'st it, else mistaking, 87.10
cost, | of more delight than hawks or horses be; 91.11
what e'er thy thoughts or thy heart's workings 93.11
or, if they sing, 'tis with so dull a cheer 97.13
or from their proud lap pluck them where they 98. 8
but sweet or color it had stol'n from thee. 99.15
that may express my love, or thy dear merit? 108. 4
for what care i who calls me well or ill, | so 112. 3
that my steel'd sense or changes right or wrong. 112. 8
that my steel'd sense or changes right or wrong. 112. 8
bird, of flow'r, or shape, which it doth /latch, 113. 6
for if it see the rud'st or gentlest sight, 113. 9
the most sweet favor or deformed'st creature, 113.10
the mountain or the sea, the day or night, | the 113.11
the mountain or the sea, the day or night, | the 113.11
the crow or dove, it shapes them to your feature 113.12
or whether doth my mind, being crown'd with you, 114. 1
or whether shall i say mine eye saith true, 114. 3
finds, | or bends with the remover to remove. 116. 4
unless my nerves were brass or hammered steel. 120. 4
or on my frailties why are frailer spies, 121. 7
or, at the least, so long as brain and heart 122. 5
lie, | made more or less by thy continual haste. 123.12
as subject to time's love, or to time's hate, 124. 3
among weeds, or flowers with flowers gather'd. 124. 4
honoring, | or laid great bases for eternity, 125. 3
which proves more short than waste or ruining? 125. 4
or if it were, it bore not beauty's name; 127. 2
or mine eyes seeing this, say this is not, | to 137.11
or, if it do, not from those lips of thine, 142. 5
or if they have, where is my judgment fled, 148. 3
or made them swear against the thing they see; 152.12
or monarch's hands that lets not bounty fall LC 41
doubt | if best were as it was, or best without. 98
or ne his manage by th' well–doing steed. 112
in thoughts, or to remain | in personal duty, 129
or forc'd examples, 'gainst her own content, 157
or my affection put to th' smallest teen, | or 192
teen, | or any of my leisures ever charmed. 193
wit well blazon'd, smil'd or made some moan. 217
or sister sanctified, of holiest note, | which 233
of burning blushes, or of weeping water, | or 304
of weeping water, | or sounding paleness; 305
or to turn white and sound at tragic shows; 308
/ORACLE 1 FR 0.0001 REL FR 1 V 0 P
/we /shall /hear /music, /wit, /and /oracle. TRO 1.03. 74
ORACLE 27 FR 0.0030 REL FR 24 V 3 P
i do believe it | against an oracle. TMP 4.01. 12
some oracle | must rectify our knowledge. 5.01.244
as we would hear an oracle. LLL 1.01.216 P
conceit, | as who should say, "i am sir oracle, MV 1.01. 93
now, from the oracle | they will bring all, WT 2.01.185
yet shall the oracle | give rest to th' minds of 2.01.190
from those you sent to th' oracle are come | an 2.03.194
and the ear–deaf'ning voice o' th' oracle, | kin 3.01. 9
when the oracle | (thus by apollo's great divine 3.01. 18
your honors all, | i do refer me to the oracle: 3.02.115
bring forth, | and in apollo's name, his oracle. 3.02.118
thence have brought | this seal'd–up oracle, by 3.02.127
there is no truth at all i' th' oracle. 3.02.140
my great profaneness 'gainst thine oracle! 3.02.154
apollo said, | is't not the tenor of his oracle, 5.01. 38
the oracle is fulfill'd; 5.02. 22 P
another elevated that the oracle was fulfill'd. 5.02. 75 P
knowing by paulina that the oracle | gave hope 5.03.126
my oracle, my prophet, my dear cousin, | i, as a R3 2.02.152
into the favor of the king, | and is his oracle. H8 3.02.104
this oracle of comfort has so pleas'd me | that 5.04. 66
bold as an oracle, and sets thersites, | a slave TRO 1.03.192
wert thou an oracle to tell me so, | i'd not 4.05.252
whom the oracle | hath doubtfully pronounc'd the TIM 4.03.121
come, | and let my grave–stone be your oracle. 5.01.219
even now, | answering the letter of the oracle, CYM 5.05.450
our master mars | /hath vouch'd his oracle, and TNK 5.04.107
ORACLES 3 FR 0.0003 REL FR 3 V 0 P
his words are bonds, his oaths are oracles, TGV 2.07. 75
my lords, these oracles | are hardly attain'd, 2H6 1.04. 70
made good, | may they not be my oracles as well, MAC 3.01. 9
ORANGE 2 FR 0.0002 REL FR 1 V 1 P
but civil count, civil as an orange, and ADO 2.01.294 P
give not this rotten orange to your friend, 4.01. 32
ORANGE–TAWNY 2 FR 0.0002 REL FR 1 V 1 P
your straw–color beard, your orange–tawny beard, MND 1.02. 94 P
cock so black of hue, | with orange–tawny bill, 3.01.126
ORANGE–WIFE 1 FR 0.0001 REL FR 0 V 1 P
in hearing a cause between an orange–wife and a COR 2.01. 70 P
ORATION 7 FR 0.0008 REL FR 4 V 3 P
after some oration fairly spoke | by a beloved MV 3.02.178
beard, | as he being dress'd to some oration." TRO 1.03.166
will sooner con an oration without book than 2.01. 17 P
is as fit as can be to serve for your oration, TIT 4.03. 96 P
can you deliver an oration to the emperor with a 4.03. 98 P
here, marcus, fold it in the oration, | for 4.03.116
in my oration, how the people take | the cruel JC 3.01.293
ORATOR 14 FR 0.0015 REL FR 13 V 1 P
be not thy tongue thy own shame's orator: ERR 3.02. 10
he's a good drum, my lord, but a naughty orator. AWW 5.03.254 P
king | prettily, methought, did play the orator. 1H6 4.01.175
to show how quaint an orator you are; 2H6 3.02.274
no, i can better play the orator. 3H6 1.02. 2
full well hath clifford play'd the orator, 2.02. 43
for warwick is a subtle orator, | and lewis a 3.01. 33
i'll play the orator as well as nestor, 3.02.188
i'll play the orator | as if the golden fee for R3 3.05. 95
read to thee | sweet poetry and tully's orator. TIT 4.01. 14
i am no orator, as brutus is; JC 3.02.217
say, | the text is old, the orator too green, VEN 806
persuade | the eyes of men without an orator; LUC 30
the orator, to deck his oratory, | will couple 815
ORATORS 5 FR 0.0005 REL FR 4 V 1 P
very good orators, when they are out, they will AYL 4.01. 75 P
gold were as good as twenty orators, | and will, R3 4.02. 38
joys, | poor breathing orators of miseries, 4.04.129
before) | my tears are now prevailing orators. TIT 3.01. 26
all orators are dumb when beauty pleadeth, LUC 268
ORATORY 6 FR 0.0006 REL FR 6 V 0 P
men | could not prevail with all their oratory, 1H6 2.02. 49
if my weak oratory | can from his mother win the R3 3.01. 37
and when /mine oratory drew /to /an end, | i bid 3.07. 20
but floods of tears will drown my oratory, | and TIT 5.03. 90
mixed, | which to her oratory adds more grace. LUC 564
the orator, to deck his oratory, | will couple 815
ORB 10 FR 0.0011 REL FR 9 V 1 P
you seem to me as dian in her orb, | as chaste ADO 4.01. 57
not the smallest orb which thou behold'st | but MV 5.01. 60
sir, does walk about the orb like the sun, it TN 3.01. 38 P
and move in that obedient orb again | where you 1H4 5.01. 17
and his fame folds in | this orb o' th' earth. COR 5.06.125
that monthly changes in her /circled orb, | lest ROM 2.02.110
that by this sister's orb | infect the air! TIM 4.03. 2
and the orb below | as hush as death, anon the HAM 2.02.485
but when he meant to quail and shake the orb, ANT 5.02. 85
lies | in the small orb of one particular tear! LC 289
ORBED 3 FR 0.0003 REL FR 3 V 0 P
in soul | as doth that orbed continent the fire TN 5.01.271
neptune's salt wash and tellus' orbed ground, HAM 3.02.156
their poor balls are tied | to th' orbed earth; LC 25
ORBS 6 FR 0.0006 REL FR 6 V 0 P
fairy queen, | to dew her orbs upon the green. MND 2.01. 9
by all the operation of the orbs, | from whom we LR 1.01.111
have empty left their orbs, and shot their fires ANT 3.13.146
the fiery orbs above and the twinn'd stones CYM 1.06. 35
after this strange starting from your orbs, 5.05.371
but in our orbs /we'll live so round and safe, PER 1.02.122
ORCHARD 17 FR 0.0019 REL FR 8 V 9 P
in a thick–pleach'd alley in mine orchard, were ADO 1.02. 10 P
bring it hither to me in the orchard. 2.03. 4 P
and tell her i and ursley | walk in the orchard, 3.01. 5
john, saw afar off in the orchard this amiable 3.03.151 P
were brought into the orchard and saw me court 5.01.237 P
o, sir, very well; here in your orchard. AYL 1.01. 41 P
we will go walk a little in the orchard, | and SHR 2.01.111
i saw't i' th' orchard. TN 3.02. 7 P
at the corner of the orchard like a bum–baily. 3.04.177 P
let him be brought into the orchard here. JN 5.07. 10
his lordship is walk'd forth into the orchard. 2H4 1.01. 4
nay, you shall see my orchard, where, in an 5.03. 1 P
walk here i' th' orchard, i'll bring her TRO 3.02. 16 P
he ran this way and leapt this orchard wall. ROM 2.01. 5
the orchard walls are high and hard to climb, 2.02. 63
'tis given out that, sleeping in my orchard, | a HAM 1.05. 35
sleeping within my orchard, | my custom always 1.05. 59
ORCHARD–END 1 FR 0.0001 REL FR 0 V 1 P
as the hunter, attends thee at the orchard–end. TN 3.04.223 P
ORCHARDS 2 FR 0.0002 REL FR 2 V 0 P
his private arbors and new–planted orchards, JC 3.02.248
heard where his plants in others' orchards grew, LC 171
ORD *(also ort*, word, worts*)*
ORD 1 FR 0.0001 REL FR 0 V 1 P
save the fall is in the ord "dissolutely." WIV 1.01.254 P
ORDAIN 2 FR 0.0002 REL FR 2 V 0 P
out of your grace devise, ordain, impose | some JN 3.01.250
thus i ordain it, | and, by mine honor, once TNK 3.06.288
ORDAIN'D 8 FR 0.0009 REL FR 8 V 0 P
far | to know the cause why music was ordain'd! SHR 3.01. 10
king is, | being ordain'd his special governor, 1H6 1.01.171
when first this order was ordain'd, my lords, 4.01. 33
wast thou ordain'd, dear father, | to lose thy 2H6 5.02. 45
for this, amongst the rest, was i ordain'd. 3H6 5.06. 58
this shoulder was ordain'd so thick to heave, 5.07. 23
titus | hath ordain'd to an honorable end, | for TIT 5.03. 22
was that mulmutius which | ordain'd our laws, CYM 3.01. 55
ORDAINED 2 FR 0.0002 REL FR 2 V 0 P
ordained is to raise this tedious siege, | and 1H6 1.02. 53
all things that we ordained festival, | turn ROM 4.05. 84
ORDAINING 1 FR 0.0001 REL FR 0 V 1 P
but fate (ordaining he should be a cuckold) held WIV 3.05.104 P
/ORDER 1 FR 0.0001 REL FR 1 V 0 P
how /order should be quell'd, and by this STM II.C 82
ORDER 89 FR 0.0100 REL FR 76 V 13 P
the several chairs of order look you scour WIV 5.05. 61
yourselves in order set; 5.05. 77
we do the denunciation lack | of outward order. MM 1.02.149
i will, as 'twere a brother of your order, 1.03. 44
worship will take order for the drabs and the 2.01.234 P
hadst thou not order? 2.02. 8
there shall be order for't. 2.02. 25
bound by my charity and my blest order, | i come 2.03. 3
the worser allow'd by order of law a furr'd gown 3.02. 7 P
i am a brother | of gracious order, late come 3.02.219
by the vow of mine order i warrant you, if my 4.02.169 P
trust not my holy order | if i pervert your 4.03.147
that should by private order else have died, | i 5.01.466
of mine oath, | a charitable duty of my order, ERR 5.01.107
whilst to take order for the wrongs i went, 5.01.146
his mother was a vot'ress of my order, | and, in MND 2.01.123
give order to my servants that they take | no MV 5.01.119
can you nominate in order now the degrees of the AYL 5.04. 88 P
therefore this order hath baptista ta'en, | that SHR 1.02.126
to learn the order of my fingering, | i must 3.01. 65
the carpets laid, and every thing in order? 4.01. 51 P
grumio gave order how it should be done. 4.03.117
i gave him no order, i gave him the stuff. 4.03.118
given order for our horses, and to–night, | when AWW 2.05. 25
i'll order take my mother shall not hear. 4.02. 55
yourself within the modest limits of order. TN 1.03. 9 P
pass | the same i am, ere ancient'st order was, WT 4.01. 10
impose | some gentle order, and then we shall be JN 3.01.251
all form is formless, order orderless, | save 3.01.253
such temperate order in so fierce a cause, 3.04. 12
that, having our fair order written down, | both 5.02. 4
order the trial, marshal, and begin. R2 1.03. 99
i | know how or which way to order these affairs 2.02.109
and, madam, there is order ta'en for you, | with 5.01. 53
uncle, help to order several powers | to oxford, 5.03.140
right | according to our threefold order ta'en? 1H4 3.01. 70
and now i live out of all order, out of all 3.03. 20 P
receive | money and order for their furniture. 3.03.202
let order die! 2H4 1.01.154
and i will take such order that thy friends 3.02.186 P
the manner and true order of the fight | this 4.04.100
teach | the act of order to a peopled kingdom. H5 1.02.189
hear the shrill whistle which doth order give 3.pr. 9
to whom the order of the siege is given, is 3.02. 65 P
throngs, | if any order might be thought upon. 4.05. 21
the devil take order now! 4.05. 22
to order peace between them — and omit | all 5.pr. 39
after that things are set in order here, | we'll 1H6 2.02. 32
for my good, | only give order for my funeral. 2.05.112
now will we take some order in the town, 3.02.126
when first this order was ordain'd, my lords, 4.01. 33
knight, | profaning this most honorable order, 4.01. 41
knight of the noble order of saint george, 4.07. 68
whiles i take order for mine own affairs. 2H6 3.01.320
until they hear the order of his death. 3.02.129
they are all in order, and march toward us. 4.02.188 P
but then are we in order when we are most out of 4.02.189 P
are we in order when we are most out of order. 4.02.190 P
let's set our men in order, | and issue forth 3H6 1.02. 69
till that the duke give order for his burial; R3 1.04.281
is clarence dead? the order was revers'd. 2.01. 87
but he, poor man, by your first order died, 2.01. 88
now will i go to take some privy order | to draw 3.05.106
and to give order that no manner person | have 3.05.108
i will take order for her keeping close. 4.02. 52
some one take order buckingham be brought | to 4.04.537
nought rebell'd, | order gave each thing view; H8 1.01. 44
there's order given for her coronation. 3.02. 46
learned and reverend fathers of his order, 4.01. 26
office, and custom, in all line of order; TRO 1.03. 88
be divided | by any voice or order of the field? 4.05. 70
aeneas | consent upon the order of their fight, 4.05. 90
by my holy order, | i thought thy disposition ROM 3.03.114
one of our order, to associate me, | here in 5.02. 6
will you go see the order of the course? JC 1.02. 25
a friend, | speak in the order of his funeral. 3.01.230
is dead, | and by that order of proscription. 4.03.180
stand not upon the order of your going, | but go MAC 3.04.118
else remains to do, | according to our order. 5.06. 6
they have already order | this night to play HAM 3.01. 20
and, but that great command o'ersways the order, 5.01.228
give order that these bodies | high on a stage 5.02.377
sir, by order of law, some year elder than this, LR 1.01. 19 P
honest iago hath ta'en order for't. OTH 5.02. 72
shall stay with us — order for sea is given, ANT 4.10. 6
see | high order in this great solemnity. 5.02.366
whereas reproof, obedient and in order, | fits PER 1.02. 42
sir, | we have given order be next our own. 2.03.110
pray order it | fitting the persons that must TNK 4.02.150
ORDER'D 1 FR 0.0001 REL FR 1 V 0 P
are men more order'd than when julius caesar CYM 2.04. 21
ORDERED 5 FR 0.0005 REL FR 5 V 0 P
art | so safely ordered that there is no soul — TMP 1.02. 29
'tis vile, unless it may be quaintly ordered, MV 2.04. 6
plain, | and thus my battle shall be ordered: R3 5.03.292
lie, | most like a soldier, ordered honorably. JC 5.05. 79
and bear his courses to be ordered | by lady PER 4.04. 47
ORDERING 3 FR 0.0003 REL FR 3 V 0 P
it, if thou hast | the ordering of the mind too, WT 2.03.106
have thou the ordering of this present time. JN 5.01. 77
strikes each in each by mutual ordering; SON 8.10
ORDERLESS 1 FR 0.0001 REL FR 1 V 0 P
all form is formless, order orderless, | save JN 3.01.253
ORDERLY 8 FR 0.0009 REL FR 6 V 2 P
the letter, very orderly, having nothing but the TGV 1.01.123 P
and gave such orderly and well–behav'd reproof WIV 2.01. 59 P
these things being bought and orderly bestowed, MV 2.02.170
you are too blunt, go to it orderly. SHR 2.01. 45
you bid me make it orderly and well, | according 4.03. 94
name, and orderly proceed | to swear him in the R2 1.03. 9
but, orderly to end where i begun, | our wills HAM 3.02.210
frame yourself | to orderly /solicits, and be CYM 2.03. 47
ORDER'S 1 FR 0.0001 REL FR 1 V 0 P
make a blush, | which is their order's robe: TNK 5.01.142
ORDERS 5 FR 0.0005 REL FR 4 V 1 P
there is pretty orders beginning, i can tell you MM 2.01.236 P
"it was the friar of orders grey, | as he forth SHR 4.01.145
send fair–play orders and make compremise, JN 5.01. 67
ere you can take due orders for a priest. 2H6 3.01.274
achievements, plots, orders, preventions, TRO 1.03.181
ORDINANCE *(also ord'nance)*
ORDINANCE 9 FR 0.0010 REL FR 9 V 0 P
by the compulsion of their ordinance | by this JN 2.01.218
pertain | by custom, and the ordinance of times, H5 2.04. 83
your mock | in second accent of his ordinance. 2.04.126
behold the ordinance on their carriages, | with 3.pr. 26
either thou wilt die by god's just ordinance R3 4.04.184
by god's fair ordinance conjoin together! 5.05. 31
when one but of my ordinance stood up | to speak COR 3.02. 12
all these things change from their ordinance, JC 1.03. 66
that slaves your ordinance, that will not see LR 4.01. 68
ORDINANT 1 FR 0.0001 REL FR 1 V 0 P
why, even in that was heaven ordinant. HAM 5.02. 48
ORDINARIES 1 FR 0.0001 REL FR 0 V 1 P
i did think thee, for two ordinaries, to be a AWW 2.03.201 P
ORDINARY 12 FR 0.0013 REL FR 8 V 4 P
the lunacy is so ordinary that the whippers are AYL 3.02.403 P
i see no more in you than in the ordinary | of 3.05. 42
wit than a christian or an ordinary man has; TN 1.03. 84 P
other day with an ordinary fool that has no more 1.05. 85 P
a lady's tears, | being an ordinary inundation; JN 5.02. 48
fits | are with his highness very ordinary. 2H4 4.04.115
an ordinary groom is for such payment. H8 5.01.172

wing | will make him fly an ordinary pitch, JC 1.01. 73
did use | to stale with ordinary oaths my love 1.02. 73
might fire the blood of ordinary men, | and turn 3.01. 37
that which ordinary men are fit for, i am LR 1.04. 34 P
and for his ordinary pays his heart | for what ANT 2.02.225
ORD'NANCE *(also ordinance)*
ORD'NANCE 4 FR 0.0004 REL FR 4 V 0 P
have i not heard great ord'nance in the field, SHR 1.02.203
a piece of ord'nance 'gainst it i have plac'd, 1H6 1.04. 15
let all the battlements their ord'nance fire. HAM 5.02.270
let ord'nance | come as the gods foresay it; CYM 4.02.145
ORD'RED 1 FR 0.0001 REL FR 1 V 0 P
all this was ord'red by the good discretion | of H8 1.01. 50
ORD'RING 2 FR 0.0002 REL FR 2 V 0 P
the gain, the ord'ring on't, is all | properly WT 2.01.169
and for the ord'ring your affairs, | to sing 4.04.139
ORDURE 1 FR 0.0001 REL FR 1 V 0 P
as gardeners do with ordure hide those roots H5 2.04. 39
/ORE 1 FR 0.0001 REL FR 0 V 1 P
this counterfeit lump of /ore will be melted, if AWW 3.06. 37 P
ORE 1 FR 0.0001 REL FR 1 V 0 P
like some ore | among a mineral of metals base, HAM 4.01. 25
ORGAN 6 FR 0.0006 REL FR 5 V 1 P
and every lovely organ of her life | shall come ADO 4.01.226
speak | his powerful sound within an organ weak; AWW 2.01.176
thy small pipe | is as the maiden's organ, TN 1.04. 33
tongue, will speak | with most miraculous organ. HAM 2.02.594
excellent voice, in this little organ, yet 3.02.368 P
could devise it so | that i might be the organ. 4.07. 70
ORGAN–PIPE 2 FR 0.0002 REL FR 2 V 0 P
that deep and dreadful organ–pipe, pronounc'd TMP 3.03. 98
and from the organ–pipe of frailty sings | his JN 5.07. 23
ORGANS 7 FR 0.0008 REL FR 5 V 2 P
said, | raise up the organs of her fantasy, WIV 5.05. 51
and given his deputation all the organs | of our MM 1.01. 20
hath not a jew hands, organs, dimensions, senses MV 3.01. 59 P
the organs, though defunct and dead before, H5 4.01. 21
as if those organs /had /deceptious functions, TRO 5.02.123
dry up in her the organs of increase, | and from LR 1.04.279
so high as it is, and moves with it own organs. ANT 2.07. 44 P
/ORGILLOUS 1 FR 0.0001 REL FR 1 V 0 P
/isles /of /greece | /the /princes /orgillous, TRO pr 2
ORIENT 7 FR 0.0008 REL FR 7 V 0 P
was wont to swell like round and orient pearls, MND 4.01. 54
i, from the orient to the drooping west 2H4 in 3
shall come again, transform'd to orient pearl, R3 4.04.322
of many doubled kisses — | this orient pearl. ANT 1.05. 41
yet sometimes falls an orient drop beside, VEN 981
bright orient pearl, alack, too timely shaded! PP 10. 3
lo in the orient when the gracious light | lifts SON 7. 1
ORIFEX 1 FR 0.0001 REL FR 1 V 0 P
admits no orifex for a point as subtle | as TRO 5.02.151
/ORIGIN 1 FR 0.0001 REL FR 1 V 0 P
/that /nature /which /contemns /it /origin LR 4.02. 32
ORIGIN 4 FR 0.0004 REL FR 4 V 0 P
(since nature cannot choose his origin), | by HAM 1.04. 26
the origin and commencement of his grief 3.01.177
as they say, from iron | came music's origin), TNK 5.04. 61
that is, to you, my origin and ender; LC 222
ORIGINAL 2 FR 0.0002 REL FR 1 V 1 P
we are their parents and original. MND 2.01.117
it hath it original from much grief, from study, 2H4 1.02.115 P
ORISONS 5 FR 0.0005 REL FR 5 V 0 P
me | are heavy orisons 'gainst this poor wretch! H5 2.02. 53
nay, stay, let's hear the orisons he makes. 3H6 1.04.110
for i have need of many orisons | to move the ROM 4.03. 3
in thy orisons | be all my sins rememb'red. HAM 3.01. 88
t' encounter me with orisons, for then | i am in CYM 1.03. 32
ORK *(also work)*
ORK 2 FR 0.0002 REL FR 0 V 2 P
and we will afterwards ork upon the cause with WIV 1.01.145 P
when i have good opportunities for the ork. 3.01. 15 P
ORLANDO 26 FR 0.0029 REL FR 10 V 16 P
understand that your younger brother, orlando, AYL 1.01.124 P
orlando, my liege, the youngest son of sir 1.02.222 P
o poor orlando! 1.02.259
yet i hate not orlando. 1.03. 34 P
run, orlando, carve on every tree | the fair, 3.02. 9
it is young orlando, that tripp'd up the 3.02.212 P
orlando? 3.02.217 P
orlando. 3.02.218 P
of fathers, when there is such a man as orlando? 3.04. 39 P
how now, orlando, where have you been all this 4.01. 39 P
give me your hand, orlando. 4.01.125 P
you must begin, "will you, orlando" — 4.01.129 P
will you, orlando, have to wife this rosalind? 4.01.130 P
but i do take thee, orlando, for my husband. 4.01.139 P
no, no, orlando, men are april when they woo, 4.01.147 P
aliena, i cannot be out of the sight of orlando. 4.01.216 P
and here much orlando! 4.03. 2 P
orlando doth commend him to you both, | and to 4.03. 91
when last the young orlando parted from you | he 4.03. 98
seeing orlando, it unlink'd itself, | and with 4.03.111
orlando did approach the man | and found it was 4.03.119
but to orlando: 4.03.125
o my dear orlando, how it grieves me to see thee 5.02. 19 P
dost thou believe, orlando, that the boy | can 5.04. 1
rosalind, | you will bestow her on orlando here? 5.04. 7
you, yours, orlando, to receive his daughter; 5.04. 20
ORLD *(also varld, vorld, world)*
ORLD 3 FR 0.0003 REL FR 0 V 3 P
it is that fery person for all the orld, as just WIV 1.01. 49 P
if you look in the maps of the orld, i warrant H5 4.07. 24 P
i will confess it to all the orld. 4.07.113 P
ORLEANCE 28 FR 0.0031 REL FR 26 V 2 P
of brabant and of orleance, shall make forth, H5 2.04. 5
you dukes of orleance, bourbon, and of berri, 3.05. 41
my lord of orleance, and my lord high constable, 3.07. 7 P
cousin orleance. 4.02. 6
charles duke of orleance, nephew to the king, 4.08. 76
guienne, champaigne, rheims, orleance, | paris, 1H6 1.01. 60
the bastard of orleance with him is join'd; 1.01. 93
lord, | retiring from the siege of orleance, 1.01.111
so you had need, for orleance is besieg'd; 1.01.157
at pleasure here we lie near orleance; 1.02. 6
bastard of orleance, thrice welcome to us. 1.02. 47
shall we give o'er orleance, or no? 1.02.125
drive them from orleance and be immortaliz'd. 1.02.148
sirrah, thou know'st how orleance is besieg'd, 1.04. 1
now it is supper–time in orleance: 1.04. 59
i must go victual orleance forthwith. 1.05. 14
pucelle is ent'red into orleance | in spite of 1.05. 36
walls, | rescu'd is orleance from the english! 1.06. 2
recover'd is the town of orleance. 1.06. 9
read, | shall be engrav'd the sack of orleance, 2.02. 15
was not the duke of orleance thy foe? 3.03. 69
orleance the bastard, charles, burgundy, 4.04. 26
beat down alanson, orleance, burgundy, | and 4.06. 14
the ireful bastard orleance, that drew blood 4.06. 16
the sword of orleance hath not made me smart; 4.06. 42
the dukes of orleance, calaber, bretagne, and 2H6 1.01. 7
/a marriage 'twixt the duke of orleance and H8 2.04.175
sir, we have known together in orleance. CYM 1.04. 35 P
/ORNAMENT 1 FR 0.0001 REL FR 1 V 0 P
and so prove | (as /ornament oft does) too WT 1.02.158
ORNAMENT 20 FR 0.0022 REL FR 19 V 1 P
sweet ornament that decks a thing divine — | ah TGV 2.01. 4
and the old ornament of his cheek hath already ADO 3.02. 46 P
the world is still deceiv'd with ornament. MV 3.02. 74
text, | hiding the grossness with fair ornament? 3.02. 80
thus ornament is but the guiled shore | to a 3.02. 97
went | still in this fashion, color, ornament, TN 3.04.382
well, | and gave the tongue a helpful ornament, 1H4 3.01.123
ought to wear | this ornament of knighthood, yea 1H6 4.01. 29
all, | gracious lavinia, rome's rich ornament, TIT 1.01. 52
brags of his substance, not of ornament; ROM 2.06. 31
thy wit, that ornament to shape and love, 3.03.130
which thou esteem'st the ornament of life, | and MAC 1.07. 42
and now | this ornament | makes me look dismal PER 5.03. 73
his show | has all the ornament of honor in't. TNK 4.02. 93
thou that art now the world's fresh ornament, SON 1. 9
who heaven itself for ornament doth use, | and 21. 3
by that sweet ornament which truth doth give! 54. 2
without all ornament, itself and true, | making 68.10
the ornament of beauty is suspect, | a crow that 70. 3
and grace | to appertainings and to ornament, LC 115
ORNAMENTS 11 FR 0.0012 REL FR 11 V 0 P
with such bedecking ornaments of praise? LLL 2.01. 79
come, tailor, let us see these ornaments; SHR 4.03. 61
for clothing me in these grave ornaments. 1H6 5.01. 54
lady's lap, | and deck my body in gay ornaments, 3H6 3.02.149
his hand — | true ornaments to know a holy man. R3 3.07. 99
rich stuffs, and ornaments of household, which H8 3.02.126
those sweet ornaments | whose circling shadows TIT 2.04. 18
cast by their grave beseeming ornaments | to ROM 1.01. 93
to help me sort such needful ornaments | as you 4.02. 34
thou seest our mistress' ornaments are chaste." LUC 322
that have profan'd their scarlet ornaments, SON 142. 6
ORODES 1 FR 0.0001 REL FR 1 V 0 P
thy pacorus, orodes, | pays this for marcus ANT 3.01. 4
ORPHAN 3 FR 0.0003 REL FR 3 V 0 P
of night, | you orphan heirs of fixed destiny, WIV 5.05. 39
to reave the orphan of his patrimony, | to wring 2H6 5.01.187
the orphan pines while the oppressor feeds, LUC 905
ORPHAN'S 1 FR 0.0001 REL FR 1 V 0 P
and many an orphan's water–standing eye — | men 3H6 5.06. 40
ORPHANS' 2 FR 0.0002 REL FR 2 V 0 P
turning the widows' tears, the orphans' cries, H5 2.04.106
then (as men report | thou orphans' father art) CYM 5.04. 40
ORPHANS 5 FR 0.0005 REL FR 5 V 0 P
orphans for their parents' timeless death — 3H6 5.06. 42
and call us orphans, wretches, castaways, | if R3 2.02. 6
were never orphans had so dear a loss. 2.02. 78
new morn | new widows howl, new orphans cry, new MAC 4.03. 5
me | but hope of orphans and unfathered fruit, SON 97.10
ORPHANTS' 1 FR 0.0001 REL FR 1 V 0 P
may have a tomb of orphants' tears wept on him! H8 3.02.399
ORPHEUS' 1 FR 0.0001 REL FR 1 V 0 P
for orpheus' lute was strung with poets' sinews, TGV 3.02. 77
ORPHEUS 3 FR 0.0003 REL FR 3 V 0 P
the poet | did feign that orpheus drew trees, MV 5.01. 80
orpheus with his lute made trees, | and the H8 3.01. 3
and moody pluto winks while orpheus plays. LUC 553
ORSINO 7 FR 0.0008 REL FR 5 V 2 P
orsino. TN 1.02. 27
orsino! 1.02. 28
from the count orsino, is it? 1.05.101 P
y' are servant to the count orsino, youth. 3.01.100
i arrest thee at the suit of count orsino. 3.04.327 P
orsino, this is that antonio | that took the 5.01. 60
orsino, noble sir, | be pleas'd that i shake off 5.01. 72
ORSINO'S 8 FR 0.0009 REL FR 4 V 4 P
we'll once more hear orsino's embassy. TN 1.05.166
in orsino's bosom. 1.05.224 P
i am bound to the count orsino's court. 2.01. 42 P
i have many enemies in orsino's court, | else 2.01. 45
i saw thee late at the count orsino's. 3.01. 37 P
gentleman of the count orsino's is return'd. 3.04. 58 P
on base and ground enough, | orsino's enemy. 5.01. 76
seen, | orsino's mistress and his fancy's queen. 5.01.388
ORT* *(also ord, word, worts*)*
ORT* 2 FR 0.0002 REL FR 0 V 2 P
the ort is (according to our meaning) WIV 1.01.254 P
fragment, some slender ort of his remainder. TIM 4.03.399 P
ORTOGRAPHY 2 FR 0.0002 REL FR 0 V 2 P
and now is he turn'd ortography — his words are ADO 2.03. 20 P
companions, such rackers of ortography, as to LLL 5.01. 19 P
ORTS 2 FR 0.0002 REL FR 2 V 0 P
the fractions of her faith, orts of her love, TRO 5.02.158
let him have time a beggar's orts to crave, LUC 985
O'S 1 FR 0.0001 REL FR 1 V 0 P
o that your face were not so full of o's! LLL 5.02. 45
OSCORBIDULCHOS 1 FR 0.0001 REL FR 0 V 1 P
oscorbidulchos volivorco. AWW 4.01. 79 P
OSIER 2 FR 0.0002 REL FR 2 V 0 P
i must up–fill this osier cage of ours | with ROM 2.03. 7
adonis made | under an osier growing by a brook, PP 6. 5
OSIERS 3 FR 0.0003 REL FR 3 V 0 P
to me were oaks, to thee like osiers bowed. LLL 4.02.108
the rank of osiers by the murmuring stream AYL 4.03. 79
to me like oaks, to thee like osiers bowed. PP 5. 4
OSPREY *(see aspray, etc.)*
OSRIC 3 FR 0.0003 REL FR 2 V 1 P
his majesty commended him to you by young osric, HAM 5.02.196 P
give them the foils, young osric. 5.02.259
why, as a woodcock to mine own springe, osric: 5.02.306
OSSA 1 FR 0.0001 REL FR 1 V 0 P
the burning zone, | make ossa like a wart! HAM 5.01.283
/OSTENT 1 FR 0.0001 REL FR 1 V 0 P
and with /th' /ostent of war will look so huge, PER 1.02. 25
OSTENT 2 FR 0.0002 REL FR 2 V 0 P
like one well studied in a sad ostent | to MV 2.02.196
signal, and ostent | quite from himself to god. H5 5.pr. 21
OSTENTARE 1 FR 0.0001 REL FR 0 V 1 P
were, replication, or rather ostentare, to show, LLL 4.02. 15 P
OSTENTATION 8 FR 0.0009 REL FR 6 V 2 P
maintain a mourning ostentation, | and on your ADO 4.01.205
with some delightful ostentation, or show, or LLL 5.01.112 P
have blown me full of maggot ostentation. 5.02.409
with war | and ostentation of despised arms? R2 2.03. 95
reason taken from me all ostentation of sorrow. 2H4 2.02. 50 P
make good this ostentation, and you shall COR 1.06. 86
bones, | no noble rite nor formal ostentation — HAM 4.05.216
have prevented | the ostentation of our love, ANT 3.06. 52
OSTENTS 1 FR 0.0001 REL FR 1 V 0 P
and such fair ostents of love | as shall MV 2.08. 44
OSTLER *(also hostler)*
OSTLER 6 FR 0.0006 REL FR 0 V 6 P
what, ostler! 1H4 2.01. 3 P
is turn'd upside down since robin ostler died. 2.01. 11 P
what, ostler! 2.01. 22 P
what, ostler! 2.01. 27 P
bid the ostler bring my gelding out of the 2.01. 96 P
out, ye rogue! shall i be your ostler? 2.02. 42 P
OSTLERS 1 FR 0.0001 REL FR 0 V 1 P
revolted tapsters, and ostlers trade–fall'n, the 1H4 4.02. 29 P
OSTRICH *(see estridge, etc., ostridge)*
OSTRIDGE 1 FR 0.0001 REL FR 0 V 1 P
but i'll make thee eat iron like an ostridge, 2H6 4.10. 28 P
OSWALD 3 FR 0.0003 REL FR 3 V 0 P
what, oswald, ho! LR 1.04.313
oswald, i say! 1.04.327
i have show'd th' unfitness — how now, oswald? 1.04.333
OTHELLO 24 FR 0.0027 REL FR 20 V 4 P
valiant othello, we must straight employ you OTH 1.03. 48
but, othello, speak. 1.03.110
say it, othello. 1.03.127
othello, the fortitude of the place is best 1.03.222 P
othello, leave some officer behind, | and he 1.03.280
lieutenant to the warlike moor othello, | is 2.01. 27
in | as to throw out our eyes for brave othello, 2.01. 38
great jove, othello guard, | and swell his sail 2.01. 77
my dear othello! 2.01.182
isle of cyprus and our noble general othello! 2.02. 12 P
have a measure to the health of black othello. 2.03. 32 P
i fear the trust othello puts him in, | on some 2.03.126
worthy othello, i am hurt to danger. 2.03.197
tell me, othello. 3.03. 68
how now, my dear othello? 3.03.279
othello! 4.01. 48
as he shall smile, othello shall go mad; 4.01.100
why, sweet othello? 4.01.239
whore of venice | that married with othello. 4.02. 90
why, then othello and desdemona return again to 4.02.222 P
who's there? othello? 5.02. 23
where should othello go? 5.02.271
that's he that was othello; here i am. 5.02.284
o thou othello, that was once so good, | fall'n 5.02.291
OTHELLO'S 10 FR 0.0011 REL FR 7 V 3 P
i saw othello's visage in his mind, | and to his OTH 1.03.252
time, to abuse othello's /ear | that he is too 1.03.395
it is othello's pleasure, our noble and valiant 2.02. 1 P
othello's occupation's gone! 3.03.357
hands, heart, | to wrong'd othello's service! 3.03.467
heaven keep the monster from othello's mind! 3.04.163
from venice to depute cassio in othello's place. 4.02.221 P
why, by making him uncapable of othello's place: 4.02.229 P
this is othello's ancient, as i take it. 5.01. 51
man but a rush against othello's breast, | and 5.02.270
/OTHER 9 FR 0.0010 REL FR 8 V 1 P
/the /other /down, /unseen, /and /full /of R2 4.01.187
/us /from /his /soul /to /love /each /other, R3 1.04.237
/on /one /and /other /side, /troyan /and /greek, TRO pr 21
/she /drinks /no /other /drink /but /tears, TIT 3.02. 37
/nor /any /other /part | belonging to a man. ROM 2.02. 41
/motley /here, | /the /other /found /out /there. LR 1.04.147
/all /thy /other /titles /thou /hast /given 1.04.149 P
and on /other grounds | christen'd and heathen, OTH 1.01. 29
and of the cannibals that each /other eat, | the 1.03.143
OTHER 621 FR 0.0702 REL FR 445 V 176 P
by any other house, or person? TMP 1.02. 42
thee more profit | than other princess' can, 1.02.173
forth, i say, there's other business for thee. 1.02.315
taught thee each hour | one thing or other. 1.02.355
quick, thou'rt best, | to answer other business. 1.02.367
there is no other shelter hereabout. 2.02. 39 P
i will pour some in thy other mouth. 2.02. 94 P
doth thy other mouth call me? 2.02. 97 P
if th' other two be brain'd like us, the state 3.02. 6 P
i have no other but a woman's reason: TGV 1.02. 23
while other men, of slender reputation, | put 1.03. 6
alphonso | with other gentlemen of good esteem 1.03. 40
one is painted, and the other out of all count. 2.01. 57 P
think, no other treasure to give your followers; 2.04. 44 P
them | upon some other pawn for fealty. 2.04. 91
her, whose worth /makes other worthies nothing: 2.04.166
the other squirrel was stol'n from me by the 4.04. 55 P
i bruis'd my shin th' other day with playing at WIV 1.01.283 P
time we have confidence, and of other wooers. 1.04.160 P
yes, and you heard what the other told me? 2.01.171 P
as any is in windsor, whoe'er be the other; 2.02.100 P
of my good parts aside, i have no other charms. 2.02.106 P
wife acquainted each other how they love me? 2.02.109 P
yet in other places she enlargeth her mirth so 2.02.222 P
marriage vow, and a thousand other her defenses, 2.02.250 P
us not be laughing–stocks to other men's humors. 3.01. 86 P
and i will one way or other make you amends. 3.01. 87 P
be sure of that — two other husbands. 3.02. 16 P
besides these, other bars he lays before me, 3.04. 7
i have turn'd away my other guests; 4.03. 10 P
i had other things to have spoken with her too 4.05. 40 P

the devil take one party and his dam the other! 4.05.107 P
while other jests are something rank on foot, 4.06. 22
while other sports are tasking of their minds, 4.06. 30
in some other, a man a beast. 5.05. 5 P
if the duke with the other dukes come not to MM 1.02. 1 P
admit no other way to save his life | (as i 2.04. 88
life | (as i subscribe not that, nor any other, 2.04. 89
the miserable have no other medicine | but only 3.01. 2
my stay must be stolen out of other affairs; 3.01.158 P
other some, he is in rome; 3.02. 89 P
one that, above all other strifes, contended 3.02.232 P
this other doth command a little door, | which 4.01. 32
are there no other tokens | between you 'greed 4.01. 40
not a jot the other, | being a murtherer, though 4.02. 61
neither in time, matter, or other circumstance. 4.02.105 P
it is no other. 4.03.117
every letter he hath writ hath disvouch'd other. 4.04. 2 P
there's other of our friends | will greet us 4.05. 12
you must walk by us on our other hand; 5.01. 17
your eye | by throwing it on any other object, 5.01. 23
if she be mad — as i believe no other — | her 5.01. 60
too, and with the other confederate companion! 5.01.348 P
lord, | i crave no other, nor no better man. 5.01.426
and therewithal | remit thy other forfeits. 5.01.520
the one so like the other | as could not be ERR 1.01. 51
and this it was (for other means was none): 1.01. 75
to him one of the other twins was bound, 1.01. 81
whilst i had been like heedful of the other. 1.01. 82
life, by some device or other | the villain is 1.02. 95
how if your husband start some other where? 2.01. 30
they can be meek that have no other cause: 2.01. 33
for god's sake send some other messenger. 2.01. 77
and he will bless that cross with other beating: 2.01. 79
the other, that at dinner they should not drop 2.02. 98 P
some other mistress hath thy sweet aspects: 2.02.111
one ne'er got me credit, the other mickle blame. 3.01. 45
some other give me thanks for kindnesses; 4.03. 5
both one and other he denies me now. 4.03. 85
one of these men is genius to the other: 5.01.333
so some gentleman or other shall scape a ADO 1.01.134 P
can afford her, that were she other than she is, 1.01.174 P
unhandsome, and being no other but as she is, i 1.01.175 P
and the other too like my lady's eldest son, 2.01. 9 P
god make men of some other mettle than earth. 2.01. 59 P
friendship is constant in all other things 2.01.175
a mountain of affection th' one with th' other. 2.01.367 P
look you for any other issue? 2.02. 30 P
good that benedick knew of it by some other, if 2.03.155 P
i would have daff'd all other respects, and made 2.03.169 P
troth, i think your other rebato were better. 3.04. 6 P
i am out of all other tune, methinks. 3.04. 43 P
you look with your eyes as other women do. 3.04. 91 P
it for my love some other way than swearing by 4.01.326 P
thee how beatrice prais'd thy wit the other day. 5.01.160 P
come let us hence, and put on other weeds, | and 5.03. 30
here comes other reck'nings. 5.04. 52
and when i liv'd, i was your other wife, | and 5.04. 60
and when you lov'd, you were my other husband. 5.04. 61
but there are other strict observances: LLL 1.01. 36
suggestions are to other as to me; 1.01.158
— of other men's secrets, i beseech you. 1.01.230 P
which each to other hath so strongly sworn. 1.01.307
catch | the other turns to a mirth–moving jest, 2.01. 71
where that and other specialties are bound: 2.01.164
do the wise think them other? 3.01. 80
not care a pin, if the other three were in. 4.03. 18 P
the other cries; 4.03.139
other slow arts entirely keep the brain; 4.03.321
the sheep: the other two concludes it — o,u. 5.01. 56 P
and among other /importunate and most serious 5.01. 99 P
will change habits, and present the other five. 5.02.539
will speak their mind in some other sort. 5.02.586 P
maintained by the owl, th' other by the cuckoo. 5.02.892 P
voice, | the other must be held the worthier. MND 1.01. 55
how happy some o'er other some can be! 1.01.226
the other slayeth me. 2.01.190
i am a man as other men are"; 3.01. 44 P
some man or other must present wall; 3.01. 67 P
and made your other love, demetrius | (who even 3.02.224
wink each at other, hold the sweet jest up; 3.02.239
and from each other look thou lead them thus, 3.02.363
swain, | that he awaking when the other do, 4.01. 66
and other of such vinegar aspect | that they'll MV 1.01. 54
more advised watch | to find the other forth, 1.01.143
may be won by some other sort than your father's 1.02.104 P
good heart as i can bid the other four farewell, 1.02.128 P
fourth for england, and other ventures he hath, 1.03. 21 P
embraced heaviness | with some delight or other. 2.08. 53
two thousand ducats in that, and other precious, 3.01. 87 P
yes, other men have ill luck too. 3.01. 97 P
one half of me is yours, the other half yours — 3.02. 16
how all the other passions fleet to air, | as 3.02.108
/hear other things: 3.04. 23
must be something else | pawn'd with the other, 3.05. 82
'mong other things | i shall disgest it. 3.05. 89
the other half | comes to the privy coffer of 4.01.353
of the duke only, 'gainst all other voice: 4.01.356
the other half comes to the general state, 4.01.371
so he will let me have | the other half in use, 4.01.383
the other, that he do record a gift, | here in 4.01.388
it must appear in other ways than words, 5.01.140
and bid him keep it better than the other. 5.01.255
while i live i'll fear no other thing | so sore, 5.01.306
thy throat till this other had pull'd out thy AYL 1.01. 60 P
ta'en thy life by some indirect means or other; 1.01.153 P
the other is daughter to the banish'd duke, 1.02.273
grounded upon no other argument | but that the 1.02.279
with reasons and the other mad without any. 1.03. 8 P
as many other mannish cowards have | that do 1.03.121
that, | he will have other means to cut you off; 2.03. 25
no man's happiness, glad of other men's good, 3.02. 75 P
and the other lives merrily because he feels no 3.02.321 P
the other knowing no burthen of heavy tedious 3.02.323 P
yourself, than seeming the lover of any other. 3.02.384 P
you have sold your own lands to see other men's; 4.01. 23 P
glass, by filling the one doth empty the other. 5.01. 43 P
consent with both that we may enjoy each other. 5.02. 9 P
and to the other | a land itself at large, a 5.04.168

i am for other than for dancing measures. 5.04.193
i will some other be, some florentine, | some SHR 1.01.204
and her withholds from me /and other more, 1.02.121
and see you read no other lectures to her. 1.02.147
well read in poetry | and other books, good ones 1.02.170
tongue, | as is the other for beauteous modesty. 1.02.253
but for these other /gawds, | unbind my hands, 2.01. 3
face | which i could fancy more than any other. 2.01. 12
latin, and other languages, as the other in 2.01. 81 P
as the other in music and mathematics. 2.01. 82 P
a kate | conformable as other household kates. 2.01.278
on one leg and a kersey boot–hose on the other, 3.02. 67 P
having no other reason | but that his beard grew 3.02.174
take that, and mend the plucking /off the other. 4.01.148
bianca | doth fancy any other but lucentio? 4.02. 2
and craves no other tribute at thy hands | but 5.02.152
and finds no other advantage in the process but AWW 1.01. 15 P
madam, i have other holy reasons, such as they 1.03. 32 P
and she herself, without other advantage, may 1.03.102 P
can 't no other, | but, i your daughter, he must 1.03.165
thy cheeks | confess it, /t' /one to th' other, 1.03.177
do other servants so? 2.03.251 P
to other regions! 2.03.283
the other, that she's in earth, from whence god 2.04. 12 P
and by other warranted testimony. 2.05. 5 P
where are my other men, monsieur? 2.05. 89
he shall suppose no other but that he is carried 3.06. 25 P
he can come no other way but by this 4.01. 1 P
for his presence must be the whip of the other. 4.03. 36 P
and how mightily some other times we drown our 4.03. 67 P
duke knows him for no other but a poor officer 4.03.198 P
and writ to me this other day to turn him out a' 4.03.199 P
a file with the duke's other letters in my tent. 4.03.204 P
what's his brother, the other captain dumaine? 4.03.282 P
i am for other business. 5.02. 34 P
thee in grace and the other brings thee out. 5.02. 50 P
which warp'd the line of every other favor, 5.03. 49
of their going to bed, and of other motions, as 5.03.263 P
that if one break, the other will hold; TN 1.05. 24 P
sir, for want of other idleness, i'll bide your 1.05. 64 P
saw him put down the other day with an ordinary 1.05. 84 P
and ask no other dowry with her but such another 2.05.184 P
i can no other answer make but thanks, | and 3.03. 14
me | to any other trust but that i am mad | or 4.03. 15
the vows | we made each other but so late ago. 5.01.215
but when in other habits you are seen, 5.01.387
if there were no other excuse why they should WT 1.01. 43 P
i' th' sun, | and bleat the one at th' other. 1.02. 68
th' other for some while a friend. 1.02.108
whiles other men have gates, and those gates 1.02.197
all other circumstances | made up to th' deed), 2.01.178
the testimony on my part no other | but what 3.02. 24
such, | so and no other, as yourself commanded; 3.02. 66
still, still so, | and own no other function. 4.04.143
we'll buy the other things anon. 4.04.274 P
but for some other reasons, my grave sir, 4.04.411
one | he chides to hell and bids the other grow 4.04.553
to me that all their other senses stuck in ears. 4.04.609 P
also, to smell out work for th' other senses. 4.04.673 P
there is no other way but to tell the king she's 4.04.688 P
with aqua–vitae or some other hot infusion; 4.04.787 P
the other, when she has obtain'd your eye, 5.01.105
and many other evidences proclaim her, with all 5.02. 38 P
not have relish'd among my other discredits. 5.02.123 P
you denied to fight with me this other day, 5.02.129 P
and coops from other lands her islanders, | even JN 2.01. 25
so, and at the other hill | command the rest to 2.01.298
why then defy each other, and pell–mell | make 2.01.406
what other harm have i, good lady, done, | but 3.01. 38
whirl about | the other four in wondrous motion. 4.02.184
arm you against your other enemies, | i'll make 4.02.249
nor met with fortune other than at feasts, 5.02. 58
when we were happy we had other names. 5.04. 8
with whom yourself, myself, and other lords, 5.07. 93
with other princes that may best be spar'd, 5.07. 97
namely, to appeal each other of high treason. R2 1.01. 27
prince, | and free from other misbegotten hate, 1.01. 33
or any other ground inhabitable | where ever 1.01. 65
the other part reserv'd i by consent, | for that 1.01.128
no, it is stopp'd with other flattering sounds, 2.01. 17
this other eden, demi–paradise, | this fortress 2.01. 42
t' other again | is my kinsman, whom the king 2.02.113
enjoy, | the other to enjoy by rage and war. 2.04. 14
therefore no dancing, girl, some other sport. 3.04. 9
amongst much other talk, that very time, | i 4.01. 14
he, from the one side to the other turning, 5.02. 18
love loving not itself, none other can. 5.03. 88
this match'd with other did, my gracious lord, 1H4 1.01. 49
the council rated me the other day in the street 1.02. 84 P
and by every other appointment to be ourselves. 1.02.175 P
there are other troyans that thou dream'st not 2.01. 69 P
so strongly that they dare not meet each other; 2.02.106
one that never spake other english in his life 2.04. 24 P
unbound the rest, and then come in the other. 2.04.183 P
me up | with like advantage on the other side, 3.01.108
much | as on the other side it takes from you. 3.01.110
the other night i fell asleep here behind the 3.03. 97 P
and said this other day you ought him a thousand 3.03.133 P
were enrich'd with any other injuries but these, 3.03.161 P
i must go write again | to other friends, and so 4.04. 41
a time | to punish this offense in other faults. 5.02. 7
other offenders we will pause upon. 5.05. 15
the big year, swoll'n with some other grief, 2H4 in 13
and not a man of them brings other news | than in 38
myself, but the cause that wit is in other men. 1.02. 10 P
my service for any other reason than to set me 1.02. 13 P
if you say i am any other than an honest man. 1.02. 85 P
all the other gifts appertinent to man, as the 1.02.171 P
and the pox pinches the other, and so both the 1.02.231 P
for the one or the other plays the rogue with my 1.02.244 P
money, and the other with current repentance. 2.01.121 P
let it alone, i'll make other shift. 2.01.156 P
master tisick, the debuty, t' other day, and, as 2.04. 85 P
and such other gambol faculties 'a has, that 2.04.250 P
for th' other, i owe her money, and whether she 2.04.339 P
and other times to see | the beachy girdle of 3.01. 49
me, there are other men fitter to go out than i. 3.02.114 P
for th' other, sir john, let me see: 3.02.120 P

of them all speaks any other word but my name. 4.03. 19 P
one time or other break some gallows' back. 4.03. 29
between his greatness and thy other brethren. 4.04. 26
with poins, and other his continual followers. 4.04. 53
by which his grace must mete the lives of other, 4.04. 77
up, and bear me hence | into some other chamber. 4.04.132
call for the music in the other room. 4.05. 4
let us withdraw into the other room. 4.05. 18
other, less fine in carat, /is more precious, 4.05.161
gape | for thee thrice wider than for other men. 5.05. 54
cut thy throat one time or other in fair terms, H5 2.01. 69 P
and other devils that suggest by treasons | do 2.02.114
of my birth, and in other particularities. 3.02.130 P
gentlemen both, you will mistake each other. 3.02.135 P
horse, and all other jades you may call beasts. 3.07. 24 P
a while, | and then i would no other company. 4.01. 32
you speak this to feel other men's minds. 4.01.126 P
and form, | creating awe and fear in other men? 4.01.247
my prains what is the name of the other river; 4.07. 29 P
of other lords and barons, knights and squires, 4.08. 78
and of all other men | but five and twenty. 4.08.105
and little loss, | on one part and on th' other? 4.08.111
and for the other i have no strength in measure, 5.02.135 P
he hath not the gift to woo in other places; 5.02.155 P
french, french englishmen, | receive each other. 5.02.368
the other lords, like lions wanting food, | do 1H6 1.02. 27
traitors have never other company. 2.01. 19
the other yet may rise against their force. 2.01. 32
and now there rests no other shift but this, 2.01. 75
spoils, | using no other weapon but his name. 2.01. 81
i'll sort some other time to visit you. 2.03. 27
nor other satisfaction do i crave, | but only, 2.03. 77
shall yield the other in the right opinion. 2.04. 42
a grave, | as witting i no other comfort have. 2.05. 16
that you elect no other king but him; 4.01. 4
with other vile and ignominious terms: 4.01. 97
it rest, | other affairs must now be managed. 4.01.181
this shouldering of each other in the court, 4.01.189
whiles they each other cross, | lives, honors, 4.03. 52
where is my other life? 4.07. 1
she vaunted 'mongst her minions t' other day, 2H6 1.03. 84
i did correct him for his fault the other day, 1.03.199 P
and other of your highness' privy council, | as 2.01.172
the other, walter whitmore, is thy share. 4.01. 14
for any that calls me other than lord mortimer. 4.06. 6 P
forefathers had no other books but the score and 4.07. 35 P
famine and no other hath slain me. 4.10. 60 P
but if thy arms be to no other end, | the king 5.01. 39
and have no other reason for this wrong | but 5.01.189
seek thee out some other chase, | for i myself 5.02. 14
nay, warwick, single out some other chase, | for 3H6 2.04. 12
the other his pale cheeks, methinks, presenteth. 2.05.100
wither one rose, and let the other flourish; 2.05.101
and come some other time to know our mind. 3.02. 17
one way or other, she is for a king, | and she 3.02. 87
i, being but a bachelor, have other some. 3.02.104
what other pleasure can the world afford? 3.02.147
for i will hence to warwick's other daughter, 4.01.120
blow, | and with the other fling it at thy face, 5.01. 51
so other foes may set upon our backs. 5.01. 61
king | in deadly hate the one against the other; R3 1.01. 35
no other harm but loss of such a lord. 1.03. 7
came, | ready to catch each other by the throat, 1.03.188
you have been factious one against the other. 2.01. 20
now cheer each other in each other's love. 2.02.114
my other self, my counsel's consistory, | my 2.02.151
which may make you and him to rue at th' other. 3.02. 14
and at the other is my good friend catesby; 3.02. 22
there's some conceit or other likes him well, 3.04. 49
star'd each on other, and look'd deadly pale; 3.07. 26
then, on the other side, i check'd my friends. 3.07.150
but we will plant some other in the throne, | to 3.07.216
which issued from my other angel husband, | and 4.01. 68
/which in their summer beauty kiss'd each other. 4.03. 13
/thy other edward dead, to quit my edward; 4.04. 64
there is no other way, | unless thou couldst put 4.04.285
unless thou couldst put on some other shape 4.04.286
crew, | and many other of great name and worth; 4.05. 16
they would restrain the one, distain the other. 5.03.322
the other moi'ty ere you ask is given; H8 1.02. 12
unfit for other life, compell'd by hunger | and 1.02. 34
compell'd by hunger | and lack of other means, 1.02. 35
he had a black mouth that said other of him. 1.03. 58
and with some other business put the king | from 2.02. 56
no other obligation? 2.03. 96
would all other women | could speak this with as 3.01. 31
they are (as all my other comforts) far hence 3.01. 90
accompanied with other | learned and reverend 4.01. 25
from the king's secretary, | the other, london. 4.01.103
the other, though unfinish'd, yet so famous, 4.02. 61
after my death i wish no other herald, | no 4.02. 69
no other speaker of my living actions | to keep 4.02. 70
is there no other way of mercy | but i must 5.02.127
what other | would you expect? 5.02.128
are under the line, they need no other penance: 5.03. 43 P
helen herself swore th' other day that troilus, TRO 1.02. 93 P
he having color enough, and the other higher, is 1.02.103 P
she came to him th' other day into the compass'd 1.02.111 P
enthron'd and spher'd | amidst the other; 1.03. 91
looks | know them from eyes of other mortals? 1.03.225
and her worth | in other arms than hers — to 1.03.272
two curs shall tame each other; 1.03.389
act | such and no other than event doth form it, 2.02.120
he hopes it is no other | but for your health 2.03.110
pride hath no other glass | to show itself but 3.03. 47
salutes each other with each other's form; 3.03.108
aleven of the clock it will go one way or other. 3.03.296 P
the one and other diomed embraces. 4.01. 15
we know each other well. 4.01. 31
we do, and long to know each other worse. 4.01. 32
so many thousand sighs | did buy each other, 4.04. 40
the edge of all extremity | pursue each other, 4.05. 69
infinite as all, | the other blank as nothing. 4.05. 81
but with my heart the other eye doth see. 5.02.108
a' th' t' other side, the policy of those crafty 5.04. 9 P
soft, here comes sleeve and t' other. 5.04. 18 P
the other side a' th' city is risen; COR 1.01. 47 P
where th' other instruments | did see and hear, 1.01.101

with other muniments and petty helps | in this 1.01.118
one affrights you, | the other makes you proud. 1.01.170
but i beseech you, | what says the other troop? 1.01.204
lean upon one crutch, and fight with t' other, 1.01.242
him, or pitying, threat'ning th' other; 1.06. 36
shall bear the business in some other fight, 1.06. 82
the one part suffered, the other will i do. 2.03.124
gap of both, and take | the one by th' other. 3.01.112
cause, the other | insult without all reason; 3.01.143
the other course | will prove too bloody; 3.01.325
in peace what each of them by th' other lose 3.02. 44
broke their sleep | to take the one the other, 4.04. 20
you, poor gentleman, take up some other station; 4.05. 30 P
had we no other quarrel else to rome but that 4.05.127
for the other has half by the entreaty and grant 4.05.199 P
a thing | made by some other deity than nature, 4.06. 91
and you'll look pale | before you find it other. 4.06.102
not to be other than one thing, not moving 4.07. 42
were author of himself, | and knew no other kin. 5.03. 37
is that the one will help to cut the other. TIT 3.01. 78
here stands my other son, a banish'd man, | and 3.01. 99
thy other banish'd son with this dear sight 3.01.256
hair, thy other hand | gnawing with thy teeth, 3.01.260
head, | and in this hand the other will i bear; 3.01.280
bait, | the other rotted with delicious /feed. 4.04. 93
is not thy coming for my other hand? 5.02. 27
both by myself and many other friends, | but he, ROM 1.01.146
this is not romeo, he's some other where. 1.01.198
examine other beauties. 1.01.228
your lady's love against some other maid | that 1.02. 97
o, be some other name! 2.02. 42
a rose | by any other word would smell as sweet; 2.02. 44
forget, | forgetting any other home but this. 2.02.175
the other did not so. 2.03. 87
i know it begins with some other letter — and 2.04.210 P
my back a' t' other side — ah, my back, my back 2.05. 50
have none shortly, for one would kill the other. 3.01. 16 P
having no other reason but because thou hast 3.01. 20 P
and with the other sends | it back to tybalt, 3.01.162
and needly will be rank'd with other griefs, 3.02.117
stuff'd, and other skins | of ill–shap'd fishes, 5.01. 43
gave | good words the other day of a bay courser TIM 1.02.211
that with your other noble parts you'll suit 2.02. 23
and so, intending other serious matters, | after 2.02.210
gentlemen, to repair some other hour, i should 3.04. 69 P
honorable lord did but try us this other day. 3.06. 3 P
when your lordship this other day sent to me, i 3.06. 42 P
he gave me a jewel th' other day, and now he has 3.06.112 P
the other, at high wish. 4.03.245
wilt thou whip thine own faults in other men? 5.01. 39
love, with other incident throes | that nature's 5.01.200
and strain what other means is left unto us | in 5.01.227
each | prescribe to other as each other's leech. 5.04. 84
war, | forgets the shows of love to other men. JC 1.02. 47
but by reflection, by some other things. 1.02. 53
set honor in one eye and death i' th' other, 1.02. 86
i cannot tell what you and other men | think of 1.02. 93
put it by thrice, every time gentler than other; 1.02.230 P
what other bond | than secret romans, that have 2.01.124
and what other oath | than honesty to honesty 2.01.126
never follow any thing | that other men begin. 2.01.152
cassius, go you into the other street, | and 3.02. 3
which, out of use and stal'd by other men, 4.01. 38
call claudio and some other of my men, | i'll 4.03.242
they could be content | to visit other places, 5.01. 9
bills | unto the legions on the other side. 5.02. 2
i myself have all the other, | and the very MAC 1.03. 14
let us speak | our free hearts each to other. 1.03.155
itself, | and falls on th' other — how now? 1.07. 28
who dares receive it other, | as we shall make 1.07. 77
eyes are made the fools o' th' other senses, 2.01. 44
that they did wake each other. 2.02. 21
the other, | as they had seen me with these 2.02. 24
who's there, in th' other devil's name? 2.03. 7 P
'tis said, they eat each other. 2.04. 18
'tis no other; 3.04. 96
thou other gold–bound brow, is like the first. 4.01.114
these are portable, | with other graces weigh'd. 4.03. 90
her walking and other actual performances, what, 5.01. 12 P
we learn no other but the confident tyrant 5.04. 8
that hath a stomach in't, which is no other, HAM 1.01.100
i think it be no other but e'en so. 1.01.108
makes us traduc'd and tax'd of other nations. 1.04. 18
and there assume some other horrible form, 1.04. 72
i saw him yesterday, or th' other day, | or then 2.01. 54
as his shirt, his knees knocking each other, 2.01. 78
and, with his other hand thus o'er his brow, 2.01. 86
i doubt it is no other but the main, | his 2.02. 56
to visit you, my lord, no other occasion. 2.02.271 P
it, | and /live the purer with the other half. 3.04.158
not there, seek him i' th' other place yourself. 4.03. 34 P
the other motive, | why to a public count i 4.07. 16
for this, sir, now shall you see the other — 5.02. 1
folded the writ up in the form of th' other, 5.02. 51
myself an enemy to all other joys | which the LR 1.01. 73
your honor, and to no other pretense of danger. 1.02. 87 P
of a prediction i read this other day, what 1.02.141 P
he flashes into one gross crime or other | that 1.03. 4
if but as /well i other accents borrow, | that 1.04. 1
but other of your insolent retinue | do hourly 1.04.202
is much o' th' savor | of other your new pranks. 1.04.238
shalt see thy other daughter will use thee 1.05. 14 P
and meeting here the other messenger, | whose 2.04. 38
some other time for that. 2.04.133
he that first lights on him | holla the other. 3.01. 55
who, with some other of the lord's dependants, 3.07. 18
one side will mock another; th' other too. 3.07. 71
going to put out | the other eye of gloucester. 4.02. 72
but, o poor gloucester, | lost he his other eye? 4.02. 81
why then your other senses grow imperfect | by 4.06. 5
but, by your favor, | how near's the other army? 4.06.212
i am only sorry | he had no other deathsman. 4.06.258
each jealous of the other, as the stung | are of 5.01. 56
say thou'lt do't, | or thrive by other means. 5.03. 34
the one the other poison'd for my sake, | and 5.03.241
that it engluts and swallows other sorrows, OTH 1.03. 57
i am glad at soul i have no other child, | for 1.03.196
wit, | the one's for use, the other useth it. 2.01.130
or from what other course you please, which the 2.01.269 P
would invent some other custom of entertainment. 2.03. 35 P
this is a more exquisite song than the other. 2.03. 99 P
a just equinox, | the one as long as th' other. 2.03.125
though other things grow fair against the sun, 2.03.376
and needs no other suitor but his likings | /to 3.01. 48
not now, sweet desdemon, some other time. 3.03. 55
and this may help to thicken other proofs | that 3.03.430
it speaks against her with the other proofs. 3.03.441
there is no other way: 3.04.107
and shut myself up in some other course, | to 3.04.121
our other healthful members even to a sense | of 3.04.147
i was the other day talking on the sea–bank with 4.01.133 P
if you think other, | remove your thought; 4.02. 13
for my lord | from any other foul unlawful touch 4.02. 84
any sense | delighted them /in any other form; 4.02.155
if 'twere no other — 4.02.168
or cassio him, or each do kill the other, 5.01. 13
his soldiership | is twice the other twain; ANT 2.01. 35
both | would each to other and all loves to both 2.02.135
other women cloy | the appetites they feed, but 2.02.235
way like a gorgon, | the other way 's a mars. 2.05.117
we'll feast each other ere we part, and let's 2.06. 60
the other three are sealing. 3.02. 3
thou hast, | they'll grind /th' /one the other. 3.05. 15
armenia | and other of his conquer'd kingdoms, i 3.06. 36
two friends | that does afflict each other! 3.06. 78
war, whose several ranges | frighted each other? 3.13. 6
come, | let's have one other gaudy night. 3.13.182
ruffian know | i have many other ways to die; 4.01. 5
let's see if other watchmen | do hear what we do 4.03. 17
look out o' th' other side your monument, | his 4.15. 8
to do that thing that ends all other deeds, 5.02. 5
my other elements | i give to baser life. 5.02.289
two other sons, who in the wars o' th' time CYM 1.01. 35
i' th' swathing clothes the other, from their 1.01. 59
by all likelihood have confounded one the other, 1.04. 51 P
the other is not a thing for sale, and only the 1.04. 84 P
the one is but frail and the other casual. 1.04. 91 P
did amplify my judgment in | other conclusions? 1.05. 18
this way, and | contemn with mows the other; 1.06. 41
and other noble friends | are partners in the 1.06.183
have heard of here, by me, | or by some other. 2.04. 78
other of them may have crook'd noses, but to owe 3.01. 36 P
if you seek us afterwards in other terms, you 3.01. 79 P
feast, | to him the other two shall minister, 3.03. 76
i am most glad | you think of other place. 3.04.141
honor untaught, | civility not seen from other; 4.02.179
all other doubts, by time let them be clear'd, 4.03. 45
no, no, alack, | there's other work in hand. 5.05.103
be demanded, | and all the other by–dependances, 5.05.390
with other spritely shows | of mine own kindred. 5.05.428
nor ask advice of any other thought | but PER 1.01. 62
some other is more fit. 2.03. 23
h'as done no more than other knights have done, 2.03. 34
who can be other in this royal presence? 2.03. 49
waste the time, which looks for other revels. 2.03. 93
come, other sorts offend as well as we. 4.02. 36 P
with other virtues, which i'll keep from boast, 4.06.184
and other chosen attractions, would allure | and 5.01. 46
brought forth, and am | no other than i appear. 5.01.105
cleon, but i am | for other service first. 5.01.254
attributes | the faculties of other instruments TNK 1.02. 68
the one of th' other may be said to water 1.03. 58
when the other presently gives it so sweet a 2.01. 42 P
one said it was an owl, | the other he said nay, 3.05. 69
you | content to take th' other to your husband? 3.06.274
the other lose his head, | and all his friends; 3.06.296
at some time of the moon than at other some, is 4.03. 2 P
/th' other, "this fire!" 4.03. 54 P
th' other curses a suing fellow and her 4.03. 55 P
of her eye hath distemper'd the other senses. 4.03. 71 P
other objects that are inserted 'tween her mind 4.03. 79 P
an addition of some other compounded odors which 4.03. 84 P
in that light which shows | the one the other. 5.03. 22
that neither could find other, get herself 5.03. 26
anon the other, then again the first, | and by 5.03.126
if the tale we have told | (for 'tis no other) ep 13
for other ruffians, as their fancies wrought, STM II.C 84
rein, | under her other was the tender boy, VEN 32
hue, | how white and red each other did destroy! 346
her other tender hand his fair cheek feels: 352
fed, | his other agents aim at like delight? 400
being nurse and feeder of the other four! 446
"long may they kiss each other for this cure! 505
lend thee light, as thou dost lend to other." 864
those eyes that taught all other eyes to see? 952
in likely thoughts the other kills thee quickly. 990
some other in their bills | would bring him 1102
of either's color was the other queen, | proving LUC 66
one sweetly flatters, th' other feareth harm, 172
without the bed her other fair hand was, | on 393
having no other pleasure of his gain | but 860
continuance tames the one, the other wild, 1097
one, | will slay the other and be nurse to none. 1162
when the one pure, the other made divine? 1164
life, | the one will live, the other being dead: 1187
weeps, the other takes in hand | no cause, but 1235
back, | brings home his lord and other company, 1584
the one doth call her his, the other his, | yet 1793
because thou lov'st the one, and i the other. PP 8. 4
other help for him i see that there is none. 17.36
and your sweet semblance to some other give. SON 13. 4
by toil, the other to complain | how far i toil, 28. 7
both find each other, and i lose both twain, 42.11
the other two, slight air and purging fire, 45. 1
the first my thought, the other my desire, 45. 3
and each doth good turns now unto the other: 47. 2
show, | the other as your bounty doth appear, 53.11
define, | as i all other in all worths surmount. 62. 8
in other accents do this praise confound | by 69. 7
good thoughts whilst other write good words, 85. 5
when other petty griefs have done their spite, 90.10
and other strains of woe, which now seem woe, 90.13
thy looks with me, thy heart in other place. 93. 4
for to no other pass my verses tend | than of 103.11
"kind," and "true" varying to other words, | and 105.10
so that other mine | thou wilt restore to be my 134. 3

OTHERGATES 1 FR 0.0001 REL FR 0 V 1 P
would have tickled you othergates than he did. TN 5.01.194 P

OTHER'S 34 FR 0.0038 REL FR 31 V 3 P
i see we still did meet each other's man, | and ERR 5.01.387
her hairs were gold, crystal the other's eyes. LLL 4.03.140
part, | neither intitled in the other's heart. 5.02.812
but in the other's silence do i see | maid's SHR 1.01. 70
to any other's, profanation. TN 1.05.217 P
of one part confirm | the other's peace. JN 2.01.360
austria and france shoot in each other's mouth. 2.01.414
each day still better other's happiness | until R2 1.01. 22
god, | embrace each other's love in banishment, 1.03.184
nor never look upon each other's face, | nor 1.03.185
the secret whispers of each other's watch. H5 4.pr. 7
each battle sees the other's umber'd face. 4.pr. 9
look pale | with envy of each other's happiness, 5.02.351
/hastings and rivers, take each other's hand, R3 2.01. 7
and award | either of you to be the other's end. 2.01. 15
now cheer each other in each other's love. 2.02.114
we know each other's faces; 3.04. 10
th' other's not come to't. TRO 1.02. 84 P
tell me another tale when th' other's come to't. 1.02. 85 P
salutes each other with each other's form; 3.03.108
let the first budger die the other's slave, COR 1.08. 5
unbuckling helms, fisting each other's throat, 4.05.125
we may, each wreathed in the other's arms | (our TIT 2.03. 25
the one is murder, and rape is the other's name, 5.02.156
i know them both; th' other's a jeweller. TIM 1.01. 8
each | prescribe to other as each other's leech. 5.04. 84
desire his jewels, and this other's house, | and MAC 4.03. 80
swords out, and tilting one at other's /breast, OTH 2.03.183
the geck and scorn | o' th' other's villainy? CYM 5.04. 68
nor yet the other's distance comfort me. PER 1.02. 10
crystals, where they view'd each other's sorrow, VEN 963
that oft they interchange each other's seat. LUC 70
far from home, wond'ring each other's chance. 1596
either was the other's mine. PHT 36

OTHERS' 24 FR 0.0027 REL FR 23 V 1 P
and yet would herein others' eyes were worse: ERR 4.02. 26
won, | save base authority from others' books. LLL 1.01. 87
no certain life achiev'd by others' death. JN 4.02.105
hath by instinct knowledge from others' eyes 2H4 1.01. 86
i seek not to wax great by others' /waning, | or 2H6 4.10. 20
and makes her pew–fellow with others' moan! R3 4.04. 58
not, but commends itself | to others' eyes; TRO 3.03.105
that death in me at others' lives may laugh. TIM 4.03.380
a corner in the thing i love | for others' uses. OTH 3.03.273
we fall, | we answer others' merits in our name, ANT 5.02.178
action to be guided by others' experiences: CYM 1.04. 45 P
blows dust in others' eyes, to spread itself; PER 1.01. 97
here, | and by relating tales of others' griefs, 1.04. 2
to eat honey like a drone | from others' labors; 2.ch. 19
is more | than others' labored meditance; TNK 1.01.136
grieving themselves to guess at others' smarts, LUC 1238
brought | by deep surmise of others' detriment, 1579
in others' works thou dost but mend the style, SON 78.11
abysm i throw all care | of others' voices, that 112.10
not by our feeling, but by others' seeing. 121. 4
for why should others' false adulterate eyes 121. 5
robb'd others' beds' revenues of their rents. 142. 8
blood | that we must curb it upon others' proof, LC 163
heard where his plants in others' orchards grew, 171

/OTHERS 3 FR 0.0003 REL FR 3 V 0 P
/copy /and /book, | /that /fashion'd /others. 2H4 2.03. 32
/and /nice | /with /others /than /with /him! 2.03. 41
/not /bolds /the /king, /with /others /whom, /i LR 5.01. 26

OTHERS 88 FR 0.0099 REL FR 76 V 12 P
because authority, though it err like others, MM 2.02.134
and dispossessing all my others parts | of 2.04. 22
little fouler than it is, | to pluck on others. 2.04.147
more nor less to others paying | than by 3.02.265
he spurs on his pow'r | to qualify in others. 4.02. 83
the gold bides still | that others touch and, ERR 2.01.111
though others have the arm, show us the sleeve: 3.02. 23
hath laugh'd at such shallow follies in others, ADO 2.03. 10 P
for others say thou dost deserve, and i 3.01.115
to correct yourself, for the example of others. 5.01.323 P
teaches them suspect | the thoughts of others! MV 1.03.162
and others, when the bagpipe sings i' th' nose, 4.01. 49
i come but in, as others do, to try with him the AYL 1.02.171 P
of men that put quarrels purposely on others, to TN 3.04.244 P
the oracle | give rest to th' minds of others — WT 2.01.191
but spoke the harm that is by others done? JN 3.01. 39
and others more, going to seek the grave | of 4.02.164
that england, that was wont to conquer others, R2 2.01. 65
whilst others come to make him lose at home. 2.02. 81
that many have and others must /sit there; 5.05. 27
faith, i ran when i saw others run. 1H4 2.04.302 P
others would say, "where, which is bullingbrook? 3.02. 49
others, like merchants, venter trade abroad; H5 1.02.192
others, like soldiers, armed in their stings, 1.02.193
and to teach others how they should prepare. 4.01.185 P
my grisly countenance made others fly, | none 1H6 1.04. 47
when others sleep upon their quiet beds, 2.01. 6
because you want the grace that others have, 5.04. 46
watch thou, and wake when others be asleep, | to 2H6 1.01.249
it | as others would ambitiously receive it. 2.03. 36
others to th' inns of court; 4.07. 2 P
that didst unworthy slaughter upon others. R3 1.02. 88
i lay unto the grievous charge of others. 1.03.325
in that file | where others tell steps with me. H8 1.02. 43
you know no more than others? 1.02. 44
others, to hear the city | abus'd extremely, and ep 5
he shall as soon read in the eyes of others | as TRO 3.03. 77
as when his virtues, aiming upon others, | heat 3.03.100
till he communicate his parts to others; 3.03.117
whiles others play the idiots in her eyes! 3.03.135
you'll ne'er be good, | nor suffer others. 4.02. 30
whiles others fish with craft for great opinion, 4.04.103
ay, if you come not in the blood of others, COR 1.06. 28
and topping all others in boasting. 2.01. 20 P
for rome, he fought | beyond the mark of others. 2.02. 89
my affairs | are servanted to others; 5.02. 83
and am not | of stronger earth than others. 5.03. 29
men of heart | look'd wond'ring each at others. 5.06. 99
this but begins the woe others must end. ROM 3.01.120
some others search. 5.03.178
being free itself, it thinks all others so. TIM 2.02.233

'bove all others? 3.03. 1
do you damn others, and let this damn you, | and 4.03.165
son, | spiteful and wrathful, who (as others do) MAC 3.05. 12
others that lesser hate him | do call it valiant 5.02. 13
as i receiv'd it, and others, whose judgments in HAM 2.02.438 P
have, | than fly to others that we know not of? 3.01. 81
allowance, o'erweigh a whole theatre of others. 3.02. 28 P
i have seen play — and heard others /praise, 3.02. 29 P
look well-favor'd | when others are more wicked; LR 2.04.257
fool to sorrow, | ang'ring itself and others. 4.01. 39
with others whom the rigor of our state | forc'd 5.01. 22
others there are | who, trimm'd in forms and OTH 1.01. 49
that they do | when they change us for others? 4.03. 97
are misthought | for things that others do; ANT 5.02.177
/this eye or ear | distinguish him from others, CYM 1.03. 10
if she went before others i have seen, as that 1.04. 72 P
that others do | (i was about to say) enjoy your 1.06. 90
but the gods made you | (unlike all others) 1.06.178
to prince it much | beyond the trick of others. 3.03. 86
you, live, | and deal with others better. 5.05.420
to make some good, but others to exceed, | and PER 2.03. 16
(millions of rates) | exceed the wine of others. TNK 1.04. 30
humors that | stick misbecomingly on others, on 5.03. 54
"for there his smell with others being mingled, VEN 691
others they think delight | in such-like 843
while others saucily | promise more speed, but LUC 1348
to think their dolor others have endured. 1582
no love toward others in that bosom sits | that SON 9.13
and die as fast as they see others grow, | and 12.12
from me far off, with others all too near. 61.14
when others would give life and bring a tomb. 83.12
then others for the breath of words respect, 85.13
who, moving others, are themselves as stone, 94. 3
others but stewards of their excellence. 94. 8
shall will in others seem right gracious, | and 135. 7
o, though i love what others do abhor, | with 150.11
with others thou shouldst not abhor my state: 150.12

OTHERWHERE 2 FR 0.0002 REL FR 2 V 0 P
i know his eye doth homage otherwhere, | or else ERR 2.01.104
excuse me, | the king has sent me otherwhere. H8 2.02. 59

OTHERWHILES 1 FR 0.0001 REL FR 1 V 0 P
otherwhiles the famish'd english, like pale 1H6 1.02. 7

OTHERWISE 38 FR 0.0043 REL FR 20 V 18 P
you were kneel'd to and importun'd otherwise TMP 2.01.129
i never knew him otherwise. TGV 2.05. 43 P
he hath stol'n, otherwise he had been executed; 4.04. 31 P
he hath kill'd, otherwise he had suffer'd for't. 4.04. 33 P
if she be otherwise, 'tis labor well bestow'd. WIV 2.01.239 P
otherwise you might slip away ere he came. 4.02. 53 P
otherwise he might put on a hat, a muffler, and 4.02. 70 P
not shortly, god forbid it should be otherwise. ADO 1.01.220 P
otherwise 'tis light, and not heavy. 3.04. 36 P
and seem'd i ever otherwise to you? 4.01. 55
which otherwise would grow into extremes. SHR in.1. 138
my maiden's name | sear'd otherwise; AWW 2.01.173
otherwise a seducer flourishes, and a poor maid 5.03.145 P
you'll find it otherwise, i assure you; TN 3.04.229 P
if it prove | she's otherwise, i'll keep my WT 2.01.134
my inward soul | persuades me it is otherwise. R2 2.02. 29
aside, thou art a beast to say otherwise. 1H4 3.03.123 P
i would it were otherwise, i would my means were 2H4 1.02.142 P
i am the sorrier, would 'twere otherwise! 5.02. 32
we hope no otherwise from your majesty. 5.02. 62
if you take the matter otherwise than is meant, H5 3.02.125 P
of it, and the modesty of it, to be otherwise. 4.01. 74 P
you find it otherwise, and henceforth let a 5.01. 77 P
are true, | otherwise i renounce all confidence. 1H6 1.02. 97
we do no otherwise than we are will'd. 1.03. 10
and otherwise will henry ne'er presume. 5.05. 22
otherwise, | he knew his man. TRO 2.01.128
would it were otherwise: 2.03. 4 P
to report otherwise were a malice that, giving COR 2.02. 32 P
sirs, | it may be i shall otherwise bethink me. JC 4.03.251
said, "'tis so," | when it prov'd otherwise? HAM 2.02.155
take this from this, if this be otherwise. 2.02.156
how otherwise? 4.07. 58
beguile | the thing i am by seeming otherwise. OTH 2.01.123
you not making it appear otherwise, for your ill CYM 1.04.161 P
was he | that (otherwise than noble nature did) 4.02.364
as your fair self, doth tune us otherwise. PER 1.01.115
and he that otherwise accounts of me, | this 2.05. 63

OTTER 3 FR 0.0003 REL FR 0 V 3 P
what beast? why, an otter. 1H4 3.03.125 P
an otter, sir john, why an otter? 3.03.126 P
an otter, sir john, why an otter? 3.03.126 P

OTTOMAN 1 FR 0.0001 REL FR 1 V 0 P
employ you | against the general enemy ottoman. OTH 1.03. 49

OTTOMITES 3 FR 0.0003 REL FR 3 V 0 P
the ottomites, reverend and gracious, | steering OTH 1.03. 33
this present wars against the ottomites. 1.03.234
that | which heaven hath forbid the ottomites? 2.03.171

O,U 1 FR 0.0001 REL FR 0 V 1 P
the sheep: the other two concludes it — o,u. LLL 5.01. 57 P

OUBLIE 3 FR 0.0003 REL FR 0 V 3 P
qu'ai-je oublie? WIV 1.04. 63 P
o seigneur dieu, je m'en oublie d' elbow. H5 3.04. 31 P
n'avez vous deja oublie ce que je vous ai 3.04. 42 P

OUCHES 1 FR 0.0001 REL FR 0 V 1 P
"your brooches, pearls, and ouches." 2H4 2.04. 48 P

OUGHT* 22 FR 0.0024 REL FR 10 V 12 P
it is spoke as a christians ought to speak. WIV 1.01.101 P
in the world that good christians ought to have. MM 2.01. 56 P
he ought to enter into a quarrel with fear and ADO 2.03.194 P
for indeed the watch ought to offend no man, and 3.03. 81 P
masters, you ought to consider with /yourselves, MND 3.01. 29 P
and we ought to look to't. 3.01. 33 P
vessel, as doublet and hose ought to show itself AYL 2.04. 7 P
your ladyship will have it as it ought to be, TN 5.01.295 P
that mercy which true prayer ought to have. R2 5.03.110
this other day you ought him a thousand pound. 1H4 3.03.134 P
affability as in discretion you ought to use me, H5 3.02.128 P
for discipline ought to be used. 3.06. 56 P
or whether that such cowards ought to wear 1H6 4.01. 28
of storm, | as every loyal subject ought to do. 3H6 4.07. 44
in my opinion, ought to be prevented. R3 2.02.131
do require our voices, we ought not to deny him. COR 2.03. 1 P
say then; 'tis true, i ought so. 3.03. 62
you ought not walk | upon a laboring day without JC 1.01. 3
and virtue of my place, | i ought to know of; 2.01.270
speak what we feel, not what we ought to say: LR 5.03.325
i must, i ought to do so, and i dare — | and TNK 2.02.205
lied so lewdly | that women ought to beat me. 4.02. 36

OUGHTST 1 FR 0.0001 REL FR 0 V 1 P
thou oughtst not to let thy horse wear a cloak, 2H6 4.07. 49 P

/OUI 1 FR 0.0001 REL FR 1 V 0 P
"/oui" away | the lag end of their lewdness and H8 1.03. 34

OUI 6 FR 0.0006 REL FR 0 V 6 P
oui, mette le au mon pocket; WIV 1.04. 54 P
je pense qu'ils sont appeles de fingres, oui, de H5 3.04. 11 P
oui. 3.04. 37 P
oui, vraiment, sauf votre grace, ainsi dit-il. 5.02.112 P
oui, dat de tongeus of de mans is be full of 5.02.119 P
oui, vraiment. 5.02.267 P

OUNCE* 6 FR 0.0006 REL FR 4 V 2 P
my sweet ounce of man's flesh, my incony jew! LLL 3.01.135
be it ounce, or cat, or bear, | pard, or boar MND 2.02. 30
nay then i must have an ounce or two of this TN 4.01. 44 P
had been the dearer by i know how much an ounce. WT 4.04.705 P
by many an ounce) he dropp'd it for his country; COR 3.01.299
give me an ounce of civet; LR 4.06.130

OUNCES 1 FR 0.0001 REL FR 1 V 0 P
dread father's, in a scale | of common ounces? TRO 2.02. 28

OUPHES 2 FR 0.0002 REL FR 2 V 0 P
we'll dress | like urchins, ouphes, and fairies, WIV 4.04. 50
strew good luck, ouphes, on every sacred room, 5.05. 57

'OUR 1 FR 0.0001 REL FR 1 V 0 P
her breeding as | she is i' th' rear 'our birth. WT 4.04.581

/OUR 41 FR 0.0046 REL FR 38 V 3 P

OUR 3264 FR 0.3689 REL FR 2885 V 379 P

/OURS 2 FR 0.0002 REL FR 2 V 0 P
my mind presumes, for his own good and /ours. SHR 1.02.213
/will /revenge /these /bitter /woes /of /ours. TIT 3.02. 3

OURS 92 FR 0.0104 REL FR 86 V 6 P
although by /confiscation they are ours, | we do MM 5.01.423
why should their liberty than ours be more? ERR 2.01. 10
his glory shall be ours, for we are the only ADO 2.01.386 P
would not show us | whiles it was ours. 4.01.222
my will is your good will | may stand with ours, 5.04. 29
to make theirs ours and ours none but our own; LLL 5.02.154
to make theirs ours and ours none but our own; 5.02.154
and in such eyes as ours appear not faults, MV 2.02.183
you will answer, | "the slaves are ours." 4.01. 98
what says lucentio to this shame of ours? SHR 3.02. 7
if ever we are nature's, these are ours. AWW 1.03.129
ours be your patience then, and yours our parts; ep 5
the imposition clear'd, | hereditary ours. WT 1.02. 75
your young prince as we | do seem to be of ours? 1.02.165
gain, the ord'ring on't, is all | properly ours. 2.01.170
this toil of ours should be a work of thine; JN 2.01. 93
as we will ours, against these saucy walls, 2.01.404
let us share thy thoughts, as thou dost ours. R2 2.01.273
words come from his mouth, ours from our breast; 5.03.102
ours of true zeal and deep integrity; 5.03.108
betwixt that holmedon and this seat of ours; 1H4 1.01. 65
o, we are undone, both we and ours for ever! 2.02. 86 P
rich reprisal is so nigh, | and yet not ours. 4.01.119
his is certain, ours is doubtful. 4.03. 4
the better part of ours are full of rest. 4.03. 27
as we will ours, and here between the armies 2H4 4.02. 62
france being ours, we'll bend it to our awe, H5 1.02.224
that grows not in a fair consent with ours; 2.02. 22
enter our gates, dispose of us and ours, | for 3.03. 49
his affections are higher mounted than ours, yet 4.01.106 P
out of doubt, be of the same relish as ours are; 4.01.109 P
herald, | i know not if the day be ours or no, 4.07. 84
four of their lords i'll change for one of ours. 1H6 1.01.151
froissard, a countryman of ours, records 1.02. 29
this day is ours, as many more shall be. 1.05. 18
fools, | to try if that our own be ours or no. 3.02. 63
all will be ours, now bloody talbot's slain. 4.07. 96
for france, 'tis ours; 2H6 1.01.106
that nothing sung but death to us and ours. 3H6 2.06. 57
but follow me, and edward shall be ours. 4.03. 25
what may befall him, to his harm and ours. 4.06. 95
her faction will be full as strong as ours. 5.03. 17
king, | as ours by murther, to make him a king! R3 1.03.197
the day is ours, the bloody dog is dead. 5.05. 2
(once weak ones) is | not ours, or not allow'd; H8 1.02. 83
know within a while | all the best men are ours; ep 13
i mean, of ours. TRO 2.02. 20
if we have lost so many tenths of ours, | to 2.02. 21
to guard a thing not ours nor worth to us | (had 2.02. 22
had with troy | as perfectly is ours as yours, 3.03.206
great troy is ours, and our sharp wars are ended 5.09. 10
then shall we hear their 'larum, and they ours. COR 1.04. 9
we may articulate | for their own good and ours. 1.09. 78
and till we call'd | both field and city ours, 2.02.121
sons, let it be your charge, as it is ours, | to TIT 2.02. 7
shall she live to betray this guilt of ours, | a 4.02.149
and ours with thine, befall what fortune will. 5.03. 3
i must up-fill this osier cage of ours | with ROM 2.03. 7
for blood of ours, shed blood of montague. 3.01.149
so is theirs and ours. TIM 3.04. 6
and ours, my lord. 3.04. 88 P
and of our athens, thine and ours, to take | the 5.01.160
ours is the fall, i fear, our foes the snare. 5.02. 17
these walls of ours | were not erected by their 5.04. 22
three parts of him | is ours already, and the JC 1.03.155
upon the next encounter yields him ours. 1.03.156
that most may claim this argument for ours? MAC 2.03.120
they not forc'd with those that should be ours, 5.05. 5
our thoughts are ours, their ends none of our HAM 3.02.213
our crown, our life, and all that we call ours, 4.05.209
is queen of us, of ours, and our fair france. LR 1.01.257
so much commend itself, you shall be ours. 2.01.114
that we can call these delicate creatures ours, OTH 3.03.269
often hurl from us, | we wish it ours again. ANT 1.02.124
and speaks as loud | as his own state and ours, 1.04. 30
both as the same, or rather ours the elder — 3.10. 13
if fortune be not ours to-day, it is | because 4.04. 4
shall want troops, | and all the haunt be ours. 4.14. 54
she soon shall know of us, by some of ours, 5.01. 57
must not so far prefer her 'fore ours of italy. CYM 1.04. 65 P
house with such | whose roof's as low as ours! 3.03. 2
no life to ours. 3.03. 26
no care of yours it is, you know 'tis ours. 5.04.100
your danger's ours. 5.05.314
and so in ours, some neighboring nation, PER 1.04. 65
whilest ours was blurted at and held a mawkin 4.03. 34
thirds his own worth (the case is each of ours), TNK 1.02. 96
garlands, | ere they have time to wish 'em ours. 2.02. 17
can be, but our imaginations | may make it ours? 2.02. 78
even in the moment that we call them ours. LUC 868
we have no good that we can say is ours, | but 873
we are their offspring, and they none of ours. 1757

OURSELF 25 FR 0.0028 REL FR 25 V 0 P
in our remove be thou at full ourself. MM 1.01. 43
we cannot weigh our brother with ourself. 2.02.126
learning is but an adjunct to ourself, | and LLL 4.03.310
ourself and bushy, /bagot /here /and /green, R2 1.04. 23
we will ourself in person to this war, | and, 1.04. 42
and we create, in absence of ourself, | our 2.01.219
because we thought ourself thy lawful king; 3.03. 74
hence, did give ourself | to barbarous license; H5 1.02.270
it was ourself thou didst abuse. 4.08. 49
we charge you, on allegiance to ourself, | to 1H6 3.01. 86
ourself, my lord protector, and the rest, 4.01.169
best, | do or undo, as if ourself were here. 2H6 3.01.196
warwick, as ourself, | shall do and undo as him 3H6 2.06.104
ourself the merchant, and this sailing pandar TRO 1.01.103
beauty than we have, | yea, overshines ourself. 1.03.158
what touches us ourself shall be last serv'd. JC 3.01. 8
we will keep ourself | till supper-time alone; MAC 3.01. 42
ourself will mingle with society, | and play the 3.04. 3
now for ourself, and for this time of meeting, HAM 1.02. 26
be as ourself in denmark. 1.02.122
i lov'd your father, and we love ourself, | and 4.07. 34
ourself, by monthly course, | with reservation LR 1.01.132
and for ourself | to show less sovereignty than CYM 3.05. 5
you their captives, which ourself have granted; 5.05. 73
and harborage for ourself, our ships, and men. PER 1.04.100

/OURSELVES 1 FR 0.0001 REL FR 1 V 0 P
/have /brought /ourselves /into /a /burning 2H4 4.01. 56

OURSELVES 119 FR 0.0134 REL FR 100 V 19 P
fall to't, yarely, or we run ourselves aground. TMP 1.01. 4 P
and all of us, ourselves, | when no man was his 5.01.212
which, with ourselves, all rest at thy dispose. TGV 4.01. 74
being known, | we'll all present ourselves; WIV 4.04. 64
and have given ourselves without scruple to hell 5.05.148 P
which sorrow is always toward ourselves, not MM 2.03. 32
both by the syracusians and ourselves, | to ERR 1.01. 14
fast'ned ourselves at either end the mast, | and 1.01. 85
as much, or more, we should ourselves complain: 2.01. 37
ourselves we do remember, sir, by you; 5.01.293
then when ourselves we see in ladies' eyes, LLL 4.03.312
we see in ladies' eyes, | with ourselves, | do 4.03.313
/let us once lose our oaths to find ourselves, 4.03.358
or else we lose ourselves to keep our oaths. 4.03.359
if overboldly we have borne ourselves | in the 5.02.734
we to ourselves prove false, | by being once 5.02.772
bring us where we may rest ourselves and feed. AYL 2.04. 73
fear not, my lord, we can contain ourselves, SHR in.1. 100
since, of ourselves, ourselves are choleric, 4.01.174
since, of ourselves, ourselves are choleric, 4.01.174
our remedies oft in ourselves do lie, | which we AWW 1.01.216
our slow designs when we ourselves are dull. 1.01.219
deservings, when of ourselves we publish them. 1.03. 7 P
ensconcing ourselves into seeming knowledge, 2.03. 4 P
we should submit ourselves to an unknown fear. 2.03. 5 P
again and suffice ourselves with the report of 3.05. 10 P
'a will betray us all unto ourselves: 4.01. 92
you barely leave our thorns to prick ourselves, 4.02. 19
in such a scarre | that we'll forsake ourselves. 4.02. 39
as we are ourselves, what things are we! 4.03. 20 P
oft our displeasures, to ourselves unjust, 5.03. 63
ourselves we do not owe; TN 1.05.310
for, boy, however we do praise ourselves, | our 2.04. 32
it is for you we speak, not for ourselves. WT 2.01.140
my best camillo! we must disguise ourselves. 4.02. 54 P
we'll have this song out anon by ourselves. 4.04.309 P
profess | ourselves to be the slaves of chance, 4.04.540
and pell-mell | make work upon ourselves, for JN 2.01.407
make such unconstant children of ourselves, | as 3.01.243
he sees | ourselves well sinewed to our defense. 5.07. 88
brow, ourselves will hear | the accuser and the R2 1.01. 16
king, | therefore we will disperse ourselves. 2.04. 4
we do debase ourselves, cousin, do we not, | to 3.03.127
and by every other appointment to be ourselves. 1H4 1.02.176 P
a head, | for, bear ourselves as even as we can, 1.03.285
and think we think ourselves unsatisfied, | till 1.03.287
forward, | on thursday we ourselves will march. 3.02.174
how in our means we should advance ourselves 2H4 1.03. 7
in his true colors, and not ourselves be seen? 2.02.170 P
beyond the river we'll encamp ourselves, | and H5 3.06.171
let's stab ourselves. 4.05. 7
even so our houses, and ourselves, and children, 5.02. 56
truce | betwixt ourselves and all our followers. 1H6 3.01.139
betwixt ourselves let us decide it then. 4.01.119
looks, | and that within ourselves we disagree, 4.01.140
though the edge hath something hit ourselves, 3H6 2.02.166
this thick-grown brake we'll shroud ourselves, 3.01. 1
and, as thou seest, ourselves in heavy plight. 3.03. 37
and with their helps only defend ourselves: 4.01. 45
in them, and in ourselves, our safety lies. 4.01. 46
and shut the gates for safety of ourselves; 4.07. 18
sirrah, leave us to ourselves, we must confer. 5.06. 6
stone a-rolling, | 'twould fall upon ourselves. H8 5.02.140
among ourselves | give him allowance for the TRO 1.03.375
to us, | when we are so unsecret to ourselves? 3.02.125
must poorly sell ourselves | with the rude 4.04. 40
not, | and sometimes we are devils to ourselves, 4.04. 95
we have power in ourselves to do it, but it is a COR 2.03. 4 P
should bring ourselves to be monstrous members. 2.03. 12 P
which we ourselves have plough'd for, sow'd, and 3.01. 71
our aediles smote, ourselves resisted? 3.01.317
ourselves, our wives, and children, on our knees 4.06. 22
will hand in hand all headlong hurl ourselves, TIT 5.03.132
this wind you talk of blows us from ourselves: ROM 1.04.104
we should think ourselves for ever perfect. TIM 1.02. 87 P
we make ourselves fools to disport ourselves, 1.02.136
we make ourselves fools to disport ourselves, 1.02.136
what we are sorry for ourselves in thee. 5.01.139

about | to find ourselves dishonorable graves. JC 1.02.138
but in ourselves, that we are underlings. 1.02.141
to ease ourselves of divers sland'rous loads, 4.01. 20
we'll along ourselves, and meet them at philippi 4.03.225
it is more worthy to leap in ourselves | than 5.05. 24
to–morrow | we'll hear ourselves again. MAC 3.04. 31
we are traitors, | and do not know ourselves; 4.02. 19
on him | together with remembrance of ourselves. HAM 1.02. 7
age | to cast beyond ourselves in our opinions, 2.01.112
and here give up ourselves, in the full bent, 2.02. 30
we'll so bestow ourselves that, seeing unseen, 3.01. 32
so please you, | we will bestow ourselves. 3.01. 43
to pay ourselves what to ourselves is debt. 3.02.193
to pay ourselves what to ourselves is debt. 3.02.193
what to ourselves in passion we propose, | the 3.02.194
we will ourselves provide. 3.03. 7
in his true nature, and we ourselves compell'd, 3.03. 62
no, nothing but ourselves. 3.04.133
to fat us, and we fat ourselves for maggots; 4.03. 22 P
finding ourselves too slow of sail, we put on a 4.06. 17 P
we are not ourselves | when nature, being LR 2.04.107
and let ourselves again but understand | that, OTH 1.03. 21
'tis in ourselves that we are thus or thus. 1.03.319 P
let's teach ourselves that honorable stop, | not 2.03. 2
and to ourselves do that | which heaven hath 2.03.170
and to defend ourselves it be a sin | when 2.03.203
and applause, transform ourselves into beasts! 2.03.292 P
time we twain | did show ourselves i' th' field, ANT 1.04. 74
we, ignorant of ourselves, | beg often our own 2.01. 5
yet, ere we put ourselves in arms, dispatch we 2.02.165
sword against sword, | ourselves alone. 3.13. 28
retire, we have engag'd ourselves too far. 4.07. 1
there is left us | ourselves to end ourselves. 4.14. 22
there is left us | ourselves to end ourselves. 4.14. 22
leave us to ourselves, and make yourself some CYM 1.01.155
people, whom we reckon | ourselves to be. 3.01. 53
be it our wives, our children, or ourselves, PER 1.04.103
well–a–day, we could scarce help ourselves. 2.01. 22 P
and ourselves | will in that kingdom spend our 5.03. 80
tell us | when we know all ourselves, and let us TNK 1.02.115
no figures of ourselves shall we ev'r see | to 2.02. 33

OUSEL *(see woosel)*

/OUT 13 FR 0.0014 REL FR 10 V 3 P
/pride /of /kingly /sway /from /out /my /heart; R2 4.01.206
/and /must /i /ravel /out | /my //weav'd–up 4.01.228
/that /i /have /worn /so /many /winters /out 4.01.258
/he /ne'er /had /borne /it /out /of /coventry; 2H4 4.01.133
that life looks through /and /will /break /out. 4.04.120
catch, and /'a knock /out either of your brains; TRO 2.01.100 P
/out /on /thee, /murderer! TIT 3.02. 54
/that /cry /out /on /the /top /of /question, HAM 2.02.340 P
/motley /here, | /the /other /found /out /there. LR 1.04.147
/if /i /had /a /monopoly /out, /they /would 1.04.153 P
/he /fastened /on /my /neck /and /bellowed /out 5.03.213
o, bear him /out o' th' air. OTH 5.01.104
i'll wake mine eyeballs /out first. CYM 3.04.101

OUT 1417 FR 0.1601 REL FR 944 V 473 P
out of our way, i say. TMP 1.01. 26 P
i am out of patience. 1.01. 55
to th' welkin's cheek, | dashes the fire out. 1.02. 5
for then thou wast not | out three years old. 1.02. 41
trunk, | and suck'd my verdure out on't. 1.02. 87
he was indeed the duke, out o' th' substitution, 1.02.103
extirpate me and mine | out of the dukedom, and 1.02.126
i, not rememb'ring how i cried out then, | will 1.02.133
out of his charity, who being then appointed 1.02.162
before the time be out? no more! 1.02.246
that made gape | the pine, and let thee out. 1.02.293
you would lift the moon out of her sphere, if 2.01.183 P
language, and thou speak'st | out of thy sleep. 2.01.212
out of that no hope | what great hope have you! 2.01.239
a space whose ev'ry cubit | seems to cry out, 2.01.258
in the dark | out of my way, unless he bid 'em; 2.02. 7
they will lay out ten to see a dead indian. 2.02. 33 P
out o' th' moon, i do assure thee. 2.02.138 P
when the butt is out, we will drink water — not 3.02. 1 P
by this hand, i'll turn my mercy out o' doors, 3.02. 70 P
out o' your wits, and hearing too? 3.02. 78 P
i am right glad that he's so out of hope. 3.03. 11
play with sparrows, | and be a boy right out. 4.01.101
of wine is, or i'll turn you out of my kingdom. 4.01.252 P
power guide us | out of this fearful country! 5.01.106
but three glasses since, we gave out split — 5.01.223
rigg'd as when | we first put out to sea. 5.01.225
last that i fear me will never out of my bones. 5.01.283 P
wear out thy youth with shapeless idleness. TGV 1.01. 8
keep tune there still, so you will sing it out. 1.02. 86
put forth their sons to seek preferment out: 1.03. 7
one is painted, and the other out of all count. 2.01. 57 P
how painted? and how out of count? 2.01. 58 P
how could he see his way to seek out you? 2.04. 94
or as one nail by strength drives out another, 2.04.193
out, out, lucetta, that will be ill–favor'd. 2.07. 54
out, out, lucetta, that will be ill–favor'd. 2.07. 54
wife | and turn her out to who will take her in: 3.01. 77
run, boy, run, run, and seek him out. 3.01.188 P
go, sirrah, find him out. come, valentine. 3.01.261
i pray thee out with't, and place it for her 3.01.335 P
out with that too; 3.01.338 P
that's monstrous. o, that that were out! 3.01.366 P
how, out of tune on the strings? 4.02. 60 P
he lov'd her out of all nick. 4.02. 76 P
"out with the dog," says one. 4.04. 20 P
"whip him out," says the third. 4.04. 21 P
me no more ado, but whips me out of the chamber. 4.04. 28 P
i should have scratch'd out your unseeing eyes, 4.04.204
eyes, | to make my master out of love with thee. 4.04.205
out at the postern by the abbey wall; 5.01. 9
such pearls as put out ladies' eyes, | for i had 5.02. 13
that they are out by lease. 5.02. 29
which, out of my neglect, was never done. 5.04. 89 P
had drunk himself out of his five sentences. WIV 1.01.175 P
well, sirs, i am almost out at heels. 1.03. 31 P
her will, out of honesty into english. 1.03. 50 P
out alas! here comes my master. 1.04. 36 P
page, i shall turn your head out of my door. 1.04.125 P
out upon't! 1.04.165 P
out of my conversation, that he dares in this 2.01. 24 P
he will print them, out of doubt; 2.01. 77 P
i will be patient; i will find out this. 2.01.126 P
here's a fellow frights english out of his wits. 2.01.139 P
i will seek out falstaff. 2.01.140 P
men — very rogues, now they be out of service. 2.01.176 P
i will stare him out of his wits; 2.02.279 P
be old and of the peace, if i see a sword out, 2.03. 45 P
he pieces out his wive's inclination; 3.02. 34 P
out upon you! 3.03.103 P
you have a friend here, convey, convey him out. 3.03.118 P
than a thousand pound he were out of the house. 3.03.124 P
ascend my chambers, search, seek, find out. 3.03.163 P
jest how my father stole two geese out of a pen, 3.04. 41 P
i'll have my brains ta'en out and butter'd, and 3.05. 7 P
on the forehead, crying, "peer out, peer out!" 4.02. 26 P
on the forehead, crying, "peer out, peer out!" 4.02. 26 P
and swears he was carried out, the last time he 4.02. 32 P
may i not go out ere he come? 4.02. 50 P
door with pistols, that none shall issue out; 4.02. 53 P
i'll go out then. 4.02. 65 P
if you go out in your own semblance, you die, 4.02. 66 P
die, sir john — unless you go out disguis'd. 4.02. 67 P
hold it out. 4.02.135 P
there was one convey'd out of my house yesterday 4.02.146 P
pluck me out all the linen. 4.02.149 P
out of my door, you witch, you rag, you baggage, 4.02.184 P
out, out! 4.02.185 P
out, out! 4.02.186 P
if i cry out thus upon no trail, never trust me 4.02.197 P
spirit of wantonness is sure scar'd out of him. 4.02.210 P
but to scrape the figures out of your husband's 4.02.216 P
out, alas, sir, cozenage! mere cozenage. 4.05. 63 P
they would melt me out of my fat drop by drop, 4.05. 97 P
search windsor castle, elves, within and out. 5.05. 56
candles, and starlight, and moonshine be out. 5.05.102
have thrust virtue out of our hearts by the head 5.05.147 P
commandements, but scrap'd one out of the table. MM 1.02. 9 P
i will, out of thine own confession, learn to 1.02. 37 P
have worn your eyes almost out in the service, 1.02.110 P
lion in a cave, | that goes not out to prey. 1.03. 23
law, | as mice by lions) hath pick'd out an act, 1.04. 64
let mine own judgment pattern out my death, 2.01. 30
he cannot, sir; he's out at elbow. 2.01. 61 P
this will last out a night in russia | when 2.01.134
you'll be glad to give out a commission for more 2.01.239 P
the valiant heart's not whipt out of his trade. 2.01.256
vantage best have took | found out the remedy. 2.02. 75
o, pardon me, my lord, it oft falls out, | to 2.04.117
but thy unkindness shall his death draw out | to 2.04.166
many a thousand grains | that issue out of dust. 3.01. 21
wilt thou be made a man out of my vice? 3.01.137
my stay must be stolen out of other affairs; 3.01.158 P
i am so out of love with life that i will sue to 3.01.171 P
but how out of this can she avail? 3.01.233 P
i have been an unlawful bawd time out of mind, 4.02. 15 P
than i meant, to pluck all fears out of you. 4.02.191 P
go in to him, and fetch him out. 4.03. 34 P
or they shall beat out my brains with billets. 4.03. 55 P
o, i will to him and pluck out his eyes! 4.03.119
come, i have found you out a stand most fit, 4.06. 10
have way, my lord, | to find this practice out. 5.01.239
him your kind pains | to find out this abuse, 5.01.247
till my tale be heard, | and hold no longer out. 5.01.366
the very mercy of the law cries out | most 5.01.407
they say best men are moulded out of faults, 5.01.439
therefore give out you are of epidamium, | lest ERR 1.02. 1
not being able to buy out his life | according 1.02. 5
dromio, come, these jests are out of season, 1.02. 68
because their business still lies out a' door. 2.01. 11
i know not thy mistress, out on thy mistress!" 2.01. 68
is wand'red forth, in care to seek me out. 2.02. 3
there ever any man thus beaten out of season, 2.02. 47
thou that keep'st me out from the house i owe? 3.01. 42
it seems thou want'st breaking, out upon thee, 3.01. 77
here's too much "out upon thee!" 3.01. 78
i could find out countries in her. 3.02.115 P
in her buttocks, i found it out by the bogs. 3.02.117 P
if any ship put out, then straight away. 3.02.185
for locking me out of my doors by day. 4.01. 18
fie, now you run this humor out of breath. 4.01. 57
now, out of doubt antipholus is mad, | else 4.03. 81
driven out of doors with it when i go from home, 4.04. 35 P
were not my doors lock'd up, and i shut out? 4.04. 70
your doors were lock'd, and you shut out. 4.04. 71
but i confess, sir, that we were lock'd out. 4.04. 99
with these nails i'll pluck out these false eyes 4.04.104
out on thee, villain, wherefore dost thou mad me 4.04.126
us, | and will not suffer us to fetch him out, 5.01.157
this woman lock'd me out this day from dinner; 5.01.218
outfacing me, | cries out, i was possess'd. 5.01.246
that he din'd not at home, but was lock'd out. 5.01.256
did he break out into tears? ADO 1.01. 24 P
is the opinion that fire cannot melt out of me; 1.01.232 P
pick out mine eyes with a ballad–maker's pen and 1.01.252 P
why are you thus out of measure sad? 1.03. 2 P
you have of late stood out against your brother, 1.03. 21 P
in every thing, and so dance out the answer. 2.01. 72 P
and god keep him out of my sight when the dance 2.01.109 P
that i had my good wit out of the "hundred merry 2.01.130 P
the world into her person, and so gives me out. 2.01.209 P
for, out a' question, you were born in a merry 2.01.332 P
no means, she mocks all her wooers out of suit. 2.01.350 P
the night, appoint her to look out at her lady's 2.02. 17 P
guts should hale souls out of men's bodies? 2.03. 60 P
and (out of all suspicion) she is virtuous. 2.03.159 P
let her wear it out with good counsel. 2.03.202 P
impossible, she may wear her heart out first. 2.03.204 P
so turns she every man the wrong side out, | and 3.01. 68
she would laugh me | out of myself, press me to 3.01. 76
can you smell him out by that? 3.02. 51 P
word is too good to paint out her wickedness. 3.02.109 P
what he is and steal out of your company. 3.03. 59 P
that the fashion wears out more apparel than the 3.03.140 P
too, that thou hast shifted out of thy tale into 3.03.142 P
she leans me out at her mistress' chamber–window 3.03.146 P
i am out of all other tune, methinks. 3.04. 43 P
if i would think my heart out of thinking, that 3.04. 84 P
they say, "when the age is in, the wit is out." 3.05. 34 P
out on thee seeming! 4.01. 56
hero, | hero itself can blot out hero's virtue. 4.01. 82
out at your window betwixt twelve and one? 4.01. 84
for it so falls out | that what we have we prize 4.01.217
out of all eyes, tongues, minds, and injuries. 4.01.243
talk with a man out at a window! 4.01.309 P
i can find out no rhyme to "lady" but "baby," an 5.02. 37 P
hast frighted the word out of his right sense, 5.02. 55 P
good morrow, masters, put your torches out. 5.03. 24
of wit–crackers cannot flout me out of my humor. 5.04.101 P
have cudgell'd thee out of thy single life, to 5.04.113 P
which out of question thou wilt be, if my cousin 5.04.115 P
well, sit you out; go home, berowne; adieu. LLL 1.01.110
i hear your grace hath sworn out house–keeping: 2.01.104
and out of heart, master; 3.01. 37 P
and out of heart you love her, being out of 3.01. 43 P
being out of heart that you cannot enjoy her. 3.01. 44 P
until the goose came out of door, | and stayed 3.01. 91
until the goose came out of door, | staying the 3.01. 97
i, costard, running out, that was safely within, 3.01.116
i will never buy and sell out of this word. 3.01.142 P
/clock, | still a–repairing, ever out of frame, 3.01.191
and, out of question, so it is sometimes: 4.01. 30
i' faith, your hand is out. 4.01.133
and if my hand be out, then belike your hand is 4.01.135
but for smelling out the odoriferous flowers of 4.02.124 P
we are much out a' th' way. 4.03. 74
then incision | would let her out in saucers. 4.03. 96
in leaden contemplation have found out | such 4.03.318
he draweth out the thread of his verbosity finer 5.01. 16 P
such eruptions and sudden breaking out of mirth, 5.01.115 P
we need more light to find your meaning out. 5.02. 21
a doubt | presence majestical would put him out; 5.02.102
the rest will /ne'er come in, if he be out. 5.02.152
out" — 5.02.164
true, out indeed. 5.02.165
"out of your favors, heavenly spirits, vouchsafe 5.02.166
they do not mark me, and that brings me out. 5.02.173
they are, with your sweet breaths puff'd out. 5.02.267
this pert berowne was out of count'nance quite. 5.02.272
berowne did swear himself out of all suit. 5.02.275
heart, | that put armado's page out of his part! 5.02.336
can any face of brass hold longer out? 5.02.395
you put our page out. 5.02.478
whole world again | cannot pick out five such, 5.02.545
you will be scrap'd out of the painted cloth for 5.02.576 P
i will not be put out of countenance. 5.02.607 P
you have put me out of countenance. 5.02.621 P
from morn till night, out of his pavilion. 5.02.654
out of a new–sad soul, that you vouchsafe | in 5.02.731
long withering out a young man's revenue. MND 1.01. 6
you should fright the ladies out of their wits, 1.02. 80 P
find you out a bed; 2.02. 39
o, i am out of breath in this fond chase! 2.02. 88
what, out of hearing gone? 2.02.152
i believe we must leave the killing out, when 3.01. 14 P
this will put them out of fear. 3.01. 22 P
find out moonshine, find out moonshine. 3.01. 54 P
find out moonshine, find out moonshine. 3.01. 54 P
but if i had wit enough to get out of this wood, 3.01.150 P
out of this wood do not desire to go; 3.01.152
this falls out better than i could devise. 3.02. 35
out, dog! 3.02. 65
out, cur! 3.02. 65
out, tawny tartar, out! 3.02.263
out, tawny tartar, out! 3.02.263
out, loathed med'cine! 3.02.264
therefore be out of hope, of question, of doubt; 3.02.279
me | to measure out my length on this cold bed. 3.02.429
fool, | i did upbraid her and fall out with her. 4.01. 50
go, one of you, find out the forester, | for now 4.01.103
my hounds are bred out of the spartan kind; 4.01.119
out of doubt he is transported. 4.02. 3 P
will tell you every thing, right as it fell out. 4.02. 32 P
for they shall hang out for the lion's claws. 4.02. 41 P
out of this silence yet i pick'd a welcome; 5.01.100
out, sword, and wound | the pap of pyramus; 5.01.296
my ventures, out of doubt | would make me sad. MV 1.01. 21
and out of doubt you do me now more wrong | in 1.01.155
in low simplicity | he lends out money gratis, 1.03. 44
a man's son may, but in the end truth will out. 2.02. 80 P
of thy old master, and inquire | my lodging out. 2.02.154
and sleep and snore, and rend apparel out — 2.05. 5
falling out that year on ash we'nsday was four 2.05. 26 P
mistress, look out at window, for all this — 2.05. 40 P
i have sent twenty out to seek for you. 2.06. 66
i pray thee let us go and find him out | and 2.08. 51
out upon it, old carrion! 3.01. 35 P
out upon her! 3.01.120 P
for, were he out of venice, i can make what 3.01.128 P
time, | to eche it and to draw it out in length, 3.02. 23
if you do love me, you will find me out. 3.02. 41
this is the fool that lent out money gratis! 3.03. 2
soul, | from out the state of hellish cruelty! 3.04. 21
not fear us, lorenzo, launcelot and i are out. 3.05. 32 P
means can carry me | out of his envy's reach, i 4.01. 10
i give you, | and find it out by proclamation; 4.01.436
she would not hold out enemy for ever | for 4.01.447
inquire the jew's house out, give him this deed, 4.02. 1
this other had pull'd out thy tongue for saying AYL 1.01. 61 P
therefore, out of my love to you, i came hither 1.01.131 P
and mine, to eke out hers. 1.02.196 P
one out of suits with fortune, | that could give 1.02.246
but, turning these jests out of service, let us 1.03. 26 P
my liege, | i cannot live out of her company. 1.03. 86
to bear your griefs yourself, and leave me out; 1.03.103
the clownish fool out of your father's court? 1.03.130
under an oak whose antique root peeps out | upon 2.01. 31
i can suck melancholy out of a song, as a weasel 2.05. 13 P
here lie i down, and measure out my grave. 2.06. 2 P
who cries out on pride | that can therein tax 2.07. 70
go find him out, | and we will nothing waste 2.07.133
find out thy brother, wheresoe'er he is; 3.01. 5
well, push him out of doors, | and let my 3.01. 15
old, cuckoldly ram, out of all reasonable match. 3.02. 82 P
out, fool! 3.02. 99 P
do lack a hind, | let him seek out rosalind. 3.02.102

seven of the nine days out of the wonder before 3.02.174 P
wonderful, and after that, out of all hooping! 3.02.193 P
pour this conceal'd man out of thy mouth, as 3.02.200 P
as wine comes out of a narrow-mouth'd bottle, 3.02.200 P
i prithee take the cork out of thy mouth that i 3.02.202 P
thou bring'st me out of tune. 3.02.248 P
you bring me out. soft, comes he not here? 3.02.251 P
goldsmiths' wives, and conn'd them out of rings? 3.02.272 P
of them all shall flout me out of my calling. 3.03.107 P
and out of you she sees herself more proper 3.05. 55
be out of love with your nativity, and almost 4.01. 35 P
very good orators, when they are out, they will 4.01. 76 P
who could be out, being before his belov'd 4.01. 81 P
not out of your apparel, and yet out of your 4.01. 87 P
out of your apparel, and yet out of your suit. 4.01. 87 P
had his brains dash'd out with a grecian club, 4.01. 98 P
a woman's wit, and it will out at the casement; 4.01.162 P
shut that, and 'twill out at the key-hole; 4.01.163 P
'twill fly with the smoke out at the chimney. 4.01.164 P
that may be chosen out of the gross band of the 4.01.194 P
as fast as you pour affection in, /it runs out. 4.01.210 P
abuses every one's eyes because his own are out, 4.01.214 P
aliena, i cannot be out of the sight of orlando. 4.01.216 P
drink, being pour'd out of a cup into a glass, 5.01. 41 P
so near the heart as your gesture cries it out, 5.02. 63 P
out of these convertites | there is much matter 5.04.184
and twice to-day pick'd out the dullest scent. SHR in.1. 24
yet would you say ye were beaten out of door, in.2. 85
sometimes you would call out for cicely hacket. in.2. 89
blow our nails together, and fast it fairly out. 1.01.108 P
(for aught i see) two and thirty, a peep out? 1.02. 33 P
yet extreme gusts will blow out fire and all; 2.01.135
my remedy is then to pluck it out. 2.01.211
that thinks with oaths to face the matter out. 2.01.289
an old rusty sword ta'en out of the town armory, 3.02. 47 P
is tir'd, my master and mistress fall'n out. 4.01. 55 P
out of their saddles into the dirt, and thereby 4.01. 57 P
he forth walked on his way" — | out, you rogue! 4.01.147
unto thee, i bid thy master cut out the gown, 4.03.126 P
i commanded the sleeves should be cut out, and 4.03.146 P
from padua and here looking out at the window. 5.01. 31 P
sir — see where he looks out of the window. 5.01. 55 P
out of hope of all but my share of the feast. 5.02.141
keep him out. AWW 1.01.114 P
be buried in highways out of all sanctified 1.01.140 P
out with't! 1.01.146 P
an old courtier, wears her cap out of fashion, 1.01.156 P
haggish age steal on, | and wore us out of act. 1.02. 30
when it was out — "let me not live," quoth he, 1.02. 58
the rest have worn me out | with several 1.02. 73
i am out a' friends, madam, and i hope to have 1.03. 39 P
a man may draw his heart out ere 'a pluck one. 1.03. 88 P
wonder that hath shot out in our latter times. 2.03. 8 P
that gave him out incurable — 2.03. 14 P
good, | to make yourself a son out of my blood. 2.03. 97
italy for picking a kernel out of a pomegranate. 2.03.259 P
a man's tongue shakes out his master's undoing. 2.04. 24 P
and out of it you'll run again, rather than 2.05. 38 P
with true observance seek to eke out that 2.05. 74
the brains of my cupid's knock'd out, and i 3.02. 15 P
son, | but i do wash his name out of my blood, 3.02. 67
but when you find him out, you have him ever 3.06. 93 P
answer to what i shall ask you out of a note. 4.03.127 P
me this other day to turn him out a' th' band. 4.03.200 P
i would repent out the remainder of nature. 4.03.243 P
he will steal, sir, an egg out of a cloister. 4.03.250 P
if you could find out a country where but women 4.03.326 P
before, because i would not fall out with thee. 4.05. 57 P
that's gone made himself much sport out of him. 4.05. 65 P
his majesty, out of a self-gracious remembrance, 4.05. 73 P
me in some grace, for you did bring me out. 5.02. 47 P
out upon thee, knave! 5.02. 48 P
thee in grace and the other brings thee out. 5.02. 50 P
while shameful hate sleeps out the afternoon. 5.03. 66
to come into me, | which i would fain shut out. 5.03.115
false, you threw it him | out of a casement. 5.03.230
and for turning away, let summer bear it out. TN 1.05. 20 P
look you now, he's out of his guard already. 1.05. 86 P
think his mother's milk were scarce out of him. 1.05.161 P
studied, and that question's out of my part. 1.05.179 P
you are now out of your text; 1.05.232 P
i will give out divers schedules of my beauty. 1.05.245 P
babbling gossip of the air | cry out "olivia!" 1.05.274
that will draw three souls out of one weaver? 2.03. 59 P
malvolio and bid him turn you out of doors, 2.03. 74 P
that ye squeak out your coziers' catches without 2.03. 89 P
out o' tune, sir! 2.03.113 P
to-day with my lady, she is much out of quiet. 2.03.133 P
cannot recover your niece, i am a foul way out. 2.03.185 P
seek him out, and play the tune the while. 2.04. 14
you know he brought me out o' favor with my lady 2.05. 8 P
with an obedient start, make out for him. 2.05. 59 P
out, scab! 2.05. 74 P
did not i say he would work it out? 2.05.127 P
are and what you would are out of my welkin — i 3.01. 57 P
only myself stood out, | for which, if i be 3.03. 35
till our very pastime, tir'd out of breath, 3.04.138 P
gentleman gives him out to be of good capacity 3.04.185 P
derives itself out of a very /competent injury; 3.04.246 P
out of my lean and low ability | i'll lend you 3.04.344
i snatch'd one half out of the jaws of death, 3.04.360
well held out, i' faith! 4.01. 5 P
out of my sight! 4.01. 49
out, hyperbolical fiend! 4.02. 25 P
and do all they can to face me out of my wits. 4.02. 93 P
that he did range the town to seek me out. 4.03. 7
can fool no more money out of me at this throw. 5.01. 41 P
taught him to face me out of his acquaintance, 5.01. 88
the faithfull'st off'rings have breath'd out 5.01.114
dearly, | him will i tear out of that cruel eye, 5.01.127
little unthought of, and speak out of my injury. 5.01.310 P
but out of question 'tis maria's hand. 5.01.347
they say it is a copy out of mine. WT 1.02.122
know't, | it will let in and out the enemy, 1.02.205
hold, | when you cast out, it still came home. 1.02.214
whereof the execution did cry out | against the 1.02.260
i learn'd it out of women's faces. 2.01. 12
brands | that calumny doth use — o, i am out — 2.01. 72
and mannerly distinguishment leave out | betwixt 2.01. 86
prison, then abound in tears | as i come out; 2.01.121
arm, out of the blank | and level of my brain — 2.03. 5
out! 2.03. 67
hence with her, out o' door! 2.03. 68
will you not push her out? 2.03. 74
your allegiance, | out of the chamber with her! 2.03.122
with these my proper hands | shall i dash out. 2.03.141
to some remote and desert place quite out | of 2.03.176
for as | thy brat hath been cast out, like to 3.02. 87
it most innocent mouth) | hal'd out to murther; 3.02.101
would have shed water out of fire ere done't; 3.02.193
or that youth would sleep out the rest; 3.03. 60 P
to see how the bear tore out his shoulder-bone, 3.03. 95 P
wipe not out the rest of thy services by leaving 4.02. 10 P
wore three-pile, but now i am out of service. 4.03. 14 P
the life to come, i sleep out the thought of it. 4.03. 30 P
dates, none — that's out of my note; 4.03. 46 P
i fear, sir, my shoulder-blade is out. 4.03. 73 P
but he was certainly whipt out of the court. 4.03. 89 P
there's no virtue whipt out of the court. 4.03. 92 P
out upon him! 4.03.101 P
if i make not this cheat bring out another, and 4.03.121 P
out, alas! 4.04.110
do plainly give you out an unstain'd shepherd, 4.04.149
we'll have this song out anon by ourselves. 4.04.309 P
i have put you out. 4.04.367
by th' pattern of mine own thoughts i cut out 4.04.382
curious business that | i leave out ceremony. 4.04.515
also, to smell out work for th' other senses. 4.04.673 P
one, i hope i shall not be flay'd out of it. 4.04.815 P
companion that e'er man | bred his hopes out of. 5.01. 12
one that gives out himself prince florizel, 5.01. 85
so out of circumstance and sudden, tells us 5.01. 90
we were all commanded out of the chamber; 5.02. 6 P
of wonder is broken out within this hour that 5.02. 24 P
being ready to leap out of himself for joy of 5.02. 49 P
out on thee, rude man, thou dost shame thy JN 1.01. 64
'a pops me out | at least from fair five hundred 1.01. 68
eyes, these brows, were moulded out of his; 2.01.100
out, insolent, thy bastard shall be king | that 2.01.122
and out of my dear love i'll give thee more 2.01.157
cull forth | out of one side her happy minion, 2.01.392
rotten carcass of old death | out of his rags! 2.01.457
nay, rather turn this day out of the week, 3.01. 87
this ungodly day | wear out the /day in peace; 3.01.110
dreading the curse that money may buy out, | and 3.01.164
out of your grace devise, ordain, impose | some 3.01.250
stuffs out his vacant garments with his form; 3.04. 97
out of the path which shall directly lead | thy 3.04.129
wrath | out of the bloody fingers' ends of john. 3.04.168
what may be wrought out of their discontent, 3.04.179
i hope your warrant will bear out the deed. 4.01. 6
so i were out of prison and kept sheep, | i 4.01. 17
turning dispiteous torture out of door? 4.01. 34
out at mine eyes in tender womanish tears. 4.01. 36
must you with hot irons burn out both mine eyes? 4.01. 39
will you put out mine eyes, | these eyes that 4.01. 56
and with hot irons must i burn them out. 4.01. 59
and told me hubert should put out mine eyes, | i 4.01. 69
my eyes are out | even with the fierce looks of 4.01. 72
or, hubert, if you will, cut out my tongue, | so 4.01.100
the breath of heaven hath blown his spirit out, 4.01.109
with this same very iron to burn them out. 4.01.124
this will break out | to all our sorrows, and 4.02.101
that thou for truth giv'st out are landed here? 4.02.130
foreknowing that the truth will fall out so. 4.02.154
i will seek them out. 4.02.169
out of my sight, and never see me more! 4.02.242
out, dunghill! dar'st thou brave a nobleman? 4.03. 87
my date of life out for his sweet live's loss. 4.03.106
there, tell the king, he may inquire us out. 4.03.115
cloak and center can | hold out this tempest. 4.03.156
nothing there holds out | but dover castle. 5.01. 30
my lord melune, let this be copied out, | and 5.02. 1
defense | cries out upon the name of salisbury! 5.02. 19
in, | that so stood out against the holy church, 5.02. 71
and now 'tis far too huge to be blown out | with 5.02. 86
have i not heard these islanders shout out 5.02.103
arms, | from out the circle of his territories. 5.02.136
to seek sweet safety out | in vaults and prisons 5.02.142
indeed your drums, being beaten, will cry out; 5.02.166
strike up our drums, to find this danger out. 5.02.179
seek out king john and fall before his feet; 5.04. 13
i in the black brow of night, | to find you out. 5.06. 18
and broke out | to acquaint you with this evil, 5.06. 24
villain, | whose bowels suddenly burst out. 5.06. 30
it would not out at windows nor at doors. 5.07. 29
out of the weak door of our fainting land. 5.07. 78
sluic'd out his innocent soul through streams of R2 1.01.103
to seek out sorrow that dwells every where. 1.02. 72
now for the rebels which stand out in ireland, 1.04. 38
for violent fires soon burn out themselves; 2.01. 34
is now leas'd out — i die pronouncing it — 2.01. 59
hast thou tapp'd out and drunkenly carous'd. 2.01.127
that their events can never fall out good. 2.01.214
if it be so, out with it boldly, man, | quick is 2.01.233
imp out our drooping country's broken wing, 2.01.292
hold out my horse, and i will first be there. 2.01.300
draws out our miles and makes them wearisome, 2.03. 5
meaning | to rase one title of your honor out. 2.03. 75
arms, | be his own carver and cut out his way, 2.03.144
to find out right with wrong — it may not be; 2.03.145
ras'd out my impress, leaving me no sign, | save 3.01. 25
to lengthen out the worst that must be spoken: 3.02.199
only to be brief | left i his title out. 3.03. 11
sun | from out the fiery portal of the east, 3.03. 64
seal of death, | that marks thee out for hell. 4.01. 26
tongue, | and in compassion weep the fire out, 5.01. 48
and piece the way out with a heavy heart. 5.01. 92
yet i'll hammer it out. 5.05. 5
choose out some secret place, some reverent room 5.06. 25
to be done | than out of anger can be uttered. 1H4 1.01.107
didst well, for wisdom cries out in the streets, 1.02. 88 P
out of my grief and my impatience | answer'd 1.03. 51
out of the bowels of the harmless earth, | which 1.03. 61
but out upon this half-fac'd fellowship! 1.03.208
jade is wrung in the withers, out of all cess. 2.01. 7 P
will she hold out water in foul way? 2.01. 84 P
the ostler bring my gelding out of the stable. 2.01. 96 P
out, ye rogue! shall i be your ostler? 2.02. 42 P
you, my lord fool, out of this nettle, danger, 2.03. 9 P
out, you mad-headed ape! 2.03. 77
ned, prithee come out of that fat room, and lend 2.04. 1 P
if i do not beat thee out of thy kingdom with a 2.04.136 P
eleven buckrom men grown out of two. 2.04.220 P
canst thou now find out to hide thee from this 2.04.264 P
what doth gravity out of his bed at midnight? 2.04.294 P
he would swear truth out of england but he would 2.04.306 P
the world pick thee out three such enemies again 2.04.367 P
and the fire of grace be not quite out of thee, 2.04.383 P
out, ye rogue! 2.04.484 P
play out the play, i have much to say in the 2.04.484 P
both which i have had, but their date is out, 2.04.503 P
and bring him out that is but woman's son | can 3.01. 46
a huge half-moon, a monstrous /cantle out. 3.01. 99
out of my blood | he'll breed revengement and a 3.02. 6
i shall be out of heart shortly, and then i 3.03. 6 P
good compass, and now i live out of all order, 3.03. 19 P
now i live out of all order, out of all compass. 3.03. 20 P
that you must needs be out of all compass, out 3.03. 22 P
of all compass, out of all reasonable compass, 3.03. 22 P
i am out of fear | of death or death's hand for 4.01.135
lay out, lay out. 4.02. 5 P
lay out, lay out. 4.02. 5 P
sons, inquire me out contracted bachelors, such 4.02. 16 P
heads, and they have bought out their services; 4.02. 22 P
rooms of them as have bought out their services, 4.02. 33 P
for indeed i had the most of them out of prison. 4.02. 41 P
well, | you speak it out of fear and cold heart. 4.03. 7
so long as out of limit and true rule | you 4.03. 39
cries out upon abuses, seems to weep | over his 4.03. 81
and in conclusion drove us to seek out | this 4.03.102
out of your sight and raise this present head, 5.01. 66
god keep lead out of me! 5.03. 34 P
i grant you i was down and out of breath, and so 5.04.146 P
and hath sent out | a speedy power to encounter 2H4 1.01.132
breaks like a fire | out of his keeper's arms, 1.01.143
that if we wrought out life 'twas ten to one, 1.01.182
a barber shall never earn sixpence out of it; 1.02. 25 P
keep his own grace, but he's almost out of mine, 1.02. 28 P
you are as a candle, the better part burnt out. 1.02.157 P
i take but two shirts out with me, and i mean 1.02.209 P
action can peep out his head but i am thrust 1.02.213 P
borrowing only lingers and lingers it out, but 1.02.237 P
not what mischief he does, if his weapon be out. 2.01. 16 P
he hath eaten me out of house and home, he hath 2.01. 74 P
but i will have some of it out again, or i will 2.01. 76 P
considerations make me out of love with my 2.02. 12 P
those that /bawl out the ruins of thy linen 2.02. 23 P
and see if thou canst find out sneak's noise. 2.04. 11 P
i'll see if i can find out sneak. 2.04. 21 P
would truncheon you out for taking their names 2.04.142 P
have you turn'd him out a' doors? 2.04.212 P
sir, and i come to draw you out by the ears. 2.04.289 P
he will drive you out of your revenge and turn 2.04.297 P
and that same word even now cries out on us. 3.01. 94
and were these inward wars once out of hand, 3.01.107
me, there are other men fitter to go out than i. 3.02.115 P
the just proportion that we gave them out. 4.01. 23
out of the speech of peace that bears such grace 4.01. 48
no, no, he cannot long hold out these pangs. 4.04.117
biggen bound | snores out the watch of night. 4.05. 28
go seek him out. 4.05. 59
have but their stings and teeth newly ta'en out; 4.05.205
purpose now | to lead out many to the holy land, 4.05.210
foreign quarrels, that action, hence borne out, 4.05.214
in a quarter bear out a knave against an honest 5.01. 48 P
devise matter enough out of this shallow to keep 5.01. 78 P
laughter the wearing out of six fashions, which 5.01. 79 P
prophecies, and to rase out | rotten opinion, 5.02.127
i can assure thee that 'a will not out, 'a. 5.03. 66 P
thou hast drawn my shoulder out of joint. 5.04. 3 P
me your doublet and stuff me out with straw. 5.05. 82 P
but light payment, to dance out of your debt. ep 20 P
piece out our imperfections with your thoughts; H5 pr 23
time | did push it out of farther question. 1.01. 5
came | and whipt th' offending adam out of him, 1.01. 29
by, | all out of work and cold for action! 1.02.114
this his mock mock out of their dear husbands; 1.02.285
see, thy fault france hath in thee found out, 2.pr. 20
fight, but i will wink and hold out mine iron. 2.01. 8 P
and chas'd your blood | out of appearance? 2.02. 76
could out of thee extract one spark of evil 2.02.101
so 'a cried out, "god, god, god!" 2.03. 18 P
they say he cried out of sack. 2.03. 27 P
as fear may teach us out of late examples | left 2.04. 12
and he is bred out of that bloody strain | that 2.04. 51
and eche out our performance with your mind. 3.pr. 35
by the means whereof 'a faces it out, but fights 3.02. 33 P
and plainly say | our mettle is bred out, and 3.05. 29
but his nose is executed, and his fire's out. 3.06.106 P
so, for fear i should be fac'd out of my way. 3.07. 82 P
by her foot, that she may tread out the oath. 3.07. 95 P
followers so far out of his knowledge! 3.07.134 P
ay, but these english are shrowdly out of beef. 3.07.152 P
evil, | would men observingly distill it out; 4.01. 5
and when the mind is quick'ned, out of doubt, 4.01. 20
though it appear a little out of fashion, 4.01. 83
his fears, out of doubt, be of the same relish 4.01.109 P
to the king wipes the crime of it out of us. 4.01.133 P
can try it out with all unspotted soldiers. 4.01.160 P
his bed, wash every mote out of his conscience; 4.01.179 P
that's a perilous shot out of an elder-gun, that 4.01.198 P
thinks thou the fiery fever will go out | with 4.01.253
that our french gallants shall to-day draw out, 4.02. 22
break out into a second course of mischief, 4.03.106
soldiers' heads | and turn them out of service. 4.03.119
/or i will fetch thy rim out at thy throat | in 4.04. 14
but it is out of my prains what is the name of 4.07. 28 P
mark you now, to take the tales out of my mouth, 4.07. 43 P
yerk out their armed heels at their dead masters 4.07. 80
your majesty's welsh plood out of your pody, i 4.07.107 P
wear if alive, i will strike it out soundly. 4.07.130 P
which your majesty is take out of the helmet of 4.08. 27 P
god, and keep you out of prawls and prabbles, 4.08. 64 P

how london doth pour out her citizens! 5.pr. 24
and out of doubt and out of question too, and 5.01. 45 P
and out of doubt and out of question too, and 5.01. 45 P
dignity, | any thing in or out of our demands, 5.02. 89
i wear out my suit. 5.02.128 P
cannot look greenly, nor gasp out my eloquence, 5.02.143 P
they do always reason themselves out again. 5.02.158 P
sad tidings bring i to you out of france, | of 1H6 1.01. 58
bedford, if thou be slack, i'll fight it out. 1.01. 99
stead whereof sharp stakes pluck'd out of hedges 1.01.117
cried out amain, | and rush'd into the bowels of 1.01.128
i am left out; 1.01.174
but long i will not be jack out of office. 1.01.175
else ne'er could they hold out so as they do. 1.02. 43
out of a great deal of old iron i chose forth. 1.02.101
what she says i'll confirm. we'll fight it out. 1.02.128
open the gates, or i'll shut thee out shortly. 1.03. 26
priest, dost thou command me to be shut out? 1.03. 30
i'll use to carry thee out of this place. 1.03. 43
out, tawny–coats! 1.03. 56
out, scarlet hypocrite! 1.03. 56
and would have armor here out of the tower, | to 1.03. 67
with my nails digg'd stones out of the ground 1.04. 45
and if i did but stir out of my bed, | ready 1.04. 55
your hearts i'll stamp out with my horse's heels 1.04.108
or tear the lions out of england's coat; 1.05. 28
why ring not out the bells aloud throughout the 1.06. 11
if all things fall out right, | i shall as 2.03. 4
my side | that any purblind eye may find it out. 2.04. 21
shall be /wip'd out in the next parliament, 2.04.117
that many have their giddy brains knock'd out; 3.01. 83
or i would see his heart out ere the priest 3.01.120
love, | and will at last break out into a flame: 3.01.190
by thrusting out a torch from yonder tower, 3.02. 23
will ye, like soldiers, come and fight it out? 3.02. 66
but gather we our forces out of hand, | and set 3.02.102
search out thy wit for secret policies, | and we 3.03. 12
lord, | and thou be thrust out like a fugitive? 3.03. 67
your private grudge, my lord of york, will out, 4.01.109
for, had the passions of thy heart burst out, 4.01.183
and strong enough to issue out and fight. 4.02. 20
and mine shall ring thy dire departure out. 4.02. 41
out, some light horsemen, and peruse their wings 4.02. 43
and give it out | that he is march'd to burdeaux 4.03. 3
cries out for noble york and somerset | to beat 4.04. 15
out of the powerful regions under earth, | help 5.03. 11
and, now it is my chance to find thee out, 5.04. 4
out, out! 5.04. 10
out, out! 5.04. 10
rancor will out. 2H6 1.01.142
and, ten to one, old joan had not gone out. 2.01. 4
thou baleful messenger, out of my sight! 3.02. 48
his eyeballs further out than when he lived, 3.02.169
and cry out for thee to close up mine eyes, | to 3.02.395
i'll have an iris that shall find thee out. 3.02.407
are we in order when we are most out of order. 4.02.190 P
break open the jails and let out the prisoners. 4.03. 16 P
the laws of england may come out of your mouth. 4.07. 6 P
biting statutes, unless his teeth be pull'd out. 4.07. 17 P
would never have given out these arms till you 4.08. 26 P
no sooner was i crept out of my cradle | but i 4.09. 3
i hid me in these woods and durst not peep out, 4.10. 3 P
or cut not out the burly–bon'd clown in chines 4.10. 57 P
wilt thou go dig a grave to find out war, | and 5.01.169
seek thee out some other chase, | for i myself 5.02. 14
in cruelty will i seek out my fame. 5.02. 60
unless he seek to thrust you out perforce. 3H6 1.01. 34
let's fight it out, and not stand cavilling thus 1.01.117
hath made her break out into terms of rage! 1.01.265
and till i root out their accursed line, | and 1.03. 32
fight it out!" 1.04. 10
but out, alas, | we bodg'd again, as i have seen 1.04. 18
breathe out invectives 'gainst the officers. 1.04. 43
flies through these wounds to seek out thee. 1.04.178
why, therefore warwick came to seek you out, 2.01.166
to blot out me, and put his own son in. 2.02. 92
nay, warwick, single out some other chase, | for 2.04. 12
to carve out dials quaintly, point by point, 2.05. 24
his cold thin drink out of his leather bottle, 2.05. 48
here burns my candle out; 2.06. 1
no way to fly, nor strength to hold out flight. 2.06. 24
air | but toiling desperately to find it out — 3.02.178
myself, | or hew my way out with a bloody axe. 3.02.181
durst the traitor breathe out so proud words? 4.01.112
brother, we will proclaim you out of hand, | the 4.07. 63
a little fire is quickly trodden out, | which, 4.08. 7
doubt | will issue out again and bid us battle. 5.01. 63
and to the latest gasp cried out for warwick, 5.02. 41
for well i wot ye blaze to burn them out. 5.04. 71
out of my sight, thou dost infect mine eyes! R3 1.02.148
shine out, fair sun, till i have bought a glass, 1.02.262
out, devil! 1.03.117
that fall out | in sharing that which you have 1.03.157
and leave out thee? 1.03.215
dabbled in blood, and he shriek'd out aloud, 1.04. 54
to give us our reward, thy conscience flies out. 1.04.130 P
it is turn'd out of towns and cities for a 1.04.141 P
for this will out, and then i must not stay. 1.04.283
i marvel that her grace did leave it out. 2.02.111
the new–heal'd wound of malice should break out, 2.02.125
and so falls it out | with rivers, vaughan, grey 3.02. 64
dispatch, the limit of your lives is out. 3.03. 8
to draw the brats of clarence out of sight, 3.05.107
hath he so long held out with me untir'd, | and 4.02. 44
inquire me out some mean poor gentleman, | whom 4.02. 53
i say again, give out | that anne, my queen, is 4.02. 56
out on /you, owls! 4.04.507
richmond in dorsetshire sent out a boat | unto 4.04.522
send out a pursuivant–at–arms | to stanley's 5.03. 59
my foreward shall be drawn out all in length, 5.03.293
give | their money out of hope they may believe, H8 pr 8
but spider–like | out of his self–drawing web, 1.01. 63
upon this french going out, took he upon him 1.01. 73
letter, | the honorable board of council out, 1.01. 79
which is budded out, | for france hath flaw'd 1.01. 94
tongues spit their duties out, and cold hearts 1.02. 61
and never seek for aid out of himself. 1.02.114
have collected | out of the duke of buckingham. 1.02.131
live in freedom, | and this man out of prison? 1.02.201
there's something more would out of thee; 1.02.202
to't, | that sure th' have worn out christendom. 1.03. 15
men than they can be | out of a foreign wisdom, 1.03. 29
beaten | a long time out of play, may bring his 1.03. 45
look out there, some of ye. 1.04. 50
(out of the great respect they bear to beauty) 1.04. 69
which they would have your grace | find out, and 1.04. 84
i were unmannerly to take you out | and not to 1.04. 95
bar, to hear | his knell rung out, his judgment, 2.01. 32
and out of ruins | made my name once more noble. 2.01.114
out of anger | he sent command to the lord mayor 2.01.150
have out of malice | to the good queen possess'd 2.01.157
when they were ready to set out for london, a 2.02. 5 P
and out of all these to restore the king, | he 2.02. 29
annual support, | out of his grace he adds. 2.03. 65
your particular fancy, | and leave me out on't. 2.03.102
and a stranger, | born out of your dominions; 2.04. 16
sovereign and pious else, could speak thee out) 2.04.141
if your business | seek me out, and that way i 3.01. 38
and that way i am wife in, | out with it boldly: 3.01. 39
my lord of york, out of his noble nature, | zeal 3.01. 62
they that must weigh out my afflictions, | they 3.01. 88
out upon ye! 3.01. 99
been, out of fondness, superstitious to him? 3.01.131
of nobleness in any person | out of himself? 3.02. 13
o, fear him not, | his spell in that is out. 3.02. 20
clear, 'tis i must snuff it, | then out it goes. 3.02. 97
straight | springs out into fast gait, then 3.02.116
whilst your great goodness, out of holy pity, 3.02.263
some of these articles, and out they shall. 3.02.304
that, out of mere ambition, you have caus'd 3.02.324
and to be | out of the king's protection. 3.02.344
out of pity taken | a load would sink a navy — 3.02.382
methinks | (out of a fortitude of soul i feel), 3.02.388
thou hast forc'd me | (out of thy honest truth) 3.02.430
found thee a way, out of his wrack, to rise in; 3.02.437
out of the pain you suffer'd, gave no ear to't. 4.02. 8
long trouble now is passing | out of this world; 4.02.163
weed, sir thomas, | and we must root him out. 5.01. 53
what, is she crying out? 5.01. 67
i will have more or scold it out of him. 5.01.173
out of which frailty | and want of wisdom, you, 5.02. 47
out of our easiness and childish pity | to one 5.02. 60
take my cause | out of the gripes of cruel men, 5.02.135
would i were fairly out on't! 5.02.144
that holy duty, out of dear respect, | his royal 5.02.154
ye, i see, | more out of malice than integrity, 5.02.180
and hit that woman, who cried out "clubs!", 5.03. 50 P
and find a way out | to let the troop pass 5.03. 84
he that will have a cake out of the wheat must TRO 1.01. 15 P
hark what good sport is out of town to–day. 1.01.113
but every thing so out of joint that he is a 1.02. 28 P
one," quoth he, "pluck't out, and give it him." 1.02.164 P
date in the pie, for then the man's date is out. 1.02.257 P
therefore this maxim out of love i teach: 1.02.292
from his deep chest laughs out a loud applause, 1.03.163
on his gorget, | shake in and out the rivet; 1.03.175
all) a man distill'd | out of our virtues, who 1.03.351
i shall cut out your tongue. 2.01.110 P
more ready to cry out, "who knows what follows?" 2.02. 13
not have slipp'd out of my contemplation. 2.03. 26 P
if she that lays thee out says thou art a fair 2.03. 32 P
wit would be out of fashion. 2.03.216 P
could not you find out that by her attributes? 3.01. 35 P
you shall piece it out with a piece of your 3.01. 51 P
this shall not hedge us out, we'll hear you sing 3.01. 60 P
you shall not bob us out of our melody. 3.01. 68 P
my cousin will fall out with you. 3.01. 85 P
falling in, after falling out, may make them 3.01.103 P
groans out for ha, ha, ha! 3.01.126
shall fight your hearts out ere i part you — 3.02. 52 P
out of those many regist'red in promise, | which 3.03. 15
greatness, once fall'n out with fortune, | must 3.03. 75
out with fortune, | must fall out with men too. 3.03. 76
who do methinks find out | some thing not worth 3.03. 90
to have done is to hang | quite out of fashion, 3.03.152
ever smiles, | and farewell goes out sighing. 3.03.169
there were wit in this head, and 'twould out — 3.03.256 P
but /he's out of tune thus. 3.03.301 P
in him when hector has knock'd out his brains, i 3.03.302 P
out of whorish loins | are pleas'd to breed out 4.01. 64
are pleas'd to breed out your inheritors. 4.01. 65
her wanton spirits look out | at every joint and 4.05. 56
out, gall! 5.01. 35 P
you will break out. 5.02. 51
will 'a swagger himself out on 's own eyes? 5.02.136 P
how hecuba cries out! 5.03. 83
be happy that my arms are out of use; 5.06. 16
never go home, here starve we out the night — 5.10. 2
and, in a word, | scare troy out of itself. 5.10. 21
your eyes, half out, weep out at pandar's fall; 5.10. 48
your eyes, half out, weep out at pandar's fall; 5.10. 48
once cannot | see what i do deliver out to each, COR 1.01.143
factions, and give out | conjectural marriages, 1.01.193
stand'st out? 1.01.241
giddy censure | will then cry out of martius, "o 1.01.269
than one voluptuously surfeit out of action. 1.03. 25 P
no, good madam, i will not out of doors. 1.03. 71 P
not out of doors? 1.03. 72 P
virgilia, turn thy solemnness out a' door, and 1.03.108 P
and four shall quickly draw out my command, 1.06. 84
for him | shall fly out of itself. 1.10. 19
conspectuities glean out of this character, if i 2.01. 65 P
you wear out a good wholesome forenoon in 2.01. 69 P
so it must fall out | to him, or our authorities 2.01.243
and out of his noble carelessness lets them 2.02. 14 P
leave nothing out for length, and make us think 2.02. 49
for requital | than we to stretch it out. 2.02. 51
if all our wits were to issue out of one skull, 2.03. 22 P
wit will not so soon out as another man's will; 2.03. 27 P
which you are out of, with a gentler spirit, 3.01. 55
at once pluck out | the multitudinous tongue; 3.01.155
i shall shake thy bones | out of thy garments. 3.01.179
i am out of breath, | confusion's near, i cannot 3.01.188
lest parties (as he is belov'd) break out, | and 3.01.313
your power well on | before you had worn it out. 3.02. 18
go see him out at gates, and follow him, | as he 3.03.138
come, come, let's see him out at gates, come. 3.03.142
bring me but out at gate. 4.01. 47
from the volscian state to find you out there. 4.03. 11 P
is almost mature for the violent breaking out. 4.03. 26 P
wife is when she's fall'n out with her husband. 4.03. 33 P
of a doit, break out | to bitterest enmity; 4.04. 17
pray get you out. 4.05. 13 P
i cannot get him out o' th' house. 4.05. 21 P
th' voice of slaves to be | hoop'd out of rome. 4.05. 78
not out of hope | (mistake me not) to save my 4.05. 79
drawn tuns of blood out of thy country's breast, 4.05. 99
thou hast beat me out | twelve several times, 4.05.121
man in blood, they will out of their burrows, 4.05.211 P
stood for rome, | and durst not once peep out. 4.06. 46
it is spoke freely out of many mouths — | how 4.06. 65
clusters, | who did hoot him out o' th' city. 4.06.123
which out of daily fortune ever taints | the 4.07. 38
one fire drives out one fire; 4.07. 54
when you have push'd out your gates the very 5.02. 39 P
can you think to blow out the intended fire your 5.02. 45 P
general has sworn you out of reprieve and pardon 5.02. 49 P
i have been blown out of your gates with sighs, 5.02. 74 P
but out, affection, | all bond and privilege of 5.03. 24
actor now | i have forgot my part, and i am out, 5.03. 41
the father tearing | his country's bowels out. 5.03.103
but with his last attempt he wip'd it out, 5.03.146
out of that i'll work | myself a former fortune. 5.03.201
let him choose | out of my files, his projects 5.06. 33
my lord, to step out of these dreary dumps, TIT 1.01.391
safe out of fortune's shot, and sits aloft, 2.01. 2
that have their alms out of the empress' chest. 2.03. 9
why dost not comfort me and help me out | from 2.03.209
hath — | out of this fell devouring receptacle, 2.03.235
reach me thy hand, that i may help thee out, 2.03.237
but out alas, here have we found him dead. 2.03.258
look, sirs, if you can find the huntsman out, 2.03.278
shall seize this prey out of his father's hands. 4.02. 96
and pull her out of acheron by the heels. 4.03. 45
thy life–blood out, if aaron now be wise, | then 4.04. 37
can couch for fear, but i will find them out, 5.02. 38
and find out /murderers in their guilty /caves; 5.02. 52
i'll find some cunning practice out of hand, 5.02. 77
thou shalt inquire him out among the goths: 5.02.123
that true hand that fought rome's quarrel out, 5.03.102
me, and turn'd weeping out | to beg relief among 5.03.105
while you live, draw your neck out of collar. ROM 1.01. 4 P
my naked weapon is out. 1.01. 33 P
shuts up his windows, locks fair daylight out, 1.01.139
out — 1.01.166
out of her favor where i am in love. 1.01.168
find those persons out | whose names are written 1.02. 35
find them out whose names are written here! 1.02. 38 P
tut, man, one fire burns out another's burning, 1.02. 45
to see it techy and fall out wi' th' dug! 1.03. 32
the date is out of such prolixity: 1.04. 3
time out a' mind the fairies' coachmakers. 1.04. 61
and then dreams he of smelling out a suit; 1.04. 78
what's he that now is going out of door? 1.05.130
turn back, dull earth, and find thy centre out. 2.01. 2
walls, | for stony limits cannot hold love out, 2.02. 67
by whose direction foundst thou out this place? 2.02. 79
a grave, | to lay one in, another out to have. 2.03. 84
this jest now, till thou hast worn out thy pump, 2.04. 62 P
i stretch it out for that word "broad," which, 2.04. 85 P
out upon you, what a man are you! 2.04.114 P
i had, my weapon should quickly have been out. 2.04.158 P
told you, my young lady bid me inquire you out; 2.04.164 P
do you not see that i am out of breath? 2.05. 30
how art thou out of breath, when thou hast 2.05. 31
to say to me that thou art out of breath? 2.05. 32
will ne'er wear out the everlasting flint; 2.06. 17
but such an eye would spy out such a quarrel? 3.01. 21 P
didst thou not fall out with a tailor for 3.01. 27 P
you pluck your sword out of his pilcher by the 3.01. 80 P
lest mine be about your ears ere it be out. 3.01. 82 P
nor tears nor prayers shall purchase out abuses; 3.01.193
die, | take him and cut him out in little stars, 3.02. 22
thy form cries out thou art; 3.03.109
i'll find out your man, | and he shall signify 3.03.169
but that a joy past joy calls out on me, | it 3.03.173
things have fall'n out, sir, so unluckily | that 3.04. 1
night's candles are burnt out, and jocund day 3.05. 9
it is the lark that sings so out of tune, 3.05. 27
then, window, let day in, and let life out. 3.05. 41
if you could find out but a man | to bear a 3.05. 96
hath sorted out a sudden day of joy, | that thou 3.05.109
out, you green–sickness carrion! 3.05.156
out, you baggage! 3.05.156
out on her, hilding! 3.05.168
therefore, out of thy long–experienc'd time, 4.01. 60
shrikes like mandrakes' torn out of the earth, 4.03. 47
as with a club, dash out my desp'rate brains? 4.03. 54
i see my cousin's ghost | seeking out romeo, 4.03. 56
i have a head, sir, that will find out logs, 4.04. 18
out, alas, she's cold, | her blood is settled, 4.05. 25
you put up your dagger, and put out your wit. 4.05.121 P
going to find a barefoot brother out, | one of 5.02. 5
yet put it out, for i would not be seen. 5.03. 2
shap'd out a man | whom this beneath world doth TIM 1.01. 43
figures are | even such as they give out. 1.01.160
to knock out an honest athenian's brains. 1.01.192 P
the strain of man's bred out | into baboon and 1.01.250
he pours it out: 1.01.276
i come to have thee thrust me out of doors. 1.02. 25
mine eyes cannot hold out water, methinks. 1.02.107 P
honor, lord lucius | (out of his free love) hath 1.02.182
great gifts, | and all out of an empty coffer; 1.02.193
would i were gently put out of office | before i 1.02.201
put out of office | before i were forc'd out! 1.02.202
thus honest fools lay out their wealth on 1.02.235
i must serve my turn | out of mine own. 2.01. 21
i'll look you out a good turn, servilius. 3.02. 60
man | when he looks out in an ungrateful shape! 3.02. 73
temper has forsook him, he's much out of health, 3.04. 72 P
tell out my blood. 3.04. 94
there's not so much left to furnish out | a 3.04.114
(/an honor in him which buys out his fault), 3.05. 17
and let out | their coin upon large interest — 3.05.106

sent to borrow of me, that my provision was out. 3.06. 16 P
other day, and now he has beat it out of my hat. 3.06.113 P
rather than render back, out with your knives, 4.01. 9
old limping sire, | with it beat out his brains! 4.01. 15
th' athenians both within and out that wall! 4.01. 38
nay, put out all your hands. 4.02. 28
i'll follow and inquire him out. 4.02. 48
nay, stay thou out for earnest. 4.03. 48
womb, | let it no more bring out ingrateful man! 4.03.188
thy heels | and skip when thou point'st out? 4.03.225
why dost thou seek me out? 4.03.236
broke the wall, that thou art out of the city? 4.03.350 P
the gods out of my misery | has sent thee 4.03.524
people | the deed of saying is quite out of use. 5.01. 26
out, rascal dogs! 5.01.115
timon, | look out and speak to friends. 5.01.128
as shall to thee blot out what wrongs were 5.01.153
to wipe out our ingratitude with loves | above 5.04. 17
who were the motives that you first went out; 5.04. 27
whom you yourselves shall set out for reproof 5.04. 57
nay, i beseech you, sir, be not out with me; JC 1.01. 16 P
yet if you be out, sir, i can mend you. 1.01. 17 P
sir, to wear out their shoes, to get myself into 1.01. 29 P
and do you now cull out a holiday? 1.01. 49
set on, and leave no ceremony out. 1.02. 11
to find out you. who's that? metellus cimber? 1.03.134
thus must i piece it out: 2.01. 51
let us not leave him out. 2.01.143
then leave him out. 2.01.152
and will he steal out of his wholesome bed | to 2.01.264
o, what a time have you chose out, brave caius, 2.01.314
thrice hath calphurnia in her sleep cried out, 2.02. 2
you shall not stir out of your house to–day. 2.02. 9
cannot live | out of the teeth of emulation. 2.03. 14
brutus, | he draws mark antony out of the way. 3.01. 26
him, | i spurn thee like a cur out of my way. 3.01. 46
some to the common pulpits, and cry out, 3.01. 80
wives, and children stare, cry out, and run, 3.01. 97
and drawing days out, that men stand upon. 3.01.100
as fire drives out fire, so pity pity — | hath 3.01.171
as rushing out of doors to be resolv'd | if 3.02.179
pluck but his name out of his heart, and turn 3.03. 34 P
which, out of use and stal'd by other men, 4.01. 38
thou dream, lucius, that thou so criedst out? 4.03.295
why did you so cry out, sirs, in your sleep? 4.03.303
their bloody sign of battle is hung out, | and 5.01. 14
stand fast, titinius; we must out and talk. 5.01. 22
carv'd out his passage | till he fac'd the slave MAC 1.02. 19
and dash'd the brains out, had i so sworn as you 1.07. 58
in heaven, | their candles are all out. 2.01. 5
they pluck out mine eyes. 2.02. 56
come hither for stealing out of a french hose. 2.03. 14 P
wild in nature, broke their stalls, flung out, 2.04. 16
if it find heaven, must find it out to–night. 3.01.141
who did strike out the light? 3.03. 19
that when the brains were out, the man would die 3.04. 78
will the line stretch out to th' crack of doom? 4.01.117
let us seek out some desolate shade, and there 4.03. 1
and yell'd out | like syllable of dolor. 4.03. 7
a rumor | of many worthy fellows that were out, 4.03.183
soldier none | that christendom gives out. 4.03.192
that would be howl'd out in the desert air, 4.03.194
out, damn'd spot! 5.01. 35 P
out, i say! 5.01. 35 P
he cannot come out on 's grave. 5.01. 64 P
send out moe horses, skirr the country round, 5.03. 35
raze out the written troubles of the brain, 5.03. 42
seyton, send out. 5.03. 49
hang out our banners on the outward walls, | the 5.05. 1
out, out, brief candle! 5.05. 23
out, out, brief candle! 5.05. 23
arm, arm, and out! 5.05. 45
bloodier villain | than terms can give thee out! 5.08. 8
our state to be disjoint and out of frame, HAM 1.02. 20
proportions are all made | out of his subject; 1.02. 33
out of the shot and danger of desire. 1.03. 35
the kettle–drum and trumpet thus bray out | the 1.04. 11
my fate cries out, | and makes each petty artere 1.04. 81
'tis given out that, sleeping in my orchard, | a 1.05. 35
or such ambiguous giving out, to note | that you 1.05.178
the time is out of joint — o cursed spite, 1.05.188
in 's rouse, | there falling out at tennis"; 2.01. 57
of bias, | by indirections find directions out. 2.01. 63
as if he had been loosed out of hell | to speak 2.01. 80
for out a' doors he went without their helps, 2.01. 96
he sent out to suppress | his nephew's levies, 2.02. 61
in hand, sends out arrests | on fortinbras, 2.02. 67
that we find out the cause of this effect, | or 2.02.101
as they fell out by time, by means, and place, 2.02.127
"lord hamlet is a prince out of thy star; 2.02.141
is to be one man pick'd out of ten thousand. 2.02.179 P
will you walk out of the air, my lord? 2.02.206 P
indeed that's out of the air. 2.02.208 P
than natural, if philosophy could find it out. 2.02.368 P
see there is not yet out of his swaddling–clouts 2.02.383 P
out, out, thou strumpet fortune! 2.02.493
out, out, thou strumpet fortune! 2.02.493
i'll have thee speak out the rest of this soon. 2.02.521 P
perhaps, | out of my weakness and my melancholy, 2.02.601
madam, it so fell out that certain players | we 3.01. 16
like sweet bells jangled, out of time and harsh; 3.01.158
you would pluck out the heart of my mystery, you 3.02.365 P
churchyards yawn and hell itself /breathes out 3.02.389
near 's as doth hourly grow | out of his brows. 3.03. 7
seen the wicked prize itself | buys out the law. 3.03. 60
look where he goes, even now, out at the portal! 3.04.136
and either /... the devil or throw him out, 3.04.169
make you to ravel all this matter out, | that i 3.04.186
whips out his rapier, cries, "a rat, a rat!" 4.01. 10
and out of haunt | this mad young man. 4.01. 18
go seek him out, speak fair, and bring the body 4.01. 36
maid, that out a maid | never departed more." 4.05. 54
burn out the sense and virtue of mine eye! 4.05.156
that he cried out 'twould be a sight indeed | if 4.07. 99
now, out of this — 4.07.106
what out of this, my lord? 4.07.106
when these are gone, | the woman will be out. 4.07.189
should have been buried out a' christian burial. 5.01. 24 P
and calves which seek out assurance in that. 5.01.116 P
you lie out on't, sir, and therefore 'tis not 5.01.123 P
trade that 'a will keep out water a great while, 5.01.171 P
in the dark | grop'd i to find out them, had my 5.02. 14
thrown out his angle for my proper life, | and 5.02. 66
of the time and, out of an habit of encounter, a 5.02.190 P
blow them to their trial, the bubbles are out. 5.02.194 P
seek it out. 5.02.312
he hath been out nine years, and away he shall LR 1.01. 32 P
out of my sight! 1.01.157
edmund, seek him out; 1.02. 97 P
find out this villain, edmund, it shall lose 1.02.114 P
for taking one's part that's out of favor. 1.04. 99 P
a dog must to kennel, he must be whipt out, when 1.04.112 P
no, boy, nothing can be made out of nothing. 1.04.132 P
so out went the candle, and we were left 1.04.217 P
let thy folly in | and thy dear judgment out! 1.04.272
beweep this cause again, i'll pluck ye out, 1.04.302
than comes from her demand out of the letter. 1.05. 3 P
that what a man cannot smell out, he may spy 1.05. 23 P
here stood he in the dark, his sharp sword out, 2.01. 38
thus out of season, threading dark–ey'd night: 2.01.119
how fell you out? say that. 2.02. 86
to go out of my dialect, which you discommend so 2.02.109 P
some time i shall sleep out, the rest i'll 2.02.156
a good man's fortune may grow out at heels. 2.02.157
thou out of heaven's benediction com'st | to the 2.02.161
and am fallen out with my more headier will, 2.04.110
out, varlet, from my sight! 2.04.187
home, and out of that provision | which shall be 2.04.205
come out o' th' storm. 2.04.309
is better than this rain–water out o' door. 3.02. 11 P
o'er our heads, | find out their enemies now. 3.02. 51
in such a night | to shut me out? 3.04. 18
keep thy foot out of brothels, thy hand out of 3.04. 96 P
foot out of brothels, thy hand out of plackets, 3.04. 96 P
you, | yet have i ventured to come seek you out, 3.04.152
seek out where thy father is, that he may be 3.05. 18 P
i will piece out the comfort with what addition 3.06. 2 P
seek out the traitor gloucester. 3.07. 3 P
pluck out his eyes. 3.07. 5 P
thy cruel nails | pluck out his poor old eyes, 3.07. 57
out, vild jelly! 3.07. 83
out, treacherous villain! 3.07. 87
go thrust him out at gates, and let him smell 3.07. 93
turn out that eyeless villain; 3.07. 96
poor tom hath been scar'd out of his good wits. 4.01. 57 P
and told me i had turn'd the wrong side out. 4.02. 9
going to put out | the other eye of gloucester. 4.02. 71
great ignorance, gloucester's eyes being out, 4.05. 9
loathed part of nature should | burn itself out. 4.06. 40
affliction till it do cry out itself | "enough, 4.06. 76
there i found 'em, there i smelt 'em out. 4.06.103 P
this great world | shall so wear out to nought. 4.06.135
the sword is out | that must destroy thee. 4.06.229
and chud ha' bin zwagger'd out of my life, 4.06.238 P
keep out, che vor' ye, or ice try whither your 4.06.240 P
out, dunghill! 4.06.243
seek him out | upon the english party. 4.06.249
you do me wrong to take me out o' th' grave: 4.07. 44
whom the rigor of our state | forc'd to cry out. 5.01. 23
goneril, | and hardly shall i carry out my side, 5.01. 61
who's in, who's out — | and take upon 's the 5.03. 15
and we'll wear out, | in a wall'd prison, packs 5.03. 17
let the trumpet sound, | and read out this. 5.03.108
and more, much more, the time will bring it out. 5.03.164
of this tough world | stretch him out longer. 5.03.316
wears out his time, much like his master's ass, OTH 1.01. 47
life, | i must show out a flag and sign of love, 1.01.156
how got she out? 1.01.169
about three several quests | to search you out. 1.02. 47
of arts inhibited and out of warrant. 1.02. 79
driven | to find out practices of cunning hell 1.03.102
of drowning thyself, it is clean out of the way. 1.03.359 P
it is impossible to bear it out. 2.01. 19
in | as to throw out our eyes for brave othello, 2.01. 38
you are pictures out /a' /doors, | bells in your 2.01.109
from frieze, | it plucks out brains and all. 2.01.127
as these strip you out of your lieutenantry, it 2.01.172 P
i prattle out of fashion, and i dote | in mine 2.01.206
for even out of that will i cause these of 2.01.274 P
not out of absolute lust (though peradventure 2.01.292
whom love hath turn'd almost the wrong side out, 2.03. 52
go out and cry a mutiny. 2.03.157
swords out, and tilting one at other's /breast, 2.03.183
there comes a fellow crying out for help, | and 2.03.226
pursue, | lest by his clamor (as it so fell out) 2.03.231
and out of her own goodness make the net | that 2.03.361
devise a mean to draw the moor | out of the way, 3.01. 38
diet, | or breed itself so out of circumstances, 3.03. 16
watch him tame, and talk him out of patience; 3.03. 23
the wars must make example | out of her best), 3.03. 66
out of his scattering and unsure observance. 3.03.151
noble nature, | out of self–bounty, be abus'd; 3.03.200
she that so young could give out such a seeming 3.03.209
i'll have the work ta'en out, | and give't iago. 3.03.296
can you inquire him out, and be edified by 3.04. 14 P
speak, is't out o' th' way? 3.04. 80
sweet bianca, | take me this work out. 3.04.180
and by and by | breaks out to savage madness. 4.01. 55
now he denies it faintly, and laughs it out. 4.01.112
she gives it out that you shall marry her. 4.01.115
this is the monkey's own giving out. 4.01.127 P
marry her, out of her own love and flattery, not 4.01.128 P
own love and flattery, not out of my promise. 4.01.129 P
i must take out the work? 4.01.151 P
some minx's token, and i must take out the work? 4.01.153 P
you had it, i'll take out no work on't. 4.01.155 P
o, she will sing the savageness out of a bear. 4.01.189 P
out of my sight! 4.01.247
nor send you out o' th' way? 4.02. 7
i have wasted myself out of my means. 4.02.186 P
knocking out his brains. 4.02.230 P
i will fashion to fall out between twelve and 4.02.236 P
or else break out in peevish jealousies, 4.03. 89
will speak, | though tongues were out of use. 5.01.110
put out the light, and then put out the light: 5.02. 7
put out the light, and then put out the light: 5.02. 7
but once put out thy light, | thou cunning'st 5.02. 10
out, strumpet! weep'st thou for him to my face? 5.02. 77
then murther's out of tune, | and sweet revenge 5.02.115
out, and alas, that was my lady's voice. 5.02.119
'twill out, 'twill out! 5.02.219
'twill out, 'twill out! 5.02.219
then must thou needs find out new heaven, new ANT 1.01. 17
out, fool, i forgive thee for a witch. 1.02. 40 P
that when old robes are worn out, there are 1.02.164 P
that i might sleep out this great gap of time 1.05. 5
made out of her impatience — which not wanted 2.02. 68
taunts | did gibe my missive out of audience. 2.02. 74
if we contend, | out of our question wipe him. 2.02. 81
to have me out of egypt, made wars here; 2.02. 95
presently be sought, | or else he seeks out us. 2.02.159
sir, we did sleep day out of countenance, and 2.02.177 P
the city cast | her people out upon her; 2.02.214
i laugh'd him out of patience; 2.05. 19
pour out the pack of matter to mine ear, | the 2.05. 54
let him not leave out | the color of her hair. 2.05.113
one another by the disposition, he cries out, 2.07. 7 P
but i'll ne'er out. 2.07. 31 P
it, and the elements once out of it, it 2.07. 45 P
sound and be hang'd, sound out! 2.07.133
of parthia | we have jaded out o' th' field. 3.01. 34
undo that prayer, by crying out as loud, | "o, 3.04. 17
his power went out in such distractions as 3.07. 76
our fortune on the sea is out of breath, | and 3.10. 24
how i convey my shame out of thine eyes | by 3.11. 52
vulgar fame, you have | luxuriously pick'd out; 3.13.120
to be furious | is to be frighted out of fear, 3.13.195
as he had power | to beat me out of egypt. 4.01. 2
tricks which sorrow shoots | out of the mind. 4.02. 15
best you saf'd the bringer | out of the host; 4.06. 26
our hour | is fully out. 4.09. 32
since the torch is out, | lie down and stray no 4.14. 46
not live to wear | all your true followers out. 4.14.134
look out o' th' other side your monument, | his 4.15. 8
lips that power, | thus would i wear them out. 4.15. 40
look | our lamp is spent, it's out. 4.15. 85
the business of this man looks out of him; 5.01. 50
and scald rhymers | ballad 's out a' tune. 5.02.216
i honor him | even out of your report. CYM 1.01. 55
yourself some comfort | out of your best advice. 1.01.156
where air comes out, air comes in; 1.02. 3 P
much like an argument that fell out last night, 1.04. 56 P
or this gentleman's opinion by this worn out. 1.04. 63 P
all of her that is out of door most rich! 1.06. 15
to my tongue | charms this report out. 1.06.117
him that broke it, it would have run all out. 2.01. 9 P
you lay out too much pains | for purchasing but 2.03. 87
outwent her, | motion and breath left out. 2.04. 85
could i find out | the woman's part in me — for 2.05. 19
if you beat us out of it, it is yours; 3.01. 80 P
what your own love will out of this advise you, 3.02. 44 P
out of your proof you speak; 3.03. 27
a pain that only seems to seek out danger | i' 3.03. 50
have done, his spirits fly out | into my story; 3.03. 90
i speak not out of weak surmises, but from proof 3.04. 23 P
poor i am stale, a garment out of fashion, | and 3.04. 51
prithee think | there's livers out of britain. 3.04.140
out, sword, and to a sore purpose! 4.01. 22 P
hercules | could have knock'd out his brains, 4.02.115
might break out and swear | he'ld fetch us in; 4.02.140
for notes of sorrow out of tune are worse | than 4.02.241
from east to occident, cry out for service, 4.02.372
us | find out the prettiest daisied plot we can, 4.02.398
yourself | so out of thought, and thereto so 4.04. 33
till it fly out and show them princes born. 4.04. 54
with mars fall out, with juno chide, | that thy 5.04. 32
look out; 5.04. 81
that | the britains have ras'd out, though with 5.05. 70
thou, king, send out | for torturers ingenious; 5.05.214
i left out one thing which the queen confess'd, 5.05.244
two on 's are as good | as i have given out him. 5.05.312
drew sleep out of mine eyes, blood from my PER 1.02. 96
speak out thy sorrows which /thou bring'st in 1.04. 58
be a day fits you, search out of the calendar, 2.01. 54 P
'twill hardly come out. 2.01.118 P
holding out gold that's by the touchstone tried; 2.02. 37
if in the world he live, we'll seek him out; 2.04. 29
cleon, for the babe | cannot hold out to tyrus. 3.01. 79
nature awakes, | a warmth /breathes out of her. 3.02. 93
says one, "wolt out?" 4.01. 61
we were never so much out of creatures. 4.02. 6 P
thou hast the harvest out of thine own report. 4.02.141 P
of eels as my giving out her beauty stirs up the 4.02.143 P
innocent | and for an honest attribute cry out, 4.03. 18
mortal vessel tears, | and yet he rides it out. 4.04. 31
but i am out of the road of rutting for ever. 4.05. 9 P
kings, | but time hath rooted out my parentage, 5.01. 92
graves, and smiling | extremity out of act. 5.01.139
fill'd, | and wishes fall out as they're will'd. 5.02. 16
do but you hold out | your helping hands, and we TNK pr 25
shall raze you out o' th' book of trespasses 1.01. 33
leave not out a jot | o' th' sacred ceremony. 1.01.130
that best knowest | how to draw out, fit to this 1.01.160
are you not out? 1.02. 26
were not spent, | rather laid out for purchase. 1.02.111
fought out together where death's self was 1.03. 40
y' are out of breath, | and this high–speeded 1.03. 82
go and find out | the bones of your dead lords, 1.04. 6
i am given out to be better lin'd than it can 2.01. 5 P
in prison, and 'twere pity they should be out. 2.01. 23 P
nobility enforce a freedom out of bondage, 2.01. 34 P
that's arcite looks out. 2.01. 48 P
out of their sight! 2.01. 52 P
hands shall never draw 'em out like lightning, 2.02. 24
put but thy head out of this window more, | and, 2.02.212
put my head out? 2.02.215
i'll throw my body out, | and leap the garden, 2.02.215
live | to knock thy brains out with my shackles. 2.02.219
to–day, i'll tickle't out | of the jades' tails 2.03. 28
and you shall see her | take a new lesson out, 2.03. 35
out upon't! 2.04. 5
and out i have brought him to a little wood | a 2.06. 3
but your silence | should break out, though i' 3.01. 62
me and pour | this oil out of your language. 3.01.103

out with't, faith! 3.03. 33
i am very cold, and all the stars are out too, 3.04. 1
and the boar, | break comely out before him; 3.05. 19
"there was three fools fell out about an howlet: 3.05. 67
by night | that seek out silent hanging. 3.05.127
maypole, and again, | ere another year run out, 3.05.146
i'll find him out to–morrow." 4.01. 69
out with the mainsail! 4.01.148
and then will she be out of love with aeneas. 4.03. 15 P
and reduce what's now out of square in her into 4.03. 95 P
to blow that nearness out that flames between ye 5.01. 10
ancient love, our kindred, | out of my memory; 5.01. 27
know my prize | must be dragg'd out of blood; 5.01. 43
out of two i should | choose one, and pray for 5.01.152
flows | out from the bowels of her holy altar 5.01.164
title of a kingdom may be tried | out of itself. 5.03. 34
temper | that breaking out in hideous violence STM II.C 132
my country's head | and give the law out there. III 8
life | in limning out a well–proportioned steed, VEN 290
things out of hope are compass'd oft with 567
with much ado the cold fault cleanly out; 694
their light blown out in some mistrustful wood, 826
against the welkin volleys out his voice; 921
where lo, two lamps burnt out in darkness lies; 1128
with modest lucrece, and wore out the night. LUC 123
"fair torch, burn out thy light, and lend it not 190
the eye of heaven is out, and misty night 356
from this fair throne to heave the owner out. 413
small lights are soon blown out, huge fires 647
lame, blind, halt, creep, cry out for thee, 902
"out, idle words, servants to shallow fools! 1016
and seems to point her out where she sits 1087
heat nor freezing cold, | will we find out; 1146
maze, | that cannot tread the way out readily, 1152
like dying coals burnt out in tedious nights. 1379
and with my knife scratch out the angry eyes 1469
little strength rings out the doleful knell: 1495
and my laments would be drawn out too long | to 1616
what he breathes out his breath drinks up again. 1666
that forc'd him on so fast | (in rage sent out, 1671
doubt, | till my bad angel fire my good one out. PP 2.14
she burnt out love, as soon as straw out–burneth 7.14
and wear their brave state out of memory: SON 15. 8
since she prick'd thee out for women's pleasure, 20.13
but out, alack, he was but one hour mine, | the 33.11
and broils root out the work of masonry, | nor 55. 6
that wear this world out to the ending doom. 55.12
pry, | to find out shames and idle hours in me, 61. 7
king | are vanishing, or vanish'd out of sight, 63. 7
o, how shall summer's honey breath hold out 65. 5
morrow, | to linger out a purpos'd overthrow. 90. 8
got | which for their habitation chose out thee, 95.10
one thing expressing, leaves out difference. 105. 8
blind, | seems seeing, but effectually is out; 113. 4
but bears it out even to the edge of doom. 116.12
how have mine eyes out of their spheres been 119. 7
doubt, | till my bad angel fire my good one out. 144.14
doth point out thee | as his triumphant prize. 151. 9
religious love put out religion's eye. LC 250

OUTBRAGG'D 1 FR 0.0001 REL FR 1 V 0 P
whose bare outbragg'd the web it seem'd to wear; LC 95

OUTBRAVE 1 FR 0.0001 REL FR 1 V 0 P
outbrave the heart most daring on the earth, MV 2.01. 28

OUTBRAVES 1 FR 0.0001 REL FR 1 V 0 P
meet, | the basest weed outbraves his dignity: SON 94.12

OUTBREAK 1 FR 0.0001 REL FR 1 V 0 P
the flash and outbreak of a fiery mind, | a HAM 2.01. 33

OUT–BREASTED 1 FR 0.0001 REL FR 1 V 0 P
and by and by out–breasted, that the sense TNK 5.03.127

OUTBREATH'D 1 FR 0.0001 REL FR 1 V 0 P
faint quittance, wearied and outbreath'd, | to 2H4 1.01.108

OUT–BURNETH 1 FR 0.0001 REL FR 1 V 0 P
burnt out love, as soon as straw out–burneth; PP 7.14

OUTCAST 3 FR 0.0003 REL FR 3 V 0 P
checks | as ovid be an outcast quite abjur'd. SHR 1.01. 33
outcast of naples, england's bloody scourge! 2H6 5.01.118
eyes, | i all alone beweep my outcast state, SON 29. 2

OUTCRAFTIED 1 FR 0.0001 REL FR 1 V 0 P
that drug–damn'd italy hath outcraftied him, CYM 3.04. 15

OUTCRIES 1 FR 0.0001 REL FR 1 V 0 P
the villain jew with outcries rais'd the duke, MV 2.08. 4

OUTCRY 2 FR 0.0002 REL FR 2 V 0 P
all run | with open outcry toward our monument. ROM 5.03.193
entombs her outcry in her lips' sweet fold. LUC 679

OUTDAR'D 1 FR 0.0001 REL FR 1 V 0 P
my height | before this outdar'd dastard? R2 1.01.190

OUTDARE *(also out–dure)*

OUTDARE 1 FR 0.0001 REL FR 1 V 0 P
and boldly did outdare | the dangers of the time 1H4 5.01. 40

OUTDARES 1 FR 0.0001 REL FR 1 V 0 P
who sensibly outdares his senseless sword | and, COR 1.04. 53

OUTDID 1 FR 0.0001 REL FR 1 V 0 P
day, | i well remember, you outdid me, cousin; TNK 3.06. 73

OUTDONE 1 FR 0.0001 REL FR 0 V 1 P
he hath in this action outdone his former deeds COR 2.01.136 P

OUT–DURE *(also outdare)*

OUT–DURE 1 FR 0.0001 REL FR 1 V 0 P
able once again | to out–dure danger. TNK 3.06. 10

OUT–DWELLS 1 FR 0.0001 REL FR 1 V 0 P
and it is marvel he out–dwells his hour, | for MV 2.06. 3

//OUT–FAC'D 1 FR 0.0001 REL FR 1 V 0 P
/was /at /last //out–fac'd /by /bullingbrook? R2 4.01.286

OUT–FAC'D 1 FR 0.0001 REL FR 0 V 1 P
but you have out–fac'd them all. LLL 5.02.623 P

OUTFAC'D 1 FR 0.0001 REL FR 0 V 1 P
with a word, outfac'd you from your prize, and 1H4 2.04.256 P

OUTFACE 6 FR 0.0006 REL FR 6 V 0 P
but we'll outface them, and outswear them too. MV 4.02. 17
have | that do outface it with their semblances. AYL 1.03.122
and outface the brow | of bragging horror; JN 5.01. 49
see if thou canst outface me with thy looks. 2H6 4.10. 46
to outface me with leaping in her grave? HAM 5.01.278
and with presented nakedness outface | the winds LR 2.03. 11

OUTFACED 1 FR 0.0001 REL FR 1 V 0 P
outfaced infant state, and done a rape | upon JN 2.01. 97

OUTFACING 3 FR 0.0003 REL FR 3 V 0 P
and with no face, as 'twere, outfacing me, ERR 5.01.245
scambling, outfacing, fashion–monging boys, ADO 5.01. 94
outfacing faults in love with love's ill rest. PP 1. 8

OUTFLY 1 FR 0.0001 REL FR 1 V 0 P
with scorn, | cannot outfly our apprehensions. TRO 2.03.115

OUT–FROWN 1 FR 0.0001 REL FR 1 V 0 P
myself could else out–frown false fortune's LR 5.03. 6

OUTGO 2 FR 0.0002 REL FR 2 V 0 P
he would outgo | his father by as much as a H8 1.02.207
the time shall not | outgo my thinking on you. ANT 3.02. 61

OUTGOES 1 FR 0.0001 REL FR 1 V 0 P
he outgoes | the very heart of kindness. TIM 1.01.274

OUTGOING 1 FR 0.0001 REL FR 1 V 0 P
so thou, thyself outgoing in thy noon, SON 7.13

OUTGROWN 1 FR 0.0001 REL FR 1 V 0 P
the prince my brother hath outgrown me far. R3 3.01.104

OUT–HERODS 1 FR 0.0001 REL FR 0 V 1 P
for o'erdoing termagant, it out–herods herod. HAM 3.02. 14 P

OUTJEST 1 FR 0.0001 REL FR 1 V 0 P
fool, who labors to outjest | his heart–strook LR 3.01. 16

OUTLAW 2 FR 0.0002 REL FR 2 V 0 P
and low, | a poor unminded outlaw sneaking home, 1H4 4.03. 58
as an outlaw in a castle keeps | and useth it to 1H6 3.01. 47

OUTLAW'D 1 FR 0.0001 REL FR 1 V 0 P
i had a son, | now outlaw'd from my blood; LR 3.04.167

OUTLAWRY 1 FR 0.0001 REL FR 1 V 0 P
that by proscription and bills of outlawry, JC 4.03.173

OUTLAWS 2 FR 0.0002 REL FR 2 V 0 P
we are held as outlaws. CYM 4.02. 67
hunt here, are outlaws, and in time | may make 4.02.138

OUTLIV'D 2 FR 0.0002 REL FR 2 V 0 P
that have outliv'd the eagle, page thy heels TIM 4.03.224
there's many a man alive that hath outliv'd TNK 5.04. 1

OUT–LIVE 2 FR 0.0002 REL FR 2 V 0 P
but him out–live, and die a violent death. 2H6 1.04. 31
but him out–live, and die a violent death." 1.04. 60

OUTLIVE 16 FR 0.0018 REL FR 13 V 3 P
to let the wretched man outlive his wealth, | to MV 4.01.269
the world, | if he outlive the envy of this day, 1H4 5.02. 66
desire should so many years outlive performance? 2H4 2.04.261 P
he let him outlive that day to see his greatness H5 4.01.184 P
outlive thy glory like my wretched self! R3 1.03.202
unwilling to outlive the good that did it; H8 4.02. 60
lavinia, live, outlive thy father's days, | and TIT 1.01.167
let not this wasp outlive, us both to sting. 2.03.132
well belov'd of caesar, | should outlive caesar. JC 2.01.157
man's memory may outlive his life half a year, HAM 3.02.132 P
but why should honor outlive honesty? OTH 5.02.245
you shall outlive the lady whom you serve. ANT 1.02. 31
and you, to outlive the age i am, | and die as i PER 5.01. 15
forth | eternal numbers to outlive long date. SON 38.12
of princes shall outlive this pow'rful rhyme, 55. 2
thee | to make him much outlive a gilded tomb, 101.11

OUTLIVES 3 FR 0.0003 REL FR 2 V 1 P
he that outlives this day, and comes safe home, H5 4.03. 41
willing misery | outlives incertain pomp, is TIM 4.03.243
for that outlives a thousand tenants. HAM 5.01. 43 P

OUTLIVING 1 FR 0.0001 REL FR 1 V 0 P
outliving beauties outward, with a mind | that TRO 3.02.162

OUTLOOK 1 FR 0.0001 REL FR 1 V 0 P
to outlook conquest and to win renown | even in JN 5.02.115

OUTLUSTRES 1 FR 0.0001 REL FR 0 V 1 P
diamond of yours outlustres many i have beheld, CYM 1.04. 73 P

OUT–NIGHT 1 FR 0.0001 REL FR 1 V 0 P
i would out–night you, did nobody come; MV 5.01. 23

OUT–PARAMOUR'D 1 FR 0.0001 REL FR 0 V 1 P
and in woman out–paramour'd the turk. LR 3.04. 91 P

OUTPEER 1 FR 0.0001 REL FR 1 V 0 P
multitudes, | could not outpeer these twain. CYM 3.06. 86

OUTPRAY 1 FR 0.0001 REL FR 1 V 0 P
our prayers do outpray his, then let them have R2 5.03.109

OUTPRIZ'D 1 FR 0.0001 REL FR 0 V 1 P
is dead, or she's outpriz'd by a trifle. CYM 1.04. 81 P

OUTRAGE 14 FR 0.0015 REL FR 13 V 1 P
sprung from the rancorous outrage of your duke ERR 1.01. 6
man | do outrage and displeasure to himself? 4.04.116
she will do a desperate outrage to herself. ADO 2.03.153 P
i fear some outrage, and i'll follow her. JN 3.04.106
in murthers and in outrage /boldly here, | but R2 3.02. 40
with this immodest clamorous outrage | to 1H6 4.01.126
my charity is outrage, life my shame, | and in R3 1.03.276
o, preposterous | and frantic outrage, end thy 2.04. 64
no outrage, peace! COR 5.06.123
times more cause than he | to do this outrage, TIT 5.03. 52
gentlemen, for shame, forbear this outrage! ROM 3.01. 87
seal up the mouth of outrage for a while, | till 5.03.216
to do upon respect such violent outrage. LR 2.04. 24
if in thy hope thou dar'st do such outrage, LUC 605

/OUTRAGEOUS 1 FR 0.0001 REL FR 1 V 0 P
/poor /heart /beats /with /outrageous /beating, TIT 3.02. 13

OUTRAGEOUS 6 FR 0.0006 REL FR 6 V 0 P
day | a most outrageous fit of madness took him, ERR 5.01.139
so strange, outrageous, and so variable | as the MV 2.08. 13
the manner of thy vile outrageous crimes, | that 1H6 3.01. 11
mov'd with remorse of these outrageous broils, 5.04. 97
the slings and arrows of outrageous fortune, HAM 3.01. 57
no outrageous thing | from vassal actors can be LUC 607

OUTRAGES 5 FR 0.0005 REL FR 5 V 0 P
provided that you do no outrages | on silly TGV 4.01. 69
much to do | to keep them from uncivil outrages. 5.04. 17
and he shall pardon thee these outrages. 3H6 5.01. 24
shall be no shelter to these outrages, | but he TIT 4.04. 22
he has been known to commit outrages | and TIM 3.05. 71

OUTRAN 1 FR 0.0001 REL FR 1 V 0 P
he, swift of foot, | outran my purpose; OTH 2.03.233

OUTRIGHT 5 FR 0.0005 REL FR 5 V 0 P
'tis ten to one it maim'd you /two outright. SHR 5.02. 62
prince harry slain outright, and both the blunts 2H4 1.01. 16
joan, this kills thy father's heart outright! 1H6 5.04. 2
nay, eleanor, then must i chide outright. 2H6 1.02. 41
kill me outright with looks, and rid my pain. SON 139.14

OUTROAR 1 FR 0.0001 REL FR 1 V 0 P
the hill of basan, to outroar | the horned herd! ANT 3.13.127

OUTRODE 1 FR 0.0001 REL FR 1 V 0 P
tidings, and, being better hors'd, | outrode me. 2H4 1.01. 36

OUTRUN 7 FR 0.0008 REL FR 5 V 2 P
being nimble–footed, he hath outrun us, | but TGV 5.03. 7
i heard say he was outrun on cotsall. WIV 1.01. 90 P
defeated the law and outrun native punishment, H5 4.01.167 P
can we outrun the heavens? good margaret, stay. 2H6 5.02. 73
it will outrun you, father, in the end. 3H6 1.02. 14
we may outrun | by violent swiftness that which H8 1.01.141
of my violent love | outrun the pauser, reason. MAC 2.03.111

OUTRUNS 3 FR 0.0003 REL FR 2 V 1 P
in a retreat he outruns any lackey; AWW 4.03.290 P
how he outruns the wind, and with what care | he VEN 681
outruns the eye that doth behold his haste, LUC 1668

OUTRUN'ST 1 FR 0.0001 REL FR 0 V 1 P
e'en so thou outrun'st grace. TIM 2.02. 88 P

OUTSCOLD 1 FR 0.0001 REL FR 1 V 0 P
we grant thou canst outscold us. JN 5.02.160

/OUTSCORN 1 FR 0.0001 REL FR 1 V 0 P
/in /his /little /world /of /man /to /outscorn LR 3.01. 10

OUTSELL 1 FR 0.0001 REL FR 1 V 0 P
her pretty action did outsell her gift, | and CYM 2.04.102

OUTSELLS 1 FR 0.0001 REL FR 1 V 0 P
and she, of all compounded, | outsells them all. CYM 3.05. 74

OUT–SHINING 1 FR 0.0001 REL FR 1 V 0 P
whose bright out–shining beams thy cloudy wrath R3 1.03.267

OUTSIDE 14 FR 0.0015 REL FR 11 V 3 P
o, what a goodly outside falsehood hath! MV 1.03.102
his life hath sold | but my outside to behold. 2.07. 68
we'll have a swashing and a martial outside, AYL 1.03.120
fortune forbid my outside have not charm'd her! TN 2.02. 18
yet for the outside of thy poverty we must make WT 4.04.632 P
inside of your purse to the outside of his hand, 4.04.803 P
you look but on the outside of this work. JN 5.02.109
outside or inside, i will not return | till my 5.02.110
were but the outside of the roman brutus, H5 2.04. 37
therefore was i created with a stubborn outside, 5.02.227 P
traffics with man's nature, | he is but outside; TIM 1.01.159
since thy outside looks so fair and warlike, LR 5.03.143
for by his rusty outside he appears | to have PER 2.02. 50
they have brought (if we judge by the outside) TNK 4.02. 74

OUTSIDES 1 FR 0.0001 REL FR 1 V 0 P
and make his wrongs | his outsides, to wear them TIM 3.05. 33

OUTSLEEP 1 FR 0.0001 REL FR 1 V 0 P
i fear we shall outsleep the coming morn | as MND 5.01.365

OUTSPEAKS 1 FR 0.0001 REL FR 1 V 0 P
that it outspeaks | possession of a subject. H8 3.02.127

OUTSPORT 1 FR 0.0001 REL FR 1 V 0 P
honorable stop, | not to outsport discretion. OTH 2.03. 3

OUTSTARE 2 FR 0.0002 REL FR 2 V 0 P
i'll follow and outstare him. H8 1.01.129
now he'll outstare the lightning: ANT 3.13.194

OUTSTAY 1 FR 0.0001 REL FR 1 V 0 P
if you outstay the time, upon mine honor, | and AYL 1.03. 88

OUTSTOOD 1 FR 0.0001 REL FR 1 V 0 P
i have outstood my time, which is material | to CYM 1.06.207

/OUTSTRETCH'D 1 FR 0.0001 REL FR 0 V 1 P
/our /monarchs /and /outstretch'd /heroes /the HAM 2.02.264 P

OUTSTRETCH'D 3 FR 0.0003 REL FR 3 V 0 P
or with an outstretch'd throat i'll tell the MM 2.04.153
and with his arms outstretch'd as he would fly TRO 3.03.167
"timon is dead, who hath outstretch'd his span: TIM 5.03. 3

OUTSTRETCHED 1 FR 0.0001 REL FR 1 V 0 P
that raught at mountains with outstretched arms, 3H6 1.04. 68

OUTSTRIKE 1 FR 0.0001 REL FR 1 V 0 P
a swifter mean | shall outstrike thought, but ANT 4.06. 35

OUTSTRIP 3 FR 0.0003 REL FR 2 V 1 P
for thou shalt find she will outstrip all praise TMP 4.01. 10
native punishment, though they can outstrip men, H5 4.01.168 P
if thou wilt outstrip death, go cross the seas, R3 4.01. 41

OUTSTRIPP'D 2 FR 0.0002 REL FR 2 V 0 P
leg, | outstripp'd the people's praises, won the TNK 2.02. 16
and though they be outstripp'd by every pen, SON 32. 6

OUTSTRIPPING 1 FR 0.0001 REL FR 1 V 0 P
outstripping crows that strive to overfly them. VEN 324

OUTSWEAR 2 FR 0.0002 REL FR 1 V 1 P
methinks i should outswear cupid. LLL 1.02. 64 P
but we'll outface them, and outswear them too. MV 4.02. 17

OUTSWEET'NED 1 FR 0.0001 REL FR 1 V 0 P
not to slander, | outsweet'ned not thy breath. CYM 4.02.224

OUTSWELL 1 FR 0.0001 REL FR 1 V 0 P
cheek | outswell the colic of puff'd aquilon; TRO 4.05. 9

OUT–TALK 1 FR 0.0001 REL FR 1 V 0 P
what, this gentleman will out–talk us all. SHR 1.02.246

OUT–TONGUE 1 FR 0.0001 REL FR 1 V 0 P
the signiory | shall out–tongue his complaints. OTH 1.02. 19

OUTVENOMS 1 FR 0.0001 REL FR 1 V 0 P
whose tongue | outvenoms all the worms of nile, CYM 3.04. 35

OUTVIED 1 FR 0.0001 REL FR 1 V 0 P
gremio is outvied. SHR 2.01.385

OUT–VILLAIN'D 1 FR 0.0001 REL FR 0 V 1 P
he hath out–villain'd villainy so far, that the AWW 4.03.273 P

OUT–VOICE 1 FR 0.0001 REL FR 1 V 0 P
shouts and claps out–voice the deep–mouth'd sea, H5 5.pr. 11

OUT–WALL 1 FR 0.0001 REL FR 1 V 0 P
that i am much more | than my out–wall, open LR 3.01. 45

/OUTWARD 1 FR 0.0001 REL FR 1 V 0 P
/showing /an /outward /pity, /yet /you /pilates R2 4.01.240

OUTWARD 55 FR 0.0062 REL FR 49 V 6 P
and executing th' outward face of royalty | with TMP 1.02.104
we do the denunciation lack | of outward order. MM 1.02.149
him hide, | though angel on the outward side! 3.02.272
that outward courtesies would fain proclaim 5.01. 15
they show well outward. ADO 1.02. 8 P
whom she hath in all outward behaviors seem'd 2.03. 97 P
he hath indeed a good outward happiness. 2.03.183 P
if half thy outward graces had been placed 4.01.101
go anticly, and show outward hideousness, | and 5.01. 96
for fame's sake, for praise, an outward part, LLL 4.01. 32
builds in the weather on the outward wall, MV 2.09. 29
so may the outward shows be least themselves — 3.02. 73
some mark of virtue on his outward parts. 3.02. 82
but like a common and an outward man | that the AWW 3.01. 11
with this thy fair and outward character. TN 1.02. 51
quickly the wrong side may be turn'd outward! 3.01. 13 P
device, | exterior form, outward accoutrement, JN 1.01.211
clapp'd on the outward eye of fickle france, 2.01.583
death, having prey'd upon the outward parts, 5.07. 15
watches on unto mine eyes, the outward watch, R2 5.05. 52
the nonce, to immask our noted outward garments.

they are our outward consciences | and preachers 1H4 1.02.180 P
he may show what outward courage he will; H5 4.01. 8
such outward things dwell not in my desires. 4.01.113 P
mistake | the outward composition of his body. 4.03. 27
that in your outward action shows itself 1H6 2.03. 75
glories, | an outward honor for an inward toil, R3 1.03. 66
there's nothing differs but the outward fame. 1.04. 79
distinguish of a man | than of his outward show, 1.04. 83
outliving beauties outward, with a mind | that 3.01. 10
if these shows be not outward, which of you TRO 3.02.162
not fearing outward force, so shall my lungs COR 1.06. 77
as well as i do know your outward favor. 3.01. 77
hang out our banners on the outward walls, | the JC 1.02. 91
tediousness the limbs and outward flourishes, MAC 5.05. 1
he that helps him take all my outward worth. HAM 2.02. 91
for when my outward action doth demonstrate LR 4.04. 10
and things outward | do draw the inward quality OTH 1.01. 61
all | is outward sorrow, though i think the king ANT 3.13. 32
think | so fair an outward and such stuff within CYM 1.01. 9
he had need mean better than his outward show 1.01. 23
us scan | the outward habit by the inward man. PER 2.02. 48
have neither in our hearts nor outward eyes 2.02. 57
she puts on outward strangeness, seems unkind: 2.03. 25
thy outward parts would move | each part in me VEN 310
whose inward ill no outward harm express'd. 435
tarquin armed to beguild | with outward honesty, LUC 91
women work, | dissembled with an outward show, 1545
neither in inward worth nor outward fair | can PP 18.38
mine eye's due is /thy outward part, | and my SON 16.11
/thy outward thus with outward praise is crown'd 46.13
outward thus with outward praise is crown'd, 69. 5
where time and outward form would show it dead. 69. 5
canopy, | with my extern the outward honoring, 108.14
painting thy outward walls so costly gay? 125. 2
146. 4

/OUTWARDLY 1 FR 0.0001 REL FR 1 V 0 P
/i /will /be /patient, /outwardly /i /will. TRO 5.02. 68

OUTWARDLY 4 FR 0.0004 REL FR 4 V 0 P
heat outwardly or breath within, i'll serve you WT 3.02.206
or that indeed | which outwardly ye show? MAC 1.03. 54
'tis mine, and this will witness outwardly, | as CYM 2.02. 35
encamp'd in hearts, but fighting outwardly. LC 203

OUTWARDS 2 FR 0.0002 REL FR 1 V 1 P
i tell you, must show fairly outwards, should HAM 2.02.374 P
o, one by nature's outwards so commended | that LC 80

OUTWARD-SAINTED 1 FR 0.0001 REL FR 1 V 0 P
this outward-sainted deputy, | whose settled MM 3.01. 88

OUTWEAR 2 FR 0.0002 REL FR 2 V 0 P
till painful study shall outwear three years, LLL 2.01. 23
the sun is high, and we outwear the day. H5 4.02. 63

/OUTWEIGHS 1 FR 0.0001 REL FR 1 V 0 P
/which /if /we /find /outweighs /ability, 2H4 1.03. 45

OUTWEIGHS 1 FR 0.0001 REL FR 1 V 0 P
if any think brave death outweighs bad life, COR 1.06. 71

OUTWENT 2 FR 0.0002 REL FR 2 V 0 P
outwent her, | motion and breath left out. CYM 2.04. 84
you outwent me, | nor could my wishes reach you.
TNK 3.06. 79

OUTWORE 1 FR 0.0001 REL FR 1 V 0 P
her song was tedious and outwore the night, VEN 841

OUTWORK 1 FR 0.0001 REL FR 1 V 0 P
venus where we see | the fancy outwork nature. ANT 2.02.201

OUTWORN 4 FR 0.0004 REL FR 4 V 0 P
deep a cunning, | may be outworn, never undone. TNK 1.03. 44
shows me a bare-bon'd death by time outworn. LUC 1761
the rich proud cost of outworn buried age; SON 64. 2
thus is his cheek the map of days outworn, 68. 1

OUTWORTHS 1 FR 0.0001 REL FR 1 V 0 P
a beggar's book | outworths a noble's blood. H8 1.01.123

OVEN 3 FR 0.0003 REL FR 2 V 1 P
the making of the cake, the heating the oven, TRO 1.01. 25 P
sorrow concealed, like an oven stopp'd, | doth TIT 2.04. 36
an oven that is stopp'd, or river stay'd, VEN 331

OVEN'S 1 FR 0.0001 REL FR 1 V 0 P
and /crickets sing at the oven's mouth, | are PER 3.ch. 7

OVER *(also o'er and compounds)*

/OVER 5 FR 0.0005 REL FR 4 V 1 P
and deliver'd /over to the king her father" — 2H6 1.01. 52 P
/tell /over /your /woes /again /by /viewing R3 4.04. 39
/why /she /dares /not /come /over /to /thee." LR 3.06. 28
/she /was /a /queen | /over /her /passion, /who, 4.03. 14
/then laid his leg | /over my thigh, and /sigh'd OTH 3.03.425

OVER 152 FR 0.0171 REL FR 98 V 54 P
and the remainder mourning over them, | brimful TMP 5.01. 13
love, | for he was more than over shoes in love. TGV 1.01. 24
for you are over boots in love, | and yet you 1.01. 25
over the boots? nay, give me not the boots. 1.01. 27
fold it over and over, | 'tis threefold too 1.01.108
fold it over and over, | 'tis threefold too 1.01.108
and when it's writ, for my sake read it over, 2.01.130
read over julia's heart (thy first best love), 5.04. 46
shalt know i will predominate over the peasant, WIV 2.02.282 P
from frogmore, over the stile, this way. 3.01. 33 P
i ha' told them over and over, they lack no 3.03. 18 P
i ha' told them over and over, they lack no 3.03. 18 P
i will give over all. 4.06. 2 P
over and above that you have suffer'd, i think 5.05.168 P
a man may go over shoes in the grime of it. ERR 3.02.104 P
when she had writ it, and was reading it over, ADO 2.03.137 P
seal with my death than repeat over to my shame. 5.01.241 P
that no man living shall come over it, for in 5.02. 7 P
to have no man come over me? 5.02. 9 P
never so truly turn'd over and over as my poor 5.02. 35 P
so truly turn'd over and over as my poor self in 5.02. 35 P
i can but say their protestation over: LLL 1.01. 33
fell over the threshold, and broke my shin. 3.01.117
berowne, read it over. where hadst thou it? 4.03.193
over hill, over dale, | thorough bush, thorough MND 2.01. 2
over hill, over dale, | thorough bush, thorough 2.01. 2
over park, over pale, | thorough flood, thorough 2.01. 4
bush, thorough brier, | over park, over pale, 2.01. 4
but all the story of the night told over, | and 5.01. 23
i have heard it over, | and it is nothing, 5.01. 77
you spurn a stranger cur | over your threshold; MV 1.03.119
gold | to pay the petty debt twenty times over. 3.02.307
and stand indebted, over and above, | in love 4.01.413
making such pitiful dole over them that all the AYL 1.02.131 P
your own safety, and give over this attempt. 1.02.179 P
they are often tarr'd over with the surgery of 3.02. 62 P
exult, and all at once, | over the wretched? 3.05. 37
of thee than a barbary cock-pigeon over his hen, 4.01.151 P
your doublet and hose pluck'd over your head, 4.01.203 P
you | to give you over at this first encounter, SHR 1.02.105
over and beside | signior baptista's liberality, 1.02.148
go hop me over every kennel home, | for you 4.03. 98
surplice of humility over the black gown of a AWW 1.03. 95 P
my stars shine darkly over me. TN 2.01. 4 P
and all those sayings will i over swear, | and 5.01.269
and given your drunken cousin rule over me, yet 5.01.305 P
shook hands, as over a vast; WT 1.01. 30 P
swear his thought over | by each particular star 1.02.424
to peer, | with heigh, the doxy over the dale! 4.03. 2
and, having flown over many knavish professions, 4.03. 99 P
over that art | which you say adds to nature, is 4.04. 90
he sings 'em over as they were gods or goddesses 4.04.208 P
that you may | (for i do fear eyes over) to 4.04.654
then 'nointed over with honey, set on the head 4.04.784 P
and dost thou now fall over to my foes? JN 3.01.127
reproach and dissolution hangeth over him. R2 2.01.258
and sent me over by berkeley, to discover | what 2.03. 33
see them delivered over | to execution and the 3.01. 29
lest you mistake the heavens are over our heads. 3.03. 17
steel | over the glittering helmet of my foe! 4.01. 51
if any plague hang over us, 'tis he. 5.03. 3
over whose acres walk'd those blessed feet 1H4 1.01. 25
i must give over this life, and i will give it 1.02. 95 P
give over this life, and i will give it over. 1.02. 96 P
charles' wain is over the new chimney, and yet 2.01. 2 P
but thou art altogether given over, and wert 3.03. 36 P
together and thrown over the shoulders like a 4.02. 44 P
seems to weep | over his /country's wrongs, and 4.03. 82
alone | the insulting hand of douglas over you, 5.04. 54
hath a little gilded over your night's exploit 2H4 1.02.149 P
i have given over, i will speak no more; 2.03. 5
found some months asleep and leapt them over. 4.04.124
the constables have deliver'd her over to me, 5.04. 4 P
urn, | tombless, with no remembrance over them. H5 1.02.229
the work ish give over, the trompet sound the 3.02. 89 P
it ish give over. 3.02. 91 P
you have shot over. 3.07.123 P
suffolk first died, and york, all haggled over, 4.06. 11
so did he turn and over suffolk's neck | he 4.06. 24
a maid yet ros'd over with the virgin crimson of 5.02.295 P
this moral ties me over to time and a hot summer 5.02.312 P
city, | and we be lords and rulers over roan, 1H6 3.02. 11
knee, | his bloody sword he brandish'd over me, 4.07. 6
i'll over then to england with this news, | and 5.03.167
and deliver'd over to the king her father, and 2H6 1.01. 59 P
and she sent over of the king of england's own 1.01. 60 P
the silly owner of the goods | weeps over them, 1.01.226
whipping, leap me over this stool and run away. 2.01.140 P
whip him till he leap over that same stool. 2.01.145 P
till the axe of death | hang over thee, as sure 2.04. 50
his guilt should be but idly posted over, 3.01.255
over whom, in time to come, i hope to reign, 4.02.130
he shall reign, but i'll be protector over him. 4.02.159 P
but stay, i'll read it over once again. 4.04. 14
face | rul'd like a wandering planet over me, 4.04. 16
with burthens, take your houses over your heads, 4.08. 30 P
and over the chair of state, where now he sits, 3H6 1.01.168
that hath authority over him that swears. 1.02. 24
pass'd over to the end they were created, 2.05. 39
mind | still ride in triumph over all mischance. 3.03. 18
that lewis of france is sending over masquers 3.03.224
shall waft them over with our royal fleet. 3.03.253
that lewis of france is sending over masquers 4.01. 94
thou hadst but power over his mortal body, | his R3 1.02. 47
eleven hours i have spent to write it over, 3.06. 5
bed, | throw over her the veil of infamy. 4.04.209
life | felt so much cold as over shoes in snow? 5.03.326
hath a witchcraft | over the king in 's tongue. H8 3.02. 19
they that bear | the cloth of honor over her, 4.01. 48
'em, | and something over to remember me by. 4.02.151
strew me over | with maiden flowers, that all 4.02.168
if he had biles — full, all over, generally? TRO 2.01. 3 P
and after it again, and over and over he comes, COR 1.03. 62 P
and after it again, and over and over he comes, 1.03. 62 P
i'll not over the threshold till my lord return 1.03. 74 P
and triumphs over chance in honor's bed. TIT 1.01.178
your desires, | saturn is dominator over mine: 2.03. 31
pray to the devils, the gods have given us over. 4.02. 48
atomi | over men's noses as they lie asleep. ROM 1.04. 58
driving back shadows over low'ring hills; 2.05. 6
weeping and wailing over tybalt's corse. 3.02.128
nor came any of his bounties over me | to mark TIM 3.02. 78
like physicians, | thrive, give him over; 3.03. 12
believe him as an enemy, and give over my trade. 4.03.454 P
that comes in triumph over pompey's blood? JC 1.01. 51
a hand | over your friend that loves you. 1.02. 36
give me your hands all over, one by one. 2.01.112
shall this our lofty scene be acted over | in 3.01.112
over thy wounds now do i prophesy | (which like 3.01.259
whilst bloody treason flourish'd over us. 3.02.192
of grief, | that it runs over even at his eyes. 5.05. 14
and, with his head over his shoulder turn'd, HAM 2.01. 94
honeying and making love | over the nasty sty! 3.04. 94
of a promis'd march | over his kingdom. 4.04. 4
good gertrude, set some watch over your son. 5.01.296
a bay trotting-horse over four-inch'd bridges, LR 3.04. 56 P
if you are so fond over her iniquity, give her OTH 4.01.197 P
i will give over my suit and repent my unlawful 4.02.198 P
let antony look over caesar's head | and speak ANT 2.02. 5
who is so full of grace that it flows over | on 5.02. 24
so tender over his occasions, true, | so feat, CYM 5.05. 87
a proportion to live quietly, and so give over. PER 4.02. 27 P
why to give over, i pray you? 4.02. 28 P
so soon as the court hurry is over, we will have TNK 2.01. 18 P
now, | by casting her black mantle over both, 5.03. 25
over one arm the lusty courser's rein, | under VEN 31
"over my altars hath he hung his lance, | his 103
when he did frown, o, had she then gave over, 571
over one shoulder doth she hang her head; 1058
if nature (sovereign mistress over wrack), | as SON 126. 5
old, | not age, but sorrow, over me hath power; LC 74
that maidens' eyes stuck over all his face. 81

OVERAWE 1 FR 0.0001 REL FR 1 V 0 P
prince, | whom like a schoolboy you may overawe.
1H6 1.01. 36

OVERBEAR 2 FR 0.0002 REL FR 2 V 0 P
egeus, i will overbear your will; MND 4.01.179
but it pleas'd your highness | to overbear it, JN 4.02. 37

OVERBEARS 1 FR 0.0001 REL FR 1 V 0 P
and overbears attaint | with cheerful semblance H5 4.pr. 39

OVERBLOWN 5 FR 0.0005 REL FR 4 V 1 P
is the storm overblown? TMP 2.02.110 P
to smile at scapes and perils overblown. SHR 5.02. 3
this ague fit of fear is overblown, | an easy R2 3.02.190
my choler being overblown | with walking once 2H6 1.03.152
seated, and domestic broils | clean overblown, R3 2.04. 61

OVERBOARD 5 FR 0.0005 REL FR 3 V 2 P
what though the mast be now blown overboard, 3H6 5.04. 3
overboard | into the tumbling billows of the R3 1.04. 19
sir, your queen must overboard. PER 3.01. 47 P
yield 'er, for she must overboard straight. 3.01. 53 P
i threw her overboard with these very arms. 5.03. 19

OVERBOLD 1 FR 0.0001 REL FR 1 V 0 P
saucy and overbold, how did you dare | to trade MAC 3.05. 3

OVERBOLDLY 1 FR 0.0001 REL FR 1 V 0 P
if overboldly we have borne ourselves | in the LLL 5.02.734

OVERBORNE 6 FR 0.0006 REL FR 5 V 1 P
hath so much overborne her that my daughter is ADO 2.03.151 P
that they have overborne their continents. MND 2.01. 92
weak shoulders, overborne with burthening grief, 1H6 2.05. 10
ay, /so the bishop be not overborne. 3.01. 53
the bishop will be overborne by thee. 5.01. 60
ever seen | an emperor in rome thus overborne, TIT 4.04. 2

OVERBULK 1 FR 0.0001 REL FR 1 V 0 P
a nursery of like evil, | to overbulk us all. TRO 1.03.320

OVERBUYS 1 FR 0.0001 REL FR 1 V 0 P
overbuys me | almost the sum he pays. CYM 1.01.146

/OVERCAME 2 FR 0.0002 REL FR 0 V 2 P
/overcame, three. LLL 4.01. 70 P
brag of "i came, saw, and /overcame." AYL 5.02. 32 P

OVERCAME 8 FR 0.0009 REL FR 4 V 4 P
videlicet, he came, /saw, and overcame: LLL 4.01. 70 P
who overcame he? 4.01. 74 P
"there, cousin, i came, saw, and overcame." 2H4 4.03. 42 P
what? wherein talbot overcame, is't so? 1H6 1.01.107
in his tent, | that day he overcame the nervii. JC 3.02.173
for brutus only overcame himself, | and no man 5.05. 56
that our last king hamlet overcame fortinbras. HAM 5.01.144 P
his brag | of "came, and saw, and overcame." CYM 3.01. 24

OVER-CANOPIED 1 FR 0.0001 REL FR 1 V 0 P
quite over-canopied with luscious woodbine, MND 2.01.251

OVER-CAREFUL 1 FR 0.0001 REL FR 1 V 0 P
for this the foolish over-careful fathers | have 2H4 4.05. 67

OVERCAST 1 FR 0.0001 REL FR 1 V 0 P
hie therefore, robin, overcast the night; MND 3.02.355

OVERCHARG'D 2 FR 0.0002 REL FR 1 V 1 P
if the ground be overcharg'd, you were best TGV 1.01.101 P
as cannons overcharg'd with double cracks, so MAC 1.02. 37

OVERCHARGED 2 FR 0.0002 REL FR 2 V 0 P
or like an overcharged gun, recoil, | and turns 2H6 3.02.331
as to him | the secrets of his overcharged soul; 3.02.376

OVERCOME 12 FR 0.0013 REL FR 9 V 3 P
to overcome. LLL 4.01. 72 P
why would you be so fond to overcome | the bonny
AYL 2.03. 7
o god, that right should thus overcome might! 2H4 5.04. 24 P
have i overcome mine enemies in this presence? 2H6 2.03. 97 P
in dreadful war mayst thou be overcome, | or 3H6 1.01.187
overcome with moss and baleful mistletoe; TIT 2.03. 95
no foes, that were enough | to overcome him. TIM 3.05. 70
be, | and overcome us like a summer's cloud, MAC 3.04.110
whereon old norway, overcome with joy, | gives HAM 2.02. 72
me, | whereas no glory's got to overcome. PER 1.04. 70
who, overcome by doubt and bloodless fear, VEN 891
here overcome, as one full of despair, | she 955

OVER-COOL 1 FR 0.0001 REL FR 0 V 1 P
for thin drink doth so over-cool their blood, 2H4 4.03. 91 P

OVER-CREDULOUS 1 FR 0.0001 REL FR 1 V 0 P
wisdom plucks me | from over-credulous haste. MAC 4.03.120

OVER-DARING 1 FR 0.0001 REL FR 1 V 0 P
the over-daring talbot | hath sullied all his 1H6 4.04. 5

OVERDONE 3 FR 0.0003 REL FR 0 V 3 P
mistress overdone. MM 2.01.200 P
nine, sir; overdone by the last. 2.01.202 P
now this overdone, or come tardy off, though it HAM 3.02. 24 P

OVERDONE'S 2 FR 0.0002 REL FR 0 V 2 P
ay, sir, by mistress overdone's means; MM 2.01. 83 P
think it were mistress overdone's own house, for 4.03. 3 P

OVER-EARNEST 1 FR 0.0001 REL FR 1 V 0 P
when you are over-earnest with your brutus, JC 4.03.122

OVER-EYEING 1 FR 0.0001 REL FR 1 V 0 P
lest, over-eyeing of his odd behavior | (for yet SHR in.1. 95

OVERFAR 1 FR 0.0001 REL FR 0 V 1 P
with such estimable wonder overfar believe that, TN 2.01. 28 P

OVERFLOW 5 FR 0.0005 REL FR 4 V 1 P
a kind overflow of kindness. ADO 1.01. 26 P
thy overflow of good converts to bad, | and thy R2 5.03. 64
and now at length they overflow their banks. PER 2.04. 24
yet i wish him | excess and overflow of power, TNK 1.03. 4
rank | perforce will force it overflow the bank. VEN 72

OVERFLOW'D 1 FR 0.0001 REL FR 1 V 0 P
tears | become a deluge, overflow'd and drown'd: TIT 3.01.229

OVERFLOWEN 1 FR 0.0001 REL FR 0 V 1 P
loath to have you overflowen with a honey-bag, MND 4.01. 16 P

OVERFLY 1 FR 0.0001 REL FR 1 V 0 P
outstripping crows that strive to overfly them. VEN 324

OVERFOND 1 FR 0.0001 REL FR 0 V 1 P
that time, overfond of the shepherd's daughter WT 5.02.117 P

OVER-FULL 1 FR 0.0001 REL FR 1 V 0 P
but, being over-full of self-affairs, | my mind MND 1.01.113

OVERGLANCE 1 FR 0.0001 REL FR 0 V 1 P
i will overglance the superscript: LLL 4.02.131 P

OVERGO 1 FR 0.0001 REL FR 1 V 0 P
moan) | to overgo thy woes and drown thy cries! R3 2.02. 61

OVERGOES 1 FR 0.0001 REL FR 1 V 0 P
a face | that overgoes my blunt invention quite, SON 103. 7

OVERGONE 1 FR 0.0001 REL FR 1 V 0 P
sad-hearted men, much overgone with care, | here
3H6 2.05.123

OVERGORG'D 1 FR 0.0001 REL FR 1 V 0 P
overgorg'd | with gobbets of thy /mother's 2H6 4.01. 84

//OVER-GREEDY 1 FR 0.0001 REL FR 1 V 0 P
/their //over-greedy /love /hath /surfeited. 2H4 1.03. 88
OVERGROWN 1 FR 0.0001 REL FR 1 V 0 P
like prisoners wildly overgrown with hair, | put H5 5.02. 43
OVER-HANDLED 1 FR 0.0001 REL FR 1 V 0 P
fall again | into your idle over-handled theme. VEN 770
/OVER-HAPPY 1 FR 0.0001 REL FR 0 V 1 P
in that we are not /over-happy, on fortune's HAM 2.02.228 P
OVERHEAD 1 FR 0.0001 REL FR 1 V 0 P
the street should see as she walk'd overhead. LLL 4.03.277
OVERHEAR 2 FR 0.0002 REL FR 2 V 0 P
by, | and overheard what you shall overhear — LLL 5.02. 95
and i will overhear their conference. MND 2.01.187
OVERHEARD 6 FR 0.0006 REL FR 2 V 4 P
i have overheard what hath pass'd between you MM 3.01.160 P
were thus much overheard by a man of mine. ADO 1.02. 10 P
who in the night overheard me confessing to this 5.01.234 P
by, | and overheard what you shall overhear — LLL 5.02. 95
i overheard him — and his practices. AYL 2.03. 26
if they have overheard me now — why, hanging. WT 4.04.626 P
OVERHEARDST 2 FR 0.0002 REL FR 2 V 0 P
say that thou overheardst us, | and bid her ADO 3.01. 6
but that thou overheardst, ere i was ware, | my ROM 2.02.103
OVERHOLD 1 FR 0.0001 REL FR 1 V 0 P
add, | that if he overhold his price so much, TRO 2.03.133
OVERJOY 1 FR 0.0001 REL FR 1 V 0 P
affords | and overjoy of heart doth minister. 2H6 1.01. 31
OVERJOY'D 2 FR 0.0002 REL FR 1 V 1 P
who, being overjoy'd with finding a bird's nest, ADO 2.01.223 P
o, she's but overjoy'd. PER 5.03. 21
OVERJOYED 1 FR 0.0001 REL FR 1 V 0 P
as being overjoyed | to see her noble lord SHR in.1. 120
OVERKIND 1 FR 0.0001 REL FR 0 V 1 P
sicilia cannot show himself overkind to bohemia. WT 1.01. 21 P
OVERKINDNESS 1 FR 0.0001 REL FR 1 V 0 P
your overkindness doth wring tears from me. ADO 5.01.293
OVERLAND 1 FR 0.0001 REL FR 1 V 0 P
of you | a conduct overland to milford-haven. CYM 3.05. 8
OVERLEATHER 1 FR 0.0001 REL FR 0 V 1 P
shoes as my toes look through the overleather. SHR in.2. 12 P
OVERLIVE 1 FR 0.0001 REL FR 1 V 0 P
that your attempts may overlive the hazard | and 2H4 4.01. 15
OVER-LONG 1 FR 0.0001 REL FR 1 V 0 P
o, hold me not with silence over-long! 1H6 5.03. 13
OVERLOOK 4 FR 0.0004 REL FR 4 V 0 P
willing you overlook this pedigree; H5 2.04. 90
into the clouds | and overlook their grafters? 3.05. 9
gates, | so york may overlook the town of york. 3H6 1.04.180
with burning eye did hotly overlook them, VEN 178
OVERLOOK'D 1 FR 0.0001 REL FR 0 V 1 P
when thou shalt have overlook'd this, give these HAM 4.06. 14 P
OVERLOOKING 1 FR 0.0001 REL FR 0 V 1 P
my lord, and bequeath'd to my overlooking. AWW 1.01. 39 P
OVERLOOKS 2 FR 0.0002 REL FR 2 V 0 P
that sways the earth this climate overlooks, JN 2.01.344
and overlooks the highest-peering hills: TIT 2.01. 8
OVERLUSTY 2 FR 0.0002 REL FR 1 V 1 P
the confident and overlusty french | do the H5 4.pr. 18
when a /man's overlusty at legs, then he wears LR 2.04. 10 P
OVERMASTER'D 1 FR 0.0001 REL FR 0 V 1 P
a woman to be overmaster'd with a piece of ADO 2.01. 61 P
OVERMATCHING 1 FR 0.0001 REL FR 1 V 0 P
and spend her strength with overmatching waves. 3H6 1.04. 21
OVER-MEASURE 1 FR 0.0001 REL FR 1 V 0 P
enough, with over-measure. COR 3.01.140
OVER-MERRY 1 FR 0.0001 REL FR 1 V 0 P
presence | may well abate the over-merry spleen, SHR in.1. 137
OVERMOUNTING 1 FR 0.0001 REL FR 1 V 0 P
my boy did drench | his overmounting spirit; 1H6 4.07. 15
OVERMUCH 2 FR 0.0002 REL FR 2 V 0 P
you tempt him overmuch. WT 5.01. 73
long, | and overmuch consum'd his royal person: R3 1.01.140
OVER-NAME 1 FR 0.0001 REL FR 0 V 1 P
i pray thee over-name them, and as thou namest MV 1.02. 36 P
OVERNIGHT 1 FR 0.0001 REL FR 1 V 0 P
madam, | if i had given you this at overnight, AWW 3.04. 23
OVER-PARTIAL 1 FR 0.0001 REL FR 1 V 0 P
if eyes, corrupt by over-partial looks, | be SON 137. 5
OVERPASS'D 1 FR 0.0001 REL FR 1 V 0 P
and like a hermit overpass'd thy days. 1H6 2.05.117
OVER-PAY 1 FR 0.0001 REL FR 1 V 0 P
which i will over-pay and pay again | when i AWW 3.07. 16
OVERPEER 2 FR 0.0002 REL FR 2 V 0 P
do overpeer the petty traffickers | that cur'sy MV 1.01. 12
bars | in yonder tower to overpeer the city, 1H6 1.04. 11
OVERPEER'D 1 FR 0.0001 REL FR 1 V 0 P
whose top-branch overpeer'd jove's spreading 3H6 5.02. 14
OVERPEERING 1 FR 0.0001 REL FR 1 V 0 P
the ocean, overpeering of his list, | eats not HAM 4.05.100
OVERPLUS 3 FR 0.0003 REL FR 3 V 0 P
our overplus of shipping will we burn, | and, ANT 3.07. 50
all thy treasure, with | his bounty overplus. 4.06. 21
will, | and will to boot, and will in overplus; SON 135. 2
OVER-PROUD 2 FR 0.0002 REL FR 2 V 0 P
lest, being over-proud in sap and blood, | with R2 3.04. 59
if you do say we think him over-proud | and TRO 2.03.123
OVERREACH 1 FR 0.0001 REL FR 1 V 0 P
we'll overreach the greybeard, gremio, | the SHR 3.02.145
OVER-READ 1 FR 0.0001 REL FR 0 V 1 P
you shall anon over-read it at your pleasure; MM 4.02.197 P
OVER-RED 1 FR 0.0001 REL FR 1 V 0 P
go prick thy face, and over-red thy fear, | thou MAC 5.03. 14
OVER-RIPEN'D 1 FR 0.0001 REL FR 1 V 0 P
like over-ripen'd corn | hanging the head at 2H6 1.02. 1
OVERROASTED 2 FR 0.0002 REL FR 1 V 1 P
than feed it with such overroasted flesh. SHR 4.01.175
overroasted rather; ready long ago. CYM 5.04.152 P
OVERRODE 1 FR 0.0001 REL FR 1 V 0 P
my lord, i overrode him on the way, | and he is 2H4 1.01. 30
/OVERRUL'D 1 FR 0.0001 REL FR 1 V 0 P
in that are one, | /not /to /be /overrul'd. LR 1.03. 16
OVERRUL'D 3 FR 0.0003 REL FR 3 V 0 P
and comes not in, overrul'd by prophecies, | i 1H4 4.04. 18
yet hath a woman's kindness overrul'd; 1H6 2.02. 50
"thus he that overrul'd i overswayed, | leading VEN 109
OVERRULE 1 FR 0.0001 REL FR 1 V 0 P
my lord, you shall overrule my mind for once. R3 3.01. 57
OVERRUN 1 FR 0.0001 REL FR 1 V 0 P
thoughts, | wherewith already france is overrun. 1H6 1.01.102
OVERRUNNING 1 FR 0.0001 REL FR 1 V 0 P
that which we run at, | and lose by overrunning. H8 1.01.143
OVERSCUTCH'D 1 FR 0.0001 REL FR 0 V 1 P
tunes to the overscutch'd huswives that he heard 2H4 3.02.317 P
OVERSEE 1 FR 0.0001 REL FR 1 V 0 P
"thou, collatine, shalt oversee this will; LUC 1205
OVERSEEN 1 FR 0.0001 REL FR 1 V 0 P
how was i overseen that thou shalt see it! LUC 1206
OVERSET 1 FR 0.0001 REL FR 1 V 0 P
calm, will overset | thy tempest-tossed body. ROM 3.05.136
OVERSHADES 1 FR 0.0001 REL FR 1 V 0 P
which overshades the mouth of that same pit TIT 2.03.273
OVER-SHINE 1 FR 0.0001 REL FR 1 V 0 P
and over-shine the earth as this the world. 3H6 2.01. 38
OVERSHINE 1 FR 0.0001 REL FR 1 V 0 P
dost overshine the gallant'st dames of rome, TIT 1.01.317
OVERSHINES 1 FR 0.0001 REL FR 1 V 0 P
beauty than we have, | yea, overshines ourself. TRO 3.01.158
OVERSHOT 2 FR 0.0002 REL FR 1 V 1 P
so study evermore is overshot: LLL 1.01.142
'tis not the first time you were overshot. H5 3.07.124 P
OVERSHUT 1 FR 0.0001 REL FR 1 V 0 P
mark the poor wretch, to overshut his troubles, VEN 680
OVERSIGHTS 1 FR 0.0001 REL FR 1 V 0 P
from me | with new lamenting ancient oversights, 2H4 2.03. 47
OVERSLIPP'D 1 FR 0.0001 REL FR 1 V 0 P
which all this time hath overslipp'd her thought LUC 1576
OVERSPREAD 1 FR 0.0001 REL FR 1 V 0 P
image of my youth, | is overspread with them; 2H4 4.04. 56
OVER-STAIN'D 1 FR 0.0001 REL FR 1 V 0 P
knows they were besmear'd and over-stain'd JN 3.01.236
OVERSWAYED 1 FR 0.0001 REL FR 1 V 0 P
"thus he that overrul'd i overswayed, | leading VEN 109
/OVERT 1 FR 0.0001 REL FR 1 V 0 P
without more wider and more /overt test | than OTH 1.03.107
OVERTA'EN 2 FR 0.0002 REL FR 2 V 0 P
york | has almost overta'en him in his growth. R3 2.04. 7
his good will | hath overta'en mine act. COR 1.09. 19
OVERTAKE 7 FR 0.0008 REL FR 5 V 2 P
and yet it cannot overtake your slow purse. TGV 1.01.126 P
when she is able to overtake seventeen years old WIV 1.01. 53 P
go, gratiano, run and overtake him; MV 4.01.452
to break a jest | upon the company you overtake? SHR 4.05. 73
wing of recompense is slow | to overtake thee. MAC 1.04. 18
the winged vengeance overtake such children. LR 3.07. 66
i'll overtake you. — speak. 5.01. 39
OVERTAKETH 1 FR 0.0001 REL FR 1 V 0 P
every sedge | he overtaketh in his pilgrimage; TGV 2.07. 30
OVER-TEDIOUS 1 FR 0.0001 REL FR 1 V 0 P
speak on, but be not over-tedious. 1H6 3.03. 43
OVERTHROW 18 FR 0.0020 REL FR 16 V 2 P
start-up hath all the glory of my overthrow. ADO 1.03. 67 P
that thine own trip shall be thine overthrow? TN 5.01.167
be minist'red, | or overthrow incurable ensues. JN 5.01. 16
that sought at oxford thy dire overthrow. R2 5.06. 16
compound, | before thy most assured overthrow; H5 4.03. 81
that plotted thus our glory's overthrow? 1H6 1.01. 24
hath the late overthrow wrought this offense? 1.02. 49
that seeks to overthrow religion | because he is 1.03. 65
we are like to have the overthrow again. 3.02.106
for i have seen our enemies' overthrow. 3.02.111
i fear thy overthrow | more than my body's 3H6 2.06. 3
though fortune's malice overthrow my state, | my 4.03. 46
his overthrow heap'd happiness upon him; H8 4.02. 64
and sudden push gives them the overthrow. JC 5.02. 5
he sweats not to overthrow your almain; OTH 2.03. 83 P
within | with bloody veins, expecting overthrow, PER 1.04. 94
not die | till mutual overthrow of mortal kind! VEN 1018
morrow, | to linger out a purpos'd overthrow. SON 90. 8
OVERTHROWN 11 FR 0.0012 REL FR 8 V 3 P
you're sham'd, y' are overthrown, y' are undone WIV 3.03. 95 P
assurance, and all the preparation overthrown. ADO 2.02. 50 P
you have overthrown alisander the conqueror! LLL 5.02.574 P
well, and overthrown | more than your enemies. AYL 1.02.254
thou art overthrown, | or charles, or something 1.02.259
are by the shrieve of yorkshire overthrown. 2H4 4.04. 99
that in this quarrel have been overthrown | and 1H6 5.04.105
by cruel cruel thee quite overthrown! ROM 4.05. 57
octavius | is overthrown by noble brutus' power, JC 5.03. 52
confess'd and prov'd, | have overthrown him. MAC 1.03.116
run | that our devices still are overthrown, HAM 3.02.212
OVERTHROWS 2 FR 0.0002 REL FR 2 V 0 P
overthrows thy joys, friends, fortune, and thy R2 3.02. 72
whose misadventur'd piteous overthrows | doth ROM pr 7
OVERTOOK 1 FR 0.0001 REL FR 1 V 0 P
along | i met and overtook a dozen captains, 2H4 2.04.358
OVERTOPP'D 1 FR 0.0001 REL FR 1 V 0 P
this pine is bark'd, | that overtopp'd them all. ANT 4.12. 24
OVERTOPPING 1 FR 0.0001 REL FR 1 V 0 P
and who | to trash for overtopping, new created TMP 1.02. 81
OVERTURE 6 FR 0.0006 REL FR 4 V 2 P
i hear there is an overture of peace. AWW 4.03. 39 P
course of honor | as she had made the overture, 5.03. 99
i bring no overture of war, no taxation of TN 1.05.208 P
judgment tried it, | without more overture. WT 2.01.172
let him be made an overture for th' wars! COR 1.09. 46
that made the overture of thy treasons to us, LR 3.07. 89
OVERTURN 1 FR 0.0001 REL FR 1 V 0 P
when wasteful war shall statues overturn, | and SON 55. 5
OVERTURN'D 1 FR 0.0001 REL FR 1 V 0 P
o god, i fear all will be overturn'd! 2H4 5.02. 19
OVER-VEIL'D 1 FR 0.0001 REL FR 1 V 0 P
whose pitchy mantle over-veil'd the earth. 1H6 2.02. 2
OVER-VIEW 1 FR 0.0001 REL FR 1 V 0 P
are we betrayed thus to thy over-view? LLL 4.03.173
OVER-WASH'D 1 FR 0.0001 REL FR 1 V 0 P
nor why her fair cheeks over-wash'd with woe. LUC 1225
OVERWATCH'D 1 FR 0.0001 REL FR 1 V 0 P
as much as we this night have overwatch'd. MND 5.01.366
OVER-WEATHER'D 1 FR 0.0001 REL FR 1 V 0 P
with over-weather'd ribs and ragged sails, MV 2.06. 18
OVERWEEN 2 FR 0.0002 REL FR 2 V 0 P
mowbray, you overween to take it so; 2H4 4.01.147
demetrius, thou dost overween in all, | and so TIT 2.01. 29
OVERWEENING 5 FR 0.0005 REL FR 4 V 1 P
overweening slave! TGV 3.01.157
here's an overweening rogue! TN 2.05. 29 P
my gage | upon this overweening traitor's foot, R2 1.01.147
whose overweening arm i have pluck'd back, | by 2H6 3.01.159
lash hence these overweening rags of france, R3 5.03.328
OVERWEIGH 1 FR 0.0001 REL FR 1 V 0 P
th' state, | will so your accusation overweigh, MM 2.04.157
OVERWHELM 2 FR 0.0002 REL FR 2 V 0 P
seek'st the greatness that will overwhelm thee. 2H4 4.05. 97
doth prop it, | would sink and overwhelm you. PER 4.06.120
OVERWHELM'D 3 FR 0.0003 REL FR 2 V 1 P
whose joy of her is overwhelm'd like mine, | and ADO 5.01. 9
a sow that hath overwhelm'd all her litter but 2H4 1.02. 11 P
if | his sorrows have so overwhelm'd his wits? TIT 4.04. 10
OVERWHELMING 1 FR 0.0001 REL FR 1 V 0 P
in tatt'red weeds, with overwhelming brows, ROM 5.01. 39
OVERWORN 1 FR 0.0001 REL FR 0 V 1 P
i might say "element," but the word is overworn. TN 3.01. 59 P
OVID 2 FR 0.0002 REL FR 1 V 1 P
as the most capricious poet, honest ovid, was AYL 3.03. 8 P
checks | as ovid be an outcast quite abjur'd. SHR 1.01. 33
OVIDIUS 1 FR 0.0001 REL FR 0 V 1 P
ovidius naso was the man. LLL 4.02.123 P
OVID'S 1 FR 0.0001 REL FR 1 V 0 P
grandsire, 'tis ovid's metamorphosis, | my TIT 4.01. 42
OW'D* 8 FR 0.0009 REL FR 6 V 2 P
did quarrel with the noblest grace she ow'd, TMP 3.01. 45
i could not have ow'd her a more rooted love. AWW 4.05. 12 P
remember since you ow'd no more to time | than i WT 5.01.219
that blood which ow'd the breadth of all this JN 4.02. 99
but, for the party that ow'd it, he might have 2H4 1.02. 4 P
slaughter of the prince that ow'd that crown, R3 4.04.142
to throw away the dearest thing he ow'd, | as MAC 1.04. 10
we on | to give obedience where 'tis truly ow'd. 5.02. 26
OW'DST 1 FR 0.0001 REL FR 1 V 0 P
that sweet sleep | which thou ow'dst yesterday. OTH 3.03.333
OWE* *(also own, etc.)*
OWE* 81 FR 0.0091 REL FR 64 V 17 P
that such an ass should owe them. TGV 5.02. 28
theirs | as they themselves would owe them. MM 1.04. 83
but only he, | owe and succeed thy weakness. 2.04.123
sir, for your kindness, i owe you a good turn. 4.02. 58 P
thou that keep'st me out from the house i owe? ERR 3.01. 42
of mine, | nor to her bed no homage do i owe: 3.02. 43
even just the sum that i do owe to you | is 4.01. 7
the money that you owe me for the chain. 4.01. 63
i owe you none, till i receive the chain. 4.01. 64
i owe you all duty. ADO 1.01.156 P
i will owe thee an answer for that, and now 3.03.101 P
for this i owe you: 5.04. 52
possess the same | which native she doth owe. LLL 1.02.106
of all perfections that a man may owe, 2.01. 6
i throw | all the power this charm doth owe. MND 2.02. 79
this wood, i have enough to serve mine owe turn. 3.01.151 P
for debt that bankrout /sleep doth sorrow owe; 3.02. 85
i owe the most, in money and in love, | and from MV 1.01.131
how to get clear of all the debts i owe. 1.01.134
i owe you much, and, like a willful youth, 1.01.146
that which i owe is lost, but if you please | to 1.01.147
the value of the sum | that he did owe him; 3.02.288
i care not for their names, they owe me nothing. AYL 2.05. 21 P
get that i wear, owe no man hate, envy no man's 3.02. 74 P
what duty they do owe their lords and husbands. SHR 5.02.131
i am not worthy of the wealth i owe, | nor dare AWW 2.05. 79
duty, such, my lord, | as you owe to your wife. 4.02. 13
who pays before, but not when he does owe it. 4.03.230
ourselves we do not owe; TN 1.05.310
a woman can bear me | and that i owe olivia. 2.04.103
too well what love women to men may owe; 2.04.105
royal bed, which owe | a moi'ty of the throne, a WT 3.02. 38
which owe the crown that thou o'ermasterest? JN 2.01.109
to pay that duty which you truly owe | to him 2.01.247
o my gentle hubert, | we owe thee much! 3.03. 20
swear by the duty that y' owe to god | (our part R2 1.03.180
know you, sir john, you owe me money, sir john, 1H4 3.03. 66 P
you owe money here besides, sir john, for your 3.03. 72 P
sirrah, do i owe you a thousand pound? 3.03.135 P
day, | england did never owe so sweet a hope, 5.02. 67
what is the gross sum that i owe thee? 2H4 2.01. 84 P
pay her the debt you owe her, and unpay the 2.01.119 P
for th' other, i owe her money, and whether she 2.04.339 P
a man can die but once, we owe god a death. 3.02.235 P
master shallow, i owe you a thousand pound. 5.05. 73 P
that owe yourselves, your lives, and services H5 1.02. 34
some upon the debts they owe, some upon their 4.01.140 P
if i owe you any thing, i will pay you in 5.01. 64 P
i owe him little duty, and less love, | and take 1H6 4.04. 34
for now we owe allegiance unto henry. 3H6 4.07. 19
the duty that i owe unto your majesty | i seal 5.07. 28
i do owe them still | my life and services. COR 2.02.133
one time will owe another. 3.01.241
but owe thy pride thyself. 3.02.130
though i owe | my revenge properly, my remission 5.02. 83
danger | which this man's life did owe you, 5.06.137
receive them then, the tribute that i owe, TIT 1.01.251
by all the duties that i owe to rome, | this 1.01.414
who now the price of his dear blood doth owe? ROM 3.01.183
i owe moe tears | to this dead man than you JC 5.03.101
from whence | you owe this strange intelligence, MAC 1.03. 76
the service and the loyalty i owe, | in doing it 1.04. 22
me strange | even to the disposition that i owe, 3.04.112
what we shall say we have, and what we owe. 5.04. 18
you owe me no subscription. LR 3.02. 18
what a /full fortune does the thick-lips owe OTH 1.01. 66
noble company | where most you owe obedience? 1.03.180
for a liberal thanks, | which i do owe you. ANT 2.06. 48
our hack'd targets like the men that owe them. 4.08. 31
against | obedience, which you owe your father. CYM 2.03.112
crook'd noses, but to owe such straight arms, 3.01. 37 P
that life, beseech you, | which i so often owe; 5.05.415
endowments which | you make more rich to owe? PER 5.01.117
this is a solemn rite | they owe bloom'd may, TNK 3.01. 3
dexter way to me | that owe it him by nature. STM III 12
'tis much to borrow, and i will not owe it; VEN 411
"fair queen," quoth he, "if any love you owe me, 523
therefore that praise which collatine doth owe LUC 82
paying more slavish tribute than they owe. 299
then thou alone kingdoms of hearts shouldst owe. SON 70.14

the true gouty landlord which doth owe them. LC 140
OWED* 5 FR 0.0005 REL FR 5 V 0 P
th' sequent issue, | hath it been owed and worn. AWW 5.03.198
into my keeping, | which is not owed to you! TIM 1.01.151
like as if that god | owed not nor made not you, STM II.C 136
i owed her, and 'tis mine that she hath kill'd." LUC 1803
o, all that borrowed motion seeming owed, LC 327
OWEN 8 FR 0.0009 REL FR 5 V 3 P
devil alone | as owen glendower for an enemy. 1H4 1.03.117
mortimer, my lord of york, and owen glendower? 2.03. 25 P
owen, owen, the same; 2.04.341 P
owen, owen, the same; 2.04.341 P
as oft as he hears | owen glendower spoke of. 3.01. 12
land within that bound, | to owen glendower; 3.01. 77
and what with owen glendower's absence thence, 4.04. 16
and, but for owen glendower, had been king, 2H6 2.02. 41
/OWES* 1 FR 0.0001 REL FR 1 V 0 P
/a /deep /well | /that /owes /two /buckets, R2 4.01.185
OWES* 26 FR 0.0029 REL FR 24 V 2 P
business, nor no sound | that the earth owes. TMP 1.02.408
a very bankrout and owes more than he's worth to ERR 4.02. 58
go, | the debt he owes will be requir'd of me. 4.04.118
i know the man; what is the sum he owes? 4.04.133
what sum owes he the jew? MV 3.02.297
such duty as the subject owes the prince, | even SHR 5.02.155
my heart | will not confess he owes the malady AWW 2.01. 9
which both thy duty owes and our power claims, 2.03.161
that all the miseries which nature owes | were 3.02.119
the jeweller that owes the ring is sent for, 5.03.296
bohemia the visitation which he justly owes him. WT 1.01. 7 P
duty which you truly owe | to him that owes it, JN 2.01.248
for all the treasure that thine uncle owes. 4.01.122
the one my duty owes, but my fair name, R2 1.01.167
to answer all the debt he owes to you | even 1H4 1.03.185
nor feels not what he owes, but by reflection; TRO 3.03. 99
retain that dear perfection which he owes ROM 2.02. 46
he owes | for ev'ry word. TIM 1.02.198
to varro and to isidore | he owes nine thousand, 2.01. 2
all these | owes their estates unto him. 3.03. 5
timon in this should pay more than he owes; 3.04. 22
be call'd desperate ones, for a madman owes 'em. 3.04.102 P
if by this crime he owes the law his life, | why 3.05. 82
will you, with those infirmities she owes, LR 1.01.202
unto the worst | owes nothing to thy blasts. 4.01. 9
since what he owes thee thou thyself dost pay. SON 79.14
OWEST* 4 FR 0.0004 REL FR 2 V 2 P
thou owest me thy love. 1H4 3.03.137 P
why, thou owest god a death. 5.01.126 P
and pay thy life thou owest me for my horse. TRO 5.06. 7
than thou knowest, | lend less than thou owest, LR 1.04.120
OWETH 1 FR 0.0001 REL FR 1 V 0 P
even such a woman oweth to her husband; SHR 5.02.156
OWGH 3 FR 0.0003 REL FR 3 V 0 P
owgh, owgh, owgh! TNK 4.01.147
owgh, owgh, owgh! 4.01.147
owgh, owgh, owgh! 4.01.147
OWING* 2 FR 0.0002 REL FR 1 V 1 P
there is more owing her than is paid, and more AWW 1.03.104 P
a black one, owing | not a hair–worth of white, TNK 5.04. 50
OWL 21 FR 0.0023 REL FR 16 V 5 P
good night, my good owl. LLL 4.01.139
compiled in praise of the owl and the cuckoo? 5.02.887 P
the one maintained by the owl, th' other by the 5.02.892 P
be /foul, | then nightly sings the staring owl, 5.02.917
the bowl, | then nightly sings the staring owl, 5.02.926
and some keep back | the clamorous owl, that MND 2.02. 6
thou ominous and fearful owl of death, | our 1H6 4.02. 15
hope | go home to bed, and like the owl by day, 3H6 5.04. 56
the owl shriek'd at thy birth, an evil sign; 5.06. 44
i bade the vile owl go learn me the tenor of the TRO 2.01. 90 P
a toad, a lezard, an owl, a puttock, or 5.01. 62 P
breeds, | unless the nightly owl or fatal raven; TIT 2.03. 97
it was the owl that shriek'd, the fatal bellman, MAC 2.02. 3
i heard the owl scream and the crickets cry. 2.02. 15
was by a mousing owl hawk'd at, and kill'd. 2.04. 13
her young ones in her nest, against the owl. 4.02. 11
they say the owl was a baker's daughter. HAM 4.05. 42 P
air, | to be a comrade with the wolf and owl — LR 2.04.210
the night to th' owl and morn to th' lark less CYM 3.06. 93
the one said it was an owl, | the other he said TNK 3.05. 68
the owl (night's herald) shrieks, 'tis very late VEN 531
OWLET *(see howlet, etc.)*
OWLS' 1 FR 0.0001 REL FR 1 V 0 P
no noise but owls' and wolves' death–boding LUC 165
OWLS 3 FR 0.0003 REL FR 3 V 0 P
there i couch when owls do cry. TMP 5.01. 90
we talk with goblins, owls, and sprites; ERR 2.02.190
out on /you, owls! R3 4.04.507
OWN *(also owe*, etc.)*
/OWN 14 FR 0.0015 REL FR 12 V 2 P
lady, i will commend you to /mine /own heart. LLL 2.01.179 P
/do /that /office /of /thine /own /good /will R2 4.01.177
/with /mine /own /tears /i /wash /away /my /balm 4.01.207
/with /mine /own /hands /i /give /away /my 4.01.208
/with /mine /own /tongue /deny /my /sacred 4.01.209
/with /mine /own /breath /release /all /duteous 4.01.210
/question /surveyors, /know /our /own /estate, 2H4 1.03. 53
/commonwealth /is /sick /of /their /own /choice, 1.03. 87
/being /now /trimm'd /in /thine /own /desires, 1.03. 94
/would /turn /their /own /perfection /to /abuse 2.03. 27
(/his /own /life /hung /upon /the /staff /he 4.01.124
how he did lap me | even in his /own garments, R3 2.01.117
/them /exclaim /against /their /own /succession? HAM 2.02.351 P
/his /own /unkindness, | /that /stripp'd /her LR 4.03. 42
OWN 815 FR 0.0921 REL FR 594 V 221 P
our cable, for our own doth little advantage. TMP 1.01. 32 P
sinner of his memory | to credit his own lie — 1.02.102
me | from mine own library with volumes that | i 1.02.167
that you have, | which first was mine own king; 1.02.342
and lodg'd thee | in mine own cell, till thou 1.02.347
know thine own meaning, but wouldst gabble like 1.02.356
the fault's your own. 2.01.136
of it own kind, all foison, all abundance, | to 2.01.164
the bottom run | by their own fear or sloth. 2.01.228
your content | tender your own good fortune? 2.01.270
of a tree with mine own hands since i was cast 2.02.123 P
face remember, | save, from my glass, mine own; 3.01. 50
have given you here a third of mine own life, 4.01. 3
and thine own acquisition | worthily purchas'd, 4.01. 13
sit then and talk with her, she is thine own. 4.01. 32
which may make this island | thine own for ever, 4.01.218
and rifted jove's stout oak | with his own bolt; 5.01. 46
all of us, ourselves, | when no man was his own. 5.01.213
two of these fellows you | must know and own, 5.01.275
and what strength i have's mine own, | which is ep 2
letter in the letter, | except mine own name; TGV 1.02.117
and with the vantage of mine own excuse | hath 1.03. 82
or your own eyes had the lights they were wont 2.01. 71 P
your own present folly, and her passing 2.01. 75 P
made them watchers of mine own heart's sorrow. 2.04.135
have i not reason to prefer mine own? 2.04.156
why, man, she is mine own, | and i as rich in 2.04.168
shape, and by your own report | a linguist, and 4.01. 54
him, | i have access my own love to prefer — 4.02. 4
i thank you for your own. 4.02. 24
and then i offer'd her mine own, who is a dog as 4.04. 57 P
i grant it, for thine own, what e'er it be. 5.04.151
never come in mine own great chamber again else, WIV 1.01.154 P
you shall have anne — fool's–head of your own. 1.04.127 P
by me, thine own true knight, | by day or night, 2.01. 14
fire of lust have melted him in his own grease. 2.01. 68 P
almost ready to wrangle with mine own honesty. 2.01. 85 P
nobody hears — mine own people, mine own people 2.02. 50 P
hears — mine own people, mine own people. 2.02. 51 P
i must very much lay open mine own imperfection; 2.02.185 P
turn another into the register of your own, that 2.02.187 P
her (i may tell you) by her own appointment; 2.02.262 P
at most odds with his own gravity and patience 3.01. 54 P
and learning, so wide of his own respect. 3.01. 58 P
and i fear not mine own shame so much as his 3.03.122 P
truly, for mine own part, i would little or 3.04. 62 P
clothes that fretted in their own grease. 3.05.114 P
why, none but mine own people. 4.02. 14 P
now he shall see his own foolery. 4.02. 37 P
if you go out in your own semblance, you die, 4.02. 66 P
not follow the imaginations of your own heart. 4.02.156 P
why, this is your own folly. 5.05.194 P
since i am put to know that your own science MM 1.01. 5
deputation all the organs | of our own pow'r. 1.01. 21
are not thine own so proper as to waste 1.01. 30
your scope is as mine own, | so to enforce or 1.01. 64
i will, out of thine own confession, learn to 1.02. 37 P
that, in the working of your own affections, 2.01. 10
have attain'd th' effect of your own purpose, 2.01. 13
let mine own judgment pattern out my death, 2.01. 30
for mine own part, i never come into any room in 2.01.208 P
who, falling in the flaws of her own youth, 2.03. 11
to a well–wish'd king | quit their own part, and 2.04. 28
whose credit with the judge, or own great place, 2.04. 92
and from this testimony of your own sex | (since 2.04.131
that you shall stifle in your own report, | and 2.04.158
for thine own bowels, which do call thee /sire, 3.01. 29
to take life | from thine own sister's shame? 3.01.139
i would require is likewise your own benefit. 3.01.155 P
do no stain to your own gracious person; 3.01.202 P
in few, bestow'd her on her own lamentation, 3.01.228 P
be but testimonied in his own bringings–forth, 3.02.145 P
if his own life answer the straitness of his 3.02.255 P
striking | kills for faults of his own liking! 3.02.268
you have occasion to use me for your own turn, 4.02. 57 P
think it were mistress overdone's own house, for 4.03. 3 P
be you judge | of your own cause. 5.01.167
not better than he, by her own report. 5.01.273 P
this finger of mine than he | dare rack his own. 5.01.315
but let my trial be mine own confession. 5.01.372
to tell sad stories of my own mishaps. ERR 1.01.120
sir, i commend you to your own content. 1.02. 32
he that commends me to mine own content, 1.02. 33
so great a charge from thine own custody? 1.02. 61
thou hast thine own form. 2.02.198
your own handwriting would tell you what i think 3.01. 14
since mine own doors refuse to entertain me, 3.01.120
be not thy tongue thy own shame's orator: 3.02. 10
what simple thief brags of his own /attaint? 3.02. 16
it is thyself, mine own self's better part: 3.02. 61
a lamp of her and run from her by her own light. 3.02. 97 P
of his own doors being shut against his entrance 4.03. 89
she did betray me to my own reproof. 5.01. 90
that you frame the season for your own harvest. ADO 1.03. 25 P
so would not i for your own sake, for i have 2.01.101 P
all hearts in love use their own tongues. 2.01.177
to the next willow, about your own business, 2.01.187 P
the argument of his own scorn by falling in love 2.03. 11 P
to put a strange face on his own perfection. 2.03. 47
says she, "by my own spirit, for i should flout 2.03.143 P
are to present the prince's own person. 3.03. 75 P
keep your fellows' counsels and your own, and 3.03. 86 P
but truly, for mine own part, if i were as 3.05. 20 P
dear my lord, if you, in your own proof, | have 4.01. 45
are our eyes our own? 4.01. 71
rightly reason'd, and in his own division, and, 5.01.224 P
give us the swords, we have bucklers of our own. 5.02. 19 P
not erect in this age his own tomb ere he dies, 5.02. 78 P
to be the trumpet of his own virtues, as i am to 5.02. 86 P
hand, | a halting sonnet of his own pure brain, 5.04. 87
here's our own hands against our hearts. 5.04. 91 P
we may lighten our own hearts and our wives' 5.04.119 P
that war against your own affections | and the LLL 1.01. 9
that his own hand may strike his honor down 1.01. 20
one who the music of his own vain tongue | doth 1.01.166
a man of fire–new words, fashion's own knight. 1.01.178
which is the duke's own person? 1.01.181 P
i myself reprehend his own person, for i am his 1.01.183 P
but i would see his own person in flesh and 1.01.184 P
that every one her own hath garnished | with 2.01. 78
your own good thoughts excuse me, and farewell. 2.01.175
thy own wish wish i thee in every place. 2.01.178
tend'ring their own worth from where they were 2.01.244
his face's own margent did cote such amazes 2.01.246
and wit's own grace to grace a learned fool. 5.02. 72
muster your wits, stand in your own defense, 5.02. 85
to make theirs ours and ours none but our own; 5.02.154
they will again be here | in their own shapes; 5.02.288
do, | if they return in their own shapes to woo? 5.02.299
for mine own part, i am, as /they say, but to 5.02.501 P
for mine own part, i know not the degree of the 5.02.506 P
for mine own part, i breathe free breath. 5.02.722 P
therefore met your loves | in their own fashion, 5.02.784
with the clamors of their own dear groans, 5.02.864
you see an ass–head of your own, do you? MND 3.01.117 P
'tis partly my own fault, | which death, or 3.02.243
eye, | steal me a while from mine own company. 3.02.436
known, | that every man should take his own, 3.02.459
like tears that did their own disgrace bewail. 4.01. 56
thou wak'st, with thine own fool's eyes peep. 4.01. 84
like a jewel, | mine own, and not mine own. 4.01.192
like a jewel, | mine own, and not mine own. 4.01.192
i take it your own business calls on you, | and MV 1.01. 63
shalt not know the sound of thine own tongue. 1.01.109
a good divine that follows his own instructions; 1.02. 15 P
one of the twenty to follow mine own teaching. 1.02. 17 P
appropriation to his own good parts that he can 1.02. 42 P
he will fence with his own shadow. 1.02. 62 P
and all for use of that which is mine own. 1.03.113
whose own hard dealings teaches them suspect 1.03.161
it is a wise father that knows his own child. 2.02. 77 P
be launcelot, thou art mine own flesh and blood. 2.02. 92 P
but, for mine own part, as i have set up my rest 2.02.102 P
and shylock, for his own part, knew the bird was 3.01. 28 P
my own flesh and blood to rebel! 3.01. 34 P
the other half yours — | mine own, i would say; 3.02. 17
for mine own part, | i have toward heaven 3.04. 26
which, better'd with his own learning, the 4.01.158 P
ring, | or your own honor to contain the ring, 5.01.201
now, by mine honor, which is yet mine own, 5.01.232
how you do leave me to mine own protection. 5.01.235
i swear to thee, even by thine own fair eyes, 5.01.242
less belov'd of her uncle than his own daughter, AYL 1.01.111 P
him, as i must for my own honor if he come in; 1.01.130 P
in that it is a thing of his own search, and 1.01.135 P
of the world, and especially of my own people, 1.01.169 P
be entreated, his own peril on his forwardness. 1.02.150 P
we pray you for your own sake to embrace your 1.02.178 P
for your own sake to embrace your own safety, 1.02.179 P
or have acquaintance with mine own desires; 1.03. 48
it was your pleasure and your own remorse. 1.03. 70
i'll have no worse a name than jove's own page, 1.03.124
should in their own confines with forked heads 2.01. 24
i have by hard adventure found mine own. 2.04. 45
ne'er be ware of mine own wit till i break my 2.04. 58 P
and wish, for her sake more than for mine own, 2.04. 76
he saves my labor by his own approach. 2.07. 8
there i shall see mine own figure. 3.02.289 P
dowry of his wife, 'tis none of his own getting. 3.03. 56 P
marry, his kisses are judas's own children. 3.04. 9 P
than thine own gladness that thou art employ'd. 3.05. 98
but it is a melancholy of mine own, compounded 4.01. 16 P
you have sold your own lands to see other men's; 4.01. 22 P
disable all the benefits of your own country; 4.01. 35 P
then, in mine own person, i die. 4.01. 93 P
there was not any man died in his own person, 4.01. 96 P
world what the bird hath done to her own nest. 4.01.204 P
abuses every one's eyes because his own are out, 4.01.214 P
well, | this is a letter of your own device. 4.03. 20
sir, an ill–favor'd thing, sir, but mine own; 5.04. 58 P
power, which were on foot | in his own conduct, 5.04.157
to mine own children in good bringing–up, | and SHR 1.01. 99
my mind presumes, for his own good and /ours. 1.02.213
pardon me, sir, the boldness is mine own, | that 2.01. 88
she is your own, else you must pardon me; 2.01.388
i'll keep mine own, despite of all the world. 3.02.142
fret, | i will be master of what is mine own. 3.02.229
why, she hath a face of her own. 4.01.100 P
he kills her in her own humor. 4.01.180 P
brav'd in mine own house with a skein of thread? 4.03.110
well, and hold your own in any case | with such 4.04. 6
and keep thy friend | under thy own life's key. AWW 1.01. 67
and so dies with feeding his own stomach. 1.01.143 P
might one do, sir, to lose it to her own liking? 1.01.150 P
till their own scorn return to them unnoted 1.02. 34
in isbel's case and mine own. 1.03. 23 P
to herself her own words to her own ears; 1.03.108 P
to herself her own words to her own ears; 1.03.108 P
eye, | safer than mine own two, more dear. 2.01.109
try, | that ministers thine own death if i die. 2.01.186
so make the choice of thy own time, for i, | thy 2.01.203
i'll never do you wrong for your own sake. 2.03. 90
me leave to use | the help of mine own eyes. 2.03.108
virtue and she | is her own dower; 2.03.144
do thine own fortunes that obedient right 2.03.160
your good will to have mine own good /fortunes. 2.04. 16 P
and make this haste as your own good proceeding, 2.04. 49
you have it from his own deliverance. 2.05. 4 P
fain would steal | what law does vouch mine own. 2.05. 82
and that with his own hand he slew the duke's 3.05. 6 P
but i hope your own grace will keep you where 3.05. 25 P
my lord, in mine own direct knowledge, without 3.06. 7 P
adversaries, when we bring him to our own tents. 3.06. 27 P
to charge in with our horse upon our own wings, 3.06. 49 P
our own wings, and to rend our own soldiers! 3.06. 49 P
we must every one be a man of his own fancy, not 4.01. 17 P
truth that e'er thine own tongue was guilty of. 4.01. 33 P
i love thee | by love's own sweet constraint, 4.02. 16
thus your own proper wisdom | brings in the 4.02. 49
merely our own traitors. 4.03. 21 P
contrives against his own nobility in his proper 4.03. 24 P
he might take a measure of his own judgments, 4.03. 33 P
the stronger part of it by her own letters, 4.03. 55 P
gallant militarist — that was his own phrase — 4.03.141 P
mine own company, chitopher, vaumond, bentii, 4.03.164 P
which are their own right by the law of nature. 4.05. 61 P
i put you to | the use of your own virtues, for 5.01. 16
our own love waking cries to see what's done, 5.03. 65
but when i had subscrib'd | to mine own fortune, 5.03. 97
mine own escape unfoldeth to my hope, | whereto TN 1.02. 19
world | till i had made mine own occasion mellow 1.02. 43
let them hang themselves in their own straps. 1.03. 13 P
nature's own sweet and cunning hand laid on. 1.05.240
behavior to his own shadow this half hour. 2.05. 17 P
but to your own most pregnant and vouchsafed ear 3.01. 89 P
to him in thine own voice, and bring me word how 4.02. 66 P

denied me mine own purse, | which i had 5.01. 90
that thine own trip shall be thine overthrow? 5.01.167
a most extracting frenzy of mine own | from my 5.01.281
i have your own letter that induc'd me to the 5.01.306 P
plaintiff and the judge | of thine own cause. 5.01.355
to your own bents dispose you; WT 1.02.179
me, let me know my trespass | by its own visage. 1.02.266
their profits | (their own particular thrifts), 1.02.311
me | even so as i mine own course have set down. 1.02.340
do't not, thou split'st thine own. 1.02.349
than one condemn'd by the king's own mouth — 1.02.445
on mine own accord i'll off, | but first i'll do 2.03. 64
accusation | than your own weak-hing'd fancy) 2.03.119
to it own protection | and favor of the climate. 2.03.178
i appeal | to your own conscience, sir, before 3.02. 46
you will not own it. 3.02. 59
i have too much believ'd mine own suspicion. 3.02.151
i'll not remember you of my own lord, | who is 3.02.230
i have of thee, thine own goodness hath made. 4.02. 12 P
for i cannot be | mine own, nor any thing to any 4.04. 44
still, still so, | and own no other function. 4.04.143
but i have it | upon his own report, and i 4.04.170
one three of them, by their own report, sir, 4.04.337 P
to her service, | or to their own perdition. 4.04.378
by th' pattern of mine own thoughts i cut out 4.04.382
dispute his own estate? 4.04.400
beseech you | of your own state take care. 4.04.448
disliken | the truth of your own seeming, that 4.04.653
and then i lost | (all mine own folly) the 5.01.135
stain your own | with oily painting. 5.03. 82
tell me, mine own, | where hast thou been 5.03.123
wrath, | and sullen presage of your own decay. JN 1.01. 28
that for thine own gain shouldst defend mine 1.01.242
our just and lineal entrance to our own; 2.01. 85
in us, that are our own great deputy, | and bear 2.01.365
have turn'd another way, | to our own vantage. 2.01.550
brought to the field | as god's own soldier, 2.01.566
hath drawn him from his own determin'd aid, 2.01.584
for your own ladies and pale-visag'd maids 5.02.154
when english measure backward their own ground 5.05. 3
who chaunts a doleful hymn to his own death, 5.07. 22
but to my own disgrace | neglected my sworn duty
R2 1.01.133
to safeguard thine own life | the best way is to 1.02. 35
and in the sentence my own life destroyed. 1.03.242
say | i was too strict to make mine own away; 1.03.244
about his marriage, nor my own disgrace, | have 2.01.168
arms, | be his own carver and cut out his way, 2.03.144
duke hath sworn his coming is | but for his own; 2.03.149
from my own windows torn my household coat, 3.01. 24
and nothing can we call our own but death, | and 3.02.152
overblown, | an easy task it is to win our own. 3.02.191
my gracious lord, i come but for mine own. 3.03.196
your own is yours, and i am yours, and all. 3.03.197
give me mine own again, 'twere no good part | to 5.01. 97
so, now i have mine own again, be gone, | that i 5.01. 99
wilt thou not hide the trespass of thine own? 5.02. 89
is he not thine own? 5.02. 94
and, for they cannot, die in their own pride. 5.05. 22
bearing their own misfortunes on the back | of 5.05. 29
thy own hand yields thy death's instrument, | go 5.05.106
the king's blood stain'd the king's own land. 5.05.110
from your own mouth, my lord, did i this deed. 5.06. 37
daub her lips with her own children's blood, 1H4 1.01. 6
balk'd in their own blood, did sir walter see 1.01. 69
hath surpris'd | to his own use he keeps, and 1.01. 94
and that same greatness too which our own hands 1.03. 12
that we at our own charge shall ransom straight 1.03. 79
tying thine ear to no tongue but thine own! 1.03.238
to bear our fortunes in our own strong arms, 1.03.298
into) for their own credit sake make all whole. 2.01. 72 P
i'll not bear my own flesh so far afoot again 2.02. 35 P
hang thyself in thine own heir-apparent garters! 2.02. 43 P
"but, for mine own part, my lord, i could be 2.03. 1 P
he loves his own barn better than he loves our 2.03. 5 P
with any tinker in his own language during my 2.04. 19 P
ago, jack, since thou sawest thine own knee? 2.04.328 P
my own knee? 2.04.329 P
partly thy mother's word, partly my own opinion, 2.04.403 P
i was never call'd so in mine own house before. 3.03. 63 P
a trust | on any soul remov'd, but on his own. 4.01. 35
for mine own part, i could be well content | to 5.01. 23
i need no more weight than mine own bowels. 5.03. 35 P
reward valor bear the sin upon their own heads. 5.04.150 P
let us not leave till all our own be won. 5.05. 44
he may keep his own grace, but he's almost out 2H4 1.02. 28 P
though he have his own lanthorn to light him. 1.02. 48 P
he stabb'd me in mine own house, most beastly, 2.01. 14 P
widow to so rough a course to come by her own? 2.01. 83 P
well spoke on, i can hear it with mine own ears. 2.02. 66 P
when your own percy, when my heart's dear harry, 2.03. 12
doth she hold her own well? 3.02.205 P
as go, and yet, for mine own part, sir, i do not 3.02.223 P
and, for mine own part, have a desire to stay 3.02.225 P
sir, i did not care, for mine own part, so much. 3.02.226 P
and told john a' gaunt he beat his own name, for 3.02.324 P
so much the worse, if your own rule be true. 4.02. 86
else, with mine own picture on the top on't 4.03. 48 P
face | of seeming sorrow, it is sure your own. 5.02. 29
a son, | hear your own dignity so much profan'd, 5.02. 93
eat a last year's pippin of mine own graffing, 5.03. 2 P
for what i have to say is of mine own making, ep 5 P
say) will (i doubt) prove mine own marring. ep 6 P
yet their own authors faithfully affirm | that H5 1.02. 43
stand for your own, unwind your bloody flag, 1.02.101
cannot defend our own doors from the dog, | let 1.02.218
by your own counsel is suppress'd and kill'd. 2.02. 80
for your own reasons turn into your bosoms, | as 2.02. 82
that you shall read | in your own losses, if he 2.04.139
and, for mine own part, i have not a case of 3.02. 4 P
for 'a never broke any man's head but his own, 3.02. 40 P
his own person kneeling at our feet but a weak 3.06.132 P
thee, constable, my mistress wears his own hair. 3.07. 61 P
a prating coxcomb, in your own conscience now? 4.01. 80 P
the king's, but every subject's soul is his own. 4.01.177 P
man that dies ill, the ill upon his own head, 4.01.187 P
sense no more can feel | but his own wringing! 4.01.236
you take it for your own fault and not mine; 4.08. 54 P
lie on heaps, | corrupting in it own fertility. 5.02. 40
fame, | despairing of his own arm's fortitude, 1H6 2.01. 17
within her quarter and mine own precinct | i was 2.01. 68
i trust ere long to choke thee with thine own, 3.02. 46
fools, | to try if that our own be ours or no. 3.02. 63
mine own is gone. 4.07. 1
upon condition i may quietly | enjoy mine own, 5.03.154
content | to be mine own attorney in this case. 5.03.166
of the king of england's own proper cost and 2H6 1.01. 61 P
wives, | and our king henry gives away his own, 1.01.130
while these do labor for their own preferment, 1.01.181
'tis thine they give away, and not their own. 1.01.221
ready to starve, and dare not touch his own. 1.01.229
while his own lands are bargain'd for and sold. 1.01.231
a day will come when york shall claim his own, 1.01.239
matter, | in thine own person answer thy abuse. 2.01. 40
what's thine own name? 2.01.121
heaping confusion on their own heads thereby! 2.01.183
many a pound of mine own proper store, | because 3.01.115
and yet herein i judge mine own wit good — 3.01.232
whiles i take order for mine own affairs. 3.01.320
thou dar'st not, for thy own. 4.01. 69
to a thing, and i was never mine own man since. 4.02. 83 P
if thou hadst been in thine own slaughter-house; 4.03. 5 P
offering their own lives in their young's 3H6 2.02. 32
to hold thine own and leave thine own with him. 2.02. 42
to hold thine own and leave thine own with him. 2.02. 42
to blot out me, and put his own son in. 2.02. 92
to greet mine own land with my wishful sight. 3.01. 14
leave | to play the broker in mine own behalf; 4.01. 63
no, but the loss of his own royal person. 4.04. 5
in the sun | and descant on mine own deformity. R3 1.01. 27
the king, on his own royal disposition | (and 1.03. 63
to royalize his blood i spent mine own. 1.03.124
my voice is now the king's, my looks mine own. 1.04.168
and are you yet to your own souls so blind 1.04.252
his tyranny for trifles, his own bastardy, | as 3.07. 9
when he had done, some followers of mine own, 3.07. 34
your right of birth, your empery, your own. 3.07.136
and prov'd the subject of mine own soul's curse, 4.01. 80
men | to turn their own points in their masters' 5.01. 24
our fathers | have in their own land beaten, 5.03.334
the father rashly slaughter'd his own son, | the 5.05. 25
our own brains and the opinion that we bring H8 pr 20
the force of his own merit makes his way — | a 1.01. 64
and his own letter, | the honorable board of 1.01. 78
as he pleases, | and for his own advantage. 1.01.193
as well | for your own quiet, as to rectify 2.04. 63
far hence | in mine own country, lords. 3.01. 91
him, how he coasts | and hedges his own way. 3.02. 39
to his own hand, in 's bedchamber. 3.02. 77
wealth hath he accumulated | to his own portion! 3.02.108
mine own ends | have been mine so, that evermore 3.02.171
good i ever labor'd | more than mine own; 3.02.192
wealth i have drawn together | for mine own ends 3.02.212
and your master) with his own hand gave me; 3.02.247
into your own hands, card'nal, by extortion; 3.02.285
what means got, i leave to your own conscience) 3.02.327
now, and provide | for thine own future safety. 3.02.421
to heaven, is all | i dare now call mine own. 3.02.454
his own opinion was his law. 4.02. 37
of his own body he was ill, and gave | the 4.02. 43
first, mine own service to your grace, the next, 4.02.115
thomas, y' are a gentleman | of mine own way; 5.01. 28
leap of danger, | and woo your own destruction. 5.01.140
in our own natures frail, and capable | of our 5.02. 46
her own shall bless her; 5.04. 30
in safety | under his own vine what he plants, 5.04. 34
all whites are ink | writing their own reproach, TRO 1.01. 57
she be not, she has the mends in her own hands. 1.01. 68 P
he shall not need it if he have his own. 1.02. 87 P
at your own house, there he unarms him. 1.02.274 P
that keeps troy on foot, | not her own sinews. 1.03.136
with truant vows to her own lips he loves, | and 1.03.270
not virtuously on his own part beheld, | do in 2.03.118
pride is his own glass, his own trumpet, his own 2.03.155 P
pride is his own glass, his own trumpet, his own 2.03.155 P
his own trumpet, his own chronicle, and whatever 2.03.155 P
that bastes his arrogance with his own seam, 2.03.185
sir, mine own company. 3.02.145
which his own will shall have desire to drink. 3.03. 46
in the eyes of others | as feel in his own fall; 3.03. 78
for my own part, i came in late. 4.02. 52 P
a priest there off'ring to it his own heart. 4.03. 9
even in the birth of our own laboring breath. 4.04. 38
to her own worth | she shall be priz'd; 4.04.133
to our own selves bend we our needful talk. 4.04.139
now, ajax, hold thine own! 4.05.114
my own searching eyes | shall find him by his 4.05.161
do buss the clouds, | must kiss their own feet. 4.05.221
will 'a swagger himself out on 's own eyes? 5.02.136 P
kill him, and we'll have corn at our own price. COR 1.01. 11 P
for corn at their own rates, whereof they say 1.01.189
their vulgar wisdoms, | of their own choice. 1.01.216
gods | lead their successes as we wish our own, 1.06. 7
the blood of others, | but mantled in your own. 1.06. 29
rome must know | the value of her own. 1.09. 21
we may articulate | for their own good and ours. 1.09. 78
ere in our own house i do shade my head, | the 2.01.195
honor, in giving him our own voices with our own 2.03. 45 P
giving him our own voices with our own tongues; 2.03. 45 P
and ran | from th' noise of our own drums." 2.03. 54
mine own desert. 2.03. 65 P
your own desert! 2.03. 66 P
ay, /not mine own desire. 2.03. 67 P
how, not your own desire? 2.03. 68 P
than as guided | by your own true affections, 2.03.231
and this shall seem, as partly 'tis, their own, 2.03.262
children is enroll'd | in jove's own book, like 3.01.291
an unnatural dam | should now eat up her own! 3.01.292
not by your own instruction, | nor by th' matter 3.02. 53
do't, | lest i surcease to honor mine own truth, 3.02.121
more holy and profound, than mine own life, | my 3.03.113
still your own foes) deliver you as most 3.03.131
that wilt revenge | thine own particular wrongs, 4.05. 86
wilt have | the leading of thine own revenges, 4.05.137
strength and weakness — thine own ways: 4.05.140
you have holp to ravish your own daughters, and 4.06. 81
for mine own part, | when i said banish him, i 4.06.139
in this action, sir, | even by your own. 4.07. 6
behalf as you have utter'd words in your own, 5.02. 25 P
so | as with a man by his own alms empoison'd, 5.06. 10
gave him way | in all his own desires; 5.06. 32
serv'd his designments | in mine own person; 5.06. 35
answering us | with our own charge, making a 5.06. 67
and his own notion — | who wears my stripes 5.06.106
unholy braggart, | 'fore your own eyes and ears? 5.06.119
his own impatience | takes from aufidius a great 5.06.144
titus, unkind and careless of thine own, | why TIT 1.01. 86
this prince in justice seizeth but his own. 1.01.281
rape call you it, my lord, to seize my own, | my 1.01.405
with his own hand did slay his youngest son, 1.01.418
tend'ring our sister's honor and our own. 1.01.476
for no name fits thy nature but thy own! 2.03.119
the whilst their own birds famish in their nests 2.03.154
and with thine own hands kill me in this place! 2.03.169
thou, poor man, hast drown'd it with thine own. 3.01.141
and yet dear too, because i bought mine own. 3.01.199
i am of age | to keep mine own, excuse it how 4.02.105
as who should say, "old lad, i am thine own." 4.02.121
and let the emperor dandle him for his own. 4.02.161
shalt thou know her by thine own proportion, 5.02.106
and will o'erreach them in their own devices, 5.02.143
like to the earth swallow her own increase. 5.02.191
to slay his daughter with his own right hand, 5.03. 37
i, measuring his affections by my own, | which ROM 1.01.126
but he, /his own affections' counsellor, | is to 1.01.147
griefs of mine own lie heavy in my breast, 1.01.186
doth add more grief to too much of mine own. 1.01.189
ay, mine own fortune in my misery. 1.02. 58
shown, | but to rejoice in splendor of mine own. 1.02.101
tut, dun's the mouse, the constable's own word. 1.04. 40
honey | is loathsome in his own deliciousness, 2.06. 12
which name i tender | as dearly as mine own — 3.01. 72
do their amorous rites | by their own beauties, 3.02. 9
still blush, as thinking their own kisses sin; 3.03. 39
on the ground, with his own tears made drunk. 3.03. 83
with blood removed but little from her own? 3.03. 96
flask, | is set afire by thine own ignorance, 3.03.133
and thou dismemb'red with thine own defense. 3.03.134
it may be so, for it is not mine own. 4.01. 36
an ill cook that cannot lick his own fingers; 4.02. 7 P
how this grace | speaks his own standing! TIM 1.01. 31
our own precedent passions do instruct us | what 1.01.133
you can with modesty speak in your own behalf; 1.02. 94 P
can we call our own than the riches of our 1.02.103 P
and entertain'd me with mine own device. 1.02.150
wrong, you bate too much of your own merits. 1.02.206
i weigh my friend's affection with mine own. 1.02.216
i must serve my turn | out of mine own. 2.01. 21
when every feather sticks in his own wing, 2.01. 30
awak'd by great occasion | to call upon his own, 2.02. 22
for my own part, i must needs confess, i have 3.02. 20 P
me so far as to use mine own words to him? 3.02. 58 P
for mine own part, | i never tasted timon in my 3.02. 76
though his right arm might purchase his own time 3.05. 76
he forfeits his own blood that spills another. 3.05. 87
for your own gifts, make yourselves prais'd; 3.06. 71 P
poor honest lord, brought low by his own heart, 4.02. 37
then the rot returns | to thine own lips again. 4.03. 66
so i shall mend mine own, by th' lack of thine. 4.03.284
thee and make thine own self the conquest of thy 4.03.337 P
needs | stand for a villain in thine own work? 5.01. 38
wilt thou whip thine own faults in other men? 5.01. 39
then do we sin against our own estate, | when we 5.01. 41
hath /sense withal | of it own fall, restraining 5.01.148
that mine own use invites me to cut down, | and 5.01.206
those enemies of timon's and mine own | whom you 5.04. 56
and for mine own part, i durst not laugh, for JC 1.02.249 P
but, for mine own part, it was greek to me. 1.02.284 P
so every bondman in his own hand bears | the 1.03.101
what need we any spur but our own cause | to 2.01.123
that keeps you in the house, and not your own. 2.02. 51
at mine own house, good lady. 2.04. 22
is there no voice more worthy than my own, | to 3.01. 49
in his own change, or by ill officers, | hath 4.02. 7
for mine own part, | i shall be glad to learn of 4.03. 53
myself have to mine own turn'd enemy. 5.03. 2
turns our swords | in our own proper entrails. 5.03. 96
there if i grow, | the harvest is your own. MAC 1.04. 33
highness' pleasure, | still to return your own. 1.06. 28
of our poison'd chalice | to our own lips. 1.07. 12
to be the same in thine own act and valor | as 1.07. 40
life, | and live a coward in thine own esteem, 1.07. 43
blood those sleepy two | of his own chamber, and 1.07. 76
that will ravin up | thine own live's means! 2.04. 29
you know your own degrees, sit down. 3.04. 1
for mine own good | all causes shall give way. 3.04.134
do) | loves for his own ends, not for you. 3.05. 13
be your dishonors, | but mine own safeties. 4.03. 30
foisons to fill up your will | of your mere own. 4.03. 89
throne | by his own interdiction stands accus'd, 4.03.107
direction, and | unspeak mine own detraction; 4.03.123
scarcely have coveted what was mine own, | at no 4.03.127
not for their own demerits, but for mine, | fell 4.03.226
the roman fool, and die | on mine own sword? 5.08. 2
the sensible and true avouch | of mine own eyes. HAM 1.01. 58
to make it truster of your own report | against 1.02.172
his greatness weigh'd, his will is not his own, 1.03. 17
dalliance treads, | and reaks not his own rede. 1.03. 51
to thine own self be true, | and it must follow, 1.03. 78
noble substance of a doubt | to his own scandal. 1.04. 38
such as it is, and for my own poor part, | i 1.05.131
is it your own inclining? 2.02.275 P
use them after your own honor and dignity — the 2.02.531 P
could force his soul so to his own conceit 2.02.553
may play the fool no where but in 's own house. 3.01.132 P
but let your own discretion be your tutor. 3.02. 16 P
to show virtue her feature, scorn her own image, 3.02. 23 P
their own enactures with themselves destroy. 3.02.197
thoughts are ours, their ends none of our own: 3.02.213
bar the door upon your own liberty if you deny 3.02.338 P
my crown, mine own ambition, and my queen. 3.03. 55
let virtue be as wax | and melt in her own fire. 3.04. 85
basket creep, | and break your own neck down. 3.04.196
to have the enginer | hoist with his own petar, 3.04.207

ah, mine own lord, what have i seen to–night! 4.01. 5
that i can keep your counsel and not mine own. 4.02. 12 P
botch the words up fit to their own thoughts, 4.05. 10
he most violent author | of his own just remove; 4.05. 81
to thine own peace. 4.07. 61
to a plurisy, | dies in his own too much. 4.07.118
lauds, | as one incapable of her own distress, 4.07.178
when she willfully seeks her own salvation? 5.01. 2 P
unless she drown'd herself in her own defense? 5.01. 7 P
is not guilty of his own death shortens not his 5.01. 20 P
of his own death shortens not his own life. 5.01. 20 P
not one now to mock your own grinning — quite 5.01.192 P
did with desp'rate hand | foredo it own life. 5.01.221
and in fine withdrew | to mine own room again, 5.02. 16
defeat | does by their own insinuation grow. 5.02. 59
why, as a woodcock to mine own springe, osric: 5.02.306
i am justly kill'd with mine own treachery. 5.02.307
make a great gap in your own honor and shake in LR 1.02. 84 P
frame the business after your own wisdom. 1.02. 99 P
often the surfeits of our own behavior — we 1.02.120 P
thou but rememb'rest me of mine own conception. 1.04. 67 P
rather blam'd as mine own jealous curiosity than 1.04. 69 P
and put'st down thine own breeches, "then they 1.04.174 P
and thereto add such reasons of your own | as 1.04.338
make your own purpose, | how in my strength you 2.01.111
unremovable and fix'd he is | in his own course. 2.04. 94
but his own disorders | deserv'd much less 2.04.199
'tis his own blame hath put himself from rest, 2.04.290
they took from me the use of mine own house, 3.03. 4 P
i had rather break mine own. 3.04. 5
prithee go in thyself, seek thine own ease. 3.04. 23
bridges, to course his own shadow for a traitor. 3.04. 57 P
hear | (if you dare venture in your own behalf) 4.02. 20
strip thy own back, | thou hotly lusts to use 4.06.161
and proceed | i' th' sway of your own will. 4.07. 19
that mine own tears | do scald like molten lead. 4.07. 46
in your own kingdom, sir. 4.07. 75
in his own grace he doth exalt himself, | more 5.03. 67
thou worse than any name, read thine own evil. 5.03.157
good i mean to do, | despite of mine own nature. 5.03.245
and | to lay the blame upon her own despair, 5.03.255
but he, as loving his own pride and purposes, OTH 1.01. 12
that, doting on his own obsequious bondage, 1.01. 46
cannot but feel this wrong as 'twere their own; 1.02. 97
in the bitter letter | after your own sense; 1.03. 69
what, in your own part, can you say to this? 1.03. 74
for i mine own gain'd knowledge should profane 1.03.384
swell his sail with thine own pow'rful breath, 2.01. 78
i will gyve thee in thine own courtship. 2.01.170 P
of fashion, and i dote | in mine own comforts. 2.01.207
for mine own part — no offense to the general, 2.03.106 P
should hazard such a place as his own second 2.03.139
he that stirs next to carve for his own rage 2.03.173
and discourse fustian with one's own shadow? 2.03.281 P
since it is as it is, mend it for your own good. 2.03.302 P
and out of her own goodness make the net | that 2.03.361
very ill at ease, | unfit for mine own purposes. 3.03. 33
to do a peculiar profit | to your own person. 3.03. 80
nor from mine own weak merits will i draw | the 3.03.187
affect many proposed matches | of her own clime, 3.03.230
is now begrim'd and black | as mine own face. 3.03.388
eyes do see them bolster | more than their own. 3.03.400
i am your own for ever. 3.03.480
he lies there, were to lie in mine own throat. 3.04. 13 P
from his very arm | puff'd his own brother — 3.04.137
who having, by their own importunate suit, | or 4.01. 26
this is the monkey's own giving out. 4.01.127 P
marry her, out of her own love and flattery, not 4.01.128 P
and his own courses will denote him so | that i 4.01.279
for your labor, 'tis a wrong in your own world, 4.03. 82 P
and speaks as loud | as his own state and ours, ANT 1.04. 30
beg often our own harms, which the wise pow'rs 2.01. 6
those wars | which fronted mine own peace. 2.02. 61
hours had bound me up | from mine own knowledge. 2.02. 91
for her own person, | it beggar'd all 2.02.197
yes, something you can deny for your own safety: 2.06. 91 P
so high as it is, and moves with it own organs. 2.07. 44 P
of it own color too. 2.07. 47 P
and mine own tongue | spleets what it speaks; 2.07.123
choose your own company, and command what cost 3.04. 37
upon his own appeal, seizes him. 3.05. 11 P
leave unexecuted | your own renowned knowledge, 3.07. 45
for our flight, | most grossly, by his own! 3.10. 28
make thine own edict for thy pains, which we 3.12. 32
in our own filth drop our clear judgments, make 3.13.113
infamous, | forgive me in thine own particular, 4.09. 20
the arm of mine own body, and the heart | where 5.01. 45
he gives me so much of mine own as i | will 5.02. 20
i cannot project mine own cause so well | to 5.02.121
that mine own servant should | parcel the sum of 5.02.162
purposes, and, being royal, | took her own way. 5.02.337
her own price | proclaims how she esteem'd him; CYM 1.01. 51
you have land enough of your own, but he added 1.02. 18 P
be weigh'd rather by her value than his own, 1.04. 16 P
rather than story him in his own hearing. 1.04. 34 P
for this time is ended, | take your own way. 1.05. 31
knows | by history, report, or his own proof, 1.06. 70
self exhibition | which your own coffers yield; 1.06.123
azure lac'd | with blue of heaven's own tinct. 2.02. 23
we will nothing pay | for wearing our own noses. 3.01. 14
by her own command | shall give thee opportunity 3.02. 18
what your own love will out of this advise you, 3.02. 44 P
speech and shows much more | his own conceiving. 3.03. 98
let thine own hands take away her life. 3.04. 27 P
and thine own? 3.04.104
virtue | which their own conscience seal'd them, 3.06. 84
and his glass to confer in his own chamber — i 4.01. 8 P
son to the queen (after his own report), | who 4.02.119
with his own single hand he'ld take us in, 4.02.121
with his own sword, | which he did wave against 4.02.149
not sooner | than thine own worth prefer thee. 4.02.386
but imogen is your own, do your best wills, 5.01. 16
more charming | with their own nobleness, which 5.03. 33
i, in mine own woe charm'd, | could not find 5.03. 68
or jump the after–inquiry on your own peril; 5.04.182 P
thyself into my grace, | and art mine own. 5.05. 95
by thine own tongue thou art condemn'd, and must 5.05.298
for mine own part unfold a dangerous speech, 5.05.313
with other spritely shows | of mine own kindred. 5.05.429
to entice his own | to evil should be done by PER 1.ch. 27
see if 'twill teach us to forget our own? 1.04. 3
and though it was mine own, part of my heritage, 2.01.123
sir, | we have given order be next our own. 2.03.110
tyre, | welcom'd and settled to his own desire. 4.ch. 2
thou hast the harvest out of thine own report. 4.02.141 P
could he speak, | would own a name too dear. 4.06.179
her neele composes | nature's own shape of bud, 5.ch. 6
mine own, helicanus — | she is not dead at 5.01.214
where, by her own most clear remembrance, she 5.03. 12
blest, and mine own! 5.03. 48
must recompense itself | with its own sweat; TNK 1.01.154
when by mine own | i may be reasonably conceiv'd 1.02. 47
or let me know | why mine own barber is unblest, 1.02. 53
other instruments | to his own nerves and act; 1.02. 69
yet what man | thirds his own worth (the case is 1.02. 96
i demand no more than your own offer, and i will 2.01. 10 P
but nothing of their own restraint and disasters 2.01. 40 P
i know mine own is but a heap of ruins, | and no 2.03. 19
well, sir, | take your own time. come, boys. 2.03. 69
to clear his own way with the mind and sword 3.01. 56
will make th' advantage of this hour | mine own; 3.06.124
look to thine own well, arcite. 3.06.131
against /thy own edict, follows thy sister, 3.06.145
the misadventure of their own eyes kill 'em; 3.06.190
by your own spotless honor — 3.06.196
in another, | by your own virtues infinite — 3.06.199
by your own eyes, by strength, | in which you 3.06.205
they are princes | as goodly as your own eyes, 3.06.276
half his own heart, set in too, that i hope 4.01. 14
i then left my angle | to his own skill, came 4.01. 60
for, and so apter | to make this cause his own. 4.02. 98
i think so, but i know not thine own will: 5.01.171
as 'twere to th' music | his own hoofs made (for 5.04. 60
more in our country than they do in their own. STM II.C 6 P
throne and sword, but given him his own name, II.C 103
the kiss shall be thine own as well as mine. VEN 117
"is thine own heart to thine own face affected? 157
"is thine own heart to thine own face affected? 157
steal thine own freedom, and complain on theft. 160
for men will kiss even by their own direction." 216
poor queen of love, in thine own law forlorn, 251
and every tongue more moving than your own, 776
from thievish ears, because it is his own? LUC 35
but she is not her own; 241
and the red rose blush at her own disgrace, 479
are nature's faults, not their own infamy." 539
thyself art mighty, for thine own sake leave me; 583
their own transgressions partially they smother: 634
that from their own misdeeds askaunce their eyes 637
till with her own white fleece her voice 678
receipt | ere he can see his own abomination. 704
or kings be breakers of their own behests? 852
at his own shadow let the thief run mad, 997
poor women's faces are their own faults' books. 1253
if tears could help, mine own would do me good. 1274
lest he should hold it her own gross abuse, 1315
once set on ringing, with his own weight goes; 1494
being from the feeling of her own grief brought 1578
"o, teach me how to make mine own excuse, | or 1653
revenged on my foe, | thine, mine, his own. 1684
so lively shown, | made me think upon mine own. PP 20.18
but thou, contracted to thine own bright eyes, SON 1. 5
within thine own bud buriest thy content, | and, 1.11
to say within thine own deep–sunken eyes | were 2. 7
and you must live drawn by your own sweet skill. 16.14
and make the earth devour her own sweet brood; 19. 2
a woman's face with nature's own hand painted 20. 1
strength's abundance weakens his own heart, | so 23. 4
and in mine own love's strength seem to decay, 23. 7
with burthen of mine own love's might. 23. 8
into my verse | thine own sweet argument, too 38. 3
what can mine own praise to mine own self bring? 39. 3
what can mine own praise to mine own self bring? 39. 3
and what is't but mine own when i praise thee? 39. 4
here | within the knowledge of mine own desert, 49.10
mine own true love that doth my rest defeat, 61.11
and for myself mine own worth do define, | as i 62. 7
mine own self–love quite contrary i read; 62.11
those same tongues that give thee so thine own, 69. 6
lie, | to do more for me than mine own desert, 72. 6
thou gav'st, thy own worth then not knowing, 87. 9
with mine own weakness being best acquainted, 88. 5
your own glass shows you when you look in it. 103.14
not mine own fears, nor the prophetic soul | of 107. 1
and the sad augurs mock their own presage, 107. 6
gor'd mine own thoughts, sold cheap what is most 110. 3
nor his own vision holds what it doth catch; 113. 8
and given to time your own dear–purchas'd right; 117. 6
that level | at my abuses reckon up their own; 121.10
o, but with mine compare thou thine own state, 142. 3
those lips that love's own hand did make 145. 1
ask'd their own wills, and made their wills obey LC 133
did in freedom stand | and was my own fee–simple 144
or forc'd examples, 'gainst her own content, 157
kept hearts in liveries, but mine own was free, 195
take all these similes to your own command, 227

OWNER 15 FR 0.0017 REL FR 13 V 2 P
'tis fit, | worthy the owner, and the owner it. WIV 5.05. 60
'tis fit, | worthy the owner, and the owner it. 5.05. 60
that stays but till her owner comes aboard, ERR 4.01. 86
stay for nought at all | but for their owner, 4.01. 92
them to sing, and restore them to the owner. ADO 2.01.233 P
and the owner of it blest | ever shall in safety MND 5.01.419
you | the owner of the house i did inquire for? AYL 4.03. 89
the owner of no one good quality worthy your AWW 3.06. 11 P
for grief is proud and makes his owner stoop. JN 3.01. 69
(who is, if every owner were well plac'd, 1H4 4.03. 94
while as the silly owner of the goods | weeps 2H6 1.01.225
climbing my walls in spite of me the owner, 4.10. 35
fit, | but, like the owner of a foul disease, HAM 4.01. 21
off me and this hand | but owner of a sword! TNK 3.01. 33
from this fair throne to heave the owner out. LUC 413

OWNER'S 2 FR 0.0002 REL FR 2 V 0 P
honor and beauty, in the owner's arms, | are LUC 27
the owner's tongue doth publish every where. SON 102. 4

OWNERS 5 FR 0.0005 REL FR 5 V 0 P
puts bars between the owners and their rights! MV 3.02. 19
craves | all dues be rend'red to their owners: TRO 2.02.174
and bid the owners quench them with their tears. TIT 5.01.134
things of like value differing in the owners TIM 1.01.170
they are the lords and owners of their faces, SON 94. 7

OWNING 1 FR 0.0001 REL FR 1 V 0 P
no father owning it (which is indeed | more WT 3.02. 88

OWN'S 1 FR 0.0001 REL FR 0 V 1 P
'twould not become him, his own's better. TRO 1.02. 91 P

OWNS 1 FR 0.0001 REL FR 1 V 0 P
not afric owns a serpent i abhor | more than thy COR 1.08. 3

OW'ST* 5 FR 0.0005 REL FR 4 V 1 P
thou dost here usurp | the name thou ow'st not, TMP 1.02.455
a husband and a son thou ow'st to me — | and R3 1.03.169
thou ow'st the worm no silk, the beast no hide, LR 3.04.104 P
ever he had on thee, who ow'st his strength, TNK 1.01. 88
nor lose possession of that fair thou ow'st, SON 18.10

OWY 1 FR 0.0001 REL FR 1 V 0 P
owy, cuppele gorge, permafoy, | peasant, unless H5 4.04. 37

OX 11 FR 0.0012 REL FR 3 V 8 P
ay, and an ox too; both the proofs are extant. WIV 5.05.120 P
take all and wean it, it may prove an ox. LLL 5.02.250
the ox hath therefore stretch'd his yoke in vain MND 2.01. 93
that differs not from the stalling of an ox? AYL 1.01. 11 P
as the ox hath his bow, sir, the horse his curb, 3.03. 79 P
barn, | my horse, my ox, my ass, my any thing; SHR 3.02.232
roasted manningtree ox with the pudding in his 1H4 2.04.452 P
then is sin struck down like an ox, and 2H6 4.02. 26 P
to an ass, were nothing, he is both ass and ox; TRO 5.01. 59 P
to an ox, were nothing, /he /is both ox and ass. 5.01. 60 P
to an ox, were nothing, /he /is both ox and ass. 5.01. 60 P

OX–BEEF 1 FR 0.0001 REL FR 0 V 1 P
giant–like ox–beef hath devour'd many a MND 3.01.192 P

OXEN 7 FR 0.0008 REL FR 5 V 2 P
six score fat oxen standing in my stalls, | and SHR 2.01.358
i think oxen and wain–ropes cannot hale them TN 3.02. 59 P
looks, | and we shall feed like oxen at a stall, 1H4 5.02. 14
the wolf, | or horse or oxen from the leopard, 1H6 1.05. 31
as market men for oxen, sheep, or horse. 5.05. 54
they fell before thee like sheep and oxen, and 2H6 4.03. 3 P
on sheep or oxen could i spend my fury. 5.01. 27

OXFORD 27 FR 0.0030 REL FR 26 V 1 P
what news from oxford? R2 5.02. 52
down their hands, | to kill the king at oxford. 5.02. 99
and told him of those triumphs held at oxford. 5.03. 14
help to order several powers | to oxford, or 5.03.141
i have from oxford sent to london | the heads of 5.06. 13
that sought at oxford thy dire overthrow. 5.06. 16
he is at oxford still, is he not? 2H4 3.02. 10 P
oxford, how haps it in this smooth discourse 3H6 3.03. 88
can oxford, that did ever fence the right, | now 3.03. 98
queen margaret, prince edward, and oxford, 3.03.109
thou and oxford, with five thousand men, | shall 3.03.234
therefore, lord oxford, to prevent the worst, 4.06. 96
and thou, brave oxford, wondrous well belov'd, 4.08. 17
sweet oxford, and my loving montague, | and all 4.08. 30
where is the post that came from valiant oxford? 5.01. 1
o cheerful colors! see where oxford comes! 5.01. 58
oxford, oxford, for lancaster! 5.01. 59
oxford, oxford, for lancaster! 5.01. 59
o, welcome, oxford, for we want thy help. 5.01. 66
and somerset, with oxford, fled to her; 5.03. 15
why, is not oxford here another anchor? 5.04. 16
thanks, gentle somerset, sweet oxford, thanks. 5.04. 58
away with oxford to hames castle straight; 5.05. 2
when oxford had me down, he rescued me, | and R3 2.01.113
oxford, redoubted pembroke, sir james blunt, 4.05. 14
my lord of oxford — you, sir william brandon — 5.03. 27
that he rais'd in you, | ipswich and oxford! H8 4.02. 59

OXFORDSHIRE 1 FR 0.0001 REL FR 1 V 0 P
in oxfordshire shalt muster up thy friends. 3H6 4.08. 18

OX–HEAD 1 FR 0.0001 REL FR 1 V 0 P
i would set an ox–head to your lion's hide, JN 2.01.292

OXLIPS 3 FR 0.0003 REL FR 3 V 0 P
where oxlips and the nodding violet grows, MND 2.01.250
bold oxlips, and | the crown imperial; WT 4.04.125
oxlips in their cradles growing, | marigolds on TNK 1.01. 10

OYES 2 FR 0.0002 REL FR 2 V 0 P
crier hobgoblin, make the fairy oyes. WIV 5.05. 41
on whose bright crest fame with her loud'st oyes TRO 4.05.143

OYSTER 7 FR 0.0008 REL FR 2 V 5 P
why then the world's mine oyster, | which i with WIV 2.02. 3
be sworn but love may transform me to an oyster,
ADO 2.03. 24 P
it, till he have made /an oyster of me, he shall 2.03. 25 P
a poor house, as your pearl in your foul oyster. AYL 5.04. 61 P
as much as an apple doth an oyster, and all one. SHR 4.02.102 P
canst tell how an oyster makes his shell? LR 1.05. 25 P
great egypt sends | this treasure of an oyster; ANT 1.05. 44

OYSTER–WENCH 1 FR 0.0001 REL FR 1 V 0 P
off goes his bonnet to an oyster–wench, | a R2 1.04. 31

PABYLON *(also babylon)*

PABYLON 1 FR 0.0001 REL FR 1 V 0 P
sing madrigals — | when as i sat in pabylon — WIV 3.01. 24

PAC'D 3 FR 0.0003 REL FR 2 V 1 P
as we pac'd along | upon the giddy footing of R3 1.04. 16
and with the same full state pac'd back again H8 4.01. 93
my lord, she's not pac'd yet, you must take some PER 4.06. 63 P

/PACE* 1 FR 0.0001 REL FR 0 V 1 P
/their /endeavor /keeps /in /the /wonted /pace; HAM 2.02.339 P

PACE* 32 FR 0.0036 REL FR 26 V 6 P
can, pace your wisdom | in that good path that i MM 4.03.132
what pace is this that thy tongue keeps? ADO 3.04. 93 P
my legs can keep no pace with my desires. MND 3.02.445
the unbated fire | that he did pace them first? MV 2.06. 12
time's pace is so hard that it seems the length AYL 3.02.316 P
and indeed he has no pace, but runs where he AWW 4.05. 67 P
on a moderate pace i have since arriv'd but TN 2.02. 3 P
and with speed so pace | to speak of perdita, WT 4.01. 23
of you, and pace softly towards my kinsman's. 4.03.112 P
with slow but stately pace kept on his course, R2 5.02. 10
of art, | and hold me pace in deep experiments. 1H4 3.01. 48
so swift a pace hath thought that even now | you H5 5.pr. 15
climb steep hills | requires slow pace at first. H8 1.01.132
it, | that never see 'em pace before, the spavin 1.03. 12
was not one doctor pace | in this man's place 2.02.121
pace 'em not in their hands to make 'em gentle, 5.02. 57
is | that by a pace goes backward with a purpose TRO 1.03.128

exampled by the first pace that is sick | of his 1.03.132
goes, that to the pace of it | i may spur on my COR 1.10. 32
i cannot bring | my tongue to such a pace. 2.03. 51
howl's his watch, thus with his stealthy pace, MAC 2.01. 54
creeps in this petty pace from day to day, | to 5.05. 20
dull ass will not mend his pace with beating, HAM 5.01. 57 P
even so my bloody thoughts, with violent pace, OTH 3.03.457
which with a snaffle | you may pace easy, but ANT 2.02. 64
and /cas'd as richly, in pace another juno; PER 5.01.111
and this high–speeded pace is but to say | that TNK 1.03. 83
in shape, in courage, color, pace, and bone. VEN 294
heavy eye, knit brow, and strengthless pace, LUC 709
then can no horse with my desire keep pace; SON 51. 9
and all–oblivious enmity | shall you pace forth; 55.10
steal from his figure, and no pace perceiv'd, 104.10
PACES 7 FR 0.0008 REL FR 5 V 2 P
travels in divers paces with divers persons. AYL 3.02.309 P
with the armed hoofs | of hostile paces. 1H4 1.01. 9
but now two paces of the vilest earth | is room 5.04. 91
lie within fifteen hundred paces of your tents. H5 3.07.126 P
rose, and with modest paces | came to the altar, H8 4.01. 82
hop forty paces through the public street; ANT 2.02.229
pale cowards, marching on with trembling paces, LUC 1391
PACIFIED 2 FR 0.0002 REL FR 0 V 2 P
ay, but he will not now be pacified. TN 3.04.281 P
thou seest i am pacified still. 1H4 3.03.173 P
PACIFY 1 FR 0.0001 REL FR 0 V 1 P
pray ye pacify yourself, sir john. 2H4 2.04. 80 P
PACING 1 FR 0.0001 REL FR 1 V 0 P
within an hour, and pacing through the forest, AYL 4.03.100
PACK* 23 FR 0.0026 REL FR 16 V 7 P
a pack of sorrows which would press you down, TGV 3.01. 20
seek shelter, pack! WIV 1.03. 82
knot, a /ging, a pack, a conspiracy against me. 4.02.118 P
time, i think, to trudge, pack, and be gone. ERR 3.02.153
and art confederate with a damned pack | to make 4.04.102
well, the most courageous fiend bids me pack. MV 2.02. 10 P
if she do bid me pack, i'll give her thanks, SHR 2.01.177
sorrow on thee and all the pack of you | that 4.03. 33
i'll be reveng'd on the whole pack of you. TN 5.01.378 P
it, and witnesses more than my pack will hold. WT 4.04.284 P
come bring away thy pack after me. 4.04.311 P
horn–ring, to keep my pack from fasting. 4.04.600 P
not able to travel with her furr'd pack, she 2H6 4.02. 48 P
god bless the prince from all the pack of you! R3 3.03. 5
honest men, | or pack to their old playfellows. H8 1.03. 33
slaves, | ere yet the fight be done, pack up. COR 1.05. 8
go pack with him, and give the mother gold, TIT 4.02.155
a pack of blessings light upon thy back, ROM 3.03.141
hence, pack! TIM 5.01.112
for form, | will pack when it begins to rain, LR 2.04. 80
pour out the pack of matter to mine ear, | the ANT 2.05. 54
provide him necessaries and pack my clothes up, TNK 2.06. 32
pack night, peep day; PP 14.29
PACK'D* 9 FR 0.0010 REL FR 8 V 1 P
goldsmith there, were he not pack'd with her, ERR 5.01.219
who i believe was pack'd in all this wrong, ADO 5.01.299
gifts she looks from me are pack'd and lock'd WT 4.04.358
the new chimney, and yet our horse not pack'd. 1H4 2.01. 3 P
our /thighs pack'd with wax, our mouths with 2H4 4.05. 76
till george be pack'd with post–horse up to R3 1.01.146
bones | of all my buried ancestors are pack'd, ROM 4.03. 41
she, eros, has | pack'd cards with caesar's, and ANT 4.14. 19
the night so pack'd, i post unto my pretty; PP 14.21
PACKET 8 FR 0.0009 REL FR 8 V 0 P
the packet is not come | where that and other LLL 2.01.163
and this small packet of greek and latin books. SHR 2.01.100
what ho! is gilliams with the packet gone? 1H4 2.03. 65
and true order of the fight | this packet, 2H4 4.04.101
the packet, cromwell, gave't you the king? H8 3.02. 76
some spirit put this paper in the packet, | to 3.02.129
made me put this main secret in the packet | i 3.02.215
finger'd their packet, and in fine withdrew | to HAM 5.02. 15
PACKETS 2 FR 0.0002 REL FR 2 V 0 P
the goodness of your intercepted packets | you H8 3.02.286
and at the door too, like a post with packets. 5.02. 32
PACK–HORSE 2 FR 0.0002 REL FR 2 V 0 P
king, | i was a pack–horse in his great affairs: R3 1.03.121
base watch of woes, sin's pack–horse, virtue's LUC 928
PACK–HORSES 1 FR 0.0001 REL FR 1 V 0 P
shall pack–horses | and hollow pamper'd jades of 2H4 2.04.163
PACKING* 8 FR 0.0009 REL FR 6 V 2 P
here's packing, with a witness, to deceive us SHR 5.01.118 P
faith, and i'll send him packing. 1H4 2.04.297 P
be packing therefore, thou that wast a knight; 1H6 4.01. 46
done, | to send me packing with an host of men: 2H6 3.01.342
and bid mine eyes be packing with my heart, 3.02.111
i'll send some packing that yet think not on't. R3 3.02. 61
this man shall set me packing; HAM 3.04.211
what, are you packing, sirrah? CYM 3.05. 80
PACKINGS 1 FR 0.0001 REL FR 1 V 0 P
either in snuffs and packings of the dukes, | or LR 3.01. 26
PACKS 1 FR 0.0001 REL FR 1 V 0 P
a wall'd prison, packs and sects of great ones, LR 5.03. 18
PACK–SADDLE 1 FR 0.0001 REL FR 0 V 1 P
or to be entomb'd in an ass's pack–saddle. COR 2.01. 89 P
PACKTHREAD 2 FR 0.0002 REL FR 1 V 1 P
and here and there piec'd with packthread. SHR 3.02. 63 P
remnants of packthread, and old cakes of roses ROM 5.01. 47
PACORUS 1 FR 0.0001 REL FR 1 V 0 P
thy pacorus, orodes, | pays this for marcus ANT 3.01. 4
/PACTION 1 FR 0.0001 REL FR 1 V 0 P
in between the /paction of these kingdoms, | to H5 5.02.365
PAD *(also bad)*
PAD 1 FR 0.0001 REL FR 0 V 1 P
you suffer for a pad conscience. WIV 3.03.219 P
PADDLE 1 FR 0.0001 REL FR 0 V 1 P
thou not see her paddle with the palm of his OTH 2.01.254 P
PADDLING 2 FR 0.0002 REL FR 2 V 0 P
but to be paddling palms and pinching fingers, WT 1.02.115
or paddling in your neck with his damn'd fingers HAM 3.04.185
PADDOCK 2 FR 0.0002 REL FR 2 V 0 P
paddock calls. MAC 1.01. 9
would from a paddock, from a bat, a gib, | such HAM 3.04.190
/PADUA 1 FR 0.0001 REL FR 1 V 0 P
all th' endeavor of a man | in speed to /padua. MV 3.04. 49
PADUA 28 FR 0.0031 REL FR 24 V 4 P
my cousin means signior benedick of padua. ADO 1.01. 36 P
letters from the doctor, | new come from padua. MV 4.01.109
came you from padua, from bellario? 4.01.119
pardon, | i must away this night toward padua, 4.01.403
it comes from padua, from bellario. 5.01.268
for the great desire i had | to see fair padua, SHR 1.01. 2
for i have pisa left | and am to padua come, as 1.01. 22
such friends as time in padua shall beget. 1.01. 45
him the best horse in padua to begin his wooing 1.01.143 P
part, | and be in padua here vincentio's son, 1.01.195
i take my leave | to see my friends in padua, 1.02. 2
gale | blows you to padua here from old verona? 1.02. 49
seas, | i come to wive it wealthily in padua; 1.02. 75
if wealthily, then happily in padua. 1.02. 76
renown'd in padua for her scolding tongue. 1.02.100
as any one | old signior gremio has in padua, 2.01.368
and make assurance here in padua | of greater 3.02.134
on the proudest he | that stops my way in padua. 3.02.235
and come to padua, careless of your life? 4.02. 79
death for any one in mantua | to come to padua. 4.02. 82
and that you look'd for him this day in padua. 4.04. 16
having come to padua | to gather in some debts, 4.04. 24
lucentio's father is arriv'd in padua, | and how 4.04. 65
and bound i am to padua, there to visit | a son 4.05. 56
i told you your son was well belov'd in padua. 5.01. 26 P
father is come from padua and here looking out 5.01. 30 P
padua affords this kindness, son petruchio. 5.02. 13
padua affords nothing but what is kind. 5.02. 14
PAEDAGOGUS 1 FR 0.0001 REL FR 1 V 0 P
by title paedagogus, that let fall | the birch TNK 3.05.110
PAGAN 6 FR 0.0006 REL FR 2 V 4 P
most beautiful pagan, most sweet jew! MV 2.03. 11 P
thyself, | and /gripple thee unto a pagan shore, JN 5.02. 36
what a pagan rascal is this! 1H4 2.03. 29 P
what pagan may that be? 2H4 2.02.154 P
their clothes are after such a pagan cut to't, H8 1.03. 14
of christians nor the gait of christian, pagan, HAM 3.02. 32 P
PAGANS 3 FR 0.0003 REL FR 3 V 0 P
of the christian cross | against black pagans, R2 4.01. 95
to chase these pagans in those holy fields, 1H4 1.01. 24
bond–slaves and pagans shall our statesmen be. OTH 1.02. 99
/PAGE 3 FR 0.0003 REL FR 1 V 2 P
i will discuss the humor of this love to /page. WIV 1.03. 95 P
i will incense /page to deal with poison; 1.03.101 P
so is alcides beaten by his /page, | and so may MV 2.01. 35
PAGE 119 FR 0.0134 REL FR 28 V 91 P
sir valentine's page; TGV 1.02. 38
weeds | as may beseem some well–reputed page. 2.07. 43
what think you of this page, my lord? 5.04.164
there is anne page, which is daughter to master WIV 1.01. 45 P
which is daughter to master /george page, which 1.01. 46 P
mistress anne page? 1.01. 47 P
between master abraham and mistress anne page. 1.01. 57 P
well, let us see honest master page. 1.01. 66 P
i will peat the door for master page. 1.01. 72 P
master page, i am glad to see you. 1.01. 81 P
how doth good mistress page? 1.01. 84 P
he hath wrong'd me, master page. 1.01.102 P
is not that so, master page? 1.01.105 P
that is, master page (fidelicet master page) and 1.01.138 P
master page (fidelicet master page) and there is 1.01.139 P
o heaven! this is mistress anne page. 1.01.190 P
the very point of it — to mistress anne page. 1.01.224 P
acquaintance with mistress anne page; 1.02. 9 P
your master's desires to mistress anne page. 1.02. 11 P
go, bear thou this letter to mistress page; 1.03. 73 P
thrift, you rogues — myself and skirted page. 1.03. 84
well, heaven send anne page no worse fortune! 1.04. 32 P
word to mistress anne page for my master in the 1.04. 83 P
himself is in love with mistress anne page; 1.04.104 P
tell–a me dat i shall have anne page for myself? 1.04.116 P
by gar, i will myself have anne page. 1.04.119 P
by gar, if i have not anne page, i shall turn 1.04.124 P
let it suffice thee, mistress page — at the 2.01. 10 P
mistress page, trust me, i was going to your 2.01. 33 P
o mistress page, give me some counsel! 2.01. 41 P
but that the name of page and ford differs! 2.01. 71 P
believe it, page, he speaks sense. 2.01.125
will you go, mistress page? 2.01.155 P
good even and twenty, good master page! 2.01.196 P
master page, will you go with us? 2.01.196 P
'tis the heart, master page, 'tis here, 'tis 2.01.227 P
though page be a secure fool, and stands so 2.01.233 P
mistress page hath her hearty commendations to 2.02. 95 P
but mistress page would desire you to send her 2.02.113 P
would desire you to send her your little page, 2.02.114 P
has a marvellous infection to the little page; 2.02.115 P
and truly master page is an honest man. 2.02.116 P
you must send her your page, no remedy. 2.02.122 P
mistress ford and mistress page, have i 2.02.152 P
page is an ass, a secure ass; 2.02.300 P
be reveng'd on falstaff, and laugh at page. 2.02.311 P
is it not true, master page? 2.03. 41 P
bodykins, master page, though i now be old and 2.03. 44 P
justices and doctors and churchmen, master page, 2.03. 47 P
in us, we are the sons of women, master page. 2.03. 49 P
it will be found so, master page. 2.03. 51 P
master guest, and master page, and eke cavaleiro 2.03. 74 P
for he speak for a jack–an–ape to anne page. 2.03. 83 P
i will bring thee where mistress anne page is, 2.03. 87 P
which i will be thy adversary toward anne page. 2.03. 95 P
ah, sweet anne page! 3.01. 40 P
o sweet anne page! 3.01. 70 P
o sweet anne page! 3.01.114 P
he promise to bring me where is anne page; 3.01.123 P
well met, mistress page. whither go you? 3.02. 9 P
has page any brains? 3.02. 30 P
of modesty from the so–seeming mistress page, 3.02. 42 P
divulge page himself for a secure and willful 3.02. 42 P
a match between anne page and my cousin slender, 3.02. 58 P
i hope i have your good will, father page. 3.02. 60 P
shall go, so shall you, master page, and you, 3.02. 82 P
mistress page, remember you your cue. 3.03. 37 P
i fear you love mistress page. 3.03. 76 P
here's mistress page at the door, sweating, and 3.03. 86 P
what's the matter, good mistress page? 3.03. 98 P
true, master page. 3.03.168 P
'tis my fault, master page. i suffer for it. 3.03.218 P
wife, come, mistress page, i pray you pardon me; 3.03.226 P
pray you go, master page. 3.03.238 P
nay, master page, be not impatient. 3.04. 71
speak to mistress page. 3.04. 77 P
good mistress page, for that i love your 3.04. 78
luck would have it, comes in one mistress page; 3.05. 84 P
farewell, mistress page. 4.01. 83 P
how near is he, mistress page? 4.02. 38 P
mistress page and i will look some linen for 4.02. 81 P
but if it prove true, master page, have you any 4.02.114 P
master page, as i am a man, there was one 4.02.145 P
what ho, mistress page! 4.02.166 P
nan page (my daughter) and my little son, | and 4.04. 48
will, | and none but he, to marry with nan page. 4.04. 85
they were nothing but about mistress anne page, 4.05. 47 P
with the dear love i bear to fair anne page, 4.06. 9
mistress page is come with me, sweet heart. 5.05. 22 P
if anne page be my daughter, she is, by this, 5.05.175 P
whoa ho, ho! father page! 5.05.177 P
came yonder at eton to marry mistress anne page, 5.05.184 P
if i did not think it had been anne page, would 5.05.187 P
vere is mistress page? 5.05.204 P
it is not anne page. 5.05.206 P
no, page, it is an epilogue or discourse, to LLL 3.01. 81
and his page a' t'other side, that handful of 4.01.147
the page, hercules. 5.01.129 P
their herald is a pretty knavish page, | that 5.02. 97
heart, | that put armado's page out of his part! 5.02.336
you put our page out. 5.02.478
armado's page, hercules; 5.02.536 P
herb), | i'll make her render up her page to me. MND 2.01.185
i'll have no worse a name than jove's own page, AYL 1.03.124
sirrah, go you to barthol'mew my page, | and see SHR in.1. 105
come, sir page, | look on me with your welkin WT 1.02.135
john, a boy, and page to thomas mowbray, duke of
2H4 3.02. 25 P
master page, good master page, sit. 5.03. 27 P
master page, good master page, sit. 5.03. 27 P
prosperity be thy page. COR 1.05. 23
where is my page? ROM 3.01. 94
where is the county's page that rais'd the watch 5.03.279
look you, here comes my master's page. TIM 2.02. 72 P
page thy heels | and skip when thou point'st out 4.03.224
a page? CYM 4.02.355
never master had | a page so kind, so duteous, 5.05. 86
thou'rt my good youth — my page; 5.05.118
thou scornful page, | there lie thy part. 5.05.228
place, | but makes antiquity for aye his page, SON 108.12
PAGEANT 10 FR 0.0011 REL FR 7 V 3 P
and, like this insubstantial pageant faded, TMP 4.01.155
ostentation, or show, or pageant, or antic, or LLL 5.01.112 P
shall we their fond pageant see? MND 3.02.114
if you will see a pageant truly play'd | between AYL 3.04. 52
a woeful pageant have we here beheld. R2 4.01.321
be slack | to play my part in fortune's pageant. 2H6 1.02. 67
the flattering index of a direful pageant; R3 4.04. 85
in all cupid's pageant there is presented no TRO 3.02. 75 P
you shall see the pageant of ajax. 3.03.272 P
'tis a pageant | to keep us in false gaze. OTH 1.03. 18
PAGEANTRY 1 FR 0.0001 REL FR 1 V 0 P
that you aptly will suppose | what pageantry, PER 5.02. 6
PAGEANTS 6 FR 0.0006 REL FR 6 V 0 P
when all our pageants of delight were play'd, TGV 4.04.159
or, as it were, the pageants of the sea, | do MV 1.01. 11
presents more woeful pageants than the scene AYL 2.07.138
day with shows, | pageants, and sights of honor. H8 4.01. 11
slanderer, he imitation calls, | he pageants us. TRO 1.03.151
these signs, | they are black vesper's pageants. ANT 4.14. 8
PAGE'S 5 FR 0.0005 REL FR 1 V 4 P
and here another to page's wife, who even now WIV 1.03. 59 P
she was in his company at page's house; 2.01.236 P
has ford's wife and page's wife acquainted each 2.02.109 P
we shall have the freer wooing at master page's. 3.02. 85 P
with, | what page's suit she hath in readiness. MV 2.04. 32
PAGES 9 FR 0.0010 REL FR 7 V 2 P
here come two of the banish'd duke's pages. AYL 5.03. 6 P
gave him their heirs as pages, followed him 1H4 4.03. 72
their dwarfish pages were | as cherubins, all H8 1.01. 22
man will work us all | from princes into pages. 2.02. 47
door 'mongst pursuivants, | pages, and footboys. 5.02. 25
that pages blush'd at him, and men of heart COR 5.06. 98
one of your lordship's pages. CYM 2.01. 41 P
pages and lights, to conduct | these knights PER 2.03.108
thy heinous hours wait on them as their pages. LUC 910
PAH *(also puh)*
PAH 3 FR 0.0003 REL FR 2 V 1 P
and smelt so? pah! HAM 5.01.200 P
pah, pah! LR 4.06.129
pah, pah! 4.06.129
PAID 65 FR 0.0073 REL FR 35 V 30 P
so: you're paid! TMP 2.01. 37 P
that no bed–right shall be paid | till hymen's 4.01. 96
some certain shot be paid and the hostess say TGV 2.05. 6 P
then i am paid; 5.04. 77
and i paid nothing for it neither, but was paid WIV 4.05. 61 P
for it neither, but was paid for my learning. 4.05. 61 P
of money, which must be paid to master /brook. 5.05.114 P
he would have paid for the nursing a thousand. MM 3.02.118 P
you have paid the heavens your function, and the 3.02.249 P
yea, and paid me richly for the practice of it. ADO 5.01.248 P
us'd so long and never paid that now men grow 5.01.311 P
of that which hath so faithfully been paid. LLL 2.01.156
redeem | the virgin tribute paid by howling troy MV 3.02. 56
when it is paid, bring your true friend along. 3.02.308
when it is paid according to the tenure. 4.01.235
he is well paid that is well satisfied, | and i, 4.01.415
and therein do account myself well paid. 4.01.417
hortensio, say thou wilt see the tailor paid. SHR 4.03.164
there is more owing her than is paid, and more AWW 1.03.104 P
and more shall be paid her than she'll demand. 1.03.104 P
thy pains not us'd must by thyself be paid. 2.01.146
are forfeited to me, and my honor's paid to him. 5.03.143 P
and pleasure will be paid, one time or another. TN 2.04. 70 P
pension of thousands to be paid from the sophy. 2.05.181 P
he hath paid you all he promis'd you. WT 4.04.239 P
may be he has paid you more, which will shame 4.04.240 P
indeed paid down | more penitence than done 5.01. 3
all my services | you have paid home. 5.03. 4
give thee thy due, thou hast paid all there. 1H4 1.02. 52 P

two i am sure i have paid, two rogues in buckrom 2.04.192 P
and with a thought seven of the eleven i paid. 2.04.218 P
the money shall be paid back again with 2.04.547 P
of an hour, paid money that i borrow'd — three 3.03. 18 P
the money is paid back again. 3.03.178 P
i have paid percy, i have made him sure. 5.03. 46 P
hot termagant scot had paid me scot and lot too. 5.04.114 P
duer paid to the hearer than the turk's tribute. 2H4 3.02.307 P
let it be cast and paid. 5.01. 20 P
the sum is paid, the traitors are agreed, | the H5 2.pr. 33
in cash, most justly paid. 2.01.115
nothing taken but paid for; 3.06.110 P
now have i paid my vow unto his soul; 1H6 2.02. 7
they set him free without his ransom paid, | in 3.03. 72
rate me at what thou wilt, thou shalt be paid. 2H6 4.01. 30
i am sure the emperor | paid ere he promis'd, H8 1.01.186
that they may have their wages duly paid 'em, 4.02.150
understand | wherefore you are not paid. TIM 2.02. 43
that part of nature | which my lord paid for, be 3.01. 62
timon's money | has paid his men their wages. 3.02. 70
ambition's debt is paid. JC 3.01. 83
your son, my lord, has paid a soldier's debt. MAC 5.09. 5
they say he parted well, and paid his score, 5.09. 18
thy madness shall be paid with weight | /till HAM 4.05.157
i am paid for't now. ANT 2.05.108
how wouldst thou have paid | my better service, 4.06. 31
death of one person can be paid but once, | and 4.14. 27
than have tidings | of any penny tribute paid. CYM 2.04. 20
come, there's no more tribute to be paid. 3.01. 34 P
paid | more pious debts to heaven than in all 3.03. 71
came our enemy, remember | he was paid for that. 4.02.246
sorry that you have paid too much, and sorry 5.04.162 P
too much, and sorry that you are paid too much; 5.04.163 P
gets | all praises, which are paid as debts, PER 4.ch. 34
honorable toil, | are paid with ice to cool 'em. TNK 1.02. 34
moan, | which i new pay as if not paid before: SON 30.12

PAIL 2 FR 0.0002 REL FR 2 V 0 P
the hall | and milk comes frozen home in pail; LLL 5.02.915
farm | i have a hundred milch–kine to the pail, SHR 2.01.357

PAILFULS 1 FR 0.0001 REL FR 0 V 1 P
same cloud cannot choose but fall by pailfuls. TMP 2.02. 24 P

PAILS 1 FR 0.0001 REL FR 1 V 0 P
great pails of puddled mire to quench the hair; ERR 5.01.173

/PAIN 1 FR 0.0001 REL FR 1 V 0 P
/light /and /portable /my /pain /seems /now, LR 3.06.108

PAIN 79 FR 0.0089 REL FR 73 V 6 P
will back descend | and turn him to no pain; WIV 5.05. 86
appears, | accountant to the law upon that pain. MM 2.04. 86
but were we burd'ned with like weight of pain, ERR 2.01. 36
if you went in pain, master, this knave would go 3.01. 65
but that most vain | which, with pain purchas'd, LLL 1.01. 73
which, with pain purchas'd, doth inherit pain: 1.01. 73
"— on pain of losing her tongue." 1.01.123 P
that shall express my true love's fasting pain. 4.03.120
and, gentle longaville, where lies thy pain? 4.03.170
but herein mean i to enrich my pain, | to have MND 1.01.250
extremely stretch'd and conn'd with cruel pain, 5.01. 80
pray thee take pain | to allay with some cold MV 2.02.185
other lives merrily because he feels no pain; AYL 3.02.322 P
of man | after his studies or his usual pain? SHR 3.01. 12
on pain of death, no person be so bold | or R2 1.03. 42
on pain to be found false and recreant, | to 1.03.106
on pain to be found false and recreant, | both 1.03.111
you, cousin herford, upon pain of life, | till 1.03.140
breathe i against thee, upon pain of life. 1.03.153
breathe truth that breathe their words in pain. 2.01. 8
be, | which i with more than with a common pain 2H4 4.05.223
till then i banish thee, on pain of death, | as 5.05. 63
or dagger, henceforward, upon pain of death. 1H6 1.03. 79 P
henceforth we banish thee, on pain of death. 4.01. 47
whom i with pain have wooed and won thereto; 5.03.138
i know no pain they can inflict upon him | will 2H6 3.01.377
disturb your rest | in pain of your dislike, or 3.02.257
in pain of your dislike, or pain of death, | yet 3.02.257
but three days longer, on the pain of death. 3.02.288
so thou wilt let me live, and feel no pain. 3.03. 4
i, | or felt that pain which i did for him once, 3H6 1.01.221
disdain, | unless the lady bona quit his pain. 3.03.128
thy mother felt more than a mother's pain, | and 5.06. 49
wert thou not banished on pain of death? R3 1.03.166
but i do find more pain in banishment | than 1.03.167
o lord, methought what pain it was to drown! 1.04. 21
of all one pain, save for a night of groans 4.04.303
fellow, and hath ta'en much pain | in the king's H8 3.02. 72
out of the pain you suffer'd, gave no ear to't. 4.02. 8
i have taken such pain to bring you together, TRO 3.02.200 P
service i have done, | in most accepted pain. 3.03. 30
with such a hell of pain and world of charge; 4.01. 58
some never–heard–of tortering pain for them. TIT 2.03.285
on pain of torture, from those bloody hands ROM 1.01. 86
once more, on pain of death, all men depart. 1.01.103
/one pain is less'ned by another's anguish; 1.02. 46
of the war | derive some pain from you. TIM 4.03.162
the labor we delight in physics pain. MAC 2.03. 50
and in this harsh world draw thy breath in pain HAM 5.02.348
found the king — in which your pain | that way, LR 3.01. 53
charg'd me on pain of perpetual displeasure 3.03. 4 P
that we the pain of death would hourly die 5.03.186
i have a pain upon my forehead, here. OTH 3.03.284
healthful members even to a sense | of pain. 3.04.148
i would not have thee linger in thy pain. 5.02. 88
/on pain of punishment, the world to weet | we ANT 1.01. 39
died of the biting of it, what pain she felt. 5.02.254 P
a pain that only seems to seek out danger | i' CYM 3.03. 50
e'er it be, | what pain it cost, what danger. 3.06. 80
pleasures here are past, so /is their pain. 4.02.290
nature should be so conversant with pain, PER 3.02. 25
and not your knowledge, your personal pain, but 3.02. 46
sir, | give me a gash, put me to present pain, 5.01.191
shrinks backward in his shelly cave with pain, VEN 1034
pain pays the income of each precious thing: LUC 334
this momentary joy breeds months of pain, | this 690
her thrall | to living death and pain perpetual; 726
leaving his spoil perplex'd in greater pain. 733
so should i have co–partners in my pain, | and 789
gain | but torment that it cannot cure his pain. 861
in spite of physic, painting, pain, and cost. PP 13.12
as take the pain but cannot pluck the pelf. 14.12

more mickle was the pain, | that nothing could 15. 9
none takes pity on thy pain. 20.20
the pain be mine, but thine shall be the praise. SON 38.14
be, | looking with pretty ruth upon my pain. 132. 4
kill me outright with looks, and rid my pain. 139.14
express | the manner of my pity–wanting pain. 140. 4
that she that makes me sin awards me pain. 141.14

PAIN'D 1 FR 0.0001 REL FR 1 V 0 P
vassal, have employ'd and pain'd | your unknown MM 5.01.386

PAINED 2 FR 0.0002 REL FR 2 V 0 P
wit | to enforce the pained impotent to smile. LLL 5.02.854
give physic to the sick, ease to the pained? LUC 901

PAINED'ST 1 FR 0.0001 REL FR 1 V 0 P
hold'st a place for which the pained'st fiend PER 4.06.163

PAINFUL 10 FR 0.0011 REL FR 8 V 2 P
there be some sports are painful, and their TMP 3.01. 1
and indeed with most painful feeling of thy MM 1.02. 37 P
if it had been painful, i would not have come. ADO 2.03.252 P
till painful study shall outwear three years, LLL 2.01. 23
commits his body | to painful labor, both by sea SHR 5.02.149
with rainy marching in the painful field; H5 4.03.111
the painful service, | the extreme dangers, and COR 4.05. 68
by many a dern and painful perch, | of pericles PER 3.ch. 15
plagu'd with cramps and gouts and painful fits, LUC 856
the painful warrior famoused for /fight, | after SON 25. 9

PAINFULLY 4 FR 0.0004 REL FR 4 V 0 P
thou didst painfully remain | a dozen years; TMP 1.02.278
as, painfully to pore upon a book | to seek the LLL 1.01. 74
who painfully with much expedient march | have JN 2.01.223
thou hast painfully discover'd; TIM 5.02. 1

PAINS 91 FR 0.0102 REL FR 70 V 21 P
since thou dost give me pains, | let me remember TMP 1.02.242
took pains to make thee speak, taught thee each 1.02.354
on whom my pains, | humanely taken, all, all 4.01.189
now you have taken the pains to set it together, TGV 1.01.116 P
to set it together, take it for your pains. 1.01.117 P
nothing but the word "noddy" for my pains. 1.01.124 P
well, sir, here is for your pains. 1.01.131 P
no, not so much as "take this for thy pains." 1.01.144 P
perchance you think too much of so much pains? 2.01.112
there's for thy pains. WIV 3.04.100
alas, it hath been great pains to you. MM 2.01.265 P
lend him your kind pains | to find out this 5.01.246
vouchsafe to take the pains | to go with us into ERR 5.01.394
fair beatrice, i thank you for your pains. ADO 2.03.249 P
i took no more pains for those thanks than you 2.03.250 P
those thanks than you take pains to thank me. 2.03.251 P
"i took no more pains for those thanks than you 2.03.259 P
those thanks than you took pains to thank me" — 2.03.260 P
"any pains that i take for you is as easy as 2.03.261 P
i thank thee for thy care and honest pains. 5.01.314
there's for thy pains. 5.01.317 P
friar, i must entreat your pains, i think. 5.04. 18
take pains, be perfit; MND 1.02.108 P
here, catch this casket, it is worth the pains. MV 2.06. 33
your grace hath ta'en great pains to qualify 4.01. 7
we freely cope your courteous pains withal. 4.01.412
that took some pains in writing, he begg'd mine, 5.01.182
yield | in lieu of all thy pains and husbandry. AYL 2.03. 65
and friends, i thank you for your pains. SHR 3.02.184
and all my pains is sorted to no proof. 4.03. 43
to those | that weigh their pains in sense, and AWW 1.01.225
my duty then shall pay me for my pains. 2.01.125
thy pains not us'd must by thyself be paid. 2.01.146
for the contents' sake are sorry for our pains. 3.02. 63
lord, how we lose our pains! 5.01. 24
but rather make you thank your pains for it. 5.01. 33
an eunuch to him, | it may be worth thy pains; TN 1.02. 57
well penn'd, i have taken great pains to con it. 1.05.174 P
alas, i took great pains to study it, and 'tis 1.05.194 P
i thank you for your pains. 1.05.283
you might have sav'd me my pains, to have taken 2.02. 6 P
there's for thy pains. 2.04. 67
no pains, sir, i take pleasure in singing, sir. 2.04. 68 P
but since you make your pleasure of your pains, 3.03. 2
to greet a man not worth her pains, much less WT 5.01.155
fall the bones that took the pains for me!), JN 1.01. 78
who, as you say, took pains to get this son, 1.01.121
that will take pains to blow a horn before her? 1.01.219
for very little pains | will bring this labor to 3.02. 9
let hell want pains enough to torture me. 4.03.138
he means to recompense the pains you take | by 5.04. 15
and plague injustice with the pains of hell. R2 3.01. 34
well have you argued, sir, and, for your pains, 4.01.150
we thank thee, gentle percy, for thy pains, 5.06. 11
thy pains, fitzwater, shall not be forgot, 5.06. 17
and, if you knew what pains | i have bestowed to 2H4 4.02. 73
like the bees, | are murd'red for our pains. 4.05. 78
his present and your pains we thank you for. H5 1.02.260
'tis good for men to love their present pains 4.01. 18
if you would take the pains but to examine the 4.01. 68 P
i have labor'd | with all my wits, my pains, and 5.02. 25
are deeply indebted for this piece of pains. 2H6 1.04. 44
'tis time to speak, my pains are quite forgot. R3 1.03.116
he is frank'd up to fatting for his pains — 1.03.313
country's fat shall pay your pains the hire; 5.03.258
i should have ta'en some pains to bring together H8 5.01.119
the gods | for our beloved mother in her pains. TIT 4.02. 47
here is for thy pains. ROM 2.04.182
farewell, be trusty, and i'll quit thy pains. 2.04.192
words have took such pains as if they labor'd TIM 3.05. 26
yet may your pains six months | be quite 4.03.144
neither wish i | you take much pains to mend. 5.01. 89
i thank you for your pains and courtesy. JC 2.02.115
thanks for your pains. MAC 1.03.117
your pains | are regist'red where every day i 1.03.150
how you shall bid god 'ield us for your pains, 1.06. 13
i commend your pains, | and every one shall 4.01. 39
turn all her mother's pains and benefits | to LR 1.04.286
on, good roderigo, i will deserve your pains. OTH 1.01.183
she gave me for my pains a world of /sighs; 1.03.159
i shall have so much experience for my pains; 2.03.367 P
masters, play here, i will content your pains; 3.01. 1
there's money for your pains. 4.02. 93
make thine own edict for thy pains, which we ANT 3.12. 32
for this pains | caesar hath hang'd him. 4.06. 14
worm of nilus there, | that kills and pains not? 5.02.244
i thank you for your pains: CYM 1.06.203

you lay out too much pains | for purchasing but 2.03. 87
you must take some pains to work her to your PER 4.06. 64 P
more of the maid to sight than husband's pains. TNK pr 8
i have put you | to too much pains, sir. 3.06. 18

PAINT 18 FR 0.0020 REL FR 12 V 6 P
does bridget paint still, pompey? ha? MM 3.02. 79 P
yea, or to paint himself? ADO 3.02. 57 P
word is too good to paint out her wickedness. 3.02.109 P
nay, never paint me now; LLL 4.01. 16
yellow hue | do paint the meadows with delight, 5.02.897
and paint your face, and use you like a fool. SHR 1.01. 65
where revenge did paint | the fearful difference JN 3.01.237
to gild refined gold, to paint the lily, | to 4.02. 11
lest, bleeding, you do paint the white rose red, 1H6 2.04. 50
when with your blood you daily paint her thus. TRO 1.01. 91
i paint him in the character. COR 5.04. 26 P
with man's blood paint the ground, gules, gules. TIM 4.03. 60
paint till a horse may mire upon your face: 4.03.148
thou canst not paint a man | so bad as is 5.01. 31
and tell her, let her paint an inch thick, to HAM 5.01.193 P
no, you shall paint when you are old. ANT 1.02. 19 P
here's something | to paint your pole withal. TNK 3.05.153
my sable ground of sin i will not paint, | to LUC 1074

PAINTED 58 FR 0.0065 REL FR 45 V 13 P
with colors fairer painted their foul ends. TMP 1.02.143
and had but this fish painted, not a holiday 2.02. 29 P
that's because the one is painted, and the other TGV 2.01. 56 P
how painted? and how out of count? 2.01. 58 P
sir, so painted to make her fair, that no man 2.01. 59 P
'tis painted about with the story of the WIV 4.05. 7 P
and let me be vildly painted, and in such great ADO 1.01.265 P
needs not the painted flourish of your praise: LLL 2.01. 14
all gentle tongues — | fie, painted rhetoric! 4.03.235
be scrap'd out of the painted cloth for this. 5.02.576 P
and therefore is wing'd cupid painted blind. MND 1.01.235
and pluck the wings from painted butterflies, 3.01.172
how low am i, thou painted maypole? 3.02.296
life more sweet | than that of painted pomp? AYL 2.01. 3
but i answer you right painted cloth, from 3.02.273 P
straight | adonis painted by a running brook, SHR in.2. 50
as lively painted as the deed was done. in.2. 56
because his painted skin contents the eye? 4.03.178
no more than were i painted i would wish | this WT 4.04.101
of war | is cold in amity and painted peace, JN 3.01.105
not painted with the crimson spots of blood. 4.02.253
away, | men are but gilded loam or painted clay. R2 1.01.179
walls | with painted imagery had said at once, 5.02. 16
as ragged as lazarus in the painted cloth, where 1H4 4.02. 25 P
with pennons painted in the blood of harflew. H5 3.05. 49
fortune is painted blind, with a muffler afore 3.06. 31 P
and she is painted also with a wheel, to signify 3.06. 32 P
painted to the hilt | in blood of those that had 3H6 1.04. 12
poor painted queen, vain flourish of my fortune! R3 1.03.240
i call'd thee then poor shadow, painted queen, 4.04. 83
your painted gloss discovers, | to men that H8 5.02.106
from cupid's shoulder pluck his painted wings, TRO 3.02. 14
in the flesh, set this in your painted cloths: 5.10. 45 P
city, which he painted | with shunless destiny; COR 2.02.111
and with that painted hope braves your TIT 2.03.126
ye alehouse painted signs! 4.02. 98
scarf, | bearing a tartar's painted bow of lath, ROM 1.04. 5
wrought he not well that painted it? TIM 1.01.197 P
but only painted, like his varnish'd friends? 4.02. 36
the skies are painted with unnumb'red sparks, JC 3.01. 63
eye of childhood | that fears a painted devil. MAC 2.02. 52
painted upon a pole, and underwrit, | "here may 5.08. 26
so, as a painted tyrant, pyrrhus stood | /and, HAM 2.02.480
it | than is my deed to my most painted word. 3.01. 52
though he be painted one way like a gorgon, ANT 2.05.116
one but painted thus | would be interpreted a CYM 3.04. 6
hung with the painted favors of their ladies, TNK 2.02. 11
so poor birds, deceiv'd with painted grapes, VEN 601
saw | shall by a painted cloth be kept in awe." LUC 245
and drop sweet balm in priam's painted wound, 1466
here feelingly she weeps troy's painted woes, 1492
"for even as subtile sinon here is painted, | so 1541
that she with painted images hath spent, | being 1577
much liker than your painted counterfeit: SON 16. 8
a woman's face with nature's own hand painted 20. 1
muse | stirr'd by a painted beauty to his verse, 21. 2
and to the painted banquet bids my heart; 47. 6
set, | and you in grecian tires are painted new; 53. 8

PAINTER 18 FR 0.0020 REL FR 13 V 5 P
and yet the painter flatter'd her a little, TGV 4.04.187
he's a god or a painter, for he makes faces. LLL 5.02.643 P
in her hairs | the painter plays the spider, and MV 3.02.121
with his pencil and the painter with his nets; ROM 1.02. 41 P
he wrought better that made the painter, and yet TIM 1.01.198 P
yonder comes a poet and a painter; 4.03.351 P
a stone–cutter or a painter could not have made LR 2.02. 58 P
you were | the ground–piece of some painter, i TNK 1.01.122
look when a painter would surpass the life | in VEN 289
which the conceited painter drew so proud, | as LUC 1371
and here and there the painter interlaces | pale 1390
some high, some low, the painter was so nice; 1412
in her the painter had anatomiz'd | time's ruin, 1450
the painter was no god to lend her those, | and 1461
in him the painter labor'd with his skill | to 1506
and chid the painter for his wondrous skill, 1528
eye hath play'd the painter and hath /stell'd SON 24. 1
for through the painter must you see his skill 24. 5

PAINTER'S 2 FR 0.0002 REL FR 2 V 0 P
red blood reek'd, to show the painter's strife, LUC 1377
and perspective it is best painter's art. SON 24. 4

PAINTING 24 FR 0.0027 REL FR 20 V 4 P
painting, sir, i have heard say, is a mystery; MM 4.02. 36 P
being members of my occupation, using painting, 4.02. 38 P
like pharaoh's soldiers in the reechy painting, ADO 3.03.134 P
your pocket like a man after the old painting; LLL 3.01. 21 P
it mourns that painting /and usurping hair 4.03.255
for native blood is counted painting now; 4.03.259
stain your own | with oily painting. WT 5.03. 83
their very labor | was to them as a painting. H8 1.01. 26
that love this painting | wherein you see me COR 1.06. 68
a piece of painting, which i do beseech | your TIM 1.01.155
painting is welcome. 1.01.156
the painting is almost the natural man; 1.01.157
this is the very painting of your fear; MAC 3.04. 60

or are you like the painting of a sorrow, | a HAM 4.07.108
(whose mother was her painting) hath betray'd CYM 3.04. 50
mind where hangs a piece | of skillful painting, LUC 1367
she throws her eyes about the painting round, 1499
in spite of physic, painting, pain, and cost. PP 13.12
painting my age with beauty of thy days. SON 62.14
why should false painting imitate his cheek, 67. 5
and their gross painting might be better us'd 82.13
i never saw that you did painting need, | and 83. 1
and therefore to your fair no painting set; 83. 2
painting thy outward walls so costly gay? 146. 4

PAINTINGS 2 FR 0.0002 REL FR 1 V 1 P
a thousand moral paintings i can show | that TIM 1.01. 90
i have heard of your paintings, well enough. HAM 3.01.142 P

PAINTS 2 FR 0.0002 REL FR 2 V 0 P
paints itself black, to imitate her brow. LLL 4.03.261
and paints the sun | with her chaste blushes! TNK 2.02.139

PAIR 47 FR 0.0053 REL FR 28 V 19 P
why, lady, love hath twenty pair of eyes. TGV 2.04. 95
to cast up, with a pair of anchoring hooks, 3.01.118
i'll do what i can to get you a pair of horns. WIV 5.01. 6 P
there went but a pair of shears between us. MM 1.02. 27 P
all that, and a pair of stocks in the town? ERR 3.01. 60
here stand a pair of honorable men, | a third is ADO 5.01.266
he hath bought a pair of cast lips of diana. AYL 3.04. 15 P
have they made a pair of stairs to marriage, 5.02. 37 P
here comes a pair of very strange beasts, which 5.04. 37 P
a pair of stocks, you rogue! SHR in.1. 2 P
a pair of old breeches thrice turn'd; 3.02. 44 P
a pair of boots that have been candle–cases, one 3.02. 45 P
would not a pair of these have bred, sir? TN 3.01. 49 P
so turtles pair | that never mean to part. WT 4.04.154
me a tawdry–lace and a pair of sweet gloves. 4.04.250 P
and here justified | by us, a pair of kings. 5.03.146
must needs want pleading for a pair of eyes. JN 4.01. 98
my subjects for a pair of carved saints, | and R2 3.03.152
till they have fretted us a pair of graves 3.03.167
if i hang, i'll make a fat pair of gallows; 1H4 2.01. 67 P
and show it a fair pair of heels and run from it 2.04. 48 P
or to take note how many pair of silk stockings 2H4 2.02. 15 P
i'll canvass thee between a pair of sheets. 2.04.225 P
i thought upon one pair of english legs | did H5 3.06.149
like to a pair of loving turtle–doves | that 1H6 2.02. 30
to call them both a pair of crafty knaves. 2H6 1.02.103
slew her brothers | a pair of bleeding hearts; R3 4.04.272
what a pair of spectacles is here! TRO 4.04. 14 P
you are a pair of strange ones. COR 2.01. 79 P
a pair of tribunes that have wrack'd for rome 5.01. 16
a pair of cursed hell–hounds and their dame. TIT 5.02.144
a pair of star–cross'd lovers take their life; ROM pr 6
play'd for a pair of stainless maidenhoods. 3.02. 13
and let him, for a pair of reechy kisses, | or HAM 3.04.184
the length and breadth of a pair of indentures? 5.01.110 P
when such a mutual pair | and such a twain can ANT 1.01. 37
/world, thou /hast a pair of chaps — no more, 3.05. 13
when vantage like a pair of twins appear'd, 3.10. 12
the earth shall clip in it | a pair so famous. 5.02.360
know not how to wish | a pair of worthier sons. CYM 5.05.356
i yet am unprovided | of a pair of bases. PER 2.01.161
shalt have my best gown to make thee a pair; 2.01.163 P
like to a pair of lions smear'd with prey, TNK 1.04. 18
they are fam'd to be a pair of absolute men. 2.01. 26 P
might well | be by a pair of kings back'd, in a 3.01. 21
blue, | a pair of maiden worlds unconquered, LUC 408
to drown /one woe, one pair of weeping eyes. 1680

PAIR'D 1 FR 0.0001 REL FR 1 V 0 P
this hour, he had pair'd | well with this lord; WT 5.01.116

PAIRS 1 FR 0.0001 REL FR 1 V 0 P
there shall the pairs of faithful lovers be MND 4.01. 91

PAIR–TAUNT–LIKE 1 FR 0.0001 REL FR 1 V 0 P
so pair–taunt–like would i o'ersway his state LLL 5.02. 67

PAJOCK *(also peacock)*

PAJOCK 1 FR 0.0001 REL FR 1 V 0 P
and now reigns here | a very, very — pajock. HAM 3.02.284

PALABRAS 1 FR 0.0001 REL FR 0 V 1 P
comparisons are odorous — palabras, neighbor ADO 3.05. 16 P

/PALACE 2 FR 0.0002 REL FR 2 V 0 P
thee, | and never from this /palace of dim night ROM 5.03.107
and thou seemest a /palace | for the crown'd PER 5.01.121

PALACE 31 FR 0.0035 REL FR 26 V 5 P
so bring us to our palace, where we'll show MM 5.01.538
and meet me in the palace wood, a mile without MND 1.02.101 P
meet presently at the palace; 4.02. 37 P
through this palace, with sweet peace, | and the 5.01.418
pray heartily he be at' palace. WT 4.04.711 P
to th' palace, and it like your worship. 4.04.716 P
the king is not at the palace. 4.04.762 P
of beads, | my gorgeous palace for a hermitage, R2 3.03.148
they, | might in thy palace perish /margaret. 2H6 3.02.100
they will by violence tear him from your palace, 3.02.246
beggary | is crept into the palace of our king, 4.01.102
this is the palace of the fearful king, | and 3H6 1.01. 25
march'd through the city to the palace gates. 1.01. 92
now my soul's palace is become a prison; 2.01. 74
and brought your prisoner to your palace gate. 3.02.119
here at the palace will i rest a while. 4.08. 33
you left poor henry at the bishop's palace, 5.01. 45
or climb my palace, till from forth this place TIT 1.01.327
so near the emperor's palace dare ye draw, | and 2.01. 46
the palace full of tongues, of eyes, and ears; 2.01.127
before the palace gate | to brave the tribune in 4.02. 35
deceit should dwell | in such a gorgeous palace! ROM 3.02. 85
they are, my lord, without the palace gate. MAC 3.01. 46
done to–night, | and something from the palace; 3.01.131
from hence to th' palace gate | make it their 3.03. 13
a tavern or a brothel | than a grac'd palace. LR 1.04.246
as where's that palace whereinto foul things OTH 3.03.137
had our great palace the capacity | to camp this ANT 4.08. 32
mount, eagle, to my palace crystalline. CYM 5.04.113
that him and his they in his palace burn; PER 5.03. 98
in the great lake that lies behind the palace, TNK 4.01. 53

PALACES 7 FR 0.0008 REL FR 5 V 2 P
the cloud–capp'd tow'rs, the gorgeous palaces, TMP 4.01.152
and poor men's cottages princes' palaces. MV 1.02. 14 P
to us, | else ruin combat with their palaces! 1H6 5.02. 7
set this diamond safe | in golden palaces, as it 5.03.170
though palaces and pyramids do slope | their MAC 4.01. 57
in palaces, treason; LR 1.02.108 P

their thoughts do hit | the roofs of palaces, CYM 3.03. 84

PALAMEDES 1 FR 0.0001 REL FR 1 V 0 P
or slain, and palamedes | sore hurt and bruised. TRO 5.05. 13

PALAMON 67 FR 0.0075 REL FR 56 V 11 P
dear palamon, dearer in love than blood, | and TNK 1.02. 1
/wi' leave, they're called | arcite and palamon. 1.04. 23
no, sir, no, that's palamon. 2.01. 49 P
like lazy clouds, whilst palamon and arcite, 2.02. 14
no, palamon, | those hopes are prisoners with us 2.02. 25
us, | and which is heaviest, palamon, unmarried. 2.02. 29
whilst palamon is with me, let me perish | if i 2.02. 61
cousin, cousin! how do you, sir? why, palamon! 2.02.131
if that will lose ye, farewell, palamon! 2.02.177
as any palamon or any living | that is a man's 2.02.181
you have told me | that i was palamon, and you 2.02.186
prince palamon, i must awhile bereave you | of 2.02.223
palamon! 2.03. 7
what happiness has palamon! 2.03. 13
but in my heart was palamon, and there, | lord, 2.04. 17
alas, | poor cousin palamon, poor prisoner! 3.01. 23
dear cousin palamon — 3.01. 43
sweet palamon — 3.01. 92
thing, | i care for nothing, and that's palamon. 3.02. 6
i should be near the place. ho, cousin palamon! 3.03. 1
palamon! 3.04. 3
here, palamon: 3.06.102
thou shalt know, palamon, i dare as well | die 3.06.128
i am palamon, | that cannot love thee, he that 3.06.138
said of me | concerning the escape of palamon? 4.01. 2
palamon has clear'd you, | and got your pardon, 4.01. 18
either this was her love to palamon, | or fear 4.01. 49
heard her | repeat this often, "palamon is gone, 4.01. 67
and between | ever was "palamon, fair palamon," 4.01. 81
and between | ever was "palamon, fair palamon," 4.01. 81
palamon," | and "palamon was a tall young man." 4.01. 82
pray did you ever hear | of one young palamon? 4.01.117
th' wood, where palamon | lies longing for me. 4.01.144
palamon | is but his foil, to him, a mere dull 4.02. 25
palamon, thou art alone | and only beautiful, 4.02. 37
now if my sister — more for palamon. 4.02. 49
methinks, of him that's first with palamon. 4.02. 90
soe'er she's about, the name palamon lards it, 4.03. 7 P
for in the next world will dido see palamon, and 4.03. 15 P
then will i make palamon a nosegay, then let him 4.03. 26 P
ever affected any man ere she beheld palamon? 4.03. 63 P
young sir her friend, the name of palamon, say 4.03. 76 P
of love as she says palamon hath sung in prison. 4.03. 82 P
all this shall become palamon, for palamon can 4.03. 86 P
this shall become palamon, for palamon can sing, 4.03. 86 P
for palamon can sing, and palamon is sweet, and 4.03. 86 P
repair to her with palamon in their mouths and 4.03. 91 P
have half persuaded her that i am palamon. 5.02. 3
will, and tell her | her palamon stays for her; 5.02. 26
come, your love palamon stays for you, child, 5.02. 41
are not you palamon? 5.02. 82
and i am glad my cousin palamon | has made so 5.02. 91
my palamon i hope will grow too, finely, | now 5.02. 95
palamon | has a most menacing aspect, his brow 5.03. 44
me, | and yet may palamon wound arcite to | the 5.03. 58
the cry's "a palamon!" 5.03. 67
still "palamon!" 5.03. 71
palamon | had the best–boding chance. 5.03. 76
they said that palamon had arcite's body 5.03. 79
that the cry | was general "a palamon!"; 5.03. 81
"palamon" still? 5.03. 90
i did think | good palamon would miscarry, yet i 5.03.101
alas, poor palamon! 5.03.104
noble palamon, | the gods will show their glory 5.04. 42
i am palamon, | one that yet loves thee dying. 5.04. 89
palamon, | your kinsman hath confess'd the right 5.04.115
we'll put on | and smile with palamon; 5.04.128

PALAMON'S 2 FR 0.0002 REL FR 2 V 0 P
but palamon's sadness is a kind of mirth, | so TNK 5.03. 51
i wore thy picture, | palamon's on the left. 5.03. 74

PALATE 10 FR 0.0011 REL FR 9 V 1 P
no motion of the liver, but the palate, | that TN 2.04. 98
our dear'st repute | with their fin'st palate; TRO 1.03.338
or brew it to a weak and colder palate, | the 4.04. 7
the drink you give me touch my palate adversely, COR 2.01. 56 P
sauce his palate | with thy most operant poison! TIM 4.03. 24
it not | to please the palate of my appetite, OTH 1.03.262
thy palate then did deign | the roughest berry ANT 1.04. 63
and to his palate doth prepare the cup. SON 114.12
keen, | with eager compounds we our palate urge, 118. 2
the one a palate hath that needs will taste, LC 167

PALATES 6 FR 0.0006 REL FR 6 V 0 P
and let their palates | be season'd with such MV 4.01. 96
be, | when that the wat'ry palates taste indeed TRO 3.02. 21
the great'st taste | most palates theirs. COR 3.01.104
and have their palates both for sweet and sour, OTH 4.03. 95
which sleeps, and never palates more the dung, ANT 5.02. 7
those palates who, not yet /two /summers younger PER 1.04. 39

PALATINE *(see palentine)*

PALATING 1 FR 0.0001 REL FR 1 V 0 P
her, | not palating the taste of her dishonor, TRO 4.01. 60

PAL'D 1 FR 0.0001 REL FR 1 V 0 P
ribb'd and pal'd in | with oaks unscalable and CYM 3.01. 19

PALE* 150 FR 0.0169 REL FR 141 V 9 P
them | as if but now they waxed pale for woe: TGV 3.01.230
for me (by this pale queen of night i swear), 4.02.100
i am pale at mine heart to see thine eyes so red MM 4.03.151 P
but, too unruly deer, he breaks the pale, | and ERR 2.01.100
look'd he or red or pale, or sad or merrily? 4.02. 4
i know it by their pale and deadly looks. 4.04. 93
ay me, poor man, how pale and wan he looks! 4.04.108
of pale distemperatures and foes to life? 5.01. 82
shall see thee, ere i die, look pale with love. ADO 1.01.247 P
as i am an honest man, he looks pale. 5.01.130 P
faults are bred | and fears by pale white shown: LLL 1.02.102
you may look pale, but i should blush, i know, 4.03.127
why look you pale? 5.02.392
the pale companion is not for our pomp. MND 1.01. 15
why is your cheek so pale? 1.01.128
bush, thorough brier, | over park, over pale, 2.01. 4
pale in her anger, washes all the air, | that 2.01.104
all fancy–sick she is and pale of cheer | with 3.02. 96
where i have seen them shiver and look pale, 5.01. 95

come, come to me, | with hands as pale as milk; 5.01.338
thou pale and common drudge | 'tween man and man MV 3.02.103
and weep, and thou must look pale and wonder. AYL 1.01.157 P
for, by this heaven, now at our sorrows pale, 1.03.104
with thy chaste eye, from thy pale sphere above, 3.02. 3
between the pale complexion of true love | and 3.04. 53
how now, my friend, why dost thou look so pale? SHR 2.01.142
for fear, i promise you, if i look pale. 2.01.143
look not pale, bianca, thy father will not frown 5.01.138 P
what, pale again? AWW 1.03.169
and pants and looks pale, as if a bear were at TN 3.04.295 P
for the red blood reigns in the winter's pale. WT 4.03. 4
the pale moon shines by night; 4.03. 16
pale primeroses, | that die unmarried, ere they 4.04.122
together with that pale, that white–fac'd shore, JN 2.01. 23
look'st thou pale, france? 3.01.195
you look pale to–day. 4.01. 28
i am the /cygnet to this pale faint swan | who 5.07. 21
pale trembling coward, there i throw my gage, R2 1.01. 69
or with pale beggar–fear impeach my height 1.01.189
is pale cold cowardice in noble breasts. 1.02. 34
thy frozen admonition | make pale our cheek, 2.01.118
comfort, my liege, why looks your grace so pale? 3.02. 75
have i not reason to look pale and dead? 3.02. 79
why should we in the compass of a pale | keep 3.04. 40
yea, look'st thou pale? 5.02. 57
my wive's brother, then his cheek look'd pale, 1H4 1.03.142
doth speak of you, his cheek looks pale, and 3.01. 9
the day looks pale | at his distemp'rature. 5.01. 2
left the liver white and pale, which is the 2H4 4.03.104 P
delivering o'er to executors pale | the lazy H5 1.02.203
fear, and with pale policy | seek to divert the 2.pr. 14
on whom, as in despite, the sun looks pale, 3.05. 17
that every wretch, pining and pale before, 4.pr. 41
and in their pale dull mouths the /gimmal'd bit 4.02. 49
whose very shores look pale | with envy of each 5.02.350
the famish'd english, like pale ghosts, 1H6 1.02. 7
i pluck this pale and maiden blossom here, 2.04. 47
for pale they look with fear, as witnessing 2.04. 63
and, by my soul, this pale and angry rose, | as 2.04.107
and pale destruction meets thee in the face. 4.02. 27
shall see thee withered, bloody, pale, and dead. 4.02. 38
how are we park'd and bounded in a pale, | a 4.02. 45
why look'st thou pale? 2H6 3.02. 27
look pale as primrose with blood–drinking sighs, 3.02. 63
of ashy semblance, meagre, pale, and bloodless, 3.02.162
these cheeks are pale for watching for your good 4.07. 85
and will you pale your head in henry's glory, 3H6 1.04.103
but sever'd in a pale clear–shining sky. 2.01. 28
the other his pale cheeks, methinks, presenteth. 2.05.100
king, | pale ashes of the house of lancaster, R3 1.02. 6
why look you pale? 1.04.170
look i so pale, lord dorset, as the rest? 2.01. 84
look'd pale when they did hear of clarence' 2.01.137
star'd each on other, and look'd deadly pale; 3.07. 26
how pale she looks, | and of an earthy cold! H8 4.02. 97
envious fever | of pale and bloodless emulation, TRO 1.03.134
respect | make livers pale and lustihood deject. 2.02. 50
wrinkles apollo's, and makes pale the morning. 2.02. 79
which, like a /bourn, a pale, a shore, confines 2.03.249
look how thy eye turns pale! 5.03. 81
of generosity | and make bold power look pale — COR 1.01.212
and faces pale | with flight and agued fear! 1.04. 37
and you'll look pale | before you find it other. 4.06.101
advanc'd above pale envy's threat'ning reach. TIT 2.01. 4
why doth your highness look so pale and wan? 2.03. 90
have i not reason, think you, to look pale? 2.03. 91
so pale did shine the moon on /pyramus | when he 2.03.231
this dear sight | struck pale and bloodless, and 3.01.257
o, take this warm kiss on thy pale cold lips, 5.03.153
who is already sick and pale with grief | that ROM 2.02. 5
why, that same pale hard–hearted wench, that 2.04. 4
so, she looks as pale as any clout in the versal 2.04.206 P
dead, | unwieldy, slow, heavy, and pale as lead. 2.05. 17
pale, pale as ashes, all bedaub'd in blood, 3.02. 55
pale, pale as ashes, all bedaub'd in blood, 3.02. 55
'tis but the pale reflex of cynthia's brow; 3.05. 20
either my eyesight fails, or thou lookest pale. 3.05. 57
your looks are pale and wild, and do import 5.01. 28
and death's pale flag is not advanced there. 5.03. 96
romeo, o, pale! 5.03.144
and her pale fire she snatches from the sun; TIM 4.03.438
calphurnia's cheek is pale, and cicero | looks JC 1.02.185
you look pale, and gaze, | and put on fear, and 1.03. 59
and wakes it now to look so green and pale | at MAC 1.07. 37
witchcraft celebrates | pale hecat's off'rings; 2.01. 52
to pieces that great bond | which keeps me pale! 3.02. 50
hands, put on your night–gown, look not so pale. 5.01. 63 P
you tremble and look pale. HAM 1.01. 53
pale, or red? 1.02.232
nay, very pale. 1.02.233
near, | and gins to pale his uneffectual fire. 1.05. 90
pale as his shirt, his knees knocking each other 2.01. 78
is sicklied o'er with the pale cast of thought, 3.01. 84
look you how pale he glares! 3.04.125
you that look pale, and tremble at this chance, 5.02.334
look you pale? OTH 5.01.104
look you pale, mistress? 5.01.105
o ill–starr'd wench, | pale as thy smock! 5.02.273
i am pale, charmian. ANT 2.05. 59
was't | that mov'd pale cassius to conspire? 2.06. 15
if you can | be pale, i beg but leave to air CYM 2.04. 96
the flower that's like thy face, pale primrose, 4.02.221
give color to my pale cheek with thy blood, 4.02.330
a distaff to a lance, gilded pale looks; 5.03. 34
with speechless tongues and semblance pale, PER 1.01. 36
if this be true which makes me pale to read it? 1.01. 75
th' moon | (which then look'd pale at parting) TNK 1.03. 53
making them red and pale with fresh variety — VEN 21
here | within the circuit of this ivory pale, 230
but now her cheek was pale, and by and by | it 347
claps her pale cheek, till clapping makes it red 468
quoth she, whereat a sudden pale, | like lawn 589
"as burning fevers, agues pale and faint, 739
she looks upon his lips, and they are pale, 1123
resembling well his pale cheeks and the blood 1169
which, in pale embers hid, lurks to aspire | and LUC 5

here pale with fear he doth premeditate | the 183
left their round turrets destitute and pale. 441
that even for anger makes the lily pale | and 478
and there the painter interlaces | pale cowards, 1391
cheeks neither red nor pale, but mingled so 1510
nor ashy pale the fear that false hearts have. 1512
and now this pale swan in her wat'ry nest 1611
from lips new waxen pale begins to blow | the 1663
he falls, and bathes the pale fear in his face, 1775
a lily pale, with damask dye to grace her, PP 7. 5
gilding pale streams with heavenly alcumy; SON 33. 4
with so dull a cheer | that leaves look pale, 97.14
tale, | ere long espied a fickle maid full pale, LC 5
hat, | hanging her pale and pined cheek beside; 32
PALE–DEAD 1 FR 0.0001 REL FR 1 V 0 P
the gum down–roping from their pale–dead eyes, H5 4.02. 48
PALE–FAC'D 5 FR 0.0005 REL FR 5 V 0 P
frighting her pale–fac'd villages with war | and R2 2.03. 94
the pale–fac'd moon looks bloody on the earth, 2.04. 10
to pluck bright honor from the pale–fac'd moon, 1H4 1.03.202
let pale–fac'd fear keep with the mean–born man,
2H6 3.01.335
affection faints not like a pale–fac'd coward, VEN 569
PALE–HEARTED 1 FR 0.0001 REL FR 1 V 0 P
that i may tell pale–hearted fear it lies, | and MAC 4.01. 85
PALENESS 3 FR 0.0003 REL FR 3 V 0 P
thy paleness moves me more than eloquence, | and
MV 3.02.106
pronouncing that the paleness of this flower 1H6 4.01.106
or of weeping water, | or sounding paleness; LC 305
PALENTINE 2 FR 0.0002 REL FR 0 V 2 P
then is there the county palentine. MV 1.02. 45 P
bad habit of frowning than the count palentine; 1.02. 60 P
PALER 4 FR 0.0004 REL FR 2 V 2 P
the daylight sick, | it looks a little paler. MV 5.01.125
come, you look paler and paler. AYL 4.03.177 P
come, you look paler and paler. 4.03.177 P
paler for sorrow than her milk–white dove, | for PP 9. 3
PALES 4 FR 0.0004 REL FR 4 V 0 P
the english beach | pales in the flood with men, H5 5.pr. 10
th' rail, | i'll peck you o'er the pales else. H8 5.03. 90
oft breaking down the pales and forts of reason, HAM 1.04. 28
what e'er the ocean pales, or sky inclips, | is ANT 2.07. 68
PALESTINE 2 FR 0.0002 REL FR 1 V 1 P
heart, | and fought the holy wars in palestine, JN 2.01. 4
walk'd barefoot to palestine for a touch of his OTH 4.03. 39 P
PALE–VISAG'D 1 FR 0.0001 REL FR 1 V 0 P
for your own ladies and pale–visag'd maids JN 5.02.154
PALFREY 4 FR 0.0004 REL FR 2 V 2 P
of the lamb, vary deserv'd praise on my palfrey. H5 3.07. 33 P
and in cheapside shall my palfrey go to grass; 2H6 4.02. 69 P
care, | is how to get my palfrey from the mare." VEN 384
"thy palfrey, as he should, | welcomes the warm 385
PALFREYS 2 FR 0.0002 REL FR 1 V 1 P
it is the prince of palfreys: H5 3.07. 27 P
provide thee two proper palfreys, black as jet, TIT 5.02. 50
PALISADOES 1 FR 0.0001 REL FR 1 V 0 P
of palisadoes, frontiers, parapets, | of 1H4 2.03. 52
PALL* 2 FR 0.0002 REL FR 2 V 0 P
and pall thee in the dunnest smoke of hell, MAC 1.05. 51
serves us well | when our deep plots do pall, HAM 5.02. 9
PALLABRIS 1 FR 0.0001 REL FR 0 V 1 P
therefore paucas pallabris, let the world slide. SHR in.1. 5 P
PALLAS 4 FR 0.0004 REL FR 4 V 0 P
apollo, pallas, jove, or mercury, | inspire me, TIT 4.01. 66
here, boy, "to pallas"; 4.03. 56
give it pallas. 4.03. 65
pallas inspire me! TNK 3.05. 94
PALL'D 1 FR 0.0001 REL FR 1 V 0 P
i'll never follow thy pall'd fortunes more. ANT 2.07. 82
PALLETS 1 FR 0.0001 REL FR 1 V 0 P
cribs, | upon uneasy pallets stretching thee, 2H4 3.01. 10
PALLIAMENT 1 FR 0.0001 REL FR 1 V 0 P
this palliament of white and spotless hue, | and TIT 1.01.182
PALLID 1 FR 0.0001 REL FR 1 V 0 P
me, | of pallid pearls and rubies red as blood, LC 198
PALM* 28 FR 0.0031 REL FR 20 V 8 P
by the barrenness, hard in the palm of the hand. ERR 3.02.121 P
and, by this virgin palm now kissing thine, | i LLL 5.02.806
for look here what i found on a palm tree. AYL 3.02.175 P
capable impressure | thy palm some moment keeps; 3.05. 24
still virginalling | upon his palm? WT 1.02.126
when his fair angels would salute my palm, | but JN 2.01.590
as now again to snatch our palm from palm, 3.01.244
as now again to snatch our palm from palm, 3.01.244
have a beard grow in the palm of my hand than he
2H4 1.02. 21 P
spirit of sense | hard as the palm of ploughman. TRO 1.01. 59
valiant lord | shall not so /stale his palm, 2.03.191
gives us more palm in beauty than we have, | yea 3.01.157
sciaticas, lime–kills i' th' palm, incurable 5.01. 22 P
and bear the palm for having bravely shed | thy COR 5.03.117
touch, | and palm to palm is holy palmers' kiss. ROM 1.05.100
touch, | and palm to palm is holy palmers' kiss. 1.05.100
you shall see him a palm in athens again, and TIM 5.01. 10
of the majestic world | and bear the palm alone. JC 1.02.131
are much condemn'd to have an itching palm, | to 4.03. 10
i, an itching palm? 4.03. 12
but do not dull thy palm with entertainment | of HAM 1.03. 64
love between them like the palm might flourish, 5.02. 40
he takes her by the palm; OTH 2.01.167 P
not see her paddle with the palm of his hand? 2.01.254 P
there's a palm presages chastity, if nothing ANT 1.02. 47 P
nay, if an oily palm be not a fruitful 1.02. 52 P
with this she seizeth on his sweating palm, VEN 25
would in thy palm dissolve, or seem to melt. 144
PALMER'S 2 FR 0.0002 REL FR 2 V 0 P
wood, | my sceptre for a palmer's walking–staff, R2 3.03.151
thy hand is made to grasp a palmer's staff | and 2H6 5.01. 97
PALMERS' 2 FR 0.0002 REL FR 2 V 0 P
touch, | and palm to palm is holy palmers' kiss. ROM 1.05.100
as palmers' chat makes short their pilgrimage. LUC 791
PALMERS 2 FR 0.0002 REL FR 2 V 0 P
where do the palmers lodge, i do beseech you? AWW 3.05. 35
have not saints lips, and holy palmers too? ROM 1.05.101
PALMS 2 FR 0.0002 REL FR 1 V 1 P
but to be paddling palms and pinching fingers, WT 1.02.115
old women, the virginal palms of your daughters, COR 5.02. 43 P
PALMY 1 FR 0.0001 REL FR 1 V 0 P
in the most high and palmy state of rome, | a HAM 1.01.113
PALPABLE 5 FR 0.0005 REL FR 4 V 1 P
them, gross as a mountain, open, palpable. 1H4 2.04.226 P
so gross | that cannot see this palpable device? R3 3.06. 11
in form as palpable | as this which now i draw. MAC 2.01. 40
a hit, a very palpable hit. HAM 5.02.281
on, | 'tis probable, and palpable to thinking. OTH 1.02. 76
PALPABLE–GROSS 1 FR 0.0001 REL FR 1 V 0 P
this palpable–gross play hath well beguil'd MND 5.01.367
PALSIED 2 FR 0.0002 REL FR 1 V 1 P
as aged, and doth beg the alms | of palsied eld; MM 3.01. 36
or with the palsied intercession of such a COR 5.02. 44 P
PALSIES 1 FR 0.0001 REL FR 0 V 1 P
in the back, lethargies, cold palsies, raw eyes, TRO 5.01. 20 P
PALSY 5 FR 0.0005 REL FR 3 V 2 P
now prisoner to the palsy, chastise thee, | and R2 2.03.104
the palsy, and not fear, provokes me. 2H6 4.07. 93
and, with a palsy fumbling on his gorget, TRO 1.03.174
'tis enough to infect the city with the palsy. STM II.C 11 P
it has infected it with the palsy, for these II.C 12 P
PALTER 5 FR 0.0005 REL FR 5 V 0 P
a whoreson dog, that shall palter with us thus! TRO 2.03.233
fo, fo, /adieu, you palter. 5.02. 48
that have spoke the word | and will not palter? JC 2.01.126
that palter with us in a double sense, | that MAC 5.08. 20
dodge | and palter in the shifts of lowness, who ANT 3.11. 63
PALT'RING 1 FR 0.0001 REL FR 1 V 0 P
this palt'ring | becomes not rome; COR 3.01. 58
PALTRY 11 FR 0.0012 REL FR 8 V 3 P
shall be our messenger to this paltry knight. WIV 2.01.159 P
of gold, a paltry ring | that she did give me, MV 5.01.147
why, thou say'st true, it is /a paltry cap, | a SHR 4.03. 81
a very dishonest paltry boy, and more a coward TN 3.04.385 P
then turn your forces from this paltry siege, JN 2.01. 54
to save a paltry life and slay bright fame, 1H6 4.06. 45
god, to shoot forth thunder | upon these paltry, 2H6 4.01.105
for underneath an alehouse' paltry sign, | the 5.02. 67
and who doth lead them but a paltry fellow, R3 5.03.323
a paltry, insolent fellow! TRO 2.03.208 P
'tis paltry to be caesar; ANT 5.02. 2
PALY 2 FR 0.0002 REL FR 2 V 0 P
and through their paly flames | each battle sees H5 4.pr. 8
fain would i go to chafe his paly lips | with 2H6 3.02.141
PAMPER 1 FR 0.0001 REL FR 1 V 0 P
nurse, | and i will pamper it with lamentation. R3 2.02. 88
PAMPER'D 1 FR 0.0001 REL FR 1 V 0 P
pack–horses | and hollow pamper'd jades of asia, 2H4 2.04.164
PAMPHLETS 1 FR 0.0001 REL FR 1 V 0 P
with written pamphlets studiously devis'd? 1H6 3.01. 2
PAMP'RED 1 FR 0.0001 REL FR 1 V 0 P
or those pamp'red animals | that rage in savage ADO 4.01. 60
PANCAKE 1 FR 0.0001 REL FR 0 V 1 P
forefinger, as a pancake for shrove tuesday, a AWW 2.02. 23 P
PANCAKES 3 FR 0.0003 REL FR 0 V 3 P
that swore by his honor they were good pancakes,
AYL 1.02. 64 P
it, the pancakes were naught and the mustard was 1.02. 66 P
ever he saw those pancakes or that mustard. 1.02. 79 P
PANDAR 9 FR 0.0010 REL FR 8 V 1 P
camillo was his help in this, his pandar. WT 2.01. 46
i cannot come to cressid but by pandar, | and TRO 1.01. 95
what cressid is, what pandar, and what we: 1.01. 99
and this sailing pandar | our doubtful hope, our 1.01.103
o gentle pandar, | from cupid's shoulder pluck 3.02. 13
bed, chamber, pandar to provide this gear! 3.02.211
the secrets of neighbor pandar | have not more 4.02. 72
coward, pandar, and the son and heir of a LR 2.02. 22 P
ah, you precious pandar! CYM 3.05. 81
PANDAR'S 3 FR 0.0003 REL FR 3 V 0 P
than in the glass of pandar's praise may be; TRO 1.02.285
as many as be here of pandar's hall, | your eyes 5.10. 47
your eyes, half out, weep out at pandar's fall; 5.10. 48
PANDARS 3 FR 0.0003 REL FR 0 V 3 P
troilus the first employer of pandars, and a ADO 5.02. 31 P
call them all pandars. TRO 3.02.202 P
women cressids, and all brokers–between pandars! 3.02.204 P
PANDARUS 17 FR 0.0019 REL FR 10 V 7 P
shall i sir pandarus of troy become, | and by my WIV 1.03. 75
i would play lord pandarus of phrygia, sir, to TN 3.01. 51 P
o pandarus, i tell thee, pandarus — | when i do TRO 1.01. 48
o pandarus, i tell thee, pandarus — | when i do 1.01. 48
good pandarus! how now, pandarus? 1.01. 69
good pandarus! how now, pandarus? 1.01. 69
what, art thou angry, pandarus? what, with me? 1.01. 73
pandarus — 1.01. 84
sweet pandarus — 1.01. 86
but pandarus — o gods! 1.01. 94
madam, your uncle pandarus. 1.02. 38 P
good morrow, uncle pandarus. 1.02. 42 P
friend, know me better, i am the lord pandarus. 3.01. 12 P
my lord pandarus, honey–sweet lord — 3.01. 65 P
my lord pandarus — 3.01. 78 P
you know all, lord pandarus. 3.01.140 P
no, pandarus, i stalk about her door, | like to 3.02. 8
PANDER 3 FR 0.0003 REL FR 1 V 2 P
of money, to whom you should have been a pander.
WIV 5.05.167 P
hand | like a base pander hold the chamber–door H5 4.05. 14
thou art the pander to her dishonor and equally CYM 3.04. 31 P
PANDERLY 1 FR 0.0001 REL FR 0 V 1 P
o you panderly rascals, there's a knot, a /ging, WIV 4.02.117 P
/PANDERS 1 FR 0.0001 REL FR 1 V 0 P
actively doth burn, | and reason /panders will. HAM 3.04. 88
PANDION 1 FR 0.0001 REL FR 1 V 0 P
king pandion, he is dead: PP 20.23
PANDULPH 2 FR 0.0002 REL FR 2 V 0 P
i pandulph, of fair milan cardinal, | and from JN 3.01.138
the cardinal pandulph is within at rest, | who 5.07. 82
PANEL 1 FR 0.0001 REL FR 0 V 1 P
then one of you will prove a shrunk panel, and AYL 3.03. 88 P
PANG 4 FR 0.0004 REL FR 4 V 0 P
in corporal sufferance finds a pang as great MM 3.01. 79
hath for your love as great a pang of heart | as TN 2.04. 90
here's the pang that pinches: H8 2.03. 1
her suff'rance made | almost each pang a death. 5.01. 69
PANG'D 1 FR 0.0001 REL FR 1 V 0 P
on, how thy memory | will then be pang'd by me. CYM 3.04. 95
PANGING 1 FR 0.0001 REL FR 1 V 0 P
'tis a sufferance panging | as soul and body's H8 2.03. 15
PANGS 15 FR 0.0017 REL FR 12 V 3 P
i suffer'd the pangs of three several deaths: WIV 3.05.108 P
and shall do till the pangs of death shake him. TN 1.05. 75 P
love, | in the sweet pangs of it remember me; 2.04. 16
can be none but by pangs of death and sepulchre. 3.04.239 P
for i do see the cruel pangs of death | right in JN 5.04. 59
no, no, he cannot long hold out these pangs. 2H4 4.04.117
see how the pangs of death do make him grin! 2H6 3.03. 24
and in the very pangs of death he cried, | like 3H6 2.03. 17
more pangs and fears than wars or women have; H8 3.02.370
their pangs of love, with other incident throes TIM 5.01.200
the pangs of despis'd love, the law's delay, HAM 3.01. 71
pitying | the pangs of barr'd affections, though CYM 1.01. 82
a touch more rare | subdues all pangs, all fears 1.01.136
make swift the pangs | of my queen's travails! PER 3.01. 13
and sweetens, in the suff'ring pangs it bears, LC 272
PANNIER 1 FR 0.0001 REL FR 0 V 1 P
the turkeys in my pannier are quite starv'd. 1H4 2.01. 26 P
PANNONIANS 2 FR 0.0002 REL FR 2 V 0 P
perfect | that the pannonians and dalmatians for CYM 3.01. 73
action | 'gainst the pannonians and dalmatians, 3.07. 3
PANSA 1 FR 0.0001 REL FR 1 V 0 P
where thou slew'st | hirtius and pansa, consuls, ANT 1.04. 58
PANSIES 1 FR 0.0001 REL FR 0 V 1 P
and there is pansies, that's for thoughts. HAM 4.05.176 P
PANT 3 FR 0.0003 REL FR 3 V 0 P
find we a time for frighted peace to pant | and 1H4 1.01. 2
shall sit and pant in your great chairs of ease, TIM 5.04. 11
i pant for life. LR 5.03.244
PANTALOON 2 FR 0.0002 REL FR 1 V 1 P
shifts | into the lean and slipper'd pantaloon, AYL 2.07.158
senis," that we might beguile the old pantaloon. SHR 3.01. 37 P
PANTED 1 FR 0.0001 REL FR 1 V 0 P
having lost her breath, she spoke, and panted, ANT 2.02.230
PANTETH 1 FR 0.0001 REL FR 1 V 0 P
in his hold–fast foot the weak mouse panteth. LUC 555
/PANTHEON 1 FR 0.0001 REL FR 1 V 0 P
and in the sacred /pantheon her espouse. TIT 1.01.242
PANTHEON 1 FR 0.0001 REL FR 1 V 0 P
ascend, fair queen, pantheon. TIT 1.01.333
PANTHER 3 FR 0.0003 REL FR 3 V 0 P
to hunt the panther and the hart with me, | with TIT 1.01.493
will rouse the proudest panther in the chase, 2.02. 21
pit | where i espied the panther fast asleep. 2.03.194
PANTHINO 2 FR 0.0002 REL FR 2 V 0 P
tell me, panthino, what sad talk was that TGV 1.03. 1
come on, panthino; 1.03. 76
/PANTING 1 FR 0.0001 REL FR 1 V 0 P
/panting forth | from goneril his mistress LR 2.04. 31
PANTING 5 FR 0.0005 REL FR 5 V 0 P
against the panting sides of his poor jade | up 2H4 1.01. 45
air, | but smother'd it within my panting bulk, R3 1.04. 40
never stood | to ease his breast with panting. COR 2.02.122
panting he lies, and breatheth in her face. VEN 62
she like a wearied lamb lies panting there; LUC 737
/PANTINGLY 1 FR 0.0001 REL FR 1 V 0 P
/the /name /of "/father" | /pantingly /forth, LR 4.03. 26
PANTLER 4 FR 0.0004 REL FR 2 V 2 P
upon | this day she was both pantler, butler, WT 4.04. 56
'a would have made a good pantler, 'a would 'a' 2H4 2.04.238 P
me, and call me pantler and bread–chipper, and i 2.04.314 P
a squire's cloth, | a pantler — not so eminent. CYM 2.03.124
PANTRY 1 FR 0.0001 REL FR 0 V 1 P
the nurse curs'd in the pantry, and every thing ROM 1.03.102 P
PANTS 4 FR 0.0004 REL FR 3 V 1 P
and pants and looks pale, as if a bear were at TN 3.04.294 P
make love's quick pants in desdemona's arms, OTH 2.01. 80
heart, and there | ride on the pants triumphing! ANT 4.08. 16
my boding heart pants, beats, and takes no rest, VEN 647
PAP 3 FR 0.0003 REL FR 2 V 1 P
him with thy bird–bolt under the left pap. LLL 4.03. 24 P
out, sword, and wound | the pap of pyramus; MND 5.01.297
ay, that left pap, | where heart doth hop. 5.01.298
/PAPER 2 FR 0.0002 REL FR 2 V 0 P
/read /o'er /this /paper /while /the /glass R2 4.01.269
bid nestor bring me spices, ink and /paper, | my PER 3.01. 65
PAPER 79 FR 0.0089 REL FR 57 V 22 P
peruse this paper, madam. TGV 1.02. 34
take the paper; 1.02. 46
to take a paper up that i let fall. 1.02. 71
and is that paper nothing? 1.02. 72
i'll kiss each several paper for amends. 1.02.105
what news then in your paper? 3.01.285 P
come, fool, come; try me in thy paper. 3.01.299 P
deliver'd you a paper that i should not: 4.04.123
will break | as easily as i do tear his paper. 4.04.131
rugby, /baillez me some paper. WIV 1.04. 88 P
for a commodity of brown paper and old ginger, MM 4.03. 5 P
her smock till she have writ a sheet of paper. ADO 2.03.133 P
now you talk of a sheet of paper, i remember a 2.03.134 P
sentences and these paper bullets of the brain 2.03.240 P
her, | for here's a paper written in his hand, 5.04. 86
give me the paper, let me read the same, | and LLL 1.01.116
he hath not eat paper, as it were; 4.02. 25 P
deliver this paper into the royal hand of the 4.02.141 P
here comes one with a paper, god give him grace 4.03. 19 P
i'll drop the paper. 4.03. 41
as would be cramm'd up in a sheet of paper, 5.02. 7
and whiter than the paper it writ on | is the MV 2.04. 13
are some shrowd contents in yond same paper 3.02.243
of any thing | that this same paper brings you. 3.02.250
unpleasant'st words | that ever blotted paper! 3.02.252
lady, | the paper as the body of my friend, 3.02.264
take your paper too, | and let me have them very SHR 1.02.150
here 'tis, here's a paper. AWW 4.03.206 P
me, | commend the paper to his gracious hand, 5.01. 31
pray you, sir, deliver me this paper. 5.02. 15 P
a paper from fortune's close–stool to give to a 5.02. 16 P
wrapp'd in a paper, which contain'd the name 5.03. 94
as many lies as will lie in thy sheet of paper, TN 3.02. 46 P
help me to a candle, and pen, ink, and paper. 4.02. 81 P
good fool, help me to some light and some paper. 4.02.106 P
good fool, some ink, paper, and light; 4.02.110 P
i will fetch you light and paper and ink. 4.02.117 P
know, | from where you do remain let paper show.
R2 1.03.250

make dust our paper, and with rainy eyes | write 3.02.146
appear | at large discoursed in this paper here. 5.06. 10
/or /else | we fortify in paper and in figures, 2H4 1.03. 56
the rest the paper tells. 2.01.135
their cheeks are paper. H5 2.02. 74
his, | sends me a paper to persuade me patience? 3H6 3.03.176
thou didst crown his warlike brows with paper, R3 1.03.174
give me some ink and paper in my tent; 5.03. 23
give me some ink and paper. 5.03. 49
is ink and paper ready? 5.03. 75
look'd he | o' th' inside of the paper? H8 3.02. 78
some spirit put this paper in the packet, | to 3.02.129
i must read this paper; 3.02.208
this paper has undone me. 3.02.210
what that contains, | that paper in your hand? 4.01. 14
i should have been beholding to your paper. 4.01. 21
deliver them this paper. COR 5.06. 2
thou knowest my lodging, get me ink and paper, ROM 5.01. 25
thou wilt give away thyself in paper shortly. TIM 1.02.242 P
good cinna, take this paper, | and look you lay JC 1.03.142
a flint, i found | this paper, thus seal'd up, 2.01. 37
unlock her closet, take forth paper, fold it, MAC 5.01. 6 P
what paper were you reading? LR 1.02. 30 P
if the matter of this paper be certain, you have 3.05. 15 P
with this ungracious paper strike the sight | of 4.06.276
why, fare thee well, i will o'erlook thy paper. 5.01. 50
dame, | or with this paper shall i /stopple it. 5.03.156
most monstrous! o! | know'st thou this paper? 5.03.161
he's busy in the paper. OTH 4.01.230
was this fair paper, this most goodly book, 4.02. 71
now here's another discontented paper, | found 5.02.314
ink and paper, charmian. ANT 1.05. 65
but come, away, | get me ink and paper. 1.05. 76
it, 'twere a paper lost | as offer'd mercy is. CYM 1.03. 3
o damn'd paper, | black as the ink that's on 3.02. 19
why tender'st thou that paper to me with | a 3.04. 11
sword, the paper | hath cut her throat already! 3.04. 32
this paper is the history of my knowledge 3.05. 99
"go get me hither paper, ink, and pen, | yet LUC 1289
first hovering o'er the paper with her quill. 1297
excellent | for every vulgar paper to rehearse? SON 38. 4
PAPER-FAC'D 1 FR 0.0001 REL FR 0 V 1 P
strook thy mother, thou paper-fac'd villain! 2H4 5.04. 10 P
PAPER-MILL 1 FR 0.0001 REL FR 0 V 1 P
and dignity, thou hast built a paper-mill. 2H6 4.07. 37 P
PAPERS 12 FR 0.0013 REL FR 11 V 1 P
and let the papers lie: TGV 1.02. 97
shall these papers lie like tell-tales here? 1.02.130
why, he comes in like a perjure, wearing papers. LLL 4.03. 46
nothing but papers, my lord. 1H4 2.04.533 P
what see you in those papers that you lose | so H5 2.02. 72
mail'd up in shame, with papers on my back, 2H6 2.04. 31
of council out, | must fetch him in he papers. H8 1.01. 80
morning | papers of state he sent me to peruse, 3.02.121
and so bestow these papers as you bade me. JC 1.03.151
rip their hearts, | their papers is more lawful. LR 4.06.261
so should my papers (yellowed with their age) SON 17. 9
tearing of papers, breaking rings a-twain, LC 6
PAPHLAGONIA 1 FR 0.0001 REL FR 1 V 0 P
philadelphos, king | of paphlagonia; ANT 3.06. 71
PAPHOS 3 FR 0.0003 REL FR 3 V 0 P
her deity | cutting the clouds towards paphos; TMP 4.01. 93
so | the dove of paphos might with the crow PER 4.ch. 32
holding their course to paphos, where their VEN 1193
PAPIST 1 FR 0.0001 REL FR 0 V 1 P
charbon the puritan and old poysam the papist, AWW 1.03. 52 P
PAPS 1 FR 0.0001 REL FR 1 V 0 P
for those milk paps, | that through the TIM 4.03.116
PAR* 2 FR 0.0002 REL FR 0 V 2 P
cargo, cargo, cargo, villianda par corbo, cargo. AWW 4.01. 66 P
doute point d'apprendre, par la grace de dieu, H5 3.04. 40 P
PARABLE 1 FR 0.0001 REL FR 0 V 1 P
get such a secret from me but by a parable. TGV 2.05. 40 P
PARACELSUS 1 FR 0.0001 REL FR 0 V 1 P
so i say, both of galen and paracelsus. AWW 2.03. 11 P
PARADISE 12 FR 0.0013 REL FR 10 V 2 P
father and a wise | makes this place paradise. TMP 4.01.124
can lay on nature is a paradise | to what we MM 3.01.130
not that adam that kept the paradise, but that ERR 4.03. 17 P
so wise | to lose an oath to win a paradise?" LLL 4.03. 71
you would for paradise break faith and troth, 4.03.141
see, | seem'd athens as a paradise to me; MND 1.01.205
although | the air of paradise did fan the house AWW 3.02.125
leaving his body as a paradise | t' envelop and H5 1.01. 30
if ye should lead her in a fool's paradise, as ROM 2.04.166 P
fiend | in mortal paradise of such sweet flesh? 3.02. 82
so wise | to break an oath, to win a paradise? PP 3.14
what largeness thinks in paradise was sawn. LC 91
PARADOX 3 FR 0.0003 REL FR 2 V 1 P
o paradox! LLL 4.03.250
you undergo too strict a paradox, | striving to TIM 3.05. 24
this was sometime a paradox, but now the time HAM 3.01.113 P
PARADOXES 2 FR 0.0002 REL FR 1 V 1 P
as stuff for these two to make paradoxes. TRO 1.03.184
these are old fond paradoxes to make fools laugh OTH 2.01.138 P
PARAGON 10 FR 0.0011 REL FR 6 V 4 P
before with such a paragon to their queen. TMP 2.01. 76 P
no; but she is an earthly paragon. TGV 2.04.146
you must say "paragon." MND 4.02. 13 P
too | expos'd this paragon to th' fearful usage WT 5.01.153
the paragon of animals! HAM 2.02.307 P
if thou with caesar paragon again | my man of ANT 1.05. 71
or, if not, | an earthly paragon! CYM 3.06. 43
that paragon, thy daughter, | for whom my heart 5.05.147
find | our paragon to all reports thus blasted, PER 4.01. 35
therefore say what a paragon she is, and thou 4.02.140 P
PARAGON'D 1 FR 0.0001 REL FR 1 V 0 P
creature | that's paragon'd o' th' world. H8 2.04.231
PARAGONS 1 FR 0.0001 REL FR 1 V 0 P
maid | that paragons description and wild fame; OTH 2.01. 62
PARAKEET *(see paraquito)*
PARALLEL 6 FR 0.0006 REL FR 6 V 0 P
and for the liberal arts | without a parallel; TMP 1.02. 74
respect and rich validity | did lack a parallel; AWW 5.03.193
the world's large spaces cannot parallel. TRO 2.02.162
my young remembrance cannot parallel | a fellow MAC 2.03. 62
to counsel cassio to this parallel course, OTH 2.03.349
where was he | that could stand up his parallel, CYM 5.04. 54
PARALLEL'D 1 FR 0.0001 REL FR 1 V 0 P
his life is parallel'd | even with the stroke MM 4.02. 79
PARALLELS 3 FR 0.0003 REL FR 2 V 1 P
for rapes and ravishments he parallels nessus. AWW 4.03.251 P
as near as the extremest ends | of parallels, as TRO 1.03.168
and delves the parallels in beauty's brow, SON 60.10
PARAMOUR 5 FR 0.0005 REL FR 3 V 2 P
and he is a very paramour for a sweet voice. MND 4.02. 12 P
a paramour is, god bless us, a thing of naught. 4.02. 13 P
books | than wanton dalliance with a paramour. 1H6 5.01. 23
a wife, | then how can margaret be thy paramour? 5.03. 82
keeps | thee here in dark to be his paramour? ROM 5.03.105
PARAMOURS 1 FR 0.0001 REL FR 1 V 0 P
encompass'd with thy lustful paramours! 1H6 3.02. 53
PARAPETS 1 FR 0.0001 REL FR 1 V 0 P
tents, | of palisadoes, frontiers, parapets, 1H4 2.03. 52
PARAQUITO 1 FR 0.0001 REL FR 1 V 0 P
come, you paraquito, answer me | directly unto 1H4 2.03. 85
PARASITE 2 FR 0.0002 REL FR 2 V 0 P
my parasite, my soldier, statesman, all. WT 1.02.168
a parasite, a keeper-back of death, | who gently R2 2.02. 70
PARASITE'S 1 FR 0.0001 REL FR 1 V 0 P
when steel grows soft as the parasite's silk, COR 1.09. 45
PARASITES 1 FR 0.0001 REL FR 1 V 0 P
most smiling, smooth, detested parasites, TIM 3.06. 94
PARASITS 1 FR 0.0001 REL FR 1 V 0 P
withal, | but idle sounds resembling parasits, VEN 848
PARCA'S 1 FR 0.0001 REL FR 1 V 0 P
troyan, | to have me fold up parca's fatal web? H5 5.01. 20
PARCEL 14 FR 0.0015 REL FR 9 V 5 P
hold that the lips is parcel of the mouth. WIV 1.01.230 P
it is a branch and parcel of mine oath, | a ERR 5.01.106
"a holy parcel of the fairest dames | that ever LLL 5.02.160
i am glad this parcel of wooers are so MV 1.02.108 P
this youthful parcel | of noble bachelors stand AWW 2.03. 52
stairs, his eloquence the parcel of a reckoning. 1H4 2.04.101 P
of beastliness, that swoll'n parcel of dropsies, 2.04.450 P
ere break the smallest parcel of this vow. 3.02.159
which now mistrust no parcel of my fear, | and 3H6 5.06. 38
as it were, a parcel of their feast, and to be COR 4.05.216 P
here comes a parcel of our hopeful booty, TIT 2.03. 49
judgments are | a parcel of their fortunes, and ANT 3.13. 32
should | parcel the sum of my disgraces by 5.02.163
coz, i would, | though parcel of myself. TNK 5.01. 24
PARCEL-BAWD 1 FR 0.0001 REL FR 0 V 1 P
parcel-bawd; MM 2.01. 63 P
PARCEL-GILT 1 FR 0.0001 REL FR 0 V 1 P
didst swear to me upon a parcel-gilt goblet, 2H4 2.01. 87 P
PARCELL'D 1 FR 0.0001 REL FR 1 V 0 P
their woes are parcell'd, mine is general. R3 2.02. 81
PARCELS 9 FR 0.0010 REL FR 7 V 2 P
had they mark'd him | in parcels as i did, would AYL 3.05.125
between these main parcels of dispatch /effected AWW 4.03. 90 P
sir, for i have about me many parcels of charge. WT 4.04.258 P
the parcels and particulars of our grief, | the 2H4 4.02. 36
importing | the several parcels of his plate, H8 3.02.125
some parcels of their power are forth already, COR 1.02. 32
whereof by parcels she had something heard, OTH 1.03.154
wind | upon his lips their silken parcels hurls. LC 87
comes | their distract parcels in combined sums. 231
PARCH 1 FR 0.0001 REL FR 1 V 0 P
and it were better parch in afric sun | than in TRO 1.03.369
PARCH'D 1 FR 0.0001 REL FR 1 V 0 P
hath thy fiery heart so parch'd thine entrails 3H6 1.04. 87
PARCHED 1 FR 0.0001 REL FR 1 V 0 P
to make his bleak winds kiss my parched lips JN 5.07. 40
PARCHING 4 FR 0.0004 REL FR 4 V 0 P
and to sun's parching heat display'd my cheeks, 1H6 1.02. 77
in winter's cold and summer's parching heat, 2H6 1.01. 81
bak'd and impasted with the parching streets, HAM 2.02.459
that knows not parching heat nor freezing cold, LUC 1145
PARCHMENT 8 FR 0.0009 REL FR 5 V 3 P
if the skin were parchment, and the blows you ERR 3.01. 13
nor brass nor stone nor parchment bears not one, WT 1.02.360
drawn with a pen | upon a parchment, and against JN 5.07. 33
with inky blots and rotten parchment bonds; R2 2.01. 64
of an innocent lamb should be made parchment? 2H6 4.02. 80 P
that parchment, being scribbled o'er, should 4.02. 80 P
but here's a parchment with the seal of caesar, JC 3.02.128
is not parchment made of sheep-skins? HAM 5.01.114 P
PAR'D 3 FR 0.0003 REL FR 2 V 1 P
but par'd my present havings, to bestow | my H8 3.02.159
to have his princely paws par'd all away. TIT 2.03.152
thou hast par'd thy wit o' both sides, and left LR 1.04.187 P
PARD 4 FR 0.0004 REL FR 4 V 0 P
make them | than pard or cat o' mountain. TMP 4.01.261
pard, or boar with bristled hair, | in thy eye MND 2.02. 31
of strange oaths, and bearded like the pard, AYL 2.07.150
pard to the hind, or step-dame to her son, | yea TRO 3.02.194
PARDIE *(see perdie, perdy)*
/PARDON 3 FR 0.0003 REL FR 3 V 0 P
/god /pardon /all /oaths /that /are /broke /to R2 4.01.214
/pardon /me, /sir, /it /was /a /black TIT 3.02. 66
/then /pardon /me /for /reprehending /thee, 3.02. 69
PARDON 311 FR 0.0351 REL FR 271 V 40 P
pardon, master, | i will be correspondent to TMP 1.02.296
and do entreat | thou pardon me my wrongs. 5.01.119
as you look | to have my pardon, trim it 5.01.294
pardon, dear madam, 'tis a passing shame | that TGV 1.02. 17
pardon the fault, i pray. 1.02. 40
pardon me, proteus, all i can is nothing | to 2.04.165
even now about it! i will pardon you. 3.02. 97
pardon me, madam, i have unadvis'd | deliver'd 4.04.122
it may not be; good madam, pardon me. 4.04.126
thou hast prevail'd, i pardon them and thee; 5.04.158
i pray you pardon me; WIV 1.01.218 P
pardon, guest-justice. 2.03. 57 P
i pray you pardon me; 3.03.224 P
wife, come, mistress page, i pray you pardon me; 3.03.227 P
pray heartly pardon me. 3.03.227 P
pardon me, wife, henceforth do what thou wilt. 4.04. 6
pardon, good father! good my mother, pardon! 5.05.216
pardon, good father! good my mother, pardon! 5.05.216
pardon is still the nurse of second woe. MM 2.01.284
i crave your honor's pardon. 2.02. 14
i do think that you might pardon him, | and 2.02. 49
to pardon him that hath from nature stol'n | a 2.04. 43
ignomy in ransom and free pardon | are of two 2.04.111
o, pardon me, my lord, it oft falls out, | to 2.04.117
sign me a present pardon for my brother, | or 2.04.152
so then you hope of pardon from lord angelo? 3.01. 1
let me ask my sister pardon. 3.01.171 P
no, pardon; 3.02.134 P
i hope it is some pardon or reprieve | for the 4.02. 71
and here comes claudio's pardon. 4.02.101
this is his pardon, purchas'd by such sin | for 4.02.108
pardon me, good father, it is against my oath. 4.02.181 P
if yet her brother's pardon be come hither. 4.03.108
hath yet the deputy sent my brother's pardon? 4.03.114
lord angelo, | for her poor brother's pardon. 5.01. 77
pardon it, | the phrase is to the matter. 5.01. 89
pardon, my lord, i will not show my face | until 5.01.169
what you have spoke i pardon. 5.01.361
o, give me pardon, | that i, your vassal, have 5.01.385
honor, you must pardon | for mariana's sake; 5.01.402
pardon me, noble lord, | i thought it was a 5.01.462
and yet here's one in place i cannot pardon. 5.01.499
so, | for we may pity, though not pardon thee. ERR 1.01. 97
i crave your pardon. 1.02. 26
invisible baldrick, all women shall pardon me. ADO 1.01.242 P
no, you shall pardon me. 2.01.126 P
but i beseech your grace pardon me, i was born 2.01.329 P
i cry you mercy, uncle. by your grace's pardon. 2.01.340 P
pardon, goddess of the night, | those that slew 5.03. 12
but pardon me, i am too sudden bold; LLL 2.01.107
to ridiculous smiling — o, pardon me, my stars! 3.01. 77 P
pardon me, madam, for i meant not so. 4.01. 13
under pardon, sir, what are the contents? 4.02.101 P
as thou art, o, pardon love this wrong, | that 4.02.117
ah, good my liege, i pray thee pardon me! 4.03.150
pardon, sir, error: 5.01.130 P
pardon me, sir, this jewel did she wear, | and 5.02.456
gentlemen and soldiers, pardon me, i will not 5.02.704 P
i do entreat your grace to pardon me. MND 1.01. 58
pardon, my lord. 4.01.141
if you pardon, we will mend. 5.01.430
i pardon thee thy life before thou ask it. MV 4.01.369
nay, take my life and all, pardon not that: 4.01.374
recant | the pardon that i late pronounced here. 4.01.392
i humbly do desire your grace of pardon, | i 4.01.402
i pray you, | not to deny me, and to pardon me. 4.01.424
only for this, i pray you pardon me. 4.01.437
pardon me, good lady, | for, by these blessed 5.01.219
pardon this fault, and by my soul i swear | i 5.01.247
pardon me, bassanio, | for, by this ring, the 5.01.258
and pardon me, my gentle gratiano, | for that 5.01.260
pardon me, i pray you. AYL 2.07.106
which you have not — but i pardon you for that, 3.02.376 P
upon the humbled neck | but first begs pardon. 3.05. 6
pardon me, dear rosalind. 4.01. 50 P
pardon me, | i am but as a guiltless messenger. 4.03. 11
of you | to pardon me yet for a night or two; SHR in.2. 119
o, pardon me, signior gremio, i would fain be 2.01. 74
pardon me, sir, the boldness is mine own, | that 2.01. 88
she is your own, else you must pardon me; 2.01.388
sir, pardon me in what i have to say — | your 4.04. 38
pardon, old father, my mistaking eyes, | that 4.05. 45
pardon, i pray thee, for my mad mistaking. 4.05. 49
pardon, sweet father. 5.01.112
pardon, dear father. 5.01.113
then pardon him, sweet father, for my sake. 5.01.130
pardon, madam; AWW 1.03.154
good madam, pardon me! 1.03.185
your pardon, noble mistress! 1.03.186
pardon, my lord, for me and for my tidings. 2.01. 61
here's a man stands that has brought his pardon. 2.01. 63
pardon, my gracious lord; 2.03.167
pray, sir, your pardon. 2.05. 78
pardon me, madam, | if i had given you this at 3.04. 22
but first i beg my pardon — the young lord 5.03. 12
let him not ask our pardon, | the nature of his 5.03. 22
blames, | dear sovereign, pardon to me. 5.03. 37
late, | like a remorseful pardon slowly carried, 5.03. 58
both, both. o, pardon! 5.03.308
pardon me, sir, your bad entertainment. TN 2.01. 33 P
would you'ld pardon me. 3.03. 24
pardon me, sweet one, even for the vows | we 5.01.214
wife, | whom for this time we pardon. WT 2.03.173
pardon | my great profaneness 'gainst thine 3.02.153
o, pardon, that i name them! 4.04. 7
your pardon, sir; 4.04.583
pardon, madam: 5.01.103
the one i have almost forgot — your pardon — 5.01.104
to pardon me all the faults i have committed to 5.02.149 P
pardon me, madam, | i may not go without you to JN 3.01. 65
purchase corrupted pardon of a man | who in that 3.01.166
who in that sale sells pardon from himself; 3.01.167
your grace shall pardon me, i will not back. 5.02. 78
pardon me | that any accent breaking from thy 5.06. 13
and exactly begg'd | your grace's pardon, and i R2 1.01.141
o my liege, | pardon me, if you please; 2.01.187
sister — cousin, i would say — pray pardon me. 2.02.105
pardon me, madam, little joy have i | to breathe 3.04. 81
i do beseech your grace to pardon me. 5.02. 60
i do beseech you pardon me, i may not show it. 5.02. 70
and beg thy pardon ere he do accuse thee. 5.02.113
my mouth, | unless a pardon ere i rise or speak. 5.03. 32
it be, | to win thy after-love i pardon thee. 5.03. 35
if thou do pardon, whosoever pray, | more sins 5.03. 83
say "pardon" first, and afterwards "stand up." 5.03.112
"pardon" should be the first word of thy speech. 5.03.114
say "pardon," king, let pity teach thee how. 5.03.116
no word like "pardon" for kings' mouths so meet. 5.03.118
dost thou teach pardon pardon to destroy? 5.03.120
dost thou teach pardon pardon to destroy? 5.03.120
speak "pardon" as 'tis current in our land, 5.03.123
pity may move thee "pardon" to rehearse. 5.03.128
pardon is all the suit i have in hand. 5.03.130
i pardon him as god shall pardon me. 5.03.131
i pardon him as god shall pardon me. 5.03.131
twice saying "pardon" doth not pardon twain, 5.03.134
twice saying "pardon" doth not pardon twain, 5.03.134
not pardon twain, | but makes one pardon strong. 5.03.135
with all my heart | i pardon him. 5.03.136
unhappy king | (whose wrongs in us god pardon!) 1H4 1.03.149

o, pardon me that i descend so low | to show the 1.03.167
behalf | (as both of you — god pardon it! 1.03.174
first, pardon me, my lord. 2.04.507
irregular, | find pardon on my true submission. 3.02. 28
god pardon thee! 3.02. 29
and pardon absolute for yourself and these 4.03. 50
pardon, and terms of love to all of you? 5.05. 3
sir, pardon, a soldier is better /accommodated 2H4 3.02. 66 P
pardon, sir, i have heard the word. 3.02. 73 P
o, pardon me, my liege! 4.05.138
give me pardon, sir. 5.03.109 P
but pardon, gentles all, | the flat unraised H5 pr 8
o, pardon! pr 15
him on, | and on his more advice we pardon him. 2.02. 43
beseeching god, and you, to pardon me. 2.02.160
my fault, but not my body, pardon, sovereign. 2.02.165
hands hold up | toward heaven, to pardon blood; 4.01.300
penitence comes after all, | imploring pardon. 4.01.305
therefore i beseech your highness pardon me. 4.08. 56 P
pardon the frankness of my mirth, if i answer 5.02.291 P
victorious talbot, pardon my abuse. 1H6 2.03. 67
pardon me, princely henry, and the rest. 4.01. 18
pardon me, gracious lord, | some sudden qualm 2H6 1.01. 53
pray, my lord, pardon me, i took ye for my lord 1.03. 11 P
it is my office, and, madam, pardon me. 2.04.102
pardon, my liege, that i have stay'd so long. 3.01. 94
make thee beg pardon for thy passed speech, 3.02.221
and here pronounce free pardon to them all 4.08. 9
who loves the king, and will embrace his pardon, 4.08. 14
and so, with thanks and pardon to you all, | i 4.09. 20
buckingham, i prithee pardon me, | that i have 5.01. 32
for thy mistaking so, we pardon thee. 5.01.128
his is the right, and therefore pardon me. 3H6 1.01.148
pardon me, margaret, pardon me, sweet son, | the 1.01.228
pardon me, margaret, pardon me, sweet son, | the 1.01.228
pardon me, god, i knew not what i did! 2.05. 69
and pardon, father, for i knew not thee! 2.05. 70
but such as i (without your special pardon) 4.01. 87
go to, we pardon thee; 4.01. 89
prevail, | i then crave pardon of your majesty. 4.06. 8
and he shall pardon thee these outrages. 5.01. 24
pardon me, edward, i will make amends; 5.01.100
sheathe thy sword, i'll pardon thee my death. 5.05. 70
o, god forgive my sins, and pardon thee! 5.06. 60
i beseech your graces both to pardon me: R3 1.01. 84
i do beseech your grace to pardon me, and withal 1.01.103
ay, and forswore himself — which jesu pardon! 1.03.135
god pardon them that are the cause thereof! 1.03.314
and shall that tongue give pardon to a slave? 2.01.104
you straight are on your knees for pardon, 2.01.125
straight are on your knees for pardon, pardon, 2.01.125
and pardon us the interruption | of thy devotion 3.07.102
i do beseech your grace to pardon me, | who, 3.07.105
i am bound by oath, and therefore pardon me. 4.01. 27
proclaim a pardon to the soldiers fled | that in 5.05. 16
but am bold'ned | under your promis'd pardon. H8 1.02. 56
with | free pardon to each man that has denied 1.02.100
every shire, | of the king's grace and pardon. 1.02.104
intercession this revokement | and pardon comes. 1.02.107
i humbly do entreat your highness' pardon, | my 4.02.104
too late, | 'tis like a pardon after execution. 4.02.121
pardon me, pardon me. TRO 1.02. 83 P
pardon me, pardon me. 1.02. 83 P
sir, pardon, 'tis for agamemnon's ears. 1.03.248
give pardon to my speech: 1.03.356
but pardon, father nestor, were your days | as 2.03.253
with the first glance that ever — pardon me — 3.02.118
my lord, i do beseech you pardon me, | 'twas not 3.02.136
o, pardon, i offend. 4.05.182
you wisest grecians, pardon me this brag. 4.05.257
good madam, pardon me, indeed i will not forth. COR 1.03. 87 P
and live you yet? o my sweet lady, pardon. 2.01.180
your honors' pardon; 2.02. 68
i minded him how royal 'twas to pardon | when it 5.01. 18
has sworn you out of reprieve and pardon. 5.02. 50 P
sighs, and conjure thee to pardon rome and thy 5.02. 75 P
pardon me, lords, 'tis the first time that ever 5.06.104
patient yourself, madam, and pardon me. TIT 1.01.121
of thee | to pardon mutius and to bury him. 1.01.363
and at my suit, sweet, pardon what is past. 1.01.431
knees, | you shall ask pardon of his majesty. 1.01.473
for fear they die before their pardon come. 3.01.175
but pardon me, sweet aunt, | and, madam, if my 4.01. 26
o, pardon me, | for when no friends are by, men 5.03.117
therefore pardon me, | and not impute this ROM 2.02.104
god pardon sin! wast thou with rosaline? 2.03. 44
pardon, good mercutio, my business was great, 2.04. 49 P
beg pardon of the prince, and call thee back 3.03.152
god pardon /him! 3.05. 82
i am too young, i pray you pardon me." 3.05.186
but, and you will not wed, i'll pardon you. 3.05.187
to fall prostrate here | and beg your pardon. 4.02. 21
pardon, i beseech you! 4.02. 21
o, pardon me for bringing these ill news, 5.01. 22
o, i beseech you pardon me, my lord, in that. TIM 1.02.213
favor, pardon me | if i speak like a captain. 3.05. 40
pardon him, sweet timandra, for his wits | are 4.03. 89
o, pardon, sir, it doth; JC 2.01.103
pardon me, caesar, for my dear dear love | to 2.02.102
pardon, caesar! 3.01. 55
caesar, pardon! 3.01. 55
pardon me, julius! 3.01.204
pardon me, caius cassius! 3.01.211
by your pardon — | i will myself into the 3.01.235
o, pardon me, thou bleeding piece of earth, 3.01.254
which, pardon me, i do not mean to read — | and 3.02.131
under your pardon. 4.03.213
implor'd your highness' pardon, and set forth MAC 1.04. 6
but i shall crave your pardon; 4.03. 20
and bow them to your gracious leave and pardon. HAM 1.02. 56
your pardon and my return shall be the end of 3.02.317 P
times | virtue itself of vice must pardon beg, 3.04.154
when i shall, first asking you pardon thereunto, 4.07. 46 P
give me your pardon, sir. 5.02.226
i will, my lord, i pray you pardon me. 5.02.291
pardon me, royal sir, | election makes not up in LR 1.01.205
i beseech you, sir, pardon me. 1.02. 36 P
i beseech you pardon me, my lord, if i be 1.04. 64 P
none of these, my lord, i beseech your pardon. 1.04. 83 P
yours | though i condemn not, yet, under pardon, 1.04.342
pardon me! 2.01. 28
i pardon that man's life. 4.06.109
pardon, dear madam, | yet to be known shortens 4.07. 8
within our power, | shall never see his pardon; 5.01. 68
good your grace, pardon me: OTH 1.03. 52
i pray you pardon me, i cannot speak. 2.03.189
good my lord, pardon me: 3.03.133
i humbly do beseech you of your pardon | for too 3.03.212
but, pardon me, i do not in position 3.03.234
pardon me, bianca. 3.04.176
if any such there be, heaven pardon him! 4.02.135
a halter pardon him! 4.02.136
o, pardon me; 'twill do me good to walk. 4.03. 2
i cry your gentle pardon; 5.01. 93
i do believe it, and i ask your pardon. 5.02.300
by your most gracious pardon, | i sing but after ANT 1.05. 72
which was as much | as to have ask'd him pardon. 2.02. 79
do | so far ask pardon as befits mine honor | to 2.02. 97
pardon what i have spoke, | for 'tis a studied, 2.02.136
come too short, | the actor may plead pardon. 2.05. 9
i crave your highness' pardon. 2.05. 98
whereon, i begg'd | his pardon for return. 3.06. 60
o, my pardon! 3.11. 61
pardon, pardon! 3.11. 68
pardon, pardon! 3.11. 68
cried he? and begg'd 'a pardon? 3.13.132
thee, cleopatra, and | weep for my pardon. 4.14. 45
o, sir, pardon me! 4.14. 80
dear my lord, pardon — i dare not, | lest i be 4.15. 22
by your pardon, sir, i was then a young CYM 1.04. 43 P
give me your pardon. 1.06.162
pray your pardon. 1.06.178
pardon me, gods! 3.06. 86
the gods hear, i hope | they'll pardon it. 4.02.379
prince, pardon me, or strike me, if you please, PER 1.02. 46
pardon old gower — this long's the text. 2.ch. 40
pardon us, sir; 3.01. 51 P
o, pardon me! TNK 1.01.117
o, pardon me! 2.03. 50
yet pardon me hard language. 3.01.106
and got your pardon, and discover'd how | and by 4.01. 19
your daughter's, | whose pardon is procur'd too; 4.01. 21
an antic 'fore the duke, | and beg his pardon." 4.01. 76
on my knees | i ask thy pardon: 4.02. 37
pardon me, | if i were there, i'ld wink. 5.03. 17
sir, pardon me, | the title of a kingdom may be 5.03. 32
you'll stand our friend to procure our pardon. STM II.C 143 P
yet pardon me, i felt a kind of fear | when as i VEN 998
o yes, dear friend, i pardon crave of thee, PP 10.11
belong | yourself to pardon of self–doing crime. SON 58.12
"'o, pardon me, in that my boast is true: LC 246

/PARDON'D 1 FR 0.0001 REL FR 1 V 0 P
ere we come to fall, | or /pardon'd being down? HAM 3.03. 50

PARDON'D 7 FR 0.0008 REL FR 7 V 0 P
and pardon'd the deceiver, dwell | in this bare TMP ep 7
as you from crimes would pardon'd be, | let your ep 19
you are pardon'd, isabel; MM 5.01.387
brother, for his sake | is he pardon'd, and, for 5.01.491
at whose request the king hath pardon'd them, JN 5.06. 35
some shall be pardon'd, and some punished: ROM 5.03.308
may one be pardon'd and retain th' offense? HAM 3.03. 56

PARDONED 4 FR 0.0004 REL FR 3 V 1 P
fast for thy offenses ere thou be pardoned. LLL 1.02.147 P
pleas'd | not to be pardoned, am content withal. R2 2.01.188
ground | till bullingbrook have pardoned thee. 5.02.117
by you being pardoned, we commit no crime | to PER 4.04. 5

PARDONER 1 FR 0.0001 REL FR 1 V 0 P
such sin | for which the pardoner himself is in. MM 4.02.109

PARDONING 2 FR 0.0002 REL FR 2 V 0 P
until thou bid me joy | by pardoning rutland, my R2 5.03. 96
mercy but murders, pardoning those that kill. ROM 3.01.197

/PARDON–ME'S 1 FR 0.0001 REL FR 0 V 1 P
these fashion–mongers, these /pardon–me's, who ROM 2.04. 33 P

PARDONNE 1 FR 0.0001 REL FR 1 V 0 P
speak it in french, king, say "pardonne moy." R2 5.03.119

PARDONNER 2 FR 0.0002 REL FR 0 V 2 P
supplie, pour l'amour de dieu, me pardonner! H5 4.04. 41 P
son jurement de pardonner aucun prisonnier; 4.04. 50 P

PARDONNEZ 1 FR 0.0001 REL FR 0 V 1 P
o, pardonnez moi! H5 4.04. 21 P

PARDONNEZ–MOI 1 FR 0.0001 REL FR 0 V 1 P
pardonnez–moi, i cannot tell wat is "like me." H5 5.02.108 P

PARDON'S 1 FR 0.0001 REL FR 1 V 0 P
pardon's the word to all. CYM 5.05.422

PARDONS 8 FR 0.0009 REL FR 6 V 2 P
for claudio's, | th' offense pardons itself. MM 5.01.534
both your pardons, | that e'er i put between WT 5.03.147
my duty, and my speech, to beg your pardons. 2H4 ep 3 P
be hang'd with your pardons about your necks? 2H6 4.08. 22 P
a gracious king that pardons all offenses H8 2.02. 67
my nobler friends, i crave their pardons. COR 3.01. 65
for they have pardons, being ask'd, as free | as 3.02. 88
a great likelihood | of both their pardons; TNK 4.01. 7

PARDON'T 1 FR 0.0001 REL FR 1 V 0 P
wrong, | but pardon't, as you are a gentleman. HAM 5.02.227

PARE 4 FR 0.0004 REL FR 1 V 3 P
let not him that plays the lion pare his nails, MND 4.02. 41 P
'tis too late to pare her nails now. AWW 5.02. 29 P
like a mad lad, | pare thy nails, dad. TN 4.02.130
that every one may pare his nails with a wooden H5 4.04. 72 P

'PAREL *(also apparel)*

'PAREL 1 FR 0.0001 REL FR 1 V 0 P
i'll bring him the best 'parel that i have, LR 4.01. 49

/PARENT 1 FR 0.0001 REL FR 0 V 1 P
/between /the /child /and /the /parent, /death, LR 1.02.145 P

PARENT 3 FR 0.0003 REL FR 3 V 0 P
like a good parent, did beget of him | a TMP 1.02. 94
all this while | between the child and parent. COR 5.03. 56
he's both their parent, and he is their grave, PER 2.03. 46

PARENTAGE 17 FR 0.0019 REL FR 16 V 1 P
he ask'd me of what parentage i was. AYL 3.04. 36 P
request, | that, upon knowledge of my parentage, SHR 2.01. 95
you might do much. | what is your parentage? TN 1.05.277
"what is your parentage?" 1.05.289
what parentage? 5.01.231
body) | i was the next by birth and parentage; 1H6 2.05. 73
graceless, wilt thou deny thy parentage? 5.04. 14
and, ignorant of his birth and parentage, 2H6 4.02.144
now provided | a gentleman of noble parentage, ROM 3.05.179
him | of whence he is, his name, and parentage. PER 2.03. 74
of whence you are, your name, and parentage. 2.03. 80
kings, | but time hath rooted out my parentage, 5.01. 92
my fortunes — parentage — good parentage — 5.01. 97
my fortunes — parentage — good parentage — 5.01. 97
i said, my lord, if you did know my parentage, 5.01. 99
report thy parentage. 5.01.129
she never would tell | her parentage; 5.01.188

PARENT'S 1 FR 0.0001 REL FR 1 V 0 P
flesh | by the defiling of her parent's bed; PER 1.01.131

PARENTS' 5 FR 0.0005 REL FR 5 V 0 P
our gentry than our parents' noble names, | in WT 1.02.393
orphans for their parents' timeless death — 3H6 5.06. 42
with their death bury their parents' strife. ROM pr 8
and the continuance of their parents' rage, pr 10
do't in your parents' eyes! TIM 4.01. 8

PARENTS 12 FR 0.0013 REL FR 10 V 2 P
those, for their parents were exceeding poor, ERR 1.01. 56
these are the parents to these children, | which 5.01.361
i have with the parents of the foresaid child or LLL 4.02.156 P
we are their parents and original. MND 2.01.117
happy the parents of so fair a child! SHR 4.05. 39
no note upon my parents, his all noble. AWW 1.03.157
for, by the honor of my parents, i | have WT 1.02.442
fame, | of parents good, of fist most valiant. H5 4.01. 46
the parents live whose children thou hast R3 4.04.393
heaven ever laid up to make parents happy | may H8 5.04. 7
obey thy parents, keep thy word's justice, swear LR 3.04. 80 P
seats we came, | our parents and us twain, CYM 5.04. 70

PARFECT 1 FR 0.0001 REL FR 0 V 1 P
say, but to parfect one man in one poor man, LLL 5.02.501 P

PARING 1 FR 0.0001 REL FR 0 V 1 P
consumes itself to the very paring, and so dies AWW 1.01.142 P

PARING–KNIFE 1 FR 0.0001 REL FR 0 V 1 P
great round beard, like a glover's paring–knife? WIV 1.04. 21 P

PARINGS 3 FR 0.0003 REL FR 2 V 1 P
some devils ask but the parings of one's nail, ERR 4.03. 71
and the very parings of our nails | shall pitch 1H6 3.01.102
here comes one o' the parings. LR 1.04.188 P

PARIS' 3 FR 0.0003 REL FR 3 V 0 P
read o'er the volume of young paris' face, | and ROM 1.03. 81
speak briefly, can you like of paris' love? 1.03. 96
bed, | acquaint her here of my son paris' love, 3.04. 16

PARIS* *(also parish*)*

/PARIS* 1 FR 0.0001 REL FR 1 V 0 P
/with /wanton /paris /sleeps — /and /that's TRO pr 10

PARIS* 76 FR 0.0086 REL FR 58 V 18 P
one, | though paris came in hope to speed alone. SHR 1.02.245
welcome to paris. AWW 1.02. 22
an intent — speak truly — | to go to paris? 1.03.219
this was your motive | for paris, was it? speak. 1.03.231
else paris, and the medicine, and the king, 1.03.233
'a was a botcher's prentice in paris, from 4.03.186 P
i did present him with the paris balls. H5 2.04.131
he'll make your paris louvre shake for it, 2.04.132
paris, guysors, poictiers, are all quite lost. 1H6 1.01. 61
is paris lost? 1.01. 65
and then depart to paris to the king, | for 3.02.128
now, governor of paris, take your oath: 4.01. 3
and now to paris in this conquering vein, | all 4.07. 95
then march to paris, royal charles of france, 5.02. 4
as did the youthful paris once to greece, | with 5.05.104
infancy | crowned in paris in despite of foes? 2H6 1.01. 94
paris is lost, the state of normandy | stands on 1.01.215
on his will | till paris was besieg'd, famish'd, 1.03.172
was crown'd in paris but at nine months old. R3 2.03. 17
that paris is returned home and hurt. TRO 1.01.109
let paris bleed, 'tis but a scar to scorn; 1.01.111
paris is gor'd with menelaus' horn. 1.01.112
she prais'd his complexion above paris. 1.02. 98 P
why, paris hath color enough. 1.02. 99 P
you, i think helen loves him better than paris. 1.02.108 P
she, "which of these hairs is paris my husband?" 1.02.163 P
and helen so blush'd, and paris so chaf'd, and 1.02.166 P
yonder comes paris, yonder comes paris. 1.02.212 P
yonder comes paris, yonder comes paris. 1.02.212 P
paris? 1.02.238 P
paris is dirt to him, and i warrant helen, to 1.02.238 P
paris should do some vengeance on the greeks. 2.02. 73
if you'll avouch 'twas wisdom paris went — | as 2.02. 84
our fire–brand brother, paris, burns us all. 2.02.110
paris should ne'er retract what he hath done, 2.02.141
paris, you speak | like one besotted on your 2.02.142
paris and troilus, you have both said well, 2.02.163
do you not follow the young lord paris? 3.01. 2 P
sir, at the request of paris my lord, who is 3.01. 31 P
i come to speak with paris from the prince 3.01. 38 P
have it, my lord, if it be not my lord paris. 3.01.100 P
'twill make us proud to be his servant, paris! 3.01.155
occasion to lie long | as /you, prince paris, 4.01. 5
hear me, paris: 4.01. 69
there is at hand | paris your brother, and 4.02. 61
now, | for thus popp'd paris in his hardiment, 4.05. 28
paris and i kiss evermore for him. 4.05. 34
no, paris is not, for you know 'tis true | that 4.05. 43
'loo, paris, 'loo! 5.07. 10 P
'loo, paris, 'loo! 5.07. 11 P
but woo her, gentle paris, get her heart, | my ROM 1.02. 16
the valiant paris seeks you for his love. 1.03. 74
o, there is a nobleman in town, one paris, that 2.04.201 P
and tell her that paris is the properer man, but 2.04.204 P
sir paris, i will make a desperate tender | of 3.04. 12
the county paris, at saint peter's church, 3.05.114
whom you know i hate, | rather than paris. 3.05.123
to go with paris to saint peter's church, | or i 3.05.154
green, so quick, so fair an eye | as paris hath. 3.05.221
if, rather than to marry county paris, | thou 4.01. 71
o, bid me leap, rather than marry paris, | from 4.01. 77
home, be merry, give consent | to marry paris. 4.01. 90
i will walk myself | to county paris, to prepare 4.02. 45
and trim her up, | i'll go and chat with paris. 4.04. 26
the county paris hath set up his rest | that you 4.05. 6
and go, sir paris. 4.05. 92
mercutio's kinsman, noble county paris! 5.03. 75
he told me paris should have married juliet. 5.03. 78

what, paris too? 5.03.144
and paris too. 5.03.156
some "juliet," and some "paris," and all run 5.03.192
sovereign, here lies the county paris slain, 5.03.195
have married her perforce | to county paris. 5.03.239
lay | the noble paris and true romeo dead. 5.03.259
inquire me first what danskers are in paris, HAM 2.01. 7
thy heat of lust, fond paris, did incur | this LUC 1473
PARISH* *(also paris*)*
PARISH* 11 FR 0.0012 REL FR 5 V 6 P
or seven, the most sufficient of your parish. MM 2.01.273 P
the parish curate, alexander; LLL 5.02.535 P
the "why" is plain as way to parish church: AYL 2.07. 52
even such kin as the parish heckfers are to the 2H4 2.02.157 P
not so, | i did beget her, all the parish knows. 1H6 5.04. 11
within the parish | saint lawrence poultney, did H8 1.02.152
do you take the court for parish garden? 5.03. 2 P
color | i'ld let a parish of such clotens blood, CYM 4.02.168
gaping till they swallow'd the whole parish, PER 2.01. 34 P
bells, steeple, church, and parish up again. 2.01. 42 P
(if i have any skill) in all the parish, | and TNK 5.02. 53
PARISHIONERS 2 FR 0.0002 REL FR 0 V 2 P
the lord for you, and so may my parishioners, LLL 4.02. 74 P
love have you wearied your parishioners withal, AYL 3.02.156 P
PARISH-TOP 1 FR 0.0001 REL FR 0 V 1 P
his brains turn o' th' toe like a parish-top. TN 1.03. 42 P
PARISIANS 1 FR 0.0001 REL FR 1 V 0 P
'tis said the stout parisians do revolt, | and 1H6 5.02. 2
PARIS-WARD 1 FR 0.0001 REL FR 1 V 0 P
their powers are marching unto paris-ward. 1H6 3.03. 30
PARITORS 1 FR 0.0001 REL FR 1 V 0 P
and great general | of trotting paritors — o my LLL 3.01.186
PARK 19 FR 0.0021 REL FR 10 V 9 P
i will cut his troat in de park; WIV 1.04.109 P
come, come, walk in the park. 3.03.224 P
word they'll meet him in the park at midnight? 4.04. 18 P
be you in the park about midnight, at herne's 5.01. 11 P
go before into the park; 5.03. 4 P
and taken following her into the park, which, LLL 1.01.208 P
it is ycliped thy park. 1.01.240 P
that i took in the park with the rational hind 1.02.118 P
for this damsel, i must keep her at the park; 1.02.131 P
the princess comes to hunt here in the park, 3.01.164
from the park let us conduct them thither; 4.03.371
over park, over pale, | thorough flood, thorough MND 2.01. 4
did i not bid thee meet me in the park, | and SHR 4.01.130
bid butler lead him forth into the park. 1H4 2.03. 72
hither | into this chiefest thicket of the park. 3H6 4.05. 3
o, thus i found her straying in the park, TIT 3.01. 88
which stands | as neptune's park, ribb'd and CYM 3.01. 19
i'll be a park, and thou shalt be my deer: VEN 231
then be my deer, since i am such a park, | no 239
PARK-CORNER 1 FR 0.0001 REL FR 1 V 0 P
your horse stands ready at the park-corner. 3H6 4.05. 19
PARK'D 1 FR 0.0001 REL FR 1 V 0 P
how are we park'd and bounded in a pale, | a 1H6 4.02. 45
PARK-GATE 1 FR 0.0001 REL FR 1 V 0 P
my coach, which stays for us | at the park-gate; MV 3.04. 83
PARKS 2 FR 0.0002 REL FR 2 V 0 P
dispark'd my parks and fell'd my forest woods, R2 3.01. 23
my parks, my walks, my manors that i had, | even 3H6 5.02. 24
PARK-WARD 1 FR 0.0001 REL FR 0 V 1 P
the pittie-ward, the park-ward — every way; WIV 3.01. 5 P
PARLE 11 FR 0.0012 REL FR 8 V 3 P
that every day with parle encounter me, | in thy TGV 1.02. 5
nature of our quarrel yet never brook'd parle, SHR 1.01.115 P
our trumpet call'd you to this gentle parle — JN 2.01.205
behold, the french amaz'd vouchsafe a parle, 2.01.226
this is the latest parle we will admit; H5 3.03. 2
ecoutez, dites-moi si je parle bien: 3.04. 17 P
il est /meilleur que l'anglois lequel je parle. 5.02.189 P
go, trumpet, to the walls, and sound a parle. 3H6 5.01. 16
rome's emperor, and nephew, break the parle, TIT 5.03. 19
so frown'd he once, when, in an angry parle, HAM 1.01. 62
at a higher rate | than a command to parle. 1.03.123
PARLER 1 FR 0.0001 REL FR 0 V 1 P
il faut que j'apprenne a parler. H5 3.04. 5 P
PARLES 1 FR 0.0001 REL FR 0 V 1 P
ete en angleterre, et tu bien parles le langage. H5 3.04. 2 P
PARLEY 24 FR 0.0027 REL FR 21 V 3 P
therefore, above the rest, we parley to you: TGV 4.01. 58
to parley with the sole inheritor | of all LLL 2.01. 5
their purpose is to parley, to court, and dance, 5.02.122
to parley or to fight, therefore prepare. JN 2.01. 78
and didst in signs again parley with sin, | yea, 4.02.238
insinuation, parley, and base truce | to arms 5.01. 68
or sound so base a parley, my teeth shall tear R2 1.01.192
through brazen trumpet send the breath of parley 3.03. 33
shame, | in such a parley should i answer thee. 1H4 3.01.201
well, by my will we shall admit no parley. 2H4 4.01.157
the town sounds a parley. H5 3.02.137 P
summon a parley, we will talk with him. 1H6 3.03. 35
a parley with the duke of burgundy! 3.03. 36
who craves a parley with the burgundy? 3.03. 37
father's castle walls | we'll crave a parley, to 5.03.130
will parley with jack cade their general. 2H6 4.04. 13
to sound retreat or parley when i command them 4.08. 4 P
break off the parley, for scarce i can refrain 3H6 2.02.110
say that the emperor requests a parley | of TIT 4.04.101
he craves a parley at your father's house, 5.01.159
they stand, and would have parley. JC 5.01. 21
that such a hideous trumpet calls to parley MAC 2.03. 82
methinks it sounds a parley to provocation. OTH 2.03. 23 P
begin | to sound a parley to his heartless foe, LUC 471
PARLEY'D 1 FR 0.0001 REL FR 1 V 0 P
this tongue hath parley'd unto foreign kings 2H6 4.07. 77
PARLEYS 1 FR 0.0001 REL FR 1 V 0 P
and, good now, | no more of these vain parleys; TNK 3.03. 10
PARLEZ 1 FR 0.0001 REL FR 0 V 1 P
le francois que vous parlez, il est /meilleur H5 5.02.189 P
PARLIAMENT 21 FR 0.0023 REL FR 19 V 2 P
a bill in the parliament for the putting down of WIV 2.01. 29 P
i am in parliament pledge for his truth | and R2 5.02. 44
to us the speaker in his parliament, | to us th' 2H4 4.02. 18
now call we our high court of parliament, | and 5.02.134
the king hath call'd his parliament, my lord. 5.05.103
shall be /wip'd out in the next parliament, 1H6 2.04.117
and therefore haste i to the parliament, 2.05.127
god speed the parliament! 3.02. 60
i summon your grace to his majesty's parliament, 2H6 2.04. 70
what, will your highness leave the parliament? 3.01.197
my mouth shall be the parliament of england. 4.07. 15 P
london, | to call a present court of parliament. 5.03. 25
the queen this day here holds her parliament, 3H6 1.01. 35
the bloody parliament shall this be call'd, 1.01. 39
lord, here in the parliament | let us assail the 1.01. 64
to make a shambles of the parliament house! 1.01. 71
bed, | until that act of parliament be repeal'd 1.01.249
was't you that revell'd in our parliament, | and 1.04. 71
to dash our late decree in parliament | touching 2.01.118
his oath enrolled in the parliament; 2.01.173
have caus'd him, by new act of parliament, | to 2.02. 91
PARLING 1 FR 0.0001 REL FR 1 V 0 P
could pick no meaning from their parling looks, LUC 100
PARLOR 2 FR 0.0002 REL FR 2 V 0 P
good margaret, run thee to the parlor, | there ADO 3.01. 1
they sit conferring by the parlor fire. SHR 5.02.102
PARLORS 1 FR 0.0001 REL FR 1 V 0 P
bells in your parlors, wild-cats in your OTH 2.01.110
PARLOUS *(also perilous)*
PARLOUS 3 FR 0.0003 REL FR 1 V 2 P
by'r lakin, a parlous fear. MND 3.01. 13 P
thou art in a parlous state, shepherd. AYL 3.02. 44 P
a parlous boy! go to, you are too shrewd. R3 2.04. 35
PARLOUSLY 1 FR 0.0001 REL FR 1 V 0 P
edify the duke | most parlously in our behalfs. TNK 2.03. 53
PARMACITI 1 FR 0.0001 REL FR 1 V 0 P
on earth | was parmaciti for an inward bruise, 1H4 1.03. 58
PAROLLES 13 FR 0.0014 REL FR 5 V 8 P
monsieur parolles, my lord calls for you. AWW 1.01.187 P
monsieur parolles, you were born under a 1.01.190 P
sweet monsieur parolles! 2.01. 39 P
o my parolles, they have married me! 2.03.272
parolles, was it not? 3.02. 85
one parolles, a filthy officer he is in those 3.05. 16 P
monsieur parolles. 3.05. 58
my lord, this is monsieur parolles, the gallant 4.03.141 P
as he vow'd to thee in thine ear, parolles." 4.03.232 P
god bless you, captain parolles. 4.03.315 P
and, parolles, live | safest in shame! 4.03.337
my name, my good lord, is parolles. 5.02. 39 P
his name's parolles. 5.03.202
PARRICIDE 1 FR 0.0001 REL FR 1 V 0 P
not confessing | their cruel parricide, filling MAC 3.01. 31
PARRICIDES 1 FR 0.0001 REL FR 1 V 0 P
'gainst parricides did all the thunder bend, LR 2.01. 46
PARROT 6 FR 0.0006 REL FR 0 V 6 P
the prophecy like the parrot, "beware the rope's ERR 4.04. 42 P
more clamorous than a parrot against rain, more AYL 4.01.151 P
fellow should have fewer words than a parrot, 1H4 2.04. 99 P
elder hath not his pole claw'd like a parrot. 2H4 2.04.259 P
the parrot will not do more for an almond than TRO 5.02.193 P
and speak parrot? OTH 2.03.279 P
PARROTS 2 FR 0.0002 REL FR 1 V 1 P
eyes, | and laugh like parrots at a bagpiper; MV 1.01. 53
grow commendable in none only but parrots. 3.05. 46 P
PARROT-TEACHER 1 FR 0.0001 REL FR 0 V 1 P
well, you are a rare parrot-teacher. ADO 1.01.138 P
PARSLEY 1 FR 0.0001 REL FR 0 V 1 P
to the garden for parsley to stuff a rabbit, and SHR 4.04.101 P
PARSNIP 1 FR 0.0001 REL FR 0 V 1 P
for what's a sorry parsnip to a good heart? STM II.C 9 P
PARSNIPS 1 FR 0.0001 REL FR 0 V 1 P
partly comes through the eating of parsnips. STM II.C 15 P
PARSON 15 FR 0.0017 REL FR 0 V 15 P
and a gentleman born, master parson, who writes WIV 1.01. 9 P
tell master parson evans i will do what i can 1.04. 33 P
he came of an errand to me from parson hugh. 1.04. 77 P
for, believe me, i hear the parson is no jester. 2.01.209 P
butter, parson hugh the welshman with my cheese, 2.02.302 P
how now, master parson? 3.01. 36 P
do you study them both, master parson? 3.01. 45 P
come to you to do a good office, master parson. 3.01. 50 P
nay, good master parson, keep in your weapon. 3.01. 73 P
shall i lose my parson? 3.01.103 P
fault with the tithe-woman if i were the parson. AWW 1.03. 85 P
jove bless thee, master parson. TN 4.02. 11 P
so i, being master parson, am master parson. 4.02. 15 P
so i, being master parson, am master parson; 4.02. 15 P
well said, master parson. 4.02. 27 P
PARSON'S 2 FR 0.0002 REL FR 2 V 0 P
and coughing drowns the parson's saw | and birds LLL 5.02.922
tickling a parson's nose as 'a lies asleep, ROM 1.04. 80
/PART 4 FR 0.0004 REL FR 3 V 1 P
/part /of /your /cares /you /give /me /with R2 4.01.194
/yet, /for /your /part, /it /not /appears /to 2H4 4.01.105
/nor /any /other /part | belonging to a man. ROM 2.02. 41
/monopoly /out, /they /would /have /part /an't. LR 1.04.153 P
PART 478 FR 0.0540 REL FR 356 V 122 P
to have no screen between this part he play'd TMP 1.02.107
for my part, the sea cannot drown me; 3.02. 13 P
nobler reason, 'gainst my fury | do i take part. 5.01. 27
which, part of it, i'll waste | with such 5.01.303
how did thy master part with madam julia? TGV 2.05. 11 P
and, ere i part with thee, confer at large | of 3.01.255
our youth got me to play the woman's part, | and 4.04.160
weep agood, | for i did play a lamentable part. 4.04.166
sir, for my part, i say the gentleman had drunk WIV 1.01.174 P
truly, for mine own part, i would little or 3.04. 62 P
to one that can my part in him advertise. MM 1.01. 41
for mine own part, i never come into any room in 2.01.208 P
to a well-wish'd king | quit their own part, and 2.04. 28
but to accuse him so, | that is your part. 4.06. 3
sweet isabel, take my part! 5.01.430
her part, poor soul! ERR 1.01.107
am better than thy dear self's better part. 2.02.123
though my cates be mean, take them in good part; 3.01. 28
which was best, we shall part with neither. 3.01. 67
plead on /her part some cause to you unknown; 3.01. 91
it is thyself, mine own self's better part: 3.02. 61
in what part of her body stands ireland? 3.02.116 P
much deserv'd on his part, and equally ADO 1.01. 12 P
now that is your grace's part. 1.01.213 P
could maintain his part but in the force of his 1.01.236 P
i will assume thy part in some disguise, | and 1.01.321
you may do the part of an honest man in it. 2.01.166 P
my lord, i have play'd the part of lady fame. 2.01.213 P
let it be thy part | to praise him more than 3.01. 18
fear you not my part of the dialogue. 3.01. 31
but truly, for mine own part, if i were as 3.05. 21 P
i might have said, "no part of it is mine; 4.01.134
for my part, i am so attir'd in wonder, | i know 4.01.144
you are almost come to part almost a fray. 5.01.114 P
not adminit any good part to intermingle with them 5.02. 64 P
for thy part, claudio, i did think to have 5.04.109 P
how canst thou part sadness and melancholy, my LLL 1.02. 7 P
which | one part of aquitaine is bound to us, 2.01.135
for fame's sake, for praise, an outward part, 4.01. 32
on thy picture, and my heart on thy every part. 4.01. 86 P
and here is part of my rhyme, and here my 4.03. 13 P
ay, or i would these hands might never part. 5.02. 57
and quite divorce his memory from his part. 5.02.150
only to part friends. 5.02.220
let's part the word. 5.02.249
heart, | that put armado's page out of his part! 5.02.336
for mine own part, i am, as /they say, but to 5.02.501 P
for mine own part, i know not the degree of the 5.02.506 P
for mine own part, i breathe free breath. 5.02.722 P
if this thou do deny, let our hands part, 5.02.811
ready. name what part i am for, and proceed. MND 1.02. 18 P
play ercles rarely, or a part to tear a cat in, 1.02. 29 P
snug, the joiner, you the lion's part. 1.02. 64 P
have you the lion's part written? 1.02. 66 P
you can play no part but pyramus; 1.02. 85 P
and for her sake i will not part with him. 2.01.137
then, for the third part of a minute, hence, 2.02. 2
you speak all your part at once, cues and all. 3.01.100 P
and from thy hated presence part i /so: 3.02. 80
in hermia's love i yield you up my part; 3.02.165
she shall not, though you take her part. 3.02.322
speak not of helena, | take not her part. 3.02.333
every man look o'er his part; 4.02. 38 P
thus have i, wall, my part discharged so; 5.01.204
the better part of my affections would | be with MV 1.01. 16
a stage, where every man must play a part, | and 1.01. 78
taken | in what part of your body pleaseth me. 1.03.151
but, for mine own part, as i have set up my rest 2.02.102 P
therefore i part with him, and part with him 2.05. 49
and part with him | to one that i would have him 2.05. 49
thus losers part. 2.07. 77
in the narrow seas that part | the french and 2.08. 28
i saw bassanio and antonio part: 2.08. 36
i, for my part, knew the tailor that made the 3.01. 26 P
and shylock, for his own part, knew the bird was 3.01. 28 P
which when you part from, lose, or give away, 3.02.172
for my part, my lord, | my purpose was not to 3.02.226
for mine own part, | i have toward heaven 3.04. 26
were in six parts, and every part a ducat, | i 4.01. 86
or the division of the twentith part | of one 4.01.329
would he were gelt that had it, for my part, 5.01.144
to part so slightly with your wive's first gift, 5.01.167
and made him swear | never to part with it, and 5.01.171
for my part, he keeps me rustically at home, or, AYL 1.01. 7 P
you shall have some part of your will. 1.01. 77 P
all the beholders take his part with weeping. 1.02.131 P
o, they take the part of a better wrastler than 1.03. 22 P
shall we part, sweet girl? 1.03. 98
"thus misery doth part | the flux of company." 2.01. 51
for my part, i had rather bear with you than 2.04. 11 P
and so he plays his part. 2.07.157
but were i not the better part made mercy, | i 3.01. 2
cleopatra's majesty, | atalanta's better part, 3.02.147
are for the most part cattle of this color; 3.02.415 P
but, for my part, | i love him not, nor hate him 3.05.126
and break but a part of the thousand part of a 4.01. 46 P
a part of the thousand part of a minute in the 4.01. 46 P
clubs cannot part them. 5.02. 41 P
you and you no cross shall part; 5.04.131
i warrant you we will play our part | as he SHR in.1. 69
but sure that part | was aptly fitted and in.1. 86
virtue and that part of philosophy | will i 1.01. 18
for who shall bear your part, | and be in padua 1.01.194
signior hortensio, come you to part the fray? 1.02. 23
i see you do not mean to part with her, | or 2.01. 64
nay then good night our part! 2.01.301
faith, gentlemen, now i play a merchant's part, 2.01.326
word, | though in some part enforced to digress, 3.02.10/
to speak on the part of virginity is to accuse AWW 1.01.136 P
have they leave | to stand on either part. 1.02. 15
but what at full i know, thou know'st no part, 2.01.132
best set thy lower part where thy nose stands. 2.03.252 P
nothing, is to be a great part of your title, 2.04. 26 P
holy seems the quarrel | upon your grace's part; 3.01. 5
for my part, i only hear your son was run away. 3.02. 43 P
brings in the champion honor on my part, 4.02. 50
the stronger part of it by her own letters, 4.03. 55 P
and thou let part so, sir andrew, would thou TN 1.03. 61 P
and you part so, mistress, i would i might never 1.03. 63 P
sound, | and all is semblative a woman's part. 1.04. 34
studied, and that question's out of my part. 1.05.179 P
my part of death, no one so true | did share it. 2.04. 57
i will not give my part of this sport for a 2.05.180 P
possibly have found in any part of illyria. 3.04.268 P
and part being prompted by your present trouble, 3.04.343
sweet sister, | we will not part from hence. 5.01.385
thanks a while, | and pay them when you part. WT 1.02. 10
we'll part the time between 's then; 1.02. 18
and i | play too, but so disgrac'd a part, whose 1.02.188
comfort | the gracious queen, part of his theme, 1.02.459
cause were not in being — part o' th' cause, 2.03. 3
and | the testimony on my part no other | but 3.02. 24
i have for the most part been air'd abroad, i 4.02. 5 P
that's likewise part of my intelligence; 4.02. 45 P
these your unusual weeds to each part of you 4.04. 1
so turtles pair | that never mean to part. 4.04.155
if thou'lt bear a part, thou shalt hear; 4.04.292 P
i can bear my part, you must know 'tis my 4.04.295 P
'tis time to part them. 4.04.344
see the play so lies | that i must bear a part. 4.04.656
and tell me for what dull part in't | you chose 5.01. 64
and answer to his part | perform'd in this wide 5.03.153
sir robert might have eat his part in me | upon JN 1.01.234
then let confusion of one part confirm | the 2.01.359
and part your mingled colors once again, | turn 2.01.389

he is the half part of a blessed man, | left to 2.01.437
whole, | hath willingly departed with a part, 2.01.563
upon which better part our pray'rs come in, | if 3.01.293
my reasonable part produces reason | how i may 3.04. 54
since all and every part of what we would | doth 4.02. 38
and to part by th' teeth | the unowed interest 4.03.146
in peace, and part this body and my soul | with 5.04. 47
the stumbling night did part our weary pow'rs? 5.05. 18
of the part of england. 5.06. 2
for in a night the best part of my pow'r, | as i 5.07. 61
the other part reserv'd i by consent, | for that R2 1.01.128
the part i had in woodstock's blood | doth more 1.02. 1
(our part therein we banish with yourselves) 1.03.181
come on, our queen, to–morrow must we part. 2.01.222
we three here part that ne'er shall meet again. 2.02.143
presently your souls must part your bodies — 3.01. 3
take leave and part, for you must part forthwith 5.01. 70
leave and part, for you must part forthwith. 5.01. 70
part us, northumberland: 5.01. 76
and must we be divided? must we part? 5.01. 81
one kiss shall stop our mouths, and dumbly part; 5.01. 95
'twere no good part | to take on me to keep and 5.01. 97
did i ever call for thee to pay thy part? 1H4 1.02. 51 P
how shall we part with them in setting forth? 1.02.167 P
he did confound the best part of an hour | in 1.03.100
yea, on his part i'll empty all these veins, 1.03.133
"but, for mine own part, my lord, i could be 2.03. 1 P
by south and east is to my part assign'd; 3.01. 74
ye me, | i'll cavil on the ninth part of a hair. 3.01.138
my daughter weeps, she'll not part with you, 3.01.192
he had his part of it, let him pay. 3.03. 75 P
meet and ne'er part till one drop down a corse. 4.01.123
the better part of ours are full of rest. 4.03. 27
for mine own part, i could be well content | to 5.01. 23
for my part, i may speak it to my shame, | i 5.01. 93
love | that are misled upon your cousin's part, 5.01.105
i'll make it greater ere i part from thee, | and 5.04. 71
the better part of valor is discretion, in the 5.04.120 P
in the which better part i have sav'd my life. 5.04.120 P
for my part, if a lie may do thee grace, | i'll 5.04.157
you are as a candle, the better part burnt out. 2H4 1.02.156 P
and every part about you blasted with antiquity? 1.02.184 P
than 'a can part young limbs and lechery; 1.02.230 P
grace, my lord, tap for tap, and so part fair. 2.01.193 P
and i could discern no part of his face from the 2.02. 80 P
marry, the immortal part needs a physician, but 2.02.104 P
i have done the part of a careful friend and a 2.04.321 P
as go, and yet, for mine own part, sir, i do not 3.02.223 P
and, for mine own part, have a desire to stay 3.02.225 P
sir, i did not care, for mine own part, so much. 3.02.226 P
and for your part, bullcalf, grow till you come 3.02.252 P
why not to him in part, and to us all | that 4.01. 97
let them have pay, and part. 4.02. 70
this part of his conjoins with my disease, | and 4.05. 63
and then imagine me taking your part, | and in 5.02. 96
'tis /all in every part. 5.05. 29 P
so that the art and practic part of life | must H5 1.01. 51
or rather swaying more upon our part | than 1.01. 73
yet | did to his predecessors part withal. 1.01. 81
for my part, i care not; 2.01. 5 P
and, for mine own part, i have not a case of 3.02. 4 P
marry, for my part, i think the duke hath lost 3.06. 99 P
and little loss, | on one part and on th' other? 4.08.111
i will make him eat some part of my leek, or i 5.01. 40 P
well that i will not part with a village of it; 5.02.174 P
endeavor for your french part of such a boy; 5.02.214 P
/reignier, duke of anjou, doth take his part; 1H6 1.01. 94
and, for myself, most part of all this night, 2.01. 67
for what you see is but the smallest part | and 2.03. 52
i'll turn my part thereof into thy throat. 2.04. 79
would some part of my young years | might but 2.05.107
pucelle hath bravely play'd her part in this, 3.03. 88
part of thy father may be sav'd in thee. 4.05. 38
no part of him but will be shame in me. 4.05. 39
have we not lost most part of all the towns, 5.04.108
be slack | to play my part in fortune's pageant. 2H6 1.02. 67
for my part, noble lords, i care not which, | or 1.03.101
loather a hundred times to part than die. 3.02.355
ay, but these rags are no part of the duke; 4.01. 47
now part them again, lest they consult about the 4.07.132 P
my sword like a great pin, ere thou and i part. 4.10. 30 P
that is too much presumption on thy part; 5.01. 38
throw in the frozen bosoms of our part | hot 5.02. 35
came on the part of york, press'd by his master; 3H6 2.05. 66
size, | to disproportion me in every part, 3.02.160
which did subdue the greatest part of spain; 3.03. 82
ay, therein clarence shall not want his part. 4.06. 57
for my part, i'll not trouble thee with words. 5.05. 5
so part we sadly in this troublous world, | to 5.05. 7
my part thereof that i have done to her. R3 1.03.307
and more /in peace my soul shall part to heaven, 2.01. 5
protest, | upon my part shall be inviolable. 2.01. 27
of, | to part the queen's proud kindred from the 2.02.150
for my part, i'll resign unto your grace | the 2.04. 70
then i see you will part but with light gifts! 3.01.118
which i presume he'll take in gentle part. 3.04. 20
lord hastings had pronounc'd your part — | i 3.04. 27
play the maid's part, still answer nay, and take 3.07. 51
and part in just proportion our small power. 5.03. 26
the least of you shall share his part thereof. 5.03.268
see his pride | peep through each part of him. H8 1.01. 69
for the most part such | to whom as great a 1.01. 76
is on me | which makes my whit'st part black. 1.01.209
i know but of a single part in aught | pertains 1.02. 41
from each | the sixt part of his substance, to 1.02. 58
sixt part of each? 1.02. 94
every tree, lop, bark, and part o' th' timber; 1.02. 96
play'd | the part my father meant to act upon 1.02.195
your graces find me here part of a huswife | (i 3.01. 24
law o'ertake ye, | you'll part away disgrac'd. 3.01. 97
time | to think upon the part of business which 3.02.145
his blessed part to heaven, and slept in peace. 4.02. 30
for my part, i'll not meddle nor make no farther TRO 1.01. 14 P
but, for my part, she is my kinswoman; 1.01. 43 P
for my part, i'll meddle nor make no more i' th' 1.01. 82 P
what heart receives from hence a conquering part 1.03.352
mater is not worth the ninth part of a sparrow. 2.01. 72 P
for my private part, | i am no more touch'd than 2.02.125
not virtuously on his own part beheld, | do in 2.03.118
shall fight your hearts out ere i part you — 3.02. 52 P
and discharging less than the tenth part of one. 3.02. 87 P
for my own part, i came in late. 4.02. 52 P
come kiss, and let us part. 4.04. 98
interview | to the expecters of our troyan part; 4.05.156
in which part of his body | shall i destroy him 4.05.242
so much, | after we part from agamemnon's tent, 4.05.285
nay, but you part in anger. 5.02. 45
a retire upon our grecian part. 5.08. 15
is gone, with one part of our roman power. COR 1.03. 97 P
and stand upon my common part with those | that 1.09. 39
a treaty find | i' th' part that is at mercy? 1.10. 7
compound with the major part of your syllables; 2.01. 59 P
it is a part | that i shall blush in acting, and 2.02.144
that's no matter, the greater part carries it, i 2.03. 37 P
the one part suffered, the other will i do. 2.03.124
where /one part does disdain with cause, the 3.01.143
that love the fundamental part of state | more 3.01.151
upon the part o' th' people, in whose power | we 3.01.209
you have put me now to such a part which never 3.02.105
perform a part | thou hast not done before. 3.02.109
you take my part from me, sir, i have the most 4.03. 50 P
for mine own part, | when i said banish him, i 4.06.139
like a dull actor now | i have forgot my part, 5.03. 41
me the duty which | to a mother's part belongs. 5.03.168
for my part, | i'll not to rome, i'll back with 5.03.197
doth more than counterpoise a full third part 5.06. 77
takes from aufidius a great part of blame. 5.06.145
i give thee thanks in part of thy deserts, | and TIT 1.01.236
too, | upon a just survey take titus' part, 1.01.446
i would not part a bachelor from the priest. 1.01.488
let's kiss and part, for we have much to do. 3.01.287
part, fools! ROM 1.01. 64
sword, | or manage it to part these men with me. 1.01. 69
cank'red with peace, to part your cank'red hate; 1.01. 95
i drew to part them. 1.01.108
came more and more, and fought on part and part, 1.01.114
came more and more, and fought on part and part, 1.01.114
till the prince came, who parted either part. 1.01.115
heart, | my will to her consent is but a part; 1.02. 17
and for thy name, which is no part of thee, 2.02. 48
being smelt, with that part cheers each part, 2.03. 25
being smelt, with that part cheers each part, 2.03. 25
i am so vex'd that every part about me quivers. 2.04.162 P
friends, part!" 3.01.165
for, ere i | could draw to part them, was stout 3.01.173
taking thy part, hath rush'd aside the law, 3.03. 26
in what vile part of this anatomy | doth my name 3.03.106
it were a grief, so brief to part with thee. 3.03.174
each part, depriv'd of supple government, 4.01.102
and yourself | had part in this fair maid, now 4.05. 67
your part in her you could not keep from death, 4.05. 69
but heaven keeps his part in eternal life. 4.05. 70
and her immortal part with angels lives. 5.01. 19
whereby we might express some part of our zeals, TIM 1.02. 86 P
let not that part of nature | which my lord paid 3.01. 61
for my own part, i must needs confess, i have 3.02. 20 P
purchase the day before for a little part, and 3.02. 47 P
for mine own part, | i never tasted timon in my 3.02. 76
we must all part | into this sea of air. 4.02. 21
thus part we rich in sorrow, parting poor. 4.02. 29
for thy part, i do wish thou wert a dog, | that 4.03. 55
it is our part and promise to th' athenians | to 5.01.120
whom, though in general part we were oppos'd, 5.02. 7
against your city, | in part for his sake mov'd. 5.02. 13
i do lack some part | of that quick spirit that JC 1.02. 28
and for mine own part, i durst not laugh, for 1.02.249 P
but, for mine own part, it was greek to me. 1.02.284 P
for my part, i have walk'd about the streets, 1.03. 46
it is the part of men to fear and tremble | when 1.03. 54
that part of tyranny that i do bear | i can 1.03. 99
and for my part, | i know no personal cause to 2.01. 10
'tis time to part. 2.01.193
for your part, | to you our swords have leaden 3.01.172
into the other street, | and part the numbers. 3.02. 4
the greater part, the horse in general, | are 4.02. 29
for mine own part, | i shall be glad to learn of 4.03. 53
this is a roman's part. 5.03. 89
away, | to part the glories of this happy day. 5.05. 81
your highness' part | is to receive our duties; MAC 1.04. 23
all harms, | was never call'd to bear my part, 3.05. 8
though the main part | pertains to you alone. 4.03.198
heaven look on, | and would not take their part? 4.03.224
so, | for it hath cow'd my better part of man! 5.08. 18
made his course t' illume that part of heaven HAM 1.01. 37
so have i heard and do in part believe it. 1.01.165
thy knotted and combined locks to part, | and 1.05. 18
i hold it fit that we shake hands and part, 1.05.128
such as it is, and for my own poor part, | i 1.05.131
his father and his friends, | and in part him." 2.01. 15
"and in part him — but," you may say, "not well 2.01. 17
that i will not more willingly part withal — 2.02.216 P
the humorous man shall end his part in peace, 2.02.322 P
and for your part, ophelia, i do wish | that 3.01. 37
who for the most part are capable of nothing but 3.02. 11 P
it was a brute part of him to kill so capital a 3.02.105 P
where you may see the /inmost part of you. 3.04. 20
or but a sickly part of one true sense | could 3.04. 80
a slave that is not twentith part the /tithe 3.04. 97
o, throw away the worser part of it, | and /live 3.04.157
against some part of poland. 4.04. 12
thought which quarter'd hath but one part wisdom 4.04. 42
i do not know from what part of the world | i 4.06. 5
what part is that, my lord? 4.07. 76
for my part, i do not lie in't, yet it is mine. 5.01.124 P
the continent of what part a gentleman would see 5.02.111 P
part them, they are incens'd. 5.02.302
to confirm, | this coronet part between you. LR 1.01.139
the contents, as in part i understand them, are 1.02. 42 P
after dinner, i will not part from thee yet. 1.04. 41 P
for taking one's part that's out of favor. 1.04. 99 P
vanity the puppet's part against the royalty of 2.02. 36 P
how now, what's the matter? part! 2.02. 44 P
a plain knave, which for my part i will not be, 2.02.112 P
send down, and take my part. 2.04.192
i have one part in my heart | that's sorry yet 3.02. 72
there is part of a power already footed: 3.03. 13 P
my tears begin to take his part so much, | they 3.06. 60
my snuff and loathed part of nature should 4.06. 39
what, in your own part, can you say to this? OTH 1.03. 74
and sufferance | on most part of their fleet. 2.01. 24
for mine own part — no offense to the general, 2.03.106 P
those legs that brought me to a part of it. 2.03.187
they were | when you yourself did part them. 2.03.239
i have lost the immortal part of myself, and 2.03.263 P
that he hath left part of his grief with me | to 3.03. 53
hath ta'en your part — to have so much to do 3.03. 73
this wretch hath part confess'd his villainy. 5.02.296
of nothing but the finest part of pure love. ANT 1.02.147 P
to the queen, | and get her /leave to part. 1.02.179
sir, you and i must part, but that's not it; 1.03. 87
to part with unhack'd edges and bear back | our 2.06. 38
we'll feast each other ere we part, and let's 2.06. 60
for my part, i am sorry it is turn'd to a 2.06.103 P
'a bears the third part of the world, man; 2.07. 90 P
the third part then is drunk. 2.07. 92
gentle lords, let's part, | you see we have 2.07.121
octavia weeps | to part from rome; 3.02. 4
you take from me a great part of myself; 3.02. 24
we will here part. 3.02. 38
for the most part, too, they are foolish that 3.03. 31
we had not rated him | his part o' th' isle. 3.06. 26
for what i have conquer'd, | i grant him part; 3.06. 35
the foul'st best fits | my latter part of life. 4.06. 38
fortune and antony part here, even here | do we 4.12. 19
if thou and nature can so gently part, | the 5.02.294
he takes his part | to draw upon an exile. CYM 1.01.165
ring i hold dear as my finger, 'tis part of it. 1.04.133 P
the dearest bodily part of your mistress, my ten 1.04.150 P
could i find out | the woman's part in me — for 2.05. 20
in man, but i affirm | it is the woman's part: 2.05. 22
that hell knows, | why, hers, in part or all; 2.05. 28
that part thou, pisanio, must act for me, if thy 3.04. 25 P
as a wren's eye, fear'd gods, a part of it! 4.02.305
from the spungy south to this part of the west, 4.02.349
imogen, | the great part of my comfort, gone; 4.03. 5
so i'll fight | against the part i come with; 5.01. 25
part shame, part spirit renew'd, that some, 5.03. 35
part shame, part spirit renew'd, that some, 5.03. 35
i have resum'd again | the part i came in. 5.03. 76
if of my freedom 'tis the main part, take | no 5.04. 16
thou scornful page, | there lie thy part. 5.05.229
for mine own part unfold a dangerous speech, 5.05.313
and though it was mine own, part of my heritage, PER 2.01.123
begin to part | their fringes of bright gold. 3.02. 99
come, the gods have done their part in you. 4.02. 70 P
being proud, swallowed some part a' th' earth. 4.04. 39
prove the thousand part | of my endurance, thou 5.01.135
you may perceive a part of him. TNK 2.01. 50 P
a wife might part us lawfully, or business, 2.02. 89
am not i | part of /your blood, part of your 2.02.185
not i | part of /your blood, part of your soul? 2.02.185
and there th' offending part burns, and the 4.03. 44 P
part burns, and the deceiving part freezes: 4.03. 44 P
your prayers, and betwixt ye | i part my wishes. 5.01. 17
get herself | some part of a good name, and many 5.03. 27
each part of him to th' all i have spoke, your 5.03.121
his part is play'd, and, though it were too 5.04.102
"you hurt my hand with wringing, let us part, VEN 421
move | each part in me that were but sensible: 436
light | do summon us to part and bid good night. 534
as fearful of him, part, through whom he rushes. 630
with cold–pale weakness numbs each feeling part: 892
this mutiny each part doth so surprise | that 1049
my part is youth, and beats these from the stage LUC 278
which once corrupted takes the worser part; 294
who, therefore angry, seems to part in sunder, 388
whiles against a thorn thou bear'st thy part 1135
when every part a part of woe doth bear. 1327
when every part a part of woe doth bear. 1327
'tis but a part of sorrow that we hear: 1328
but kneel with me and help to bear thy part, 1830
grief in heart | he with thee doth bear a part. PP 20.54
who with his fear is put besides his part, | or SON 23. 2
suffic'd, | and by a part of all thy glory live. 37.12
sing, | when thou art all the better part of me? 39. 2
clear eye's moiety and the dear heart's part — 46.12
mine eye's due is /thy outward part, | and my 46.13
and in his thoughts of love doth share a part. 47. 8
whence at pleasure thou mayst come and part, 48.12
to guard the lawful reasons on thy part: 49.12
in all external grace you have some part, | but 53.13
eye, | and all my soul, and all my every part; 62. 2
review | the very part was consecrate to thee: 74. 6
my spirit is thine, the better part of me. 74. 8
although in me each part will be forgotten. 81. 4
upon thy part i can set down a story | of faults 88. 6
governs me to go about | doth part his function, 113. 3
of his quick objects hath the mind no part, 113. 7
till each to raz'd oblivion yield his part | of 122. 7
grace, | and suit thy pity like in every part. 132.12
and play the mother's part, kiss me, be kind: 143.12
my nobler part to my gross body's treason; 151. 6
stand | and was my own fee–simple (not in part), LC 144

PARTAKE 8 FR 0.0009 REL FR 6 V 2 P
(not meaning to partake with me in danger) TN 5.01. 87
and yet partake no venom (for his knowledge | is WT 2.01. 41
your exultation | partake to every one. 5.03.132
you may partake of any thing we say: R3 1.01. 89
what, what, what? let's partake. COR 4.05.174 P
and by and by thy bosom shall partake | the JC 2.01.305
would not let him partake in the glory of the ANT 3.05. 9 P
not, | when i against myself with thee partake? SON 149. 2

PARTAKEN 1 FR 0.0001 REL FR 0 V 1 P
if she had partaken of my flesh, and cost me the AWW 4.05. 10 P

PARTAKER 3 FR 0.0003 REL FR 3 V 0 P
wish me partaker in thy happiness | when thou TGV 1.01. 14
for your partaker pole, and you yourself, | i'll 1H6 2.04.100
shall beseech you, sir, | to let me be partaker. ANT 1.04. 83

PARTAKERS 1 FR 0.0001 REL FR 1 V 0 P
us withal, | make us partakers of a little gain, 1H6 2.01. 52

PARTAKES 1 FR 0.0001 REL FR 1 V 0 P
and our mind partakes her private actions | to PER 1.01.152

PART–CREATED 1 FR 0.0001 REL FR 1 V 0 P

o'er, and leaves his part–created cost | a naked 2H4 1.03. 60
/PARTED 1 FR 0.0001 REL FR 1 V 0 P
/were /in /her /eyes, /which, /parted /thence, LR 4.03. 21
PARTED 44 FR 0.0049 REL FR 35 V 9 P
but now he parted hence to embark for milan. TGV 1.01. 71
in earnest, they parted very fairly in jest. 2.05. 13 P
this ring i gave him when he parted from me, 4.04. 97
me, her assistant or go–between parted from me. WIV 2.02.263 P
then, | who parted with me to go fetch a chain, ERR 5.01.221
thou know'st we parted, but perhaps, my son, 5.01.322
like to a double cherry, seeming parted, | but MND 3.02.209
methinks i see these things with parted eye, 4.01.189
you, the wall is down that parted their fathers. 5.01.352 P
proverb is very well parted between my master MV 2.02.149 P
he wrung bassanio's hand, and so they parted. 2.08. 49
are sever'd lips, | parted with sugar breath; 3.02.119
you would not then have parted with the ring. 5.01.202
how parted he with thee? AYL 3.02.223 P
when last the young orlando parted from you | he 4.03. 98
and so we measur'd swords and parted. 5.04. 87 P
when his disguise and he is parted, tell me what AWW 3.06.104 P
what said our cousin when you parted with him? R2 1.04. 10
you promis'd, when you parted with the king, 2.02. 2
'a parted ev'n just between twelve and one, ev'n H5 2.03. 12 P
arms, | yet parted but the shadow with his hand. 3H6 1.04. 69
why, warwick, when we parted, | thou call'dst me 4.03. 30
he parted frowning from me, as if ruin | leap'd H8 3.02.205
so she parted, | and with the same full state 4.01. 92
life | and able means, we had not parted thus. 4.02.153
they had parted so much honesty among 'em — 5.02. 28
writes me that man, how dearly ever parted, TRO 3.03. 96
and parted thus you and your argument. 4.05. 29
my country's love | than when i parted hence, COR 5.06. 72
till the prince came, who parted either part. ROM 1.01.115
they say he parted well, and paid his score, MAC 5.09. 18
and france in choler parted? LR 1.02. 23
parted you in good terms? 1.02.156 P
what thing was that | which parted from you? 4.06. 68
for they were parted | with foul and violent OTH 2.01. 33
of /the sea and skies | parted our fellowship. 2.01. 93
the day had broke | before we parted. 3.01. 33
was not that cassio parted from my wife? 3.03. 37
what, are the brothers parted? ANT 3.02. 1
that have my heart parted betwixt two friends 3.06. 77
they were parted | by gentlemen at hand. CYM 1.01.163
and parted with | pray'rs for the provider. 3.06. 51
how parted with your /brothers? 5.05.386
when we with tears parted pentapolis, | the king PER 5.03. 38
PARTHIA 7 FR 0.0008 REL FR 7 V 0 P
in parthia did i take thee prisoner, | and then JC 5.03. 37
if we compose well here, to parthia. ANT 2.02. 15
he shall to parthia. 2.03. 33
o, come, ventidius, | you must to parthia. 2.03. 42
now, darting parthia, art thou strook, and now 3.01. 1
the ne'er–yet–beaten horse of parthia | we have 3.01. 33
great media, parthia, and armenia | he gave to 3.06. 14
PARTHIAN 5 FR 0.0005 REL FR 5 V 0 P
hath with his parthian force | extended asia; ANT 1.02.100
whilst yet with parthian blood thy sword is warm 3.01. 6
shall i do that which all the parthian darts, 4.14. 70
or, like the parthian, i shall flying fight — CYM 1.06. 20
flies like a parthian quiver from our rages, TNK 2.02. 50
PARTHIANS 1 FR 0.0001 REL FR 1 V 0 P
sword is warm, | the fugitive parthians follow. ANT 3.01. 7
PARTIAL 8 FR 0.0009 REL FR 8 V 0 P
out my death, | and nothing come in partial. MM 2.01. 31
i am not partial to infringe our laws; ERR 1.01. 4
a partial slander sought i to avoid, | and in R2 1.03.241
canst thou, o partial sleep, give /then repose 2H4 3.01. 26
of partial indulgence | to their benumbed wills, TRO 2.02.178
since nature makes them partial, should o'erhear HAM 3.03. 32
i cannot be so partial, goneril, | to the great LR 1.04.311
worthy blame, | as well as fancy, partial might. PP 18. 4
PARTIALIZE 1 FR 0.0001 REL FR 1 V 0 P
should nothing privilege him nor partialize R2 1.01.120
PARTIALLY 2 FR 0.0002 REL FR 2 V 0 P
if partially affin'd, or /leagu'd in office, OTH 2.03.218
their own transgressions partially they smother: LUC 634
PARTICIPATE 2 FR 0.0002 REL FR 2 V 0 P
clad | which from the womb i did participate. TN 5.01.238
and, mutually participate, did minister | unto COR 1.01.103
PARTICIPATION 2 FR 0.0002 REL FR 1 V 1 P
princely privilege | with vile participation. 1H4 3.02. 87
with the participation of society that they 2H4 5.01. 69 P
PARTICLE 2 FR 0.0002 REL FR 1 V 1 P
and every particle and utensil labell'd to my TN 1.05.246 P
if he do break the smallest particle | of any JC 2.01.139
PARTI–COATED 1 FR 0.0001 REL FR 1 V 0 P
which parti–coated presence of loose love | put LLL 5.02.766
PARTI–COLOR'D 1 FR 0.0001 REL FR 1 V 0 P
did in eaning time | fall parti–color'd lambs, MV 1.03. 88
/PARTICULAR 1 FR 0.0001 REL FR 0 V 1 P
/let /me /question /more /in /particular. HAM 2.02.239 P
PARTICULAR 54 FR 0.0061 REL FR 41 V 13 P
and the particular accidents gone by | since i TMP 5.01.306
that no particular scandal once can touch | but MM 4.04. 27
they would swear down each particular saint, 5.01.243
recount their particular duties afterwards. ADO 4.01. 3 P
together trans–shape thy particular virtues, yet 5.01.171 P
that i should love a bright particular star AWW 1.01. 86
and required office | on my particular. 2.05. 61
i knew in what particular action to try him. 3.06. 17 P
ay, and the particular confirmations, point from 4.03. 61 P
you let me answer to the particular of the 4.03.182 P
their profits | (their own particular thrifts), WT 1.02.311
over | by each particular star in heaven and 1.02.425
your doing | (so singular in each particular) 4.04.144
commonwealth, | i make my quarrel in particular. 2H4 4.01. 94
i will have it in a particular ballad else, with 4.03. 48 P
read, | with every course in his particular. 4.04. 90
doth any name particular belong | unto the 4.05.232
upon my particular knowledge of his directions. H5 3.02. 78 P
to lay apart their particular functions and 3.07. 38 P
perfection of a good and particular mistress. 3.07. 47 P
to answer the particular endings of his soldiers 4.01.156 P
whose tenures and particular effects | you have 5.02. 72
here i am, thou particular fellow. 2H6 4.02.112 P
make yourself mirth with your particular fancy, H8 2.03.101
but by particular consent proceeded | under your 2.04.222
as 'twere in love's particular, be more | to me, 3.02.189
many beasts of their particular additions: TRO 1.02. 20 P
although particular, shall give a scantling | of 1.03.341
than i | as far as toucheth my particular, | yet 2.02. 9
but value dwells not in particular will, | it 2.02. 53
yet is the kindness but particular, | 'twere 4.05. 20
that wilt revenge | thine own particular wrongs, COR 4.05. 86
yet i wish, sir | (i mean for your particular), 4.07. 13
who loved him | in a most dear particular. 5.01. 3
in hourly synod about thy particular prosperity, 5.02. 69 P
but what particular rarity? TIM 1.01. 4
away | of him that, his particular to foresee, 4.03.159
yet our old love made a particular force, | and 5.02. 8
whereby he does receive | particular addition, MAC 3.01. 99
in what particular thought to work i know not, HAM 1.01. 67
it be, | why seems it so particular with thee? 1.02. 75
it | as he in his particular act and place | may 1.03. 26
so, oft it chances in particular men, | that for 1.04. 23
take corruption | from that particular fault: 1.04. 36
and each particular hair to stand an end, | like 1.05. 19
than your particular demands will touch it. 2.01. 12
inform her full of my particular fear, | and LR 1.04.337
for his particular, i'll receive him gladly, 2.04.292
for these domestic and particular broils | are 5.01. 30
for my particular grief | is of so flood–gate OTH 1.03. 55
my more particular, | and that which most with ANT 1.03. 54
the world should note | something particular. 3.13. 22
infamous, | forgive me in thine own particular, 4.09. 20
lies | in the small orb of one particular tear! LC 289
PARTICULARITIES 2 FR 0.0002 REL FR 1 V 1 P
of my birth, and in other particularities. H5 3.02.130 P
particularities and petty sounds | to cease! 2H6 5.02. 44
PARTICULARIZE 1 FR 0.0001 REL FR 0 V 1 P
an inventory to particularize their abundance; COR 1.01. 21 P
PARTICULARLY 2 FR 0.0002 REL FR 2 V 0 P
who hath done | to thee particularly, and to all COR 4.05. 66
my free drift | halts not particularly, but TIM 1.01. 46
PARTICULARS 11 FR 0.0012 REL FR 6 V 5 P
give us particulars of thy preservation, | how TMP 5.01.135
ay and no to these particulars is more than to AYL 3.02.227 P
and examine me upon the particulars of my life. 1H4 2.04.377 P
the parcels and particulars of our grief, | the 2H4 4.02. 36
may soon bring his particulars therein to a TRO 1.02.114 P
he's to make his requests by particulars, COR 2.03. 43 P
i know | all the particulars of vice so grafted MAC 4.03. 51
parts, | that all particulars of duty know, LR 1.04.264
but how, but how? give me particulars. ANT 1.02. 56 P
more particulars | must justify my knowledge. CYM 2.04. 78
but these particulars are not my measure, | all SON 91. 7
PARTIES 15 FR 0.0017 REL FR 9 V 6 P
from the two parties, forsooth. WIV 4.05.105 P
o lord, sir, the parties themselves, the actors, LLL 5.02.499 P
but when the parties were met themselves, one of AYL 5.04.100 P
too mighty, | and in his parties, his alliance. WT 2.03. 21
these promises are fair, the parties sure, | and 1H4 3.01. 1
for then both parties nobly are subdued, | and 2H4 4.02. 90
that divided was | into two parties, is now 1H6 5.02. 12
witness whereof the parties interchangeably" — TRO 3.02. 58 P
conjectural marriages, making parties strong, COR 1.01.194
their cause is calling both the parties knaves. 2.01. 79 P
lest parties (as he is belov'd) break out, | and 3.01.313
the same intent wherein | you wish'd us parties, 5.06. 13
bring forth the parties of suspicion. ROM 5.03.222
in the marriage than the love of the parties. ANT 2.06.119 P
and though it be allowed in meaner parties CYM 2.03.116
//PARTI–EY'D 1 FR 0.0001 REL FR 1 V 0 P
my father, //parti–ey'd? LR 4.01. 10
PARTING 32 FR 0.0036 REL FR 28 V 4 P
this parting strikes poor lovers dumb. TGV 2.02. 20
a jew would have wept to have seen our parting; 2.03. 12 P
look you, wept herself blind at my parting. 2.03. 13 P
chid the hasty–footed time | for parting us — o MND 3.02.201
my moans, | for parting my fair pyramus and me! 5.01.189
for so your father charg'd me at our parting; SHR 1.01.213
that at the parting all the church did echo. 3.02.179
grow to you, and our parting is a tortur'd body. AWW 2.01. 36 P
have procur'd his leave | for present parting; 2.05. 56
month behind the gest | prefix'd for 's parting; WT 1.02. 42
his tears proclaim'd his, parting with her; 5.01.160
and say, what store of parting tears were shed? R2 1.04. 5
did grace our hollow parting with a tear. 1.04. 9
more than with parting from my lord the king. 2.02. 13
shed | upon the parting of your wives and you. 1H4 3.01. 94
and peace, no war, befall thy parting soul! 1H6 2.05.115
though parting be a fretful corrosive, | it is 2H6 3.02.403
more than my body's parting with my soul. 3H6 2.06. 4
slightly shakes his parting guest by th' hand, TRO 3.03.166
kindly, | for it is parting from us. 4.04. 61
parting is such sweet sorrow, | that i shall say ROM 2.02.184
thus part we rich in sorrow, parting poor. TIM 4.02. 29
if not, why then this parting was well made. JC 5.01.118
if not, 'tis true this parting was well made. 5.01.121
the soul and body rive not more in parting ANT 4.13. 5
to air yourself, | such parting were too petty. CYM 1.01.111
give him that parting kiss which i had set 1.03. 34
which are often the sadness of parting, as the 5.04.160 P
when you caught hurt in parting two that fought; PER 4.01. 87
(which then look'd pale at parting) when our TNK 1.03. 53
"adieu," | the honey fee of parting tend'red is: VEN 538
yet at my parting sweetly did she smile, | in PP 14. 7
PARTISAN 2 FR 0.0002 REL FR 1 V 1 P
shall i strike it with my partisan? HAM 1.01.140
me no service as a partisan i could not heave. ANT 2.07. 13 P
PARTISANS 3 FR 0.0003 REL FR 3 V 0 P
clubs, bills, and partisans! ROM 1.01. 73
beseeming ornaments | to wield old partisans, in 1.01. 94
and make him with our pikes and partisans | a CYM 4.02.399
PARTITION 4 FR 0.0004 REL FR 3 V 1 P
seeming parted, | but yet an union in partition, MND 3.02.210
it is the wittiest partition that ever i heard 5.01.167 P
as chaff, | and good from bad find no partition. 2H4 4.01.194
not | partition make with spectacles so precious CYM 1.06. 37
PARTLET 2 FR 0.0002 REL FR 1 V 1 P
unroosted | by thy dame partlet here. WT 2.03. 76
how now, dame partlet the hen? 1H4 3.03. 52 P
PARTLY 36 FR 0.0040 REL FR 21 V 15 P
and partly, seeing you are beautified | with TGV 4.01. 53
partly that i have need of such a youth | that 4.04. 64
pompey, you are partly a bawd, pompey, howsoever MM 2.01.219 P
partly for that her promised proportions | came 5.01.219
i partly think | a due sincerity governed his 5.01.445
and partly by his oaths, which first possess'd ADO 3.03.156 P
first possess'd them, partly by the dark night, 3.03.156 P
great persuasion, and partly to save your life, 5.04. 95 P
'tis partly my own fault, | which death, or MND 3.02.243
you may partly hope that your father got you not MV 3.05. 10 P
i partly guess; for i have lov'd ere now. AYL 2.04. 24
and that i partly know the instrument | that TN 5.01.122
whereof being by circumstances partly laid open, WT 3.02. 18 P
(for him, i partly know his mind) to find thee 5.03.142
thou art my son i have partly thy mother's word, 1H4 2.04.403 P
partly thy mother's word, partly my own opinion, 2.04.403 P
as partly touching or concerning the disciplines H5 3.02. 96 P
partly to satisfy my opinion, and partly for the 3.02. 98 P
my opinion, and partly for the satisfaction, 3.02. 99 P
pistol, i do partly understand your meaning. 3.06. 50 P
but now you partly may perceive my mind. 3H6 3.02. 66
for god doth know, and you may partly see, | how R3 3.07.235
i partly know the man; 4.02. 41
i do but partly know, sir, it is music in parts. TRO 3.01. 18 P
it to please his mother, and to be partly proud, COR 1.01. 39 P
and this shall seem, as partly 'tis, their own, 2.03.262
of death | is partly to behold my lady's face, ROM 5.03. 29
and partly credit things that do presage. JC 5.01. 78
i but believe it partly, | for i am fresh of 5.01. 89
and most wise consent | (as partly i find it is) OTH 1.01.122
a sin), | but partly led to diet my revenge, 2.01.294
for he partly begs | to be desir'd to give. ANT 3.13. 66
i partly feel thee. 5.02.322
i partly know him, 'tis | cloten, the son o' th' CYM 4.02. 64
shake, which partly comes through the eating of STM II.C 14 P
doth part his function, and is partly blind, SON 113. 3
PARTNER 16 FR 0.0018 REL FR 10 V 6 P
wishing me with him, partner of his fortune. TGV 1.03. 59
your partner, as i hear, must die to–morrow, MM 2.03. 37
receive some instruction from my fellow partner. 4.02. 18 P
have been always call'd a merciful man, partner. ADO 3.03. 62 P
go, good partner, go, get you to francis seacole 3.05. 57 P
marry, that am i and my partner. 4.02. 4 P
prithee be my present partner in this business, WT 4.02. 51 P
habited as it becomes | the partner of your bed. 4.04.547
roan | and will be partner of your weal or woe. 1H6 3.02. 92
sweet partner, | i must not yet forsake you. H8 1.04.103
my partner in this action, | you must report to COR 5.03. 2
the last | i seem'd his follower, not partner, 5.06. 38
my noble partner | you greet with present grace, MAC 1.03. 54
deliver thee, my dearest partner of greatness, 1.05. 11 P
i, | your partner in the cause 'gainst which he ANT 2.02. 59
to be thy partner in this shameful doom." LUC 672
PARTNER'D 1 FR 0.0001 REL FR 1 V 0 P
to be partner'd | with tomboys hir'd with that CYM 1.06.121
PARTNER'S 1 FR 0.0001 REL FR 1 V 0 P
look how our partner's rapt. MAC 1.03.142
PARTNERS 6 FR 0.0006 REL FR 6 V 0 P
my vows are equal partners with thy vows. 1H6 3.02. 85
you shall have | two noble partners with you, H8 5.02.202
my noble partners and myself thus pray | all 5.04. 5
or | /vouchsaf'd to think he had partners. ANT 1.04. 8
then, noble partners, | the rather for i 2.02. 22
noble friends | are partners in the business. CYM 1.06.184
PARTRIDGE 2 FR 0.0002 REL FR 1 V 1 P
and then there's a partridge wing sav'd, for the ADO 2.01.149 P
who finds the partridge in the puttock's nest 2H6 3.02.191
PART'S 1 FR 0.0001 REL FR 1 V 0 P
as shall with either part's agreement stand? SHR 4.04. 50
PARTS' 1 FR 0.0001 REL FR 0 V 1 P
course from the inwards to the parts' extremes. 2H4 4.03.107 P
/PARTS 1 FR 0.0001 REL FR 1 V 0 P
a man of sovereign /parts, /peerless esteem'd, LLL 2.01. 44
PARTS 117 FR 0.0132 REL FR 94 V 23 P
peace, stand aside, the company parts. TGV 4.02. 81
examin'd my parts with most judicious iliads; WIV 1.03. 60 P
setting the attraction of my good parts aside, i 2.02.106 P
come, and remember your parts. 5.04. 2 P
and dispossessing all my others parts | of MM 2.04. 22
have by this play'd their parts with beatrice, ADO 3.02. 77 P
for which of my bad parts didst thou first fall 5.02. 60 P
for which of my good parts did you first suffer 5.02. 65 P
an animal, only sensible in the duller parts; LLL 4.02. 27 P
for those parts that do fructify in us more than 4.02. 29
is to me some praise that i thy parts admire. 4.02.114
the extreme parts of time extremely forms | all 5.02.740
but masters, here are your parts, and i am to MND 1.02. 99 P
every mother's son, and rehearse your parts. 3.01. 73 P
to vow, and swear, and superpraise my parts, 3.02.153
to his own good parts that he can shoe him MV 1.02. 42 P
parts that become thee happily enough | and in 2.02.182
some mark of virtue on his outward parts. 3.02. 82
but when this ring | parts from this finger, 3.02.184
from this finger, then parts life from hence; 3.02.184
in six thousand ducats | were in six parts, and 4.01. 86
mules, | you use in abject and in slavish parts, 4.01. 92
an envious emulator of every man's good parts, a AYL 1.01.144 P
my better parts | are all thrown down, and that 1.02.249
commend | the parts and graces of the wrastler 2.02. 13
and one man in his time plays many parts, | his 2.07.142
thus rosalind of many parts | by heavenly synod 3.02.149
that will divide a minute into a thousand parts, 4.01. 45 P
my lessons make no music in three parts. SHR 3.01. 60
should well agree with our external parts? 5.02.168
thy father's moral parts | mayst thou inherit AWW 1.02. 21
what is infirm from your sound parts shall fly, 2.01.167
ours be your patience then, and yours our parts; ep 5
the parts that fortune hath bestow'd upon her, TN 2.04. 83
your travel, | being skilless in these parts; 3.03. 9
upon some stubborn and uncourteous parts | we 5.01.361
thee, by all the parts of man | which honor does WT 1.02.400
'tis in three parts. 4.04.293 P
mine eye hath well examined his parts, | and JN 1.01. 89
than arm thy constant and thy nobler parts 3.01.291
words, | remembers me of all his gracious parts, 3.04. 96
death, having prey'd upon the outward parts, 5.07. 15
three parts of that receipt i had for callice R2 1.01.126
a stain | upon the beauty of all parts besides, 1H4 3.01.186

the perilous narrow ocean parts asunder. H5 pr 22
into a thousand parts divide one man, | and make pr 24
put into parts, doth keep in one consent, 1.02.181
to view the sick and feeble parts of france; 2.04. 22
have in these parts from morn till even fought, 3.01. 20
leaving their earthly parts to choke your clime, 4.03.102
notice of the numbers dead | on both our parts. 4.07.118
your mightiness on both parts best can witness. 5.02. 28
to her dispraise those parts in me that you love 5.02.200 P
and, banding themselves in contrary parts, | do 1H6 3.01. 81
to be our regent in these parts of france; 4.01.163
from being regent | i' th' parts of france, till 2H6 1.01. 67
and therefore i will take the nevils' parts, 1.01.240
would (but that they dare not) take our parts. 4.02.187
reigns in the hearts of all our present parts. 5.02. 87
to richmond, in the parts where he abides. R3 4.02. 49
you, that have so fair parts of woman on you, H8 2.03. 27
and thy parts | sovereign and pious else, could 2.04.140
thee and all thy best parts bound together) 3.02.258
from all parts they are coming, | as if we kept 5.03. 68
the still and mental parts, | that do contrive TRO 1.03.200
that 'twixt his mental and his active parts 2.03.174
and thy parts of nature | thrice fam'd beyond, 2.03.242
confines | /thy spacious and dilated parts. 2.03.250
i do but partly know, sir, it is music in parts. 3.01. 18 P
till he communicate his parts to others; 3.03.117
how novelty may move, and parts with /person, 4.04. 79
the mutinous parts | that envied his receipt; COR 1.01.111
where being three parts melted away with rotten 2.03. 32 P
of rome, | or rudely visit them in parts remote, 4.05.142
rather to show a noble grace to both parts 5.03.121
affliction is enamor'd of thy parts, | and thou ROM 3.03. 2
stuff'd, as they say, with honorable parts, 3.05.181
that sits next him, now parts bread with him, TIM 1.02. 47 P
that with your other noble parts you'll suit 2.02. 23
good parts in thee! 3.01. 37 P
my lords, if not for any parts in him — 3.05. 75
three parts of him | is ours already, and the JC 1.03.154
strife | shall cumber all the parts of italy; 3.01.264
caesar's better parts | shall be crown'd in 3.02. 51
in the secret parts of fortune? HAM 2.02.235 P
one part wisdom | and ever three parts coward — 4.04. 43
your sum of parts | did not together pluck such 4.07. 73
/crown i' th' middle and gav'st away both parts, LR 1.04.161 P
my train are men of choice and rarest parts, 1.04.263
he that parts us shall bring a brand from heaven 5.03. 22
my parts, my title, and my perfect soul | shall OTH 1.02. 31
and to his honors and his valiant parts | did i 1.03.253
mark, and /denotement of her parts and graces. 2.03.318 P
and have not those soft parts of conversation 3.03.264
none our parts so poor | but was a race of ANT 1.03. 36
mean, if on both parts | this be not cherish'd. 3.02. 32
ne'er stood between, | praying for both parts. 3.04. 14
that she hath all courtly parts more exquisite CYM 3.05. 71
perform | all parts of his subjection loyally. 4.03. 19
knights come from all parts of the world to just PER 2.01.110 P
i hear say you're of honorable parts, and are 4.06. 81 P
and make a batt'ry through his /deafen'd parts, 5.01. 47
how came you in these parts? 5.01.169
tell me | news from all parts o' th' world. TNK 3.04. 13
they come from all parts of the dukedom to him. 4.01.136
thy outward parts would move | each part in me VEN 435
is to me some praise, that i thy parts admire. PP 5.10
reason none, | if what parts, can so remain." PHT 48
in singleness the parts that thou shouldst bear. SON 8. 8
hides your life, and shows not half your parts. 17. 4
there reigns love and all love's loving parts, 31. 3
who all their parts of me to thee did give: 31.11
more, | entitled in /thy parts do crowned sit, 37. 7
which parts the shore where two contracted new 56.10
those parts of thee that the world's eye doth 69. 1
and when in his fair parts she did abide, | she LC 83
"'my parts had pow'r to charm a sacred /nun, 260

PART'ST 1 FR 0.0001 REL FR 1 V 0 P
thou part'st a fair fray. LLL 5.02.484

PARTY 48 FR 0.0054 REL FR 37 V 11 P
canst thou bring me to the party? TMP 3.02. 59 P
myself (fidelicet myself) and the three party is WIV 1.01.140 P
the devil take one party and his dam the other! 4.05.106 P
for the nomination of the party /writing to the LLL 4.02.134 P
the party is gone" — 5.02.671
the party 'gainst the which he doth contrive MV 4.01.352
pride | that can therein tax any private party? AYL 2.07. 71
for i must be | a party in this alteration, WT 1.02.383
not a party to | the anger of the king, nor 2.02. 59
pushes 'gainst our heart — the party tried, 3.02. 2
are you a party in this business? 4.04.812 P
world, | upon the right and party of her son? JN 1.01. 34
whose party do the townsmen yet admit? 2.01.361
to brag and stamp and swear | upon my party! 3.01.123
i know | our party may well meet a prouder foe. 5.01. 79
southern gentlemen in arms | upon his party. R2 3.02.203
knees, | which on thy royal party granted once, 3.03.115
three knights upon our party slain to-day, | a 1H4 5.05. 6
put on his ugliest mask | to fright our party. 2H4 1.01. 67
for from his metal was his party steeled, 1.01.116
but, for the party that ow'd it, he might have 1.02. 4 P
nobly are subdued, | and neither party loser. 4.02. 91
but dare maintain the party of the truth, 1H6 2.04. 32
pole, | will i upon thy party wear this rose. 2.04.123
to fight on edward's party for the crown, | and R3 1.03.137
forward | upon his party for the gain thereof; 3.02. 47
my prayers on the adverse party fight, | and 4.04.191
him, they came from buckingham | upon his party. 4.04.526
there's not the meanest spirit on our party TRO 2.02.156
by th' ears, and he | upon my party, i'd revolt, COR 1.01.234
i saw our party to their trenches driven, | and 1.06. 12
are hearing a matter between party and party, if 2.01. 73 P
are hearing a matter between party and party, if 2.01. 73 P
sir, 'tis fit | you make strong party, or defend 3.02. 94
always factionary on the party of your general. 5.02. 29 P
for whom we stand | a special party, have by TIT 1.01. 21
could | but win the noble brutus to our party — JC 1.03.141
your party in converse, him you would sound, HAM 2.01. 42
upon his party 'gainst the duke of albany? LR 2.01. 26
him an intelligent party to the advantages of 3.05. 11 P
i should show | what party i do follow. 4.05. 40
seek him out | upon the english party. 4.06.250
this trash | to be a party in this injury. OTH 5.01. 86
i would not be the party that should desire you ANT 5.02.246 P
to the king's party there's no going. CYM 4.04. 9
and implore | her power unto our party. TNK 5.01. 76
sense — | thy adverse party is thy advocate — SON 35.10
be, | where neither party is nor true nor kind: LC 186

PARTY-VERDICT 1 FR 0.0001 REL FR 1 V 0 P
whereto thy tongue a party-verdict gave. R2 1.03.234

PAS 1 FR 0.0001 REL FR 0 V 1 P
leur noces, il n'est pas la coutume de france. H5 5.02.259 P

/PASH* 1 FR 0.0001 REL FR 1 V 0 P
my armed fist | i'll /pash him o'er the face. TRO 2.03.203

PASH* 1 FR 0.0001 REL FR 1 V 0 P
thou want'st a rough pash and the shoots that i WT 1.02.128

PASHED 1 FR 0.0001 REL FR 1 V 0 P
his beam, | upon the pashed corses of the kings TRO 5.05. 10

PASHFUL *(also bashful)*

PASHFUL 1 FR 0.0001 REL FR 0 V 1 P
come, wherefore should you be so pashful? H5 4.08. 70 P

/PASS 1 FR 0.0001 REL FR 1 V 0 P
and in a /pass of practice | requite him for HAM 4.07.138

PASS 140 FR 0.0158 REL FR 109 V 31 P
by line and level" is an excellent pass of pate; TMP 4.01.244 P
and, for the ways are dangerous to pass, | i do TGV 4.03. 24
please you, i'll tell you as we pass along, 5.04.168
be avis'd, sir, and pass good humors. WIV 1.01.166 P
the anchor is deep. will that humor pass? 1.03. 51 P
nobody but has his fault — but let that pass. 1.04. 15 P
own, that i may pass with a reproof the easier, 2.02.188 P
to see thee there, to see thee pass thy puncto, 2.03. 26 P
what's brought to pass under the profession of 4.02.175 P
when evil deeds have their permissive pass, MM 1.03. 38
the laws | that thieves do pass on thieves? 2.01. 23
if you live to see this come to pass, say pompey 2.01.242 P
vantage on the duke, | he shall not pass you. 4.06. 12
kick, being kick'd, and, being at that pass, ERR 3.01. 17
kneel to the duke before he pass the abbey. 5.01.129
your oath is pass'd to pass away from these. LLL 1.01. 49
for what is inward between us, let it pass. 5.01. 97 P
of great import indeed too — but let that pass; 5.01.101 P
but, sweet heart, let that pass. 5.01.105 P
but let that pass. 5.01.108 P
limb or joint, shall pass pompey the great; 5.01.128 P
when in that moment (so it came to pass) MND 3.02. 33
how came these things to pass? 4.01. 78
of themselves, they may pass for excellent men. 5.01.216 P
made him, and therefore let him pass for a man. MV 1.02. 56 P
a thing not in his power to bring to pass, | but 1.03. 92
so shall we pass along | and never stir AYL 1.03.113
if it do come to pass | that any man turn ass, 2.05. 50
that o'er the green corn-field did pass, | in 5.03. 18
though it pass your patience and mine to endure SHR 1.01.126 P
her father's liking, which to bring to pass, 3.02.129
ere three days pass, which hath as long lov'd me 4.02. 38
day, | to pass assurance of a dow'r in marriage 4.02.118
him, | and pass my daughter a sufficient dower, 4.04. 45
we'll pass the business privately and well. 4.04. 57
sigh, | till i be brought to such a silly pass! 5.02.124
hath told the thievish minutes how they pass, AWW 2.01.166
it might pass: 2.03.203 P
uses a known truth to pass a thousand nothings 2.05. 30 P
and common speech | gives him a worthy pass. 2.05. 53
lack advice so much | as letting her pass so. 3.04. 20
for it will come to pass | that every braggart 4.03.335
am sure i lack thee, may pass for a wise man. TN 1.05. 35 P
but he will not pass his word for twopence that 1.05. 80 P
nay, and thou pass upon me, i'll no more with 3.01. 42 P
for it comes to pass oft that a terrible oath, 3.04.179 P
i had a pass with him, rapier, scabbard, and all 3.04.274 P
i know not what i shall incur to pass it, WT 2.02. 55
as this world goes, to pass for honest. 2.03. 73
let me pass | the same i am, ere ancient'st 4.01. 9
accident, | should pass this way as you did. 4.04. 20
but if you fondly pass our proffer'd offer, JN 2.01.258
and crack'd crowns, | and pass them current too. 1H4 2.03. 94
that daff'd the world aside | and bid it pass? 4.01. 97
if it pass against us, | we lose the better half H5 1.01. 7
the narrow seas | to give you gentle pass; 2.pr. 39
if we may pass, we will; 3.06.160
pass our accept and peremptory answer. 5.02. 82
but your request shall make me let it pass. 5.02.344
i have no power to let her pass, | my hand would 1H6 5.03. 60
be so — | what ransom must i pay before i pass? 5.03. 73
till thou speak, thou shalt not pass from hence. 2H6 1.04. 27
let never day nor night unhallowed pass, | but 2.01. 83
no, stir not for your lives, let her pass by. 2.04. 18
disturb him not, let him pass peaceably. 3.03. 25
as for these silken-coated slaves, i pass not, 4.02.128
quake, | shake he his weapon at us and pass by. 4.08. 18
may pass into the presence of a king, | lo, i 5.01. 65
proclaim'd | in every borough as we pass along, 3H6 2.01.195
did i let pass th' abuse done to my niece? 3.03.188
my noble queen, let former grudges pass, | and 3.03.195
peace, | have no delight to pass away the time, R3 1.01. 25
my lord, stand back, and let the coffin pass. 1.02. 38
a glass, | that i may see my shadow as i pass. 1.02.263
for curses never pass | the lips of those that 1.03.284
my lord, will't please you pass along? 3.01.136
and so agree | the play may pass, if they be H8 pr 11
and it's come to pass | this tractable obedience 1.02. 63
you, if these fair ladies | pass away frowning. 1.04. 33
pray you pass on. 2.04.131
behold | the lady anne pass from her coronation? 4.01. 3
if your will pass, | i shall both find your 5.02. 94
when they pass back from the christening. 5.03. 74
find a way out | to let the troop pass fairly; 5.03. 85
a most unspotted lily shall she pass | to th' 5.04. 61
up here and see them as they pass toward ilion? TRO 1.02.178 P
you them all by their names as they pass by, but 1.02.183 P
were i alone to pass the difficulties, | and had 2.02.139
please it our general pass strangely by him, 3.03. 39
put on | a form of strangeness as we pass along. 3.03. 51
they pass by strangely. 3.03. 71
please you | that i may pass this doing. COR 2.02.139
pass no further. 3.01. 24
if you will pass | to where you are bound, you 3.01. 53
you may not pass, you must return; 5.02. 5
therefore, fellow, | i must have leave to pass. 5.02. 23
words in your own, you should not pass here; 5.02. 26 P
true under him, must say you cannot pass. 5.02. 33 P
my lord, you pass not here. TIT 1.01.290
shows | pass the remainder of our hateful days? 3.01.132
and that you'll say ere half an hour pass. 3.01.191
i will frown as i pass by, and let them take it ROM 1.01. 40 P
i'll tell thee as we pass, but this i pray, 2.03. 63
set, | for then thou canst not pass to mantua, 3.03.149
smiles and still invites | all that pass by. TIM 2.01. 12
but wrong to stir me up, | let me pass quietly. 3.04. 54
become your lips as they pass thorough them. 5.01.195
not a man | shall pass his quarter, or offend 5.04. 60
pass by and curse thy fill, but pass and stay 5.04. 73
thy fill, but pass and stay not here thy gait." 5.04. 73
to see great pompey pass the streets of rome; JC 1.01. 42
he is a dreamer, let us leave him. pass. 1.02. 24
as they pass by, pluck casca by the sleeve, 1.02.179
here will i stand till caesar pass along, | and 2.03. 11
my stand, | to see him pass on to the capitol. 2.04. 26
honesty | that they pass by me as the idle wind, 4.03. 68
that it might please you to give quiet pass HAM 2.02. 77
you know, "it came to pass, as most like it was" 2.02.418
between the pass and fell incensed points | of 5.02. 61
i pray you pass with your best violence; 5.02.298
has his daughters brought him to this pass? LR 3.04. 63
though well we may not pass upon his life 3.07. 24
this trusty servant | shall pass between us. 4.02. 19
thus might he pass indeed; 4.06. 47
pass. 4.06. 94 P
gentleman, go your gait, and let poor voke pass. 4.06.238 P
o, let him pass, he hates him | that would upon 5.03.314
indignity | which patience could not pass. OTH 2.03.246
let him not pass, | but kill him rather. 5.02.241
on, there, pass along! ANT 3.01. 37
as my farthest band | shall pass on thy approof. 3.02. 27
a prophesying fear | of what hath come to pass; 4.14.121
that the strait pass was damm'd | with dead men CYM 5.03. 11
so let it pass. PER 2.03. 35
it will come to that pass if strangers be STM II.C 4 P
as scorning it should pass | to wash the foul VEN 982
the boy he should not pass those grounds. PP 9. 8
that time when thou shalt strangely pass, | and SON 49. 5
for to no other pass my verses tend | than of 103.11
then in the number let me pass untold, | though 136. 9

PASSA 1 FR 0.0001 REL FR 1 V 0 P
let him play | qui passa o' th' bells and bones. TNK 3.05. 86

PASSABLE 2 FR 0.0002 REL FR 1 V 1 P
the virtue of your name | is not here passable. COR 5.02. 13
his body's a passable carcass, if he be not hurt CYM 1.02. 9 P

PASSADO 3 FR 0.0003 REL FR 0 V 3 P
the passado he respects not, the duello he LLL 1.02.178 P
ah, the immortal passado, the punto reverso, the ROM 2.04. 26 P
come, sir, your passado. 3.01. 85 P

PASSAGE 38 FR 0.0043 REL FR 35 V 3 P
in | now in the stirring passage of the day, | a ERR 3.01. 99
leaves the wind, | all unseen, can passage find; LLL 4.03.104
father — o, that "had," how sad a passage 'tis! AWW 1.01. 18 P
as long as there is a passage in my throat and TN 1.03. 39 P
in whose easiest passage | look for no less than WT 3.02. 90
it not a crime | to me, or my swift passage, 4.01. 5
whose passage, vex'd with thy impediment, JN 2.01.336
the mouth of passage shall we fling wide ope, 2.01.449
through the false passage of thy throat thou R2 1.01.125
the sullen passage of thy weary steps | esteem 1.03.265
track | of his bright passage to the occident. 3.03. 67
may tear a passage thorough the flinty ribs | of 5.05. 20
us | will cut their passage through the force of H5 2.02. 16
might but redeem the passage of your age! 1H6 2.05.108
here is the best and safest passage in? 3.02. 22
the hollow passage of my poison'd voice, | by 5.04.121
hath stopp'd the passage where thy words should 3H6 1.03. 22
ope | and give sweet passage to my sinful soul! 2.03. 41
unless our halberds did shut up his passage. 4.03. 20
if | the passage and whole /carriage /of /this TRO 2.03.131
down before him, and leave his passage poll'd. COR 4.05.202 P
and | with bloody passage led your wars even to 5.06. 75
rome, | keep then this passage to the capitol, TIT 1.01. 12
the fearful passage of their death-mark'd love, ROM pr 9
what, are my doors oppos'd against my passage? TIM 3.04. 79
carv'd out his passage | till he fac'd the slave MAC 1.02. 19
stop up th' access and passage to remorse, 1.05. 44
when he is fit and season'd for his passage? HAM 3.03. 86
to have prov'd most royal, and, for his passage, 5.02.398
for if such actions may have passage free, OTH 1.02. 98
what ho! no watch? no passage? murther, murther! 5.01. 37
hereafter find | it is no act of common passage, CYM 3.04. 91
made good the passage, cried to those that fled, 5.03. 23
yet in the passage | the gods have been most TNK 5.04.114
which to his speech did honey passage yield, VEN 452
struggling for passage, earth's foundation 1047
to make more vent for passage of her breath, LUC 1040
leaves the wind | all unseen gan passage find, PP 16. 6

PASSAGES 10 FR 0.0011 REL FR 7 V 3 P
one that countermands | the passages of alleys, ERR 4.02. 38
believe such impossible passages of grossness. TN 3.02. 72 P
a long apprenticehood | to foreign passages, and R2 1.03.272
from whence this stream through muddy passages 5.03. 62
but thou dost in thy passages of life | make me 1H4 3.02. 8
the severals and unhidden passages | of his true H5 1.01. 86
and there is gallant and most prave passages. 3.06. 93 P
hind'red, oft, | the passages made toward it. H8 2.04.166
by time, | and that i see, in passages of proof, HAM 4.07.112
i will, between the passages of this project, TNK 4.03. 99 P

PASSANT 1 FR 0.0001 REL FR 0 V 1 P
it agrees well, passant. WIV 1.01. 20 P

PASS'D 45 FR 0.0050 REL FR 39 V 6 P
and so conclusions pass'd the careers. WIV 1.01.179 P
so cried and shriek'd at it, that it pass'd. 1.01.297 P
to know what hath pass'd between me and ford's 3.05. 62 P
overheard what hath pass'd between you and your MM 3.01.160 P
knowing what hath pass'd between you and claudio ADO 5.02. 48 P
your oaths are pass'd, and now subscribe your LLL 1.01. 19
your oath is pass'd to pass away from these. 1.01. 49
did point you to buy them, along as you pass'd; 2.01.245
is my doom | which i have pass'd upon her; AYL 1.03. 84
thousand crowns | to what is pass'd already. AWW 3.07. 36

hath newly pass'd between this youth and me. TN 5.01.155
practice hath most shrewdly pass'd upon thee; 5.01.352
justly weigh'd | that have on both sides pass'd. 5.01.368
your gallery | have we pass'd through, not WT 5.03. 11
and thus still doing, thus he pass'd along. R2 5.02. 21
remember, as thou read'st, thy promise pass'd. 5.03. 51
was like, and had indeed against us pass'd, H5 1.01. 3
'tis certain he hath pass'd the river somme. 3.05. 1
pass'd over to the end they were created, 3H6 2.05. 39
thou seest what's pass'd, go fear thy king 3.03.226
well have we pass'd and now repass'd the seas, 4.07. 5
hath pass'd in safety through the narrow seas, 4.08. 3
o, i have pass'd a miserable night, | so full of R3 1.04. 2
i pass'd, methought, the melancholy flood, 1.04. 45
voice, and that not pass'd me but | by learned H8 1.02. 70
but pray how pass'd it? 2.01. 10
as he pass'd along, | how earnestly he cast his 5.02. 11
and all the rest so laugh'd, that it pass'd. TRO 1.02.167 P
for they pass'd by me | as misers do by beggars, 3.03.142
and handkerchers, | upon him as he pass'd; COR 2.01.265
of his choler, | and pass'd him unelected. 2.03.199
hath he not pass'd the noble and the common? 3.01. 29
that being pass'd for consul with full voice, 3.03. 59
i have pass'd | my word and promise to the TIT 1.01.468
in the people's ears, there nought hath pass'd, 4.04. 7
where i may read who pass'd that passing fair? ROM 1.01.236
no villainous bounty yet hath pass'd my heart; TIM 2.02.173
of any promise that hath pass'd from him. JC 2.01.140
last conference, pass'd in probation with you: MAC 3.01. 79
sieges, /fortunes, | that i have pass'd. OTH 1.03.131
she lov'd me for the dangers i had pass'd, | and 1.03.167
men should be, | till he hath pass'd necessity. PER 2.ch. 6
skill, pass'd slightly | his careless execution, TNK 1.03. 28
thou hast pass'd by the ambush of young days, SON 70. 9
as i by yours, y' have pass'd a hell of time, 120. 6

PASSED 3 FR 0.0003 REL FR 3 V 0 P
and passed sentence may not be recall'd | but to ERR 1.01.147
moon, | and the imperial vot'ress passed on, MND 2.01.163
make thee beg pardon for thy passed speech, 2H6 3.02.221

PASSENGER 3 FR 0.0003 REL FR 3 V 0 P
fellows, stand fast; i see a passenger. TGV 4.01. 1
law, | have some unhappy passenger in chase. 5.04. 15
never did passenger in summer's heat | more VEN 91

PASSENGERS 4 FR 0.0004 REL FR 4 V 0 P
no outrages | on silly women or poor passengers. TGV 4.01. 70
and beat our watch and rob our passengers, R2 5.03. 9
felonious thief that fleec'd poor passengers, 2H6 3.01.129
with sorrow snares relenting passengers; 3.01.227

PASSES 12 FR 0.0013 REL FR 7 V 5 P
your passes, stoccadoes, and i know not what. WIV 2.01.225 P
why, this passes, master ford. 4.02.122 P
this passes! 4.02.137 P
like pow'r divine, | hath look'd upon my passes. MM 5.01.370
she passes praise, then praise too short doth LLL 4.03.237
to make no stain a stain | as passes coloring. WT 2.02. 18
he passes some humors and careers. H5 2.01.126 P
the common body | to yield what passes here. COR 2.02. 54
he passes. TIM 1.01. 12
but i have that within which passes show, HAM 1.02. 85
that in a dozen passes between yourself and him, 5.02.166 P
a gaudy shadow | that old time, as he passes by, TNK 2.02.104

PASSETH 1 FR 0.0001 REL FR 1 V 0 P
eye, | and passeth by with stiff unbowed knee, 2H6 3.01. 16

PASSING 36 FR 0.0040 REL FR 31 V 5 P
dear madam, 'tis a passing shame | that i TGV 1.02. 17
own present folly, and her passing deformity: 2.01. 75 P
is she not passing fair? 4.04.148
deny | the jury, passing on the prisoner's life, MM 2.01. 19
cousin, you apprehend passing shrewdly. ADO 2.01. 81 P
spied a blossom passing fair | playing in the LLL 4.03.101
for oberon is passing fell and wrath, | because MND 2.01. 20
i will be bitter with him and passing short. AYL 3.05.138
it will be pastime passing excellent, | if it be SHR in.1. 67
you are passing welcome, | and so i pray you all 2.01.112
no, not a whit, i find you passing gentle: 2.01.242
thou art pleasant, gamesome, passing courteous, 2.01.245
though he be blunt, i know him passing wise; 3.02. 24
my falcon now is sharp and passing empty, | and 4.01.190
'tis passing good, i prithee let me have it. 4.03. 18
of the vapians passing the equinoctial of TN 2.03. 24 P
this is a passing merry one and goes to the tune WT 4.04.288 P
passing these flats, are taken by the tide — JN 5.06. 40
believe me, i am passing light in spirit. 2H4 4.02. 85
and our air shakes them passing scornfully. H5 4.02. 42
precinct | i was employ'd in passing to and fro, 1H6 2.01. 69
o passing traitor, perjur'd and unjust! 3H6 5.01.106
lip, a bonny eye, a passing pleasing tongue; R3 1.01. 94
say his long trouble now is passing | out of H8 4.02.162
discretion, | yet are they passing cowardly. COR 1.01.203
this valley fits the purpose passing well. TIT 2.03. 84
show me a mistress that is passing fair, | what ROM 1.01.234
where i may read who pass'd that passing fair? 1.01.236
must die, | passing through nature to eternity. HAM 1.02. 73
and no more, | the which he loved passing well." 2.02.408
i have a daughter that i love passing well. 2.02.412 P
in faith 'twas strange, 'twas passing strange; OTH 1.03.160
short ears, straight legs and passing strong, VEN 297
to one sore sick that hears the passing bell. 702
deep conceit is such | as, passing all conceit, PP 8. 8
was ever may, | spied a blossom passing fair, 16. 3

PASSIO 1 FR 0.0001 REL FR 1 V 0 P
/hysterica passio, down, thou climbing sorrow, LR 2.04. 57

/PASSION 3 FR 0.0003 REL FR 3 V 0 P
/alas, /the /tender /boy, /in /passion /mov'd, TIT 3.02. 48
/did /put /me | /into /a /tow'ring /passion. HAM 5.02. 80
/she /was /a /queen | /over /her /passion, /who, LR 4.03. 14

PASSION 115 FR 0.0130 REL FR 96 V 19 P
allaying both their fury and my passion | with TMP 1.02.393
your father's in some passion | that works him 4.01.143
that relish all as sharply | passion as they, be 5.01. 24
how now? what means this passion at his name? TGV 1.02. 16
got's will, and his passion of my heart! WIV 3.01. 62 P
but till this afternoon his passion | ne'er ERR 5.01. 47
each one with ireful passion, with drawn swords, 5.01.151
if my passion change not shortly, god forbid it ADO 1.01.219 P
never counterfeit of passion came so near the 2.03.105 P
so near the life of passion as she discovers it. 2.03.105 P
why, what effects of passion shows she? 2.03.107 P
and counsel him to fight against his passion, 3.01. 83
their counsel turns to passion, which before 5.01. 23
but with this i passion to say wherewith" — LLL 1.01.260 P
sighs reek from you, noted well your passion. 4.03.138
it did move him to passion, and therefore let's 4.03.198
you spend your passion on a mispris'd mood. MND 3.02. 74
tears | the passion of loud laughter never shed. 5.01. 70
this passion, and the death of a dear friend, 5.01.288 P
here she comes, and her passion ends the play. 5.01.315 P
i never heard a passion so confus'd, | so MV 2.08. 12
/mistress of passion, sways it to the mood | of 4.01. 51
what passion hangs these weights upon my tongue? AYL 1.02.257
company | abruptly, as my passion now makes me, 2.04. 41
this shepherd's passion | is much upon my 2.04. 60
for every passion something and for no passion 3.02.413 P
something and for no passion truly any thing, as 3.02.413 P
complexion that it was a passion of earnest. 4.03.170 P
all made of passion, and all made of wishes, 5.02. 95
you break into some merry passion | and so SHR in.1. 97
a re, to plead hortensio's passion; 3.01. 74
and therefore be not — cock's passion, silence! 4.01.118 P
where love's strong passion is impress'd in AWW 1.03.133
against the proclamation of thy passion, | to 1.03.174
cox my passion! 5.02. 41 P
o, then unfold the passion of my love, TN 1.04. 24
the cunning of her passion | invites me in this 2.02. 22
methought it did relieve my passion much, | more 2.04. 4
can bide the beating of so strong a passion | as 2.04. 94
pride, | nor wit nor reason can my passion hide. 3.01.152
with the same havior that your passion bears 3.04.206
methinks his words do from such passion fly 3.04.373
let thy fair wisdom, not thy passion, sway | in 4.01. 52
fear you his tyrannous passion more, alas, WT 2.03. 28
cast your good counsels | upon his passion. 4.04.496
a notable passion of wonder appear'd in them; 5.02. 16 P
merriment — | a passion hateful to my purposes; JN 3.03. 47
then with a passion would i shake the world, 3.04. 39
his passion is so ripe, it needs must break. 4.02. 79
forgive the comment that my passion made | upon 4.02.263
for i must speak in passion, and i will do it in 1H4 2.04.386 P
not in pleasure but in passion; 2.04.416 P
having this distemp'rature, | in passion shook. 3.01. 34
this strained passion doth you wrong, my lord. 2H4 1.01.161
if you give o'er | to stormy passion, must 1.01.165
unto whose grace our passion is as subject | as H5 1.02.242
free from gross passion, or of mirth or anger, 2.02.132
attaint | with any passion of inflaming /love, 1H6 5.05. 82
to tell the passion of my sovereign's heart, 3H6 3.03. 62
this is it that makes me bridle passion, | and 4.04. 19
quench, | or but allay, the fire of passion. H8 1.01.149
to the hot passion of distemp'red blood | than TRO 2.02.169
even such a passion doth embrace my bosom: 3.02. 35
with that which here his passion doth express? 5.02.162
your passion draws ears hither. 5.02.181
shed, | a mother's tears in passion for her son; TIT 1.01.106
but passion lends them power, time means, to ROM 2.pr. 13
passion! 2.01. 7
ere i was ware, | my true–love passion; 2.02.104
i feel my master's passion. TIM 3.01. 56
and with such sober and unnoted passion | he did 3.05. 21
then, brutus, i have much mistook your passion, JC 1.02. 48
passion, i see, is catching, /for mine eyes, 3.01.283
you shall offend him and extend his passion. MAC 3.04. 56
macduff, this noble passion, | child of 4.03.114
eyes of heaven, | and passion in the gods." HAM 2.02.518
here, | but in a fiction, in a dream of passion, 2.02.552
had he the motive and /the /cue for passion 2.02.561
as i may say, whirlwind of your passion, you 3.02. 7 P
periwig–pated fellow tear a passion to totters, 3.02. 9 P
what to ourselves in passion we propose, | the 3.02.194
the passion ending, doth the purpose lose. 3.02.195
that, laps'd in time and passion, lets go by 3.04.107
thought and afflictions, passion, hell itself, 4.05.188
smooth every passion | that in the natures of LR 2.02. 75
for those that mingle reason with your passion 2.04.234
'twixt two extremes of passion, joy and grief, 5.03.199
and passion, having my best judgment collied, OTH 2.03.206
from the heart, | that passion cannot rule. 3.03.124
i see, /sir, you are eaten up with passion; 3.03.391
herself in such shadowing passion without some 4.01. 40 P
grief | (a passion most /unsuiting such a man), 4.01. 77
concerning this, sir — o well–painted passion! 4.01.257
this the nature | whom passion could not shake? 4.01.266
some bloody passion shakes your very frame. 5.02. 44
/whose every passion fully strives | to make ANT 1.01. 50
your speech is passion; 2.02. 12
what's thy passion? 3.10. 5
by such poor passion as the maid that milks 4.15. 74
the quality of her passion shall require, | lest 5.01. 63
this borrowed passion stands for true old woe; PER 4.04. 24
eye, o coz, | what passion would enclose thee! TNK 3.01. 30
thou shouldst perceive my passion, if these 3.01. 31
'tis your passion | that thus mistakes, the 3.01. 48
not made in passion neither, but good heed. 3.06.232
and, trembling in her passion, calls it balm, VEN 27
and swelling passion doth provoke a pause. 218
passion on passion deeply is redoubled: 832
passion on passion deeply is redoubled: 832
all entertain'd, each passion labors so, | that 969
the life and feeling of her passion | she hoards LUC 1317
such passion her assails | that patience is 1562
my woe too sensible thy passion maketh | more 1678
hast thou, the master mistress of my passion; SON 20. 2
"for lo his passion, but an art of craft, | even LC 295

/PASSIONATE 2 FR 0.0002 REL FR 2 V 0 P
i am amazed at your /passionate words. MND 3.02.220
/and /cannot /passionate /our /tenfold /grief TIT 3.02. 6

PASSIONATE 6 FR 0.0006 REL FR 3 V 3 P
"poor forlorn proteus, passionate proteus: TGV 1.02.121
child, make passionate my sense of hearing. LLL 3.01. 1 P
she is sad and passionate at your highness' tent JN 2.01.544
nephew, what means this passionate discourse, 2H6 1.01.104
i hope this passionate humor of mine will change R3 1.04.118 P
of your quality, come, a passionate speech. HAM 2.02.432 P

PASSIONING 1 FR 0.0001 REL FR 1 V 0 P
'twas ariadne passioning | for theseus' perjury TGV 4.04.167

PASSION'S 3 FR 0.0003 REL FR 3 V 0 P
to check their folly, passion's solemn tears. LLL 5.02.118
give me that man | that is not passion's slave, HAM 3.02. 72
no object but her passion's strength renews; LUC 1103

PASSIONS 20 FR 0.0022 REL FR 18 V 2 P
dimensions, senses, affections, passions; MV 3.01. 60 P
how all the other passions fleet to air, | as 3.02.108
for your passions | have to the full appeach'd. AWW 1.03.190
till that his passions, like a whale on ground, 2H4 4.04. 40
for, had the passions of thy heart burst out, 1H6 4.01.183
of all base passions, fear is most accurs'd. 5.02. 18
do breed love's settled passions in my heart, 5.05. 4
but his passions moves me so | that hardly can i 3H6 1.04.150
whose passions and whose plots have broke their COR 4.04. 19
and plead my passions for lavinia's love. TIT 2.01. 36
then be my passions bottomless with them! 3.01.217
our own precedent passions do instruct us | what TIM 1.01.133
i am | of late with passions of some difference, JC 1.02. 40
as oft as any passions under heaven | that does HAM 2.01.102
her passions are made of nothing but the finest ANT 1.02.146 P
the passions of the mind, | that have their PER 1.02. 11
variable passions throng her constant woe, | as VEN 967
dumbly she passions, franticly she doteth, | she 1059
catching all passions in his craft of will, LC 126
that they their passions likewise lent me | of 199

PASSIVE 1 FR 0.0001 REL FR 1 V 0 P
affords | to such as may the passive drugs of it TIM 4.03.254

PASSPORT 3 FR 0.0003 REL FR 3 V 0 P
look on his letter, madam, here's my passport. AWW 3.02. 56
let him depart, his passport shall be made, H5 4.03. 36
a passport too! PER 3.02. 66

PASSY–MEASURES 1 FR 0.0001 REL FR 0 V 1 P
then he's a rogue, and a passy–measures /pavin. TN 5.01.200 P

/PAST 3 FR 0.0003 REL FR 3 V 0 P
/past /and /to /come /seems /best; 2H4 1.03.108
though less than yours in /past, must o'ertop TRO 3.03.164
/what's /past /and /what's /to /come /is 4.05.166

PAST 154 FR 0.0174 REL FR 121 V 33 P
past the mid season. TMP 1.02.239
an act | whereof what's past is prologue, what 2.01.253
here shroud till the dregs of the storm be past. 2.02. 41 P
no matter, since i feel | the best is past. 3.03. 51
loss, and patience | says, it is past her cure. 5.01.141
back | and ask remission for my folly past. TGV 1.02. 65
'tis past the hour, sir, that sir hugh promis'd WIV 2.03. 4 P
my riots past, my wild societies, | and tells me 3.04. 8
'tis past eight already, sir. 3.05.132 P
and such a one were past cure of the thing you MM 2.01.111 P
he's now past it, yet (and i say to thee) he 3.02.182 P
reakless, and fearless of what's past, present, 4.02.144 P
that life is better life, past fearing death, 5.01.397
now he's there, past thought of human reason. ERR 5.01.189
o, she misus'd me past the endurance of a block; ADO 2.01.239 P
it is past the infinite of thought. 2.03.101 P
forbear till this company be past. LLL 1.02.126 P
great reason: for past care is still past cure. 5.02. 28
great reason: for past care is still past cure. 5.02. 28
your cue is past; MND 3.01.101 P
thou driv'st me past the bounds | of maiden's 3.02. 65
saint valentine is past; 4.01.139
past the wit of man to say what dream it was. 4.01.205 P
his hour is almost past. MV 2.06. 2
way, | he did entreat me, past all saying nay, 3.02.229
past all expressing. 3.05. 73
is it not past two a' clock? AYL 4.03. 1 P
why, i am past my gamouth long ago. SHR 3.01. 71
ray'd with the yellows, past cure of the fives, 3.02. 53 P
our strength as weak, our weakness past compare, 5.02.174
be found in the calendar of my past endeavors, AWW 1.03. 5 P
a senseless help when help past sense we deem. 2.01.124
my art is not past power, nor you past cure. 2.01.158
my art is not past power, nor you past cure. 2.01.158
they say miracles are past, and we have our 2.03. 1 P
for doing i am past, as i will by thee, in what 2.03.233 P
the troop is past. 3.05. 93
may token to the future our past deeds. 4.02. 63
'tis past, my liege, | and i beseech your 5.03. 4
the bitter past, more welcome is the sweet. 5.03.334
past question, for thou seest it will not /curl TN 1.03. 98 P
a wrack past hope he was. 5.01. 79
not you seen, camillo | (but that's past doubt; WT 1.02.268
he so troubles me, | 'tis past enduring. 2.01. 2
then 'twere past all doubt | you'd call your 2.03. 81
of our dear services | past and to come) that 2.03.151
to do so) my past life | hath been as continent, 3.02. 33
as you were past all shame | (those of your fact 3.02. 84
(those of your fact are so), so past all truth; 3.02. 85
what's gone and what's past help | should be 3.02.222
and what's past help | should be past grief. 3.02.223
i have a kinsman not past three quarters of a 4.03. 80 P
boy, i am past moe children, but thy sons and 5.02.126 P
which was so strongly urg'd past my defense. JN 1.01.258
indeed we fear'd his sickness was past cure. 4.02. 86
all murthers past do stand excus'd in this; 4.03. 51
writ in remembrance more than things long past. R2 2.01. 14
things past redress are now with me past care. 2.03.171
things past redress are now with me past care. 2.03.171
nay, that's past praying for, i have pepper'd 1H4 2.04.191 P
your lordship, though not clean past your youth, 2H4 1.02. 97 P
'tis one a' clock, and past. 3.01. 34
what perils past, what crosses to ensue, | would 3.01. 55
mouldy, stay at home till you are past service; 3.02.251 P
the heat is past, follow no further now; 4.03. 24
of other, | turning past evils to advantages. 4.04. 78
of indigent faint souls past corporal toil, | a H5 1.01. 16
either past or not arriv'd to pith and puissance 3.pr. 21
the interim, by rememb'ring you 'tis past. 5.pr. 43
saint davy's day is past. 5.01. 2 P
what's past and what's to come she can descry. 1H6 1.02. 57
for grief that they are past recovery; 2H6 1.01.116
here comes a man, let's stay till he be past. 3H6 3.01. 12
brittany, | till storms be past of civil enmity. 4.06. 98
harp not on that string, madam, that is past. R3 4.04.364
hereafter time, for time past wrong'd by thee. 4.04.390
my lord, the enemy is past the marsh, | after 5.03.345
the lord help, | they vex me past my patience. H8 2.04.131
must no more call it york–place, that's past; 4.01. 95
but now i am past all comforts here but prayers. 4.02.123
you know he has not past three or four hairs on TRO 1.02.112 P

i took the blow — unless it swell past hiding, 1.02.269 P
swell past hiding, and then it's past watching. 1.02.270 P
those scraps are good deeds past, which are 3.03.148
though they are made and moulded of things past, 3.03.177
well, well, 'tis done, 'tis past. 5.02. 97
scaling his present bearing with his past, COR 2.03.249
better put in hazard | than stay, past doubt, 2.03.257
present, but the loss | of what is past. 3.02. 72
the main blaze of it is past, but a small thing 4.03. 20 P
with pride, ambitious past all thinking, 4.06. 31
subtle ground, | i have tumbled past the throw; 5.02. 21
and at my suit, sweet, pardon what is past. TIT 1.01.431
kinsmen, his sorrows are past remedy, | but /... 4.03. 31
these wrongs unspeakable, past patience, | or 5.03.126
for you and i are past our dancing days. ROM 1.05. 31
not to be talk'd on, yet they are past compare. 2.05. 43 P
but that a joy past joy calls out on me, | it 3.03.173
come weep with me, past hope, past /cure, past 4.01. 45
weep with me, past hope, past /cure, past help! 4.01. 45
weep with me, past hope, past /cure, past help! 4.01. 45
it strains me past the compass of my wits. 4.01. 47
his days and times are past, | and my reliances TIM 2.01. 21
on forfeiture, my lord, six weeks | and past. 2.02. 31
now lord timon's happy hours are done and past, 3.02. 6 P
the law, which is past depth | to those that, 3.05. 12
i should not urge thy duty past thy might; JC 4.03.261
that it was he in the times past which held you MAC 3.01. 76
all pressures past | that youth and observation HAM 1.05.100
my fault is past, but, o, what form of prayer 3.03. 51
repent what's past, avoid what is to come, | and 3.04.150
he thought, | by this had thought been past. LR 4.06. 45
meanest wretch, | past speaking of in a king! 4.06.205
'tis past, and so am i. 5.03.165
until some half hour past, when i was arm'd. 5.03.194
o, she deceives me | past thought! OTH 1.01.166
when remedies are past, the griefs are ended 1.03.202
to mourn a mischief that is past and gone | is 1.03.204
not past a pint, as i am a soldier. 2.03. 66 P
ay, past all surgery. 2.03.260 P
of such mortal kind | that nor my service past, 3.04.116
things that are past are done with me. ANT 1.02. 97
she is cunning past man's thought. 1.02.145
to the deserver | till his deserts are past, 1.02.187
were one such, | it's past the size of dreaming. 5.02. 97
past grace? obedience? CYM 1.01.136
past hope, and in despair, that way past grace. 1.01.137
past hope, and in despair, that way past grace. 1.01.137
for certainties | either are past remedies, or, 1.06. 97
th' great, | thou art past the tyrant's stroke; 4.02.265
their pleasures here are past, so /is their pain 4.02.290
it strikes me, past | the hope of comfort. 4.03. 8
of what's past, is, and to come, the discharge. 5.04.168 P
any thing | that's due to all the villains past, 5.05.212
bethought what was past, what might succeed. PER 1.02. 83
kindness | makes my past miseries sports. 5.03. 41
talk more of this when the solemnity is past. TNK 2.01. 13 P
she's lost | past all cure. 4.01.140
my day's delight is past, my horse is gone, VEN 380
my will is strong, past reason's weak removing: LUC 243
by thine inclination | to all sins past, and all 923
since that my case is past the help of law. 1022
rage sent out, recall'd in rage, being past), 1671
suppose thou dost defend me | from what is past: 1685
although i know my years be past the best, | i PP 1. 6
when i behold the violet past prime, | and sable SON 12. 3
i summon up remembrance of things past, | i sigh 30. 2
hue, | finding thy worth a limit past my praise, 82. 6
not wond'ring at the present, nor the past, 123.10
past reason hunted, and no sooner had, | past 129. 6
past reason hated as a swallowed bait | on 129. 7
although she knows my days are past the best, 138. 6
past cure i am, now reason is past care, | and 147. 9
past cure i am, now reason is past care, | and 147. 9

PAST–CURE 1 FR 0.0001 REL FR 1 V 0 P
to prostitute our past–cure malady | to empirics AWW 2.01.121

PASTE 5 FR 0.0005 REL FR 4 V 1 P
which serves as paste and cover to our bones. R2 3.02.154
and with your blood and it i'll make a paste, TIT 5.02.187
paste, | and of the paste a coffin i will rear, 5.02.188
and in that paste let their vile heads be bak'd. 5.02.200
to the eels when she put 'em i' th' paste alive; LR 2.04.123 P

PASTER *(also pasture)*

PASTER 1 FR 0.0001 REL FR 1 V 0 P
it is the paster lards the brother's sides, TIM 4.03. 12

/PASTERNS 1 FR 0.0001 REL FR 0 V 1 P
with any that treads but on four /pasterns. H5 3.07. 12 P

PASTERS' 1 FR 0.0001 REL FR 1 V 0 P
her pasters' grass with faithful english blood. R2 3.03.100

PASTIES 1 FR 0.0001 REL FR 1 V 0 P
and make two pasties of your shameful heads, TIT 5.02.189

PASTIME 15 FR 0.0017 REL FR 13 V 2 P
whose pastime | is to make midnight mushrumps, TMP 5.01. 38
stream, | and make a pastime of each weary step, TGV 2.07. 35
we will with some strange pastime solace them, LLL 4.03.374
to see no pastime i. AYL 5.04.195
it will be pastime passing excellent, | if it be SHR in.1. 67
husht, master, here's some good pastime toward; 1.01. 68
began, | on the catastrophe and heel of pastime, AWW 1.02. 57
pleasure and his penance, till our very pastime, TN 3.04.138 P
and make itself a pastime | to harder bosoms! WT 1.02.152
make their pastime at my sorrow: 2.03. 24
did you assay him | to any pastime? HAM 3.01. 15
be shook with danger | and think it pastime. 4.07. 33
ha? | mak'st thou this shame thy pastime? LR 2.04. 6
make pastime with us a day or two, or longer. CYM 3.01. 77 P
if you but favor, our country pastime made is. TNK 3.05.102

PASTIMES 3 FR 0.0003 REL FR 3 V 0 P
we have had pastimes here and pleasant game. LLL 5.02.360
in the other's arms | (our pastimes done), TIT 2.03. 26
what pastimes are they? TNK 2.03. 66

PASTORAL 1 FR 0.0001 REL FR 0 V 1 P
comedy, history, pastoral, pastoral–comical, HAM 2.02.397 P

PASTORAL–COMICAL 1 FR 0.0001 REL FR 0 V 1 P
pastoral, pastoral–comical, historical–pastoral, HAM 2.02.397 P

PASTORALS 1 FR 0.0001 REL FR 1 V 0 P
as i have seen them do | in whitsun pastorals. WT 4.04.134

PASTORS 1 FR 0.0001 REL FR 1 V 0 P
do not, as some ungracious pastors do, | show me HAM 1.03. 47

PAST–PROPORTION 1 FR 0.0001 REL FR 1 V 0 P
sum | the past–proportion of his infinite, | and TRO 2.02. 29

PASTRY 1 FR 0.0001 REL FR 1 V 0 P
they call for dates and quinces in the pastry. ROM 4.04. 2

PAST–SAVING 1 FR 0.0001 REL FR 0 V 1 P
what a past–saving slave is this! AWW 4.03.138 P

PASTURE *(also paster, etc.)*

PASTURE 12 FR 0.0013 REL FR 10 V 2 P
here's too small a pasture for such store of TGV 1.01. 99 P
you sheep, and i pasture: LLL 2.01.221
so you grant pasture for me. 2.01.222
full of the pasture, jumps along by him | and AYL 2.01. 53
what is he that shall buy his flock and pasture? 2.04. 88
buy thou the cottage, pasture, and the flock, 2.04. 92
that good pasture makes fat sheep; 3.02. 27 P
they sell the pasture now to buy the horse, H5 2.pr. 5
show us here | the mettle of your pasture; 3.01. 27
like the stag, when snow the pasture sheets, ANT 1.04. 65
so graze, as you find pasture. CYM 5.04. 2
for our milk | will relish of the pasture, and TNK 1.02. 77

PASTY 2 FR 0.0002 REL FR 0 V 2 P
come, we have a hot venison pasty to dinner. WIV 1.01.195 P
if ye pinch me like a pasty, i can say no more. AWW 4.03.123 P

/PAT 1 FR 0.0001 REL FR 1 V 0 P
now might i do it /pat, now 'a is a–praying; HAM 3.03. 73

PAT 5 FR 0.0005 REL FR 1 V 4 P
pat, pat; MND 3.01. 2 P
pat, pat; 3.01. 2 P
you shall see it will fall pat as i told you. 5.01.187 P
could | come pat betwixt too early and too late H8 2.03. 84
/edgar — pat! LR 1.02.134 P

PATCH* 13 FR 0.0014 REL FR 10 V 3 P
thou scurvy patch! TMP 3.02. 63
mome, malt–horse, capon, coxcomb, idiot, patch! ERR 3.01. 32
what patch is made our porter? 3.01. 36
patch grief with proverbs, make misfortune drunk ADO 5.01. 17
so were there a patch set on learning, to see LLL 4.02. 31
the patch is kind enough, but a huge feeder, MV 2.05. 46
lord your son with a patch of velvet on 's face. AWW 4.05. 95 P
velvet knows, but 'tis a goodly patch of velvet. 4.05. 97 P
and begin to patch up thine old body for heaven? 2H4 2.04.233 P
what soldiers, patch? MAC 5.03. 15
we go to gain a little patch of ground | that HAM 4.04. 18
should patch a wall t' expel the /winter's flaw! 5.01.216
if you'll patch a quarrel, | as matter whole you ANT 2.02. 52

PATCH–BREECH 1 FR 0.0001 REL FR 0 V 1 P
what, patch–breech, i say! PER 2.01. 14 P

/PATCH'D 1 FR 0.0001 REL FR 0 V 1 P
i had — but man is but /a /patch'd fool, if he MND 4.01.209 P

PATCH'D 7 FR 0.0008 REL FR 4 V 3 P
any thing that's mended is but patch'd; TN 1.05. 48 P
that transgresses is but patch'd with sin, and 1.05. 48 P
and sin that amends is but patch'd with virtue. 1.05. 49 P
patch'd with foul moles and eye–offending marks, JN 3.01. 47
than did the fault before it was so patch'd. 4.02. 34
this must be patch'd | with cloth of any color. COR 3.01.251
but | you patch'd up your excuses. ANT 2.02. 56

PATCHERY 2 FR 0.0002 REL FR 1 V 1 P
here is such patchery, such juggling, and such TRO 2.03. 71 P
know his gross patchery, love him, feed him, TIM 5.01. 96

PATCHES* 5 FR 0.0005 REL FR 5 V 0 P
a crew of patches, rude mechanicals, | that work MND 3.02. 9
as patches set upon a little breach | discredit JN 4.02. 32
do botch and bungle up damnation | with patches, H5 2.02.116
and patches will i get unto these cudgell'd 5.01. 88
a king of shreds and patches — | save me, and HAM 3.04.102

PATE 30 FR 0.0034 REL FR 17 V 13 P
by line and level" is an excellent pass of pate; TMP 4.01.244 P
there is either liquor in his pate, or money in WIV 2.01.190 P
for she will /score your fault upon my pate: ERR 1.02. 65
i have some marks of yours upon my pate: 1.02. 82
back, slave, or i will break thy pate across. 2.01. 78
as the plain bald pate of father time himself. 2.02. 70 P
ay, and let none enter, lest i break your pate. 2.02.218
breaking here, and i'll break your knave's pate. 3.01. 74
rap me well, or i'll knock your knave's pate. SHR 1.02. 12
and through the instrument my pate made way, 2.01.154
i would i had, so i had broke thy pate, | and AWW 2.01. 66
taken | by any understanding pate but thine? WT 1.02.223
that broker that still breaks the pate of faith, JN 2.01.568
as good deed as drink to break the pate on thee, 1H4 2.01. 30 P
shot here, here's no scoring but upon the pate. 5.03. 31 P
tell him i'll knock his leek about his pate H5 4.01. 54
of my leek, or i will peat his pate four days. 5.01. 41 P
hold you, there is a groat to heal your pate. 5.01. 59 P
god buy you, and keep you, and heal your pate. 5.01. 67 P
will turn white, a curl'd pate will grow bald, a 5.02.160 P
do pelt so fast at one another's pate | that 1H6 3.01. 82
and chop away that factious pate of his. 2H6 5.01.135
lay the serving–creature's dagger on your pate. ROM 4.05.118 P
the learned pate | ducks to the golden fool. TIM 4.03. 17
who calls me villain, breaks my pate across, HAM 2.02.572
this might be the pate of a politician, which 5.01. 78 P
to have his fine pate full of fine dirt? 5.01.107 P
singeing his pate against the burning zone, 5.01.282
comes from my pate as birdlime does from frieze, OTH 2.01.126
you have broke his pate with your bowl. CYM 2.01. 7 P

PATENS 1 FR 0.0001 REL FR 1 V 0 P
is thick inlaid with patens of bright gold. MV 5.01. 59

PATENT 4 FR 0.0004 REL FR 2 V 2 P
ere i will yield my virgin patent up | unto his MND 1.01. 80
which he thinks is a patent for his sauciness, AWW 4.05. 66 P
over her iniquity, give her patent to offend, OTH 4.01.198 P
and so my patent back again is swerving. SON 87. 8

PATERNAL 1 FR 0.0001 REL FR 1 V 0 P
here i disclaim all my paternal care, LR 1.01.113

PATES 2 FR 0.0002 REL FR 2 V 0 P
fat paunches have lean pates; LLL 1.01. 26
and | to melt the city leads upon your pates, COR 4.06. 82

PATH 15 FR 0.0017 REL FR 15 V 0 P
in that good path that i would wish it go, | and MM 4.03.133
out of the path which shall directly lead | thy JN 3.04.129
go tread the path that thou shalt ne'er return: R3 1.01.117
away, | and that my path were even to the crown, 3.07.157
keep then the path, | for emulation hath a TRO 3.03.155
must we pursue, and i have found the path: TIT 2.01.111
from forth day's path and titan's /fiery wheels. ROM 2.03. 4
for if thou path, thy native semblance on, | not JC 2.01. 83
himself the primrose path of dalliance treads, HAM 1.03. 50
here is a path to't; CYM 3.06. 18
this funeral path brings to your household's TNK 1.05. 11
and where there is a path of ground i'll venture 2.06. 33
will be honest, | she has the path before her. 5.02. 23
the path is smooth that leadeth on to danger. VEN 788
she treads the path that she untreads again; 908

PATHETICAL 3 FR 0.0003 REL FR 1 V 2 P
of a child, most pretty and pathetical! LLL 1.02. 98 P
ah, heavens, it is /a most pathetical nit! 4.01.148
think you the most pathetical break–promise, and AYL 4.01.192 P

PATHS 5 FR 0.0005 REL FR 4 V 1 P
in their so sacred paths he dares to tread | in WIV 4.04. 60
his sprite, | in the church–way paths to glide. MND 5.01.382
if we walk not in the trodden paths, our very AYL 1.03. 15 P
but tread the stranger paths of banishment. R2 1.03.143
strain | that haunted us in our familiar paths. H5 2.04. 52

PATHWAY 1 FR 0.0001 REL FR 1 V 0 P
thou showest the naked pathway to thy life, R2 1.02. 31

PATHWAYS 1 FR 0.0001 REL FR 1 V 0 P
should, without eyes, see pathways to his will! ROM 1.01.172

/PATIENCE 2 FR 0.0002 REL FR 2 V 0 P
/patience /and /sorrow /strove | /who /should LR 4.03. 16
grow, /patience! CYM 4.02. 58

PATIENCE 201 FR 0.0227 REL FR 176 V 25 P
i am out of patience. TMP 1.01. 55
by your patience, | i needs must rest me. 3.03. 3
irreparable is the loss, and patience | says, it 5.01.140
have patience, gentle julia. TGV 2.02. 1
and think my patience, more than thy desert, 3.01.159
i do entreat your patience | to hear me speak 4.04.111
love, lend me patience to forbear a while. 5.04. 27
abusing of god's patience and the king's english WIV 1.04. 5 P
his own gravity and patience that ever you saw. 3.01. 54 P
pray you use your patience in good time. 3.01. 82 P
and patience to this his distemper he is in now. 4.02. 28 P
your wisdom, daughter, in your close patience. MM 4.03.118
keep me in patience, and with ripened time 5.01.116
scope of justice, | my patience here is touch'd. 5.01.235
patience unmov'd! ERR 2.01. 32
with urging helpless patience would relieve me; 2.01. 39
this fool–begg'd patience in thee will be left. 2.01. 41
have patience, sir, o, let it not be so! 3.01. 85
be rul'd by me, depart in patience, | and let us 3.01. 94
have patience, i beseech. 4.02. 16
my master preaches patience to him, and the 5.01.174
god give me patience!" ADO 2.03.148 P
is but prolong'd, have patience and endure. 4.01.254
like mine, | and bid him speak of patience; 5.01. 10
yet to me, | and i of him will gather patience. 5.01. 19
no, 'tis all men's office to speak patience | to 5.01. 27
gentlemen both, we will not wake your patience. 5.01.102
i know not how to pray your patience, | yet i 5.01.271
god grant us patience! LLL 1.01.195 P
god i have as little patience as another man, 1.02.165 P
o me, with what strict patience have i sat, | to 4.03.163
i'll stay with patience, but the time is long. 5.02.835
then let us teach our trial patience, | because MND 1.01.152
master mustardseed, i know your patience well. 3.01.192 P
me past the bounds | of maiden's patience. 3.02. 66
a virgin and extort | a poor soul's patience, 3.02.161
her, | and she in mild terms begg'd my patience, 4.01. 58
sweet friends, your patience for my long abode; MV 2.06. 21
i do oppose | my patience to his fury, and am 4.01. 11
silence, and her patience | speak to the people, AYL 1.03. 78
and never cried, "have patience, good people!" 3.02.157 P
patience herself would startle at this letter, 4.03. 13
find a time, audrey, patience, gentle audrey. 5.01. 1 P
all humbleness, all patience, and impatience, 5.02. 97
patience once more, whiles our compact is urg'd: 5.04. 5
sir, by your patience. 5.04.180
your patience and your virtue well deserves it; 5.04.187
though it pass your patience and mine to endure SHR 1.01.126 P
petruchio, patience, i am grumio's pledge. 1.02. 45
hear me with patience. 1.02.237
for patience she will prove a second grissel, 2.01.295
patience, good katherine, and baptista too. 3.02. 21
patience, i pray you, 'twas a fault unwilling. 4.01.156
think upon patience. AWW 3.02. 48
you are, you must have the patience to hear it. 4.03.115 P
ours be your patience then, and yours our parts; ep 5
by your patience, no. TN 2.01. 3 P
she sat like patience on a monument, | smiling 2.04.114
nay, patience, or we break the sinews of our 2.05. 75 P
blush, and tyranny | tremble at patience. WT 3.02. 32
take your patience to you, | and i'll say 3.02.231
your patience this allowing, | i turn my glass, 4.01. 15
o, patience! 5.03. 46
patience, good lady, comfort, gentle constance! JN 3.04. 22
yet can i not of such tame patience boast | as R2 1.01. 52
call it not patience, gaunt, it is despair. 1.02. 29
that which in mean men we entitle patience | is 1.02. 33
and prick my tender patience to those thoughts 2.01.207
smiles, | the badges of his grief and patience, 5.02. 33
patience is stale, and i am weary of it. 5.05.103
for accordingly | you tread upon my patience; 1H4 1.03. 4
drives him beyond the bounds of patience. 1.03.200
enough | to put him quite besides his patience. 3.01.177
and spoke it on purpose to try my patience. 2H4 2.04.308 P
to remember, not to have patience to shift me — 5.05. 21 P
to pray your patience for it and to promise you ep 9 P
who, prologue–like, your humble patience pray, H5 pr 33
linger your patience on, and we'll digest | th' 2.pr. 31
though patience be a tir'd /mare, yet she will 2.01. 23 P
god of his mercy give | you patience to endure, 2.02.180
by your patience, aunchient pistol: 3.06. 30 P
have patience, noble duke, i may not open, | the 1H6 1.03. 18
but only, with your patience, that we may 2.03. 78
priest, this place commands my patience, | or 3.01. 8
patience, good lady, wizards know their times. 2H6 1.04. 15
i pray thee sort thy heart to patience, | these 2.04. 68
patience is for poltroons, such as he. 3H6 1.01. 62
renowned queen, with patience calm the storm, 3.03. 38

his, | sends me a paper to persuade me patience? 3.03.176
nor i, but stoop with patience to my fortune. 5.05. 6
mean time, have patience. R3 1.01.116
with patience, noble lord, as prisoners must; 1.01.126
have patience, madam, there's no doubt his 1.03. 1
lest to thy harm thou move our patience. 1.03.247
no, | i must have patience to endure the load; 3.07.230
by your patience, | i may not suffer you to 4.01. 15
too venturous | in tempting of your patience; H8 1.02. 55
in all the rest show'd a most noble patience. 2.01. 36
the lord help, | they vex me past my patience. 2.04.131
yet will i add an honor — a great patience. 3.01.137
good sir, have patience. 3.02.458
patience, be near me still, and set me lower; 4.02. 76
softly, gentle patience. 4.02. 82
patience, is that letter | i caus'd you write 4.02.127
nay, patience, | you must not leave me yet. 4.02.165
you must take | your patience to you, and be 5.01.105
must be fulfill'd, and i attend with patience. 5.02. 19
lay all the weight ye can upon my patience, | i 5.02.101
patience herself, what goddess e'er she be, TRO 1.01. 27
hector, whose patience | is as a virtue fix'd, 1.02. 4
bid them have patience, she shall come anon. 4.04. 52
hold, patience! 5.02. 29
you have not patience, come. 5.02. 42
my will and all offenses | a guard of patience. 5.02. 54
you have sworn patience. 5.02. 62
i am all patience. 5.02. 64
i did swear patience. 5.02. 84
patience awhile, you'st hear the belly's answer. COR 1.01.126
indeed no, by your patience; 1.03. 74 P
by your patience, | if 'gainst yourself you be 1.09. 55
will rob you of a great deal of patience. 2.01. 29 P
set up the bloody flag against all patience, and 2.01. 75 P
coriolanus, patience! 3.01.190
patience, prince saturninus. TIT 1.01.203
under your patience, gentle emperess, | 'tis 2.03. 66
why, i have patience to endure all this. 2.03. 88
patience, dear niece. 3.01.138
these wrongs unspeakable, past patience, | or 5.03.126
patience perforce with willful choler meeting ROM 1.05. 89
hear me with patience but to speak a word. 3.05.159
i do beseech you, sir, have patience. 5.01. 27
and let mischance be slave to patience. 5.03.221
and bear this work of heaven with patience. 5.03.261
you have to say | i will with patience hear, and JC 1.02.169
can i bear that with patience, | and not my 2.01.301
have patience, gentle friends, i must not read 3.02.140
hear me with patience. 3.02.245
once, | i have the patience to endure it now. 4.03.192
arming myself with patience | to stay the 5.01.105
your patience so predominant in your nature MAC 3.01. 86
you must have patience, madam. 4.02. 2
devotion, patience, courage, fortitude, | i have 4.03. 94
ay, my lord, they stay upon your patience. HAM 3.02.107 P
flame of thy distemper | sprinkle cool patience. 3.04.124
be you content to lend your patience to us, 4.05.211
strengthen your patience in our last night's 5.01.294
see, | till then in patience our proceeding be. 5.01.299
i pray you, sir, take patience. LR 2.04.138
you heavens, give me that patience, patience i 2.04.271
heavens, give me that patience, patience i need! 2.04.271
no, i will be the pattern of all patience, | i 3.02. 37
where is the patience now | that you so oft have 3.06. 58
sir, by your patience, | i hold you but a 5.03. 59
patience, good sir. OTH 1.01.104
yet (by your gracious patience) | i will a round 1.03. 89
takes, | patience her injury a mock'ry makes. 1.03.207
to pay grief, must of poor patience borrow. 1.03.215
let it not gall your patience, good iago, | that 2.01. 97
indignity | which patience could not pass. 2.03.246
how poor are they that have not patience! 2.03.370
watch him tame, and talk him out of patience; 3.03. 23
patience, i say; your mind /perhaps may change. 3.03.452
marry, patience, | or i shall say y' are all in 4.01. 87
i will be found most cunning in my patience; 4.01. 90
in some place of my soul | a drop of patience; 4.02. 53
patience, thou young and rose–lipp'd cherubin — 4.02. 63
patience awhile, good cassio. 5.01. 87
with patience more | than savages could suffer. ANT 1.04. 60
i laugh'd him out of patience; 2.05. 19
and that night | i laugh'd him into patience; 2.05. 20
good madam, patience. 2.05. 62
good your highness, patience. 2.05.106
pray you | be ever known to patience. 3.06. 98
patience is sottish, and impatience does 4.15. 79
you lean'd unto his sentence with what patience CYM 1.01. 78
beseech your patience. 1.01.153
no, faith; not so much as his patience. 1.02. 7 P
have patience, sir, | and take your ring again, 2.04.113
quite besides | the government of patience! 2.04.150
good lady, | hear me with patience. 3.04.112
i do note | that grief and patience, rooted in 4.02. 57
to bear with patience | such griefs as you PER 1.02. 65
i shall with aged patience bear your yoke. 2.04. 48
patience, good sir, do not assist the storm. 3.01. 19
patience, good sir, | even for this charge. 3.01. 26
patience then, | and think you now are all in 4.04. 50
look | like patience gazing on kings' graves, 5.01.138
patience, good sir! | or here i'll cease. 5.01.144
so, on your patience evermore attending, | new 5.03.101
i do think they have patience to make any TNK 2.01. 23 P
gods please — to hold here a brave patience, 2.02. 59
here, with a little patience, | we shall live 2.02. 85
i thank him for his gentle patience, | he's a 5.02. 43
and with our patience anger tott'ring fortune, 5.04. 20
where thou with patience must my will abide — LUC 486
that lose half with greater patience bear it 1158
mild patience bid fair lucrece speak | to the 1268
so mild that patience seem'd to scorn his woes. 1505
that patience is quite beaten from her breast; 1563
and patience, tame to sufferance, bide each SON 58. 7
my tongue–tied patience with too much disdain, 140. 2
/PATIENT 2 FR 0.0002 REL FR 2 V 0 P
boats dare sail | upon her /patient breast, TRO 1.03. 36
/i /will /be /patient, /outwardly /i /will. 5.02. 68
PATIENT 88 FR 0.0099 REL FR 70 V 18 P
nay, good, be patient. TMP 1.01. 15 P
and for your sake | am i this patient log–man. 3.01. 67
be patient, for the prize i'll bring thee to 4.01.205
i'll be as patient as a gentle stream, | and TGV 2.07. 34
come, come, | be patient; 5.03. 2
i will be patient; i will find out this. WIV 2.01.126 P
hath shown himself a wise and patient churchman. 2.03. 55 P
thou must be patient. MM 4.03.152 P
if so, be patient, sister. ERR 2.01. 9
good sir, be patient. 4.04. 18
nay, 'tis for me to be patient: 4.04. 19 P
be patient, for i will not let him stir | till i 5.01.102
you are not pinch's patient, are you, sir? 5.01.295
a present remedy, at least a patient sufferance. ADO 1.03. 8 P
sir, sir, be patient. 4.01.143
still have i borne it with a patient shrug, MV 1.03.109
sweet masters, be patient, for your father's AYL 1.01. 63 P
be patient, gentlemen, i choose her for myself. SHR 2.01.302
me give away myself | to this most patient, 3.02.195
be patient, to–morrow't shall be mended, | and 4.01.176
i, | thy resolv'd patient, on thee still rely. AWW 2.01.204
well, i must be patient, there is no fettering 2.03.237 P
i must be patient. 5.03.219
sweet sir toby, be patient for to–night. TN 2.03.131 P
alas, sir, be patient. 4.02.103 P
i must be patient till the heavens look | with WT 2.01.106
he is more patient | than when you left him; JN 5.07. 11
and patient underbearing of his fortune, | as R2 1.04. 29
and thou, too careless patient as thou art, 2.01. 97
how long shall i be patient? 2.01.163
have ever made me sour my patient cheek, | or 2.01.169
sweet york, be patient. hear me, gentle liege. 5.03. 91
am as poor as job, my lord, but not so patient. 2H4 1.02.127 P
but how i should be your patient to follow your 1.02.129 P
be patient, princes, you do know these fits 4.04.114
good corporal, be patient here. H5 2.01. 27 P
be patient, for you shall remain with us. 3.05. 66
but only in patient stillness while his rider 3.07. 23 P
be patient, lords, and give them leave to speak. 1H6 4.01. 82
be patient, york. 5.04.113
madam, be patient. 2H6 1.03. 65
be patient, gentle nell, forget this grief. 2.04. 26
he doth revive again. madam, be patient. 3.02. 36
be patient, gentle earl of westmerland. 3H6 1.01. 61
be patient, gentle queen, and i will stay. 1.01.214
who can be patient in such extremes? 1.01.215
why art thou patient, man? 1.04. 89
me have | some patient leisure to excuse myself. R3 1.02. 82
i can no longer hold me patient. 1.03.156
be patient, they are friends — ratcliffe and 3.05. 21
either be patient and entreat me fair, | or with 4.04.152
no, my good lord, therefore be patient. 5.01. 2
be patient yet. H8 2.04. 73
pray, sir, be patient; 5.03. 12
be the physician that should be the patient. TRO 2.03.214 P
by jove, | i will be patient. 5.02. 47
were i as patient as the midnight sleep, | by COR 3.01. 85
nay, pray be patient. 5.01. 33
and patient fools, | whose children he hath 5.06. 51
patient yourself, madam, and pardon me. TIT 1.01.121
the which if you with patient ears attend, ROM pr 13
therefore be patient, take no note of him; 1.05. 71
be patient, for the world is broad and wide. 3.03. 16
the livelong day, with patient expectation, | to JC 1.01. 41
only be patient till we have appeas'd | the 3.01.179
be patient till the last. 3.02. 12
will you be patient? 3.02.149
how does your patient, doctor? MAC 5.03. 37
therein the patient | must minister to himself. 5.03. 45
that patient merit of th' unworthy takes, | when HAM 3.01. 73
we must be patient, but i cannot choose but weep 4.05. 68 P
anon, as patient as the female dove, | when that 5.01.286
pray, sir, be patient. LR 1.04.261
i can be patient, i can stay with regan, | i and 2.04.230
bear free and patient thoughts. 4.06. 80
thou must be patient; 4.06.178
you must awhile be patient. OTH 3.04.129
apart, | confine yourself but in a patient list. 4.01. 75
and let | patient octavia plough thy visage up ANT 4.12. 38
your lordship is the most patient man in loss, CYM 2.03. 1 P
but not every man patient after the noble temper 2.03. 4 P
if you'll be patient, i'll no more be mad; 2.03.103
sir, be patient. 2.04.130
expect even here, where is a kingly patient, PER 5.01. 71
nay, i'll be patient. 5.01.145
"the patient dies while the physician sleeps, LUC 904
whilst like a willing patient i will drink SON 111. 9
playing patient sports in unconstrained gyves? LC 242
PATIENTLY 21 FR 0.0023 REL FR 18 V 3 P
have learn'd me how to brook this patiently. TGV 5.03. 4
i do; and bear the shame most patiently. MM 2.03. 20
if you take it not patiently, why, your mettle 3.02. 76 P
perchance you will not bear them patiently. ERR 1.02. 86
that could endure the toothache patiently, ADO 5.01. 36
if you will patiently dance in our round | and MND 2.01.140
i'll keep my oath, | patiently to bear my wroth. MV 2.09. 78
if they will patiently receive my medicine. AYL 2.07. 61
and i embrace this fortune patiently, | since 1H4 5.05. 12
watchful fires | sit patiently and inly ruminate H5 4.pr. 24
therefore patiently and yielding. 5.02.274 P
then patiently hear my impatience. R3 4.04.157
march patiently along; TRO 5.09. 7
your clemency, | we beg your hearing patiently. HAM 3.02.151
shake patiently my great affliction off. LR 4.06. 36
for since patiently and constantly thou hast CYM 3.05.117 P
good heavens, | hear patiently my purpose: 5.01. 22
and to that destiny have patiently | laid up my TNK 2.02. 5
sedges, | as patiently i was attending sport, 4.01. 55
you must ev'n take it patiently. 4.01.115
sword, | swearing, unless i took all patiently, LUC 1641
PATIENT'S 3 FR 0.0003 REL FR 2 V 1 P
sit, my preserver, by thy patient's side, | and AWW 2.03. 47
brings his physic | after his patient's death. H8 3.02. 41
the surgeon's box, or the patient's wound. TRO 5.01. 11 P
PATIENTS 1 FR 0.0001 REL FR 0 V 1 P
de knight, de lords, de gentlemen, my patients. WIV 2.03. 93 P
PATRICIAN 1 FR 0.0001 REL FR 0 V 1 P
i am known to be a humorous patrician, and one COR 2.01. 47 P
PATRICIANS 15 FR 0.0017 REL FR 13 V 2 P
accounted poor citizens, the patricians good. COR 1.01. 15 P
charitable care | have the patricians of you. 1.01. 66
the gods, not the patricians, make it, and 1.01. 73
where great patricians shall attend and shrug, 1.09. 4
my head, | the good patricians must be visited, 2.01.196
o /good but most unwise patricians! 3.01. 91
patricians! 3.01.185
the people against the senators, patricians, and 4.03. 14 P
the senators and patricians love him too; 4.07. 30
is worth of consuls, senators, patricians, | a 5.04. 53
subscrib'd by th' consuls and patricians, 5.06. 81
noble patricians, patrons of my right, | defend TIT 1.01. 1
patricians, draw your swords, and sheathe them 1.01.204
patricians and plebeians, we create | lord 1.01.231
lest then the people, and patricians too, | upon 1.01.445
PATRICK 1 FR 0.0001 REL FR 1 V 0 P
yes, by saint patrick, but there is, horatio, HAM 1.05.136
PATRICK'S 3 FR 0.0003 REL FR 3 V 0 P
at friar patrick's cell, | where i intend holy TGV 4.03. 43
silvia at friar patrick's cell should meet me. 5.01. 3
intend confession | at patrick's cell this even, 5.02. 42
PATRIMONY 4 FR 0.0004 REL FR 4 V 0 P
to me now, | give me bianca for my patrimony. SHR 4.04. 22
pity him, | bereft and gelded of his patrimony. R2 2.01.237
to reave the orphan of his patrimony,,| to wring 2H6 5.01.187
take thou my soldiers, prisoners, patrimony; LR 5.03. 75
PATROCLUS' 3 FR 0.0003 REL FR 2 V 1 P
achilles is my lord, i am patroclus' knower, and TRO 2.03. 53 P
go bear patroclus' body to achilles, | and bid 5.05. 17
patroclus' wounds have rous'd his drowsy blood, 5.05. 32
/PATROCLUS 1 FR 0.0001 REL FR 0 V 1 P
/and, /as /aforesaid, /patroclus /is /a /fool. TRO 2.03. 59 P
PATROCLUS 22 FR 0.0024 REL FR 11 V 11 P
with him patroclus | upon a lazy bed the TRO 1.03.146
now play him me, patroclus, | arming to answer 1.03.170
cries, "o, enough, patroclus, | or give me ribs 1.03.176
there's for you, patroclus. 2.01.116 P
then tell me, patroclus, what's achilles? 2.03. 45 P
thy knower, patroclus. 2.03. 48 P
then tell me, patroclus, what art thou? 2.03. 49 P
i am patroclus' knower, and patroclus is a fool. 2.03. 54 P
a fool, and this patroclus is a fool positive. 2.03. 65 P
come, patroclus, i'll speak with nobody. 2.03. 69 P
here comes patroclus. 2.03.103 P
hear you, patroclus: 2.03.112
how now, patroclus! 3.03. 65
go call thersites hither, sweet patroclus. 3.03.234
his presence, let patroclus make demands to me; 3.03.271 P
to him, patroclus. 3.03.273 P
patroclus kisses you. 4.05. 33
patroclus, let us feast him to the height. 5.01. 3
my sweet patroclus, i am thwarted quite | from 5.01. 37
away, patroclus! 5.01. 47
patroclus will give me any thing for the 5.02.192 P
patroclus ta'en or slain, and palamedes | sore 5.05. 13
PATRON 10 FR 0.0011 REL FR 9 V 1 P
twenty years | have i been patron to antipholus, ERR 5.01.328
earth's god, and body's fost'ring patron" — LLL 1.01.221 P
i'll plead for you | as for my patron, stand you SHR 1.02.155
you ever | the patron of my life and liberty. 4.02.114
down, | call warwick patron, and be penitent? 3H6 5.01. 27
patron of virtue, rome's best champion, TIT 1.01. 65
best senses | acknowledge thee their patron, and TIM 1.02.124
as my great patron thought on in my prayers — LR 1.01.142
my worthy arch and patron, comes to–night. 2.01. 59
"o thou clear god, and patron of all light, VEN 860
PATRONAGE 2 FR 0.0002 REL FR 2 V 0 P
keeps | and useth it to patronage his theft. 1H6 3.01. 48
sir, as well as you dare patronage | the envious 3.04. 32
PATRONESS 3 FR 0.0003 REL FR 3 V 0 P
this is | the patroness of heavenly harmony. SHR 3.01. 5
behold our patroness, the life of rome! COR 5.05. 1
divinest patroness, and /midwife gentle | to PER 3.01. 11
PATRONS 1 FR 0.0001 REL FR 1 V 0 P
noble patricians, patrons of my right, | defend TIT 1.01. 1
PATRUM 1 FR 0.0001 REL FR 0 V 1 P
i have some of 'em in limbo patrum, and there H8 5.03. 64 P
PATTERN 17 FR 0.0019 REL FR 17 V 0 P
let mine own judgment pattern out my death, MM 2.01. 30
pattern in himself to know, | grace to stand, 3.02.263
which is more | than history can pattern, though WT 3.02. 36
by th' pattern of mine own thoughts i cut out 4.04.382
so we could find some pattern of our shame. JN 3.04. 16
memory | shall as a pattern or a measure live, 2H4 4.04. 76
bliss, | and is a pattern of celestial peace. 1H6 5.05. 65
deeds, | behold this pattern of thy butcheries. R3 1.02. 54
a pattern to all princes living with her, | and H8 5.04. 22
a pattern, president, and lively warrant | for TIT 5.03. 44
no, i will be the pattern of all patience, | i LR 3.02. 37
thou cunning'st pattern of excelling nature, | i OTH 5.02. 11
on my head no toy | but was her pattern, her TNK 1.03. 72
and by this pattern | not /one of you should STM II.C 82
even so this pattern of the worn–out age LUC 1350
allow | for beauty's pattern to succeeding men. SON 19.12
drawn after you, you pattern of all those. 98.12
PATTERN'D 2 FR 0.0002 REL FR 2 V 0 P
pattern'd by that the poet here describes, | by TIT 4.01. 57
when pattern'd by thy fault foul sin may say LUC 629
PATTERNS 3 FR 0.0003 REL FR 2 V 1 P
before, and he is one of the patterns of love. AYL 4.01.100 P
the patterns that by god and by french fathers H5 2.04. 61
and knew the patterns of his foul beguiling, LC 170
PATTLE *(also battle)*
PATTLE 1 FR 0.0001 REL FR 0 V 1 P
fought a most prave pattle here in france. H5 4.07. 95 P
PAUCA 6 FR 0.0006 REL FR 1 V 5 P
pauca verba; sir john, good worts. WIV 1.01.120 P
pauca, pauca. 1.01.132 P
pauca, pauca. 1.01.132 P
but vir /sapit qui pauca loquitur. LLL 4.02. 80 P
pauca verba. 4.02.165 P
and — pauca, there's enough too! H5 2.01. 79
PAUCAS 1 FR 0.0001 REL FR 0 V 1 P
therefore paucas pallabris, let the world slide. SHR in.1. 5 P
PAUL 5 FR 0.0005 REL FR 5 V 0 P
villains, set down the corse, or, by saint paul, R3 1.02. 36
or, by saint paul, i'll strike thee to my foot, 1.02. 41
by holy paul, they love his grace but lightly 1.03. 45

now by saint paul i swear | i will not dine 3.04. 76
by the apostle paul, shadows to–night | have 5.03.216

PAULINA 16 FR 0.0018 REL FR 13 V 3 P

thou ne'er shalt see | thy wife paulina more." WT 3.03. 36
good paulina, | who hast the memory of hermione, 5.01. 49
i'll have no wife, paulina. 5.01. 69
never, paulina, so be bless'd my spirit! 5.01. 71
my true paulina, | we shall not marry till thou 5.01. 81
and rings of his that paulina knows. 5.02. 66 P
'twixt joy and sorrow was fought in paulina! 5.02. 74 P
which is in the keeping of paulina — a piece 5.02. 95 P
o grave and good paulina, the great comfort 5.03. 1
o paulina, | we honor you with trouble; 5.03. 8
but yet, paulina, | hermione was not so much 5.03. 27
o sweet paulina, | make me to think so twenty 5.03. 70
do, paulina; 5.03. 75
knowing by paulina that the oracle | gave hope 5.03.126
o, peace, paulina! 5.03.135
good paulina, | lead us from hence, where we may 5.03.151

PAULINA'S 1 FR 0.0001 REL FR 0 V 1 P

here comes the lady paulina's steward, he can WT 5.02. 26 P

PAUL'S *(also powle's)*

PAUL'S 4 FR 0.0004 REL FR 2 V 2 P

this oily rascal is known as well as paul's. 1H4 2.04.526 P
i bought him in paul's, and he'll buy me a horse 2H4 1.02. 52 P
load, | taken from paul's to be interred there; R3 1.02. 30
that it may be to–day read o'er in paul's. 3.06. 3

PAUNCH 3 FR 0.0003 REL FR 1 V 2 P

batter his skull, or paunch him with a stake, TMP 3.02. 90
what, a coward, sir john paunch? 1H4 2.02. 66 P
'zounds, ye fat paunch, and ye call me coward, 2.04.144 P

PAUNCHES 1 FR 0.0001 REL FR 1 V 0 P

fat paunches have lean pates; LLL 1.01. 26

PAUSE 43 FR 0.0048 REL FR 41 V 2 P

and (without any pause or staggering) take this WIV 3.03. 12 P
no marvel though she pause — | they can be meek ERR 2.01. 32
pause awhile, | and let my counsel sway you in ADO 4.01.200
take time to pause, and by the next new moon — MND 1.01. 83
pause there, morocco, | and weigh thy value with MV 2.07. 24
too long a pause for that which you find there. 2.09. 53
tarry, pause a day or two | before you hazard, 3.02. 1
why doth the jew pause? take thy forfeiture. 4.01.335
and while i pause, serve in your harmony. SHR 3.01. 14
gentle lord, | we coldly pause for thee; JN 2.01. 53
peace, lady, pause, or be more temperate. 2.01.195
hadst thou but shook thy head or made a pause 4.02.231
then pause not; 5.01. 14
may be i will go with you, but yet i'll pause, R2 2.03.168
stay, and pause a while. 1H4 1.03.129
there did he pause, but let me tell the world, 5.02. 65
other offenders we will pause upon. 5.05. 15
and pause us, till these rebels, now afoot, 2H4 4.04. 9
a night is but small breath, and little pause, H5 2.04.145
pause, and take thy breath; 1H6 4.06. 4
why dost thou pause? 2H6 5.02. 19
i vow to god above | i'll never pause again, 3H6 2.03. 30
breathe we, lords, good fortune bids us pause, 2.06. 31
it were no less, but yet i'll make a pause. 3.02. 10
and twenty times made pause to sob and weep, R3 1.02.161
nay, do not pause: 1.02.179
give me some little breath, some pause, dear 4.02. 24
justles roughly by | all time of pause, rudely TRO 4.04. 35
and i have seen thee pause and take thy breath, 4.05.192
pause, if thou wilt. 5.06. 14
i pause for a reply. JC 3.02. 34 P
and i must pause till it come back to me. 3.02.107
so, after pyrrhus' pause, | a roused vengeance HAM 2.02.487
off this mortal coil, | must give us pause. 3.01. 67
i stand in pause where i shall first begin, 3.03. 42
sending him away must seem | deliberate pause. 4.03. 9
steps in to cassio and entreats his pause; OTH 2.03.229
being done, there is no pause. 5.02. 82
yet pause awhile, | yon knight doth sit too PER 2.03. 53
then mightst thou pause, for then i were not for VEN 137
and swelling passion doth provoke a pause. 218
sad pause and deep regard beseems the sage; LUC 277
eye | he rouseth up himself, and makes a pause; 541

PAUSER 1 FR 0.0001 REL FR 1 V 0 P

of my violent love | outrun the pauser, reason. MAC 2.03.111

PAUSES 1 FR 0.0001 REL FR 1 V 0 P

tell him he mocks | the pauses that he makes. ANT 5.01. 3

PAUSING 1 FR 0.0001 REL FR 1 V 0 P

pausing for means to mourn some newer way. LUC 1365

PAUSINGLY 1 FR 0.0001 REL FR 1 V 0 P

with demure confidence | this pausingly ensu'd: H8 1.02.168

PAUVRE 1 FR 0.0001 REL FR 1 V 0 P

paysans, la pauvre gens de france, | poor market 1H6 3.02. 14

PAVAN *(see pavin)*

PAV'D 2 FR 0.0002 REL FR 1 V 1 P

and my way shall be pav'd with english faces. H5 3.07. 81 P
but when the way was made | and pav'd with gold, H8 1.01.188

PAVED 3 FR 0.0003 REL FR 3 V 0 P

her brother's ghost his paved bed would break, MM 5.01.435
o, if the streets were paved with thine eyes, LLL 4.03.274
or mead, | by paved fountain or by rushy brook, MND 2.01. 84

/PAVEMENT 1 FR 0.0001 REL FR 1 V 0 P

/lie /there /for /pavement /to /the /abject TRO 3.03.162

PAVEMENT 2 FR 0.0002 REL FR 2 V 0 P

the marble pavement closes, he is enter'd | his CYM 5.04.120
as he thus went counting | the flinty pavement, TNK 5.04. 59

PAVILION 6 FR 0.0006 REL FR 5 V 1 P

come to our pavilion — boyet is dispos'd. LLL 2.01.250
the princess at her pavilion in the posteriors 5.01. 88 P
from morn till night, out of his pavilion. 5.02.654
them, and anon | desire them all to my pavilion. H5 4.01. 27
to our pavilion shall i lead you, sir. TRO 1.03.305
she did lie | in her pavilion — cloth of gold, ANT 2.02.199

PAVILION'D 1 FR 0.0001 REL FR 1 V 0 P

and lie pavilion'd in the fields of france. H5 1.02.129

/PAVILIONS 1 FR 0.0001 REL FR 1 V 0 P

/greeks /do /pitch | /their /brave /pavilions. TRO pr 15

/PAVIN 1 FR 0.0001 REL FR 0 V 1 P

then he's a rogue, and a passy–measures /pavin. TN 5.01.201 P

PAW 3 FR 0.0003 REL FR 3 V 0 P

by the tongue, | a cased lion by the mortal paw, JN 3.01.259
the lion dying thrusteth forth his paw, | and R2 5.01. 29
with the bear's fell paw | hath clapp'd his tail 2H6 5.01.153

PAWN 26 FR 0.0029 REL FR 17 V 9 P

here is her oath for love, her honor's pawn: TGV 1.03. 47
them | upon some other pawn for fealty. 2.04. 91
sir, you should lay my countenance to pawn. WIV 2.02. 6 P
come, lay their swords to pawn. 3.01.110 P
these ducats pawn i for my father here. ERR 5.01.390
i'll pawn the little blood which i have left WT 2.03.166
this young man in pawn till i bring it you. 4.04.808 P
as he says, your pawn till it be brought you. 4.04.823 P
much strength | as to take up mine honor's pawn, R2 1.01. 74
redeem from broking pawn the blemish'd crown, 2.01.293
there is my honor's pawn, | engage it to the 4.01. 55
in proof whereof, there is my honor's pawn, 4.01. 70
on, i must be fain to pawn both my plate and the 2H4 2.01.141 P
i' faith, i am loath to pawn my plate, so god 2.01.154 P
well, you shall have it, though i pawn my gown. 2.01.158 P
alas, sweet wife, my honor is at pawn, | and, 2.03. 7
go to ward, | they'll pawn their swords /for my 2H6 5.01.113
thereon i pawn my credit and mine honor. 3H6 3.03.116
that he would pawn his fortunes | to hopeless COR 3.01. 15
lord, | pawn me to this your honor, she is his. TIM 1.01.147
ages love | security, i'll pawn my victories, 3.05. 80
my life i never held but as /a pawn | to wage LR 1.01.155
i dare pawn down my life for him that he hath 1.02. 86 P
pawn their experience to their present pleasure, ANT 1.04. 32
i dare thereupon pawn the moi'ty of my estate to CYM 1.04.108 P
and pawn mine honor for their safety. 1.06.194

PAWN'D 10 FR 0.0011 REL FR 9 V 1 P

till he hath pawn'd his horses to mine host of WIV 2.01. 96 P
must be something else | pawn'd with the other, MV 3.05. 82
have i not pawn'd to you my majesty? JN 3.01. 98
i pawn'd thee none. 2H4 4.02.112
hath pawn'd an open hand in sign of love; 3H6 4.02. 9
france | hath pawn'd the sicils and jerusalem, 5.07. 39
for which your honor and your faith is pawn'd, R3 4.02. 89
garter, blemish'd, pawn'd his knightly virtue; 4.04.370
him, and i pawn'd | mine honor for his truth; COR 5.06. 20
of the worn–out age | pawn'd honest looks, but LUC 1351

PAWNING 1 FR 0.0001 REL FR 1 V 0 P

make, | pawning his honor to obtain his lust, LUC 156

PAWNS 1 FR 0.0001 REL FR 1 V 0 P

to lie like pawns lock'd up in chests and trunks JN 5.02.141

PAWS 3 FR 0.0003 REL FR 3 V 0 P

wretch | that trembles under his devouring paws; 3H6 1.03. 13
to have his princely paws par'd all away. TIT 2.03.152
devouring time, blunt thou the lion's paws, SON 19. 1

PAX 2 FR 0.0002 REL FR 2 V 0 P

for he hath stol'n a pax, and hanged must 'a be H5 3.06. 40
the doom of death | for pax of little price. 3.06. 45

/PAY 1 FR 0.0001 REL FR 1 V 0 P

i /pay thy poverty, and not thy will. ROM 5.01. 76

PAY 150 FR 0.0169 REL FR 117 V 33 P

he shall pay for him that hath him, and that TMP 2.02. 77 P
i will pay thy graces | home both in word and 5.01. 70
take all, pay all, go to bed when she list, rise WIV 2.02.118 P
shall have my horses, but i'll make them pay; 4.03. 9 P
make us pay down for our offense by weight | the MM 1.02.121
disguised | pay with falsehood false exacting, 3.02.281
to pay the saddler for my mistress' crupper? ERR 1.02. 56
if i should pay your worship those again, 1.02. 85
yes, to pay a fine for a periwig, and recover 2.02. 75 P
either consent to pay this sum for me | or i 4.01. 72
consent to pay thee that i never had! 4.01. 74
here's that, i warrant you, will pay them all. 4.04. 10
and, knowing how the debt grows, i will pay it. 4.04.121
if any friend will pay the sum for him, | he 5.01.131
my life, | and pay the sum that may deliver me. 5.01.285
debt | pay him the due of honey–tongued boyet. LLL 5.02.334
which now in some slight measure it will pay, MND 3.02. 86
and swore he would pay him again when he was MV 1.02. 81 P
he keep his day, | or he shall pay for this. 2.08. 26
pay him six thousand, and deface the bond; 3.02.299
gold | to pay the petty debt twenty times over. 3.02.307
pray god bassanio come | to see me pay his debt, 3.03. 36
i will be bound to pay it ten times o'er, | on 4.01.211
i'll pay it instantly with all my heart. 4.01.281
pay the bond thrice | and let the christian go. 4.01.318
and thou shalt have to pay for it of us. AYL 2.04. 93
you will not pay for the glasses you have burst? SHR in.1. 7 P
tailor, i'll pay thee for thy gown to–morrow, 4.03.166
my duty then shall pay me for my pains. AWW 2.01.125
which i will over–pay and pay again | when i 3.07. 16
choose thou thy husband, and i'll pay thy dower, 5.03.328
which we will pay, | with strife to please you, ep 3
to pay this debt of love but to a brother, | how TN 1.01. 33
i prithee (and i'll pay thee bounteously) 1.02. 52
i'll pay thy pleasure then. 2.04. 69
are shuffled off with such uncurrent pay; 3.03. 16
i be lapsed in this place, | i shall pay dear. 3.03. 37
of sicilia means to pay bohemia the visitation WT 1.01. 6 P
you pay a great deal too dear for what's given 1.01. 17 P
thanks a while, | and pay them when you part. 1.02. 10
so you shall pay your fees | when you depart, 1.02. 53
if this prove true, they'll pay for't. 2.01.146
and you shall pay well for 'em. 4.04.314 P
lie, but we pay them for it with stamped coin, 4.04.724 P
our abbeys and our priories shall pay | this JN 1.01. 48
then | to pay that duty which you truly owe | to 2.01.247
and with advantage means to pay thy love; 3.03. 22
o, let us pay the time but needful woe, | since 5.07.110
god for his richard hath in heavenly pay | a R2 3.02. 60
if we prevail, their heads shall pay for it. 3.02.126
to pay their aweful duty to our presence? 3.03. 76
did i ever call for thee to pay thy part? 1H4 1.02. 51 P
i throw off | and pay the debt i never promised, 1.02.209
till he hath found a time to pay us home. 1.03.288
spleen, | to fight against me under percy's pay, 3.02.126
he had his part of it, let him pay. 3.03. 75 P
i'll not pay a denier. 3.03. 79 P
knows at what time to promise, when to pay. 4.03. 53
soul | shall pay full dearly for this encounter, 5.01. 84
yet, i would be loath to pay him before his day. 5.01.127 P
we, as the spring of all, shall pay for all. 5.02. 23
thee, | who never promiseth but he means to pay. 5.04. 43
pay her the debt you owe her, and unpay the 2H4 2.01.118 P
you'll pay me all together? 2.01.159 P
pay the musicians, sirrah. 2.04.373 P
let them have pay, and part. 4.02. 70
shall, o dear father, pay thee plenteously. 4.05. 40
i meant indeed to pay you with this, which if ep 10 P
bate me some, and i will pay you some, and (as ep 14 P
you'll pay me the eight shillings i won of you H5 2.01. 94 P
a noble shalt thou have, and present pay, | and 2.01.107
forgive, | although my body pay the price of it. 2.02.154
the /word is "pitch and pay"; 2.03. 49
you pay him then. 4.01.197 P
five hundred poor i have in yearly pay, | who 4.01.298
i owe you any thing, i will pay you in cudgels; 5.01. 64 P
his ransom there is none but i shall pay: 1H6 1.01.148
my body shall | pay recompense, if you will 5.03. 19
be so — | what ransom must i pay before i pass? 5.03. 73
why speak'st thou not? what ransom must i pay? 5.03. 77
swear | to pay him tribute and submit thyself, 5.04.130
through the realm | for soldiers' pay in france, 2H6 3.01. 62
and, being protector, stay'd the soldiers' pay, 3.01.105
i never robb'd the soldiers of their pay, | nor 3.01.108
what, think you much to pay two thousand crowns, 4.01. 18
he that made us pay one and twenty fifteens, and 4.07. 22 P
head on his shoulders, unless he pay me tribute. 4.07.121 P
but she shall pay to me her maidenhead ere they 4.07.122 P
you shall have pay and every thing you wish. 5.01. 47
with promise of high pay and great rewards; 3H6 2.01.134
shall have wars, and pay for their presumption. 4.01.114
and, that once gotten, doubt not of large pay. 4.07. 88
discharge the common sort | with pay and thanks, 5.05. 88
country's fat shall pay your pains the hire; R3 5.03.258
for which i pay 'em | a thousand thanks, and H8 1.04. 73
the honor of it | does pay the act of it, as i' 3.02.182
let us pay betimes | a moi'ty of that mass of TRO 2.02.106
words pay no debts, give her deeds; 3.02. 55 P
howsoever, he shall pay for me ere he has me. 3.03.297 P
and pay thy life thou owest me for my horse. 5.06. 7
heart consent to take | a bribe to pay my sword. COR 1.09. 38
he tumble down, | and pay you for your voices. 4.06.136
o, were the sum of these that i should pay TIT 5.03.158
countless and infinite, yet would i pay them! 5.03.159
your lives shall pay the forfeit of the peace. ROM 1.01. 97
i'll pay that doctrine, or else die in debt. 1.01.238
night, | and pay no worship to the garish sun. 3.02. 25
i'll pay the debt and free him. TIM 1.01.103
if i should pay you for't as 'tis extoll'd, | it 1.01.167
worthy of thee, and to pay thee for thy labor. 1.01.225 P
having lacks a half | to pay your present debts. 2.02.145
timon in this should pay more than he owes; 3.04. 22
methinks he should the sooner pay his debts, 3.04. 75
there's gold to pay thy soldiers, | make large 4.03.127
i did send | to you for gold to pay my legions, JC 4.03. 76
to this dead man than you shall see me pay. 5.03.102
to herald thee into his sight, | not pay thee. MAC 1.03.103
more is thy due than more than all can pay. 1.04. 21
pay his breath | to time and mortal custom. 4.01. 99
may kindly say | our duties did his welcome pay. 4.01.132
that you have ta'en these tenders for true pay, HAM 1.03.106
and scape /detecting, i will pay the theft. 3.02. 89
to pay ourselves what to ourselves is debt. 3.02.193
to pay five ducats, five, i would not farm it; 4.04. 20
sentence and the sorrow | that, to pay grief, OTH 1.03.215
he could not | but pay me terms of honor, cold ANT 3.04. 7
hence safe | does pay thy labor richly; 4.14. 37
which i will be ever to pay and yet pay still. CYM 1.04. 37 P
which i will be ever to pay and yet pay still. 1.04. 37 P
and we will nothing pay | for wearing our own 3.01. 13
why should we pay tribute? 3.01. 42 P
his pocket, we will pay him tribute for light; 3.01. 44 P
first pay me for the nursing of thy sons, | and 5.05.322
promising | to pay our wonted tribute, from the 5.05.462
or pay you with unthankfulness in thought, | be PER 1.04.102
low fortunes better, | i'll pay your bounties; 2.01.143
have fresh ones, what e'er we pay for them. 4.02. 11 P
thy sacred physic shall receive such pay | as 5.01. 74
may, and the athenians pay it | to th' heart of TNK 3.01. 3
justice of affection, | i'll pay thee soundly. 3.06. 52
else, | to call the maids and pay the minstrels, 4.01.111
and must needs be by | to give the service pay. 5.03. 32
one sweet kiss shall pay this comptless debt. VEN 84
but when her lips were ready for his pay, | he 89
so thou wilt buy, and pay, and use good dealing, 514
me, | and pay them at thy leisure, one by one. 518
the petty streams that pay a daily debt | to LUC 649
which happies those that pay the willing loan; SON 6. 6
moan, | which i new pay as if not paid before: 30.12
since what he owes thee thou thyself dost pay. 79.14

PAYEST 1 FR 0.0001 REL FR 1 V 0 P

free thee from the tribute which thou payest, TMP 2.01.293

PAYING 9 FR 0.0010 REL FR 6 V 3 P

and (as i say) paying for them very honestly; MM 2.01.102 P
more nor less to others paying | than by 3.02.265
have broke off, | not paying me a welcome. MND 5.01. 99
and since in paying it, it is impossible i MV 3.02.318 P
paying the fine of rated treachery | even with a JN 5.04. 37
o, i do not like that paying back, 'tis a double 1H4 3.03.179 P
obey, | paying what ransom the insulter willeth; VEN 550
paying more slavish tribute than they owe. LUC 299
lose all, and more, by paying too much rent, SON 125. 6

PAYMENT 15 FR 0.0017 REL FR 12 V 3 P

the payment of a hundred thousand crowns, LLL 2.01.129
/on payment of a hundred thousand crowns, | to 2.01.144
fair payment for foul words is more than due. 4.01. 19
if he come to–morrow, i'll give him his payment. AYL 1.01.160 P
too little payment for so great a debt. SHR 5.02.154
you tarry longer, | i shall give worse payment. TN 4.01. 20
even with the bloody payment of your deaths. 1H4 1.03.186
and yet that were but light payment, to dance 2H4 ep 20 P
i will give treason his payment into plows, i H5 4.08. 14 P
with downright payment show'd unto my father. 3H6 1.04. 32
an ordinary groom is for such payment. H8 5.01.172
he humbly prays your speedy payment. TIM 2.02. 28
there's payment, hence! 5.01.113
that the proportion both of thanks and payment MAC 1.04. 19
with such black payment as thou hast pretended; LUC 576

PAYMENTS 1 FR 0.0001 REL FR 0 V 1 P

you shall be call'd to no more payments, fear no CYM 5.04.158 P

PAYS 29 FR 0.0032 REL FR 24 V 5 P

he that dies pays all debts. TMP 3.02.131 P
haste still pays haste, and leisure answers MM 5.01.410

sense, | it pays the hearing double recompense. MND 3.02.180
and he repents not that he pays your debt; MV 4.01.279
after he scores, he never pays the score. AWW 4.03.224
he ne'er pays after–debts, take it before, | and 4.03.226
who pays before, but not when he does owe it. 4.03.230
he pays you as surely as your feet hits the TN 3.04.277 P
and the old saying is, the third pays for all. 5.01. 37 P
where fearing dying pays death servile breath. R2 3.02.185
the proud soul ne'er pays but to the proud. 1H4 1.03. 9
base is the slave that pays. H5 2.01. 96
edward for edward pays a dying debt. R3 4.04. 21
but that he pays himself with being proud. COR 1.01. 33 P
he is so kind that he now | pays interest for't; TIM 1.02.200
five thousand drops pays that. 3.04. 96
the loyalty i owe, | in doing it, pays itself. MAC 1.04. 23
and thy free awe | pays homage to us — thou HAM 4.03. 62
else so thy cheek pays shame | when ANT 1.01. 31
and for his ordinary pays his heart | for what 2.02.225
pacorus, orodes, | pays this for marcus crassus. 3.01. 5
pays dear for my offenses. CYM 1.01.106
overbuys me | almost the sum he pays. 1.01.147
to the spectators, the dish pays the shot. 5.04.156 P
to which love's eyes pays tributary gazes, | nor VEN 632
let, | till every minute pays the hour his debt. LUC 329
pain pays the income of each precious thing: 334
he robs thee of, and pays it thee again. SON 79. 8
me, | he pays the whole, and yet am i not free. 134.14

PAYSANS 1 FR 0.0001 REL FR 1 V 0 P
paysans, la pauvre gens de france, | poor market 1H6 3.02. 14

PAY'T 1 FR 0.0001 REL FR 0 V 1 P
and i'll pay't as valorously as i may, that sall H5 3.02.116 P

/PEACE 4 FR 0.0004 REL FR 3 V 1 P
/nor /do /i /as /an /enemy /to /peace | /troop 2H4 4.01. 61
/peace, /fool, /i /have /not /done. TRO 2.03. 56 P
/peace, /tender /sapling, /thou /art /made /of TIT 3.02. 50
/peace, /who /comes /here? HAM 5.02. 80

PEACE 566 FR 0.0639 REL FR 450 V 116 P
to silence, and work the peace of the present, TMP 1.01. 22 P
prithee peace. 2.01. 9
prithee peace. 2.01.128
yea, all the creatures, | against your peace. 3.03. 75
we wish your peace. 4.01.163
peace, here she comes. TGV 2.01. 93 P
peace! we'll hear him. 4.01. 9
peace, villain. 4.01. 39
ay; but peace, let's hear 'em. 4.02. 38 P
peace, stand aside, the company parts. 4.02. 81
but well, when i discourse of love and peace. 5.02. 17
but better indeed, when you hold /your peace. 5.02. 18
of gloucester, justice of peace and coram. WIV 1.01. 6 P
peace, i pray you. 1.01.136 P
he's a justice of peace in his country, simple 1.01.218 P
a justice of peace sometime may be beholding to 1.01.273 P
peace, i pray you. 1.04. 80 P
been a great fighter, though now a man of peace. 2.03. 43 P
though i now be old and of the peace, if i see a 2.03. 45 P
i am sworn of the peace. 2.03. 53 P
peace, i say, gallia and gaul, french and welsh, 3.01. 97 P
peace, i say! 3.01.100 P
follow me, /lads of peace; 3.01.111 P
peace be with you, sir. 3.05. 56 P
peace your tattlings! what is "fair," william? 4.01. 25 P
i pray you peace. 4.01. 31 P
peace! 4.01. 56 P
prithee hold thy peace. 4.01. 73 P
heaven grant us its peace, but not the king of MM 1.02. 4 P
relish the petition well that prays for peace. 1.02. 16 P
ho! peace be in this place! 1.04. 6
peace and prosperity! who is't that calls? 1.04. 15
what ho! peace here; grace and good company! 3.01. 44
peace be with you! 3.02.260 P
peace, ho, be here! 4.03.106
o, peace, the friar is come. 4.06. 9
no, my good lord, | nor wish'd to hold my peace. 5.01. 79
but peace be with him! 5.01.396
peace, doting wizard, peace! i am not mad. ERR 4.04. 58
peace, doting wizard, peace! i am not mad. 4.04. 58
peace, fool, thy master and his man are here, 5.01.178
he do fear god, 'a must necessarily keep peace; ADO 2.03.194 P
if he break the peace, he ought to enter into a 2.03.194 P
why then depart in peace, and let the child wake 3.03. 69 P
peace, stir not. 3.03. 96 P
pray thee, fellow, peace. 4.02. 44 P
i pray thee peace. 5.01. 34
i shall meet, and till then peace be with him. 5.01.193 P
peace, i will stop your mouth. 5.04. 98 P
peace! LLL 1.01.226 P
the treason and you go in peace away together. 4.03.190
men of peace, well encount'red. 5.01. 34 P
peace, the peal begins. 5.01. 43 P
encounters mounted are | against your peace. 5.02. 83
nothing but peace and gentle visitation. 5.02.179
nothing but peace and gentle visitation. 5.02.181
peace, for i will not have to do with you. 5.02.428
peace, peace, forbear: 5.02.439
peace, peace, forbear: 5.02.439
peace, i have done. 5.02.483
i wish you the peace of mind, most royal 5.02.531 P
peace! 5.02.650 P
monster's view, and all things shall be peace. MND 3.02.377
bless, | through this palace, with sweet peace, 5.01.418
well, peace be with you! MV 4.01.448
peace ho! 5.01.109
peace, fool, he's not thy kinsman. AYL 2.04. 67
peace, i say. good even to /you, friend. 2.04. 69
peace, you dull fool, i found them on a tree. 3.02.115 P
peace, | here comes my sister reading, stand 3.02.123
peace ho! 5.04.125
peace, tranio! SHR 1.01. 72
hortensio, peace! 1.02. 93
peace, grumio, it is the rival of my love. 1.02.141
peace, sirrah! 1.02.161
marry, peace it bodes, and love, and quiet life, 5.02.108
to offer war where they should kneel for peace, 5.02.162
bless him at home in peace, whilst i from far AWW 3.04. 10
i hear there is an overture of peace. 4.03. 39 P
nay, i assure you a peace concluded. 4.03. 40 P
peace, you rogue, no more o' that. TN 1.05. 29 P
my words are as full of peace as matter. 1.05.210 P
"hold thy peace, thou knave," knight? 2.03. 65 P
it begins, "hold thy peace." 2.03. 69 P
i shall never begin if i hold my peace. 2.03. 70 P
for the love o' god, peace! 2.03. 85 P
o, peace! 2.05. 30 P
peace, i say! 2.05. 34 P
peace, peace! 2.05. 38 P
peace, peace! 2.05. 38 P
o, peace! 2.05. 42 P
o, peace, peace! 2.05. 51 P
o, peace, peace! 2.05. 51 P
o peace, peace, peace! now, now. 2.05. 57 P
o peace, peace, peace! now, now. 2.05. 57 P
o peace, peace, peace! now, now. 2.05. 57 P
silence be drawn from us with cars, yet peace. 2.05. 64 P
o, peace, and the spirit of humors intimate 2.05. 84 P
peace, peace, we must deal gently with him. 3.04. 95 P
peace, peace, we must deal gently with him. 3.04. 95 P
prithee hold thy peace, this is not the way. 3.04.108 P
i will make your peace with him if i can. 3.04.269 P
uncivil and unjust extent | against thy peace. 4.01. 54
what ho, i say! peace in this prison! 4.02. 18 P
and too doubtful soul | may live at peace. 4.03. 28
pursue him, and entreat him to a peace; 5.01.380
sir, to have held my peace until | you had drawn WT 1.02. 28
o, peace, paulina! 5.03.135
bear mine to him, and so depart in peace. JN 1.01. 23
the peace of heaven is theirs that lift their 2.01. 35
that right in peace which here we urge in war, 2.01. 47
peace be to france — if france in peace permit 2.01. 84
if france in peace permit | our just and lineal 2.01. 84
not, bleed france, and peace ascend to heaven, 2.01. 86
proud contempt that beats his peace to heaven. 2.01. 88
peace be to england, if that war return | from 2.01. 89
from france to england, there to live in peace. 2.01. 90
peace! 2.01.134
good my mother, peace. 2.01.163
peace, lady, pause, or be more temperate. 2.01.195
made | for bloody power to rush upon your peace. 2.01.221
leave your children, wives, and you in peace. 2.01.257
peace, no more. 2.01.293
of one part confirm | the other's peace. 2.01.360
and i shall show you peace and fair–fac'd league 2.01.417
war | to a most base and vile–concluded peace. 2.01.586
gone to swear a peace? 3.01. 1
of war | is cold in amity and painted peace, 3.01.105
this ungodly day | wear out the /day in peace; 3.01.110
lady constance, peace! 3.01.112
war, war, no peace! 3.01.113
peace is to me a war. 3.01.113
sound of words | was deep–sworn faith, peace, 3.01.231
hands | to clap this royal bargain up of peace, 3.01.235
of smiling peace to march a bloody host, | and 3.01.246
than keep in peace that hand which thou dost 3.01.261
the fat ribs of peace | must by the hungry now 3.03. 9
lo! now! now see the issue of your peace. 3.04. 21
o fair affliction, peace! 3.04. 36
peace; 4.01.126
i'll make a peace between your soul and you. 4.02.250
keep the peace, i say. 4.03. 93
and snarleth in the gentle eyes of peace; 4.03.150
me, | and i have made a happy peace with him, 5.01. 63
perchance the cardinal cannot make your peace; 5.01. 74
hand, | it may lie gently at the foot of peace, 5.02. 76
to tell me john hath made | his peace with rome? 5.02. 92
what is that peace to me? 5.02. 92
because that john hath made his peace with rome? 5.02. 96
there end thy brave, and turn thy face in peace; 5.02.159
may think the remnant of my thoughts | in peace, 5.04. 47
and brings from him such offers of our peace 5.07. 84
set on you | to wake our peace, which in our R2 1.03.132
might from our quiet confines fright fair peace, 1.03.137
in peace was never gentle lamb more mild, | than 2.01.174
more hath he spent in peace than they in wars. 2.01.255
and fright our native peace with self–borne arms 2.03. 80
warrant they have made peace with bullingbrook. 3.02.127
peace have they made with him indeed, my lord. 3.02.128
would they make peace? 3.02.133
their souls, their peace is made | with heads, 3.02.137
but ere the crown he looks for live in peace, 3.03. 95
change the complexion of her maid–pale peace 3.03. 98
hold thy peace. 3.04. 47
sweet peace conduct his sweet soul to the bosom 4.01.103
peace shall go sleep with turks and infidels, 4.01.139
and in this seat of peace tumultuous wars 4.01.140
peace, foolish woman. 5.02. 80
i will not peace. what is the matter, aumerle? 5.02. 81
so as thou liv'st in peace, die free from strife 5.06. 27
find we a time for frighted peace to pant | and 1H4 1.01. 2
peace, cousin, say no more. 1.03.187
peace, ye fat–kidney'd rascal! 2.02. 5 P
peace, ye fat–guts, lie down. 2.02. 31 P
peace, good pint–pot, peace, good ticklebrain. 2.04.397 P
peace, good pint–pot, peace, good ticklebrain. 2.04.397 P
peace, cousin percy, you will make him mad. 3.01. 51
peace, she sings. 3.01.244 P
and shake the peace and safety of our throne. 3.02.117
the cankers of a calm world and a long peace. 4.02. 30 P
you conjure from the breast of civil peace 4.03. 43
to sue his livery and beg his peace, | with 4.03. 62
and made us doff our easy robes of peace, | to 5.01. 12
peace, chewet, peace! 5.01. 29 P
peace, chewet, peace! 5.01. 29 P
i speak of peace, while covert enmity | under 2H4 in 9
all you that kiss my lady peace at home, that 1.02.207 P
what is the matter? keep the peace here, ho! 2.01. 61 P
pray thee peace. 2.01.118 P
peace! 2.02.122 P
peace, good doll, do not speak like a 2.04.234 P
and one of the king's justices of the peace. 3.02. 58 P
it well befits you should be of the peace. 3.02. 90 P
go to, peace, mouldy, you shall go. 3.02.116 P
peace, fellow, peace, stand aside, know you 3.02.119 P
peace, fellow, peace, stand aside, know you 3.02.119 P
god send us peace! 3.02.293 P
say on, my lord of westmerland, in peace, | what 4.01. 29
whose see is by a civil peace maintain'd, 4.01. 42
beard the silver hand of peace hath touch'd, 4.01. 43
learning and good letters peace hath tutor'd, 4.01. 44
the dove, and very blessed spirit of peace, 4.01. 46
out of the speech of peace that bears such grace 4.01. 48
not to break peace, or any branch of it, | but 4.01. 85
of it, | but to establish here a peace indeed, 4.01. 86
and knit our powers to the arm of peace. 4.01.175
/and either end in peace, which god so frame! 4.01.178
me | that no conditions of our peace can stand. 4.01.182
if we can make our peace | upon such large terms 4.01.183
our peace shall stand as firm as rocky mountains 4.01.186
our peace will, like a broken limb united, 4.01.220
and both against the peace of heaven and him 4.02. 29
i am not here against your father's peace, | but 4.02. 31
and deliver to the army | this news of peace. 4.02. 70
i have bestowed to breed this present peace, 4.02. 74
the word of peace is rend'red. 4.02. 87
a peace is of the nature of a conquest, | for 4.02. 89
but peace puts forth her olive every where. 4.04. 87
and to bloodshed, | wounding supposed peace. 4.05.195
and grant it may with thee in true peace live! 4.05.219
health, peace, and happiness to my royal father! 4.05.226
thou bring'st me happiness and peace, son john, 4.05.227
well, peace be with him that hath made us heavy! 5.02. 25
peace be with us, lest we be heavier! 5.02. 26
that guards the peace and safety of your person? 5.02. 88
that war, or peace, or both at once, may be | as 5.02.138
so get you hence in peace; H5 1.02.294
for peace itself should not so dull a kingdom 2.04. 16
o, peace, prince dolphin! 2.04. 29
in peace there's nothing so becomes a man | as 3.01. 3
gor'd the gentle bosom of peace with pillage and 4.01.165 P
the slave, a member of the country's peace, 4.01.281
what watch the king keeps to maintain the peace, 4.01.283
god's peace, i would not lose so great an honor 4.03. 31
to order peace between them — and omit | all 5.pr. 39
peace to this meeting, wherefore we are met! 5.02. 1
why that the naked, poor, and mangled peace, 5.02. 34
that i may know the let why gentle peace 5.02. 65
if, duke of burgundy, you would the peace, 5.02. 68
you must buy that peace | with full accord to 5.02. 70
the peace, | which you before so urg'd, lies in 5.02. 75
cease these jars and rest your minds in peace. 1H6 1.01. 44
by guileful fair words peace may be obtain'd. 1.01. 77
thus contumeliously should break the peace! 1.03. 58
peace, mayor, thou know'st little of my wrongs. 1.03. 59
one that still motions war and never peace, 1.03. 63
this day against god's peace and the king's, we 1.03. 75 P
and prosperous be thy life in peace and war! 2.05.114
and peace, no war, befall thy parting soul! 2.05.115
usurer, | froward by nature, enemy to peace, 3.01. 18
who preferreth peace | more than i do, except i 3.01. 33
hold your slaught'ring hands and keep the peace. 3.01. 87
or who should study to prefer a peace, | if holy 3.01.110
then be at peace, except ye thirst for blood. 3.01.117
yet, pucelle, hold thy peace, | if talbot do but 3.02. 58
quiet yourselves, i pray, and be at peace. 4.01.115
and then your highness shall command a peace. 4.01.117
and therefore, as we hither came in peace, | so 4.01.160
so let us still continue peace, and love. 4.01.161
but if you frown upon this proffer'd peace, 4.02. 9
excellence | to have a godly peace concluded of 5.01. 5
to draw conditions of a friendly peace, | which 5.01. 38
peace be amongst them if they turn to us, | else 5.02. 6
i kiss these fingers for eternal peace, | and 5.03. 48
and peace established between these realms. 5.03. 92
have earnestly implor'd a general peace 5.04. 98
shall we at last conclude effeminate peace? 5.04.107
if we conclude a peace, | it shall be with such 5.04.113
and suffer you to breathe in fruitful peace, 5.04.127
still, | for here we entertain a solemn peace. 5.04.175
france | as his alliance will confirm our peace, 5.05. 42
bliss, | and is a pattern of celestial peace. 5.05. 65
here are the articles of contracted peace 2H6 1.01. 40
peace, son, and show some reason, buckingham, 1.03.113
peace, headstrong warwick! 1.03.175
image of pride, why should i hold my peace? 1.03.176
i prithee peace, | good queen, and whet not on 2.01. 32
let me be blessed for the peace i make | against 2.01. 35
and go in peace, humphrey, no less belov'd 2.03. 26
gone, | may honorable peace attend thy throne! 2.03. 38
peace to his soul, if god's good pleasure be! 3.03. 26
thou hast appointed justices of peace, to call 4.07. 41 P
that will forsake thee and go home in peace. 4.08. 10
to know the reason of these arms in peace; 5.01. 18
thus war hath given thee peace, for thou art 5.02. 29
peace with his soul, heaven, if it be thy will! 5.02. 30
to lose thy youth in peace, and to achieve | the 5.02. 46
sons, peace! 3H6 1.01.119
peace thou! and give king henry leave to speak. 1.01.120
or live in peace abandon'd and despis'd! 1.01.188
in war | as he is fam'd for mildness, peace, and 2.01.156
and thou this day hadst kept thy chair in peace. 2.06. 20
peace, impudent and shameless warwick, | proud 3.03.156
crown, | as likely to be blest in peace and war; 4.06. 35
not mutinous in peace, yet bold in war; 4.08. 10
peace, willful boy, or i will charm your tongue. 5.05. 31
that thou mightst repossess the crown in peace, 5.07. 19
having my country's peace and brothers' loves. 5.07. 36
why, i, in this weak piping time of peace, R3 1.01. 24
say then my peace is made. 1.02.197
on thee, the troubler of the poor world's peace! 1.03.220
peace, master marquess, you are malapert, | your 1.03.254
peace, peace, for shame! if not, for charity. 1.03.272
peace, peace, for shame! if not, for charity. 1.03.272
and there awake god's gentle–sleeping peace. 1.03.287
make peace with god, for you must die, my lord. 1.04.249
souls | to counsel me to make my peace with god, 1.04.251
and more /in peace my soul shall part to heaven, 2.01. 5
since i have made my friends at peace on earth. 2.01. 6
here | to make the blessed period of this peace. 2.01. 44
made peace of enmity, fair love of hate, 2.01. 51
desire | to reconcile me to his friendly peace. 2.01. 60
first, madam, i entreat true peace of you, 2.01. 63
i prithee peace, my soul is full of sorrow. 2.01. 97
peace, children, peace, the king doth love you 2.02. 17
children, peace, the king doth love you well. 2.02. 17
i hope the king made peace with all of us, | and 2.02.132

the peace of england, and our persons' safety, 3.05. 45
your discipline in war, wisdom in peace, | your 3.07. 16
i to my grave, where peace and rest lie with me! 4.01. 94
infer fair england's peace by this alliance. 4.04.343
to reap the harvest of perpetual peace | by this 5.02. 15
sleep, richmond, sleep in peace and wake in joy. 5.03.150
you sleep in peace, the tyrant being slain; 5.03.256
enrich the time to come with smooth–fac'd peace, 5.05. 33
would with treason wound this fair land's peace! 5.05. 39
now civil wounds are stopp'd, peace lives again; 5.05. 40
the peace between the french and us not values H8 1.01. 88
dashing the garment of this peace, aboded | the 1.01. 93
a proper title of a peace, and purchas'd | at a 1.01. 98
king's course, | and break the foresaid peace. 1.01.190
'gainst me, that i cannot take peace with; 2.01. 85
god's peace be with him! 2.01.111
heav'n's peace be with him! 2.02.129
peace to your highness! 3.01. 23
too far), | offers, as i do, in a sign of peace, 3.01. 66
within me | a peace above all earthly dignities, 3.02.379
still in thy right hand carry gentle peace | to 3.02.445
the rod, and bird of peace, and all such emblems 4.01. 89
his blessed part to heaven, and slept in peace. 4.02. 30
peace be with him! 4.02. 75
spirits of peace, where are ye? 4.02. 83
as you wish christian peace to souls departed, 4.02.156
place, | defacers of a public peace than i do. 5.02. 76
the merry songs of peace to all his neighbors. 5.04. 35
nor shall this peace sleep with her; 5.04. 39
peace, plenty, love, truth, terror, | that were 5.04. 47
peace, you ungracious clamors! TRO 1.01. 89
peace, rude sounds! 1.01. 89
peace, for shame, peace! 1.02.230 P
peace, for shame, peace! 1.02.230 P
that's their /fame in peace. 1.03.236
but peace, aeneas, | peace, troyan, lay thy 1.03.239
peace, troyan, lay thy finger on thy lips! 1.03.240
peace, fool! 2.01. 82 P
i would have peace and quietness, but the fool 2.01. 83 P
no more words, thersites, peace! 2.01.113 P
i will hold my peace when achilles' /brach bids 2.01.114 P
the wound of peace is /surety, | /surety secure, 2.02. 14
peace, sister, peace! 2.02.103
peace, sister, peace! 2.02.103
to see great hector in his weeds of peace, | to 3.03.239
peace, drums! 5.09. 2
have, you curs, | that like nor peace nor war? COR 1.01.169
all the peace you make in their cause is calling 2.01. 78 P
peace, peace, peace! 3.01.187
peace, peace, peace! 3.01.187
peace, peace, peace! 3.01.187
stay, hold, peace! 3.01.187
hear me, people, peace! 3.01.191
peace! 3.01.192
peace, peace! 3.01.216
peace, peace! 3.01.216
peace! 3.01.272
he shall answer, by a lawful form | (in peace), 3.01.324
ordinance stood up | to speak of peace or war. 3.02. 13
in peace what each of them by th' other lose 3.02. 44
that it shall hold companionship in peace | with 3.02. 49
our large temples with the shows of peace, | and 3.03. 36
list to your tribunes. audience! peace, i say! 3.03. 40
well, say. peace ho! 3.03. 41
peace! 3.03. 75
peace, peace, be not so loud. 4.02. 12
peace, peace, be not so loud. 4.02. 12
come, come, peace. 4.02. 29
this peace is nothing but to rust iron, increase 4.05.219 P
i, it exceeds peace as far as day does night; 4.05.221 P
peace is a very apoplexy, lethargy, mull'd, deaf 4.05.223 P
cannot be denied but peace is a great maker of 4.05.228 P
the present peace | and quietness of the people, 4.06. 2
but commanding peace | even with the same 4.07. 43
i beseech you peace; 5.03. 78
and cry, "be blest | for making up this peace!" 5.03.140
make true wars, | i'll frame convenient peace. 5.03.191
good sir, | what peace you'll make, advise me. 5.03.197
arms, | could not have made this peace. 5.03.209
we have made peace | with no less honor to the 5.06. 78
peace both, and hear me speak. 5.06.110
peace ho! 5.06.123
no outrage, peace! 5.06.123
stand, aufidius, | and trouble not the peace. 5.06.127
plead your deserts in peace and humbleness. TIT 1.01. 45
and sleep in peace, slain in your country's wars 1.01. 91
in peace and honor rest you here, my sons, 1.01.150
in peace and honor rest you here, my sons! 1.01.156
in peace and honor live lord titus long! 1.01.157
these lovers will not keep the peace. 2.01. 37
however these disturbers of our peace | buzz in 4.04. 6
"peace, tawny slave, half me and half thy dame. 5.01. 27
peace, villain, peace!" 5.01. 33
peace, villain, peace!" 5.01. 33
for peace, for love, for league, and good to 5.03. 23
i do but keep the peace. ROM 1.01. 68
what, drawn and talk of peace? 1.01. 70
rebellious subjects, enemies to peace, 1.01. 81
cank'red with peace, to part your cank'red hate; 1.01. 95
your lives shall pay the forfeit of the peace. 1.01. 97
think, | for men so old as we to keep the peace. 1.02. 3
enough of this, i pray thee hold thy peace. 1.03. 49
peace, i have done. 1.03. 59
peace, peace, mercutio, peace! 1.04. 95
peace, peace, mercutio, peace! 1.04. 95
peace, peace, mercutio, peace! 1.04. 95
dwell upon thine eyes, peace in thy breast! 2.02.186
would i were sleep and peace, so sweet to rest! 2.02.187
well, peace be with you, sir, here comes my man. 3.01. 56
the unruly spleen | of tybalt deaf to peace, but 3.01.158
peace, you mumbling fool! 3.05.173
peace ho, for shame! 4.05. 65
to lie discolor'd by this place of peace? 5.03.143
a glooming peace this morning with it brings, 5.03.305
and returns in peace | most rich in timon's nod. TIM 1.01. 61
my father's age, | and call him to long peace. 1.02. 3
religion to the gods, peace, justice, truth, 4.01. 16
let us first see peace in athens. 4.03.456 P

peace and content be here! 5.01.127
too savage, doth root up | his country's peace. 5.01.166
make war breed peace, make peace stint war, make 5.04. 83
make war breed peace, make peace stint war, make 5.04. 83
peace ho, caesar speaks. JC 1.02. 1
bid every noise be still; peace yet again! 1.02. 14
peace, count the clock. 2.01.192
heaven nor earth have been at peace to–night. 2.02. 1
let's all cry, "peace, freedom, and liberty!" 3.01.110
thy death, | to see thy antony making his peace, 3.01.197
peace, silence! brutus speaks. 3.02. 54
peace ho! 3.02. 54
peace, let us hear what antony can say. 3.02. 71
peace ho, let us hear him. 3.02. 72
peace there, hear the noble antony. 3.02.207 P
peace ho, hear antony, most noble antony! 3.02.234 P
peace ho! 3.02.246 P
peace, peace, you durst not so have tempted him. 4.03. 59
peace, peace, you durst not so have tempted him. 4.03. 59
may, | lovers in peace, lead on our days to age! 5.01. 94
peace then, no words. 5.05. 7
peace, the charm's wound up. MAC 1.03. 37
nor keep peace between | th' effect and /it! 1.05. 46
prithee peace! 1.07. 45
peace! 2.02. 2
put rancors in the vessel of my peace | only for 3.01. 66
whom we, to gain our peace, have sent to peace, 3.02. 20
whom we, to gain our peace, have sent to peace, 3.02. 20
but peace! 3.06. 21
uproar the universal peace, confound | all unity 4.03. 99
the tyrant has not batter'd at their peace? 4.03.178
they were well at peace when i did leave 'em. 4.03.179
peace, break thee off! HAM 1.01. 40
itself should gape | and bid me hold my peace. 1.02.245
the humorous man shall end his part in peace, 2.02.323 P
peace! 3.04. 34
this is th' imposthume of much wealth and peace, 4.04. 27
lord, | so you will not o'errule me to a peace. 4.07. 60
to thine own peace. 4.07. 61
as peace should still her wheaten garland wear 5.02. 41
i have a voice and president of peace | to /keep 5.02.249
peace, kent! LR 1.01.121
so be my grave my peace, as here i give | her 1.01.125
peace be with burgundy! 1.01.247
and sometimes i am whipt for holding my peace. 1.04.185 P
keep peace, upon your lives! 2.02. 48
peace, sirrah! 2.02. 68
peace, smulkin, peace, thou fiend! 3.04.140 P
peace, smulkin, peace, thou fiend! 3.04.140 P
peace, peace, this piece of toasted cheese will 4.06. 89 P
peace, peace, this piece of toasted cheese will 4.06. 89 P
when the thunder would not peace at my bidding, 4.06.102 P
little bless'd with the soft phrase of peace; OTH 1.03. 82
a moth of peace, and he go to the war, | the 1.03.256
and practicing upon his peace and quiet | even 2.01.310
to put up in peace what already i have foolishly 4.02.179 P
peace, and be still! 5.02. 46
peace, you were best. 5.02.161
/'zounds, hold your peace. 5.02.219
i peace? 5.02.219
servant, making peace or war | as thou affects. ANT 1.03. 70
those wars | which fronted mine own peace. 2.02. 61
and though i make this marriage for my peace, 2.03. 40
shall make thy peace for moving me to rage, 2.05. 70
fly, | and make your peace with caesar. 3.11. 6
prithee peace. 3.13. 12
peace, what noise? 4.03. 12
peace, i say. | what should this mean? 4.03. 14
the time of universal peace is near. 4.06. 4
peace! | hark further. 4.09. 10
hence, saucy eunuch, peace! 4.14. 25
peace! 4.15. 13
peace, peace, iras! 4.15. 72
peace, peace, iras! 4.15. 72
peace, peace! 5.02.308
peace, peace! 5.02.308
peace, | dear lady daughter, peace! CYM 1.01.153
peace, | dear lady daughter, peace! 1.01.154
plenty and peace breeds cowards; 3.06. 21
now peace be here, | poor house, that keep'st 3.06. 35
peace, | i'll give no wound to thee. 5.01. 20
be fortunate and flourish in peace and plenty." 5.04.144 P
peace, peace, see further. 5.05.124
peace, peace, see further. 5.05.124
peace, my lord, hear, hear — 5.05.227
be fortunate and flourish in peace and plenty." 5.05.442 P
whose issue | promises britain peace and plenty. 5.05.458
well, | my peace we will begin. 5.05.459
above do tune | the harmony of this peace. 5.05.467
publish we this peace | to all our subjects. 5.05.478
of great jupiter | our peace we'll ratify; 5.05.483
bloody hands were wash'd) with such a peace. 5.05.485
so i bequeath a happy peace to you | and all PER 1.01. 50
peace, peace, and give experience tongue. 1.02. 37
peace, peace, and give experience tongue. 1.02. 37
when signior sooth here does proclaim peace, 1.02. 44
peace to the lords of tyre! 1.03. 29
white flags display'd, they bring us peace, 1.04. 72
welcome is peace, if he on peace consist; 1.04. 83
welcome is peace, if he on peace consist; 1.04. 83
here to have death in peace is all he'll crave. 2.01. 11
peace be at your labor, honest fishermen. 2.01. 52
and tyrus stands | in a litigious peace. 3.03. 3
me, | but, not to be a troubler of your peace, 5.01.151
and now flurted | by peace, for whom he fought, TNK 1.02. 19
that peace might purge | for her repletion, and 1.02. 23
peace be to you | as i pursue this war! 1.03. 24
peace sleep with him! 1.05. 12
her, | and fluently persuade her to a peace. 3.05. 87
peace, hear me! STM II.C 1 P
peace ho, peace, i charge you keep the peace! II.C 28
peace ho, peace, i charge you keep the peace! II.C 28
peace ho, peace, i charge you keep the peace! II.C 28
peace i say, peace! II.C 35 P
peace i say, peace! II.C 35 P
peace, peace, silence, peace! II.C 50 P
peace, peace, silence, peace! II.C 50 P
peace, peace, silence, peace! II.C 50 P

plague on them, they will not hold their peace. II.C 53 P
peace, peace! II.C 60 P
peace, peace! II.C 60 P
you do offend you cry upon, | that is the peace; II.C 62
that could have topp'd the peace, as now you II.C 64
the peace wherein you have till now grown up II.C 65
that you like rebels lift against the peace II.C 109
lift against the peace | lift up for peace, and II.C 110
afar, | how he in peace is wounded, not in war. LUC 831
"o, peace," quoth lucrece, "if it should be told 1284
and for the peace of you i hold such strife | as SON 75. 3
and peace proclaims olives of endless age. 107. 8
love's arms are peace, 'gainst rule, 'gainst LC 271

PEACE–A 1 FR 0.0001 REL FR 0 V 1 P
peace–a your tongue. — speak–a your tale. WIV 1.04. 81 P

PEACEABLE 2 FR 0.0002 REL FR 0 V 2 P
the most peaceable way for you, if you do take a ADO 3.03. 57 P
so to be call'd for his peaceable reign and good PER 2.01.103 P

PEACEABLY 2 FR 0.0002 REL FR 1 V 1 P
thou and i are too wise to woo peaceably. ADO 5.02. 72 P
disturb him not, let him pass peaceably. 2H6 3.03. 25

PEACEFUL 14 FR 0.0015 REL FR 14 V 0 P
water keep | a peaceful progress to the ocean. JN 2.01.340
march | so many miles upon her peaceful bosom, R2 2.03. 93
measure our confines with such peaceful steps? 3.02.125
souls | may make a peaceful and a sweet retire H5 4.03. 86
sword, | how many would the peaceful city quit, 5.pr. 33
wars | will turn unto a peaceful comic sport, 1H6 2.02. 45
that peaceful truce shall be proclaim'd in 5.04.117
wounds | deliver'd up again with peaceful words? 2H6 1.01.122
smooth the frowns of war with peaceful looks. 3H6 2.06. 32
his looks are full of peaceful majesty, | his 4.06. 71
peaceful commerce from dividable shores, | the TRO 1.03.105
in the day's glorious walk or peaceful night, PER 1.02. 4
you return to us, | peaceful and comfortable! 1.02. 36
and in a peaceful hour doth cry, 'kill, kill!' VEN 652

PEACEMAKER 1 FR 0.0001 REL FR 0 V 1 P
your if is the only peacemaker; AYL 5.04.103 P

PEACEMAKERS 2 FR 0.0002 REL FR 2 V 0 P
for blessed are the peacemakers on earth. 2H6 2.01. 34
pray think us | those we profess, peacemakers, H8 3.01.167

PEACE–PARTED 1 FR 0.0001 REL FR 1 V 0 P
and such rest to her | as to peace–parted souls. HAM 5.01.238

PEACES 1 FR 0.0001 REL FR 1 V 0 P
hold your peaces. WT 2.01.139

PEACH 1 FR 0.0001 REL FR 0 V 1 P
if i be ta'en, i'll peach for this. 1H4 2.02. 44 P

PEACH–COLOR'D 2 FR 0.0002 REL FR 0 V 2 P
for some four suits of peach–color'd satin, MM 4.03. 11 P
and those that were thy peach–color'd once, or 2H4 2.02. 16 P

PEACHES 1 FR 0.0001 REL FR 0 V 1 P
satin, which now peaches him a beggar. MM 4.03. 11 P

PEACOCK *(also pajock)*

PEACOCK 3 FR 0.0003 REL FR 2 V 1 P
"fly pride," says the peacock: ERR 4.03. 80
and like a peacock sweep along his tail; 1H6 3.03. 6
'a stalks up and down like a peacock — a stride TRO 3.03.251 P

PEACOCK'S 1 FR 0.0001 REL FR 0 V 1 P
fanning in his face with a peacock's feather. H5 4.01.201 P

PEACOCKS 1 FR 0.0001 REL FR 1 V 0 P
/her peacocks fly amain. TMP 4.01. 74

PEAK 2 FR 0.0002 REL FR 2 V 0 P
times nine, | shall he dwindle, peak, and pine; MAC 1.03. 23
muddy–mettled rascal, peak | like john–a–dreams, HAM 2.02.567

PEAKING 1 FR 0.0001 REL FR 0 V 1 P
/brook, but the peaking cornuto her husband, WIV 3.05. 70 P

PEAL 4 FR 0.0004 REL FR 3 V 1 P
peace, the peal begins. LLL 5.01. 43 P
and rouse the prince, and ring a hunter's peal, TIT 2.02. 5
i promised your grace a hunter's peal. 2.02. 13
drowsy hums | hath rung night's yawning peal, MAC 3.02. 43

PEALS 1 FR 0.0001 REL FR 1 V 0 P
whether those peals of praise be his or no, | so MV 3.02.145

'PEAR *(also appear)*

'PEAR 1 FR 0.0001 REL FR 1 V 0 P
it shall as level to your judgment 'pear | as HAM 4.05.152

PEAR* *(also bear*)*

PEAR* 5 FR 0.0005 REL FR 1 V 4 P
wits till i were as crestfall'n as a dried pear. WIV 4.05.100 P
ill, it eats drily, marry, 'tis a wither'd pear; AWW 1.01.162 P
better, marry, yet 'tis a wither'd pear. 1.01.163 P
i hope your majesty is pear me testimony and H5 4.08. 35 P
she were | an open/–arse, thou a pop'rin pear! ROM 2.01. 38

PEARD *(also beard)*

PEARD 2 FR 0.0002 REL FR 0 V 2 P
i like not when a oman has a great peard. WIV 4.02.193 P
i spy a great peard under his muffler. 4.02.194 P

PEARL 26 FR 0.0029 REL FR 23 V 3 P
as twenty seas, if all their sand were pearl, TGV 2.04.170
a sea of melting pearl, which some call tears; 3.01.226
like sapphire, pearl, and rich embroidery, WIV 5.05. 71
enough for a flint, pearl enough for a swine: LLL 4.02. 89 P
will you have me, or your pearl again? 5.02.458
decking with liquid pearl the bladed grass | (a MND 1.01.211
here, | and hang a pearl in every cowslip's ear. 2.01. 15
a poor house, as your pearl in your foul oyster. AYL 5.04. 61 P
their harness studded all with gold and pearl. SHR in.2. 42
fine linen, turkey cushions boss'd with pearl, 2.01.353
what 'cerns it you if i wear pearl and gold? 5.01. 75 P
this pearl she gave me, i do feel't and see't, TN 4.03. 2
the intertissued robe of gold and pearl, | the H5 4.01.262
wedges of gold, great anchors, heaps of pearl, R3 1.04. 26
shall come again, transform'd to orient pearl, 4.04.322
her bed is india, there she lies, a pearl; TRO 1.01.100
why, she is a pearl, | whose price hath launch'd 2.02. 81
i will be bright, and shine in pearl and gold, TIT 2.01. 19
this is the pearl that pleas'd your empress' eye 5.01. 42
i see thee compass'd with thy kingdom's pearl, MAC 5.09. 22
hamlet, this pearl is thine, | here's to thy HAM 5.02.282
threw a pearl away | richer than all his tribe; OTH 5.02.347
of many doubled kisses — | this orient pearl. ANT 1.05. 41
and wip'd the brinish pearl from her bright eyes LUC 1213
bright orient pearl, alack, too timely shaded! PP 10. 3
but those tears are pearl which thy love sheeds, SON 34.13

/PEARLS 2 FR 0.0002 REL FR 2 V 0 P
this, and these /pearls, to me sent longaville. LLL 5.02. 53
/thence, | /as /pearls /from /diamonds /dropp'd. LR 4.03. 22

PEARLS 12 FR 0.0013 REL FR 10 V 2 P
those are pearls that were his eyes: TMP 1.02.399
but pearls are fair; TGV 5.02. 11
black men are pearls in beauteous ladies' eyes. 5.02. 12
such pearls as put out ladies' eyes, | for i had 5.02. 13
and lac'd with silver, set with pearls, down ADO 3.04. 20 P
was wont to swell like round and orient pearls, MND 4.01. 54
those heaven–moving pearls from his poor eyes, JN 2.01.169
"your brooches, pearls, and ouches." 2H4 2.04. 48 P
of gold, and hail | rich pearls upon thee. ANT 2.05. 46
being prison'd in her eye like pearls in glass, VEN 980
those round clear pearls of his, that move thy LUC 1553
me, | of pallid pearls and rubies red as blood, LC 198
PEARLY 1 FR 0.0001 REL FR 1 V 0 P
with pearly sweat resembling dew of night. LUC 396
PEARS 1 FR 0.0001 REL FR 0 V 1 P
is like one of our french wither'd pears, it AWW 1.01.161 P
PEAS 2 FR 0.0002 REL FR 0 V 2 P
had rather have a handful or two of dried peas. MND 4.01. 38 P
peas and beans are as dank here as a dog, and 1H4 2.01. 8 P
/PEASANT 1 FR 0.0001 REL FR 1 V 0 P
/proud /majesty /a /subject, /state /a /peasant. R2 4.01.252
PEASANT 21 FR 0.0023 REL FR 18 V 3 P
how now, you whoreson peasant, | where have you
TGV 4.04. 43
then | she's fled unto that peasant valentine; 5.02. 35
shalt know i will predominate over the peasant, WIV 2.02.282 P
hence, prating peasant! fetch thy master home. ERR 2.01. 81
and sent my peasant home | for certain ducats; 5.01.231
you have train'd me like a peasant, obscuring AYL 1.01. 68 P
when they do homage to this simple peasant. SHR in.1. 135
you peasant swain! 4.01.129
this have i rumor'd through the peasant towns 2H4 in 33
fire | even to the dullest peasant in his camp, 1.01.113
whose hours the peasant best advantages. H5 4.01.284
peasant, unless thou give me crowns, brave 4.04. 38
so do our vulgar drench their peasant limbs | in 4.07. 77
like peasant footboys do they keep the walls, 1H6 3.02. 69
and like me to the peasant boys of france, | to 4.06. 48
peasant, avaunt! 5.04. 21
o, what a rogue and peasant slave am i! HAM 2.02.550
that the toe of the peasant comes so near the 5.01.140 P
give me thy sword. a peasant stand up thus? LR 3.07. 80
wherefore, bold peasant, | /durst thou support a 4.06.231
and suit myself | as does a britain peasant; CYM 5.01. 24
PEASANTRY 1 FR 0.0001 REL FR 1 V 0 P
how much low peasantry would then be gleaned MV 2.09. 46
PEASANTS 8 FR 0.0009 REL FR 7 V 1 P
that our superfluous lackeys and our peasants, H5 4.02. 26
so worthless peasants bargain for their wives, 1H6 5.05. 53
is a ragged multitude | of hinds and peasants, 2H6 4.04. 33
and you, base peasants, do ye believe him? 4.08. 21 P
a scum of britains and base lackey peasants, R3 5.03.317
how many prodigal bits have slaves and peasants TIM 2.02.165
from the hard hands of peasants their vile trash JC 4.03. 74
which heartless peasants did so well resemble, LUC 1392
PEASCOD 4 FR 0.0004 REL FR 0 V 4 P
your mother, and to master peascod, your father. MND 3.01.187 P
remember the wooing of a peascod instead of her,
AYL 2.04. 51 P
as a squash is before 'tis a peascod, or a TN 1.05.157 P
that's a sheal'd peascod. LR 1.04.200 P
PEASCOD–TIME 1 FR 0.0001 REL FR 0 V 1 P
thee these twenty–nine years, come peascod–time,
2H4 2.04.383 P
PEASE 2 FR 0.0002 REL FR 2 V 0 P
of wheat, rye, barley, fetches, oats, and pease; TMP 4.01. 61
this fellow pecks up wit as pigeons pease, | and LLL 5.02.315
PEASEBLOSSOM 5 FR 0.0005 REL FR 2 V 3 P
peaseblossom! MND 3.01.162
peaseblossom. 3.01.185
good master peaseblossom, i shall desire you of 3.01.188 P
where's peaseblossom? 4.01. 5 P
scratch my head, peaseblossom. 4.01. 7 P
PEAT* *(also beat, etc.)*
PEAT* 3 FR 0.0003 REL FR 1 V 2 P
i will peat the door for master page. WIV 1.01. 72 P
a pretty peat! SHR 1.01. 78
of my leek, or i will peat his pate four days. H5 5.01. 41 P
PEATEN 1 FR 0.0001 REL FR 0 V 1 P
and has been grievously peaten as an old oman. WIV 4.04. 21 P
PEBBLE *(also pibble*, etc.)*
PEBBLE 3 FR 0.0003 REL FR 2 V 1 P
a pebble. WIV 4.01. 34 P
have fill'd their pockets full of pebble stones; 1H6 3.01. 80
that on th' unnumb'red idle pebble chafes, LR 4.06. 21
PEBBLES 2 FR 0.0002 REL FR 2 V 0 P
flints, and pebbles should be thrown on her. HAM 5.01.231
like wrinkled pebbles in a /glassy stream, | you TNK 1.01.112
PECK* *(also pick*, pitch*)*
PECK* 9 FR 0.0010 REL FR 6 V 3 P
in the circumference of a peck, hilt to point, WIV 3.05.111 P
when beasts most graze, birds best peck, and men
LLL 1.01.236 P
truly, a peck of provender; MND 4.01. 31 P
so doves do peck the falcon's piercing talons, 3H6 1.04. 41
and doves will peck in safeguard of their brood. 2.02. 18
th' rail, | i'll peck you o'er the pales else. H8 5.03. 90
and bring in | the crows to peck the eagles. COR 3.01.139
my heart upon my sleeve | for daws to peck at: OTH 1.01. 65
in that mood | the dove will peck the estridge; ANT 3.13.196
PECK'D 1 FR 0.0001 REL FR 1 V 0 P
to tell | what crows have peck'd them here. CYM 5.03. 93
PECKS 2 FR 0.0002 REL FR 2 V 0 P
this fellow pecks up wit as pigeons pease, | and LLL 5.02.315
and pecks of crows in the foul fields of thebes. TNK 1.01. 42
PECULIAR 9 FR 0.0010 REL FR 8 V 1 P
groping for trouts in a peculiar river. MM 1.02. 90 P
any, | in will peculiar and in self–admission. TRO 2.03.166
the single and peculiar life is bound | with all HAM 3.03. 11
and duty, | but seeming so, for my peculiar end; OTH 1.01. 60
or sue to you to do a peculiar profit | to your 3.03. 79
unproper beds | which they dare swear peculiar; 4.01. 69
and so much | for my peculiar care. CYM 5.05. 83
their nobleness peculiar to them, gives | the TNK 5.03. 87
with pure aspects did him peculiar duties. LUC 14
/PECUS 1 FR 0.0001 REL FR 0 V 1 P
precor gelida quando /pecus /omne sub umbra LLL 4.02. 93 P

PEDANT 8 FR 0.0009 REL FR 5 V 3 P
constable, | a domineering pedant o'er the boy, LLL 3.01.177
the pedant, judas machabeus; 5.02.536 P
the pedant, the braggart, the hedge–priest, the 5.02.542 P
but, wrangling pedant, this is | the patroness SHR 3.01. 4
how fiery and forward our pedant is! 3.01. 48
but i have cause to pry into this pedant. 3.01. 87
master, a mercantant, or a pedant, | i know not 4.02. 63
like a pedant that keeps a school i' th' church. TN 3.02. 75 P
PEDANTICAL 1 FR 0.0001 REL FR 1 V 0 P
figures pedantical — these summer flies | have LLL 5.02.408
PEDASCULE 1 FR 0.0001 REL FR 1 V 0 P
pedascule, i'll watch you better yet. SHR 3.01. 50
PEDIGREE 4 FR 0.0004 REL FR 4 V 0 P
willing you overlook this pedigree; H5 2.04. 90
he | from john of gaunt doth bring his pedigree, 1H6 2.05. 77
you tell a pedigree | of threescore and two 3H6 3.03. 92
right, | now buckler falsehood with a pedigree? 3.03. 99
PEDLAR 6 FR 0.0006 REL FR 3 V 3 P
he is wit's pedlar, and retails his wares | at LLL 5.02.317
sly's son of burton–heath, by birth a pedlar, by SHR in.2. 19 P
if you did but hear the pedlar at the door, you WT 4.04.181 P
pedlar, let's have the first choice. 4.04.312 P
come to the pedlar, | money's a meddler, | that 4.04.321
i had rather be a pedlar: R3 1.03.148
PEDLAR'S 3 FR 0.0003 REL FR 1 V 2 P
the pedlar's silken treasury and have pour'd it WT 4.04.350
let me pocket up my pedlar's excrement. 4.04.714 P
she was indeed a pedlar's daughter, and sold 2H6 4.02. 45 P
PEDLARS 1 FR 0.0001 REL FR 0 V 1 P
you have of these pedlars, that have more in WT 4.04.215 P
/PEDRO 2 FR 0.0002 REL FR 0 V 2 P
in this letter that don /pedro of arragon comes ADO 1.01. 1 P
i find here that don /pedro hath bestow'd much 1.01. 10 P
PEDRO 4 FR 0.0004 REL FR 0 V 4 P
his part, and equally rememb'red by don pedro. ADO 1.01. 13 P
don pedro is approach'd. 1.01. 95 P
look, don pedro is return'd to seek you. 1.01.202 P
me a meet hour to draw don pedro and the count 2.02. 34 P
PEDS *(also beds)*
PEDS 1 FR 0.0001 REL FR 1 V 0 P
there will we make our peds of roses, | and a WIV 3.01. 19
PEEL'D *(also pil'd*, pill'd)*
PEEL'D 1 FR 0.0001 REL FR 1 V 0 P
peel'd priest, dost thou command me to be shut 1H6 1.03. 30
PEEP* 21 FR 0.0023 REL FR 18 V 3 P
thou wak'st, with thine own fool's eyes peep. MND 4.01. 84
some that will evermore peep through their eyes, MV 1.01. 52
(for aught i see) two and thirty, a peep out? SHR 1.02. 33 P
through flinty tartar's bosom would peep forth AWW 4.04. 7
dangerous action can peep out his head but i am 2H4 1.02.213 P
ay, where thou dar'st not peep. 2H6 2.01. 41
i hid me in these woods and durst not peep out, 4.10. 3 P
see his pride | peep through each part of him. H8 1.01. 69
stood for rome, | and durst not once peep out. COR 4.06. 46
and peep about | to find ourselves dishonorable JC 1.02.137
nor heaven peep through the blanket of the dark MAC 1.05. 53
forth at your eyes your spirits wildly peep, HAM 3.04.119
that treason can but peep to what it would, 4.05.125
no vessel can peep forth, but 'tis as soon ANT 1.04. 53
i'll force | the wine peep through their scars. 3.13.190
peep through thy marble mansion, help, | or we CYM 5.04. 87
on, | under whose brim the gaudy sun would peep;
VEN 1088
night's black bosom should not peep again. LUC 788
crystal walls each little mote will peep; 1251
pack night, peep day; PP 14.29
wherethrough the sun | delights to peep, to gaze SON 24.12
PEEP'D 3 FR 0.0003 REL FR 2 V 1 P
the ale–wive's petticoat and so peep'd through. 2H4 2.02. 83 P
this league | peep'd harms that menac'd him — H8 1.01.183
some beauty peep'd through lettice of sear'd age LC 14
PEEPING 4 FR 0.0004 REL FR 4 V 0 P
the court of his eye, peeping thorough desire: LLL 2.01.235
who, peeping forth this tumult to behold, | are LUC 447
leave thy peeping, | mock with thy tickling 1089
all sleeping, | nymphs /back peeping fearfully. PP 17.28
PEEPS 3 FR 0.0003 REL FR 3 V 0 P
under an oak whose antique root peeps out | upon
AYL 2.01. 31
and the true blood which peeps fairly through't, WT 4.04.148
and faintly through a rusty beaver peeps. H5 4.02. 44
PEER* 17 FR 0.0019 REL FR 13 V 4 P
o peer! TMP 4.01.222 P
on the forehead, crying, "peer out, peer out!" WIV 4.02. 26 P
on the forehead, crying, "peer out, peer out!" 4.02. 26 P
when daffadils begin to peer, | with heigh, the WT 4.03. 1
thanks, noble peer! R2 5.05. 67
how bloodily the sun begins to peer | above yon 1H4 5.01. 1
what peer hath been suborn'd to grate on you? 2H4 4.01. 90
no prince nor peer shall have just cause to say, 5.02.144
no, | for yet a many of your horsemen peer | and H5 4.07. 85
i trow, | or be inferior to the proudest peer. 1H6 5.01. 57
heart, | pernicious protector, dangerous peer, 2H6 2.01. 21
becomes | so good a quarrel and so bad a peer. 2.01. 28
the proudest peer in the realm shall not wear a 4.07.119 P
back'd by the power of warwick, that false peer, 3H6 1.01. 52
"king stephen was and–a worthy peer, | his OTH 2.03. 89
this king unto him took a peer, | who died and PER 1.ch. 21
but king nor peer to such a peerless dame. LUC 21
PEER'D 1 FR 0.0001 REL FR 1 V 0 P
peer'd forth the golden window of the east, | a ROM 1.01.119
PEERETH 1 FR 0.0001 REL FR 1 V 0 P
clouds, | so honor peereth in the meanest habit. SHR 4.03.174
PEERING *(also piring)*
PEERING 4 FR 0.0004 REL FR 4 V 0 P
but flora, | peering in april's front. WT 4.04. 3
like a proud river peering o'er his bounds? JN 3.01. 23
the hollow eyes of death | i spy life peering, R2 2.01.271
like a dive–dapper peering through a wave, | who VEN 86
/PEERLESS 1 FR 0.0001 REL FR 1 V 0 P
a man of sovereign /parts, /peerless esteem'd, LLL 2.01. 44
PEERLESS 8 FR 0.0009 REL FR 8 V 0 P
so perfect and so peerless, are created | of TMP 3.01. 47
the most peerless piece of earth, i think, WT 5.01. 94
as she liv'd peerless, | so her dead likeness, i 5.03. 14
her peerless feature, joined with her birth, 1H6 5.05. 68
it is a peerless kinsman. MAC 1.04. 58

the world to weet | we stand up peerless. ANT 1.01. 40
might stand peerless by this slaughter. PER 4.ch. 40
but king nor peer to such a peerless dame. LUC 21
PEERS' 1 FR 0.0001 REL FR 1 V 0 P
and all the peers', for surety of our leagues. H5 5.02.372
PEERS* 40 FR 0.0045 REL FR 40 V 0 P
me, till i have pleas'd | my discontented peers! JN 4.02.127
need | some messenger betwixt me and the peers, 4.02.179
o, haste thee to the peers, | throw this report 4.02.260
most mighty liege, and my companion peers, R2 1.03. 93
besides himself, are all the english peers, 3.04. 88
then hear me, gracious sovereign, and you peers, H5 1.02. 33
see you, my princes and my noble peers, | these 2.02. 84
his princes and his peers to servitude, | his 2.02.171
the english are embattled, you french peers. 4.02. 14
princes french, and peers, health to you all! 5.02. 8
that two such noble peers as ye should jar! 1H6 3.01. 70
this late dissension grown betwixt the peers 3.01.188
my gracious prince, and honorable peers, 3.04. 1
regard, | king henry's peers and chief nobility 4.01.146
after the slaughter of so many peers, | so many 5.04.103
in sight of england and her lordly peers, 2H6 1.01. 11
brave peers of england, pillars of the state, 1.01. 75
o peers of england, shameful is this league, 1.01. 98
the peers agreed, and henry was well pleas'd 1.01.218
and humphrey with the peers be fall'n at jars: 1.01.253
salisbury and warwick are no simple peers. 1.03. 74
and all the peers and nobles of the realm | have 1.03.126
good queen, and whet not on these furious peers, 2.01. 33
the king and all the peers are here at hand. 3.02. 10
our people and our peers are both misled, | our 3H6 3.03. 35
methinks these peers of france should smile at 3.03. 91
you peers, continue this united league. R3 2.01. 2
and, princely peers, a happy time of day! 2.01. 48
between these swelling wrong–incensed peers. 2.01. 52
you cloudy princes and heart–sorrowing peers 2.02.112
fatal and ominous to noble peers! 3.03. 10
now, noble peers, the cause why we are met | is 3.04. 1
where be the bending peers that flattered thee? 4.04. 95
and so his peers upon this evidence | have found H8 2.01. 26
which of the peers | have uncontemn'd gone by 3.02. 9
first, all you peers of greece, go to my tent; TRO 4.05.271
think of this, good peers, | but as a thing of MAC 3.04. 95
you shall not need, my fellow peers of tyre, PER 1.03. 10
when peers thus knit, a kingdom ever stands. 2.04. 58
who o'er the white sheet peers her whiter chin, LUC 472
PEESEL 1 FR 0.0001 REL FR 0 V 1 P
good captain peesel, be quiet, 'tis very late, 2H4 2.04.161 P
PEEVISH 29 FR 0.0032 REL FR 24 V 5 P
no, trust me, she is peevish, sullen, froward, TGV 3.01. 68
why, this it is to be a peevish girl, | that 5.02. 49
he is something peevish that way; WIV 1.04. 14 P
why, thou peevish sheep, | what ship of ERR 4.01. 93
what wilt thou do, thou peevish officer? 4.04.114
and creep into the jaundies | by being peevish? MV 1.01. 86
'tis but a peevish boy — yet he talks well — AYL 3.05.110
and when she is froward, peevish, sullen, sour, SHR 5.02.157
besides, virginity is peevish, proud, idle, made AWW 1.01.144 P
run after that same peevish messenger, | the TN 1.05.300
being wrong'd as we are by this peevish town, JN 2.01.402
desperate here, a peevish self–will'd harlotry, 1H4 3.01.196
what a wretched and peevish fellow is this king H5 3.07.132 P
i scorn thee and thy fashion, peevish boy. 1H6 2.04. 76
you of my household, leave this peevish broil, 3.01. 92
presume | to send such peevish tokens to a king. 5.03.186
what a peevish fool was that of crete | that 3H6 5.06. 18
should all but answer for that peevish brat? R3 1.03.193
what an indirect and peevish course | is this of 3.01. 31
king, | when richmond was a little peevish boy. 4.02. 97
the gods are deaf to hot and peevish vows; TRO 5.03. 16
a peevish self/–will'd harlotry it is. ROM 4.02. 14
a peevish schoolboy, worthless of such honor, JC 5.01. 61
why should we in our peevish opposition | take HAM 1.02.100
speak | any beginning to this peevish odds; OTH 2.03.185
or else break out in peevish jealousies, 4.03. 89
he's strange and peevish. CYM 1.06. 54
if the peevish baggage would but give way to PER 4.06. 19 P
if your peevish chastity, which is not worth a 4.06.122 P
PEEVISH/–FOND 1 FR 0.0001 REL FR 1 V 0 P
and be not peevish/–fond in great designs. R3 4.04.417
PEEVISHLY 1 FR 0.0001 REL FR 0 V 1 P
come, sir, you peevishly threw it to her; TN 2.02. 13 P
PEG 1 FR 0.0001 REL FR 1 V 0 P
oak | and peg thee in his knotty entrails till TMP 1.02.295
PEG–A–RAMSEY 1 FR 0.0001 REL FR 0 V 1 P
we are politicians, malvolio's a peg–a–ramsey, TN 2.03. 76 P
PEGASUS 3 FR 0.0003 REL FR 2 V 1 P
genoa, | where we were lodgers at the pegasus. SHR 4.04. 5
the clouds | to turn and wind a fiery pegasus, 1H4 4.01.109
le cheval volant, the pegasus, chez les narines H5 3.07. 14 P
PEGS 1 FR 0.0001 REL FR 1 V 0 P
but i'll set down the pegs that make this music, OTH 2.01.200
PEIZE 2 FR 0.0002 REL FR 2 V 0 P
i speak too long, but 'tis to peize the time, MV 3.02. 22
lest leaden slumber peize me down to–morrow, R3 5.03.105
PEIZED 1 FR 0.0001 REL FR 1 V 0 P
the world, who of itself is peized well, | made JN 2.01.575
PELF 3 FR 0.0003 REL FR 3 V 0 P
immortal gods, i crave no pelf, | i pray for no TIM 1.02. 62
all perishen of man, of pelf, | ne aught PER 2.ch. 35
as take the pain but cannot pluck the pelf. PP 14.12
PELICAN 3 FR 0.0003 REL FR 3 V 0 P
son, | that blood already, like the pelican, R2 2.01.126
and, like the kind life–rend'ring pelican, HAM 4.05.147
this flesh begot | those pelican daughters. LR 3.04. 75
PELION 2 FR 0.0002 REL FR 1 V 1 P
be a giantess, and lie under mount pelion. WIV 2.01. 80 P
mountain you have made | t' o'ertop old pelion, HAM 5.01.253
PELLA 1 FR 0.0001 REL FR 1 V 0 P
you have condemn'd and noted lucius pella | for JC 4.03. 2
PELLETED 2 FR 0.0002 REL FR 2 V 0 P
by the /discandying of this pelleted storm, ANT 3.13.165
brine | that seasoned woe had pelleted in tears, LC 18
PELL–MELL 5 FR 0.0005 REL FR 5 V 0 P
pell–mell, down with them! LLL 4.03.365
other, and pell–mell | make work upon ourselves, JN 2.01.406
for a time | of pell–mell havoc and confusion. 1H4 5.01. 82
march on, join bravely, let us to it pell–mell; R3 5.03.312

to't, luxury, pell–mell, for i lack soldiers. LR 4.06.117
PELOPONNESUS 1 FR 0.0001 REL FR 1 V 0 P
toward peloponnesus are they fled. ANT 3.10. 30
PELOPS' 1 FR 0.0001 REL FR 1 V 0 P
far sweeter, | smoother than pelops' shoulder! TNK 4.02. 21
PELT 3 FR 0.0003 REL FR 3 V 0 P
do pelt so fast at one another's pate | that 1H6 3.01. 82
the chidden billow seems to pelt the clouds, OTH 2.01. 12
another, smother'd, seems to pelt and swear, LUC 1418
PELTING* 7 FR 0.0008 REL FR 7 V 0 P
for every pelting, petty officer | would use his MM 2.02.112
hath every pelting river made so proud | that MND 2.01. 91
it — | like to a tenement or pelting farm. R2 2.01. 60
we have had pelting wars since you refus'd | the TRO 4.05.267
poor pelting villages, sheep–cotes, and mills, LR 2.03. 18
that bide the pelting of this pitiless storm, 3.04. 29
thou bring'st such pelting scurvy news TNK 2.02.266
PEMBROKE 9 FR 0.0010 REL FR 9 V 0 P
pembroke, look to't. JN 1.01. 30
pembroke and stafford, you in our behalf | go 3H6 4.01.130
i have fought with pembroke and his fellows, 4.03. 54
at pembroke or at /ha'rford–west in wales. R3 4.05. 10
oxford, redoubted pembroke, sir james blunt, 4.05. 14
the earl of pembroke keeps his regiment; 5.03. 29
no less flowing | than marchioness of pembroke; H8 2.03. 63
the marchioness of pembroke? 2.03. 94
the marchioness of pembroke? 3.02. 90
/PEN* 1 FR 0.0001 REL FR 1 V 0 P
/of /author's /pen /or /actor's /voice, /but TRO pr 24
PEN* 40 FR 0.0045 REL FR 26 V 14 P
side–stitches, that shall pen thy breath up; TMP 1.02.326
jest how my father stole two geese out of a pen, WIV 3.04. 41 P
with a ballad–maker's pen and hang me up at the ADO 1.01.252 P
bid him bring his pen and inkhorn to the jail. 3.05. 58 P
from my snow–white pen the ebon–colored ink LLL 1.01.243 P
write, pen, for i am for whole volumes in folio. 1.02.184 P
marvellous well for the pen. 4.02.152 P
never durst poet touch a pen to write | until 4.03.343
the poet's pen | turns them to shapes and gives MND 5.01. 15
for if i do, i'll mar the young clerk's pen. MV 5.01.237
to give great charlemain a pen in 's hand | and AWW 2.01. 77
and i will presently pen down my dilemmas, 3.06. 75 P
hermit of prague, that never saw pen and ink, TN 4.02. 13 P
at my hand, help me to a candle, and pen, ink, 4.02. 81 P
a semicircle, | or a half–moon made with a pen. WT 2.01. 11
form, drawn with a pen | upon a parchment, and JN 5.07. 32
for his nose was as sharp as a pen, and 'a H5 2.03. 16 P
thus far, with rough and all–unable pen, | our ep 1
verbatim to rehearse the method of my pen. 1H6 3.01. 13
i'll call for pen and ink, and write my mind. 5.03. 66
hang him with his pen and inkhorn about his neck
2H6 4.02.110 P
than breath or pen can give expressure to. TRO 3.03.204
heaven guide thy pen to print thy sorrows plain, TIT 4.01. 75
give me pen and ink. 4.03.106 P
and find delight writ there with beauty's pen; ROM 1.03. 82
out of plackets, thy pen from lenders' books, LR 3.04. 97 P
away with her, | and pen her up. CYM 1.01.153
your neck, sir, is pen, book, and counters; 5.04.169 P
she would with rich and constant pen | vail to PER 4.ch. 28
"go get me hither paper, ink, and pen, | yet LUC 1289
which this time's pencil, or my pupil pen, SON 16.10
nor draw no lines there with thine antique pen; 19.10
and though they be outstripp'd by every pen, 32. 6
my verse | as every alien pen hath got my use, 78. 3
deserves the travail of a worthier pen, | yet 79. 6
you still shall live (such virtue hath my pen) 81.13
lean penury within that pen doth dwell | that to 84. 5
affords | in polish'd form of well–refined pen. 85. 8
and gives thy pen both skill and argument. 100. 8
i see their antique pen would have express'd 106. 7
PENALTIES 2 FR 0.0002 REL FR 2 V 0 P
awakes me all the enrolled penalties | which MM 1.02.166
been this day acquitted | of grievous penalties, MV 4.01.410
PENALTY 12 FR 0.0013 REL FR 9 V 3 P
and an express command, under penalty, to MM 4.02.166 P
levied | to quit the penalty and to ransom him. ERR 1.01. 22
let's see the penalty. LLL 1.01.123 P
who devis'd this penalty? 1.01.124 P
to fright them hence with that dread penalty. 1.01.127
thou mayst with better face | exact the penalty. MV 1.03.137
and where thou now exacts the penalty, | which 4.01. 22
the law, | the penalty and forfeit of my bond. 4.01.207
of the law | hath full relation to the penalty, 4.01.248
he shall have nothing but the penalty. 4.01.322
here feel we not the penalty of adam, | the AYL 2.01. 5
in penalty alike, and 'tis not hard, i think, ROM 1.02. 2
PENANCE 19 FR 0.0021 REL FR 15 V 4 P
my penance is, to call lucetta back | and ask TGV 1.02. 64
i have done penance for contemning love, | whose 2.04.129
as he in penance wander'd through the forest; 5.02. 38
'tis your penance but to hear | the story of 5.04.170
impose me to what penance your invention | can ADO 5.01.273
and bide the penance of each three years' day. LLL 1.01.115
suffer him to take no delight nor no penance, 1.02.129 P
i go woolward for penance. 5.02.711 P
from which ling'ring penance | of such misery MV 4.01.271
and make her bear the penance of her tongue? SHR 1.01. 89
for our pleasure and his penance, till our very TN 3.04.138 P
shall, after three days' open penance done, 2H6 2.03. 11
now thou dost penance too. 2.04. 20
let not her penance exceed the king's commission 2.04. 75
madam, your penance done, throw off this sheet, 2.04.105
i would i were, | they should find easy penance. H8 1.04. 17
the penance lies on you, if these fair ladies 1.04. 32
are under the line, they need no other penance: 5.03. 43 P
nor double penance, to correct correction. SON 111.12
PENCE 7 FR 0.0008 REL FR 3 V 4 P
for one shot of five pence, thou shalt have five TGV 2.05. 9 P
me two shilling and two pence a–piece of yead WIV 1.01.157 P
hadst thou not fifteen pence? 2.02. 14
she say i am not fourteen pence on the score for SHR in.2. 23 P
yet sell your face for five pence and 'tis dear. JN 1.01.153
seven groats and two pence. 2H4 1.02.235 P
forty pence, no. H8 2.03. 89
PENCIL 4 FR 0.0004 REL FR 3 V 1 P
and over–stain'd | with slaughter's pencil — JN 3.01.237
the fisher with his pencil and the painter with ROM 1.02. 41 P
that life repair | which this time's pencil, or SON 16.10
beauty no pencil, beauty's truth to lay; 101. 7
PENCILL'D 3 FR 0.0003 REL FR 3 V 0 P
these pencill'd figures are | even such as they TIM 1.01.159
kind | which sometime show well, pencill'd. TNK 5.03. 13
to pencill'd pensiveness and color'd sorrow; LUC 1497
PENCILS 1 FR 0.0001 REL FR 1 V 0 P
ware pencils /ho! LLL 5.02. 43
PENDANT 5 FR 0.0005 REL FR 5 V 0 P
with ribands pendant, flaring 'bout her head; WIV 4.06. 42
violence round about | the pendant world; MM 3.01.125
hath made his pendant bed and procreant cradle. MAC 1.06. 8
there, on the pendant boughs her crownet weeds HAM 4.07.172
or lion, | a /tower'd citadel, a pendant rock, ANT 4.14. 4
PENDRAGON 1 FR 0.0001 REL FR 1 V 0 P
i read | that stout pendragon in his litter sick 1H6 3.02. 95
PENDULOUS 1 FR 0.0001 REL FR 1 V 0 P
now all the plagues that in the pendulous air LR 3.04. 67
/PENE 1 FR 0.0001 REL FR 1 V 0 P
/pene gelidus timor occupat artus: 2H6 4.01.117
PENELOPE 1 FR 0.0001 REL FR 0 V 1 P
you would be another penelope: COR 1.03. 82 P
PENETRABLE 3 FR 0.0003 REL FR 3 V 0 P
but penetrable to your kind entreaties, | albeit R3 3.07.225
so i shall, | if it be made of penetrable stuff, HAM 3.04. 36
no penetrable entrance to her plaining: LUC 559
PENETRATE 5 FR 0.0005 REL FR 2 V 3 P
and penetrate the breasts | of ever–angry bears. TMP 1.02.288
could penetrate her uncompassionate sire; TGV 3.01.233
they say it will penetrate. CYM 2.03. 12 P
if you can penetrate her with your fingering, so 2.03. 14 P
if this penetrate, i will consider your music 2.03. 27 P
PENETRATIVE 1 FR 0.0001 REL FR 1 V 0 P
his face subdu'd | to penetrative shame, whilst ANT 4.14. 75
PENITENCE 6 FR 0.0006 REL FR 6 V 0 P
by penitence th' eternal's wrath's appeas'd: TGV 5.04. 81
and try your penitence, if it be sound, | or MM 2.03. 22
paid down | more penitence than done trespass. WT 5.01. 4
fear, and not love, begets his penitence. R2 5.03. 56
since that my penitence comes after all, H5 4.01.304
clifford, repent in bootless penitence. 3H6 2.06. 70
PENITENT 14 FR 0.0015 REL FR 10 V 4 P
they being penitent, | the sole drift of my TMP 5.01. 28
hangman is a more penitent trade than your bawd
MM 4.02. 50 P
the desire of the penitent to be so bar'd before 4.02.176 P
and so deep sticks it in my penitent heart 5.01.475
pray, | are penitent for your default to–day. ERR 1.02. 52
i from thee departed | thy penitent reform'd. WT 1.02.239
besides, the penitent king, my master, hath sent 4.02. 6 P
me with the remembrance of that penitent (as 4.02. 22 P
didst ever hear a man so penitent? 2H6 3.02. 4
down, | call warwick patron, and be penitent? 3H6 5.01. 27
me too, | to see you are become so penitent. R3 1.02.220
in faith, he's penitent; OTH 3.03. 63
as i may, | i'll play the penitent to you; ANT 2.02. 92
me | the penitent instrument to pick that bolt, CYM 5.04. 10
PENITENTIAL 1 FR 0.0001 REL FR 1 V 0 P
me | with bitter fasts, with penitential groans, TGV 2.04.131
PENITENTLY 1 FR 0.0001 REL FR 0 V 1 P
hath he borne himself penitently in prison? MM 4.02.140 P
PENITENTS 1 FR 0.0001 REL FR 1 V 0 P
of enjoin'd penitents | there's four or five, to AWW 3.05. 94
/PENKER 1 FR 0.0001 REL FR 1 V 0 P
go thou to friar /penker; R3 3.05.104
PENKNIFE 1 FR 0.0001 REL FR 0 V 1 P
as great aim level at the edge of a penknife. 2H4 3.02.267 P
PENN'D 7 FR 0.0008 REL FR 5 V 2 P
nor to their penn'd speech render we no grace, LLL 5.02.147
their shallow shows and prologue vildly penn'd, 5.02.305
o, never will i trust to speeches penn'd, | nor 5.02.402
for besides that it is excellently well penn'd, TN 1.05.174 P
makes welsh as sweet as ditties highly penn'd, 1H4 3.01.206
and penn'd by no worse man than giraldo, TNK 4.03. 12 P
found yet moe letters sadly penn'd in blood, LC 47
PENNER 1 FR 0.0001 REL FR 1 V 0 P
at whose great feet i offer up my penner. TNK 3.05.124
PENNING 1 FR 0.0001 REL FR 0 V 1 P
mark but the penning of it. LR 4.06.139 P
PENNONS 1 FR 0.0001 REL FR 1 V 0 P
with pennons painted in the blood of harflew. H5 3.05. 49
PENN'WORTH 1 FR 0.0001 REL FR 0 V 1 P
i had a great penn'worth on't to give half my TNK 4.03. 67 P
/PENNY 1 FR 0.0001 REL FR 0 V 1 P
by my /penny of observation. LLL 3.01. 27 P
PENNY 21 FR 0.0023 REL FR 7 V 14 P
ay, and her father is make her a petter penny. WIV 1.01. 61 P
i will not lend thee a penny. 2.02. 2 P
not a penny. 2.02. 5 P
"one penny." LLL 3.01.139 P
and i had but one penny in the world, thou 5.01. 71 P
i have given him a penny and he renders me the AYL 2.05. 28 P
nay, by saint jamy, | i hold you a penny, | a SHR 3.02. 83
you beg a single penny more. AWW 5.02. 37 P
what penny hath rome borne? JN 5.02. 97
whose tongue shall ask me for one penny cost 1H4 1.03. 91
not a penny, not a penny, you are too impatient 2H4 1.02.225 P
not a penny, not a penny, you are too impatient 1.02.225 P
i' th' court is better than a penny in purse. 5.01. 31 P
cut | with edge of penny cord and vile reproach. H5 3.06. 48
pay, | nor ever had one penny bribe from france. 2H6 3.01.109
england seven halfpenny loaves sold for a penny; 4.02. 66 P
i have, | to the last penny, 'tis the king's. H8 3.02.452
/i will buy nine sparrows for a penny, and his TRO 2.01. 71 P
no, truly, sir, not a penny. ROM 2.04.183 P
than have tidings | of any penny tribute paid. CYM 2.04. 20
o, the charity of a penny cord! 5.04.167 P
PENNYWORTH 7 FR 0.0008 REL FR 2 V 5 P
we'll fit the /hid–fox with a pennyworth. ADO 2.03. 42
sir, your pennyworth is good, and your goose be LLL 3.01.102
that i have a poor pennyworth in the english. MV 1.02. 71 P
though the pennyworth on his side be the worst, WT 4.04.635 P
of ned, i give thee this pennyworth of sugar, 1H4 2.04. 23 P
the sugar thou gavest me, 'twas a pennyworth, 2.04. 59 P
and one poor pennyworth of sugar–candy to make 3.03.159 P
PENNYWORTHS 2 FR 0.0002 REL FR 2 V 0 P
may make cheap pennyworths of their pillage 2H6 1.01.222
you take your pennyworths now; ROM 4.05. 4
PENS* 4 FR 0.0004 REL FR 4 V 0 P
your pens to lances, and your tongue divine | to 2H4 4.01. 51
son, | and private in his chamber pens himself, ROM 1.01.138
one that excels the quirks of blazoning pens, OTH 2.01. 63
wears | he pens her piteous clamors in her head, LUC 681
PENSE 6 FR 0.0006 REL FR 1 V 5 P
and "honi soit qui mal y pense" write | in WIV 5.05. 69
je pense qu'ils sont appeles de fingres, oui, de H5 3.04. 10 P
je pense que je suis le bon ecolier; 3.04. 13 P
il est trop difficile, madame, comme je pense. 3.04. 27 P
je pense que vous etes le gentilhomme de bonne 4.04. 2 P
tombe entre les mains d'un chevalier, je pense, 4.04. 56 P
PENSION 3 FR 0.0003 REL FR 1 V 2 P
of this sport for a pension of thousands to be TN 2.05.181 P
and my pension shall seem the more reasonable. 2H4 1.02.246 P
pension beg | to keep base life afoot. LR 2.04.214
PENSIONERS 2 FR 0.0002 REL FR 1 V 1 P
has been earls, nay (which is more) pensioners; WIV 2.02. 77 P
the cowslips tall her pensioners be, | in their MND 2.01. 10
PENSIV'D 1 FR 0.0001 REL FR 1 V 0 P
of pensiv'd and subdu'd desires the tender, LC 219
PENSIVE 2 FR 0.0002 REL FR 2 V 0 P
that you stand pensive as half malecontent? 3H6 4.01. 10
my leisure serves me, pensive daughter, now. ROM 4.01. 39
PENSIVENESS 1 FR 0.0001 REL FR 1 V 0 P
to pencill'd pensiveness and color'd sorrow; LUC 1497
PENT 8 FR 0.0009 REL FR 7 V 1 P
let me not be pent up, sir; LLL 1.02.155 P
and, in thy closet pent up, rue my shame, | and 2H6 2.04. 24
being pent from liberty, as i am now, | if two R3 1.04.258
that my pent heart may have some scope to beat, 4.01. 34
the son of clarence have i pent up close, | his 4.03. 36
pent to linger | but with a grain a day, i would COR 3.03. 89
left | a liquid prisoner pent in walls of glass, SON 5.10
and yet thou wilt, for i, being pent in thee, 133.13
PENTAPOLIS 5 FR 0.0005 REL FR 4 V 1 P
this /is call'd pentapolis, and our king the PER 2.01. 99 P
the sum of this, | brought hither to pentapolis, 3.ch. 34
did wed | at pentapolis the fair thaisa. 5.03. 4
when we with tears parted pentapolis, | the king 5.03. 38
your daughter, | shall marry her at pentapolis. 5.03. 72
PENTECOST 3 FR 0.0003 REL FR 3 V 0 P
for at pentecost, | when all our pageants of TGV 4.04.158
you know since pentecost the sum is due, | and ERR 4.01. 1
come pentecost as quickly as it will, | some ROM 1.05. 36
PENTHESILEA 1 FR 0.0001 REL FR 0 V 1 P
good night, penthesilea. TN 2.03.177 P
PENTHOUSE 3 FR 0.0003 REL FR 2 V 1 P
stand thee close then under this penthouse, for ADO 3.03.103 P
this is the penthouse under which lorenzo MV 2.06. 1
night nor day | hang upon his penthouse lid; MAC 1.03. 20
PENTHOUSE–LIKE 1 FR 0.0001 REL FR 0 V 1 P
with your hat penthouse–like o'er the shop of LLL 3.01. 17 P
PENT–UP 2 FR 0.0002 REL FR 2 V 0 P
so looks the pent–up lion o'er the wretch | that 3H6 1.03. 12
close pent–up guilts, | rive your concealing LR 3.02. 57
PENURIOUS 1 FR 0.0001 REL FR 1 V 0 P
doth daily make revolt | in my penurious band. TIM 4.03. 93
/PENURY 1 FR 0.0001 REL FR 1 V 0 P
ache, /penury, and imprisonment | can lay on MM 3.01.129
PENURY 6 FR 0.0006 REL FR 4 V 2 P
have i spent, that i should come to such penury? AYL 1.01. 39 P
knowing no burthen of heavy tedious penury. 3.02.324 P
then crushing penury | persuades me i was better R2 5.05. 34
noting this penury, to myself i said, | "an" if ROM 5.01. 49
and most poorest shape | that ever penury, in LR 2.03. 8
lean penury within that pen doth dwell | that to SON 84. 5
/PEOPLE 2 FR 0.0002 REL FR 1 V 1 P
/the /common /people /swarm /like /summer /flies
3H6 2.06. 8
/who /is /conductor /of /his /people? LR 4.07. 87 P
PEOPLE 193 FR 0.0218 REL FR 157 V 36 P
durst not, | so dear the love my people bore me; TMP 1.02.141
all abundance, | to feed my innocent people. 2.01.165
(for, certes, these are people of the island), 3.03. 30
o brave new world | that has such people in't! 5.01.184
nobody hears — mine own people, mine own people
WIV 2.02. 51 P
hears — mine own people, mine own people. 2.02. 51 P
why, none but mine own people. 4.02. 14 P
the nature of our people, | our city's MM 1.01. 9
i love the people, | but do not like to stage me 1.01. 67
sith 'twas my fault to give the people scope, 1.03. 35
of your order, | visit both prince and people; 1.03. 45
if these be good people in a commonweal that do 2.01. 42 P
be quiet, people. wherefore throng you hither? ERR 5.01. 38
good people, enter and lay hold on him. 5.01. 91
these people saw the chain about his neck. 5.01.259
as in a sanctuary, and people sin upon purpose, ADO 2.01.259 P
both, | possess the people in messina here | how 5.01.281
the people fall a–hooting. LLL 4.02. 59
rest, | but seek the weary beds of people sick. 5.02.822
i pray you, let none of your people stir me; MND 4.01. 38 P
my people do already know my mind, | and will MV 3.04. 37
you drop manna in the way | of starved people. 5.01.295
and especially of my own people, who best know AYL 1.01.170 P
but that the people praise her for her virtues, 1.02.280
and her patience | speak to the people, and they 1.03. 79
why do people love you? 2.03. 5
and never cried, "have patience, good people!" 3.02.157 P
who of my people hold him in delay? TN 1.05.104 P
your fooling grows old, and people dislike it. 1.05.111 P
seven of my people, with an obedient start, make 2.05. 58 P
belike you slew great number of his people? 3.03. 29
let some of my people have a special care of him 3.04. 62 P
are all the people mad? 4.01. 27
to frown | upon sir toby and the lighter people; 5.01.339
and | my people did expect my hence departure WT 1.02.450
borne shall cool the hearts | of all his people, JN 3.04.150
of all his people shall revolt from him, | and 3.04.165
land, | i find the people strangely fantasied, 4.02.144
our people quarrel with obedience, | swearing 5.01. 9
observ'd his courtship to the common people, R2 1.04. 24
these same thoughts people this little world, 5.05. 9
in humors like the people of this world: 5.05. 10
thus play i in one person many people, | and 5.05. 31
taken, | a thousand of his people butchered, 1H4 1.01. 42
we love our people well, even those we love 5.01.104

good people, bring a rescue or two. 2H4 2.01. 56 P
be no more so familiarity with such poor people, 2.01.100 P
the people fear me, for they do observe 4.04.121
take pity of your town and of your people, H5 3.03. 28
and give our vineyards to a barbarous people. 3.05. 4
whiles a more frosty people | sweat drops of 3.05. 24
my people are with sickness much enfeebled, | my 3.06.145
charge, | among the people gather up a tenth. 1H6 5.05. 93
his valor, coin, and people, in the wars? 2H6 1.01. 79
what though the common people favor him, 1.01.158
have made thee fear'd and honor'd of the people; 1.01.198
abrook | the abject people gazing on thy face, 2.04. 11
and when i start, the envious people laugh, 2.04. 35
i thank you, good people — there shall be no 4.02. 72 P
it is to you, good people, that i speak, | over 4.02.129
the rascal people, thirsting after prey, | join 4.04. 51
the people liberal, valiant, active, wealthy, 4.07. 63
our people and our peers are both misled, | our 3H6 3.03. 35
the common people by numbers swarm to us. 4.02. 2
and that the people of this blessed land | may 4.06. 21
to london, | and many giddy people flock to him. 4.08. 5
the people were not used | to be spoke to but by R3 3.07. 29
good wine, good welcome, | can make good people.
H8 1.04. 7
all good people, | you that thus far have come 2.01. 55
all good people, | pray for me! 2.01.131
freely | the beauty of her person to the people. 4.01. 68
which when the people | had the full view of, 4.01. 70
then rose again and bow'd her to the people; 4.01. 85
hark, do you not hear the people cry "troilus"? TRO 1.02.225 P
know caius martius is chief enemy to the people. COR 1.01. 8 P
agrippa, one that hath always lov'd the people. 1.01. 52 P
when we were chosen tribunes for the people — 1.01.254
the dearth is great, | the people mutinous; 1.02. 11
not according to the prayer of the people, for 2.01. 4 P
will be large cicatrices to show the people, 2.01.148 P
his wounds | to th' people, beg their stinking 2.01.236
we must suggest the people in what hatred | he 2.01.245
soaring insolence | shall teach the people — 2.01.255
proud, and loves not the common people. 2.02. 6 P
many great men that have flatter'd the people, 2.02. 8 P
and displeasure of the people is as bad as that 2.02. 22 P
having been supple and courteous to the people, 2.02. 26 P
masters a' th' people, | we do request your 2.02. 51
a kinder value of the people than | he hath 2.02. 59
he loves your people, | but tie him not to be 2.02. 64
but your people, | i love them as they weigh — 2.02. 73
masters of the people, | your multiplying spawn 2.02. 77
then remains | that you do speak to the people. 2.02.135
sir, the people | must have their voices; 2.02.139
and might well | be taken from the people. 2.02.146
we recommend to you, tribunes of the people, 2.02.151
you see how he intends to use the people. 2.02.155
if he would incline to the people, there was 2.03. 38 P
you have not indeed lov'd the common people. 2.03. 93 P
flatter my sworn brother, the people, to earn a 2.03. 96 P
him joy, and make him good friend to the people! 2.03.135 P
the people do admit you and are summon'd | to 2.03.143
we stay here for the people. 2.03.150
will you dismiss the people? 2.03.154
will be there before the stream o' th' people; 2.03.261
behold, these are the tribunes of the people, 3.01. 21
the people are incens'd against him. 3.01. 32
the people cry you mock'd them; 3.01. 42
scandall'd the suppliants for the people, call'd 3.01. 44
too much of that | for which the people stir. 3.01. 53
the people are abus'd, set on. 3.01. 58
you speak a' th' people | as if you were a god, 3.01. 80
'twere well | we let the people know't. 3.01. 83
though there the people had more absolute pow'r, 3.01.116
why shall the people give | one that speaks thus 3.01.118
what should the people do with these bald 3.01.164
go call the people, in whose name myself 3.01.173
you, tribunes | to th' people! 3.01.190
hear me, people, peace! 3.01.191
what is the city but the people? 3.01.198
true, | the people are the city. 3.01.199
upon the part o' th' people, in whose power | we 3.01.209
by the tribunes' leave, and yours, good people, 3.01.280
now it lies you on to speak | to th' people; 3.02. 53
enforce him with his envy to the people, | and 3.03. 3
assemble presently the people hither; 3.03. 12
draw near, ye people. 3.03. 39
for which you are a traitor to the people. 3.03. 66
the fires i' th' lowest hell fold in the people! 3.03. 68
mark you this, people? 3.03. 74
from time to time | envied against the people, 3.03. 95
doth distribute it — in the name a' th' people, 3.03. 99
as enemy to the people and his country. 3.03.118
the people against the senators, patricians, and 4.03. 14 P
ripe aptness to take all power from the people, 4.03. 24 P
the cruelty and envy of the people, | permitted 4.05. 74
the present peace | and quietness of the people, 4.06. 3
the people | deserve such pity of him as the 4.06.109
and their people | will be as rash in the repeal 4.07. 31
and | intends t' appear before the people, 5.06. 7
we must proceed as we do find the people. 5.06. 15
the people will remain uncertain whilst | 'twixt 5.06. 16
ere he express himself or move the people | with 5.06. 54
know that the people of rome, for whom we stand
TIT 1.01. 20
titus andronicus, the people of rome, | whose 1.01.179
people of rome, and people's tribunes here, | i 1.01.217
rome, | the people will accept whom he admits. 1.01.222
lest then the people, and patricians too, | upon 1.01.445
you heavy people, circle me about, | that i may 3.01.276
'tis he the common people love so much; 4.04. 73
you sad–fac'd men, people and sons of rome, | by 5.03. 67
but, gentle people, give me aim a while, | for 5.03.149
o, the people in the street cry "romeo," | some ROM 5.03.191
together with the common /lag of people — what TIM 3.06. 81 P
but in the plainer and simpler kind of people 5.01. 25
i do fear the people | choose caesar for their JC 1.02. 79
hand thus, and then the people fell a–shouting. 1.02.223 P
if the tag–rag people did not clap him and hiss 1.02.258 P
people and senators, be not affrighted; 3.01. 82
and leave us, publius, lest that the people, 3.01. 92
know you how much the people may be mov'd | by 3.01.234
how the people take | the cruel issue of these 3.01.293
belike they had some notice of the people, | how 3.02.270
the people 'twixt philippi and this ground | do 4.03.204
do face him there, | these people at our back. 4.03.212
banners flout the sky | and fan our people cold. MAC 1.02. 50
golden opinions from all sorts of people, 1.07. 33
but strangely–visited people, | all swoll'n and 4.03.150
the tyrant's people on both sides do fight, 5.07. 25
the people muddied, | thick and unwholesome in HAM 4.05. 81
you strike my people, | and your disorder'd LR 1.04.255
go, go, my people. 1.04.272
house | should many people under two commands 2.04.241
the old man and 's people | cannot be well 2.04.288
call up all my people! OTH 1.01.141
on the brow o' th' sea | stand ranks of people, 2.01. 54
and could almost read | the thoughts of people. 3.04. 58
the streets and note | the qualities of people. ANT 1.01. 54
dear goddess, hear that prayer of the people! 1.02. 71 P
our slippery people, | whose love is never 1.02.185
the people love me, and the sea is mine; 2.01. 9
the city cast | her people out upon her; 2.02.214
the people knows it, and have now receiv'd | his 3.06. 22
reapers, people | ingross'd by swift impress. 3.07. 35
to be trusted but in the keeping of wise people; 5.02.266 P
to their approvers they are people such | that CYM 2.04. 25
which to shake off | becomes a warlike people, 3.01. 52
dost thou find the inclination of the people, PER 4.02. 97 P
are met together | before the people all, 5.01.243
and cur'st the world | o' th' plurisy of people! TNK 5.01. 66
that hath outliv'd | the love o' th' people, yea 5.04. 2
look how the world's poor people are amazed | at VEN 925
much like a press of people at a door, | throng LUC 1301
PEOPLED 5 FR 0.0005 REL FR 4 V 1 P
i had peopled else | this isle with calibans. TMP 1.02.350
i better brook than flourishing peopled towns: TGV 5.04. 3
no, the world must be peopled. ADO 2.03.242 P
peopled with wolves, thy old inhabitants! 2H4 4.05.137
teach | the act of order to a peopled kingdom. H5 1.02.189
PEOPLE'S 23 FR 0.0026 REL FR 23 V 0 P
that thinks he hath done well in people's eyes, MV 3.02.142
but is he gracious in the people's eye? 3H6 3.03.117
nor how to study for the people's welfare, | nor 4.03. 39
stand these poor people's friend, and urge the H8 4.02.157
tribunes | endue you with the people's voice. COR 2.03.139
we were establish'd | the people's magistrates. 3.01.201
the noble tribunes are the people's mouths, 3.01.270
menenius, | be you then as the people's officer. 3.01.328
if you submit you to the people's voices, 3.03. 44
i' th' people's name, | i say it shall be so. 3.03.104
the people's enemy is gone, is gone! 3.03.136
go whip him 'fore the people's eyes — his 4.06. 61
and to my fortunes and the people's favor TIT 1.01. 54
rather than rob me of the people's hearts! 1.01.207
i will restore to thee | the people's hearts, 1.01.211
people of rome, and people's tribunes here, | i 1.01.217
what time i threw the people's suffrages | on 4.03. 19
of our peace | buzz in the people's ears, there 4.04. 7
o, he sits high in all the people's hearts; JC 1.03.157
yet wild, the people's hearts brimful of fear, OTH 2.03.214
for which the people's prayers still fall upon PER 3.03. 19
leg, | outstripp'd the people's praises, won the TNK 2.02. 16
and had their epitaphs, the people's curses. 2.02.110
PEOPLES 1 FR 0.0001 REL FR 1 V 0 P
'tis hymen peoples every town, | high wedlock AYL 5.04.143
PEPIN *(also pippen)*
PEPIN 2 FR 0.0002 REL FR 2 V 0 P
king pepin, which deposed childeric, | did, as H5 1.02. 65
had been councillors | to pepin or clotharius, H8 1.03. 10
PEPIN'S 1 FR 0.0001 REL FR 1 V 0 P
king pepin's title and hugh capet's claim, H5 1.02. 87
PEPPER 1 FR 0.0001 REL FR 0 V 1 P
i warrant there's vinegar and pepper in't. TN 3.04.144 P
PEPPER–BOX 1 FR 0.0001 REL FR 0 V 1 P
into a halfpenny purse, nor into a pepper–box. WIV 3.05.147 P
PEPPERCORN 1 FR 0.0001 REL FR 0 V 1 P
of a church is made of, i am a peppercorn, a 1H4 3.03. 8 P
PEPPER'D 3 FR 0.0003 REL FR 0 V 3 P
past praying for, i have pepper'd two of them. 1H4 2.04.191 P
have led my ragamuffins where they are pepper'd; 5.03. 36 P
i am pepper'd, i warrant, for this world. ROM 3.01. 99 P
PEPPER–GINGERBREAD
1 FR 0.0001 REL FR 1 V 0 P
and such protest of pepper–gingerbread, | to 1H4 3.01.255
PER 5 FR 0.0005 REL FR 4 V 1 P
say he is a very man per se and stands alone. TRO 1.02. 15 P
calm these fits, | per stygia, per manes vehor. TIT 2.01.135
calm these fits, | per stygia, per manes vehor. 2.01.135
"piu per dolcera que per forca." PER 2.02. 27
"piu per dolcera que per forca." 2.02. 27
PERADVENTURE 15 FR 0.0017 REL FR 3 V 12 P
which peradventure prings goot discretions with WIV 1.01. 44 P
if peradventure he shall ever return to have MM 3.01.203 P
if peradventure | he speak against me on the 4.06. 5
for an answer, if peradventure this be true. ADO 1.02. 23 P
a comparison or two on me, which peradventure, 2.01.147 P
peradventure, to make it the more gracious, i MND 4.01.218 P
peradventure this is not fortune's work neither, AYL 1.02. 51 P
king | yet speaks, and peradventure may recover. JN 5.06. 31
peradventure i will with ye to the court. 2H4 3.02.295 P
peradventure i shall think you do not use me H5 3.02.126 P
some, peradventure, have on them the guilt of 4.01.161 P
good toward you peradventure than is in your 4.08. 4 P
though peradventure some of the best of 'em were
COR 2.01. 92 P
when peradventure thou wert accus'd by the ass; TIM 4.03.331 P
(though peradventure | i stand accomptant for as OTH 2.01.292
PERADVENTURES 1 FR 0.0001 REL FR 0 V 1 P
that peradventures shall tell you another tale, WIV 1.01. 77 P
PERCEIV'D 16 FR 0.0018 REL FR 9 V 7 P
are all these things perceiv'd in me? TGV 2.01. 33 P
they are all perceiv'd without ye. 2.01. 34 P
but the changes i perceiv'd in the king and WT 5.02. 10 P
perceiv'd northumberland did lean to him, | the 1H4 4.03. 67
to marry since i perceiv'd the first white hair 2H4 1.02.241 P
as i perceiv'd his grace would fain have done, H5 1.01. 85
when he perceiv'd me shrink and on my knee, 1H6 4.07. 5
when he perceiv'd the common herd was glad he JC 1.02.263 P
as i perceiv'd it (i must tell you that) HAM 2.02.133
i have perceiv'd a most faint neglect of late, LR 1.04. 68 P
whose welcome i perceiv'd had poison'd mine — 2.04. 39
duke, that my charity be not of him perceiv'd. 3.03. 16 P
till we perceiv'd both how you were wrong led ANT 3.06. 80
which was when i perceiv'd thee — that thou PER 5.01.127
but yet perceiv'd not | who made the sound, the TNK 4.01. 60
steal from his figure, and no pace perceiv'd, SON 104.10
PERCEIVE 104 FR 0.0117 REL FR 78 V 26 P
i perceive these lords | at this encounter do so TMP 5.01.153
i perceive i must be fain to bear with you. TGV 1.01.120 P
why? couldst thou perceive so much from her? 1.01.134 P
sir, i could perceive nothing at all from her; 1.01.136 P
and that thou mayst perceive how well i like it, 1.03. 35
why, do you not perceive the jest? 2.01.153 P
but did you perceive her earnest? 2.01.157 P
and, that thou mayst perceive my fear of this, 3.01. 33
i perceive you delight not in music. 4.02. 66 P
perceive how i might be knighted. WIV 2.01. 55 P
ha, do i perceive dat? 3.01.115 P
i do begin to perceive that i am made an ass. 5.05.119 P
i do perceive | these poor informal women are no MM 5.01.235
when i perceive your grace, like pow'r divine, 5.01.369
mightst thou perceive austerely in his eye ERR 4.02. 2
proudly, if i perceive the love come from her; ADO 2.03.226 P
then i well perceive you are not nigh: MND 2.02.155
now i perceive they have conjoin'd all three 3.02.193
bond, for i perceive | a weak bond holds you. 3.02.267
now i perceive that she hath made compare 3.02.290
you shall perceive them make a mutual stand, MV 5.01. 77
term, and then they perceive not how time moves.
AYL 3.02.332 P
bear to women (as i perceive by your simp'ring, ep 15 P
and now i well perceive | you have but jested SHR 2.01. 19
now i perceive thou art a reverent father. 4.05. 48
i perceive, by this demand, you are not AWW 4.03. 43 P
i perceive, sir, by /the general's looks, we 4.03.239 P
that you may well perceive i have not wrong'd 4.04. 1
but i perceive in you so excellent a touch of TN 2.01. 12 P
and stable bearing | as i perceive she does. 4.03. 20
by that | i do perceive it hath offended you. 5.01.213
though you perceive me not how i give line. WT 1.02.181
didst perceive it? 1.02.216
that he shall not perceive | but that you have 4.04.562
you perceive she stirs. 5.03.103
and well shall you perceive how willingly | i JN 4.02. 45
now i perceive the devil understands welsh, 1H4 3.01.229
then you perceive the body of our kingdom | how 2H4 3.01. 38
when you perceive his blood inclin'd to mirth; 4.04. 38
for god doth know, so shall the world perceive, 5.05. 57
i cannot perceive how, unless you give me your 5.05. 81 P
i do perceive he is not the man that he would H5 3.06. 82 P
if any noise or soldier you perceive | near to 1H6 2.01. 2
you perceive my mind? 2.02. 59
your honors shall perceive how i will work | to 3.03. 27
by the sound of drum you may perceive | their 3.03. 29
let him perceive how ill we brook his treason, 4.01. 74
if they perceive dissension in our looks, | and 4.01.139
then i perceive that will be verified | henry 5.01. 30
thou shalt well perceive | that neither in birth 5.01. 58
for i perceive i am thy prisoner. 5.03. 74
for by his death we do perceive his guilt, | and 2H6 2.03.101
by this i shall perceive the commons' mind, 3.01.374
but now you partly may perceive my mind. 3H6 3.02. 66
my mind will never grant what i perceive | your 3.02. 67
what shall we do if we perceive | lord hastings R3 3.01.191
what of his heart perceive you in his face | by 3.04. 54
when they once perceive | the least rub in your H8 2.01.128
perceive i speak sincerely, and high note's 2.03. 59
i may perceive | these cardinals trifle with me; 2.04.236
"perceive | my king is tangled in affection to 3.02. 34
lest hector or my father should perceive me, | i TRO 1.01. 36
a maiden battle then? o, i perceive you. 4.05. 87
you shall perceive | whether i blush or no; COR 1.09. 69
may they perceive 's intent! 2.02.156
did you perceive | he did solicit you in free 2.03.199
you shall perceive that a jack guardant cannot 5.02. 62 P
full well shalt thou perceive how much i dare. TIT 2.01. 44
dost thou not perceive | that rome is but a 3.01. 53
you shall perceive how you | mistake my fortunes TIM 2.02.183
but i perceive | men must learn now with pity to 3.02. 85
i perceive our masters may throw their caps at 3.04.100 P
so do you too, where you perceive them thick. JC 1.01. 71
and i perceive you feel | the dint of pity. 3.02.193
(which should perceive nothing but love from us) 4.02. 44
for i perceive | but cold demeanor in octavio's 5.02. 3
are those my tents where i perceive the fire? 5.03. 13
you, but can perceive no truth in your report. MAC 5.01. 2 P
didst perceive? HAM 3.02.287 P
i now perceive, it was not altogether your LR 3.05. 5 P
no tearing, lady, i perceive you know it. 5.03.158
do you perceive in all this noble company OTH 1.03.179
father, | i do perceive here a divided duty: 1.03.181
if more thou dost perceive, let me know more; 3.03.239
you shall by that perceive him and his means. 3.03.249
did you perceive how he laugh'd at his vice? 4.01.171 P
do you perceive the gastness of her eye? 5.01.106
to do, for i perceive | four feasts are toward. ANT 2.06. 72
when you above perceive me like a crow, | that CYM 3.03. 12
i perceive he was a wise fellow and had good PER 1.03. 3 P
well, i perceive | i shall not be hang'd now, 1.03. 25
we perceive | our losses fall so thick we must TNK pr 31
to school, may we perceive | walking in thebes! 1.02. 14
perceive you none that do arouse your pity, 1.02. 30
you may perceive a part of him. 2.01. 50 P
thou shouldst perceive my passion, if these 3.01. 31
i perceive | you would fain be at that fight. 3.06. 59
yet i might perceive, | ere i departed, a great 4.01. 5
when i might well perceive | 'twas one that sung 4.01. 57
she comes, you shall perceive her behavior. 4.03. 9 P
if you perceive | her mood inclining that way 5.02. 33
mark | you shall perceive how horrible a shape STM II.C 92
"now of this dark night i perceive the reason: VEN 727
when i perceive that men as plants increase, SON 15. 5
PERCEIVES 4 FR 0.0004 REL FR 4 V 0 P
by this lord angelo perceives he's safe; MM 5.01.494
where it perceives it is but faintly borne. R2 1.03.281
when he perceives the envious clouds are bent 3.03. 65
the king in this perceives him, how he coasts H8 3.02. 38

PERCEIVE'T 2 FR 0.0002 REL FR 2 V 0 P
i perceive't. MM 2.02.125
he's very knowing, | i do perceive't. ANT 3.03. 24
PERCEIVETH 1 FR 0.0001 REL FR 0 V 1 P
who perceiveth our natural wits too dull to AYL 1.02. 52 P
PERCEIVING 1 FR 0.0001 REL FR 1 V 0 P
his love, perceiving how he was enrag'd, | grew VEN 317
PERCEIV'ST 1 FR 0.0001 REL FR 1 V 0 P
this thou perceiv'st, which makes thy love more SON 73.13
PERCH 4 FR 0.0004 REL FR 4 V 0 P
make it | their perch and not their terror. MM 2.01. 4
wrens make prey where eagles dare not perch. R3 1.03. 70
by many a dern and painful perch, | of pericles PER 3.ch. 15
pie, | may on our bridehouse perch or sing, | or TNK 1.01. 22
PERCHANCE 51 FR 0.0057 REL FR 45 V 6 P
i'll fall flat, | perchance he will not mind me. TMP 2.02. 17
perchance you think too much of so much pains? TGV 2.01.112
strange tenor — perchance of the duke's death, MM 4.02.200 P
death, perchance entering into some monastery, 4.02.201 P
perchance, publicly, she'll be asham'd. 5.01.276 P
perchance you will not bear them patiently. ERR 1.02. 86
perchance i will be there as soon as you. 4.01. 39
you may think perchance that i think you are in ADO 3.04. 81 P
perchance light in the light. i desire her name. LLL 2.01.199
perchance till after theseus' wedding–day. MND 2.01.139
gentles, perchance you wonder at this show; 5.01.127
may now perchance both quake and tremble here, 5.01.221
if they but hear perchance a trumpet sound, | or MV 5.01. 75
perchance he's hurt i' th' battle. AWW 3.05. 87 P
perchance he is not drown'd — what think you, TN 1.02. 5
it is perchance that you yourself were saved. 1.02. 6
o my poor brother! and so perchance may he be. 1.02. 7
unless, perchance, you come to me again | to 1.05.281
frown the while, and perchance wind up my watch, 2.05. 59 P
perchance are to this business purblind? WT 1.02.228
vain dew | perchance shall dry your pities; 2.01.110
nay, it perchance will sparkle in your eyes; JN 4.01.114
when perchance it frowns | more upon humor than 4.02.213
perchance the cardinal cannot make your peace; 5.01. 74
foul wares, | and think perchance they'll sell; TRO 1.03.359
lest perchance he think | we dare not move the 2.03. 81
perchance, my lord, i show more craft than love, 3.02.153
perchance she weeps because they kill'd her TIT 3.01.114
perchance because she knows them innocent. 3.01.115
perchance she cannot meet him — that's not so. ROM 2.05. 3
perchance some single vantages you took, | when TIM 2.02.129
what you have spoke, it may be so perchance. MAC 4.03. 11
perchance even there where i did find my doubts. 4.03. 25
watch to–night, | perchance 'twill walk again. HAM 1.02.242
as i perchance hereafter shall think meet | to 1.05.171
or, perchance, | "i saw him enter such a house 2.01. 57
die, to sleep, | to sleep, perchance to dream! 3.01. 64
want true color — tears perchance for blood. 3.04.130
no more, perchance, does mine, nor his, nor hers LR 2.02. 91
perchance | she have restrain'd the riots of 2.04.142
whereof, perchance, these are but furnishings — 3.01. 29
hath mov'd me, | and shall perchance do good: 5.03.201
though i perchance am vicious in my guess | (as OTH 3.03.145
perchance, iago, i will ne'er go home. 5.02.197
fulvia perchance is angry; ANT 1.01. 20
perchance? 1.01. 25
perchance to–morrow | you'll serve another 4.02. 27
which first, perchance, she'll prove on cats and CYM 1.05. 38
perchance he spoke not, but, | like a 2.05. 15
perchance his boast of lucrece' sov'reignty LUC 36
perchance that envy of so rich a thing, 39
PERCH'D 1 FR 0.0001 REL FR 1 V 0 P
two mighty eagles fell, and there they perch'd, JC 5.01. 80
PERCIES 1 FR 0.0001 REL FR 1 V 0 P
during whose reign the percies of the north, 1H6 2.05. 67
PERCUSSION 1 FR 0.0001 REL FR 1 V 0 P
and | the thunder–like percussion of thy sounds, COR 1.04. 59
PERCY 49 FR 0.0055 REL FR 39 V 10 P
lord northumberland, his son young harry percy, R2 2.02. 53
it is my son, young harry percy, | sent from my 2.03. 21
i thank thee, gentle percy, and be sure | i 2.03. 45
we thank thee, gentle percy, for thy pains, 5.06. 11
young harry percy, and brave archibald, | that 1H4 1.01. 53
lay, | and call'd mine percy, his plantagenet! 1.01. 89
which harry percy here at holmedon took, | were, 1.03. 24
what e'er lord harry percy then had said | to 1.03. 71
thou dost belie him, percy, thou dost belie him; 1.03.113
and "gentle harry percy" and "kind cousin" — 1.03.254
i'll play percy, and that damn'd brawn shall 2.04.109 P
that same mad fellow of the north, percy, and he 2.04.336 P
again as that fiend douglas, that spirit percy, 2.04.368 P
sit, cousin percy, sit, good cousin hotspur, 3.01. 7
peace, cousin percy, you will make him mad. 3.01. 51
to–morrow, cousin percy, you and i | and my good 3.01. 82
fie, cousin percy, how you cross my father! 3.01.145
tell her that she and my aunt percy | shall 3.01.194
as slow | as hot lord percy is on fire to go. 3.01.264
and even as i was then is percy now. 3.02. 96
percy, northumberland, | the archbishop's grace 3.02.118
percy is but my factor, good my lord, | to 3.02.147
the land is burning, percy stands on high, | and 3.03.203
make haste, percy is already in the field. 4.02. 74 P
i fear the power of percy is too weak | to wage 4.04. 19
but there is mordake, vernon, lord harry percy, 4.04. 24
for if lord percy thrive not, ere the king 4.04. 36
with all the world | in praise of henry percy. 5.01. 87
percy! 5.02. 96
i have paid percy, i have made him sure. 5.03. 46 P
hal, if percy be alive, thou gets not my sword, 5.03. 50 P
well, if percy be alive, i'll pierce him. 5.03. 56 P
i saw him hold lord percy at the point, | with 5.04. 21
boys | seek percy and thyself about the field, 5.04. 32
my name is harry percy. 5.04. 61
i am the prince of wales, and think not, percy, 5.04. 63
reign | of harry percy and the prince of wales. 5.04. 67
no, percy, thou art dust, | and food for — 5.04. 85
for worms, brave percy. 5.04. 87
and by, | till then in blood by noble percy lie. 5.04.110
of this gunpowder percy though he be dead. 5.04.122 P
there is percy. 5.04.140 P
if not, let him kill the next percy himself. 5.04.141 P
why, percy i kill'd myself, and saw thee dead. 5.04.144
the noble percy slain, and all his men | upon 5.05. 19
down | the never–daunted percy to the earth, 2H4 1.01.110
times, | and be like them to percy troublesome. 2.03. 4
when your own percy, when my heart's dear harry, 2.03. 12
since | this percy was the man nearest my soul, 3.01. 61
PERCY'S 9 FR 0.0010 REL FR 8 V 1 P
think you, coz, | of this young percy's pride? 1H4 1.01. 92
yet no farther wise | than harry percy's wife; 2.03.108
i am not yet of percy's mind, the hotspur of the 2.04.101 P
spleen, | to fight against me under percy's pay, 3.02.126
i will redeem all this on percy's head, | and in 3.02.132
and that young harry percy's spur was cold. 2H4 1.01. 42
said he young harry percy's spur was cold? 1.01. 49
and i my percy's death ere thou report'st it. 1.01. 75
yet, for all this, say not that percy's dead. 1.01. 93
PERDIE *(also perdy)*
PERDIE 3 FR 0.0003 REL FR 3 V 0 P
perdie, your doors were lock'd, and you shut out ERR 4.04. 71
"my lady is unkind, perdie." TN 4.02. 75
that runs away, | the fool no knave, perdie. LR 2.04. 85
PERDITA 8 FR 0.0009 REL FR 8 V 0 P
lost for ever, perdita | i prithee call't. WT 3.03. 33
and with speed so pace | to speak of perdita, 4.01. 24
thou dear'st perdita, | with these forc'd 4.04. 40
your hand, my perdita. 4.04.154
hark, perdita! | i'll hear you by and by. 4.04.506
my prettiest perdita! 4.04.584
o perdita! 4.04.660
turn, good lady, | our perdita is found. 5.03.121
PERDITION 10 FR 0.0011 REL FR 6 V 4 P
not so much perdition as an hair | betid to any TMP 1.02. 30
and do pronounce by me | ling'ring perdition 3.03. 77
this shall end without the perdition of souls. TN 3.04.289 P
to her service, | or to their own perdition. WT 4.04.378
the perdition of th' athversary hath been very H5 3.06. 98 P
where reason can revolt | without perdition, and TRO 5.02.145
sir, his definement suffers no perdition in you, HAM 5.02.112 P
importing the mere perdition of the turkish OTH 2.02. 3 P
perdition catch my soul, | but i do love thee! 3.03. 90
to lose't or give't away were such perdition 3.04. 67
PERDONATO 1 FR 0.0001 REL FR 1 V 0 P
mi perdonato, gentle master mine; SHR 1.01. 25
/PERDU 1 FR 0.0001 REL FR 1 V 0 P
/to /watch — /poor /perdu! LR 4.07. 34
PERDU 2 FR 0.0002 REL FR 2 V 0 P
o seigneur! le jour est perdu, tout est perdu! H5 4.05. 2
o seigneur! le jour est perdu, tout est perdu! 4.05. 2
PERDURABLE 2 FR 0.0002 REL FR 1 V 1 P
o perdurable shame! H5 4.05. 7
deserving with cables of perdurable toughness. OTH 1.03.338 P
PERDURABLY 1 FR 0.0001 REL FR 1 V 0 P
for the momentary trick | be perdurably fin'd? MM 3.01.114
PERDY *(also perdie)*
PERDY 2 FR 0.0002 REL FR 2 V 0 P
in thy hateful lungs, yea, in thy maw, perdy; H5 2.01. 49
why then belike he likes it not, perdy. HAM 3.02.294
PERE 1 FR 0.0001 REL FR 0 V 1 P
dat is as it shall please de roi mon pere. H5 5.02.247 P
PEREGRINATE 1 FR 0.0001 REL FR 0 V 1 P
too odd as it were, too peregrinate, as i may LLL 5.01. 14 P
PEREMPTORILY 1 FR 0.0001 REL FR 0 V 1 P
then, peremptorily i speak it, there is virtue 1H4 2.04.429 P
PEREMPTORY 13 FR 0.0014 REL FR 12 V 1 P
to go — | excuse it not, for i am peremptory. TGV 1.03. 71
what peremptory eagle–sighted eye | dares look LLL 4.03.222
his humor is lofty, his discourse peremptory, 5.01. 10 P
i am as peremptory as she proud–minded; SHR 2.01.131
himself | in mortal fury half so peremptory, JN 2.01.454
sir, your presence is too bold and peremptory, 1H4 1.03. 17
pass our accept and peremptory answer. H5 5.02. 82
is your priesthood grown peremptory? 2H6 2.01. 23
how proud, how peremptory, and unlike himself? 3.01. 8
course, | where peremptory warwick now remains. 3H6 4.08. 59
that with his peremptory "shall," being but COR 3.01. 94
then, | for we are peremptory to dispatch | this 3.01.284
yea, mistress, are you so peremptory? PER 2.05. 73
PERFECT *(also perfit, etc.)*
/PERFECT 1 FR 0.0001 REL FR 1 V 0 P
/in /thy /dumb /action /will /i /be /as /perfect TIT 3.02. 40
PERFECT 54 FR 0.0061 REL FR 46 V 8 P
upon him, his complexion is perfect gallows. TMP 1.01. 30 P
so perfect and so peerless, are created | of 3.01. 47
of time, | and how he cannot be a perfect man, TGV 1.03. 20
for since the substance of your perfect self 4.02.123
her hair is auburn, mine is perfect yellow: 4.04.189
were man | but constant, he were perfect; 5.04.111
her cause and yours | i'll perfect him withal, MM 4.03.141
for yourself, pray heaven you then | be perfect. 5.01. 82
i knew he was not in his perfect wits. ERR 5.01. 42
but i hope i was perfect. LLL 5.02.559 P
o helen, goddess, nymph, perfect, divine! MND 3.02.137
so holy and so perfect is my love, | and in such AYL 3.05. 99
wants, | he does it under name of perfect love; SHR 4.03. 12
i will return perfect courtier, in the which my AWW 1.01.207 P
ere i can perfect mine intents, to kneel. 4.04. 4
thou art perfect then, our ship hath touch'd WT 3.03. 1
took something good | to make a perfect woman, 5.01. 15
his parts, | and finds them perfect richard. JN 1.01. 90
therefore, since law itself is perfect wrong, 3.01.189
thou hast a perfect thought. 5.06. 6
thou art perfect. 1H4 2.04. 35 P
these swelling heavens | i am too perfect in, 3.01.200
come, kate, thou art perfect in lying down. 3.01.226 P
but the true and perfect image of life indeed. 5.04.119 P
king richard might create a perfect guess | that 2H4 3.01. 88
our men more perfect in the use of arms, | our 4.01.153
to choose for wealth and not for perfect love. 1H6 5.05. 50
three glorious suns, each one a perfect sun, 3H6 2.01. 26
can neither call it perfect day nor night. 2.05. 4
so prosper i, as i swear perfect love! R3 2.01. 16
from her shall read the perfect /ways of honor, H8 5.04. 37
the grief is fine, full, perfect, that i taste, TRO 4.04. 3
we should think ourselves for ever perfect. TIM 1.02. 87 P
in his life, | which in his death were perfect. MAC 3.01.107
acquaint you with the perfect spy o' th' time, 3.01.129
i had else been perfect, | whole as the marble, 3.04. 20
though in your state of honor i am perfect. 4.02. 66
such coz'nage — is't not perfect conscience, HAM 5.02. 67
that, sons at perfect age and fathers declin'd, LR 1.02. 72 P
plainly, | i fear i am not in my perfect mind. 4.07. 62
and my perfect soul | shall manifest me rightly. OTH 1.02. 31
world | of one entire and perfect chrysolite, 5.02.145
and let it look | like perfect honor. ANT 1.03. 80
and thy most perfect goodness | her assur'd CYM 1.06.158
i am perfect | that the pannonians and 3.01. 72
false oaths prevail'd | before my perfect honor, 3.03. 67
i am perfect what: 4.02.118
apollo, perfect me in the characters! PER 3.02. 67
you are perfect. TNK 2.05. 15
now i am perfect. 3.06. 88
and once made perfect, never lost again." VEN 408
whose perfect white | show'd like an april daisy LUC 394
to say | the perfect ceremony of love's /rite, SON 23. 6
creating every bad a perfect best | as fast as 114. 7
PERFECTED 3 FR 0.0003 REL FR 3 V 0 P
being once perfected how to grant suits, | how TMP 1.02. 79
and perfected by the swift course of time. TGV 1.03. 23
admit the means | how things are perfected. H5 1.01. 69
PERFECTER 1 FR 0.0001 REL FR 0 V 1 P
understood to be a perfecter giber for the table COR 2.01. 82 P
PERFECTEST 1 FR 0.0001 REL FR 0 V 1 P
silence is the perfectest herald of joy; ADO 2.01.306 P
/PERFECTION 2 FR 0.0002 REL FR 1 V 1 P
/would /turn /their /own /perfection /to /abuse 2H4 2.03. 27
no /perfection in reversion shall have a praise TRO 3.02. 92 P
PERFECTION 27 FR 0.0030 REL FR 23 V 4 P
i would with such perfection govern, sir, | t' TMP 2.01.168
to clothe mine age with angel–like perfection, TGV 2.04. 66
her true perfection, or my false transgression, 2.04.197
of such divine perfection, as sir proteus. 2.07. 13
is by, | and feed upon the shadow of perfection. 3.01.177
and a man of such perfection | as we do in our 4.01. 55
it will grow to a most prosperous perfection. MM 3.01.260 P
to put a strange face on his own perfection. ADO 2.03. 47
are | to their right praise and true perfection! MV 5.01.108
whose dear perfection hearts that scorn'd to AWW 5.03. 18
to die, even when they to perfection grow! TN 2.04. 41
whose fullness of perfection lies in him. JN 2.01.440
praise and perfection of a good and particular H5 3.07. 47 P
vouchsafe, divine perfection of a woman, | of R3 1.02. 75
match'd not the high perfection of my loss. 4.04. 66
vowing more than the perfection of ten, and TRO 3.02. 86 P
retain that dear perfection which he owes ROM 2.02. 46
smoke and lukewarm water | is your perfection. TIM 3.06. 90
that will confess perfection so could err OTH 1.03.100
she is indeed perfection. 2.03. 28 P
panted, | that she did make defect perfection, ANT 2.02.231
whose full perfection all the world amazes, VEN 634
and pure perfection with impure defeature, 736
bee, | have no perfection of my summer left, LUC 837
but no perfection is so absolute, | that some 853
grows | holds in perfection but a little moment; SON 15. 2
and right perfection wrongfully disgrac'd, | and 66. 7
PERFECTIONS 9 FR 0.0010 REL FR 9 V 0 P
but when i look on her perfections, | there is TGV 2.04.211
of all perfections that a man may owe, LLL 2.01. 6
her sweet perfections with one self king! TN 1.01. 38
methinks i feel this youth's perfections | with 1.05.296
the chief perfections of that lovely dame | (had 1H6 5.05. 12
all her perfections challenge sovereignty: 3H6 3.02. 86
on mount of all the age | for her perfections — HAM 4.07. 29
sit, | to knit in her their best perfections. PER 1.01. 11
for he's no man on whom perfections wait | that, 1.01. 79
PERFECTLY 3 FR 0.0003 REL FR 1 V 2 P
of her custom, so perfectly he is her ape. WT 5.02. 99 P
my fair cousin, how perfectly i love her, and H5 5.02.284 P
had with troy | as perfectly is ours as yours, TRO 3.03.206
PERFECTNESS 2 FR 0.0002 REL FR 2 V 0 P
is this your perfectness? be gone, you rogue! LLL 5.02.174
the prince will in the perfectness of time 2H4 4.04. 74
/PERFECT'ST 1 FR 0.0001 REL FR 1 V 0 P
desire (of /perfect'st love being made) | shall SON 51.10
PERFECT'ST 1 FR 0.0001 REL FR 0 V 1 P
and i have learn'd by the perfect'st report, MAC 1.05. 2 P
PERFIDIOUS 5 FR 0.0005 REL FR 4 V 1 P
me — that a brother should | be so perfidious! TMP 1.02. 68
light, a most perfidious and drunken monster! 2.02.150 P
he's quoted for a most perfidious slave, | with AWW 5.03.205
men fear the french would prove perfidious, | to H8 1.02.156
o thou most perfidious | that ever gently look'd TNK 3.01. 35
PERFIDIOUSLY 1 FR 0.0001 REL FR 1 V 0 P
perfidiously | he has betray'd your business, COR 5.06. 90
PERFIT *(also perfect, etc.)*
PERFIT 5 FR 0.0005 REL FR 2 V 3 P
french–crown–color beard, your perfit yellow. MND 1.02. 96 P
take pains, be perfit; 1.02.109 P
and such fellows are perfit in the great H5 3.06. 70 P
by heaven, we come to him in perfit love, | and R3 3.07. 90
rest you said | thou hast been godlike perfit, PER 5.01.206
PERFITLY 1 FR 0.0001 REL FR 0 V 1 P
and this they con perfitly in the phrase of war, H5 3.06. 75 P
/PERFORCE 3 FR 0.0003 REL FR 3 V 0 P
/was /force /perforce /compell'd /to /banish 2H4 4.01.114
/her /material /sap, /perforce /must /wither, LR 4.02. 35
/humanity /must /perforce /prey /on /itself, 4.02. 49
PERFORCE 46 FR 0.0052 REL FR 43 V 3 P
require | my dukedom of thee, which perforce, i TMP 5.01.133
do, | perforce, against all checks, rebukes, and WIV 3.04. 80
into my house, and took perforce | my ring away. ERR 4.03. 94
and take perforce my husband from the abbess. 5.01.117
but she perforce withholds the loved boy, MND 2.01. 26
perforce i must confess | i thought you lord of 2.02.131
and thy fair virtue's force (perforce) doth move 3.01.140
of thy misprision must perforce ensue | some 3.02. 90
he hath taken away from thy father perforce, i AYL 1.02. 20 P
he that perforce robs lions of their hearts JN 1.01.268
and force perforce | keep stephen langton, 3.01.142
and royalties | pluck'd from my arms perforce — R2 2.03.121
hearts of men, they must perforce have melted, 5.02. 35
o'er | to stormy passion, must perforce decay. 2H4 1.01.165
perforce a third | must take up us. 1.03. 72
and these unseasoned hours perforce must add 3.01.105
(as, force perforce, the age will pour it in), 4.04. 46
light and weightless down | perforce must move. 4.05. 34
i must perforce compound | with /mistful eyes, H5 4.06. 33
constancy, for he perforce must do thee right, 5.02.154 P

how i am brav'd, and must perforce endure it! 1H6 2.04.115
and force perforce i'll make him yield the crown 2H6 1.01.258
unless he seek to thrust you out perforce. 3H6 1.01. 34
and made him to resign his crown perforce. 1.01.142
away with her, go bear her hence perforce. 5.05. 68
i must perforce. farewell. R3 1.01.116
but by his mother was perforce withheld. 3.01. 30
and from her jealous arms pluck him perforce. 3.01. 36
and yet must | perforce be their acquaintance. H8 1.02. 47
her times of preservation, which perforce | i, 3.02.147
power), | must make perforce an universal prey, TRO 1.03.123
you must perforce accomplish as you may. TIT 2.01.107
now perforce we will enjoy | that nice–preserved 2.03.134
so that perforce you must needs stay a time. 4.03. 42
patience perforce with willful choler meeting ROM 1.05. 89
betroth'd and would have married her perforce 5.03.238
these hot tears, which break from me perforce, LR 1.04.298
to take't again perforce! monster ingratitude! 1.05. 39 P
this weaves itself perforce into my business. 2.01. 15
thou hast no weapon, and perforce must suffer. OTH 5.02.256
when perforce he could not | but pay me terms of ANT 3.04. 6
i must perforce | have shown to thee such a 5.01. 37
honor, | which he to seek of me again, perforce, CYM 3.01. 71
rank | perforce will force it overflow the bank. VEN 72
with foul offenders thou perforce must bear, LUC 612
perforce am thine, and all that is in me. SON 133.14
PERFORM 43 FR 0.0048 REL FR 35 V 8 P
to perform an act | whereof what's past is TMP 2.01.252
for yet ere supper–time must i perform | much 3.01. 95
your last service | did worthily perform; 4.01. 36
exacting, | and perform an old contracting. MM 3.02.282
you should refuse to perform your father's will, MV 1.02. 93 P
where you are, they are coming to perform it. AYL 1.02.116 P
the wrastling, and they are ready to perform it. 1.02.146 P
of the two fled hence | be left her to perform. WT 2.01.196
by this sword | thou wilt perform my bidding. 2.03.169
mark and perform it — seest thou? 2.03.170
what they did | than to perform it first. 3.02. 57
or "what good love may i perform for you?" JN 4.01. 49
will the hateful commons perform for us, R2 2.02.138
the which if he be pleas'd i shall perform, | i 1H4 3.02.154
i will perform with a most christian care. 2H4 4.02.115
this oath i willingly take and will perform. 3H6 1.01.201
and what god will, that let your king perform; 3.01.100
sister, | i will perform it to enfranchise you. R3 1.01.110
they did perform | beyond thought's compass, H8 1.01. 35
yet reserve an ability that they never perform; TRO 3.02. 86 P
though he perform | to th' utmost of a man, and COR 1.01.267
perform a part | thou hast not done before. 3.02.109
and with thy weapon nothing dar'st perform! TIT 2.01. 59
for me, most wretched, to perform the like. 5.03. 45
i did | would i perform if i might have my will. 5.03.188
where and what time thou wilt perform the rite, ROM 2.02.146
promise me friendship, but perform none. TIM 4.03. 73 P
if thou dost perform, confound thee, for thou 4.03. 75 P
what cannot you and i perform upon | th' MAC 1.07. 69
shall, my lord, | perform what you command us. 3.01.126
a sound, | while you perform your antic round; 4.01.130
we will perform in measure, time, and place. 5.09. 39
branches — it is to act, to do, to perform; HAM 5.01. 12 P
i'll perform it | to the last article. OTH 3.03. 21
this if she perform, | she shall not sue unheard ANT 3.12. 23
i bid thee do, to perform it directly and truly, CYM 3.05.112 P
i dare be bound he's true and shall perform 4.03. 18
let us with care perform his great behest. 5.04.122
which, to preserve mine honor, i'll perform. PER 2.02. 16
fell storm | shall for itself itself perform. 3.ch. 54
or perform my bidding, or thou livest in woe; 5.01.247
to perform thy just command, | i here confess 5.03. 1
the sports | once ended, we'll perform. TNK 2.03. 59
PERFORMANCE 17 FR 0.0019 REL FR 10 V 7 P
thy will by my performance shall be serv'd. AWW 2.01.202
desire should so many years outlive performance? 2H4 2.04.261 P
and eche out our performance with your mind. H5 3.pr. 35
tell you, expects performance of your promises. 2H6 1.04. 2 P
his father by as much as a performance | does an H8 1.02.208
but his performance, as he is now, nothing. 4.02. 42
than the performance of our heaving spleens, | i TRO 2.02.196
piece it out with a piece of your performance. 3.01. 52 P
lovers swear more performance than they are able 3.02. 84 P
be so lov'd and the performance so loath'd? 5.10. 39 P
performance is ever the duller for his act, TIM 5.01. 24
performance is a kind of will or testament 5.01. 28
to think that or our cause or our performance JC 2.01.135
the desire, but it takes away the performance. MAC 2.03. 30 P
that our drift look through our bad performance, HAM 4.07.151
in his offense | should my performance perish. ANT 3.01. 27
performance shall follow. PER 4.02. 63 P
PERFORMANCES 2 FR 0.0002 REL FR 0 V 2 P
her walking and other actual performances, what, MAC 5.01. 12 P
your words and performances are no kin together. OTH 4.02.183 P
/PERFORM'D 1 FR 0.0001 REL FR 1 V 0 P
/not /daughters, /what /have /you /perform'd? LR 4.02. 40
PERFORM'D 39 FR 0.0044 REL FR 36 V 3 P
perform'd to point the tempest that i bade thee? TMP 1.02.194
ariel, thy charge | exactly is perform'd; 1.02.238
hast promis'd, | which is not yet perform'd me. 1.02.244
the figure of this harpy hast thou | perform'd, 3.03. 84
let this be duly perform'd, with a thought that MM 4.02.124 P
for now our observation is perform'd, | and MND 4.01.104
part | was aptly fitted and naturally perform'd. SHR in.1. 87
which once perform'd, let all the world say no, 3.02.141
the now–born brief, | and be perform'd to–night. AWW 2.03.180
and so | the king's will be perform'd! WT 2.01.115
old man does when the business is perform'd, and 4.04.822 P
and have perform'd | a saint–like sorrow. 5.01. 1
of something wildly | by us perform'd before. 5.01.130
in doing and now newly perform'd by that rare 5.02. 96 P
perform'd in this wide gap of time since first 5.03.154
made to heaven, first be to heaven perform'd, JN 3.01.266
and who perform'd | the bloody office of his R2 4.01. 4
swore him assistance, and perform'd it too. 1H4 4.03. 65
lord, | to see perform'd the tenure of my word. 2H4 5.05. 71
thus joan de pucelle hath perform'd her word. 1H6 1.06. 3
i have perform'd my task, and was espous'd; 2H6 1.01. 9
provide | to see her coronation be perform'd. 1.01. 74
and that's not suddenly to be perform'd, | but 2.02. 67
a charge, lord york, that i will see perform'd. 3.01.321
that's soon perform'd, because i am a subject. 3H6 3.02. 54
dead, | and i would have it suddenly perform'd. R3 4.02. 19
which perform'd, the choir, | with all the H8 4.01. 90
a little of that worthy work perform'd | by COR 2.02. 45
father, how we have perform'd | our roman rites. TIT 1.01.142
ruthful to hear, yet piteously perform'd. 5.01. 66
when caesar says, "do this," it is perform'd. JC 1.02. 10
murthers have been perform'd | too terrible for MAC 3.04. 76
our achievements, though perform'd at height, HAM 1.04. 21
but let this same be presently perform'd | even 5.02.393
i have perform'd | your pleasure and my promise. ANT 5.02.203
to see perform'd the dreaded act which thou | so 5.02.331
posthumus hath | to cymbeline perform'd. CYM 5.04. 76
this was well ask'd, 'twas so well perform'd. PER 2.03. 99
of kindness | perform'd to your sole daughter. 4.03. 39
PERFORMED 1 FR 0.0001 REL FR 1 V 0 P
thyself, | and may not be performed by thyself, JN 3.01.269
PERFORMER 1 FR 0.0001 REL FR 0 V 1 P
attributed to the true and exact performer, i AWW 3.06. 61 P
PERFORMERS 2 FR 0.0002 REL FR 2 V 0 P
sons of tamora | performers of this heinous, TIT 4.01. 80
for three performers are the file when all | the CYM 5.03. 30
PERFORMING 1 FR 0.0001 REL FR 0 V 1 P
ask some tears in the true performing of it. MND 1.02. 25 P
PERFORMS 2 FR 0.0002 REL FR 1 V 1 P
like brabbler the hound, but when he performs, TRO 5.01. 92 P
one that but performs | the bidding of the ANT 3.13. 86
PERFORM'T 2 FR 0.0002 REL FR 2 V 0 P
and as prone to mischief | as able to perform't) H8 1.01.161
perform't, or else we damn thee." ANT 1.01. 24
PERFUM'D 7 FR 0.0008 REL FR 4 V 3 P
or, as 'twere perfum'd by a fen. TMP 2.01. 49 P
the courtier's hands are perfum'd with civet. AYL 3.02. 64 P
too, | and let me have them very well perfum'd; SHR 1.02.151
than in the perfum'd chambers of the great, 2H4 3.01. 12
whose sweet smell the air shall be perfum'd, 2H6 1.01.255
marry, a perfum'd one! OTH 4.01.146 P
of thy face excelling | comes breath perfum'd, VEN 444
PERFUME 13 FR 0.0014 REL FR 10 V 3 P
count sent me — they are an excellent perfume. ADO 3.04. 63 P
and with her breath she did perfume the air. SHR 1.01.175
for she is sweeter than perfume itself | to whom 1.02.152
necklace amber, | perfume for a lady's chamber; WT 4.04.223
the lily, | to throw a perfume on the violet, JN 4.02. 12
whose smoke like incense doth perfume the sky. TIT 1.01.145
when thou wast in thy gilt and thy perfume, they TIM 4.03.302 P
the perfume and suppliance of a minute — | no HAM 1.03. 9
their perfume lost, | take these again, for to 3.01. 98
no hide, the sheep no wool, the cat no perfume. LR 3.04.105 P
a strange invisible perfume hits the sense | of ANT 2.02.212
where, phoenix–like, | they died in perfume. TNK 1.03. 71
and will perfume me finely against the wedding. 5.02. 89
PERFUMED 3 FR 0.0003 REL FR 3 V 0 P
he was perfumed like a milliner, | and 'twixt 1H4 1.03. 36
and so perfumed that | the winds were love–sick ANT 2.02.193
a dye | as the perfumed tincture of the roses, SON 54. 6
PERFUMER 1 FR 0.0001 REL FR 0 V 1 P
being entertain'd for a perfumer, as i was ADO 1.03. 58 P
PERFUMES 9 FR 0.0010 REL FR 7 V 2 P
wine, and it perfumes the blood ere one can say, 2H4 2.04. 27 P
hug their diseas'd perfumes, and have forgot TIM 4.03.207
all the perfumes of arabia will not sweeten this MAC 5.01. 51 P
hast thou not learn'd me how | to make perfumes? CYM 1.05. 13
her breathing that | perfumes the chamber thus. 2.02. 19
and | perfumes to kill the smell o' th' prison; TNK 3.01. 86
things needful — files and shirts and perfumes. 3.03. 48
three april perfumes in three hot junes burn'd, SON 104. 7
and in some perfumes is there more delight 130. 7
PERGE 2 FR 0.0002 REL FR 0 V 2 P
perge, good master holofernes, perge, so it LLL 4.02. 53 P
good master holofernes, perge, so it shall 4.02. 53 P
/PERHAPS 2 FR 0.0002 REL FR 2 V 0 P
a king — perhaps — /perhaps — R3 4.02. 98
patience, i say; your mind /perhaps may change. OTH 3.03.452
PERHAPS 45 FR 0.0050 REL FR 37 V 8 P
if happ'ly won, perhaps a hapless gain; TGV 1.01. 32
with child, perhaps? MM 1.02.156
perhaps some merchant hath invited him, | and ERR 2.01. 4
thou know'st we parted, but perhaps, my son, 5.01.322
this wedding–day | perhaps is but prolong'd, ADO 4.01.254
is but a colt, and your love perhaps a hackney. LLL 3.01. 32 P
qualm, perhaps. 5.02.279
auditor, | an actor too perhaps, if i see cause. MND 3.01. 80
you perhaps may think, | because she is 3.02.303
perhaps i will return immediately. MV 2.05. 52
perhaps you mark'd not what's the pith of all. SHR 1.01.166
a servant to use his master so, being perhaps 1.02. 32 P
she may perhaps call him half a score knaves or 1.02.110 P
and perhaps with more successful words | than 1.02.157
perhaps him and her, sir; what have you to do? 1.02.224
of my fate might perhaps distemper yours; TN 2.01. 4 P
say that some lady, as perhaps there is, | hath 2.04. 89
as it might be, perhaps, were i a woman, | i 2.04.108
for thou perhaps mayst move | that heart, which 3.01.163
for he perhaps shall need | some messenger JN 4.02.178
perhaps they had ere this, but that they stay R2 2.01.289
so perhaps did yours. H5 3.07. 50 P
i have perhaps some shallow spirit of judgment; 1H6 2.04. 16
your grace may starve, perhaps, before that time 3.02. 48
perhaps i shall be rescu'd by the french, | and 5.03.104
and so, perhaps, he doth; 3H6 2.06. 64
perhaps thou wilt object my holy oath: 5.01. 89
and perhaps | may move your hearts to pity if R3 1.03.347
a king — perhaps — /perhaps — 4.02. 98
ay, and perhaps receive much honor by him. TRO 3.03.226
perhaps thy childishness will move him more COR 5.03.157
throw my books, and fly — | causeless, perhaps. TIT 4.01. 26
perhaps, she cull'd it from among the rest. 4.01. 44
perhaps you have learn'd it without book. ROM 1.02. 59 P
which give some soil, perhaps, to my behaviors; JC 1.02. 42
i, perhaps, speak this | before a willing 1.03.112
perhaps he loves you now, | and now no soil nor HAM 1.03. 14
t' assume a pleasing shape, yea, and perhaps, 2.02.600
his purgation would perhaps plunge him into more 3.02.306 P
which may to you, perhaps, seem much unsinow'd, 4.07. 10
/gain–giving, as would perhaps trouble a woman. 5.02.216 P
perhaps he sees it not, or his good nature OTH 2.03.133
although perhaps | it may be heard at court that CYM 4.02.136
perhaps they will but please themselves upon her PER 4.01.100
when i (perhaps) compounded am with clay, | do SON 71.10
PERIAPTS 1 FR 0.0001 REL FR 1 V 0 P
now help, ye charming spells and periapts, | and 1H6 5.03. 2
PERICLES 34 FR 0.0038 REL FR 33 V 1 P
prince pericles — PER 1.01. 25
prince pericles, touch not, upon thy life, | for 1.01. 87
my lord, prince pericles is fled. 1.01.160
unless thou say prince pericles is dead. 1.01.164
till pericles be dead, | my heart can lend no 1.01.168
here must i kill king pericles, and if i do it 1.03. 2 P
i come | with message unto princely pericles, 1.03. 32
"keep it, my pericles, it hath been a shield 2.01.126
a gentleman of tyre, my name, pericles, | my 2.03. 81
names himself pericles, | a gentleman of tyre, 2.03. 86
if that you love prince pericles, forbear. 2.04. 42
painful perch, | of pericles the careful search, 3.ch. 16
if king pericles | come not home in twice six 3.ch. 30
the seas–toss'd pericles appears to speak. 3.ch. 60
i, king pericles, have lost | this queen, worth 3.02. 70
if thou livest, pericles, thou hast a heart 3.02. 76
heavenly jewels | which pericles hath lost, 3.02. 99
but since king pericles, | my wedded lord, i 3.04. 8
imagine pericles arriv'd at tyre, | welcom'd and 4.ch. 1
when noble pericles shall demand his child? 4.03. 13
will fly hence | and open this to pericles. 4.03. 23
and as for pericles, | what should he say? 4.03. 40
pericles | is now again thwarting /the wayward 4.04. 9
and pericles, in sorrow all devour'd, | with 4.04. 25
let pericles believe his daughter's dead, | and 4.04. 46
of heavy pericles think this his bark; 5.ch. 22
i am the daughter to king pericles, | if good 5.01.178
to king pericles, | if good king pericles be. 5.01.179
i am pericles of tyre; 5.01.204
and another /life | to pericles thy father. 5.01.208
you are, you are — o royal pericles! 5.03. 14
o my lord, | are you not pericles? 5.03. 32
in pericles, his queen and daughter, seen, 5.03. 87
name | of pericles to rage the city turn, | that 5.03. 97
PERIGENIA 1 FR 0.0001 REL FR 1 V 0 P
through the glimmering night | from perigenia, MND 2.01. 78
PERIGORT 1 FR 0.0001 REL FR 1 V 0 P
between lord perigort and the beauteous heir LLL 2.01. 41
PERIL *(also apperil)*
PERIL 44 FR 0.0049 REL FR 38 V 6 P
i fear not mine own shame so much as his peril. WIV 3.03.123 P
to do't, | i'll take it as a peril to my soul, MM 2.04. 65
pleas'd you to do't at peril of your soul, 2.04. 67
office, as you will answer it at your peril." 4.02.126 P
stay, on thy peril; i alone will go. MND 2.02. 87
know, | lest, to thy peril, thou aby it dear. 3.02.175
without the peril of the athenian law — 4.01.153
and then there is the peril of waters, winds, MV 1.03. 24 P
and to be in peril of my life with the edge of a 2.02.164 P
forfeiture, | to be so taken at thy peril, jew. 4.01.344
be entreated, his own peril on his forwardness. AYL 1.02.150 P
more free from peril than the envious court? 2.01. 4
charg'd, | in peril to incur your former malady, SHR in.2. 122
no part, | i knowing all my peril, thou no art. AWW 2.01.133
most provident in peril, bind himself | (courage TN 1.02. 12
lord, | on your displeasure's peril and on mine, WT 2.03. 45
on thy soul's peril and thy body's torture, 2.03.181
philip of france, on peril of a curse, | let go JN 3.01.191
know | the peril of our curses light on thee 3.01.295
as full of peril and adventerous spirit | as to 1H4 1.03.191
chok'd the respect of likely peril fear'd, | and 2H4 1.01.184
fly | towards fronting peril and oppos'd decay! 4.04. 66
fears | thou seest with peril i have answered; 4.05.196
for thousands more, that yet suspect no peril, 2H6 3.01.152
must edward fall, which peril heaven forefend! 3H6 2.01.191
death, | but that the extreme peril of the case, R3 3.05. 44
and take thy office from thee on my peril. 4.01. 25
if without peril it be possible, | sweet blunt, 5.03. 39
/seeks his praise more than he fears his peril, TRO 1.03.267
a lawful form | (in peace), to his utmost peril. COR 3.01.324
in peril of precipitation | from off the rock 3.03.102
there lies more peril in thine eye | than twenty ROM 2.02. 71
other means is left unto us | in our dear peril. TIM 5.01.228
wast thou not charg'd at peril — LR 3.07. 52
him, if he do resist | subdue him at his peril. OTH 1.02. 81
there stand i in much peril. 5.01. 21
next day's fate, | which promises royal peril. ANT 4.08. 35
upon his peril, that i have reserv'd | to myself 5.02.143
i had rather seel my lips than to my peril 5.02.146
you know the peril. CYM 1.01. 80
though peril to my modesty, not death on't, | i 3.04.152
to the face of peril | myself i'll dedicate. 5.01. 28
or jump the after–inquiry on your own peril; 5.04.182 P
peril and want contending, they have skiff'd TNK 1.03. 37
PERILOUS *(also parlous, etc.)*
PERILOUS 13 FR 0.0014 REL FR 12 V 1 P
o perilous mouths, | that bear in them one and MM 2.04.172
this gentle offer of the perilous time. JN 4.03. 13
a perilous gash, a very limb lopp'd off — | and 1H4 4.01. 43
withal | in the adventure of this perilous day. 5.02. 95
the perilous narrow ocean parts asunder. H5 pr 22
that's a perilous shot out of an elder–gun, that 4.01.197 P
o, 'tis a perilous boy, | bold, quick, ingenious R3 3.01.154
you know a sword employ'd is perilous, | and TRO 2.02. 40
a perilous knock — and it cried bitterly. ROM 1.03. 54
submitting me unto the perilous night; JC 1.03. 47
cleanse the stuff'd bosom of that perilous stuff MAC 5.03. 44
girl, | unsifted in such perilous circumstance. HAM 1.03.102
body hath a tail | more perilous than the head. CYM 4.02.145
/PERILS 1 FR 0.0001 REL FR 1 V 0 P
/you /knew /he /walk'd /o'er /perils, /on /an 2H4 1.01.170
PERILS 7 FR 0.0008 REL FR 6 V 1 P
to smile at scapes and perils overblown. SHR 5.02. 3
mule, if you prattle me into these perils. AWW 4.01. 43 P
what perils past, what crosses to ensue, | would 2H4 3.01. 55
it from their soul, though perils did | abound, H8 3.02.194
disclos'd, | and open perils surest answered. JC 4.01. 47
resolv'd | to meet all perils very constantly. 5.01. 91
content, | to put the by–past perils in her way? LC 158
/PERIOD 2 FR 0.0002 REL FR 2 V 0 P

/my /point /and /period /will /be /throughly LR 4.07. 95
/this /would /have /seem'd /a /period | /to 5.03.205
PERIOD 15 FR 0.0017 REL FR 13 V 2 P
a pretty period! TGV 2.01.116
this is the period of my ambition. WIV 3.03. 45 P
methinks there would be no period to the jest, 4.02.221 P
thy sight | my worldly business makes a period. 2H4 4.05.230
the period of thy tyranny approacheth. 1H6 4.02. 17
happy, | and prove the period of their tyranny, 2H6 3.01.149
now here a period of tumultuous broils. 3H6 5.05. 1
o, let me make the period to my curse! R3 1.03.237
here | to make the blessed period of this peace. 2.01. 44
there's his period, | to sheathe his knife in us H8 1.02.209
o bloody period! OTH 5.02.357
may be it is the period of your duty; ANT 4.02. 25
and time is at his period. 4.14.107
then had they seen the period of their ill! LUC 380
she puts the period often from his place, | and 565
PERIODS 2 FR 0.0002 REL FR 2 V 0 P
pale, | make periods in the midst of sentences, MND 5.01. 96
him up, which failing, | periods his comfort. TIM 1.01. 99
PERISH 39 FR 0.0044 REL FR 37 V 2 P
ship wrack'd, | and his great person perish. TMP 1.02.237
wrack, | which cannot perish having thee aboard, TGV 1.01.149
die, perish! MM 3.01.143
great things laboring perish in their birth. LLL 5.02.520
word | is that vile name to perish on my sword! MND 2.02.107
tranio, i burn, i pine, i perish, tranio, | if i SHR 1.01.155
'twill bring you gain, or perish on the seas. 2.01.329
who, on my life, | did perish with the infant. WT 5.01. 44
and yet we strike not, but securely perish. R2 2.01.266
and where they would be safe, they perish. H5 4.01.173 P
perish the man whose mind is backward now! 4.03. 72
so perish they | that grudge one thought against 1H6 3.01.174
perish, base prince, ignoble duke of york! 3.01.177
or else let talbot perish with this shame. 3.02. 57
and perish ye, with your audacious prate! 4.01.124
they, | might in thy palace perish /margaret. 2H6 3.02.100
many simple souls | should perish by the sword! 4.04. 11
or i with grief and extreme age shall perish R3 4.04.186
i shall perish | under device and practice. H8 1.01.203
and flourish'd, | i'll hang my head and perish. 3.01.153
not to let | thy hopeful service perish too. 3.02.419
diomed, | to reinforcement, or we perish all. TRO 5.05. 16
our good city | cleave in the midst and perish. COR 3.02. 28
all trades in rome, | and occupations perish! 4.01. 14
valiant ignorance, | and perish constant fools. 4.06.105
let her rot, and perish, and be damn'd to-night, OTH 4.01.181 P
much tall youth | that else must perish here. ANT 2.06. 8
in his offense | should my performance perish. 3.01. 27
or this, or perish. CYM 3.05.101
he scap'd the land to perish at the sea. PER 1.03. 28
of noble minds) | in us two here shall perish; TNK 2.02. 53
me, let me perish | if i think this our prison! 2.02. 61
and so perish | without your noble hand to close 2.02. 92
you perish instantly | for breaking prison, and 3.06.113
as i love most, and in that faith will perish, 3.06.163
for express will, all the world must perish. 3.06.229
shall any thing that loves me perish for me? 3.06.241
so did i tarquin, so my troy did perish. LUC 1547
harsh, featureless, and rude, barrenly perish: SON 11.10
PERISH'D 6 FR 0.0006 REL FR 4 V 2 P
poor souls, they perish'd. TMP 1.02. 9
not a hair perish'd; 1.02.217
having in that perish'd vessel the dowry of his MM 3.01.217 P
but as an intent | that perish'd by the way. 5.01.453
we maids that have our livers perish'd, crack'd TNK 4.03. 23 P
that which perish'd should | go to't unsentenc'd 5.01.156
PERISHEN 1 FR 0.0001 REL FR 1 V 0 P
all perishen of man, of pelf, | ne aught PER 2.ch. 35
PERISHEST 1 FR 0.0001 REL FR 0 V 1 P
of this female, or, clown, thou perishest; AYL 5.01. 51 P
PERISHETH 1 FR 0.0001 REL FR 1 V 0 P
about, | and talbot perisheth by your default. 1H6 4.04. 28
PERISHING 2 FR 0.0002 REL FR 2 V 0 P
and duty in his service perishing. MND 5.01. 86
his perishing root with the increasing vine. CYM 4.02. 60
PERIWIG 2 FR 0.0002 REL FR 1 V 1 P
his love, | i'll get me such a color'd periwig. TGV 4.04.191
to pay a fine for a periwig, and recover the ERR 2.02. 75 P
PERIWIG-PATED 1 FR 0.0001 REL FR 0 V 1 P
to hear a robustious periwig-pated fellow tear a HAM 3.02. 9 P
PERJUR'D 29 FR 0.0032 REL FR 28 V 1 P
thou subtile, perjur'd, false, disloyal man, TGV 4.02. 95
cannot be) | i do detest false perjur'd proteus. 5.04. 39
o perjur'd woman! ERR 5.01.212
there did this perjur'd goldsmith swear me down 5.01.227
for you'll prove perjur'd if you make me stay. LLL 2.01.113
nay, to be perjur'd, which is worst of all; 3.01.194
am i the first that have been perjur'd so? 4.03. 49
would from my forehead wipe a perjur'd note: 4.03.123
you'll not be perjur'd, 'tis a hateful thing; 4.03.155
nor god, nor i, delights in perjur'd men. 5.02.346
no, no, my lord, your grace is perjur'd much, 5.02.790
so the boy love is perjur'd every where; MND 1.01.241
arm, you heavens, against these perjur'd kings! JN 3.01.107
set armed discord 'twixt these perjur'd kings! 3.01.111
thou art perjur'd too, | and sooth'st up 3.01.120
if he be perjur'd, see you now, his reputation H5 4.07.140 P
now, perjur'd henry, wilt thou kneel for grace, 3H6 2.02. 81
o passing traitor, perjur'd and unjust! 5.01.106
lascivious edward, and thou perjur'd george, 5.05. 34
is come — false, fleeting, perjur'd clarence, R3 1.04. 55
i mean in perjur'd witness, than your master, H8 5.01.136
no faith, no honesty in men, all perjur'd, | all ROM 3.02. 86
thou perjur'd, and thou simular of virtue | that LR 3.02. 54
o perjur'd woman, thou dost stone my heart, OTH 5.02. 63
goodly and gallant shall be false and perjur'd CYM 3.04. 63
this mild image drew | for perjur'd sinon, whose LUC 1521
and till action, lust | is perjur'd, murd'rous, SON 129. 3
i am perjur'd most, | for all my vows are oaths 152. 6
more perjur'd eye, | to swear against the truth 152.13
PERJURE 2 FR 0.0002 REL FR 2 V 0 P
why, he comes in like a perjure, wearing papers. LLL 4.03. 46
but want will perjure | the ne'er-touch'd vestal ANT 3.12. 30
PERJURED 1 FR 0.0001 REL FR 1 V 0 P
one's right hand | is perjured to the bosom? TGV 5.04. 68
PERJURIES 1 FR 0.0001 REL FR 1 V 0 P
at lovers' perjuries, | they say, jove laughs. ROM 2.02. 92
PERJURY 23 FR 0.0026 REL FR 21 V 2 P
my oath | provokes me to this threefold perjury. TGV 2.06. 5
for theseus' perjury and unjust flight; 4.04.168
and all those oaths | descended into perjury, to 5.04. 49
how oft hast thou with perjury cleft the root? 5.04.103
not add to her damnation | a sin of perjury; ADO 4.01.173
why, this is flat perjury, to call a prince's 4.02. 42 P
persuade my heart to this false perjury? LLL 4.03. 60
some salve for perjury. 4.03.285
thus pour the stars down plagues for perjury. 5.02.394
now, to our perjury to add more terror, | we are 5.02.470
you are attaint with faults and perjury: 5.02.819
shall i lay perjury upon my soul? MV 4.01.229
week, | this day of shame, oppression, perjury. JN 3.01. 88
virgins with the broken seals of perjury; H5 4.01.164 P
and there's for twitting me with perjury. 3H6 5.05. 40
aloud, "what scourge for perjury | can this dark R3 1.04. 50
perjury, perjury, in the highest degree; 5.03.196
perjury, perjury, in the highest degree; 5.03.196
thy dear love sworn but hollow perjury, ROM 3.03.128
take heed of perjury, thou art on thy death-bed. OTH 5.02. 51
of theft, | guilty of perjury and subornation, LUC 919
false creeping craft and perjury should thrust 1517
persuade my heart to this false perjury? PP 3. 3
/PERK 2 FR 0.0002 REL FR 2 V 0 P
la car, | one gilbert /perk, his /chancellor — H8 1.01.219
sir gilbert /perk his chancellor, and john car, 2.01. 20
PERK'D 1 FR 0.0001 REL FR 1 V 0 P
than to be perk'd up in a glist'ring grief | and H8 2.03. 21
PERKES 1 FR 0.0001 REL FR 0 V 1 P
of woncote against clement perkes a' th' hill. 2H4 5.01. 39 P
PERMAFOY 1 FR 0.0001 REL FR 1 V 0 P
owy, cuppele gorge, permafoy, | peasant, unless H5 4.04. 37
PERMANENT 1 FR 0.0001 REL FR 1 V 0 P
forward, not permanent, sweet, not lasting, HAM 1.03. 8
PERMISSION 4 FR 0.0004 REL FR 3 V 1 P
protest | he speaks by leave and by permission; JC 3.01.239
of caesar, | and say you do't by our permission; 3.01.247
which mark antony | (by our permission) is 3.02. 59
lust of the blood and a permission of the will. OTH 1.03.334 P
PERMISSIVE 1 FR 0.0001 REL FR 1 V 0 P
when evil deeds have their permissive pass, MM 1.03. 38
PERMIT 14 FR 0.0015 REL FR 14 V 0 P
shall we thus permit | a blasting and a MM 5.01.121
if france in peace permit | our just and lineal JN 2.01. 84
to plashy too, | but time will not permit. R2 2.02.121
will you permit that i shall stand condemn'd | a 2.03.119
who doth permit the base contagious clouds | to 1H4 1.02.198
if that my fading breath permit | and death 1H6 2.05. 61
to me, wishing me to permit | john de la car, my H8 1.02.161
but by your voices, will not so permit me; COR 2.03.169
heart | will not permit mine eyes once to behold TIT 2.03.218
and permit | the curiosity of nations to deprive LR 1.02. 3
the weight we must convey with 's will permit, ANT 3.01. 36
you some permit | to second ills with ills, each CYM 5.01. 13
or if thou wilt permit the sun to climb | his LUC 775
anon permit the basest clouds to ride | with SON 33. 5
PERMITTED 3 FR 0.0003 REL FR 2 V 1 P
by this time, had the king permitted us, | one R2 1.03.194
permitted by our dastard nobles, who | have all COR 4.05. 75
may rather seem to steal in than be permitted. TNK 4.03. 75 P
PERNICIOUS 21 FR 0.0023 REL FR 19 V 2 P
be much believ'd, | and most pernicious purpose! MM 2.04.150
i went | to this pernicious caitiff deputy — 5.01. 88
thou foolish friar, and thou pernicious woman, 5.01.241
this pernicious slave, | forsooth, took on him ERR 5.01.242
have been troubled with a pernicious suitor. ADO 1.01.129 P
set eye upon the pernicious and indubitate LLL 4.01. 66 P
on the casque | of thy adverse pernicious enemy. R2 1.03. 82
with too much urging your pernicious lives, 3.01. 4
plot | to rid the realm of this pernicious blot? 4.01.325
thou art a most pernicious usurer, | froward by 1H6 3.01. 17
forsaken your pernicious faction | and join'd 4.01. 59
pernicious protector, dangerous peer, | that 2H6 2.01. 21
hell, | pernicious blood-sucker of sleeping men! 3.02.226
and, not reform'd, may prove pernicious. H8 5.02. 54
that quench the fire of your pernicious rage ROM 1.01. 84
let this pernicious hour | stand aye accursed in MAC 4.01.133
deeper, grows with more pernicious root | than 4.03. 85
o most pernicious woman! HAM 1.05.105
that will with two pernicious daughters join LR 3.02. 22
may his pernicious soul | rot half a grain a day OTH 5.02.155
o thou pernicious caitiff! 5.02.318
PERNICIOUSLY 1 FR 0.0001 REL FR 1 V 0 P
all the commons | hate him perniciously, and, o' H8 2.01. 50
PERORATION 1 FR 0.0001 REL FR 1 V 0 P
this peroration with such circumstance? 2H6 1.01.105
PERPEND 5 FR 0.0005 REL FR 3 V 2 P
perpend. WIV 2.01.115
learn of the wise, and perpend: AYL 3.02. 67 P
therefore perpend, my princess, and give ear. TN 5.01.299 P
perpend my words, o signieur dew, and mark: H5 4.04. 8
perpend. HAM 2.02.105
PERPENDICULAR 1 FR 0.0001 REL FR 0 V 1 P
runs a' horseback up a hill perpendicular — 1H4 2.04.344 P
PERPENDICULARLY 1 FR 0.0001 REL FR 1 V 0 P
altitude | which thou hast perpendicularly fell. LR 4.06. 54
PERPETUAL 25 FR 0.0028 REL FR 21 V 4 P
to the perpetual wink for aye might put | this TMP 2.01.285
that it may stand till the perpetual doom | in WIV 5.05. 58
perpetual durance? MM 3.01. 66
ay, just, perpetual durance — a restraint, 3.01. 67
winters more respect | than a perpetual honor. 3.01. 76
and a perpetual succession for it perpetually. AWW 4.03.280 P
and still winter | in storm perpetual, could not WT 3.02.213
their death appear (unto | our shame perpetual). 3.02.238
to push destruction and perpetual shame | out of JN 5.07. 77
o, thou art a perpetual triumph, an everlasting 1H4 3.03. 41 P
to be scour'd to nothing with perpetual motion. 2H4 1.02.220 P
why, 'twere perpetual shame. 3H6 5.04. 51
write of, | unto the kingdom of perpetual night. R3 1.04. 47
in the air | and be not fix'd in doom perpetual, 4.04. 12
to reap the harvest of perpetual peace | by this 5.02. 15
lives of men, as if | 'twere a perpetual spoil; COR 2.02.120
thine and albany's /issue | be this perpetual. LR 1.01. 67
me on pain of perpetual displeasure neither to 3.03. 4 P
to hold you in perpetual amity, | to make you ANT 2.02.124
no matter, would it were perpetual night, | and TNK 3.02. 3
her thrall | to living death and pain perpetual; LUC 726
may set at noon and make perpetual night. 784
act will be | my fame and thy perpetual infamy.' 1638
the spirit of love with a perpetual dullness: SON 56. 8
which from love's fire took heat perpetual, 154.10
PERPETUALLY 4 FR 0.0004 REL FR 3 V 1 P
that /shake not, though they blow perpetually. SHR 2.01.141
and a perpetual succession for it perpetually. AWW 4.03.281 P
why cloud they not their sights perpetually, PER 1.01. 74
her tears should drop on them perpetually. LUC 686
PERPETUAL-SOBER 1 FR 0.0001 REL FR 1 V 0 P
exceptless rashness, | you perpetual-sober gods! TIM 4.03.496
PERPETUITY 3 FR 0.0003 REL FR 3 V 0 P
our thanks, | and yet we should, for perpetuity, WT 1.02. 5
tyranny, | coupled in bonds of perpetuity, | two 1H6 4.07. 20
rather | groan so in perpetuity than be cur'd CYM 5.04. 6
PERPLEX 1 FR 0.0001 REL FR 1 V 0 P
what canst thou say but will perplex thee more, JN 3.01.222
PERPLEX'D 5 FR 0.0005 REL FR 5 V 0 P
i am perplex'd, and know not what to say. JN 3.01.221
would be interpreted a thing perplex'd | beyond CYM 3.04. 7
betide to cloten, but remain | perplex'd in all. 4.03. 41
why stands he so perplex'd? 5.05.108
leaving his spoil perplex'd in greater pain. LUC 733
PERPLEXED 3 FR 0.0003 REL FR 3 V 0 P
i rest perplexed with a thousand cares. 1H6 5.05. 95
but, being wrought, | perplexed in the extreme; OTH 5.02.346
who, like a king perplexed in his throne, | by VEN 1043
PERPLEXITY 3 FR 0.0003 REL FR 1 V 2 P
and all our house in a great perplexity, yet did TGV 2.03. 9 P
doctor, in perplexity and doubtful dilemma. WIV 4.05. 84 P
avaunt, perplexity! LLL 5.02.298
PERSECUTED 1 FR 0.0001 REL FR 0 V 1 P
practices he hath persecuted time with hope, and AWW 1.01. 14 P
PERSECUTIONS 1 FR 0.0001 REL FR 1 V 0 P
outface | the winds and persecutions of the sky. LR 2.03. 12
PERSECUTOR 1 FR 0.0001 REL FR 1 V 0 P
a persecutor i am sure thou art. 3H6 5.06. 31
PERSEUS' 1 FR 0.0001 REL FR 1 V 0 P
the two moist elements, | like perseus' horse. TRO 1.03. 42
PERSEUS 2 FR 0.0002 REL FR 1 V 1 P
it is a beast for perseus. H5 3.07. 21 P
as hot as perseus, spur thy phrygian steed, TRO 4.05.186
PERSEVER 9 FR 0.0010 REL FR 7 V 2 P
i'll say as they say, and persever so, | and in ERR 2.02.215
persever, counterfeit sad looks, | make mouths MND 3.02.237
and will you persever to enjoy her? AYL 5.02. 4 P
instruct my daughter how she shall persever, AWW 3.07. 37
ever | my love, as it begins, shall so persever. 4.02. 37
persever not, but hear me, mighty kings. JN 2.01.421
but to persever | in obstinate condolement is a HAM 1.02. 92
i will persever in my course of loyalty, though LR 3.05. 21 P
persever in that clear way thou goest, | and the PER 4.06.106
PERSEVERANCE 2 FR 0.0002 REL FR 2 V 0 P
perseverance, dear my lord, | keeps honor bright TRO 3.03.150
bounty, perseverance, mercy, lowliness, MAC 4.03. 93
PERSEVERS 1 FR 0.0001 REL FR 1 V 0 P
ay, and perversely she persevers so. TGV 3.02. 28
PERSIA 1 FR 0.0001 REL FR 1 V 0 P
not, but that i am bound | to persia, and want ERR 4.01. 4
PERSIAN 2 FR 0.0002 REL FR 1 V 1 P
that slew the sophy and a persian prince | that MV 2.01. 25
you will say they are persian, but let them be LR 3.06. 81 P
PERSIST 1 FR 0.0001 REL FR 1 V 0 P
thus to persist | in doing wrong extenuates not TRO 2.02.186
PERSISTED 1 FR 0.0001 REL FR 1 V 0 P
compel us to lament | our most persisted deeds. ANT 5.01. 30
PERSISTENCY 1 FR 0.0001 REL FR 0 V 1 P
thou and falstaff, for obduracy and persistency. 2H4 2.02. 47 P
PERSISTIVE 1 FR 0.0001 REL FR 1 V 0 P
jove | to find persistive constancy in men? TRO 1.03. 21
PERSISTS 1 FR 0.0001 REL FR 1 V 0 P
for he persists | as if his life lay on't. AWW 3.07. 42
/PERSON 3 FR 0.0003 REL FR 3 V 0 P
/committed /by /your /person /and /your R2 4.01.224
/we /are /denied /access /unto /his /person 2H4 4.01. 78
how novelty may move, and parts with /person, TRO 4.04. 79
PERSON 149 FR 0.0168 REL FR 117 V 32 P
by any other house, or person? TMP 1.02. 42
ship wrack'd, | and his great person perish. 1.02.237
thou mightst call him | a goodly person. 1.02.417
will guard your person while you take your rest, 2.01.197
and yet she takes exceptions at your person. TGV 5.02. 3
it is that fery person for all the orld, as just WIV 1.01. 49 P
authentic in your place and person, generally 2.02.227 P
belike having receiv'd wrong by some person, is 3.01. 53 P
how i may formally in person bear | like a true MM 1.03. 47
is a more respected person than any of us all. 2.01.166 P
finding yourself desir'd of such a person, 2.04. 91
do no stain to your own gracious person; 3.01.202 P
at thy garden-house | in her imagin'd person. 5.01.213
that friar lodowick to be a dishonest person? 5.01.261 P
have won his grace to come in person hither, ERR 5.01.116
anon i'm sure the duke himself in person | comes 5.01.119
officer | to go in person with me to my house. 5.01.234
of beatrice that puts the world into her person, ADO 2.01.209 P
are to present the prince's own person. 3.03. 75 P
which is the duke's own person? LLL 1.01.181 P
i myself reprehend his own person, for i am his 1.01.183 P
i would see his own person in flesh and blood. 1.01.185 P
thee at liberty, enfreedoming thy person: 3.01.124 P
god give you good morrow, master person. 4.02. 82 P
master person, quasi //pers-one. 4.02. 83 P
good master person, be so good as read me this 4.02. 90 P
the party /writing to the person written unto: 4.02.135 P
our person misdoubts it; 4.03.192
or to present, the person of moonshine. MND 3.01. 61 P
yea, and the best person too; 4.02. 11 P
be assur'd | my purse, my person, my extremest MV 1.01.138
well, in her person, i say i will not have you. AYL 4.01. 91 P
then, in mine own person, i die. 4.01. 93 P
there was not any man died in his own person, 4.01. 97 P
and the shape of nature | a gracious person. TN 1.05.262
from our free person she should be confin'd, WT 2.01.194
that the queen | appear in person here in court. 3.02. 10
hath made thy person for the thrower-out | of my 3.03. 29
forgiveness, | as 'twere i' th' father's person; 4.04.550

pains, much less | th' adventure of her person? 5.01.156
a graceful gentleman, against whose person | (so 5.01.171
all punish'd in the person of this child, | and JN 2.01.189
and bear possession of our person here, | lord 2.01.366
good reverend father, make my person yours, 3.01.224
no person be so bold | or daring–hardy as to R2 1.03. 42
we will ourself in person to this war, | and, 1.04. 42
words by you, | here comes his grace in person. 2.03. 82
true faith of heart | to his most royal person; 3.03. 38
thus play i in one person many people, | and 5.05. 31
fire | that staggers thus my person. 5.05.109
harry percy then had said | to such a person, 1H4 1.03. 72
thus did i keep my person fresh and new, | my 3.02. 55
the king himself in person is set forth, | or 4.01. 91
thou | that counterfeit'st the person of a king? 5.04. 28
her serve your uses both in purse and in person. 2H4 2.01.116 P
here doth he wish his person, with such powers 4.01. 10
i then did use the person of your father, | the 5.02. 73
that guards the peace and safety of your person? 5.02. 88
place, | my person, or my liege's sovereignty. 5.02.101
not to come near our person by ten mile. 5.05. 65
therefore take heed how you impawn our person, H5 1.02. 21
yesterday, | that rail'd against our person. 2.02. 41
care | and tender preservation of our person, 2.02. 59
you have conspir'd against our royal person, 2.02.167
touching our person seek we no revenge, | but we 2.02.174
his own person kneeling at our feet but a weak 3.06.132 P
a friend to alanson, and an enemy to our person. 4.07.157 P
matter, | in thine own person answer thy abuse. 2H6 2.01. 40
that he should come about your royal person, 3.01. 26
from meaning treason to our royal person | as is 3.01. 70
if those that care to keep your royal person 3.01.173
they say, in care of your most royal person, 3.02.254
so might your grace's person be in danger. 4.04. 45
such | as are of better person than myself, 3H6 3.02.167
first, to do greetings to thy royal person, 3.03. 52
myself in person will straight follow you. 4.01.133
tent | but to defend his person from night–foes? 4.03. 22
no, but the loss of his own royal person. 4.04. 5
long, | and overmuch consum'd his royal person: R3 1.01.140
denier, | i do mistake my person all this while! 1.02.252
there's many a gentle person made a jack. 1.03. 72
nay, for a need, thus far come near my person: 3.05. 85
and to give order that no manner person | have 3.05.108
the dark night can afford | be to thy person, 5.03. 81
is he in person ready? H8 1.01.117
in person | i'll hear him his confessions 1.02. 5
which neither know | my faculties nor person, 1.02. 73
not friended by his wish, to your high person; 1.02.140
you charge not in your spleen a noble person 1.02.174
'em, by his person | more worthy this place than 1.04. 78
as suits | the greatness of his person. 2.01.100
against your sacred person — in god's name 2.04. 41
present state, | or touch of her good person? 2.04.156
i left no reverend person in this court; 2.04.221
for no dislike i' th' world against the person 2.04.224
the stamp of nobleness in any person | out of 3.02. 12
to th' good of your most sacred person and | the 3.02.173
freely | the beauty of her person to the people. 4.01. 68
will triumph o'er my person, which i weigh not, 5.01.124
and shade thy person | under their blessed wings 5.01.160
in troy, whosoever, and a proper man of person. TRO 1.02.193 P
untent his person and share th' air with us? 2.03.168
of paris my lord, who is there in person; 3.01. 31 P
safe–conduct for his person of the magnanimous 3.03.276 P
is the prince there in person? 4.01. 3
how honor would become such a person, that it COR 1.03. 10 P
fear | /lesser his person than an ill report; 1.06. 70
that hath beside well in his person wrought | to 2.03.246
upon the earth he hated | your person most; 3.01. 15
theirs, so far | as thou hast power and person. 3.02. 86
even to my person, than i thought he would 4.07. 9
the country, our dear nurse, or else thy person, 5.03.110
serv'd his designments | in mine own person; 5.06. 35
favor of my country | commit myself, my person, TIT 1.01. 59
to attend the emperor's person carefully. 2.02. 8
hadst thou in person ne'er offended me, | even 2.03.161
what names the writing person hath here writ. ROM 1.02. 43 P
that calls our person from our morning rest? 5.03.189
there is no harm intended to your person, | nor JC 3.01. 90
were the grac'd person of our banquo present, MAC 3.04. 40
that macduff denies his person | at our great 3.04.127
fell cruelty, | which is too nigh your person. 4.02. 72
if it assume my noble father's person, | i'll HAM 1.02.243
will nothing stick our person to arraign | in 4.05. 93
let him go, gertrude, do not fear our person: 4.05.123
my lord, the opposition of your person in trial. 5.02.171 P
the mischief of your person it would scarcely LR 1.02.163 P
against the grace and person of my master, 2.02.131
himself in person there? 4.05. 2
bore the commission of my place and person, 5.03. 64
if none appear to prove upon thy person | thy 5.03. 91
he hath a person and a smooth dispose | to be OTH 1.03.397
to do a peculiar profit | to your own person. 3.03. 80
for her own person, | it beggar'd all ANT 2.02.197
ever won | more in their officer than person. 3.01. 17
us, why should not we | be there in person? 3.07. 6
can he be there in person? 3.07. 56
death of one person can be paid but once, | and 4.14. 27
your lady's person. is she ready? CYM 2.03. 81
more respect than my noble and natural person, 3.05.136 P
i create you | companions to our person, and 5.05. 21
was wife to your place, | abhorr'd your person. 5.05. 40
some marks | of secret on her person, that he 5.05.206
this was a goodly person, | till the disaster PER 5.01. 36
the duke himself | will be in person there. TNK 2.03. 66
your person | without hypocrisy i may not wish 3.01. 94
your person i am friends with, | and i could 3.06. 39
wife that greeteth thee, | health to thy person; LUC 1305
her well, | and set her person forth to sale. PP 18.12

PERSONAGE 3 FR 0.0003 REL FR 2 V 1 P
and with her personage, her tall personage, MND 3.02.292
and with her personage, her tall personage, 3.02.292
of what personage and years is he? TN 1.05.155 P

PERSONAGES 1 FR 0.0001 REL FR 0 V 1 P
and honorable personages than the commission of AWW 2.03.261 P

/PERSONAL 1 FR 0.0001 REL FR 0 V 1 P
/danger /that /his /personal /return /was /most LR 4.03. 6 P

PERSONAL 14 FR 0.0015 REL FR 13 V 1 P
/importunes personal conference with his grace. LLL 2.01. 32
their encounters (though not personal) hath been WT 1.01. 27 P
here, | when he was personal in the irish war. 1H4 4.03. 88
only, we want a little personal strength; 2H4 4.04. 8
in personal action, yet prodigious grown, | and JC 1.03. 77
i know no personal cause to spurn at him, | but 2.01. 11
thy personal venture in the rebels' fight, | his MAC 1.03. 91
giving to you no further personal power | to HAM 1.02. 36
in personal suit to make me his lieutenant, OTH 1.01. 9
with my personal eye | will i look to't. 2.03. 5
whipt with rods, dares me to personal combat, ANT 4.01. 3
and not your knowledge, your personal pain, but PER 3.02. 46
do make my cause | your personal hazard. TNK 5.01. 74
or to remain | in personal duty, following where LC 130

PERSONALLY 3 FR 0.0003 REL FR 3 V 0 P
nobleman, | so vulgarly and personally accus'd, MM 5.01.160
and therefore personally i lay my claim | to my R2 2.03.135
i could not personally deliver to her | what you H8 5.01. 62

PERSONATE 1 FR 0.0001 REL FR 1 V 0 P
one do i personate of lord timon's frame, | whom TIM 1.01. 69

PERSONATED 1 FR 0.0001 REL FR 0 V 1 P
he shall find himself most feelingly personated. TN 2.03.159 P

PERSONATES 1 FR 0.0001 REL FR 1 V 0 P
lofty cedar, royal cymbeline, | personates thee; CYM 5.05.454

PERSONATING 1 FR 0.0001 REL FR 1 V 0 P
it must be a personating of himself; TIM 5.01. 34

//PERS–ONE 1 FR 0.0001 REL FR 0 V 1 P
master person, quasi //pers–one. LLL 4.02. 83 P

PERSON'S 3 FR 0.0003 REL FR 3 V 0 P
and as his person's mighty, | must it be violent WT 1.02.453
tend'ring my person's safety, hath appointed R3 1.01. 44
you tender more your person's honor than | your H8 2.04.116

PERSONS' 1 FR 0.0001 REL FR 1 V 0 P
the peace of england, and our persons' safety, R3 3.05. 45

PERSONS 19 FR 0.0021 REL FR 11 V 8 P
sir, change persons with me, ere you make that MM 5.01.336 P
have indeed comprehended two aspicious persons, ADO 3.05. 46 P
travels in divers paces with divers persons. AYL 3.02.309 P
and we have our philosophical persons, to make AWW 2.03. 2 P
is there no respect of place, persons, nor time TN 2.03. 91 P
jests, | the quality of persons, and the time; 3.01. 63
one face, one voice, one habit, and two persons, 5.01.216
is aboard, tender your persons to his presence, WT 4.04.796 P
a sort of naughty persons, lewdly bent, | under 2H6 2.01.163
ye see | the very persons of our noble story H8 pr 26
or proclaim | there's difference in no persons. 1.01.139
we live not to be grip'd by meaner persons. 2.02.135
wit | to make a seemly answer to such persons. 3.01.178
find those persons out | whose names are written ROM 1.02. 35
sent to find those persons whose names are here 1.02. 42 P
he may not, as unvalued persons do, | carve for HAM 1.03. 19
at a breakfast, and but twelve persons there; ANT 2.02.180 P
despisings of our persons, and such poutings, TNK 3.06. 33
order it | fitting the persons that must use it. 4.02.151

PERSPECTIVE 3 FR 0.0003 REL FR 3 V 0 P
contempt his scornful perspective did lend me, AWW 5.03. 48
a natural perspective, that is and is not! TN 5.01.217
and perspective it is best painter's art. SON 24. 4

PERSPECTIVELY 1 FR 0.0001 REL FR 0 V 1 P
yes, my lord, you see them perspectively: H5 5.02.320 P

PERSPECTIVES 1 FR 0.0001 REL FR 1 V 0 P
like perspectives, which rightly gaz'd upon R2 2.02. 18

PERSPICUOUS 1 FR 0.0001 REL FR 1 V 0 P
true, the purpose is perspicuous as substance, TRO 1.03.324

PERSUADE 37 FR 0.0041 REL FR 32 V 5 P
only | professes to persuade) the king his son's TMP 2.01.236
cease to persuade, my loving proteus: TGV 1.01. 1
sir hugh, persuade me not; WIV 1.01. 1 P
let that persuade thee there's something 3.03. 68 P
and discourse, | and well she can persuade. MM 1.02.186
do you persuade yourself that i respect you? 4.01. 52
i | persuade this rude wretch willingly to die. 4.03. 81
nay, rather persuade him to hold his hands. ERR 4.04. 22 P
persuade my heart to this false perjury? LLL 4.03. 60
if your love do not persuade you to come, let MV 3.02.321 P
that feelingly persuade me what i am." AYL 2.01. 11
persuade him that he hath been lunatic, | and SHR in.1. 63
we will persuade him, be it possible, | to put 3.02.125
and they should sooner persuade harry of england H5 5.02.278 P
do, | let me persuade you to forbear a while. 1H6 3.01.105
courageous bedford, let us now persuade you. 3.02. 93
let me persuade you take a better course. 4.01.132
but your discretions better can persuade | than 4.01.158
my thoughts that labor to persuade my soul 2H6 3.02.137
his, | sends me a paper to persuade me patience? 3H6 3.03.176
i, but we shall soon persuade | both him and all 4.07. 33
persuade the queen to send the duke of york R3 3.01. 33
i persuade me, from her | will fall some H8 3.02. 50
cassandra, call my father to persuade. TRO 5.03. 30
if i cannot persuade thee | rather to show a COR 5.03.120
hadst thou thy wits and didst persuade revenge, HAM 4.05.169
persuade me to the murther of your lordship, LR 2.01. 44
persuade me rather to be slave and sumpter | to 2.04.216
yet, i persuade myself, to speak the truth OTH 2.03.223
that dost almost persuade | justice to break her 5.02. 16
could i persuade him to become a freeman, | he TNK 2.06. 24
her, | and fluently persuade her to a peace. 3.05. 87
but by a kiss thought to persuade him there; VEN 1114
beauty itself doth of itself persuade | the eyes LUC 29
weak–built hopes persuade him to abstaining: 130
persuade my heart to this false perjury? PP 3. 3
my glass shall not persuade me i am old, | so SON 22. 1

/PERSUADED 1 FR 0.0001 REL FR 1 V 0 P
/i /should /be /false /persuaded | /i /had LR 1.04.233

PERSUADED 21 FR 0.0023 REL FR 15 V 6 P
when he is earth'd, hath here almost persuaded TMP 2.01.234
nought but mine eye | could have persuaded me; TGV 5.04. 65
how i persuaded, how i pray'd, and kneel'd, MM 5.01. 93
but i persuaded them, if they lov'd benedick, ADO 3.01. 41
of greatest port, have all persuaded with him, MV 3.02.281
have so mightily persuaded him from a first. AYL 1.02.206 P
the best persuaded of himself, so cramm'd (as he TN 2.03.150 P
i have persuaded him the youth's a devil. 3.04.293 P
done in fight, and persuaded us to do the like. 1H4 2.04.307 P
who then persuaded you to stay at home? 2H4 2.03. 15
since we are well persuaded | we carry not a H5 2.02. 20
are you now persuaded | that talbot is but 1H6 2.03. 61
him off, | persuaded him from any further act: 2H6 5.03. 10
a wise stout captain, and soon persuaded! 3H6 4.07. 30
o, be persuaded! TRO 5.03. 19
nay, these are almost thoroughly persuaded; COR 1.01.201
she is persuaded i will marry her, out of her OTH 4.01.128 P
nor am i yet persuaded to put up in peace what 4.02.179 P
to be believ'd | of one persuaded well of. CYM 2.04.132
i am persuaded this question, sick between 's, TNK 3.01.113
have half persuaded her that i am palamon. 5.02. 3

PERSUADES 6 FR 0.0006 REL FR 5 V 1 P
and wrangle with my reason that persuades me TN 4.03. 14
pure innocence | persuades when speaking fails. WT 2.02. 40
my inward soul | persuades me it is otherwise. R2 2.02. 29
penury | persuades me i was better when a king; 5.05. 35
it persuades him, and disheartens him; MAC 2.03. 33 P
this act persuades me | that this remotion of LR 2.04.113

PERSUADING 3 FR 0.0003 REL FR 1 V 2 P
at my elbow, persuading me not to kill the duke. R3 1.04.146 P
exceeding wise, fair–spoken, and persuading; H8 4.02. 52
me from my profession, by persuading me to it. TIM 4.03.451 P

PERSUASION 20 FR 0.0022 REL FR 14 V 6 P
(for he's a spirit of persuasion, only TMP 2.01.235
where you may temper her by your persuasion | to TGV 3.02. 64
whose persuasion is | i come about my brother. MM 4.01. 46
nor persuasion can with ease attempt you, i will 4.02.190 P
i will not die to–day for any man's persuasion. 4.03. 60 P
with what persuasion did he tempt thy love? ERR 4.02. 13
i yield upon great persuasion, and partly to ADO 5.04. 95 P
a good persuasion; MND 1.01.156
wives | as prisoners to her womanly persuasion. SHR 5.02.120
that my deserts to you | can lack persuasion? TN 3.04.349
lords | by his persuasion are again fall'n off, JN 5.05. 11
thee the spirit of persuasion and him the ears 1H4 1.02.152 P
one that no persuasion can do good upon. 3.01.197
can lift your blood up with persuasion. 5.02. 78
or that persuasion could but thus convince me TRO 3.02.164
not be, by the persuasion of his new feasting. TIM 3.06. 7 P
and the persuasion of his augurers | may hold JC 2.01.200
a great deal abus'd in too bold a persuasion, CYM 1.04.114 P
if i were ripe for your persuasion, you | have TNK 1.03. 91
so cross him with their opposite persuasion, LUC 286

PERSUASIONS 2 FR 0.0002 REL FR 2 V 0 P
by fair persuasions, mix'd with sug'red words, 1H6 3.03. 18
the best persuasions to the contrary | fail not H8 5.01.147

PERSUASIVELY 1 FR 0.0001 REL FR 1 V 0 P
persuasively and cunningly. TNK 3.05. 92

PERT 2 FR 0.0002 REL FR 2 V 0 P
this pert berowne was out of count'nance quite. LLL 5.02.272
awake the pert and nimble spirit of mirth, MND 1.01. 13

PERTAIN 2 FR 0.0002 REL FR 2 V 0 P
if she pertain to life let her speak too. WT 5.03.113
and all wide–stretched honors that pertain | by H5 2.04. 82

PERTAINING 1 FR 0.0001 REL FR 1 V 0 P
points of ignorance | pertaining thereunto, as H8 1.03. 27

PERTAINS 5 FR 0.0005 REL FR 5 V 0 P
for intermission | no more pertains to me, my MV 3.02.200
a single part in aught | pertains to th' state; H8 1.02. 42
though the main part | pertains to you alone. MAC 4.03.199
more than pertains to feats of broils and battle OTH 1.03. 87
the birthright of this beauty | truly pertains TNK 3.06. 32

PERTINENT 2 FR 0.0002 REL FR 2 V 0 P
"good" should be pertinent, | but so it is, it WT 1.02.221
but yet my caution was more pertinent | than the COR 2.02. 63

PERTLY 2 FR 0.0002 REL FR 2 V 0 P
appear, and pertly! TMP 4.01. 58
for yonder walls, that pertly front your town, TRO 4.05.219

PERTURBATION 4 FR 0.0004 REL FR 1 V 3 P
disquiet, horror, and perturbation follows her. ADO 2.01.260 P
from study, and perturbation of the brain. 2H4 1.02.116 P
o polish'd perturbation! 4.05. 23
a great perturbation in nature, to receive at MAC 5.01. 9 P

PERTURBATIONS 1 FR 0.0001 REL FR 1 V 0 P
thee, | now fills thy sleep with perturbations. R3 5.03.161

PERTURB'D 2 FR 0.0002 REL FR 1 V 1 P
the perturb'd court | for my being absent? CYM 3.04.105
i think she has a perturb'd mind, which i cannot TNK 4.03. 59 P

PERTURBED 1 FR 0.0001 REL FR 1 V 0 P
rest, rest, perturbed spirit! HAM 1.05.182

PERUSAL 2 FR 0.0002 REL FR 2 V 0 P
he falls to such perusal of my face | as 'a HAM 2.01. 87
in me | worthy perusal stand against thy sight, SON 38. 6

PERUS'D 8 FR 0.0009 REL FR 7 V 1 P
o, very well, i have perus'd the note. SHR 1.02.144
our fair appointments may be well perus'd. R2 3.03. 53
have you perus'd the letters from the pope, 1H6 5.01. 1
i have perus'd her well; H8 2.03. 75
i have with exact view perus'd thee, hector, TRO 4.05.232
and for so much as i have perus'd, i find it not LR 1.02. 38 P
this picture she advisedly perus'd, | and chid LUC 1527
which she perus'd, sigh'd, tore, and gave the LC 44

PERUSE 15 FR 0.0017 REL FR 14 V 1 P
peruse this paper, madam. TGV 1.02. 34
madam, please you peruse this letter — | pardon 4.04.121
peruse the traders, gaze upon the buildings, ERR 1.02. 13
come go with me, peruse this as thou goest. MV 2.04. 38
peruse them well. AWW 2.03. 61
pray you peruse that letter. TN 5.01.330
peruse this writing here, and thou shalt know R2 5.03. 49
us, that we may peruse the men | we should have 2H4 4.02. 94
some light horsemen, and peruse their wings. 1H6 4.02. 43
morning | papers of state he sent me to peruse, H8 3.02.121
let me peruse this face. ROM 5.03. 74
will not peruse the foils, so that, with ease, HAM 4.07.136
comfortable beams i may | peruse this letter. LR 2.02.165
by his side, and i to peruse him by items. CYM 1.04. 6 P
she thinks not so; peruse this writing else. PER 2.05. 41

PERUSED 1 FR 0.0001 REL FR 1 V 0 P
have you with heed perused | what i have written COR 5.06. 61

PERUSING 1 FR 0.0001 REL FR 1 V 0 P
both they and we, perusing o'er these notes, JN 5.02. 5

PERVERSE 4 FR 0.0004 REL FR 4 V 0 P
if i were covetous, ambitious, or perverse, | as 1H6 3.01. 29
well | to bear with their perverse objections; 4.01.129
i'll frown and be perverse, and say thee nay, ROM 2.02. 96

perverse it shall be where it shows most toward, VEN 1157
PERVERSELY 1 FR 0.0001 REL FR 1 V 0 P
ay, and perversely she persevers so. TGV 3.02. 28
PERVERSENESS 1 FR 0.0001 REL FR 1 V 0 P
what, to perverseness? TN 5.01.112
PERVERT 3 FR 0.0003 REL FR 3 V 0 P
not my holy order | if i pervert your course. MM 4.03.148
let's follow him and pervert the present wrath CYM 2.04.151
and new pervert a reconciled maid!" LC 329
PERVERTED 1 FR 0.0001 REL FR 0 V 1 P
he hath perverted a young gentlewoman here in AWW 4.03. 14 P
PESANT 1 FR 0.0001 REL FR 0 V 1 P
oon pesant, by gar. WIV 5.05.206 P
PESEECH *(also beseech)*
PESEECH 1 FR 0.0001 REL FR 0 V 1 P
i peseech you heartily, scurvy, lousy knave, at H5 5.01. 22 P
PESTER 1 FR 0.0001 REL FR 1 V 0 P
he hath not fail'd to pester us with message HAM 1.02. 22
PESTER'D 1 FR 0.0001 REL FR 1 V 0 P
blame | his pester'd senses to recoil and start, MAC 5.02. 23
PESTIFEROUS 2 FR 0.0002 REL FR 1 V 1 P
army and made such pestiferous reports of men AWW 4.03.306 P
thy lewd, pestiferous, and dissentious pranks, 1H6 3.01. 15
PESTILENCE 14 FR 0.0015 REL FR 11 V 3 P
to walk alone, like one that had the pestilence; TGV 2.01. 22 P
he is sooner caught than the pestilence, and the ADO 1.01. 87 P
methought she purg'd the air of pestilence! TN 1.01. 19
suppose | devouring pestilence hangs in our air, R2 1.03.284
his clouds on our behalf | armies of pestilence, 3.03. 87
a pestilence | that does infect the land; H8 5.01. 45
a pestilence on him! TRO 4.02. 21
now the red pestilence strike all trades in rome COR 4.01. 13
where the infectious pestilence did reign, ROM 5.02. 10
a pestilence on him for a mad rogue! HAM 5.01.179 P
i'll pour this pestilence into his ear — | that OTH 2.03.356
the most infectious pestilence upon thee! ANT 2.05. 61
on our side like the token'd pestilence, | where 3.10. 9
life–poisoning pestilence, and frenzies wood, VEN 740
PESTILENT 7 FR 0.0008 REL FR 3 V 4 P
they are | most pestilent to th' hearing, and, H8 1.02. 49
what a pestilent knave is this same! ROM 4.05.144 P
to me but a foul and pestilent congregation of HAM 2.02.302 P
with pestilent speeches of his father's death, 4.05. 91
a pestilent gall to me! LR 1.04.114 P
a pestilent complete knave, and the woman hath OTH 2.01.247 P
i will contend | even with his pestilent scythe. ANT 3.13.193
PEST'RED 2 FR 0.0002 REL FR 1 V 1 P
being cold, | to be so pest'red with a popingay, 1H4 1.03. 50
the poor world is pest'red with such water–flies TRO 5.01. 33 P
PEST'RING 1 FR 0.0001 REL FR 1 V 0 P
behold | dissentious numbers pest'ring streets, COR 4.06. 7
PETAR 1 FR 0.0001 REL FR 1 V 0 P
to have the enginer | hoist with his own petar, HAM 3.04.207
PETER 33 FR 0.0037 REL FR 8 V 25 P
peter simple, you say your name is? WIV 1.04. 15 P
this letter then to friar peter give; MM 4.03.137
i would friar peter — 4.06. 9
deliver i up my apes, and away to saint peter. ADO 2.01. 47 P
first, good peter quince, say what the play MND 1.02. 8 P
now, good peter quince, call forth your actors 1.02. 14 P
here, peter quince. 1.02. 43 P
here, peter quince. 1.02. 59 P
here, peter quince. 1.02. 62 P
peter quince! 3.01. 7 P
peter quince! 4.01.202 P
i will get peter quince to write a ballet of 4.01.214 P
and peter turph, and henry pimpernell, | and SHR in.2. 94
peter, didst ever see the like? 4.01.179 P
and if his name be george, i'll call him peter; JN 1.01.186
peter bullcalf o' th' green! 2H4 3.02.172 P
and i'll pledge you all, and a fig for peter! 2H6 2.03. 67 P
here, peter, i drink to thee, and be not afraid. 2.03. 68 P
be merry, peter, and fear not thy master. 2.03. 70 P
peter, forsooth. 2.03. 81 P
peter? what more? 2.03. 82 P
and therefore, peter, have at thee with a 2.03. 89 P
hold, peter, hold! i confess, i confess treason. 2.03. 93 P
o peter, thou hast prevail'd in right! 2.03. 98 P
peter! ROM 2.04.104 P
my fan, peter. 2.04.106 P
good peter, to hide her face, for her fan's the 2.04.107 P
ay, a thousand times. peter! 2.04.214 P
peter, stay at the gate. 2.05. 20 P
now, by saint peter's church and peter too, | he 3.05.116
call peter, he will show thee where they are. 4.04. 17
logs, | and never trouble peter for the matter. 4.04. 19
that have the office opposite to saint peter, OTH 4.02. 91
PETER'S 4 FR 0.0004 REL FR 4 V 0 P
there was no link to color peter's hat, | and SHR 4.01.134
the county paris, at saint peter's church, ROM 3.05.114
now, by saint peter's church and peter too, | he 3.05.116
to go with paris to saint peter's church, | or i 3.05.154
PETIT 1 FR 0.0001 REL FR 0 V 1 P
petit monsieur, que dit–il? H5 4.04. 49 P
PETITION 24 FR 0.0027 REL FR 21 V 3 P
do relish the petition well that prays for peace MM 1.02. 15 P
you | to give this poor petition to the king, AWW 5.01. 19
here's a petition from a florentine, | who hath 5.03.130
do not receive affliction | at my petition; WT 3.02.224
but your petition | is yet unanswer'd. 5.01.228
of england than a general petition of monarchs. H5 5.02.279 P
and that is my petition, noble lord. 1H6 4.01.101
of your office, is the point | of my petition. H8 1.02. 17
my next poor petition | is, that his noble grace 4.02.138
look'd | you would have given me your petition, 5.01.118
to shame the seal of my petition to thee | in TRO 4.04.122
consort with me in loud and dear petition, 5.03. 9
and a petition granted them — a strange one, COR 1.01.210
it was a bare petition of a state | to one whom 5.01. 20
does reason our petition with more strength 5.03.176
region, | i pray you deliver him this petition. TIT 4.03. 14
thy full petition at the hand of brutus! JC 2.01. 58
from me my slow leave | by laborsome petition, HAM 1.02. 59
friends in rome | petition us at home. ANT 1.02.183
o, my petition was | set down in ice, which, by TNK 1.01.106
begging in our eyes | to make petition clear. 1.01.157
if you grant not | my sister her petition, in 1.01.201
among intermingle your petition of grace and 4.03. 89 P
ne'er ent'red wanton sound) to my petition, 5.01.148
PETITIONARY 2 FR 0.0002 REL FR 0 V 2 P
i prithee now, with most petitionary vehemence, AYL 3.02.189 P
to pardon rome and thy petitionary countrymen. COR 5.02. 76 P
PETITION'D 1 FR 0.0001 REL FR 1 V 0 P
petition'd all the gods | for my prosperity! COR 2.01.170
PETITIONER 3 FR 0.0003 REL FR 2 V 1 P
o vain petitioner! LLL 5.02.207
i am but a poor petitioner of our whole township 2H6 1.03. 23 P
these both put off, a poor petitioner, | a R3 3.07.183
PETITIONERS 3 FR 0.0003 REL FR 3 V 0 P
let us that are poor petitioners speak too. SHR 2.01. 72
petitioners for blood thou ne'er put'st back. 3H6 5.05. 80
her eyes petitioners to his eyes suing, | his VEN 356
PETITIONS 7 FR 0.0008 REL FR 5 V 2 P
all their petitions are as freely theirs | as MM 1.04. 82
should exhibit their petitions in the street? 4.04. 10 P
he would not stay at your petitions, made | his WT 1.02.215
melted by the windy breath | of soft petitions, JN 2.01.478
and my requests, and my petitions, to eat, look H5 5.01. 23 P
what, urge you your petitions in the street? JC 3.01. 11
since in our terrene state petitions are not TNK 1.03. 14
/PETO 1 FR 0.0001 REL FR 0 V 1 P
/bardolph, /peto, and gadshill shall rob those 1H4 1.02.162 P
PETO 7 FR 0.0008 REL FR 1 V 6 P
peto! 1H4 2.02. 21 P
you fought fair, so did you, peto, so did you, 2.04.299 P
no, my good lord, banish peto, banish bardolph, 2.04.474 P
in the morning, and so good morrow, peto. 2.04.549 P
go, peto, to horse, to horse, for thou and i 3.03.197
bid my lieutenant peto meet me at town's end. 4.02. 9 P
peto, how now, what news? 2H4 2.04.354 P
PETRARCH 1 FR 0.0001 REL FR 0 V 1 P
is he for the numbers that petrarch flow'd in. ROM 2.04. 39 P
PETRUCHIO 33 FR 0.0037 REL FR 28 V 5 P
and my good friend petruchio! SHR 1.02. 21 P
ben venuto, molto honorato signor mio petruchio. 1.02. 26 P
petruchio, patience, i am grumio's pledge. 1.02. 45
petruchio, shall i then come roundly to thee, 1.02. 59
petruchio, since we are stepp'd thus far in, | i 1.02. 83
i can, petruchio, help thee to a wife | with 1.02. 85
tarry, petruchio, i must go with thee, | for in 1.02.117
now shall my friend petruchio do me grace, | and 1.02.131
petruchio, stand by a while. 1.02.142
it so, | petruchio, i shall be your ben venuto. 1.02.280
petruchio is my name, antonio's son, | a man 2.01. 68
saving your tale, petruchio, i pray | let us 2.01. 71
signior petruchio, will you go with us, | or 2.01.166
but here she comes, and now, petruchio, speak. 2.01.181
now, signior petruchio, how speed you with my 2.01.281
hark, petruchio, she says she'll see thee hang'd 2.01.300
god send you joy, petruchio! 2.01.319
that katherine and petruchio should be married, 3.02. 2
upon my life, petruchio means but well, 3.02. 22
why, petruchio is coming in a new hat and an old 3.02. 43 P
who? that petruchio came? 3.02. 77 P
ay, that petruchio came. 3.02. 78 P
i warrant him, petruchio is kated. 3.02.245
ay, mistress, and petruchio is the master, 4.02. 56
signior petruchio, fie, you are to blame. 4.03. 48
petruchio, go thy ways, the field is won. 4.05. 23
well, petruchio, this has put me in heart. 4.05. 77
brother petruchio, sister katherina, | and thou, 5.02. 6
padua affords this kindness, son petruchio. 5.02. 13
o, o, petruchio, tranio hits you now. 5.02. 57
now, in good sadness, son petruchio, | i think 5.02. 63
now fair befall thee, good petruchio! 5.02.111
marry, that, i think, be young petruchio. ROM 1.05.131
PETRUCHIO'S 3 FR 0.0003 REL FR 2 V 1 P
know | one rich enough to be petruchio's wife SHR 1.02. 67
and say, "lo, there is mad petruchio's wife, 3.02. 19
is it not news to /hear of petruchio's coming? 3.02. 33 P
PETTER *(also better, bettre)*
PETTER 4 FR 0.0004 REL FR 0 V 4 P
it is petter that friends is the sword, and end WIV 1.01. 42 P
ay, and her father is make her a petter penny. 1.01. 60 P
nay, it is petter yet. 1.02. 7 P
the world, know to be no petter than a fellow, H5 5.01. 7 P
PETTICOAT 8 FR 0.0009 REL FR 3 V 5 P
ought to show itself courageous to petticoat; AYL 2.04. 7 P
of the forest, like fringe upon a petticoat. 3.02.336 P
myself, | yea, all my raiment, to my petticoat, SHR 2.01. 5
holes in the ale–wive's petticoat and so peep'd 2H4 2.02. 82 P
battle as thou hast done in a woman's petticoat? 3.02.155 P
that you might still have worn the petticoat, 3H6 5.05. 23
your old smock brings forth a new petticoat, and ANT 1.02.168 P
but this poor petticoat and two coarse smocks. TNK 5.02. 84
PETTICOATS 2 FR 0.0002 REL FR 0 V 2 P
paths, our very petticoats will catch them. AYL 1.03. 15 P
of lawn, nor for gowns, petticoats, nor caps, OTH 4.03. 74 P
PETTINESS 1 FR 0.0001 REL FR 0 V 1 P
to re–answer, his pettiness would bow under. H5 3.06.129 P
/PETTISH 1 FR 0.0001 REL FR 1 V 0 P
yea, watch | his /pettish /lines, his ebbs, /his TRO 2.03.130
PETTITOES 1 FR 0.0001 REL FR 0 V 1 P
he would not stir his pettitoes till he had both WT 4.04.607 P
PETTY 34 FR 0.0038 REL FR 32 V 2 P
and i for such like petty crimes as these. TGV 4.01. 50
petty officer | would use his heaven for thunder MM 2.02.112
do overpeer the petty traffickers | that cur'sy MV 1.01. 12
gold | to pay the petty debt twenty times over. 3.02.307
(these petty brands | that calumny doth use — o WT 2.01. 71
is as a meeting of the petty gods, | and you the 4.04. 4
commoners and inland petty spirits muster me all 2H4 4.03.110 P
and pretty traps to catch the petty thieves. H5 1.02.177
dowry, | some petty and unprofitable dukedoms. 3.pr. 31
quite, | except some petty towns of no import. 1H6 1.01. 91
tut, these are petty faults to faults unknown, 2H6 3.01. 64
fight | be counterpois'd with such a petty sum! 4.01. 22
particularities and petty sounds | to cease! 5.02. 44
arm of mine hath chastised | the petty rebel, R3 4.04.332
with other muniments and petty helps | in this COR 1.01.118
power, | but was a petty servant to the state, 2.03.178
adore, | this petty brabble will undo us all. TIT 2.01. 62
and we petty men | walk under his huge legs, and JC 1.02.136
creeps in this petty pace from day to day, | to MAC 5.05. 20
and makes each petty artere in this body | as HAM 1.04. 82
each small annexment, petty consequence, 3.03. 21
petticoats, nor caps, nor any petty exhibition; OTH 4.03. 74 P
to mend the petty present, i will piece | her ANT 1.05. 45
have donn'd his helm | for such a petty war. 2.01. 34
and bind up | the petty difference, we yet not 2.01. 49
i was of late as petty to his ends | as is the 3.12. 8
exactly valued, | not petty things admitted. 5.02.140
to air yourself, | such parting were too petty. CYM 1.01.111
no more, you petty spirits of region low, 5.04. 93
the petty wrens of tharsus will fly hence | and PER 4.03. 22
fee, | he held such petty bondage in disdain, VEN 394
the petty streams that pay a daily debt | to LUC 649
if all these petty ills shall change thy good, 656
when other petty griefs have done their spite, SON 90.10
PEU 2 FR 0.0002 REL FR 0 V 2 P
un peu, madame. H5 3.04. 3 P
par la grace de dieu, et en peu de temps. 3.04. 41 P
PEW 1 FR 0.0001 REL FR 0 V 1 P
knives under his pillow, and halters in his pew, LR 3.04. 55 P
PEW–FELLOW 1 FR 0.0001 REL FR 1 V 0 P
and makes her pew–fellow with others' moan! R3 4.04. 58
PEWTER 2 FR 0.0002 REL FR 1 V 1 P
pewter and brass, and all things that belongs SHR 2.01.355
lady, a long lease for the clinking of pewter. 1H4 2.04. 46 P
PEWTERER'S 1 FR 0.0001 REL FR 0 V 1 P
you with the motion of a pewterer's hammer, come 2H4 3.02.262 P
PHAETON 5 FR 0.0005 REL FR 5 V 0 P
why, phaeton (for thou art merops' son), | wilt TGV 3.01.153
down, down i come, like glist'ring phaeton, R2 3.03.178
now phaeton hath tumbled from his car, | and 3H6 1.04. 33
that phaeton should check thy fiery steeds, 2.06. 12
as phaeton would whip you to the west, | and ROM 3.02. 3
PHANTASIME 1 FR 0.0001 REL FR 1 V 0 P
a phantasime, a monarcho, and one that makes LLL 4.01. 99
/PHANTASIMES 1 FR 0.0001 REL FR 0 V 1 P
lisping, affecting /phantasimes, these new ROM 2.04. 29 P
PHANTASIMES 1 FR 0.0001 REL FR 0 V 1 P
i abhor such fanatical phantasimes, such LLL 5.01. 18 P
PHANTASMA 1 FR 0.0001 REL FR 1 V 0 P
is | like a phantasma or a hideous dream. JC 2.01. 65
PHARAMOND 3 FR 0.0003 REL FR 3 V 0 P
but this, which they produce from pharamond: H5 1.02. 37
and pharamond | the founder of this law and 1.02. 41
years | after defunction of king pharamond, 1.02. 58
PHARAOH'S 2 FR 0.0002 REL FR 0 V 2 P
them like pharaoh's soldiers in the reechy ADO 3.03.133 P
then pharaoh's /lean kine are to be lov'd. 1H4 2.04.473 P
PHARSALIA 1 FR 0.0001 REL FR 1 V 0 P
ay, and to wage this battle at pharsalia, ANT 3.07. 31
PHEASANT 2 FR 0.0002 REL FR 0 V 2 P
advocate's the court–word for a pheasant. WT 4.04.742 P
none, sir; i have no pheasant cock, nor hen. 4.04.744 P
PHEAZAR 1 FR 0.0001 REL FR 0 V 1 P
an emperor — caesar, keiser, and pheazar. WIV 1.03. 10 P
PHEBE 17 FR 0.0019 REL FR 16 V 1 P
o phebe, phebe, phebe! AYL 2.04. 43
o phebe, phebe, phebe! 2.04. 43
o phebe, phebe, phebe! 2.04. 43
sweet phebe, do not scorn me, do not, phebe; 3.05. 1
sweet phebe, do not scorn me, do not, phebe; 3.05. 1
o dear phebe, | if ever (as that ever may be 3.05. 27
sweet phebe — 3.05. 83
sweet phebe, pity me. 3.05. 84
phebe, with all my heart. 3.05.136
my gentle phebe did bid me give you this. 4.03. 7
i know not the contents, | but phebe did write it. 4.03. 22
of sighs and tears, | and so am i for phebe. 5.02. 85
of faith and service, | and so am i for phebe. 5.02. 90
and so am i for phebe. 5.02. 99
as you love phebe, meet. 5.02.119 P
you say that you'll have phebe, if she will? 5.04. 16
keep you your word, phebe, that you'll marry me, 5.04. 21
PHEBE'S 1 FR 0.0001 REL FR 1 V 0 P
yet heard too much of phebe's cruelty. AYL 4.03. 38
PHEBES 1 FR 0.0001 REL FR 1 V 0 P
she phebes me. AYL 4.03. 39
PHEESE *(also feaz'd, pheeze)*
PHEESE 1 FR 0.0001 REL FR 1 V 0 P
and he be proud with me, i'll pheese his pride. TRO 2.03.205
PHEEZE 1 FR 0.0001 REL FR 0 V 1 P
i'll pheeze you, in faith. SHR in.1. 1 P
PHIBBUS' *(also phoebus')*
PHIBBUS' 1 FR 0.0001 REL FR 1 V 0 P
and phibbus' car | shall shine from far, | and MND 1.02. 35
PHILADELPHOS 1 FR 0.0001 REL FR 1 V 0 P
philadelphos, king | of paphlagonia; ANT 3.06. 70
/PHILARIO'S 1 FR 0.0001 REL FR 1 V 0 P
my residence in rome at one /philario's, | who CYM 1.01. 97
PHILARMONUS 1 FR 0.0001 REL FR 1 V 0 P
philarmonus! CYM 5.05.433
PHILEMON 1 FR 0.0001 REL FR 1 V 0 P
philemon, ho! PER 3.02. 1
PHILEMON'S 1 FR 0.0001 REL FR 0 V 1 P
my visor is philemon's roof, within the house is ADO 2.01. 96 P
/PHILIP 1 FR 0.0001 REL FR 1 V 0 P
king /philip, determine what we shall do JN 2.01.149
PHILIP 17 FR 0.0019 REL FR 14 V 3 P
a year and a quarter old come philip and jacob. MM 3.02.202 P
joseph, nicholas, philip, walter, sugarsop, and SHR 4.01. 90 P
where is nathaniel, gregory, philip? 4.01.122
philip of france, in right and true behalf | of JN 1.01. 7
philip, my liege, so is my name begun, | philip, 1.01.158
philip, good old sir robert's wive's eldest son. 1.01.159
kneel thou down philip, but rise more great, 1.01.161
good leave, good philip. 1.01.231
philip? 1.01.231
philip of france, if thou be pleas'd withal, 2.01.531
philip of france, on peril of a curse, | let go 3.01.191
king philip, listen to the cardinal. 3.01.198
philip, what say'st thou to the cardinal? 3.01.202
do so, king philip, hang no more in doubt. 3.01.219
head lie there, | while philip breathes. 3.02. 4
philip, make up. 3.02. 5
his father was called philip of macedon, as i H5 4.07. 20 P
PHILIPPAN 1 FR 0.0001 REL FR 1 V 0 P
on him, whilst | i wore his sword philippan. ANT 2.05. 23
PHILIPPE 2 FR 0.0002 REL FR 2 V 0 P
the crown, had issue, philippe, a daughter, 2H6 2.02. 35

son | of edmund mortimer, who married philippe, 2.02. 49
PHILIPPI 14 FR 0.0015 REL FR 14 V 0 P
bending their expedition toward philippi. JC 4.03.170
you think | of marching to philippi presently? 4.03.197
the people 'twixt philippi and this ground | do 4.03.204
him off | if at philippi we do face him there, 4.03.211
along ourselves, and meet them at philippi. 4.03.225
to tell thee thou shalt see me at philippi. 4.03.283
ay, at philippi. 4.03.285
why, i will see thee at philippi then. 4.03.286
they mean to warn us at philippi here, 5.01. 5
hands, | who to philippi here consorted us. 5.01. 82
and, this last night, here in philippi fields. 5.05. 19
who at philippi the good brutus ghosted, | there ANT 2.06. 13
wept | when at philippi he found brutus slain. 3.02. 56
he at philippi kept | his sword e'en like a 3.11. 35
PHILIP'S 1 FR 0.0001 REL FR 1 V 0 P
nor yet saint philip's daughters, were like thee 1H6 1.02.143
PHILLIDA 1 FR 0.0001 REL FR 1 V 0 P
of corn and versing love | to amorous phillida. MND 2.01. 68
PHILOMEL 5 FR 0.0005 REL FR 5 V 0 P
his philomel must lose her tongue to–day, | thy TIT 2.03. 43
that could have better sew'd than philomel. 2.04. 43
this is the tragic tale of philomel, | and 4.01. 47
for worse than philomel you us'd my daughter, 5.02.194
lays, | as philomel in summer's front doth sing, SON 102. 7
PHILOMELA 3 FR 0.0003 REL FR 3 V 0 P
fair philomela, why, she but lost her tongue, TIT 2.04. 38
ravish'd and wrong'd as philomela was, | forc'd 4.01. 52
while philomela sits and sings, i sit and mark, PP 14.17
PHILOMELE 5 FR 0.0005 REL FR 5 V 0 P
philomele, with melody | sing in our sweet MND 2.02. 13
philomele, with melody, etc. 2.02. 24
leaf's turn'd down | where philomele gave up. CYM 2.02. 46
lamenting philomele had ended | the well–tun'd LUC 1079
"come, philomele, that sing'st of ravishment, 1128
PHILOMELS 1 FR 0.0001 REL FR 1 V 0 P
two emulous philomels beat the ear o' th' night TNK 5.03.124
PHILOSOPHER 10 FR 0.0011 REL FR 4 V 6 P
for there was never yet philosopher | that could ADO 5.01. 35
prove the weeping philosopher when he grows old, MV 1.02. 49 P
such a one is a natural philosopher. AYL 3.02. 32 P
the heathen philosopher, when he had a desire to 5.01. 33 P
how now, philosopher? TIM 1.01.215 P
like a lawyer, sometime like a philosopher, with 2.02.110 P
sometime the philosopher. 2.02.122 P
first let me talk with this philosopher. LR 3.04.154
noble philosopher, your company. 3.04.172
i will keep still with my philosopher. 3.04.176
PHILOSOPHER'S 1 FR 0.0001 REL FR 0 V 1 P
i'll make him a philosopher's two stones to me. 2H4 3.02.329 P
PHILOSOPHERS 1 FR 0.0001 REL FR 0 V 1 P
for divers philosophers hold that the lips is WIV 1.01.229 P
PHILOSOPHICAL 1 FR 0.0001 REL FR 0 V 1 P
are past, and we have our philosophical persons, AWW 2.03. 2 P
PHILOSOPHY 14 FR 0.0015 REL FR 12 V 2 P
and die, | with all these living in philosophy. LLL 1.01. 32
hast any philosophy in thee, shepherd? AYL 3.02. 21 P
virtue and that part of philosophy | will i SHR 1.01. 18
to suck the sweets of sweet philosophy. 1.01. 28
then give me leave to read philosophy, | and 3.01. 13
preach some philosophy to make me mad, | and JN 3.04. 51
thought | unfit to hear moral philosophy. TRO 2.02.167
adversity's sweet milk, philosophy, | to comfort ROM 3.03. 55
hang up philosophy! 3.03. 57
unless philosophy can make a juliet, | displant 3.03. 58
of your philosophy you make no use, | if you JC 4.03.145
even by the rule of that philosophy | by which i 5.01.100
than are dreamt of in your philosophy. HAM 1.05.167
than natural, if philosophy could find it out. 2.02.367 P
PHILOSTRATE 2 FR 0.0002 REL FR 2 V 0 P
go, philostrate, | stir up the athenian youth to MND 1.01. 11
call philostrate. 5.01. 38
PHILOTEN 3 FR 0.0003 REL FR 3 V 0 P
this maid | hight philoten, and it is said | for PER 4.ch. 18
still | this philoten contends in skill | with 4.ch. 30
this so darks | in philoten all graceful marks, 4.ch. 36
PHILOTUS 1 FR 0.0001 REL FR 1 V 0 P
and, sir, philotus too! TIM 3.04. 6
PHLEGMATIC 1 FR 0.0001 REL FR 0 V 1 P
i beseech you be not so phlegmatic. WIV 1.04. 75 P
/PHOEBE 1 FR 0.0001 REL FR 1 V 0 P
that like the stately /phoebe 'mongst her nymphs TIT 1.01.316
PHOEBE 2 FR 0.0002 REL FR 2 V 0 P
a title to phoebe, to luna, to the moon. LLL 4.02. 38
when phoebe doth behold | her silver visage in MND 1.01.209
PHOEBUS' *(also phibbus')*
PHOEBUS' 10 FR 0.0011 REL FR 10 V 0 P
i shall think or phoebus' steeds are founder'd TMP 4.01. 30
where phoebus' fire scarce thaws the icicles, MV 2.01. 5
th' wanton spoil | of phoebus' burning kisses — COR 2.01.218
fiery–footed steeds, | towards phoebus' lodging; ROM 3.02. 2
full thirty times hath phoebus' cart gone round HAM 3.02.155
radiant fire | on /flick'ring phoebus' front — LR 2.02.108
that am with phoebus' amorous pinches black, ANT 1.05. 28
it, were it carbuncled | like holy phoebus' car. 4.08. 29
so, had it been a carbuncle | of phoebus' wheel; CYM 5.05.190
the sweet melodious sound | that phoebus' lute, PP 8.10
PHOEBUS 12 FR 0.0013 REL FR 11 V 1 P
day, | before the wheels of phoebus, round about ADO 5.03. 26
they can behold | bright phoebus in his strength WT 4.04.124
moon and the seven stars, and not by phoebus, he 1H4 1.02. 15 P
silken streamers the young phoebus /fanning. H5 3.pr. 6
sweats in the eye of phoebus, and all night 4.01.273
o phoebus! 3H6 2.06. 11
when she coldly eyes | the youthful phoebus. TRO 1.03.230
and golden phoebus never be beheld | of eyes ANT 5.02.317
heaven's gate sings, | and phoebus gins arise, CYM 2.03. 21
from the blest eye | of holy phoebus, but TNK 1.01. 46
phoebus, when | he broke his whipstock and 1.02. 85
to phoebus thou | add'st flames, hotter than his 5.01. 90
PHOENICIA 1 FR 0.0001 REL FR 1 V 0 P
he assign'd | syria, cilicia, and phoenicia. ANT 3.06. 16
PHOENICIANS 1 FR 0.0001 REL FR 1 V 0 P
egyptians | and the phoenicians go a–ducking; ANT 3.07. 64
PHOENIX' 3 FR 0.0003 REL FR 3 V 0 P
arabia | there is one tree, the phoenix' throne, TMP 3.03. 23
saw his right | flaming in the phoenix' sight; PHT 35
death is now the phoenix' nest, | and the 56
PHOENIX 15 FR 0.0017 REL FR 15 V 0 P
one phoenix | at this hour reigning there. TMP 3.03. 23
from the mart | home to your house, the phoenix, ERR 1.02. 75
your worship's wife, my mistress at the phoenix; 1.02. 88
my house was at the phoenix? 2.02. 11
could not love me | were man as rare as phoenix. AYL 4.03. 17
a phoenix, captain, and an enemy, | a guide, a AWW 1.01.168
that took the phoenix and her fraught from candy TN 5.01. 61
a phoenix that shall make all france afeard. 1H6 4.07. 93
my ashes, as the phoenix, may bring forth | a 3H6 1.04. 35
the bird of wonder dies, the maiden phoenix, H8 5.04. 40
a naked gull, | which flashes now a phoenix. TIM 2.01. 32
phoenix and the turtle fled | in a mutual flame PHT 23
made this threne | to the phoenix and the dove, 50
and burn the long–liv'd phoenix in her blood; SON 19. 4
his phoenix down began but to appear | like LC 93
PHOENIX–LIKE 1 FR 0.0001 REL FR 1 V 0 P
the like innocent cradle, where, phoenix–like, TNK 1.03. 70
PHOTINUS 1 FR 0.0001 REL FR 1 V 0 P
in rome | that photinus an eunuch and your maids ANT 3.07. 14
PHRASE 28 FR 0.0031 REL FR 13 V 15 P
what phrase is this? WIV 1.01.149 P
a fico for the phrase! 1.03. 30 P
'tis not a soldier–like phrase — but i say, 2.01. 13 P
pardon it, | the phrase is to the matter. MM 5.01. 90
gallant militarist — that was his own phrase — AWW 4.03.142 P
write from it, if you can, in hand or phrase, TN 5.01.332
it comes of accommodo, very good, a good phrase. 2H4 3.02. 72 P
phrase call you it? 3.02. 73 P
by this day, i know not the phrase, but i will 3.02. 74 P
and this they con perfitly in the phrase of war, H5 3.06. 75 P
save the phrase is a little variations. 4.07. 17 P
when these suns | (for so they phrase 'em) by H8 1.01. 34
sodden business! there's a stew'd phrase indeed! TRO 3.01. 41 P
for i am proverb'd with a grandsire phrase, ROM 1.04. 37
or (not to crack the wind of the poor phrase, HAM 1.03.108
and with swinish phrase | soil our addition, and 1.04. 19
or by pronouncing of some doubtful phrase, | as 1.05.175
according to the phrase or the addition | of man 2.01. 47
beautified ophelia" — that's an ill phrase, a 2.02.111 P
ophelia" — that's an ill phrase, a vile phrase, 2.02.111 P
a vile phrase, "beautified" is a vile phrase. 2.02.112 P
nor no matter in the phrase that might indict 2.02.443 P
whose phrase of sorrow | conjures the wand'ring 5.01.255
the phrase would be more germane to the matter, 5.02.158 P
in better phrase and matter than thou didst. LR 4.06. 8
little bless'd with the soft phrase of peace; OTH 1.03. 82
rail thou in fulvia's phrase, and taunt my ANT 1.02.107
and precious phrase by all the muses fil'd. SON 85. 4
PHRASELESS 1 FR 0.0001 REL FR 1 V 0 P
"'o, then advance of yours that phraseless hand, LC 225
PHRASES 5 FR 0.0005 REL FR 2 V 3 P
cat–a–mountain looks, your red–lattice phrases, WIV 2.02. 27 P
that hath a mint of phrases in his brain; LLL 1.01.165
taffata phrases, silken terms precise, 5.02.406
her very phrases! TN 2.05. 91 P
good phrases are surely, and ever were, very 2H4 3.02. 70 P
/PHRYGIA 1 FR 0.0001 REL FR 1 V 0 P
/athenian /bay | /put /forth /toward /phrygia, TRO pr 7
PHRYGIA 2 FR 0.0002 REL FR 0 V 2 P
i would play lord pandarus of phrygia, sir, to TN 3.01. 51 P
becomes him better than any man in all phrygia. TRO 1.02.123 P
PHRYGIAN 5 FR 0.0005 REL FR 5 V 0 P
when thou shalt lack, | base phrygian turk! WIV 1.03. 88
as hot as perseus, spur thy phrygian steed, TRO 4.05.186
the fall of every phrygian stone will cost | a 4.05.223
thus proudly /pight upon our phrygian plains, 5.10. 24
that piteous looks to phrygian shepherds lent; LUC 1502
/PHRYNIA 1 FR 0.0001 REL FR 1 V 0 P
/phrynia and /timandra had gold of him. TIM 5.01. 5
PHTHISIC *(see tisick)*
PHYSIC 39 FR 0.0044 REL FR 33 V 6 P
caius, that calls himself doctor of physic? WIV 3.01. 4 P
for 'tis a physic | that's bitter to sweet end. MM 4.06. 7
the most wholesome physic of thy health–giving LLL 1.01.233 P
my physic says ay. 2.01.188
i will physic your rankness, and yet give no AYL 1.01. 86 P
not cast away my physic but on those that are 3.02.358 P
sweet practicer, thy physic i will try, | that AWW 2.01.185
ease, will day by day | come here for physic. 3.01. 19
i know my physic will work with him. TN 2.03.173 P
physic for't there's none. WT 1.02.200
that, for the health and physic of our right, JN 5.02. 21
in poison there is physic, and these news, 2H4 1.01.137
be sick with joy, he'll recover without physic. 4.05. 15 P
and i will see what physic the tavern affords. 1H6 3.01.147
'tis time to give 'em physic, their diseases H8 1.03. 36
and he brings his physic | after his patient's 3.02. 40
that gentle physic given in time had cur'd me; 4.02.122
this contagious sickness, | farewell all physic! 5.02. 62
man, | for that will physic the great myrmidon, TRO 1.03.377
to jump a body with a dangerous physic | that's COR 3.01.154
the violent fit a' th' time craves it as physic 3.02. 33
hark ye, lords, you see i have given her physic, TIT 4.02.162
remedies | within thy help and holy physic lies. ROM 2.03. 52
soft, take thy physic first — thou too — and TIM 3.06.100
throw physic to the dogs, i'll none of it. MAC 5.03. 47
this physic but prolongs thy sickly days. HAM 3.03. 96
take physic, pomp, | expose thyself to feel what LR 3.04. 33
for it doth physic love — of his content, | all CYM 3.02. 34
learning, physic, must | all follow this and 4.02.268
sharp physic is the last. PER 1.01. 72
'tis known, i ever | have studied physic; 3.02. 32
diseases have been sold dearer than physic — 4.06. 98
thy sacred physic shall receive such pay | as 5.01. 74
we should give her physic till we find that — TNK 5.02. 29
give physic to the sick, ease to the pained? LUC 901
in spite of physic, painting, pain, and cost. PP 13.12
nor can thy shame give physic to my grief, SON 34. 9
desire is death, which physic did except. 147. 8
as compound love to physic your cold breast. LC 259
PHYSICAL 2 FR 0.0002 REL FR 2 V 0 P
the blood i drop is rather physical | than COR 1.05. 18
and is it physical | to walk unbraced and suck JC 2.01.261
/PHYSICIAN 1 FR 0.0001 REL FR 1 V 0 P
/i /take /not /on /me /here /as /a /physician, 2H4 4.01. 60
PHYSICIAN 22 FR 0.0024 REL FR 13 V 9 P
sees you but is a physician to comment on your TGV 2.01. 40 P
you have show'd yourself a wise physician, and WIV 2.03. 54 P
doctor caius, the renown'd french physician. 3.01. 61 P
cast away your child on a fool, and a physician? 3.04. 97 P
since the physician at your father's died? AWW 1.02. 70
myself your loyal servant, your physician, WT 2.03. 54
this we prescribe, though no physician; R2 1.01.154
and i care not if i do become your physician. 2H4 1.02.125 P
the immortal part needs a physician, but that 2.02.104 P
'tis butts, | the king's physician. H8 5.02. 11
he will be the physician that should be the TRO 2.03.213 P
which time i will make a lip at the physician. COR 2.01.116 P
trust not the physician, | his antidotes are TIM 4.03.431
more needs she the divine than the physician. MAC 5.01. 74
kill thy physician, and /the fee bestow | upon LR 1.01.163
to die, when death is our physician. OTH 1.03.310 P
for her physician tells me | she hath pursu'd ANT 5.02.354
than be cur'd | by th' sure physician, death, CYM 5.04. 7
who worse than a physician | would this report 5.05. 27
thou speak'st like a physician, helicanus, PER 1.02. 67
"the patient dies while the physician sleeps, LUC 904
my reason, the physician to my love, | angry SON 147. 5
PHYSICIAN'S 3 FR 0.0003 REL FR 3 V 0 P
charge — | a poor physician's daughter my wife! AWW 2.03.115
a poor physician's daughter — thou dislik'st 2.03.123
in the physician's mind | to help him to his R2 1.04. 59
PHYSICIANS 8 FR 0.0009 REL FR 7 V 1 P
for your physicians have expressly charg'd, | in SHR in.2. 121
he hath abandon'd his physicians, madam, under AWW 1.01. 13 P
he and his physicians | are of a mind; 1.03.237
of those physicians that first wounded thee. R2 2.01. 99
thence | he was much fear'd by his physicians. 1H4 4.01. 24
and his physicians fear him mightily. R3 1.01.137
his friends, like physicians, | thrive, give him TIM 3.03. 11
no news but health from their physicians know; SON 140. 8
PHYSICK'D 1 FR 0.0001 REL FR 1 V 0 P
not physick'd by respect might turn our blood STM III 13
PHYSICS 2 FR 0.0002 REL FR 1 V 1 P
indeed, physics the subject, makes old hearts WT 1.01. 38 P
the labor we delight in physics pain. MAC 2.03. 50
PHYSIOGNOMY *(also fisnomy)*
PHYSIOGNOMY 1 FR 0.0001 REL FR 1 V 0 P
o, what art | of physiognomy might one behold! LUC 1395
/PIA 1 FR 0.0001 REL FR 0 V 1 P
nourish'd in the womb of /pia /mater, and LLL 4.02. 69 P
PIA 2 FR 0.0002 REL FR 0 V 2 P
one of thy kin has a most weak pia mater. TN 1.05.115 P
and his pia mater is not worth the ninth part of TRO 2.01. 71 P
PIBBLE* *(also bibble, pebble, etc.)*
PIBBLE* 2 FR 0.0002 REL FR 0 V 2 P
he is a stone, a very pibble stone, and has no TGV 2.03. 10 P
no tiddle taddle nor pibble babble in pompey's H5 4.01. 71 P
PIBBLED 1 FR 0.0001 REL FR 1 V 0 P
as the waves make towards the pibbled shore, SON 60. 1
PIBBLES 2 FR 0.0002 REL FR 1 V 1 P
deliver'd such a show'r of pibbles, that i was H8 5.03. 57 P
then let the pibbles on the hungry beach COR 5.03. 58
PIBLE 1 FR 0.0001 REL FR 0 V 1 P
he has pray his pible well, dat he is no come. WIV 2.03. 7 P
PICARDY 2 FR 0.0002 REL FR 2 V 0 P
artois, | wallon, and picardy are friends to us, 1H6 2.01. 10
lord, and picardy | hath slain their governors, 2H6 4.01. 88
PICK* *(also peck*, pitch*)*
PICK* 19 FR 0.0021 REL FR 7 V 12 P
pistol, did you pick master slender's purse? WIV 1.01.151 P
pick out mine eyes with a ballad–maker's pen and ADO 1.01.252 P
whole world again | cannot pick out five such, LLL 5.02.545
ask questions and sing, pick his teeth and sing. AWW 3.02. 7 P
we may pick a thousand sallets ere we light on 4.05. 14 P
and pick strong matter of revolt and wrath | out JN 3.04.167
could the world pick thee out three such enemies 1H4 2.04.367 P
and now you pick a quarrel to beguile me of it. 3.03. 67 P
house is turn'd bawdy–house, they pick pockets. 3.03. 99 P
quit you with gud leve, as i may pick occasion; H5 3.02.103 P
i can eat grass, or pick a sallet another while, 2H6 4.10. 8 P
slaves, as high | as i could pick my lance. COR 1.01.200
he could not stay to pick them in a pile | of 5.01. 25
chill pick your teeth, zir. LR 4.06.244 P
not to pick bad from bad, but by bad mend. OTH 4.03.105
me | the penitent instrument to pick that bolt, CYM 5.04. 10
our youths we could pick up some pretty estate, PER 4.02. 32 P
all day long but pick flowers with proserpine. TNK 4.03. 25 P
could pick no meaning from their parling looks, LUC 100
PICKAXE 1 FR 0.0001 REL FR 1 V 0 P
"a pickaxe and a spade, a spade, | for and a HAM 5.01. 94
PICKAXES 1 FR 0.0001 REL FR 1 V 0 P
flies, as deep | as these poor pickaxes can dig; CYM 4.02.389
PICKBONE 1 FR 0.0001 REL FR 0 V 1 P
and black george barnes, and francis pickbone, 2H4 3.02. 20 P
/PICK'D 1 FR 0.0001 REL FR 0 V 1 P
/me /drunk, /and /afterward /pick'd /my /pocket. WIV 1.01.127 P
PICK'D 18 FR 0.0020 REL FR 9 V 9 P
at pick'd leisure, | which shall be shortly, TMP 5.01.247
behavior hath this flemish drunkard pick'd (with WIV 2.01. 24 P
law, | as mice by lions) hath pick'd out an act, MM 1.04. 64
out of this silence yet i pick'd a welcome; MND 5.01.100
pick'd from the chaff and ruin of the times | to MV 2.09. 48
and twice to–day pick'd out the dullest scent. SHR in.1. 24
time of lethargy i pick'd and cut most of their WT 4.04.614 P
have you inquir'd yet who pick'd my pocket? 1H4 3.03. 53 P
a hair, and i'll be sworn my pocket was pick'd. 3.03. 60 P
in mine inn but i shall have my pocket pick'd? 3.03. 81 P
here behind the arras and had my pocket pick'd. 3.03. 98 P
you confess then you pick'd my pocket? 3.03.168 P
pick'd from the worm–holes of long–vanish'd days H5 2.04. 86
false vows with him, | like empty purses pick'd; TIM 4.02. 12
is to be one man pick'd out of ten thousand. HAM 2.02.179 P
the age is grown so pick'd that the toe of the 5.01.140 P
vulgar fame, you have | luxuriously pick'd out; ANT 3.13.120
force him think i have pick'd the lock and ta'en CYM 2.02. 41
PICKED 2 FR 0.0002 REL FR 1 V 1 P
he is too picked, too spruce, too affected, too LLL 5.01. 13 P

and catechize | my picked man of countries. JN 1.01.193
PICKERS 1 FR 0.0001 REL FR 0 V 1 P
and do still, by these pickers and stealers. HAM 3.02.336 P
PICKING 5 FR 0.0005 REL FR 1 V 4 P
beaten in italy for picking a kernel out of a AWW 2.03.258 P
i know by the picking on 's teeth. WT 4.04.753 P
thou variest no more from picking of purses than 1H4 2.01. 50 P
charge an honest woman with picking thy pocket! 3.03.156 P
weary | of dainty and such picking grievances, 2H4 4.01.196
PICKLE 3 FR 0.0003 REL FR 2 V 1 P
how cam'st thou in this pickle? TMP 5.01.281
have been in such a pickle since i saw you last 5.01.282 P
stew'd in brine, | smarting in ling'ring pickle. ANT 2.05. 66
PICKLE-HERRING 1 FR 0.0001 REL FR 0 V 1 P
here — a plague o' these pickle-herring! TN 1.05.121 P
PICKLOCK 1 FR 0.0001 REL FR 0 V 1 P
sir, a strange picklock, which we have sent to MM 3.02. 17 P
PICK-PURSE 3 FR 0.0003 REL FR 0 V 3 P
no, it is false, if it is a pick-purse. WIV 1.01.160 P
think he is not a pick-purse nor a horse-stealer AYL 3.04. 22 P
at hand, quoth pick-purse. 1H4 2.01. 48 P
PICK-PURSES 1 FR 0.0001 REL FR 1 V 0 P
are pick-purses in love, and we deserve to die. LLL 4.03.205
PICKS 1 FR 0.0001 REL FR 1 V 0 P
love breaks through, and picks them all at last. VEN 576
PICK-THANKS 1 FR 0.0001 REL FR 1 V 0 P
by smiling pick-thanks and base newsmongers, | i 1H4 3.02. 25
PICKT-HATCH 1 FR 0.0001 REL FR 0 V 1 P
to your manor of pickt-hatch! WIV 2.02. 18 P
PICTUR'D 2 FR 0.0002 REL FR 1 V 1 P
i have not seen him so pictur'd. CYM 5.04.179 P
to find where your true image pictur'd lies, SON 24. 6
PICTURE 49 FR 0.0055 REL FR 32 V 17 P
of our catch, play'd by the picture of nobody. TMP 3.02.127 P
'tis but her picture i have yet beheld, | and TGV 2.04.209
vouchsafe me yet your picture for my love, | the 4.02.120
the picture that is hanging in your chamber; 4.02.121
i claim the promise for her heavenly picture. 4.04. 87
o, he sends you for a picture? 4.04.115
ursula, bring my picture there. 4.04.117
here is her picture: 4.04.184
and then you may come and see the picture, she WIV 2.02. 87 P
what, have you got the picture of old adam new ERR 4.03. 13 P
i will go get her picture. ADO 2.03.264 P
my lips on thy foot, my eyes on thy picture, and LLL 4.01. 85 P
o, he hath drawn my picture in his letter! 5.02. 38
he is a proper man's picture, but, alas, who can MV 1.02. 72 P
the one of them contains my picture, prince: 2.07. 11
of these three contains her heavenly picture. 2.07. 48
like to take dust, like mistress mall's picture? TN 1.03.127 P
will draw the curtain and show you the picture. 1.05.233 P
did you never see the picture of "we three"? 2.03. 17 P
here, wear this jewel for me, 'tis my picture. 3.04.208
means i saw whose purse was best in picture, and WT 4.04.603 P
another, | as like hermione as is her picture, 5.01. 74
kindred, are going to see the queen's picture. 5.02.174 P
else, with mine own picture on the top on't 2H4 4.03. 48 P
to me, | for in my gallery thy picture hangs; 1H6 2.03. 37
were but his picture left amongst you here, | it 4.07. 83
draw this curtain and let's see your picture. TRO 3.02. 47 P
why, thou picture of what thou seemest, and idol 5.01. 6 P
had i but seen thy picture in this plight, | it TIT 3.01.103
myself, | the vigor and the picture of my youth: 4.02.108
a picture, sir. when comes your book forth? TIM 1.01. 26
how lik'st thou this picture, apemantus? 1.01.195 P
ducats a-piece for his picture in little. HAM 2.02.366 P
look here upon this picture, and on this, | the 3.04. 53
besides, his picture | i will send far and near, LR 2.01. 81
nature did) | hath alter'd that good picture? CYM 4.02.365
he began | his mistress' picture, which by his 5.05.175
/yon king's to me like to my father's picture, PER 2.03. 37
hairs, i have drawn her picture with my voice. 4.02. 95 P
upon my right side still i wore thy picture, TNK 5.03. 73
"fie, liveless picture, cold and senseless stone VEN 211
mine eye | the picture of an angry chafing boar, 662
while she, the picture of pure piety, | like a LUC 542
this picture she advisedly perus'd, | and chid 1527
that she concludes the picture was belied. 1533
with my love's picture then my eye doth feast, SON 47. 5
so, either by thy picture or my love, | thyself 47. 9
thy picture in my sight | awakes my heart to 47.13
"many there were that did his picture get | to LC 134
PICTURE-LIKE 1 FR 0.0001 REL FR 0 V 1 P
no better than picture-like to hang by th' wall, COR 1.03. 11 P
PICTURE'S 1 FR 0.0001 REL FR 1 V 0 P
eye my heart /thy picture's sight would bar, SON 46. 3
PICTURES 8 FR 0.0009 REL FR 8 V 0 P
all the pictures fairest lin'd | are but black AYL 3.02. 92
and hang it round with all my wanton pictures. SHR in.1. 47
dost thou love pictures? in.2. 49
the sleeping and the dead | are but as pictures; MAC 2.02. 51
without the which we are pictures, or mere HAM 4.05. 86
you are pictures out /a' /doors, | bells in your OTH 2.01.109
such and such pictures; CYM 2.02. 25
averring notes | of chamber-hanging, pictures, 5.05.204
PID *(also bid*)*
PID 1 FR 0.0001 REL FR 0 V 1 P
and when i give the watch-ords, do as i pid you. WIV 5.04. 3 P
PIE* *(also maggot-pies)*
PIE* 9 FR 0.0010 REL FR 4 V 5 P
by cock and pie, you shall not choose, sir! WIV 1.01.303 P
cap, | a custard-coffin, a bauble, a silken pie. SHR 4.03. 82
date is better in your pie and your porridge AWW 1.01.159 P
by cock and pie, sir, you shall not away 2H4 5.01. 1 P
no man's pie is freed | from his ambitious H8 1.01. 52
and then to be bak'd with no date in the pie, TRO 1.02.257 P
why, there they are, both baked in this pie; TIT 5.03. 60
sir, in a lenten pie, that is something stale ROM 2.04.132 P
raven, nor /chough /hoar, | nor chatt'ring pie, TNK 1.01. 21
PIEC'D 4 FR 0.0004 REL FR 2 V 2 P
one girth six times piec'd, and a woman's SHR 3.02. 60 P
and here and there piec'd with packthread. 3.02. 62 P
or all of it, with our displeasure piec'd, | and LR 1.01.199
yet their purpos'd trim | piec'd not his grace, LC 119
/PIECE 1 FR 0.0001 REL FR 1 V 0 P
this is a /piece of malice. H8 5.02. 8
PIECE 100 FR 0.0113 REL FR 54 V 46 P
thy mother was a piece of virtue, and | she said TMP 1.02. 56
fool there but would give a piece of silver. 2.02. 29 P
lest he transform me to a piece of cheese! WIV 5.05. 82 P
i were chok'd with a piece of toasted cheese. 5.05.139 P
thou'rt a three-pil'd piece, i warrant thee. MM 1.02. 32 P
i do it for some piece of money, and go through 2.01.270 P
to be overmaster'd with a piece of valiant dust? ADO 2.01. 61 P
the most dangerous piece of lechery that ever 3.03.167 P
as pretty a piece of flesh as any is in messina, 4.02. 82 P
why, sir, is this such a piece of study? LLL 1.02. 50 P
a very good piece of work, i assure you, and a MND 1.02. 13 P
in respect of a good piece of flesh indeed! AYL 3.02. 66 P
'tis a very excellent piece of work, madam lady; SHR 1.01.253 P
a piece of ice. 4.01. 14 P
what say you to a piece of beef and mustard? 4.03. 23
thou wert as witty a piece of eve's flesh as any TN 1.05. 28 P
now, good cesario, but that piece of song, 2.04. 2
were never for a piece of beauty rarer, | nor in WT 4.04. 32
and thou, fresh piece | of excellent witchcraft, 4.04.422
the prince himself is about a piece of iniquity: 4.04.678 P
i thought it were a piece of honesty to acquaint 4.04.680 P
the most peerless piece of earth, i think, 5.01. 94
a piece many years in doing and now newly 5.02. 96 P
and with our company piece the rejoicing? 5.02.108 P
o royal piece, | there's magic in thy majesty, 5.03. 38
grief from you as he | will piece up in himself. 5.03. 56
and piece the way out with a heavy heart. R2 5.01. 92
never call a true piece of gold a counterfeit. 1H4 2.04.491 P
i'll murder all his wardrop, piece by piece, 5.03. 27
i'll murder all his wardrop, piece by piece, 5.03. 27
i would make him eat a piece of my sword. 5.04.153 P
and 'a would manage you his piece thus, and 'a 2H4 3.02.282 P
piece out our imperfections with your thoughts; H5 pr 23
i knew by that piece of service the men would 3.02. 46 P
there's not a piece of feather in our host — 4.03.112
'tis as arrant a piece of knavery, mark you now, 4.07. 2 P
i will tell him a little piece of my desires. 5.01. 13 P
a piece of ord'nance 'gainst it i have plac'd, 1H6 1.04. 15
are deeply indebted for this piece of pains. 2H6 1.04. 44
and such a piece of service will you do, | if 5.01.155
but then i sigh, and, with a piece of scripture, R3 1.03.333
suborn | to do this piece of /ruthless butchery, 4.03. 5
to be thus jaded by a piece of scarlet, H8 3.02.280
all were woven | so strangely in one piece. 4.01. 81
that mould up such a mighty piece as this is, 5.04. 26
you shall piece it out with a piece of your TRO 3.01. 51 P
piece it out with a piece of your performance. 3.01. 52 P
up | the lees and dregs of a flat tamed piece; 4.01. 63
five hundred, and their friends to piece 'em. COR 2.03.212
that /for /th' poorest piece | will bear the 3.03. 32
ways, go give that changing piece | to him that TIT 1.01.309
will beget | a very excellent piece of villainy. 2.03. 7
and 'tis known i am a pretty piece of flesh. ROM 1.01. 29 P
good thou, save me a piece of marchpane, and, as 1.05. 8 P
let's see your piece. TIM 1.01. 28
'tis a good piece. 1.01. 28
a piece of painting, which i do beseech | your 1.01.155
and yet he's but a filthy piece of work. 1.01.199 P
when dinner's done, | show me this piece. 1.01.246
soul, and just of the same piece | is every 3.02. 64
only i will promise him an excellent piece. 5.01. 19
thus must i piece it out: JC 2.01. 51
a piece of work that will make sick men whole. 2.01.327
o, pardon me, thou bleeding piece of earth, 3.01.254
and question this most bloody piece of work, MAC 2.03.128
a piece of him. HAM 1.01. 19
what /a piece of work is a man! 2.02.303 P
god your voice, like a piece of uncurrent gold, 2.02.427 P
will the king hear this piece of work? 3.02. 46 P
'tis a knavish piece of work, but what of that? 3.02.240 P
i will piece out the comfort with what addition LR 3.06. 2 P
peace, this piece of toasted cheese will do't. 4.06. 89 P
o ruin'd piece of nature! 4.06.134
there's a poor piece of gold for thee. OTH 3.01. 24 P
a likely piece of work, that you should find it 4.01.151 P
had then been left unseen a wonderful piece of work, ANT 1.02.154 P
i will piece | her opulent throne with kingdoms. 1.05. 45
let not the piece of virtue which is set 3.02. 28
an antony were nature's piece 'gainst fancy, 5.02. 99
a piece of work | so bravely done, so rich, that CYM 2.04. 72
to let an arrogant piece of flesh threat us, 4.02.127
find, and be embrac'd by a piece of tender air; 5.04.140 P
find, and be embrac'd by a piece of tender air; 5.05.437 P
the piece of tender air, thy virtuous daughter, 5.05.446
take in your arms this piece | of your dead PER 3.01. 17
i have gone through for this piece you see. 4.02. 43 P
when nature fram'd this piece, she meant thee a 4.02.139 P
such a piece of slaughter | the sun and moon 4.03. 2
fare thee well, thou art a piece of virtue, and 4.06.111
i beseech your honor one piece for me. 4.06.117 P
she were a thornier piece of ground than she is, 4.06.144 P
that knew me | would say it was my best piece; TNK 2.05. 14
this is that scornful piece, that scurvy hilding 3.05. 42
is not this piece too strait? 3.06. 86
kill this cousin, | on any piece the earth has. 3.06.263
and what broken piece of matter soe'er she's 4.03. 6 P
you must bring a piece of silver on the tip of 4.03. 20 P
commend me to her, and, to piece her portion, 5.04. 31
at last she calls to mind where hangs a piece LUC 1366
to this well-painted piece is lucrece come, | to 1443
PIECES 39 FR 0.0044 REL FR 25 V 14 P
noble creature in her) | dash'd all to pieces! TMP 1.02. 8
is well-nigh worn to pieces with age to show WIV 2.01. 21 P
he pieces out his wive's inclination; 3.02. 34 P
cut me to pieces with thy keen conceit; LLL 5.02.399
gown, but i did not bid him cut it to pieces. SHR 4.03.127 P
cassocks, lest they shake themselves to pieces. AWW 4.03.169 P
he was torn to pieces with a bear. WT 5.02. 63 P
cut him to pieces. JN 4.03. 93
us, | except like curs to tear us all to pieces. R2 2.02.139
touch ground | and dash themselves to pieces. 2H4 4.01. 18
bend it to our awe, | or break it all to pieces. H5 1.02.225
steel, | and spurn in pieces posts of adamant; 1H6 1.04. 52
hew them to pieces, hack their bones asunder, 4.07. 47
break thou in pieces and consume to ashes, 5.04. 92
and on the pieces of the broken wand | were 2H6 1.02. 28
if they fall, they dash themselves to pieces. R3 1.03.259
are crack'd in pieces by malignant death, | and 2.02. 52
reft, | rush all to pieces on thy rocky bosom. 4.04.235
cut me to pieces, volsces, men and lads, | stain COR 5.06.111
tear him to pieces! 5.06.120 P
it beats as it would fall in twenty pieces. ROM 2.05. 49
a thousand pieces. TIM 3.06. 21 P
a thousand pieces? 3.06. 22 P
tear him to pieces, he's a conspirator. JC 3.03. 28 P
all your thunderbolts, | dash him to pieces! 4.03. 82
hand | cancel and tear to pieces that great bond MAC 3.02. 49
own honor and shake in pieces the heart of his LR 1.02. 85 P
caitiff, to pieces shake, | that under covert 3.02. 55
i'll tear her all to pieces. OTH 3.03.431
bruised pieces, go, | you have been nobly borne. ANT 4.14. 42
to pieces with me! CYM 3.04. 53
thy garments cut to pieces before /her face: 4.01. 18 P
though light, take pieces for the figure's sake; 5.04. 25
pieces of gold 'gainst this which then he wore 5.05.183
a strong wind will blow it to pieces, they are PER 4.02. 19 P
i cannot be bated one doit of a thousand pieces. 4.02. 52 P
heavens infuse | in their best-temper'd pieces, TNK 1.03. 10
i'll set it down | he's torn to pieces. 3.02. 18
livers perish'd, crack'd to pieces with love, we 4.03. 24 P
PIE-CORNER 1 FR 0.0001 REL FR 0 V 1 P
'a comes /continuantly to pie-corner (saving 2H4 2.01. 26 P
PIED* 4 FR 0.0004 REL FR 3 V 1 P
what a pied ninny's this! TMP 3.02. 63
when daisies pied and violets blue | and LLL 5.02.894
all the eanlings which were streak'd and pied MV 1.03. 79
comment appelez-vous le pied et la robe? H5 3.04. 50 P
PIEDNESS 1 FR 0.0001 REL FR 1 V 0 P
there is an art which in their piedness shares WT 4.04. 87
PIER 1 FR 0.0001 REL FR 1 V 0 P
seen | the well-appointed king at /hampton pier H5 3.pr. 4
PIERC'D 8 FR 0.0009 REL FR 7 V 1 P
the preyful princess pierc'd and prick'd a LLL 4.02. 56
and if one should be pierc'd, which is the one? 4.02. 84 P
i, | pierc'd through the heart with your stern MND 3.02. 59
pierc'd to the soul with slander's venom'd spear R2 1.01.171
whose loss hath pierc'd him deep and scarr'd his TIT 4.04. 31
that pierc'd the fearful hollow of thine ear; ROM 3.05. 3
it pierc'd me thorough, | and though you call my PER 4.03. 35
lie | (a closet never pierc'd with crystal eyes) SON 46. 6
/PIERCE* 1 FR 0.0001 REL FR 0 V 1 P
/did /your /letters /pierce /the /queen /to /any LR 4.03. 9 P
PIERCE* 24 FR 0.0027 REL FR 22 V 2 P
even | ambition cannot pierce a wink beyond, TMP 2.01.242
dart of love | can pierce a complete bosom. MM 1.03. 3
honest plain words best pierce the ear of grief, LLL 5.02.753
as it should pierce a hundred thousand hearts; MND 2.01.160
can no prayers pierce thee? MV 4.01.126
with sweetest touches pierce your mistress' ear, 5.01. 67
hearing how our plaints and prayers do pierce, R2 5.03.127
sir pierce of exton, who | lately came from the 5.05.100
well, if percy be alive, i'll pierce him. 1H4 5.03. 56 P
i come to pierce it, or to give thee mine. 3H6 2.01.203
her tears will pierce into a marble heart; 3.01. 38
can curses pierce the clouds and enter heaven? R3 1.03.194
woes will make them sharp and pierce like mine. 4.04.125
let some graver eye | pierce into that — but i H8 1.01. 68
air | may pierce the head of the great combatant TRO 4.05. 5
when by and by the din of war gan pierce | his COR 2.02.115
he is able to pierce a corslet with his eye, 5.04. 20 P
and pierce the inmost centre of the earth; TIT 4.03. 12
holy vestments bleeding, | shall pierce a jot. TIM 4.03.127
father's curse | pierce every sense about thee! LR 1.04.301
how far your eyes may pierce i cannot tell: 1.04.345
arm it in rags, a pigmy's straw does pierce it. 4.06.167
dart of chance | could neither graze nor pierce? OTH 4.01.268
my bended hook shall pierce | their slimy jaws; ANT 2.05. 12
PIERCED 1 FR 0.0001 REL FR 1 V 0 P
the bruis'd heart was pierced through the /ear. OTH 1.03.219
PIERCES 2 FR 0.0002 REL FR 2 V 0 P
which pierces so, that it assaults | mercy TMP ep 17
and it pierces and sharpens the stomach. PER 4.01. 28
PIERCETH 1 FR 0.0001 REL FR 1 V 0 P
thus most invectively he pierceth through | the AYL 2.01. 58
PIERCING 13 FR 0.0014 REL FR 11 V 2 P
of piercing a hogshead! LLL 4.02. 87 P
and say she uttereth piercing eloquence; SHR 2.01.176
still-peering air | that sings with piercing, do AWW 3.02.111
good comfort as it is | now piercing to my soul. WT 5.03. 34
boastful neighs | piercing the night's dull ear; H5 4.pr. 11
ay, sharp and piercing, to maintain his truth, 1H6 2.04. 70
so doves do peck the falcon's piercing talons, 3H6 1.04. 41
have been as piercing as the midday sun | to 5.02. 17
and provide more piercing statutes daily to COR 1.01. 84 P
my soul's hate, aufidius, | piercing our romans; 1.05. 11
with piercing steel at bold mercutio's breast, ROM 3.01.159
for piercing steel, and darts envenomed, | shall JC 5.03. 76
brand not my forehead with thy piercing light, LUC 1091
PIERS 1 FR 0.0001 REL FR 1 V 0 P
piring in maps for ports and piers and roads; MV 1.01. 19
PIES* 2 FR 0.0002 REL FR 1 V 1 P
i must have saffron to color the warden pies; WT 4.03. 46 P
and chatt'ring pies in dismal discords sung; 3H6 5.06. 48
PIETY 7 FR 0.0008 REL FR 6 V 1 P
thou villain, thou art full of piety, as shall ADO 4.02. 79 P
and how his piety | does my deeds make the WT 3.02.171
fetch'd | from glist'ring semblances of piety; H5 2.02.117
for king and commonweal | were piety in thine, TIT 1.01.115
o cruel, irreligious piety! 1.01.130
piety, and fear, | religion to the gods, peace, TIM 4.01. 15
while she, the picture of pure piety, | like a LUC 542
PIG* *(also big)*
PIG* 8 FR 0.0009 REL FR 5 V 3 P
the capon burns, the pig falls from the spit; ERR 1.02. 44
"the pig," quoth i, "is burn'd": 2.01. 66
some men there are love not a gaping pig; MV 4.01. 47
be rend'red | why he cannot abide a gaping pig; 4.01. 54
town's name where alexander the pig was born? H5 4.07. 13 P
why, i pray you, is not "pig" great? 4.07. 15 P
the pig, or the great, or the mighty, or the 4.07. 16 P
so cries a pig prepared to the spit. TIT 4.02.146
PIGEON-EGG 1 FR 0.0001 REL FR 0 V 1 P
purse of wit, thou pigeon-egg of discretion. LLL 5.01. 74 P
PIGEON-LIVER'D 1 FR 0.0001 REL FR 1 V 0 P
for it cannot be | but i am pigeon-liver'd, and HAM 2.02.577
PIGEONS 12 FR 0.0013 REL FR 3 V 9 P
this fellow pecks up wit as pigeons pease, | and LLL 5.02.315

o, ten times faster venus' pigeons fly | to seal MV 2.06. 5
he will put on us, as pigeons feed their young. AYL 1.02. 93 P
and as pigeons bill, so wedlock would be 3.03. 81 P
for william cook — are there no young pigeons? 2H4 5.01. 17 P
some pigeons, davy, a couple of short–legg'd 5.01. 26 P
ay, of my pigeons, sir, nothing else. TIT 4.03. 88 P
i am going with my pigeons to the tribunal plebs 4.03. 92 P
let him deliver the pigeons to the emperor from 4.03. 96 P
ado, | but give your pigeons to the emperor. 4.03.103
then deliver up your pigeons, and then look for 4.03.111 P
you a letter and a couple of pigeons here. 4.04. 44 P
PIGHT *(also pitch'd, etc.)*
/PIGHT 1 FR 0.0001 REL FR 1 V 0 P
thus proudly /pight upon our phrygian plains, TRO 5.10. 24
PIGHT 1 FR 0.0001 REL FR 1 V 0 P
and found him pight to do it, with curst speech LR 2.01. 65
PIG–LIKE 1 FR 0.0001 REL FR 1 V 0 P
pig–like he whines | at the sharp rowel, which TNK 5.04. 69
PIGMIES 2 FR 0.0002 REL FR 1 V 1 P
do you any embassage to the pigmies, rather than ADO 2.01.269 P
by east and north–east to the king of pigmies, TNK 3.04. 15
PIGMY 1 FR 0.0001 REL FR 1 V 0 P
to whip this dwarfish war, this pigmy arms, JN 5.02.135
PIGMY'S 1 FR 0.0001 REL FR 1 V 0 P
arm it in rags, a pigmy's straw does pierce it. LR 4.06.167
PIG–NUTS 1 FR 0.0001 REL FR 1 V 0 P
and i with my long nails will dig thee pig–nuts, TMP 2.02.168
PIGROGROMITUS 1 FR 0.0001 REL FR 0 V 1 P
when thou spok'st of pigrogromitus, of the TN 2.03. 23 P
PIKE* 4 FR 0.0004 REL FR 2 V 2 P
sword, pike, knife, gun, or need of any engine, TMP 2.01.162
come off the breach with his pike bent bravely, 2H4 2.04. 50 P
if the young dace be a bait for the old pike, i 3.02.331 P
trail'st thou the puissant pike? H5 4.01. 40
PIKES 9 FR 0.0010 REL FR 7 V 2 P
margaret, you must put in the pikes with a vice, ADO 5.02. 21 P
your naked infants spitted upon pikes, | whiles H5 3.03. 38
he wanted pikes to set before his archers; 1H6 1.01.116
soldiers should have toss'd me on their pikes, 3H6 1.01.244
let us revenge this with our pikes, ere we COR 1.01. 23 P
trail your steel pikes. 5.06.150
and make him with our pikes and partisans | a CYM 4.02.399
grin like lions | upon the pikes o' th' hunters. 5.03. 39
of bristly pikes that ever threat his foes, VEN 620
/PILATE 1 FR 0.0001 REL FR 1 V 0 P
/though /some /of /you, /with /pilate, /wash R2 4.01.239
PILATE 1 FR 0.0001 REL FR 1 V 0 P
how fain, like pilate, would i wash my hands R3 1.04.272
/PILATES 1 FR 0.0001 REL FR 1 V 0 P
/yet /you /pilates | /have /here /deliver'd /me R2 4.01.240
PILCH 1 FR 0.0001 REL FR 0 V 1 P
what /ho, pilch! PER 2.01. 12 P
PILCHER 1 FR 0.0001 REL FR 0 V 1 P
pluck your sword out of his pilcher by the ears? ROM 3.01. 80 P
PILCHERS 1 FR 0.0001 REL FR 0 V 1 P
as like husbands as pilchers are to herrings, TN 3.01. 34 P
PIL'D* *(also peel'd)*
PIL'D* 4 FR 0.0004 REL FR 2 V 2 P
lief be a list of an english kersey as be pil'd, MM 1.02. 33 P
english kersey as be pil'd, as thou art pil'd, 1.02. 34 P
whose foundation | is pil'd upon his faith, and WT 1.02.430
for this they have engrossed and pil'd up | the 2H4 4.05. 70
PILE* 9 FR 0.0010 REL FR 8 V 1 P
some thousands of these logs, and pile them up, TMP 3.01. 10
up those logs that you are enjoin'd to pile! 3.01. 17
pray give me that, | i'll carry it to the pile. 3.01. 25
left cheek is a cheek of two pile and a half, AWW 4.05. 97 P
heels, | or pile ten hills on the tarpeian rock, COR 3.02. 3
he could not stay to pick them in a pile | of 5.01. 25
that we may hew his limbs and on a pile | ad TIT 1.01. 97
and with our swords, upon a pile of wood, 1.01.128
now pile your dust upon the quick and dead, HAM 5.01.251
PILES 2 FR 0.0002 REL FR 2 V 0 P
what piles of wealth hath he accumulated | to H8 3.02.107
distinctly ranges, | in heaps and piles of ruin. COR 3.01.206
PILFERING 1 FR 0.0001 REL FR 1 V 0 P
our inland from the pilfering borderers. H5 1.02.142
/PILF'RINGS 1 FR 0.0001 REL FR 1 V 0 P
/for /pilf'rings /and /most /common /trespasses LR 2.02.144
PILGRIM 9 FR 0.0010 REL FR 7 V 2 P
a true–devoted pilgrim is not weary | to measure TGV 2.07. 9
"i am saint jaques' pilgrim, thither gone. AWW 3.04. 4
look, here comes a pilgrim. 3.05. 30 P
god save you, pilgrim! 3.05. 32 P
if you will tarry, holy pilgrim, | but till the 3.05. 39
if you shall please so, pilgrim. 3.05. 44
come, pilgrim, i will bring you | where you 3.05. 93
good pilgrim, you do wrong your hand too much, ROM 1.05. 97
ay, pilgrim, lips that they must use in pray'r. 1.05.102
PILGRIMAGE 18 FR 0.0020 REL FR 17 V 1 P
every sedge | he overtaketh in his pilgrimage; TGV 2.07. 30
for that's the utmost of his pilgrimage. MM 2.01. 36
their blood | to undergo such maiden pilgrimage; MND 1.01. 75
same | to whom you swore a secret pilgrimage, MV 1.01.120
the life of man | runs his erring pilgrimage, AYL 3.02.130
her pretense is a pilgrimage to saint jaques le AWW 4.03. 48 P
two men | that vow a long and weary pilgrimage. R2 1.03. 49
age, | but stop no wrinkle in his pilgrimage; 1.03.230
it so, | which finds it an enforced pilgrimage. 1.03.264
his time is spent, our pilgrimage must be. 2.01.154
in prison hast thou spent a pilgrimage, | and 1H6 2.05.116
time saw | in lasting labor of his pilgrimage! ROM 4.05. 45
from first to last | told him our pilgrimage. LR 5.03.197
heart | that i would all my pilgrimage dilate, OTH 1.03.153
as palmers' chat makes short their pilgrimage. LUC 791
"why work'st thou mischief in thy pilgrimage, 960
still, | attending on his golden pilgrimage: SON 7. 8
i abide) | intend a zealous pilgrimage to thee, 27. 6
PILGRIMS' 1 FR 0.0001 REL FR 1 V 0 P
saints have hands that pilgrims' hands do touch, ROM 1.05. 99
PILGRIMS 2 FR 0.0002 REL FR 1 V 1 P
there are pilgrims going to canterbury with rich 1H4 1.02.126 P
my lips, two blushing pilgrims, ready stand | to ROM 1.05. 95
PILL 1 FR 0.0001 REL FR 1 V 0 P
your grave masters are, | and pill by law. TIM 4.01. 12
PILLAGE 6 FR 0.0006 REL FR 5 V 1 P
which pillage they with merry march bring home H5 1.02.195
gentle bosom of peace with pillage and robbery. 4.01.166 P
not born | to be the pillage of a giglot wench." 1H6 4.07. 41
may make cheap pennyworths of their pillage 2H6 1.01.222
to–day, | thy sons make pillage of her chastity, TIT 2.03. 44
like straggling slaves for pillage fighting, LUC 428
PILLAR 5 FR 0.0005 REL FR 5 V 0 P
law, | whereof you are a well–deserving pillar, MV 4.01.239
when we have here her base and pillar by us. TRO 4.05.212
him | the triple pillar of the world transform'd ANT 1.01. 12
from dis to daedalus, from post to pillar, | is TNK 3.05.115
fair and knightly strength to touch the pillar, 3.06.295
PILLARS 4 FR 0.0004 REL FR 4 V 0 P
and set it down | with gold on lasting pillars: TMP 5.01.208
brave peers of england, pillars of the state, 2H6 1.01. 75
and call them pillars that will stand to us; 3H6 2.03. 51
these ruin'd pillars, out of pity taken | a load H8 3.02.382
PILL'D *(also peel'd, pil'd*)*
PILL'D 6 FR 0.0006 REL FR 6 V 0 P
the skillful shepherd pill'd me certain wands, MV 1.03. 84
the commons hath he pill'd with grievous taxes, R2 2.01.246
rather than i would be so pill'd esteem'd: 1H6 1.04. 33
in sharing that which you have pill'd from me! R3 1.03.158
ay me, the bark pill'd from the lofty pine, LUC 1167
so must my soul, her bark being pill'd away. 1169
PILLICOCK 1 FR 0.0001 REL FR 0 V 1 P
pillicock sat on pillicock–hill, alow! LR 3.04. 76 P
PILLICOCK–HILL 1 FR 0.0001 REL FR 0 V 1 P
pillicock sat on pillicock–hill, alow! LR 3.04. 76 P
PILLORY 2 FR 0.0002 REL FR 1 V 1 P
i have stood on the pillory for geese he hath TGV 4.04. 32 P
as on a pillory, looking through the lute, SHR 2.01.156
PILLOW 20 FR 0.0022 REL FR 18 V 2 P
one turf shall serve as pillow for us both, MND 2.02. 41
a lover | as ever sigh'd upon a midnight pillow. AYL 2.04. 27
bed, | and here i'll fling the pillow, there the SHR 4.01.201
set me the crown upon my pillow here. 2H4 4.05. 5
why doth the crown lie there upon his pillow, 4.05. 21
where is the crown? who took it from my pillow? 4.05. 57
a good soft pillow for that good white head H5 4.01. 14
and whispers to his pillow as to him | the 2H6 3.02.375
a book of prayers on their pillow lay, | which R3 4.03. 14
fair queen, fair thoughts be your fair pillow! TRO 3.01. 46 P
and make his dead trunk pillow to our lust. TIT 2.03.130
sung thee asleep, his loving breast thy pillow; 5.03.163
that hath laid knives under his pillow, and LR 3.04. 54 P
have i my pillow left unpress'd in rome, ANT 3.13.106
when resty sloth | finds the down pillow hard. CYM 3.06. 35
who is this | thou mak'st thy bloody pillow? 4.02.363
lay the babe | upon the pillow. PER 3.01. 68
a pillow for his head. 5.01.236
under, | coz'ning the pillow of a lawful kiss; LUC 387
and on that pillow lay | where thou wast wont to 1620
PILLOWS 3 FR 0.0003 REL FR 3 V 0 P
pluck stout men's pillows from below their heads TIM 4.03. 33
which unwip'd we found | upon their pillows. MAC 2.03.104
to their deaf pillows will discharge their 5.01. 73
PILLS 2 FR 0.0002 REL FR 1 V 1 P
when i was sick, you gave me bitter pills, | and TGV 2.04.149
swallow'd snowballs for pills to cool the reins. WIV 3.05. 23 P
PILOT 9 FR 0.0010 REL FR 9 V 0 P
be pilot to me, and thy places shall | still WT 1.02.448
yet lives our pilot still. 3H6 5.04. 6
i am no pilot, yet, wert thou as far | as that ROM 2.02. 82
thou desperate pilot, now at once run on | the 5.03.117
and his pilot | of very expert and approv'd OTH 2.01. 48
these letters give, iago, to the pilot, | and by 3.02. 1
king to tharsus — think /his pilot thought, PER 4.04. 18
where's the pilot? TNK 4.01.150
desire my pilot is, beauty my prize, | then who LUC 279
PILOT'S 3 FR 0.0003 REL FR 3 V 0 P
or four and twenty times the pilot's glass AWW 2.01.165
for once allow'd the skillful pilot's charge? 3H6 5.04. 20
here i have a pilot's thumb, | wrack'd as MAC 1.03. 28
PILOTS 1 FR 0.0001 REL FR 1 V 0 P
two traded pilots 'twixt the dangerous /shores TRO 2.02. 64
PIMPERNELL 1 FR 0.0001 REL FR 1 V 0 P
greece, | and peter turph, and henry pimpernell, SHR in.2. 94
/PIN 1 FR 0.0001 REL FR 1 V 0 P
will she get the upshoot by cleaving the /pin. LLL 4.01.136
PIN 17 FR 0.0019 REL FR 10 V 7 P
from a pound to a pin? TGV 1.01.108
a round hose, madam, now's not worth a pin, 2.07. 55
tut, a pin! this shall be answer'd. WIV 1.01.114 P
no indeed, sir, not of a pin; MM 2.01. 96 P
if you should need a pin, | you could not with 2.02. 45
down for your deliverance | as frankly as a pin. 3.01.105
nail, | a rush, a hair, a drop of blood, a pin, ERR 4.03. 72
by the world, i would not care a pin, if the LLL 4.03. 18 P
scratch thee but with a pin, and there remains AYL 3.05. 21
eyes | blind with the pin and web but theirs, WT 1.02.291
embracing, as if she would pin her to her heart, 5.02. 77 P
comes at the last and with a little pin | bores R2 3.02.169
and swallow my sword like a great pin, ere thou 2H6 4.10. 29 P
fo, fo, come, tell a pin. you are forsworn. TRO 5.02. 22
the very pin of his heart cleft with the blind ROM 2.04. 15 P
he gives the web and the pin, /squinies the eye, LR 3.04.117 P
let's see, | i feel this pin prick. 4.07. 55
PIN–BUTTOCK 1 FR 0.0001 REL FR 0 V 1 P
the pin–buttock, the quatch–buttock, the AWW 2.02. 18 P
PINCH *(also pinse)*
PINCH 25 FR 0.0028 REL FR 23 V 2 P
each pinch more stinging | than bees that made TMP 1.02.329
but they'll nor pinch, | fright me with 2.02. 4
and, fairy–like, to pinch the unclean knight; WIV 4.04. 58
let the supposed fairies pinch him sound, | and 4.04. 62
to pinch her by the hand, and, on that token, 4.06. 44
there pinch the maids as blue as bilberry; 5.05. 45
pinch them, arms, legs, backs, shoulders, sides, 5.05. 54
and, as you trip, still pinch him to your time. 5.05. 92
pinch him, fairies, mutually! 5.05. 99
pinch him for his villainy! 5.05.100
pinch him, and burn him, and turn him about, 5.05.101
suck our breath, or pinch us black and blue. ERR 2.02.192
good doctor pinch, you are a conjurer, 4.04. 47
along with them | they brought one pinch, a 5.01.238
if ye pinch me like a pasty, i can say no more. AWW 4.03.123 P
save how to gall and pinch this bullingbrook, 1H4 1.03.229
when thou dost pinch thy bearer, thou dost sit 2H4 4.05. 29
not rascal–like, to fall down with a pinch, 1H6 4.02. 49
pinch wanton on your cheek, call you his mouse, HAM 3.04.183
the wolf and owl — | necessity's sharp pinch. LR 2.04.211
as they pinch one another by the disposition, he ANT 2.07. 6 P
the stroke of death is as a lover's pinch, 5.02.295
there cannot be a pinch in death | more sharp CYM 1.01.130
do i pinch you? TNK 3.06. 55
since i know | their lives but pinch 'em. 5.03.133
PINCH'D 10 FR 0.0011 REL FR 8 V 2 P
thou shalt be pinch'd | as thick as honeycomb, TMP 1.02.328
thou art pinch'd for't now, sebastian. 5.01. 74
i shall be pinch'd to death. 5.01.276
and pinch'd the lily–tincture of her face, TGV 4.04.155
what, have i pinch'd you, signior gremio? SHR 2.01.371
my design, and i | remain a pinch'd thing; WT 2.01. 51
you might have pinch'd a placket, it was 4.04.609 P
is with a kind of colic pinch'd and vex'd | by 1H4 3.01. 28
who having pinch'd a few and made them cry, 3H6 2.01. 16
if you chance to be pinch'd with the colic, you COR 2.01. 74 P
PINCHES 5 FR 0.0005 REL FR 4 V 1 P
toe to crown he'll fill our skins with pinches, TMP 4.01.233
(whose inward pinches therefore are most strong) 5.01. 77
galls the one, and the pox pinches the other, 2H4 1.02.231 P
here's the pang that pinches: H8 2.03. 1
that am with phoebus' amorous pinches black, ANT 1.05. 28
PINCHING 2 FR 0.0002 REL FR 2 V 0 P
but to be paddling palms and pinching fingers, WT 1.02.115
in this our pinching cave, shall we discourse CYM 3.03. 38
PINCH'S 1 FR 0.0001 REL FR 1 V 0 P
you are not pinch's patient, are you, sir? ERR 5.01.295
PINCH–SPOTTED 1 FR 0.0001 REL FR 1 V 0 P
and more pinch–spotted make them | than pard or TMP 4.01.260
PIN'D 3 FR 0.0003 REL FR 2 V 1 P
she pin'd in thought, | and with a green and TN 2.04.112
for whom, and not for tybalt, juliet pin'd. ROM 5.03.236
into france, sir, the fool hath much pin'd away. LR 1.04. 74 P
PINDARUS 9 FR 0.0010 REL FR 9 V 0 P
and pindarus is come | to do you salutation from JC 4.02. 4
your master, pindarus, | in his own change, or 4.02. 6
pindarus, | bid our commanders lead their 4.02. 47
go, pindarus, get higher on that hill; 5.03. 20
far from this country pindarus shall run, 5.03. 49
with pindarus his bondman, on this hill. 5.03. 56
what, pindarus? where art thou, pindarus? 5.03. 72
what, pindarus? where art thou, pindarus? 5.03. 72
and i will seek for pindarus the while. 5.03. 79
PINE* 23 FR 0.0026 REL FR 23 V 0 P
her most unmitigable rage, | into a cloven pine; TMP 1.02.277
that made gape | the pine, and let thee out. 1.02.293
by the spurs pluck'd up | the pine and cedar. 5.01. 48
the mind shall banquet, though the body pine; LLL 1.01. 25
to love, to wealth, to pomp, i pine and die, 1.01. 31
tranio, i burn, i pine, i perish, tranio, | if i SHR 1.01.155
go to flint castle, there i'll pine away — | a R2 3.02.209
within a loathsome dungeon, there to pine, | was 1H6 2.05. 57
droops this lofty pine and hangs his sprays, 2H6 2.03. 45
infects the sound pine and diverts his grain TRO 1.03. 8
times nine, | shall he dwindle, peak, and pine; MAC 1.03. 23
all which we pine for now. 3.06. 37
where yond pine does stand | i shall discover ANT 4.12. 1
and this pine is bark'd, | that overtopp'd them 4.12. 23
that by the top doth take the mountain pine CYM 4.02.175
makes both my body pine and soul to languish, PER 1.02. 32
do surfeit by the eye and pine the maw; VEN 602
infamy, | but i alone, alone must sit and pine, LUC 795
ay me, the bark pill'd from the lofty pine, 1167
thus do i pine and surfeit day by day, | or SON 75.13
why dost thou pine within and suffer dearth, 146. 3
and let that pine to aggravate thy store; 146.10
it break, with bleeding groans they pine, | and LC 275
PINED 2 FR 0.0002 REL FR 2 V 0 P
pity the dearth that i have pined in, | by TGV 2.07. 16
hat, | hanging her pale and pined cheek beside; LC 32
PINES* 7 FR 0.0008 REL FR 7 V 0 P
you may as well forbid the mountain pines | to MV 4.01. 75
behind the tuft of pines i met them; WT 2.01. 34
he fires the proud tops of the eastern pines R2 3.02. 42
shivering cold and sickness pines the clime; 5.01. 77
the orphan pines while the oppressor feeds, LUC 905
he ten times pines that pines beholding food, 1115
he ten times pines that pines beholding food, 1115
PINETH 1 FR 0.0001 REL FR 1 V 0 P
that cloy'd with much, he pineth still for more. LUC 98
PINFOLD 2 FR 0.0002 REL FR 0 V 2 P
you mistake; i mean the pound — a pinfold. TGV 1.01.107 P
if i had thee in lipsbury pinfold, i would make LR 2.02. 9 P
PINING 2 FR 0.0002 REL FR 2 V 0 P
that every wretch, pining and pale before, H5 4.pr. 41
eyes, | see, see the pining malady of france! 1H6 3.03. 49
PINION 2 FR 0.0002 REL FR 2 V 0 P
pinion him like a thief, bring him before us. LR 3.07. 23
hither | he sends so poor a pinion of his wing, ANT 3.12. 4
PINION'D 2 FR 0.0002 REL FR 1 V 1 P
to go loose any longer, you must be pinion'd. WIV 4.02.123 P
will not wait pinion'd at your master's court, ANT 5.02. 53
PINK* 3 FR 0.0003 REL FR 1 V 2 P
nay, i am the very pink of courtesy. ROM 2.04. 57 P
pink for flower. 2.04. 58 P
of the vine, | plumpy bacchus with pink eyne! ANT 2.07.114
PINK'D 1 FR 0.0001 REL FR 0 V 1 P
upon me till her pink'd porringer fell off her H8 5.03. 48 P
PINKS 1 FR 0.0001 REL FR 1 V 0 P
maiden pinks, of odor faint, | daisies TNK 1.01. 4
PINNACE 3 FR 0.0003 REL FR 3 V 0 P
sail like my pinnace to these golden shores. WIV 1.03. 80
for, whilst our pinnace anchors in the downs, 2H6 4.01. 9
being captain of a pinnace, threatens more 4.01.107
PINN'D 1 FR 0.0001 REL FR 1 V 0 P
yet seem shut, we have but pinn'd with rushes, COR 1.04. 18
PIN'S 1 FR 0.0001 REL FR 1 V 0 P
i do not set my life at a pin's fee, | and for HAM 1.04. 65
PINS' 2 FR 0.0002 REL FR 0 V 2 P
in their bellies no bigger than pins' heads, and 1H4 4.02. 22 P
the element (which show like pins' heads to her) 2H4 4.03. 53 P
/PINS 1 FR 0.0001 REL FR 1 V 0 P
my wretchedness unto a row of /pins, | they will R2 3.04. 26
PINS 7 FR 0.0008 REL FR 5 V 2 P
unless you have a codpiece to stick pins on. TGV 2.07. 56

this gallant pins the wenches on his sleeve; LLL 5.02.321
pins and poking–sticks of steel; WT 4.04.226
give crowns like pins! 2H4 2.04.174 P
his back, and the whole frame stands upon pins. 3.02.144 P
the kitchen malkin pins | her richest lockram COR 2.01.208
in their numb'd and mortified arms | pins, LR 2.03. 16
PINSE *(also pinch)*
PINSE 1 FR 0.0001 REL FR 0 V 1 P
your desires, and fairies will not pinse you. WIV 5.05.130 P
PINT 2 FR 0.0002 REL FR 0 V 2 P
score a pint of bastard in the half–moon," or so 1H4 2.04. 27 P
not past a pint, as i am a soldier. OTH 2.03. 66 P
PINT–POT 1 FR 0.0001 REL FR 0 V 1 P
peace, good pint–pot, peace, good ticklebrain. 1H4 2.04.397 P
PIONED 1 FR 0.0001 REL FR 1 V 0 P
thy banks with pioned and twilled brims, | which TMP 4.01. 64
PIONER 2 FR 0.0002 REL FR 2 V 0 P
a worthy pioner! HAM 1.05.163
there might you see the laboring pioner LUC 1380
PIONERS 2 FR 0.0002 REL FR 1 V 1 P
have the pioners given o'er? H5 3.02. 87 P
pioners and all, had tasted her sweet body, | so OTH 3.03.346
/PIOUS 1 FR 0.0001 REL FR 1 V 0 P
unless you play the /pious innocent | and for an PER 4.03. 17
PIOUS 10 FR 0.0011 REL FR 9 V 1 P
now, pious sir, | you will demand of me why i do MM 1.03. 16
and is not this course pious? H8 2.02. 36
and thy parts | sovereign and pious else, could 2.04.141
and he whose pious breath seeks to convert you, TIM 4.03.141
in pious rage the two delinquents tear, | that MAC 3.06. 12
of the most pious edward with such grace | that 3.06. 27
breathing like sanctified and pious bonds, | the HAM 1.03.130
the first row of the pious chanson will show you 2.02.419 P
visage | and pious action we do sugar o'er | the 3.01. 47
paid | more pious debts to heaven than in all CYM 3.03. 72
PIP *(see peep*)*
PIPE 14 FR 0.0015 REL FR 9 V 5 P
now had he rather hear the tabor and the pipe; ADO 2.03. 15 P
when shepherds pipe on oaten straws | and merry LLL 5.02.903
thy small pipe | is as the maiden's organ, TN 1.04. 32
would never dance again after a tabor and pipe; WT 4.04.183 P
rumor is a pipe | blown by surmises, jealousies, 2H4 in 15
hoof is more musical than the pipe of hermes. H5 3.07. 17 P
now crack thy lungs, and split thy brazen pipe. TRO 4.05. 7
with my drum, into a pipe | small as an eunuch, COR 3.02.113
and, kinsmen, then we may go pipe for justice. TIT 4.03. 24
that they are not a pipe for fortune's finger HAM 3.02. 70
will you play upon this pipe? 3.02.351 P
think i am easier to be play'd on than a pipe? 3.02.370 P
my shepherd's pipe can sound no deal, | my PP 17.17
and stops /her pipe in growth of riper days: SON 102. 8
PIPERS 1 FR 0.0001 REL FR 0 V 1 P
strike up, pipers. ADO 5.04.129 P
PIPES 7 FR 0.0008 REL FR 5 V 2 P
playing on pipes of corn and versing love | to MND 2.01. 67
treble, pipes | and whistles in his sound. AYL 2.07.162
these pipes and these conveyances of our blood COR 5.01. 54
faith, we may put up our pipes and be gone. ROM 4.05. 96 P
your statue spouting blood in many pipes, | in JC 2.02. 85
then put up your pipes in your bag, for i'll OTH 3.01. 19 P
the spring that those shrunk pipes had fed, LUC 1455
PIPE–WINE 1 FR 0.0001 REL FR 0 V 1 P
think i shall drink in pipe–wine first with him; WIV 3.02. 89 P
PIPING 2 FR 0.0002 REL FR 2 V 0 P
therefore the winds, piping to us in vain, | as MND 2.01. 88
why, i, in this weak piping time of peace, R3 1.01. 24
PIPPEN *(also pepin)*
PIPPEN 2 FR 0.0002 REL FR 1 V 1 P
that was a man when king pippen of france was a LLL 4.01.120 P
touch | is powerful to araise king pippen, nay, AWW 2.01. 76
PIPPIN 1 FR 0.0001 REL FR 0 V 1 P
eat a last year's pippin of mine own graffing, 2H4 5.03. 2 P
PIPPINS 1 FR 0.0001 REL FR 0 V 1 P
there's pippins and cheese to come. WIV 1.02. 12 P
PIRATE 8 FR 0.0009 REL FR 6 V 2 P
thou conclud'st like the sanctimonious pirate, MM 1.02. 8 P
fever | one ragozine, a most notorious pirate, 4.03. 71
notable pirate, thou salt–water thief! TN 5.01. 69
antonio never yet was thief or pirate, | though 5.01. 74
more | than bargulus the strong illyrian pirate. 2H6 4.01.108
straightway /calm'd and boarded with a pirate. 4.09. 33
a pirate of very warlike appointment gave us HAM 4.06. 16 P
roguing thieves serve the great pirate valdes, PER 4.01. 96
PIRATES 9 FR 0.0010 REL FR 8 V 1 P
water–thieves and land–thieves, i mean pirates, MV 1.03. 24 P
pirates may make cheap pennyworths of their 2H6 1.01.222
and suffolk dies by pirates. 4.01.138
hear me, you wrangling pirates, that fall out R3 1.03.157
word | menecrates and menas, famous pirates, ANT 1.04. 48
and i must | rid all the sea of pirates; 2.06. 36
or that these pirates, | not enough barbarous, PER 4.02. 65
do't, | a crew of pirates came and rescued me; 5.01.174
high winds, strong pirates, shelves and sands, LUC 335
PIRING *(also peering)*
PIRING 1 FR 0.0001 REL FR 1 V 0 P
piring in maps for ports and piers and roads; MV 1.01. 19
PIRITHOUS' 1 FR 0.0001 REL FR 1 V 0 P
you talk of pirithous' and theseus' love: TNK 1.03. 55
PIRITHOUS 6 FR 0.0006 REL FR 6 V 0 P
pirithous, | lead on the bride. TNK 1.01.207
pirithous, | keep the feast full, bate not an 1.01.219
assurance | that we, more than his pirithous, 1.03. 95
prince pirithous | obtained his liberty; 2.02.244
pirithous, | dispose of this fair gentleman. 2.05. 31
them, | that truly noble prince pirithous, 4.01. 13
PISA 14 FR 0.0015 REL FR 12 V 2 P
pisa, renowned for grave citizens, | gave me my SHR 1.01. 10
for i have pisa left | and am to padua come, as 1.01. 21
some neapolitan, or meaner man of pisa. 1.01.205
of pisa, sir, son to vincentio. 2.01.103
a mighty man of pisa; 2.01.104
within rich pisa walls, as any one | old signior 2.01.367
son unto vincentio of pisa, "/sigeia tellus," 3.01. 32 P
our turn — | and he shall be vincentio of pisa, 3.02.133
first, tell me, have you ever been at pisa? 4.02. 93
ay, sir, in pisa have i often been, | pisa 4.02. 94
often been, | pisa renowned for grave citizens. 4.02. 95
come, sir, we will better it in pisa. 4.04. 71
my name is call'd vincentio, my dwelling pisa, 4.05. 55
lucentio that his father is come from pisa, and 5.01. 28 P
PISANIO 25 FR 0.0028 REL FR 22 V 3 P
but, good pisanio, | when shall we hear from him CYM 1.03. 22
how now, pisanio? 1.05. 29
fare thee well, pisanio; 1.05. 84
what ho, pisanio! 1.06.139
what ho, pisanio! 1.06.148
what ho, pisanio! 1.06.155
how now, pisanio? 2.03.136
how now, pisanio? 3.02. 24
hear'st thou, pisanio? 3.02. 48
then, true pisanio, | who long'st like me to see 3.02. 52
pisanio! 3.04. 3
"thy mistress, pisanio, hath play'd the strumpet 3.04. 21 P
that part thou, pisanio, must act for me, if thy 3.04. 25 P
that man of hers, pisanio, her old servant, | i 3.05. 54
pisanio, thou that stand'st so for posthumus! 3.05. 56
when from the mountain top pisanio show'd thee, 3.06. 5
should meet, if pisanio have mapp'd it truly. 4.01. 2 P
pisanio, | i'll now taste of thy drug. 4.02. 37
pisanio, | all curses madded hecuba gave the 4.02.312
damn'd pisanio | hath with his forged letters 4.02.317
hath with his forged letters (damn'd pisanio!) 4.02.318
pisanio might have kill'd thee at the heart 4.02.322
pisanio? 4.02.323
o pisanio, | every good servant does not all 5.01. 5
"if pisanio | have," said she, "given his 5.05.245
PISANIO'S 1 FR 0.0001 REL FR 1 V 0 P
this is pisanio's deed, and cloten. CYM 4.02.329
PISH *(also push*)*
PISH 4 FR 0.0004 REL FR 1 V 3 P
pish! H5 2.01. 41 P
pish for thee, iceland dog! 2.01. 42
pish! OTH 2.01.263 P
pish! 4.01. 42 P
PISMIRES 1 FR 0.0001 REL FR 1 V 0 P
nettled and stung with pismires, when i hear 1H4 1.03.240
PISS 2 FR 0.0002 REL FR 1 V 1 P
jove, or who can blame me to piss my tallow? WIV 5.05. 14 P
now to be frampal, now to piss o' th' nettle! TNK 3.05. 57
PISSING–CONDUIT 1 FR 0.0001 REL FR 0 V 1 P
the pissing–conduit run nothing but claret wine 2H6 4.06. 3 P
PISSING–WHILE 1 FR 0.0001 REL FR 0 V 1 P
a pissing–while, but all the chamber smelt him. TGV 4.04. 19 P
PISTOL 40 FR 0.0045 REL FR 5 V 35 P
rascals, bardolph, nym, and pistol. WIV 1.01.125 P
pistol! 1.01.147 P
pistol, did you pick master slender's purse? 1.01.151 P
is this true, pistol? 1.01.159 P
no quips now, pistol! 1.03. 41 P
pistol him, pistol him! TN 2.05. 37 P
pistol him, pistol him! 2.05. 37 P
speed and with his pistol kills a sparrow flying 1H4 2.04.346 P
thou gets not my sword, but take my pistol, if 5.03. 51 P
welcome, ancient pistol. 2H4 2.04.111 P
here, pistol, i charge you with a cup of sack, 2.04.111 P
no more, pistol, i would not have you go off 2.04.136 P
discharge yourself of our company, pistol. 2.04.137 P
no, good captain pistol, not here, sweet captain 2.04.138 P
pistol, i would be quiet. 2.04.185 P
there's one pistol come from the court with news 5.03. 81 P
how now, pistol? 5.03. 83 P
what wind blew you hither, pistol? 5.03. 85 P
sir john, i am thy pistol and thy friend, | and 5.03. 93
then, pistol, lay thy head in furies' lap. 5.03.106
when pistol lies, do this, and fig me like | the 5.03.118
pistol, i will double–charge thee with dignities 5.03.124 P
o sweet pistol! 5.03.132 P
come, pistol, utter more to me, and withal 5.03.133 P
is dead that you and pistol beat amongst you. 5.04. 17 P
come here, pistol, stand behind me. 5.05. 10 P
pistol speaks nought but truth. 5.05. 38
come, lieutenant pistol, come, bardolph. 5.05. 89 P
what, are ancient pistol and you friends yet? H5 2.01. 3 P
here comes ancient pistol and his wife. 2.01. 26 P
how now, mine host pistol? 2.01. 28 P
if you grow foul with me, pistol, i will scour 2.01. 56 P
mine host pistol, you must come to my master, 2.01. 81 P
for pistol, he hath a killing tongue and a quiet 3.02. 34 P
he is call'd aunchient pistol. 3.06. 18 P
by your patience, aunchient pistol: 3.06. 30 P
aunchient pistol, i do partly understand your 3.06. 50 P
my name is pistol call'd. 4.01. 62
pragging knave, pistol, which you and yourself, 5.01. 6 P
god pless you, aunchient pistol! 5.01. 17 P
PISTOL–PROOF 1 FR 0.0001 REL FR 0 V 1 P
she is pistol–proof, sir; 2H4 2.04.116 P
PISTOL'S 3 FR 0.0003 REL FR 2 V 1 P
sir, ancient pistol's below, and would speak 2H4 2.04. 69 P
for i can take, and pistol's cock is up, | and H5 2.01. 52
if i can get him within my pistol's length, PER 1.01.166
PISTOLS 1 FR 0.0001 REL FR 0 V 1 P
ford's brothers watch the door with pistols, WIV 4.02. 52 P
/PIT 1 FR 0.0001 REL FR 1 V 0 P
/and /soon /lie /richard /in /an /earthy /pit! R2 4.01.219
PIT 20 FR 0.0022 REL FR 17 V 3 P
are all couch'd in a pit hard by herne's oak, WIV 5.03. 13 P
follow me into the pit, and when i give the 5.04. 3 P
she is fall'n | into a pit of ink, that the wide ADO 4.01.140
they'll fill a pit as well as better. 1H4 4.02. 66 P
and when they show'd me this abhorred pit, TIT 2.03. 98
lust, | and tumble me into some loathsome pit, 2.03.176
straight will i bring you to the loathsome pit 2.03.193
in this detested, dark, blood–drinking pit. 2.03.224
and shows the ragged entrails of this pit: 2.03.230
into the swallowing womb | of this deep pit, 2.03.240
which overshades the mouth of that same pit 2.03.273
this is the pit, and this the elder–tree. 2.03.277
sirs, drag them from the pit unto the prison, 2.03.283
what, are they in this pit? 2.03.286
our enemies have beat us to the pit. JC 5.05. 23
and at the pit of acheron | meet me i' th' MAC 3.05. 15
conscience and grace, to the profoundest pit! HAM 4.05.133
a pit of clay for to be made | for such a guest 5.01. 96
a pit of clay for to be made | /for /such /a 5.01.120
there is the sulphurous pit, burning, scalding, LR 4.06.128
PITCH* *(also peck*, pick*)*
/PITCH* 1 FR 0.0001 REL FR 1 V 0 P
/fresh /and /yet /unbruised /greeks /do /pitch TRO pr 14
PITCH* 32 FR 0.0036 REL FR 27 V 5 P
sky, it seems, would pour down stinking pitch, TMP 1.02. 3
me with urchin–shows, pitch me i' th' mire, 2.02. 5
she lov'd not the savor of tar nor of pitch, 2.02. 52
raze the sanctuary | and pitch our evils there? MM 2.02.171
i think they that touch pitch will be defil'd. ADO 3.03. 57 P
i am toiling in a pitch — pitch that defiles — LLL 4.03. 3 P
i am toiling in a pitch — pitch that defiles — 4.03. 3 P
there, | of what validity and pitch soe'er, TN 1.01. 12
how high a pitch his resolution soars! R2 1.01.109
known to many in our land by the name of pitch. 1H4 2.04.412 P
this pitch (as ancient writers do report) doth 2.04.413 P
the /word is "pitch and pay"; H5 2.03. 49
here, | it is of such a spacious lofty pitch, 1H6 2.03. 55
between two hawks, which flies the higher pitch, 2.04. 11
nails | shall pitch a field when we are dead. 3.01.103
place barrels of pitch upon the fatal stake, 5.04. 57
and what a pitch she flew above the rest! 2H6 2.01. 6
and bears his thoughts above his falcon's pitch. 2.01. 12
and convers'd with such | as, like to pitch, 2.01.192
here pitch our battle, hence we will not budge. 3H6 5.04. 66
seduc'd the pitch and height of his degree | to R3 3.07.188
here pitch our tent, even here in bosworth field 5.03. 1
to be fashion'd | into what pitch he please. H8 2.02. 49
and mount her pitch, whom thou in triumph long TIT 2.01. 14
bound | i cannot bound a pitch above dull woe; ROM 1.04. 21
wing | will make him fly an ordinary pitch, JC 1.01. 73
and enterprises of great pitch and moment | with HAM 3.01. 85
so will i turn her virtue into pitch, | and out OTH 2.03.360
and pitch between her arms to anger thee. TNK 2.02.217
vultur thought doth pitch the price so high VEN 551
but when from highmost pitch, with weary car, SON 7. 9
spirits taught to write | above a mortal pitch, 86. 6
PITCH–BALLS 1 FR 0.0001 REL FR 1 V 0 P
with two pitch–balls stuck in her face for eyes; LLL 3.01.197
PITCH'D *(also pight, pitched)*
PITCH'D 4 FR 0.0004 REL FR 3 V 1 P
they have pitch'd a toil: LLL 4.03. 2 P
on either hand thee there are squadrons pitch'd, 1H6 4.02. 23
loss of some pitch'd battle against warwick? 3H6 4.04. 4
the lands thou hast | lie in a pitch'd field. TIM 1.02.225
PITCHED 2 FR 0.0002 REL FR 2 V 0 P
have i not in a pitched battle heard | loud SHR 1.02.205
hedges | they pitched in the ground confusedly, 1H6 1.01.118
PITCHERS 2 FR 0.0002 REL FR 2 V 0 P
for you know | pitchers have ears, and i have SHR 4.04. 52
pitchers have ears. R3 2.04. 37
PITCHY 5 FR 0.0005 REL FR 5 V 0 P
the cozen'd thoughts | defiles the pitchy night; AWW 4.04. 24
whose pitchy mantle over–veil'd the earth. 1H6 2.02. 2
light, | but i will sort a pitchy day for thee; 3H6 5.06. 85
so did the merciless and pitchy night | fold in VEN 821
which blow these pitchy vapors from their biding LUC 550
/PITEOUS 1 FR 0.0001 REL FR 1 V 0 P
/told /the /most /piteous /tale /of /lear /and LR 5.03.215
PITEOUS 25 FR 0.0028 REL FR 23 V 2 P
tell your piteous heart | there's no harm done. TMP 1.02. 14
and piteous plainings of the pretty babes, ERR 1.01. 72
down his innocent nose | in piteous chase; AYL 2.01. 40
importance 'twere | most piteous to be wild), i WT 2.01.182
o, the most piteous cry of the poor souls! 3.03. 90 P
or in thy piteous heart plant thou thine ear, R2 5.03.126
or piteous they will look, like drowned mice. 1H6 1.02. 12
tears, | and say, "alas, it was a piteous deed!" 3H6 1.04.163
o piteous spectacle! 2.05. 73
to hear the piteous moan that rutland made R3 1.02.157
the most arch deed of piteous massacre | that 4.03. 2
at hand, | ensues his piteous and unpitied end. 4.04. 74
whose misadventur'd piteous overthrows | doth ROM pr 7
a piteous corse, a bloody piteous corse, | pale, 3.02. 54
a piteous corse, a bloody piteous corse, | pale, 3.02. 54
piteous predicament! 3.03. 86
but the true ground of all these piteous woes 5.03.180
o piteous spectacle! JC 3.02.198 P
and with a look so piteous in purport | as if he HAM 2.01. 79
he rais'd a sigh so piteous and profound | as it 2.01. 91
lest with this piteous action you convert | my 3.04.128
yea, and a woeful and a piteous nullity. TNK 3.05. 55
but for thy piteous lips no more had seen. VEN 504
wears | he pens her piteous clamors in her head, LUC 681
that piteous looks to phrygian shepherds lent; 1502
PITEOUSLY 2 FR 0.0002 REL FR 2 V 0 P
ruthful to hear, yet piteously perform'd. TIT 5.01. 66
was "antony," | and word it, prithee, piteously. ANT 4.13. 9
PITFALL 1 FR 0.0001 REL FR 1 V 0 P
the net nor lime, | the pitfall nor the gin. MAC 4.02. 35
PITH 7 FR 0.0008 REL FR 7 V 0 P
and that's my pith | of business 'twixt you and MM 1.04. 70
perhaps you mark'd not what's the pith of all. SHR 1.01.166
past or not arriv'd to pith and puissance; H5 3.pr. 21
height, | the pith and marrow of our attribute. HAM 1.04. 22
let it feed | even on the pith of life. 4.01. 23
since these arms of mine had seven years' pith, OTH 1.03. 83
palm, | the president of pith and livelihood, VEN 26
PITHLESS 1 FR 0.0001 REL FR 1 V 0 P
and pithless arms, like to a withered vine 1H6 2.05. 11
PITHY 1 FR 0.0001 REL FR 1 V 0 P
more pleasant, pithy, and effectual, | than hath SHR 3.01. 68
PITIE 1 FR 0.0001 REL FR 0 V 1 P
o, prenez misericorde! ayez pitie de moi! H5 4.04. 12 P
PITIED 19 FR 0.0021 REL FR 19 V 0 P
i pitied thee, | took pains to make thee speak, TMP 1.02.353
shall be lamented, pitied, and excus'd | of ADO 4.01.216
and know what 'tis to pity and be pitied, | let AYL 2.07.117
and therefore know how far i may be pitied. AWW 5.03.161
receive much better | than to be pitied of thee. WT 3.02.234
melted, | and barbarism itself have pitied him. R2 5.02. 36
win him, | for she's a woman to be pitied much. 3H6 3.01. 36
and pitied me, and kindly kiss'd my cheek; R3 2.02. 24
but all | was either pitied in him or forgotten. H8 2.01. 29
witness, | yet freshly pitied in our memories. 5.02. 66
the gracious duncan | was pitied of macbeth; MAC 3.06. 4
her mood will needs be pitied. HAM 4.05. 3
to my bosom | be as well neighbor'd, pitied, and LR 1.01.119
my mourning and importun'd tears hath pitied. 4.04. 26
for i know your plight is pitied | of him that ANT 5.02. 33

in our name, | are therefore to be pitied. 5.02.179
pitied nor hated, to the face of peril | myself CYM 5.01. 28
next, i pitied him; TNK 2.04. 11
it grows, | thy pity may deserve to pitied be. SON 142.12
PITIEDST 1 FR 0.0001 REL FR 1 V 0 P
thou pitiedst rutland, i will pity thee. 3H6 2.06. 74
PITIES 6 FR 0.0006 REL FR 5 V 1 P
o, ay; and pities them. TGV 5.02. 26
vain dew | perchance shall dry your pities; WT 2.01.110
a begging prince what beggar pities not? R3 1.04.267
if any power pities wretched tears, | to that i TIT 3.01.208
if any one relieves or pities him, | for the 5.03.181
here's a night pities neither wise men nor fools LR 3.02. 12 P
PITIFUL 32 FR 0.0036 REL FR 23 V 9 P
alas, i should be a pitiful lady! WIV 3.03. 53 P
me, and knows me, | how pitiful i deserve" — ADO 5.02. 29
making such pitiful dole over them that all the AYL 1.02.130 P
that pitiful rumor may report my flight | to AWW 3.02.127
the ballad is very pitiful, and as true. WT 4.04.281 P
but though my case be a pitiful one, i hope i 4.04.815 P
good ground, be pitiful and hurt me not! JN 4.03. 2
as i have done, thou wouldst be more pitiful. R2 5.02.103
precious rich crown for a pitiful bald crown! 1H4 2.04.382 P
i did never see such pitiful rascals. 4.02. 64 P
who should be pitiful, if you be not? 1H6 3.01.109
together with the pitiful complaints | of such 4.01. 57
women are soft, mild, pitiful, and flexible; 3H6 1.04.141
be pitiful, dread lord, and grant it then. 3.02. 32
or edward's soft and pitiful, like mine: R3 1.03.140
never | (but where he meant to ruin) pitiful. H8 4.02. 40
let all pitiful goers–between be call'd to the TRO 3.02.200 P
no, | nothing so kind, but something pitiful! TIT 2.03.156
in my cheeks, | be pitiful to my condemned sons, 3.01. 8
up, | for well you know this is a pitiful case. ROM 4.05. 99
pitiful sight! 5.03.174
our hearts you see not, they are pitiful; JC 3.01.169
night, | scarf up the tender eye of pitiful day, MAC 3.02. 47
all swoll'n and ulcerous, pitiful to the eye, 4.03.151
and shows a most pitiful ambition in the fool HAM 3.02. 44 P
a sight most pitiful in the meanest wretch, LR 4.06.204
'twas pitiful, 'twas wondrous pitiful. OTH 1.03.161
'twas pitiful, 'twas wondrous pitiful. 1.03.161
'tis pitiful; 5.02.210
heart to hear what pitiful cries they made to us PER 2.01. 21 P
let there bechance him pitiful mischances | to LUC 976
pitiful thrivers, in their gazing spent? SON 125. 8
PITIFUL–HEARTED 1 FR 0.0001 REL FR 0 V 1 P
kiss a dish of butter, pitiful–hearted titan, 1H4 2.04.121 P
PITIFULLY 4 FR 0.0004 REL FR 1 V 3 P
trust me, he beat him most pitifully. WIV 4.02.201 P
my lords, | as you are great, be pitifully good. TIM 3.05. 52
should be, which pitifully disaster the cheeks. ANT 2.07. 16 P
blow it to pieces, they are so pitifully sodden. PER 4.02. 19 P
PITILESS 4 FR 0.0004 REL FR 4 V 0 P
a fiend, a fairy, pitiless and rough; ERR 4.02. 35
must you be therefore proud and pitiless? AYL 3.05. 40
offended me, | even for his sake am i pitiless. TIT 2.03.162
that bide the pelting of this pitiless storm, LR 3.04. 29
PITS 1 FR 0.0001 REL FR 1 V 0 P
these lovely caves, these round enchanting pits, VEN 247
PITTANCE 1 FR 0.0001 REL FR 1 V 0 P
are like to have a thin and slender pittance. SHR 4.04. 61
PITTIE–WARD 1 FR 0.0001 REL FR 0 V 1 P
marry, sir, the pittie–ward, the park–ward — WIV 3.01. 5 P
PITTIKINS 1 FR 0.0001 REL FR 1 V 0 P
'od's pittikins! CYM 4.02.293
/PITY 4 FR 0.0004 REL FR 3 V 1 P
/showing /an /outward /pity, /yet /you /pilates R2 4.01.240
/do /those /villains /pity /who /are /punish'd LR 4.02. 54
/let /pity /not /be /believ'd!" 4.03. 29
for all the whole world — /'ud's /pity, who OTH 4.03. 75 P
PITY 254 FR 0.0287 REL FR 215 V 39 P
alack, for pity! TMP 1.02.132
to sigh | to th' winds, whose pity, sighing back 1.02.150
pity move my father | to be inclin'd my way! 1.02.447
sir, have pity, | i'll be his surety. 1.02.475
stone, and has no more pity in him than a dog. TGV 2.03. 11 P
pity the dearth that i have pined in, | by 2.07. 16
madam, i pity much your grievances, | which 4.03. 37
i cannot choose | but pity her. 4.04. 78
wherefore shouldst thou pity her? 4.04. 78
'tis pity love should be so contrary; 4.04. 83
why do i pity him | that with his very heart 4.04. 93
because i love him, i must pity him. 4.04. 96
'twere pity two such friends should be long foes 5.04.118
i will not say, pity me — 'tis not a WIV 2.01. 12 P
there will be pity taken on you. MM 1.02.109 P
be not a bawd's house, it is pity of her life, 2.01. 77 P
yet show some pity. 2.02. 99
for then i pity those i do not know, | which a 2.02.101
'tis pity of him. 2.03. 42
if my brother wrought by my pity, it should not 3.02.210 P
th' one has my pity; 4.02. 61
excludes all pity from our threat'ning looks: ERR 1.01. 10
so, | for we may pity, though not pardon thee. 1.01. 97
that takes pity on decay'd men and gives them 4.03. 26 P
'tis pity that thou liv'st | to walk where any 5.01. 27
they seem to pity the lady. ADO 2.03.222 P
if i do not take pity of her, i am a villain; 2.03.262 P
yea, or else it were pity but they should suffer 3.03. 2 P
thee, but, by this light, i take thee for pity. 5.04. 93 P
not wounding, pity would not let me do't; LLL 4.01. 27
sir, it were pity you should get your living by 5.02.496 P
ay me, for pity! MND 2.02.147
come hither as a lion, it were pity of my life. 3.01. 43 P
the more the pity that some honest neighbors 3.01.145 P
this you should pity rather than despise. 3.02.235
if you have any pity, grace, or manners, | you 3.02.241
her dotage now i do begin to pity. 4.01. 47
into this place, 'twere pity on my life. 5.01.226
beshrew my heart, but i pity the man. 5.01.290 P
no, that were pity. MV 2.02.200
uncapable of pity, void and empty | from any 4.01. 5
glancing an eye of pity on his losses, | that 4.01. 27
the more pity, that fools may not speak wisely AYL 1.02. 86 P
in pity of the challenger's youth i would fain 1.02.159 P
and pity her for her good father's sake; 1.02.281
speak to the people, and they pity her. 1.03. 79
fair sir, i pity her, | and wish, for her sake 2.04. 75
and know what 'tis to pity and be pitied, | let 2.07.117
of drops that sacred pity hath engend'red; 2.07.123
though it be pity to see such a sight, it well 3.02.242 P
comes, | afflict me with thy mocks, pity me not, 3.05. 33
not, | as till that time i shall not pity thee. 3.05. 34
sweet phebe, pity me. 3.05. 84
do you pity him? 4.03. 66 P
no, he deserves no pity. 4.03. 66 P
e la mi, show pity, or i die." SHR 3.01. 78
qualities, there commendations go with pity: AWW 1.01. 43 P
that i wish well. 'tis pity — 1.01.179
what's pity? 1.01.180 P
then give pity | to her whose state is such that 1.03.213
name of justice, | without all terms of pity. 2.03.166
i'll have no more pity of his age than i would 2.03.240 P
'tis pity he is not honest. 3.05. 82
i do pity his distress in my /similes of comfort 5.02. 24 P
of air and earth, | but you should pity me! TN 1.05.276
and we do not, it is pity of our lives. 2.05. 12 P
i pity you. 3.01.123
a vulgar proof | that very oft we pity enemies. 3.01.125
will thereto add | 'tis pity she's not honest — WT 2.01. 68
aside, have done | like offices of pity. 2.03.189
my misery, yet with eyes | of pity, not revenge! 3.02.123
i'll take it up for pity — yet i'll tarry till 3.03. 76 P
i cannot say 'tis pity | she lacks instructions, 4.04.581
which though it be great pity, yet it is 4.04.775 P
you pity not the state, nor the remembrance | of 5.01. 25
by the windy breath | of soft petitions, pity, JN 2.01.478
this is pity now, | that, hang'd and drawn and 2.01.507
and is't not pity, o my grieved friends, | that 5.02. 24
for him, | unless you call it good to pity him, R2 2.01.236
what pity is it | that he had not so trimm'd and 3.04. 55
that you in pity may dissolve to dew | and wash 5.01. 9
forget to pity him, lest thy pity prove | a 5.03. 57
lest thy pity prove | a serpent that will sting 5.03. 57
speak with me, pity me, open the door! 5.03. 77
say "pardon," king, let pity teach thee how. 5.03.116
pity may move thee "pardon" to rehearse. 5.03.128
and that it was great pity, so it was, | this 1H4 1.03. 59
were't not for laughing, i should pity him. 2.02.110
that he is old, the more the pity, his white 2.04.468 P
zeal, | my father, in kind heart and pity mov'd, 4.03. 64
he hath a tear for pity, and a hand | open as 2H4 4.04. 31
take pity of your town and of your people, H5 3.03. 28
where — o for pity! 4.pr. 49
was, | again, in pity of my hard distress, 1H6 2.05. 87
henry, | pity the city of london, pity us! 3.01. 77
henry, | pity the city of london, pity us! 3.01. 77
for god's sake pity my case. 2H6 1.03.214 P
pity was all the fault that was in me; 3.01.125
in great affairs, | too full of foolish pity; 3.01.225
which makes me hope you are not void of pity. 4.07. 64
henceforth i will not have to do with pity. 5.02. 56
sweet clifford, pity me! 3H6 1.03. 36
such pity as my rapier's point affords. 1.03. 37
thou hast one son, for his sake pity me, | lest 1.03. 40
lenity | and harmful pity must be laid aside. 2.02. 10
were it not pity that this goodly boy | should 2.02. 34
had slept, | and we, in pity of the gentle king, 2.02.161
o, pity, god, this miserable age! 2.05. 88
o, pity, pity, gentle heaven, pity! 2.05. 96
o, pity, pity, gentle heaven, pity! 2.05. 96
o, pity, pity, gentle heaven, pity! 2.05. 96
the foe is merciless, and will not pity; 2.06. 25
for at their hands i have deserv'd no pity. 2.06. 26
thou pitiedst rutland, i will pity thee. 2.06. 74
'twere pity they should lose their father's 3.02. 31
not that i pity henry's misery, | but seek 3.03.264
and 'twere pity | to sunder them that yoke so 4.01. 22
my pity hath been balm to heal their wounds, 4.08. 41
i, that have neither pity, love, nor fear. 5.06. 68
more pity that the eagles should be mew'd, R3 1.01.132
no beast so fierce but knows some touch of pity. 1.02. 71
may move your hearts to pity if you mark him. 1.03.348
my friend, i spy some pity in thy looks. 1.04.263
poor heart, adieu, i pity thy complaining. 4.01. 87
pity, you ancient stones, those tender babes 4.01. 98
tear–falling pity dwells not in this eye. 4.02. 65
loves me, | and if i die no soul will pity me. 5.03.201
i myself | find in myself no pity to myself? 5.03.203
those that can pity, here | may (if they think H8 pr 5
you that thus far have come to pity me, | hear 2.01. 56
o, this is full of pity! 2.01.137
the avaunt, it is a pity | would move a monster. 2.03. 10
so much the more | must pity drop upon her. 2.03. 18
and justice, | and to bestow your pity on me; 2.04. 14
have me | (if you have any justice, any pity, 3.01.116
shipwrack'd upon a kingdom, where no pity, | no 3.01.149
whilst your great goodness, out of holy pity, 3.02.263
out of pity taken | a load would sink a navy — 3.02.382
that his noble grace would have some pity | upon 4.02.139
out of our easiness and childish pity | to one 5.02. 60
and would, as i shall pity, i could help! TRO 4.03. 11
let's leave the hermit pity with our mother, 5.03. 45
that you might leave pricking it for pity. COR 1.03. 86 P
within my view, | and wrath o'erwhelm'd my pity. 1.09. 86
people | deserve such pity of him as the wolf 4.06.110
when i said banish him, i said 'twas pity. 4.06.140
and his injury | the jailer to his pity. 5.01. 65
shall poison rather | than pity note how much. 5.02. 87
'longs more pride | than pity to our prayers. 5.03.171
'tis pity they should take him for a stag. TIT 2.03. 71
do thou entreat her show a woman's pity. 2.03.147
the lion, mov'd with pity, did endure | to have 2.03.151
for pity of mine age, whose youth was spent | in 3.01. 2
if they did mark, | they would not pity me; 3.01. 35
her life was beastly and devoid of pity, | and, 5.03.199
and, being dead, let birds on her take pity. 5.03.200
both, | and pity 'tis you liv'd at odds so long. ROM 1.02. 5
is there no pity sitting in the clouds, | that 3.05.196
'tis pity bounty had not eyes behind, | that man TIM 1.02.163
a wrench — would all were well — 'tis pity — 2.02.209
men must learn now with pity to dispense, | for 3.02. 86
for pity is the virtue of the law, | and none 3.05. 8
i am thy friend, and pity thee, dear timon. 4.03. 98
how dost thou pity him whom thou dost trouble? 4.03. 99
pity not honor'd age for his white beard, | he 4.03.112
eyes, | are not within the leaf of pity writ, 4.03.118
speaks it, | in pity of our aged and our youth, 5.01.176
and pity to the general wrong of rome — | as JC 3.01.170
as fire drives out fire, so pity pity — | hath 3.01.171
as fire drives out fire, so pity pity — | hath 3.01.171
all pity chok'd with custom of fell deeds; 3.01.269
and i perceive you feel | the dint of pity. 3.02.194
and pity, like a naked new–born babe, | striding MAC 1.07. 21
for unkindness | than pity for mischance. 3.04. 42
pity me not, but lend thy serious hearing | to HAM 1.05. 5
that he's mad, 'tis true, 'tis true 'tis pity, 2.02. 97
'tis true 'tis pity, | and pity 'tis 'tis true. 2.02. 98
and the more pity that great folk should have 5.01. 26 P
i desir'd their leave that i might pity him, LR 3.03. 3 P
o pity! 3.06. 58
treasons to us, | who is too good to pity thee. 3.07. 90
in pity of his misery, to dispatch | his nighted 4.05. 12
and feeling sorrows, | am pregnant to good pity. 4.06.223
these white flakes | did challenge pity of them. 4.07. 30
i should ev'n die with pity | to see another 4.07. 52
makes us tremble, | touches us not with pity. 5.03.233
and i lov'd her that she did pity them. OTH 1.03.168
'tis pity of him. 2.03.125
and 'tis great pity that the noble moor | should 2.03.138
but yet the pity of it, iago! 4.01.195 P
o iago, the pity of it, iago! 4.01.196 P
it were pity to cast them away for nothing, ANT 1.02.138 P
'tis pity of him. 1.04. 71
pity me, charmian, | but do not speak to me. 2.05.118
each heart in rome does love and pity you; 3.06. 92
he | does pity, as constrained blemishes, | not 3.13. 59
our care and pity is so much upon you, | that we 5.02.188
story is | no less in pity than his glory which 5.02.362
it had been pity you should have been put CYM 1.04. 40 P
i am bound to wonder, i am bound | to pity too. 1.06. 82
what do you pity, sir? 1.06. 82
wrack discern you in me | deserves your pity? 1.06. 85
why do you pity me? 1.06. 89
my heart | with pity that doth make me sick. 1.06.119
tear, took pity | from most true wretchedness. 3.04. 60
yet left in heaven as small a drop of pity | as 4.02.304
came crying 'mongst his foes, | a thing of pity! 5.04. 47
which care of them, not pity of myself — | who PER 1.02. 29
for them to play upon, entreats you pity him. 2.01. 61
now, by the gods, i pity his misfortune, | and 2.03. 90
/lone bosom | inflame too nicely, nor let pity, 4.01. 6
you live as ye do makes pity in your lovers; 4.02.119 P
seldom but that pity begets you a good opinion, 4.02.120 P
o, pity, duke! TNK 1.01. 47
that equally canst poise sternness with pity, 1.01. 86
my brother's heart, and warm it to some pity, 1.01.128
perceive you none that do arouse your pity, 1.02. 30
yes, i pity | decays where e'er i find them, but 1.02. 31
'tis pity they are in prison, and 'twere pity 2.01. 22 P
in prison, and 'twere pity they should be out. 2.01. 22 P
thou shalt have pity of us both, o theseus, | if 3.06.172
alas, the pity! 3.06.185
yet that i will be woman, and have pity, | my 3.06.191
by that you would have pity in another, | by 3.06.198
you are a right woman, sister, you have pity, 3.06.215
their knees | begg'd with such handsome pity, 4.01. 9
nothing but my pity. 4.01. 42
alas, what pity it is! 4.01. 94
'tis pity love should be so tyrannous. 4.02.146
o, what pity | enough for such a chance! 5.03. 59
infinite pity | that four such eyes should be so 5.03.144
we expire, | and not without men's pity; 5.04. 5
"o, pity," gan she cry, "flint–hearted boy, VEN 95
"pity," she cries, "some favor, some remorse!" 257
for pity now she can no more detain him; 577
which knows no pity, but is still severe; 1000
and straight, in pity of his tender years, 1091
this moves in him more rage and lesser pity | to LUC 468
soft pity enters at an iron gate. 595
that thou shalt see thy state, and pity mine." 644
to make him moan, but pity not his moans; 977
round clear pearls of his, that move thy pity, 1553
ditty, | that to hear it was great pity. PP 20.12
none takes pity on thy pain. 20.20
flattering, | "pity but he were a king!" 20.40
pity the world, or else this glutton be, | to SON 1.13
pity me then, and wish i were renew'd, | whilst 111. 8
pity me then, dear friend, and i assure ye 111.13
ye | even that your pity is enough to cure me. 111.14
your love and pity doth th' impression fill 112. 1
grace, | and suit thy pity like in every part. 132.12
root pity in thy heart, that, when it grows, 142.11
it grows, | thy pity may deserve to pitied be. 142.12
have of my suffering youth some feeling pity LC 178
PITYING 6 FR 0.0006 REL FR 6 V 0 P
succeeding, truly pitying | my father's loss, H8 2.01.112
our mistress' sorrows we were pitying. 2.03. 53
ransoming him, or pitying, threat'ning th' other COR 1.06. 36
pitying | the pangs of barr'd affections, though CYM 1.01. 81
and ever since, as pitying lucrece' woes, LUC 1747
thine eyes i love, and they, as pitying me, SON 132. 1
PITY–PLEADING 1 FR 0.0001 REL FR 1 V 0 P
her pity–pleading eyes are sadly fixed | in the LUC 561
PITY'S 2 FR 0.0002 REL FR 2 V 0 P
pity's sleeping: TIM 4.03.485
for pity's sake and true gentility's, | hear and TNK 1.01. 25
PITY–WANTING 1 FR 0.0001 REL FR 1 V 0 P
express | the manner of my pity–wanting pain. SON 140. 4
PIU 1 FR 0.0001 REL FR 1 V 0 P
"piu per dolcera que per forca." PER 2.02. 27
PIUS 1 FR 0.0001 REL FR 1 V 0 P
surnamed pius | for many good and great deserts TIT 1.01. 23
PIZZLE 1 FR 0.0001 REL FR 0 V 1 P
you dried neat's tongue, you bull's pizzle, you 1H4 2.04.245 P
PLAC'D 23 FR 0.0026 REL FR 21 V 2 P
which since i know they virtuously are plac'd, TGV 4.03. 38
planted and plac'd and possess'd by my master ADO 3.03.150 P
like my master's, be | plac'd in contempt! TN 1.05.288
(who is, if every owner were well plac'd, 1H4 4.03. 94
well plac'd. H5 3.07.118 P
plac'd behind | with purpose to relieve and 1H6 1.01.132
a piece of ord'nance 'gainst it i have plac'd, 1.04. 15

words sweetly plac'd and /modestly directed. 5.03.179
thou shalt be plac'd as viceroy under him, | and 5.04.131
were plac'd the heads of edmund duke of somerset 2H6 1.02. 29
and plac'd a choir of such enticing birds | that 1.03. 89
hath plac'd thy beauty's image and thy virtue. 3H6 3.03. 64
two women plac'd together makes cold weather. H8 1.04. 22
side | they have plac'd their men of trust? COR 1.06. 52
doubt and suspect, alas, are plac'd too late; TIM 4.03.512
upon my head they plac'd a fruitless crown, MAC 3.01. 60
and i'll be plac'd (so please you) in the ear HAM 3.01.184
it, gave't th' impression, plac'd it safely, 5.02. 52
my resolution's plac'd, and i have nothing | of ANT 5.02.238
ungentle fortune | have plac'd me in this sty, PER 4.06. 97
her, and plac'd her | here in diana's temple. 5.03. 24
how she came plac'd here in the temple; 5.03. 67
in love, | there a nay is plac'd without remove. PP 17. 8

/PLACE 5 FR 0.0005 REL FR 5 V 0 P

/thy /land, | /come /place /him /here /by /me, LR 1.04.142
/robed /man /of /justice, /take /thy /place, 3.06. 36
/corruption /in /the /place! 3.06. 55
/and /her /father | /requires /a /fitter /place. 5.03. 59
hast likewise blest a /place | with thy sole TNK 3.01. 10

PLACE 442 FR 0.0499 REL FR 363 V 79 P

springs, brine–pits, barren place and fertile. TMP 1.02.338
upon our guard, | or that we quit this place. 2.01.322
den, | the most opportune place, the strong'st 4.01. 26
whom i give thee pow'r) here to this place. 4.01. 38
here on this grass–plot, in this very place, 4.01. 73
father and a wise | makes this place paradise. 4.01.124
being awake, enforce them to this place; 5.01.100
worth, | and you an officer fit for the place. TGV 1.02. 45
never welcome to a place till some certain shot 2.05. 6 P
out with't, and place it for her chief virtue. 3.01.335 P
no more adhere and keep place together than the WIV 2.01. 62 P
by mistaking the place where i erected it. 2.02.217 P
admittance, authentic in your place and person, 2.02.227 P
i never heard a man of his place, gravity, and 3.01. 57 P
have i not, at de place i did appoint? 3.01. 93 P
this is the place appointed. 3.01. 95 P
me | to look into the bottom of my place. MM 1.01. 78
though you change your place, you need not 1.02.107 P
whether the tyranny be in his place, | or in his 1.02.163
my absolute power and place here in vienna, 1.03. 13
ho! peace be in this place! 1.04. 6
a novice of this place, and the fair sister | to 1.04. 19
upon his place, | and with full line of his 1.04. 55
had time coher'd with place, or place with 2.01. 11
time coher'd with place, or place with wishing, 2.01. 11
long have you been in this place of constable? 2.01.259 P
do you your office, or give up your place, | and 2.02. 13
dispose of her | to some more fitter place; 2.02. 17
o place, o form, | how often dost thou with thy 2.04. 12
whose credit with the judge, or own great place, 2.04. 92
my vouch against you, and my place i' th' state, 2.04.156
and the place answer to convenience. 3.01.248 P
to stead up your appointment, go in your place. 3.01.251 P
at that place call upon me, and dispatch with 3.01.265 P
o place and greatness! 4.01. 59
shrift and advise him for a better place. 4.02.208 P
your provost knows the place where he abides, 5.01.252
respect to your great place! 5.01.292
sit you down, | we'll borrow place of him. 5.01.362
and yet here's one in place i cannot pardon. 5.01.499
we shall employ thee in a worthier place. 5.01.531
or that, or any place that harbors men. ERR 1.01.136
in what safe place you have bestow'd my money; 1.02. 78
if thou hadst been dromio to–day in my place, 3.01. 46
i'll meet you at that place some hour hence. 3.01.122
he took this place for sanctuary, | and it shall 5.01. 94
vale, | the place of /death and sorry execution, 5.01.121
and all that are assembled in this place | that 5.01.397
you to heaven, here's no place for you maids." ADO 2.01. 46 P
dost thou not suspect my place? 4.02. 74 P
to specify, when time and place shall serve, 5.01.256 P
fit in his place and time. LLL 1.01. 98
then for the place where? 1.01.240 P
but to the place where? 1.01.244 P
thy own wish wish i thee in every place. 2.01.178
most rude melancholy, valor gives thee place. 3.01. 68
and to that place the sharp athenian law MND 1.01.162
in that same place thou hast appointed me 1.01.177
lysander and myself will fly this place. 1.01.203
what worser place can i beg in your love | (and 2.01.208
love | (and yet a place of high respect with me) 2.01.209
and the ill counsel of a desert place | with the 2.01.218
a marvail's convenient place for our rehearsal. 3.01. 3 P
but i will not stir from this place, do what 3.01.122 P
thou seest these lovers seek a place to fight; 3.02.354
thou run'st before me, shifting every place, 3.02.423
should as lion come in strife | into this place, 5.01.226
grace, | will we sing, and bless this place. 5.01.400
not in one bottom trusted, | nor to one place; MV 1.01. 43
means | to hold a rival place with one of them, 1.01.174
day, | in such a place, such sum or sums as are 1.03.147
i be misconst'red in the place i go to, | and 2.02.188
i think they call the place, a very dangerous 3.01. 4 P
jessica | in place of lord bassanio and myself. 3.04. 39
know | a many fools, that stand in better place, 3.05. 68
go give him courteous conduct to this place. 4.01.148
you are welcome, take your place. 4.01.170
rain from heaven | upon the place beneath. 4.01.186
with his hinds, bars me the place of a brother, AYL 1.01. 20 P
here, for here is the place appointed for the 1.02.145 P
only in the world i fill up a place, which may 1.02.192 P
in friendship counsel you | to leave this place. 1.02.262
to the which place a poor sequest'red stag, 2.01. 33
show me the place. 2.01. 66
this is no place, this house is but a butchery; 2.03. 27
when i was at home, i was in a better place, but 2.04. 17 P
can in this desert place buy entertainment, 2.04. 72
i like this place, | and willingly could waste 2.04. 94
are you native of this place? 3.02.338 P
to meet me in this place of the forest and to 3.03. 45 P
west of this place, down in the neighbor bottom, 4.03. 78
left on your right hand brings you to the place. 4.03. 80
as how i came into that desert place — | /in 4.03.141
as firmly as yourself were still in place, | yea SHR 1.02.156
you shall supply the bridegroom's place, | and 3.02.249
thou shouldst have heard in how miry a place, 4.01. 75 P
the taming–school! what, is there such a place? 4.02. 55
and i had thee in place where, thou shouldst 4.03.150 P
and place your hands below your husband's foot; 5.02.177
that they take place when virtue's steely bones AWW 1.01.103
the court's a learning place, and he is one — 1.01.177
him | he us'd as creatures of another place, 1.02. 42
i fill a place, i know't. 1.02. 69
why, what place make you special, when you put 2.02. 5 P
from lowest place /when virtuous things proceed, 2.03.125
the place is dignified by th' doer's deed. 2.03.126
that time and place with this deceit so lawful 3.07. 38
faithfully confirm'd by the rector of the place. 4.03. 59 P
be the officer at a place there call'd mile–end, 4.03.269 P
there's place and means for every man alive. 4.03.339
to which place | we have convenient convoy. 4.04. 9
not three hours' travel from this very place. TN 1.02. 23
give us the place alone, we will hear this 1.05.218 P
is there no respect of place, persons, nor time 2.03. 91 P
let all the rest give place. 2.04. 79
say | my love can give no place, bide no denay. 2.04.124
them i know my place as i would they should do 2.05. 54 P
out, | for which, if i be lapsed in this place, 3.03. 36
that screws me from my true place in your favor, 5.01.123
embrace me till each circumstance | of place, 5.01.252
like a cipher | (yet standing in rich place), i WT 1.02. 7
which i'll not call a creature of thy place, 2.01. 83
to some remote and desert place quite out | of 2.03.176
that thou commend it strangely to some place 2.03.182
hurried | here to this place, i' th' open air, 3.02.105
this place is famous for the creatures | of prey 3.03. 12
thou shalt accompany us to the place, where we 4.02. 47 P
than herself, | too noble for this place. 4.04.159
have you thought on | a place whereto you'll go? 4.04.537
the place of your dwelling? 4.04.718 P
let's from this place. 5.03.146
would i might never stir from off this place, JN 1.01.145
and he that stands upon a slipp'ry place | makes 3.04.137
as thus to drop them still upon one place, R2 3.03.166
here in this place | i'll set a bank of rue, 3.04.104
fellow, give place, here is no longer stay. 5.05. 95
choose out some secret place, some reverent room 5.06. 25
after them and appoint them a place of meeting, 1H4 1.02.170 P
said | to such a person, and in such a place, 1.03. 72
in richard's time — what do you call the place? 1.03.242
to the wars, and thy place shall be honorable. 2.04.544 P
i'll have the current in this place damm'd up, 3.01.100
thy place in council thou hast rudely lost, 3.02. 32
but a braver place | in my heart's love hath no 4.01. 7
when yet you were in place and in account 5.01. 37
doth this become your place, your time, and 2H4 2.01. 66
with me as my dog, and he holds his place, for 2.02.107 P
at the old place, my lord, in eastcheap. 2.02.148 P
there, | or it will seek me in another place, 2.03. 49
or to the place of diff'rence call the swords 4.01.179
but you misuse the reverence of your place, 4.02. 23
of what condition are you, and of what place? 4.03. 2 P
knight is your degree, and your place the dale. 4.03. 6 P
and the dungeon your place, a place deep enough; 4.03. 8 P
and the dungeon your place, a place deep enough; 4.03. 8 P
thou hast a better place in his affection | than 4.04. 22
which, as immediate from thy place and blood, 4.05. 42
your highness pleased to forget my place, | the 5.02. 77
what i have done that misbecame my place, | my 5.02.100
figure may | attest in little place a million, H5 pr 16
day and cry all, "we died at such a place" — 4.01.138 P
art thou aught else but place, degree, and form, 4.01.246
will it give place to flexure and low bending? 4.01.255
now in london place him — | as yet the 5.pr. 35
it was in a place where i could not breed no 5.01. 10 P
each hath his place and function to attend: 1H6 1.01.173
reignier, stand thou as dolphin in my place; 1.02. 61
i'll use to carry thee out of this place. 1.03. 43
draw, men, for all this privileged place — 1.03. 46
where is best place to make our batt'ry next? 1.04. 65
'tis sure they found some place | but weakly 2.01. 73
with long continuance in a settled place. 2.05.106
priest, this place commands my patience, | or 3.01. 8
occasions | at eltam place i told your majesty. 3.01.155
take heed, be wary how you place your words, 3.02. 3
lord, | we will bestow you in some better place, 3.02. 88
we'll set thy statue in some holy place, | and 3.03. 14
france were no place for henry's warriors, | nor 3.03. 22
and in our coronation take your place. 3.04. 27
doth stop my cornets, were in talbot's place! 4.03. 25
place barrels of pitch upon the fatal stake, 5.04. 57
and greatness of his place be grief to us, | yet 2H6 1.01.173
if somerset be unworthy of the place, | let york 1.03.105
and at his pleasure will resign my place. 1.03.121
though in this place most master wear no 1.03.146
next, if i be appointed for the place, | my lord 1.03.167
them | for single combat in convenient place, 1.03.208
from thence, unto the place of execution. 2.03. 6
as place duke humphrey for the king's protector? 3.01.250
nor let the rain of heaven wet this place | to 3.02.341
is term'd the civill'st place of all this isle: 4.07. 61
alas, he hath no home, no place to fly to; 4.08. 38
give place! 5.01.104
henry had none, but did usurp the place. 3H6 1.02. 25
and rear it in the place your father's stands. 2.06. 86
in this self place where now we mean to stand. 3.01. 11
thy place is fill'd, thy sceptre wrung from thee 3.01. 16
to strengthen and support king edward's place. 3.01. 52
to take their rooms, ere i can place myself: 3.02.132
for i have heard that she was there in place. 4.01.103
for choosing me when clarence is in place. 4.06. 31
shadow | to henry's body, and supply his place; 4.06. 50
his currish riddles sorts not with this place. 5.05. 26
for he was fitter for that place than earth. R3 1.02.108
and thou unfit for any place, but hell. 1.02.109
yes, one place else, if you will hear me name it 1.02.110
never came poison from so sweet a place. 1.02.146
when you have done, repair to crosby place. 1.03.344
to those whose dealings have deserv'd the place 3.01. 49
and those who have the wit to claim the place. 3.01. 50
i do not like the tower, of any place. 3.01. 68
did julius caesar build that place, my lord? 3.01. 69
he did, my gracious lord, begin that place, 3.01. 70
thou didst usurp my place, and dost thou not 4.04.109
for him, which buys | a place next to the king. H8 1.01. 66
his mind and place | infecting one another, yea, 1.01.161
arise, and take place by us. 1.02. 10
let me say | 'tis but the fate of place, and the 1.02. 75
place you that side, i'll take the charge of 1.04. 20
his person | more worthy this place than myself, 1.04. 79
i would not be so sick though for his place. 2.02. 82
that | a woman of less place might ask by law: 2.02.111
doctor pace | in this man's place before him? 2.02.122
the most convenient place that i can think of 2.02.137
o, 'tis a tender place, and i must leave her. 2.02.143
you sign your place and calling, in full seeming 2.04.108
for if | it did take place, "i do," quoth he, 3.02. 34
bade me enjoy it, with the place and honors, 3.02.248
more is chosen | lord chancellor in your place. 3.02.394
the queen | to a prepar'd place in the choir, 4.01. 64
as not thus to suffer | a man of his place, and 5.02. 30
both in his private conscience and his place, 5.02. 75
than but once think his place becomes thee not. 5.02.168
is this a place to roar in? 5.03. 7 P
they fell on, i made good my place; 5.03. 54 P
here, here's an excellent place, here we may see TRO 1.02.181 P
the which, most mighty for thy place and sway, 1.03. 60
centre | observe degree, priority, and place, 1.03. 86
but by degree, stand in authentic place? 1.03.108
in full as proud a place | as broad achilles; 1.03.189
they place before his hand that made the engine, 1.03.208
we fear to warrant in our native place! 2.02. 96
we dare not move the question of our place, | or 2.03. 82
those honors | that are without him, as place, 3.03. 82
keeps place with thought and almost, like the 3.03.199
let me be privileg'd by my place and message, 4.04.130
in what place of the field doth calchas keep? 4.05.278
this place is dangerous, | the time right deadly 5.02. 38
more attain'd than by | a place below the first; COR 1.01.266
the people, when he shall stand for his place. 2.01.149 P
nay, keep your place. 2.02. 66
a place of potency and sway o' th' state, | if 2.03.182
in his person wrought | to be set high in place, 2.03.247
here's no place for you; 4.05. 8 P
here's no place for you. 4.05. 30 P
till from forth this place | i lead espous'd my TIT 1.01.327
he that would vouch it in any place but here. 1.01.360
these two have 'ticed me hither to this place: 2.03. 92
and with thine own hands kill me in this place! 2.03.169
a very fatal place it seems to me. 2.03.202
ay, such a place there is where we did hunt | (o 4.01. 55
heir, | and substituted in the place of mine, 4.02.159
from the place where you behold us pleading, 5.03.130
the measure done, i'll watch her place of stand, ROM 1.05. 50
and the place death, considering who thou art, 2.02. 64
by whose direction foundst thou out this place? 2.02. 79
either withdraw unto some private place, | or 3.01. 51
together with the terror of the place — | as in 4.03. 38
to lie discolor'd by this place of peace? 5.03.143
this is the place, there where the torch doth 5.03.171
as the time and place | doth make against me, of 5.03.224
post he came from mantua | to this same place, 5.03.274
sirrah, what made your master in this place? 5.03.280
angry at him, | that might have known my place. TIM 3.03. 14
the place which i have feasted, does it now 3.04. 82
meat cool ere we can agree upon the first place; 3.06. 68 P
make the hoar leprosy ador'd, place thieves, 4.03. 36
this place? 4.03.204
as i took note of the place, it cannot be far 5.01. 1
by all description this should be the place. 5.03. 1
and land, | in every place, save here in italy. JC 1.03. 88
which, by the right and virtue of my place, | i 2.01.269
i'll get me to a place more void, and there 2.04. 37
sirrah, give place. 3.01. 10
but there's but one in all doth hold his place. 3.01. 65
tell him, so please him come unto this place, 3.01.140
no place will please me so, no mean of death, 3.01.161
of his dying, a place in the commonwealth, as 3.02. 43 P
i fear there will a worse come in his place. 3.02.111
look, in this place ran cassius' dagger through; 3.02.174
we'll burn his body in the holy place, | and 3.02.254
no use, | if you give place to accidental evils. 4.03.146
good reasons must of force give place to better: 4.03.203
where the place? MAC 1.01. 6
nor time, nor place, | did then adhere, and yet 1.07. 51
but screw your courage to the sticking place, 1.07. 60
why did you bring these daggers from the place? 2.02. 45
but this place is too cold for hell. 2.03. 16 P
a falcon, tow'ring in her pride of place, | was 2.04. 12
here is a place reserv'd, sir. 3.04. 45
in a place | from whence himself does fly? 4.02. 7
in no place so unsanctified | where such as thou 4.02. 81
we will perform in measure, time, and place. 5.09. 39
barnardo hath my place. | give you good night. HAM 1.01. 17
as he in his particular act and place | may give 1.03. 26
the very place puts toys of desperation, 1.04. 75
as they fell out by time, by means, and place, 2.02.127
get you a place. 3.02. 91
it will but skin and film the ulcerous place, 3.04.147
bestow this place on us a little while. 4.01. 4
not there, seek him i' th' other place yourself. 4.03. 35 P
no place indeed should murther sanctuarize, 4.07.127
which nor our nature nor our place can bear, LR 1.01.171
grace, | i would prefer him to a better place. 1.01.274
i will place you where you shall hear us confer 1.02. 90 P
my frame of nature | from the fix'd place; 1.04.269
o sir, fly this place, | intelligence is given 2.01. 20
no place | that guard and most unusual vigilance 2.03. 3
what's he that hath so much thy place mistook 2.04. 12
ere i was risen from the place that showed | my 2.04. 29
to no more | will i give place or notice. 2.04.249
here is the place, my lord; 3.04. 1
from that place | i shall no leading need. 4.01. 77
come on, sir, here's the place; 4.06. 11
he led me to that place. 4.06. 79
not, time and place will be fruitfully offer'd. 4.06.264 P
deliver me, and supply the place for your labor. 4.06.268 P
for i am mainly ignorant | what place this is, 4.07. 65
found my brother's way | to the forfended place? 5.01. 11
bore the commission of my place and person, 5.03. 64

maugre thy strength, place, youth, and eminence, 5.03.132
the dark and vicious place where thee he got 5.03.173
i know my price, i am worth no worse a place. OTH 1.01. 11
my spirits and my place have in their power | to 1.01.103
it seems not meet, nor wholesome to my place, 1.01.145
neither my place, nor aught i heard of business, 1.03. 53
you best know the place. 1.03.121
the fortitude of the place is best known to you; 1.03.222 P
wife, | due reference of place and exhibition, 1.03.237
to get his place and to plume up my will | in 1.03.393
him to be unworthy of his place that does those 2.03.101 P
should hazard such a place as his own second 2.03.139
have you forgot all place of sense and duty? 2.03.167
drunkenness to give place to the devil wrath: 2.03.297 P
as the time, the place, and the condition of 2.03.300 P
i will ask him for my place again, he shall tell 2.03.303 P
her help to put you in your place again. 2.03.319 P
that, i being absent and my place supplied, | my 3.03. 17
emilia here, | i give thee warrant of thy place. 3.03. 20
although 'tis fit that cassio have his place — 3.03.246
she haunts me in every place. 4.01.133 P
cassio shall have my place. 4.01.261
i should have found in some place of my soul | a 4.02. 52
what place? 4.02.138
from venice to depute cassio in othello's place. 4.02.221 P
why, by making him uncapable of othello's place: 4.02.230 P
the time, the place, the torture, o, enforce it! 5.02.369
the while i'll place you, then the boy shall ANT 2.07.110
a lower place, note well, | may make too great 3.01. 12
one of my place in syria, his lieutenant, | for 3.01. 18
from which place | we may the number of the 3.09. 2
conquer, | and earns a place i' th' story. 3.13. 46
in) | bestow'd his lips on that unworthy place, 3.13. 84
conquest, shall | hang in what place you please. 5.02.136
i'll place it | upon this fairest prisoner. CYM 1.01.122
that it is place which lessens and sets off, 3.03. 13
which attends | in place of greater state. 3.03. 78
came from horse, the place | was near at hand. 3.04. 1
this place? 3.04.103
i am most glad | you think of other place. 3.04.141
our good minds | by this rude place we live in. 3.06. 65
i am near to th' place where they should meet, 4.01. 1 P
in this place we left them. 4.02.107
make distinction | of place 'tween high and low. 4.02.249
accommodated by the place, more charming | with 5.03. 32
married your royalty, was wife to your place, 5.05. 39
that place them on the truth of girls and boys. 5.05.107
in suit the place of 's bed and win this ring 5.05.185
but nor the time nor place | will serve our long 5.05.391
he would have well becom'd this place, and 5.05.406
/to place upon the volume of your deeds, | as in PER 2.03. 3
daughter, so you are — here take your place. 2.03. 18
sir, yonder is your place. 2.03. 23
here is a thing too young for such a place, 3.01. 15
which makes /her both th' /heart and place | of 4.ch. 10
nor never shall do in such a place as this, she 4.05. 2 P
know this house to be a place of such resort, 4.06. 79 P
parts, and are the governor of this place. 4.06. 81 P
come bring me to some private place. 4.06. 90 P
would set me free from this unhallowed place, 4.06.100
thou hold'st a place for which the pained'st 4.06.163
gods | would safely deliver me from this place! 4.06.180
if i can place thee, i will. 4.06.193 P
here we her place, | and to her father turn our 5.ch. 11
first, what is your place? 5.01. 20
i am the governor of this place you lie before. 5.01. 21
from the deck | you may discern the place. 5.01.115
shall we make worthy uses of this place | that TNK 2.02. 69
this place | is our inheritance. 2.02. 83
had not the loving gods found this place for us, 2.02.108
no, but from this place to remove your lordship; 2.02.261
and happiness prefer me to a place | where i may 2.03. 81
what made you seek this place, sir? 2.05. 25
i have seen you move in such a place, which well 3.01. 63
i should be near the place. ho, cousin palamon! 3.03. 1
a place prepar'd for those that sleep in honor, 3.06. 99
compassion to 'em both, how would you place it? 3.06.213
three fair knights, appear again in this place, 3.06.292
the place | was knee–deep where she sat; 4.01. 82
that stands | in the /first place with arcite, 4.02. 76
'tis a sore life they have i' th' tother place, 4.03. 32 P
got maids with child, they are in this place. 4.03. 42 P
confine her to a place where the light may 4.03. 74 P
and i' th' self–same place | to seat something i 5.01. 27
stroke laments | the place whereon it falls, and 5.03. 5
in this place first you fought; 5.04. 99
and him bind by my place | to give the smooth STM III 10
proud, | because the cry remaineth in one place, VEN 885
with this she falleth in the place she stood, 1121
through little vents and crannies of the place LUC 310
and in thy dead arms do i mean to place him, 517
she puts the period often from his place, | and 565
keep still possession of thy gloomy place, 803
the murd'rous knife, and, as it left the place, 1735
which seems to weep upon the tainted place, 1746
and bids lucretius give his sorrow place, | and 1773
treasure thou some place | with beauty's SON 6. 3
in the world doth spend | shifts but his place, 9.10
as soon as think the place where he would be. 44. 8
each changing place with that which goes before, 60. 3
and my sick muse doth give another place. 79. 4
light, | and place my merit in the eye of scorn, 88. 2
thy looks with me, thy heart in other place. 93. 4
of age, | nor gives to necessary wrinkles place, 108.11
thy black is fairest in my judgment's place. 131.12
my heart knows the wide world's common place? 137.10
anon their gazes lend | to every place at once, LC 27
love lack'd a dwelling and made him her place; 82
all aids, themselves made fairer by their place, 117
playing the place which did no form receive, 241
all vows and consecrations giving place. 263
that th' unexperient gave the tempter place, 318

PLACED 6 FR 0.0006 REL FR 6 V 0 P
if half thy outward graces had been placed ADO 4.01.101
true, | shall she be placed in my constant soul. MV 2.06. 57
your father's head, which clifford placed there; 3H6 2.06. 53
our archers shall be placed in the midst; R3 5.03.295
bodies | high on a stage be placed to the view, HAM 5.02.378
like stones of worth they thinly placed are, SON 52. 7

PLACENTIO 1 FR 0.0001 REL FR 0 V 1 P
signior placentio and his lovely nieces; ROM 1.02. 66 P

PLACE'S 1 FR 0.0001 REL FR 1 V 0 P
he bears him on the place's privilege, | or 1H6 2.04. 86

PLACES 36 FR 0.0040 REL FR 25 V 11 P
sometime i'ld divide, | and burn in many places; TMP 1.02.199
i think, hath appointed them contrary places; WIV 2.01.209 P
yet in other places she enlargeth her mirth so 2.02.222 P
i have directed you to wrong places. 3.01.108 P
should aid him, i will search impossible places. 3.05.148 P
an abstract for the remembrance of such places, 4.02. 63 P
war–thoughts | have left their places vacant, in ADO 1.01.302
and take your places, ladies. MND 5.01. 84
a voyage, he hath strange places cramm'd | with AYL 2.07. 40
but in all places else /your master lucentio. SHR 1.01.244
wants | for to supply the places at the table, 3.02.247
you know your places well; AWW 3.01. 21
same knave | that leads him to these places. 3.05. 83
to fight with him, hurt him in eleven places — TN 3.02. 35 P
me, and thy places shall | still neighbor mine. WT 1.02.448
oath, | places remote enough are in bohemia, 3.03. 31
all places that the eye of heaven visits | are R2 1.03.275
how many nobles then should hold their places, 2H4 5.02. 17
you know your places. H5 4.03. 78
he hath not the gift to woo in other places; 5.02.155 P
that follows our places stops the mouth of all 5.02.272 P
sirs, take your places and be vigilant. 1H6 2.01. 1
lords, take your places; 2H6 3.02. 19
for living murmurers | there's places of rebuke. H8 2.02.131
alas, our places, | the way of our profession is 3.01.156
that in these several places of the city | you COR 1.01.185
all places yields to him ere he sits down, | and 4.07. 28
you, therefore, draw nigh and take your places. TIT 5.03. 24
your diet shall be in all places alike. TIM 3.06. 67 P
they could be content | to visit other places, JC 5.01. 9
and you whose places are the nearest, know | we MAC 1.04. 36
in many places | gives me superfluous death. HAM 4.05. 95
change places, and, handy–dandy, which is the LR 4.06.153 P
to such whose places under us require, | our ANT 1.02.195
i think he would change places with his officer; CYM 5.04.175 P
and little stars shot from their fixed places, LUC 1525

PLACETH 1 FR 0.0001 REL FR 1 V 0 P
friend no less | than those she placeth highest! COR 1.05. 24

PLACING 2 FR 0.0002 REL FR 2 V 0 P
town, | placing therein some expert officers, 1H6 3.02.127
down, | i have the placing of the british crown. CYM 3.05. 65

PLACK *(also black)*

PLACK 1 FR 0.0001 REL FR 0 V 1 P
great–uncle edward the plack prince of wales, as H5 4.07. 94 P

PLACKET 2 FR 0.0002 REL FR 0 V 2 P
you might have pinch'd a placket, it was WT 4.04.610 P
curse depending on those that war for a placket. TRO 2.03. 20 P

PLACKETS 3 FR 0.0003 REL FR 1 V 2 P
dread prince of plackets, king of codpieces, LLL 3.01.184
they wear their plackets where they should bear WT 4.04.243 P
foot out of brothels, thy hand out of plackets, LR 3.04. 97 P

PLAGU'D 2 FR 0.0002 REL FR 2 V 0 P
and god, not we, hath plagu'd thy bloody deed. R3 1.03.180
is plagu'd with cramps and gouts and painful LUC 856

PLAGUE 98 FR 0.0110 REL FR 62 V 36 P
a plague upon this howling! TMP 1.01. 36 P
a plague upon the tyrant that i serve! 2.02.162
i will plague them all, | even to roaring. 4.01.192
come what plague could have come after it. ADO 2.03. 82 P
o plague right well prevented! 3.02.133 P
it is a plague | that cupid will impose for my LLL 3.01.201
they have the plague, and caught it of your eyes 5.02.421
i'll plague him, i'll torture him. MV 3.01.116 P
'twas pretty, though a plague, | to see him AWW 1.01. 92
a plague upon him! 4.03.116 P
i'll no more drumming, a plague of all drums! 4.03.298 P
what a plague means my niece to take the death TN 1.03. 1 P
here — a plague o' these pickle–herring! 1.05.120 P
even so quickly may one catch the plague? 1.05.295
plague on't, and i thought he had been valiant, 3.04.283 P
but god hath made her sin and her the plague JN 2.01.185
plagued for her | and with her plague, her sin; 2.01.187
a plague upon her! 2.01.190
i feel | the different plague of each calamity. 3.04. 60
and plague injustice with the pains of hell. R2 3.01. 34
if any plague hang over us, 'tis he. 5.03. 3
what a plague have i to do with a buff jerkin? 1H4 1.02. 45 P
a plague upon it, it is in gloucestershire — 1.03.243
a plague on thee! 2.01. 27 P
a plague upon you both! 2.02. 20 P
a plague upon it when thieves cannot be true one 2.02. 27 P
a plague upon you all! 2.02. 28 P
what a plague mean ye to colt me thus? 2.02. 37 P
a plague of all cowards, i say, and a vengeance 2.04.114 P
a plague of all cowards! 2.04.117 P
a plague of all cowards, i say still. 2.04.134 P
a plague upon such backing! 2.04.150 P
a plague of all cowards, still say i. 2.04.155 P
a plague of all cowards! 2.04.170 P
a plague of sighing and grief, it blows a man up 2.04.332 P
of a welsh hook — what a plague call you him? 2.04.339 P
well as another man, a plague on my bringing up! 2.04.497 P
and uncle worcester — a plague upon it! 3.01. 5
smell whereof shall breed a plague in france. H5 4.03.103
a plague upon that villain somerset, | that thus 1H6 4.03. 9
or we will plague thee with incessant wars. 5.04.154
a plague upon them! 2H6 3.02.309
to plague thee for thy foul misleading me. 3H6 5.01. 97
by heaven, brat, i'll plague ye for that word. 5.05. 27
ay, thou wast born to be a plague to men. 5.05. 28
a plague upon you all! R3 1.03. 58
if heaven have any grievous plague in store 1.03.216
plague of your policy! H8 3.02.259
how do you plague me! TRO 1.01. 94
the plague of greece upon thee, thou mongrel 2.01. 12 P
a plague of opinion! 3.03.264 P
a plague upon antenor! 4.02. 76 P
a plague upon antenor! 4.02. 87 P
o plague and madness! 5.02. 35
wilt believe me, but a plague break thy neck — 5.04. 32 P
for our gentlemen, | the common file (a plague! COR 1.06. 43
"i pray, sir" — plague upon't! 2.03. 50
the hoarded plague a' th' gods | requite your 4.02. 11
and the gods will plague thee | that thou 5.03.166
a plague a' both houses! ROM 3.01. 91
a plague a' both your houses! 3.01. 99 P
a plague a' both your houses! 3.01.106
a plague upon him, dog! TIM 2.02. 49 P
if thou wilt not promise, the gods plague thee, 4.03. 74 P
be as a planetary plague when jove | will o'er 4.03.109
plague all, | that your activity may defeat and 4.03.162
plague, plague! 4.03.197
plague, plague! 4.03.197
the plague of company light upon thee! 4.03.352 P
a plague on thee, thou art too bad to curse! 4.03.360
thank them, and would send them back the plague, 5.01.137
be alcibiades your plague, you his, | and last 5.01.189
what is amiss, plague and infection mend! 5.01.221
a plague consume you, wicked caitiffs left! 5.04. 71
pray to the gods to intermit the plague | that JC 1.01. 54
being taught, return | to plague th' inventor. MAC 1.07. 10
marry, i'll give thee this plague for thy dowry: HAM 3.01.134 P
my virtue or my plague, be it either which — 4.07. 13
should i | stand in the plague of custom, and LR 1.02. 3
a plague upon your epileptic visage! 2.02. 81
plague! 2.04. 95
'tis the time's plague, when madmen lead the 4.01. 46
pleasant vices | make instruments to plague us: 5.03.172
a plague upon you, murderers, traitors all! 5.03.270
fertile climate dwell, | plague him with flies. OTH 1.01. 71
(as i confess it is my nature's plague | to spy 3.03.146
yet 'tis the plague /of great ones, 3.03.273
even then this forked plague is fated to us 3.03.276
(as 'tis the strumpet's plague | to beguile many 4.01. 96
the very devils cannot plague them better. CYM 2.05. 35
a plague on them, they ne'er come but i look to PER 2.01. 25 P
a plague on them, they will not hold their peace STM II.C 53 P
may say, the plague is banish'd by thy breath. VEN 510
some one | become the public plague of many moe? LUC 1479
many fall, | to plague a private sin in general? 1484
drink up the monarch's plague, this flattery? SON 114. 2
erred, | and to this false plague are they now 137.14
only my plague thus far i count my gain, | that 141.13

PLAGUED 3 FR 0.0003 REL FR 3 V 0 P
say, | that he is not only plagued for her sin, JN 2.01.184
issue, plagued for her | and with her plague, 2.01.186
i shall be plagued. TRO 5.02.105

PLAGUES 14 FR 0.0015 REL FR 14 V 0 P
heaven and fortune still rewards with plagues. TGV 4.03. 31
light wenches may prove plagues to men forsworn; LLL 4.03.382
thus pour the stars down plagues for perjury. 5.02.394
th' ambition in my love thus plagues itself: AWW 1.01. 90
wander, | what plagues and what portents! TRO 1.03. 96
i say, at once, let your brief plagues be mercy, 5.10. 8
herd of — biles and plagues | plaster you o'er, COR 1.04. 31
which oft the angry mab with blisters plagues, ROM 1.04. 75
plagues incident to men, | your potent and TIM 4.01. 21
thy saints for aye | be crown'd with plagues, 5.01. 53
now all the plagues that in the pendulous air LR 3.04. 67
thou whom the heav'ns' plagues | have humbled to 4.01. 64
that all the plagues of hell should at one time CYM 1.06.111
of plagues, of dearths, or seasons' quality; SON 14. 4

PLAGUE–SORE 1 FR 0.0001 REL FR 1 V 0 P
a plague–sore, or embossed carbuncle, | in my LR 2.04.224

PLAGUING 1 FR 0.0001 REL FR 1 V 0 P
a plaguing mischief light on charles and thee! 1H6 5.03. 39

PLAGUY 1 FR 0.0001 REL FR 1 V 0 P
he is so plaguy proud that the death–tokens of TRO 2.03.177

PLAIN* *(also complain, etc., explain)*

/PLAIN* 1 FR 0.0001 REL FR 1 V 0 P
/sorrow | /the /king /hath /cause /to /plain. LR 3.01. 39

PLAIN* 101 FR 0.0114 REL FR 72 V 29 P
and prompt me, plain and holy innocence! TMP 3.01. 82
one of them | is a plain fish, and no doubt 5.01.266
and, that my love may appear plain and free, TGV 5.04. 82
a plain kerchief, sir john. WIV 3.03. 59 P
to be received plain, i'll speak more gross: MM 2.04. 82
by a rule as plain as the plain bald pate of ERR 2.02. 69 P
a rule as plain as the plain bald pate of father 2.02. 69 P
conclude hairy men plain dealers without wit. 2.02. 86 P
why, 'tis a plain case: 4.03. 23 P
he was wont to speak plain and to the purpose ADO 2.03. 18 P
i meant plain holy–thistle. 3.04. 80 P
be brief — only to the plain form of marriage, 4.01. 2 P
o sir, plantan, a plain plantan: LLL 3.01. 73 P
to make plain | some obscure precedence that 3.01. 81
this will i send and something else more plain 4.03.119
for, sir, to tell you plain, | i'll find a 4.03.268
that some plain man recount their purposes. 5.02.177
well, better wits have worn plain statute–caps. 5.02.281
and to confirm it plain, | you gave me this: 5.02.452
my scutcheon plain declares that i am alisander" 5.02.564
judas machabeus clipt is plain judas. 5.02.599 P
honest plain words best pierce the ear of grief, 5.02.753
but wonder on till truth make all things plain. MND 5.01.128
or, as you would say in plain terms, gone to MV 2.02. 65 P
prolixity or crossing the plain highway of talk, 3.01. 12 P
i was always plain with you, and so now i speak 3.05. 3 P
thee understand a plain man in his plain meaning 3.05. 57 P
understand a plain man in his plain meaning: 3.05. 58 P
but with all brief and plain conveniency | let 4.01. 82
you were to blame, i must be plain with you, 5.01.166
the "why" is plain as way to parish church: AYL 2.07. 52
spake you not these words plain, "sirrah, knock SHR 1.02. 40 P
why then i'll tell her plain | she sings as 2.01.170
lie, in faith, for you are call'd plain kate, 2.01.185
all this chat aside, | thus in plain terms: 2.01.269
smock, | creaking my shoes on the plain masonry, AWW 2.01. 31
but the plain single vow that is vow'd true. 4.02. 22
if it appear not plain and prove untrue, 5.03.317
mark it, cesario, it is old and plain. TN 2.04. 43
as plain as i see you now. 3.02. 10 P
and, to be plain, | i think there is not half a WT 4.04.174
we are but plain fellows, sir. 4.04.721 P
(for you seem to be honest plain men) what you 4.04.794 P
up higher to the plain, where we'll set forth JN 2.01.295
he speaks plain cannon–fire, and smoke, and 2.01.462
face | of plain old form is much disfigured, 4.02. 22

my brother gloucester, plain well–meaning soul, R2 2.01.128
we march | upon the grassy carpet of this plain. 3.03. 50
mark now how a plain tale shall put you down. 1H4 2.04.255 P
and of so easy and so plain a stop | that the 2H4 in 17
then plain and right must my possession be, 4.05.222
for it is plain pocketing up of wrongs. H5 3.02. 50 P
brave soldier, doth he lie, | larding the plain; 4.06. 8
but in plain shock and even play of battle, 4.08.109
find me such a plain king that thou wouldst 5.02.124 P
i speak to thee plain soldier. 5.02.149 P
take a fellow of plain and uncoin'd constancy, 5.02.153 P
which is so plain that exeter doth wish | his 1H6 3.01.199
no more but plain and bluntly "to the king"? 4.01. 51
for, to be plain, | they, knowing dame eleanor's 2H6 1.02. 96
what plain proceedings is more plain than this? 2.02. 53
what plain proceedings is more plain than this? 2.02. 53
to tell thee plain, i aim to lie with thee. 3H6 3.02. 69
to tell you plain, i had rather lie in prison. 3.02. 70
be plain, queen margaret, and tell thy grief; 3.03. 19
simple plain clarence, i do love thee so | that R3 1.01.118
but the plain devil and dissembling looks? 1.02.236
cannot a plain man live and think no harm, | but 1.03. 51
shall i be plain? 4.02. 18
plain and not honest is too harsh a style. 4.04.360
i will lead forth my soldiers to the plain, 5.03.291
you are a sectary, | that's the plain truth. H8 5.02.106
grecian tents do stand | hollow upon this plain, TRO 1.03. 80
ay, ay, ay, ay, 'tis too plain a case. 4.04. 29 P
the moral of my wit | is "plain and true"; 4.04.108
laid falsely | i' th' plain way of his merit. COR 3.01. 61
way, and runs like swallows o'er the plain. TIT 2.02. 24
let them not speak a word, the guilt is plain, 2.03.301
this sandy plot is plain; 4.01. 69
heaven guide thy pen to print thy sorrows plain, 4.01. 75
be plain, good son, and homely in thy drift, ROM 2.03. 55
me all) a plain blunt man | that love my friend, JC 3.02.218
there are no tricks in plain and simple faith; 4.02. 22
i would not, in plain terms, from this time HAM 1.03.132
telling it, and deliver a plain message bluntly. LR 1.04. 33 P
goose, /and i had you upon sarum plain, | i'ld 2.02. 83
sir, 'tis my occupation to be plain: 2.02. 92
an honest mind and plain, he must speak truth! 2.02. 99
if not, he's plain. 2.02.100
beguil'd you in a plain accent was a plain knave 2.02.111 P
you in a plain accent was a plain knave, which 2.02.111 P
chill be plain with you. 4.06.242 P
knavery's plain face is never seen till us'd. OTH 2.01.312
what's dumb in show i'll plain with speech. PER 3.ch. 14
sweet bottom grass and high delightful plain, VEN 236
and all this dumb play had his acts made plain 359
o, learn to love, the lesson is but plain, | and 407
their smoothness, like a goodly champaign plain, LUC 1247
such signs of truth in his plain face she spied, 1532
yet sometime "tarquin" was pronounced plain, 1786
in true plain words by thy true–telling friend; SON 82.12

PLAIN–DEALING 5 FR 0.0005 REL FR 1 V 4 P
in plain–dealing, pompey, i shall have you whipt MM 2.01.249 P
not be denied but i am a plain–dealing villain. ADO 1.03. 32 P
now to plain–dealing, lay these glozes by: LLL 4.03.367
to thyself, like a honest plain–dealing man? 2H6 4.02.104 P
not so well as plain–dealing, which will not TIM 1.01.211 P

PLAINER 4 FR 0.0004 REL FR 3 V 1 P
the plainer dealer, the sooner lost; ERR 2.02. 88 P
follow me then | to plainer ground. MND 3.02.404
but beseech your grace | be plainer with me, let WT 1.02.265
and but in the plainer and simpler kind of TIM 5.01. 25

PLAINEST 2 FR 0.0002 REL FR 2 V 0 P
or rather do i not in plainest truth | tell you MND 2.01.200
i took him for the plainest harmless creature R3 3.05. 25

PLAINING 2 FR 0.0002 REL FR 2 V 0 P
after our sentence plaining comes too late. R2 1.03.175
no penetrable entrance to her plaining: LUC 559

PLAININGS 1 FR 0.0001 REL FR 1 V 0 P
and piteous plainings of the pretty babes, ERR 1.01. 72

/PLAINLY 1 FR 0.0001 REL FR 1 V 0 P
/hear /me /more /plainly. 2H4 4.01. 66

PLAINLY 21 FR 0.0023 REL FR 16 V 5 P
plainly conceive, i love you. MM 2.04.141
nay, he strook so plainly, i could too well feel ERR 2.01. 52 P
but i must tell thee plainly, claudio undergoes ADO 5.02. 57 P
and tell them plainly he is snug the joiner. MND 3.01. 45 P
now my foes tell me plainly i am an ass; TN 5.01. 18 P
plainly as heaven sees earth and earth sees WT 1.02.315
do plainly give you out an unstain'd shepherd, 4.04.149
and tell him plainly | the self–same sun that 4.04.443
plainly denouncing vengeance upon john. JN 3.04.159
all | speak plainly your opinions of our hopes. 2H4 1.03. 3
at us, and plainly say | our mettle is bred out, H5 3.05. 28
i mind to tell him plainly what i think. 3H6 4.01. 8
which plainly signified | that i should snarl, 5.06. 76
an honest tale speeds best being plainly told. R3 4.04.358
then plainly to her tell my loving tale. 4.04.359
his noble carelessness lets them plainly see't. COR 2.02. 15 P
lords, how plainly | i have borne this business. 5.03. 3
then plainly know my heart's dear love is set ROM 2.03. 57
and, to deal plainly, | i fear i am not in my LR 4.07. 61
plainly spoken! TNK 3.01.105
halt — | but plainly say thou lov'st her well, PP 18.11

PLAINNESS 11 FR 0.0012 REL FR 11 V 0 P
and now in plainness do confess to thee, | that SHR 1.01.152
your plainness and your shortness please me well 4.04. 39
therefore with frank and with uncurbed plainness H5 1.02.244
then for the truth and plainness of the case, 1H6 2.04. 46
thy deeds, thy plainness, and thy house–keeping, 2H6 1.01.191
with truth and plainness i do wear mine bare. TRO 4.04.106
let pride, which she calls plainness, marry her. LR 1.01.129
to plainness honor's bound, | when majesty falls 1.01.148
which in this plainness | harbor more craft and 2.02.101
in honest plainness thou hast heard me say | my OTH 1.01. 97
enjoy thy plainness, | it nothing ill becomes ANT 2.06. 78

/PLAINS 1 FR 0.0001 REL FR 1 V 0 P
/now /on /dardan /plains | /the /fresh /and /yet TRO pr 13

PLAINS 7 FR 0.0008 REL FR 7 V 0 P
did sir walter see | on holmedon's plains. 1H4 1.01. 70
safer shall he be upon the sandy plains | than 2H6 1.04. 36
safer shall he be upon the sandy plains | than 1.04. 68
his branches | to all the plains about him. H8 5.04. 54
thus proudly /pight upon our phrygian plains, TRO 5.10. 24
bring him to th' plains, his learning makes no TNK 2.03. 54
swains, | all our merry meetings on the plains, PP 17.30

PLAIN–SONG 4 FR 0.0004 REL FR 3 V 1 P
and the lark, | the plain–song cuckoo grey, MND 3.01.131
is too hot, that is the very plain–song of it. H5 3.02. 6 P
the plain–song is most just; 3.02. 7
may bring his plain–song | and have an hour of H8 1.03. 45

PLAINTFUL 1 FR 0.0001 REL FR 1 V 0 P
a plaintful story from a sist'ring vale, | my LC 2

PLAINTIFF 2 FR 0.0002 REL FR 1 V 1 P
not under white and black, this plaintiff here, ADO 5.01.305 P
thou shalt be both the plaintiff and the judge TN 5.01.354

PLAINTIFFS 1 FR 0.0001 REL FR 0 V 1 P
come, bring away the plaintiffs. ADO 5.01.253 P

PLAINTS 4 FR 0.0004 REL FR 4 V 0 P
hearing how our plaints and prayers do pierce, R2 5.03.127
bootless are plaints, and cureless are my wounds 3H6 2.06. 23
with remorse | to hear and see her plaints, her 3.01. 41
that she her plaints a little while doth stay, LUC 1364

PLAIT *(see plat, etc., plighted*)*

PLANCHED 1 FR 0.0001 REL FR 1 V 0 P
and to that vineyard is a planched gate, | that MM 4.01. 30

PLANE 1 FR 0.0001 REL FR 1 V 0 P
rest, spreads like a plane | fast by a brook, TNK 2.06. 5

PLANET 9 FR 0.0010 REL FR 8 V 1 P
no, i was not born under a rhyming planet, nor i ADO 5.02. 40 P
it is a bawdy planet, that will strike | where WT 1.02.201
there's some ill planet reigns; 2.01.105
face | rul'd like a wandering planet over me, 2H6 4.04. 16
and therefore is the glorious planet sol | in TRO 1.03. 89
reinforcement struck | corioles like a planet. COR 2.02.114
if i do wake, some planet strike me down, | that TIT 2.04. 14
but now | (as if some planet had unwitted men), OTH 2.03.182
now the fleeting moon | no planet is of mine. ANT 5.02.241

PLANETARY 2 FR 0.0002 REL FR 1 V 1 P
be as a planetary plague when jove | will o'er TIM 4.03.109
by an enforc'd obedience of planetary influence; LR 1.02.125 P

/PLANETS 1 FR 0.0001 REL FR 1 V 0 P
corrects the /ill /aspects /of /planets /evil, TRO 1.03. 92

PLANETS 7 FR 0.0008 REL FR 7 V 0 P
shall we curse the planets of mishap | that 1H6 1.01. 23
combat with adverse planets in the heavens! 1.01. 54
be opposite all planets of good luck | to my R3 4.04.402
the heavens themselves, the planets, and this TRO 1.03. 85
but when the planets | in evil mixture to 1.03. 94
nights are wholesome, then no planets strike, HAM 1.01.162
the senate–house of planets all did sit, | to PER 1.01. 10

PLANKS 2 FR 0.0002 REL FR 2 V 0 P
to crouch in litter of your stable planks, | to JN 5.02.140
not fight by sea, | trust not to rotten planks. ANT 3.07. 62

PLANT 24 FR 0.0027 REL FR 22 V 2 P
ears | and plant in tyrants mild humility. LLL 4.03.346
know | it is in us to plant thine honor where AWW 2.03.156
i will plant you two, and let the fool make a TN 2.03.173 P
self–born hour | to plant and o'erwhelm custom. WT 4.01. 9
knowest the way | to plant unrightful kings, R2 5.01. 63
or in thy piteous heart plant thou thine ear, 5.03.126
amongst a grove the very straightest plant, 1H4 1.01. 82
and plant this thorn, this canker, bullingbrook? 1.03.176
plant neighborhood and christian–like accord H5 5.02.353
they labored to plant the rightful heir, | i 1H6 2.05. 80
i'll plant plantagenet, root him up who dares. 3H6 1.01. 48
this may plant courage in their quailing breasts 2.03. 54
that this his love was an /eternal plant, 3.03.124
how sweet a plant have you untimely cropp'd! 5.05. 62
and plant your joys in living edward's throne. R3 2.02.100
but we will plant some other in the throne, | to 3.07.216
plant love among 's! COR 3.03. 35
full soon the canker death eats up that plant. ROM 2.03. 30
i have begun to plant thee, and will labor | to MAC 1.04. 28
i will advise you where to plant yourselves, 3.01.128
without miracle | should never plant in me. LR 1.01.223
so that if we will plant nettles or sow lettuce, OTH 1.03.321 P
plant those that have revolted in the vant, ANT 4.06. 8
in this place, | in which i'll plant a pyramid; TNK 3.06.293

PLANTAGE 1 FR 0.0001 REL FR 1 V 0 P
as true as steel, as plantage to the moon, | as TRO 3.02.177

PLANTAGENET 41 FR 0.0046 REL FR 39 V 2 P
arthur plantagenet, lays most lawful claim | to JN 1.01. 9
great, | arise sir richard, and plantagenet. 1.01.162
the very spirit of plantagenet! 1.01.167
of him it holds, stands young plantagenet, | son 2.01.238
lay, | and call'd mine percy, his plantagenet! 1H4 1.01. 89
is thine, and henry plantagenet is thine"; H5 5.02.240 P
plantagenet, i will, and like thee, /nero, 1H6 1.04. 95
i pluck this white rose with plantagenet. 2.04. 36
no, plantagenet; 2.04. 64
hath not thy rose a thorn, plantagenet? 2.04. 69
where false plantagenet dare not be seen. 2.04. 74
turn not thy scorns this way, plantagenet. 2.04. 77
richard plantagenet, my lord, will come. 2.05. 18
richard plantagenet, my friend, is he come? 2.05. 34
father's sake, | in honor of a true plantagenet, 2.05. 52
plantagenet, i see, must hold his tongue, | lest 3.01. 61
which in the right of richard plantagenet | we 3.01.149
rise, richard, like a true plantagenet, | and 3.01.171
my mother a plantagenet — 2H6 4.02. 42 P
unless plantagenet, duke of york, be king, | and 3H6 1.01. 40
i'll plant plantagenet, root him up who dares. 1.01. 48
plantagenet, of thee and these thy sons, | thy 1.01. 95
plantagenet shall speak first. 1.01.121
plantagenet, for all the claim thou lay'st, 1.01.152
richard plantagenet, | enjoy the kingdom after 1.01.174
long live king henry! plantagenet, embrace him. 1.01.202
plantagenet, i come, plantagenet! 1.03. 49
plantagenet, i come, plantagenet! 1.03. 49
yield to our mercy, proud plantagenet. 1.04. 30
but how is it that great plantagenet | is 1.04. 99
field, | that we, the sons of brave plantagenet, 2.01. 35
o warwick, warwick, that plantagenet, | which 2.01.101
edward plantagenet, arise a knight, | and learn 2.02. 61
plantagenet. R3 1.02.142
when gallant–springing brave plantagenet, | that 1.04.221
famous plantagenet, most gracious prince, | lend 3.07.100
my niece plantagenet, | led in the hand of her 4.01. 1
edward plantagenet, why art thou dead? 4.04. 19
plantagenet doth quit plantagenet, | edward for 4.04. 20
plantagenet doth quit plantagenet, | edward for 4.04. 20
and little ned plantagenet, his son? 4.04.146

PLANTAGENETS 2 FR 0.0002 REL FR 2 V 0 P
to think | i come one way of the plantagenets. JN 5.06. 11
of the timeless deaths | of these plantagenets, R3 1.02.118

PLANTAIN *(see plantan, plantin)*

PLANTAN 5 FR 0.0005 REL FR 2 V 3 P
o sir, plantan, a plain plantan: LLL 3.01. 73 P
o sir, plantan, a plain plantan: 3.01. 73 P
no l'envoy, no salve, sir, but a plantan! 3.01. 74 P
true, and i for a plantan; 3.01.108
your plantan leaf is excellent for that. ROM 1.02. 51

PLANTATION 1 FR 0.0001 REL FR 1 V 0 P
had i plantation of this isle, my lord — TMP 2.01.144

PLANTED 9 FR 0.0010 REL FR 7 V 2 P
planted and plac'd and possess'd by my master ADO 3.03.150 P
a man in all the world's new fashion planted, LLL 1.01.164
the fool hath planted in his memory | an army of MV 3.05. 66
elect, | anointed, crowned, planted many years, R2 4.01.127
but he hath so planted his honors in their eyes COR 2.02. 29 P
you are but newly planted in your throne; TIT 1.01.444
thy temples should be planted presently | with 2.03. 62
which would be planted newly with the time, | as MAC 5.09. 31
yet at the first | i saw the treasons planted. ANT 1.03. 26

PLANTEST 1 FR 0.0001 REL FR 1 V 0 P
thou plantest scandal and displacest laud. LUC 887

PLANTETH 1 FR 0.0001 REL FR 1 V 0 P
for it engenders choler, planteth anger, | and SHR 4.01.172

PLANTIN *(also plantan)*

PLANTIN 1 FR 0.0001 REL FR 1 V 0 P
these poor slight sores | need not a plantin; TNK 1.02. 61

PLANTING 1 FR 0.0001 REL FR 1 V 0 P
planting oblivion, beating reason back, VEN 557

PLANTS* 17 FR 0.0019 REL FR 15 V 2 P
growing, | plants with goodly burthen bowing; TMP 4.01.113
and such barren plants are set before us, that LLL 4.02. 28
abuses our young plants with carving "rosalind" AYL 3.02.360 P
pray god the plants thou graft'st may never grow R2 3.04.101
/her royal stock graft with ignoble plants, R3 3.07.127
old barren plants, to wail it with their age. 4.04.394
to his music plants and flowers | ever sprung, H8 3.01. 6
in safety | under his own vine what he plants, 5.04. 34
he watered his new plants with dews of flattery, COR 5.06. 22
is the powerful grace that lies | in plants, ROM 2.03. 16
some o' their plants are ill rooted already, the ANT 2.07. 1 P
how dares the plants look up to heaven, from PER 1.02. 55
herbs for their smell, and sappy plants to bear: VEN 165
not, | green plants bring not forth their dye; PP 17.26
sing, | trees did grow and plants did spring; 20. 6
when i perceive that men as plants increase, SON 15. 5
heard where his plants in others' orchards grew, LC 171

PLASH 1 FR 0.0001 REL FR 1 V 0 P
a shallow plash to plunge him in the deep, | and SHR 1.01. 23

PLASHY 3 FR 0.0003 REL FR 3 V 0 P
with all good speed at plashy visit me. R2 1.02. 66
sirrah, get thee to plashy, to my sister 2.02. 90
i should to plashy too, | but time will not 2.02.120

PLASTER 5 FR 0.0005 REL FR 4 V 1 P
the sore, | when you should bring the plaster. TMP 2.01.140
and let him have some plaster, or some loam, or MND 3.01. 68 P
should seek a plaster by contemn'd revolt, | and JN 5.02. 13
biles and plagues | plaster you o'er, that you COR 1.04. 32
venom'd sores the only sovereign plaster; VEN 916

PLASTERER 1 FR 0.0001 REL FR 1 V 0 P
villain, thy father was a plasterer, | and thou 2H6 4.02.132

PLAST'RING 1 FR 0.0001 REL FR 1 V 0 P
harlot's cheek, beautied with plast'ring art, HAM 3.01. 50

PLAT *(also plighted*)*

PLAT 1 FR 0.0001 REL FR 1 V 0 P
her hair, nor loose nor tied in formal plat, LC 29

/PLATE 1 FR 0.0001 REL FR 1 V 0 P
/plate /sin with gold, | and the strong lance of LR 4.06.165

PLATE 10 FR 0.0011 REL FR 6 V 4 P
city | is richly furnished with plate and gold, SHR 2.01.347
our assistance we do seize to us | the plate, R2 2.01.161
we seize into our hands | his plate, his goods, 2.01.210
fain to pawn both my plate and the tapestry of 2H4 2.01.141 P
i am loath to pawn my plate, so god save me law! 2.01.154 P
importing | the several parcels of his plate, H8 3.02.125
remove the court–cupboard, look to the plate. ROM 1.05. 7 P
kindnesses from him, as money, plate, jewels, TIM 3.02. 21 P
of money, plate, and jewels | i am possess'd of; ANT 5.02.138
'tis plate of rare device, and jewels | of rich CYM 1.06.189

PLATED 2 FR 0.0002 REL FR 2 V 0 P
hither | thus plated in habiliments of war, R2 1.03. 28
of the war | have glow'd like plated mars, now ANT 1.01. 4

PLATES 1 FR 0.0001 REL FR 1 V 0 P
were | as plates dropp'd from his pocket. ANT 5.02. 92

PLATFORM 3 FR 0.0003 REL FR 3 V 0 P
my lord, upon the platform where we watch. HAM 1.02.213
upon the platform 'twixt aleven and twelf | i'll 1.02.251
to th' platform, masters, come, let's set the OTH 2.03.120

PLATFORMS 1 FR 0.0001 REL FR 1 V 0 P
and lay new platforms to endamage them. 1H6 2.01. 77

PLATS 1 FR 0.0001 REL FR 1 V 0 P
that plats the manes of horses in the night, ROM 1.04. 89

PLATTED 1 FR 0.0001 REL FR 1 V 0 P
upon her head a platted hive of straw, | which LC 8

PLAUSIBLE 1 FR 0.0001 REL FR 0 V 1 P
answer his requiring with a plausible obedience, MM 3.01.244 P

PLAUSIBLY 1 FR 0.0001 REL FR 1 V 0 P
the romans plausibly did give consent | to LUC 1854

PLAUSIVE 3 FR 0.0003 REL FR 2 V 1 P
his plausive words | he scatter'd not in ears, AWW 1.02. 53
it must be a very plausive invention that 4.01. 26 P
o'er–leavens | the form of plausive manners — HAM 1.04. 30

PLAUTUS 1 FR 0.0001 REL FR 0 V 1 P
cannot be too heavy, nor plautus too light, for HAM 2.02.400 P

/PLAY 2 FR 0.0002 REL FR 2 V 0 P
/that /our /play | /leaps /o'er /the /vaunt /and TRO pr 26
/to /what /may /be /digested /in /a /play. pr 29

PLAY 310 FR 0.0350 REL FR 213 V 97 P
play the men. TMP 1.01. 10 P
what foul play had we, that we came from thence? 1.02. 60
by foul play (as thou say'st) were we heav'd 1.02. 62
he will shoot no more, but play with sparrows, 4.01.100
sweet lord, you play me false. 5.01.172
should wrangle, | and i would call it fair play. 5.01.175
what is this maid with whom thou wast at play? 5.01.185

you would have them always play but one thing? TGV 4.02. 70 P
i would always have one play but one thing. 4.02. 72
a man's servant shall play the cur with him, 4.04. 1 P
our youth got me to play the woman's part, | and 4.04.160
weep agood, | for i did play a lamentable part. 4.04.166
master slender is let the boys leave to play. WIV 4.01. 12 P
go your ways and play, go. 4.01. 79 P
when she will play with reason and discourse, MM 1.02.185
far from heart — play with all virgins so. 1.04. 33
so play the foolish throngs with one that 2.04. 24
this would make mercy swear and play the tyrant. 3.02.195 P
for if we two be one, and thou play false, | i ERR 2.02.142
dromio, play the porter well. 2.02.211
or do you play the flouting jack, to tell us ADO 1.01.183 P
when he would play the noble beast in love. 5.04. 47
therefore play, music. 5.04.121 P
words | that aged ears play truant at his tales, LLL 2.01. 74
that we must stand and play the murtherer in? 4.01. 8
and he from forage will incline to play. 4.01. 91
"all hid, all hid," an old infant play. 4.03. 76
and nestor play at push–pin with the boys, | and 4.03.167
i will play three myself. 5.01.143 P
or i will play | on the tabor to the worthies, 5.01.153
play, music, then! 5.02.211
since you can cog, i'll play no more with you. 5.02.235
faith, unless you play the honest troyan, the 5.02.675 P
time, | play'd foul play with our oaths. 5.02.756
our wooing doth not end like an old play: 5.02.874
that's too long for a play. 5.02.878
to play in our enterlude before the duke and the MND 1.02. 5 P
good peter quince, say what the play treats on; 1.02. 8 P
our play is the most lamentable comedy and most 1.02. 11 P
i could play ercles rarely, or a part to tear a 1.02. 29 P
let not me play a woman; 1.02. 47 P
you shall play it in a mask, and you may speak 1.02. 49 P
and i may hide my face, let me play thisby too. 1.02. 51 P
no, no, you must play pyramus; 1.02. 55 P
robin starveling, you must play thisby's mother. 1.02. 60 P
and i hope here is a play fitted. 1.02. 65 P
let me play the lion too. 1.02. 70 P
you can play no part but pyramus; 1.02. 85 P
therefore you must needs play pyramus. 1.02. 88 P
what beard were i best to play it in? 1.02. 91 P
and then you will play barefac'd. 1.02. 98 P
a bill of properties, such as our play wants. 1.02.106 P
doth the moon shine that night we play our play? 3.01. 51 P
doth the moon shine that night we play our play? 3.01. 52 P
of the great chamber window (where we play) open 3.01. 57 P
what, a play toward? 3.01. 79
were met together to rehearse a play | intended 3.02. 11
and i will sing it in the latter end of a play, 4.01.217 P
if he come not, then the play is marr'd. 4.02. 5 P
short and the long is, our play is preferr'd. 4.02. 39 P
is there no play | to ease the anguish of a 5.01. 36
a play there is, my lord, some ten words long, 5.01. 61
which is as brief as i have known a play; 5.01. 62
for in all the play | there is not one word apt, 5.01. 64
what are they that do play it? 5.01. 71
their unbreathed memories | with this same play, 5.01. 75
i will hear that play; 5.01. 81
here she comes, and her passion ends the play. 5.01.315 P
for your play needs no excuse. 5.01.355 P
this palpable–gross play hath well beguil'd 5.01.367
a stage, where every man must play a part, | and MV 1.01. 78
let me play the fool: 1.01. 79
if hercules and lichas play at dice | which is 2.01. 32
if a christian do not play the knave and get 2.03. 12 P
you shall please to play the thieves for wives, 2.06. 23
for the close night doth play the runaway, | and 2.06. 47
we'll play with them the first boy for a 3.02.213 P
how every fool can play upon the word! 3.05. 43 P
if two gods should play some heavenly match, 3.05. 79
pageants than the scene | wherein we play in. AYL 2.07.139
and under that habit play the knave with him. 3.02.296 P
say | i'll prove a busy actor in their play. 3.04. 59
at this letter, | and play the swaggerer: 4.03. 14
an instrument, and play false strains upon thee? 4.03. 68 P
play, music! 5.04.178
'tis true that a good play needs no epilogue. ep 4 P
insinuate with you in the behalf of a good play! ep 9 P
men, to like as much of this play as please you; ep 14 P
between you and the women the play may please. ep 17 P
i warrant you we will play our part | as he SHR in.1. 69
there is a lord will hear you play to–night; in.1. 93
(for yet his honor never heard a play), | you in.1. 96
even as the waving sedges play with wind. in.2. 53
amendment, | are come to play a pleasant comedy, in.2. 130
therefore they thought it good you hear a play, in.2. 134
marry, i will, let them play it. in.2. 137 P
my lord, you nod, you do not mind the play. 1.01.249
faith, gentlemen, now i play a merchant's part, 2.01.326
take you your instrument, play you the whiles, 3.01. 22
hark, hark, i hear the minstrels play. 3.02.183
while i play the good husband at home, my son 5.01. 68 P
and death should have play for lack of work. AWW 1.01. 21 P
i play the noble huswife with the time, | to 2.02. 60
and fortune play upon thy prosperous helm | as 3.03. 7
so lust doth play | with what it loathes for 4.04. 24
the king's a beggar, now the play is done; ep 1
if music be the food of love, play on, | give me TN 1.01. 1
fangs of malice i swear) i am not that i play. 1.05.184 P
seek him out, and play the tune the while. 2.04. 14
perchance wind up my watch, or play with my — 2.05. 60 P
shall i play my freedom at tray–trip, and become 2.05.190 P
i would play lord pandarus of phrygia, sir, to 3.01. 51 P
this fellow is wise enough to play the fool, 3.01. 60
'tis not for gravity to play at cherry–pit with 3.04.116 P
tertio, is a good play, and the old saying is, 5.01. 36 P
but that's all one, our play is done, | and 5.01.407
go play, boy, play. WT 1.02.187
go play, boy, play. 1.02.187
and i | play too, but so disgrac'd a part, whose 1.02.188
go play, boy, play. 1.02.190
go play, boy, play. 1.02.190
go play, mamillius, thou'rt an honest man. 1.02.211
yea, a very trick | for them to play at will. 2.01. 52
no, like a bank, for love to lie and play on; 4.04.130
methinks i play as i have seen them do | in 4.04.133

appointed, as if | the scene you play were mine. 4.04.593
i see the play so lies | that i must bear a part 4.04.655
and if she did play false, the fault was hers, JN 1.01.118
one that will play the devil, sir, with you, 2.01.135
doth play | upon the dancing banners of the 2.01.307
i'd play incessantly upon these jades, | even 2.01.385
play fast and loose with faith? 3.01.242
it is apparent foul play and 'tis shame | that 4.02. 93
according to the fair play of the world, | let 5.02.118
can sick men play so nicely with their names? R2 2.01. 84
i play the torturer by small and small | to 3.02.198
or shall we play the wantons with our woes | and 3.03.164
madam, we'll play at bowls. 3.04. 3
thus play i in one person many people, | and 5.05. 31
to play with mammets and to tilt with lips. 1H4 2.03. 92
and bid you play it off. 2.04. 17 P
be so valiant as to play the coward with thy 2.04. 47 P
i'll play percy, and that damn'd brawn shall 2.04.109 P
damn'd brawn shall play dame mortimer his wife. 2.04.110 P
we be merry, shall we have a play extempore? 2.04.280 P
do thou stand for me, and i'll play my father. 2.04.434 P
play out the play, i have much to say in the 2.04.484 P
play out the play, i have much to say in the 2.04.484 P
so, | and those musicians that shall play to you 3.01.223
hand, | as ever off'red foul play in a state. 3.02.169
wind | doth play the trumpet to his purposes, 5.01. 4
you shall find no boy's play here, i can tell 5.04. 76 P
wav'ring multitude, | can play upon it. 2H4 in 20
well, thus we play the fools with the time, and 2.02.142 P
chaps, and you play the saucy cuttle with me. 2.04.130 P
let them play. 2.04.227 P
play, sirs. 2.04.227 P
lately here in the end of a displeasing play, to ep 9 P
gently to hear, kindly to judge, our play. H5 pr 34
play a set | shall strike his father's crown 1.02.262
force a play: 2.pr. 32
we'll not offend one stomach with our play. 2.pr. 40
fumble with the sheets, and play with flowers, 2.03. 14 P
play with your fancies: 3.pr. 7
for when /lenity and cruelty play for a kingdom, 3.06.112 P
french | do the low–rated english play at dice; 4.pr. 19
valor than this roaring devil i' th' old play, 4.04. 71 P
but in plain shock and even play of battle, 4.08.109
doth fortune play the huswife with me now? 5.01. 80
play on the lute, beholding the towns burn: 1H6 1.04. 96
king | prettily, methought, did play the orator. 4.01.175
be slack | to play my part in fortune's pageant. 2H6 1.02. 67
but mine is made the prologue to their play; 3.01.151
wilt thou on thy death–bed play the ruffian, 5.01.164
no, i can better play the orator. 3H6 1.02. 2
i'll play the orator as well as nestor, 3.02.188
leave | to play the broker in mine own behalf; 4.01. 63
belike she minds to play the amazon. 4.01.106
that i should snarl, and bite, and play the dog. 5.06. 77
and seem a saint, when most i play the devil. R3 1.03.337
i'll play the orator | as if the golden fee for 3.05. 95
play the maid's part, still answer nay, and take 3.07. 51
ah, buckingham, now do i play the touch, | to 4.02. 8
and the beholders of this frantic play, | th' 4.04. 68
under our tents i'll play the ease–dropper, | to 5.03.221
and so agree | the play may pass, if they be H8 pr 11
they | that come to hear a merry, bawdy play, pr 14
beaten | a long time out of play, may bring his 1.03. 45
yes, if i make my play. 1.04. 46
every thing that heard him play, | even the 3.01. 9
(out of thy honest truth) to play the woman. 3.02.430
simony was fair play; 4.02. 36
cause the musicians play me that sad note | i 4.02. 78
charles, i will play no more to–night, | my 5.01. 56
nor shall not, when my fancy's on my play. 5.01. 60
to me you cannot reach you play the spaniel, 5.02.161
marshalsea shall hold ye play these two months. 5.03. 86
'tis ten to one this play can never please | all ep 1
are like to hear | for this play at this time, ep 9
now play me nestor, hem, and stroke thy beard, TRO 1.03.165
now play him me, patroclus, | arming to answer 1.03.170
who play they to? 3.01. 21 P
at whose request do these men play? 3.01. 29 P
if i confess much, you will play the tyrant. 3.02.119
whiles others play the idiots in her eyes! 3.03.135
i'll play the hunter for thy life | with all my 4.01. 18
nor play at subtile games — fair virtues all, 4.04. 87
o, 'tis fair play. 5.03. 43
fool's play, by heaven, hector. 5.03. 43
i must have you play the idle huswife with me COR 1.03. 70 P
rather say, i play | the man i am. 3.02. 15
and if thy stumps will let thee play the scribe. TIT 2.04. 4
so, now bring them in, for i'll play the cook, 5.02.204
come, musicians, play. ROM 1.05. 25
day, night, work, play, |,alone, in company, 3.05.176
me this bloody knife | shall play the umpeer, 4.01. 63
me alone, | i'll play the huswife for this once. 4.02. 43
and madly play with my forefathers' joints, 4.03. 51
and you will have me live, play "heart's ease." 4.05.103 P
o, play me some merry dump to comfort me. 4.05.107 P
not a dump we, 'tis no time to play now. 4.05.109 P
if our betters play at that game, we must not TIM 1.02. 12
which doth seldom | play the recanter, feeling 5.01.146
wouldst not play false, | and yet wouldst MAC 1.05. 21
mingle with society, | and play the humble host. 3.04. 4
o, i could play the woman with mine eyes, | and 4.03.230
why should i play the roman fool, and die | on 5.08. 1
for they are actions that a man might play, HAM 1.02. 84
all is not well, | i doubt some foul play. 1.02.255
for the play, i remember, pleas'd not the 2.02.436 P
cried in the top of mine — an excellent play, 2.02.439 P
him, friends, we'll hear a play to–morrow. 2.02.535 P
can you play "the murther of gonzago"? 2.02.537 P
that guilty creatures sitting at a play | have 2.02.589
play something like the murther of my father 2.02.595
already order | this night to play before him. 3.01. 21
that he may play the fool no where but in 's own 3.01.132 P
after the play | let his queen–mother all alone 3.01.181
o, there be players that i have seen play — and 3.02. 29 P
and let those that play your clowns speak no 3.02. 39 P
question of the play be then to be consider'd. 3.02. 43 P
there is a play to–night before the king, | one 3.02. 75
'a steal aught the whilst this play is playing, 3.02. 88

they are coming to the play. 3.02. 90
this show imports the argument of the play. 3.02.140 P
i'll mark the play. 3.02.148 P
madam, how like you this play? 3.02.229 P
what do you call the play? 3.02.236 P
this play is the image of a murther done in 3.02.238 P
give o'er the play. 3.02.268 P
strooken deer go weep, | the hart ungalled play, 3.02.272
will you play upon this pipe? 3.02.350 P
you would play upon me, you would seem to know 3.02.364 P
you fret me, /yet you cannot play upon me. 3.02.372 P
beg | your sudden coming o'er to play with you. 4.07.105
the breeding, but to play at loggats with them? 5.01. 92 P
to my brains, | they had begun the play. 5.02. 31
know if your pleasure hold to play with laertes, 5.02.198 P
to laertes before you fall to play. 5.02.207 P
and will this brother's wager frankly play. 5.02.253
i'll play this bout first, set it by a while. 5.02.284
sung, | that such a king should play bo–peep, LR 1.04.177
do me no foul play, friends. 3.07. 31
bad is the trade that must play fool to sorrow, 4.01. 38
i thus would play and trifle with your reverence OTH 1.01.132
you rise to play, and go to bed to work. 2.01.115
now again you are most apt to play the sir in. 2.01.174 P
and what's he then that says i play the villain? 2.03.336
even as her appetite shall play the god | with 2.03.347
masters, play here, i will content your pains; 3.01. 1
i will play the swan, | and die in music. 5.02.247
now, play one scene | of excellent dissembling, ANT 1.03. 78
as i may, | i'll play the penitent to you; 2.02. 92
if thou dost play with him at any game, | thou 2.03. 26
my arm is sore, best play with mardian. 2.05. 4
come, you'll play with me, sir? 2.05. 6
i'll give thee leave | to play till doomsday. 5.02.232
crown's /awry, | i'll mend it, and then play — 5.02.319
that play with all infirmities for gold | which CYM 1.06.124
cadwal and i | will play the cook and servant, 3.06. 30
therein i must play the workman. 4.01. 6 P
us, | play judge and executioner all himself, 4.02.128
to our rock, | you and fidele play the cooks. 4.02.164
and do not play in wench–like words with that 4.02.230
shall 's have a play of this? 5.05.228
hath made the ball | for them to play upon, PER 2.01. 61
unless you play the /pious innocent | and for an 4.03. 17
attribute cry out, | "she died by foul play." 4.03. 19
while our /scene must play | his daughter's woe 4.04. 48
here our play has ending. 5.03.102
and a good play | (whose modest scenes blush on TNK pr 3
we pray our play may be so; pr 9
if this play do not keep | a little dull time pr 30
you play the child extremely. 2.02.204
let the plough play to–day, i'll tickle't out 2.03. 28
play o' th' virginals? 3.03. 34
and let him play | qui passa o' th' bells and 3.05. 85
i think he might be brought to play at tennis. 5.02. 56
why, play at stoolball: 5.02. 74
go to dinner, | and then we'll play at cards. 5.02.108
never fortune | did play a subtler game. 5.04.113
i would now ask ye how ye like the play, | but, ep 1
be bold to play, our sport is not in sight; VEN 124
and all this dumb play had his acts made plain 359
it off, and being gone, | play with his locks; 1090
dwell | will play the tyrants to the very same, SON 5. 3
hang on such thorns, and play as wantonly, 54. 7
to play the watchman ever for thy sake. 61.12
as with your shadow i with these did play. 98.14
and play the mother's part, kiss me, be kind: 143.12

/PLAY'D 1 FR 0.0001 REL FR 1 V 0 P

/that /play'd /on /her /ripe /lip /seem'd /not LR 4.03. 20

PLAY'D 53 FR 0.0060 REL FR 39 V 14 P

to have no screen between this part he play'd TMP 1.02.107
this part he play'd | and him he play'd it for, 1.02.108
mad, and play'd | some tricks of desperation. 1.02.209
of our catch, play'd by the picture of nobody. 3.02.126 P
done little better than play'd the jack with us. 4.01.197 P
and i have play'd the sheep in losing him. TGV 1.01. 73
when all our pageants of delight were play'd, 4.04.159
since i pluck'd geese, play'd truant, and whipt WIV 5.01. 25 P
heaven shield my mother play'd my father fair! MM 3.01.140
my lord, i have play'd the part of lady fame. ADO 2.01.213 P
have by this play'd their parts with beatrice, 3.02. 77 P
time, | play'd foul play with our oaths. LLL 5.02.756
and it was play'd | when i from thebes came last MND 5.01. 50
indeed he hath play'd on this prologue like a 5.01.122 P
if he that writ it had play'd pyramus and hang'd 5.01.358 P
my lady his mother play'd false with a smith. MV 1.02. 44 P
at an instant, learn'd, play'd, eat together, AYL 1.03. 74
if you will see a pageant truly play'd | between 3.04. 52
since once he play'd a farmer's eldest son. SHR in.1. 84
wherein have you play'd the knave with fortune AWW 5.02. 30 P
if this were play'd upon a stage now, i could TN 3.04.127 P
geck and gull | that e'er invention play'd on? 5.01.344
or else a fool | that seest a game play'd home, WT 1.02.248
if industriously | i play'd the fool, it was my 1.02.257
though devis'd | and play'd to take spectators. 3.02. 37
assured loss before the match be play'd. JN 3.01.336
to win this easy match play'd for a crown? 5.02.106
who on the french ground play'd a tragedy, H5 1.02.106
these the wretches that we play'd at dice for? 4.05. 8
and myself have play'd | the interim, by 5.pr. 42
if sir john falstaff had not play'd the coward. 1H6 1.01.131
when they shall hear how we have play'd the men. 1.06. 16
pucelle hath bravely play'd her part in this, 3.03. 88
beshrew the winners, for they play'd me false! 2H6 3.01.184
full well hath clifford play'd the orator, 3H6 2.02. 43
were play'd in jest by counterfeiting actors? 2.03. 28
i would have play'd | the part my father meant H8 1.02.194
so, bassianus, you have play'd your prize. TIT 1.01.399
i play'd the cheater for thy father's hand, 5.01.111
play'd for a pair of stainless maidenhoods. ROM 3.02. 13
think, | if i had play'd the desk or table–book, HAM 2.02.136
my lord, you play'd once i' th' university, you 3.02. 99 P
think i am easier to be play'd on than a pipe? 3.02.370 P
as would store the world they play'd for. OTH 4.03. 85 P
as well a woman with an eunuch play'd | as with ANT 2.05. 5
half the bulk o' th' world play'd as i pleas'd, 3.11. 64
but that my master rather play'd than fought CYM 1.01.162
pisanio, hath play'd the strumpet in my bed; 3.04. 21 P

but being play'd upon before your time, | hell PER 1.01. 84
his part is play'd, and, though it were too TNK 5.04.102
like golden threads play'd with her breath — LUC 400
my curtal dog, that wont to have play'd, | plays PP 17.19
mine eye hath play'd the painter and hath SON 24. 1
PLAY'DST 1 FR 0.0001 REL FR 1 V 0 P
and i fear | thou play'dst most foully for't; MAC 3.01. 3
PLAYED 2 FR 0.0002 REL FR 2 V 0 P
well bandied both, a set of wit well played. LLL 5.02. 29
a stranger pyramus than e'er played here. MND 3.01. 88
/PLAYER 1 FR 0.0001 REL FR 0 V 1 P
/the /poet /and /the /player /went /to /cuffs HAM 2.02.355 P
PLAYER 5 FR 0.0005 REL FR 4 V 1 P
there is not one word apt, one player fitted. MND 5.01. 65
and, like a strutting player, whose conceit TRO 1.03.153
life's but a walking shadow, a poor player, MAC 5.05. 24
is it not monstrous that this player here, | but HAM 2.02.551
nor tripp'd neither, you base football player. LR 1.04. 86 P
/PLAYERS 1 FR 0.0001 REL FR 0 V 1 P
/should /grow /themselves /to /common /players HAM 2.02.349 P
PLAYERS 22 FR 0.0024 REL FR 6 V 16 P
now name the rest of the players. MND 1.02. 39 P
for when the players are all dead, there need 5.01.356 P
and all the men and women merely players; AYL 2.07.140
players | that offer service to your lordship. SHR in.1. 77
your honor's players, hearing your amendment, in.2. 129
one of these harlotry players as ever i see! 1H4 2.04.396 P
as they use to do the players in the theatre, i JC 1.02.260 P
entertainment the players shall receive from you HAM 2.02.316 P
what players are they? 2.02.326 P
there are the players. 2.02.369 P
garb, /lest /my extent to the players, which, i 2.02.373 P
he comes to tell me of the players, mark it. 2.02.387 P
my lord, will you see the players well bestow'd? 2.02.522 P
i'll have these players | play something like 2.02.594
madam, it so fell out that certain players | we 3.01. 16
but if you mouth it, as many of our players do, 3.02. 3 P
o, there be players that i have seen play — and 3.02. 28 P
bid the players make haste. 3.02. 49 P
be the players ready? 3.02.106 P
the players cannot keep /counsel, they'll tell 3.02.141 P
shoes, get me a fellowship in a cry of players? 3.02.278 P
players in your huswifery, and huswives in your OTH 2.01.112
PLAYETH 1 FR 0.0001 REL FR 1 V 0 P
and lulls him whilst she playeth on her back, TIT 4.01. 99
PLAYFELLOW 8 FR 0.0009 REL FR 8 V 0 P
farewell, sweet playfellow, pray thou for us; MND 1.01.220
not cross'd the eyes | of my young playfellow. WT 1.02. 80
my gracious lord, | shall i be your playfellow? 2.01. 3
old sullen playfellow | for tender princes — R3 4.01.101
be familiar with | my playfellow, your hand, ANT 3.13.125
you bred him as my playfellow, and he is | a man CYM 1.01.145
a bedfellow, | in marriage pleasures playfellow; PER 1.ch. 34
once with a time when i enjoy'd a playfellow; TNK 1.03. 50
PLAYFELLOWS 2 FR 0.0002 REL FR 2 V 0 P
affliction | be playfellows to keep you company! 2H6 3.02.302
honest men, | or pack to their old playfellows. H8 1.03. 33
PLAY–FERES 1 FR 0.0001 REL FR 0 V 1 P
maids have been her companions and play–feres, TNK 4.03. 91 P
PLAYHOUSE 2 FR 0.0002 REL FR 1 V 1 P
there is the playhouse now, there must you sit, H5 2.pr. 36
that thunder at a playhouse and fight for bitten H8 5.03. 60 P
PLAYING 15 FR 0.0017 REL FR 12 V 3 P
th' other day with playing at sword and dagger WIV 1.01.283 P
passing fair | playing in the wanton air: LLL 4.03.102
playing on pipes of corn and versing love | to MND 2.01. 67
given him sixpence a day for playing pyramus, 4.02. 22 P
if all the year were playing holidays, | to 1H4 1.02.204
eggs, | playing the mouse in absence of the cat, H5 1.02.172
news | by playing it to me with so sour a face. ROM 2.05. 24
so o'erdone is from the purpose of playing, HAM 3.02. 20 P
'a steal aught the whilst this play is playing, 3.02. 88
there, | my music playing far off, i will betray ANT 2.05. 11
'tis better playing with a lion's whelp | than 3.13. 94
but | playing o'er business in his hand, another TNK 1.03. 31
passing fair, | playing in the wanton air. PP 16. 4
playing the place which did no form receive, LC 241
playing patient sports in unconstrained gyves? 242
PLAYING–DAY 1 FR 0.0001 REL FR 0 V 1 P
'tis a playing–day, i see. WIV 4.01. 9 P
PLAY'S 1 FR 0.0001 REL FR 1 V 0 P
the play's the thing | wherein i'll catch the HAM 2.02.604
PLAYS 29 FR 0.0032 REL FR 20 V 9 P
he plays false, father. TGV 4.02. 59 P
plays such fantastic tricks before high heaven MM 2.02.121
the music plays, vouchsafe some motion to it. LLL 5.02.216
that, when he plays at tables, chides the dice 5.02.326
and let not him that plays the lion pare his MND 4.02. 40 P
in her hairs | the painter plays the spider, and MV 3.02.121
and one man in his time plays many parts, | his AYL 2.07.142
and so he plays his part. 2.07.157
and good plays prove the better by the help of ep 6 P
hark, apollo plays, | and twenty caged SHR in.2. 35
he plays o' th' viol–de–gamboys, and speaks TN 1.03. 25 P
thy mother plays, and i | play too, but so WT 1.02.187
stays in his course and plays the alchymist, JN 3.01. 78
whiles warm life plays in that infant's veins, 3.04.132
plays fondly with her tears and smiles in R2 3.02. 9
or is it fantasy that plays upon our eyesight? 1H4 5.04.135
for the one or the other plays the rogue with my 2H4 1.02.244 P
both of a bigness, and 'a plays at quoits well, 2.04.245 P
as plays the sun upon the glassy streams, 1H6 5.03. 62
my heart itself plays "my heart is full." ROM 4.05.106 P
master" and the cap | plays in the right hand, TIM 2.01. 19
he loves no plays, | as thou dost, antony; JC 1.02.203
mace upon my boy, | that plays thee music? 4.03.269
he that plays the king shall be welcome — his HAM 2.02.319 P
free of speech, sings, plays, and dances /well; OTH 3.03.185
'a plays and tumbles, driving the poor fry PER 2.01. 30 P
new plays and maidenheads are near akin — TNK pr 1
and moody pluto winks while orpheus plays. LUC 553
play'd, | plays not at all, but seems afraid; PP 17.20
PLAY'ST 2 FR 0.0002 REL FR 2 V 0 P
that play'st so subtilly with a king's repose. H5 4.01.258
music play'st | upon that blessed wood whose SON 128. 1
PLEA 11 FR 0.0012 REL FR 11 V 0 P
the plea of no less weight | than aquitaine, a LLL 2.01. 7
in law, what plea so tainted and corrupt | but, MV 3.02. 75
but none can drive him from the envious plea 3.02.282
though justice be thy plea, consider this, 4.01.198
thus much | to mitigate the justice of thy plea, 4.01.203
that is my brother's plea and none of mine, JN 1.01. 67
that to your sword you will bequeath this plea, TNK 3.01.115
no rightful plea might plead for justice there. LUC 1649
and 'gainst myself a lawful plea commence. SON 35.11
eyes), | but the defendant doth that plea deny, 46. 7
how with this rage shall beauty hold a plea, 65. 3
PLEACH'D 1 FR 0.0001 REL FR 1 V 0 P
and see | thy master thus with pleach'd arms, ANT 4.14. 73
PLEACHED 1 FR 0.0001 REL FR 1 V 0 P
us, | and bid her steal into the pleached bower, ADO 3.01. 7
PLEAD 50 FR 0.0056 REL FR 47 V 3 P
to plead for love deserves more fee than hate. TGV 1.02. 48
sir thurio, fear not you, i will so plead, 4.02. 82
to plead for that which i would not obtain, | to 4.04.100
plead a new state in thy unrival'd merit, | to 5.04.144
for which i would not plead, but that i must; MM 2.02. 31
for which i must not plead, but that i am | at 2.02. 32
he cannot plead his estimation with you; 4.02. 26 P
i profess, i will plead against it with my life. 4.02.179 P
merchant of syracusa, plead no more. ERR 1.01. 3
plead you to me, fair dame? 2.02.147
plead on /her part some cause to you unknown; 3.01. 91
in his eye | that he did plead in earnest? 4.02. 3
if he were mad, he would not plead so coldly. 5.01.273
in such a presence here to plead my thoughts; MND 1.01. 61
to her, i'll plead for you | as for my patron, SHR 1.02.154
here i swear | i'll plead for you myself, but 2.01. 15
a re, to plead hortensio's passion; 3.01. 74
your majesty, may plead | for amplest credence. AWW 1.02. 10
you need but plead your honorable privilege. 4.05. 90 P
war | plead for our interest and our being here. JN 5.02.165
and plead his love–suit to her gentle heart? H5 5.02.101
humbler, | it fitteth not a prelate so to plead. 1H6 3.01. 57
o henry, let me plead for gentle suffolk! 2H6 3.02.289
if thou dost plead for him, | thou wilt but add 3.02.291
us'd to command, untaught to plead for favor. 4.01.122
if not, our swords shall plead it in the field. 3H6 1.01.103
been | an earnest advocate to plead for him. R3 1.03. 86
withal obdurate, do not hear him plead; 1.03.346
as if the golden fee for which i plead | were 3.05. 96
and if you plead as well for them | as i can say 3.07. 52
plead what i will be, not what i have been; 4.04.414
will help me nothing | to plead mine innocence; H8 1.01.208
land, who are assembled | to plead your cause. 2.04. 61
plead my successive title with your swords. TIT 1.01. 4
plead your deserts in peace and humbleness. 1.01. 45
my nephew mutius' deeds do plead for him, | he 1.01.356
brother, for in that name doth nature plead — 1.01.370
son | did graciously plead for his funerals; 1.01.381
prince bassianus, leave to plead my deeds, 1.01.424
and plead my passions for lavinia's love. 2.01. 36
ah, lucius, for thy brothers let me plead. 3.01. 30
yet plead i must, | and bootless unto them. 3.01. 35
then go successantly, and plead to him. 4.04.113
that he may never more false title plead, | nor TIM 4.03.154
that his virtues | will plead like angels, MAC 1.07. 19
come too short, | the actor may plead pardon. ANT 2.05. 9
shall plead for me and tell my loving tale. LUC 480
no rightful plea might plead for justice there. 1649
who plead for love and look for recompense SON 23.11
my heart doth plead that thou in him dost lie 46. 5
PLEADED 3 FR 0.0003 REL FR 3 V 0 P
then pleaded i for you. ERR 4.02. 11
if he suppose that i have pleaded truth, | from 1H6 2.04. 29
his accusations | he pleaded still not guilty, H8 2.01. 13
PLEADER 1 FR 0.0001 REL FR 1 V 0 P
sure if you | would be your country's pleader, COR 5.01. 36
PLEADERS 1 FR 0.0001 REL FR 1 V 0 P
have made them mules, silenc'd their pleaders, COR 2.01.247
PLEADETH 1 FR 0.0001 REL FR 1 V 0 P
all orators are dumb when beauty pleadeth, LUC 268
PLEADING 10 FR 0.0011 REL FR 9 V 1 P
mistook by me, | pleading for a lover's fee. MND 3.02.113
must needs want pleading for a pair of eyes. JN 4.01. 98
love, | pleading so wisely in excuse of it! 2H4 4.05.180
and it be but for pleading so well for his life. 2H6 4.07.107 P
from the place where you behold us pleading, TIT 5.03.130
/i will be deaf to pleading and excuses, | nor ROM 3.01.192
said, impatience chokes her pleading tongue, VEN 217
that love–sick love by pleading may be blest; 328
her pleading hath deserv'd a greater fee; 609
there pleading might you see grave nestor stand, LUC 1401
PLEADS 4 FR 0.0004 REL FR 4 V 0 P
pleads he in earnest? R2 5.03.100
pleads your fair usage, and to diomed | you TRO 4.04.119
and she for him pleads strongly to the moor, OTH 2.03.355
pleads, in a wilderness where are no laws, | to LUC 544
PLEASANCE 2 FR 0.0002 REL FR 1 V 1 P
that we should, with joy, pleasance, revel, and OTH 2.03.292 P
youth is full of pleasance, age is full of care, PP 12. 2
PLEASANT 35 FR 0.0039 REL FR 30 V 5 P
limb, nor beauty, | to make thy riches pleasant. MM 3.01. 38
you are pleasant, sir, and speak apace. 3.02.113 P
he's return'd, and as pleasant as ever he was. ADO 1.01. 37 P
by my troth, most pleasant. how both did fit it! LLL 4.01.129
pleasant without scurrility, witty without 5.01. 3 P
we have had pastimes here and pleasant game. 5.02.360
rated them | at courtship, pleasant jest, and 5.02.780
amendment, | are come to play a pleasant comedy, SHR in.2. 130
lombardy, | the pleasant garden of great italy, 1.01. 4
your ancient, trusty, pleasant servant grumio. 1.02. 47
for thou art pleasant, gamesome, passing 2.01.245
that i have been thus pleasant with you both. 3.01. 58
more pleasant, pithy, and effectual, | than hath 3.01. 68
like pleasant travellers, to break a jest | upon 4.05. 72
as it hath been to us rare, pleasant, speedy, WT 3.01. 13
down, or a very pleasant thing indeed and sung 4.04.189 P
his body to that pleasant country's earth, | and R2 4.01. 98
why, here it is, welcome these pleasant days! 2H4 5.03.141
we are glad the dolphin is so pleasant with us, H5 1.02.259
and tell the pleasant prince this mock of his 1.02.281
else | but like a pleasant slumber in thy lap? 2H6 3.02.390
i am glad | your grace is grown so pleasant. H8 1.04. 90
come, you are pleasant. 2.03. 93
well, sweet queen, you are pleasant with me. TRO 3.01. 62 P
upon the north side of this pleasant chase; TIT 2.03.255
and then awake as from a pleasant sleep. ROM 4.01.106
i have upon a high and pleasant hill | feign'd TIM 1.01. 63
this castle hath a pleasant seat, the air MAC 1.06. 1
and our practices | pleasant and helpful to him! HAM 2.02. 39
most he should dislike seems pleasant to him; LR 4.02. 10
and of our pleasant vices | make instruments to 5.03.171
exceeding pleasant; CYM 1.06. 59
stray lower, where the pleasant fountains lie. VEN 234
month of may, | sitting in a pleasant shade, PP 20. 3
not that the summer is less pleasant now | than SON 102. 9
PLEASANTLY 1 FR 0.0001 REL FR 1 V 0 P
think'st thou to catch my life so pleasantly TRO 4.05.249
PLEASANT–SPIRITED 1 FR 0.0001 REL FR 0 V 1 P
by my troth, a pleasant–spirited lady. ADO 2.01.341 P
PLEASANT'ST 1 FR 0.0001 REL FR 1 V 0 P
the pleasant'st angling is to see the fish | cut ADO 3.01. 26
/PLEAS'D 1 FR 0.0001 REL FR 1 V 0 P
/and /thou /with /all /pleas'd, /that /hast /all R2 4.01.217
PLEAS'D 86 FR 0.0097 REL FR 76 V 10 P
i' th' state | to what tune pleas'd his ear, TMP 1.02. 85
wilt thou be pleas'd to hearken once again to 3.02. 38 P
if you be pleas'd, retire into my cell, | and 4.01.161
but she would be best pleas'd | to be so ang'red TGV 1.02. 99
i fear me, he will scarce be pleas'd withal. 2.07. 67
nor of heaven nor earth, for these are pleas'd; 5.04. 80
unloose this tied–up justice when you pleas'd: MM 1.03. 32
pleas'd you to do't at peril of your soul, 2.04. 67
my mirth it much displeas'd, but pleas'd my woe. 4.01. 13
the heavens were so pleas'd that thou wert but LLL 5.01. 75 P
i am best pleas'd with that. 5.02.229
it pleas'd them to think me worthy of pompey the 5.02.505 P
if you be well pleas'd with this, | and hold MV 3.02.135
madam, it is, so you stand pleas'd withal. 3.02.209
and am well pleas'd | to wish it back on you. 3.04. 43
and i be pleas'd to give ten thousand ducats 4.01. 45
if you had pleas'd to have defended it | with 5.01.204
shouldst have better pleas'd me with this deed AYL 1.02.227
food he eats, | and pleas'd with what he gets, 2.05. 41
as many of you as had beards that pleas'd me, ep 19 P
if she and i be pleas'd, what's that to you? SHR 2.01.303
she will be pleas'd, then wherefore should i 4.04.106
might do her | a shrewd turn, if she pleas'd. AWW 3.05. 68
if the heavens had been pleas'd, would we had so TN 2.01. 20 P
be pleas'd that i shake off these names you give 5.01. 73
since these good men are pleas'd, let them come WT 4.04.341 P
if not, my senses, better pleas'd with madness, 4.04.484
philip of france, if thou be pleas'd withal, JN 2.01.531
if heaven be pleas'd that you must use me ill, 4.01. 55
i am best pleas'd to be from such a deed. 4.01. 85
"once again" (but that your highness pleas'd) 4.02. 3
but it pleas'd your highness | to overbear it, 4.02. 36
to overbear it, and we are all well pleas'd, 4.02. 37
me, till i have pleas'd | my discontented peers! 4.02.126
not, i, pleas'd | not to be pardoned, am content R2 2.01.187
with nothing shall be pleas'd, till he be eas'd 5.05. 40
the which if he be pleas'd i shall perform, | i 1H4 3.02.154
it pleas'd your majesty to turn your looks | of 5.01. 30
whose music, to my thinking, pleas'd the king. 2H4 5.05.108
heaven and our lady gracious hath it pleas'd 1H6 1.02. 74
and henry was well pleas'd | to change two 2H6 1.01.218
nay, be not angry, i am pleas'd again. 1.02. 55
and it hath pleas'd him that three times to–day 5.03. 18
before it pleas'd his majesty | to raise my 3H6 4.01. 67
o' th' combination drew | as himself pleas'd; H8 1.01.170
the king | is pleas'd you shall to th' tower, 1.01.213
long, be pleas'd yourself to say | how far you 2.04.211
if heaven had pleas'd to have given me longer 4.02.152
this oracle of comfort has so pleas'd me | that 5.04. 66
are pleas'd to breed out your inheritors. TRO 4.01. 65
pleas'd with this dainty bait, thus goes to bed. 5.08. 20
was pleas'd to let him seek danger where he was COR 1.03. 12 P
corioles walls, | and made what work i pleas'd. 1.08. 9
are well pleas'd | to make thee consul. 2.02.132
if thou be pleas'd with this my sudden choice, TIT 1.01.318
is the pearl that pleas'd your empress' eye, 5.01. 42
it hath pleas'd the gods to remember my father's TIM 1.02. 2
taste, touch, all, pleas'd from thy table rise; 1.02.126
according as he pleas'd and displeas'd them, as JC 1.02.259 P
play, i remember, pleas'd not the million, 'twas HAM 2.02.436 P
but heaven hath pleas'd it so | to punish me 3.04.173
been born than not t' have pleas'd me better. LR 1.01.234
it pleas'd the king his master very late | to 2.02.116
it hath pleas'd the devil drunkenness to give OTH 2.03.296 P
had it pleas'd heaven | to try me with 4.02. 47
you may be pleas'd to catch at mine intent | by ANT 2.02. 41
be pleas'd to tell us | (for this is from the 2.06. 29
pleas'd fortune does of marcus crassus' death 3.01. 2
look upon you | but when you are well pleas'd. 3.03. 4
half the bulk o' th' world play'd as i pleas'd, 3.11. 64
subject to, | when't pleas'd you to employ me. CYM 1.01.173
cloys his beak, | as when his god is pleas'd. 5.04.119
be pleas'd awhile: 5.05.356
the strict fates had pleas'd you had brought her PER 3.03. 8
pray be pleas'd | to show in generous terms your TNK 3.01. 53
been merry, | and have pleas'd /ye with a derry, 3.05.139
if we have pleas'd /thee too | and have done as 3.05.142
never so pleas'd, sir. 3.05.149
all the chaste nights i have ever pleas'd you — 3.06.200
i hope she's pleas'd, | her signs were gracious. 5.01.172
if't pleas'd his rider | to put pride in him. 5.04. 57
would you be pleas'd | to find a nation of such STM II.C 130
if pleas'd themselves, others they think delight VEN 843
a nurse's song ne'er pleas'd her babe so well. 974
grief best is pleas'd with grief's society; LUC 1111
who in despite of view is pleas'd to dote; SON 141. 4
PLEASE' 1 FR 0.0001 REL FR 1 V 0 P
please' your highness, posts | from those you WT 2.03.193
/PLEASE 3 FR 0.0003 REL FR 3 V 0 P
/may /it /please /you, /lords, /to /grant /the R2 4.01.154
/please /you, /draw /near. LR 4.07. 24
/if /you /please, | /be't at her father's. OTH 1.03.239
PLEASE 409 FR 0.0462 REL FR 314 V 95 P
please you, farther. TMP 1.02. 65
please you, sir, | do not omit the heavy offer 2.01.193
will't please you taste of what is here? 3.03. 42
on a trice, so please you, | even in a dream, 5.01.238

please you draw near. 5.01.319
or else my project fails, | which was to please. ep 13
please you repeat their names, i'll show my mind TGV 1.02. 7
come, come, will't please you go? 1.02.137
to–morrow, may it please you, don alphonso 1.03. 39
may't please your lordship, 'tis a word or two 1.03. 52
please you deliberate a day or two. 1.03. 73
i will write | (please you command) a thousand 2.01.114
please you, i'll write your ladyship another. 2.01.129
sake read it over, | and if it please you, so; 2.01.131
if it please me, madam, what then? 2.01.132
why, if it please you, take it for your labor; 2.01.133
where, if it please you, you may intercept him. 3.01. 43
please it your grace, there is a messenger 3.01. 52
in what you please; i'll do what i can. 4.04. 42
madam, please you peruse this letter — | pardon 4.04.121
please you, i'll tell you as we pass along, 5.04.168
will't please your worship to come in, sir? WIV 1.01.266 P
not so, and't please your worship. 2.02. 35 P
if it please your honor, i am the poor duke's MM 2.01. 47 P
if it please your honor, i know not well what 2.01. 53 P
sir, if it please your honor, this is not so. 2.01. 85 P
yes, and't please you, sir. 2.01.196 P
to your honor, | please but your honor hear me. 2.02. 28
it, would much better please me | than to demand 2.04. 32
please you to do't, | i'll take it as a peril to 2.04. 64
as many as you please. 3.01. 51 P
and much please the absent duke, if peradventure 3.01.203 P
years' continuance, may it please your honor. 3.02.197 P
so please you, this friar hath been with him, 3.02.212 P
will't please you walk aside? 4.01. 58
look, if it please you, on this man condemn'd 5.01.444
had rather it would please you i might be whipt. 5.01.506 P
please you, i'll meet with you upon the mart, ERR 1.02. 27
it seems he hath great care to please his wife. 2.01. 56
since that my beauty cannot please his eye, 2.01.114
what please yourself, sir; 3.02.170
go home with it, and please your wife withal, 3.02.173
and i will please you what you will demand. 4.04. 49
may it please your grace, antipholus, my husband 5.01.136
please it your grace lead on? ADO 1.01.159 P
make cur'sy and say, "father, as it please you." 2.01. 53 P
cur'sy and say, "father, as it please me." 2.01. 56 P
i may say so when i please. 2.01. 92 P
and when please you to say so? 2.01. 93 P
her hair shall be of what color it please god. 2.03. 35 P
if it please you — yet count claudio may hear, 3.02. 85 P
let me say no, my liege, and if you please: LLL 1.01. 50
study me how to please the eye indeed | by 1.01. 80
me, an't shall please you: i am anthony dull. 1.01.270 P
so please your grace, the packet is not come 2.01.163
so it shall please you to abrogate squirility. 4.02. 54 P
did they please you, sir nathaniel? 4.02.150 P
it shall please you to gratify the table with a 4.02.154 P
for i must tell thee it will please his grace 5.01.102 P
please it you, | as much in private, and i'll 5.02.240
please it your majesty | command me any service 5.02.311
and utters it again when god doth please. 5.02.316
there, an't shall please you, a foolish mild man 5.02.580 P
and therewithal to win me, if you please, 5.02.848
of pyramus and thisby that will never please. MND 3.01. 10 P
and those things do best please me | that befall 3.02.120
so please your grace, the prologue is address'd. 5.01.106
will it please you to see the epilogue, or to 5.01.352 P
but if you please | to shoot another arrow that MV 1.01.147
if it please you to dine with us. 1.03. 32 P
of launcelot, an't please your mastership. 2.02. 59 P
studied in a sad ostent | to please his grandam, 2.02.197
and it shall please you to break up this, it 2.04. 10 P
when you shall please to play the thieves for 2.06. 23
ready, so please your grace. 4.01. 2
i am not bound to please thee with my answers. 4.01. 65
so please my lord the duke and all the court 4.01.380
i will not till i please. AYL 1.01. 66 P
so please you, he is here at the door, and 1.01. 91 P
and, if it please your ladyships, you may see 1.02.114 P
ay, my liege, so please you give us leave. 1.02.157 P
my voice is ragged, i know i cannot please you. 2.05. 16 P
i do not desire you to please me, i do desire 2.05. 17 P
more at your request than to please myself. 2.05. 23 P
his wealth and ease | a stubborn will to please, 2.05. 53
to blow on whom i please, for so fools have; 2.07. 49
so please you, for i never heard it yet; 4.03. 37
believe then, if you please, that i can do 5.02. 59 P
would send me word he cut it to please himself: 5.04. 74 P
men, to like as much of this play as please you; ep 14 P
between you and the women the play may please. ep 17 P
"will't please your lordship cool your hands?" SHR in.1. 58
an't please your honor, players | that offer in.1. 77
so please your lordship to accept our duty. in.1. 82
will't please your /lordship drink a cup of sack in.2. 2
will't please your honor taste of these in.2. 3
will't please your mightiness to wash your hands in.2. 76
yea, and to marry her, if her dowry please. 1.02.184
please ye we may contrive this afternoon | and 1.02.274
but learn my lessons as i please myself. 3.01. 20
old fashions please me best; 3.01. 80
if it would please him come and marry her!" 3.02. 20
no, nor to–morrow — not till i please myself. 3.02.209
for me, i'll not be gone till i please myself. 3.02.212
even to the uttermost, as i please, in words. 4.03. 80
this is the house, please it you that i call? 4.04. 1
and if you please to like | no worse than i, 4.04. 32
plainness and your shortness please me well. 4.04. 39
and be it moon, or sun, or what you please; 4.05. 13
and if you please to call it a rush–candle, 4.05. 14
in token of which duty, if he please, | my hand 5.02.178
may it please you, madam, that he bid helen come AWW 1.03. 66 P
and virtuous mistress | fall, when love please! 2.03. 58
please it your majesty, i have done already. 2.03. 68
no better, if you please. 2.03. 84
thine honor where | we please to have it grow. 2.03.157
if you shall please so, pilgrim. 3.05. 44
please it this matron and this gentle maid | to 3.05. 97
as't please your lordship. i'll leave you. 3.06.109
that it will please you | to give this poor 5.01. 18
so please your majesty, my master hath been an 5.03.238 P
yes, so please your majesty. 5.03.258 P
with strife to please you, day exceeding day. ep 4
so please my lord, i might not be admitted, TN 1.01. 23
and it would please you to take leave of her, 2.03.100 P
he is not here, so please your lordship, that 2.04. 8 P
if it please the eye of one, it is with me as 3.04. 22 P
with me as the very true sonnet is, "please one, 3.04. 23 P
true sonnet is, "please one, and please all." 3.04. 23 P
pray, sir, put your sword up, if you please. 3.04.321 P
though it please you to be one of my friends. 5.01. 25 P
even what it please my lord, that shall become 5.01.116
think of me as you please. 5.01.309 P
my lord, so please you, these things further 5.01.316
shall crown th' alliance on't, so please you, 5.01.318
and we'll strive to please you every day. 5.01.408
please your highness | to take the urgent hour. WT 1.02.464
please you t' accept it — that the queen is 2.01.131
so please you, madam, | to put apart these your 2.02. 12
please your ladyship | to visit the next room, 2.02. 44
please you, come something nearer. 2.02. 53
madam, if't please the queen to send the babe, 2.02. 54
these lords, my noble fellows, if they please, 2.03.143
so please you, sir, their speed | hath been 2.03.197
and honor 'fore | who please to come and hear. 3.02. 42
which may, if fortune please, both breed thee, 3.03. 48
i, that please some, try all, both joy and 4.01. 1
little but bowling) it will please plentifully. 4.04.331 P
will't please you, sir, be gone? 4.04.446
if you may please to think i love the king | and 4.04.521
and't please you, sir, to undertake the business 4.04.806 P
please you, great sir, | bohemia greets you from 5.01.180
please you to interpose, fair madam, kneel, 5.03.119
and if thou please, | thou mayst befriend me so JN 5.06. 9
and wish (so please my sovereign) ere i move, R2 1.01. 45
o my liege, | pardon me, if you please; 2.01.187
to please the king i did, to please myself | i 2.02. 5
king i did, to please myself | i cannot do it; 2.02. 5
unless you please to enter in the castle, | and 2.03.160
speak with you, may it please you to come down. 3.03.177
but thou shouldst please me better wouldst thou 3.04. 20
my lord, will't please you to fall to? 5.05. 98
that, when he please again to be himself, 1H4 1.02.200
so please your majesty, i would i could | quit 3.02. 18
with some fine color that may please the eye 5.01. 75
please it your honor knock but at the gate, 2H4 1.01. 5
falstaff, and't please your lordship. 1.02. 59 P
and't please your lordship, i hear his majesty 1.02.103 P
a kind of lethargy, and't please your lordship, 1.02.112 P
rather, and't please you, it is the disease of 1.02.121 P
most worshipful lord, and't please your grace, i 2.01. 69 P
please it your grace | to go to bed. 3.01. 98
here, and't please you. 3.02.101 P
yea, and't please you. 3.02.105 P
four of which you please. 3.02.242 P
gaultree forest, and't shall please your grace. 4.01. 2
please you, lords, | in sight of both our 4.01.176
if this may please you, | discharge your powers 4.02. 60
i know it will well please them. 4.02. 71
and, good my lord, so please you, let our trains 4.02. 93
order of the fight | this packet, please it you, 4.04.101
will't please your grace to go along with us? 4.05. 19
and't please your worship, there's one pistol 5.03. 80 P
may't please your majesty to give us leave H5 1.02.237
ay, so please your majesty. 3.06. 90 P
as, if god please, they shall — my ransom then 4.03.120
of famous memory, an't please your majesty, and 4.07. 93 P
and't please your majesty, 'tis the gage of one 4.07.122 P
and't please your majesty, a rascal that 4.07.125 P
and a villain else, and't please your majesty, 4.07.133 P
and please god of his grace that i might see. 4.07.164 P
he is my dear friend, and please you. 4.07.166 P
and please your majesty, let his neck answer for 4.08. 43 P
is it not lawful, and please your majesty, to 4.08.117 P
dat is as it shall please de roi mon pere. 5.02.247 P
nay, it will please him well, kate; 5.02.248 P
it shall please him, kate. 5.02.249 P
so please you. 5.02.325 P
now, quiet soul, depart when heaven please, 1H6 3.02.110
yes, if it please your majesty, my liege. 3.04. 15
yet call th' embassadors, and as you please, 5.01. 24
no shape but his can please your dainty eye. 5.03. 38
and if my father please, i am content. 5.03.127
my daughter shall be henry's, if he please. 5.03.156
my lords, and please you, 'tis not so, | i did 5.04. 10
so, now dismiss your army when ye please; 5.04.173
my lord protector, so it please your grace, 2H6 1.01. 39
they please us well. 1.01. 63
mine is, and't please your grace, against john 1.03. 16 P
please it your majesty, this is the man | that 1.03.181
and't shall please your majesty, i never said 1.03.187 P
born blind, and't please your grace. 2.01. 75
saunder simpcox, and if it please you, master. 2.01.122
yes, my lord, if it please your grace. 2.01.135
please it your majesty, | this is the day 2.03. 47
so please your highness to behold the fight. 2.03. 51
so please your grace, we'll take her from the 2.04. 17
and't please your grace, here my commission 2.04. 76
am i given in charge, may't please your grace. 2.04. 80
and when he please to make commotion, | 'tis to 3.01. 29
i will, my lord, so please his majesty. 3.01.315
please it your grace to be advertised | the duke 4.09. 23
so please it you, my lord, 'twere not amiss | he 5.01. 76
to effect this marriage, so it please my lord. 3H6 2.06. 98
may it please your highness to resolve me now, 3.02. 19
please you dismiss me, either with ay or no. 3.02. 78
our dukedom till god please to send the rest. 4.07. 47
and please your worship, brakenbury, | you may R3 1.01. 88
which if thou please to hide in this true breast 1.02.175
that it may please you leave these sad designs 1.02.210
and may direct his course as please himself, 2.02.129
then where you please, and shall be thought most 3.01. 66
my lord, will't please you pass along? 3.01.136
the better that your lordship please to ask. 3.02. 97
would it might please your grace, | on our 3.07.114
to–morrow may it please you to be crown'd? 3.07.242
even when you please, for you will have it so. 3.07.243
please you; | but i had rather kill two enemies. 4.02. 70
may it please you to resolve me in my suit. 4.02.117
what, may it please you, shall i do at salisbury 4.04.453
good, my liege, to please you with the hearing, 4.04.457
where and what time your majesty shall please. 4.04.489
whither, if it please you, we may now withdraw 5.05. 11
here, so please you. H8 1.01.116
ay, please your grace. 1.01.117
that he would please to alter the king's course, 1.01.189
please you, sir, | i know but of a single part 1.02. 40
please your highness note | this dangerous 1.02.138
they rested, | i think would better please 'em. 1.04. 13
sweet ladies, will it please you sit? 1.04. 19
an't please your grace, sir thomas bullen's 1.04. 92
to be fashion'd | into what pitch he please. 2.02. 49
him, so i'll stand, | if the king please; 2.02. 52
receive | if you might please to stretch it. 2.03. 33
please you, sir, | the king, your father, was 2.04. 44
serve your will as't please | yourself pronounce 2.04.114
highness | that it shall please you to declare, 2.04.146
so please your highness, | the question did at 2.04.212
so please your highness, | the queen being 2.04.231
and't please your grace, the two great cardinals 3.01. 16
may it please you, noble madam, to withdraw 3.01. 27
(if you please | to trust us in your business), 3.01.172
may it please your highness | to hear me speak 4.02. 46
please your honors, | the chief cause concerns 5.02. 37
may it please your grace — 5.02.169
no, sir, it does not please me. 5.02.169
will these please you? 5.02.203
and't please your honor, | we are but men; 5.03. 74
'tis ten to one this play can never please | all ep 1
his experienc'd tongue, yet let it please both, TRO 1.03. 68
please it our great general | to call together 2.03.259
please it our general pass strangely by him, 3.03. 39
let's have your company, or, if you please, 4.01. 40
please you walk in, my lords. 4.03. 12
so please you, save the thanks this prince 4.04.117
princes, enough, so please you. 4.05.117
for his country, he did it to please his mother, COR 1.01. 39 P
but, and't please you, deliver. 1.01. 95 P
please you to march, | and four shall quickly 1.06. 83
therefore please you, | most reverend and grave 2.02. 41
please you | to hear cominius speak? 2.02. 61
please you | that i may pass this doing. 2.02.138
please it your honors | to call me to your 5.06.138
me, andronicus, doth this motion please thee? TIT 1.01.243
and it please your majesty | to hunt the panther 1.01.492
discord's ground, the music would not please. 2.01. 70
may it please you, | my grandsire, well advis'd, 4.02. 9
then let the ladies tattle what they please. 4.02.168
bid him demand what pledge will please him best. 4.04.106
say on, and if it please me which thou speak'st, 5.01. 59
and if it please thee? 5.01. 61
but would it please thee, good andronicus, | to 5.02.111
please you, therefore, draw nigh and take your 5.03. 24
'twill fill your stomachs, please you eat of it. 5.03. 29
will't please you eat? 5.03. 54
will't please your highness feed? 5.03. 54
so please you step aside, | i'll know his ROM 1.01.156
in a fair lady's ear, | such as would please; 1.05. 24
so please you, let me now be left alone, | and 4.03. 9
please you, my lord, there are certain ladies TIM 1.02.116 P
attends you, | please you to dispose yourselves. 1.02.156
may it please your honor, lord lucius | (out of 1.02.181
please you, my lord, that honorable gentleman, 1.02.186 P
please it your lordship, he hath put me off | to 2.02. 19
please you, gentlemen, | the time is unagreeable 2.02. 39
please your lordship, here is the wine. 3.01. 30 P
may it please your honor, my lord hath sent — 3.02. 30 P
dost please thyself in't? 4.03.238
if thou couldst please me with speaking to me, 4.03.346 P
therefore so please thee to return with us, 5.01.159
that whoso please | to stop affliction, let him 5.01.209
to–morrow, if you please to speak with me, | i JC 1.02.304
if it will please caesar | to be so good to 2.04. 28
tell him, so please him come unto this place, 3.01.140
no place will please me so, no mean of death, 3.01.161
when it shall please my country to need my death 3.02. 46 P
vaunting true, | and it shall please me well. 4.03. 53
so please you, we will stand and watch your 4.03.249
ay, my lord, an't please you. 4.03.258
so please you, it is true; MAC 1.05. 34
it was, so please your highness. 3.01. 74
may't please your highness sit. 3.04. 38
whom you may say (if't please you) fleance 3.06. 6
key | (as, and't please heaven, he shall not), 3.06. 19
the english force, so please you. 5.03. 18
so please you, something touching the lord HAM 1.03. 89
there put on him | what forgeries you please: 2.01. 20
if it will please you | to show us so much 2.02. 21
that it might please you to give quiet pass 2.02. 77
gracious, so please you, | we will bestow 3.01. 42
my lord, do as you please, | but, if you hold it 3.01.180
and i'll be plac'd (so please you) in the ear 3.01.184
finger | to sound what stop she please. 3.02. 71
if it shall please you to make me a wholesome 3.02.315 P
will't please you go, my lord? 4.04. 30
'a shall, sir, and/'t please him. 4.06. 9 P
if it please his majesty, it is the breathing 5.02.173 P
so please your lordship, none. LR 1.02. 27 P
if it shall please you to suspend your 1.02. 80 P
put on what weary negligence you please, | you 1.03. 12
so please you — 1.04. 45 P
own purpose, | how in my strength you please. 2.01.112
with you, goodman boy, /and you please! 2.02. 45 P
tempt me again | to die before you please! 4.06.219
so please your majesty | that we may wake the 4.07. 16
will't please your highness walk? 4.07. 82
if you please | to get good guard and go along OTH 1.01.178
please it your grace, on to the state affairs. 1.03.190
it not | to please the palate of my appetite, 1.03.262
so please your grace, my ancient; 1.03.283
or from what other course you please, which the 2.01.269 P
yet, if you please to /hold him off awhile, 3.03.248
i nothing but to please his fantasy. 3.03.299
if it might please you, to enforce no further ANT 2.02. 99
will't please you hear me? 2.05. 41
if caesar please, our master | will leap to be 3.13. 50
it much would please him, | that of his fortunes 3.13. 67

till we do please | to daff't for our repose, 4.04. 12
please you retire to your chamber? 4.04. 35
is to–day by sea, | we please them not by land. 4.10. 2
do not please sharp fate | to grace it with your 4.14.135
but please your thoughts | in feeding them with 4.15. 52
if thou please | to take me to thee, as i was to 5.01. 9
if he please | to give me conquer'd egypt for my 5.02. 18
to caesar i will speak what you shall please, 5.02. 69
if it might please ye — 5.02. 78
conquest, shall | hang in what place you please. 5.02.136
please your highness, | i will from hence to–day CYM 1.01. 79
may it please you | to take them in protection? 1.06.192
if you please | to greet your lord with writing, 1.06.205
please you, madam. 2.02. 1
please you, read, | and you shall find me, 3.04. 18
please you, sir, | her chambers are all lock'd, 3.05. 42
so please you, leave me, | stick to your journal 4.02. 9
you health. so please you, sir. 4.02. 31
but first, and't please the gods, | i'll hide my 4.02.387
follow you, | so please you entertain me. 4.02.394
so please your majesty, | the roman legions, all 4.03. 23
she confess'd | i will report, so please you. 5.05. 34
we did, so please your highness. 5.05. 62
in private, if you please | to give me hearing. 5.05.115
to glad your ear and please your eyes. PER 1.ch. 4
prince, pardon me, or strike me, if you please, 1.02. 46
since he's gone, the king's seas must please: 1.03. 27
air | were all too little to content and please, 1.04. 35
now, by the gods, he could not please me better. 2.03. 72
yes, if't please your majesty. 2.05. 91
in silken bags, | to please the fool and death. 3.02. 42
moreover, if you please, a niece of mine | shall 3.04. 15
they will but please themselves upon her, | not 4.01.100
if it please the gods to defend you by men, then 4.02. 90 P
now please you wit | the epitaph is for marina 4.04. 31
please you to name it. 4.06. 70 P
shall be discover'd, please you sit and hark. 5.ch. 24
if the gods please — to hold here a brave TNK 2.02. 59
and me too, | even when you please, of life. 2.02.225
he has as much to please a woman in him | (if he 2.04. 9
a woman in him | (if he please to bestow it so) 2.04. 10
i am proud to please you. 2.05. 4
your attendance | cannot please heaven, and i 3.01.111
will't please you arm, sir? 3.06. 35
so let me be most traitor, and ye please me. 3.06.167
please her appetite, | and do it home; 5.02. 36
that sure shall please the gods | sooner than 5.04. 11
how many tales to please me hath she coined, PP 7. 9
i tell the day, to please him, thou art bright, SON 28. 9
if my slight muse do please these curious days, 38.13
me, so it please thee hold | that nothing me, a 136.11
ill, | th' uncertain sickly appetite to please. 147. 4

PLEASED 5 FR 0.0005 REL FR 5 V 0 P
appear | among the buzzing pleased multitude, MV 3.02.180
be pleased then | to pay that duty which you JN 2.01.246
your highness pleased to forget my place, | the 2H4 5.02. 77
and sends the poor well pleased from my gate. 2H6 4.10. 23
what, are you both pleased? PER 2.05. 88

PLEASE–MAN 1 FR 0.0001 REL FR 1 V 0 P
some carry–tale, some please–man, some slight LLL 5.02.463

PLEASES 19 FR 0.0021 REL FR 9 V 10 P
the better that it pleases your good worship to WIV 1.04.135 P
i know not which pleases me better, that my 3.03.178 P
for he both pleases men and angers them, and ADO 2.01.141 P
it pleases your worship to say so, but we are 3.05. 19 P
that sport best pleases that doth /least know LLL 5.02.516
he that speaks them pleases those that hear. AYL 3.05.112
it pleases him to call you so; 4.01. 66 P
content you, if what pleases you contents you, 5.02.117 P
howe'er it pleases you to take it so, | the ring AWW 5.03. 88
i could tell to thee — as to one it pleases me, 2H4 2.02. 41 P
preserve it, as long as it pleases his grace, H5 4.07.108 P
command in anjou what your honor pleases. 1H6 5.03.147
and if what pleases him shall pleasure you. 3H6 3.02. 22
does buy and sell his honor as he pleases, | and H8 1.01.192
as hector pleases. TRO 4.05.119
but that that likes not you pleases me best. 5.02.103 P
it pleases time and fortune to lie heavy | upon TIM 3.05. 10
the justice of it pleases; OTH 4.01.209 P
port even where | the heavenly limiter pleases. TNK 5.01. 30

PLEASEST 2 FR 0.0002 REL FR 2 V 0 P
and how thou pleasest, god, dispose the day! H5 4.03.133
if thou pleasest not, | i yield thee up my life. ANT 5.01. 11

PLEASE'T 1 FR 0.0001 REL FR 1 V 0 P
please't your highness | to grace us with your MAC 3.04. 43

PLEASETH 18 FR 0.0020 REL FR 15 V 3 P
pleaseth you walk with me down to his house, | i ERR 4.01. 12
special honors it pleaseth his greatness to LLL 5.01.106 P
taken | in what part of your body pleaseth me. MV 1.03.151
it is in the fields, it pleaseth me well; AYL 3.02. 18 P
come, | and nothing pleaseth but rare accidents. 1H4 1.02.207
and she will sing the song that pleaseth you, 3.01.213
pleaseth your lordship | to meet his grace just 2H4 4.01.223
pleaseth your grace to answer them directly 4.02. 52
pleaseth your grace | to appoint some of your H5 5.02. 78
what wills lord talbot pleaseth burgundy. 1H6 3.02.130
shall do and undo as him pleaseth best. 3H6 2.06.105
i know it pleaseth neither of us well. R3 1.01.113
which pleaseth god above | and all good men of 3.07.109
pleaseth your majesty to give me leave, | i'll 4.04.487
when it pleaseth their deities to take the wife ANT 1.02.162 P
pleaseth your highness, ay. CYM 1.05. 5
it pleaseth you, my royal father, to express PER 2.02. 8
it pleaseth me so well that i will see you wed, 2.05. 92

/PLEASING 1 FR 0.0001 REL FR 1 V 0 P
/my /aunt /merry /with /some /pleasing /tale. TIT 3.02. 47

PLEASING 23 FR 0.0026 REL FR 21 V 2 P
under | the pleasing punishment that women bear) ERR 1.01. 46
ear, | that never object pleasing in thine eye, 2.02.115
pierc'd and prick'd a pretty pleasing pricket; LLL 4.02. 56
was no thought of pleasing you when she was AYL 3.02.266 P
no, my good lord, it is more pleasing stuff. SHR in.2. 139
more quaint, more pleasing, nor more commendable 4.03.102
of a cheerful look, a pleasing eye, and a most 1H4 2.04.423 P
charming your blood with pleasing heaviness, 3.01.215
so your dislikes, to whom i would be pleasing, 3H6 4.01. 73
chamber | to the lascivious pleasing of a lute. R3 1.01. 13
lip, a bonny eye, a passing pleasing tongue; 1.01. 94
a pleasing cordial, princely buckingham, | is 2.01. 41
can make seem pleasing to her tender years? 4.04.342
we are convented | upon a pleasing treaty, and COR 2.02. 55
in pleasing smiles such murderous tyranny. TIT 2.03.267
that blabb'd them with such pleasing eloquence, 3.01. 83
sport, | she sounded almost at my pleasing tale, 5.01.119
a very pleasing night to honest men. JC 1.03. 43
/dev'l hath power | t' assume a pleasing shape, HAM 2.02.600
fed | with such delightful pleasing harmony. PER 2.05. 28
relish your nimble notes to pleasing ears, LUC 1126
who all in one, one pleasing note do sing: SON 8.12
that music hath a far more pleasing sound; 130.10

PLEASURE 196 FR 0.0221 REL FR 152 V 44 P
i come | to answer thy best pleasure; TMP 1.02.190
i am full of pleasure, | let us be jocund. 3.02.116
thy thoughts i cleave to. what's thy pleasure? 4.01.165
i wait upon his pleasure. TGV 2.04.117
service | it is your pleasure to command me in. 4.03. 10
what i do is to pleasure you, coz. WIV 1.01.243 P
grace's will, | i come to know your pleasure. MM 1.01. 26
is't your worship's pleasure i shall do with 2.01.183 P
i'll know | his pleasure, may be he will relent. 2.02. 3
i am come to know your pleasure. 2.04. 31
what pleasure was he given to? 3.02.234 P
you shall anon over–read it at your pleasure; 4.02.197 P
and punish them to your height of pleasure. 5.01.240
prison, | and see our pleasure herein executed. 5.01.521
you take pleasure then in the message? ADO 2.03.253 P
as we do the minstrels, draw to pleasure us. 5.01.129 P
the duke's pleasure is that you keep costard LLL 1.02.127 P
his forbidden gates, | to know his pleasure; 2.01. 27
at your sweet pleasure, for the mountain. 5.01. 85 P
the king's most sweet pleasure and affection to 5.01. 87 P
when i had at my pleasure taunted her, | and she MND 4.01. 57
the object and the pleasure of mine eye, | is 4.01.170
will you pleasure me? MV 1.03. 7 P
notwithstanding, use your pleasure; 3.02.321 P
me how to remember any extraordinary pleasure. AYL 1.02. 7 P
it was your pleasure and your own remorse. 1.03. 70
no profit grows where is no pleasure ta'en. SHR 1.01. 39
shall you have to court her at your pleasure. 1.01. 54
sir, to your pleasure humbly i subscribe; 1.01. 81
in brief, sir, sith it your pleasure is, | and i 1.01.211
nor hast thou pleasure to be cross in talk; 2.01.249
but is this true, or is it else your pleasure, 4.05. 71
what is your pleasure, madam? AWW 1.03.137
your pleasure, sir? 2.03.185 P
even to the world's pleasure and the increase of 2.04. 36 P
o'erflow with joy | and pleasure drown the brim. 2.04. 47
you presently | attend his further pleasure. 2.04. 53
be it his pleasure. 3.01. 16
whisper with the general, and know his pleasure. 4.03.297 P
glove, my lord, she goes off and on at pleasure. 5.03.278 P
know, | to make the even truth in pleasure flow. 5.03.326
no pains, sir, i take pleasure in singing, sir. TN 2.04. 68 P
i'll pay thy pleasure then. 2.04. 69
sir, and pleasure will be paid, one time or 2.04. 70 P
but since you make your pleasure of your pains, 3.03. 2
he attends your ladyship's pleasure. 3.04. 59 P
carry it thus, for our pleasure and his penance, 3.04.137 P
it is his highness' pleasure that the queen WT 3.02. 9
world can match | the pleasure of that madness. 5.03. 73
to do your pleasure and continue friends. JN 3.01.252
but that your royal pleasure must be done, 4.02. 17
call it a travel that thou tak'st for pleasure. R2 1.03.262
the pleasure that some fathers feed upon | is my 2.01. 79
meeting, wherein it is at our pleasure to fail; 1H4 1.02.171 P
that takes from thee | thy stomach, pleasure, 2.03. 41
not in pleasure but in passion; 2.04.415 P
and deliver him | up to his pleasure, ransomless 5.05. 28
than will do me good, for no man's pleasure, i. 2H4 2.04.120 P
what is your good pleasure with me? 3.02. 59 P
now are we well prepar'd to know the pleasure H5 1.02.234
would desire the duke to use his good pleasure, 3.06. 55 P
god's will, and his pleasure, captain, i beseech 4.08. 2 P
at pleasure here we lie near orleance; 1H6 1.02. 6
our pleasure is | that richard be restored to 3.01.157
although you break it when your pleasure serves. 5.04.164
it was the pleasure of my lord the king. 2H6 1.01.138
hast thou not worldly pleasure at command 1.02. 45
'tis his highness' pleasure | you do prepare to 1.02. 56
and at his pleasure will resign my place. 1.03.121
at your pleasure, my good lord. 1.04. 78
his highness' pleasure is to talk with him. 2.01. 71
with every several pleasure in the world; 3.02.363
peace to his soul, if god's good pleasure be! 3.03. 26
set, | it is our pleasure one of them depart; 4.01.140
art thou a messenger, or come of pleasure? 5.01. 16
keep | than in possession any jot of pleasure. 3H6 2.02. 53
and what your pleasure is shall satisfy me. 3.02. 20
and if what pleases him shall pleasure you. 3.02. 22
what other pleasure can the world afford? 3.02.147
we may surprise and take him at our pleasure? 4.02. 17
for that it made my imprisonment a pleasure; 4.06. 11
ay, such a pleasure as incaged birds | conceive, 4.06. 12
such as befits the pleasure of the court? 5.07. 44
he sends to know your lordship's pleasure, | if R3 3.02. 15
his gracious pleasure any way therein. 3.04. 17
leaving this, what is your grace's pleasure? 3.07.108
your grace may do your pleasure. 4.02. 21
mighty liege, tell me your highness' pleasure, 4.04.447
'tis his highness' pleasure | you shall to th' H8 1.01.206
be done, and the king's pleasure | by me obey'd! 1.01.215
by my life, | this is against our pleasure. 1.02. 68
in which we come | to know your royal pleasure. 2.02. 70
th' name of god, | your pleasure be fulfill'd! 2.04. 57
your pleasure, madam? 2.04. 69
a known friend, 'gainst his highness' pleasure 3.01. 85
that ne'er dream'd a joy beyond his pleasure; 3.01.135
hear the king's pleasure, cardinal! 3.02.228
lord cardinal, the king's further pleasure is — 3.02.337
but i pray you, | what is your pleasure with me? 4.02.114
he attends your highness' pleasure. 5.01. 83
is my duty | t' attend your highness' pleasure. 5.01. 91
'tis his highness' pleasure | and our consent, 5.02. 87
there to remain till the king's further pleasure 5.02.125
at your pleasure. TRO 1.02.180 P
i shall split all | in pleasure of my spleen." 1.03.178
for pleasure and revenge | have ears more deaf 2.02.171
if any thing more than your sport and pleasure 2.03.108
at whose pleasure, friend? 3.01. 23 P
you speak your fair pleasure, sweet queen. 3.01. 48 P
if you take it as a pleasure to you in being so. COR 2.01. 32 P
now talk at pleasure of your safety. TIT 4.02.134
wings | he can at pleasure stint their melody; 4.04. 86
madam, depart at pleasure, leave us here. 5.02.145
to know our farther pleasure in this case, | to ROM 1.01.101
my house and welcome on their pleasure stay. 1.02. 37
suffer every knave to use me at his pleasure! 2.04.156 P
i saw no man use you at his pleasure; 2.04.157 P
i will not budge for no man's pleasure, i. 3.01. 55
here, sir, what is your pleasure? TIM 2.01. 14
your lordship speaks your pleasure. 3.01. 33 P
say, that i cannot pleasure such an honorable 3.02. 56 P
that i do bear | i can shake off at pleasure. JC 1.03.100
i but in the suburbs | of your good pleasure? 2.01.286
do reek and smoke, | fulfill your pleasure. 3.01.159
you, we will stand and watch your pleasure. 4.03.249
to make their audit at your highness' pleasure, MAC 1.06. 27
he hath been in unusual pleasure, and | sent 2.01. 13
attend those men | our pleasure? 3.01. 45
only it spoils the pleasure of the time. 3.04. 97
what's your gracious pleasure? 5.03. 30
or in th' incestious pleasure of his bed, | at HAM 3.03. 90
my lord, guarded, to know your pleasure. 4.03. 14
sends to know if your pleasure hold to play with 5.02.198 P
to my purposes, they follow the king's pleasure. 5.02.201 P
no less in space, validity, and pleasure, | than LR 1.01. 81
for thee, friend, 'tis the /duke's pleasure, 2.02.152
then let fall | your horrible pleasure. 3.02. 19
do as i bid thee, or rather do thy pleasure; 4.01. 47
self–reproving — bring his constant pleasure. 5.01. 4
methinks our pleasure might have been demanded 5.03. 62
if't be your pleasure and most wise consent OTH 1.01.121
him, thou dost thyself a pleasure, me a sport. 1.03.369 P
it is othello's pleasure, our noble and valiant 2.02. 1 P
so much was his pleasure should be proclaim'd. 2.02. 8 P
pleasure and action make the hours seem short. 2.03.379
what is your pleasure? 4.02. 25
what is your pleasure, madam? how is't with you? 4.02.110
and one), you may take him at your pleasure. 4.02.237 P
should stretch | without some pleasure now. ANT 1.01. 47
at your noble pleasure. 1.02.112
the present pleasure, | by revolution low'ring, 1.02.124
what's your pleasure, sir? 1.02.131 P
say our pleasure, | to such whose places under 1.02.194
pawn their experience to their present pleasure, 1.04. 32
what's your highness' pleasure? 1.05. 8
i take no pleasure | in aught an eunuch has. 1.05. 9
for my peace, | i' th' east my pleasure lies. 2.03. 41
whom | he may at pleasure whip, or hang, or 3.13.150
yours, | bestow it at your pleasure, and believe 5.02.182
i have perform'd | your pleasure and my promise. 5.02.204
i dedicate myself to your sweet pleasure, | more CYM 1.06.136
of him and might not spend them at my pleasure. 2.01. 5 P
what's your lordship's pleasure? 2.03. 80
me of my lawful pleasure she restrain'd, | and 2.05. 9
i know your master's pleasure and he mine: 3.01. 84
what pleasure, sir, /find /we in life, to lock 4.04. 2
our pleasure his full fortune doth confine, 5.04.110
your pleasure was my /mere offense, my 5.05.334
man sing | may to your wishes pleasure bring, PER 1.ch. 14
i am at your grace's pleasure. 2.03.111
it is your grace's pleasure to commend, | not my 2.05. 29
honor, | or tie my pleasure up in silken bags, 3.02. 41
ay, and you shall live in pleasure. 4.02. 76 P
boult, take her away, use her at thy pleasure. 4.06.141 P
youth and pleasure, | still as she tasted, TNK 2.02.239
me, great mars, | some token of thy pleasure. 5.01. 61
bless me with a sign | of thy great pleasure. 5.01.129
well, well then, at your pleasure. 5.03. 34
when he was by, the birds such pleasure took, VEN 1101
that all love's pleasure shall not match his woe 1140
having no other pleasure of his gain | but LUC 860
"thy secret pleasure turns to open shame, | thy 890
"why should the private pleasure of some one 1478
and would not take her meaning nor her pleasure. PP 11.12
all our pleasure known to us poor swains, | all 17.29
or else receiv'st with pleasure thine annoy? SON 8. 4
since she prick'd thee out for women's pleasure, 20.13
from whence at pleasure thou mayst come and part 48.12
for blunting the fine point of seldom pleasure. 52. 4
in thought control your times of pleasure, | or 58. 2
not blame your pleasure, be it ill or well. 58.14
better'd that the world may see my pleasure; 75. 8
and every humor hath his adjunct pleasure, 91. 5
from thee, the pleasure of the fleeting year! 97. 2
and the just pleasure lost, which is so deemed 121. 3
yet fear her, o thou minion of her pleasure, 126. 9

PLEASURE'S 3 FR 0.0003 REL FR 3 V 0 P
shake the head | to hear of pleasure's name — LR 4.06.121
yet neither pleasure's art can joy my spirits, PER 1.02. 9
shows, | that are quick–ey'd pleasure's foes! TNK 1.05. 8

/PLEASURES 1 FR 0.0001 REL FR 1 V 0 P
/or /find /fault, /do /as /your /pleasures /are, TRO pr 30

PLEASURES 44 FR 0.0049 REL FR 41 V 3 P
what's dead, | and makes my labors pleasures. TMP 3.01. 7
it is admirable pleasures and fery honest WIV 4.04. 80 P
where all those pleasures live that art would LLL 4.02.110
remote from all the pleasures of the world; 5.02.796
so to your pleasures, | i am for other than for AYL 5.04.192
day, | attended with the pleasures of the world, JN 3.03. 35
never to taste the pleasures of the world, 4.03. 68
such barren pleasures, rude society, | as thou 1H4 3.02. 14
and hate the idle pleasures of these days. R3 1.01. 31
and all the pleasures you usurp are mine. 1.03.172
what are their pleasures? H8 1.04. 64
thanks, and pray 'em take their pleasures. 1.04. 74
what are your pleasures with me, reverent lords? 3.01. 26
my lords, you speak your pleasures. 3.02. 13
but their pleasures | must be fulfill'd, and i 5.02. 18
dance attendance on their lordships' pleasures, 5.02. 31
has done half an hour, to know your pleasures. 5.02. 41
the pleasures such a beauty brings with it, TRO 2.02.147

the reins and be angry at your pleasures; COR 2.01. 31 P
share a bounteous time | in different pleasures. TIM 1.01.255
bears that office to signify their pleasures. 1.02.120 P
you have done our pleasures much grace, fair 1.02.146
fates, we will know your pleasures. JC 3.01. 98
and to your heirs for ever — common pleasures, 3.02.250
convey your pleasures in a spacious plenty, MAC 4.03. 71
by your companies | to draw him on to pleasures, HAM 2.02. 15
us, | put your dread pleasures more into command 2.02. 28
'tis not in thee | to grudge my pleasures, to LR 2.04.174
until their greater pleasures first be known 5.03. 2
i kiss the instrument of their pleasures. OTH 4.01.218
their pleasures here are past, so /is their pain CYM 4.02.290
flow'rs are like the pleasures of the world; 4.02.296
a bedfellow, | in marriage pleasures playfellow; PER 1.ch. 34
where is read | nothing but curious pleasures, 1.01. 16
your child | (which pleasures fits a husband, 1.01.129
here pleasures court mine eyes, and mine eyes 1.02. 6
and all those pleasures | that woo the wills of TNK 2.02.100
this garden has a world of pleasures in't. 2.02.118
where all those pleasures live that art can PP 5. 6
and we will all the pleasures prove | that hills 19. 2
and if these pleasures may thee move, | then 19.15
these pretty pleasures might me move | to live 19.19
for summer and his pleasures wait on thee, | and SON 97.11
and laboring in moe pleasures to bestow them LC 139
PLEATS 1 FR 0.0001 REL FR 1 V 0 P
estate, | hiding base sin in pleats of majesty; LUC 93
PLEBEIANS 8 FR 0.0009 REL FR 6 V 2 P
with the plebeians swarming at their heels, | go H5 5.pr. 27
that with the fusty plebeians hate thine honors, COR 1.09. 7
as the hungry plebeians would the noble martius. 2.01. 9 P
being the herdsmen of the beastly plebeians. 2.01. 95 P
you are plebeians, | if they be senators; 3.01.101
the plebeians have got your fellow tribune, 5.04. 36
patricians and plebeians, we create | lord TIT 1.01.231
and hoist thee up to the shouting plebeians! ANT 4.12. 34
PLEBEII 1 FR 0.0001 REL FR 1 V 0 P
malignantly remain | fast foe to th' plebeii, COR 2.03.184
PLEBS 1 FR 0.0001 REL FR 0 V 1 P
am going with my pigeons to the tribunal plebs, TIT 4.03. 93 P
PLEDGE 22 FR 0.0024 REL FR 20 V 2 P
petruchio, patience, i am grumio's pledge. SHR 1.02. 45
i am in parliament pledge for his truth | and R2 5.02. 44
i pledge your grace, and, if you knew what pains 2H4 4.02. 73
come, | i'll pledge you a mile to th' bottom." 5.03. 54
there is my pledge, accept it, somerset. 1H6 4.01.120
bear her this jewel, pledge of my affection. 5.01. 47
i' faith, and i'll pledge you all, and a fig for 2H6 2.03. 66 P
what pledge have we of thy firm loyalty? 3H6 3.03.239
and here, to pledge my vow, i give my hand. 3.03.250
here's to your ladyship, and pledge it, madam, H8 1.04. 47
now the pledge, now, now, now! TRO 5.02. 65 P
o pretty, pretty pledge! 5.02. 77
bid him demand what pledge will please him best.
TIT 4.04.106
my heart is thirsty for that noble pledge. JC 4.03.160
our duties, and the pledge. MAC 3.04. 91
thus bray out | the triumph of his pledge. HAM 1.04. 12
and many treasons, | there is my pledge. LR 5.03. 93
with that recognizance and pledge of love OTH 5.02.214
bear him ashore. i'll pledge it for him, pompey. ANT 2.07. 85
i thank both him and you, and pledge him freely. PER 2.03. 78
well, sir, i'll pledge you. TNK 3.03. 16
you'll pledge her? 3.03. 38
PLEDGES 4 FR 0.0004 REL FR 3 V 1 P
all my sons, | as pledges of my fealty and love; 2H6 5.01. 50
he loves his pledges dearer than his life. TIT 3.01.291
let the emperor give his pledges | unto my 5.01.163
pledges the breath of him in a divided draught, TIM 1.02. 47 P
PLEINES 1 FR 0.0001 REL FR 0 V 1 P
langues des hommes sont pleines de tromperies. H5 5.02.116 P
PLENITUDE 1 FR 0.0001 REL FR 1 V 0 P
"in him a plenitude of subtle matter, | applied LC 302
PLENTEOUS 11 FR 0.0012 REL FR 10 V 1 P
even so her plenteous womb | expresseth his full MM 1.04. 43
that i shall think it a most plenteous crop | to AYL 3.05.101
hanging the head at ceres' plenteous load? 2H6 1.02. 2
may send forth plenteous tears to drown the R3 2.02. 70
wishes towards you | honor and plenteous safety) H8 1.01.104
come freely | to gratulate thy plenteous bosom. TIM 1.02.125
in the last conflict, and made plenteous wounds! 3.05. 65
from forth thy plenteous bosom, one poor root! 4.03.186
my plenteous joys, | wanton in fullness, seek to MAC 1.04. 33
with plenteous rivers and wide-skirted meads, LR 1.01. 65
of so high and plenteous wit and invention! OTH 4.01.190 P
PLENTEOUSLY 1 FR 0.0001 REL FR 1 V 0 P
shall, o dear father, pay thee plenteously. 2H4 4.05. 40
PLENTIES 1 FR 0.0001 REL FR 1 V 0 P
dear nurse of arts, plenties, and joyful births, H5 5.02. 35
PLENTIFUL 5 FR 0.0005 REL FR 1 V 4 P
being, as it is, so plentiful an excrement? ERR 2.02. 78 P
if reasons were as plentiful as blackberries, i 1H4 2.04.239 P
gum, and that they have a plentiful lack of wit, HAM 2.02.199 P
work | more plentiful than tools to do't — CYM 5.03. 9
'a keeps a plentiful shrievaltry, and 'a made my STM II.C 42 P
PLENTIFULLY 3 FR 0.0003 REL FR 1 V 2 P
depart, | if fairings come thus plentifully in. LLL 5.02. 2
this nothing that he so plentifully gives me, AYL 1.01. 17 P
little but bowling) it will please plentifully. WT 4.04.331 P
PLENTY 16 FR 0.0018 REL FR 12 V 4 P
earth's increase, foison plenty, | barns and TMP 4.01.110
but as there is no more plenty in it, it goes AYL 3.02. 20 P
in delay there lies no plenty, | then come kiss TN 2.03. 50
with smiling plenty, and fair prosperous days! R3 5.05. 34
peace, plenty, love, truth, terror, | that were H8 5.04. 47
he has made too much plenty with /'em. TIM 3.05. 66
hang'd himself on th' expectation of plenty. MAC 2.03. 5 P
convey your pleasures in a spacious plenty, 4.03. 71
plenty and peace breeds cowards; CYM 3.06. 21
be fortunate and flourish in peace and plenty." 5.04.144 P
be fortunate and flourish in peace and plenty." 5.05.442 P
whose issue | promises britain peace and plenty. 5.05.458
a city on whom plenty held full hand, | for PER 1.04. 22
but rather famish them amid their plenty, VEN 20
he with her plenty press'd, she faint with 545
a swallowing gulf that even in plenty wanteth. LUC 557
PLENTY'S 1 FR 0.0001 REL FR 1 V 0 P
let those cities that of plenty's cup | and her PER 1.04. 52
PLESS *(also bless, etc.)*
PLESS 8 FR 0.0009 REL FR 0 V 8 P
got pless your house here! WIV 1.01. 73 P
/jeshu pless my soul! 3.01. 11 P
pless my soul! 3.01. 15 P
/god pless you from his mercy sake, all of you! 3.01. 42 P
god pless your majesty! H5 3.06. 87 P
god pless it, and preserve it, as long as it 4.07.108 P
god pless you, aunchient pistol! 5.01. 17 P
you scurvy, lousy knave, god pless you! 5.01. 18 P
PLESSED 1 FR 0.0001 REL FR 0 V 1 P
'od's plessed will! WIV 1.01.264 P
PLESSING 1 FR 0.0001 REL FR 0 V 1 P
here is got's plessing, and your friend, and WIV 1.01. 75 P
PLEURISY *(see plurisy)*
PLIANT 1 FR 0.0001 REL FR 1 V 0 P
took once a pliant hour, and found good means OTH 1.03.151
PLIED 1 FR 0.0001 REL FR 1 V 0 P
indeed he plied them both with excellent praises ANT 3.02. 14
PLIES 4 FR 0.0004 REL FR 4 V 0 P
he plies the duke at morning and at night, | and MV 3.02.277
he plies her hard, and much rain wears the 3H6 3.02. 50
thou not guess wherefore she plies thee thus? TIT 4.01. 15
fool | plies desdemona to repair his fortune, OTH 2.03.354
PLIGHT* 17 FR 0.0019 REL FR 16 V 1 P
myself in better plight for a lender than you WIV 2.02.166 P
plight me the full assurance of your faith, TN 4.03. 26
be with me, for you see | my plight requires it. WT 2.01.118
and, as thou seest, ourselves in heavy plight. 3H6 3.03. 37
to keep her constancy in plight and youth, TRO 3.02.161
had i but seen thy picture in this plight, | it TIT 3.01.103
and rather comfort his distressed plight | than 4.04. 32
as seemeth by his plight, of the revolt | the MAC 1.02. 2
lord whose hand must take my plight shall carry LR 1.01.101
bid her alight, | and her troth plight, | and 3.04.123
for i know your plight is pitied | of him that ANT 5.02. 33
loyall'st husband that did e'er plight troth. CYM 1.01. 96
rather than have 'em | freed of this plight, and TNK 1.04. 34
i am in plight," there shall be at your choice 3.01. 88
"shall plight your honorable faiths to me | with LUC 1690
in howling wise, to see my doleful plight. PP 17.22
how can i then return in happy plight | that am SON 28. 1
PLIGHTED* *(also plat, etc.)*
PLIGHTED* 4 FR 0.0004 REL FR 4 V 0 P
and quick berowne hath plighted faith to me. LLL 5.02.283
give thee her hand, for sign of plighted faith. 1H6 5.03.162
time shall unfold what plighted cunning hides, LR 1.01.280
him, be plighted with | a love that grows as you TNK 5.03.110
PLIGHTER 1 FR 0.0001 REL FR 1 V 0 P
this kingly seal | and plighter of high hearts! ANT 3.13.126
PLOD 4 FR 0.0004 REL FR 3 V 1 P
plod away i' th' hoof! WIV 1.03. 82
that barefoot plod i the cold ground upon, AWW 3.04. 6
patience be a tir'd /mare, yet she will plod — H5 2.01. 24 P
if one of mean affairs | may plod it in a week, CYM 3.02. 51
PLODDED 2 FR 0.0002 REL FR 2 V 0 P
and plodded like a man for working-days; H5 1.02.277
bare-headed plodded by my foot-cloth mule | and
2H6 4.01. 54
PLODDERS 1 FR 0.0001 REL FR 1 V 0 P
small have continual plodders ever won, | save LLL 1.01. 86
PLODDING 2 FR 0.0002 REL FR 2 V 0 P
why, universal plodding poisons up | the nimble LLL 4.03.301
luggage | plodding to th' ports and coasts for STM II.C 76
PLODS 1 FR 0.0001 REL FR 1 V 0 P
plods /dully on, to bear that weight in me, | as SON 50. 6
PLOOD *(also blood, etc.)*
PLOOD 1 FR 0.0001 REL FR 0 V 1 P
your majesty's welsh plood out of your pody, i H5 4.07.107 P
PLOODY 1 FR 0.0001 REL FR 0 V 1 P
for your green wound and your ploody coxcomb. H5 5.01. 42 P
/PLOT 2 FR 0.0002 REL FR 2 V 0 P
/we /first /survey /the /plot, /then /draw /the 2H4 1.03. 42
/the /plot /of /situation /and /the /model, 1.03. 51
PLOT 51 FR 0.0057 REL FR 39 V 12 P
dost thou like the plot, trinculo? TMP 3.02.109 P
since they did plot | the means that dusky dis 4.01. 88
the minute of their plot | is almost come. 4.01.141
as thou hast lent me wit to plot this drift. TGV 2.06. 43
myself am one made privy to the plot. 3.01. 12
i will lay a plot to try that, and we will yet WIV 3.03.190 P
but let our plot go forward. 4.04. 12
what is your plot? 4.04. 46
to this her mother's plot | she, seemingly 4.06. 32
the provost knows our purpose and our plot. MM 4.05. 2
this green plot shall be our stage, this MND 3.01. 3 P
why then to-night | let us assay our plot, which AWW 3.07. 44
who cannot be crush'd with a plot? 4.03.325 P
patience, or we break the sinews of our plot! TN 2.05. 76 P
there is a plot against my life, my crown; WT 2.01. 47
that he did plot the duke of gloucester's death, R2 1.01.100
nor never by advised purpose meet | to plot, 1.03.189
this blessed plot, this earth, this realm, this 2.01. 50
is there no plot | to rid the realm of this 4.01.324
i'll lay | a plot shall show us all a merry day. 4.01.334
to ambition, they do plot | unlikely wonders: 5.05. 18
why, it cannot choose but be a noble plot. 1H4 1.03.279
thou layest the plot how. 2.01. 52 P
unsorted, and your whole plot too light for the 2.03. 13 P
lord, our plot is a good plot as ever was laid, 2.03. 17 P
lord, our plot is a good plot as ever was laid, 2.03. 17 P
a good plot, good friends, and full of 2.03. 18 P
an excellent plot, very good friends. 2.03. 19 P
of york commends the plot and the general course 2.03. 21 P
the plot is laid. 1H6 2.03. 4
my words | on any plot of ground in christendom. 2.04. 89
a pretty plot, well chosen to build upon! 2H6 1.04. 56
and in this private plot be we the first | that 2.02. 60
these are the limbs o' th' plot. H8 1.01.220
agent of our cardinal, | to second all his plot. 3.02. 60
it is a purpos'd thing, and grows by plot, | to COR 3.01. 38
call't not a plot. 3.01. 41
yet, were there but this single plot to lose, 3.02.102
you do but plot your deaths | by this device. TIT 2.01. 78
steed, | and wand'red hither to an obscure plot, 2.03. 77
tongues | plot some device of further misery, 3.01.134
this sandy plot is plain; 4.01. 69
ravish a maid, or plot the way to do it, 5.01.129
fight for a plot | whereon the numbers cannot HAM 4.04. 62
i'ld turn it all | to thy suggestion, plot, and LR 2.01. 73
i have o'erheard a plot of death upon him. 3.06. 89
a plot upon her virtuous husband's life, | and 4.06.272
she hath sold me, and i fall | under this plot. ANT 4.12. 49
us | find out the prettiest daisied plot we can, CYM 4.02.398
this plot of death when sadly she had laid, LUC 1212
why should my heart think that a several plot, SON 137. 9
PLOT-PROOF 1 FR 0.0001 REL FR 1 V 0 P
the blank | and level of my brain — plot-proof; WT 2.03. 6
PLOTS 15 FR 0.0017 REL FR 13 V 2 P
then she plots, then she ruminates, then she WIV 2.02.306 P
good plots, they are laid, and our revolted 3.02. 38 P
to unburthen all my plots and purposes | how to MV 1.01.133
to cull the plots of best advantages. JN 2.01. 40
john lays you plots; 3.04.146
plots have i laid, inductions dangerous, | by R3 1.01. 32
that do conspire my death with devilish plots 3.04. 60
achievements, plots, orders, preventions, TRO 1.03.181
passions and whose plots have broke their sleep COR 4.04. 19
and many unfrequented plots there are, | fitted TIT 2.01.115
to ruminate strange plots of dire revenge; 5.02. 6
serves us well | when our deep plots do pall, HAM 5.02. 9
more mischance | on plots and errors happen. 5.02.395
a mother hourly coining plots, a wooer | more CYM 2.01. 59
whoever plots the sin, thou 'point'st the season LUC 879
PLOTTED 9 FR 0.0010 REL FR 9 V 0 P
one) had plotted with them | to take my life. TMP 5.01.273
means | plotted and 'greed on for my happiness. TGV 2.04.183
ay, marry, am i, sir; and now 'tis plotted. SHR 1.01.188
dead time when gloucester's death was plotted, R2 4.01. 10
but what i know | is ruminated, plotted, and set 1H4 1.03.274
that plotted thus our glory's overthrow? 1H6 1.01. 24
was by york and talbot | too rashly plotted. 4.04. 3
will not conclude their plotted tragedy. 2H6 3.01.153
that the subtile traitor | this day had plotted, R3 3.05. 38
PLOTTER 1 FR 0.0001 REL FR 1 V 0 P
chief architect and plotter of these woes. TIT 5.03.122
PLOUGH 6 FR 0.0006 REL FR 4 V 2 P
to hold the plough for her sweet love three year LLL 5.02.884 P
draught-oxen, and make you plough up the wars. TRO 2.01.107 P
let the volsces | plough rome and harrow italy, COR 5.03. 34
sooner this sword shall plough thy bowels up. TIT 4.02. 87
and let | patient octavia plough thy visage up ANT 4.12. 38
let the plough play to-day, i'll tickle't out TNK 2.03. 28
PLOUGH'D 3 FR 0.0003 REL FR 2 V 1 P
of civil wounds plough'd up with neighbors' R2 1.03.128
which we ourselves have plough'd for, sow'd, and COR 3.01. 71
of ground than she is, she shall be plough'd. PER 4.06.145 P
PLOUGHED 1 FR 0.0001 REL FR 1 V 0 P
he ploughed her, and she cropp'd. ANT 2.02.228
PLOUGH-IRONS 1 FR 0.0001 REL FR 0 V 1 P
the smith's note for shoeing and plough-irons. 2H4 5.01. 19 P
PLOUGHMAN 4 FR 0.0004 REL FR 4 V 0 P
the ploughman lost his sweat, and the green corn MND 2.01. 94
whilst the heavy ploughman snores, | all with 5.01.373
spirit of sense | hard as the palm of ploughman. TRO 1.01. 59
to cheer the ploughman with increaseful crops, LUC 958
PLOUGHMEN'S 1 FR 0.0001 REL FR 1 V 0 P
straws | and merry larks are ploughmen's clocks; LLL 5.02.904
PLOUGH'ST 1 FR 0.0001 REL FR 1 V 0 P
that rig'st the bark and plough'st the foam, TIM 5.01. 50
PLOUGH-TORN 1 FR 0.0001 REL FR 1 V 0 P
dry up thy marrows, vines, and plough-torn leas, TIM 4.03.193
PLOW *(also blow*, etc.)*
PLOW 1 FR 0.0001 REL FR 0 V 1 P
by cheshu, i think 'a will plow up all, if there H5 3.02. 63 P
PLOWS 1 FR 0.0001 REL FR 0 V 1 P
i will give treason his payment into plows, i H5 4.08. 14 P
/PLUCK 2 FR 0.0002 REL FR 2 V 0 P
/set /up /do /not /pluck /my /cares /down: R2 4.01.195
/to /pluck /a /kingdom /down | /and /set 2H4 1.03. 49
PLUCK 115 FR 0.0130 REL FR 94 V 21 P
thy hand, | and pluck my magic garment from me.
TMP 1.02. 24
i'll pluck thee berries; 2.02.160
i here could pluck his highness' frown upon you 5.01.127
a team of horse shall not pluck that from me; TGV 3.01.267 P
pluck the borrow'd veil of modesty from the WIV 3.02. 41 P
pluck me out all the linen. 4.02.149 P
little fouler than it is, | to pluck on others. MM 2.04.147
than i meant, to pluck all fears out of you. 4.02.191 P
o, i will to him and pluck out his eyes! 4.03.119
did not i pluck thee by the nose for thy 5.01.339 P
help us in, sirrah, we'll pluck a crow together. ERR 3.01. 83
with these nails i'll pluck out these false eyes 4.04.104
pluck off the bull's horns and set them in my ADO 1.01.263 P
pluck up, my heart, and be sad. 5.01.203 P
is sworn | ne'er to pluck thee from thy /thorn; LLL 4.03.110
youth unmeet, | youth so apt to pluck a sweet. 4.03.112
to pluck this crawling serpent from my breast! MND 2.02.146
and pluck the wings from painted butterflies, 3.01.172
pluck the young sucking cubs from the she-bear, MV 2.01. 29
and pluck commiseration of /his /state | from 4.01. 30
nor pluck it from his finger, for the wealth 5.01.173
my remedy is then to pluck it out. SHR 2.01.211
she waded through the dirt to pluck him off me; 4.01. 78 P
you pluck my foot awry. 4.01.147
pluck up thy spirits, look cheerfully upon me. 4.03. 38
thee may furnish, and my prayers pluck down, AWW 1.01. 69
a man may draw his heart out ere 'a pluck one. 1.03. 89 P
to pluck his indignation on thy head | by the 3.02. 30
may rather pluck on laughter than revenge, | if TN 5.01.366
pluck but off these rags; WT 4.03. 52 P
sweetheart's hat | and pluck it o'er your brows, 4.04.651
either push on or pluck back thy business there; 4.04.737 P
but they will pluck away his natural cause | and JN 3.04.156
and pluck nights from me, but not lend a morrow;
R2 1.03.228
you pluck a thousand dangers on your head, | you 2.01.205
which i have sworn to weed and pluck away. 2.03.167
and when they from thy bosom pluck a flower, 3.02. 19
to pluck him headlong from the usurped throne. 5.01. 65
and wilt thou pluck my fair son from mine age, 5.02. 92
and from the common'st creature pluck a glove 5.03. 17
to pluck bright honor from the pale-fac'd moon, 1H4 1.03.202
and pluck up drowned honor by the locks, | so he 1.03.205

nettle, danger, we pluck this flower, safety. 2.03. 10 P
that i did pluck allegiance from men's hearts, 3.02. 52
go pluck him by the elbow, i must speak with him 2H4 1.02. 69 P
pluck down my officers, break my decrees, | for 4.05.117
to pluck down justice from your aweful bench? 5.02. 86
opposed numbers | pluck their hearts from them. H5 4.01.292
or they will pluck | the gay new coats o'er the 4.03.117
from off this brier pluck a white rose with me. 1H6 2.04. 30
pluck a red rose from off this thorn with me. 2.04. 33
i pluck this white rose with plantagenet. 2.04. 36
i pluck this red rose with young somerset, | and 2.04. 37
stay, lords and gentlemen, and pluck no more, 2.04. 39
i pluck this pale and maiden blossom here, 2.04. 47
prick not your finger as you pluck it off, 2.04. 49
in sign whereof i pluck a white rose too. 2.04. 58
that you on my behalf would pluck a flower. 2.04.129
and pluck the crown from feeble henry's head. 2H6 5.01. 2
let's pluck him down. 3H6 1.01. 59
can pluck the diadem from faint henry's head, 2.01.153
tut, were it farther off, i'll pluck it down. 3.02.195
and from her jealous arms pluck him perforce. R3 3.01. 36
in | so far in blood that sin will pluck on sin. 4.02. 64
pluck off a little, | i would not be a young H8 2.03. 40
from cupid's shoulder pluck his painted wings, TRO 3.02. 14
doth one pluck down another, and together | die 3.03. 86
see him pluck aufidius down by th' hair; COR 1.03. 30
would pluck reproof and rebuke from every ear 2.02. 33 P
at once pluck out | the multitudinous tongue; 3.01.155
pursue him to his house and pluck him thence, 3.01.307
seeking means | to pluck away their power, as 3.03. 96
and to pluck from them their tribunes for ever. 4.03. 24 P
but hope to pluck a dainty doe to ground. TIT 2.02. 26
i have no strength to pluck thee to the brink. 2.03.241
to pluck proud lucius from the warlike goths. 4.04.110
will you pluck your sword out of his pilcher by ROM 3.01. 80 P
and pluck the mangled tybalt from his shroud, 4.03. 52
pluck the grave wrinkled senate from the bench, TIM 4.01. 5
pluck the lin'd crutch from thy old limping sire 4.01. 14
pluck stout men's pillows from below their heads 4.03. 33
as they pass by, pluck casca by the sleeve, JC 1.02.179
pluck down benches. 3.02.258 P
pluck down forms, windows, any thing. 3.02.259 P
pluck but his name out of his heart, and turn 3.03. 33 P
they pluck out mine eyes. MAC 2.02. 56
pluck from the memory a rooted sorrow, | raze 5.03. 41
you would pluck out the heart of my mystery, you HAM 3.02.365 P
did not together pluck such envy from him | as 4.07. 74
pluck them asunder. 5.01.264
beweep this cause again, i'll pluck ye out, LR 1.04.302
pluck out his eyes. 3.07. 5 P
most ignobly done | to pluck me by the beard. 3.07. 36
thy cruel nails | pluck out his poor old eyes, 3.07. 57
may all the building in my fancy pluck | upon my 4.02. 85
more, | to pluck the common bosom on his side, 5.03. 49
the hand could pluck her back that shov'd her on ANT 1.02.127
mine ear must pluck it thence. 1.05. 42
can from the lap of egypt's widow pluck | the 2.01. 37
off, pluck off, | the sevenfold shield of ajax 4.14. 37
should from my lips | pluck a hard sentence. CYM 5.05.289
i should pluck | all ladies' scandal on me. TNK 1.01.191
the flow'r that i would pluck | and put between 1.03. 66
wicked, all my sins | could never pluck upon me. 2.03. 7
who dost pluck | with hand armipotent from forth 5.01. 53
courageously to pluck him from his horse. VEN 30
pluck down the rich, enrich the poor with 1150
to pluck the quills from ancient ravens' wings, LUC 949
as take the pain but cannot pluck the pelf. PP 14.12
sworn | ne'er to pluck thee from thy /thorn, 16.12
youth unmeet, | youth, so apt to pluck a sweet. 16.14
not from the stars do i my judgment pluck, | and SON 14. 1
pluck the keen teeth from the fierce tiger's 19. 3
from their proud lap pluck them where they grew; 98. 8
thou goest onwards, still will pluck thee back, 126. 6
PLUCK'D 40 FR 0.0045 REL FR 31 V 9 P
and by the spurs pluck'd up | the pine and cedar TMP 5.01. 47
since i pluck'd geese, play'd truant, and whipt WIV 5.01. 25 P
in the suburbs of vienna must be pluck'd down. MM 1.02. 96 P
was (as they say) pluck'd down in the suburbs; 2.01. 65 P
your doublet and hose pluck'd over your head, AYL 4.01.203 P
and with her golden hand hath pluck'd on france JN 3.01. 57
and that high royalty was ne'er pluck'd off; 4.02. 5
of his banish'd years | pluck'd four away. R2 1.03.211
and royalties | pluck'd from my arms perforce — 2.03.121
the cloak of night being pluck'd from off their 3.02. 45
are pluck'd up root and all by bullingbrook, | i 3.04. 52
together, i pluck'd this glove from his helm. H5 4.07.155 P
stead whereof sharp stakes pluck'd out of hedges 1H6 1.01.117
whose overweening arm i have pluck'd back, | by 2H6 3.01.159
confess who set thee up and pluck'd thee down, 3H6 5.01. 26
my remembrance brutish wrath | sinfully pluck'd, R3 2.01.120
and pluck'd two crutches from my feeble hands, 2.02. 58
have i pluck'd off to grace thy brows withal. 5.05. 6
youth with comeliness pluck'd all gaze his way; COR 1.03. 7 P
from him pluck'd | either his gracious promise, 2.03.192
i may be pluck'd into the swallowing womb | of TIT 2.03.239
growing feathers pluck'd from caesar's wing JC 1.01. 72
the crown, he pluck'd me ope his doublet, and 1.02.265 P
sir, their hats are pluck'd about their ears, 2.01. 73
and as he pluck'd his cursed steel away, | mark 3.02.177
have pluck'd my nipple from his boneless gums, MAC 1.07. 57
stroke which since | hath pluck'd him after. LR 4.02. 78
as if he pluck'd up kisses by the roots | that OTH 3.03.423
now he tells how she pluck'd him to my chamber. 4.01.141 P
when i have pluck'd thy rose, | i cannot give it 5.02. 13
an argument that he is pluck'd, when hither | he ANT 3.12. 3
may be she pluck'd it off | to send it me. CYM 2.04.104
which grows to the stalk, never pluck'd yet, i PER 4.06. 42 P
a dove's motion when the head's pluck'd off; TNK 1.01. 98
fast, | or being early pluck'd is sour to taste. VEN 528
though the rose have prickles, yet 'tis pluck'd! 574
this said, his guilty hand pluck'd up the latch, LUC 358
who pluck'd the knife from lucrece' side, 1807
rose, fair flower, untimely pluck'd, soon vaded, PP 10. 1
pluck'd in the bud, and vaded in the spring! 10. 2
PLUCKER–DOWN 1 FR 0.0001 REL FR 1 V 0 P
thou setter–up and plucker–down of kings, 3H6 2.03. 37
PLUCKING 6 FR 0.0006 REL FR 6 V 0 P
plucking the grass to know where sits the wind, MV 1.01. 18
take that, and mend the plucking /off the other. SHR 4.01.148
more straining on for plucking back, not WT 4.04.465
his friends | that, plucking to unfix an enemy, 2H4 4.01.206
herbs as these | are meet for plucking up, and TIT 3.01.178
plucking the entrails of an offering forth, JC 2.02. 39
PLUCKS 13 FR 0.0014 REL FR 12 V 1 P
dead, | and liberty plucks justice by the nose; MM 1.03. 29
i fear, the angle that plucks our son thither. WT 4.02. 46 P
whose valor plucks dead lions by the beard; JN 2.01.138
for the fift harry from curb'd license plucks 2H4 4.05.130
beholding him, plucks comfort from his looks. H5 4.pr. 42
and from the cross–row plucks the letter g, R3 1.01. 55
ajax employ'd plucks down achilles' plumes. TRO 1.03.385
and with a silken thread plucks it back again, ROM 2.02.180
his power, and modest wisdom plucks me | from MAC 4.03.119
plucks off my beard and blows it in my face, HAM 2.02.573
as from the body of contraction plucks | the 3.04. 46
from frieze, | it plucks out brains and all. OTH 2.01.127
who plucks the bud before one leaf put forth? VEN 416
PLUCK'ST 1 FR 0.0001 REL FR 1 V 0 P
bid thee crop a weed, thou pluck'st a flower. VEN 946
PLUCK'T 1 FR 0.0001 REL FR 0 V 1 P
one," quoth he, "pluck't out, and give it him." TRO 1.02.164 P
PLUE *(also blue)*
PLUE 1 FR 0.0001 REL FR 0 V 1 P
coal of fire, sometimes plue and sometimes red, H5 3.06.105 P
PLUM 4 FR 0.0004 REL FR 4 V 0 P
and it grandame will | give it a plum, a cherry, JN 2.01.162
hang him, plum porridge! TNK 2.03. 72
the mellow plum doth fall, the green sticks fast VEN 527
like a green plum that hangs upon a tree, | and PP 10. 5
PLUM–BROTH 1 FR 0.0001 REL FR 1 V 0 P
even the very plum–broth | and marrow of my TNK 3.05. 5
PLUM'D 1 FR 0.0001 REL FR 1 V 0 P
all plum'd like estridges, that with the wind 1H4 4.01. 98
PLUME 7 FR 0.0008 REL FR 7 V 0 P
as diminish | one dowle that's in my plume. TMP 3.03. 65
could i, with boot, change for an idle plume, MM 2.04. 11
what plume of feathers is he that indited this LLL 4.01. 94
he, | that with the plume; AWW 3.05. 78
there stuck no plume in any english crest | that JN 2.01.317
to get his place and to plume up my will | in OTH 1.03.393
he vails his tail that, like a falling plume, VEN 314
/PLUMED 1 FR 0.0001 REL FR 1 V 0 P
/with /plumed /helm /thy /state /begins /to LR 4.02. 57
PLUMED 1 FR 0.0001 REL FR 1 V 0 P
farewell the plumed troops and the big wars OTH 3.03.349
PLUME–PLUCK'D 1 FR 0.0001 REL FR 1 V 0 P
i come to thee | from plume–pluck'd richard, who R2 4.01.108
PLUMES 5 FR 0.0005 REL FR 4 V 1 P
how he jets under his advanc'd plumes! TN 2.05. 32 P
everlasting shame | sits mocking in our plumes. H5 4.05. 5
we'll pull his plumes and take away his train, 1H6 3.03. 7
ajax employ'd plucks down achilles' plumes. TRO 1.03.385
your enemies, with nodding of their plumes, COR 3.03.126
PLUMMET 3 FR 0.0003 REL FR 2 V 1 P
i'll seek him deeper than e'er plummet sounded, TMP 3.03.101
and deeper than did ever plummet sound | i'll 5.01. 56
ignorance itself is a plummet o'er me. WIV 5.05.163 P
PLUMP 2 FR 0.0002 REL FR 1 V 1 P
him thy harry's company — banish plump jack, 1H4 2.04.479 P
my flesh is soft and plump, my marrow burning, VEN 142
PLUMPY 1 FR 0.0001 REL FR 1 V 0 P
of the vine, | plumpy bacchus with pink eyne! ANT 2.07.114
PLUMS 1 FR 0.0001 REL FR 1 V 0 P
mass, thou lov'dst plums well, that wouldst 2H6 2.01. 99
PLUM–TREE 2 FR 0.0002 REL FR 1 V 1 P
a plum–tree, master. 2H6 2.01. 95
eyes purging thick amber and plum–tree gum, and HAM 2.02.198 P
PLUNG'D 2 FR 0.0002 REL FR 2 V 0 P
all but mariners | plung'd in the foaming brine, TMP 1.02.211
thou wouldst have plung'd thyself | in general TIM 4.03.255
PLUNGE 5 FR 0.0005 REL FR 3 V 2 P
being o'er shoes in blood, plunge in the deep, MND 3.02. 48
a shallow plash to plunge him in the deep, | and SHR 1.01. 23
do not plunge thyself too far in anger, lest AWW 2.03.211 P
to those that, without heed, do plunge into't. TIM 3.05. 13
would perhaps plunge him into more choler. HAM 3.02.306 P
PLUNGED 1 FR 0.0001 REL FR 1 V 0 P
as i was, i plunged in | and bade him follow; JC 1.02.105
PLUNGES 1 FR 0.0001 REL FR 1 V 0 P
nor diff'ring plunges | disroot his rider whence TNK 5.04. 74
PLUNGING 1 FR 0.0001 REL FR 1 V 0 P
like an unpractic'd swimmer plunging still, LUC 1098
PLURAL 2 FR 0.0002 REL FR 1 V 1 P
better have none | than plural faith, which is TGV 5.04. 52
what is your genitive case plural, william? WIV 4.01. 57 P
PLURISY 2 FR 0.0002 REL FR 2 V 0 P
still, | for goodness, growing to a plurisy, HAM 4.07.117
and cur'st the world | o' th' plurisy of people! TNK 5.01. 66
PLUS 2 FR 0.0002 REL FR 0 V 2 P
chevalier, je pense, le plus brave, vaillant, et H5 4.04. 56 P
answer you, la plus belle katherine du monde, 5.02.216 P
PLUTO 5 FR 0.0005 REL FR 4 V 1 P
for, by the dreadful pluto, if thou dost not, TRO 4.04.127
nor i, by pluto; 5.02.102 P
pluto and hell! COR 1.04. 36
no, my good lord, but pluto sends you word, | if TIT 4.03. 38
and moody pluto winks while orpheus plays. LUC 553
/PLUTO'S 1 FR 0.0001 REL FR 1 V 0 P
knows almost every /grain /of /pluto's /gold, TRO 3.03.197
PLUTO'S 4 FR 0.0004 REL FR 3 V 1 P
see her damn'd first, to pluto's damned lake, by 2H4 2.04.156 P
strong as pluto's gates: TRO 5.02.153
then, when you come to pluto's region, | i pray TIT 4.03. 13
a heart | dearer than pluto's mine, richer than JC 4.03.102
PLUTUS 2 FR 0.0002 REL FR 2 V 0 P
plutus himself, | that knows the tinct and AWW 5.03.101
plutus, the god of gold, | is but his steward. TIM 1.01.276
PLY 6 FR 0.0006 REL FR 6 V 0 P
shepherd, ply her hard. AYL 3.05. 76
keep house and ply his book, welcome his friends SHR 1.01.196
go ply thy needle, meddle not with her. 2.01. 25
see here he comes, and i must ply my theme. TIT 5.02. 80
and let him ply his music. HAM 2.01. 70
ply desdemona well, and you are sure on't. OTH 4.01.106
PO 2 FR 0.0002 REL FR 2 V 0 P
and apennines, | the pyrenean and the river po, JN 1.01.203
more famous yet 'twixt po and silver trent. TNK pr 12
POACH *(see potch)*
/POCKET 1 FR 0.0001 REL FR 0 V 1 P
/me /drunk, /and /afterward /pick'd /my /pocket. WIV 1.01.127 P
POCKET 33 FR 0.0037 REL FR 10 V 23 P
ay, or very falsely pocket up his report. TMP 2.01. 68 P
he will carry this island home in his pocket, 2.01. 92 P
oui, mette le au mon pocket; WIV 1.04. 54 P
the hand in the pocket and extracting /it MM 3.02. 47 P
in my cousin's hand, stol'n from her pocket, ADO 5.04. 89
your hands in your pocket like a man after the LLL 3.01. 20 P
wear prayer–books in my pocket, look demurely, MV 2.02.192
i think i have his letter in my pocket. AWW 4.03.201 P
put your grace in your pocket, sir, for this TN 5.01. 32 P
let me pocket up my pedlar's excrement. WT 4.04.713 P
well, ruffian, i must pocket up these wrongs, JN 3.01.200
have you inquir'd yet who pick'd my pocket? 1H4 3.03. 53 P
a hair, and i'll be sworn my pocket was pick'd. 3.03. 60 P
in mine inn but i shall have my pocket pick'd? 3.03. 81 P
here behind the arras and had my pocket pick'd. 3.03. 98 P
charge an honest woman with picking thy pocket! 3.03.156 P
any thing in thy pocket but tavern–reckonings, 3.03.158 P
if thy pocket were enrich'd with any other 3.03.160 P
will stand to it, you will not pocket up wrong. 3.03.163 P
you confess then you pick'd my pocket? 3.03.168 P
take from another's pocket to put into mine; H5 3.02. 50 P
or i have another leek in my pocket, which you 5.01. 62 P
h'as a book in his pocket with red letters in't. 2H6 4.02. 90 P
brings 'a victory in his pocket? COR 2.01.123 P
i put it in the pocket of my gown. JC 4.03.253
diadem stole, | and put it in his pocket — HAM 3.04.101
that terrible dispatch of it into your pocket? LR 1.02. 33 P
found in the pocket of the slain roderigo, | and OTH 5.02.309
discontented paper, | found in his pocket too; 5.02.315
in alexandria you | did pocket up my letters; ANT 2.02. 73
were | as plates dropp'd from his pocket. 5.02. 92
or put the moon in his pocket, we will pay him CYM 3.01. 44 P
letter of my master's | then in my pocket, which 5.05.280
POCKETING 1 FR 0.0001 REL FR 0 V 1 P
for it is plain pocketing up of wrongs. H5 3.02. 51 P
POCKETS 6 FR 0.0006 REL FR 2 V 4 P
if but one of his pockets could speak, would it TMP 2.01. 66 P
search his pockets. 1H4 2.04.531 P
house is turn'd bawdy–house, they pick pockets. 3.03. 99 P
familiar with men's pockets as their gloves or H5 3.02. 48 P
have fill'd their pockets full of pebble stones; 1H6 3.01. 80
let's see these pockets; LR 4.06.256
POCKY 1 FR 0.0001 REL FR 0 V 1 P
before 'a die — as we have many pocky corses, HAM 5.01.166 P
PODY *(also body)*
PODY 2 FR 0.0002 REL FR 0 V 2 P
if there be any pody in the house, and in the WIV 3.03.210 P
your majesty's welsh plood out of your pody, i H5 4.07.107 P
POEM 1 FR 0.0001 REL FR 0 V 1 P
scene individable, or poem unlimited; HAM 2.02.399 P
POESY 5 FR 0.0005 REL FR 4 V 1 P
ay, much is the force of heaven–bred poesy. TGV 3.02. 71
facility, and golden cadence of poesy, caret. LLL 4.02.122 P
talk, | music and poesy use to quicken you, SHR 1.01. 36
our poesy is as a /gum, which /oozes | from TIM 1.01. 21
my use, | and under thee their poesy disperse. SON 78. 4
/POET 1 FR 0.0001 REL FR 0 V 1 P
/unless /the /poet /and /the /player /went /to HAM 2.02.355 P
POET 16 FR 0.0018 REL FR 8 V 8 P
never durst poet touch a pen to write | until LLL 4.03.343
and the poet | are of imagination all compact. MND 5.01. 7
therefore the poet | did feign that orpheus drew MV 5.01. 79
goats, as the most capricious poet, honest ovid, AYL 3.03. 8 P
now, if thou wert a poet, i might have some hope 3.03. 26 P
the poet makes a most excellent description of H5 3.06. 37 P
pattern'd by that the poet here describes, | by TIT 4.01. 57
not worth my thinking. how now, poet? TIM 1.01.214 P
art not a poet? 1.01.220 P
yonder comes a poet and a painter; 4.03.351 P
i am cinna the poet, i am cinna the poet. JC 3.03. 29 P
i am cinna the poet, i am cinna the poet. 3.03. 29 P
and a poet never went | more famous yet 'twixt TNK pr 11
a learned poet says, unless by th' tail | and 3.05. 49
the age to come would say, "this poet lies, SON 17. 7
yet what of thee thy poet doth invent | he robs 79. 7
POETICAL 4 FR 0.0004 REL FR 0 V 4 P
truly, i would the gods had made thee poetical. AYL 3.03. 16 P
i do not know what "poetical" is: 3.03. 17 P
wish then that the gods had made me poetical? 3.03. 24 P
took great pains to study it, and 'tis poetical. TN 1.05.195 P
POETRY 10 FR 0.0011 REL FR 6 V 4 P
very unlearned, neither savoring of poetry, wit, LLL 4.02.159 P
for all the world like cutler's poetry | upon a MV 5.01.149
for the truest poetry is the most feigning, and AYL 3.03. 19 P
most feigning, and lovers are given to poetry; 3.03. 20 P
what they swear in poetry may be said as lovers 3.03. 21 P
delight | in music, instruments, and poetry, SHR 1.01. 93
her turn, well read in poetry | and other books, 1.02.169
an edge, | nothing so much as mincing poetry. 1H4 3.01.132
read to thee | sweet poetry and tully's orator. TIT 4.01. 14
if music and sweet poetry agree, | as they must PP 8. 1
POET'S 5 FR 0.0005 REL FR 5 V 0 P
the poet's eye, in a fine frenzy rolling, | doth MND 5.01. 12
the poet's pen | turns them to shapes and gives 5.01. 15
as cerberus at the thracian poet's feet. TIT 2.04. 51
and your true rights be term'd a poet's rage, SON 17.11
did exceed | the barren tender of a poet's debt; 83. 4
POETS' 1 FR 0.0001 REL FR 1 V 0 P
for orpheus' lute was strung with poets' sinews, TGV 3.02. 77
POETS 6 FR 0.0006 REL FR 6 V 0 P
and all that poets feign of bliss and joy. 3H6 1.02. 31
with that sour ferryman which poets write of, R3 1.04. 46
scribes, bards, poets, cannot | think, speak, ANT 3.02. 16
one god is god of both (as poets feign), | one PP 8.13
but since he died and poets better prove, SON 32.13
than both your poets can in praise devise. 83.14
POICTIERS 6 FR 0.0006 REL FR 6 V 0 P
to ireland, poictiers, anjou, touraine, maine, JN 1.01. 11
for /anjou and fair touraine, maine, poictiers, 2.01.487
poictiers, and anjou, these five provinces, 2.01.528
paris, guysors, poictiers, are all quite lost. 1H6 1.01. 61

this dastard, at the battle of poictiers, | when 4.01. 19
maine, blois, poictiers, and tours, are won away 4.03. 45
POINS 20 FR 0.0022 REL FR 2 V 18 P
he kept company with the wild prince and poins; WIV 3.02. 73 P
poins! 1H4 1.02.106 P
poins! poins, and be hang'd! poins! 2.02. 4 P
poins! poins, and be hang'd! poins! 2.02. 4 P
poins! poins, and be hang'd! poins! 2.02. 4 P
where's poins, hal? 2.02. 7 P
poins! 2.02. 20 P
ned poins and i will walk lower. 2.02. 61 P
and the prince and poins be not two arrant 2.02. 99 P
no more valor in that poins than in a wild duck. 2.02.101 P
poins! 2.04. 85 P
and poins there? 2.04.143 P
banish bardolph, banish poins, but for sweet 2.04.475 P
shall i tell thee one thing, poins? 2H4 2.02. 32 P
be not too familiar with poins, for he misuses 2.02.127 P
here will be the prince and master poins anon, 2.04. 16 P
they say poins has a good wit. 2.04.239 P
and art not thou poins his brother? 2.04.284 P
by heaven, poins, i feel me much to blame | so 2.04.361
with poins, and other his continual followers. 4.04. 53
'POINT *(also appoint, etc.)*
'POINT 1 FR 0.0001 REL FR 1 V 0 P
woo a thousand, 'point the day of marriage, SHR 3.02. 15
/POINT* 2 FR 0.0002 REL FR 2 V 0 P
/and /are /at /point | /to /show /their /open LR 3.01. 33
/my /point /and /period /will /be /throughly 4.07. 95
POINT* 145 FR 0.0164 REL FR 122 V 23 P
perform'd to point the tempest that i bade thee? TMP 1.02.194
and most poor matters | point to rich ends. 3.01. 4
(how sharp the point of this remembrance is!) 5.01.138
ay, there's the point, sir. WIV 1.01.222 P
the very point of it — to mistress anne page. 1.01.223 P
in the circumference of a peck, hilt to point, 3.05.111 P
our satisfaction have | touching that point. MM 1.01. 83
this is the point. 1.04. 49
err'd in this point which now you censure him, 2.01. 15
but to the point. 2.01. 97 P
let me know the point. 3.01. 72
obedience, agree with his demands to the point; 3.01.245 P
take upon a knive's point and choke a daw withal ADO 2.03.255 P
hath no man's dagger here a point for me? 4.01.109
pray you examine him upon that point. 5.01.313 P
no point, with my knife. LLL 2.01.190
did point you to buy them, along as you pass'd; 2.01.245
"no point," quoth i; 5.02.277
and so grow to a point. MND 1.02. 10 P
and touching now the point of human skill, 2.02.119
the thorny point | of bare distress hath ta'en AYL 2.07. 94
now must the world point at poor katherine, SHR 3.02. 18
so that from point to point now have you heard AWW 3.01. 1
so that from point to point now have you heard 3.01. 1
her story true, even to the point of her death. 4.03. 56 P
the particular confirmations, point from point, 4.03. 62 P
the particular confirmations, point from point, 4.03. 62 P
let us from point to point this story know, | to 5.03.325
let us from point to point this story know, | to 5.03.325
he does obey every point of the letter that i TN 3.02. 77 P
like to th' egyptian thief at point of death, 5.01.118
the fail | of any point in't shall not only be WT 2.03.171
and it you cannot thrust a bodkin's point. 3.03. 86 P
but that's not to the point. 3.03. 90 P
i'll point you where you shall have such 4.04.526
the which shall point you forth at every sitting 4.04.561
whence they gape and point | at your industrious JN 2.01.375
turn face to face and bloody point to point; 2.01.390
turn face to face and bloody point to point; 2.01.390
and with thy blessings steel my lance's point, R2 1.03. 74
lent | shall point on me and gild my banishment. 1.03.147
where it was forged, with my rapier's point. 4.01. 40
to prove it on thee to the extremest point | of 4.01. 47
takes on the point of honor to support | so 5.03. 11
watch, | whereto my finger, like a dial's point, 5.05. 53
cut's saddle, put a few flocks in the point. 1H4 2.01. 6 P
here i lay, and thus i bore my point. 2.04.195 P
if then thou be son to me, here lies the point: 2.04.406 P
then to the point. 4.03. 89
'tis a point of friendship. 5.01.122 P
too long | if life did ride upon a dial's point, 5.02. 83
i saw him hold lord percy at the point, | with 5.04. 21
honor, for a silken point | i'll give my barony. 2H4 1.01. 53
yea, marry, there's the point! 1.03. 18
divine | to a loud trumpet and a point of war? 4.01. 52
and hides a sword, from hilts unto the point, H5 2.pr. 9
of the military discipline, that is the point. 3.02.101 P
je ne doute point d'apprendre, par la grace de 3.04. 40 P
o signieur dew, thou diest on point of fox, 4.04. 9
ma foi, je ne veux point que vous abaissez votre 5.02.254 P
and humble service till the point of death. 1H6 3.01.167
stands on a tickle point now they are gone. 2H6 1.01.216
but what a point, my lord, your falcon made, 2.01. 5
see how the giddy multitude do point | and nod 2.04. 21
that cardinal beauford is at point of death; 3.02.369
ne'er shall this blood be wiped from thy point, 4.10. 69
such pity as my rapier's point affords. 3H6 1.03. 37
that valiant clifford with his rapier's point 1.04. 80
with the steely point of clifford's lance; 2.03. 16
to carve out dials quaintly, point by point, 2.05. 24
to carve out dials quaintly, point by point, 2.05. 24
my breast can better brook thy dagger's point 5.06. 27
but that thy brothers beat aside the point. R3 1.02. 96
you may, sir, 'tis a point of wisdom. 1.04. 98 P
and point by point the treasons of his master H8 1.02. 7
and point by point the treasons of his master 1.02. 7
of your office, is the point | of my petition. 1.02. 16
note | this dangerous conception in this point, 1.02.139
to this point hast thou heard him | at any time 1.02.145
i speak my good lord card'nal to this point, 2.04.167
suddenly an answer | in such a point of weight, 3.01. 71
but in this point | all his tricks founder, and 3.02. 39
touch'd the highest point of all my greatness, 3.02.223
enjoy | at ample point all that i did possess, TRO 3.03. 89
admits no orifex for a point as subtle | as 5.02.151
rome and her rats are at the point of battle, COR 1.01.162
as the main point of this our after-meeting, 2.02. 39
whom with all praise i point at, saw him fight, 2.02. 90
you are at point to lose your liberties. 3.01.193
in this point charge him home, that he affects 3.03. 1
almost at point to enter. 5.04. 61
bids thee christen it with thy dagger's point. TIT 4.02. 70
i'll broach the tadpole on my rapier's point. 4.02. 85
got, | he dies upon my scimitar's sharp point, 4.02. 91
true, 'tis true, witness my knive's sharp point. 5.03. 63
and from her bosom took the enemy's point, 5.03.111
who, all as hot, turns deadly point to point, ROM 3.01.160
who, all as hot, turns deadly point to point, 3.01.160
there's a fearful point! 4.03. 32
that did spit his body | upon a rapier's point. 4.03. 57
how oft when men are at the point of death 5.03. 88
since riches point to misery and contempt? TIM 4.02. 32
this angry flood, | and swim to yonder point?" JC 1.02.104
but ere we could arrive the point propos'd, 1.02.110
things | unto the climate that they point upon. 1.03. 32
here, as i point my sword, the sun arises, 2.01.106
but was indeed | sway'd from the point, by 3.01.219
either led or driven, as we point the way; 4.01. 23
point against point, rebellious arm 'gainst arm, MAC 1.02. 56
point against point, rebellious arm 'gainst arm, 1.02. 56
all our service | in every point twice done, and 1.06. 15
which is now | our point of second meeting. 3.01. 85
ten thousand warlike men | already at a point, 4.03.135
armed at point exactly, cap–a–pe, | appears HAM 1.02.200
as your business and desire shall point you, 1.05.129
to this point i stand, | that both the worlds i 4.05.134
i'll touch my point | with this contagion, that, 4.07.146
for here lies the point: 5.01. 10 P
the point envenom'd too! 5.02.321
that stands | aloof from th' entire point. LR 1.01.240
to let him keep | at point a hundred knights; 1.04.324
ay, there's the point; OTH 3.03.228
scorn | to point his slow /unmoving finger at! 4.02. 55
yet i hope, i hope, | they do not point on me. 5.02. 46
there's the point. ANT 2.06. 31
your best love draw to that point which seeks 3.04. 21
have nick'd his captainship, at such a point, 3.13. 8
even to the point of envy, if 'twere made CYM 2.03.128
the fam'd cassibelan, who was once at point | (o 3.01. 30
outcraftied him, | and he's at some hard point. 3.04. 16
well then, here's the point: 3.04.153
the due of honor in no point omit. 3.05. 11
and in that point | i will conclude to hate her, 3.05. 77
even before, i was | at point to sink for food. 3.06. 17
and in a time | when fearful wars point at me; 4.03. 7
and thy lopp'd branches point | thy two sons 5.05.454
tell him | o'er, point by point, for yet he PER 5.01.225
tell him | o'er, point by point, for yet he 5.01.225
i must no more believe thee in this point TNK 1.03. 87
but the point is this — | an end, and that is 3.02. 37
with javeling's point a churlish swine to gore, VEN 616
better proof than thy spear's point can enter; 626
and seems to point her out where she sits LUC 1087
for blunting the fine point of seldom pleasure. SON 52. 4
doth point out thee | as his triumphant prize. 151. 9
POINT–BLANK 2 FR 0.0002 REL FR 0 V 2 P
as a cannon will shoot point–blank twelve score. WIV 3.02. 33 P
art thou within point–blank of our jurisdiction 2H6 4.07. 26 P
POINT–DEVICE 1 FR 0.0001 REL FR 0 V 1 P
you are rather point–device in your AYL 3.02.382 P
POINT–DEVISE 2 FR 0.0002 REL FR 0 V 2 P
such insociable and point–devise companions, LLL 5.01. 18 P
i will be point–devise the very man. TN 2.05.163 P
'POINTED 3 FR 0.0003 REL FR 3 V 0 P
i'll not be tied to hours nor 'pointed times, SHR 3.01. 19
signior lucentio, this is the 'pointed day, 3.02. 1
a husband i have 'pointed, | but do not know him TNK 5.01.151
POINTED 6 FR 0.0006 REL FR 5 V 1 P
why, being son to me, art thou so pointed at? 1H4 2.04.407 P
that evermore they pointed | to th' good of your H8 3.02.172
of space had pointed him sharp as my needle; CYM 1.03. 19
me and death" — and pointed to this brace — PER 2.01.127
no more shake | our pointed javelins, whilst the TNK 2.02. 49
as from a promontory | pointed in heaven, should 4.02. 23
'POINTING 1 FR 0.0001 REL FR 1 V 0 P
'pointing to each his thunder, rain, and wind, SON 14. 6
POINTING 3 FR 0.0003 REL FR 2 V 1 P
is pointing still, in cleansing them from tears. R2 5.05. 54
find hector's purpose | pointing on him. TRO 1.03.331
go to, leave your pointing. TNK 2.01. 51 P
POINTING–STOCK 1 FR 0.0001 REL FR 1 V 0 P
was made a wonder and a pointing–stock | to 2H6 2.04. 46
POINTS 28 FR 0.0031 REL FR 19 V 9 P
but then exactly do | all points of my command. TMP 1.02.501
by this i think the dial points at five. ERR 5.01.118
this fellow doth not stand upon points. MND 5.01.118 P
that i did suit me all points like a man? AYL 1.03.116
that is one of the points in the which women 3.02.390 P
with two broken points; SHR 3.02. 48 P
so, neither, but i am resolv'd on two points — TN 1.05. 23 P
points more than all the lawyers in bohemia can WT 4.04.205 P
yea, at all points, and longs to enter in. R2 1.03. 2
but took all their seven points in my target, 1H4 2.04.202 P
their points being broken — 2.04.214 P
god's light, with two points on your shoulder? 2H4 2.04.133 P
come we to full points here? 2.04.184
brother, wherefore stand you on nice points? 3H6 4.07. 58
men | to turn their own points in their masters' R3 5.01. 24
with all their honorable points of ignorance H8 1.03. 26
but the sharp thorny points | of my alleged 2.04.225
be at once to all the points a' th' compass. COR 2.03. 24 P
obeys his points | as if he were his officer. 4.06.125
his /agile arm beats down their fatal points, ROM 3.01.166
lord, | for any benefit that points to me, TIM 4.03.519
to you our swords have leaden points, mark JC 3.01.173
smiles upon me, | and points at them for his. MAC 4.01.124
between the pass and fell incensed points | of HAM 5.02. 61
you the sourest points with sweetest terms, ANT 2.02. 24
you mingle eyes | with one that ties his points? 3.13.157
thy relation | to points that seem impossible, PER 5.01.124
points on me graciously with fair aspect, | and SON 26.10
'POINT'ST 1 FR 0.0001 REL FR 1 V 0 P
plots the season, thou 'point'st the season; LUC 879
POINT'ST 1 FR 0.0001 REL FR 1 V 0 P
thy heels | and skip when thou point'st out? TIM 4.03.225
POIS'D 3 FR 0.0003 REL FR 3 V 0 P
our imputation shall be oddly pois'd | in this TRO 1.03.339
both merits pois'd, each weighs nor less nor 4.01. 66
by, | herself pois'd with herself in either eye; ROM 1.02. 95
POISE 8 FR 0.0009 REL FR 7 V 1 P
soul, | were equal poise of sin and charity. MM 2.04. 68
and poise the cause in justice' equal scales, 2H6 2.01.200
so is the equal poise of this fell war. 3H6 2.05. 13
for the great swinge and rudeness of his poise, TRO 1.03.207
scale of reason to poise another of sensuality, OTH 1.03.327 P
it shall be full of poise and difficult weight, 3.03. 82
that equally canst poise sternness with pity, TNK 1.01. 86
and his full poise | becomes the rider's load. 5.04. 81
POISING 1 FR 0.0001 REL FR 1 V 0 P
dream | we, poising us in her defective scale, AWW 2.03.154
POIS'NED 5 FR 0.0005 REL FR 5 V 0 P
transports his pois'ned shot, may miss our name, HAM 4.01. 43
it is the pois'ned cup, it is too late. 5.02.292
i am pois'ned. 5.02.310
thy mother's pois'ned. 5.02.319
whom thou hast pois'ned too. PER 4.03. 10
POIS'NING 1 FR 0.0001 REL FR 0 V 1 P
upon the talk of the pois'ning? HAM 3.02.289 P
/POISON 1 FR 0.0001 REL FR 1 V 0 P
/come /hither /purposely /to /poison /me. TIT 3.02. 73
POISON 83 FR 0.0093 REL FR 72 V 11 P
(like poison given to work a great time after) TMP 3.03.105
i will incense /page to deal with poison; WIV 1.03.101 P
false, | i do digest the poison of thy flesh, ERR 2.02.143
the poison of that lies in you to temper. ADO 2.02. 21 P
i have drunk poison whiles he utter'd it. 5.01.246
if you poison us, do we not die? MV 3.01. 66 P
he will practice against thee by poison, entrap AYL 1.01.150 P
i will deal in poison with thee, or in bastinado 5.01. 54 P
i his lady, | i would poison that vile rascal. AWW 3.05. 84
what dish a' poison has she dress'd him! TN 2.05.112 P
that should not work | maliciously, like poison; WT 1.02.321
camillo for the minister to poison | my friend 3.02.160
sweet, sweet, sweet poison for the age's tooth, JN 1.01.213
of that fell poison which assaileth him. 5.07. 9
and there the poison | is as a fiend confin'd to 5.07. 46
his heart–blood | which breath'd this poison. R2 1.01.173
they love not poison that do poison need, | nor 5.06. 38
they love not poison that do poison need, | nor 5.06. 38
to filthy tunes, let a cup of sack be my poison. 1H4 2.02. 46 P
in poison there is physic, and these news, 2H4 1.01.137
hide not thy poison with such sug'red words. 2H6 3.02. 45
poison be their drink! 3.02.321
bring the strong poison that i bought of him. 3.03. 18
would it were mortal poison for thy sake! R3 1.02.145
never came poison from so sweet a place. 1.02.146
never hung poison on a fouler toad. 1.02.147
but look'd not on the poison of their hearts. 3.01. 14
all goodness | is poison to thy stomach. H8 3.02.283
a mind | that shall remain a poison where it is; COR 3.01. 87
not poison any further. 3.01. 88
them not lick | the sweet which is their poison. 3.01.157
ingrate forgetfulness shall poison rather | than 5.02. 86
eye, | and the rank poison of the old will die. ROM 1.02. 50
poison hath residence and medicine power; 2.03. 24
and that bare vowel i shall poison more | than 3.02. 46
hadst thou no poison mix'd, no sharp–ground 3.03. 44
you could find out but a man | to bear a poison, 3.05. 97
what if it be a poison which the friar 4.03. 24
i said, | "an' if a man did need a poison now, 5.01. 50
let me have | a dram of poison, such 5.01. 60
there is thy gold, worse poison to men's souls, 5.01. 80
i sell thee poison, thou hast sold me none. 5.01. 83
come, cordial and not poison, go with me | to 5.01. 85
poison, i see, hath been his timeless end. 5.03.162
lips, | haply some poison yet doth hang on them, 5.03.165
and here he writes that he did buy a poison | of 5.03.288
turn to nutriment | when he is turn'd to poison? TIM 3.01. 59
(as their friendship) may | be merely poison! 4.01. 32
sauce his palate | with thy most operant poison! 4.03. 25
will o'er some high–vic'd city hang his poison 4.03.110
would poison were obedient and knew my mind! 4.03.296 P
his antidotes are poison, and he slays | moe 4.03.432
nor steel, nor poison, | malice domestic, MAC 3.02. 24
they do but jest, poison in jest — no offense HAM 3.02.234 P
o, this is the poison of deep grief, it springs 4.05. 75
served, | it is a poison temper'd by himself. 5.02.328
the potent poison quite o'er–crows my spirit. 5.02.353
if you have poison for me, i will drink it. LR 4.07. 71
rouse him, make after him, poison his delight, OTH 1.01. 68
subdue and poison this young maid's affections? 1.03.112
the moor already changes with my poison: 3.03.325
poison, or fire, or suffocating streams, | i'll 3.03.389
get me some poison, iago, this night. 4.01.204 P
do it not with poison; 4.01.207 P
hath yet but life, | and not a serpent's poison. ANT 1.02.194
now i feed myself | with most delicious poison. 1.05. 27
and poison it in the source, and the first stone 3.13.160
if they had swallow'd poison, 'twould appear 5.02.345
thou'rt poison to my blood. CYM 1.01.128
such boil'd stuff | as well might poison poison. 1.06.126
such boil'd stuff | as well might poison poison. 1.06.126
and we will fear no poison, which attends | in 3.03. 77
prevented it, she had | ta'en off by poison. 5.05. 47
o, give me cord, or knife, or poison, | some 5.05.213
get thee from my sight, | thou gav'st me poison. 5.05.237
on sweetest flowers, yet they poison breed. PER 1.01.133
poison and treason are the hands of sin, | ay, 1.01.139
behold, | here's poison and here's gold; 1.01.155
the poison of pure spirits, might, like women, TNK 2.02. 75
arcite, thou mightst now poison me. 3.03. 8
the bottom poison, and the top o'erstraw'd VEN 1143
"i will not poison thee with my attaint, | nor LUC 1072
drugs poison him that so fell sick of you. SON 118.14
POISON'D 17 FR 0.0019 REL FR 17 V 0 P
thou wouldst have poison'd good camillo's honor, WT 3.02.188
the king, i fear, is poison'd by a monk. JN 5.06. 23
poison'd — ill fare! 5.07. 35
stead of homage sweet, | but poison'd flattery? H5 4.01.251
the hollow passage of my poison'd voice, | by 1H6 5.04.121
my valor's poison'd | with only suff'ring stain COR 1.10. 17
commends th' ingredience of our poison'd chalice MAC 1.07. 11
in the poison'd entrails throw; 4.01. 5

whose welcome i perceiv'd had poison'd mine — LR 2.04. 39
and her sister | by her is poison'd; 5.03.228
the one the other poison'd for my sake, | and 5.03.241
poison'd then. ANT 5.02.340
o, would | our viands had been poison'd, or at CYM 5.05.156
it poison'd me. 5.05.243
pure | doth in her poison'd closet yet endure." LUC 1659
if it be poison'd, 'tis the lesser sin | that SON 114.13
his poison'd me, and mine did him restore. LC 301
POISONED 4 FR 0.0004 REL FR 4 V 0 P
some poisoned by their wives, some sleeping R2 3.02.159
i would have him poisoned with a pot of ale. 1H4 1.03.233
and then when poisoned hours had bound me up ANT 2.02. 90
the poisoned fountain clears itself again, | and LUC 1707
POISONER 1 FR 0.0001 REL FR 1 V 0 P
i must be the poisoner | of good polixenes, and WT 1.02.352
POISONOUS 13 FR 0.0014 REL FR 13 V 0 P
thou poisonous slave, got by the devil himself TMP 1.02.319
end | as all the poisonous potions in the world, 1H4 5.04. 56
be poisonous too, and kill thy forlorn queen. 2H6 3.02. 77
thee curse this poisonous bunch–back'd toad. R3 1.03.245
helps, are very poisonous | where the disease is COR 3.01.220
might condemn us, | as poisonous of your honor. 5.03.135
it up again | with poisonous spite and envy. TIM 1.02.139
whereof | doth, like a poisonous mineral, gnaw OTH 2.01.297
the poisonous damp of night dispunge upon me, ANT 4.09. 13
commanded of me these most poisonous compounds, CYM 1.05. 8
false italian | (as poisonous tongu'd as handed) 3.02. 5
the poisonous simple sometime is compacted | in LUC 530
knit poisonous clouds about his golden head. 777
POISONS 9 FR 0.0010 REL FR 8 V 1 P
poisons more deadly than a mad dog's tooth. ERR 5.01. 70
why, universal plodding poisons up | the nimble LLL 4.03.301
whose tongue more poisons than the adder's tooth 3H6 1.04.112
'a poisons him i' th' garden for his estate. HAM 3.02.261 P
black or white, | tooth that poisons if it bite; LR 3.06. 67
dangerous conceits are in their natures poisons, OTH 3.03.326
the object poisons sight, | let it be hid. 5.02.364
doth think she has | strange ling'ring poisons. CYM 1.05. 34
oft importun'd me | to temper poisons for her, 5.05.250
POITIERS *(see poictiers)*
POKE 1 FR 0.0001 REL FR 1 V 0 P
and then he drew a dial from his poke, | and, AYL 2.07. 20
POKING–STICKS 1 FR 0.0001 REL FR 1 V 0 P
pins and poking–sticks of steel; WT 4.04.226
POLACK 4 FR 0.0004 REL FR 4 V 0 P
to be a preparation 'gainst the polack; HAM 2.02. 63
so levied, as before, against the polack, | with 2.02. 75
why then the polack never will defend it. 4.04. 23
you from the polack wars, and you from england, 5.02.376
/POLACKS 1 FR 0.0001 REL FR 1 V 0 P
he smote the sledded /polacks on the ice. HAM 1.01. 63
POLAND 5 FR 0.0005 REL FR 4 V 1 P
and he supposes me travell'd to poland — | for MM 1.03. 14
the tallow in them will burn a poland winter: ERR 3.02. 99 P
against some part of poland. HAM 4.04. 12
goes it against the main of poland, sir, | or 4.04. 15
fortinbras, with conquest come from poland, | to 5.02.350
POLD *(also bold)*
POLD 1 FR 0.0001 REL FR 0 V 1 P
be pold, i pray you. WIV 5.04. 2 P
POLE* 25 FR 0.0028 REL FR 19 V 6 P
by the north pole, i do challenge thee. LLL 5.02.693 P
will not fight with a pole like a northren man; 5.02.694 P
amounts not to fifteen thousand pole, half of AWW 4.03.167 P
elder hath not his pole claw'd like a parrot. 2H4 2.04.259 P
proud pole, i will, and scorn both him and thee. 1H6 2.04. 78
away, away, good william de la pole! 2.04. 80
for your partaker pole, and you yourself, | i'll 2.04.100
have with thee, pole. 2.04.114
thee, | against proud somerset and william pole, 2.04.122
fie, de la pole, disable not thyself. 5.03. 67
the french king charles, and william de la pole, 2H6 1.01. 44 P
and william de la pole, first duke of suffolk. 1.02. 30
i tell thee, pole, when in the city tours | thou 1.03. 50
the duke of suffolk, william de la pole. 4.01. 45
and sooner dance upon a bloody pole | than stand 4.01.127
see if his head will stand steadier on a pole, 4.07. 96 P
we are the greater pole, and in true fear | they COR 3.01.134
that we have procur'd | set down by th' pole? 3.03. 10
painted upon a pole, and underwrit, | "here may MAC 5.08. 26
yond same star that's westward from the pole HAM 1.01. 36
nor will it yield to norway or the pole | a 4.04. 21
as white as snow, | /all flaxen was his pole, 4.05.196
and quench the guards of th' ever–fixed pole; OTH 2.01. 15
of the war, | the soldier's pole is fall'n! ANT 4.15. 65
here's something | to paint your pole withal. TNK 3.05.153
POLE–AXE *(see poll–axe)*
POLECAT *(see poulcat, etc.)*
POLE–CLIPT 1 FR 0.0001 REL FR 1 V 0 P
thy pole–clipt vineyard, | and thy sea–marge, TMP 4.01. 68
POLEMON 1 FR 0.0001 REL FR 1 V 0 P
polemon and amyntas, | the kings of mede and ANT 3.06. 74
POLES 1 FR 0.0001 REL FR 0 V 1 P
head, and bring them both upon two poles hither. 2H6 4.07.112 P
POLI 1 FR 0.0001 REL FR 1 V 0 P
magni dominator poli, | tam lentus audis scelera TIT 4.01. 81
POLICIES 1 FR 0.0001 REL FR 1 V 0 P
search out thy wit for secret policies, | and we 1H6 3.03. 12
/POLICY 1 FR 0.0001 REL FR 0 V 1 P
i will o'errun thee with /policy; AYL 5.01. 56 P
POLICY 46 FR 0.0052 REL FR 37 V 9 P
both strength of limb, and policy of mind, ADO 4.01.198
and 'tis some policy | to have one show worse LLL 5.02.512
if she be curst, it is for policy, | for she's SHR 2.01.292
is there no military policy how virgins might AWW 1.01.121 P
some laudable attempt either of valor or policy. TN 3.02. 29 P
way, it must be with valor, for policy i hate. 3.02. 31 P
smacks it not something of the policy? JN 2.01.396
that were some love, but little policy. R2 5.01. 84
never did bare and rotten policy | color her 1H4 1.03.108
offer, | and it proceeds from policy, not love. 2H4 4.01.146
turn him to any cause of policy, | the gordian H5 1.01. 45
nation lose | the name of hardiness and policy. 1.02.220
fear, and with pale policy | seek to divert the 2.pr. 14
through which our policy must make a breach. 1H6 3.02. 2
it is your policy | to save your subjects from 5.04.159
his wits, | to keep by policy what henry got? 2H6 1.01. 84
me seemeth then it is no policy, | respecting 3.01. 23
that he should die is worthy policy, | but yet 3.01.235
but, in my mind, that were no policy: 3.01.238
if york, with all his far–fet policy, | had been 3.01.293
by devilish policy art thou grown great | and, 4.01. 83
with pow'rful policy strengthen themselves, 3H6 1.02. 58
'tis but his policy to counterfeit, | because he 2.06. 65
it is his policy | to haste thus fast, to find 5.04. 62
plague of your policy! H8 3.02.259
they tax our policy, and call it cowardice, TRO 1.03.197
life | with all my force, pursuit, and policy. 4.01. 19
the policy of those crafty swearing rascals, 5.04. 9 P
they set me up, in policy, that mongril cur, 5.04. 12 P
barbarism, and policy grows into an ill opinion. 5.04. 17 P
i have heard you say | honor and policy, like COR 3.02. 42
you adopt your policy, how is it less or worse 3.02. 48
desperation | is all the policy, strength, and 4.06.127
'tis policy and stratagem must do | that you TIT 2.01.104
o lord, sir, 'tis a deed of policy. 4.02.148
to dispense, | for policy sits above conscience. TIM 3.02. 87
hunts not the trail of policy so sure | as it HAM 2.02. 47
"this policy and reverence of age makes the LR 1.02. 46 P
a punishment more in policy than in malice, even OTH 2.03.274 P
lady, | that policy may either last so long, 3.03. 14
which not wanted | shrowdness of policy too — i ANT 2.02. 69
i think the policy of that purpose made more in 2.06.118 P
good end | for lawful policy remains enacted. LUC 529
by, | wherein deep policy did him disguise, 1815
thus policy in love, t' anticipate | the ills SON 118. 9
it fears not policy, that heretic, | which works 124. 9
POLISH'D 2 FR 0.0002 REL FR 2 V 0 P
o polish'd perturbation! 2H4 4.05. 23
affords | in polish'd form of well–refined pen. SON 85. 8
POLITIC 16 FR 0.0018 REL FR 5 V 11 P
am i politic? WIV 3.01.101 P
which maintain'd so politic a state of evil that ADO 5.02. 63 P
nor the lawyer's, which is politic; AYL 4.01. 14 P
a lady, i have been politic with my friend, 5.04. 45 P
it is not politic in the commonwealth of nature AWW 1.01.126 P
you, interpreter, you must seem very politic. 4.01. 21 P
i will be proud, i will read politic authors, i TN 2.05.161 P
with silence, nephew, be thou politic. 1H6 2.05.101
famously enrich'd | with politic grave counsel; R3 2.03. 20
bites his lip with a politic regard, as who TRO 3.03.254 P
knew not what he did when he made man politic; TIM 3.03. 29 P
of such a nature is his politic love. 3.03. 34 P
convocation of politic worms are e'en at him. HAM 4.03. 20 P
'tis politic and safe to let him keep | at point LR 1.04.323
no farther off | than in a politic distance. OTH 3.03. 13
hours, | but all alone stands hugely politic, SON 124.11
POLITICIAN 4 FR 0.0004 REL FR 2 V 2 P
i had as lief be a brownist as a politician. TN 3.02. 32 P
pismires, when i hear | of this vile politician, 1H4 1.03.241
this might be the pate of a politician, which HAM 5.01. 78 P
and, like a scurvy politician, seem | to see the LR 4.06.171
POLITICIANS 1 FR 0.0001 REL FR 0 V 1 P
my lady's a cataian, we are politicians, TN 2.03. 75 P
POLITICLY 2 FR 0.0002 REL FR 2 V 0 P
thus have i politicly begun my reign, | and 'tis SHR 4.01.188
'tis politicly done, | to send me packing with 2H6 3.01.341
POLIXENES 15 FR 0.0017 REL FR 13 V 2 P
i must be the poisoner | of good polixenes, and WT 1.02.353
for 'tis polixenes | has made thee swell thus. 2.01. 61
have mistook, my lady, | polixenes for leontes. 2.01. 82
camillo and polixenes | laugh at me; 2.03. 23
is none of mine, | it is the issue of polixenes. 2.03. 94
in committing adultery with polixenes, king of 3.02. 15 P
sir, before polixenes | came to your court, how 3.02. 46
for polixenes | (with whom i am accus'd), i do 3.02. 61
you had a bastard by polixenes, | and i but 3.02. 83
"hermione is chaste, polixenes blameless, 3.02.132 P
i'll reconcile me to polixenes, | new woo my 3.02.155
the minister to poison | my friend polixenes; 3.02.161
that thou betrayedst polixenes, 'twas nothing — 3.02.185
being indeed the issue | of king polixenes) it 3.03. 44
son of polixenes, with his princess (she | the 5.01. 86
POLL *(see pole*)*
POLL–AXE 1 FR 0.0001 REL FR 0 V 1 P
that holds his poll–axe sitting on a close–stool LLL 5.02.577 P
POLL'D 2 FR 0.0002 REL FR 1 V 1 P
down before him, and leave his passage poll'd. COR 4.05.202 P
the poll'd bachelor — | whose youth, like TNK 5.01. 85
POLLUTE 2 FR 0.0002 REL FR 2 V 0 P
absolute, | that some impurity doth not pollute. LUC 854
he shall not boast who did thy stock pollute 1063
POLLUTED 3 FR 0.0003 REL FR 3 V 0 P
but you, that are polluted with your lusts, 1H6 5.04. 43
they are polluted off'rings, more abhorr'd TRO 5.03. 17
of that polluted prison where it breathed. LUC 1726
POLLUTION 4 FR 0.0004 REL FR 3 V 1 P
her body stoop | to such abhorr'd pollution. MM 2.04.183
and i say, the pollution holds in the exchange, LLL 4.02. 46 P
a beauteous wall | doth oft close in pollution, TN 1.02. 49
it, | but with my body my poor soul's pollution? LUC 1157
POLONIUS' 1 FR 0.0001 REL FR 1 V 0 P
and whispers | for good polonius' death; HAM 4.05. 83
POLONIUS 4 FR 0.0004 REL FR 2 V 2 P
what says polonius? HAM 1.02. 57
hamlet in madness hath polonius slain, | and 4.01. 34
now, hamlet, where's polonius? 4.03. 16 P
where is polonius? 4.03. 32 P
POLTROONS 1 FR 0.0001 REL FR 1 V 0 P
patience is for poltroons, such as he. 3H6 1.01. 62
POLYDAMAS 1 FR 0.0001 REL FR 1 V 0 P
the fierce polydamas | hath beat down menon; TRO 5.05. 6
POLYDORE 8 FR 0.0009 REL FR 8 V 0 P
this polydore, | the heir of cymbeline and CYM 3.03. 86
you, polydore, have prov'd best woodman and 3.06. 28
would, polydore, thou hadst not done't! 4.02.155
polydore, | i love thee brotherly, but envy much 4.02.157
i'll stay | till hasty polydore return, and 4.02.165
my ingenious instrument | (hark, polydore), it 4.02.187
and let us, polydore, though now our voices 4.02.235
this gentleman, whom i call polydore, | most 5.05.357
POLYXENA 1 FR 0.0001 REL FR 1 V 0 P
much | to throw down hector than polyxena. TRO 3.03.208
POLYXENES 1 FR 0.0001 REL FR 1 V 0 P
polyxenes is slain, | amphimachus and thoas TRO 5.05. 11
POMANDER 1 FR 0.0001 REL FR 0 V 1 P
stone, not a ribbon, glass, pomander, brooch, WT 4.04.598 P
POMEGRANATE *(also pomgarnet)*
POMEGRANATE 2 FR 0.0002 REL FR 1 V 1 P
italy for picking a kernel out of a pomegranate. AWW 2.03.259 P
nightly she sings on yond pomegranate tree. ROM 3.05. 4
POMEWATER 1 FR 0.0001 REL FR 0 V 1 P
in blood, ripe as the pomewater, who now hangeth LLL 4.02. 4 P
/POMFRET 1 FR 0.0001 REL FR 1 V 0 P
/king /richard, /scrap'd /from /pomfret /stones; 2H4 1.01.205
POMFRET 13 FR 0.0014 REL FR 13 V 0 P
with me | from forth the streets of pomfret, JN 4.02.148
you must to pomfret, not unto the tower. R2 5.01. 52
from my heart" — | meaning the king at pomfret. 5.04. 10
from whence she came, | and him to pomfret; 2H6 2.02. 26
lord rivers and lord grey are sent to pomfret, R3 2.04. 42
to–morrow are let blood at pomfret castle, | and 3.01.183
the kindred of the queen, must die at pomfret. 3.02. 50
the lords at pomfret, when they rode from london 3.02. 83
your friends at pomfret, they do need the priest 3.02.114
o pomfret, pomfret! 3.03. 9
o pomfret, pomfret! 3.03. 9
to–day at pomfret bloodily were butcher'd, | and 3.04. 90
soul to–morrow, | rivers, that died at pomfret! 5.03.140
POMGARNET *(also pomegranate)*
POMGARNET 1 FR 0.0001 REL FR 0 V 1 P
look down into the pomgarnet, ralph. 1H4 2.04. 38 P
POMMEL 1 FR 0.0001 REL FR 0 V 1 P
the pommel of caesar's falchion. LLL 5.02.614 P
/POMP 1 FR 0.0001 REL FR 1 V 0 P
/all /pomp /and /majesty /i /do /forswear; R2 4.01.211
POMP 31 FR 0.0035 REL FR 30 V 1 P
to love, to wealth, to pomp, i pine and die, LLL 1.01. 31
the pale companion is not for our pomp. MND 1.01. 15
with pomp, with triumph, and with revelling. 1.01. 19
life more sweet | than that of painted pomp? AYL 2.01. 3
which i take to be too little for pomp to enter. AWW 4.05. 52 P
nor the pomp that may | be thereat gleaned, for WT 4.04.488
us, | to this unlook'd–for, unprepared pomp. JN 2.01.560
clamors of hell, be measures to our pomp? 3.01.304
therefore, to be possess'd with double pomp, 4.02. 9
my towns | with dreadful pomp of stout invasion! 4.02.173
beast, | the imminent decay of wrested pomp. 4.03.154
scoffing his state and grinning at his pomp, R2 3.02.163
from whence set forth in pomp | she came adorned 5.01. 78
nor the tide of pomp | that beats upon the high H5 4.01.264
myself | for living idly here in pomp and ease, 1H6 1.01.142
to think upon my pomp shall be my hell. 2H6 2.04. 41
why, what is pomp, rule, reign, but earth and 3H6 5.02. 27
men might say | till this time pomp was single, H8 1.01. 15
only to show his pomp as well in france | as 1.01.163
still growing in a majesty and pomp, the which 2.03. 7
will, much better | she ne'er had known pomp! 2.03. 13
vain pomp and glory of this world, i hate ye! 3.02.365
but safer triumph is this funeral pomp, | that TIT 1.01.176
as this pomp shows to a little oil and root. TIM 1.02.135
to have his pomp, and all what state compounds, 4.02. 35
willing misery | outlives incertain pomp, is 4.03.243
no, let the candied tongue lick absurd pomp, HAM 3.02. 60
take physic, pomp, | expose thyself to feel what LR 3.04. 33
pride, pomp, and circumstance of glorious war! OTH 3.03.354
o, behold, | how pomp is followed! ANT 5.02.151
it suffers not in smiling pomp, nor falls SON 124. 6
/POMPAE 1 FR 0.0001 REL FR 1 V 0 P
"me /pompae provexit apex." PER 2.02. 30
POMPEIUS 3 FR 0.0003 REL FR 3 V 0 P
sextus pompeius | /hath given the dare to caesar ANT 1.02.183
sextus pompeius | makes his approaches to the 1.03. 45
having in sicily | sextus pompeius spoil'd, we 3.06. 25
POMPEY 81 FR 0.0091 REL FR 31 V 50 P
pompey. MM 2.01.214 P
the beastliest sense you are pompey the great. 2.01.219 P
pompey, you are partly a bawd, pompey, howsoever 2.01.219 P
you are partly a bawd, pompey, howsoever you 2.01.220 P
how would you live, pompey? 2.01.224 P
what do you think of the trade, pompey? 2.01.225 P
but the law will not allow it, pompey; 2.01.228 P
no, pompey. 2.01.232 P
see this come to pass, say pompey told you so. 2.01.243 P
thank you, good pompey; 2.01.244 P
if i do, pompey, i shall beat you to your tent, 2.01.248 P
in plain–dealing, pompey, i shall have you whipt 2.01.249 P
so for this time, pompey, fare you well. 2.01.250 P
how now, noble pompey? 3.02. 43 P
art going to prison, pompey? 3.02. 61 P
why, 'tis not amiss, pompey. 3.02. 63 P
for debt, pompey? 3.02. 64 P
farewell, good pompey. 3.02. 69 P
commend me to the prison, pompey. 3.02. 69 P
you will turn good husband now, pompey, you will 3.02. 70 P
no indeed will i not, pompey, it is not the wear 3.02. 74 P
i will pray, pompey, to increase your bondage. 3.02. 75 P
adieu, trusty pompey. 3.02. 77 P
does bridget paint still, pompey? ha? 3.02. 79 P
then, pompey, nor now. 3.02. 82 P
go to kennel, pompey, go. 3.02. 85 P
limb or joint, shall pass pompey the great; LLL 5.01.128 P
them to think me worthy of pompey the great; 5.02.506 P
the swain, pompey the great; 5.02.535 P
"i pompey am" — 5.02.547
"i pompey am" — 5.02.548
"i pompey am, pompey surnam'd the big" — 5.02.550
"i pompey am, pompey surnam'd the big" — 5.02.550
"pompey surnam'd the great, | that oft in field 5.02.552
would say, "thanks, pompey," i had done. 5.02.556
great thanks, great pompey. 5.02.557 P
to a halfpenny, pompey proves the best worthy. 5.02.560 P
pompey the great — 5.02.570 P
stand aside, good pompey. 5.02.587 P
him and hang'd for pompey that is dead by him. 5.02.681 P
most rare pompey! 5.02.683 P
renowned pompey! 5.02.684 P
greater than great, great, great, great pompey! 5.02.686 P
pompey the huge! 5.02.686 P

pompey is mov'd. 5.02.688 P
most resolute pompey! 5.02.699 P
do you not see pompey is uncasing for the combat 5.02.701 P
pompey hath made the challenge. 5.02.706 P
but to examine the wars of pompey the great, you H5 4.01. 69 P
savage islanders | pompey the great; 2H6 4.01.138
you cruel men of rome, | knew you not pompey? JC 1.01. 37
to see great pompey pass the streets of rome; 1.01. 42
who rated him for speaking well of pompey; 2.01.216
witness that against my will | (as pompey was) 5.01. 74
throw | pompey the great and all his dignities ANT 1.02.188
the condemn'd pompey, | rich in his father's 1.03. 49
pompey is strong at sea, | and it appears he is 1.04. 36
pompey | thrives in our idleness. 1.04. 75
and great pompey | would stand and make his eyes 1.05. 31
know, worthy pompey, | that what they do delay, 2.01. 2
when you hear no more words of pompey, return it 2.02.105 P
i did not think to draw my sword 'gainst pompey, 2.02.153
of us must pompey presently be sought, | or else 2.02.158
thou canst not fear us, pompey, with thy sails; 2.06. 24
i have heard it, pompey, | and am well studied 2.06. 46
that will i, pompey. 2.06. 61
thy father, pompey, would ne'er have made this 2.06. 82 P
pompey doth this day laugh away his fortune. 2.06.104 P
pompey, a word. 2.07. 37
with the health that pompey gives him, else he 2.07. 51 P
no, pompey, i have kept me from the cup. 2.07. 66
bear him ashore. i'll pledge it for him, pompey. 2.07. 85
pompey, good night. 2.07.119
they have dispatch'd with pompey, he is gone; 3.02. 2
but he hath wag'd | new wars 'gainst pompey; 3.04. 4
caesar and lepidus have made wars upon pompey. 3.05. 5 P
made use of him in the wars 'gainst pompey, 3.05. 8 P
him of letters he had formerly wrote to pompey; 3.05. 11 P
of that his officer | that murd'red pompey. 3.05. 19
at pharsalia, | where caesar fought with pompey. 3.07. 32
are those that often have 'gainst pompey fought; 3.07. 37

POMPEY'S 10 FR 0.0011 REL FR 9 V 1 P
taddle nor pibble babble in pompey's camp. H5 4.01. 71 P
that comes in triumph over pompey's blood? JC 1.01. 51
by this they stay for me | in pompey's porch; 1.03.126
repair to pompey's porch, where you shall find 1.03.147
that done, repair to pompey's theatre. 1.03.152
that now on pompey's basis /lies along | no 3.01.115
even at the base of pompey's statue | (which all 3.02.188
for pompey's name strikes more | than could his ANT 1.04. 54
since pompey's feast, as menas says, is troubled 3.02. 5
nay, you were a fragment | of cneius pompey's — 3.13.118

POMPION *(see pumpion, etc.)*

POMPION 1 FR 0.0001 REL FR 0 V 1 P
one man in one poor man, pompion the great, sir. LLL 5.02.502 P

/POMPOUS 1 FR 0.0001 REL FR 1 V 0 P
/t' /undeck /the /pompous /body /of /a /king; R2 4.01.250

POMPOUS 2 FR 0.0002 REL FR 2 V 0 P
and thrown into neglect the pompous court? AYL 5.04.182
breast | of this most pompous marriage–feast. PER 3.ch. 4

POMPS 1 FR 0.0001 REL FR 0 V 1 P
what needs these feasts, pomps, and vainglories? TIM 1.02.242 P

/POND 1 FR 0.0001 REL FR 1 V 0 P
/froze /them /up, | /as /fish /are /in /a /pond. 2H4 1.01.200

POND 3 FR 0.0003 REL FR 3 V 0 P
cast, he would appear | a pond as deep as hell. MM 3.01. 93
do cream and mantle like a standing pond, | and MV 1.01. 89
and his pond fish'd by his next neighbor — by WT 1.02.195

PONDER 1 FR 0.0001 REL FR 1 V 0 P
this tempest will not give me leave to ponder LR 3.04. 24

PONDEROUS 4 FR 0.0004 REL FR 4 V 0 P
strings | most ponderous and substantial things! MM 3.02.276
if your more ponderous and settled project | may WT 4.04.524
hath op'd his ponderous and marble jaws | to HAM 1.04. 50
sure my love's | more ponderous than my tongue. LR 1.01. 78

PONDS 1 FR 0.0001 REL FR 0 V 1 P
know strange fowl light upon neighboring ponds. CYM 1.04. 89 P

PONIARD 1 FR 0.0001 REL FR 1 V 0 P
give me the poniard; TIT 2.03.120

PONIARDS 4 FR 0.0004 REL FR 1 V 3 P
she speaks poniards, and every word stabs. ADO 2.01.247 P
faith, for seventeen poniards are at thy bosom. AWW 4.01. 76 P
stab poniards in our flesh till all were told, 3H6 2.01. 98
it, six french rapiers and poniards, with their HAM 5.02.149 P

PONT 1 FR 0.0001 REL FR 1 V 0 P
king of pont; ANT 3.06. 72

PONTIC 1 FR 0.0001 REL FR 1 V 0 P
like to the pontic sea, | whose icy current and OTH 3.03.453

PONTIFICAL 1 FR 0.0001 REL FR 1 V 0 P
and new, | my presence, like a robe pontifical, 1H4 3.02. 56

PONTON 1 FR 0.0001 REL FR 1 V 0 P
call'd the brave lord ponton de santrailles, 1H6 1.04. 28

PONTUS *(see pont)*

POOL 4 FR 0.0004 REL FR 2 V 2 P
i' th' filthy–mantled pool beyond your cell, TMP 4.01.182
ay, but to lose our bottles in the pool — 4.01.208 P
drinks the green mantle of the standing pool; LR 3.04.134 P
in a great pool a swan's nest. CYM 3.04.139

/POOLE 2 FR 0.0002 REL FR 2 V 0 P
/yes, /poole. 2H6 4.01. 70
/poole? 4.01. 70

POOLE 2 FR 0.0002 REL FR 2 V 0 P
poole! 2H6 4.01. 70
sir poole! 4.01. 70

POOP 2 FR 0.0002 REL FR 1 V 1 P
thou bearest the lantern in the poop, but 'tis 1H4 3.03. 26 P
the poop was beaten gold, | purple the sails, ANT 2.02.192

POOP'D 1 FR 0.0001 REL FR 0 V 1 P
ay, she quickly poop'd him, she made him PER 4.02. 24 P

/POOR 13 FR 0.0014 REL FR 9 V 4 P
no, your /poor disposer's sick. TRO 3.01. 92 P
/thy /niece /and /i, /poor /creatures, /want TIT 3.02. 5
/this /poor /right /hand /of /mine | /is /left 3.02. 7
/when /thy /poor /heart /beats /with /outrageous 3.02. 13
/the /tears /that /thy /poor /eyes /let /fall 3.02. 18
/poor /harmless /fly, | /that, /with /his 3.02. 63
/alas, /poor /man, /grief /has /so /wrought /on 3.02. 79
/foul /fiend /haunts /poor /tom /in /the /voice LR 3.06. 29 P
/she /kick'd /the /poor /king /her /father. 3.06. 48 P
/fiends /have /been /in /poor /tom /at /once: 4.01. 59 P
/the /poor /distressed /lear's /i' /th' /town, 4.03. 38
/alack, /poor /gentleman! 4.03. 47
/to /watch — /poor /perdu! 4.07. 34

POOR 696 FR 0.0786 REL FR 525 V 171 P
poor souls, they perish'd. TMP 1.02. 9
than prospero, master of a full poor cell, | and 1.02. 20
me (poor man) my library | was dukedom large 1.02.109
the dukedom yet unbow'd (alas, poor milan!) 1.02.115
and let's make further search | for my poor son. 2.01.324
a most poor credulous monster! 2.02.146 P
but that the poor monster's in drink. 2.02.158 P
monster, to make a wonder of a poor drunkard! 2.02.166 P
and most poor matters | point to rich ends. 3.01. 3
poor worm, thou art infected! 3.01. 31
the poor monster's my subject, and he shall not 3.02. 36 P
prospero, his dukedom | in a poor isle; 5.01.212
your highness and your train | to my poor cell, 5.01.302
poor wounded name: TGV 1.02.111
"poor forlorn proteus, passionate proteus: 1.02.121
this parting strikes poor lovers dumb. 2.02. 20
with falsehood, cowardice, and poor descent, 3.02. 32
my riches are these poor habiliments, | of which 4.01. 13
no outrages | on silly women or poor passengers. 4.01. 70
alas, poor proteus, thou hast entertain'd | a 4.04. 91
alas, poor fool, why do i pity him | that with 4.04. 93
poor gentlewoman, my master wrongs her much. 4.04.141
acted with my tears | that my poor mistress, 4.04.170
alas, poor lady, desolate and left! 4.04.174
yet i live like a poor gentleman born. WIV 1.01.276 P
and high and low beguiles the rich and poor. 1.03. 86
he woos both high and low, both rich and poor, 2.01.113
hang him, poor cuckoldly knave! 2.02.270 P
yet i wrong him to call him poor. 2.02.271 P
i think you have kill'd the poor woman. 4.02.188 P
in their hearts the poor unvirtuous fat knight 4.02.217 P
as you see, like a poor old man, but i came from 5.01. 16 P
from her, master /brook, like a poor old woman. 5.01. 17 P
gods have hot backs, what shall poor men do? 5.05. 12 P
and as poor as job? 5.05.156 P
of business 'twixt you and your poor brother. MM 1.04. 71
what poor ability's in me | to do him good? 1.04. 75
your honor, i am the poor duke's constable, and 2.01. 47 P
your worship think me the poor duke's officer. 2.01.177 P
a tapster, a poor widow's tapster. 2.01.198 P
truly, sir, i am a poor fellow that would live. 2.01.223 P
sir, in my poor opinion, they will to't then. 2.01.233 P
but yet, poor claudio! 2.01.285
whose rate are either rich or poor | as fancy 2.02.150
as much for my poor brother as myself: 2.04. 99
fear the soft and tender fork | of a poor worm. 3.01. 17
if thou art rich, thou'rt poor, | for, like an 3.01. 25
and the poor beetle, that we tread upon, | in 3.01. 78
uprighteously do a poor wrong'd lady a merited 3.01.200 P
how heavily this befell to the poor gentlewoman. 3.01.218 P
in death to take this poor maid from the world! 3.01.232 P
honor untainted, the poor mariana advantag'd, 3.01.254 P
i have labor'd for the poor gentleman to the 3.02.251 P
for my poor self, | i am combined by a sacred 4.03.143
poor soul, | she speaks this in th' infirmity of 5.01. 46
lord angelo, | for her poor brother's pardon. 5.01. 77
he sends a warrant | for my poor brother's head. 5.01.103
perceive | these poor informal women are no more 5.01.236
but o, poor souls, | come you to seek the lamb 5.01.297
those, for their parents were exceeding poor, ERR 1.01. 56
her part, poor soul! 1.01.107
th' alluring beauty took | from my poor cheek? 2.01. 90
poor i am but his stale. 2.01.101
alas, poor women! 3.02. 21
before the judgment carries poor souls to hell. 4.02. 40
o that thou wert not, poor distressed soul! 4.04. 59
ay me, poor man, how pale and wan he looks! 4.04.108
god help, poor souls, how idlely do they talk! 4.04.129
to fetch my poor distracted husband hence. 5.01. 39
hast thou so crack'd and splitted my poor tongue 5.01.309
alas, poor hurt fowl! ADO 2.01.202 P
i thank it — poor fool, it keeps on the windy 2.01.314 P
a sport of it, and torment the poor lady worse. 2.03.157 P
for when rich villains have need of poor ones, 3.03.114 P
ones, poor ones may make what price they will. 3.03.114 P
to say so, but we are the poor duke's officers; 3.05. 20 P
and though i be but a poor man, i am glad to 3.05. 27 P
and dispose | for henceforth of poor claudio. 5.01.295
turn'd over and over as my poor self in love. 5.02. 35 P
alas, poor heart, if you spite it for my sake, i 5.02. 68 P
alone now seek to spill | the poor deer's blood, LLL 4.01. 35
but if thou strive, poor soul, what art thou 4.01. 92
sometime to lean upon my poor shoulder, and with 5.01.103 P
things seem foolish and rich things but poor. 5.02.378
but to parfect one man in one poor man, pompion 5.02.502 P
alas, poor machabeus, how hath he been baited! 5.02.631 P
the honest troyan, the poor wench is cast away. 5.02.676 P
wishes and tears, poor fancy's followers. MND 1.01.155
to conjure tears up in a poor maid's eyes | with 3.02.158
a virgin and extort | a poor soul's patience, 3.02.161
to join with men in scorning your poor friend? 3.02.216
from these that my poor company detest. 3.02.434
a knavish lad, | thus to make poor females mad. 3.02.441
and what poor duty cannot do, noble respect 5.01. 91
and through wall's chink, poor souls, they are 5.01.133
but mark, poor knight, | what dreadful dole is 5.01.277
and poor men's cottages princes' palaces. MV 1.02. 13 P
and swear that i have a poor pennyworth in the 1.02. 71 P
no master, sir, but a poor man's son. 2.02. 51 P
is an honest exceeding poor man and, god be 2.02. 52 P
here's my son, sir, a poor boy — 2.02.122 P
not a poor boy, sir, but the rich jew's man, 2.02.123 P
say it, though old man, yet poor man, my father. 2.02.140 P
to become | the follower of so poor a gentleman. 2.02.148
deny not, | it will go hard with poor antonio. 3.02.290
for the poor rude world | hath not her fellow. 3.05. 82
which is a pound of this poor merchant's flesh, 4.01. 23
of the twentith part | of one poor scruple, nay, 4.01.330
me by will but poor a thousand crowns, and, as AYL 1.01. 2 P
god made, a poor unworthy brother of yours, with 1.01. 33 P
or give me the poor allottery my father left me 1.01. 73 P
yonder they lie, the poor old man, their father, 1.02.130 P
o poor orlando! 1.02.259
o my poor rosalind, whither wilt thou go? 1.03. 90
i'll put myself in poor and mean attire, | and 1.03.111
and yet it irks me the poor dappled fools, 2.01. 22
to the which place a poor sequest'red stag, 2.01. 33
"poor deer," quoth he, "thou mak'st a testament 2.01. 47
upon that poor and broken bankrupt there?" 2.01. 57
but, poor old man, thou prun'st a rotten tree, 2.03. 63
alas, poor shepherd! 2.04. 44
that your poor friends must woo your company? 2.07. 10
there is an old poor man, | who after me hath 2.07.129
poor men alone? 3.03. 56 P
nothing, is to have rich eyes and poor hands. 4.01. 24 P
the poor world is almost six thousand years old, 4.01. 94 P
alas, poor shepherd! 4.03. 65
a poor virgin, sir, an ill–favor'd thing, sir, 5.04. 57 P
a poor humor of mine, sir, to take that that no 5.04. 58 P
sir, in a poor house, as your pearl in your foul 5.04. 60 P
(brach merriman, the poor cur, is emboss'd), SHR in.1. 17
no better than a poor and loathsome beggar. in.1. 123
poor girl, she weeps. 2.01. 24
let us that are poor petitioners speak too. 2.01. 72
now must the world point at poor katherine, 3.02. 18
me, | as i can change these poor accoutrements, 3.02.119
and swears, and rates, that she, poor soul, 4.01.184
our purses shall be proud, our garments poor, 4.03.171
worse | for this poor furniture and mean array. 4.03.180
bless our poor virginity from underminers and AWW 1.01.120 P
his humility, | in their poor praise he humbled. 1.02. 45
not unknown to you, madam, i am a poor fellow. 1.03. 13 P
'tis not so well that i am poor, though many of 1.03. 16 P
my poor body, madam, requires it. 1.03. 28 P
that would suffer her poor knight surpris'd 1.03.115 P
my friends were poor, but honest, so's my love. 1.03.195
how shall they credit | a poor unlearned virgin, 1.03.240
sir, i am a poor friend of yours that loves you. 2.02. 43 P
charge — | a poor physician's daughter my wife! 2.03.115
a poor physician's daughter — thou dislik'st 2.03.123
for thy sake, and my poor doing eternal; 2.03.233 P
poor lord, is't i | that chase thee from thy 3.02.102
for with the dark, poor thief, i'll steal away. 3.02.129
alas, poor lady! 3.05. 63
your oaths | are words and poor conditions, but 4.02. 30
sat i' th' stocks all night, poor gallant knave. 4.03.102 P
and the commanders very poor rogues, upon my 4.03.133 P
"poor rogues," i pray you say. 4.03.154 P
truth's a truth, the rogues are marvellous poor. 4.03.157 P
him for no other but a poor officer of mine, and 4.03.198 P
his qualities being at this poor price, i need 4.03.276 P
under my poor instructions yet must suffer 4.04. 27
you | to give this poor petition to the king, 5.01. 19
the carp as you may, for he looks like a poor, 5.02. 23 P
fair grace and speech | of the poor suppliant, 5.03.134
a seducer flourishes, and a poor maid is undone. 5.03.146 P
i am a poor man, and at your majesty's command. 5.03.251 P
o my poor brother! and so perchance may he be. TN 1.02. 7
when you, and those poor number saved with you, 1.02. 10
'tis, | poor lady, she were better love a dream. 2.02. 26
and i (poor monster) fond as much on him; 2.02. 34
what thriftless sighs shall poor olivia breathe? 2.02. 39
not a friend greet | my poor corpse, where my 2.04. 62
o world, how apt the poor are to be proud! 3.01.127
he started one poor heart of mine, in thee. 4.01. 59
they say, poor gentleman, he's much distract. 5.01.280
alas, poor fool, how have they baffled thee! 5.01.369
says, "my poor prisoner, | i am innocent as you. WT 2.02. 26
come on, poor babe. 2.03.185
on thy side, | poor thing, condemn'd to loss! 2.03.192
to have him kill a king — poor trespasses, 3.02.189
come, poor babe. 3.03. 15
person for the thrower–out | of my poor babe, 3.03. 30
poor wretch, | that for thy mother's fault art 3.03. 49
that got this than the poor thing is here. 3.03. 76 P
o, the most piteous cry of the poor souls! 3.03. 90 P
first, how the poor souls roar'd, and the sea 3.03. 99 P
and how the poor gentleman roar'd, and the bear 3.03.100 P
alack, poor soul, thou hast need of more rags to 4.03. 54 P
alas, poor man, a million of beating may come to 4.03. 59 P
alas, poor soul! 4.03. 71 P
with a swain's wearing, and me, poor lowly maid, 4.04. 9
god, | golden apollo, a poor humble swain, | as 4.04. 30
i think | you have heard of my poor services, i' 4.04.516
i am a poor fellow, sir. 4.04.630 P
i am a poor fellow, sir. i know ye well enough. 4.04.638 P
who now | has these poor men in question. 5.01.198
o my poor father! 5.01.202
heirs of your kingdoms, my poor house to visit, 5.03. 6
if i had thought the sight of my poor image 5.03. 57
his mother shames him so, poor boy, he weeps. JN 2.01.166
those heaven–moving pearls from his poor eyes, 2.01.169
thy sins are visited in this poor child, | the 2.01.179
the word "maid," cheats the poor maid of that, 2.01.572
yet, | like a poor beggar, raileth on the rich. 2.01.592
bonds, | because my poor child is a prisoner. 3.04. 75
many a poor man's son would have lien still, 4.01. 50
and find th' inheritance of this poor child, 4.02. 97
my heart hath one poor string to stay it by, 5.07. 55
wooing poor craftsmen with the craft of smiles R2 1.04. 28
though death be poor, it ends a mortal woe. 2.01.152
nor the prevention of poor bullingbrook | about 2.01.167
alas, poor duke, the task he undertakes | is 2.02.145
evermore thank's the exchequer of the poor, 2.03. 65
when my poor heart no measure keeps in grief; 3.04. 8
poor queen, so that thy state might be no worse, 3.04.102
alack, poor richard, where rode he the whilst? 5.02. 22
it is no more | than my poor life must answer. 5.02. 83
poor boy, thou art amaz'd. 5.02. 85
i was a poor groom of thy stable, king, | when 5.05. 72
for the poor abuses of the time want countenance 1H4 1.02.156 P
poor jade is wrung in the withers, out of all 2.01. 6 P
is the next way to give poor jades the bots. 2.01. 9 P
poor fellow never joy'd since the price of oats 2.01. 12 P
a hundred upon poor four of us. 2.04.162 P
not two or three and fifty upon poor old jack, 2.04.187 P
such poor, such bare, such lewd, such mean 3.02. 13
he? alas, he is poor, he hath nothing. 3.03. 76 P
poor? 3.03. 77 P
and one poor pennyworth of sugar–candy to make 3.03.159 P
and what should poor jack falstaff do in the 3.03.165 P
methinks they are exceeding poor and bare, too 4.02. 69 P

and low, | a poor unminded outlaw sneaking home, 4.03. 58
made to my father, while his blood was poor, 4.03. 76
of fickle changelings and poor discontents, 5.01. 76
poor jack, farewell! 5.04.103
against the panting sides of his poor jade | up 2H4 1.01. 45
i am as poor as job, my lord, but not so patient 1.02.126 P
is a long one for a poor lone woman to bear, and 2.01. 32 P
your grace, i am a poor widow of eastcheap, and 2.01. 70 P
asham'd to enforce a poor widow to so rough a 2.01. 82 P
be no more so familiarity with such poor people, 2.01.100 P
my lord, this is a poor /mad soul, and she says 2.01.104 P
of your reputation, and satisfy the poor woman. 2.01.131 P
i do now remember the poor creature, small beer. 2.02. 10 P
a /borrower's cap, "i am the king's poor cousin, 2.02.116 P
grant that, my poor virtue, grant that. 2.04. 46 P
what, you poor, base, rascally, cheating, 2.04.124 P
for tearing a poor whore's ruff in a bawdy–house 2.04.145 P
alas, poor ape, how thou sweat'st! 2.04.216 P
she's in hell already, and burns poor souls; 2.04.339 P
sir, a poor esquire of this county, and one of 3.02. 57 P
have i, in my poor and old motion, the 4.03. 33 P
and no food — | such are the poor, in health; 4.04.106
o my poor kingdom, sick with civil blows! 4.05.133
but 'tis no matter, this poor show doth better, 5.05. 13 P
the poor mechanic porters crowding in | their H5 1.02.200
we never valu'd this poor seat of england, | and 1.02.269
ah, poor heart! 2.01.118 P
me | are heavy orisons 'gainst this poor wretch! 2.02. 53
hence, | poor miserable wretches, to your death; 2.02.178
on the poor souls for whom this hungry war 2.04.104
poor we call them in their native lords! 3.05. 26
for our losses, his exchequer is too poor; 3.06.130 P
alas, poor harry of england! 3.07.130 P
the poor condemned english, | like sacrifices, 4.pr. 22
be ransom'd, and a many poor men's lives sav'd. 4.01.122 P
some upon their wives left poor behind them, 4.01.139 P
that a poor and a private displeasure can do 4.01.198 P
five hundred poor i have in yearly pay, | who 4.01.298
do but behold yond poor and starved band, | and 4.02. 16
and their poor jades | lob down their heads, 4.02. 46
their poor bodies | must lie and fester. 4.03. 87
god, why should they mock poor fellows thus? 4.03. 92
and my poor soldiers tell me, yet ere night, 4.03.116
why that the naked, poor, and mangled peace, 5.02. 34
notwithstanding the poor and untempering effect 5.02.224 P
he may mean more than we poor men do know: 1H6 1.02.122
thus are poor servitors, | when others sleep 2.01. 5
to visit her poor castle where she lies, | that 2.02. 41
poor gentleman, his wrong doth equal mine. 2.05. 22
as he will have me, how am i so poor? 3.01. 30
poor market folks that come to sell their corn. 3.02. 15
mean and right poor, for that pure blood of mine 4.06. 23
poor boy, he smiles, methinks, as who should say 4.07. 27
duke of anjou and maine, yet is he poor, | and 5.03. 95
a poor earl's daughter is unequal odds, | and 5.05. 34
that he should be so abject, base, and poor, 5.05. 49
unto the poor king reignier, whose large style 2H6 1.01.111
i am but a poor petitioner of our whole township 1.03. 23 P
poor soul, god's goodness hath been great to 2.01. 82
sent his poor queen to france, from whence she 2.02. 25
the truth and innocence of this poor fellow, 2.03.103
felonious thief that fleec'd poor passengers, 3.01.129
so the poor chicken should be sure of death. 3.01.251
thus is poor suffolk ten times banished, | once 3.02.357
but wherefore grieve i at an hour's poor loss, 3.02.381
to call poor men before them about matters they 4.07. 42 P
long sitting to determine poor men's causes 4.07. 88
and sends the poor well pleased from my gate. 4.10. 23
kent, | took odds to combat a poor famish'd man. 4.10. 44
a poor esquire of kent, that loves his king. 5.01. 75
poor clifford, how i scorn his worthless threats 3H6 1.01.101
poor queen, how love to me and to her son | hath 1.01.264
in vain thou speak'st, poor boy; 1.03. 21
alas, poor york, but that i hate thee deadly, 1.04. 84
hath that poor monarch taught thee to insult? 1.04.124
and grac'd thy poor sire with his bridal day, 2.02.155
so many weeks ere the poor fools will ean, | so 2.05. 36
dens, | poor harmless lambs abide their enmity. 2.05. 75
poor queen and son, your labor is but lost; 3.01. 32
that she, poor wretch, for grief can speak no 3.01. 47
o margaret, thus 'twill be, and thou, poor soul, 3.01. 53
this is the cause that i, poor margaret, | with 3.03. 30
renowned prince, how shall poor henry live, 3.03.214
alas, poor clarence! 4.01. 59
ay, by my faith, for a poor earl to give. 5.01. 32
you left poor henry at the bishop's palace, 5.01. 45
all these the enemies to our poor bark. 5.04. 28
in my eye | where my poor young was lim'd, was 5.06. 17
my poor boy, icarus; 5.06. 21
how my sword weeps for the poor king's death! 5.06. 63
poor key–cold figure of a holy king, | pale R3 1.02. 5
ghost | to hear the lamentations of poor anne, 1.02. 9
life | i pour the helpless balm of my poor eyes. 1.02. 13
even so thy breast encloseth my poor heart: 1.02.204
and if thy poor devoted servant may | but beg 1.02.206
tower, | and edward, my poor son, at tewksbury. 1.03.119
poor clarence did forsake his father, warwick, 1.03.134
and for his meed, poor lord, he is mewed up. 1.03.138
on thee, the troubler of the poor world's peace! 1.03.220
poor painted queen, vain flourish of my fortune! 1.03.240
and say poor margaret was a prophetess! 1.03.300
o, spare my guiltless wife and my poor children! 1.04. 72
the bitter sentence of poor clarence' death? 1.04.186
but he, poor man, by your first order died, 2.01. 88
who told me how the poor soul did forsake | the 2.01.110
speak unto myself | for him, poor soul. 2.01.129
ah, poor clarence! 2.01.134
is lighted on poor hastings' wretched head! 3.04. 93
these both put off, a poor petitioner, | a 3.07.183
go, go, poor soul, i envy not thy glory, | to 4.01. 63
poor heart, adieu, i pity thy complaining. 4.01. 87
adieu, poor soul, that tak'st thy leave of it! 4.01. 90
inquire me out some mean poor gentleman, | whom 4.02. 53
ah, my poor princes! 4.04. 9
life, blind sight, poor mortal–living ghost, 4.04. 26
i call'd thee then poor shadow, painted queen, 4.04. 83
joys, | poor breathing orators of miseries, 4.04.129
and the dire death of my poor sons and brothers? 4.04.143
like a poor bark of sails and tackling reft, 4.04.234
too deep and dead, poor infants, in their graves 4.04.363
poor clarence, by thy guile betray'd to death! 5.03.133
for want of means, poor rats, had hang'd 5.03.331
and make poor england weep in streams of blood! 5.05. 37
minister communication of | a most poor issue? H8 1.01. 87
i am the shadow of poor buckingham, | whose 1.01.224
they have done my poor house grace; 1.04. 73
now, poor edward bohun. 2.01.103
alas, poor lady! | she's a stranger now again. 2.03. 16
for | i am a most poor woman, and a stranger, 2.04. 15
be their business | with me, a poor weak woman, 3.01. 20
you speak truth, for their poor mistress' sake; 3.01. 47
alas, poor wenches, where are now your fortunes? 3.01.148
great graces | heap'd upon me, poor undeserver, 3.02.175
is that poor man that hangs on princes' favors! 3.02.367
i am a poor fall'n man, unworthy now | to be thy 3.02.413
alas, poor man! 4.02. 16
worms, and my poor name | banish'd the kingdom! 4.02.126
my next poor petition | is, that his noble grace 4.02.138
stand these poor people's friend, and urge the 4.02.157
pray'rs remember | th' estate of my poor queen. 5.01. 74
calumnious tongues | than i myself, poor man. 5.01.113
it, | that am a poor and humble subject to you? 5.02.200
of four foot | (you see the poor remainder) 5.03. 20
himself? alas, poor troilus, i would he were! TRO 1.02. 72 P
alas, poor chin! many a wart is richer. 1.02.141 P
what, am i poor of late? 3.03. 74
most dear in the esteem, | and poor in worth! 3.03.130
alas, poor wretch! 4.02. 31 P
a poor /capocchia! 4.02. 31 P
o poor gentleman! 4.02. 87 P
ah, how the poor world is pest'red with such 5.01. 33 P
ah, poor our sex! 5.02.109
how poor andromache shrills her dolors forth! 5.03. 84
here's a letter come from yond poor girl. 5.03. 99 P
thus is the poor agent despis'd! 5.10. 36 P
we are accounted poor citizens, the patricians COR 1.01. 15 P
they say poor suitors have strong breaths; 1.01. 60 P
daily to chain up and restrain the poor. 1.01. 85 P
that rubbing the poor itch of your opinion 1.01.165
lay here in corioles | at a poor man's house; 1.09. 83
i request you | to give my poor host freedom. 1.09. 87
in what enormity is martius poor in, that you 2.01. 16 P
he's poor in no one fault, but stor'd with all. 2.01. 18 P
you are ambitious for poor knaves' caps and legs 2.01. 68 P
my desire yet to trouble the poor with begging. 2.03. 70 P
to my poor unworthy notice, | he mock'd us when 2.03.158
a marv'llous poor one. 4.05. 27 P
pray you, poor gentleman, take up some other 4.05. 29 P
for one poor grain or two, to leave unburnt 5.01. 27
for one poor grain or two? 5.01. 28
this is a poor epitome of yours, | which by th' 5.03. 68
and to poor we | thine enmity's most capital; 5.03.103
when she, poor hen, fond of no second brood, 5.03.162
in a male tiger, that shall our poor city find. 5.04. 29 P
tribunes, and me, a poor competitor. TIT 1.01. 63
had, | behold the poor remains, alive and dead! 1.01. 81
so long, | poor i was slain when bassianus died. 2.03.171
womb | of this deep pit, poor bassianus' grave. 2.03.240
poor bassianus here lies murthered. 2.03.263
for thou, poor man, hast drown'd it with thine 3.01.141
alas, poor heart, that kiss is comfortless | as 3.01.250
make poor men's cattle break their necks, | set 5.01.132
although the cheer be poor, | 'twill fill your 5.03. 28
the poor remainder of andronici | will hand in 5.03.131
how many thousand times hath these poor lips, 5.03.167
o, she is rich in beauty, only poor | that, when ROM 1.01.215
at my poor house look to behold this night 1.02. 24
like a poor prisoner in his twisted gyves, | and 2.02.179
alas, poor romeo, he is already dead, stabb'd 2.04. 13 P
break, my heart, poor bankrout, break at once! 3.02. 57
ah, poor my lord, what tongue shall smooth thy 3.02. 98
poor ropes, you are beguil'd, | both you and i, 3.02.132
is my poor heart, so for a kinsman vex'd. 3.05. 95
poor soul, thy face is much abus'd with tears. 4.01. 29
but one, poor one, one poor and loving child, 4.05. 46
but one, poor one, one poor and loving child, 4.05. 46
i see that thou art poor. 5.01. 58
then be not poor, but break it, and take this. 5.01. 74
than these poor compounds that thou mayest not 5.01. 82
poor living corse, clos'd in a dead man's tomb! 5.02. 30
that he did buy a poison | of a poor pothecary, 5.03.289
his lady's lie, | poor sacrifices of our enmity! 5.03.304
poor rogues, and usurers' men, bawds between TIM 2.02. 59 P
when he was poor, | imprison'd, and in scarcity 2.02.224
no matter what, he's poor, and that's revenge 3.04. 62 P
by the righteous gods, | i am as poor as you. 4.02. 5
and his poor self, | a dedicated beggar to the 4.02. 12
and we, poor mates, stand on the dying deck, 4.02. 20
thus part we rich in sorrow, parting poor. 4.02. 29
poor honest lord, brought low by his own heart, 4.02. 37
and thatch your poor thin roofs | with burthens 4.03.145
from forth thy plenteous bosom, one poor root! 4.03.186
a poor unmanly melancholy sprung | from change 4.03.203
if thou wilt curse, thy father (that poor rag) 4.03.271
and compounded thee | poor rogue hereditary. 4.03.274
it is some poor fragment, some slender ort of 4.03.399 P
an honest poor servant of yours. 4.03.475
nev'r did poor steward wear a truer grief | for 4.03.480
and whilst this poor wealth lasts | to entertain 4.03.488
he likewise enrich'd poor straggling soldiers 5.01. 6
impression | interprets for my poor ignorance. 5.04. 69
fault | assemble all the poor men of your sort; JC 1.01. 57
than that poor brutus, with himself at war, 1.02. 46
poor man, i know he would not be a wolf, | but 1.03.104
when that the poor have cried, caesar hath wept; 3.02. 91
poor soul, his eyes are red as fire with weeping 3.02.115
there, | and none so poor to do him reverence. 3.02.120
show you sweet caesar's wounds, poor, poor, dumb 3.02.225
sweet caesar's wounds, poor, poor, dumb mouths, 3.02.225
poor knave, i blame thee not, thou art 4.03.241
come, poor remains of friends, rest on this rock 5.05. 1
were poor and single business to contend MAC 1.06. 16
"i would," | like the poor cat i' th' adage? 1.07. 45
whilest our poor malice | remains in danger of 3.02. 14
for the poor wren, | the most diminutive of 4.02. 9
poor bird, thou'dst never fear the net nor lime, 4.02. 34
poor birds they are not set for. 4.02. 36
now, god help thee, poor monkey! 4.02. 59 P
poor prattler, how thou talk'st! 4.02. 64 P
and wisdom | to offer up a weak, poor, innocent 4.03. 16
bleed, bleed, poor country! 4.03. 31
yet my poor country | shall have more vices than 4.03. 46
snow, and the poor state | esteem him as a lamb, 4.03. 53
is thine and my poor country's to command: 4.03.132
alas, poor country, | almost afraid to know 4.03.164
which the poor heart would fain deny, and dare 5.03. 28
life's but a walking shadow, a poor player, 5.05. 24
with which she followed my poor father's body, HAM 1.02.148
the same, my lord, and your poor servant ever. 1.02.162
or (not to crack the wind of the poor phrase, 1.03.108
alas, poor ghost! 1.05. 4
upon a wretch whose natural gifts were poor | to 1.05. 51
ay, thou poor ghost, whiles memory holds a seat 1.05. 96
such as it is, and for my own poor part, | i 1.05.131
and soldiers, | give me one poor request. 1.05.142
and what so poor a man as hamlet is | may do, t' 1.05.184
look where sadly the poor wretch comes reading. 2.02.168
beggar that i am, i am /even poor in thanks — 2.02.272 P
rich gifts wax poor when givers prove unkind. 3.01.100
why should the poor be flatter'd? 3.02. 59
memory, | of violent birth, but poor validity, 3.02.189
the poor advanc'd makes friends of enemies. 3.02.205
poor ophelia | divided from herself and her fair 4.05. 84
pull'd the poor wretch from her melodious lay 4.07.182
too much of water hast thou, poor ophelia, | and 4.07.185
alas, poor yorick, i knew him, horatio, a fellow 5.01.184 P
wronged, | his madness is poor hamlet's enemy. 5.02.239
a love that makes breath poor, and speech unable LR 1.01. 60
then poor cordelia! 1.01. 76
fairest cordelia, that art most rich being poor, 1.01.250
and with what poor judgment he hath now cast her 1.01.291 P
honest–hearted fellow, and as poor as the king. 1.04. 19 P
if thou be'st as poor for a subject as he's for 1.04. 21 P
as he's for a king, /th' art poor enough. 1.04. 22 P
poor pelting villages, sheep–cotes, and mills, 2.03. 18
poor turlygod! 2.03. 20
poor tom! 2.03. 20
arrant whore, | ne'er turns the key to th' poor. 2.04. 53
you see me here, you gods, a poor old man, | as 2.04.272
a poor, infirm, weak, and despis'd old man; 3.02. 20
poor fool and knave, i have one part in my heart 3.02. 72
no squire in debt, nor no poor knight; 3.02. 88
poor naked wretches, wheresoe'er you are, | that 3.04. 28
fathom and half, fathom and half! poor tom! 3.04. 38 P
a spirit, a spirit! he says his name's poor tom. 3.04. 42 P
who gives any thing to poor tom? 3.04. 51 P
do poor tom some charity, whom the foul fiend 3.04. 60 P
of silks betray thy poor heart to woman. 3.04. 95 P
unaccommodated man is no more but such a poor, 3.04.107 P
wheat, and hurts the poor creature of earth. 3.04.119 P
poor tom, that eats the swimming frog, the toad, 3.04.129 P
poor tom's a–cold. 3.04.147 P
he said it would be thus, poor banish'd man. 3.04.164
poor tom, thy horn is dry. 3.06. 75 P
thy cruel nails | pluck out his poor old eyes, 3.07. 57
yet, poor old heart, he holp the heavens to rain 3.07. 62
'tis poor mad tom. 4.01. 26
poor tom's a–cold. i cannot daub it further. 4.01. 52
poor tom hath been scar'd out of his good wits. 4.01. 57 P
give me thy arm; | poor tom shall lead thee. 4.01. 79
but, o poor gloucester, | lost he his other eye? 4.02. 80
in it a jewel | well worth a poor man's taking. 4.06. 29
a poor unfortunate beggar. 4.06. 68
a most poor man, made tame to fortune's blows, 4.06.221
gentleman, go your gait, and let poor voke pass. 4.06.237 P
my fire, and wast thou fain, poor father, | to 4.07. 37
if e'er your grace had speech with man so poor, 5.01. 38
and hear poor rogues | talk of court news; 5.03. 13
and my poor fool is hang'd! 5.03.306
than these thin habits and poor likelihoods | of OTH 1.03.108
to pay grief, must of poor patience borrow. 1.03.215
if this poor trash of venice, whom i trace | for 2.01.303
i have very poor and unhappy brains for drinking 2.03. 33 P
how poor are they that have not patience! 2.03.370
there's a poor piece of gold for thee. 3.01. 23 P
not enriches him, | and makes me poor indeed. 3.03.161
poor and content is rich, and rich enough, | but 3.03.172
but riches fineless is as poor as winter | to 3.03.173
to him that ever fears he shall be poor. 3.03.174
poor lady, she'll run mad | when she shall lack 3.03.317
one is too poor, too weak for my revenge. 3.03.443
jealousy must /conster | poor cassio's smiles, 4.01.102
alas, poor caitiff! 4.01.108
alas, poor rogue, i think, /i' /faith, she loves 4.01.111
all at one side | and sing it like poor barbary. 4.03. 33
"the poor soul sat /sighing by a sycamore tree, 4.03. 40
gentlemen, let's go see poor cassio dress'd. 5.01.124
poor desdemon! 5.02.204
none our parts so poor | but was a race of ANT 1.03. 36
mine honesty | shall not make poor my greatness, 2.02. 93
though thou think me poor, i am the man | will 2.07. 64
so the poor third is up, till death enlarge his 3.05. 12 P
hither | he sends so poor a pinion of his wing, 3.12. 4
birthday, | i had thought t' have held it poor; 3.13.185
poor antony! 4.01. 16
poor enobarbus did | before thy face repent! 4.09. 9
of many thousand kisses the poor last | i lay 4.15. 20
by such poor passion as the maid that milks 4.15. 74
a poor egyptian yet; 5.01. 52
what poor an instrument | may do a noble deed! 5.02.236
poor venomous fool, | be angry, and dispatch. 5.02.305
herself | unto a poor but worthy gentleman. CYM 1.01. 7
as i my poor self did exchange for you, | to 1.01.119
sir, you o'errate my poor kindness, i was glad i 1.04. 38 P
alas, poor princess, | thou divine imogen, what 2.01. 56
give | is telling you that i am poor of thanks, 2.03. 89
and his shipping | (poor ignorant baubles!) 3.01. 27
we poor unfledg'd | have never wing'd from view 3.03. 27
poor i am stale, a garment out of fashion, | and 3.04. 51
thus may poor fools | believe false teachers. 3.04. 84
will poor folks lie, | that have afflictions on 3.06. 9
be here, | poor house, that keep'st thyself! 3.06. 36
the dish, | poor tributary rivers as sweet fish. 4.02. 36

poor sick fidele! 4.02.166
flies, as deep | as these poor pickaxes can dig; 4.02.389
blest beams, remaining | so long a poor unknown. 4.04. 43
hath my poor boy done aught but well, | whose 5.04. 35
or we poor ghosts will cry | to th' shining 5.04. 88
poor shadows of elysium, hence, and rest | upon 5.04. 97
poor wretches that depend | on greatness' favor 5.04.127
that the poor soldier that so richly fought, 5.05. 3
never saw | such noble fury in so poor a thing; 5.05. 8
promis'd nought | but beggary and poor looks. 5.05. 10
did company these three | in poor beseeming; 5.05.409
oppression, and the poor worm doth die for't. PER 1.01.102
i am thinking of the poor men that were cast 2.01. 18 P
alas, poor souls, it griev'd my heart to hear 2.01. 20 P
and tumbles, driving the poor fry before him, 2.01. 31 P
in the net, like a poor man's right in the law; 2.01.117 P
dives, | so up and down the poor ship drives. 3.ch. 50
yet for the love | of this poor infant, this 3.01. 41
get fire and meat for these poor men. 3.02. 3
poor maid, | born in a tempest when my mother 4.01. 17
you between, | and save poor me, the weaker. 4.01. 90
we have but poor three, and they can do no more 4.02. 7 P
'tis not our bringing up of poor bastards — as 4.02. 14 P
the poor transylvanian is dead that lay with the 4.02. 22 P
poor lady, say no more. TNK 1.01.101
i freely lend | to do these poor queens service. 1.01.199
with him | my poor chin too, for 'tis not 1.02. 54
these poor slight sores | need not a plantin; 1.02. 60
i know | his ocean needs not my poor drops, yet 1.03. 7
cabin'd | in many as dangerous as poor a corner, 1.03. 36
venture, | and in some poor disguise be there. 2.03. 79
in thy rumination | that i, poor man, might 3.01. 12
alas, | poor cousin palamon, poor prisoner! 3.01. 23
alas, | poor cousin palamon, poor prisoner! 3.01. 23
is blown abroad, help me, thy poor well–willer, 3.05.116
poor wench, go weep, for whosoever wins | loses 4.02.155
what stuff's here? poor soul! 4.03. 17 P
she is horribly in love with him, poor beast, 5.02. 62
but this poor petticoat and two coarse smocks. 5.02. 84
alas, poor chicken! 5.02. 96
poor servant, thou hast lost. 5.03. 72
alas, poor palamon! 5.03.104
whose lives (for this poor comfort) are laid 5.04. 14
is merely to the undoing of poor prentices, for STM II.C 8 P
alas, poor things, what is it you have got, II.C 68
much advantage the poor handicrafts of the city. II.C 71 P
with their poor luggage | plodding to th' ports II.C 75
what were thy lips the worse for one poor kiss? VEN 207
poor queen of love, in thine own law forlorn, 251
he stamps, and bites the poor flies in his fume. 316
that they have murd'red this poor heart of mine, 502
the poor fool prays her that he may depart. 578
even so poor birds, deceiv'd with painted grapes 601
as those poor birds that helpless berries saw. 604
mark the poor wretch, to overshut his troubles, 680
"by this, poor wat, far off upon a hill, 697
look how the world's poor people are amazed | at 925
this solemn sympathy poor venus noteth, | over 1057
"alas, poor world, what treasure hast thou lost! 1075
down the rich, enrich the poor with treasures; 1150
"poor flow'r," quoth she, "this was thy father's 1177
that they prove bankrout in this poor rich gain. LUC 140
poor wretches have remorse in poor abuses, 269
poor wretches have remorse in poor abuses, 269
but all these poor forbiddings could not stay 323
may feel her heart (poor citizen!) 465
his bow | to strike a poor unseasonable doe. 581
wolf hath seiz'd his prey, the poor lamb cries, 677
feeble desire, all recreant, poor, and meek, 710
poor wasting monuments of lasting moans. 798
the poor, lame, blind, halt, creep, cry out for 902
one poor retiring minute in an age | would 962
poor grooms are sightless night, kings glorious 1013
"poor hand, why quiver'st thou at this decree? 1030
poor helpless help, the treasure stol'n away, 1056
"and for, poor bird, thou sing'st not in the day 1142
as the poor frighted deer that stands at gaze, 1149
it, | but with my body my poor soul's pollution? 1157
poor lucrece' cheeks unto her maid seem so | as 1217
poor women's faces are their own faults' books. 1253
poor women's faults that they are so fulfill'd 1258
to the poor counterfeit of her complaining: 1269
"poor instrument," quoth she, "without a sound, 1464
to tell them all with one poor tired tongue. 1617
"mine enemy was strong, my poor self weak | (and 1646
that my poor beauty had purloin'd his eyes, 1651
which speechless woe of his poor she attendeth, 1674
their oaths, should right poor ladies' harms." 1694
more than "he" her poor tongue could not speak, 1718
her blood, in poor revenge, held it in chase; 1736
"poor broken glass, i often did behold | in thy 1758
words, so thick come in his poor heart's aid, 1784
all our pleasure known to us poor swains, | all PP 17.29
poor corydon must live alone, | other help for 17.35
she, poor bird, as all forlorn, | lean'd her 20. 9
which wit so poor as mine | may make seem bare, SON 26. 5
these poor rude lines of thy deceased lover, 32. 4
so then i am not lame, poor, nor despis'd, 37. 9
to leave poor me thou hast the strength of laws, 49.13
o, what excuse will my poor beast then find, 51. 5
why should poor beauty indirectly seek | roses 67. 7
clay, | do not so much as my poor name rehearse, 71.11
spite of him, i'll live in this poor rhyme, 107.11
that poor retention could not so much hold, 122. 9
and take thou my oblation, poor but free, 125.10
whilst my poor lips, which should that harvest 128. 7
then my friend's heart let my poor heart bail; 133.10
not prizing her poor infant's discontent; 143. 8
poor soul, the centre of my sinful earth, | /... 146. 1
pride, | he is contented thy poor drudge to be, 151.11
sometime diverted their poor balls are tied | to LC 24
POORER 5 FR 0.0005 REL FR 3 V 2 P
which might be felt, that we, the poorer born, AWW 1.01.182
and our esteem | was made much poorer by it; 5.03. 2
i have often wish'd myself poorer, that i might TIM 1.02.101 P
her die twenty times upon far poorer moment. ANT 1.02.142 P
and lust, the thief, far poorer than before. LUC 693
POOREST 8 FR 0.0009 REL FR 8 V 0 P
the poorest service is repaid with thanks, | and SHR 4.03. 45
how many thousand of my poorest subjects | are 2H4 3.01. 4
and make me as the poorest vassal is | that doth 4.05.175
the last is for my men (they are the poorest, H8 4.02.148
that, being one o' th' lowest, basest, poorest, COR 1.01.157
that /for /th' poorest piece | will bear the 3.03. 32
to take the basest and most poorest shape | that LR 2.03. 7
beggars | are in the poorest thing superfluous. 2.04.265
POOR–JOHN 2 FR 0.0002 REL FR 0 V 2 P
a kind of not–of–the–newest poor–john. TMP 2.02. 27 P
if thou hadst, thou hadst been poor–john. ROM 1.01. 31 P
POORLY 7 FR 0.0008 REL FR 7 V 0 P
not, | to look so poorly and to speak so fair? R2 3.03.128
their ragged curtains poorly are let loose, H5 4.02. 41
must poorly sell ourselves | with the rude TRO 4.04. 40
be not lost | so poorly in your thoughts. MAC 2.02. 69
myself, and let me die, | stealing so poorly. CYM 4.02. 16
but poorly rich, so wanteth in his store, | that LUC 97
the counterfeit | is poorly imitated after you; SON 53. 6
POOR'ST 2 FR 0.0002 REL FR 2 V 0 P
caius, rome is thine, | thou art poor'st of all; COR 4.07. 57
be shown | for poor'st diminutives, for dolts, ANT 4.12. 37
POOTHER *(also pudder)*
POOTHER 1 FR 0.0001 REL FR 1 V 0 P
such a poother | as if that whatsoever god who COR 2.01.218
POPE 19 FR 0.0021 REL FR 19 V 0 P
here comes the holy legate of the pope. JN 3.01.135
and from pope innocent the legate here, | do in 3.01.139
name, | pope innocent, i do demand of thee. 3.01.146
to charge me to an answer, as the pope. 3.01.151
so tell the pope, all reverence set apart | to 3.01.159
alone do me oppose | against the pope, and count 3.01.171
from this my hand, as holding of the pope, 5.01. 3
up, | upon your stubborn usage of the pope; 5.01. 18
well, | upon your oath of service to the pope, 5.01. 23
the legate of the pope hath been with me, | and 5.01. 62
in spite of pope or dignities of church, | here 1H6 1.03. 50
thou wilt answer this before the pope. 1.03. 52
have you perus'd the letters from the pope, 5.01. 1
would choose him pope and carry him to rome, 2H6 1.03. 62
him | to him that made him proud, the pope. H8 2.02. 55
here, | before you all, appeal unto the pope, 2.04.119
the cardinal's letters to the pope miscarried, 3.02. 30
"to th' pope"? 3.02.220
packets | you writ to th' pope against the king. 3.02.287
POPEDOM 1 FR 0.0001 REL FR 1 V 0 P
(indeed to gain the popedom | and fee my friends H8 3.02.212
POPILIUS 3 FR 0.0003 REL FR 3 V 0 P
what enterprise, popilius? JC 3.01. 14
what said popilius lena? 3.01. 15
popilius lena speaks not of our purposes, | for 3.01. 23
POPINGAY 1 FR 0.0001 REL FR 1 V 0 P
being cold, | to be so pest'red with a popingay, 1H4 1.03. 50
POPISH 1 FR 0.0001 REL FR 1 V 0 P
with twenty popish tricks and ceremonies, TIT 5.01. 76
POPP'D 2 FR 0.0002 REL FR 2 V 0 P
now, | for thus popp'd paris in his hardiment, TRO 4.05. 28
popp'd in between th' election and my hopes, HAM 5.02. 65
POPPY 1 FR 0.0001 REL FR 1 V 0 P
not poppy, nor mandragora, | nor all the drowsy OTH 3.03.330
POP'RIN 1 FR 0.0001 REL FR 1 V 0 P
she were | an open/–arse, thou a pop'rin pear! ROM 2.01. 38
POPS 1 FR 0.0001 REL FR 1 V 0 P
'a pops me out | at least from fair five hundred JN 1.01. 68
POPULAR 6 FR 0.0006 REL FR 4 V 2 P
o'er–priz'd all popular rate, in my false TMP 1.02. 92
or art thou base, common, and popular? H5 4.01. 38
flamens | do press among the popular throngs, COR 2.01.214
counterfeit the bewitchment of some popular man, 2.03.101 P
his popular "shall," against a graver bench 3.01.106
and, in a violent popular ignorance, given your 5.02. 40 P
POPULARITY 2 FR 0.0002 REL FR 2 V 0 P
streets, | enfeoff'd himself to popularity, 1H4 3.02. 69
sequestration | from open haunts and popularity. H5 1.01. 59
POPULOUS 6 FR 0.0006 REL FR 6 V 0 P
and for because the world is populous, | and R2 5.05. 3
a wilderness is populous enough, | so suffolk 2H6 3.02.360
the fire | is spied in populous cities. OTH 1.01. 77
there's many a beast then in a populous city, 4.01. 63
of heaven, | rais'd by your populous troops. ANT 3.06. 50
i doubt not but this populous city will | yield PER 4.06.186
PORCH 4 FR 0.0004 REL FR 3 V 1 P
'tis ready, sir, here in the porch. WIV 1.04. 61 P
though calved i' th' porch o' th' capitol! COR 3.01.239
by this they stay for me | in pompey's porch; JC 1.03.126
repair to pompey's porch, where you shall find 1.03.147
PORCHES 1 FR 0.0001 REL FR 1 V 0 P
and in the porches of my ears did pour | the HAM 1.05. 63
PORCUPINE *(see porpentine)*
PORE 2 FR 0.0002 REL FR 2 V 0 P
as, painfully to pore upon a book | to seek the LLL 1.01. 74
can you still dream and pore and thereon look? 4.03.294
PORING 1 FR 0.0001 REL FR 1 V 0 P
when creeping murmur and the poring dark | fills H5 4.pr. 2
PORK 2 FR 0.0002 REL FR 0 V 2 P
yes, to smell pork, to eat of the habitation MV 1.03. 33 P
jews to christians, you raise the price of pork. 3.05. 36 P
PORK–EATERS 1 FR 0.0001 REL FR 0 V 1 P
if we grow all to be pork–eaters, we shall not MV 3.05. 24 P
PORN *(also born)*
PORN 3 FR 0.0003 REL FR 0 V 3 P
ay, he was porn at monmouth, captain gower. H5 4.07. 11 P
think it is in macedon where alexander is porn. 4.07. 23 P
tell you there is good men porn at monmouth. 4.07. 52 P
PORPAS 1 FR 0.0001 REL FR 0 V 1 P
as much when i saw the porpas how he bounc'd and
PER 2.01. 24 P
PORPENTINE 8 FR 0.0009 REL FR 7 V 1 P
bring it, i pray you, to the porpentine, | for ERR 3.01.116
i thought to have ta'en you at the porpentine; 3.02.167
your breach of promise to the porpentine: 4.01. 49
promising to bring it to the porpentine, | where 5.01.222
sir, he din'd with her there, at the porpentine. 5.01.276
were almost like a sharp–quill'd porpentine; 2H6 3.01.363
do not, porpentine, do not, my fingers itch. TRO 2.01. 26 P
end, | like quills upon the fearful porpentine. HAM 1.05. 20
PORPOISE *(see porpas)*
PORRIDGE 9 FR 0.0010 REL FR 2 V 7 P
he receives comfort like cold porridge. TMP 2.01. 10 P
as lief you would tell me of a mess of porridge. WIV 3.01. 63 P
at dinner they should not drop in his porridge. ERR 2.02. 99 P
rather pray a month with mutton and porridge. LLL 1.01.303 P
your pie and your porridge than in your cheek; AWW 1.01.159 P
they want their porridge and their fat 1H6 1.02. 9
porridge after meat! TRO 1.02.242 P
set ratsbane by his porridge, made him proud of LR 3.04. 55 P
hang him, plum porridge! TNK 2.03. 72
PORRINGER 2 FR 0.0002 REL FR 1 V 1 P
why, this was moulded on a porringer — | a SHR 4.03. 64
me till her pink'd porringer fell off her head, H8 5.03. 48 P
/PORT* 1 FR 0.0001 REL FR 1 V 0 P
/have /to /the /port /of /athens /sent /their TRO pr 3
PORT* 17 FR 0.0019 REL FR 16 V 1 P
by something showing a more swelling port | than MV 1.01.124
and the magnificoes | of greatest port, have all 3.02.281
keep house and port and servants, as i should. SHR 1.01.203
tranio, "regia," bearing my port, "celsa senis," 3.01. 36 P
at the saint francis here beside the port. AWW 3.05. 36
i have from le port blanc, | a bay in britain, R2 2.01.277
assume the port of mars, and at his heels H5 pr 6
and bear the name and port of gentlemen? 2H6 4.01. 19
at the port, lord, i'll give her to thy hand, TRO 4.04.111
come, to the port. 4.04.136
then is all safe, the anchor in the port. TIT 4.04. 38
no port is free, no place | that guard and most LR 2.03. 3
makes his approaches to the port of rome; ANT 1.03. 46
riveted trim, | and at the port expect you. 4.04. 23
with our sprightly port make the ghosts gaze. 4.14. 52
sails that must these vessels port even where TNK 5.01. 29
into whose port | ne'er ent'red wanton sound) to 5.01.147
/PORTABLE 1 FR 0.0001 REL FR 1 V 0 P
/how /light /and /portable /my /pain /seems /now
LR 3.06.108
PORTABLE 2 FR 0.0002 REL FR 2 V 0 P
like an engine | not portable, lie under this TRO 2.03.135
all these are portable, | with other graces MAC 4.03. 89
PORTAGE* 2 FR 0.0002 REL FR 2 V 0 P
let it pry through the portage of the head H5 3.01. 10
thy loss is more than can thy portage quit PER 3.01. 35
PORTAL 4 FR 0.0004 REL FR 4 V 0 P
sun | from out the fiery portal of the east, R2 3.03. 64
look where he goes, even now, out at the portal! HAM 3.04.136
once more the ruby–color'd portal open'd, VEN 451
as each unwilling portal yields him way, LUC 309
PORTANCE 2 FR 0.0002 REL FR 2 V 0 P
you | th' apprehension of his present portance, COR 2.03.224
thence | and portance in my /travel's history; OTH 1.03.139
PORTCULLIS'D 1 FR 0.0001 REL FR 1 V 0 P
doubly portcullis'd with my teeth and lips, R2 1.03.167
PORTEND 4 FR 0.0004 REL FR 0 V 4 P
what should that alphabetical position portend? TN 2.05.119 P
what think you they portend? 1H4 2.04.322 P
in the sun and moon portend no good to us. LR 1.02.104 P
o, these eclipses do portend these divisions! 1.02.136 P
PORTENDOUS *(also portentous)*
PORTENDOUS 1 FR 0.0001 REL FR 1 V 0 P
black and portendous must this humor prove, ROM 1.01.141
PORTENDS 3 FR 0.0003 REL FR 3 V 0 P
and it portends alone | the fall of antony! ANT 3.13.154
what cloten's being here to us portends, | or CYM 4.02.182
there vanish'd in the sunbeams, which portends 4.02.350
PORTENT 1 FR 0.0001 REL FR 1 V 0 P
and a portent | of broached mischief to the 1H4 5.01. 20
PORTENTOUS *(also portendous)*
PORTENTOUS 2 FR 0.0002 REL FR 2 V 0 P
they are portentous things | unto the climate JC 1.03. 31
well may it sort that this portentous figure HAM 1.01.109
PORTENTS 4 FR 0.0004 REL FR 4 V 0 P
o, what portents are these? 1H4 2.03. 62
wander, | what plagues and what portents! TRO 1.03. 96
these does she apply for warnings and portents JC 2.02. 80
these are portents; OTH 5.02. 45
PORTER* 17 FR 0.0019 REL FR 7 V 10 P
i know not how i may deserve to be your porter. WIV 2.02.175 P
dromio, play the porter well. ERR 2.02.211
master, shall i be porter at the gate? 2.02.217
what patch is made our porter? 3.01. 36
the porter for this time, sir, and my name is 3.01. 43
the town gates on his back like a porter; LLL 1.02. 72 P
porter, remember what i gave in charge, | and 1H6 2.03. 1
good master porter, i belong to th' larder. H8 5.03. 4 P
do you hear, master porter? 5.03. 28 P
achilles! a drayman, a porter, a very camel. TRO 1.02.249 P
has the porter his eyes in his head, that he COR 4.05. 11 P
and sowl the porter of rome gates by th' ears. 4.05.201 P
let the porter let in susan grindstone and nell. ROM 1.05. 9 P
no porter at his gate, | but rather one that TIM 2.01. 10
if a man were porter of hell gate, he should MAC 2.03. 2 P
i pray you remember the porter. 2.03. 21 P
thou shouldst have said, "good porter, turn the LR 3.07. 64
PORTERS* 2 FR 0.0002 REL FR 2 V 0 P
the poor mechanic porters crowding in | their H5 1.02.200
where are these porters? H8 5.03. 69
PORTIA 23 FR 0.0026 REL FR 23 V 0 P
her name is portia, nothing undervalu'd | to MV 1.01.165
to cato's daughter, brutus' portia. 1.01.166
to furnish thee to belmont, to fair portia. 1.01.182
now | for princes to come view fair portia. 2.07. 43
they come | as o'er a brook to see fair portia. 2.07. 47
portia, adieu. 2.07. 76
how much unlike art thou to portia! 2.09. 56
friends and countrymen, | sweet portia, welcome. 3.02.224
o sweet portia, | here are a few of the 3.02.250
and portia one, there must be something else 3.05. 81
the voice, | or i am much deceiv'd, of portia. 5.01.111
sweet portia, | if you did know to whom i gave 5.01.192
portia, forgive me this enforced wrong, | and in 5.01.240
there you shall find that portia was the doctor, 5.01.269
portia! JC 2.01.234
why, so i do. good portia, go to bed. 2.01.260
kneel not, gentle portia. 2.01.278
more, | portia is brutus' harlot, not his wife. 2.01.287
portia, go in a while, | and by and by thy bosom 2.01.304
no man bears sorrow better. portia is dead. 4.03.147
ha? portia? 4.03.148
portia, art thou gone? 4.03.166

why, farewell, portia. 4.03.190
PORTIA'S 2 FR 0.0002 REL FR 2 V 0 P
fair portia's counterfeit! MV 3.02.115
for never shall you lie by portia's side | with 3.02.305
PORTIGAL *(also portugal)*
PORTIGAL 1 FR 0.0001 REL FR 1 V 0 P
to any german province, spain or portigal, | nay STM II.C 128
PORTION 8 FR 0.0009 REL FR 6 V 2 P
with him, the portion and sinew of her fortune, MM 3.01.221 P
what prodigal portion have i spent, that i AYL 1.01. 38 P
and all things answerable to this portion. SHR 2.01.359
to him, and will make | her portion equal his. WT 4.04.386
wife | and have no portion in the choice myself. 1H6 5.03.125
wealth hath he accumulated | to his own portion! H8 3.02.108
give but that portion which yourself propos'd, LR 1.01.242
commend me to her, and, to piece her portion, TNK 5.04. 31
PORTLY 7 FR 0.0008 REL FR 5 V 2 P
view gilded my foot, sometimes my portly belly. WIV 1.03. 62 P
there where your argosies with portly sail MV 1.01. 9
our own hands | have holp to make so portly. 1H4 1.03. 13
a goodly portly man, i' faith, and a corpulent, 2.04.422 P
shall find him by his large and portly size. TRO 4.05.162
alone, | 'a bears him like a portly gentleman; ROM 1.05. 66
shore, | a portly sail of ships make hitherward. PER 1.04. 61
PORTOTARTAROSSA 1 FR 0.0001 REL FR 0 V 1 P
hush, hush! hoodman comes! portotartarossa. AWW 4.03.118 P
PORTRAIT 1 FR 0.0001 REL FR 1 V 0 P
the portrait of a blinking idiot, | presenting MV 2.09. 54
/PORTRAITURE 1 FR 0.0001 REL FR 1 V 0 P
/my /cause /i /see | /the /portraiture /of /his. HAM 5.02. 78
/PORTS* 1 FR 0.0001 REL FR 1 V 0 P
/secret /feet | /in /some /of /our /best /ports, LR 3.01. 33
PORTS* 11 FR 0.0012 REL FR 11 V 0 P
piring in maps for ports and piers and roads; MV 1.01. 19
are to a wise man ports and happy havens. R2 1.03.276
that keep'st the ports of slumber open wide | to 2H4 4.05. 24
he touch'd the ports desir'd, | and for an old TRO 2.02. 76
so, let the ports be guarded; COR 1.07. 1
i accuse | the city ports by this hath enter'd, 5.06. 6
/descend, and open your uncharged ports. TIM 5.04. 55
all the other, | and the very ports they blow, MAC 1.03. 15
all ports i'll bar, the villain shall not scape; LR 2.01. 80
to the ports | the discontents repair, and men's ANT 1.04. 39
luggage | plodding to th' ports and coasts for STM II.C 76
PORTUGAL *(also portigal)*
PORTUGAL 1 FR 0.0001 REL FR 0 V 1 P
an unknown bottom, like the bay of portugal. AYL 4.01.208 P
POS'D 1 FR 0.0001 REL FR 1 V 0 P
tell ten — i have pos'd him. TNK 3.05. 79
POSE 1 FR 0.0001 REL FR 1 V 0 P
then i shall pose you quickly. MM 2.04. 51
POSIED 1 FR 0.0001 REL FR 1 V 0 P
crack'd many a ring of posied gold and bone, LC 45
POSIES 4 FR 0.0004 REL FR 4 V 0 P
peds of roses, | and a thousand fragrant posies. WIV 3.01. 20
in pabylon — | and a thousand vagram posies. 3.01. 25
and to 'em spoke | the prettiest posies — "thus TNK 4.01. 90
bed of roses, | with a thousand fragrant posies, PP 19.10
POSITION 5 FR 0.0005 REL FR 3 V 2 P
what should that alphabetical position portend? TN 2.05.119 P
i do not strain at the position — | it is TRO 3.03.112
(as it is a most pregnant and unforc'd position) OTH 2.01.236 P
i do not in position | distinctly speak of her, 3.03.234
in manners this was false position. TNK 3.05. 51
POSITIVE 3 FR 0.0003 REL FR 1 V 2 P
for it is as positive as the earth is firm that WIV 3.02. 48 P
'tis positive against all exceptions, lords, H5 4.02. 25
a fool, and this patroclus is a fool positive. TRO 2.03. 65 P
POSITIVELY *(also possitable)*
POSITIVELY 2 FR 0.0002 REL FR 2 V 0 P
dear lord, | before i positively speak in this R3 4.02. 25
that i have positively said, "'tis so," | when HAM 2.02.154
POSSE 1 FR 0.0001 REL FR 1 V 0 P
"aio /te, aeacida, romanos vincere posse." 2H6 1.04. 62
POSSESS 35 FR 0.0039 REL FR 31 V 4 P
remember | first to possess his books; TMP 3.02. 92
i will possess him with yellowness, for the WIV 1.03.101 P
if aught possess thee from me, it is dross, ERR 2.02.177
both, | possess the people in messina here | how ADO 5.01.281
for still her cheeks possess the same | which LLL 1.02.105
o, i am yours, and all that i possess! 5.02.383
possess us, possess us, tell us something of him TN 2.03.138 P
possess us, possess us, tell us something of him 2.03.138 P
her sainted spirit | again possess her corpse, WT 5.01. 58
why seek'st thou to possess me with these fears? JN 4.02.203
'tis in reversion that i do possess — | but R2 2.02. 38
to have | the present benefit which i possess, 2.03. 14
nor did the french possess the salique land H5 1.02. 56
no man should possess him with any appearance of 4.01.110 P
soldiers' hearts, | possess them not with fear! 4.01.290
possess it, york, | for this is thine and not 3H6 1.01. 26
to sanctuary, and good thoughts possess thee! R3 4.01. 93
which you have promised i shall possess. 4.02. 91
madam, such good dreams | possess your fancy. H8 4.02. 94
enjoy | at ample point all that i did possess, TRO 3.03. 89
hand, | and by the way possess thee what she is. 4.04.112
and possess me | some harlot's spirit! COR 3.02.111
(our pastimes done), possess a golden slumber, TIT 2.03. 26
unless some fit or frenzy do possess her; 4.01. 17
so shall you share all that he doth possess, ROM 1.03. 93
which shall possess them with the heaviest sound MAC 4.03.202
rank and gross in nature | possess it merely. HAM 1.02.137
possess it, i'll make answer. ANT 2.07.101
i will possess you of that ship and treasure. 3.11. 21
possess | the high throne in his heart. TNK 1.03. 95
them, cut their throats, possess their houses, STM II.C 120
what they have not, that which they possess, LUC 135
the old bees die, the young possess their hive: 1769
till manly shame bids him possess his breath, 1777
yet neither may possess the claim they lay. 1794
POSSESS'D 45 FR 0.0050 REL FR 37 V 8 P
thy conscience | is so possess'd with guilt. TMP 1.02.472
so much of bad already hath possess'd them. TGV 3.01.207
and that i have possess'd him my most stay | can MM 4.01. 43
that spirit's possess'd with haste | that wounds 4.02. 88
i am possess'd with an adulterate blot; ERR 2.02.140
possess'd with such a gentle sovereign grace, 3.02.160
mistress, both man and master is possess'd: 4.04. 92
outfacing me, | cries out, i was possess'd. 5.01.246
cousin, and she were not possess'd with a fury, ADO 1.01.191 P
and plac'd and possess'd by my master don john, 3.03.150 P
partly by his oaths, which first possess'd them, 3.03.156 P
as well deriv'd as he, | as well possess'd; MND 1.01.100
is he yet possess'd | how much ye would? MV 1.03. 64
i have possess'd your grace of what i purpose, 4.01. 35
of all he dies possess'd | unto his son lorenzo 4.01.389
after his death, of all he dies possess'd of. 5.01.293
you would have her after you have possess'd her. AYL 4.01.144 P
possess'd with the glanders and like to mose in SHR 3.02. 50 P
he is sure possess'd, madam. TN 3.04. 9 P
and legion himself possess'd him, yet i'll speak 3.04. 86 P
therefore, to be possess'd with double pomp, JN 4.02. 9
double coronation | i have possess'd you with, 4.02. 41
possess'd with rumors, full of idle dreams, 4.02.145
deposing thee before thou wert possess'd, R2 2.01.107
which art possess'd now to depose thyself. 2.01.108
whereof our uncle gaunt did stand possess'd. 2.01.162
are all scattered and possess'd with fear | so 1H4 2.02.105
because the king is certainly possess'd | of all 4.01. 40
and that we now possess'd | the utmost man of 2H4 1.03. 64
'tis known already that i am possess'd | with 1H6 5.04.138
unless you be possess'd with devilish spirits 2H6 4.07. 75
whereof the king my brother was possess'd. R3 3.01.196
to the good queen possess'd him with a scruple H8 2.01.158
possess'd he is with greatness, | and speaks not TRO 2.03.170
myself | from certain and possess'd conveniences 3.03. 7
is the senate possess'd of this? COR 2.01.132 P
mean while am i possess'd of that is mine. TIT 1.01.408
but not possess'd it, and, though i am sold, ROM 3.02. 27
ah me, how sweet is love itself possess'd, 5.01. 10
since i am still possess'd | of those effects HAM 3.03. 53
of money, plate, and jewels | i am possess'd of; ANT 5.02.139
and like him possess'd | with fire malevolent, TNK 5.04. 62
and, if possess'd, as soon decay'd and done, LUC 23
for thou art so possess'd with murd'rous hate, SON 10. 5
like him, like him with friends possess'd, 29. 6
POSSESSED 2 FR 0.0002 REL FR 2 V 0 P
and thou possessed with a thousand wrongs; JN 3.03. 41
may be possessed with some store of crowns, 3H6 2.05. 57
/POSSESSES 2 FR 0.0002 REL FR 1 V 1 P
the most precious square of sense /possesses, LR 1.01. 74
/who /since /possesses /chambermaids /and 4.01. 62 P
POSSESSES 2 FR 0.0002 REL FR 2 V 0 P
what a strange drowsiness possesses them! TMP 2.01.199
instructions enter | where folly now possesses? CYM 1.05. 48
POSSESSETH 2 FR 0.0002 REL FR 2 V 0 P
weakness possesseth me, and i am faint. JN 5.03. 17
sin of self–love possesseth all mine eye, | and SON 62. 1
POSSESSING 2 FR 0.0002 REL FR 2 V 0 P
possessing or pursuing no delight | save what is SON 75.11
farewell, thou art too dear for my possessing, 87. 1
POSSESSION 36 FR 0.0040 REL FR 31 V 5 P
take but possession of her with a touch — | i TGV 5.04.130
contract | i got possession of julietta's bed. MM 1.02.146
for ever hous'd where it gets possession. ERR 3.01.106
man, | to yield possession to my holy prayers, 4.04. 55
how long hath this possession held the man? 5.01. 44
the virtue that possession would not show us ADO 4.01.221
and in possession twenty thousand crowns. SHR 2.01.122
when i should take possession of the bride, AWW 2.05. 26
our strong possession and our right for us. JN 1.01. 39
your strong possession much more than your right 1.01. 40
rage, | and stalk in blood to our possession? 2.01.266
and bear possession of our person here, | lord 2.01.366
his words do take possession of my bosom. 4.01. 32
and him, | broke the possession of a royal bed, R2 3.01. 13
yields | to the possession of thy royal hand. 4.01.110
the crown, | had still kept loyal to possession, 1H4 3.02. 43
then plain and right must my possession be, 2H4 4.05.222
us, | we lose the better half of our possession; H5 1.01. 8
athversary was have possession of the pridge, 3.06. 94 P
je quand sur le possession de france, et quand 5.02.181 P
et quand vous avez le possession de moi — let 5.02.182 P
i mean to take possession of my right. 3H6 1.01. 44
keep | than in possession any jot of pleasure. 2.02. 53
to london | to see these honors in possession. 2.06.110
that it outspeaks | possession of a subject. H8 3.02.128
now to deliver her possession up | on terms of TRO 2.02.152
i have abandon'd troy, left my possession, 3.03. 5
as i say, spacious in the possession of dirt. HAM 5.02. 88 P
from the possession of this heavenly sight! OTH 5.02.278
in thy possession lies | a lass unparallel'd. ANT 5.02.315
of thy late master's garments in thy possession? CYM 3.05.124 P
i, that took possession | first with mine eye of TNK 2.02.167
lent | in the possession of his beauteous mate; LUC 18
keep still possession of thy gloomy place, 803
nor lose possession of that fair thou ow'st, SON 18.10
/mad in pursuit and in possession so, | had, 129. 9
POSSESSIONS 5 FR 0.0005 REL FR 5 V 0 P
likes | (only for his possessions are so huge), TGV 2.04.175
for me and my possessions she esteems not. 3.01. 79
considers she my possessions? 5.02. 25
for his possessions, | although by /confiscation MM 5.01.422
of such possessions, and so high esteem, SHR in.2. 15
POSSESSOR 2 FR 0.0002 REL FR 2 V 0 P
wrought in his behalf) | the third possessor; MV 1.03. 74
lewis, | that henry, sole possessor of my love, 3H6 3.03. 24
/POSSET 1 FR 0.0001 REL FR 1 V 0 P
and with a sudden vigor it doth /posset | and HAM 1.05. 68
POSSET 2 FR 0.0002 REL FR 0 V 2 P
go, and we'll have a posset for't soon at night, WIV 1.04. 8 P
thou shalt eat a posset to–night at my house, 5.05.171 P
POSSETS 1 FR 0.0001 REL FR 1 V 0 P
i have drugg'd their possets, | that death and MAC 2.02. 6
POSSIBILITIES 1 FR 0.0001 REL FR 0 V 1 P
seven hundred pounds, and possibilities, is goot WIV 1.01. 64 P
POSSIBILITY 4 FR 0.0004 REL FR 2 V 2 P
and to the possibility of thy soldiership will AWW 3.06. 82 P
with the very extremest inch of possibility; 2H4 4.03. 35 P
for more, | be cast from possibility of all. 1H6 5.04.146
o brother, speak with possibility, | and do not TIT 3.01.214
/POSSIBLE 1 FR 0.0001 REL FR 0 V 1 P
/is't /possible? HAM 2.02.357 P
POSSIBLE 60 FR 0.0067 REL FR 33 V 27 P
as little by such toys as may be possible: TGV 1.02. 79
'tis not possible. MM 3.02.124 P
is't possible? ADO 1.01. 74 P
very easily possible. 1.01. 75 P
is it possible disdain should die while she hath 1.01.120 P
is't possible? sits the wind in that corner? 2.03. 98 P
of her love, 'tis very possible he'll scorn it, 2.03.179 P
is it possible that any villainy should be so 3.03.110 P
ask if it were possible any villainy should be 3.03.112 P
it were as possible for me to say i lov'd 4.01.270 P
as the rest of the court can possible devise." LLL 1.01.131 P
it is not possible. MND 4.02. 7 P
is it possible | a cur can lend three thousand MV 1.03.121
is it possible, on such a sudden, you should AYL 1.03. 27 P
can it be possible that no man saw them? 2.02. 1
is it possible? 3.02.188 P
is't possible that on so little acquaintance you 5.02. 1 P
is it possible | that love should of a sudden SHR 1.01.146
true, | i never thought it possible or likely. 1.01.149
not possible; 1.01.194
we will persuade him, be it possible, | to put 3.02.125
is't possible you will away to–night? 3.02.189
is't possible, friend litio, that mistress 4.02. 1
is it possible he should know what he is, and be AWW 4.01. 44 P
thinks it were not possible with well–weighing 4.03.179 P
is't possible? TN 3.04.126 P
is't possible that my deserts to you | can lack 3.04.348
thou dost make possible things not so held, WT 1.02.139
to save the innocent — any thing possible. 2.03.167
it shall be possible. 2.03.168
may this be possible? may this be true? JN 5.04. 21
it is not possible, it cannot be, | the king 1H4 5.02. 4
conscience will make any possible satisfaction, 2H4 ep 21 P
may it be possible that foreign hire | could out H5 2.02.100
is it possible dat i sould love de enemy of 5.02.169 P
it is not possible you should love the enemy of 5.02.171 P
ask me what question thou canst possible, | and 1H6 1.02. 87
if without peril it be possible, | sweet blunt, R3 5.03. 39
being now seen possible enough, got credit, H8 1.01. 37
is't possible the spells of france should juggle 1.03. 1
is't possible? TRO 4.02. 74 P
is't possible? 4.04. 32
not possible. COR 4.06. 57
if it be possible for you to displace it with 5.04. 4 P
is't possible that so short a time can alter the 5.04. 9 P
is't possible the world should so much differ, TIM 3.01. 46
is't possible? JC 4.03. 38
is't possible a young maid's wits | should be as HAM 4.05.160
is't possible? 5.02. 25
is't not possible to understand in another 5.02.125 P
nay, it is possible enough to judgment. OTH 1.03. 9
with him? why, 'tis not possible. 2.01.220 P
is't possible? 2.03.287 P
is't possible, my lord? 3.03.358
is't possible? 3.04. 68
is't possible? 4.01. 42 P
is't possible? 4.02. 87
that possible strength might meet, would seek us CYM 4.02.160
'twas possible | they might have been recovered. TNK 1.04. 26
i do not think it possible our friendship 2.02.114
POSSIBLY 3 FR 0.0003 REL FR 2 V 1 P
when possibly i can, i will return. TGV 2.02. 3
that you could possibly have found in any part TN 3.04.267 P
how possibly preserved, and who to thank PER 5.03. 57
POSSITABLE *(also positively)*
POSSITABLE 1 FR 0.0001 REL FR 0 V 1 P
you must speak possitable, if you can carry her WIV 1.01.236 P
POST* 62 FR 0.0070 REL FR 53 V 9 P
can have no note, unless the sun were post — TMP 2.01.248
receiving them from such a worthless post. TGV 1.01.153
shipp'd, and thou art to post after with oars. 2.03. 34 P
i from my mistress come to you in post: ERR 1.02. 63
if i return, i shall be post indeed, | for she 1.02. 64
go hie thee presently, post to the road, | and 3.02.147
that stole your meat, and you'll beat the post. ADO 2.01.200 P
i post from love; good lover, let me go. LLL 4.03.186
see | quick cupid's post that comes so mannerly. MV 2.09.100
tell him there's a post come from my master, 5.01. 46 P
why then 'tis good to be a post. AYL 4.01. 9 P
his highness comes post from marsellis, of as AWW 4.05. 80 P
he'll stand at your door like a sheriff's post, TN 1.05.148 P
i am no fee'd post, lady; 1.05.284
i have dispatch'd in post | to sacred delphos, WT 2.01.182
myself on every post | proclaim'd a strumpet; 3.02.101
this afternoon will post | to consummate this JN 5.07. 94
which else would post until it had return'd R2 1.01. 56
itself, | away with me in post to ravenspurgh; 2.01.296
post you to london and you will find it so, | i 3.04. 90
spur post, and get before him to the king, | and 5.02.112
came | a post from wales loaden with heavy news, 1H4 1.01. 37
if i be not sent away post, i will see you again 2H4 2.04.378 P
and that was against a post when he was drunk. H5 3.02. 41 P
take therefore shipping, post, my lord, to 1H6 5.05. 87
york, | to be the post, in hope of his reward. 2H6 1.04. 77
why com'st thou in such post? 3H6 1.02. 48
me, | my brother montague shall post to london. 1.02. 55
mount you, my lord, towards berwick post amain. 2.05.128
warwick, this is some post to us or thee. 3.03.162
then, england's messenger, return in post, | and 3.03.222
where is the post that came from valiant oxford? 5.01. 1
where is the post that came from montague? 5.01. 5
to london, all in post, and, as i guess, | to 5.05. 84
shall be that straight shall post to /ludlow. R3 2.02.142
and with all speed post with him toward the 3.02. 17
mayor towards guildhall hies him in all post. 3.05. 73
light–foot friend post to the duke of norfolk; 4.04.440
post to salisbury; 4.04.444
your highness told me i should post before. 4.04.455
and at the door too, like a post with packets. H8 5.02. 32
your native town you enter'd like a post, | and COR 5.06. 49
marcus, the post is come. TIT 4.03. 78
vault, | and presently took post to tell it you. ROM 5.01. 21
and then in post he came from mantua | to this 5.03.273
post back with speed, and tell him what hath JC 3.01.287
as thick as tale | /came post with post, and MAC 1.03. 98
as thick as tale | /came post with post, and 1.03. 98
to post | with such dexterity to incestious HAM 1.02.156
my duty kneeling, came there a reeking post, LR 2.04. 30
post speedily to my lord your husband, show him 3.07. 1 P
the post unsanctified | of murtherous lechers; 4.06.274

away to britain | post i in this design. CYM 5.05.192
time | post /on the lame feet of my rhyme, PER 4.ch. 48
we will post | to athens /'fore our army. TNK 1.04. 48
from dis to daedalus, from post to pillar, | is 3.05.115
from the besieged ardea all in post, | borne by LUC 1
and in a desp'rate rage | post hither, this vile 220
swift subtle post, carrier of grisly care, 926
the post attends, and she delivers it, 1333
the night so pack'd, i post unto my pretty; PP 14.21
were i with her, the night would post too soon, 14.25
POSTED 6 FR 0.0006 REL FR 6 V 0 P
and posted day and night | to meet you on the 1H4 5.01. 35
his guilt should be but idly posted over, 2H6 3.01.255
nor posted off their suits with slow delays; 3H6 4.08. 40
and | is posted, as the agent of our cardinal, H8 3.02. 59
faith, he is posted hence on serious matter. LR 4.05. 8
the swiftest harts have posted you by land, CYM 2.04. 27
POSTERIOR 2 FR 0.0002 REL FR 0 V 2 P
the posterior of the day, most generous sir, is LLL 5.01. 91 P
of time, some show in the posterior of this day, 5.01.119 P
POSTERIORS 1 FR 0.0001 REL FR 0 V 1 P
at her pavilion in the posteriors of this day, LLL 5.01. 89 P
POSTERITY 14 FR 0.0015 REL FR 14 V 0 P
whose joy is nothing else | but fair posterity) WT 4.04.409
and for amends to his posterity, | at our JN 2.01. 6
king, | cut off the sequence of posterity, 2.01. 96
posterity, await for wretched years, | when at 1H6 1.01. 48
to age, | as 'twere retail'd to all posterity, R3 3.01. 77
what then? | he'ld make an end of thy posterity. COR 4.02. 26
severity | cuts beauty off from all posterity. ROM 1.01.220
was said | it should not stand in thy posterity, MAC 3.01. 4
grave, | seeming to bury that posterity, VEN 758
that my posterity, sham'd with the note, | shall LUC 208
leaving no posterity, | 'twas not their PHT 59
the tomb, | of his self-love, to stop posterity? SON 3. 8
depart, | leaving thee living in posterity? 6.12
even in the eyes of all posterity | that wear 55.11
POSTERN 3 FR 0.0003 REL FR 3 V 0 P
out at the postern by the abbey wall; TGV 5.01. 9
wounds th' unsisting postern with these strokes. MM 4.02. 89
to thread the postern of a small needle's eye." R2 5.05. 17
POSTERNS 3 FR 0.0003 REL FR 3 V 0 P
and will by twos and threes at several posterns WT 1.02.438
to command | the keys of all the posterns. 1.02.464
how came the posterns | so easily open? 2.01. 52
POSTERS 1 FR 0.0001 REL FR 1 V 0 P
hand in hand, | posters of the sea and land, MAC 1.03. 33
POST–HASTE 3 FR 0.0003 REL FR 3 V 0 P
and hath sent post–haste | to entreat your R2 1.04. 55
in haste, post–haste, are come to join with you; 3H6 2.01.139
of this post–haste and romage in the land. HAM 1.01.107
POST–HORSE 2 FR 0.0002 REL FR 2 V 0 P
drooping west | (making the wind my post–horse), 2H4 in 4
george be pack'd with post–horse up to heaven. R3 1.01.146
POST–HORSES 1 FR 0.0001 REL FR 1 V 0 P
get me ink and paper, | and hire post–horses; ROM 5.01. 26
POSTHUMUS' 1 FR 0.0001 REL FR 0 V 1 P
it is posthumus' hand, i know't. CYM 3.05.108 P
POSTHUMUS 30 FR 0.0034 REL FR 23 V 7 P
to his protection, calls him posthumus leonatus, CYM 1.01. 41
for you, posthumus, | so soon as i can win th' 1.01. 74
it is your fault that i have lov'd posthumus: 1.01.144
leonatus posthumus." 3.02. 47 P
where is posthumus? 3.04. 4
so thou, posthumus, | wilt lay the leaven on all 3.04. 61
and thou, posthumus, | that didst set up my 3.04. 87
yea, happily, near | the residence of posthumus; 3.04.148
since the exile of posthumus, most retir'd 3.05. 36
pisanio, thou that stand'st so for posthumus! 3.05. 56
love, she's flown | to her desir'd posthumus. 3.05. 62
on | the low posthumus slanders so her judgment 3.05. 76
is she with posthumus? 3.05. 87
to the bare fortune of that beggar posthumus, 3.05.119 P
even there, thou villain posthumus, will i kill 3.05.132 P
the very garment of posthumus in more respect 3.05.135 P
so more equal ballasting | to thee, posthumus. 3.06. 78
posthumus, thy head, which now is growing upon 4.01. 15 P
the garments of posthumus? 4.02.308
o posthumus, alas, | where is thy head? 4.02.320
my throes, | that from me was posthumus ripp'd, 5.04. 45
like hardiment posthumus hath | to cymbeline 5.04. 75
then shall posthumus end his miseries, britain 5.04.143 P
the good posthumus | (what should i say? 5.05.157
this posthumus, | most like a noble lord in love 5.05.170
i am posthumus, | that kill'd thy daughter — 5.05.217
every villain | be call'd posthumus leonatus, 5.05.224
o my lord posthumus, | you ne'er kill'd imogen 5.05.230
see, | posthumus anchors upon imogen; 5.05.393
then shall posthumus end his miseries, britain 5.05.440 P
POSTING 4 FR 0.0004 REL FR 4 V 0 P
but this exceeding posting day and night | must AWW 5.01. 1
runs posting on in bullingbrook's proud joy, R2 5.05. 59
rides on the posting winds and doth belie | all CYM 3.04. 36
till i return, of posting is no need. SON 51. 4
POSTMASTER'S 2 FR 0.0002 REL FR 0 V 2 P
and 'tis a postmaster's boy. WIV 5.05.188 P
and yet it was not anne, but a postmaster's boy. 5.05.199 P
POST–POST–HASTE 1 FR 0.0001 REL FR 1 V 0 P
write from us to him, post–post–haste. dispatch! OTH 1.03. 46
POSTS* 12 FR 0.0013 REL FR 10 V 2 P
posts | from those you sent to th' oracle are WT 2.03.193
what, are there no posts dispatch'd for ireland? R2 2.02.103
the posts come tiring on, | and not a man of 2H4 in 37
get posts and letters, and make friends with 1.01.214
and there are twenty weak and wearied posts 2.04.356
i have found'red ninescore and odd posts, and 4.03. 36 P
steel, | and spurn in pieces posts of adamant; 1H6 1.04. 52
tidings, as swiftly as the posts could run, 3H6 2.01.109
and posts, like the commandment of a king, TRO 1.03. 93
our posts shall be swift and intelligent betwixt LR 3.07. 11 P
met'st thou my posts? ANT 1.05. 61
away he posts | with unchaste purpose, and with CYM 5.05.283
POSTSCRIPT 2 FR 0.0002 REL FR 1 V 1 P
here is yet a postscript. TN 2.05.173 P
and in a postscript here, he says, "alone." HAM 4.07. 52
POSTURE 5 FR 0.0005 REL FR 5 V 0 P
her natural posture! WT 5.03. 23
human powers, | and gave him graceful posture. COR 2.01.221
the posture of your blows are yet unknown; JC 5.01. 33
boy my greatness | i' th' posture of a whore. ANT 5.02.221
and puts himself in posture | that acts my words CYM 3.03. 94
POSTURES 2 FR 0.0002 REL FR 2 V 0 P
in most strange postures | we have seen him set H8 3.02.118
minerva, | postures beyond brief nature; CYM 5.05.165
POSY 3 FR 0.0003 REL FR 2 V 1 P
whose posy was | for all the world like cutler's MV 5.01.148
what talk you of the posy or the value? 5.01.151
is this a prologue, or the posy of a ring? HAM 3.02.152 P
POT 13 FR 0.0014 REL FR 6 V 7 P
note, | while greasy joan doth keel the pot. LLL 5.02.920
note, | while greasy joan doth keel the pot. 5.02.929
for god's sake, a pot of small ale. SHR in.2. 1 P
and once again a pot o' th' smallest ale. in.2. 75
now, were not i a little pot and soon hot, my 4.01. 6 P
i would have him poisoned with a pot of ale. 1H4 1.03.233
give all my fame for a pot of ale and safety. H5 3.02. 13 P
and here's a pot of good double beer, neighbor. 2H6 2.03. 64 P
the three–hoop'd pot shall have ten hoops, and i 4.02. 66 P
serv'd me instead of a quart pot to drink in; 4.10. 14 P
a more temperate fire under the pot of her eyes. TRO 1.02.147 P
to th' pot, i warrant him. COR 1.04. 47
got, | boil thou first i' th' charmed pot. MAC 4.01. 9
POTABLE 1 FR 0.0001 REL FR 1 V 0 P
precious, | preserving life in med'cine potable; 2H4 4.05.162
POTATIONS 2 FR 0.0002 REL FR 1 V 1 P
be, to forswear thin potations and to addict 2H4 4.03.124 P
hath to–night carous'd | potations pottle–deep; OTH 2.03. 54
POTATO 1 FR 0.0001 REL FR 0 V 1 P
with his fat rump and potato finger, tickles TRO 5.02. 56 P
POTATOES 1 FR 0.0001 REL FR 0 V 1 P
let the sky rain potatoes; WIV 5.05. 19 P
POTCH 1 FR 0.0001 REL FR 1 V 0 P
true sword to sword, i'll potch at him some way, COR 1.10. 15
POTENCY 6 FR 0.0006 REL FR 6 V 0 P
i would to heaven i had your potency, | and you MM 2.02. 67
the cardinal's malice and his potency | together H8 1.01.105
powers, | presuming on their changeful potency. TRO 4.04. 97
a place of potency and sway o' th' state, | if COR 2.03.182
devil or throw him out, | with wondrous potency. HAM 3.04.170
bear, | our potency made good, take thy reward. LR 1.01.172
POTENT 20 FR 0.0022 REL FR 19 V 1 P
thee, | by help of her more potent ministers, TMP 1.02.275
what would my potent master? here i am. 4.01. 34
op'd, and let 'em forth | by my so potent art. 5.01. 50
well money'd, and his friends | potent at court. WIV 4.04. 89
a land itself at large, a potent dukedom. AYL 5.04.169
but such a headstrong potent fault it is | that TN 3.04.204
a lady's "verily" is | as potent as a lord's. WT 1.02. 51
no man so potent breathes upon the ground | but 1H4 4.01. 11
i do believe | (induc'd by potent circumstances) H8 2.04. 76
fine, | too subtile, potent, tun'd too sharp in TRO 3.02. 24
the reasons are more potent and heroical. 3.03.192
your potent and infectious fevers heap | on TIM 4.01. 22
here's another, | more potent than the first. MAC 4.01. 76
as he is very potent with such spirits, | abuses HAM 2.02.602
the potent poison quite o'er–crows my spirit. 5.02.353
most potent, grave, and reverend signiors, | my OTH 1.03. 76
where indeed they are most potent in potting; 2.03. 77 P
and gives his potent regiment to a trull | that ANT 3.06. 95
a valiant race thy harsh | and potent injuries. CYM 5.04. 84
o you most potent gods! PER 3.02. 63
POTENTATES 3 FR 0.0003 REL FR 2 V 1 P
to me | with commendation from great potentates, TGV 2.04. 79
dost thou infamonize me among potentates? LLL 5.02.678 P
but kings and mightiest potentates must die, 1H6 3.02.136
POTENTIAL 3 FR 0.0003 REL FR 3 V 0 P
were very pregnant and potential spirits | to LR 2.01. 76
and hath in his effect a voice potential | as OTH 1.02. 13
o most potential love! LC 264
POTENTLY 2 FR 0.0002 REL FR 1 V 1 P
you are potently oppos'd, and with a malice | of H8 5.01.134
though i most powerfully and potently believe, HAM 2.02.201 P
POTENTS 1 FR 0.0001 REL FR 1 V 0 P
you equal potents, fiery kindled spirits! JN 2.01.358
POTHECARY *(also apothecary)*
POTHECARY 2 FR 0.0002 REL FR 2 V 0 P
that he did buy a poison | of a poor pothecary, ROM 5.03.289
give this to the pothecary, | and tell me how it PER 3.02. 9
POTHER *(see poother, pudder)*
POTION 6 FR 0.0006 REL FR 5 V 1 P
o hated potion, hence! MND 3.02.264
i could do this, and that with no rash potion, WT 1.02.319
may minister the potion of imprisonment to me in 2H4 1.02.127 P
a sleeping potion, which so took effect | as i ROM 5.03.244
damned dane, | drink /off this potion! HAM 5.02.326
that ministers a potion unto me | that thou PER 1.02. 68
POTION'S 1 FR 0.0001 REL FR 1 V 0 P
being the time the potion's force should cease. ROM 5.03.249
/POTIONS 1 FR 0.0001 REL FR 1 V 0 P
/constrain'd | /as /men /drink /potions, /that 2H4 1.01.197
POTIONS 4 FR 0.0004 REL FR 3 V 1 P
no, he gives me the potions and the motions. WIV 3.01.102 P
end | as all the poisonous potions in the world, 1H4 5.04. 56
potions of eisel 'gainst my strong infection, SON 111.10
what potions have i drunk of siren tears 119. 1
POTPAN 2 FR 0.0002 REL FR 0 V 2 P
where's potpan, that he helps not to take away? ROM 1.05. 1 P
anthony and potpan! 1.05. 10 P
POTS 2 FR 0.0002 REL FR 1 V 1 P
and wild half–can that stabb'd pots, and i think MM 4.03. 18 P
green earthen pots, bladders, and musty seeds, ROM 5.01. 46
POTTER'S 1 FR 0.0001 REL FR 1 V 0 P
my thoughts are whirled like a potter's wheel, 1H6 1.05. 19
POTTING 1 FR 0.0001 REL FR 0 V 1 P
where indeed they are most potent in potting; OTH 2.03. 77 P
POTTLE 3 FR 0.0003 REL FR 0 V 3 P
but i'll give you a pottle of burnt sack to give WIV 2.01.214 P
go, brew me a pottle of sack finely. 3.05. 29 P
a vomit ere the next pottle can be fill'd. OTH 2.03. 84 P
POTTLE–DEEP 1 FR 0.0001 REL FR 1 V 0 P
hath to–night carous'd | potations pottle–deep; OTH 2.03. 54
POTTLE–POT 1 FR 0.0001 REL FR 0 V 1 P
yea, sir, in a pottle–pot. 2H4 5.03. 64 P
POTTLE-POT'S 1 FR 0.0001 REL FR 0 V 1 P
such a matter to get a pottle–pot's maidenhead? 2H4 2.02. 78 P
POUCH 2 FR 0.0002 REL FR 2 V 0 P
tester i'll have in pouch when thou shalt lack, WIV 1.03. 87
with spectacles on nose and pouch on side, | his AYL 2.07.159
POULCAT 1 FR 0.0001 REL FR 0 V 1 P
you rag, you baggage, you poulcat, you runnion! WIV 4.02.185 P
POULCATS 2 FR 0.0002 REL FR 0 V 2 P
poulcats? WIV 4.01. 28 P
there are fairer things than poulcats sure. 4.01. 29 P
POULTER'S 1 FR 0.0001 REL FR 0 V 1 P
heels for a rabbit–sucker or a poulter's hare. 1H4 2.04.437 P
POULTICE 1 FR 0.0001 REL FR 1 V 0 P
is this the poultice for my aching bones? ROM 2.05. 63
POULTNEY 1 FR 0.0001 REL FR 1 V 0 P
within the parish | saint lawrence poultney, did H8 1.02.153
POUNCET–BOX 1 FR 0.0001 REL FR 1 V 0 P
finger and his thumb he held | a pouncet–box, 1H4 1.03. 38
POUND* *(see pun)*
POUND* 54 FR 0.0061 REL FR 23 V 31 P
'twere best pound you. TGV 1.01.104 P
less than a pound shall serve me for carrying 1.01.105 P
you mistake; i mean the pound — a pinfold. 1.01.107 P
from a pound to a pin? 1.01.108
did her grandsire leave her seven hundred pound? WIV 1.01. 59 P
than a thousand pound he were out of the house. 3.03.124 P
a hundred pound in gold more than your loss. 4.06. 5
a man of fourscore pound a year; MM 2.01.123 P
i buy a thousand pound a year! i buy a rope! ERR 4.01. 21
will cost him a thousand pound ere 'a be cur'd. ADO 1.01. 90 P
and 'twere a thousand pound more than 'tis, for 3.05. 24 P
be nominated for an equal pound | of your fair MV 1.03.149
a pound of man's flesh taken from a man | is not 1.03.165
me | that i shall hardly spare a pound of flesh 3.03. 33
which is a pound of this poor merchant's flesh, 4.01. 23
the pound of flesh which i demand of him | is 4.01. 99
by this the jew may claim | a pound of flesh, to 4.01.232
a pound of that same merchant's flesh is thine, 4.01.299
the words expressly are "a pound of flesh." 4.01.307
then thy bond, take thou thy pound of flesh, 4.01.308
thou less nor more | but just a pound of flesh. 4.01.326
if thou tak'st more | or less than a just pound, 4.01.327
i would not lose the dog for twenty pound. SHR in.1. 21
what if a man bring him a hundred pound or two, 5.01. 21 P
i had rather than forty pound i were at home. TN 5.01.177 P
tods, every tod yields pound and odd shilling; WT 4.03. 33 P
three pound of sugar, five pound of currants, 4.03. 38 P
three pound of sugar, five pound of currants, 4.03. 38 P
at least from fair five hundred pound a year. JN 1.01. 69
a half–fac'd groat five hundred pound a year! 1.01. 94
your face hath got five hundred pound a year, 1.01.152
bid her send me presently a thousand pound. R2 2.02. 91
i will give thee for it a thousand pound. 1H4 2.04. 61 P
would give a thousand pound i could run as fast 2.04.147 P
have ta'en a thousand pound this day morning. 2.04.159 P
and money lent you, four and twenty pound. 3.03. 74 P
three or four bonds of forty pound a–piece, and 3.03.102 P
this other day you ought him a thousand pound. 3.03.134 P
sirrah, do i owe you a thousand pound? 3.03.135 P
a thousand pound, hal? 3.03.136 P
lend me a thousand pound to furnish me forth? 2H4 1.02.223 P
let it be ten pound, if thou canst. 2.01.147 P
i have three pound to free mouldy and bullcalf. 3.02.244 P
bestow'd the thousand pound i borrow'd of you. 5.05. 12 P
master shallow, i owe you a thousand pound. 5.05. 73 P
many a pound of mine own proper store, | because 2H6 3.01.115
i'll give a thousand pound to look upon him. 3.03. 13
and one shilling to the pound, the last subsidy. 4.07. 23 P
to which title | a thousand pound a year, annual H8 2.03. 64
and yet will he, within three pound, lift as TRO 1.02.116 P
our walls | rather than they shall pound us up; COR 1.04. 17
i'll take the ghost's word for a thousand pound. HAM 3.02.287 P
i had a hundred pound on't; CYM 2.01. 3 P
butter at alevenpence a pound, meal at nine STM II.C 2 P
POUNDS 17 FR 0.0019 REL FR 6 V 11 P
will desire, and seven hundred pounds of moneys, WIV 1.01. 50 P
seven hundred pounds, and possibilities, is goot 1.01. 64 P
i sit at ten pounds a week. 1.03. 8 P
looks handsome in three hundred pounds a year! 3.04. 33
make you a hundred and fifty pounds jointure. 3.04. 49 P
his cudgel, and twenty pounds of money, which 5.05.113 P
are you of fourscore pounds a year? MM 2.01.195 P
ninescore and seventeen pounds, of which he made 4.03. 6 P
keep your hundred pounds to yourself, he shall SHR 5.01. 23 P
four pounds of pruins, and as many of raisins o' WT 4.03. 48 P
fifty soldiers, three hundred and odd pounds. 1H4 4.02. 14 P
a score of good ewes may be worth ten pounds. 2H4 3.02. 51 P
king beside, | a thousand pounds by th' year. H5 1.01. 19
too early and too late | for any suit of pounds; H8 2.03. 85
a thousand pounds a year for pure respect? 2.03. 95
will (too late) | tie leaden pounds to 's heels. COR 3.01.312
yearly three thousand pounds, which, by thee, CYM 3.01. 9
POUR* 38 FR 0.0043 REL FR 24 V 14 P
sky, it seems, would pour down stinking pitch, TMP 1.02. 3
i will pour some in thy other mouth. 2.02. 94 P
let me pour in some sack to the thames water; WIV 3.05. 21 P
thus pour the stars down plagues for perjury. LLL 5.02.394
bob, | and on her withered dewlop pour the ale. MND 2.01. 50
that thou mightst pour this conceal'd man out of AYL 3.02.199 P
that as fast as you pour affection in, /it runs 4.01.210 P
sieve | i still pour in the waters of my love AWW 1.03.203
and from your sacred vials pour your graces WT 5.03.122
day, | i would into thy bosom pour my thoughts. JN 3.03. 53
not without a storm, | pour down thy weather. 4.02.109
(as, force perforce, the age will pour it in), 2H4 4.04. 46
dites–moi l'anglois pour le bras. H5 3.04. 21 P
et non pour les dames de honneur d'user. 3.04. 54 P
les seigneurs de france pour tout le monde. 3.04. 56 P
c'est assez pour une fois: allons–nous a diner. 3.04. 61 P
o, je vous supplie, pour l'amour de dieu, me 4.04. 40 P
pour les ecus que vous /lui promettez, il est 4.04. 51 P
how london doth pour out her citizens! 5.pr. 24
dames et demoiselles pour etre baisees devant 5.02.258 P
is not be de fashon pour les ladies of france — 5.02.261 P
life | i pour the helpless balm of my poor eyes. R3 1.02. 13

me, threefold distress'd, | pour all your tears. 2.02. 87
force him with /praises — pour in, pour /in, TRO 2.03.223 P
pour in, pour /in, his ambition is dry. 2.03.224 P
that i may pour my spirits in thine ear, | and MAC 1.05. 26
pour in sow's blood, that hath eaten | her nine 4.01. 64
pour the sweet milk of concord into hell, 4.03. 98
and with him pour we, in our country's purge, 5.02. 28
and in the porches of my ears did pour | the HAM 1.05. 63
pour on, i will endure. LR 3.04. 18
i'll pour this pestilence into his ear — | that OTH 2.03.356
and pour our treasures into foreign laps; 4.03. 88
the gold i give thee will i melt and pour | down ANT 2.05. 34
pour out the pack of matter to mine ear, | the 2.05. 54
of noble race, | who pour their bounty on her; PER 5.ch. 10
be rough with me and pour | this oil out of your TNK 3.01.102
my well, | and mine i pour your ocean all among: LC 256
POUR'D 7 FR 0.0008 REL FR 5 V 2 P
drink, being pour'd out of a cup into a glass, AYL 5.01. 41 P
of color, weight, and heat, pour'd all together, AWW 2.03.119
the pedlar's silken treasury and have pour'd it WT 4.04.350
i pour'd forth tears in vain | to save your TIT 2.03.163
defense, | and pour'd them down before him. MAC 1.03.100
'a pour'd a flagon of rhenish on my head once. HAM 5.01.180 P
your honor has through ephesus pour'd forth PER 3.02. 43
POUREST 2 FR 0.0002 REL FR 2 V 0 P
which thou pourest down from these swelling 1H4 3.01.199
pourest in the open ulcer of my heart | her eyes TRO 1.01. 53
POURING 2 FR 0.0002 REL FR 2 V 0 P
came pouring like the tide into a breach, | with H5 1.02.149
and pouring war | into the bowels of ungrateful COR 4.05.129
POURQUOI 2 FR 0.0002 REL FR 0 V 2 P
pourquoi, my dear knight? TN 1.03. 90 P
what is "pourquoi"? 1.03. 91 P
POURS 3 FR 0.0003 REL FR 3 V 0 P
hovers in the sky | and pours down mischief. JN 3.02. 3
he pours it out: TIM 1.01.276
usuring senate | pours into captains' wounds? 3.05.110
POUR'ST 1 FR 0.0001 REL FR 1 V 0 P
that pour'st into my verse | thine own sweet SON 38. 2
POUT 1 FR 0.0001 REL FR 1 V 0 P
and then | we pout upon the morning, are unapt COR 5.01. 52
POUTED 1 FR 0.0001 REL FR 1 V 0 P
boy, | who blush'd and pouted in a dull disdain, VEN 33
POUTINGS 1 FR 0.0001 REL FR 1 V 0 P
despisings of our persons, and such poutings, TNK 3.06. 33
/POUTS 1 FR 0.0001 REL FR 1 V 0 P
thou /pouts /upon thy fortune and thy love. ROM 3.03.144
POVERTY 24 FR 0.0027 REL FR 18 V 6 P
riches, poverty, | and use of service, none; TMP 2.01.151
what with the gallows, and what with poverty, i MM 1.02. 83 P
o poverty in wit, kingly–poor flout! LLL 5.02.269
i am a fool, and full of poverty. 5.02.380
eye and wrinkled brow | an age of poverty; MV 4.01.271
so much | to think my poverty is treacherous. AYL 1.03. 65
is my love, | and in such a poverty of grace, 3.05.100
giddiness of it in question, the poverty of her, 5.02. 6 P
for the outside of thy poverty we must make an WT 4.04.632 P
faith, for their poverty, i know not where they 1H4 4.02. 70 P
of imprisonment to me in respect of poverty, but 2H4 1.02.128 P
sound | with hollow poverty and emptiness. 1.03. 75
and the truth is, poverty hath distracted her. 2.01.107 P
back, | and in her heart she scorns our poverty. 2H6 1.03. 81
of birth, | yet so much is my poverty of spirit, R3 3.07.159
but poverty could never draw 'em from me), H8 4.02.149
my poverty, but not my will, consents. ROM 5.01. 75
i /pay thy poverty, and not thy will. 5.01. 76
air, | with his disease of all–shunn'd poverty, TIM 4.02. 14
you houseless poverty, | nay, get thee in. LR 3.04. 26
head, | steep'd me in poverty to the very lips, OTH 4.02. 50
all poverty was scorn'd, and pride so great, PER 1.04. 30
although thou steal thee all my poverty; SON 40.10
alack, what poverty my muse brings forth, | that 103. 1
POW 1 FR 0.0001 REL FR 0 V 1 P
true? pow, waw. COR 2.01.142 P
POWDER 9 FR 0.0010 REL FR 6 V 3 P
with swifter spleen than powder can enforce, JN 2.01.448
good enough to toss, food for powder, food for 1H4 4.02. 66 P
to toss, food for powder, food for powder; 4.02. 66 P
i'll give you leave to powder me and eat me too 5.04.112 P
let me go grind their bones to powder small, TIT 5.02.198
and in their triumph die, like fire and powder, ROM 2.06. 10
like powder in a skilless soldier's flask, | is 3.03.132
as violently as hasty powder fir'd | doth hurry 5.01. 64
being dried with grief, will break to powder, ANT 4.09. 17
POWDER'D 1 FR 0.0001 REL FR 0 V 1 P
ever your fresh whore and your powder'd bawd, an MM 3.02. 59 P
POWD'RING–TUB 1 FR 0.0001 REL FR 1 V 0 P
and from the powd'ring–tub of infamy | fetch H5 2.01. 75
/POWER 1 FR 0.0001 REL FR 1 V 0 P
/from /france /there /comes /a /power | /into LR 3.01. 30
POWER 319 FR 0.0360 REL FR 297 V 22 P
had i been any god of power, i would | have sunk TMP 1.02. 10
was the duke of milan and | a prince of power. 1.02. 55
but what my power might else exact — like one 1.02. 99
some heavenly power guide us | out of this 5.01.105
and deal in her command without her power. 5.01.271
have some malignant power upon my life; TGV 3.01.240
my absolute power and place here in vienna, MM 1.03. 13
if power change purpose, what our seemers be. 1.03. 54
my power? alas, i doubt — 1.04. 77
shall then have no power to stand against us. 4.04. 13 P
some blessed power deliver us from hence! ERR 4.03. 44
their pride | against that power that bred it. ADO 3.01. 11
by that fatherly and kindly power | that you 4.01. 74
whose edge hath power to cut, whose will still LLL 2.01. 50
it should none spare that come within his power. 2.01. 51
most power to do most harm, least knowing ill; 2.01. 58
i fear these stubborn lines lack power to move. 4.03. 53
courses as swift as thought in every power, 4.03.327
and gives to every power a double power, | above 4.03.328
and gives to every power a double power, | above 4.03.328
since all the power thereof it doth apply | to 5.02. 77
and within his power | to leave the figure or MND 1.01. 50
i know not by what power i am made bold, | nor 1.01. 59
and ere a man hath power to say "behold!" 1.01.147
leave you your power to draw, | and i shall have 2.01.197
draw, | and i shall have no power to follow you. 2.01.198
i throw | all the power this charm doth owe. 2.02. 79
flower | hath such force and blessed power. 4.01. 74
my good lord, i wot not by what power | (but by 4.01.164
not by what power | (but by some power it is), 4.01.165
a thing not in his power to bring to pass, | but MV 1.03. 92
methinks it should have power to steal both his 3.02.125
int'rest here | have power to bid you welcome. 3.02.222
lord, | if law, authority, and power deny not, 3.02.289
upon my power i may dismiss this court, | unless 4.01.104
his sceptre shows the force of temporal power, 4.01.190
and earthly power doth then show likest god's 4.01.196
there is no power in venice | can alter a decree 4.01.218
i swear | there is no power in the tongue of man 4.01.241
entreat some power to change this currish jew. 4.01.292
to a modest gaze, | by the sweet power of music; 5.01. 79
you meet in some fresh cheek the power of fancy, AYL 3.05. 29
eyne | have power to raise such love in mine, 4.03. 51
address'd a mighty power, which were on foot 5.04.156
able for thine enemy | rather in power than use, AWW 1.01. 66
what power is it which mounts my love so high, 1.01.220
of my dear father's gift stands chief in power, 2.01.112
my art is not past power, nor you past cure. 2.01.158
hand | what husband in thy power i will command. 2.01.194
and debile minister, great power, great 2.03. 34 P
whom both sovereign power and father's voice | i 2.03. 54
thou hast power to choose, and they none to 2.03. 56
ever whilst i live, | into your guiding power. 2.03.104
which to defeat, | i must produce my power. 2.03.150
which both thy duty owes and our power claims, 2.03.161
all the intelligence in his power against you, 3.06. 31 P
but have no power | to give it from me. 4.02. 40
majesty's ear, | if he would spend his power. 5.01. 8
and aid me with that store of power you have 5.01. 20
had she such power, | she had just cause. WT 5.01. 60
i will prove so, sir, to my power. 5.02.169 P
made | for bloody power to rush upon your peace. JN 2.01.221
with strength, and power confronted power: 2.01.330
with strength, and power confronted power: 2.01.330
not that i have the power to clutch my hand 2.01.589
then, by the lawful power that i have, | thou 3.01.172
is no tongue hath power to curse him right. 3.01.183
and raise the power of france upon his head, 3.01.193
and from his holiness use all your power | to 5.01. 6
and tempt us not to bear above our power! 5.06. 38
tell thee, hubert, half my power this night, 5.06. 39
for gnarling sorrow hath less power to bite R2 1.03.292
that he, our hope, might have retir'd his power, 2.02. 46
for us to levy power | proportionable to the 2.02.124
what power the duke of york had levied there, 2.03. 34
behind, | and in my loyal bosom lies his power. 2.03. 98
because my power is weak and all ill left; 2.03.154
that power that made you king | hath power to 3.02. 27
hath power to keep you king in spite of all. 3.02. 28
strong and great in substance and in power. 3.02. 35
how far off lies your power? 3.02. 63
york | hath power enough to serve our turn. 3.02. 90
and all goes worse than i have power to tell. 3.02.120
where is the duke my father with his power? 3.02.143
my father hath a power, inquire of him, | and 3.02.186
scroop, where lies our uncle with his power? 3.02.192
that power i have, discharge, and let them go 3.02.211
even at his feet to lay my arms and power, 3.03. 39
if not, i'll use the advantage of my power, 3.03. 42
forthwith a power of english shall we levy, 1H4 1.01. 22
that men of your nobility and power | did gage 1.03.172
and then the power of scotland, and of york, 1.03.280
if thou have power to raise him, bring him 3.01. 59
i'll be sworn i have power to shame him hence. 3.01. 60
henry bullingbrook made head | against my power; 3.01. 64
to meet your father and the scottish power, | as 3.01. 84
who leads his power? 4.01. 18
he /cannot draw his power this fourteen days. 4.01.126
the king with mighty and quick–raised power 4.04. 12
whose power was in the first proportion, | and 4.04. 15
i fear the power of percy is too weak | to wage 4.04. 19
king | dismiss his power he means to visit us, 4.04. 37
then this remains, that we divide our power. 5.05. 34
hath sent out | a speedy power to encounter you, 2H4 1.01.133
upon the power and puissance of the king. 1.03. 9
flatt'ring himself in project of a power | much 1.03. 29
of an house | beyond his power to build it, who, 1.03. 59
one power against the french, | and one against 1.03. 71
you speak as having power to do wrong, but 2.01.129 P
so that his power, like to a fangless lion, 4.01.216
our navy is address'd, our power collected, 4.04. 5
with a great power of english and of scots, 4.04. 98
and by whose power i well might lodge a fear 4.05.207
father, | the image of his power lay then in me, 5.02. 74
the majesty and power of law and justice, | the 5.02. 78
and in your power soft silencing your son. 5.02. 97
making defeat on the full power of france, H5 1.02.107
help | and yours, the noble sinews of our power, 1.02.223
thus comes the english with full power upon us, 2.04. 1
go down upon him, you have power enough, | and 3.05. 53
my live, and my living, and my uttermost power. 3.06. 9 P
king, | and take with you free power to ratify, 5.02. 86
if i now had him brought into my power. 1H6 1.04. 37
is come with a great power to raise the siege. 1.04.103
at all times will you have my power alike? 2.01. 55
we'll follow them with all the power we have. 2.02. 33
my forces and my power of men are yours. 3.03. 83
and i'll withdraw me and my bloody power. 4.02. 8
that he is march'd to burdeaux with his power 4.03. 4
i have no power to let her pass, | my hand would 5.03. 60
god, whose name and power | thou tremblest at, 2H6 1.04. 25
and each of them had twenty times their power, 2.04. 61
until a power be rais'd to put them down. 4.04. 40
and with a puissant and a mighty power | of 4.09. 25
should raise so great a power without his leave, 5.01. 21
back'd by the power of warwick, that false peer, 3H6 1.01. 52
'tis not thy southern power | of essex, norfolk, 1.01.155
their power, i think, is thirty thousand strong. 2.01.177
methinks the power that edward hath in field 4.08. 35
queen from france hath brought a puissant power; 5.02. 31
away, away, to meet the queen's great power! 5.02. 50
thou hadst but power over his mortal body, | his R3 1.02. 47
but you have power in me as in a kinsman. 3.01.109
is in the field, and still his power increaseth. 4.03. 48
greatest strength and power that he can make, 4.04.450
where is thy power then, to beat him back? 4.04.479
to the rebels, and their power grows strong. 4.04.505
is with a mighty power landed at milford | is 4.04.533
and towards london do they bend their power, 4.05. 17
six or seven thousand is their utmost power. 5.03. 10
and part in just proportion our small power. 5.03. 26
least | south from the mighty power of the king. 5.03. 38
bid him bring his power | before sunrising, lest 5.03. 60
call up lord stanley, bid him bring his power. 5.03.290
will he bring his power? 5.03.342
effect wants not | a minister in his power. H8 1.01.108
and i | have not the power to muzzle him, 1.01.121
you have half our power. 1.02. 11
by commission and main power, took 'em from me, 2.02. 6 P
yea, with a spitting power, and made to tremble 2.04.184
your brain, and every function of your power, 3.02.187
by which power | you maim'd the jurisdiction of 3.02.311
by your power legative within this kingdom 3.02.339
i have no power to speak, sir. 3.02.373
ye | power as he was a councillor to try him, 5.02.178
then every thing include itself in power, TRO 1.03.119
power into will, will into appetite, | and 1.03.120
wolf | (so doubly seconded with will and power), 1.03.122
the fever whereof all our power is sick. 1.03.139
and had as ample power as i have will, | paris 2.02.140
we must with all our main of power stand fast; 2.03.262
of generosity | and make bold power look pale — COR 1.01.212
it will in time | win upon power, and throw 1.01.220
"they have press'd a power, but it is not known 1.02. 9
some parcels of their power are forth already, 1.02. 32
is gone, with one part of our roman power. 1.03. 98 P
revenge | wrench up thy power to th' highest. 1.08. 11
good addition | to th' fairness of my power. 1.09. 73
our office may, | during his power, go sleep. 2.01.223
that to 's power he would | have made them mules 2.01.246
we have power in ourselves to do it, but it is a 2.03. 4 P
but it is a power that we have no power to do; 2.03. 5 P
but it is a power that we have no power to do; 2.03. 5 P
when he had no power, | but was a petty servant 2.03.177
bruising to you | when he hath power to crush? 2.03.203
no, nor power, but that | which they have given 3.01. 73
if he have power, | then vail your ignorance; 3.01. 97
not having the power to do the good it would, 3.01.160
be meet, | and throw their power i' th' dust. 3.01.170
he that would take from you all your power. 3.01.181
people, in whose power | we were elected theirs, 3.01.209
his trident, | or jove for 's power to thunder. 3.01.256
trial | than the severity of the public power, 3.01.268
i would have had you put your power well on 3.02. 17
dispos'd | ere they lack'd power to cross you. 3.02. 23
theirs, so far | as thou hast power and person. 3.02. 86
him home, that he affects | tyrannical power. 3.03. 2
and power i' th' truth a' th' cause. 3.03. 18
and to wind | yourself into a power tyrannical, 3.03. 65
those whose great power must try him — even 3.03. 80
seeking means | to pluck away their power, as 3.03. 96
and in the power of us the tribunes, we, | even 3.03.100
have the power still | to banish your defenders, 3.03.127
now we have shown our power, | let us seem 4.02. 3
i would i had the power | to say so to my 4.02. 15
ripe aptness to take all power from the people, 4.03. 23 P
mars, i tell thee, | we have a power on foot; 4.05.119
with aufidius, leads a power 'gainst rome, | and 4.06. 67
and power, unto itself most commendable, | hath 4.07. 51
'tis a spell, you see, of much power. 5.02. 96 P
traitor, if rome have law, or we have power, TIT 1.01.403
if any power pities wretched tears, | to that i 3.01.208
head, and with a power | of high–resolved men, 4.04. 63
but passion lends them power, time means, to ROM 2.pr. 13
poison hath residence and medicine power; 2.03. 24
if all else fail, myself have power to die. 3.05.242
breath, | hath had no power yet upon thy beauty: 5.03. 93
a greater power than we can contradict | hath 5.03.153
all these spirits thy power | hath conjur'd to TIM 1.01. 6
what a mental power | this eye shoots forth! 1.01. 31
i myself would have no power; 1.02. 36 P
is, | being of no power to make his wishes good. 1.02.196
paid for, be of any power | to expel sickness, 3.01. 62
of me, because i have no power to be kind. 3.02. 54 P
the world, apemantus, if it lay in thy power? 4.03.322 P
in their rough power | has uncheck'd theft. 4.03.443
that you had power and wealth | to requite me by 4.03.521
allow'd with absolute power, and thy good name 5.01.162
as slept within the shadow of your power | have 5.04. 6
ere thou hadst power or we had cause of fear, 5.04. 15
bars, | never lacks power to dismiss itself. JC 1.03. 97
hand bears | the power to cancel his captivity. 1.03.102
is when it disjoins | remorse from power; 2.01. 19
nor the power of speech | to stir men's blood; 3.02.222
antony | come down upon us with a mighty power, 4.03.169
octavius | is overthrown by noble brutus' power, 5.03. 52
with barefac'd power sweep him from my sight, MAC 3.01.118
tell me, thou unknown power — 4.01. 69
trains hath sought to win me | into his power, 4.03.119
for that i saw the tyrant's power afoot. 4.03.185
come go we to the king, our power is ready, 4.03.236
of woman | shall e'er have power upon thee." 5.03. 7
do we but find the tyrant's power to–night, 5.06. 7
no fairy takes, nor witch hath power to charm, HAM 1.01.163
giving to you no further personal power | to 1.02. 36
o wicked wit and gifts that have the power | so 1.05. 44
might, by the sovereign power you have of us, 2.02. 27
gods, | in general synod take away her power! 2.02.494
and the /dev'l hath power | t' assume a pleasing 2.02.599
for the power of beauty will sooner transform 3.01.110 P
as my great power thereof may give thee sense, 4.03. 59
i do invest you jointly with my power, LR 1.01.130
dread to speak | when power to flattery bows? 1.01.148
to come betwixt our sentence and our power, 1.01.170
who sways, not as it hath power, but as it is 1.02. 51 P
that thou hast power to shake my manhood thus, 1.04.297
there is part of a power already footed: 3.03. 13 P
yet our power | shall do a court'sy to our wrath 3.07. 25
whose power | will close the eye of anguish. 4.04. 14
who have the power | to seal th' accuser's lips. 4.06.169

the battle done, and they within our power, 5.01. 67
this old majesty, | to him our absolute power. 5.03.301
my spirits and my place have in their power | to OTH 1.01.103
the power and corrigible authority of this lies 1.03.325 P
if i have any grace or power to move you, | his 3.03. 46
your power and your command is taken off, | and 5.02.331
as both truth and malice | have power to utter. ANT 1.02.109
upon his son, who, high in name and power, 1.02.189
that keep you here, | i have no power upon you; 1.03. 23
my greatness, nor my power | work without it. 2.02. 93
what power is in agrippa, | if i would say, 2.02.140
the power of caesar, and | his power unto 2.02.142
power of caesar, and | his power unto octavia. 2.02.143
the jove of power make me most weak, most weak, 3.04. 29
impossible | strange that his power should be. 3.07. 57
his whole action grows | not in the power on't. 3.07. 69
his power went out in such distractions as 3.07. 76
very action speaks | in every power that moves. 3.12. 36
and chides as he had power | to beat me out of 4.01. 1
had i great juno's power, | the strong-wing'd 4.15. 34
had my lips that power, | thus would i wear them 4.15. 39
and franchise | shall, by the power we hold, be CYM 3.01. 57
but my mother, having power of his testiness, 4.01. 21 P
thou knowest i have power | to take thy life PER 1.02. 56
stuff'd the hollow vessels with their power | to 1.04. 67
which shows that beauty hath his power and will, 2.02. 34
o, you have heard something of my power, and so 4.06. 87 P
name | was given me by one that had some power, 5.01.148
through whom the gods have shown their power; 5.03. 60
hast much more power on him | than ever he had TNK 1.01. 87
'tis in our power | (unless we fear that apes 1.02. 42
assured | beyond its power there's nothing; 1.02. 65
yet i wish him | excess and overflow of power, 1.03. 4
torrents whose roaring tyranny and power | i' 1.03. 38
that with thy power hast turn'd | green neptune 5.01. 49
and implore | her power unto our party. 5.01. 76
who hast power | to call the fiercest tyrant 5.01. 77
what godlike power | hast thou not power upon? 5.01. 89
what godlike power | hast thou not power upon? 5.01. 90
'twas thy power | to put life into dust: 5.01.109
what disorder | his power could give his will, 5.04. 67
lent | of dread, of justice, power and command, STM II.C 99
is the provision of the power above | fitted and III 3
and, hearing him, thy power had lost his power. VEN 944
and, hearing him, thy power had lost his power. 944
having solicited th' eternal power | that his LUC 345
by heaven and earth, and all the power of both, 572
when more is felt than one hath power to tell. 1288
before the which is drawn the power of greece, 1368
he hath no power to ask her how she fares. 1594
thy sorrow to my sorrow lendeth | another power; 1677
sea, | but sad mortality o'ersways their power, SON 65. 2
who in thy power | dost hold time's fickle glass 126. 1
for since each hand hath put on nature's power, 127. 5
thy face hath not the power to make love groan; 131. 6
use power with power and slay me not by art. 139. 4
use power with power and slay me not by art. 139. 4
old, | not age, but sorrow, over me hath power; LC 74
art, | threw my affections in his charmed power, 146
POWERFUL 10 FR 0.0011 REL FR 8 V 2 P
o powerful love, that in some respects makes a WIV 5.05. 4 P
touch | is powerful to araise king pippen, nay, AWW 2.01. 76
speak | his powerful sound within an organ weak; 2.01.176
some powerful spirit instruct the kites and WT 2.03.186
and knock are too powerful on the highway. 4.03. 28 P
with all their powerful friends, are fled to him R2 2.02. 55
out of the powerful regions under earth, | help 1H6 5.03. 11
distinction, with a broad and powerful fan, TRO 1.03. 27
o, mickle is the powerful grace that lies | in ROM 2.03. 15
the powerful venus well hath grac'd her altar, TNK 5.04.105
POWERFULLY 1 FR 0.0001 REL FR 0 V 1 P
though i most powerfully and potently believe, HAM 2.02.201 P
POWERLESS 1 FR 0.0001 REL FR 1 V 0 P
i give you welcome with a powerless hand, | but JN 2.01. 15
/POWERS 2 FR 0.0002 REL FR 1 V 1 P
/and /cornwall's /powers /you /heard /not? LR 4.03. 48
/the /powers /of /the /kingdom /approach /apace. 4.07. 92 P
POWERS 58 FR 0.0065 REL FR 54 V 4 P
the sudden surprise of my powers, drove the WIV 5.05.124 P
to flatter up these powers of mine with rest, LLL 5.02.814
and, all my powers, address your love and might MND 2.02.143
and there is such confusion in my powers, | as, MV 3.02.177
thy conceit is nearer death than thy powers. AYL 2.06. 9 P
against) i am assisted | by wicked powers. WT 5.03. 91
i'll send those powers o'er to your majesty. JN 3.03. 70
now powers from home and discontents at home 4.03.151
like a kind host, the dolphin and his powers. 5.01. 32
and he hath promis'd to dismiss the powers | led 5.01. 64
uncle, help to order several powers | to oxford, R2 5.03.140
son your only mean | for powers in scotland, 1H4 1.03.262
where you and douglas and our powers at once, 1.03.296
the powers of us may serve so great a day. 4.01.132
and you too, but my powers are there already. 4.02. 55 P
proper to madmen, led his powers to death, | and 2H4 1.03. 32
look to see his father | bring up his powers; 2.03. 14
the powers that you already have sent forth 3.01.100
with such powers | as might hold sortance with 4.01. 10
and knit our powers to the arm of peace. 4.01.175
you, | discharge your powers unto their several 4.02. 61
call in the powers, good cousin westmerland. 4.03. 25
if we, with thrice such powers left at home, H5 1.02.217
returns us that his powers are yet not ready 3.03. 46
their powers are marching unto paris-ward. 1H6 3.03. 30
now let us on, my lords, and join our powers, 3.03. 90
and keep not back your powers in dalliance. 5.02. 5
sorrow and grief have vanquish'd all my powers; 2H6 2.01.179
is fled, my lord, and all his powers do yield, 4.09. 10
if secret powers | suggest but truth to my 3H6 4.06. 68
those powers that the queen | hath rais'd in 5.03. 7
sweetness | for the capacity of my ruder powers. TRO 3.02. 25
and all my powers do their bestowing lose, 3.02. 37
when we will tempt the frailty of our powers, 4.04. 96
own, | that both our powers, with smiling fronts COR 1.06. 8
him | were slily crept into his human powers, 2.01.220
reports the volsces with two several powers 4.06. 39
the highest degree | he hath abus'd your powers. 5.06. 85
all thy powers | shall make their harbor in our TIM 5.04. 52
brutus and cassius | are levying powers; JC 4.01. 42
to stay the providence of some high powers 5.01.106
merciful powers, | restrain in me the cursed MAC 2.01. 7
heavenly powers, restore him! HAM 3.01.141 P
my operant powers their functions leave to do, 3.02.174
good sir, whose powers are these? 4.04. 9
the enemy's in view, draw up your powers. LR 5.01. 51
he led our powers, | bore the commission of my 5.03. 63
amen to that, sweet powers! OTH 2.01.195
equality of two domestic powers | breed ANT 1.03. 47
my powers are crescent, and my auguring hope 2.01. 10
but, o you powers! PER 1.01. 72
let it suffice the greatness of your powers | to 2.01. 8
we cannot but obey | the powers above us. 3.03. 10
the powers of all women will be with us. TNK 3.06.194
hand will honor | the very powers that love 'em. 5.01. 7
o all you heavenly powers, where is /your mercy? 5.03.139
and therein heartens up his servile powers, LUC 295
the powers to whom i pray abhor this fact, | how 349
POWLE'S *(also paul's)*
POWLE'S 1 FR 0.0001 REL FR 1 V 0 P
we may as well push against powle's as stir 'em. H8 5.03. 16
/POW'R 1 FR 0.0001 REL FR 1 V 0 P
now, if this suit lay in bianca's /pow'r, | how OTH 4.01.107
POW'R 45 FR 0.0050 REL FR 43 V 2 P
his art is of such pow'r, | it would control my TMP 1.02.372
entertainment till | mine enemy has more pow'r. 1.02.467
they now are in my pow'r; 3.03. 90
(o'er whom i give thee pow'r) here to this place 4.01. 38
and ev'n that pow'r which gave me first my oath TGV 2.06. 4
deputation all the organs | of our own pow'r. MM 1.01. 21
a pow'r i have, but of what strength and nature 1.01. 79
assay the pow'r you have. 1.04. 76
that in himself which he spurs on his pow'r | to 4.02. 82
at the gates, | there to give up their pow'r. 4.03.132
when i perceive your grace, like pow'r divine, 5.01.369
make rash remonstrance of my hidden pow'r | than 5.01.392
transform me then, and to your pow'r i'll yield. ERR 3.02. 40
reach them, nor | shall she, within my pow'r. WT 2.03. 26
gap, since it is in my pow'r | to o'erthrow law, 4.01. 7
(as it must be) by th' pow'r of the king. 4.04. 37
pow'r no jot | hath she to change our loves. 5.01.217
let him that was the cause of this have pow'r 5.03. 54
a greater pow'r than we denies all this, | and JN 2.01.368
never such a pow'r | for any foreign preparation 4.02.110
for in a night the best part of my pow'r, | as i 5.07. 61
till we meet warwick with his foreign pow'r. 3H6 4.01.149
and of wisdom | o'ertopping woman's pow'r. H8 2.04. 88
my heart dropp'd love, my pow'r rain'd honor, 3.02.185
though there the people had more absolute pow'r, COR 3.01.116
had i the pow'r that some say dian had, | thy TIT 2.03. 61
now will i to the goths and raise a pow'r, | to 3.01.299
laugh to scorn | the pow'r of man; MAC 4.01. 80
nay, had i pow'r, i should | pour the sweet milk 4.03. 97
it, when none can call our pow'r to accompt? 5.01. 38 P
the english pow'r is near, led on by malcolm, 5.02. 1
leave her, sir, for, by the pow'r that made me, LR 1.01.207
prescrib'd his pow'r, | confin'd to exhibition? 1.02. 24
all the pow'r of his wits have given way to his 3.06. 4 P
he does not feel, feel your pow'r quickly; 4.01. 69
thou hast not half that pow'r to do me harm | as OTH 5.02.162
and, breathless, pow'r breathe forth. ANT 2.02.232
take my pow'r i' th' court for yours. CYM 1.06.179
would cease | the present pow'r of life, but in 5.05.256
the pow'r that i have on you is to spare you; 5.05.418
whereto he'll infuse pow'r and press you forth TNK 1.01. 73
they that have pow'r to hurt and will do none, SON 94. 1
dark'ning thy pow'r to lend base subjects light? 100. 4
o, from what pow'r hast thou this pow'rful might 150. 1
"'my parts had pow'r to charm a sacred /nun, LC 260
POW'RFUL 12 FR 0.0013 REL FR 12 V 0 P
and 'tis pow'rful — think it — | from east, WT 1.02.202
you're pow'rful at it. 2.01. 28
with pow'rful policy strengthen themselves, 3H6 1.02. 58
and kept low shrubs from winter's pow'rful wind. 5.02. 15
take not the quarrel from his pow'rful arm; R3 1.04.217
wing, | for a charm of pow'rful trouble, | like MAC 4.01. 18
you fen-suck'd fogs, drawn by the pow'rful sun, LR 2.04.167
that with some mixtures pow'rful o'er the blood, OTH 1.03.104
swell his sail with thine own pow'rful breath, 2.01. 78
have not sent | his pow'rful mandate to you: ANT 1.01. 22
of princes shall outlive this pow'rful rhyme, SON 55. 2
o, from what pow'r hast thou this pow'rful might 150. 1
/POW'RS 1 FR 0.0001 REL FR 1 V 0 P
/york /is /up | /with //well-appointed /pow'rs. 2H4 1.01.190
POW'RS 25 FR 0.0028 REL FR 25 V 0 P
they are both in either's pow'rs; TMP 1.02.451
for which foul deed | the pow'rs, delaying (not 3.03. 73
if pow'rs divine | behold our human actions (as WT 3.02. 28
the higher pow'rs forbid! 3.02.202
france, shall we knit our pow'rs, | and lay this JN 2.01.398
under whose conduct came those pow'rs of france 4.02.129
even at my gates, with ranks of foreign pow'rs; 4.02.244
the stumbling night did part our weary pow'rs? 5.05. 18
in your right spheres, | where be your pow'rs? 5.07. 75
think you not that the pow'rs we bear with us H5 2.02. 15
whose dismal tune bereft my vital pow'rs; 2H6 3.02. 41
then, buckingham, i do dismiss my pow'rs. 5.01. 44
are mounted | where pow'rs are your retainers, H8 2.04.113
bid him set on his pow'rs betimes before, | and JC 4.03.307
and the pow'rs above | put on their instruments. MAC 4.03.238
he may enguard his dotage with their pow'rs, LR 1.04.326
hasten his musters and conduct his pow'rs. 4.02. 16
the british pow'rs are marching hitherward. 4.04. 21
but are my brother's pow'rs set forth? 4.05. 1
which the wise pow'rs | deny us for our good; ANT 2.01. 6
the pow'rs that he already hath in gallia | will CYM 3.05. 24
the want is but to put those pow'rs in motion 4.03. 31
and so, great pow'rs, | if you will take this 5.04. 26
the fingers of the pow'rs above do tune | the 5.05.466
/... these rebel pow'rs that thee array, | why SON 146. 2
POX 23 FR 0.0026 REL FR 2 V 21 P
a pox o' your throat, you bawling, blasphemous, TMP 1.01. 40 P
a pox o' that! 2.01. 78 P
a pox o' your bottle! 3.02. 79 P
pox of your love-letters! TGV 3.01.380 P
a pox o' your throats! MM 4.03. 24 P
show your knave's visage, with a pox to you! 5.01.353 P
a pox of that jest! LLL 5.02. 46
a pox on't, let it go, 'tis but a drum. AWW 3.06. 46 P
a pox upon him for me, he's more and more a cat. 4.03.263 P
a pox on him, he's a cat still. 4.03.275 P
pox on't, i'll not meddle with him. TN 3.04.280 P
what a pox have i to do with my hostess of the 1H4 1.02. 47 P
galls the one, and the pox pinches the other, 2H4 1.02.231 P
a pox of this gout! 1.02.243 P
or, a gout of this pox! 1.02.244 P
a pox damn you, you muddy rascal, is that all 2.04. 39 P
eye of that proverb with "a pox of the devil." H5 3.07.120 P
the pox of such antic, lisping, affecting ROM 2.04. 28 P
a pox of wrinkles! TIM 4.03.149
a pox of drowning thyself, it is clean out of OTH 1.03.358 P
a pox on't! CYM 2.01. 18 P
now the pox upon her green-sickness for me! PER 4.06. 13 P
no way to be rid on't but by the way to the pox. 4.06. 16 P
POYS *(also boys*)*
POYS 1 FR 0.0001 REL FR 0 V 1 P
kill the poys and the luggage! H5 4.07. 1 P
POYSAM 1 FR 0.0001 REL FR 0 V 1 P
charbon the puritan and old poysam the papist, AWW 1.03. 52 P
PRABBLES *(also brabble, pribbles)*
PRABBLES 4 FR 0.0004 REL FR 0 V 4 P
motion if we leave our pribbles and prabbles, WIV 1.01. 55 P
leave your prabbles, oman. 4.01. 50 P
swearings and starings, pribbles and prabbles? 5.05.160 P
and keep you out of prawls and prabbles, and H5 4.08. 65 P
PRACTIC 1 FR 0.0001 REL FR 1 V 0 P
so that the art and practic part of life | must H5 1.01. 51
/PRACTIC'D 1 FR 0.0001 REL FR 1 V 0 P
/had /no /legs /that /practic'd /not /his /gait; 2H4 2.03. 23
PRACTIC'D 12 FR 0.0013 REL FR 11 V 1 P
the children must | be practic'd well to this, WIV 4.04. 66
throttle their practic'd accent in their fears, MND 5.01. 97
as now they are, and making practic'd smiles, WT 1.02.116
practic'd upon the easy-yielding spirit of this 2H4 2.01.114 P
wouldst thou have practic'd on me, for thy use H5 2.02. 99
have practic'd dangerously against your state, 2H6 2.01.167
seeming | has practic'd on man's life! LR 3.02. 57
that thou hast practic'd on her with foul charms OTH 1.02. 73
how intend you, practic'd? ANT 2.02. 40
i never practic'd it. PER 2.01. 67
to have practic'd more the whipstock than the 2.02. 51
and my true eyes have never practic'd how | to LUC 748
/PRACTICE 1 FR 0.0001 REL FR 1 V 0 P
/and /by /still /practice /learn /to /know /thy TIT 3.02. 45
PRACTICE 64 FR 0.0072 REL FR 53 V 11 P
there shall he practice tilts and tournaments, TGV 1.03. 30
and thy advice this night i'll put in practice: 3.02. 88
in | as art and practice hath enriched any MM 1.01. 12
of her virtue to practice his judgment with the 3.01.163 P
made in crimes, | making practice on the times, 3.02.274
against his honor | in hateful practice. 5.01.107
this needs must be a practice. 5.01.123
have way, my lord, | to find this practice out. 5.01.239
ere i learn love, i'll practice to obey. ERR 2.01. 29
in practice let us put it presently. ADO 1.01.328
two helps, will so practice on benedick that, in 2.01.382 P
adverse issue it can, i will put it in practice. 2.02. 52 P
the practice of it lives in john the bastard, 4.01.188
despite his nice fence and his active practice, 5.01. 75
yea, and paid me richly for the practice of it. 5.01.248 P
to put in practice that | which each to other LLL 1.01.306
these bragging jacks, | which i will practice. MV 3.04. 78
thee, he will practice against thee by poison, AYL 1.01.150 P
sirs, i will practice on this drunken man. SHR in.1. 36
and practice rhetoric in your common talk, 1.01. 35
on them to look and practice by myself. 1.01. 83
proceed in practice with my younger daughter; 2.01.164
shall sweet bianca practice how to bride it? 3.02.251
which, as the dearest issue of his practice, AWW 2.01.106
and the practice in the chape of his dagger. 4.03.143 P
and hope both teaching him the practice) | to a TN 1.02. 13
this is a practice | as full of labor as a wise 3.01. 65
this practice hath most shrewdly pass'd upon 5.01.352
to my kingly guest | unclasp'd my practice, quit WT 3.02.167
which, though i will not practice to deceive, JN 1.01.214
the practice and the purpose of the king; 4.03. 63
if thou love me, practice an answer. 1H4 2.04.375 P
let them practice and converse with spirits. 1H6 2.01. 25
shadow | whereon to practice your severity. 2.03. 47
esteem | he be approv'd in practice culpable. 2H6 3.02. 22
i shall perish | under device and practice. H8 1.01.204
practice your eyes with tears! TRO 2.02.108
i will practice the insinuating nod and be off COR 2.03. 99 P
be caught | with cautelous baits and practice. 4.01. 33
i'll find some cunning practice out of hand, TIT 5.02. 77
that heaven should practice stratagems | upon so ROM 3.05.209
older in practice, abler than yourself | to make JC 4.03. 31
i do not, till you practice them on me. 4.03. 88
this disease is beyond my practice; MAC 5.01. 59 P
but even his mother shall uncharge the practice, HAM 4.07. 67
and in a /pass of practice | requite him for 4.07.138
into france i have been in continual practice. 5.02.211 P
the foul practice | hath turn'd itself on me. 5.02.317
to thy suggestion, plot, and damned practice; LR 2.01. 73
he did bewray his practice, and receiv'd | this 2.01.107
remotion of the duke and her | is practice only. 2.04.115
this is practice, gloucester. 5.03.152
mere prattle, without practice, | is all his OTH 1.01. 26
or some unhatch'd practice | made demonstrable 3.04.141
fall'n in the practice of a /damned slave, 5.02.292
yet if you there | did practice on my state, ANT 2.02. 39
and no practice had | in the brave squares of 3.11. 39
shall from this practice but make hard your CYM 1.05. 24
and, to be brief, my practice so prevail'd, 5.05.199
in those that practice them they are, my lord. PER 2.03.104
together with my practice, made familiar | to me 3.02. 34
must be quench'd with some present practice. 4.02.125 P
to put in practice either, alas, it was a spite PP 15. 7
talk, | lest she some subtile practice smell — 18. 9
PRACTICED 1 FR 0.0001 REL FR 1 V 0 P
i never practiced | upon man's wife, nor would TNK 5.01.100
PRACTICER 2 FR 0.0002 REL FR 2 V 0 P
sweet practicer, thy physic i will try, | that AWW 2.01.185
a practicer | of arts inhibited and out of OTH 1.02. 78
PRACTICERS 1 FR 0.0001 REL FR 1 V 0 P

and therefore, finding barren practicers, LLL 4.03.322
PRACTICES 14 FR 0.0015 REL FR 13 V 1 P
no, we detest such vile base practices. TGV 4.01. 71
i overheard him — and his practices. AYL 2.03. 26
under whose practices he hath persecuted time AWW 1.01. 14 P
i doubt | my uncle practices more harm to me. JN 4.01. 20
and sworn unto the practices of france | to kill H5 2.02. 90
law, | and god acquit them of their practices! 2.02.144
pretend | malicious practices against his state. 1H6 4.01. 7
upon my life, began her devilish practices; 2H6 3.01. 46
bid him recount | the fore–recited practices, H8 1.02.127
how came | his practices to light? 3.02. 29
their practices | must bear the same proportion, 5.01.128
heavens make our presence and our practices HAM 2.02. 38
whose foolish honesty | my practices ride easy. LR 1.02.182
driven | to find out practices of cunning hell OTH 1.03.102
PRACTICING 3 FR 0.0003 REL FR 2 V 1 P
banished | for practicing to steal away a lady, TGV 4.01. 46
yonder i' the sun practicing behavior to his own TN 2.05. 17 P
and practicing upon his peace and quiet | even OTH 2.01.310
PRACTISANTS 1 FR 0.0001 REL FR 1 V 0 P
here ent'red pucelle and her practisants. 1H6 3.02. 20
PRAECLARISSIMUS 1 FR 0.0001 REL FR 0 V 1 P
latin, praeclarissimus filius noster henricus, H5 5.02.341 P
PRAEMUNIRE 1 FR 0.0001 REL FR 1 V 0 P
fall into th' compass of a praemunire — | that H8 3.02.340
PRAETOR'S 1 FR 0.0001 REL FR 1 V 0 P
and look you lay it in the praetor's chair, JC 1.03.143
PRAETORS 1 FR 0.0001 REL FR 1 V 0 P
of senators, of praetors, common suitors, | will JC 2.04. 35
PRAGGING *(also bragging)*
PRAGGING 1 FR 0.0001 REL FR 0 V 1 P
beggarly, lousy, pragging knave, pistol, which H5 5.01. 6 P
PRAGUE 1 FR 0.0001 REL FR 0 V 1 P
as the old hermit of prague, that never saw pen TN 4.02. 13 P
PRAIN *(also brain, etc.)*
PRAIN 2 FR 0.0002 REL FR 0 V 2 P
and there is also another device in my prain, WIV 1.01. 43 P
i pray you remember in your prain. 4.01. 36 P
PRAINS 3 FR 0.0003 REL FR 0 V 3 P
and let us knog our prains together to be WIV 3.01.119 P
but it is out of my prains what is the name of H5 4.07. 29 P
also being a little intoxicates in his prains, 4.07. 37 P
/PRAIS'D 1 FR 0.0001 REL FR 0 V 1 P
/prais'd women's modesty; WIV 2.01. 58 P
PRAIS'D 34 FR 0.0038 REL FR 20 V 14 P
for good things should be prais'd. TGV 3.01.347 P
/god be prais'd for my jealousy! WIV 2.02.309 P
i shall be rather prais'd for this than mock'd; 3.02. 47 P
but mine, and mine i lov'd, and mine i prais'd, ADO 4.01.136
thee how beatrice prais'd thy wit the other day. 5.01.159 P
well, prais'd be the gods for thy foulness! AYL 3.03. 40 P
hearing thy mildness prais'd in every town, SHR 2.01.191
that she whom all men prais'd and whom myself, AWW 5.03. 53
jove and my stars be prais'd! TN 2.05.173 P
now god be prais'd, that to believing souls 2H6 2.01. 64
god and your arms be prais'd, victorious friends R3 5.05. 1
she prais'd his complexion above paris. TRO 1.02. 98 P
if she prais'd him above, his complexion is 1.02.102 P
if that the prais'd himself bring the praise 1.03.242
the lord be prais'd! 3.01. 8 P
which she hath prais'd him with above compare ROM 3.05.238
"when we for recompense have prais'd the vild, TIM 1.01. 15
for your own gifts, make yourselves prais'd; 3.06. 72 P
that prais'd my lord such–a–one's horse, when 'a HAM 5.01. 84 P
and prais'd be rashness for it — let us know 5.02. 7
of wisdom | than prais'd for harmful mildness. LR 1.04.344
fellow | who, having been prais'd for bluntness, 2.02. 96
well prais'd! how if she be black and witty? OTH 2.01.131
the soothsayer that you prais'd so to th' queen? ANT 1.02. 3 P
much, but i ha' prais'd ye | when you have well 2.06. 76
(which rare it is to do) most prais'd, most CYM 1.01. 47
i prais'd her as i rated her: so do i my stone. 1.04. 77 P
will execute in the clothes that she so prais'd) 3.05.143 P
great jupiter be prais'd! 5.03. 84
hint, | and (not dispraising whom we prais'd; 5.05.173
the niggard prodigal that prais'd her so — | in LUC 79
hearing you prais'd, i say, "'tis so, 'tis true, SON 85. 9
tomb, | and to be prais'd of ages yet to be. 101.12
preach'd pure maid, and prais'd cold chastity. LC 315
PRAISE' 1 FR 0.0001 REL FR 1 V 0 P
that self–sovereignty | only for praise' sake, LLL 4.01. 37
/PRAISE 1 FR 0.0001 REL FR 0 V 1 P
i have seen play — and heard others /praise, HAM 3.02. 29 P
PRAISE 190 FR 0.0214 REL FR 145 V 45 P
praise in departing. TMP 3.03. 39
for thou shalt find she will outstrip all praise 4.01. 10
/is /it mine /eye, or valentinus' praise, | her TGV 2.04.196
flatter and praise, commend, extol their graces; 3.01.102
"item, she will often praise her liquor." 3.01.345 P
to praise his faith which i would have 4.04.102
you that by the way, i praise heaven for it. WIV 1.04.141 P
such a sickly creature, i give heaven praise. 3.04. 59 P
first he did praise my beauty, then my speech. ERR 4.02. 15
methinks she's too low for a high praise, too ADO 1.01.172 P
too brown for a fair praise, and too little for 1.01.172 P
fair praise, and too little for a great praise; 1.01.173 P
thus far can i praise him: 2.01.378 P
to praise him more than ever man did merit. 3.01. 19
the duchess of milan's gown that they praise so. 3.04. 16 P
and reverent youth, and i praise god for you. 5.01.316 P
then write me a sonnet in praise of my beauty? 5.02. 4 P
wise man among twenty that will praise himself. 5.02. 74 P
speak you this in my praise, master? LLL 1.02. 24 P
in thy condign praise. 1.02. 25 P
i will praise an eel with the same praise. 1.02. 26 P
i will praise an eel with the same praise. 1.02. 26 P
needs not the painted flourish of your praise: 2.01. 14
in spending your wit in the praise of mine. 2.01. 19
with such bedecking ornaments of praise? 2.01. 79
first praise me, and again say no? 4.01. 14
where fair is not, praise cannot mend the brow. 4.01. 17
hand, though foul, shall have fair praise. 4.01. 23
that more for praise than purpose meant to kill. 4.01. 29
for fame's sake, for praise, an outward part, 4.01. 32
as i for praise alone now seek to spill | the 4.01. 34
only for praise — and praise we may afford | to 4.01. 39
and praise we may afford | to any lady that 4.01. 39
sir, i praise the lord for you, and so may my 4.02. 73 P
which is to me some praise that i thy parts 4.02.114
that sings heaven's praise with such an earthly 4.02.118
when shall you hear that i | will praise a hand, 4.03.182
to things of sale a seller's praise belongs: 4.03.236
she passes praise, then praise too short doth 4.03.237
passes praise, then praise too short doth blot. 4.03.237
i praise god for you, sir. 5.01. 2 P
much in the letters, nothing in the praise. 5.02. 40
days) | in courtesy gives undeserving praise. 5.02.366
men have compiled in praise of the owl and the 5.02.886 P
to follow me and praise my eyes and face? MND 3.02.223
well, and i remember him worthy of thy praise. MV 1.02.121 P
far | the substance of my praise doth wrong this 3.02.127
whether those peals of praise be his or no, | so 3.02.145
nay, let me praise you while i have a stomach. 3.05. 87
are | to their right praise and true perfection! 5.01.108
but that the people praise her for her virtues, AYL 1.02.280
your praise is come too swiftly home before you. 2.03. 9
wearing thy hearer in thy mistress' praise, 2.04. 38
best brine a maiden can season her praise in. AWW 1.01. 49 P
his humility, | in their poor praise he humbled. 1.02. 45
in argument of praise, or to the worth | of the 3.05. 59
that ever nature had praise for creating. 4.05. 10 P
i praise god for you. 5.02. 55 P
i will on with my speech in your praise, and TN 1.05.190 P
i forgive you the praise. 1.05.193 P
were you sent hither to praise me? 1.05.249 P
for, boy, however we do praise ourselves, | our 2.04. 32
she did praise my leg being cross–garter'd, and 2.05.167 P
sir, they praise me and make an ass of me. 5.01. 17 P
may, though they cannot praise us, as little WT 1.01. 15 P
cram 's with praise, and make 's | as fat as 1.02. 91
praise her but for this her without–door form 2.01. 69
much surpassing | the common praise it bears. 3.01. 3
well could i bear that england had this praise, JN 3.04. 15
whilst i, by looking on the praise of him, | see 1H4 1.01. 84
art thou then, to praise him so for running! 2.04.351 P
i laud them, i praise them. 3.03.192 P
sun in march, | this praise doth nourish agues. 4.01.112
with all the world | in praise of henry percy. 5.01. 87
making you ever better than his praise | by 5.02. 58
by still dispraising praise valued with you, 5.02. 59
adieu, and take thy praise with thee to heaven! 5.04. 99
thou hast a sigh to blow away this praise, 2H4 1.01. 80
good cheer, | and praise god for the merry year, 5.03. 18
and make /her chronicle as rich with praise | as H5 1.02.163
ay, i praise god, and i have merited some love 3.06. 23 P
of the lamb, vary deserv'd praise on my palfrey. 3.07. 33 P
once writ a sonnet in his praise and began thus: 3.07. 39 P
is the prescript praise and perfection of a good 3.07. 46 P
let him cry, "praise and glory on his head!" 4.pr. 31
or take that praise from god | which is his only 4.08.115
shall in procession sing her endless praise. 1H6 1.06. 20
this is the latest glory of thy praise | that i, 4.02. 33
good wishes, praise, and prayers | shall suffolk 5.03.173
solicit henry with her wondrous praise; 5.03.190
tale | is but a preface of her worthy praise. 5.05. 11
that would annoy our foot | is worthy praise; 2H6 3.01. 68
to entertain my vows of thanks and praise! 4.09. 14
nor should thy prowess want praise and esteem, 5.02. 22
days, | to sin's rebuke and my creator's praise. 3H6 4.06. 44
that we may praise thee in the victory! R3 5.03.114
him in eye | still him in praise, and being H8 1.01. 31
see what this child does, and praise my maker. 5.04. 68
not, as they term it, praise her, but i would TRO 1.01. 44 P
is too flaming a praise for a good complexion. 1.02.104 P
than in the glass of pandar's praise may be; 1.02.285
the worthiness of praise distains his worth, 1.03.241
that the prais'd himself bring the praise forth; 1.03.242
that breath fame blows, that praise, sole pure, 1.03.244
and /seeks his praise more than he fears his 1.03.267
so to be valiant, is no praise at all. 2.02.145
but in the deed, devours the deed in the praise. 2.03.157 P
or covetous of praise — 2.03.237
praise him that gat thee, she that gave thee 2.03.241
i will not praise thy wisdom, | which, like a 2.03.248
i must needs praise him. 3.01. 7 P
praise us as we are tasted, allow us as we prove 3.02. 90 P
in reversion shall have a praise in present; 3.02. 93 P
all, with one consent, praise new–born gawds, 3.03.176
do deeds worth praise, and tell you them at 5.03. 93
sir, praise me not; COR 1.05. 16
her blood, | when she does praise me grieves me. 1.09. 15
whom with all praise i point at, saw him fight, 2.02. 90
so, | to have my praise for this, perform a part 3.02.109
and in his praise | have (almost) stamp'd the 5.02. 21
call all your tribes together, praise the gods, 5.05. 2
and fame's eternal date, for virtue's praise! TIT 1.01.168
digress too much, | citing my worthless praise. 5.03.117
when no friends are by, men praise themselves. 5.03.118
sir, your jewel | hath suffered under praise. TIM 1.01.165
man | can justly praise but what he does affect. 1.02.215
when the means are gone that buy this praise, 2.02.169
the breath is gone whereof this praise is made. 2.02.170
praise his most vicious strain, | and call it 4.03.213
i come to bury caesar, not to praise him. JC 3.02. 74
we'll put on those shall praise your excellence, HAM 4.07.131
the argument of your praise, balm of your age, LR 1.01.215
being the worst | stands in some rank of praise. 2.04.258
you shall not write my praise. OTH 2.01.116
wouldst write of me, if thou shouldst praise me? 2.01.117
come, how wouldst thou praise me? 2.01.124
what miserable praise hast thou for her that's 2.01.139 P
but what praise couldst thou bestow on a 2.01.144 P
as you shall prove us, praise us. 5.01. 66
you praise yourself | by laying defects of ANT 2.02. 54
though i lose | the praise of it by telling, you 2.06. 43
i will praise any man that will praise me, 2.06. 88 P
i will praise any man that will praise me, 2.06. 88 P
would you praise caesar, say "caesar," go no 3.02. 13
see him rouse himself | to praise my noble act. 5.02.285
where each of us fell in praise of our country CYM 1.04. 57 P
this (and praise | be given to your remembrance) 2.04. 92
clotens blood, | and praise myself for charity. 4.02.169
that he deserv'd the praise o' th' world, | as 5.04. 50
hearing us praise our loves of italy | for 5.05.161
made scruple of his praise, and wager'd with him 5.05.182
soul | embold'ned with the glory of her praise, PER 1.01. 4
oft the wrack | of earned praise, marina's life 4.ch. 13
characters express | a general praise to her, 4.03. 45
i dare not praise | my feat in horsemanship, yet TNK 2.05. 12
if i could praise | each part of him to th' all 5.03.120
to praise the clear unmatched red and white LUC 11
therefore that praise which collatine doth owe 82
which is to me some praise, that i thy parts PP 5.10
to sing heaven's praise with such an earthly 5.14
there | where thy desert may merit praise, | by 18.15
were an all–eating shame, and thriftless praise. SON 2. 8
how much more praise deserv'd thy beauty's use, 2. 9
i will not praise that purpose not to sell. 21.14
the pain be mine, but thine shall be the praise. 38.14
what can mine own praise to mine own self bring? 39. 3
and what is't but mine own when i praise thee? 39. 4
your praise shall still find room, | even in the 55.10
to subjects worse have given admiring praise. 59.14
'tis thee (myself) that for myself i praise, 62.13
outward thus with outward praise is crown'd, 69. 5
in other accents do this praise confound | by 69. 7
yet this thy praise cannot be so thy praise | to 70.11
yet this thy praise cannot be so thy praise | to 70.11
and hang more praise upon deceased i | than 72. 7
no praise to thee but what in thee doth live. 79.12
and in the praise thereof spends all his might, 80. 3
hue, | finding thy worth a limit past my praise, 82. 6
than both your poets can in praise devise. 83.14
which can say more | than this rich praise, that 84. 2
being fond on praise, which makes your praises 84.14
while comments of your praise, richly compil'd, 85. 2
and to the most of praise add something more, 85.10
cannot dispraise but in a kind of praise, 95. 7
nor praise the deep vermilion in the rose, 98.10
because he needs no praise, wilt thou be dumb? 101. 9
than when it hath my added praise beside. 103. 4
in praise of ladies dead and lovely knights, 106. 4
have eyes to wonder, but lack tongues to praise. 106.14
white weighs down the airy scale of praise. LC 226
PRAISED 8 FR 0.0009 REL FR 5 V 3 P
base, is now | the praised of the king, who, so AWW 2.03.172
praised! WT 3.02.137
he is not — god be praised and blessed! H5 3.06. 10 P
praised be god, and not our strength, for it! 4.07. 87
to be ashamed of your majesty, praised be god, 4.07.114 P
of warwick, here is — praised be god for it! 4.08. 20 P
my bright hair and scratch my praised cheeks, TRO 4.02.107
diamonds | of a most praised water doth appear, PER 3.02.101
/PRAISES 1 FR 0.0001 REL FR 0 V 1 P
force him with /praises — pour in, pour /in, TRO 2.03.223 P
PRAISES 31 FR 0.0035 REL FR 29 V 2 P
worth | comes all the praises that i now bestow) TGV 2.04. 72
o, flatter me; for love delights in praises. 2.04.148
making the bold wag by their praises bolder. LLL 5.02.108
hath heard your praises, and this night he means AYL 2.03. 22
the rather will i spare my praises towards him, AWW 2.01.103
our praises are our wages. WT 1.02. 94
o doricles, | your praises are too large. 4.04.147
as praises, of whose taste the wise are /fond, R2 2.01. 18
trimm'd up your praises with a princely tongue, 1H4 5.02. 56
ev'n as your horse bears your praises, who would H5 3.07. 76 P
oft have i heard his praises in pursuit, | but 3H6 2.01.149
and whatever praises itself but in the deed, TRO 2.03.156 P
the present eye praises the present object. 3.03.180
she is as far high–soaring o'er thy praises | as 4.04.124
which, to the spire and top of praises vouch'd, COR 1.09. 24
should be dieted | in praises sauc'd with lies. 1.09. 53
said | my praises made thee first a soldier, so, 3.02.108
his wonders and his praises do contend | which MAC 1.03. 92
thy praises in his kingdom's great defense, 1.03. 99
whose worth, if praises may go back again, HAM 4.07. 27
got praises of the king | for him attempting who LR 2.02.121
he plied them both with excellent praises. ANT 3.02. 14
thine uncle | (famous in caesar's praises, no CYM 3.01. 6
her face the book of praises, where is read PER 1.01. 15
marina gets | all praises, which are paid as 4.ch. 34
leg, | outstripp'd the people's praises, won the TNK 2.02. 16
and decks with praises collatine's high name, LUC 108
fond on praise, which makes your praises worse. SON 84.14
since all alike my songs and praises be | to one 105. 3
so all their praises are but prophecies | of 106. 9
to know my shames and praises from your tongue; 112. 6
PRAISEST 1 FR 0.0001 REL FR 0 V 1 P
thou praisest the worst best. OTH 2.01.143 P
PRAISEWORTHY 1 FR 0.0001 REL FR 0 V 1 P
i myself will bear witness, is praiseworthy. ADO 5.02. 88 P
PRAISING 12 FR 0.0013 REL FR 11 V 1 P
which must be done by praising me as much | as TGV 3.02. 54
so much for praising myself, who, i myself will ADO 5.02. 87 P
upon the tomb, | praising her when i am /dumb. 5.03. 10
thou spend'st such high–day wit in praising him. MV 2.09. 98
this comes too near the praising of myself, 3.04. 22
praising the proud disdainful shepherdess | that AYL 3.04. 50
praising what is lost | makes the remembrance AWW 5.03. 19
seal of my petition to thee | in praising her. TRO 4.04.123
i blame you not for praising caesar so, | but JC 3.01.214
in praising antony i have disprais'd caesar. ANT 2.05.107
by praising him here who doth hence remain! SON 39.14
praising thy worth, despite his cruel hand. 60.14
PRANCING 1 FR 0.0001 REL FR 1 V 0 P
trimm'd like a younker prancing to his love! 3H6 2.01. 24
PRANK 1 FR 0.0001 REL FR 1 V 0 P
for they do prank them in authority, | against COR 3.01. 23
PRANK'D 1 FR 0.0001 REL FR 1 V 0 P
poor lowly maid, | most goddess–like prank'd up. WT 4.04. 10
PRANKS 10 FR 0.0011 REL FR 8 V 2 P
and shrive you of a thousand idle pranks. ERR 2.02.208
that nature pranks her in attracts my soul. TN 2.04. 86
and hear thou there how many fruitless pranks 4.01. 55
all, every word, yea, and his son's pranks too; WT 4.04.700 P
thy lewd, pestiferous, and dissentious pranks, 1H6 3.01. 15
tell him his pranks have been too broad to bear HAM 3.04. 2
is much o' th' savor | of other your new pranks. LR 1.04.238
but does foul pranks which fair and wise ones do OTH 2.01.142
in venice they do let /god see the pranks | they 3.03.202
and eye become the pranks and friskins of her TNK 4.03. 80 P
PRAT 2 FR 0.0002 REL FR 0 V 2 P
come, mother prat, come give me your hand. WIV 4.02.182 P

i'll prat her. 4.02.184 P
/PRATE 1 FR 0.0001 REL FR 1 V 0 P
you gods, i /prate, | and the most noble mother COR 5.03. 48
PRATE 14 FR 0.0015 REL FR 10 V 4 P
lords that can prate | as amply and TMP 2.01.263
we must give folks leave to prate; WIV 1.04.121 P
i cannot cog, i cannot prate, mistress ford. 3.03. 48 P
to prate and talk for life and honor 'fore | who WT 3.02. 41
with his innocent prate | he will awake my mercy JN 4.01. 25
justice hath done nothing but prate to me of the 2H4 3.02.305 P
and perish ye, with your audacious prate! 1H6 4.01.124
tut, tut, my lord, we will not stand to prate; R3 1.03.349
what do you prate of service? COR 3.03. 83
yet here he lets me prate | like one i' th' 5.03.159
fear | the very stones prate of my whereabout, MAC 2.01. 58
and, if thou prate of mountains, let them throw HAM 5.01.280
dost thou prate, rogue? OTH 2.03.150 P
i am | to those that prate and have done, no TNK 5.01.119
PRATED 1 FR 0.0001 REL FR 1 V 0 P
nay, but he prated, | and spoke such scurvy and OTH 1.02. 6
PRATER 1 FR 0.0001 REL FR 0 V 1 P
a speaker is but a prater, a rhyme is but a H5 5.02.158 P
PRATING 12 FR 0.0013 REL FR 6 V 6 P
body, | disguised cheaters, prating mountebanks, ERR 1.02.101
hence, prating peasant! fetch thy master home. 2.01. 81
clerk, | a prating boy, that begg'd it as a fee. MV 5.01.164
thou shalt think on prating whilst thou liv'st! SHR 4.03.113
leave your prating. WT 4.04.340 P
is an ass and a fool, and a prating coxcomb, is H5 4.01. 77 P
be an ass and a fool, and a prating coxcomb, in 4.01. 79 P
this little prating york | was not incensed by R3 3.01.151
why stay we prating here? COR 1.01. 47 P
when 'twas a little prating thing — o, there is ROM 2.04.200 P
who was in life a foolish prating knave. HAM 3.04.215
to love him still for prating — let not thy OTH 2.01.224 P
PRAT'ST 3 FR 0.0003 REL FR 1 V 2 P
why prat'st thou to thyself, and answer'st not? ERR 2.02.193
thou prat'st, and prat'st; COR 4.05. 48 P
thou prat'st, and prat'st; 4.05. 48 P
PRATTLE 8 FR 0.0009 REL FR 7 V 1 P
but i prattle | something too wildly, and my TMP 3.01. 57
he had some cause | to prattle for himself. MM 5.01.182
mule, if you prattle me into these perils. AWW 4.01. 43 P
what great ones do the less will prattle of) TN 1.02. 33
next, | thinking his prattle to be tedious, R2 5.02. 26
pranks, | as very infants prattle of thy pride. 1H6 3.01. 16
mere prattle, without practice, | is all his OTH 1.01. 26
i prattle out of fashion, and i dote | in mine 2.01.206
PRATTLER 1 FR 0.0001 REL FR 0 V 1 P
poor prattler, how thou talk'st! MAC 4.02. 64 P
PRATTLING 2 FR 0.0002 REL FR 1 V 1 P
prithee no more prattling. WIV 5.01. 1 P
your prattling nurse | into a rapture lets her COR 2.01.206
PRAVE *(also brave)*
PRAVE 4 FR 0.0004 REL FR 0 V 4 P
'a utt'red as prave words at the pridge as you H5 3.06. 63 P
and there is gallant and most prave passages. 3.06. 93 P
can tell your majesty, the duke is a prave man. 3.06. 96 P
fought a most prave pattle here in france. 4.07. 95 P
PRAWLS *(also brawls)*
PRAWLS 1 FR 0.0001 REL FR 0 V 1 P
and keep you out of prawls and prabbles, and H5 4.08. 65 P
PRAWNS 1 FR 0.0001 REL FR 0 V 1 P
telling us she had a good dish of prawns, 2H4 2.01. 96 P
/PRAY 5 FR 0.0005 REL FR 4 V 1 P
/softly, /pray. 2H4 4.04.132
/i /pray /god /he /be /not, /i /say. R3 3.04. 58
and of all christians' souls, /i /pray /god. HAM 4.05.200 P
/i /pray /you /go | /along /with /me. LR 4.03. 54
/i /pray /talk /me /of /cassio. OTH 3.04. 92
PRAY 778 FR 0.0879 REL FR 498 V 280 P
i pray now keep below. TMP 1.01. 11 P
i pray thee mark me — that a brother should 1.02. 67
i pray thee mark me. 1.02. 88
and now i pray you, sir, | for still 'tis 1.02.175
no, pray thee. 1.02.371
alas, now pray you | work not so hard. 3.01. 15
pray set it down, and rest you. 3.01. 18
pray now rest yourself, | he's safe for these 3.01. 20
pray give me that, | i'll carry it to the pile. 3.01. 24
follow, i pray you. 3.03.109
pray you tread softly, that the blind mole may 4.01.194
pray you look in. 5.01.167
and on a love–book pray for my success? TGV 1.01. 19
upon some book i love i'll pray for thee. 1.01. 20
pardon the fault, i pray. 1.02. 40
and pray her to a fault for which i chid her. 1.02. 52
therefore i pray you go. 1.03. 89
pray heav'n he prove so when you come to him! 2.07. 79
sir thurio, give us leave, i pray, a while, | we 3.01. 1
when would you use it? pray, sir, tell me that. 3.01.123
i pray thee let me feel thy cloak upon me. 3.01.136
why, sir, i'll strike nothing. i pray you — 3.01.203 P
if so — i pray thee breathe it in mine ear, 3.01.241
i pray thee, launce, and if thou seest my boy, 3.01.259
i pray thee out with't, and place it for her 3.01.335 P
i pray you, why is it? 4.02. 27 P
pray you, where lies sir proteus? 4.02.136 P
i pray you be my mean | to bring me where to 4.04.108
i pray thee let me look on that again. 4.04.125
therefore i pray you stand not to discourse, 5.02. 44
peace, i pray you. WIV 1.01.136 P
i pray you pardon me; 1.01.218 P
i pray you, sir, walk in. 1.01.281 P
nay, pray you lead the way. 1.01.305 P
not i, sir, pray you keep on. 1.01.308 P
i pray you, sir. 1.01.311 P
i pray you be gone. 1.02. 11 P
i pray thee go to the casement, and see if you 1.04. 2 P
pray you go and vetch me in my closet /une 1.04. 45 P
peace, i pray you. 1.04. 80 P
come near the house, i pray you. 1.04.133 P
and i pray, how does good mistress anne? 2.01.164 P
sir — i pray come a little nearer this ways. 2.02. 44 P
i pray your worship come a little nearer this 2.02. 48 P
heaven forgive you, and all of us, i pray — 2.02. 57 P
but i pray thee tell me this: 2.02.108 P
he has pray his pible well, dat he is no come. 2.03. 7 P
i pray you bear witness that me have stay six or 2.03. 35 P
i pray you now, good master slender's servingman 3.01. 1 P
pray you give me my gown, or else keep it in 3.01. 34 P
i pray you let–a me speak a word with your ear. 3.01. 79 P
pray you use your patience in good time. 3.01. 81 P
pray you let us not be laughing–stocks to other 3.01. 85 P
well, i will smite his noddles. pray you follow. 3.01.125 P
cheer at home, and i pray you all go with me. 3.02. 52 P
pray you do so, she's a very tattling woman. 3.03. 91 P
pray heaven it be not so, that you have such a 3.03.112 P
pray you come near. 3.03.149 P
i pray you pardon me; 3.03.224 P
wife, come, mistress page, i pray you pardon me; 3.03.226 P
pray heartly pardon me. 3.03.227 P
pray you go, master page. 3.03.238 P
i pray you now remembrance to–morrow on the 3.03.239 P
pray you a word with you. 3.04. 34 P
pray you, uncle, tell mistress anne the jest how 3.04. 39 P
and i pray thee, once to–night | give my sweet 3.04. 99
i pray you ask him some questions in his 4.01. 16 P
i pray you peace. 4.01. 30 P
i pray you remember in your prain. 4.01. 35 P
pray you mark; 4.01. 42 P
i pray you have your remembrance, child. 4.01. 46 P
pray heaven it be not full of knight again. 4.02.112 P
master ford, you must pray, and not follow the 4.02.155 P
pray you, sir, was't not the wise woman of 4.05. 26 P
and what says she, i pray, sir? 4.05. 35 P
be pold, i pray you. 5.04. 2 P
pray you lock hand in hand; 5.05. 77
i pray you come, hold up the jest no higher. 5.05.105
and leave you your jealousies too, i pray you. 5.05.132 P
to what, i pray? MM 1.02. 48 P
who's that, i pray thee? 1.02. 63 P
i pray she may; 1.02.187 P
i pray you answer him. 1.04. 14
i pray you home to dinner with me. 2.01.278 P
pray you do. 2.02. 2
pray you be gone. 2.02. 66
pray heaven she win him! 2.02.125
when i would pray and think, i think and pray 2.04. 1
think, i think and pray | to several subjects. 2.04. 1
i'll pray a thousand prayers for thy death, | no 3.01.145
i will pray, pompey, to increase your bondage. 3.02. 75 P
to call upon you, and i pray you your name? 3.02.158 P
farewell, good friar, i prithee pray for me. 3.02.180 P
i pray you, sir, of what disposition was the 3.02.230 P
i pray you tell me, hath any body inquir'd for 4.01. 16 P
i pray you be acquainted with this maid, | she 4.01. 50
pray, sir, by your good favor — for surely, sir 4.02. 32 P
pray you let's hear. 4.02.119 P
pray, sir, in what? 4.02.163 P
pray, master barnardine, awake till you are 4.03. 32 P
to advise you, comfort you, and pray with you. 4.03. 52 P
madness, pray heaven his wisdom be not tainted! 4.04. 4 P
pray you take note of it; 5.01. 80
for yourself, pray heaven you then | be perfect. 5.01. 81
pray you, my lord, give me leave to question, 5.01.270 P
and pray thee take this mercy to provide | for 5.01.484
but we that know what 'tis to fast and pray, ERR 1.02. 51
tell me this, i pray: 1.02. 53
i pray you jest, sir, as you sit at dinner. 1.02. 62
i pray you, master, tell me. 2.02. 21
but i pray, sir, why am i beaten? 2.02. 39 P
if it be, sir, i pray you eat none of it. 2.02. 60 P
nay, not sound, i pray you. 2.02. 92 P
pray god our cheer | may answer my good will and 3.01. 19
i pray thee let me in. 3.01. 78
bring it, i pray you, to the porpentine, | for 3.01.116
i pray you, sir, receive the money now, | for 3.02.176
i pray you see him presently discharg'd, | for 4.01. 32
nay, come, i pray you, sir, give me the chain: 4.01. 45
the hour steals on, i pray you, sir, dispatch. 4.01. 52
i pray you let me see it. 4.01. 58
i pray you, sir, my ring, or else the chain; 4.03. 77
i, sir, am dromio, pray let me stay. 5.01.337
i pray you, is signior mountanto return'd from ADO 1.01. 30 P
i pray you, how many hath he kill'd and eaten in 1.01. 42 P
but i pray you, who is his companion? 1.01. 81 P
no, i pray thee speak in sober judgment. 1.01.170 P
i pray thee tell me truly how thou lik'st her. 1.01.177 P
i pray you, what is he? 2.01.136 P
i pray you dissuade him from her, she is no 2.01.164 P
i pray you leave me. 2.01.197 P
i pray thee sing, and let me woo no more. 2.03. 48
nay, pray thee come, | or, if thou wilt hold 2.03. 52
and i pray god his bad voice bode no mischief. 2.03. 81 P
i pray thee get us some excellent music; 2.03. 85 P
how, how, i pray you? 2.03.113 P
i pray you tell benedick of it, and hear what 'a 2.03.170 P
i pray you be not angry with me, madam, 3.01. 94
there be any impediment, i pray you discover it. 3.02. 93 P
i pray you watch about signior leonato's door, 3.03. 91 P
no, pray thee, good meg, i'll wear this. 3.04. 8 P
brief, i pray you, for you see it is a busy time 3.05. 4 P
nay, i pray you let me go. 4.01.294 P
pray write down borachio. yours, sirrah? 4.02. 12 P
pray thee, fellow, peace. 4.02. 44 P
i pray thee cease thy counsel, | which falls 5.01. 3
i pray thee peace. 5.01. 34
i pray you choose another subject. 5.01.136 P
i know not how to pray your patience, | yet i 5.01.271
that were impossible — but i pray you both, 5.01.280
pray you examine him upon that point. 5.01.312 P
pray thee, sweet mistress margaret, deserve well 5.02. 1 P
and so i pray thee call beatrice; 5.02. 16 P
and i pray thee now tell me, for which of my bad 5.02. 59 P
i had rather pray a month with mutton and LLL 1.01.302 P
pray you, do my commendations — i would be glad 2.01.181 P
sir, i pray you a word. what lady is that same? 2.01.194
pray you, sir, whose daughter? 2.01.201
pray you, sir, how much carnation ribbon may a 3.01.145 P
her, to watch for her, | to pray for her, go to! 3.01.201
i will love, write, sigh, pray, sue, groan: 3.01.204
pray you, which is the head lady? 4.01. 42 P
ah, good my liege, i pray thee pardon me! 4.03.150
sans "sans," i pray you. 5.02.416
farewell, sweet playfellow, pray thou for us; MND 1.01.220
pray you, if it be, give it me, for i am slow of 1.02. 66 P
i pray you fail me not. 1.02.106 P
i pray thee give it me. 2.01.248
pray, masters, fly, masters! 3.01.105 P
i pray thee, gentle mortal, sing again. 3.01.137
i pray you commend me to mistress squash, your 3.01.186 P
i pray thee, tell me then that he is well. 3.02. 77
i pray you, though you mock me, /gentlemen, 3.02.299
pray you, leave your curtsy, good mounsieur. 4.01. 20 P
but, i pray you, let none of your people stir me 4.01. 38 P
i pray you all, stand up. 4.01.141
no epilogue, i pray you; 5.01.355 P
i pray you have in mind where we must meet. MV 1.01. 71
i pray you, good bassanio, let me know it, | and 1.01.135
i pray thee over–name them, and as thou namest 1.02. 36 P
i pray thee set a deep glass of rhenish wine on 1.02. 95 P
and i pray god grant them a fair departure. 1.02.110 P
eat with you, drink with you, nor pray with you. 1.03. 37 P
pray you tell me this: 1.03.162
and for my love i pray you wrong me not. 1.03.170
therefore i pray you lead me to the caskets | to 2.01. 23
man, you, i pray you, which is the way to master 2.02. 33 P
master young gentleman, i pray you, which is the 2.02. 39 P
but i pray you, ergo, old man, ergo, i beseech 2.02. 57 P
young gentleman, but i pray you tell me, is my 2.02. 71 P
pray you, sir, stand up. 2.02. 81 P
pray you let's have no more fooling about it, 2.02. 83 P
i pray thee, good leonardo, think on this: 2.02.169
pray thee take pain | to allay with some cold 2.02.185
i pray thee let us go and find him out | and 2.08. 51
quick, i pray thee, draw the curtain straight; 2.09. 1
no more, i pray thee. 2.09. 96
i pray you tarry, pause a day or two | before 3.02. 1
i pray you tell me how my good friend doth. 3.02.233
i pray thee hear me speak. 3.03. 11
pray god bassanio come | to see me pay his debt, 3.03. 35
bring them i pray thee with imagin'd speed 3.04. 52
and what hope is that, i pray thee? 3.05. 9 P
i pray thee understand a plain man in his plain 3.05. 57 P
no, pray thee, let it serve for table–talk; 3.05. 88
i pray you think you question with the jew: 4.01. 70
we do pray for mercy, | and that same prayer 4.01.200
i pray you let me look upon the bond. 4.01.225
i pray thee pursue sentence. 4.01.298
i pray you give me leave to go from hence, | i 4.01.395
i pray you know me when we meet again; 4.01.419
grant me two things, i pray you, | not to deny 4.01.423
only for this, i pray you pardon me. 4.01.437
most thankfully, | and so i pray you tell him; 4.02. 10
i pray you show my youth old shylock's house. 4.02. 11
your name, i pray you, friend? 5.01. 27
i pray you, is my master yet return'd? 5.01. 34
but go we in, i pray thee, jessica, | and 5.01. 36
my friend /stephano, signify, i pray you, 5.01. 51
i pray you leave me. AYL 1.01. 78 P
i pray thee, rosalind, sweet my coz, be merry. 1.02. 1 P
we pray you for your own sake to embrace your 1.02.178 P
fare you well! pray heaven i be deceiv'd in you! 1.02.197 P
and pray you tell me this: 1.02.268
i pray you bear with me, i cannot go no further. 2.04. 9 P
i pray you, one of you question yond man | if he 2.04. 64
i pray thee, if it stand with honesty, | buy 2.04. 91
pardon me, i pray you. 2.07.106
i pray you mar no more trees with writing 3.02.259 P
i pray you mar no moe of my verses with reading 3.02.261 P
i pray you, what is't a' clock? 3.02.299 P
so love–shak'd, i pray you tell me your remedy. 3.02.367 P
and therefore i pray the gods make me honest. 3.03. 33 P
nay, pray be cover'd. 3.03. 76 P
and why, i pray you? 3.05. 35
sweet youth, i pray you chide a year together, 3.05. 64
i pray you do not fall in love with me, | for i 3.05. 72
pray thee marry us. 4.01.127 P
pray you (if you know) | where in the purlieus 4.03. 75
i pray you tell it. 4.03. 97
i pray you, will you take him by the arm? 4.03.162
i pray you tell your brother how well i 4.03.166 P
pray you draw homewards. 4.03.177 P
but i pray you commend my counterfeiting to him. 4.03.181 P
pray you no more of this, 'tis like the howling 5.02.109 P
let's be no stoics nor no stocks, i pray, | or SHR 1.01. 31
i pray you, sir, is it your will | to make a 1.01. 57
but a word, i pray. 1.01.114 P
what's that, i pray? 1.01.119 P
i pray, sir, tell me, is it possible | that love 1.01.146
i pray, awake, sir; 1.01.178
pray what's the news? 1.01.224 P
i pray you, sir, let him go while the humor 1.02.107 P
not her that chides, sir, at any hand, i pray. 1.02.225
sir, i pray, are not the streets as free | for 1.02.231
pray have you not a daughter | call'd katherina, 2.01. 42
i pray | let us that are poor petitioners speak 2.01. 71
pray accept his service. 2.01. 83 P
lucentio is your name, of whence, i pray? 2.01.102
and so i pray you all to think yourselves. 2.01.113
i pray you do. 2.01.168
good master, take it not unkindly, pray, | that 3.01. 57
all ready; and therefore, i pray thee, news. 4.01. 52 P
patience, i pray you, 'twas a fault unwilling. 4.01.156
i pray you, husband, be not so disquiet. 4.01.168
now tell me, i pray, | you that durst swear that 4.02. 11
what countryman, i pray? 4.02. 77
my life, sir? how, i pray? for that goes hard. 4.02. 80
i pray you let it stand. 4.03. 44
i pray you stand good father to me now, | give 4.04. 21
i pray the gods she may with all my heart! 4.04. 67
i pray thee moralize them. 4.04. 81 P
forward, i pray, since we have come so far, 4.05. 12
pardon, i pray thee, for my mad mistaking. 4.05. 49
i pray you tell signior lucentio that his father 5.01. 27 P
pray what do you think is his name? 5.01. 79 P
now pray thee, love, stay. 5.01.148
pray you sit down, | for now we sit to chat as 5.02. 10
i pray you tell me what you meant by that. 5.02. 27
pray god, sir, your wife send you not a worse. 5.02. 84
pray you leave me. AWW 1.03.125 P
home | and pray god's blessing into thy attempt. 1.03.254
i pray you, sir, are you a courtier? 2.02. 40 P

i pray you. come, sirrah.		2.04. 55
i pray you make us friends, i will pursue the		2.05. 13 P
pray you, sir, who's his tailor?		2.05. 16 P
pray, sir, your pardon.		2.05. 78
i pray you stay not, but in haste to horse.		2.05. 87
by what observance, i pray you?		3.02. 5 P
pray you, gentlemen, | i have felt so many		3.02. 48
where is my son, i pray you?		3.02. 51
his name, i pray you?		3.05. 48
o, pray, pray, pray! manka revania dulche.		4.01. 78 P
o, pray, pray, pray! manka revania dulche.		4.01. 78 P
o, pray, pray, pray! manka revania dulche.		4.01. 78 P
then pray you tell me, | if i should swear by		4.02. 24
"poor rogues," i pray you say.		4.03.154 P
i pray you, sir, put it up again.		4.03.216 P
yet, i pray you:		4.04. 30
let us go see your son, i pray you.		4.05.102 P
pray you, sir, deliver me this paper.		5.02. 15 P
pray you, sir, use the carp as you may, for he		5.02. 22 P
now pray you let me see it;		5.03. 81
i pray you yet | (since you lack virtue, i will		5.03.221
what ring was yours, i pray you?		5.03.225
how, i pray you?		5.03.244 P
i pray you bring your hand to th' butt'ry–bar,	TN	1.03. 69 P
fetch him off, i pray you, he speaks nothing but		1.05.106 P
i pray you tell me if this be the lady of the		1.05.171 P
i pray you keep it in.		1.05.196 P
o, by your leave, i pray you:		3.01.106
i pray you let us satisfy our eyes | with the		3.03. 22
pray god he be not bewitch'd!		3.04.101 P
say his prayers, good sir toby, get him to pray.		3.04.119 P
i pray you, sir, what is he?		3.04.234 P
pray you, sir, do you know of this matter?		3.04.259 P
pray god defend me!		3.04.302 P
pray god he keep his oath!		3.04.310 P
pray, sir, put your sword up, if you please.		3.04.321 P
come, sir, i pray you go.		3.04.358
pray you peruse that letter.		5.01.330
pray now | what color are your eyebrows?	WT	2.01. 12
pray you sit by us, | and tell 's a tale.		2.01. 22
pray you then, | conduct me to the queen.		2.02. 6
is't lawful, pray you, to see her women?		2.02. 11
i pray now call her. | withdraw yourselves.		2.02. 14
pray you, emilia;		2.02. 33
i pray you do not push me, i'll be gone.		2.03.125
i pray thee, good camillo, be no more		4.02. 1 P
offer me no money, i pray you, that kills my		4.03. 83 P
pray you bid | these unknown friends to 's		4.04. 64
pray so;		4.04.139
but come, our dance, i pray.		4.04.153
pray, good shepherd, what fair swain is this		4.04.166
pray now buy some.		4.04.260 P
pray you now buy it.		4.04.272 P
pray let's see these four threes of herdsmen.		4.04.335 P
pray you once more, | is not your father grown		4.04.396
therefore, i pray you, | as you have ever been		4.04.492
pray you a word.		4.04.661
pray heartily he be at' palace.		4.04.711 P
what, pray you, became of antigonus, that		5.02. 59 P
madam, kneel, | and pray your mother's blessing.		5.03.120
pray that their burthens may not fall this day,	JN	3.01. 90
made hard with kneeling, i do pray to thee,		3.01.310
husband, i cannot pray that thou mayst win;		3.01.331
uncle, i needs must pray that thou mayst lose;		3.01.332
grandame, i will pray | (if ever i remember to		3.03. 14
i pray you bear me hence | from forth the noise		5.04. 44
most heartily i pray | your highness to assign	R2	1.01.150
pray god we may make haste and come too late!		1.04. 64
sister — cousin, i would say — pray pardon me.		2.02.105
guard it, i pray thee, with a lurking adder,		3.02. 20
pray god the plants thou graft'st may never grow		3.04.101
i know she is come to pray for your foul sin.		5.03. 82
if thou do pardon, whosoever pray, | more sins		5.03. 83
we pray with heart and soul, and all beside;		5.03.104
come, my old son, i pray god make thee new.		5.03.146
but soft, i pray you, did king richard then	1H4	1.03.155
i pray thee lend me thine.		2.01. 38 P
of it, i pray thee keep that for the hangman,		2.01. 63 P
sooner than drink, and drink sooner than pray;		2.01. 79 P
i lie, for they pray continually to their saint,		2.01. 79 P
or rather, not pray to her, but prey on her, for		2.01. 81 P
anon, sir. pray stay a little, my lord.		2.04. 57 P
pray god you have not murd'red some of them.		2.04.189 P
watch to–night, pray to–morrow.		2.04.277 P
my lord, i pray you hear me.		3.03. 91 P
nay, and i do, i pray god my girdle break.		3.03.151 P
pray god my news be worth a welcome, lord.		4.01. 87
pray god you do.		4.03.113
pray god his tongue be hotter!	2H4	1.02. 34 P
i pray you, sir, then set your knighthood and		1.02. 83 P
i pray you let me speak with you.		1.02.109 P
but look you pray, all you that kiss my lady		1.02.207 P
i pray you all | speak plainly your opinions of		1.03. 2
i pray you, since my exion is ent'red and my		2.01. 29 P
pray thee peace.		2.01.118 P
pray thee, sir john, let it be but twenty nobles		2.01.153 P
i pray thee, loving wife, and gentle daughter,		2.03. 1
shut the door, i pray you.		2.04. 78 P
pray ye pacify yourself, sir john.		2.04. 80 P
since when, i pray you, sir?		2.04.132 P
pray thee go down, good ancient.		2.04.151 P
pray thee go down.		2.04.155 P
i pray thee, jack, i pray thee do not draw.		2.04.202 P
i pray thee, jack, i pray thee do not draw.		2.04.202 P
i pray thee, jack, be quiet, the rascal's gone.		2.04.208 P
and so i pray you go in with me to dinner.		3.02.189 P
i pray you take me up, and bear me hence | into		4.04.131
i pray thee now deliver them like a man of this		5.03. 97 P
but i pray god the fruit of her womb miscarry.		5.04. 12 P
to pray your patience for it and to promise you		ep 9 P
you — but, indeed, to pray for the queen.		ep 17 P
who, prologue–like, your humble patience pray,	H5	pr 33
my learned lord, we pray you to proceed, | and		1.02. 9
pray thee, corporal, stay.		3.02. 3 P
i pray you, and beseech you, that you will.		4.01. 82 P
i pray you, what thinks he of our estate?		4.01. 96 P
god's will, i pray thee wish not one man more.		4.03. 23
i pray thee bear my former answer back:		4.03. 90
why, i pray you, is not "pig" great?		4.07. 15 P
pray thee go seek him, and bring him to my tent.		4.07.167 P
for you, and i pray you to serve god, and keep		4.08. 64 P
i humbly pray them to admit th' excuse | of time		5.pr. 3
i pray you fall to;		5.01. 37 P
bite, i pray you, it is good for your green		5.01. 41 P
eat, i pray you.		5.01. 49 P
nay, pray you throw none away, the skin is good		5.01. 54 P
to see leeks hereafter, i pray you mock at 'em,		5.01. 56 P
speak, my fair, and fairly, i pray thee.		5.02.168 P
i pray you then, in love and dear alliance,		5.02.345
go'st | except it be to pray against thy foes.	1H6	1.01. 43
pray god she prove not masculine ere long, | if		2.01. 22
for what are you, i pray, | but one imperious in		3.01. 43
pray, uncle gloucester, mitigate this strife.		3.01. 88
quiet yourselves, i pray, and be at peace.		4.01.115
why, what, i pray, is margaret more than that?		5.05. 36
uncle of winchester, i pray read on.	2H6	1.01. 56
i pray, my lord, pardon me, i took ye for my		1.03. 11 P
pray god the duke of york excuse himself!		1.03.178
and so i pray you go in god's name, and leave us		1.04. 9 P
now pray, my lord, let's see the devil's writ.		1.04. 57
i pray, my lords, let me compound this strife.		2.01. 56
drink, and pray for me, i pray you, for i think		2.03. 72 P
and pray for me, i pray you, for i think i have		2.03. 73 P
o lord bless me, i pray god, for i am never able		2.03. 77 P
i pray thee sort thy heart to patience, | these		2.04. 68
entreat her not the worse in that i pray | you		2.04. 81
and i pray you all | proceed no straiter 'gainst		3.02. 19
pray god he may acquit him of suspicion!		3.02. 25
i pray thee, buckingham, go and meet him, | and		4.09. 36
doornail, i pray god i may never eat grass more.		4.10. 41 P
priests pray for enemies, but princes kill.		5.02. 71
o, let me pray before i take my death!	3H6	1.03. 35
to thee i pray;		1.03. 36
but say, i pray, what nobleman is that | that		4.03. 9
and pray that i may repossess the crown.		4.05. 29
god, i pray him, | that none of you may live his	R3	1.03.211
to pray for them that have done scath to us.		1.03.316
i pray you tell me.		1.04. 8
i pray you, uncle, give me this dagger.		3.01.110
pray god, i say, i prove a needless coward!		3.02. 88
i pray you all, tell me what they deserve | that		3.04. 59
master lieutenant, pray you, by your leave,		4.01. 13
gapes, hell burns, fiends roar, saints pray,		4.04. 75
cancel his bond of life, dear god, i pray,		4.04. 77
the wronged heirs of york do pray for thee.		5.03.137
thy adversary's wife doth pray for thee.		5.03.166
i pray you, who, my lord?	H8	1.01. 49
pray give me favor, sir:		1.01.168
pray look to't;		1.02.101
now i would pray our monsieurs | to think an		1.03. 21
pray sit between these ladies.		1.04. 24
and pray receive 'em nobly and conduct 'em		1.04. 58
thanks, and pray 'em take their pleasures.		1.04. 74
pray tell 'em thus much from me:		1.04. 77
pray speak what has happen'd.		2.01. 6
but pray how pass'd it?		2.01. 10
pray tell him | you met him half in heaven.		2.01. 87
all good people, | pray for me!		2.01.132
pray god he do, he'll never know himself else.		2.02. 22
we had need pray, | and heartily, for our		2.02. 44
pray god he be not angry.		2.02. 63
but i pray you, | what think you of a duchess?		2.03. 37
now i pray god, amen!		2.03. 56
whose health and royalty i pray for.		2.03. 73
pray do not deliver | what here y' have heard to		2.03.106
pray you keep your way;		2.04.129
pray you pass on.		2.04.131
pray their graces | to come near.		3.01. 18
pray speak in english.		3.01. 46
speak like honest men (pray god ye prove so!),		3.01. 69
pray hear me.		3.01.142
pray think us | those we profess, peacemakers,		3.01.166
and pray forgive me;		3.01.175
pray do my service to his majesty;		3.01.179
i pray you tell me, | if what i now pronounce		3.02.162
that sun, i pray, may never set!		3.02.415
who may that be, i pray you?		4.01.108
she is going, wench. pray, pray.		4.02. 99
she is going, wench. pray, pray.		4.02. 99
but i pray you, | what is your pleasure with me?		4.02.113
i most humbly pray you to deliver | this to my		4.02.129
the fruit she goes with | i pray for heartily,		5.01. 21
your highness | most heartily to pray for her.		5.01. 66
to pray for her?		5.01. 67
pray you arise, | my good and gracious lord of		5.01. 91
pray heaven he sound not my disgrace!		5.02. 13
pray heaven the king may never find a heart		5.02. 77
pray, sir, be patient;		5.03. 12
my noble partners and myself thus pray | all		5.04. 5
pray you speak no more to me, i will leave all	TRO	1.01. 87 P
is this great agamemnon's tent, i pray you?		1.03.216
what's your affairs, i pray you?		1.03.247
then tell me, i pray thee, what's thersites?		2.03. 46 P
pray you a word.		3.01. 1 P
pray you content you.		3.02.143
pray you come in.		4.02. 40
pray thee get thee in.		4.02. 85 P
stand fair, i pray thee, let me look on thee.		4.05.235
i pray you let us see you in the field;		4.05.266
you are moved, prince, let us depart, i pray,		5.02. 36
behold, i pray you!		5.02. 40
i pray you stay.		5.02. 43
be sent | to pray achilles see us at our tent.		5.09. 8
speak, i pray you.	COR	1.01. 56
pray follow.		1.01.251
i pray you, daughter, sing, or express yourself		1.03. 1 P
why, i pray you?		1.03. 80 P
true, on mine honor, and so i pray go with us.		1.03.101 P
pray now, no more.		1.09. 13
i pray you | ('tis south the city mills) bring		1.10. 30
pray you, who does the wolf love?		2.01. 7 P
pray now, no more.		2.01.169
pray now, sit down.		2.02. 74
pray you go fit you to the custom, and | take to		2.02.142
"i pray, sir" — plague upon't!		2.03. 50
pray you speak to 'em, i pray you, | in		2.03. 59
pray you speak to 'em, i pray you, | in		2.03. 59
well then, i pray, your price a' th' consulship?		2.03. 73 P
kindly, sir, i pray let me ha't.		2.03. 76 P
pray you now, if it may stand with the tune of		2.03. 85 P
we pray the gods he may deserve your loves.		2.03.157
pray you be gone.		3.01.249
pray you let's to him.		3.01.334
pray be counsell'd.		3.02. 28
pray be content.		3.02.130
pray you let us go.		3.02.142
with a voice as free | as i do pray the gods.		3.03. 74
know, i pray you —		3.03. 87
i pray you come.		4.01. 50
pray let's go.		4.02. 36
now, pray, sir, get you gone;		4.02. 37
pray go to the door.		4.05. 8 P
pray get you out.		4.05. 13 P
pray you avoid the house.		4.05. 22 P
pray you, poor gentleman, take up some other		4.05. 29 P
pray you avoid.		4.05. 30 P
on our knees, | are bound to pray for you both.		4.06. 23
pray now, your news?		4.06. 87
pray, your news?		4.06. 88
pray let's go.		4.06.160
nay, pray be patient.		5.01. 33
pray you go to him.		5.01. 39
how can we, for our country pray, | whereto we		5.03.107
you, and pray you | stand to me in this cause.		5.03.198
take it up, i pray thee, | and give the king	TIT	2.03. 46
i pray you let us hence, | and let her joy her		2.03. 82
and pray the roman gods confound you both!		4.02. 6
come let us go and pray to all the gods | for		4.02. 46
pray to the devils, the gods have given us over.		4.02. 48
region, | i pray you deliver him this petition.		4.03. 14
go get you gone, and pray be careful all, | and		4.03. 21
i pray thee do on them some violent death,		5.02.108
for what, i pray thee?	ROM	1.02. 52
god gi' god–den. i pray, sir, can you read?		1.02. 57 P
but, i pray, can you read any thing you see?		1.02. 60 P
if you be not of the house of montagues, i pray,		1.02. 80 P
enough of this, i pray thee hold thy peace.		1.03. 49
and stint thou too, i pray thee, nurse, say i.		1.03. 58
they pray — grant thou, lest faith turn to		1.05.104
i'll tell thee as we pass, but this i pray,		2.03. 63
i pray thee chide me not.		2.03. 85
i pray you, sir, what saucy merchant was this,		2.04.145 P
pray you, sir, a word:		2.04.162 P
nay, come, i pray thee speak, good, good nurse,		2.05. 28
i pray thee, good mercutio, let's retire.		3.01. 1
i pray you tell my lord and father, madam, | i		3.05.120
i am too young, i pray you pardon me."		3.05.186
i pray thee leave me to myself to–night, | for i		4.03. 2
pray you put up your dagger, and put out your		4.05.121 P
o, pray let's see't. for the lord timon, sir?	TIM	1.01. 13
pray entertain them, give them guide to us.		1.01.243
pray you let us in.		1.01.255
pray sit, more welcome are ye to my fortunes		1.02. 19
i crave no pelf, | i pray for no man but myself.		1.02. 63
i pray let them be admitted.		1.02.121 P
pray you, | how goes the world, that i am thus		2.02. 35
pray draw near.		2.02. 45
pray you walk near, i'll speak with you anon.		2.02.123
pray is my lord ready to come forth?		3.04. 34 P
we attend his lordship; pray signify so much.		3.04. 37 P
i pray you, upon what?		3.06. 57 P
no more, i pray — and he's a steward.		4.03.498
i pray you do my greeting.		5.01.212
pray to the gods to intermit the plague | that	JC	1.01. 54
i pray you do.		1.02. 27
but soft, i pray you; what, did caesar swound?		1.02.251
if thou dost bend, and pray, and fawn for him,		3.01. 45
if i could pray to move, prayers would move me;		3.01. 59
no more, i pray you.		4.03.166
i pray you, sirs, lie in my tent and sleep;		4.03.246
cousins, a word, i pray you.	MAC	1.03.127
i pray you remember the porter.		2.03. 20 P
to pray for this good man, and for his issue,		3.01. 88
so shall i, love, and so, i pray, be you.		3.02. 29
pray you keep seat.		3.04. 53
pray you sit still.		3.04.107
i pray you speak not.		3.04.116
thither macduff | is gone to pray the holy king,		3.06. 30
my dearest coz, | i pray you school yourself.		4.02. 15
run away, i pray you!		4.02. 85
i pray you, | let not my jealousies be your		4.03. 28
comes the king forth, i pray you?		4.03.140
pray god it be, sir.		5.01. 58 P
let's do't, i pray, and i this morning know	HAM	1.01.174
we pray you throw to earth | this unprevailing		1.02.106
i pray thee stay with us, go not to wittenberg.		1.02.119
i pray you all, | if you have hitherto conceal'd		1.02.245
is, and for my own poor part, | i will go pray.		1.05.132
and still your fingers on your lips, i pray.		1.05.187
pray god your voice, like a piece of uncurrent		2.02.427 P
i pray you now receive them.		3.01. 94
speak the speech, i pray you, as i pronounc'd it		3.02. 1 P
pray you avoid it.		3.02. 14 P
i pray you.		3.02.353 P
arm you, i pray you, to this speedy viage, | for		3.03. 24
pray can i not, | though inclination be as sharp		3.03. 38
pray you be round /with /him.		3.04. 5
i pray you haste in this.		4.01. 37
pray you make haste.		4.03. 57
how purpos'd, sir, i pray you?		4.04. 11
nay, pray you mark.		4.05. 28 P
pray you mark.		4.05. 35 P
pray let's have no words of this, but when they		4.05. 46 P
her close, give her good watch, i pray you.		4.05. 74
i pray you give me leave.		4.05.114
pray you, love, remember.		4.05.176 P
i pray you go with me.		4.05.220
i pray thee, good horatio, wait upon him.		5.01.293
i will, my lord, i pray you pardon me.		5.02.291
i pray you pass with your best violence;		5.02.298
pray you let us /hit together;	LR	1.01.303 P
wind me into him, i pray you.		1.02. 98 P
i pray you have a continent forbearance till the		1.02.166 P
pray ye go, there's my key.		1.02.169 P

pray you away. 1.02.175 P
pray, sir, be patient. 1.04.261
pray you, content. 1.04.313
not i. pray you, what are they? 2.01. 9 P
pray do not, sir. 2.02.155
i pray you, sir, take patience. 2.04.138
therefore i pray you | that to our sister you do 2.04.150
i pray you, father, being weak, seem so. 2.04.201
things toward, edmund, pray you be careful. 3.03. 20 P
i'll pray, and then i'll sleep. 3.04. 27
pray, innocent, and beware the foul fiend. 3.06. 7 P
if you do find him, pray you give him this; 4.05. 33
you, | i pray desire her call her wisdom to her. 4.05. 35
well pray you, father. 4.06.219
pray do not mock me. 4.07. 58
i pray weep not. 4.07. 70
pray you now forget, and forgive; 4.07. 83
'tis most convenient, pray go with us. 5.01. 36
pray that the right may thrive. 5.02. 2
and pray, and sing, and tell old tales, and 5.03. 12
pray you undo this button. 5.03.310
pray you lead on. OTH 1.01.180
but i pray you, sir, | are you fast married? 1.02. 10
i pray you hear her speak. 1.03.175
pray /heaven he be; 2.01. 34
i pray you, sir, go forth, | and give us truth 2.01. 57
here, at the door; i pray you call them in. 2.03. 46 P
i pray you, after the lieutenant, go. 2.03.137
i pray you, sir, hold your hand. 2.03.151 P
i pray you pardon me, i cannot speak. 2.03.189
are these, i pray you, wind instruments? 3.01. 6 P
pray you come in. 3.01. 53
i am to pray you not to strain my speech | to 3.03.218
slander her and torture me, | never pray more; 3.03.369
pray you let cassio be receiv'd again. 3.04. 88
pray heaven it be state matters, as you think, 3.04.155
why, i pray you? 3.04.195
i pray you bring me on the way a little, | and 3.04.197
and yet she'll kneel and pray; 4.02. 23
pray you, chuck, come hither. 4.02. 24
i pray you turn the key and keep our counsel. 4.02. 94
i pray you be content; 4.02.165
i pray you look upon her. 5.01.108
will you, i pray, demand that demi–devil | why 5.02.301
what? not to pray? 5.02.305
i pray you, in your letters, | when you shall 5.02.340
pray then, foresee me one. ANT 1.02. 16 P
pray you stand farther from me. 1.03. 18
nay, pray you, seek no color for your going, 1.03. 32
but pray you stir no embers up. 2.02. 13
pray you hasten | your generals after. 2.04. 1
what, i pray you? 2.06. 69
pray you, is he married to cleopatra? 2.06.108 P
pray ye, sir? 2.06.113 P
when i shall pray, "o, bless my lord and husband 3.04. 16
pray you | be ever known to patience. 3.06. 97
pray you look not sad, | nor make replies of 3.11. 17
leave me, i pray, a little; 3.11. 22
pray you now, | nay, do so; 3.11. 22
i have lost command, | therefore i pray you. 3.11. 24
a conqueror that will pray in aid for kindness 5.02. 27
pray you tell him | i am his fortune's vassal, 5.02. 28
nay, pray you, sir. 5.02.108
i pray you rise, rise, egypt. 5.02.115
give it nothing, i pray you, for it is not worth 5.02.269 P
but pray you tell me, | is she sole child to th' CYM 1.01. 55
be brief, i pray you. 1.01.101
pray walk awhile. 1.01.176
some half hour hence, | pray you speak with me. 1.01.177
was born, and i pray you be better acquainted. 1.04.121 P
pray let us follow 'em. 1.04.171 P
i pray you, sir, | deliver with more openness 1.06. 87
pray you — | since doubting things go ill often 1.06. 94
pray your pardon. 1.06.178
pray, what is't? 1.06.184
i pray you spare me. 2.03. 95
in a true hate, to pray they have their will: 2.05. 34
else, sir, no more tribute, pray you now. 3.01. 45 P
and men in dangerous bonds pray not alike; 3.02. 37
i pray his absence | proceed by swallowing that; 3.05. 57
pray draw near. 3.06. 92
i pray draw near. 3.06. 95
pray you trust me here, | i'll rob none but 4.02. 14
pray, be not sick, | for you must be our huswife 4.02. 44
pray you away, | let me alone with him. 4.02. 69
pray you fetch him hither. 4.02.251
pray how far thither? 4.02.292
pray, sir, to th' army. 4.04. 31
blest pray you be, | that, after this strange 5.05.370
and we'll pray for you. PER 1.04. 98
arise, i pray you, rise. 1.04. 98
for that i am a man, pray you see me buried. 2.01. 77
i pray you let me see it. 2.01.120
i pray you give her air. 3.02. 91
no, i pray you, | i'll not bereave you of your 4.01. 30
go, i pray you, | walk, and be cheerful once 4.01. 38
pray walk softly, do not heat your blood. 4.01. 48
pray, but be not tedious, for | the gods are 4.01. 68
why to give over, i pray you? 4.02. 28 P
pray you come hither a while. 4.02.115 P
pray you, will you go with us? 4.02.149 P
pray you, without any more virginal fencing, 4.06. 57 P
i pray greet him fairly. 5.01. 10
pray you turn your eyes upon me. 5.01.101
first, sir, i pray, | what is your title? 5.01.202
bound, | the interim, pray you, all confound. 5.02. 14
we pray our play may be so; TNK pr 9
pray you kneel not; 1.01. 54
the helmeted bellona use them | and pray for me, 1.01. 76
pray stand up, | your grief is written in your 1.01.109
pray you say nothing, pray you. 1.01.119
pray you say nothing, pray you. 1.01.119
pray have good comfort. 1.01.129
pray stand up. 1.01.205
get you and pray the gods | for success and 1.01.208
feast, of which i pray you | make no abatement. 1.01.224
pray, forward. 2.02.122
pray you, whither go you? 2.03. 60
pray observe her goodness. 2.05. 35
pray be pleas'd | to show in generous terms your 3.01. 53
i pray you | take comfort and be strong. 3.01. 99
pray hold your promise; 3.01.100
nay, pray you — | you talk of feeding me to 3.01.118
pray sit down then, and let me entreat you | by 3.03. 13
pray thee tell me, cousin, | where got'st thou 3.06. 53
pray heaven it hold so! 4.01. 16
pray go on, sir. 4.01. 65
pray did you ever hear | of one young palamon? 4.01.116
pray speak, | you that have seen them, what they 4.02. 71
pray speak him, friend. 4.02. 91
pray order it | fitting the persons that must 4.02.150
i should | choose one, and pray for his success, 5.01.153
pray bring her in | and let's see how she is. 5.02. 24
you'll find it so. she comes. pray /humor her. 5.02. 40
know best, i pray them he | be made your lot. 5.03. 39
pray, how does she? 5.04. 25
pray yet stay a while, | and let me look upon ye ep 3
i pray you hence, and leave me here alone, | for VEN 382
that for his prey to pray he doth begin, | as if LUC 342
the powers to whom i pray abhor this fact, | how 349
so will i pray that thou mayst have thy will, SON 143.13

PRAY'D 14 FR 0.0015 REL FR 12 V 2 P
how i persuaded, how i pray'd, and kneel'd, MM 5.01. 93
swore, how she pray'd that never pray'd before; SHR 4.01. 79 P
swore, how she pray'd that never pray'd before; 4.01. 79 P
your mother well hath pray'd, and prove you true R2 5.03.145
had not churchmen pray'd, | his thread of life 1H6 1.01. 33
english, thus they pray'd | to tell your grace, H8 1.04. 65
her fair eyes to heaven, and pray'd devoutly; 4.01. 84
that was sent to me from the council pray'd me 5.02. 2
you have pray'd well to–day. COR 5.04. 55
pray'd you | to hold your hand more close. TIM 2.02.138
have you pray'd to–night, desdemon? OTH 5.02. 25
she restrain'd, | and pray'd me oft forbearance; CYM 2.05. 10
she pray'd me to excuse her keeping close, 3.05. 46
(i fast and pray'd for their intelligence) thus: 4.02.347

PRAYER 36 FR 0.0040 REL FR 27 V 9 P
is despair, | unless i be reliev'd by prayer, TMP ep 16
his worst fault is, that he is given to prayer; WIV 1.04. 13 P
will not miss you morning nor evening prayer, as 2.02. 99 P
unless you have the grace by your fair prayer MM 1.04. 69
events, with a prayer they may prove prosperous, 3.02.238 P
amen, amen, to that fair prayer, say i — | and MND 2.02. 62
the more my prayer, the lesser is my grace. 2.02. 89
lest the devil cross my prayer, for here he MV 3.01. 20 P
vow | to live in prayer and contemplation, 3.04. 28
and that same prayer doth teach us all to render 4.01.201
in vain, said many | a prayer upon her grave. WT 5.03.141
that mercy which true prayer ought to have. R2 5.03.110
as he is fam'd for mildness, peace, and prayer. 3H6 2.01.156
but if an humble prayer may prevail, | i then 4.06. 7
to your good prayer will scarcely say amen. R3 1.03. 21
to hear her prayer for them, as now for us! 3.03. 20
and see, a book of prayer in his hand — | true 3.07. 98
hath turn'd my feigned prayer on my head, | and 5.01. 21
book than thou learn /a prayer without book. TRO 2.01. 18 P
what, art thou devout? wast thou in prayer? 2.03. 35 P
not according to the prayer of the people, for COR 2.01. 4 P
in bootless prayer have they been held up, | and TIT 3.01. 75
being thus frighted, swears a prayer or two, ROM 1.04. 87
and what's in prayer but this twofold force, HAM 3.03. 48
but, o, what form of prayer | can serve my turn? 3.03. 51
to draw from her a prayer of earnest heart OTH 1.03.152
fasting and prayer, | much castigation, exercise 3.04. 40
but while i say one prayer! 5.02. 83
good isis, hear me this prayer, though thou deny ANT 1.02. 68 P
dear goddess, hear that prayer of the people! 1.02. 70 P
undo that prayer, by crying out as loud, | "o, 3.04. 17
prays, and destroys the prayer, no midway 3.04. 19
for so bad a prayer as his | was never yet for 4.09. 26
if you require a little space for prayer, | i PER 4.01. 67
but in the midst of his unfruitful prayer, LUC 344
for these dead birds sigh a prayer. PHT 67

PRAYER–BOOK 1 FR 0.0001 REL FR 1 V 0 P
and look you get a prayer–book in your hand, R3 3.07. 47

PRAYER–BOOKS 1 FR 0.0001 REL FR 1 V 0 P
wear prayer–books in my pocket, look demurely, MV 2.02.192

PRAYER'S 1 FR 0.0001 REL FR 1 V 0 P
then move not while my prayer's effect i take. ROM 1.05.106

PRAYERS' 1 FR 0.0001 REL FR 1 V 0 P
do not move, though grant for prayers' sake. ROM 1.05.105

/PRAYERS 3 FR 0.0003 REL FR 2 V 1 P
wind were but long enough /to /say /my /prayers, WIV 4.05.103 P
/and /all /their /prayers /and /love | /were 2H4 4.01.135
/as /begging /hermits /in /their /holy /prayers. TIT 3.02. 41

PRAYERS 88 FR 0.0099 REL FR 72 V 16 P
all lost! to prayers, to prayers! all lost! TMP 1.01. 51 P
all lost! to prayers, to prayers! all lost! 1.01. 51 P
the king and prince at prayers! 1.01. 54
chiefly that i might set it in my prayers — 3.01. 35
commend thy grievance to my holy prayers, | for TGV 1.01. 17
ere she sleep, has thrice her prayers said, WIV 5.05. 50
but with true prayers, | that shall be up at MM 2.02.151
ere sun–rise, prayers from preserved souls, 2.02.153
way going to temptation, | where prayers cross. 2.02.159
i'll pray a thousand prayers for thy death, | no 3.01.145
ever the duke return (as our prayers are he may) 3.02.155 P
i would desire you to clap into your prayers; 4.03. 42 P
man, | to yield possession to my holy prayers, ERR 4.04. 55
with wholesome syrups, drugs, and holy prayers, 5.01.104
and never rise until my tears and prayers | have 5.01.115
i say my prayers aloud. ADO 2.01.104 P
o that my prayers could such affection move! MND 1.01.197
i'll follow him no more with bootless prayers. MV 3.03. 20
can no prayers pierce thee? 4.01.126
how then might your prayers move? AYL 4.03. 55
thee may furnish, and my prayers pluck down, AWW 1.01. 69
when thou hast leisure, say thy prayers; 1.01.213 P
you had my prayers to lead them on, and to keep 2.04. 17 P
do so ever, though i took him at 's prayers. 2.05. 42 P
shut his bosom | against our borrowing prayers. 3.01. 9
unless her prayers, whom heaven delights to hear 3.04. 27
get him to say his prayers, good sir toby, get TN 3.04.118 P
my prayers, minx! 3.04.120 P
add proof unto mine armor with thy prayers, R2 1.03. 73
unto my mother's prayers i bend my knee. 5.03. 97
eyes do drop no tears, his prayers are in jest, 5.03.101
his prayers are full of false hypocrisy, | ours 5.03.107
our prayers do outpray his, then let them have 5.03.109
hearing how our plaints and prayers do pierce, 5.03.127
say thy prayers, and farewell. 1H4 5.01.124 P
and concludes in hearty prayers | that your 2H4 4.01. 14
i know thee not, old man, fall to thy prayers. 5.05. 47
and therefore he scorns to say his prayers, lest H5 3.02. 38 P
they have said their prayers, and they stay for 4.02. 56
the church's prayers made him so prosperous. 1H6 1.01. 32
i would prevail, if prayers might prevail, | to 3.01. 67
praise, and prayers | shall suffolk ever have of 5.03.173
love till death, my humble thanks, my prayers — 3H6 3.02. 62
with earnest prayers all to that effect. R3 2.02. 15
a book of prayers on their pillow lay, | which 4.03. 14
my prayers on the adverse party fight, | and 4.04.191
the prayers of holy saints and wronged souls, 5.03.241
their curses now | live where their prayers did; H8 1.02. 63
me, | make of your prayers one sweet sacrifice, 2.01. 77
my vows and prayers | yet are the king's; 2.01. 88
nor my prayers | are not words duly hallowed, 2.03. 67
yet prayers and wishes | are all i can return. 2.03. 69
he has my heart yet and shall have my prayers 3.01.180
but now i am past all comforts here but prayers. 4.02.123
my good mistress will | remember in my prayers. 5.01. 78
men's prayers then would seek you, not their 5.02.118
i have said my prayers, and devil envy say amen. TRO 2.03. 21 P
speedy strength, and visit her with my prayers; COR 1.03. 79 P
the prayers of priests nor times of sacrifice, 1.10. 21
take my prayers with you. 4.02. 44
thou barr'st us | our prayers to the gods, which 5.03.105
'longs more pride | than pity to our prayers. 5.03.171
dear heart, for heaven shall hear our prayers, TIT 3.01.210
i, that with base prayers | i should repent the 5.03.185
nor tears nor prayers shall purchase out abuses; ROM 3.01.193
if i could pray to move, prayers would move me; JC 3.01. 59
but they did say their prayers, and address'd MAC 2.02. 22
i'll send my prayers with him. 3.06. 49
put on with holy prayers, and 'tis spoken, | to 4.03.154
let not thy mother lose her prayers, hamlet, | i HAM 1.02.118
for charitable prayers, | /shards, flints, and 5.01.230
as my great patron thought on in my prayers — LR 1.01.142
with lunatic bans, sometime with prayers, 2.03. 19
so find we profit | by losing of our prayers. ANT 2.01. 8
before the gods my knee shall bow my prayers 2.03. 3
and on it said a century of prayers | (such as i CYM 4.02.391
which the people's prayers still fall upon you, PER 3.03. 19
madam, my thanks and prayers. 3.03. 34
come say your prayers. 4.01. 65
her master reasons, her prayers, her knees, that 4.06. 8 P
as cold as a snowball, saying his prayers too. 4.06.140 P
to close mine eyes, | or prayers to the gods. TNK 2.02. 94
next hear my prayers. 3.06.210
and before the gods | tender their holy prayers. 5.01. 2
i'll leave you to your prayers, and betwixt ye 5.01. 16
but she with vehement prayers urgeth still LUC 475
his ear her prayers admits, but his heart 558
sweet boy, but yet, like prayers divine, | i SON 108. 5

PRAYING 7 FR 0.0008 REL FR 5 V 2 P
we have been praying for our husbands' welfare, MV 5.01.114
of life in thee, from praying to purse–taking. 1H4 1.02.103 P
nay, that's past praying for, i have pepper'd 2.04.191 P
but praying, to enrich his watchful soul. R3 3.07. 77
they shall be praying nuns, not weeping queens; 4.04.202
wherein my letters, praying on his side, JC 4.03. 4
ne'er stood between, | praying for both parts. ANT 3.04. 14

PRAY'R 2 FR 0.0002 REL FR 2 V 0 P
vouchsafe my pray'r | may know if you remain TMP 1.02.423
ay, pilgrim, lips that they must use in pray'r. ROM 1.05.102

PRAY'RS 10 FR 0.0011 REL FR 10 V 0 P
upon which better part our pray'rs come in, | if JN 3.01.293
pray'rs and tears have mov'd me, gifts could 2H6 4.07. 68
if when you make your pray'rs, | god should be 4.07.114
if my deep pray'rs cannot appease thee, | but R3 1.04. 69
almost forgot my pray'rs to content him? H8 3.01.132
my pray'rs to heaven for you, my loyalty, 3.02.177
but my pray'rs | for ever and for ever shall be 3.02.426
and in thy pray'rs remember | th' estate of my 5.01. 73
and parted with | pray'rs for the provider. CYM 3.06. 52
sir, | as i shall here make trial of my pray'rs, TNK 1.01.193

/PRAYS 2 FR 0.0002 REL FR 2 V 0 P
have no more strength than her weak /prays. MND 3.02.250
he looks sadly, | and /prays the moor be safe; OTH 2.01. 33

PRAYS 19 FR 0.0021 REL FR 13 V 6 P
relish the petition well that prays for peace. MM 1.02. 16 P
and prays that you will hie you home to dinner. ERR 1.02. 90
my heart prays for him, though my tongue do 4.02. 28
and he heartily prays some occasion may detain ADO 1.01.150 P
he is no hypocrite, but prays from his heart. 1.01.151 P
beats her heart, tears her hair, prays, curses: 2.03.147 P
where she kneels and prays | for happy wedlock MV 5.01. 31
your father prays you leave your books, | and SHR 3.01. 82
toby, my lady prays you to have a care of him. TN 3.04. 92 P
he prays but faintly, and would be denied, | we R2 5.03.103
he prays you to save his life. H5 4.04. 44 P
who prays continually for richmond's good. R3 5.03. 84
own, and humbly prays you | that with your other TIM 2.02. 22
he humbly prays your speedy payment. 2.02. 28
you thus, | and prays you to believe him. OTH 1.03. 42
prays, and destroys the prayer, no midway ANT 3.04. 19
the poor fool prays her that he may depart. VEN 578
decays, | the guilty rebel for remission prays. LUC 714
light, | she prays she never may behold the day: 746

PRAY'ST 1 FR 0.0001 REL FR 1 V 0 P
thou pray'st not well. HAM 5.01.259

PREACH 4 FR 0.0004 REL FR 4 V 0 P
preach some philosophy to make me mad, | and JN 3.04. 51
i have heard you preach | that malice was a 1H6 3.01.127
i will preach to thee. LR 4.06.180
for fear of harms that preach in our behoof. LC 165

PREACH'D 3 FR 0.0003 REL FR 2 V 1 P
caves, | where manners ne'er were preach'd! TN 4.01. 49
but to have divinity preach'd there! PER 4.05. 4 P
he preach'd pure maid, and prais'd cold chastity LC 315

PREACHERS 1 FR 0.0001 REL FR 1 V 0 P
outward consciences | and preachers to us all, H5 4.01. 9

PREACHES 1 FR 0.0001 REL FR 1 V 0 P
my master preaches patience to him, and the ERR 5.01.174

PREACHING 1 FR 0.0001 REL FR 1 V 0 P
form and cause conjoin'd, preaching to stones, HAM 3.04.126
PREACHMENT 1 FR 0.0001 REL FR 1 V 0 P
and made a preachment of your high descent? 3H6 1.04. 72
PREAD *(also bread)*
PREAD 1 FR 0.0001 REL FR 0 V 1 P
to me, and prings me pread and salt yesterday, H5 5.01. 9 P
PREAMBULATE 1 FR 0.0001 REL FR 0 V 1 P
arts–man, preambulate, we will be singuled from LLL 5.01. 81 P
PRECEDENCE 2 FR 0.0002 REL FR 2 V 0 P
some obscure precedence that hath tofore been LLL 3.01. 82
"but yet," it does allay | the good precedence; ANT 2.05. 51
PRECEDENT *(also president*)*
PRECEDENT 7 FR 0.0008 REL FR 7 V 0 P
'twill be recorded for a precedent, | and many MV 4.01.220
lest barbarism (making me the precedent) WT 2.01. 84
the precedent was full as long a–doing, | and R3 3.06. 7
our own precedent passions do instruct us | what TIM 1.01.133
part the /tithe | of your precedent lord, a vice HAM 3.04. 98
once, | or thy precedent services are all | but ANT 4.14. 83
who ever shunn'd by precedent | the destin'd ill LC 155
PRECEDING 2 FR 0.0002 REL FR 2 V 0 P
of six preceding ancestors, that gem, AWW 5.03.196
as harbingers preceding still the fates | and HAM 1.01.122
PRECEPT 1 FR 0.0001 REL FR 1 V 0 P
in action all of precept, he did show me | the MM 4.01. 39
PRECEPTIAL 1 FR 0.0001 REL FR 1 V 0 P
before | would give preceptial med'cine to rage, ADO 5.01. 24
PRECEPTS 8 FR 0.0009 REL FR 7 V 1 P
and my father's precepts | i therein do forget. TMP 3.01. 58
i will bestow some precepts of this virgin AWW 3.05.100
those precepts cannot be serv'd; 2H4 5.01. 13 P
as send precepts to the leviathan | to come H5 3.03. 26
me | with precepts that would make invincible COR 4.01. 10
and never learn'd | the icy precepts of respect, TIM 4.03.258
and these few precepts in thy memory | look thou HAM 1.03. 58
what are precepts worth | of stale example? LC 267
/PRECHIA 1 FR 0.0001 REL FR 1 V 0 P
che non te /vede, che non te /prechia. LLL 4.02. 98
PRECINCT 1 FR 0.0001 REL FR 1 V 0 P
within her quarter and mine own precinct | i was 1H6 2.01. 68
/PRECIOUS 1 FR 0.0001 REL FR 1 V 0 P
/it /sends /some /precious /instance /of /itself HAM 4.05.163
PRECIOUS 79 FR 0.0089 REL FR 71 V 8 P
no, precious creature, | i had rather crack my TMP 3.01. 25
for love is still most precious in itself, | and TGV 2.06. 24
with juice of balm and every precious flow'r; WIV 5.05. 62
may counterpoise this rich and precious gift? ADO 4.01. 28
shall come apparell'd in more precious habit, 4.01.227
yourself, held precious in the world's esteem, LLL 2.01. 4
it adds a precious seeing to the eye: 4.03.330
that he did hold me dear | as precious eyesight, 5.02.445
nymph, divine and rare, | precious, celestial? MND 3.02.227
two stones, two rich and precious stones, MV 2.08. 20
two thousand ducats in that, and other precious, 3.01. 87 P
in that, and other precious, precious jewels. 3.01. 87 P
thy words are too precious to be cast away upon AYL 1.03. 4 P
wears yet a precious jewel in his head; 2.01. 14
by so much is a horn more precious than to want. 3.03. 63 P
what, is the jay more precious than the lark, SHR 4.03.175
your precious self had then not cross'd the eyes WT 1.02. 79
this jealousy | is for a precious creature: 1.02.452
loss of his most precious queen and children are 4.02. 24 P
my father will grant precious things as trifles. 5.01.222
would he do so, i'ld beg your precious mistress, 5.01.223
go together, | you precious winners all; 5.03.131
turning with splendor of his precious eye | the JN 3.01. 79
hair, | any annoyance in that precious sense! 4.01. 93
we hold our time too precious to be spent | with 5.02.161
tend'ring the precious safety of my prince, R2 1.01. 32
is crack'd, and all the precious liquor spilt, 1.02. 19
to set | the precious jewel of thy home return. 1.03.267
this precious stone set in the silver sea, 2.01. 46
and threat the glory of my precious crown. 3.03. 90
and thy precious rich crown for a pitiful bald 1H4 2.04.381 P
to blame | so idly to profane the precious time, 2H4 2.04.362
other, less fine in carat, /is more precious, 4.05.161
in an urn more precious | than the rich–jewell'd 1H6 1.06. 24
hand, | and set a precious crown upon thy head, 5.03.119
the precious image of our dear redeemer, | you R3 2.01.124
protest, | was it so precious to me as 'tis now. 3.02. 80
made precious by the foil | of england's chair, 5.03.250
as well wherein 'tis precious of itself | as in TRO 2.02. 55
no more my grief, in such a precious loss. 4.04. 10
and look'd upon things precious as they were COR 2.02.125
returns with precious lading to the bay | from TIT 1.01. 72
a precious ring that lightens all this hole, 2.03.227
the precious treasure of his eyesight lost. ROM 1.01.233
this precious book of love, this unbound lover, 1.03. 87
thence from her dead finger | a precious ring — 5.03. 31
o, what a precious comfort 'tis to have so many TIM 1.02.104 P
yellow, glittering, precious gold? 4.03. 26
those precious motives, those strong knots of MAC 4.03. 27
things were, | that were most precious to me. 4.03.223
that from a shelf the precious diadem stole, HAM 3.04.100
joys | which the most precious square of sense LR 1.01. 74
can buy this unpriz'd precious maid of me. 1.01.259
is strange | and can make vild things precious. 3.02. 71
rings, | their precious stones new lost; 5.03.191
make it a darling like your precious eye. OTH 3.04. 66
precious villain! 5.02.235
my precious queen, forbear, | and give true ANT 1.03. 73
have not seen the most precious diamond that is, CYM 1.04. 75 P
not | partition make with spectacles so precious 1.06. 37
the precious note of it with a base slave, | a 2.03.122
it from the queen, | what's in't is precious. 3.04.189
for he believes | it is a thing most precious. 3.05. 59
ah, you precious pandar! 3.05. 81
thou precious varlet, | my tailor made them not. 4.02. 83
which he said was precious | and cordial to me, 4.02.326
such precious deeds in one that promis'd nought 5.05. 9
you was not thought by me | a precious thing. 5.05.242
my precious maid, | those best affections that TNK 1.03. 8
were i to lose one — they are equal precious — 5.01.155
whose precious taste her thirsty lips well knew, VEN 543
hath dropp'd a precious jewel in the flood, | or 824
pain pays the income of each precious thing: LUC 334
weeds take root with precious flow'rs, | the 870
for precious friends hid in death's dateless SON 30. 6
i have no precious time at all to spend, | nor 57. 3
thy dial how thy precious minutes waste; 77. 2
and precious phrase by all the muses fil'd. 85. 4
thou art the fairest and most precious jewel. 131. 4
PRECIOUS–DEAR 1 FR 0.0001 REL FR 1 V 0 P
holds honor far more precious–dear than life. TRO 5.03. 28
PRECIOUS–JUICED 1 FR 0.0001 REL FR 1 V 0 P
with baleful weeds and precious–juiced flowers. ROM 2.03. 8
PRECIOUSLY 1 FR 0.0001 REL FR 1 V 0 P
now | must by us both be spent most preciously. TMP 1.02.241
PRECIOUS–PRINCELY
1 FR 0.0001 REL FR 1 V 0 P
found it too precious–princely for a grave. JN 4.03. 40
PRECIPIT 1 FR 0.0001 REL FR 1 V 0 P
you take a precipit for no leap of danger, | and H8 5.01.139
PRECIPITANCE 1 FR 0.0001 REL FR 1 V 0 P
that with cords, knives, drams, precipitance, TNK 1.01.142
PRECIPITATING 1 FR 0.0001 REL FR 1 V 0 P
air | (so many fathom down precipitating), LR 4.06. 50
PRECIPITATION 2 FR 0.0002 REL FR 2 V 0 P
that the precipitation might down stretch COR 3.02. 4
in peril of precipitation | from off the rock 3.03.102
/PRECISE 1 FR 0.0001 REL FR 1 V 0 P
/to /hold /your /honor /more /precise /and /nice 2H4 2.03. 40
PRECISE 5 FR 0.0005 REL FR 2 V 3 P
i can do to keep the terms of my honor precise. WIV 2.02. 22 P
and he was ever precise in promise–keeping. MM 1.02. 75 P
lord angelo is precise; 1.03. 50
but precise villains they are, that i am sure of 2.01. 54 P
taffata phrases, silken terms precise, LLL 5.02.406
PRECISELY 6 FR 0.0006 REL FR 2 V 4 P
even as one would say precisely, "thus i would TGV 4.04. 5 P
therefore precisely, can you carry your good WIV 1.01.230 P
tell me precisely of what complexion. LLL 1.02. 81 P
and indeed such a fellow, to say precisely, were AWW 2.02. 12 P
he knows | he cannot so precisely weed this land 2H4 4.01.203
of thinking too precisely on th' event — | a HAM 4.04. 41
PRECISENESS 1 FR 0.0001 REL FR 1 V 0 P
is all your strict preciseness come to this? 1H6 5.04. 67
PRECISIAN 1 FR 0.0001 REL FR 0 V 1 P
for though love use reason for his precisian, he WIV 2.01. 5 P
PRE–CONTRACT 1 FR 0.0001 REL FR 1 V 0 P
he is your husband on a pre–contract: MM 4.01. 71
PRECOR 1 FR 0.0001 REL FR 0 V 1 P
precor gelida quando /pecus /omne sub umbra LLL 4.02. 93 P
PRECURRER 1 FR 0.0001 REL FR 1 V 0 P
harbinger, | foul precurrer of the fiend, PHT 6
PRECURSE 1 FR 0.0001 REL FR 1 V 0 P
and even the like precurse of /fear'd events, HAM 1.01.121
PRECURSORS 1 FR 0.0001 REL FR 1 V 0 P
the precursors | o' th' dreadful thunder–claps, TMP 1.02.201
PREDECEAS'D 1 FR 0.0001 REL FR 0 V 1 P
worn as a memorable trophy of predeceas'd valor,
H5 5.01. 72 P
PREDECEASE 1 FR 0.0001 REL FR 1 V 0 P
if children predecease progenitors, | we are LUC 1756
PREDECESSOR 1 FR 0.0001 REL FR 1 V 0 P
in the right | of your great predecessor, king H5 1.02.248
PREDECESSORS 4 FR 0.0004 REL FR 3 V 1 P
yet | did to his predecessors part withal. H5 1.01. 81
is worth all your predecessors since deucalion, COR 2.01. 91 P
and | take to you, as your predecessors have, 2.02.143
the sacred store–house of his predecessors | and MAC 2.04. 34
PREDESTINATE 1 FR 0.0001 REL FR 0 V 1 P
other shall scape a predestinate scratch'd face. ADO 1.01.134 P
PREDICAMENT 3 FR 0.0003 REL FR 3 V 0 P
in which predicament i say thou stand'st; MV 4.01.357
to show the line and the predicament | wherein 1H4 1.03.168
piteous predicament! ROM 3.03. 86
PREDICT 1 FR 0.0001 REL FR 1 V 0 P
go well, | by oft predict that i in heaven find: SON 14. 8
PREDICTION 3 FR 0.0003 REL FR 1 V 2 P
and great prediction | of noble having and of MAC 1.03. 55
this villain of mine comes under the prediction; LR 1.02.110 P
brother, of a prediction i read this other day, 1.02.140 P
PREDICTIONS 1 FR 0.0001 REL FR 1 V 0 P
for these predictions | are to the world in JC 2.02. 28
PREDOMINANCE 3 FR 0.0003 REL FR 2 V 1 P
an observing kind | his humorous predominance; TRO 2.03.129
is't night's predominance, or the day's shame, MAC 2.04. 8
and treachers by spherical predominance; LR 1.02.123 P
PREDOMINANT 5 FR 0.0005 REL FR 4 V 1 P
when he was predominant. AWW 1.01.197 P
that will strike | where 'tis predominant; WT 1.02.202
foul subornation is predominant, | and equity 2H6 3.01.145
and where the worser is predominant, | full soon ROM 2.03. 29
your patience so predominant in your nature MAC 3.01. 86
PREDOMINATE 2 FR 0.0002 REL FR 1 V 1 P
shalt know i will predominate over the peasant, WIV 2.02.282 P
up, | let your close fire predominate his smoke, TIM 4.03.143
PREECHES *(also breeches)*
PREECHES 1 FR 0.0001 REL FR 0 V 1 P
/quae's, and your quod's, you must be preeches. WIV 4.01. 79 P
PRE–EMINENCE 2 FR 0.0002 REL FR 2 V 0 P
of more pre–eminence than fish and fowls, | are ERR 2.01. 23
pre–eminence, and all the large effects | that LR 1.01.131
PRE–EMPLOY'D 1 FR 0.0001 REL FR 1 V 0 P
whom i employ'd was pre–employ'd by him: WT 2.01. 49
PREFACE 2 FR 0.0002 REL FR 2 V 0 P
tale | is but a preface of her worthy praise. 1H6 5.05. 11
'twas an excellent dance, and for a preface, | i TNK 3.05.150
PREFER 21 FR 0.0023 REL FR 19 V 2 P
have i not reason to prefer mine own? TGV 2.04.156
and i will help thee to prefer her too: 2.04.157
him, | i have access my own love to prefer — 4.02. 4
you, know any such, | prefer them hither; SHR 1.01. 97
or who should study to prefer a peace, | if holy 1H6 3.01.110
and i will love thee and prefer thee for it. R3 4.02. 81
that prefer | a noble life before a long, and COR 3.01.152
this before all the world do i prefer, | this TIT 4.02.109
and ne'er prefer his injuries to his heart, | to TIM 3.05. 34
go | and presently prefer his suit to caesar. JC 3.01. 28
ay, if messala will prefer me to you. 5.05. 62
grace, | i would prefer him to a better place. LR 1.01.274
of modern seeming do prefer against him. OTH 1.03.109
by the means i shall then have to prefer them; 2.01.278 P
you must not so far prefer her 'fore ours of CYM 1.04. 65 P
vantages that may | prefer you to his daughter. 2.03. 46
not sooner | than thine own worth prefer thee. 4.02.386
ere i arise, i will prefer my sons; 5.05.326
who is the first that doth prefer himself? PER 2.02. 17
and happiness prefer me to a place | where i may TNK 2.03. 81
that shall prefer and undertake my troth.' LC 280
PREFERMENT 11 FR 0.0012 REL FR 7 V 4 P
put forth their sons to seek preferment out: TGV 1.03. 7
if it be preferment | to leave a rich jew's MV 2.02.146
to me, | in the preferment of the eldest sister. SHR 2.01. 93
life in me, would preferment drop on my head. WT 5.02.114 P
while these do labor for their own preferment, 2H6 1.01.181
preferment falls on him that cuts him off. LR 4.05. 38
preferment goes by letter and affection, | and OTH 1.01. 36
move the king | to any shape of thy preferment, CYM 1.05. 71
for thy relief nor my voice for thy preferment. 3.05.115 P
and true preferment shall tender itself to thee. 3.05.154 P
profit, but my wish hath a preferment in't. 5.04.206 P
PREFERMENTS 2 FR 0.0002 REL FR 2 V 0 P
she may help you to many fair preferments, | and R3 1.03. 94
stands in the gap and trade of moe preferments, H8 5.01. 36
PREFERR'D 12 FR 0.0013 REL FR 11 V 1 P
whose sovereignty so oft thou hast preferr'd TGV 2.06. 15
short and the long is, our play is preferr'd. MND 4.02. 39 P
and hath preferr'd thee, if it be preferment MV 2.02.146
although in writing i preferr'd | the manner of 1H6 3.01. 10
us | in our opinions she should be preferr'd. 5.05. 61
why somerset should be preferr'd in this. 2H6 1.03.114
because my book preferr'd me to the king; 4.07. 72
newly preferr'd from the king's secretary, | the H8 4.01.102
why then preferr'd you not your sums and bills TIM 3.04. 49
i'll have preferr'd him | a chalice for the HAM 4.07.159
and hated | for being preferr'd so well. CYM 2.03.131
boy, he's preferr'd | by thee to us, and he 4.02.400
PREFERRETH 1 FR 0.0001 REL FR 1 V 0 P
who preferreth peace | more than i do, except i 1H6 3.01. 33
PREFERRING 1 FR 0.0001 REL FR 1 V 0 P
to you, preferring you before her father, | so OTH 1.03.187
PREFERS 1 FR 0.0001 REL FR 1 V 0 P
of so quick condition | that it prefers itself, MM 1.01. 54
PREFER'ST 1 FR 0.0001 REL FR 1 V 0 P
but thou prefer'st thy life before thine honor; 3H6 1.01.246
PREFIGURING 1 FR 0.0001 REL FR 1 V 0 P
of this our time, all you prefiguring, | and, SON 106.10
PREFIX'D 4 FR 0.0004 REL FR 4 V 0 P
the hour draws on | prefix'd by angelo. MM 4.03. 79
month behind the gest | prefix'd for 's parting; WT 1.02. 42
and the hour prefix'd | for her delivery to this TRO 4.03. 1
this quarrel | sleep till the hour prefix'd, and TNK 3.06.304
PREFIXED 1 FR 0.0001 REL FR 1 V 0 P
all alone, | at the prefixed hour of her waking, ROM 5.03.253
PREFORMED 1 FR 0.0001 REL FR 1 V 0 P
their natures, and preformed faculties, | to JC 1.03. 67
PREGNANCY 1 FR 0.0001 REL FR 0 V 1 P
pregnancy is made a tapster, and his quick wit 2H4 1.02.170 P
PREGNANT* 16 FR 0.0018 REL FR 11 V 5 P
y' are as pregnant in | as art and practice hath MM 1.01. 11
'tis very pregnant, | the jewel that we find, we 2.01. 23
wherein the pregnant enemy does much. TN 2.02. 28
to your own most pregnant and vouchsafed ear. 3.01. 89 P
"odors," "pregnant," and "vouchsafed"; 3.01. 90 P
if ever truth were pregnant by circumstance. WT 5.02. 30 P
the grecians are most prompt and pregnant — TRO 4.04. 88
how pregnant sometimes his replies are! HAM 2.02.209 P
and crook the pregnant hinges of the knee 3.02. 61
death | were very pregnant and potential spirits LR 2.01. 76
and feeling sorrows, | am pregnant to good pity. 4.06.223
(as it is a most pregnant and unforc'd position) OTH 2.01.236 P
'twere pregnant they should square between ANT 2.01. 45
o, 'tis pregnant, pregnant! CYM 4.02.325
o, 'tis pregnant, pregnant! 4.02.325
dionyza hath | the pregnant instrument of wrath PER 4.ch. 44
PREGNANTLY 1 FR 0.0001 REL FR 1 V 0 P
blows of fortune's | more pregnantly than words. TIM 1.01. 92
PREJUDICATES 1 FR 0.0001 REL FR 1 V 0 P
our dearest friend | prejudicates the business, AWW 1.02. 8
PREJUDICE 4 FR 0.0004 REL FR 4 V 0 P
powers, | and seek how we may prejudice the foe. 1H6 3.03. 91
through their amity | breed him some prejudice; H8 1.01.182
be to the prejudice of her present state, | or 2.04.155
gives | the prejudice of disparity, value's TNK 5.03. 88
PREJUDICIAL 1 FR 0.0001 REL FR 1 V 0 P
think you 'twere prejudicial to his crown? 3H6 1.01.144
PRELATE 9 FR 0.0010 REL FR 9 V 0 P
creep | of that same noble prelate well belov'd, 1H4 1.03.267
to meet northumberland and the prelate scroop, 5.05. 37
you would desire the king were made a prelate; H5 1.01. 40
arrogant winchester, that haughty prelate, 1H6 1.03. 23
no, prelate, such is thy audacious wickedness, 3.01. 14
and am not i a prelate of the church? 3.01. 46
humbler, | it fitteth not a prelate so to plead. 3.01. 57
proud prelate, in thy face | i see thy fury. 2H6 1.01.142
sir edward courtney and the haughty prelate, R3 4.04.500
PREMEDITATE 1 FR 0.0001 REL FR 1 V 0 P
here pale with fear he doth premeditate | the LUC 183
PREMEDITATED 3 FR 0.0003 REL FR 2 V 1 P
to greet me with premeditated welcomes; MND 5.01. 94
on them the guilt of premeditated and contriv'd H5 4.01.162 P
com'st thou with deep premeditated lines, | with 1H6 3.01. 1
PREMEDITATING 1 FR 0.0001 REL FR 1 V 0 P
your premeditating | more than their actions; TNK 1.01.136
PREMEDITATION 1 FR 0.0001 REL FR 1 V 0 P
a cold premeditation for my purpose! 3H6 3.02.133
PREMISED 1 FR 0.0001 REL FR 1 V 0 P
and the premised flames of the last day | knit 2H6 5.02. 41
PREMISES 3 FR 0.0003 REL FR 3 V 0 P
which was, that he, in lieu o' th' premises, TMP 1.02.123
here is my hand, the premises observ'd, | thy AWW 2.01.201
't has done, upon the premises, but justice; H8 2.01. 63
PRENEZ 1 FR 0.0001 REL FR 0 V 1 P
o, prenez misericorde! ayez pitie de moi! H5 4.04. 12 P
PRENOMINATE 2 FR 0.0002 REL FR 2 V 0 P
as to prenominate in nice conjecture | where TRO 4.05.250
having ever seen in the prenominate crimes | the HAM 2.01. 43
PRENTICE 3 FR 0.0003 REL FR 0 V 3 P
'a was a botcher's prentice in paris, from AWW 4.03.185 P
from a prince to a prentice? 2H4 2.02.174 P
my accuser is my prentice, and when i did 2H6 1.03.198 P

/PRENTICES 1 FR 0.0001 REL FR 0 V 1 P
how say you now, /prentices? STM II.C 22 P
PRENTICES 5 FR 0.0005 REL FR 0 V 5 P
fight for credit of the prentices. 2H6 2.03. 71 P
is merely to the undoing of poor prentices, for STM II.C 9 P
prentices simple, down with him! II.C 22 P
prentices simple, prentices simple! II.C 23 P
prentices simple, prentices simple! II.C 23 P
PRENZIE 2 FR 0.0002 REL FR 2 V 0 P
the prenzie angelo? MM 3.01. 93
body to invest and cover | in prenzie guards! 3.01. 96
PREOCCUPIED 1 FR 0.0001 REL FR 1 V 0 P
preoccupied with what you rather must do | than COR 2.03.232
PREORDAIN'D 1 FR 0.0001 REL FR 0 V 1 P
again to execute their preordain'd faculties, TNK 4.03. 72 P
PREORDINANCE 1 FR 0.0001 REL FR 1 V 0 P
and turn preordinance and first decree | into JC 3.01. 38
PREPARATION 28 FR 0.0031 REL FR 17 V 11 P
to press with so little preparation upon you. WIV 2.02.156 P
me dat you make grand preparation for a duke de 4.05. 87 P
divines, and have all charitable preparation. MM 3.02.209 P
for indeed he hath made great preparation. ADO 1.01.278 P
assurance, and all the preparation overthrown. 2.02. 49 P
we have not made good preparation. MV 2.04. 4
put myself into my mortal preparation; AWW 3.06. 76 P
dismount thy tuck, be yare in thy preparation, TN 3.04.224 P
all preparation for a bloody siege | and JN 2.01.213
never such a pow'r | for any foreign preparation 4.02.111
speedily, | with strong and mighty preparation. 1H4 4.01. 93
of this most dreadful preparation, | shake in H5 2.pr. 13
rivets up, | give dreadful note of preparation. 4.pr. 14
lost wherein such preparation was gain'd; 4.01.182 P
take my leave, | to go about my preparation. 1H6 1.01.166
these three lead on this preparation | whither COR 1.02. 15
they are in a most warlike preparation, and hope 4.03. 17 P
so, | would have inform'd for preparation. MAC 1.05. 33
your royal preparation | makes us hear something 5.03. 57
to be a preparation 'gainst the polack; HAM 2.02. 63
you are going, to a most /festinate preparation; LR 3.07. 10 P
our preparation stands | in expectation of them. 4.04. 22
the turkish preparation makes for rhodes, | so OTH 1.03. 14
with a most mighty preparation makes for cyprus. 1.03.221 P
i'll raise the preparation of a war | shall ANT 3.04. 26
their preparation is to-day by sea, | we please 4.10. 1
that's the way | to fool their preparation, and 5.02.225
your preparation can affront no less | than what CYM 4.03. 29
PREPARATIONS 3 FR 0.0003 REL FR 2 V 1 P
war-like, court-like, and learned preparations. WIV 2.02.228 P
but that defenses, musters, preparations, H5 2.04. 18
it, | is the main motive of our preparations, HAM 1.01.105
PREPAR'D 34 FR 0.0038 REL FR 29 V 5 P
bring him his confessor, let him be prepar'd, MM 2.01. 35
he's not prepar'd for death. 2.02. 84
i have hope to live, and am prepar'd to die. 3.01. 4
me desire to know how you find claudio prepar'd. 3.02.239 P
she may be the better prepar'd for an answer, if ADO 1.02. 22 P
i am arm'd and well prepar'd. MV 4.01.264
i'll go seek the duke, his banket is prepar'd. AYL 2.05. 62 P
and have prepar'd great store of wedding cheer, SHR 3.02.186
prepar'd i was not | for such a business; AWW 2.05. 61
our waggon is prepar'd, and time revives us. 4.04. 34
fast by, but not prepar'd | for this design. WT 4.04.501
let them be welcome then, we are prepar'd. JN 2.01. 83
he is prepar'd, and reason too he should — 5.02.130
and is well prepar'd | to whip this dwarfish war 5.02.134
why then the champions are prepar'd, and stay R2 1.03. 5
mine ear is open, and my heart prepar'd, | the 3.02. 93
we are prepar'd. 1H4 2.03. 35 P
i, | make fearful musters and prepar'd defense, 2H4 in 12
now are we well prepar'd to know the pleasure H5 1.02.234
i am prepar'd; 1H6 1.02. 98
the queen | to a prepar'd place in the choir, H8 4.01. 64
you'll find | th' have not prepar'd for us. COR 1.02. 30
for they are prepar'd | with accusations, as i 3.02.139
me, | who am prepar'd against your territories, 4.05.134
for that i am prepar'd and full resolv'd, TIT 2.01. 57
the fiery tybalt, with his sword prepar'd, ROM 1.01.109
therefore, good brutus, be prepar'd to hear; JC 1.02. 66
will not, come when you are next prepar'd for. OTH 4.01.160 P
but be prepar'd to know | the purposes i bear; ANT 1.03. 66
i came before you here a man prepar'd | to take 2.06. 40
go, make thee ready, | our letters are prepar'd. 3.03. 38
hearing that you prepar'd for war, acquainted 3.06. 58
refusing him at sea, | being prepar'd for land. 3.07. 40
a place prepar'd for those that sleep in honor, TNK 3.06. 99
PREPARE 67 FR 0.0075 REL FR 59 V 8 P
spirit, | we must prepare to meet with caliban. TMP 4.01.166
therefore prepare yourself to death. MM 3.01.167 P
well, go, prepare yourself. 4.02. 69
and i will have more time to prepare me, or they 4.03. 54 P
who do prepare to meet him at the gates, | there 4.03.131
prepare, madam, prepare! LLL 5.02. 81
prepare, madam, prepare! 5.02. 81
go bid them prepare. 5.02.509 P
boyet, prepare, i will away to-night. 5.02.727
prepare, i say. 5.02.729
upon that day either prepare to die | for MND 1.01. 86
will you prepare you for this masque to-night? MV 2.04. 22
go in, sirrah, bid them prepare for dinner. 3.05. 46 P
then bid them prepare dinner! 3.05. 50 P
you must prepare your bosom for his knife — 4.01.245
most learned judge! a sentence! come, prepare! 4.01.304
therefore prepare thee to cut off the flesh. 4.01.324
and ceremoniously let us prepare | some welcome 5.01. 37
go you and prepare aliena; AYL 5.02. 15 P
of white, stuck all with yew, | o, prepare it! TN 2.04. 56
prepare you, lords, | summon a session, that we WT 2.03.201
prepare | to see the life as lively mock'd as 5.03. 18
to parley or to fight, therefore prepare. JN 2.01. 78
come, boy, prepare yourself. 4.01. 89
for when you should be told they do prepare, 4.02.114
sometimes queen, prepare thee hence for france. R2 5.01. 37
my lord, prepare, the king comes on apace. 1H4 5.02. 89
and to teach others how they should prepare. H5 4.01.185 P
bid him prepare, for i will cut his throat. 4.04. 32
'fore the king | seems to prepare his way. 5.pr. 13
prepare we for our marriage; 5.02.370
you do prepare to ride unto saint albons, 2H6 1.02. 57
and i'll prepare | my tear-stain'd eyes to see 2.04. 15
behalf | go levy men, and make prepare for war; 3H6 4.01.131
prepare you, lords, for edward is at hand, 5.04. 60
never, my lord, therefore prepare to die. R3 1.04.180
prepare her ears to hear a wooer's tale; 4.04.327
be — | prepare thy battle early in the morning, 5.03. 88
prepare there, | the duke is coming. H8 2.01. 97
and to prepare the ways | you have for dignities 3.02.328
you must prepare to fight without achilles. TRO 2.03.227
prepare thy brow to frown. know'st thou me yet? COR 4.05. 63
back to rome, and prepare for your execution. 5.02. 48 P
titus, prepare thy aged eyes to weep, | or, if TIT 3.01. 59
and now prepare your throats. 5.02.196
nay, gentlemen, prepare not to be gone, | we ROM 1.05.121
do so, and bid my sweet prepare to chide. 3.03.162
prepare her, wife, against this wedding-day. 3.04. 32
paris, to prepare up him | against to-morrow. 4.02. 45
every one prepare | to follow this fair corse 4.05. 92
then, timon, presently prepare thy grave; TIM 4.03.377
in, and prepare: 5.02. 16
bid them prepare within; JC 2.02.118
prepare the body then, and follow us. 3.01.253
if you have tears, prepare to shed them now. 3.02.169
prepare to lodge their companies to-night. 4.03.140
prepare you, generals. 5.01. 12
therefore prepare you. HAM 3.03. 2
therefore prepare thyself, | the bark is ready, 4.03. 43
prepare for dinner. LR 1.03. 26
prepare my horses. 1.04.258
and by those fearful objects to prepare | this PER 1.01. 43
prepare for mirth, for mirth becomes a feast. 2.03. 7
a present murderer does prepare | for good 4.ch. 38
bid him with speed prepare to carry it, | the LUC 1294
against this coming end you should prepare, SON 13. 3
and to his palate doth prepare the cup. 114.12
PREPARED 5 FR 0.0005 REL FR 5 V 0 P
where they prepared | a rotten carcass of a butt TMP 1.02.145
we have with a leaven'd and prepared choice MM 1.01. 51
so cries a pig prepared to the spit. TIT 4.02.146
with his prepared sword he charges home | my LR 2.01. 51
plough thy visage up | with her prepared nails. ANT 4.12. 39
PREPAREDLY 1 FR 0.0001 REL FR 1 V 0 P
that she preparedly may frame herself | to th' ANT 5.01. 55
PREPARES 4 FR 0.0004 REL FR 4 V 0 P
king that he | prepares for some attempt of war. MAC 3.06. 39
to bid the wind a base he now prepares, | and VEN 303
her maid is gone, and she prepares to write, LUC 1296
she modestly prepares to let them know | her 1607
PREPARING 2 FR 0.0002 REL FR 1 V 1 P
the dolphin is preparing hitherward, | where JN 5.07. 59
thou art preparing fire for us; COR 5.02. 71 P
PREPOSTEROUS 5 FR 0.0005 REL FR 3 V 2 P
preposterous ass, that never read so far | to SHR 3.01. 9
luck, being in so preposterous estate as we are. WT 5.02.148 P
devil" were alike, | and both preposterous; 3H6 5.06. 5
o, preposterous | and frantic outrage, end thy R3 2.04. 63
and take again such preposterous discoveries! TRO 5.01. 23 P
PREPOSTEROUSLY 3 FR 0.0003 REL FR 2 V 1 P
you prescribe to yourself very preposterously. WIV 2.02.241 P
that wrought upon thee so preposterously | hath H5 2.02.112
that it could so preposterously be stain'd, | to SON 109.11
PREPOST'ROUS 2 FR 0.0002 REL FR 0 V 2 P
obscene and most prepost'rous event that draweth LLL 1.01.242 P
conduct us to most prepost'rous conclusions. OTH 1.03.329 P
PREPOST'ROUSLY 2 FR 0.0002 REL FR 2 V 0 P
do best please me | that befall prepost'rously. MND 3.02.121
for nature so prepost'rously to err | (being not OTH 1.03. 62
PREROGATIFES 1 FR 0.0001 REL FR 0 V 1 P
and aunchient prerogatifes and laws of the wars H5 4.01. 67 P
PREROGATIV'D 1 FR 0.0001 REL FR 1 V 0 P
prerogativ'd are they less than the base; OTH 3.03.274
PREROGATIVE 9 FR 0.0010 REL FR 8 V 1 P
outward face of royalty | with all prerogative. TMP 1.02.105
then give me leave to have prerogative, | and SHR 3.01. 6
the great prerogative and rite of love, | which, AWW 2.04. 41
niece, give me this prerogative of speech" — TN 2.05. 70 P
our prerogative | calls not your counsels, but WT 2.01.163
detract so much from that prerogative | as to be 1H6 5.04.142
prerogative of age, crowns, sceptres, laurels, TRO 1.03.107
insisting on the old prerogative | and power i' COR 3.03. 17
life | to take prerogative and tithe of knees STM III 9
PRESAGE 8 FR 0.0009 REL FR 7 V 1 P
away, | let it presage the ruin of your love, MV 3.02.173
bears in his visage no great presage of cruelty. TN 3.02. 65 P
wrath, | and sullen presage of your own decay. JN 1.01. 28
but that it doth presage some ill event. 1H6 4.01.191
my dreams presage some joyful news at hand. ROM 5.01. 2
and partly credit things that do presage. JC 5.01. 78
this ill presage advisedly she marketh: VEN 457
and the sad augurs mock their own presage, SON 107. 6
PRESAGERS 1 FR 0.0001 REL FR 1 V 0 P
and dumb presagers of my speaking breast, | who SON 23.10
PRESAGES 5 FR 0.0005 REL FR 4 V 1 P
i have a mind presages me such thrift | that i MV 1.01.175
abortives, presages, and tongues of heaven, JN 3.04.158
if heart's presages be not vain, | we three here R2 2.02.142
whose face between her forks presages snow; LR 4.06.119
there's a palm presages chastity, if nothing ANT 1.02. 47 P
PRESAGETH 2 FR 0.0002 REL FR 1 V 1 P
my mind presageth happy gain and conquest. 3H6 5.01. 71
e'en as the o'erflowing nilus presageth famine. ANT 1.02. 49 P
PRESAGING 1 FR 0.0001 REL FR 1 V 0 P
as henry's late presaging prophecy | did glad my 3H6 4.06. 92
PRESCIENCE 4 FR 0.0004 REL FR 3 V 1 P
and by my prescience | i find my zenith doth TMP 1.02.180
forestall prescience, and esteem no act | but TRO 1.03.199
vex not his prescience, be attentive. ANT 1.02. 21 P
which in her prescience she controlled still, LUC 727
PRESCRIB'D 1 FR 0.0001 REL FR 1 V 0 P
prescrib'd his pow'r, | confin'd to exhibition? LR 1.02. 24
PRESCRIBE 4 FR 0.0004 REL FR 3 V 1 P
methinks you prescribe to yourself very WIV 2.02.240 P
this we prescribe, though no physician; R2 1.01.154
each | prescribe to other as each other's leech. TIM 5.04. 84
prescribe not us our duty. LR 1.01.276
PRESCRIPT 2 FR 0.0002 REL FR 1 V 1 P
which is the prescript praise and perfection of H5 3.07. 46 P
do not exceed | the prescript of this scroll. ANT 3.08. 5
PRESCRIPTION 4 FR 0.0004 REL FR 2 V 2 P
to make prescription for a kingdom's worth. 3H6 3.03. 94
you, and i'll go along | by your prescription; H8 1.01.151
the most sovereign prescription in galen is but COR 2.01.116 P
and then have we a prescription to die, when OTH 1.03.309 P
PRESCRIPTIONS 3 FR 0.0003 REL FR 2 V 1 P
you know my father left me some prescriptions AWW 1.03.221
be your patient to follow your prescriptions, 2H4 1.02.129 P
angry that his prescriptions are not kept, SON 147. 6
PRESCRIPTS 1 FR 0.0001 REL FR 1 V 0 P
and then i prescripts gave her, | that she HAM 2.02.142
/PRESENCE 2 FR 0.0002 REL FR 2 V 0 P
/she /took /them, /read /them /in /my /presence, LR 4.03. 11
is't not a goodly /presence? PER 5.01. 66
PRESENCE 107 FR 0.0121 REL FR 95 V 12 P
repair me with thy presence, silvia; TGV 5.04. 11
and me, when he approacheth to your presence. 5.04. 32
with men | but in the presence of the prioress; MM 1.04. 11
in obsequious fondness | crowd to his presence, 2.04. 29
bear a fair presence, though your heart be ERR 3.02. 13
of such enchanting presence and discourse, 3.02.161
i promised your presence and the chain, | but 4.01. 23
convert to disdain, if you come in her presence. ADO 1.01.123 P
excepting your worship's presence, ha' ta'en a 3.05. 31 P
a doubt | presence majestical would put him out; LLL 5.02.102
here is like to be a good presence of worthies: 5.02.533 P
which parti-coated presence of loose love | put 5.02.766
in such a presence here to plead my thoughts; MND 1.01. 61
do, as a monster, fly my presence thus. 2.02. 97
and from thy hated presence part i /so: 3.02. 80
hecat's team | from the presence of the sun, 5.01.385
with no less presence, but with much more love, MV 3.02. 54
madam, although i speak it in your presence, 3.04. 1
young men, of excellent growth and presence. AYL 1.02.122 P
haply my presence | may well abate the SHR in.1. 136
for his presence must be the whip of the other. AWW 4.03. 36 P
of power you have | to come into his presence. 5.01. 21
therefore in my presence still smile, dear my TN 2.05.177 P
yet of your royal presence i'll adventure | the WT 1.02. 38
of my body, from his presence | i am barr'd, 3.02. 97
flaunts, behold | the sternness of his presence? 4.04. 24
tender your persons to his presence, whisper him 4.04.796 P
beheld), desires access | to your high presence. 5.01. 88
lord of thy presence and no land beside? JN 1.01.137
it ill beseems this presence to cry aim | to 2.01.196
lord of our presence, angiers, and of you. 2.01.367
up | her presence would have interrupted much. 2.01.542
the king by me requests your presence straight. 4.03. 22
then call them to our presence; R2 1.01. 15
come i appellant to this princely presence. 1.01. 34
what presence must not know, | from where you do 1.03.249
whereon thou tread'st the presence strow'd, 1.03.289
your presence makes us rich, most noble lord. 2.03. 63
to pay their aweful duty to our presence? 3.03. 76
in all this presence that hath mov'd me so. 4.01. 32
'tis very true, you were in presence then, | and 4.01. 62
worst in this royal presence may i speak, | yet 4.01.115
would god that any in this noble presence | were 4.01.117
thou hast a traitor in thy presence there. 5.03. 40
sir, your presence is too bold and peremptory, 1H4 1.03. 17
had i so lavish of my presence been, | so 3.02. 39
even in the presence of the crowned king. 3.02. 54
my presence, like a robe pontifical, | ne'er 3.02. 56
being with his presence glutted, gorg'd, and 3.02. 84
no, my good lord, he is in presence here. 2H4 4.04. 17
not here in presence. H5 1.02. 2
unless the dolphin be in presence here, | to 2.04.111
victory | we with our stately presence glorify, 1H6 1.01. 21
the presence of a king engenders love | amongst 3.01.180
in presence of the kings of france and sicil, 2H6 1.01. 6
but 'tis my presence that doth trouble ye; 1.01.141
all in this presence are thy betters, warwick. 1.03.111
have i overcome mine enemies in this presence? 2.03. 98 P
go call our uncle to our presence straight. 3.02. 15
and that my sovereign's presence makes me mild, 3.02.219
if from this presence thou dar'st go with me. 3.02.228
wrathful weapons drawn | here in our presence? 3.02.238
be it known unto thee by these presence, even 4.07. 30 P
presence, even the presence of lord mortimer, 4.07. 30 P
may pass into the presence of a king, | lo, i 5.01. 65
what's he approacheth boldly to our presence? 3H6 3.03. 44
for 'tis thy presence that exhales this blood R3 1.02. 58
and sent to warn them to his royal presence. 1.03. 39
to who in all this presence speaks your grace? 1.03. 54
i will avouch't in presence of the king. 1.03.114
that is hardly borne | /by any in this presence, 2.01. 59
this, | to be so flouted in this royal presence? 2.01. 79
and no man in the presence | but his red color 2.01. 85
which by my presence might have been concluded. 3.04. 25
makes me most forward in this princely presence 3.04. 64
best, now worst, | as presence did present them: H8 1.01. 30
salisbury, | made suit to come in 's presence; 1.02.197
'em nobly and conduct 'em | into our presence, 1.04. 59
the two great cardinals | wait in the presence. 3.01. 17
i' th' presence | he would say untruths, and be 4.02. 37
and in my presence | they are too thin and base 5.02.159
i have receiv'd much honor by your presence, 5.04. 71
and her presence | shall quite strike off all TRO 3.03. 28
i will put on his presence, let patroclus make 3.03.271 P
and that not in the presence | of dreaded COR 3.03. 97
rome | desires to be admitted to your presence. TIT 5.01.153
and by her presence still renew his sorrows. 5.03. 42
show a fair presence and put off these frowns, ROM 1.05. 73
this vault a feasting presence full of light. 5.03. 86
in the presence of thy corse? JC 3.01.199
supper, sir, | and i'll request your presence. MAC 3.01. 15
he fail'd | his presence at the tyrant's feast, 3.06. 22
be something scanter of your maiden presence, HAM 1.03.121
heavens make our presence and our practices 2.02. 38
this presence knows, | and you must needs have 5.02.228
forbear his presence until some little time hath LR 1.02.161 P
by you invited, do attend your presence. OTH 3.03.281
you wrong this presence, therefore speak no more ANT 2.02.109
your presence needs must puzzle antony, | take 3.07. 10
that will not be denied your highness' presence. 5.02.234
the offender, | and take him from our presence. CYM 5.05.301

to glad her presence, | the senate–house of PER 1.01. 9
your presence glads our days. 2.03. 21
who can be other in this royal presence? 2.03. 49
blest a /place | with thy sole presence. TNK 3.01. 11
be as thy presence is gracious and kind, | or to SON 10.11
he live, | and with his presence grace impiety, 67. 2
PRESENCES 1 FR 0.0001 REL FR 1 V 0 P
your royal presences be rul'd by me: JN 2.01.377
/PRESENT* 3 FR 0.0003 REL FR 3 V 0 P
/yes, /if /this /present /quality /of /war — 2H4 1.03. 36
/things /present /worst. 1.03.108
/from /the /king /or /in /the /present /time, 4.01.106
PRESENT* 259 FR 0.0292 REL FR 214 V 45 P
and work the peace of the present, we will not TMP 1.01. 22 P
and then i'll bring thee to the present business 1.02.136
he's a present for any emperor that ever trod on 2.02. 70 P
for some of you there present | are worse than 3.03. 35
confines call'd to enact | my present fancies. 4.01.122
and myself present | as i was sometime milan. 5.01. 85
your own present folly, and her passing TGV 2.01. 75 P
but she did scorn a present that i sent her. 3.01. 92
he must carry for a present to his lady. 4.02. 79 P
to deliver him as a present to mistress silvia 4.04. 7 P
thanks is good enough for such a present. 4.04. 50 P
the folly of my soul dares not present itself; WIV 2.02.244 P
being known, | we'll all present ourselves; 4.04. 64
must my sweet nan present the fairy queen; 4.06. 20
besides, i'll make a present recompense. 4.06. 55
sign me a present pardon for my brother, | or MM 2.04.152
if not, use him for the present and dismiss him. 4.02. 25 P
and fearless of what's past, present, or to come 4.02.144 P
you are to do me both a present and a dangerous 4.02.161 P
i will give him a present shrift and advise him 4.02.207 P
my present business calls me from you now. ERR 1.02. 29
therefore make present satisfaction, | or i'll 4.01. 5
i am not furnish'd with the present money: 4.01. 34
besides this present instance of his rage, | is 4.03. 87
and sure (unless you send some present help) 5.01.176
and till this present hour | my heavy burthen 5.01.402
he meant to take the present time by the top, ADO 1.02. 15 P
if not a present remedy, at least a patient 1.03. 8 P
are to present the prince's own person. 3.03. 75 P
th' endeavor of this present breath may buy LLL 1.01. 5
what present hast thou there? 4.03.187
that the king would have me present the princess 5.01.110 P
you shall present before her the nine worthies. 5.01.117 P
say none so fit as to present the nine worthies. 5.01.123 P
will you find men worthy enough to present them? 5.01.125 P
he shall present hercules in minority; 5.01.133 P
will change habits, and present the other five. 5.02.539
and say he comes to disfigure, or to present, MND 3.01. 61 P
some man or other must present wall; 3.01. 67 P
with lime and rough–cast, doth present | wall, 5.01.131
that i, one /snout by name, present a wall; 5.01.156
this lanthorn doth the horned moon present — 5.01.239
this lanthorn doth the horned moon present; 5.01.244
estate | upon the fortune of this present year: MV 1.01. 44
i money nor commodity | to raise a present sum; 1.01.179
i am debating of my present store, | and, by the 1.03. 53
supply your present wants, and take no doit | of 1.03.140
i have brought him a present. 2.02.101 P
give him a present! 2.02.105 P
give me your present to one master bassanio, who 2.02.108 P
he had | the present money to discharge the jew, 3.02.273
that holds this present question in the court? 4.01.172
absent argument | of my revenge, thou present. AYL 3.01. 4
let's present him to the duke like a roman 4.02. 3 P
and mark what object did present itself | under 4.03.103
and therefore take the present time, | with a 5.03. 30
and now by present profession a tinker? SHR in.2. 20 P
and say you would present her at the leet, in.2. 87
i do present you with a man of mine, | cunning 2.01. 55
door | upon entreaty have a present alms, | if 4.03. 5
'twere deadly sickness or else present death. 4.03. 14
this, | and urge her to a present answer back. AWW 2.02. 64
his present gift | shall furnish me to those 2.03.289
have procur'd his leave | for present parting; 2.05. 56
be but your lordship present at his examination, 3.06. 28 P
if i were to live this present hour, i will tell 4.03.160 P
thou shalt present me as an eunuch to him, | it TN 1.02. 56
look you, sir, such a one i was this present. 1.05.234 P
present mirth hath present laughter; 2.03. 48
present mirth hath present laughter; 2.03. 48
and part being prompted by your present trouble, 3.04.343
i'll make division of my present with you. 3.04.346
come | taint the condition of this present hour, 5.01.357
and many a man there is (even at this present, WT 1.02.192
so, without | my present vengeance taken. 1.02.281
present our services to a fine new prince | one 2.01. 17
but if one present | th' abhorr'd ingredient to 2.01. 42
madam, i must | be present at your conference. 2.02. 16
for present vengeance, | take it on her. 2.03. 22
though a present death | had been more merciful. 2.03.184
look grimly | and threaten present blusters. 3.03. 4
and make stale | the glistering of this present, 4.01. 14
prithee be my present partner in this business, 4.02. 51 P
and present yourself | that which you are, 4.04. 67
crowns what you are doing in the present deeds, 4.04.145
and five or six honest wives that were present. 4.04.271 P
and there present yourself and your fair 4.04.544
to him will i present them, there may be matter 4.04.841 P
for present comfort, and for future good, | to 5.01. 32
as every present time doth boast itself | above 5.01. 96
you, sir, were you present at this relation? 5.02. 1 P
nay, present your hand. 5.03.107
for the present time's so sick, | that present JN 5.01. 14
that present med'cine must be minist'red, | or 5.01. 15
have thou the ordering of this present time. 5.01. 77
joy absent, grief is present for that time. R2 1.03.259
join with the present sickness that i have, 2.01.132
to have | the present benefit which i possess, 2.03. 14
inferior breath, | and he himself not present? 4.01.129
within this coffin i present | thy buried fear. 5.06. 30
the pupil age of this present twelve a' clock at 1H4 2.04. 94 P
yet oftentimes it doth present harsh rage, 3.01.181
his present want | seems more than we shall find 4.01. 44
out of your sight and raise this present head, 5.01. 66
this present enterprise set off his head, | i do 5.01. 88
this present grief had wip'd it from my mind. 2H4 1.01.211
our present musters grow upon the file | to five 1.03. 10
whether our present five and twenty thousand 1.03. 16
of every minute's instance (present now) | hath 4.01. 83
form | and present execution of our wills — 4.01.172
this land | as his misdoubts present occasion. 4.01.204
i have bestowed to breed this present peace, 4.02. 74
confederates | to york, to present execution. 4.03. 74
feign, | o, let me in my present wildness die, 4.05.152
his present and your pains we thank you for. H5 1.02.260
a noble shalt thou have, and present pay, | and 2.01.107
we'll give them present audience. 2.04. 67
i did present him with the paris balls. 2.04.131
les mots que vous m'avez appris des a present. 3.04. 26 P
'tis good for men to love their present pains 4.01. 18
hark how our steeds for present service neigh! 4.02. 8
that whoso draws a sword, 'tis present death, 1H6 3.04. 39
to present your highness with the man. 2H6 2.01. 67
york doth present himself unto your highness. 5.01. 59
lo, i present your grace a traitor's head, | the 5.01. 66
reigns in the hearts of all our present parts. 5.02. 87
london, | to call a present court of parliament. 5.03. 25
from whence this present day he is delivered? R3 1.01. 69
if heaven will take the present at our hands. 1.01.120
northumberland, then present, wept to see it. 1.03.186
therefore present to her — as sometimes 4.04.274
the fear of that holds off my present aid. 4.05. 5
do through the clouds behold this present hour, 5.01. 8
as draw the eye to flow, | we now present. H8 pr 5
i was then present, saw them salute on horseback 1.01. 8
best, now worst, | as presence did present them: 1.01. 30
still him in praise, and being present both, 1.01. 31
from liberty, to look on | the business present. 1.01.206
he is attach'd, | call him to present trial. 1.02.211
whom once more i present unto your highness. 2.02. 97
the king is present: 2.04. 95
be to the prejudice of her present state, | or 2.04.155
whereupon we are | now present here together: 2.04.203
got your leave | to make this present summons. 2.04.220
but par'd my present havings, to bestow | my 3.02.159
i'm very sorry | to sit here at this present, 5.02. 44
whose present courage may beat down our foes, TRO 2.02.201
in reversion shall have a praise in present; 3.02. 93 P
then what they do in present, | though less than 3.03.163
the present eye praises the present object. 3.03.180
the present eye praises the present object. 3.03.180
present the fair steed to my lady cressid. 5.05. 2
the present wars devour him! COR 1.01.258
singularity, he goes | upon this present action. 1.01.279
and that you not delay the present, but, 1.06. 60
to desire | the present consul and last general 2.02. 43
you | th' apprehension of his present portance, 2.03.224
scaling his present bearing with his past, 2.03.249
theirs, martius is worthy | of present death. 3.01.211
mine ears, present me | death on the wheel, or 3.02. 1
not what is dangerous present, but the loss | of 3.02. 71
a din confus'd | enforce the present execution 3.03. 21
shall i be charg'd no further than this present? 3.03. 42
i think, that shall set them in present action. 4.03. 47 P
and present | my throat to thee and to thy 4.05. 95
the present peace | and quietness of the people, 4.06. 2
'tis present death i beg, and one thing more TIT 2.03.173
do, and with his gifts present | your lordships, 4.02. 14
but give them to his master for a present. 4.03. 76
give me some present counsel, or, behold, ROM 4.01. 61
this shall free thee from this present shame, 4.01.118
now, | whose sale is present death in mantua, 5.01. 51
her, | whose present grace to present slaves and TIM 1.01. 71
present grace to present slaves and servants 1.01. 71
three talents on the present; in future, all. 1.01.141
when, for some trifling present, you have bid me 2.02.136
having lacks a half | to pay your present debts. 2.02.145
will hardly stop the mouth | of present dues. 2.02.148
doubting your present assistance therein. 3.01. 20 P
h'as only sent his present occasion now, my lord 3.02. 34 P
for these my present friends, as they are to me 3.06. 82 P
eye, i will present | my honest grief unto him; 4.03.469
either in hope or present, i'd exchange | for 4.03.520
what have you now to present unto him? 5.01. 17
his expedition promises | present approach. 5.02. 4
for this present, | i would not (so with love i JC 1.02.165
i did present myself | even in the aim and very 1.03. 51
go bid the priests do present sacrifice, | and 2.02. 5
as by our hands and this our present act | you 3.01.166
go pronounce his present death, | and with his MAC 1.02. 64
my noble partner | you greet with present grace, 1.03. 55
present fears | are less than horrible 1.03.137
transported me beyond | this ignorant present, 1.05. 57
and take the present horror from the time, 2.01. 59
present him eminence both with eye and tongue: 3.02. 31
will venom breed, | no teeth for th' present. 3.04. 30
were the grac'd person of our banquo present, 3.04. 40
herein | this present object made probation. HAM 1.01.156
to that effect, | the present death of hamlet. 4.03. 65
we'll put the matter to the present push. 5.01.295
will you require in present dower with her, | or LR 1.01.192
i have this present evening from my sister 2.01.101
and why you answer | this present summons? 5.03.121
and vain is it | that we present us to him. 5.03.295
our present business | is general woe. 5.03.319
yet, for necessity of present life, | i must OTH 1.01.155
side, | upon some present business of the state, 1.02. 90
so justly to your grave ears i'll present | how 1.03.124
this present wars against the ottomites. 1.03.234
though true advantage never present itself; 2.01.244 P
feasting from this present hour of five till the 2.02. 9 P
to move you, | his present reconciliation take; 3.03. 47
that nor my service past, nor present sorrows, 3.04.116
the present pleasure, | by revolution low'ring, ANT 1.02.124
as have not thrived | upon the present state, 1.03. 52
pawn their experience to their present pleasure, 1.04. 32
land i can be able | to front this present time. 1.04. 79
to mend the petty present, i will piece | her 1.05. 45
were to remember that the present need | speaks 2.02.101
for 'tis a studied, not a present thought, | by 2.02.137
us | (for this is from the present) how you take 2.06. 30
stage us, and present | our alexandrian revels: 5.02.217
mingled sums | to buy a present for the emperor; CYM 1.06.187
is material | to th' tender of our present. 1.06.208
quake in the present winter's state, and wish 2.04. 5
and it gave me present hunger | to feed again, 2.04.137
let's follow him and pervert the present wrath 2.04.151
'fore noble lucius | present yourself, desire 3.04.173
command our present numbers | be muster'd; 4.02.343
her son gone, | so needful for this present! 4.03. 8
these present wars shall find i love my country, 4.03. 43
i speak against my present profit, but my wish 5.04.205 P
wet cheeks | were present when she finish'd. 5.05. 36
would cease | the present pow'r of life, but in 5.05.256
i'll present myself. PER 1.03. 29
and stay your coming to present themselves. 2.02. 3
but his present is | a withered branch, that's 2.02. 42
a present murderer does prepare | for good 4.ch. 38
must be quench'd with some present practice. 4.02.125 P
sir, | give me a gash, put me to present pain, 5.01.191
your present kindness | makes my past miseries 5.03. 40
their surfeit | that craves a present med'cine, TNK 1.01.191
do here present this machine, or this frame. 3.05.113
put thyself | upon thy present guard — 3.06.122
she and i at this present stood unfeignedly on 4.03. 68 P
you must be present, | you are the victor's meed 5.03. 15
give them our present justice, since i know 5.03.132
not /one of you here present, | had there such STM II.C 62
so, | that every present sorrow seemeth chief, VEN 970
hind'ring their present fall by this dividing; LUC 551
were | to view thy present trespass in another. 632
with circumstances strong | of present death, 1263
see) | some present speed to come and visit me. 1307
each present lord began to promise aid, | as 1696
love, | thyself away are present still with me, SON 47.10
for we, which now behold these present days, 106.13
crowning the present, doubting of the rest? 115.12
not wond'ring at the present, nor the past, 123.10
spend | revenge upon myself with present moan? 149. 8
PRESENT–ABSENT 1 FR 0.0001 REL FR 1 V 0 P
these present–absent with swift motion slide. SON 45. 4
PRESENTATION 2 FR 0.0002 REL FR 1 V 1 P
and under the presentation of that he shoots his AYL 5.04.107 P
queen, | the presentation of but what i was; R3 4.04. 84
PRESENTED 17 FR 0.0019 REL FR 16 V 1 P
when i presented ceres, | i thought to have told TMP 4.01.167
should be presented at our tent to us. LLL 5.02.307
"great hercules is presented by this imp, 5.02.588
who pyramus presented, in their sport, | forsook MND 3.02. 14
presented thee more hideous than thou art. JN 4.02.266
rage | presented to the tears of soft remorse. 4.03. 50
the image of the king whom i presented, | and 2H4 5.02. 79
presented them unto the gazing moon | so many H5 4.pr. 27
their huge and proper life | be here presented. 5.pr. 6
where i hope ere long | to be presented, by your 1H6 4.01.172
cupid's pageant there is presented no monster. TRO 3.02. 75 P
my hearth, | presented to my knife his throat. COR 5.06. 30
hath presented to you | four milk–white horses, TIM 1.02.182
the marbled mansion all above | never presented! 4.03.192
i thrice presented him a kingly crown, | which JC 3.02. 96
and with presented nakedness outface | the winds LR 2.03. 11
thee, | to take advantage on presented joy; VEN 405
PRESENTETH 4 FR 0.0004 REL FR 4 V 0 P
dog, and bush of thorn, | presenteth moonshine; MND 5.01.136
the other his pale cheeks, methinks, presenteth. 3H6 2.05.100
presenteth to mine eye | the picture of an angry VEN 661
that this huge stage presenteth nought but shows SON 15. 3
PRESENTING 1 FR 0.0001 REL FR 1 V 0 P
of a blinking idiot, | presenting me a schedule! MV 2.09. 55
/PRESENTLY 2 FR 0.0002 REL FR 2 V 0 P
/and /bitter /fool | /will /presently /appear: LR 1.04.145
/shall /attend /you /presently /at /your /tent. 5.01. 33
PRESENTLY 154 FR 0.0174 REL FR 118 V 36 P
should presently extirpate me and mine | out of TMP 1.02.125
presently? 4.01. 42
and presently, i prithee. 5.01.101
will scratch the nurse | and presently, all TGV 1.02. 59
when you fasted, it was presently after dinner; 2.01. 29 P
i will send him hither to you presently. 2.04. 86
must use, | and then i'll presently attend you. 2.04.189
madcap, i'll to the alehouse with you presently; 2.05. 9 P
now presently i'll give her father notice | of 2.06. 36
him, | and presently go with me to my chamber, 2.07. 83
come, answer not, but to it presently, | i am 2.07. 89
gone, | and this way comes he with it presently, 3.01. 42
let us into the city presently | to sort some 3.02. 90
this, | that presently you hie you home to bed. 4.02. 94
and will employ thee in some service presently. 4.04. 41
go presently, and take this ring with thee, 4.04. 71
but mount you presently and meet with me | upon 5.02. 45
and would needs speak with you presently. WIV 3.03. 88 P
sure he is by this — or will be presently. 4.01. 3 P
nay, but he'll be here presently. 4.02. 97 P
i will presently to saint luke's; MM 3.01.264 P
dispatch it presently, the hour draws on 4.03. 78
this shall be done, good father, presently. 4.03. 82
go hie thee presently, post to the road, | and ERR 3.02.147
i pray you see him presently discharg'd, | for 4.01. 32
honor and mine honesty | against thee presently, 5.01. 31
pestilence, and the taker runs presently mad. ADO 1.01. 88 P
thou wilt be like a lover presently, | and tire 1.01.306
in practice let us put it presently. 1.01.328
i will presently go learn their day of marriage. 2.02. 56 P
i'll make her come, i warrant you, presently. 3.01. 14
him go, and presently call the rest of the watch 3.03. 29 P
presently away, | for to strange sores strangely 4.01.251
will you come presently? 5.02.100 P
familiar, | and to the chapel let us presently. 5.04. 71
meet presently at the palace; MND 4.02. 37 P
go presently inquire, and so will i, | where MV 1.01.183
knave, and presently | i'll be with you. 1.03.176
come about, | bassanio presently will go aboard. 2.06. 65
his oath, | and comes to his election presently. 2.09. 3
this favor | he presently become a christian; 4.01.387
padua, | and it is meet i presently set forth. 4.01.404
come, you and i will thither presently, | and in 4.01.455
i will here be with thee presently, and if i AYL 2.06. 11 P
nature presently distill'd | helen's cheek, but 3.02.144
you shall go see your pupils presently. SHR 2.01.107
my boy shall fetch the scrivener presently. 4.04. 59
but presently | do thine own fortunes that AWW 2.03.159

you presently | attend his further pleasure. 2.04. 52
you | that presently you take your way for home, 2.05. 64
and i will presently pen down my dilemmas, 3.06. 74 P
way till he take leave, and presently after him. TN 3.04.198 P
send one presently to sir toby. 5.01.173 P
i'll presently | acquaint the queen of your most WT 2.02. 45
quit presently the chapel, or resolve you | for 5.03. 86
for at saint mary's chapel presently | the rites JN 2.01.538
with purpose presently to leave this war. 5.07. 86
wants, | for we will make for ireland presently. R2 1.04. 52
bid her send me presently a thousand pound. 2.02. 91
your men, | and meet me presently at berkeley. 2.02.119
since presently your souls must part your bodies 3.01. 3
woes, | but presently prevent the ways to wail; 3.02.179
they will away presently. 1H4 2.01. 60 P
hand, | for we shall presently have need of you. 3.02. 3
he presently, as greatness knows itself, | steps 4.03. 74
the king will bid you battle presently. 5.02. 30
you shall have letters of me presently. 2H4 2.01.178
you must away to court, sir, presently, | a 2.04.371
good husband, come home presently. H5 2.01. 89 P
fluellen, you must come presently to the mines; 3.02. 54 P
to appoint some of your council presently | to 5.02. 79
presently we'll try; 1H6 1.02.149
that will i show you presently. 2.03. 60
presently, | and then do execution on the watch. 3.02. 34
mean | shall be transported presently to france. 5.01. 40
one, | and means to give you battle presently. 5.02. 13
is, | but we will presently provide for them. 5.02. 15
delay, | i'll to the duke of suffolk presently. 2H6 1.01.171
yes, my good lord, i'll follow presently. 1.02. 60
send for his master with a pursuivant presently. 1.03. 35 P
then send for one presently. 2.01.136
i'll call him presently, my noble lord. 3.02. 18
him, i will make myself a knight presently. 4.02.120 P
say, and strike off his head presently, and then 4.07.110 P
marry, presently. 4.07.128 P
brother, thou shalt to london presently, | and 3H6 1.02. 36
unsheathe your sword, and dub him presently. 2.02. 59
i will away towards barnet presently, | and bid 5.01.110
mourner, | and presently repair to crosby house; R3 1.02.212
of york | unto his princely brother presently? 3.01. 34
if you will presently take horse with him, | and 3.02. 16
i will resolve you herein presently. 4.02. 26
presently the duke | said, 'twas the fear indeed H8 1.02.157
presently | he did unseal them, and the first he 3.02. 78
to render up the great seal presently | into our 3.02.229
the king | shall understand it presently. 5.02. 10
i shall be with you presently, good master puppy 5.03. 29 P
i shall, and bring his answer presently. TRO 2.03.139
i'll bring her to the grecian presently; 4.03. 6
and presently, when you have drawn your number,
COR 2.03.253
assemble presently the people hither; 3.03. 12
to–morrow, to–day, presently; 4.05.214 P
behold now presently, and swound for what's to 5.02. 67 P
do it presently! 5.06.120 P
thy temples should be planted presently | with TIT 2.03. 62
days, | but send the midwife presently to me. 4.02.166
go take him away and hang him presently. 4.04. 45
not die | so sweet a death as hanging presently. 5.01.146
go fetch them hither to us presently. 5.03. 59
and with this knife i'll help it presently. ROM 4.01. 54
when presently through all thy veins shall run 4.01. 95
vault, | and presently took post to tell it you. 5.01. 21
our spirit, | he shall be executed presently. TIM 3.05.102
we shall to't presently. 3.06. 35 P
then, timon, presently prepare thy grave; 4.03.377
go | and presently prefer his suit to caesar. JC 3.01. 28
i'll fetch him presently. 3.01.142
and let us presently go sit in council, | how 4.01. 45
you think | of marching to philippi presently? 4.03.197
heaven given his hand, | they presently amend. MAC 4.03.145
i'll board him presently. HAM 2.02.170
that presently | they have proclaim'd their 2.02.591
and the queen too, and that presently. 3.02. 48 P
the queen would speak with you, and presently. 3.02.375 P
but let this same be presently perform'd | even 5.02.393
i will seek him, sir, presently; LR 1.02.101 P
of intermission, | which presently they read; 2.04. 34
wife, i'ld speak with them — | now, presently. 2.04.117
do thou meet me presently at the harbor. OTH 2.01.214 P
man, by and by a fool, and presently a beast! 2.03.306 P
i'll send her to you presently; 3.01. 36
/yes, presently: 5.02. 52
of us must pompey presently be sought, | or else ANT 2.02.158
the good gods will mock me presently, | when i 3.04. 15
'gainst pompey, presently denied him rivality, 3.05. 8 P
more, domitius, | my lord desires you presently; 3.05. 21
to dorothy my woman hie thee presently, CYM 2.03.138
and provide me presently | a riding–suit, no 3.02. 75
return, and bring him | to dinner presently. 4.02.166
good mariner, | i'll bring the body presently. PER 3.01. 81
my masters, you shall have your money presently. 4.02. 54 P
me leave a word, and i'll have done presently. 4.06. 47 P
when the other presently gives it so sweet a TNK 2.01. 42 P
lord arcite, you must presently to th' duke; 2.02.221
i'll presently | provide him necessaries and 2.06. 31
say "ay," and all shall presently advance. 3.05.134
and safely presently | into your bush again, sir 3.06.110
when presently | she slipp'd away, and to the 4.01. 96
i told her, presently, and kiss'd her twice. 5.02. 6
your fit comes, fit her home, and presently. 5.02. 11
and presently | backward the jade comes o'er, 5.04. 80
who in their pride do presently abuse it; LUC 864
the moon being clouded presently is miss'd, 1007
bud, | a brittle glass that's broken presently: PP 13. 4
PRESENTMENT 2 FR 0.0002 REL FR 2 V 0 P
upon the heels of my presentment, sir. TIM 1.01. 27
the counterfeit presentment of two brothers. HAM 3.04. 54
PRESENTS* *(also pursents)*
PRESENTS* 15 FR 0.0017 REL FR 10 V 5 P
not only bought many presents to give her, but WIV 2.02.198 P
i have in doing good a remedy presents itself. MM 3.01.199 P
dies in the zeal of that which it presents. LLL 5.02.518
he presents hector of troy; 5.02.534 P
"be it known unto all men by these presents." AYL 1.02.124 P
presents more woeful pageants than the scene 2.07.138
he presents no mark to the enemy, the foeman may
2H4 3.02.265 P
presents well worthy rome's imperious lord: TIT 1.01.250
sons | presents that i intend to send them both. 4.01.116
let the presents | be worthily entertain'd. TIM 1.02.184
toward the north | he first presents his fire, JC 2.01.110
who is the second that presents himself? PER 2.02. 23
and that work presents itself to th' doing: TNK 1.01.151
the year) presents me with | a brace of horses; 3.01. 19
presents /thy shadow to my sightless view, SON 27.10
PRESENT'ST 1 FR 0.0001 REL FR 1 V 0 P
and thou present'st a pure unstained prime. SON 70. 8
PRESERVATION 6 FR 0.0006 REL FR 6 V 0 P
but for the miracle | (i mean our preservation), TMP 2.01. 7
give us particulars of thy preservation, | how 5.01.135
care | and tender preservation of our person, H5 2.02. 59
were't not that by great preservation | we live R3 3.05. 36
nature does require | her times of preservation, H8 3.02.147
fairer | than those for preservation cas'd, or CYM 5.03. 22
PRESERVATIVE 1 FR 0.0001 REL FR 0 V 1 P
and, to this preservative, of no better report COR 2.01.117 P
/PRESERV'D 1 FR 0.0001 REL FR 1 V 0 P
virtue /preserv'd from fell destruction's blast, PER 5.03. 89
PRESERV'D 9 FR 0.0010 REL FR 9 V 0 P
i was preserv'd to serve this noble count. TN 5.01.256
me, mine own, | where hast thou been preserv'd? WT 5.03.124
being, have preserv'd | myself to see the issue. 5.03.127
rather than life preserv'd with infamy. 1H6 4.05. 33
men's flesh preserv'd so whole do seldom win. 2H6 3.01.301
must gently be preserv'd, cherish'd, and kept. R3 2.02.119
that have preserv'd her welfare in my blood, TIT 5.03.110
what cannot be preserv'd when fortune takes, OTH 1.03.206
preserv'd the britains, was the romans' bane." CYM 5.03. 58
/PRESERVE 1 FR 0.0001 REL FR 1 V 0 P
/than /will /preserve /just /so /much /strength TIT 3.02. 2
PRESERVE 30 FR 0.0034 REL FR 25 V 5 P
o, a cherubin | thou wast that did preserve me. TMP 1.02.153
now, good angels | preserve the king! 2.01.307
commonwealth of nature to preserve virginity. AWW 1.01.127 P
of my sheets | (which to preserve is sleep, WT 1.02.328
had said at once, | "jesu preserve /thee! R2 5.02. 17
well, there is sixpence to preserve thee. 2H4 2.02. 95 P
o, the lord preserve thy grace! 2.04.291 P
god pless it, and preserve it, as long as it H5 4.07.108 P
with "god preserve the good duke humphrey!" 2H6 1.01.162
jesus preserve your royal majesty! 1.02. 70
and to preserve my sovereign from his foe, | say 3.01.271
(whom god preserve better than you would wish!)
R3 1.03. 59
the gods preserve our noble tribunes! COR 3.03.143
the gods preserve you both! 4.06. 20
the gods preserve ye! TIM 1.01.162
heaven preserve you! MAC 4.02. 72
whiles i may scape | i will preserve myself, and LR 2.03. 6
if to preserve this vessel for my lord | from OTH 4.02. 83
to that point which seeks | best to preserve it. ANT 3.04. 22
so the gods preserve thee! 5.01. 60
a dram, you cannot preserve it from tainting. CYM 1.04.136 P
preserve? 1.05. 13
which, to preserve mine honor, i'll perform. PER 2.02. 16
the fates, | to foster it, not ever to preserve. 4.03. 15
the good gods preserve you! 4.06.107
hail, reverent sir! the gods preserve you! 5.01. 14
the gods preserve you! 5.01. 39
her, yet i'll preserve | the honor of affection, TNK 3.06.268
from her, | but still preserve her in this way. 5.02.106
feeding on that which doth preserve the ill, SON 147. 3
PRESERVED 3 FR 0.0003 REL FR 3 V 0 P
ere sun–rise, prayers from preserved souls, MM 2.02.153
of men's impossibilities, have preserved thee. LR 4.06. 74
how possibly preserved, and who to thank PER 5.03. 57
PRESERVER 3 FR 0.0003 REL FR 3 V 0 P
my true preserver, and a loyal sir | to him thou TMP 5.01. 69
sit, my preserver, by thy patient's side, | and AWW 2.03. 47
preserver of my father, now of me, | the WT 4.04.586
PRESERVERS 1 FR 0.0001 REL FR 1 V 0 P
the gods have made | preservers of my throne. CYM 5.05. 2
PRESERVING 2 FR 0.0002 REL FR 2 V 0 P
precious, | preserving life in med'cine potable; 2H4 4.05.162
a choking gall, and a preserving sweet. ROM 1.01.194
PRESIDENT* *(also precedent)*
/PRESIDENT* 1 FR 0.0001 REL FR 0 V 1 P
step aside, and i'll show thee a /president. 1H4 2.04. 33 P
PRESIDENT* 14 FR 0.0015 REL FR 13 V 1 P
thy case, dear friend, | shall be my president: TMP 2.01.291
example my digression by some mighty president.
LLL 1.02.117 P
return the president to these lords again, JN 5.02. 3
may be a president and witness good | that thou R2 2.01.130
for shame, my liege, make them your president! 3H6 2.02. 33
have you a president | of this commission? H8 1.02. 91
your grace has given a president of wisdom 2.02. 85
a pattern, president, and lively warrant | for TIT 5.03. 44
i have a voice and president of peace | to /keep HAM 5.02.249
the country gives me proof and president | of LR 2.03. 13
war, | and, as the president of my kingdom, will ANT 3.07. 17
a president | which not to read would show the CYM 3.01. 74
palm, | the president of pith and livelihood, VEN 26
the president whereof in lucrece view, LUC 1261
PRESS* 35 FR 0.0039 REL FR 27 V 8 P
a pack of sorrows which would press you down, TGV 3.01. 20
for he cares not what he puts into the press, WIV 2.01. 78 P
to press with so little preparation upon you. 2.02.156 P
neither press, coffer, chest, trunk, well, vault 4.02. 61 P
me | out of myself, press me to death with wit. ADO 3.01. 76
why should he stay, whom love doth press to go? MND 3.02.184
what love could press lysander from my side? 3.02.185
his back, | enow to press a royal merchant down, MV 4.01. 29
you press me far, and therefore i will yield. 4.01.425
i press in here, sir, amongst the rest of the AYL 5.04. 55 P
press me not, beseech you, so. WT 1.02. 19
in their throng and press to that last hold, JN 5.07. 19
i have misus'd the king's press damnably. 1H4 4.02. 12 P
i press me none but good householders, /yeomen's 4.02. 14 P
no humble suitors press to speak for right, | no 3H6 3.01. 19
o my lord, | press not a falling man too far! H8 3.02.333
would shake the press | and make 'em reel before 4.01. 78
go break among the press, and find a way out 5.03. 84
of your pretty encounters, press it to death. TRO 3.02.209 P
flamens | do press among the popular throngs, COR 2.01.214
should be so bold to press to heaven in my young TIT 4.03. 91 P
and thou and romeo press /one heavy bier! ROM 3.02. 60
this, | to press before thy father to a grave? 5.03.215
who is it in the press that calls on me? JC 1.02. 15
and that great men shall press | for tinctures, 2.02. 88
what caesar doth, what suitors press to him. 2.04. 15
he is address'd; press near and second him. 3.01. 29
nay, press not so upon me, stand far off. 3.02.167
did softly press the rushes ere he waken'd | the CYM 2.02. 13
the banks, or for | the press of boats or pride. 2.04. 72
whereto he'll infuse pow'r and press you forth TNK 1.01. 73
much like a press of people at a door, | throng LUC 1301
about him were a press of gaping faces, | which 1408
prove unjust, | press never thou to choose anew. PP 18.22
do not press | my tongue–tied patience with too SON 140. 1
/PRESS'D* 1 FR 0.0001 REL FR 1 V 0 P
/forth, /as /if /it /press'd /her /heart; LR 4.03. 26
PRESS'D* 17 FR 0.0019 REL FR 15 V 2 P
come, sister, i am press'd down with conceit — ERR 4.02. 65
half that wish the wisher's eyes be press'd! MND 2.02. 65
for every man that bullingbrook hath press'd R2 3.02. 58
i am press'd to death through want of speaking! 3.04. 72
i press'd me none but such toasts–and–butter, 1H4 4.02. 20 P
all the gibbets and press'd the dead bodies. 4.02. 37 P
from london by the king was i press'd forth; 3H6 2.05. 64
came on the part of york, press'd by his master; 2.05. 66
did throng | and press'd in with this caution. H8 2.04.187
the large achilles, on his press'd bed lolling, TRO 1.03.162
"they have press'd a power, but it is not known COR 1.02. 9
being press'd to th' war, | even when the navel 3.01.122
which thou wilt propagate to have it press'd ROM 1.01.187
this while with leaden thoughts been press'd, OTH 3.04.177
wanting form, | is press'd with deeper matter. TNK 1.01.109
i had my load before, now press'd with bearing: VEN 430
he with her plenty press'd, she faint with 545
PRESSED 1 FR 0.0001 REL FR 1 V 0 P
sing while thou on pressed flowers dost sleep. MND 3.01.159
PRESSES 4 FR 0.0004 REL FR 3 V 1 P
and in the coffers, and in the presses, heaven WIV 3.03.212 P
him of that humor | that presses him from sleep. WT 2.03. 39
that presses them and learns them first to bear, ROM 1.04. 93
o, it presses to my memory | like damned guilty 3.02.110
PRESSING 2 FR 0.0002 REL FR 1 V 1 P
a punk, my lord, is pressing to death, whipping, MM 5.01.522 P
under her breast | (worthy her pressing) lies a CYM 2.04.135
PRESS–MONEY 1 FR 0.0001 REL FR 0 V 1 P
there's your press–money. LR 4.06. 87 P
PRESSURE 1 FR 0.0001 REL FR 0 V 1 P
age and body of the time his form and pressure. HAM 3.02. 24 P
PRESSURES 1 FR 0.0001 REL FR 1 V 0 P
all pressures past | that youth and observation HAM 1.05.100
PREST 2 FR 0.0002 REL FR 2 V 0 P
may by me be done, | and i am prest unto it; MV 1.01.160
instrument of wrath | prest for this blow. PER 4.ch. 45
PRESTER 1 FR 0.0001 REL FR 0 V 1 P
bring you the length of prester john's foot, ADO 2.01.268 P
PRESUME 22 FR 0.0024 REL FR 20 V 2 P
dare you presume to harbor wanton lines? TGV 1.02. 42
let none presume | to wear an undeserved dignity MV 2.09. 39
us not, "regia," presume not, "celsa senis," SHR 3.01. 44 P
left legs and not presume to touch a hair of my 4.01. 93 P
i do presume, sir, that you are not fall'n AWW 5.01. 12
which i presume shall render you no blame, | but 5.01. 32
jest, | i presume not that i am the thing i was, 2H4 5.05. 56
durst not presume to look once in the face. 1H6 1.01.140
that doth presume to boast of gentle blood. 4.01. 44
i dare presume, sweet prince, he thought no harm 4.01.179
i will not so presume | to send such peevish 5.03.185
and otherwise will henry ne'er presume. 5.05. 22
dare he presume to scorn us in this manner? 3H6 3.03.178
thou been kill'd when first thou didst presume, 5.06. 35
which i presume he'll take in gentle part. R3 3.04. 20
i presume | that, as my hand has open'd bounty H8 3.02.183
for i presume brave hector would not lose | so TRO 2.02.203
this, i presume, will wake him. 2.02.213
as, if it can, i will presume in you — | to 3.02.159
and presume to know | what's done i' th' capitol COR 1.01.191
do not presume too much upon my love, | i may do
JC 4.03. 63
presume not on thy heart when mine is slain, SON 22.13
PRESUMES 2 FR 0.0002 REL FR 2 V 0 P
my mind presumes, for his own good and /ours. SHR 1.02.213
because thine eye | presumes to reach, all the PER 1.01. 33
PRESUMING 3 FR 0.0003 REL FR 3 V 0 P
fool, | presuming on an ague's privilege, R2 2.01.116
powers, | presuming on their changeful potency. TRO 4.04. 97
either presuming them to have some force, | or TNK 1.01.194
PRESUMPTION 6 FR 0.0006 REL FR 6 V 0 P
but most it is presumption in us when | the help AWW 2.01.151
let my presumption not provoke thy wrath, | for 1H6 2.03. 70
grove | shall lose his head for his presumption. 2H6 1.02. 34
that is too much presumption on thy part; 5.01. 38
shall have wars, and pay for their presumption. 3H6 4.01.114
thy son i kill'd for his presumption. 5.06. 34
PRESUMPTUOUS 5 FR 0.0005 REL FR 5 V 0 P
him not | by any token of presumptuous suit, AWW 1.03.198
presumptuous priest, this place commands my 1H6 3.01. 8
presumptuous vassals, are you not asham'd | with 4.01.125
presumptuous dame, ill–nurtur'd eleanor, | art 2H6 1.02. 42
which makes thee thus presumptuous and proud, 3H6 1.01.157
PRESUPPOS'D 1 FR 0.0001 REL FR 1 V 0 P
and in such forms which here were presuppos'd TN 5.01.350
/PRESURMISE 1 FR 0.0001 REL FR 1 V 0 P
/it /was /your /presurmise | /that /in /the 2H4 1.01.168
PRET 1 FR 0.0001 REL FR 0 V 1 P
commande a vous dire que vous faites vous pret; H5 4.04. 35 P
PRETEND 6 FR 0.0006 REL FR 6 V 0 P
and none your foes but such as shall pretend 1H6 4.01. 6
pretend some alteration in good will? 4.01. 54
why shall we fight if you pretend no title? 3H6 4.07. 57
right, | whom you pretend to honor and adore, TIT 1.01. 42
alas the day, | what good could they pretend? MAC 2.04. 24
the contract you pretend with that base wretch, CYM 2.03.113
PRETENDED 3 FR 0.0003 REL FR 3 V 0 P
of their disguising and pretended flight, | who, TGV 2.06. 37
not any thing | in the pretended celebration. TNK 1.01.210

with such black payment as thou hast pretended; LUC 576
PRETENDERS 1 FR 0.0001 REL FR 1 V 0 P
he of the two pretenders that best loves me TNK 5.01.158
PRETENDING 2 FR 0.0002 REL FR 1 V 1 P
pretending in her discoveries of dishonor; MM 3.01.227 P
her, still pretending | the satisfaction of her CYM 5.05.250
PRETENSE 10 FR 0.0011 REL FR 6 V 4 P
hath made me publisher of this pretense. TGV 3.01. 47
her pretense is a pilgrimage to saint jaques le AWW 4.03. 48 P
the pretense whereof being by circumstances WT 3.02. 17 P
under pretense to see the queen his aunt | (for H8 1.01.177
and the pretense for this | is nam'd, your wars 1.02. 59
against the undivulg'd pretense i fight | of MAC 2.03.131
your honor, and to no other pretense of danger. LR 1.02. 87 P
curiosity than as a very pretense and purpose of 1.04. 70 P
thou abus'd | so many miles with a pretense? CYM 3.04.103
and make pretense of wrong that i have done him;
PER 1.02. 91
PRETENSES 1 FR 0.0001 REL FR 1 V 0 P
to keep your great pretenses veil'd till when COR 1.02. 20
PRETEXT 1 FR 0.0001 REL FR 1 V 0 P
and my pretext to strike at him admits | a good COR 5.06. 19
PRETTIER 1 FR 0.0001 REL FR 1 V 0 P
i'll prove the prettier fellow of the two, | and MV 3.04. 64
PRETTIEST 10 FR 0.0011 REL FR 6 V 4 P
but kate, the prettiest kate in christendom, SHR 2.01.187
this is the prettiest low–born lass that ever WT 4.04.156
he has the prettiest love–songs for maids, so 4.04.193 P
my prettiest perdita! 4.04.584
one of the prettiest touches of all, and that 5.02. 82 P
it is the prettiest villain, she fetches her TRO 3.02. 33 P
thou wast the prettiest babe that e'er i nurs'd. ROM 1.03. 60
and she hath the prettiest sententious of it, of 2.04.211 P
us | find out the prettiest daisied plot we can, CYM 4.02.398
and to 'em spoke | the prettiest posies — "thus TNK 4.01. 90
PRETTILY 7 FR 0.0008 REL FR 6 V 1 P
not, sith so prettily | he couples it to his TGV 1.02.123
lysander riddles very prettily. MND 2.02. 53
how prettily th' young swain seems to wash | the WT 4.04.366
i promise you, the king | prettily, methought, 1H6 4.01.175
uncle, | he prettily and aptly taunts himself: R3 3.01.134
how prettily she's amiss! TNK 4.03. 28 P
still she entreats, and prettily entreats, | for VEN 73
PRETTINESS 1 FR 0.0001 REL FR 1 V 0 P
itself, | she turns to favor and to prettiness. HAM 4.05.189
/PRETTY 3 FR 0.0003 REL FR 1 V 2 P
/that, /with /his /pretty /buzzing /melody, TIT 3.02. 64
/pretty! what say you, hugh rebeck? ROM 4.05.133 P
/pretty too! what say you, james soundpost? 4.05.136 P
PRETTY 134 FR 0.0151 REL FR 84 V 50 P
a pretty period! TGV 2.01.116
why, my pretty youth? 4.02. 58 P
master /george page, which is pretty virginity. WIV 1.01. 46 P
what news? how does pretty mistress anne? 1.04.137 P
in truth, sir, and she is pretty, and honest, 1.04.139 P
where had you this pretty weathercock? 3.02. 18 P
'od's heartlings, that's a pretty jest indeed! 3.04. 57 P
there is pretty orders beginning, i can tell you MM 2.01.236 P
o pretty isabella, i am pale at mine heart to 4.03.151 P
i can tell thee pretty tales of the duke. 4.03.166 P
and piteous plainings of the pretty babes, ERR 1.01. 72
of excellent discourse, | pretty and witty; 3.01.110
i remember a pretty jest your daughter told /us ADO 2.03.135 P
thus, pretty lady, | i am sorry for thy much 4.01. 98
as pretty a piece of flesh as any is in messina, 4.02. 82 P
what a pretty thing man is when he goes in his 5.01.199 P
pretty and apt. LLL 1.02. 18 P
i pretty, and my saying apt? 1.02. 19 P
or i apt, and my saying pretty? 1.02. 20 P
thou pretty, because little. 1.02. 21 P
little pretty, because little. wherefore apt? 1.02. 22 P
of a child, most pretty and pathetical! 1.02. 97 P
the meaning, pretty ingenious? 3.01. 58 P
pierc'd and prick'd a pretty pleasing pricket; 4.02. 56
'tis pretty; 4.02. 89 P
their herald is a pretty knavish page, | that 5.02. 97
madam, and pretty mistresses, give ear: 5.02.286
which she with pretty and with swimming gait MND 2.01.130
pretty soul, she durst not lie | near this 2.02. 76
stood now within the pretty flouriets' eyes 4.01. 55
see | the pretty follies that themselves commit, MV 2.06. 37
in such a night | did pretty jessica (like a 5.01. 21
the cow's dugs that her pretty chopp'd hands had AYL 2.04. 50 P
you are full of pretty answers; 3.02.270 P
where dwell you, pretty youth? 3.02.334 P
'tis pretty, sure, and very probable, | that 3.05. 11
it is a pretty youth — not very pretty — | but 3.05.113
it is a pretty youth — not very pretty — | but 3.05.113
there was a pretty redness in his lip, | a 3.05.120
i prithee, pretty youth, let me /be better 4.01. 1 P
and by all pretty oaths that are not dangerous, 4.01.189 P
coz, my pretty little coz, that thou didst know 4.01.205 P
ay, sir, i have a pretty wit. 5.01. 29 P
in spring time, the only pretty /ring time, 5.03. 19
nonino, | these pretty country folks would lie, 5.03. 24
a pretty peat! SHR 1.01. 78
farewell, pretty lady, | you must hold the AWW 1.01. 77
'twas pretty, though a plague, | to see him 1.01. 92
with a world | of pretty, fond, adoptious 1.01.174
for two ordinaries, to be a pretty wise fellow. 2.03.202 P
trip no further, pretty sweeting; TN 2.03. 42
you were pretty lordings then? WT 1.02. 62
the pretty dimples of his chin and cheek, his 2.03.102
may, if fortune please, both breed thee, pretty, 3.03. 48
a very pretty barne! 3.03. 70 P
a pretty one, a very pretty one: 3.03. 71 P
a pretty one, a very pretty one: 3.03. 71 P
this is a merry ballad, but a very pretty one. 4.04.286 P
never | must i behold my pretty arthur more. JN 3.04. 89
puts on his pretty looks, repeats his words, 3.04. 95
and, pretty child, sleep doubtless and secure 4.01.129
and make some pretty match with shedding tears?
R2 3.03.165
that pretty welsh | which thou pourest down from 1H4 3.01.198
yea, i thank your pretty sweet wit for it. 2H4 1.02.206 P
and for thy walls, a pretty slight drollery, or 2.01.144 P
of mutton, and any pretty little tiny kickshaws, 5.01. 28 P
and pretty traps to catch the petty thieves. H5 1.02.177
the pretty and sweet manner of it forc'd | those 4.06. 28
a pretty plot, well chosen to build upon! 2H6 1.04. 56
the pretty vaulting sea refus'd to drown me, 3.02. 94
this pretty lad will prove our country's bliss. 3H6 4.06. 70
we say that shore's wife hath a pretty foot, | a R3 1.01. 93
in the faultless blood of pretty rutland — 1.03.177
my pretty cousins, you mistake me both: 2.02. 8
i prithee, pretty york, who told thee this? 2.04. 31
rough cradle for such little pretty ones! 4.01.100
not so much at the hair as at his pretty answer. TRO 1.02.155 P
what makes this pretty abruption? 3.02. 65 P
pretty, i' faith. 3.02.135 P
it shall not speak of your pretty encounters, 3.02.208 P
sleep kill those pretty eyes, | and give as soft 4.02. 4
o pretty, pretty pledge! 5.02. 77
o pretty, pretty pledge! 5.02. 77
i shall tell you | a pretty tale. COR 1.01. 90
i'll swear 'tis a very pretty boy. 1.03. 58 P
and he hath cut those pretty fingers off | that TIT 2.04. 42
is torn from forth that pretty hollow cage, 3.01. 84
and bid thee bear his pretty tales in mind, 5.03.165
and 'tis known i am a pretty piece of flesh. ROM 1.01. 29 P
thou knowest my daughter's of a pretty age. 1.03. 10
of my dug and felt it bitter, pretty fool, | to 1.03. 31
the pretty wretch left crying and said, "ay." 1.03. 44
and, pretty fool, it stinted and said, "ay." 1.03. 48
it is a pretty mocking of the life. TIM 1.01. 35
thou there under thy cloak, pretty flaminius? 3.01. 14 P
my pretty cousin, | blessing upon you! MAC 4.02. 25
all my pretty ones? 4.03.216
what, all my pretty chickens, and their dam, 4.03.218
how do you, pretty lady? HAM 4.05. 41
pretty ophelia! 4.05. 56
how now, my pretty knave, how dost thou? LR 1.04. 96 P
thou wast a pretty fellow when thou hadst no 1.04.191 P
stars are no moe than seven is a pretty reason. 1.05. 35 P
on each side her | stood pretty dimpled boys, ANT 2.02.202
hast thou the pretty worm of nilus there, | that 5.02.243
of him, but had | most pretty things to say. CYM 1.03. 26
with every thing that pretty is, my lady sweet, 2.03. 25
her pretty action did outsell her gift, | and 2.04.102
should tread a course | pretty and full of view; 3.04.147
woman it pretty self) into a waggish courage, 3.04.157
a pretty moral. PER 2.01. 35
a pretty moral; 2.02. 45
chequins were as pretty a proportion to live 4.02. 27 P
our youths we could pick up some pretty estate, 4.02. 32 P
why lament you, pretty one? 4.02. 68 P
that i am pretty. 4.02. 69
now, pretty one, how long have you been at this 4.06. 66 P
but i protest to thee, pretty one, my authority 4.06. 88 P
what shows, | what minstrelsy, and pretty din, 5.02. 7
but was her pattern, her affections (pretty, TNK 1.03. 72
this is a pretty color, will't not do | rarely 2.02.129
wrastling and running. — 'tis a pretty fellow. 2.03. 67
a pretty brown wench 'tis. 3.03. 39
pretty soul! 4.01. 69
pretty soul, | how do ye? 5.02. 69
for to a pretty ear she tunes her tale. VEN 74
that in each cheek appears a pretty dimple; 242
a pretty while these pretty creatures stand, LUC 1233
a pretty while these pretty creatures stand, 1233
the night so pack'd, i post unto my pretty; PP 14.21
these pretty pleasures might me move | to live 19.19
those pretty wrongs that liberty commits | when SON 41. 1
be, | looking with pretty ruth upon my pain. 132. 4
knows | her pretty looks have been mine enemies, 139.10
PREVAIL 23 FR 0.0026 REL FR 20 V 3 P
the world can more prevail in man's commendation
TN 3.02. 37 P
if word nor oath | prevail not, go and see. WT 3.02.204
wherein my hope is i shall so prevail | to force 4.04.664
where how he did prevail i shame to speak. JN 1.01.104
if we prevail, their heads shall pay for it. R2 3.02.126
"if wishes would prevail with me, | my purpose H5 3.02. 15
heavens, can you suffer hell so to prevail? 1H6 1.05. 9
sleeping or waking, must i still prevail, | or 2.01. 56
men | could not prevail with all their oratory, 2.02. 49
thy grave admonishments prevail with me. 2.05. 98
i would prevail, if prayers might prevail, | to 3.01. 67
i would prevail, if prayers might prevail, | to 3.01. 67
god forbid any malice should prevail, | that 2H6 3.02. 23
well, seeing gentle words will not prevail, 4.02.174
but if an humble prayer may prevail, | i then 3H6 4.06. 7
york's dread curse prevail so much with heaven R3 1.03.190
i am strong–fram'd, he cannot prevail with me. 1.04.150 P
they shall no more prevail than we give way to. H8 5.01.143
especially his mother, may prevail with him. COR 5.04. 6 P
let me, upon my knee, prevail in this. JC 2.02. 54
whose ministers would prevail | under the ANT 3.13. 23
you shall prevail, | were it to woo my daughter, PER 5.01.261
how insolence and strong hand should prevail, STM II.C 81
PREVAIL'D 24 FR 0.0027 REL FR 22 V 2 P
you have prevail'd, my lord; TGV 3.02. 46
thou hast prevail'd, i pardon them and thee; 5.04.158
you have prevail'd. ERR 3.01.107
height, forsooth, she hath prevail'd with him. MND 3.02.293
which often hath no less prevail'd than so | on WT 2.01. 54
since then my office hath so far prevail'd, H5 5.02. 29
but reignier, king of naples, that prevail'd. 1H6 5.04. 78
thus suffolk hath prevail'd, and thus he goes, 5.05.103
the dolphin hath prevail'd beyond the seas, 2H6 1.03.125
o peter, thou hast prevail'd in right! 2.03. 99 P
his, | and have prevail'd as much on him as you. R3 1.01.131
and that have prevail'd | upon my body with 3.04. 61
/unroof'd the city | ere so prevail'd with me; COR 1.01.219
but how prevail'd you? 1.06. 45
most dangerously you have with him prevail'd, 5.03.188
the ladies have prevail'd, | the volscians are 5.04. 40
rise, titus, rise, my empress hath prevail'd. TIT 1.01.459
as it hath much prevail'd on your condition, | i JC 2.01.254
thou and those thy scars had once prevail'd | to ANT 4.05. 2
me directly to understand you have prevail'd, i CYM 1.04.159 P
hath prevail'd | on thy too ready hearing? 3.02. 5
whose false oaths prevail'd | before my perfect 3.03. 66
and, to be brief, my practice so prevail'd, 5.05.199
they that nev'r begg'd | but they prevail'd, had TNK 4.01. 27
PREVAILED 1 FR 0.0001 REL FR 1 V 0 P
will sourly leave her till /she have prevailed? SON 41. 8
PREVAILETH 1 FR 0.0001 REL FR 0 V 1 P
the spite of man prevaileth against me. 2H6 1.03.214 P
PREVAILING 3 FR 0.0003 REL FR 2 V 1 P
love — | a sin prevailing much in youthful men, ERR 5.01. 52
they nothing doubt prevailing, and to make it COR 1.03.100 P
before) | my tears are now prevailing orators. TIT 3.01. 26
PREVAILMENT 1 FR 0.0001 REL FR 1 V 0 P
of strong prevailment in unhardened youth. MND 1.01. 35
PREVAILS 4 FR 0.0004 REL FR 4 V 0 P
beam stands sure, whose rightful cause prevails. 2H6 2.01.201
sometime the flood prevails, and then the wind; 3H6 2.05. 9
with whom /an upright zeal to right prevails 5.01. 78
prince's doom, | it helps not, it prevails not. ROM 3.03. 60
PREVENT 30 FR 0.0034 REL FR 25 V 5 P
thou didst prevent me; TMP 1.02.350
for i would prevent | the loose encounters of TGV 2.07. 40
prevent; WIV 2.01.117
i will prevent this, detect my wife, be reveng'd 2.02.310 P
it wants matter to prevent so gross o'erreaching 5.05.136 P
woes, | but presently prevent the ways to wail; R2 3.02.179
prevent it, resist it, let it not be so, | lest 4.01.148
if god prevent not, i purpose so. 5.02. 55
and, to prevent the worst, sir michael, speed; 1H4 4.04. 35
and so both the degrees prevent my curses. 2H4 1.02.232 P
but, to prevent the tyrant's violence | (for 3H6 4.04. 29
therefore, lord oxford, to prevent the worst, 4.06. 96
will touch us all too near, if god prevent not. R3 2.03. 26
unless thou tell me how i may prevent it. ROM 4.01. 51
as that is desperate which we would prevent. 4.01. 70
i'll teach them to prevent wild alcibiades' TIM 5.01.203
then lest he may, prevent. JC 2.01. 28
which to prevent, | let antony and caesar fall 2.01.160
i must prevent thee, cimber. 3.01. 35
might fall, so to prevent | the time of life — 5.01.104
so shall my anticipation prevent your discovery, HAM 2.02.294 P
which for to prevent, | i have in quick 3.01.167
how to prevent the fiend, and to kill vermin. LR 3.04.159 P
lest it see more, prevent it. 3.07. 83
which to prevent he made a law, | to keep her PER 1.ch. 35
we prevent | the loathsome misery of age, TNK 5.04. 6
her, | which cunning love did wittily prevent: VEN 471
post hither, this vile purpose to prevent? LUC 220
i could prevent this storm, and shun thy wrack! 966
urge, | as to prevent our maladies unseen, | we SON 118. 3
PREVENTED 20 FR 0.0022 REL FR 17 V 3 P
o plague right well prevented! ADO 3.02.133 P
if worthier friends had not prevented me. MV 1.01. 61
she hath prevented me. SHR 5.02. 49
her intents, | which thus she hath prevented. AWW 3.04. 22
that caesar himself could not have prevented, if 3.06. 53 P
with gait and entrance — but we are prevented. TN 3.01. 83 P
how near, | which way to be prevented, if to be; WT 1.02.405
this might have been prevented and made whole JN 1.01. 35
myself, | prevented from a damned enterprise. H5 2.02.164
but that i am prevented, | i should have begg'd 1H6 4.01. 71
in my opinion, ought to be prevented. R3 2.02.131
for i, too fond, might have prevented this. 3.04. 81
something against our meanings, have prevented; 3.05. 55
the gods have well prevented it, and rome | sits COR 4.06. 36
o nurse, how shall this be prevented? ROM 3.05.204
that future strife | may be prevented now. LR 1.01. 45
and have prevented | the ostentation of our love ANT 3.06. 51
fury, for one death | might have prevented many. 4.12. 42
but that her flight prevented it, she had CYM 5.05. 46
recount it to you, | but see, i am prevented. PER 5.01. 64
PREVENTION 6 FR 0.0006 REL FR 6 V 0 P
nor the prevention of poor bullingbrook | about R2 2.01.167
but what prevention? H5 1.01. 21
but god be thanked for prevention, | which /i in 2.02.158
snar'd, | nor never seek prevention of thy foes. 2H6 2.04. 57
were dim enough | to hide thee from prevention. JC 2.01. 85
casca, be sudden, for we fear prevention. 3.01. 19
PREVENTIONS 1 FR 0.0001 REL FR 1 V 0 P
achievements, plots, orders, preventions, TRO 1.03.181
PREVENTS 3 FR 0.0003 REL FR 1 V 2 P
fortune, and prevents the slander of his wife. AYL 4.01. 61 P
many a good hanging prevents a bad marriage; TN 1.05. 19 P
forcibly prevents | our lock'd embrasures, TRO 4.04. 36
PREVENT'ST 1 FR 0.0001 REL FR 1 V 0 P
so thou prevent'st his scythe and crooked knife. SON 100.14
PREWARN 1 FR 0.0001 REL FR 1 V 0 P
/... | comets prewarn, whose havoc in vast field TNK 5.01. 51
/PREY 2 FR 0.0002 REL FR 2 V 0 P
whiles kites and buzzards /prey at liberty. R3 1.01.133
/humanity /must /perforce /prey /on /itself, LR 4.02. 49
PREY 47 FR 0.0053 REL FR 43 V 4 P
lion in a cave, | that goes not out to prey. MM 1.03. 23
law, | setting it up to fear the birds of prey, 2.01. 2
and would have reft the fishers of their prey, ERR 1.01.115
thee, thou lamb, that standest as his prey; LLL 4.01. 89
away, | and you sat smiling at his cruel prey. MND 2.02.150
yea, mock the lion when 'a roars for prey, | to MV 2.01. 30
to prey on nothing that doth seem as dead. AYL 4.03.118
of her nature became as a prey to her grief; AWW 4.03. 51 P
if one should be a prey, how much the better TN 3.01.128
for the creatures | of prey that keep upon't. WT 3.03. 13
not pray to her, but prey on her, for they ride 1H4 2.01. 81 P
for once the eagle (england) being in prey, | to H5 1.02.169
the french might have a good prey of us, if he 4.04. 76 P
food, | do rush upon us as their hungry prey. 1H6 1.02. 28
and give her as a prey to law and shame, | that 2H6 2.01.194
the rascal people, thirsting after prey, | join 4.04. 51
and made a prey for carrion kites and crows 5.02. 11
be thou a prey unto the house of york, | and die 3H6 1.01.185
and so he walks, insulting o'er his prey, | and 1.03. 14
that to my foes this body must be prey, | yet 2.03. 39
that wrens make prey where eagles dare not perch
R3 1.03. 70
heart, | without control, lusted to make a prey. 3.05. 84
about, | and left thee but a very prey to time, 4.04.106
thy broken faith hath made the prey for worms. 4.04.386
power), | must make perforce an universal prey, TRO 1.03.123
tigers must prey, and rome affords no prey | but TIT 3.01. 55
and rome affords no prey | but me and mine. 3.01. 55
shall seize this prey out of his father's hands. 4.02. 96
but throw her forth to beasts and birds to prey: 5.03.198
downward look on us | as we were sickly prey. JC 5.01. 86

itself in a celestial bed | and prey on garbage. HAM 1.05. 57
in greediness, dog in madness, lion in prey. LR 3.04. 94 P
and let her down the wind | to prey at fortune. OTH 3.03.263
and gnats of nile | have buried them for prey! ANT 3.13.167
subtle as the fox for prey, | like warlike as CYM 3.03. 40
like to a pair of lions smear'd with prey, TNK 1.04. 18
why may't not be | they have made prey of him? 3.02. 13
till either gorge be stuff'd, or prey be gone; VEN 58
she feedeth on the steam as on a prey, | and 63
now quick desire hath caught the yielding prey, 547
if he had spoke, the wolf would leave his prey, 1097
that for his prey to pray he doth begin, | as if LUC 342
as the grim lion fawneth o'er his prey, | sharp 421
the wolf hath seiz'd his prey, the poor lamb 677
balk | the prey wherein by nature they delight, 697
care, | art left the prey of every vulgar thief. SON 48. 8
the prey of worms, my body being dead, | the 74.10

PREY'D 1 FR 0.0001 REL FR 1 V 0 P
death, having prey'd upon the outward parts, JN 5.07. 15

PREYED 1 FR 0.0001 REL FR 1 V 0 P
the wolves have preyed, and look, the gentle day ADO 5.03. 25

PREYFUL 1 FR 0.0001 REL FR 1 V 0 P
the preyful princess pierc'd and prick'd a LLL 4.02. 56

/PREYS 1 FR 0.0001 REL FR 1 V 0 P
when valor /preys /on reason, | it eats the ANT 3.13.198

PREYS 4 FR 0.0004 REL FR 4 V 0 P
consuming means, soon preys upon itself. R2 2.01. 39
cur | preys on the issue of his mother's body, R3 4.04. 57
night's black agents to their preys do rouse. MAC 3.02. 53
rich preys make true men thieves; VEN 724

PRIAM 24 FR 0.0027 REL FR 24 V 0 P
but priam found the fire ere he his tongue, 2H4 1.01. 74
more, | as priam was for all his valiant sons. 3H6 2.05.120
a prince call'd hector — priam is his father — TRO 1.03.261
as toucheth my particular, | yet, dread priam, 2.02. 10
give us a prince of blood, a son of priam, | in 3.03. 26
by priam and the general state of troy. 4.02. 67
life shall be as safe | as priam is in ilion. 4.04.116
the youngest son of priam, a true knight, | not 4.05. 96
lay hold upon him, priam, hold him fast, | he is 5.03. 59
which you do here forbid me, royal priam. 5.03. 75
o priam, yield not to him! 5.03. 76
who shall tell priam so, or hecuba? 5.10. 15
there is a word will priam turn to stone, | make 5.10. 18
sons, | half of the number that king priam had, TIT 1.01. 80
hellish pyrrhus | old grandsire priam seeks." HAM 2.02.464
pyrrhus at priam drives, in rage strikes wide, 2.02.472
declining on the milky head | of reverent priam, 2.02.479
pyrrhus' bleeding sword | now falls on priam. 2.02.492
"lo here weeps hecuba, here priam dies, | here LUC 1485
had doting priam check'd his son's desire, 1490
story | the credulous old priam after slew; 1522
as priam him did cherish, | so did i tarquin, so 1546
"look, look how list'ning priam wets his eyes, 1548
priam, why art thou old, and yet not wise? 1550

PRIAMI 3 FR 0.0003 REL FR 1 V 2 P
hic steterat priami regia celsa senis." SHR 3.01. 29
and that lucentio that comes a-wooing, "priami," 3.01. 35 P
i trust you not, "hic steterat priami," take 3.01. 43 P

/PRIAM'S 1 FR 0.0001 REL FR 1 V 0 P
/priam's //six-gated /city, | /dardan /and TRO pr 15

PRIAM'S 14 FR 0.0015 REL FR 12 V 2 P
done, done fond, | was this king priam's joy?" AWW 1.03. 73
drew priam's curtain in the dead of night, | and 2H4 1.01. 72
at priam's royal table do i sit, | and when fair TRO 1.01. 29
i am no more touch'd than all priam's sons; 2.02.126
let us to priam's hall | to greet the warriors. 3.01.148
you are in love | with one of priam's daughters. 3.03.194
son, | a cousin-german to great priam's seed; 4.05.121
a bastard son of priam's. 5.07. 15 P
when subtile greeks surpris'd king priam's troy. TIT 5.03. 84
especially when he speaks of priam's slaughter. HAM 2.02.448 P
of skillful painting, made for priam's troy, LUC 1367
staring on priam's wounds with her old eyes, 1448
and drop sweet balm in priam's painted wound, 1466
so priam's trust false sinon's tears doth 1560

PRIAMUS 2 FR 0.0002 REL FR 2 V 0 P
yours, | you valiant offspring of great priamus. TRO 2.02.207
my retire, | not priamus and hecuba on knees, 5.03. 54

PRIAPUS 1 FR 0.0001 REL FR 0 V 1 P
she's able to freeze the god priapus, and undo a PER 4.06. 4 P

PRIBBLES *(also brabble, prabbles)*

PRIBBLES 2 FR 0.0002 REL FR 0 V 2 P
motion if we leave our pribbles and prabbles, WIV 1.01. 55 P
swearings and starings, pribbles and prabbles? 5.05.160 P

PRICE 33 FR 0.0037 REL FR 22 V 11 P
and held in idle price to haunt assemblies MM 1.03. 9
ones, poor ones may make what price they will. ADO 3.03.115 P
"what's the price of this inkle?" LLL 3.01.138 P
we can afford no more at such a price. 5.02.223
price you yourselves; what buys your company? 5.02.224
of christians will raise the price of hogs. MV 3.05. 24 P
jews to christians, you raise the price of pork. 3.05. 36 P
his qualities being at this poor price, i need AWW 4.03.276 P
make trivial price of serious things we have, 5.03. 61
so, | he might have bought me at a common price. 5.03.190
but falls into abatement and low price | even in TN 1.01. 13
if you hold your life at any price, betake you 3.04.230 P
fellow never joy'd since the price of oats rose, 1H4 2.01. 12 P
and golden times, and happy news of price. 2H4 5.03. 96
forgive, | although my body pay the price of it. H5 2.02.154
the doom of death | for pax of little price. 3.06. 45
whose price hath launch'd above a thousand ships TRO 2.02. 82
add, | that if he overhold his price so much, 2.03.133
kill him, and we'll have corn at our own price. COR 1.01. 11 P
well then, i pray, your price a' th' consulship? 2.03. 73 P
the price is, to ask it kindly. 2.03. 75 P
buy | their mercy at the price of one fair word, 3.03. 91
of them | as jewels purchas'd at an easy price, TIT 3.01.198
who now the price of his dear blood doth owe? ROM 3.01.183
if i do so, it will be of more price, | being 4.01. 27
did hold her so, | but now her price is fallen. LR 1.01.197
i know my price, i am worth no worse a place. OTH 1.01. 11
it is a great price | for a small vice. 4.03. 69
her own price | proclaims how she esteem'd him; CYM 1.01. 51
what's her price, boult? PER 4.02. 50 P
the price and garland | to crown the question's TNK 5.03. 16
which some will say | weakens his price, and 5.04. 52
vultur thought doth pitch the price so high VEN 551

PRICELESS 1 FR 0.0001 REL FR 1 V 0 P
what priceless wealth the heavens had him lent LUC 17

/PRICK 1 FR 0.0001 REL FR 0 V 1 P
/prick /him. 2H4 3.02.110 P

PRICK 31 FR 0.0035 REL FR 19 V 12 P
let the mark have a prick in't, to mete at, if LLL 4.01.132
if you prick us, do we not bleed? MV 3.01. 64 P
find, | must find love's prick and rosalind. AYL 3.02.112
you barely leave our thorns to prick ourselves, AWW 4.02. 19
and prick my tender patience to those thoughts R2 2.01.207
but how if honor prick me off when i come on? 1H4 5.01.130 P
for they never prick their finger but they say, 2H4 2.02.112 P
shadow will serve for summer, prick him, for we 3.02.133 P
shall i prick him, sir john? 3.02.142 P
prick him no more. 3.02.145 P
shall i prick him, sir? 3.02.151 P
prick the woman's tailor. 3.02.160 P
come prick bullcalf till he roar again. 3.02.175 P
live honestly by the prick of their needles but H5 2.01. 34 P
i would prick your guts a little in good terms, 2.01. 58 P
prick not your finger as you pluck it off, 1H6 2.04. 49
and made an evening at the noontide prick. 3H6 1.04. 34
do not honor him so much | to prick thy finger, 1.04. 55
can so young a thorn begin to prick? 5.05. 13
scruple, and prick, on certain speeches utter'd H8 2.04.172
prick love for pricking, and you beat love down. ROM 1.04. 28
hand of the dial is now upon the prick of noon. 2.04.113 P
spur but our own cause | to prick us to redress? JC 2.01.124
prick him down, antony. 4.01. 3
have no spur | to prick the sides of my intent, MAC 1.07. 26
go prick thy face, and over-red thy fear, | thou 5.03. 14
in her bosom lodge | to prick and sting her. HAM 1.05. 88
let's see, | i feel this pin prick. LR 4.07. 55
a needle, that i might prick | the goer-back. CYM 1.01.168
o for a prick now, like a nightingale, | to put TNK 3.04. 25
fair, | ere he arrive his weary noontide prick, LUC 781

PRICK'D 16 FR 0.0018 REL FR 10 V 6 P
like unback'd colts, they prick'd their ears, TMP 4.01.176
princess pierc'd and prick'd a pretty pleasing LLL 4.02. 56
of forty fancies prick'd in't for a feather: SHR 3.02. 69 P
the fiend hath prick'd down bardolph 2H4 2.04.332 P
i was prick'd well enough before, and you could 3.02.111 P
you need not to have prick'd me, there are other 3.02.114 P
had been a man's tailor, he'd 'a' prick'd you. 3.02.153 P
what, dost thou roar before thou art prick'd? 3.02.178 P
prick'd on by public wrongs sustain'd in france, 1H6 3.02. 78
worm | prick'd from the lazy finger of a /maid. ROM 1.04. 69
will you be prick'd in number of our friends, JC 3.01.216
many then shall die, their names are prick'd. 4.01. 1
and took his voice who should be prick'd to die 4.01. 16
thereto prick'd on by a most emulate pride, HAM 1.01. 83
far | (prick'd to't by foolish honesty and love) OTH 3.03.412
but since she prick'd thee out for women's SON 20.13

PRICK-EAR'D 1 FR 0.0001 REL FR 1 V 0 P
thou prick-ear'd cur of iceland! H5 2.01. 42

PRICKET 6 FR 0.0006 REL FR 2 V 4 P
'twas not a haud credo, 'twas a pricket. LLL 4.02. 12 P
the deer was not a haud credo, 'twas a pricket. 4.02. 21 P
that, 'twas a pricket that the princess kill'd. 4.02. 48 P
/call /i the deer the princess kill'd a pricket. 4.02. 52 P
pierc'd and prick'd a pretty pleasing pricket; 4.02. 56
from thicket, | or pricket sore, or else sorel; 4.02. 59

PRICKING 5 FR 0.0005 REL FR 4 V 1 P
briers, sharp furzes, pricking goss, and thorns, TMP 4.01.180
that you might leave pricking it for pity. COR 1.03. 86 P
prick love for pricking, and you beat love down. ROM 1.04. 28
by the pricking of my thumbs, | something wicked MAC 4.01. 44
what cares he now for curb or pricking spur, VEN 285

PRICKLES 1 FR 0.0001 REL FR 1 V 0 P
what though the rose have prickles, yet 'tis VEN 574

PRICKS 12 FR 0.0013 REL FR 10 V 2 P
way, and mount | their pricks at my footfall; TMP 2.02. 12
my duty pricks me on to utter that | which, else TGV 3.01. 8
i (as my ever-esteemed duty pricks me on) have LLL 1.01.266 P
she's too hard for you at pricks, sir, challenge 4.01.138
'tis some odd humor pricks him to this fashion; SHR 3.02. 72
the which he pricks and wounds | with many JN 5.07. 17
to know what pricks you on | to take advantage R2 2.03. 78
well, 'tis no matter, honor pricks me on. 1H4 5.01.129 P
(although small pricks | to their subsequent TRO 1.03.343
rude, too boist'rous, and it pricks like thorn. ROM 1.04. 26
numb'd and mortified arms | pins, wooden pricks, LR 2.03. 16
and griping it, the needle his finger pricks, LUC 319

PRICK-SONG 1 FR 0.0001 REL FR 0 V 1 P
he fights as you sing prick-song, keeps time, ROM 2.04. 21 P

PRICK'ST 1 FR 0.0001 REL FR 0 V 1 P
there thou prick'st her with a thistle. ADO 3.04. 76 P

PRICK'T 1 FR 0.0001 REL FR 1 V 0 P
will you prick't with your eye? LLL 2.01.189

/PRIDE 1 FR 0.0001 REL FR 1 V 0 P
/the /pride /of /kingly /sway /from /out /my R2 4.01.206

PRIDE 124 FR 0.0140 REL FR 113 V 11 P
and, may i say to thee, this pride of hers, TGV 3.01. 72
wherein (let no man hear me) i take pride, MM 2.04. 10
"fly pride," says the peacock: ERR 4.03. 80
that advance their pride | against that power ADO 3.01. 10
stand i condemn'd for pride and scorn so much? 3.01.108
contempt, farewell, and maiden pride, adieu! 3.01.109
all pride is willing pride, and yours is so. LLL 2.01. 36
all pride is willing pride, and yours is so. 2.01. 36
proud with his form, in his eye pride expressed; 2.01.237
o short-liv'd pride! 4.01. 15
now much beshrew my manners and my pride, | if MND 2.02. 54
my pride fell with my fortunes, | i'll ask him AYL 1.02.252
who cries out on pride | that can therein tax 2.07. 70
the greatest of my pride is to see my ewes graze 3.02. 76 P
he's proud — and yet his pride becomes him. 3.05.114
nor bitterness | were in his pride or sharpness; AWW 1.02. 37
i love thee so, that, maugre all thy pride, TN 3.01.151
and for we think the eagle-winged pride | of R2 1.03.129
side, | for time hath set a blot upon my pride. 3.02. 81
and, for they cannot, die in their own pride. 5.05. 22
since pride must have a fall, and break the neck 5.05. 88
thy kingly doom and sentence of his pride. 5.06. 23
and pride of their contention did take horse, 1H4 1.01. 60
who is sweet fortune's minion and her pride, 1.01. 83
think you, coz, | of this young percy's pride? 1.01. 92
pride, haughtiness, opinion, and disdain, | the 3.01.183
and now their pride and mettle is asleep, 4.03. 22
men of all sorts take a pride to gird at me. 2H4 1.02. 6 P
or swell my thoughts to any strain of pride, 4.05.170
with half their forces the full pride of france, H5 1.02.112
free from vainness and self-glorious pride; 5.pr. 20
pranks, | as very infants prattle of thy pride. 1H6 3.01. 16
that hardly we escap'd the pride of france. 3.02. 40
and from the pride of gallia rescued thee. 4.06. 15
and, commendable prov'd, let's die in pride. 4.06. 57
died | my icarus, my blossom, in his pride. 4.07. 16
though humphrey's pride | and greatness of his 2H6 1.01.172
pride went before, ambition follows him. 1.01.180
the pride of suffolk and the cardinal, | with 1.01.201
first, for i cannot flatter thee in pride; 1.03.166
image of pride, why should i hold my peace? 1.03.176
at beauford's pride, at somerset's ambition, 2.02. 71
thus eleanor's pride dies in her youngest days. 2.03. 46
ay, and allay this thy abortive pride: 4.01. 60
what hath broach'd this tumult but thy pride? 3H6 2.02.159
have we mow'd down in tops of all their pride! 5.07. 4
and richard falls in height of all his pride! R3 5.03.176
did almost sweat to bear | the pride upon them, H8 1.01. 25
but i can see his pride | peep through each part 1.01. 68
this priest has no pride in him? 2.02. 81
is cramm'd with arrogancy, spleen, and pride. 2.04.110
my high-blown pride | at length broke under me, 3.02.361
the seeded pride | that hath to this maturity TRO 1.03.316
than in the pride and salt scorn of his eyes, 1.03.370
pride alone | must /tarre the mastiffs on, as 1.03.389
but, by my head, 'tis pride. 2.03. 88 P
how doth pride grow? 2.03.151 P
i know not what pride is. 2.03.152 P
pride is his own glass, his own trumpet, his own 2.03.155 P
and speaks not to himself but with a pride 2.03.171
that were to enlard his fat-already pride, | and 2.03.195
and he be proud with me, i'll pheese his pride. 2.03.205
shall pride carry it? 2.03.218 P
to use between your strangeness and his pride, 3.03. 45
pride hath no other glass | to show itself but 3.03. 47
hath no other glass | to show itself but pride; 3.03. 48
how one man eats into another's pride, | while 3.03.136
while pride is fasting in his wantonness! 3.03.137
valor and pride excel themselves in hector, 4.05. 79
and that which looks like pride is courtesy. 4.05. 82
especially in pride. COR 2.01. 19 P
because you talk of pride now — will you not be 2.01. 25 P
you talk of pride: 2.01. 38 P
enforce his pride, | and his old hate unto you; 2.03.219
thy mother rather feel thy pride than fear | thy 3.02.126
but owe thy pride thyself. 3.02.130
o'ercome with pride, ambitious past all thinking 4.06. 31
whether /'twas pride, | which out of daily 4.07. 37
to his surname coriolanus 'longs more pride 5.03.170
and took some pride | to do myself this wrong; 5.06. 36
and chastised with arms | our enemies' pride; TIT 1.01. 33
we will afflict the emperor in his pride. 4.03. 63
let two more summers wither in their pride, ROM 1.02. 10
and 'tis much pride | for fair without the fair 1.03. 89
sour cold habit on | to castigate thy pride, TIM 4.03.240
pride and wrath would confound thee and make 4.03.336 P
a falcon, tow'ring in her pride of place, | was MAC 2.04. 12
thereto prick'd on by a most emulate pride, HAM 1.01. 83
let pride, which she calls plainness, marry her. LR 1.01.129
and with strain'd pride | to come betwixt our 1.01.169
this is a slave whose easy-borrowed pride 2.04.185
but he, as loving his own pride and purposes, OTH 1.01. 12
'tis pride that pulls the country down, | /then 2.03. 95
pride, pomp, and circumstance of glorious war! 3.03.354
as salt as wolves in pride, and fools as gross 3.03.404
the banks, or for | the press of boats or pride. CYM 2.04. 72
all poverty was scorn'd, and pride so great, PER 1.04. 30
even in the height and pride of all his glory, 2.04. 6
if't pleas'd his rider | to put pride in him. TNK 5.04. 58
steps, | with gentle majesty and modest pride; VEN 278
loseth his pride, and never waxeth strong. 420
sith in thy pride so fair a hope is slain. 762
and as their captain, so their pride doth grow, LUC 298
swell in their pride, the onset still expecting. 432
smoking with pride, march'd on, to make his 438
thou loathed in their shame, they in thy pride. 662
while lust is in his pride, no exclamation | can 705
who in their pride do presently abuse it; 864
yet in the eddy boundeth in his pride | back to 1669
began to clothe his wit in state and pride, 1809
devil, | wooing his purity with her fair pride. PP 2. 8
and in themselves their pride lies buried, | for SON 25. 7
blest, | by new unfolding his imprison'd pride. 52.12
why is my verse so barren of new pride? 76. 1
boat, | he of tall building and of goodly pride. 80.12
and having thee, of all men's pride i boast: 91.12
the purple pride | which on thy soft cheek for 99. 3
in pride of all his growth | a vengeful canker 99.12
that, having such a scope to show her pride, 103. 2
from the forests shook three summers' pride, 104. 4
devil, | wooing his purity with her foul pride. 144. 8
proud of this pride, | he is contented thy poor 151.10
proclaim'd in her a careless hand of pride; LC 30
did livery falseness in a pride of truth. 105

PRIDES 1 FR 0.0001 REL FR 1 V 0 P
ambitions, covetings, change of prides, disdain, CYM 2.05. 25

PRIDGE *(also bridge)*

PRIDGE 6 FR 0.0006 REL FR 0 V 6 P
is an aunchient lieutenant there at the pridge, H5 3.06. 13 P
prave words at the pridge as you shall see in a 3.06. 64 P
and i must speak with him from the pridge. 3.06. 86 P
exeter has very gallantly maintain'd the pridge. 3.06. 91 P
athversary was have possession of the pridge, 3.06. 94 P
and the duke of exeter is master of the pridge. 3.06. 95 P

PRIE 1 FR 0.0001 REL FR 0 V 1 P
je te prie, m'enseignez; H5 3.04. 4 P

PRIED 1 FR 0.0001 REL FR 1 V 0 P
i pried me through the crevice of a wall, | when TIT 5.01.114

PRIEF *(also breff, brief*)*

PRIEF 1 FR 0.0001 REL FR 0 V 1 P
i will make a prief of it in my note-book, and WIV 1.01.144 P

PRIES 1 FR 0.0001 REL FR 1 V 0 P

which pries not to th' interior, but, like the MV 2.09. 28
/PRIEST 1 FR 0.0001 REL FR 1 V 0 P
/am /i /both /priest /and /clerk? R2 4.01.173
PRIEST 59 FR 0.0066 REL FR 40 V 19 P
a scurvy jack–a–nape priest to meddle or make — WIV 1.04.110 P
by gar, i vill kill de jack priest; 1.04.117 P
though the priest o' th' town commended him for 2.01.145 P
sir hugh the welsh priest and caius the french 2.01.201 P
by gar, he is de coward jack priest of de vorld; 2.03. 31 P
scurvy jack–dog priest! 2.03. 63 P
by gar, me vill kill de priest, for he speak for 2.03. 82 P
my priest? 3.01.104 P
and at the dean'ry, where a priest attends, 4.06. 31
bring you the maid, you shall not lack a priest. 4.06. 53
with a priest that lacks latin, and a rich man AYL 3.02.319 P
and have a good priest that can tell you what 3.03. 85 P
sister, you shall be the priest, and marry us. 4.01.124 P
there's a girl goes before the priest, and 4.01.140 P
faith, the priest was good enough, for all the 5.01. 3 P
to want the bridegroom when the priest attends SHR 3.02. 5
when the priest | should ask if katherine should 3.02.158
that, all amaz'd, the priest let fall the book, 3.02.161
such a cuff | that down fell priest and book, 3.02.164
down fell priest and book, and book and priest. 3.02.164
the old priest of saint luke's church is at your 4.04. 88 P
to th' church take the priest, clerk, and some 4.04. 94 P
saint luke's to bid the priest be ready to come 4.04.103 P
and swiftly, sir, for the priest is ready. 5.01. 1 P
although before the solemn priest i have sworn, AWW 2.03.269
had rather go with sir priest than sir knight. TN 3.04.271 P
kept in a dark house, visited by the priest, 5.01.342
the hand deliver'd | of great apollo's priest; WT 3.02.128
and lay me | where no priest shovels in dust. 4.04.458
that no italian priest | shall tithe or toll in JN 3.01.153
are led so grossly by this meddling priest, 3.01.163
peel'd priest, dost thou command me to be shut 1H6 1.03. 30
priest, beware your beard, | i mean to tug it 1.03. 47
presumptuous priest, this place commands my 3.01. 8
am i not protector, saucy priest? 3.01. 45
or i would see his heart out ere the priest 3.01.120
i gave a noble to the priest | the morn that i 5.04. 23
now by god's mother, priest, i'll shave your 2H6 2.01. 50
york and impious beauford, that false priest, 2.04. 53
say but the word, and i will be his priest. 3.01.272
ere you can take due orders for a priest. 3.01.274
what, talking with a priest, lord chamberlain? R3 3.02.113
friends at pomfret, they do need the priest, 3.02.114
o, now i need the priest that spake to me! 3.04. 87
that blind priest, like the eldest son of H8 2.02. 20
this priest has no pride in him? 2.02. 81
this just and learned priest, card'nal campeius, 2.02. 96
thou art a proud traitor, priest. 3.02.252
your long coat, priest, protects you, thou 3.02.276
helenus is a priest. TRO 1.02.225 P
you are for dreams and slumbers, brother priest, 2.02. 37
a priest there off'ring to it his own heart. 4.03. 9
gods, | sith priest and holy water are so near, TIT 1.01.323
i would not part a bachelor from the priest. 1.01.488
i tell thee, churlish priest, | a minist'ring HAM 5.01.240
should he make me | live, like diana's priest, CYM 1.06.133
i here, thy priest, | am humbled 'fore thine TNK 5.01.142
some blind priest for the purpose that will 5.02. 78
let the priest in surplice white, | that PHT 13
PRIESTHOOD 2 FR 0.0002 REL FR 2 V 0 P
is your priesthood grown peremptory? 2H6 2.01. 23
chaplain, away, thy priesthood saves thy life. 3H6 1.03. 3
PRIEST–LIKE 2 FR 0.0002 REL FR 2 V 0 P
wherein, priest–like, thou | hast cleans'd my WT 1.02.237
suppler souls | than in our priest–like fasts: COR 5.01. 56
PRIESTLY 1 FR 0.0001 REL FR 1 V 0 P
thee, whiles i say | a priestly farewell to her. PER 3.01. 69
PRIESTS 15 FR 0.0017 REL FR 12 V 3 P
like god bel's priests in the old church–window, ADO 3.03.135 P
where the sad and solemn priests | sing still H5 4.01.301
and all the priests and friars in my realm 1H6 1.06. 19
priests pray for enemies, but princes kill. 2H6 5.02. 71
the prayers of priests nor times of sacrifice, COR 1.10. 21
our very priests must become mockers if they 2.01. 84 P
will lug your priests and servants from your TIM 4.03. 32
nor sight of priests in holy vestments bleeding, 4.03.126
swear priests and cowards, and men cautelous, JC 2.01.129
go bid the priests do present sacrifice, | and 2.02. 5
when priests are more in word than matter; LR 3.02. 81
that the holy priests | bless her when she is ANT 2.02.238
are worse | than priests and fanes that lie. CYM 4.02.242
our cavalleria, and make our swearers priests. PER 4.06. 12 P
when my maiden priests are met together | before 5.01.242
PRIG 2 FR 0.0002 REL FR 0 V 2 P
prig, for my life, prig! WT 4.03.101 P
prig, for my life, prig! 4.03.101 P
PRIMAL 2 FR 0.0002 REL FR 2 V 0 P
it hath the primal eldest curse upon't, | a HAM 3.03. 37
it hath been taught us from the primal state ANT 1.04. 41
/PRIME 1 FR 0.0001 REL FR 1 V 0 P
though not his /prime consent, he did not flow PER 4.03. 27
PRIME 22 FR 0.0024 REL FR 22 V 0 P
and prospero the prime duke, being so reputed TMP 1.02. 72
my prime request, | which i do last pronounce, 1.02.426
bud, | losing his verdure, even in the prime, TGV 1.01. 49
nonino, | for love is crowned with the prime, AYL 5.03. 32
all | that happiness and prime can happy call. AWW 2.01.182
lest you be cropp'd before you come to prime. R2 5.02. 51
how well resembles it the prime of youth, 3H6 2.01. 23
cropp'd the golden prime of this sweet prince R3 1.02.247
that from the prime creation e'er she framed." 4.03. 19
thy prime of manhood daring, bold, and venturous 4.04.171
think how thou stab'st me in my prime of youth 5.03.119
i not made you | the prime man of the state? H8 3.02.162
were they as prime as goats, as hot as monkeys, OTH 3.03.403
and our prime cousin, yet unhard'ned in | the TNK 1.02. 2
flowers that are not gath'red in their prime VEN 131
they wither in their prime, prove nothing worth: 418
sith in his prime death doth my love destroy, 1163
spring, | to add a more rejoicing to the prime, LUC 332
thee | calls back the lovely april of her prime, SON 3.10
when i behold the violet past prime, | and sable 12. 3
and thou present'st a pure unstained prime. 70. 8
bearing the wanton burthen of the prime, | like 97. 7
PRIMER 1 FR 0.0001 REL FR 1 V 0 P
for | there is no primer baseness. H8 1.02. 67
PRIMERO 2 FR 0.0002 REL FR 1 V 1 P
prosper'd since i forswore myself at primero. WIV 4.05.102 P
and left him at primero | with the duke of H8 5.01. 7
PRIMEROSES *(also primrose)*
PRIMEROSES 2 FR 0.0002 REL FR 2 V 0 P
pale primeroses, | that die unmarried, ere they WT 4.04.122
the violets, cowslips, and the primeroses, CYM 1.05. 83
PRIMEST 1 FR 0.0001 REL FR 1 V 0 P
before the primest creature | that's paragon'd H8 2.04.230
PRIMITIVE 1 FR 0.0001 REL FR 0 V 1 P
the primitive statue and oblique memorial of TRO 5.01. 54 P
PRIMO 1 FR 0.0001 REL FR 0 V 1 P
primo, secundo, tertio, is a good play, and the TN 5.01. 36 P
PRIMOGENITY 1 FR 0.0001 REL FR 1 V 0 P
shores, | the primogenity and due of birth, TRO 1.03.106
PRIMROSE *(also primeroses)*
PRIMROSE 7 FR 0.0008 REL FR 6 V 1 P
i | upon faint primrose beds were wont to lie, MND 1.01.215
look pale as primrose with blood–drinking sighs, 2H6 3.02. 63
that go the primrose way to th' everlasting MAC 2.03. 19 P
himself the primrose path of dalliance treads, HAM 1.03. 50
the flower that's like thy face, pale primrose, CYM 4.02.221
primrose, first–born child of ver, | merry TNK 1.01. 7
"witness this primrose bank whereon i lie, VEN 151
PRIM'ST 3 FR 0.0003 REL FR 3 V 0 P
the prim'st for this proceeding, and the number TNK 1.01.161
beauteous morn | (the prim'st of all the year) 3.01. 19
and he is | doubtless the prim'st of men. 5.03. 70
PRIMY 1 FR 0.0001 REL FR 1 V 0 P
blood, | a violet in the youth of primy nature, HAM 1.03. 7
PRINCE' 2 FR 0.0002 REL FR 2 V 0 P
show'dst a subject's shine, i a true prince'. PER 1.02.124
good alive, | and to fulfill his prince' desire, 2.ch. 21
/PRINCE 4 FR 0.0004 REL FR 3 V 1 P
this swears he, as he is /a /prince, /is just, R2 3.03.119
/speak, /prince /of /ithaca, /and /be't /of TRO 1.03. 70
/hobbididence, /prince /of /dumbness; LR 4.01. 60 P
/a /man, /a /prince, /by /him /so /benefited! 4.02. 45
PRINCE 371 FR 0.0419 REL FR 275 V 96 P
the king and prince at prayers! TMP 1.01. 54
was the duke of milan and | a prince of power. 1.02. 55
i am, in my condition, | a prince, miranda; 3.01. 60
for more assurance that a living prince | does 5.01.108
know, worthy prince, sir valentine, my friend, TGV 3.01. 10
he kept company with the wild prince and poins; WIV 3.02. 73 P
of your order, | visit both prince and people; MM 1.03. 45
o worthy prince, dishonor not your eye | by 5.01. 22
o prince, i conjure thee, as thou believ'st 5.01. 48
believe it, royal prince, | if he be less, he's 5.01. 57
noble prince, | as there comes light from heaven 5.01.224
then, good prince, | no longer session hold upon 5.01.370
hither, isabel, | your friar is now your prince. 5.01.382
slandering a prince deserves it. 5.01.524
justice, sweet prince, against that woman there! ERR 5.01.197
being reconcil'd to the prince your brother: ADO 1.01.155 P
the prince and count claudio, walking in a 1.02. 8 P
the prince discover'd to claudio that he lov'd 1.02. 11 P
the prince your brother is royally entertain'd 1.03. 43 P
a musty room, comes me the prince and claudio, 1.03. 59 P
agreed upon that the prince should woo hero for 1.03. 62 P
if the prince do solicit you in that kind, you 2.01. 67 P
if the prince be too important, tell him there 2.01. 70 P
'tis certain so, the prince woos for himself. 2.01.174
it one way, for the prince hath got your hero. 2.01.191 P
did you think the prince would have serv'd you 2.01.195 P
go you to the prince your brother; 2.02. 22 P
proof enough to misuse the prince, to vex 2.02. 28 P
a kind of zeal both to the prince and claudio — 2.02. 36 P
the prince and monsieur love! 2.03. 35 P
proposing with the prince and claudio. 3.01. 3
so says the prince and my new–trothed lord. 3.01. 38
if you meet the prince in the night, you may 3.03. 76 P
marry, not without the prince be willing, for 3.03. 80 P
i should first tell thee how the prince, claudio 3.03.149 P
two of them did, the prince and claudio, but the 3.03.154 P
madam, withdraw, the prince, the count, signior 3.04. 95 P
sweet prince, you learn me noble thankfulness. 4.01. 30
sweet prince, why speak not you? 4.01. 63
is this the prince? 4.01. 70
love | is very much unto the prince and claudio, 4.01.246
write down prince john a villain. 4.02. 41 P
prince john is this morning secretly stol'n away 4.02. 61 P
so shall the prince, | and all of them that thus 5.01. 43
here comes the prince and claudio hastily. 5.01. 45
sweet prince, let me go no farther to mine 5.01.230 P
accus'd, the prince and claudio mightily abus'd, 5.02. 97 P
so are the prince and claudio, who accus'd her 5.04. 2
the prince and claudio promis'd by this hour 5.04. 13
you had from me, | from claudio, and the prince. 5.04. 26
here comes the prince and claudio. 5.04. 33
good morrow, prince; 5.04. 35
why then your uncle and the prince and claudio 5.04. 75
i'll tell thee what, prince: 5.04.100 P
prince, thou art sad, get thee a wife, get thee 5.04.122 P
as jewels in crystal for some prince to buy, LLL 2.01.243
dread prince of plackets, king of codpieces, 3.01.184
makes sport | to the prince and his book–mates. 4.01.100
first, there is the neapolitan prince. MV 1.02. 39 P
come from a fift, the prince of morocco, who 1.02.125 P
who brings word the prince his master will be 1.02.126 P
yourself, renowned prince, then stood as fair 2.01. 20
that slew the sophy and a persian prince | that 2.01. 25
the several caskets to this noble prince. 2.07. 2
the one of them contains my picture, prince: 2.07. 11
take it, prince, and if my form lie there, 2.07. 61
the prince of arragon hath ta'en his oath, | and 2.09. 2
behold, there stand the caskets, noble prince. 2.09. 4
some oration fairly spoke | by a beloved prince, 3.02.179
such duty as the subject owes the prince, | even SHR 5.02.155
you, i can serve as great a prince as you are. AWW 4.05. 37 P
what prince is that? 4.05. 41 P
the black prince, sir, alias the prince of 4.05. 42 P
sir, alias the prince of darkness, alias the 4.05. 42 P
but sure he is the prince of the world; 4.05. 49 P
comfort of your young prince mamillius: WT 1.01. 35 P
are you so fond of your young prince as we | do 1.02.164
give scandal to the blood o' th' prince my son 1.02.330
present our services to a fine new prince | one 2.01. 17
leave out | betwixt the prince and beggar. 2.01. 87
the mother to a hopeful prince, here standing 3.02. 40
the prince your son, with mere conceit and fear 3.02.144
the death | of the young prince, whose honorable 3.02.195
when saw'st thou the prince florizel, my son? 4.02. 26 P
sir, it is three days since i saw the prince. 4.02. 29 P
i have serv'd prince florizel, and in my time 4.03. 13 P
i knew him once a servant of the prince. 4.03. 88 P
that knew'st this was the prince, and wouldst 4.04.459
the prince himself is about a piece of iniquity: 4.04.678 P
and a means to do the prince my master good; 4.04.834 P
one that gives out himself prince florizel, 5.01. 85
had our prince, | jewel of children, seen this 5.01.115
your mother was most true to wedlock, prince, 5.01.124
their country quitted | with this young prince. 5.01.193
the old man and his son aboard the prince; 5.02.115 P
and then the prince, my brother, and the 5.02.142 P
me your good report to the prince my master. 5.02.151 P
i will swear to the prince thou art as honest a 5.02.156 P
i'll swear to the prince thou art a tall fellow 5.02.164 P
to him that owes it, namely this young prince, JN 2.01.248
speak then, prince dolphin, can you love this 2.01.524
good morrow, little prince. 4.01. 9
as little prince, having so great a title | to 4.01. 10
having so great a title | to be more prince, as 4.01. 11
but you at your sick service had a prince. 4.01. 52
made it no conscience to destroy a prince. 4.02.229
who kill'd this prince? 4.03.103
thou art more deep damn'd than prince lucifer. 4.03.122
to your proceedings, yet believe me, prince, | i 5.02. 11
hail, noble prince of france! 5.02. 68
where is my prince, the dolphin? 5.05. 9
and brought prince henry in their company, | at 5.06. 34
be of good comfort, prince, for you are born 5.07. 25
let it be so, and you, my noble prince, | with 5.07. 96
tend'ring the precious safety of my prince, R2 1.01. 32
of whom thy father, prince of wales, was first. 2.01.172
such wrongs are borne | in him, a royal prince, 2.01.239
and myself | rescued the black prince, that 2.03.101
you have misled a prince, a royal king, | a 3.01. 8
myself, a prince by fortune of my birth, | near 3.01. 16
most mighty prince, my lord northumberland, 3.03.172
my lord, some two days since i saw the prince, 5.03. 13
hail, royal prince! 5.05. 67
it is a conquest for a prince to boast of. 1H4 1.01. 77
comparative, rascalliest, sweet young prince. 1.02. 81 P
i prithee leave the prince and me alone, i will 1.02.149 P
hears may be believ'd, that the true prince may 1.02.155 P
and that same sword–and–buckler prince of wales, 1.03.230
i prithee, good prince — hal! 2.02. 40 P
and the prince and poins be not two arrant 2.02. 99 P
that though i be but prince of wales, yet i am 2.04. 10 P
you, prince of wales! 2.04.139 P
should i turn upon the true prince? 2.04.270 P
the lion will not touch the true prince. 2.04.272 P
for a valiant lion, and thou for a true prince. 2.04.275 P
o jesu, my lord the prince! 2.04.284 P
you will not touch the true prince, no, fie! 2.04.301 P
i'll tickle ye for a young prince, i' faith. 2.04.444 P
the prince of wales and i | must have some 3.02. 1
o jesu, i have heard the prince tell him, i know 3.03. 83 P
the prince is a jack, a sneak–up. 3.03. 85 P
i dare, but as thou art prince, i fear thee as i 3.03.146 P
is marching hitherwards, with him prince john. 4.01. 89
son, | the nimble–footed madcap prince of wales, 4.01. 95
against the bosom of the prince of wales. 4.01.121
the prince of wales, lord john of lancaster, 4.04. 29
the prince of wales doth join with all the world 5.01. 86
and, prince of wales, so dare we venture thee, 5.01.101
the prince of wales stepp'd forth before the 5.02. 45
and, which became him like a prince indeed, | he 5.02. 60
did i hear | of any prince so wild a liberty. 5.02. 71
the prince of wales from such a field as this, 5.04. 12
it is the prince of wales that threatens thee, 5.04. 42
i am the prince of wales, and think not, percy, 5.04. 63
reign | of harry percy and the prince of wales. 5.04. 67
prince harry slain outright, and both the blunts 2H4 1.01. 16
young prince john | and westmerland and stafford 1.01. 17
if the prince put thee into my service for any 1.02. 12 P
the juvenal, the prince your master, whose chin 1.02. 19 P
that committed the prince for striking him about 1.02. 56 P
you have misled the youthful prince. 1.02.144 P
the young prince hath misled me. 1.02.145 P
you follow the young prince up and down, like 1.02.163 P
the box of the year that the prince gave you, he 1.02.195 P
he gave it like a rude prince, and you took it 1.02.195 P
well, god send the prince a better companion! 1.02.199 P
god send the companion a better prince! 1.02.201 P
to my lord of lancaster, this to the prince, 1.02.239 P
when the prince broke thy head for liking his 2.01. 89 P
and harry prince of wales | are near at hand. 2.01.134
a prince should not be so loosely studied as to 2.02. 7 P
king nearest his father, harry prince of wales, 2.02.120 P
from a prince to a prentice? 2.02.174 P
the prince once set a dish of apple–johns before 2.04. 4 P
here will be the prince and master poins anon, 2.04. 15 P
sirrah, what humor's the prince of? 2.04.236 P
why does the prince love him so then? 2.04.243 P
able body, for the which the prince admits him. 2.04.252 P
for the prince himself is such another, the 2.04.253 P
no man's too good to serve 's prince, and let it 3.02.237 P
the prince, lord john and duke of lancaster. 4.01. 28
hath the prince john a full commission, | in 4.01.160
the prince is here at hand. 4.01.223
hereof comes it that prince harry is valiant, 4.03.117 P
gloucester, | where is the prince your brother? 4.04. 13
chance thou art not with the prince thy brother? 4.04. 20
the prince but studies his companions | like a 4.04. 68
the prince will in the perfectness of time 4.04. 74
prince john your son doth kiss your grace's hand 4.04. 83
sweet prince, speak low, | the king your father 4.05. 16
we left the prince my brother here, my liege, 4.05. 51
the prince of wales, where is he? 4.05. 53
the prince hath ta'en it hence. 4.05. 59
my lord, i found the prince in the next room, 4.05. 82

this shallow to keep prince harry in continual 5.01. 79 P
here comes the prince. 5.02. 42
how might a prince of my great hopes forget | so 5.02. 68
no prince nor peer shall have just cause to say, 5.02.144
and so the prince obscur'd his contemplation H5 1.01. 63
and your great–uncle's, edward the black prince, 1.02.105
the prince our master | says that you savor too 1.02.249
and tell the pleasant prince this mock of his 1.02.281
and you, prince dolphin, with all swift dispatch 2.04. 6
o, peace, prince dolphin! 2.04. 29
that black name, edward, black prince of wales; 2.04. 56
arrayed in flames like to the prince of fiends, 3.03. 16
prince dolphin, you shall stay with us in roan. 3.05. 64
provided of both as any prince in the world. 3.07. 9 P
it is the prince of palfreys: 3.07. 27 P
white hand of my lady, he's a gallant prince. 3.07. 94 P
great–uncle edward the plack prince of wales, as 4.07. 94 P
none do you like but an effeminate prince, 1H6 1.01. 35
and lookest to command the prince and realm. 1.01. 38
where's the prince dolphin? i have news for him. 1.02. 46
to crown himself king and suppress the prince. 1.03. 68
and ere that we will suffer such a prince, | so 3.01. 97
for, sweet prince, | and if your grace mark 3.01.151
welcome, high prince, the mighty duke of york! 3.01.176
perish, base prince, ignoble duke of york! 3.01.177
but ere we go, regard this dying prince, | the 3.02. 86
my gracious prince, and honorable peers, 3.04. 1
this is my servant, hear him, noble prince. 4.01. 80
i dare presume, sweet prince, he thought no harm 4.01.179
as i would embrace | the christian prince, king 5.03.172
the first, edward the black prince, prince of 2H6 2.02. 11
first, edward the black prince, prince of wales; 2.02. 11
edward the black prince died before his father, 2.02. 18
that virtuous prince, the good duke humphrey. 2.02. 74
think i am thy married wife | and thou a prince, 2.04. 29
wife, | and he a prince, and ruler of the land; 2.04. 43
yet so he rul'd, and such a prince he was, | as 2.04. 44
stay, whitmore, for thy prisoner is a prince, 4.01. 44
how well you love your prince and country: 4.09. 16
and so do i, victorious prince of york. 3H6 1.01. 21
what wrong is this unto the prince your son! 1.01.176
why, that is spoken like a toward prince. 2.02. 66
and lewis a prince soon won with moving words. 3.01. 34
with this my son, prince edward, henry's heir, 3.03. 31
yet here prince edward stands, king henry's son. 3.03. 73
and thou no more art prince than she is queen. 3.03. 80
and after that wise prince, henry the fift, 3.03. 85
queen margaret, prince edward, and oxford, 3.03.109
renowned prince, how shall poor henry live, 3.03.214
and prince shall follow with a fresh supply. 3.03.237
that if our queen and this young prince agree, 3.03.241
that young prince edward marries warwick's 4.01.117
o brave young prince! 5.04. 52
deathsmen, you have rid this sweet young prince! 5.05. 67
so come to you, and yours, as to this prince! 5.05. 82
king henry and the prince his son are gone; 5.06. 89
hath she forgot already that brave prince, R3 1.02.239
cropp'd the golden prime of this sweet prince 1.02.247
edward thy son, that now is prince of wales, 1.03.198
for edward our son, that was prince of wales, 1.03.199
a begging prince what beggar pities not? 1.04.267
a careful mother | of the young prince your son. 2.02. 97
forthwith from ludlow the young prince be fet 2.02.121
that it is meet so few should fetch the prince. 2.02.139
my lord, whoever journeys to the prince, | for 2.02.146
part the queen's proud kindred from the prince. 2.02.150
i long with all my heart to see the prince. 2.04. 4
how doth the prince? 2.04. 40
welcome, sweet prince, to london, to your 3.01. 1
sweet prince, the untainted virtue of your years 3.01. 7
the tender prince | would fain have come with me 3.01. 28
this prince hath neither claim'd it nor deserv'd 3.01. 51
the prince my brother hath outgrown me far. 3.01.104
he for his father's sake so loves the prince 3.01.165
god bless the prince from all the pack of you! 3.03. 5
ah ha, my lord, this prince is not an edward! 3.07. 71
would this virtuous prince | take on his grace 3.07. 78
two props of virtue for a christian prince, | to 3.07. 96
famous plantagenet, most gracious prince, | lend 3.07.100
this edward, whom our manners call the prince. 3.07.191
call him again, sweet prince, accept their suit. 3.07.221
pure heart's love, to greet the tender prince. 4.01. 4
how doth the prince and my young son of york? 4.01. 14
true, noble prince. 4.02. 15
that edward still should live true noble prince! 4.02. 16
the slaughter of the prince that ow'd that crown 4.04.142
like a most royal prince | restor'd me to my H8 2.01.113
was reputed for | a prince most prudent, of an 2.04. 46
the wisest prince that there had reign'd by many 2.04. 49
princess dowager | and widow to prince arthur. 3.02. 71
in daily thanks, that gave us such a prince, 5.02.150
if a prince | may be beholding to a subject, i 5.02.190
how now, prince troilus, wherefore not a–field? TRO 1.01.105
brave troilus, the prince of chivalry! 1.02.229 P
may one that is a herald and a prince | do a 1.03.218
here in troy | a prince call'd hector — priam 1.03.261
to speak with paris from the prince troilus. 3.01. 39 P
fair prince, here is good broken music. 3.01. 49 P
prince troilus, i have lov'd you night and day 3.02.114
they will almost | give us a prince of blood, a 3.03. 26
is the prince there in person? 4.01. 3
occasion to lie long | as /you, prince paris, 4.01. 5
is not prince troilus here? 4.02. 47
the young prince will go mad. 4.02. 75 P
please you, save the thanks this prince expects. 4.04.117
o, be not mov'd, prince troilus. 4.04.129
the prince must think me tardy and remiss, 4.04.141
so now, fair prince of troy, i bid good night. 5.01. 71
you are moved, prince, let us depart, i pray, 5.02. 36
what hath she done, prince, that can /soil our 5.02.134
have with you, prince. 5.02.185
patience, prince saturninus. TIT 1.01.203
content thee, prince, i will restore to thee 1.01.210
this prince in justice seizeth but his own. 1.01.281
sent by the heavens for prince saturnine, 1.01.335
prince bassianus, leave to plead my deeds, 1.01.424
for you, prince bassianus, i have pass'd | my 1.01.468
and rouse the prince, and ring a hunter's peal, 2.02. 5
the wand'ring prince and dido once enjoyed, 2.03. 22
and hear the sentence of your moved prince. ROM 1.01. 88
till the prince came, who parted either part. 1.01.115
more than prince of cats. 2.04. 19 P
the prince expressly hath | forbid this bandying 3.01. 88
the prince will doom thee death | if thou art 3.01.134
o noble prince, i can discover all | the unlucky 3.01.142
o prince! 3.01.147
prince, as thou art true, | for blood of ours, 3.01.148
beg for justice, which thou, prince, must give: 3.01.180
not romeo, prince, he was mercutio's friend; 3.01.184
fault our law calls death, but the kind prince, 3.03. 25
beg pardon of the prince, and call thee back 3.03.152
go tell the prince, run to the capulets, | raise 5.03.177
hold him in safety till the prince come hither. 5.03.183
we name hereafter | the prince of cumberland; MAC 1.04. 39
the prince of cumberland! 1.04. 48
"lord hamlet is a prince out of thy star; HAM 2.02.141
charge | led by a delicate and tender prince, 4.04. 48
good night, sweet prince, | and flights of 5.02.359
the prince of darkness is a gentleman. LR 3.04.143 P
conspirant 'gainst this high illustrious prince, 5.03.136
worthy prince, i know't. 5.03.179
i liv'd, the greatest prince o' th' world, | the ANT 4.15. 54
in simple and low things to prince it much CYM 3.03. 85
as being our foe, | yet bury him as a prince. 4.02.251
he was a prince. 5.05.291
most worthy prince, as yours, is true guiderius; 5.05.358
young prince of tyre, you have at large received PER 1.01. 1
prince pericles — 1.01. 25
and all good men, as every prince should do; 1.01. 51
prince pericles, touch not, upon thy life, | for 1.01. 87
young prince of tyre, | though by the tenor of 1.01.110
and therefore instantly this prince must die, 1.01.148
we hate the prince | of tyre, and thou must kill 1.01.155
my lord, prince pericles is fled. 1.01.160
unless thou say prince pericles is dead. 1.01.164
prince, pardon me, or strike me, if you please, 1.02. 46
fit counsellor and servant for a prince, | who 1.02. 63
who by thy wisdom makes a prince thy servant, 1.02. 64
a better prince and benign lord, | that will 2.ch. 3
and he, good prince, having all lost, | by waves 2.ch. 33
to have bereft a prince of all his fortunes; 2.01. 9
a prince of macedon, my royal father, | and the 2.02. 24
wrong not your prince you love. 2.04. 25
but if the prince do live, let us salute him, 2.04. 27
if that you love prince pericles, forbear. 2.04. 42
this prince, the fair–betrothed of your daughter 5.03. 71
prince palamon, i must awhile bereave you | of TNK 2.02.223
prince pirithous | obtained his liberty; 2.02.244
mean keeper of his prison, | and he a prince. 2.04. 4
this; but far off, prince. 2.05. 5
i like him better, prince, i shall not then 2.05. 47
them, | that truly noble prince pirithous, 4.01. 13
and quick sweetness, | has this young prince! 4.02. 14
should be a stout man, by his face a prince 4.02. 77
i guess he is a prince too, | and, if it may be, 4.02. 91
this miserable prince, that cuts away | a life 5.03.142
i'll close thine eyes, prince; 5.04. 96

PRINCE–LIKE 1 FR 0.0001 REL FR 1 V 0 P

the wrongs he did me | were nothing prince–like; CYM 5.05.293

PRINCELY 82 FR 0.0092 REL FR 77 V 5 P

was | the ivy which had hid my princely trunk, TMP 1.02. 86
surely a princely testimony, a goodly count, ADO 4.01.315 P
submissive fall his princely feet before, | and LLL 4.01. 90
any of these princely suitors that are already MV 1.02. 34 P
as kate this chamber with her princely gait? SHR 2.01.259
frequent to his princely exercises than formerly WT 4.02. 32 P
nor keep his princely heart from richard's hand. JN 1.01.267
if that the dolphin there, thy princely son, 2.01.484
death, made proud with pure and princely beauty! 4.03. 35
come i appellant to this princely presence. R2 1.01. 34
than was that young and princely gentleman. 2.01.175
you debase your princely knee | to make the base 3.03.190
but neither my good word nor princely favor. 5.06. 42
and hold their level with thy princely heart? 1H4 3.02. 17
for thou hast lost thy princely privilege | with 3.02. 86
trimm'd up your praises with a princely tongue, 5.02. 56
belike then my appetite was not princely got, 2H4 2.02. 9 P
i would think thee a most princely hypocrite. 2.02. 54 P
here come i from our princely general | to know 4.01.139
i take your princely word for these redresses. 4.02. 66
comes sneaking, and so sucks her princely eggs, H5 1.02.171
of valor as of kindness, | princely in both. 4.03. 16
to our most fair and princely cousin katherine; 5.02. 4
which of this princely train | call ye the 1H6 2.02. 34
and rise created princely duke of york. 3.01.172
the princely charles of france, thy countryman. 3.03. 38
pardon me, princely henry, and the rest. 4.01. 18
thou princely leader of our english strength, 4.03. 17
beauty's princely majesty is such, | 'confounds 5.03. 70
hath gain'd thy daughter princely liberty. 5.03.140
upon thy princely warrant, i descend | to give 5.03.143
worth | to be the princely bride of such a lord, 5.03.152
no princely commendations to my king? 5.03.176
done | in entertainment to my princely queen. 2H6 1.01. 72
the princely warwick, and the nevils all, 4.01. 91
and not to grace an aweful princely sceptre. 5.01. 98
do right unto this princely duke of york, | or i 3H6 1.01.166
i wonder how our princely father scap'd; 2.01. 1
your princely father and my loving lord! 2.01. 47
nay, if thou be that princely eagle's bird, 2.01. 91
i mean our princely father, duke of york. 2.06. 51
whose arms gave shelter to the princely eagle, 5.02. 12
and kiss your princely nephew, brothers both. 5.07. 27
o princely buckingham, i'll kiss thy hand | in R3 1.03.279
that princely novice, was struck dead by thee? 1.04.222
when that our princely father york | blest his 1.04.235
now, princely buckingham, seal thou this league 2.01. 29
a pleasing cordial, princely buckingham, | is 2.01. 41
and, princely peers, a happy time of day! 2.01. 48
among this princely heap, if any here | by false 2.01. 54
but now two mirrors of his princely semblance 2.02. 51
of york | unto his princely brother presently? 3.01. 34
dear | to princely richard and to buckingham. 3.02. 68
and for my sister and her princely sons, | be 3.03. 21
makes me most forward in this princely presence 3.04. 64
my princely father, then had wars in france, 3.05. 88
i tender not thy beauteous princely daughter! 4.04.405
but tell me, where is princely richmond now? 4.05. 9
yet in bestowing, madam, | he was most princely: H8 4.02. 57
by me | sends you his princely commendations, 4.02.118
grace | and princely care foreseeing those fell 5.01. 49
all princely graces | that mould up such a 5.04. 25
let me confirm my princely brother's greeting: TRO 4.05.174
at menelaus' tent, most princely troilus. 4.05.279
that now | refus'd most princely gifts, am bound COR 1.09. 80
princely shall be thy usage every way. TIT 1.01.266
warrants these words in princely courtesy. 1.01.272
were gracious in those princely eyes of thine, 1.01.429
to have his princely paws par'd all away. 2.03.152
y' are fall'n into a princely hand, fear nothing ANT 5.02. 22
then | the princely blood flows in his cheek, he CYM 3.03. 93
into contempt the suits | of princely fellows, 3.04. 90
thou blazon'st | in these two princely boys! 4.02.171
our foe was princely, | and though you took his 4.02.249
cadwal, arviragus, | your younger princely son. 5.05.360
which foreshow'd our princely eagle, | th' 5.05.473
i thought it princely charity to grieve for them PER 1.02.100
i come | with message unto princely pericles, 1.03. 32
beseeching you | to give her princely training, 3.03. 16
and reverend welcome to her princely guest, LUC 90
wrong'st his honor, wound'st his princely name. 599
thy princely office how canst thou fulfill, 628

PRINCE'S 29 FR 0.0032 REL FR 16 V 13 P

wars, | and i to thee engag'd a prince's word, ERR 5.01.162
why, he is the prince's jester, a very dull fool ADO 2.01.137 P
the prince's fool! 2.01.204 P
had been myself, that i was the prince's jester, 2.01.243 P
in them, being chosen for the prince's watch. 3.03. 6 P
are to bid any man stand, in the prince's name. 3.03. 26 P
is bidden, he is none of the prince's subjects. 3.03. 32 P
to meddle with none but the prince's subjects. 3.03. 34 P
are to present the prince's own person. 3.03. 75 P
we charge you, in the prince's name, stand! 3.03.164 P
is this the prince's brother? 4.01. 70
i charge you in the prince's name accuse these 4.02. 38 P
sir, that don john, the prince's brother, was a 4.02. 40 P
perjury, to call a prince's brother villain. 4.02. 42 P
let him write down the prince's officer coxcomb. 4.02. 71 P
as a false favorite doth his prince's name, | in 2H4 4.02. 25
the prince's espials have informed me | how the 1H6 1.04. 8
burnt | unto the prince's heart of calydon. 2H6 1.01.235
enjoys, | is far beyond a prince's delicates — 3H6 2.05. 51
which of you, if you were a prince's son, R3 1.04.257
dangerous | it is to get upon a prince's right? TIT 2.01. 64
this gentleman, the prince's near ally, | my ROM 3.01.109
i charge thee in the prince's name, obey. 3.01.140
what is the prince's doom? 3.03. 4
i bring thee tidings of the prince's doom. 3.03. 8
what less than dooms–day is the prince's doom? 3.03. 9
displant a town, reverse a prince's doom, | it 3.03. 59
to, and will abide it with | a prince's courage. CYM 3.04.184
to this world | that ever was prince's child. PER 3.01. 31

PRINCES' 6 FR 0.0006 REL FR 5 V 1 P

and poor men's cottages princes' palaces. MV 1.02. 14 P
and princes' courts be fill'd with my reproach. 2H6 3.02. 69
is that poor man that hangs on princes' favors! H8 3.02.367
if there be such a dart in princes' frowns, PER 1.02. 53
air | how many worthy princes' bloods were shed 1.02. 88
great princes' favorites their fair leaves SON 25. 5

/PRINCES 2 FR 0.0002 REL FR 2 V 0 P

your daughter here the /princes left for dead, ADO 4.01.202
/isles /of /greece | /the /princes /orgillous, TRO pr 2

PRINCES 112 FR 0.0126 REL FR 105 V 7 P

which princes, would they, may not disannul, ERR 1.01.144
like favorites | made proud by princes, that ADO 3.01. 10
would the two princes lie, and claudio lie, 4.01.152
to burn the errors that these princes hold 4.01.163
there is some strange misprision in the princes. 4.01.185
princes and counties! 4.01.315 P
i thank you, princes, for my daughter's death; 5.01.268
now | for princes to come view fair portia. MV 2.07. 43
the cost of princes on unworthy shoulders? AYL 2.07. 76
act was worth the audience of kings and princes, WT 5.02. 80 P
hark, the kings and the princes, our kindred, 5.02.173 P
to these two princes, if you marry them. JN 2.01.445
it likes us well, young princes; 2.01.533
with other princes that may best be spar'd, 5.07. 97
now these her princes are come home again, 5.07.115
princes and noble lords, | what answer shall i R2 4.01. 19
of all the court and princes of my blood; 1H4 3.02. 35
if die, brave death, when princes die with us! 5.02. 86
a guard too wanton for the head | which princes, 2H4 1.01.149
tell me how many good young princes would do so, 2.02. 30 P
be patient, princes, you do know these fits 4.04.114
speak lower, princes, for the king recovers. 4.04.129
sweet princes, what i did, i did in honor, | led 5.02. 35
and, princes all, believe me, i beseech you, 5.02.122
a kingdom for a stage, princes to act, | and H5 pr 3
see you, my princes and my noble peers, | these 2.02. 84
his princes and his peers to servitude, | his 2.02.171
and, princes, look you strongly arm to meet him. 2.04. 49
and all our princes captiv'd by the hand | of 2.04. 55
up, princes, and, with spirit of honor edged 3.05. 38
high dukes, great princes, barons, lords, and 3.05. 46
now forth, lord constable and princes all, | and 3.05. 67
both, | commend me to the princes in our camp; 4.01. 25
to horse, you gallant princes! 4.02. 15
god buy you, princes all; 4.03. 6
for many of our princes (woe the while!) 4.07. 75
their peasant limbs | in blood of princes, and 4.07. 78
of princes, in this number, | and nobles bearing 4.08. 81
the rest are princes, barons, lords, knights, 4.08. 89
and, princes french, and peers, health to you 5.02. 8
so are you, princes english, every one. 5.02. 11
you english princes all, i do salute you. 5.02. 22
go with the princes, or stay here with us? 5.02. 91
as princes do their courts, when they are cloy'd 1H6 2.05.105
dismay not, princes, at this accident, | nor 3.03. 1
when foreign princes shall be certified | that 4.01.144
for princes should be free. 5.03.114
than all the princes in the land beside. 2H6 1.01.176
the spirit of putting down kings and princes — 4.02. 36 P
priests pray for enemies, but princes kill. 5.02. 71
princes have but their titles for their glories, R3 1.04. 78

you cloudy princes and heart–sorrowing peers 2.02.112
the princes both make high account of you — 3.02. 69
and do not doubt, right noble princes both, 3.05. 64
have any time recourse unto the princes. 3.05.109
to gratulate the gentle princes there. 4.01. 10
old sullen playfellow | for tender princes — 4.01.102
ah, my poor princes! 4.04. 9
and both the princes had been breathing here, 4.04.384
of butchered princes fight in thy behalf. 5.03.122
as great embassadors | from foreign princes. H8 1.04. 56
man will work us all | from princes into pages. 2.02. 47
given a president of wisdom | above all princes, 2.02. 86
the hearts of princes kiss obedience, | so much 3.01.162
or else | to foreign princes, "ego et rex meus" 3.02.314
that sweet aspect of princes, and their ruin, 3.02.369
stomach, ever ranking | himself with princes; 4.02. 35
a pattern to all princes living with her, | and 5.04. 22
princes: TRO 1.03. 1
nor, princes, is it matter new to us | that we 1.03. 10
why then, you princes, | do you with cheeks 1.03. 17
kings, princes, lords! 1.03.264
now, princes, for the service i have done, | th' 3.03. 1
let him be sent, great princes, | and he shall 3.03. 27
him, | as if he were forgot, and, princes all, 3.03. 40
princes, enough, so please you. 4.05.117
welcome, brave hector, welcome, princes all. 5.01. 70
o, courage, courage, princes! 5.05. 30
princes, that strive by factions and by friends TIT 1.01. 18
lord lucius, and you princes of the goths, | the 5.01.156
him | some of the chiefest princes of the goths. 5.02.125
themselves blaze forth the death of princes. JC 2.02. 31
how like a deer, strooken by many princes, 3.01.209
cell, | that thou so many princes at a shot | so HAM 5.02.366
the princes, france and burgundy, | great rivals LR 1.01. 45
thus kent, o princes, bids you all adieu, 1.01.186
tales i have told you | of courts, of princes, CYM 3.03. 15
till it fly out and show them princes born. 4.04. 54
breathe not where princes are. 5.05.238
these gentle princes | (for such and so they are 5.05.336
your servant, princes. 5.05.425
sinful dame | made many princes thither frame PER 1.ch. 32
yon sometimes famous princes, like thyself, 1.01. 34
are arms to princes and bring joys to subjects. 1.02. 74
and there are princes and knights come from all 2.01.109 P
so, for princes are | a model which heaven makes 2.02. 10
so princes their renowns if not respected. 2.02. 13
you are princes and my guests. 2.03. 8
had princes sit like stars about his throne, 2.03. 39
princes in this should live like gods above, 2.03. 59
and princes not doing so are like to gnats, 2.03. 62
princes, it is too late to talk of love, | and 2.03.112
i can tell you they are princes. TNK 2.01. 20 P
mercy on these princes. 3.06.211
they are princes | as goodly as your own eyes, 3.06.275
are you content too, princes? 3.06.279
ye | now usage like to princes and to friends. 3.06.306
must now be soil'd | with blood of princes? 4.02. 60
spirit do incite | the princes to their proof! 5.03. 57
for princes are the glass, the school, the book, LUC 615
wind, | or say with princes if it shall go well, SON 14. 7
of princes shall outlive this pow'rful rhyme, 55. 2

PRINCESS' 2 FR 0.0002 REL FR 2 V 0 P
thee more profit | than other princess' can, TMP 1.02.173
hisperia, the princess' gentlewoman, | confesses AYL 2.02. 10

PRINCESS 61 FR 0.0069 REL FR 44 V 17 P
his only heir | and princess no worse issued. TMP 1.02. 59
or vainly comes th' admired princess hither. LLL 1.01.140
fair princess, welcome to the court of navarre. 2.01. 90
dear princess, were not his requests so far 2.01.149
you may not come, fair princess, within my gates 2.01.171
the princess comes to hunt here in the park, 3.01.164
that, 'twas a pricket that the princess kill'd. 4.02. 48 P
/call /i the deer the princess kill'd a pricket. 4.02. 52 P
the preyful princess pierc'd and prick'd a 4.02. 56
there is no certain princess that appears; 4.03.154
to congratulate the princess at her pavilion in 5.01. 88 P
that the king would have me present the princess 5.01.111 P
and learned gentleman, before the princess, i 5.01.122 P
what would you with the princess? 5.02.178
the princess bids you tell | how many inches 5.02.192
fair sir, god save you! where's the princess? 5.02.310
my faith and this the princess i did give; 5.02.454
let me kiss | this princess of pure white, this MND 3.02.144
fair princess, you have lost much good sport. AYL 1.02. 99 P
the challenger, the princess calls for you. 1.02.165 P
no, fair princess; 1.02.170 P
cesario is your servant's name, fair princess. TN 3.01. 97
therefore perpend, my princess, and give ear. 5.01.299 P
tak'st up the princess by that forced baseness WT 2.03. 79
there present yourself and your fair princess 4.04.544
kisses the hands | of your fresh princess; 4.04.551
son of polixenes, with his princess (she | the 5.01. 86
his princess, say you, with him? 5.01. 93
and your fair princess — goddess! 5.01.131
she lifted the princess from the earth, and so 5.02. 76 P
the princess hearing of her mother's statue, 5.02. 94 P
prince, my brother, and the princess, my sister, 5.02.143 P
holds hand with any princess of the world. JN 2.01.494
(the best i had, a princess wrought it me) | and 4.01. 43
dat is de princess. H5 5.02.120 P
the princess is the better englishwoman. 5.02.121 P
the rather, gentle princess, because i love thee 5.02.202 P
my royal cousin, teach you our princess english? 5.02.282 P
say, gentle princess, would you not suppose 1H6 5.03.110
to marry princess margaret for your grace; 2H6 1.01. 4
wrong not her birth, she is a royal princess. R3 4.04.212
acquaint the princess | with the sweet silent 4.04.329
but princess dowager | and widow to prince H8 3.02. 70
become of katherine, | the princess dowager? 4.01. 23
off | from ampthill, where the princess lay — 4.01. 28
make way there for the princess. 5.03. 87
to the high and mighty princess of england, 5.04. 3 P
to the happiness of england, | an aged princess; 5.04. 57
kind and dear princess! LR 4.07. 28
and fitting for a princess | descended of so ANT 5.02.326
he that hath miss'd the princess is a thing CYM 1.01. 16
comes the gentleman, | the queen, and princess. 1.01. 69
most mighty princess, that i have adventur'd 1.06.172
alas, poor princess, | thou divine imogen, what 2.01. 56
the princess. 2.03. 85
belied a lady, | the princess of this country; 5.02. 3
and here the bracelet of the truest princess 5.05.416
a most virtuous princess. PER 2.05. 34
yet a princess | to equal any single crown a' 4.03. 7
justify in knowledge | she is thy very princess. 5.01.218
to ask the spotted princess how she fares. LUC 721

PRINCIPAL 10 FR 0.0011 REL FR 5 V 5 P
and love, | forgive a moi'ty of the principal, MV 4.01. 26
give me my principal, and let me go. 4.01.336
shall i not have barely my principal? 4.01.342
remember any of the principal evils that he laid AYL 3.02.351 P
there were none principal, they were all like 3.02.353 P
and the principal itself not much the worse. AWW 1.01.148 P
herself | but with her most vild principal — WT 2.01. 92
stand, | culling the principal of all the deer. 3H6 3.01. 4
hath your principal made known unto you who i am PER 4.06. 82 P
who is my principal? 4.06. 84 P

PRINCIPALITIES 1 FR 0.0001 REL FR 1 V 0 P
thy wishes to the brim | with principalities. ANT 3.13. 19

PRINCIPALITY 1 FR 0.0001 REL FR 1 V 0 P
if not divine, | yet let her be a principality, TGV 2.04.152

PRINCIPALS 1 FR 0.0001 REL FR 1 V 0 P
the very principals did seem to rend, | and all PER 3.02. 16

PRINCIPLE 2 FR 0.0002 REL FR 1 V 1 P
that need must needs infer this principle, JN 3.01.213
the first humane principle i would teach them 2H4 4.03.123 P

PRINCIPLES 1 FR 0.0001 REL FR 1 V 0 P
these warlike principles | do not throw from you AWW 2.01. 1

PRINCOX 1 FR 0.0001 REL FR 1 V 0 P
you are a princox, go, | be quiet, or — more ROM 1.05. 86

PRINGS *(also brings)*

PRINGS 2 FR 0.0002 REL FR 0 V 2 P
which peradventure prings goot discretions with WIV 1.01. 44 P
to me, and prings me pread and salt yesterday, H5 5.01. 9 P

PRINT 16 FR 0.0018 REL FR 9 V 7 P
which any print of goodness wilt not take, TMP 1.02.352
all this i speak in print, for in print i found TGV 2.01.169 P
this i speak in print, for in print i found it. 2.01.169 P
he will print them, out of doubt; WIV 2.01. 77 P
thy neck into a yoke, wear the print of it, and ADO 1.01.201 P
heart, like an agot, with your print impressed, LLL 2.01.236
i will do it, sir, in print. 3.01.172 P
o sir, we quarrel in print, by the book — as AYL 5.04. 90 P
although the print be little, the whole matter WT 2.03. 99
i love a ballet in print, a–life, for then we 4.04.260 P
for she did print your royal father off, 5.01.125
that leaves the print of blood where e'er it JN 4.03. 26
heaven guide thy pen to print thy sorrows plain, TIT 4.01. 75
must wear the print of his remembrance on't, CYM 2.03. 43
tend'rer cheek receives her soft hand's print, VEN 353
and meant thereby | thou shouldst print more, SON 11.14

PRINTED 2 FR 0.0002 REL FR 2 V 0 P
deny | the story that is printed in her blood? ADO 4.01.122
o, could this kiss be printed in thy hand, 2H6 3.02.343

PRINTING 2 FR 0.0002 REL FR 1 V 1 P
printing their proud hoofs i' th' receiving H5 pr 27
the tally, thou hast caus'd printing to be us'd, 2H6 4.07. 36 P

PRINTLESS 1 FR 0.0001 REL FR 1 V 0 P
and ye that on the sands with printless foot TMP 5.01. 34

PRINTS 1 FR 0.0001 REL FR 1 V 0 P
are, | and credulous to false prints. MM 2.04.130

PRIORESS 1 FR 0.0001 REL FR 1 V 0 P
with men | but in the presence of the prioress; MM 1.04. 11

PRIORIES 1 FR 0.0001 REL FR 1 V 0 P
our abbeys and our priories shall pay | this JN 1.01. 48

PRIORITY 2 FR 0.0002 REL FR 2 V 0 P
and this centre | observe degree, priority, and TRO 1.03. 86
we must follow you, | right worthy you priority. COR 1.01.247

PRIORY 1 FR 0.0001 REL FR 1 V 0 P
this is some priory, in, or we are spoil'd! ERR 5.01. 37

PRISCIAN 1 FR 0.0001 REL FR 0 V 1 P
/bone /for /bene, priscian a little scratch'd, LLL 5.01. 28 P

PRISER 1 FR 0.0001 REL FR 1 V 0 P
the bonny priser of the humorous duke? AYL 2.03. 8

/PRISON 5 FR 0.0005 REL FR 1 V 4 P
/beats /in /this /hollow /prison /of /my /flesh, TIT 3.02. 10
/that /she /sends /you /to /prison /hither? HAM 2.02.241 P
/prison, /my /lord? 2.02.242 P
/denmark's /a /prison. 2.02.243 P
/to /me /it /is /a /prison. 2.02.251 P

PRISON 92 FR 0.0104 REL FR 66 V 26 P
rock, | who hadst deserv'd more than a prison. TMP 1.02.362
me, | might i but through my prison once a day 1.02.491
space enough | have i in such a prison. 1.02.494
that to close prison he commanded her, | with TGV 3.01.237
and carried to prison was worth five thousand of MM 1.02. 61 P
claudio to prison? 'tis not so. 1.02. 66 P
yonder man is carried to prison. 1.02. 86 P
signior claudio, led by the provost to prison; 1.02.115 P
bear me to prison, where i am committed. 1.02.117
not to be weary with you, he's in prison. 1.04. 25
the afflicted spirits | here in the prison. 2.03. 5
take him to prison, officer. 3.02. 31
art going to prison, pompey? 3.02. 61 P
commend me to the prison, pompey. 3.02. 69 P
go, away with him to prison. 3.02.190 P
away with her to prison! 3.02.205 P
here is in our prison a common executioner, who 4.02. 8 P
hath he borne himself penitently in prison? 4.02.140 P
he hath evermore had the liberty of the prison; 4.02.148 P
here in the prison, father, | there died this 4.03. 69
to prison with her! 5.01.121
she and that friar, | i saw them at the prison. 5.01.135
slander to th' state! | away with him to prison. 5.01.323
i met you at the prison, in the absence of the 5.01.328 P
away with him to prison! 5.01.345 P
away with him to prison! 5.01.346 P
for testimony whereof, one in the prison, | that 5.01.465
take him to prison, | and see our pleasure 5.01.520
on, officer, to prison till it come. ERR 4.01.108
paradise, but that adam that keeps the prison; 4.03. 18 P
thou shalt to prison. LLL 1.02.158 P
shall break the locks | of prison gates; MND 1.02. 34
stay, officer, he shall not go to prison. SHR 5.01. 95 P
i say he shall go to prison. 5.01. 97 P
i do not like her now, | to prison with her; AWW 5.03.282
she does abuse our ears. to prison with her! 5.03.294
what ho, i say! peace in this prison! TN 4.02. 18 P
away with her, to prison! WT 2.01.103
shall know your mistress | has deserv'd prison, 2.01.120
the keeper of the prison, call to him; 2.02. 1
good for thee, | what dost thou then in prison? 2.02. 4
will, | in the vild prison of afflicted breath. JN 3.04. 19
so i were out of prison and kept sheep, | i 4.01. 17
this is the prison. what is he lies here? 4.03. 34
this prison where i live unto the world; R2 5.05. 2
of this hard world, my ragged prison walls; 5.05. 21
for indeed i had the most of them out of prison. 1H4 4.02. 42 P
and roughly send to prison | th' immediate heir 2H4 5.02. 70
is in base durance and contagious prison, 5.05. 34
in prison hast thou spent a pilgrimage, | and 1H6 2.05.116
hell our prison is. 4.07. 58
away with them to prison; 2H6 1.03.218 P
you four, from hence to prison back again; 2.03. 5
go, lead the way, i long to see my prison. 2.04.110
thou hast put them in prison, and because they 4.07. 43 P
lord, | i'll yield myself to prison willingly, 4.09. 42
ah, let me live in prison all my days, | and 3H6 1.03. 43
now my soul's palace is become a prison; 2.01. 74
to tell you plain, i had rather lie in prison. 3.02. 70
o thou bloody prison! R3 3.03. 9
live in freedom, | and this man out of prison? H8 1.02.201
there is a slave, whom we have put in prison, COR 4.06. 38
before this earthy prison of their bones, | that TIT 1.01. 99
sirs, drag them from the pit unto the prison, 2.03.283
shut up in prison, kept without my food, | whipt ROM 1.02. 55
to prison, eyes, ne'er look on liberty! 3.02. 58
is wealthy too, | whom he redeem'd from prison. TIM 3.03. 4
/an anchor's cheer in prison be my scope! HAM 3.02.219
come let's away to prison: LR 5.03. 8
in a wall'd prison, packs and sects of great 5.03. 18
go follow them to prison. 5.03. 27
wife and me | to hang cordelia in the prison, 5.03.254
to prison, till fit time | of law and course of OTH 1.02. 85
though forfeiters you cast in prison, yet | you CYM 3.02. 38
a prison, or a debtor that not dares | to stride 3.03. 34
alas, the prison i keep, though it be for great TNK 2.01. 2 P
'tis pity they are in prison, and 'twere pity 2.01. 22 P
the prison itself is proud of 'em; 2.01. 24 P
me, let me perish | if i think this our prison! 2.02. 62
let's think this prison holy sanctuary | to keep 2.02. 71
never till now i was in prison, arcite. 2.02.132
base, | my father the mean keeper of his prison, 2.04. 3
hour the whoobub | will be all o'er the prison. 2.06. 36
and | perfumes to kill the smell o' th' prison; 3.01. 86
you perish instantly | for breaking prison, and 3.06.114
cannot love thee, he that broke thy prison — 3.06.139
of love as she says palamon hath sung in prison. 4.03. 82 P
and in her vaulty prison stows the day. LUC 119
o, had they in that darksome prison died, | then 379
his true respect will prison false desire, | and 642
of that polluted prison where it breathed. 1726
prison my heart in thy steel bosom's ward, | but SON 133. 9

PRISON'D 3 FR 0.0003 REL FR 3 V 0 P
we make a choir, as doth the prison'd bird, CYM 3.03. 43
the hand, | a lily prison'd in a jail of snow, VEN 362
being prison'd in her eye like pearls in glass, 980

/PRISONER 1 FR 0.0001 REL FR 1 V 0 P
what /was't /that /prisoner told me | when i TNK 1.04. 21

PRISONER 81 FR 0.0091 REL FR 72 V 9 P
'twere to be a judge, | and what a prisoner. MM 2.02. 70
and the prisoner the very debt of your calling. 3.02.250 P
i am going to visit the prisoner. fare you well. 3.02.258 P
and bred, one that is a prisoner nine years old. 4.02.131 P
now, sir, how do you find the prisoner? 4.03. 66
this is another prisoner that i sav'd, | who 5.01.487
thou jailer, thou, | i am thy prisoner. ERR 4.04.110
he is my prisoner, and you shall not have him. 4.04.112
he is my prisoner; 4.04.117
and take her hearing prisoner with the force ADO 1.01.324
i discharge thee of thy prisoner, and i thank 5.01.319 P
i would take desire prisoner, and ransom him to LLL 1.02. 61 P
cage of rushes i am sure you /are not prisoner. AYL 3.02.371 P
force me to keep you as a prisoner, | not like a WT 1.02. 52
my prisoner? 1.02. 55
to be your prisoner should import offending, 1.02. 57
says, "my poor prisoner, | i am innocent as you. 2.02. 26
this child was prisoner to the womb and is | by 2.02. 57
produce the prisoner. 3.02. 8
arthur ta'en prisoner? JN 3.04. 7
bonds, | because my poor child is a prisoner. 3.04. 75
are not you griev'd that arthur is his prisoner? 3.04.123
now prisoner to the palsy, chastise thee, | and R2 2.03.104
is doom'd a prisoner by proud bullingbrook. 5.01. 4
thee, | unless thou yield thee as my prisoner. 1H4 5.03. 10
the hulk sir john, | is prisoner to your son. 2H4 1.01. 20
that noble worcester | so soon ta'en prisoner, 1.01.126
to fill king edward's fame with prisoner kings, H5 1.02.162
chariot into roan | bring him our prisoner. 3.05. 55
o no, he lives, but is took prisoner, | and lord 1H6 1.01.145
how wert thou handled, being prisoner? 1.04. 24
the earl of bedford had a prisoner | call'd the 1.04. 27
if thou be he, then art thou prisoner. 2.03. 33
prisoner? to whom? 2.03. 34
and was he not in england prisoner? 3.03. 70
be what thou wilt, thou art my prisoner. 5.03. 45
keeping them prisoner underneath /her wings. 5.03. 57
for i perceive i am thy prisoner. 5.03. 74
see, reignier, see, thy daughter prisoner! 5.03.131
lord cardinal, he is your prisoner. 2H6 3.01.187
master, this prisoner freely give i thee, | and 4.01. 12
stay, whitmore, for thy prisoner is a prince, 4.01. 44
upon thine honor, is he prisoner? 5.01. 42
upon mine honor, he is prisoner. 5.01. 43
and brought your prisoner to your palace gate. 3H6 3.02.119
ay, almost slain, for he is taken prisoner, 4.04. 7
is prisoner to the bishop here, at whose hands 4.05. 5
but warwick's king is edward's prisoner. 5.01. 39
is prisoner to the foe, his state usurp'd, | his 5.04. 77
then was i going prisoner to the tower, | by the R3 3.02.100
ague | stay'd me a prisoner in my chamber when H8 1.01. 5
the whole time | i was my chamber's prisoner. 1.01. 13
the ceremony | of bringing back the prisoner. 2.01. 5

you be convey'd to th' tower a prisoner; 5.02.124
you have a troyan prisoner call'd antenor, TRO 3.03. 18
bastard margarelon | hath doreus prisoner, | and 5.05. 8
i saw him prisoner; COR 1.09. 84
give us the proudest prisoner of the goths, TIT 1.01. 96
now, madam, are you prisoner to an emperor; 1.01.258
whom thou in triumph long | hast prisoner held, 2.01. 15
like a poor prisoner in his twisted gyves, | and ROM 2.02.179
often | drowns him and takes his valor prisoner. TIM 3.05. 68
in parthia did i take thee prisoner, | and then JC 5.03. 37
we must not. a noble prisoner! 5.04. 15
insane root | that takes the reason prisoner? MAC 1.03. 85
a hideous crash | takes prisoner pyrrhus' ear; HAM 2.02.477
of our ship, so i alone became their prisoner. 4.06. 20 P
what, a prisoner? LR 4.06.190
then am i the prisoner, and his bed my jail; 4.06.266 P
you shall close prisoner rest, | till that the OTH 5.02.335
you're my prisoner, but | your jailer shall CYM 1.01. 72
i'll place it | upon this fairest prisoner. 1.01.123
takes prisoner the wild motion of mine eye, 1.06.103
his manacles, bring your prisoner to the king. 5.04.191 P
yea, though thou do demand a prisoner, | the 5.05. 99
alas, | poor cousin palamon, poor prisoner! TNK 3.01. 23
and the prisoner — | not to be held ungrateful 4.01. 21
leading him prisoner in a red rose chain; VEN 110
know | her honor is ta'en prisoner by the foe, LUC 1608
and when the judge is robb'd, the prisoner dies. 1652
left | a liquid prisoner pent in walls of glass, SON 5.10

PRISONER'S 2 FR 0.0002 REL FR 1 V 1 P
deny | the jury, passing on the prisoner's life, MM 2.01. 19
every soldier to cut his prisoner's throat. H5 4.07. 10 P

PRISONERS' 1 FR 0.0001 REL FR 1 V 0 P
of prisoners' ransom, and of soldiers slain, 1H4 2.03. 54

/PRISONERS 1 FR 0.0001 REL FR 1 V 0 P
/come, /bring /forth /the /prisoners. R3 3.03. 1

PRISONERS 37 FR 0.0041 REL FR 33 V 4 P
all prisoners, sir, | in the line–grove which TMP 5.01. 9
sure, i think she holds them prisoners still. TGV 2.04. 92
it is not for prisoners to be too silent in LLL 1.02.163 P
wives | as prisoners to her womanly persuasion. SHR 5.02.120
of prisoners, hotspur took | mordake earl of 1H4 1.01. 70
the prisoners | which he in this adventure hath 1.01. 92
those prisoners in your highness' name demanded, 1.03. 23
my liege, i did deny no prisoners, | but i 1.03. 29
my prisoners in your majesty's behalf. 1.03. 48
why, yet he doth deny his prisoners, | but with 1.03. 77
send me your prisoners with the speediest means, 1.03.120
send us your prisoners, or you will hear of it. 1.03.124
he will, forsooth, have all my prisoners, | and 1.03.140
same noble scots | that are your prisoners — 1.03.213
those prisoners you shall keep. 1.03.218
then once more to your scottish prisoners: 1.03.259
will go to hazard with me for twenty prisoners? H5 3.07. 86 P
then every soldier kill his prisoners, | give 4.06. 37
what prisoners of good sort are taken, uncle? 4.08. 75
like prisoners wildly overgrown with hair, | put 5.02. 43
beside five hundred prisoners of esteem, | lets 1H6 3.04. 8
were there surpris'd and taken prisoners. 4.01. 26
i come to know what prisoners thou hast ta'en, 4.07. 56
for prisoners ask'st thou? 4.07. 58
break open the jails and let out the prisoners. 2H6 4.03. 16 P
with patience, noble lord, as prisoners must; R3 1.01.126
and with them sir thomas vaughan, prisoners. 2.04. 43
my sword, my chariot, and my prisoners, TIT 1.01.249
ransomless here we set our prisoners free. 1.01.274
take thou my soldiers, prisoners, patrimony; LR 5.03. 75
have threaten'd | our prisoners with the sword. CYM 5.05. 78
rather have 'em | prisoners to us than death. TNK 1.04. 37
mean time, look tenderly to the two prisoners. 2.01. 20 P
we are prisoners | i fear for ever, cousin. 2.02. 3
palamon, | those hopes are prisoners with us. 2.02. 26
get many more such prisoners and such daughters, 2.06. 38
the prisoners have their lives. 4.01. 28

PRISON–HOUSE 1 FR 0.0001 REL FR 1 V 0 P
forbid | to tell the secrets of my prison–house, HAM 1.05. 14

PRISONMENT 2 FR 0.0002 REL FR 2 V 0 P
life, | but hold himself safe in his prisonment. JN 3.04.161
signs | of prisonment were off me and this hand TNK 3.01. 32

PRISONNIER 1 FR 0.0001 REL FR 0 V 1 P
son jurement de pardonner aucun prisonnier; H5 4.04. 51 P

PRISONS 4 FR 0.0004 REL FR 4 V 0 P
seek sweet safety out | in vaults and prisons, JN 5.02.143
as is our wretches fett'red in our prisons; H5 1.02.243
let prisons swallow 'em, | debts wither 'em to TIM 4.03.530
cheer'd, | make not your thoughts your prisons; ANT 5.02.185

PRISTINE 2 FR 0.0002 REL FR 1 V 1 P
disciplines of the pristine wars of the romans. H5 3.02. 81 P
and purge it to a sound and pristine health, | i MAC 5.03. 52

/PRITHEE 1 FR 0.0001 REL FR 1 V 0 P
/then, /prithee, get thee away. LR 4.01. 41

PRITHEE 228 FR 0.0257 REL FR 141 V 87 P
i prithee, | remember i have done thee worthy TMP 1.02.246
prithee peace. 2.01. 9
i prithee spare. 2.01. 25
prithee peace. 2.01.128
prithee no more; thou dost talk nothing to me. 2.01.171
prithee say on. 2.01.228
do not torment me, prithee. 2.02. 71 P
prithee do not turn me about, my stomach is not 2.02.114 P
i prithee be my god. 2.02.149
i prithee let me bring thee where crabs grow; 2.02.167
i prithee now lead the way without any more 2.02.173 P
lo, lo, again! bite him to death, i prithee. 3.02. 34 P
prithee stand further off. 3.02. 83 P
prithee, my king, be quiet. 4.01.215
and presently, i prithee. 5.01.101
prithee hold thy peace. WIV 4.01. 73 P
prithee no more prattling. 5.01. 1 P
i prithee, lucio, do me this kind service: MM 1.02.176
therefore i prithee | supply me with the habit, 1.03. 45
what, i prithee, might be the cause? 3.02.133 P
farewell, good friar, i prithee pray for me. 3.02.180 P
but say, i prithee, is he coming home? ERR 2.01. 55
marry, i prithee do, to make sport withal. AYL 1.02. 26 P
prithee, who is't that thou mean'st? 1.02. 81 P
thou hast not, cousin, | prithee be cheerful. 1.03. 94
i prithee, shepherd, if that love or gold | can 2.04. 71
more, more, i prithee more. 2.05. 9 P
more, i prithee more. 2.05. 12 P
more, i prithee more. 2.05. 14 P
i prithee who? 3.02.183 P
nay, i prithee now, with most petitionary 3.02.189 P
i prithee tell me who is it quickly, and speak 3.02.197 P
i prithee take the cork out of thy mouth that i 3.02.202 P
cry "holla" to /thy tongue, i prithee; 3.02.244 P
i prithee, who doth he trot withal? 3.02.312 P
i prithee recount some of them. 3.02.357 P
do, i prithee, but yet have the grace to 3.04. 2 P
i prithee, pretty youth, let me /be better 4.01. 1 P
nay, prithee be cover'd. 5.01. 17 P
i prithee, sister kate, untie my hands. SHR 2.01. 21
o kate, content thee, prithee be not angry. 3.02.215
i prithee, good grumio, tell me, how goes the 4.01. 33 P
i prithee go, and get me some repast; 4.03. 15
'tis passing good, i prithee let me have it. 4.03. 18
prithee, kate, let's stand aside and see the end 5.01. 61 P
i prithee, lady, have a better cheer; AWW 3.02. 64
i prithee do not strive against my vows. 4.02. 14
prithee allow the wind. 5.02. 8 P
prithee get thee further. 5.02. 13 P
foh, prithee stand away. 5.02. 16 P
i prithee (and i'll pay thee bounteously) TN 1.02. 52
ay, prithee sing. 2.04. 50
presence still smile, dear my sweet, i prithee." 2.05.177 P
i prithee tell me what thou think'st of me. 3.01.138
prithee hold thy peace, this is not the way. 3.04.108 P
i prithee vent thy folly somewhere else, | thou 4.01. 10
i prithee now ungird thy strangeness and tell me 4.01. 15 P
i prithee, foolish greek, depart from me. 4.01. 18
i prithee, gentle friend, | let thy fair wisdom, 4.01. 51
nay, come, i prithee. 4.01. 64
nay, i prithee put on this gown and this beard, 4.02. 1 P
i prithee be gone. 4.02.119 P
prithee read i' thy right wits. 5.01.297 P
prithee be content. 5.01.351
i prithee tell me; WT 1.02. 91
prithee. 2.02. 16
prithee bring me | to the dead bodies of my 3.02.234
lost for ever, perdita | i prithee call't. 3.03. 34
fatal country sicilia, prithee speak no more, 4.02. 20 P
prithee be my present partner in this business, 4.02. 50 P
i prithee darken not | the mirth o' th' feast. 4.04. 41
prithee bring him in, and let him approach 4.04.211 P
prithee let him. 4.04.414
nay, prithee dispatch. 4.04.640 P
dispatch, i prithee. 4.04.644 P
prithee no more; 5.01.119
prithee, son, do; 5.02.152 P
i prithee, lady, go away with me. JN 3.04. 20
and i prithee, sweet wag, when thou art a king, 1H4 1.02. 16 P
that thou art heir apparent — but i prithee, 1.02. 58 P
hal, i prithee trouble me no more with vanity; 1.02. 81 P
john, i prithee leave the prince and me alone, i 1.02.149 P
i prithee, tom, beat cut's saddle, put a few 2.01. 5 P
i prithee lend me thy lantern, to see my gelding 2.01. 34 P
i prithee, good prince — hal! 2.02. 40 P
ned, prithee come out of that fat room, and lend 2.04. 1 P
come, i prithee do thou stand in some by–room, 2.04. 29 P
i prithee call in falstaff. 2.04.109 P
prithee let him alone, we shall have more anon. 2.04.207 P
prithee do, jack. 2.04.296 P
prithee let her alone, and list to me. 3.03. 95 P
nay, prithee be gone. 3.03.174 P
i prithee tell me, doth he keep his bed? 4.01. 21
i prithee lend me thy sword. 5.03. 43
hal, i prithee give me leave to breathe a while. 5.03. 44 P
i prithee lend me thy sword. 5.03. 49 P
i prithee, | harry, withdraw thyself, thou 5.04. 1
i prithee speak, we will not trust our eyes 5.04.136
prithee put up. H5 2.01.104 P
prithee, honey–sweet husband, let me bring thee 2.03. 1 P
discourse, i prithee, on this turret's top. 1H6 1.04. 26
what tidings send our scouts? i prithee speak. 5.02. 10
i prithee give me leave to curse a while. 5.03. 43
deny me not, i prithee, gentle joan. 5.04. 20
i prithee peace, | good queen, and whet not on 2H6 2.01. 32
stanley, i prithee go, and take me hence, | i 2.04. 91
whither goes vaux so fast? what news, i prithee? 3.02.367
buckingham, i prithee pardon me, | that i have 5.01. 32
i prithee grieve, to make me merry, york. 3H6 1.04. 86
i prithee give no limits to my tongue, | i am a 2.02.119
keeper, i prithee sit by me awhile. R3 1.04. 73
nay, i prithee stay a little. 1.04.117 P
i prithee peace, my soul is full of sorrow. 2.01. 97
how, my young york? i prithee let me hear it. 2.04. 26
i prithee, pretty york, who told thee this? 2.04. 31
i prithee hear me speak. 4.04.180
my lord chamberlain, | prithee come hither. H8 1.04. 91
prithee call gardiner to me, my new secretary. 2.02.115
well–beloved servant, cranmer, | prithee return; 2.04.240
serve the king, and — prithee lead me in. 3.02.450
prithee, good griffith, tell me how he died. 4.02. 9
prithee to bed, and in thy pray'rs remember 5.01. 73
prithee let's walk. 5.01.116
ay, ay, prithee now. TRO 3.01.107 P
i prithee now, to bed. 4.02. 7
prithee tarry, | you men will never tarry. 4.02. 15
prithee be silent, /boy, i profit not by thy 5.01. 14 P
i prithee do not hold me to mine oath, | bid me 5.02. 26
i prithee stay. 5.02. 42
i prithee, diomed, visit me no more. 5.02. 74
i prithee come. 5.02.106
prithee, virgilia, turn thy solemnness out a' COR 1.03.107 P
now, mars, i prithee make us quick in work, 1.04. 10
i prithee, noble friend, home to thy house; 3.01.233
i prithee now, my son, | go to them, with this 3.02. 72
prithee now, | go, and be rul'd; 3.02. 89
prithee now, say you will, and go about it. 3.02. 98
i prithee now, sweet son, as thou hast said | my 3.02.107
nay, i prithee, woman — 4.01. 12
prithee call my master to him. 4.05. 21 P
prithee tell my master what a strange guest he 4.05. 34 P
prithee, fellow, remember my name is menenius, 5.02. 28 P
i prithee, noble lord, | join with me to forbid TIM 1.01.126
prithee let my meat make thee silent. 1.02. 37 P
i prithee let's be provided to show them 1.02.179
i prithee but repair to me next morning. 2.02. 25
prithee, apemantus, read me the superscription 2.02. 78 P
prithee no more. 2.02.163
prithee, man, look cheerly. 2.02.214
(prithee be not sad, | thou art true and honest; 2.02.220
i prithee beat thy drum and get thee gone. 4.03. 97
thy back, i prithee. 4.03.395
i prithee, boy, run to the senate–house; JC 2.04. 1
prithee listen well; 2.04. 17
of old, i prithee | hold thou my sword–hilts, 5.05. 27
i prithee, strato, stay thou by thy lord. 5.05. 44
prithee peace! MAC 1.07. 45
dear duff, i prithee contradict thyself, | and 2.03. 89
so prithee go with me. 3.02. 56
prithee see there! 3.04. 67
i prithee do not mock me, fellow student, | i HAM 1.02.177
prithee say on, he's for a jig or a tale of 2.02.500 P
prithee no more. 2.02.520 P
i prithee, when thou seest that act afoot, 3.02. 78
prithee, horatio, tell me one thing. 5.01.195 P
i prithee take thy fingers from my throat. 5.01.260
prithee tell him, so much the rent of his land LR 1.04.134 P
prithee, nuncle, keep a schoolmaster that can 1.04.179 P
then i prithee be merry, thy wit shall not go 1.05. 11 P
prithee, if thou lov'st me, tell me. 2.02. 6 P
i prithee, daughter, do not make me mad. 2.04.218
prithee go in thyself, seek thine own ease. 3.04. 23
prithee, nuncle, be contented, 'tis a naughty 3.04.110 P
prithee, nuncle, tell me whether a madman be a 3.06. 9 P
good friend, i prithee take him in thy arms; 3.06. 88
i prithee put them off. 4.07. 8
prithee away. 5.03.269
break, heart, i prithee break! 5.03.313
i prithee, let thy wife attend on her, | and OTH 1.03.296
i prithee, good iago, | go to the bay and 2.01.207
prithee keep up thy quillets. 3.01. 23 P
i prithee call him back. 3.03. 51
i prithee name the time, but let it not | exceed 3.03. 62
prithee no more; 3.03. 75
i prithee speak to me as to thy thinkings, | as 3.03.131
i prithee do so. 3.04.140
prithee bear some charity to my wit, do not 4.01.119 P
prithee say true. 4.01.124 P
prithee come; will you? 4.01.168 P
prithee to–night | lay on my bed my 4.02.104
prithee unpin me — have grace and favor /in 4.03. 21
prithee shroud me | in one of these same sheets. 4.03. 24
prithee dispatch. 4.03. 33
"— willow, willow" — | prithee hie thee; 4.03. 50 P
prithee, emilia, | go know of cassio where he 5.01.116
prithee, how many boys and wenches must i have? ANT 1.02. 36 P
prithee tell her but a worky–day fortune. 1.02. 53 P
i prithee turn aside, and weep for her, | then 1.03. 76
look, prithee, charmian, | how this herculean 1.03. 83
prithee, friend, | pour out the pack of matter 2.05. 53
guess at her years, i prithee. 3.03. 26
prithee peace. 3.13. 12
was "antony," | and word it, prithee, piteously. 4.13. 9
too late, good diomed. call my guard, i prithee. 4.14.128
prithee go hence, | or i shall show the cinders 5.02.172
nay, i prithee take it, | it is an earnest of a CYM 1.05. 64
awake by four o' th' clock, | i prithee call me. 2.02. 7
prithee speak, | how many /score of miles may we 3.02. 66
away, i prithee, | do as i bid thee. 3.02. 80
prithee dispatch, | the lamb entreats the 3.04. 95
prithee think | there's livers out of britain. 3.04.139
prithee away, | there's more to be consider'd; 3.04.180
away, i prithee. 3.04.184
prithee, fair youth, | think us no churls; 3.06. 63
i prithee to our rock, | you and fidele play the 4.02.163
prithee have done, | and do not play in 4.02.229
prithee say. 5.05. 36
prithee, valiant youth, | deny't again. 5.05.289
rise, prithee rise. PER 1.02. 60
and i prithee tell me, how dost thou find the 4.02. 96 P
what, prithee? 4.06. 37 P
prithee tell me one thing first. 4.06.156 P
prithee speak. 5.01.119
prithee kill me. TNK 2.02.263
prithee take mine, good cousin. 3.06. 65
i prithee run | and tell me how it goes. 5.03. 70
i prithee lay attention to the cry; 5.03. 91
thing | i shall be glad of, prithee tell her so. 5.04. 30

PRIVACY 3 FR 0.0003 REL FR 2 V 1 P
fie, privacy? WIV 4.05. 23 P
of this my privacy | i have strong reasons. TRO 3.03.190
but 'gainst your privacy | the reasons are more 3.03.191

PRIVATE 74 FR 0.0083 REL FR 65 V 9 P
the private wound is deepest: TGV 5.04. 71
no, my good lord; it was by private message. MM 5.01.460
that should by private order else have died, | i 5.01.466
haply, in private. ERR 5.01. 60
in private? ADO 3.02. 84 P
in private then. LLL 5.02.229
you, | as much in private, and i'll bid adieu. 5.02.241
one word in private with you ere i die. 5.02.254
i have some private schooling for you both. MND 1.01.116
pride | that can therein tax any private party? AYL 2.07. 71
but in respect that it is private, it is a very 3.02. 16 P
for private quarrel 'twixt your duke and him, SHR 4.02. 84
only he desires | some private speech with you. AWW 2.05. 57
let me enjoy my private. TN 3.04. 89 P
but he is a devil in private brawl. 3.04.236 P
in private brabble did we apprehend him. 5.01. 65
whose private with me of the dolphin's love | is JN 4.03. 16
gaunt's rebukes, nor england's private wrongs, R2 2.01.166
with some few private friends upon this coast. 3.03. 4
wales and i | must have some private conference, 1H4 3.02. 2
cannot put him to a private soldier that is the 2H4 3.02.166 P
at this, i shall be sent for in private to him. 5.05. 77 P
that a poor and a private displeasure can do H5 4.01.198 P
must kings neglect, that private men enjoy! 4.01.237
in private will i talk with thee apart. 1H6 1.02. 69
your private grudge, my lord of york, will out, 4.01.109
let not your private discord keep away | the 4.04. 22
retain but privilege of a private man? 5.04.136
and in this private plot be we the first | that 2H6 2.02. 60

land, | while i myself will lead a private life, 3H6 4.06. 42
that no man shall have private conference | (of R3 1.01. 86
the state takes notice of the private difference H8 1.01.101
let's think in private more. 2.01.169
i left him private, | full of sad thoughts and 2.02. 14
thrust yourselves | into my private meditations? 2.02. 65
give us but an hour | of private conference. 2.02. 80
first i began in private | with you, my lord of 2.04.207
to withdraw | into your private chamber, we 3.01. 28
i was | from any private malice in his end, 3.02.268
both in his private conscience and his place, 5.02. 75
tower, | where, being but a private man again, 5.02. 90
for my private part, | i am no more touch'd than TRO 2.02.125
and with private soul | did in great ilion thus 4.05.111
to show you, which shall be yours in private. COR 2.03. 77 P
he had wounds, which he could show in private; 2.03.166
to awaken his regard | for 's private friends. 5.01. 24
never admitted | a private whisper, no, not with 5.03. 7
suits, | nor from the state nor private friends, 5.03. 18
for we'll | hear nought from rome in private. 5.03. 93
saucy controller of my private steps! TIT 2.03. 60
say, | when i have walked like a private man, 4.04. 75
son, | and private in his chamber pens himself, ROM 1.01.138
either withdraw unto some private place, | or 3.01. 51
should fall | for private faults in them. TIM 5.04. 26
but for your private satisfaction, | because i JC 2.02. 73
what private griefs they have, alas, i know not, 3.02.213
his private arbors and new–planted orchards, 3.02.248
very oft of late | given private time to you, HAM 1.03. 92
let me ask you one word in private. LR 3.04.160
fear, | to manage private and domestic quarrel? OTH 2.03.215
not almost a fault | t' incur a private check. 3.03. 67
what, | to kiss in private? 4.01. 2
'tis not a time | for private stomaching. ANT 2.02. 9
heavens and earth, | a private man in athens: 3.12. 15
you, sir, in private, if you please | to give me CYM 5.05.115
and our mind partakes her private actions | to PER 1.01.152
who either by public war or private treason 1.02.104
not a man in private conference | or council has 2.04. 17
come bring me to some private place. 4.06. 90 P
o unfelt sore, crest–wounding private scar! LUC 828
shame, | thy private feasting to a public fast, 891
"why should the private pleasure of some one 1478
many fall, | to plague a private sin in general? 1484
when every private widow well may keep, | by SON 9. 7

PRIVATELY 7 FR 0.0008 REL FR 4 V 3 P
if you handled her privately, she would sooner MM 5.01.275 P
speak it privately. MV 2.04. 20
we'll pass the business privately and well. SHR 4.04. 57
for she hath privately twice or thrice a day, WT 5.02.105 P
he hears nought privately that comes from troy. TRO 1.03.249
be it as you shall privately determine, | either OTH 1.03.275
the duke himself came privately in the night, TNK 2.01. 46 P

PRIVATES 2 FR 0.0002 REL FR 1 V 1 P
and what have kings, that privates have not too, H5 4.01.238
faith, her privates we. HAM 2.02.234 P

/PRIVILEG'D 1 FR 0.0001 REL FR 0 V 1 P
/he /is /a /privileg'd /man. TRO 2.03. 57 P

PRIVILEG'D 4 FR 0.0004 REL FR 4 V 0 P
tongue, | i am a king, and privileg'd to speak. 3H6 2.02.120
by all the laws of war y' are privileg'd. H8 1.04. 52
let me be privileg'd by my place and message, TRO 4.04.130
and, privileg'd by age, desires to know | in LC 62

PRIVILEGE 34 FR 0.0038 REL FR 31 V 3 P
desert, | is privilege for thy departure hence. TGV 3.01.160
and it shall privilege him from your hands ERR 5.01. 95
as under privilege of age to brag | what i have ADO 5.01. 60
on my privilege i have with the parents of the LLL 4.02.156 P
i beg the ancient privilege of athens: MND 1.01. 41
your virtue is my privilege. 2.01.220
a privilege never to see me more. 3.02. 79
hadst thou not the privilege of antiquity upon AWW 2.03.209 P
you need but plead your honorable privilege. 4.05. 90 P
hatred | the child–bed privilege denied, which WT 3.02.103
some sins do bear their privilege on earth, JN 1.01.261
sir, sir, impatience hath his privilege. 4.03. 32
should nothing privilege him nor partialize R2 1.01.120
fool, | presuming on an ague's privilege, 2.01.116
else | but only they have privilege to live. 2.01.158
for thou hast lost thy princely privilege | with 1H4 3.02. 86
of blood, | and an adopted name of privilege, 5.02. 18
he bears him on the place's privilege, | or 1H6 2.04. 86
priest | should ever get that privilege of me. 3.01.121
that warranteth by law to be thy privilege. 5.04. 61
retain but privilege of a private man? 5.04.136
we should infringe the holy privilege | of R3 3.01. 41
you break no privilege nor charter there. 3.01. 54
man, | or that we women had men's privilege | of TRO 3.02.128
up | their rotten privilege and custom 'gainst COR 1.10. 23
all bond and privilege of nature, break! 5.03. 25
why, there's the privilege your beauty bears. TIT 4.02.116
hair, | nor age nor honor shall shape privilege; 4.04. 57
yes, sir, but anger hath a privilege. LR 2.02. 70
behold, it is my privilege, | the privilege of 5.03.129
is my privilege, | the privilege of mine honors, 5.03.130
for blame, | to privilege dishonor in thy name? LUC 621
that you yourself may privilege your time | to SON 58.10
take heed, dear heart, of this large privilege, 95.13

PRIVILEGED 1 FR 0.0001 REL FR 1 V 0 P
draw, men, for all this privileged place — 1H6 1.03. 46

PRIVILEGES 1 FR 0.0001 REL FR 1 V 0 P
and have you nuns no farther privileges? MM 1.04. 1

PRIVILEGIO 2 FR 0.0002 REL FR 1 V 1 P
of her, cum privilegio ad imprimendum solum; SHR 4.04. 93 P
they may, cum privilegio, "/oui" away | the lag H8 1.03. 34

PRIVILY 4 FR 0.0004 REL FR 3 V 1 P
give me your hand, | i'll privily away. MM 1.01. 67
norfolk, | and tell him privily of our intent. 3H6 1.02. 39
him — privily | deals with our cardinal, and, H8 1.01.183
i will look him and privily relieve him. LR 3.03. 14 P

PRIVITY 1 FR 0.0001 REL FR 1 V 0 P
he upon him | (without the privity o' th' king) H8 1.01. 74

PRIVY 15 FR 0.0017 REL FR 13 V 2 P
myself am one made privy to the plot. TGV 3.01. 12
to her, told me what privy marks i had about me, ERR 3.02.142 P
half | comes to the privy coffer of the state, MV 4.01.354
ay, and privy | to this their late escape. WT 2.01. 94
no, by my life, | privy to none of this. 2.01. 96
the dead men's blood, the privy maidens' groans, H5 2.04.107
and other of your highness' privy council, | as 2H6 2.01.172
or, if he were not privy to those faults, | yet, 3.01. 47
rise, | and yet the king not privy to my drift, 3H6 1.02. 46
now will i go to take some privy order | to draw R3 3.05.106
is the banket ready | i' th' privy chamber? H8 1.04. 99
house, | and one, already, of the privy council. 4.01.112
know, and to the marriage | her nurse is privy; ROM 5.03.266
if thou art privy to thy country's fate, | which HAM 1.01.133
none but your sheets are privy to your wishes. ANT 1.02. 41 P

PRIVY–KITCHEN 1 FR 0.0001 REL FR 0 V 1 P
and his face is lucifer's privy–kitchen, where 2H4 2.04.333 P

PRIZ'D 9 FR 0.0010 REL FR 8 V 1 P
excellent a wit | as she is priz'd to have — as ADO 3.01. 90
hearts, | to have the touches dearest priz'd. AYL 3.02.152
if you priz'd my lady's favor at any thing more TN 2.03.121 P
beggar the estimation which you priz'd | richer TRO 2.02. 91
to her own worth | she shall be priz'd; 4.04.134
the people than | he hath hereto priz'd them at. COR 2.02. 60
is caesar with antonius priz'd so slight? ANT 1.01. 56
she gave it me, and said | she priz'd it once. CYM 2.04.104
if i priz'd life so much | as to deny my act; TNK 3.02. 23

PRIZE* 53 FR 0.0060 REL FR 45 V 8 P
with volumes that | i prize above my dukedom. TMP 1.02.168
lest too light winning | make the prize light. 1.02.453
else i' th' world, | do love, prize, honor you. 3.01. 73
for the prize i'll bring thee to | shall 4.01.205
a prize, a prize, a prize! TGV 5.04.121
a prize, a prize, a prize! 5.04.121
a prize, a prize, a prize! 5.04.121
she is my prize, or ocean whelm them all! WIV 2.02.137
that what we have we prize not to the worth ADO 4.01.218
is that my prize? MV 2.09. 60
like one of two contending in a prize, | that 3.02.141
alone again, i'll never wrestle for prize more. AYL 1.01.161 P
'tis deeds must win the prize, and he of both SHR 2.01.342
for life, i prize it | as i weigh grief, which i WT 3.02. 42
no life | (i prize it not a straw), but for mine 3.02.110
a prize, a prize! 4.03. 31 P
a prize, a prize! 4.03. 31 P
i would not prize them | without her love; 4.04.375
a gallant prize? 1H4 1.01. 75
word, outfac'd you from your prize, and have it, 2.04.257 P
forth | shall bring this prize in very easily. 2H4 3.01.101
the mighty sender, doth he prize you at. H5 2.04.119
a goodly prize, fit for the devil's grace! 1H6 5.03. 33
therefore bring forth the soldiers of our prize, 2H6 4.01. 8
i lost mine eye in laying the prize aboard, 4.01. 25
my lord, a prize, a prize! 4.07. 20 P
my lord, a prize, a prize! 4.07. 20 P
it is war's prize to take all vantages, | and 3H6 1.04. 59
methinks 'tis prize enough to be his son. 2.01. 20
made prize and purchase of his wanton eye, R3 3.07.187
men prize the thing ungain'd more than it is. TRO 1.02.289
you'll confess /he brought home worthy prize — 2.02. 86
he is my prize, i will not look upon. 5.06. 10
see here these movers that do prize their hours COR 1.05. 4
whose loves i prize | as the dead carcasses of 3.03.121
so, bassianus, you have play'd your prize. TIT 1.01.399
camp | but i do prize it at my love before | the TIM 5.01.181
but, i assure you, | a prize no less in worth. JC 5.04. 27
and oft 'tis seen the wicked prize itself | buys HAM 3.03. 59
metal as my sister, | and prize me at her worth. LR 1.01. 70
occasions, noble gloucester, of some prize, 2.01.120
a proclaim'd prize! 4.06.226
if it prove lawful prize, he's made for ever. OTH 1.02. 51
to make prize with you | of things that ANT 5.02.183
my father's sons, then had my prize | been less, CYM 3.06. 76
a prize, a prize! PER 4.01. 93 P
a prize, a prize! 4.01. 93 P
you know my prize | must be dragg'd out of blood TNK 5.01. 42
arm your prize, | i know you will not loose her. 5.03.135
desire my pilot is, beauty my prize, | then who LUC 279
for truth proves thievish for a prize so dear. SON 48.14
bound for the prize of all–too–precious you, 86. 2
doth point out thee | as his triumphant prize. 151.10

PRIZED 1 FR 0.0001 REL FR 1 V 0 P
in the owners | are prized by their masters. TIM 1.01.171

PRIZER *(see priser)*

PRIZER 1 FR 0.0001 REL FR 1 V 0 P
'tis precious of itself | as in the prizer. TRO 2.02. 56

PRIZES 5 FR 0.0005 REL FR 4 V 1 P
the world, | prizes not quantity of dirty lands; TN 2.04. 82
know | she prizes not such trifles as these are. WT 4.04.357
favor — | prizes of accident as oft as merit, TRO 3.03. 83
prizes the virtue that appears in cassio, | and OTH 2.03.134
and to see how he prizes the foolish woman your 4.01.176 P

PRIZEST 1 FR 0.0001 REL FR 1 V 0 P
faint–hearted woodvile, prizest him 'fore me? 1H6 1.03. 22

PRIZING 1 FR 0.0001 REL FR 1 V 0 P
not prizing her poor infant's discontent; SON 143. 8

PROBABLE 10 FR 0.0011 REL FR 9 V 1 P
(which to you shall seem probable) of every TMP 5.01.249
'tis pretty, sure, and very probable, | that AYL 3.05. 11
apology you think | may make it probable need. AWW 2.04. 51
and clap upon you two or three probable lies. 3.06. 98 P
the least of all these signs were probable. 2H6. 3.02.178
how probable i do not know — that martius, COR 4.06. 66
on, | 'tis probable, and palpable to thinking. OTH 1.02. 76
most probable | that so she died; ANT 5.02.353
it may be probable she lost it; CYM 2.04.115
yet is't not probable | to come alone, either he 4.02.141

PROBAL 1 FR 0.0001 REL FR 1 V 0 P
probal to thinking, and indeed the course | to OTH 2.03.338

PROBATION 7 FR 0.0008 REL FR 6 V 1 P
i (in probation of a sisterhood) | was sent to MM 5.01. 72
and all probation will make up full clear, 5.01.157
that suffers under probation: TN 2.05.130 P
last conference, pass'd in probation with you: MAC 3.01. 79
herein | this present object made probation. HAM 1.01.156
it | that the probation bear no hinge nor loop OTH 3.03.365
which for more probation | i can with ease CYM 5.05.362

/PROCEED 2 FR 0.0002 REL FR 1 V 1 P
/so /we /shall /proceed | /without /suspicion. R2 4.01.156
/proceed, /thersites. TRO 2.03. 57 P

PROCEED 73 FR 0.0082 REL FR 55 V 18 P
mum then, and no more. — proceed. TMP 3.02. 51 P
stand farther. — come, proceed. 3.02. 86
muse not that i thus suddenly proceed; TGV 1.03. 64
which i was much unwilling to proceed in, | but 2.01.106
well, proceed. 3.01.352 P
very well, sir, proceed. WIV 2.02.190 P
reprieve thee from thy fate, it should proceed. MM 3.01.144
form, | we shall proceed with angelo. 4.03.101
proceed. 5.01. 87
mended again. the matter; proceed. 5.01. 91
proceed, solinus, to procure my fall, | and by ERR 1.01. 1
seen more, and heard more, proceed accordingly. ADO 3.02.122 P
proceed, sweet cupid, thou hast thump'd him with LLL 4.03. 22 P
o, some authority how to proceed; 4.03.283
proceed, good alexander. 5.02.567
ready. name what part i am for, and proceed. MND 1.02. 18 P
well, proceed. 1.02. 57 P
proceed, moon. 5.01.256 P
law | cannot impugn you as you do proceed. MV 4.01.179
a well–deserving pillar, | proceed to judgment. 4.01.240
proceed. AYL 3.02.239 P
proceed, proceed. i'll give her. 3.03. 71 P
proceed, proceed. i'll give her. 3.03. 71 P
proceed, proceed. 5.04.197
proceed, proceed. 5.04.197
proceed in practice with my younger daughter; SHR 2.01.164
proceed. 4.03.138 P
if thou proceed | as high as word, my deed shall AWW 2.01.209
from lowest place /when virtuous things proceed, 2.03.125
of the house, that i may proceed in my speech. TN 1.05.181 P
since we so openly | proceed in justice, which WT 3.02. 6
therefore proceed. 3.02.108
the sessions shall proceed; 3.02.141
proceed; | no foot shall stir. 5.03. 97
name, and orderly proceed | to swear him in the R2 1.03. 9
my learned lord, we pray you to proceed, | and H5 1.02. 9
hat, | if thou proceed in this thy insolence. 1H6 1.03. 37
proceed no straiter 'gainst our uncle gloucester 2H6 3.02. 20
hath given them heart and courage to proceed. 4.04. 35
where nothing can proceed that toucheth us R3 3.02. 23
proceed thus rashly in the villain's death, 3.05. 43
lady mine, proceed. H8 1.02. 17
proceed. 1.02.188
yet | but from this lady may proceed a gem | to 2.03. 78
be't so; proceed. 2.04. 5
that thus you should proceed to put me off, 2.04. 21
madam, | it's fit this royal session do proceed, 2.04. 66
it fits we thus proceed, or else no witness 5.01.107
before we proceed any further, hear me speak. COR 1.01. 1 P
would you proceed especially against caius 1.01. 26 P
in our counsels, | and know how we proceed. 1.02. 3
proceed, cominius. 2.02. 81
and temp'rately proceed to what you would | thus 3.01.218
proceed by process, | lest parties (as he is 3.01.312
not martius, we'll proceed | in our first way. 3.01.331
we must proceed as we do find the people. 5.06. 15
proceed directly. JC 3.03. 19 P
we will proceed no further in this business: MAC 1.07. 31
so proceed you. HAM 2.02.465 P
but wilt thou hear now how i did proceed? 5.02. 27
where, if you violently proceed against him, LR 1.02. 83 P
and proceed | i' th' sway of your own will. 4.07. 18
i humbly beseech you proceed to th' affairs of OTH 1.03.220
proceed you in your tears. 4.01.256
hell | but that i did proceed upon just grounds 5.02.138
the ships behold, | and so proceed accordingly. ANT 3.09. 4
proceed. CYM 2.04. 66
i pray his absence | proceed by swallowing that; 3.05. 58
proceed. 5.05. 42
we might proceed to /cancel of your days; PER 1.01.113
your hurly | cannot proceed but by obedience. STM II.C 114
and doth so far proceed | that what is vile LUC 251
showing their birth and where they did proceed? SON 76. 8

/PROCEEDED 1 FR 0.0001 REL FR 1 V 0 P
me | why you /proceeded not against these feats, HAM 4.07. 6

PROCEEDED 12 FR 0.0013 REL FR 12 V 0 P
leaven'd and prepared choice | proceeded to you; MM 1.01. 52
proceeded well, to stop all good proceeding! LLL 1.01. 95
proceeded further — cut me off the heads | of 1H4 4.03. 85
and your good graces both have well proceeded, R3 3.05. 48
how far i have proceeded, | or how far further H8 2.04. 90
but by particular consent proceeded | under your 2.04.222
thou like us from our first swath proceeded TIM 4.03.252
you | what hath proceeded worthy note to–day. JC 1.02.181
caesar when i strook him, | have thus proceeded. 3.01.183
how calm and gentle i proceeded still | in all ANT 5.01. 75
having thus far proceeded | (unless thou CYM 1.05. 15
you, having proceeded but | by both your wills. 2.04. 55

PROCEEDERS 1 FR 0.0001 REL FR 1 V 0 P
quick proceeders, marry! SHR 4.02. 11

PROCEEDING 28 FR 0.0031 REL FR 27 V 1 P
some sly trick blunt thurio's dull proceeding. TGV 2.06. 41
and here an engine fit for my proceeding! 3.01.138
life answer the straitness of his proceeding, it MM 3.02.256 P
proceeded well, to stop all good proceeding! LLL 1.01. 95
for it appears, by manifest proceeding, | that MV 4.01.358
and make this haste as your own good proceeding, AWW 2.04. 49
which on your just proceeding i'll keep off — 5.03.236
up to th' deed), doth push on this proceeding. WT 2.01.179
siege | and merciless proceeding by these french JN 2.01.214
is this proceeding just and honorable? 2H4 4.02.110
i like this fair proceeding of the king's. 5.05. 97
if little faults, proceeding on distemper, H5 2.02. 54
usurp'st, | of benefit proceeding from our king, 1H6 5.04.152
are daily seen | by our proceeding in hostility, 5.04.162
all planets of good luck | to my proceeding, if R3 4.04.403
anon advise you | further in the proceeding. H8 1.02.108
assurance | of equal friendship and proceeding. 2.04. 18
i have an interest in your heart's proceeding; ROM 3.01.188
love | to your proceeding bids me tell you this; JC 2.02.103
proceeding from the heat–oppressed brain? MAC 2.01. 39
see, | till then in patience our proceeding be. HAM 5.01.299
then necessity | will call discreet proceeding. LR 1.04.214
with th' ancient of war on our proceeding. 5.01. 32
who e'er he be that in this foul proceeding OTH 1.03. 65
(for such proceeding i am charg'd withal) | i 1.03. 93
to such proceeding | who ever but his PER 4.03. 25

the prim'st for this proceeding, and the number TNK 1.01.161
the goddess venus | commend we our proceeding, 5.01. 75
PROCEEDINGS 19 FR 0.0021 REL FR 17 V 2 P
and afterward determine our proceedings. TGV 3.02. 96
to these violent proceedings all my neighbors WIV 3.02. 44 P
me unpregnant | and dull to all proceedings. MM 4.04. 21
to curse the fair proceedings of this day. JN 3.01. 97
blush | and glow with shame of your proceedings, 4.01.113
what says the world | to your proceedings? 4.02.133
zeal and an unurg'd faith | to your proceedings, 5.02. 11
to the king, and lay open all our proceedings. 1H4 2.03. 31 P
of our proceedings kept the earl from hence, 4.01. 65
what plain proceedings is more plain than this? 2H6 2.02. 53
were but a feigned friend to our proceedings. 3H6 4.02. 11
with all your just proceedings in this /cause. R3 3.05. 66
in the divorce his contrary proceedings | are H8 3.02. 26
follow me, sirs, and my proceedings eye, | it is TRO 5.07. 7
of our proceedings here on th' market-place; COR 2.02.159
face | for testimony of her foul proceedings. TIT 5.03. 8
them, fair coz, | i'll maintain my proceedings. TNK 3.01. 53
i were dumb, yet his proceedings teach thee. VEN 406
like the proceedings of a drunken brain, | full 910
PROCEEDS 9 FR 0.0010 REL FR 9 V 0 P
that what in time proceeds | may token to the AWW 4.02. 62
offer, | and it proceeds from policy, not love. 2H4 4.01.146
and listen after humphrey, how he proceeds. 2H6 1.03.149
which i think proceeds | from wayward sickness R3 1.03. 28
but it proceeds or comes from them to you, | and COR 1.01.153
i know from whence this same device proceeds. TIT 4.04. 52
his eye drops fire, no water thence proceeds; LUC 1552
such childish humor from weak minds proceeds; 1825
and thence this slander, as i think, proceeds. SON 131.14
PROCESS 19 FR 0.0021 REL FR 18 V 1 P
in brief, to set the needless process by — MM 5.01. 92
that which long process could not arbitrate. LLL 5.02.743
wife, | tell her the process of antonio's end, MV 4.01.274
advantage in the process but only the losing of AWW 1.01. 15 P
is | by law and process of great nature thence WT 2.02. 58
the tediousness and process of my travel. R2 2.03. 12
to run, | finish the process of his sandy hour, 1H6 4.02. 36
when thou shalt tell the process of their death. R3 4.03. 32
lest that the process of thy kindness | last 4.04.254
sweet at first t' acquire — after this process, H8 2.03. 9
in the course | and process of this time, you 2.04. 38
witness the process of your speech, wherein TRO 4.01. 9
proceed by process, | lest parties (as he is COR 3.01.312
of denmark | is by a forged process of my death HAM 1.05. 37
arras i'll convey myself | to hear the process. 3.03. 29
mayst not coldly set | our sovereign process, 4.03. 63
was my hint to speak — such was my process — OTH 1.03.142
where's fulvia's process? ANT 1.01. 28
turn'd | in process of the seasons have i seen, SON 104. 6
PROCESSION 3 FR 0.0003 REL FR 3 V 0 P
come, go /we in procession to the village; H5 4.08.113
shall in procession sing her endless praise. 1H6 1.06. 20
here comes the townsmen on procession, | to 2H6 2.01. 66
PROCESS-SERVER 1 FR 0.0001 REL FR 0 V 1 P
been since an ape-bearer, then a process-server, WT 4.03. 96 P
/PROCLAIM 1 FR 0.0001 REL FR 1 V 0 P
/whose /warp'd /looks /proclaim | /what /store LR 3.06. 53
PROCLAIM 44 FR 0.0049 REL FR 40 V 4 P
the setting of thine eye and cheek proclaim | a TMP 2.01.229
well, i will proclaim myself what i am. WIV 3.05.143 P
as those cheek-roses | proclaim you are no less! MM 1.04. 17
proclaim an enshield beauty ten times louder 2.04. 80
i will proclaim thee, angelo, look for't! 2.04.151
and why should we proclaim it in an hour before 4.04. 8 P
will not proclaim against her maiden loss, | how 4.04. 24
that outward courtesies would fain proclaim 5.01. 15
proclaim it, provost, round about the city, | if 5.01.508
yet once again proclaim it publicly, | if any ERR 5.01.130
make friends, invite, and proclaim the banes, SHR 3.02. 16
i am not an imposture that proclaim | myself AWW 2.01.155
whom i proclaim a man of truth, of mercy; WT 3.02.157
and many other evidences proclaim her, with all 5.02. 38 P
and to proclaim | arthur of britain england's JN 2.01.310
on wednesday next we solemnly proclaim | our R2 4.01.319
then | proclaim my brother edmund mortimer 1H4 1.03.156
rather proclaim it, westmerland, through my host H5 4.03. 34
and then i will proclaim young henry king. 1H6 1.01.169
in dumb significants proclaim your thoughts: 2.04. 26
fellow, what miracle dost thou proclaim? 2H6 2.01. 58
proclaim them traitors that are up with cade, 4.02.177
if you'll not here proclaim yourself our king, 3H6 4.07. 54
brother, we will proclaim you out of hand, | the 4.07. 63
and once again proclaim us king of england. 4.08. 53
hands, | i here proclaim myself thy mortal foe; 5.01. 94
proclaim a pardon to the soldiers fled | that in R3 5.05. 16
or proclaim | there's difference in no persons. H8 1.01.138
the grecians began to proclaim barbarism, and TRO 5.04. 16 P
proclaim our honors, lords, with trump and drum. TIT 1.01.275
i do proclaim | one honest man — mistake me not TIM 4.03.496
run hence, proclaim, cry it about the streets. JC 3.01. 79
i will proclaim my name about the field. 5.04. 3
proclaim no shame | when the compulsive ardure HAM 3.04. 85
roughly awake, i here proclaim was madness. 5.02.232
by his authority i will proclaim it, | that he LR 2.01. 60
his delight, | proclaim him in the streets; OTH 1.01. 69
and to proclaim it civilly were like | a ANT 3.13.129
hath sent | me to proclaim the truth, and i am 4.14.126
when signior sooth here does proclaim peace, PER 1.02. 44
fetch breath that may proclaim them louder, that 1.04. 15
proclaim that i can sing, weave, sew, and dance, 4.06.183
for use me so he shall, or i'll proclaim him, TNK 2.06. 30
havoc in vast field | unearthed skulls proclaim, 5.01. 52
PROCLAIM'D 30 FR 0.0034 REL FR 23 V 7 P
you let it be proclaim'd betimes i' th' morn. MM 4.04. 15 P
mile of my court" — hath this been proclaim'd? LLL 1.01.120 P
it was proclaim'd a year's imprisonment to be 1.01.287 P
well, it was proclaim'd damsel. 1.01.291 P
is so varied too, for it was proclaim'd virgin. 1.01.294 P
him, | hath publish'd and proclaim'd it openly. SHR 4.02. 85
you might have heard it else proclaim'd about. 4.02. 87
this satisfaction | the by-gone day proclaim'd. WT 1.02. 32
myself on every post | proclaim'd a strumpet; 3.02.102
him, whose daughter | his tears proclaim'd his, 5.01.160
why have you not proclaim'd northumberland | and R2 2.02. 56
was not he proclaim'd | by richard, that dead is 1H4 1.03.145
proclaim'd at market-crosses, read in churches, 5.01. 73
join'd with an enemy proclaim'd, and from his H5 2.02.168
peaceful truce shall be proclaim'd in france, 1H6 5.04.117
and i proclaim'd a coward through the world! 2H6 4.01. 43
for king of england shalt thou be proclaim'd 3H6 2.01.194
sound trumpet, edward shall be here proclaim'd. 4.07. 69
hath any well-advised friend proclaim'd | reward R3 4.04.515
thou art proclaim'd fool, i think. TRO 2.01. 25 P
this, sir, is proclaim'd through all our host: 2.01.121
they have proclaim'd their malefactions: HAM 2.02.592
i heard myself proclaim'd, | and by the happy LR 2.03. 1
a proclaim'd prize! 4.06.226
nothing less | than i have here proclaim'd thee. 5.03. 95
so much was his pleasure should be proclaim'd. OTH 2.02. 8 P
sons /he /there proclaim'd the /kings of kings: ANT 3.06. 13
the combat's consummation is proclaim'd | by the TNK 5.03. 94
saw her, and | even then proclaim'd your fancy. 5.04.118
proclaim'd in her a careless hand of pride; LC 30
PROCLAIMED 3 FR 0.0003 REL FR 2 V 1 P
contrary to thy established proclaimed edict and LLL 1.01.259 P
because your lordship was proclaimed traitor. R2 2.03. 30
and be it death proclaimed through our host | to H5 4.08.114
PROCLAIMETH 1 FR 0.0001 REL FR 1 V 0 P
and still proclaimeth, as he comes along, | his 2H6 4.09. 28
PROCLAIMING 1 FR 0.0001 REL FR 1 V 0 P
the more proclaiming | our suit shall be TNK 1.01.174
PROCLAIMS 10 FR 0.0011 REL FR 8 V 2 P
proclaims you for a man replete with mocks, LLL 5.02.843
in the hottest day prognostication proclaims), WT 4.04.788 P
jack cade proclaims himself lord mortimer, 2H6 4.04. 28
proclaims him king, and many fly to him. 3H6 2.02. 71
gaudy, | for the apparel oft proclaims the man, HAM 1.03. 72
drop of blood that's calm proclaims me bastard, 4.05.118
take the hint | which my despair proclaims: ANT 3.11. 19
her own price | proclaims how she esteem'd him; CYM 1.01. 52
the house you dwell in proclaims you to be a PER 4.06. 77 P
and peace proclaims olives of endless age. SON 107. 8
PROCLAMATION 22 FR 0.0024 REL FR 11 V 11 P
there is a proclamation that you are vanish'd. TGV 3.01.217 P
according to our proclamation, gone? 3.02. 12
but most of all agreeing with the proclamation. MM 1.02. 79 P
you have not heard of the proclamation, have you 1.02. 93 P
what proclamation, man? 1.02. 94 P
warranted need, give him a better proclamation. 3.02.144 P
did you hear the proclamation? LLL 1.01.284 P
i give you, | and find it out by proclamation; MV 4.01.436
against the proclamation of thy passion, | to AWW 1.03.174
he was, i heard the proclamation. 1H4 1.03.147
strife | but to make open proclamation. 1H6 1.03. 71
come, fellow soldier, make thou proclamation. 3H6 4.07. 70
is proclamation made, that who finds edward 5.05. 9
such proclamation hath been made, my lord. R3 4.04.517
i hear of none but the new proclamation | that's H8 1.03. 17
toadstool! learn me the proclamation. TRO 2.01. 21 P
the proclamation! 2.01. 24 P
i say, the proclamation! 2.01. 31 P
owl go learn me the tenor of the proclamation, 2.01. 91 P
the bloody proclamation to escape, | that LR 5.03.184
he offer'd to cut a caper at the proclamation, PER 4.02.108 P
or how can well that proclamation sound | when STM II.C 117
PROCLAMATIONS 2 FR 0.0002 REL FR 2 V 0 P
these proclamations, | so forcing faults upon WT 3.01. 15
be chosen with proclamations to-day, | to-morrow TIT 1.01.190
PROCONSUL 1 FR 0.0001 REL FR 1 V 0 P
he creates | lucius proconsul; CYM 3.07. 8
PROCRASTINATE 1 FR 0.0001 REL FR 1 V 0 P
wend, | but to procrastinate his liveless end. ERR 1.01.158
PROCREANT 1 FR 0.0001 REL FR 1 V 0 P
hath made his pendant bed and procreant cradle. MAC 1.06. 8
PROCREANTS 1 FR 0.0001 REL FR 1 V 0 P
leave procreants alone, and shut the door; OTH 4.02. 28
PROCREATION 1 FR 0.0001 REL FR 1 V 0 P
whose procreation, residence, and birth | scarce TIM 4.03. 4
PROCRUS 2 FR 0.0002 REL FR 2 V 0 P
not shafalus to procrus was so true. MND 5.01.198
as shafalus to procrus, i to you. 5.01.199
PROCULEIUS 5 FR 0.0005 REL FR 5 V 0 P
none about caesar trust but proculeius. ANT 4.15. 48
come hither, proculeius. 5.01. 61
where's dolabella, | to second proculeius? 5.01. 70
my name is proculeius. 5.02. 12
proculeius, | what thou hast done thy master 5.02. 64
PROCURATOR 1 FR 0.0001 REL FR 1 V 0 P
for france, | as procurator to your excellence, 2H6 1.01. 3
/PROCUR'D 1 FR 0.0001 REL FR 1 V 0 P
and now, to tempt, all liberty /procur'd. LC 252
PROCUR'D 4 FR 0.0004 REL FR 3 V 1 P
king, and have procur'd his leave | for present AWW 2.05. 55
i have procur'd thee, jack, a charge of foot. 1H4 3.03.186 P
of all the voices that we have procur'd | set COR 3.03. 9
your daughter's, | whose pardon is procur'd too; TNK 4.01. 21
/PROCURE 1 FR 0.0001 REL FR 1 V 0 P
/procure /your /sureties /for /your /days /of R2 4.01.159
PROCURE 18 FR 0.0020 REL FR 13 V 5 P
that you'll procure the vicar | to stay for me WIV 4.06. 48
i am sorry that such sorrow i procure, | and so MM 5.01.474
proceed, solinus, to procure my fall, | and by ERR 1.01. 1
procure me music ready when he wakes, | to make SHR in.1. 50
and those that you'll procure from king leontes? WT 4.04.621
i'll procure this fat rogue a charge of foot, 1H4 2.04.545 P
you should procure him better assurance than 2H4 1.02. 31 P
town, | something i must do to procure me grace. 1H6 1.04. 7
and procure | that lady margaret do vouchsafe to 5.05. 88
all these could not procure me any scathe | so 2H6 2.04. 62
amongst the loving welshmen canst procure, 3H6 2.01.180
might corrupt minds procure knaves as corrupt H8 5.01.132
and to procure safe-conduct for his person of TRO 3.03.275 P
and to procure safe-conduct from agamemnon. 3.03.287 P
by one that i'll procure to come to thee, ROM 2.02.145
the injuries that they themselves procure | must LR 2.04.303
to virtuous desdemona | procure me some access. OTH 3.01. 36
you'll stand our friend to procure our pardon. STM II.C 143 P
PROCURE-A 1 FR 0.0001 REL FR 0 V 1 P
and i shall procure-a you de good guest: WIV 2.03. 91 P
PROCURES 3 FR 0.0003 REL FR 2 V 1 P
procures she still? MM 3.02. 55 P
what unaccustom'd cause procures her hither? ROM 3.05. 67
with sighs so deep procures to weep, | in PP 17.21
PROCURING 1 FR 0.0001 REL FR 0 V 1 P
sadness of parting, as the procuring of mirth. CYM 5.04.160 P
PRODIGAL 24 FR 0.0027 REL FR 17 V 7 P
painted about with the story of the prodigal, WIV 4.05. 8 P
calve's-skin that was kill'd for the prodigal; ERR 4.03. 19 P
be now as prodigal of all dear grace | as nature LLL 2.01. 9
and spend his prodigal wits in bootless rhymes, 5.02. 64
wherein my time something too prodigal | hath MV 1.01.129
in hate, to feed upon | the prodigal christian. 2.05. 15
how like a younger or a prodigal | the scarfed 2.06. 14
how like the prodigal doth she return, | with 2.06. 17
a bankrout, a prodigal, who dare scarce show his 3.01. 45 P
what prodigal portion have i spent, that i AYL 1.01. 38 P
he's a very fool and a prodigal. TN 1.03. 24 P
then he compass'd a motion of the prodigal son, WT 4.03. 97 P
when the tongue's office should be prodigal | to R2 1.03.256
stoop with oppression of their prodigal weight; 3.04. 31
or the story of the prodigal, or the german 2H4 2.01.145 P
my noble gossips, y' have been too prodigal. H8 5.04. 12
how many prodigal bits have slaves and peasants TIM 2.02.165
you must consider that a prodigal course | is 3.04. 12
i, that i was | no prodigal. 4.03.278
the chariest maid is prodigal enough | if she HAM 1.03. 36
how prodigal the soul | lends the tongue vows. 1.03.116
dearth of daughters and of sons, | be prodigal: VEN 755
the niggard prodigal that prais'd her so — | in LUC 79
if that one be prodigal, | bountiful they will PP 20.37
PRODIGALITY 1 FR 0.0001 REL FR 1 V 0 P
fram'd in the prodigality of nature — | young, R3 1.02.243
PRODIGALLY 1 FR 0.0001 REL FR 1 V 0 P
beside | and prodigally gave them all to you. LLL 2.01. 12
PRODIGAL'S 1 FR 0.0001 REL FR 0 V 1 P
a sore eye, thou tossel of a prodigal's purse, TRO 5.01. 32 P
PRODIGALS 1 FR 0.0001 REL FR 0 V 1 P
and fifty totter'd prodigals lately come from 1H4 4.02. 34 P
PRODIGIES 5 FR 0.0005 REL FR 5 V 0 P
cause | and call them meteors, prodigies, and JN 3.04.157
nor we disturb'd with prodigies on earth. TIT 1.01.101
when these prodigies | do so conjointly meet, JC 1.03. 28
it may be these apparent prodigies, | the 2.01.198
amazed | at apparitions, signs, and prodigies, VEN 926
PRODIGIOUS 7 FR 0.0008 REL FR 5 V 2 P
receiv'd my proportion, like the prodigious son, TGV 2.03. 3 P
nor mark prodigious, such as are | despised in MND 5.01.412
lame, foolish, crooked, swart, prodigious, JN 3.01. 46
it, | prodigious, and untimely brought to light, R3 1.02. 22
it is prodigious, there will come some change; TRO 5.01. 93 P
prodigious birth of love it is to me | that i ROM 1.05.140
me, | in personal action, yet prodigious grown, JC 1.03. 77
PRODIGIOUSLY 1 FR 0.0001 REL FR 1 V 0 P
lest that their hopes prodigiously be cross'd; JN 3.01. 91
PRODIGY 4 FR 0.0004 REL FR 4 V 0 P
monument, | some comet or unusual prodigy? SHR 3.02. 96
now hath my soul brought forth her prodigy, R2 2.02. 64
a prodigy of fear, and a portent | of broached 1H4 5.01. 20
and where's that valiant crook-back prodigy, 3H6 1.04. 75
PRODITOR 1 FR 0.0001 REL FR 1 V 0 P
i do, thou most usurping proditor, | and not 1H6 1.03. 31
PRODUC'D 2 FR 0.0002 REL FR 2 V 0 P
in open market-place produc'd they me | to be a 1H6 1.04. 40
their arguments | be now produc'd and heard. H8 2.04. 68
PRODUCE 18 FR 0.0020 REL FR 17 V 1 P
all things in common nature should produce TMP 2.01.160
you can produce acquittances | for such a sum LLL 2.01.160
which to defeat, | i must produce my power. AWW 2.03.150
us, whom we must produce for an interpreter. 4.01. 6 P
but loath am to produce | so bad an instrument. 5.03.201
than they | should not produce fair issue. WT 2.01.150
(not able to produce more accusation | than your 2.03.118
produce the prisoner. 3.02. 8
shall i produce the men? JN 1.01. 46
i can produce | a will that bars the title of 2.01.191
but this, which they produce from pharamond: H5 1.02. 37
produce the grand sum of his sins, the articles H8 3.02.293
i may | produce his body to the market-place, JC 3.01.228
though thou didst produce | my very character), LR 2.01. 71
i can produce a champion that will prove | what 5.01. 43
produce the bodies, be they alive or dead. 5.03.231
for more probation | i can with ease produce. CYM 5.05.363
produce. TNK 3.05.136
PRODUCES 1 FR 0.0001 REL FR 1 V 0 P
my reasonable part produces reason | how i may JN 3.04. 54
PRODUCING 2 FR 0.0002 REL FR 2 V 0 P
an evil soul producing holy witness | is like a MV 1.03. 99
producing forth the cruel ministers | of this MAC 5.09. 34
PRODUCTED 1 FR 0.0001 REL FR 1 V 0 P
to be producted (as, if i stay, i shall) OTH 1.01.146
PROFACE 1 FR 0.0001 REL FR 0 V 1 P
proface! 2H4 5.03. 28 P
PROFANATION 3 FR 0.0003 REL FR 1 V 2 P
and void of all profanation in the world that MM 2.01. 55 P
wit in them, | but in the less foul profanation. 2.02.128
to any other's, profanation. TN 1.05.217 P
PROFAN'D 7 FR 0.0008 REL FR 7 V 0 P
though his false finger have profan'd the ring, TGV 4.04.136
a son, | hear your own dignity so much profan'd, 2H4 5.02. 93
profan'd, dishonor'd, and the third usurp'd. R3 4.04.367
thy george, profan'd, hath lost his lordly honor 4.04.369
evil, | when virtue is profan'd in such a devil! LUC 847
but is profan'd, if not lives in disgrace. SON 127. 8
that have profan'd their scarlet ornaments, 142. 6
PROFANE 18 FR 0.0020 REL FR 16 V 2 P
paths he dares to tread | in shape profane. WIV 4.04. 61
thy reply, i profane my lips on thy foot, my LLL 4.01. 84 P
o most profane coxcomb! 4.03. 82
o, let no noble eye profane a tear | for me, if R2 1.03. 59
that my tongue | should so profane the word, 1.04. 13
"grace" | in an ungracious mouth is but profane. 2.03. 89
unless he do profane, steal, or usurp. 3.03. 81
which our profane hours here have thrown down. 5.01. 25
to blame | so idly to profane the precious time, 2H4 2.04.362
so surfeit-swell'd, so old, and so profane; 5.05. 50
may these same instruments, which you profane, COR 1.09. 41

if i profane with my unworthiest hand | this ROM 1.05. 93
we should profane the service of the dead | to HAM 5.01.236
what profane wretch art thou? OTH 1.01.114
for i mine own gain'd knowledge should profane 1.03.384
is he not a most profane and liberal counsellor? 2.01.163 P
profane fellow! CYM 2.03.124
lest i (too much profane) should do it wrong, SON 89.11

PROFANED 1 FR 0.0001 REL FR 1 V 0 P
had his great name profaned with their scorns, 1H4 3.02. 64

PROFANELY 2 FR 0.0002 REL FR 1 V 1 P
and that highly — not to speak it profanely, HAM 3.02. 30 P
and that which we profanely term our fortunes STM III 2

PROFANENESS 1 FR 0.0001 REL FR 1 V 0 P
my great profaneness 'gainst thine oracle! WT 3.02.154

PROFANERS 1 FR 0.0001 REL FR 1 V 0 P
profaners of this neighbor–stained steel — ROM 1.01. 82

PROFANING 1 FR 0.0001 REL FR 1 V 0 P
knight, | profaning this most honorable order, 1H6 4.01. 41

PROFESS 26 FR 0.0029 REL FR 18 V 8 P
and crown what i profess with kind event | if i TMP 3.01. 69
and i profess requital to a hair's breadth, not WIV 4.02. 3 P
by the saint whom i profess, i will plead MM 4.02.179 P
yet i profess curing it by counsel. AYL 3.02.404 P
and since you do profess to be a suitor, | you SHR 1.02.270
i read that i profess, the art to love. 4.02. 8
my father, | in what he did profess, well found. AWW 2.01.102
whether dost thou profess thyself — a knave or 4.05. 22 P
let me hear | what you profess. WT 4.04.369
so we profess | ourselves to be the slaves of 4.04.539
me from my tale, | for i profess not talking; 1H4 5.02. 91
i do profess | you speak not like yourself, who H8 2.04. 84
pray think us | those we profess, peacemakers, 3.01.167
your wish, my lord, | for i profess you have it. 3.02. 44
i do profess | that for your highness' good i 3.02.190
hear me profess sincerely: COR 1.03. 21 P
you know | that i profess myself in banqueting JC 1.02. 77
i conjure you, by that which you profess | (how MAC 4.01. 50
that i profess | myself an enemy to all other LR 1.01. 72
what dost thou profess? 1.04. 11 P
i do profess to be no less than i seem, to serve 1.04. 13 P
some soul, | and such a one do i profess myself. OTH 1.01. 55
so much i challenge that i may profess | due to 1.03.188
her nothing, though i profess myself her adorer, CYM 1.04. 68 P
i now | profess myself the winner of her honor, 2.04. 53
but profess | had that was well worth watching), 2.04. 67

PROFESS'D 8 FR 0.0009 REL FR 4 V 4 P
at any thing which profess'd to make him rejoice MM 3.02.236 P
hath to the public ear | profess'd the contrary. 4.02.100
as being a profess'd tyrant to their sex? ADO 1.01.169 P
me, how long have you profess'd apprehension? 3.04. 68 P
by a man which ever | profess'd to him, why, his WT 1.02.456
a sin–absolver, and my friend profess'd, | to ROM 3.03. 50
i must you con | that you are thieves profess'd, TIM 4.03.426
i have profess'd me thy friend, and i confess me OTH 1.03.336 P

PROFESSED 1 FR 0.0001 REL FR 1 V 0 P
to your professed bosoms i commit him, | but yet LR 1.01.272

PROFESSES 8 FR 0.0009 REL FR 4 V 4 P
only | professes to persuade) the king his son's TMP 2.01.236
and now she professes a hot–house; MM 2.01. 65 P
he professes to have receiv'd no sinister 3.02.242 P
he professes not keeping of oaths; AWW 4.03.252 P
me, who professes | myself your loyal servant, WT 2.03. 53
he professes not answering. TRO 3.03.268 P
war, | the day almost itself professes yours, MAC 5.07. 27
who professes | to clear his own way with the TNK 3.01. 55

PROFESSEST 1 FR 0.0001 REL FR 1 V 0 P
for what thou professest, a baboon, could he PER 4.06.178

PROFESSION 21 FR 0.0023 REL FR 9 V 12 P
to pass under the profession of fortune–telling. WIV 4.02.175 P
here as i was in our house of profession. MM 4.03. 2 P
and now by present profession a tinker? SHR in.2. 21 P
sir, in his profession, and it was his great AWW 1.01. 26 P
which was the great'st | of his profession, that 1.03.244
one that, in her sex, her years, profession, 2.01. 83
and therein am i constant to my profession. WT 4.04.683 P
are content to do the profession some grace, 1H4 2.01. 71 P
beseems | a man of thy profession and degree; 1H6 3.01. 20
honor than | your high profession spiritual; H8 2.04.117
the way of our profession is against it; 3.01.157
h'as almost charm'd me from my profession, by TIM 4.03.450 P
day without the sign | of your profession? JC 1.01. 5
they hold up adam's profession. HAM 5.01. 31 P
of mine honors, | my oath, and my profession. LR 5.03.131
of nature's, have subdu'd me | in my profession? CYM 5.02. 6
neither is our profession any trade, it's no PER 4.02. 38 P
and do me the kindness of our profession, she 4.06. 7 P
how long have you been of this profession? 4.06. 72 P
/she makes our profession as it were to stink 4.06.135 P
go with me | before the god of our profession. TNK 5.01. 38

PROFESSION'S 1 FR 0.0001 REL FR 1 V 0 P
love, | for my profession's sacred from above. 1H6 1.02.114

PROFESSIONS 4 FR 0.0004 REL FR 1 V 3 P
you go against the hair of your professions. WIV 2.03. 41 P
having flown over many knavish professions, he WT 4.03. 99 P
is boundless theft | in limited professions. TIM 4.03.428
have let in some of all professions that go the MAC 2.03. 18 P

PROFESSORS 3 FR 0.0003 REL FR 3 V 0 P
might quench the zeal | of all professors else, WT 5.01.108
should reign among professors of one faith. 1H6 5.01. 14
woe upon ye | and all such false professors! H8 3.01.115

PROFFER 7 FR 0.0008 REL FR 7 V 0 P
this fawning greyhound then did proffer me! 1H4 1.03.252
and for the proffer of my lord your master, | i 1H6 5.01. 41
this proffer is absurd and reasonless. 5.04.137
to you | which daily she was bound to proffer. CYM 3.05. 49
he may my proffer take for an offense, | since PER 2.03. 68
or he refus'd to take /her figured proffer, PP 4.10
be thou not slack | to proffer, though she put 18.24

PROFFER'D 5 FR 0.0005 REL FR 5 V 0 P
but if you fondly pass our proffer'd offer, JN 2.01.258
gifts before him, proffer'd him their oaths, 1H4 4.03. 71
but if you frown upon this proffer'd peace, 1H6 4.02. 9
royal self | this proffer'd benefit of dignity; R3 3.07.196
refuse not, mighty lord, this proffer'd love. 3.07.202

PROFFERED 1 FR 0.0001 REL FR 1 V 0 P
the proffered means of succors and redress. R2 3.02. 32

PROFFERER 1 FR 0.0001 REL FR 1 V 0 P
they would have the profferer construe "ay." TGV 1.02. 56

PROFFERS 2 FR 0.0002 REL FR 2 V 0 P
proffers not took reap thanks for their reward. AWW 2.01.147
proffers his only daughter to your grace | in 1H6 5.01. 19

PROFICIENT 1 FR 0.0001 REL FR 0 V 1 P
i am so good a proficient in one quarter of an 1H4 2.04. 18 P

/PROFIT 1 FR 0.0001 REL FR 1 V 0 P
/the /state /and /profit /of /this /land; R2 4.01.225

PROFIT 41 FR 0.0046 REL FR 31 V 10 P
made thee more profit | than other princess' can TMP 1.02.172
wood, and serves in offices | that profit us. 1.02.313
you taught me language, and my profit on't | is, 1.02.363
both work | ere this rude beast will profit. MM 3.02. 33
have no more profit of their shining nights LLL 1.01. 90
and their daughters profit very greatly under 4.02. 75 P
snail–slow in profit, and he sleeps by day MV 2.05. 47
since that the trade and profit of the city 3.03. 30
and report speaks goldenly of his profit. AYL 1.01. 6 P
if you like upon report | the soil, the profit, 2.04. 98
if that an eye may profit by a tongue, | then 4.03. 83
no profit grows where is no pleasure ta'en. SHR 1.01. 39
now, mistress, profit you in what you read? 4.02. 6
sir, i profit in the knowledge of myself, and by TN 5.01. 19 P
and my profit therein the heaping friendships. WT 4.02. 19 P
the noisome weeds which without profit suck R2 3.04. 38
while they do tend the profit of the land. 2H6 1.01.204
the land | and common profit of his country! 1.01.206
in england | but little for my profit; H8 3.01. 83
sacred person and | the profit of the state. 3.02.174
be silent, /boy, i profit not by thy talk. TRO 5.01. 14 P
when we may profit meet, and come too late. TIM 5.01. 42
profit again should hardly draw me here. MAC 5.03. 62
a while | for the supply and profit of our hope, HAM 2.02. 24
both in reputation and profit, was better both 2.02.330 P
ground | that hath in it no profit but the name. 4.04. 19
such /a snipe | but for my sport and profit. OTH 1.03.386
or sue to you to do a peculiar profit | to your 3.03. 79
i thank you for this profit, and from hence 3.03.379
if you dare do yourself a profit and a right. 4.02.232 P
so find we profit | by losing of our prayers. ANT 2.01. 7
'tis not my profit that does lead mine honor; 2.07. 76
thus | draws us a profit from all things we see; CYM 3.03. 18
nor seek for danger | where there's no profit. 4.02.163
i speak against my present profit, but my wish 5.04.205 P
world so soon | to yield thee so much profit. PER 4.01. 4
wherein my death might yield her any profit, 4.01. 80
despise profit where you have most gain. 4.02.118 P
a good opinion, and that opinion a mere profit. 4.02.121 P
more, the profit of excess | is but to surfeit, LUC 138
shall profit thee, and much enrich thy book. SON 77.14

PROFITABLE 3 FR 0.0003 REL FR 2 V 1 P
a man | is not so estimable, profitable neither, MV 1.03.166
sir, was profitable, and much fool may you find AWW 2.04. 35 P
year | with profitable labor to his grave: H5 4.01.277

PROFITABLY 2 FR 0.0002 REL FR 0 V 2 P
my mouth, that i might answer thee profitably. TIM 2.02. 77 P
and the impediment most profitably remov'd, OTH 2.01.279 P

PROFITED 2 FR 0.0002 REL FR 1 V 1 P
read, and profited | in strange concealments, 1H4 3.01.164
has not the boy profited? 2H4 2.02. 84 P

PROFITING 2 FR 0.0002 REL FR 1 V 1 P
men their creation mar | in profiting by them. MM 2.04.128
of persuasion and him the ears of profiting, 1H4 1.02.153 P

PROFITLESS 3 FR 0.0003 REL FR 3 V 0 P
which falls into mine ears as profitless | as ADO 5.01. 4
and gain | to wake and wage a danger profitless. OTH 1.03. 30
profitless usurer, why dost thou use | so great SON 4. 7

PROFIT'S 2 FR 0.0002 REL FR 2 V 0 P
that will not trust thee but for profit's sake? 1H6 3.03. 63
that profit's yet to come 'tween me and you. OTH 2.03. 10

PROFITS 8 FR 0.0009 REL FR 7 V 1 P
husband says my son profits nothing in the world WIV 4.01. 15 P
his natural edge | with profits of the mind — MM 1.04. 61
this nor hurts him, nor profits you a jot. 4.03.123
eyes | to see alike mine honor as their profits WT 1.02.310
be | unto the camp, and profits will accrue. H5 2.01.112
ill blows the wind that profits nobody. 3H6 2.05. 55
employ'd you where high profits might come home,
H8 3.02.158
if they not thought the profits of my death LR 2.01. 75

/PROFOUND 1 FR 0.0001 REL FR 0 V 1 P
and through the most /profound and /winnow'd HAM 5.02.192 P

PROFOUND 16 FR 0.0018 REL FR 11 V 5 P
of your hips has the most profound sciatica? MM 1.02. 59 P
in most profound earnest, and, i'll warrant you, ADO 5.01.195 P
a gig, | and profound salomon to tune a jig, LLL 4.03.166
vildly compiled, profound simplicity. 5.02. 52
with such a zealous laughter, so profound, 5.02.116
opinion | of wisdom, gravity, profound conceit, MV 1.01. 92
with a magician, most profound in his art, and AYL 5.02. 61 P
no, my profound heart; TN 1.05.183 P
or the profound seas hides | in unknown fadoms, WT 4.04.490
when such profound respects do pull you on. JN 3.01.318
more holy and profound, than mine own life, | my
COR 3.03.113
the moon | there hangs a vap'rous drop profound, MAC 3.05. 24
he rais'd a sigh so piteous and profound | as it HAM 2.01. 91
matter in these sighs, these profound heaves — 4.01. 1
but a most thick and profound melancholy. TNK 4.03. 49 P
in so profound abysm i throw all care | of SON 112. 9

PROFOUNDEST 1 FR 0.0001 REL FR 1 V 0 P
conscience and grace, to the profoundest pit! HAM 4.05.133

PROFOUNDLY 1 FR 0.0001 REL FR 0 V 1 P
why sigh you so profoundly? TRO 4.02. 80 P

PROGENITORS 4 FR 0.0004 REL FR 4 V 0 P
titles | usurp'd from you and your progenitors. H5 1.02. 95
like true subjects, sons of your progenitors, 1H6 4.01.166
our great progenitors had conquered? 5.04.110
if children predecease progenitors, | we are LUC 1756

PROGENY 5 FR 0.0005 REL FR 5 V 0 P
and though the mourning brow of progeny | forbid
LLL 5.02.744
and this same progeny of evils comes | from our MND 2.01.115
thee, | doubting thy birth and lawful progeny. 1H6 3.03. 61
swain, | but issued from the progeny of kings; 5.04. 38
that was the whip of your bragg'd progeny | thou COR 1.08. 12

PROGNE 1 FR 0.0001 REL FR 1 V 0 P
and worse than progne i will be reveng'd. TIT 5.02.195

PROGNOSTICATE 1 FR 0.0001 REL FR 1 V 0 P
or else of thee this i prognosticate: SON 14.13

PROGNOSTICATION 2 FR 0.0002 REL FR 0 V 2 P
in the hottest day prognostication proclaims), WT 4.04.788 P
an oily palm be not a fruitful prognostication, ANT 1.02. 53 P

PROGRESS 13 FR 0.0014 REL FR 12 V 1 P
and so in progress to be hatch'd and born, | are MM 2.02. 97
of that and all the progress, more and less, AWW 5.03.331
water keep | a peaceful progress to the ocean. JN 2.01.340
that silverly doth progress on thy cheeks. 5.02. 46
team | begins his golden progress in the east. 1H4 3.01.219
happiest youth, viewing his progress through, 2H4 3.01. 54
the king is now in progress towards saint albons 2H6 1.04. 72
i' th' progress of this business, | ere a H8 2.04.176
in all the progress | both of my life and office 5.02. 67
for no pulse | shall keep his native progress, ROM 4.01. 97
i cannot by the progress of the stars | give JC 2.01. 2
how a king may go a progress through the guts of HAM 4.03. 31 P
know | time's thievish progress to eternity. SON 77. 8

PROGRESSION 1 FR 0.0001 REL FR 0 V 1 P
accidentally, or by the way of progression, hath LLL 4.02.140 P

PROH 1 FR 0.0001 REL FR 1 V 0 P
proh deum, medius fidius, ye are all dunces! TNK 3.05. 11

PROHIBIT 1 FR 0.0001 REL FR 0 V 1 P
a merry meeting may be wish'd, god prohibit it! ADO 5.01.326 P

PROHIBITION 1 FR 0.0001 REL FR 1 V 0 P
there is a prohibition so divine | that cravens CYM 3.04. 77

PROIN *(also prune*)*

PROIN 1 FR 0.0001 REL FR 1 V 0 P
do men proin | the straight young boughs that TNK 3.06.242

PROJECT 12 FR 0.0013 REL FR 11 V 1 P
and sends me forth | (for else his project dies) TMP 2.01.299
yet always bending | towards their project. 4.01.175
now does my project gather to a head: 5.01. 1
my sails | must fill, or else my project fails, ep 12
nor take no shape nor project of affection, ADO 3.01. 55
the king's disease — my project may deceive me, AWW 1.01.228
if your more ponderous and settled project | may WT 4.04.524
flatt'ring himself in project of a power | much 2H4 1.03. 29
off | all fears attending on so dire a project. TRO 2.02.134
therefore this project | should have a back or HAM 4.07.152
i cannot project mine own cause so well | to ANT 5.02.121
between the passages of this project, come in TNK 4.03. 99 P

PROJECTION 1 FR 0.0001 REL FR 1 V 0 P
which, of a weak and niggardly projection, H5 2.04. 46

PROJECT'S 1 FR 0.0001 REL FR 1 V 0 P
our project's life this shape of sense assumes: TRO 1.03.384

PROJECTS 1 FR 0.0001 REL FR 1 V 0 P
out of my files, his projects to accomplish, COR 5.06. 33

PROLIXIOUS 1 FR 0.0001 REL FR 1 V 0 P
lay by all nicety and prolixious blushes | that MM 2.04.162

PROLIXITY 2 FR 0.0002 REL FR 1 V 1 P
any slips of prolixity or crossing the plain MV 3.01. 11 P
the date is out of such prolixity: ROM 1.04. 3

/PROLOGUE 2 FR 0.0002 REL FR 2 V 0 P
/a /prologue /arm'd, /but /not /in /confidence TRO pr 23
/nor /no //without–book /prologue, /faintly ROM 1.04. 7

PROLOGUE 19 FR 0.0021 REL FR 8 V 11 P
an act | whereof what's past is prologue, what TMP 2.01.253
as it were, spoke the prologue of our comedy; WIV 3.05. 74 P
their shallow shows and prologue vildly penn'd, LLL 5.02.305
write me a prologue, and let the prologue seem MND 3.01. 17 P
and let the prologue seem to say we will do no 3.01. 17 P
we will have such a prologue, and it shall be 3.01. 23 P
therefore another prologue must tell he is not a 3.01. 34 P
so please your grace, the prologue is address'd. 5.01.106
he hath rid his prologue like a rough colt; 5.01.119 P
hath play'd on this prologue like a child on a 5.01.122 P
unhandsome than to see the lord the prologue. AYL ep 3 P
much as will serve to be prologue to an egg and 1H4 1.02. 21 P
but mine is made the prologue to their play; 2H6 3.01.151
the fates | and prologue to the omen coming on, HAM 1.01.123
is this a prologue, or the posy of a ring? 3.02.152 P
each toy seems prologue to some great amiss, 4.05. 18
or i could make a prologue to my brains, | they 5.02. 30
an index and obscure prologue to the history of OTH 2.01.258 P
'tis evermore /the prologue to his sleep. 2.03.129

PROLOGUE–LIKE 1 FR 0.0001 REL FR 1 V 0 P
who, prologue–like, your humble patience pray, H5 pr 33

PROLOGUES 3 FR 0.0003 REL FR 2 V 1 P
which are the only prologues to a bad voice? AYL 5.03. 13 P
thus he his special nothing ever prologues. AWW 2.01. 92
as happy prologues to the swelling act | of the MAC 1.03.128

PROLONG 3 FR 0.0003 REL FR 3 V 0 P
i would prolong a while the traitor's life. 3H6 1.04. 52
power | to expel sickness, but prolong his hour! TIM 3.01. 63
a better, to prolong | your old loves to us. TNK ep 16

PROLONG'D 4 FR 0.0004 REL FR 4 V 0 P
that by misfortunes was my life prolong'd, | to ERR 1.01.119
this wedding–day | perhaps is but prolong'd, ADO 4.01.254
as else i would be, were the day prolong'd. R3 3.04. 45
by med'cine life may be prolong'd, yet death CYM 5.05. 29

PROLONGS 1 FR 0.0001 REL FR 1 V 0 P
this physic but prolongs thy sickly days. HAM 3.03. 96

PROMETHEAN 3 FR 0.0003 REL FR 3 V 0 P
whence doth spring the true promethean fire. LLL 4.03.300
they sparkle still the right promethean fire; 4.03.348
i know not where is that promethean heat | that OTH 5.02. 12

PROMETHEUS 1 FR 0.0001 REL FR 1 V 0 P
eyes | than is prometheus tied to caucasus. TIT 2.01. 17

PROMETTEZ 1 FR 0.0001 REL FR 0 V 1 P
pour les ecus que vous /lui promettez, il est H5 4.04. 52 P

/PROMIS'D 1 FR 0.0001 REL FR 1 V 0 P
/grace /in /mind | /of /what /you /promis'd /me. R3 4.02.111

PROMIS'D 61 FR 0.0069 REL FR 38 V 23 P
let me remember thee what thou hast promis'd, TMP 1.02.243
but she i mean is promis'd by her friends | unto TGV 3.01.106
the hour, sir, that sir hugh promis'd to meet. WIV 2.03. 5 P
well, i promis'd you a dinner. 3.03.223 P
can for them all three, for so i have promis'd, 3.04.107 P
he promis'd to meet me two hours since, and he MM 1.02. 74 P
he promis'd her marriage. 3.02.200 P
upon this time have i promis'd here to meet. 4.01. 17 P
sister, you know he promis'd me a chain; ERR 2.01.106
is that the chain you promis'd me to–day? 4.03. 47
or, for my diamond, the chain you promis'd, 4.03. 69
and for the same he promis'd me a chain: 4.03. 84
for indeed i promis'd to eat all of his killing. ADO 1.01. 44 P
the prince and claudio promis'd by this hour 5.04. 13

that you to–day promis'd to tell me of? MV 1.01.121
who hath promis'd to meet me in this place of AYL 3.03. 44 P
i have promis'd to make all this matter even: 5.04. 18
i promis'd to inquire carefully | about a SHR 1.02.165
hath promis'd me to help /me to another, | a 1.02.172
i promis'd we would be contributors | and bear 1.02.214
receive | the confirmation of my promis'd gift, AWW 2.03. 50
his highness hath promis'd me to do it, and, to 4.05. 74 P
do you know he promis'd me marriage? 5.03.255 P
but he has promis'd me, as he is a gentleman and TN 3.04.308 P
and for that i promis'd you, i'll be as good as 3.04.322 P
i was promis'd them against the feast, but they WT 4.04.235 P
he hath promis'd you more than that, or there be 4.04.237 P
he hath paid you all he promis'd you. 4.04.239 P
you promis'd me a tawdry–lace and a pair of 4.04.249 P
after i have done what i promis'd? 4.04.810 P
and he hath promis'd to dismiss the powers | led JN 5.01. 64
you promis'd, when you parted with the king, R2 2.02. 2
i promis'd you redress of these same grievances 2H4 4.02.113
here i promis'd you i would be, and here i ep 13 P
the courses of his youth promis'd it not. H5 1.01. 24
coronets, | promis'd to harry and his followers. 2.pr. 11
it to in change promis'd to wear it in his cap. 4.08. 29 P
i promis'd to strike him, if he did. 4.08. 30 P
her aid she promis'd, and assur'd success; 1H6 1.02. 82
you promis'd knighthood to our forward son, 3H6 2.02. 58
i am sure the emperor | paid ere he promis'd, H8 1.01.186
but am bold'ned | under your promis'd pardon. 1.02. 56
they promis'd me eternal happiness, | and 4.02. 90
earth below | fails in the promis'd largeness. TRO 1.03. 5
so rich advantage of a promis'd glory | as 2.02.204
wife, | that is another's lawful promis'd love. TIT 1.01.298
love | by humble message and by promis'd means. TIM 5.04. 20
no, i am promis'd forth. JC 1.02.289 P
of cawdor to me | promis'd no less to them? MAC 1.03.120
ignorant of what greatness is promis'd thee. 1.05. 13 P
cawdor, and shalt be | what thou art promis'd. 1.05. 16
as the weird women promis'd, and i fear | thou 3.01. 2
craves the conveyance of a promis'd march | over HAM 4.04. 3
you tumbled me, | you promis'd me to wed.'" 4.05. 63
is this the promis'd end? LR 5.03.264
and here speak with me, | the which he promis'd. OTH 4.01. 81
to have the courtesy your cradle promis'd, | but CYM 4.04. 28
such precious deeds in one that promis'd nought 5.05. 9
so he thrived | that he is promis'd to be wived PER 5.02. 10
estate your daughter in what i have promis'd. TNK 2.01. 11 P
assuage, | 'tis promis'd in the charity of age. LC 70

/PROMISE 1 FR 0.0001 REL FR 1 V 0 P
/my /lord, /your /promise /for /the /earldom — R3 4.02.102

PROMISE 108 FR 0.0122 REL FR 79 V 29 P
thou did promise | to bate me a full year. TMP 1.02.249
it is my promise, | and they expect it from me. 4.01. 41
and promise you calm seas, auspicious gales, 5.01.315
i claim the promise for her heavenly picture. TGV 4.04. 87
have you receiv'd no promise of satisfaction at WIV 2.02.209 P
he promise to bring me where is anne page; 3.01.122 P
not by my consent, i promise you. 3.02. 71 P
i mine, to build upon a foolish woman's promise. 3.05. 42 P
likewise hath | made promise to the doctor. 4.06. 34
to his bed, give him promise of satisfaction. MM 3.01.263 P
there have i made my promise upon the heavy 4.01. 34
your breach of promise to the porpentine: ERR 4.01. 49
borne himself beyond the promise of his age, ADO 1.01. 14 P
i do not like thy look, i promise thee. 4.02. 45 P
keep promise, love. look, here comes helena. MND 1.01.179
i fear it, i promise you. 3.01. 28 P
i promise you your kindred hath made my eyes 3.01.194 P
alack, | i fear my thisby's promise is forgot! 5.01.173
if thou keep promise, i shall end this strife, MV 2.03. 20
the second, silver, which this promise carries, 2.07. 6
promise me life, and i'll confess the truth. 3.02. 34
rather threaten'st than dost promise aught, 3.02.105
with oaths of love, at last, if promise last, 3.02.205
i got a promise of this fair one here | to have 3.02.206
therefore, i promise you, i fear you. 3.05. 3 P
or i, i promise thee. AYL 1.02.140 P
but justly, as you have exceeded all promise, 1.02.244
rosalind, i come within an hour of my promise. 4.01. 43 P
break an hour's promise in love! 4.01. 44 P
if you break one jot of your promise, or come 4.01.190 P
beware my censure, and keep your promise. 4.01.196 P
from you | he left a promise to return again 4.03. 99
that you might excuse | his broken promise, and 4.03.154
and yet i'll promise thee she shall be rich, SHR 1.02. 62
suitors, | and will not promise her to any man, 1.02.260
for fear, i promise you, if i look pale. 2.01.143
now i promise you | you have show'd a tender 2.01.285
mine from all the world, | by your firm promise; 2.01.385
i must believe my master, else, i promise you, 3.01. 54
fee, | but, if i help, what do you promise me? AWW 2.01.190
to whom i promise | a counterpoise; 2.03.174
for the promise of his life and in the highest 3.06. 29 P
and then to break promise with him and make a TN 2.03.128 P
nothing of that wonderful promise, to read him 3.04.264 P
which methought did promise | most venerable 3.04.362
cesario, you do not keep promise with me. 5.01.103
of the greatest promise that ever came into my WT 1.01. 36 P
is this your promise? go to, hold your tongue. JN 4.01. 96
remember, as thou read'st, thy promise pass'd. R2 5.03. 51
this in the name of god i promise here, | the 1H4 3.02.153
know the king | knows at what time to promise, 4.03. 53
hope, | eating the air, and promise of supply, 2H4 1.03. 28
patience for it and to promise you a better. ep 10 P
and (as most debtors do) promise you infinitely; ep 15 P
between the promise of his greener days | and H5 2.04.136
'tis hereafter to know, but now to promise. 5.02.213 P
do but now promise, kate, you will endeavor for 5.02.213 P
my lord of york, i promise you, the king 1H6 4.01.174
with promise of high pay and great rewards; 3H6 2.01.134
promise them such rewards | as victors wear at 2.03. 52
her | with promise of his sister and what else, 3.01. 51
i promise you, i scarcely know myself. R3 2.03. 2
i'll claim that promise at your grace's hand. 3.01.197
my lord, i claim the gift, my due by promise, 4.02. 88
enemies | and promise them success and victory. 4.04.194
i promise you, my soul is very jocund | in the 5.03.232
i cannot promise | but that you shall sustain H8 3.02. 4
out of those many regist'red in promise, | which TRO 3.03. 15
could promise to himself | a thought of added 4.05.144
he will spend his mouth and promise, like 5.01. 91 P
it is your former promise. COR 1.01.238
from him pluck'd | either his gracious promise, 2.03.193
nay, temperately; your promise. 3.03. 67
is this the promise that you made your mother? 3.03. 86
have pass'd | my word and promise to the emperor TIT 1.01.469
and mine, i promise you; 2.03.196
i promise you, but for your company, | i would ROM 3.04. 6
my hand to thee, mine honor on my promise. TIM 1.01.148
i promise you, my lord, you mov'd me much. 1.02.113
promise me friendship, but perform none. 4.03. 73 P
if thou wilt not promise, the gods plague thee, 4.03. 74 P
only i will promise him an excellent piece. 5.01. 19
to promise is most courtly and fashionable; 5.01. 27
it is our part and promise to th' athenians | to 5.01.120
o rome, i make thee promise, | if the redress JC 2.01. 56
of any promise that hath pass'd from him. 2.01.140
make gallant show and promise of their mettle; 4.02. 24
his absence, sir, | lays blame upon his promise. MAC 3.04. 43
that keep the word of promise to our ear, | and 5.08. 21
extinct in both | even in their promise, as it HAM 1.03.119
i promise you, the effects he writes of succeed LR 1.02.143 P
i cannot speak of this. come now, your promise. OTH 3.04. 48
what promise, chuck? 3.04. 49
own love and flattery, not out of my promise. 4.01.129 P
from antony win cleopatra, promise, | and in our ANT 3.12. 27
i have perform'd | your pleasure and my promise. 5.02.204
i cross'd the seas on purpose and on promise CYM 1.06.202
willing spirits | that promise noble service; 4.02.339
who did promise | to yield me often tidings. 4.03. 38
most unlike our courtiers, | as good as promise! 5.04.137
is at hand to seal | the promise of his wrath. TNK 1.02. 93
but have you a full promise of her? 2.01. 13 P
pray hold your promise; 3.01.100
that gave her promise faithfully she would | be 3.05. 43
upon this promise did he raise his chin, | like VEN 85
while others saucily | promise more speed, but LUC 1349
each present lord began to promise aid, | as 1696
why didst thou promise such a beauteous day, SON 34. 1

PROMISE–BREACH 1 FR 0.0001 REL FR 1 V 0 P
of sacred chastity and of promise–breach, MM 5.01.405

PROMISE–BREAKER 2 FR 0.0002 REL FR 1 V 1 P
and endless liar, an hourly promise–breaker, the AWW 3.06. 10 P
i do hate thee | worse than a promise–breaker. COR 1.08. 2

PROMISE–CRAMM'D 1 FR 0.0001 REL FR 0 V 1 P
i eat the air, promise–cramm'd — you cannot HAM 3.02. 94 P

PROMISED 14 FR 0.0015 REL FR 13 V 1 P
partly for that her promised proportions | came MM 5.01.219
i promised your presence and the chain, | but ERR 4.01. 23
i have promised to study three years with the LLL 1.02. 35 P
the boy | can do all this that he hath promised? AYL 5.04. 2
in padua | of greater sums than i have promised. SHR 3.02.135
as to my ample hope was promised | before i drew JN 5.02.112
i throw off | and pay the debt i never promised, 1H4 1.02.209
that thus delays my promised supply | of 1H6 4.03. 10
the sum of money which i promised | should be 5.01. 52
this they have promised, to show your highness 2H6 1.02. 78
from giving aid which late i promised. 3H6 3.03.148
which you have promised i shall possess. R3 4.02. 91
i promised your grace a hunter's peal. TIT 2.02. 13
in half an hour she promised to return. ROM 2.05. 2

PROMISEDST 1 FR 0.0001 REL FR 1 V 0 P
'twas i indeed thou promisedst to strike, | and H5 4.08. 41

PROMISE–KEEPING 1 FR 0.0001 REL FR 0 V 1 P
and he was ever precise in promise–keeping. MM 1.02. 76 P

PROMISES 24 FR 0.0027 REL FR 19 V 5 P
my mind promises with my habit, no loss shall MM 3.01.177 P
of his frailty) many deceiving promises of life, 3.02.246 P
if you do keep your promises in love | but AYL 1.02.243
hopes of her good that her education promises; AWW 1.01. 40 P
and most oft there | where most it promises; 2.01.143
their promises, enticements, oaths, tokens, and 3.05. 18 P
these promises are fair, the parties sure, | and 1H4 3.01. 1
they are, | if promises be kept on every hand, 3.02.168
die, | if hell and treason hold their promises, H5 2.pr. 29
thy promises are like adonis' garden, | that one 1H6 1.06. 6
tell you, expects performance of your promises. 2H6 1.04. 2 P
that promises no element | in such a business. H8 1.01. 48
by my life, | that promises moe thousands; 2.03. 97
his promises were, as he then was, mighty; 4.02. 41
'tis a girl | promises boys hereafter. 5.01.166
yet now promises | upon this land a thousand 5.04. 18
and fill his aged ears | with golden promises, TIT 4.04. 97
his promises fly so beyond his state | that what TIM 1.02.197
his expedition promises | present approach. 5.02. 3
the higher nilus swells, | the more it promises; ANT 2.07. 21
quite forgo | the way which promises assurance, 3.07. 46
next day's fate, | which promises royal peril. 4.08. 35
whose issue | promises britain peace and plenty. CYM 5.05.458
fairer promises | in such a body yet i never TNK 4.02.118

PROMISETH 3 FR 0.0003 REL FR 3 V 0 P
ripe | the bloom that promiseth a mighty fruit. JN 2.01.473
thee, | who never promiseth but he means to pay. 1H4 5.04. 43
face, which promiseth | successful fortune, 3H6 2.02. 40

PROMISING 6 FR 0.0006 REL FR 5 V 1 P
promising to bring it to the porpentine, | where ERR 5.01.222
love and credence | upon thy promising fortune. AWW 3.03. 3
and of other motions, as promising her marriage, 5.03.264 P
a course more promising | than a wild dedication WT 4.04.565
promising is the very air o' th' time; TIM 5.01. 22
empire, promising | to pay our wonted tribute, CYM 5.05.461

PROMONTORY 7 FR 0.0008 REL FR 6 V 1 P
the strong–bas'd promontory | have i made shake, TMP 5.01. 46
since once i sat upon a promontory, | and heard MND 2.01.149
like one that stands upon a promontory | and 3H6 3.02.135
chase, | and climb the highest promontory top. TIT 2.02. 22
the earth, seems to me a sterile promontory; HAM 2.02.299 P
or blue promontory | with trees upon't that nod ANT 4.14. 5
hence, as from a promontory | pointed in heaven, TNK 4.02. 22

PROMOTION 4 FR 0.0004 REL FR 4 V 0 P
where none will sweat but for promotion, | and AYL 2.03. 60
to do this deed, | promotion follows. WT 1.02.357
the high promotion of his grace of canterbury, H8 5.02. 23
the most you sought was her promotion, | for ROM 4.05. 71

PROMOTIONS 3 FR 0.0003 REL FR 3 V 0 P
her rich | in titles, honors, and promotions, JN 2.01.492
while great promotions | are daily given to R3 1.03. 79
home | to high promotions and great dignity. 4.04.314

PROMPT 13 FR 0.0014 REL FR 11 V 2 P
and prompt me, plain and holy innocence! TMP 3.01. 82
out of breath, prompt us to have mercy on him; TN 3.04.139 P
my voice shall sound as you do prompt mine ear, 2H4 5.02.119
not read the story, | that i may prompt them; H5 5.pr. 2
the grecians are most prompt and pregnant — TRO 4.04. 88
ready, when time shall prompt them, to make road COR 3.01. 5
come, come, we'll prompt you. 3.02.106
and prompt me that my tongue may utter forth TIT 5.03. 12
by love, that first did prompt me to inquire; ROM 2.02. 80
thee always for a towardly prompt spirit — give TIM 3.01. 35 P
i do agnize | a natural and prompt alacrity | i OTH 1.03.232
him, i am prompt | to lay my crown at 's feet, ANT 3.13. 75
all replication prompt and reason strong, | for LC 122

PROMPTED 4 FR 0.0004 REL FR 4 V 0 P
and part being prompted by your present trouble, TN 3.04.343
in his descent than shall my prompted sword TRO 5.02.175
i have | prompted you in the ebb of your estate TIM 2.02.141
prompted to my revenge by heaven and hell, HAM 2.02.584

PROMPTEMENT 1 FR 0.0001 REL FR 0 V 1 P
non, je reciterai a vous promptement: H5 3.04. 44 P

/PROMPTER 1 FR 0.0001 REL FR 1 V 0 P
/faintly /spoke | /after /the /prompter, /for ROM 1.04. 8

PROMPTER 1 FR 0.0001 REL FR 1 V 0 P
i should have known it | without a prompter. OTH 1.02. 84

PROMPTING 2 FR 0.0002 REL FR 2 V 0 P
all prompting me how fair young hero is, ADO 1.01.304
such fiery numbers as the prompting eyes | of LLL 4.03.319

PROMPTS 5 FR 0.0005 REL FR 5 V 0 P
it goes on, i see, | as my soul prompts it. TMP 1.02.421
heart sues, and prompts my tongue to speak. R3 1.02.170
th' advantage of the time prompts me aloud | to TRO 3.03. 2
nor by th' matter which your heart prompts you, COR 3.02. 54
and nature prompts them | in simple and low CYM 3.03. 84

PROMPTURE 1 FR 0.0001 REL FR 1 V 0 P
though he hath fall'n by prompture of the blood, MM 2.04.178

PRONE 7 FR 0.0008 REL FR 6 V 1 P
youth | there is a prone and speechless dialect, MM 1.02.183
i am not prone to weeping, as our sex | commonly WT 2.01.108
and as prone to mischief | as able to perform't) H8 1.01.160
beget young gibbets, i never saw one so prone. CYM 5.04.199 P
which speaks him prone to labor, never fainting TNK 4.02.129
o that prone lust should stain so pure a bed! LUC 684
nor tender feeling to base touches prone, | nor SON 141. 6

PRONONCER 1 FR 0.0001 REL FR 0 V 1 P
je ne voudrais prononcer ces mots devant les H5 3.04. 55 P

PRONONCEZ 1 FR 0.0001 REL FR 0 V 1 P
vous prononcez les mots aussi droit que les H5 3.04. 38 P

PRONOUN 1 FR 0.0001 REL FR 0 V 1 P
articles are borrow'd of the pronoun, and be WIV 4.01. 40 P

PRONOUNC'D 12 FR 0.0013 REL FR 9 V 3 P
organ–pipe, pronounc'd | the name of prosper; TMP 3.03. 98
good sentences, and well pronounc'd. MV 1.02. 10 P
his followers, whose condemnation is pronounc'd. H5 3.06.135 P
forthwith that edward be pronounc'd a traitor, 3H6 4.06. 54
or who pronounc'd | the bitter sentence of poor R3 1.04.185
lord hastings had pronounc'd your part — | i 3.04. 27
after your way his tale pronounc'd shall bury COR 5.06. 57
for which attempt the judges have pronounc'd TIT 3.01. 50
hath doubtfully pronounc'd the throat shall cut, TIM 4.03.122
all mortal consequences have pronounc'd me thus: MAC 5.03. 5
fortune's state would treason have pronounc'd. HAM 2.02.511
speech, i pray you, as i pronounc'd it to you, 3.02. 1 P

/PRONOUNCE 1 FR 0.0001 REL FR 1 V 0 P
/pronounce but "love" and "/dove"; ROM 2.01. 10

PRONOUNCE 29 FR 0.0032 REL FR 26 V 3 P
which i do last pronounce, is (o you wonder!) TMP 1.02.427
and do pronounce by me | ling'ring perdition 3.03. 76
pronounce a sentence on your brother's life; MM 2.04. 62
sir, i will pronounce your sentence: LLL 1.01.300 P
"det," when he should pronounce "debt" — 5.01. 21 P
pronounce that sentence then on me, my liege, AYL 1.03. 85
pronounce thee a gross lout, a mindless slave, WT 1.02.301
this sessions (to our great grief we pronounce) 3.02. 1
till this time my tongue did ne'er pronounce, JN 3.01.307
which i with some unwillingness pronounce: R2 1.03.149
ride, | the which in every language i pronounce, 2H4 in 7
and here pronounce free pardon to them all 2H6 4.08. 9
i do pronounce him in that very shape | he shall H8 1.01.196
tongue could ever | pronounce dishonor of her — 2.03. 4
as't please | yourself pronounce their office. 2.04.115
if what i now pronounce you have found true; 3.02.163
we do here pronounce, | upon the part o' th' COR 3.01.208
let them pronounce the steep tarpeian death, 3.03. 88
if thou dost love, pronounce it faithfully; ROM 2.02. 94
pronounce this sentence then: 2.03. 79
go pronounce his present death, | and with his MAC 1.02. 64
but wherefore could not i pronounce "amen"? 2.02. 28
pronounce it for me, sir, to all our friends, 3.04. 7
the devil himself could not pronounce a title 5.07. 8
i am tame, sir. pronounce. HAM 3.02.310 P
pronounce | the beggary of his change; CYM 1.06.114
do here pronounce | by th' very truth of it, i 2.03.107
that i am to pronounce augustus caesar | (caesar 3.01. 62
in caesar's name pronounce i 'gainst thee; 3.01. 66

PRONOUNCED 2 FR 0.0002 REL FR 2 V 0 P
recant | the pardon that i late pronounced here. MV 4.01.392
yet sometime "tarquin" was pronounced plain, LUC 1786

PRONOUNCES 1 FR 0.0001 REL FR 1 V 0 P
to him, and pronounces | ruin to thebes; TNK 1.02. 91

PRONOUNCING 3 FR 0.0003 REL FR 3 V 0 P
is now leas'd out — i die pronouncing it — R2 2.01. 59
pronouncing that the paleness of this flower 1H6 4.01.106
or by pronouncing of some doubtful phrase, | as HAM 1.05.175

PRONOUNS 1 FR 0.0001 REL FR 0 V 1 P
now, william, some declensions of your pronouns. WIV 4.01. 75 P

/PROOF 1 FR 0.0001 REL FR 1 V 0 P
/in /thy /just /proof /repeals /and /reconciles LR 3.06.113

PROOF 77 FR 0.0087 REL FR 59 V 18 P
such another proof will make me cry "baa." TGV 1.01. 93 P
we'll leave a proof, by that which we will do, WIV 4.02.104
proof? MM 4.02. 42 P
of lord angelo, came not to an undoubtful proof. 4.02.137 P
this is an accident of hourly proof, | which i ADO 2.01.181
what proof shall i make of that? 2.02. 27 P
proof enough to misuse the prince, to vex 2.02. 28 P
dear my lord, if you, in your own proof, | have 4.01. 45
but what was true, and very full of proof. 5.01.105
i urge this childhood proof, | because what MV 1.01.144
you have seen cruel proof of this man's strength AYL 1.02.174 P
ay, to the proof, as mountains are for winds, SHR 2.01.140
and all my pains is sorted to no proof. 4.03. 43
make your proof. TN 1.05. 61 P
want of other idleness, i'll bide your proof. 1.05. 65 P
for 'tis a vulgar proof | that very oft we pity 3.01.124
approbation than ever proof itself would have 3.04.181 P
are like to find him in the proof of his valor. 3.04.266 P
for i am proof against that title and what shame WT 4.04.840 P
bear no credit, | were not the proof so nigh. 5.01.180
add proof unto mine armor with thy prayers, R2 1.03. 73
in proof whereof, there is my honor's pawn, 4.01. 70
as, for proof, now: 1H4 1.02. 33 P
well, we leave that to the proof. 2.02. 69 P
dare | to gentle exercise and proof of arms. 5.02. 54
none of these demure boys come to any proof, for 2H4 4.03. 91 P
only this proof i'll of thy valor make, | in 1H6 1.02. 94
call we to mind, and mark but this for proof: 3.03. 68
in argument and proof of which contract, | bear 5.01. 46
this speedy and quick appearance argues proof 5.03. 8
not fear the sword, for his coat is of proof. 2H6 4.02. 61 P
as by proof we see | the water swell before a R3 2.03. 43
armed in proof and led by shallow richmond. 5.03.219
in that very shape | he shall appear in proof. H8 1.01.197
troilus will stand to the proof, if you'll prove TRO 1.02.129 P
reproof of chance | lies the true proof of men: 1.03. 34
a proof of strength she could not publish more, 5.02.113
amorous troyan, | and am her knight by proof. 5.05. 5
so much | that proof is call'd impossibility. 5.05. 29
and fight | with hearts more proof than shields. COR 1.04. 25
should be so tyrannous and rough in proof! ROM 1.01.170
and, in strong proof of chastity well arm'd, 1.01.210
sweet, | and i am proof against their enmity. 2.02. 73
exactest auditors, | and set me on the proof. TIM 2.02.157
whose proof nor yells of mothers, maids, nor 4.03.125
but 'tis a common proof | that lowliness is JC 2.01. 21
i have made strong proof of my constancy, 2.01.299
the proof of it will turn to redder drops. 5.01. 49
till that bellona's bridegroom, lapp'd in proof, MAC 1.02. 54
on mars's armor forg'd for proof eterne | with HAM 2.02.490
a paradox, but now the time gives it proof. 3.01.114 P
now what my /love is, proof hath made you know, 3.02.169
so | that it be proof and bulwark against sense. 3.04. 38
by time, | and that i see, in passages of proof, 4.07.112
that might hold | if this did blast in proof. 4.07.154
the country gives me proof and president | of LR 2.03. 13
i'll put't in proof, | and when i have stol'n 4.06.185
of whom his eyes had seen the proof | at rhodes, OTH 1.01. 28
to vouch this is no proof, | without more wider 1.03.106
and on the proof, there is no more but this — 3.03.191
i speak not yet of proof. 3.03.196
give me the ocular proof, | or, by the worth of 3.03.360
i'll have some proof. 3.03.386
i will make proof of thine. 5.01. 26
through proof of harness to my heart, and there ANT 4.08. 15
knows | by history, report, or his own proof, CYM 1.06. 70
let proof speak. 3.01. 76
out of your proof you speak; 3.03. 27
but from proof as strong as my grief and as 3.04. 24 P
naked breast | stepp'd before targes of proof, 5.05. 5
that i return'd with simular proof enough | to 5.05.200
spirit do incite | the princes to their proof! TNK 5.03. 57
are better proof than thy spear's point can VEN 626
i never more will grind | on newer proof, to try SON 110.11
down, | and on just proof surmise accumulate; 117.10
a bliss in proof, and prov'd, /a very woe, 129.11
blood | that we must curb it upon others' proof, LC 163
PROOFS 14 FR 0.0015 REL FR 10 V 4 P
ay, and an ox too; both the proofs are extant. WIV 5.05.120 P
if the devil have given thee proofs for sin, MM 3.02. 30
we have ten proofs to one that blood hath the ADO 2.03.164 P
my fore–past proofs, howe'er the matter fall, AWW 5.03.121
is his wife, | that ring's a thousand proofs. 5.03.199
(all proofs sleeping else | but what your WT 3.02.112
you see, there is such unity in the proofs. 5.02. 32 P
come, i'll drink no proofs nor no bullets. 2H4 2.04.118 P
and proofs as clear as founts in july when | we H8 1.01.154
contrary | urg'd on the examinations, proofs, 2.01. 16
confirmations strong | as proofs of holy writ; OTH 3.03.324
and this may help to thicken other proofs | that 3.03.430
it speaks against her with the other proofs. 3.03.441
many bulwarks builded | of proofs new–bleeding, LC 153
PROP 6 FR 0.0006 REL FR 4 V 2 P
boy was the very staff of my age, my very prop. MV 2.02. 67 P
a cudgel or a hovel–post, a staff, or a prop? 2.02. 69 P
you take my house when you do take the prop 4.01.375
sweet duke of york, our prop to lean upon, | now 3H6 2.01. 68
nor has no friends | so much as but to prop him? CYM 1.05. 60
house, but for this virgin that doth prop it, PER 4.06.119
PROPAGATE 4 FR 0.0004 REL FR 4 V 0 P
my low and humble name to propagate | with any AWW 2.01.197
which thou wilt propagate to have it press'd ROM 1.01.187
of this sphere | to propagate their states. TIM 1.01. 67
from whence an issue i might propagate, | are PER 1.02. 73
PROPAGATION 1 FR 0.0001 REL FR 1 V 0 P
only for propagation of a dow'r | remaining in MM 1.02.150
PROPEND 1 FR 0.0001 REL FR 1 V 0 P
i propend to you | in resolution to keep helen TRO 2.02.190
PROPENSION 1 FR 0.0001 REL FR 1 V 0 P
your full consent | gave wings to my propension, TRO 2.02.133
PROPER 63 FR 0.0071 REL FR 46 V 17 P
said, "as proper a man as ever went on four legs TMP 2.02. 60 P
valor men hang and drown | their proper selves. 3.03. 60
by my beard, will we, for he is a proper man. TGV 4.01. 10
are not thine own so proper as to waste MM 1.01. 30
like rats that ravin down their proper bane, | a 1.02.129
/sire, | the mere effusion of thy proper loins, 3.01. 30
he should pursue | faults proper to himself. 5.01.110
mouth, | and in the witness of his proper ear, 5.01.308
out | most audible, even from his proper tongue, 5.01.408
a proper squire! ADO 1.03. 52 P
he is a very proper man. 2.03.182 P
excuse | that which appears in proper nakedness? 4.01.175
a proper saying! 4.01.309 P
a proper man as one shall see in a summer's day; MND 1.02. 86 P
he is a proper man's picture, but, alas, who can MV 1.02. 72 P
that the comparison | may stand more proper, my 3.02. 46
three proper young men, of excellent growth and AYL 1.02.121 P
had not that been as proper? 3.02.307 P
and out of you she sees herself more proper 3.05. 55
he'll make a proper man. 3.05.115
a proper stripling, and an amorous! SHR 1.02.143
thus your own proper wisdom | brings in the AWW 4.02. 49
his own nobility in his proper stream o'erflows 4.03. 25 P
an advertisement to a proper maid in florence, 4.03.213 P
your wife is like to reap a proper man. TN 3.01.133
you, | here at my house and at my proper cost. 5.01.319
the bastard brains with these my proper hands WT 2.03.140
some proper man, i hope. JN 1.01.250
with great imagination | proper to madmen, led 2H4 1.03. 32
and that i am a proper fellow of my hands, and 2.02. 67 P
a proper gentlewoman, sir, and a kinswoman of my 2.02.155 P
in his true, native, and most proper shape, 4.01. 37
bold, | that dares do justice on my proper son; 5.02.109
which cannot in their huge and proper life | be H5 5.pr. 5
o, charles the dolphin is a proper man, | no 1H6 5.03. 37
king of england's own proper cost and charges, 2H6 1.01. 61 P
a proper jest, and never heard before, | that 1.01.132
many a pound of mine own proper store, | because 3.01.115
the man is a proper man, of mine honor; 4.02. 95 P
cannot) | myself to be a marv'llous proper man. R3 1.02.254
the noble isle doth want /her proper limbs; 3.07.125
a proper title of a peace, and purchas'd | at a H8 1.01. 98
in troy, whosoever, and a proper man of person. TRO 1.02.193 P
you now | the issue of your proper wisdoms rate, 2.02. 89
you | (like one that means his proper harm) in COR 1.09. 57
provide thee two proper palfreys, black as jet, TIT 5.02. 50
as proper men as ever trod upon neat's–leather JC 1.01. 25 P
difference, | conceptions only proper to myself, 1.02. 41
turns our swords | in our own proper entrails. 5.03. 96
o proper stuff! MAC 3.04. 59
by heaven it is as proper to our age | to cast HAM 2.01.111
thrown out his angle for my proper life, | and 5.02. 66
fault undone, the issue of it being so proper. LR 1.01. 18 P
proper deformity /shows not in the fiend | so 4.02. 60
though our proper son | stood in your action. OTH 1.03. 69
in /me defunct) and proper satisfaction; 1.03.264
cassio's a proper man. 1.03.392
this lodovico is a proper man. 4.03. 35
'tis proper i obey him; 5.02.196
a proper man. ANT 3.03. 38
wilt lay the leaven on all proper men; CYM 3.04. 62
when i have slain thee with my proper hand, 4.02. 97
upon my soul, a proper man! TNK 2.05. 16
PROPERER 3 FR 0.0003 REL FR 1 V 2 P
you are a thousand times a properer man | than AYL 3.05. 51
and tell her that paris is the properer man, but ROM 2.04.204 P
and what better or properer can we call our own TIM 1.02.102 P
PROPER–FALSE 1 FR 0.0001 REL FR 1 V 0 P
how easy is it for the proper–false | in women's TN 2.02. 29
PROPERLY 4 FR 0.0004 REL FR 3 V 1 P
or, to speak more properly, stays me here at AYL 1.01. 8 P
gain, the ord'ring on't, is all | properly ours. WT 2.01.170
or if you will, to speak more properly, | i will JN 2.01.514
though i owe | my revenge properly, my remission COR 5.02. 84
PROPER'ST 1 FR 0.0001 REL FR 0 V 1 P
a sigh, thou wast the proper'st man in italy. ADO 5.01.172 P
PROPERTIED 3 FR 0.0003 REL FR 2 V 1 P
they have here propertied me, keep me in TN 4.02. 91 P
i am too high–born to be propertied, | to be a JN 5.02. 79
his voice was propertied | as all the tuned ANT 5.02. 83
PROPERTIES 5 FR 0.0005 REL FR 4 V 1 P
go get us properties | and tricking for our WIV 4.04. 78
of government the properties to unfold | would MM 1.01. 3
the mean time i will draw a bill of properties, MND 1.02.105 P
subdues and properties to his love and tendance TIM 1.01. 57
hard, | whereto his invis'd properties did tend; LC 212
PROPERTY 16 FR 0.0018 REL FR 13 V 3 P
i should love thee but as a property. WIV 3.04. 10
whose liquor hath this virtuous property, | to MND 3.02.367
that the property of rain is to wet and fire to AYL 3.02. 26 P
time, or flinch in property | of what i spoke, AWW 2.01.187
the property by what /it is should go, | not by 2.03.130
sweet love, i see, changing his property, R2 3.02.135
the second property of your excellent sherris is 2H4 4.03.102 P
do not talk of him | but as a property. JC 4.01. 40
love, | whose violent property fordoes itself, HAM 2.01.100
upon whose property and most dear life | a 2.02.570
thy natural magic and dire property | on 3.02.259
hath made it in him a property of easiness. 5.01. 67 P
care, | propinquity and property of blood, | and LR 1.01.114
by which the property of youth and maidhood OTH 1.01.172
he comes too short of that great property ANT 1.01. 58
property was thus appalled, | that the self was PHT 37
PROPHECIES 9 FR 0.0010 REL FR 9 V 0 P
ant, | of the dreamer merlin and his prophecies, 1H4 3.01.148
and comes not in, overrul'd by prophecies, | i 4.04. 18
to frustrate prophecies, and to rase out 2H4 5.02.127
for i will buzz abroad such prophecies | that 3H6 5.06. 86
by drunken prophecies, libels, and dreams, | to R3 1.01. 33
he hearkens after prophecies and dreams, | and 1.01. 54
that was he | that fed him with his prophecies? H8 2.01. 23
gazed, | infusing them with dreadful prophecies: VEN 928
so all their praises are but prophecies | of SON 106. 9
PROPHECY 14 FR 0.0015 REL FR 10 V 4 P
and, in requital of your prophecy, hark you: MM 2.01.245 P
or rather, the prophecy like the parrot, "beware ERR 4.04. 42 P
mistress (let my prophecy | come home to ye!), WT 4.04.648
did speak these words, now prov'd a prophecy? 2H4 3.01. 69
the spirit of deep prophecy she hath, 1H6 1.02. 55
and now i fear that fatal prophecy | which in 3.01.194
as henry's late presaging prophecy | did glad my 3H6 4.06. 92
clarence closely be mew'd up | about a prophecy, R3 1.01. 39
not consulting, broke | into a general prophecy: H8 1.01. 92
to this | by a vain prophecy of nicholas henton. 1.02.147
my prophecy is but half his journey yet, | for TRO 4.05.218
virtue, | he hath a heavenly gift of prophecy, MAC 4.03.157
i'll speak a prophecy ere i go: LR 3.02. 80 P
this prophecy merlin shall make, for i live 3.02. 95 P
PROPHESIED 5 FR 0.0005 REL FR 5 V 0 P
i prophesied, if a gallows were on land, | this TMP 5.01.217
it hath been prophesied to me many years, | i 2H4 4.05.236
i prophesied france will be lost ere long. 2H6 1.01.146
no man but prophesied revenge for it. R3 1.03.185
harry, that prophesied thou shouldst be king, 5.03.129
PROPHESIER 1 FR 0.0001 REL FR 0 V 1 P
deceiv'd me like a double–meaning prophesier. AWW 4.03.100 P
PROPHESY 20 FR 0.0022 REL FR 18 V 2 P
what of her ensues | i list not prophesy; WT 4.01. 26
the streets | do prophesy upon it dangerously. JN 4.02.186
king, | and if you crown him, let me prophesy, R2 4.01.136
o, i could prophesy, | but that the earthy and 1H4 5.04. 83
the which observ'd, a man may prophesy, | with a 2H4 3.01. 82
and here i prophesy: 1H6 2.04.124
verified | henry the fift did sometime prophesy: 5.01. 31
shall find their deaths, if york can prophesy. 2H6 2.02. 76
my thoughts do hourly prophesy | mischance unto 3.02.283
and thus i prophesy, that many a thousand 3H6 5.06. 37
i prophesy the fearfull'st time to thee | that R3 3.04.104
did prophesy that richmond should be king, 4.02. 96
thou didst prophesy the time would come | that i 4.04. 79
over thy wounds now do i prophesy | (which like JC 3.01.259
i will prophesy, he comes to tell me of the HAM 2.02.386 P
but i do prophesy th' election lights | on 5.02.355
methought thy very gait did prophesy | a royal LR 5.03.176
divine of this unity, i would not prophesy so. ANT 2.06.117 P
i prophesy thy death, my living sorrow, | if VEN 671
"since thou art dead, lo here i prophesy, 1135
PROPHESYING 2 FR 0.0002 REL FR 2 V 0 P
and prophesying, with accents terrible, | of MAC 2.03. 57
she had a prophesying fear | of what hath come ANT 4.14.120
/PROPHET 1 FR 0.0001 REL FR 1 V 0 P
/how /chance /the /prophet /could /not /at /that R3 4.02.100
PROPHET 13 FR 0.0014 REL FR 11 V 2 P
and like a prophet | looks in a glass that shows MM 2.02. 94
which your prophet the nazarite conjur'd the MV 1.03. 34 P
a prophet i, madam, and i speak the truth the AWW 1.03. 58 P
and here's a prophet that i brought with me JN 4.02.147
did not the prophet | say that before 5.01. 25
methinks i am a prophet new inspir'd, | and thus R2 2.01. 31
no prophet will i trust, if she prove false. 1H6 1.02.150
a prophet to the fall of all our foes! 3.02. 32
die, prophet, in thy speech: 3H6 5.06. 57
my oracle, my prophet, my dear cousin, | i, as a R3 2.02.152
where every flower | did, as a prophet, weep TRO 1.02. 10
prophet may you be! 3.02.183
and is myself | am like a prophet suddenly enrapt 5.03. 65
PROPHETESS 4 FR 0.0004 REL FR 4 V 0 P
join'd, | a holy prophetess new risen up, | is 1H6 1.04.102
france, triumph in thy glorious prophetess! 1.06. 8
and say poor margaret was a prophetess! R3 1.03.300
sorrow, | remember margaret was a prophetess." 5.01. 27
PROPHETIC 6 FR 0.0006 REL FR 6 V 0 P
now hear me speak with a prophetic spirit; JN 3.04.126
and i will fill them with prophetic tears. TRO 2.02.102
you stop our way | with such prophetic greeting? MAC 1.03. 78
o my prophetic soul! | my uncle? HAM 1.05. 40
in her prophetic fury sew'd the work; OTH 3.04. 72
nor the prophetic soul | of the wide world, SON 107. 1
PROPHETICALLY 2 FR 0.0002 REL FR 1 V 1 P
every man | prophetically do forethink thy fall. 1H4 3.02. 38
and is so prophetically proud of an heroical TRO 3.03.248 P
PROPHET–LIKE 1 FR 0.0001 REL FR 1 V 0 P
then prophet–like | they hail'd him father to a MAC 3.01. 58
PROPHET'S 1 FR 0.0001 REL FR 1 V 0 P
o, had thy grandsire with a prophet's eye | seen R2 2.01.104
PROPHETS 4 FR 0.0004 REL FR 4 V 0 P
and lean–look'd prophets whisper fearful change, R2 2.04. 11
his champions are the prophets and apostles, 2H6 1.03. 57
jesters do oft prove prophets. LR 5.03. 71
our reasons are not prophets | when oft our TNK 5.03.102
PROPINQUITY 1 FR 0.0001 REL FR 1 V 0 P
care, | propinquity and property of blood, | and LR 1.01.114
PROPONTIC 1 FR 0.0001 REL FR 1 V 0 P
due on | to the propontic and the hellespont, OTH 3.03.456
PROPORTION 24 FR 0.0027 REL FR 18 V 6 P
i have receiv'd my proportion, like the TGV 2.03. 3 P
where there was no proportion held in love. WIV 5.05.222
in any proportion, or in any language. MM 1.02. 22 P
there must be needs a like proportion | of MV 3.04. 14
a pale | keep law and form and due proportion, R2 3.04. 41
is | when time is broke, and no proportion kept! 5.05. 43
whose power was in the first proportion, | and 1H4 4.04. 15
the just proportion that we gave them out. 2H4 4.01. 23
but thou ('gainst all proportion) didst bring in H5 2.02.109
which must proportion the losses we have borne, 3.06.126 P
were against all proportion of subjection. 4.01.146 P
and large proportion of his strong–knit limbs. 1H6 2.03. 21
part | and least proportion of humanity. 2.03. 53
bear that proportion to my flesh and blood | as 2H6 1.01.233
thee | in courage, courtship, and proportion; 1.03. 54
i, that am curtail'd of this fair proportion, R3 1.01. 18
not | usurp the just proportion of my sorrow? 4.04.110
and part in just proportion our small power. 5.03. 26
their practices | must bear the same proportion, H8 5.01.129
insisture, course, proportion, season, form, TRO 1.03. 87
shalt thou know her by thine own proportion, TIT 5.02.106
keeps time, distance, and proportion; ROM 2.04. 22 P
that the proportion both of thanks and payment MAC 1.04. 19
were as pretty a proportion to live quietly, and PER 4.02. 27 P
PROPORTIONABLE 1 FR 0.0001 REL FR 1 V 0 P
us to levy power | proportionable to the enemy R2 2.02.125
PROPORTION'D 3 FR 0.0003 REL FR 3 V 0 P
proportion'd as one's thought would wish a man, ROM 3.05.182
proportion'd to our cause, must be as great | as ANT 4.15. 5
make war against proportion'd course of time; LUC 774
PROPORTIONS 6 FR 0.0006 REL FR 6 V 0 P
partly for that her promised proportions | came MM 5.01.219
extended or contracted all proportions | to a AWW 5.03. 51
but lay down our proportions to defend | against H5 1.02.137
therefore let our proportions for these wars 1.02.304

so the proportions of defense are fill'd; 2.04. 45
and full proportions are all made | out of his HAM 1.02. 32
/PROPOS'D 1 FR 0.0001 REL FR 1 V 0 P
at many leisures i /propos'd. TIM 2.02.128
PROPOS'D 6 FR 0.0006 REL FR 6 V 0 P
one, | and yet we ventur'd for the gain propos'd 2H4 1.01.183
but, now thy beauty is propos'd my fee, | my R3 1.02.169
in the lily–beds | propos'd for the deserver! TRO 3.02. 13
but ere we could arrive the point propos'd, JC 1.02.110
give but that portion which yourself propos'd, LR 1.01.242
woe, | before, a joy propos'd, behind, a dream. SON 129.12
PROPOSE 10 FR 0.0011 REL FR 9 V 1 P
will she hide her, | to listen our propose. ADO 3.01. 12
shall win the wager which we will propose. SHR 5.02. 69
a self–gracious remembrance, did first propose. AWW 4.05. 74 P
be now the father and propose a son, | hear your 2H4 5.02. 92
whilst i propose the self–same words to thee, 3H6 5.05. 20
i propose not merely to myself | the pleasures TRO 2.02.146
would i propose to achieve her whom i love. TIT 2.01. 80
propose the oath, my lord. HAM 1.05.152
what to ourselves in passion we propose, | the 3.02.194
wherein the /toged consuls can propose | as OTH 1.01. 25
PROPOSED 3 FR 0.0003 REL FR 3 V 0 P
all, | according to their firm proposed natures. H5 5.02.334
not to affect many proposed matches | of her own OTH 3.03.229
and when great treasure is the meed proposed, LUC 132
PROPOSER 1 FR 0.0001 REL FR 0 V 1 P
what more dear a better proposer can charge you HAM 2.02.286 P
PROPOSES 1 FR 0.0001 REL FR 0 V 1 P
is running away, when fear proposes the safety. AWW 1.01.202 P
PROPOSING 1 FR 0.0001 REL FR 1 V 0 P
proposing with the prince and claudio. ADO 3.01. 3
PROPOSITION 1 FR 0.0001 REL FR 1 V 0 P
the ample proposition that hope makes | in all TRO 1.03. 3
PROPOSITIONS 1 FR 0.0001 REL FR 0 V 1 P
as to resolve the propositions of a lover. AYL 3.02.233 P
PROPOUND 1 FR 0.0001 REL FR 1 V 0 P
who did propound | to his bold ends honor and TNK 1.02. 16
PROPOUNDED 1 FR 0.0001 REL FR 1 V 0 P
as by your grace shall be propounded him. 2H6 1.02. 81
PROPP'D 1 FR 0.0001 REL FR 1 V 0 P
for, being not propp'd by ancestry, whose grace H8 1.01. 59
PROPRE 1 FR 0.0001 REL FR 0 V 1 P
"le chien est retourne a son propre vomissement, H5 3.07. 64 P
PROPRIETY 2 FR 0.0002 REL FR 2 V 0 P
fear | that makes thee strangle thy propriety. TN 5.01.147
bell, it frights the isle | from her propriety. OTH 2.03.176
PROPS 3 FR 0.0003 REL FR 3 V 0 P
two props of virtue for a christian prince, | to R3 3.07. 96
known, | the ratifiers and props of every word, HAM 4.05.106
in me, | since thy best props are warp'd! TNK 3.02. 32
PROPUGNATION 1 FR 0.0001 REL FR 1 V 0 P
what propugnation is in one man's valor | to TRO 2.02.136
PROROGUE 4 FR 0.0004 REL FR 4 V 0 P
i hear thou must, and nothing may prorogue it, ROM 4.01. 48
that sleep and feeding may prorogue his honor ANT 2.01. 26
taken sustenance | but to prorogue his grief. PER 5.01. 26
prorogue this business we are going about, and TNK 1.01.196
PROROGUED 1 FR 0.0001 REL FR 1 V 0 P
than death prorogued, wanting of thy love. ROM 2.02. 78
PROSCRIPTION 3 FR 0.0003 REL FR 3 V 0 P
to die | in our black sentence and proscription. JC 4.01. 17
that by proscription and bills of outlawry, 4.03.173
is dead, | and by that order of proscription. 4.03.180
PROSCRIPTIONS 1 FR 0.0001 REL FR 1 V 0 P
senators that died | by their proscriptions, JC 4.03.178
PROSE 2 FR 0.0002 REL FR 1 V 1 P
these numbers will i tear, and write in prose! LLL 4.03. 55
soft, here follows prose. TN 2.05.142 P
PROSECUTE 4 FR 0.0004 REL FR 4 V 0 P
why should not i then prosecute my right? MND 1.01.105
that will the king severely prosecute | 'gainst R2 2.01.244
that we will prosecute by good advice | mortal TIT 4.01. 92
plight | than prosecute the meanest or the best 4.04. 33
PROSECUTION 1 FR 0.0001 REL FR 1 V 0 P
see behind me | th' inevitable prosecution of ANT 4.14. 65
PROSELYTES 1 FR 0.0001 REL FR 1 V 0 P
make proselytes | of who she but bid follow. WT 5.01.108
PROSERPINA 1 FR 0.0001 REL FR 1 V 0 P
o proserpina, | for the flow'rs now, that, WT 4.04.116
PROSERPINA'S 1 FR 0.0001 REL FR 0 V 1 P
greatness as cerberus is at proserpina's beauty, TRO 2.01. 34 P
PROSERPINE 1 FR 0.0001 REL FR 0 V 1 P
all day long but pick flowers with proserpine. TNK 4.03. 25 P
PROSPECT 6 FR 0.0006 REL FR 5 V 1 P
life, | into the eye and prospect of his soul, ADO 4.01.229
between me and the full prospect of my hopes. TN 3.04. 82 P
here | before the eye and prospect of your town, JN 2.01.208
their chiefest prospect murd'ring basilisks! 2H6 3.02.324
king | stands not within the prospect of belief, MAC 1.03. 74
i think, | to bring them to that prospect; OTH 3.03.398
PROSPER* *(also prospero)*
PROSPER* 24 FR 0.0027 REL FR 17 V 7 P
marriage, and we prosper well in our return. TMP 2.01. 73 P
on prosper fall and make him | by inch–meal a 2.02. 2
now prosper works upon thee. 2.02. 80 P
organ–pipe, pronounc'd | the name of prosper; 3.03. 99
to whose falls —" | heaven prosper the right! WIV 3.01. 30 P
heaven prosper our sport! 5.02. 12 P
that have stood by and seen our wishes prosper, MV 3.02.187
prosper well in this, | and thou shalt live as TN 1.04. 38
prosper you, sweet sir! WT 4.03.118 P
as your good flock shall prosper. 4.04. 70
more sins for this forgiveness prosper may. R2 5.03. 84
god prosper your affairs! 2H4 3.02.292 P
prosper this realm, keep it from civil broils, 1H6 1.01. 53
prosper our colors in this dangerous fight! 4.02. 56
love, | but prosper better than the troyan did. 5.05.106
they prosper best of all when i am thence. 3H6 2.05. 18
so prosper i, as i swear perfect love! R3 2.01. 16
as i intend to prosper and repent, | so thrive i 4.04.397
's heirs | (tell you the duke) shall prosper. H8 1.02.169
well may you prosper! LR 1.01.282
i grow, i prosper: 1.02. 21
kind gods, forgive me that, and prosper him! 3.07. 92
fairies and gods | prosper it with thee! 4.06. 30
be us'd in every trade, we shall never prosper. PER 4.02. 12 P
PROSPER'D 1 FR 0.0001 REL FR 0 V 1 P
i never prosper'd since i forswore myself at WIV 4.05.101 P
PROSPERITIES 1 FR 0.0001 REL FR 1 V 0 P
cup | and her prosperities so largely taste, PER 1.04. 53
/PROSPERITY 1 FR 0.0001 REL FR 1 V 0 P
/like /to /my /followers /in /prosperity, R2 4.01.280
PROSPERITY 14 FR 0.0015 REL FR 11 V 3 P
peace and prosperity! who is't that calls? MM 1.04. 15
therefore welcome the sour cup of prosperity! LLL 1.01.313 P
a jest's prosperity lies in the ear | of him 5.02.861
you come | to give their bed joy and prosperity. MND 2.01. 73
and bless it to all fair prosperity. 4.01. 90
night, | thou hate and terror to prosperity, JN 3.04. 28
into the purse of rich prosperity | as lewis 5.02. 61
so now prosperity begins to mellow | and drop R3 4.04. 1
prosperity be thy page. COR 1.05. 23
petition'd all the gods | for my prosperity! 2.01.171
in hourly synod about thy particular prosperity, 5.02. 69 P
thou saw'st them, when i had prosperity. TIM 4.03. 78
a satire against the softness of prosperity, 5.01. 35
there were no expectation of our prosperity. OTH 2.01.280 P
PROSPERITY'S 1 FR 0.0001 REL FR 1 V 0 P
you know, | prosperity's the very bond of love, WT 4.04.573
PROSPERO *(also prosper*)*
PROSPERO 11 FR 0.0012 REL FR 11 V 0 P
i am, nor that i am more better | than prospero, TMP 1.02. 20
and prospero the prime duke, being so reputed 1.02. 72
you did supplant your brother prospero. 2.01.271
prospero my lord shall know what i have done. 2.01.326
when prospero is destroy'd. 3.02.146
three | from milan did supplant good prospero, 3.03. 70
sir king, | the wronged duke of milan, prospero. 5.01.107
but how should prospero | be living, and be here 5.01.119
if thou beest prospero, | give us particulars of 5.01.134
certain | that i am prospero and that very duke 5.01.159
prospero, his dukedom | in a poor isle; 5.01.211
PROSPEROUS 24 FR 0.0027 REL FR 20 V 4 P
bless this twain, that they may prosperous be, TMP 4.01.104
she hath prosperous art | when she will play MM 1.02.184
it will grow to a most prosperous perfection. 3.01.260 P
with a prayer they may prove prosperous, and let 3.02.238 P
increas'd | by prosperous voyages i often made ERR 1.01. 40
and fortune play upon thy prosperous helm | as AWW 3.03. 7
sir, be prosperous | in more than this deed does WT 2.03.189
thence | (a prosperous south–wind friendly) we 5.01.161
god in thy good cause make thee prosperous! R2 1.03. 78
and our induction full of prosperous hope. 1H4 3.01. 2
the church's prayers made him so prosperous. 1H6 1.01. 32
and prosperous be thy life in peace and war! 2.05.114
with smiling plenty, and fair prosperous days! R3 5.05. 34
from thy endless goodness send prosperous life, H8 5.04. 2 P
menenius, and with most prosperous approbation. COR 2.01.103 P
be strong and prosperous | in this resolve. ROM 4.01.122
live and be prosperous, and farewell, good 5.03. 42
you | to the protection of the prosperous gods, TIM 5.01.183
thane of cawdor lives | a prosperous gentleman; MAC 1.03. 73
still hath been both grave and prosperous) | in 3.01. 21
to my unfolding lend your prosperous ear, | and OTH 1.03.244
of all 'say'd yet, mayst thou prove prosperous! PER 1.01. 59
if that thy prosperous and artificial /feat 5.01. 72
leave her, | and the gods make her prosperous! 5.01. 79
PROSPEROUSLY 2 FR 0.0002 REL FR 1 V 1 P
to know | that prosperously i have attempted, COR 5.06. 74
could not so prosperously be deliver'd of. HAM 2.02.211 P
PROSPERS 1 FR 0.0001 REL FR 1 V 0 P
by that which knitteth souls and prospers loves, MND 1.01.172
PROSP'ROUS 2 FR 0.0002 REL FR 2 V 0 P
and may our oaths well kept and prosp'rous be! H5 5.02.374
prove this a prosp'rous day, the three–nook'd ANT 4.06. 5
PROSTITUTE 2 FR 0.0002 REL FR 2 V 0 P
to prostitute our past–cure malady | to empirics AWW 2.01.121
again | and prostitute me to the basest groom PER 4.06.190
PROSTRATE 6 FR 0.0006 REL FR 5 V 1 P
i will fall prostrate at his feet, | and never ERR 5.01.114
teacheth this prostrate and exterior bending. 2H4 4.05.148
mean time look gracious on thy prostrate thrall. 1H6 1.02.117
be you prostrate and grovel on the earth. 2H6 1.04. 10 P
by holy lawrence to fall prostrate here | and ROM 4.02. 20
and, being prostrate, thus he bade me say: JC 3.01.125
PROTECT 14 FR 0.0015 REL FR 12 V 2 P
now the melancholy god protect thee, and the TN 2.04. 73 P
the lord protect him! 1H6 1.03. 9
why should he then protect our sovereign, | he 2H6 1.01.165
marry, the lord protect him, for he's a good man 1.03. 4 P
protector, see to't well, protect yourself. 2.01. 52
must you, sir john, protect my lady here? 2.04. 79
king | had virtuous uncles to protect his grace. R3 2.03. 21
the lord protect him from that kingly title! 4.01. 19
god and your majesty | protect mine innocence, H8 5.01.141
god protect thee! 5.04. 10
that you protect this course and put it on | by LR 1.04.208
the gods protect you, | and bless the good CYM 1.01.128
the gods of greece protect you! PER 1.04. 97
the which the gods protect thee /from! 2.01.129
PROTECTED 2 FR 0.0002 REL FR 2 V 0 P
that love to be protected | under the wings of 2H6 1.03. 37
years | should be to be protected like a child. 2.03. 29
PROTECTION 13 FR 0.0014 REL FR 13 V 0 P
how you do leave me to mine own protection. MV 5.01.235
then leaving her | in the protection of his son, TN 1.02. 38
to it own protection | and favor of the climate. WT 2.03.178
whose protection | is most divinely vow'd upon JN 2.01.236
myself and beauford had him in protection, | and 2H6 3.02.180
eyes, | yet, in protection of their tender ones, 3H6 2.02. 28
put your main cause into the king's protection, H8 3.01. 93
and to be | out of the king's protection. 3.02.344
you | to the protection of the prosperous gods, TIM 5.01.183
thou shalt meet | both welcome and protection. LR 3.06. 92
the king he takes the babe | to his protection, CYM 1.01. 41
may it please you | to take them in protection? 1.06.193
to your protection i commend me, gods, | from 2.02. 8
/PROTECTOR 1 FR 0.0001 REL FR 1 V 0 P
or thou or i, somerset, will be /protector, 2H6 1.01.178
PROTECTOR 47 FR 0.0053 REL FR 42 V 5 P
what e'er we like, thou art protector, | and 1H6 1.01. 37
villains, answer you so the lord protector? 1.03. 8
there's none protector of the realm but i. 1.03. 12
open the gates unto the lord protector, | or 1.03. 27
and not protector, of the king or realm. 1.03. 32
religion | because he is protector of the realm, 1.03. 66
am i not protector, saucy priest? 3.01. 45
is not his grace protector to the king? 3.01. 60
yield, my lord protector, yield, winchester, 3.01.112
and now, lord protector, view the letter | sent 4.01. 48
ourself, my lord protector, and the rest, 4.01.169
and so, my lord protector, see them guarded 5.01. 48
therefore, my lord protector, give consent 5.05. 23
my lord protector, so it please your grace, 2H6 1.01. 39
so, there goes our protector in a rage. 1.01.147
gloss, | he will be found a dangerous protector. 1.01.164
if gloucester be displac'd, he'll be protector. 1.01.177
my lord protector, 'tis his highness' pleasure 1.02. 56
my lord protector will come this way by and by, 1.03. 2 P
the duke of suffolk and not my lord protector. 1.03. 9 P
pardon me, i took ye for my lord protector. 1.03. 12 P
"to my lord protector"? 1.03. 13 P
beside the haughty protector, have we beauford 1.03. 68
your grace | to be protector of his excellence? 1.03.119
madam, i am protector of the realm, | and at his 1.03.120
my lord protector will, i doubt it not, | see 1.04. 45
a sorry breakfast for my lord protector. 1.04. 75
pernicious protector, dangerous peer, | that 2.01. 21
against this proud protector with my sword! 2.01. 36
protector, see to't well, protect yourself. 2.01. 52
and so, my lord protector, by this means | your 2.01.174
henry will to himself | protector be, and god 2.03. 24
than when thou wert protector to thy king. 2.03. 27
and thou a prince, protector of this land, 2.04. 29
and, being protector, stay'd the soldiers' pay, 3.01.105
'tis well known that, whiles i was protector, 3.01.124
as place duke humphrey for the king's protector? 3.01.250
he shall reign, but i'll be protector over him. 4.02.159 P
the lord protector lost it, and not i; 3H6 1.01.111
seas, | the duke is made protector of the realm, 1.01.240
and i choose clarence only for protector. 4.06. 37
is it concluded he shall be protector? R3 1.03. 14
my lord protector needs will have it so. 3.01.141
thou protector of this damned strumpet, 3.04. 74
not as protector, steward, substitute, | or 3.07.133
i mean the lord protector. 4.01. 18
who seem'd my good protector, and, being here, PER 1.02. 82
PROTECTOR'S 6 FR 0.0006 REL FR 6 V 0 P
and the protector's wife, belov'd of him? 2H6 1.02. 44
under the wings of our protector's grace, 1.03. 38
as that proud dame, the lord protector's wife: 1.03. 76
my lord protector's hawks do tow'r so well; 2.01. 10
of lady eleanor, the protector's wife, | the 2.01.165
who knows the lord protector's mind herein? R3 3.04. 7
PROTECTORS 2 FR 0.0002 REL FR 2 V 0 P
whom we have left protectors of the king, | with 3H6 1.02. 57
i make you both protectors of this land, | while 4.06. 41
PROTECTORSHIP 3 FR 0.0003 REL FR 3 V 0 P
an't like your lordly lord's protectorship. 2H6 2.01. 30
and did he not, in his protectorship, | levy 3.01. 60
in your protectorship you did devise | strange 3.01.121
PROTECTRESS 1 FR 0.0001 REL FR 1 V 0 P
she is protectress of her honor too; OTH 4.01. 14
PROTECTS 3 FR 0.0003 REL FR 3 V 0 P
despite the bearard that protects the bear. 2H6 5.01.210
priest, protects you, thou shouldst feel | my H8 3.02.276
the law | protects not us; CYM 4.02.126
PROTEST 56 FR 0.0063 REL FR 37 V 19 P
when i protest true loyalty to her, | she twits TGV 4.02. 7
to think upon her woes i do protest | that i 4.04.144
inherit first, for i protest mine never shall. WIV 2.01. 73 P
none, i protest; 2.01.214 P
and, i protest to you, bestow'd much on her; 2.02.194 P
i protest i love the duke as i love myself. MM 5.01.341 P
mean, | my wife (but, i protest, without desert) ERR 3.01.112
you, | but i protest he had the chain of me, 5.01. 2
i protest i love thee. ADO 4.01.280 P
happy hour, i was about to protest i lov'd you. 4.01.284 P
much of my heart that none is left to protest. 4.01.287 P
do me right, or i will protest your cowardice. 5.01.147 P
not, i, | but i protest i love to hear him lie, LLL 1.01.175
i do protest i never heard of it; 2.01.157
yet as pure | as the unsallied lily, i protest, 5.02.352
i do forswear them, and i here protest, | by 5.02.410
for, i protest, the schoolmaster is exceeding 5.02.528 P
or on diana's altar to protest | for aye MND 1.01. 89
i have a wife who i protest i love; MV 4.01.290
mind, for i protest her frown might kill me. AYL 4.01.110 P
no, i protest, i know not the contents, | phebe 4.03. 21
wealthiest | that i protest i simply am a maid. AWW 2.03. 67
to swear by him whom i protest to love | that i 4.02. 28
my meaning in't, i protest, was very honest in 4.03.218 P
i protest i take these wise men that crow so at TN 1.05. 88 P
my lord, i do protest — 5.01.170
then you'll think | (which i protest against) i WT 5.03. 90
i do protest i never lov'd myself | till now JN 2.01.501
which, i protest, hath very much beguil'd | the R2 2.03. 11
i protest my soul is full of woe | that blood 5.06. 45
and such protest of pepper–gingerbread, | to 1H4 3.01.255
for i protest | i have not sought the day of 5.01. 25
for i protest we are well fortified, | and 1H6 4.02. 19
king lewis, i here protest in sight of heaven, 3H6 3.03.181
but i protest | as yet i do not. R3 1.01. 52
this interchange of love, i here protest, | upon 2.01. 26
/do yours, | and never in my days, i do protest, 3.02. 79
yet, i protest, | were i alone to pass the TRO 2.02.138
full of protest, of oath and big compare, 3.02.175
that, on mine honor, here do i protest. TIT 1.01.477
i protest unto thee — ROM 2.04.172 P
will tell her, sir, that you do protest, which, 2.04.177 P
i do protest i never injuried thee, | but love 3.01. 68
yet, i protest, | for his right noble mind, TIM 3.02. 79
do, /villains, do, since you protest to do't. 4.03.434
i will protest | he speaks by leave and by JC 3.01.238
i inhabit then, protest me | the baby of a girl. MAC 3.04.104
that even now | protest their first of manhood. 5.02. 11
the lady doth protest too much, methinks. HAM 3.02.230 P
i protest, | maugre thy strength, place, youth, LR 5.03.131
i protest, in the sincerity of love and honest OTH 2.03.327 P
nothing but what i protest intendment of doing. 4.02.202 P
but yet i protest i have dealt most directly in 4.02.208 P
i do | protest my ears were never better fed PER 2.05. 27

but i protest to thee, pretty one, my authority 4.06. 88 P
the which, by cupid's bow she doth protest, | he VEN 581
PROTESTATION 7 FR 0.0008 REL FR 6 V 1 P
here is a coil with protestation! TGV 1.02. 96
i can but say their protestation over: LLL 1.01. 33
but to your protestation; WT 4.04.368
nor i have no cunning in protestation; H5 5.02.144 P
say i, to fashion in | my sequent protestation: TRO 4.04. 66
task hath not said, | the protestation stops. LUC 1700
and to his protestation urg'd the rest, | who, 1844
PROTESTATIONS 2 FR 0.0002 REL FR 1 V 1 P
i know they are stuff'd with protestations, TGV 4.04.129
"upon his many protestations to marry me when AWW 5.03.139 P
PROTESTED 1 FR 0.0001 REL FR 0 V 1 P
after we had embrac'd, kiss'd, protested, and, WIV 3.05. 73 P
PROTESTER 1 FR 0.0001 REL FR 1 V 0 P
ordinary oaths my love | to every new protester; JC 1.02. 74
PROTESTING 1 FR 0.0001 REL FR 1 V 0 P
she vied so fast, protesting oath on oath, SHR 2.01.309
PROTESTINGS 1 FR 0.0001 REL FR 1 V 0 P
yet in the mids of all her pure protestings, PP 7.11
PROTESTS 3 FR 0.0003 REL FR 1 V 2 P
protests to my husband he is now here, and hath WIV 4.02. 33 P
he protests he will not hurt you. TN 3.04.300 P
but he protests he loves you, | and needs no OTH 3.01. 47
PROTEUS' 1 FR 0.0001 REL FR 1 V 0 P
but truer stars did govern proteus' birth: TGV 2.07. 74
PROTEUS 55 FR 0.0062 REL FR 51 V 4 P
cease to persuade, my loving proteus: TGV 1.01. 1
think on thy proteus, when thou, happ'ly, seest 1.01. 12
sweet proteus, no; 1.01. 56
sir proteus! 'save you! saw you my master? 1.01. 70
what think'st thou of the gentle proteus? 1.02. 14
why not on proteus, as of all the rest? 1.02. 20
and sent, i think, from proteus. 1.02. 38
indeed i bid the base for proteus. 1.02. 94
and here is writ "love–wounded proteus." 1.02.110
twice, or thrice, was "proteus" written down: 1.02.114
"poor forlorn proteus, passionate proteus: 1.02.121
"poor forlorn proteus, passionate proteus: 1.02.121
'twas of his nephew proteus, your son. 1.03. 3
for all these exercises | he said that proteus, 1.03. 12
with them shall proteus go — | and in good time 1.03. 43
sir proteus, your /father calls for you: 1.03. 88
you have learn'd, like sir proteus, to wreathe 2.01. 19 P
to have when you chid at sir proteus for going 2.01. 72 P
sir proteus, you are stay'd for. 2.02. 19
and am going with sir proteus to the imperial's 2.03. 4 P
yet hath sir proteus (for that's his name) 2.04. 67
welcome, dear proteus! 2.04.100
ay, proteus, but that life is alter'd now: 2.04.128
o gentle proteus, love's a mighty lord, | and 2.04.136
pardon me, proteus, all i can is nothing | to 2.04.165
good proteus, go with me to my chamber, | in 2.04.184
may undertake | a journey to my loving proteus. 2.07. 7
of such divine perfection, as sir proteus. 2.07. 13
better forbear till proteus make return. 2.07. 14
if proteus like your journey when you come, | no 2.07. 65
of love, | warrant me welcome to my proteus. 2.07. 71
now tell me, proteus, what's your will with me? 3.01. 3
proteus, i thank thee for thine honest care, 3.01. 22
how now, sir proteus? 3.02. 11
proteus, the good conceit i hold of thee | (for 3.02. 17
and, proteus, we dare trust you in this kind, 3.02. 56
therefore, sweet proteus, my direction–giver, 3.02. 89
how now, sir proteus, are you crept before us? 4.02. 18
doth this sir proteus that we talk on | often 4.02. 73
sir proteus, as i take it. 4.02. 90
sir proteus, gentle lady, and your servant. 4.02. 91
pray you, where lies sir proteus? 4.02.136 P
alas, poor proteus, thou hast entertain'd | a 4.04. 91
from my master, sir proteus, madam. 4.04.114
belike she thinks that proteus hath forsook her? 4.04.146
sir proteus, what says silvia to my suit? 5.02. 1
how now, sir proteus? 5.02. 31
rather than have false proteus rescue me. 5.04. 35
cannot be) | i do detest false perjur'd proteus. 5.04. 39
when proteus cannot love where he's belov'd! 5.04. 45
all men but proteus. 5.04. 54
proteus, | i am sorry i must never trust thee 5.04. 68
o proteus, let this habit make thee blush! 5.04.104
come, proteus, 'tis your penance but to hear 5.04.170
change shapes with proteus for advantages, | and 3H6 3.02.192
PROTRACT 2 FR 0.0002 REL FR 2 V 0 P
else ne'er could he so long protract his speech. 1H6 1.02.120
and not protract with admiration what | is now CYM 4.02.232
PROTRACTIVE 1 FR 0.0001 REL FR 1 V 0 P
else | but the protractive trials of great jove TRO 1.03. 20
/PROUD 2 FR 0.0002 REL FR 2 V 0 P
/proud /majesty /a /subject, /state /a /peasant. R2 4.01.252
/when /through /proud /london /he /came /sighing 2H4 1.03.104

PROUD 230 FR 0.0260 REL FR 198 V 32 P
rich scarf to my proud earth — why hath thy TMP 4.01. 82
kiss, | and, of so great a favor growing proud, TGV 2.04.161
proud, disobedient, stubborn, lacking duty, 3.01. 69
"item, she is proud." 3.01.337 P
but man, proud man, | dress'd in a little brief MM 2.02.117
my wife, not meanly proud of two such boys, ERR 1.01. 58
i must not seem proud; ADO 2.03.229 P
like favorites | made proud by princes, that 3.01. 10
and mine that i was proud on, mine so much 4.01.137
why should proud summer boast | before the birds LLL 1.01.102
i am less proud to hear you tell my worth | than 2.01. 17
proud of employment, willingly i go. 2.01. 35
proud with his form, in his eye pride expressed; 2.01.237
and make him proud to make me proud that jests! 5.02. 66
and make him proud to make me proud that jests! 5.02. 66
ill met by moonlight, proud titania. MND 2.01. 60
hath every pelting river made so proud | that 2.01. 91
where art thou, proud demetrius? speak thou now. 3.02.401
i am more proud to be sir rowland's son, | his AYL 1.02.232
longing and liking, proud, fantastical, apish, 3.02.411 P
praising the proud disdainful shepherdess | that 3.04. 50
and the red glow of scorn and proud disdain, 3.04. 54
must you be therefore proud and pitiless? 3.05. 40
no, faith, proud mistress, hope not after it. 3.05. 45
look on him better, | and be not proud; 3.05. 78
but sure he's proud — and yet his pride becomes 3.05.114
nor the courtier's, which is proud; 4.01. 12 P
she calls me proud, and that she could not love 4.03. 16
as i have lov'd this proud disdainful haggard. SHR 4.02. 39
our purses shall be proud, our garments poor, 4.03.171
besides, virginity is peevish, proud, idle, made AWW 1.01.144 P
his humble ambition, proud humility; 1.01.171
low ranks, | making them proud of his humility, 1.02. 44
proud scornful boy, unworthy this good gift, 2.03.151
find what it is to be proud of thy bondage. 2.03.227 P
our virtues would be proud, if our faults whipt 4.03. 72 P
i see you what you are, you are too proud; TN 1.05.250
i will be proud, i will read politic authors, i 2.05.161 P
o world, how apt the poor are to be proud! 3.01.127
the proud control of fierce and bloody war, | to JN 1.01. 17
their proud contempt that beats his peace to 2.01. 88
like a proud river peering o'er his bounds? 3.01. 23
i will instruct my sorrows to be proud, | for 3.01. 68
for grief is proud and makes his owner stoop. 3.01. 69
the sun is in the heaven, and the proud day, 3.03. 34
death, made proud with pure and princely beauty! 4.03. 35
the unowed interest of proud swelling state. 4.03.147
shall, | lie at the proud foot of a conqueror, 5.07.113
report of fashions in proud italy, | whose R2 2.01. 21
he fires the proud tops of the eastern pines 3.02. 42
proud bullingbrook, i come | to change blows 3.02.188
on yon proud man should take it off again | with 3.03.135
swell'st thou, proud heart? 3.03.140
to make the base earth proud with kissing it. 3.03.191
is a foul traitor to proud herford's king, | and 4.01.135
is doom'd a prisoner by proud bullingbrook. 5.01. 4
bare–headed, lower than his proud steed's neck, 5.02. 19
runs posting on in bullingbrook's proud joy, 5.05. 59
so proud that bullingbrook was on his back! 5.05. 84
this hand hath made him proud with clapping him. 5.05. 86
of that proud man that did usurp his back? 5.05. 89
which the proud soul ne'er pays but to the proud 1H4 1.03. 9
the proud soul ne'er pays but to the proud. 1.03. 9
and disdain'd contempt | of this proud king, who 1.03.184
tell me flatly i am no proud jack like falstaff, 2.04. 11 P
i was not born a yielder, thou proud scot, | and 5.03. 11
than those proud titles thou hast won of me. 5.04. 79
printing their proud hoofs i' th' receiving H5 pr 27
or, like to men proud of destruction, | defy us 3.03. 4
proud of their numbers and secure in soul, | the 4.pr. 17
no, thou proud dream, | that play'st so subtilly 4.01.257
thy wife is proud, she holdeth thee in awe, 1H6 1.01. 39
now am i like that proud insulting ship | which 1.02.138
proud pole, i will, and scorn both him and thee. 2.04. 78
thee, | against proud somerset and william pole, 2.04.122
who in proud heart | doth stop my cornets, were 4.03. 24
it warm'd thy father's heart with proud desire 4.06. 11
but with a proud majestical high scorn | he 4.07. 39
he speaks with such a proud commanding spirit. 4.07. 88
proud prelate, in thy face | i see thy fury. 2H6 1.01.142
as stout and proud as he were lord of all, 1.01.187
and make a show of love to proud duke humphrey, 1.01.241
nor shall proud lancaster usurp my right, | nor 1.01.244
do vex me half so much | as that proud dame, the 1.03. 76
yea, i it was, proud frenchwoman. 1.03.140
against this proud protector with my sword! 2.01. 36
that erst did follow thy proud chariot–wheels 2.04. 13
how proud, how peremptory, and unlike himself? 3.01. 8
say, if thou dar'st, proud lord of warwickshire, 3.02.201
murther of a guiltless king | and lofty, proud, 4.01. 96
small things make base men proud. 4.01.106
kerns | is marching hitherward in proud array, 4.09. 27
iden, farewell, and be proud of thy victory. 4.10. 72 P
is to remove proud somerset from the king, 5.01. 36
proud northern lord, clifford of cumberland, 5.02. 6
which makes thee thus presumptuous and proud, 3H6 1.01.157
yield to our mercy, proud plantagenet. 1.04. 30
i would assay, proud queen, to make thee blush. 1.04.118
needs not, nor it boots thee not, proud queen, 1.04.125
'tis beauty that doth oft make women proud, 1.04.128
the proud insulting queen, | with clifford and 2.01.168
and of their feather many moe proud birds, 2.01.170
go rate thy minions, proud insulting boy! 2.02. 84
while proud ambitious edward, duke of york, 3.03. 27
proud setter–up and puller–down of kings! 3.03.157
durst the traitor breathe out so proud words? 4.01.112
speak like a subject, proud ambitious york! 5.05. 17
my proud heart sues, and prompts my tongue to R3 1.02.170
i hate not you for her proud arrogance. 1.03. 24
a weeder–out of his proud adversaries, | a 1.03.122
of, | to part the queen's proud kindred from the 2.02.150
the queen's sons and brothers haught and proud! 2.03. 28
now thy proud neck bears half my burthen'd yoke, 4.04.111
thy age confirm'd, proud, subtle, sly, and 4.04.172
spur your proud horses hard, and ride in blood; 5.03.340
so i leave him | to him that made him proud, the H8 2.02. 55
which | i find at such proud rate, that it 3.02.127
thou art a proud traitor, priest. 3.02.252
proud lord, thou liest! 3.02.252
in full as proud a place | as broad achilles; TRO 1.03.189
were he not proud, we all should share with him. 1.03.367
yes, lion–sick, sick of proud heart. 2.03. 86 P
why should a man be proud? 2.03.151 P
he that is proud eats up himself. 2.03.154 P
i do hate a proud man, as i do hate the 2.03.158 P
he is so plaguy proud that the death–tokens of 2.03.177
shall the proud lord | that bastes his arrogance 2.03.184
and he be proud with me, i'll pheese his pride. 2.03.205
if he were proud — 2.03.236
'twill make us proud to be his servant, paris! 3.01.155
and 'tis a burthen | which i am proud to bear. 3.03. 37
feed arrogance and are the proud man's fees. 3.03. 49
and is so prophetically proud of an heroical 3.03.248 P
it would discredit the blest gods, proud man, 4.05.247
proud diomed, believe, | i come to lose my arm, 5.03. 95
i do disdain thy courtesy, proud troyan. 5.06. 15
but that he pays himself with being proud. COR 1.01. 34 P
it to please his mother, and to be partly proud, 1.01. 39 P
one affrights you, | the other makes you proud. 1.01.170
he is a lion | that i am proud to hunt. 1.01.236
was ever man so proud as is this martius? 1.01.252
he is grown | too proud to be so valiant. 1.01.259
you blame martius for being proud? 2.01. 33 P
should discover a brace of unmeriting, proud, 2.01. 44 P
yet you must be saying martius is proud; 2.01. 90 P
he has more cause to be proud. 2.01.146 P
i as little question | as he is proud to do't. 2.01.231
but he's vengeance proud, and loves not the 2.02. 6 P
with a proud heart he wore his humble weeds. 2.03.153
strike the proud cedars 'gainst the fiery sun, 5.03. 60
proud and ambitious tribune, canst thou tell? TIT 1.01.202
proud saturnine, interrupter of the good | that 1.01.208
how proud i am of thee and of thy gifts | rome 1.01.254
agree these deeds with that proud brag of thine, 1.01.306
farewell, proud rome, till lucius come again; 3.01.290
and make proud saturnine and his emperess | beg 3.01.297
for this proud mock i'll be thy slaughter–man, 4.04. 58
to pluck proud lucius from the warlike goths. 4.04.110
that i know thee well | for our proud empress, 5.02. 26
is she not proud? ROM 3.05.143
not proud you have, but thankful that you have. 3.05.146
proud can i never be of what i hate, | but 3.05.147
"proud," and "i thank you," and "i thank you not 3.05.150
and yet "not proud," mistress minion you? 3.05.151
thank me no thankings, nor proud me no prouds, 3.05.152
thou art proud, apemantus. TIM 1.01.188 P
feasts are too proud to give thanks to the gods. 1.02. 61
and i am proud, say, that my occasions have 2.02.191 P
when i have laid proud athens on a heap — 4.03.102
whereof thy proud child, arrogant man, is puff'd 4.03.180
art thou proud yet? 4.03.276
before proud athens he's set down by this, 5.03. 9
fret till your proud heart break; JC 4.03. 42
be lion–mettled, proud, and take no care | who MAC 4.01. 90
oppressor's wrong, the proud man's contumely, HAM 3.01. 70
i am very proud, revengeful, ambitious, with 3.01.123 P
o proud death, | what feast is toward in thine 5.02.364
a base, proud, shallow, beggarly, three–suited, LR 2.02. 16 P
by his porridge, made him proud of heart, to 3.04. 56 P
spouse, set not thy sweet heart on proud array. 3.04. 83 P
proud in heart and mind; 3.04. 85 P
tyrant's rage, | and frustrate his proud will. 4.06. 64
to as proud a fortune | as this that i have OTH 1.02. 23
she that was ever fair, and never proud, | had 2.01.148
i will give thee, | and make thy fortunes proud; ANT 2.05. 69
for he seems | proud and disdainful, harping on 3.13.142
fashion, | and make death proud to take us. 4.15. 88
the story | proud cleopatra, when she met her CYM 2.04. 70
right proud | of that most delicate lodging. 2.04.135
thetis, being proud, swallowed some part a' th' PER 4.04. 39
who made too proud the bed, took leave o' th' TNK 1.03. 52
the prison itself is proud of 'em; 2.01. 24 P
our fiery horses | like proud seas under us! 2.02. 20
i am proud to please you. 2.05. 4
emily my sovereign), how far | i may be proud. 3.01. 17
shows him hardy, fearless, proud of dangers. 4.02. 80
to hear there a proud lady and a proud city–wife 4.03. 51 P
a proud lady and a proud city–wife howl together 4.03. 51 P
and rein his proud head to the saddle–bow; VEN 14
o, be not proud, nor brag not of thy might, 113
a breeding jennet, lusty, young, and proud, 260
for nothing else with his proud sight agrees. 288
lack, | save a proud rider on so proud a back. 300
lack, | save a proud rider on so proud a back. 300
being proud, as females are, to see him woo her, 309
but the blunt boar, rough bear, or lion proud, 884
clapping their proud tails to the ground below, 923
reck'ning his fortune at such high proud rate LUC 19
suggested this proud issue of a king; 37
his hand, as proud of such a dignity, | smoking 437
the flesh being proud, desire doth fight with 712
to ruinate proud buildings with thy hours, | and 944
those proud lords to blame | make weak–made 1259
which the conceited painter drew so proud, | as 1371
which bleeding under pyrrhus' proud foot lies. 1449
for adon's sake, a youngster proud and wild, PP 9. 4
thy youth's proud livery, so gaz'd on now, SON 2. 3
making a couplement of proud compare | with sun 21. 5
stars | of public honor and proud titles boast, 25. 2
the rich proud cost of outworn buried age; 64. 2
his, | and, proud of many, lives upon his gains? 67.12
now proud as an enjoyer, and anon | doubting the 75. 5
yet be most proud of that which i compile, 78. 9
was it the proud full sail of his great verse, 86. 1
or from their proud lap pluck them where they 98. 8
eyes straight, though thy proud heart go wide. 140.14
thy proud heart's slave and vassal wretch to be: 141.12
that is so proud thy service to despise, | when 149.10
proud of this pride, | he is contented thy poor 151.10
proud of subjection, noble by the sway, | what LC 108
PROUDER 8 FR 0.0009 REL FR 7 V 1 P
heart | of prouder stuff than that of beatrice. ADO 3.01. 50
i know you would be prouder of the work | than MV 3.04. 8
i know | our party may well meet a prouder foe. JN 5.01. 79
his crest that prouder than blue iris bends. TRO 1.03.379
and now is the cur ajax prouder than the cur 5.04. 14 P
use thee not so hardly | as prouder livers do. CYM 3.03. 9
prouder than rustling in unpaid–for silk: 3.03. 24
richer than wealth, prouder than garments' cost, SON 91.10
PROUDEST 14 FR 0.0015 REL FR 11 V 3 P
as sip on a cup with the proudest of them all, WIV 2.02. 76 P
the proudest of them shall well hear of it. ADO 4.01.192
i'll bring mine action on the proudest he | that SHR 3.02.234
that thou and the proudest of you all shall find 4.01. 87 P
here, | it would amaze the proudest of you all. 1H6 4.07. 84
i trow, | or be inferior to the proudest peer. 5.01. 57
the proudest peer in the realm shall not wear a 2H6 4.07.119 P
best, | the proudest he that holds up lancaster, 3H6 1.01. 46
thee, | or any he the proudest of thy sort. 2.02. 97
the proudest of you all | have been beholding to R3 2.01.129
now let me see the proudest | he, that dares H8 5.02.165
give us the proudest prisoner of the goths, TIT 1.01. 96
will rouse the proudest panther in the chase, 2.02. 21
is) | the humble as the proudest sail doth bear, SON 80. 6
PROUD–HEARTED 1 FR 0.0001 REL FR 1 V 0 P
and so, proud–hearted warwick, i defy thee, 3H6 5.01. 98
PROUDLIER 1 FR 0.0001 REL FR 1 V 0 P
he bears himself more proudlier, | even to my COR 4.07. 8
PROUDLY 11 FR 0.0012 REL FR 10 V 1 P
they say i will bear myself proudly, if i ADO 2.03.225 P

their birthrights proudly on their backs, | to JN 2.01. 70
so proudly as if he disdain'd the ground. R2 5.05. 83
in me | hath proudly flow'd in vanity till now; 2H4 5.02.130
let me speak proudly: H5 4.03.108
question her proudly, let thy looks be stern. 1H6 1.02. 62
french, | he left me proudly, as unworthy fight. 4.07. 43
and by that knot looks proudly on the crown, R3 4.03. 42
a little proudly, and great deal misprising TRO 4.05. 74
thus proudly /pight upon our phrygian plains, 5.10. 24
as those whose beauties proudly make them cruel; SON 131. 2

PROUD–MINDED 1 FR 0.0001 REL FR 1 V 0 P
i am as peremptory as she proud–minded; SHR 2.01.131
PROUD–PIED 1 FR 0.0001 REL FR 1 V 0 P
when proud–pied april (dress'd in all his trim) SON 98. 2
PROUDS 1 FR 0.0001 REL FR 1 V 0 P
thank me no thankings, nor proud me no prouds, ROM 3.05.152
PROUD'ST 1 FR 0.0001 REL FR 1 V 0 P
cut off the proud'st conspirator that lives. TIT 4.04. 26
PROVAND *(also provender)*
PROVAND 1 FR 0.0001 REL FR 1 V 0 P
war, who have their provand | only for bearing COR 2.01.251
PROV'D 40 FR 0.0045 REL FR 29 V 11 P
and rather prov'd the sliding of your brother MM 2.04.115
all this time have prov'd there is no time for ERR 2.02.100 P
it is prov'd already that you are little better ADO 4.02. 20 P
as shall be prov'd upon thee by good witness. 4.02. 79 P
it is prov'd my lady hero hath been falsely 5.02. 96 P
well prov'd, wit! LLL 4.03. 5 P
well prov'd again a' my side! 4.03. 7 P
a kissing traitor. how art thou prov'd judas? 5.02.600 P
and true she is, as she hath prov'd herself; MV 2.06. 55
some prescriptions | of rare and prov'd effects, AWW 1.03.222
o that it could be prov'd | that some 1H4 1.01. 86
did speak these words, now prov'd a prophecy? 2H4 3.01. 69
and, commendable prov'd, let's die in pride. 1H6 4.06. 57
that e'er i prov'd thee false or fear'd thy 2H6 3.01.205
a fox, | by nature prov'd an enemy to the flock, 3.01.258
as humphrey, prov'd by reasons, to my liege. 3.01.260
might happily have prov'd far worse than his. 3.01.306
it will be prov'd to thy face that thou hast men 4.07. 38 P
seeing thou hast prov'd so unnatural a father! 3H6 1.01.218
and prov'd the subject of mine own soul's curse, R3 4.01. 80
ulysses, is not prov'd worth a blackberry. TRO 5.04. 12 P
now in first seeing he had prov'd himself a man. COR 1.03. 17 P
he prov'd best man i' th' field, and for his 2.02. 97
for such faults | as shall be prov'd upon you? 3.03. 47
accursed, if the /fault be prov'd in them — TIT 2.03.291
if it be prov'd! 2.03.292
't 'as been prov'd. TIM 1.02. 49 P
spent, | as if he had but prov'd an argument. 3.05. 23
that thou hast prov'd lucilius' saying true. JC 5.05. 59
but treasons capital, confess'd and prov'd, MAC 1.03.115
said, "'tis so," | when it prov'd otherwise? HAM 2.02.155
'tis too much prov'd — that with devotion's 3.01. 46
to have prov'd most royal, and, for his passage, 5.02.398
she was in love, and he she lov'd prov'd mad, OTH 4.03. 27
you have seen and prov'd a fairer former fortune ANT 1.02. 33
have prov'd best woodman and | are master of the CYM 3.06. 28
or his description | prov'd us unspeaking sots. 5.05.178
she hath assay'd as much as may be prov'd. VEN 608
and worse essays prov'd thee my best of love. SON 110. 8
a bliss in proof, and prov'd, /a very woe, 129.11
/PROVE 1 FR 0.0001 REL FR 1 V 0 P
/which /to /prove /fruit | /hope /gives /not /so 2H4 1.03. 39
PROVE 267 FR 0.0301 REL FR 206 V 61 P
if you prove a mutineer — the next tree! TMP 3.02. 36 P
this will prove a brave kingdom to me, where i 3.02.144 P
like to lose your hair, and prove a bald jerkin. 4.01.237 P
if this prove | a vision of the island, one dear 5.01.175
so, by your circumstance, i fear you'll prove. TGV 1.01. 37
it shall go hard but i'll prove it by another. 1.01. 85 P
i fear she'll prove as hard to you in telling 1.01.139 P
i cannot now prove constant to myself, | without 2.06. 31
pray heav'n he prove so when you come to him! 2.07. 79
i'll prove it: 3.01.359 P
longer than i prove loyal to your grace | let me 3.02. 20
unless i prove false traitor to myself. 4.04.105
his dove will prove, his gold will hold, | and WIV 1.03. 98
ay, but if it prove true, master page, have you 4.02.114 P
prove it before these varlets here, thou MM 2.01. 86 P
varlets here, thou honorable man, prove it. 2.01. 87 P
prove this, thou wicked hannibal, or i'll have 2.01.178 P
to your tent, and prove a shrewd caesar to you; 2.01.248 P
guides me most, | i'll prove a tyrant to him. 2.04.169
mercy to thee would prove itself a bawd, | 'tis 3.01.149
but yet, sir, i would prove — 3.02. 29 P
thee proofs for sin, | thou wilt prove his. 3.02. 31
with a prayer they may prove prosperous, and let 3.02.238 P
painting, do prove my occupation a mystery; 4.02. 38 P
this may prove worse than hanging. 5.01.360 P
if it prove so, i will be gone the sooner. ERR 1.02.103
you may prove it by my long ears. 4.04. 29 P
i'll prove mine honor and mine honesty | against 5.01. 30
prove that ever i lose more blood with love than ADO 1.01.250 P
this faith, thou wilt prove a notable argument. 1.01.256 P
thither, this may prove food to my displeasure. 1.03. 66 P
shall we go prove what's to be done? 1.03. 73 P
lord, lest i should prove the mother of fools. 2.01.286 P
if it prove so, then loving goes by haps: 3.01.105
we are like to prove a goodly commodity, being 3.03.177 P
prove you that any man with me convers'd | at 4.01.181
i'll prove it on his body, if he dare, | despite 5.01. 74
these oaths and laws will prove an idle scorn. LLL 1.01.309
to prove you a cipher. 1.02. 56 P
where now his knowledge must prove ignorance. 2.01.103
for you'll prove perjur'd if you make me stay. 2.01.113
and, if you prove it, i'll repay it back, | or 2.01.158
all those three i will prove. 3.01. 38 P
what wilt thou prove? 3.01. 39 P
to myself forsworn, to thee i'll faithful prove; 4.02.107
where i will prove those verses to be very 4.02.158 P
a woman i forswore, but i will prove, | thou 4.03. 62
i'll prove her fair, or talk till doomsday here. 4.03.270
good berowne, now prove | our loving lawful, and 4.03.280
or keeping what is sworn, you will prove fools. 4.03.353
light wenches may prove plagues to men forsworn; 4.03.382
all the power thereof it doth apply | to prove, 5.02. 78
take all and wean it, it may prove an ox. 5.02.250
we to ourselves prove false, | by being once 5.02.772
that he may prove | more fond on her than she MND 2.01.265
bearing the badge of faith to prove them true? 3.02.127
to prove him false that says i love thee not. 3.02.253
if thou say so, withdraw, and prove it too. 3.02.255
he might yet recover, and yet prove an ass. 5.01.311 P
i fear he will prove the weeping philosopher MV 1.02. 48 P
to prove whose blood is reddest, his or mine. 2.01. 7
i would it might prove the end of his losses. 3.01. 18 P
prove it so, | let fortune go to hell for it, 3.02. 20
i'll prove the prettier fellow of the two, | and 3.04. 64
how prove you that, in the great heap of your AYL 1.02. 68 P
then one of you will prove a shrunk panel, and 3.03. 88 P
say | i'll prove a busy actor in their play. 3.04. 59
i knew what you would prove; 4.01.183 P
and good plays prove the better by the help of ep 6 P
beloved of me, and that my deeds shall prove. SHR 1.02.176
and that his bags shall prove. 1.02.177
sir, give him head, i know he'll prove a jade. 1.02.247
what, will my daughter prove a good musician? 2.01.144
i think she'll sooner prove a soldier, | iron 2.01.145
for patience she will prove a second grissel, 2.01.295
'tis like you'll prove a jolly surly groom, 3.02.213
and may you prove, sir, master of your art! 4.02. 9
you, sweet dear, prove mistress of my heart! 4.02. 10
sew'd up again, and that i'll prove upon thee, 4.03.147 P
fellows, and like to prove most sinewy swordmen. AWW 2.01. 59 P
and i shall prove | a lover of thy drum, hater 3.03. 10
with this deceit so lawful | may prove coherent. 3.07. 39
if it should prove | that thou art so inhuman — 5.03.115
that thou art so inhuman — 'twill not prove so; 5.03.116
if you shall prove | this ring was ever hers, 5.03.124
prove that i husbanded her bed in florence, 5.03.126
fairer prove your honor | than in my thought it 5.03.183
if it appear not plain and prove untrue, 5.03.317
think they have thee do very oft prove fools; TN 1.05. 34 P
good madonna, give me leave to prove you a fool. 1.05. 58 P
for still we prove | much in our vows, but 2.04.117
so false, i am loath to prove reason with them. 3.01. 25 P
i will prove it legitimate, sir, upon the oaths 3.02. 14 P
often prove | rough and unhospitable. 3.03. 10
prove true, imagination, o, prove true, | that i 3.04.375
prove true, imagination, o, prove true, | that i 3.04.375
o, if it prove, | tempests are kind and salt 3.04.383
great lubber, the world, will prove a cockney. 4.01. 15 P
lest it should bite its master, and so prove WT 1.02.157
which if you seek to prove, | i dare not stand 1.02.443
lest your justice | prove violence, in the which 2.01.128
if it prove | she's otherwise, i'll keep my 2.01.133
if this prove true, they'll pay for't. 2.01.146
if i prove honey–mouth'd, let my tongue blister; 2.02. 31
th' journey | prove as successful to the queen 3.01. 12
this is fairy gold, boy, and 'twill prove so. 3.03.123 P
bring out another, and the shearers prove sheep, 4.03.121 P
i will prove so, sir, to my power. 5.02.169 P
ay, by any means prove a tall fellow. 5.02.170 P
the which if he can prove, 'a pops me out | at JN 1.01. 68
proves the king, | to him will we prove loyal. 2.01.271
doth not the crown of england prove the king? 2.01.273
one must prove greatest. 2.01.332
that give you cause to prove my saying true. 3.01. 28
and prove a deadly bloodshed but a jest, 4.03. 55
do not prove me so; 4.03. 90
tongue speaks, my right drawn sword may prove. R2 1.01. 46
look what i speak, my life shall prove it true: 1.01. 87
besides i say, and will in battle prove, | or 1.01. 92
to prove myself a loyal gentleman | even in the 1.01.148
arm, | to prove him, in defending of myself, | a 1.03. 23
here do stand in arms | to prove by god's grace, 1.03. 37
to prove the duke of norfolk, thomas mowbray, 1.03.107
things sweet to taste prove in digestion sour. 1.03.236
and these stones | prove armed soldiers, ere her 3.02. 25
to prove it on thee to the extremest point | of 4.01. 47
it will the woefullest division prove | that 4.01.146
lest thy pity prove | a serpent that will sting 5.03. 57
mother well hath pray'd, and prove you true. 5.03.145
my brain i'll prove the female to my soul, | my 5.05. 6
(for recreation sake) prove a false thief, for 1H4 1.02.155 P
to prove that true | needs no more but one 1.03. 95
the blessed sun of heaven prove a micher and eat 2.04.408 P
the son of england prove a thief and take purses 2.04.409 P
my faith, i am afraid he would prove the better 5.04.124 P
prove that ever i dress myself handsome till thy 2H4 2.04.279 P
and thou shalt prove a shelter to thy friends, 4.04. 42
say) will (i doubt) prove mine own marring. ep 6 P
and thou must therefore needs prove a good H5 5.02.206 P
no prophet will i trust, if she prove false. 1H6 1.02.150
pray god she prove not masculine ere long, | if 2.01. 22
remedy) | i mean to prove this lady's courtesy. 2.02. 58
and that i'll prove on better men than somerset, 2.04. 98
teach, | but prove a chief offender in the same? 3.01.130
prove them, and i lie open to the law; 2H6 1.03.156
to prove him a knave and myself an honest man; 2.03. 86 P
happy, | and prove the period of their tyranny, 3.01.149
nay then, this spark will prove a raging fire, 3.01.302
the first i warrant thee, if dreams prove true. 5.01.195
prove it, henry, and thou shalt be king. 3H6 1.01.131
i'll prove the contrary, if you'll hear me speak 1.02. 20
to prove him tyrant this reason may suffice, 3.03. 71
tell him, in hope he'll prove a widower shortly, 3.03.227
him, in hope he'll prove a widower shortly, 4.01. 99
marriage | i may not prove inferior to yourself. 4.01.122
this pretty lad will prove our country's bliss. 4.06. 70
since i cannot prove a lover | to entertain R3 1.01. 28
i am determined to prove a villain | and hate 1.01. 30
days, | which here you urge to prove us enemies, 1.03.145
i fear, i fear 'twill prove a giddy world. 2.03. 5
pray god, i say, i prove a needless coward! 3.02. 88
prove me, my gracious lord. 4.02. 68
hoping the consequence | will prove as bitter, 4.04. 7
so deal with him as i prove true to you. 4.04.497
thou — will our friends prove all true? 5.03.213
when these so noble benefits shall prove | not H8 1.02.115
men fear the french would prove perfidious, | to 1.02.156
'twould prove the verity of certain words 1.02.159
and prove it too, against mine honor aught — 2.04. 39
prove but our marriage lawful, by my life | and 2.04.227
speak like honest men (pray god ye prove so!), 3.01. 69
and, not reform'd, may prove pernicious. 5.02. 54
but to prove to you that helen loves him: TRO 1.02.118 P
but to prove to you that helen loves troilus — 1.02.127 P
will stand to the proof, if you'll prove it so. 1.02.129 P
and may that soldier a mere recreant prove, 1.03.287
i'll prove this troth with my three drops of 1.03.301
us as we are tasted, allow us as we prove. 3.02. 91 P
if ever you prove false one to another, since i 3.02.199 P
my dreams will sure prove ominous to the day. 5.03. 6
now prove good seconds: COR 1.04. 43
advanc'd and darts, | we prove this very hour. 1.06. 62
trumpets shall | i' th' field prove flatterers, 1.09. 43
the other course | will prove too bloody; 3.01.326
it | that my revengeful services may prove | as 4.05. 89
and that to prove more fortunes | th' art tir'd, 4.05. 93
a soldier's head | which will not prove a whip. 4.06.134
good faith, i'll prove him, | speed how it will. 5.01. 60
that thou mayst prove | to shame unvulnerable, 5.03. 72
wouldst thou have me prove myself a bastard? TIT 2.03.148
to prove thou hast a true–divining heart, 2.03.214
which i wish may prove | more stern and bloody 5.02.202
black and portendous must this humor prove, ROM 1.01.141
if thou swear'st, | thou mayest prove false. 2.02. 92
i'll prove more true | than those that have 2.02.100
lest that thy love prove likewise variable. 2.02.111
may prove a beauteous flow'r when next we meet. 2.02.122
for this alliance may so happy prove | to turn 2.03. 91
grant i may never prove so fond, | to trust man TIM 1.02. 64
so it may prove an argument of laughter | to th' 3.03. 20
it could not else be i should prove so base | to 3.05. 93
my sword | i'll prove the lie thou speak'st. MAC 5.07. 11
i would fain prove so. HAM 2.02.131
rich gifts wax poor when givers prove unkind. 3.01.100
for 'tis a question left us yet to prove, 3.02.202
and our mere defects | prove our commodities. LR 4.01. 21
our wishes on the way | may prove effects. 4.02. 15
there's my gauntlet, i'll prove it on a giant. 4.06. 90 P
i can produce a champion that will prove | what 5.01. 43
jesters do oft prove prophets. 5.03. 71
let the drum strike, and prove my title thine. 5.03. 81
if none appear to prove upon thy person | thy 5.03. 91
best spirits are bent | to prove upon thy heart, 5.03.141
if it prove lawful prize, he's made for ever. OTH 1.02. 51
and i dare think he'll prove to desdemona | a 2.01.290
when i doubt, prove; 3.03.190
if i do prove her haggard, | though that her 3.03.260
villain, be sure thou prove my love a whore; 3.03.359
so prove it | that the probation bear no hinge 3.03.364
each drop she falls would prove a crocodile. 4.01.246
i knew | that stroke would prove the worst! 4.01.274
as you shall prove us, praise us. 5.01. 66
of their amity shall prove the immediate author ANT 2.06.129 P
prove such a wife | as my thoughts make thee, 3.02. 25
prove this a prosp'rous day, the three–nook'd 4.06. 5
now to that name my courage prove my title! 5.02.288
expected to prove so worthy as since he hath CYM 1.04. 2 P
first, perchance, she'll prove on cats and dogs, 1.05. 38
but when to my good lord i prove untrue, | i'll 1.05. 86
nor like to be) | that this will prove a war; 2.04. 17
as honest, then | my purpose would prove well. 3.04.119
grant, heavens, that which i fear | prove false! 3.05. 53
what he learns by this | may prove his travel, 3.05.103
for true to thee | were to prove false, which i 3.05.158
so, if i prove a good repast to the spectators, 5.04.155 P
thou mayst say, | and prove it in thy feeling. 5.05. 68
my tears that fall | prove holy water on thee! 5.05.269
but i will prove that two on 's are as good | as 5.05.311
of all 'say'd yet, mayst thou prove prosperous! PER 1.01. 59
that will prove aweful both in deed and word. 2.ch. 4
me, | this sword shall prove he's honor's enemy. 2.05. 64
prove that i cannot, take me home again | and 4.06.189
prove the thousand part | of my endurance, thou 5.01.135
i'll prove it in my shackles, with these hands TNK 3.01. 39
honorable, | how good they'll prove, i know not. 4.01. 31
even now | to tie the rider she begins to prove. VEN 40
they wither in their prime, prove nothing worth: 418
all is imaginary she doth prove, | he will not 597
that they prove bankrout in this poor rich gain. LUC 140
when they in thee the like offenses prove. 613
since men prove beasts, let beasts bear gentle 1148
but i will prove, | thou being a goddess, i PP 3. 5
to myself forsworn, to thee i'll constant prove; 5. 3
unless thy lady prove unjust, | press never thou 18.21
and we will all the pleasures prove | that hills 19. 2
"thou single wilt prove none." SON 8.14
or to thyself at least kind–hearted prove: 10.12
not show my head where thou mayst prove me. 26.14
but since he died and poets better prove, 32.13
o absence, what a torment wouldst thou prove, 39. 9
quite, | for you in me can nothing worthy prove; 72. 4
and prove thee virtuous, though thou art 88. 4
since my appeal says i did strive to prove | the 117.13
in things of great receipt with ease we prove 136. 7
lest guilty of my faults thy sweet self prove: 151. 4
which yet men prove | against strange maladies a 153. 7
came there for cure, and this by that i prove: 154.13
PROVED 2 FR 0.0002 REL FR 2 V 0 P
of venice, | if it be proved against an alien, MV 4.01.349
if this be error and upon me proved, | i never SON 116.13
PROVENDER *(also provand)*
PROVENDER 6 FR 0.0006 REL FR 5 V 1 P
truly, a peck of provender; MND 4.01. 31 P
and give their fasting horses provender, | and H5 4.02. 58
and have their provender tied to their mouths, 1H6 1.02. 11
for that | i do appoint him store of provender. JC 4.01. 30
for nought but provender, and when he's old, OTH 1.01. 48
th' accounts | of all his hay and provender. TNK 5.02. 59
PROVER 1 FR 0.0001 REL FR 0 V 1 P
make that demand of the prover, it suffices me TRO 2.03. 67 P
PROVERB 13 FR 0.0014 REL FR 6 V 7 P
and thereof comes the proverb: TGV 3.01.304 P
to make one mad, let the proverb go with me: WIV 3.05.151 P
have at you with a proverb — shall i set in my ERR 3.01. 51
and the country proverb known, | that every man MND 3.02.458
the old proverb is very well parted between my MV 2.02.149 P

find — | a proverb never stale in thrifty mind. 2.05. 55
might we lay th' old proverb to your charge, WT 2.03. 97
you are the hare of whom the proverb goes, JN 2.01.137
or any such proverb so little kin to the purpose H5 3.07. 68 P
i will cap that proverb with "there is flattery 3.07.114 P
the very eye of that proverb with "a pox of the 3.07.119 P
the ancient proverb will be well effected: 2H6 3.01.170
grass grows" — the proverb is something musty. HAM 3.02.344 P
PROVERB'D 1 FR 0.0001 REL FR 1 V 0 P
for i am proverb'd with a grandsire phrase, ROM 1.04. 37
PROVERBS 5 FR 0.0005 REL FR 2 V 3 P
no, he gives me the proverbs and the no–verbs. WIV 3.01.105 P
patch grief with proverbs, make misfortune drunk ADO 5.01. 17
for he was never yet a breaker of proverbs. 1H4 1.02.119 P
you are the better at proverbs, by how much "a H5 3.07.121 P
sigh'd forth proverbs — | that hunger broke COR 1.01.205
PROVES 18 FR 0.0020 REL FR 14 V 4 P
this proves me still a sheep. TGV 1.01. 82 P
this proves that thou canst not read. 3.01.297 P
love's tongue proves dainty bacchus gross in LLL 4.03.336
else none at all in aught proves excellent. 4.03.351
this proves you wise and rich, for in my eye — 5.02.379
to a halfpenny, pompey proves the best worthy. 5.02.560 P
and so far blameless proves my enterprise, MND 3.02.350
but o, how vild an idol proves this god! TN 3.04.365
but he that proves the king, | to him will we JN 2.01.270
being touch'd and tried, | proves valueless. 3.01.101
so god help montague as he proves true! 3H6 4.01.143
expressly proves | that no man is the lord of TRO 3.03.114
goose, proves thee far and wide a broad goose. ROM 2.04. 86 P
it proves not so: JC 5.01. 4
this proves me base. ANT 5.02.300
what proves you? TNK 2.05. 9
for truth proves thievish for a prize so dear. SON 48.14
which proves more short than waste or ruining? 125. 4
PROVETH 2 FR 0.0002 REL FR 2 V 0 P
this proveth edward's love and warwick's honesty 3H6 3.03.180
yet hasty marriage seldom proveth well. 4.01. 18
PROVEXIT 1 FR 0.0001 REL FR 1 V 0 P
"me /pompae provexit apex." PER 2.02. 30
PROVIDE 33 FR 0.0037 REL FR 27 V 6 P
to none, | you must provide to bottom it on me; TGV 3.02. 53
i'll provide you a chain, and i'll do what i can WIV 5.01. 5 P
provide your block and your axe to–morrow, four MM 4.02. 52 P
and pray thee take this mercy to provide | for 5.01.484
such as sea–faring men provide for storms; ERR 1.01. 80
you, niece, provide yourself; AYL 1.03. 87
provide the feast, father, and bid the guests, SHR 2.01.316
provide this messenger. AWW 3.04. 40
go, go, provide. 5.01. 38
go, fellow, get thee home, provide some carts, R2 2.02.106
provide us all things necessary, and meet me 1H4 1.02.191 P
is, | but we will presently provide for them. 1H6 5.02. 15
us in, and with all speed provide | to see her 2H6 1.01. 73
the deed, | and i'll provide his executioner, 3.01.276
provide me soldiers, lords, | whiles i take 3.01.319
i will provide thee. 3H6 4.01. 60
to provide | a salve for any sore that may 4.06. 87
now, and provide | for thine own future safety. H8 3.02.420
bed, chamber, pandar to provide this gear! TRO 3.02.211
and provide more piercing statutes daily to COR 1.01. 83 P
provide thee two proper palfreys, black as jet, TIT 5.02. 50
he commands us to provide, and give great gifts, TIM 1.02.192
my cook and i'll provide. 3.04.117
your vessels and your spells provide, | your MAC 3.05. 18
t' hold what distance | his wisdom can provide. 3.06. 45
we will ourselves provide. HAM 3.03. 7
traverse, go, provide thy money. OTH 1.03.371 P
provide your going, | choose your own company, ANT 3.04. 36
and provide me presently | a riding–suit, no CYM 3.02. 75
we'll sure provide. PER 2.01.162 P
keep close | till i provide him files and food, TNK 2.06. 7
provide him necessaries and pack my clothes up, 2.06. 32
that did not better for my life provide | than SON 111. 3
PROVIDED 31 FR 0.0035 REL FR 23 V 8 P
my lord, i cannot be so soon provided: TGV 1.03. 72
provided that you do no outrages | on silly 4.01. 69
i have provided for you. MM 2.03. 17
hath he provided this music? ADO 1.02. 2 P
to our law | immediately provided in that case. MND 1.01. 45
i am provided of a torch–bearer. MV 2.04. 23
provided that your fortune | achiev'd her 3.02.207
two things provided more, that for this favor 4.01.386
provided that you weed your better judgments AYL 2.07. 45
and so we will, provided that he win her. SHR 1.02.216
provided that, when he's remov'd, your highness WT 1.02.335
he was provided to do us good. 4.04.829 P
what men provided? JN 5.02. 98
provided that my banishment repeal'd | and lands R2 3.03. 40
in another place, | and find me worse provided. 2H4 2.03. 50
have you provided me here half a dozen 3.02. 93 P
followers | shall all be very well provided for, 5.05. 99
you are as well provided of both as any prince H5 3.07. 9 P
master hume, we are therefore provided. 2H6 1.04. 3 P
for i myself am not so well provided | as else i R3 3.04. 44
more than, i fear, you are provided for. H8 5.02. 92
and having now provided | a gentleman of noble ROM 3.05.178
themselves have provided that i shall have much TIM 1.02. 89 P
i prithee let's be provided to show them 1.02.179
what i shall say i have provided for him. 5.01. 33
he that's coming | must be provided for; MAC 1.05. 67
now or whensoever, provided i be so able as now. HAM 5.02.202 P
you yet, nor am provided | for your fit welcome. LR 2.04.232
i have spoke already, and it is provided; ANT 5.02.195
provided i have your commendation for my more CYM 1.04.154 P
provided | that none but i and my companion maid PER 5.01. 76
PROVIDENCE 6 FR 0.0006 REL FR 5 V 1 P
by providence divine. TMP 1.02.159
but by immortal providence she's mine. 5.01.189
the providence that's in a watchful state TRO 3.03.196
to stay the providence of some high powers JC 5.01.106
us, whose providence | should have kept short, HAM 4.01. 17
there is special providence in the fall of a 5.02.220 P
PROVIDENT 2 FR 0.0002 REL FR 2 V 0 P
most provident in peril, bind himself | (courage TN 1.02. 12
it fits us then to be as provident | as fear may H5 2.04. 11
PROVIDENTLY 1 FR 0.0001 REL FR 1 V 0 P
feed, | yea, providently caters for the sparrow, AYL 2.03. 44
PROVIDER 1 FR 0.0001 REL FR 1 V 0 P
and parted with | pray'rs for the provider. CYM 3.06. 52
PROVIDES 1 FR 0.0001 REL FR 1 V 0 P
o, 'tis an accident that heaven provides! MM 4.03. 77
PROVINCE 5 FR 0.0005 REL FR 4 V 1 P
will unpeople the province with continency. MM 3.02.174 P
as he had lost some province and a region WT 1.02.369
say 'tis not so, a province i will give thee, ANT 2.05. 68
a caterpillar, | and so inflict our province. PER 5.01. 61
to any german province, spain or portigal, | nay STM II.C 128
PROVINCES 6 FR 0.0006 REL FR 6 V 0 P
poictiers, and anjou, these five provinces, JN 2.01.528
lewis have blanch, and blanch those provinces? 3.01. 3
with us, | but be extirped from our provinces. 1H6 3.03. 24
those provinces these arms of mine did conquer, 2H6 1.01.120
and seiz'd upon their towns and provinces. 3H6 1.01.109
we have kiss'd away | kingdoms and provinces. ANT 3.10. 8
PROVINCIAL 2 FR 0.0002 REL FR 1 V 1 P
his subject am i not, | nor here provincial. MM 5.01.316
with /two provincial roses on my raz'd shoes, HAM 3.02.276 P
PROVING 2 FR 0.0002 REL FR 2 V 0 P
proving from world's minority their right: LUC 67
proving his beauty by succession thine! SON 2.12
PROVISION 10 FR 0.0011 REL FR 9 V 1 P
i have with such provision in mine art | so TMP 1.02. 28
bear) | had made provision for her following me, ERR 1.01. 47
we shall be short in our provision, | 'tis now ROM 4.02. 38
sent to borrow of me, that my provision was out. TIM 3.06. 16 P
for provision | to shield thee from disasters of LR 1.01.173
home, and out of that provision | which shall be 2.04.205
that will to some provision | give thee quick 3.06. 96
you | that for our gold we may provision have, PER 5.01. 56
and give you gold for such provision | as our 5.01.257
fortunes | is the provision of the power above STM III 3
PROVISO 1 FR 0.0001 REL FR 1 V 0 P
his prisoners, | but with proviso and exception, 1H4 1.03. 78
PROVOCATION 2 FR 0.0002 REL FR 0 V 2 P
let there come a tempest of provocation, i will WIV 5.05. 21 P
methinks it sounds a parley to provocation. OTH 2.03. 23 P
PROVOCATIONS 1 FR 0.0001 REL FR 1 V 0 P
love's provocations, zeal, a mistress' task, TNK 1.04. 41
PROVOK'D 14 FR 0.0015 REL FR 12 V 2 P
thither provok'd and instigated by his distemper WIV 3.05. 76 P
nor heady–rash, provok'd with raging ire, ERR 5.01.216
god | (so my untruth had not provok'd him to it) R2 2.02.101
peace | more than i do, except i be provok'd? 1H6 3.01. 34
yet know, my lord, i was provok'd by him, | and 4.01.104
how will their grudging stomachs be provok'd 4.01.141
(and not provok'd by any suitor else), | aiming, R3 1.03. 64
told me the king, provok'd to it by the queen, 2.02. 21
not soon provok'd, nor being provok'd soon TRO 4.05. 99
soon provok'd, nor being provok'd soon calm'd; 4.05. 99
provok'd by him, you cannot) the great danger COR 5.06.136
break her wheel, | provok'd by my offense. ANT 4.15. 45
being so far provok'd as i was in france, i CYM 1.04. 67 P
"'tis not my fault, the boar provok'd my tongue, VEN 1003
PROVOKE 19 FR 0.0021 REL FR 16 V 3 P
what this ecstasy | may now provoke them to. TMP 3.03.109
and i will provoke him to't, or let him wag. WIV 2.03. 70 P
to make bad good, and good provoke to harm. MM 4.01. 15
rebuke me not for that which you provoke: LLL 5.02.347
no had, my lord? why, did you provoke me? JN 4.02.207
let my presumption not provoke thy wrath, | for 1H6 2.03. 70
provoke us hither now to slaughter thee. R3 1.04.225
since you provoke me, shall be most notorious. H8 3.02.288
wilt thou provoke me? then have at thee, boy! ROM 5.03. 70
what three things does drink especially provoke? MAC 2.03. 26 P
the need we have to use you did provoke | our HAM 2.02. 3
that to provoke in him, | are many simples LR 4.04. 13
and happily may strike at you — provoke him, OTH 2.01.273 P
provoke not battle | till we have done at sea. ANT 3.08. 3
for he did provoke me | with language that would CYM 5.05.293
liking took, | and her to incest did provoke — PER 1.ch. 26
one sin, i know, another doth provoke: 1.01.137
and swelling passion doth provoke a pause. VEN 218
the bloody spur cannot provoke him on | that SON 50. 9
PROVOKED 3 FR 0.0003 REL FR 3 V 0 P
i was provoked by her sland'rous tongue, | that R3 1.02. 97
thou wast provoked by thy bloody mind, | that 1.02. 99
but 'twas thy beauty that provoked me. 1.02.180
PROVOKER 1 FR 0.0001 REL FR 0 V 1 P
drink, sir, is a great provoker of three things. MAC 2.03. 25 P
PROVOKES 10 FR 0.0011 REL FR 7 V 3 P
my tale provokes that question. TMP 1.02.140
my oath | provokes me to this threefold perjury. TGV 2.06. 5
heaving of my lungs provokes me to ridiculous LLL 3.01. 77 P
of this oppressed child | religiously provokes. JN 2.01.246
provokes the mightiest hulk against the tide, 1H6 5.05. 6
the palsy, and not fear, provokes me. 2H6 4.07. 93
unnatural | provokes this deluge most unnatural. R3 1.02. 61
provokes itself and like the current flies TIM 1.01. 24
lechery, sir, it provokes, and unprovokes: MAC 2.03. 29 P
it provokes the desire, but it takes away the 2.03. 29 P
PROVOKETH 1 FR 0.0001 REL FR 1 V 0 P
beauty provoketh thieves sooner than gold. AYL 1.03.110
PROVOKING 2 FR 0.0002 REL FR 1 V 1 P
but a provoking merit, set a–work by a LR 3.05. 7 P
and spoke such scurvy and provoking terms OTH 1.02. 7
/PROVOK'ST 1 FR 0.0001 REL FR 1 V 0 P
/that /thou /provok'st /thyself /to /cast /him 2H4 1.03. 96
PROVOK'ST 2 FR 0.0002 REL FR 2 V 0 P
and that thou oft provok'st, yet grossly fear'st MM 3.01. 18
drink tears, that thou provok'st such weeping? VEN 949
PROVOST 24 FR 0.0027 REL FR 16 V 8 P
signior claudio, led by the provost to prison; MM 1.02.115 P
the provost hath | a warrant for 's execution. 1.04. 73
where is the provost? 2.01. 32
now, what's the matter, provost? 2.02. 6
hail to you, provost! so i think you are. 2.03. 1
i am the provost. what's your will, good friar? 2.03. 2
provost, a word with you. 3.01. 50 P
provost, a word with you. 3.01.174 P
provost, my brother angelo will not be alter'd, 3.02.207 P
of the night | envelop you, good provost! 4.02. 74
this is a gentle provost: 4.02. 86
as near the dawning, provost, as it is, | you 4.02. 94
there is written in your brow, provost, honesty 4.02.154 P
will i write letters to angelo | (the provost, 4.03. 94
good even. friar, where's the provost? 4.03.149 P
the provost knows our purpose and our plot. 4.05. 2
your provost knows the place where he abides, 5.01.252
the rascal i spoke of, here with the provost. 5.01.284 P
where is the provost? 5.01.345 P
first, provost, let me bail these gentle three. 5.01.357
go with him, provost. 5.01.379
provost, how came it claudio was beheaded | at 5.01.457
proclaim it, provost, round about the city, | if 5.01.508
thanks, provost, for thy care and secrecy, | we 5.01.530
/PROVULGATE 1 FR 0.0001 REL FR 1 V 0 P
i shall /provulgate — i fetch my life and being OTH 1.02. 21
PROWESS 3 FR 0.0003 REL FR 3 V 0 P
nor should thy prowess want praise and esteem, 2H6 5.02. 22
fift, | who by his prowess conquered all france: 3H6 3.03. 86
the which no sooner had his prowess confirm'd MAC 5.09. 7
PRUDENCE 2 FR 0.0002 REL FR 2 V 0 P
put | this ancient morsel, this sir prudence, TMP 2.01.286
good prudence, smatter with your gossips, go. ROM 3.05.171
PRUDENT 4 FR 0.0004 REL FR 3 V 1 P
thought among the prudent he would quickly have TN 1.03. 32 P
o prudent discipline! JN 2.01.413
was reputed for | a prince most prudent, of an H8 2.04. 46
that seem like prudent helps, are very poisonous COR 3.01.220
PRUINS *(also prunes*)*
PRUINS 5 FR 0.0005 REL FR 0 V 5 P
your honors' reverence) for stew'd pruins. MM 2.01. 90 P
and longing (as i said) for pruins; 2.01. 99 P
cracking the stones of the foresaid pruins — 2.01.107 P
four pounds of pruins, and as many of raisins o' WT 4.03. 48 P
lives upon mouldy stew'd pruins and dried cakes. 2H4 2.04.147 P
PRUNE* *(also proin, pruins)*
PRUNE* 2 FR 0.0002 REL FR 1 V 1 P
which makes him prune himself, and bristle up 1H4 1.01. 98
no more faith in thee than in a stew'd prune, 3.03.113 P
PRUNES* 2 FR 0.0002 REL FR 1 V 1 P
(three veneys for a dish of stew'd prunes) and, WIV 1.01.285 P
prunes the immortal wing and cloys his beak, CYM 5.04.118
PRUNING 2 FR 0.0002 REL FR 2 V 0 P
who, all for want of pruning, with intrusion ERR 2.02.179
joan, or spend a minute's time | in pruning me? LLL 4.03.181
PRUN'ST 1 FR 0.0001 REL FR 1 V 0 P
but, poor old man, thou prun'st a rotten tree, AYL 2.03. 63
PRY 8 FR 0.0009 REL FR 8 V 0 P
but i have cause to pry into this pedant. SHR 3.01. 87
whence | the eye of reason may pry in upon us. 1H4 4.01. 72
of safety, and withal to pry | into his title, 4.03.103
let it pry through the portage of the head H5 3.01. 10
asleep, | to pry into the secrets of the state, 2H6 1.01.250
speak and look back, and pry on every side, R3 3.05. 6
dost return to pry | in what i farther shall ROM 5.03. 33
thee | so far from home into my deeds to pry, SON 61. 6
PRY'ST 1 FR 0.0001 REL FR 1 V 0 P
of eyes, | why pry'st thou through my window? LUC 1089
P'S 1 FR 0.0001 REL FR 0 V 1 P
and her t's, and thus makes she her great p's. TN 2.05. 88 P
PSALMIST 1 FR 0.0001 REL FR 0 V 1 P
death, as the psalmist saith, is certain to all, 2H4 3.02. 37 P
PSALMS 3 FR 0.0003 REL FR 0 V 3 P
together than the hundred psalms to the tune of WIV 2.01. 63 P
amongst them, and he sings psalms to hornpipes. WT 4.03. 44 P
i would i were a weaver, i could sing psalms, or 1H4 2.04.133 P
PSALTERIES 1 FR 0.0001 REL FR 1 V 0 P
the trumpets, sackbuts, psalteries, and fifes, COR 5.04. 49
PTOLOMIES' 1 FR 0.0001 REL FR 0 V 1 P
i have heard the ptolomies' pyramises are very ANT 2.07. 34 P
PTOLOMIES 1 FR 0.0001 REL FR 1 V 0 P
the circle of the ptolomies for her heirs, | now ANT 3.12. 18
PTOLOMY 3 FR 0.0003 REL FR 3 V 0 P
nor the queen of ptolomy | more womanly than he; ANT 1.04. 6
is not | amiss to tumble on the bed of ptolomy, 1.04. 17
to ptolomy he assign'd | syria, cilicia, and 3.06. 15
PUBLIC 40 FR 0.0045 REL FR 37 V 3 P
wives | yet once again (to make us public sport) WIV 4.04. 13
or whether that the body public be | a horse MM 1.02.159
lord angelo hath to the public ear | profess'd 4.02. 99
cannot but yield you forth to public thanks, 5.01. 7
and then, with public accusation, uncover'd ADO 4.01.305 P
he shall endure such public shame as the rest of LLL 1.01.131 P
nor thrust your head into the public street | to MV 2.05. 32
so near our public court as twenty miles, | thou AYL 1.03. 44
and this our life, exempt from public haunt, 2.01. 15
come follow us, | we are to speak in public; WT 2.01.197
and sit at chiefest stern of public weal. 1H6 1.01.177
they me | to be a public spectacle to all: 1.04. 41
prick'd on by public wrongs sustain'd in france, 3.02. 78
join we together, for the public good, | in what 2H6 1.01.199
attire | have cost a mass of public treasury. 1.03.131
place, | defacers of a public peace than i do. H8 5.02. 76
shall find | no public benefit which you receive COR 1.01.152
innovator, | a foe to th' public weal. 3.01.175
trial | than the severity of the public power, 3.01.268
we talk here in the public haunt of men. ROM 3.01. 50
which now the public body, which doth seldom TIM 5.01.145
but shall be remedied to your public laws | at 5.04. 62
and public reasons shall be rendered | of JC 3.02. 7
let him go up into the public chair, | we'll 3.02. 63
that gave me public leave to speak of him. 3.02.220
motive, | why to a public count i might not go, HAM 4.07. 17
o thou public commoner, | i should make very OTH 4.02. 73
hop forty paces through the public street; ANT 2.02.229
made his will, and read it | to public ear; 3.04. 5
this in the public eye? 3.06. 11
caesar, | not by a public minister of justice, 3.06. 20
'twas a contention in public, which may, without CYM 1.04. 54 P
who either by public war or private treason PER 1.02.104
honor | in public question with their swords. TNK 3.06.222
shame, | thy private feasting to a public fast, LUC 891
some one | become the public plague of many moe? 1479
stars | of public honor and proud titles boast, SON 25. 2
shame, | nor thou with public kindness honor me, 36.11
than public means which public manners breeds. 111. 4

than public means which public manners breeds. 111. 4
PUBLICAN 1 FR 0.0001 REL FR 1 V 0 P
how like a fawning publican he looks! MV 1.03. 41
PUBLICATION 1 FR 0.0001 REL FR 1 V 0 P
and, in the publication, make no strain | but TRO 1.03.326
PUBLICLY 10 FR 0.0011 REL FR 7 V 3 P
i'll warrant they'll have him publicly sham'd, WIV 4.02.220 P
to the jest, should he not be publicly sham'd. 4.02.222 P
injunctions i am bound | to enter publicly. MM 4.03. 97
perchance, publicly, she'll be asham'd. 5.01.276 P
this town, | beheaded publicly for his offense. ERR 5.01.127
yet once again proclaim it publicly, | if any 5.01.130
as she hath | been publicly accus'd, so shall WT 2.03.204
the deed, | o, know you yet he doth it publicly. R3 1.04.216
it hath already publicly been read, | and on all H8 2.04. 3
in chairs of gold | were publicly enthron'd. ANT 3.06. 5
PUBLICOLA 2 FR 0.0002 REL FR 2 V 0 P
the noble sister of publicola, | the moon of COR 5.03. 64
justeius, | publicola, and caelius, are for sea; ANT 3.07. 73
/PUBLISH 1 FR 0.0001 REL FR 1 V 0 P
/and /publish /the /occasion /of /our /arms. 2H4 1.03. 86
PUBLISH 9 FR 0.0010 REL FR 6 V 3 P
in, | and publish it that she is dead indeed. ADO 4.01.204
trial shall better publish his commendation." MV 4.01.165 P
deservings, when of ourselves we publish them. AWW 1.03. 7 P
that, yet thus far i will boldly publish her: TN 2.01. 28 P
a proof of strength she could not publish more, TRO 5.02.113
we have this hour a constant will to publish LR 1.01. 43
publish we this peace | to all our subjects. CYM 5.05.478
and so to publish tarquin's foul offense; LUC 1852
the owner's tongue doth publish every where. SON 102. 4
PUBLISH'D 4 FR 0.0004 REL FR 4 V 0 P
him, | hath publish'd and proclaim'd it openly. SHR 4.02. 85
knowledge, that | you thus have publish'd me! WT 2.01. 98
his second marriage shall be publish'd, and H8 3.02. 68
/durst thou support a publish'd traitor? LR 4.06.232
PUBLISHED 1 FR 0.0001 REL FR 1 V 0 P
to–day, | if he be guilty, as 'tis published. 2H6 3.02. 17
PUBLISHER 2 FR 0.0002 REL FR 2 V 0 P
hath made me publisher of this pretense. TGV 3.01. 47
or why is collatine the publisher | of that rich LUC 33
PUBLISHING 1 FR 0.0001 REL FR 1 V 0 P
shall i not lie in publishing a truth? TRO 5.02.119
PUBLIUS 20 FR 0.0022 REL FR 20 V 0 P
of the same house publius and quintus were, COR 2.03.241
no, publius and sempronius, you must do it, TIT 4.03. 10
o publius, is not this a heavy case, | to see 4.03. 25
publius, how now? 4.03. 36
publius, publius, what hast thou done? 4.03. 69
publius, publius, what hast thou done? 4.03. 69
when publius shot, | the bull, being gall'd, 4.03. 71
come, marcus, let us go. publius, follow me. 4.03.121
publius, come hither! 5.02.151
fie, publius, fie, thou art too much deceiv'd. 5.02.155
name, | and therefore bind them, gentle publius. 5.02.157
and look where publius is come to fetch me. JC 2.02.108
welcome, publius. 2.02.109
desiring thee that publius cimber may | have an 3.01. 53
to beg enfranchisement for publius cimber. 3.01. 57
where's publius? 3.01. 85
publius, good cheer, | there is no harm intended 3.01. 89
so tell them, publius. 3.01. 91
and leave us, publius, lest that the people, 3.01. 92
upon condition publius shall not live, | who is 4.01. 4
PUCELLE 13 FR 0.0014 REL FR 13 V 0 P
excellent pucelle, if thy name be so, | let me 1H6 1.02.110
the dolphin, with one joan de pucelle join'd, 1.04.101
pucelle or puzzel, dolphin or dogfish, | your 1.04.107
pucelle is ent'red into orleance | in spite of 1.05. 36
thus joan de pucelle hath perform'd her word. 1.06. 3
but joan de pucelle shall be france's saint. 1.06. 29
but what's that pucelle whom they term so pure? 2.01. 20
here ent'red pucelle and her practisants. 3.02. 20
pucelle, that witch, that damned sorceress, 3.02. 38
yet, pucelle, hold thy peace, | if talbot do but 3.02. 58
but where is pucelle now? 3.02.121
speak, pucelle, and enchant him with thy words. 3.03. 40
pucelle hath bravely play'd her part in this, 3.03. 88
PUCK 5 FR 0.0005 REL FR 5 V 0 P
those, that hobgoblin call you, and sweet puck, MND 2.01. 40
my gentle puck, come hither. 2.01.148
and, gentle puck, take this transformed scalp 4.01. 64
and, as i am an honest puck, | if we have 5.01.431
else the puck a liar call. 5.01.435
PUDDER *(also poother)*
PUDDER 1 FR 0.0001 REL FR 1 V 0 P
that keep this dreadful pudder o'er our heads, LR 3.02. 50
PUDDING 5 FR 0.0005 REL FR 0 V 5 P
and young drop–heir that kill'd lusty pudding, MM 4.03. 15 P
friar's mouth, nay, as the pudding to his skin. AWW 2.02. 27 P
manningtree ox with the pudding in his belly, 1H4 2.04.453 P
yield the crow a pudding one of these days. H5 2.01. 87 P
bless'd pudding! OTH 2.01.253 P
PUDDINGS 3 FR 0.0003 REL FR 0 V 3 P
sat in the stocks for puddings he hath stol'n, TGV 4.04. 31 P
as sure as his guts are made of puddings. WIV 2.01. 32 P
and, moreo'er, puddings and flap–jacks, and thou PER 2.01. 82 P
PUDDLE 3 FR 0.0003 REL FR 3 V 0 P
ay, kennel, puddle, sink, whose filth and dirt 2H6 4.01. 71
the stale of horses and the gilded puddle ANT 1.04. 62
and not the puddle in thy sea dispersed. LUC 658
PUDDLED 2 FR 0.0002 REL FR 2 V 0 P
great pails of puddled mire to quench the hair; ERR 5.01.173
cyprus to him, | hath puddled his clear spirit; OTH 3.04.143
PUDDLE'S 1 FR 0.0001 REL FR 1 V 0 P
thy sea within a puddle's womb is hearsed, | and LUC 657
PUDENCY 1 FR 0.0001 REL FR 1 V 0 P
it with | a pudency so rosy the sweet view on't CYM 2.05. 11
PUERITIA 1 FR 0.0001 REL FR 0 V 1 P
ba, pueritia, with a horn added. LLL 5.01. 49 P
PUFF 4 FR 0.0004 REL FR 2 V 2 P
lady, i think 'a be, but goodman puff of barson. 2H4 5.03. 89 P
puff? 5.03. 91 P
puff i' thy teeth, most recreant coward base! 5.03. 92
throngs, and puff | to win a vulgar station; COR 2.01.214
PUFF'D 9 FR 0.0010 REL FR 7 V 2 P
a puff'd man? WIV 5.05.152 P
they are, with your sweet breaths puff'd out. LLL 5.02.267
have i not heard the sea, puff'd up with winds, SHR 1.02.201
who, great and puff'd up with this retinue, doth 2H4 4.03.111 P
cheek | outswell the colic of puff'd aquilon; TRO 4.05. 9
thy proud child, arrogant man, is puff'd, TIM 4.03.180
whiles, /like a puff'd and reckless libertine, HAM 1.03. 49
whose spirit with divine ambition puff'd | makes 4.04. 49
from his very arm | puff'd his own brother — OTH 3.04.137
PUFFING 3 FR 0.0003 REL FR 3 V 0 P
like foggy south, puffing with wind and rain? AYL 3.05. 50
puffing at all, winnows the light away, | and TRO 1.03. 28
when he bestrides the lazy puffing clouds, | and ROM 2.02. 31
PUFFS 2 FR 0.0002 REL FR 2 V 0 P
and, being anger'd, puffs away from thence, ROM 1.04.102
puffs forth another wind that fires the torch. LUC 315
PUGGING 1 FR 0.0001 REL FR 1 V 0 P
doth set my pugging tooth an edge, | for a quart WT 4.03. 7
PUH *(also pah)*
PUH 1 FR 0.0001 REL FR 1 V 0 P
affection, puh! HAM 1.03.101
PUIS 1 FR 0.0001 REL FR 1 V 0 P
rien puis? l'air et feu? H5 4.02. 5
PUISNE *(also puny)*
PUISNE 1 FR 0.0001 REL FR 0 V 1 P
the heart of his lover, as a puisne tilter, that AYL 3.04. 43 P
PUISSANCE 10 FR 0.0011 REL FR 9 V 1 P
cousin, go draw our puissance together. JN 3.01.339
upon the power and puissance of the king. 2H4 1.03. 9
and come against us in full puissance, | need 1.03. 77
have of their puissance made a little taste. 2.03. 52
divide one man, | and make imaginary puissance; H5 pr 25
us deliver | our puissance into the hand of god, 2.02.190
past or not arriv'd to pith and puissance; 3.pr. 21
with a staff, but that my puissance holds it up. 2H6 4.02.163 P
whose puissance on either side | shall be well R3 5.03.299
not dreams we stand before your puissance, TNK 1.01.155
/PUISSANT 1 FR 0.0001 REL FR 1 V 0 P
/his /grief /grew /puissant /and /the /strings LR 5.03.217
PUISSANT 9 FR 0.0010 REL FR 8 V 1 P
and with your puissant arm renew their feats. H5 1.02.116
trail'st thou the puissant pike? 4.01. 40
je vous supplie, mon tres puissant seigneur. 5.02.256 P
and with a puissant and a mighty power | of 2H6 4.09. 25
me | the queen is coming with a puissant host, 3H6 2.01.207
by this at daintry, with a puissant troop. 5.01. 6
queen from france hath brought a puissant power; 5.02. 31
on the western coast | rideth a puissant navy; R3 4.04.434
high, most mighty, and most puissant caesar, JC 3.01. 33
PUKE–STOCKING 1 FR 0.0001 REL FR 0 V 1 P
agate–ring, puke–stocking, caddis–garter, 1H4 2.04. 70 P
PUKING 1 FR 0.0001 REL FR 1 V 0 P
mewling and puking in the nurse's arms. AYL 2.07.144
PULCHER 1 FR 0.0001 REL FR 0 V 1 P
pulcher. WIV 4.01. 27 P
PULING 4 FR 0.0004 REL FR 3 V 1 P
to speak puling, like a beggar at hallowmas. TGV 2.01. 25 P
he, like a puling cuckold, would drink up | the TRO 4.01. 62
leave this faint puling, and lament as i do, COR 4.02. 52
man, | and then to have a wretched puling fool, ROM 3.05.183
PULL 12 FR 0.0013 REL FR 9 V 3 P
i'll pull thee by the lesser legs. TMP 2.02.103 P
unbind my hands, i'll pull them off myself, SHR 2.01. 4
only doth backward pull | our slow designs when AWW 1.01.218
for thou hast to pull at a smack a' th' contrary 2.03.225 P
when such profound respects do pull you on. JN 3.01.318
we'll pull his plumes and take away his train, 1H6 3.03. 7
now go some and pull down the savoy; 2H6 4.07. 1 P
let them pull all about mine ears, present me COR 3.02. 1
and pull her out of acheron by the heels. TIT 4.03. 45
what, man, ne'er pull your hat upon your brows; MAC 4.03.208
i pull in resolution, and begin | to doubt th' 5.05. 41
pull off my boots; LR 4.06.173
PULL'D 8 FR 0.0009 REL FR 4 V 4 P
houses of resort in the suburbs be pull'd down? MM 1.02.102 P
you censure him, | and pull'd the law upon you. 2.01. 16
till this other had pull'd out thy tongue for AYL 1.01. 61 P
bookish rule hath pull'd fair england down. 2H6 1.01.259
biting statutes, unless his teeth be pull'd out. 4.07. 17 P
there was the weight that pull'd me down. H8 3.02.407
you pull'd me by the cloak, would you speak with JC 1.02.215 P
pull'd the poor wretch from her melodious lay HAM 4.07.182
PULLER–DOWN 1 FR 0.0001 REL FR 1 V 0 P
proud setter–up and puller–down of kings! 3H6 3.03.157
PULLET–SPERM 1 FR 0.0001 REL FR 0 V 1 P
i'll no pullet–sperm in my brewage. WIV 3.05. 31 P
PULLING 1 FR 0.0001 REL FR 0 V 1 P
flavius, for pulling scarfs off caesar's images, JC 1.02.285 P
PULLS 3 FR 0.0003 REL FR 2 V 1 P
two pulls at once — | his lady banish'd, and a 2H6 2.03. 41
'tis pride that pulls the country down, | /then OTH 2.03. 95
so /hales and pulls me. 4.01.140 P
PULL'T 1 FR 0.0001 REL FR 1 V 0 P
pull't off, i say. MAC 5.03. 54
PULPIT 4 FR 0.0004 REL FR 4 V 0 P
go to the pulpit, brutus. JC 3.01. 84
and in the pulpit, as becomes a friend, | speak 3.01.229
pardon — | i will myself into the pulpit first, 3.01.236
speak | in the same pulpit whereto i am going, 3.01.250
PULPITS 1 FR 0.0001 REL FR 1 V 0 P
some to the common pulpits, and cry out, JC 3.01. 80
PULSE 10 FR 0.0011 REL FR 10 V 0 P
me, and return | or ere your pulse twice beat. TMP 5.01.103
thy pulse | beats as of flesh and blood; 5.01.113
give me your hand, and let me feel your pulse. ERR 4.04. 52
and, gazing in mine eyes, feeling my pulse, 5.01.244
daughter and mother | so strive upon your pulse. AWW 1.03.169
have i commandement on the pulse of life? JN 4.02. 92
my heart beats thicker than a feverous pulse, TRO 3.02. 36
for no pulse | shall keep his native progress, ROM 4.01. 96
my pulse, as yours, doth temperately keep time, HAM 3.04.140
have you a working pulse, and are no fairy? PER 5.01.153
PULSES 1 FR 0.0001 REL FR 1 V 0 P
he bends her fingers, holds her pulses hard, VEN 476
PULSIDGE 1 FR 0.0001 REL FR 0 V 1 P
your pulsidge beats as extraordinarily as heart 2H4 2.04. 23 P
PUMP 2 FR 0.0002 REL FR 0 V 2 P
why then is my pump well flower'd. ROM 2.04. 60 P
now, till thou hast worn out thy pump, that, 2.04. 62 P
PUMPION 1 FR 0.0001 REL FR 0 V 1 P
unwholesome humidity, this gross wat'ry pumpion. WIV 3.03. 41 P
PUMPIONS 1 FR 0.0001 REL FR 0 V 1 P
true, and pumpions together. STM II.C 16 P
PUMPS 2 FR 0.0002 REL FR 1 V 1 P
to your beards, new ribands to your pumps; MND 4.02. 37 P
and gabr'el's pumps were all unpink'd i' th' SHR 4.01.133
PUN 1 FR 0.0001 REL FR 0 V 1 P
he would pun thee into shivers with his fist, as TRO 2.01. 39 P
PUNCHED 1 FR 0.0001 REL FR 1 V 0 P
body | by thee was punched full of deadly holes. R3 5.03.125
PUNCTO 1 FR 0.0001 REL FR 0 V 1 P
there, to see thee pass thy puncto, thy stock, WIV 2.03. 26 P
PUNISH 21 FR 0.0023 REL FR 19 V 2 P
that which i must speak | must either punish me, MM 5.01 31
and punish them to your height of pleasure. 5.01.240
you, punish me not with your hard thoughts, AYL 1.02.183 P
above | punish my life for tainting of my love! TN 5.01.138
for me less easy to commit | than you to punish. WT 1.02. 59
the rod of heaven, | to punish my mistreadings. 1H4 3.02. 11
a time | to punish this offense in other faults. 5.02. 7
to punish you by the heels would amend the 2H4 1.02.123 P
so may your highness, and yet punish too. H5 2.02. 48
god punish me | with hate in those where i R3 2.01. 34
nay, before, | or god will punish me. H8 2.04. 75
a' th' people | as if you were a god, to punish; COR 3.01. 81
before you punish him, where he heard this, 4.06. 53
hath pleas'd it so | to punish me with this, and HAM 3.04.174
but i will punish home. LR 3.04. 16
to punish me for what you make me do | seems ANT 2.05.100
bid that welcome | which comes to punish us, and 4.14.137
and we punish it | seeming to bear it lightly. 4.14.137
and punish that before that he would punish. PER 1.02. 33
and punish that before that he would punish. 1.02. 33
gods for murder seemed so content | to punish, 5.03.100
/PUNISH'D 2 FR 0.0002 REL FR 2 V 0 P
/common /trespasses | /are /punish'd /with. LR 2.02.145
/do /those /villains /pity /who /are /punish'd 4.02. 54
PUNISH'D 19 FR 0.0021 REL FR 15 V 4 P
if i have too austerely punish'd you, | your TMP 4.01. 1
whose high imperious thoughts have punish'd me TGV 2.04.130
methinks his flesh is punish'd, he shall have no WIV 4.04. 23 P
why they are not so punish'd and cur'd is, that AYL 3.02.402 P
rather | let me be punish'd, that have minded WT 3.02.225
flesh and blood is not to be punish'd by him. 4.04.695 P
all punish'd in the person of this child, | and JN 2.01.189
thou shalt be punish'd for thus frighting me, 3.01. 11
let him be punish'd, sovereign, lest example H5 2.02. 45
of our person, | would have him punish'd. 2.02. 60
that here men are punish'd for before–breach of 4.01.170 P
me | to watch the coming of my punish'd duchess. 2H6 2.04. 7
may not be punish'd with my thwarting stars, 3H6 4.06. 22
of a state | to one whom they had punish'd. COR 5.01. 21
all are punish'd. ROM 5.03.295
how i am punish'd | with a sore distraction. HAM 5.02.229
she's punish'd for her truth, and undergoes, CYM 3.02. 7
and subjects punish'd that ne'er thought offense PER 1.02. 28
it is enough my hearing shall be punish'd | with TNK 5.03. 7
PUNISHED 2 FR 0.0002 REL FR 1 V 1 P
thou shalt be heavily punished. LLL 1.02.150 P
some shall be pardon'd, and some punished: ROM 5.03.308
PUNISHES 1 FR 0.0001 REL FR 0 V 1 P
no more, whose very naming punishes me with the WT 4.02. 21 P
PUNISHMENT 24 FR 0.0027 REL FR 16 V 8 P
hope, to betray him to another punishment? WIV 3.03.196 P
their permissive pass, | and not the punishment. MM 1.03. 39
he should receive his punishment in thanks: 1.04. 28
under | the pleasing punishment that women bear) ERR 1.01. 46
nay, that were a punishment too good for them, ADO 3.03. 4 P
you let it be rememb'red in his punishment. 5.01.307 P
to receive the meed of punishment, by thy sweet LLL 1.01.267 P
vows for thee broke deserve not punishment. 4.03. 61
defeated the law and outrun native punishment, H5 4.01.167 P
i never gave them condign punishment. 2H6 3.01.130
and yet his punishment was bitter death. R3 2.01.106
th' contrary | the foulness is the punishment. H8 3.02.183
death, | as punishment for his most wicked life. TIT 5.03.145
judicious punishment! LR 3.04. 74
quit the house on purpose that their punishment 4.02. 93
a punishment more in policy than in malice, even OTH 2.03.273 P
/on pain of punishment, the world to weet | we ANT 1.01. 39
you call it) deserve more — a punishment too. CYM 1.04.119 P
on them, knowing 'tis | a punishment or trial? 3.06. 11
was my /mere offense, my punishment | itself, 5.05.334
having receiv'd the punishment before | for that 5.05.343
o, 'twas a studied punishment, a death | beyond TNK 2.03. 4
in troth, a very grievous punishment, as one 4.03. 45 P
vows for thee broke deserve not punishment. PP 3. 4
PUNISHMENTS 1 FR 0.0001 REL FR 0 V 1 P
i'll devise thee brave punishments for him. ADO 5.04.128 P
PUNK 4 FR 0.0004 REL FR 1 V 3 P
this punk is one of cupid's carriers. WIV 2.02.135
my lord, she may be a punk; MM 5.01.179 P
marrying a punk, my lord, is pressing to death, 5.01.522 P
as your french crown for your taffety punk, as AWW 2.02. 22 P
PUNTO 1 FR 0.0001 REL FR 0 V 1 P
the immortal passado, the punto reverso, the hay ROM 2.04. 26 P
PUNY *(also puisne)*
PUNY 6 FR 0.0006 REL FR 5 V 1 P
and twenty of these puny lies i'll tell, | that MV 3.04. 74
a puny subject strikes | at thy great glory. R2 3.02. 86
while i question my puny drawer to what end he 1H4 2.04. 30 P
did flesh his puny sword in frenchmen's blood! 1H6 4.07. 36
and boys with stones | in puny battle slay me. COR 4.04. 6
but every puny whipster gets my sword. OTH 5.02.244
PUPIL 12 FR 0.0013 REL FR 9 V 3 P
he being her pupil, to become her tutor. TGV 2.01.138
at the father's of a certain pupil of mine, LLL 4.02.154 P
with the parents of the foresaid child or pupil, 4.02.157 P
a nurse, | too far in years to be a pupil now. R2 1.03.171
of goodman adam to the pupil age of this present 1H4 2.04. 94 P
which calls me pupil or hath read to me? 3.01. 45
shall king henry be a pupil still | under the 2H6 1.03. 46
his pupil age | man–ent'red thus, he waxed like COR 2.02. 98
for doting, not for loving, pupil mine. ROM 2.03. 82

have i not been | thy pupil long? CYM 1.05. 12
me thy pupil, | youngest follower of thy drum, TNK 5.01. 56
which this time's pencil, or my pupil pen, SON 16.10
PUPIL-LIKE 1 FR 0.0001 REL FR 1 V 0 P
to be o'erpow'r'd, and wilt thou, pupil-like, R2 5.01. 31
PUPILS 2 FR 0.0002 REL FR 2 V 0 P
you shall go see your pupils presently. SHR 2.01.107
that pupils lacks she none of noble race, | who PER 5.ch. 9
PUPPET 8 FR 0.0009 REL FR 5 V 3 P
o exceeding puppet! TGV 2.01. 95 P
fie, fie, you counterfeit, you puppet, you! MND 3.02.288
"puppet"? 3.02.289
and marry him to a puppet or an aglet-baby, or SHR 1.02. 79 P
belike you mean to make a puppet of me. 4.03.103
why, true, he means to make a puppet of thee. 4.03.104
says your worship means to make a puppet of her. 4.03.106 P
thou, an egyptian puppet, shall be shown | in ANT 5.02.208
PUPPET'S 1 FR 0.0001 REL FR 0 V 1 P
and take vanity the puppet's part against the LR 2.02. 36 P
PUPPETS 1 FR 0.0001 REL FR 0 V 1 P
your love, if i could see the puppets dallying. HAM 3.02.247 P
PUPPIES 4 FR 0.0004 REL FR 0 V 4 P
they would have drown'd a blind bitch's puppies, WIV 3.05. 11 P
very wisely, puppies! WT 4.04.706 P
drown cats and blind puppies! OTH 1.03.336 P
as many inches as you have oceans. puppies! CYM 1.02. 21 P
PUPPY 4 FR 0.0004 REL FR 1 V 3 P
one that i brought up of a puppy; TGV 4.04. 3 P
may stroke him as gently as a puppy greyhound. 2H4 2.04. 98 P
i take it, is a kind of puppy | to th' old dam, H8 1.01.175
shall be with you presently, good master puppy. 5.03. 30 P
PUPPY-DOG 1 FR 0.0001 REL FR 0 V 1 P
of the roman disciplines, than is a puppy-dog. H5 3.02. 73 P
PUPPY-DOGS 1 FR 0.0001 REL FR 1 V 0 P
lions | as maids of thirteen do of puppy-dogs! JN 2.01.460
PUPPY-HEADED 1 FR 0.0001 REL FR 0 V 1 P
myself to death at this puppy-headed monster. TMP 2.02.154 P
PURBLIND 6 FR 0.0006 REL FR 5 V 1 P
this wimpled, whining, purblind, wayward boy, LLL 3.01.179
perchance are to this business purblind? WT 1.02.228
my side | that any purblind eye may find it out. 1H6 2.04. 21
many hands and no use, or purblind argus, all TRO 1.02. 29 P
one nickname for her purblind son and /heir, ROM 2.01. 12
"and when thou hast on foot the purblind hare, VEN 679
PURCHAS'D 13 FR 0.0014 REL FR 10 V 3 P
and thine own acquisition | worthily purchas'd, TMP 4.01. 14
that i have purchas'd at an infinite rate, and WIV 2.02.205 P
i have purchas'd as many diseases under her roof MM 1.02. 46 P
purchas'd by such sin | for which the pardoner 4.02.108
but that most vain | which, with pain purchas'd, LLL 1.01. 73
were purchas'd by the merit of the wearer! MV 2.09. 43
and you shall see 'tis purchas'd by the weight, 3.02. 89
you have among you many a purchas'd slave, 4.01. 90
with die and drab i purchas'd this caparison, WT 4.03. 27 P
for what in me was purchas'd | falls upon thee 2H4 4.05.199
a peace, and purchas'd | at a superfluous rate! H8 1.01. 98
of them | as jewels purchas'd at an easy price, TIT 3.01.198
hereditary, | rather than purchas'd; ANT 1.04. 14
/PURCHASE 1 FR 0.0001 REL FR 0 V 1 P
if there were wealth enough for the /purchase, CYM 1.04. 83 P
PURCHASE 35 FR 0.0039 REL FR 27 V 8 P
choleric, and purchase me another dry basting. ERR 2.02. 62 P
they are worse fools to purchase mocking so. LLL 5.02. 59
than you could purchase in so remov'd a dwelling AYL 3.02.342 P
upon some toy | you have desire to purchase; TN 3.03. 45
a good report — after fourteen years' purchase. 4.01. 23 P
purse is not hot enough to purchase your spice. WT 4.03.119 P
purchase the sight again of dear sicilia | and 4.04.511
purchase corrupted pardon of a man | who in that JN 3.01.166
is purchase of a heavy curse from rome, | or the 3.01.205
go, say i sent thee forth to purchase honor, R2 1.03.282
thou shalt have a share in our purchase, as i am 1H4 2.01. 92 P
ball of wildfire, there's no purchase in money. 3.03. 40 P
they will steal any thing, and call it purchase. H5 3.02. 42 P
favor | may haply purchase him a box a' th' ear. 4.07.173
and purchase friends and give to courtezans, 2H6 1.01.223
enough to purchase such another island, | so 3.03. 3
for by that loss i will not purchase them. 3H6 3.02. 73
unless abroad they purchase great alliance? 3.03. 70
which i will purchase with my duteous service; R3 2.01. 64
made prize and purchase of his wanton eye, 3.07.187
which she shall purchase with still-lasting war. 4.04.344
do this and purchase us thy lasting friends." TIT 2.03.275
nor tears nor prayers shall purchase out abuses; ROM 3.01.193
that i should purchase the day before for a TIM 3.02. 47 P
though his right arm might purchase his own time 3.05. 76
silver hairs | will purchase us a good opinion, JC 2.01.145
the purchase made, the fruits are to ensue; OTH 2.03. 9
enough to purchase what you have made known. ANT 5.02.148
the purchase is to make men glorious, | et bonum PER 1.ch. 9
i sought the purchase of a glorious beauty, 1.02. 72
were not spent, | rather laid out for purchase. TNK 1.02.111
to purchase name, and do my ablest service | to 2.05. 26
save what is bought, and yet i purchase cheaply, 5.03.113
which purchase if thou make, for fear of slips, VEN 515
would purchase thee a thousand thousand friends, LUC 963
PURCHASED 1 FR 0.0001 REL FR 0 V 1 P
how hast thou purchased this experience? LLL 3.01. 26 P
PURCHASES 1 FR 0.0001 REL FR 0 V 1 P
vouchers vouch him no more of his purchases, and HAM 5.01.109 P
PURCHASETH 1 FR 0.0001 REL FR 1 V 0 P
that | which simpleness and merit purchaseth. ADO 3.01. 70
PURCHASING 3 FR 0.0003 REL FR 2 V 1 P
in purchasing the semblance of my soul, | from MV 3.04. 20
you, and not without his true purchasing. COR 2.01.140 P
out too much pains | for purchasing but trouble. CYM 2.03. 88
PURE 98 FR 0.0110 REL FR 90 V 8 P
and women too, but innocent and pure; TMP 2.01.156
the water nectar, and the rocks pure gold. TGV 2.04.171
his tears pure messengers sent from his heart, 2.07. 77
my herald thoughts in thy pure bosom rest them, 3.01.144
but neither bended knees, pure hands held up, 3.01.231
one, lady, if you knew his pure heart's truth, 4.02. 88
upon whose grave thou vow'dst pure chastity. 4.03. 21
against my soul's pure truth, why labor you, ERR 3.02. 37
thou pure impiety and impious purity! ADO 4.01.104
hand, | a halting sonnet of his own pure brain, 5.04. 87
pure, pure /idolatry. LLL 4.03. 73
pure, pure /idolatry. 4.03. 73
by heaven, all dry-beaten with pure scoff! 5.02.263
honor, yet as pure | as the unsallied lily, i 5.02.351
welcome, pure wit! 5.02.484
that pure congealed white, high taurus' snow, MND 3.02.141
let me kiss | this princess of pure white, this 3.02.144
proof, | because what follows is pure innocence. MV 1.01.145
than with safety of a pure blush thou mayst in AYL 1.02. 28 P
me hath many a weary step | limp'd in pure love; 2.07.131
warrant you, with pure love and troubled brain, 4.03. 3 P
speed her foot again, | led hither by pure love. AWW 3.04. 38
sake | did i expose myself (pure for his love) TN 5.01. 83
the silence often of pure innocence | persuades WT 2.02. 39
in pure white robes, | like very sanctity, she 3.03. 22
his thin bestained cloak | with our pure honors, JN 4.03. 25
death, made proud with pure and princely beauty! 4.03. 35
and his pure brain | (which some suppose the 5.07. 2
and his pure soul unto his captain christ, R2 4.01. 99
see now whether pure fear and entire cowardice 2H4 2.04.325 P
have, in my pure and immaculate valor, taken sir 4.03. 37 P
conscience wash'd | as pure as sin with baptism. H5 1.02. 32
though in pure truth it was corrupt and naught, 1.02. 73
if your pure maidens fall into the hand | of hot 3.03. 20
he is pure air and fire; 3.07. 21 P
but what's that pucelle whom they term so pure? 1H6 2.01. 20
blush for pure shame to counterfeit our roses, 2.04. 66
for that pure blood of mine | which thou didst 4.06. 23
yes, my good lord, a pure unspotted heart, 5.03.182
and yet, forsooth, she is a virgin pure. 5.04. 83
god knows, of pure devotion, being call'd | a 2H6 2.01. 87
alas, sir, we did it for pure need. 2.01.154
from scotland am i stol'n, even of pure love, 3H6 3.01. 13
on pure heart's love, to greet the tender prince R3 4.01. 4
a thousand pounds a year for pure respect? H8 2.03. 95
and fair virtue | than this pure soul shall be. 5.04. 25
fame blows, that praise, sole pure, transcends. TRO 1.03.244
that most pure spirit of sense, behold itself, 3.03.106
but let desert in pure election shine, | and, TIT 1.01. 16
to turn your households' rancor to pure love. ROM 2.03. 92
lips, | who, even in pure and vestal modesty, 3.03. 38
for i will /raise her statue in pure gold, 5.03.299
and morsels unctious, greases his pure mind, TIM 4.03.195
all villains that do stand by thee are pure. 4.03.361
with an hundred spouts, | did run pure blood; JC 2.02. 78
black macbeth | will seem as pure as snow, and MAC 4.03. 53
his virtues else, be they as pure as grace, | as HAM 1.04. 33
be thou as chaste as ice, as pure as snow, thou 3.01.135 P
a mineral of metals base, | shows itself pure: 4.01. 27
her brother that, in pure kindness to his horse, LR 2.04.125 P
in simple and pure soul i come to you. OTH 1.01.107
who has that breast so pure | /but /some 3.03.138
and pure grief | shore his old thread in twain. 5.02.205
of nothing but the finest part of pure love. ANT 1.02.147 P
you had of her pure honor gains or loses | your CYM 2.04. 59
pure surprise and fear | made me to quit the PER 3.02. 17
pure dian, | /i bless thee for thy vision, and 5.03. 68
i am sure | it has a noble breeder and a pure, TNK pr 10
the poison of pure spirits, might, like women, 2.02. 75
pure red and white, for yet no beard has blest 4.02.107
white as chaste, and pure | as wind-fann'd snow, 5.01.139
pure shame and aw'd resistance made him fret, VEN 69
"pure lips, sweet seals in my soft lips 511
forgetting shame's pure blush and honor's wrack. 558
and pure perfection with impure defeature. 736
with pure aspects did him peculiar duties. LUC 14
in their pure ranks his traitor eye encloses, 73
pure thoughts are dead and still, | while lust 167
offer pure incense to so pure a shrine: 194
offer pure incense to so pure a shrine: 194
doth confound and kill | all pure effects, and 251
but with a pure appeal seeks to the heart, 293
sometime is compacted | in a pure compound; 531
while she, the picture of pure piety, | like a 542
from a pure heart command thy rebel will; 625
o that prone lust should stain so pure a bed! 684
pure chastity is rifled of her store, | and lust 692
find | some purer chest to close so pure a mind. 761
of mine | as i ere this was pure to collatine. 826
shall gush pure streams to purge my impure tale. 1078
when the one pure, the other made divine? 1164
but still pure | doth in her poison'd closet yet 1658
may my pure mind with the foul act dispense, 1704
some of her blood still pure and red remain'd, 1742
yet in the mids of all her pure protestings, PP 7.11
and thou present'st a pure unstained prime. SON 70. 8
even to thy pure and most most loving breast. 110.14
he preach'd pure maid, and prais'd cold chastity LC 315
/PURELY 1 FR 0.0001 REL FR 1 V 0 P
/troth, | /strain'd /purely /from /all /hollow TRO 4.05.169
PURER 4 FR 0.0004 REL FR 4 V 0 P
where should he find it purer than in blanch? JN 2.01.429
it, | and /live the purer with the other half. HAM 3.04.158
the meanest bird | that flies i' th' purer air! PER 4.06.102
find | some purer chest to close so pure a mind. LUC 761
PUREST 6 FR 0.0006 REL FR 6 V 0 P
the purest treasure mortal times afford | is R2 1.01.177
the purest spring is not so free from mud | as i 2H6 3.01.101
that's curdied by the frost from purest snow COR 5.03. 66
thou bright defiler | of hymen's purest bed! TIM 4.03.383
the purest of their wives | is foul as slander. OTH 4.02. 18
jollity, | and purest faith unhappily forsworn, SON 66. 4
PURGATION 6 FR 0.0006 REL FR 3 V 3 P
now you will be my purgation and let me loose. LLL 3.01.126 P
if their purgation did consist in words, | they AYL 1.03. 53
man doubt that, let him put me to my purgation. 5.04. 44 P
course, | even to the guilt or the purgation. WT 3.02. 7
and fair purgation to the world than malice, H8 5.02.187
to put him to his purgation would perhaps plunge HAM 3.02.306 P
PURGATIVE 1 FR 0.0001 REL FR 1 V 0 P
what rhubarb, cyme, or what purgative drug, MAC 5.03. 55
PURGATORY 2 FR 0.0002 REL FR 1 V 1 P
walls, | but purgatory, torture, hell itself. ROM 3.03. 18
i should venture purgatory for't. OTH 4.03. 77 P
PURG'D 9 FR 0.0010 REL FR 9 V 0 P
methought she purg'd the air of pestilence! TN 1.01. 19
be by some certain king purg'd and depos'd. JN 2.01.372
shall these hands, so lately purg'd of blood, 3.01.239
by heaven, my soul is purg'd from grudging hate, R3 2.01. 9
being purg'd, a fire sparkling in lovers' eyes, ROM 1.01.191
thus from my lips, by thine, my sin is purg'd. 1.05.107
ere humane statute purg'd the gentle weal; MAC 3.04. 75
my days of nature | are burnt and purg'd away. HAM 1.05. 13
and that your rage | would not be purg'd, she ANT 4.14.124
/PURGE 1 FR 0.0001 REL FR 1 V 0 P
/and /purge /th' /obstructions /which /begin /to 2H4 4.01. 65
PURGE 22 FR 0.0024 REL FR 19 V 3 P
and i will purge thy mortal grossness so, | that MND 3.01.160
to purge him of that humor | that presses him WT 2.03. 38
aboard a new ship to purge melancholy and air 4.04.763 P
purge all infection from our air whilest you 5.01.169
let's purge this choler without letting blood. R2 1.01.153
as well as i am doubtless i can purge | myself 1H4 3.02. 20
i'll grow less, for i'll purge and leave sack, 5.04.164 P
now, neighbor confines, purge you of your scum! 2H4 4.05.123
to purge this field of such a hilding foe; H5 4.02. 29
whereof you cannot easily purge yourself. 2H6 3.01.135
and from his bosom purge this black despair! 3.03. 23
and then, to purge his fear, i'll be thy death. 3H6 5.06. 88
you cannot with such freedom purge yourself H8 5.01.102
people, hoping | to purge himself with words. COR 5.06. 8
and here i stand both to impeach and purge ROM 5.03.226
and with him pour we, in our country's purge, MAC 5.02. 28
and purge it to a sound and pristine health, | i 5.03. 52
of rest, would purge | by any desperate change. ANT 1.03. 53
we would purge the land of these drones, that PER 2.01. 46 P
that peace might purge | for her repletion, and TNK 1.02. 23
gush pure streams to purge my impure tale." LUC 1078
we sicken to shun sickness when we purge; SON 118. 4
PURGED 2 FR 0.0002 REL FR 2 V 0 P
you must be purged too, your sins are rack'd, LLL 5.02.818
and but in purged judgment trusting neither? H5 2.02.136
PURGER 1 FR 0.0001 REL FR 1 V 0 P
thou purger of the earth, draw thy fear'd sword TNK 1.01. 48
PURGERS 1 FR 0.0001 REL FR 1 V 0 P
we shall be call'd purgers, not murderers. JC 2.01.180
PURGING 3 FR 0.0003 REL FR 2 V 1 P
their eyes purging thick amber and plum-tree gum HAM 2.02.198 P
to take him in the purging of his soul, | when 3.03. 85
the other two, slight air and purging fire, SON 45. 1
PURIFIED 1 FR 0.0001 REL FR 1 V 0 P
so applied, | his venom in effect is purified. LUC 532
PURIFIES 1 FR 0.0001 REL FR 1 V 0 P
sin, | thus purifies itself and turns to grace. LLL 5.02.776
PURIFY 1 FR 0.0001 REL FR 1 V 0 P
the spots whereof could weeping purify, | her LUC 685
PURIFYING 1 FR 0.0001 REL FR 0 V 1 P
in ten, madam, which is a purifying a' th' song. AWW 1.03. 83 P
PURITAN 7 FR 0.0008 REL FR 0 V 7 P
for young charbon the puritan and old poysam the AWW 1.03. 52 P
though honesty be no puritan, yet it will do no 1.03. 93 P
marry, sir, sometimes he is a kind of puritan. TN 2.03.140 P
what, for being a puritan? 2.03.143 P
the dev'l a puritan that he is, or any thing 2.03.147 P
but one puritan amongst them, and he sings WT 4.03. 44 P
that she would make a puritan of the devil, if PER 4.06. 9 P
PURITY 12 FR 0.0013 REL FR 11 V 1 P
drive her then from the ward of her purity, her WIV 2.02.248 P
thou pure impiety and impious purity! ADO 4.01.104
all purity, all trial, all observance; AYL 5.02. 98
sully | the purity and whiteness of my sheets WT 1.02.327
mine own thoughts i cut out | the purity of his. 4.04.383
unmatchable, | shall give a holiness, a purity, JN 4.03. 53
and weight | of such a winnowed purity in love! TRO 3.02.167
i love thee in so strain'd a purity | that the 4.04. 24
who dares | in purity of manhood stand upright TIM 4.03. 14
breaths make sick | the life of purity, the LUC 780
devil, | wooing his purity with her fair pride. PP 2. 8
devil, | wooing his purity with her foul pride. SON 144. 8
PURL'D 1 FR 0.0001 REL FR 1 V 0 P
thin winding breath, which purl'd up to the sky. LUC 1407
PURLIEUS 1 FR 0.0001 REL FR 1 V 0 P
where in the purlieus of this forest stands | a AYL 4.03. 76
PURLOIN'D 1 FR 0.0001 REL FR 1 V 0 P
that my poor beauty had purloin'd his eyes, LUC 1651
PURPLE 18 FR 0.0020 REL FR 17 V 1 P
pense" write | in em'rald tuffs, flow'rs purple, WIV 5.05. 70
before milk-white, now purple with love's wound, MND 2.01.167
with purple grapes, green figs, and mulberries; 3.01.167
flower of this purple dye, | hit with cupid's 3.02.102
to open | the purple testament of bleeding war; R2 3.03. 94
upon hell-fire and dives that liv'd in purple; 1H4 3.03. 32 P
came edward to my side | with purple falchion, 3H6 1.04. 12
the one his purple blood right well resembles, 2.05. 99
may such purple tears be alway shed | from those 5.06. 64
the purple sap from her sweet brother's body, R3 4.04.277
with purple fountains issuing from your veins — ROM 1.01. 85
purple the sails, and so perfumed that | the ANT 2.02.193
the purple violets, and marigolds | shall as a PER 4.01. 15
power hast turn'd | green neptune into purple, TNK 5.01. 50
whose wonted lily white | with purple tears, VEN 1054
a purple flow'r sprung up, check'red with white, 1168
and from the purple fountain brutus drew | the LUC 1734
the purple pride | which on thy soft cheek for SON 99. 3
PURPLE-COLOR'D 1 FR 0.0001 REL FR 1 V 0 P
even as the sun with purple-color'd face | had VEN 1
PURPLED 2 FR 0.0002 REL FR 2 V 0 P
our lusty english, all with purpled hands, JN 2.01.322
whilst your purpled hands do reek and smoke, JC 3.01.158
PURPLE-HU'D 1 FR 0.0001 REL FR 0 V 1 P
of these mad mustachio purple-hu'd malt-worms, 1H4 2.01. 75 P
PURPLE-IN-GRAIN 1 FR 0.0001 REL FR 0 V 1 P
orange-tawny beard, your purple-in-grain beard, MND 1.02. 94 P
PURPLES 1 FR 0.0001 REL FR 1 V 0 P
and long purples | that liberal shepherds give a HAM 4.07.169
PURPORT 1 FR 0.0001 REL FR 1 V 0 P
and with a look so piteous in purport | as if he HAM 2.01. 79
/PURPOS'D 1 FR 0.0001 REL FR 1 V 0 P
/your /purpos'd /low /correction | /is /such /as LR 2.02.142
PURPOS'D 18 FR 0.0020 REL FR 17 V 1 P

you have spoken truer than you purpos'd. TMP 2.01. 20 P
and oftentimes have purpos'd to forbid | sir TGV 3.01. 26
when lo, to interrupt my purpos'd rest, | toward LLL 5.02. 91
of sorrow justle it | from what it purpos'd; 5.02.749
worn, | our purpos'd hunting shall be set aside. MND 4.01.183
twice did he turn his back, and purpos'd so; AYL 4.03.127
the archbishopric of toledo, this is purpos'd. H8 2.01.164
what was purpos'd | concerning his imprisonment 5.02.184
it is a purpos'd thing, and grows by plot, | to COR 3.01. 38
whose end is purpos'd by the mighty gods? JC 2.02. 27
how purpos'd, sir, i pray you? HAM 4.04. 11
let my disclaiming from a purpos'd evil | free 5.02.241
so am i purpos'd. LR 2.04.293
sorrows, | nor purpos'd merit in futurity, | can OTH 3.04.117
(whom | he purpos'd to his wive's sole son — a CYM 1.01. 5
in which time she purpos'd, | by watching, 5.05. 52
morrow, | to linger out a purpos'd overthrow. SON 90. 8
yet their purpos'd trim | piec'd not his grace, LC 118

PURPOSE 220 FR 0.0248 REL FR 173 V 47 P

one midnight | fated to th' purpose, did antonio TMP 1.02.129
the ministers for th' purpose hurried thence 1.02.131
if you but knew how you the purpose cherish 2.01.224
forgo the purpose | that you resolv'd t' effect. 3.03. 12
the sole drift of my purpose doth extend | not a 5.01. 29
love, lend me wings to make my purpose swift, TGV 2.06. 42
and here's the ladder for the purpose. 3.01.152
but to the purpose — for we cite our faults 4.01. 51
have you importun'd her to such a purpose? WIV 2.02.212 P
to what purpose have you unfolded this to me? 2.02.218 P
now, sir john, here is the heart of my purpose: 2.02.224 P
he'll tell me all his purpose. 4.04. 77
assist me in my purpose, | and, as i am a 4.06. 3
the purpose why, is here; 4.06. 21
i knew of your purpose; 5.05.201 P
near to the speech we had to such a purpose. MM 1.02. 78 P
hath a purpose | more grave and wrinkled than 1.03. 4
if power change purpose, what our seemers be. 1.03. 54
have attain'd th' effect of your own purpose, 2.01. 13
to the purpose: 2.01.115 P
'tis for a good purpose. 2.01.149 P
on mine honor, | my words express my purpose. 2.04.148
be much believ'd, | and most pernicious purpose! 2.04.150
angelo had never the purpose to corrupt her; 3.01.162 P
the provost knows our purpose and our plot. 4.05. 2
to do it, | he says, to veil full purpose. 4.06. 4
his purpose surfeiting, he sends a warrant | for 5.01.102
joint by joint, but we will know his purpose. 5.01.312
slower foot came on, | that brain'd my purpose. 5.01.396
and told thee to what purpose and what end. ERR 4.01. 97
on purpose shut the doors against his way. 4.03. 91
and people sin upon purpose, because they would ADO 2.01.259 P
he was wont to speak plain and to the purpose 2.03. 19 P
is, | as hush'd on purpose to grace harmony! 2.03. 39
in brief, since i do purpose to marry, i will 5.04.105 P
think nothing to any purpose that the world can 5.04.106 P
vouchsafe to read the purpose of my coming, LLL 2.01.109
that more for praise than purpose meant to kill. 4.01. 29
and i will have an apology for that purpose. 5.01.136 P
their purpose is to parley, to court, and dance, 5.02.122
you, and purpose now | to lead you to our court; 5.02.343
forms | all causes to the purpose of his speed, 5.02.741
of this their purpose hither to this wood, | and MND 4.01.161
with purpose to be dress'd in an opinion | of MV 1.01. 91
the devil can cite scripture for his purpose. 1.03. 98
for we have friends | that purpose merriment. 2.02.203
my purpose was not to have seen you here, | but 3.02.227
i have possess'd your grace of what i purpose, 4.01. 35
for the intent and purpose of the law | hath 4.01.247
myself notice of my brother's purpose herein, AYL 1.01.139 P
have you no song, forester, for this purpose? 4.02. 6 P
(for now i speak to some purpose) that i know 5.02. 53 P
bed | on purpose trimm'd up for semiramis. SHR in.2. 39
such is his noble purpose, and, believe't, | the AWW 3.02. 70
count solicits her | in the unlawful purpose. 3.05. 70
now i see | the bottom of your purpose. 3.07. 29
seem to know, is to know straight our purpose: 4.01. 19 P
and knowing i had no such purpose? 4.01. 36 P
come, come, to th' purpose. 5.03.241 P
what's that to th' purpose? TN 1.03. 21 P
my purpose is indeed a horse of that color. 2.03.167 P
she sends him on purpose, that i may appear 3.04. 66 P
of my negligence, nothing of my purpose. 3.04.256 P
dearest, thou never spok'st | to better purpose. WT 1.02. 89
but once before i spoke to th' purpose? 1.02.100
i have spoke to th' purpose twice: 1.02.106
and to come) that you do change this purpose, 2.03.151
will speak, that you must change this purpose, 4.04. 39
as little skill to fear as i have purpose | to 4.04.152
(which i do guess | you do not purpose to him) 4.04.469
i not purpose it. | i think, camillo? 4.04.472
if you will not change your purpose | but 4.04.542
from all direction, purpose, course, intent — JN 2.01.580
yet am i sworn, and i did purpose, boy, | with 4.01.123
and go | between his purpose and his conscience, 4.02. 77
the practice and the purpose of the king; 4.03. 63
be said, | they saw we had a purpose of defense. 5.01. 76
with purpose presently to leave this war. 5.07. 86
nor never by advised purpose meet | to plot, R2 1.03.188
o, to what purpose dost thou hoard thy words, 1.03.253
that had not god, for some strong purpose, 5.02. 34
if god prevent not, i purpose so. 5.02. 55
but this our purpose now is twelve month old, 1H4 1.01. 28
we must neglect | our holy purpose to jerusalem. 1.01.102
"the purpose you undertake is dangerous" — why, 2.03. 7 P
"the purpose you undertake is dangerous, the 2.03. 10 P
that you did nothing purpose 'gainst the state, 5.01. 43
in every thing the purpose must weigh with the 2H4 2.02.176 P
and spoke it on purpose to try my patience. 2.04.308 P
but this is mere digression from my purpose. 4.01.138
and had a purpose now | to lead out many to the 4.05.209
but to the purpose, and so to the venture. ep 7 P
/end in one purpose, and be all well borne H5 1.02.212
as two yoke-devils sworn to either's purpose, 2.02.106
with me, | my purpose should not fail with me, 3.02. 16
any such proverb so little kin to the purpose. 3.07. 68 P
for they purpose not their death when they 4.01.157 P
their death when they purpose their services. 4.01.158 P
with purpose to relieve and follow them, 1H6 1.01.133
purpose to answer what thou canst object. 3.01. 7
your purpose is both good and reasonable; 5.01. 36
this man | of purpose to obscure my noble birth. 5.04. 22
over, | because his purpose is not executed. 2H6 3.01.256
by them, | yet did i purpose as they do entreat; 3.02.282
a cold premeditation for my purpose! 3H6 3.02.133
how he doth stand affected to our purpose, | and R3 3.01.171
but for his purpose in the coronation, | i have 3.04. 15
the manner and the purpose of his treasons, 3.05. 58
indeed, left nothing fitting for your purpose 3.07. 18
smil'd and said, "the better for our purpose." 5.03.274
as a performance | does an irresolute purpose. H8 1.02.209
and | does purpose honor to you no less flowing 2.03. 62
this is of purpose laid by some that hate me 5.02. 14
that by a pace goes backward with a purpose | it TRO 1.03.128
me take a trumpet, | and to this purpose speak: 1.03.264
name, | relates in purpose only to achilles. 1.03.323
true, the purpose is perspicuous as substance, 1.03.324
find hector's purpose | pointing on him. 1.03.330
me, | 'twas not my purpose thus to beg a kiss. 3.02.137
we'll execute your purpose, and put on | a form 3.03. 50
his purpose meets you; 4.01. 37
she is to do, | and haste her to the purpose. 4.03. 5
or do you purpose | a victor shall be known? 4.05. 66
alone | till accident or purpose bring you to't. 4.05.262
from my great purpose in to-morrow's battle. 5.01. 38
it is the purpose that makes strong the vow, 5.03. 23
vow, | but vows to every purpose must not hold; 5.03. 24
but, since it serves my purpose, i will venture COR 1.01. 91
fought, and did | retire to win our purpose. 1.06. 50
when you speak best unto the purpose, it is not 2.01. 86 P
than have him hold that purpose and to put it 2.01.240
our purpose to them, and to our noble consul 2.02.152
purpose so barr'd, it follows | nothing is done 3.01.148
barr'd, it follows | nothing is done to purpose. 3.01.149
ask'd, as free | as words to little purpose. 3.02. 89
and i had purpose | once more to hew thy target 4.05.119
i purpose not to wait on fortune till | these 5.03.119
this valley fits the purpose passing well. TIT 2.03. 84
for what purpose, love? ROM 2.02.130
thy purpose marriage, send me word to-morrow, 2.02.144
thisby a grey eye or so, but not to the purpose. 2.04. 43 P
to supper to him of purpose to have him spend TIM 3.01. 25 P
speak'st with every tongue | to every purpose! 4.03.389
clean from the purpose of the things themselves. JC 1.03. 35
this shall make | our purpose necessary, and not 2.01.178
i fear our purpose is discovered. 3.01. 17
misgiving still | falls shrewdly to the purpose. 3.01.146
visitings of nature | shake my fell purpose, nor MAC 1.05. 46
heels, and had a purpose | to be his purveyor; 1.06. 21
infirm of purpose! 2.02. 49
the flighty purpose never is o'ertook | unless 4.01.145
this deed i'll do before this purpose cool. 4.01.154
scarcely hears | of this his nephew's purpose — HAM 1.02. 30
any thing, but to th' purpose. 2.02.278 P
black as his purpose, did the night resemble 2.02.453
and drive his purpose into these delights. 3.01. 27
so o'erdone is from the purpose of playing, 3.02. 20 P
purpose is but the slave to memory, | of violent 3.02.188
the passion ending, doth the purpose lose. 3.02.195
is but to whet thy almost blunted purpose. 3.04.111
and, for /that purpose, i'll anoint my sword. 4.07.140
venom'd stuck, | our purpose may hold there. 4.07.162
if thou answerest me not to the purpose, confess 5.01. 38 P
and the king hold his purpose, i will win for 5.02.176 P
mean time we shall express our darker purpose. LR 1.01. 36
glib and oily art | to speak and purpose not, 1.01.225
proceed against him, mistaking his purpose, it 1.02. 83 P
as a very pretense and purpose of unkindness. 1.04. 70 P
suspend thy purpose, if thou didst intend | to 1.04.276
opposite i stood | to his unnatural purpose, in 2.01. 50
make your own purpose, | how in my strength you 2.01.111
the night before there was no purpose in them 2.04. 3
good sir, to th' purpose. 2.04.181
quit the house on purpose that their punishment 4.02. 93
know of the duke if his last purpose hold, | or 5.01. 1
well, | the better shall my purpose work on him. OTH 1.03.391
he, swift of foot, | outran my purpose; 2.03.233
if it be not for some purpose of import, 3.03.316
reason to believe now than ever (i mean purpose, 4.02.213 P
that there he dropp'd it for a special purpose 5.02.322
let our officers | have notice what we purpose. ANT 1.02.177
i am sorry to give breathing to my purpose — 1.03. 14
may i never | (to this good purpose, that so 2.02.144
that call'd me timelier than my purpose hither; 2.06. 51
the policy of that purpose made more in the 2.06.118 P
'tis a brave army, | and full of purpose. 4.03. 12
go and say | we purpose her no shame. 5.01. 62
with so mortal a purpose as then each bore, upon CYM 1.04. 41 P
you bear a graver purpose, i hope. 1.04.139 P
i cross'd the seas on purpose and on promise 1.06.202
fellow, | albeit he comes on angry purpose now; 2.03. 56
she hath my letter for the purpose; 3.04. 29 P
whereunto i never | purpose return. 3.04.107
as honest, then | my purpose would prove well. 3.04.119
out, sword, and to a sore purpose! 4.01. 23 P
have you dream'd of late of this war's purpose? 4.02.345
good heavens, | hear patiently my purpose: 5.01. 22
nay, nay, to th' purpose. 5.05.178
dreading that her purpose | was of more danger, 5.05.253
away he posts | with unchaste purpose, and with 5.05.284
a fitment for | the purpose i then follow'd. 5.05.410
and on set purpose let his armor rust | until PER 2.02. 54
madam, if this you purpose as ye speak, 3.04. 12
melt thee, but be | a soldier to thy purpose. 4.01. 8
diana aid my purpose! 4.02.148
i will make them acquainted with your purpose, 4.06.198 P
my purpose was for tharsus, there to strike 5.01.252
that way he takes | i purpose is my way too. TNK 2.06. 18
but that's all one, 'tis nothing to our purpose. 5.02. 32
blind priest for the purpose that will venture 5.02. 78
(for to that honest purpose it was meant ye), ep 14
far from the purpose of his coming thither, | he LUC 113
post hither, this vile purpose to prevent? 220
way, | for in thy bed i purpose to destroy thee. 514
yet for the self-same purpose seek a knife; 1047
by adding one thing to my purpose nothing. SON 20.12
i will not praise that purpose not to sell. 21.14
you are so strongly in my purpose bred | that 112.13
she keeps thee to this purpose, that her skill 126. 7
bait | on purpose laid to make the taker mad: 129. 8

PURPOSE-CHANGER 1 FR 0.0001 REL FR 1 V 0 P

in the ear | with that same purpose-changer, JN 2.01.567

PURPOSED 3 FR 0.0003 REL FR 3 V 0 P

great clerks have purposed | to greet me with MND 5.01. 93
a pause | when i spake darkly what i purposed, JN 4.02.232
world | the noble change that i have purposed! 2H4 4.05.154

/PURPOSELY 1 FR 0.0001 REL FR 1 V 0 P

/come /hither /purposely /to /poison /me. TIT 3.02. 73

PURPOSELY 3 FR 0.0003 REL FR 2 V 1 P

conduct, purposely to take | his brother here, AYL 5.04.157
of men that put quarrels purposely on others, to TN 3.04.243 P
for purposely therefore | left i the court, to 2H6 2.03. 52

PURPOSES 40 FR 0.0045 REL FR 39 V 1 P

i endow'd thy purposes | with words that made TMP 1.02.357
the heavens give safety to your purposes! MM 1.01. 73
that some plain man recount their purposes. LLL 5.02.177
to unburthen all my plots and purposes | how to MV 1.01.133
camp i'll show, | their force, their purposes; AWW 4.01. 85
will have fulfill'd their secret purposes; WT 5.01. 36
secure | and confident from foreign purposes, JN 2.01. 28
the better act of purposes mistook | is to 3.01.274
merriment — | a passion hateful to my purposes; 3.03. 47
to sound the purposes of all their hearts, 4.02. 48
start away, | and lend no ear unto my purposes. 1H4 1.03.217
is certainly possess'd | of all our purposes. 4.01. 41
early shall mine uncle | bring him our purposes. 4.03.111
wind | doth play the trumpet to his purposes, 5.01. 4
to us and /to our purposes confin'd | we come 2H4 4.01.173
blood, | my father's purposes have been mistook, 4.02. 56
nature, | and to our purposes he lives no more. 5.02. 5
policy | seek to divert the english purposes. H5 2.pr. 15
our purposes god justly hath discover'd, | and i 2.02.151
more than could | my studied purposes requite, H8 3.02.168
and is very likely to load our purposes | with TIM 5.01. 14
let not our looks put on our purposes, | but JC 2.01.225
popilius lena speaks not of our purposes, | for 3.01. 23
to-morrow, as he purposes. MAC 1.05. 60
so is it, if thou knew'st our purposes. HAM 4.03. 47
i am constant to my purposes, they follow the 5.02.200 P
purposes mistook | fall'n on th' inventors' 5.02.384
beseech you | to understand my purposes aright, LR 1.04.239
might not you | transport her purposes by word? 4.05. 20
ask him his purposes, why he appears | upon this 5.03.118
but he, as loving his own pride and purposes, OTH 1.01. 12
frank appearance | their purposes toward cyprus. 1.03. 39
very ill at ease, | unfit for mine own purposes. 3.03. 33
but be prepar'd to know | the purposes i bear; ANT 1.03. 67
is shorter, | my purposes do draw me much about. 2.04. 8
have we | our written purposes before us sent, 2.06. 4
shall bereave yourself | of my good purposes, 5.02.131
she levell'd at our purposes, and, being royal, 5.02.336
why gone, | nor when she purposes return. CYM 4.03. 15
(in despite | of heaven and men) her purposes; 5.05. 59

PURPOSETH 2 FR 0.0002 REL FR 2 V 0 P

but that, it seems, he little purposeth: LLL 2.01.141
he purposeth to athens, whither, with what haste ANT 3.01. 35

PURPOSING 1 FR 0.0001 REL FR 1 V 0 P

here, purposing the bastard to destroy, | came 1H6 4.06. 25

/PURR 1 FR 0.0001 REL FR 0 V 1 P

/purr /the /cat /is /grey. LR 3.06. 45 P

PURR 1 FR 0.0001 REL FR 0 V 1 P

here is a purr of fortune's, sir, or of AWW 5.02. 19 P

PURS'D 1 FR 0.0001 REL FR 0 V 1 P

she purs'd up his heart upon the river of cydnus ANT 2.02.187 P

/PURSE 1 FR 0.0001 REL FR 0 V 1 P

/put /money /enough /in /your /purse. OTH 1.03.381 P

PURSE 78 FR 0.0088 REL FR 38 V 40 P

and yet it cannot overtake your slow purse. TGV 1.01.126 P
open your purse, that the money and the matter 1.01.129 P
of her purse she shall not, for that i'll keep 3.01.350 P
here, youth, there is my purse; 4.04.176
pistol, did you pick master slender's purse? WIV 1.01.152 P
she has all the rule of her husband's purse. 1.03. 53 P
she bears the purse too; 1.03. 68 P
liquor in his pate, or money in his purse, when 2.01.191 P
there's my purse, i am yet thy debtor. 2.02.132 P
he cannot creep into a halfpenny purse, nor into 3.05.146 P
turkish tapestry | there is a purse of ducats; ERR 4.01.105
the desk, the purse! 4.02. 29
went'st not thou to her for a purse of ducats? 4.04. 87
this purse of ducats i receiv'd from you, | and 5.01.385
and money enough in his purse, such a man would ADO 2.01. 15 P
had of thy master, thou halfpenny purse of wit, LLL 5.01. 74 P
eye of honor, be assur'd | my purse, my person, MV 1.01.138
and i will go and purse the ducats straight, 1.03.174
have him help to waste | his borrowed purse. 2.05. 51
for i think you have no money in your purse. AYL 2.04. 14 P
crowns in my purse i have, and goods at home, SHR 1.02. 57
take this purse of gold, | and let me buy your AWW 3.07. 14
hold thee, there's my purse. 4.05. 44 P
keep your purse; TN 1.05.284
hold, sir, here's my purse. 3.03. 38
why i your purse? 3.03. 43
my necessity | makes me to ask you for my purse? 3.04.335
denied me mine own purse, | which i had 5.01. 90
your purse is not hot enough to purchase your WT 4.03.118 P
means i saw whose purse was best in picture, and 4.04.603 P
'twas nothing to geld a codpiece of a purse; 4.04.611 P
i had not left a purse alive in the whole army. 4.04.618 P
the inside of your purse to the outside of his 4.04.803 P
hand as deep | into the purse of rich prosperity JN 5.02. 61
a purse of gold most resolutely snatch'd on 1H4 1.02. 33 P
where shall we take a purse to-morrow, jack? 1.02. 98 P
what money is in my purse? 2H4 1.02.234 P
no remedy against this consumption of the purse; 1.02.237 P
her serve your uses both in purse and in person. 2.01.116 P
i' th' court is better than a penny in purse. 5.01. 31 P
that he should, for a foreign purse, so sell H5 2.02. 10
and crowns for convoy put into his purse. 4.03. 37
agrees not with the leanness of his purse. 2H6 1.01.112
o, in the duke of gloucester's purse. R3 1.04.128 P
when he opens his purse to give us our reward, 1.04.129 P
it made me once restore a purse of gold that (by 1.04.140 P

there is my purse to cure that blow of thine. 4.04.514
thou, trumpet, there's my purse. TRO 4.05. 6
eye, thou tossel of a prodigal's purse, thou? 5.01. 32 P
nor will he know his purse, or yield me this, TIM 1.02.194
father, | and kept his credit with his purse; 3.02. 68
'tis deepest winter in lord timon's purse; 3.04. 14
costly thy habit as thy purse can buy, | but not HAM 1.03. 70
i had my father's signet in my purse, | which 5.02. 49
his purse is empty already: 5.02.130 P
open this purse and take | what it contains. LR 3.01. 45
here, take this purse, thou whom the heav'ns' 4.01. 64
here, friend, 's another purse; 4.06. 28
eyes in your head, nor no money in your purse? 4.06.146 P
eyes are in a heavy case, your purse in a light, 4.06.147 P
villain, take my purse: 4.06.246
who hast had my purse | as if the strings were OTH 1.01. 2
put money in thy purse; 1.03.340 P
i say put money in thy purse. 1.03.341 P
love to the moor — put money in thy purse — 1.03.343 P
sequestration — put but money in thy purse. 1.03.346 P
in their wills — fill thy purse with money. 1.03.347 P
therefore put money in thy purse. 1.03.352 P
thus do i ever make my fool my purse; 1.03.383
and didst contract and purse thy brow together, 3.03.113
who steals my purse steals trash; 3.03.157
me, i had rather have lost my purse | full of 3.04. 25
in your despite, upon your purse — revenge it. CYM 1.06.135
give me thy hand, here's my purse. 3.05.123 P
this cloten was a fool, an empty purse, | there 4.02.113
purse and brain both empty; 5.04.163 P
for being too light, the purse too light, being 5.04.165 P
pain, but even | your purse, still open, hath PER 3.02. 47

PURSE–BEARER 1 FR 0.0001 REL FR 1 V 0 P
i'll be your purse–bearer and leave you | for an TN 3.03. 47

PURSENTS *(also presents*)*

PURSENTS 1 FR 0.0001 REL FR 1 V 0 P
it is vara fine, | for every one pursents three. LLL 5.02.488

PURSES 11 FR 0.0012 REL FR 4 V 7 P
our purses shall be proud, our garments poor, SHR 4.03.171
i pick'd and cut most of their festival purses; WT 4.04.615 P
for their love | lies in their purses, and whoso R2 2.02.130
for we that take purses go by the moon and the 1H4 1.02. 14 P
and traders riding to london with fat purses. 1.02.127 P
go, i will stuff your purses full of crowns; 1.02.132 P
no more from picking of purses than giving 2.01. 51 P
hot livers and cold purses. 2.04.323 P
son of england prove a thief and take purses? 2.04.410 P
o'ercharging your free purses with large fines; 1H6 1.03. 64
false vows with him, | like empty purses pick'd; TIM 4.02. 12

PURSE–TAKING 1 FR 0.0001 REL FR 0 V 1 P
of life in thee, from praying to purse–taking. 1H4 1.02.103 P

PURSU'D 11 FR 0.0012 REL FR 9 V 2 P
i have pursu'd her as love hath pursu'd me, WIV 2.02.200 P
i have pursu'd her as love hath pursu'd me, 2.02.201 P
fled | into this abbey, whither we pursu'd them, ERR 5.01.155
had we pursu'd that life, | and our weak spirits WT 1.02. 71
our bending author hath pursu'd the story, | in H5 ep 2
while we pursu'd the horsemen of the north, | he 3H6 1.01. 2
or lambs pursu'd by hunger–starved wolves. 1.04. 5
where eagerly his sickness | pursu'd him still, H8 4.02. 25
would i might never | o'ertake pursu'd success, ANT 5.02.103
tells me | she hath pursu'd conclusions infinite 5.02.355
so the revenge alone pursu'd me. CYM 4.02.157

/PURSUE 1 FR 0.0001 REL FR 0 V 1 P
/will /they /pursue /the /quality /no /longer HAM 2.02.346 P

PURSUE 36 FR 0.0040 REL FR 32 V 4 P
clap on more sails, pursue; WIV 2.02.136
conscience, pursue him with any further revenge? 4.02.208 P
our natures do pursue, | like rats that ravin MM 1.02.128
that with such vehemency he should pursue 5.01.109
place the sharp athenian law | cannot pursue us. MND 1.01.163
the wood will he to–morrow night | pursue her; 1.01.248
she shall pursue it with the soul of love. 2.01.182
therefore pursue me not. 2.01.188
i pray thee pursue sentence. MV 4.01.298
bush, | and then pursue me as you draw your bow. SHR 5.02. 47
you make us friends, i will pursue the amity. AWW 2.05. 14 P
fell and cruel hounds, | e'er since pursue me. TN 1.01. 22
nay, pursue him now, lest the device take air 3.04.131 P
niece that i cannot pursue with any safety this 4.02. 70 P
pursue him, and entreat him to a peace; 5.01.380
strike up our drums, pursue the scatt'red stray; 2H4 4.02.120
let us pursue him ere the writs go forth. 2H6 5.03. 26
ah, hark, the fatal followers do pursue, | and i 3H6 1.04. 22
some troops pursue the bloody–minded queen, 2.06. 33
hath a thousand sons | that one by one pursue. TRO 3.03.157
the edge of all extremity | pursue each other, 4.05. 69
and dear petition, | pursue we him on knees; 5.03. 10
shame | pursue thy life, and live aye with thy 5.10. 34
pursue him to his house and pluck him thence, COR 3.01.307
/than ling'ring languishment | must we pursue, TIT 2.01.111
both here and hence pursue me lasting strife, HAM 3.02.222
pursue him, ho! go after. by no means what? LR 2.01. 43
comes too short | which can pursue th' offender. 2.01. 89
myself the crying fellow did pursue, | lest by OTH 2.03.230
edge to edge | a' th' world, i would pursue it. ANT 2.02.116
fortune pursue thee! 3.12. 25
i will pursue her | even to augustus' throne. CYM 3.05.100
peace be to you | as i pursue this war! TNK 1.03. 25
no; but unjust | if thou pursue that sight. 2.02.193
pursue these fearful creatures o'er the downs, VEN 677
ear, | to hearken if his foes pursue him still. 699

PURSUED 4 FR 0.0004 REL FR 4 V 0 P
weary self, | pursued my humor not pursuing his, ROM 1.01.129
can vengeance be pursued further than death? 5.03. 55
hath your noble father slain | pursued my life. HAM 4.07. 5
is he pursued? LR 2.01.109

PURSUERS 2 FR 0.0002 REL FR 2 V 0 P
he was so bruis'd | that the pursuers took him. 1H4 5.05. 22
keep, | to stop the loud pursuers in their yell, VEN 688

PURSUES 9 FR 0.0010 REL FR 9 V 0 P
like a shadow flies when substance love pursues, WIV 2.02.207
that that flies, and flying what pursues." 2.02.208
nay, but hear me, | your sense pursues not mine. MM 2.04. 74
the dove pursues the griffin; MND 2.01.232
speed, | when cowardice pursues and valor flies. 2.01.234
i wot your love pursues | a banish'd traitor. R2 2.03. 59
to fly the boar before the boar pursues | were R3 3.02. 28
but, howsomever thou pursues this act, | taint HAM 1.05. 84
they fright him, yet he still pursues his fear. LUC 308

PURSUEST 2 FR 0.0002 REL FR 2 V 0 P
go, | and find not her whom thou pursuest. CYM 3.05.160
else, if thou pursuest her, | be as that cursed TNK 2.02.198

PURSUING 4 FR 0.0004 REL FR 4 V 0 P
pursuing that that flies, and flying what WIV 2.02.208
than boys pursuing summer butterflies, | or COR 4.06. 94
weary self, | pursued my humor not pursuing his, ROM 1.01.129
possessing or pursuing no delight | save what is SON 75.11

PURSUIT 19 FR 0.0021 REL FR 19 V 0 P
slow in pursuit; MND 4.01.123
way | to hide us from pursuit that will be made AYL 1.03.136
and yet she writes, | pursuit would be but vain. AWW 3.04. 25
arguments of fear, | set forth in your pursuit. TN 3.03. 13
now, have you left pursuit? 2H4 4.03. 71
turn head, and stop pursuit; H5 2.04. 69
here sound retreat, and cease our hot pursuit. 1H6 2.02. 3
from clifford's and northumberland's pursuit. 3H6 2.01. 3
oft have i heard his praises in pursuit, | but 2.01.149
and weak we are and cannot shun pursuit. 2.03. 13
for death doth hold us in pursuit. 2.05.127
and make pursuit where he did mean no chase. R3 3.02. 30
what he hath done, | nor faint in the pursuit. TRO 2.02.142
for thy life | with all my force, pursuit, and 4.01. 19
haply so long until | the follow'd make pursuit? TNK 1.02. 52
make slow pursuit, or altogether balk | the prey LUC 696
with swift pursuit to venge this wrong of mine, 1691
/mad in pursuit and in possession so, | had, SON 129. 9
in pursuit of the thing she would have stay; 143. 4

PURSUIVANT 2 FR 0.0002 REL FR 1 V 1 P
send for his master with a pursuivant presently. 2H6 1.03. 34 P
i now repent i told the pursuivant, | as too R3 3.04. 88

PURSUIVANT–AT–ARMS 1 FR 0.0001 REL FR 1 V 0 P
send out a pursuivant–at–arms | to stanley's R3 5.03. 59

PURSUIVANTS 2 FR 0.0002 REL FR 2 V 0 P
and these grey locks, the pursuivants of death, 1H6 2.05. 5
who holds his state at door 'mongst pursuivants, H8 5.02. 24

PURSY 2 FR 0.0002 REL FR 2 V 0 P
and pursy insolence shall break his wind | with TIM 5.04. 12
for in the fatness of these pursy times | virtue HAM 3.04.153

PURUS 1 FR 0.0001 REL FR 1 V 0 P
"integer vitae, scelerisque purus, | non eget TIT 4.02. 20

PURVEYOR 1 FR 0.0001 REL FR 1 V 0 P
heels, and had a purpose | to be his purveyor; MAC 1.06. 22

PUSH* *(also pish)*

PUSH* 25 FR 0.0028 REL FR 21 V 4 P
and made a push at chance and sufferance. ADO 5.01. 38
well, push him out of doors, | and let my AYL 3.01. 15
up to th' deed), doth push on this proceeding. WT 2.01.179
will you not push her out? 2.03. 74
i pray you do not push me, i'll be gone. 2.03.125
one that will either push on or pluck back thy 4.04.737 P
least they desire (upon this push) to trouble 5.03.129
again | to push destruction and perpetual shame JN 5.07. 77
and stand the push | of every beardless vain 1H4 3.02. 66
can make a head | to push against a kingdom, 4.01. 81
i stand the push of your one thing that you will 2H4 2.02. 37 P
time | did push it out of farther question. H5 1.01. 5
as manhood shall compound. push home. 2.01. 98
we may as well push against powle's as stir 'em. H8 5.03. 16
valor | to stand the push and enmity of those TRO 2.02.137
therefore i will push montague's men from the ROM 1.01. 17 P
push, did you see my cap? TIM 3.06.109 P
and sudden push gives them the overthrow. JC 5.02. 5
in ourselves | than tarry till they push us. 5.05. 25
on their crowns, | and push us from our stools. MAC 3.04. 81
this push | will cheer me ever, or /disseat me 5.03. 20
we'll put the matter to the present push. HAM 5.01.295
thou not /say, when i did push thee back — PER 5.01.126
i am in labor | to push your name, your ancient TNK 5.01. 26
to push grief on, and back the same grief draw. LUC 1673

PUSH'D 2 FR 0.0002 REL FR 1 V 1 P
when you have push'd out your gates the very COR 5.02. 39 P
backward she push'd him, as she would be thrust, VEN 41

PUSHES 2 FR 0.0002 REL FR 2 V 0 P
even pushes 'gainst our heart — the party tried WT 3.02. 2
what pushes are we wenches driven to | when TNK 2.04. 6

PUSH–PIN 1 FR 0.0001 REL FR 1 V 0 P
and nestor play at push–pin with the boys, | and LLL 4.03.167

PUSILLANIMITY 1 FR 0.0001 REL FR 0 V 1 P
is the badge of pusillanimity and cowardice; 2H4 4.03.105 P

/PUT 6 FR 0.0006 REL FR 4 V 2 P
/am /thus /bold /to /put /your /grace /in /mind R3 4.02.110
/athenian /bay | /put /forth /toward /phrygia, TRO pr 7
/the /bravery /of /his /grief /did /put /me HAM 5.02. 79
/put your bonnet to his right use, 'tis for the 5.02. 92 P
/put /in /his /legs. LR 2.02.150
/put /money /enough /in /your /purse. OTH 1.03.380 P

PUT 519 FR 0.0586 REL FR 367 V 152 P
you have | put the wild waters in this roar, TMP 1.02. 2
lov'd, and to him put | the manage of my state, 1.02. 69
the strangeness of your story put | heaviness in 1.02.306
and hast put thyself | upon this island as a spy 1.02.455
put thy sword up, traitor, | who mak'st a show 1.02.470
as fresh as when we put them on first in afric, 2.01. 70 P
'twere a kibe, | 'twould put me to my slipper; 2.01.277
to the perpetual wink for aye might put | this 2.01.285
do you put tricks upon 's with salvages and men 2.02. 58 P
grace she ow'd, | and put it to the foil. 3.01. 46
even here i will put off my hope, and keep it 3.03. 7
your rye–straw hats put on, | and these fresh 4.01.136
put off that gown, trinculo. 4.01.227 P
monster, come put some lime upon your fingers, 4.01.245 P
rigg'd as when | we first put out to sea. 5.01.225
put forth their sons to seek preferment out: TGV 1.03. 7
being in love, cannot see to put on your hose. 2.01. 77 P
and thy advice this night i'll put in practice: 3.02. 88
such pearls as put out ladies' eyes, | for i had 5.02. 13
but i'll ne'er put my finger in the fire, and WIV 1.04. 85 P
puts into the press, when he would put us two. 2.01. 79 P
yet i cannot put off my opinion so easily. 2.01.234 P
and has threat'ned to put me into everlasting 3.03. 30 P
go fetch me a quart of sack — put a toast in't. 3.05. 3 P
shall i put him into the basket again? 4.02. 47 P
otherwise he might put on a hat, a muffler, and 4.02. 71 P
put on the gown the while. 4.02. 83 P
since i am put to know that your own science MM 1.01. 5
they put forth to steal. 1.02. 14 P
too, but that a wise burgher put in for them. 1.02.100 P
they do you wrong to put you so oft upon't. 2.01.266 P
why do you put these sayings upon me? 2.02.133
penitence, if it be sound, | or hollowly put on. 2.03. 23
true made | as to put metal in restrained means 2.04. 48
of two usuries, the merriest was put down, and 3.02. 6 P
friar, till eating and drinking be put down. 3.02.103 P
and his use was to put a ducat in her clack–dish 3.02.126 P
put not yourself into amazement how these things 4.02.204 P
be so good, sir, to rise and be put to death. 4.03. 27 P
put them in secret holds, both barnardine and 4.03. 87
and put your trial in the villain's mouth 5.01.302
a fool, | to put the finger in the eye and weep, ERR 2.02.204
i know not what use to put her to but to make a 3.02. 96 P
if any bark put forth, come to the mart, | where 3.02.150
if any ship put out, then straight away. 3.02.185
that the bark expedition put forth to–night, and 4.03. 38 P
that you would put me to this shame and trouble, 5.01. 14
had hoisted sail and put to sea to–day. 5.01. 21
who put unluckily into this bay | against the 5.01.125
yea, and a case to put it into. ADO 1.01.182 P
in practice let us put it presently. 1.01.328
you have put him down, lady, you have put him 2.01.283 P
have put him down, lady, you have put him down. 2.01.284 P
adverse issue it can, i will put it in practice. 2.02. 52 P
to put a strange face on his own perfection. 2.03. 47
their detractions and can put them to mending. 2.03.230 P
margaret, you must put in the pikes with a vice, 5.02. 20 P
good morrow, masters, put your torches out. 5.03. 24
come let us hence, and put on other weeds, | and 5.03. 30
park, which, put together, is in manner and form LLL 1.01.208 P
to put in practice that | which each to other 1.01.306
and how easy it is to put "years" to the word 1.02. 52 P
sweet, put up this — 'twill be thine another 4.01.107
why, she that bears the bow. | finely put off! 4.01.110
finely put on! 4.01.113
finely put on indeed! 4.01.116
lord, how the ladies and i have put him down! 4.01.141
put l to sore, then sorel jumps from thicket, 4.02. 58
daughters be capable, i will put it to them: 4.02. 80 P
i could put thee in comfort: 4.03. 50
a doubt | presence majestical would put him out; 5.02.102
heart, | that put armado's page out of his part! 5.02.336
you put our page out. 5.02.478
but we will put it, as they say, to fortuna de 5.02.530 P
i will not be put out of countenance. 5.02.607 P
forward, for we have put thee in countenance. 5.02.619 P
you have put me out of countenance. 5.02.621 P
presence of loose love | put on by us, if, in 5.02.767
i'll put a girdle round about the earth | in MND 2.01.175
this will put them out of fear. 3.01. 21 P
your vows to her and me, put in two scales, 3.02.132
the man should be put into the lanthorn. 5.01.247 P
letters deliver'd, put the liveries to making, MV 2.02.116 P
if i do not put on a sober habit, | talk with 2.02.190
i would entreat you rather to put on | your 2.02.201
turning his face, he put his hand behind him, 2.08. 47
the seeming truth which cunning times put on 3.02.100
and when she put it on, she made me vow | that i 4.01.442
or four loving lords have put themselves into AYL 1.01.101 P
which he will put on us, as pigeons feed their 1.02. 93 P
i'll put myself in poor and mean attire, | and 1.03.111
and therefore put i on the countenance | of 2.07.108
so you may put a man in your belly. 3.02.204 P
upon a foul slut were to put good meat into an 3.03. 36 P
open his lips when he put it into his mouth, 5.01. 34 P
therefore put you in your best array, bid your 5.02. 71 P
man doubt that, let him put me to my purgation. 5.04. 43 P
his brother here, and put him to the sword; 5.04.158
the duke hath put on a religious life, | and 5.04.181
in sweet clothes, rings put upon his fingers, SHR in.1. 38
ashore, | we could at once put us in readiness, 1.01. 43
it is best | put finger in the eye, and she knew 1.01. 79
on, | and i for my escape have put on his; 1.01.230
a herald, kate? o, put me in thy books! 2.01.224
go to my chamber, put on clothes of mine. 3.02.113
to put on better ere he go to church. 3.02.126
well, petruchio, this has put me in heart. 4.05. 77
a hundred marks, my kate does put her down. 5.02. 35
that had put such difference betwixt their two AWW 1.03.111 P
and put you in the catalogue of those | that 1.03.143
sir, i shall now put you to the height of your 2.02. 1 P
when you put off that with such contempt? 2.02. 6 P
any manners, he may easily put it off at court. 2.02. 9 P
he that cannot make a leg, put off 's cap, kiss 2.02. 10 P
o lord, sir! — nay, put me to't, i warrant you. 2.02. 48 P
day, | great mars, i put myself into thy file; 3.03. 9
nay, good my lord, put him to't; 3.06. 1 P
put myself into my mortal preparation; 3.06. 76 P
and would not put my reputation now | in any 3.07. 6
i must put you into a butter–woman's mouth and 4.01. 41 P
and on your finger in the night i'll put 4.02. 61
i pray you, sir, put it up again. 4.03.216 P
if i put any tricks upon 'em, sir, they shall be 4.05. 60 P
by, i put you to | the use of your own virtues, 5.01. 15
dost thou put upon me at once both the office of 5.02. 48 P
that she would never put it from her finger, 5.03.109
i'll put in bail, my liege. 5.03.285
when did i see thee so put down? TN 1.03. 81 P
i think, unless you see canary put me down. 1.03. 83 P
and't be thy will, put me into good fooling! 1.05. 32 P
i saw him put down the other day with an 1.05. 84 P
that you should put your lord into a desperate 2.02. 7 P
i would have men of such constancy put to sea, 2.04. 76 P
put thyself into the trick of singularity. 2.05.151 P
why, thou hast put him in such a dream, that 2.05.193 P
yes, being kept together and put to use. 3.01. 50 P
taste your legs, sir, put them to motion. 3.01. 78 P
your dormouse valor, to put fire in your heart, 3.02. 20 P
put thyself into the trick of singularity"; 3.04. 70 P
some kind of men that put quarrels purposely on 3.04.243 P
put up your sword. 3.04.312
pray, sir, put your sword up, if you please. 3.04.321 P
come, my young soldier, put up your iron; 4.01. 39 P
nay, i prithee put on this gown and this beard, 4.02. 1 P

well, i'll put it on, and i will dissemble 4.02. 4 P
put your grace in your pocket, sir, for this 5.01. 32 P
saint bennet, sir, may put you in mind — one, 5.01. 39 P
but in conclusion put strange speech upon me. 5.01. 67
though you have put me into darkness, and given 5.01.303 P
that induc'd me to the semblance i put on; 5.01.307 P
to put on yellow stockings and to frown | upon 5.01.338
to make us say, | "this is put forth too truly." WT 1.02. 14
tougher, brother, | than you can put us to't. 1.02. 16
you put me off with limber vows; 1.02. 47
this entertainment | may a free face put on, 1.02.112
myself, i'll put | my fortunes to your service, 1.02.439
to put apart these your attendants, i | shall 2.02. 13
that forced baseness | which he has put upon't! 2.03. 80
put on thee by my lord, thou ne'er shalt see 3.03. 35
and you shall help to put him i' th' ground. 3.03.136 P
me, and these detestable things put upon me. 4.03. 62 P
that's the rogue that put me into this apparel. 4.03.104 P
unroll'd, and my name put in the book of virtue! 4.03.122 P
i'll not put | the dibble in earth to set one 4.04. 99
to fear as i have purpose | to put you to't. 4.04.153
i have put you out. 4.04.367
some hangman must put on my shroud and lay me 4.04.457
i am put to sea | with her who here i cannot 4.04.498
eternity and could put breath into his work, 5.02. 98 P
that e'er i put between your holy looks | my ill 5.03.148
and put the same into young arthur's hand, | thy JN 1.01. 14
i put you o'er to heaven and to my mother. 1.01. 62
your just demands, | hath put himself in arms. 2.01. 57
down our just–borne arms | we'll put thee down, 2.01.346
and put my eyeballs in thy vaulty brows, | and 3.04. 30
will you put out mine eyes, | these eyes that 4.01. 56
and told me hubert should put out mine eyes, | i 4.01. 69
you, | what ever torment you do put me to. 4.01. 83
your sword is bright, sir, put it up again. 4.03. 79
put up thy sword betime, | or i'll so maul you 4.03. 98
thyself, | put but a little water in a spoon, 4.03.131
grow great by your example and put on | the 5.01. 52
put spirit in the french; 5.04. 2
and put his cause and quarrel | to the disposing 5.07. 91
and happily may your sweet self put on | the 5.07.101
put we our quarrel to the will of heaven, | who, R2 1.02. 6
put into his hands | that knows no touch to tune 1.03.164
now put it, god, in the physician's mind | to 1.04. 59
to the traitor lives, the true man's put to death. 5.03. 73
lament, | and put on sullen black incontinent. 5.06. 48
to put down richard, that sweet lovely rose, 1H4 1.03.175
cut's saddle, put a few flocks in the point. 2.01. 5 P
mark now how a plain tale shall put you down. 2.04.255 P
enough | to put him quite besides his patience. 3.01.177
where hateful death put on his ugliest mask | to 2H4 1.01. 66
come, we will all put forth, body and goods. 1.01.186
if the prince put thee into my service for any 1.02. 12 P
had as live they would put ratsbane in my mouth 1.02. 42 P
he hath put all my substance into that fat belly 2.01. 75 P
i put thee now to thy book–oath. 2.01.103 P
put on two leathern jerkins and aprons, and wait 2.02.171 P
put not you on the visage of the times, | and be 2.03. 3
and they will put on two of our jerkins and 2.04. 16 P
alas, put up your naked weapons, put up your 2.04.206 P
your naked weapons, put up your naked weapons. 2.04.207 P
i cannot put him to a private soldier that is 3.02.166 P
put me a caliver into wart's hand, bardolph. 3.02.270 P
now) | hath put us in these ill–beseeming arms, 4.01. 84
and put the world's whole strength | into one 4.05. 44
royal liege, | accusing it, i put it on my head, 4.05.165
god put /it in thy mind to take it hence, | that 4.05.178
appears | that i will deeply put the fashion on 5.02. 52
put into parts, doth keep in one consent, H5 1.02.181
i may, and to put forth | my rightful hand in a 1.02.292
nym, show thy valor, and put up your sword. 2.01. 44 P
good bardolph, put thy face between his sheets, 2.01. 83 P
prithee put up. 2.01.104 P
i put my hand into the bed and felt them, and 2.03. 23 P
take from another's pocket to put into mine; 3.02. 50 P
our scions, put in wild and savage stock, 3.05. 7
use his good pleasure, and put him to execution; 3.06. 55 P
and crowns for convoy put into his purse. 4.03. 37
our fertile france, put up her lovely visage? 5.02. 37
with hair, | put forth disorder'd twigs; 5.02. 44
marry, if you would put me to verses, or to 5.02.132 P
put off your maiden blushes, avouch the thoughts 5.02.234 P
queen, | to put a golden sceptre in thy hand, 1H6 5.03.118
put forth thy hand, reach at the glorious gold. 2H6 1.02. 11
had not your man put up the fowl so suddenly, 2.01. 44
and, had i first been put to speak my mind, | i 3.01. 43
are up | and put the englishmen unto the sword. 3.01.284
you put sharp weapons in a madman's hands. 3.01.347
be, | and henry put apart, the next for me. 3.01.383
the elder of them, being put to nurse, | was by 4.02.142
until a power be rais'd to put them down. 4.04. 40
moreover, thou hast put them in prison, and 4.07. 43 P
to seek to put me down and reign thyself. 3H6 1.01.200
to blot out me, and put his own son in. 2.02. 92
in hewing rutland when his leaves put forth, 2.06. 48
our treasure seiz'd, our soldiers put to flight, 3.03. 36
did i put henry from his native right? 3.03.190
laid aside, | and i am ready to put armor on. 3.03.230
are done, | and i am ready to put armor on." 4.01.105
well, well, put up your sword. R3 1.02.196
is put unto the trust of richard gloucester, | a 1.03. 12
let me put in your minds, if you forget, | what 1.03.130
of you | had so much grace to put it in my mind. 2.01.121
god bless thee, and put meekness in thy breast, 2.02.107
it should be put | to no apparent likelihood of 2.02.135
clouds are seen, wise men put on their cloaks; 2.03. 32
this day those enemies are put to death, | and i 3.02.103
tell them how edward put to death a citizen 3.05. 76
these both put off, a poor petitioner, | a 3.07.183
unless thou couldst put on some other shape 4.04.286
put in her tender heart th' aspiring flame | of 4.04.328
and put thy fortune to the arbitrement | of 5.03. 89
put in their hands thy bruising irons of wrath, 5.03.110
if you do sweat to put a tyrant down, | you 5.03.255
to them 'longing, have put off | the spinsters, H8 1.02. 32
i put it to your care. 1.02.102
hath into monstrous habits put the graces | that 1.02.122
his duty) would | have put his knife into him." 1.02.199

and with some other business put the king | from 2.02. 56
that thus you should proceed to put me off, 2.04. 21
by some of these | the queen is put in anger. 2.04.162
put your main cause into the king's protection, 3.01. 93
put my sick cause into his hands that hates me? 3.01.118
a noble spirit | as yours was put into you, ever 3.01.170
there (on my conscience, put unwittingly)? 3.02.123
some spirit put this paper in the packet, | to 3.02.129
made me put this main secret in the packet | i 3.02.215
now, | while 'tis hot, i'll put it to the issue. 5.01.176
when we first put this dangerous stone a–rolling 5.02.139
and in my vambrace put my withered brawns, | and TRO 1.03.297
i know not, 'tis put to lott'ry. 2.01.128
you draw backward, we'll put you i' th' fills. 3.02. 45 P
and put on | a form of strangeness as we pass 3.03. 50
i will put on his presence, let patroclus make 3.03.270 P
tullus aufidius, that will put you to't. COR 1.01.229
now put your shields before your hearts, and 1.04. 24
'gainst yourself you be incens'd, we'll put you 1.09. 56
nor on him put | the napless vesture of humility 2.01.233
than have him hold that purpose and to put it 2.01.240
if he be put upon't, and that's as easy | as to 2.01.256
for i cannot | put on the gown, stand naked, and 2.02.137
put them not to't. 2.02.141
we are to put our tongues into those wounds and 2.03. 6 P
this mutiny were better put in hazard | than 2.03.256
shall it be put to that? 3.01.232
put not your worthy rage into your tongue; 3.01.240
i would have had you put your power well on 3.02. 17
for the whole state, i would put mine armor on, 3.02. 34
which else would put you to your fortune and 3.02. 60
you have put me now to such a part which never 3.02.105
put him to choler straight, he hath been us'd 3.03. 25
we need not put new matter to his charge. 3.03. 76
there is a slave, whom we have put in prison, 4.06. 38
will you be put in mind of his blind fortune, 5.06.117
masters all, be quiet, | put up your swords. 5.06.134
be candidatus then and put it on, | and help to TIT 1.01.185
openly, | and basely put it up without revenge? 1.01.433
for shame, put up. 2.01. 53
put up your swords, you know not what you do. ROM 1.01. 65
put up thy sword, | or manage it to part these 1.01. 68
give me a case to put my visage in, | a visor 1.04. 29
show a fair presence and put off these frowns, 1.05. 73
gentle mercutio, put thy rapier up. 3.01. 84
let me be ta'en, let me be put to death, | i am 3.05. 17
one who, to put thee from thy heaviness, | hath 3.05.108
herself alone, | may be put from her by society. 4.01. 14
faith, we may put up our pipes and be gone. 4.05. 96 P
honest good fellows, ah, put up, put up, | for 4.05. 98
honest good fellows, ah, put up, put up, | for 4.05. 98
pray you put up your dagger, and put out your 4.05.121 P
you put up your dagger, and put out your wit. 4.05.121 P
you with an iron wit, and put up my iron dagger. 4.05.124 P
put this in any liquid thing you will | and 5.01. 77
yet put it off, for i would not be seen. 5.03. 2
thee, youth, | put not another sin upon my head, 5.03. 62
his land's put to their books. TIM 1.02.200
would i were gently put out of office | before i 1.02.201
you gone, | put on a most importunate aspect, 2.01. 28
he hath put me off | to the succession of new 2.02. 19
you took, | when my indisposition put you back, 2.02.130
me, | i would have put my wealth into donation, 3.02. 83
than he that has no house to put his head in? 3.04. 64 P
put in now, titus. 3.04. 84 P
they have e'en put my breath from me, the slaves 3.04.103
many my near occasions did urge me to put off; 3.06. 11 P
nay, put out all your hands. 4.02. 28
put up thy gold. 4.03.108
put armor on thine ears and on thine eyes, 4.03.124
chamberlain, | will put thy shirt on warm? 4.03.223
if thou didst put this sour cold habit on | to 4.03.239
who in spite put stuff | to some she–beggar and 4.03.272
the common wrack, | as common bruit doth put it. 5.01.193
and do you now put on your best attire? JC 1.01. 48
he put it by with the back of his hand thus, and 1.02.222 P
was't, and he put it by thrice, every time 1.02.229 P
and, as i told you, he put it by once; 1.02.239 P
then he put it by again; 1.02.241 P
he put it the third time by; 1.02.243 P
scarfs off caesar's images, are put to silence. 1.02.286 P
besides — i ha' not since put up my sword — 1.03. 19
and put on fear, and cast yourself in wonder, 1.03. 60
and then i grant we put a sting in him | that at 2.01. 16
let not our looks put on our purposes, | but 2.01.225
remember | the first time ever caesar put it on; 3.02.171
and put a tongue | in every wound of caesar, 3.02.228
lepidus | have put to death an hundred senators. 4.03.175
i put it in the pocket of my gown. 4.03.253
they | put on my brows this wreath of victory, 5.03. 82
and you shall put | this night's great business MAC 1.05. 67
what not put upon | his spungy officers, who 1.07. 70
let's briefly put on manly readiness, | and meet 2.03.133
when first they put the name of king upon me, 3.01. 57
crown, | and put a barren sceptre in my gripe, 3.01. 61
put rancors in the vessel of my peace | only for 3.01. 66
and i will put that business in your bosoms, 3.01.103
in a ring, | enchanting all that you put in. 4.01. 43
then, alas, | do i put up that womanly defense, 4.02. 78
for even now | i put myself to thy direction, 4.03.122
put on with holy prayers, and 'tis spoken, | to 4.03.154
and the pow'rs above | put on their instruments. 4.03.239
wash your hands, put on your night–gown, look 5.01. 62 P
i'll put it on. 5.03. 34
come, put mine armor on; 5.03. 48
event, and put we on | industrious soldiership. 5.04. 15
if it be so — as so 'tis put on me, | and that HAM 1.03. 94
think meet | to put an antic disposition on — 1.05.172
and there put on him | what forgeries you please 2.01. 19
you must not put another scandal on him, | that 2.01. 29
death, that thus hath put him | so much from th' 2.02. 8
us, | put your dread pleasures more into command 2.02. 28
at my beck than i have thoughts to put them in, 3.01.125 P
for me to put him to his purgation would perhaps 3.02.305 P
my lord, put your discourse into some frame, and 3.02.308 P
for we will fetters put about this fear, | which 3.03. 25
diadem stole, | and put it in his pocket — 3.04.101

gives a frock or livery, | that aptly is put on. 3.04.165
yet must not we put the strong law on him. 4.03. 3
too slow of sail, we put on a compell'd valor, 4.06. 18 P
and you must put me in your heart for friend, 4.07. 2
we'll put on those shall praise your excellence, 4.07.131
i'll put another question to thee. 5.01. 37 P
we'll put the matter to the present push. 5.01.295
he should those bearers put to sudden death, 5.02. 46
of deaths put on by cunning and /forc'd cause, 5.02.383
stage, | for he was likely, had he been put on, 5.02.397
why so earnestly seek you to put up that letter? LR 1.02. 28
put on what weary negligence you please, | you 1.03. 12
to serve him truly that will put me in trust, to 1.04. 14 P
that you protect this course and put it on | by 1.04.208
and put away | these dispositions which of late 1.04.220
why, to put 's head in, not to give it away to 1.05. 30 P
'tis they have put him on the old man's death, 2.01. 99
and put upon him such a deal of man | that 2.02.120
to the eels when she put 'em i' th' paste alive; 2.04.123 P
who put my man i' th' stocks? 2.04.182
'tis his own blame hath put himself from rest, 2.04.290
he that has a house to put 's head in has a good 3.02. 25 P
going to put out | the other eye of gloucester. 4.02. 71
thy friendly hand | put strength enough to't. 4.06.231
i prithee put them off. 4.07. 8
of sleep | we put fresh garments on him. 4.07. 21
for shame, put on your gown; OTH 1.01. 86
or put upon you what restraint or grievance 1.02. 15
condition | put into circumscription and confine 1.02. 27
to put my father in impatient thoughts | by 1.03.242
put money in thy purse; 1.03.339 P
i say put money in thy purse. 1.03.341 P
love to the moor — put money in thy purse — 1.03.343 P
sequestration — put but money in thy purse. 1.03.345 P
therefore put money in thy purse. 1.03.352 P
the ship is here put in. 2.01. 25
who has put in? 2.01. 65
o gentle lady, do not put me to't, | for i am 2.01.118
did justly put on the vouch of very malice 2.01.146 P
so, yet that i put the moor | at least into a 2.01.300
fleet, every man put himself into triumph; 2.02. 4 P
am i to put our cassio in some action | that may 2.03. 60
were well | the general were put in mind of it. 2.03.132
christian shame, put by this barbarous brawl. 2.03.172
that men should put an enemy in their mouths to 2.03.290 P
importune her help to put you in your place 2.03.319 P
when devils will the blackest sins put on, 2.03.351
then put up your pipes in your bag, for i'll 3.01. 19 P
i do repent me that i put it to you. 3.03.392
and will upon the instant put thee to't: 3.03.471
it were enough | to put him to ill thinking. 3.04. 29
this is a trick to put me from my suit. 3.04. 87
if any wretch have put this in your head, | let 4.02. 15
and put in every honest hand a whip | to lash 4.02.142
nor am i yet persuaded to put up in peace what 4.02.179 P
you shall think yourself bound to put it on him. 4.02.241 P
wear thy good rapier bare, and put it home. 5.01. 2
put out the light, and then put out the light: 5.02. 7
put out the light, and then put out the light: 5.02. 7
but once put out thy light, | thou cunning'st 5.02. 10
yet, ere we put ourselves in arms, dispatch we ANT 2.02.165
then put my tires and mantles on him, whilst | i 2.05. 22
but mark antony | put me to some impatience. 2.06. 42
and, when we are put off, fall to their throats: 2.07. 72
chariots, and | put garlands on thy head. 3.01. 11
antony, | and put yourself under his shroud, 3.13. 71
come, good fellow, put thine iron on. 4.04. 3
go, put on thy defenses. 4.04. 10
sea is given, | they have put forth the haven — 4.10. 7
put color in thy cheek. 4.14. 69
die, | not cowardly put off my helmet to | my 4.15. 56
and put your children | to that destruction 5.02.131
acknowledg'd, | put we i' th' roll of conquest. 5.02.181
go put it to the haste. 5.02.196
give me my robe, put on my crown, i have 5.02.280
had been pity you should have been put together, CYM 1.04. 40 P
yes, to be put to the arbiterment of swords, and 1.04. 49 P
would i had put my estate and my neighbor's on 1.04.123 P
winning will put any man into courage. 2.03. 7 P
you put me to forget a lady's manners | by being 2.03.105
with a blanket, or put the moon in his pocket, 3.01. 43 P
all color here | did put the yoke upon 's; 3.01. 51
who was the first of britain which did put | his 3.01. 59
put thyself | into a havior of less fear, ere 3.04. 8
husband, shall be thought | put on for villainy; 3.04. 56
and /make me put into contempt the suits | of 3.04. 89
fortune put them into my hand! 4.01. 23 P
seek us through | and put us to our answer. 4.02.161
and put | my clouted brogues from off my feet, 4.02.213
the want is but to put those pow'rs in motion 4.03. 31
my faults, i never | had liv'd to put on this; 5.01. 9
gods, put the strength o' th' leonati in me! 5.01. 31
you have put me into rhyme. 5.03. 63
and then a mind put in't, either our brags 5.05.176
those arts they have as i | could put into them. 5.05.339
sin, | ay, and the targets to put off the shame; PER 1.01.140
he, doing so, put forth to seas, | where when 2.ch. 27
come put it on, keep thee warm. 2.01. 79 P
if put upon you, make the judgment good | that 4.06. 93
in your supposing once more put your sight: 5.ch. 21
sir, there is a barge put off from meteline, 5.01. 3
sir, | give me a gash, put me to present pain, 5.01.191
some god hath put his mercy in your manhood, TNK 1.01. 72
when our friends don their helms, or put to sea, 1.03. 19
that i would pluck | and put between my breasts 1.03. 67
two souls | put in two noble bodies, let 'em 2.02. 65
put but thy head out of this window more, | and, 2.02.212
put my head out? 2.02.215
ay, do but put | a fescue in her fist, and you 2.03. 33
like a nightingale, | to put my breast against! 3.04. 26
i have put you | to too much pains, sir. 3.06. 17
nor put off | this great adventure to a second 3.06.118
put thyself | upon thy present guard — 3.06.121
and there shall we be put in a cauldron of lead 4.03. 36 P
let us put it in execution; 4.03.100 P
force and great feat | must put my garland on, 5.01. 44
'twas thy power | to put life into dust: 5.01.110
if't pleas'd his rider | to put pride in him. 5.04. 58

the visages of bridegrooms we'll put on | and 5.04.127
you'll put down strangers, | kill them, cut STM II.C 119
who plucks the bud before one leaf put forth? VEN 416
but gold that's put to use more gold begets." 768
"and therefore would he put his bonnet on, 1087
put fear to valor, courage to the coward. 1158
hast thou put on his shape to do him shame? LUC 597
coming from thee, i could not put him back, 843
to put in practice either, alas, it was a spite PP 15. 7
slack | to proffer, though she put thee back. 18.24
it be day, | that which with scorn she put away. 18.30
who with his fear is put besides his part, | or SON 23. 2
for that same groan doth put this in my mind: 50.13
hath put a spirit of youth in every thing, 98. 3
for since each hand hath put on nature's power, 127. 5
have put on black, and loving mourners be, 132. 3
is not, | to put fair truth upon so foul a face? 137.12
what eyes hath love put in my head, | which have 148. 1
to serve their eyes, and in it put their mind, LC 135
content, | to put the by–past perils in her way? 158
or my affection put to th' smallest teen, | or 192
religious love put out religion's eye. 250

PUTREFIED 2 FR 0.0002 REL FR 2 V 0 P
most putrefied core, so fair without, | thy TRO 5.08. 1
abide, | blushing at that which is so putrefied. LUC 1750

PUTREFY 1 FR 0.0001 REL FR 1 V 0 P
they would but stink, and putrefy the air. 1H6 4.07. 90

/PUTS 1 FR 0.0001 REL FR 1 V 0 P
he /puts on sackcloth, and to sea. PER 4.04. 29

PUTS 49 FR 0.0055 REL FR 41 V 8 P
for he cares not what he puts into the press, WIV 2.01. 78 P
a name | now puts the drowsy and neglected act MM 1.02.170
he puts transgression to't. 3.02. 95 P
is there any ships puts forth to–night? ERR 4.03. 35 P
of beatrice that puts the world into her person, ADO 2.01.208 P
loud, | puts the wretch that lies in woe | in MND 5.01.377
the scarfed bark puts from her native bay, MV 2.06. 15
puts bars between the owners and their rights! 3.02. 19
then she puts you to entreaty, and there begins AYL 4.01. 79 P
life, | puts my apparel and my count'nance on, SHR 1.01.229
but puts it off to a compell'd restraint; AWW 2.04. 43
me and as mine honesty puts it to utterance. WT 1.01. 20 P
doings of the world, | sometime puts forth. 1.02.254
as rank as any flax–wench that puts to | before 1.02.277
a sickness | which puts some of us in distemper, 1.02.385
no harm, good man" — puts him off, slights him, 4.04.199 P
puts on his pretty looks, repeats his words, JN 3.04. 95
stuff | as puts me from my faith. 1H4 3.01.153
but peace puts forth her olive every where. 2H4 4.04. 87
head, | for york in justice puts his armor on. 3H6 2.02.130
in him stuff that puts him to these ends; H8 1.01. 58
whose figure even this instant cloud puts on 1.01.225
to–day he puts forth | the tender leaves of 3.02.352
she came and puts me her white hand to his TRO 1.02.119 P
agamemnon, | thy topless deputation he puts on, 1.03.152
here tend the savage strangeness he puts on, 2.03.126
his back, | wherein he puts alms for oblivion, 3.03.146
where injury of chance | puts back leave–taking, 4.04. 34
mutiners, | your valor puts well forth; COR 1.01.251
and such a one as he, who puts his "shall," 3.01.105
for it is you that puts us to our shifts. TIT 4.02.176
a while, | for nature puts me to a heavy task. 5.03.150
being black, puts us in mind they hide the fair. ROM 1.01.231
your steward puts me off, my lord, | and i am TIM 2.02. 31
that puts odds | among the rout of nations, i 4.03. 43
however he puts on this tardy form. JC 1.02.299
which puts upon them | suspicion of the deed. MAC 2.04. 26
the very place puts toys of desperation, HAM 1.04. 75
get from him why he puts on this confusion, 3.01. 2
whereon his brains still beating puts him thus 3.01.174
she puts her tongue a little in her heart, | and OTH 2.01.106
i fear the trust othello puts him in, | on some 2.03.126
puts to him all the learnings that his time CYM 1.01. 43
and puts himself in posture | that acts my words 3.03. 94
so puts himself unto the shipman's toil, | with PER 1.03. 23
almost puts | faith in a fever, and deifies TNK 1.02. 65
she puts on outward strangeness, seems unkind: VEN 310
she puts the period often from his place, | and LUC 565
and puts apparel on my tottered loving, | to SON 26.11

PUT'ST 3 FR 0.0003 REL FR 2 V 1 P
petitioners for blood thou ne'er put'st back. 3H6 5.05. 80
the rod, and put'st down thine own breeches, LR 1.04.174 P
thou usurer, that put'st forth all to use, | and SON 134.10

PUT'T 1 FR 0.0001 REL FR 1 V 0 P
i'll put't in proof, | and when i have stol'n LR 4.06.185

PUTTER *(also butter)*

PUTTER 3 FR 0.0003 REL FR 0 V 3 P
seese is not good to give putter; WIV 5.05.140 P
your belly is all putter. 5.05.141 P
"seese" and "putter"! 5.05.142 P

PUTTER–ON 2 FR 0.0002 REL FR 2 V 0 P
and by some putter–on | that will be damn'd WT 2.01.141
most bitterly on you as putter–on | of these H8 1.02. 24

PUTTER–OUT 1 FR 0.0001 REL FR 1 V 0 P
each putter–out of five for one will bring us TMP 3.03. 48

PUTTING 17 FR 0.0019 REL FR 9 V 8 P
in the parliament for the putting down of men. WIV 2.01. 29 P
it now, | by putting on the destin'd livery. MM 2.04.138
had now, for putting the hand in the pocket and 3.02. 46 P
there's a simple putting off. AWW 2.02. 41 P
even with the swiftness of putting on. TN 2.05.172 P
for putting on so new a fashion'd robe. JN 4.02. 27
more sir johns, and, putting off his hat, said, 2H4 2.04. 6 P
else, putting all affairs else in oblivion, as 5.05. 26 P
of god, | putting it straight in expedition. H5 2.02.191
with the spirit of putting down kings and 2H6 4.02. 36 P
so putting him to rage, | you should have ta'en COR 2.03.197
(harp on that still) but by our putting on; 2.03.252
if he were putting to my house the brand | that 4.06.115
say, | "two may keep counsel, putting one away"? ROM 2.04.197
woods | by putting on the cunning of a carper. TIM 4.03.209
conscionable than in putting on the mere form of OTH 2.01.239 P
for his quick hunting, stand the putting on, 2.01.304

PUTTING–BY 1 FR 0.0001 REL FR 0 V 1 P
and at every putting–by mine honest neighbors JC 1.02.230 P

PUTTING–ON 1 FR 0.0001 REL FR 0 V 1 P
awakens me with this unwonted putting–on, MM 4.02.117 P

PUTTOCK 2 FR 0.0002 REL FR 1 V 1 P
an owl, a puttock, or a herring without a roe, i TRO 5.01. 62 P
i chose an eagle, | and did avoid a puttock. CYM 1.01.140

PUTTOCK'S 1 FR 0.0001 REL FR 1 V 0 P
who finds the partridge in the puttock's nest 2H6 3.02.191

PUZZEL 1 FR 0.0001 REL FR 1 V 0 P
pucelle or puzzel, dolphin or dogfish, | your 1H6 1.04.107

PUZZLE 1 FR 0.0001 REL FR 1 V 0 P
your presence needs must puzzle antony, | take ANT 3.07. 10

PUZZLED 1 FR 0.0001 REL FR 0 V 1 P
which thou art more puzzled than the egyptians TN 4.02. 43 P

PUZZLES 1 FR 0.0001 REL FR 1 V 0 P
bourn | no traveller returns, puzzles the will, HAM 3.01. 79

PYGMALION'S 1 FR 0.0001 REL FR 0 V 1 P
is there none of pygmalion's images newly made MM 3.02. 45 P

PYGMY *(see pigmies, pigmy)*

PY'R *(also by'r)*

PY'R 1 FR 0.0001 REL FR 0 V 1 P
yes, py'r lady. WIV 1.01. 28 P

PYRAMID 3 FR 0.0003 REL FR 3 V 0 P
o' th' nile | by certain scales i' th' pyramid; ANT 2.07. 18
in this place, | in which i'll plant a pyramid; TNK 3.06.293
arcite's body | within an inch o' th' pyramid, 5.03. 80

PYRAMIDES 1 FR 0.0001 REL FR 1 V 0 P
make | my country's high pyramides my gibbet, ANT 5.02. 61

PYRAMIDS 2 FR 0.0002 REL FR 2 V 0 P
though palaces and pyramids do slope | their MAC 4.01. 57
thy pyramids built up with newer might | to me SON 123. 2

PYRAMIS 1 FR 0.0001 REL FR 1 V 0 P
a statelier pyramis to her i'll rear | than 1H6 1.06. 21

PYRAMISES 1 FR 0.0001 REL FR 0 V 1 P
the ptolomies' pyramises are very goodly things; ANT 2.07. 35 P

PYRAMUS' 1 FR 0.0001 REL FR 0 V 1 P
you, pyramus' father; MND 1.02. 63 P

/PYRAMUS 1 FR 0.0001 REL FR 1 V 0 P
so pale did shine the moon on /pyramus | when he TIT 2.03.231

PYRAMUS 43 FR 0.0048 REL FR 13 V 30 P
and most cruel death of pyramus and thisby. MND 1.02. 12 P
you, nick bottom, are set down for pyramus. 1.02. 20 P
what is pyramus? a lover, or a tyrant? 1.02. 22 P
it is the lady that pyramus must love. 1.02. 46 P
ah pyramus, my lover dear! 1.02. 53 P
no, no, you must play pyramus; 1.02. 55 P
you can play no part but pyramus; 1.02. 85 P
for pyramus is a sweet–fac'd man; 1.02. 86 P
therefore you must needs play pyramus. 1.02. 89 P
in this comedy of pyramus and thisby that will 3.01. 9 P
pyramus must draw a sword to kill himself; 3.01. 10 P
swords, and that pyramus is not kill'd indeed; 3.01. 19 P
tell them that i pyramus am not pyramus, but 3.01. 20 P
tell them that i pyramus am not pyramus, but 3.01. 21 P
you know, pyramus and thisby meet by moonlight. 3.01. 49 P
for pyramus and thisby (says the story) did talk 3.01. 63 P
that cranny shall pyramus and thisby whisper. 3.01. 70 P
pyramus, you begin. 3.01. 74 P
speak, pyramus. thisby, stand forth. 3.01. 81 P
a stranger pyramus than e'er played here. 3.01. 88
"most radiant pyramus, most lily–white of hue, 3.01. 93
i'll meet thee, pyramus, at ninny's tomb." 3.01. 97
that you answer to pyramus. 3.01. 99 P
pyramus, enter. 3.01.100 P
who pyramus presented, in their sport, | forsook 3.02. 14
fear, | and left sweet pyramus translated there; 3.02. 32
my next is, "most fair pyramus." 4.01.201 P
in all athens able to discharge pyramus but he. 4.02. 8 P
given him sixpence a day for playing pyramus, 4.02. 22 P
sixpence a day in pyramus, or nothing. 4.02. 24 P
"a tedious brief scene of young pyramus | and 5.01. 56
for pyramus therein doth kill himself. 5.01. 67
this man is pyramus, if you would know; 5.01.129
anon comes pyramus, sweet youth and tall, | and 5.01.144
through which the lovers, pyramus and thisby, 5.01.159
pyramus draws near the wall. silence! 5.01.169 P
my moans, | for parting my fair pyramus and me! 5.01.189
and then came pyramus. 5.01.270 P
out, sword, and wound | the pap of pyramus; 5.01.297
should not use a long one for such a pyramus. 5.01.317 P
a mote will turn the balance, which pyramus, 5.01.318 P
o pyramus, arise! 5.01.326
writ it had play'd pyramus and hang'd himself in 5.01.358 P

PYRENEAN 1 FR 0.0001 REL FR 1 V 0 P
and apennines, | the pyrenean and the river po, JN 1.01.203

PYRRHUS' 4 FR 0.0004 REL FR 4 V 0 P
a hideous crash | takes prisoner pyrrhus' ear; HAM 2.02.477
so, after pyrrhus' pause, | a roused vengeance 2.02.487
with less remorse than pyrrhus' bleeding sword 2.02.491
which bleeding under pyrrhus' proud foot lies. LUC 1449

PYRRHUS 9 FR 0.0010 REL FR 8 V 1 P
but it must grieve young pyrrhus now at home TRO 3.03.209
"the rugged pyrrhus, like th' hyrcanian beast — HAM 2.02.450
beast —" | 'tis not so, it begins with pyrrhus: 2.02.451 P
"the rugged pyrrhus, he whose sable arms, 2.02.452
the hellish pyrrhus | old grandsire priam seeks. 2.02.463
pyrrhus at priam drives, in rage strikes wide, 2.02.472
as a painted tyrant, pyrrhus stood | /and, like 2.02.480
when she saw pyrrhus make malicious sport | in 2.02.513
and rail on pyrrhus that hath done him wrong, LUC 1467

PYTHAGORAS' 1 FR 0.0001 REL FR 0 V 1 P
i was never so berhym'd since pythagoras' time, AYL 3.02.176 P

PYTHAGORAS 3 FR 0.0003 REL FR 1 V 2 P
in my faith | to hold opinion with pythagoras, MV 4.01.131
what is the opinion of pythagoras concerning TN 4.02. 50 P
th' opinion of pythagoras ere i will allow of 4.02. 58 P

QUADRANGLE 1 FR 0.0001 REL FR 1 V 0 P
with walking once about the quadrangle, | i come 2H6 1.03.153

/QUAE 1 FR 0.0001 REL FR 0 V 1 P
it is qui, /quae, quod: WIV 4.01. 77 P

/QUAE'S 1 FR 0.0001 REL FR 0 V 1 P
if you forget your qui's, your /quae's, and your WIV 4.01. 78 P

QUAFF 1 FR 0.0001 REL FR 1 V 0 P
and quaff carouses to our mistress' health, SHR 1.02.275

QUAFF'D 2 FR 0.0002 REL FR 2 V 0 P
mates | after a storm, quaff'd off the muscadel, SHR 3.02.172
that tyranny, which never quaff'd but blood, 2H4 4.05. 85

QUAFFING 1 FR 0.0001 REL FR 0 V 1 P
that quaffing and drinking will undo you. TN 1.03. 14 P

QUAGMIRE 2 FR 0.0002 REL FR 1 V 1 P
and make a quagmire of your mingled brains. 1H6 1.04.109
/ford and whirlpool, o'er bog and quagmire; LR 3.04. 53 P

QU'AI–JE 1 FR 0.0001 REL FR 0 V 1 P
qu'ai–je oublie? WIV 1.04. 63 P

QUAIL 4 FR 0.0004 REL FR 4 V 0 P
and thrum, | quail, crush, conclude, and quell! MND 5.01.287
and let not search and inquisition quail | to AYL 2.02. 20
but when he meant to quail and shake the orb, ANT 5.02. 85
and my false spirits | quail to remember — give CYM 5.05.149

QUAILING 2 FR 0.0002 REL FR 2 V 0 P
for, as he writes, there is no quailing now, 1H4 4.01. 39
may plant courage in their quailing breasts, 3H6 2.03. 54

QUAILS 2 FR 0.0002 REL FR 1 V 1 P
honest fellow enough, and one that loves quails, TRO 5.01. 52 P
and his quails ever | beat mine, inhoop'd, at ANT 2.03. 38

QUAINT 11 FR 0.0012 REL FR 10 V 1 P
my quaint ariel, | hark in thine ear. TMP 1.02.317
that quaint in green she shall be loose enrob'd, WIV 4.06. 41
but for a fine, quaint, graceful, and excellent ADO 3.04. 22 P
and the quaint mazes in the wanton green | for MND 2.01. 99
hoots and wonders | at our quaint spirits. 2.02. 7
a fine bragging youth, and tell quaint lies, MV 3.04. 69
the quaint musician, amorous litio, | all for my SHR 3.02.147
more quaint, more pleasing, nor more commendable 4.03.102
for though he seem with forged quaint conceit 1H6 4.01.102
to show how quaint an orator you are; 2H6 3.02.274
faint, | daisies smell–less, yet most quaint, TNK 1.01. 5

QUAINTLY 6 FR 0.0006 REL FR 6 V 0 P
the lines are very quaintly writ, | but (since TGV 2.01.122
why then a ladder, quaintly made of cords, | to 3.01.117
'tis vile, unless it may be quaintly ordered, MV 2.04. 6
to carve out dials quaintly, point by point, 3H6 2.05. 24
but breathe his faults so quaintly | that they HAM 2.01. 31
spent | with your fine fancies quaintly /eche: PER 3.ch. 13

QUAK'D 2 FR 0.0002 REL FR 1 V 1 P
i quak'd for fear, lest the lunatic knave would WIV 3.05.103 P
ladies shall be frighted | and, gladly quak'd, COR 1.09. 6

QUAKE 16 FR 0.0018 REL FR 15 V 1 P
o, i do fear thee, claudio, and i quake, | lest MM 3.01. 73
in venice, thou wilt quake for this shortly. ADO 1.01.272 P
lysander, look how i do quake with fear. MND 2.02.148
may now perchance both quake and tremble here, 5.01.221
never saw i | wretches so quake: WT 5.01.199
but they will quake and tremble all this day. JN 3.01. 18
whose bloody deeds shall make all europe quake. 1H6 1.01.156
henry the fift, that made all france to quake, 2H6 4.08. 17
yet that, by you depos'd, you quake like rebels? R3 1.03.161
cousin, canst thou quake and change thy color, 3.05. 1
revenge, which makes the foul offender quake. TIT 5.02. 40
/business /as /the day | would quake to look on. HAM 3.02.392
quake in the present winter's state, and wish CYM 2.04. 5
upon the sea, | shook as the earth did quake; PER 3.02. 15
one would swear he saw them quake and tremble. LUC 1393
for sinon in his fire doth quake with cold, 1556

QUAKES 2 FR 0.0002 REL FR 2 V 0 P
when i do stare, see how the subject quakes. LR 4.06.108
whereat each tributary subject quakes, | as when VEN 1045

QUAKING 2 FR 0.0002 REL FR 2 V 0 P
is in expectation, | yet quaking and unsettled. TNK 5.03.106
bids them leave quaking, bids them fear no more VEN 899

QUALIFICATION 1 FR 0.0001 REL FR 0 V 1 P
whose qualification shall come into no true OTH 2.01.275 P

QUALIFIED 8 FR 0.0009 REL FR 4 V 4 P
so qualified as may beseem | the spouse of any SHR 4.05. 66
with thoughts so qualified as your charities WT 2.01.113
humor | rests by you only to be qualified. JN 5.01. 13
some little time hath qualified the heat of his LR 1.02.161 P
ordinary men are fit for, i am qualified in, and 1.04. 35 P
and that was craftily qualified too — and OTH 2.03. 40 P
constant, qualified, and less attemptable than CYM 1.04. 60 P
stay, | his rage of lust by gazing qualified; LUC 424

QUALIFIES 1 FR 0.0001 REL FR 1 V 0 P
time qualifies the spark and fire of it. HAM 4.07.113

QUALIFY 9 FR 0.0010 REL FR 9 V 0 P
hot fire, | but qualify the fire's extreme rage, TGV 2.07. 22
so to enforce or qualify the laws | as to your MM 1.01. 65
he spurs on his pow'r | to qualify in others. 4.02. 83
all this amazement can i qualify, | when after ADO 5.04. 67
your grace hath ta'en great pains to qualify MV 4.01. 7
your discontenting father strive to qualify, WT 4.04.532
success in a bad cause, | can qualify the same? TRO 2.02.118
is no addition but a rebel | to qualify a rebel? STM II.C 119
though absence seem'd my flame to qualify! SON 109. 2

QUALIFYING 1 FR 0.0001 REL FR 1 V 0 P
my love admits no qualifying dross, | no more my TRO 4.04. 9

QUALITE 1 FR 0.0001 REL FR 0 V 1 P
que vous etes le gentilhomme de bonne qualite. H5 4.04. 3 P

/QUALITIES 1 FR 0.0001 REL FR 1 V 0 P
and knows all /qualities, with a learned spirit, OTH 3.03.259

QUALITIES 27 FR 0.0030 REL FR 17 V 10 P
and show'd thee all the qualities o' th' isle, TMP 1.02.337
and qualities | beseeming such a wife as your TGV 3.01. 65
she hath more qualities than a water–spaniel, 3.01.272 P
withal, | are men endu'd with worthy qualities. 5.04.153
your own sake, for i have many ill qualities. ADO 2.01.102 P
eyes, | so i, admiring of his qualities. MND 1.01.231
in graces, and in qualities of breeding; MV 2.07. 33
and hiding from me all gentleman–like qualities. AYL 1.01. 70 P
her wondrous qualities and mild behavior, | am SHR 2.01. 50
an unclean mind carries virtuous qualities, AWW 1.01. 42 P
his might only where qualities were level; 1.03.113 P
his qualities being at this poor price, i need 4.03.276 P
will, according to your strengths and qualities, 2H4 5.05. 69
and bless us with her former qualities. H5 5.02. 67
to fill the world with vicious qualities. 1H6 5.04. 35
thou art alone | (if thy rare qualities, sweet H8 2.04.138
nor his qualities. TRO 1.02. 88 P
plants, herbs, stones, and their true qualities; ROM 2.03. 16
at my dearest cost | in qualities of the best. TIM 1.01.125
the streets and note | the qualities of people. ANT 1.01. 54
together with the adornment of my qualities. CYM 3.05.137 P
a shop of all the qualities that man | loves 5.05.166
boult, has she any qualities? PER 4.02. 46 P
necessity of qualities can make her be refus'd. 4.02. 49 P
a little of all noble qualities: TNK 2.05. 10
both favor, savor, hue, and qualities, | whereat VEN 747
"his qualities were beauteous as his form, | for LC 99

/QUALITY 3 FR 0.0003 REL FR 1 V 2 P
/yes, /if /this /present /quality /of /war — 2H4 1.03. 36
/and /light /a /quality /that /it /is /but /a HAM 2.02.262 P
/they /pursue /the /quality /no /longer /than 2.02.347 P
QUALITY 59 FR 0.0066 REL FR 49 V 10 P
bidding, task | ariel, and all his quality. TMP 1.02.193
it is the quality o' th' climate. 2.01.200
as we do in our quality much want — TGV 4.01. 56
of what quality was your love then? WIV 2.02.214 P
destiny, | attend your office and your quality. 5.05. 40
what quality are they of? MM 2.01. 58 P
yourself, | hate counsels not in such a quality. MV 3.02. 6
the quality of mercy is not strain'd, | it 4.01.184
the owner of no one good quality worthy your AWW 3.06. 11 P
soul, | in your fine frame hath love no quality? 4.02. 4
jests, | the quality of persons, and the time; TN 3.01. 63
albeit the quality of the time and quarrel 3.03. 31
it would allay the burning quality | of that JN 5.07. 8
the quality and hair of our attempt | brooks no 1H4 4.01. 61
good name, | because you are not of our quality, 4.03. 36
as might hold sortance with his quality, | the 2H4 4.01. 11
indeed, | concurring both in name and quality. 4.01. 87
which swims against your stream of quality. 5.02. 34
best | neighbor'd by fruit of baser quality; H5 1.01. 62
what is thy name? i know thy quality. 3.06.137
squires, | and gentlemen of blood and quality. 4.08. 90
looks we fairly hope | have lost their quality, 5.02. 19
hitting a grosser quality, is cried up | for our H8 1.02. 84
approach, | with the whole quality wherefore. TRO 4.01. 45
the grecian youths are full of quality; 4.04. 76
creatures as | of grave and austere quality, TIM 1.01. 54
know you the quality of lord timon's fury? 3.06.107 P
that /scolds against the quality of flesh | and 4.03.156
why birds and beasts from quality and kind, JC 1.03. 64
to monstrous quality — why, you shall find 1.03. 68
that will be thaw'd from the true quality | with 3.01. 41
of whose true-fix'd and resting quality | there 3.01. 61
come give us a taste of your quality, come, a HAM 2.02.432 P
in hamlet's hearing, for a quality | wherein, 4.07. 72
more composition and fierce quality | than doth, LR 1.02. 12
the quality of nothing hath not such need to 1.02. 33 P
lord, | you know the fiery quality of the duke, 2.04. 92
what "quality"? 2.04. 96
not believe | with how deprav'd a quality — o 2.04.137
"if any man of quality or degree within the 5.03.110 P
your name, your quality? 5.03.120
subdu'd | even to the very quality of my lord. OTH 1.03.251
and such things else of quality and respect | as 1.03.282
to the general, nor any man of quality — i hope 2.03.107 P
fife, | the royal banner, and all quality, 3.03.353
whose quality, going on, | the sides o' th' ANT 1.02.191
outward | do draw the inward quality after them, 3.13. 33
the quality of her passion shall require, | lest 5.01. 63
flat, for taking a beggar without less quality. CYM 1.04. 23 P
of your knowing to a stranger of his quality. 1.04. 30 P
not his kinsmen | in blood unless in quality. TNK 1.02. 79
men of great quality, as may be judg'd | by 1.04. 14
else grant | the file and quality i hold i may 5.01.161
so, but alters to | the quality of his thoughts; 5.03. 48
or kills his life or else his quality. LUC 875
her grief, but not her grief's true quality. 1313
"what is the quality of my offense, | being 1702
of plagues, of dearths, or seasons' quality; SON 14. 4
each stone's dear nature, worth, and quality. LC 210
QUALM *(also calm*)*
QUALM 3 FR 0.0003 REL FR 2 V 1 P
it is the only thing for a qualm. ADO 3.04. 75 P
qualm, perhaps. LLL 5.02.279
some sudden qualm hath struck me at the heart, 2H6 1.01. 54
QUALMISH 1 FR 0.0001 REL FR 1 V 0 P
i am qualmish at the smell of leek. H5 5.01. 21
QUALTITIE 1 FR 0.0001 REL FR 0 V 1 P
qualtitie! H5 4.04. 4 P
QUAM 1 FR 0.0001 REL FR 1 V 0 P
but so, | "redime te captum quam queas minimo." SHR 1.01.162
QUAND 2 FR 0.0002 REL FR 0 V 2 P
je quand sur le possession de france, et quand H5 5.02.181 P
et quand vous avez le possession de moi — let 5.02.182 P
QUANDO 1 FR 0.0001 REL FR 0 V 1 P
precor gelida quando /pecus /omne sub umbra LLL 4.02. 93 P
QUANTITIES 1 FR 0.0001 REL FR 0 V 1 P
if i were saw'd into quantities, i should make 2H4 5.01. 62 P
QUANTITY 13 FR 0.0014 REL FR 11 V 2 P
he is not quantity enough for that worthy's LLL 5.01.130 P
things base and vile, holding no quantity, MND 1.01.232
away, thou rag, thou quantity, thou remnant, SHR 4.03.111
the world, | prizes not quantity of dirty lands; TN 2.04. 82
my view, | retaining but a quantity of life, JN 5.04. 23
here, | in quantity equals not one of yours. 1H4 3.01. 96
poor straggling soldiers with | great quantity. TIM 5.01. 7
ingratitude with loves | above their quantity. 5.04. 18
to set on some quantity of barren spectators to HAM 3.02. 41 P
/for women's fear and love hold quantity, | in 3.02.167
but it reserv'd some quantity of choice, | to 3.04. 75
could not with all their quantity of love | make 5.01.270
how much the quantity, the weight as much, | as CYM 4.02. 17
/QUARE 1 FR 0.0001 REL FR 0 V 1 P
/quare chirrah, not sirrah? LLL 5.01. 33 P
/QUARREL 3 FR 0.0003 REL FR 3 V 0 P
/from /heaven /his /quarrel /and /his /cause; 2H4 1.01.206
/paris /sleeps — /and /that's /the /quarrel. TRO pr 10
and fortune, on his damned /quarrel smiling, MAC 1.02. 14
QUARREL 95 FR 0.0107 REL FR 64 V 31 P
did quarrel with the noblest grace she ow'd, TMP 3.01. 45
but i shall as soon quarrel at it as any man in WIV 1.01.291 P
the lady beatrice hath a quarrel to you. ADO 2.01.236 P
to enter into a quarrel with fear and trembling. 2.03.195 P
nay, do not quarrel with us, good old man. 5.01. 50
in a false quarrel there is no true valor. 5.01.120 P
a quarrel ho already! what's the matter? MV 5.01.146
jealous in honor, sudden, and quick in quarrel, AYL 2.07.151
and found the quarrel was upon the seventh cause 5.04. 49 P
how did you find the quarrel on the seventh 5.04. 67 P
o sir, we quarrel in print, by the book — as 5.04. 90 P
when seven justices could not take up a quarrel, 5.04. 99 P
the nature of our quarrel yet never brook'd SHR 1.01.114 P
for in a quarrel since i came ashore | i kill'd 1.01.231
grumio, rise, we will compound this quarrel. 1.02. 27
for private quarrel 'twixt your duke and him, 4.02. 84
holy seems the quarrel | upon your grace's part; AWW 3.01. 4
albeit the quality of the time and quarrel TN 3.03. 31
no man hath any quarrel to me. 3.04.227 P
i have his horse to take up the quarrel. 3.04.292 P
he hath better bethought him of his quarrel, and 3.04.298 P
and let no quarrel nor no brawl to come | taint 5.01.356
our people quarrel with obedience, | swearing JN 5.01. 9
and put his cause and quarrel | to the disposing 5.07. 91
put we our quarrel to the will of heaven, | who, R2 1.02. 6
god's is the quarrel, for god's substitute, 1.02. 37
what man thou com'st, and what thy quarrel. 1.03. 13
and what's thy quarrel? 1.03. 33
and now you pick a quarrel to beguile me of it. 1H4 3.03. 67 P
o, would the quarrel lay upon our heads, | and 5.02. 47
commonwealth, | i make my quarrel in particular. 2H4 4.01. 94
and heir from heir shall hold his quarrel up 4.02. 48
my father, | the quarrel of a true inheritor. 4.05.168
which daily grew to quarrel and to bloodshed, 4.05.194
war nor no known quarrel were in question) | but H5 2.04. 17
his cause being just and his quarrel honorable. 4.01.128 P
of the king's laws in now the king's quarrel. 4.01.171 P
let it be a quarrel between us, if you live. 4.01.205 P
acknowledge it, i will make it my quarrel. 4.01.210 P
say | this quarrel will drink blood another day. 1H6 2.04.133
the quarrel toucheth none but us alone, 4.01.118
quite to forget this quarrel, and the cause. 4.01.136
that in this quarrel have been overthrown | and 5.04.105
becomes | so good a quarrel and so bad a peer. 2H6 2.01. 28
left i the court, to see this quarrel tried. 2.03. 53
thrice is he arm'd that hath his quarrel just; 3.02.233
what is your quarrel? 3H6 1.02. 5
no quarrel, but a slight contention. 1.02. 6
and in that quarrel use it to the death. 2.02. 65
this deadly quarrel daily doth beget! 2.05. 91
because in quarrel of the house of york | the 3.02. 6
my quarrel and this english queen's are one. 3.03.216
it is a quarrel most unnatural, | to be reveng'd R3 1.02.134
it is a quarrel just and reasonable, | to be 1.02.136
to fight | in quarrel of the house of lancaster. 1.04.204
take not the quarrel from his pow'rful arm; 1.04.217
yet, if that quarrel, fortune, do divorce | it H8 2.03. 14
what's the quarrel? TRO 2.01. 89 P
cannot distaste the goodness of a quarrel 2.02.123
and enmity of those | this quarrel would excite? 2.02.138
a good quarrel to draw emulous factions and 2.03. 73 P
not for the worth that hangs upon our quarrel. 2.03.207
had we no other quarrel else to rome but that COR 4.05.127
in wrongful quarrel you have slain your son. TIT 1.01.293
in a bad quarrel slain a virtuous son. 1.01.342
ye draw, | and maintain such a quarrel openly? 2.01. 47
for all my blood in rome's great quarrel shed, 3.01. 4
that true hand that fought rome's quarrel out, 5.03.102
the quarrel is between our masters and us their ROM 1.01. 19 P
quarrel, i will back thee. 1.01. 33 P
do you quarrel, sir? 1.01. 52 P
quarrel, sir? no, sir. 1.01. 53 P
who set this ancient quarrel new abroach? 1.01.104
if i see occasion in a good quarrel, and the law 2.04.160 P
thou wilt quarrel with a man that hath a hair 3.01. 17 P
thou wilt quarrel with a man for cracking nuts, 3.01. 19 P
but such an eye would spy out such a quarrel? 3.01. 22 P
and i were so apt to quarrel as thou art, any 3.01. 31 P
bid him bethink | how nice the quarrel was, and 3.01.154
and since the quarrel | will bear no color for JC 2.01. 28
of goodness | be like our warranted quarrel! MAC 4.03.137
beware | of entrance to a quarrel, but being in, HAM 1.03. 66
but greatly to find quarrel in a straw | when 4.04. 55
insolent retinue | do hourly carp and quarrel, LR 1.04.203
speak yet, how grew your quarrel? 2.02. 61 P
upon your chin, | i'ld shake it on this quarrel. 3.07. 77
to quarrel with your great opposeless wills, 4.06. 38
he'll be as full of quarrel and offense | as my OTH 2.03. 50
fear, | to manage private and domestic quarrel? 2.03.215
a quarrel, but nothing wherefore. 2.03.289 P
quarrel no more, but be prepar'd to know | the ANT 1.03. 66
if you'll patch a quarrel, | as matter whole you 2.02. 52
is mended) my quarrel was not altogether slight. CYM 1.04. 47 P
this quarrel | sleep till the hour prefix'd, and TNK 3.06.303
to end the quarrel? 4.02. 57
QUARRELL'D 1 FR 0.0001 REL FR 0 V 1 P
thou hast quarrell'd with a man for coughing in ROM 3.01. 24 P
QUARRELLER 1 FR 0.0001 REL FR 0 V 1 P
that he's a fool, he's a great quarreller; TN 1.03. 30 P
QUARRELLING 7 FR 0.0008 REL FR 3 V 4 P
if he could right himself with quarrelling, ADO 5.01. 51
yet more quarrelling with occasion! MV 3.05. 55 P
coward to allay the gust he hath in quarrelling, TN 1.03. 32 P
been beaten as addle as an egg for quarrelling. ROM 3.01. 24 P
and yet thou wilt tutor me from quarrelling! 3.01. 30 P
and set quarrelling | upon the head of valor; TIM 3.05. 27
ay, or drinking, fencing, swearing, quarrelling, HAM 2.01. 25
QUARRELLOUS 1 FR 0.0001 REL FR 1 V 0 P
saucy, and | as quarrellous as the weasel; CYM 3.04.159
QUARREL'S 2 FR 0.0002 REL FR 1 V 1 P
take heed, the quarrel's most ominous to us. TRO 5.07. 20 P
bold in the quarrel's right, rous'd to th' LR 2.01. 54
/QUARRELS 1 FR 0.0001 REL FR 1 V 0 P
/and /the /best /quarrels, /in /the /heat, /are LR 5.03. 56
QUARRELS 18 FR 0.0020 REL FR 12 V 6 P
in the managing of quarrels you may say he is ADO 2.03.190 P
i am th' unhappy subject of these quarrels. MV 5.01.238
undone three tailors, i have had four quarrels, AYL 5.04. 47 P
of men that put quarrels purposely on others, to TN 3.04.243 P
the nobles hath he fin'd | for ancient quarrels, R2 2.01.248
to busy giddy minds | with foreign quarrels, 2H4 4.05.214
be friends, we have french quarrels enow, if you H5 4.01.223 P
and prabbles, and quarrels and dissensions, and, 4.08. 65 P
shall change all griefs and quarrels into love. 5.02. 20
that fill the court with quarrels, talk, and H8 1.03. 20
but with a pride | that quarrels at self-breath. TRO 2.03.172
this day all quarrels die, andronicus. TIT 1.01.465
that for her love such quarrels may be broach'd, 2.01. 67
i'll go fetch thy sons | to back thy quarrels, 2.03. 54
parle, | these quarrels must be quietly debated. 5.03. 20
head is as full of quarrels as an egg is full of ROM 3.01. 22 P
quarrels unjust against the good and loyal, MAC 4.03. 83
quarrels consume us, envy of ill men | crave our TNK 2.02. 90
QUARRELSOME 3 FR 0.0003 REL FR 1 V 2 P
this is call'd the countercheck quarrelsome; AYL 5.04. 81 P
the fift, the countercheck quarrelsome; 5.04. 95 P
my master is grown quarrelsome. SHR 1.02. 13
QUARRIES 1 FR 0.0001 REL FR 1 V 0 P
rough quarries, rocks, /and hills whose /heads OTH 1.03.141
QUARRY 3 FR 0.0003 REL FR 3 V 0 P
i'd make a quarry | with thousands of these COR 1.01.198
were on the quarry of these murther'd deer | to MAC 4.03.206
this quarry cries on havoc. HAM 5.02.364
QUART 4 FR 0.0004 REL FR 1 V 3 P
go fetch me a quart of sack — put a toast in't. WIV 3.05. 3 P
edge, | for a quart of ale is a dish for a king. WT 4.03. 8
by the mass, you'll crack a quart together, ha, 2H4 5.03. 62 P
serv'd me instead of a quart pot to drink in; 2H6 4.10. 14 P
QUARTER 21 FR 0.0023 REL FR 9 V 12 P
i may quarter, coz. WIV 1.01. 24 P
it is marring indeed, if he quarter it. 1.01. 26 P
if he has a quarter of your coat, there is but 1.01. 28 P
within a quarter of an hour. 4.04. 5 P
is a year and a quarter old come philip and MM 3.02.201 P
so he would keep fair quarter with his bed! ERR 2.01.108
why, an hour in clamor and a quarter in rheum; ADO 5.02. 83 P
yard, three-quarters, half-yard, quarter, nail! SHR 4.03.108
of honor again into his native quarter, be AWW 3.06. 66 P
keep good quarter and good care to-night; JN 5.05. 20
so good a proficient in one quarter of an hour, 1H4 2.04. 18 P
to a bawdy-house not above once in a quarter — 3.03. 17 P
once or twice in a quarter bear out a knave 2H4 5.01. 48 P
whereof take you one quarter into france, | and H5 1.02.215
within her quarter and mine own precinct | i was 1H6 2.01. 68
fee-simple of my life for an hour and a quarter. ROM 3.01. 33 P
not a man | shall pass his quarter, or offend TIM 5.04. 60
known her continue in this a quarter of an hour. MAC 5.01. 30 P
in quarter, and in terms like bride and groom OTH 2.03.180
follow the noise so far as we have quarter; ANT 4.03. 21
were he | a quarter carrier of that honor which TNK 1.02.108
QUARTER'D 9 FR 0.0010 REL FR 8 V 1 P
and quarter'd in her heart! JN 2.01.506
hang'd and drawn and quarter'd, there should be 2.01.508
where is lord stanley quarter'd, do you know? R3 5.03. 34
the hope o' th' strond, where she was quarter'd. H8 5.03. 53 P
with thousands of these quarter'd slaves, as COR 1.01.199
they mean this night in sardis to be quarter'd. JC 4.02. 28
a thought which quarter'd hath but one part HAM 4.04. 42
i, that with my sword | quarter'd the world, and ANT 4.14. 58
behold their quarter'd fires, have both their CYM 4.04. 18
QUARTERED 1 FR 0.0001 REL FR 1 V 0 P
their infants quartered with the hands of war; JC 3.01.268
QUARTERING 1 FR 0.0001 REL FR 1 V 0 P
lean famine, quartering steel, and climbing fire 1H6 4.02. 11
QUARTERS 6 FR 0.0006 REL FR 2 V 4 P
but her name /and three quarters, that's an ell ERR 3.02.109 P
that's an ell and three quarters, will not 3.02.110 P
kinsman not past three quarters of a mile hence, WT 4.03. 80 P
stand till he be three quarters and a dram dead; 4.04.785 P
had all your quarters been as safely kept | as 1H6 2.01. 63
blow, | all the quarters that they know | i' th' MAC 1.03. 16
QUARTS 1 FR 0.0001 REL FR 1 V 0 P
she brought stone jugs and no seal'd quarts. SHR in.2. 88
QUASI 1 FR 0.0001 REL FR 0 V 1 P
master person, quasi //pers-one. LLL 4.02. 83 P
QUAT 1 FR 0.0001 REL FR 1 V 0 P
have rubb'd this young quat almost to the sense, OTH 5.01. 11
QUATCH-BUTTOCK 1 FR 0.0001 REL FR 0 V 1 P
the pin-buttock, the quatch-buttock, the AWW 2.02. 18 P
QUE 18 FR 0.0020 REL FR 1 V 17 P
il faut que j'apprenne a parler. H5 3.04. 4 P
je pense que je suis le bon ecolier; 3.04. 13 P
de tous les mots que vous m'avez appris des a 3.04. 26 P
les mots aussi droit que les natifs d'angleterre 3.04. 38 P
vous deja oublie ce que je vous ai enseigne? 3.04. 42 P
je pense que vous etes le gentilhomme de bonne 4.04. 2 P
que dit-il, monsieur? 4.04. 33 P
commande a vous dire que vous faites vous pret; 4.04. 34 P
petit monsieur, que dit-il? 4.04. 49 P
pour les ecus que vous /lui promettez, il est 4.04. 51 P
et je m'estime heureux que je tombe entre les 4.04. 55 P
que dit-il? que je suis semblable a les anges? 5.02.111 P
que dit-il? que je suis semblable a les anges? 5.02.111 P
sauf votre honneur, le francois que vous parlez, 5.02.188 P
il est /meilleur que l'anglois lequel je parle. 5.02.189 P
ma foi, je ne veux point que vous abaissez votre 5.02.254 P
your majesty entendre bettre que moi. 5.02.264 P
"piu per dolcera que per forca." PER 2.02. 27
QUEAN 4 FR 0.0004 REL FR 0 V 4 P
a witch, a quean, an old cozening quean! WIV 4.02.172 P
a witch, a quean, an old cozening quean! 4.02.172 P
horn, as a scolding quean to a wrangling knave, AWW 2.02. 26 P
villain's head, throw the quean in the channel. 2H4 2.01. 47 P
QUEAS 1 FR 0.0001 REL FR 1 V 0 P
but so, | "redime te captum quam queas minimo." SHR 1.01.162
/QUEASINESS 1 FR 0.0001 REL FR 1 V 0 P
/and /they /did /fight /with /queasiness, 2H4 1.01.196
QUEASY 3 FR 0.0003 REL FR 2 V 1 P
despite of his quick wit and his queasy stomach, ADO 2.01.383 P
and i have one thing, of a queasy question, LR 2.01. 17
who, queasy with his insolence | already, will ANT 3.06. 20
/QUEEN 4 FR 0.0004 REL FR 2 V 2 P
/the /ravish'd /helen, /menelaus' /queen, TRO pr 9
that's good, "/mobled /queen" /is /good. HAM 2.02.504 P
/pierce /the /queen /to /any /demonstration /of LR 4.03. 9 P
/it /seem'd /she /was /a /queen | /over /her 4.03. 13
QUEEN 444 FR 0.0501 REL FR 398 V 46 P
gone forth, i'll make you | the queen of naples. TMP 1.02.450
before with such a paragon to their queen. 2.01. 76 P
the marriage of your daughter, who is now queen. 2.01. 99 P
she that is queen of tunis; 2.01.246
true, my brother's daughter 's queen of tunis, 2.01.255
his daughter and i will be king and queen — 3.02.107 P
thou thyself dost air — the queen o' th' sky, 4.01. 70
why hath thy queen | summon'd me hither, to this 4.01. 82
as thou dost know, | do now attend the queen? 4.01. 88
highest queen of state, | great juno, comes, i 4.01.101
both in naples, | the king and queen there! 5.01.150
for me (by this pale queen of night i swear), TGV 4.02.100

my nan shall be the queen of all the fairies, WIV 4.04. 71
must my sweet nan present the fairy queen; 4.06. 20
our radiant queen hates sluts and sluttery. 5.05. 46
weight | than aquitaine, a dowry for a queen. LLL 2.01. 8
that was a woman when queen guinover of britain 4.01.123 P
o queen of queens, how far dost thou excel | no 4.03. 39
and by that fire which burn'd the carthage queen MND 1.01.173
and i serve the fairy queen, | to dew her orbs 2.01. 8
our queen and all her elves come here anon. 2.01. 17
take heed the queen come not within his sight; 2.01. 19
do no wrong, | come not near our fairy queen. 2.02. 12
here, | so near the cradle of the fairy queen? 3.01. 78
i'll to my queen and beg her indian boy; 3.02.375
but first i will release the fairy queen. 4.01. 70
now, my titania, wake you, my sweet queen. 4.01. 75
come, my queen, take hands with me, | and rock 4.01. 85
then, my queen, in silence sad | trip we after 4.01. 95
we will, fair queen, | up to the mountain's top, 4.01.109
except to steal your thoughts, my gentle queen. MV 2.01. 12
master of my servants, | queen o'er myself; 3.02.169
and thou, thrice-crowned queen of night, survey AYL 3.02. 2
as dear | as anna to the queen of carthage was: SHR 1.01.154
'save you, fair queen! AWW 1.01.106 P
/diana /no queen of virgins, that would suffer 1.03.114 P
but 'tis that miracle and queen of gems | that TN 2.04. 85
seen, | orsino's mistress and his fancy's queen. 5.01.388
tongue-tied our queen? speak you. WT 1.02. 27
we were, fair queen, | two lads that thought 1.02. 62
lest you say | your queen and i are devils. 1.02. 82
will take again your queen as yours at first, 1.02.336
feasts, keep with bohemia | and with your queen. 1.02.345
that you have touch'd his queen | forbiddenly. 1.02.416
and comfort | the gracious queen, part of his 1.02.459
hark ye, | the queen your mother rounds apace: 2.01. 16
beseech your highness call the queen again. 2.01.126
ones suffer, | yourself, your queen, your son. 2.01.129
that the queen is spotless | i' th' eyes of 2.01.131
pray you then, | conduct me to the queen. 2.02. 7
the queen receives | much comfort in't; 2.02. 25
commend my best obedience to the queen. 2.02. 34
acquaint the queen of your most noble offer, 2.02. 46
i'll to the queen. 2.02. 53
madam, if't please the queen to send the babe, 2.02. 54
of | (if any be) the trespass of the queen. 2.02. 61
i say, i come | from your good queen. 2.03. 58
good queen? 2.03. 59
good queen, my lord, good queen, i say good 2.03. 60
queen, my lord, good queen, i say good queen, 2.03. 60
queen, my lord, good queen, i say good queen, 2.03. 60
the good queen | (for she is good) hath brought 2.03. 65
but this most cruel usage of your queen | (not 2.03.117
th' journey | prove as successful to the queen 3.01. 12
it is his highness' pleasure that the queen 3.02. 9
"hermione, queen to the worthy leontes, king of 3.02. 12 P
this news is mortal to the queen. 3.02.148
new woo my queen, recall the good camillo, 3.02.156
the queen, the queen, | the sweet'st, dear'st 3.02.200
the queen, the queen, | the sweet'st, dear'st 3.02.200
the love i bore your queen — lo, fool again! 3.02.228
me | to the dead bodies of my queen and son. 3.02.235
of his most precious queen and children are even 4.02. 24 P
of the petty gods, | and you the queen on't. 4.04. 5
sooth, she is | the queen of curds and cream. 4.04.161
being now awake, i'll queen it no inch farther, 4.04.449
holy | than to rejoice the former queen is well? 5.01. 30
give me the office | to choose you a queen. 5.01. 78
not a month | 'fore your queen died, she was 5.01.226
the mantle of queen hermione's; 5.02. 33 P
but we came | to see the statue of our queen. 5.03. 10
dear queen, that ended when i but began, | give 5.03. 45
shall be king | that thou mayst be a queen, and JN 2.01.123
her dowry shall weigh equal with a queen; 2.01.486
since last i went to france to fetch his queen. R2 1.01.131
come on, our queen, to-morrow must we part. 2.01.222
then, thrice-gracious queen, | more than your 2.02. 24
why, is he not with the queen? 2.03. 25
made a divorce betwixt his queen and him, 3.01. 12
uncle, you say the queen is at your house, | for 3.01. 36
poor queen, so that thy state might be no worse, 3.04.102
seen, | in the remembrance of a weeping queen. 3.04.107
have any resting for her true king's queen. 5.01. 6
good sometimes queen, prepare thee hence for 5.01. 37
weep not, sweet queen, for trickling tears are 1H4 2.04.391
god's sake, lords, convey my /tristful queen, 2.04.393
sung by a fair queen in a summer's bow'r, | with 3.01.207
you — but, indeed, to pray for the queen. 2H4 ep 17 P
till satisfied | that fair queen isabel, his H5 1.02. 81
therefore, queen of all, katherine, break thy 5.02.245 P
that i kiss your hand, and i call you my queen. 5.02.252 P
that here i kiss her as my sovereign queen. 5.02.358
he doth intend she shall be england's queen. 1H6 5.01. 45
your bondage happy, to be made a queen? 5.03.111
to be a queen in bondage is more vile | than is 5.03.112
i'll undertake to make thee henry's queen, | to 5.03.117
that marg'ret may be england's royal queen. 5.05. 24
henry is able to enrich his queen, | and not to 5.05. 51
and not to seek a queen to make him rich: 5.05. 52
conclude with me | that margaret shall be queen, 5.05. 78
king henry's faithful and anointed queen. 5.05. 91
margaret shall now be queen, and rule the king; 5.05.107
deliver up my title in the queen | to your most 2H6 1.01. 12
the fairest queen that ever king receiv'd. 1.01. 16
welcome, queen margaret, | i can express no 1.01. 17
long live queen margaret, england's happiness! 1.01. 37
and crown her queen of england ere the thirtieth 1.01. 48 P
done | in entertainment to my princely queen. 1.01. 72
his new bride and england's dear-bought queen, 1.01.252
where as the king and queen do mean to hawk. 1.02. 58
here 'a comes, methinks, and the queen with him. 1.03. 6 P
am i a queen in title and in style, | and must 1.03. 48
strangers in court do take her for the queen. 1.03. 79
good queen, and whet not on these furious peers, 2.01. 33
sent his poor queen to france, from whence she 2.02. 25
why, now is henry king and margaret queen, | and 2.03. 39
meant him any ill, nor the king, nor the queen; 2.03. 89 P
that these great lords, and margaret our queen, 3.01.207
to be a queen, and crown'd with infamy! 3.02. 71
be poisonous too, and kill thy forlorn queen. 3.02. 77
ungentle queen, to call him gentle suffolk! 3.02.290
cease, gentle queen, these execrations, | and 3.02.305
when i have feasted with queen margaret? 4.01. 58
thy lips that kiss'd the queen shall sweep the 4.01. 75
i go of message from the queen to france; 4.01.114
lie, | until the queen his mistress bury it. 4.01.143
so will the queen, that living held him dear. 4.01.147
see, buckingham, somerset comes with th' queen. 5.01. 83
the queen this day here holds her parliament, 3H6 1.01. 35
come, cousin, let us tell the queen these news. 1.01.182
here comes the queen, whose looks bewray her 1.01.211
be patient, gentle queen, and i will stay. 1.01.214
poor queen, how love to me and to her son | hath 1.01.264
the queen with all the northern earls and lords 1.02. 49
the army of the queen mean to besiege us. 1.02. 64
the army of the queen hath got the field. 1.04. 1
i would assay, proud queen, to make thee blush. 1.04.118
needs not, nor it boots thee not, proud queen, 1.04.125
see, ruthless queen, a hapless father's tears! 1.04.156
arm | of unrelenting clifford and the queen; 2.01. 58
the ruthless queen gave him to dry his cheeks 2.01. 61
toward saint albons to intercept the queen, 2.01.114
who look'd full gently on his warlike queen, 2.01.123
the king unto the queen; 2.01.137
the proud insulting queen, | with clifford and 2.01.168
me | the queen is coming with a puissant host, 2.01.207
the queen hath best success when you are absent. 2.02. 74
for margaret my queen, and clifford too, | have 2.05. 16
but love to go | whither the queen intends. 2.05.139
some troops pursue the bloody-minded queen, 2.06. 33
france, | and ask the lady bona for thy queen. 2.06. 90
my queen and son are gone to france for aid; 3.01. 28
poor queen and son, your labor is but lost; 3.01. 32
and she shall be my love or else my queen. 3.02. 88
say that king edward take thee for his queen? 3.02. 89
i know i am too mean to be your queen, | and yet 3.02. 97
you cavil, widow, i did mean my queen. 3.02. 99
answer no more, for thou shalt be my queen. 3.02.106
fair queen of england, worthy margaret, | sit 3.03. 1
great albion's queen in former golden days; 3.03. 7
why, say, fair queen, whence springs this deep 3.03. 12
be plain, queen margaret, and tell thy grief; 3.03. 19
renowned queen, with patience calm the storm, 3.03. 38
and why not queen? 3.03. 78
and thou no more art prince than she is queen. 3.03. 80
queen margaret, prince edward, and oxford, 3.03.109
draw near, queen margaret, and be a witness 3.03.138
and as for you yourself, our quondam queen, 3.03.153
i like it well that our fair queen and mistress 3.03.167
and yours, fair queen? 3.03.171
my noble queen, let former grudges pass, | and 3.03.195
but by thy help to this distressed queen? 3.03.213
this noble queen | and prince shall follow with 3.03.236
that if our queen and this young prince agree, 3.03.241
should not become my wife and england's queen. 4.01. 26
majesty | to raise my state to title of a queen, 4.01. 68
but what said henry's queen? 4.01.102
that margaret your queen and my son edward | be 4.06. 60
the queen from france hath brought a puissant 5.02. 31
those powers that the queen | hath rais'd in 5.03. 7
the queen is valued thirty thousand strong, 5.03. 14
and see our gentle queen how well she fares. 5.05. 89
clarence and gloucester, love my lovely queen, 5.07. 26
and his noble queen | well strook in years, fair R3 1.01. 91
queen margaret saw | thy murd'rous falchion 1.02. 93
maid | than a great queen with this condition, 1.03.107
small joy have i in being england's queen. 1.03.109
ere you were queen, ay, or your husband king, 1.03.120
in me | that i enjoy, being the queen thereof. 1.03.153
a little joy enjoys the queen thereof, | for i 1.03.154
if not, that i am queen, you bow like subjects, 1.03.160
thyself a queen, for me that was a queen, 1.03.201
thyself a queen, for me that was a queen, 1.03.201
die neither mother, wife, nor england's queen! 1.03.208
poor painted queen, vain flourish of my fortune! 1.03.240
teach me to be your queen, and you my subjects: 1.03.251
and tell them 'tis the queen and her allies 1.03.329
good morrow to my sovereign king and queen, 2.01. 47
not | how that the guilty kindred of the queen 2.01.136
told me the king, provok'd to it by the queen, 2.02. 21
i, | the queen your mother and your brother york 3.01. 27
persuade the queen to send the duke of york 3.01. 33
the kindred of the queen, must die at pomfret. 3.02. 50
there to be crowned richard's royal queen. 4.01. 32
nor mother, wife, nor england's counted queen. 4.01. 46
and die ere men can say, "god save the queen!" 4.01. 62
give out | that anne, my queen, is sick and like 4.02. 57
i call'd thee then poor shadow, painted queen, 4.04. 83
a queen in jest, only to fill the scene. 4.04. 91
and kneels, and says, "god save the queen"? 4.04. 94
for queen, a very caitiff crown'd with care; 4.04.101
york's wife, and queen of sad mischance, | these 4.04.114
and do intend to make her queen of england. 4.04.264
even he that makes her queen. 4.04.266
and by that loss your daughter is made queen. 4.04.308
say she shall be a high and mighty queen. 4.04.347
withal say that the queen hath heartily 4.05. 7
under pretense to see the queen his aunt | (for H8 1.01.177
to the good queen possess'd him with a scruple 2.01.158
the queen shall be acquainted | forthwith for 2.02.107
deliver this with modesty to th' queen. 2.02.136
troth and maidenhead, | i would not be a queen. 2.03. 24
yes, troth, and troth. you would not be a queen? 2.03. 34
bow'd would hire me, | old as i am, to queen it. 2.03. 37
i would not be a queen | for all the world. 2.03. 45
that would not be a queen, that would she not, 2.03. 91
the queen is comfortless, and we forgetful | in 2.03.105
say, katherine queen of england, come into the 2.04. 10 P
katherine queen of england, etc. 2.04. 12 P
thinking that | we are a queen (or long have 2.04. 71
the queen is obstinate, | stubborn to justice, 2.04.121
katherine queen of england, come into the court. 2.04.126 P
speak thee out) | the queen of earthly queens. 2.04.142
by some of these | the queen is put in anger. 2.04.162
world against the person | of the good queen, 2.04.225
katherine our queen, before the primest creature 2.04.230
the queen being absent, 'tis a needful fitness 2.04.232
made to the queen to call back her appeal | she 2.04.235
katherine no more | shall be call'd queen, but 3.02. 70
the queen's queen? 3.02. 95
this day was view'd in open as his queen, 3.02.404
stand close, the queen is coming. 4.01. 36
having brought the queen | to a prepar'd place 4.01. 63
she had all the royal makings of a queen, | as 4.01. 87
were those that went on each side of the queen? 4.01.100
yet like | a queen, and daughter to a king, 4.02.172
now, lovell, from the queen what is the news? 5.01. 61
pray'rs remember | th' estate of my poor queen. 5.01. 74
is the queen deliver'd? 5.01.162
sir, your queen | desires your visitation, and 5.01.166
give her an hundred marks. i'll to the queen. 5.01.170
and to your royal grace and the good queen, | my 5.04. 4
ye must all see the queen, and she must thank ye 5.04. 73
queen hecuba and helen. TRO 1.02. 1
queen hecuba laugh'd that her eyes ran o'er. 1.02.142 P
he brought a grecian queen, whose youth and 2.02. 78
what treason were it to the ransack'd queen, 2.02.150
especially to you, fair queen, fair thoughts be 3.01. 45 P
you speak your fair pleasure, sweet queen. 3.01. 48 P
i have business to my lord, dear queen. 3.01. 58 P
well, sweet queen, you are pleasant with me. 3.01. 62 P
go to, sweet queen, go to — commends himself 3.01. 66 P
sweet queen, sweet queen, that's a sweet queen 3.01. 70 P
sweet queen, sweet queen, that's a sweet queen 3.01. 70 P
sweet queen, that's a sweet queen — i' faith — 3.01. 71 P
what says my sweet queen, my very very sweet 3.01. 79 P
says my sweet queen, my very very sweet queen? 3.01. 80 P
what says my sweet queen? 3.01. 84 P
now, sweet queen. 3.01. 95 P
in love with a thing you have, sweet queen. 3.01. 98 P
not i, honey-sweet queen. 3.01.141 P
farewell, sweet queen. 3.01.145 P
i will, sweet queen. 3.01.147 P
here is a letter from queen hecuba, | a token 5.01. 39
now, by the jealous queen of heaven, that kiss COR 5.03. 46
the eldest son of this distressed queen. TIT 1.01.103
the self-same gods that arm'd the queen of troy 1.01.136
his tent | may favor tamora, the queen of goths 1.01.139
(when goths were goths and tamora was queen), 1.01.140
clear up, fair queen, that cloudy countenance; 1.01.263
can make you greater than the queen of goths. 1.01.269
and therefore, lovely tamora, queen of goths, 1.01.315
speak, queen of goths, dost thou applaud my 1.01.321
if saturnine advance the queen of goths, | she 1.01.330
ascend, fair queen, pantheon. 1.01.333
how comes it that the subtile queen of goths 1.01.392
and make them know what 'tis to let a queen 1.01.454
to wanton with this queen, | this goddess, this 2.01. 21
believe me, queen, your /swart cimmerian | doth 2.03. 72
o tamora, be call'd a gentle queen, | and with 2.03.168
beg at the gates, like tarquin and his queen. 3.01.298
confederate with the queen and her two sons; 5.01.108
and, would you represent our queen aright, | it 5.02. 89
and in the emperor's court | there is a queen, 5.02.105
welcome, dread queen; 5.03. 26
o then i see queen mab hath been with you. ROM 1.04. 53
the queen that bore thee, | oft'ner upon her MAC 4.03.109
the queen, my lord, is dead. 5.05. 16
of this dead butcher and his fiend-like queen, 5.09. 35
therefore our sometime sister, now our queen, HAM 1.02. 8
the will of my most seeming virtuous queen. 1.05. 46
of life, of crown, of queen, at once dispatch'd, 1.05. 75
or my dear majesty your queen here, think, | if 2.02.135
know the good king and queen have sent for you. 2.02.281 P
secrecy to the king and queen moult no feather. 2.02.295 P
"but who, ah woe, had seen the mobled queen" — 2.02.502
"the mobled queen"? 2.02.503 P
and the queen too, and that presently. 3.02. 48 P
the queen, your mother, in most great affliction 3.02.311 P
my lord, the queen would speak with you, and 3.02.374 P
my crown, mine own ambition, and my queen. 3.03. 55
you are the queen, your husband's brother's wife 3.04. 15
for who, that's but a queen, fair, sober, wise, 3.04.189
the queen his mother | lives almost by his looks 4.07. 11
these to your majesty, this to the queen. 4.07. 37
here comes the king, | the queen, the courtiers. 5.01.218
the king and queen and all are coming down. 5.02.203 P
the queen desires you to use some gentle 5.02.206 P
the queen carouses to thy fortune, hamlet. 5.02.289
look to the queen there ho! 5.02.303
how does the queen? 5.02.308
wretched queen, adieu! 5.02.333
is queen of us, of ours, and our fair france. LR 1.01.257
though that the queen on special cause is here, 4.06.215
with him i sent the queen, | my reason all the 5.03. 51
as i am egypt's queen, | thou blushest, antony, ANT 1.01. 29
fie, wrangling queen! 1.01. 48
come, my queen, | last night you did desire it. 1.01. 54
the soothsayer that you prais'd so to th' queen? 1.02. 3 P
not he, the queen. 1.02. 79
i must from this enchanting queen break off; 1.02.128
the cause of our expedience to the queen, | and 1.02.178
now, my dearest queen — 1.03. 17
o, never was there queen | so mightily betrayed! 1.03. 24
most sweet queen — 1.03. 31
hear me, queen: 1.03. 41
she's dead, my queen. 1.03. 59
my precious queen, forbear, | and give true 1.03. 73
nor the queen of ptolomy | more womanly than he; 1.04. 6
last thing he did, dear queen, | he kiss'd — 1.05. 39
a certain queen to caesar in a mattress. 2.06. 70
ay, dread queen. 3.03. 8
of lower syria, cyprus, lydia, | absolute queen. 3.06. 11
do, most dear queen. 3.11. 26
the queen, my lord, the queen. 3.11. 42
the queen, my lord, the queen. 3.11. 42
most noble sir, arise, the queen approaches. 3.11. 46
sir, the queen. 3.11. 50
the queen | of audience nor desire shall fail, 3.12. 20
the queen shall then have courtesy, so she 3.13. 15
come on, my queen, | there's sap in't yet. 3.13.190
before, | and let the queen know of our /gests. 4.08. 2
i made these wars for egypt, and the queen, 4.14. 15
i come, my queen! 4.14. 50
my queen and eros | have by their brave 4.14. 97
one word, sweet queen: 4.15. 45

the queen my mistress, | confin'd in all she has 5.01. 52
caesar sends greeting to the queen of egypt, 5.02. 9
if your master | would have a queen his beggar, 5.02. 16
royal queen! 5.02. 37
o cleopatra! thou art taken, queen. 5.02. 38
and take a queen | worth many babes and beggars! 5.02. 47
for the queen, | i'll take her to my guard. 5.02. 66
which is the queen of egypt? 5.02.112
good queen, let us entreat you. 5.02.158
no, dear queen, | for we intend so to dispose 5.02.185
where's the queen? 5.02.197
adieu, good queen, i must attend on caesar. 5.02.206
show me, my women, like a queen; 5.02.227
where's the queen? 5.02.320
so is the queen, | that most desir'd the match. CYM 1.01. 11
comes the gentleman, | the queen, and princess. 1.01. 69
my queen, my mistress! 1.01. 92
thither write, my queen, | and with mine eyes 1.01. 99
that mightst have had the sole son of my queen! 1.01.138
it was his queen, his queen! 1.03. 5
it was his queen, his queen! 1.03. 5
the queen, madam, | desires your highness' 1.03. 37
get them dispatch'd, | i will attend the queen. 1.03. 40
or she that bore you was no queen, and you 1.06.127
fight with me because of the queen my mother. 2.01. 19 P
to your mistress, | attend the queen and us; 2.03. 62
come, our queen. 2.03. 63
here is a box, i had it from the queen, | what's 3.04.188
but, my gentle queen, | where is our daughter? 3.05. 29
know him, 'tis | cloten, the son o' th' queen. 4.02. 65
thou shalt know | i am son to th' queen. 4.02. 93
son to the queen (after his own report), | who 4.02.119
my queen | upon a desperate bed, and in a time 4.03. 5
now for the counsel of my son and queen! 4.03. 27
happiness, i must report | the queen is dead. 5.05. 27
my queen, my life, my wife! 5.05.226
i had it from the queen. 5.05.242
i left out one thing which the queen confess'd, 5.05.244
the queen, sir, very oft importun'd me | to 5.05.249
wrought by th' hand | of his queen mother, which 5.05.362
which | we were dissuaded by our wicked queen, 5.05.463
come, queen a' th' feast — | for, daughter, so PER 2.03. 17
by juno, that is queen of marriage, | all viands 2.03. 30
his queen, with child, makes her desire — 3.ch. 40
how does my queen? 3.01. 7
in your arms this piece | of your dead queen. 3.01. 18
here's all that is left living of your queen: 3.01. 20
sir, your queen must overboard. 3.01. 47 P
as you think meet. most wretched queen! 3.01. 54
have lost | this queen, worth all our mundane 3.02. 71
gentlemen, this queen will live. 3.02. 92
o your sweet queen! 3.03. 7
his woeful queen we leave at ephesus, | unto 4.ch. 3
hail, madam, and my queen! 5.03. 49
will you deliver | how this dead queen relives? 5.03. 64
yet there, my queen, | we'll celebrate their 5.03. 79
in pericles, his queen and daughter, seen, 5.03. 87
o queen emilia, | fresher than may, sweeter TNK 3.01. 4
on, where she sticks | the queen of flowers. 5.01. 45
hail, sovereign queen of secrets, who hast power 5.01. 77
o sacred, shadowy, cold, and constant queen, 5.01.137
therefore, most modest queen, | he of the two 5.01.157
by this the love–sick queen began to sweat, VEN 175
poor queen of love, in thine own law forlorn, 251
these mine eyes, true leaders to their queen, 503
"fair queen," quoth he, "if any love you owe me, 523
but all in vain, good queen, it will not be; 607
where their queen | means to immure herself, and 1193
of either's color was the other queen, | proving LUC 66
the silver–shining queen he would distain; 786
looks as none could look but beauty's queen. PP 4. 4
then fell she on her back, fair queen, and 4.13
eye, | yet not so wistly as this queen on him. 6.12
sound | that phoebus' lute, the queen of music, 8.10
fair was the morn when the fair queen of love, 9. 1
she, silly queen, with more than love's good 9. 7
was seen | 'twixt this turtle and his queen: PHT 31
as on the finger of a throned queen | the basest SON 96. 5

QUEEN–MOTHER 1 FR 0.0001 REL FR 1 V 0 P
let his queen–mother all alone entreat him | to HAM 3.01.182

QUEEN'S 33 FR 0.0037 REL FR 29 V 4 P
berowne, one of the strange queen's lords. LLL 4.02.130 P
a letter to a sequent of the stranger queen's, 4.02.139 P
at the good queen's entreaty. WT 1.02.220
at the queen's be't; 1.02.221
passion more, alas, | than the queen's life? 2.03. 29
he | the sacred honor of himself, his queen's, 2.03. 85
mere conceit and fear | of the queen's speed, is 3.02.145
i might have look'd upon my queen's full eyes, 5.01. 53
be such | as, walk'd your first queen's ghost, 5.01. 80
be when your first queen's again in breath; 5.01. 83
at the relation of the queen's death (with the 5.02. 84 P
kindred, are going to see the queen's picture. 5.02.173 P
and stain'd the beauty of a fair queen's cheeks R2 3.01. 14
my quarrel and this english queen's are one. 3H6 3.03.216
away, away, to meet the queen's great power! 5.02. 50
is no man /is secure | but the queen's kindred, R3 1.01. 72
and that the queen's kindred are made 1.01. 95
we are the queen's abjects, and must obey. 1.01.106
of, | to part the queen's proud kindred from the 2.02.150
and the queen's sons and brothers haught and 2.03. 28
by the suggestion of the queen's allies; 3.02.101
us and the emperor (the queen's great nephew), H8 2.02. 25
in affection to | a creature of the queen's, 3.02. 36
the late queen's gentlewoman? 3.02. 94
the queen's queen? 3.02. 95
the queen's in labor, | they say in great 5.01. 18
and my queen's a squire | more tight at this ANT 4.04. 14
and tell the fishes he's the queen's son, cloten CYM 4.02.153
he was a queen's son, boys, | and though he came 4.02.244
by the queen's dram she swallow'd. 5.05.381
make swift the pangs | of my queen's travails! PER 3.01. 14
my queen's square brows, | her stature to an 5.01.108
but tell me now | my drown'd queen's name, as in 5.01.205

QUEENS 13 FR 0.0014 REL FR 13 V 0 P
o queen of queens, how far dost thou excel | no LLL 4.03. 39
present deeds, | that all your acts are queens. WT 4.04.146
before the kings and queens of france. 1H6 1.06. 27
that chair where kings and queens were crown'd, 2H6 1.02. 38
say, what art thou talk'st of kings and queens? 3H6 3.01. 55
and reverend looker–on of two fair queens. R3 4.01. 30
they shall be praying nuns, not weeping queens; 4.04.202
speak thee out) | the queen of earthly queens. H8 2.04.142
kings, queens, and states, | maids, matrons, nay CYM 3.04. 37
we are three queens, whose sovereigns fell TNK 1.01. 39
think | of rotten kings or blubber'd queens? 1.01.180
i freely lend | to do these poor queens service. 1.01.199
queens, | follow your soldier. 1.01.210

QUELL 6 FR 0.0006 REL FR 6 V 0 P
the least whereof would quell a lover's hope, TGV 4.02. 13
and thrum, | quail, crush, conclude, and quell! MND 5.01.287
either to quell the dolphin utterly, | or bring 1H6 1.01.163
to quell the rebels and their complices. 2H6 5.01.212
that your activity may defeat and quell | the TIM 4.03.163
who shall bear the guilt | of our great quell? MAC 1.07. 72

QUELL'D 1 FR 0.0001 REL FR 1 V 0 P
how /order should be quell'd, and by this STM II.C 82

QUENCH 31 FR 0.0035 REL FR 30 V 1 P
as seek to quench the fire of love with words. TGV 2.07. 20
i do not seek to quench your love's hot fire, 2.07. 21
great pails of puddled mire to quench the hair; ERR 5.01.173
death | will quench the wonder of her infamy. ADO 4.01.239
and with saciety seeks to quench his thirst. SHR 1.01. 24
and the thing she took to quench it | she would WT 4.04. 61
come, quench your blushes, and present yourself 4.04. 67
might quench the zeal | of all professors else, 5.01.107
to ashes, ere our blood shall quench that fire. JN 3.01.345
and quench /his fiery indignation | even in the 4.01. 63
scarce serves to quench my furnace–burning heart 3H6 2.01. 80
burns me up with flames that tears would quench. 2.01. 84
which, being suffer'd, rivers cannot quench. 4.08. 8
if with the sap of reason you would quench, | or H8 1.01.148
my lord and me — | which god's dew quench! 2.04. 80
sought their malice) | to quench mine honor; 5.02. 16
this is the way to kindle, not to quench. COR 3.01.196
look thee, here's water to quench it. 5.02. 72 P
and bid the owners quench them with their tears. TIT 5.01.134
that quench the fire of your pernicious rage ROM 1.01. 84
and quench the fire, the room is grown too hot. 1.05. 28
and quench the guards of th' ever–fixed pole; OTH 2.01. 15
if i quench thee, thou flaming minister, | i can 5.02. 8
dost thou think in time | she will not quench, CYM 1.05. 47
that were to blow at fire in hope to quench it, PER 1.04. 4
dreadful thunders, gently quench | thy nimble, 3.01. 5
doth quench the maiden burning of his cheeks; VEN 50
they burn too, i'll quench them with my tears. 192
to quench the coal which in his liver glows. LUC 47
who in a salt–wav'd ocean quench their light, 1231
and with my tears quench troy that burns so long 1468

QUENCH'D 7 FR 0.0008 REL FR 5 V 2 P
in all reason should have quench'd her love) MM 3.01.241 P
quench'd in the chaste beams of the wat'ry moon, MND 2.01.162
moist hesperus hath quench'd her sleepy lamp, AWW 2.01.164
what hath quench'd them hath given me fire. MAC 2.02. 2
have buoy'd up | and quench'd the stelled fires; LR 3.07. 61
so being thus quench'd | of hope, not longing, mine CYM 5.05.195
of hers must be quench'd with some present PER 4.02.124 P

QUENCHED 1 FR 0.0001 REL FR 1 V 0 P
this brand she quenched in a cool well by, SON 154. 9

QUENCHING 2 FR 0.0002 REL FR 1 V 1 P
quenching my familiar smile with an austere TN 2.05. 65 P
quenching the flame of bold rebellion | even 2H4 in 26

QUENCHLESS 2 FR 0.0002 REL FR 2 V 0 P
i dare your quenchless fury to more rage. 3H6 1.04. 28
are balls of quenchless fire to burn thy city. LUC 1554

QUERN 1 FR 0.0001 REL FR 1 V 0 P
skim milk, and sometimes labor in the quern, MND 2.01. 36

QUEST 10 FR 0.0011 REL FR 9 V 1 P
might bear him company in the quest of him: ERR 1.01.129
in quest of them (unhappy), ah, lose myself. 1.02. 40
strond, | and many jasons come in quest of her. MV 1.01.172
if lusty love should go in quest of beauty, JN 2.01.426
what lawful quest have given their verdict up R3 1.04.184
ay, marry, is't — crowner's quest law. HAM 5.01. 22 P
dower with her, | or cease your quest of love? LR 1.01.193
and sail and high expense | can stead the quest. PER 3.ch. 21
this title is impanelled | a quest of thoughts, SON 46.10
had, having, and in quest to have, extreme, | a 129.10

QUESTANT 1 FR 0.0001 REL FR 1 V 0 P
to wed it, when | the bravest questant shrinks. AWW 2.01. 16

/QUESTION 6 FR 0.0006 REL FR 3 V 3 P
/question /surveyors, /know /our /own /estate, 2H4 1.03. 53
/let /me /question /more /in /particular. HAM 2.02.239 P
/that /cry /out /on /the /top /of /question, 2.02.340 P
/player /went /to /cuffs /in /the /question. 2.02.356 P
/made /she /no /verbal /question? LR 4.03. 24
/the /question /of /cordelia /and /her /father 5.03. 58

QUESTION 152 FR 0.0171 REL FR 105 V 47 P
my tale provokes that question. TMP 1.02.140
but that is not the question: WIV 1.01.220 P
the question is concerning your marriage. 1.01.220 P
disarm them, and let them question. 3.01. 76 P
my daughter will i question how she loves you, 3.04. 90
though first in question, is thy secondary. MM 1.01. 46
but in the loss of question), that you, his 2.04. 90
wise? why, no question but he was. 3.02.138 P
my lord, give me leave to question, you shall 5.01.271 P
that's a question; how shall we try it? ERR 5.01.422
do you question me, as an honest man should do, ADO 1.01.166 P
i will send for him, and question him yourself. 1.02. 19 P
for, out a' question, you were born in a merry 2.01.332 P
a commodity in question, i warrant you. 3.03.179 P
let me but move one question to your daughter, 4.01. 73
question: 5.02. 82 P
in the true course of all the question. 5.04. 6
which out of question thou wilt be, if my cousin 5.04.115 P
how needless was it then | to ask the question? LLL 2.01.117
and, out of question, so it is sometimes: 4.01. 30
i do, sans question. 5.01. 86 P
therefore, fair hermia, question your desires, MND 1.01. 67
therefore be out of hope, of question, of doubt; 3.02.279
more wrong | in making question of my uttermost MV 1.01.156
and i no question make | to have it of my trust, 1.01.184
i pray you think you question with the jew: 4.01. 70
you may as well use question with the wolf | why 4.01. 73
that holds this present question in the court? 4.01.172
i'll stay no longer question. 4.01.346
one of you question yond man | if he for gold AYL 2.04. 64
as yet to question you about your fortunes. 2.07.172
duke yesterday, and had much question with him. 3.04. 36 P
neither call the giddiness of it in question, 5.02. 5 P
after some question with him, was converted 5.04.161
let me ask a question. AWW 1.01.112 P
more should i question thee, and more i must — 2.01.205
your constable, it will fit any question. 2.02. 31 P
i will be a fool in question, hoping to be the 2.02. 39 P
rather than suffer question for your residence. 2.05. 38 P
i'll question her. 3.05. 32 P
no question. TN 1.03. 87 P
past question, for thou seest it will not /curl 1.03. 98 P
that you call in question the continuance of his 1.04. 6 P
it is, in contempt of question, her hand. 2.05. 88 P
make the trial of it in any constant question. 4.02. 49 P
but out of question 'tis maria's hand. 5.01.347
i'll question you | of my lord's tricks and WT 1.02. 60
make that thy question, and go rot! 1.02.324
avoid what's grown than question how 'tis born. 1.02.433
we are) have some question with the shepherd; 4.02. 48 P
who now | has these poor men in question. 5.01.198
"i shall beseech you" — that is question now; JN 1.01.195
"no, sir," says question, "i, sweet sir, at 1.01.199
and so, ere answer knows what question would, 1.01.200
my liege, this haste was hot in question, | and 1H4 1.01. 34
me | directly unto this question that i ask. 2.03. 86
i must not have you henceforth question me 2.03.103
while i question my puny drawer to what end he 2.04. 30 P
a question not to be ask'd. 2.04.408 P
a question to be ask'd. 2.04.410 P
and breed a kind of question in our cause. 4.01. 68
to devour the way, | staying no longer question. 2H4 1.01. 48
he that was in question for the robb'ry? 1.02. 60 P
the question then, lord hastings, standeth thus: 1.03. 15
so the question stands. 4.01. 53
i muse you make so slight a question. 4.01.165
question your royal thoughts, make the case 5.02. 91
time | did push it out of farther question. H5 1.01. 5
war nor no known quarrel were in question) | but 2.04. 17
question your grace the late embassadors, | with 2.04. 31
king | come here himself to question our delay; 2.04.142
full fain heard some question 'tween you tway. 3.02.119 P
and out of doubt and out of question too, and 5.01. 46 P
you'll question this gentlewoman about me; 5.02.198 P
question her proudly, let thy looks be stern. 1H6 1.02. 62
ask me what question thou canst possible, | and 1.02. 87
question, my lords, no further of the case, 2.01. 72
the truth | about a certain question in the law 4.01. 95
no question of that; 2H6 4.02. 57 P
ay, there's the question; 4.02.141
took him, | to question of his apprehension. 3H6 3.02.122
and let your reason with your choler question H8 1.01.130
which might | induce you to the question on't? 2.04.152
the question did at first so stagger me, 2.04.213
justice and the truth o' th' question carries 5.01.130
this is her question. TRO 1.02.159 P
that's true, make no question of that. 1.02.160 P
the first sword was drawn about this question, 2.02. 18
and on the cause and question now in hand | have 2.02.164
i'll decline the whole question: 2.03. 52 P
we dare not move the question of our place, | or 2.03. 82
no question. 2.03.146 P
too, if she call your activity in question. 3.02. 57 P
'tis like he'll question me | why such 3.03. 42
sir, | during all question of the gentle truce; 4.01. 12
in this i do not call your faith in question 4.04. 84
gods, proud man, | to answer such a question. 4.05.248
that he will give them make i as little question COR 2.01.230
no question ask'd him by any of the senators but 4.05.193 P
now question me no more, we are espied. TIT 2.03. 48
way | to call hers, exquisite, in question more. ROM 1.01.229
stay not to question, for the watch is coming. 5.03.158
he last ask'd the question. TIM 2.02. 59 P
might change his nature, there's the question. JC 2.01. 13
the question of his death is enroll'd in the 3.02. 38 P
here, | and call in question our necessities. 4.03.165
or are you aught | that man may question? MAC 1.03. 43
when i burnt in desire to question them further, 1.05. 4 P
and question this most bloody piece of work, 2.03.128
grows worse and worse, | question enrages him. 3.04.117
that was and is the question of these wars. HAM 1.01.111
by this encompassment and drift of question 2.01. 10
niggard of question, but of our demands | most 3.01. 13
to be, or not to be, that is the question: 3.01. 55
time some necessary question of the play be then 3.02. 43 P
for 'tis a question left us yet to prove, 3.02.202
go, go, you question with a wicked tongue. 3.04. 12
will not debate the question of this straw. 4.04. 26
to earth, | that i must call't in question. 4.05.218
i'll put another question to thee. 5.01. 38 P
when you are ask'd this question next, say "a 5.01. 58 P
but since, so jump upon this bloody question, 5.02.375
i'd have it come to question. LR 1.03. 13
and i have one thing, of a queasy question, 2.01. 17
hadst been set i' th' stocks for that question, 2.04. 65 P
particular broils | are not the question here. 5.01. 31
thy great employment | will not bear question; 5.03. 33
so may he with more facile question bear it, OTH 1.03. 23
and such fair question | as soul to soul 1.03.113
now will i question cassio of bianca, | a 4.01. 93
there be some such, no question. 4.03. 63
your being in egypt | might be my question. ANT 2.02. 40
if we contend, | out of our question wipe him. 2.02. 81
world oppos'd, he being | the mered question. 3.13. 10
and had (besides this gentleman in question) CYM 1.01. 34
doctor, | thou ask'st me such a question. 1.05. 11
home, i grant | we were to question farther; 2.04. 52
further to question me of your king's departure. PER 1.03. 11
success i dare not | make any timorous question; TNK 1.03. 3
yes, 'tis a question | to me that know not. 2.03. 61
i am persuaded this question, sick between 's, 3.01.113
honor | in public question with their swords. 3.06.222
neither heard i one question | of your name or 4.01. 15
business withal, fits it to every question. 4.03. 8 P

give me the victory of this question, which | is 5.01.127
you leave dispute | that are above our question. 5.04.136
things that ever stood in such a question. STM II.C 21
then of thy beauty do i question make | that SON 12. 9
nor dare i question with my jealious thought 57. 9
and controversy hence a question takes, LC 110
all kind of arguments and question deep, | all 121
and yet do question make | what i should do 321
QUESTIONABLE 1 FR 0.0001 REL FR 1 V 0 P
thou com'st in such a questionable shape | that HAM 1.04. 43
QUESTION'D 6 FR 0.0006 REL FR 6 V 0 P
i am question'd by my fears of what may chance WT 1.02. 11
hast found mine, | but how, is to be question'd; 5.03.139
where this is question'd send our letters, with H8 1.02. 99
it is not to be question'd | that they had 2.04. 50
still question'd me the story of my life | from OTH 1.03.129
thereto so o'ergrown, | cannot be question'd. CYM 4.04. 34
QUESTIONED 2 FR 0.0002 REL FR 2 V 0 P
many holiday and lady terms | he questioned me, 1H4 1.03. 47
for after supper long he questioned | with LUC 122
QUESTIONEDST 1 FR 0.0001 REL FR 1 V 0 P
o' th' haven, | and questionedst every sail. CYM 1.03. 2
QUESTIONING 1 FR 0.0001 REL FR 1 V 0 P
we sing, | feed yourselves with questioning; AYL 5.04.138
QUESTIONLESS 2 FR 0.0002 REL FR 2 V 0 P
that i should questionless be fortunate! MV 1.01.176
she questionless with her sweet harmony, | and PER 5.01. 45
QUESTION'S 5 FR 0.0005 REL FR 4 V 1 P
fie, what a question's that, | if thou wert near MV 3.04. 79
studied, and that question's out of my part. TN 1.05.179 P
whither? why, what a question's that! TNK 2.03. 61
since that | your question's with your equal, 3.01. 55
and garland | to crown the question's title. 5.03. 17
QUESTIONS 14 FR 0.0015 REL FR 7 V 7 P
here cease more questions. TMP 1.02.184
you ask him some questions in his accidence. WIV 4.01. 16 P
long of you that spur me with such questions. LLL 2.01.118
i will not stay thy questions. MND 2.01.235
from whence you have studied your questions. AYL 3.02.274 P
a bountiful answer that fits all questions. AWW 2.02. 16 P
will your answer serve fit to all questions? 2.02. 20 P
an answer of such fitness for all questions? 2.02. 29 P
mend the ruff and sing, ask questions and sing, 3.02. 7 P
that shall make answer to such questions | as by 2H6 1.02. 80
it is enough, i'll think upon the questions. 1.02. 82
that is, make questions, and by them answer. OTH 3.04. 17 P
these are strange questions. TNK 4.01. 35
but this very day | i ask'd her questions, and 4.01. 38
QUESTRISTS 1 FR 0.0001 REL FR 1 V 0 P
hot questrists after him, met him at gate, | who LR 3.07. 17
/QUESTS 1 FR 0.0001 REL FR 1 V 0 P
with these false and most contrarious /quests MM 4.01. 61
QUESTS 1 FR 0.0001 REL FR 1 V 0 P
the senate hath sent about three several quests OTH 1.02. 46
QUEUBUS 1 FR 0.0001 REL FR 0 V 1 P
the vapians passing the equinoctial of queubus. TN 2.03. 24 P
QUI 7 FR 0.0008 REL FR 5 V 2 P
it is qui, /quae, quod: WIV 4.01. 77 P
and "honi soit qui mal y pense" write | in 5.05. 69
but vir /sapit qui pauca loquitur. LLL 4.02. 80 P
qui vous la? H5 4.01. 35
qui la? 1H6 3.02. 13
"qui me alit, me extinguit." PER 2.02. 33
let him play | qui passa o' th' bells and bones. TNK 3.05. 86
/QUICK 1 FR 0.0001 REL FR 1 V 0 P
/nimble /stroke | /of /quick /cross /lightning? LR 4.07. 34
QUICK 107 FR 0.0121 REL FR 82 V 25 P
fetch us in fuel, and be quick, thou'rt best, TMP 1.02.366
i'll not show him | where the quick freshes are. 3.02. 67
incite them to quick motion, for i must | bestow 4.01. 39
with their high wrongs i am strook to th' quick, 5.01. 25
shall make it | go quick away — the story of my 5.01.305
beshrew me, but you have a quick wit. TGV 1.01.125 P
more than quick words do move a woman's mind. 3.01. 91
you have a quick ear. 4.02. 63 P
alas, i had rather be set quick i' th' earth, WIV 3.04. 86
quick, quick! 4.02. 82 P
quick, quick! 4.02. 82 P
brief, short, quick, snap. 4.05. 3 P
ay; come; quick. 4.05. 43 P
our haste from hence is of so quick condition MM 1.01. 53
break off thy song, and haste thee quick away. 4.01. 7
hence hath offense his quick celerity, | when it 4.02.110
quick, dispatch, and send the head to angelo. 4.03. 92
how dearly would it touch thee to the quick, ERR 2.02.130
that, in despite of his quick wit and his queasy ADO 2.01.383 P
thy wit is as quick as the greyhound's mouth — 5.02. 11 P
but is there no quick recreation granted? LLL 1.01.161
and therefore apt, because quick. 1.02. 23 P
that an eel is quick. 1.02. 28 P
i do say thou art quick in answers; 1.02. 29 P
on serious business craving quick dispatch, 2.01. 31
you must not be so quick. 2.01.117
a sweet touch, a quick venue of wit — snip, 5.01. 59 P
venue of wit — snip, snap, quick and home. 5.01. 60 P
and quick berowne hath plighted faith to me. 5.02.283
she's quick, the child brags in her belly 5.02.676 P
jaquenetta that is quick by him and hang'd for 5.02.681 P
so quick bright things come to confusion. MND 1.01.149
the ear more quick of apprehension makes; 3.02.178
quick, come! 3.02.256
quick, quick, i pray thee, draw the curtain MV 2.09. 1
quick, quick, i pray thee, draw the curtain 2.09. 1
see | quick cupid's post that comes so mannerly. 2.09.100
jealous in honor, sudden, and quick in quarrel, AYL 2.07.151
quick proceeders, marry! SHR 4.02. 11
if the quick fire of youth light not your mind, AWW 4.02. 5
one that's dead is quick — | and now behold the 5.03.303
o spirit of love, how quick and fresh art thou, TN 1.01. 9
for thy assailant is quick, skillful, and deadly 3.04.225 P
not to be buried, | but quick and in mine arms. WT 4.04.132
to have an open ear, a quick eye, and a nimble 4.04.671 P
quick is mine ear to hear of good towards him. R2 2.01.234
guts away as nimbly, with as quick dexterity, 1H4 2.04.259 P
come, quick, quick, that i may lay my head in 3.01.227 P
quick, quick, that i may lay my head in thy lap. 3.01.227 P
and his quick wit wasted in giving reckonings; 2H4 1.02.170 P
it, makes it apprehensive, quick, forgetive, 4.03. 99 P
the mercy that was quick in us but late, | by H5 2.02. 79
and shall our quick blood, spirited with wine, 3.05. 21
in the quick forge and working-house of thought, 5.pr. 23
and something lean to cutpurse of quick hand. 5.01. 86
this speedy and quick appearance argues proof 1H6 5.03. 8
a breach that craves a quick expedient stop! 2H6 3.01.288
my eye's too quick, my heart o'erweens too much, 3H6 3.02.144
or earth gape open wide and eat him quick, | as R3 1.02. 65
and cheer his grace with quick and merry eyes. 1.03. 5
then give way, dull clouds, to my quick curses! 1.03.195
boy, | bold, quick, ingenious, forward, capable: 3.01.155
mad'st quick conveyance with her good aunt anne. 4.04.283
your reasons are too shallow and too quick. 4.04.361
highness | would give it quick consideration, H8 1.02. 66
a woman of quick sense. TRO 4.05. 54
now, mars, i prithee make us quick in work, COR 1.04. 10
that wound beyond their feeling to the quick. TIT 4.02. 28
but, titus, i have touch'd thee to the quick; 4.04. 36
hath not so green, so quick, so fair an eye | as ROM 3.05.220
thy drugs are quick. 5.03.120
shall demonstrate these quick blows of fortune's TIM 1.01. 91
th' art quick, | but yet i'll bury thee; 4.03. 45
part | of that quick spirit that is in antony. JC 1.02. 29
he was quick mettle when he went to school. 1.02.296
observe his looks, | i'll tent him to the quick. HAM 2.02.597
i have in quick determination | thus set it down 3.01.168
but to the quick of th' ulcer: 4.07.123
'tis for the dead, not for the quick, therefore 5.01.126 P
'tis a quick lie, sir, 'twill away again from me 5.01.128 P
now pile your dust upon the quick and dead, 5.01.251
be buried quick with her, and so will i. 5.01.279
but yaw neither, in respect of his quick sail. 5.02.115 P
to some provision | give thee quick conduct. LR 3.06. 97
make love's quick pants in desdemona's arms, OTH 2.01. 80
whom i trace | for his quick hunting, stand the 2.01.304
quick, quick, fear nothing; 5.01. 3
quick, quick, fear nothing; 5.01. 3
forth weeds | when our quick winds lie still, ANT 1.02.110
under us require, | our quick remove from hence. 1.02.196
quick, and return. 1.03. 5
lieutenant, | for quick accumulation of renown, 3.01. 19
o, quick, or i am gone. 4.15. 31
quick, quick, good hands. 5.02. 39
quick, quick, good hands. 5.02. 39
the quick comedians | extemporally will stage us 5.02.216
quick. 5.02.283
walk with leonine, the air is quick there, | and PER 4.01. 27
for | the gods are quick of ear, and i am sworn 4.01. 69
of what a fiery sparkle and quick sweetness, TNK 4.02. 13
nimbly she fastens (o, how quick is love!); VEN 38
eyes are grey, and bright, and quick in turning; 140
now quick desire hath caught the yielding prey, 547
in youth, quick bearing and dexterity; LUC 1389
mars his sword nor war's quick fire shall burn SON 55. 7
so far from variation or quick change? 76. 2
of his quick objects hath the mind no part, 113. 7
QUICK-ANSWER'D 1 FR 0.0001 REL FR 1 V 0 P
ready in gibes, quick-answer'd, saucy, and | as CYM 3.04.158
QUICK-CONCEIVING 1 FR 0.0001 REL FR 1 V 0 P
and to your quick-conceiving discontents | i'll 1H4 1.03.189
QUICKEN 9 FR 0.0010 REL FR 9 V 0 P
him out | and quicken his embraced heaviness MV 2.08. 52
talk, | music and poesy use to quicken you, SHR 1.01. 36
quicken a rock, and make you dance canary | with AWW 2.01. 74
my words are dull, o, quicken them with thine! R3 4.04.124
to quicken your increase, i will beget | mine 4.04.297
thou dost ravish from my chin | will quicken, LR 3.07. 39
plague is fated to us | when we do quicken. OTH 3.03.277
the shambles, | that quicken even with blowing. 4.02. 67
when thou hast liv'd, | quicken with kissing. ANT 4.15. 39
QUICKEN'D 1 FR 0.0001 REL FR 1 V 0 P
quicken'd with youthful spleen and warlike rage, 1H6 4.06. 13
QUICKENS 2 FR 0.0002 REL FR 2 V 0 P
the mistress which i serve quickens what's dead, TMP 3.01. 6
by the fire | that quickens nilus' slime, i go ANT 1.03. 69
QUICKER 2 FR 0.0002 REL FR 2 V 0 P
your hands than mine are quicker for a fray; MND 3.02.342
for when these quicker elements are gone | in SON 45. 5
QUICK-EY'D 1 FR 0.0001 REL FR 1 V 0 P
shows, | that are quick-ey'd pleasure's foes! TNK 1.05. 8
QUICKLIER 1 FR 0.0001 REL FR 0 V 1 P
blown down, man will quicklier be blown up. AWW 1.01.124 P
/QUICKLY 2 FR 0.0002 REL FR 2 V 0 P
/and /tears /will /quickly /melt /thy /life TIT 3.02. 51
/send /quickly /down /to /tame /these /vild LR 4.02. 47
QUICKLY 123 FR 0.0139 REL FR 80 V 43 P
quickly, spirit, | thou shalt ere long be free. TMP 5.01. 86
of words, gentlemen, and quickly shot off. TGV 2.04. 33 P
i'll quickly cross | by some sly trick blunt 2.06. 40
you would quickly learn to know him by his voice 4.02. 89
and there dwells one mistress quickly, which is WIV 1.02. 3 P
depeche, quickly. 1.04. 54 P
my nursh-a quickly tell me so mush. 3.02. 65 P
quickly, quickly! is the buck-basket — 3.03. 2 P
quickly, quickly! is the buck-basket — 3.03. 2 P
go take up these clothes here quickly. 3.03.146 P
quickly, come. 3.03.148 P
we send that foolish carrion, mistress quickly, 3.03.194 P
break their talk, mistress quickly, my kinsman 3.04. 22 P
here's mistress quickly, sir, to speak with you. 3.05. 19 P
i must carry her word quickly. 3.05. 47 P
quickly, dispatch. 4.02.110 P
send quickly to sir john, to know his mind. 4.04. 83
her to the deanery, and dispatch it quickly. 5.03. 3 P
then i shall pose you quickly. MM 2.04. 51
a bawd, | 'tis best that thou diest quickly. 3.01.150
dispatch with angelo, that it may be quickly. 3.01.267 P
tell him he must awake, and that quickly too. 4.03. 30 P
for, did i think thou wouldst not quickly die, ADO 4.01.124
o for your reason! quickly, sir — i long! LLL 5.02.244
call them forth quickly, we will do so. 5.02.889 P
four days will quickly steep themselves in night MND 1.01. 7
four nights will quickly dream away the time; 1.01. 8
look'st cheerly, and i'll be with thee quickly. AYL 2.06. 15 P
i prithee tell me who is it quickly, and speak 3.02.198 P
who quickly fell before him, in which hurtling 4.03.131
went they not quickly, i should die with SHR 3.02.241
home, | i quickly were dissolved from my hive, AWW 1.02. 66
not in heaven, whither god send her quickly! 2.04. 12 P
in earth, from whence god send her quickly! 2.04. 13 P
of my daughter, | that she may quickly come. 5.03. 76
the prudent he would quickly have the gift of a TN 1.03. 33 P
even so quickly may one catch the plague? 1.05.295
how quickly the wrong side may be turn'd outward 3.01. 13 P
nicely with words may quickly make them wanton. 3.01. 15 P
thou art sir topas the curate, do it quickly. 4.02. 3 P
or will not else thy craft so quickly grow, 5.01.166
but quickly now. WT 4.04.341 P
speak quickly, or i shoot. JN 5.06. 1
though this be all, do not so quickly go; R2 1.02. 64
what is six winters? they are quickly gone. 1.03.260
that is not quickly buzz'd into his ears? 2.01. 26
o, then how quickly should this arm of mine, 2.03.103
what say'st thou, mistress quickly? 1H4 3.03. 92 P
you took occasion to be quickly wooed | to gripe 5.01. 56
which cannot choose but bring him quickly on. 5.02. 44
i arrest you at the suit of mistress quickly. 2H4 2.01. 45 P
wife, come in then and call me gossip quickly? 2.01. 95 P
lord, but old mistress quickly and mistress doll 2.02.152 P
i' good faith — "neighbor quickly," says he — 2.04. 87 P
was by then — "neighbor quickly," says he, 2.04. 89 P
how quickly nature falls into revolt | when gold 4.05. 65
with so weak a wind | that it will quickly drop; 4.05.100
that he is married to nell quickly, and H5 2.01. 18 P
hold, the quondam quickly | for the only she; 2.01. 78
you come of women, come in quickly to sir john. 2.01.118 P
and quickly bring us word of england's fall. 3.05. 68
gunpowder, | and quickly will return an injury. 4.07.181
be it spoken, i should quickly leap into a wife. 5.02.139 P
burst them open, if that you come not quickly. 1H6 1.03. 28
and interchanging blows i quickly shed | some of 4.06. 19
henry is youthful and will quickly yield. 5.03. 99
we'll quickly hoise duke humphrey from his seat. 2H6 1.01.169
would make thee quickly hop without thy head. 1.03.137
come on, sirrah, off with your doublet quickly. 2.01.148 P
these few days' wonder will be quickly worn. 2.04. 69
lord, these faults are easy, quickly answer'd; 3.01.133
"a staff is quickly found to beat a dog." 3.01.171
this gloucester should be quickly rid the world, 3.01.233
go bid her hide him quickly from the duke. 5.01. 84
but when the duke is slain, they'll quickly fly. 3H6 1.01. 69
and that will quickly dry thy melting tears. 1.04.174
they are already or quickly will be landed. 4.01.132
a little fire is quickly trodden out, | which, 4.08. 7
they are at hand, and you shall quickly know. 5.01. 15
we'll quickly rouse the traitors in the same. 5.01. 65
come quickly, montague, or i am dead. 5.02. 39
tread on the sand, why, there you quickly sink; 5.04. 30
this fair alliance quickly shall call home | to R3 4.04.313
you may guess quickly what. H8 2.01. 7
and four shall quickly draw out my command, COR 1.06. 84
i strike quickly, being mov'd. ROM 1.01. 6 P
but thou art not quickly mov'd to strike. 1.01. 7 P
come pentecost as quickly as it will, | some 1.05. 36
or if thou thinkest i am too quickly won, | i'll 2.02. 95
i had, my weapon should quickly have been out. 2.04.158 P
give it in a breath, | how quickly were it gone! TIM 2.02.154
done, then 'twere well | it were done quickly. MAC 1.07. 2
sign that i should quickly have a new father. 4.02. 62 P
keep it not from me, quickly let me have it. 4.03.200
thy story quickly. 5.05. 29
to a nunn'ry, go, and quickly too. HAM 3.01.139 P
he does not feel, feel your pow'r quickly; LR 4.01. 69
quickly send | (be brief in it) to th' castle, 5.03.245
he'll strike, and quickly too. 5.03.286
bianca's /pow'r, | how quickly should you speed! OTH 4.01.108
own world, and you might quickly make it right. 4.03. 82 P
bring in the banket quickly; ANT 1.02. 12
i am quickly ill, and well, | so antony loves. 1.03. 72
let his shames quickly | drive him to rome. 1.04. 72
bring me word quickly. 2.05.114
he could so quickly cut the ionian sea, | and 3.07. 22
i know he'll quickly fly my friendship too. CYM 5.03. 62
i shall, | unless thou wouldst grieve quickly. 5.05.170
ay, she quickly poop'd him, she made him PER 4.02. 24 P
what you do quickly | is not done rashly; TNK 1.01.134
i would quickly teach thee | what 'twere to 2.02.209
will be seen, | and quickly, yours or mine. 3.06. 35
i'll tell you quickly. 4.01. 52
bring 'em in | quickly, by any means, i long to 4.02. 65
haste you made | if you have done so quickly. 5.04. 42
who, being look'd on, ducks as quickly in; VEN 87
are they not quickly told, and quickly gone? 520
are they not quickly told, and quickly gone? 520
in likely thoughts the other kills thee quickly. 990
in her light chariot, quickly is convey'd, 1192
addict to vice, | quickly him they will entice; PP 20.42
and his love-kindling fire did quickly steep SON 153. 3
"but quickly on this side the verdict went: LC 113
QUICK'NED 1 FR 0.0001 REL FR 1 V 0 P
and when the mind is quick'ned, out of doubt, H5 4.01. 20
/QUICKNESS 1 FR 0.0001 REL FR 1 V 0 P
must send thee hence | /with /fiery /quickness; HAM 4.03. 43
QUICK'NING 2 FR 0.0002 REL FR 2 V 0 P
methinks i see a quick'ning in his eye. MM 5.01.495
whereon hyperion's quick'ning fire doth shine: TIM 4.03.184
QUICK-RAISED 1 FR 0.0001 REL FR 1 V 0 P
the king with mighty and quick-raised power 1H4 4.04. 12
QUICKSAND 1 FR 0.0001 REL FR 1 V 0 P
what clarence but a quicksand of deceit? 3H6 5.04. 26
QUICKSANDS 1 FR 0.0001 REL FR 1 V 0 P
these quicksands, lepidus, | keep off them, for ANT 2.07. 59
QUICK-SHIFTING 1 FR 0.0001 REL FR 1 V 0 P
there appears | quick-shifting antics, ugly in LUC 459
QUICKSILVER 2 FR 0.0002 REL FR 1 V 1 P
the rogue fled from me like quicksilver. 2H4 2.04.229 P
that swift as quicksilver it courses through HAM 1.05. 66
QUICK'ST 1 FR 0.0001 REL FR 1 V 0 P
and on our quick'st decrees | th' inaudible and AWW 5.03. 40
QUICK-WITTED 1 FR 0.0001 REL FR 1 V 0 P
how likes gremio these quick-witted folks? SHR 5.02. 38
QUID 2 FR 0.0002 REL FR 1 V 1 P
satis quid sufficit. LLL 5.01. 1 P
i cry you mercy, 'tis but quid for quo. 1H6 5.03.109

QUIDDITIES 2 FR 0.0002 REL FR 0 V 2 P
what, in thy quips and thy quiddities? 1H4 1.02. 45 P
where be his quiddities now, his quillities, his HAM 5.01. 99 P
QUIER'D *(also choir, quire, etc.)*
QUIER'D 1 FR 0.0001 REL FR 1 V 0 P
which quier'd with my drum, into a pipe | small COR 3.02.113
/QUIET 1 FR 0.0001 REL FR 1 V 0 P
/are /enforc'd /from /our /most /quiet /there 2H4 4.01. 71
QUIET 85 FR 0.0096 REL FR 70 V 15 P
as i hope | for quiet days, fair issue, and long TMP 4.01. 24
prithee, my king, be quiet. 4.01.215
be you quiet, monster. 4.01.235 P
i am glad he is so quiet. WIV 1.04. 89 P
as jove himself does, jove would never be quiet, MM 2.02.111
we bid be quiet when we hear it cry; ERR 2.01. 35
i will depart in quiet, | and in despite of 3.01.107
be quiet, people. wherefore throng you hither? 5.01. 38
be quiet and depart, thou shalt not have him. 5.01.112
is here, a man may live as quiet in hell as in a ADO 2.01.258 P
speak like an ancient and most quiet watchman, 3.03. 40 P
as another man, and therefore i can be quiet. LLL 1.02.166 P
and now, so you will let me quiet go, | to MND 3.02.314
of fortune | into so quiet and so sweet a style. AYL 2.01. 20
the gain i seek is, quiet /in the match. SHR 2.01.330
no doubt but he hath got a quiet catch. 2.01.331
father, be quiet, he shall stay my leisure. 3.02.217
nay, let them go, a couple of quiet ones. 3.02.240
marry, peace it bodes, and love, and quiet life, 5.02.108
to–day with my lady, she is much out of quiet. TN 2.03.133 P
that thought to fill his grave in quiet; WT 4.04.454
one minute, nay, one quiet breath of rest. JN 3.04.134
men away, | and i will sit as quiet as a lamb; 4.01. 79
truth hath a quiet breast. R2 1.03. 96
might from our quiet confines fright fair peace, 1.03.137
lie | in earth as quiet as thy father's skull; 4.01. 69
and says to his wife, "fie upon this quiet life! 1H4 2.04.105 P
the lag end of my life | with quiet hours; 5.01. 25
th' unquiet time for your quiet o'erposting that 2H4 1.02.150 P
good captain peesel, be quiet, 'tis very late, 2.04.161 P
for god's sake be quiet. 2.04.178 P
pistol, i would be quiet. 2.04.185 P
i pray thee, jack, be quiet, the rascal's gone. 2.04.208 P
to thee it shall descend with better quiet, 4.05.187
capet, | could not keep quiet in his conscience, H5 1.02. 79
he hath a killing tongue and a quiet sword; 3.02. 34 P
quiet thy cudgel, thou dost see i eat. 5.01. 52 P
when others sleep upon their quiet beds, 1H6 2.01. 6
now, quiet soul, depart when heaven please, 3.02.110
quiet yourselves, i pray, and be at peace. 4.01.115
sweet aunt, be quiet, 'twas against her will. 2H6 1.03.143
thy greatest help is quiet, gentle nell. 2.04. 67
court | and may enjoy such quiet walks as these? 4.10. 17
and thou shalt reign in quiet while thou liv'st. 3H6 1.01.173
would bring white hairs unto a quiet grave. 2.05. 40
cannot be quiet scarce a breathing while | but R3 1.03. 60
i shall not sleep in quiet at the tower. 3.01.142
it, | and so god give you quiet rest to–night! 5.03. 43
quiet untroubled soul, awake, awake! 5.03.157
wife, | that never slept a quiet hour with thee, 5.03.160
thou quiet soul, sleep thou a quiet sleep, 5.03.164
thou quiet soul, sleep thou a quiet sleep, 5.03.164
my wolsey, | the quiet of my wounded conscience, H8 2.02. 74
as well | for your own quiet, as to rectify 2.04. 63
dignities, | a still and quiet conscience. 3.02.380
let's sit down quiet | for fear we wake her; 4.02. 81
i wish your highness | a quiet night, and my 5.01. 77
masters all, be quiet, | put up your swords. COR 5.06.133
have thrice disturb'd the quiet of our streets, ROM 1.01. 91
go, | be quiet, or — more light, more light! 1.05. 87
for shame, | i'll make you quiet. 1.05. 88
upon receipt thereof, | soon sleep in quiet. 3.05. 99
never at quiet! MAC 2.03. 16 P
have you had quiet guard? HAM 1.01. 10
that it might please you to give quiet pass 2.02. 77
grating so harshly all his days of quiet | with 3.01. 3
good my lord, be quiet. 5.01.265
an hour of quiet /shortly shall we see, | till 5.01.298
/bravery dost thou come | to start my quiet. OTH 1.01.101
of spirit so still and quiet that her motion 1.03. 95
and practicing upon his peace and quiet | even 2.01.310
it were not for your quiet nor your good, | nor 3.03.152
the lethargy must have his quiet course; 4.01. 53
this life is best, | if quiet life be best; CYM 3.03. 30
quiet consummation have, | and renowned be thy 4.02.280
where grief should sleep, can breed me quiet? PER 1.02. 5
be quiet then, as men should be, | till he hath 2.ch. 5
quiet and gentle thy conditions! 3.01. 29
new sea–farer, | i would it would be quiet. 3.01. 42
hence and bring | that that shall quiet all. TNK 3.03. 50
run | into the quiet closure of my breast, | and VEN 782
the staring ruffian shall it keep in quiet, 1149
must'ring to the quiet cabinet | where their LUC 442
"her house is sack'd, her quiet interrupted, 1170
mind, | for thee, and for myself, no quiet find. SON 27.14
QUIETER 1 FR 0.0001 REL FR 0 V 1 P
the house will be the quieter. TN 3.04.134 P
QUIETLY 10 FR 0.0011 REL FR 9 V 1 P
so shall you quietly enjoy your hope, | and SHR 3.02.136
upon condition i may quietly | enjoy mine own, 1H6 5.03.153
your grace shall well and quietly enjoy. 5.03.159
i took an oath that he should quietly reign. 3H6 1.02. 15
parle, | these quarrels must be quietly debated. TIT 5.03. 20
but wrong to stir me up, | let me pass quietly. TIM 3.04. 54
and let the foes quietly cut their throats 3.05. 44
wherein we saw thee quietly interr'd, | hath HAM 1.04. 49
were as pretty a proportion to live quietly, and PER 4.02. 27 P
"lie quietly, and hear a little more, | nay, do VEN 709
QUIETNESS 7 FR 0.0008 REL FR 6 V 1 P
arm'd | to suffer, with a quietness of spirit, MV 4.01. 12
blood, | and stablish quietness on every side. 1H6 5.01. 10
ay, but give me worship and quietness, | i like 3H6 4.03. 16
i would have peace and quietness, but the fool TRO 2.01. 83 P
the present peace | and quietness of the people, COR 4.06. 3
and quietness, grown sick of rest, would purge ANT 1.03. 53
o, quietness, lady! 4.15. 68
QUIETUS 2 FR 0.0002 REL FR 2 V 0 P
when he himself might his quietus make | with a HAM 3.01. 74
must be, | and her quietus is to render thee. SON 126.12
QU'IL 1 FR 0.0001 REL FR 0 V 1 P
encore qu'il est contre son jurement de H5 4.04. 50 P
QUILL* 5 FR 0.0005 REL FR 4 V 1 P
note so true, | the wren with little quill — MND 3.01.128
we may deliver our supplications in the quill. 2H6 1.03. 3 P
first hovering o'er the paper with her quill. LUC 1297
how far a modern quill doth come too short, SON 83. 7
reserve their character with golden quill | and 85. 3
QUILLETS 5 FR 0.0005 REL FR 4 V 1 P
some tricks, some quillets, how to cheat the LLL 4.03.284
but in these nice sharp quillets of the law, 1H6 2.04. 17
and do not stand on quillets how to slay him; 2H6 3.01.261
title plead, | nor sound his quillets shrilly; TIM 4.03.155
prithee keep up thy quillets. OTH 3.01. 23 P
QUILLITIES 1 FR 0.0001 REL FR 0 V 1 P
where be his quiddities now, his quillities, his HAM 5.01.100 P
QUILLS 2 FR 0.0002 REL FR 2 V 0 P
end, | like quills upon the fearful porpentine. HAM 1.05. 20
to pluck the quills from ancient ravens' wings, LUC 949
QU'ILS 1 FR 0.0001 REL FR 0 V 1 P
je pense qu'ils sont appeles de fingres, oui, de H5 3.04. 10 P
QUILT 1 FR 0.0001 REL FR 0 V 1 P
how now, blown jack? how now, quilt? 1H4 4.02. 49 P
QUINAPALUS 1 FR 0.0001 REL FR 0 V 1 P
for what says quinapalus? TN 1.05. 35 P
QUINCE 8 FR 0.0009 REL FR 0 V 8 P
first, good peter quince, say what the play MND 1.02. 8 P
now, good peter quince, call forth your actors 1.02. 14 P
here, peter quince. 1.02. 43 P
here, peter quince. 1.02. 59 P
here, peter quince. 1.02. 62 P
peter quince! 3.01. 7 P
peter quince! 4.01.202 P
i will get peter quince to write a ballet of 4.01.214 P
QUINCES 1 FR 0.0001 REL FR 1 V 0 P
they call for dates and quinces in the pastry. ROM 4.04. 2
QUINTAIN 1 FR 0.0001 REL FR 1 V 0 P
that which here stands up | is but a quintain, a AYL 1.02.251
QUINTESSENCE 2 FR 0.0002 REL FR 1 V 1 P
read to know | the quintessence of every sprite AYL 3.02.139
yet, to me, what is this quintessence of dust? HAM 2.02.308 P
QUINTUS 1 FR 0.0001 REL FR 1 V 0 P
of the same house publius and quintus were, COR 2.03.241
QUIP 2 FR 0.0002 REL FR 0 V 2 P
this is call'd the quip modest. AYL 5.04. 75 P
the second, the quip modest; 5.04. 93 P
QUIPS 4 FR 0.0004 REL FR 1 V 3 P
and, notwithstanding all her sudden quips, | the TGV 4.02. 12
no quips now, pistol! WIV 1.03. 41 P
shall quips and sentences and these paper ADO 2.03.240 P
what, in thy quips and thy quiddities? 1H4 1.02. 45 P
QUIRE *(also choir, quier'd)*
QUIRE 1 FR 0.0001 REL FR 1 V 0 P
and then the whole quire hold their hips and MND 2.01. 55
QUIRING 1 FR 0.0001 REL FR 1 V 0 P
still quiring to the young–ey'd cherubins; MV 5.01. 62
QUIRK 1 FR 0.0001 REL FR 0 V 1 P
belike this is a man of that quirk. TN 3.04.245 P
QUIRKS 4 FR 0.0004 REL FR 2 V 2 P
chance have some odd quirks and remnants of wit ADO 2.03.236 P
i have felt so many quirks of joy and grief AWW 3.02. 49
one that excels the quirks of blazoning pens, OTH 2.01. 63
of our profession, she has me her quirks, her PER 4.06. 7 P
QUI'S 1 FR 0.0001 REL FR 0 V 1 P
if you forget your qui's, your /quae's, and your WIV 4.01. 78 P
QUIS 3 FR 0.0003 REL FR 0 V 3 P
videsne quis venit? LLL 5.01. 30 P
quis, quis, thou consonant? 5.01. 52 P
quis, quis, thou consonant? 5.01. 52 P
/QUIT 1 FR 0.0001 REL FR 1 V 0 P
conscience, | /to /quit /him /with /this /arm? HAM 5.02. 68
QUIT 48 FR 0.0054 REL FR 42 V 6 P
the very rats | instinctively have quit it. TMP 1.02.148
in the foaming brine, and quit the vessel; 1.02.211
upon our guard, | or that we quit this place. 2.01.322
to a well–wish'd king | quit their own part, and MM 2.04. 28
like doth quit like, and measure still for 5.01.411
but, for those earthly faults, i quit them all, 5.01.483
levied | to quit the penalty and to ransom him. ERR 1.01. 22
of friends, | to quit me of them throughly. ADO 4.01.200
to quit the fine for one half of his goods, | i MV 4.01.381
till thou canst quit thee by thy brother's mouth AYL 3.01. 11
hortensio will be quit with thee by changing. SHR 3.01. 92
though yet he never harm'd me, here i quit him. AWW 5.03.299
unclasp'd my practice, quit his fortunes here WT 3.02.167
quit presently the chapel, or resolve you | for 5.03. 86
i could | quit all offenses with as clear excuse 1H4 3.02. 19
thou art not, i think thou art quit for that. 2H4 2.04.342 P
he that dies this year is quit for the next. 3.02.238 P
god quit you in his mercy! H5 2.02.166
now, captain macmorris, have you quit the mines? 3.02. 87 P
captens bath, and i sall quit you with gud leve, 3.02.103 P
let us quit all, | and give our vineyards to a 3.05. 3
your great seats now quit you of great shames. 3.05. 47
by him, at all adventures, so we were quit here. 4.01.116 P
sword, | how many would the peaceful city quit, 5.pr. 33
disdain, | unless the lady bona quit his pain. 3H6 3.03.128
plantagenet doth quit plantagenet, | edward for R3 4.04. 20
/thy other edward dead, to quit my edward; 4.04. 64
god safely quit her of her burthen, and | with H8 5.01. 70
spite, | to be full quit of those my banishers, COR 4.05. 83
to quit the bloody wrongs upon her foes. TIT 1.01.141
farewell, be trusty, and i'll quit thy pains. ROM 4.04.192
long live so, and so die. i am quit. TIM 4.03.396
avaunt, and quit my sight! MAC 3.04. 92
hit, | or quit in answer of the third exchange, HAM 5.02.269
now quit you well. LR 2.01. 30
the sparks of nature, | to quit this horrid act. 3.07. 87
him, | and quit the house on purpose that their 4.02. 93
to thy sinking, for | thy dearest quit thee. ANT 3.13. 65
that will take rewards | and say "god quit you!" 3.13.124
or torture, | as he shall like, to quit me. 3.13.151
took such sorrow | that he quit being, and his CYM 1.01. 38
o, of this contradiction you shall now be quit. 5.04.166 P
let's quit this ground, | and smoke the temple 5.05.397
thy loss is more than can thy portage quit PER 3.01. 35
surprise and fear | made me to quit the house. 3.02. 18
quit me of these cold gyves, give me a sword, TNK 3.01. 72
then i shall quit you. 3.06. 24
nor youth all quit, but, spite of heaven's fell LC 13
QUITE 94 FR 0.0106 REL FR 87 V 7 P
humanely taken, all, all lost, quite lost; TMP 4.01.190
love | is by a newer object quite forgotten. TGV 2.04.195
the nurse, and quite athwart | goes all decorum. MM 1.03. 30
but this virtuous maid | subdues me quite. 2.02.185
but it is impossible to extirp it quite, friar, 3.02.103 P
this deed unshapes me quite, makes me unpregnant 4.04. 20
and may it be that you have quite forgot | a ERR 3.02. 1
make rich the ribs, but bankrout quite the wits. LLL 1.01. 27
these be the stops that hinder study quite, 1.01. 70
what say you, lords? why, this was quite forgot. 1.01.141
and younger hearings are quite ravished, | so 2.01. 75
and quite divorce his memory from his part. 5.02.150
this pert berowne was out of count'nance quite. 5.02.272
thrust thy sharp wit quite through my ignorance, 5.02.398
either i mistake your shape and making quite, MND 2.01. 32
quite over–canopied with luscious woodbine, 2.01.251
thou hast mistaken quite, | and laid the 3.02. 88
quite dumb? 5.01.327
had your husband's ring, | had quite miscarried. MV 5.01.251
and breaks them bravely, quite traverse, athwart AYL 3.04. 42 P
checks | as ovid be an outcast quite abjur'd. SHR 1.01. 33
would all the world but he had quite forsworn! 4.02. 35
would quite confound distinction, yet stands off AWW 2.03.120
wise /men, folly–fall'n, quite taint their wit. TN 3.01. 68
for the harlot king | is quite beyond mine arm, WT 2.03. 5
to some remote and desert place quite out | of 2.03.176
ship–boy's semblance hath disguis'd me quite. JN 4.03. 4
figur'd quite o'er with burning meteors. 5.02. 53
grievous taxes, | and quite lost their hearts; R2 2.01.247
ancient quarrels, and quite lost their hearts. 2.01.248
waste of idle hours hath quite thrown down. 3.04. 66
ere thou bid good night, to quite their griefs, 5.01. 43
the turkeys in my pannier are quite starv'd. 1H4 2.01. 27 P
and the fire of grace be not quite out of thee, 2.04.383 P
enough | to put him quite besides his patience. 3.01.177
quite from the flight of all thy ancestors. 3.02. 31
the fortune of the day quite turn'd from him, 5.05. 18
my gracious lord, you look beyond him quite: 2H4 4.04. 67
great sort, quite from the answer of his degree. H5 4.07.136 P
signal, and ostent | quite from himself to god. 5.pr. 22
and there my rendezvous is quite cut off. 5.01. 83
paris, guysors, poictiers, are all quite lost. 1H6 1.01. 61
france is revolted from the english quite, 1.01. 90
is not quite exempt | from envious malice of thy 3.01. 25
be quite degraded, like a hedge–born swain 4.01. 43
quite to forget this quarrel, and the cause. 4.01.136
and i forgive and quite forget old faults, | and 3H6 3.03.200
till warwick or himself be quite suppress'd. 4.03. 6
they quite forget their loss of liberty. 4.06. 15
'tis time to speak, my pains are quite forgot. R3 1.03.116
and from a mouth of honor quite cry down | this H8 1.01.137
calm of states | quite from their fixure! TRO 1.03.101
shall quite strike off all service i have done, 3.03. 29
to have done is to hang | quite out of fashion, 3.03.152
i am thwarted quite | from my great purpose in 5.01. 37
o'ercover'd quite with dead men's rattling bones ROM 4.01. 82
by cruel cruel thee quite overthrown! 4.05. 57
as 'tis extoll'd, | it would unclew me quite. TIM 1.01.168
the infinite malady | crust you quite o'er! 3.06. 99
may your pains six months | be quite contrary. 4.03.145
take the bridge quite away | of him that, his 4.03.158
people | the deed of saying is quite out of use. 5.01. 26
and he looks | quite through the deeds of men. JC 1.02.203
quite from the main opinion he held once | of 2.01.196
here, quite confounded with this mutiny. 3.01. 86
than traitors' arms, | quite vanquish'd him. 3.02.186
what? quite unmann'd in folly? MAC 3.04. 72
th' observ'd of all observers, quite, quite down HAM 3.01.154
observ'd of all observers, quite, quite down! 3.01.154
to mock your own grinning — quite chop–fall'n? 5.01.192 P
the potent poison quite o'er–crows my spirit. 5.02.353
and constrains the garb | quite from his nature. LR 2.02. 98
and light behaviors | quite in the wrong. OTH 4.01.103
he's almost slain, and roderigo quite dead. 5.01.114
that either makes me, or foredoes me quite. 5.01.129
not yet quite dead? 5.02. 86
to forget them quite | were to remember that the ANT 2.02.100
quite forgo | the way which promises assurance, 3.07. 45
piece 'gainst fancy, | condemning shadows quite. 5.02.100
shall quite unpeople her | of liegers for her CYM 1.05. 79
quite besides | the government of patience! 2.04.149
for cloten | is quite forgot. 4.02.244
but think her bond of chastity quite crack'd, 5.05.207
i have forgot it quite; TNK 4.03. 11 P
to me deserving | than i can quite or speak of. 5.04. 35
authority quite silenc'd by your brawl, | and STM II.C 78
and then my little heart were quite undone, | in VEN 783
that patience is quite beaten from her breast; LUC 1563
all my merry jigs are quite forgot, | all my PP 17. 5
check'd with frost and lusty leaves quite gone, SON 5. 7
foil'd, | is from the book of honor rased quite, 25.11
mine own self–love quite contrary i read; 62.11
after my death, dear love, forget me quite, 72. 3
a face | that overgoes my blunt invention quite, 103. 7
QUITS 3 FR 0.0003 REL FR 3 V 0 P
well, angelo, your evil quits you well. MM 5.01.496
your master quits you; TN 5.01.321
your children's children quits it in your age. R3 5.03.262
QUITTAL 1 FR 0.0001 REL FR 1 V 0 P
wife, | as in revenge or quittal of such strife; LUC 236
QUITTANCE 6 FR 0.0006 REL FR 5 V 1 P
in any bill, warrant, quittance, or obligation, WIV 1.01. 10 P
omittance is no quittance. AYL 3.05.133
state, | rend'ring faint quittance, wearied and 2H4 1.01.108
sooner than quittance of desert and merit, H5 2.02. 34
as fitting best to quittance their deceit 1H6 2.01. 14
giver a return exceeding | all use of quittance. TIM 1.01.280
QUITTED 1 FR 0.0001 REL FR 1 V 0 P
having both their country quitted | with this WT 5.01.192
QUITTING 1 FR 0.0001 REL FR 1 V 0 P
quitting thee thereby of ten thousand shames, 2H6 3.02.218
QUIVER* 5 FR 0.0005 REL FR 2 V 3 P
cupid have not spent all his quiver in venice, ADO 1.01.272 P

show — there was a little quiver fellow, and 'a 2H4 3.02.281 P
why dost thou quiver, man? 2H6 4.07. 92 P
the green leaves quiver with the cooling wind TIT 2.03. 14
flies like a parthian quiver from our rages, TNK 2.02. 50
QUIVERING 1 FR 0.0001 REL FR 1 V 0 P
fine foot, straight leg, and quivering thigh, ROM 2.01. 19
QUIVERS 1 FR 0.0001 REL FR 0 V 1 P
i am so vex'd that every part about me quivers. ROM 2.04.162 P
QUIVER'ST 1 FR 0.0001 REL FR 1 V 0 P
"poor hand, why quiver'st thou at this decree?" LUC 1030
QUO 3 FR 0.0003 REL FR 3 V 0 P
i cry you mercy, 'tis but quid for quo. 1H6 5.03.109
glorious, | et bonum quo antiquius, eo melius. PER 1.ch. 10
quo usque tandem? here is a woman wanting. TNK 3.05. 38
QUOD 2 FR 0.0002 REL FR 1 V 1 P
it is qui, /quae, quod: WIV 4.01. 77 P
"et opus exegi, quod nec jovis ira, nec ignis" TNK 3.05. 88
QUOD'S 1 FR 0.0001 REL FR 0 V 1 P
your /quae's, and your quod's, you must be WIV 4.01. 78 P
QUOIFS *(also coif)*
QUOIFS 1 FR 0.0001 REL FR 1 V 0 P
golden quoifs and stomachers | for my lads to WT 4.04.224
QUOINT *(see coint)*
QUOIT 1 FR 0.0001 REL FR 0 V 1 P
quoit him down, bardolph, like a shove–groat 2H4 2.04.192 P
QUOITS 1 FR 0.0001 REL FR 0 V 1 P
both of a bigness, and 'a plays at quoits well, 2H4 2.04.245 P
QUONDAM 6 FR 0.0006 REL FR 4 V 2 P
a whole bookful of these quondam carpet–mongers,
ADO 5.02. 32 P
i did converse this quondam day with a companion
LLL 5.01. 6 P
hold, the quondam quickly | for the only she; H5 2.01. 78
this is the quondam king; 3H6 3.01. 23
and as for you yourself, our quondam queen, 3.03.153
your quondam wife swears still by venus' glove. TRO 4.05.179
QUONIAM 1 FR 0.0001 REL FR 1 V 0 P
quoniam he seemeth in minority, | ergo i come LLL 5.02.592
QUOTE *(also cote*, etc.)*
QUOTE 2 FR 0.0002 REL FR 0 V 2 P
and how quote you my folly? TGV 2.04. 18 P
i quote it in your jerkin. 2.04. 19 P
QUOTED 3 FR 0.0003 REL FR 3 V 0 P
he's quoted for a most perfidious slave, | with AWW 5.03.205
quoted, and sign'd to do a deed of shame, | this JN 4.02.222
thee, hector, | and quoted joint by joint. TRO 4.05.233
QUOTH *(also keth)*
QUOTH 117 FR 0.0132 REL FR 100 V 17 P
"lord," quoth he? TMP 3.02. 32 P
"friend," quoth i, "you mean to whip the dog?" TGV 4.04. 25 P
"ay, marry, do i," quoth he. 4.04. 26 P
"you do him the more wrong," quoth i, "'twas i 4.04. 27 P
"the humor of it," quoth 'a! WIV 2.01.138 P
"'tis dinner–time," quoth i: ERR 2.01. 62
quoth he. 2.01. 62
"your meat doth burn," quoth i: 2.01. 63
quoth he. 2.01. 63
quoth i: 2.01. 64
quoth he; 2.01. 64
"the pig," quoth i, "is burn'd": 2.01. 66
quoth he. 2.01. 66
"my mistress, sir," quoth i: 2.01. 67
quoth who? 2.01. 69
quoth my master. 2.01. 70
"i know," quoth he, "no house, no wife, no 2.01. 71
air, quoth he, thy cheeks may blow; LLL 4.03.107
did they, quoth you? 4.03.217
"for," quoth the king, "an angel shalt thou see; 5.02.103
"veal," quoth the dutchman. is not veal a calf? 5.02.247
"no point," quoth i; 5.02.277
"poor deer," quoth he, "thou mak'st a testament AYL 2.01. 47
"'tis right," quoth he, "thus misery doth part 2.01. 51
"ay," quoth jaques, | "sweep on, you fat and 2.01. 54
"good morrow, fool," quoth i. 2.07. 18
"no, sir," quoth he, | "call me not fool till 2.07. 18
thus we may see," quoth he, "how the world wags. 2.07. 23
"be serviceable to my son," quoth he, | although SHR 1.01.214
quoth she, "i'll fume with them." 2.01.152
by gogs–wouns," quoth he, and swore so loud, 3.02.160
"now take them up," quoth he, "if any list." 3.02.165
quoth he, as if | he had been aboard, carousing 3.02.170
when it was out — "let me not live," quoth he, AWW 1.02. 58
"was this fair face the cause," quoth she, 1.03. 70
one in ten, quoth 'a? 1.03. 85 P
quoth he. R2 5.04. 4
lend me thy lantern, quoth he! 1H4 2.01. 40 P
at hand, quoth pick–purse. 2.01. 48 P
as fair as — at hand, quoth the chamberlain; 2.01. 49 P
sirrah, quoth 'a, we shall "do nothing but eat, 2H4 5.03. 16 P
quoth i, "what, man? H5 2.03. 17 P
"tell him," quoth she, "my mourning weeds are 3H6 4.01.104
"ay," quoth my uncle gloucester, | "small herbs R3 2.04. 12
"thanks, gentle citizens and friends," quoth i, 3.07. 38
"be thou," quoth i, "accurs'd | for making me, 4.01. 71
thus," quoth dighton, "lay the gentle babes." 4.03. 9
thus," quoth forrest, "girdling one another 4.03. 10
which /once," quoth forrest, "almost chang'd my 4.03. 15
"when he," quoth she, "shall split thy heart 5.01. 26
"if," quoth he, "i for this had been committed H8 1.02.193
"i do," quoth he, "perceive | my king is tangled 3.02. 34
quoth she, "here's but two and fifty hairs on TRO 1.02.157 P
"two and fifty hairs," quoth he, "and one white. 1.02.161 P
"jupiter," quoth she, "which of these hairs is 1.02.163 P
"the fork'd one," quoth he, "pluck't out, and 1.02.164 P
"sweet," quoth 'a! 5.01. 75 P
"true is it, my incorporate friends," quoth he, COR 1.01.130
shake, quoth the dove–house; ROM 1.03. 33
"yea," quoth he, "dost thou fall upon thy face? 1.03. 41
quoth he; 1.03. 47
"yea," quoth my husband, "fall'st upon thy face? 1.03. 55
"for himself to mar," quoth 'a! 2.04.118 P
quoth i. MAC 1.03. 5
"quoth she, 'before you tumbled me, | you HAM 4.05. 62
"good friend," quoth he, | "say the firm roman ANT 1.05. 42
"ay me," quoth venus, "young, and so unkind, VEN 187
"i know not love," quoth he, "nor will not know 409
quoth she, "hast thou a tongue? 427
quoth she, "in earth or heaven, | or in the 493
"fair queen," quoth he, "if any love you owe me, 523
"good night," quoth she, and, ere he says "adieu 537
quoth she, whereat a sudden pale, | like lawn 589
"thou hadst been gone," quoth she, "sweet boy, 613
"no matter where," quoth he, | "leave me, and 715
quoth she. 717
"i am," quoth he, "expected of my friends, | and 718
"in night," quoth she, "desire sees best of all. 720
"nay then," quoth adon, "you will fall again 769
"no, no," quoth she, "sweet death, i did but 997
"o jove," quoth she, "how much a fool was i | to 1015
and yet," quoth she, "behold two adons dead! 1070
"wonder of time," quoth she, "this is my spite, 1133
"poor flow'r," quoth she, "this was thy father's 1177
quoth he, "she took me kindly by the hand, | and LUC 253
"so, so," quoth he, "these lets attend the time, 330
quoth he, "i must deflow'r: 348
"lucrece," quoth he, "this night i must enjoy 512
quoth she, "reward not hospitality | with such 575
"have done," quoth he, "my uncontrolled tide 645
"thou art," quoth she, "a sea, a sovereign king, 652
"no more," quoth he, "by heaven, i will not hear 667
"for day," quoth she, "night's scapes doth open 747
"in vain," quoth she, "i live, and seek in vain 1044
"you mocking birds," quoth she, "your tunes 1121
"to kill myself," quoth she, "alack, what were 1156
"my girl," quoth she, "on what occasion break 1270
peace," quoth lucrece, "if it should be told, 1284
"poor instrument," quoth she, "without a sound, 1464
"it cannot be," quoth she, "that so much guile" 1534
fool," quoth she, "his wounds will not be sore." 1568
"few words," quoth she, "shall fit the trespass 1613
some hard–favor'd groom of thine,' quoth he, 1632
you fair lords," quoth she | (speaking to those 1688
"o, speak," quoth she, | "how may this forced 1700
no," quoth she, "no dame hereafter living | by 1714
"o," quoth lucretius, "i did give that life 1800
"woe, woe," quoth collatine, "she was my wife, 1802
"thou wronged lord of rome," quoth he, "arise, 1818
"o jove," quoth she, "why was not i a flood?" PP 6.14
"once," quoth she, "did i see a fair sweet youth 9. 9
in my thigh," quoth she, "here was the sore." 9.12
"even thus," quoth she, "the warlike god 11. 5
"even thus," quoth she, "the warlike god unlac'd 11. 7
"even thus," quoth she, "he seized on my lips," 11. 9
"farewell," quoth she, "and come again to–morrow 14. 5
"air," quoth he, "thy cheeks may blow, | air, 16. 9
QUOTIDIAN 2 FR 0.0002 REL FR 0 V 2 P
he seems to have the quotidian of love upon him. AYL 3.02.365 P
he is so shak'd of a burning quotidian tertian, H5 2.01.119 P
R 2 FR 0.0002 REL FR 0 V 2 P
ay, nurse, what of that? both with an r. ROM 2.04.208 P
r is for the — no, i know it begins with some 2.04.209 P
/RABBIT 1 FR 0.0001 REL FR 0 V 1 P
away, you whoreson upright /rabbit, away! 2H4 2.02. 85 P
RABBIT 2 FR 0.0002 REL FR 0 V 2 P
thin/–bellied doublet like a rabbit on a spit; LLL 3.01. 19 P
to the garden for parsley to stuff a rabbit, and SHR 4.04.101 P
RABBIT–SUCKER 1 FR 0.0001 REL FR 0 V 1 P
by the heels for a rabbit–sucker or a poulter's 1H4 2.04.437 P
RABBLE 10 FR 0.0011 REL FR 9 V 1 P
go bring the rabble | (o'er whom i give thee TMP 4.01. 37
and at his heels a rabble of his companions, WIV 3.05. 75 P
and a rabble more | of vild confederates. ERR 5.01.236
and follow'd with a rabble that rejoice | to see 2H6 2.04. 32
there's a trim rabble let in. H8 5.03. 71
the rabble should have first /unroof'd the city COR 1.01.218
the nature of our seats and make the rabble 3.01.136
'twas you incens'd the rabble; 4.02. 33
the rabble call him lord, | and, as the world HAM 4.05.103
and your disorder'd rabble make servants of LR 1.04.256
RABBLEMENT 1 FR 0.0001 REL FR 0 V 1 P
still as he refus'd it, the rabblement howted, JC 1.02.244 P
RABBLE'S 1 FR 0.0001 REL FR 1 V 0 P
and to be baited with the rabble's curse. MAC 5.08. 29
RABLE 1 FR 0.0001 REL FR 1 V 0 P
fable, | we are a merry rout, or else a rable, TNK 3.05.106
RACE* *(also razes)*
RACE* 17 FR 0.0019 REL FR 16 V 1 P
but thy vild race | (though thou didst learn) TMP 1.02.358
and now i give my sensual race the rein. MM 2.04.160
herd, | or race of youthful and unhandled colts, MV 5.01. 72
a race or two of ginger, but that i may beg; WT 4.03. 47 P
a bark of baser kind | by bud of nobler race. 4.04. 95
mouth | sound on into the drowsy race of night; JN 3.03. 39
thou art | and never of the nevils' noble race. 2H6 3.02.215
forespent with toil, as runners with a race, | i 3H6 2.03. 1
live and beget a happy race of kings! R3 5.03.152
hate may grow | to the whole race of mankind, TIM 4.01. 40
beauteous and swift, the minions of their race, MAC 2.04. 15
our parts so poor | but was a race of heaven. ANT 1.03. 37
rome, | forborne the getting of a lawful race, 3.13.107
longer exercise | upon a valiant race thy harsh CYM 5.04. 83
that pupils lacks she none of noble race, | who PER 5.ch. 9
lest his race | should show i' th' world too TNK 5.03.117
shall neigh (no dull flesh) in his fiery race, SON 51.11
RACK* 16 FR 0.0018 REL FR 15 V 1 P
what i command, i'll rack thee with old cramps, TMP 1.02.369
pageant faded, | leave not a rack behind. 4.01.156
idle dream | and rack thee in their fancies. MM 4.01. 64
to th' rack with him! 5.01.311
this finger of mine than he | dare rack his own. 5.01.315
lack'd and lost, | why then we rack the value; ADO 4.01.220
me choose, | for as i am, i live upon the rack. MV 3.02. 25
upon the rack, bassanio! 3.02. 26
ay, but i fear you speak upon the rack, | where 3.02. 32
even like a man new haled from the rack, | so 1H6 2.05. 3
without the rack. TRO 1.02.138 P
a silence in the heavens, the rack stand still, HAM 2.02.484
that would upon the rack of this tough world LR 5.03.315
thou hast set me on the rack. OTH 3.03.335
even with a thought | the rack dislimns, and ANT 4.14. 10
to ride | with ugly rack on his celestial face, SON 33. 6
RACK'D 5 FR 0.0005 REL FR 5 V 0 P
you must be purged too, your sins are rack'd, LLL 5.02.818
that shall be rack'd, even to the uttermost, MV 1.01.181
how have the hours rack'd and tortur'd me, TN 5.01.219
the commons hast thou rack'd, the clergy's bags 2H6 1.03.128
say he be taken, rack'd, and tortured, | i know 3.01.376
RACKERS 1 FR 0.0001 REL FR 0 V 1 P
companions, such rackers of ortography, as to LLL 5.01. 19 P
RACKET 1 FR 0.0001 REL FR 0 V 1 P
with thee when thou keepest not racket there; 2H4 2.02. 20 P
RACKETS 1 FR 0.0001 REL FR 1 V 0 P
when we have match'd our rackets to these balls, H5 1.02.261
RACKING 1 FR 0.0001 REL FR 1 V 0 P
sun, | not separated with the racking clouds, 3H6 2.01. 27
RACKS 2 FR 0.0002 REL FR 1 V 1 P
racks? WT 3.02.176
at the strappado, or all the racks in the world, 1H4 2.04.237 P
RADDOCK 1 FR 0.0001 REL FR 1 V 0 P
the raddock would, | with charitable bill (o CYM 4.02.224
RADIANCE 3 FR 0.0003 REL FR 3 V 0 P
in his bright radiance and collateral light AWW 1.01. 88
for, by the sacred radiance of the sun, | the LR 1.01.109
weak sights their sickly radiance do amend; LC 214
RADIANT 8 FR 0.0009 REL FR 7 V 1 P
our radiant queen hates sluts and sluttery. WIV 5.05. 46
"most radiant pyramus, most lily–white of hue, MND 3.01. 93
most radiant, exquisite, and unmatchable beauty TN 1.05.170 P
so /lust, though to a radiant angel link'd, HAM 1.05. 55
like the wreath of radiant fire | on /flick'ring LR 2.02.107
to hide me from the radiant sun, and solace | i' CYM 1.06. 86
closes, he is enter'd | his radiant roof. 5.04.121
unite | his favor with the radiant cymbeline, 5.05.475
RADISH *(also redish)*
RADISH 1 FR 0.0001 REL FR 0 V 1 P
not with fifty of them, i am a bunch of radish. 1H4 2.04.186 P
RAFE 2 FR 0.0002 REL FR 1 V 1 P
there were none fine but adam, rafe, and gregory SHR 4.01.136
rafe mouldy! 2H4 3.02. 98 P
RAFT 1 FR 0.0001 REL FR 1 V 0 P
son | that floated with thee on the fatal raft? ERR 5.01.349
RAG 5 FR 0.0005 REL FR 4 V 1 P
out of my door, you witch, you rag, you baggage, WIV 4.02.185 P
might, | but surely, master, not a rag of money. ERR 4.04. 86
away, thou rag, thou quantity, thou remnant, SHR 4.03.111
thou rag of honor! R3 1.03.232
if thou wilt curse, thy father (that poor rag) TIM 4.03.271
RAGAMUFFINS 1 FR 0.0001 REL FR 0 V 1 P
i have led my ragamuffins where they are 1H4 5.03. 36 P
RAG'D 2 FR 0.0002 REL FR 2 V 0 P
young hot colts being rag'd do rage the more. R2 2.01. 70
in war was never lion rag'd more fierce, | in 2.01.173
/RAGE 2 FR 0.0002 REL FR 2 V 0 P
/the /impetuous /blasts /with /eyeless /rage LR 3.01. 8
/not /to /a /rage, /patience /and /sorrow 4.03. 16
RAGE 135 FR 0.0152 REL FR 133 V 2 P
ministers, | and in her most unmitigable rage, TMP 1.02.276
hot fire, | but qualify the fire's extreme rage, TGV 2.07. 22
know'st, being stopp'd, impatiently doth rage; 2.07. 26
besides this present instance of his rage, | is ERR 4.03. 87
and did not i in rage depart from thence? 4.04. 76
that since have felt the vigor of his rage. 4.04. 78
when as your husband all in rage to–day | came 4.04.137
passion | ne'er brake into extremity of rage. 5.01. 48
rings, jewels, any thing his rage did like. 5.01.144
animals | that rage in savage sensuality. ADO 4.01. 61
before | would give preceptial med'cine to rage, 5.01. 24
food for his rage, repasture for his den." LLL 4.01. 93
yet i have a trick | of the old rage. 5.02.417
tearing the thracian singer in their rage." MND 5.01. 49
when lion rough in wildest rage doth roar. 5.01.222
of spirit, | the very tyranny and rage of his. MV 4.01. 13
nought so stockish, hard, and full of rage, 5.01. 81
rage like an angry boar chafed with sweat? SHR 1.02.202
into a most hideous opinion of his rage, skill, TN 3.04.194 P
dagger of lath, | in his rage and his wrath, 4.02.127
or shall we give the signal to our rage, | and JN 2.01.265
and in their rage, i having hold of both, | they 3.01.329
wrath, | a rage whose heat hath this condition, 3.01.341
thy rage shall burn thee up, and thou shalt turn 3.01.344
throw this report on their incensed rage, | and 4.02.261
made | upon thy feature, for my rage was blind, 4.02.264
that ever wall–ey'd wrath or staring rage 4.03. 49
lest i, by marking of your rage, forget | your 4.03. 85
doth he still rage? 5.07. 11
ire, | in rage, deaf as the sea, hasty as fire. R2 1.01. 19
rage must be withstood, | give me his gage. 1.01.173
young hot colts being rag'd do rage the more. 2.01. 70
enjoy, | the other to enjoy by rage and war. 2.04. 14
so high above his limits swells the rage | of 3.02.109
the rage be his, whilst on the earth i rain | my 3.03. 59
if nothing else, with rage | to be o'erpow'r'd, 5.01. 30
the rod, | and fawn on rage with base humility, 5.01. 33
when i was dry with rage and extreme toil, 1H4 1.03. 31
yet oftentimes it doth present harsh rage, 3.01.181
in rage dismiss'd my father from the court, 4.03.100
and that the king before the douglas' rage 2H4 in 31
led on by bloody youth, guarded with rage, | and 4.01. 34
when rage and hot blood are his counsellors, 4.04. 63
inflame thy noble liver, | and make thee rage. 5.05. 32
disguise fair nature with hard–favor'd rage; H5 3.01. 8
abate thy rage, abate thy manly rage, | abate 3.02. 23
abate thy rage, abate thy manly rage, | abate 3.02. 23
thy manly rage, | abate thy rage, great duke! 3.02. 24
good bawcock, bate thy rage; 3.02. 25
and with wild rage | yerk out their armed heels 4.07. 79
and left us to the rage of france his sword. 1H6 4.06. 3
quicken'd with youthful spleen and warlike rage, 4.06. 13
if i to–day die not with frenchmen's rage, 4.06. 34
rough deeds of rage and stern impatience; 4.07. 8
none, | dizzy–ey'd fury and great rage of heart 4.07. 11
that i in rage might shoot them at your faces! 4.07. 80
so, there goes our protector in a rage. 2H6 1.01.147
from treason's secret knife and traitors' rage 3.01.174
send succors, lords, and stop the rage betime, 3.01.285
and this fell tempest shall not cease to rage 3.01.351
thy words move rage and not remorse in me. 4.01.112
who in rage forgets | aged contusions and all 5.03. 2
hath made her break out into terms of rage! 3H6 1.01.265
i dare your quenchless fury to more rage. 1.04. 28
bid'st thou me rage? 1.04.143
and when the rage allays, the rain begins. 1.04.146
wailing our losses, whiles the foe doth rage, 2.03. 26
that was in thy rage. R3 1.02.187

and in that shame still live my sorrow's rage! 1.03.277
my brother's love, the devil, and my rage. 1.04.223
me a foe — | if i /unwittingly, or in my rage, 2.01. 57
your rage mistakes us. H8 3.01.101
as rous'd with rage, with rage doth sympathize, TRO 1.03. 52
as rous'd with rage, with rage doth sympathize, 1.03. 52
on, you heavens, effect your rage with speed! 5.10. 6
so putting him to rage, | you should have ta'en COR 2.03.197
nature is, he fall in rage | with their refusal, 2.03.258
put not your worthy rage into your tongue; 3.01.240
whose rage doth rend | like interrupted waters, 3.01.247
this tiger-footed rage, when it shall find | the 3.01.310
my lords, when you shall know (as in this rage, 5.06.135
my rage is gone, | and i am struck with sorrow. 5.06.146
if the winds rage, doth not the sea wax mad, TIT 3.01.222
the emperor in his rage will doom her death. 4.02.114
and the continuance of their parents' rage, ROM pr 10
that quench the fire of your pernicious rage 1.01. 84
doth much excuse the appertaining rage | to such 3.01. 63
and in this rage, with some great kinsman's bone 4.03. 53
he's flung in rage from this ingrateful seat TIM 4.02. 45
bring in thy ranks, but leave without thy rage; 5.04. 39
have seen | th' ambitious ocean swell, and rage, JC 1.03. 7
do, | stir up their servants to an act of rage, 2.01.176
stir | your hearts and minds to mutiny and rage, 3.02.122
in pious rage the two delinquents tear, | that MAC 3.06. 12
pyrrhus at priam drives, in rage strikes wide, HAM 2.02.472
when he is drunk asleep, or in his rage, | or in 3.03. 89
how much i had to do to calm his rage! 4.07.192
till the speed of his rage goes slower; LR 1.02.167 P
the king is in high rage. 2.04.296
rage, blow! 3.02. 1
lest his ungovern'd rage dissolve the life 4.04. 19
when misery could beguile the tyrant's rage, 4.06. 63
be comforted, good madam, the great rage, | you 4.07. 77
he that stirs next to carve for his own rage OTH 2.03.173
as men in rage strike those that wish them best, 2.03.243
shall make thy peace for moving me to rage, ANT 2.05. 70
when one so great begins to rage, he's hunted 4.01. 7
me, | alcides, thou mine ancestor, thy rage. 4.12. 44
and that your rage | would not be purg'd, she 4.14.123
yet | the fire of rage is in him, and 'twere CYM 1.01. 77
my holy duty) what | his rage can do on me. 1.01. 88
while, | till that his rage and anger be forgot, PER 1.02.107
took it in rage, though calm'd have given't 2.01.132
could i rage and roar | as doth the sea she lies 3.03. 10
name | of pericles to rage the city turn, | that 5.03. 97
leaden-footed | till his great rage be off him. TNK 1.02. 85
to call the fiercest tyrant from his rage, | and 5.01. 78
burneth more hotly, swelleth with more rage; VEN 332
as life for honor in fell battle's rage, | honor LUC 145
not wake, and in a desp'rate rage | post hither, 219
stay, | his rage of lust by gazing qualified; 424
this moves in him more rage and lesser pity | to 468
in ajax' eyes blunt rage and rigor roll'd, | but 1398
and in their rage such signs of rage they bear, 1419
and in their rage such signs of rage they bear, 1419
that forc'd him on so fast | (in rage sent out, 1671
(in rage sent out, recall'd in rage, being past) 1671
day | and barren rage of death's eternal cold? SON 13.12
and your true rights be term'd a poet's rage, 17.11
or some fierce thing replete with too much rage, 23. 3
rased, | and brass eternal slave to mortal rage; 64. 4
how with this rage shall beauty hold a plea, 65. 3
all quit, but, spite of heaven's fell rage, LC 13
this said, in top of rage the lines she rents, 55
for when we rage, advice is often seen | by 160

RAGES 14 FR 0.0015 REL FR 11 V 3 P
you did but see how it chafes, how it rages, how WT 3.03. 89 P
the dolphin rages at our very heels. JN 5.07. 80
and you know, in his rages, and his furies, and H5 4.07. 34 P
fled, | and warwick rages like a chafed bull. 3H6 2.05.126
parts | kingdom'd achilles in commotion rages, TRO 2.03.175
with aufidius, rages | upon our territories, and COR 4.06. 76
desire not | t' allay my rages and revenges with 5.03. 85
fear, | we sent to thee to give thy rages balm, TIM 5.04. 16
for like the hectic in my blood he rages, | and HAM 4.03. 66
fury of his heart, when the foul fiend rages, LR 3.04.131 P
go in and cheer the king, he rages, none | dare CYM 3.05. 67
o' th' sun, | nor the furious winter's rages, 4.02.259
flies like a parthian quiver from our rages, TNK 2.02. 50
wrath, envy, treason, rape, and murther's rages, LUC 909

RAGETH 1 FR 0.0001 REL FR 0 V 1 P
which at this instant so rageth in him, that LR 1.02.162 P

RAGG'D 1 FR 0.0001 REL FR 1 V 0 P
round about an oak, with great ragg'd horns, WIV 4.04. 31

/RAGGED 1 FR 0.0001 REL FR 1 V 0 P
and richard but a /ragged fatal rock? 3H6 5.04. 27

RAGGED 24 FR 0.0027 REL FR 19 V 5 P
some whirlwind bear | unto a ragged, fearful, TGV 1.02.118
with over-weather'd ribs and ragged sails, MV 2.06. 18
my voice is ragged, i know i cannot please you. AYL 2.05. 15 P
a wretched ragged man, o'ergrown with hair, 4.03.106
the rest were ragged, old, and beggarly, | yet, SHR 4.01.137
of this hard world, my ragged prison walls; R2 5.05. 21
slaves as ragged as lazarus in the painted cloth 1H4 4.02. 25 P
more dishonorable ragged than an old feaz'd 4.02. 31 P
and this worm-eaten /hold of ragged stone, 2H4 in 35
thou art a very ragged wart. 3.02.141 P
wart, you see what a ragged appearance it is. 3.02.261 P
i will beg | a ragged and forestall'd remission. 5.02. 38
with four or five most vile and ragged foils H5 4.pr. 50
their ragged curtains poorly are let loose, 4.02. 41
and would not dash me with their ragged sides, 2H6 3.02. 98
and sent the ragged soldiers wounded home. 4.01. 90
his army is a ragged multitude | of hinds and 4.04. 32
the rampant bear chain'd to the ragged staff, 5.01.203
rude ragged nurse, old sullen playfellow | for R3 4.01.101
and shows the ragged entrails of this pit: TIT 2.03.230
and on the ragged stones beat forth our souls, 5.03.133
the studded bridle on a ragged bough | nimbly VEN 37
fast, | thy smoothing titles to a ragged name, LUC 892
then let not winter's ragged hand deface | in SON 6. 1

RAGGEDNESS 1 FR 0.0001 REL FR 1 V 0 P
your /loop'd and window'd raggedness, defend you
LR 3.04. 31

RAGGED'ST 1 FR 0.0001 REL FR 1 V 0 P
the ragged'st hour that time and spite dare 2H4 1.01.151

RAGING 21 FR 0.0023 REL FR 20 V 1 P
rock, | and throw it thence into the raging sea. TGV 1.02.119
thereof the raging fire of fever bred, | and ERR 5.01. 75
nor heady-rash, provok'd with raging ire, 5.01.216
"the raging rocks | and shivering shocks | shall MND 1.02. 31
and where two raging fires meet together, | they SHR 2.01.132
and time it is, when raging war is /done, | to 5.02. 2
rancorous spite, more furious raging broils, 1H6 4.01.185
how the young whelp of talbot's, raging wood, 4.07. 35
nay then, this spark will prove a raging fire, 2H6 3.01.302
where, from thy sight, i should be raging mad, 3.02.394
for raging wind blows up incessant showers, 3H6 1.04.145
even where his raging eye or savage heart, R3 3.05. 83
what raging of the sea! TRO 1.03. 97
nation | to curb those raging appetites that are 2.02.181
who, raging with thy tears, and they with them, ROM 3.05.135
still in motion | of raging waste? TIM 2.01. 4
but we have reason to cool our raging motions, OTH 1.03.330 P
and, being troubled with a raging tooth, | i 3.03.414
make raging battery upon shores of flint." PER 4.04. 43
with waters | that drift-winds force to raging. TNK 5.03.100
it shall be raging mad and silly mild, | make VEN 1151

RAGOZINE 3 FR 0.0003 REL FR 3 V 0 P
this morning of a cruel fever | one ragozine, a MM 4.03. 71
the deputy with the visage | of ragozine, more 4.03. 76
you home | the head of ragozine for claudio's, 5.01.533

RAGS 15 FR 0.0017 REL FR 8 V 7 P
yet you, rogue, will ensconce your rags, your WIV 2.02. 26 P
her rags and the tallow in them will burn a ERR 3.02. 98 P
what shalt thou exchange for rags? LLL 4.01. 83 P
pluck but off these rags; WT 4.03. 53 P
thou hast need of more rags to lay on thee, 4.03. 54 P
rotten carcass of old death | out of his rags! JN 2.01.457
the duke of suffolk muffled up in rags? 2H6 4.01. 46
ay, but these rags are no part of the duke; 4.01. 47
lash hence these overweening rags of france, R3 5.03.328
in thy rags thou know'st none, but art despis'd TIM 4.03.303 P
fellow tear a passion to totters, to very rags, HAM 3.02. 10 P
fathers that wear rags | do make their children LR 2.04. 48
arm it in rags, a pigmy's straw does pierce it. 4.06.167
taught me to shift | into a madman's rags, t' 5.03.188
whose rags sham'd gilded arms, whose naked CYM 5.05. 4

RAH 1 FR 0.0001 REL FR 0 V 1 P
"rah, tah, tah," would 'a say, "bounce," would 2H4 3.02.283 P

RAIL* 31 FR 0.0035 REL FR 18 V 13 P
did not her kitchen maid rail, taunt, and scorn ERR 4.04. 74
and sometime rail thou like demetrius; MND 3.02.362
till thou canst rail the seal from off my bond, MV 4.01.139
i'll rail against all the first-born of egypt. AYL 2.05. 60 P
and we two will rail against our mistress the 3.02.278 P
can a woman rail thus? 4.03. 42 P
door, | and rail upon the hostess of the house, SHR in.2. 86
he begin once, he'll rail in his rope-tricks. 1.02.112 P
say that she rail, why then i'll tell her plain 2.01.170
and if she chance to nod i'll rail and brawl, 4.01.206
an allow'd fool, though he do nothing but rail; TN 1.05. 95 P
and why rail i on this commodity? JN 2.01.587
well, whiles i am a beggar, i will rail, | and 2.01.593
why do i rail on thee, | since thou, created to R2 5.05. 90
that i, in all despite, might rail at him, 3H6 2.06. 81
tell-tale women | rail on the lord's anointed. R3 4.04.151
you i' th' chamblet, get up o' th' rail, | i'll H8 5.03. 89
i shall sooner rail thee into wit and holiness, TRO 2.01. 16 P
he beats me, and i rail at him. 2.03. 3 P
good thersites, come in and rail. 2.03. 24 P
that i might rail at him to ease my mind! TIT 2.04. 35
there would be none left to rail upon thee, and TIM 1.02.239 P
nay, and you begin to rail on society once, i am 1.02.244 P
such may rail against great buildings. 3.04. 64 P
thus to rail on one that is neither known of LR 2.02. 26 P
/faith, i must, she'll rail in the streets else. OTH 4.01.163 P
rail thou in fulvia's phrase, and taunt my ANT 1.02.107
no, let me speak, and let me rail so high, 4.15. 43
to commix | with winds that sailors rail at. CYM 4.02. 56
"in vain i rail at opportunity, | at time, at LUC 1023
and rail on pyrrhus that hath done him wrong, 1467

RAIL'D 10 FR 0.0011 REL FR 5 V 5 P
most, | forsworn my company, and rail'd at me, TGV 3.02. 4
rail'd at herself, that she should be so ADO 2.03.141 P
because i have rail'd so long against marriage; 2.03.237 P
thou hast rail'd on thyself. AYL 1.01. 62 P
sun, | and rail'd on lady fortune in good terms, 2.07. 16
yesterday, | that rail'd against our person. H5 2.02. 41
that rail'd upon me till her pink'd porringer H8 5.03. 47 P
that i could beat him, whilst he rail'd at me. TRO 2.03. 5 P
being down, insulted, rail'd, | and put upon him LR 2.02.119
i rail'd on thee, fearing my love's decesse. VEN 1002

RAILER 1 FR 0.0001 REL FR 1 V 0 P
take that, the likeness of this railer here. 3H6 5.05. 38

RAILEST 2 FR 0.0002 REL FR 1 V 1 P
thou grumblest and railest every hour on TRO 2.01. 32 P
why railest thou on thy birth? ROM 3.03.119

RAILETH 1 FR 0.0001 REL FR 1 V 0 P
yet, | like a poor beggar, raileth on the rich. JN 2.01.592

RAILING 8 FR 0.0009 REL FR 5 V 3 P
seems his sleeps were hind'red by thy railing, ERR 5.01. 71
call you this railing? AYL 4.03. 43
did you ever hear such railing? 4.03. 46 P
nor no railing in a known discreet man, though TN 1.05. 95 P
as tedious | as a tired horse, a railing wife, 1H4 3.01.158
i speak not to that railing hecate, | but unto 1H6 3.02. 64
my liege, his railing is intolerable. 2H6 3.01.172
i am a rascal, a scurvy railing knave, a very TRO 5.04. 28 P

RAILS 6 FR 0.0006 REL FR 3 V 3 P
so rails against all married mankind; WIV 4.02. 23 P
he hates our sacred nation, and he rails, | even MV 1.03. 48
making a sermon of continency to her, and rails, SHR 4.01.184
factious feasts, rails on our state of war, TRO 1.03.191
tenor of the proclamation, and he rails upon me. 2.01. 91 P
see how yond justice rails upon yond simple LR 4.06.152 P

RAIMENT 8 FR 0.0009 REL FR 7 V 1 P
have took upon me | such an immodest raiment —
TGV 5.04.106
what raiment will your honor wear to-day? SHR in.2. 4
ne'er ask me what raiment i'll wear, for i have in.2. 8 P
yea, all my raiment, to my petticoat, | or what 2.01. 5
our raiment | and state of bodies would bewray COR 5.03. 94
to wear them like his raiment, carelessly, | and TIM 3.05. 33
knees i beg | that you'll vouchsafe me raiment, LR 2.04.156
thee | is but the seemly raiment of my heart, SON 22. 6

/RAIN 2 FR 0.0002 REL FR 2 V 0 P
/the //to-and-fro-conflicting /wind /and /rain. LR 3.01. 11
/have /seen | /sunshine /and /rain /at /once; 4.03. 18

RAIN 65 FR 0.0073 REL FR 54 V 11 P
heavens rain grace | on that which breeds TMP 3.01. 75
let the sky rain potatoes; WIV 5.05. 18 P
is't not drown'd i' th' last rain? MM 3.02. 49 P
then under this penthouse, for it drizzles rain, ADO 3.03.104 P
your mistresses dare never come in rain, | for LLL 4.03.266
belike for want of rain; MND 1.01.130
in measure rain thy joy, scant this excess! MV 3.02.112
it droppeth as the gentle rain from heaven 4.01.185
that the property of rain is to wet and fire to AYL 3.02. 26 P
like foggy south, puffing with wind and rain? 3.05. 50
more clamorous than a parrot against rain, more 4.01.152 P
gift | to rain a shower of commanded tears, | an SHR in.1. 125
lady, the heavens rain odors on you! TN 3.01. 84 P
that youth's a rare courtier — "rain odors," 3.01. 86 P
tine boy, | with hey ho, the wind and the rain, 5.01.390
but a toy, | for the rain it raineth every day. 5.01.392
men shut their gate, | for the rain, etc. 5.01.396
could i never thrive, | for the rain, etc. 5.01.400
still had drunken heads, | for the rain, etc. 5.01.404
being as like | as rain to water, or devil to JN 2.01.128
shall rain their drift of bullets on this town. 2.01.412
will rain hot vengeance on offenders' heads. R2 1.02. 8
his, whilst on the earth i rain | my waters — 3.03. 59
to rain upon remembrance with mine eyes, | that 2H4 2.03. 59
how now, rain within doors, and none abroad? 4.05. 9
constrain'd to watch in darkness, rain, and cold 1H6 2.01. 7
if talbot do but thunder, rain will follow. 3.02. 59
nor let the rain of heaven wet this place | to 2H6 3.02.341
and when the rage allays, the rain begins. 3H6 1.04.146
plies her hard, and much rain wears the marble. 3.02. 50
their cheeks | like trees bedash'd with rain — R3 1.02.163
rain, to lay this wind, or my heart will be TRO 4.04. 53 P
out of their burrows, like conies after rain, COR 4.05.212 P
to them | as unrelenting flint to drops of rain. TIT 2.03.141
o earth, i will befriend thee more with rain, 3.01. 16
rain sacrificial whisperings in his ear, | make TIM 1.01. 81
in thunder, lightning, or in rain? MAC 1.01. 2
it will be rain to-night. 3.03. 16
is there not rain enough in the sweet heavens HAM 3.03. 45
for form, | will pack when it begins to rain, LR 2.04. 80
spout, rain! 3.02. 14
nor rain, wind, thunder, fire are my daughters. 3.02. 15
such groans of roaring wind and rain, i never 3.02. 47
wit — | with heigh-ho, the wind and the rain — 3.02. 75
fit, | though the rain it raineth every day." 3.02. 77
poor old heart, he holp the heavens to rain. 3.07. 62
when the rain came to wet me once, and the wind 4.06.101 P
be, she makes a show'r of rain as well as jove. ANT 1.02.151 P
thick cloud, and rain, that i may say | the gods 5.02.299
hear | the rain and wind beat dark december, how
CYM 3.03. 37
wind, rain, and thunder, remember earthly man PER 2.01. 2
who cannot feel nor see the rain, being in't, TNK 1.01.120
the whole week's not fair | if any day it rain. 3.01. 66
rain added to a river that is rank | perforce VEN 71
more than flint, for stone at rain relenteth. 200
to shelter thee from tempest and from rain: 238
with tears which chorus-like her eyes did rain. 360
"love comforteth like sunshine after rain, | but 799
through the flood-gates breaks the silver rain, 959
but like a stormy day, now wind, now rain, 965
this windy tempest, till it blow up rain, | held LUC 1788
'pointing to each his thunder, rain, and wind, SON 14. 6
to dry the rain on my storm-beaten face, | for 34. 6
the sea, all water, yet receives rain still, 135. 9
storming her world with sorrow's wind and rain. LC 7

RAINBOW 3 FR 0.0003 REL FR 1 V 2 P
myself into all the colors of the rainbow; WIV 4.05.115 P
hath ribbons of all the colors i' th' rainbow; WT 4.04.204 P
or add another hue | unto the rainbow, or with JN 4.02. 14

RAINBOWS 1 FR 0.0001 REL FR 1 V 0 P
blue circles stream'd, like rainbows in the sky. LUC 1587

RAIN'D 7 FR 0.0008 REL FR 7 V 0 P
rain'd from the wounds of slaughtered englishmen
R2 3.03. 44
it rain'd down fortune show'ring on your head, 1H4 5.01. 47
my heart dropp'd love, my pow'r rain'd honor, H8 3.02.185
and in his grave rain'd many a tear" — | fare HAM 4.05.167
had they rain'd | all kind of sores and shames OTH 4.02. 48
on that unworthy place, | as it rain'd kisses. ANT 3.13. 85
which long have rain'd, making her cheeks all VEN 83

RAINETH 3 FR 0.0003 REL FR 3 V 0 P
but a toy, | for the rain it raineth every day. TN 5.01.392
fit, | though the rain it raineth every day." LR 3.02. 77
even as the wind is hush'd before it raineth, VEN 458

RAINING 4 FR 0.0004 REL FR 4 V 0 P
raining the tears of lamentation | for the LLL 5.02.809
harden lust, though marble /wear with raining. LUC 560
from thee, that down thy cheeks are raining? 1271
no flood by raining slaketh. 1677

RAINOLD 1 FR 0.0001 REL FR 1 V 0 P
that harry duke of herford, rainold lord cobham, R2 2.01.279

RAINS 2 FR 0.0002 REL FR 2 V 0 P
sunset of my brother's son | it rains downright. ROM 3.05.128
at last it rains, and busy winds give o'er: LUC 1790

RAIN-WATER 1 FR 0.0001 REL FR 0 V 1 P
is better than this rain-water out o' door. LR 3.02. 11 P

RAINY 4 FR 0.0004 REL FR 4 V 0 P
and with rainy eyes | write sorrow on the bosom R2 3.02.146
with rainy marching in the painful field; H5 4.03.111
that both mine eyes were rainy like to his; TIT 5.01.117
give not a windy night a rainy morrow, | to SON 90. 7

RAIS'D 27 FR 0.0030 REL FR 25 V 2 P
which rais'd in me | an undergoing stomach, to TMP 1.02.156
he hath rais'd the wall, and houses too. 2.01. 88 P
i did say so, | when first i rais'd the tempest. 5.01. 6
with it when i sleep, rais'd with it when i sit, ERR 4.04. 35 P
the villain jew with outcries rais'd the duke, MV 2.08. 4
thou know'st she has rais'd me from my sickly AWW 2.03.111
a spirit rais'd from depth of under ground, 2H6 1.02. 79
until a power be rais'd to put them down. 4.04. 40
i was the chief that rais'd him to the crown, 3H6 3.03.262

hath rais'd in gallia have arriv'd our coast, 5.03. 8
by him that rais'd me to this careful height R3 1.03. 82
one rais'd in blood, and one in blood 5.03.247
who first rais'd head against usurping richard, H8 2.01.108
ever by your grace, whose hand has rais'd me. 2.02.119
those twins of learning that he rais'd in you, 4.02. 58
rais'd only that the weaker sort may wish | good COR 4.06. 70
i rais'd him, and i pawn'd | mine honor for his 5.06. 20
is the county's page that rais'd the watch? ROM 5.03.279
and my estate deserves an heir more rais'd TIM 1.01.119
he rais'd a sigh so piteous and profound | as it HAM 2.01. 91
he rais'd the house with loud and coward cries. LR 2.04. 43
harder than the stones whereof 'tis rais'd, 3.02. 64
and many of the consuls, rais'd and met, | are OTH 1.02. 43
hath rais'd me from my bed, nor doth the general 1.03. 54
look if my gentle love be not rais'd up! 2.03.250
of heaven, | rais'd by your populous troops. ANT 3.06. 50
if thy unworthiness rais'd love in me, | more SON 150.13
/RAISE 1 FR 0.0001 REL FR 1 V 0 P
for i will /raise her statue in pure gold, ROM 5.03.299
RAISE 49 FR 0.0055 REL FR 44 V 5 P
said, | raise up the organs of her fantasy, WIV 5.05. 51
be–gar, i'll raise all windsor. 5.05.210 P
true, | let me in safety raise me from my knees, MM 5.01.231
i money nor commodity | to raise a present sum; MV 1.01.179
i cannot instantly raise up the gross | of full 1.03. 55
mark me now, now will i raise the waters. 2.02. 49 P
of christians will raise the price of hogs. 3.05. 24 P
jews to christians, you raise the price of pork. 3.05. 36 P
eyne | have power to raise such love in mine, AYL 4.03. 51
began to scold and raise up such a storm | that SHR 1.01.172
for this business | will raise us all. WT 2.01.198
and raise the power of france upon his head, JN 3.01.193
o, if you raise this house against this house, R2 4.01.145
if thou have power to raise him, bring him 1H4 3.01. 59
out of your sight and raise this present head, 5.01. 66
will raise your highness such a mighty sum | as H5 1.02.133
are yet not ready | to raise so great a siege. 3.03. 47
son, and from her blood raise up | issue to me, 5.02.348
let's raise the siege; 1H6 1.02. 13
ordained is to raise this tedious siege, | and 1.02. 53
this night the siege assuredly i'll raise: 1.02.130
leave off delays, and let us raise the siege. 1.02.146
is come with a great power to raise the siege. 1.04.103
haps it i seek not to advance | or raise myself, 3.01. 32
mouths | to raise a mutiny betwixt yourselves. 4.01.131
then will i raise aloft the milk–white rose, 2H6 1.01.254
whom we raise, | we will make fast within a 1.04. 21
should raise so great a power without his leave, 5.01. 21
king, | and raise his issue like a loving sire; 3H6 2.02. 22
majesty | to raise my state to title of a queen, 4.01. 68
and when the morning sun shall raise his car 4.07. 80
i'll learn to conjure and raise devils, but i'll TRO 2.03. 6 P
hie to the goths and raise an army there, | and TIT 3.01.285
now will i to the goths and raise a pow'r, | to 3.01.299
him | to raise a spirit in his mistress' circle, ROM 2.01. 24
name | i conjure only but to raise up him. 2.01. 29
run to the capulets, | raise up the montagues; 5.03.178
raise me this beggar, and deny't that lord, TIM 4.03. 9
for i can raise no money by vile means. JC 4.03. 71
it may be i shall raise you by and by | on 4.03.247
shall raise such artificial sprites | as by the MAC 3.05. 27
was first fram'd flesh | to raise my fortunes. LR 4.06.228
raise all my kindred. OTH 1.01.167
and raise some special officers of /night. 1.01.182
i'll raise the preparation of a war | shall ANT 3.04. 26
/aulis meet us with | the forces you can raise, TNK 1.01.213
raise me a devil now, and let him play | qui 3.05. 85
upon this promise did he raise his chin, | like VEN 85
with sighs that burning lungs did raise; LC 228
RAISED 2 FR 0.0002 REL FR 2 V 0 P
him, | lead to the sagittary the raised search; OTH 1.01.158
those are the raised father and his friends. 1.02. 29
RAISES 1 FR 0.0001 REL FR 0 V 1 P
but it raises the greater war between him and ANT 2.07. 9 P
RAISING 6 FR 0.0006 REL FR 6 V 0 P
mind, your reason | for raising this sea–storm? TMP 1.02.177
till, raising of more aid, | we came again to ERR 5.01.153
to bring me down | must answer for your raising? AWW 2.03.113
speed, | to save our heads by raising of a head, 1H4 1.03.284
raising up wicked spirits from under ground, 2H6 2.01.170
whip him 'fore the people's eyes — his raising, COR 4.06. 61
RAISINS 1 FR 0.0001 REL FR 0 V 1 P
of pruins, and as many of raisins o' th' sun. WT 4.03. 48 P
RAK'D 1 FR 0.0001 REL FR 1 V 0 P
days, | nor from the dust of old oblivion rak'd, H5 2.04. 87
RAKE 4 FR 0.0004 REL FR 4 V 0 P
sweet lady, let me rake it from the earth. TGV 4.02.115
even in your hearts, there will he rake for it. H5 2.04. 98
name of thrift, | does he rake this together? H8 3.02.110
thee i'll rake up, the post unsanctified | of LR 4.06.274
RAKES 1 FR 0.0001 REL FR 0 V 1 P
this with our pikes, ere we become rakes; COR 1.01. 23 P
RALPH 1 FR 0.0001 REL FR 0 V 1 P
look down into the pomgarnet, ralph. 1H4 2.04. 38 P
RAM 7 FR 0.0008 REL FR 6 V 1 P
old, cuckoldly ram, out of all reasonable match. AYL 3.02. 82 P
the green neptune | a ram and bleated; WT 4.04. 29
so that the ram that batters down the wall, TRO 1.03.206
an old black ram | is tupping your white ewe. OTH 1.01. 88
ram thou thy fruitful tidings in mine ears, ANT 2.05. 24
be the ram to batter | the fortress of it; 3.02. 30
that yet remains upon her breast | (rude ram, to LUC 464
RAMBURES 2 FR 0.0002 REL FR 2 V 0 P
jacques chatillion, rambures, vaudemont, H5 3.05. 43
the master of the cross–bows, lord rambures, 4.08. 94
RAMM'D 2 FR 0.0002 REL FR 1 V 1 P
ramm'd me in with foul shirts and smocks, socks, WIV 3.05. 89 P
have we ramm'd up our gates against the world. JN 2.01.272
RAMPALLIAN 1 FR 0.0001 REL FR 0 V 1 P
you rampallian! 2H4 2.01. 59 P
RAMPANT 1 FR 0.0001 REL FR 1 V 0 P
the rampant bear chain'd to the ragged staff, 2H6 5.01.203
RAMPING 3 FR 0.0003 REL FR 3 V 0 P
a ramping fool, to brag and stamp and swear JN 3.01.122
raven, | a couching lion and a ramping cat, 1H4 3.01.151
under whose shade the ramping lion slept, 3H6 5.02. 13
RAMPIR'D 1 FR 0.0001 REL FR 1 V 0 P
against our rampir'd gates and they shall ope, TIM 5.04. 47
RAMPS 1 FR 0.0001 REL FR 1 V 0 P
sheets, | whiles he is vaulting variable ramps, CYM 1.06.134
RAM'S 1 FR 0.0001 REL FR 1 V 0 P
down fell both the ram's horns in the court, TIT 4.03. 73
RAMS 6 FR 0.0006 REL FR 4 V 2 P
rank, | in end of autumn turned to the rams, MV 1.03. 81
or is your gold and silver ewes and rams? 1.03. 95
to bring the ewes and the rams together, and to AYL 3.02. 79 P
any thing so sudden but the fight of two rams, 5.02. 31 P
week to go, like rams | in the old time of war, H8 4.01. 77
breed not, | my rams speed not, all is amiss; PP 17. 2
RAMSTON 1 FR 0.0001 REL FR 1 V 0 P
sir thomas erpingham, sir john ramston, | sir R2 2.01.283
RAM–TENDER 1 FR 0.0001 REL FR 0 V 1 P
an old sheep–whistling rogue, a ram–tender, to WT 4.04.777 P
RAN 34 FR 0.0038 REL FR 26 V 8 P
by the salt rheum that ran between france and it ERR 3.02.128 P
arm, that i, amaz'd, ran from her as a witch. 3.02.144 P
she that would be your wife now ran from you. 4.04.148
and immediately | ran hither to your grace, whom 5.01.252
he had, my lord, and when he ran in here, 5.01.258
told you all the wealth i had | ran in my veins: MV 3.02.255
shadow ere himself, | and ran dismayed away. 5.01. 9
how i cried, how the horses ran away, how her SHR 4.01. 80 P
low–born lass that ever | ran on the green–sord. WT 4.04.157
ran fearfully among the trembling reeds, | and 1H4 1.03.105
you are lions too, you ran away upon instinct, 2.04.300 P
faith, i ran when i saw others run. 2.04.302 P
the goats ran from the mountains, and the herds 3.01. 38
i ran from shrewsbury, my noble lord, | where 2H4 1.01. 65
me, as you did when you ran away by gadshill. 2.04.307 P
cowardly rascals that ran from the battle ha' H5 4.07. 6 P
so griev'd him, | that he ran mad, and died. H8 2.02.129
queen hecuba laugh'd that her eyes ran o'er. TRO 1.02.143 P
and ran | from th' noise of our own drums." COR 2.03. 53
than when these fellows ran about the streets, 4.06. 28
read that hecuba of troy | ran mad for sorrow. TIT 4.01. 21
he ran this way and leapt this orchard wall. ROM 2.01. 5
which way ran he that kill'd mercutio? 3.01.137
tybalt, that murtherer, which way ran he? 3.01.138
on him, | and then i ran away to call the watch. 5.03.285
look, in this place ran cassius' dagger through; JC 3.02.174
statue | (which all the while ran blood) great 3.02.189
that ran through caesar's bowels, search this 5.03. 42
there ran a rumor | of many worthy fellows that MAC 4.03.182
i ran it through, even from my boyish days | to OTH 1.03.132
the fresh streams ran by her, and murmur'd her 4.03. 44
he ran upon the boar with his sharp spear, | who VEN 1112
to simois' reedy banks the red blood ran, LUC 1437
he rose and ran away, ah, fool too froward! PP 4.14
RANCOR 6 FR 0.0006 REL FR 5 V 1 P
uncover'd slander, unmitigated rancor — o god, ADO 4.01.306 P
it issues from the rancor of a villain, | a R2 1.01.143
rancor will out. 2H6 1.01.142
the broken rancor of your high–swoll'n hates, R3 2.02.117
this sudden stab of rancor i misdoubt; 3.02. 87
to turn your households' rancor to pure love. ROM 2.03. 92
RANCOROUS 5 FR 0.0005 REL FR 5 V 0 P
sprung from the rancorous outrage of your duke ERR 1.01. 6
seen decipher'd there | more rancorous spite, 1H6 4.01.185
respecting what a rancorous mind he bears | and 2H6 3.01. 24
that shall be scoured in his rancorous heart 3.02.199
courtesy, | i must be held a rancorous enemy. R3 1.03. 50
RANCOR'S 1 FR 0.0001 REL FR 1 V 0 P
and charity chas'd hence by rancor's hand; 2H6 3.01.144
RANCORS 1 FR 0.0001 REL FR 1 V 0 P
put rancors in the vessel of my peace | only for MAC 3.01. 66
RANDOM 1 FR 0.0001 REL FR 1 V 0 P
it goes, | i writ at random, very doubtfully. TGV 2.01.111
RANDON 4 FR 0.0004 REL FR 4 V 0 P
and /the great care of goods at randon left, ERR 1.01. 42
he talks at randon; sure the man is mad. 1H6 5.03. 85
to see, | but hatefully at randon dost thou hit. VEN 940
at randon from the truth vainly express'd; SON 147.12
/RANG'D 1 FR 0.0001 REL FR 1 V 0 P
/him /where /most /trade /of /danger /rang'd; 2H4 1.01.174
RANG'D 3 FR 0.0003 REL FR 3 V 0 P
else had she with her father rang'd along. AYL 1.03. 68
and the wide arch | of the rang'd empire fall! ANT 1.01. 34
that is my home of love, if i have rang'd, SON 109. 5
RANGE 8 FR 0.0009 REL FR 8 V 0 P
that he did range the town to seek me out. TN 4.03. 7
then thieves and robbers range abroad unseen R2 3.02. 39
wherein you range under this subtile king! 1H4 1.03.169
heart, | in liberty of bloody hand, shall range, H5 3.03. 12
i saw him in the battle range about, | and 3H6 2.01. 11
born, | and range with humble livers in content, H8 2.03. 20
so let high–sighted tyranny range on, | till JC 2.01.118
it safe with us | to let his madness range. HAM 3.03. 2
RANGERS 1 FR 0.0001 REL FR 1 V 0 P
and makes | diana's rangers false themselves, CYM 2.03. 69
RANGES 3 FR 0.0003 REL FR 2 V 1 P
athwart his affection ranges evenly with mine. ADO 2.02. 7 P
and bury all, which yet distinctly ranges, | in COR 3.01.205
war, whose several ranges | frighted each other? ANT 3.13. 5
RANGING 2 FR 0.0002 REL FR 2 V 0 P
if once i find thee ranging, | hortensio will be SHR 3.01. 91
and caesar's spirit, ranging for revenge, | with JC 3.01.270
/RANK* 5 FR 0.0005 REL FR 5 V 0 P
/to /diet /rank /minds /sick /of /happiness, 2H4 4.01. 64
/when /rank /thersites /opes /his /mastic /jaws, TRO 1.03. 73
/a /gallant /horse /fall'n /in /first /rank, 3.03.161
had not impressure made | /of /our /rank /feud; 4.05.132
abuse him to the moor in the /rank garb | (for i OTH 2.01.306
RANK* 47 FR 0.0053 REL FR 43 V 4 P
while other jests are something rank on foot, WIV 4.06. 22
he would give't thee, from this rank offense, MM 3.01. 99
fall as jacob's hire, the ewes, being rank, | in MV 1.03. 80
and rank me with the barbarous multitudes. 2.09. 33
nay, if i keep not my rank — AYL 1.02.107 P
of all opinion that grows rank in them | that i 2.07. 46
it is the right butter–women's rank to market. 3.02. 98 P
the rank of osiers by the murmuring stream 4.03. 79
for all this, though it be as rank as a fox. TN 2.05.124 P
a name | as rank as any flax–wench that puts to WT 1.02.277
how foul it is, what rank diseases grow, | and 2H4 3.01. 39
in equal rank with the best govern'd nation, 5.02.137
hemlock, and rank femetary | doth root upon, H5 5.02. 45
wanting the scythe withal, uncorrected, rank, 5.02. 50
let that one article rank with the rest, | and 5.02.346
to rank our chosen truth with such a show | as H8 pr 18
what, so rank? 1.02.186
he's a rank weed, sir thomas, | and we must root 5.01. 52
how rank soever rounded in with danger. TRO 1.03.196
up | in rank achilles must or now be cropp'd 1.03.318
eye, | and the rank poison of the old will die. ROM 1.02. 50
but one | that unassailable holds on his rank, JC 3.01. 69
who else must be let blood, who else is rank; 3.01.152
not i' th' worst rank of manhood, say't, | and i MAC 3.01.102
things rank and gross in nature | possess it HAM 1.02.136
and they in france of the best rank and station 1.03. 73
marry, none so rank | as may dishonor him, take 2.01. 20
thou mixture rank, of midnight weeds collected, 3.02.257
o, my offense is rank, it smells to heaven, | it 3.03. 36
to live | in the rank sweat of an enseamed bed, 3.04. 92
whiles rank corruption, mining all within, 3.04.148
forth | in rank and not–to–be–endur'd riots. LR 1.04.204
being the worst | stands in some rank of praise. 2.04.258
crown'd with rank /femiter and furrow–weeds, 4.04. 3
foh, one may smell in such, a will most rank, OTH 3.03.232
but let the world rank me in register | a ANT 4.09. 21
rank of gross diet, shall we be enclouded, | and 5.02.212
would he had been one of my rank! CYM 2.01. 15 P
lust and rank thoughts, hers, hers; 2.05. 24
and somewhat better than your rank i'll use you. TNK 2.05. 43
rain added to a river that is rank | perforce VEN 71
to thy fair flower add the rank smell of weeds: SON 69.12
words come hindmost) holds his rank before. 85.12
a healthful state | which, rank of goodness, 118.12
by their rank thoughts my deeds must not be 121.12
which shall above that idle rank remain | beyond 122. 3
to blush at speeches rank, to weep at woes, | or LC 307
RANK'D 4 FR 0.0004 REL FR 4 V 0 P
my fortunes every way as fairly rank'd | (if not MND 1.01.101
that were embattailed and rank'd in kent. JN 4.02.200
and needly will be rank'd with other griefs, ROM 3.02.117
base o' th' mount | is rank'd with all deserts, TIM 1.01. 65
RANKER 3 FR 0.0003 REL FR 2 V 1 P
or i should think my honesty ranker than my wit. AYL 4.01. 84 P
the compost on the weeds | to make them ranker. HAM 3.04.152
it yield to norway or the pole | a ranker rate, 4.04. 22
RANKEST 2 FR 0.0002 REL FR 1 V 1 P
i do forgive | thy rankest fault — all of them; TMP 5.01.132
there was the rankest compound of villainous WIV 3.05. 92 P
RANKING 1 FR 0.0001 REL FR 1 V 0 P
stomach, ever ranking | himself with princes; H8 4.02. 34
RANKLE 2 FR 0.0002 REL FR 2 V 0 P
fell sorrow's tooth doth never rankle more R2 1.03.302
his venom tooth will rankle to the death. R3 1.03.290
RANKLY 1 FR 0.0001 REL FR 1 V 0 P
by a forged process of my death | rankly abus'd; HAM 1.05. 38
RANKNESS 3 FR 0.0003 REL FR 2 V 1 P
i will physic your rankness, and yet give no AYL 1.01. 86 P
leaving our rankness and irregular course, JN 5.04. 54
stifled | with the mere rankness of their joy. H8 4.01. 59
RANKS 21 FR 0.0023 REL FR 21 V 0 P
and bow'd his eminent top to their low ranks, AWW 1.02. 43
even at my gates, with ranks of foreign pow'rs; JN 4.02.244
and fill up | her enemies' ranks — i must 5.02. 29
from forth the ranks of many thousand french, R2 2.03.102
shall now, in mutual well–beseeming ranks, 1H4 1.01. 14
why, all our ranks are broke. H5 4.05. 6
our ranks are broke, and ruin follows us. 3H6 2.03. 10
cruel way | through ranks of greekish youth, and TRO 4.05.185
bring in thy ranks, but leave without thy rage; TIM 5.04. 39
in ranks and squadrons and right form of war, JC 2.02. 20
he finds thee in the stout norweyan ranks, MAC 1.03. 95
yours in the ranks of death. LR 4.02. 25
on the brow o' th' sea | stand ranks of people, OTH 2.01. 54
when it hath blown his ranks into the air, | and 3.04.135
how, with his banners and his well–paid ranks, ANT 3.01. 32
in their pure ranks his traitor eye encloses, LUC 73
whose ranks of blue veins, as his hand did scale 440
that in their smoky ranks his smoth'red light 783
and their ranks began | to break upon the galled 1439
than | retire again, till meeting greater ranks, 1441
brought | to march in ranks of better equipage; SON 32.12
RANK–SCENTED 1 FR 0.0001 REL FR 1 V 0 P
for the mutable, rank–scented meiny, let them COR 3.01. 66
/RANSACK 1 FR 0.0001 REL FR 1 V 0 P
/and /their /vow /is /made | /to /ransack /troy, TRO pr 8
RANSACK'D 4 FR 0.0004 REL FR 3 V 1 P
my bed shall be abus'd, my coffers ransack'd, my WIV 2.02.293 P
i would have ransack'd | the pedlar's silken WT 4.04.349
what treason were it to the ransack'd queen, TRO 2.02.150
but robb'd and ransack'd by injurious theft. LUC 838
RANSACKING 1 FR 0.0001 REL FR 1 V 0 P
is now in england ransacking the church, JN 3.04.172
RANSOM 55 FR 0.0062 REL FR 50 V 5 P
sorrow | be a sufficient ransom for offense, | i TGV 5.04. 75
ignomy in ransom and free pardon | are of two MM 2.04.111
a dishonor'd life | with ransom of such shame. 4.04. 32
levied | to quit the penalty and to ransom him. ERR 1.01. 22
and ransom him to any french courtier for a new LLL 1.02. 62 P
rescue in the first assault or ransom afterward. AWW 1.03.116 P
that laboring art can never ransom nature | from 2.01.118
o, ransom, ransom! do not hide mine eyes. 4.01. 67
o, ransom, ransom! do not hide mine eyes. 4.01. 67
in stubborn jewry | of the world's ransom, R2 2.01. 56
that we at our own charge shall ransom straight 1H4 1.03. 79
penny cost | to ransom home revolted mortimer. 1.03. 92
and when i urg'd the ransom once again | of my 1.03.141
he said he would not ransom mortimer, | forbade 1.03.219
deliver them up without their ransom straight, 1.03.260
of prisoners' ransom, and of soldiers slain, 2.03. 54
wales, | there without ransom to lie forfeited; 4.03. 96
fear, | and for achievement offer us his ransom. H5 3.05. 60
send | to know what willing ransom he will give. 3.05. 63
bid him therefore consider of his ransom, which 3.06.126 P
my ransom is this frail and worthless trunk; 3.06.154
if for thy ransom thou wilt now compound, 4.03. 80
shall — my ransom then | will soon be levied. 4.03.120
come thou no more for ransom, gentle herald, 4.03.122
thou wilt once more come again for a ransom. 4.03.129 P
signieur, thou do give to me | egregious ransom. 4.04. 11

and for his ransom he will give you two hundred 4.04. 45 P
is this the king we sent to for his ransom? 4.05. 9
i have fin'd these bones of mine for ransom? 4.07. 69
com'st thou again for ransom? 4.07. 70
his ransom there is none but i shall pay: 1H6 1.01.148
his crown shall be the ransom of my friend; 1.01.150
they set him free without his ransom paid, | in 3.03. 72
be so — | what ransom must i pay before i pass? 5.03. 73
why speak'st thou not? what ransom must i pay? 5.03. 77
wilt thou accept of ransom, yea or no? 5.03. 80
that is her ransom; 5.03.157
and lowly words were ransom for their fault. 2H6 3.01.127
the world shall not be ransom for thy life. 3.02.297
here shall they make their ransom on the sand, 4.01. 10
what is my ransom, master? let me know. 4.01. 15
be not so rash, take ransom, let him live. 4.01. 28
and as for these whose ransom we have set, | it 4.01.139
and hither have they sent it for her ransom. 3H6 5.07. 40
the ransom of my bold attempt | shall be this R3 5.03.265
and that shall be the ransom for their fault. TIT 3.01.156
to ransom my two nephews from their death; 3.01.172
i will send his ransom, | and being enfranchis'd TIM 1.01.105
use me well, | you shall have ransom. LR 4.06.192
futurity, | can ransom me into his love again, OTH 3.04.118
lucky, men did ransom lives | of me for jests; ANT 3.13.179
nothing but our lives | may be call'd ransom, CYM 5.05. 80
obey, | paying what ransom the insulter willeth; VEN 550
and they are rich, and ransom all ill deeds. SON 34.14
mine ransoms yours, and yours must ransom me. 120.14
RANSOM'D 5 FR 0.0005 REL FR 1 V 4 P
look'd as they had heard of a world ransom'd, or WT 5.02. 15 P
so should he be sure to be ransom'd, and a many H5 4.01.122 P
heard the king say he would not be ransom'd. 4.01.191 P
when our throats are cut, he may be ransom'd, 4.01.193 P
my boy, a britain born, | let him be ransom'd. CYM 5.05. 85
RANSOMED 1 FR 0.0001 REL FR 1 V 0 P
for him was i exchang'd and ransomed. 1H6 1.04. 29
RANSOMING 1 FR 0.0001 REL FR 1 V 0 P
ransoming him, or pitying, threat'ning th' other COR 1.06. 36
RANSOMLESS 2 FR 0.0002 REL FR 2 V 0 P
him | up to his pleasure, ransomless and free. 1H4 5.05. 28
ransomless here we set our prisoners free. TIT 1.01.274
RANSOM'S 1 FR 0.0001 REL FR 1 V 0 P
for me, my ransom's death. CYM 5.03. 80
RANSOMS 2 FR 0.0002 REL FR 2 V 0 P
whose ransoms did the general coffers fill; JC 3.02. 89
mine ransoms yours, and yours must ransom me. SON 120.14
RAN'ST 3 FR 0.0003 REL FR 1 V 2 P
and sword on thy side, and yet thou ran'st away; 1H4 2.04.317 P
when thou ran'st up gadshill in the night to 3.03. 38 P
tours | thou ran'st a–tilt in honor of my love 2H6 1.03. 51
RANT 1 FR 0.0001 REL FR 1 V 0 P
and thou'lt mouth, | i'll rant as well as thou. HAM 5.01.284
RANTING 1 FR 0.0001 REL FR 0 V 1 P
look where my ranting host of the garter comes. WIV 2.01.189 P
RAP 3 FR 0.0003 REL FR 1 V 2 P
and rap me well, or i'll knock your knave's pate SHR 1.02. 12
he bid me knock him and rap him soundly, sir. 1.02. 31 P
rap me here; 1.02. 41 P
RAPE 17 FR 0.0019 REL FR 17 V 0 P
and done a rape | upon the maiden virtue of the JN 2.01. 97
it, | but i would have the soil of her fair rape TRO 2.02.148
thou and thy faction shall repent this rape. TIT 1.01.404
rape call you it, my lord, to seize my own, | my 1.01.405
are, | fitted by kind for rape and villainy. 2.01.116
and treats of tereus' treason and his rape — 4.01. 48
and rape, i fear, was root of thy annoy. 4.01. 49
lord junius brutus sware for lucrece' rape, 4.01. 91
the news, | for villains mark'd with rape. 4.02. 9
where bloody murther or detested rape | can 5.02. 37
lo by thy side where rape and murder stands; 5.02. 45
rape and murder, therefore called so | 'cause 5.02. 62
show me a villain that hath done a rape, | and i 5.02. 94
nay, nay, let rape and murder stay with me, | or 5.02.134
the one is murder, and rape is the other's name, 5.02.156
wrath, envy, treason, rape, and murther's rages, LUC 909
greece, | for helen's rape the city to destroy, 1369
RAPES 3 FR 0.0003 REL FR 2 V 1 P
for rapes and ravishments he parallels nessus. AWW 4.03.251 P
by nature made for murthers and for rapes. TIT 4.01. 58
for i must talk of murthers, rapes, and 5.01. 63
RAPIER 22 FR 0.0024 REL FR 8 V 14 P
ariel, | fetch me the hat and rapier in my cell. TMP 5.01. 84
come, take–a your rapier, and come after my heel
WIV 1.04. 59 P
rugby, my rapier! 1.04. 69 P
the frenchman hath good skill in his rapier. 2.01.223 P
take your rapier, jack, i vill tell you how i 2.03. 13 P
villainy, take your rapier. 2.03. 16 P
master starve–lackey the rapier and dagger man, MM 4.03. 14 P
do excel thee in my rapier as much as thou didst LLL 1.02. 74 P
therefore too much odds for a spaniard's rapier. 1.02.177 P
adieu, valor, rust, rapier, be still, drum, for 1.02.181 P
dubb'd with unhatch'd rapier and on carpet TN 3.04.235 P
i had a pass with him, rapier, scabbard, and all 3.04.274 P
give me my rapier, boy. 2H4 2.04.201 P
i will scour you with my rapier, as i may, in H5 2.01. 57 P
till i have sheath'd | my rapier in his bosom, TIT 2.01. 54
fetch me my rapier, boy. ROM 1.05. 55
gentle mercutio, put thy rapier up. 3.01. 84
whips out his rapier, cries, "a rat, a rat!" HAM 4.01. 10
defense, | and for your rapier most especial, 4.07. 98
rapier and dagger. 5.02.145 P
wear thy good rapier bare, and put it home. OTH 5.01. 2
there | that does command my rapier from my hip,
TNK 1.02. 56
RAPIER'S 5 FR 0.0005 REL FR 5 V 0 P
where it was forged, with my rapier's point. R2 4.01. 40
such pity as my rapier's point affords. 3H6 1.03. 37
that valiant clifford with his rapier's point 1.04. 80
i'll broach the tadpole on my rapier's point. TIT 4.02. 85
that did spit his body | upon a rapier's point. ROM 4.03. 57
/RAPIERS 1 FR 0.0001 REL FR 0 V 1 P
/that /many /wearing /rapiers /are /afraid /of HAM 2.02.343 P
RAPIERS 1 FR 0.0001 REL FR 0 V 1 P
as i take it, six french rapiers and poniards, HAM 5.02.149 P
RAPINE 3 FR 0.0003 REL FR 3 V 0 P
task, | so thou destroy rapine and murder there. TIT 5.02. 59
rapine and murther, you are welcome too. 5.02. 83
thee, | good rapine, stab him, he is a ravisher. 5.02.103
RAPS 1 FR 0.0001 REL FR 1 V 0 P
what, dear sir, | thus raps you? are you well? CYM 1.06. 51
RAPT 8 FR 0.0009 REL FR 7 V 1 P
being transported | and rapt in secret studies. TMP 1.02. 77
i was much rapt in this, | and apprehended here TRO 3.03.123
more dances my rapt heart | than when i first my COR 4.05.116
you are rapt, sir, in some work, some dedication TIM 1.01. 19
i am rapt and cannot cover | the monstrous bulk 5.01. 64
and of royal hope, | that he seems rapt withal; MAC 1.03. 57
look how our partner's rapt. 1.03.142
whiles i stood rapt in the wonder of it, came 1.05. 6 P
/RAPTURE 1 FR 0.0001 REL FR 1 V 0 P
and, spite of all the /rapture of the sea, PER 2.01.155
RAPTURE 2 FR 0.0002 REL FR 2 V 0 P
for in this rapture i shall surely speak | the TRO 3.02.130
nurse | into a rapture lets her baby cry | while COR 2.01.207
RAPTURES 1 FR 0.0001 REL FR 1 V 0 P
her brain–sick raptures | cannot distaste the TRO 2.02.122
RARE 65 FR 0.0073 REL FR 47 V 18 P
fair encounter | of two most rare affections! TMP 3.01. 75
so rare a wond'red father and a wise | makes 4.01.123
some rare noteworthy object in thy travel. TGV 1.01. 13
jars | with triumphs, mirth, and rare solemnity. 5.04.161
well, you are a rare parrot–teacher. ADO 1.01.138 P
a good hare–finder and vulcan a rare carpenter? 1.01.185 P
so rare a gentleman as signior benedick. 3.01. 91
and your gown's a most rare fashion, i' faith. 3.04. 15 P
in the rare semblance that i lov'd it first. 5.01.252
a rare talent! LLL 4.02. 62 P
most rare pompey! 5.02.683 P
to call me goddess, nymph, divine and rare, MND 3.02.226
i have had a most rare vision. 4.01.205 P
bassanio, who indeed gives rare new liveries. MV 2.02.109 P
o rare fortune! 2.02.111 P
could not love me | were man as rare as phoenix. AYL 4.03. 17
is not this a rare fellow, my lord? 5.04.104 P
some prescriptions | of rare and prov'd effects, AWW 1.03.222
contemplation makes a rare turkey–cock of him. TN 2.05. 30 P
that youth's a rare courtier — "rain odors," 3.01. 86 P
we shall have a rare letter from him; 3.02. 56 P
cannot with such magnificence — in so rare — i WT 1.01. 13 P
none rare, my lord. 1.02.367
as she's rare, | must it be great; 1.02.452
as it hath been to us rare, pleasant, speedy, 3.01. 13
something rare | even then will rush to 3.01. 20
a man, who hath a daughter of most rare note. 4.02. 42 P
now newly perform'd by that rare italian master, 5.02. 97 P
o rare! 1H4 1.02. 64 P
of the thieves, and so become a rare hangman. 1.02. 68 P
come, | and nothing pleaseth but rare accidents. 1.02.207
rare words! 3.03.205
to give their censure of these rare reports. 1H6 2.03. 10
created, for his rare success in arms, | great 4.07. 62
your wondrous rare description, noble earl, | of 5.05. 1
gentleman is learn'd, and a most rare speaker, H8 1.02.111
thou art alone | (if thy rare qualities, sweet 2.04.138
then there's achilles, a rare enginer! TRO 2.03. 7 P
and by his rare example made the coward | turn COR 2.02.104
where it draws blood, no cataplasm so rare, HAM 4.07.143
beyond what can be valued, rich or rare, | no LR 1.01. 57
(as his composure must be rare indeed | whom ANT 1.04. 22
o, rare for antony! 2.02.205
rare egyptian! 2.02.218
liv'd in court | (which rare it is to do) most CYM 1.01. 47
a touch more rare | subdues all pangs, all fears 1.01.135
if she be furnish'd with a mind so rare, | she 1.06. 16
judgment | in the election of a sir so rare, 1.06.175
'tis plate of rare device, and jewels | of rich 1.06.189
her judgment | that what's else rare is chok'd; 3.05. 77
thou diedst, a most rare boy, of melancholy. 4.02.208
o rare one, | be not, as is our fangled world, a 5.04.133
o rare instinct! 5.05.381
fate, fair creature, | rare as you seem to be. PER 3.02.104
most rare. 3.02.106
marks, | that cleon's wife, with envy rare, | a 4.ch. 37
yet do effect | rare issues by their operance, TNK 1.03. 63
'tis a rare one. 2.02.153
is't but a rare one? 2.02.154
and nods, and hums, | and then cries, "rare!" 3.05. 16
with that thy rare green eye — which never yet 5.01.144
and all things rare | that heaven's air in this SON 21. 7
therefore are feasts so solemn and so rare, 52. 5
summer's welcome thrice more wish'd, more rare. 56.14
i think my love as rare | as any she belied with 130.13
RARELY 13 FR 0.0014 REL FR 11 V 2 P
how wise, how noble, young, how rarely featur'd, ADO 3.01. 60
doth not my wit become me rarely? 3.04. 70 P
i could play ercles rarely, or a part to tear a MND 1.02. 29 P
so rarely kind, are as interpreters | of my WT 5.01.150
how rarely does it meet with this time's guise, TIM 4.03.465
rarely, rarely: ANT 4.04. 11
rarely, rarely: 4.04. 11
o rarely base! 5.02.158
could be so rarely and exactly wrought, | since CYM 2.04. 75
no better choice, and think me rarely to wed. PER 5.01. 69
will't not do | rarely upon a skirt, wench? TNK 2.02.130
king of pigmies, | for he tells fortunes rarely. 3.04. 16
ye have danc'd rarely, wenches. 3.05.159
RARENESS 3 FR 0.0003 REL FR 2 V 1 P
a feast, | and wan by rareness such solemnity. 1H4 3.02. 59
and his infusion of such dearth and rareness as, HAM 5.02.117 P
of common passage, but | a strain of rareness; CYM 3.04. 92
RARER 4 FR 0.0004 REL FR 4 V 0 P
the rarer action is | in virtue than in TMP 5.01. 27
were never for a piece of beauty rarer, | nor in WT 4.04. 32
we'll have thee, as our rarer monsters are, MAC 5.08. 25
a rarer spirit never | did steer humanity; ANT 5.01. 31
RAREST 11 FR 0.0012 REL FR 7 V 4 P
and the rarest that e'er came there. TMP 2.01.100 P
'tis the rarest argument of wonder that hath AWW 2.03. 7 P
men, that she is | the rarest of all women. WT 5.01.112
he is simply the rarest man i' th' world. COR 4.05.161 P
my train are men of choice and rarest parts, LR 1.04.263
than any the rarest of our ladies in france. CYM 1.04. 61 P
forget that rarest treasure of your cheek, 3.04.160
this is the rarest dream that e'er dull'd sleep PER 5.01.161
rarest sounds! do ye not hear? 5.01.231
i warrant her, she'll do the rarest gambols. TNK 3.05. 75
whose rarest havings made the blossoms dote, LC 235
RARIETIES 1 FR 0.0001 REL FR 0 V 1 P
as many vouch'd rarieties are. TMP 2.01. 61 P
RARIETY 1 FR 0.0001 REL FR 0 V 1 P
but the rariety of it is — which is indeed TMP 2.01. 59 P
RARITIES 1 FR 0.0001 REL FR 1 V 0 P
brow, | feeds on the rarities of nature's truth, SON 60.11
/RARITY 1 FR 0.0001 REL FR 1 V 0 P
/sorrow /would /be /a /rarity /most /beloved, LR 4.03. 23
RARITY 3 FR 0.0003 REL FR 2 V 1 P
villainy so far, that the rarity redeems him. AWW 4.03.274 P
but what particular rarity? TIM 1.01. 4
beauty, truth, and rarity, | grace in all PHT 53
RAR'ST 1 FR 0.0001 REL FR 1 V 0 P
best of all | amongst the rar'st of good ones), CYM 5.05.160
/RASCAL 1 FR 0.0001 REL FR 0 V 1 P
/you /rascal! TRO 2.03. 55 P
RASCAL 57 FR 0.0064 REL FR 20 V 37 P
this wide–chopp'd rascal — would thou mightst TMP 1.01. 57
what a damn'd epicurean rascal is this! WIV 2.02.287 P
hang him, dishonest rascal! 3.03.185 P
my lord, here comes the rascal i spoke of, here MM 5.01.283 P
this is the rascal; this is he i spoke of. 5.01.304
you bald–pated, lying rascal, you must be hooded 5.01.352 P
noblest deer hath them as huge as the rascal. AYL 3.03. 58 P
i bade the rascal knock upon your gate, | and SHR 1.02. 37
while she did call me rascal fiddler | and 2.01.157
and bring along these rascal knaves with thee? 4.01.131
where is the rascal cook? 4.01.162
i his lady, | i would poison that vile rascal. AWW 3.05. 84
ladyship takes delight in such a barren rascal. TN 1.05. 84 P
"madam, why laugh you at such a barren rascal? 5.01.375 P
and where some stretch–mouth'd rascal would, as
WT 4.04.196 P
peace, ye fat–kidney'd rascal! 1H4 2.02. 6 P
the rascal hath remov'd my horse, and tied him i 2.02. 11 P
if the rascal have not given me medicines to 2.02. 18 P
and i were now by this rascal, i could brain him 2.03. 23 P
what a pagan rascal is this! 2.03. 29 P
well, that rascal hath good mettle in him, he 2.04.349 P
why, what a rascal art thou then, to praise him 2.04.351 P
this oily rascal is known as well as paul's. 2.04.526 P
impudent, emboss'd rascal, if there were any 3.03.157 P
a pox damn you, you muddy rascal, is that all 2H4 2.04. 39 P
hang him, swaggering rascal! 2.04. 71 P
away, you cutpurse rascal! 2.04.128 P
away, you bottle–ale rascal! 2.04.131 P
i cannot endure such a fustian rascal. 2.04.189 P
a rascal! to brave me? 2.04.215 P
a rascal bragging slave! 2.04.228 P
thou damn'd tripe–visag'd rascal, and the child 5.04. 8 P
come, you thin thing, come, you rascal. 5.04. 30 P
and a basterd, and a knave, and a rascal. H5 3.02.123 P
this is an arrant counterfeit rascal, i remember 3.06. 61 P
a rascal that swagger'd with me last night; 4.07.125 P
pointing–stock | to every idle rascal follower. 2H6 2.04. 47
and reap the harvest which that rascal sow'd. 3.01.381
the rascal people, thirsting after prey, | join 4.04. 51
no, no, i am a rascal, a scurvy railing knave, a TRO 5.04. 28 P
thou rascal, that art worst in blood to run, COR 1.01.159
'tis most just | that thou turn rascal; TIM 4.03.217
rascal thieves, | here's gold. 4.03.428
out, rascal dogs! 5.01.115
to lock such rascal counters from his friends, JC 4.03. 80
a dull and muddy–mettled rascal, peak | like HAM 2.02.567
do you bandy looks with me, you rascal? LR 1.04. 84 P
a knave, a rascal, an eater of broken meats; 2.02. 15 P
draw, you rascal! 2.02. 35 P
draw, you rascal! 2.02. 38 P
you cowardly rascal, nature disclaims in thee: 2.02. 54 P
thou rascal beadle, hold thy bloody hand! 4.06.160
/'zounds, you rogue! you rascal! OTH 2.03.145 P
here comes a flattering rascal, upon him | will CYM 1.05. 27
a banish'd rascal; 2.01. 39 P
no, nor thy tailor, rascal, | who is thy 4.02. 81
thee | unto the base bed of some rascal groom, LUC 671
RASCALLIEST 1 FR 0.0001 REL FR 0 V 1 P
art indeed the most comparative, rascalliest, 1H4 1.02. 80 P
RASCAL–LIKE 1 FR 0.0001 REL FR 1 V 0 P
not rascal–like, to fall down with a pinch, 1H6 4.02. 49
/RASCALLY 1 FR 0.0001 REL FR 0 V 1 P
a /rascally yea–forsooth knave, to bear a 2H4 1.02. 36 P
RASCALLY 10 FR 0.0011 REL FR 0 V 10 P
time the jealious rascally knave her husband WIV 2.02.265 P
that blind rascally boy that abuses every one's AYL 4.01.213 P
decay'd, ingenious, foolish, rascally knave. AWW 5.02. 24 P
have the niggardly rascally sheep–biter come by TN 2.05. 5 P
away, you rascally althaea's dream, away! 2H4 2.02. 87 P
you poor, base, rascally, cheating, lack–linen 2.04.124 P
ah, rascally slave! 2.04.222 P
manhood, what an arrant, rascally, beggarly, H5 4.08. 34 P
the rascally, scald, beggarly, lousy, pragging 5.01. 5 P
a whoreson rascally tisick so troubles me, and TRO 5.03.101 P
RASCAL'S 2 FR 0.0002 REL FR 0 V 2 P
i pray thee, jack, be quiet, the rascal's gone. 2H4 2.04.208 P
the rascal's drunk; 2.04.213 P
RASCALS 18 FR 0.0020 REL FR 7 V 11 P
and against your cony–catching rascals, bardolph WIV 1.01.124 P
o you panderly rascals, there's a knot, a /ging, 4.02.117 P
go, rascals, go, and fetch my supper in. SHR 4.01.139
words are very rascals since bonds disgrac'd TN 3.01. 21 P
but what talk we of these traitorly rascals, WT 4.04.792 P
i did never see such pitiful rascals. 1H4 4.02. 64 P
you make fat rascals, mistress doll. 2H4 2.04. 41 P
and the cowardly rascals that ran from the H5 4.07. 6 P
lean raw–bon'd rascals! 1H6 1.02. 35
a sort of vagabonds, rascals, and runaways, | a R3 5.03.316
you'll leave your noise anon, ye rascals; H8 5.03. 1 P
look for ale and cakes here, you rude rascals? 5.03. 11 P
the policy of those crafty swearing rascals, TRO 5.04. 10 P
they did budge | from rascals worse than they. COR 1.06. 45
i can tell you news — news, you rascals! 4.05.173 P
i'll once more feast the rascals. TIM 3.04.112
thou wealth again, | rascals should have't. 4.03.218
to lash the rascals naked through the world OTH 4.02.143
RAS'D 3 FR 0.0003 REL FR 3 V 0 P

ras'd out my imprese, leaving me no sign, | save R2 3.01. 25
that | the britains have ras'd out, though with CYM 5.05. 70
as from thence | sorrow were ever ras'd, and PER 1.01. 17
RASE* *(also raze, etc.)*
/RASE* 1 FR 0.0001 REL FR 1 V 0 P
stanley did dream the boar did /rase our helms, R3 3.04. 82
RASE* 3 FR 0.0003 REL FR 3 V 0 P
meaning | to rase one title of your honor out. R2 2.03. 75
prophecies, and to rase out | rotten opinion, 2H4 5.02.127
all, | and rase their faction and their family, TIT 1.01.451
RASED* 3 FR 0.0003 REL FR 3 V 0 P
he dreamt the boar had rased off his helm. R3 3.02. 11
foil'd, | is from the book of honor rased quite, SON 25.11
when sometime lofty towers i see down rased, 64. 3
/RASH* 1 FR 0.0001 REL FR 1 V 0 P
in his anointed flesh /rash boarish fangs. LR 3.07. 58
RASH* 37 FR 0.0041 REL FR 34 V 3 P
make not too rash a trial of him, for | he's TMP 1.02.468
lest i might be too rash. MM 2.02. 9
first, here's young master rash, he's in for a 4.03. 4 P
make rash remonstrance of my hidden pow'r | than 5.01.392
tarry, rash wanton! am not i thy lord? MND 2.01. 63
this is not well, rash and unbridled boy, | to AWW 3.02. 28
our rash faults | make trivial price of serious 5.03. 60
i could do this, and that with no rash potion, WT 1.02.319
blood | that hot rash haste so indirectly shed. JN 2.01. 49
rash, inconsiderate, fiery voluntaries, | with 2.01. 67
his rash fierce blaze of riot cannot last, | for R2 2.01. 33
with shallow jesters, and rash bavin wits, 1H4 3.02. 61
work as strong | as aconitum or rash gunpowder. 2H4 4.04. 48
be not so rash, take ransom, let him live. 2H6 4.01. 28
leisure to salute you, | my matter is so rash. TRO 4.02. 60
not rash like his accusers, and thus answered: COR 1.01.129
their people | will be as rash in the repeal, as 4.07. 32
was it well done of rash virginius | to slay his TIT 5.03. 36
it is too rash, too unadvis'd, too sudden, | too ROM 2.02.118
must i give way and room to your rash choler? JC 4.03. 39
when that rash humor which my mother gave me 4.03.120
o, what a rash and bloody deed is this! HAM 3.04. 27
thou wretched, rash, intruding fool, farewell! 3.04. 31
for though i am not splenitive /and rash, | yet 5.01.261
and soundest of his time hath been but rash; LR 1.01.296 P
will you wish on me, when the rash mood is on. 2.04.169
sir, he's rash and very sudden in choler, and OTH 2.01.272 P
why do you speak so startingly and rash? 3.04. 79
thou art rash as fire to say | that she was 5.02.134
where is this rash and most unfortunate man? 5.02.283
fear not slander, censure rash. CYM 4.02.272
whether he should follow | his rash oath, or the TNK 4.01. 11
is alive, | her rash suspect she doth extenuate, VEN 1010
o rash false heat, wrapp'd in repentant cold, LUC 48
chin, | the reason of this rash alarm to know, 473
appeal, | not to seducing lust, thy rash relier. 639
can curb his heat, or rein his rash desire, 706
RASH–EMBRAC'D 1 FR 0.0001 REL FR 1 V 0 P
as doubtful thoughts, and rash–embrac'd despair, MV 3.02.109
RASHER 1 FR 0.0001 REL FR 0 V 1 P
not shortly have a rasher on the coals for money MV 3.05. 25 P
RASH–LEVIED 1 FR 0.0001 REL FR 1 V 0 P
than buckingham and his rash–levied strength. R3 4.03. 50
RASHLY 6 FR 0.0006 REL FR 6 V 0 P
was by york and talbot | too rashly plotted. 1H6 4.04. 3
proceed thus rashly in the villain's death, R3 3.05. 43
the father rashly slaughter'd his own son, | the 5.05. 25
rashly — | and prais'd be rashness for it — HAM 5.02. 6
what you do quickly | is not done rashly; TNK 1.01.135
that oath was rashly made, and in your anger, 3.06.227
RASHNESS 10 FR 0.0011 REL FR 9 V 1 P
man | (a rashness that i ever yet have shunn'd), TGV 3.01. 30
have show'd too much | the rashness of a woman; WT 3.02.221
advantage is a better soldier than rashness. H5 3.06.120 P
this is the fruits of rashness! R3 2.01.135
who cannot condemn rashness in cold blood? TIM 3.05. 53
forgive my general and exceptless rashness, 4.03.495
and prais'd be rashness for it — let us know HAM 5.02. 7
consideration check | this hideous rashness. LR 1.01.151
your /reproof | were well deserv'd of rashness. ANT 2.02.122
for the white | reprove the brown for rashness, 3.11. 14
RASING 1 FR 0.0001 REL FR 1 V 0 P
memory, | rasing the characters of your renown, 2H6 1.01.101
RASURE *(see razure)*
RAT 10 FR 0.0011 REL FR 7 V 3 P
what if my house be troubled with a rat, | and i MV 4.01. 44
since pythagoras' time, that i was an irish rat, AYL 3.02.177 P
'zounds, a dog, a rat, a mouse, a cat, to ROM 3.01.100 P
thither sail, | and, like a rat without a tail, MAC 1.03. 9
how now? a rat? dead, for a ducat, dead! HAM 3.04. 24
whips out his rapier, cries, "a rat, a rat!" 4.01. 10
whips out his rapier, cries, "a rat, a rat!" 4.01. 10
swallows the old rat and the ditch–dog; LR 3.04.132 P
why should a dog, a horse, a rat, have life, 5.03.307
she is serv'd | as i would serve a rat." CYM 5.05.248
RAT–CATCHER 1 FR 0.0001 REL FR 0 V 1 P
tybalt, you rat–catcher, will you walk? ROM 3.01. 75 P
/RATCLIFFE 1 FR 0.0001 REL FR 1 V 0 P
/ratcliffe, come hither. R3 4.04.444
RATCLIFFE 11 FR 0.0012 REL FR 11 V 0 P
here comes sir richard ratcliffe and the duke. R3 2.01. 46
sir richard ratcliffe, let me tell thee this: 3.03. 2
lovel and ratcliffe, look that it be done: 3.04. 78
they are friends — ratcliffe and lovel. 3.05. 21
ratcliffe, thyself — or catesby — where is he? 4.04.441
ratcliffe! 5.03. 66
ratcliffe, about the mid of night come to my 5.03. 77
ratcliffe, my lord, 'tis i. 5.03.209
o ratcliffe, i have dream'd a fearful dream! 5.03.212
o ratcliffe, i fear, i fear! 5.03.214
ratcliffe! 5.03.281
/RATE* 1 FR 0.0001 REL FR 1 V 0 P
/then /must /we /rate /the /cost /of /the 2H4 1.03. 44
RATE* 32 FR 0.0036 REL FR 31 V 1 P
o'er–priz'd all popular rate, in my false TMP 1.02. 92
my son is lost and (in my rate) she too, | who 2.01.110
that i have purchas'd at an infinite rate, and WIV 2.02.205 P
whose rate are either rich or poor | as fancy MM 2.02.150
thy substance, valued at the highest rate, ERR 1.01. 23
i'll serve you, sir, five hundred at the rate. 4.04. 14
i am a spirit of no common rate; MND 3.01.154
moan to be abridg'd | from such a noble rate, MV 1.01.127
the rate of usance here with us in venice. 1.03. 45
then, let me see, the rate — 1.03.104
for all that life can rate | worth name of life AWW 2.01.179
it, and she reckon'd it | at her life's rate. 5.03. 91
with her modern grace, | subdu'd me to her rate. 5.03.217
upon or near the rate of thirty thousand. 2H4 4.01. 22
what, rate, rebuke, and roughly send to prison 5.02. 70
fast | before he'll buy again at such a rate. 1H6 3.02. 43
why do you rate my lord of suffolk thus? 2H6 3.02. 56
rate me at what thou wilt, thou shalt be paid. 4.01. 30
for all the rest is held at such a rate | as 3H6 2.02. 51
go rate thy minions, proud insulting boy! 2.02. 84
a peace, and purchas'd | at a superfluous rate! H8 1.01. 99
which | i find at such proud rate, that it 3.02.127
you now | the issue of your proper wisdoms rate, TRO 2.02. 89
you are to blame, my lord, to rate her so. ROM 3.05.169
there shall no figure at such rate be set | as 5.03.301
set your entreatments at a higher rate | than a HAM 1.03.122
it yield to norway or the pole | a ranker rate, 4.04. 22
as we rate boys who, being mature in knowledge, ANT 1.04. 31
i purchase cheaply, | as i do rate your value. TNK 5.03.114
but back retires to rate the boar for murther. VEN 906
reck'ning his fortune at such high proud rate LUC 19
but as they open, they all rate his ill, | which 304
RATED* 16 FR 0.0018 REL FR 14 V 2 P
and in our maiden council rated them | at LLL 5.02.779
oft | in the rialto you have rated me | about my MV 1.03.107
if thou beest rated by thy estimation, | thou 2.07. 26
now, | affection is not rated from the heart. SHR 1.01.160
paying the fine of rated treachery | even with a JN 5.04. 37
lord of the council rated me the other day in 1H4 1.02. 84 P
rated mine uncle from the council–board, | in 4.03. 99
thence, | who with them was a rated sinew too, 4.04. 17
then check'd and rated by northumberland, | did 2H4 3.01. 68
rage | be thus upbraided, chid, and rated at, 2H6 3.01.175
great reason that my noble lord be rated | for TIT 2.03. 81
'tis rated | as those which sell would give; TIM 1.01.168
that i might so have rated my expense | as i had 2.02.126
who rated him for speaking well of pompey; JC 2.01.216
we had not rated him | his part o' th' isle. ANT 3.06. 25
i prais'd her as i rated her: so do i my stone. CYM 1.04. 77 P
RATES* 6 FR 0.0006 REL FR 6 V 0 P
and rails, and swears, and rates, that she, poor SHR 4.01.184
for corn at their own rates, whereof they say COR 1.01.189
even thus he rates the babe — | "for i must TIT 5.01. 33
one of them rates | all that is won and lost. ANT 3.11. 69
that thy adulteries | rates and revenges. CYM 5.04. 34
the very lees of such (millions of rates) TNK 1.04. 29
/RATHER 2 FR 0.0002 REL FR 2 V 0 P
/but /rather /show /a /while /like /fearful /war 2H4 4.01. 63
/i /had /rather /lose /the /battle /than /that LR 5.01. 18
RATHER 335 FR 0.0378 REL FR 239 V 96 P
and rather like a dream than an assurance | that TMP 1.02. 45
have follow'd it, | or it hath drawn me rather. 1.02.395
being rather new dy'd than stain'd with salt 2.01. 64 P
daughter, | but rather loose her to an african, 2.01.126
thou let'st thy fortune sleep — die, rather; 2.01.216
of bellowing | like bulls, or rather lions. 2.01.312
i had rather crack my sinews, break my back, 3.01. 26
bring a corollary, | rather than want a spirit. 4.01. 58
i rather think | you have not sought her help, 5.01.141
or stole it, rather. 5.01.300
i rather would entreat thy company | to see the TGV 1.01. 5
sake, i rather chose | to cross my friend in his 3.01. 17
of you, | but rather to beget more love in you. 3.01. 97
and why not death, rather than living torment? 3.01.170
eyes, | for i had rather wink than look on them. 5.02. 14
rather than have false proteus rescue me. 5.04. 35
i had rather than forty shillings i had my book WIV 1.01.198 P
i had rather walk here, i thank you. 1.01.282 P
i'll rather be unmannerly than troublesome. 1.01.312 P
i had rather be a giantess, and lie under mount 2.01. 79 P
i had rather hear them scold than fight. 2.01.231 P
i will rather trust a fleming with my butter, 2.02.302 P
whether had you rather lead mine eyes, or eye 3.02. 3 P
i had rather, forsooth, go before you like a man 3.02. 5 P
i shall be rather prais'd for this than mock'd; 3.02. 47 P
i had rather than a thousand pound he were out 3.03.123 P
never stand "you had rather" and "you had rather 3.03.126 P
stand "you had rather" and "you had rather." 3.03.126 P
alas, i had rather be set quick i' th' earth, 3.04. 86
any extremity rather than a mischief. 4.02. 74 P
i rather will suspect the sun with /cold | than 4.04. 7
but rather wishing a more strict restraint MM 1.04. 4
the rather for i now must make you know | i am 1.04. 22
yet | let us be keen, and rather cut a little, 2.01. 5
but rather tell me, | when i, that censure him, 2.01. 28
thou rather with thy sharp and sulphurous bolt 2.02.115
which had you rather, that the most just law 2.04. 52
this, | i had rather give my body than my soul. 2.04. 56
and rather prov'd the sliding of your brother 2.04.115
i had rather my brother die by the law than my 3.01.189 P
rather rejoicing to see another merry, than 3.02.235 P
and would not rather | make rash remonstrance of 5.01.391
but i had rather it would please you i might be 5.01.506 P
rather approach'd too late: ERR 1.02. 43
leave battering, i had rather have it a head. 2.02. 36 P
nay, rather persuade him to hold his hands. 4.04. 22 P
respect your end, or rather, the prophecy like 4.04. 42 P
i had rather hear my dog bark at a crow than a ADO 1.01.131 P
i had rather be a canker in a hedge than a rose 1.03. 27 P
on his face, i had rather lie in the woollen! 2.01. 30 P
rather than hold three words' conference with 2.01.270 P
i would rather have one of your father's getting 2.01.322 P
and now had he rather hear the tabor and the 2.03. 14 P
her, rather than she will bate one breath of her 2.03.176 P
too that she will rather die than give any sign 2.03.227 P
rather i will go to benedick | and counsel him 3.01. 82
we will rather sleep than talk, we know what 3.03. 37 P
thou shouldst rather ask if it were possible any 3.03.112 P
which i had rather seal with my death than 5.01.240 P
i had rather pray a month with mutton and LLL 1.01.302 P
he rather means to lodge you in the field, 2.01. 85
which we much rather had depart withal, | and 2.01.146
minime, honest master, or rather, master, no. 3.01. 60
were, replication, or rather ostentare, to show, 4.02. 15 P
untrained, or rather unlettered, or ratherest 4.02. 18 P
or rather, as horace says in his — what, my 4.02.101 P
i must rather give it the rein, for it runs 5.02.657 P
rather your eyes must with his judgment look. MND 1.01. 57
or rather do i not in plainest truth | tell you 2.01.200
i had rather give his carcass to my hounds. 3.02. 64
this you should pity rather than despise. 3.02.235
i had rather have a handful or two of dried peas 4.01. 37 P
night, | did scare away, or rather did affright; 5.01.141
and let my liver rather heat with wine | than my MV 1.01. 81
i had rather be married to a death's–head with a 1.02. 51 P
i had rather he should shrive me than wive me. 1.02.130 P
but lend it rather to thine enemy, | who, if he 1.03.135
for me, | i'll rather dwell in my necessity. 1.03.155
man's son" — or rather an honest woman's son, 2.02. 16 P
i would entreat you rather to put on | your 2.02.201
which rather threaten'st than dost promise aught 3.02.105
that he would rather have antonio's flesh | than 3.02.286
you'll ask me why i rather choose to have | a 4.01. 40
had been her husband rather than a christian! 4.01.297
whether till the next night she had rather stay, 5.01.302
i rather will subject me to the malice | of a AYL 2.03. 36
part, i had rather bear with you than bear you. 2.04. 11 P
you are rather point–device in your 3.02.382 P
i had rather hear you chide than this man woo. 3.05. 65
i had rather have a fool to make me merry than 4.01. 28 P
or rather, bottomless — that as fast as you 4.01.209 P
the rather for i have some sport in hand, SHR in.1. 91
to cart her rather; 1.01. 55
which i have bettered rather than decreas'd. 2.01.118
you would entreat me rather go than stay. 3.02.192
and rather than it shall, i will be free, | even 4.03. 79
it up where it wanted rather than lack it where AWW 1.01. 9 P
lest it be rather thought you affect a sorrow 1.01. 52 P
able for thine enemy | rather in power than use, 1.01. 66
when he was retrograde, i think rather. 1.01.198 P
frank nature, rather curious than in haste, 1.02. 20
the rather will i spare my praises towards him, 2.01.103
i had rather be in this choice than throw 2.03. 78 P
disdain | rather corrupt me ever! 2.03.116
when rather from our acts we them derive | than 2.03.136
acquaintance with thee, or rather my knowledge, 2.03.228 P
rather than suffer question for your residence. 2.05. 38 P
and rather muse than ask why i entreat you, 2.05. 65
the rather for i think i know your hostess | as 3.05. 42
of the sallet, or rather the herb of grace. 4.05. 17 P
but rather make you thank your pains for it. 5.01. 33
bounds, | rather than make unprofited return. TN 1.04. 22
your approach rather to wonder at you than to 1.05.198 P
me in manners the rather to express myself. 2.01. 15 P
but i think it rather consists of eating and 2.03. 11 P
i had rather than forty shillings i had such a 2.03. 20 P
they were blanks, rather than fill'd with me! 3.01.104
i had rather hear you to solicit that | than 3.01.109
but rather reason thus with reason fetter: 3.01.155
love, | the rather by these arguments of fear, 3.03. 12
i am one that had rather go with sir priest than 3.04.271 P
i had rather than forty pound i were at home. 5.01.177 P
may rather pluck on laughter than revenge, | if 5.01.366
and i had rather glib myself than they | should WT 2.01.149
i had rather you did lack than i, my lord, 2.01.158
but rather follow | our forceful instigation? 2.01.162
nay, rather, good my lords, be second to me. 2.03. 27
i beseech you, rather | let me be punish'd, that 3.02.224
rags to lay on thee, rather than have these off. 4.03. 55 P
which does mend nature — change it rather; 4.04. 96
or rather, thou art she | in thy not chiding; 5.03. 25
whether hadst thou rather be a faulconbridge, JN 1.01.134
the rather that you give his offspring life, 2.01. 13
more than we of france, | rather lost more. 2.01.343
nay, rather turn this day out of the week, 3.01. 87
or rather then set forward, for 'twill be | two 4.03. 19
whom he hath us'd rather for sport than need) 5.02.175
he will the rather do it when he sees 5.07. 87
but i had rather | you would have bid me argue R2 1.03.237
nay rather, every tedious stride i make | will 1.03.268
me rather had my heart might feel your love 3.03.192
i heard you say that you had rather refuse | the 4.01. 15
but soft, but see, or rather do not see, | my 5.01. 7
sure | i will from henceforth rather be myself, 1H4 1.03. 5
the cords, the ladder, or the hangman rather? 1.03.166
the commonwealth, or rather, not pray to her, 2.01. 81 P
rather let me have it as you are a false thief. 2.01. 93 P
i had rather be a kitten and cry mew | than one 3.01.127
i had rather hear a brazen canstick turn'd, | or 3.01.129
i had rather live | with cheese and garlic in a 3.01.159
i had rather hear lady, my brach, howl in irish. 3.01.235 P
but rather drows'd and hung their eyelids down, 3.02. 81
i rather of his absence make this use: 4.01. 76
rather, and't please you, it is the disease of 2H4 1.02.120 P
nay, rather damn them with | king cerberus, and 2.04.167
why rather, sleep, liest thou in smoky cribs, 3.01. 9
sir, i do not care, but rather, because i am 3.02.224 P
or rather swaying more upon our part | than H5 1.01. 73
and rather choose to hide them in a net | than 1.02. 93
i had rather have my horse to my mistress. 3.07. 57 P
rather proclaim it, westmerland, through my host 4.03. 34
the moon, or rather the sun and not the moon; 5.02.163 P
mock me mercifully, the rather, gentle princess, 5.02.202 P
rather with their teeth | the walls they'll tear 1H6 1.02. 39
rather than i would be so pill'd esteem'd: 1.04. 33
care is no cure, but rather corrosive, | for 3.03. 3
fall down with a pinch, | but rather, moody–mad; 4.02. 50
rather than life preserv'd with infamy. 4.05. 33
ay, rather than i'll shame my mother's womb. 4.05. 35
i'll rather keep | that which i have than, 5.04.144
i rather would have lost my life betimes | than 2H6 3.01.297
no, rather let my head | stoop to the block than 4.01.124
or rather, of stealing a cade of herrings. 4.02. 33 P
rather than bloody war shall cut them short, 4.04. 12
rather than have made that savage duke thine 3H6 1.01.224
nay then whip me; he'll rather give her two. 3.02. 28
to tell you plain, i had rather lie in prison. 3.02. 70
i rather wish you foes than hollow friends. 4.01.139
and i the rather wain me from despair | for love 4.04. 17
nay rather, wilt thou draw thy forces hence, 5.01. 25
i had rather chop this hand off at a blow, | and 5.01. 50
nay, take away this scolding crook–back, rather. 5.05. 30
my good lord — my lord, i should say rather. 5.06. 2

i had rather be a country servant maid | than a R3 1.03.106
i had rather be a pedlar: 1.03.148
that i would rather hide me from my greatness — 3.07.161
please you; | but i had rather kill two enemies. 4.02. 71
alas, i rather hate myself | for hateful deeds 5.03.189
had rather have us win than him they follow: 5.03.244
i had rather want those than my head. H8 3.02.309
concerning his imprisonment was rather | (if 5.02.185
i had rather be such a man as troilus than TRO 1.02.244 P
force should be right, or rather, right and 1.03.116
or rather, the neapolitan bone–ache! 2.03. 18 P
i had rather be a tick in a sheep than such a 3.03.311 P
(or rather call my thought a certain knowledge) 4.01. 42
troilus had rather troy were borne to greece 4.01. 47
i will rather leave to see hector than not to 5.01. 95 P
rather think this not cressid. 5.02.133
you are all resolv'd rather to die than to COR 1.01. 4 P
i had rather had eleven die nobly for their 1.03. 24 P
he had rather see the swords and hear a drum 1.03. 55 P
our walls | rather than they shall pound us up; 1.04. 17
the blood i drop is rather physical | than 1.05. 18
i had rather be their servant in my way | than 2.01.203
he would miss it rather | than carry it but by 2.01.237
rather our state's defective for requital | than 2.02. 50
which the rather | we shall be blest to do, if 2.02. 57
i would you rather had been silent. 2.02. 61
i had rather have my wounds to heal again | than 2.02. 69
i had rather have one scratch my head i' th' sun 2.02. 75
he had rather venture all his limbs for honor 2.02. 80
of their choice is rather to have my hat than my 2.03. 98 P
rather than fool it so, | let the high office 2.03.121
preoccupied with what you rather must do | than 2.03.232
rather say, i play | the man i am. 3.02. 15
and you will rather show our general louts | how 3.02. 66
although i know thou hadst rather | follow thine 3.02. 90
let | thy mother rather feel thy pride than fear 3.02.126
such as become a soldier | rather than envy you. 3.03. 57
blush that the world goes well, who rather had, 4.06. 5
ingrate forgetfulness shall poison rather | than 5.02. 86
rather to show a noble grace to both parts 5.03.121
rather than rob me of the people's hearts! TIT 1.01.207
and rather comfort his distressed plight | than 4.04. 32
no, coz, i rather weep. ROM 1.01.183
whom you know i hate, | rather than paris. 3.05.123
if, rather than to marry county paris, | thou 4.01. 71
o, bid me leap, rather than marry paris, | from 4.01. 77
you had rather be at a breakfast of enemies than TIM 1.02. 76 P
but rather one that smiles and still invites 2.01. 11
i'd rather than the worth of thrice the sum 3.03. 22
rather than render back, out with your knives, 4.01. 9
i had rather be alone. 4.03.100
stomach finds meat, or, rather, where i eat it. 4.03.294 P
i had rather be a beggar's dog than apemantus. 4.03.356 P
and rather woo | those that would mischief me 4.03.467
thou rather shalt enforce it with thy smile 5.04. 45
brutus had rather be a villager | than to repute JC 1.02.172
i rather tell thee what is to be fear'd | than 1.02.211
had you rather caesar were living, and die all 3.02. 23 P
i rather choose | to wrong the dead, to wrong 3.02.125
i had rather be a dog, and bay the moon, | than 4.03. 27
i had rather coin my heart | and drop my blood 4.03. 72
i had rather have | such men my friends than 5.04. 28
i'll rather kill myself. 5.05. 7
and that which rather thou dost fear to do MAC 1.05. 24
(whereto the rather shall his day's hard journey 1.07. 62
this my hand will rather | the multitudinous 2.02. 58
rather than so, come fate into the list, | and 3.01. 70
who may i rather challenge for unkindness | than 3.04. 41
if th' hadst rather hear it from our mouths, 4.01. 62
let us rather | hold fast the mortal sword, and 4.03. 2
which was to my belief witness'd the rather, 4.03.184
or rather say, the cause of this defect, | for HAM 2.02.102
and makes us rather bear those ills we have, 3.01. 80
you shall command, or, rather, as you say, my 3.02.323 P
the rather, if you could devise it so | that i 4.07. 69
let it fall rather, though the fork invade | the LR 1.01.144
which i have rather blam'd as mine own jealous 1.04. 69 P
i had rather be any kind o' thing than a fool, 1.04.185 P
no, rather i abjure all roofs, and choose | to 2.04.208
persuade me rather to be slave and sumpter | to 2.04.216
or rather a disease that's in my flesh, | which 2.04.222
i had rather break mine own. 3.04. 5
do as i bid thee, or rather do thy pleasure; 4.01. 47
madam, i had rather — 4.05. 22
would hourly die | rather than die at once!), 5.03.187
by heaven, i rather would have been his hangman.
OTH 1.01. 34
men do their broken weapons rather use | than 1.03.174
i had rather to adopt a child than get it. 1.03.191
seek thou rather to be hang'd in compassing thy 1.03.359 P
i had rather have this tongue cut from my mouth 2.03.221
and i return'd /the rather | for that i heard 2.03.233
i will rather sue to be despis'd than to deceive 2.03.277 P
for thy solicitor shall rather die | than give 3.03. 27
i had rather be a toad | and live upon the vapor 3.03.270
me, i had rather have lost my purse | full of 3.04. 25
device, iago, and rather, as it seems to me now, 4.02.176 P
let him not pass, | but kill him rather. 5.02.242
i had rather heat my liver with drinking. ANT 1.02. 24 P
hereditary, | rather than purchas'd; 1.04. 14
partners, | the rather for i earnestly beseech, 2.02. 23
did he not rather | discredit my authority with 2.02. 48
neglected, rather; 2.02. 89
but i had rather fast from all, four days, 2.07.102
rather makes choice of loss | than gain which 3.01. 23
she shows a body rather than a life, | a statue, 3.03. 20
both as the same, or rather ours the elder — 3.10. 13
you | where rather i'll expect victorious life 4.02. 43
swoonds rather, for so bad a prayer as his | was 4.09. 26
rather a ditch in egypt | be gentle grave unto 5.02. 57
rather on nilus' mud | lay me stark–nak'd, and 5.02. 58
rather make | my country's high pyramides my 5.02. 60
know | we will extenuate rather than enforce. 5.02.125
i had rather seel my lips than to my peril 5.02.146
crush him together rather than unfold | his CYM 1.01. 26
no, i rather added | a lustre to it. 1.01.142
but that my master rather play'd than fought 1.01.162
he must be weigh'd rather by her value than his 1.04. 15 P
rather than story him in his own hearing. 1.04. 33 P
rather shunn'd to go even with what i heard than 1.04. 44 P
but i make my wager rather against your 1.04.110 P
i shall flying fight — | rather, directly fly. 1.06. 21
i had rather not be so noble as i am. 2.01. 18 P
which i had rather | you felt than make't my 2.03.110
but rather, all; 2.05. 28
all gold and silver rather turn to dirt, | as 3.06. 53
the rather (saving reverence of the word) for 4.01. 4 P
i had rather | have skipp'd from sixteen years 4.02.198
but dead rather; 4.02.356
and rather father thee than master thee. 4.02.395
or rather fairer | than those for preservation 5.03. 21
made | rather to wonder at the things you hear 5.03. 54
since he had rather | groan so in perpetuity 5.04. 5
you rather, mine being yours; 5.04. 26
overroasted rather; ready long ago. 5.04.152 P
i had rather thou shouldst live while nature 5.05.151
i had rather than twice the worth of her she had PER 4.06. 1 P
i could wish him to be my master, or rather, my 4.06.160 P
were not spent, | rather laid out for purchase. TNK 1.02.111
her spirits would sojourn (rather dwell on) 1.03. 77
rather than a gap | should be in their dear 1.04. 8
our richest balms, | rather than niggard, waste; 1.04. 32
rather than have 'em | freed of this plight, and 1.04. 33
but forty thousand fold we had rather have 'em 1.04. 36
but say that one | had rather combat me? 2.02.197
i had rather both, | so neither for my sake 4.02. 68
where the light may rather seem to steal in than 4.03. 75 P
i had rather see a wren hawk at a fly | than 5.03. 2
the calkins | did rather tell than trample; 5.04. 56
which he frets at rather | than any jot obeys; 5.04. 70
but rather famish them amid their plenty, VEN 20
him go, | rather than triumph in so false a foe. LUC 77
and rather make them born to our desire | than SON 123. 7

RATHEREST 1 FR 0.0001 REL FR 0 V 1 P
unlettered, or ratherest unconfirmed fashion, to LLL 4.02. 18 P

RATIFIED 4 FR 0.0004 REL FR 3 V 1 P
here are only numbers ratified, but, for the LLL 4.02.121 P
until confirm'd, sign'd, ratified by you. MV 3.02.148
and they were ratified | as he cried, "thus let H8 1.01.170
compact | well ratified by law and heraldy, HAM 1.01. 87

RATIFIERS 1 FR 0.0001 REL FR 1 V 0 P
known, | the ratifiers and props of every word, HAM 4.05.106

RATIFY 4 FR 0.0004 REL FR 4 V 0 P
afore heaven, | i ratify this my rich gift. TMP 4.01. 8
king, | and take with you free power to ratify, H5 5.02. 86
(with him above | to ratify the work) we may MAC 3.06. 33
of great jupiter | our peace we'll ratify; CYM 5.05.483

RATING 1 FR 0.0001 REL FR 1 V 0 P
rating myself at nothing, you shall see | how MV 3.02.257

RATIONAL 2 FR 0.0002 REL FR 0 V 2 P
took in the park with the rational hind costard. LLL 1.02.118 P
loss of virginity is rational increase, and AWW 1.01.128 P

RATO–LORUM 1 FR 0.0001 REL FR 0 V 1 P
ay, and rato–lorum too; WIV 1.01. 8 P

RATS 8 FR 0.0009 REL FR 7 V 1 P
the very rats | instinctively have quit it. TMP 1.02.147
have made you four tall fellows skip like rats. WIV 2.01.229 P
like rats that ravin down their proper bane, | a MM 1.02.129
for want of means, poor rats, had hang'd R3 5.03.331
rome and her rats are at the point of battle, COR 1.01.162
take these rats thither | to gnaw their garners. 1.01.249
like rats, oft bite the holy cords a–twain LR 2.02. 74
but mice and rats, and such small deer, | have 3.04.138

RATSBANE 3 FR 0.0003 REL FR 1 V 2 P
as live they would put ratsbane in my mouth as 2H4 1.02. 42 P
had been a little ratsbane for thy sake! 1H6 5.04. 29
in his pew, set ratsbane by his porridge, made LR 3.04. 55 P

RATTLE 1 FR 0.0001 REL FR 1 V 0 P
(as loud as thine) rattle the welkin's ear, JN 5.02.172

RATTLES 1 FR 0.0001 REL FR 1 V 0 P
on their heads, | and rattles in their hands. WIV 4.04. 52

RATTLING 5 FR 0.0005 REL FR 5 V 0 P
to the dread rattling thunder | have i given TMP 5.01. 44
i read as much as from the rattling tongue | of MND 5.01.102
quite with dead men's rattling bones, | with ROM 4.01. 82
ear, | make mingle with our rattling taborines, ANT 4.08. 37
and shake the orb, | he was as rattling thunder. 5.02. 86

RAUGHT *(also reach'd)*

RAUGHT 5 FR 0.0005 REL FR 5 V 0 P
and raught not to five weeks when he came to LLL 4.02. 40
he smil'd me in the face, raught me his hand, H5 4.06. 21
this staff of honor raught, there let it stand, 2H6 2.03. 43
that raught at mountains with outstretched arms, 3H6 1.04. 68
the hand of death hath raught him. ANT 4.09. 29

RAV'D 1 FR 0.0001 REL FR 1 V 0 P
absolute madness could so far have rav'd | to CYM 4.02.135

RAVE 4 FR 0.0004 REL FR 4 V 0 P
why, what's the matter? does he rave? TN 3.04. 10
stamp, rave, and fret, that i may sing and dance 3H6 1.04. 91
there let him stand and rave and cry for food. TIT 5.03.180
let him have time against himself to rave, | let LUC 982

/RAVEL 1 FR 0.0001 REL FR 1 V 0 P
/and /must /i /ravel /out | /my //weav'd–up R2 4.01.228

RAVEL 2 FR 0.0002 REL FR 2 V 0 P
him, | lest it should ravel and be good to none, TGV 3.02. 52
make you to ravel all this matter out, | that i HAM 3.04.186

RAVELL'D 1 FR 0.0001 REL FR 1 V 0 P
sleep that knits up the ravell'd sleave of care, MAC 2.02. 34

RAVEN *(see ravin, etc.)*

RAVEN 17 FR 0.0019 REL FR 14 V 3 P
an amber–color'd raven was well noted. LLL 4.03. 86
who will not change a raven for a dove? MND 2.02.114
waits, | as doth a raven on a sick–fall'n beast, JN 4.03.153
a clip–wing'd griffin and a moulten raven, | a 1H4 3.01.150
for he's disposed as the hateful raven. 2H6 3.01. 76
the raven rook'd her on the chimney's top, | and 3H6 5.06. 47
the raven chides blackness. TRO 2.03.211 P
i would croak like a raven, i would bode, i 5.02.191 P
breeds, | unless the nightly owl or fatal raven; TIT 2.03. 97
'tis true, the raven doth not hatch a lark, 2.03.149
did ever raven sing so like a lark | that gives 3.01.158
dove–feather'd raven! ROM 3.02. 76
the raven himself is hoarse | that croaks the MAC 1.05. 38
the croaking raven doth bellow for revenge. HAM 3.02.254 P
as doth the raven o'er the infectious house, OTH 4.01. 21
nor | the boding raven, nor /chough /hoar, | nor TNK 1.01. 20
therefore my mistress' eyes are raven black, SON 127. 9

RAVEN–COLORED 1 FR 0.0001 REL FR 1 V 0 P
hence, | and let her joy her raven–colored love; TIT 2.03. 83

RAVENING 2 FR 0.0002 REL FR 2 V 0 P
wolvish ravening lamb! ROM 3.02. 76
fill'd and running — ravening first the lamb, CYM 1.06. 49

RAVENOUS 7 FR 0.0008 REL FR 7 V 0 P
are wolvish, bloody, starv'd, and ravenous. MV 4.01.138
nor with thy sweets comfort his ravenous sense, R2 3.02. 13
i wish some ravenous wolf had eaten thee! 1H6 5.04. 31
for he's inclin'd as is the ravenous wolves. 2H6 3.01. 78
this ravenous tiger, this accursed devil; TIT 5.03. 5
as for that ravenous tiger tamora, | no funeral 5.03.195
and men like ravenous fishes | would feed on STM II.C 86

RAVEN'S 5 FR 0.0005 REL FR 5 V 0 P
with raven's feather from unwholesome fen | drop
TMP 1.02.322
love, | to spite a raven's heart within a dove. TN 5.01.131
came he right now to sing a raven's note, 2H6 3.02. 40
whiter than new snow upon a raven's back. ROM 3.02. 19
night, that dawning | may bare the raven's eye! CYM 2.02. 49

RAVENS' 2 FR 0.0002 REL FR 2 V 0 P
him, black and shining | like ravens' wings; TNK 4.02. 84
to pluck the quills from ancient ravens' wings, LUC 949

RAVENS 6 FR 0.0006 REL FR 5 V 1 P
young ravens must have food. WIV 1.03. 35 P
take that, and he that doth the ravens feed, AYL 2.03. 43
powerful spirit instruct the kites and ravens WT 2.03.186
some say that ravens foster forlorn children TIT 2.03.153
and in their steads do ravens, crows, and kites JC 5.01. 84
who endured | the beaks of ravens, talents of TNK 1.01. 41

RAVENSPURGH 9 FR 0.0010 REL FR 9 V 0 P
itself, | away with me in post to ravenspurgh; R2 2.01.296
uplifted arms is safe arriv'd | at ravenspurgh. 2.02. 51
way | from ravenspurgh to cotshall will be found 2.03. 9
is gone to ravenspurgh | to offer service to the 2.03. 31
then with directions to repair to ravenspurgh. 2.03. 35
when you and he came back from ravenspurgh —
1H4 1.03.248
when i from france set foot at ravenspurgh, 3.02. 95
was poor, | upon the naked shore at ravenspurgh, 4.03. 77
from ravenspurgh haven before the gates of york, 3H6 4.07. 8

RAVES 2 FR 0.0002 REL FR 1 V 1 P
cudgelling that he raves in saying nothing. TRO 3.03.249 P
into the madness wherein now he raves, | and all HAM 2.02.150

RAVIN 3 FR 0.0003 REL FR 3 V 0 P
like rats that ravin down their proper bane, | a MM 1.02.129
'twere | i met the ravin lion when he roar'd AWW 3.02.117
that will ravin up | thine own live's means! MAC 2.04. 28

RAVIN'D 1 FR 0.0001 REL FR 1 V 0 P
maw and gulf | of the ravin'd salt–sea shark, MAC 4.01. 24

RAVISH 15 FR 0.0017 REL FR 12 V 3 P
tongue | doth ravish like enchanting harmony; LLL 1.01.167
hair | should ravish doters with a false aspect: 4.03.256
o, then his lines would ravish savage ears | and 4.03.345
lines, | able to ravish any dull conceit; 1H6 5.05. 15
her sight did ravish, but her grace in speech, 2H6 1.01. 32
ravish your wives and daughters before your 4.08. 30 P
ravish our daughters? R3 5.03.337
you have holp to ravish your own daughters, and COR 4.06. 81
ravish a maid, or plot the way to do it, TIT 5.01.129
these hairs which thou dost ravish from my chin LR 3.07. 38
with that suit upon my back will i ravish her; CYM 3.05.138 P
faith, i must ravish her, or she'll disfurnish PER 4.06. 11 P
take manhood to her, | and seek to ravish me. TNK 2.02.259
"with rotten damps ravish the morning air; LUC 778
touch | upon the lute doth ravish human sense; PP 8. 6

/RAVISH'D 2 FR 0.0002 REL FR 2 V 0 P
/whose /strong /immures | /the /ravish'd /helen, TRO pr 9
/ravish'd our sides, like age, must run to rust, TNK 2.02. 22

RAVISH'D 9 FR 0.0010 REL FR 7 V 2 P
now is his soul ravish'd! ADO 2.03. 58 P
almost with ravish'd list'ning, could not find H8 1.02.120
who 'twas that cut thy tongue and ravish'd thee. TIT 2.04. 2
ravish'd and wrong'd as philomela was, | forc'd 4.01. 52
they cut thy sister's tongue, and ravish'd her, 5.01. 92
what, was she ravish'd? tell who did the deed. 5.03. 53
they ravish'd her, and cut away her tongue, 5.03. 57
whom they have ravish'd must by me be slain. PER 4.01.102
must either get her ravish'd or be rid of her. 4.06. 5 P

RAVISHED *(also yravished)*

RAVISHED 3 FR 0.0003 REL FR 3 V 0 P
and younger hearings are quite ravished, | so LLL 2.01. 75
night | from perigenia, whom he ravished? MND 2.01. 78
and they it were that ravished our sister. TIT 5.03. 99

RAVISHER 4 FR 0.0004 REL FR 3 V 1 P
may be said to be a ravisher, so it cannot be COR 4.05.228 P
thee, | good rapine, stab him, he is a ravisher. TIT 5.02.103
with close–tongu'd treason and the ravisher! LUC 770
thou ravisher, thou traitor, thou false thief, 888

RAVISHING 2 FR 0.0002 REL FR 2 V 0 P
bow'r, | with ravishing division, to her lute. 1H4 3.01.208
with tarquin's ravishing /strides, towards his MAC 2.01. 55

RAVISHMENT 2 FR 0.0002 REL FR 2 V 0 P
in bloody death and ravishment delighting, | nor LUC 430
"come, philomele, that sing'st of ravishment, 1128

RAVISHMENTS 1 FR 0.0001 REL FR 0 V 1 P
for rapes and ravishments he parallels nessus. AWW 4.03.251 P

RAV'NOUS 2 FR 0.0002 REL FR 2 V 0 P
(for he is equal rav'nous | as he is subtile, H8 1.01.159
as rav'nous fishes, do a vessel follow | that is 1.02. 79

RAW 15 FR 0.0017 REL FR 10 V 5 P
your doublet and hose, this raw rheumatic day? WIV 3.01. 47 P
the snow | and marian's nose looks red and raw; LLL 5.02.924
a thousand raw tricks of these bragging jacks, MV 3.04. 77
thou art raw. AYL 3.02. 72 P
then, raw as he is (and in the hottest day WT 4.04.787 P
such as it is, being tender, raw, and young, R2 2.03. 42
is not their climate foggy, raw, and dull, | on H5 3.05. 16
in to my tent, the dew is raw and cold. R3 5.03. 46
cold palsies, raw eyes, dirt–rotten livers, TRO 5.01. 20 P
for once, upon a raw and gusty day, | the JC 1.02.100
your weak condition to the raw cold morning. 2.01.236
since yet thy cicatrice looks raw and red HAM 4.03. 60
that she may not be raw in her entertainment. PER 4.02. 55 P
i first appear, though rude, and raw, and muddy, TNK 3.05.122
eyes, though sod in tears, look'd red and raw, LUC 1592

RAW–BON'D 1 FR 0.0001 REL FR 1 V 0 P

lean raw–bon'd rascals! 1H6 1.02. 35
RAWER 1 FR 0.0001 REL FR 0 V 1 P
we wrap the gentleman in our more rawer breath? HAM 5.02.123 P
RAWLY 1 FR 0.0001 REL FR 0 V 1 P
they owe, some upon their children rawly left. H5 4.01.141 P
RAWNESS 1 FR 0.0001 REL FR 1 V 0 P
why in that rawness left you wife and child, MAC 4.03. 26
RAY 1 FR 0.0001 REL FR 1 V 0 P
for in her ray and brightness | the herd hath TRO 1.03. 47
RAY'D *(also beray'd)*
RAY'D 2 FR 0.0002 REL FR 0 V 2 P
sped with spavins, ray'd with the yellows, past SHR 3.02. 53 P
was ever man so ray'd? 4.01. 3 P
RAYS 5 FR 0.0005 REL FR 5 V 0 P
when their fresh rays have smote | the night of LLL 4.03. 27
with those clear rays which she infus'd on me 1H6 1.02. 85
bulk | take up the rays o' th' beneficial sun, H8 1.01. 56
reflect on rome as /titan's rays on earth, | and TIT 1.01.226
as in thy red rays thou dost sink to–night, | so JC 5.03. 61
RAZ'D 4 FR 0.0004 REL FR 2 V 2 P
ay, that he raz'd. MM 1.02. 11 P
with /two provincial roses on my raz'd shoes, HAM 3.02.277 P
that full issue | for which i raz'd my likeness. LR 1.04. 4
till each to raz'd oblivion yield his part | of SON 122. 7
RAZE *(also rase*, etc.)*
RAZE 3 FR 0.0003 REL FR 3 V 0 P
shall we desire to raze the sanctuary | and MM 2.02.170
raze out the written troubles of the brain, MAC 5.03. 42
shall raze you out o' th' book of trespasses TNK 1.01. 33
RAZES *(also race*)*
RAZES 1 FR 0.0001 REL FR 0 V 1 P
have a gammon of bacon and two razes of ginger, 1H4 2.01. 24 P
RAZETH 1 FR 0.0001 REL FR 1 V 0 P
razeth your cities, and subverts your towns, 1H6 2.03. 65
RAZOR 1 FR 0.0001 REL FR 1 V 0 P
and what this fourteen years no razor touch'd, PER 5.03. 75
RAZORABLE 1 FR 0.0001 REL FR 1 V 0 P
till new–born chins | be rough and razorable; TMP 2.01.250
RAZOR'S 1 FR 0.0001 REL FR 1 V 0 P
are as keen | as is the razor's edge invisible, LLL 5.02.257
RAZORS 1 FR 0.0001 REL FR 1 V 0 P
these words are razors to my wounded heart. TIT 1.01.314
RAZURE 1 FR 0.0001 REL FR 1 V 0 P
the tooth of time | and razure of oblivion. MM 5.01. 13
RE 5 FR 0.0005 REL FR 2 V 3 P
ut, re, sol, la, mi, fa. LLL 4.02.100 P
a re, to plead hortensio's passion; SHR 3.01. 74
d sol re, one cliff, two notes have i; 3.01. 77
i will carry no crotchets, i'll re you, i'll fa ROM 4.05.118 P
and you re us and fa us, you note us. 4.05.120 P
REACH 31 FR 0.0035 REL FR 30 V 1 P
i cannot reach so high. TGV 1.02. 84
wilt thou reach stars, because they shine on 3.01.156
but that my nails can reach unto thine eyes. MND 3.02.298
means can carry me | out of his envy's reach, i MV 4.01. 10
grapes, and if my royal fox | could reach them. AWW 2.01. 72
they should not laugh if i could reach them, nor WT 2.03. 25
beyond the infinite and boundless reach | of JN 4.03.117
lift me up | to reach at victory above my head, R2 1.03. 72
from forth thy reach he would have laid thy 2.01.106
what may the king's whole battle reach unto? 1H4 4.01.129
put forth thy hand, reach at the glorious gold. 2H6 1.02. 11
above the reach or compass of thy thought? 1.02. 46
by marrying her which i must reach unto. R3 1.01.159
and live with richmond, from the reach of hell. 4.01. 42
what envy reach you? H8 2.02. 88
reach a chair. 4.02. 3
to me you cannot reach you play the spaniel, 5.02.161
and like a mountain cedar reach his branches 5.04. 53
there's all the reach of it. TRO 4.04.108
advanc'd above pale envy's threat'ning reach. TIT 2.01. 4
reach me thy hand, that i may help thee out, 2.03.237
ay, madam, from the reach of these my hands. ROM 3.05. 85
one may reach deep enough and yet | find little. TIM 3.04. 15
truth, | and thus do we of wisdom and of reach, HAM 2.01. 61
to grosser issues nor to larger reach | than to OTH 3.03.219
because thine eye | presumes to reach, all the PER 1.01. 33
when canst thou reach it? 3.01. 75
'hath set a mark which nature could not reach to TNK 1.04. 43
they stand a grise above the reach of report. 2.01. 28 P
you outwent me, | nor could my wishes reach you. 3.06. 80
reach thy hand; 5.04. 91
REACH'D *(also raught)*
REACH'D 1 FR 0.0001 REL FR 1 V 0 P
proud a fortune | as this that i have reach'd; OTH 1.02. 24
REACHES 3 FR 0.0003 REL FR 3 V 0 P
and dogged york, that reaches at the moon, 2H6 3.01.158
and't may be said | it reaches far, and where H8 1.01.111
with thoughts beyond the reaches of our souls? HAM 1.04. 56
REACHETH 1 FR 0.0001 REL FR 1 V 0 P
that reacheth from the restful english court R2 4.01. 12
REACHING 2 FR 0.0002 REL FR 2 V 0 P
great men have reaching hands; 2H6 4.07. 81
shield | is a black ethiope reaching at the sun; PER 2.02. 20
/READ 9 FR 0.0010 REL FR 9 V 0 P
/but /that /you /read | /these /accusations, R2 4.01.222
/a /troop | /to /read /a /lecture /of /them? 4.01.232
/lord, /dispatch, /read /o'er /these /articles. 4.01.243
/read /o'er /this /paper /while /the /glass 4.01.269
/i'll /read /enough, | /when /i /do /see /the 4.01.273
/me /that /glass, /and /therein /will /i /read. 4.01.276
/and /go /read /with /thee | /sad /stories TIT 3.02. 82
/and /thou /shalt /read /when /mine /begin /to 3.02. 85
/she /took /them, /read /them /in /my /presence, LR 4.03. 11
READ 204 FR 0.0230 REL FR 154 V 50 P
and when it's writ, for my sake read it over, TGV 2.01.130
i read your fortune in your eye. 2.04.143
let me read them. 3.01.289 P
fie on thee, jolthead, thou canst not read. 3.01.291 P
this proves that thou canst not read. 3.01.298 P
read on. 3.01.326 P
read over julia's heart (thy first best love), 5.04. 46
here, read, read; WIV 2.01. 54 P
here, read, read; 2.01. 54 P
is like a good thing, being often read, | grown MM 2.04. 8
if i read it not truly, my ancient skill 4.02.154 P
let not my sister read it in your eye; ERR 3.02. 9
and let her read it in thy looks at board: 3.02. 18
or george seacole, for they can write and read. ADO 3.03. 12 P
fortune, but to write and read comes by nature. 3.03. 15 P
how well he's read, to reason against reading! LLL 1.01. 94
give me the paper, let me read the same, | and 1.01.116
as i have read, sir, and the best of them too. 1.02. 84 P
vouchsafe to read the purpose of my coming, 2.01.109
we will read it, i swear. 4.01. 58
person, be so good as read me this letter. 4.02. 90 P
i beseech you read it. 4.02. 92 P
once more i'll read the ode that i have writ. 4.03. 97
i beseech your grace let this letter be read: 4.03.191
berowne, read it over. where hadst thou it? 4.03.193
for aught that i could ever read, | could ever MND 1.01.132
then read the names of the actors; 1.02. 9 P
i read as much as from the rattling tongue | of 5.01.102
i'll read the writing. MV 2.07. 64
i will read it. 2.09. 55
here is a letter, read it at your leisure. 5.01.267
for here i read for certain that my ships | are 5.01.287
write, | teaching all that read to know | the AYL 3.02.138
i have heard him read many lectures against it, 3.02.347 P
and see you read no other lectures to her. SHR 1.02.147
what will you read to her? 1.02.153
what e'er i read to her, i'll plead for you | as 1.02.154
her turn, well read in poetry | and other books, 1.02.169
that never read so far | to know the cause why 3.01. 9
then give me leave to read philosophy, | and 3.01. 13
yet read the gamouth of hortensio. 3.01. 72
now, mistress, profit you in what you read? 4.02. 6
what, master, read you? first resolve me that. 4.02. 7
i read that i profess, the art to love. 4.02. 8
read it. 4.03.131 P
you shall read it in what–do–ye–call there. AWW 2.03. 22 P
read it again. 3.04. 3
is taken, and it shall be read to his face. 4.03.114 P
shall i read it to you? 4.03.206 P
nay, i'll read it first, by your favor. 4.03.217 P
o, i have read it; TN 1.05.228 P
i will be proud, i will read politic authors, i 2.05.161 P
here's the challenge, read it. 3.04.143 P
ay, is't! i warrant him. do but read. 3.04.146 P
that wonderful promise, to read him by his form, 3.04.264 P
open't and read it. 5.01.289 P
no, madam, i do but read madness. 5.01.294 P
prithee read i' thy right wits. 5.01.297 P
but to read his right wits is to read thus; 5.01.298 P
but to read his right wits is to read thus; 5.01.299 P
read it you, sirrah. 5.01.301 P
infection | that e'er was heard or read! WT 1.02.424
read the indictment. 3.02. 11
break the holy seal | nor read the secrets in't. 3.02.130
break up the seals, and read. 3.02.131
hast thou read truth? 3.02.138
yet i can read waiting–gentlewoman in the scape. 3.03. 72 P
upon the water as he'll stand and read | as 4.04.173
do you not read some tokens of my son | in the JN 1.01. 87
can in this book of beauty read, "i love," | her 2.01.485
who hath read or heard | of any kindred action 3.04. 13
read here, young arthur. 4.01. 33
can you not read it? 4.01. 37
or have you read, or heard, or could you think? 4.03. 42
i do repent me, read not my name there, | my R2 5.03. 52
i'll read you matter deep and dangerous, | as 1H4 1.03.190
let's see what they be. read them. 2.04.534 P
keep close, we'll read it at more advantage. 2.04.542 P
which calls me pupil or hath read to me? 3.01. 45
exceedingly well read, and profited | in strange 3.01.164
for therein should we read | the very bottom and 4.01. 49
proclaim'd at market–crosses, read in churches, 5.01. 73
i cannot read them now. 5.02. 80
i have read the cause of his effects in galen, 2H4 1.02.116 P
have you read o'er the /letters that i sent you? 3.01. 36
o god, that one might read the book of fate, 3.01. 45
here at more leisure may your highness read, 4.04. 89
for you shall read that my great–grandfather H5 1.02.146
read them, and know i know your worthiness. 2.02. 69
what read you there | that have so cowarded and 2.02. 74
that you shall read | in your own losses, if he 2.04.138
of wales, as i have read in the chronicles, 4.07. 94 P
vouchsafe to those that have not read the story, 5.pr. 1
upon the which, that every one may read, | shall 1H6 2.02. 14
for once i read | that stout pendragon in his 3.02. 94
dimm'd mine eyes, that i can read no further. 2H6 1.01. 55
uncle of winchester, i pray read on. 1.01. 56
i never read but england's kings have had 1.01.128
john southwell, read you; 1.04. 12 P
as i have read, laid claim unto the crown, | and 2.02. 40
he can write and read and cast accompt. 4.02. 86 P
but stay, i'll read it over once again. 4.04. 14
and because they could not read, thou hast 4.07. 44 P
that it may be to–day read o'er in paul's. R3 3.06. 3
that you read | the cardinal's malice and his H8 1.01.104
i read in 's looks | matter against me, and his 1.01.125
whilst our commission from rome is read, | let 2.04. 1
it hath already publicly been read, | and on all 2.04. 3
wherein was read | how that the cardinal did 3.02. 31
read o'er this, | and, after, this, and then to 3.02.201
i must read this paper; 3.02.208
you may read the rest. 4.01. 19
from her shall read the perfect /ways of honor, 5.04. 37
is | he shall as soon read in the eyes of others TRO 3.03. 77
o, like a book of sport thou'lt read me o'er; 4.05.239
let me read. 5.03.100
say we read lectures to you, | how youngly he COR 2.03.235
whence men have read | his fame unparallel'd, 5.02. 15
having read it, | bid them repair to th' 5.06. 2
read it not, noble lords, | but tell the traitor 5.06. 83
read to her sons than she hath read to thee TIT 4.01. 13
read to her sons than she hath read to thee 4.01. 13
and i have read that hecuba of troy | ran mad 4.01. 20
but thou art deeper read, and better skill'd; 4.01. 33
lavinia, shall i read? 4.01. 46
o, do ye read, my lord, what she hath writ? 4.01. 77
it well, | i read it in the grammar long ago. 4.02. 23
where i may read who pass'd that passing fair? ROM 1.01.236
god gi' god–den. i pray, sir, can you read? 1.02. 57 P
but, i pray, can you read any thing you see? 1.02. 60 P
stay, fellow, i can read. 1.02. 63 P
read o'er the volume of young paris' face, | and 1.03. 81
thy love did read by rote that could not spell. 2.03. 88
read me the superscription of these letters, i TIM 2.02. 78 P
canst not read? 2.02. 80 P
of their love, | ever to read them thine. 5.01.155
some beast read this; 5.03. 4
what's on this tomb | i cannot read; 5.03. 6
give so much light that i may read by them. JC 2.01. 45
if thou read this, o caesar, thou mayest live; 2.03. 15
hail, caesar! read this schedule. 3.01. 3
o caesar, read mine first; 3.01. 6
read it, great caesar. 3.01. 7
delay not, caesar, read it instantly. 3.01. 9
which, pardon me, i do not mean to read — | and 3.02.131
we'll hear the will. read it, mark antony. 3.02.138
patience, gentle friends, i must not read it. 3.02.140
read the will, we'll hear it, antony. 3.02.147
you shall read us the will, caesar's will. 3.02.148
the will, read the will! 3.02.156 P
you will compel me then to read the will? 3.02.157
where every day i turn | the leaf to read them. MAC 1.03.152
as a book, where men | may read strange matters. 1.05. 63
it, write upon't, read it, afterwards seal it, 5.01. 7 P
and at our more considered time we'll read, HAM 2.02. 81
what do you read, my lord? 2.02.191 P
i mean, the matter that you read, my lord. 2.02.195 P
read on this book, | that show of such an 3.01. 43
here's the commission, read it at more leisure. 5.02. 26
brother, of a prediction i read this other day, LR 1.02.140 P
of intermission, | which presently they read; 2.04. 34
i'll read, and answer. 4.02. 87
read thou this challenge; 4.06.138 P
read. 4.06.143 P
stay till i have read the letter. 5.01. 47
let the trumpet sound, | and read out this. 5.03.108
thou worse than any name, read thine own evil. 5.03.157
have you not read, roderigo, | of some such OTH 1.01.173
you shall yourself read in the bitter letter 1.03. 68
and could almost read | the thoughts of people. 3.04. 57
infinite book of secrecy | a little i can read. ANT 1.02. 11
and at thy sovereign leisure read | the garboils 1.03. 60
read not my blemishes in the world's report. 2.03. 5
made his will, and read it | to public ear; 3.04. 4
his virtue | by her election may be truly read, CYM 1.01. 53
so far i read aloud — | but even the very 1.06. 26
i have read three hours then. 2.02. 3
which not to read would show the britains cold. 3.01. 75
read, and tell me | how far 'tis thither. 3.02. 49
o boys, this story | the world may read in me: 3.03. 56
which to read | would be even mortal to me. 3.04. 17
please you, read, | and you shall find me, 3.04. 18
to write and read | be henceforth treacherous! 4.02.316
who is't can read a woman? 5.05. 48
read, and declare the meaning. 5.05.434
in their lives | have read it for restoratives. PER 1.ch. 8
where is read | nothing but curious pleasures, 1.01. 15
scorning advice, read the conclusion then; 1.01. 56
which read and not expounded, 'tis decreed, | as 1.01. 57
if this be true which makes me pale to read it? 1.01. 75
you cannot read it there. TNK 1.01.111
judge by the outside) | i never saw nor read of. 4.02. 75
nor would the libels read | of liberal wits. 5.01.101
can he write and read too? 5.02. 57
nor read the subtle shining secrecies | writ in LUC 101
where subjects' eyes do learn, do read, do look. 616
must he in thee read lectures of such shame? 618
face, | and tarquin's eye may read the mot afar, 830
how tarquin must be us'd, read it in me: 1195
in them i read such art | as truth and beauty SON 14.10
o, learn to read what silent love hath writ: 23.13
theirs for their style i'll read, his for his 32.14
mine own self–love quite contrary i read; 62.11
nay, if you read this line, remember not | the 71. 5
READER 1 FR 0.0001 REL FR 1 V 0 P
of their thoughts | to every ticklish reader! TRO 4.05. 61
READIEST 4 FR 0.0004 REL FR 3 V 1 P
you, which is the readiest way | to the house of SHR 1.02.219
the readiest way to make the wench amends | is R3 1.01.155
rome's readiest champions, repose you here in TIT 1.01.151
draught, is the readiest man to kill him; TIM 1.02. 48 P
READILY 2 FR 0.0002 REL FR 2 V 0 P
in our fortunes made | may readily be stopp'd. 2H6 5.02. 83
maze, | that cannot tread the way out readily, LUC 1152
READINESS 15 FR 0.0017 REL FR 11 V 4 P
to–morrow be in readiness to go — | excuse it TGV 1.03. 70
i thought, by the readiness in the office, you MM 2.01.261 P
with, | what page's suit she hath in readiness. MV 2.04. 32
ashore, | we could at once put us in readiness, SHR 1.01. 43
your ships already are in readiness. 1H6 3.01.185
royal commanders, be in readiness, | for with a 3H6 2.02. 67
but he's deceiv'd, we are in readiness. 5.04. 64
is, my liege, and all things are in readiness. R3 5.03. 52
i am joyful to hear of their readiness, and am COR 4.03. 46 P
every thing | in readiness for hymenaeus stand, TIT 1.01.325
here, my lord, in readiness. TIM 1.02.166 P
let's briefly put on manly readiness, | and meet MAC 2.03.133
now, yet it /will come — the readiness is all. HAM 5.02.222 P
our chariots and our horsemen be in readiness. CYM 3.05. 23
they are here in readiness. 4.02.336
READING 21 FR 0.0023 REL FR 13 V 8 P
how now? what letter are you reading there? TGV 1.03. 51
now will he be swing'd for reading my letter — 3.01.382 P
and my uncle's fool, reading the challenge, ADO 1.01. 41 P
when she had writ it, and was reading it over, 2.03.136 P
it, and for your writing and reading, let that 3.03. 21 P
trust not my reading, nor my observations, 4.01.165
how well he's read, to reason against reading! LLL 1.01. 94
what, longaville, and reading! 4.03. 43
here comes my sister reading, stand aside. AYL 3.02.124
of my verses with reading them ill–favoredly. 3.02.262 P
such as his reading | and manifest experience AWW 1.03.222
for on the reading it he chang'd almost into 4.03. 5 P
spirit of humors intimate reading aloud to him! TN 2.05. 85 P
you should fashion, wrest, or bow your reading, H5 1.02. 14
here is ulysses, | i'll interrupt his reading. TRO 3.03. 93
what are you reading? 3.03. 95
not the leaf turn'd down | where i left reading? JC 4.03.274

look where sadly the poor wretch comes reading. HAM 2.02.168
what paper were you reading? LR 1.02. 30 P
she hath been reading late | the tale of tereus; CYM 2.02. 44
and often reading what contents it bears; LC 19
READINS 1 FR 0.0001 REL FR 0 V 1 P
that has cozen'd all the hosts of readins, of WIV 4.05. 78 P
READS 2 FR 0.0002 REL FR 2 V 0 P
he reads much, | he is a great observer, and he JC 1.02.201
and when he reads | thy personal venture in the MAC 1.03. 90
READ'ST 1 FR 0.0001 REL FR 1 V 0 P
remember, as thou read'st, thy promise pass'd. R2 5.03. 51
/READY 1 FR 0.0001 REL FR 1 V 0 P
/let /us /make /ready /straight. TRO 4.04.144
READY 151 FR 0.0170 REL FR 102 V 49 P
and make yourself ready in your cabin for the TMP 1.01. 25 P
i am ready now, | approach, my ariel. 1.02.187
open and show riches | ready to drop upon me, 3.02.142
madam, | dinner is ready, and your father stays. TGV 1.02.128
'tis ready, sir, here in the porch. WIV 1.04. 61 P
it makes me almost ready to wrangle with mine 2.01. 85 P
my heart is ready to crack with impatience. 2.02.288 P
robert, be ready here hard by in the brew–house, 3.03. 10 P
be ready, claudio, for your death to–morrow. MM 3.01.106
go to your knees, and make ready. 3.01.170 P
the hand, | who hath a story ready for your ear. 4.01. 55
pounds, of which he made five marks ready money. 4.03. 7 P
very ready, sir. 4.03. 38 P
my lord, will you walk? dinner is ready. ADO 2.03.210 P
five a' clock, cousin, 'tis time you were ready. 3.04. 53 P
i'll wait upon them, i am ready. 3.05. 56 P
call her forth, brother, here's the friar ready. 5.04. 39
ready. name what part i am for, and proceed. MND 1.02. 18 P
ready. 3.01.163
here, villain, drawn and ready. where art thou? 3.02.402
ready. 4.01. 6
ready. 4.01. 9
ready. 4.01. 18
hasted that supper be ready at the farthest by MV 2.02.115 P
ready, so please your grace. 4.01. 2
he is ready at the door; he comes, my lord. 4.01. 15
i have them ready. 4.01.256
i have it ready for thee, here it is. 4.01.337
the wrastling, and they are ready to perform it. AYL 1.02.146 P
ready, sir, but his will hath in it a more 1.02.202 P
procure me music ready when he wakes, | to make SHR in.1. 50
and if he chance to speak, be ready straight, in.1. 52
some one be ready with a costly suit, | and ask in.1. 59
on thee, | each in his office ready at thy beck. in.2. 34
ay, sir, they be ready; 3.02.205 P
there's fire ready, and therefore, good grumio, 4.01. 39 P
is supper ready, the house trimm'd, rushes 4.01. 46 P
all ready; and therefore, i pray thee, news. 4.01. 52 P
are they all ready? 4.01. 95 P
now, my spruce companions, is all ready, and all 4.01.113 P
all things is ready. how near is our master? 4.01.115 P
agreement | me shall you find ready and willing 4.04. 34
home, | and bid bianca make her ready straight; 4.04. 63
to bid the priest be ready to come against you 4.04.103 P
and swiftly, sir, for the priest is ready. 5.01. 1 P
please, | my hand is ready, may it do him ease. 5.02.179
are you ready, sir? TN 2.04. 49 P
i'll get 'em all three all ready. 3.01. 91 P
that i am ready to distrust mine eyes | and 4.03. 13
my ships are ready, and | my people did expect WT 1.02.449
being ready to leap out of himself for joy of 5.02. 49 P
and ready mounted are they to spit forth | their JN 2.01.211
and even at hand a drum is ready brac'd | that 5.02.169
be ready, as your lives shall answer it, | at R2 1.01.198
be ready to direct these home alarms. 1.01.205
i, who ready here do stand in arms | to prove by 1.03. 36
lords, be ready all. 4.01.320
my father glendower is not ready yet, | nor 1H4 3.01. 86
go make ready breakfast; 3.03.170 P
see what a ready tongue suspicion hath! 2H4 1.01. 84
the answer is as ready as a /borrower's cap, "i 2.02.115 P
if my heart be not ready to burst — well, sweet 2.04.379 P
we ready are to try our fortunes | to the last 4.02. 43
which i could with a ready guess declare, H5 1.01. 96
returns us that his powers are yet not ready 3.03. 46
all things are ready, if our minds be so. 4.03. 71
bed, | ready they were to shoot me to the heart. 1H6 1.04. 56
ah, thou shalt find us ready for thee still; 2.04.104
ready to starve, and dare not touch his own. 2H6 1.01.229
and ready are the appellant and defendant, | the 2.03. 49
that have a sword, and yet am ready to famish! 4.10. 2 P
our army is ready; 3H6 1.01.256
laid aside, | and i am ready to put armor on. 3.03.230
are done, | and i am ready to put armor on." 4.01.105
your horse stands ready at the park–corner. 4.05. 19
lords, for edward is at hand, | ready to fight; 5.04. 61
came, | ready to catch each other by the throat, R3 1.03.188
is all things ready for the royal time? 3.04. 4
ready with every nod to tumble down | into the 3.04.100
and both are ready in their offices | at any 3.05. 10
is ink and paper ready? 5.03. 75
is he in person ready? H8 1.01.117
is the banket ready | i' th' privy chamber? 1.04. 98
see the barge be ready; 2.01. 98
when they were ready to set out for london, a 2.02. 4 P
we are ready | to use our utmost studies in your 3.01.173
is he ready | to come abroad? 3.02. 82
let some o' th' guard be ready there. 5.02.130
and bid the cheek be ready with a blush | modest TRO 1.03.228
more ready to cry out, "who knows what follows?" 2.02. 13
she's making her ready, she'll come straight. 3.02. 30 P
ajax is ready. 3.03. 35
they are at hand and ready to effect it. 4.02. 68
my lord, is the lady ready? 4.04. 49
but make you ready your stiff bats and clubs, COR 1.01.161
we never yet made doubt but rome was ready | to 1.02. 18
by the din of war gan pierce | his ready sense; 2.02.116
ready, when time shall prompt them, to make road 3.01. 5
i have; 'tis ready. 3.03. 10
and ready for this hint | when we shall hap to 3.03. 23
have you an army ready, say you? 4.03. 42 P
intended fire your city is ready to flame in, 5.02. 46 P
they shall be ready at your highness' will, | to TIT 2.03.297
and see them ready against their mother comes. 5.02.205
the feast is ready which the careful titus 5.03. 21
ay, boy, ready. ROM 1.05. 11 P
ready stand | to smooth that rough touch with a 1.05. 95
will you be ready? 3.04. 22
come, is the bride ready to go to church? 4.05. 33
ready to go, but never to return. 4.05. 34
ready for his friends. TIM 1.02.230
pray is my lord ready to come forth? 3.04. 35 P
are we all ready? JC 3.01. 31
be ready, gods, with all your thunderbolts, 4.03. 81
we, at the height, are ready to decline. 4.03.217
our army lies, ready to give up the ghost. 5.01. 88
go bid thy mistress, when my drink is ready, MAC 2.01. 31
i laid their daggers ready, | he could not miss 2.02. 11
come go we to the king, our power is ready, 4.03.236
go make you ready. HAM 3.02. 45 P
be the players ready? 3.02.106 P
the bark is ready, and the wind at help, | th' 4.03. 44
if his fitness speaks, mine is ready; 5.02.201 P
me not stay a jot for dinner, go get it ready. LR 1.04. 9 P
be my horses ready? 1.05. 33 P
how now, are the horses ready? 1.05. 48 P
ready, my lord. 1.05. 49 P
and bring you where both fire and food is ready. 3.04.153
is, that he may be ready for our apprehension. 3.05. 19 P
there is a litter ready, lay him in't, | and 3.06. 90
all the same, and they are ready | to–morrow, or 5.03. 52
hold it in, | for i am almost ready to dissolve, 5.03.204
your commission's ready; ANT 2.03. 42
go, make thee ready, | our letters are prepar'd. 3.03. 37
he shall in time be ready. 5.01. 72
your lady's person. is she ready? CYM 2.03. 81
hath prevail'd | on thy too ready hearing? 3.02. 6
ready in gibes, quick–answer'd, saucy, and | as 3.04.158
come more, for more you're ready; 4.03. 30
come, sir, are you ready for death? 5.04.151 P
overroasted rather; ready long ago. 5.04.152 P
if you be ready for that, you are well cook'd. 5.04.153 P
thus ready for the way of life or death, | i PER 1.01. 54
are ready now | to eat those little darlings 1.04. 43
are the knights ready to begin the triumph? 2.02. 1
return them, we are ready; 2.02. 4
beneath the hatches, caulk'd and bitum'd ready. 3.01. 71 P
i am ready, keeper. TNK 2.02.222
sweet, you must be ready — | and you, emilia — 2.05. 48
but when her lips were ready for his pay, | he VEN 89
one of my husband's men | bid thou be ready, by LUC 1292
REAK *(also reaking, reaks, recketh)*
REAK 3 FR 0.0003 REL FR 3 V 0 P
i reak not though i end my life to–day. TRO 5.06. 26
that's all i reak. CYM 4.02.154
i reak not if the wolves would jaw me, so | he TNK 3.02. 7
REAKING 1 FR 0.0001 REL FR 1 V 0 P
with you, | reaking as little what betideth me, TGV 4.03. 40
REAKLESS *(also reckless)*
REAKLESS 3 FR 0.0003 REL FR 2 V 1 P
careless, reakless, and fearless of what's past, MM 4.02.143 P
so flies the reakless shepherd from the wolf; 3H6 5.06. 7
you grave but reakless senators, have you thus COR 3.01. 92
REAKS 2 FR 0.0002 REL FR 2 V 0 P
and little reaks to find the way to heaven | by AYL 2.04. 81
dalliance treads, | and reaks not his own rede. HAM 1.03. 51
REAL 3 FR 0.0003 REL FR 3 V 0 P
is't real that i see? AWW 5.03.306
it must omit | real necessities, and give way COR 3.01.147
his real habitude gave life and grace | to LC 114
REALLY 2 FR 0.0002 REL FR 0 V 2 P
you will to't, sir, really. HAM 5.02.126 P
i would i were really that i am deliver'd to be. TNK 2.01. 7 P
REALM 53 FR 0.0060 REL FR 47 V 6 P
of lust and late–walking through the realm. WIV 5.05.145 P
and the truth of all this realm | is fled to heaven; JN 4.03.144
confess thy treasons ere thou fly the realm; R2 1.03.198
we are enforc'd to farm our royal realm, | the 1.04. 45
plot, this earth, this realm, this england, 2.01. 50
the earl of wiltshire hath the realm in farm. 2.01.256
plot | to rid the realm of this pernicious blot? 4.01.325
though he divide the realm and give thee half, 5.01. 60
he doth fill fields with harness in the realm, 1H4 3.02.101
now when the lords and barons of the realm 4.03. 66
art now one of the greatest men in this realm. 2H4 5.03. 88 P
unjustly gloze | to be the realm of france, and H5 1.02. 41
law | was not devised for the realm of france; 1.02. 55
and lookest to command the prince and realm. 1H6 1.01. 38
prosper this realm, keep it from civil broils, 1.01. 53
there's none protector of the realm but i. 1.03. 12
and not protector, of the king or realm. 1.03. 32
religion | because he is protector of the realm, 1.03. 66
and all the priests and friars in my realm 1.06. 19
so much applauded through the realm of france? 2.02. 36
to slay your sovereign and destroy the realm. 3.01.114
peers, | hearing of your arrival in this realm, 3.04. 2
themselves, and lost the realm of france! 4.01.147
of all his wars within the realm of france? 4.07. 71
it were enough to fright the realm of france! 4.07. 82
the utter loss of all the realm of france. 5.04.112
but i will rule both her, the king, and realm. 5.05.108
with all the learned council of the realm, 2H6 1.01. 89
behooves it us to labor for the realm. 1.01.182
art thou not second woman in the realm? 1.02. 43
madam, i am protector of the realm, | and at his 1.03.120
and all the peers and nobles of the realm | have 1.03.126
man | to be your regent in the realm of france. 1.03.161
seiz'd on the realm, depos'd the rightful king, 2.02. 24
god and king henry govern england's realm. 2.03. 30
give up your staff, sir, and the king his realm. 2.03. 31
levy great sums of money through the realm | for 3.01. 61
for swallowing the treasure of the realm. 4.01. 74
all the realm shall be in common, and in 4.02. 68 P
burn all the records of the realm, my mouth 4.07. 14 P
the youth of the realm in erecting a grammar 4.07. 33 P
/but to maintain the king, the realm, and you? 4.07. 70
proudest peer in the realm shall not wear a head 4.07.120 P
first shall war unpeople this my realm; 3H6 1.01.126
seas, | the duke is made protector of the realm, 1.01.240
i and ten thousand in this luckless realm | had 2.06. 18
his realm a slaughter–house, his subjects slain, 5.04. 78
till richard wear the garland of the realm. R3 3.02. 40
a wise council to them | of every realm, that H8 2.04. 52
the whole realm by your teaching and your 5.02. 51
this realm dismantled was | of jove himself, and HAM 3.02.282
then shall the realm of albion | come to great LR 3.02. 85
you twain | rule in this realm, and the gor'd 5.03.321
REALMS 7 FR 0.0008 REL FR 6 V 1 P
combine your hearts in one, your realms in one! H5 5.02.360
between the realms of england and of france. 1H6 5.01. 6
and peace established between these realms. 5.03. 92
methinks the realms of england, france, and 2H6 1.01.232
i weigh'd the danger which my realms stood in H8 2.04.198
hot ardent zeal would set whole realms on fire; TIM 3.03. 33 P
realms and islands were | as plates dropp'd from ANT 5.02. 91
RE–ANSWER 1 FR 0.0001 REL FR 0 V 1 P
which in weight to re–answer, his pettiness H5 3.06.128 P
REAP 14 FR 0.0015 REL FR 14 V 0 P
our corn's to reap, for yet our tithe's to sow. MM 4.01. 75
they that reap must sheaf and bind, | then to AYL 3.02.107
proffers not took reap thanks for their reward. AWW 2.01.147
your wife is like to reap a proper man. TN 3.01.133
but little vantage shall i reap thereby; R2 1.03.218
and reap the harvest which that rascal sow'd. 2H6 3.01.381
to thee | as now i reap at thy too cruel hand! 3H6 1.04.166
and of our labors thou shalt reap the gain. 5.07. 20
king, | we are to reap the harvest of his son. R3 2.02.116
to reap the harvest of perpetual peace | by this 5.02. 15
which thou shalt thereby reap is such a name COR 5.03.143
holp to reap the fame | which he did end all his 5.06. 35
which you might from relation likewise reap, CYM 2.04. 86
my poor lips, which should that harvest reap, SON 128. 7
REAP'D 3 FR 0.0003 REL FR 3 V 0 P
sow'd cockle reap'd no corn, | and justice LLL 4.03.380
and his chin new reap'd | show'd like a 1H4 1.03. 34
how have i reap'd it? H8 3.02.204
REAPERS 1 FR 0.0001 REL FR 1 V 0 P
your mariners are /muleters, reapers, people ANT 3.07. 35
REAPING 1 FR 0.0001 REL FR 1 V 0 P
/autumn it was | that grew the more by reaping. ANT 5.02. 88
REAPS 1 FR 0.0001 REL FR 1 V 0 P
after the man | that the main harvest reaps. AYL 3.05.103
/REAR* 1 FR 0.0001 REL FR 1 V 0 P
/there /for /pavement /to /the /abject /rear, TRO 3.03.162
REAR* 11 FR 0.0012 REL FR 11 V 0 P
and when i rear my hand, do you the like, | to TMP 2.01.295
die, | and for her sake do i rear up her boy; MND 2.01.136
no! i'll not rear | another's issue. WT 2.03.192
her breeding so | she is i' th' rear 'our birth. 4.04.581
shall thy old dugs once more a traitor rear? R2 5.03. 90
a statelier pyramis to her i'll rear | than 1H6 1.06. 21
rear up his body, wring him by the nose. 2H6 3.02. 34
and rear it in the place your father's stands. 3H6 2.06. 86
paste, | and of the paste a coffin i will rear, TIT 5.02.188
and keep you in the rear of your affection, HAM 1.03. 34
but let us rear | the higher our opinion, that ANT 2.01. 35
REAR'D 6 FR 0.0006 REL FR 6 V 0 P
and our weak spirits ne'er been higher rear'd WT 1.02. 72
form | have bench'd and rear'd to worship, who 1.02.314
but from their ashes shall be rear'd | a phoenix 1H6 4.07. 92
grow in the veins of actions highest rear'd, TRO 1.03. 6
rome, | and rear'd aloft the bloody battle–axe, TIT 3.01.168
the ocean, his rear'd arm | crested the world, ANT 5.02. 82
/REARLY 1 FR 0.0001 REL FR 1 V 0 P
do, very /rearly, i must be abroad else, | to TNK 4.01.110
REARS 2 FR 0.0002 REL FR 2 V 0 P
casca, you are the first that rears your hand. JC 3.01. 30
anon he rears upright, curvets, and leaps, | as VEN 279
REARWARD 5 FR 0.0005 REL FR 4 V 1 P
myself would, on the rearward of reproaches, ADO 4.01.126
'a came /ever in the rearward of the fashion, 2H4 3.02.316 P
now in the rearward comes the duke and his. 1H6 3.03. 33
but with a rearward following tybalt's death, ROM 3.02.121
come in the rearward of a conquer'd woe; SON 90. 6
/REASON 3 FR 0.0003 REL FR 1 V 2 P
/for, /by /my /fay, /i /cannot /reason. HAM 2.02.265 P
/knowledge, /and /reason, /i /should /be /false LR 1.04.233
/suddenly /gone /back, /know /you /no /reason? 4.03. 2 P
REASON 303 FR 0.0342 REL FR 215 V 88 P
mind, your reason | for raising this sea–storm? TMP 1.02.176
that this coil | would not infect his reason? 1.02.208
request, monster, i will do reason, any reason. 3.02.119 P
request, monster, i will do reason, any reason. 3.02.120 P
yet, with my nobler reason, 'gainst my fury | do 5.01. 26
fumes that mantle | their clearer reason. 5.01. 68
so much admire | that they devour their reason, 5.01.155
your reason? TGV 1.02. 22
i have no other but a woman's reason: 1.02. 23
'tis you that have the reason. 2.01.144 P
have i not reason to prefer mine own? 2.04.156
that makes me, reasonless, to reason thus? 2.04.198
and that's the reason i love him so little. 2.04.206
there is no reason but i shall be blind. 2.04.212
lest it should burn above the bounds of reason. 2.07. 23
if it be so, i shall do that that is reason. WIV 1.01.211 P
do as it shall become one that would do reason. 1.01.234 P
that, upon your request, cousin, in any reason. 1.01.241 P
"ask me no reason why i love you, for though 2.01. 4 P
for though love use reason for his precisian, he 2.01. 5 P
reason, you rogue, reason; 2.02. 15 P
reason, you rogue, reason; 2.02. 15 P
in despite of the teeth of all rhyme and reason, 5.05.126 P
when she will play with reason and discourse, MM 1.02.185
reason thus with life: 3.01. 6
(that in all reason should have quench'd her 3.01.241 P
he shows his reason for that: 4.04. 11 P
yet reason dares her no, | for my authority 4.04. 25
nor do not banish reason | for inequality, but 5.01. 64
but let your reason serve | to make the truth 5.01. 65
are not mad | have sure more lack of reason. 5.01. 68
it imports no reason | that with such vehemency 5.01.108
and the wherefore is neither rhyme nor reason? ERR 2.02. 48
your reason? 2.02. 61 P
for what reason? 2.02. 90 P
but your reason was not substantial, why there 2.02.104 P
to know the reason of this strange restraint. 3.01. 97
what, are you mad, that you do reason so? 3.02. 53
how fondly dost thou reason! 4.02. 57
hath he not reason to turn back an hour in a day 4.02. 62

the reason that i gather he is mad, | besides 4.03. 86
now he's there, past thought of human reason. 5.01.189
you should hear reason. ADO 1.03. 5 P
you have no reason, i do it freely. 4.01.258 P
there thou speak'st reason; 5.01. 41
why, no, no more than reason. 5.04. 74
troth, no, no more than reason. 5.04. 77
how well he's read, to reason against reading! LLL 1.01. 94
in reason nothing. 1.01. 99
color, methinks sampson had small reason for it. 1.02. 88 P
master, against the reason of white and red. 1.02.107 P
a yielding 'gainst some reason in my breast, 2.01.151
all liberal reason i will yield unto. 2.01.167
your reason? 2.01.233
great reason: for past care is still past cure. 5.02. 28
i know the reason, lady, why you ask. 5.02.243
o for your reason! quickly, sir — i long! 5.02.244
what reason have you for't? 5.02.709 P
the will of man is by his reason sway'd; MND 2.02.115
and reason says you are the worthier maid. 2.02.116
so i, being young, till now ripe not to reason; 2.02.118
skill, | reason becomes the marshal to my will, 2.02.120
you should have little reason for that. 3.01.143 P
reason and love keep little company together 3.01.143 P
more than cool reason ever comprehends. 5.01. 6
but yet in courtesy, in all reason, we must stay 5.01.255 P
and what's his reason? MV 3.01. 58 P
i did, my lord, | and i have reason for it. 3.02.231
his reason well i know: 3.03. 21
much that the moor should be more than reason; 3.05. 41 P
it, | in reason he should never come to heaven! 3.05. 78
as there is no firm reason to be rend'red | why 4.01. 53
so can i give no reason, nor i will not, | more 4.01. 59
the reason is, your spirits are attentive; 5.01. 70
wits too dull to reason of such goddesses, /and AYL 1.02. 53 P
by reason of his absence, there is nothing 2.04. 85
and you will not be answer'd with reason, i must 2.07.100 P
for not being at court? your reason. 3.02. 39 P
neither rhyme nor reason can express how much. 3.02.398 P
and the reason why they are not so punish'd and 3.02.402 P
by my faith, you have great reason to be sad. 4.01. 22 P
sigh'd but they ask'd one another the reason; 5.02. 36 P
no sooner knew the reason but they sought the 5.02. 36 P
that reason wonder may diminish | how thus we 5.04.139
i hope this reason stands for my excuse. SHR in.2. 124
for what reason, i beseech you? 1.02.233
for this reason, if you'll know, | that she's 1.02.233
i see no reason but suppos'd lucentio | must get 2.01.407
having no other reason | but that his beard grew 3.02.174
my heart as great, my reason haply more, | to 5.02.171
tell me thy reason why thou wilt marry. AWW 1.03. 27 P
is this all your worship's reason? 1.03. 31 P
if you have reason, be brief. TN 1.05.200 P
thy exquisite reason, dear knight? 2.03.144 P
i have no exquisite reason for't, but i have 2.03.145 P
reason for't, but i have reason good enough. 2.03.146 P
for every reason excites to this, that my lady 2.05.165 P
thy reason, man? 3.01. 22 P
so false, i am loath to prove reason with them. 3.01. 25 P
pride, | nor wit nor reason can my passion hide. 3.01.152
but rather reason thus with reason fetter: 3.01.155
but rather reason thus with reason fetter: 3.01.155
thy reason, dear venom, give thy reason. 3.02. 2 P
thy reason, dear venom, give thy reason. 3.02. 2 P
you must needs yield your reason, sir andrew. 3.02. 3 P
sir, upon the oaths of judgment and reason. 3.02. 15 P
thee so, for i will show thee no reason for't." 3.04.152 P
and wrangle with my reason that persuades me 4.03. 14
reason my son | should choose himself a wife, WT 4.04.406
himself a wife, but as good reason | the father 4.04.407
if my reason | will thereto be obedient, i have 4.04.482
will thereto be obedient, i have reason; 4.04.483
is all as monstrous to our human reason | as my 5.01. 41
that which may | unfurnish me of reason. 5.01.123
no, i have no reason for it; JN 1.01. 66
my reasonable part produces reason | how i may 3.04. 54
then, have i reason to be fond of grief? 3.04. 98
our griefs, and not our manners, reason now. 4.03. 29
but there is little reason in your grief; 4.03. 30
therefore 'twere reason you had manners now. 4.03. 31
he is prepar'd, and reason too he should — 5.02.130
teach thy necessity to reason thus: R2 1.03.277
what was his reason? 2.03. 28
have i not reason to look pale and dead? 3.02. 79
i see no reason why thou shouldst be so 1H4 1.02. 10 P
if he fight longer than he sees reason, i'll 1.02.185 P
and 'tis no little reason bids us speed, | to 1.03.283
me | whither i go, nor reason whereabout. 2.03.104
come, tell us your reason; 2.04.233 P
come, your reason, jack, your reason. 2.04.235 P
come, your reason, jack, your reason. 2.04.235 P
give you a reason on compulsion? 2.04.238 P
i would give no man a reason upon compulsion, i. 2.04.240 P
shalt find me tractable to any honest reason; 3.03.173 P
whence | the eye of reason may pry in upon us. 4.01. 72
service for any other reason than to set me off, 2H4 1.02. 13 P
as thou art hath in reason taken from me all 2.02. 49 P
the reason? 2.02. 51 P
i see no reason in the law of nature but i may 3.02.331 P
then reason will our hearts should be as good. 4.01.155
yea, every idle, nice, and wanton reason, 4.01.189
hear him but reason in divinity, | and, H5 1.01. 38
'tis a subject for a sovereign to reason on, and 3.07. 36 P
therefore, when he sees reason of fears, as we 4.01.108 P
yet, in reason, no man should possess him with 4.01.110 P
they do always reason themselves out again. 5.02.157 P
we have consented to all terms of reason. 5.02.330 P
the reason mov'd these warlike lords to this 1H6 2.05. 70
you have great reason to do richard right, 3.01.153
i see no reason, if i wear this rose, | that any 4.01.152
the lists | by reason of his adversary's odds. 5.05. 33
there's reason he should be displeas'd at it. 2H6 1.01.155
peace, son, and show some reason, buckingham, 1.03.113
then give me leave | to show some reason, of no 1.03.163
i see no reason why a king of years | should be 2.03. 28
'tis york that hath more reason for his death. 3.01.245
and good reason; 4.02.162 P
and ask him what's the reason of these arms. 4.09. 37
to know the reason of these arms in peace; 5.01. 18
and have no other reason for this wrong | but 5.01.189
and reason too: 3H6 2.02. 93
to prove him tyrant this reason may suffice, 3.03. 71
then 'tis but reason that i be releas'd | from 3.03.147
tell me some reason why the lady grey | should 4.01. 25
both him and all his brothers unto reason. 4.07. 34
had i not reason, think ye, to make haste, | and 5.06. 72
i will not reason what is meant hereby, R3 1.04. 93
no, we'll reason with him. 1.04.160 P
you cannot reason (almost) with a man | that 2.03. 39
lord mayor, the reason we have sent — 3.05. 18
while we reason here, | a royal battle might be 4.04.535
great reason why — | lest i revenge. 5.03.185
and let your reason with your choler question H8 1.01.130
if with the sap of reason you would quench, | or 1.01.148
main power, took 'em from me, with this reason: 2.02. 7 P
of their souls | by reason guide his execution. TRO 1.03.210
what merit's in that reason which denies | the 2.02. 24
bear the great sway of his affairs with reason, 2.02. 35
priest, | you fur your gloves with reason. 2.02. 38
and reason flies the object of all harm. 2.02. 41
do set | the very wings of reason to his heels 2.02. 44
nay, if we talk of reason, | /let's shut our 2.02. 46
fat their thoughts | with this cramm'd reason: 2.02. 49
reason and respect | make livers pale and 2.02. 49
so madly hot that no discourse of reason, | nor 2.02.116
and much the reason | why we ascribe it to him; 2.03.116
blind fear, that seeing reason leads, finds 3.02. 71 P
footing than blind reason stumbling without fear 3.02. 72 P
where reason can revolt | without perdition, and 5.02.144
and loss assume all reason | without revolt. 5.02.145
in manacles, | then reason safely with you. COR 1.09. 58
cause, the other | insult without all reason; 3.01.144
reason: 4.05.231 P
but reason with the fellow, | before you punish 4.06. 52
does reason our petition with more strength 5.03.176
to do myself this reason and this right. TIT 1.01.279
great reason that my noble lord be rated | for 2.03. 81
have i not reason, think you, to look pale? 2.03. 91
but yet let reason govern thy lament. 3.01.218
if there were reason for these miseries, | then 3.01.219
and wilt thou have a reason for this coil? 3.01.224
had he not reason, lord demetrius? 4.02. 39
your reason, mighty lord? 5.03. 40
a reason mighty, strong, and effectual, | a 5.03. 43
having no other reason but because thou hast ROM 3.01. 20 P
place, | or reason coldly of your grievances, 3.01. 52
the reason that i have to love thee | doth much 3.01. 62
till thou shalt know the reason of my love, 3.01. 70
now do you know the reason of this haste. 4.01. 15
hold, no reason | can sound his state in safety. TIM 2.01. 12
the reason of this? 2.02.102 P
and one that knows what belongs to reason; 3.01. 36 P
his affections sway'd | more than his reason. JC 2.01. 21
and reason to my love is liable. 2.02.104
and show the reason of our caesar's death. 3.01.237
beasts, | and men have lost their reason. 3.02.105
methinks there is much reason in his sayings. 3.02.108
your reason? 4.03.198
let's reason with the worst that may befall. 5.01. 96
insane root | that takes the reason prisoner? MAC 1.03. 85
and the receipt of reason | a limbeck only. 1.07. 66
of my violent love | outrun the pauser, reason. 2.03.111
have i not reason, beldams as you are? 3.05. 2
where the flight | so runs against all reason. 4.02. 14
you cannot speak of reason to the dane | and HAM 1.02. 44
to reason most absurd, whose common theme | is 1.02.103
o god, a beast, that wants discourse of reason, 1.02.150
oft breaking down the pales and forts of reason, 1.04. 28
which might deprive your sovereignty of reason, 1.04. 73
and be not from his reason fall'n thereon, | let 2.02.165
hits on, which reason and /sanity could not so 2.02.210 P
how noble in reason! 2.02.304 P
now see /that noble and most sovereign reason, 3.01.157
actively doth burn, | and reason /panders will. 3.04. 88
that capability and godlike reason | to fust in 4.04. 38
excitements of my reason and my blood, | and let 4.04. 58
sir, | what is the reason that you use me thus? 5.01.289
must be a faith that reason without miracle LR 1.01.222
wisdom of nature can reason it thus and thus, 1.02.105 P
the reason why the seven stars are no moe than 1.05. 34 P
stars are no moe than seven is a pretty reason. 1.05. 36 P
i know what reason | i have to think so. 2.04.129
for those that mingle reason with your passion 2.04.234
o, reason not the need! 2.04.264
he has some reason, else he could not beg. 4.01. 31
reason in madness! 4.06.175
my reason all the same, and they are ready 5.03. 52
stay yet, hear reason. 5.03. 82
what is the reason of this terrible summons? OTH 1.01. 82
with such loud reason to the cyprus wars 1.01.150
this cannot be | by no assay of reason; 1.03. 18
had not one scale of reason to poise another of 1.03.327 P
but we have reason to cool our raging motions, 1.03.330 P
thine hath no less reason. 1.03.367 P
and yet his trespass, in our common reason 3.03. 64
for now i shall have reason | to show the love 3.03.193
give me a living reason she's disloyal. 3.03.409
which i have greater reason to believe now than 4.02.213 P
is it within reason and compass? 4.02.218 P
i will hear further reason for this. 4.02.244 P
if you can, your reason? ANT 2.03. 13
though my reason | sits in the wind against me. 3.10. 35
that would make his will | lord of his reason. 3.13. 4
when valor /preys /on reason, | it eats the 3.13.198
late, for that's the reason i was up so early. CYM 2.03. 34 P
i am not very sick, | since i can reason of it. 4.02. 14
heard you say, | love's reason's without reason. 4.02. 22
but in all safe reason | he must have some 4.02.131
to th' east, | my father hath a reason for't. 4.02.256
no reason i, since of your lives you set | so 4.04. 48
it fits thee not | to ask the reason why, PER 1.01.157
now do i see he had some reason for't; 1.03. 7 P
we have no reason to desire it, | commended to 1.03. 36
her reason to herself is only known, | which 2.05. 5
my commission | is not to reason of the deed, 4.01. 83
and reason has no manners | to say it is not you TNK 1.03. 48
in will | /o'er–wrastling strength in reason. 1.04. 45
what the reason of it is, i know not. 2.01. 47 P
i love him beyond love and beyond reason, | or 2.06. 11
a cuff, my stomach | not reconcil'd by reason. 3.01.105
in your anger, | your reason will not hold it. 3.06.228
i am a fool, my reason is lost in me; 4.02. 34
planting oblivion, beating reason back, VEN 557
me go, | you have no reason to withhold me so." 612
"now of this dark night i perceive the reason: 727
when reason is the bawd to lust's abuse. 792
respect and reason, wait on wrinkled age! LUC 275
chin, | the reason of this rash alarm to know, 473
but as reproof and reason beat it dead, | by thy 489
thou that spurn'st at right, at law, at reason, 880
strike, | let reason rule things worthy blame, PP 18. 3
reason, in itself confounded, | saw division PHT 41
love hath reason, reason none, | if what parts, 47
love hath reason, reason none, | if what parts, 47
yet then my judgment knew no reason why | my SON 115. 3
past reason hunted, and no sooner had, | past 129. 6
past reason hated as a swallowed bait | on 129. 7
my reason, the physician to my love, | angry 147. 5
past cure i am, now reason is past care, | and 147. 9
flesh stays no farther reason, | but, rising at 151. 8
all replication prompt and reason strong, | for LC 122
though reason weep and cry, 'it is thy last.' 168
even there resolv'd my reason into tears, 296

REASONABLE 19 FR 0.0021 REL FR 6 V 13 P
will shortly fill the reasonable /shores | that TMP 5.01. 81
ay, sir, you shall find me reasonable. WIV 1.01.210 P
i will marry her upon any reasonable demands. 1.01.226 P
if he be of any reasonable stature, he may creep 3.03.130 P
intelligence is true, my jealousy is reasonable. 4.02.149 P
he hath left to be known a reasonable creature. ADO 1.01. 71 P
i have a reasonable good ear in music. MND 4.01. 28 P
am glad this parcel of wooers are so reasonable, MV 1.02.109 P
old, cuckoldly ram, out of all reasonable match. AYL 3.02. 83 P
father grown incapable | of reasonable affairs? WT 4.04.398
(who wants but something to be a reasonable man) 4.04.605 P
my reasonable part produces reason | how i may JN 3.04. 54
of all compass, out of all reasonable compass, 1H4 3.03. 22 P
and my pension shall seem the more reasonable. 2H4 1.02.247 P
upon | that may with reasonable swiftness add H5 1.02.306
hath been very great, reasonable great. 3.06. 99 P
measure, yet a reasonable measure in strength. 5.02.135 P
your purpose is both good and reasonable; 1H6 5.01. 36
it is a quarrel just and reasonable, | to be R3 1.02.136

REASONABLY 2 FR 0.0002 REL FR 2 V 0 P
may reasonably die, and never rise | to do him 1H4 1.03. 74
by mine own | i may be reasonably conceiv'd; TNK 1.02. 48

REASON'D 3 FR 0.0003 REL FR 2 V 1 P
rightly reason'd, and in his own division, and, ADO 5.01.224 P
i reason'd with a frenchman yesterday, | who MV 2.08. 27
why is this reason'd? LR 5.01. 28

REASONING 2 FR 0.0002 REL FR 0 V 2 P
what are you reasoning with yourself? TGV 2.01.141 P
but this reasoning is not in the fashion to MV 1.02. 21 P

REASONLESS 2 FR 0.0002 REL FR 2 V 0 P
that makes me, reasonless, to reason thus? TGV 2.04.198
this proffer is absurd and reasonless. 1H6 5.04.137

REASON'S 6 FR 0.0006 REL FR 6 V 0 P
and that hath dazzled my reason's light; TGV 2.04.210
his requests so far | from reason's yielding, LLL 2.01.150
oil and fire, too strong for reason's force, AWW 5.03. 7
yet nature's tears are reason's merriment. ROM 4.05. 83
heard you say, | love's reason's without reason. CYM 4.02. 22
my will is strong, past reason's weak removing: LUC 243

REASONS 67 FR 0.0075 REL FR 56 V 11 P
there is reasons and causes for it. WIV 3.01. 48 P
moe reasons for this action | at our more MM 1.03. 48
shall ne'er weigh more reasons in her balance. ADO 5.01.207 P
your reasons at dinner have been sharp and LLL 5.01. 2 P
his reasons are as two grains of wheat hid in MV 1.01.115 P
come, lame me with reasons. AYL 1.03. 6 P
should be lam'd with reasons and the other mad 1.03. 8 P
sufficeth my reasons are both good and weighty. SHR 1.01.248
madam, i have other holy reasons, such as they AWW 1.03. 32 P
you heard | the fundamental reasons of this war, 3.01. 2
lord, | the reasons of our state i cannot yield, 3.01. 10
my reasons are most strong, and you shall know 4.02. 59
way to–morrow, | i'll give him reasons for't. TN 1.05.306
do not extort thy reasons from this clause, 3.01.153
but for some other reasons, my grave sir, WT 4.04.411
strong reasons makes strange actions. JN 3.04.182
some reasons of this double coronation | i have 4.02. 40
which for some reasons i would not have seen. R2 5.02. 62
which for some reasons, sir, i mean to see. 5.02. 63
lay him down such reasons for this adventure 1H4 1.02.150 P
for divers reasons | which i shall send you 1.03.262
if reasons were as plentiful as blackberries, i 2.04.239 P
but many thousand reasons hold me back. 2H4 2.03. 66
for your own reasons turn into your bosoms, | as H5 2.02. 82
most of all these reasons bindeth us | in our 1H6 5.05. 60
which fear, if better reasons can supplant, | i 2H6 3.01. 37
as humphrey, prov'd by reasons, to my liege. 3.01.260
but i have reasons strong and forcible. 3H6 1.02. 3
for divers unknown reasons, i beseech you, R3 1.02.217
with what a sharp–provided wit he reasons! 3.01.132
thou know'st our reasons urg'd upon the way; 3.01.160
encourage him, and tell him all our reasons; 3.01.175
your reasons are too shallow and too quick. 4.04.361
o no, my reasons are too deep and dead — | too 4.04.362
alleged | many sharp reasons to defeat the law. H8 2.01. 14
the sharp thorny points | of my alleged reasons, 2.04.226
fell mischiefs | our reasons laid before him, 5.01. 50
and inches so diminutive | as fears and reasons? TRO 2.02. 32
no marvel though you bite so sharp /at reasons, 2.02. 33
here are your reasons: 2.02. 38
the reasons you allege do more conduce | to the 2.02.168
of this my privacy | i have strong reasons. 3.03.191
the reasons are more potent and heroical. 3.03.192
i'll give my reasons, | more worthier than their COR 3.01.119
rages and revenges with | your colder reasons. 5.03. 86
will move him more | than can our reasons. 5.03.158
shall bury | his reasons with his body. 5.06. 58
"these are their reasons, they are natural"; JC 1.03. 30
he loves me well, and i have given him reasons; 2.01.219
this hope, that you shall give me reasons | why, 3.01.221

our reasons are so full of good regard | that 3.01.224
and public reasons shall be rendered | of 3.02. 7
i will hear cassius, and compare their reasons, 3.02. 9
and will no doubt with reasons answer you. 3.02.215
good reasons must of force give place to better: 4.03.203
the common eye | for sundry weighty reasons. MAC 3.01.125
o, for two special reasons, | which may to you, HAM 4.07. 9
larded with many several sorts of reasons, 5.02. 20
and thereto add such reasons of your own | as LR 1.04.338
and yet he hath given me satisfying reasons. OTH 5.01. 9
she has me her quirks, her reasons, her master PER 4.06. 8 P
her reasons, her master reasons, her prayers, 4.06. 8 P
our reasons are not prophets | when oft our TNK 5.03.102
with self–same hand, self reasons, and self STM II.C 85
was | shall reasons find of settled gravity — SON 49. 8
to guard the lawful reasons on thy part: 49.12
halt, | against thy reasons making no defense. 89. 4

REAVE 2 FR 0.0002 REL FR 2 V 0 P
had you that craft to reave her | of what should AWW 5.03. 86
to reave the orphan of his patrimony, | to wring 2H6 5.01.187

REAVES 1 FR 0.0001 REL FR 1 V 0 P
or butcher sire that reaves his son of life: VEN 766

REBATE 1 FR 0.0001 REL FR 1 V 0 P
but doth rebate and blunt his natural edge MM 1.04. 60

REBATO 1 FR 0.0001 REL FR 0 V 1 P
troth, i think your other rebato were better. ADO 3.04. 6 P

REBECK 1 FR 0.0001 REL FR 0 V 1 P
/pretty! what say you, hugh rebeck? ROM 4.05.133 P

/REBEL 1 FR 0.0001 REL FR 1 V 0 P
you, | or let a /rebel lead you to your deaths? 2H6 4.08. 13

REBEL 23 FR 0.0026 REL FR 22 V 1 P
my own flesh and blood to rebel! MV 3.01. 34 P
will, | what is she but a foul contending rebel, SHR 5.02.159
both young and old rebel, | and all goes worse R2 3.02.119
then i see | a very valiant rebel of the name. 1H4 5.04. 62
a famous rebel art thou, colevile. 2H4 4.03. 63
if any rebel or vain spirit of mine | did with 4.05.171
provok'd | to willful disobedience, and rebel! 1H6 4.01.142
and fight against that monstrous rebel cade, 2H6 5.01. 62
my lords, look where the sturdy rebel sits, 3H6 1.01. 50
arm of mine hath chastised | the petty rebel, R3 4.04.332
to think that caesar bears such rebel blood JC 3.01. 40
merciless macdonwald | (worthy to be a rebel, MAC 1.02. 10
or did line the rebel | with hidden help and 1.03.112
that in the natures of their lords rebel, LR 2.02. 76
present pleasure, | and so rebel to judgment. ANT 1.04. 33
upon me, | that life, a very rebel to my will, 4.09. 14
cause, | and not to be a rebel to her state; PER 2.05. 62
what rebel captain, | as mutines are incident, STM II.C 114
when there is no addition but a rebel | to II.C 118
is no addition but a rebel | to qualify a rebel? II.C 119
from a pure heart command thy rebel will; LUC 625
decays, | the guilty rebel for remission prays. 714
/... these rebel pow'rs that thee array, | why SON 146. 2

REBELL'D 2 FR 0.0002 REL FR 2 V 0 P
to the disposing of it nought rebell'd, | order H8 1.01. 43
the body's members | rebell'd against the belly; COR 1.01. 97

//REBEL–LIKE 1 FR 0.0001 REL FR 1 V 0 P
/over /her /passion, /who, /most //rebel–like, LR 4.03. 14

REBELLING 1 FR 0.0001 REL FR 1 V 0 P
sky–planted, batters all rebelling coasts? CYM 5.04. 96

/REBELLION 2 FR 0.0002 REL FR 2 V 0 P
/for /that /same /word, /rebellion, /did /divide 2H4 1.01.194
/this /word, /rebellion, /it /had /froze /them 1.01.199

REBELLION 28 FR 0.0031 REL FR 24 V 4 P
for the rebellion of a codpiece to take away the MM 3.02.115 P
now, god delay our rebellion! AWW 4.03. 19 P
your majesty to make it | natural rebellion, 5.03. 6
one | who, in rebellion with himself, will have WT 1.02.355
thy first, | is in thyself rebellion to thyself; JN 3.01.289
rebellion, flat rebellion! 3.01.298
rebellion, flat rebellion! 3.01.298
unthread the rude eye of rebellion, | and 5.04. 11
in gross rebellion and detested treason. R2 2.03.109
kind | cherish rebellion and are rebels all. 2.03.147
rebellion lay in his way, and he found it. 1H4 5.01. 28 P
to face the garment of rebellion | with some 5.01. 74
thus ever did rebellion find rebuke. 5.05. 1
rebellion in this land shall lose his sway, 5.05. 41
quenching the flame of bold rebellion | even 2H4 in 26
he told me that rebellion had bad luck, | and 1.01. 41
that rebellion | had met ill luck? 1.01. 50
than the name of rebellion can tell how to make 1.02. 77 P
if that rebellion | came like itself, in base 4.01. 32
book | of forg'd rebellion with a seal divine. 4.01. 92
meet for rebellion /and /such /acts /as /yours. 4.02.117
bringing rebellion broached on his sword, | how H5 5.pr. 32
'twas by rebellion against his king. 3H6 1.01.133
loyalty, and almost appears | in loud rebellion. H8 1.02. 29
of this most wise rebellion, thou goest foremost COR 1.01.158
'gainst our senate | the cockle of rebellion, 3.01. 70
in a rebellion, | when what's not meet, but what 3.01.166
that thy rebellion looks so giant–like? HAM 4.05.122

REBELLION'S 1 FR 0.0001 REL FR 1 V 0 P
king | shall falter under foul rebellion's arms. R2 3.02. 26

REBELLIOUS 11 FR 0.0012 REL FR 11 V 0 P
apply | hot and rebellious liquors in my blood, AYL 2.03. 49
if this rebellious earth | have any resting for R2 5.01. 5
with which he yoketh your rebellious necks, 1H6 2.03. 64
nor be rebellious to the crown of england, 5.04.171
rebellious hinds, the filth and scum of kent, 2H6 4.02.122
rebellious subjects, enemies to peace, ROM 1.01. 81
point against point, rebellious arm 'gainst arm, MAC 1.02. 56
rebellious dead, rise never till the wood | of 4.01. 97
rebellious to his arm, lies where it falls, HAM 2.02.470
rebellious hell, | if thou canst mutine in a 3.04. 82
rebellious to oppose; TNK 1.02.101

REBEL'S 2 FR 0.0002 REL FR 2 V 0 P
there is not now a rebel's sword unsheath'd, 2H4 4.04. 86
/quarrel smiling, | show'd like a rebel's whore. MAC 1.02. 15

REBELS' 4 FR 0.0004 REL FR 3 V 1 P
on, | and rebels' arms triumph in massacres! 1H4 5.04. 14
of bold rebellion | even with the rebels' blood. 2H4 in 27
makes your grace to the rebels' supplication? 2H6 4.04. 8 P
thy personal venture in the rebels' fight, | his MAC 1.03. 91

REBELS 29 FR 0.0032 REL FR 24 V 5 P
rebels it at these years? MV 3.01. 35 P
now for the rebels which stand out in ireland, R2 1.04. 38
kind | cherish rebellion and are rebels all. 2.03.147
though rebels wound thee with their horses' 3.02. 7
is that the rebels have consum'd with fire | our 5.06. 2
a hundred thousand rebels die in this. 1H4 3.02.160
that douglas and the english rebels met | the 3.02.165
god be thank'd for these rebels, they offend 3.03.191 P
he calls us rebels, traitors, and will scourge 5.02. 39
do not the rebels need soldiers? 2H4 1.02. 74 P
grace says that which his flesh rebels against. 2.04.350 P
cheering a rout of rebels with your drum, 4.02. 9
but for you rebels, look to taste the due | meet 4.02.116
and pause us, till these rebels, now afoot, 4.04. 9
to signify that rebels there are up | and put 2H6 3.01.283
the rebels are in southwark; 4.04. 27
these kentish rebels would be soon appeas'd! 4.04. 42
farewell, my lord, trust not the kentish rebels. 4.04. 57
the tower to defend the city from the rebels. 4.05. 5 P
the rebels have assay'd to win the tower. 4.05. 8
to quell the rebels and their complices. 5.01.212
yet that, by you depos'd, you quake like rebels? R3 1.03.161
safe–conducting the rebels from their ships? 4.04.482
hour more competitors | flock to the rebels, and 4.04.505
yet to beat down these rebels here at home. 4.04.530
think thy slave man rebels, and by thy virtue TIM 4.03.390
youth to itself rebels, though none else near. HAM 1.03. 44
and sweating devil here | that commonly rebels. OTH 3.04. 43
that you like rebels lift against the peace STM II.C 109

REBOUND 1 FR 0.0001 REL FR 1 V 0 P
by the rebound of yours, a grief that /smites ANT 5.02.104

REBUKABLE 1 FR 0.0001 REL FR 1 V 0 P
rebukable | and worthy shameful check it were, ANT 4.04. 30

REBUK'D 3 FR 0.0003 REL FR 2 V 1 P
tell him we could have rebuk'd him at harflew, H5 3.06.121 P
and under him | my genius is rebuk'd, as it is MAC 3.01. 55
so i return rebuk'd to my content, | and gain by SON 119.13

REBUKE 20 FR 0.0022 REL FR 17 V 3 P
rebuke me not for that which you provoke: LLL 5.02.347
o, why rebuke you him that loves you so? MND 3.02. 43
does not the stone rebuke me | for being more WT 5.03. 37
and to rebuke the usurpation | of thy unnatural JN 2.01. 9
yield, | rebuke and dread correction wait on us, 1H4 5.01.111
thus ever did rebellion find rebuke. 5.05. 1
i never knew yet but rebuke and check was the 2H4 4.03. 31 P
i had forestall'd this dear and deep rebuke 4.05.140
rate, rebuke, and roughly send to prison | th' 5.02. 70
days, | to sin's rebuke and my creator's praise. 3H6 4.06. 44
for living murmurers | there's places of rebuke. H8 2.02.131
pluck reproof and rebuke from every ear that COR 2.02. 33 P
more pertinent | than the rebuke you give it. 2.02. 64
receives rebuke from norway, and, in fine, HAM 2.02. 69
my manners tell me | we have your wrong rebuke. OTH 1.01.130
arm, the best of you | shall sink in my rebuke. 2.03.209
a good rebuke, | which might have well becom'd ANT 3.07. 25
the gods rebuke me, but it is tidings | to wash 5.01. 27
the god of this great vast, rebuke these surges, PER 3.01. 1
gives it so sweet a rebuke that i could wish TNK 2.01. 43 P

REBUKES 4 FR 0.0004 REL FR 4 V 0 P
against all checks, rebukes, and manners, | i WIV 3.04. 80
why bear you these rebukes, and answer not? ERR 5.01. 89
not gaunt's rebukes, nor england's private R2 2.01.166
so tender of rebukes that words are /strokes, CYM 3.05. 40

REBUS'D 1 FR 0.0001 REL FR 0 V 1 P
is there any man has rebus'd your worship? SHR 1.02. 7 P

RECALL 3 FR 0.0003 REL FR 3 V 0 P
new woo my queen, recall the good camillo, WT 3.02.156
or blood–consuming sighs recall his life, | i 2H6 3.02. 61
we here below | recall not what we give, and PER 3.01. 25

RECALL'D 4 FR 0.0004 REL FR 4 V 0 P
and let them be recall'd from their exile; TGV 5.04.155
and passed sentence may not be recall'd | but to ERR 1.01.147
if henry were recall'd to life again, | these 1H6 1.01. 66
(in rage sent out, recall'd in rage, being past) LUC 1671

RECANT 1 FR 0.0001 REL FR 1 V 0 P
or else i do recant | the pardon that i late MV 4.01.391

RECANTATION 2 FR 0.0002 REL FR 0 V 2 P
and master did well to make his recantation. AWW 2.03.187 P
recantation? my lord? my master? 2.03.188 P

RECANTER 1 FR 0.0001 REL FR 1 V 0 P
which doth seldom | play the recanter, feeling TIM 5.01.146

RECANTING 2 FR 0.0002 REL FR 2 V 0 P
tear | the slavish motive of recanting fear, R2 1.01.193
recanting goodness, sorry ere 'tis shown; TIM 1.02. 17

RECEIPT 13 FR 0.0014 REL FR 11 V 2 P
villain, thou didst deny the gold's receipt, ERR 2.02. 17
wife | disburse the sum on the receipt thereof. 4.01. 38
in so unseeming to confess receipt | of that LLL 2.01.155
that at the receipt of your letter i am very MV 4.01.151 P
that his good receipt | shall for my legacy be AWW 1.03.244
three parts of that receipt i had for callice R2 1.01.126
we have the receipt of fern–seed, we walk 1H4 2.01. 87 P
for such receipt of learning is black–friars; H8 2.02.138
the mutinous parts | that envied his receipt; COR 1.01.112
it, | that romeo should, upon receipt thereof, ROM 3.05. 98
and the receipt of reason | a limbeck only. MAC 1.07. 66
drunken desire must vomit his receipt | ere he LUC 703
in things of great receipt with ease we prove SON 136. 7

RECEIPTS 1 FR 0.0001 REL FR 1 V 0 P
on 's bed of death | many receipts he gave me; AWW 2.01.105

RECEIV'D 76 FR 0.0086 REL FR 56 V 20 P
of whom i have | receiv'd a second life; TMP 5.01.195
i have receiv'd my proportion, like the TGV 2.03. 3 P
but she receiv'd my dog? 4.04. 51 P
marry, she hath receiv'd your letter — for the WIV 2.02. 81 P
meed, i am sure, i have receiv'd none, unless 2.02.204 P
have you receiv'd no promise of satisfaction at 2.02.209 P
belike having receiv'd wrong by some person, is 3.01. 53 P
i have receiv'd from her another ambassy of 3.05.129 P
eld | receiv'd and did deliver to our age | this 4.04. 37
grossness of the foppery into a receiv'd belief, 5.05.125 P
it in the common ear, | and so it is receiv'd. MM 1.03. 16
professes to have receiv'd no sinister measure 3.02.242 P
you receiv'd no gold? ERR 2.02. 9
and, gentle master, i receiv'd no gold; 4.04. 98
that i this day of him receiv'd the chain, 5.01.228
this purse of ducats i receiv'd from you, | and 5.01.385
that he had receiv'd a thousand ducats of don ADO 4.02. 47 P
receiv'd that sum, yet there remains unpaid | a LLL 2.01.133
but here without you shall be so receiv'd | as 2.01.172
we have receiv'd your letters full of love; 5.02.777
not that, i hope, which you receiv'd of me. MV 5.01.185
the gift doth stretch itself as 'tis receiv'd, AWW 2.01. 4
under the influence of the most receiv'd star, 2.01. 55 P
but women were that had receiv'd so much shame, 4.03.327 P
shall (as i express it) | be so receiv'd. WT 3.02. 28
ancient'st order was, | or what is now receiv'd. 4.01. 11
offend me more than the stripes i have receiv'd, 4.03. 57 P
london hath receiv'd, | like a kind host, the JN 5.01. 31
that mowbray hath receiv'd eight thousand nobles R2 1.01. 88
but ere i last receiv'd the sacrament | i did 1.01.139
receiv'd intelligence | that harry duke of 2.01.278
i must acquaint you that i have receiv'd 2H4 4.01. 7
how did this offer seem receiv'd, my lord? H5 1.01. 82
receiv'd the golden earnest of our death; 2.02.169
the fairest queen that ever king receiv'd. 2H6 1.01. 16
receiv'd deep scars in france and normandy? 1.01. 87
within this half hour, hath receiv'd his sight, 2.01. 62
the sea receiv'd it, | and so i wish'd thy body 3.02.108
for strokes receiv'd and many blows repaid 3H6 2.03. 3
and i, who at his hands receiv'd my life, | have 2.05. 67
i have this day receiv'd a traitor's judgment, H8 2.01. 58
my conscience first receiv'd a tenderness, 2.04.171
with all his covent honorably receiv'd him; 4.02. 19
i have receiv'd much honor by your presence, 5.04. 71
he receiv'd in the repulse of tarquin seven COR 2.01.149 P
from whom i have receiv'd not only greetings, 2.01.197
as if i had receiv'd them for the hire | of 2.02.149
you have receiv'd many wounds for your country. 2.03.106 P
marks of merit, wounds receiv'd for 's country. 2.03.164
bend like his | that hath receiv'd an alms! 3.02.120
the romans, | "this we receiv'd"; 5.03.138
deer | that hath receiv'd some unrecuring wound. TIT 3.01. 90
i'll hunt with him, and let them be receiv'd, TIM 1.02.190
i have receiv'd some small kindnesses from him, 3.02. 20 P
hands from whom | you have receiv'd your grief; 5.04. 24
a word, lucilius, | how he receiv'd you; JC 4.02. 14
the king hath happily receiv'd, macbeth, | the MAC 1.03. 89
will it not be receiv'd, | when we have mark'd 1.07. 74
and is receiv'd | of the most pious edward with 3.06. 26
but how hath she | receiv'd his love? HAM 2.02.129
but it was — as i receiv'd it, and others, 2.02.437 P
he receiv'd them | of him that brought them. 4.07. 40
lord, who hath receiv'd you | at fortune's alms. LR 1.01.277
his practice, and receiv'd | this hurt you see, 2.01.107
i have receiv'd a letter this night — 'tis 3.03. 10 P
i have receiv'd a hurt; 3.07. 95
receiv'd | from him that fled some strange OTH 2.03.244
had thought you had receiv'd some bodily wound; 2.03.267 P
pray you let cassio be receiv'd again. 3.04. 88
told me she hath receiv'd them and return'd me 4.02.188 P
in fulvia's death, how mine receiv'd shall be. ANT 1.03. 65
it, and have now receiv'd | his accusations. 3.06. 22
since i receiv'd command to do this business | i CYM 3.04. 99
confiscate all, so soon | as i have receiv'd it. 5.05.324
having receiv'd the punishment before | for that 5.05.343
i have receiv'd from many a several fair, LC 206

RECEIVE 99 FR 0.0112 REL FR 82 V 17 P
being in the way, | did in your name receive it; TGV 1.02. 40
and once again i do receive thee honest. 5.04. 78
at, and i shall not only receive this villainous WIV 2.02.294 P
enter, | and there receive her approbation. MM 1.02.178
he should receive his punishment in thanks: 1.04. 28
denial which he is most glad to receive. 3.01.166 P
i would be glad to receive some instruction from 4.02. 17 P
you, | and then receive my money for the chain. ERR 3.02.175
i pray you, sir, receive the money now, | for 3.02.176
clock | i shall receive the money for the same: 4.01. 11
i owe you none, till i receive the chain. 4.01. 64
sent to thee, to receive the meed of punishment, LLL 1.01.266 P
mean time receive such welcome at my hand | as 2.01.168
eyes | i did receive fair speechless messages. MV 1.01.164
leave, | i come by note, to give and to receive. 3.02.140
have | a weight of carrion flesh than to receive 4.01. 41
if they will patiently receive my medicine. AYL 2.07. 61
you, yours, orlando, to receive his daughter; 5.04. 20
good duke, receive thy daughter, | hymen from 5.04.111
we here receive it | a certainty, vouch'd from AWW 1.02. 4
tender your supposed aid, | he would receive it? 1.03.237
our hearts receive your warnings. 2.01. 22
a second time receive | the confirmation of my 2.03. 49
my wish receive, | which great love grant, and 2.03. 84
and would never | receive the ring again. 5.03.101
receive it so. TN 2.02. 11 P
(as i know his youth will aptly receive it) into 3.04.193 P
what old or newer torture | must i receive, WT 3.02.178
do not receive affliction | at my petition; 3.02.223
which i receive much better | than to be pitied 3.02.233
receive thy lance, and god defend the right! R2 1.03.101
could the noble mortimer | receive so many, and 1H4 1.03.111
and there receive | money and order for their 3.03.201
says he, "receive those that are civil, for," 2H4 2.04. 89 P
on, therefore take heed what guests you receive. 2.04. 93 P
receive," says he, "no swaggering companions." 2.04. 93 P
i shall receive money a' thursday, shalt have a 2.04.274 P
that the fix'd sentinels almost receive | the H5 4.pr. 6
french, french englishmen, | receive each other. 5.02.368
if thou receive me for thy warlike mate. 1H6 1.02. 92
you shall first receive | the sum of money which 5.01. 51
where reignier sooner will receive than give. 5.05. 47
receive the sentence of the law for /sins | such 2H6 2.03. 3
it | as others would ambitiously receive it. 2.03. 36
thou didst receive the sacrament to fight | in R3 1.04.203
and here receive we from our father stanley 5.02. 5
and pray receive 'em nobly and conduct 'em H8 1.04. 58
me, | this from a dying man receive as certain: 2.01.125
of your soft cheveril conscience would receive 2.03. 32
receive him, | and see him safe i' th' tower. 5.02.131
what he shall receive of us in duty | gives us TRO 3.01.156
ay, and perhaps receive much honor by him. 3.03.226
in kissing, do you render or receive? 4.05. 36
he, | "that i receive the general food at first COR 1.01.131
veins | from me receive that natural competency 1.01.139
all | from me do back receive the flour of all, 1.01.145
no public benefit which you receive | but it 1.01.152
for the nobles receive so to heart the 4.03. 21 P

receive them then, the tribute that i owe, TIT 1.01.251
receive him then to favor, saturnine, | that 1.01.421
they humbly at my feet | receive my tears, and 3.01. 42
receive the blood, and when that they are dead, 5.02.197
let him receive no sust'nance; 5.03. 6
both | receive in either by this dear encounter. ROM 2.06. 29
with more than common thanks i will receive it. TIM 1.02.208
temper, do receive you in | with all kind love, JC 3.01.175
he did receive his letters, and is coming, | and 3.01.279
death, shall receive the benefit of his dying, a 3.02. 42 P
your highness' part | is to receive our duties; MAC 1.04. 24
who dares receive it other, | as we shall make 1.07. 77
whereby he does receive | particular addition, 3.01. 98
do faithful homage and receive free honors; 3.06. 36
receive what cheer you may, | the night is long 4.03.239
to receive at once the benefit of sleep and do 5.01. 9 P
your visitation shall receive such thanks | as HAM 2.02. 25
admit no messengers, receive no tokens. 2.02.144
the players shall receive from you. 2.02.316 P
did he receive you well? 3.01. 10
i pray you now receive them. 3.01. 94
i will receive it, sir, with all diligence of 5.02. 91 P
time | i do receive your offer'd love like love, 5.02.251
we look from his age to receive not alone the LR 1.01.296 P
my sister may receive it much more worse | to 2.02.148
receive attendance | from those that she calls 2.04.243
for his particular, i'll receive him gladly, 2.04.292
let's meet him and receive him. OTH 2.01.180
therefore, as i am bound, | receive it from me. 3.03.196
we must receive him | according to the honor of CYM 2.03. 57
receive it from me then: 3.01. 65
receive it friendly; 3.05. 13
must or for britains slay us or receive us | for 4.04. 5
either expound now, or receive your sentence. PER 1.01. 90
that thou wouldst tremble to receive thyself. 1.02. 69
will do graciously, i will thankfully receive. 4.06. 61 P
thy sacred physic shall receive such pay | as 5.01. 74
you shall receive all dues | fit for the honor TNK 2.05. 60
receive you her, you him, be plighted with | a 5.03.110
to trust those tables that receive thee more: SON 122.12
playing the place which did no form receive, LC 241

/RECEIVED 1 FR 0.0001 REL FR 1 V 0 P
/lear /and /him | /that /ever /ear /received, LR 5.03.216

RECEIVED 7 FR 0.0008 REL FR 7 V 0 P
to be received plain, i'll speak more gross: MM 2.04. 82
more, i have received | a certain instance that 2H4 3.01.102
and be received for the emperor's heir, | and TIT 4.02.158
i have received letters from great rome | which 5.01. 2
first man | that e'er received gift from him; TIM 3.03. 17
i have here received letters | that young JC 4.03.167
you have at large received | the danger of the PER 1.01. 1

RECEIVER 1 FR 0.0001 REL FR 1 V 0 P
that his time | could make him the receiver of, CYM 1.01. 44

RECEIVES 16 FR 0.0018 REL FR 13 V 3 P
he receives comfort like cold porridge. TMP 2.01. 10 P
what maintenance he from his friends receives, TGV 1.03. 68
for he this very day receives letters of strange MM 4.02.200 P
the queen receives | much comfort in't; WT 2.02. 25
receives not thy nose court–odor from me? 4.04.733 P
what heart receives from hence a conquering part TRO 1.03.352
receives and renders back | his figure and his 3.03.122
the basin that receives your guilty blood. TIT 5.02.183
none | can truly say he gives if he receives. TIM 1.02. 11
receives rebuke from norway, and, in fine, HAM 2.02. 69
his tend'rer cheek receives her soft hand's VEN 353
eye | receives the scroll without or yea or no, LUC 1340
thence comes it that my name receives a brand, SON 111. 5
when not to be receives reproach of being, | and 121. 2
the sea, all water, yet receives rain still, 135. 9
applied to cautels, all strange forms receives, LC 303

RECEIVEST 2 FR 0.0002 REL FR 2 V 0 P
thou receivest | thy full petition at the hand JC 2.01. 57
then if for my love thou my love receivest, | i SON 40. 5

RECEIVE'T 2 FR 0.0002 REL FR 2 V 0 P
why, let the war receive't in valiant gore, TIM 3.05. 83
follow me, and receive't. ANT 2.03. 43

RECEIVETH 1 FR 0.0001 REL FR 1 V 0 P
thy capacity | receiveth as the sea, nought TN 1.01. 11

RECEIVING 7 FR 0.0008 REL FR 6 V 1 P
receiving them from such a worthless post. TGV 1.01.153
by so receiving a dishonor'd life | with ransom MM 4.04. 31
to one of your receiving | enough is shown; TN 3.01.120
point you where you shall have such receiving WT 4.04.526
their proud hoofs i' th' receiving earth; H5 pr 27
of opening my lips and receiving the bad air. JC 1.02.250 P
receiving /nought by elements so slow | but SON 44.13

RECEIV'ST 2 FR 0.0002 REL FR 2 V 0 P
thou that which thou receiv'st not gladly, | or SON 8. 3
or else receiv'st with pleasure thine annoy? 8. 4

RECEPTACLE 3 FR 0.0003 REL FR 3 V 0 P
o sacred receptacle of my joys, | sweet cell of TIT 1.01. 92
hath — | out of this fell devouring receptacle, 2.03.235
place — | as in a vault, an ancient receptacle, ROM 4.03. 39

RECEPTACLES 1 FR 0.0001 REL FR 1 V 0 P
empty | old receptacles, or common shores, of PER 4.06.175

RECHATE 1 FR 0.0001 REL FR 0 V 1 P
that i will have a rechate winded in my forehead ADO 1.01.240 P

RECIPROCAL 1 FR 0.0001 REL FR 0 V 1 P
"let our reciprocal vows be rememb'red. LR 4.06.262 P

RECIPROCALLY 1 FR 0.0001 REL FR 1 V 0 P
infecting one another, yea, reciprocally, | only H8 1.01.162

RECITE 1 FR 0.0001 REL FR 1 V 0 P
lest the world should task you to recite | what SON 72. 1

RECITERAI 2 FR 0.0002 REL FR 0 V 2 P
non, je reciterai a vous promptement: H5 3.04. 44 P
je reciterai une autre fois ma lecon ensemble: 3.04. 57 P

RECKETH *(also reak, etc.)*

RECKETH 1 FR 0.0001 REL FR 1 V 0 P
what recketh he his rider's angry stir, | his VEN 283

RECKLESS *(also reakless)*

RECKLESS 3 FR 0.0003 REL FR 3 V 0 P
eglamour | than for the love of reckless silvia. TGV 5.02. 52
hath so incens'd that i am reckless what | i do MAC 3.01.109
whiles, /like a puff'd and reckless libertine, HAM 1.03. 49

RECK'NING 11 FR 0.0012 REL FR 8 V 3 P
for truth is truth | to th' end of reck'ning. MM 5.01. 46
i am ill at reck'ning, it fitteth the spirit of LLL 1.02. 40 P
pity you should get your living by reck'ning, 5.02.497 P
by this reck'ning he is more shrew than she. SHR 4.01. 85 P
take from them now | the sense of reck'ning, /if H5 4.01.291
may stand in number, though in reck'ning none. ROM 1.02. 33
and at length | how goes our reck'ning? TIM 2.02.150
no reck'ning made, but sent to my account | with HAM 1.05. 78
o weary reck'ning! OTH 3.04.176
informs the tapster to inflame the reck'ning. TNK 3.05.130
reck'ning his fortune at such high proud rate LUC 19

RECK'NINGS 1 FR 0.0001 REL FR 1 V 0 P
here comes other reck'nings. ADO 5.04. 52

RECKON 8 FR 0.0009 REL FR 5 V 3 P
i reckon this always, that a man is never undone TGV 2.05. 4 P
whereof i reckon | the casting forth to crows WT 3.02.190
quarrels enow, if you could tell how to reckon. H5 4.01.224 P
i have no more to reckon, he to spend. TIM 3.04. 56
time | before we reckon with your several loves, MAC 5.09. 27
i have not art to reckon my groans, but that i HAM 2.02.121 P
people, whom we reckon | ourselves to be. CYM 3.01. 52
that level | at my abuses reckon up their own; SON 121.10

RECKON'D 6 FR 0.0006 REL FR 6 V 0 P
maid, | nor no such men as you have reckon'd up, SHR in.2. 92
it, and she reckon'd it | at her live's rate. AWW 5.03. 90
was reckon'd one | the wisest prince that there H8 2.04. 48
beggary in the love that can be reckon'd. ANT 1.01. 15
as 'tis no better reckon'd, but of those | who CYM 3.06. 54
we prove | among a number one is reckon'd none: SON 136. 8

RECKONING 13 FR 0.0014 REL FR 6 V 7 P
to call young claudio to a reckoning for it. ADO 5.04. 9
signs | have brought about the annual reckoning. LLL 5.02.798
dead than a great reckoning in a little room. AYL 3.03. 15 P
call'd her to a reckoning many a time and oft. 1H4 1.02. 49 P
stairs, his eloquence the parcel of a reckoning. 2.04.101 P
in reckoning up the several devils' names | that 3.01.155
or i will tear the reckoning from his heart. 3.02.152
a trim reckoning! 5.01.135 P
the king himself hath a heavy reckoning to make, H5 4.01.135 P
but her brain to set down her reckoning; TRO 3.03.254 P
of honorable reckoning are you both, | and pity ROM 1.02. 4
a heavy reckoning for you, sir. CYM 5.04.157 P
but reckoning time, whose million'd accidents SON 115. 5

RECKONINGS 3 FR 0.0003 REL FR 0 V 3 P
they are both the confirmer of false reckonings. AYL 3.04. 32 P
and his quick wit wasted in giving reckonings; 2H4 1.02.171 P
or the magnanimous, are all one reckonings, save H5 4.07. 17 P

RECLAIM'D 2 FR 0.0002 REL FR 2 V 0 P
that hath reclaim'd | to your obedience fifty 1H6 3.04. 5
since this same wayward girl is so reclaim'd. ROM 4.02. 47

RECLAIMS 1 FR 0.0001 REL FR 1 V 0 P
and beauty, that the tyrant oft reclaims, 2H6 5.02. 54

RECLUSIVE 1 FR 0.0001 REL FR 1 V 0 P
in some reclusive and religious life, | out of ADO 4.01.242

RECOGNIZANCE 1 FR 0.0001 REL FR 1 V 0 P
with that recognizance and pledge of love OTH 5.02.214

RECOGNIZANCES 1 FR 0.0001 REL FR 0 V 1 P
with his statutes, his recognizances, his fines, HAM 5.01.105 P

RECOIL 6 FR 0.0006 REL FR 6 V 0 P
methoughts i did recoil | twenty–three years, WT 1.02.154
of my revenges that way | recoil upon me: 2.03. 20
glass, | or like an overcharged gun, recoil, 2H6 3.02.331
a good and virtuous nature may recoil | in an MAC 4.03. 19
blame | his pester'd senses to recoil and start, 5.02. 23
queen, and you | recoil from your great stock. CYM 1.06.128

RECOILING 1 FR 0.0001 REL FR 1 V 0 P
her will, recoiling to her better judgment, OTH 3.03.236

RECOLLECT 1 FR 0.0001 REL FR 1 V 0 P
and from their wat'ry empire recollect | all PER 2.01. 50

RECOLLECTED 1 FR 0.0001 REL FR 1 V 0 P
more than light airs and recollected terms | of TN 2.04. 5

RECOMFORTED 1 FR 0.0001 REL FR 1 V 0 P
tide, | as the recomforted through th' gates. COR 5.04. 48

RECOMFORTURE 1 FR 0.0001 REL FR 1 V 0 P
selves of themselves, to your recomforture. R3 4.04.425

RECOMMEND 1 FR 0.0001 REL FR 1 V 0 P
we recommend to you, tribunes of the people, COR 2.02.151

RECOMMENDED 1 FR 0.0001 REL FR 1 V 0 P
which i had recommended to his use | not half an TN 5.01. 91

RECOMMENDS 2 FR 0.0002 REL FR 2 V 0 P
nimbly and sweetly recommends itself | unto our MAC 1.06. 2
with his free duty recommends you thus, | and OTH 1.03. 41

RECOMPENS'D 3 FR 0.0003 REL FR 3 V 0 P
such love | could be but recompens'd, though you TN 1.05.253
care | to have them recompens'd as thought on. WT 4.04.520
so shall his father's wrongs be recompens'd. 1H6 3.01.160

RECOMPENSE 30 FR 0.0034 REL FR 25 V 5 P
besides, i'll make a present recompense. WIV 4.06. 55
hereafter, it may compel him to her recompense; MM 3.01.252 P
do not recompense me in making me a cuckold. 5.01.516 P
no, truly, but in friendly recompense. ADO 5.04. 83
ay, that is study's godlike recompense. LLL 1.01. 58
sense, | it pays the hearing double recompense. MND 3.02.180
yet fortune cannot recompense me better | than AYL 2.03. 75
but do not look for further recompense | than 3.05. 97
more truly labor | to recompense your love. AWW 4.04. 18
my master, not myself, lacks recompense. TN 1.05.285
it were a bad recompense for your love, to lay 2.01. 7 P
give a dog and in recompense desire my dog again 5.01. 6 P
in recompense whereof he hath married her. 5.01.364
(as recompense of our dear services | past and WT 2.03.150
he means to recompense the pains you take | by JN 5.04. 15
it shall be still thy true love's recompense. R2 2.03. 49
shall be your love and labor's recompense. 2.03. 62
hence, | then will i think upon a recompense. 1H6 1.02.116
my body shall | pay recompense, if you will 5.03. 19
time prompts me aloud | to call for recompense. TRO 3.03. 3
they know the corn | was not our recompense, COR 3.01.121
"when we for recompense have prais'd the vild, TIM 1.01. 15
our dinner will not recompense this long stay; 3.06. 33 P
together with a recompense more fruitful | than 5.01.150
that swiftest wing of recompense is slow | to MAC 1.04. 17
your recompense is still | that i regard it not. CYM 2.03. 92
my recompense is thanks, that's all, | yet my PER 3.04. 17
bootless toil must recompense itself | with its TNK 1.01.153
think either, | well done, a noble recompense. 3.06. 24
who plead for love and look for recompense SON 23.11

RECOMPT *(also recount)*

RECOMPT 1 FR 0.0001 REL FR 1 V 0 P
if we should recompt | our baleful news, and at 3H6 2.01. 96

RECONCIL'D 9 FR 0.0010 REL FR 7 V 2 P
being reconcil'd to the prince your brother: ADO 1.01.155 P
we are reconcil'd, and the first view shall kill AWW 5.03. 21
(as thou call'st him) and reconcil'd king, my WT 4.02. 23 P
king john hath reconcil'd | himself to rome, his JN 5.02. 69
now york and lancaster are reconcil'd. 3H6 1.01.204
i shall be reconcil'd to him again. R3 1.04.179
that i have reconcil'd your friends and you. TIT 1.01.467
reconcil'd my thoughts | to thy good truth and MAC 4.03.116
a cuff, my stomach | not reconcil'd by reason. TNK 3.01.105

RECONCILE 9 FR 0.0010 REL FR 9 V 0 P
i'll reconcile me to polixenes, | new woo my WT 3.02.155
nor reconcile | this low'ring tempest of your R2 1.03.186
a mean | to reconcile you all unto the king. 2H6 4.08. 69
and i, i hope, shall reconcile them all. 3H6 1.01.273
desire | to reconcile me to his friendly peace. R3 2.01. 60
no, our suit | is that you reconcile them: COR 5.03.136
to blaze your marriage, reconcile your friends, ROM 3.03.151
things at once | 'tis hard to reconcile. MAC 4.03.139
your ears unto your eyes i'll reconcile. PER 4.04. 22

RECONCILED 1 FR 0.0001 REL FR 1 V 0 P
and new pervert a reconciled maid!" LC 329

RECONCILEMENT 1 FR 0.0001 REL FR 1 V 0 P
and will no reconcilement | till by some elder HAM 5.02.247

RECONCILER 1 FR 0.0001 REL FR 1 V 0 P
me most weak, most weak, | /your reconciler! ANT 3.04. 30

/RECONCILES 1 FR 0.0001 REL FR 1 V 0 P
/just /proof /repeals /and /reconciles /thee. LR 3.06.113

RECONCILES 1 FR 0.0001 REL FR 0 V 1 P
reconciles them to his entreaty, and himself to ANT 2.07. 7 P

RECONCILIATION 1 FR 0.0001 REL FR 1 V 0 P
to move you, | his present reconciliation take; OTH 3.03. 47

/RECORD 1 FR 0.0001 REL FR 1 V 0 P
/if /thy /offenses /were /upon /record, | /would R2 4.01.230

RECORD 24 FR 0.0027 REL FR 23 V 1 P
notes | tune my distresses and record my woes. TGV 5.04. 6
to fine the faults whose fine stands in record, MM 2.02. 40
my villainy they have upon record, which i had ADO 5.01.240 P
record it with your high and worthy deeds. 5.01.269
the other, that he do record a gift, | here in MV 4.01.388
o, that record is lively in my soul! TN 5.01.246
first, heaven be the record to my speech, | in R2 1.01. 30
is it upon record, or else reported R3 3.01. 72
upon record, my gracious lord. 3.01. 74
brief abstract and record of tedious days, 4.04. 28
and in record left them the heirs of shame. 5.03.335
whereof we have record, trial did draw | bias TRO 1.03. 14
we have record that very well it can, | and COR 4.06. 50
am of thee and of thy gifts | rome shall record, TIT 1.01.255
strange, | which manifold record not matches? TIM 1.01. 5
when men revolted shall upon record | bear ANT 4.09. 8
instruction got upon me | a nobleness in record; 4.14. 99
the record of what injuries you did us, | though 5.02.118
a sland'rous epitaph | as record of fair act; CYM 3.03. 53
is there record of any two that lov'd | better TNK 2.02.112
so should my shame still rest upon record, | and LUC 1643
shall burn | the living record of your memory. SON 55. 8
o, that record could with a backward look, 59. 5
part | of thee, thy record never can be miss'd. 122. 8

RECORDATION 2 FR 0.0002 REL FR 2 V 0 P
heaven, | for recordation to my noble husband. 2H4 2.03. 61
to make a recordation to my soul | of every TRO 5.02.116

RECORDED 7 FR 0.0008 REL FR 6 V 1 P
i (now the voice of the recorded law) MM 2.04. 61
that are recorded in this schedule here. LLL 1.01. 18
'twill be recorded for a precedent, | and many MV 4.01.220
wherein my soul recorded | the history of all R3 3.05. 27
let me be recorded by the righteous gods, | i am TIM 4.02. 4
to day, | to the last syllable of recorded time; MAC 5.05. 21
fetch my gold and have our two wagers recorded. CYM 1.04.168 P

RECORDER* 2 FR 0.0002 REL FR 1 V 1 P
on this prologue like a child on a recorder — a MND 5.01.123 P
not used | to be spoke to but by the recorder. R3 3.07. 30

RECORDERS 2 FR 0.0002 REL FR 0 V 2 P
come, the recorders! HAM 3.02.292 P
o, the recorders! 3.02.345 P

RECORDS 5 FR 0.0005 REL FR 4 V 1 P
records | england all olivers and rolands bred 1H6 1.02. 29
away, burn all the records of the realm, my 2H6 4.07. 14 P
i'll wipe away all trivial fond records, | all HAM 1.05. 99
mute, | that still records with moan; PER 4.ch. 27
for thy records and what we see doth lie, | made SON 123.11

RECOUNT *(also recompt)*

RECOUNT 12 FR 0.0013 REL FR 8 V 4 P
once in a month recount what thou hast been, TMP 1.02.262
and you shall recount their particular duties ADO 4.01. 2 P
by the world, i recount no fable: LLL 5.01.106 P
that some plain man recount their purposes. 5.02.177
him, | and by the way let's recount our dreams. MND 4.01.199
i prithee recount some of them. AYL 3.02.357 P
bid him recount | the fore–recited practices, H8 1.02.126
by, | and you recount your sorrows to a stone. TIT 3.01. 29
and of these times, | i shall recount hereafter. JC 1.02.165
recount the occasion of my sudden /and /more HAM 4.07. 46 P
sit, sir, i will recount it to you, | but see, i PER 5.01. 63
recount, i do beseech thee. 5.01.141

RECOUNTED 1 FR 0.0001 REL FR 1 V 0 P
when i have heard your king's desert recounted, 3H6 3.03.132

/RECOUNTING 1 FR 0.0001 REL FR 1 V 0 P
/ever /ear /received, /which /in /recounting, LR 5.03.216

RECOUNTING 1 FR 0.0001 REL FR 1 V 0 P
of /thy fair health, recounting it to me. SON 45.12

RECOUNTMENTS 1 FR 0.0001 REL FR 1 V 0 P
tears our recountments had most kindly bath'd, AYL 4.03.140

RECOUNTS 1 FR 0.0001 REL FR 1 V 0 P
recounts most horrid sights seen by the watch. JC 2.02. 16

RECOURSE 4 FR 0.0004 REL FR 3 V 1 P
that no man hath recourse to her by night. TGV 3.01.112
sack to give me recourse to him and tell him my WIV 2.01.215 P
have any time recourse unto the princes. R3 3.05.109
their eyes o'ergalled with recourse of tears, TRO 5.03. 55

RECOVER* 28 FR 0.0031 REL FR 12 V 16 P
if i can recover him, and keep him tame, and get TMP 2.02. 68 P
if i can recover him, and keep him tame, i will 2.02. 76 P
if all the wine in my bottle will recover him, i 2.02. 93 P
i swam, ere i could recover the shore, five and 3.02. 14 P
if we recover that, we are sure enough. TGV 5.01. 12
no time for a man to recover his hair that grows ERR 2.02. 72 P

and recover the lost hair of another man. 2.02. 75 P
/e'en no time to recover hair lost by nature. 2.02.103 P
substantial, why there is no time to recover. 2.02.105 P
with the help of a surgeon he might yet recover, MND 5.01.310 P
if i cannot recover your niece, i am a foul way TN 2.03.184 P
she will recover. WT 3.02.150
king | yet speaks, and peradventure may recover. JN 5.06. 31
recover breath, tell us how near is danger R2 5.03. 47
be sick with joy, he'll recover without physic. 2H4 4.05. 14 P
that so he might recover what was lost. 1H6 2.05. 32
yet to recover them would lose my life. 2H6 4.07. 66
we are, | we might recover all our loss again. 3H6 5.02. 30
will soon recover his accustom'd health. R3 1.03. 2
when they are in great danger, i recover them. JC 1.01. 24 P
but to recover of us, by strong hand | and terms HAM 1.01.102
why do you go about to recover the wind of me, 3.02.346 P
'a shall recover his wits there, or, if 'a do 5.01.150 P
are more ways to recover the general again. OTH 2.03.272 P
a little while, | he will recover straight. 4.01. 57
come on then, he may recover yet. ANT 4.09. 33
that do die of it do seldom or never recover. 5.02.248 P
be minist'red to nature | that can recover him. PER 3.02. 9
RECOVERABLE 1 FR 0.0001 REL FR 1 V 0 P
like the sun's, but not, like his, recoverable, TIM 3.04. 13
RECOVER'D 14 FR 0.0015 REL FR 4 V 10 P
we have here recover'd the most dangerous piece ADO 3.03.167 P
brief, i recover'd him, bound up his wound, AYL 4.03.150
she hath recover'd the king, and undone me. AWW 3.02. 20 P
of that drum, but it is not to be recover'd. 3.06. 57 P
it might have been recover'd. 3.06. 58 P
it is to be recover'd. 3.06. 60 P
i would swear i recover'd it. 4.01. 62 P
kill him whom you have recover'd, desire it not. TN 2.01. 38 P
then recover'd again with aqua–vitae or some WT 4.04.786 P
recover'd is the town of orleance. 1H6 1.06. 9
arms till you had recover'd your ancient freedom 2H6 4.08. 26 P
by what safe means the crown may be recover'd. 3H6 4.07. 52
how came you thus recover'd? OTH 2.03.295 P
which i have /here recover'd from the moor. 5.02.240
RECOVERED 6 FR 0.0006 REL FR 6 V 0 P
lost, and recovered in a day again! 1H6 3.02.115
nor grieve that roan is so recovered: 3.03. 2
dead, | who was by good appliance recovered. PER 3.02. 86
found there rich jewels, recovered her, and 5.03. 24
look, thaisa is | recovered. 5.03. 28
'twas possible | they might have been recovered. TNK 1.04. 27
/RECOVERIES 1 FR 0.0001 REL FR 0 V 1 P
/and /the /recovery /of /his /recoveries, to HAM 5.01.107 P
RECOVERIES 1 FR 0.0001 REL FR 0 V 1 P
his fines, his double vouchers, his recoveries. HAM 5.01.106 P
RECOVERS 3 FR 0.0003 REL FR 3 V 0 P
look, he recovers. AYL 4.03.160
unto my sick desires, | who then recovers. AWW 4.02. 36
speak lower, princes, for the king recovers. 2H4 4.04.129
/RECOVERY 1 FR 0.0001 REL FR 0 V 1 P
/and /the /recovery /of /his /recoveries, to HAM 5.01.106 P
RECOVERY 8 FR 0.0009 REL FR 5 V 3 P
him not in fee–simple, with fine and recovery, WIV 4.02.211 P
may he not do it by fine and recovery? ERR 2.02. 74 P
him fast, | and bear him home for his recovery. 5.01. 41
move me to undertake the recovery of this drum, AWW 4.01. 35 P
for grief that they are past recovery; 2H6 1.01.116
use means for her recovery. 3H6 5.05. 45
that the death–tokens of it | cry "no recovery." TRO 2.03.178
i will use | my utmost skill in his recovery, PER 5.01. 76
RECOVERY'S 1 FR 0.0001 REL FR 1 V 0 P
nothing we'll omit | that bears recovery's name. PER 5.01. 54
RECOV'RY 1 FR 0.0001 REL FR 0 V 1 P
to be made than alone the recov'ry of the king, AWW 2.03. 36 P
RECREANT 14 FR 0.0015 REL FR 14 V 0 P
come, recreant, come, thou child, | i'll whip MND 3.02.409
and hang a calve's–skin on those recreant limbs. JN 3.01.129
and hang a calve's–skin on those recreant limbs. 3.01.131
and hang a calve's–skin on those recreant limbs. 3.01.133
and hang a calve's–skin on his recreant limbs. 3.01.199
a recreant and most degenerate traitor, | which R2 1.01.144
a caitive recreant to my cousin herford! 1.02. 53
on pain to be found false and recreant, | to 1.03.106
on pain to be found false and recreant, | both 1.03.111
puff i' thy teeth, most recreant coward base! 2H4 5.03. 92
and may that soldier a mere recreant prove, TRO 1.03.287
either thou | must as a foreign recreant be led COR 5.03.114
hear me, recreant, | on thine allegiance, hear LR 1.01.166
feeble desire, all recreant, poor, and meek, LUC 710
RECREANTS 2 FR 0.0002 REL FR 1 V 1 P
distrustful recreants, | fight till the last 1H6 1.02.126
but you are all recreants and dastards, and 2H6 4.08. 27 P
RECREATE 2 FR 0.0002 REL FR 2 V 0 P
to walk abroad and recreate yourselves. JC 3.02.251
to recreate himself when he hath song, | the VEN 1095
RECREATION 8 FR 0.0009 REL FR 5 V 3 P
sweet recreation barr'd, what doth ensue | but ERR 5.01. 78
but is there no quick recreation granted? LLL 1.01.161
at their game, and we will to our recreation. 4.02.166 P
and make him a common recreation, do not think i TN 2.03.135 P
and tears shed there | shall be my recreation. WT 3.02.240
that the true prince may (for recreation sake) 1H4 1.02.155 P
most fit | for your best health and recreation. R3 3.01. 67
it is a recreation to be by | and hear him mock CYM 1.06. 75
RECTIFIER 1 FR 0.0001 REL FR 1 V 0 P
and i, that am the rectifier of all, | by title TNK 3.05.109
RECTIFY 3 FR 0.0003 REL FR 3 V 0 P
some oracle | must rectify our knowledge. TMP 5.01.245
as to rectify | what is unsettled in the king. H8 2.04. 63
i meant to rectify my conscience — which | i 2.04.204
RECTOR 1 FR 0.0001 REL FR 0 V 1 P
faithfully confirm'd by the rector of the place. AWW 4.03. 59 P
RECTORSHIP 1 FR 0.0001 REL FR 1 V 0 P
to cry | against the rectorship of judgment? COR 2.03.205
RECURE 1 FR 0.0001 REL FR 1 V 0 P
which to recure, we heartily solicit | your R3 3.07.130
RECURED 1 FR 0.0001 REL FR 1 V 0 P
until live's composition be recured | by those SON 45. 9
RECURES 1 FR 0.0001 REL FR 1 V 0 P
a smile recures the wounding of a frown. VEN 465
RED 96 FR 0.0108 REL FR 79 V 17 P
by this hat, then he in the red face had it; WIV 1.01.170 P
am pale at mine heart to see thine eyes so red; MM 4.03.152 P
look'd he or red or pale, or sad or merrily? ERR 4.02. 4
my love is most immaculate white and red. LLL 1.02. 91 P
if she be made of white and red, | her faults 1.02. 99
master, against the reason of white and red. 1.02.108 P
and therefore red, that would avoid dispraise, 4.03.260
debtor, | my red dominical, my golden letter: 5.02. 44
the snow | and marian's nose looks red and raw; 5.02.924
of color like the red rose on triumphant brier, MND 3.01. 94
even till the eastern gate, all fiery red, 3.02.391
than there is between red wine and rhenish. MV 3.01. 41 P
and the red glow of scorn and proud disdain, AYL 3.04. 54
a little riper and more lusty red | than that 3.05.121
betwixt the constant red and mingled damask. 3.05.123
on the other, gart'red with a red and blue list; SHR 3.02. 68 P
such war of white and red within her cheeks! 4.05. 30
whose red and white | nature's own sweet and TN 1.05.239
as, item, two lips, indifferent red; 1.05.247 P
for the red blood reigns in the winter's pale. WT 4.03. 4
them sprightly, | and let's be red with mirth. 4.04. 54
with eyes as red as new–enkindled fire, | and JN 4.02.163
give me a cup of sack to make my eyes look red, 1H4 2.04.385 P
my lord, through a red lattice, and i could 2H4 2.02. 80 P
i warrant you, is as red as any rose, in good 2.04. 25 P
with red wheat, davy. 5.01. 16 P
sometimes plue and sometimes red, but his nose H5 3.06.105 P
we shall your tawny ground with your red blood 3.06.161
pluck a red rose from off this thorn with me. 1H6 2.04. 33
i pluck this red rose with young somerset, | and 2.04. 37
lest, bleeding, you do paint the white rose red, 2.04. 50
shall dye your white rose in a bloody red. 2.04. 61
shall send between the red rose and the white 2.04.126
red, master, red as blood. 2H6 2.01.108
red, master, red as blood. 2.01.108
beauford's red sparkling eyes blab his heart's 3.01.154
h'as a book in his pocket with red letters in't. 4.02. 90 P
o' th' ear, and that will make 'em red again. 4.07. 87 P
the red rose and the white are on his face, 3H6 2.05. 97
as red as fire? nay then, her wax must melt. 3.02. 51
but his red color hath forsook his cheeks. R3 2.01. 86
their lips were four red roses on a stalk, 4.03. 12
we will unite the white rose and the red. 5.05. 19
the red wine first must rise | in their fair H8 1.04. 43
a red murrion a' thy jade's tricks! TRO 2.01. 19 P
well | in characters as red as mars his heart 5.02.164
backs red, and faces pale | with flight and COR 1.04. 37
now the red pestilence strike all trades in rome 4.01. 13
sit in gold, his eye | red as 'twould burn rome; 5.01. 64
yet do thy cheeks look red as titan's face TIT 2.04. 31
and, waving our red weapons o'er our heads, JC 3.01.109
soul, his eyes are red as fire with weeping. 3.02.115
as in thy red rays thou dost sink to–night, | so 5.03. 61
so in his red blood cassius' day is set! 5.03. 62
seas incarnadine, | making the green one red. MAC 2.02. 60
pale, or red? HAM 1.02.232
since yet thy cicatrice looks raw and red 4.03. 60
to have a thousand with red burning spits | come LR 3.06. 15
blood, sir, white and red, you shall see a rose, PER 4.06. 34 P
pure red and white, for yet no beard has blest TNK 4.02.107
his red lips, after fights, are fit for ladies. 4.02.111
he that will not see a red herring at a harry STM II.C 1 P
more white and red than doves or roses are: VEN 10
making them red and pale with fresh variety — 21
she red and hot as coals of glowing fire, | he 35
fire, | he red for shame, but frosty in desire. 36
being red, she loves him best, and being white, 77
scorning his churlish drum and ensign red, 107
leading him prisoner in a red rose chain; 110
though mine be not so fair, yet are they red — 116
red cheeks and fiery eyes blaze forth her wrong; 219
hue, | how white and red each other did destroy! 346
like a red morn, that ever yet betoken'd | wrack 453
her pale cheek, till clapping makes it red; 468
whose frothy mouth bepainted all with red, 901
heavy heart's lead, melt at mine eyes' red fire! 1073
to praise the clear unmatched red and white LUC 11
then virtue claims from beauty beauty's red, 59
shame assail'd, the red should fence the white. 63
argued by beauty's red and virtue's white; 65
first red as roses that on lawn we lay, | then 258
and the red rose blush at her own disgrace, 479
that two red fires in both their faces blazed; 1353
the red blood reek'd, to show the painter's 1377
being throng'd bears back, all boll'n and red, 1417
to simois' reedy banks the red blood ran, 1437
cheeks neither red nor pale, but mingled so 1510
so | that blushing red no guilty instance gave, 1511
eyes, though sod in tears, look'd red and raw, 1592
some of her blood still pure and red remain'd, 1742
and blood untainted still doth red abide, 1749
a third, nor red nor white, had stol'n of both, SON 99.10
coral is far more red than her lips' red; 130. 2
coral is far more red than her lips' red; 130. 2
i have seen roses damask'd, red and white, | but 130. 5
me, | of pallid pearls and rubies red as blood, LC 198
REDBREAST 1 FR 0.0001 REL FR 0 V 1 P
way to turn tailor, or be redbreast teacher. 1H4 3.01.260 P
REDDER 1 FR 0.0001 REL FR 1 V 0 P
the proof of it will turn to redder drops. JC 5.01. 49
REDDEST 1 FR 0.0001 REL FR 1 V 0 P
to prove whose blood is reddest, his or mine. MV 2.01. 7
REDE 1 FR 0.0001 REL FR 1 V 0 P
dalliance treads, | and reaks not his own rede. HAM 1.03. 51
REDEEM 23 FR 0.0026 REL FR 20 V 3 P
took your brother's life, /or, to redeem him, MM 2.04. 53
redeem thy brother | by yielding up thy body to 2.04.163
redeem your brother from the angry law; 3.01.201 P
assist him, it shall redeem you from your gyves; 4.02. 11 P
who, wanting guilders to redeem their lives, ERR 1.01. 8
alas, i sent you money to redeem you, | by 4.04. 83
when he did redeem | the virgin tribute paid by MV 3.02. 55
unless you do redeem it by some laudable attempt TN 3.02. 28 P
sea's enrag'd and foamy mouth | did i redeem. 5.01. 79
"o that these hands could so redeem my son | as JN 3.04. 71
redeem from broking pawn the blemish'd crown, R2 2.01.293
then | be emptied to redeem a traitor home? 1H4 1.03. 86
yet time serves wherein you may redeem | your 1.03.180
so he that doth redeem her thence might wear 1.03.206
i will redeem all this on percy's head, | and in 3.02.132
and, but my going, nothing can redeem it. 2H4 2.03. 8
weening to redeem | and have install'd me in the 1H6 2.05. 88
might but redeem the passage of your age! 2.05.108
embassage | from my redeemer to redeem me hence; R3 2.01. 4
let me redeem my brothers both from death. TIT 3.01.180
before the time that romeo | come to redeem me? ROM 4.03. 32
it is a chance which does redeem all sorrows LR 5.03.267
and straight redeem | in gentle numbers time so SON 100. 5
REDEEM'D 6 FR 0.0006 REL FR 6 V 0 P
could you make | which you have not redeem'd; WT 5.01. 3
thou hast redeem'd thy lost opinion, | and 1H4 5.04. 48
in fine, redeem'd i was as i desir'd. 1H6 1.04. 34
soldiers, this day have you redeem'd your lives, 2H6 4.09. 15
is wealthy too, | whom he redeem'd from prison. TIM 3.03. 4
hath the king | five times redeem'd from death. CYM 1.05. 63
REDEEMED 1 FR 0.0001 REL FR 1 V 0 P
all seals and symbols of redeemed sin, | his OTH 2.03.344
REDEEMER 2 FR 0.0002 REL FR 2 V 0 P
embassage | from my redeemer to redeem me hence; R3 2.01. 4
the precious image of our dear redeemer, | you 2.01.124
REDEEMING 3 FR 0.0003 REL FR 3 V 0 P
at once, | than that a sister, by redeeming him, MM 2.04.107
redeeming time when men think least i will. 1H4 1.02.217
engaging and redeeming of himself | with such a TRO 5.05. 39
REDEEMS 3 FR 0.0003 REL FR 2 V 1 P
villainy so far, that the rarity redeems him. AWW 4.03.274 P
for from him | dear life redeems you. WT 5.03.103
who redeems nature from the general curse LR 4.06.206
REDEEM'ST 1 FR 0.0001 REL FR 1 V 0 P
hated all mankind, | and thou redeem'st thyself. TIM 4.03.500
/REDELIVER 1 FR 0.0001 REL FR 0 V 1 P
the gates, and /redeliver our authorities there? MM 4.04. 6 P
REDELIVER 1 FR 0.0001 REL FR 1 V 0 P
of yours | that i have longed long to redeliver. HAM 3.01. 93
/REDEMPTION 1 FR 0.0001 REL FR 1 V 0 P
you, as you hope /to /have /redemption | /by R3 1.04.189
REDEMPTION 9 FR 0.0010 REL FR 8 V 1 P
mercy | is nothing kin to foul redemption. MM 2.04.113
duke, | you bid me seek redemption of the devil. 5.01. 29
mistress, redemption, the money in his desk? ERR 4.02. 46
condemn'd into everlasting redemption for this. ADO 4.02. 57 P
o villains, vipers, damn'd without redemption! R2 3.02.129
who died within the year of our redemption H5 1.02. 60
which held thee dearly as his soul's redemption, 3H6 2.01.102
of my redemption thence | and portance in my OTH 1.03.138
anon | th' assistants made a brave redemption, TNK 5.03. 82
RED–EY'D 1 FR 0.0001 REL FR 1 V 0 P
(better the red–ey'd god of war nev'r /ware), TNK 2.02. 21
RED–FAC'D 1 FR 0.0001 REL FR 0 V 1 P
for bardolph, he is white–liver'd and red–fac'd; H5 3.02. 32 P
RED–HIPP'D 1 FR 0.0001 REL FR 0 V 1 P
and kill me a red–hipp'd humble–bee on the top MND 4.01. 11 P
RED–HOT 3 FR 0.0003 REL FR 3 V 0 P
told you, sir, they were red–hot with drinking, TMP 4.01.171
the iron of itself, though heat red–hot, JN 4.01. 61
that must round my brow | were red–hot steel, to R3 4.01. 60
REDIME 1 FR 0.0001 REL FR 1 V 0 P
but so, | "redime te captum quam queas minimo." SHR 1.01.162

REDISH *(also radish)*
REDISH 1 FR 0.0001 REL FR 0 V 1 P
he was for all the world like a fork'd redish, 2H4 3.02.311 P
RED–LATTICE 1 FR 0.0001 REL FR 0 V 1 P
cat–a–mountain looks, your red–lattice phrases, WIV 2.02. 27 P
RED–LOOK'D 1 FR 0.0001 REL FR 1 V 0 P
and never to my red–look'd anger be | the WT 2.02. 32
REDNESS 1 FR 0.0001 REL FR 1 V 0 P
there was a pretty redness in his lip, | a AYL 3.05.120
RED–NOSE 1 FR 0.0001 REL FR 0 V 1 P
albons, or the red–nose innkeeper of daventry. 1H4 4.02. 46 P
REDOUBLED 4 FR 0.0004 REL FR 4 V 0 P
and let thy blows, doubly redoubled, | fall like R2 1.03. 80
and on my head | my shames redoubled! 1H4 3.02.144
so they | doubly redoubled strokes upon the foe. MAC 1.02. 38
passion on passion deeply is redoubled: VEN 832
REDOUBTED 5 FR 0.0005 REL FR 5 V 0 P
valor's excrement | to render them redoubted! MV 3.02. 88
so far be mine, my most redoubted lord, | as my R2 3.03.198
my most redoubted father, | it is most meet we H5 2.04. 14
lord regent, and redoubted burgundy, | by whose 1H6 2.01. 8
oxford, redoubted pembroke, sir james blunt, R3 4.05. 14
REDOUND 1 FR 0.0001 REL FR 1 V 0 P
as all things shall redound unto your good. 2H6 4.09. 47
RED–PLAGUE 1 FR 0.0001 REL FR 1 V 0 P
the red–plague rid you | for learning me your TMP 1.02.364
REDRESS 30 FR 0.0034 REL FR 28 V 2 P
that if any crave redress of injustice, they MM 4.04. 9 P
not being believ'd, | or wring redress from you. 5.01. 32
here of the fox, | good night to your redress! 5.01.299
no, i defy all counsel, all redress, | but that JN 3.04. 23
but that which ends all counsel, true redress: 3.04. 24
things past redress are now with me past care. R2 2.03.171
the proffered means of succors and redress. 3.02. 32
i beseech you i may have redress against them. 2H4 2.01.108 P
there is no need of any such redress, | or if 4.01. 95
i promis'd you redress of these same grievances 4.02.113
house, | i doubt not but with honor to redress. 1H6 2.05.126
and no way canst thou turn thee for redress, 4.02. 25
no hope to have redress? 5.03. 18
no, not a man comes for redress of thee; 3H6 3.01. 20
but cheerly seek how to redress their harms. 5.04. 2
to what you would | thus violently redress. COR 3.01.219
and now he writes to heaven for his redress. TIT 4.04. 13
sound | with speedy help doth lend redress." ROM 4.05.143
that thou wilt use the wars as thy redress | and TIM 5.04. 51
be factious for redress of all these griefs, JC 1.03.118
speak, strike, redress!" 2.01. 47
"speak, strike, redress!" 2.01. 55
if the redress will follow, thou receivest | thy 2.01. 57
spur but our own cause | to prick us to redress? 2.01.124
amiss | that caesar and his senate must redress? 3.01. 32
and what i can redress, | as i shall find the MAC 4.03. 9
to have found a safe redress, but now grow LR 1.04.206

is but a heap of ruins, | and no redress there. TNK 2.03. 20
and tell thy grief, that we may give redress. LUC 1603
ground, | as broken glass no cement can redress: PP 13.10
REDRESS'D 3 FR 0.0003 REL FR 2 V 1 P
if it be confess'd, it is not redress'd. WIV 1.01.104 P
each several article herein redress'd, | all 2H4 4.01.168
these griefs shall be with speed redress'd, 4.02. 59
REDRESSES 2 FR 0.0002 REL FR 2 V 0 P
i take your princely word for these redresses. 2H4 4.02. 66
not scape censure, nor the redresses sleep, LR 1.04.210
RED–TAIL'D 1 FR 0.0001 REL FR 0 V 1 P
king than by that red–tail'd humble–bee i speak AWW 4.05. 6 P
REDUCE 4 FR 0.0004 REL FR 3 V 1 P
which to reduce into our former favor | you are H5 5.02. 63
all springs reduce their currents to mine eyes, R3 2.02. 68
that would reduce these bloody days again, | and 5.05. 36
and reduce what's now out of square in her into TNK 4.03. 95 P
REECHY 3 FR 0.0003 REL FR 2 V 1 P
like pharaoh's soldiers in the reechy painting, ADO 3.03.134 P
her richest lockram 'bout her reechy neck, COR 2.01.209
and let him, for a pair of reechy kisses, | or HAM 3.04.184
REED 3 FR 0.0003 REL FR 2 V 1 P
the change of man and boy | with a reed voice, MV 3.04. 67
i had as live have a reed that will do me no ANT 2.07. 12 P
and eat, | to thee the reed is as the oak. CYM 4.02.267
RE–EDIFIED 2 FR 0.0002 REL FR 2 V 0 P
which, since, succeeding ages have re–edified. R3 3.01. 71
stood, | which i have sumptuously re–edified. TIT 1.01.351
REEDS 5 FR 0.0005 REL FR 5 V 0 P
with hair up–staring (then like reeds, not hair) TMP 1.02.213
beard like winter's drops | from eaves of reeds. 5.01. 17
ran fearfully among the trembling reeds, | and 1H4 1.03.105
the far shore, thick set with reeds and sedges, TNK 4.01. 54
the rushes and the reeds | had so encompass'd it 4.01. 61
REEDY 1 FR 0.0001 REL FR 1 V 0 P
to simois' reedy banks the red blood ran, LUC 1437
REEK 7 FR 0.0008 REL FR 5 V 2 P
is as hateful to me as the reek of a lime–kill. WIV 3.03. 79 P
saw sighs reek from you, noted well your passion LLL 4.03.138
how under my oppression i did reek | when i H8 2.04.209
breath i hate | as reek a' th' rotten fens, COR 3.03.121
whilst your purpled hands do reek and smoke, JC 3.01.158
of action hath made you reek as a sacrifice. CYM 1.02. 2 P
her face doth reek and smoke, her blood doth VEN 555
REEK'D 1 FR 0.0001 REL FR 1 V 0 P
the red blood reek'd, to show the painter's LUC 1377
REEKING 6 FR 0.0006 REL FR 6 V 0 P
and draw their honors reeking up to heaven, H5 4.03.101
he did | run reeking o'er the lives of men, as COR 2.02.119
sprinkles in your faces | your reeking villainy. TIM 3.06. 93
except they meant to bathe in reeking wounds, MAC 1.02. 39
my duty kneeling, came there a reeking post, LR 2.04. 30
"o night, thou furnace of foul reeking smoke! LUC 799
REEKS 1 FR 0.0001 REL FR 1 V 0 P
than in the breath that from my mistress reeks. SON 130. 8
REEKY 1 FR 0.0001 REL FR 1 V 0 P
with reeky shanks and yellow /chapless skulls; ROM 4.01. 83
REEL 4 FR 0.0004 REL FR 3 V 1 P
shake the press | and make 'em reel before 'em. H8 4.01. 79
i will make my very house reel to–night. COR 2.01.111 P
to reel the streets at noon, and stand the ANT 1.04. 20
ye make my faith reel. TNK 3.06.212
REELETH 1 FR 0.0001 REL FR 1 V 0 P
car, | like feeble age he reeleth from the day, SON 7.10
REELING 3 FR 0.0003 REL FR 2 V 1 P
and trinculo is reeling ripe. TMP 5.01.279
it is a reeling world indeed, my lord, | and i R3 3.02. 38
of meat, depart reeling with too much drink; CYM 5.04.161 P
REELS 4 FR 0.0004 REL FR 4 V 0 P
and fleckled darkness like a drunkard reels ROM 2.03. 3
wassail, and the swagg'ring up–spring reels; HAM 1.04. 9
drink thou; increase the reels. ANT 2.07. 94
fortune, | who, at her certain'st, reels. TNK 5.04. 21
REFELL'D 1 FR 0.0001 REL FR 1 V 0 P
how he refell'd me, and how i replied | (for MM 5.01. 94
REFER 3 FR 0.0003 REL FR 2 V 1 P
only refer yourself to this advantage: MM 3.01.245 P
your honors all, | i do refer me to the oracle: WT 3.02.115
her, | for i'll refer me to all things of sense, OTH 1.02. 64
REFERENCE 5 FR 0.0005 REL FR 5 V 0 P
something that hath a reference to my state: AYL 1.03.127
all that he is hath reference to your highness. AWW 5.03. 29
things, having full reference | to one consent, H5 1.02.205
wife, | due reference of place and exhibition, OTH 1.03.237
make your full reference freely to my lord, ANT 5.02. 23
REFERR'D 2 FR 0.0002 REL FR 1 V 1 P
and referr'd me to the coming on of time with MAC 1.05. 8 P
hath referr'd herself | unto a poor but worthy CYM 1.01. 6
REFIGUR'D 1 FR 0.0001 REL FR 1 V 0 P
art, | if ten of thine ten times refigur'd thee, SON 6.10
REFIN'D 1 FR 0.0001 REL FR 1 V 0 P
god, | that in a christian climate souls refin'd R2 4.01.130
REFINED 2 FR 0.0002 REL FR 2 V 0 P
is haunted | with a refined traveller of spain, LLL 1.01.163
to gild refined gold, to paint the lily, | to JN 4.02. 11
REFLECT 4 FR 0.0004 REL FR 2 V 2 P
reflect i not on thy baseness court–contempt? WT 4.04.733 P
reflect on rome as /titan's rays on earth, | and TIT 1.01.226
reflect upon him accordingly, as you value your CYM 1.06. 23 P
a thousand times, and now no more reflect, VEN 1130
REFLECTING 1 FR 0.0001 REL FR 1 V 0 P
(as 'twere in scorn of eyes) reflecting gems, R3 1.04. 31
REFLECTION 6 FR 0.0006 REL FR 4 V 2 P
nor feels not what he owes, but by reflection; TRO 3.03. 99
for the eye sees not itself | but by reflection, JC 1.02. 53
cannot see yourself | so well as by reflection, 1.02. 68
as whence the sun gins his reflection MAC 1.02. 25
but i have seen small reflection of her wit. CYM 1.02. 31 P
upon fools, lest the reflection should hurt her. 1.02. 33 P
REFLECTS 1 FR 0.0001 REL FR 1 V 0 P
whether it is that she reflects so bright | that LUC 376
REFLEX 2 FR 0.0002 REL FR 2 V 0 P
may never glorious sun reflex his beams | upon 1H6 5.04. 87
'tis but the pale reflex of cynthia's brow; ROM 3.05. 20
REFORM 3 FR 0.0003 REL FR 2 V 1 P
takes on him to reform | some certain edicts and 1H4 4.03. 78
and, as we hear you do reform yourselves, | we 2H4 5.05. 68
o, reform it altogether. HAM 3.02. 38 P
REFORMATION 6 FR 0.0006 REL FR 5 V 1 P
that fault, | right joyful of your reformation. LLL 5.02.869
my reformation, glitt'ring o'er my fault, 1H4 1.02.213
never came reformation in a flood | with such a H5 1.01. 33
for your captain is brave, and vows reformation. 2H6 4.02. 65 P
the reformation of our travell'd gallants, H8 1.03. 19
which reformation must be sudden too, | my noble 5.02. 55
REFORM'D 5 FR 0.0005 REL FR 3 V 2 P
our sexton hath reform'd signior leonato of the ADO 5.01.254 P
i from thee departed | thy penitent reform'd. WT 1.02.239
what you would have reform'd that is not well, JN 4.02. 44
and, not reform'd, may prove pernicious. H8 5.02. 54
i hope we have reform'd that indifferently with HAM 3.02. 36 P
REFORMED 1 FR 0.0001 REL FR 1 V 0 P
they are reformed, civil, full of good, | and TGV 5.04.156
REFRACTORY 1 FR 0.0001 REL FR 1 V 0 P
that are | most disobedient and refractory. TRO 2.02.182
REFRAIN 5 FR 0.0005 REL FR 5 V 0 P
nay, ask me if i can refrain from love, | for i JN 2.01.525
for scarce i can refrain | the execution of my 3H6 2.02.110
who could refrain, | that had a heart to love, MAC 2.03.116
refrain /to–night, | and that shall lend a kind HAM 3.04.165
complain, | scarce i could from tears refrain; PP 20.16
REFRESH 6 FR 0.0006 REL FR 5 V 1 P
these sweet thoughts do even refresh my labors, TMP 3.01. 14
was it not to refresh the mind of man | after SHR 3.01. 11
you weary those that refresh us. WT 4.04.335 P
and labor shall refresh itself with hope | to do H5 2.02. 37
shall we refresh us, sir, upon your shore, | and PER 5.01.256
found, | as vaded gloss no rubbing will refresh, PP 13. 8
REFRESH'D 1 FR 0.0001 REL FR 1 V 0 P
come on refresh'd, new–added, and encourag'd; JC 4.03.209
REFRESHING 2 FR 0.0002 REL FR 2 V 0 P
diffusest honey–drops, refreshing show'rs, | and TMP 4.01. 79
with this refreshing, able once again | to TNK 3.06. 9
REFT 6 FR 0.0006 REL FR 6 V 0 P
and would have reft the fishers of their prey, ERR 1.01.115
reft of his brother, but retain'd his name — 1.01.128
nor my bad life reft me so much of friends, ADO 4.01.196
like a poor bark of sails and tackling reft, R3 4.04.234
was by the rough seas reft of ships and men, PER 2.03. 84
since he himself is reft from her by death. VEN 1174
REFTS 1 FR 0.0001 REL FR 1 V 0 P
of succession, as | thou refts me of my lands. CYM 3.03.103
REFUGE 7 FR 0.0008 REL FR 7 V 0 P
i will for refuge straight to bristow castle: R2 2.02.135
who, sitting in the stocks, refuge their shame, 5.05. 26
leap o'er the walls for refuge in the field. 1H6 2.02. 25
i did imagine what would be her refuge. 5.04. 69
their latest refuge | was to send him; COR 5.03. 11
must i be his last refuge? TIM 3.03. 11
or (at the least) this refuge let me find: LUC 1654
REFUSAL 1 FR 0.0001 REL FR 1 V 0 P
is, he fall in rage | with their refusal, both COR 2.03.259
REFUS'D 12 FR 0.0013 REL FR 7 V 5 P
to carry that which i would have refus'd, | to TGV 4.04.101
in this very manner refus'd, and upon the grief ADO 4.02. 63 P
o, that a lady, of one man refus'd, | should of MND 2.02.133
he hath refus'd it in the open court; MV 4.01.338
the pretty vaulting sea refus'd to drown me, 2H6 3.02. 94
we have had pelting wars since you refus'd | the TRO 4.05.267
that now | refus'd most princely gifts, am bound COR 1.09. 80
and still as he refus'd it, the rabblement JC 1.02.244 P
breath because caesar refus'd the crown, that it 1.02.247 P
the common herd was glad he refus'd the crown, 1.02.264 P
necessity of qualities can make her be refus'd. PER 4.02. 49 P
or he refus'd to take /her figured proffer, PP 4.10
REFUSE 34 FR 0.0038 REL FR 29 V 5 P
since mine own doors refuse to entertain me, ERR 3.01.120
that would refuse so fair an offer'd chain. 3.02.181
as to refuse | so rare a gentleman as signior ADO 3.01. 90
refuse me, hate me, torture me to death! 4.01.184
me in this case, | if i refuse to wed demetrius. MND 1.01. 64
choose who i would, nor refuse who i dislike; MV 1.02. 24 P
that i cannot choose one, nor refuse none? 1.02. 26 P
you should refuse to perform your father's will, 1.02. 93 P
will, if you should refuse to accept him. 1.02. 94 P
which did refuse three thousand ducats of me, 5.01.211
but if you do refuse to marry me, | you'll give AYL 5.04. 13
that you'll marry her | if she refuse me; 5.04. 24
refuse it not, it hath no tongue to vex you; TN 3.04.209
if thou refuse | and wilt encounter with my WT 2.03.138
your father, | being none of his, refuse him. JN 1.01.127
heaven's offer we refuse, | the proffered means R2 3.02. 31
i heard you say that you had rather refuse | the 4.01. 15
those | that for my surety will refuse the boys! 2H6 5.01.121
refuse not, mighty lord, this proffer'd love. R3 3.07.202
if you refuse it — as, in love and zeal, 3.07.208
from my soul | refuse you for my judge, whom, H8 2.04. 82
that again | i do refuse you for my judge, and 2.04.118
i do refuse it, | and stand upon my common part COR 1.09. 38
if you refuse your aid | in this so never–needed 5.01. 33
which they did refuse | and cannot now accept, 5.03. 14
so thou refuse to drink my dear sons' blood. TIT 3.01. 22
deny thy father and refuse thy name; ROM 2.02. 34
a kingly crown, | which he did thrice refuse. JC 3.02. 97
wholesome wisdom | he might not but refuse you. OTH 3.01. 47
that she should love this fellow, and refuse me! CYM 1.02. 26 P
which if you shall refuse, when i am dead, | for PER 2.01. 76
if she refuse me, yet my grave will wed me, TNK 3.06.284
do you refuse it? STM II.C 17
that in the very refuse of thy deeds | there is SON 150. 6
REFUSED 2 FR 0.0002 REL FR 2 V 0 P
but, be refused, | let the white death sit on AWW 2.03. 70
but one must be refused; PP 15. 9
REFUSES 2 FR 0.0002 REL FR 2 V 0 P
and that sword he refuses, | if it but hold, i TNK 3.06. 14
he that she refuses | must die then. 3.06.280
REFUSEST 1 FR 0.0001 REL FR 1 V 0 P
by willful taste of what thyself refusest. SON 40. 8
REFUSING 3 FR 0.0003 REL FR 3 V 0 P
refusing her grand hests, she did confine thee, TMP 1.02.274
or else, refusing me, to wed this shepherd; AYL 5.04. 22
shall fall you for refusing him at sea, | being ANT 3.07. 39
/REGAL 2 FR 0.0002 REL FR 2 V 0 P
/i /have /shook /off /the /regal /thoughts R2 4.01.163
/that /wore | /their /crownets /regal, /from TRO pr 6
REGAL 10 FR 0.0011 REL FR 9 V 1 P
in god's name i'll ascend the regal throne. R2 4.01.113
under him, | and still enjoy thy regal dignity. 1H6 5.04.132
within point–blank of our jurisdiction regal. 2H6 4.07. 27 P
of the fearful king, | and this the regal seat. 3H6 1.01. 26
york, | usurps the regal title and the seat | of 3.03. 28
did i impale him with the regal crown? 3.03.189
and see him seated in the regal throne. 4.03. 64
have shaken edward from the regal seat, | and 4.06. 2
likely in time to bless a regal throne. 4.06. 74
my waned state for henry's regal crown. 4.07. 4
REGAN 18 FR 0.0020 REL FR 16 V 2 P
daughter, | our dearest regan, wife of cornwall? LR 1.01. 68
duke of cornwall and regan his duchess will be 2.01. 4 P
th' night, i' th' haste, | and regan with him. 2.01. 25
nor i, assure thee, regan. 2.01.104
regan, i think /you are; 2.04.129
beloved regan, | thy sister's naught. 2.04.133
o regan, she hath tied | sharp–tooth'd 2.04.134
with how deprav'd a quality — o regan! 2.04.137
never, regan: 2.04.158
no, regan, thou shalt never have my curse. 2.04.170
regan, i have good hope | thou didst not know 2.04.188
o regan, will you take her by the hand? 2.04.194
i can be patient, i can stay with regan, | i and 2.04.230
regan, said you so? 2.04.254
'tis a wild night, | my regan counsels well. 2.04.309
o regan, goneril! 3.04. 19
then let them anatomize regan; 3.06. 76 P
regan, i bleed apace, | untimely comes this hurt 3.07. 97
REGARD 49 FR 0.0055 REL FR 43 V 6 P
full many a lady | i have ey'd with best regard, TMP 3.01. 40
the honor and regard of such a father. TGV 2.04. 60
thyself) | regard thy danger, and along with me. 3.01.258
vail your regard | upon a wrong'd — i would MM 5.01. 20
your worth is very dear in my regard. MV 1.01. 62
you | you have show'd a tender fatherly regard, SHR 2.01.286
no regard? 4.01.126
and after a demure travel of regard — telling TN 2.05. 53 P
smile with an austere regard of control — 2.05. 66 P
you throw a strange regard upon me, and by that 5.01.212
who have sped the better | by my regard, but WT 1.02.390
i thank my liege that in regard of me | he R2 1.03.216
where will doth mutiny with wit's regard. 2.01. 28
sick in the world's regard, wretched and low, 1H4 4.03. 57
is of so little regard in these costermongers' 2H4 1.02.168 P
the king is full of grace and fair regard. H5 1.01. 22
and in regard of causes now in hand, | which i 1.01. 77
scorn and defiance, slight regard, contempt, 2.04.117
but ere we go, regard this dying prince, | the 1H6 3.02. 86
that for a toy, a thing of no regard, | king 4.01.145
your loss is great, so your regard should be; 4.05. 22
that, in regard king henry gives consent, | of 5.04.124
turn this way, henry, and regard them not. 3H6 1.01.189
when did he regard | the stamp of nobleness in H8 3.02. 11
nay, but regard him well. TRO 2.01. 61 P
all, | lay negligent and loose regard upon him. 3.03. 41
what things there are | most /abject in regard, 3.03.128
bites his lip with a politic regard, as who 3.03.254 P
let them | regard me as i do not flatter, and COR 3.01. 67
i offered to awaken his regard | for 's private 5.01. 23
once, i am sworn not to give regard to you. TIM 1.02.245 P
our reasons are so full of good regard | that JC 3.01.224
such as he is, full of regard and honor. 4.02. 12
regard titinius, | and tell me what thou not'st 5.03. 21
without all remedy | should be without regard: MAC 3.02. 12
feed, and regard him not. 3.04. 57
with this regard their currents turn awry, | and HAM 3.01. 86
him | as did that one, and that, in my regard, 4.07. 75
and in the most exact regard support | the LR 1.04.265
in which regard, | though i do hate him as i do OTH 1.01.153
main and th' aerial blue | an indistinct regard. 2.01. 40
your recompense is still | that i regard it not. CYM 2.03. 93
where nor gain | made him regard, or loss TNK 1.03. 30
and, as the gods regard ye, fight with justice. 5.01. 15
then love's deep groans i never shall regard, VEN 377
sad pause and deep regard beseems the sage; LUC 277
which drives the creeping thief to some regard; 305
showed deep regard and smiling government. 1400
in whose fresh regard | weak sights their sickly LC 213
REGARDED 7 FR 0.0008 REL FR 5 V 2 P
myself | to be regarded in her sun–bright eye. TGV 3.01. 88
he talk'd very wisely, but i regarded him not, 1H4 1.02. 86 P
as the cuckoo is in june, | heard, not regarded; 3.02. 76
small curs are not regarded when they grin, 2H6 3.01. 18
virtue is not regarded in handicrafts–men. 4.02. 10 P
let him be regarded | as the most noble corse COR 5.06.142
apace, | and see how i regarded caius cassius. JC 5.03. 88
REGARDFULLY 1 FR 0.0001 REL FR 1 V 0 P
minion, whom the world | voic'd so regardfully? TIM 4.03. 82
REGARDING 1 FR 0.0001 REL FR 1 V 0 P
duty, | neither regarding that she is my child, TGV 3.01. 70
REGARDS 7 FR 0.0008 REL FR 5 V 2 P
your niece regards me with an eye of favor. ADO 5.04. 22
he respects not, the duello he regards not: LLL 1.02.179 P
cries out in the streets, and no man regards it. 1H4 1.02. 89 P
here's beauford, that regards nor god nor king, 1H6 1.03. 60
let him, | as he regards his aged father's life. TIT 5.02.130
on such regards of safety and allowance | as HAM 2.02. 79
when it is mingled with regards that stands LR 1.01.239
REGENERATE 1 FR 0.0001 REL FR 1 V 0 P
whose youthful spirit, in me regenerate, | doth R2 1.03. 70
REGENT 19 FR 0.0021 REL FR 19 V 0 P
regent of love–rhymes, lord of folded arms, LLL 3.01.181
why, cousin, wert thou regent of the world, | it R2 2.01.109
from the most gracious regent of this land, 2.03. 77
me they concern, regent i am of france. 1H6 1.01. 84
lord regent, and redoubted burgundy, | by whose 2.01. 8
to be our regent in the realm of france; 4.01.163
the regent hath with talbot broke his word, 4.06. 2
the regent conquers, and the frenchmen fly. 5.03. 1
lord regent, i do greet your excellence | with 5.04. 94
we here discharge your grace from being regent 2H6 1.01. 66
when thou wert regent for our sovereign, | have 1.01.197
let york be regent, i will yield to him. 1.03.106
man | to be your regent in the realm of france. 1.03.161
let somerset be regent o'er the french, 1.03.205
that somerset be sent as regent thither: 3.01.290
had been the regent there in stead of me, | he 3.01.294

thy fortune, york, hadst thou been regent there, 3.01.305
i know not, but | here's the regent, sir, of PER 5.01.186
and pretty din, | the regent made in metelin, 5.02. 8
REGENTSHIP 1 FR 0.0001 REL FR 1 V 0 P
then let him be denay'd the regentship. 2H6 1.03.104
REGIA 3 FR 0.0003 REL FR 1 V 2 P
hic steterat priami regia celsa senis." SHR 3.01. 29
is my man tranio, "regia," bearing my port, 3.01. 35 P
take heed he hear us not, "regia," presume not, 3.01. 44 P
REGIMENT 8 FR 0.0009 REL FR 6 V 2 P
you shall find in the regiment of the spinii one AWW 2.01. 42 P
i know you are the muskos' regiment, | and i 4.01. 69
the earl of pembroke keeps his regiment; R3 5.03. 29
his regiment lies half a mile at least | south 5.03. 37
a pursuivant–at–arms | to stanley's regiment, 5.03. 60
good lords, conduct him to his regiment. 5.03.103
and gives his potent regiment to a trull | that ANT 3.06. 95
in her into their former law and regiment. TNK 4.03. 96 P
REGIMENTS 1 FR 0.0001 REL FR 1 V 0 P
forth | in best appointment all our regiments. JN 2.01.296
REGINA 1 FR 0.0001 REL FR 0 V 1 P
erga te mentis integritas, regina serenissima — H8 3.01. 40 P
REGION 17 FR 0.0019 REL FR 15 V 2 P
she is a region in guiana, all gold and bounty. WIV 1.03. 69 P
he is of too high a region, he knows too much. 3.02. 73 P
in thrilling region of thick–ribbed ice; MM 3.01.122
every region near | seem all one mutual cry. MND 4.01.116
as he had lost some province and a region WT 1.02.369
now, | from every region, apes of idleness! 2H4 4.05.122
and made to tremble | the region of my breast, H8 2.04.185
then, when you come to pluto's region, | i pray TIT 4.03. 13
would through the airy region stream so bright ROM 2.02. 21
the dreadful thunder | doth rend the region; HAM 2.02.487
i should 'a' fatted all the region kites | with 2.02.579
though the fork invade | the region of my heart; LR 1.01.145
scorns | that dwell in every region of his face, OTH 4.01. 83
no more, you petty spirits of region low, CYM 5.04. 93
from bourn to bourn, region to region. PER 4.04. 4
from bourn to bourn, region to region. 4.04. 4
the region cloud hath mask'd him from me now. SON 33.12
REGIONS 8 FR 0.0009 REL FR 8 V 0 P
'twixt which regions | there is some space. TMP 2.01.256
to other regions! AWW 2.03.283
by whose approach the regions of artois, 1H6 2.01. 9
out of the powerful regions under earth, | help 5.03. 11
all the regions | do smilingly revolt, and who COR 4.06.102
down, | but keep the hills and upper regions. JC 5.01. 3
to seek through the regions of the earth | for CYM 1.01. 20
to pentapolis, | yravished the regions round, PER 3.ch. 35
REGISTER 5 FR 0.0005 REL FR 4 V 1 P
turn another into the register of your own, that WIV 2.02.187 P
but let the world rank me in register | a ANT 4.09. 21
dim register and notary of shame! LUC 765
what's new to speak, what now to register, SON 108. 3
cried, "o false blood, thou register of lies, LC 52
REGISTERS 1 FR 0.0001 REL FR 1 V 0 P
thy registers and thee i both defy, | not SON 123. 9
REGIST'RED 4 FR 0.0004 REL FR 4 V 0 P
lives, | live regist'red upon our brazen tombs, LLL 1.01. 2
but say, my lord, it were not regist'red, R3 3.01. 75
out of those many regist'red in promise, | which TRO 3.03. 15
pains | are regist'red where every day i turn MAC 1.03.151
REGREET 4 FR 0.0004 REL FR 4 V 0 P
unyoke this seizure and this kind regreet? JN 3.01.241
feasts, so i regreet | the daintiest last, to R2 1.03. 67
fields | shall not regreet our fair dominions, 1.03.142
nor never write, regreet, nor reconcile | this 1.03.186
REGREETS 1 FR 0.0001 REL FR 1 V 0 P
lord, | from whom he bringeth sensible regreets: MV 2.09. 89
REGRESS 1 FR 0.0001 REL FR 0 V 1 P
thou shalt have egress and regress — said i WIV 2.01.218 P
REGUERDON 1 FR 0.0001 REL FR 1 V 0 P
my foot, | and, in reguerdon of that duty done, 1H6 3.01.169
REGUERDON'D 1 FR 0.0001 REL FR 1 V 0 P
or been reguerdon'd with so much as thanks, 1H6 3.04. 23
REGULAR 1 FR 0.0001 REL FR 1 V 0 P
of regular justice in your city's bounds, | but TIM 5.04. 61
REHEARSAL 3 FR 0.0003 REL FR 2 V 1 P
a marvail's convenient place for our rehearsal. MND 3.01. 3 P
it | with sweet rehearsal of my morning's dream. 2H6 1.02. 24
this rehearsal | (which, /ev'ry innocent wots TNK 1.03. 78
REHEARS'D 3 FR 0.0003 REL FR 3 V 0 P
which, when i saw rehears'd, i must confess, MND 5.01. 68
incurr'd | the danger formerly by me rehears'd. MV 4.01.362
for those defects i have before rehears'd, SHR 1.02.124
REHEARSE 15 FR 0.0017 REL FR 10 V 5 P
rehearse that once more. TGV 3.01.357 P
for that which now torments me to rehearse: 4.01. 26
there will we rehearse; MND 1.02.103 P
and there we may rehearse most obscenely and 1.02.107 P
every mother's son, and rehearse your parts. 3.01. 73 P
were met together to rehearse a play | intended 3.02. 11
first, rehearse your song by rote, | to each 5.01.397
which will have matter to rehearse, though WT 5.02. 62 P
pity may move thee "pardon" to rehearse. R2 5.03.128
verbatim to rehearse the method of my pen. 1H6 3.01. 13
let's rehearse by any means | before the ladies TNK 2.03. 56
and every fair with his fair doth rehearse, SON 21. 4
excellent | for every vulgar paper to rehearse? 38. 4
clay, | do not so much as my poor name rehearse, 71.11
and tongues to be your being shall rehearse, 81.11
REIGN 47 FR 0.0053 REL FR 43 V 4 P
thus have i politicly begun my reign, | and 'tis SHR 4.01.188
happy star reign now! WT 1.02.363
where we do reign, we will alone uphold JN 3.01.157
advantage shall step forth | to check his reign, 3.04.152
nor can one england brook a double reign | of 1H4 5.04. 66
of the first–born cain | reign in all bosoms, 2H4 1.01.158
for all my reign hath been but as a scene 4.05.197
in th' eleventh year of the last king's reign H5 1.01. 2
during the time edward the third did reign. 1H6 1.02. 31
since henry monmouth first began to reign, 2.05. 23
during whose reign the percies of the north, 2.05. 67
(succeeding his father bullingbrook) did reign, 2.05. 83
should reign among professors of one faith. 5.01. 14
this edmund, in the reign of bullingbrook, | as 2H6 2.02. 39
till lionel's issue fails, his should not reign. 2.02. 56
over whom, in time to come, i hope to reign, 4.02.130
i am content he shall reign, but i'll be 4.02.159 P
but claret wine this first year of our reign. 4.06. 4 P
for yet may england curse my wretched reign. 4.09. 49
to aspire unto the crown and reign as king. 3H6 1.01. 53
but that the next heir should succeed and reign. 1.01.146
let me for this my life–time reign as king. 1.01.171
and thou shalt reign in quiet while thou liv'st. 1.01.173
to seek to put me down and reign thyself. 1.01.200
as thou shalt reign but by their sufferance. 1.01.234
i took an oath that he should quietly reign. 1.02. 15
would break a thousand oaths to reign one year. 1.02. 17
what is pomp, rule, reign, but earth and dust? 5.02. 27
no, no, by god's good grace his son shall reign. R3 2.03. 10
and make (no doubt) us happy by his reign. 3.07.170
your brother's son shall never reign our king, 3.07.215
twenty of the dog–days now reign in 's nose; H8 5.03. 42 P
couch his limbs, there golden sleep doth reign. ROM 2.03. 38
where the infectious pestilence did reign, 5.02. 10
sun, hide thy beams, timon hath done his reign. TIM 5.01.223
banquo's issue ever | reign in this kingdom? MAC 4.01.103
better macbeth | than such an one to reign. 4.03. 66
from your orbs, | you may reign in them now! CYM 5.05.372
i'll show you those in troubles reign, | losing PER 2.ch. 7
for his peaceable reign and good government. 2.01.103 P
that best know how to rule and how to reign, 2.04. 38
our son and daughter shall in tyrus reign. 5.03. 82
that all the faults which in thy reign are made LUC 804
ruin, beauty's wrack, and grim care's reign; 1451
and each (though enemies to /either's reign) SON 28. 5
all men are bad and in their badness reign. 121.14
"that he did in the general bosom reign | of LC 127
/REIGN'D 1 FR 0.0001 REL FR 1 V 0 P
/the /regal /thoughts | /wherewith /i /reign'd? R2 4.01.164
REIGN'D 7 FR 0.0008 REL FR 7 V 0 P
after edward the third's death reign'd as king 2H6 2.02. 20
the issue of the next son should have reign'd. 2.02. 32
the spavin | /and springhalt reign'd among 'em. H8 1.03. 13
the wisest prince that there had reign'd by many 2.04. 49
our jovial star reign'd at his birth, and in CYM 5.04.105
though in my nature reign'd | all frailties that SON 109. 9
free, | and reign'd commanding in his monarchy. LC 196
REIGNED 1 FR 0.0001 REL FR 1 V 0 P
at whose conception, till lucina reigned, PER 1.01. 8
/REIGNIER 3 FR 0.0003 REL FR 3 V 0 P
/reignier, duke of anjou, doth take his part; 1H6 1.01. 94
alanson, /reignier, compass him about, | and 4.04. 27
/reignier, her father, to the king of france 3H6 5.07. 38
REIGNIER 10 FR 0.0011 REL FR 9 V 1 P
reignier, stand thou as dolphin in my place; 1H6 1.02. 61
reignier, is't thou that thinkest to beguile me? 1.02. 65
see, reignier, see, thy daughter prisoner! 5.03.131
thanks, reignier, happy for so sweet a child, 5.03.148
reignier of france, i give thee kingly thanks, 5.03.163
so farewell, reignier! 5.03.169
but reignier, king of naples, that prevail'd. 5.04. 78
where reignier sooner will receive than give. 5.05. 47
margaret, daughter unto reignier king of naples, 2H6 1.01. 47 P
unto the poor king reignier, whose large style 1.01.111
REIGNING 2 FR 0.0002 REL FR 2 V 0 P
one phoenix | at this hour reigning there. TMP 3.03. 24
i do | to th' freshest things now reigning, and WT 4.01. 13
REIGNS 15 FR 0.0017 REL FR 13 V 2 P
lord, lord! to see what folly reigns in us! TGV 1.02. 15
she | reigns in my blood and will rememb'red be. LLL 4.03. 94
fortune reigns in gifts of the world, not in the AYL 1.02. 41 P
there's some ill planet reigns; WT 2.01.105
for the red blood reigns in the winter's pale. 4.03. 4
a weather–bitten conduit of many kings' reigns. 5.02. 56 P
hostility and civil tumult reigns | between my JN 4.02.247
reigns solely in the breast of every man. H5 2.pr. 4
reigns in the hearts of all our present parts. 2H6 5.02. 87
still breathes, edward still lives and reigns; R3 1.01.161
that reigns in galled eyes of weeping souls, 4.04. 53
of nature | reigns that which would be fear'd. MAC 3.01. 50
of jove himself, and now reigns here | a very, HAM 3.02.283
"for where love reigns, disturbing jealousy VEN 649
and there reigns love and all love's loving SON 31. 3
REIGN'ST 1 FR 0.0001 REL FR 1 V 0 P
o thou that from eleven to ninety reign'st | in TNK 5.01.130
REIN 15 FR 0.0017 REL FR 13 V 2 P
do not give dalliance | too much the rein. TMP 4.01. 52
and now i give my sensual race the rein. MM 2.04.160
sweet lord longaville, rein thy tongue. LLL 5.02.656 P
i must rather give it the rein, for it runs 5.02.657 P
when she will take the rein i let her run, | but WT 2.03. 51
what rein can hold licentious wickedness | when H5 3.03. 22
where every horse bears his commanding rein R3 2.02.128
and bears his head | in such a rein, in full as TRO 1.03.189
spur them to ruthful work, rein them from ruth. 5.03. 48
or the hard rein which both of them hath borne LR 3.01. 27
and rein his proud head to the saddle–bow; VEN 14
over one arm the lusty courser's rein, | under 31
breaketh his rein, and to her straight goes he. 264
tree, | servilely master'd with a leathern rein! 392
can curb his heat, or rein his rash desire, LUC 706
REIN'D 1 FR 0.0001 REL FR 1 V 0 P
he cannot | be rein'd again to temperance; COR 3.03. 28
REINFORC'D 1 FR 0.0001 REL FR 1 V 0 P
the french have reinforc'd their scatter'd men. H5 4.06. 36
REINFORCE 1 FR 0.0001 REL FR 1 V 0 P
or betimes | let's reinforce, or fly. CYM 5.02. 18
REINFORCEMENT 2 FR 0.0002 REL FR 2 V 0 P
diomed, | to reinforcement, or we perish all. TRO 5.05. 16
off, | and with a sudden reinforcement struck COR 2.02.113
REINS* 4 FR 0.0004 REL FR 1 V 3 P
swallow'd snowballs for pills to cool the reins. WIV 3.05. 23 P
he will bear you easily, and reins well. TN 3.04.324 P
from giving reins and spurs to my free speech, R2 1.01. 55
your dispositions the reins and be angry at your COR 2.01. 30 P
REITERATE 1 FR 0.0001 REL FR 1 V 0 P
which to reiterate were sin | as deep as that, WT 1.02.283
REJECT 1 FR 0.0001 REL FR 1 V 0 P
she shall challenge this, you will reject her. LLL 5.02.438
REJECTED 1 FR 0.0001 REL FR 1 V 0 P
then woo thyself, be of thyself rejected; VEN 159
REJOIC'D 1 FR 0.0001 REL FR 1 V 0 P
ne'er mother | rejoic'd deliverance more. CYM 5.05.370
REJOICE 26 FR 0.0029 REL FR 18 V 8 P
that rejoice | to hear the solemn curfew: TMP 5.01. 39
o, rejoice | beyond a common joy, and set it 5.01.206
i'll after, to rejoice in the boy's correction. TGV 3.01.384 P
my husband will not rejoice so much at the abuse WIV 5.03. 7 P
any thing which profess'd to make him rejoice; MM 3.02.236 P
embrace thy brother there, rejoice with him. ERR 5.01.414
gold, | and all europa shall rejoice at thee, ADO 5.04. 45
as to rejoice at friends but newly found. LLL 5.02.751
the condition of my estate, to rejoice in yours. AYL 1.02. 16 P
holy | than to rejoice the former queen is well? WT 5.01. 30
rejoice, you men of angiers, ring your bells, JN 2.01.312
i should rejoice now at this happy news, | and 2H4 4.04.109
which /i in sufferance heartily will rejoice, H5 2.02.159
never did faithful subject more rejoice | at the 2.02.161
why then rejoice therefore. 3.06. 52
aunchient, it is not a thing to rejoice at; 3.06. 53 P
and follow'd with a rabble that rejoice | to see 2H6 2.04. 32
or shall they last, and we rejoice in them? R3 4.02. 6
i should freelier rejoice in that absence COR 1.03. 3 P
you, you'll rejoice | that he is thus cut off. 5.06.137
shown, | but to rejoice in splendor of mine own. ROM 1.02.101
child, | but one thing to rejoice and solace in, 4.05. 47
to see caesar, and to rejoice in his triumph. JC 1.01. 31 P
wherefore rejoice? 1.01. 32
as he was fortunate, i rejoice at it; 3.02. 25 P
expel, | for now reviving joy bids her rejoice, VEN 977
REJOICER 1 FR 0.0001 REL FR 1 V 0 P
to those that would and cannot, a rejoicer. TNK 5.01.121
REJOICES 2 FR 0.0002 REL FR 1 V 1 P
it rejoices me, that i hope i shall see him ere AWW 4.05. 84 P
am not | one that rejoices in the common wrack, TIM 5.01.192
REJOICETH 1 FR 0.0001 REL FR 0 V 1 P
it rejoiceth my intellect. LLL 5.01. 60 P
REJOICING 6 FR 0.0006 REL FR 3 V 3 P
but my rejoicing | at nothing can be more. TMP 3.01. 93
rather rejoicing to see another merry, than MM 3.02.235 P
and with our company piece the rejoicing? WT 5.02.108 P
lose the dues of rejoicing by being ignorant of MAC 1.05. 12 P
made lud's–town with rejoicing fires bright, CYM 3.01. 32
spring, | to add a more rejoicing to the prime, LUC 332
REJOICINGLY 1 FR 0.0001 REL FR 0 V 1 P
she hath despis'd me rejoicingly, and i'll be CYM 3.05.145 P
REJOINDURE 1 FR 0.0001 REL FR 1 V 0 P
rudely beguiles our lips | of all rejoindure, TRO 4.04. 36
REJOURN 1 FR 0.0001 REL FR 0 V 1 P
and then rejourn the controversy of threepence COR 2.01. 71 P
RELAPSE 2 FR 0.0002 REL FR 2 V 0 P
of mischief, | killing in relapse of mortality. H5 4.03.107
must be look'd to, | for her relapse is mortal. PER 3.02.109
RELATE 10 FR 0.0011 REL FR 10 V 0 P
relate your wrongs. MM 5.01. 26
for interim to our studies shall relate, | in LLL 1.01.171
(without your special pardon) | dare not relate. 3H6 4.01. 88
treasons of his master | he shall again relate. H8 1.02. 8
forth, and with bold spirit relate what you, 1.02.129
to relate the manner, | were on the quarry of MAC 4.03.205
thoughts speculative their unsure hopes relate, 5.04. 19
when you shall these unlucky deeds relate, OTH 5.02.341
state | this heavy act with heavy heart relate. 5.02.371
i nill relate, action may | conveniently the PER 3.ch. 55
RELATES 1 FR 0.0001 REL FR 1 V 0 P
name, | relates in purpose only to achilles. TRO 1.03.323
RELATING 1 FR 0.0001 REL FR 1 V 0 P
here, | and by relating tales of others' griefs, PER 1.04. 2
RELATION 9 FR 0.0010 REL FR 7 V 2 P
not a relation for a breakfast, nor | befitting TMP 5.01.164
of the law | hath full relation to the penalty, MV 4.01.248
you, sir, were you present at this relation? WT 5.02. 2 P
was when, at the relation of the queen's death 5.02. 84 P
push) to trouble | your joys with like relation. 5.03.130
(with whom relation | durst never meddle) in the TRO 3.03.201
o, relation! | too nice, and yet too true. MAC 4.03.173
which you might from relation likewise reap, CYM 2.04. 86
and make /my senses credit thy relation | to PER 5.01.123
RELATIONS 1 FR 0.0001 REL FR 1 V 0 P
augures and understood relations have | by MAC 3.04.123
RELATIVE 1 FR 0.0001 REL FR 1 V 0 P
i'll have grounds | more relative than this — HAM 2.02.604
RELEAS'D 5 FR 0.0005 REL FR 3 V 2 P
he hath releas'd him, isabel, from the world, MM 4.03.115
or by what means gots thou to be releas'd? 1H6 1.04. 25
of maine shall be releas'd and deliver'd /over 2H6 1.01. 51 P
/of maine shall be releas'd and deliver'd over 1.01. 59 P
then 'tis but reason that i be releas'd | from 3H6 3.03.147
/RELEASE 1 FR 0.0001 REL FR 1 V 0 P
/mine /own /breath /release /all /duteous /oaths R2 4.01.210
RELEASE 6 FR 0.0006 REL FR 6 V 0 P
they cannot boudge till your release. TMP 5.01. 11
go, release them, ariel. 5.01. 30
but release me from my bands | with the help of ep 9
intemperate lust, | release my brother; MM 5.01. 99
and then i will her charmed eye release | from MND 3.02.376
but first i will release the fairy queen. 4.01. 70
RELEASING 2 FR 0.0002 REL FR 2 V 0 P
and from her twining arms doth urge releasing. VEN 256
the charter of thy worth gives thee releasing; SON 87. 3
RELENT 16 FR 0.0018 REL FR 16 V 0 P
i do relent. what would thou more of man? WIV 2.02. 30
i'll know | his pleasure, may be he will relent. MM 2.02. 3
he will relent. 2.02.124
relent, sweet hermia, and, lysander, yield | thy MND 1.01. 91
and dull–ey'd fool | to shake the head, relent, MV 3.03. 15
my sighs and tears, and will not once relent? 1H6 3.01.108
for shame, my lord of winchester, relent! 3.01.132
her words, | or nature makes me suddenly relent. 3.03. 59
me, | and could it not enforce them to relent, 2H6 4.04. 17
and therefore yet relent, and save my life. 4.07.117
will ye relent | and yield to mercy whilst 'tis 4.08. 11
relent, and save your souls. R3 1.04.256
relent? no: 'tis cowardly and womanish. 1.04.261
not to relent is beastly, savage, devilish. 1.04.262
but fierce andronicus would not relent. TIT 2.03.165
can you hear a good man groan | and not relent, 4.01.124
RELENTETH 1 FR 0.0001 REL FR 1 V 0 P
more than flint, for stone at rain relenteth. VEN 200
RELENTING 3 FR 0.0003 REL FR 3 V 0 P
with sorrow snares relenting passengers; 2H6 3.01.227
relenting fool, and shallow, changing woman! R3 4.04.431

heart | in such relenting dew of lamentations, LUC 1829
RELENTS 1 FR 0.0001 REL FR 0 V 1 P
her tears, is wash'd with them, but relents not. MM 3.01.230 P
RELIANCES 1 FR 0.0001 REL FR 1 V 0 P
and my reliances on his fracted dates | have TIM 2.01. 22
RELICS 3 FR 0.0003 REL FR 3 V 0 P
we do bury | th' incensing relics of it. AWW 5.03. 25
the bits and greasy relics | of her o'er–eaten TRO 5.02.159
for tinctures, stains, relics, and cognizance. JC 2.02. 89
RELIEF 14 FR 0.0015 REL FR 12 V 2 P
i will give him some relief, if it be but for TMP 2.02. 68 P
honor, | how true a gentleman you send relief, MV 3.04. 6
where ever sorrow is, relief would be. AYL 3.05. 86
zeal | in the relief of this oppressed child JN 2.01.245
and, to relief of lazars, and weak age | of H5 1.01. 15
away, for your relief! 2H6 5.02. 88
it shall be eas'd if france can yield relief. 3H6 3.03. 20
out | to beg relief among rome's enemies, | who TIT 5.03.106
and my relief | must not be toss'd and turn'd to TIM 2.01. 25
for this relief much thanks. HAM 1.01. 8
abus'd, and my relief | must be to loathe her. OTH 3.03.267
my means for thy relief nor my voice for thy CYM 3.05.114 P
"within this limit is relief enough, | sweet VEN 235
th' offender's sorrow lends but weak relief | to SON 34.11
RELIER 1 FR 0.0001 REL FR 1 V 0 P
appeal, | not to seducing lust, thy rash relier. LUC 639
RELIEV'D 12 FR 0.0013 REL FR 10 V 2 P
is despair, | unless i be reliev'd by prayer, TMP ep 16
reliev'd him with such sanctity of love, | and TN 3.04.361
we might guess they reliev'd us humanely; COR 1.01. 18 P
who hath reliev'd you? HAM 1.01. 17
grown | by desperate appliance are reliev'd, 4.03. 10
be as well neighbor'd, pitied, and reliev'd, LR 1.01.119
me), the king my old master must be reliev'd. 3.03. 18 P
if we be not reliev'd within this hour, | we ANT 4.09. 1
who are in this | reliev'd, but not betray'd. 5.02. 41
such, i mean, | where they should be reliev'd. CYM 3.06. 8
by you reliev'd, would force me to my duty; PER 3.03. 22
many, | and, being low, never reliev'd by any. VEN 708
RELIEVE 15 FR 0.0017 REL FR 12 V 3 P
basis bowed, | as stooping to relieve him. TMP 2.01.122
will not give a doit to relieve a lame beggar, 2.02. 32 P
with urging helpless patience would relieve me; ERR 2.01. 39
my fortunes were more able to relieve her; AYL 2.04. 77
help, that by this token | i would relieve her. AWW 5.03. 86
methought it did relieve my passion much, | more TN 2.04. 4
virtue in my tears, | that might relieve you! JN 5.07. 45
with purpose to relieve and follow them, 1H6 1.01.133
what authority surfeits /on would relieve us. COR 1.01. 17 P
from the bone | ere thou relieve the beggar. TIM 4.03.529
i will look him and privily relieve him. LR 3.03. 14 P
and did relieve me | to see this gracious season CYM 5.05.400
and finding little comfort to relieve them, | i PER 1.02. 99
but to relieve them of their heavy load; 1.04. 91
give me, | for such kindness must relieve me: 5.02. 4
RELIEVES 1 FR 0.0001 REL FR 1 V 0 P
if any one relieves or pities him, | for the TIT 5.03.181
RELIEVETH 1 FR 0.0001 REL FR 1 V 0 P
he cheers the morn, and all the earth relieveth; VEN 484
RELIEVING 1 FR 0.0001 REL FR 1 V 0 P
to and fro, | about relieving of the sentinels. 1H6 2.01. 70
/RELIGION 1 FR 0.0001 REL FR 1 V 0 P
/bishop | /turns /insurrection /to /religion. 2H4 1.01.201
RELIGION 15 FR 0.0017 REL FR 11 V 4 P
i think, or in any religion. MM 1.02. 23 P
it is religion to be thus forsworn: LLL 4.03.360
in religion, | what damned error but some sober MV 3.02. 77
with no less religion than if thou wert indeed AYL 4.01.197 P
howsome'er their hearts are sever'd in religion, AWW 1.03. 53 P
it is religion that doth make vows kept, | but JN 3.01.279
kept, | but thou hast sworn against religion, 3.01.280
name not religion, for thou lov'st the flesh, 1H6 1.01. 41
that seeks to overthrow religion | because he is 1.03. 65
when the devout religion of mine eye | maintains ROM 1.02. 88
religion groans at it. TIM 3.02. 76
religion to the gods, peace, justice, truth, 4.01. 16
and sweet religion makes | a rhapsody of words. HAM 3.04. 47
(which my love makes religion to obey), | i tell ANT 5.02.199
but i see you have some religion in you, that CYM 1.04.137 P
RELIGION'S 1 FR 0.0001 REL FR 1 V 0 P
religious love put out religion's eye. LC 250
RELIGIONS 1 FR 0.0001 REL FR 1 V 0 P
yellow slave | will knit and break religions, TIM 4.03. 35
RELIGIOUS 21 FR 0.0023 REL FR 19 V 2 P
in some reclusive and religious life, | out of ADO 4.01.242
but indeed an old religious uncle of mine taught AYL 3.02.344 P
where, meeting with an old religious man, 5.04.160
the duke hath put on a religious life, | and 5.04.181
religious in mine error, i adore | the sun, that AWW 1.03.205
thou lov'st her, | thy love's to me religious; 2.03.183
a coward, a most devout coward, religious in it. TN 3.04.389 P
with all religious strength of sacred vows. JN 3.01.229
and cloister thee in some religious house. R2 5.01. 23
seem they religious? H5 2.02.130
awe, | more than god or religious churchmen may. 1H6 1.01. 40
methinks my lord should be religious, | and know 3.01. 54
when holy and devout religious men | are at R3 3.07. 92
made me, | with thy religious truth and modesty, H8 4.02. 74
i know you wise, religious, | and, let me tell 5.01. 28
not only good and wise but most religious; 5.02.151
i do not, | yet, for i know thou art religious, TIT 5.01. 74
religious canons, civil laws are cruel; TIM 4.03. 61
most holy and religious fear it is | to keep HAM 3.03. 8
hath dear religious love stol'n from mine eye SON 31. 6
religious love put out religion's eye. LC 250
RELIGIOUSLY 7 FR 0.0008 REL FR 5 V 2 P
done this in the fear of god, very religiously; LLL 4.02.148 P
winter's sisterhood kisses not more religiously, AYL 3.04. 16 P
of this oppressed child | religiously provokes. JN 2.01.246
do in his name religiously demand | why thou 3.01.140
our souls religiously confirm thy words. 4.03. 73
and justly and religiously unfold | why the law H5 1.02. 10
slain | religiously they ask a sacrifice: TIT 1.01.124
RELINQUISH'D 1 FR 0.0001 REL FR 0 V 1 P
to be relinquish'd of the artists — AWW 2.03. 10 P
RELIQUES 2 FR 0.0002 REL FR 2 V 0 P
idolatrous fancy | must sanctify his reliques. AWW 1.01. 98
shall we go see the reliques of this town? TN 3.03. 19
RELIQUIT 1 FR 0.0001 REL FR 1 V 0 P
terras astraea reliquit; TIT 4.03. 4
RELISH* 20 FR 0.0022 REL FR 12 V 8 P
that relish all as sharply | passion as they, be TMP 5.01. 23
to relish a love–song, like a robin–redbreast; TGV 2.01. 20 P
i do not relish well | their loud applause and MM 1.01. 69
do relish the petition well that prays for peace 1.02. 15 P
finding him, and relish it with good observance. AYL 3.02.234 P
what relish is in this? TN 4.01. 60
relish a truth like us, inform yourselves | we WT 2.01.167
you, some relish of the saltness of time in you, 2H4 1.02. 98 P
out of doubt, be of the same relish as ours are; H5 4.01.109 P
now, ulysses, i begin to relish thy advice, TRO 1.03.386
th' imaginary relish is so sweet | that it 3.02. 19
home that will not | be grafted to your relish. COR 2.01.189
i have no relish of them, but abound | in the MAC 4.03. 95
our old stock but we shall relish of it. HAM 3.01.117 P
act | that has no relish of salvation in't — 3.03. 92
from us till our oldness cannot relish them. LR 1.02. 48 P
you may relish him more in the soldier than in OTH 2.01.165 P
let what is here contain'd relish of love, | of CYM 3.02. 30
for our milk | will relish of the pasture, and TNK 1.02. 77
relish your nimble notes to pleasing ears, LUC 1126
RELISH'D 2 FR 0.0002 REL FR 1 V 1 P
it would not have relish'd among my other WT 5.02.122 P
that never relish'd of a base descent. PER 2.05. 60
RELIVES 1 FR 0.0001 REL FR 1 V 0 P
will you deliver | how this dead queen relives? PER 5.03. 64
RELUME 1 FR 0.0001 REL FR 1 V 0 P
promethean heat | that can thy light relume. OTH 5.02. 13
RELY 5 FR 0.0005 REL FR 5 V 0 P
thou hast, | rely upon it till my tale be heard, MM 5.01.365
i, | thy resolv'd patient, on thee still rely. AWW 2.01.204
bade me rely on him as on my father, | and he R3 2.02. 25
he doth rely on none, | but carries on the TRO 2.03.163
i'll guard them from | if thereon you rely. ANT 5.02.133
RELYING 1 FR 0.0001 REL FR 1 V 0 P
as one relying on your lordship's will, | and TGV 1.03. 61
REMAIN 74 FR 0.0083 REL FR 65 V 9 P
thou didst painfully remain | a dozen years; TMP 1.02.278
may know if you remain upon this island, | and 1.02.424
for trouble being gone, comfort should remain; ADO 1.01.101 P
thou shalt remain here, whether thou wilt or no. MND 3.01.153
here therefore for a while i will remain. 3.02. 83
to helen is it home return'd, | there to remain. 3.02.173
at large discourse, while here they do remain. 5.01.151
remain there but an hour, nor speak to me. AWW 4.02. 58
let his nobility remain in 's court. 4.05. 50 P
your lordship to remain with me till they meet 4.05. 86 P
remain thou still in darkness. TN 4.02. 57 P
my design, and i | remain a pinch'd thing; WT 2.01. 51
does when the business is perform'd, and remain, 4.04.822 P
know, | from where you do remain let paper show. R2 1.03.250
be it known unto you | i do remain as neuter. 2.03.159
there remain, | and fortify it strongly 'gainst H5 3.03. 52
be patient, for you shall remain with us. 3.05. 66
they set the same, and there it doth remain, 3H6 2.01. 66
here in this country where we now remain. 3.01. 75
and thou shalt still remain the duke of york. 5.01. 28
there to remain till the king's further pleasure H8 5.02.125
as i have made ye one, lords, one remain: 5.02.214
that only like a gulf it did remain | i' th' COR 1.01. 98
let's fetch him off, or make remain alike. 1.04. 62
if he should still malignantly remain | fast foe 2.03.183
a mind | that shall remain a poison where it is; 3.01. 87
shall remain? 3.01. 88
you so remain. 3.01.201
and here remain with your uncertainty! 3.03.124
while i remain above the ground, you shall 4.01. 51
the people will remain uncertain whilst | 'twixt 5.06. 16
single sole of it is worn, the jest may remain, ROM 2.04. 63 P
here will i remain | with worms that are thy 5.03.108
of men, and remain a beast with the beasts? TIM 4.03.325 P
yet remain assur'd | that he's a made–up villain 5.01. 97
and constant do remain to keep him so. JC 3.01. 73
and we beseech you bend you to remain | here in HAM 1.02.115
my words fly up, my thoughts remain below: 3.03. 97
remain this ample third of our fair kingdom, LR 1.01. 80
and let me still remain | the true blank of 1.01.158
not in this land shall he remain uncaught; 2.01. 57
neither can be encoy'd | if both remain alive: 5.01. 59
if cassio do remain, | he hath a daily beauty in OTH 5.01. 18
and i, hence fleeting, here remain with thee. ANT 1.03.104
for't cannot be | we shall remain in friendship, 2.02.113
not for himself, | remain in't as thou mayst. 2.06. 29
you, | that we remain your friend, and so adieu. 5.02.189
dolabella, | i shall remain your debtor. 5.02.205
i will remain | the loyall'st husband that did CYM 1.01. 95
remain, remain thou here, | while sense can keep 1.01.117
remain, remain thou here, | while sense can keep 1.01.117
i dare lay mine honor | he will remain so. 1.01.175
if she remain unseduc'd, you not making it 1.04.160 P
if none will do, let her remain; 2.03. 16 P
king as i am bold her honor | will remain hers. 2.04. 3
all the remain is "welcome!" 3.01. 85
remain here in the cave, | we'll come to you 4.02. 1
betide to cloten, but remain | perplex'd in all. 4.03. 40
/unscissor'd shall this hair of mine remain, PER 3.03. 29
if she remain, | whom they have ravish'd must by 4.01.101
those that remain with you could wish their TNK 5.03. 35
love's gentle spring doth always fresh remain, VEN 801
"so thy surviving husband shall remain | the LUC 519
the scar that will despite of cure remain, 732
be, | to have their unseen sin remain untold; 753
remain | cave–keeping evils that obscurely sleep 1249
of what she was, no semblance did remain. 1453
one knight loves both, and both in thee remain. PP 8.14
inconstancy | more in women than in men remain. 17.12
reason none, | if what parts, can so remain." PHT 48
so shall those blots that do with me remain, SON 36. 3
by praising him here who doth hence remain! 39.14
which shall above that idle rank remain | beyond 122. 3
in thoughts, or to remain | in personal duty, LC 129
REMAIN'D 5 FR 0.0005 REL FR 4 V 1 P
where would you had remain'd until this time, ERR 4.04. 66
continuing, this mystery remain'd undiscover'd. WT 5.02.120 P
not sensible of fire, remain'd unscorch'd. JC 1.03. 18
some of her blood still pure and red remain'd, LUC 1742
which remain'd the foil | of this false jewel, LC 153
REMAINDER 10 FR 0.0011 REL FR 8 V 2 P
and the remainder mourning over them, | brimful TMP 5.01. 13
which is as dry as the remainder biscuit | after AYL 2.07. 39
i would repent out the remainder of nature. AWW 4.03.243 P
in my debt, | upon remainder of a dear account, R2 1.01.130
of four foot | (you see the poor remainder) H8 5.03. 20
nor the remainder viands | we do not throw in TRO 2.02. 70
shows | pass the remainder of our hateful days? TIT 3.01.132
the poor remainder of andronici | will hand in 5.03.131
fragment, some slender ort of his remainder. TIM 4.03.399 P
thus it remains, and the remainder thus. HAM 2.02.104
REMAINDERS 3 FR 0.0003 REL FR 2 V 1 P
and cut th' entail from all remainders, and a AWW 4.03.280 P
and the remainders that shall still depend, | to LR 1.04.250
and bless the good remainders of the court! CYM 1.01.129
REMAINETH 3 FR 0.0003 REL FR 3 V 0 P
remaineth none but mad–brain'd salisbury, | and 1H6 1.02. 15
remaineth nought but to inter our brethren, TIT 1.01.146
proud, | because the cry remaineth in one place, VEN 885
REMAINING 6 FR 0.0006 REL FR 6 V 0 P
dow'r | remaining in the coffer of her friends, MM 1.02.151
if any spark of life be yet remaining, | down, 3H6 5.06. 66
are we undone, cast off, nothing remaining? TIM 4.02. 2
remaining now in gallia? CYM 3.07. 12
blest beams, remaining | so long a poor unknown. 4.04. 42
and both she thinks too long with her remaining. LUC 1572
/REMAINS 1 FR 0.0001 REL FR 1 V 0 P
/what /more /remains? R2 4.01.222
REMAINS 42 FR 0.0047 REL FR 35 V 7 P
then no more remains | but that: MM 1.01. 7
ladies follow her, and but one visor remains. ADO 2.01.158 P
yet there remains unpaid | a hundred thousand LLL 2.01.133
nothing remains but that i kindle the boy AYL 1.01.172 P
where remains he? 3.02.223 P
with a pin, and there remains | some scar of it; 3.05. 21
if love have touch'd you, nought remains but so, SHR 1.01.161
by his authority he remains here, which he AWW 4.05. 65 P
norfolk, for thee remains a heavier doom, R2 1.03.148
should, | where now remains a sweet reversion, 1H4 4.01. 53
then this remains, that we divide our power. 5.05. 34
for me nothing remains. 1H6 1.01.174
but there remains a scruple in that too; 5.03. 93
what now remains, my lords, for us to do | but 3H6 4.03. 60
what then remains, we being thus arriv'd | from 4.07. 7
course, | where peremptory warwick now remains. 4.08. 59
to kimmalton, | where she remains now sick. H8 4.01. 35
and | to send for titus lartius, it remains, COR 2.02. 38
it then remains | that you do speak to the 2.02.134
remains | that, in th' official marks invested, 2.03.139
only that name remains; 4.05. 73
and his name remains | to th' ensuing age 5.03.147
had, | behold the poor remains, alive and dead! TIT 1.01. 81
and what remains will hardly stop the mouth | of TIM 2.02.147
i hope it remains not unkindly with your 3.06. 36 P
come, poor remains of friends, rest on this rock JC 5.05. 1
malice | remains in danger of her former tooth. MAC 3.02. 15
we | shall take upon 's what else remains to do, 5.06. 5
and now remains | that we find out the cause of HAM 2.02.100
thus it remains, and the remainder thus. 2.02.104
this bad begins and worse remains behind. 3.04.179
part of myself, and what remains is bestial. OTH 2.03.264 P
remains the censure of this hellish villain, 5.02.368
but my full heart | remains in use with you. ANT 1.03. 44
all happiness, that remains loyal to his vow, CYM 3.02. 46 P
i nothing know where she remains, why gone, 4.03. 14
what face remains alive that's worth the viewing VEN 1076
his hand, that yet remains upon her breast LUC 463
good end | for lawful policy remains enacted. 529
she there remains a hopeless castaway; 744
and that is this, and this with thee remains. SON 74.14
and so much less of shame in me remains | by how LC 188
REMARKABLE 2 FR 0.0002 REL FR 1 V 1 P
and there is nothing left remarkable | beneath ANT 4.15. 67
and more remarkable in single oppositions; CYM 4.01. 13 P
REMARK'D 1 FR 0.0001 REL FR 1 V 0 P
speak of two | the most remark'd i' th' kingdom. H8 5.01. 33
REMEDIATE 1 FR 0.0001 REL FR 1 V 0 P
be aidant and remediate | in the good man's LR 4.04. 17
REMEDIED 2 FR 0.0002 REL FR 2 V 0 P
for things that are not to be remedied. 1H6 3.03. 4
but shall be remedied to your public laws | at TIM 5.04. 62
REMEDIES 8 FR 0.0009 REL FR 8 V 0 P
our remedies oft in ourselves do lie, | which we AWW 1.01.216
tenderly apply to her | some remedies for life. WT 3.02.153
tears show their love, but want their remedies. R2 3.03.203
his remedies are tame: COR 4.06. 2
both our remedies | within thy help and holy ROM 2.03. 51
seeking to give | losses their remedies." LR 2.02.170
when remedies are past, the griefs are ended OTH 1.03.202
for certainties | either are past remedies, or, CYM 1.06. 97
REMEDY 62 FR 0.0070 REL FR 47 V 15 P
i must, where is no remedy. TGV 2.02. 2
there is no remedy; WIV 1.03. 33 P
you must send her your page, no remedy. 2.02.122 P
here is no remedy. 5.05.231
well, what remedy? 5.05.236
the death of claudio — | but there's no remedy. MM 2.01.281
there is no remedy. 2.01.285
maiden, no remedy. 2.02. 48
vantage best have took | found out the remedy. 2.02. 75
is there no remedy? 3.01. 60
none, but such remedy as, to save a head, | to 3.01. 61
i have in doing good a remedy presents itself. 3.01.198 P
if there be no remedy for it but that you will 3.02. 1 P
lovest, | and i will fit thee with the remedy. ADO 1.01.319
if not a present remedy, at least a patient 1.03. 8 P
wak'st, if she be by, | beg of her for remedy. MND 3.02.109
which death, or absence, soon shall remedy. 3.02.244
apply | /to your eye, | gentle lover, remedy. 3.02.452
no remedy, my lord, when walls are so willful to 5.01.208 P
yet i know no wise remedy how to avoid it. AYL 1.01. 25 P
so love–shak'd, i pray you tell me your remedy. 3.02.368 P
knew the reason but they sought the remedy: 5.02. 37 P
i know my remedy; SHR in.1. 11 P

my remedy is then to pluck it out. 2.01.211
there is a remedy, approv'd, set down, | to cure AWW 1.03.228
since you set up your rest 'gainst remedy. 2.01.135
there is no remedy, sir, but you must die. 4.03.303 P
and both shall cease, without your remedy. 5.03.164
if it will not, what remedy? TN 1.05. 51 P
there's no remedy, sir, he will fight with you 3.04.296 P
sir andrew, there's no remedy, the gentleman 3.04.305 P
but there's no remedy, i shall answer it. 3.04.333
no remedy. | have you done there? WT 4.04.656
no remedy but you will — give me the office 5.01. 77
is there no remedy? JN 4.01. 90
i can get no remedy against this consumption of 2H4 1.02.236 P
well then, alone (since there's no remedy) | i 1H6 2.02. 57
rome shall remedy this. 3.01. 51
suffolk, what remedy? 5.03.132
yes, there is remedy enough, my lord. 5.03.135
but i will remedy this gear ere long, | or sell 2H6 3.01. 91
i did steer | toward this remedy, whereupon we H8 2.04.202
if entreaties | will render you no remedy, this 5.01.150
sickness found, ulysses, | what is the remedy? TRO 1.03.141
no remedy. 4.04. 55
there's no remedy, | unless, by not so doing, COR 3.02. 26
we may, | till time beget some careful remedy. TIT 4.03. 30
kinsmen, his sorrows are past remedy, | but /... 4.03. 31
i'll to the friar to know his remedy; ROM 3.05.241
if what thou speak'st speak not of remedy. 4.01. 67
and if thou darest, i'll give thee remedy. 4.01. 76
things without all remedy | should be without MAC 3.02. 11
thus, | that, open'd, lies within our remedy. HAM 2.02. 18
shame itself doth speak | for instant remedy. LR 1.04.247
why, there's no remedy. OTH 1.01. 35
the remedy then born — discover to me | what CYM 1.06. 98
alack, no remedy!) 3.04.162
there is no remedy. TNK 2.02.274
me, but enjoy't till | i may enforce my remedy. 3.01.123
the remedy indeed to do me good | is to let LUC 1028
and for this sin there is no remedy, | it is so SON 62. 3
growing a bath and healthful remedy | for men 154.11
/REMEMBER 2 FR 0.0002 REL FR 2 V 0 P
/yet /i /well /remember | /the /favors /of R2 4.01.167
/lest /we /remember /still /that /we /have /none TIT 3.02. 30
REMEMBER 207 FR 0.0234 REL FR 143 V 64 P
good, yet remember whom thou hast aboard. TMP 1.01. 19 P
canst thou remember | a time before we came unto 1.02. 38
let me remember thee what thou hast promis'd, 1.02.243
remember i have done thee worthy service, | told 1.02.247
the ditty does remember my drown'd father. 1.02.406
i remember | you did supplant your brother 2.01.270
no woman's face remember, | save, from my glass, 3.01. 49
remember | first to possess his books; 3.02. 91
that shall be by and by. i remember the story. 3.02.147 P
but remember | (for that's my business to you) 3.03. 68
company | some few odd lads you remember not. 5.01.255
nay, i remember the trick you serv'd me, when i TGV 4.04. 34 P
from me, | to bind him to remember my good will; 4.04. 98
for though i cannot remember what i did when you WIV 1.01.171 P
o, i should remember him. 1.04. 28 P
mistress page, remember you your cue. 3.03. 37 P
i pray you remember in your prain. 4.01. 35 P
remember, william, focative is caret. 4.01. 53 P
remember, son slender, my /daughter. 5.02. 2 P
come, and remember your parts. 5.04. 1 P
remember, jove, thou wast a bull for thy europa, 5.05. 3 P
practice hath enriched any | that we remember. MM 1.01. 13
but, soft and low, | "remember now my brother." 4.01. 69
i remember you, sir, by the sound of your voice; 5.01.327 P
and do you remember what you said of the duke? 5.01.330 P
i am sure you both of you remember me. ERR 5.01.292
ourselves we do remember, sir, by you; 5.01.293
daughter, remember what i told you. ADO 2.01. 66 P
i remember. 2.02. 15 P
i remember a pretty jest your daughter told /us 2.03.134 P
i remember his name. 3.03.127 P
but, masters, remember that i am an ass; 4.02. 76 P
"which, as i remember, hight costard" — LLL 1.01.255 P
i am much deceived but i remember the style. 4.01. 96
i do beseech thee remember thy courtesy; 5.01. 98 P
i remember. MND 2.01.154
do you not remember, lady, in your father's time MV 1.02.112 P
i remember him well, and i remember him worthy 1.02.120 P
well, and i remember him worthy of thy praise. 1.02.120 P
as i remember, adam, it was upon this fashion AYL 1.01. 1 P
not learn me how to remember any extraordinary 1.02. 6 P
i remember, when i was in love i broke my sword 2.04. 46 P
and i remember the kissing of her batler and the 2.04. 49 P
and i remember the wooing of a peascod instead 2.04. 51 P
i was an irish rat, which i can hardly remember. 3.02.178 P
can you remember any of the principal evils that 3.02.351 P
i do now remember a saying, "the fool doth think 5.01. 30 P
i do remember in this shepherd boy | some lively 5.04. 26
this fellow i remember | since once he play'd a SHR in.1. 83
signior baptista may remember me | near twenty 4.04. 3
if i can remember thee, i will think of thee at AWW 1.01.188 P
when thou hast none, remember thy friends. 1.01.213 P
you remember | the daughter of this lord? 5.03. 42
love, | in the sweet pangs of it remember me; TN 2.04. 16
remember who commended thy yellow stockings, and 2.05.153 P
i say, remember. 2.05.155 P
i do remember. 3.03. 48
"remember who commended thy yellow stockings" — 3.04. 47 P
that face of his i do remember well, | yet, when 5.01. 51
and yet, alas, now i remember me, | they say, 5.01.279
but do you remember? 5.01.374 P
i'll not remember you of my own lord, | who is WT 3.02.230
now may be | in fair bohemia, and remember well, 4.01. 21
remember "ston'd," and "flay'd alive." 4.04.804 P
whilest i remember | her and her virtues, i 5.01. 6
words that follow'd | should be "remember mine." 5.01. 67
remember since you ow'd no more to time | than i 5.01.219
i will pray | (if ever i remember to be holy) JN 3.03. 15
remember. 3.03. 69
yet i remember, when i was in france, | young 4.01. 14
on this ascension–day, remember well, | upon 5.01. 22
i shall remember more. R2 1.02. 65
make | will but remember me what a deal of world 1.03.269
that is not forgot | which ne'er i did remember. 2.03. 38
comfort, my liege, remember who you are. 3.02. 82
or not remember what i must be now! 3.03.139
it doth remember me the more of sorrow; 3.04. 14
i do remember well | the very time aumerle and 4.01. 60
remember, as thou read'st, thy promise pass'd. 5.03. 51
but i remember, when the fight was done, | when 1H4 1.03. 30
and now i remember me, his name is falstaff. 2.04.425 P
and yet i must remember you, my lord, | we were 5.01. 32
studied as to remember so weak a composition. 2H4 2.02. 8 P
my troth, i do now remember the poor creature, 2.02. 10 P
a disgrace is it to me to remember thy name, or 2.02. 13 P
a death's–head, do not bid me remember mine end. 2.04.235 P
by — | you, cousin nevil, as i may remember — 3.01. 66
do you remember since we lay all night in the 3.02.194 P
i remember at mile–end green, when i lay at 3.02.279 P
i do remember him at clement's inn, like a man 3.02.308 P
we do remember, but our argument | is all too 5.02. 23
and not to deliberate, not to remember, not to 5.05. 21 P
do you not remember, 'a saw a flea stick upon H5 2.03. 40 P
arrant counterfeit rascal, i remember him now; 3.06. 62 P
but he'll remember with advantages | what feats 4.03. 50
remember, lords, your oaths to henry sworn: 1H6 1.01.162
i do remember it, and here take my leave, | to 1.01.165
gone, | remember to avenge me on the french." 1.04. 94
porter, remember what i gave in charge, | and 2.03. 1
i do remember how my father said | a stouter 3.04. 18
remember where we are — | in france, amongst a 4.01.137
fond man, remember that thou hast a wife, | then 5.03. 81
but still remember what the lord hath done. 2H6 2.01. 84
remember it, and let it make thee crestfall'n, 4.01. 59
no, warwick, i remember it to my grief, | and, 3H6 1.01. 93
i do remember them too well: R3 1.03.117
o, but remember this another day, | when he 1.03.298
remember our reward when the deed's done. 1.04.123 P
i will never more remember | our former hatred, 2.01. 23
o, remember, god, | to hear her prayer for them, 3.03. 19
i do remember me, henry the sixt | did prophesy 4.02. 95
sorrow, | remember margaret was a prophetess." 5.01. 27
time | forbids to dwell upon, yet remember this: 5.03.239
remember whom you are to cope withal — | a sort 5.03.315
i remember | of such a time, being my sworn H8 1.02.190
you remember | how under my oppression i did 2.04.208
memory, i yet remember | some of these articles, 3.02.303
'em, | and something over to remember me by. 4.02.151
remember me | in all humility unto his highness. 4.02.160
and in thy pray'rs remember | th' estate of my 5.01. 73
my good mistress will | remember in my prayers. 5.01. 78
i shall remember this bold language. 5.02.119
do. | remember your bold life too. 5.02.120
you'll remember your brother's excuse? TRO 3.01.142 P
will you remember? 5.02. 12
remember? yes. 5.02. 13
what shall she remember? 5.02. 16
but, if you do remember, | i send it through the COR 1.01.134
we met here both to thank and to remember | with 2.02. 47
if he remember | a kinder value of the people 2.02. 58
fellow, remember my name is menenius, always 5.02. 28 P
or, if you'ld ask, remember this before: 5.03. 79
for a noble man | still to remember wrongs? 5.03.155
remember, boys, i pour'd forth tears in vain TIT 2.03.163
gregory, remember thy washing blow. ROM 1.01. 62 P
that shall she, marry, i remember it well. 1.03. 22
let me stand here till thou remember it. 2.02.171
i do remember an apothecary — | and hereabouts 5.01. 37
as i remember, this should be the house. 5.01. 55
i do remember well where i should be, | and 5.03.149
pleas'd the gods to remember my father's age, TIM 1.02. 2
and now i remember, my lord, you gave | good 1.02.210
i shall remember: JC 1.02. 9
was more foolery yet, if i could remember it. 1.02.287 P
but all remember | what you have said, and show 2.01.222
remember that you call on me to–day; 2.02.122
be near me, that i may remember you. 2.02.123
i remember | the first time ever caesar put it 3.02.170
remember march, the ides of march remember: 4.03. 18
remember march, the ides of march remember: 4.03. 18
i pray you remember the porter. MAC 2.03. 20 P
threescore and ten i can remember well, | within 2.04. 1
but i remember now | i am in this earthly world 4.02. 74
i cannot but remember such things were, | that 4.03.222
heaven and earth, | must i remember? HAM 1.02.143
and remember well | what i have said to you. 1.03. 84
remember me. 1.05. 91
remember thee! 1.05. 95
remember thee! 1.05. 97
remember me." 1.05.111
for the play, i remember, pleas'd not the 2.02.436 P
i remember one said there were no sallets in the 2.02.441 P
pray you, love, remember. 4.05.176 P
other — | you do remember all the circumstance? 5.02. 2
remember it, my lord! 5.02. 3
i beseech you remember. 5.02.104 P
remember him hereafter as my honorable friend. LR 1.01. 27 P
remember what i have said. 1.03. 21
wind and rain, i never | remember to have heard. 3.02. 48
i do remember now. 4.06. 75
the trick of that voice i do well remember; 4.06.106
i remember thine eyes well enough. 4.06.136 P
old unhappy traitor, | briefly thyself remember; 4.06.229
for your sisters | have (as i do remember) done 4.07. 73
i remember a mass of things, but nothing OTH 2.03.288 P
lay on my bed my wedding–sheets — remember; 4.02.105
quite | were to remember that the present need ANT 2.02.101
remember, | if e'er thou look'st on majesty. 3.03. 17
for i remember now | how he's employ'd; 5.01. 71
we shall remember | as things but done by chance 5.02.119
you do remember | this stain upon her? CYM 2.04.138
remember, sir, my liege, | the kings your 3.01. 16
came our enemy, remember | he was paid for that. 4.02.245
and my false spirits | quail to remember — give 5.05.149
remember me at court, where i was taught | of 5.05.193
and, to remember what he does, | build his PER 2.ch. 13
remember earthly man | is but a substance that 2.01. 2
you'll remember from whence you had them. 2.01.151 P
that i was shipp'd at sea i well remember, 3.04. 5
thy oath remember, thou hast sworn to do't. 4.01. 1
remember what i have said. 4.01. 46
as i can remember, by my troth, | i never did 4.01. 73
e'er since i can remember. 4.06. 73 P
to my just belief, | i'll well remember you. 5.01.239
can you remember what i call'd the man? 5.03. 52
remember that your fame | knolls in the ear o' TNK 1.01.133
and | thou shalt remember nothing more than what 1.01.185
remember me | to our all–royal brother, for 1.03. 11
"remember what your fathers were, and conquer!" 2.02. 36
steward's daughter — | do you remember her? 3.03. 30
sister | had her share too, as i remember, 3.03. 37
go thy ways, i'll remember thee, i'll fit thee! 3.05. 58
day, | i well remember, you outdid me, cousin; 3.06. 73
you had indeed, | a bright bay, i remember. 3.06. 78
good sir, remember. 4.01. 3
this line, remember not | the hand that writ it, SON 71. 5
to keep an adjunct to remember thee | were to 122.13
REMEMBERED 3 FR 0.0003 REL FR 3 V 0 P
the world, | but we in it shall be remembered — H5 4.03. 59
for death remembered should be like a mirror, PER 1.01. 45
knife, | too base of thee to be remembered. SON 74.12
/REMEMBERS 1 FR 0.0001 REL FR 1 V 0 P
/tune, /remembers | /what /we /are /come /about, LR 4.03. 39
REMEMBERS 3 FR 0.0003 REL FR 2 V 1 P
words, | remembers me of all his gracious parts, JN 3.04. 96
and he no more remembers his mother now than an COR 5.04. 16 P
the skill i have | remembers not these garments; LR 4.07. 66
REMEMBER'ST 1 FR 0.0001 REL FR 1 V 0 P
remember'st thou any that have died on't? ANT 5.02.249
REMEMBER'T 1 FR 0.0001 REL FR 0 V 1 P
to ask him one thing, i'll remember't anon.) CYM 3.05.131 P
REMEMBRANCE 64 FR 0.0072 REL FR 50 V 14 P
tell me, that | hath kept with thy remembrance. TMP 1.02. 44
an assurance | that my remembrance warrants. 1.02. 46
turn'd you to, | which is from my remembrance! 1.02. 65
although this lord of weak remembrance, this 2.01.232
(how sharp the point of this remembrance is!) 5.01.138
keep this remembrance for thy julia's sake. TGV 2.02. 5
so the remembrance of my former love | is by a 2.04.194
i pray you now remembrance to–morrow on the WIV 3.03.239 P
i pray you have your remembrance, child. 4.01. 46 P
an abstract for the remembrance of such places, 4.02. 62 P
for the remembrance of my father's death. LLL 5.02.810
to me now | as the remembrance of an idle gaud MND 4.01.167
that lies in woe | in remembrance of a shroud. 5.01.378
take some remembrance of us, as a tribute, | not MV 4.01.422
for your father's remembrance, be at accord. AYL 1.01. 64 P
the remembrance of her father never approaches AWW 1.01. 49 P
and these great tears grace his remembrance more 1.01. 80
his good remembrance, sir, | lies richer in your 1.02. 48
the time of his remembrance to this very instant 4.03.109 P
out of a self–gracious remembrance, did first 4.05. 73 P
what is lost | makes the remembrance dear. 5.03. 20
keep fresh | and lasting in her sad remembrance. TN 1.01. 31
i seem to drown her remembrance again with more. 2.01. 31 P
my remembrance is very free and clear from any 3.04.227 P
own | from my remembrance clearly banish'd his. 5.01.282
me with the remembrance of that penitent (as WT 4.02. 22 P
grace and remembrance be to you both, | and 4.04. 76
nor the remembrance | of his most sovereign name 5.01. 25
which has | my evils conjur'd to remembrance, 5.03. 40
out, | and keep it safe for our remembrance. JN 5.02. 2
unkind remembrance! 5.06. 12
writ in remembrance more than things long past. R2 2.01. 14
seen, | in the remembrance of a weeping queen. 3.04.107
to rain upon remembrance with mine eyes, | that 2H4 2.03. 59
and history his loss | to new remembrance; 4.01.202
with this remembrance, that you use the same 5.02.115
awake remembrance of these valiant dead, | and H5 1.02.115
urn, | tombless, with no remembrance over them. 1.02.229
all this from my remembrance brutish wrath R3 2.01.119
thou drown the sad remembrance of those wrongs 4.04.252
ay, if yourself's remembrance wrong yourself. 4.04.421
jocund | in the remembrance of so fair a dream. 5.03.233
may give me | remembrance of my father–in–law, H8 3.02. 8
more than remembrance of my father's death. TIT 3.01.240
let it not cumber your better remembrance. TIM 3.06. 46 P
my young remembrance cannot parallel | a fellow MAC 2.03. 62
let your remembrance apply to banquo, | present 3.02. 30
to satisfy my remembrance the more strongly. 5.01. 33 P
on him | together with remembrance of ourselves. HAM 1.02. 7
such thanks | as fits a king's remembrance. 2.02. 26
there's rosemary, that's for remembrance; 4.05.175 P
in madness, thoughts and remembrance fitted. 4.05.178 P
this was her first remembrance from the moor. OTH 3.03.291
this is from some mistress, some remembrance; 3.04.186
which seem'd to tell them his remembrance lay ANT 1.05. 57
only, | lest my remembrance suffer ill report; 2.02.156
must wear the print of his remembrance on't, CYM 2.03. 43
whose remembrance | is yet fresh in their grief. 2.04. 14
(and praise | be given to your remembrance), the 2.04. 93
(whose remembrance yet | lives in men's eyes, 3.01. 2
you see, not wore him | from my remembrance. 4.04. 24
by her own most clear remembrance, she | made PER 5.03. 12
bereft, | nor it nor no remembrance what it was: SON 5.12
i summon up remembrance of things past, | i sigh 30. 2
REMEMBRANCER 2 FR 0.0002 REL FR 2 V 0 P
sweet remembrancer! MAC 3.04. 36
and the remembrancer of her to hold | the CYM 1.05. 77
REMEMBRANCES 5 FR 0.0005 REL FR 5 V 0 P
let us not burthen our remembrances with | a TMP 5.01.199
by our remembrances of days foregone, | such AWW 1.03.134
in place, we did commend | to your remembrances; COR 2.03.248
call me to your remembrances. TIM 3.05. 91
lord, i have remembrances of yours | that i have HAM 3.01. 92
REMEMB'RED 28 FR 0.0031 REL FR 19 V 9 P
you being then (if you be rememb'red) cracking MM 2.01.106 P
i telling you then (if you be rememb'red) that 2.01.110 P
his part, and equally rememb'red by don pedro. ADO 1.01. 13 P
you let it be rememb'red in his punishment. 5.01.306 P
she | reigns in my blood and will rememb'red be. LLL 4.03. 94
marry, well rememb'red. MV 2.08. 26
is not so sharp | as friend rememb'red not. AYL 2.07.189
and, now i am rememb'red, scorn'd at me. 3.05.131
but if you be rememb'red, | i did not bid you SHR 4.03. 96
and what i saw, to my good use i rememb'red. WT 4.04.604 P
the grave, | but not rememb'red in thy epitaph! 1H4 5.04.101

bell, | rememb'red tolling a departing friend. 2H4 1.01.103
my lord, my humble duty rememb'red, i will not 2.01.125 P
we will accite | (as i before rememb'red) all 5.02.142
be in their flowing cups freshly rememb'red. H5 4.03. 55
if your majesties is rememb'red of it, the 4.07. 98 P
now, by my troth, if i had been rememb'red, | i R3 2.04. 23
if i could 'a' rememb'red a gilt counterfeit, TRO 2.03. 25 P
and they smart | to hear themselves rememb'red. COR 1.09. 29
be you rememb'red, marcus, she's gone, she's TIT 4.03. 5
i have rememb'red me, thou s' hear our counsel. ROM 1.03. 9
which craves to be rememb'red | with those five TIM 2.02.228
in thy orisons | be all my sins rememb'red. HAM 3.01. 89
"let our reciprocal vows be rememb'red. LR 4.06.262 P
o, be rememb'red, no outrageous thing | from LUC 607
but if thou live rememb'red not to be, | die SON 3.13
for thy sweet love rememb'red such wealth brings 29.13
that our night of woe might have rememb'red | my 120. 9
REMEMB'REST 4 FR 0.0004 REL FR 3 V 1 P
if thou rememb'rest aught ere thou cam'st here, TMP 1.02. 51
thou rememb'rest | since once i sat upon a MND 2.01.148
if thou rememb'rest not the slightest folly AYL 2.04. 34
thou but rememb'rest me of mine own conception.
LR 1.04. 67 P
REMEMB'RING 5 FR 0.0005 REL FR 5 V 0 P
i, not rememb'ring how i cried out then, | will TMP 1.02.133
rememb'ring that my love to her is dead; TGV 2.06. 28
as in a soul rememb'ring my good friends, | and, R2 2.03. 47
the interim, by rememb'ring you 'tis past. H5 5.pr. 43
there, | rememb'ring how i love thy company. ROM 2.02.173
/REMERCIMENTS 1 FR 0.0001 REL FR 0 V 1 P
mes genoux /je vous donne mille /remerciments; H5 4.04. 55 P
REMISS 5 FR 0.0005 REL FR 4 V 1 P
belike, thinking me remiss in mine office, MM 4.02.116 P
he means, my lord, that we are too remiss, R2 3.02. 33
that thus we die, while remiss traitors sleep. 1H6 4.03. 29
the prince must think me tardy and remiss, TRO 4.04.141
he, being remiss, | most generous, and free from HAM 4.07.134
REMISSION 5 FR 0.0005 REL FR 5 V 0 P
back | and ask remission for my folly past. TGV 1.02. 65
i find an apt remission in myself; MM 5.01.498
i will beg | a ragged and forestall'd remission. 2H4 5.02. 38
my remission lies | in volscian breasts. COR 5.02. 84
decays, | the guilty rebel for remission prays. LUC 714
REMISSNESS 1 FR 0.0001 REL FR 1 V 0 P
either now, or by remissness new conceiv'd, MM 2.02. 96
REMIT 4 FR 0.0004 REL FR 4 V 0 P
as to remit | their saucy sweetness that do coin MM 2.04. 44
and therewithal | remit thy other forfeits. 5.01.520
i remit both twain. LLL 5.02.459
i do remit these young men's heinous faults. TIT 1.01.484
REMNANT 5 FR 0.0005 REL FR 5 V 0 P
where i thought the remnant of mine age | should TGV 3.01. 74
away, thou rag, thou quantity, thou remnant, SHR 4.03.111
where i may think the remnant of my thoughts JN 5.04. 46
the remnant northward lying off from trent. 1H4 3.01. 78
thou bloodless remnant of that royal blood, | be R3 1.02. 7
REMNANTS 3 FR 0.0003 REL FR 2 V 1 P
some odd quirks and remnants of wit broken on me
ADO 2.03.236 P
leave those remnants | of fool and feather that H8 1.03. 24
remnants of packthread, and old cakes of roses ROM 5.01. 47
REMONSTRANCE 1 FR 0.0001 REL FR 1 V 0 P
make rash remonstrance of my hidden pow'r | than
MM 5.01.392
REMORSE 30 FR 0.0034 REL FR 25 V 5 P
expell'd remorse and nature, whom, with TMP 5.01. 76
river with as little remorse as they would have WIV 3.05. 10 P
if so your heart were touch'd with that remorse MM 2.02. 54
my sisterly remorse confutes mine honor, | and i 5.01.100
shall on her behalf | change slander to remorse; ADO 4.01.211
thou'lt show thy mercy and remorse more strange
MV 4.01. 20
it was your pleasure and your own remorse. AYL 1.03. 70
without any mitigation or remorse of voice? TN 2.03. 90 P
breath | of soft petitions, pity, and remorse, JN 2.01.478
rage | presented to the tears of soft remorse. 4.03. 50
it seem | like rivers of remorse and innocency. 4.03.110
what says monsieur remorse? 1H4 1.02.113 P
mov'd with remorse of these outrageous broils, 1H6 5.04. 97
thy words move rage and not remorse in me. 2H6 4.01.112
i feel remorse in myself with his words; 4.07.105 P
and nero will be tainted with remorse | to hear 3H6 3.01. 40
thought of them would have stirr'd up remorse, 5.05. 64
"judgment" hath bred a kind of remorse in me. R3 1.04.108 P
of heart | and gentle, kind, effeminate remorse, 3.07.211
hence both are gone with conscience and remorse 4.03. 20
in our sister work | some touches of remorse? TRO 2.02.115
throat shall cut, | and mince it sans remorse. TIM 4.03.123
is when it disjoins | remorse from power; JC 2.01. 19
stop up th' access and passage to remorse, MAC 1.05. 44
with less remorse than pyrrhus' bleeding sword HAM 2.02.491
a servant that he bred, thrill'd with remorse, LR 4.02. 73
abandon all remorse; OTH 3.03.369
command, | and to obey shall be in me remorse, 3.03.468
"pity," she cries, "some favor, some remorse!" VEN 257
poor wretches have remorse in poor abuses, LUC 269
REMORSEFUL 4 FR 0.0004 REL FR 4 V 0 P
valiant, wise, remorseful, well accomplish'd: TGV 4.03. 13
late, | like a remorseful pardon slowly carried, AWW 5.03. 58
and remorseful day | is crept into the bosom of 2H6 4.01. 1
these eyes, which never shed remorseful tear — R3 1.02.155
REMORSELESS 4 FR 0.0004 REL FR 4 V 0 P
even so remorseless have they borne him hence; 2H6 3.01.213
stern, obdurate, flinty, rough, remorseless. 3H6 1.04.142
remorseless, treacherous, lecherous, kindless HAM 2.02.581
fixed | in the remorseless wrinkles of his face; LUC 562
REMOTE 9 FR 0.0010 REL FR 9 V 0 P
remote from all the pleasures of the world; LLL 5.02.796
from athens is her house remote seven leagues; MND 1.01.159
it | to some remote and desert place quite out WT 2.03.176
oath, | places remote enough are in bohemia, 3.03. 31
cause — | to grace the gentry of a land remote, JN 5.02. 31
broils | to be commenc'd in stronds afar remote. 1H4 1.01. 4
of rome, | or rudely visit them in parts remote, COR 4.05.142
hearts remote, yet not asunder; PHT 29
from limits far remote, where thou dost stay. SON 44. 4
REMOTION 2 FR 0.0002 REL FR 1 V 1 P
all thy safety were remotion and thy defense TIM 4.03.342 P
me | that this remotion of the duke and her | is LR 2.04.114
REMOV'D 22 FR 0.0024 REL FR 13 V 9 P
see you the fornicatress be remov'd. MM 2.02. 23
what, remov'd? MND 2.02.151
but mountains may be remov'd with earthquakes, AYL 3.02.185 P
you could purchase in so remov'd a dwelling. 3.02.342 P
upon a lie seven times remov'd (bear your body 5.04. 68 P
entertainment, your inclining cannot be remov'd. AWW 3.06. 39 P
he hence remov'd last night, and with more haste 5.01. 23
provided that, when he's remov'd, your highness WT 1.02.335
are germane to him (though remov'd fifty times) 4.04.774 P
death of hermione, visited that remov'd house. 5.02.107 P
o, be remov'd from him, and answer well! JN 3.01.218
i have remov'd falstaff's horse, and he frets 1H4 2.02. 1 P
the rascal hath remov'd my horse, and tied him i 2.02. 11 P
and dear a trust | on any soul remov'd, but on 4.01. 35
was, for that (young richard thus remov'd, 1H6 2.05. 71
and like a mountain, not to be remov'd. 2.05.103
then deputy of ireland, who remov'd, | earl H8 2.01. 42
since which she was remov'd to kimmalton, 4.01. 34
and the impediment most profitably remov'd, OTH 2.01.279 P
but things remov'd that hidden in /thee lie! SON 31. 8
upon the farthest earth remov'd from thee, | for 44. 6
and yet this time remov'd was summer's time, 97. 5
REMOVE 37 FR 0.0041 REL FR 35 V 2 P
wine afore, it will go near to remove his fit. TMP 2.02. 75 P
i must remove | some thousands of these logs, 3.01. 9
in our remove be thou at full ourself. MM 1.01. 43
o, come, let us remove, | the sight of lovers AYL 3.04. 56
him that mov'd you hither | remove you hence. SHR 2.01.196
the moon | as or by oath remove or counsel shake WT 1.02.428
to't) once remove | the root of his opinion, 2.03. 89
o nation, that thou couldst remove! JN 5.02. 33
of my pow'r, | as i upon advantage did remove, 5.07. 62
i would remove these tedious stumbling–blocks, 2H6 1.02. 64
his arms are only to remove from thee | the duke 4.09. 29
is to remove proud somerset from the king, 5.01. 36
the cure is to | remove these thoughts from you; H8 2.04.102
before 's, for the remove | bring up your army; COR 1.02. 28
but their children's end, nought could remove, ROM pr 11
unless good counsel may the cause remove. 1.01.142
with the join–stools, remove the court–cupboard, 1.05. 6 P
you, to remove that siege of grief from her, 5.03.237
good god betimes remove | the means that makes MAC 4.03.162
remove from her the means of all annoyance, 5.01. 76
till birnan wood remove to dunsinane | i cannot 5.03. 2
once more remove, good friends. HAM 1.05.163
he most violent author | of his own just remove; 4.05. 81
there was no purpose in them | of this remove. LR 2.04. 4
if you think other, | remove your thought; OTH 4.02. 14
cannot remove nor choke the strong conception 5.02. 55
under us require, | our quick remove from hence. ANT 1.02.196
come on then, and remove him. CYM 4.02.257
no, but from this place to remove your lordship; TNK 2.02.261
from his soft bosom never to remove | till he VEN 81
the sun doth burn my face, i must remove." 186
remove your siege from my unyielding heart, | to 423
if but for fear of this, thy will remove: LUC 614
in love, | there a nay is plac'd without remove. PP 17. 8
love and am beloved | where i may not remove, SON 25.14
finds, | or bends with the remover to remove. 116. 4
and did thence remove | to spend her living in LC 237
REMOVED 11 FR 0.0012 REL FR 11 V 0 P
who is so far from italy removed | i ne'er again TMP 2.01.111
you | how i have ever lov'd the life removed, MM 1.03. 8
to shine | (those clouds removed) upon our LLL 5.02.206
and grew a twenty years removed thing | while TN 5.01. 89
removed from thy sin–conceiving womb. JN 2.01.182
sin and her the plague | on this removed issue, 2.01.186
crest | that is removed by a staff of france; 2.01.318
with blood removed but little from her own? ROM 3.03. 96
action | it waves you to a more removed ground, HAM 1.04. 61
grant them removed and grant that this your STM II.C 72
where i may not remove, nor be removed. SON 25.14
REMOVEDNESS 1 FR 0.0001 REL FR 0 V 1 P
my service which look upon his removedness; WT 4.02. 36 P
REMOVER 1 FR 0.0001 REL FR 1 V 0 P
finds, | or bends with the remover to remove. SON 116. 4
REMOVES 3 FR 0.0003 REL FR 3 V 0 P
loves | woo contrary, deceiv'd by these removes. LLL 5.02.135
she moves me not, or not removes, at least, SHR 1.02. 72
who hath for four or five removes come short AWW 5.03.131
REMOVING 5 FR 0.0005 REL FR 2 V 3 P
but now thy uncle is removing hence, | as 1H6 2.05.104
can be so determinate as the removing of cassio. OTH 4.02.227 P
how do you mean, removing him? 4.02.228 P
marry, the removing of the strangers, which STM II.C 70 P
my will is strong, past reason's weak removing: LUC 243
/REMUNERATE 1 FR 0.0001 REL FR 1 V 0 P
/yes, /and /will /nobly /him /remunerate. TIT 1.01.398
REMUNERATION 12 FR 0.0013 REL FR 1 V 11 P
there is remuneration, for the best ward of mine LLL 3.01.131 P
now will i look to his remuneration. 3.01.136 P
remuneration! 3.01.136 P
three farthings — remuneration. 3.01.138 P
"no, i'll give you a remuneration": 3.01.140 P
remuneration: 3.01.140 P
ribbon may a man buy for a remuneration? 3.01.146 P
o, what is a remuneration? 3.01.147 P
better than remuneration, aleven–pence–farthing 3.01.170 P
remuneration! 3.01.172 P
there is the very remuneration i had of thy 5.01. 73 P
virtue seek | remuneration for the thing it was; TRO 3.03.170
REND *(also rents*)*
REND 13 FR 0.0014 REL FR 12 V 1 P
i will rend an oak | and peg thee in his knotty TMP 1.02.294
whose dear sake thou didst then rend thy faith TGV 5.04. 47
and sleep and snore, and rend apparel out — MV 2.05. 5
our own wings, and to rend our own soldiers! AWW 3.06. 49 P
that they suppos'd i could rend bars of steel, 1H6 1.04. 51
and from thy burgonet i'll rend thy bear, | and 2H6 5.01.208
and so he comes, to rend his limbs asunder. 3H6 1.03. 15
we must not rend our subjects from our laws, H8 1.02. 93
rend and deracinate | the unity and married calm TRO 1.03. 99
whose rage doth rend | like interrupted waters, COR 3.01.247
the dreadful thunder | doth rend the region; HAM 2.02.487
great, and let not | a leaner action rend us. ANT 2.02. 19
the very principals did seem to rend, | and all PER 3.02. 16
RENDER 43 FR 0.0048 REL FR 39 V 4 P
action | at our more leisure shall i render you; MM 1.03. 49
nothing, unless you render her again. ADO 4.01. 29
hand, claudio shall render me a dear account. 4.01.333 P
nor to their penn'd speech render we no grace, LLL 5.02.147
and what is mine my love shall render him. MND 1.01. 96
herb), | i'll make her render up her page to me. 2.01.185
valor's excrement | to render them redoubted! MV 3.02. 88
see thou render this | into my /cousin's hands, 3.04. 49
and that same prayer doth teach us all to render 4.01.201
what mercy can you render him, antonio? 4.01.378
to render it | upon his death unto the gentleman 4.01.383
perforce, i will render thee again in affection. AYL 1.02. 20 P
and he did render him the most unnatural | that 4.03.122
which i presume shall render you no blame, | but AWW 5.01. 32
that it shall render vengeance and revenge R2 4.01. 67
account | that he shall render every glory up, 1H4 3.02.150
leave | freely to render what we have in charge? H5 1.02.238
if my father render fair return, | it is against 2.04.127
i | can nothing render but allegiant thanks, H8 3.02.176
you | to render up the great seal presently 3.02.229
if entreaties | will render you no remedy, this 5.01.150
to calchas' house, and there to render him, TRO 4.01. 38
in kissing, do you render or receive? 4.05. 36
we render you the tenth, to be ta'en forth, COR 1.09. 34
greater devotion than they can render it him, 2.02. 19 P
store, | that thou wilt never render to me more! TIT 1.01. 95
tears | i render for my brethren's obsequies; 1.01.160
i could render one. TIM 2.02.103 P
rather than render back, out with your knives, 4.01. 9
and send forth us to make their sorrowed render, 5.01.149
render me worthy of this noble wife! JC 2.01.303
let each man render me his bloody hand. 3.01.184
and tormenting flames | must render up myself. HAM 1.05. 4
to caesar will i render | my legions and my ANT 3.10. 32
render to me some corporal sign about her, CYM 2.04.119
report should render him hourly to your ear | as 3.04.150
may drive us to a render | where we have liv'd, 4.04. 11
take | no stricter render of me than my all. 5.04. 17
that this gentleman may render | of whom he had 5.05.135
to wrong the wronger till he render right, | to LUC 943
no art, | but mutual render, only me for thee. SON 125.12
must be, | and her quietus is to render thee. 126.12
but yield them up where i myself must render: LC 221
RENDER'D 2 FR 0.0002 REL FR 2 V 0 P
whereof | the king is render'd lost. AWW 1.03.230
it were a mock | apt to be render'd, for some JC 2.02. 97
RENDERED 2 FR 0.0002 REL FR 2 V 0 P
and public reasons shall be rendered | of JC 3.02. 7
reasons, | when severally we hear them rendered. 3.02. 10
RENDERS 4 FR 0.0004 REL FR 3 V 1 P
given him a penny and he renders me the beggarly
AYL 2.05. 29 P
and that's the dearest grace it renders you — 1H4 3.01.180
which renders good for bad, blessings for curses R3 1.02. 69
receives and renders back | his figure and his TRO 3.03.122
RENDEZVOUS 4 FR 0.0004 REL FR 3 V 1 P
a rendezvous, a home to fly unto, | if that the 1H4 4.01. 57
that is my rest, that is the rendezvous of it. H5 2.01. 16 P
and there my rendezvous is quite cut off. 5.01. 83
you know the rendezvous. HAM 4.04. 4
/REND'RED 1 FR 0.0001 REL FR 0 V 1 P
of this day, to be /rend'red by our /assistance, LLL 5.01.120 P
REND'RED 9 FR 0.0010 REL FR 9 V 0 P
's | than this for whom we rend'red up this woe. ADO 5.03. 33
as there is no firm reason to be rend'red | why MV 4.01. 53
slept in his face and rend'red such aspect | as 1H4 3.02. 82
that freely rend'red me these news for true. 2H4 1.01. 27
the word of peace is rend'red. 4.02. 87
hear | a fearful battle rend'red you in music; H5 1.01. 44
craves | all dues be rend'red to their owners: TRO 2.02.174
this way, my lord, the castle's gently rend'red: MAC 5.07. 24
she rend'red life, | thy name so buried in her. ANT 4.14. 33
REND'RING 2 FR 0.0002 REL FR 2 V 0 P
how shalt thou hope for mercy, rend'ring none? MV 4.01. 88
state, | rend'ring faint quittance, wearied and 2H4 1.01.108
RENEGADO 1 FR 0.0001 REL FR 0 V 1 P
malvolio is turn'd heathen, a very renegado; TN 3.02. 70 P
/RENEGE 1 FR 0.0001 REL FR 1 V 0 P
/renege, affirm, and turn their halcyon beaks LR 2.02. 78
RENEGES 1 FR 0.0001 REL FR 1 V 0 P
the buckles on his breast, reneges all temper, ANT 1.01. 8
RENEW 13 FR 0.0014 REL FR 12 V 1 P
the enchanted herbs | that did renew old aeson. MV 5.01. 14
and with your puissant arm renew their feats. H5 1.02.116
hark, countrymen, either renew the fight, | or 1H6 1.05. 27
live | to bear his image and renew his glories! 3H6 5.04. 54
that doth renew swifter than blood decays! TRO 3.02.163
renew, renew! 5.05. 6
renew, renew! 5.05. 6
shall he die, | and i'll renew me in his fall. COR 5.06. 48
and by her presence still renew his sorrows. TIT 5.03. 42
but then renew i could not, like the moon; TIM 4.03. 69
creatures, would even renew me with your eyes. CYM 3.02. 42 P
renew thy strength; 5.05.150
sweet love, renew thy force, be it not said SON 56. 1
RENEW'D 4 FR 0.0004 REL FR 3 V 1 P
our house, let our old acquaintance be renew'd. 2H4 3.02.294 P
give renew'd fire to our extincted spirits, OTH 2.01. 81
part shame, part spirit renew'd, that some, CYM 5.03. 35
pity me then, and wish i were renew'd, | whilst SON 111. 8
RENEWEST 1 FR 0.0001 REL FR 1 V 0 P
whose fresh repair if now thou not renewest, SON 3. 3
RENEWS 1 FR 0.0001 REL FR 1 V 0 P
no object but her passion's strength renews; LUC 1103
RENOUNCE 5 FR 0.0005 REL FR 5 V 0 P
are true, | otherwise i renounce all confidence. 1H6 1.02. 97
renounce your soil, give sheep in lions' stead: 1.05. 29
him, | i here renounce him and return to henry. 3H6 3.03.194
this world i do renounce, and in your sights LR 4.06. 35
win the moor, were/'t to renounce his baptism, OTH 2.03.343
RENOUNCEMENT 1 FR 0.0001 REL FR 1 V 0 P
by your renouncement an immortal spirit, | and MM 1.04. 35
RENOUNCING 1 FR 0.0001 REL FR 1 V 0 P
renouncing clean | the faith they have in tennis H8 1.03. 29
RENOWM'D 1 FR 0.0001 REL FR 1 V 0 P
dost thou with him | that is renowm'd for faith? ROM 3.05. 62
RENOWMED 3 FR 0.0003 REL FR 3 V 0 P

honor hath he got | against renowmed douglas! 1H4 3.02.107
renowmed titus, more than half my soul — TIT 1.01.373
renowmed lucius, from our troops i stray'd | to 5.01. 20
RENOWN 24 FR 0.0027 REL FR 21 V 3 P
milan, | of whom so often i have heard renown, TMP 5.01.193
high honor, and renown | to hymen, god of every AYL 5.04.145
here in florence, of a most chaste renown, and AWW 4.03. 15 P
what e'er the course, the end is the renown. 4.04. 36
the things of fame | that do renown this city. TN 3.03. 24
to outlook conquest and to win renown | even in JN 5.02.115
that this same child of honor and renown, | this 1H4 3.02.139
it more | than as your honor and as your renown, 2H4 4.05.145
of auvergne, | with modesty admiring thy renown, 1H6 2.02. 39
thou never hadst renown, nor canst not lose it. 4.05. 40
tide, | so am i driven by breath of her renown, 5.05. 7
memory, | rasing the characters of your renown, 2H6 1.01.101
like men born to renown by life or death. 3H6 1.04. 8
stay we no longer, dreaming of renown, | but 2.01.199
hector, | she is a theme of honor and renown, TRO 2.02.199
to hang by th' wall, if renown made it not stir, COR 1.03. 12 P
renown and grace is dead, | the wine of life is MAC 2.03. 94
he was a wight of high renown, | and thou art OTH 2.03. 93
lieutenant, | for quick accumulation of renown, ANT 3.01. 19
by wounding his belief in her renown | with CYM 5.05.202
the king | of every virtue gives renown to men! PER 1.01. 14
such strong renown as time shall never — 3.02. 48
that /dignifies the renown of a bawd, no less 4.06. 39 P
once do frown, | then farewell his great renown; PP 20.46
/RENOWN'D 1 FR 0.0001 REL FR 1 V 0 P
threefold /renown'd | for hardy and undoubted 3H6 5.07. 5
RENOWN'D 7 FR 0.0008 REL FR 4 V 3 P
doctor caius, the renown'd french physician. WIV 3.01. 61 P
there she lost a noble and renown'd brother, in MM 3.01.219 P
his honor in marrying the renown'd claudio — ADO 2.02. 24 P
renown'd in padua for her scolding tongue. SHR 1.02.100
thou, most fine, most honor'd, most renown'd, 2H4 4.05.163
chance doth throw upon him — | ajax renown'd! TRO 3.03.132
thus then, thou most renown'd: ANT 3.13. 53
RENOWNED 28 FR 0.0031 REL FR 27 V 1 P
duke menaphon, your most renowned uncle. ERR 5.01.369
renowned duke, vouchsafe to take the pains | to 5.01.394
renowned pompey! LLL 5.02.684 P
happy be theseus, our renowned duke! MND 1.01. 20
blow in from every coast | renowned suitors, and MV 1.01.169
yourself, renowned prince, then stood as fair 2.01. 20
pisa, renowned for grave citizens, | gave me my SHR 1.01. 10
often been, | pisa renowned for grave citizens. 4.02. 95
what wilt thou do, renowned faulconbridge? JN 4.03.101
lift up thy brow, renowned salisbury, | and with 5.02. 54
renowned for their deeds as far from home, | for R2 2.01. 53
the blood and courage that renowned them | runs H5 1.02.118
renowned talbot doth expect my aid, | and i am 1H6 4.03. 12
him aid, | while he, renowned noble gentleman, 4.04. 24
yes, your renowned name. shall flight abuse it? 4.05. 41
myself | the title of this most renowned duke, 2H6 5.01.176
thy death, | or die renowned by attempting it. 3H6 2.01. 88
renowned queen, with patience calm the storm, 3.03. 38
renowned prince, how shall poor henry live, 3.03.214
was my great father–in–law, renowned warwick, R3 1.04. 49
sir walter herbert, a renowned soldier, | sir 4.05. 12
welcome to rome, renowned coriolanus! COR 2.01.166
welcome to rome, renowned coriolanus! 2.01.167
the good gods forbid | that our renowned rome, 3.01.289
to rome, | renowned titus, flourishing in arms. TIT 1.01. 38
leave unexecuted | your own renowned knowledge,
ANT 3.07. 45
consummation have, | and renowned be thy grave!
CYM 4.02.281
a knight of sparta, my renowned father, | and PER 2.02. 18
RENOWNS 1 FR 0.0001 REL FR 1 V 0 P
so princes their renowns if not respected. PER 2.02. 13
RENT* 12 FR 0.0013 REL FR 10 V 2 P
year, i'll rent the fairest house in it after MM 2.01.241 P
did these rent lines show some love of thine? LLL 4.03.216
and will you rent our ancient love asunder, | to MND 3.02.215
lean, rent, and beggar'd by the strumpet wind! MV 2.06. 19
france should have torn and rent my very heart 2H6 1.01.126
rents the thorns, and is rent with the thorns, 3H6 3.02.175
these nails should rent that beauty from my R3 1.02.126
rent off thy silver hair, thy other hand TIT 3.01.260
see what a rent the envious casca made; JC 3.02.175
and shrieks that rent the air | are made, not MAC 4.03.168
tell him, so much the rent of his land comes to. LR 1.04.134 P
lose all, and more, by paying too much rent, SON 125. 6
RENTS* *(also rend, etc.)*
/RENTS* 1 FR 0.0001 REL FR 1 V 0 P
/my /manors, /rents, /revenues /i /forgo; R2 4.01.212
RENTS* 4 FR 0.0004 REL FR 4 V 0 P
what are thy rents? H5 4.01.243
that rents the thorns, and is rent with the 3H6 3.02.175
robb'd others' beds' revenues of their rents. SON 142. 8
this said, in top of rage the lines she rents, LC 55
REPAID 5 FR 0.0005 REL FR 5 V 0 P
for here he doth demand to have repaid | a LLL 2.01.142
the poorest service is repaid with thanks, | and SHR 4.03. 45
for strokes receiv'd and many blows repaid 3H6 2.03. 3
marry, as for clarence, he is well repaid; R3 1.03.312
ill art thou repaid | for that good hand thou TIT 3.01.234
REPAIR* 49 FR 0.0055 REL FR 42 V 7 P
love doth to her eyes repair, | to help him of TGV 4.02. 46
repair me with thy presence, silvia; 5.04. 11
none but only a repair i' th' dark, | and that i MM 4.01. 42
fair | a sunny look of his would soon repair. ERR 2.01. 99
good signior benedick, repair to leonato's, ADO 1.01.276 P
all senses to that sense did make their repair, LLL 2.01.240
therefore change favors, and, when they repair, 5.02.292
other do, | may all to athens back again repair, MND 4.01. 67
repair thy wit, good youth, or it will fall | to MV 4.01.141
could i repair what she will wear in me, | as i SHR 3.02.118
what holier than, for royalty's repair, | for WT 5.01. 31
some speedy messenger bid her repair | to our JN 2.01.554
even in the instant of repair and health, | the 3.04.113
bid him repair to us to ely house | to see this R2 2.01.216
then with directions to repair to ravenspurgh. 2.03. 35
to line and new repair our towns of war | with H5 2.04. 7
name, to repair to your several dwelling–places, 1H6 1.03. 77 P
and to repair my honor lost for him, | i here 3H6 3.03.193
in, | for hither will our friends repair to us. 4.07. 15
that we could hear no news of his repair? 5.01. 20
mourner, | and presently repair to crosby house; R3 1.02.212
when you have done, repair to crosby place. 1.03.344
times to repair our nature | with comforting H8 5.01. 3
hive | to whom the foragers shall all repair, TRO 1.03. 82
myself again, | repair to th' senate–house. COR 2.03.148
have drawn your number, | repair to th' capitol. 2.03.254
bid them repair to th' market–place, where i, 5.06. 3
bid him repair to me, and bring with him | some TIT 5.02.124
'tis my father's mind | that i repair to rome, i 5.03. 2
i prithee but repair to me next morning. TIM 2.02. 25
gentlemen, to repair some other hour, i should 3.04. 68 P
repair to pompey's porch, where you shall find JC 1.03.147
that done, repair to pompey's theatre. 1.03.152
and repair thou to me with as much speed as thou
HAM 4.06. 23 P
i will forestall their repair hither, and say 5.02.218 P
and i'll repair the misery thou dost bear | with LR 4.01. 76
repair those violent harms that my two sisters 4.07. 27
fool | plies desdemona to repair his fortune, OTH 2.03.354
repair there to me. 3.02. 4
to the ports | the discontents repair, and men's ANT 1.04. 39
that shouldst repair my youth, thou heap'st | a CYM 1.01.132
mangled, whose repair and franchise | shall, by 3.01. 56
thou givest me somewhat to repair myself; PER 2.01.122
here he does but repair it. 4.02.111 P
and let them repair to her with palamon in their TNK 4.03. 91 P
to this urn let those repair | that are either PHT 65
whose fresh repair if now thou not renewest, SON 3. 3
which to repair should be thy chief desire. 10. 8
so should the lines of life that life repair 16. 9
REPAIR'D 2 FR 0.0002 REL FR 1 V 1 P
been often burst and now repair'd with knots; SHR 3.02. 59 P
times | repair'd with double riches of content. R3 4.04.319
REPAIRING 1 FR 0.0001 REL FR 1 V 0 P
being opposites of such repairing nature. 2H6 5.03. 22
REPAIRS 3 FR 0.0003 REL FR 3 V 0 P
it much repairs me | to talk of your good father AWW 1.02. 30
the brow of youth, | repairs him with occasion? 2H6 5.03. 5
o'erlabor'd sense | repairs itself by rest. CYM 2.02. 12
REPASS'D 1 FR 0.0001 REL FR 1 V 0 P
well have we pass'd and now repass'd the seas, 3H6 4.07. 5
REPAST 4 FR 0.0004 REL FR 2 V 2 P
where, if (before repast) it shall please you to LLL 4.02.154 P
i prithee go, and get me some repast; SHR 4.03. 15
pelican, | repast them with my blood. HAM 4.05.148
so, if i prove a good repast to the spectators, CYM 5.04.155 P
REPASTURE 1 FR 0.0001 REL FR 1 V 0 P
food for his rage, repasture for his den." LLL 4.01. 93
REPAY 5 FR 0.0005 REL FR 4 V 1 P
i think to repay that money will be a biting WIV 5.05.169 P
and, if you prove it, i'll repay it back, | or LLL 2.01.158
sport, | if you repay me not on such a day, | in MV 1.03.146
with dull unwillingness to repay a debt, | which R3 2.02. 92
all | wherein i should your great deserts repay, SON 117. 2
REPAYING 1 FR 0.0001 REL FR 1 V 0 P
it might have since been answer'd in repaying TN 3.03. 33
REPAYS 3 FR 0.0003 REL FR 3 V 0 P
repays he my deep service | with such contempt? R3 4.02.119
no meed but he repays | sevenfold above itself; TIM 1.01.277
even this repays me. ANT 3.11. 71
REPEAL 9 FR 0.0010 REL FR 8 V 1 P
him so, | when she for thy repeal was suppliant, TGV 3.01.236
cancel all grudge, repeal thee home again, 5.04.143
i will repeal thee, or, be well assur'd, 2H6 3.02.349
repeal daily any wholesome act establish'd COR 1.01. 82 P
the time thrust forth | a cause for thy repeal, 4.01. 41
their people | will be as rash in the repeal, as 4.07. 32
repeal him with the welcome of his mother. 5.05. 5
may | have an immediate freedom of repeal. JC 3.01. 54
i sue for exil'd majesty's repeal, | let him LUC 640
REPEAL'D 6 FR 0.0006 REL FR 6 V 0 P
whose banish'd sense | thou hast repeal'd, a AWW 2.03. 49
provided that my banishment repeal'd | and lands R2 3.03. 40
this, | if he may be repeal'd to try his honor. 4.01. 85
all rest under gage | till norfolk be repeal'd. 4.01. 87
repeal'd he shall be, | and, though mine enemy, 4.01. 87
bed, | until that act of parliament be repeal'd 3H6 1.01.249
REPEALING 1 FR 0.0001 REL FR 1 V 0 P
ear | for the repealing of my banish'd brother? JC 3.01. 51
/REPEALS 1 FR 0.0001 REL FR 1 V 0 P
/in /thy /just /proof /repeals /and /reconciles LR 3.06.113
REPEALS 2 FR 0.0002 REL FR 2 V 0 P
the banish'd bullingbrook repeals himself, | and R2 2.02. 49
that she repeals him for her body's lust, | and OTH 2.03.357
REPEAT 18 FR 0.0020 REL FR 14 V 4 P
kneel, and repeat it. TMP 3.02. 40 P
please you repeat their names, i'll show my mind TGV 1.02. 7
seal with my death than repeat over to my shame.
ADO 5.01.241 P
last of the five vowels, if "you" repeat them; LLL 5.01. 53 P
i will repeat them — a,e,i — 5.01. 55 P
for i the ballad will repeat, | which men full AWW 1.03. 60
for what i have i need not to repeat, | and what R2 3.04. 17
memory | that may repeat and history his loss 2H4 4.01.201
repeat their semblance often on the seas, | that 1H6 5.03.193
lo, ere i can repeat this curse again, | within R3 4.01. 77
repeat your will and take it. H8 1.02. 13
and am right sorry to repeat what follows. 5.01. 96
great, | the name of help grew odious to repeat. PER 1.04. 31
thou speak'st like /him's untutor'd to repeat: 1.04. 74
'twould be too tedious to repeat, | but the main 5.01. 28
repeat my wishes | to our great lord, of whose TNK 1.03. 1
only i heard her | repeat this often, "palamon 4.01. 67
he doth again repeat, and that they swore. LUC 1848
REPEATED 3 FR 0.0003 REL FR 3 V 0 P
she is too mean | to have her name repeated. AWW 3.05. 61
of grief, and those repeated | vexations of it! CYM 1.06. 4
for vice repeated is like the wand'ring wind, PER 1.01. 96
REPEATING 1 FR 0.0001 REL FR 1 V 0 P
and, in the last repeating, troublesome, | being JN 4.02. 19
REPEATS 1 FR 0.0001 REL FR 1 V 0 P
puts on his pretty looks, repeats his words, JN 3.04. 95
REPEAT'ST 1 FR 0.0001 REL FR 1 V 0 P
these evils thou repeat'st upon thyself | hath MAC 4.03.112
REPEL 2 FR 0.0002 REL FR 2 V 0 P
i did repel his letters, and denied | his access HAM 2.01.106
foul words and frowns must not repel a lover; VEN 573
REPELL'D 1 FR 0.0001 REL FR 1 V 0 P
and he repell'd, a short tale to make, | fell HAM 2.02.146
REPENT 61 FR 0.0069 REL FR 50 V 11 P
i kill'd a man, whose death i much repent, | but TGV 4.01. 27
why, ne'er repent it, if it were done so. 4.01. 30
enough /to /say /my /prayers, i would repent. WIV 4.05.103 P
repent you, fair one, of the sin you carry? MM 2.03. 19
i do confess it, and repent it, father. 2.03. 29
but lest you do repent | as that the sin hath 2.03. 30
i do repent me as it is an evil, | and take the 2.03. 35
yet did repent me, after more advice, | for 5.01.464
i do repent | the tedious minutes i with her MND 2.02.111
that you should here repent you, | the actors 5.01.115
i never did repent for doing good, | nor shall MV 3.04. 10
then i'll repent, | and wish, for all that, that 3.04. 72
repent but you that you shall lose your friend, 4.01.278
are, and indeed i do marry that i may repent. AWW 1.03. 37 P
since i cannot yet find in my heart to repent. 2.05. 12 P
i would repent out the remainder of nature. 4.03.243 P
do not repent these things, for they are heavier WT 3.02.208
when i shall come to know them, | i do repent. 3.02.220
and then we shall repent each drop of blood JN 2.01. 48
look to that, devil, lest that france repent, 3.01.196
i repent. 4.02.103
i do repent me, read not my name there, | my R2 5.03. 52
well, i'll repent, and that suddenly, while i am 1H4 3.03. 5 P
and then i shall have no strength to repent. 3.03. 7 P
repent at idle times as thou mayst and so 2H4 2.02.129 P
and i repent my fault more than my death, H5 2.02.152
england shall repent his folly, see his weakness 3.06.124 P
i must repent. 3.06.152
clifford, repent in bootless penitence. 3H6 2.06. 70
and i repent | my part thereof that i have done R3 1.03.306
i say, | for i repent me that the duke is slain. 1.04.278
i now repent i told the pursuivant, | as too 3.04. 88
which after–hours gives leisure to repent. 4.04.293
as i intend to prosper and repent, | so thrive i 4.04.397
i shall surely speak | the thing i shall repent. TRO 3.02.131
almost all | repent in their election. COR 2.03.255
repent what you have spoke. 3.02. 37
thou and thy faction shall repent this rape. TIT 1.01.404
prayers | i should repent the evils i have done. 5.03.186
life i did, | i do repent it from my very soul. 5.03.190
that you shall all repent the loss of mine. ROM 3.01.191
where i have learnt me to repent the sin | of 4.02. 17
then i repent not. TIM 1.01.184 P
o, yet i do repent me of my fury, | that i did MAC 2.03.106
yet what can it, when one can not repent? HAM 3.03. 66
repent what's past, avoid what is to come, | and 3.04.150
for this same lord, | i do repent; 3.04.173
is my fortune, that i must repent to be just! LR 3.05. 10 P
with her country forms, | and happily repent. OTH 3.03.238
i do repent me that i put it to you. 3.03.392
over my suit and repent my unlawful solicitation 4.02.198 P
thy former light restore, | should i repent me; 5.02. 10
repent that e'er thy tongue | hath so betray'd ANT 2.07. 77
i repent me much | that so i harried him. 3.03. 39
let him repent | thou wast not made his daughter 3.13.134
poor enobarbus did | before thy face repent! 4.09. 10
so had you saved | the noble imogen to repent, CYM 5.01. 10
must i repent, | i cannot do it better than in 5.04. 13
he will repent the breadth of his great voyage, PER 4.01. 36
and then too late she will repent | that thus PP 18.27
though thou repent, yet i have still the loss: SON 34.10
REPENTANCE 8 FR 0.0009 REL FR 6 V 2 P
who by repentance is not satisfied | is nor of TGV 5.04. 79
and then comes repentance, and with his bad legs ADO 2.01. 78 P
money, and the other with current repentance. 2H4 2.01.121 P
and true repentance | of all your dear offenses! H5 2.02.180
thou wilt mind | thy followers of repentance; 4.03. 85
foretold should be his last, full of repentance, H8 4.02. 27
pardon, and set forth | a deep repentance. MAC 1.04. 7
try what repentance can. HAM 3.03. 65
REPENTANT 4 FR 0.0004 REL FR 4 V 0 P
out, | and strew'd repentant ashes on his head. JN 4.01.110
and wet his grave with my repentant tears) | i R3 1.02.215
o rash false heat, wrapp'd in repentant cold, LUC 48
i know repentant tears ensue the deed, 502
REPENTED 3 FR 0.0003 REL FR 3 V 0 P
judgment hath | repented o'er his doom. MM 2.02. 12
not seem too dear, | howe'er repented after. AWW 3.07. 28
repented | the evils she hatch'd were not CYM 5.05. 59
REPENTING 1 FR 0.0001 REL FR 0 V 1 P
wedding, and repenting, is as a scotch jig, a ADO 2.01. 73 P
REPENTS 3 FR 0.0003 REL FR 2 V 1 P
and he repents not that he pays your debt; MV 4.01.279
check'd him for it, and the young lion repents, 2H4 1.02.197 P
woe, that too late repents! LR 1.04.257
REPETITION 10 FR 0.0011 REL FR 8 V 2 P
and the first view shall kill | all repetition. AWW 5.03. 22
je m'en fais la repetition de tous les mots que H5 3.04. 25 P
but repetition of what thou hast marr'd, | that R3 1.03.164
faults (with surplus) to tire in repetition. COR 1.01. 46 P
whose repetition will be dogg'd with curses; 5.03.144
/mine, | with repetition of my /romeo's /name. ROM 2.02.163
the repetition in a woman's ear | would murther MAC 2.03. 85
call | and give them repetition to the /life. PER 5.01.246
troubled, | make verbal repetition of her moans; VEN 831
be told, | the repetition cannot make it less; LUC 1285
REPETITIONS 1 FR 0.0001 REL FR 1 V 0 P
to cry aim | to these ill–tuned repetitions. JN 2.01.197
REPIN'D 1 FR 0.0001 REL FR 1 V 0 P
when corn was given them gratis, you repin'd, COR 3.01. 43
REPINE 2 FR 0.0002 REL FR 2 V 0 P
let henry fret, and all the world repine. 1H6 5.02. 20
had not his clouded with his brow's repine; VEN 490
REPINING 1 FR 0.0001 REL FR 1 V 0 P
but what the repining enemy commends, | that TRO 1.03.243
REPLANT 1 FR 0.0001 REL FR 1 V 0 P
bona, | and replant henry in his former state. 3H6 3.03.198
REPLENISH 1 FR 0.0001 REL FR 1 V 0 P
the more she saw the blood his cheeks replenish, LUC 1357
REPLENISH'D 1 FR 0.0001 REL FR 1 V 0 P
so, | the most replenish'd villain in the world, WT 2.01. 79
REPLENISHED 2 FR 0.0002 REL FR 1 V 1 P
his intellect is not replenished; LLL 4.02. 26 P
the most replenished sweet work of nature | that R3 4.03. 18
REPLETE 9 FR 0.0010 REL FR 9 V 0 P

proclaims you for a man replete with mocks, LLL 5.02.843
if not to thy estate, | a balance more replete. AWW 2.03.176
his sparkling eyes, replete with wrathful fire, 1H6 1.01. 12
all france will be replete with mirth and joy, 1.06. 15
so full replete with choice of all delights, 5.05. 17
lend me a heart replete with thankfulness! 2H6 1.01. 20
her looks doth argue her replete with modesty, 3H6 3.02. 84
or some fierce thing replete with too much rage, SON 23. 3
incapable of more, replete with you, | my most 113.13
REPLETION 1 FR 0.0001 REL FR 1 V 0 P
that peace might purge | for her repletion, and TNK 1.02. 24
REPLICATION 4 FR 0.0004 REL FR 2 V 2 P
as it were, replication, or rather ostentare, to LLL 4.02. 15 P
banks | to hear the replication of your sounds JC 1.01. 46
what replication should be made by the son of a HAM 4.02. 13 P
all replication prompt and reason strong, | for LC 122
REPLIED 9 FR 0.0010 REL FR 9 V 0 P
how he refell'd me, and how i replied | (for MM 5.01. 94
the boy replied, "an angel is not evil; LLL 5.02.105
roundly replied. SHR 5.02. 21
i replied, | men fear the french would prove H8 1.02.155
it /tauntingly replied | to th' discontented COR 1.01.110
he replied, | it was a bare petition of a state 5.01. 19
he replied, | "thou unpossessing bastard, dost LR 2.01. 66
she replied, | it should be better he became her ANT 2.02.220
"madam, ere i was up," replied the maid, | "the LUC 1277
REPLIES 10 FR 0.0011 REL FR 8 V 2 P
before i speak, too threat'ningly replies. AWW 2.03. 81
and he replies, "thanks, agamemnon." TRO 3.03.261 P
how pregnant sometimes his replies are! HAM 2.02.209 P
the moor replies | that he you hurt is of great OTH 3.01. 44
look not sad, | nor make replies of loathness; ANT 3.11. 18
thus she replies: VEN 385
echo replies, | as if another chase were in the 695
to whom she speaks, and he replies with howling. 918
thus he replies: LUC 477
replies her husband, "do not take away | my 1796
REPLIEST 1 FR 0.0001 REL FR 1 V 0 P
how oddly thou repliest! ROM 2.05. 59
REPLY 24 FR 0.0027 REL FR 18 V 6 P
for want of idle time, could not again reply; TGV 2.01.166
what reply? MM 3.02. 47 P
thus expecting thy reply, i profane my lips on LLL 4.01. 84 P
my lord, i shall reply amazedly, | half sleep, MND 4.01.146
reply, reply. MV 3.02. 66
reply, reply. 3.02. 66
this is call'd the reply churlish. AYL 5.04. 77 P
the third, the reply churlish; 5.04. 93 P
you were straited | for a reply, at least if you WT 4.04.355
thine ears, and make reply | without a tongue, JN 3.03. 49
tongue, | before i make reply to aught you say. R2 2.03. 73
we will not now be troubled with reply. 1H4 5.01.113
i will not undergo this sneap without reply. 2H4 2.01.123 P
reply not to me with a fool–born jest, | presume 5.05. 55
to give me hearing what i shall reply. 1H6 3.01. 28
fair lords, take leave and stand not to reply. 3H6 4.08. 23
why, so i did, but look'd for no reply. R3 1.03.236
reply not in how many fadoms deep | they lie TRO 1.01. 50
speak not, reply not, do not answer me! ROM 3.05.163
and with their faint reply this answer join: TIM 3.03. 25
i pause for a reply. JC 3.02. 34 P
why, 'tis a loving and a fair reply. HAM 1.02.121
but of our demands | most free in his reply. 3.01. 14
well, i could reply: ANT 3.07. 6
REPLYING 2 FR 0.0002 REL FR 2 V 0 P
think | tongue–tied ambition, not replying, R3 3.07.145
replying shrilly to the well–tun'd horns, | as TIT 2.03. 18
/REPORT 2 FR 0.0002 REL FR 1 V 1 P
/making /just /report | /of /how /unnatural /and LR 3.01. 37
/report /is /changeable. 4.07. 91 P
REPORT 151 FR 0.0170 REL FR 107 V 44 P
ay, or very falsely pocket up his report. TMP 2.01. 68 P
if in naples | i should report this now, would 3.03. 28
kind, | because we know, on valentine's report, TGV 3.02. 57
shape, and by your own report | a linguist, and 4.01. 54
now, the report goes she has all the rule of her WIV 1.03. 52 P
of her own youth, | hath blister'd her report. MM 2.03. 12
that you shall stifle in your own report, | and 2.04.158
some report a sea–maid spawn'd him; 3.02.108 P
you better, sir, if i may live to report you. 3.02.162 P
volumes of report | run with these false and 4.01. 60
not better than he, by her own report. 5.01.273 P
persons with me, ere you make that my report. 5.01.337 P
by computation and mine host's report, | i could ERR 2.02. 4
and that is false thou dost report to us. 5.01.179
valor, | goes foremost in report through italy. ADO 3.01. 97
marry, sir, they have committed false report; 5.01.215 P
i saw | is my report to his great worthiness. LLL 2.01. 63
sort, | rising and cawing at the gun's report, MND 3.02. 22
his tongue to conceive, nor his heart to report, 4.01.213 P
if my gossip report be an honest woman of her MV 3.01. 7 P
and report speaks goldenly of his profit. AYL 1.01. 6 P
if you like upon report | the soil, the profit, 2.04. 97
of that report which i so oft have heard. SHR 2.01. 53
by report | i know him well. 2.01.104
and sullen, | and now i find report a very liar; 2.01.244
why does the world report that kate doth limp? 2.01.252
and, for the good report i hear of you, | and 4.04. 28
i shall report it so. AWW 2.04. 55
know it before the report come. 3.02. 23 P
that pitiful rumor may report my flight | to 3.02.127
and suffice ourselves with the report of it. 3.05. 11 P
from the report that goes upon your goodness, 5.01. 13
unless it be to report your lord's taking of TN 2.02. 10 P
commendation with woman than report of valor. 3.02. 38 P
set upon aguecheek a notable report of valor, 3.04.192 P
give fools money get themselves a good report — 4.01. 23 P
i shall report, | for most it caught me, the WT 3.01. 3
o sir, i shall be hated to report it! 3.02.143
the report of her is extended more than can be 4.02. 42 P
but i have it | upon his own report, and i 4.04.170
though i report it | that should be silent. 4.04.177
one three of them, by their own report, sir, 4.04.337 P
that which i shall report will bear no credit, 5.01.179
which lames report to follow it and undoes 5.02. 57 P
and to give me your good report to the prince my 5.02.151 P
for ere thou canst report, i will be there; JN 1.01. 25
throw this report on their incensed rage, | and 4.02.261
report of fashions in proud italy, | whose R2 2.01. 21
but i shall grieve you to report the rest. 2.02. 95
you, let not his report | come current for an 1H4 1.03. 67
(as ancient writers do report) doth defile, so 2.04.413 P
such as fear the report of a caliver worse than 4.02. 19 P
court, stand my good lord in your good report. 2H4 4.03. 83 P
whose glory fills the world with loud report. 1H6 2.02. 43
i see report is fabulous and false. 2.03. 18
whether it be through force of your report, | my 5.05. 79
let this my sword report what speech forbears. 2H6 4.10. 54
of salisbury, who can report of him, | that 5.03. 1
or whether 'twas report of her success, | or 3H6 2.01.125
the day, | if warwick be so near as men report. 4.03. 8
or, if she be accus'd on true report, | bear R3 1.03. 27
such news, my lord, as grieves me to report. 2.04. 39
or with the clamorous report of war | thus will 4.04.153
flatter my sorrow with report of it; 4.04.246
and process of this time, you can report, | and H8 2.04. 38
if he know | that i am free of your report, he 2.04. 99
that man i' th' world who shall report he has 2.04.135
an engine | not portable, lie under this report: TRO 2.03.135
could be content to give him good report for't, COR 1.01. 33 P
then his good report should have been my son; 1.03. 20 P
i, sir, | half an hour since brought my report. 1.06. 21
fear | /lesser his person than an ill report; 1.06. 70
but i'll report it | where senators shall mingle 1.09. 2
more cruel to your good report than grateful 1.09. 54
of no better report than a horse–drench. 2.01.118 P
them at all into their estimation and report. 2.02. 28 P
to report otherwise were a malice that, giving 2.02. 31 P
to report | a little of that worthy work 2.02. 44
gave me his clothes made a false report of him. 4.05.151 P
eyes — his raising, | nothing but his report. 4.06. 62
the slave's report is seconded, and more, | more 4.06. 63
you must report to th' volscian lords, how 5.03. 3
yes, mercy, if you report him truly. 5.04. 25 P
are, | that my report is just and full of truth. TIT 5.03.115
wrong'st it more than tears with that report. ROM 4.01. 32
men report | thou dost affect my manners, and TIM 4.03.198
a just and true report that goes of his having. 5.01. 16
are his files | as full as thy report? 5.02. 2
brutus, thrusting this report | into his ears; JC 5.03. 74
he can report, | as seemeth by his plight, of MAC 1.02. 1
i must report they were | as cannons overcharg'd 1.02. 36
who did report | that very frankly he confess'd 1.04. 4
and i have learn'd by the perfect'st report, 1.05. 2 P
and this report | hath so exasperate /the king 3.06. 37
you, but can perceive no truth in your report. 5.01. 2 P
that, sir, which i will not report after her. 5.01. 14 P
host, and make discovery | err in report of us. 5.04. 7
lord, | i should report that which i say i saw, 5.05. 30
to make it truster of your own report | against HAM 1.02.172
epitaph than their ill report while you live. 2.02.526 P
and gave you such a masterly report | for art 4.07. 96
this report of his | did hamlet so envenom with 4.07.102
report me and my cause aright | to the 5.02.339
i would not take this from report; LR 4.06.141
so was i bid report here to the state | by OTH 1.03. 15
if you do find me foul in her report, | the 1.03.117
more of this matter cannot i report. 2.03.240
you inquire him out, and be edified by report? 3.04. 15 P
she said so; i must needs report the truth. 5.02.128
storms and tempests than almanacs can report. ANT 1.02.149 P
if in mirth, report | that i am sudden sick. 1.03. 4
shalt thou have report | how 'tis abroad. 1.04. 35
only, | lest my remembrance suffer ill report; 2.02.156
triumphant lady, if report be square to her. 2.02.184 P
read not my blemishes in the world's report. 2.03. 5
i made no such report. 2.05. 57
bid him | report the feature of octavia, her 2.05.112
let me report to him | your sweet dependancy, 5.02. 25
this i'll report, dear lady. 5.02. 32
truly, she makes a very good report o' th' worm; 5.02.255 P
princess is a thing | too bad for bad report; CYM 1.01. 17
i honor him | even out of your report. 1.01. 55
may, without contradiction, suffer the report. 1.04. 56 P
who knows | by history, report, or his own proof 1.06. 70
to my tongue | charms this report out. 1.06.117
is as far | from thy report as thou from honor, 1.06.146
to try your taking of a false report, which hath 1.06.173
is gold for you, | sell me your good report. 2.03. 83
or to report of you | what i shall think is good 2.03. 84
saw i figures | so likely to report themselves. 2.04. 83
and my report was once | first with the best of 3.03. 57
report should render him hourly to your ear | as 3.04.150
and am right sorry that i must report ye | my 3.05. 3
experience, o, thou disprov'st report! 4.02. 34
son to the queen (after his own report), | who 4.02.119
then (as men report | thou orphans' father art) 5.04. 39
report it. 5.05. 16
happiness, i must report | the queen is dead. 5.05. 26
than a physician | would this report become? 5.05. 28
what she confess'd | i will report, so please 5.05. 34
drawn by report, advent'rous by desire, | tell PER 1.01. 35
report what a sojourner we have; 4.02.137 P
thou hast the harvest out of thine own report. 4.02.141 P
than it gives a good report to a number to be 4.06. 40 P
report thy parentage. 5.01.129
it can appear to me report is a true speaker. TNK 2.01. 6 P
they stand a grise above the reach of report. 2.01. 28 P
as thou being mine, mine is thy good report. SON 36.14
and therefore have i slept in your report, 83. 5
praise, | naming thy name blesses an ill report. 95. 8
as thou being mine, mine is thy good report. 96.14
REPORTED 16 FR 0.0018 REL FR 11 V 5 P
meddler, | as he's reported by this gentleman; MM 5.01.146
and a coward, as you then reported him to be? 5.01.334 P
is she so hot a shrew as she's reported? SHR 4.01. 21 P
so 'tis reported, sir. AWW 1.02. 3
it is reported that he has taken their great'st 3.05. 5 P
as 'tis reported, for the king had married him 3.05. 53
i have heard her reported to be a woman of an 2H6 1.04. 6 P
it is reported, mighty sovereign, | that good 3.02.122
tyrants themselves wept when it was reported. R3 1.03.184
or else reported | successively from age to age, 3.01. 72
nor none so bad but well may be reported. 4.04.458
all is confirm'd, my lord, which was reported. MAC 5.03. 31
it is reported thou didst eat strange flesh, ANT 1.04. 67
before gave audience, | as 'tis reported, so. 3.06. 19
so 'tis reported; CYM 5.03. 87
i heard them reported in the battle to be the TNK 2.01. 29 P
REPORTER 1 FR 0.0001 REL FR 0 V 1 P
or my reporter devis'd well for her. ANT 2.02.188 P
REPORTEST 1 FR 0.0001 REL FR 0 V 1 P
a notable lubber — as thou reportest him to be. TGV 2.05. 45 P
REPORTING 2 FR 0.0002 REL FR 2 V 0 P
your knowledge, nor | concern me the reporting. WT 4.04.504
seem | like lies disdain'd in the reporting. PER 5.01.119
REPORTINGLY 1 FR 0.0001 REL FR 1 V 0 P
and i | believe it better than reportingly. ADO 3.01.116
REPORTS 19 FR 0.0021 REL FR 15 V 4 P
is marvellous little beholding to your reports, MM 4.03.160 P
uncle, | whom he reports to be a great magician, AYL 5.04. 33
to him i live, and observe his reports for me. AWW 2.01. 45 P
serves the count | reports but coarsely of her. 3.05. 57
creatures, not daring the reports of my tongue. 4.01. 30 P
such pestiferous reports of men very nobly held, 4.03.306 P
i'll fill these dogged spies with false reports; JN 4.01.128
stuffing the ears of men with false reports. 2H4 in 8
the tongue offends not that reports his death, 1.01. 97
to give their censure of these rare reports. 1H6 2.03. 10
reports the volsces with two several powers COR 4.06. 39
alcibiades reports it; TIM 5.01. 4
bring me no more reports, let them fly all. MAC 5.03. 1
all my reports go with the modest truth, | nor LR 4.07. 5
(as in these cases where the aim reports, | 'tis OTH 1.03. 6
and your reports have set the murder on. 5.02.187
and men's reports | give him much wrong'd. ANT 1.04. 39
and have my learning from some true reports 2.02. 47
find | our paragon to all reports thus blasted, PER 4.01. 35
REPORT'ST 2 FR 0.0002 REL FR 2 V 0 P
as thou report'st thyself, was then her servant, TMP 1.02.271
and i my percy's death ere thou report'st it. 2H4 1.01. 75
REPOSAL 1 FR 0.0001 REL FR 1 V 0 P
against thee, would the reposal | of any trust, LR 2.01. 68
REPOSE 29 FR 0.0032 REL FR 29 V 0 P
this is a strange repose, to be asleep | with TMP 2.01.213
whiles we stood here securing your repose, 2.01.310
retire into my cell, | and there repose. 4.01.162
company, | upon whose faith and honor i repose. TGV 4.03. 26
(travelling some journey) to repose him here. SHR in.1. 76
castle, | and there repose you for this night. R2 2.03.161
give /then repose | to the wet //sea–boy in an 2H4 3.01. 26
that play'st so subtilly with a king's repose. H5 4.01.258
well, for this night we will repose us here; 2H6 2.01.196
consent, | for on thy fortune i repose myself. 3H6 4.06. 47
your highness shall repose you at the tower; R3 3.01. 65
to repair our nature | with comforting repose, H8 5.01. 4
where, ere we do repose us, we will write | to COR 1.09. 74
readiest champions, repose you here in rest, TIT 1.01.151
soldiers and rome's servitors | repose in fame; 1.01.353
and so repose, sweet gold, for their unrest, 2.03. 8
as sweet repose and rest | come to thy heart as ROM 2.02.123
noble cassius, | good night, and good repose. JC 4.03.233
thoughts that nature | gives way to in repose! MAC 2.01. 9
good repose the while! 2.01. 29
sport and repose lock from me day and night, HAM 3.02.217
repose you there, while i to this hard house LR 3.02. 63
our foster–nurse of nature is repose, | the 4.04. 12
till we do please | to daff't for our repose, ANT 4.04. 13
hours | shake off the golden slumber of repose. PER 3.02. 23
here she exclaims against repose and rest, | and LUC 757
betray'd the hours thou gav'st me to repose? 933
the dear repose for limbs with travel tired, SON 27. 2
doth teach that ease and that repose to say, 50. 3
REPOSED 1 FR 0.0001 REL FR 1 V 0 P
in his clear bed might have reposed still! LUC 382
REPOSETH 1 FR 0.0001 REL FR 1 V 0 P
the king reposeth all his confidence in thee. R2 2.04. 6
REPOSING 3 FR 0.0003 REL FR 2 V 1 P
lest, reposing too far in his virtue, which he AWW 3.06. 13 P
sorrow breaks seasons and reposing hours, R3 1.04. 76
his right cheek | reposing on a cushion. CYM 4.02.212
REPOSSESS 4 FR 0.0004 REL FR 4 V 0 P
her suit is now to repossess those lands, 3H6 3.02. 4
and pray that i may repossess the crown. 4.05. 29
for if edward repossess the crown, | 'tis like 4.06. 99
that thou mightst repossess the crown in peace, 5.07. 19
REPREHEND 4 FR 0.0004 REL FR 3 V 1 P
i myself reprehend his own person, for i am his LLL 1.01.183 P
but a dream, | gentles, do not reprehend. MND 5.01.429
and that you come to reprehend my ignorance. R3 3.07.113
for sharply he did think to reprehend her, VEN 470
REPREHENDED 3 FR 0.0003 REL FR 3 V 0 P
you should for that have reprehended him. ERR 5.01. 57
she never reprehended him but mildly, | when he 5.01. 87
which when i saw, i reprehended them, | and R3 3.07. 27
/REPREHENDING 1 FR 0.0001 REL FR 1 V 0 P
/then /pardon /me /for /reprehending /thee, TIT 3.02. 69
REPREHENDS 1 FR 0.0001 REL FR 1 V 0 P
and then she reprehends her mangling eye, | that VEN 1065
REPRESENT 3 FR 0.0003 REL FR 3 V 0 P
did represent my master's blushing cheeks, 1H6 4.01. 93
of that great shadow i did represent: 2H6 1.01. 14
and, would you represent our queen aright, | it TIT 5.02. 89
REPRIEVE 6 FR 0.0006 REL FR 5 V 1 P
that in his reprieve, | longer or shorter, he MM 2.04. 39
my bending down | reprieve thee from thy fate, 3.01.144
i hope it is some pardon or reprieve | for the 4.02. 71
grant, reprieve him from the wrath | of greatest AWW 3.04. 28
has sworn you out of reprieve and pardon. COR 5.02. 49 P
send | thy token of reprieve. LR 5.03.250
REPRIEVES 2 FR 0.0002 REL FR 0 V 2 P
friends for three reprieves for you and your WIV 2.02. 7 P
his friends still wrought reprieves for him; MM 4.02.135 P
REPRISAL 1 FR 0.0001 REL FR 1 V 0 P
on fire | to hear this rich reprisal is so nigh, 1H4 4.01.118
REPROACH 25 FR 0.0028 REL FR 24 V 1 P
for that he knew you, might reproach your life, MM 5.01.421
who can blot that name | with any just reproach? ADO 4.01. 81
my young master doth expect your reproach. MV 2.05. 20 P
reproach and dissolution hangeth over him. R2 2.01.258
cut | with edge of penny cord and vile reproach. H5 3.06. 48
reproach and everlasting shame | sits mocking in 4.05. 4
o, whither shall we fly from this reproach? 1H6 1.01. 97
or else reproach be talbot's greatest fame! 3.02. 76

in confutation of which rude reproach, | and in 4.01. 98
and not deface your honor with reproach? 5.05. 29
wouldst have me rescue thee from this reproach? 2H6 2.04. 64
that's bad enough, for i am but reproach; 2.04. 96
and princes' courts be fill'd with my reproach. 3.02. 69
reproach and beggary | is crept into the palace 4.01.101
but if black scandal or foul–fac'd reproach R3 3.07.231
all whites are ink | writing their own reproach, TRO 1.01. 57
and see their blood or die with this reproach. TIT 4.01. 94
dames even thus, | all guiltless, meet reproach. OTH 4.01. 47
reproach, disdain, and deadly enmity, | yet LUC 503
thou back'st reproach against long–living laud, 622
will couple my reproach to tarquin's shame; 816
and undeserv'd reproach to him allotted | that 824
reproach is stamp'd in collatinus' face, | and 829
when not to be receives reproach of being, | and SON 121. 2
by how much of me their reproach contains. LC 189

REPROACHES 2 FR 0.0002 REL FR 2 V 0 P
myself would, on the rearward of reproaches, ADO 4.01.126
they vent reproaches | most bitterly on you as H8 1.02. 23

REPROACHFUL 2 FR 0.0002 REL FR 2 V 0 P
o monstrous! what reproachful words are these? TIT 1.01.308
thrust those reproachful speeches down his 2.01. 55

REPROACHFULLY 1 FR 0.0001 REL FR 1 V 0 P
and shall i then be us'd reproachfully? 2H6 2.04. 97

REPROACH'S 1 FR 0.0001 REL FR 1 V 0 P
when life is sham'd and death reproach's debtor. LUC 1155

REPROBANCE 1 FR 0.0001 REL FR 1 V 0 P
angel from his side, | and fall to reprobance. OTH 5.02.209

REPROBATE 3 FR 0.0003 REL FR 2 V 1 P
this reprobate till he were well inclin'd, | and MM 4.03. 74
deliver me from the reprobate thought of it, i LLL 1.02. 61 P
by reprobate desire thus madly led, | the roman LUC 300

/REPROOF 1 FR 0.0001 REL FR 1 V 0 P
your /reproof | were well deserv'd of rashness. ANT 2.02.121

REPROOF 19 FR 0.0021 REL FR 11 V 8 P
and well–behav'd reproof to all uncomeliness, WIV 2.01. 59 P
that i may pass with a reproof the easier, sith 2.02.188 P
of the benefit defends the deceit from reproof. MM 3.01.258 P
she did betray me to my own reproof. ERR 5.01. 90
this is call'd the reproof valiant. AYL 5.04. 79 P
the fourth, the reproof valiant; 5.04. 94 P
potent fault it is | that it but mocks reproof. TN 3.04.205
and in the reproof of this lives the jest. 1H4 1.02.190 P
done, | without the taste of danger and reproof. 3.01.173
me beg | as, in reproof of many tales devis'd, 3.02. 23
your reproof is something too round, i should be H5 4.01.203 P
silence, | or bitterly to speak in your reproof, R3 3.07.142
that cannot brook the accent of reproof. 4.04.159
in the reproof of chance | lies the true proof TRO 1.03. 33
would pluck reproof and rebuke from every ear COR 2.02. 33 P
whom you yourselves shall set out for reproof TIM 5.04. 57
whereas reproof, obedient and in order, | fits PER 1.02. 42
it shall no longer grieve without reproof. 2.04. 19
but as reproof and reason beat it dead, | by thy LUC 489

REPROVABLE 1 FR 0.0001 REL FR 0 V 1 P
set a–work by a reprovable badness in himself. LR 3.05. 7 P

REPROV'D 1 FR 0.0001 REL FR 1 V 0 P
after your highness had reprov'd the duke H8 1.02.189

REPROV'DST 1 FR 0.0001 REL FR 1 V 0 P
art one, | who now reprov'dst me for't — PER 1.02. 95

REPROVE 7 FR 0.0008 REL FR 5 V 2 P
'tis so, i cannot reprove it; ADO 2.03.232 P
what grace hast thou thus to reprove | these LLL 4.03.151
discreet man, though he do nothing but reprove. TN 1.05. 96 P
and york, | reprove my allegation if you can, 2H6 3.01. 40
if to reprove you for this suit of yours, | so R3 3.07.148
for the white | reprove the brown for rashness, ANT 3.11. 14
"what have you urg'd that i cannot reprove? VEN 787

REPROVES 1 FR 0.0001 REL FR 1 V 0 P
there's something in me that reproves my fault; TN 3.04.203

REPROVING 2 FR 0.0002 REL FR 2 V 0 P
the worst is but denial and reproving. LUC 242
and thou shalt find it merits not reproving, SON 142. 4

REPUGN 1 FR 0.0001 REL FR 1 V 0 P
when stubbornly he did repugn the truth | about 1H6 4.01. 94

REPUGNANCY 1 FR 0.0001 REL FR 1 V 0 P
quietly cut their throats | without repugnancy? TIM 3.05. 45

REPUGNANT 1 FR 0.0001 REL FR 1 V 0 P
lies where it falls, | repugnant to command. HAM 2.02.471

REPULSE 5 FR 0.0005 REL FR 3 V 2 P
do not, for one repulse, forgo the purpose TMP 3.03. 12
take no repulse, what ever she doth say; TGV 3.01.100
except you mean with obstinate repulse | to slay 1H6 3.01.113
he receiv'd in the repulse of tarquin seven COR 2.01.149 P
a repulse, though your attempt (as you call it) CYM 1.04.118 P

REPURCHAS'D 1 FR 0.0001 REL FR 1 V 0 P
throne, | repurchas'd with the blood of enemies. 3H6 5.07. 2

REPUTATION 50 FR 0.0056 REL FR 24 V 26 P
home, | while other men, of slender reputation, TGV 1.03. 6
dispose, | my goods, my lands, my reputation; 2.07. 87
i will keep the havior of reputation. WIV 1.03. 78 P
from the ward of her purity, her reputation, her 2.02.249 P
my coffers ransack'd, my reputation gnawn at, 2.02.293 P
all your senses to you, defend your reputation, 3.03.119 P
in chief | for that her reputation was disvalued MM 5.01.221
herein you war against your reputation, | and ERR 3.01. 86
this touches me in reputation. 4.01. 71
of very reverent reputation, sir, | of credit 5.01. 5
made this match, and his friend's reputation, ADO 2.02. 38 P
her, | as best befits her wounded reputation, 4.01.241
wrong, | and wrong the reputation of your name, LLL 2.01.154
you will lose your reputation. 5.02.703 P
your reputation shall not therefore be mispris'd AYL 1.02.180 P
seeking the bubble reputation | even in the 2.07.152
and would not put my reputation now | in any AWW 3.07. 6
upon my reputation and credit and as i hope to 4.03.133 P
what his reputation is with the duke; 4.03.177 P
what is his reputation with the duke? 4.03.197 P
have answer'd to his reputation with the duke, 4.03.248 P
your reputation comes too short for my daughter, 5.03.176 P
turn then my freshest reputation to | a savor WT 1.02.420
mortal times afford | is spotless reputation; R2 1.01.178
dear for her reputation through the world, | is 2.01. 58
land, | wherein thou liest in reputation sick, 2.01. 96
but answer in th' effect of your reputation, and 2H4 2.01.130 P
his reputation is as arrant a villain and a jack H5 4.07.140 P
like a tall man that respects thy reputation. R3 1.04.153 P
alive | and case thy reputation in thy tent, TRO 3.03.187
i see my reputation is at stake, | my fame is 3.03.227
my reputation stain'd | with tybalt's slander — ROM 3.01.111
seeing his reputation touch'd to death, | he did TIM 3.05. 19
their residence, both in reputation and profit, HAM 2.02.330 P
matter | that you unlace your reputation thus, OTH 2.03.194
reputation, reputation, reputation! 2.03.262 P
reputation, reputation, reputation! 2.03.262 P
reputation, reputation, reputation! 2.03.262 P
o, i have lost my reputation! 2.03.263 P
my reputation, iago, my reputation! 2.03.264 P
my reputation, iago, my reputation! 2.03.265 P
there is more sense in that than in reputation. 2.03.268 P
reputation is an idle and most false imposition; 2.03.268 P
you have lost no reputation at all, unless you 2.03.270 P
i have offended reputation, | a most unnoble ANT 3.11. 49
against your confidence than her reputation; CYM 1.04.111 P
fiend | of hell would not in reputation change. PER 4.06.164
us not, | having our ancient reputation with us, TNK 3.03. 11
laud, | and mak'st fair reputation but a bawd. LUC 623
"let my good name, that senseless reputation, 820

REPUTE 10 FR 0.0011 REL FR 7 V 3 P
how will the world repute me | for undertaking TGV 2.07. 59
anthony dull, a man of good repute, carriage, LLL 1.01.268 P
let them be men of good repute and carriage. 1.02. 69 P
and will repute you ever | the patron of my life SHR 4.02.113
wars | that all in england did repute him dead; 1H4 5.01. 54
and in my conscience do repute his grace | the 2H6 5.01.177
for here the troyans taste our dear'st repute TRO 1.03.337
my foes i do repute you every one, | so trouble TIT 1.01.366
villager | than to repute himself a son of rome JC 1.02.173
at all, unless you repute yourself such a loser. OTH 2.03.271 P

/REPUTED 1 FR 0.0001 REL FR 1 V 0 P
/the /earl /of /herford /was /reputed /then 2H4 4.01.129

REPUTED 8 FR 0.0009 REL FR 6 V 2 P
the prime duke, being so reputed | in dignity, TMP 1.02. 72
and not without desert so well reputed. TGV 2.04. 57
i am not so reputed. ADO 2.01.207 P
that therefore only are reputed wise | for MV 1.01. 96
yet his brother is reputed one of the best that AWW 4.03.289 P
or the reputed son of cordelion, | lord of thy JN 1.01.136
father, was reputed for | a prince most prudent, H8 2.04. 45
but withal | a woman well reputed, cato's JC 2.01.295

REPUTELESS 1 FR 0.0001 REL FR 1 V 0 P
and left me in reputeless banishment, | a fellow 1H4 3.02. 44

REPUTES 2 FR 0.0002 REL FR 2 V 0 P
he reputes me a cannon, and the bullet, that's LLL 3.01. 64
which rome reputes to be a heinous sin, | yield TIT 1.01.448

REPUTING 1 FR 0.0001 REL FR 1 V 0 P
faults, | yet, by reputing of his high descent, 2H6 3.01. 48

REQUEST 67 FR 0.0075 REL FR 49 V 18 P
my prime request, | which i do last pronounce, TMP 1.02.426
at thy request, monster, i will do reason, any 3.02.119 P
and did request me to importune you | to let him TGV 1.03. 13
you writ them, sir, at my request, | but i will 2.01.126
swear), | i am so far from granting thy request, 4.02.101
do a greater thing than that, upon your request, WIV 1.01.241 P
i will marry her, sir, at your request; 1.01.245 P
i'll tell him yet of angelo's request, | and fit MM 2.04.186
novelty is only in request, and, as it is, as 3.02.224 P
then ginger was not much in request, for the old 4.03. 8 P
upon his mere request, | being come to knowledge 5.01.152
and i am to entreat you, request you, and desire MND 1.02.100 P
i would wish you," or "i would request you," or 3.01. 40 P
fond | to come abroad with him at his request. MV 3.03. 10
to fill up your grace's request in my stead. 4.01.161 P
more at your request than to please myself. AYL 2.05. 23 P
this liberty is all that i request, | that, upon SHR 2.01. 94
but did you not request to have it cut? 4.03.121
answer the time of request. AWW 1.01.155 P
at your request! yes, nightingales answer daws. TN 3.04. 35 P
good master fabian, grant me another request. 5.01. 2 P
were there necessity in your request, although WT 1.02. 22
at my request he would not. 1.02. 87
this your request | is altogether just; 3.02.116
'tis in request, i can tell you. 4.04.290 P
at your request | my father will grant precious 5.01.221
heartily request | th' enfranchisement of arthur JN 4.02. 51
at whose request the king hath pardon'd them, 5.06. 35
have some countenance at his friend's request. 2H4 5.01. 45 P
but your request shall make me let it pass. H5 5.02.344
ay, if thou wilt say ay to my request; 3H6 3.02. 79
vouchsafe, at our request, to stand aside, 3.03.110
my lord of somerset, at my request, | see that 4.03. 51
now, catesby, what says your lord to my request? R3 3.07. 58
my desert | unmeritable shuns your high request. 3.07.155
the late request that you did sound me in. 4.02. 84
what says your highness to my just request? 4.02. 94
the king's request that i would visit you, | who H8 4.02.116
why will he not upon our fair request | untent TRO 2.03.167
be led | at your request a little from himself. 2.03.181
at whose request do these men play? 3.01. 28 P
sir, at the request of paris my lord, who is 3.01. 30 P
i request you | to give my poor host freedom. COR 1.09. 86
we do request your kindest ears, and after, 2.02. 52
the custom of request you have discharg'd. 2.03.142
"we did request it, | we are the greater pole, 3.01.133
i'll try whether my old wit be in request | with 3.01.250
since that to both | it stands in like request? 3.02. 51
being now in no request of his country. 4.03. 35 P
watch him | till he be dieted to my request, 5.01. 57
that, if you fail in our request, the blame 5.03. 90
your request? 5.03. 93
if it were so that our request did tend | to 5.03.132
i gave thee mine before thou didst request it; ROM 2.02.128
let the request be fifty talents. TIM 2.02.193 P
what ill request did brutus make to thee? JC 5.05. 11
supper, sir, | and i'll request your presence. MAC 3.01. 15
and soldiers, | give me one poor request. HAM 1.05.142
or came it by request, and such fair question OTH 1.03.113
'tis done at your request. 3.03.474
let me request you /off, our graver business ANT 2.07.120
for antony, | i have no ears to his request. 3.12. 20
t' entreat your grace but in a small request, CYM 1.06.181
let his virtue join | with my request, which 5.05. 89
what's your request? deliver you for all. TNK 1.01. 38
she would request to know your heaviness." LUC 1283
at this request, with noble disposition | each 1695

REQUESTED 3 FR 0.0003 REL FR 2 V 1 P
as if he did contemn what he requested | should COR 2.02.157
goodness not to do more than she is requested. OTH 2.03.322 P
but, as you requested, | yourself shall go ANT 3.04. 24

REQUESTING 1 FR 0.0001 REL FR 0 V 1 P
requesting your lordship to supply his instant TIM 3.02. 35 P

REQUEST'S 2 FR 0.0002 REL FR 2 V 0 P
small as nothing, for request's sake only, | he TRO 2.03.169
say my request's unjust, | and spurn me back; COR 5.03.164

REQUESTS 14 FR 0.0015 REL FR 10 V 4 P
door, mistress ford, and requests your company. WIV 3.03. 25 P
were not his requests so far | from reason's LLL 2.01.149
thou now requests but moonshine in the water. 5.02.208
i will both hear and grant you your requests. JN 4.02. 46
the king by me requests your presence straight. 4.03. 22
at my desires, and my requests, and my petitions H5 5.01. 23 P
then say at once what is it thou requests. R3 2.01. 99
and be not easily won to our requests: 3.07. 50
prince, | lend favorable ear to our requests, 3.07.101
calchas shall have | what he requests of us. TRO 3.03. 32
he's to make his requests by particulars, COR 2.03. 43 P
say that the emperor requests a parley | of TIT 4.04.101
make thy requests to thy friend. TIM 1.01.269 P
he lessons his requests, and to thee sues | to ANT 3.12. 13

REQUICK'NED 1 FR 0.0001 REL FR 1 V 0 P
spirit | requick'ned what in flesh was fatigate, COR 2.02.117

REQUIEM 2 FR 0.0002 REL FR 2 V 0 P
dead | to sing a requiem and such rest to her HAM 5.01.237
swan, | lest the requiem lack his right. PHT 16

/REQUIR'D 1 FR 0.0001 REL FR 0 V 1 P
/return /was /most /requir'd /and /necessary. LR 4.03. 6 P

REQUIR'D 9 FR 0.0010 REL FR 8 V 1 P
and when i have requir'd | some heavenly music TMP 5.01. 51
go, | the debt he owes will be requir'd of me. ERR 4.04.118
behind, restraining | from course requir'd; WT 1.02.245
confess | i lov'd him as in honor he requir'd; 3.02. 63
it is requir'd | you do awake your faith. 5.03. 94
of state he sent me to peruse, | as i requir'd; H8 3.02.122
my fortunes and my friends at stake requir'd | i COR 3.02. 63
now for want of these requir'd conveniences, her OTH 2.01.231 P
to lend me arms and aid when i requir'd them, ANT 2.02. 88

REQUIRE 24 FR 0.0027 REL FR 20 V 4 P
and require | my dukedom of thee, which perforce TMP 5.01.132
is to desire and require her to solicit your WIV 1.02. 10 P
satisfaction i would require is likewise your MM 3.01.155 P
in more than this deed does require! WT 2.03.190
'twill require | a strong faith to conceal it. H8 2.01.144
in humblest manner i require your highness 2.04.145
he | (i mean the bishop) did require a respite, 2.04.178
and nature does require | her times of 3.02.146
those charges | which will require your answer, 5.01.104
he will require them | as if he did contemn what COR 2.02.156
once if he do require our voices, we ought not 2.03. 1 P
now all the service i require of them | is that TIT 3.01. 77
the gods require our thanks. TIM 3.06. 69 P
always thought | that i require a clearness: MAC 3.01.132
but in best time | we will require her welcome. 3.04. 6
will you require in present dower with her, | or LR 1.01.192
i do require them of you, so to use them | as we 5.03. 43
to such whose places under us require, | our ANT 1.02.195
shall i say to caesar | what you require of him? 3.13. 66
the quality of her passion shall require, | lest 5.01. 63
if you require a little space for prayer, | i PER 4.01. 67
require him he advance it o'er our heads; TNK 1.01. 93
there | require of him the hearts of lions and 5.01. 39
spend, | nor services to do, till you require. SON 57. 4

REQUIRED 2 FR 0.0002 REL FR 1 V 1 P
the ministration and required office | on my AWW 2.05. 60
there is more better opportunity to be required, H5 3.02.139 P

/REQUIRES 1 FR 0.0001 REL FR 1 V 0 P
/and /her /father | /requires /a /fitter /place. LR 5.03. 59

REQUIRES 14 FR 0.0015 REL FR 11 V 3 P
my poor body, madam, requires it. AWW 1.03. 28 P
hence, it requires haste of your lordship. 4.03. 94 P
be with me, for you see | my plight requires it. WT 2.01.118
and to be so still requires nothing but secrecy. 3.03.125 P
that your estate requires and mine can yield. 3H6 3.03.150
for it requires the royal debt it lent you. R3 2.02. 95
appliance only | which your disease requires. H8 1.01.125
climb steep hills | requires slow pace at first. 1.01.132
requires nor child nor woman's face to see. COR 5.03.130
it requires swift foot. TIM 5.01.228
and he requires your haste–post–haste appearance OTH 1.02. 37
this hand of yours requires | a sequester from 3.04. 39
thee, and | requires to live in egypt, which not ANT 3.12. 12
promise, | and in our name, what she requires; 3.12. 28

REQUIRETH 1 FR 0.0001 REL FR 1 V 0 P
brother, the time and case requireth haste, 3H6 4.05. 18

REQUIRING 4 FR 0.0004 REL FR 3 V 1 P
for fish, | nor fetch in firing | at requiring, TMP 2.02.182
answer his requiring with a plausible obedience, MM 3.01.244 P
a jove, | that if requiring fail he will compel; H5 2.04.101
which shall be then | beyond further requiring. TNK 1.03. 26

REQUISITE 1 FR 0.0001 REL FR 0 V 1 P
a good nose is requisite also, to smell out work WT 4.04.672 P

REQUISITES 1 FR 0.0001 REL FR 0 V 1 P
and hath all those requisites in him that folly OTH 2.01.246 P

REQUIT 1 FR 0.0001 REL FR 1 V 0 P
expos'd unto the sea (which hath requit it) TMP 3.03. 71

REQUITAL 7 FR 0.0008 REL FR 4 V 3 P
in requital whereof, henceforth carry your TGV 1.01.145 P
and, i profess requital to a hair's breadth, not WIV 4.02. 3 P
and, in requital of your prophecy, hark you: MM 2.01.244 P
to public thanks, | forerunning more requital. 5.01. 8
be bold you do so grow in my requital | as AWW 5.01. 5
strength | to make a more requital to your love! JN 2.01. 34
rather our state's defective for requital | than COR 2.02. 50

REQUITE 26 FR 0.0029 REL FR 23 V 3 P
i will requite you with as good a thing, | at TMP 5.01.169
which to requite, command me while i live. TGV 3.01. 23
and, benedick, love on, i will requite thee, ADO 3.01.111
and i do with an eye of love requite her. 5.04. 24
love me to madness, i shall never requite him. MV 1.02. 65 P
thou shalt find i will most kindly requite. AYL 1.01.138 P
shall be for me, and, to requite you further, AWW 3.05. 99
fool, i'll requite it in the highest degree. TN 4.02.118 P

captain, for his life, and i will thee requite. H5 3.06. 49
and i'll requite it | with sweet rehearsal of my 2H6 1.02. 23
stanley, i will requite thy forwardness. 3H6 4.05. 23
be thou sure, i'll well requite thy kindness, 4.06. 10
if fortune serve me, i'll requite this kindness. 4.07. 78
at his return | no doubt he will requite it. H8 2.01. 46
more than could | my studied purposes requite, 3.02.168
hoarded plague a' th' gods | requite your love! COR 4.02. 12
and will with deeds requite thy gentleness; TIT 1.01.237
if lucius live, he will requite your wrongs, 1.01.296
of me now, | that i'll requite it last? TIM 3.03. 19
wealth | to requite me by making rich yourself. 4.03.522
why, how shall i requite you? 5.01. 73
i will requite your loves. HAM 1.02.250
/pass of practice | requite him for your father. 4.07.139
let heaven requite it with the serpent's curse! OTH 4.02. 16
for a fee, | the gods requite his charity!" PER 3.02. 75
the gods requite you all, and make her thankful! TNK 5.04. 36
REQUITED 5 FR 0.0005 REL FR 2 V 3 P
why, it must be requited. ADO 2.03.224 P
tongue, | else with the like i had requited him. 1H6 2.05. 50
are you set a–work, and how ill requited! TRO 5.10. 38 P
shed for my thankless country are requited | but COR 4.05. 70
but i requited him for his lie, and, i think, MAC 2.03. 39 P
REQUITES 2 FR 0.0002 REL FR 2 V 0 P
for edward's sake, and see how he requites me! R3 1.04. 68
ingrateful rome requites with foul contempt, TIT 5.01. 12
RERE–MICE 1 FR 0.0001 REL FR 1 V 0 P
some war with rere–mice for their leathren wings MND 2.02. 4
RE–SALUTE 2 FR 0.0002 REL FR 2 V 0 P
to re–salute his country with his tears, | tears TIT 1.01. 75
i will not re–salute the streets of rome, | or 1.01.326
RESCU'D 5 FR 0.0005 REL FR 5 V 0 P
was't you he rescu'd? AYL 4.03.133
walls, | rescu'd is orleance from the english! 1H6 1.06. 2
i gave thee life, and rescu'd thee from death. 4.06. 5
perhaps i shall be rescu'd by the french, | and 5.03.104
and from the bishop's huntsmen rescu'd him; 3H6 4.06. 84
RESCUE 28 FR 0.0031 REL FR 24 V 4 P
and rescue you from him | that would have forc'd TGV 5.04. 21
rather than have false proteus rescue me. 5.04. 35
wilt thou suffer them | to make a rescue? ERR 4.04.111
rescue thy mistress if thou be a man. SHR 3.02.237
surpris'd without rescue in the first assault or AWW 1.03.115 P
here comes the man, sir, that did rescue me. TN 5.01. 50
rescue those breathing lives to die in beds, JN 2.01.419
and there | where honorable rescue and defense 5.02. 18
in this fair rescue thou hast brought to me. 1H4 5.04. 50
a rescue! a rescue! 2H4 2.01. 55 P
a rescue! a rescue! 2.01. 55 P
good people, bring a rescue or two. 2.01. 56 P
spur to the rescue of the noble talbot, | who 1H6 4.03. 19
and, in advantage ling'ring, looks for rescue, 4.04. 19
too late comes rescue, he is ta'en or slain; 4.04. 42
the bastard to destroy, | came in strong rescue. 4.06. 26
had york and somerset brought rescue in, | we 4.07. 33
wouldst have me rescue thee from this reproach? 2H6 2.04. 64
unless thou rescue him from foul despair? 3H6 3.03.215
rescue, my lord of norfolk, rescue, rescue! R3 5.04. 1
rescue, my lord of norfolk, rescue, rescue! 5.04. 1
rescue, my lord of norfolk, rescue, rescue! 5.04. 1
rescue, fair lord, or else the day is lost! 5.04. 6
that you | have holp to make this rescue? COR 3.01.275
that in the rescue of lavinia | with his own TIT 1.01.417
to rescue my two brothers from their death, 3.01. 49
no rescue? LR 4.06.190
seize her, but | your comfort makes the rescue. ANT 3.11. 48
RESCUED 6 FR 0.0006 REL FR 6 V 0 P
my lord, i rescued her; JN 3.02. 7
and myself | rescued the black prince, that R2 2.03.101
and from the pride of gallia rescued thee. 1H6 4.06. 15
and, in the end being rescued, i have seen | him 2H6 3.01.364
when oxford had me down, he rescued me, | and R3 2.01.113
do't, | a crew of pirates came and rescued me; PER 5.01.174
RESCUES 1 FR 0.0001 REL FR 1 V 0 P
how well this yielding rescues thee from shame! LLL 1.01.118
RESCUING 1 FR 0.0001 REL FR 1 V 0 P
my uncles both are slain in rescuing me; 3H6 1.04. 2
RESEMBLANCE 3 FR 0.0003 REL FR 1 V 2 P
not a resemblance, but a certainty; MM 4.02.188 P
of the creature in resemblance of the mother; WT 5.02. 36 P
and his resemblance, being not like the duke. R3 3.07. 11
RESEMBLE 9 FR 0.0010 REL FR 6 V 3 P
you in the rest, we will resemble you in that. MV 3.01. 68 P
in count'nance somewhat doth resemble you. SHR 4.02.100
if i could make that resemble something in me! TN 2.05.120 P
in face, in gait, in speech, he doth resemble. 2H6 3.01.373
for up and down she doth resemble thee. TIT 5.02.107
and would most resemble sweet instruments hung TIM 1.02. 98 P
did the night resemble | when he lay couched in HAM 2.02.453
which heartless peasants did so well resemble, LUC 1392
such cherubins as your sweet self resemble, SON 114. 6
RESEMBLED 3 FR 0.0003 REL FR 2 V 1 P
though it was said she much resembled me, was TN 2.01. 26 P
i thought king henry had resembled thee | in 2H6 1.03. 53
had he not resembled | my father as he slept, i MAC 2.02. 12
RESEMBLES 4 FR 0.0004 REL FR 4 V 0 P
how well resembles it the prime of youth, 3H6 2.01. 23
the one his purple blood right well resembles, 2.05. 99
nor the inward man | resembles that it was. HAM 2.02. 7
another | not more resembles that sweet rosy lad CYM 5.05.121
RESEMBLETH 1 FR 0.0001 REL FR 1 V 0 P
o, how this spring of love resembleth | the TGV 1.03. 84
RESEMBLING 7 FR 0.0008 REL FR 7 V 0 P
soonest tempt, resembling spirits of light. LLL 4.03.253
me with a counterfeit | resembling majesty, JN 3.01.100
withal, | but idle sounds resembling parasits, VEN 848
resembling well his pale cheeks and the blood 1169
with pearly sweat resembling dew of night. LUC 396
resembling strong youth in his middle age, | yet SON 7. 6
resembling sire, and child, and happy mother, 8.11
RE–SEND 1 FR 0.0001 REL FR 1 V 0 P
tokens and letters which she did re–send, | and AWW 3.06.115
RESERVATION 5 FR 0.0005 REL FR 4 V 1 P
me | in heedfull'st reservation to bestow them, AWW 1.03.225
to make some reservation of your wrongs. 2.03.245 P
feels, | making /not reservation of yourselves, COR 3.03.130
with reservation of an hundred knights | by you LR 1.01.133
but kept a reservation to be followed | with 2.04.252
RESERV'D 14 FR 0.0015 REL FR 12 V 2 P
order else have died, | i have reserv'd alive. MM 5.01.467
the other part reserv'd i by consent, | for that R2 1.01.128
only reserv'd, you claim no interest | in any of 1H6 5.04.167
only reserv'd their factor to buy souls | and R3 4.04. 72
that hast thus lovingly reserv'd | the cordial TIT 1.01.165
here is a place reserv'd, sir. MAC 3.04. 45
but it reserv'd some quantity of choice, | to HAM 3.04. 75
nay, he reserv'd a blanket, else we had been all LR 3.04. 65 P
peril, that i have reserv'd | to myself nothing. ANT 5.02.143
that i some lady trifles have reserv'd, 5.02.165
not what you have reserv'd, nor what 5.02.180
but nothing | (always reserv'd my holy duty) CYM 1.01. 87
honor of hers which you imagine so reserv'd. 1.04.131 P
reserv'd the stalk and gave him all my flower. LC 147
RESERVE 11 FR 0.0012 REL FR 7 V 4 P
reserve them till a merrier hour than this: ERR 1.02. 69
what is yours to bestow is not yours to reserve. TN 1.05.189 P
able, and yet reserve an ability that they never TRO 3.02. 85 P
but reserve still to give, lest your deities be TIM 3.06. 72 P
if he covetously reserve it, how shall 's get it 4.03.405 P
each man's censure, but reserve thy judgment. HAM 1.03. 69
reserve thy state, | and in thy best LR 1.01.149
should reserve | my crack'd one to more care. CYM 4.04. 49
once again, reserve | that excellent complexion, PER 4.01. 39
reserve them for my love, not for their rhyme, SON 32. 7
reserve their character with golden quill | and 85. 3
RESERVED 1 FR 0.0001 REL FR 1 V 0 P
all her deserving | is a reserved honesty, and AWW 3.05. 62
RESERVES 1 FR 0.0001 REL FR 1 V 0 P
that she reserves it evermore about her | to OTH 3.03.295
RESIDE 3 FR 0.0003 REL FR 3 V 0 P
floods, or to reside | in thrilling region of MM 3.01.121
if thou wouldst not reside | but where one TIM 5.01.110
/i /would /not there reside, | to put my father OTH 1.03.241
RESIDENCE 9 FR 0.0010 REL FR 7 V 2 P
a forted residence 'gainst the tooth of time MM 5.01. 12
rather than suffer question for your residence. AWW 2.05. 39 P
souls | that to their everlasting residence, JN 2.01.284
blood | with fury from his native residence. R2 2.01.119
poison hath residence and medicine power; ROM 2.03. 24
whose procreation, residence, and birth | scarce TIM 4.03. 4
their residence, both in reputation and profit, HAM 2.02.329 P
my residence in rome at one /philario's, | who CYM 1.01. 97
yea, happily, near | the residence of posthumus; 3.04.148
RESIDENT 2 FR 0.0002 REL FR 2 V 0 P
that hath so long been resident in france? 1H6 3.04. 14
divine, | be resident in men like one another, 3H6 5.06. 82
/RESIDES 1 FR 0.0001 REL FR 1 V 0 P
between our ilium and where she /resides, | let TRO 1.01.101
RESIDES 5 FR 0.0005 REL FR 4 V 1 P
my heart fly to your service, there resides, TMP 3.01. 65
moated grange, resides this dejected mariana. MM 3.01.265 P
resides not in that man that does not think) WT 1.02.272
(between whose endless jar justice resides) TRO 1.03.117
i have a kind of self resides with you; 3.02.148
RESIDING 4 FR 0.0004 REL FR 3 V 1 P
and, there residing, the tenderness of her AWW 4.03. 51 P
that thou, residing here, goes yet with me; ANT 1.03.103
no more than my residing here at rome | might be 2.02. 37
will keep our honors, | it is for our residing; TNK 1.02. 38
RESIDUE 1 FR 0.0001 REL FR 1 V 0 P
the residue of your fortune, | go to my cave and AYL 2.07.196
/RESIGN 3 FR 0.0003 REL FR 3 V 0 P
/thought /you /had /been /willing /to /resign. R2 4.01.190
/are /you /contented /to /resign /the /crown? 4.01.200
/therefore /no /no, /for /i /resign /to /thee. 4.01.202
RESIGN 19 FR 0.0021 REL FR 19 V 0 P
thy dukedom i resign, and do entreat | thou TMP 5.01.118
wilt thou resign them and lay down thy arms? JN 2.01.154
take but my shame, | and i resign my gage. R2 1.01.176
he bids you then resign | your crown and kingdom H5 2.04. 93
and at his pleasure will resign my place. 2H6 1.03.121
resign it then and leave thine insolence. 1.03.122
as willingly do i the same resign | as ere thy 2.03. 33
to be, or what thou art | resign to death; 3.01.334
and made him to resign his crown perforce. 3H6 1.01.142
for he could not so resign his crown | but that 1.01.145
henry of lancaster, resign thy crown. 1.01.164
crown, | i here resign my government to thee, 4.06. 24
resign thy chair, and where i stand kneel thou, 5.05. 19
i'll resign unto your grace | the seal i keep, R3 2.04. 70
it is your fault that you resign | the supreme 3.07.117
to–morrow yield up rule, resign my life, | and TIT 1.01.191
vile earth, to earth resign, end motion here, ROM 3.02. 59
for us, we will resign, | during the life of LR 5.03.299
where they resign their office and their light VEN 1039
/RESIGNATION 1 FR 0.0001 REL FR 1 V 0 P
/the /resignation /of /thy /state /and /crown R2 4.01.179
RESIGN'D 3 FR 0.0003 REL FR 3 V 0 P
hath broken his staff, resign'd his stewardship, R2 2.02. 59
lords, | resign'd the crown to henry the fourth, 3H6 1.01.139
that thus i have resign'd to you my charge. R3 1.04. 97
RESIST 12 FR 0.0013 REL FR 12 V 0 P
i will resist such entertainment till | mine TMP 1.02.466
a fool, | if she had not a spirit to resist. SHR 3.02.221
prevent it, resist it, let it not be so, | lest R2 4.01.148
but how, my lord, shall we resist it now? H5 1.01. 6
it boots not to resist both wind and tide. 3H6 4.03. 59
to their benumbed wills, resist the same, TRO 2.02.179
him, if he do resist | subdue him at his peril. OTH 1.02. 80
those that would die or e'er resist are grown CYM 5.03. 50
for going on death's net, whom none resist. PER 1.01. 40
our men be vanquish'd ere they do resist, | and 1.02. 27
if wars, we are unable to resist. 1.04. 84
these cates resist me, he not thought upon. 2.03. 29
RESISTANCE 6 FR 0.0006 REL FR 4 V 2 P
have vanquish'd the resistance of her youth, ADO 4.01. 46
unfold to us some warlike resistance. AWW 1.01.117 P
feathers turn back in any show of resistance. 2H4 2.04.100 P
unarm'd, and can | smell where resistance is. TNK 3.02. 17
pure shame and aw'd resistance made him fret, VEN 69
such danger to resistance did belong | that LUC 1265
RESISTED 5 FR 0.0005 REL FR 5 V 0 P
thou that so stoutly hath resisted me, | give me 3H6 2.05. 79
he hath resisted law, | and therefore law shall COR 3.01.266
our aediles smote, ourselves resisted? 3.01.317
name strikes more | than could his war resisted. ANT 1.04. 55
look | for fury not to be resisted. CYM 3.01. 67
RESISTETH 1 FR 0.0001 REL FR 1 V 0 P
he now obeys, and now no more resisteth, | while VEN 563
RESISTING 1 FR 0.0001 REL FR 1 V 0 P
bent | against the brows of this resisting town. JN 2.01. 38
RESISTS 2 FR 0.0002 REL FR 1 V 1 P
what, resists he? help him, lucio. MM 5.01.350 P
revolt, and who resists | are mock'd for valiant COR 4.06.103
RESOLUTE 12 FR 0.0013 REL FR 8 V 4 P
or that the resolute acting of /your blood MM 2.01. 12
most resolute pompey! LLL 5.02.699 P
but he is resolute. AYL 1.01.141 P
you are resolute then? TN 1.05. 21 P
do what ye dare, we are as resolute. 1H6 3.01. 91
but always resolute in most extremes. 4.01. 38
not resolute, except so much were done, | for 2H6 3.01.267
and therefore am i bold and resolute. 4.04. 60
then leave me not, my lords, be resolute, | i 3H6 1.01. 43
therefore be resolute. 5.04. 61
i thought thou hadst been resolute. R3 1.04.113 P
be bloody, bold, and resolute: MAC 4.01. 79
RESOLUTELY 3 FR 0.0003 REL FR 1 V 2 P
ort is (according to our meaning) "resolutely." WIV 1.01.255 P
purse of gold most resolutely snatch'd on monday 1H4 1.02. 34 P
thrice–noble suffolk, 'tis resolutely spoke. 2H6 3.01.266
RESOLUTES 1 FR 0.0001 REL FR 1 V 0 P
there | shark'd up a list of lawless resolutes, HAM 1.01. 98
RESOLUTION 31 FR 0.0035 REL FR 27 V 4 P
think you i can a resolution fetch | from MM 3.01. 81
not satisfy your resolution with hopes that are 3.01.168 P
my leave, | in resolution as i swore before. SHR 4.02. 43
your resolution cannot hold when 'tis | oppos'd WT 4.04. 36
lest resolution drop | out at mine eyes in JN 4.01. 35
and put on | the dauntless spirit of resolution. 5.01. 53
how high a pitch his resolution soars! R2 1.01.109
and resolution thus fubb'd as it is with the 1H4 1.02. 60 P
withal | how terrible in constant resolution, H5 2.04. 35
thoughts, | and change misdoubt to resolution; 2H6 3.01.332
be witness that no want of resolution in me, but 4.08. 62 P
be it with resolution then to fight. 3H6 2.02. 77
and in this resolution, i defy thee, | not 2.02.170
with resolution, wheresoe'er i meet thee | (as i 5.01. 95
and in this resolution here we leave you. R3 3.07.218
ere a determinate resolution, he | (i mean the H8 2.04.177
to you | in resolution to keep helen still, TRO 2.02.191
breaking his oath and resolution like | a twist COR 5.06. 94
thy resolution mock'd! TIT 3.01.238
no help, | do thou but call my resolution wise, ROM 4.01. 53
and let us swear our resolution. JC 2.01.113
i pull in resolution, and begin | to doubt th' MAC 5.05. 41
and thus the native hue of resolution | is HAM 3.01. 83
would unstate myself to be in a due resolution. LR 1.02.100 P
on that, | and fix most firm thy resolution. OTH 5.01. 5
my resolution and my hands i'll trust, | none ANT 4.15. 49
no friend | but resolution and the briefest end. 4.15. 91
be sick, | but that my resolution helps me. CYM 3.06. 4
my will is back'd with resolution. LUC 352
my resolution, love, shall be thy boast, | by 1193
my resolution, husband, do thou take, | mine 1200
RESOLUTION'S 1 FR 0.0001 REL FR 1 V 0 P
my resolution's plac'd, and i have nothing | of ANT 5.02.238
/RESOLV'D 1 FR 0.0001 REL FR 1 V 0 P
before her beauty, | /resolv'd to carry her. AWW 3.07. 19
RESOLV'D 44 FR 0.0049 REL FR 38 V 6 P
forgo the purpose | that you resolv'd t' effect. TMP 3.03. 13
i am resolv'd that thou shalt spend some time TGV 1.03. 66
i now am full resolv'd to take a wife | and turn 3.01. 76
to him, and now is he resolv'd to die. MM 3.02.248 P
for how i firmly am resolv'd you know: SHR 1.01. 49
i am resolv'd. 1.01. 90
well, gentlemen, | i am thus resolv'd: 2.01.393
i, | thy resolv'd patient, on thee still rely. AWW 2.01.204
so, neither, but i am resolv'd on two points — TN 1.05. 22 P
he's irremovable, | resolv'd for flight. WT 4.04.508
kings of our fear, until our fears, resolv'd, JN 2.01.371
from a resolv'd and honorable war | to a most 2.01.585
he was not so resolv'd when last we spake R2 2.03. 29
up | and hangs resolv'd correction in the arm 2H4 4.01.211
we would be resolv'd, | before we hear him, of H5 1.02. 4
now are we well resolv'd, and by god's help 1.02.222
and therefore are we certainly resolv'd | to 1H6 5.01. 37
hast, | i am resolv'd for death /or dignity. 2H6 5.01.194
i am resolv'd to bear a greater storm | than any 5.01.198
until i be resolv'd | where our right valiant 3H6 2.01. 9
i am resolv'd | that clifford's manhood lies 2.02.124
last, i firmly am resolv'd | you shall have aid. 3.03.219
ah, that thy father had been so resolv'd! 5.05. 22
you are all resolv'd rather to die than to COR 1.01. 4 P
resolv'd, resolv'd. 1.01. 6 P
resolv'd, resolv'd. 1.01. 6 P
are you all resolv'd to give your voices? 2.03. 36 P
madam, stand resolv'd, but hope withal | the TIT 1.01.135
and resolv'd withal | to do myself this reason 1.01.278
for that i am prepar'd and full resolv'd, 2.01. 57
if he be so resolv'd, | i can o'ersway him; JC 2.01.202
and be resolv'd | how caesar hath deserv'd to 3.01.131
as rushing out of doors to be resolv'd | if 3.02.179
let me be resolv'd. 4.02. 14
spirit, and resolv'd | to meet all perils very 5.01. 90
we are resolv'd, my lord. MAC 3.01.138
to be once in doubt | is /once to be resolv'd. OTH 3.03.180
i have myself resolv'd upon a course | which has ANT 3.11. 9
thou art resolv'd? PER 4.01. 12
i am resolv'd. 4.01. 12
then i am resolv'd, i will not go. TNK 2.02.269
i am resolv'd: 2.03. 21
she is resolv'd no longer to restrain him, VEN 579
even there resolv'd my reason into tears, LC 296
RESOLVE 33 FR 0.0037 REL FR 30 V 3 P
which shall be shortly, single i'll resolve you TMP 5.01.248
i am now going to resolve him. MM 3.01.189 P
amaz'd, but this shall absolutely resolve you. 4.02.209 P
my coming, | and suddenly resolve me in my suit. LLL 2.01.110
shall we resolve to woo these girls of france? 4.03.368

count atomies as to resolve the propositions of AYL 3.02.232 P
glad that you thus continue your resolve | to SHR 1.01. 27
nor is your firm resolve unknown to me, | in the 2.01. 92
what, master, read you? first resolve me that. 4.02. 7
the chapel, or resolve you | for more amazement. WT 5.03. 86
i will resolve for scotland; 2H4 2.03. 67
resolve on this: 1H6 1.02. 91
let us resolve to scale their flinty bulwarks. 2.01. 27
if with a lady of so high resolve | (as is fair 5.05. 75
resolve thee, richard, claim the english crown. 3H6 1.01. 49
may it please your highness to resolve me now, 3.02. 19
now, sister, let us hear your firm resolve. 3.03.129
i go, hastings and montague, | resolve my doubt. 4.01.135
i will resolve you herein presently. R3 4.02. 26
dar'st thou resolve to kill a friend of mine? 4.02. 69
may it please you to resolve me in my suit. 4.02.117
my letter will resolve him of my mind. 4.05. 20
do | that you affect, and so must you resolve, TIT 2.01.105
my lord the emperor, resolve me this: 5.03. 35
be strong and prosperous | in this resolve. ROM 4.01.123
resolve yourselves apart, | i'll come to you MAC 3.01.137
melt, | thaw, and resolve itself into a dew! HAM 1.02.130
resolve me with all modest haste which way LR 2.04. 25
yet in two, | as you will live, resolve it you. PER 1.01. 71
resolve your angry father if my tongue | did 2.05. 68
he can resolve you. 5.01. 1
man that can, in aught you would, | resolve you. 5.01. 13
that can | from first to last resolve you. 5.03. 61

RESOLVED 6 FR 0.0006 REL FR 6 V 0 P
and he wants wit that wants resolved will | to TGV 2.06. 12
i am resolved, 'tis but a three years' fast: LLL 1.01. 24
a monk, i tell you, a resolved villain, | whose JN 5.06. 29
long since we were resolved of your truth, 1H6 3.04. 20
how now, my hardy, stout, resolved mates, | are R3 1.03.339
and be resolved he lives to govern us, | or, PER 2.04. 31

RESOLVEDLY 1 FR 0.0001 REL FR 1 V 0 P
less, | resolvedly more leisure shall express. AWW 5.03.332

RESOLVES 2 FR 0.0002 REL FR 2 V 0 P
how yet resolves the governor of the town? H5 3.03. 1
whose liquid surge resolves | the moon into salt TIM 4.03.439

RESOLVETH 1 FR 0.0001 REL FR 1 V 0 P
resolveth from his figure 'gainst the fire? JN 5.04. 25

RESOLVING 1 FR 0.0001 REL FR 1 V 0 P
yet ever to obtain his will resolving, | though LUC 129

RESORT 15 FR 0.0017 REL FR 12 V 3 P
of all the fair resort of gentlemen | that every TGV 1.02. 4
worth, | and kept severely from resort of men, 3.01.108
why then i would resort to her by night. 3.01.110
we talk on | often resort unto this gentlewoman? 4.02. 74
shall all our houses of resort in the suburbs be MM 1.02.101 P
liv'st | to walk where any honest men resort. ERR 5.01. 28
to get the cause of my son's resort thither. WT 4.02. 50 P
what men of name resort to him? R3 4.05. 11
at some hours in the night spirits resort — ROM 4.03. 44
lord, | join with me to forbid him her resort, TIM 1.01.127
and what men to-night | have had resort to you; JC 2.01.276
that she should lock herself from /his resort, HAM 2.02.143
know this house to be a place of such resort, PER 4.06. 80 P
foes, | and merry fools to mock at him resort; LUC 989
thou mak'st faults graces that to thee resort. SON 96. 4

RESORTED 1 FR 0.0001 REL FR 1 V 0 P
men of great worth resorted to this forest, AYL 5.04.155

RESORTERS 1 FR 0.0001 REL FR 0 V 1 P
for you that your resorters stand upon sound PER 4.06. 24 P

RESOUND 1 FR 0.0001 REL FR 1 V 0 P
how sighs resound through heartless ground, PP 17.23

RESOUNDS 2 FR 0.0002 REL FR 2 V 0 P
that it resounds | as if it felt with scotland, MAC 4.03. 6
whose hollow womb resounds like heaven's thunder VEN 268

RESPEAKING 1 FR 0.0001 REL FR 1 V 0 P
shall bruit again, | respeaking earthly thunder. HAM 1.02.128

RESPECT 109 FR 0.0123 REL FR 76 V 33 P
if you respect them, best to take them up. TGV 1.02.131
win her with gifts, if she respect not words: 3.01. 89
be /kiss'd fasting, in respect of her breath." 3.01.324 P
(though you respect not aught your servant doth) 5.04. 20
if it were not for one trifling respect, i could WIV 2.01. 45 P
and learning, so wide of his own respect. 3.01. 58 P
heaven | with less respect than we do minister MM 2.02. 86
and six or seven winters more respect | than a 3.01. 75
do you persuade yourself that i respect you? 4.01. 52
respect to your great place! 5.01.292
respice finem, respect your end, or rather, the ERR 4.04. 41 P
troth 's but a night-gown /in respect of yours: ADO 3.04. 18 P
that more than all the world i did respect her. LLL 5.02.437
hector was but a troyan in respect of this. 5.02.636 P
or else misgraffed in respect of years — MND 1.01.137
love | (and yet a place of high respect with me) 2.01.209
for you in my respect are all the world. 2.01.224
cannot do, noble respect | takes it in might, 5.01. 91
you have too much respect upon the world. MV 1.01. 74
talk with respect, and swear but now and then, 2.02.191
nothing is good, i see, without respect; 5.01. 99
i attend them with all respect and duty. AYL 1.02.167 P
shepherd, in respect of itself, it is a good 3.02. 13 P
but in respect that it is a shepherd's life, it 3.02. 14 P
in respect that it is solitary, i like it very 3.02. 15 P
but in respect that it is private, it is a very 3.02. 16 P
now, in respect it is in the fields, it pleaseth 3.02. 17 P
but in respect it is not in the court, it is 3.02. 18 P
in respect of a good piece of flesh indeed! 3.02. 66 P
'fore me, i speak in respect — AWW 2.03. 27 P
not a hilding, hold me no more in your respect. 3.06. 4 P
indeed he is not for your lordship's respect. 3.06.101 P
whose high respect and rich validity | did lack 5.03.192
is there no respect of place, persons, nor time TN 2.03. 91 P
me with a more exalted respect than any one else 2.05. 27 P
i will respect thee as a father, if | thou WT 1.02.461
my uncle's will in this respect is mine. JN 2.01.510
to tread down fair respect of sovereignty, | and 3.01. 58
to say what good respect i have of thee. 3.03. 28
you hold too heinous a respect of grief. 3.04. 90
frowns | more upon humor than advis'd respect. 4.02.214
fought | between compulsion and a brave respect! 5.02. 44
the love of him, and this respect besides, | for 5.04. 41
peace | as we with honor and respect may take, 5.07. 85
so it be new, there's no respect how vile — R2 2.01. 25
with solemn reverence, throw away respect, 3.02.172
and therefore lost that title of respect | which 1H4 1.03. 8
in respect of the love i bear your house." 2.03. 2 P
in the respect of the love he bears our house: 2.03. 4 P
he holds your temper in a high respect, | and 3.01.168
king, | if you vouchsafe me hearing and respect. 4.03. 31
john, | but now i do respect thee as my soul. 5.04. 20
chok'd the respect of likely peril fear'd, | and 2H4 1.01.184
of imprisonment to me in respect of poverty, but 1.02.128 P
deliver'd with good respect. 2.02.101 P
/begun upon an honorable respect, and worn as a H5 5.01. 71 P
this, in respect, a child, | and men ne'er spend 3H6 5.05. 56
nothing that i respect, my gracious lord. R3 1.03.295
(out of the great respect they bear to beauty) H8 1.04. 69
a thousand pounds a year for pure respect? 2.03. 95
as you respect the common good, the state | of 3.02.290
yet should find respect | for what they have 5.02.110
that holy duty, out of dear respect, | his royal 5.02.154
well, well, my lords, respect him, | take him, 5.02.188
reason and respect | make livers pale and TRO 2.02. 49
dispose | without observance or respect of any, 2.03.165
let me not shame respect, but give me leave | to 5.03. 73
on both sides more respect. COR 3.01.180
my country's good with a respect more tender, 3.03.112
to break our necks, they respect not us. 5.04. 33 P
it is my will, the which if thou respect, | show ROM 1.05. 72
with me, | in one respect i'll thy assistant be; 2.03. 90
he does deny him (in respect of his) | what TIM 3.02. 74
and never learn'd | the icy precepts of respect, 4.03.258
sir, in respect of a fine workman, i am but, as JC 1.01. 10 P
heard | where many of the best respect in rome 1.02. 59
for mine honor, and have respect to mine honor, 3.02. 15 P
with courtesy and with respect enough, | but not 4.02. 15
by me as the idle wind, | which i respect not. 4.03. 69
thou art a fellow of a good respect; 5.05. 45
use him, | with all respect and rites of burial. 5.05. 77
fortune nothing | takes from his high respect. MAC 3.06. 29
there's the respect | that makes calamity of so HAM 3.01. 67
but yaw neither, in respect of his quick sail. 5.02.115 P
my love should kindle to inflam'd respect. LR 1.01.255
but, in respect of that, i would fain think it 1.02. 64 P
to do upon respect such violent outrage. 2.04. 24
nature's above art in that respect. 4.06. 86 P
education both do learn me | how to respect you; OTH 1.03.184
and such things else of quality and respect | as 1.03.282
his worthiness | does challenge much respect. 2.01.211
i may say so in this respect, for that he hath 2.03.316 P
and comforts of sudden respect and acquaintance, 4.02.190 P
in my respect than all the hairs above thee, CYM 2.03.135
of posthumus in more respect than my noble and 3.05.135 P
or council has respect with him but he. PER 2.04. 18
who shall not be more dear to my respect | than 3.03. 33
and true gentility's, | hear and respect me! TNK 1.01. 26
thrive with fair ones, | hear and respect me! 1.01. 28
this is virtue | of no respect in thebes. 1.02. 36
not physick'd by respect might turn our blood STM III 13
true valor still a true respect should have; LUC 201
respect and reason, wait on wrinkled age! 275
his true respect will prison false desire, | and 642
such harmless creatures have a true respect | to 1347
to show me worthy of /thy sweet respect: SON 26.12
in our two loves there is but one respect, 36. 5
then others for the breath of words respect, 85.13
what merit do i in myself respect, | that is so 149. 9

RESPECTED 12 FR 0.0013 REL FR 3 V 9 P
and it like you, the house is a respected house; MM 2.01.162 P
next, this is a respected fellow; 2.01.163 P
and his mistress is a respected woman. 2.01.164 P
his wife is a more respected person than any of 2.01.165 P
to come that she was ever respected with man, 2.01.168 P
she was respected with him before he married 2.01.170 P
i respected with her before i was married to her 2.01.175 P
if ever i was respected with her, or she with me 2.01.176 P
is not then respected | for what before it was. COR 3.01.305
only their ends | you have respected; 5.03. 5
when we banish'd him, we respected not them; 5.04. 32 P
so princes their renowns if not respected. PER 2.02. 13

RESPECTING 6 FR 0.0006 REL FR 6 V 0 P
and i am mean indeed, respecting you. SHR 5.02. 32
is none worthy, | respecting her that's gone. WT 5.01. 35
respecting what a rancorous mind he bears | and 2H6 3.01. 24
respecting this our marriage with the dowager, H8 2.04.181
full of respects, yet nought at all respecting, VEN 911
children's tears nor mothers' groans respecting, LUC 431

RESPECTIVE 4 FR 0.0004 REL FR 4 V 0 P
in her, | but i can make respective in myself, TGV 4.04.195
should have been respective and have kept it. MV 5.01.156
'tis too respective and too sociable | for your JN 1.01.188
away to heaven, respective lenity, | and ROM 3.01.123

RESPECTIVELY 1 FR 0.0001 REL FR 0 V 1 P
flaminius, you are very respectively welcome, TIM 3.01. 8 P

/RESPECTS 1 FR 0.0001 REL FR 1 V 0 P
since that /respects /of /fortune are his love, LR 1.01.248

RESPECTS 19 FR 0.0021 REL FR 14 V 5 P
since she respects my mistress' love so much. TGV 4.04.182
what should it be that he respects in her, | but 4.04.194
in love | who respects friend? 5.04. 54
love, that in some respects makes a beast a man; WIV 5.05. 5 P
i would have daff'd all other respects, and made ADO 2.03.169 P
the passado he respects not, the duello he LLL 1.02.179 P
but more devout than this /in our respects 5.02.782
and she respects me as her only son. MND 1.01.160
for my respects are better than they seem, | and AWW 2.05. 66
when such profound respects do pull you on. JN 3.01.318
and yet in some respects i grant i cannot go. 2H4 1.02.167 P
like a tall man that respects thy reputation. R3 1.04.152 P
but the respects thereof are nice and trivial, 3.07.175
she will /be rul'd | in all respects by me; ROM 3.04. 14
marriage move | are base respects of thrift, but HAM 3.02.183
you shall do small respects, show too bold LR 2.02.130
for and a daughter who | he not respects at all. CYM 1.06.155
full of respects, yet nought at all respecting, VEN 911
sum, | call'd to that audit by advis'd respects; SON 49. 4

RESPECT'ST 1 FR 0.0001 REL FR 1 V 0 P
that thou respect'st not spilling edward's blood R2 2.01.131

RESPICE 1 FR 0.0001 REL FR 0 V 1 P
mistress, respice finem, respect your end, or ERR 4.04. 41 P

RESPITE 6 FR 0.0006 REL FR 5 V 1 P
effect, i crave but four days' respite; MM 4.02.160 P
after some respite, will return to callice; 1H6 4.01.170
soul, | is the determin'd respite of my wrongs. R3 5.01. 19
he | (i mean the bishop) did require a respite, H8 2.04.178
this respite shook | the bosom of my conscience, 2.04.182
forty days longer we do respite you; PER 1.01.116

RESPITES 1 FR 0.0001 REL FR 1 V 0 P
that respites me a life whose very comfort | is MM 2.03. 41

RESPONSIVE 1 FR 0.0001 REL FR 0 V 1 P
dear to fancy, very responsive to the hilts, HAM 5.02.151 P

/REST* 4 FR 0.0004 REL FR 3 V 1 P
/i /find /myself /a /traitor /with /the /rest; R2 4.01.248
/sort /you /with /the /rest /of /my /servants; HAM 2.02.268 P
/you /lie /down /and /rest /upon /the /cushions? LR 3.06. 34
/this /rest /might /yet /have /balm'd /thy 3.06. 98

REST* 352 FR 0.0397 REL FR 299 V 53 P
hast dispos'd, | and all the rest o' th' fleet. TMP 1.02.226
and for the rest o' th' fleet | (which i 1.02.232
you do keep from me | the rest o' th' island. 1.02.344
will guard your person while you take your rest, 2.01.197
for all the rest, | they'll take suggestion as a 2.01.287
pray set it down, and rest you. 3.01. 18
pray now rest yourself, | he's safe for these 3.01. 20
by your patience, | i needs must rest me. 3.03. 4
sit down, and rest. 3.03. 6
lime upon your fingers, and away with the rest. 4.01.246 P
her sovereign aid, | and rest myself content. 5.01.144
every man shift for all the rest, and let no man 5.01.256 P
where you shall take your rest | for this one 5.01.302
why not on proteus, as of all the rest? TGV 1.02. 20
why, he, of all the rest, hath never mov'd me. 1.02. 27
yet he, of all the rest, i think best loves ye. 1.02. 28
and there i'll rest, as after much turmoil | a 2.07. 37
my herald thoughts in thy pure bosom rest them, 3.01.144
therefore, above the rest, we parley to you: 4.01. 58
which, with ourselves, all rest at thy dispose. 4.01. 74
and so, good rest. 4.02.132
the good humor is to steal at a minute's rest. WIV 1.03. 28 P
drawn him and the rest of their company from 4.02. 34 P
captain and all the rest from their functions; MM 1.02. 13 P
this very man, having eaten the rest (as i said) 2.01.101 P
there rest. 2.03. 36
and fit his mind to death, for his soul's rest. 2.04.187
thy best of rest is sleep, | and that thou oft 3.01. 17
rest you well. 4.03.176 P
he that sets up his rest to do more exploits ERR 4.03. 27 P
going to bed and says, "god give you good rest!" 4.03. 33 P
well, sir, there rest in your foolery. 4.03. 34 P
and life-preserving rest | to be disturb'd, 5.01. 83
presently call the rest of the watch together, ADO 3.03. 29 P
you swore to that, berowne, and to the rest. LLL 1.01. 53
such public shame as the rest of the court can 1.01.131 P
who are the rest? 2.01. 55
her, fellow, by the rest that have no heads. 4.01. 44 P
for the rest of the worthies? 5.01.142 P
when lo, to interrupt my purpos'd rest, | toward 5.02. 91
i make no doubt | the rest will /ne'er come in, 5.02.152
to flatter up these powers of mine with rest, 5.02.814
a twelvemonth shall you spend, and never rest, 5.02.821
the rest i'll give to be to you translated. MND 1.01.191
to the rest — yet my chief humor is for a 1.02. 28 P
now name the rest of the players. 1.02. 39 P
set your heart at rest; 2.01.121
then to your offices, and let me rest. 2.02. 8
we'll rest us, hermia, if you think it good, 2.02. 37
for i upon this bank will rest my head. 2.02. 40
sleep give thee all his rest! 2.02. 64
i in dark uneven way, | and here will rest me. 3.02.418
here will i rest me till the break of day. 3.02.446
for all the rest, | let lion, moonshine, wall, 5.01.149
this is the greatest error of all the rest. 5.01.246 P
owner of it blest | ever shall in safety rest. 5.01.420
and thankfully rest debtor for the first. MV 1.01.152
rest you fair, good signior, | your worship was 1.03. 59
me, is my boy, god rest his soul, alive or dead? 2.02. 71 P
own part, as i have set up my rest to run away, 2.02.103 P
so i will not rest till i have run some ground. 2.02.103 P
and i must to lorenzo and the rest, | but we 2.02.205
there is some ill a-brewing towards my rest, 2.05. 17
fie, fie, gratiano, where are all the rest? 2.06. 62
if we are like you in the rest, we will resemble 3.01. 67 P
nerissa and the rest, stand all aloof. 3.02. 42
the rest aloof are the dardanian wives, | with 3.02. 58
stay, | nor rest be interposer 'twixt us twain. 3.02.327
i rest much bounden to you; AYL 1.02.286
bring us where we may rest ourselves and feed. 2.04. 73
you have too courtly a wit for me, i'll rest. 3.02. 70 P
wilt thou rest damn'd? 3.02. 71 P
god rest you merry, sir. 5.01. 59 P
amongst the rest of the country copulatives, to 5.04. 55 P
the rest will comfort, for thy counsel 's sound. SHR 1.01.164
must stead us all, and me amongst the rest; 1.02.264
to whom we all rest generally beholding. 1.02.272
if that be jest, then all the rest was so. 2.01. 22
i may have welcome 'mongst the rest that woo, 2.01. 96
woo, | and free access and favor as the rest; 2.01. 97
but let it rest. 3.01. 56
philip, walter, sugarsop, and the rest; 4.01. 90 P
the rest were ragged, old, and beggarly, | yet, 4.01.137
why then the beef, and let the mustard rest. 4.03. 26
my cake is dough, but i'll in among the rest, 5.01.140
the rest have worn me out | with several AWW 1.02. 73
amongst the rest, | there is a remedy, approv'd, 1.03.227
since you set up your rest 'gainst remedy. 2.01.135
but rest | unquestion'd welcome and undoubted 2.01.207
thanks, sir; all the rest is mute. 2.03. 77
creature as a maid, | i can create the rest. 2.03.143
let the rest go. 2.03.148
o, you should not rest | between the elements of TN 1.05.274
let all the rest give place. 2.04. 79
of a flea, i'll eat the rest of th' anatomy. 3.02. 62 P
to do you rest, a thousand deaths would die. 5.01.133
were you a woman, as the rest goes even, | i 5.01.239
the oracle | give rest to th' minds of others — WT 2.01.191
nor night, nor day, no rest. 2.03. 1
a moi'ty of my rest | might come to me again. 2.03. 8
he took good rest to-night; 2.03. 10
both breed thee, pretty, | and still rest thine. 3.03. 49

or that youth would sleep out the rest; 3.03. 61 P
wipe not out the rest of thy services by leaving 4.02. 11 P
which so drew the rest of the herd to me that 4.04.608 P
at the other hill | command the rest to stand. JN 2.01.299
though you, and all the rest so grossly led, 3.01.168
one minute, nay, one quiet breath of rest. 3.04.134
if what in rest you have in right you hold, 4.02. 55
sings | his soul and body to their lasting rest. 5.07. 24
the cardinal pandulph is within at rest, | who 5.07. 82
we make, | to rest without a spot for evermore. 5.07.107
us rue, | if england to itself do rest but true. 5.07.118
as for the rest appeal'd, | it issues from the R2 1.01.142
and all the rest revolted faction traitors? 2.02. 57
but i shall grieve you to report the rest. 2.02. 95
these differences shall all rest under gage 4.01. 86
your differences shall all rest under gage 4.01.105
here let us rest, if this rebellious earth 5.01. 5
once more, adieu, the rest let sorrow say. 5.01.102
my lord, you told me you would tell the rest, 5.02. 1
fest'red joint cut off, the rest rest sound, 5.03. 85
fest'red joint cut off, the rest rest sound, 5.03. 85
this let alone will all the rest confound. 5.03. 86
with all the rest of that consorted crew, 5.03.138
take hence the rest, and give them burial here. 5.05.118
amongst the rest demanded | my prisoners in your 1H4 1.03. 47
at such a time, with all the rest retold, | may 1.03. 73
falstaff and the rest of the thieves are at the 2.04. 87 P
and unbound the rest, and then come in the other 2.04.182 P
him keep with, the rest banish. 2.04.431 P
thee behind the arras, the rest walk up above. 2.04.500 P
down, | and rest your gentle head upon her lap, 3.01.212
the better part of ours are full of rest. 4.03. 27
and all the rest | to whom they are directed. 4.04. 3
men | upon the foot of fear, fled with the rest, 5.05. 20
him abated, all the rest | turn'd on themselves, 2H4 1.01.117
say i am an old man, you should give me rest. 1.02.217 P
the rest the paper tells. 2.01.135
because the rest of the low countries have /made 2.02. 21 P
it be book'd with the rest of this day's deeds, 4.03. 47 P
warning to all the rest of this little kingdom, 4.03.108 P
lest rest and lying still might make them look 4.05.211
as i have done the rest of my misleaders, | not 5.05. 64
that is my rest, that is the rendezvous of it. H5 2.01. 16 P
gets him to rest, cramm'd with distressful bread 4.01.270
the rest are princes, barons, lords, knights, 4.08. 89
let that one article rank with the rest, | and 5.02.346
cease these jars and rest your minds in peace. 1H6 1.01. 44
most of the rest slaughter'd or took likewise. 1.01.147
age, | let dying mortimer here rest himself. 2.05. 2
but, as the rest, so fell that noble earl | and 2.05. 90
the rest i wish thee gather; 2.05. 96
breast, | and what i do imagine, let that rest. 2.05.119
as will the rest, so willeth winchester. 3.01.161
hecate, | but unto thee, alanson, and the rest. 3.02. 65
if dolphin and the rest will be but rul'd. 3.03. 8
charles and the rest will take thee in their 3.03. 77
pardon me, princely henry, and the rest. 4.01. 18
nay, let it rest where it began at first. 4.01.121
ourself, my lord protector, and the rest, 4.01.169
and if i /wist he did — but let it rest, 4.01.180
charles, and the rest, it is enacted thus: 5.04.123
shall i, for lucre of the rest unvanquish'd, 5.04.141
i rest perplexed with a thousand cares. 5.05. 95
so let her rest; 2H6 1.03. 92
well, to the rest: 1.04. 63
and what a pitch she flew above the rest! 2.01. 6
but, to the rest. 2.02. 43
and you, my sovereign lady, with the rest, 3.01.161
and charge that no man should disturb your rest 3.02.256
i cannot rest | until the white rose that i wear 3H6 1.02. 32
let noble warwick, cobham, and the rest, | whom 1.02. 56
or, with the rest, where is your darling, 1.04. 78
cry, | the rest stand all aloof and bark at him. 2.01. 17
body | might in the ground be closed up in rest! 2.01. 76
for all the rest is held at such a rate | as 2.02. 51
and spite of spite needs must i rest awhile. 2.03. 5
my flock, | so many hours must i take my rest, 2.05. 32
come, york and richard, warwick and the rest, 2.06. 29
but for the rest: 3.03. 92
against your majesty | than all the rest, 4.01.109
you twain, of all the rest, | are near to 4.01.135
to rest mistrustful where a noble heart | hath 4.02. 8
never to lie and take his natural rest | till 4.03. 5
guess thou the rest; 4.04. 28
there shall i rest secure from force and fraud. 4.04. 33
of gloucester, lord hastings, and the rest, 4.05. 16
like that richmond with the rest shall down. 4.06.100
brother richard, lord hastings, and the rest, 4.07. 1
our dukedom till god please to send the rest. 4.07. 47
shall rest in london till we come to him. 4.08. 22
here at the palace will i rest a while. 4.08. 33
the doubt is that he will seduce the rest. 4.08. 37
sweet rest his soul! 5.02. 48
and, if the rest be true which i have heard, 5.06. 55
for this, amongst the rest, was i ordain'd. 5.06. 58
clarence, thy turn is next, and then the rest, 5.06. 90
rest you, whiles i lament king henry's corse. R3 1.02. 32
ill rest betide the chamber where thou liest! 1.02.112
i will, my lord. god give your grace good rest! 1.04. 75
look i so pale, lord dorset, as the rest? 2.01. 84
and at northampton they do rest to–night. 2.04. 2
well, let them rest. 3.01.157
the rest that love me, rise, and follow me. 3.04. 79
which hitherto hath held /my eyes from rest; 4.01. 81
i to my grave, where peace and rest lie with me! 4.01. 94
foes to my rest and my sweet sleep's disturbers, 4.02. 73
well, let that rest. dorset is fled to richmond. 4.02. 85
rest thy unrest on england's lawful earth, 4.04. 29
then would i hide my bones, not rest them here. 4.04. 33
yield me not thy light, nor, night, thy rest! 4.04.401
to salisbury, the rest march on with me. 4.04.538
it, | and so god give you quiet rest to–night! 5.03. 43
in all the rest show'd a most noble patience. H8 2.01. 36
you may read the rest. 4.01. 19
it is, and all the rest are countesses. 4.01. 53
while her grace sate down | to rest a while, 4.01. 66
so may he rest, his faults lie gently on him! 4.02. 31

many good–nights, my lord! i rest your servant. 5.01. 55
is my father, and all the rest are his sons." TRO 1.02.162 P
paris so chaf'd, and all the rest so laugh'd, 1.02.167 P
they pass by, but mark troilus above the rest. 1.02.184 P
my rest and negligence befriends thee now, | but 5.06. 17
rest, sword, thou hast thy fill of blood and 5.08. 4
would all the rest were so! COR 1.01. 53 P
never bearing | like labor with the rest, where 1.01.101
the rest | shall bear the business in some other 1.06. 81
the rest will serve | for a short holding. 1.07. 3
devise with thee | where thou shalt rest, that 4.01. 39
have all forsook me, hath devour'd the rest, 4.05. 76
alarbus goes to rest, and we survive | to TIT 1.01.133
in peace and honor rest you here, my sons, 1.01.150
readiest champions, repose you here in rest, 1.01.151
in peace and honor rest you here, my sons! 1.01.156
rest on my word, and let not discontent | daunt 1.01.267
speak thou no more, if all the rest will speed. 1.01.372
perhaps, she cull'd it from among the rest. 4.01. 44
but let her rest in her unrest a while. 4.02. 31
well, god give her good rest! 4.02. 63
for this time all the rest depart away. ROM 1.01. 98
ye say honestly, rest you merry! 1.02. 62 P
rest you merry! 1.02. 81 P
susan and she — god rest all christian souls! 1.03. 18
by my fay, it waxes late, | i'll to my rest. 1.05.127
as sweet repose and rest | come to thy heart as 2.02.123
would i were sleep and peace, so sweet to rest! 2.02.187
that last is true — the sweeter rest was mine. 2.03. 43
me hereafter, dry–beat the rest of the eight. 3.01. 79 P
get thee to bed and rest, for thou hast need. 4.03. 13
the county paris hath set up his rest | that you 4.05. 6
up his rest | that you shall rest but little. 4.05. 7
o, here | will i set up my everlasting rest, 5.03.110
that calls our person from our morning rest? 5.03.189
with one man beckon'd from the rest below, TIM 1.01. 74
may prove an argument of laughter | to th' rest, 3.03. 21
the rest of your fees, o gods — the senators of 3.06. 79 P
and all the rest look like a chidden train: JC 1.02.184
i think we are too bold upon your rest. 2.01. 86
here, under leave of brutus and the rest | (for 3.02. 81
are full of rest, defense, and nimbleness. 4.03.202
which we will niggard with a little rest. 4.03.228
i know young bloods look for a time of rest. 4.03.262
that i may rest assur'd | whether yond troops 5.03. 17
poor remains of friends, rest on this rock. 5.05. 1
night hangs upon mine eyes, my bones would rest, 5.05. 41
so call the field to rest, and let's away, | to 5.05. 80
in viewing o'er the rest o' th' self–same day, MAC 1.03. 94
the rest is labor, which is not us'd for you. 1.04. 44
leave all the rest to me. 1.05. 73
heap'd up to them, | we rest your ermites. 1.06. 20
what, sir, not yet at rest? 2.01. 12
th' other senses, | or else worth all the rest. 2.01. 45
the rest | that are within the note of 3.03. 9
heaven rest them now! 4.03.227
fancies, | that keep her from her rest. 5.03. 39
rest, rest, perturbed spirit! HAM 1.05.182
rest, rest, perturbed spirit! 1.05.182
that you voutsafe your rest here in our court 2.02. 13
go to your rest, at night we'll feast together. 2.02. 84
i'll have thee speak out the rest of this soon. 2.02.521 P
shall live, the rest shall keep as they are. 3.01.149 P
o, confound the rest! 3.02.177
if the rest of my fortunes turn turk with me — 3.02.275 P
are all the rest come back? 4.07. 49
a woman, sir, but, rest her soul, she's dead. 5.01.135 P
to sing a requiem and such rest to her | as to 5.01.237
which have solicited — the rest is silence. 5.02.358
and flights of angels sing thee to thy rest! 5.02.360
and thought to set my rest | on her kind nursery LR 1.01.123
the sway, revenue, execution of the rest, 1.01.137
time i shall sleep out, the rest i'll whistle. 2.02.156
'tis his own blame hath put himself from rest, 2.04.290
a small spark, all the rest on 's body cold. 3.04.112 P
now, good my lord, lie here and rest awhile. 3.06. 82
above the rest, be gone. 4.01. 48
rest you. 4.06.255
instant way | where they shall rest for ever. 5.03.151
hands, | both you of my inclining, and the rest. OTH 1.02. 82
my lord shall never rest, | i'll watch him tame, 3.03. 22
you shall close prisoner rest, | till that the 5.02.335
rest you happy! ANT 1.01. 62
and quietness, grown sick of rest, would purge 1.03. 53
with the arm'd rest, courtiers of beauteous 2.06. 17
and, with the rest full–mann'd, from th' head of 3.07. 51
canidius and the rest | that fell away have 4.06. 15
middle of my heart | is warm'd by th' rest — CYM 1.06. 28
which i (the factor for the rest) have done | in 1.06.188
o'erlabor'd sense | repairs itself by rest. 2.02. 12
we'll leave you for this time, go in, and rest. 4.02. 43
are the file when all | the rest do nothing — 5.03. 31
to th' shining synod of the rest | against thy 5.04. 89
and rest | upon your never–withering banks of 5.04. 97
within our law, | as dangerous as the rest. PER 1.01. 89
the rest (hark in thine ear) as black as incest, 1.02. 76
my dionyza, shall we rest us here, | and by 1.04. 1
was not best | longer for him to make his rest. 2.ch. 26
till then, rest your debtor. 2.01.143
marshal, the rest, as they deserve their grace. 2.03. 19
therefore each one betake him to his rest; 2.03.114
if in his grave he rest, we'll find him there; 2.04. 30
action may | conveniently the rest convey, 3.ch. 56
the gods | make up the rest upon you! 3.03. 5
of her virginity, and make the rest malleable. 4.06.142 P
as in the rest you said | thou hast been godlike 5.01.205
let me rest. 5.01.235
do our longing stay | to hear the rest untold. 5.03. 84
higher than all the rest, spreads like a plane TNK 2.06. 5
where's the rest o' th' music? 3.05. 31
we, and all our might, | rest at your service. ep 18
my boding heart pants, beats, and takes no rest, VEN 647
in his bedchamber to be barr'd of rest. 784
lo here the gentle lark, weary of rest, | from 853
lo in this hollow cradle take thy rest, | my 1185
fight, | and every one to rest himself betakes, LUC 125
"but if thou yield, i rest thy secret friend: 526
here she exclaims against repose and rest, | and 757

"disturb his hours of rest with restless trances 974
where thou wast wont to rest thy weary head, 1621
so should my shame still rest upon record, | and 1643
and to his protestation urg'd the rest, | who, 1844
outfacing faults in love with love's ill rest. PP 1. 8
good night, good rest. 14. 1
she bade good night that kept my rest away, 14. 2
doth cite each moving sense from idle rest, 14.15
turtle's loyal breast | to eternity doth rest. PHT 58
and all the rest forgot for which he toil'd. SON 25.12
plight | that am debarr'd the benefit of rest? 28. 2
mine own true love that doth my rest defeat, 61.11
death's second self, that seals up all in rest. 73. 8
wherein it finds a joy above the rest, | but 91. 6
crowning the present, doubting of the rest? 115.12

'RESTED *(also arrested, etc.)*

'RESTED 3 FR 0.0003 REL FR 3 V 0 P
not know the matter, he is 'rested on the case. ERR 4.02. 42
but /'a's in a suit of buff which 'rested him, 4.02. 45
money, | to warrant thee, as i am 'rested for. 4.04. 3

RESTED 3 FR 0.0003 REL FR 3 V 0 P
it rested in your grace | to unloose this MM 1.03. 31
in whom the title rested, were suppress'd. 1H6 2.05. 92
should find a running banket, ere they rested, H8 1.04. 12

RESTEM 1 FR 0.0001 REL FR 1 V 0 P
and now they do restem | their backward course, OTH 1.03. 37

RESTETH* 3 FR 0.0003 REL FR 3 V 0 P
to strive for that which resteth in my choice. SHR 3.01. 17
while you are thus employ'd, what resteth more, 3H6 1.02. 44
that with the king here resteth in his tent? 4.03. 10

RESTFUL 2 FR 0.0002 REL FR 2 V 0 P
that reacheth from the restful english court R2 4.01. 12
tir'd with all these, for restful death i cry: SON 66. 1

RESTING* 4 FR 0.0004 REL FR 3 V 1 P
have any resting for her true king's queen. R2 5.01. 6
resting well assur'd | they ne'er did service COR 3.01.121
of whose true–fix'd and resting quality | there JC 3.01. 61
the glory of the action, and not resting here, ANT 3.05. 10 P

RESTITUTION 4 FR 0.0004 REL FR 3 V 1 P
a child of conscience, he makes restitution. WIV 5.05. 29 P
garrisons, | and never ask'd for restitution. 2H6 3.01.118
pawn his fortunes | to hopeless restitution, so COR 3.01. 16
he calls me to a restitution large | of gold and OTH 5.01. 15

RESTIVE *(see resty)*

RESTLESS 6 FR 0.0006 REL FR 6 V 0 P
and blown with restless violence round about MM 3.01.124
that stands upon the rolling restless stone — H5 3.06. 29
they often feel a world of restless cares; R3 1.04. 81
of the mind to lie | in restless ecstasy. MAC 3.02. 22
his hours of rest with restless trances, LUC 974
my restless discord loves no stops nor rests; 1124

RESTORATION 1 FR 0.0001 REL FR 1 V 0 P
restoration hang | thy medicine on my lips, and LR 4.07. 25

RESTORATIVE 1 FR 0.0001 REL FR 1 V 0 P
on them, | to make me die with a restorative. ROM 5.03.166

RESTORATIVES 1 FR 0.0001 REL FR 1 V 0 P
in their lives | have read it for restoratives. PER 1.ch. 8

/RESTOR'D 1 FR 0.0001 REL FR 1 V 0 P
/were /you /not /restor'd | /to /all /the /duke 2H4 4.01.108

RESTOR'D 14 FR 0.0015 REL FR 14 V 0 P
and all their lands restor'd to /them again AYL 5.04.164
to see her noble lord restor'd to health, | who SHR in.1. 121
o how we joy to see your wit restor'd! in.2. 77
hath through me restor'd the king to his health. AWW 2.03. 64
that you are well restor'd, my lord, i'm glad. 2.03.147
and lands restor'd again be freely granted. R2 3.03. 41
restor'd again | to all his lands and signories. 4.01. 88
and, till thou be restor'd, thou art a yeoman. 1H6 2.04. 95
hast thou been long blind and now restor'd? 2H6 2.01. 74
a most royal prince | restor'd me to my honors; H8 2.01.114
i did not think a week could have restor'd | my TNK 3.06. 5
sir, she's well restor'd, | and to be married 5.04. 27
he restor'd her | as your stol'n jewel, and 5.04.118
all losses are restor'd, and sorrows end. SON 30.14

RESTORE 20 FR 0.0022 REL FR 14 V 6 P
my charms i'll break, their senses i'll restore, TMP 5.01. 31
which perforce, i know, | thou must restore. 5.01.134
claudio, that you wrong'd, look you restore. MM 5.01.525
them to sing, and restore them to the owner. ADO 2.01.232 P
god restore you to health! 5.01.324 P
if then the king your father will restore | but LLL 2.01.137
we be friends, | and robin shall restore amends. MND 5.01.438
heaven restore thee! TN 3.04. 46 P
malvolio, thy wits the heavens restore! 4.02. 95 P
your banish'd honors and restore yourselves 1H4 1.03.181
that could restore this cripple to his legs 2H6 2.01.131
it made me once restore a purse of gold that (by R3 1.04.140 P
and out of all these to restore the king, | he H8 2.02. 29
i will restore to thee | the people's hearts, TIT 1.01.210
traitor, restore lavinia to the emperor. 1.01.296
heavenly powers, restore him! HAM 3.01.141 P
i can again thy former light restore, | should i OTH 5.02. 9
heaven restore me! CYM 1.01.148
mine | thou wilt restore to be my comfort still: SON 134. 4
his poison'd me, and mine did him restore. LC 301

RESTORED 6 FR 0.0006 REL FR 6 V 0 P
which to his former strength may be restored 2H4 3.01. 42
tokens home | of our restored love and amity. 4.02. 65
parliament, | either to be restored to my blood, 1H6 2.05.128
is | that richard be restored to his blood. 3.01.158
let richard be restored to his blood, | so shall 3.01.159
your creatures, who by you have been restored; PER 3.02. 45

RESTORES 1 FR 0.0001 REL FR 1 V 0 P
in our captain's brain | restores his heart. ANT 3.13.198

RESTORING 1 FR 0.0001 REL FR 1 V 0 P
wisdom | in the restoring his bereaved sense? LR 4.04. 9

/RESTRAIN 1 FR 0.0001 REL FR 1 V 0 P
/could /restrain | /the //stiff–borne /action. 2H4 1.01.176

RESTRAIN 6 FR 0.0006 REL FR 5 V 1 P
such as we see when men restrain their breath 1H4 2.03. 61
they would restrain the one, distain the other. R3 5.03.322
daily to chain up and restrain the poor. COR 1.01. 84 P
restrain in me the cursed thoughts that nature MAC 2.01. 8
cannot restrain | from the excess of laughter. OTH 4.01. 98
she is resolv'd no longer to restrain him, VEN 579

RESTRAIN'D 6 FR 0.0006 REL FR 4 V 2 P
being restrain'd to keep him from stumbling, SHR 3.02. 58 P
you have restrain'd yourself within the list of AWW 2.01. 51 P

should by the cormorant belly be restrain'd, COR 1.01.121
providence | should have kept short, restrain'd, HAM 4.01. 18
she have restrain'd the riots of your followers, LR 2.04.143
me of my lawful pleasure she restrain'd, | and CYM 2.05. 9
RESTRAINED 3 FR 0.0003 REL FR 2 V 1 P
as to put metal in restrained means | to make a MM 2.04. 48
thou wert immured, restrained, captivated, bound LLL 3.01.125 P
messenger, | should have him thus restrained. LR 2.02.147
RESTRAINING 2 FR 0.0002 REL FR 2 V 0 P
behind, restraining | from course requir'd; WT 1.02.244
of it own fall, restraining aid to timon, | and TIM 5.01.148
RESTRAINS 2 FR 0.0002 REL FR 2 V 0 P
and your great love to me restrains you thus. TRO 3.03.221
his eye, which late this mutiny restrains, LUC 426
RESTRAIN'ST 1 FR 0.0001 REL FR 1 V 0 P
that thou restrain'st from me the duty which COR 5.03.167
RESTRAINT 14 FR 0.0015 REL FR 13 V 1 P
whence comes this restraint? MM 1.02.124
by the immoderate use | turns to restraint. 1.02.128
but rather wishing a more strict restraint 1.04. 4
ay, just, perpetual durance — a restraint, 3.01. 67
to know the reason of this strange restraint. ERR 3.01. 97
but puts it off to a compell'd restraint; AWW 2.04. 43
me, | madding my eagerness with her restraint, 5.03.213
add | my love, without retention or restraint, TN 5.01. 81
whose restraint | doth move the murmuring lips JN 4.02. 52
curb'd license plucks | the muzzle of restraint, 2H4 4.05.131
or put upon you what restraint or grievance OTH 1.02. 15
jealousies, | throwing restraint upon us; 4.03. 90
you the keys | that lock up your restraint. CYM 1.01. 74
nothing of their own restraint and disasters. TNK 2.01. 40 P
RESTS 1 FR 0.0001 REL FR 0 V 1 P
are tir'd, gives them a sob and 'rests them; ERR 4.03. 25 P
RESTS* 17 FR 0.0019 REL FR 15 V 2 P
now, thus it rests: WIV 4.06. 34
and here it rests, that you'll procure the vicar 4.06. 48
one thing more rests, that thyself execute — SHR 1.01.246
humor | rests by you only to be qualified. JN 5.01. 13
nought rests for me in this tumultuous strife 1H6 1.03. 70
and now there rests no other shift but this, 2.01. 75
what you command that rests in me to do. 3H6 3.02. 45
and now what rests but, in night's coverture, 4.02. 13
and now what rests but that we spend the time 5.07. 42
traitors, away, he rests not in this tomb. TIT 1.01.349
never hopes more heaven than rests in thee, 2.03. 41
he rests his minim rests, one, two, and the ROM 2.04. 22 P
he rests his minim rests, one, two, and the 2.04. 22 P
since the affairs of men rests still incertain, JC 5.01. 95
that spirit upon whose weal depends and rests HAM 3.03. 14
what rests? 3.03. 64
my restless discord loves no stops nor rests; LUC 1124
RESTY 3 FR 0.0003 REL FR 3 V 0 P
dull and long–continued truce | is resty grown. TRO 1.03.263
when resty sloth | finds the down pillow hard. CYM 3.06. 34
rise, resty muse, my love's sweet face survey, SON 100. 9
RESUM'D 1 FR 0.0001 REL FR 1 V 0 P
i have resum'd again | the part i came in. CYM 5.03. 75
RESUME 4 FR 0.0004 REL FR 4 V 0 P
resume that spirit when you were wont to say, COR 4.01. 16
that i'll resume the shape which thou dost think LR 1.04.309
had to take from 's, to resume | we have again. CYM 3.01. 15
juno would | resume her ancient fit of jealousy TNK 1.02. 22
/RESUMES 1 FR 0.0001 REL FR 1 V 0 P
nor /resumes no care | of what is to continue. TIM 2.02. 4
RESURRECTIONS 1 FR 0.0001 REL FR 0 V 1 P
(got deliver to a joyful resurrections!) WIV 1.01. 52 P
RE–SURVEY 2 FR 0.0002 REL FR 2 V 0 P
with better heed | to re–survey them, we will H5 5.02. 81
and shalt by fortune once more re–survey | these SON 32. 3
RETAIL 2 FR 0.0002 REL FR 2 V 0 P
more than he haply may retail from me. 2H4 1.01. 32
to whom i will retail my conquest won, | and she R3 4.04.335
RETAIL'D 1 FR 0.0001 REL FR 1 V 0 P
to age, | as 'twere retail'd to all posterity, R3 3.01. 77
RETAILS 1 FR 0.0001 REL FR 1 V 0 P
and retails his wares | at wakes and wassails, LLL 5.02.317
RETAIN 8 FR 0.0009 REL FR 8 V 0 P
thy shape invisible retain thou still. TMP 4.01.185
but longer did we not retain much hope; ERR 1.01. 65
retain but privilege of a private man? 1H6 5.04.136
retain that dear perfection which he owes ROM 2.02. 46
may one be pardon'd and retain th' offense? HAM 3.03. 56
only we shall retain | the name, and all th' LR 1.01.135
now | that you so oft have boasted to retain? 3.06. 59
and retain anew | her charitable heart, now hard TNK 1.02. 24
RETAIN'D 2 FR 0.0002 REL FR 2 V 0 P
reft of his brother, but retain'd his name — ERR 1.01.128
my sworn servant, | the duke retain'd him his. H8 1.02.192
RETAINERS 1 FR 0.0001 REL FR 1 V 0 P
are mounted | where pow'rs are your retainers, H8 2.04.113
RETAINING 1 FR 0.0001 REL FR 1 V 0 P
my view, | retaining but a quantity of life, JN 5.04. 23
RETAINS 1 FR 0.0001 REL FR 1 V 0 P
and still retains | more of the maid to sight TNK pr 7
RETELL 1 FR 0.0001 REL FR 0 V 1 P
thee often, and i retell thee again and again, i OTH 1.03.365 P
RETENTION 4 FR 0.0004 REL FR 4 V 0 P
they lack retention. TN 2.04. 96
add | my love, without retention or restraint, 5.01. 81
king | to some retention /and /appointed /guard, LR 5.03. 47
that poor retention could not so much hold, SON 122. 9
RETENTIVE 2 FR 0.0002 REL FR 2 V 0 P
free, and must my house | be my retentive enemy? TIM 3.04. 81
can be retentive to the strength of spirit; JC 1.03. 95
RETINUE 2 FR 0.0002 REL FR 1 V 1 P
great and puff'd up with this retinue, doth any 2H4 4.03.112 P
but other of your insolent retinue | do hourly LR 1.04.202
RETIR'D 9 FR 0.0010 REL FR 8 V 1 P
mind | with that which, but by being so retir'd, TMP 1.02. 91
he is of late much retir'd from court and is WT 4.02. 32 P
that he, our hope, might have retir'd his power, R2 2.02. 46
with works of war, retir'd himself | to italy, 4.01. 96
whereupon | he is retir'd, to ripe his growing 2H4 4.01. 13
or is he but retir'd to make him strong? 2H6 4.09. 9
i have retir'd me to a wasteful cock | and set TIM 2.02.162
hearing you were retir'd, your friends fall'n 5.01. 59
of posthumus, most retir'd | hath her life been; CYM 3.05. 36
RETIRE 39 FR 0.0044 REL FR 37 V 2 P
if you be pleas'd, retire into my cell, | and TMP 4.01.161
and thence retire me to my milan, where | every 5.01.311
advance the colors of my love, | and not retire. WIV 3.04. 82
all his behaviors did make their retire | to the LLL 2.01.234
you must retire yourself | into some covert. WT 4.04.649
heaven, | and with a blessed and unvex'd retire, JN 2.01.253
the onset and retire | of both your armies, 2.01.326
the french fight coldly, and retire themselves. 5.03. 13
backward their own ground | in faint retire. 5.05. 4
upon our soldiers, we will retire to callice. H5 3.03. 56
but he is enforced to retire, and the duke of 3.06. 95 P
may make a peaceful and a sweet retire | from 4.03. 86
our english troops retire, i cannot stay them; 1H6 1.05. 2
it will not be, retire into your trenches. 1.05. 33
if thou retire, the dolphin, well appointed, 4.02. 21
my gracious lord, retire to killingworth, 2H6 4.04. 39
and when the hardiest warriors did retire, 3H6 1.04. 14
but ne'er till now his scandal of retire. 2.01.150
to see a sunshine day | that cries "retire!" 2.01.188
sea | forc'd to retire by fury of the wind. 2.05. 8
mars | beck'ning with fiery truncheon my retire, TRO 5.03. 53
thou dost miscall retire. 5.04. 20
a retire upon our grecian part. 5.08. 15
beseech you give me leave to retire myself. COR 1.03. 27
foolish in our stands | nor cowardly in retire. 1.06. 3
fought, and did | retire to win our purpose. 1.06. 50
i pray thee, good mercutio, let's retire. ROM 3.01. 1
retire we to our chamber. MAC 2.02. 63
as i say, retire with me to my lodging, from LR 1.02.168 P
retire thee, go where thou art billeted. OTH 2.03.380
please you retire to your chamber? ANT 4.04. 35
retire, we have engag'd ourselves too far. 4.07. 1
they do retire. 4.07. 8
a retire; CYM 5.03. 40
o, retire, | for honor's sake, and safely TNK 3.06.109
charm, | doth too too oft betake him to retire, LUC 174
both, | that to his borrowed bed he make retire, 573
let him return, and flatt'ring thoughts retire; 641
and than | retire again, till meeting greater 1441
RETIRED 3 FR 0.0003 REL FR 3 V 0 P
you are retired, | as if you were a feasted one WT 4.04. 62
flight, | and like a bated and retired flood, JN 5.04. 53
he is retired to antium. COR 3.01. 11
RETIREMENT 5 FR 0.0005 REL FR 4 V 1 P
spake against your grace | in your retirement, i MM 5.01.130
a comfort of retirement lives in this. 1H4 4.01. 56
lest your retirement do amaze your friends. 5.04. 6
any retirement, any sequestration | from open H5 1.01. 58
is in his retirement marvellous distemp'red. HAM 3.02.301 P
RETIRES 7 FR 0.0008 REL FR 7 V 0 P
and thou hast talk'd | of sallies and retires, 1H4 2.03. 51
in self–same key | retires to chiding fortune. TRO 1.03. 54
if none, he'll say in troy when he retires, 1.03.281
he that retires, i'll take him for a volsce, COR 1.04. 28
rush against othello's breast, | and he retires. OTH 5.02.271
but back retires to rate the boar for murther. VEN 906
each one by him enforc'd retires his ward; LUC 303
RETIRING 3 FR 0.0003 REL FR 3 V 0 P
lord, | retiring from the siege of orleance, 1H6 1.01.111
compulsive course | nev'r /feels retiring ebb, OTH 3.03.455
one poor retiring minute in an age | would LUC 962
RETOLD 2 FR 0.0002 REL FR 2 V 0 P
not be | without much shame retold or spoken of. 1H4 1.01. 46
at such a time, with all the rest retold, | may 1.03. 73
/RETORT 1 FR 0.0001 REL FR 1 V 0 P
/i /will /retort /the /sum /in /equipage. WIV 2.02. 1
RETORT 5 FR 0.0005 REL FR 3 V 2 P
unjust | thus to retort your manifest appeal, MM 5.01.301
this is call'd the retort courteous. AYL 5.04. 72 P
the first, the retort courteous; 5.04. 92 P
i do retort the "solus" in thy bowels, | for i H5 2.01. 51
and they retort that heat again | to the first TRO 3.03.101
RETORTS 1 FR 0.0001 REL FR 1 V 0 P
it back to tybalt, whose dexterity | retorts it. ROM 3.01.164
RETOURNE 1 FR 0.0001 REL FR 0 V 1 P
"le chien est retourne a son propre vomissement, H5 3.07. 64 P
RETRACT 1 FR 0.0001 REL FR 1 V 0 P
paris should ne'er retract what he hath done, TRO 2.02.141
RETRAIT 3 FR 0.0003 REL FR 2 V 1 P
the trumpet sounds retrait, the day is our. 1H4 5.04.159
and for a retrait, how swiftly will this feeble 2H4 3.02.267 P
retrait is made and execution stay'd. 4.03. 72
RETREAT 6 FR 0.0006 REL FR 2 V 4 P
let us make an honorable retreat, though not AYL 3.02.161 P
in a retreat he outruns any lackey; AWW 4.03.290 P
ish give over, the trompet sound the retreat. H5 3.02. 89 P
here sound retreat, and cease our hot pursuit. 1H6 2.02. 3
any be so bold to sound retreat or parley when i 2H6 4.08. 4 P
whose warlike ears could never brook retreat, 3H6 1.01. 5
RETROGRADE 2 FR 0.0002 REL FR 1 V 1 P
when he was retrograde, i think rather. AWW 1.01.198 P
it is most retrograde to our desire, | and we HAM 1.02.114
/RETURN 1 FR 0.0001 REL FR 0 V 1 P
/danger /that /his /personal /return /was /most LR 4.03. 6 P
RETURN 213 FR 0.0240 REL FR 176 V 37 P
marriage, and we prosper well in our return. TMP 2.01. 74 P
me, and return | or ere your pulse twice beat. 5.01.102
or else return no more into my sight. TGV 1.02. 47
when possibly i can, i will return. 2.02. 3
if you turn not, you will return the sooner. 2.02. 4
better forbear till proteus make return. 2.07. 14
return, return, and make thy love amends. 4.02. 99
return, return, and make thy love amends. 4.02. 99
again, | or ne'er return again into my sight. 4.04. 60
if ever he return, and i can speak to him, i MM 3.01.192 P
he shall ever return to have hearing of this 3.01.204 P
but if ever the duke return (as our prayers are 3.02.154 P
o, you hope the duke will return no more; 3.02.164 P
the contents of this is the return of the duke. 4.02.196 P
make a swift return, | for i would commune with 4.03.103
'tis that he sent me of the duke's return. 4.03.138
happy return be to your royal grace! 5.01. 3
which consummate, | return him here again. 5.01.379
boys, | made daily motions for our home return: ERR 1.01. 59
and then return and sleep within mine inn, | for 1.02. 14
if i return, i shall be post indeed, | for she 1.02. 64
by thee, and this thou didst return from him: 2.02.157
where i will walk till thou return to me. 3.02.151
or else you may return without your money. 4.01. 44
from home, welcom'd home with it when i return; 4.04. 37 P
/on saturday we will return to france. LLL 4.01. 6
but to return to the verses: 4.02.150 P
will they return? 5.02.290
do, | if they return in their own shapes to woo? 5.02.299
land | to fetch me trifles, and return again, MND 2.01.133
which is indeed to return to their home, and to MV 1.02.102 P
i do expect return | of thrice three times the 1.03.158
return in haste, for i do feast to–night | my 2.02.171
us at my lodging, and return | all in an hour. 2.04. 2
perhaps i will return immediately. 2.05. 52
how like the prodigal doth she return, | with 2.06. 17
him he would make some speed | of his return; 2.08. 38
and manage of my house | until my lord's return. 3.04. 26
here, | until her husband and my lord's return. 3.04. 30
and we will nothing waste till you return. AYL 2.07.134
he left a promise to return again | within an 4.03. 99
in oblivion and thou return unexperienc'd to thy SHR 4.01. 83 P
love, | will we return unto thy father's house, 4.03. 53
i will return perfect courtier, in the which my AWW 1.01.207 P
till their own scorn return to them unnoted 1.02. 34
to return | and find your grace in health. 2.01. 6
return you thither? 3.02. 72
gone, | he will return, and hope i may that she, 3.04. 36
let's return again and suffice ourselves with 3.05. 10 P
but return with an invention and clap upon you 3.06. 97 P
and then to return and swear the lies he forges. 4.01. 23 P
he travel higher, or return again into france? 4.03. 42 P
that my lord your son was upon his return home, 4.05. 70 P
send for your ring, i will return it home, | and 5.03.223
but from her handmaid do return this answer: TN 1.01. 24
bounds, | rather than make unprofited return. 1.04. 22
i will return again into the house and desire 3.04.241 P
stay you by this gentleman till my return. 3.04.258 P
that to my home i will no more return | till JN 2.01. 21
if that war return | from france to england, 2.01. 89
hither return all gilt with frenchmen's blood. 2.01.316
our colors do return in those same hands | that 2.01.319
o fair return of banish'd majesty! 3.01.321
deliver him to safety, and return, | for i must 4.02.158
return, and tell him so. 4.03. 27
would not my lords return to me again | after 5.01. 37
return the president to these lords again, 5.02. 3
i will not return | till my attempt so much be 5.02.110
and instantly return with me again | to push 5.07. 76
and both return back to their chairs again. R2 1.03.120
while we return these dukes what we decree. 1.03.122
the hopeless word of "never to return" | breathe 1.03.152
return again, and take an oath with thee. 1.03.178
return with welcome home from banishment. 1.03.212
to set | the precious jewel of thy home return. 1.03.267
o, call back yesterday, bid time return, | and 3.02. 69
crowns | than bullingbrook's return to england, 4.01. 17
from whence he intercepted did return | to be 1H4 1.03.151
shall i return this answer to the king? 4.03.106
impawn'd | some surety for a safe return again, 4.03.109
ever i dress myself handsome till thy return — 2H4 2.04.280 P
at your return visit our house, let our old 3.02.293 P
as i return, i will fetch off these justices. 3.02.301 P
i'll be acquainted with him if i return, and't 3.02.328 P
world, | he might return to vasty tartar back, H5 2.02.123
shall chide your trespass and return your mock 2.04.125
if my father render fair return, | it is against 2.04.127
to grace himself at his return into london under 3.06. 68 P
gunpowder, | and quickly will return an injury. 4.07.181
and therefore tell her i return great thanks, 1H6 2.02. 51
return thee therefore with a flood of tears, 3.03. 56
come, come, return; 3.03. 76
return, thou wandering lord! 3.03. 76
after some respite, will return to callice; 4.01.170
he that flies so will ne'er return again. 4.05. 19
be gone, i say, for, till you do return, | i 5.05. 94
when from saint albons we do make return, 2H6 1.02. 83
but now return we to the false duke humphrey. 3.01.322
with the rude multitude till i return. 3.02.135
when i return with victory /from the field 3H6 1.01.261
him, | i here renounce him and return to henry. 3.03.194
then, england's messenger, return in post, | and 3.03.222
but i return his sworn and mortal foe. 3.03.257
how could he stay till warwick made return? 4.01. 5
be sent for, to return from france with speed; 4.06. 61
go tread the path that thou shalt ne'er return: R3 1.01.117
grave, | and then return lamenting to my love. 1.02.261
go, fellow, go, return unto thy lord, | bid him 3.02. 19
i shall return before your lordship thence. 3.02.120
return, good catesby, to the gracious duke, 3.07. 65
and so once more return and tell his grace. 3.07. 91
fled | that in submission will return to us, 5.05. 17
at his return | no doubt he will requite it. H8 2.01. 45
yet prayers and wishes | are all i can return. 2.03. 70
when you are call'd, return. 2.04.130
well–beloved servant, cranmer, | prithee return; 2.04.240
the threshold till my lord return from the wars. COR 1.03. 75 P
the fourth would return for conscience' sake to 2.03. 33 P
will you hence | before the tag return, whose 3.01.247
you must return and mend it. 3.02. 26
return to th' tribunes. 3.02. 36
i'll return consul, | or never trust to what my 3.02.135
and say that martius | return me, as cominius is 5.01. 42
you may not pass, you must return; 5.02. 5
tears of true joy for his return to rome. TIT 1.01. 76
and return | captive to thee and to thy roman 1.01.110
joy | shed on this earth for thy return to rome. 1.01.162
and gratulate his safe return to rome, | the 1.01.221
this will i do, and soon return again. 5.02.131
to twinkle in their spheres till they return. ROM 2.02. 17
in half an hour she promised to return. 2.05. 2
how shall that faith return again to earth, 3.05.206
ready to go, but never to return. 4.05. 34
dost return to pry | in what i farther shall 5.03. 33
but breeds the giver a return exceeding | all TIM 1.01.279
to your free heart, i do return those talents, 1.02. 6
you have bid me | return so much, i have shook 2.02.137
heads, and i am here | no richer in return. 2.02.203
but now return, | and with their faint reply 3.03. 24

gifts, | expecting in return twenty for one? 4.03.510
therefore so please thee to return with us, 5.01.159
i like this well, he will return again. 5.01.204
let us return, | and strain what other means is 5.01.226
and so return to you, and nothing else? JC 2.04. 12
highness' pleasure, | still to return your own. MAC 1.06. 28
being taught, return | to plague th' inventor. 1.07. 9
adieu, | till you return at night. 3.01. 35
may soon return to this our suffering country 3.06. 48
it, afterwards seal it, and again return to bed; 5.01. 8 P
your leave and favor to return to france, | from HAM 1.02. 51
most fair return of greetings and desires. 2.02. 60
your pardon and my return shall be the end of 3.02.317 P
of my sudden /and /more /strange return. 4.07. 47 P
to what base uses we may return, horatio! 5.01.202 P
i | return those duties back as are right fit, LR 1.01. 97
get you gone, | and hasten your return. 1.04.340
you | that to our sister you do make return. 2.04.151
return you to my sister. 2.04.158
you will return and sojourn with my sister, 2.04.203
return to her? 2.04.207
return with her? 2.04.211
return with her? 2.04.215
denied me to come in) return, and force | their 3.02. 66
is nothing done, if he return the conqueror; 4.06.265 P
if ever i return to you again, | i'll bring you 5.02. 3
and a little more wit, return again to venice. OTH 2.03.368 P
bade him anon return and here speak with me, 4.01. 80
i obey the mandate, | and will return to venice. 4.01.260
if she will return me my jewels, i will give 4.02.197 P
othello and desdemona return again to venice. 4.02.223 P
he says he will return incontinent, | and hath 4.03. 12
quick, and return. ANT 1.03. 5
hear no more words of pompey, return it again. 2.02.105 P
whereon, i begg'd | his pardon for return. 3.06. 60
if from the field i shall return once more | to 3.13.173
hour, | we must return to th' court of guard. 4.09. 2
i shall but lend my diamond till your return. CYM 1.04.143 P
return he cannot, nor | continue where he is. 1.05. 53
shall short my word | by length'ning my return. 1.06.201
answer made | the speediness of your return. 2.04. 31
from our hence–going | and our return, to excuse 3.02. 64
whereunto i never | purpose return. 3.04.107
safe mayst thou wander, safe return again! 3.05.105
i'll stay | till hasty polydore return, and 4.02.165
his body's hostage | for his return. 4.02.186
why gone, | nor when she purposes return. 4.03. 15
a leg of rome shall not return to tell | what 5.03. 92
end, i think you'll never return to tell one. 5.04.184 P
so thou never return | unless thou say prince PER 1.01.163
and keep your mind, till you return to us, 1.02. 35
lading's in our haven, | and then return to us. 1.02. 50
now message must return from whence it came. 1.03. 35
return them, we are ready; 2.02. 4
if in which time expir'd he not return, | i 2.04. 47
whom if you find, and win unto return, | you 2.04. 52
that calls me traitor, i return the lie. 2.05. 57
your master will be dead ere you return, 3.02. 7
there's no hope she will return. 4.01. 98
and you pray the gods | for success and return; TNK 1.01.209
feast's solemnity | shall want till your return. 1.01.222
when ye return, who wins i'll settle here; 3.06.307
they may return and settle again to execute 4.03. 71 P
see the dew–bedabbled wretch | turn, and return, VEN 704
return again in haste, | thou seest our LUC 321
let him return, and flatt'ring thoughts retire; 641
unless thou couldst return to make amends? 961
but long she thinks till he return again, | and 1359
how can i then return in happy plight | that am SON 28. 1
till i return, of posting is no need. 51. 4
when they see | return of love, more blest may 56.12
return, forgetful muse, and straight redeem | in 100. 5
rang'd, | like him that travels i return again, 109. 6
so i return rebuk'd to my content, | and gain by 119.13

/RETURN'D 2 FR 0.0002 REL FR 2 V 0 P
which had /return'd | to the inheritance of HAM 1.01. 91
/was /this /before /the /king /return'd? LR 4.03. 37

RETURN'D 54 FR 0.0061 REL FR 40 V 14 P
in vain, | mars's hot minion is return'd again; TMP 4.01. 98
see it be return'd, | or else return no more TGV 1.02. 46
i would the duke we talk of were return'd again. MM 3.02.173 P
would he were return'd! 3.02.178 P
how chance thou art return'd so soon? ERR 1.02. 42
return'd so soon! 1.02. 43
neither my husband nor the slave return'd, 2.01. 1
rope's end, sir, and to that end am i return'd. 4.04. 16
he with none return'd. 5.01.232
signior mountanto return'd from the wars or no? ADO 1.01. 30 P
o, he's return'd, and as pleasant as ever he was 1.01. 37 P
look, don pedro is return'd to seek you. 1.01.202 P
but now i am return'd, and that war–thoughts 1.01.301
my herald is return'd. LLL 3.01. 69
and now to helen is it home return'd, | there to MND 3.02.172
i pray you, is my master yet return'd? MV 5.01. 34
are they return'd? 5.01.116
as soon as you, | and even but now return'd; 5.01.272
and her will is, it should be so return'd. TN 2.02. 14 P
gentleman of the count orsino's is return'd. 3.04. 58 P
are they return'd to the court? WT 5.02. 93 P
which else would post until it had return'd R2 1.01. 56
when he is return'd, | against aumerle we will 4.01. 89
my uncle is return'd, | deliver up my lord of 1H4 5.02. 27
i hear his majesty is return'd with some 2H4 1.02.104 P
here is return'd my lord of westmerland. 4.01.222
talbot, my life, my joy, again return'd? 1H6 1.04. 23
and answer was return'd that he will come. 2.05. 20
are not the speedy scouts return'd again | that 4.03. 1
they are return'd, my lord, and give it out 4.03. 3
he is return'd in his opinions, which | have H8 3.02. 64
that cranmer is return'd with welcome, 3.02.400
who return'd her thanks | in the great'st 5.01. 64
nations speak aloud | to have her back return'd. TRO 2.02.186
a cruel war i sent him, from whence he return'd, COR 1.03. 14 P
martius | return me, as cominius is return'd, 5.01. 42
i am return'd your soldier; 5.06. 70
five times he hath return'd | bleeding to rome, TIT 1.01. 33
with honor and with fortune is return'd, | from 1.01. 67
till all these mischiefs be return'd again, 3.01.273
and yesternight | return'd my letter back. ROM 5.03.252
and the best half should have return'd to him, TIM 3.02. 84
lordship that i return'd you an empty messenger. 3.06. 37 P
/are not | those in commission yet return'd? MAC 1.04. 2
norway, my good lord, | are joyfully return'd. HAM 2.02. 41
hamlet return'd shall know you are come home. 4.07.130
followed the old man forth. he is return'd. LR 2.04.295
and i return'd /the rather | for that i heard OTH 2.03.233
receiv'd them and return'd me expectations and 4.02.189 P
on th' instant, i will be return'd forthwith. 4.03. 7 P
that i return'd with simular proof enough | to CYM 5.05.200
boult's return'd. PER 4.02. 92 P
your two contending lovers are return'd, | and TNK 4.02. 66
by those swift messengers return'd from thee, SON 45.10

RETURNED 3 FR 0.0003 REL FR 3 V 0 P
shall share the good of our returned fortune, AYL 5.04.174
that paris is returned home and hurt. TRO 1.01.109
if he be now returned, | as /checking at his HAM 4.07. 61

RETURNEST 1 FR 0.0001 REL FR 1 V 0 P
that thou returnest no greeting to thy friends? R2 1.03.254

RETURNETH 2 FR 0.0002 REL FR 1 V 1 P
with the heart there cools and ne'er returneth 2H6 3.02.166
was buried, alexander returneth to dust, the HAM 5.01.209 P

RETURNING 5 FR 0.0005 REL FR 3 V 2 P
for her, writ to my lady mother i am returning, AWW 4.03. 89 P
and, he returning to break our necks, they COR 5.04. 33 P
the games are done, and caesar is returning. JC 1.02.178
no more, | returning were as tedious as go o'er. MAC 3.04.137
we shall be returning | ere you can end this TNK 1.01.223

RETURNS 16 FR 0.0018 REL FR 15 V 1 P
must think, which never | returns us thanks. AWW 1.01.186
she returns this ring to you, sir. TN 2.02. 5 P
for news to go for ireland, | but none returns. R2 2.02.124
northumberland, say thus the king returns: 3.03.121
returns us that his powers are yet not ready H5 3.03. 46
but, my lord, | when returns cranmer? H8 3.02. 63
but he returns | splitting the air with noise. COR 5.06. 50
spoils, | returns the good andronicus to rome, TIT 1.01. 37
returns with precious lading to the bay | from 1.01. 72
and returns in peace | most rich in timon's nod. TIM 1.01. 61
all | my honor to you, upon his good returns. 3.05. 81
then the rot returns | to thine own lips again. 4.03. 65
ay, madam, but returns again to–night. MAC 3.02. 2
from whose bourn | no traveller returns, puzzles HAM 3.01. 79
when he returns from hunting, | i will not speak LR 1.03. 7
from the best, | the worst returns to laughter. 4.01. 6

RE–UNITED 1 FR 0.0001 REL FR 1 V 0 P
great | was re–united to the crown of france. H5 1.02. 85

REVANIA 1 FR 0.0001 REL FR 0 V 1 P
o, pray, pray, pray! manka revania dulche. AWW 4.01. 78 P

REVEAL 7 FR 0.0008 REL FR 6 V 1 P
reveal yourself to him. MM 5.01. 28
treasons, we still see them reveal themselves, AWW 4.03. 22 P
madam, i have a secret to reveal. 1H6 5.03.100
reveal the damn'd contriver of this deed. TIT 4.01. 36
no, you will reveal it. HAM 1.05.119
reveal how thou at sea didst lose thy wife. PER 5.01.244
for breaking prison, and i, if you reveal me, TNK 3.06.114

REVEAL'D 5 FR 0.0005 REL FR 5 V 0 P
in complete glory she reveal'd herself; 1H6 1.02. 83
and god in justice hath reveal'd to us | the 2H6 2.03.102
reveal'd myself unto him, | until some half hour LR 5.03.193
all those beauties in her | reveal'd to mankind. TNK 2.02.169
nev'r reveal'd secret, for i knew none — would 5.01. 99

REVEALING 1 FR 0.0001 REL FR 1 V 0 P
revealing day through every cranny spies, | and LUC 1086

REVEALS 1 FR 0.0001 REL FR 1 V 0 P
what occasion now | reveals before 'tis ripe, TN 5.01.154

REVEL 16 FR 0.0018 REL FR 14 V 2 P
and ask him why, that hour of fairy revel, | in WIV 4.04. 59
face | revel and feast it at my house to–day, ERR 4.04. 62
go to the feast, revel and domineer, | carouse SHR 3.02.224
house, | and revel it as bravely as the best, 4.03. 54
this harness'd masque and unadvised revel, JN 5.02.132
revel the night, rob, murder, and commit | the 2H4 4.05.125
you cannot revel into dukedoms there. H5 1.02.253
to revel it with him and his new bride. 3H6 3.03.225
to revel it with him and his new bride." 4.01. 95
heart | to revel in the entrails of my lambs. R3 4.04.229
like conies after rain, and revel all with him. COR 4.05.212 P
heaven's eye, | and revel in lavinia's treasury. TIT 2.01.131
being our kinsman, if we revel much: ROM 3.04. 26
this heavy–headed revel east and west | makes us HAM 1.04. 17
with joy, pleasance, revel, and applause, OTH 2.03.292 P
and wastes | the lamps of night in revel; ANT 1.04. 5

REVELL'D 3 FR 0.0003 REL FR 3 V 0 P
who all this while hath revell'd in the night, R2 3.02. 48
was't you that revell'd in our parliament, | and 3H6 1.04. 71
his father revell'd in the heart of france, 2.02.150

REVELLER 2 FR 0.0002 REL FR 2 V 0 P
honor, | join'd with a masker and a reveller! JC 5.01. 62
he is call'd | the britain reveller. CYM 1.06. 61

REVELLERS 2 FR 0.0002 REL FR 1 V 1 P
you moonshine revellers, and shades of night, WIV 5.05. 38
the revellers are ent'ring, brother, make good ADO 2.01. 84 P

REVELLING 3 FR 0.0003 REL FR 3 V 0 P
i know we shall have revelling to–night; ADO 1.01.320
with pomp, with triumph, and with revelling. MND 1.01. 19
still revelling like lords till all be gone; 2H6 1.01.224

REVELRY 1 FR 0.0001 REL FR 1 V 0 P
dignity, | and fall into our rustic revelry. AYL 5.04.177

REVELS 19 FR 0.0021 REL FR 15 V 4 P
our revels now are ended. TMP 4.01.148
for revels, dances, masks, and merry hours LLL 4.03.376
the king doth keep his revels here to–night; MND 2.01. 18
in our round | and see our moonlight revels, go 2.01.141
what revels are in hand? 5.01. 36
solemnity, | in nightly revels and new jollity. 5.01.370
in masques and revels sometimes altogether. TN 1.03.114 P
shall we /set about some revels? 1.03.136 P
and entreat | an hour of revels with 'em. H8 1.04. 72
his fearful date | with this night's revels, and ROM 1.04.109
see, antony, that revels long a–nights, | is JC 2.02.116
where joy most revels, grief doth most lament; HAM 3.02.198
to what sport and revels his /addiction leads OTH 2.02. 5 P
'tis a night of revels, the gallants desire it. 2.03. 43 P
stage us, and present | our alexandrian revels: ANT 5.02.218
waste the time, which looks for other revels. PER 2.03. 93
abandoner of revels, mute, contemplative, TNK 5.01.138
love keeps his revels where there are but twain; VEN 123
for there it revels, and when that decays, | the LUC 713

REVENG'D 41 FR 0.0046 REL FR 29 V 12 P
more to be reveng'd on eglamour | than for the TGV 5.02. 51
how shall i be reveng'd on him? WIV 2.01. 30 P
for reveng'd i will be! 2.01. 31 P
how shall i be reveng'd on him? 2.01. 66 P
let's be reveng'd on him: 2.01. 93 P
detect my wife, be reveng'd on falstaff, and 2.02.311 P
on whom to–night i will be reveng'd, and i will 5.01. 28 P
well, i'll be reveng'd as i may. ADO 2.01.209 P
her silence flouts me, and i'll be reveng'd. SHR 2.01. 29
but i will in to be reveng'd for this villainy. 5.01.136 P
i'll be reveng'd on the whole pack of you. TN 5.01.378 P
he does, he does, we'll be reveng'd on him. 1H4 1.03.291
i'll be reveng'd of her. 2H4 2.04.154 P
endur'd, | but we will be reveng'd sufficiently. 1H6 1.04. 58
it irks his heart he cannot be reveng'd. 1.04.105
if i be not, heavens be reveng'd on me! 3H6 1.01. 57
reveng'd may she be on that hateful duke, 1.01.266
be thou reveng'd on men, and let me live. 1.03. 20
how shall bona be reveng'd | but by thy help to 3.03.212
i would i were, to be reveng'd on thee. R3 1.02.133
to be reveng'd on him that loveth thee. 1.02.135
to be reveng'd on him that kill'd my husband. 1.02.137
and withal whet me | to be reveng'd on rivers, 1.03.332
the duke, | to be reveng'd on him. H8 3.02. 9
a pow'r, | to be reveng'd on rome and saturnine. TIT 3.01.300
a rape, | and i am sent to be reveng'd on him. 5.02. 95
and worse than progne i will be reveng'd. 5.02.195
we will be reveng'd! JC 3.02.203 P
caesar, thou art reveng'd, | even with the sword 5.03. 45
so 'a goes to heaven, | and so am i reveng'd. HAM 3.03. 75
only i'll be reveng'd | most throughly for my 4.05.136
the king now bears will be reveng'd home; LR 3.03. 12 P
for when i am reveng'd upon my charm, | i have ANT 4.12. 16
be reveng'd, | or she that bore you was no queen CYM 1.06.126
reveng'd? 1.06.128
how should i be reveng'd? 1.06.129
if it be true, | how should i be reveng'd? 1.06.132
i'll be reveng'd. | "his mean'st garment"! well. 2.03.155
hate her, nay indeed, | to be reveng'd upon her. 3.05. 79
i fear 'twill be reveng'd. 4.02.154
by whose example thou reveng'd mayst be. LUC 1194

/REVENGE 1 FR 0.0001 REL FR 1 V 0 P
/as /will /revenge /these /bitter /woes /of TIT 3.02. 3

REVENGE 160 FR 0.0180 REL FR 139 V 21 P
if thy greatness will | revenge it on him — for TMP 3.02. 54
julia, | as in revenge of thy ingratitude, | i TGV 1.02.107
sighs, | for, in revenge of my contempt of love, 2.04.133
/in /my /head which be humors of revenge. WIV 1.03. 90 P
wilt thou revenge? 1.03. 91
together to be revenge on this same scall, 3.01.119 P
conscience, pursue him with any further revenge? 4.02.208 P
might in the times to come have ta'en revenge, MM 4.04. 30
choose your revenge yourself, | impose me to ADO 5.01.272
have giv'n her cousin, | and so dies my revenge. 5.01.292
as in revenge, have suck'd up from the sea MND 2.01. 89
i'll find demetrius and revenge this spite. 3.02.420
will feed nothing else, it will feed my revenge. MV 3.01. 54 P
and if you wrong us, shall we not revenge? 3.01. 67 P
revenge. 3.01. 69 P
why, revenge. 3.01. 71 P
and no satisfaction, no revenge, nor no ill luck 3.01. 94 P
not seek an absent argument | of my revenge, AYL 3.01. 4
but kindness, nobler ever than revenge, | and 4.03.128
and weep, | till i can find occasion of revenge. SHR 2.01. 36
both my revenge and hate | loosing upon thee, in AWW 2.03.164
vice in him will my revenge find notable cause TN 2.03.153 P
may rather pluck on laughter than revenge, | if 5.01.366
my misery, yet with eyes | of pity, not revenge! WT 3.02.123
jealousies | to bloody thoughts and to revenge, 3.02.159
brib'd | to do him justice, and revenge on you. JN 2.01.172
where revenge did paint | the fearful difference 3.01.237
done, | doth lay it open to urge on revenge. 4.03. 38
hand, | by giving it the worship of revenge. 4.03. 72
behind | to do the office for thee of revenge, 5.07. 71
let heaven revenge, for i may never lift | an R2 1.02. 40
lament we may, but not revenge /thee dead. 1.03. 58
that it shall render vengeance and revenge 4.01. 67
revenge the jeering and disdain'd contempt | of 1H4 1.03.183
and thou shalt find a king that will revenge 5.03. 12
man | the aptest way for safety and revenge. 2H4 1.01.213
drive you out of your revenge and turn all to a 2.04.297 P
rouse up revenge from ebon den with fell 5.05. 37
touching our person seek we no revenge, | but we H5 2.02.174
i will most horribly revenge — i eat and eat — 5.01. 47 P
i take thy groat in earnest of revenge. 5.01. 63
for none would strike a stroke in his revenge. 1H6 1.05. 35
behold | what ruin happened in revenge of him, 2.02. 11
now shine it like a comet of revenge, | a 3.02. 31
let no words, but deeds, revenge this treason! 3.02. 49
fly, to revenge my death, if i be slain. 4.05. 18
fly, to revenge my death when i am dead; 4.06. 30
my death's revenge, thy youth, and england's 4.06. 39
and care not who they sting in his revenge. 2H6 3.02.127
and therefore to revenge it shalt thou die, 4.01. 26
therefore, when merchant–like i sell revenge, 4.01. 41
if he revenge it not, yet will his friends; 4.01.146
think therefore on revenge and cease to weep. 4.04. 3
and you both have vow'd revenge | on him, his 3H6 1.01. 55
as shall revenge his death before i stir. 1.01.100
they seek revenge, and therefore will not yield. 1.01.190
and thine | were not revenge sufficient for me; 1.03. 26
lest in revenge thereof, sith god is just, | he 1.03. 41
forth | a bird that will revenge upon you all; 1.04. 36
blows and revenge for me. 2.01. 86
withhold revenge, dear god! 2.02. 7
clangor heard from far, | "warwick, revenge! 2.03. 19
brother, revenge my death!" 2.03. 19
mine | or fortune given me measure of revenge. 2.03. 32
and this for rutland, both bound to revenge, 2.04. 3
i will revenge his wrong to lady bona, | and 3.03.197
misery, | but seek revenge on edward's mockery. 3.03.265
nor forward of revenge, though they much err'd. 4.08. 46
which this blood mad'st, revenge his death! R3 1.02. 62
which this blood drink'st, revenge his death! 1.02. 63

which god revenge! 1.03.136
no man but prophesied revenge for it. 1.03.185
god will revenge it. 2.01.139
god will revenge it, whom i will importune 2.02. 14
i am hungry for revenge, | and now i cloy me 4.04. 61
hour, | even for revenge mock my destruction! 5.01. 9
great reason why — | lest i revenge. 5.03.186
by oath he menac'd | revenge upon the cardinal. H8 1.02.138
and merely to revenge him on the emperor | for 2.01.162
for pleasure and revenge | have ears more deaf TRO 2.02.171
hope of revenge shall hide our inward woe. 5.10. 31
let us revenge this with our pikes, ere we COR 1.01. 22 P
in hunger for bread, not in thirst for revenge. 1.01. 25 P
for thy revenge | wrench up thy power to th' 1.08. 10
that wilt revenge | thine own particular wrongs, 4.05. 85
and vows revenge as spacious as between | the 4.06. 68
though i owe | my revenge properly, my remission 5.02. 84
a kiss | long as my exile, sweet as my revenge! 5.03. 45
with opportunity of sharp revenge | upon the TIT 1.01.137
openly, | and basely put it up without revenge? 1.01.433
without controlment, justice, or revenge? 2.01. 68
blood and revenge are hammering in my head. 2.03. 39
revenge it, as you love your mother's life, | or 2.03.114
because the law hath ta'en revenge on them. 3.01.117
or else to heaven she heaves them for revenge. 4.01. 40
what god will have discovered for revenge. 4.01. 74
mortal revenge upon these traitorous goths, 4.01. 93
but yet so just that he will not revenge. 4.01.128
revenge the heavens for old andronicus! 4.01.129
if you will have revenge from hell, you shall. 4.03. 39
who threats, in course of this revenge, to do 4.04. 67
and say i am revenge, sent from below | to join 5.02. 3
to ruminate strange plots of dire revenge; 5.02. 6
tell him revenge is come to join with him, | and 5.02. 7
i am revenge, sent from th' infernal kingdom 5.02. 30
revenge, which makes the foul offender quake. 5.02. 40
art thou revenge? 5.02. 41
now give some surance that thou art revenge — 5.02. 46
o sweet revenge, now do i come to thee, | and, 5.02. 67
for now he firmly takes me for revenge, | and, 5.02. 73
again, | and cleave to no revenge but lucius. 5.02.136
revenge now goes | to lay a complot to betray 5.02.146
i know thou dost, and, sweet revenge, farewell. 5.02.148
and calls herself revenge, and thinks me mad. 5.02.185
now judge what /cause had titus to revenge 5.03.125
romeo, | who had but newly entertain'd revenge, ROM 3.01.171
what, he's poor, and that's revenge enough. TIM 3.04. 63 P
to revenge is no valor, but to bear. 3.05. 39
not square to take | on those that are, revenge; 5.04. 37
and caesar's spirit, ranging for revenge, | with JC 3.01.270
revenge! 3.02.204 P
most noble caesar! we'll revenge his death. 3.02.243
come, | revenge yourselves alone on cassius, 4.03. 94
thou mayst revenge. MAC 3.03. 18
let's make us med'cines of our great revenge 4.03.214
so art thou to revenge, when thou shalt hear. HAM 1.05. 7
revenge his foul and most unnatural murther. 1.05. 25
the thoughts of love, | may sweep to my revenge. 1.05. 31
prompted to my revenge by heaven and hell, 2.02.584
the croaking raven doth bellow for revenge. 3.02.254 P
why, this is /hire /and /salary, not revenge. 3.03. 79
inform against me, | and spur my dull revenge! 4.04. 33
dear father, is't writ in your revenge | that, 4.05.142
hadst thou thy wits and didst persuade revenge, 4.05.169
for her perfections — but my revenge will come. 4.07. 29
sanctuarize, | revenge should have no bounds. 4.07.128
should stir me most | to my revenge, but in my 5.02.246
i will have my revenge ere i depart his house. LR 3.05. 1 P
show'dst the king, | and to revenge thine eyes. 4.02. 96
us be conjunctive in our revenge against him. OTH 1.03.368 P
she that being ang'red, her revenge being nigh, 2.01.152
a sin), | but partly led to diet my revenge, 2.01.294
one is too poor, too weak for my revenge. 3.03.443
till that a capable and wide revenge | swallow 3.03.459
we have some grace, | yet have we some revenge. 4.03. 93
my great revenge | had stomach for them all. 5.02. 74
out of tune, | and sweet revenge grows harsh. 5.02.116
in your despite, upon your purse — revenge it. CYM 1.06.135
my grief and as certain as i expect my revenge. 3.04. 25 P
me rejoicingly, and i'll be merry in my revenge. 3.05.145 P
my revenge is now at milford; 3.05.155 P
so the revenge alone pursu'd me. 4.02.157
the gods revenge it upon me and mine | to the PER 3.03. 24
as wakes my vengeance and revenge for 'em. TNK 1.01. 58
wife, | as in revenge or quittal of such strife; LUC 236
revenge on him that made me stop my breath. 1180
her blood, in poor revenge, held it in chase; 1736
is it revenge to give thyself a blow | for his 1823
we will revenge the death of this true wife." 1841
spend | revenge upon myself with present moan? SON 149. 8
REVENGED 4 FR 0.0004 REL FR 4 V 0 P
wrong, | and i will be revenged on them all. TIT 5.02. 97
and am i then revenged, | to take him in the HAM 3.03. 84
be suddenly revenged on my foe, | thine, mine, LUC 1683
breath, | and live to be revenged on her death. 1778
REVENGEFUL 9 FR 0.0010 REL FR 8 V 1 P
and never brandish more revengeful steel | over R2 4.01. 50
stay thy revengeful hand, thou hast no cause to 5.03. 42
foes | tell our devotion with revengeful arms? 3H6 2.01.164
if thy revengeful heart cannot forgive, | lo R3 1.02.173
you know his nature, | that he's revengeful; H8 1.01.109
use it | that my revengeful services may prove COR 4.05. 89
and with revengeful war | take wreak on rome for TIT 4.03. 33
i am very proud, revengeful, ambitious, with HAM 3.01.124 P
to chase injustice with revengeful arms: LUC 1693
REVENGEMENT 1 FR 0.0001 REL FR 1 V 0 P
he'll breed revengement and a scourge for me; 1H4 3.02. 7
REVENGER 1 FR 0.0001 REL FR 1 V 0 P
of marcus crassus' death | make me revenger. ANT 3.01. 3
REVENGERS 1 FR 0.0001 REL FR 1 V 0 P
wherefore my father should revengers want, ANT 2.06. 11
REVENGE'S 1 FR 0.0001 REL FR 1 V 0 P
then which way shall i find revenge's cave? TIT 3.01.270
REVENGES 15 FR 0.0017 REL FR 12 V 3 P
grace of the duke, revenges to your heart, | and MM 4.03.135
though my revenges were high bent upon him | and
AWW 5.03. 10
the whirligig of time brings in his revenges. TN 5.01.377 P
his revenges must | in that be made more bitter. WT 1.02.456
the very thought of my revenges that way 2.03. 19
wilt have | the leading of thine own revenges, COR 4.05.137
think to front his revenges with the easy groans 5.02. 42 P
not | t' allay my rages and revenges with | your 5.03. 85
if thy revenges hunger for that food | which TIM 5.04. 32
revenges burn in them; MAC 5.02. 3
i will have such revenges on you both | that all LR 2.04.279
the revenges we are bound to take upon your 3.07. 7 P
revenges, hers; CYM 2.05. 24
i would revenges, | that possible strength might 4.02.159
that thy adulteries | rates and revenges. 5.04. 34
REVENGING 1 FR 0.0001 REL FR 1 V 0 P
burns with revenging fire, whose hopeful colors 2H6 4.01. 97
REVENGINGLY 1 FR 0.0001 REL FR 1 V 0 P
and the air on't | revengingly enfeebles me, or CYM 5.02. 4
/REVENGIVE 1 FR 0.0001 REL FR 1 V 0 P
the /revengive gods | 'gainst parricides did all LR 2.01. 45
REVENUE 18 FR 0.0020 REL FR 11 V 7 P
lorded, | not only with what my revenue yielded, TMP 1.02. 98
long withering out a young man's revenue. MND 1.01. 6
of great revenue, and she hath no child. 1.01.158
in beard is a younger brother's revenue — then AYL 3.02.378 P
house and all the revenue that was old sir 5.02. 11 P
caparison, and my revenue is the silly cheat. WT 4.03. 27 P
this juggling witchcraft with revenue cherish, JN 3.01.169
the revenue whereof shall furnish us | for our R2 1.04. 46
crown, | as the ripe revenue and due of birth, R3 3.07.158
of this action | for the whole world's revenue. TRO 2.02.206
folly and ignorance, be thine in great revenue! 2.03. 29 P
thee | that no revenue hast but thy good spirits HAM 3.02. 58
the sway, revenue, execution of the rest, LR 1.01.137
you should enjoy half his revenue for ever, and 1.02. 53 P
i wake him, you should enjoy half his revenue." 1.02. 56 P
ward to the son, and the son manage his revenue. 1.02. 74 P
and, being, that we detain | all his revenue. ANT 3.06. 30
if i would lose it for a revenue | of any king's CYM 2.03.143
/REVENUES 1 FR 0.0001 REL FR 1 V 0 P
/my /manors, /rents, /revenues /i /forgo; R2 4.01.212
REVENUES 6 FR 0.0006 REL FR 5 V 1 P
whose lands and revenues enrich the new duke; AYL 1.01.102 P
us | the plate, coin, revenues, and moveables, R2 2.01.161
barely in title, not in revenues. 2.01.226
she bears a duke's revenues on her back, | and 2H6 1.03. 80
to have th' expense and waste of his revenues. LR 2.01.100
robb'd others' beds' revenues of their rents. SON 142. 8
REVERB 1 FR 0.0001 REL FR 1 V 0 P
whose low sounds | reverb no hollowness. LR 1.01.154
REVERBERATE 2 FR 0.0002 REL FR 2 V 0 P
hallow your name to the reverberate hills, | and TN 1.05.272
that shall reverberate all as loud as thine. JN 5.02.170
REVERB'RATE 1 FR 0.0001 REL FR 1 V 0 P
like an arch, reverb'rate | the voice again, or, TRO 3.03.120
REVERENC'D 2 FR 0.0002 REL FR 2 V 0 P
and have thee reverenc'd like a blessed saint. 1H6 3.03. 15
and therein reverenc'd for their lawful king. 5.04.140
/REVERENCE 1 FR 0.0001 REL FR 1 V 0 P
/whose /reverence /even /the //head–lugg'd /bear
LR 4.02. 42
REVERENCE 44 FR 0.0049 REL FR 35 V 9 P
(saving your honors' reverence) for stew'd MM 2.01. 90 P
cannot sure hide himself in such reverence. ADO 2.03.120 P
you would have me say, "saving your reverence, a 3.04. 32 P
my reverence, calling, nor divinity, | if this 4.01.168
me | that i am forc'd to lay my reverence by, 5.01. 64
that cur'sy to them, do them reverence, | as MV 1.01. 13
who, saving your reverence, is the devil himself 2.02. 26 P
he (saving your worship's reverence) are scarce 2.02.131 P
coming before me is nearer to his reverence. AYL 1.01. 51 P
and with a low submissive reverence | say, "what SHR in.1. 53
i charge thee by thy reverence | here to unfold, TN 5.01.151
them) and the reverence | of the grave wearers. WT 3.01. 5
all reverence set apart | to him and his usurp'd JN 3.01.159
the fair reverence of your highness curbs me R2 1.01. 54
which fear, not reverence, makes thee to except. 1.01. 72
what reverence he did throw away on slaves, 1.04. 27
not flesh and blood | with solemn reverence, 3.02.172
besides a clergyman | of holy reverence, who, i 3.03. 29
it, but that he is, saving your reverence, a 1H4 2.04.469 P
encircled you to hear with reverence | your 2H4 4.02. 6
but you misuse the reverence of your place, 4.02. 23
of what your reverence shall incite us to. H5 1.02. 20
for i am sorry that with reverence | i did not 1H6 2.03. 71
madam, be still — with reverence may i say — 2H6 3.02.207
and, in thy reverence and thy chair–days, thus 5.02. 48
save that, for reverence to some alive, | i give R3 3.07.193
a saucy fellow, | deserve we no more reverence? H8 4.02.101
but reverence to your calling makes me modest. 5.02.104
ay, | i ask, that i might waken reverence, | and TRO 1.03.227
it be | that thou adorest and hast in reverence, TIT 5.01. 83
foam, | settlest admired reverence in a slave. TIM 5.01. 51
all kind love, good thoughts, and reverence. JC 3.01.176
there, | and none so poor to do him reverence. 3.02.120
"this policy and reverence of age makes the LR 1.02. 46 P
you beastly knave, know you no reverence? 2.02. 69
my two sisters | have in thy reverence made. 4.07. 28
thus would play and trifle with your reverence. OTH 1.01.132
in the due reverence of a sacred vow | i here 3.03.461
the rather (saving reverence of the word) for CYM 4.01. 5 P
those that i reverence, those i fear — the wise 4.02. 95
have one dust, yet reverence | (that angel of 4.02.247
we do not look for reverence but for love, | and PER 1.04. 99
throne, | and he the sun for them to reverence; 2.03. 40
do reverence; | she is a goddess, arcite! TNK 2.02.134
REVEREND 44 FR 0.0049 REL FR 38 V 6 P
yonder is a most reverend gentleman, who, belike
WIV 3.01. 52 P
she is a virtuous and a reverend lady: ERR 5.01.134
to let him lack a reverend estimation, for i MV 4.01.162 P
here 'tis, most reverend doctor, here it is. 4.01.226
that all is done in reverend care of her, | and, SHR 4.01.204
a sad face, a reverend carriage, a slow tongue, TN 3.04. 72 P
reverend sirs, | for you there's rosemary and WT 4.04. 73
good reverend father, make my person yours, JN 3.01.224
sir, | my reverend father, let it not be so! 3.01.249
leads ancient lords and reverend bishops on | to 1H4 3.02.104
lordship to have a reverend care of your health. 2H4 1.02.100 P
i am bound to thee, reverend feeble. 3.02.170 P
you, reverend father, and these noble lords 4.01. 38
and their most reverend heads dash'd to the H5 3.03. 37
for i will touch thee but with reverend hands. 1H6 5.03. 47
twelve barons, and twenty reverend bishops, | i 2H6 1.01. 8
with reverend fathers and well–learned bishops. R3 3.05.100
he is within, with two right reverend fathers, 3.07. 61
and reverend looker–on of two fair queens. 4.01. 30
of the right reverend cardinal of york. H8 1.01. 51
this business | our reverend cardinal carried. 1.01.100
most learned reverend sir, into our kingdom, 2.02. 76
these reverend fathers, men | of singular 2.04. 58
by all the reverend fathers of the land | and 2.04.206
i left no reverend person in this court; 2.04.221
upon my soul, two reverend cardinal virtues; 3.01.103
come, reverend fathers, | bestow your counsels 3.01.181
learned and reverend fathers of his order, 4.01. 26
what two reverend bishops | were those that went 4.01. 99
where the reverend abbot | with all his covent 4.02. 18
and thou most reverend for /thy stretch'd–out TRO 1.03. 61
most reverend nestor, i am glad to clasp thee. 4.05.204
with those that say you are reverend grave men, COR 2.01. 61 P
most reverend and grave elders, to desire | the 2.02. 42
now, afore god, this reverend holy friar, | all ROM 4.02. 31
for i know your reverend ages love | security, TIM 3.05. 79
by two of their most reverend senate, greet thee 5.01.129
as you are old and reverend, should be wise. LR 1.04.240
most reverend signior, do you know my voice? OTH 1.01. 93
the ottomites, reverend and gracious, | steering 1.03. 33
most potent, grave, and reverend signiors, | my 1.03. 76
in reverend cerimon there well appears | the PER 5.03. 93
and reverend welcome to her princely guest, LUC 90
a reverend man that graz'd his cattle nigh, LC 57
/REVEREND'ST 1 FR 0.0001 REL FR 1 V 0 P
love before | the /reverend'st throat in athens. TIM 5.01.182
REVERENT 22 FR 0.0024 REL FR 17 V 5 P
a very reverent body: ERR 3.02. 90 P
of very reverent reputation, sir, | of credit 5.01. 5
to see a reverent syracusian merchant, | who put 5.01.124
speaks like a most thankful and reverent youth, ADO 5.01.316 P
is no staff more reverent than one tipp'd with 5.04.123 P
very reverent sport, truly, and done in the LLL 4.02. 1 P
now i perceive thou art a reverent father. SHR 4.05. 48
and now by law, as well as reverent age, | i may 4.05. 60
out some secret place, some reverent room, R2 5.06. 25
the pudding in his belly, that reverent vice, 1H4 2.04.453 P
thou art reverent | touching thy spiritual 1H6 3.01. 49
the reverent care i bear unto my lord | made me 2H6 3.01. 34
if ancient sorrow be most reverent, | give mine R3 4.04. 35
what are your pleasures with me, reverent lords? H8 3.01. 26
for by my fathers' reverent tomb i vow | they TIT 2.03.296
o reverent tribunes! 3.01. 23
come, come, thou reverent man of rome, | and 5.03.137
declining on the milky head | of reverent priam, HAM 2.02.479
stubborn ancient knave, you reverent braggart, LR 2.02.126
hail, reverent sir! the gods preserve you! PER 5.01. 14
reverent appearer, no, | i threw her overboard 5.03. 18
reverent sir, | the gods can have no mortal 5.03. 61
REVERENTLY 3 FR 0.0003 REL FR 3 V 0 P
chide him for faults, and do it reverently, 2H4 4.04. 37
how may i reverently worship thee enough? 1H6 1.02.145
northumberland, i hold thee reverently. 3H6 2.02.109
REVERS'D 1 FR 0.0001 REL FR 1 V 0 P
is clarence dead? the order was revers'd. R3 2.01. 87
REVERSE 3 FR 0.0003 REL FR 2 V 1 P
puncto, thy stock, thy reverse, thy distance, WIV 2.03. 26 P
unbind my sons, reverse the doom of death, | and TIT 3.01. 24
displant a town, reverse a prince's doom, | it ROM 3.03. 59
REVERSION 4 FR 0.0004 REL FR 3 V 1 P
as were our england in reversion his, | and he R2 1.04. 35
'tis in reversion that i do possess — | but 2.02. 38
should, | where now remains a sweet reversion, 1H4 4.01. 53
no /perfection in reversion shall have a praise TRO 3.02. 92 P
REVERSO 1 FR 0.0001 REL FR 0 V 1 P
the immortal passado, the punto reverso, the hay ROM 2.04. 26 P
REVERTED 2 FR 0.0002 REL FR 1 V 1 P
in her forehead, arm'd and reverted, making war ERR 3.02.123 P
/a /wind, | would have reverted to my bow again, HAM 4.07. 23
RE–VIEW 1 FR 0.0001 REL FR 1 V 0 P
in whose company | i shall re–view sicilia, for WT 4.04.666
REVIEW 1 FR 0.0001 REL FR 1 V 0 P
thou dost review | the very part was consecrate SON 74. 5
REVIEWEST 1 FR 0.0001 REL FR 1 V 0 P
when thou reviewest this, thou dost review | the SON 74. 5
REVIL'D 2 FR 0.0002 REL FR 2 V 0 P
sans fable, she herself revil'd you there. ERR 4.04. 73
and his eye revil'd | me as his abject object; H8 1.01.126
REVILE 1 FR 0.0001 REL FR 1 V 0 P
and did not she herself revile me there? ERR 4.04. 72
REVISITS 1 FR 0.0001 REL FR 1 V 0 P
steel | revisits thus the glimpses of the moon, HAM 1.04. 53
/REVIV'D 1 FR 0.0001 REL FR 1 V 0 P
/that /need /to /be /reviv'd /and /breath'd /in 2H4 4.01.112
REVIV'D 5 FR 0.0005 REL FR 5 V 0 P
that talbot's name might be in thee reviv'd, 1H6 4.05. 3
how well my comfort is reviv'd by this! ROM 3.03.165
in my lips | that i reviv'd and was an emperor. 5.01. 9
is not this boy reviv'd from death? CYM 5.05.120
for many years thought dead, are now reviv'd, 5.05.456
REVIVE 10 FR 0.0011 REL FR 8 V 2 P
and so stop the air | by which he should revive; MM 2.04. 26
but with my breath i can revive it, boy. JN 4.01.111
henry is dead, and never shall revive. 1H6 1.01. 18
methinks i should revive the soldiers' hearts, 3.02. 97
he doth revive again. madam, be patient. 2H6 3.02. 36
o clifford, how thy words revive my heart! 3H6 1.01.163
those gracious words revive my drooping thoughts 3.03. 21
revive, look up, or i will die with thee! ROM 4.05. 20
being dead many years, shall after revive, be CYM 5.04.142 P
being dead many years, shall after revive, be 5.05.439 P
REVIVES 4 FR 0.0004 REL FR 4 V 0 P
our waggon is prepar'd, and time revives us. AWW 4.04. 34
revives two greater in the heirs of life; 2H4 4.01.198
yet he revives. LR 4.06. 47
glow, | even as a dying coal revives with wind, VEN 338
REVIVETH 1 FR 0.0001 REL FR 1 V 0 P
for looks kill love, and love by looks reviveth: VEN 464
REVIVING 3 FR 0.0003 REL FR 3 V 0 P
from you great rome shall suck | reviving blood, JC 2.02. 88

spirits a time, | to be more fresh, reviving. CYM 1.05. 42
expel, | for now reviving joy bids her rejoice, VEN 977
REVOK'D 1 FR 0.0001 REL FR 1 V 0 P
by jupiter, | this shall not be revok'd. LR 1.01.179
REVOKE 4 FR 0.0004 REL FR 4 V 0 P
revoke that doom of mercy, for 'tis clifford, 3H6 2.06. 46
and on a safer judgment all revoke | your COR 2.03.218
enemy, and revoke | your sudden approbation. 2.03.250
revoke thy gift, | or, whilst i can vent clamor LR 1.01.164
REVOKEMENT 1 FR 0.0001 REL FR 1 V 0 P
that through our intercession this revokement H8 1.02.106
REVOLT 43 FR 0.0048 REL FR 40 V 3 P
and cannot soon revolt and change your mind. TGV 3.02. 59
for the revolt of mine is dangerous — that is WIV 1.03.102 P
excess | as gravity's revolt to /wantonness. LLL 5.02. 74
sums of gold to corrupt him to a revolt." AWW 4.03.180 P
to ask you if gold will corrupt him to revolt. 4.03.277 P
that suffer surfeit, cloyment, and revolt, | but TN 2.04. 99
and blessed shall he be that doth revolt | from JN 3.01.174
o foul revolt of french inconstancy! 3.01.322
of all his people shall revolt from him, | and 3.04.165
and pick strong matter of revolt and wrath | out 3.04.167
the faiths of men ne'er stained with revolt; 4.02. 6
our discontented counties do revolt; 5.01. 8
should seek a plaster by contemn'd revolt, | and 5.02. 13
and will, i fear, revolt on herford's side. R2 2.02. 89
revolt our subjects? 3.02.100
then let not him be slandered with revolt. 1H4 1.03.112
how quickly nature falls into revolt | when gold 2H4 4.05. 65
for this revolt of thine, methinks, is like H5 2.02.141
what? doth my uncle burgundy revolt? 1H6 4.01. 64
'tis said the stout parisians do revolt, | and 5.02. 2
the king is merciful, if you revolt. 2H6 4.02.125
all will revolt from me and turn to him. 3H6 1.01.151
thou wilt revolt and fly to him, i fear. R3 4.04.477
if i revolt, off goes young george's head; 4.05. 4
where reason can revolt | without perdition, and TRO 5.02.144
and loss assume all reason | without revolt. 5.02.146
and he | upon my party, i'd revolt, to make COR 1.01.234
all the regions | do smilingly revolt, and who 4.06.103
lucius, | and will revolt from me to succor him. TIT 4.04. 80
or my true heart with treacherous revolt | turn ROM 4.01. 58
the want whereof doth daily make revolt | in my TIM 4.03. 92
by his plight, of the revolt | the newest state. MAC 1.02. 2
both more and less have given him the revolt, 5.04. 12
fetches, | the images of revolt and flying off. LR 2.04. 90
leave), | i say again, hath made a gross revolt, OTH 1.01.134
draw | the smallest fear or doubt of her revolt, 3.03.188
blood to think on't, and flush youth revolt. ANT 1.04. 52
alexas did revolt, and went to jewry on 4.06. 11
o antony, | nobler than my revolt is infamous, 4.09. 19
hell should at one time | encounter such revolt. CYM 1.06.112
by thy revolt, o husband, shall be thought | put 3.04. 55
but i must tell you, now my thoughts revolt, PER 1.01. 78
since that my life on thy revolt doth lie; SON 92.10
REVOLTED 12 FR 0.0013 REL FR 10 V 2 P
and our revolted wives share damnation together.
WIV 3.02. 39 P
should all despair | that have revolted wives, WT 1.02.199
and all the rest revolted faction traitors? R2 2.02. 57
penny cost | to ransom home revolted mortimer. 1H4 1.03. 92
revolted mortimer! 1.03. 93
sons to younger brothers, revolted tapsters, and 4.02. 29 P
france is revolted from the english quite, 1H6 1.01. 90
by means whereof the towns each day revolted? 2H6 3.01. 63
farewell, revolted fair! TRO 5.02.186
the kings that have revolted, and the soldier ANT 4.05. 4
plant those that have revolted in the vant, 4.06. 8
when men revolted shall upon record | bear 4.09. 8
REVOLTING 4 FR 0.0004 REL FR 4 V 0 P
curse, | a mother's curse, on her revolting son. JN 3.01.257
and make a dearth in this revolting land. R2 3.03.163
and with them scourge the bad revolting stars 1H6 1.01. 4
the false revolting normans thorough thee 2H6 4.01. 87
REVOLTS 6 FR 0.0006 REL FR 6 V 0 P
and you degenerate, you ingrate revolts, | you JN 5.02.151
lead me to the revolts of england here. 5.04. 7
their mutinies and revolts, wherein they show'd COR 3.01.126
revolts from true birth, stumbling on abuse. ROM 2.03. 20
now minutely revolts upbraid his faith–breach; MAC 5.02. 18
for barbarous and unnatural revolts | during CYM 4.04. 6
REVOLUTION 4 FR 0.0004 REL FR 3 V 1 P
and see the revolution of the times | make 2H4 3.01. 46
here's fine revolution, and we had the trick to HAM 5.01. 90 P
by revolution low'ring, does become | the ANT 1.02.125
they, | or whether revolution be the same. SON 59.12
REVOLUTIONS 1 FR 0.0001 REL FR 0 V 1 P
ideas, apprehensions, motions, revolutions. LLL 4.02. 67 P
REVOLVE 4 FR 0.0004 REL FR 3 V 1 P
"if this fall into thy hand, revolve. TN 2.05.143 P
company, | i may revolve and ruminate my grief. 1H6 5.05.101
save such as doth revolve | and ruminate himself TRO 2.03.187
and you may then revolve what tales i have told CYM 3.03. 14
REVOLVING 2 FR 0.0002 REL FR 2 V 0 P
revolving this will teach thee how to curse. R3 4.04.123
as one of which doth tarquin lie revolving | the LUC 127
REWARD 38 FR 0.0043 REL FR 25 V 13 P
i desire nothing but the reward of a villain. ADO 5.01.243 P
is "old dog" my reward? AYL 1.01. 82 P
proffers not took reap thanks for their reward. AWW 2.01.147
with | reward did threaten and encourage him, WT 3.02.164
this two and thirty years, god reward me for it! 1H4 3.03. 48 P
let them that should reward valor bear the sin 5.04.149 P
i'll follow, as they say, for reward. 5.04.162 P
he that rewards me, god reward him! 5.04.163 P
but rebuke and check was the reward of valor. 2H4 4.03. 32 P
yet never have you tasted our reward, | or been 1H6 3.04. 22
here, hume, take this reward. 2H6 1.02. 85
york, | to be the post, in hope of his reward. 1.04. 77
come, fellow, follow us for thy reward. 2.03.105
i will reward you for this venturous deed. 3.02. 9
therefore thus will i reward thee: 4.03. 6 P
shall have a thousand crowns for his reward. 4.08. 67
we give thee for reward a thousand marks, | and 5.01. 79
there's thy reward, be gone. 3H6 3.03.233
who finds edward | shall have a high reward, and 5.05. 10
remember our reward when the deed's done. R3 1.04.123 P
/'zounds, he dies! i had forgot the reward. 1.04.126 P
when he opens his purse to give us our reward, 1.04.130 P
who shall reward you better for my life | than 1.04.230
reward to him that brings the traitor in? 4.04.516
you are, not to reward | what you have done, COR 1.09. 26
these that survive let rome reward with love; TIT 1.01. 82
look for thy reward | among the nettles at the 2.03.271
up your pigeons, and then look for your reward. 4.03.112 P
let them be receiv'd, | not without fair reward. TIM 1.02.191
you gods, reward them! 2.02.213
bear, | our potency made good, take thy reward. LR 1.01.172
the gods reward your kindness! 3.06. 5 P
make the moor thank me, love me, and reward me,
OTH 2.01.308
i will reward thee | once for thy sprightly ANT 4.07. 14
i am | the heir of his reward, which i will add CYM 5.05. 13
to bar heaven's shaft, but sin had his reward. PER 2.04. 15
of monstrous lust the due and just reward. 5.03. 86
she, "reward not hospitality | with such black LUC 575
REWARDED 3 FR 0.0003 REL FR 2 V 1 P
your fellows, for they are but lightly rewarded. LLL 1.02.152 P
and am i thus rewarded? H8 3.01.133
one see 'em all rewarded. TNK 3.05.152
REWARDER 1 FR 0.0001 REL FR 1 V 0 P
a liberal rewarder of his friends; R3 1.03.123
REWARDING 1 FR 0.0001 REL FR 0 V 1 P
ward of mine honor is rewarding my dependants. LLL 3.01.132 P
REWARDS 10 FR 0.0011 REL FR 8 V 2 P
heaven and fortune still rewards with plagues. TGV 4.03. 31
he that rewards me, god reward him! 1H4 5.04.163 P
with promise of high pay and great rewards; 3H6 2.01.134
promise them such rewards | as victors wear at 2.03. 52
no doubt | in time will find their fit rewards. H8 3.02.245
would give, rewards | his deeds with doing them, COR 2.02.127
his honesty rewards him in itself, | it must not TIM 1.01.130
a man that fortune's buffets and rewards | hast HAM 3.02. 67
soaks up the king's countenance, his rewards, 4.02. 16 P
to let a fellow that will take rewards | and say ANT 3.13.123
REWORD 1 FR 0.0001 REL FR 1 V 0 P
and /i the matter will reword, which madness HAM 3.04.143
REWORDED 1 FR 0.0001 REL FR 1 V 0 P
from off a hill whose concave womb reworded | a LC 1
REX 2 FR 0.0002 REL FR 1 V 1 P
filius noster henricus, rex angliae, et heres H5 5.02.341 P
"ego et rex meus" | was still inscrib'd; H8 3.02.314
REYNALDO 3 FR 0.0003 REL FR 3 V 0 P
give him this money and these notes, reynaldo. HAM 2.01. 1
you shall do marvell's wisely, good reynaldo, 2.01. 3
do you mark this, reynaldo? 2.01. 15
REYNOLD *(see rainold)*
RHAPSODY 1 FR 0.0001 REL FR 1 V 0 P
and sweet religion makes | a rhapsody of words. HAM 3.04. 48
RHEIMS 3 FR 0.0003 REL FR 2 V 1 P
that hath been long studying at rheims, as SHR 2.01. 80 P
guienne, champaigne, rheims, orleance, | paris, 1H6 1.01. 60
the dolphin charles is crowned king in rheims; 1.01. 92
RHENISH 4 FR 0.0004 REL FR 1 V 3 P
set a deep glass of rhenish wine on the contrary MV 1.02. 96 P
than there is between red wine and rhenish. 3.01. 42 P
and, as he drains his draughts of rhenish down, HAM 1.04. 10
'a pour'd a flagon of rhenish on my head once. 5.01.180 P
RHESUS' 1 FR 0.0001 REL FR 1 V 0 P
with sleight and manhood stole to rhesus' tents 3H6 4.02. 20
RHETORIC 8 FR 0.0009 REL FR 7 V 1 P
the heart's still rhetoric disclosed with eyes, LLL 2.01.229
sweet smoke of rhetoric! 3.01. 63
"did not the heavenly rhetoric of thine eye, 4.03. 58
all gentle tongues — | fie, painted rhetoric! 4.03.235
for it is a figure in rhetoric that drink, being AYL 5.01. 41 P
and practice rhetoric in your common talk, SHR 1.01. 35
did not the heavenly rhetoric of thine eye, PP 3. 1
what strained touches rhetoric can lend, | thou, SON 82.10
RHEUM 15 FR 0.0017 REL FR 12 V 3 P
and the rheum | for ending thee no sooner. MM 3.01. 31
by the salt rheum that ran between france and it ERR 3.02.128 P
why, an hour in clamor and a quarter in rheum; ADO 5.02. 83 P
that did void your rheum upon my beard | and MV 1.03.117
why holds thine eye that lamentable rheum, JN 3.01. 22
how now, foolish rheum? 4.01. 33
eyes, | for villainy is not without such rheum, 4.03.108
awak'd the sleeping rheum, and so by chance R2 1.04. 8
the alps doth spit and void his rheum upon. H5 3.05. 52
and i have a rheum in mine eyes too, and such an TRO 5.03.104 P
at a few drops of women's rheum, which are | as COR 5.06. 45
threat'ning the flames | with bisson rheum, a HAM 2.02.506
i have a salt and sorry rheum offends me; OTH 3.04. 51
that year indeed, he was troubled with a rheum; ANT 3.02. 57
beguile | the gout and rheum, that in lag hours TNK 5.04. 8
RHEUMATIC 5 FR 0.0005 REL FR 2 V 3 P
your doublet and hose, this raw rheumatic day? WIV 3.01. 47 P
the air, | that rheumatic diseases do abound. MND 2.01.105
i' good truth, as rheumatic as two dry toasts, 2H4 2.04. 57 P
but then he was rheumatic, and talk'd of the H5 2.03. 38 P
o'erworn, despised, rheumatic, and cold, VEN 135
RHEUMS 1 FR 0.0001 REL FR 1 V 0 P
is he not stupid | with age and alt'ring rheums? WT 4.04.399
RHEUMY 1 FR 0.0001 REL FR 1 V 0 P
and tempt the rheumy and unpurged air | to add JC 2.01.266
RHINOCEROS 1 FR 0.0001 REL FR 1 V 0 P
the arm'd rhinoceros, or th' hyrcan tiger, MAC 3.04.100
RHODES 6 FR 0.0006 REL FR 6 V 0 P
of whom his eyes had seen the proof | at rhodes, OTH 1.01. 29
the turkish preparation makes for rhodes, | so 1.03. 14
that, as it more concerns the turk than rhodes, 1.03. 22
th' abilities | that rhodes is dress'd in — if 1.03. 26
nay, in all confidence, he's not for rhodes. 1.03. 31
with due course toward the isle of rhodes, 1.03. 34
RHODOPE'S 1 FR 0.0001 REL FR 1 V 0 P
i'll rear | than rhodope's /of memphis ever was. 1H6 1.06. 22
RHUBARB 1 FR 0.0001 REL FR 1 V 0 P
what rhubarb, cyme, or what purgative drug, MAC 5.03. 55
RHYM'D 1 FR 0.0001 REL FR 0 V 1 P
you might have rhym'd. HAM 3.02.285 P
RHYME 35 FR 0.0039 REL FR 19 V 16 P
some love of yours hath writ to you in rhyme. TGV 1.02. 76
about him, fairies, sing a scornful rhyme, | and WIV 5.05. 91
in despite of the teeth of all rhyme and reason, 5.05.125 P
and the wherefore is neither rhyme nor reason? ERR 2.02. 48
marry, i cannot show it in rhyme; ADO 5.02. 36 P
i can find out no rhyme to "lady" but "baby," an 5.02. 37 P
rhyme to "lady" but "baby," an innocent rhyme; 5.02. 38 P
for "scorn," "horn," a hard rhyme; 5.02. 38 P
for "school," "fool," a babbling rhyme: 5.02. 39 P
something then in rhyme. LLL 1.01. 99
a dangerous rhyme, master, against the reason of 1.02.107 P
some extemporal god of rhyme, for i am sure i 1.02.183 P
it hath taught me to rhyme and to be mallicholy; 4.03. 13 P
and here is part of my rhyme, and here my 4.03. 14 P
when shall you see me write a thing in rhyme, 4.03.179
as much love in rhyme | as would be cramm'd up 5.02. 6
nor woo in rhyme, like a blind harper's song! 5.02.405
i'll rhyme you so eight years together, dinners AYL 3.02. 96 P
neither rhyme nor reason can express how much. 3.02.398 P
through the army with this rhyme in 's forehead. AWW 4.03.234 P
that can rhyme themselves into ladies' favors, H5 5.02.156 P
is but a prater, a rhyme is but a ballad; 5.02.158 P
there was never a truer rhyme. TRO 4.04. 21 P
a rhyme i learnt even now | of one i danc'd ROM 1.05.142
speak but one rhyme, and i am satisfied; 2.01. 9
ha, ha! how vildly doth this cynic rhyme! JC 4.03.133
will you rhyme upon't, | and vent it for a CYM 5.03. 55
you have put me into rhyme. 5.03. 63
time | post /on the lame feet of my rhyme, PER 4.ch. 48
with means more blessed than my barren rhyme? SON 16. 4
you should live twice, in it and in my rhyme. 17.14
reserve them for my love, not for their rhyme, 32. 7
of princes shall outlive this pow'rful rhyme, 55. 2
and beauty making beautiful old rhyme | in 106. 3
spite of him, i'll live in this poor rhyme, 107.11
RHYMERS 2 FR 0.0002 REL FR 2 V 0 P
and scald rhymers | ballad 's out a' tune. ANT 5.02.215
than those old nine which rhymers invocate, SON 38.10
RHYMES 10 FR 0.0011 REL FR 9 V 1 P
whose composed rhymes | should be full–fraught TGV 3.02. 69
o, rhymes are guards on wanton cupid's hose: LLL 4.03. 56
i heard your guilty rhymes, observ'd your 4.03.137
and spend his prodigal wits in bootless rhymes, 5.02. 64
thou, lysander, thou hast given her rhymes, MND 1.01. 28
are you so much in love as your rhymes speak? AYL 3.02.396 P
to whom he sung, in rude harsh–sounding rhymes,
JN 4.02.150
when their rhymes, | full of protest, of oath TRO 3.02.174
times, | when wit's more ripe, accept my rhymes, PER 1.ch. 12
shalt have thy trespass cited up in rhymes, LUC 524
RHYMING 2 FR 0.0002 REL FR 0 V 2 P
nay, i was rhyming; TGV 2.01.143 P
no, i was not born under a rhyming planet, nor i ADO 5.02. 40 P
RIALTO 5 FR 0.0005 REL FR 1 V 4 P
moreover, upon the rialto, he hath a third at MV 1.03. 19 P
what news on the rialto? 1.03. 38 P
a time and oft | in the rialto you have rated me 1.03.107
now what news on the rialto? 3.01. 1 P
who dare scarce show his head on the rialto; 3.01. 46 P
RIB 2 FR 0.0002 REL FR 2 V 0 P
to rib her cerecloth in the obscure grave. MV 2.07. 51
then join you with them, like a rib of steel, 2H4 2.03. 54
RIBALD 1 FR 0.0001 REL FR 1 V 0 P
wak'd by the lark, hath rous'd the ribald crows, TRO 4.02. 9
RIBAND *(also ribbon, etc.)*
RIBAND 2 FR 0.0002 REL FR 1 V 1 P
another for tying his new shoes with old riband? ROM 3.01. 29 P
a very riband in the cap of youth, | yet needful HAM 4.07. 77
RIBANDS 3 FR 0.0003 REL FR 2 V 1 P
with ribands pendant, flaring 'bout her head; WIV 4.06. 42
to your beards, new ribands to your pumps; MND 4.02. 36 P
where be your ribands, maids? TNK 3.05. 28
RIBAUDRED 1 FR 0.0001 REL FR 1 V 0 P
yon ribaudred nag of egypt | (whom leprosy ANT 3.10. 10
RIBB'D 1 FR 0.0001 REL FR 1 V 0 P
ribb'd and pal'd in | with oaks unscalable and CYM 3.01. 19
RIBBON *(also riband, etc.)*
RIBBON 2 FR 0.0002 REL FR 0 V 2 P
how much carnation ribbon may a man buy for a LLL 3.01.145 P
not a counterfeit stone, not a ribbon, glass, WT 4.04.598 P
RIBBONS 2 FR 0.0002 REL FR 0 V 2 P
he hath ribbons of all the colors i' th' rainbow WT 4.04.204 P
be the bondage of certain ribbons and gloves. 4.04.233 P
RIB–BREAKING 1 FR 0.0001 REL FR 0 V 1 P
is there yet another dotes upon rib–breaking? AYL 1.02.143 P
RIBS 17 FR 0.0019 REL FR 12 V 5 P
which was before barr'd up with ribs of iron! ADO 4.01.151
and dainty bits | make rich the ribs, but LLL 1.01. 27
vailing her high top lower than her ribs | to MV 1.01. 28
you may tell every finger i have with my ribs. 2.02.107 P
with over–weather'd ribs and ragged sails, 2.06. 18
him, and broke three of his ribs, that there is AYL 1.02.127 P
i heard breaking of ribs was sport for ladies. 1.02.138 P
the flinty ribs of this contemptuous city. JN 2.01.384
the fat ribs of peace | must by the hungry now 3.03. 9
go to the rude ribs of that ancient castle; R2 3.03. 32
may tear a passage thorough the flinty ribs | of 5.05. 20
call in ribs, call in tallow. 1H4 2.04.111 P
unless you call three fingers in the ribs bare. 4.02. 74 P
enough, patroclus, | or give me ribs of steel! TRO 1.03.177
and make my seated heart knock at my ribs, MAC 1.03.136
thought t' have yerk'd him here under the ribs. OTH 1.02. 5
what ribs of oak, when mountains melt on them, 2.01. 8
RICE* 3 FR 0.0003 REL FR 1 V 2 P
five pound of currants, rice — what will this WT 4.03. 38 P
what will this sister of mine do with rice? 4.03. 39 P
and rice ap thomas, with a valiant crew, | and R3 4.05. 15
RICH 180 FR 0.0203 REL FR 154 V 26 P
did give us, with | rich garments, linens, TMP 1.02.164
a sea–change | into something rich and strange. 1.02.402
and most poor matters | point to rich ends. 3.01. 4
afore heaven, | i ratify this my rich gift. 4.01. 8
most bounteous lady, thy rich leas | of wheat, 4.01. 60
approach, rich ceres, her to entertain. 4.01. 75
rich scarf to my proud earth — why hath thy 4.01. 82
what think'st thou of the rich mercatio? TGV 1.02. 12
and i as rich in having such a jewel | as twenty 2.04.169
and sure the match | were rich and honorable; 3.01. 64
and high and low beguiles the rich and poor. WIV 1.03. 86
he woos both high and low, both rich and poor, 2.01.113
like sapphire, pearl, and rich embroidery, 5.05. 71
whose rate are either rich or poor | as fancy MM 2.02.150
if thou art rich, thou'rt poor, | for, like an 3.01. 25

d when thou art old and rich, | thou hast 3.01. 36
clining their rich aspect to the hot breath of ERR 3.02.135 P
h she shall be, that's certain; ADO 2.03. 30 P
were possible any villainy should be so rich; 3.03.113 P
when rich villains have need of poor ones, 3.03.113 P
ay counterpoise this rich and precious gift? 4.01. 28
e law, go to, and a rich fellow enough, go to, 4.02. 83 P
d dainty bits | make rich the ribs, but LLL 1.01. 27
eet hearts, we shall be rich ere we depart, 5.02. 1
auties no richer than rich taffata. 5.02.159
r duty is so rich, so infinite, | that we may 5.02.199
ings seem foolish and rich things but poor. 5.02.378
s proves you wise and rich, for in my eye — 5.02.379
your rich wisdom to excuse or hide | the 5.02.732
er womb then rich with my young squire) MND 2.01.131
from a voyage, rich with merchandise. 2.01.134
ace | with the rich worth of your virginity. 2.01.219
ny your love (so rich within his soul) | and 3.02.229
e signiors and rich burghers on the flood, MV 1.01. 10
y, sir, but the rich jew's man, that would, 2.02.123 P
preferment | to leave a rich jew's service, 2.02.147
ver so rich a gem | was set in worse than gold 2.07. 54
o stones, two rich and precious stones, 2.08. 20
d courteous breath), | gifts of rich value. 2.09. 91
th a ship of rich lading wrack'd on the narrow 3.01. 3 P
nes more fair, ten thousand times more rich, 3.02.154
om the rich jew, a special deed of gift, 5.01.292
tin, and a rich man that hath not the gout; AYL 3.02.319 P
thing, is to have rich eyes and poor hands. 4.01. 24 P
hank god" — a good answer. art rich? 5.01. 25 P
h honesty dwells like a miser, sir, in a poor 5.04. 59 P
ough her father be very rich, any man is so SHR 1.01.124 P
d yet i'll promise thee she shall be rich, 1.02. 62
omise thee she shall be rich, | and very rich. 1.02. 63
now | one rich enough to be petruchio's wife 1.02. 67
thin rich pisa walls, as any one | old signior 2.01.367
r 'tis the mind that makes the body rich; 4.03.172
am poor, though many of the rich are damn'd, AWW 1.03. 17 P
r name, and no legacy is so rich as honesty. 3.05. 13 P
is ring he holds | in most rich choice; 3.07. 26
hose high respect and rich validity | did lack 5.03.192
w will she love when the rich golden shaft TN 1.01. 34
ve–thoughts lie rich when canopied with bow'rs 1.01. 40
my watch, or play with my — some rich jewel. 2.05. 60 P
e a cipher | (yet standing in rich place), i WT 1.02. 7
est a game play'd home, the rich stake drawn, 1.02.248
was told me i should be rich by the fairies. 3.03.117 P
en make /your garden rich in gillyvors, | and 4.04. 98
s garments are rich, but he wears them not 4.04.749 P
d left them | more rich for what they yielded. 5.01. 55
our choice is not so rich in worth as beauty, 5.01.214
hen the rich blood of kings is set on fire! JN 2.01.351
all gild her bridal bed and make her rich | in 2.01.491
d this rich fair town | we make him lord of. 2.01.552
t, | like a poor beggar, raileth on the rich. 2.01.592
il, | and say there is no sin but to be rich; 2.01.594
d being rich, my virtue then shall be | to say 2.01.595
omp, | to guard a title that was rich before, 4.02. 10
s youth | the rich advantage of good exercise. 4.02. 60
and as deep | into the purse of rich prosperity 5.02. 61
hereto, when they shall know what men are rich,
R2 1.04. 49
our presence makes us rich, most noble lord. 2.03. 63
ch men look sad, and ruffians dance and leap, 2.04. 12
oing to canterbury with rich offerings, and 1H4 1.02.126 P
d thy precious rich crown for a pitiful bald 2.04.382 P
dent, | to rob me of so rich a bottom here. 3.01.104
hat call you rich? 3.03. 78 P
set so rich a main | on the nice hazard of 4.01. 47
n fire | to hear this rich reprisal is so nigh, 4.01.118
nd make thee rich for doing me such wrong. 2H4 1.01. 90
nd takes away the stomach — such are the rich, 4.04.107
t | like a rich armor worn in heat of day, 4.05. 30
od, you have here goodly dwelling and rich. 5.03. 6 P
nd make /her chronicle as rich with praise | as H5 1.02.163
weat drops of gallant youth in our rich fields! 3.05. 25
nd not to seek a queen to make him rich: 1H6 5.05. 52
dare not say from the rich cardinal | and from 2H6 1.02. 94
im, | and like rich hangings in a homely house, 5.03. 12
heep | than doth a rich embroider'd canopy | to 3H6 2.05. 44
ch stuffs, and ornaments of household, which H8 3.02.126
he rich stream | of lords and ladies, having 4.01. 62
a rich chair of state, opposing freely | the 4.01. 67
he do, the rich shall have more. TRO 1.02.198 P
y itself | lies rich in virtue and unmingled. 1.03. 30
nd doth think it rich | to hear the wooden 1.03.154
ot lose | so rich advantage of a promis'd glory 2.02.204
ome thing not worth in me such rich beholding 3.03. 91
robber's haste | crams his rich thiev'ry up, 4.04. 43
ny wholesome act establish'd against the rich, COR 1.01. 83 P
he gods sent not | corn for the rich men only. 1.01.208
s big as thou art, | were not so rich a jewel. 1.04. 56
ll, | gracious lavinia, rome's rich ornament, TIT 1.01. 52
, she is rich in beauty, only poor | that, when ROM 1.01.215
ny master is the great rich capulet, and if you 1.02. 79 P
f night | as a rich jewel in an ethiop's ear — 1.05. 46
eauty too rich for use, for earth too dear! 1.05. 47
s set | on the fair daughter of rich capulet. 2.03. 58
ir, and let rich /music's tongue | unfold the 2.06. 27
onceit, more rich in matter than in words, 2.06. 30
when but love's shadows are so rich in joy! 5.01. 11
he world affords no law to make thee rich; 5.01. 73
s rich shall romeo's by his lady's lie, | poor 5.03.303
and rich. here is a water, look ye. TIM 1.01. 18
and returns in peace | most rich in timon's nod. 1.01. 62
e is gone happy, and has left me rich. 1.02. 4
aults that are rich are fair. 1.02. 13
ich men sin, and i eat root. 1.02. 71
hou art a soldier, therefore seldom rich, | it 1.02.222
and e'en as if your lord should wear rich jewels 3.04. 23
nterest — i myself | rich only in large hurts. 3.05.108
hus part we rich in sorrow, parting poor. 4.02. 29
ich only to be wretched, thy great fortunes 4.02. 43
usuring kindness, and, as rich men deal gifts, 4.03.509
wealth | to requite me by making rich yourself. 4.03.522
go, live rich and happy, | but thus condition'd: 4.03.525
yet rich conceit | taught thee to make vast 5.04. 77
made rich | with the most noble blood of all JC 3.01.155

bequeathing it as a rich legacy | unto their 3.02.136
the tyrant's grasp, | and the rich east to boot. MAC 4.03. 37
but not express'd in fancy, rich, not gaudy, HAM 1.03. 71
compos'd | as made these things more rich. 3.01. 98
rich gifts wax poor when givers prove unkind. 3.01.100
beyond what can be valued, rich or rare, | no LR 1.01. 57
fairest cordelia, that art most rich being poor, 1.01.250
thou dost bear | with something rich about me. 4.01. 77
and spend your rich opinion for the name | of a OTH 2.03.195
poor and content is rich, and rich enough, | but 3.03.172
poor and content is rich, and rich enough, | but 3.03.172
rich in his father's honor, creeps apace | into ANT 1.03. 50
of gold, and hail | rich pearls upon thee. 2.05. 46
all of her that is out of door most rich! CYM 1.06. 15
to see this vaulted arch and the rich crop | of 1.06. 33
and jewels | of rich and exquisite form, their 1.06.190
sweet air, with admirable rich words to it — 2.03. 18 P
a piece of work | so bravely done, so rich, that 2.04. 73
you have me, rich, and i will never fail 3.04.178
no wonder, | when rich ones scarce tell true. 3.06. 12
branches, which | distinction should be rich in. 5.05.384
i can compare our rich misers to nothing so PER 2.01. 29 P
having | rich tire about you, should at these 3.02. 22
doth appear, | to make the world twice rich. 3.02.102
or when | she would with rich and constant pen 4.ch. 28
his banners sable, trimm'd with rich expense, 5.ch. 19
endowments which | you make more rich to owe? 5.01.117
found there rich jewels, recovered her, and 5.03. 24
spur, | for rich caparisons or trappings gay? VEN 286
that she will draw his lips' rich treasure dry. 552
rich preys make true men thieves; 724
pluck down the rich, enrich the poor with 1150
of that rich jewel he should keep unknown | from LUC 34
perchance that envy of so rich a thing, 39
but poorly rich, so wanteth in his store, | that 97
that they prove bankrout in this poor rich gain. 140
the merchant fears, ere rich at home he lands." 336
sets you most rich in youth before my sight, SON 15.10
sun and moon, with earth and sea's rich gems, 21. 6
wishing me like to one more rich in hope, 29. 5
and they are rich, and ransom all ill deeds. 34.14
so am i as the rich whose blessed key | can 52. 1
the rich proud cost of outworn buried age; 64. 2
which can say more | than this rich praise, that 84. 2
the teeming autumn, big with rich increase, 97. 6
that love is merchandiz'd whose rich esteeming 102. 3
so thou, being rich in will, add to thy will 135.11
within be fed, without be rich no more: 146.12

/RICHARD 7 FR 0.0008 REL FR 7 V 0 P
/fetch /hither /richard, /that /in /common /view R2 4.01.155
/and /soon /lie /richard /in /an /earthy /pit! 4.01.219
/save /king /henry, /unking'd /richard /says, 4.01.220
/with /the /blood | /of /fair /king /richard, 2H4 1.01.205
/thy /glutton /bosom /of /the /royal /richard, 1.03. 98
/they /that, /when /richard /liv'd, /would /have 1.03.101
/of /which /disease | /our /late /king /richard 4.01. 58

RICHARD 149 FR 0.0168 REL FR 147 V 2 P
we came in with richard conqueror. SHR in.1. 4 P
his parts, | and finds them perfect richard. JN 1.01. 90
great, | arise sir richard, and plantagenet. 1.01.162
i am thy grandame, richard, call me so. 1.01.168
and come, richard, we must speed | for france, 1.01.178
"good den, sir richard!" 1.01.185
king richard cordelion was thy father. 1.01.253
and they shall say, when richard me begot, | if 1.01.274
richard, that robb'd the lion of his heart, 2.01. 3
sir richard, what think you? 4.03. 41
this news was brought to richard but even now. 5.03. 12
hither | before king richard in his royal lists? R2 1.03. 32
to god of heaven, king richard, and to me — 1.03. 40
though richard my live's counsel would not hear, 2.01. 15
o richard! 2.01.184
to so sweet a guest | as my sweet richard. 2.02. 9
as well assured richard their king is dead. 2.04. 17
ah, richard! 2.04. 18
god for his richard hath in heavenly pay | a 3.02. 60
richard not far from hence hath hid his head. 3.03. 6
the lord northumberland | to say king richard. 3.03. 8
king richard lies | within the limits of yon 3.03. 25
methinks king richard and myself should meet 3.03. 54
march on, and mark king richard how he looks. 3.03. 61
see, see, king richard doth himself appear, | as 3.03. 62
give richard leave to live till richard die? 3.03.174
give richard leave to live till richard die? 3.03.174
why dost thou say king richard is depos'd? 3.04. 77
king richard, he is in the mighty hold | of 3.04. 83
and with that odds he weighs king richard down. 3.04. 89
i come to thee | from plume–pluck'd richard, who 4.01.108
noble to be upright judge | of noble richard! 4.01.119
king richard's tomb, | and not king richard; 5.01. 13
what, is my richard both in shape and mind 5.01. 26
alack, poor richard, where rode he the whilst? 5.02. 22
men's eyes | did scowl on gentle richard. 5.02. 28
and love to richard | is a strange brooch in 5.05. 65
richard of burdeaux, by me hither brought. 5.06. 33
was not he proclaim'd | by richard, that dead is 1H4 1.03.146
you, did king richard then | proclaim my brother 1.03.155
to put down richard, that sweet lovely rose, 1.03.175
as thou art to this hour was richard then | when 3.02. 94
o no, my nephew must not know, sir richard, 5.02. 1
years gone | since richard and northumberland, 2H4 3.01. 58
even to the eyes of richard | gave him defiance. 3.01. 64
when richard, with his eye brimful of tears, 3.01. 67
this | king richard might create a perfect guess 3.01. 88
one, richard earl of cambridge, and the second, H5 2.pr. 23
then, richard earl of cambridge, there is yours; 2.02. 66
by the name of richard earl of cambridge. 2.02.146 P
suffolk, | sir richard ketly, davy gam, esquire; 4.08.104
was not thy father, richard earl of cambridge, 1H6 2.04. 90
farewell, ambitious richard. 2.04.114
richard plantagenet, my lord, will come. 2.05. 18
and even since then hath richard been obscur'd, 2.05. 26
richard plantagenet, my friend, is he come? 2.05. 34
your nephew, late–despised richard, comes. 2.05. 36
depos'd his nephew richard, edward's son, | the 2.05. 64
was, for that (young richard thus remov'd, 2.05. 71
which in the right of richard plantagenet | we 3.01.149
you have great reason to do richard right, 3.01.153

is | that richard be restored to his blood. 3.01.158
let richard be restored to his blood, | so shall 3.01.159
if richard will be true, not that alone | but 3.01.162
rise, richard, like a true plantagenet, | and 3.01.171
and so thrive richard as thy foes may fall! 3.01.173
well didst thou, richard, to suppress thy voice; 4.01.182
that richard duke of york | was rightful heir 2H6 1.03.183
and left behind him richard, his only son, | who 2.02. 19
harmless richard was murthered traitorously. 2.02. 27
for richard, the first son's heir, being dead, 2.02. 31
married richard earl of cambridge, who was | to 2.02. 45
long live our sovereign richard, england's king! 2.02. 63
richard shall live to make the earl of warwick 2.02. 81
i thank you, richard. 5.03. 16
richard hath best deserv'd of all my sons. 3H6 1.01. 17
resolve thee, richard, claim the english crown. 1.01. 49
true, clifford, that's richard duke of york. 1.01. 83
for richard, in the view of many lords, 1.01.138
richard plantagenet, | enjoy the kingdom after 1.01.174
richard, enough; 1.02. 35
thou, richard, shalt to the duke of norfolk, 1.02. 38
edward and richard, you shall stay with me, | my 1.02. 54
three times did richard make a lane to me, | and 1.04. 9
warriors did retire, | richard cried, "charge! 1.04. 15
richard, i bear thy name, i'll venge thy death, 2.01. 87
nor now my scandal, richard, dost thou hear; 2.01.151
king edward, valiant richard, montague, | stay 2.01.198
now, richard, i am with thee here alone: 2.04. 5
edward and richard, like a brace of greyhounds 2.05.129
come, york and richard, warwick and the rest, 2.06. 29
your brother richard mark'd him for the grave, 2.06. 40
richard, i will create thee duke of gloucester, 2.06.103
richard, be duke of gloucester. 2.06.109
field | this lady's husband, sir richard grey, 3.02. 2
well, say there is no kingdom then for richard; 3.02.146
yea, brother richard, are you offended too? 4.01. 19
now, brother richard, will you stand by us? 4.01.145
richard and hastings. 4.03. 29
he was convey'd by richard, duke of gloucester, 4.06. 81
now, brother richard, lord hastings, and the 4.07. 1
and, richard, do not frown upon my faults, | for 5.01.101
and richard but a /ragged fatal rock? 5.04. 27
hold, richard, hold, for we have done too much. 5.05. 43
is that devil's butcher, | hard–favor'd richard? 5.05. 78
richard, where art thou? 5.05. 78
where's richard gone? 5.05. 83
yea, richard, when i know; R3 1.01. 52
is put unto the trust of richard gloucester, | a 1.03. 12
richard! 1.03.233
here comes sir richard ratcliffe and the duke. 2.01. 46
richard of york, how fares our loving brother? 3.01. 96
till richard wear the garland of the realm. 3.02. 40
dear | to princely richard and to buckingham. 3.02. 68
sir richard ratcliffe, let me tell thee this: 3.03. 2
richard the second here was hack'd to death; 3.03. 12
for standing by when richard stabb'd her son. 3.03. 17
then curs'd she richard, then curs'd she 3.03. 18
o bloody richard! 3.04.103
their country's good | cry, "god save richard, 3.07. 22
some ten voices cried, "god save king richard!" 3.07. 36
your /wisdoms and your love to richard" — | and 3.07. 40
long live richard, england's worthy king! 3.07.240
go thou to richard, and good angels tend thee! 4.01. 92
and thy assistance, is king richard seated; 4.02. 4
i had an edward, till a richard kill'd him; 4.04. 40
i had a /harry, till a richard kill'd him: 4.04. 41
thou hadst an edward, till a richard kill'd him; 4.04. 42
thou hadst a richard, till a richard kill'd him. 4.04. 43
thou hadst a richard, till a richard kill'd him. 4.04. 43
i had a richard too, and thou didst kill him; 4.04. 44
hadst a clarence too, and richard kill'd him. 4.04. 46
richard yet lives, hell's black intelligencer, 4.04. 71
for my daughters, richard, | they shall be 4.04.201
and not be richard that hath done all this. 4.04.287
as long as hell and richard likes of it. 4.04.354
will not king richard let me speak with him? 5.01. 1
let us be lead within thy bosom, richard, | and 5.03.147
richard, thy wife, that wretched anne thy wife, 5.03.159
and richard falls in height of all his pride! 5.03.176
richard loves richard; 5.03.183
richard loves richard; 5.03.183
to–morrow's vengeance on the head of richard. 5.03.206
have strook more terror to the soul of richard 5.03.217
their souls whose bodies richard murther'd 5.03.230
richard except, those whom we fight against 5.03.243
father meant to act upon | th' usurper richard, H8 1.02.196
who first rais'd head against usurping richard, 2.01.108
richard du champ. CYM 4.02.377

/RICHARD'S 1 FR 0.0001 REL FR 1 V 0 P
/thou /live /in /richard's /seat /to /sit, R2 4.01.218

RICHARD'S 17 FR 0.0019 REL FR 17 V 0 P
nor keep his princely heart from richard's hand. JN 1.01.267
lives or dies, true to king richard's throne, R2 1.03. 86
from richard's night to bullingbrook's fair day. 3.02.218
on both his knees doth kiss king richard's hand, 3.03. 36
the fresh green lap of fair king richard's land, 3.03. 47
and who sits here that is not richard's subject? 4.01.122
thou map of honor, thou king richard's tomb, 5.01. 12
threw dust and rubbish on king richard's head. 5.02. 6
but that is lost for being richard's friend; 5.02. 42
in richard's time — what do you call the place? 1H4 1.03.242
staff of office did i break | in richard's time, 5.01. 35
i richard's body have interred new, | and on it H5 4.01.295
solemn priests | sing still for richard's soul. 4.01.302
but that i'll give my voice on richard's side R3 3.02. 53
there to be crowned richard's royal queen. 4.01. 32
o, when, i say, i look'd on richard's face, 4.01. 70
awake and think our wrongs in richard's bosom 5.03.144

RICH–BUILT 1 FR 0.0001 REL FR 1 V 0 P
burnt the shining glory | of rich–built ilion, LUC 1524

RICH'D (*also enrich'd*)

RICH'D 1 FR 0.0001 REL FR 1 V 0 P
with shadowy forests and with champains rich'd, LR 1.01. 64

RICHER 19 FR 0.0021 REL FR 16 V 3 P
signify that craft, being richer than innocency, MM 3.02. 9 P
beauties no richer than rich taffata. LLL 5.02.159
lies richer in your thoughts than on his tomb. AWW 1.02. 49
himself commended, | no richer than his honor. WT 3.02.170

whose veins bound richer blood than lady blanch? JN 2.01.431
had nobles richer and more loyal subjects, H5 1.02.127
yet i am richer than my base accusers, | that H8 2.01.104
and more and richer, when he strains that lady. 4.01. 46
alas, poor chin! many a wart is richer. TRO 1.02.141 P
which you priz'd | richer than sea and land? 2.02. 92
heads, and i am here | no richer in return. TIM 2.02.203
dearer than pluto's mine, richer than gold: JC 4.03.102
show itself more richer to signify this to the HAM 3.02.304 P
richer than that which four successive kings 5.02.273
even for want of that for which i am richer — LR 1.01.230
threw a pearl away | richer than all his tribe; OTH 5.02.348
richer than doing nothing for a /bable; CYM 3.03. 23
and, for i am richer than to hang by th' walls, 3.04. 52
richer than wealth, prouder than garments' cost, SON 91.10
RICHES 24 FR 0.0027 REL FR 22 V 2 P
riches, poverty, | and use of service, none; TMP 2.01.151
the clouds methought would open and show riches 3.02.141
honor, riches, marriage–blessing, | long 4.01.106
my riches are these poor habiliments, | of which TGV 4.01. 13
and 'tis the very riches of thyself | that now i WIV 3.04. 17
thou bear'st thy heavy riches but a journey, MM 3.01. 27
limb, nor beauty, | to make thy riches pleasant. 3.01. 38
o then belike you fancy riches more: SHR 2.01. 16
with too much riches it confound itself; R2 3.04. 60
that's all the riches i got in his service. H5 2.03. 44 P
sweet is the country, because full of riches, 2H6 4.07. 62
times | repair'd with double riches of content. R3 4.04.319
no, not for all the riches under heaven. H8 2.03. 35
are without him, as place, riches, and favor — TRO 3.03. 82
we call our own than the riches of our friends? TIM 1.02.103 P
since riches point to misery and contempt? 4.02. 32
the riches of the ship is come on shore! OTH 2.01. 83
but riches fineless is as poor as winter | to 3.03.173
is not there, who was indeed | the riches of it. CYM 3.04. 71
my riches to the earth from whence they came; PER 1.01. 52
for riches strew'd herself even in her streets; 1.04. 23
endowments greater | than nobleness and riches. 3.02. 28
and for that riches where is my deserving? SON 87. 6
and husband nature's riches from expense; 94. 6
RICHEST 8 FR 0.0009 REL FR 8 V 0 P
"all hail, the richest beauties on the earth!" LLL 5.02.158
love's stories written in love's richest book. MND 2.02.122
did astonish the survey | of richest eyes, whose AWW 5.03. 17
no, it will hang upon my richest robes, | and 2H6 2.04.108
her richest lockram 'bout her reechy neck, COR 2.01.209
in us, | his countenance, like richest alchymy, JC 1.03.159
convent in their behoof, our richest balms, TNK 1.04. 31
for she was sought by spirits of richest coat, LC 236
RICH–JEWELL'D 1 FR 0.0001 REL FR 1 V 0 P
than the rich–jewell'd coffer of darius, 1H6 1.06. 25
RICH–LEFT 1 FR 0.0001 REL FR 1 V 0 P
those rich–left heirs that let their fathers lie CYM 4.02.226
RICHLY 14 FR 0.0015 REL FR 12 V 2 P
yea, and paid me richly for the practice of it. ADO 5.01.248 P
in belmont is a lady richly left, | and she is MV 1.01.161
a vessel of our country richly fraught. 2.08. 30
argosies | are richly come to harbor suddenly. 5.01.277
city | is richly furnished with plate and gold, SHR 2.01.347
wears her cap out of fashion, richly suited, but AWW 1.01.157 P
hand, whose worth and honesty | is richly noted; WT 5.03.145
richly in both, if justice had her right. R2 2.01.227
away their shilling | richly in two short hours. H8 pr 13
hence safe | does pay thy labor richly; ANT 4.14. 37
desert, am bound | to load thy merit richly. CYM 1.05. 74
that the poor soldier that so richly fought, 5.05. 3
her eyes as jewel–like | and /cas'd as richly, PER 5.01.111
while comments of your praise, richly compil'd, SON 85. 2
/RICHMOND 2 FR 0.0002 REL FR 2 V 0 P
/richmond! R3 4.02.103
/not /live /long /after /i /saw /richmond. 4.02.107
RICHMOND 33 FR 0.0037 REL FR 33 V 0 P
arthur duke of britain | and earl of richmond, JN 2.01.552
my liege, it is young henry, earl of richmond. 3H6 4.06. 67
glad my heart with hope of this young richmond, 4.06. 93
'tis like that richmond with the rest shall down 4.06.100
the countess richmond, good my lord of derby, R3 1.03. 20
and live with richmond, from the reach of hell. 4.01. 42
go thou to richmond, and good fortune guide thee 4.01. 91
is fled | to richmond, in the parts where he 4.02. 49
well, let that rest. dorset is fled to richmond. 4.02. 85
if she convey | letters to richmond, you shall 4.02. 93
did prophesy that richmond should be king, 4.02. 96
king, | when richmond was a little peevish boy. 4.02. 97
for i know the britain richmond aims | at young 4.03. 40
morton is fled to richmond, | and buckingham, 4.03. 46
ely with richmond troubles me more near | than 4.03. 49
'tis thought that richmond is their admiral; 4.04.437
richmond is on the seas. 4.04.462
ay, thou wouldst be gone to join with richmond; 4.04.490
richmond in dorsetshire sent out a boat | unto 4.04.522
that the earl of richmond | is with a mighty 4.04.532
sir christopher, tell richmond this from me: 4.05. 1
but tell me, where is princely richmond now? 4.05. 9
be cheerful, richmond, for the wronged souls 5.03.121
king henry's issue, richmond, comforts thee. 5.03.123
sleep, richmond, sleep in peace and wake in joy. 5.03.150
armed in proof and led by shallow richmond. 5.03.219
good morrow, richmond! 5.03.223
richmond and victory! 5.03.270
what said northumberland as touching richmond? 5.03.271
why, what is that to me | more than to richmond? 5.03.286
seeking for richmond in the throat of death. 5.04. 5
courageous richmond, well hast thou acquit thee. 5.05. 3
division, | o, now let richmond and elizabeth, 5.05. 29
RICHMOND'S 2 FR 0.0002 REL FR 2 V 0 P
who prays continually for richmond's good. R3 5.03. 84
god and good angels fight on richmond's side, 5.03.175
RICHMONDS 1 FR 0.0001 REL FR 1 V 0 P
i think there be six richmonds in the field; R3 5.04. 11
RICHNESS 1 FR 0.0001 REL FR 1 V 0 P
his richness | and costliness of spirit look'd TNK 5.03. 96
RID* *(also ridden)*
RID* 35 FR 0.0039 REL FR 25 V 10 P
the red–plague rid you | for learning me your TMP 1.02.364
love with life that i will sue to be rid of it. MM 3.01.172 P
together, and thank god you are rid of a knave. ADO 3.03. 30 P
he hath rid his prologue like a rough colt; MND 5.01.119 P
wed her, bed her, and rid the house of her! SHR 1.01.144 P
that till the father rid his hands of her, 1.01.181
then we are rid of litio. 4.02. 49
i would we were well rid of this knavery. TN 4.02. 67 P
am glad at heart | to be so rid o' th' business. WT 3.03. 15
care, | and what loss is it to be rid of care? R2 3.02. 96
plot | to rid the realm of this pernicious blot? 4.01.325
"have i no friend will rid me of this living 5.04. 2
i am the king's friend, and will rid his foe. 5.04. 11
i cannot rid my hands of him. 2H4 1.02.202 P
so we be rid of them, do with /'em what thou 1H6 4.07. 94
this gloucester should be quickly rid the world, 2H6 3.01.233
world, | to rid us from the fear we have of him. 3.01.234
deathsmen, you have rid this sweet young prince! 3H6 5.05. 67
and will, no doubt, shortly be rid of me. R3 4.01. 86
and soon i'll rid you from the fear of them. 4.02. 77
as to one | that would be rid of such an enemy. TRO 4.05.164
mean | to rid her from this second marriage, ROM 5.03.241
give it the beasts, to be rid of the men. TIM 4.03.323 P
rid me these villains from your companies; 5.01.101
we are blest that rome is rid of him. JC 3.02. 70
are rid like madmen through the gates of rome. 3.02.269
on any chance, | to mend it, or be rid on't. MAC 3.01.113
let her who would be rid of him devise | his LR 5.01. 64
and i must | rid all the sea of pirates; ANT 2.06. 36
how many /score of miles may we well rid CYM 3.02. 67
must either get her ravish'd or be rid of her. PER 4.06. 5 P
there's no way to be rid on't but by the way to 4.06. 15 P
one would marry a leprous witch to be rid on't, TNK 4.03. 47 P
honor thyself to rid me of this shame, | for if LUC 1031
kill me outright with looks, and rid my pain. SON 139.14
RIDDANCE 2 FR 0.0002 REL FR 1 V 1 P
a gentle riddance. MV 2.07. 78
a good riddance. TRO 2.01.120 P
RIDDEN *(also rid*)*
RIDDEN 2 FR 0.0002 REL FR 0 V 2 P
am i ridden with a welsh goat too? WIV 5.05.137 P
i had, i saw well chosen, ridden, and furnish'd. H8 2.02. 2 P
RIDDLE 8 FR 0.0009 REL FR 5 V 3 P
much upon this riddle runs the wisdom of the MM 3.02.229 P
some enigma, some riddle — come, thy l'envoy — LLL 3.01. 71
no egma, no riddle, no l'envoy, no salve in the 3.01. 72 P
so there's my riddle: AWW 5.03.303
a fustian riddle! TN 2.05.108 P
hoy–day, a riddle! R3 4.04.459
o ho, i know the riddle. — i will go. LR 5.01. 37
his wife, | his riddle told not, lost his life. PER 1.ch. 38
RIDDLE–LIKE 1 FR 0.0001 REL FR 1 V 0 P
but riddle–like lives sweetly where she dies! AWW 1.03.217
RIDDLES 5 FR 0.0005 REL FR 3 V 2 P
you have not the book of riddles about you, have WIV 1.01.202 P
book of riddles? 1.01.203 P
lysander riddles very prettily. MND 2.02. 53
his currish riddles sorts not with this place. 3H6 5.05. 26
with macbeth | in riddles and affairs of death; MAC 3.05. 5
RIDDLING 3 FR 0.0003 REL FR 3 V 0 P
this is a riddling merchant for the nonce: 1H6 2.03. 57
riddling confession finds but riddling shrift. ROM 2.03. 56
riddling confession finds but riddling shrift. 2.03. 56
RIDE 59 FR 0.0066 REL FR 41 V 18 P
into the fire, to ride | on the curl'd clouds. TMP 1.02.191
surges under him, | and ride upon their backs. 2.01.116
be | a horse whereon the governor doth ride, MM 1.02.160
disdain and scorn ride sparkling in her eyes, ADO 3.01. 51
and two men ride of a horse, one must ride 3.05. 37 P
two men ride of a horse, one must ride behind. 3.05. 37 P
or wilt thou ride? SHR in.2. 41
that ride upon the violent speed of fire, | fly AWW 3.02.109
i'll ride home to–morrow, sir toby. TN 1.03. 89 P
i'll ride your horse as well as i ride you. 3.04.290 P
i'll ride your horse as well as i ride you. 3.04.291 P
you may ride 's | with one soft kiss a thousand WT 1.02. 94
my lord, no leave take i, for i will ride, | as R2 1.03.251
old, | i doubt not but to ride as fast as york. 5.02.115
good sweet honey lord, ride with us to–morrow. 1H4 1.02.160 P
prey on her, for they ride up and down on her, 2.01. 81 P
come, wilt thou see me ride? 2.03.100
have thirty miles to ride yet ere dinner–time. 3.03.198
too long | if life did ride upon a dial's point, 5.02. 83
upon my tongues continual slanders ride, | the 2H4 in 6
or i will ride thee a' nights like the mare. 2.01. 76 P
i think i am as like to ride the mare, if i have 2.01. 78 P
we'll ride all night. 5.03.131 P
as it were, to ride day and night, and not to 5.05. 20 P
on, and for a sovereign's sovereign to ride on; H5 3.07. 37 P
they that ride so, and ride not warily, fall 3.07. 56 P
they that ride so, and ride not warily, fall 3.07. 57 P
ride thou unto the horsemen on yond hill. 4.07. 57
you do prepare to ride unto saint albons, 2H6 1.02. 57
i go. come, nell, thou wilt ride with us? 1.02. 59
when thou didst ride in triumph through the 2.04. 14
thou dost ride in a foot–cloth, dost thou not? 4.07. 46 P
of maces, will we ride through the streets, and 4.07.135 P
mind | still ride in triumph over all mischance. 3H6 3.03. 18
spur your proud horses hard, and ride in blood; R3 5.03.340
that swore to ride before him to the field. TRO 4.04.142
the venom'd vengeance ride upon our swords, 5.03. 47
ride, ride, messala, ride, and give these bills JC 5.02. 1
ride, ride, messala, ride, and give these bills 5.02. 1
messala, ride, and give these bills | unto the 5.02. 1
ride, ride, messala, let them all come down. 5.02. 6
ride, ride, messala, let them all come down. 5.02. 6
ride you this afternoon? MAC 3.01. 19
is't far you ride? 3.01. 23
infected be the air whereon they ride, | and 4.01.138
whose foolish honesty | my practices ride easy. LR 1.02.182
i can keep honest counsel, ride, run, mar a 1.04. 32 P
than thou owest, | ride more than thou goest, 1.04.121
to ride on a bay trotting–horse over four–inch'd 3.04. 56 P
six shirts to his body — horse to ride, and 3.04.137
heart, and there | ride on the pants triumphing! ANT 4.08. 16
seeing this goodly vessel ride before us, | i PER 5.01. 18
must needs entreat you | this afternoon to ride, TNK 2.05. 46
"he s' buy me a white cut, forth for to ride, 3.04. 22
anon permit the basest clouds to ride | with SON 33. 5
whilst he upon your soundless deep doth ride, 80.10
be anchor'd in the bay where all men ride, | why 137. 6
sometimes her levell'd eyes their carriage ride, LC 22
"well could he ride, and often men would say, 106
RIDER 12 FR 0.0013 REL FR 10 V 2 P
not till it leave the rider in the mire. LLL 2.01.120
the ape his keeper, the tired horse his rider. 4.02.127 P
and throw the rider headlong in the lists, | a R2 1.02. 52
which his aspiring rider seem'd to know, | with 5.02. 9
in patient stillness while his rider mounts him. H5 3.07. 23 P
save one that had | a rider like myself, who CYM 4.04. 39
if't pleas'd his rider | to put pride in him. TNK 5.04. 57
plunges | disroot his rider whence he grew, but 5.04. 75
even now | to tie the rider she begins to prove. VEN 40
lack, | save a proud rider on so proud a back. 300
the wretch did know | his rider lov'd not speed, SON 50. 8
'that horse his mettle from his rider takes; LC 107
RIDER'S 2 FR 0.0002 REL FR 2 V 0 P
and his full poise | becomes the rider's load. TNK 5.04. 82
what recketh he his rider's angry stir, | his VEN 283
RIDERS 1 FR 0.0001 REL FR 0 V 1 P
manage, and to that end riders dearly hir'd; AYL 1.01. 13 P
RIDES 9 FR 0.0010 REL FR 6 V 3 P
'tis true she rides me and i long for grass. ERR 2.02.200
to her need i have | a vessel rides fast by, but WT 4.04.501
he that rides at high speed and with his pistol 1H4 2.04.345 P
the devil rides upon a fiddlestick. 2.04.487 P
and rides the wild–mare with the boys, and jumps 2H4 2.04.246 P
strong as the axle–tree | on which heaven rides, TRO 1.03. 67
but he rides well, | and his great love, sharp MAC 1.06. 22
rides on the posting winds and doth belie | all CYM 3.04. 36
mortal vessel tears, | and yet he rides it out. PER 4.04. 31
RIDEST 1 FR 0.0001 REL FR 1 V 0 P
so ridest thou triumphing in my woe. LLL 4.03. 34
RIDETH 1 FR 0.0001 REL FR 1 V 0 P
on the western coast | rideth a puissant navy; R3 4.04.434
RIDGE 1 FR 0.0001 REL FR 0 V 1 P
in as high a flow as the ridge of the gallows. 1H4 1.02. 38 P
RIDGES 4 FR 0.0004 REL FR 4 V 0 P
afoot | even to the frozen ridges of the alps, R2 1.01. 64
and ridges hors'd | with variable complexions, COR 2.01.211
whose ridges with the meeting clouds contend: VEN 820
the battle sought | with swelling ridges, and LUC 1439
RIDICULOUS 16 FR 0.0018 REL FR 10 V 6 P
a most ridiculous monster, to make a wonder of a TMP 2.02.165 P
of my lungs provokes me to ridiculous smiling — LLL 3.01. 77 P
and his general behavior vain, ridiculous, and 5.01. 12 P
that in this spleen ridiculous appears, | to 5.02.117
and their rough carriage so ridiculous, | should 5.02.306
and what in us hath seem'd ridiculous — | as 5.02.759
how many actions most ridiculous | hast thou AYL 2.04. 30
at the court are as ridiculous in the country as 3.02. 46 P
you with this ridiculous boldness before my lady TN 3.04. 37 P
a name | so slight, unworthy, and ridiculous, JN 3.01.150
to garnish, | is wasteful and ridiculous excess. 4.02. 16
(right ill dispos'd, in brawl ridiculous) | the H5 4.pr. 51
though they be never so ridiculous | (nay, let H8 1.03. 3
and with ridiculous and /awkward action, | which TRO 1.03.149
encounter such ridiculous subjects as you are. COR 2.01. 85 P
despair and hope makes thee ridiculous: VEN 988
RIDING 7 FR 0.0008 REL FR 5 V 2 P
or whether, riding on the balls of mine, | seem MV 3.02.117
hill, my master riding behind my mistress — SHR 4.01. 67 P
and traders riding to london with fat purses. 1H4 1.02.127 P
this man was riding | from alcibiades to timon's TIM 5.02. 9
were you but riding forth to air yourself, CYM 1.01.110
i have heard of riding wagers, | where horses 3.02. 71
'gainst whose shore | riding, her fortunes PER 5.03. 11
RIDING–ROBES 1 FR 0.0001 REL FR 1 V 0 P
but who comes in such haste in riding–robes? JN 1.01.217
RIDING–RODS 1 FR 0.0001 REL FR 1 V 0 P
him, | and if my legs were two such riding–rods, JN 1.01.140
RIDING–SUIT 1 FR 0.0001 REL FR 1 V 0 P
and provide me presently | a riding–suit, no CYM 3.02. 76
RIDS 2 FR 0.0002 REL FR 2 V 0 P
will thither straight, for willingness rids way, 3H6 5.03. 21
of death too, | that rids our dogs of languish? ANT 5.02. 42
RIEN 1 FR 0.0001 REL FR 1 V 0 P
rien puis? l'air et feu? H5 4.02. 5
RIFLE 1 FR 0.0001 REL FR 1 V 0 P
if not, we'll make you sit, and rifle you. TGV 4.01. 4
RIFLED 2 FR 0.0002 REL FR 2 V 0 P
pure chastity is rifled of her store, | and lust LUC 692
of that true type hath tarquin rifled me. 1050
RIFT 3 FR 0.0003 REL FR 3 V 0 P
within which rift | imprison'd, thou didst TMP 1.02.277
that even your ears | should rift to hear me, WT 5.01. 66
and that slain men | should solder up the rift. ANT 3.04. 32
RIFTED 1 FR 0.0001 REL FR 1 V 0 P
and rifted jove's stout oak | with his own bolt; TMP 5.01. 45
RIG 1 FR 0.0001 REL FR 1 V 0 P
and that is it | hath made me rig my navy, at ANT 2.06. 20
RIGG'D 3 FR 0.0003 REL FR 3 V 0 P
a rotten carcass of a butt, not rigg'd, | nor TMP 1.02.146
and bravely rigg'd as when | we first put out to 5.01.224
our great navy's rigg'd. ANT 3.05. 19
RIGGISH 1 FR 0.0001 REL FR 1 V 0 P
holy priests | bless her when she is riggish. ANT 2.02.239
/RIGHT 2 FR 0.0002 REL FR 2 V 0 P
/your /noble /and /right //well–rememb'red 2H4 4.01.110
/this /poor /right /hand /of /mine | /is /left TIT 3.02. 7
RIGHT 372 FR 0.0420 REL FR 307 V 65 P
i am right glad that he's so out of hope. TMP 3.03. 11
play with sparrows, | and be a boy right out. 4.01.101
when one's right hand | is perjured to the bosom TGV 5.04. 67
to whose falls —" | heaven prosper the right! WIV 3.01. 30 P
thou hast the right arch'd beauty of the brow 3.03. 56 P
this is strange. who hath got the right anne? 5.05.211 P
you are therein in the right. MM 2.01. 97 P
he's in the right, constable. 2.01.160 P
and do him right that, answering one foul wrong, 2.02.103
thou'rt i' th' right, girl, more o' that. 2.02.129
do me the common right | to let me see them, and 2.03. 5
hooking both right and wrong to th' appetite, 2.04.176
it is the right of it; 3.02. 58 P
be the due of a bawd, why, 'tis his right. 3.02. 67 P
nothing goes right — we would, and we would not 4.04. 34
right. 5.01. 85

it may be right, but you are i' the wrong | to 5.01. 86
but, if thou live to see like right bereft, ERR 2.01. 40
right, sir, i'll tell you when, and you'll tell 3.01. 39
first he denied you had in him no right. 4.02. 7
why, here begins his morning story right: 5.01.357
most in the company of the right noble claudio. ADO 1.01. 84 P
any, i will do myself the right to trust none; 1.01.244 P
marry, it is your brother's right hand. 1.03. 49 P
o plague right well prevented! 3.02.133 P
call up the right master constable. 3.03.166 P
and it be the right husband and the right wife; 3.04. 36 P
and it be the right husband and the right wife; 3.04. 36 P
the man deserve of me that would right her! 4.01.262 P
if he could right himself with quarrelling, 5.01. 51
you say not right, old man. 5.01. 73
do me right, or i will protest your cowardice. 5.01.147 P
"right," says she, "a great gross one." 5.01.162 P
give her the right you should have giv'n her 5.01.291
hast frighted the word out of his right sense, 5.02. 56 P
whom right and wrong | have chose as umpeer of LLL 1.01.168
in my correction, and god defend the right! 1.01.214 P
we will give up our right in aquitaine, | and 2.01.139
out being watch'd that it may still go right! 3.01.193
they sparkle still the right promethean fire; 4.03.348
a right description of our sport, my lord. 5.02.521
for it stands too right. 5.02.565
most true, 'tis right; you were so, alisander. 5.02.569
and i will right myself like a soldier. 5.02.724 P
that fault, | right joyful of your reformation. 5.02.869
yield | thy crazed title to my certain right. MND 1.01. 92
mine, and all my right of her | i do estate unto 1.01. 97
why should not i then prosecute my right? 1.01.105
am a right maid for my cowardice. 3.02.302
now follow, if thou dar'st, to try whose right, 3.02.336
will tell you every thing, right as it fell out. 4.02. 31 P
and this the cranny is, right and sinister, 5.01.163
offer to choose, and choose the right casket, MV 1.02. 93 P
bars me the right of voluntary choosing. 2.01. 16
turn up on your right hand at the next turning, 2.02. 41 P
am right loath to go; 2.05. 16
how shall i know if i do choose the right? 2.07. 10
if i fail | of the right casket, never in my 2.09. 12
could teach you | how to choose right, but 3.02. 11
to do a great right, do a little wrong, | and 4.01.216
are | to their right praise and true perfection! 5.01.108
"'tis right," quoth he, "thus misery doth part AYL 2.01. 51
be, | and buy it with your gold right suddenly. 2.04.100
if it do him right, | then he hath wrong'd 2.07. 84
man, | thou art right welcome as thy /master is. 2.07.198
it is the right butter–women's rank to market. 3.02. 98 P
ripe, and that's the right virtue of the medlar. 3.02.120 P
but i answer you right painted cloth, from 3.02.273 P
right! 3.03. 53 P
would not have my right rosalind of this mind, 4.01.109 P
left on your right hand brings you to the place. 4.03. 80
faith, i should have been a woman by right. 4.03.176 P
if you be gentlemen, | do me this right: SHR 1.02.237
the base is right, 'tis the base knave that jars 3.01. 47
minola, | as if he were the right vincentio. 4.02. 70
you are i' th' right, sir, 'tis for my mistress. 4.03.156 P
imagine 'twere the right vincentio. 4.04. 12
right true it is, your son lucentio here | doth 4.04. 40
dare swear this is the right vincentio. 5.01.100 P
lucentio, | right son to the right vincentio, 5.01.115
lucentio, | right son to the right vincentio, 5.01.115
right, i mean you. 5.02. 31
life, | an aweful rule, and right supremacy; 5.02.109
and it was his great right to be so — gerard de AWW 1.01. 27 P
moderate lamentation is the right of the dead, 1.01. 55 P
right, so i say. 2.03. 13 P
right, as 'twere a man assur'd of a — 2.03. 17 P
to thine own fortunes that obedient right 2.03.160
which are their own right by the law of nature. 4.05. 61 P
and a half, but his right cheek is worn bare. 4.05. 98 P
know thy constellation is right apt | for this TN 1.04. 35
th' art i' th' right. 2.03.119 P
then think you right: i am not what i am. 3.01.141
be not amaz'd, right noble is his blood. 5.01.264
prithee read i' thy right wits. 5.01.297 P
but to read his right wits is to read thus; 5.01.298 P
which i doubt not but to do myself much right, 5.01.308 P
you scarce can right me throughly, then, to say WT 2.01. 99
or death, upon the earth | of its right father. 3.03. 46
here and there, | i then do most go right. 4.03. 18
toward the sea–side, go on the right hand, i 4.04.825 P
in right and true behalf | of thy deceased JN 1.01. 7
land, | thy nephew and right royal sovereign. 1.01. 15
world, | upon the right and party of her son? 1.01. 34
our strong possession and our right for us. 1.01. 39
strong possession much more than your right, 1.01. 40
something about, a little from the right, | in 1.01.170
shadowing their right under your wings of war. 2.01. 14
noble boy! who would not do thee right? 2.01. 18
all angiers, and the right thou hast in france, 2.01. 22
that right in peace which here we urge in war, 2.01. 47
england was geffrey's right, | and this is 2.01.105
to look into the blots and stains of right. 2.01.114
i'll smoke your skin–coat and i catch you right. 2.01.139
maine, | in right of arthur do i claim of thee. 2.01.153
to in this right hand, whose protection | is 2.01.236
most divinely vow'd upon the right | of him 2.01.237
for him, and in his right, we hold this town. 2.01.268
till you compound whose right is worthiest, | we 2.01.281
we for the worthiest hold the right from both. 2.01.282
god and our right! 2.01.299
say, shall the current of our right roam on? 2.01.335
know him in us, that here hold up his right. 2.01.364
in her right we came, | which we, god knows, 2.01.548
no tongue hath power to curse him right. 3.01.183
when law can do no right, | let it be lawful 3.01.185
you, in the right of lady blanch your wife, 3.04.142
what in rest you have in right you hold, 4.02. 55
the life, the right, and truth of all this realm 4.03.144
that, for the health and physic of our right, 5.02. 21
and on our actions set the name of right | with 5.02. 67
you taught me how to know the face of right, 5.02. 88
the cruel pangs of death | right in thine eye. 5.04. 60
and happy newness, that intends old right. 5.04. 61
now, you stars that move in your right spheres, 5.07. 74
tongue speaks, my right drawn sword may prove. R2 1.01. 46
cousin of herford, as thy cause is right, | so 1.03. 55
receive thy lance, and god defend the right! 1.03.101
now, by my seat's right royal majesty, | wert 2.01.120
right, you say true: 2.01.145
richly in both, if justice had her right. 2.01.227
whom conscience and my kinred bids to right. 2.02.115
it stands your grace upon to do him right. 2.03.138
and labor'd all i could to do him right; 2.03.142
to find out right with wrong — it may not be; 2.03.145
and for the right of that | we all have strongly 2.03.149
must fall, for heaven still guards the right. 3.02. 62
his noble cousin is right welcome hither, | and 3.03.122
and to thy worth will add right worthy gains. 5.06. 12
forgot, | right noble is thy merit, well i wot. 5.06. 18
shall we divide our right | according to our 1H4 3.01. 69
for of no right, nor color like to right, | he 3.02.100
for of no right, nor color like to right, | he 3.02.100
nor claim no further than your new–fall'n right, 5.01. 44
this is the right fencing grace, my lord, tap 2H4 2.01.192 P
not his craft's master, he doth not do it right. 3.02.279 P
with grant of our most just and right desires, 4.02. 40
therefore let me have right, and let desert 4.03. 55 P
then plain and right must my possession be, 4.05.222
you are right justice, and you weigh this well, 5.02.102
why, now you have done me right. 5.03. 72 P
"do me right, | and dub me knight, | samingo." 5.03. 73
o god, that right should thus overcome might! 5.04. 24 P
a hundred almshouses right well supplied; H5 1.01. 17
whose right | suits not in native colors with 1.02. 16
to hold in right and title of the female; 1.02. 89
may i with right and conscience make this claim? 1.02. 96
/blood and sword and fire, to win your right; 1.02.131
in the right | of your great predecessor, king 1.02.247
nym, thou hast spoke the right. 2.01.123
vile and ragged foils | (right ill dispos'd, in 4.pr. 51
being in his right wits and his good judgments, 4.07. 47 P
nay, that's right; 5.01. 1 P
right joyous are we to behold your face, | most 5.02. 9
for he perforce must do thee right, because he 5.02.154 P
for thee, and for the right | of english henry, 1H6 2.01. 35
if all things fall out right, | i shall as 2.03. 4
and say withal, i think he held the right. 2.04. 38
shall yield the other in the right opinion. 2.04. 42
which in the right of richard plantagenet | we 3.01.149
you have great reason to do richard right, 3.01.153
and saint george, talbot and england's right, 4.02. 55
mean and right poor, for that pure blood of mine 4.06. 23
nor shall proud lancaster usurp my right, | nor 2H6 1.01.244
which now they hold by force and not by right; 2.02. 30
here let them end it, and god defend the right! 2.03. 55
o peter, thou hast prevail'd in right! 2.03. 99 P
came he right now to sing a raven's note, 3.02. 40
from ireland thus comes york to claim his right, 5.01. 1
to wring the widow from her custom'd right, 5.01.188
as i in justice and true right express it. 5.02. 25
by words or blows here let us win our right. 3H6 1.01. 37
i mean to take possession of my right. 1.01. 44
his is the right, and therefore pardon me. 1.01.148
king henry, be thy title right or wrong, | lord 1.01.159
do right unto this princely duke of york, | or i 1.01.166
your right depends not on his life or death. 1.02. 11
and if thou tell'st the heavy story right, 1.04.160
and here's to right our gentle–hearted king. 1.04.176
where our right valiant father is become. 2.01. 10
thou shalt know this strong right hand of mine 2.01.152
draw thy sword in right. 2.02. 62
say, henry, shall i have my right, or no? 2.02.126
if that be right which warwick says is right, 2.02.131
if that be right which warwick says is right, 2.02.131
there is no wrong, but every thing is right. 2.02.132
the one his purple blood right well resembles, 2.05. 99
if this right hand would buy two hours' life 2.06. 80
no humble suitors press to speak for right, | no 3.01. 19
he, on his right, asking a wife for edward. 3.01. 44
right gracious lord, i cannot brook delay. 3.02. 18
can oxford, that did ever fence the right, | now 3.03. 98
did i put henry from his native right? 3.03.190
do me but right, and you must all confess | that 4.01. 69
to save, at least, the heir of edward's right; 4.04. 32
for 'tis my right, | and henry but usurps the 4.07. 65
and whosoe'er gainsays king edward's right, | by 4.07. 74
with whom /an upright zeal to right prevails 5.01. 78
and thou usurp'st my father's right and mine. 5.05. 37
and seek their ruin that usurp'd our right? 5.06. 73
valiant, wise, and (no doubt) right royal — R3 1.02.244
this sorrow that i have, by right is yours, 1.03.171
so just is god, to right the innocent. 1.03.181
right, as snow in harvest. 1.04.242
i'll win our ancient right in france again, | or 3.01. 92
and do not doubt, right noble princes both, 3.05. 64
being the right idea of your father, | both in 3.07. 13
he is within, with two right reverend fathers, 3.07. 61
of thy devotion and right christian zeal. 3.07.103
your right of birth, your empery, your own. 3.07.136
me, | the right and fortune of his happy stars, 3.07.172
right well, dear madam. 4.01. 15
say that right for right | hath dimm'd your 4.04. 15
say that right for right | hath dimm'd your 4.04. 15
should be branded, if that right were right, 4.04.141
should be branded, if that right were right, 4.04.141
he was in the right, and so indeed it is. 5.03.275
of the right reverend cardinal of york. H8 1.01. 51
sir, i desire you do me right and justice, | and 2.04. 13
yet i know | a way, if it take right, in spite 3.02.219
glad your grace has made that right use of it. 3.02.386
still in thy right hand carry gentle peace | to 3.02.445
a right good husband (let him be a noble), | and 4.02.146
and urge the king | to do me this last right. 4.02.158
and am right sorry to repeat what follows. 5.01. 96
and am right glad to catch this good occasion 5.01.109
'tis the right ring, by heav'n! 5.02.138
force should be right, or rather, right and TRO 1.03.116
or rather, right and wrong | (between whose 1.03.116
'tis agamemnon right! 1.03.164
'tis nestor right. 1.03.170
a free determination | 'twixt right and wrong; 2.02.171
this thrice worthy and right valiant lord 2.03.190
when right with right wars who shall be most 3.02.172
when right with right wars who shall be most 3.02.172
right with right wars who shall be most right! 3.02.172
desir'd my cressid in right great exchange, 3.03. 21
place is dangerous, | the time right deadly. 5.02. 39
we must follow you, | right worthy you priority. COR 1.01.247
ever right. 2.01.191
'tis right. 2.01.236
he's right noble. | let him be call'd for. 2.02.129
o sir, you are not right. 2.03. 48
so | i' th' right and strength a' th' commons," 3.03. 14
noble patricians, patrons of my right, | defend TIT 1.01. 1
friends, followers, favorers of my right, | if 1.01. 9
and in the capitol and senate's right, | whom 1.01. 41
that have been thus forward in my right, | i 1.01. 56
in right and service of their noble country. 1.01.197
romans, do me right. 1.01.203
to do myself this reason and this right. 1.01.279
dangerous | it is to jet upon a prince's right? 2.01. 64
mother's hand shall right your mother's wrong. 2.03.121
and swear unto my soul to right your wrongs. 3.01.278
just — a verse in horace, right, you have it. 4.02. 24
to join with him and right his heinous wrongs. 5.02. 4
to slay his daughter with his own right hand, 5.03. 37
right glad i am he was not at this fray. ROM 1.01.117
a right good mark–man! and she's fair i love. 1.01.206
a right fair mark, fair coz, is soonest hit. 1.01.207
or if not so, then here i hit it right — | our 2.03. 41
right. 2.04. 59 P
right, if doing nothing be death by th' law. TIM 1.01.194 P
right welcome, sir! 1.01.253
master" and the cap | plays in the right hand, 2.01. 19
parts you'll suit | in giving him his right. 2.02. 24
why, this hits right; 3.01. 6 P
i am right glad that his health is well, sir; 3.01. 13 P
for his right noble mind, illustrious virtue, 3.02. 80
though his right arm might purchase his own time 3.05. 76
will make | black white, foul fair, wrong right, 4.03. 29
nations, i will make thee | do thy right nature. 4.03. 45
come on my right hand, for this ear is deaf, JC 1.02.213
need of him, | you have right well conceited. 1.03.162
which, by the right and virtue of my place, | i 2.01.269
in ranks and squadrons and right form of war, 2.02. 20
i only speak right on. 3.02.223
upon the right hand i, keep thou the left. 5.01. 18
and the right valiant banquo walk'd too late, MAC 3.06. 5
there would be hands uplifted in my right; 4.03. 42
shall with my cousin, your right noble son, 5.06. 3
why, right, you are in the right, | and so, HAM 1.05.126
why, right, you are in the right, | and so, 1.05.126
spite, | that ever i was born to set it right! 1.05.189
you say right, sir, a' monday morning, 'twas 2.02.387 P
am i not i' th' right, old jephthah? 2.02.410 P
my honor'd lord, you know right well you did, 3.01. 96
lord, this courtesy is not of the right breed. 3.02.315 P
commune with your grief, | or you deny me right. 4.05.204
it falls right. 4.07. 70
your lordship is right welcome back to denmark. 5.02. 81
/put your bonnet to his right use, 'tis for the 5.02. 92 P
i | return those duties back as are right fit, LR 1.01. 97
right noble burgundy, | when she was dear to us, 1.01.195
bold in the quarrel's right, rous'd to th' 2.01. 54
your graces are right welcome. 2.01.129
when every case in law is right; 3.02. 87
love, dear love, and our ag'd father's right. 4.04. 28
pray that the right may thrive. 5.02. 2
th' hast spoken right, 'tis true. 5.03.174
an inviting eye; and yet methinks right modest. OTH 2.03. 24 P
this is my ancient, this is my right hand, and 2.03.114 P
you are in the right. 2.03.333 P
if you dare do yourself a profit and a right. 4.02.233 P
own world, and you might quickly make it right. 4.03. 82 P
by hercules, i think i am i' th' right. ANT 3.07. 67
go on: right royal. 3.13. 55
he is a god and knows | what is most right. 3.13. 61
like a right gipsy, hath at fast and loose 4.12. 28
right proud | of that most delicate lodging. CYM 2.04.135
and am right sorry that i must report ye | my 3.05. 3
his right cheek | reposing on a cushion. 4.02.211
our fealty and tenantius' right | with honor to 5.04. 73
and am right glad he is not standing here | to 5.05.296
in the net, like a poor man's right in the law; PER 2.01.117 P
you are right courteous knights. 2.03. 27
'tis right — those, those. | they are not dead? TNK 1.04. 23
with thy twinkling eyes look right and straight 3.05.117
up, and under me | i had a right good horse. 3.06. 77
(if there be a right in seeing | and first 3.06.147
you are a right woman, sister, you have pity, 3.06.215
not right? 4.01. 45
three or four days | i'll make her right again. 5.02.105
upon my right side still i wore thy picture, 5.03. 73
go we hence, | right joyful, with some sorrow. 5.03.135
a right good creature, more to me deserving 5.04. 34
thou art a right good man, and while i live, 5.04. 97
kinsman hath confess'd the right o' th' lady 5.04.116
self–same hand, self reasons, and self right, STM II.C 85
can thy right hand seize love upon thy left? VEN 158
being judge in love, she cannot right her cause. 220
thou art the next of blood, and 'tis thy right. 1184
proving from world's minority their right: LUC 67
to the rough beast that knows no gentle right, 545
'tis thou that spurn'st at right, at law, at 880
to wrong the wronger till he render right, | to 943
this helpless smoke of words doth me no right. 1027
their oaths, should right poor ladies' harms." 1694
my better angel is a man (right fair), | my PP 2. 3
swan, | lest the requiem lack his right. PHT 16
that the turtle saw his right | flaming in the 34
my heart mine eye the freedom of that right. SON 46. 4
and my heart's right /thy inward love of heart. 46.14
and right perfection wrongfully disgrac'd, | and 66. 7
the right of sepulchres, were shorn away, | to 68. 6
that for thy right myself will bear all wrong. 88.14
that my steel'd sense or changes right or wrong. 112. 8
and given to time your own dear–purchas'd right; 117. 6
shall will in others seem right gracious, | and 135. 7
in things right true my heart and eyes have 137.13

the better angel is a man right fair, | the 144. 3
sometimes they do extend | their view right on; LC 26
RIGHTEOUS 6 FR 0.0006 REL FR 6 V 0 P
daughter | in such a righteous fashion as i do, WIV 3.04. 79
this shall ye do, so help you righteous god! 1H6 4.01. 8
should be good men, their affairs as righteous. H8 3.01. 22
rome and the righteous heavens be my judge, TIT 1.01.426
seal with a righteous kiss | a dateless bargain ROM 5.03.114
let me be recorded by the righteous gods, | i am TIM 4.02. 4
RIGHTEOUSLY 1 FR 0.0001 REL FR 0 V 1 P
love to me were so righteously temper'd as mine AYL 1.02. 14 P
RIGHTFUL 14 FR 0.0015 REL FR 12 V 2 P
most rightful judge! MV 4.01.301
for the deposing of a rightful king. R2 5.01. 50
my rightful hand in a well–hallow'd cause. H5 1.02.293
they labored to plant the rightful heir, | i 1H6 2.05. 80
with charles, the rightful king of france." 4.01. 60
the duke of york was rightful heir to the crown. 2H6 1.03. 27 P
of york say he was rightful heir to the crown? 1.03. 29 P
york | was rightful heir unto the english crown 1.03.184
beam stands sure, whose rightful cause prevails. 2.01.201
seiz'd on the realm, depos'd the rightful king, 2.02. 24
that shall salute our rightful sovereign | with 2.02. 61
reign, | for i am rightful heir unto the crown. 4.02.131
the rightful heir to england's royal seat. 5.01.178
no rightful plea might plead for justice there. LUC 1649
RIGHTFULLY 1 FR 0.0001 REL FR 1 V 0 P
'gainst all the world will rightfully maintain. 2H4 4.05.224
RIGHT–HAND 1 FR 0.0001 REL FR 0 V 1 P
the city, i mean of us a' th' right–hand file? COR 2.01. 23 P
RIGHTLY 26 FR 0.0029 REL FR 18 V 8 P
voice of her behavior (to be english'd rightly) WIV 1.03. 48 P
rightly reason'd, and in his own division, and, ADO 5.01.224 P
and he it was that might rightly say, veni, vidi LLL 4.01. 67 P
be chosen by any rightly but one who you shall MV 1.02. 32 P
any rightly but one who you shall rightly love. 1.02. 33 P
if i heard you rightly, | the duke hath put on a AYL 5.04.180
doth to our rose of youth rightly belong; AWW 1.03.130
sav'd by believing rightly can ever believe such TN 3.02. 72 P
which rightly gaz'd upon | show nothing but R2 2.02. 18
choler, my lord, if rightly taken. 1H4 2.04.324 P
no, if rightly taken, halter. 2.04.325 P
i am assur'd, if i be measur'd rightly, | your 2H4 5.02. 65
thy name is gualtier, being rightly sounded. 2H6 4.01. 37
for few men rightly temper with the stars; 3H6 4.06. 29
he tells you rightly. H8 3.01. 97
disgest things rightly | touching the weal a' COR 1.01.150
if thou consider rightly of the matter, | caesar JC 3.02.109
you may be rightly just, | what ever i shall MAC 4.03. 30
rightly to be great | is not to stir without HAM 4.04. 53
that justly think'st and hast most rightly said! LR 1.01.183
late transport you | from what you rightly are. 1.04.222
and my perfect soul | shall manifest me rightly. OTH 1.02. 32
i shall be furnish'd to inform you rightly ANT 1.04. 77
thou hast been rightly honest — so hast thou — 4.02. 11
by the holy gods | i cannot rightly say. PER 3.04. 8
slow, | they rightly do inherit heaven's graces, SON 94. 5
/RIGHTS 1 FR 0.0001 REL FR 1 V 0 P
/casualties, /gave /her /dear /rights | /to /his LR 4.03. 44
RIGHTS 22 FR 0.0024 REL FR 21 V 1 P
puts bars between the owners and their rights! MV 3.02. 19
will for ever | do thee all rights of service. AWW 4.02. 17
to enforce these rights so forcibly withheld. JN 1.01. 18
royalties, and rights | of this oppressed boy. 2.01.176
the royalties and rights of banish'd herford? R2 2.01.190
take herford's rights away, and take from time 2.01.195
time | his charters and his customary rights; 2.01.196
if you do wrongfully seize herford's rights, 2.01.201
my rights and royalties | pluck'd from my arms 2.03.120
and given my treasures and my rights of thee 1H4 2.03. 45
deck'd in thy rights as thou art stall'd in mine R3 1.03.205
then, in the name of god and all these rights, 5.03.263
as, let 'em have their rights, they are ever H8 4.01. 9
rights by rights fouler, strengths by strengths COR 4.07. 55
rights by rights fouler, strengths by strengths 4.07. 55
me conjure you, by the rights of our fellowship, HAM 2.02.284 P
i have some rights, of memory in this kingdom, 5.02.389
in my rights, | by me invested, he compeers the LR 5.03. 68
you, to your rights, | with boot, and such 5.03.301
which by the rights of time thou needs must have VEN 759
by all our country rights in rome maintained, LUC 1838
and your true rights be term'd a poet's rage, SON 17.11
RIGOL 2 FR 0.0002 REL FR 2 V 0 P
that from this golden rigol hath divorc'd | so 2H4 4.05. 36
face | of that black blood a wat'ry rigol goes, LUC 1745
RIGOR 10 FR 0.0011 REL FR 10 V 0 P
and follows close the rigor of the statute, | to MM 1.04. 67
awake), i tell you | 'tis rigor and not law. WT 3.02.114
heart, | and like as rigor of tempestuous gusts 1H6 5.05. 5
let him have all the rigor of the law. 2H6 1.03.196
or more than common fear of clifford's rigor, 3H6 2.01.126
his time, | unto the rigor of severest law. ROM 5.03.269
with others whom the rigor of our state | forc'd LR 5.01. 22
since her best work is ruin'd with thy rigor." VEN 954
in ajax' eyes blunt rage and rigor roll'd, | but LUC 1398
thou canst not then use rigor in my jail: SON 133.12
RIGOROUS 3 FR 0.0003 REL FR 3 V 0 P
have seal'd his rigorous statutes with their ERR 1.01. 9
great pains to qualify | his rigorous course; MV 4.01. 8
down the tarpeian rock | with rigorous hands. COR 3.01.266
RIGOROUSLY 1 FR 0.0001 REL FR 1 V 0 P
whose maiden blood, thus rigorously effus'd, 1H6 5.04. 52
RIG'ST 1 FR 0.0001 REL FR 1 V 0 P
'tis thou that rig'st the bark and plough'st the TIM 5.01. 50
RIM 1 FR 0.0001 REL FR 1 V 0 P
/or i will fetch thy rim out at thy throat | in H5 4.04. 14
RINALDO 2 FR 0.0002 REL FR 2 V 0 P
rinaldo, you did never lack advice so much | as AWW 3.04. 19
write, write, rinaldo, | to this unworthy 3.04. 29
RIND 2 FR 0.0002 REL FR 2 V 0 P
sweetest nut hath sourest rind, | such a nut is AYL 3.02.109
within the infant rind of this weak flower ROM 2.03. 23
/RING* 1 FR 0.0001 REL FR 1 V 0 P
in spring time, the only pretty /ring time, AYL 5.03. 19
RING* 153 FR 0.0173 REL FR 133 V 20 P
sea–nymphs hourly ring his knell: TMP 1.02.403
go presently, and take this ring with thee, TGV 4.04. 71
give her that ring and therewithal | this letter 4.04. 85
this ring i gave him when he parted from me, 4.04. 97
madam, he sends your ladyship this ring. 4.04.132
though his false finger have profan'd the ring, 4.04.136
charg'd me to deliver a ring to madam silvia, 5.04. 89 P
where is that ring, boy? 5.04. 91
why, this is the ring i gave to julia. 5.04. 93
this is the ring you sent to silvia. 5.04. 95
but how cam'st thou by this ring? 5.04. 96
once to–night | give my sweet nan this ring. WIV 3.04.100
sing, | like to the garter's compass, in a ring. 5.05. 66
do you not hear it ring? ERR 4.02. 51
give me the ring of mine you had at dinner, | or 4.03. 68
i pray you, sir, my ring, or else the chain; 4.03. 77
a ring he hath of mine worth forty ducats, | and 4.03. 83
into my house, and took perforce | my ring away. 4.03. 95
came to my house, and took away my ring — | the 4.04.138
ring — | the ring i saw upon his finger now — 4.04.139
he did, and from my finger snatch'd that ring. 5.01.277
'tis true, my liege, this ring i had of her. 5.01.278
a death's face in a ring. LLL 5.02.612 P
one of them show'd me a ring that he had of your MV 3.01.118 P
let us all ring fancy's knell. 3.02. 70
i give them with this ring, | which when you 3.02.171
but when this ring | parts from this finger, 3.02.183
and for your love i'll take this ring from you. 4.01.427
this ring, good sir, alas, it is a trifle! 4.01.430
the dearest ring in venice will i give you, 4.01.435
good sir, this ring was given me by my wife, 4.01.441
and know how well i have deserv'd this ring, 4.01.446
my lord bassanio, let him have the ring. 4.01.449
give him the ring, and bring him, if thou canst, 4.01.453
upon more advice | hath sent you here this ring, 4.02. 7
his ring i do accept most thankfully, | and so i 4.02. 9
i'll see if i can get my husband's ring, | which 4.02. 13
of gold, a paltry ring | that she did give me, 5.01.147
i gave my love a ring, and made him swear 5.01.170
off, | and swear i lost the ring defending it. 5.01.178
my lord bassanio gave his ring away | unto the 5.01.179
what ring gave you, my lord? 5.01.184
you see my finger | hath not the ring upon it, 5.01.188
ne'er come in your bed | until i see the ring! 5.01.191
if you did know to whom i gave the ring, | if 5.01.193
if you did know for whom i gave the ring, | and 5.01.194
and would conceive for what i gave the ring, 5.01.195
the ring, | and how unwillingly i left the ring, 5.01.196
when nought would be accepted but the ring, 5.01.197
if you had known the virtue of the ring, | or 5.01.199
or half her worthiness that gave the ring, | or 5.01.200
ring, | or your own honor to contain the ring, 5.01.201
you would not then have parted with the ring. 5.01.202
i'll die for't but some woman had the ring! 5.01.208
and begg'd the ring, the which i did deny him, 5.01.212
the ring of me to give the worthy doctor. 5.01.222
which, but for him that had your husband's ring, 5.01.250
here, lord bassanio, swear to keep this ring. 5.01.256
for, by this ring, the doctor lay with me. 5.01.259
thing | so sore, as keeping safe nerissa's ring. 5.01.307
he that runs fastest gets the ring. SHR 1.01.140 P
sirrah, and you'll not knock, i'll ring it. 1.02. 16
bring | their fiery torcher his diurnal ring, AWW 2.01.162
"when thou canst get the ring upon my finger, 3.02. 57 P
a ring the county wears, | that downward hath 3.07. 22
this ring he holds | in most rich choice; 3.07. 25
ere she seems as won, | desires this ring; 3.07. 32
give me that ring. 4.02. 39
mine honor's such a ring, | my chastity's the 4.02. 45
here, take my ring! 4.02. 51
when back again this ring shall be deliver'd; 4.02. 60
finger in the night i'll put | another ring, 4.02. 62
he hath given her his monumental ring, and 4.03. 17 P
such a ring as this, | the last that e'er i took 5.03. 78
this ring was mine, and, when i gave it helen, 5.03. 83
you to take it so, | the ring was never hers. 5.03. 89
and would never | receive the ring again. 5.03.101
mystery more science | than i have in this ring. 5.03.104
win me to believe, | more than to see this ring. 5.03.120
if you shall prove | this ring was ever hers, 5.03.125
o, behold this ring, | whose high respect and 5.03.191
she hath that ring of yours. 5.03.209
she got the ring, | and i had that which any 5.03.217
send for your ring, i will return it home, | and 5.03.223
what ring was yours, i pray you? 5.03.225
know you this ring? this ring was his of late. 5.03.227
know you this ring? this ring was his of late. 5.03.227
my lord, i do confess the ring was hers. 5.03.231
this ring you say was yours? 5.03.270
this ring was mine, i gave it his first wife. 5.03.279
thou tell'st me where thou hadst this ring, 5.03.283
the jeweller that owes the ring is sent for, 5.03.296
there is your ring, | and, look you, here's your 5.03.310
"when from my finger you can get this ring | and 5.03.312
he left this ring behind him, | would i or not. TN 1.05.301
she returns this ring to you, sir. 2.02. 5 P
she took the ring of me, i'll none of it. 2.02. 12 P
i left no ring with her. 2.02. 17
none of my lord's ring? 2.02. 24
you did here, | a ring in chase of you; 3.01.113
rejoice, you men of angiers, ring your bells, JN 2.01.312
and ring these fingers with thy household worms, 3.04. 31
hold, take my ring. R2 2.02. 92
i know not how oft, that that ring was copper! 1H4 3.03. 84 P
yea, if he said my ring was copper. 3.03.142 P
such order that thy friends shall ring for thee. 2H4 3.02.186 P
and bid the merry bells ring to thine ear | that 4.05.111
why ring not out the bells aloud throughout the 1H6 1.06. 11
and mine shall ring thy dire departure out. 4.02. 41
ring bells aloud, burn bonfires clear and bright 2H6 5.01. 3
vouchsafe to wear this ring. R3 1.02.201
look how my ring encompasseth thy finger, | even 1.02.203
render you no remedy, this ring | deliver them, H8 5.01.150
by virtue of that ring, i take my cause | out of 5.02.134
this is the king's ring. 5.02.137
'tis the right ring, by heav'n! 5.02.138
when that a ring of greeks have /hemm'd thee in, TRO 4.05.193
and rouse the prince, and ring a hunter's peal, TIT 2.02. 5
a precious ring that lightens all this hole, 2.03.227
weed, | no mournful bell shall ring her burial, 5.03.197
give this ring to my true knight, | and bid him ROM 3.02.142
here, sir, a ring she bid me give you, sir. 3.03.163
thence from her dead finger | a precious ring — 5.03. 31
a ring that i must use | in dear employment — 5.03. 31
then make a ring about the corpse of caesar, JC 3.02.158
a ring, stand round. 3.02.164
ring the alarum–bell! MAC 2.03. 74
ring the bell. 2.03. 80
sing, | like elves and fairies in a ring, 4.01. 42
ring the alarum–bell! 5.05. 50
uncurrent gold, be not crack'd within the ring. HAM 2.02.428
is this a prologue, or the posy of a ring? 3.02.152
(as fear not but you shall), show her this ring, LR 3.01. 47
your ring may be stol'n too: CYM 1.04. 90
notwithstanding, i fear not my ring. 1.04. 98
pawn the moi'ty of my estate to your ring, which 1.04.109
will lay you ten /thousand ducats to your ring, 1.04.128
my ring i hold dear as my finger, 'tis part of 1.04.133
here's my ring. 1.04.146
was mine in britain, for the ring is won. 2.04. 45
winner of her honor, | together with your ring; 2.04. 54
tasted her in bed, my hand | and ring is yours; 2.04. 58
and take your ring again, 'tis not yet won. 2.04.114
back my ring! 2.04.118
'tis true — nay, keep the ring — 'tis true. 2.04.123
gentleman may render | of whom he had this ring. 5.05.136
by villainy | i got this ring. 5.05.143
in suit the place of 's bed and win this ring 5.05.185
than i did truly find her, stakes this ring, 5.05.188
but your ring first, | and here the bracelet of 5.05.415
the king my father gave you such a ring. PER 5.03. 39
be bold to ring the bell. TNK 3.02. 20
crack'd many a ring of posied gold and bone, LC 45
RING–CARRIER 1 FR 0.0001 REL FR 0 V 1
and your courtesy, for a ring–carrier! AWW 3.05. 92
RING'D 1 FR 0.0001 REL FR 1 V 0
talbot, | who, ring'd about with bold adversity, 1H6 4.04. 14
RINGING 4 FR 0.0004 REL FR 3 V 1
sir, which i caught with ringing in the king's 2H4 3.02.182
thy old groans yet ringing in mine ancient ears; ROM 2.03. 74
once set on ringing, with his own weight goes; LUC 1494
merit praise, | by ringing in thy lady's ear. PP 18.16
RINGLEADER 1 FR 0.0001 REL FR 1 V 0
the ringleader and head of all this rout, | have 2H6 2.01.166
RINGLETS 2 FR 0.0002 REL FR 2 V 0
by moonshine do the green sour ringlets make, TMP 5.01. 37
to dance our ringlets to the whistling wind, MND 2.01. 86
RING'S 1 FR 0.0001 REL FR 1 V 0
is his wife, | that ring's a thousand proofs. AWW 5.03.199
RINGS* 18 FR 0.0020 REL FR 15 V 3
in their houses, bearing thence | rings, jewels, ERR 5.01.144
than the bell rings and the widow weeps. ADO 5.02. 79
her fantasy | with bracelets of thy hair, rings, MND 1.01. 33
that they did give the rings away to men; MV 4.02. 16
nor master would take aught | but the two rings. 5.01.184
goldsmiths' wives, and conn'd them out of rings? AYL 3.02.272
in sweet clothes, rings put upon his fingers, SHR in.1. 38
we will have rings and things, and fine array; 2.01.323
with silken coats and caps, and golden rings, 4.03. 55
strength'ned by interchangement of your rings, TN 5.01.159
but a handkerchief and rings of his that paulina WT 5.02. 66
habit | met i my father with his bleeding rings, LR 5.03.190
who's that which rings the bell? OTH 2.03.161
rings she made | of rushes that grew by, and to TNK 4.01. 88
this dismal cry rings sadly in her ear, VEN 889
then little strength rings out the doleful knell LUC 1495
no deal, | my wether's bell rings doleful knell, PP 17.18
tearing of papers, breaking rings a–twain, LC 6
RINGWOOD 1 FR 0.0001 REL FR 1 V 0
sir actaeon he, with ringwood at thy heels — WIV 2.01.118
RINSING *(see wrenching*, wrinching)*
RIOT 16 FR 0.0018 REL FR 12 V 4
the council shall hear it, it is a riot. WIV 1.01. 35
it is not meet the council hear a riot; 1.01. 36
there is no fear of got in a riot. 1.01. 37
to hear the fear of got, and not to hear a riot. 1.01. 39
"the riot of the tipsy bacchanals, | tearing the MND 5.01. 48
and make a riot on the gentle brow | of true JN 3.01.247
his rash fierce blaze of riot cannot last, | for R2 2.01. 33
see riot and dishonor stain the brow | of my 1H4 1.01. 85
for when his headstrong riot hath no curb, 2H4 4.04. 62
what wilt thou do when riot is thy care? 4.05.135
to maintain it, | nor cease his flow of riot. TIM 2.02. 3
they may strive, | and drown themselves in riot! 4.01. 28
wouldst have plung'd thyself | in general riot, 4.03.256
ever you can make, | whose discipline is riot. STM II.C 113
"it shall be sparing, and too full of riot, VEN 1147
who lead thee in their riot even there | where SON 41.11
RIOTER 1 FR 0.0001 REL FR 1 V 0
he's a sworn rioter; TIM 3.05. 67
RIOTING 1 FR 0.0001 REL FR 1 V 0
when rioting in alexandria you | did pocket up ANT 2.02. 72
RIOTOUS 11 FR 0.0012 REL FR 11 V 0
save that his riotous youth with dangerous sense MM 4.04. 29
and therefore shall it charm thy riotous tongue. 2H6 4.01. 64
who slew to–day a riotous gentleman | lately R3 2.01.101
have been oppress'd | with riotous feeders, when TIM 2.02.159
haste | than young laertes, in a riotous head, HAM 4.05.102
his knights grow riotous, and himself upbraids LR 1.03. 6
with their manners, | shows like a riotous inn. 1.04.244
was he not companion with the riotous knights 2.01. 94
horse goes to't | with a more riotous appetite. 4.06.123
riotous madness, | to be entangled with those ANT 1.03. 29
then what a rough and riotous charge have you STM II.C 55
RIOTS 7 FR 0.0008 REL FR 7 V 0
my riots past, my wild societies, | and tells me WIV 3.04. 8
when that my care could not withhold thy riots, 2H4 4.05.134
wast, | the tutor and the feeder of my riots. 5.05. 62
his hours fill'd up with riots, banquets, sports H5 1.01. 56
forth | in rank and not–to–be–endur'd riots. LR 1.04.204
she have restrain'd the riots of your followers, 2.04.143
with their superfluous riots, hear these tears! PER 1.04. 54
RIP 2 FR 0.0002 REL FR 2 V 0
to know our enemies' minds, we rip their hearts, LR 4.06.260
from thy heart, or rip | thy heart to find it. CYM 3.05. 86
/RIPE 2 FR 0.0002 REL FR 2 V 0
/play'd /on /her /ripe /lip /seem'd /not /to LR 4.03. 20
wench, | even /ripe for marriage /rite; PER 4.ch. 17
RIPE 42 FR 0.0047 REL FR 36 V 6

and trinculo is reeling ripe. TMP 5.01.279
his head unmellowed, but his judgment ripe; TGV 2.04. 70
and when the doctor spies his vantage ripe, | to WIV 4.06. 43
in blood, ripe as the pomewater, who now hangeth LLL 4.02. 4 P
things growing are not ripe until their season, MND 2.02.117
so i, being young, till now ripe not to reason; 2.02.118
o, how ripe in show | thy lips, those kissing 3.02.139
there is a brief how many sports are ripe. 5.01. 42
yet, to supply the ripe wants of my friend, MV 1.03. 63
and so, from hour to hour, we ripe and ripe, AYL 2.07. 26
and so, from hour to hour, we ripe and ripe, 2.07. 26
for you'll be rotten ere you be half ripe, and 3.02.120 P
favor, and bestows himself | like a ripe sister; 4.03. 87
a ripe age. is thy name william? 5.01. 20 P
boy, with me, my thoughts are ripe in mischief. TN 5.01.129
what occasion now | reveals before 'tis ripe, 5.01.154
and love as mine), | without ripe moving to't? WT 1.02.332
that yon green boy shall have no sun to ripe JN 2.01.472
his passion is so ripe, it needs must break. 4.02. 79
who, when they see the hour's ripe on earth, R2 1.02. 7
some unborn sorrow, ripe in fortune's womb, | is 2.02. 10
when time is ripe, which will be suddenly, 1H4 1.03.294
he is retir'd, to ripe his growing fortunes, 2H4 4.01. 13
thee with my honors | before thy hour be ripe? 4.05. 96
ripe for exploits and mighty enterprises. H5 1.02.121
good to bruise an injury till it were full ripe. 3.06.123 P
o, let them keep it till thy sins be ripe, | and R3 1.03.218
crown, | as the ripe revenue and due of birth, 3.07.158
he was a scholar, and a ripe and good one; H8 4.02. 51
and there the strawy greeks, ripe for his edge, TRO 5.05. 24
that they are in a ripe aptness to take all COR 4.03. 23 P
the tartness of his face sours ripe grapes. 5.04. 18 P
ere we may think her ripe to be a bride. ROM 1.02. 11
fevers heap | on athens, ripe for stroke! TIM 4.01. 23
our legions are brimful, our cause is ripe: JC 4.03.215
macbeth | is ripe for shaking, and the pow'rs MAC 4.03.238
work him | to an exploit, now ripe in my device, HAM 4.07. 64
fruits that blossom first will first be ripe. OTH 2.03.377
when wit's more ripe, accept my rhymes, | and PER 1.ch. 12
if i were ripe for your persuasion, you | have TNK 1.03. 91
his complexion | is, as a ripe grape, ruddy. 4.02. 96
that did my ripe thoughts in my brain inhearse, SON 86. 3
RIPELY 1 FR 0.0001 REL FR 1 V 0 P
it fits us therefore ripely | our chariots and CYM 3.05. 22
RIPEN 3 FR 0.0003 REL FR 3 V 0 P
which elder days shall ripen and confirm | to R2 2.03. 43
and wholesome berries thrive and ripen best H5 1.01. 61
earth, | and ripen justice in this commonweal. TIT 1.01.227
RIPENED 4 FR 0.0004 REL FR 4 V 0 P
and with ripened time | unfold the evil which is MM 5.01.116
bower, | where honeysuckles, ripened by the sun, ADO 3.01. 8
were growing time once ripened to my will. 1H6 2.04. 99
and, in his full and ripened years, himself, R3 2.03. 14
RIPENESS 2 FR 0.0002 REL FR 2 V 0 P
blessings, | which time shall bring to ripeness. H8 5.04. 20
even as their coming hither, | ripeness is all. LR 5.02. 11
RIPENING 1 FR 0.0001 REL FR 1 V 0 P
this bud of love, by summer's ripening breath, ROM 2.02.121
RIPENS 3 FR 0.0003 REL FR 3 V 0 P
and, as my fortune ripens with thy love, | it R2 2.03. 48
heart | and ripens in the sunshine of his favor, 2H4 4.02. 12
it ripens towards it. ANT 2.07. 97
RIPER 3 FR 0.0003 REL FR 3 V 0 P
a little riper and more lusty red | than that AYL 3.05.121
die, | but as the riper should by time decease, SON 1. 3
and stops /her pipe in growth of riper days: 102. 8
RIPE–RED 1 FR 0.0001 REL FR 1 V 0 P
bring him mulberries and ripe–red cherries: VEN 1103
RIPEST 2 FR 0.0002 REL FR 2 V 0 P
the ripest fruit first falls, and so doth he; R2 2.01.153
now humble as the ripest mulberry | that will COR 3.02. 79
RIPING 1 FR 0.0001 REL FR 1 V 0 P
but stay the very riping of the time; MV 2.08. 40
RIPP'D 3 FR 0.0003 REL FR 3 V 0 P
was from his mother's womb | untimely ripp'd. MAC 5.08. 16
than to hang by th' walls, | i must be ripp'd. CYM 3.04. 53
my throes, | that from me was posthumus ripp'd, 5.04. 45
RIPPING 1 FR 0.0001 REL FR 1 V 0 P
ripping up the womb | of your dear mother JN 5.02.152
RIPS 1 FR 0.0001 REL FR 1 V 0 P
that which rips my bosom | almost to th' heart's TNK 1.02. 61
/RISE 1 FR 0.0001 REL FR 1 V 0 P
/that /rise /thus /nimbly /by /a /true /king's R2 4.01.318
RISE 89 FR 0.0100 REL FR 81 V 8 P
go to bed when she list, rise when she list, all WIV 2.02.119 P
some rise by sin, and some by virtue fall; MM 2.01. 38
you must rise and be hang'd, master barnardine! 4.03. 21 P
be so good, sir, to rise and be put to death. 4.03. 27 P
and never rise until my tears and prayers | have ERR 5.01.115
wake my cousin beatrice, and desire her to rise. ADO 3.04. 2 P
rise, grumio, rise, we will compound this SHR 1.02. 27
grumio, rise, we will compound this quarrel. 1.02. 27
kneel thou down philip, but rise more great, JN 1.01.161
an' never will i rise up from the ground | till R2 5.02.116
my mouth, | unless a pardon ere i rise or speak. 5.03. 32
rise up, good aunt. 5.03. 92
his weary joints would gladly rise, i know, 5.03.105
die, and never rise | to do him wrong or any way 1H4 1.03. 74
rise from the ground like feathered mercury, 4.01.106
how if he should counterfeit too and rise? 5.04.123 P
why may not he rise as well as i? 5.04.126 P
let me no more from this obedience rise, | which 2H4 4.05.146
but i will rise there with so full a glory H5 1.02.278
but like a lackey, from the rise to set, 4.01.272
doth rise and help hyperion to his horse, | and 4.01.275
make him burst his lead and rise from death. 1H6 1.01. 64
the other yet may rise against their force. 2.01. 32
rise, richard, like a true plantagenet, | and 3.01.171
and rise created princely duke of york. 3.01.172
the commons haply rise, to save his life; 2H6 3.01.240
rise up sir john mortimer. 4.02.120 P
rise up a knight. 5.01. 78
with whom the kentishmen will willingly rise; 3H6 1.02. 41
more, | but that i seek occasion how to rise, 1.02. 45
ere my knee rise from the earth's cold face, | i 2.03. 35
the scatt'red foe that hopes to rise again; 2.06. 93
ay, now begins a second storm to rise, | for 3.03. 47
i will not rise, unless your highness hear me. R3 2.01. 98
go, bid thy master rise and come to me, | and we 3.02. 31
the rest that love me, rise, and follow me. 3.04. 79
rise, and lend thine ear. 4.02. 79
the red wine first must rise | in their fair H8 1.04. 43
and fearing he would rise (he was so virtuous), 2.02.127
found thee a way, out of his wrack, to rise in; 3.02.437
shall star–like rise as great in fame as she was 5.04. 46
your fair sword, | you bid them rise and live. TRO 5.03. 42
plains, | let titan rise as early as he dare, 5.10. 25
who's like to rise, | who thrives, and who COR 1.01.192
'twas very faintly he said, "rise"; 5.01. 66
rise, marcus, rise. TIT 1.01.383
rise, marcus, rise. 1.01.383
rise, titus, rise, my empress hath prevail'd. 1.01.459
rise, titus, rise, my empress hath prevail'd. 1.01.459
doth rise and fall between thy rosed lips, 2.04. 24
for juliet's sake, for her sake, rise and stand; ROM 3.03. 89
taste, touch, all, pleas'd from thy table rise; TIM 1.02.126
wherefore rise you now? JC 2.01.234
move | the stones of rome to rise and mutiny. 3.02.230
early to–morrow will we rise, and hence. 4.03.230
as from your graves rise up, and walk like MAC 2.03. 79
gentlemen, rise, his highness is not well. 3.04. 51
but now they rise again | with twenty mortal 3.04. 79
dead, rise never till the wood | of birnan rise, 4.01. 97
rise never till the wood | of birnan rise, and 4.01. 98
the field, i have seen her rise from her bed, 5.01. 5 P
/foul deeds will rise, | though all the earth HAM 1.02.256
lo here i lie, | never to rise again. 5.02.319
you rise to play, and go to bed to work. OTH 2.01.115
the town will rise. 2.03.162
do not rise yet. 3.03.462
say to me, whose fortunes shall rise higher, ANT 2.03. 16
merit thou wilt hear me, | rise from thy stool. 2.07. 56
to business that we love we rise betime, | and 4.04. 20
i pray you rise, rise, egypt. 5.02.115
i pray you rise, rise, egypt. 5.02.115
rise, and fade. CYM 5.04.106
rise, prithee rise. PER 1.02. 60
rise, prithee rise. 1.02. 60
alike to groves, being topp'd, they higher rise. 1.04. 9
arise, i pray you, rise. 1.04. 98
this day i'll rise, or else add ill to ill. 2.01.166
rise, th' art my child. 5.01.213
sad lady, rise. TNK 1.01. 35
let us rise | and bow before the goddess. 5.01.135
that hostler | must rise betime that cozens him. 5.02. 60
god himself installs, | but rise 'gainst god? STM II.C 106
and she by her good will | will never rise, so VEN 480
nay, do not struggle, for thou shalt not rise. 710
o, how her fear did make her color rise! LUC 257
wounding itself to death, rise up and fall, 466
the morning rise | doth cite each moving sense PP 14.14
rise, resty muse, my love's sweet face survey, SON 100. 9
her "love" for whose dear love i rise and fall. 151.14
RISEN 5 FR 0.0005 REL FR 4 V 1 P
speak, | and sits as one new risen from a dream. SHR 4.01.186
join'd, | a holy prophetess new risen up, | is 1H6 1.04.102
the other side a' th' city is risen; COR 1.01. 47 P
ere i was risen from the place that showed | my LR 2.04. 29
know that our griefs are risen to the top, | and PER 2.04. 23
RISES 7 FR 0.0008 REL FR 4 V 3 P
the humor rises; WIV 1.03. 56 P
to bed wi' th' sun | and with him rises weeping. WT 4.04.106
the manner of his gait, | he rises on the toe. TRO 4.05. 15
is this | that rises like the issue of a king, MAC 4.01. 87
the king rises. HAM 3.02.265 P
my gorge rises at it. 5.01.187 P
the younger rises when the old doth fall. LR 3.03. 25
RISETH 1 FR 0.0001 REL FR 1 V 0 P
who riseth from a feast | with that keen MV 2.06. 8
/RISING 1 FR 0.0001 REL FR 1 V 0 P
/doth /enlarge /his /rising /with /the /blood 2H4 1.01.204
RISING 20 FR 0.0022 REL FR 17 V 3 P
so their rising senses | begin to chase the TMP 5.01. 66
with me | upon the rising of the mountain foot TGV 5.02. 46
hard | against the steep–up rising of the hill? LLL 4.01. 2
sort, | rising and cawing at the gun's report, MND 3.02. 22
for it shall strew the footsteps of my rising. JN 1.01.216
and, rising so again, | when i shall meet him in 3.04. 86
shall see us rising in our throne, the east, R2 3.02. 50
with | a rising sigh he wisheth you in heaven. 1H4 3.01. 10
from the rising of the lark to the lodging of H5 3.07. 32 P
vain, | as hating thee, /are rising up in arms; 2H6 4.01. 93
and stop the rising of blood–sucking sighs, 3H6 4.04. 22
so excellent in art, and still so rising, | that H8 4.02. 62
they are rising, they are rising. COR 4.05.233 P
they are rising, they are rising. 4.05.234 P
even from /hyperion's rising in the east, TIT 5.02. 56
o me, my heart! my rising heart! but down! LR 2.04.121
i see two comforts rising, two mere blessings, TNK 2.02. 58
rising 'gainst him that god himself installs, STM II.C 105
round rising hillocks, brakes obscure and rough, VEN 237
but, rising at thy name, doth point out thee SON 151. 9
/RITE 2 FR 0.0002 REL FR 2 V 0 P
wench, | even /ripe for marriage /rite; PER 4.ch. 17
to say | the perfect ceremony of love's /rite, SON 23. 6
RITE 10 FR 0.0011 REL FR 10 V 0 P
may | with full and holy rite be minist'red, TMP 4.01. 17
yearly will i do this rite. ADO 5.03. 23
they rose up early to observe | the rite of may; MND 4.01.133
the great prerogative and rite of love, | which, AWW 2.04. 41
no funeral rite, nor man in mourning weed, | no TIT 5.03.196
where and what time thou wilt perform the rite, ROM 2.02.146
to cross my obsequies and true love's rite? 5.03. 20
bones, | no noble rite nor formal ostentation — HAM 4.05.216
the soldiers' music and the rite of war | speak 5.02.399
this is a solemn rite | they owe bloom'd may, TNK 3.01. 2
RITES 21 FR 0.0023 REL FR 20 V 1 P
goes on crutches till love have all his rites. ADO 2.01.358 P
and do all rites | that appertain unto a burial. 4.01.207
when after that the holy rites are ended, | i'll 5.04. 68
straight shall our nuptial rites be solemniz'd; MV 2.09. 6
we'll begin these rites, | as we do trust AYL 5.04.197
to speak the ceremonial rites of marriage? SHR 3.02. 6
the rites of marriage shall be solemniz'd. JN 2.01.539
by that, and all the rites of knighthood else, R2 1.01. 75
for doing these fair rites of tenderness. 1H4 5.04. 98
do we all holy rites: H5 4.08.122
i must not yield to any rites of love, | for my 1H6 1.02.113
god give us leisure for these rites of love! R3 5.03.101
stand gracious to the rites that we intend! TIT 1.01. 78
father, how we have perform'd | our roman rites. 1.01.143
there shall we consummate our spousal rites. 1.01.337
lovers can see to do their amorous rites | by ROM 3.02. 8
have all true rites and lawful ceremonies. JC 3.01.241
use him, | with all respect and rites of burial. 5.05. 77
and with such maimed rites? HAM 5.01.219
the rites for why i love him are bereft me, OTH 1.03.257
than a gap | should be in their dear rites, we TNK 1.04. 9
RIVAGE 1 FR 0.0001 REL FR 1 V 0 P
but think | you stand upon the rivage and behold H5 3.pr. 14
RIVAL 5 FR 0.0005 REL FR 5 V 0 P
my foolish rival, that her father likes | (only TGV 2.04.174
and take this shadow up, | for 'tis thy rival. 4.04.198
i know you two are rival enemies. MND 4.01.142
means | to hold a rival place with one of them, MV 1.01.174
peace, grumio, it is the rival of my love. SHR 1.02.141
RIVAL–HATING 1 FR 0.0001 REL FR 1 V 0 P
with rival–hating envy, set on you | to wake our R2 1.03.131
RIVALITY 1 FR 0.0001 REL FR 0 V 1 P
presently denied him rivality, would not let him ANT 3.05. 8 P
RIVALL'D 1 FR 0.0001 REL FR 1 V 0 P
with this king | hath rivall'd for our daughter. LR 1.01.191
RIVALS 8 FR 0.0009 REL FR 7 V 1 P
you both are rivals, and love hermia; MND 3.02.155
and now both rivals, to mock helena. 3.02.156
and lead these testy rivals so astray | as one 3.02.358
mistress and be happy rivals in bianca's love, SHR 1.01.117 P
more, | suitors to her and rivals in my love; 1.02.122
slaves and servants | translates his rivals. TIM 1.01. 72
the rivals of my watch, bid them make haste. HAM 1.01. 13
great rivals in our youngest daughter's love, LR 1.01. 46
RIV'D 2 FR 0.0002 REL FR 2 V 0 P
the scolding winds | have riv'd the knotty oaks, JC 1.03. 6
brutus hath riv'd my heart. 4.03. 85
RIVE 6 FR 0.0006 REL FR 6 V 0 P
sacrament | to rive their dangerous artillery 1H6 4.02. 29
as wedged with a sigh, would rive in twain, TRO 1.01. 35
blunt wedges rive hard knots; 1.03.316
with a bolt | that should but rive an oak. COR 5.03.153
rive your concealing continents, and cry | these LR 3.02. 58
the soul and body rive not more in parting ANT 4.13. 5
RIVELL'D 1 FR 0.0001 REL FR 0 V 1 P
and the rivell'd fee–simple of the tetter, take TRO 5.01. 22 P
RIVER 25 FR 0.0028 REL FR 17 V 8 P
man, if the river were dry, i am able to fill it TGV 2.03. 52 P
rogues slighted me into the river with as little WIV 3.05. 9 P
groping for trouts in a peculiar river. MM 1.02. 90 P
hath every pelting river made so proud | that MND 2.01. 91
and apennines, | the pyrenean and the river po, JN 1.01.203
like a proud river peering o'er his bounds? 3.01. 23
see how this river comes me cranking in, | and 1H4 3.01. 97
the river hath thrice flowed, no ebb between, 2H4 4.04.125
and did seat the french | beyond the river sala, H5 1.02. 63
'tis certain he hath pass'd the river somme. 3.05. 1
beyond the river we'll encamp ourselves, | and 3.06.171
there is a river in macedon, and there is also 4.07. 26 P
and there is also moreover a river at monmouth. 4.07. 27 P
my prains what is the name of the other river; 4.07. 29 P
should the approach of this wild river break, H8 3.02.198
as the tercel, for all the ducks i' th' river. TRO 3.02. 53 P
fly not, for shouldst thou take the river styx, 5.04. 19
alas, a crimson river of warm blood, | like to a TIT 2.04. 22
breath, | no, nor the fruitful river in the eye, HAM 1.02. 80
purs'd up his heart upon the river of cydnus. ANT 2.02.187 P
give me mine angle, we'll to th' river; 2.05. 10
rain added to a river that is rank | perforce VEN 71
an oven that is stopp'd, or river stay'd, 331
jet, | which one by one she in a river threw, LC 38
each cheek a river running from a fount | with 283
RIVERS 28 FR 0.0031 REL FR 27 V 1 P
"to shallow rivers, to whose falls | melodious WIV 3.01. 17
"to shallow rivers, to whose falls —" | heaven 3.01. 29
you say he has been thrown in the rivers, and 4.04. 20 P
it seem | like rivers of remorse and innocency. JN 4.03.110
nor let my kingdom's rivers take their course 5.07. 38
which makes the silver rivers drown their shores R2 3.02.107
why, brother rivers, are you yet to learn | what 3H6 4.04. 2
which, being suffer'd, rivers cannot quench. 4.08. 8
she may, lord rivers! R3 1.03. 92
and, rivers, so were you. 1.03.128
with thy scorns drew'st rivers from his eyes, 1.03.175
rivers and dorset, you were standers–by, | and 1.03.209
and withal whet me | to be reveng'd on rivers, 1.03.332
/hastings and rivers, take each other's hand, 2.01. 7
of you, and you, lord rivers, and of dorset, 2.01. 67
my uncle rivers talk'd how i did grow | more 2.04. 11
lord rivers and lord grey are sent to pomfret, 2.04. 42
and so falls it out | with rivers, vaughan, grey 3.02. 65
th' adulterate hastings, rivers, vaughan, grey, 4.04. 69
where is the gentle rivers, vaughan, grey? 4.04.147
her uncle rivers, ay (and for her sake!), 4.04.282
and edward's children, grey and rivers, | holy 5.01. 3
soul to–morrow, | rivers, that died at pomfret! 5.03.140
i send it through the rivers of your blood, COR 1.01.135
with plenteous rivers and wide–skirted meads, LR 1.01. 65
the dish, | poor tributary rivers as sweet fish. CYM 4.02. 36
it doth divide | in two slow rivers, that the LUC 1738
by shallow rivers, by whose falls | melodious PP 19. 7
RIVET 2 FR 0.0002 REL FR 2 V 0 P
on his gorget, | shake in and out the rivet; TRO 1.03.175
note, | for i mine eyes will rivet to his face, HAM 3.02. 85
RIVETED 3 FR 0.0003 REL FR 3 V 0 P
and so riveted with faith unto your flesh. MV 5.01.169
early though't be, have on their riveted trim, ANT 4.04. 22
why should i write this down, that's riveted, CYM 2.02. 43
RIVETS 2 FR 0.0002 REL FR 2 V 0 P
knights, | with busy hammers closing rivets up, H5 4.pr. 13
i'll frush it and unlock the rivets all, | but TRO 5.06. 29
RIVO 1 FR 0.0001 REL FR 0 V 1 P
"rivo!" 1H4 2.04.111 P
ROAD 14 FR 0.0015 REL FR 10 V 4 P
my father at the road | expects my coming, there TGV 1.01. 53
i must unto the road, to disembark | some 2.04.187

go hie thee presently, post to the road, | and ERR 3.02.147
run smoothly in the even road of a blank verse, ADO 5.02. 34 P
wall, | even in the force and road of casualty. MV 2.09. 30
certain that my ships | are safely come to road. 5.01.288
enforce | a thievish living on the common road? AYL 2.03. 33
an argosy | that now is lying in marsellis road. SHR 2.01.375
villainous house in all london road for fleas. 1H4 2.01. 15 P
this doll tearsheet should be some road. 2H4 2.02.166 P
who will make road upon us | with all advantages H5 1.02.138
shall prompt them, to make road | upon 's again. COR 3.01. 5
you know the very road into his kindness, | and 5.01. 59
but i am out of the road of rutting for ever. PER 4.05. 9 P
ROADS 2 FR 0.0002 REL FR 2 V 0 P
piring in maps for ports and piers and roads; MV 1.01. 19
at last, with easy roads, he came to leicester, H8 4.02. 17
ROAD-WAY 1 FR 0.0001 REL FR 0 V 1 P
the world keeps the road-way better than thine: 2H4 2.02. 58 P
ROAM 3 FR 0.0003 REL FR 3 V 0 P
say, shall the current of our right roam on? JN 2.01.335
and lusty lads roam here and there | so merrily, 2H4 5.03. 20
roam thither then. 1H6 3.01. 51
ROAMING 3 FR 0.0003 REL FR 3 V 0 P
roaming clean through the bounds of asia, | and, ERR 1.01.133
or daphne roaming through a thorny wood, SHR in.2. 57
"o mistress mine, where are you roaming? TN 2.03. 39
ROAN* 16 FR 0.0018 REL FR 15 V 1 P
when bullingbrook rode on roan barbary, | that R2 5.05. 78
what horse? roan? a crop-ear, is it not? 1H4 2.03. 69
that roan shall be my throne. 2.03. 70
"give my roan horse a drench," says he, and 2.04.107 P
and in a captive chariot into roan | bring him H5 3.05. 54
prince dolphin, you shall stay with us in roan. 3.05. 64
is roan yielded up? 1H6 1.01. 65
these are the city-gates, the gates of roan, 3.02. 1
city, | and we be lords and rulers over roan, 3.02. 11
now, roan, i'll shake thy bulwarks to the ground 3.02. 17
and once again we'll sleep secure in roan. 3.02. 19
torch | that joineth roan unto her countrymen, 3.02. 27
here will i sit before the walls of roan | and 3.02. 91
roan hangs her head for grief | that such a 3.02.124
but see his exequies fulfill'd in roan. 3.02.133
nor grieve that roan is so recovered: 3.03. 2
ROAR* 30 FR 0.0034 REL FR 20 V 10 P
you have | put the wild waters in this roar, TMP 1.02. 2
make thee roar | that beasts shall tremble at 1.02.370
sure it was the roar | of a whole herd of lions. 2.01.315
hark, they roar! 4.01.261
thus dost thou hear the nemean lion roar LLL 4.01. 88
i will roar, that i will do any man's heart good MND 1.02. 70 P
i will roar, that i will make the duke say, "let 1.02. 71 P
i will make the duke say, "let him roar again; 1.02. 72 P
let him roar again." 1.02. 73 P
voice so that i will roar you as gently as any 1.02. 82 P
i will roar you and 'twere any nightingale. 1.02. 83 P
neigh, and bark, and grunt, and roar, and burn, 3.01.110
when lion rough in wildest rage doth roar. 5.01.222
have i not in my time heard lions roar? SHR 1.02.200
o, tremble! for you hear the lion roar. JN 2.01.294
and if the devil come and roar for them, | i 1H4 1.03.125
with | king cerberus, and let the welkin roar. 2H4 2.04.168
come prick bullcalf till he roar again. 3.02.176 P
what, dost thou roar before thou art prick'd? 3.02.178 P
and makes him roar these accusations forth. 1H6 3.01. 40
gapes, hell burns, fiends roar, saints pray, R3 4.04. 75
is this a place to roar in? H8 5.03. 7 P
but i fear | they'll roar him in again. COR 4.06.124
as we shall make our griefs and clamor roar MAC 1.07. 78
fadoms to the sea | and hears it roar beneath. HAM 1.04. 78
that were wont to set the table on a roar? 5.01.191 P
nay, lay thee down and roar; OTH 5.02.198
me spurn the sea | if it could so roar to me. CYM 5.05.295
could i rage and roar | as doth the sea she lies PER 3.03. 10
let all the dukes and all the devils roar, | he TNK 2.06. 1
ROAR'D 14 FR 0.0015 REL FR 8 V 6 P
us, | to cry to th' sea, that roar'd to us; TMP 1.02.149
well roar'd, lion. MND 5.01.265 P
i met the ravin lion when he roar'd | with sharp AWW 3.02.117
first, how the poor souls roar'd, and the sea WT 3.03. 99 P
and how the poor gentleman roar'd, and the bear 3.03.100 P
how the fat rogue roar'd! 1H4 2.02.111 P
with as quick dexterity, and roar'd for mercy, 2.04.259 P
and roar'd for mercy, and still run and roar'd, 2.04.260 P
there roar'd the sea, and trumpet-clangor sounds 2H4 5.05. 40
and made the forest tremble when they roar'd. 3H6 5.07. 12
when | some certain of your brethren roar'd, and COR 2.03. 53
tears | he whin'd and roar'd away your victory, 5.06. 97
this torture should be roar'd in dismal hell. ROM 3.02. 44
the torrent roar'd, and we did buffet it | with JC 1.02.107
ROARERS 1 FR 0.0001 REL FR 0 V 1 P
what cares these roarers for the name of king? TMP 1.01. 17 P
ROARING 27 FR 0.0030 REL FR 22 V 5 P
of sulphurous roaring the most mighty neptune TMP 1.02.204
i will plague them all, | even to roaring. 4.01.193
sea and the azur'd vault | set roaring war; 5.01. 44
with strange and several noises | of roaring, 5.01.233
do it extempore, for it is nothing but roaring. MND 1.02. 69 P
enrobe the roaring waters with my silks, | and, MV 1.01. 34
both roaring louder than the sea or weather. WT 3.03.101 P
whose foot spurns back the ocean's roaring tides JN 2.01. 24
talks as familiarly of roaring lions | as maids 2.01.459
so, by a roaring tempest on the flood, | a whole 3.04. 1
as to o'erwalk a current roaring loud | on the 1H4 1.03.192
thee as i fear the roaring of the lion's whelp. 3.03.147 P
more valor than this roaring devil i' th' old H5 4.04. 71 P
have batt'red me like roaring cannon-shot, | and 1H6 3.03. 79
from the tongue of roaring typhon dropp'd, TRO 1.03.160
roaring for troilus, who hath done to-day | mad 5.05. 37
and, in roaring for a chamber-pot, dismiss the COR 2.01. 76 P
chain me with roaring bears, | or hide me ROM 4.01. 80
far | than empty tigers or the roaring sea. 5.03. 39
of bedlam beggars, who, with roaring voices, LR 2.03. 14
such groans of roaring wind and rain, i never 3.02. 47
but if /thy flight lay toward the roaring sea, 3.04. 10
caesar dead, | he cried almost to roaring; ANT 3.02. 55
in | with oaks unscalable and roaring waters, CYM 3.01. 20
he had not apprehension | of roaring terrors; 4.02.111
torrents whose roaring tyranny and power | i' TNK 1.03. 38
as through an arch the violent roaring tide LUC 1667
ROARS 6 FR 0.0006 REL FR 6 V 0 P
now the hungry /lion roars, | and the wolf MND 5.01.371
yea, mock the lion when 'a roars for prey, | to MV 2.01. 30
but great men tremble when the lion roars, | and 2H6 3.01. 19
hark how troy roars! TRO 5.03. 83
and roars | as doth the lion in the capitol — JC 1.03. 74
that roars so loud and thunders in the index? HAM 3.04. 52
ROAST 5 FR 0.0005 REL FR 3 V 2 P
where he doth nothing but roast malt-worms. 2H4 2.04.334 P
suffolk, the new-made duke that rules the roast, 2H6 1.01.109
come in, tailor, here you may roast your goose. MAC 2.03. 15 P
roast me in sulphur! OTH 5.02.279
he roast eggs! TNK 2.03. 73
ROASTED 5 FR 0.0005 REL FR 3 V 2 P
when roasted crabs hiss in the bowl, | then LLL 5.02.925
bowl, | in very likeness of a roasted crab, MND 2.01. 48
that roasted manningtree ox with the pudding in 1H4 2.04.452 P
roasted in wrath and fire, | and thus o'er-sized HAM 2.02.461
eight wild-boars roasted whole at a breakfast, ANT 2.02.179 P
ROAST-MEAT 1 FR 0.0001 REL FR 0 V 1 P
poop'd him, she made him roast-meat for worms. PER 4.02. 25 P
/ROB 1 FR 0.0001 REL FR 1 V 0 P
/and /rob /in /the /behalf /of /charity. TRO 5.03. 22
ROB 37 FR 0.0041 REL FR 24 V 13 P
when 's god's asleep, he'll rob his bottle. TMP 2.02.151 P
than to fashion a carriage to rob love from any. ADO 1.03. 30 P
didst rob it of some taste of tediousness. MV 2.03. 3
must i rob the law? JN 4.03. 78
mine age, | and rob me of a happy mother's name? R2 5.02. 93
and beat our watch and rob our passengers, 5.03. 9
who, i rob? i a thief? not i, by my faith. 1H4 1.02.138 P
and gadshill shall rob those men that we have 1.02.163 P
have the booty, if you and i do not rob them, 1.02.165 P
i am accurs'd to rob in that thieve's company. 2.02. 10 P
i'll starve ere i'll rob a foot further. 2.02. 21 P
'zounds, will they not rob us? 2.02. 65 P
could thou and i rob the thieves and go merrily 2.02. 94 P
wilt thou rob this leathern-jerkin, 2.04. 69 P
indent, | to rob me of so rich a bottom here. 3.01.104
rob me the exchequer the first thing thou doest, 3.03.183 P
revel the night, rob, murder, and commit | the 2H4 4.05.125
and when the dusky sky began to rob | my 2H6 3.02.104
and i should rob the deathsman of his fee, 3.02.217
drones suck not eagles' blood, but rob beehives. 4.01.109
and like a thief to come to rob my grounds, 4.10. 34
vow | to do a murd'rous deed, to rob a man, | to 5.01.185
glory, | and rob his temples of the diadem, 3H6 1.04.104
business | should rob my bed-mate of my company. TRO 4.01. 6
on martius shall | of his demerits rob cominius. COR 1.01.272
thief of occasion will rob you of a great deal 2.01. 29 P
rather than rob me of the people's hearts! TIT 1.01.207
so should i rob my sweet sons of their fee. 2.03.179
are poison, and he slays | moe than you rob. TIM 4.03.433
love not yourselves, away, | rob one another. 4.03.445
but for your words, they rob the hybla bees, JC 5.01. 34
and yet i know not how conceit may rob | the LR 4.06. 42
i'll rob none but myself, and let me die, CYM 4.02. 15
of these drones, that rob the bee of her honey. PER 2.01. 47 P
i will rob tellus of her weed | to strow thy 4.01. 13
trips, | and all is but to rob thee of a kiss. VEN 723
lurk'd like two thieves, to rob him of his fair. 1086
ROBA 1 FR 0.0001 REL FR 0 V 1 P
she was then a bona roba. 2H4 3.02.205 P
/ROBAS 1 FR 0.0001 REL FR 0 V 1 P
knew where the bona /robas were and had the best 2H4 3.02. 23 P
ROBB'D 26 FR 0.0029 REL FR 22 V 4 P
these three have robb'd me, and this demi-devil TMP 5.01.272
the knight may be robb'd. WIV 4.05. 16 P
i am robb'd, sir, and beaten; WT 4.03. 61 P
what manner of fellow was he that robb'd you? 4.03. 84 P
richard, that robb'd the lion of his heart, JN 2.01. 3
by some damn'd hand was robb'd and ta'en away. 5.01. 41
if he have robb'd these men, | he shall be 1H4 2.04.521
o, harry, thou hast robb'd me of my youth! 5.04. 77
i never robb'd the soldiers of their pay, | nor 2H6 3.01.108
that robb'd my soldiers of their heated spleen; 3H6 2.01.124
have robb'd my strong-knit sinews of their 2.03. 4
these ears (for, where i am robb'd and bound, H8 2.04.147
robb'd this bewailing land | of noble buckingham 3.02.255
hath robb'd many beasts of their particular TRO 1.02. 19 P
devil | that robb'd andronicus of his good hand; TIT 5.01. 41
/'zounds, sir, y' are robb'd! OTH 1.01. 86
the robb'd that smiles steals something from the 1.03.208
he that is robb'd, not wanting what is stol'n, 3.03.342
let him not know't, and he's not robb'd at all. 3.03.343
she has robb'd me of my sword. ANT 4.14. 23
this is his sword, | i robb'd his wound of it; 5.01. 25
envy much | thou hast robb'd me of this deed. CYM 4.02.159
and every beauty robb'd of his effect. VEN 1132
but robb'd and ransack'd by injurious theft. LUC 838
and when the judge is robb'd, the prisoner dies. 1652
robb'd others' beds' revenues of their rents. SON 142. 8
ROBBER 1 FR 0.0001 REL FR 1 V 0 P
thou art a robber, | a law-breaker, a villain. CYM 4.02. 74
ROBBER'S 2 FR 0.0002 REL FR 2 V 0 P
injurious time now with a robber's haste | crams TRO 4.04. 42
with robber's hands my hospitable favors | you LR 3.07. 40
ROBBERS 6 FR 0.0006 REL FR 5 V 1 P
then thieves and robbers range abroad unseen R2 3.02. 39
of money, be assail'd by robbers and die in many H5 4.01.152 P
so true men yield, with robbers so o'ermatch'd. 3H6 1.04. 64
and what makes robbers bold but too much lenity? 2.06. 22
large-handed robbers your grave masters are, TIM 4.01. 11
of all this world | but for supporting robbers, JC 4.03. 23
ROBBERY 6 FR 0.0006 REL FR 4 V 2 P
thieves for their robbery have authority | when MM 2.02.175
have in this robbery lost three hundred marks. 1H4 2.04.520
hal, to the news at court for the robbery, lad, 3.03.175 P
gentle bosom of peace with pillage and robbery. H5 4.01.166 P
thou think | i'll grace thee with that robbery, COR 5.06. 88
a storm or robbery (call it what you will) CYM 3.03. 62
ROBBING 6 FR 0.0006 REL FR 4 V 2 P
to watch, like one that fears robbing; TGV 2.01. 25 P
but by the robbing of the banish'd duke. R2 2.01.261
is like to be executed for robbing a church, one H5 3.06.101 P
unless by robbing of your friends and us. 2H6 4.08. 40
what tell'st thou me of robbing? OTH 1.01.105
green, | robbing no old to dress his beauty new, SON 68.12
ROBB'RY 3 FR 0.0003 REL FR 2 V 1 P
he that was in question for the robb'ry? 2H4 1.02. 60 P
i do forgive thy robb'ry, gentle thief, SON 40. 9
and to his robb'ry had annex'd thy breath, | but 99.11
ROBB'ST 1 FR 0.0001 REL FR 1 V 0 P
griefs are thine, | thou robb'st me of a moi'ty. AWW 3.02. 66
ROBE 18 FR 0.0020 REL FR 16 V 2 P
fairies, | finely attired in a robe of white. WIV 4.04. 72
the marshal's truncheon, nor the judge's robe, MM 2.02. 61
sure this robe of mine | does change my WT 4.04.134
o, well did he become that lion's robe, | that JN 2.01.141
robe, | that did disrobe the lion of that robe! 2.01.142
for putting on so new a fashion'd robe. 4.02. 27
not a buff jerkin a most sweet robe of durance? 1H4 1.02. 42 P
and new, | my presence, like a robe pontifical, 3.02. 56
comment appelez-vous le pied et la robe? H5 3.04. 50 P
the intertissued robe of gold and pearl, | the 4.01.262
my robe, | and my integrity to heaven, is all H8 3.02.452
what should i don this robe and trouble you? TIT 1.01.189
give me my robe, for i will go. JC 2.02.107
like a giant's robe | upon a dwarfish thief. MAC 5.02. 21
where late the diadem stood, and for a robe, HAM 2.02.507
give me my robe, put on my crown, i have ANT 5.02.280
make a blush, | which is their order's robe: TNK 5.01.142
or as the wardrobe which the robe doth hide, SON 52.10
/ROBED 1 FR 0.0001 REL FR 1 V 0 P
/thou /robed /man /of /justice, /take /thy LR 3.06. 36
ROBERT 24 FR 0.0027 REL FR 13 V 11 P
falstaffs, he shall not abuse robert shallow, WIV 1.01. 3 P
believe me, robert shallow, esquire, saith he is 1.01.106 P
what, john! what, robert! 3.03. 1 P
as i told you before, john and robert, be ready 3.03. 10 P
robert! 3.03.145 P
son, | as i suppose, to robert faulconbridge, JN 1.01. 52
if old sir robert did beget us both, | and were 1.01. 80
o old sir robert, father, on my knee | i give 1.01. 82
or day | when i was got, sir robert was away! 1.01.166
my brother robert, old sir robert's son? 1.01.224
why scorn'st thou at sir robert? 1.01.228
sir robert might have eat his part in me | upon 1.01.234
sir robert could do well — marry, to confess — 1.01.236
sir robert could not do it; 1.01.237
sir robert never holp to make this leg. 1.01.240
son, | i have disclaim'd sir robert and my land, 1.01.247
sir john norbery, sir robert waterton, and R2 2.01.284
i am robert shallow, sir, a poor esquire of this 2H4 3.02. 57 P
to see you well, good master robert shallow. 3.02. 85 P
and there will i visit master robert shallow, 4.03.129 P
you must excuse me, master robert shallow. 5.01. 3 P
i'll follow you, good master robert shallow. 5.01. 60 P
master robert shallow, choose what office thou 5.03.123 P
sir robert brakenbury, and sir william brandon. R3 5.05. 14
ROBERT'S 9 FR 0.0010 REL FR 9 V 0 P
had my shape | and i had his, sir robert's his, JN 1.01.139
philip, good old sir robert's wive's eldest son. 1.01.159
my brother robert, old sir robert's son? 1.01.224
is it sir robert's son that you seek so? 1.01.226
sir robert's son! 1.01.227
ay, thou unreverend boy, | sir robert's son! 1.01.228
he is sir robert's son, and so art thou. 1.01.229
madam, i was not old sir robert's son; 1.01.233
but, mother, i am not sir robert's son, | i have 1.01.246
ROBES 18 FR 0.0020 REL FR 14 V 4 P
robes; LLL 4.01. 83 P
and offer me disguis'd in sober robes | to old SHR 1.02.132
see not your bride in these unreverent robes, 3.02.112
in pure white robes, | like very sanctity, she WT 3.03. 22
were best say these robes are not gentlemen born 5.02.132 P
for there he is in his robes, burning, burning. 1H4 3.03. 33 P
and made us doff our easy robes of peace, | to 5.01. 12
they'll be in fresher robes, or they will pluck H5 4.03.117
away with these disgraceful wailing robes! 1H6 1.01. 86
thy scarlet robes as a child's bearing-cloth 1.03. 42
no, it will hang upon my richest robes, | and 2H6 2.04.108
to an impatient child that hath new robes | and ROM 3.02. 30
is, | /in thy best robes, uncovered on the bier, 4.01.110
why do you dress me | in borrowed robes? MAC 1.03.109
lest our old robes sit easier than our new! 2.04. 38
robes and furr'd gowns hide all. LR 4.06.165
therein, that when old robes are worn out, there ANT 1.02.164 P
give me my robes. PER 5.01.222
ROBIN 20 FR 0.0022 REL FR 12 V 8 P
by the bare scalp of robin hood's fat friar, TGV 4.01. 36
i warrant. what, robin, i say! WIV 3.03. 4 P
here comes little robin. 3.03. 21 P
robin starveling, the tailor. MND 1.02. 58 P
robin starveling, you must play thisby's mother. 1.02. 60 P
and knavish sprite | call'd robin goodfellow. 2.01. 34
hie therefore, robin, overcast the night; 3.02.355
welcome, good robin. 4.01. 46
robin, take off this head. 4.01. 80
we be friends, | and robin shall restore amends. 5.01.438
they live like the old robin hood of england. AYL 1.01.116 P
"hey, robin, jolly robin, | tell me how thy lady TN 4.02. 72
"hey, robin, jolly robin, | tell me how thy lady 4.02. 72
is turn'd upside down since robin ostler died. 1H4 2.01. 10 P
and had robin nightwork by old nightwork before 2H4 3.02.208 P
"and robin hood, scarlet, and john." 5.03.103
here, robin, and if i die, i give thee my apron; 2H6 2.03. 74 P
end — "for bonny sweet robin is all my joy." HAM 4.05.187
my fam'd works makes lighter | than robin hood!" TNK pr 21
i can sing "the broom," | and "bonny robin." 4.01.108
ROBIN-REDBREAST 1 FR 0.0001 REL FR 0 V 1 P
to relish a love-song, like a robin-redbreast; TGV 2.01. 21 P
ROBS 9 FR 0.0010 REL FR 9 V 0 P
she robs thee of thy name, | and thou wilt show AYL 1.03. 80
he that perforce robs lions of their hearts JN 1.01.268
which robs my tongue from breathing native R2 1.03.173
with his great attraction | robs the vast sea; TIM 4.03.437
he robs himself that spends a bootless grief. OTH 1.03.209
name | robs me of that which not enriches him, 3.03.160
like a thief, | that robs thee of thy goodness! PER 4.06.115
to that sweet thief which sourly robs from me. SON 35.14

of thee thy poet doth invent | he robs thee of, 79. 8
ROBUSTIOUS 2 FR 0.0002 REL FR 0 V 2 P
the mastiffs in robustious and rough coming on, H5 3.07.148 P
to the soul to hear a robustious periwig-pated HAM 3.02. 9 P
ROCHESTER 1 FR 0.0001 REL FR 0 V 1 P
gadshill lies to-night in rochester. 1H4 1.02.129 P
ROCHFORD 1 FR 0.0001 REL FR 1 V 0 P
the viscount rochford — one of her highness' H8 1.04. 93
ROCK* 40 FR 0.0045 REL FR 38 V 2 P
and here you sty me | in this hard rock, whiles TMP 1.02.343
wast thou | deservedly confin'd into this rock, 1.02.361
my cellar is in a rock by th' sea-side, where my 2.02.134 P
i'll get thee | young scamels from the rock. 2.02.172
bear | unto a ragged, fearful, hanging rock, TGV 1.02.118
leagues, | we were encount'red by a mighty rock, ERR 1.01.101
are as coy and wild | as haggards of the rock. ADO 3.01. 36
and rock the ground whereon these sleepers be. MND 4.01. 86
quicken a rock, and make you dance canary | with
AWW 2.01. 74
then death rock me asleep, abridge my doleful 2H4 2.04.197
and rock his brains | in cradle of the rude 3.01. 19
as fearfully as doth a galled rock | o'erhang H5 3.01. 12
shore, | or turn our stern upon a dreadful rock? 2H6 3.02. 91
in his moan, the ship splits on the rock, 3H6 5.04. 10
and richard but a /ragged fatal rock? 5.04. 27
bestride the rock, the tide will wash you off, 5.04. 31
lo, where comes that rock | that i advise your H8 1.01.113
and make my vouch as strong | as shore of rock. 1.01.158
as doth a rock against the chiding flood, 3.02.197
bear him to th' rock tarpeian, and from thence COR 3.01.212
lay hands upon him, | and bear him to the rock. 3.01.222
he shall be thrown down the tarpeian rock | with 3.01.265
heels, | or pile ten hills on the tarpeian rock, 3.02. 3
to th' rock, to th' rock with him! 3.03. 75
to th' rock, to th' rock with him! 3.03. 75
of precipitation | from off the rock tarpeian, 3.03.103
he's the rock, the oak not to be wind-shaken. 5.02.111 P
for now i stand as one upon a rock, | environ'd TIT 3.01. 93
poor remains of friends, rest on this rock. JC 5.05. 1
whole as the marble, founded as the rock, | as MAC 3.04. 21
sleep rock thy brain, | and never come mischance HAM 3.02.227
a double set | if drink rock not his cradle. OTH 2.03.131
or lion, | a /tower'd citadel, a pendant rock, ANT 4.14. 4
we house i' th' rock, yet use thee not so hardly CYM 3.03. 8
this rock and these demesnes have been my world, 3.03. 70
i'll throw't into the creek | behind our rock, 4.02.152
i prithee to our rock, | you and fidele play the 4.02.163
think that you are upon a rock, and now | throw 5.05.262
and there's a rock lies watching under water; TNK 3.04. 6
throbbing heart shall rock thee day and night; VEN 1186
ROCK'D 1 FR 0.0001 REL FR 1 V 0 P
which strook her sad, and then it faster rock'd, LUC 262
ROCKS 22 FR 0.0024 REL FR 20 V 2 P
the water nectar, and the rocks pure gold. TGV 2.04.171
"the raging rocks | and shivering shocks | shall MND 1.02. 31
and not bethink me straight of dangerous rocks, MV 1.01. 31
there is the peril of waters, winds, and rocks. 1.03. 25 P
the dreadful touch | of merchant-marring rocks? 3.02.271
mountains and rocks | more free from motion, no,
JN 2.01.452
spits forth death and mountains, rocks and seas, 2.01.458
the splitting rocks cow'r'd in the sinking sands 2H6 3.02. 97
o, i could hew up rocks and fight with flint, 5.01. 24
as the rocks cheer them that fear their wrack: 3H6 2.02. 5
from shelves and rocks that threaten us with 5.04. 23
than with ruthless waves, with sands and rocks. 5.04. 36
weep seas, live in fire, eat rocks, tame tigers; TRO 3.02. 78 P
on | the dashing rocks thy sea-sick weary bark! ROM 5.03.118
rough quarries, rocks, /and hills whose /heads OTH 1.03.141
the gutter'd rocks and congregated sands, 2.01. 69
surges, crack'd | as easily 'gainst our rocks. CYM 3.01. 29
alas, the seas hath cast me on the rocks, PER 2.01. 5
tame tempests, | and make the wild rocks wanton.
TNK 2.03. 17
huge rocks, high winds, strong pirates, shelves LUC 335
there will we sit upon the rocks, | and see the PP 19. 5
days, | when rocks impregnable are not so stout, SON 65. 7
ROCKY 5 FR 0.0005 REL FR 5 V 0 P
whose rocky shore beats back the envious siege R2 2.01. 62
peace shall stand as firm as rocky mountains. 2H4 4.01.186
reft, | rush all to pieces on thy rocky bosom. R3 4.04.235
beat at thy rocky and wrack-threat'ning heart, LUC 590
eyes | what rocky heart to water will not wear? LC 291
ROCKY-HARD 1 FR 0.0001 REL FR 1 V 0 P
and thy sea-marge, sterile and rocky-hard, TMP 4.01. 69
ROD 13 FR 0.0014 REL FR 7 V 6 P
and presently, all humbled, kiss the rod! TGV 1.02. 59
use, in time the rod | /becomes more mock'd than MM 1.03. 26
as being forsaken, or to bind him up a rod, as ADO 2.01.219 P
yet it had not been amiss the rod had been made, 2.01.227 P
and the rod he might have bestow'd on you, who, 2.01.229 P
come, thou child, | i'll whip thee with a rod. MND 3.02.410
take the correction, mildly kiss the rod, | and R2 5.01. 32
for the hot vengeance, and the rod of heaven, 1H4 3.02. 10
and that the earl of surrey, with the rod. H8 4.01. 39
the rod, and bird of peace, and all such emblems 4.01. 89
her enemies, you have been a rod to her friends; COR 2.03. 92 P
would i had a rod in my mouth, that i might TIM 2.02. 76 P
for when thou gav'st them the rod, and put'st LR 1.04.174 P
RODE 15 FR 0.0017 REL FR 14 V 1 P
alack, poor richard, where rode he the whilst? R2 5.02. 22
when bullingbrook rode on roan barbary, | that 5.05. 78
rode he on barbary? 5.05. 81
i learn'd in worcester, as i rode along, | he 1H4 4.01.125
why should that gentleman that rode by travers 2H4 1.01. 55
fellow that had stol'n | the horse he rode on, 1.01. 58
and helter-skelter have i rode to thee, | and 5.03. 94
and gentle, and you rode like a kern of ireland, H5 3.07. 53 P
the king himself is rode to view their battle. 4.03. 2
my gracious sovereign, as i rode from callice, 1H6 4.01. 9
lords at pomfret, when they rode from london, R3 3.02. 83
/carriage /of /this /action | rode on his tide. TRO 2.03.132
betossed soul | did not attend him as we rode? ROM 5.03. 77
the other day of a bay courser | i rode on. TIM 1.02.212
why, one that rode to 's execution, man, | could CYM 3.02. 70
RODERIGO 27 FR 0.0030 REL FR 21 V 6 P
for, sir, | it is as sure as you are roderigo, OTH 1.01. 56
my name is roderigo. 1.01. 95
this thou shalt answer; i know thee, roderigo. 1.01.119
now, roderigo, | where didst thou see her? 1.01.162
have you not read, roderigo, | of some such 1.01.173
on, good roderigo, i will deserve your pains. 1.01.183
you, roderigo! come, sir, i am for you. 1.02. 58
go to, farewell. do you hear, roderigo? 1.03.376 P
villainous thoughts, roderigo! 2.01.260 P
now, my sick fool roderigo, | whom love hath 2.03. 51
how now, roderigo? 2.03.136
how now, roderigo? 2.03.362
how now, roderigo? 4.02.172 P
will you hear me, roderigo? 4.02.181 P
give me thy hand, roderigo. 4.02.206 P
but, roderigo, if thou hast that in thee indeed, 4.02.212 P
live roderigo, | he calls me to a restitution 5.01. 14
my friend and my dear countryman | roderigo! 5.01. 90
no — yes, sure — /o /heaven, roderigo! 5.01. 90
roderigo! 5.01. 97
dark | by roderigo and fellows that are scap'd. 5.01.113
he's almost slain, and roderigo quite dead. 5.01.114
hath kill'd a young venetian | call'd roderigo. 5.02.113
roderigo kill'd? | and cassio kill'd? 5.02.113
found in the pocket of the slain roderigo, | and 5.02.309
death of cassio to be undertook | by roderigo. 5.02.312
roderigo meant t' have sent this damned villain; 5.02.316
RODERIGO'S 1 FR 0.0001 REL FR 1 V 0 P
there is besides, in roderigo's letter, | how he OTH 5.02.324
RODORIGO 1 FR 0.0001 REL FR 0 V 1 P
my name is sebastian, which i call'd rodorigo; TN 2.01. 17 P
RODS 3 FR 0.0003 REL FR 3 V 0 P
look you, i am /whipt and scourg'd with rods, 1H4 1.03.239
the king hath wasted all his rods | on late 2H4 4.01.213
my messenger | he hath whipt with rods, dares me
ANT 4.01. 3
ROE* 5 FR 0.0005 REL FR 3 V 2 P
ay, fleeter than the roe. SHR in.2. 48
or a herring without a roe, i would not care; TRO 5.01. 62 P
without his roe, like a dried herring: ROM 2.04. 37 P
or as the fleet-foot roe that's tir'd with VEN 561
or at the roe which no encounter dare; 676
ROES 1 FR 0.0001 REL FR 1 V 0 P
whip to our tents, as roes /run o'er land. LLL 5.02.309
ROGER 5 FR 0.0005 REL FR 5 V 0 P
witch, | with roger bolingbrook, the conjurer? 2H6 1.02. 76
edmund had issue, roger earl of march; 2.02. 37
roger had issue, edmund, anne, and eleanor. 2.02. 38
she was heir | to roger earl of march, who was 2.02. 48
thy grandfather, roger mortimer, earl of march: 3H6 1.01.106
ROGERO 1 FR 0.0001 REL FR 0 V 1 P
the news, rogero? WT 5.02. 21 P
ROGUE 79 FR 0.0089 REL FR 13 V 66 P
i never heard such a drawling, affecting rogue. WIV 2.01.142 P
reason, you rogue, reason; 2.02. 15 P
you'll not bear a letter for me, you rogue? 2.02. 20 P
and yet you, rogue, will ensconce your rags, 2.02. 26 P
hang him, mechanical salt-butter rogue! 2.02.278 P
away, you rogue, away! i am sleepy. MM 4.03. 28 P
you rogue, i have been drinking all night, i am 4.03. 43 P
"once to behold," rogue. LLL 5.02.168 P
is this your perfectness? be gone, you rogue! 5.02.174
a pair of stocks, you rogue! SHR in.1. 2 P
here comes the rogue. 1.01.221
he forth walked on his way" — | out, you rogue! 4.01.147
come hither, you rogue. 5.01. 48 P
damnable both-sides rogue! AWW 4.03.222 P
peace, you rogue, no more o' that. TN 1.05. 29 P
here's an overweening rogue! 2.05. 29 P
'slight, i could so beat the rogue! 2.05. 33 P
ah, rogue! 2.05. 36 P
"thou kill'st me like a rogue and a villain." 3.04.162 P
then he's a rogue, and a passy-measures /pavin. 5.01.200 P
i hate a drunken rogue. 5.01.201 P
knavish professions, he settled only in rogue. WT 4.03.100 P
that's the rogue that put me into this apparel. 4.03.103 P
not a more cowardly rogue in all bohemia. 4.03.105 P
an old sheep-whistling rogue, a ram-tender, to 4.04.777 P
let him call me rogue for being so far officious 4.04.839 P
that this same fat rogue will tell us when we 1H4 1.02.187 P
this, if i scape hanging for killing that rogue. 2.02. 15 P
out, ye rogue! shall i be your ostler? 2.02. 42 P
you lie, ye rogue, 'tis going to the king's 2.02. 56 P
how the fat rogue roar'd! 2.02.111 P
what a frosty-spirited rogue is this! 2.03. 20 P
away, you rogue, dost thou not hear them call? 2.04. 78 P
give me a cup of sack, rogue. 2.04.118 P
you rogue, here's lime in this sack too. 2.04.124 P
i am a rogue if i drunk to-day. 2.04.152 P
i am a rogue if i were not at half-sword with a 2.04.164 P
you rogue, they were bound, every man of them, 2.04.178 P
out, ye rogue! 2.04.484 P
i'll procure this fat rogue a charge of foot, 2.04.545 P
or the other plays the rogue with my great toe. 2H4 1.02.245 P
thou bastardly rogue! 2.01. 50 P
ah, thou honeyseed rogue! 2.01. 52 P
do, do, thou rogue! 2.01. 58 P
it is the foul-mouth'd'st rogue in england. 2.04. 72 P
away, you mouldy rogue, away! 2.04.125 P
hang him, rogue! 2.04.146 P
ah, you sweet little rogue, you! 2.04.216 P
ah, rogue! 2.04.218 P
i will toss the rogue in a blanket. 2.04.222 P
the rogue fled from me like quicksilver. 2.04.228 P
swing'd for this — you blue-bottle rogue, you 5.04. 20 P
come, you rogue, come bring me to a justice. 5.04. 26 P
away, you rogue! H5 2.01. 86 P
a fool, a rogue, that now and then goes to the 3.06. 67 P
belong to th' gallows, and be hang'd, ye rogue! H8 5.03. 7 P
male varlot, you rogue! what's that? TRO 5.01. 16 P
that same diomed's a false-hearted rogue, a most 5.01. 88 P
would i could meet that rogue diomed! 5.02.190 P
a scurvy railing knave, a very filthy rogue. 5.04. 29 P
a braggart, a rogue, a villain, that fights by ROM 3.01.101 P
and compounded thee | poor rogue hereditary. TIM 4.03.274
away, thou tedious rogue! 4.03.369
rogue, rogue, rogue! 4.03.374
rogue, rogue, rogue! 4.03.374
rogue, rogue, rogue! 4.03.374
for the satirical rogue says here that old men HAM 2.02.196 P
o, what a rogue and peasant slave am i! 2.02.550
a pestilence on him for a mad rogue! 5.01.179 P
glass-gazing, superserviceable, finical rogue; LR 2.02. 19 P
draw, you rogue, for though it be night, yet the 2.02. 31 P
draw, you rogue, or i'll so carbonado your 2.02. 37 P
stand, rogue, stand, you neat slave! 2.02. 41 P
/'zounds, you rogue! you rascal! OTH 2.03.145 P
dost thou prate, rogue? 2.03.150 P
alas, poor rogue, i think, /i' /faith, she loves 4.01.111
villain, | some busy and insinuating rogue, 4.02.131
rogue, thou hast liv'd too long. ANT 2.05. 73
to the choleric fisting of every rogue | thy ear PER 4.06.167
ROGUERY 2 FR 0.0002 REL FR 0 V 2 P
there is nothing but roguery to be found in 1H4 2.04.125 P
roguery! TRO 5.02. 19 P
ROGUE'S 2 FR 0.0002 REL FR 0 V 2 P
her as the key of the cuckoldly rogue's coffer, WIV 2.02.274 P
and yet i am bewitch'd with the rogue's company. 1H4 2.02. 17 P
ROGUES 21 FR 0.0023 REL FR 8 V 13 P
rogues, hence, avaunt, vanish like hailstones; WIV 1.03. 81
french thrift, you rogues — myself and skirted 1.03. 84
are a yoke of his discarded men — very rogues, 2.01.176 P
the rogues slighted me into the river with as 3.05. 9 P
y' are a baggage, the slys are no rogues. SHR in.1. 3 P
off with my boots, you rogues! 4.01.144
and the commanders very poor rogues, upon my AWW 4.03.133 P
"poor rogues," i pray you say. 4.03.154 P
truth's a truth, the rogues are marvellous poor. 4.03.157 P
to turn true man and to leave these rogues, i am 1H4 2.02. 23 P
give me my horse, you rogues, give me my horse, 2.02. 29 P
sure i have paid, two rogues in buckrom suits. 2.04.192 P
four rogues in buckrom let drive at me — 2.04.196 P
what's become of the wenching rogues? TRO 5.04. 33 P
what's the matter, you dissentious rogues, COR 1.01.164
poor rogues, and usurers' men, bawds between TIM 2.02. 59 P
i would i might go to hell among the rogues. JC 1.02.268 P
such smiling rogues as these, | like rats, oft LR 2.02. 73
none of these rogues and cowards | but ajax is 2.02.124
to hovel thee with swine and rogues forlorn | in 4.07. 38
and hear poor rogues | talk of court news; 5.03. 13
ROGUING 1 FR 0.0001 REL FR 1 V 0 P
these roguing thieves serve the great pirate PER 4.01. 96
/ROGUISH 1 FR 0.0001 REL FR 1 V 0 P
/his /roguish /madness | /allows /itself /to LR 3.07.104
ROI 3 FR 0.0003 REL FR 1 V 2 P
heard these islanders shout out | "vive le roi!" JN 5.02.104
dat is as it shall please de roi mon pere. H5 5.02.247 P
notre tres cher fils henri, roi d'angleterre, 5.02.339 P
ROINISH *(see roynish)*
ROISTING 1 FR 0.0001 REL FR 1 V 0 P
i have a roisting challenge sent amongst | the TRO 2.02.208
ROLANDS *(also rowland)*
ROLANDS 1 FR 0.0001 REL FR 1 V 0 P
england all olivers and rolands bred | during 1H6 1.02. 30
ROLL 9 FR 0.0010 REL FR 6 V 3 P
varying in subjects as the eye doth roll | to LLL 5.02.764
and make his eyeballs roll with wonted sight. MND 3.02.369
do show | i am not in the roll of common men. 1H4 3.01. 42
where's the roll? 2H4 3.02. 96 P
where's the roll? 3.02. 96 P
where's the roll? 3.02. 97 P
for you're fatal then | when your eyes roll so. OTH 5.02. 38
acknowledg'd, | put we i' th' roll of conquest. ANT 5.02.181
deep woes roll forward like a gentle flood, LUC 1118
ROLL'D 2 FR 0.0002 REL FR 2 V 0 P
or as the snake roll'd in a flow'ring bank, 2H6 3.01.228
in ajax' eyes blunt rage and rigor roll'd, | but LUC 1398
ROLLED 1 FR 0.0001 REL FR 1 V 0 P
the /snake lies rolled in the cheerful sun, TIT 2.03. 13
ROLLING 6 FR 0.0006 REL FR 6 V 0 P
the poet's eye, in a fine frenzy rolling, | doth MND 5.01. 12
wrinkled brows, with nods, with rolling eyes. JN 4.02.192
that stands upon the rolling restless stone — H5 3.06. 29
and in his rolling eyes sits victory, | as if TNK 4.02.108
rolling his greedy eyeballs in his head. LUC 368
more bright than theirs, less false in rolling, SON 20. 5
ROLLS 4 FR 0.0004 REL FR 1 V 3 P
is fixed upon a spherical stone, which rolls, H5 3.06. 36 P
stone, which rolls, and rolls, and rolls. 3.06. 36 P
stone, which rolls, and rolls, and rolls. 3.06. 36 P
is made master | o' th' rolls, and the king's H8 5.01. 35
ROMAGE 1 FR 0.0001 REL FR 1 V 0 P
of this post-haste and romage in the land. HAM 1.01.107
ROMAN 96 FR 0.0108 REL FR 84 V 12 P
the face of an old roman coin, scarce seen. LLL 5.02.613 P
in whom | the ancient roman honor more appears MV 3.02.295
present him to the duke like a roman conqueror, AYL 4.02. 3 P
grissel, | and roman lucrece for her chastity; SHR 2.01.296
i think we do know the sweet roman hand. TN 3.04. 28 P
were but the outside of the roman brutus, H5 2.04. 37
look you, of the roman disciplines, than is a 3.02. 73 P
the disciplines of the war, the roman wars, in 3.02. 97 P
a roman sworder and bandetto slave | murder'd 2H6 4.01.135
staves as lift them | against the roman state, COR 1.01. 69
you), | and titus lartius, a most valiant roman, 1.02. 14
is gone, with one part of our roman power. 1.03. 98 P
the roman gods | lead their successes as we wish 1.06. 6
our guider, come, to th' roman camp conduct us. 1.07. 7
i would i were a roman, for i cannot, | being a 1.10. 4
he bestrid | an o'erpress'd roman, and i' th' 2.02. 93
i am a roman, and my services are, as you are, 4.03. 4 P
i would not be a roman, of all nations; 4.05.175 P
powers | are ent'red in the roman territories, 4.06. 40
do they still fly to th' roman? 4.07. 1
you are a roman, are you? 5.02. 36 P
if | the roman ladies bring not comfort home, 5.04. 38
voice, | in election for the roman empery, TIT 1.01. 22
stay, roman brethren! 1.01.104
return | captive to thee and to thy roman yoke; 1.01.111
father, how we have perform'd | our roman rites. 1.01.143
suum /cuique is our roman justice: 1.01.280
and here i swear by all the roman gods, | sith 1.01.322
thou art a roman, be not barbarous: 1.01.378
in rome, | a roman now adopted happily, | and 1.01.463
there will the lovely roman ladies troop; 2.01.113
madam, now shall ye see | our roman hunting. 2.02. 20
what roman lord it was durst do the deed; 4.01. 62
and kneel, sweet boy, the roman hector's hope, 4.01. 88

and pray the roman gods confound you both! 4.02. 6
i would we had a thousand roman dames | at such 4.02. 41
have with my knife carved in roman letters, 5.01.139
goths, | the roman emperor greets you all by me, 5.01.157
he is a noble roman, and well given. JC 1.02.197
a roman. 1.03. 41
of life | that should be in a roman you do want, 1.03. 58
yourself | which every noble roman bears of you. 2.01. 93
every drop of blood | that every roman bears, 2.01.137
purposes, | but bear it as our roman actors do, 2.01.226
intended to your person, | nor to no roman else. 3.01. 91
thy master is a wise and valiant roman, | i 3.01.138
who is here so rude that would not be a roman? 3.02. 31 P
to every roman citizen he gives, | to every 3.02.241
be a dog, and bay the moon, | than such a roman. 4.03. 28
if that thou be'st a roman, take it forth. 4.03.103
now as you are a roman tell me true. 4.03.187
then like a roman bear the truth i tell: 4.03.188
think not, thou noble roman, | that ever brutus 5.01.110
run, | where never roman shall take note of him. 5.03. 50
this was the noblest roman of them all: 5.05. 68
why should i play the roman fool, and die | on MAC 5.08. 1
did squeak and gibber in the roman streets. HAM 1.01.116
i am more an antique roman than a dane. 5.02.341
do /you triumph, roman? do you triumph? OTH 4.01.118 P
on the sudden | a roman thought hath strook him. ANT 1.02. 83
how this herculean roman does become | the 1.03. 84
"say the firm roman to great egypt sends | this 1.05. 43
what | made all–honor'd, honest, roman brutus, 2.06. 16
to the young roman boy she hath sold me, and i 4.12. 48
a roman by a roman | valiantly vanquish'd. 4.15. 57
a roman by a roman | valiantly vanquish'd. 4.15. 57
let's do't after the high roman fashion, | and 4.15. 87
have need | t' employ you towards this roman. CYM 2.03. 63
story | proud cleopatra, when she met her roman, 2.04. 70
my body's mark'd | with roman swords, and my 3.03. 57
some roman courtezan? 3.04.123
lucius the roman, comes to milford–haven 3.04.142
she hath not appear'd | before the roman, nor to 3.05. 31
i saw jove's bird, the roman eagle, wing'd 4.02.348
my divination) | success to th' roman host. 4.02.352
the roman emperor's letters, | sent by a consul 4.02.384
the roman legions, all from gallia drawn, | are 4.03. 24
with a supply | of roman gentlemen, by the 4.03. 26
that when they hear their roman horses neigh, 4.04. 17
great the slaughter is | here made by th' roman; 5.03. 79
a roman, | who had not now been drooping here, 5.03. 89
knaves desire to live, for all he be a roman; 5.04.201 P
a roman with a roman's heart can suffer. 5.05. 81
britain harm, | though he have serv'd a roman. 5.05. 91
he is a roman, no more kin to me | than i to 5.05.112
and when came you to serve our roman captive? 5.05.385
and to the roman empire, promising | to pay our 5.05.461
for the roman eagle, | from south to west on 5.05.470
let | a roman and a british ensign wave 5.05.480
lust–breathed tarquin leaves the roman host, LUC 3
well was he welcom'd by the roman dame, | within 51
led, | the roman lord marcheth to lucrece' bed. 301
this said, he shakes aloft his roman blade, 505
and softly cried, 'awake, thou roman dame, | and 1628
"courageous roman, do not steep thy heart | in 1828
to rouse our roman gods with invocations | that 1831
ROMANO 1 FR 0.0001 REL FR 0 V 1 P
by that rare italian master, julio romano, who, WT 5.02. 97 P
ROMANOS 1 FR 0.0001 REL FR 1 V 0 P
"aio /te, aeacida, romanos vincere posse." 2H6 1.04. 62
ROMAN'S 2 FR 0.0002 REL FR 2 V 0 P
this is a roman's part. JC 5.03. 89
a roman with a roman's heart can suffer. CYM 5.05. 81
ROMANS' 1 FR 0.0001 REL FR 1 V 0 P
preserv'd the britains, was the romans' bane." CYM 5.03. 58
ROMANS 51 FR 0.0057 REL FR 47 V 4 P
will imitate the honorable romans in brevity." 2H4 2.02.123 P
disciplines of the pristine wars of the romans. H5 3.02. 82 P
my soul's hate, aufidius, | piercing our romans; COR 1.05. 11
we are come off | like romans, neither foolish 1.06. 2
not romans, as they are not, | though calved i' 3.01.238
break out, | and sack great rome with romans. 3.01.314
i hope to see romans as cheap as volscians. 4.05.233 P
but do not say | for that, "forgive our romans." 5.03. 44
that our request did tend | to save the romans, 5.03.133
the romans, | "this we receiv'd"; 5.03.137
tabors and cymbals, and the shouting romans, 5.04. 50
to the antiates | than shame to th' romans; 5.06. 80
romans, friends, followers, favorers of my right TIT 1.01. 9
and, romans, fight for freedom in your choice. 1.01. 17
romans, make way! 1.01. 64
romans, of five and twenty valiant sons, | half 1.01. 79
romans, do me right. 1.01.203
deserts, | romans, forget your fealty to me. 1.01.257
romans, let us go; 1.01.273
have you heard the truth, what say you, romans? 5.03.128
speak, romans, speak, and if you say we shall, 5.03.135
thanks, gentle romans, may i govern so, | to 5.03.147
ay, and that tongue of his that bade the romans JC 1.02.125
for romans now | have thews and limbs like to 1.03. 80
but that he sees the romans are but sheep; 1.03.105
he were no lion, were not romans hinds. 1.03.106
some certain of the noblest–minded romans | to 1.03.122
what other bond | than secret romans, that have 2.01.125
you have said, and show yourselves true romans. 2.01.223
by all the gods that romans bow before, | i here 2.01.320
and many lusty romans | came smiling and did 2.02. 78
pipes, | in which so many smiling romans bath'd, 2.02. 86
stoop, romans, stoop, | and let us bathe our 3.01.105
romans, countrymen, and lovers, hear me for my 3.02. 13 P
you gentle romans — 3.02. 72
friends, romans, countrymen, lend me your ears! 3.02. 73
are yet two romans living such as these? 5.03. 98
the last of all the romans, fare thee well! 5.03. 99
clock, and, romans, yet ere night | we shall try 5.03.109
and make the hearts of romans serve your ends! ANT 3.02. 37
his honor | against the romans with cassibelan, CYM 1.01. 30
some dozen romans of us and your lord | (the 1.06.185
or look upon our romans, whose remembrance | is 2.04. 14
till the injurious romans did extort | this 3.01. 47
cymbeline | i was confederate with the romans. 3.03. 68
the romans | must or for britains slay us or 4.04. 4
due fall on me by | the hands of romans! 4.04. 47
or we are romans and will give you that | like 5.03. 26
you look like romans, | and not o' th' court of 5.05. 24
he with the romans was esteemed so | as seely LUC 1811
the romans plausibly did give consent | to 1854
ROME 285 FR 0.0322 REL FR 268 V 17 P
other some, he is in rome; MM 3.02. 89 P
it was enjoin'd him in rome for want of linen; LLL 5.02.712 P
visitation was with me a young doctor of rome. MV 4.01.153 P
two, | but then up farther, and as far as rome, SHR 4.02. 75
that i have room with rome to curse a while! JN 3.01.180
his head, | unless he do submit himself to rome. 3.01.194
is purchase of a heavy curse from rome, | or the 3.01.205
that's the curse of rome. 3.01.207
king john hath reconcil'd | himself to rome, his 5.02. 70
church, | the great metropolis and see of rome; 5.02. 72
to tell me john hath made | his peace with rome? 5.02. 92
because that john hath made his peace with rome? 5.02. 96
what penny hath rome borne? 5.02. 97
say, with the hook–nos'd fellow of rome, "there, 2H4 4.03. 41 P
like to the senators of th' antique rome, | with H5 5.pr. 26
hath, | exceeding the nine sibyls of old rome: 1H6 1.02. 56
rome shall remedy this. 3.01. 51
would choose him pope and carry him to rome, 2H6 1.03. 62
rome, the nurse of judgment, | invited by your H8 2.02. 93
the court of rome commanding, you, my lord 2.02.104
whilst our commission from rome is read, | let 2.04. 1
consistory, | yea, the whole consistory of rome. 2.04. 93
abhor | this dilatory sloth and tricks of rome. 2.04.238
cardinal campeius | is stol'n away to rome, hath 3.02. 57
speedily i wish | to hear from rome. 3.02. 90
gain the popedom | and fee my friends in rome). 3.02.213
then, that in all you writ to rome, or else | to 3.02.313
to furnish rome, and to prepare the ways | you 3.02.328
the senators of rome are this good belly, | and COR 1.01.148
rome and her rats are at the point of battle, 1.01.162
that they of rome are ent'red in our counsels, 1.02. 2
that could be brought to bodily act ere rome 1.02. 5
enemy | (who is of rome worse hated than of you) 1.02. 13
we never yet made doubt but rome was ready | to 1.02. 18
in the hatching, | it seem'd, appear'd to rome. 1.02. 22
ere (almost) rome | should know we were afoot. 1.02. 24
got in fear, | though you were born in rome!" 1.03. 34
of the south light on you, | you shames of rome! 1.04. 31
this will i carry to rome. 1.05. 1 P
holding corioles in the name of rome, | even 1.06. 37
thank the gods | our rome hath such a soldier." 1.09. 9
rome must know | the value of her own. 1.09. 20
us, we will write | to rome of our success. 1.09. 75
send us to rome | the best, with whom we may 1.09. 76
what they are that must | be hostages for rome. 1.10. 29
testy magistrates (alias fools) as any in rome. 2.01. 45 P
know, rome, that all alone martius did fight 2.01.162
welcome to rome, renowned coriolanus! 2.01.166
welcome to rome, renowned coriolanus! 2.01.167
/you are three | that rome should dote on; 2.01.187
i doubt not but | our rome will cast upon thee. 2.01.202
when tarquin made a head for rome, he fought 2.02. 88
this palt'ring | becomes not rome; 3.01. 59
as they are, | though in rome litter'd; 3.01.238
the good gods forbid | that our renowned rome, 3.01.289
what has he done to rome that's worthy death? 3.01.296
break out, | and sack great rome with romans. 3.01.314
come home belov'd | of all the trades in rome. 3.02.134
th' honor'd gods | keep rome in safety, and the 3.03. 34
to take | from rome all season'd office, and to 3.03. 64
but since he hath | serv'd well for rome — 3.03. 83
tarpeian, never more | to enter our rome gates. 3.03.104
and can show /for rome | her enemies' marks upon 3.03.110
the red pestilence strike all trades in rome, 4.01. 13
to banish him that strook more blows for rome 4.02. 19
good man, the wounds that he does bear for rome! 4.02. 28
the capitol exceed | the meanest house in rome, 4.02. 40
what's the news in rome? 4.03. 10 P
there hath been in rome strange insurrections; 4.03. 13 P
tell you most strange things from rome, all 4.03. 41 P
th' voice of slaves to be | hoop'd out of rome. 4.05. 78
had we no other quarrel else to rome but that 4.05.127
war | into the bowels of ungrateful rome, | like 4.05.130
your territories, | though not for rome itself. 4.05.135
whether to knock against the gates of rome, | or 4.05.141
and sowl the porter of rome gates by th' ears. 4.05.201 P
it, and rome | sits safe and still without him. 4.06. 36
were inshell'd when martius stood for rome, 4.06. 45
with aufidius, leads a power 'gainst rome, | and 4.06. 67
he'll shake | your rome about your ears. 4.06. 99
if they | should say, "be good to rome," they 4.06.112
you have brought | a trembling upon rome, such 4.06.119
and defense | that rome can make against them. 4.06.128
sir, i beseech you, think you he'll carry rome? 4.07. 27
sits down, | and the nobility of rome are his. 4.07. 29
i think he'll be to rome | as is the aspray to 4.07. 33
when, caius, rome is thine, | thou art poor'st 4.07. 56
himself a name a' th' fire | of burning rome. 5.01. 15
a pair of tribunes that have wrack'd for rome 5.01. 16
make trial what your love can do | for rome, 5.01. 41
good will | must have that thanks from rome, 5.01. 46
sit in gold, his eye | red as 'twould burn rome; 5.01. 64
from rome. 5.02. 4
you'll see your rome embrac'd with fire before 5.02. 7
if you have heard your general talk of rome 5.02. 9
then you should hate rome, as he does. 5.02. 38 P
therefore back to rome, and prepare for your 5.02. 48 P
conjure thee to pardon rome and thy petitionary 5.02. 75 P
this man, aufidius, | was my belov'd in rome; 5.02. 93
we will before the walls of rome to–morrow | set 5.03. 1
your ears against | the general suit of rome; 5.03. 6
whom with a crack'd heart i have sent to rome, 5.03. 9
let the volsces | plough rome and harrow italy, 5.03. 34
these eyes are not the same i wore in rome. 5.03. 38
the moon of rome, chaste as the icicle | that's 5.03. 65
for we'll | hear nought from rome in private. 5.03. 93
that, if thou conquer rome, the benefit | which 5.03.142
so we will home to rome, | and die among our 5.03.172
you have won a happy victory to rome; 5.03.186
i'll not to rome, i'll back with you, and pray 5.03.198
finger, there is some hope the ladies of rome, 5.04. 6 P
a merrier day did never yet greet rome, | no, 5.04. 42
behold our patroness, the life of rome! 5.05. 1
when he had carried rome and that we look'd 5.06. 42
led your wars even to | the gates of rome. 5.06. 76
up, | for certain drops of salt, your city rome, 5.06. 92
last | that ware the imperial diadem of rome, TIT 1.01. 6
son, | were gracious in the eyes of royal rome, 1.01. 11
know that the people of rome, for whom we stand 1.01. 20
pius | for many good and great deserts to rome. 1.01. 24
since first he undertook | this cause of rome, 1.01. 32
five times he hath return'd | bleeding to rome, 1.01. 34
spoils, | returns the good andronicus to rome, 1.01. 37
rome, be as just and gracious unto me | as i am 1.01. 60
and brought to yoke, the enemies of rome. 1.01. 69
hail, rome, victorious in thy mourning weeds! 1.01. 70
tears of true joy for his return to rome. 1.01. 76
these that survive let rome reward with love; 1.01. 82
sufficeth not that we are brought to rome | to 1.01.109
oppose not scythia to ambitious rome; 1.01.132
and with loud 'larums welcome them to rome. 1.01.147
joy | shed on this earth for thy return to rome. 1.01.162
kind rome, that hast thus lovingly reserv'd 1.01.165
gracious triumpher in the eyes of rome! 1.01.170
titus andronicus, the people of rome, | whose 1.01.179
on, | and help to set a head on headless rome. 1.01.186
rome, i have been thy soldier forty years, | and 1.01.193
people of rome, and people's tribunes here, | i 1.01.217
and gratulate his safe return to rome, | the 1.01.221
reflect on rome as /titan's rays on earth, | and 1.01.226
grace, | and here in sight of rome to saturnine, 1.01.246
am of thee and of thy gifts | rome shall record, 1.01.255
thou com'st not to be made a scorn in rome; 1.01.265
what, villain boy, | barr'st me my way in rome? 1.01.291
was none in rome to make a stale | but saturnine 1.01.304
sons, | to ruffle in the commonwealth of rome. 1.01.313
dost overshine the gallant'st dames of rome, 1.01.317
bride, | and will create thee emperess of rome. 1.01.320
i will not re–salute the streets of rome, | or 1.01.326
and here in sight of heaven to rome i swear, 1.01.329
i saw, | to be dishonored by my sons in rome! 1.01.385
of goths | is of a sudden thus advanc'd in rome? 1.01.393
traitor, if rome have law, or we have power, 1.01.403
but let the laws of rome determine all, | mean 1.01.407
by all the duties that i owe to rome, | this 1.01.414
deeds | a father and a friend to thee and rome. 1.01.423
rome and the righteous heavens be my judge, 1.01.426
the gods of rome forfend | i should be author to 1.01.434
which rome reputes to be a heinous sin, | yield 1.01.448
titus, i am incorporate in rome, | a roman now 1.01.462
more | be so dishonored in the court of rome. 2.01. 52
in rome | how furious and impatient they be, 2.01. 75
rome could afford no tribunes like to these. 3.01. 44
that rome is but a wilderness of tigers? 3.01. 54
and rome affords no prey | but me and mine. 3.01. 55
for they have fought for rome, and all in vain; 3.01. 73
for hands to do rome service is but vain. 3.01. 80
which of your hands hath not defended rome, 3.01.167
the woefull'st man that ever liv'd in rome. 3.01.289
farewell, proud rome, till lucius come again; 3.01.290
a pow'r, | to be reveng'd on rome and saturnine. 3.01.300
ay, when my father was in rome she did. 4.01. 7
for these base bondmen to the yoke of rome. 4.01.109
youth, | the hope of rome, for so he bid me say; 4.02. 13
lords, was't not a happy star | led us to rome, 4.02. 33
or some of you shall smoke for it in rome. 4.02.111
rome will despise her for this foul escape. 4.02.113
shaken with sorrows in ungrateful rome. 4.03. 17
ah, rome! 4.03. 18
war | take wreak on rome for this ingratitude, 4.03. 34
ever seen | an emperor in rome thus overborne, 4.04. 2
sweet scrolls to fly about the streets of rome! 4.04. 16
as who would say, in rome no justice were. 4.04. 20
in hope thyself should govern rome and me. 4.04. 60
rome never had more cause. 4.04. 62
even so mayest thou the giddy men of rome. 4.04. 87
i have received letters from great rome | which 5.01. 2
and wherein rome hath done you any scath, | let 5.01. 7
ingrateful rome requites with foul contempt, 5.01. 12
there is a messenger from rome | desires to be 5.01.152
welcome, aemilius, what's the news from rome? 5.01.155
look round about the wicked streets of rome, 5.02. 98
who leads towards rome a band of warlike goths, 5.02.113
'tis my father's mind | that i repair to rome, i 5.03. 2
peace, for love, for league, and good to rome. 5.03. 23
you sad–fac'd men, people and sons of rome, | by 5.03. 67
let rome herself be bane unto herself, | and she 5.03. 73
fatal engine in | that gives our troy, our rome, 5.03. 87
come, come, thou reverent man of rome, | and 5.03.137
what tributaries follow him to rome, | to grace JC 1.01. 33
o you hard hearts, you cruel men of rome, | knew 1.01. 36
to see great pompey pass the streets of rome; 1.01. 42
heard | where many of the best respect in rome 1.02. 59
rome, thou hast lost the breed of noble bloods! 1.02.151
could they say, till now, that talk'd of rome, 1.02.154
now is it rome indeed and room enough, | when 1.02.156
th' eternal devil to keep his state in rome | as 1.02.160
than to repute himself a son of rome | under 1.02.173
the great opinion | that rome holds of his name; 1.02.319
what trash is rome? 1.03.108
shall rome, etc. 2.01. 47
"shall rome, etc." 2.01. 51
shall rome stand under one man's awe? 2.01. 52
what, rome? 2.01. 52
my ancestors did from the streets of rome | the 2.01. 53
o rome, i make thee promise, | if the redress 2.01. 56
soul of rome! 2.01.321
signifies that from you great rome shall suck 2.02. 87
with the most boldest and best hearts of rome. 3.01.121
and pity to the general wrong of rome — | as 3.01.170
caesar did write for him to come to rome. 3.01.278
he lies to–night within seven leagues of rome. 3.01.286
here is a mourning rome, a dangerous rome, | no 3.01.288
here is a mourning rome, a dangerous rome, | no 3.01.288
rome, | no rome of safety for octavius yet; 3.01.289
i lov'd caesar less, but that i lov'd rome more. 3.02. 22 P
as i slew my best lover for the good of rome, i 3.02. 45 P
we are blest that rome is rid of him. 3.02. 70
he hath brought many captives home to rome, 3.02. 88
there's not a nobler man in rome than antony. 3.02.116

move | the stones of rome to rise and mutiny. 3.02.230
sir, octavius is already come to rome. 3.02.262
are rid like madmen through the gates of rome. 3.02.269
led in triumph | thorough the streets of rome? 5.01.109
roman, | that ever brutus will go bound to rome; 5.01.111
the sun of rome is set. 5.03. 63
it is impossible that ever rome | should breed 5.03.100
in the most high and palmy state of rome, | a HAM 1.01.113
when roscius was an actor in rome — 2.02.391 P
news, my good lord, from rome. ANT 1.01. 18
let rome in tiber melt, and the wide arch | of 1.01. 33
common liar, who | thus speaks of him at rome; 1.01. 61
name cleopatra as she is call'd in rome. 1.02.106
too | of many our contriving friends in rome 1.02.182
makes his approaches to the port of rome; 1.03. 46
let his shames quickly | drive him to rome. 1.04. 73
i know they are in rome together, | looking for 2.01. 19
mark antony is every hour in rome | expected. 2.01. 29
welcome to rome. 2.02. 28
no more than my residing here at rome | might be 2.02. 37
merchandise which thou hast brought from rome 2.05.104
to scourge th' ingratitude that despiteful rome 2.06. 22
then, to send | measures of wheat to rome. 2.06. 37
octavia weeps | to part from rome; 3.02. 4
madam, in rome; 3.03. 8
contemning rome, he has done all this and more 3.06. 1
let rome be thus | inform'd. 3.06. 19
but you are come | a market–maid to rome, and 3.06. 51
welcome to rome, | nothing more dear to me. 3.06. 85
each heart in rome does love and pity you; 3.06. 92
and 'tis said in rome | that photinus an eunuch 3.07. 13
sink rome, and their tongues rot | that speak 3.07. 15
while he was yet in rome, | his power went out 3.07. 75
have i my pillow left unpress'd in rome, 3.13.106
wouldst thou be window'd in great rome, and see 4.14. 72
for her life in rome | would be eternal in our 5.01. 65
me to the shouting varlotry | of censuring rome? 5.02. 57
puppet, shall be shown | in rome as well as i. 5.02.209
show attend this funeral, | and then to rome. 5.02.365
my residence in rome at one /philario's, | who CYM 1.01. 97
madam, a noble gentleman of rome, | comes from 1.06. 10
so like you, sir, ambassadors from rome; 2.03. 54
him | and his succession granted rome a tribute, 3.01. 8
our good deed, | though rome be therefore angry. 3.01. 58
he is in rome. 3.05. 91
but what from rome? 4.02.336
a leg of rome shall not return to tell | what 5.03. 92
it was in rome — accurs'd | the mansion where! 5.05.154
good my lord of rome, | call forth your 5.05.425
so fares it with this fault–full lord of rome, LUC 715
and never be forgot in mighty rome | th' 1644
"thou wronged lord of rome," quoth he, "arise, 1818
(since rome herself in them doth stand disgraced 1833
by all our country rights in rome maintained, 1838
to show her bleeding body thorough rome, | and 1851

ROMEO 118 FR 0.0133 REL FR 106 V 12 P
o, where is romeo? ROM 1.01.116
this is not romeo, he's some other where. 1.01.198
why, romeo, art thou mad? 1.02. 53
nay, gentle romeo, we must have you dance. 1.04. 13
young romeo is it? 1.05. 64
'tis he, that villain romeo. 1.05. 64
his name is romeo, and a montague, | the only 1.05.136
now romeo is belov'd and loves again, | alike 2.pr. 5
romeo! my cousin romeo! romeo! 2.01. 3
romeo! my cousin romeo! romeo! 2.01. 3
romeo! my cousin romeo! romeo! 2.01. 3
romeo! 2.01. 7
o, romeo, that she were, o that she were | an 2.01. 37
romeo, good night, i'll to my truckle–bed, 2.01. 39
o romeo, romeo, wherefore art thou romeo? 2.02. 33
o romeo, romeo, wherefore art thou romeo? 2.02. 33
o romeo, romeo, wherefore art thou romeo? 2.02. 33
so romeo would, were he not romeo call'd, 2.02. 45
so romeo would, were he not romeo call'd, 2.02. 45
romeo, doff thy name, | and for thy name, which 2.02. 47
henceforth i never will be romeo. 2.02. 51
art thou not romeo, and a montague? 2.02. 60
o gentle romeo, | if thou dost love, pronounce 2.02. 93
three words, dear romeo, and good night indeed. 2.02.142
hist, romeo, hist! 2.02.158
romeo! 2.02.163
romeo! 2.02.167
our romeo hath not been in bed to–night. 2.03. 42
where the dev'l should this romeo be? 2.04. 1
romeo will answer it. 2.04. 9 P
alas, poor romeo, he is already dead, stabb'd 2.04. 13 P
here comes romeo, here comes romeo. 2.04. 36 P
here comes romeo, here comes romeo. 2.04. 36 P
signior romeo, bon jour! 2.04. 43 P
now art thou sociable, now art thou romeo; 2.04. 90 P
of you tell me where i may find the young romeo? 2.04.119 P
you, but young romeo will be older when you have 2.04.120 P
romeo, will you come to your father's? 2.04.140 P
doth not rosemary and romeo begin both with a 2.04.207 P
romeo! 2.05. 39 P
here's such a coil! come, what says romeo? 2.05. 65
romeo shall thank thee, daughter, for us both. 2.06. 22
mercutio, thou consortest with romeo — 3.01. 45 P
romeo, the love i bear thee can afford | no 3.01. 60
o romeo, romeo, brave mercutio is dead! 3.01.116
o romeo, romeo, brave mercutio is dead! 3.01.116
romeo, away, be gone! 3.01.132
here lies the man, slain by young romeo, | that 3.01.144
romeo that spoke him fair, bid him bethink | how 3.01.153
romeo he cries aloud, | "hold, friends! 3.01.164
but by and by comes back to romeo, | who had but 3.01.170
and, as he fell, did romeo turn and fly. 3.01.174
romeo slew tybalt, romeo must not live. 3.01.181
romeo slew tybalt, romeo must not live. 3.01.181
romeo slew him, he slew mercutio; 3.01.182
not romeo, prince, he was mercutio's friend; 3.01.184
let romeo hence in haste, | else, when he is 3.01.194
and romeo | leap to these arms untalk'd of and 3.02. 6
night, come, romeo, come, thou day in night, 3.02. 17
give me my romeo, and, when i shall die, | take 3.02. 21
the cords | that romeo bid thee fetch? 3.02. 35
romeo can, | though heaven cannot. 3.02. 40
o romeo, romeo! 3.02. 41
o romeo, romeo! 3.02. 41
romeo! 3.02. 42
hath romeo slain himself? 3.02. 45
and thou and romeo press /one heavy bier! 3.02. 60
is romeo slaught'red? 3.02. 65
tybalt is gone, and romeo banished, | romeo that 3.02. 69
romeo that kill'd him, he is banished. 3.02. 70
shame come to romeo! 3.02. 90
"tybalt is dead, and romeo banished." 3.02.112
"romeo is banished," to speak that word, | is 3.02.122
is father, mother, tybalt, romeo, juliet, | all 3.02.123
"romeo is banished"! 3.02.124
beguil'd, | both you and i, for romeo is exil'd. 3.02.133
and death, not romeo, take my maidenhead! 3.02.137
i'll find romeo | to comfort you, i wot well 3.02.138
hark ye, your romeo will be here at night. 3.02.140
romeo, come forth, come forth, thou fearful man: 3.03. 1
heaven and may look on her, | but romeo may not. 3.03. 33
courtship lives | in carrion flies than romeo; 3.03. 35
but romeo may not, he is banished. 3.03. 40
arise, one knocks. good romeo, hide thyself. 3.03. 71
romeo, arise, | thou wilt be taken. 3.03. 74
where's romeo? 3.03. 82
up, | and tybalt calls, and then on romeo cries, 3.03.101
romeo is coming. 3.03.158
be much in years | ere i again behold my romeo! 3.05. 47
that same villain romeo. 3.05. 80
indeed i never shall be satisfied | with romeo, 3.05. 94
that romeo should, upon receipt thereof, | soon 3.05. 98
do, i swear | it shall be romeo, whom you know i 3.05.122
romeo is banished, and all the world to nothing 3.05.213
shall romeo by my letters know our drift, | and 4.01.114
night | shall romeo bear thee hence to mantua. 4.01.117
because he married me before to romeo? 4.03. 27
i wake before the time that romeo | come to 4.03. 31
and there die strangled ere my romeo comes? 4.03. 35
i see my cousin's ghost | seeking out romeo, 4.03. 56
romeo, romeo, romeo! 4.03. 58
romeo, romeo, romeo! 4.03. 58
romeo, romeo, romeo! 4.03. 58
what says romeo? 5.02. 3
who bare my letter then to romeo? 5.02. 13
she will beshrew me much that romeo | hath had 5.02. 26
and keep her at my cell till romeo come — 5.02. 29
romeo. 5.03.129
romeo! 5.03.139
romeo, o, pale! 5.03.144
where is my romeo? 5.03.150
o, the people in the street cry "romeo," | some 5.03.191
and romeo dead, and juliet, dead before, | warm 5.03.196
romeo, there dead, was husband to that juliet, 5.03.231
mean time i writ to romeo, | that he should 5.03.246
cell, | till i conveniently could send to romeo. 5.03.256
lay | the noble paris and true romeo dead. 5.03.259
of more woe | than this of juliet and her romeo. 5.03.310

/ROMEO'S 1 FR 0.0001 REL FR 1 V 0 P
/mine, | with repetition of my /romeo's /name. ROM 2.02.163

ROMEO'S 13 FR 0.0014 REL FR 13 V 0 P
it was. what sadness lengthens romeo's hours? ROM 1.01.163
tybalt, here slain, whom romeo's hand did slay! 3.01.152
but romeo's name speaks heavenly eloquence. 3.02. 33
o god, did romeo's hand shed tybalt's blood? 3.02. 71
when theirs are dry, for romeo's banishment. 3.02.131
romeo's a dishclout to him. 3.05.219
god join'd my heart and romeo's, thou our hands, 4.01. 55
and ere this hand, by thee to romeo's seal'd, 4.01. 56
here's romeo's man, we found him in the 5.03.182
here is a friar, and /slaughter'd romeo's man, 5.03.199
she, there dead, /that romeo's faithful wife. 5.03.232
where's romeo's man? 5.03.271
as rich shall romeo's by his lady's lie, | poor 5.03.303

ROME'S 24 FR 0.0027 REL FR 24 V 0 P
am i rome's slave? JN 5.02. 97
ever thou wise words, | and for rome's good. COR 4.02. 22
or capitulate | again with rome's mechanics. 5.03. 83
all, | gracious lavinia, rome's rich ornament, TIT 1.01. 52
patron of virtue, rome's best champion, 1.01. 65
rome's readiest champions, repose you here in 1.01.151
whose fortunes rome's best citizens applaud! 1.01.164
them not | till saturninus be rome's emperor. 1.01.205
create | lord saturninus rome's great emperor, 1.01.232
rome's royal mistress, mistress of my heart, 1.01.241
presents well worthy rome's imperious lord: 1.01.250
here none but soldiers and rome's servitors 1.01.352
this siren that will charm rome's saturnine, 2.01. 23
rome's royal emperess, | unfurnish'd of her 2.03. 55
for all my blood in rome's great quarrel shed, 3.01. 4
our empress' shame, and stately rome's disgrace! 4.02. 60
rome's emperor, and nephew, break the parle, 5.03. 19
speak, rome's dear friend, as erst our ancestor, 5.03. 80
here's rome's young captain, let him tell the 5.03. 94
that true hand that fought rome's quarrel out, 5.03.102
out | to beg relief among rome's enemies, | who 5.03.106
lucius, all hail, rome's royal emperor! 5.03.141
lucius, all hail, rome's gracious governor! 5.03.146
to heal rome's harms, and wipe away her woe! 5.03.148

ROMISH 1 FR 0.0001 REL FR 1 V 0 P
in his court to mart | as in a romish stew, and CYM 1.06.152

RONDURE *(also rounder*)*

RONDURE 1 FR 0.0001 REL FR 1 V 0 P
that heaven's air in this huge rondure hems. SON 21. 8

RONYON *(also runnion)*

RONYON 1 FR 0.0001 REL FR 1 V 0 P
the rump–fed ronyon cries. MAC 1.03. 6

ROOD 5 FR 0.0005 REL FR 4 V 1 P
an early stirrer, by the rood! 2H4 3.02. 3 P
you may jest on, but, by the holy rood, | i do R3 3.02. 75
no, by the holy rood, | she could have run and 4.04.166
nay, by th' rood, | she could have run and ROM 1.03. 36
no, by the rood, not so: HAM 3.04. 14

/ROOF 2 FR 0.0002 REL FR 2 V 0 P
and swearing till my very /roof was dry | with MV 3.02.204
/that /every /day /under /his /household /roof R2 4.01.282

ROOF 16 FR 0.0018 REL FR 11 V 5 P
as many diseases under her roof as come to — MM 1.02. 47 P
my visor is philemon's roof, within the house is ADO 2.01. 96 P
the roof of this court is too high to be yours, LLL 2.01. 92 P
within this roof | the enemy of all your graces AYL 2.03. 17
to my teeth, my tongue to the roof of my mouth, SHR 4.01. 7 P
him, | and underneath that consecrated roof, TN 4.03. 25
my tongue cleave to my roof within my mouth, R2 5.03. 31
your roof were not sufficient to contain't. 1H6 2.03. 56
flat, | to bring the roof to the foundation, COR 3.01.204
this majestical roof fretted with golden fire, HAM 2.02.301 P
should have ascended to the roof of heaven, ANT 3.06. 49
the roof o' th' chamber | with golden cherubins CYM 2.04. 87
closes, he is enter'd | his radiant roof. 5.04.121
like goodly buildings left without a roof | soon PER 2.04. 36
that for our crowned heads we have no roof TNK 1.01. 52
seeking that beauteous roof to ruinate, | which SON 10. 7

ROOF'D 1 FR 0.0001 REL FR 1 V 0 P
here had we now our country's honor roof'd, MAC 3.04. 39

ROOF'S 1 FR 0.0001 REL FR 1 V 0 P
house with such | whose roof's as low as ours! CYM 3.03. 2

ROOFS 4 FR 0.0004 REL FR 4 V 0 P
the singing masons building roofs of gold, | the H5 1.02.198
and thatch your poor thin roofs | with burthens TIM 4.03.145
no, rather i abjure all roofs, and choose | to LR 2.04.208
their thoughts do hit | the roofs of palaces, CYM 3.03. 84

ROOK'D 1 FR 0.0001 REL FR 1 V 0 P
the raven rook'd her on the chimney's top, | and 3H6 5.06. 47

ROOKS 2 FR 0.0002 REL FR 2 V 0 P
when turtles tread, and rooks and daws, | and LLL 5.02.905
maggot–pies and choughs and rooks brought forth MAC 3.04.124

ROOKY 1 FR 0.0001 REL FR 1 V 0 P
and the crow | makes wing to th' rooky wood; MAC 3.02. 51

ROOM 45 FR 0.0050 REL FR 31 V 14 P
blow till thou burst thy wind, if room enough! TMP 1.01. 8 P
strew good luck, ouphes, on every sacred room, WIV 5.05. 57
because it is an open room and good for winter. MM 2.01.131 P
i never come into any room in a tap–house, but i 2.01.209 P
they must be bound and laid in some dark room. ERR 4.04. 94
as i was smoking a musty room, comes me the ADO 1.03. 59 P
revellers are ent'ring, brother, make good room. 2.01. 85 P
room for the incens'd worthies! LLL 5.02.697 P
but room, fairy! MND 2.01. 58
make room, and let him stand before our face. MV 4.01. 16
dead than a great reckoning in a little room. AYL 3.03. 15 P
place, | and let bianca take her sister's room. SHR 3.02.250
from my hive, | to give some laborers room. AWW 1.02. 67
come, we'll have him in a dark room and bound. TN 3.04.135 P
please your ladyship | to visit the next room, WT 2.02. 45
to make room for him in my husband's bed. JN 1.01.255
that i have room with rome to curse a while! 3.01.180
grief fills the room up of my absent child, 3.04. 93
go thou and fill another room in hell. R2 5.05.107
out some secret place, some reverent room, 5.06. 25
prithee come out of that fat room, and lend me 1H4 2.04. 1 P
but, sirrah, there's no room for faith, truth, 3.03.153 P
two paces of the vilest earth | is room enough. 5.04. 92
the room where they supp'd is too hot, they'll 2H4 2.04. 13 P
call for the music in the other room. 4.05. 4
let us withdraw into the other room. 4.05. 18
my lord, i found the prince in the next room, 4.05. 82
story, | in little room confining mighty men, H5 ep 3
in stead whereof let this supply the room: 3H6 2.06. 54
i'll throw thy body in another room, | and 5.06. 92
him into the malmsey–butt in the next room. R3 1.04.156 P
we shall have | great store of room, no doubt, H8 5.03. 73
give room! ROM 1.05. 26
and quench the fire, the room is grown too hot. 1.05. 28
when every room | hath blaz'd with lights and TIM 2.02.160
now is it rome indeed and room enough, | when JC 1.02.156
room for antony, most noble antony. 3.02.166 P
stand back; room, bear back! 3.02.168 P
must i give way and room to your rash choler? 4.03. 39
room ho! tell antony, brutus is ta'en. 5.04. 16
i'll lug the guts into the neighbor room. HAM 3.04.212
and in fine withdrew | to mine own room again, 5.02. 16
you must forsake this room and go with us. OTH 5.02.330
i have yet | room for six scotches more. ANT 4.07. 10
your praise shall still find room, | even in the SON 55.10

ROOMS 3 FR 0.0003 REL FR 2 V 1 P
vacant, in their rooms | come thronging soft and ADO 1.01.302
to fill up the rooms of them as have bought out 1H4 4.02. 32 P
issue of their bodies | to take their rooms, ere 3H6 3.02.132

/ROOT* 1 FR 0.0001 REL FR 0 V 1 P
or my heart will be blown up by /th' /root. TRO 4.04. 54 P

ROOT* 47 FR 0.0053 REL FR 45 V 2 P
disdain to root the summer–swelling flow'r | and TGV 2.04.162
how oft hast thou with perjury cleft the root? 5.04.103
and that's a good root. WIV 4.01. 54 P
you should take true root but by the fair ADO 1.03. 23 P
under an oak whose antique root peeps out | upon AYL 2.01. 31
once remove | the root of his opinion, which is WT 2.03. 90
or seven fair branches springing from one root. R2 1.02. 13
one flourishing branch of his most royal root, 1.02. 18
i will go root away | the noisome weeds which 3.04. 37
are pluck'd up root and all by bullingbrook, | i 3.04. 52
which should not find a ground to root upon 2H4 3.01. 91
and rank femetary | doth root upon, while that H5 5.02. 46
spring crestless yeomen from so deep a root? 1H6 2.04. 85
i'll plant plantagenet, root him up who dares. 3H6 1.01. 48
and till i root out their accursed line, | and 1.03. 32
increase, | we set the axe to thy usurping root; 2.02.165
but set his murth'ring knife unto the root 2.06. 49
whereof the root was fix'd in virtue's ground, 3.03.125
why grow the branches when the root is gone? R3 2.02. 41
we should take root here where we sit, or sit H8 1.02. 87
though we leave it with a root, thus hack'd, 1.02. 97
his greatness is a–ripening, nips his root, 3.02.357
weed, sir thomas, | and we must root him out. 5.01. 53
a curse begin at very root on 's heart, | that COR 2.01.185
weeded from my heart | a root of ancient envy. 4.05.103
and rape, i fear, was root of thy annoy. TIT 4.01. 49
rich men sin, and i eat root. TIM 1.02. 71
as this pomp shows to a little oil and root. 1.02.135
from forth thy plenteous bosom, one poor root! 4.03.186
o, a root, dear thanks! 4.03.192
be as a cantherizing to the root o' th' tongue, 5.01.133
too savage, doth root up | his country's peace. 5.01.165
or have we eaten on the insane root | that takes MAC 1.03. 84
but that myself should be the root and father 3.01. 5

shark, | root of hemlock digg'd i' th' dark, 4.01. 25
bid the tree | unfix his earth–bound root? 4.01. 96
deeper, grows with more pernicious root | than 4.03. 85
a grief that /smites | my very heart at root. ANT 5.02.105
i cannot delve him to the root: CYM 1.01. 28
his perishing root with the increasing vine. 4.02. 60
love of mine | will take more root within him. TNK 2.06. 28
would root these beauties as he roots the mead. VEN 636
but low shrubs wither at the cedar's root. LUC 665
the branches of another root are rotted, | and 823
weeds take root with precious flow'rs, | the 870
and broils root out the work of masonry, | nor SON 55. 6
root pity in thy heart, that, when it grows, 142.11
ROOTED 8 FR 0.0009 REL FR 5 V 3 P
i could not have ow'd her a more rooted love. AWW 4.05. 12 P
and there rooted betwixt them then such an WT 1.01. 23 P
thy truth and thy integrity is rooted | in us, H8 5.01.114
pluck from the memory a rooted sorrow, | raze MAC 5.03. 41
some o' their plants are ill rooted already, the ANT 2.07. 2 P
to know if your affiance | were deeply rooted, CYM 1.06.164
that grief and patience, rooted in them both, 4.02. 57
kings, | but time hath rooted out my parentage, PER 5.01. 92
ROOTEDLY 1 FR 0.0001 REL FR 1 V 0 P
they all do hate him | as rootedly as i. TMP 3.02. 95
ROOTETH 1 FR 0.0001 REL FR 1 V 0 P
that westward rooteth from this city side, | so ROM 1.01.122
ROOTING 1 FR 0.0001 REL FR 1 V 0 P
thou elvish–mark'd, abortive, rooting hog! R3 1.03.227
ROOTS* 16 FR 0.0018 REL FR 14 V 2 P
be | the fresh–brook mussels, wither'd roots, TMP 1.02.464
as gardeners do with ordure hide those roots H5 2.04. 39
must by the roots be hewn up yet ere night. 3H6 5.04. 69
i'll make you feed on berries and on roots, TIT 4.02.177
earth, yield me roots! TIM 4.03. 23
roots, you clear heavens! 4.03. 28
behold, the earth hath roots; 4.03.417
can you eat roots and drink cold water? 5.01. 74
weed | that roots itself in ease on lethe wharf, HAM 1.05. 33
as if he pluck'd up kisses by the roots | that OTH 3.03.423
he cut our roots in characters, | and sauc'd our CYM 4.02. 49
which fence the roots they grow by and defend PER 1.02. 31
that sets seeds and roots of shame and iniquity. 4.06. 86 P
to water | their intertangled roots of love, but TNK 1.03. 59
they bring in strange roots, which is merely to STM II.C 8 P
would root these beauties as he roots the mead. VEN 636
ROPE 10 FR 0.0011 REL FR 8 V 2 P
of the present, we will not hand a rope more. TMP 1.01. 23 P
hanging, make the rope of his destiny our cable, 1.01. 31 P
buy thou a rope, and bring it home to me. ERR 4.01. 20
i buy a thousand pound a year! i buy a rope! 4.01. 21
thou drunken slave, i sent thee for a rope, 4.01. 96
why, sir, i gave the money for the rope. 4.04. 12
five hundred ducats, villain, for a rope? 4.04. 13
that i was sent for nothing but a rope! 4.04. 91
winchester goose, i cry, "a rope! 1H6 1.03. 53
a rope!" 1.03. 53
ROPE–MAKER 1 FR 0.0001 REL FR 1 V 0 P
god and the rope–maker bear me witness | that i ERR 4.04. 90
ROPERY 1 FR 0.0001 REL FR 0 V 1 P
was this, that was so full of his ropery? ROM 2.04.146 P
ROPE'S 5 FR 0.0005 REL FR 4 V 1 P
house, go thou | and buy a rope's end; ERR 4.01. 16
you sent me for a rope's end as soon: 4.01. 98
to a rope's end, sir, and to that end am i 4.04. 16
like the parrot, "beware the rope's end." 4.04. 43 P
i see that men make rope's in such a scarre AWW 4.02. 38
ROPES 2 FR 0.0002 REL FR 2 V 0 P
poor ropes, you are beguil'd, | both you and i, ROM 3.02.132
galling | his kingly hands haling ropes, | and, PER 4.01. 54
ROPE–TRICKS 1 FR 0.0001 REL FR 0 V 1 P
he begin once, he'll rail in his rope–tricks. SHR 1.02.112 P
ROPING 1 FR 0.0001 REL FR 1 V 0 P
let us not hang like roping icicles | upon our H5 3.05. 23
ROSALIND 58 FR 0.0065 REL FR 24 V 34 P
can you tell if rosalind, the duke's daughter, AYL 1.01.105 P
i pray thee, rosalind, sweet my coz, be merry. 1.02. 1 P
but heavenly rosalind! 1.02.289
why, cousin, why, rosalind! 1.03. 1 P
o my poor rosalind, whither wilt thou go? 1.03. 90
rosalind lacks then the love | which teacheth 1.03. 96
o rosalind, these trees shall be my books, | and 3.02. 5
to western inde, | no jewel is like rosalind. 3.02. 89
wind, | through all the world bears rosalind. 3.02. 91
fairest lin'd | are but black to rosalind. 3.02. 93
be kept in mind | but the fair of rosalind." 3.02. 95
do lack a hind, | let him seek out rosalind. 3.02.102
cat will after kind, | so be sure will rosalind. 3.02.104
must be lin'd, | so must slender rosalind. 3.02.106
sheaf and bind, | then to cart with rosalind. 3.02.108
nut hath sourest rind, | such a nut is rosalind. 3.02.110
find, | must find love's prick and rosalind. 3.02.112
thus rosalind of many parts | by heavenly synod 3.02.149
rosalind is your love's name? 3.02.263 P
plants with carving "rosalind" on their barks; 3.02.361 P
all, forsooth, /deifying the name of rosalind. 3.02.363 P
on the trees, wherein rosalind is so admir'd? 3.02.393 P
by the white hand of rosalind, i am that he, 3.02.395 P
would but call me rosalind and come every day to 3.02.427 P
nay, you must call me rosalind. 3.02.434 P
good day and happiness, dear rosalind! 4.01. 30 P
my fair rosalind, i come within an hour of my 4.01. 42 P
pardon me, dear rosalind. 4.01. 50 P
and my rosalind is virtuous. 4.01. 63 P
and i am your rosalind. 4.01. 65 P
but he hath a rosalind of a better leer than you 4.01. 67 P
to me now, and i were your very very rosalind? 4.01. 71 P
am not i your rosalind? 4.01. 88 P
i would not have my right rosalind of this mind, 4.01.109 P
now i will be your rosalind in a more coming–on 4.01.112 P
then love me, rosalind. 4.01.115 P
will you, orlando, have to wife this rosalind? 4.01.131 P
you must say, "i take thee, rosalind, for wife." 4.01.135 P
i take thee, rosalind, for wife. 4.01.137 P
but will my rosalind do so? 4.01.157 P
for these two hours, rosalind, i will leave thee 4.01.177 P
ay, sweet rosalind. 4.01.187 P
and the most unworthy of her you call rosalind, 4.01.194 P
religion than if thou wert indeed my rosalind; 4.01.198 P
and to that youth he calls his rosalind | he 4.03. 92
and cried, in fainting, upon rosalind. 4.03.149
youth | that he in sport doth call his rosalind. 4.03.156
back | how you excuse my brother, rosalind. 4.03.180
for look you, here comes my rosalind. 5.02. 16 P
to–morrow i cannot serve your turn for rosalind? 5.02. 49 P
if you do love rosalind so near the heart as 5.02. 62 P
and to rosalind, if you will. 5.02. 73 P
and i for rosalind. 5.02. 87
and i for rosalind. 5.02. 92
and so am i for rosalind. 5.02.101
as you love rosalind, meet. 5.02.119 P
you say, if i bring in your rosalind, | you will 5.04. 6
if there be truth in sight, you are my rosalind. 5.04.119
ROSALINDA 1 FR 0.0001 REL FR 1 V 0 P
every sentence end, | will i 'rosalinda' write, AYL 3.02.137
/ROSALINE 1 FR 0.0001 REL FR 1 V 0 P
/rosaline, by good hap. LLL 2.01.210
ROSALINE 18 FR 0.0020 REL FR 16 V 2 P
name her name, | and rosaline they call her. LLL 3.01.167
from monsieur berowne to one lady rosaline. 4.01. 53
to a lady of france that he call'd rosaline. 4.01.105
hand of the most beauteous lady rosaline." 4.02.133 P
who sees the heavenly rosaline, | that, like a 4.03.217
but, rosaline, you have a favor too? 5.02. 30
hold, rosaline, this favor thou shalt wear, 5.02.130
thine, | so shall berowne take me for rosaline. 5.02.133
rosaline, | what did the russian whisper in your 5.02.442
my fair niece rosaline, /and livia; ROM 1.02. 69 P
sups the fair rosaline whom thou so loves, 1.02. 83
god pardon sin! wast thou with rosaline? 2.03. 44
with rosaline? 2.03. 45
is rosaline, that thou didst love so dear, | so 2.03. 66
hath wash'd thy sallow cheeks for rosaline! 2.03. 70
thou and these woes were all for rosaline. 2.03. 78
thou chidst me oft for loving rosaline. 2.03. 81
same pale hard–hearted wench, that rosaline, 2.04. 4
ROSALINE'S 1 FR 0.0001 REL FR 1 V 0 P
i conjure thee by rosaline's bright eyes, | by ROM 2.01. 17
ROSCIUS 2 FR 0.0002 REL FR 1 V 1 P
what scene of death hath roscius now to act? 3H6 5.06. 10
when roscius was an actor in rome — HAM 2.02.391 P
ROS'D 1 FR 0.0001 REL FR 0 V 1 P
being a maid yet ros'd over with the virgin H5 5.02.295 P
ROSE* 73 FR 0.0082 REL FR 64 V 9 P
be a canker in a hedge than a rose in his grace, ADO 1.03. 28 P
at christmas i no more desire a rose | than wish LLL 1.01.105
to those fresh morning drops upon the rose, | as 4.03. 26
but earthlier happy is the rose distill'd, MND 1.01. 76
fall in the fresh lap of the crimson rose, | and 2.01.108
of color like the red rose on triumphant brier, 3.01. 94
no doubt they rose up early to observe | the 4.01.132
therefore, my sweet rose, my dear rose, be merry AYL 1.02. 23 P
my sweet rose, my dear rose, be merry. 1.02. 23 P
rose at an instant, learn'd, play'd, eat 1.03. 74
he that sweetest rose will find, | must find 3.02.111
what said the wench when he rose again? SHR 3.02.166
doth to our rose of youth rightly belong; AWW 1.03.130
that in mine ear i durst not stick a rose | lest JN 1.01.142
lilies boast, | and with the half–blown rose. 3.01. 54
or rather do not see, | my fair rose wither; R2 5.01. 8
to put down richard, that sweet lovely rose, 1H4 1.03.175
fellow never joy'd since the price of oats rose, 2.01. 13 P
but we rose both at an instant and fought a long 5.04.147 P
i warrant you, is as red as any rose, in good 2H4 2.04. 25 P
from off this brier pluck a white rose with me. 1H6 2.04. 30
pluck a red rose from off this thorn with me. 2.04. 33
i pluck this white rose with plantagenet. 2.04. 36
i pluck this red rose with young somerset, | and 2.04. 37
giving my verdict on the white rose side. 2.04. 48
lest, bleeding, you do paint the white rose red, 2.04. 50
in sign whereof i pluck a white rose too. 2.04. 58
shall dye your white rose in a bloody red. 2.04. 61
hath not thy rose a canker, somerset? 2.04. 68
hath not thy rose a thorn, plantagenet? 2.04. 69
and, by my soul, this pale and angry rose, | as 2.04.107
pole, | will i upon thy party wear this rose. 2.04.123
shall send between the red rose and the white 2.04.126
tongue, | upbraided me about the rose i wear, 4.01. 91
i see no reason, if i wear this rose, | that any 4.01.152
then will i raise aloft the milk–white rose, 2H6 1.01.254
he rose against him, being his sovereign, | and 3H6 1.01.141
rest | until the white rose that i wear be dy'd 1.02. 33
the red rose and the white are on his face, 2.05. 97
wither one rose, and let the other flourish; 2.05.101
we will unite the white rose and the red. R3 5.05. 19
the duke being at the rose, within the parish H8 1.02.152
at length her grace rose, and with modest paces 4.01. 82
then rose again and bow'd her to the people; 4.01. 85
before the sun rose he was harness'd light, TRO 1.02. 8
that which we call a rose | by any other word ROM 2.02. 43
friend demand why brutus rose against caesar, JC 3.02. 20 P
th' expectation and rose of the fair state, HAM 3.01.152
takes off the rose | from the fair forehead of 3.04. 42
"then up he rose and donn'd his clo'es, | and 4.05. 52
o rose of may! 4.05.158
when i have pluck'd thy rose, | i cannot give it OTH 5.02. 13
tell him he wears the rose | of youth upon him; ANT 3.13. 20
against the blown rose may they stop their nose 3.13. 39
white and red, you shall see a rose, and she PER 4.06. 35 P
shall see a rose, and she were a rose indeed, if 4.06. 35 P
of all flow'rs | methinks a rose is best. TNK 2.02.136
but one rose! 5.01.165
leading him prisoner in a red rose chain; VEN 110
what though the rose have prickles, yet 'tis 574
like lawn being spread upon the blushing rose, 590
his breath and beauty set | gloss on the rose, 936
and the red rose blush at her own disgrace, LUC 479
i know what thorns the growing rose defends, | i 492
of day, | and ere i rose was tarquin gone away. 1281
he rose and ran away, ah, fool too froward! PP 4.14
sweet rose, fair flower, untimely pluck'd, soon 10. 1
that thereby beauty's rose might never die, SON 1. 2
the rose looks fair, but fairer we it deem | for 54. 3
seek | roses of shadow, since his rose is true? 67. 8
which, like a canker in the fragrant rose, 95. 2
nor praise the deep vermilion in the rose, 98.10
save thou, my rose, in it thou art my all. 109.14
ROSE CHEEK'D 2 FR 0.0002 REL FR 2 V 0 P
bring down rose–cheek'd youth | to the /tub–fast TIM 4.03. 87
rose–cheek'd adonis hied him to the chase; VEN 3
ROSED 1 FR 0.0001 REL FR 1 V 0 P
doth rise and fall between thy rosed lips, TIT 2.04. 24
ROSE–LIPP'D 1 FR 0.0001 REL FR 1 V 0 P
patience, thou young and rose–lipp'd cherubin — OTH 4.02. 63
ROSEMARY 7 FR 0.0008 REL FR 3 V 4 P
sirs, | for you there's rosemary and rue; WT 4.04. 74
doth not rosemary and romeo begin both with a ROM 2.04.206 P
sententious of it, of you and rosemary, that it 2.04.212 P
and stick your rosemary | on this fair corse, 4.05. 79
there's rosemary, that's for remembrance; HAM 4.05.175 P
pins, wooden pricks, nails, sprigs of rosemary; LR 2.03. 16
up, my dish of chastity with rosemary and bays! PER 4.06.151 P
ROSENCRANTZ 7 FR 0.0008 REL FR 5 V 2 P
welcome, dear rosencrantz and guildenstern! HAM 2.02. 1
thanks, rosencrantz and gentle guildenstern. 2.02. 33
thanks, guildenstern and gentle rosencrantz. 2.02. 34
ah, rosencrantz! 2.02.225 P
rosencrantz and guildenstern hold their course 4.06. 27 P
so guildenstern and rosencrantz go to't. 5.02. 56
that rosencrantz and guildenstern are dead. 5.02.371
ROSES 36 FR 0.0040 REL FR 35 V 1 P
the air hath starv'd the roses in her cheeks, TGV 4.04.154
there will we make our peds of roses, | and a WIV 3.01. 19
blow like sweet roses in this summer air. LLL 5.02.293
fair ladies mask'd are roses in their bud; 5.02.295
are angels /vailing clouds, or roses blown. 5.02.297
how chance the roses there do fade so fast? MND 1.01.129
clear | as morning roses newly wash'd with dew; SHR 2.01.173
but when you have our roses, | you barely leave AWW 4.02. 18
for women are as roses, whose fair flow'r TN 2.04. 38
cesario, by the roses of the spring, | by 3.01.149
was crow, | gloves as sweet as damask roses, WT 4.04.220
the fewest roses are cropp'd from the tree 1H6 2.04. 41
mean time your cheeks do counterfeit our roses; 2.04. 62
blush for pure shame to counterfeit our roses, 2.04. 66
i'll find friends to wear my bleeding roses, 2.04. 72
their lips were four red roses on a stalk, R3 4.03. 12
the roses in thy lips and cheeks shall fade | to ROM 4.01. 99
and old cakes of roses | were thinly scattered, 5.01. 47
with /two provincial roses on my raz'd shoes, HAM 3.02.277 P
that even her art sisters the natural roses; PER 5.ch. 7
roses, their sharp spines being gone, | not TNK 1.01. 1
with cherry lips and cheeks of damask roses, 4.01. 74
do bear thy yoke | as 'twere a wreath of roses, 5.01. 96
more white and red than doves or roses are: VEN 10
this silent war of lilies and of roses, | which LUC 71
first red as roses that on lawn we lay, | then 258
lay, | then white as lawn, the roses took away. 259
there will i make thee a bed of roses, | with a PP 19. 9
roses have thorns, and silver fountains mud, SON 35. 2
a dye | as the perfumed tincture of the roses, 54. 6
sweet roses do not so, | of their sweet deaths 54.11
poor beauty indirectly seek | roses of shadow, 67. 8
the roses fearfully on thorns did stand, | /one 99. 8
i have seen roses damask'd, red and white, | but 130. 5
white, | but no such roses see i in her cheeks, 130. 6
who glaz'd with crystal gate the glowing roses LC 286
ROSE–WATER 1 FR 0.0001 REL FR 1 V 0 P
full of rose–water and bestrew'd with flowers, SHR in.1. 56
ROSS 3 FR 0.0003 REL FR 3 V 0 P
the lords of ross, beaumond, and willoughby, R2 2.02. 54
cotshall will be found | in ross and willoughby, 2.03. 10
here come the lords of ross and willoughby, 2.03. 57
ROSSE 1 FR 0.0001 REL FR 1 V 0 P
the worthy thane of rosse. MAC 1.02. 45
/ROSSILLION 1 FR 0.0001 REL FR 1 V 0 P
it is the count /rossillion, my good lord, AWW 1.02. 18
ROSSILLION 12 FR 0.0013 REL FR 6 V 6 P
the count rossillion cannot be my brother: AWW 1.03.155
are you companion to the count rossillion? 2.03.192 P
thou shalt have none, rossillion, none in france 3.02.101
no, come thou home, rossillion, | whence honor 3.02.120
the count rossillion. know you such a one? 3.05. 49
go tell the count rossillion, and my brother, 4.01. 89
what will count rossillion do then? 4.03. 41 P
heed of the allurement of one count rossillion, 4.03.215 P
and the captain of his horse, count rossillion. 4.03.295 P
writ to diana in behalf of the count rossillion? 4.03.321 P
marry, as i take it, to rossillion, | whither i 5.01. 28
now is the count rossillion a widower, his vows 5.03.141 P
ROSY 4 FR 0.0004 REL FR 4 V 0 P
it with | a pudency so rosy the sweet view on't CYM 2.05. 11
not more resembles that sweet rosy lad | who 5.05.121
her lily hand her rosy cheek lies under, LUC 386
though rosy lips and cheeks | within his bending SON 116. 9
ROT 20 FR 0.0022 REL FR 18 V 2 P
to lie in cold obstruction, and to rot; MM 3.01.118
in the spring of love, thy love–springs rot? ERR 3.02. 3
and then, from hour to hour, we rot and rot; AYL 2.07. 27
and then, from hour to hour, we rot and rot; 2.07. 27
make that thy question, and go rot! WT 1.02.324
and if i do not, may my hands rot off, | and R2 4.01. 49
as fest'red members rot but by degree, | till 1H6 3.01.191
an unwholesome dish, | are like to rot untasted. TRO 2.03.121
i'll speak no more but "vengeance rot you all!" TIT 5.01. 58
thy lips rot off! TIM 4.03. 64
then the rot returns | to thine own lips again. 4.03. 65
i would my tongue could rot them off! 4.03.365
how long will a man lie i' th' earth ere he rot? HAM 5.01.164 P
no further, sir, a man may rot even here. LR 5.02. 8
ay, let her rot, and perish, and be damn'd OTH 4.01.181 P
his pernicious soul | rot half a grain a day! 5.02.156
the varying tide, | to rot itself with motion. ANT 1.04. 47
and their tongues rot | that speak against us! 3.07. 15
the south–fog rot him! CYM 2.03.131
that are not gath'red in their prime | rot, and VEN 132
ROTE 4 FR 0.0004 REL FR 3 V 1 P
first, rehearse your song by rote, | to each MND 5.01.397
will learn you by rote where services were done H5 3.06. 71 P
thy love did read by rote that could not spell. ROM 2.03. 88
set in a note–book, learn'd, and conn'd by rote, JC 4.03. 98
ROTED 1 FR 0.0001 REL FR 1 V 0 P
but with such words that are but roted in | your COR 3.02. 55
ROTTED 3 FR 0.0003 REL FR 3 V 0 P

hath rotted ere his youth attain'd a beard. MND 2.01. 95
bait, | the other rotted with delicious /feed. TIT 4.04. 93
the branches of another root are rotted, | and LUC 823
ROTTEN 41 FR 0.0046 REL FR 28 V 13 P
they prepared | a rotten carcass of a butt, not TMP 1.02.146
as if it had lungs, and rotten ones. 2.01. 48 P
be detected with a jealious rotten bell–wether; WIV 3.05.109 P
would else have married me to the rotten medlar. MM 4.03.174 P
give not this rotten orange to your friend, ADO 4.01. 32
the sweet war–man is dead and rotten, sweet LLL 5.02.660 P
cheek, | a goodly apple rotten at the heart. MV 1.03.101
but, poor old man, thou prun'st a rotten tree, AYL 2.03. 63
for you'll be rotten ere you be half ripe, and 3.02.119 P
you say, there's small choice in rotten apples. SHR 1.01.135 P
so that the muster–file, rotten and sound, upon AWW 4.03.166 P
which is rotten | as ever oak or stone was sound WT 2.03. 90
thing to talk on when thou art dead and rotten, 3.03. 81 P
that shakes the rotten carcass of old death JN 2.01.456
with inky blots and rotten parchment bonds; R2 2.01. 64
never did bare and rotten policy | color her 1H4 1.03.108
a rotten case abides no handling. 2H4 4.01.159
and rotten times that you shall look upon, 4.04. 60
and to rase out | rotten opinion, who hath writ 5.02.128
and have their heads crush'd like rotten apples! H5 3.07.145 P
and hung their rotten coffins up in chains, | it 3H6 1.03. 28
and drop into the rotten mouth of death. R3 4.04. 2
then the rotten diseases of the south, the TRO 5.01. 18 P
up | their rotten privilege and custom 'gainst COR 1.10. 23
being three parts melted away with rotten dews, 2.03. 32 P
hence, rotten thing! 3.01.178
breath i hate | as reek a' th' rotten fens, 3.03.121
and resolution like | a twist of rotten silk, 5.06. 95
earth, | thus i enforce thy rotten jaws to open, ROM 5.03. 47
sun, draw from the earth | rotten humidity; TIM 4.03. 2
something is rotten in the state of denmark. HAM 1.04. 90
faith, if 'a be not rotten before 'a die — as 5.01.165 P
he's dead and rotten. LR 5.03.286
not fight by sea, | trust not to rotten planks. ANT 3.07. 62
continual action are even as good as rotten. PER 4.02. 9 P
think | of rotten kings or blubber'd queens? TNK 1.01.180
thousand blossoms, | because they may be rotten? 3.06.244
"shall rotten damps ravish the morning air; LUC 778
shall rotten death make conquest of the stronger 1767
way, | hiding thy brav'ry in their rotten smoke? SON 34. 4
or you survive when i in earth am rotten, | from 81. 2
ROTTENNESS 2 FR 0.0002 REL FR 2 V 0 P
sound rottenness! JN 3.04. 26
for gold | which rottenness can lend nature; CYM 1.06.125
ROTTING 1 FR 0.0001 REL FR 1 V 0 P
though mean and mighty, rotting | together, have CYM 4.02.246
ROTUNDITY 1 FR 0.0001 REL FR 1 V 0 P
strike flat the thick rotundity o' th' world! LR 3.02. 7
ROUEN *(see roan*)*
//ROUGE–MOUNT 1 FR 0.0001 REL FR 1 V 0 P
/and /call'd /it //rouge–mount, /at /which /name R3 4.02.105
/ROUGH 2 FR 0.0002 REL FR 2 V 0 P
/no /enemy | /but /winter /and /rough /weather. AYL 2.05. 45
/there | /by /the /rough /torrent /of /occasion, 2H4 4.01. 72
ROUGH 78 FR 0.0088 REL FR 67 V 11 P
till new–born chins | be rough and razorable; TMP 2.01.250
but this rough magic | i here abjure; 5.01. 50
flow'r | and make rough winter everlastingly. TGV 2.04.163
'em, they are very ill–favor'd rough things. WIV 1.01.299 P
a fiend, a fairy, pitiless and rough; ERR 4.02. 35
ay, but not rough enough. 5.01. 58
when he demean'd himself rough, rude, and wildly 5.01. 88
and their rough carriage so ridiculous, | should LLL 5.02.306
he hath rid his prologue like a rough colt; MND 5.01.119 P
when lion rough in wildest rage doth roar. 5.01.222
from brassy bosoms and rough hearts of flints, MV 4.01. 31
my father's rough and envious disposition AYL 1.02.241
see | no enemy | but winter and rough weather. 2.05. 8
she's too rough for me. SHR 1.01. 55
/whe'er she is as rough | as are the swelling 1.02. 73
me, | for i am rough, and woo not like a babe. 2.01.137
'twas told me you were rough and coy and sullen, 2.01.243
and by what rough enforcement | you got it from AWW 5.03.107
often prove | rough and unhospitable. TN 3.03. 11
the fiend is rough, and will not be roughly us'd 3.04.111 P
thou want'st a rough pash and the shoots that i WT 1.02.128
thou'rt like to have | a lullaby too rough. 3.03. 55
mind (if it be not too rough for some that know 4.04.330 P
you are rough and hairy. 4.04.722 P
the grappling vigor and rough frown of war | is JN 3.01.104
to me for justice and rough chastisement; R2 1.01.106
we must supplant those rough rug–headed kerns, 2.01.156
these high wild hills and rough uneven ways 2.03. 4
not all the water in the rough rude sea | can 3.02. 54
a poor widow to so rough a course to come by her 2H4 2.01. 83 P
daughter, | give even way unto my rough affairs; 2.03. 2
we shall be winnow'd with so rough a wind | that 4.01.192
the flesh'd soldier, rough and hard of heart, H5 3.03. 11
the mastiffs in robustious and rough coming on, 3.07.148 P
teems | but hateful docks, rough thistles, 5.02. 52
our tongue is rough, coz, and my condition is 5.02.286 P
thus far, with rough and all–unable pen, | our ep 1
rough deeds of rage and stern impatience; 1H6 4.07. 8
the tongue and makes the senses rough. 5.03. 71
well–proportion'd beard made rough and rugged, 2H6 3.02.175
suffolk's imperial tongue is stern and rough, 4.01.121
in any case, be not too rough in terms, | for he 4.09. 44
come, bloody clifford, rough northumberland, | i 3H6 1.04. 27
stern, obdurate, flinty, rough, remorseless. 1.04.142
of sweet young rutland, by rough clifford slain. 2.01. 63
keep our course (though the rough wind say no) 5.04. 22
rough cradle for such little pretty ones! R3 4.01.100
place, and the rough brake | that virtue must go H8 1.02. 75
come, you have been too rough, something too COR 3.02. 25
you have been too rough, something too rough; 3.02. 25
never known before | but to be rough, unswayable 5.06. 25
should be so tyrannous and rough in proof! ROM 1.01.170
it is too rough, | too rude, too boist'rous, and 1.04. 25
if love be rough with you, be rough with love; 1.04. 27
if love be rough with you, be rough with love; 1.04. 27
to smooth that rough touch with a tender kiss. 1.05. 96
i have, in this rough work, shap'd out a man TIM 1.01. 43
in their rough power | has uncheck'd theft. 4.03.443
'twas a rough night. MAC 2.03. 61
so that it follows, i am rough and lecherous. LR 1.02.131 P
the tyranny of the open night's too rough | for 3.04. 2
rough quarries, rocks, /and hills whose /heads OTH 1.03.141
be a little angry for my so rough usage; CYM 4.01. 20 P
and yet as rough, | their royal blood enchaf'd, 4.02.173
till the rough seas, that spares not any man, PER 2.01.131
garment through the rough seams of the waters. 2.01.149 P
was by the rough seas reft of ships and men, 2.03. 84
they were too rough | that threw her in the sea. 3.02. 79
the rough and woeful music that we have, | cause 3.02. 88
this afternoon to ride, but 'tis a rough one. TNK 2.05. 46
be rough with me and pour | this oil out of your 3.01.102
all foul means | of boist'rous and rough jad'ry, 5.04. 72
then what a rough and riotous charge have you STM II.C 55
round rising hillocks, brakes obscure and rough, VEN 237
but the blunt boar, rough bear, or lion proud, 884
to the rough beast that knows no gentle right, LUC 545
but chide rough winter that the flow'r hath 1255
rough winds do shake the darling buds of may, SON 18. 3
ROUGH–CAST 3 FR 0.0003 REL FR 2 V 1 P
or some loam, or some rough–cast about him, to MND 3.01. 69 P
this man, with lime and rough–cast, doth present 5.01.131
this loam, this rough–cast, and this stone doth 5.01.161
ROUGHER 2 FR 0.0002 REL FR 2 V 0 P
but had a rougher task in hand | than to drive ADO 1.01.299
his rougher /accents for malicious sounds, | but COR 3.03. 55
ROUGHEST 2 FR 0.0002 REL FR 2 V 0 P
time and the hour runs through the roughest day. MAC 1.03.147
deign | the roughest berry on the rudest hedge; ANT 1.04. 64
ROUGH–GROWN 1 FR 0.0001 REL FR 1 V 0 P
in men, as in a rough–grown grove, remain LUC 1249
ROUGH–HEW 1 FR 0.0001 REL FR 1 V 0 P
shapes our ends, | rough–hew them how we will — HAM 5.02. 11
ROUGHLY 6 FR 0.0006 REL FR 5 V 1 P
as roughly as my modesty would let me. ERR 5.01. 59
fiend is rough, and will not be roughly us'd. TN 3.04.111 P
and roughly send to prison | th' immediate heir 2H4 5.02. 70
justles roughly by | all time of pause, rudely TRO 4.04. 34
winds of heaven | visit her face too roughly. HAM 1.02.142
and exception | roughly awake, i here proclaim 5.02.232
ROUGHNESS 1 FR 0.0001 REL FR 1 V 0 P
doth affect | a saucy roughness, and constrains LR 2.02. 97
ROUND* 87 FR 0.0098 REL FR 77 V 10 P
a round hose, madam, now's not worth a pin, TGV 2.07. 55
does he not wear a great round beard, like a WIV 1.04. 20 P
walk round about an oak, with great ragg'd horns 4.04. 31
round about the oak | of herne the hunter, let 5.05. 75
be, | to guide our measure round about the tree. 5.05. 79
so long that nineteen zodiacs have gone round MM 1.02.168
and blown with restless violence round about 3.01.124
proclaim it, provost, round about the city, | if 5.01.508
am i so round with you, as you with me, | that ERR 2.01. 82
skirts, round underborne with a bluish tinsel; ADO 3.04. 21 P
songs of woe, | round about her tomb they go. 5.03. 15
round about | dapples the drowsy east with spots 5.03. 26
if you will patiently dance in our round | and MND 2.01.140
i'll put a girdle round about the earth | in 2.01.175
i'll follow you, i'll lead you about a round, 3.01.106
was wont to swell like round and orient pearls, 4.01. 54
his doublet in italy, his round hose in france, MV 1.02. 75 P
three thousand ducats — 'tis a good round sum. 1.03.103
forked heads | have their round haunches gor'd. AYL 2.01. 25
and the big round tears | cours'd one another 2.01. 38
in fair round belly with good capon lin'd, 2.07.154
and hang it round with all my wanton pictures. SHR in.1. 47
he that is giddy thinks the world turns round. 5.02. 20
"he that is giddy thinks the world turns round": 5.02. 26
and water once a day her chamber round | with TN 1.01. 28
sir toby, i must be round with you. 2.03. 95 P
why, you whoreson round man, what's the matter? 1H4 2.04.140 P
with a white head and something a round belly. 2H4 1.02.189 P
chamber, at the round table by a sea–coal fire, 2.01. 88 P
will now take my leave of these six dry, round, 2.04. 8 P
your reproof is something too round, i should be H5 4.01.203 P
thousand of the french | was round encompassed, 1H6 1.01.114
my body round engirt with misery — | for what's 2H6 3.01.200
that gold must round engirt these brows of mine, 5.01. 99
or as a bear, encompass'd round with dogs, | who 3H6 2.01. 15
head | be round impaled with a glorious crown. 3.02.171
of golden metal that must round my brow | were R3 4.01. 59
let it go round. H8 1.04. 97
on your heads | clap round fines for neglect. 5.03. 80
expectation whirls me round; TRO 3.02. 18
empale him with your weapons round about, | in 5.07. 5
and thou, and i, sit round about some fountain, TIT 3.01.123
a scroll, and written round about. 4.02. 18
look round about the wicked streets of rome, 5.02. 98
not half so big as a round little worm | prick'd ROM 1.04. 68
my lord, in heart; and let the health go round. TIM 1.02. 53
i must be round with him, now he comes from 2.02. 8
but when he once attains the upmost round, | he JC 2.01. 24
a ring, stand round. 3.02.164 P
time is come round, | and where i did begin, 5.03. 23
titinius is enclosed round about | with horsemen 5.03. 28
all that impedes thee from the golden round, MAC 1.05. 28
anon we'll drink a measure | the table round. 3.04. 12
round about the cauldron go; 4.01. 4
and wears upon his baby–brow the round | and top 4.01. 88
a sound, | while you perform your antic round; 4.01.130
send out moe horses, skirr the country round, 5.03. 35
no, i went round to work, | and my young HAM 2.02.139
and bowl the round nave down the hill of heaven 2.02.496
let her be round with him, | and i'll be plac'd 3.01.183
full thirty times hath phoebus' cart gone round 3.02.155
pray you be round /with /him. 3.04. 5
being thus benetted round with /villainies — 5.02. 29
i will a round unvarnish'd tale deliver | of my OTH 1.03. 90
thee, and on every hand, | enwheel thee round! 2.01. 87
above, | you elements that clip us round about, 3.03.464
cup us till the world go round, | cup us till ANT 2.07.117
go round, | cup us till the world go round! 2.07.118
is't long or round? 3.03. 29
round, even to faultiness. 3.03. 30
the round world | should have shook lions into 5.01. 15
the noise is round about us. CYM 4.04. 1
does the world go round? 5.05.232
but in our orbs /we'll live so round and safe, PER 1.02.122
to pentapolis, | yravished the regions round, 3.ch. 35
arm'd long and round, and on his thigh a sword TNK 4.02. 85
aged cramp | had screw'd his square foot round, 5.01.111
round rising hillocks, brakes obscure and rough, VEN 237
these lovely caves, these round enchanting pits, 247
"o fairest mover on this mortal round, | would 368
which in round drops upon their whiteness stood. 1170
left their round turrets destitute and pale. LUC 441
and turn the giddy round of fortune's wheel; 952
she throws her eyes about the painting round, 1499
those round clear pearls of his, that move thy 1553
and round about her tear–distained eye | blue 1586
she will not stick to round me on th' ear, | to PP 18.51
ROUNDED* 5 FR 0.0005 REL FR 5 V 0 P
and our little life | is rounded with a sleep. TMP 4.01.158
for she his hairy temples then had rounded MND 4.01. 51
own soldier, rounded in the ear | with that same JN 2.01.566
how rank soever rounded in with danger. TRO 1.03.196
careless tresses | a /wreath of bulrush rounded; TNK 4.01. 84
ROUNDEL 1 FR 0.0001 REL FR 1 V 0 P
come, now a roundel and a fairy song; MND 2.02. 1
ROUNDER* *(also rondure)*
ROUNDER* 2 FR 0.0002 REL FR 2 V 0 P
i'll wear a boot, to make it somewhat rounder. TGV 5.02. 6
'tis not the rounder of your old–fac'd walls JN 2.01.259
ROUNDEST 1 FR 0.0001 REL FR 0 V 1 P
he answer'd me in the roundest manner, he would LR 1.04. 54 P
ROUND–FAC'D 1 FR 0.0001 REL FR 1 V 0 P
he's round–fac'd, and when he smiles | he shows TNK 4.02.135
ROUND–HOOF'D 1 FR 0.0001 REL FR 1 V 0 P
round–hoof'd, short–jointed, fetlocks shag and VEN 295
ROUNDING 1 FR 0.0001 REL FR 1 V 0 P
here with me already, whisp'ring, rounding: WT 1.02.217
ROUNDLY 10 FR 0.0011 REL FR 6 V 4 P
shall we clap into't roundly, without hawking or AYL 5.03. 11 P
petruchio, shall i then come roundly to thee, SHR 1.02. 59
that take it on you at the first so roundly. 3.02.214
hap what hap may, i'll roundly go about her; 4.04.107
roundly replied. 5.02. 21
this tongue that runs so roundly in thy head R2 2.01.122
well, how then? come, roundly, roundly. 1H4 1.02. 22 P
well, how then? come, roundly, roundly. 1.02. 22 P
have done any thing indeed too, and roundly too. 2H4 3.02. 18 P
and fell so roundly to a large confession, | to TRO 3.02.154
ROUNDS 5 FR 0.0005 REL FR 5 V 0 P
with rounds of waxen tapers on their heads, WIV 4.04. 51
wet, | the many–color'd iris, rounds thine eye? AWW 1.03.152
hark ye, | the queen your mother rounds apace: WT 2.01. 16
crown | that rounds the mortal temples of a king R2 3.02.161
what rounds, what bounds, what course, what stop LC 109
ROUND–WOMB'D 1 FR 0.0001 REL FR 0 V 1 P
whereupon she grew round–womb'd, and had indeed, LR 1.01. 14 P
ROUS'D 7 FR 0.0008 REL FR 7 V 0 P
which so rous'd up with boist'rous untun'd drums R2 1.03.134
rous'd on the sudden from their drowsy beds, 1H6 2.02. 23
as rous'd with rage, with rage doth sympathize, TRO 1.03. 52
wak'd by the lark, hath rous'd the ribald crows, 4.02. 9
patroclus' wounds have rous'd his drowsy blood, 5.05. 32
in the quarrel's right, rous'd to th' encounter, LR 2.01. 54
hark, the game is rous'd! CYM 3.03. 98
ROUSE* *(also carouses)*
ROUSE* 31 FR 0.0035 REL FR 27 V 4 P
"for the heavens, rouse up a brave mind," says MV 2.02. 12 P
shall we rouse the night–owl in a catch that TN 2.03. 58 P
and rouse from sleep that fell anatomy | which JN 3.04. 40
rouse up thy youthful blood, be valiant and live R2 1.03. 83
to rouse his wrongs and chase them to the bay. 2.03.128
stirs | to rouse a lion than to start a hare! 1H4 1.03.198
therefore rouse up fear and trembling, and do 2H4 4.03. 14 P
rouse up revenge from ebon den with fell 5.05. 37
do all expect that you should rouse yourself, H5 1.02.123
when i do rouse me in my throne of france. 1.02.275
nym, rouse thy vaunting veins; 2.03. 4
named, | and rouse him at the name of crispian. 4.03. 43
we'll quickly rouse the traitors in the same. 3H6 5.01. 65
troy, | to rouse a grecian that is true in love. TRO 1.03.279
sweet, rouse yourself, and the weak wanton cupid 3.03.222
rouse him and give him note of our approach, 4.01. 44
and rouse the prince, and ring a hunter's peal, TIT 2.02. 5
will rouse the proudest panther in the chase, 2.02. 21
what, rouse thee, man! ROM 3.03.135
juliet, on thursday early will i rouse ye; 4.01. 42
the morning comes | to rouse thee from thy bed, 4.01.108
night's black agents to their preys do rouse. MAC 3.02. 53
would at a dismal treatise rouse and stir | as 5.05. 12
and the king's rouse the heaven shall bruit HAM 1.02.127
the king doth wake to–night and takes his rouse, 1.04. 8
there was 'a gaming, there o'ertook in 's rouse, 2.01. 56
rouse him, make after him, poison his delight, OTH 1.01. 68
'fore /god, they have given me a rouse already. 2.03. 64 P
i see him rouse himself | to praise my noble act ANT 5.02.284
no dog shall rouse thee, though a thousand bark. VEN 240
to rouse our roman gods with invocations | that LUC 1831
/ROUSED 1 FR 0.0001 REL FR 1 V 0 P
/mounted /and /both /roused /in /their /seats, 2H4 4.01.116
ROUSED 1 FR 0.0001 REL FR 1 V 0 P
pause, | a roused vengeance sets him new a–work, HAM 2.02.488
ROUSETH 1 FR 0.0001 REL FR 1 V 0 P
dead–killing eye | he rouseth up himself, and LUC 541
ROUSILLON *(see rossillion)*
ROUSSI 2 FR 0.0002 REL FR 2 V 0 P
beaumont, grandpre, roussi, and faulconbridge, H5 3.05. 44
grandpre and roussi, faulconbridge and foix, 4.08. 99
ROUT* 14 FR 0.0015 REL FR 14 V 0 P
and that supposed by the common rout | against ERR 3.01.101
and after me, i know, the rout is coming. SHR 3.02.181
cheering a rout of rebels with your drum, 2H4 4.02. 9
with charles, alanson, and that traitorous rout. 1H6 4.01.173
the ringleader and head of all this rout, | have 2H6 2.01.166
all is on the rout, | fear frames disorder, and 5.02. 31
that puts odds | among the rout of nations, i TIM 4.03. 44
profess myself in banqueting | to all the rout, JC 1.02. 78

give me to know | how this foul rout began; OTH 2.03.210
anon | a rout, confusion thick. CYM 5.03. 41
now sleep yslacked hath the rout, | no din but PER 3.ch. 1
we are a merry rout, or else a rable, | or TNK 3.05.106
out, | we'll make thee laugh and all this rout. 3.05.147
are incident, by his name | can still the rout? STM II.C 116
ROUTED 1 FR 0.0001 REL FR 1 V 0 P
and the shelters whither | the routed fly; ANT 3.01. 9
ROUTS* 2 FR 0.0002 REL FR 2 V 0 P
came like itself, in base and abject routs, 2H4 4.01. 33
nothing routs us but | the villainy of our fears CYM 5.02. 12
ROVE 1 FR 0.0001 REL FR 1 V 0 P
full | of the wars' surfeits to go rove with one COR 4.01. 46
ROVER 1 FR 0.0001 REL FR 1 V 0 P
next to thyself and my young rover, he's WT 1.02.176
ROW 2 FR 0.0002 REL FR 1 V 1 P
my wretchedness unto a row of /pins, | they will R2 3.04. 26
the first row of the pious chanson will show you HAM 2.02.419 P
ROWEL 2 FR 0.0002 REL FR 2 V 0 P
who ne'er wore rowel | nor iron on his heel! CYM 4.04. 39
pig–like he whines | at the sharp rowel, which TNK 5.04. 70
ROWEL–HEAD 1 FR 0.0001 REL FR 1 V 0 P
sides of his poor jade | up to the rowel–head, 2H4 1.01. 46
ROWLAND *(also rolands)*
ROWLAND 7 FR 0.0008 REL FR 5 V 2 P
give the like notice | to valentius, rowland, MM 4.05. 8
i am the youngest son of sir rowland de boys. AYL 1.01. 57 P
liege, the youngest son of sir rowland de boys. 1.02.223 P
my father lov'd sir rowland as his soul, | and 1.02.235
o you memory | of old sir rowland! 2.03. 4
i am the second son of old sir rowland, | that 5.04.152
"child rowland to the dark tower came, | his LR 3.04.182
ROWLAND'S 4 FR 0.0004 REL FR 2 V 2 P
i am more proud to be sir rowland's son, | his AYL 1.02.232
a liking with old sir rowland's youngest son? 1.03. 28 P
if that you were the good sir rowland's son, 2.07.191
that was old sir rowland's will i estate upon 5.02. 11 P
ROY 2 FR 0.0002 REL FR 1 V 1 P
harry le roy. H5 4.01. 49 P
le roy? 4.01. 50
/ROYAL 1 FR 0.0001 REL FR 1 V 0 P
/thy /glutton /bosom /of /the /royal /richard, 2H4 1.03. 98
ROYAL 222 FR 0.0251 REL FR 206 V 16 P
all our trim, freshly beheld | our royal, good, TMP 5.01.237
that shall catch | your royal fleet far off. 5.01.317
attends the emperor in his royal court. TGV 1.03. 27
will give thee time to leave our royal court, 3.01.165
happy return be to your royal grace! MM 5.01. 3
justice, o royal duke! 5.01. 20
believe it, royal prince, | if he be less, he's 5.01. 57
blessed be your royal grace! 5.01.137
lord, and i have heard | your royal ear abus'd. 5.01.139
this paper into the royal hand of the king; LLL 4.02.141 P
my poor shoulder, and with his royal finger, 5.01.103 P
much expense of thy royal sweet breath as will 5.02.523 P
you the peace of mind, most royal couplement. 5.02.531 P
i will kiss thy royal finger, and take leave. 5.02.882 P
more than to us | wait in your royal walks, your MND 5.01. 31
how doth that royal merchant, good antonio? MV 3.02.239
his back, | enow to press a royal merchant down, 4.01. 29
for 'tis | the royal disposition of that beast AYL 4.03.117
lives not his epitaph | as in your royal speech. AWW 1.02. 51
o, will you eat | no grapes, my royal fox? 2.01. 70
grapes, and if my royal fox | could reach them. 2.01. 71
humbly entreating from your royal thoughts | a 2.01.127
to choose from forth the royal blood of france, 2.01.196
stay, royal sir. 5.03.295
sport royal, i warrant you. TN 2.03.172 P
more mature dignities and royal necessities made WT 1.01. 25 P
yet of your royal presence i'll adventure | the 1.02. 38
the one for ever earn'd a royal husband; 1.02.107
hail, most royal sir! 1.02.366
my royal liege, | he is not guilty of her coming 2.03.144
our sovereign lord the king, thy royal husband: 3.02. 17 P
a fellow of the royal bed, which owe | a moi'ty 3.02. 38
sir, royal sir, forgive a foolish woman. 3.02.227
must know | the royal fool thou cop'st with — 4.04.424
for she did print your royal father off, 5.01.125
most royal sir, from thence; 5.01.159
o royal piece, | there's magic in thy majesty, 5.03. 38
hand, | thy nephew and right royal sovereign. JN 1.01. 15
we'll lay before this town our royal bones, 2.01. 41
we bear, | or add a royal number to the dead, 2.01.347
why stand these royal fronts amazed thus? 2.01.356
your royal presences be rul'd by me: 2.01.377
this royal hand and mine are newly knit, | and 3.01.226
between our kingdoms and our royal selves, | and 3.01.232
hands | to clap this royal bargain up of peace, 3.01.235
but that your royal pleasure must be done, 4.02. 17
one flourishing branch of his most royal root, R2 1.02. 18
hither | before king richard in his royal lists? 1.03. 32
right, | so be thy fortune in this royal fight! 1.03. 56
lay on our royal sword your banish'd hands; 1.03.179
we are enforc'd to farm our royal realm, | the 1.04. 45
this royal throne of kings, this sceptred isle, 2.01. 40
this nurse, this teeming womb of royal kings, 2.01. 51
chasing the royal blood | with fury from his 2.01.118
now, by my seat's right royal majesty, | wert 2.01.120
such wrongs are borne | in him, a royal prince, 2.01.239
you have misled a prince, a royal king, | a 3.01. 8
and him, | broke the possession of a royal bed, 3.01. 13
earth, | and do thee favors with my royal hands. 3.02. 11
true faith of heart | to his most royal person; 3.03. 38
that stands upon your royal grandsire's bones, 3.03.106
knees, | which on thy royal party granted once, 3.03.115
yields | to the possession of thy royal hand. 4.01.110
worst in this royal presence may i speak, | yet 4.01.115
hail, royal prince! 5.05. 67
to look upon my sometimes royal master's face. 5.05. 75
that jade hath eat bread from my royal hand, 5.05. 85
as full of valure as of royal blood! 5.05.113
nor thou cam'st not of the blood royal, if thou 1H4 1.02.141 P
give him as much as will make him a royal man, 2.04.291 P
towns | between that royal field of shrewsbury 2H4 in 34
will not stick to say his face is a face royal. 1.02. 23 P
he may keep it still at a face royal, for a 1.02. 25 P
that, were our royal faiths martyrs in love, 4.01.191
o my royal father! 4.04.112
down, royal state! 4.05.120
thus, my most royal liege, | accusing it, i put 4.05.164
health, peace, and happiness to my royal father! 4.05.226
nay more, to spurn at your most royal image, 5.02. 89
question your royal thoughts, make the case 5.02. 91
god save thy grace, king hal! my royal hal! 5.05. 41
thee guard and keep, most royal imp of fame! 5.05. 45
and i, my royal sovereign. H5 2.02. 65
you have conspir'd against our royal person, 2.02.167
behold | the royal captain of this ruin'd band 4.pr. 29
upon his royal face there is no note | how dread 4.pr. 35
more help, could fight this royal battle! 4.03. 75
here was a royal fellowship of death! 4.08.101
majesties | unto this bar and royal interview, 5.02. 27
that face to face, and royal eye to eye, | you 5.02. 30
me, | if i demand, before this royal view, 5.02. 32
my royal cousin, teach you our princess english? 5.02.281 P
and, for your royal birth, | inferior to none 1H6 3.01. 95
then march to paris, royal charles of france, 5.02. 4
you, | if happy england's royal king be free. 5.03.115
and i again, in henry's royal name, | as deputy 5.03.160
that marg'ret may be england's royal queen. 5.05. 24
voice, | "jesu maintain your royal excellence!" 2H6 1.01.161
jesus preserve your royal majesty! 1.02. 70
i do beseech your royal majesty, | let him have 1.03.195
i humbly thank your royal majesty. 1.03.211
that he should come about your royal person, 3.01. 26
from meaning treason to our royal person | as is 3.01. 70
if those that care to keep your royal person 3.01.173
man, | and find no harbor in a royal heart. 3.01.336
his behalf | is slander to your royal dignity. 3.02.209
they say, in care of your most royal person, 3.02.254
swear | to spoil the city and your royal court. 4.04. 53
the rightful heir to england's royal seat. 5.01.178
the next degree is england's royal throne; 3H6 2.01.193
royal commanders, be in readiness, | for with a 2.02. 67
my royal father, cheer these noble lords, | and 2.02. 78
there to be crowned england's royal king; 2.06. 88
first, to do greetings to thy royal person, 3.03. 52
shall waft them over with our royal fleet. 3.03.253
wherefore else guard we his royal tent | but to 4.03. 21
no, but the loss of his own royal person. 4.04. 5
once more we sit in england's royal throne, 5.07. 1
long, | and overmuch consum'd his royal person: R3 1.01.140
thou bloodless remnant of that royal blood, | be 1.02. 7
valiant, wise, and (no doubt) right royal — 1.02.244
good time of day unto your royal grace! 1.03. 18
and sent to warn them to his royal presence. 1.03. 39
his royal grace | (whom god preserve better than 1.03. 58
the king, on his own royal disposition | (and 1.03. 63
but not, as i am, royal. 1.04.165
this, | to be so flouted in this royal presence? 2.01. 79
for it requires the royal debt it lent you. 2.02. 95
where it seems best unto your royal self. 3.01. 63
duke | in the seat royal of this famous isle? 3.01.164
in god's name speak, when is the royal day? 3.04. 3
is all things ready for the royal time? 3.04. 4
cry, "god save richard, england's royal king!" 3.07. 22
birth, | the lineal glory of your royal house, 3.07.121
/her royal stock graft with ignoble plants, 3.07.127
the royal tree hath left us royal fruit, | which 3.07.167
the royal tree hath left us royal fruit, | which 3.07.167
take to your royal self | this proffer'd benefit 3.07.195
then i salute you with this royal title — 3.07.239
there to be crowned richard's royal queen. 4.01. 32
i have no moe sons of the royal blood | for thee 4.04.200
virtuous and fair, royal and gracious. 4.04.205
wrong not her birth, she is a royal princess. 4.04.212
here, | a royal battle might be won and lost. 4.04.536
the true succeeders of each royal house, | by 5.05. 30
all was royal; H8 1.01. 42
here i'll make | my royal choice. 1.04. 86
like a most royal prince | restor'd me to my 2.01.113
in which we come | to know your royal pleasure. 2.02. 70
madam, | it's fit this royal session do proceed, 2.04. 66
but with thanks to god for such | a royal lady, 2.04.154
i confess your royal graces | show'r'd on me 3.02.166
truth | toward the king, my ever royal master, 3.02.273
am sure have shown at full their royal minds — 4.01. 8
a royal train, believe me. 4.01. 37
she had all the royal makings of a queen, | as 4.01. 87
my royal nephew, and your name capuchius. 4.02.110
now good angels | fly o'er thy royal head, and 5.01.160
his royal self in judgment comes to hear | the 5.02.155
and to your royal grace and the good queen, | my 5.04. 4
this royal infant — heaven still move about her 5.04. 17
at priam's royal table do i sit, | and when fair TRO 1.01. 29
which you do here forbid me, royal priam. 5.03. 75
a most royal one: COR 4.03. 43 P
i minded him how royal 'twas to pardon | when it 5.01. 18
son, | were gracious in the eyes of royal rome, TIT 1.01. 11
rome's royal mistress, mistress of my heart, 1.01.241
rome's royal emperess, | unfurnish'd of her 2.03. 55
touch not the boy, he is of royal blood. 5.01. 49
lucius, all hail, rome's royal emperor! 5.03.141
noble, worthy, royal timon! TIM 2.02.168
royal cheer, i warrant you. 3.06. 49 P
caesar was mighty, bold, royal, and loving. JC 3.01.127
o royal caesar! 3.02.244 P
prediction | of noble having and of royal hope, MAC 1.03. 56
to give thee from our royal master thanks, 1.03.101
banquo, banquo, | our royal master's murther'd! 2.03. 87
your royal father's murther'd. 2.03.100
most royal sir, fleance is scap'd. 3.04. 19
my royal lord, | you do not give the cheer. 3.04. 31
highness | to grace us with your royal company? 3.04. 44
thy royal father | was a most sainted king; 4.03.108
your royal preparation | makes us hear something 5.03. 57
call thee hamlet, | king, father, royal dane. HAM 1.04. 45
let not the royal bed of denmark be | a couch 1.05. 82
where i found, horatio — | ah, royal knavery! 5.02. 19
to have prov'd most royal, and, for his passage, 5.02.398
royal lear, | whom i have ever honor'd as my LR 1.01.139
most royal majesty, | i crave no more than hath 1.01.193
pardon me, royal sir, | election makes not up in 1.01.205
royal king, | give but that portion which 1.01.241
you are a royal one, and we obey you. 4.06.201
how does my royal lord? how fares your majesty? 4.07. 43
thy very gait did prophesy | a royal nobleness. 5.03.177
my life and being | from men of royal siege, and OTH 1.02. 22
the royal banner, and all quality, | pride, pomp 3.03.353
royal wench! ANT 2.02.226
go on: right royal. 3.13. 55
to–day, and knew'st | the royal occupation, thou 4.04. 17
next day's fate, | which promises royal peril. 4.08. 35
royal egypt! | empress! 4.15. 70
royal queen! 5.02. 37
never be beheld | of eyes again so royal! 5.02.318
a princess | descended of so many royal kings. 5.02.327
she levell'd at our purposes, and, being royal, 5.02.336
thanks, royal sir. CYM 3.05. 1
royal sir, | since the exile of posthumus, most 3.05. 35
for she's fair and royal, | and that she hath 3.05. 70
their royal blood enchaf'd, as the rud'st wind 4.02.174
his royal bird | prunes the immortal wing and 5.04.117
lord in love and one | that had a royal lover, 5.05.172
the lofty cedar, royal cymbeline, | personates 5.05.453
royal antiochus, on what cause i know not, PER 1.03. 19
it pleaseth you, my royal father, to express 2.02. 8
a prince of macedon, my royal father, | and the 2.02. 24
who can be other in this royal presence? 2.03. 49
hail, royal sir! 5.01. 40
you are, you are — o royal pericles! 5.03. 14
being gone, | not royal in their smells alone, TNK 1.01. 2
most royal brother — 3.06.195
good friend, be royal. 4.02.154
you royal germane foes, that this day come | to 5.01. 9
ROYALIZE 1 FR 0.0001 REL FR 1 V 0 P
to royalize his blood i spent mine own. R3 1.03.124
ROYALLY 8 FR 0.0009 REL FR 6 V 2 P
your brother is royally entertain'd by leonato, ADO 1.03. 43 P
hath been royally attorney'd with interchange of WT 1.01. 27 P
be so my care | to have you royally appointed, 4.04.592
the castle royally is mann'd, my lord, | against R2 3.03. 21
royally! | why, it contains no king? 3.03. 23
sorrow so royally in you appears | that i will 2H4 5.02. 51
us concerns | to answer royally in our defenses. H5 2.04. 3
come in, and let us banquet royally, | after 1H6 1.06. 30
ROYALTIES 6 FR 0.0006 REL FR 6 V 0 P
of temporal royalties | he thinks me now TMP 1.02.110
and thine usurp | the dominations, royalties, JN 2.01.176
the royalties and rights of banish'd herford? R2 2.01.190
my rights and royalties | pluck'd from my arms 2.03.120
and by the royalties of both your bloods, 3.03.107
further scope | than for his lineal royalties, 3.03.113
ROYALTY 24 FR 0.0027 REL FR 22 V 2 P
and executing th' outward face of royalty | with TMP 1.02.104
sweet royalty, bestow on me the sense of hearing LLL 5.02.664 P
besides, i have stay'd | to tire your royalty. WT 1.02. 15
and that high royalty was ne'er pluck'd off; JN 4.02. 5
up | from forth this morsel of dead royalty! 4.03.143
of soul | to stranger blood, to foreign royalty. 5.01. 11
king, | for thus his royalty doth speak in me: 5.02.129
but a clod | and module of confounded royalty. 5.07. 58
setting aside his high blood's royalty, | and R2 1.01. 58
king, | and lay aside my high blood's royalty, 1.01. 71
mingled his royalty with cap'ring fools, | had 1H4 3.02. 63
did give him that same royalty he wears, | and 4.03. 55
king at /hampton pier | embark his royalty; H5 3.pr. 5
and, as a branch and member of this royalty, 5.02. 5
isle, | and this the royalty of albion's king? 2H6 1.03. 45
shall lose the royalty of england's throne. R3 3.04. 40
lo here this long–usurped royalty | from the 5.05. 4
whose health and royalty i pray for. H8 2.03. 73
and in his royalty of nature | reigns that which MAC 3.01. 49
to the succeeding royalty he leaves | the 4.03.155
puppet's part against the royalty of her father. LR 2.02. 37 P
but that your royalty | holds idleness your ANT 1.03. 91
should frame them | to royalty unlearn'd, honor CYM 4.02.178
married your royalty, was wife to your place, 5.05. 39
ROYALTY'S 1 FR 0.0001 REL FR 1 V 0 P
what holier than, for royalty's repair, | for WT 5.01. 31
ROYNISH 1 FR 0.0001 REL FR 1 V 0 P
my lord, the roynish clown, at whom so oft AYL 2.02. 8
RUB 13 FR 0.0014 REL FR 11 V 2 P
you rub the sore, | when you should bring the TMP 2.01.139
go, sir, rub your chain with crumbs. TN 2.03.119 P
blow each dust, each straw, each little rub, JN 3.04.128
which gape and rub the elbow at the news | of 1H4 5.01. 77
not now | but every rub is smoothed on our way. H5 2.02.188
view, | what rub or what impediment there is, 5.02. 33
once perceive | the least rub in your fortunes, H8 2.01.129
so, so, rub on and kiss the mistress. TRO 3.02. 49 P
coriolanus | deserv'd this so dishonor'd rub, COR 3.01. 60
ay, there's the rub, | for in that sleep of HAM 3.01. 64
here, hamlet, take my napkin, rub thy brows. 5.02.288
rub him about the temples. OTH 4.01. 52
why do you rub my kiss off? TNK 5.02. 88
RUBB'D 3 FR 0.0003 REL FR 3 V 0 P
one rubb'd his elbow thus, and fleer'd, and LLL 5.02.109
well knows, | will not be rubb'd nor stopp'd. LR 2.02.154
i have rubb'd this young quat almost to the OTH 5.01. 11
RUBBING 3 FR 0.0003 REL FR 3 V 0 P
i fear too much rubbing. LLL 4.01.139
that rubbing the poor itch of your opinion COR 1.01.165
found, | as vaded gloss no rubbing will refresh, PP 13. 8
RUBBISH 2 FR 0.0002 REL FR 2 V 0 P
threw dust and rubbish on king richard's head. R2 5.02. 6
what rubbish and what offal? JC 1.03.109
RUBIED 1 FR 0.0001 REL FR 1 V 0 P
her inkle, silk, /twin with the rubied cherry, PER 5.ch. 8
RUBIES 5 FR 0.0005 REL FR 4 V 1 P
impression of keen whips i'ld wear as rubies, MM 2.04.101
all o'er embellish'd with rubies, carbuncles, ERR 3.02.135 P
those be rubies, fairy favors, | in those MND 2.01. 12
rubies unparagon'd, | how dearly they do't! CYM 2.02. 17
me, | of pallid pearls and rubies red as blood, LC 198
RUBIOUS 1 FR 0.0001 REL FR 1 V 0 P
diana's lip | is not more smooth and rubious; TN 1.04. 32
RUBS 5 FR 0.0005 REL FR 3 V 2 P
nay, 'a rubs himself with civet. ADO 3.02. 50 P
'twill make me think the world is full of rubs, R2 3.04. 4
o, this is well. he rubs the vein of him. TRO 2.03.200
to leave no rubs nor botches in the work — MAC 3.01.133
look how she rubs her hands. 5.01. 26 P
RUBY 2 FR 0.0002 REL FR 2 V 0 P

(which like dumb mouths do ope their ruby lips JC 3.01.260
and keep the natural ruby of your cheeks, | when MAC 3.04.114
RUBY–COLOR'D 1 FR 0.0001 REL FR 1 V 0 P
once more the ruby–color'd portal open'd, VEN 451
RU'D 1 FR 0.0001 REL FR 1 V 0 P
was ever son so ru'd a father's death? 3H6 2.05.109
RUDDER 2 FR 0.0002 REL FR 2 V 0 P
with all their sixty, fly and turn the rudder. ANT 3.10. 3
my heart was to thy rudder tied by th' strings, 3.11. 57
RUDDINESS 1 FR 0.0001 REL FR 1 V 0 P
the ruddiness upon her lip is wet; WT 5.03. 81
RUDDOCK *(see raddock)*
RUDDY 2 FR 0.0002 REL FR 2 V 0 P
as dear to me as are the ruddy drops | that JC 2.01.289
his complexion | is, as a ripe grape, ruddy. TNK 4.02. 96
RUDE 74 FR 0.0083 REL FR 67 V 7 P
let go that rude uncivil touch, | thou friend of TGV 5.04. 60
both work | ere this rude beast will profit. MM 3.02. 33
i | persuade this rude wretch willingly to die. 4.03. 81
when he demean'd himself rough, rude, and wildly
ERR 5.01. 88
but by and by rude fishermen of corinth | by 5.01.352
most rude melancholy, valor gives thee place. LLL 3.01. 68
that, like a rude and savage man of inde, | at 4.03.218
which the rude multitude call the afternoon. 5.01. 89 P
for our rude transgression | some fair excuse. 5.02.431
that the rude sea grew civil at her song, | and MND 2.01.152
hour, | a crew of patches, rude mechanicals, 3.02. 9
why are you grown so rude? 3.02.262
thou art too wild, too rude, and bold of voice MV 2.02.181
for the poor rude world | hath not her fellow. 3.05. 82
or else a rude despiser of good manners, | that AYL 2.07. 92
art not seen, | although thy breath be rude. 2.07.179
that twenty such rude boys might tend upon | and AWW 3.02. 82
from the rude sea's enrag'd and foamy mouth TN 5.01. 78
out on thee, rude man, thou dost shame thy JN 1.01. 64
were harbor'd in their rude circumference. 2.01.262
to whom he sung, in rude harsh–sounding rhymes, 4.02.150
and consequently thy rude hand to act | the deed 4.02.240
in my form, | which, howsoever rude exteriorly, 4.02.257
unthread the rude eye of rebellion, | and 5.04. 11
which he hath left so shapeless and so rude. 5.07. 27
not all the water in the rough rude sea | can R2 3.02. 54
go to the rude ribs of that ancient castle; 3.03. 32
how dares thy harsh rude tongue sound this 3.04. 74
where rude misgoverned hands from windows' tops 5.02. 5
how now, what means death in this rude assault? 5.05.105
was by the rude hands of that welshman taken, 1H4 1.01. 41
attempts, | such barren pleasures, rude society, 3.02. 14
set | on bloody courses, the rude scene may end, 2H4 1.01.159
prince gave you, he gave it like a rude prince, 1.02.195 P
brains | in cradle of the rude imperious surge, 3.01. 20
to the wet //sea–boy in an hour so rude, | and 3.01. 27
his companies unletter'd, rude, and shallow, H5 1.01. 55
in confutation of which rude reproach, | and in 1H6 4.01. 98
with the rude multitude till i return. 2H6 3.02.135
'tis like the commons, rude unpolish'd hinds, 3.02.271
of hinds and peasants, rude and merciless. 4.04. 33
why, rude companion, whatsoe'er thou be, | i 4.10. 31
if one so rude and of so mean condition | may 5.01. 64
what means this scene of rude impatience? R3 2.02. 38
rude ragged nurse, old sullen playfellow | for 4.01.101
of a rude stream that must for ever hide me. H8 3.02.364
her wonted greatness, | to use so rude behavior. 4.02.103
ye rude slaves, leave your gaping. 5.03. 2 P
look for ale and cakes here, you rude rascals? 5.03. 11 P
peace, rude sounds! TRO 1.01. 89
and the rude son should strike his father dead; 1.03.115
rude, in sooth, in good sooth, very rude. 3.01. 56 P
rude, in sooth, in good sooth, very rude. 3.01. 56 P
with the rude brevity and discharge of one. 4.04. 41
too rude, too boist'rous, and it pricks like ROM 1.04. 26
and, touching hers, make blessed my rude hand. 1.05. 51
in man as well as herbs, grace and rude will; 2.03. 28
my blood for your rude brawls doth lie 3.01.189
o rude unthankfulness! 3.03. 24
who is here so rude that would not be a roman? JC 3.02. 31 P
wag thy tongue | in noise so rude against me? HAM 3.04. 40
you are not worth the dust which the rude wind LR 4.02. 30
rude am i in my speech, | and little bless'd OTH 1.03. 81
whose rude throats | th' immortal jove's dread 3.03.355
our good minds | by this rude place we live in. CYM 3.06. 65
rude and impatient, then, like chastity, | she TNK 2.02.141
may rude wind never hurt thee! 2.02.275
i first appear, though rude, and raw, and muddy, 3.05.122
retire, | beaten away by brain–sick rude desire. LUC 175
that yet remains upon her breast | (rude ram, to 464
harsh, featureless, and rude, barrenly perish: SON 11.10
these poor rude lines of thy deceased lover, 32. 4
advance | as high as learning my rude ignorance. 78.14
savage, extreme, rude, cruel, not to trust, 129. 4
RUDE–GROWING 1 FR 0.0001 REL FR 1 V 0 P
whose mouth is covered with rude–growing briers,
TIT 2.03.199
RUDELIEST 1 FR 0.0001 REL FR 1 V 0 P
thou art the rudeliest welcome to this world PER 3.01. 30
RUDELY 8 FR 0.0009 REL FR 7 V 1 P
yet you began rudely. TN 1.05.212 P
thy place in council thou hast rudely lost, 1H4 3.02. 32
i, that am rudely stamp'd, and want love's R3 1.01. 16
rudely beguiles our lips | of all rejoindure, TRO 4.04. 35
of rome, | or rudely visit them in parts remote, COR 4.05.142
bed, | throwing his mantle rudely o'er his arm, LUC 170
of love's coy touch, shall rudely tear thee; 669
and maiden virtue rudely strumpeted, | and right SON 66. 6
RUDENESS 6 FR 0.0006 REL FR 4 V 2 P
the rudeness that hath appear'd in me have i TN 1.05.214 P
for the great swinge and rudeness of his poise, TRO 1.03.207
mars his idiot! do, rudeness, do, camel, do, do. 2.01. 53 P
this rudeness is a sauce to his good wit, JC 1.02.300
whose rudeness | answer'd my steps too loud. CYM 4.02.214
his rudeness so with his authoriz'd youth | did LC 104
RUDER 3 FR 0.0003 REL FR 3 V 0 P
the bolder to salute my king | with ruder terms, 2H6 1.01. 30
sweetness | for the capacity of my ruder powers. TRO 3.02. 25
here | that ruder tongues distinguish villager, TNK 3.05.104
RUDESBY 2 FR 0.0002 REL FR 2 V 0 P
heart | unto a mad–brain rudesby full of spleen, SHR 3.02. 10
rudesby, be gone! TN 4.01. 51
RUDEST 1 FR 0.0001 REL FR 1 V 0 P
deign | the roughest berry on the rudest hedge; ANT 1.04. 64
RUDIMENTS 3 FR 0.0003 REL FR 3 V 0 P
and hath been tutor'd in the rudiments | of many AYL 5.04. 31
fingering, | i must begin with rudiments of art, SHR 3.01. 66
have my rudiments | been labor'd so long with ye TNK 3.05. 3
RUD'ST 2 FR 0.0002 REL FR 2 V 0 P
as the rud'st wind | that by the top doth take CYM 4.02.174
for if it see the rud'st or gentlest sight, SON 113. 9
RUE* 18 FR 0.0020 REL FR 16 V 2 P
sirs, | for you there's rosemary and rue; WT 4.04. 74
thou shalt rue this hour within this hour. JN 3.01.323
well then, france shall rue. 3.01.325
nought shall make us rue, | if england to itself 5.07.117
and all too soon, i fear, the king shall rue. R2 1.03.205
here in this place | i'll set a bank of rue, 3.04.105
rue, even for ruth, here shortly shall be seen, 3.04.106
thou shalt rue this treason with thy tears, | if 1H6 3.02. 36
and, in thy closet pent up, rue my shame, | and 2H6 2.04. 24
by his soul, thou and thy house shall rue it. 3H6 1.01. 94
shall rue the hour that ever thou wast born. 5.06. 43
which may make you and him to rue at th' other. R3 3.02. 14
if you deny them, all the land will rue it. 3.07.222
victorious titus, rue the tears i shed, | a TIT 1.01.105
and what not done, that thou hast cause to rue, 5.01.109
"you'll rue the time | that clogs me with this MAC 3.06. 42
there's rue for you, and here's some for me; HAM 4.05.181 P
you may wear your rue with a difference. 4.05.183 P
RUFF 5 FR 0.0005 REL FR 1 V 4 P
upon his boot and sing, mend the ruff and sing, AWW 3.02. 7 P
not live, but i will murther your ruff for this. 2H4 2.04.135 P
tearing a poor whore's ruff in a bawdy–house? 2.04.145 P
have him here to–morrow with his best ruff on. PER 4.02.103 P
and you in ruff of your opinions cloth'd, | what STM II.C 79
RUFFIAN 15 FR 0.0017 REL FR 13 V 2 P
ruffian! TGV 5.04. 60
thee, | by ruffian lust should be contaminate? ERR 2.02.133
talk with a ruffian at her chamber–window, | who ADO 4.01. 91
lunatic, | a madcap ruffian and a swearing jack, SHR 2.01.288
fruitless pranks | this ruffian hath botch'd up, TN 4.01. 56
well, ruffian, i must pocket up these wrongs, JN 3.01.200
that grey iniquity, that father ruffian, that 1H4 2.04.454 P
who take the ruffian /billows by the top, 2H4 3.01. 22
all, | swear like a ruffian, and demean himself 2H6 1.01.188
wilt thou on thy death–bed play the ruffian, 5.01.164
thy chair–days, thus | to die in ruffian battle? 5.02. 49
but let the ruffian boreas once enrage | the TRO 1.03. 38
this ancient ruffian, sir, whose life i have LR 2.02. 62 P
let the old ruffian know | i have many other ANT 4.01. 4
the staring ruffian shall it keep in quiet, VEN 1149
RUFFIAN'D 1 FR 0.0001 REL FR 1 V 0 P
if it hath ruffian'd so upon the sea, | what OTH 2.01. 7
RUFFIANS 4 FR 0.0004 REL FR 3 V 1 P
rich men look sad, and ruffians dance and leap, R2 2.04. 12
make curl'd–pate ruffians bald, | and let the TIM 4.03.160
to do you service and you think we are ruffians, OTH 1.01.110 P
for other ruffians, as their fancies wrought, STM II.C 84
RUFFIN 1 FR 0.0001 REL FR 1 V 0 P
have you a ruffin that will swear, drink, dance, 2H4 4.05.124
RUFFLE* 5 FR 0.0005 REL FR 5 V 0 P
sons, | to ruffle in the commonwealth of rome. TIT 1.01.313
were an antony | would ruffle up your spirits, JC 3.02.228
on, and the /bleak winds | do sorely ruffle; LR 2.04.301
hospitable favors | you should not ruffle thus. 3.07. 41
sometime a blusterer that the ruffle knew | of LC 58
RUFFLING 1 FR 0.0001 REL FR 1 V 0 P
to deck thy body with his ruffling treasure. SHR 4.03. 60
RUFFS 1 FR 0.0001 REL FR 1 V 0 P
with ruffs and cuffs, and fardingales, and SHR 4.03. 56
RUGBY 15 FR 0.0017 REL FR 0 V 15 P
what, john rugby! WIV 1.04. 1 P
what, john rugby! 1.04. 39 P
vere is dat knave rugby? 1.04. 55 P
what, john rugby! john! 1.04. 56 P
you are john rugby, and you are jack rugby. 1.04. 58 P
you are john rugby, and you are jack rugby. 1.04. 59 P
rugby, my rapier! 1.04. 68 P
rugby, /baillez me some paper. 1.04. 87 P
rugby, come to the court with me. 1.04.123 P
follow my heels, rugby. 1.04.125 P
jack rugby! 2.03. 1 P
by gar, jack rugby, he is dead already, if he be 2.03. 8 P
come at my heels, jack rugby. 2.03. 98 P
jack rugby — mine host de jarteer — have i not 3.01. 91 P
go home, john rugby, i come anon. 3.02. 86 P
RUGGED 5 FR 0.0005 REL FR 5 V 0 P
well–proportion'd beard made rough and rugged, 2H6 3.02.175
gentle my lord, sleek o'er your rugged looks, MAC 3.02. 27
approach thou like the rugged russian bear, 3.04. 99
"the rugged pyrrhus, like th' hyrcanian beast — HAM 2.02.450
"the rugged pyrrhus, he whose sable arms, 2.02.452
RUG–HEADED 1 FR 0.0001 REL FR 1 V 0 P
we must supplant those rough rug–headed kerns, R2 2.01.156
/RUIN 3 FR 0.0003 REL FR 3 V 0 P
/husks | /and /formless /ruin /of /oblivion; TRO 4.05.167
me, should stop my way, | /but /by /my /ruin. 5.03. 58
consequence, | attends the boist'rous /ruin. HAM 3.03. 22
RUIN 40 FR 0.0045 REL FR 40 V 0 P
pick'd from the chaff and ruin of the times | to MV 2.09. 48
away, | let it presage the ruin of your love, 3.02.173
good youth, or it will fall | to cureless ruin. 4.01.142
your ruin — marry her, | and with my best WT 4.04.530
soul, | kneeling before this ruin of sweet life, JN 4.03. 65
cry woe, destruction, ruin, and decay: R2 3.02.102
whose ruin you /have sought, that to her laws H5 2.02.176
behold | what ruin happened in revenge of him, 1H6 2.02. 11
defac'd | by wasting ruin of the cruel foe. 3.03. 46
there comes the ruin, there begins confusion. 4.01.194
alone, | tend'ring my ruin and assail'd of none, 4.07. 10
to us, | else ruin combat with their palaces! 5.02. 7
come, thou new ruin of old clifford's house: 2H6 5.02. 61
disgrace, | and utter ruin of the house of york. 3H6 1.01.254
our ranks are broke, and ruin follows us. 2.03. 10
and seek their ruin that usurp'd our right? 5.06. 73
i see the ruin of my house: R3 2.04. 49
soul, | death, desolation, ruin, and decay. 4.04.409
and weigh thee down to ruin, shame, and death! 5.03.148
ye tell me what ye wish for both — my ruin. H8 3.01. 98
from me, as if ruin | leap'd from his eyes. 3.02.205
ye appear in every thing may bring my ruin! 3.02.242
that sweet aspect of princes, and their ruin, 3.02.369
never | (but where he meant to ruin) pitiful. 4.02. 40
disobedience, fed | the ruin of the state. COR 3.01.118
distinctly ranges, | in heaps and piles of ruin. 3.01.206
and safeguard | of what that want might ruin. 3.02. 69
come all to ruin, let | thy mother rather feel 3.02.125
else | triumphantly tread on thy country's ruin, 5.03.116
heaven, | and bow this feeble ruin to the earth; TIT 3.01.207
the noble ruin of her magic, antony, | claps on ANT 3.10. 18
this mortal house i'll ruin, | do caesar what he 5.02. 51
the ruin speaks that sometime | it was a worthy CYM 4.02.354
left without a roof | soon fall to ruin — your PER 2.04. 37
meet you no ruin but the soldier in | the cranks TNK 1.02. 27
to him, and pronounces | ruin to thebes; 1.02. 92
sister, | i find no anger to 'em, nor no ruin: 3.06.189
their lives | might breed the ruin of my name, 3.06.240
in her the painter had anatomiz'd | time's ruin, LUC 1451
decay, | ruin hath taught me thus to ruminate, SON 64.11
RUINATE 3 FR 0.0003 REL FR 3 V 0 P
i will not ruinate my father's house, | who gave 3H6 5.01. 83
to ruinate proud buildings with thy hours, | and LUC 944
seeking that beauteous roof to ruinate, | which SON 10. 7
/RUIN'D 1 FR 0.0001 REL FR 1 V 0 P
bare /ruin'd choirs, where late the sweet birds SON 73. 4
RUIN'D 12 FR 0.0013 REL FR 12 V 0 P
in me that can be found, | by him not ruin'd? ERR 2.01. 97
the breath of parley | into his ruin'd ears, and R2 3.03. 34
her fruit–trees all unprun'd, her hedges ruin'd, 3.04. 45
hope and expectation of thy time | is ruin'd, 1H4 3.02. 37
the royal captain of this ruin'd band | walking H5 4.pr. 29
and see the noble ruin'd man you speak of. H8 2.01. 54
these ruin'd pillars, out of pity taken | a load 3.02.382
mark but my fall, and that that ruin'd me: 3.02.439
all broken implements of a ruin'd house. TIM 4.02. 16
o ruin'd piece of nature! LR 4.06.134
since her best work is ruin'd with thy rigor." VEN 954
and ruin'd love, when it is built anew, | grows SON 119.11
RUINING 1 FR 0.0001 REL FR 1 V 0 P
which proves more short than waste or ruining? SON 125. 4
/RUINOUS 1 FR 0.0001 REL FR 1 V 0 P
shall love, in /building, grow so /ruinous? ERR 3.02. 4
RUINOUS 5 FR 0.0005 REL FR 3 V 2 P
lest, growing ruinous, the building fall | and TGV 5.04. 9
why, no, you ruinous butt, you whoreson TRO 5.01. 28 P
i stray'd | to gaze upon a ruinous monastery, TIT 5.01. 21
is yond despis'd and ruinous man my lord? TIM 4.03.459
and all ruinous disorders follow us disquietly LR 1.02.113 P
RUIN'S 1 FR 0.0001 REL FR 1 V 0 P
breach in nature | for ruin's wasteful entrance; MAC 2.03.114
RUINS 8 FR 0.0009 REL FR 7 V 1 P
what ruins are in me that can be found, | by him ERR 2.01. 96
that /bawl out the ruins of thy linen shall 2H4 2.02. 24 P
and all the ruins of distressful times R3 4.04.318
and out of ruins | made my name once more noble.
H8 2.01.114
thou art the ruins of the noblest man | that JC 3.01.256
what strange ruins, | since first we went to TNK 1.02. 13
i know mine own is but a heap of ruins, | and no 2.03. 19
to whose weak ruins muster troops of cares, | to LUC 720
RUL'D 34 FR 0.0038 REL FR 28 V 6 P
we'll do thee homage and be rul'd by thee, TGV 4.01. 64
and i beseech you be rul'd by your well–willers. WIV 1.01. 71 P
be rul'd by him. MM 4.06. 4
be rul'd by me, depart in patience, | and let us ERR 3.01. 94
niece, i trust you will be rul'd by your father. ADO 2.01. 51 P
to be rul'd by my conscience, i should stay with MV 2.02. 22 P
from the jew, i should be rul'd by the fiend, 2.02. 25 P
would thou'dst be rul'd by me! TN 4.01. 64
your royal presences be rul'd by me: JN 2.01.377
wrath–kindled /gentlemen, be rul'd by me, R2 1.01.152
had they been rul'd by me, | you should have won 2H4 4.03. 66
be thou rul'd by me. 1H6 1.04. 5
if dolphin and the rest will be but rul'd. 3.03. 8
yet so he rul'd, and such a prince he was, | as 2H6 2.04. 44
face | rul'd like a wandering planet over me, 4.04. 16
you shall have four /and you'll be rul'd by him. 3H6 3.02. 30
why, this it is, when men are rul'd by women: R3 1.01. 62
and were they to be rul'd, and not to rule, 2.03. 29
be rul'd by him, lord ajax. TRO 2.03.257
prithee now, | go, and be rul'd; COR 3.02. 90
my lord, be rul'd by me, be won at last, TIT 1.01.442
be rul'd by me, forget to think of her. ROM 1.01.225
i think she will /be rul'd | in all respects by 3.04. 13
henceforward i am ever rul'd by you. 4.02. 22
it shall be said his judgment rul'd our hands; JC 2.01.147
so to–day, | if cassius might have rul'd. 5.01. 47
be rul'd, you shall not go. HAM 1.04. 81
will you be rul'd by me? 4.07. 59
my lord, i will be rul'd, | the rather, if you 4.07. 68
you should be rul'd and led | by some discretion LR 2.04.148
but, sir, be you rul'd by me. OTH 2.01.263 P
either be rul'd by me, or i'll make you — | man PER 2.05. 83
we'll be rul'd by you, master more, if you'll STM II.C 142 P
"but if thou needs wilt hunt, be rul'd by me, VEN 673
RULE 57 FR 0.0064 REL FR 49 V 8 P
there be that can rule naples | as well as he TMP 2.01.262
goes she has all the rule of her husband's purse WIV 1.03. 52 P
by what rule, sir? ERR 2.02. 68 P
by a rule as plain as the plain bald pate of 2.02. 69 P
yet in such rule that the venetian law | cannot MV 4.01.178
life, | an aweful rule, and right supremacy; SHR 5.02.109
or seek for rule, supremacy, and sway, | when 5.02.163
be said in't, 'tis against the rule of nature. AWW 1.01.136 P
you would not give means for this uncivil rule. TN 2.03.123 P
and given your drunken cousin rule over me, yet 5.01.304 P
what? canst not rule her? WT 2.03. 46
honor — trust it, | he shall not rule me. 2.03. 50
so long as out of limit and true rule | you 1H4 4.03. 39
so much the worse, if your own rule be true. 2H4 4.02. 86
creatures that by a rule in nature teach | the H5 1.02.188
let senses rule; 2.03. 49
the imputation of his wickedness, by your rule, 4.01.149 P
margaret shall now be queen, and rule the king; 1H6 5.05.107
but i will rule both her, the king, and realm. 5.05.108
whose bookish rule hath pull'd fair england down 2H6 1.01.259

let them obey that knows not how to rule; 5.01. 6
not fit to govern and rule multitudes, | which 5.01. 94
dar'st not, no, nor canst not rule a traitor. 5.01. 95
thou shalt rule no more | o'er him whom heaven 5.01.104
for though usurpers sway the rule a while, | yet 3H6 3.03. 76
away with scrupulous wit! now arms must rule. 4.07. 61
why, what is pomp, rule, reign, but earth and 5.02. 27
and were they to be rul'd, and not to rule, R3 2.03. 29
and so leisurely | that, if his rule were true, 2.04. 20
ever belov'd and loving may his rule be; H8 2.01. 92
an army cannot rule 'em. 5.03. 77
the specialty of rule hath been neglected, | and TRO 1.03. 78
to square the general sex | by cressid's rule. 5.02.133
delight, | if there be rule in unity itself, 5.02.141
their mouths, why rule you not their teeth? COR 3.01. 36
suffer't, and live with such as cannot rule, 3.01. 40
by friends | ambitiously for rule and empery, TIT 1.01. 19
to–morrow yield up rule, resign my life, | and 1.01.191
where is thy leather apron and thy rule? JC 1.01. 7
even by the rule of that philosophy | by which i 5.01.100
his distemper'd cause | within the belt of rule. MAC 5.02. 16
kings, | a cutpurse of the empire and the rule, HAM 3.04. 99
(since now we will divest us both of rule, LR 1.01. 49
i might well delay | by rule of knighthood, i 5.03.146
you twain | rule in this realm, and the gor'd 5.03.321
my blood begins my safer guides to rule, | and OTH 2.03.205
from the heart, | that passion cannot rule. 3.03.124
that to come | shall all be done by th' rule. ANT 2.03. 7
your rule direct to any; PER 1.02.109
that best know how to rule and how to reign, 2.04. 38
even by the rule you have among yourselves, STM II.C 46
the dev'l cannot rule them. II.C 54 P
you | to lead those that the dev'l cannot rule. II.C 56
hath bid him rule, and will'd you to obey; II.C 100
could rule them both without ten women's wit." VEN 1008
strike, | let reason rule things worthy blame, PP 18. 3
love's arms are peace, 'gainst rule, 'gainst LC 271
RULED 1 FR 0.0001 REL FR 1 V 0 P
such as cannot rule, | nor ever will be ruled. COR 3.01. 41
RULER 6 FR 0.0006 REL FR 6 V 0 P
as doth a ruler with unlawful oaths, | or one 1H6 5.05. 30
himself | unlike the ruler of a commonweal. 2H6 1.01.189
wife, | and he a prince, and ruler of the land; 2.04. 43
'tis meet that lucky ruler be employ'd — 3.01.291
be'st found | on any ground that i am ruler of, 3.02.296
o'er him whom heaven created for thy ruler. 5.01.105
RULERS 1 FR 0.0001 REL FR 1 V 0 P
city, | and we be lords and rulers over roan, 1H6 3.02. 11
/RULES 1 FR 0.0001 REL FR 1 V 0 P
/in /military /rules, /humors /of /blood, | /he 2H4 2.03. 30
RULES 7 FR 0.0008 REL FR 7 V 0 P
to /change true rules for /odd inventions. SHR 3.01. 81
good lord, what madness rules in brain–sick men, 1H6 4.01.111
suffolk, the new–made duke that rules the roast, 2H6 1.01.109
lady, you know no rules of charity, | which R3 1.02. 68
so could err | against all rules of nature, and OTH 1.03.101
is taken off, | and cassio rules in cyprus. 5.02.332
mechanic slaves | with greasy aprons, rules, and ANT 5.02.210
RULING 2 FR 0.0002 REL FR 1 V 1 P
ruling in large and ample empery | o'er france H5 1.02.226
of their captivity than i of ruling athens. TNK 2.01. 38 P
RUMBLE 1 FR 0.0001 REL FR 1 V 0 P
rumble thy bellyful! LR 3.02. 14
RUMINAT 1 FR 0.0001 REL FR 0 V 1 P
gelida quando /pecus /omne sub umbra ruminat —
LLL 4.02. 94 P
RUMINATE 8 FR 0.0009 REL FR 8 V 0 P
that you may ruminate. TGV 1.02. 49
sit patiently and inly ruminate | the morning's H5 4.pr. 24
company, | i may revolve and ruminate my grief. 1H6 5.05.101
dangerous for /him | to ruminate on this so far, H8 1.02.180
such as doth revolve | and ruminate himself, TRO 2.03.188
to ruminate strange plots of dire revenge; TIT 5.02. 6
as thou dost ruminate, and give thy worst of OTH 3.03.132
decay, | ruin hath taught me thus to ruminate, SON 64.11
RUMINATED 2 FR 0.0002 REL FR 2 V 0 P
be, but what i know | is ruminated, plotted, and 1H4 1.03.274
not a present thought, | by duty ruminated. ANT 2.02.138
RUMINATES 2 FR 0.0002 REL FR 0 V 2 P
then she plots, then she ruminates, then she WIV 2.02.306 P
ruminates like an hostess that hath no TRO 3.03.252 P
RUMINATION 2 FR 0.0002 REL FR 1 V 1 P
in which /my often rumination wraps me in a most
AYL 4.01. 19 P
in thy rumination | that i, poor man, might TNK 3.01. 11
RUMMAGE *(see romage)*
RUMOR 17 FR 0.0019 REL FR 17 V 0 P
that pitiful rumor may report my flight | to AWW 3.02.127
(for to a vision so apparent rumor | cannot be WT 1.02.270
from forth the noise and rumor of the field, JN 5.04. 45
the vent of hearing when loud rumor speaks? 2H4 in 2
and who but rumor, who but only i, | make in 11
rumor is a pipe | blown by surmises, jealousies, in 15
why is rumor here? in 22
rumor doth double, like the voice and echo, 3.01. 97
great is the rumor of this dreadful knight, 1H6 2.03. 7
rumor it abroad | that anne, my wife, is very R3 4.02. 50
to the lord mayor straight | to stop the rumor, H8 2.01.152
let every feeble rumor shake your hearts! COR 3.03.125
does the rumor hold for true that he's | so full TIM 5.01. 3
i heard a bustling rumor, like a fray, | and the JC 2.04. 18
when we hold rumor | from what we fear, yet know
MAC 4.02. 19
there ran a rumor | of many worthy fellows that 4.03.182
belike 'tis but a rumor. good night to you. ANT 4.03. 5
RUMOR'D 2 FR 0.0002 REL FR 2 V 0 P
this have i rumor'd through the peasant towns 2H4 in 33
and it is rumor'd, | cominius, martius your old COR 1.02. 11
RUMORER 1 FR 0.0001 REL FR 1 V 0 P
go see this rumorer whipt. COR 4.06. 48
RUMOR'S 2 FR 0.0002 REL FR 2 V 0 P
but this from rumor's tongue | i idly heard — JN 4.02.123
from rumor's tongues | they bring smooth 2H4 in 39
RUMORS 3 FR 0.0003 REL FR 2 V 1 P
possess'd with rumors, full of idle dreams, JN 4.02.145
that fill his ears with such dissentious rumors. R3 1.03. 46
and which i hear from common rumors, now lord TIM 3.02. 5 P
RUMP 1 FR 0.0001 REL FR 0 V 1 P
luxury, with his fat rump and potato finger, TRO 5.02. 55 P
RUMP–FED 1 FR 0.0001 REL FR 1 V 0 P
the rump–fed ronyon cries. MAC 1.03. 6
/RUN 3 FR 0.0003 REL FR 3 V 0 P
whip to our tents, as roes /run o'er land. LLL 5.02.309
/which /way /the /stream /of /time /doth /run, 2H4 4.01. 70
/eyes /let /fall | /may /run /into /that /sink, TIT 3.02. 19
RUN 200 FR 0.0226 REL FR 131 V 69 P
fall to't, yarely, or we run ourselves aground. TMP 1.01. 4 P
deep, | to run upon the sharp wind of the north, 1.02.254
do so near the bottom run | by their own fear or 2.01.227
we'll not run, monsieur monster. 3.02. 18 P
trinculo, run into no further danger. 3.02. 68 P
run, boy, run, run, and seek him out. TGV 3.01.188 P
run, boy, run, run, and seek him out. 3.01.188 P
run, boy, run, run, and seek him out. 3.01.188 P
thou must run to him, for thou hast stay'd so 3.01.378 P
makes him run through all th' sins: 5.04.112
you, if you run the nuthook's humor on me — WIV 1.01.167 P
i will run no base humor. 1.03. 77 P
run in here, good young man; 1.04. 37 P
a woman would run through fire and water for 3.04.103 P
run up, sir john. 4.02. 79 P
run away with the cozeners; 4.05. 66 P
fly, run, hue and cry, villain! 4.05. 91 P
when night–dogs run, all sorts of deer are 5.05.238
which have for long run by the hideous law, | as MM 1.04. 63
some run from brakes of ice and answer none, 2.01. 39
run with these false and most contrarious 4.01. 61
make a lamp of her and run from her by her own ERR 3.02. 97 P
as from a bear a man would run for life, | so 3.02.154
fie, now you run this humor out of breath. 4.01. 57
run, master, run! 5.01. 36
run, master, run! 5.01. 36
you will never run mad, niece. ADO 1.01. 93 P
good margaret, run thee to the parlor, | there 3.01. 1
whose names yet run smoothly in the even road of 5.02. 33 P
well run, dice! LLL 5.02.233
hath this brave /manage, this career, been run. 5.02.482
run away for shame, alisander. 5.02.579 P
the course of true love never did run smooth; MND 1.01.134
i'll run from thee and hide me in the brakes, 2.01.227
run when you will; 2.01.230
for beasts that meet me run away for fear. 2.02. 95
and run through fire i will for thy sweet sake. 2.02.103
why do they run away? 3.01.112 P
my legs are longer though, to run away. 3.02.343
well run, thisby. 5.01.266 P
that do run | by the triple hecat's team | from 5.01.383
i should not see the sandy hour–glass run | but MV 1.01. 25
will serve me to run from this jew my master. 2.02. 2 P
use your legs, take the start, run away." 2.02. 6 P
"honest launcelot /gobbo, do not run, scorn 2.02. 9 P
up a brave mind," says the fiend, "and run." 2.02. 13 P
and, to run away from the jew, i should be rul'd 2.02. 25 P
i will run, fiend; 2.02. 31 P
my heels are at your commandement, i will run. 2.02. 32 P
as i have set up my rest to run away, so i will 2.02.103 P
so i will not rest till i have run some ground. 2.02.104 P
him, i will run as far as god has any ground. 2.02.110 P
hour, | for lovers ever run before the clock. 2.06. 4
go, gratiano, run and overtake him; 4.01.452
and with an unthrift love did run from venice, 5.01. 16
brook such disgrace well as he shall run into, AYL 1.01.134 P
folly | that ever love did make thee run into, 2.04. 35
we that are true lovers run into strange capers; 2.04. 54 P
run, run, orlando, carve on every tree | the 3.02. 9
run, run, orlando, carve on every tree | the 3.02. 9
my heel with no greater a run but my head and my
SHR 4.01. 16 P
thus the bowl should run, | and not unluckily 4.05. 24
not how i have deserv'd to run into my lord's AWW 2.05. 34 P
you have made shift to run into't, boots and 2.05. 36 P
and out of it you'll run again, rather than 2.05. 38 P
you shall hear i am run away; 3.02. 22 P
say i, madam, if he run away, as i hear he does. 3.02. 40 P
for my part, i only hear your son was run away. 3.02. 44 P
boy the count, have i run into this danger. 4.03.301 P
run after that same peevish messenger, | the TN 1.05.300
when the image of it leaves him he must run mad. 2.05.194 P
when she will take the rein i let her run, | but WT 2.03. 51
done, | and then run mad indeed — stark mad! 3.02.183
but look'd big and spit at him, he'ld have run. 4.03.106 P
since my desires | run not before mine honor, 4.04. 34
well, | made to run even upon even ground, JN 2.01.576
what can go well, when we have run so ill? 3.04. 5
run more fast. 4.02.269
and run | to meet displeasure farther from the 5.01. 59
and calmly run on in obedience | even to our 5.04. 56
even so must i run on, and even so stop. 5.07. 67
were i tied to run afoot | even to the frozen R2 1.01. 63
head | should run thy head from thy unreverent 2.01.123
show it a fair pair of heels and run from it? 1H4 2.04. 48 P
thousand pound i could run as fast as thou canst 2.04.148 P
and roar'd for mercy, and still run and roar'd, 2.04.260 P
faith, i ran when i saw others run. 2.04.302 P
rascal hath good mettle in him, he will not run. 2.04.350 P
and here the smug and silver trent shall run 3.01.101
i am afraid my daughter will run mad, | so much 3.01.143
nay, if you melt, then will she run mad. 3.01.209
i run before king harry's victory, | who in a 2H4 in 23
o, run, doll, run, run, good doll. 2.04.389 P
o, run, doll, run, run, good doll. 2.04.389 P
o, run, doll, run, run, good doll. 2.04.389 P
will this feeble the woman's tailor run off! 3.02.269 P
save those to god, that run before our business. H5 1.02.303
the first stroke, i'll run him up to the hilts, 2.01. 64 P
the king hath run bad humors on the knight, 2.01.121 P
had any apprehension, they would run away. 3.07.136 P
that run winking into the mouth of a russian 3.07.143 P
do not run away. 4.05. 6
if thou spy'st any, run and bring me word, | and 1H6 1.04. 19
dogs, | now, like to whelps, we crying run away. 1.05. 26
sheep run not half so treacherous from the wolf, 1.05. 30
lance, | and run a–tilt at death within a chair? 3.02. 51
given, | like to a trusty squire did run away; 4.01. 23
for ere the glass, that now begins to run, 4.02. 35
stay, | if the first hour i shrink and run away. 4.05. 31
the commonwealth hath daily run to wrack, | the 2H6 1.03.124
whipping, leap me over this stool and run away. 2.01.141 P
it made me laugh to see the villain run. 2.01.152
run to my lord of suffolk; 3.02. 1
run, go, help, help! o henry, ope thine eyes! 3.02. 35
the pissing–conduit run nothing but claret wine 4.06. 3 P
seen a hot o'erweening cur | run back and bite, 5.01.152
that beggars mounted run their horse to death. 3H6 1.04.127
tidings, as swiftly as the posts could run, 2.01.109
thereby to see the minutes how they run: 2.05. 25
but yet i run before my horse to market: R3 1.01.160
what need'st thou run so many miles about, 4.04.460
by violent swiftness that which we run at, | and H8 1.01.142
the fire that mounts the liquor till't run o'er 1.01.144
duke of buckingham | is run in your displeasure. 1.02.110
they must either | (for so run the conditions) 1.03. 24
when he has run his course and sleeps in 3.02.398
did her eyes run o'er too? TRO 1.02.147 P
and those biles did run — say so — did not the 2.01. 5 P
run — say so — did not the general run then? 2.01. 6 P
and too little brain, these two may run mad, but 5.01. 49 P
thou rascal, that art worst in blood to run, COR 1.01.159
i saw him run after a gilded butterfly, and when 1.03. 60 P
how have you run | from slaves that apes would 1.04. 35
he did | run reeking o'er the lives of men, as 2.02.119
i'll run away till i am bigger, but then i'll 5.03.128
how, turn thy back and run? ROM 1.01. 35 P
she could have run and waddled all about; 1.03. 37
wisely and slow, they stumble that run fast. 2.03. 94
torments him so, that he will sure run mad. 2.04. 5
black eye, run through the ear with a love–song, 2.04. 14 P
nay, if our wits run the wild–goose chase, i am 2.04. 71 P
run to my study. 3.03. 76
when presently through all thy veins shall run 4.01. 95
that living mortals, hearing them, run mad — 4.03. 48
you love your child so ill | that you run mad, 4.05. 76
say | a madman's mercy bid thee run away. 5.03. 67
now at once run on | the dashing rocks thy 5.03.117
go tell the prince, run to the capulets, | raise 5.03.177
and all run | with open outcry toward our 5.03.192
run to your houses, fall upon your knees, | pray JC 1.01. 53
in antonio's way | when he doth run his course. 1.02. 4
would run to these and these extremities; 2.01. 31
now bid me run, | and i will strive with things 2.01.324
with an hundred spouts, | did run pure blood; 2.02. 78
i prithee, boy, run to the senate–house; 2.04. 1
run to the capitol, and nothing else? 2.04. 11
run, lucius, and commend me to my lord, | say i 2.04. 44
run hence, proclaim, cry it about the streets. 3.01. 79
wives, and children stare, cry out, and run, 3.01. 97
fight, | to wind, to stop, to run directly on, 4.01. 32
my life is run his compass. 5.03. 25
far from this country pindarus shall run, 5.03. 49
hold thou my sword–hilts, whilest i run on it. 5.05. 28
turn away thy face, | while i do run upon it. 5.05. 48
i held the sword, and he did run on it. 5.05. 65
run away, i pray you! MAC 4.02. 85
"run barefoot up and down, threat'ning the HAM 2.02.505
our wills and fates do so contrary run | that 3.02.211
of his intent, you should run a certain course; LR 1.02. 82 P
ride, run, mar a curious tale in telling it, and 1.04. 32 P
and the creature run from the cur? 4.06.157 P
run, run, o, run! 5.03.248
run, run, o, run! 5.03.248
run, run, o, run! 5.03.248
run from her guardage to the sooty bosom | of OTH 1.02. 70
lady, she'll run mad | when she shall lack it. 3.03.317
emilia, run you to the citadel, | and tell my 5.01.126
nay then i'll run. ANT 2.05. 73
cowards | to run and show their shoulders. 3.11. 8
run one before, | and let the queen know of our 4.08. 1
my death, and run into't | as to a lover's bed. 4.14.100
him that broke it, it would have run all out. CYM 2.01. 9 P
than the sands | that run i' th' clock's behalf. 3.02. 73
(lads more like to run | the country base than 5.03. 19
is living, let the time run on | to good or bad. 5.05.128
now our sands are almost run, | more a little, PER 5.02. 1
/ravish'd our sides, like age, must run to rust, TNK 2.02. 22
and run | swifter than wind upon a field of corn 2.03. 76
what e'er you are, you run the best, and wrastle 2.05. 3
he cannot run, the jingling of his gyves | might 3.02. 14
maypole, and again, | ere another year run out, 3.05.146
yet doubtless | she would run mad for this man. 4.02. 12
me | whether i lov'd, i had run mad for arcite; 4.02. 48
i prithee run | and tell me how it goes. 5.03. 70
run and inquire. 5.03. 72
and whe'er he run or fly they know not whether; VEN 304
"lest the deceiving harmony should run | into 781
at his own shadow let the thief run mad, LUC 997
to kiss and clip me till i run away! PP 11.14
towards thee i'll run, and give him leave to go. SON 51.14
RUNAGATE 3 FR 0.0003 REL FR 3 V 0 P
white–liver'd runagate, what doth he there? R3 4.04.464
where that same banish'd runagate doth live, ROM 3.05. 89
more noble than that runagate to your bed, | and CYM 1.06.137
RUNAGATES 2 FR 0.0002 REL FR 2 V 0 P
i cannot find those runagates, that villain CYM 4.02. 62
those runagates? 4.02. 63
RUNAWAY 2 FR 0.0002 REL FR 2 V 0 P
thou runaway, thou coward, art thou fled? MND 3.02.405
for the close night doth play the runaway, | and MV 2.06. 47
RUNAWAY'S 1 FR 0.0001 REL FR 1 V 0 P
that /th' runaway's eyes may wink, and romeo ROM 3.02. 6
RUNAWAYS 3 FR 0.0003 REL FR 3 V 0 P
quail | to bring again these foolish runaways. AYL 2.02. 21
heels, | and that we are most lofty runaways. H5 3.05. 35
a sort of vagabonds, rascals, and runaways, | a R3 5.03.316
RUNG 6 FR 0.0006 REL FR 6 V 0 P
none since the curfew rung. MM 4.02. 75
enter, go in, the market bell is rung. 1H6 3.02. 16
bar, to hear | his knell rung out, his judgment, H8 2.01. 32
and you have rung it lustily, my lords — TIT 2.02. 14
the curfew–bell hath rung, 'tis three a' clock. ROM 4.04. 4
drowsy hums | hath rung night's yawning peal, MAC 3.02. 43
RUNNER 1 FR 0.0001 REL FR 1 V 0 P
'tis sport to maul a runner. ANT 4.07. 14
RUNNERS 1 FR 0.0001 REL FR 1 V 0 P
forespent with toil, as runners with a race, | i 3H6 2.03. 1

RUNNING 22 FR 0.0024 REL FR 16 V 6 P
by running fast. ERR 4.02. 30
i, costard, running out, that was safely within, LLL 3.01.116
do not run, scorn running with thy heels." MV 2.02. 9 P
tongues in trees, books in the running brooks, AYL 2.01. 16
straight | adonis painted by a running brook, SHR in.2. 50
so is running away, when fear proposes the AWW 1.01.202 P
she would not live | the running of one glass. WT 1.02.306
and the argument shall be thy running away. 1H4 2.04.282 P
art thou then, to praise him so for running! 2.04.352 P
so | he seem'd in running to devour the way, 2H4 1.01. 47
that makes a still–stand, running neither way. 2.03. 64
the farced title running 'fore the king, | the H5 4.01.263
when arm in arm they both came swiftly running, 1H6 2.02. 29
some of these | should find a running banket, H8 1.04. 12
to this course | which you are running here. 2.04.218
the which | you were now running o'er. 3.02.139
besides the running banquet of two beadles that 5.03. 65 P
and you get it, you shall get it by running. LR 4.06.203 P
that tub | both fill'd and running — ravening CYM 1.06. 49
wrastling and running. — 'tis a pretty fellow. TNK 2.03. 67
the glass is running now that cannot finish 5.01. 18
each cheek a river running from a fount | with LC 283
RUNNION *(also ronyon)*
RUNNION 1 FR 0.0001 REL FR 0 V 1 P
you rag, you baggage, you poulcat, you runnion! WIV 4.02.185 P
/RUNS 1 FR 0.0001 REL FR 1 V 0 P
/keep /their /fur /dry, /unbonneted /he /runs, LR 3.01. 14
RUNS 44 FR 0.0049 REL FR 33 V 11 P
his tears runs down his beard like winter's TMP 5.01. 16
much upon this riddle runs the wisdom of the MM 3.02.229 P
a hound that runs counter, and yet draws ERR 4.02. 39
pestilence, and the taker runs presently mad. ADO 1.01. 88 P
like a lapwing, runs | close by the ground, to 3.01. 24
runs not this speech like iron through your 5.01.245
give it the rein, for it runs against hector. LLL 5.02.657 P
the life of man | runs his erring pilgrimage, AYL 3.02.130
a woman's thought runs before her actions. 4.01.141 P
as fast as you pour affection in, /it runs out. 4.01.210 P
he that runs fastest gets the ring. SHR 1.01.140 P
which runs himself, and catches for his master. 5.02. 53
indeed he has no pace, but runs where he will. AWW 4.05. 67 P
how runs the stream? TN 4.01. 60
which else runs tickling up and down the veins, JN 3.03. 44
this tongue that runs so roundly in thy head R2 2.01.122
and that my fortune runs against the bias. 3.04. 5
runs posting on in bullingbrook's proud joy, 5.05. 59
that runs a' horseback up a hill perpendicular 1H4 2.04.343 P
and runs me up | with like advantage on the 3.01.107
of land, | and then he runs straight and even. 3.01.113
thus runs the bill. H5 1.01. 19
courage that renowned them | runs in your veins; 1.02.119
they seem to threaten | runs far before them. 2.04. 71
smooth runs the water where the brook is deep, 2H6 3.01. 53
and as the dam runs lowing up and down, 3.01.214
my mother's blood | runs on the dexter cheek, TRO 4.05.128
way, and runs like swallows o'er the plain. TIT 2.02. 24
a great natural that runs lolling up and down to ROM 2.04. 92 P
of grief, | that it runs over even at his eyes. JC 5.05. 14
time and the hour runs through the roughest day. MAC 1.03.147
where the flight | so runs against all reason. 4.02. 14
some must sleep, | thus runs the world away. HAM 3.02.274
this lapwing runs away with the shell on his 5.02.185 P
go thy hold when a great wheel runs down a hill, LR 2.04. 72 P
the knave turns fool that runs away, | the fool 2.04. 84
the fountain from the which my current runs | or OTH 4.02. 59
tainted with extremes) runs through his body, TNK 4.02.101
"sometime he runs among a flock of sheep, | to VEN 685
and homeward through the dark laund runs apace, 813
and as she runs, the bushes in the way, | some 871
this way she runs, and now she will no further, 905
he runs, and chides his vanish'd loath'd delight LUC 742
lo as a careful huswife runs to catch | one of SON 143. 1
RUN'ST 5 FR 0.0005 REL FR 3 V 2 P
to shun, | and yet run'st toward him still. MM 3.01. 13
why, how now, dromio, where run'st thou so fast?
ERR 3.02. 71 P
for well i wot | thou run'st before me, shifting MND 3.02.423
therefore, if thou art mov'd, thou run'st away. ROM 1.01. 10 P
so run'st thou after that which flies from thee, SON 143. 9
RUPTURE 1 FR 0.0001 REL FR 0 V 1 P
it is a rupture that you may easily heal; MM 3.01.235 P
RUPTURES 1 FR 0.0001 REL FR 0 V 1 P
south, the guts–griping, ruptures, /catarrhs, TRO 5.01. 18 P
RURAL 2 FR 0.0002 REL FR 2 V 0 P
thou | these rural latches to his entrance open, WT 4.04.438
here is a rural fellow | that will not be denied ANT 5.02.233
RUSH* 19 FR 0.0021 REL FR 18 V 1 P
let them from forth a sawpit rush at once | with WIV 4.04. 54
a rush, a hair, a drop of blood, a pin, | a nut, ERR 4.03. 72
by the same example | will rush into the state. MV 4.01.222
lean upon a rush, | the cicatrice and capable AYL 3.05. 22
were it better i should rush in thus: SHR 3.02. 91
punk, as tib's rush for tom's forefinger, as a AWW 2.02. 23 P
rare | even then will rush to knowledge. WT 3.01. 21
made | for bloody power to rush upon your peace.
JN 2.01.221
rush forth | and bind the boy which you shall 4.01. 3
a rush will be a beam | to hang thee on; 4.03.129
rush on his host, as doth the melted snow | upon H5 3.05. 50
we will rush on them. 1H6 1.02. 18
food, | do rush upon us as their hungry prey. 1.02. 28
reft, | rush all to pieces on thy rocky bosom. R3 4.04.235
they all rush by | and leave you /hindmost; TRO 3.03.159
hid in an auger–hole, may rush and seize us? MAC 2.03.122
man but a rush against othello's breast, | and OTH 5.02.270
and spurns | the rush that lies before him; ANT 3.05. 17
it sin | to rush into the secret house of death 4.15. 81
RUSH–CANDLE 1 FR 0.0001 REL FR 1 V 0 P
and if you please to call it a rush–candle, SHR 4.05. 14
RUSH'D 5 FR 0.0005 REL FR 5 V 0 P
he rush'd into my house, and took perforce | my ERR 4.03. 94
so with civil and uncivil arms | be rush'd upon! R2 3.03.103
and rush'd into the bowels of the battle. 1H6 1.01.129
with this, my weapon drawn, i rush'd upon him, TIT 5.01. 37
taking thy part, hath rush'd aside the law, ROM 3.03. 26
RUSHES* 15 FR 0.0017 REL FR 11 V 4 P
in which cage of rushes i am sure you /are not AYL 3.02.371 P
the house trimm'd, rushes strew'd, cobwebs swept
SHR 4.01. 46 P
she bids you on the wanton rushes lay you down, 1H4 3.01.211
more rushes, more rushes. 2H4 5.05. 1 P
more rushes, more rushes. 5.05. 1 P
fins of lead, | and hews down oaks with rushes. COR 1.01.181
yet seem shut, we have but pinn'd with rushes, 1.04. 18
tickle the senseless rushes with their heels. ROM 1.04. 36
their fatal points, | and 'twixt them rushes; 3.01.167
did softly press the rushes ere he waken'd | the CYM 2.02. 13
the rushes and the reeds | had so encompass'd it TNK 4.01. 61
rings she made | of rushes that grew by, and to 4.01. 89
and forth she rushes, snorts, and neighs aloud. VEN 262
as fearful of him, part, through whom he rushes. 630
he takes it from the rushes where it lies, | and LUC 318
RUSHING 7 FR 0.0008 REL FR 7 V 0 P
to the citizens | by rushing in their houses, ERR 5.01.143
comes rushing on this woeful land at once! R2 2.02. 99
so, rushing in the bowels of the french, | he 1H6 4.07. 42
rushing on us, should do your age some mischief. JC 3.01. 93
as rushing out of doors to be resolv'd | if 3.02.179
lest this great sea of joys rushing upon me PER 5.01.192
rushing from forth a cloud, bereaves our sight, LUC 373
RUSHLING *(also rustling)*
RUSHLING 1 FR 0.0001 REL FR 0 V 1 P
all musk, and so rushling, i warrant you, in WIV 2.02. 67 P
RUSHY 1 FR 0.0001 REL FR 1 V 0 P
or mead, | by paved fountain or by rushy brook, MND 2.01. 84
RUSSET 2 FR 0.0002 REL FR 2 V 0 P
in russet yeas and honest kersey noes. LLL 5.02.413
but look the morn in russet mantle clad | walks HAM 1.01.166
RUSSET–PATED 1 FR 0.0001 REL FR 1 V 0 P
or russet–pated choughs, many in sort, | rising MND 3.02. 21
RUSSIA 3 FR 0.0003 REL FR 2 V 1 P
this will last out a night in russia | when MM 2.01.134
some say he is with the emperor of russia; 3.02. 88 P
the emperor of russia was my father. WT 3.02.119
RUSSIAN 5 FR 0.0005 REL FR 4 V 1 P
confronted were with four | in russian habit; LLL 5.02.368
dance, | nor never more in russian habit wait. 5.02.401
what did the russian whisper in your ear? 5.02.443
into the mouth of a russian bear and have their H5 3.07.144 P
approach thou like the rugged russian bear, MAC 3.04. 99
RUSSIANS 3 FR 0.0003 REL FR 3 V 0 P
thus, | like muscovites or russians, as i guess. LLL 5.02.121
a mess of russians left us but of late. 5.02.361
how, madam? russians? 5.02.362
RUST 13 FR 0.0014 REL FR 10 V 3 P
adieu, valor, rust, rapier, be still, drum, for LLL 1.02.181 P
rust, sword! AWW 4.03.337
how he glisters | through my rust! WT 3.02.171
nay, after that, consume away in rust, | but for JN 4.01. 65
his glittering arms he will commend to rust, R2 3.03.116
eaten to death with a rust than to be scour'd to 2H4 1.02.219 P
to my blade | shall rust upon my weapon, till 3H6 1.03. 51
this peace is nothing but to rust iron, increase COR 4.05.219 P
there rust, and let me die. ROM 5.03.170
your bright swords, for the dew will rust them. OTH 1.02. 59
and on set purpose let his armor rust | until PER 2.02. 54
/ravish'd our sides, like age, must run to rust, TNK 2.02. 22
foul cank'ring rust the hidden treasure frets, VEN 767
RUSTED 1 FR 0.0001 REL FR 1 V 0 P
but here's a vengeful sword, rusted with ease, 2H6 3.02.198
RUSTIC 3 FR 0.0003 REL FR 3 V 0 P
dignity, | and fall into our rustic revelry. AYL 5.04.177
of that kind | our rustic garden's barren, and i WT 4.04. 84
yield, rustic mountaineer. CYM 4.02.100
RUSTICALLY 1 FR 0.0001 REL FR 0 V 1 P
for my part, he keeps me rustically at home, or, AYL 1.01. 7 P
RUSTICS 1 FR 0.0001 REL FR 0 V 1 P
how now, rustics, whither are you bound? WT 4.04.715 P
RUSTLE 1 FR 0.0001 REL FR 0 V 1 P
i hear his straw rustle. MM 4.03. 36 P
RUSTLING *(also rushling)*
RUSTLING 2 FR 0.0002 REL FR 1 V 1 P
of shoes nor the rustling of silks betray thy LR 3.04. 95 P
prouder than rustling in unpaid–for silk: CYM 3.03. 24
RUSTS 1 FR 0.0001 REL FR 1 V 0 P
upon, while that the coulter rusts | that should H5 5.02. 46
/RUSTY 1 FR 0.0001 REL FR 0 V 1 P
/how /comes /it? /do /they /grow /rusty? HAM 2.02.337 P
RUSTY 9 FR 0.0010 REL FR 6 V 3 P
an old rusty sword ta'en out of the town armory, SHR 3.02. 46 P
distaff–women manage rusty bills | against thy R2 3.02.118
as it is with the rusty curb of old father antic 1H4 1.02. 61 P
and faintly through a rusty beaver peeps. H5 4.02. 44
like a rusty mail | in monumental mock'ry. TRO 3.03.152
come at last, and 'tis turn'd to a rusty armor. PER 2.01.119 P
for by his rusty outside he appears | to have 2.02. 50
though it be rusty, and the charity | of one TNK 3.01. 73
softer than wax, and yet as iron rusty: PP 7. 4
RUTH 5 FR 0.0005 REL FR 5 V 0 P
rue, even for ruth, here shortly shall be seen, R2 3.04.106
spur them to ruthful work, rein them from ruth. TRO 5.03. 48
would the nobility lay aside their ruth | and COR 1.01.197
boar, | deep in the thigh, a spectacle of ruth! PP 9.11
be, | looking with pretty ruth upon my pain. SON 132. 4
RUTHFUL 3 FR 0.0003 REL FR 3 V 0 P
o that my death would stay these ruthful deeds! 3H6 2.05. 95
spur them to ruthful work, rein them from ruth. TRO 5.03. 48
ruthful to hear, yet piteously perform'd. TIT 5.01. 66
/RUTHLESS 1 FR 0.0001 REL FR 1 V 0 P
suborn | to do this piece of /ruthless butchery, R3 4.03. 5
RUTHLESS 11 FR 0.0012 REL FR 10 V 1 P
why, what a ruthless thing is this in him, for MM 3.02.114 P
and ruthless slaughters as are daily seen | by 1H6 5.04.161
the ruthless flint doth cut my tender feet, 2H6 2.04. 34
ay, to such mercy as his ruthless arm | with 3H6 1.04. 31
see, ruthless queen, a hapless father's tears! 1.04.156
the ruthless queen gave him to dry his cheeks 2.01. 61
and what is edward but a ruthless sea? 5.04. 25
the brothers | more than with ruthless waves, 5.04. 36
the woods are ruthless, dreadful, deaf, and dull TIT 2.01.128
forc'd in the ruthless, vast, and gloomy woods? 4.01. 53
thee, | ruthless bears they will not cheer thee. PP 20.22
RUTLAND 14 FR 0.0015 REL FR 14 V 0 P
and, madam, you must call him rutland now. R2 5.02. 43
until thou bid me joy | by pardoning rutland, my 5.03. 96
with the rest, where is your darling, rutland? 3H6 1.04. 78
in the harmless blood | of sweet young rutland, 2.01. 63
'twas you that kill'd young rutland, was it not? 2.02. 98
as thou didst kill our tender brother rutland, 2.02.115
and this for rutland, both bound to revenge, 2.04. 3
and this the hand that slew thy brother rutland, 2.04. 7
in hewing rutland when his leaves put forth, 2.06. 48
thou pitiedst rutland, i will pity thee. 2.06. 74
york and young rutland could not satisfy. 2.06. 84
to hear the piteous moan that rutland made R3 1.02.157
in the faultless blood of pretty rutland — 1.03.177
i had a rutland too, thou /holp'st to kill him. 4.04. 45
RUTLAND'S 3 FR 0.0003 REL FR 3 V 0 P
that not a tear can fall for rutland's death? 3H6 1.04. 88
these tears are my sweet rutland's obsequies, 1.04.147
did to thy father, steep'd in rutland's blood — R3 4.04.275
RUT–TIME 1 FR 0.0001 REL FR 0 V 1 P
send me a cool rut–time, jove, or who can blame WIV 5.05. 14 P
RUTTING 1 FR 0.0001 REL FR 0 V 1 P
but i am out of the road of rutting for ever. PER 4.05. 9 P
RUTTISH 1 FR 0.0001 REL FR 0 V 1 P
foolish idle boy, but for all that very ruttish. AWW 4.03.216 P
RYCAS 1 FR 0.0001 REL FR 1 V 0 P
and rycas, and three better lads nev'r danc'd TNK 2.03. 38
RYE 2 FR 0.0002 REL FR 2 V 0 P
lady, thy rich leas | of wheat, rye, barley, TMP 4.01. 61
between the acres of the rye, | with a hey, and AYL 5.03. 22
RYE–STRAW 1 FR 0.0001 REL FR 1 V 0 P
your rye–straw hats put on, | and these fresh TMP 4.01.136
'S* *(also as*, his, is, these, us)*
/'S* 3 FR 0.0003 REL FR 2 V 1 P
for /'s apparel is built upon his back, and the 2H4 3.02.143 P
for honor | than /one /on /'s ears to hear it? COR 2.02. 81
the moon | to stand /'s auspicious mistress. LR 2.01. 40
'S* 175 FR 0.0197 REL FR 123 V 52 P
to the present business | which now's upon 's; TMP 1.02.137
true, my brother's daughter 's queen of tunis, 2.01.255
do you put tricks upon 's with salvages and men 2.02. 58 P
when 's god's asleep, he'll rob his bottle. 2.02.151 P
if you trouble him any more in 's tale, by this 3.02. 48 P
spirit, | how fares the king and 's followers? 5.01. 7
there's not a hair on 's head but 'tis a TGV 3.01.192 P
he, he — i can never hit on 's name. WIV 3.02. 24 P
the provost hath | a warrant for 's execution. MM 1.04. 74
but tuesday night last gone, in 's garden–house, 5.01.229
whence he came, lest he catch cold on 's feet. ERR 3.01. 37
by my troth 's not so good, and i warrant your ADO 3.04. 9 P
by my troth 's but a night–gown /in respect of 3.04. 18 P
clap 's into "light a' love"; 3.04. 44 P
and hymen now with luckier issue speed 's | than 5.03. 32
therefore to 's seemeth it a needful course, LLL 2.01. 25
will ne'er wear hair on 's face that had it. MV 5.01.158
invite the duke and all 's contented followers. AYL 5.02. 15 P
the rest will comfort, for thy counsel 's sound. SHR 1.01.164
the note lies in 's throat if he say i said so. 4.03.132 P
to give great charlemain a pen in 's hand | and AWW 2.01. 77
on 's bed of death | many receipts he gave me; 2.01.104
he that cannot make a leg, put off 's cap, kiss 2.02. 10 P
where great additions swell 's, and virtue none, 2.03.127
he, sir, 's a good workman, a very good tailor. 2.05. 18 P
do so ever, though i took him at 's prayers. 2.05. 41 P
how he would woo, | as if she sate in 's heart. 4.02. 70
through the army with this rhyme in 's forehead. 4.03.234 P
let his nobility remain in 's court. 4.05. 50 P
lord your son with a patch of velvet on 's face. 4.05. 95 P
he come, for sure the man is tainted in 's wits. TN 3.04. 13 P
sir, he will fight with you for 's oath sake. 3.04.297 P
we'll part the time between 's then; WT 1.02. 18
month behind the gest | prefix'd for 's parting; 1.02. 42
temptations have since then been born to 's: 1.02. 77
cram 's with praise, and make 's | as fat as 1.02. 91
praise, and make 's | as fat as tame things. 1.02. 91
you may ride 's | with one soft kiss a thousand 1.02. 94
why, happy man be 's dole! 1.02.163
shall 's attend you there? 1.02.178
thinks she has been sluic'd in 's absence, | and 1.02.194
many thousand on 's | have the disease, and 1.02.206
i saw his heart in 's face. 1.02.447
pray you sit by us, | and tell 's a tale. 2.01. 23
the trick of 's frown, his forehead, nay, the 2.03.101
what you have underta'en to do in 's absence. 3.02. 78
we have in hand are angry, | and frown upon 's. 3.03. 6
mercy on 's, a barne? 3.03. 69 P
you bid | these unknown friends to 's welcome, 4.04. 65
him that he use no scurrilous words in 's tunes. 4.04.214 P
i know by the picking on 's teeth. 4.04.753 P
this is a match, | and made between 's by vows. 5.03.138
sits on 's horseback at mine hostess' door, JN 2.01.289
come give 's some sack. 2H4 2.04.180 P
no man's too good to serve 's prince, and let it 3.02.237 P
i read in 's looks | matter against me, and his H8 1.01.125
'neither the king nor 's heirs | (tell you the 1.02.168
salisbury, | made suit to come in 's presence; 1.02.197
another spread on 's breast, mounting his eyes, 1.02.205
hath a witchcraft | over the king in 's tongue. 3.02. 19
to his own hand, in 's bedchamber. 3.02. 77
fret the string, | the master–cord on 's heart! 3.02.106
it may well be, | there is a mutiny in 's mind. 3.02.120
with all the business | i writ to 's holiness. 3.02.222
twenty of the dog–days now reign in 's nose; 5.03. 42 P
well, i'll make 's excuse. TRO 3.01. 90 P
he wears his tongue in 's arms. 3.03.270 P
i would they had broke 's neck! 4.02. 76 P
will 'a swagger himself out on 's own eyes? 5.02.136 P
if they set down before 's, for the remove COR 1.02. 28
one on 's father's moods. 1.03. 66 P
follow 's. 1.04. 42
and shut your gates upon 's. 1.07. 6
would i | wash my fierce hand in 's heart. 1.10. 27
on 's brows. 2.01.124 P
that dark spirit, in 's nervy arm doth lie, 2.01.160
a curse begin at very root on 's heart, | that 2.01.185
that to 's power he would | have made them mules 2.01.246
may they perceive 's intent! 2.02.156
by his looks, methinks, | 'tis warm at 's heart. 2.03.152
marks of merit, wounds receiv'd for 's country. 2.03.164
shall prompt them, to make road | upon 's again. 3.01. 6
his trident, | or jove for 's power to thunder. 3.01.256

will (too late) | tie leaden pounds to 's heels. 3.01.312
plant love among 's! 3.03. 35
sanctifies himself with 's hand, and turns up 4.05.195 P
shall 's to the capitol? 4.06.147
to awaken his regard | for 's private friends. 5.01. 24
help, yet do not | upbraid 's with our distress. 5.01. 35
no man in the world | more bound to 's mother, 5.03.159
nay, behold 's! 5.03.173
there is no crossing him in 's humor, | else i TIM 1.02.160
with two stones moe than 's artificial one. 2.02.111 P
he covetously reserve it, how shall 's get it? 4.03.405 P
the morning comes upon 's. JC 2.01.221
trifles, to betray 's | in deepest consequence. MAC 1.03.125
there's one did laugh in 's sleep, and one cried 2.02. 20
in that heart | courage to make 's love known? 2.03.118
ay, my good lord. our time does call upon 's. 3.01. 36
he cannot come out on 's grave. 5.01. 64 P
we | shall take upon 's what else remains to do, 5.06. 5
there was 'a gaming, there o'ertook in 's rouse, HAM 2.01. 56
not turn'd his color and has tears in 's eyes. 2.02.520 P
may play the fool no where but in 's own house. 3.01.132 P
looks, and my father died within 's two hours. 3.02.127 P
endure | hazard so near 's as doth hourly grow 3.03. 6
no, let 's come in. 4.05.114
fellow might be in 's time a great buyer of land 5.01.104 P
all 's golden words are spent. 5.02.130 P
himself, there are no tongues else for 's turn. 5.02.184 P
this fellow has banish'd two on 's daughters, LR 1.04.102 P
if a man's brains were in 's heels, were't not 1.05. 8 P
why one's nose stands i' th' middle on 's face? 1.05. 20 P
to keep one's eyes of either side 's nose, that 1.05. 22 P
why, to put 's head in, not to give it away to 1.05. 30 P
go tell the duke, and 's wife, i'ld speak with 2.04.116
the old man and 's people | cannot be well 2.04.288
he that has a house to put 's head in has a good 3.02. 25 P
here's three on 's are sophisticated. 3.04.105 P
a small spark, all the rest on 's body cold. 3.04.113 P
here, friend, 's another purse; 4.06. 28
and take upon 's the mystery of things | as if 5.03. 16
come, mistress, you must tell 's another tale. OTH 5.01.125
by heaven, i saw my handkerchief in 's hand. 5.02. 62
time calls upon 's. ANT 2.02.157
way like a gorgon, | the other way 's a mars. 2.05.117
show 's the way, sir. 2.06. 81
and shall, sir, give 's your hand. 2.07.127
the weight we must convey with 's will permit, 3.01. 36
he has a cloud in 's face. 3.02. 51
you requested, | yourself shall go between 's. 3.04. 25
his heart, take from his brain, from 's time, 3.07. 11
i am prompt | to lay my crown at 's feet, and 3.13. 76
laugh at 's while we strut | to our confusion. 3.13.114
before the sun shall see 's, we'll spill the 4.08. 3
this last day was | a shrewd one to 's. 4.09. 5
and scald rhymers | ballad 's out a' tune. 5.02.216
his daughter, and the heir of 's kingdom (whom CYM 1.01. 4
minist'red, | and in 's spring became a harvest; 1.01. 46
as the fits and stirs of 's mind | could best 1.03. 12
let there be covenants drawn between 's. 1.04.143 P
(your lord, i mean) laughs from 's free lungs; 1.06. 68
be, will 's free hours languish for | assured 1.06. 72
caius lucius | will do 's commission throughly. 2.04. 12
which then they had to take from 's, to resume 3.01. 15
all color here | did put the yoke upon 's; 3.01. 51
madam, 's enough for you — and too much too. 3.02. 69
why, one that rode to 's execution, man, | could 3.02. 70
and thus i set my foot on 's neck," even then 3.03. 92
that's false to 's bed? 3.04. 44
say, where shall 's lay him? 4.02.233
i know the shape of 's leg; 4.02.309
and so extort from 's that | which we have done, 4.04. 12
beard came to, | in doing this for 's country. 5.03. 18
your death has eyes in 's head then; 5.04.178 P
in suit the place of 's bed and win this ring 5.05.185
safely, had it | been all the worth of 's car. 5.05.191
shall 's have a play of this? 5.05.228
i cut off 's head, | and am right glad he is not 5.05.295
but i will prove that two on 's are as good | as 5.05.311
or, dead, give 's cause to mourn his funeral, PER 2.04. 32
at ephesus, | unto diana there 's a votaress. 4.ch. 4
shall 's go hear the vestals sing? 4.05. 7 P
sir, lead 's the way. 5.03. 84
(unless we fear that apes can tutor 's) to | be TNK 1.02. 43
in 's bosom. 1.03. 17
some of thebes have told 's | they are sisters' 1.04. 15
boys in athens | blow wind i' th' breech on 's, 2.03. 47
see the sports, then every man to 's tackle! 2.03. 55
lest this match between 's | be cross'd ere met. 3.01. 97
i am persuaded this question, sick between 's, 3.01.113
let 's die together, at one instant, duke. 3.06.177
in 's face appears | all the fair hopes of what 4.02. 98
as ever he may go upon 's legs, for in the next 4.03. 14 P
he lisps in 's neighing able to entice | a 5.02. 66
S'* *(also shall, so)*
S'* 3 FR 0.0003 REL FR 3 V 0 P
rome, such as was never | s' incapable of help. COR 4.06.120
i have rememb'red me, thou s' hear our counsel. ROM 1.03. 9
"he s' buy me a white cut, forth for to ride, TNK 3.04. 22
SA' *(also save*)*
SA' 2 FR 0.0002 REL FR 0 V 2 P
so god sa' me, 'tis shame to stand still, it is H5 3.02.110 P
there ish nothing done, so christ sa' me law! 3.02.113 P
SA 4 FR 0.0004 REL FR 0 V 4 P
sa, sa, sa, sa. LR 4.06.203 P
sa, sa, sa, sa. 4.06.203 P
sa, sa, sa, sa. 4.06.203 P
sa, sa, sa, sa. 4.06.203 P
SABA 1 FR 0.0001 REL FR 1 V 0 P
saba was never | more covetous of wisdom and H8 5.04. 23
SABAOTH 1 FR 0.0001 REL FR 1 V 0 P
and by our holy sabaoth have i sworn | to have MV 4.01. 36
SABBATH 1 FR 0.0001 REL FR 1 V 0 P
come the next sabbath, and i will content you. R3 3.02.111
SABLE 7 FR 0.0008 REL FR 7 V 0 P
i have seen it in his life, | a sable silver'd. HAM 1.02.241
"the rugged pyrrhus, he whose sable arms, 2.02.452
his banners sable, trimm'd with rich expense, PER 5.ch. 19
till sable night, mother of dread and fear, LUC 117
my sable ground of sin i will not paint, | to 1074
that thy sable gender mak'st | with the breath PHT 18
and sable curls /all silver'd o'er with white; SON 12. 4
SABLE-COLORED 1 FR 0.0001 REL FR 0 V 1 P
it is, besieged with sable-colored melancholy, i LLL 1.01.231 P
SABLES 2 FR 0.0002 REL FR 1 V 1 P
wear black, for i'll have a suit of sables. HAM 3.02.130 P
than settled age his sables and his weeds, 4.07. 80
SACIETY *(also satiety)*
SACIETY 3 FR 0.0003 REL FR 3 V 0 P
and with saciety seeks to quench his thirst. SHR 1.01. 24
a mere saciety of commendations; TIM 1.01.166
"and yet not cloy thy lips with loath'd saciety, VEN 19
SACK* 55 FR 0.0062 REL FR 8 V 47 P
upon a butt of sack which the sailors heav'd TMP 2.02.121 P
my man-monster hath drown'd his tongue in sack. 3.02. 13 P
coward that hath drunk so much sack as i to-day? 3.02. 28 P
this can sack and drinking do. 3.02. 79 P
you love sack, and so do i; WIV 2.01. 9 P
you a pottle of burnt sack to give me recourse 2.01.215 P
sent your worship a morning's draught of sack. 2.02.147 P
are whole, and let burnt sack be the issue. 3.01.109 P
go fetch me a quart of sack — put a toast in't. 3.05. 3 P
let me pour in some sack to the thames water; 3.05. 21 P
go, brew me a pottle of sack finely. 3.05. 29 P
and to taverns, and sack, and wine, and 5.05.159 P
please your /lordship drink a cup of sack? SHR in.2. 2
i ne'er drank sack in my life; in.2. 6 P
come, i'll go burn some sack, 'tis too late to TN 2.03.190 P
art so fat-witted with drinking of old sack, and 1H4 1.02. 3 P
unless hours were cups of sack, and minutes 1.02. 7 P
what says sir john sack and sugar? 1.02.113 P
to filthy tunes, let a cup of sack be my poison. 2.02. 46 P
give me a cup of sack, boy. 2.04.115 P
give me a cup of sack, rogue. 2.04.118 P
you rogue, here's lime in this sack too. 2.04.124 P
is worse than a cup of sack with lime in it. 2.04.126 P
give me a cup of sack. 2.04.152 P
thou stolest a cup of sack eighteen years ago, 2.04.314 P
give me a cup of sack to make my eyes look red, 2.04.385 P
that huge bombard of sack, that stuff'd 2.04.451 P
is he good, but to taste sack and drink it? 2.04.455 P
if sack and sugar be a fault, god help the 2.04.470 P
item, sack, two gallons ... 5s.8d.. 2.04.537 P
item, anchoves and sack after supper ... 2s.6d.. 2.04.538 P
of bread to this intolerable deal of sack! 2.04.541 P
but the sack that thou hast drunk me would have 3.03. 44 P
fill me a bottle of sack. 4.02. 2 P
there's that will sack a city. 5.03. 54 P
for i'll purge and leave sack, and live cleanly 5.04.164 P
and sackcloth, but in new silk and old sack. 2H4 1.02.198 P
steep this letter in sack and make him eat it. 2.02.135 P
pistol, i charge you with a cup of sack, do you 2.04.112 P
come give 's some sack. 2.04.180 P
give me some sack, and, sweet heart, lie thou 2.04.183
some sack, francis. 2.04.281 P
that skill in the weapon is nothing without sack 4.03.114 P
till sack commences it and sets it in act and 4.03.116 P
thin potations and to addict themselves to sack. 4.03.125 P
wages, about the sack he lost at /hinckley fair? 5.01. 24 P
the mass, i have drunk too much sack at supper. 5.03. 14 P
they say he cried out of sack. H5 2.03. 27 P
read, | shall be engrav'd the sack of orleance, 1H6 2.02. 15
our sacks shall be a mean to sack the city, 3.02. 10
thy knee, | or sack this country with a mutiny. 5.01. 62
horner, i drink to you in a cup of sack; 2H6 2.03. 60 P
break out, | and sack great rome with romans. COR 3.01.314
tell me, that i may sack | the hateful mansion. ROM 3.03.107
but if he sack fair athens, | and take our TIM 5.01.171
SACKBUTS 1 FR 0.0001 REL FR 1 V 0 P
the trumpets, sackbuts, psalteries, and fifes, COR 5.04. 49
SACKCLOTH 2 FR 0.0002 REL FR 1 V 1 P
marry, not in ashes and sackcloth, but in new 2H4 1.02.198 P
he /puts on sackcloth, and to sea. PER 4.04. 29
SACK'D 1 FR 0.0001 REL FR 1 V 0 P
"her house is sack'd, her quiet interrupted, LUC 1170
SACKED 1 FR 0.0001 REL FR 1 V 0 P
quoth she, | "why the grecians sacked troy? AWW 1.03. 71
SACKERSON 1 FR 0.0001 REL FR 0 V 1 P
i have seen sackerson loose twenty times, and WIV 1.01.295 P
SACKS 2 FR 0.0002 REL FR 2 V 0 P
more sacks to the mill! LLL 4.03. 79
our sacks shall be a mean to sack the city, 1H6 3.02. 10
SACRAMENT 8 FR 0.0009 REL FR 7 V 1 P
do, i'll take the sacrament on't, how and which AWW 4.03.136 P
may know wherefore we took the sacrament, | and JN 5.02. 6
but ere i last receiv'd the sacrament | i did R2 1.01.139
you shall not only take the sacrament | to bury 4.01.328
a dozen of them here have ta'en the sacrament, 5.02. 97
ten thousand french have ta'en the sacrament 1H6 4.02. 28
thou didst receive the sacrament to fight | in R3 1.04.203
us, | and then, as we have ta'en the sacrament, 5.05. 18
/SACRED 1 FR 0.0001 REL FR 1 V 0 P
/mine /own /tongue /deny /my /sacred /state, R2 4.01.209
SACRED 55 FR 0.0062 REL FR 55 V 0 P
no valentine indeed, for sacred silvia. TGV 3.01.212
in their so sacred paths he dares to tread | in WIV 4.04. 60
strew good luck, ouphes, on every sacred room, 5.05. 57
my poor self, | i am combined by a sacred vow, MM 4.03.144
of sacred chastity and of promise-breach, 5.01.405
justice, most sacred duke, against the abbess! ERR 5.01.133
he hates our sacred nation, and he rails, | even MV 1.03. 48
of drops that sacred pity hath engend'red; AYL 2.07.123
sacred and sweet was all i saw in her. SHR 1.01.176
o my most sacred lady, | temptations have since WT 1.02. 76
i have dispatch'd in post | to sacred delphos, 2.01.183
for he | the sacred honor of himself, his 2.03. 85
their sacred wills be done! 3.03. 7
against whose person | (so sacred as it is) i 5.01.172
and from your sacred vials pour your graces 5.03.122
can taste the free breath of a sacred king? JN 3.01.148
with all religious strength of sacred vows. 3.01.229
such neighbor nearness to our sacred blood R2 1.01.119
one, | were as seven vials of his sacred blood, 1.02. 12
one vial full of edward's sacred blood, | one 1.02. 17
when such a sacred king should hide his head! 3.03. 9
can gripe the sacred handle of our sceptre, 3.03. 80
but dust was thrown upon his sacred head, 5.02. 30
first, to thy sacred state wish i all happiness. 5.06. 6
god and his angels guard your sacred throne, H5 1.02. 7
love, | for my profession's sacred from above. 1H6 1.02.114
doth but usurp the sacred name of knight, 4.01. 40
his weapons holy saws of sacred writ, | his 2H6 1.03. 58
against your sacred person — in god's name H8 2.04. 41
to th' good of your most sacred person and | the 3.02.173
who from the sacred ashes of her honor | shall 5.04. 45
my sacred aunt, should by my mortal sword | be TRO 4.05.134
o sacred receptacle of my joys, | sweet cell of TIT 1.01. 92
and in the sacred /pantheon her espouse. 1.01.242
with her sacred wit | to villainy and vengeance 2.01.120
make sacred even his stirrup, and through him TIM 1.01. 82
and dip their napkins in his sacred blood; JC 3.02.133
the sacred store-house of his predecessors | and MAC 2.04. 34
our hands | unite comutual in most sacred bands. HAM 3.02.160
for, by the sacred radiance of the sun, | the LR 1.01.109
in the due reverence of a sacred vow | i here OTH 3.03.461
where be the sacred vials thou shouldst fill ANT 1.03. 63
the honor is sacred which he talks on now, 2.02. 85
joy and all comfort in your sacred breast! PER 1.02. 34
thy sacred physic shall receive such pay | as 5.01. 74
leave not out a jot | o' th' sacred ceremony. TNK 1.01.131
heavy cheers, | sacred vials fill'd with tears, 1.05. 5
let the temples | burn bright with sacred fires, 5.01. 3
o sacred, shadowy, cold, and constant queen, 5.01.137
and, sacred silver mistress, lend thine ear 5.01.146
of her holy altar | with sacred act advances: 5.01.165
her sacred temple spotted, spoil'd, corrupted, LUC 1172
sight, | serving with looks his sacred majesty, SON 7. 4
tan sacred beauty, blunt the sharp'st intents, 115. 7
"'my parts had pow'r to charm a sacred /nun, LC 260
SACRIFIC'D 2 FR 0.0002 REL FR 2 V 0 P
than jephthah when he sacrific'd his daughter. 3H6 5.01. 91
life | be sacrific'd some hour before his time, ROM 5.03.268
SACRIFICE 22 FR 0.0024 REL FR 20 V 2 P
altar of her beauty | you sacrifice your tears, TGV 3.02. 73
i stand for sacrifice; MV 3.02. 57
ay, sacrifice them all | here to this devil, to 4.01.286
i'll sacrifice the lamb that i do love, | to TN 5.01.130
o, the sacrifice! WT 3.01. 6
bear 'em, | the back is sacrifice to th' load. H8 1.02. 50
me, | make of your prayers one sweet sacrifice, 2.01. 77
vows, gifts, tears, and love's full sacrifice, TRO 1.02.282
ere the first sacrifice, within this hour, | we 4.02. 64
abhorr'd | than spotted livers in the sacrifice. 5.03. 18
encount'ring, | may give you thankful sacrifice. COR 1.06. 9
the prayers of priests nor times of sacrifice, 1.10. 21
a pile | ad /manes fratrum sacrifice his flesh TIT 1.01. 98
slain | religiously they ask a sacrifice: 1.01.124
vain | to save your brother from the sacrifice, 2.03.164
go bid the priests do present sacrifice, | and JC 2.02. 5
to do | a murther, which i thought a sacrifice. OTH 5.02. 65
why, sir, give the gods a thankful sacrifice. ANT 1.02.161 P
of action hath made you reek as a sacrifice. CYM 1.02. 2 P
thither, | and do upon mine altar sacrifice. PER 5.01.241
but in no wise | till he had done his sacrifice, 5.02. 12
must be the sacrifice | to my unhappy beauty? TNK 4.02. 63
SACRIFICERS 1 FR 0.0001 REL FR 1 V 0 P
let's be sacrificers, but not butchers, caius. JC 2.01.166
SACRIFICES 7 FR 0.0008 REL FR 7 V 0 P
beds, | that here come sacrifices for the field. JN 2.01.420
they come like sacrifices in their trim, | and 1H4 4.01.113
like sacrifices, by their watchful fires | sit H5 4.pr. 23
his lady's lie, | poor sacrifices of our enmity! ROM 5.03.304
upon such sacrifices, my cordelia, | the gods LR 5.03. 20
and smoke the temple with our sacrifices. CYM 5.05.398
knights, kinsmen, lovers, yea, my sacrifices, TNK 5.01. 34
SACRIFICIAL 1 FR 0.0001 REL FR 1 V 0 P
rain sacrificial whisperings in his ear, | make TIM 1.01. 81
SACRIFICING 2 FR 0.0002 REL FR 2 V 0 P
which blood, like sacrificing abel's, cries, R2 1.01.104
and entrails feed the sacrificing fire, | whose TIT 1.01.144
SACRILEGIOUS 2 FR 0.0002 REL FR 2 V 0 P
most sacrilegious murther hath broke ope | the MAC 2.03. 67
than myself, | a sacrilegious thief, to do't. CYM 5.05.220
SACRING 1 FR 0.0001 REL FR 1 V 0 P
i'll startle you | worse than the sacring bell, H8 3.02.295
/SAD 1 FR 0.0001 REL FR 1 V 0 P
/sad /stories /chanced /in /the /times /of /old. TIT 3.02. 83
SAD 186 FR 0.0210 REL FR 154 V 32 P
isle, and sitting, | his arms in this sad knot. TMP 1.02.224
what sad talk was that | wherewith my brother TGV 1.03. 1
servant, you are sad. 2.04. 8 P
sad sighs, deep groans, nor silver-shedding 3.01.232
where thou shalt find me sad and solitary. 4.04. 89
is it sad, and few words? MM 3.02. 51 P
to tell sad stories of my own mishaps. ERR 1.01.120
y' are sad, signior balthazar, pray god our 3.01. 19
look'd he or red or pale, or sad or merrily? 4.02. 4
this week he hath been heavy, sour, sad, | and 5.01. 45
but speak you this with a sad brow? ADO 1.01.183 P
why are you thus out of measure sad? 1.03. 2 P
i must be sad when i have cause, and smile at no 1.03. 13 P
and claudio, hand in hand in sad conference. 1.03. 60 P
why, how now, count, wherefore are you sad? 2.01.289 P
not sad, my lord. 2.01.290 P
the count is neither sad, nor sick, nor merry, 2.01.293 P
she is never sad but when she sleeps, and not 2.01.343 P
sad but when she sleeps, and not ever sad then; 2.01.344 P
if he be sad, he wants money. 3.02. 20 P
pluck up, my heart, and be sad. 5.01.204 P
if your love | can labor aught in sad invention, 5.01.283
prince, thou art sad, get thee a wife, get thee 5.04.122 P
a great sign, sir, that he will look sad. LLL 1.02. 3 P
he made her melancholy, sad, and heavy, | and so 5.02. 14
amaz'd, my lord? why looks your highness sad? 5.02.391
persever, counterfeit sad looks, | make mouths MND 3.02.237
here she comes, curst and sad. 3.02.439
in silence sad | trip we after night's shade. 4.01. 95
friend, would go near to make a man look sad. 5.01.289 P
in sooth, i know not why i am so sad; MV 1.01. 1
my ventures, out of doubt | would make me sad. 1.01. 22
that such a thing bechanc'd would make me sad? 1.01. 38
antonio | is sad to think upon his merchandise. 1.01. 40
therefore my merchandise makes me not sad. 1.01. 45
then let us say you are sad | because you are 1.01. 47
and say you are merry | because you are not sad. 1.01. 50

man must play a part, | and mine a sad one. 1.01. 79
like one well studied in a sad ostent | to 2.02.196
better part, | sad lucretia's modesty. AYL 3.02.148
speak sad brow and true maid. 3.02.214 P
why, 'tis good to be sad and say nothing. 4.01. 8 P
by my faith, you have great reason to be sad. 4.01. 22 P
and your experience makes you sad. 4.01. 27 P
make me merry than experience to make me sad — 4.01. 29 P
and at that sight shall sad apollo weep, | so SHR in.2. 59
first were we sad, fearing you would not come, 3.02. 98
father — o, that "had," how sad a passage 'tis! AWW 1.01. 18 P
keep fresh | and lasting in her sad remembrance. TN 1.01. 31
death, | and in sad cypress let me be laid. 2.04. 52
o, where | sad true lover never find my grave, 2.04. 65
he is sad and civil, | and suits well for a 3.04. 5
mad as he, | if sad and merry madness equal be. 3.04. 15
i sent for thee upon a sad occasion. 3.04. 18 P
sad, lady? 3.04. 20 P
i could be sad. 3.04. 20 P
as, a sad face, a reverend carriage, a slow 3.04. 72 P
merry, or sad, shall't be? WT 2.01. 23
a sad tale's best for winter. 2.01. 25
goes all the day, | your sad tires in a mile–a. 4.03.126
my father and the gentlemen are in sad talk, and 4.04.310 P
she is sad and passionate at your highness' tent JN 2.01.544
be these sad signs confirmers of thy words? 3.01. 24
cousin, look not sad, | thy grandame loves thee, 3.03. 2
you are sad. 4.01. 11
methinks nobody should be sad but i. 4.01. 13
young gentlemen would be as sad as night, | only 4.01. 15
why look you sad? 5.01. 44
let not the world see fear and sad distrust 5.01. 46
/were born to see so sad an hour as this, 5.02. 26
i did not think to be so sad to–night | as this 5.05. 15
thy sad aspect | hath from the number of his R2 1.03.209
my death's sad tale may yet undeaf his ear. 2.01. 16
madam, your majesty is too much sad. 2.02. 1
howe'er it be, | i cannot but be sad; 2.02. 30
so heavy sad, | as, /though on thinking on no 2.02. 30
rich men look sad, and ruffians dance and leap, 2.04. 12
and tell sad stories of the death of kings: 3.02.156
that my sad look | should grace the triumph of 3.04. 98
at that sad stop, my lord, | where rude 5.02. 4
but that sad dog | that brings me food to make 5.05. 70
where they did spend a sad and bloody hour, | as 1H4 1.01. 56
yea, there thou mak'st me sad, and mak'st me sin 1.01. 78
look how we can, or sad or merrily, 5.02. 12
i tell thee it is not meet that i should be sad, 2H4 2.02. 40 P
to call my friend — i could be sad, and sad 2.02. 42 P
my friend — i could be sad, and sad indeed too. 2.02. 42 P
oath and a jest with a sad brow will do with a 5.01. 82 P
yet be sad, good brothers, | for, by my faith, 5.02. 49
why then be sad, | but entertain no more of it, 5.02. 53
and their gesture sad, | investing lank–lean H5 4.pr. 25
where the sad and solemn priests | sing still 4.01.301
sad tidings bring i to you out of france, | of 1H6 1.01. 58
methinks your looks are sad, your cheer appal'd. 1.02. 48
my troublous dreams this night doth make me sad.
2H6 1.02. 22
gloucester's case | with sad unhelpful tears, 3.01.218
why is he so sad? 3H6 2.01. 8
our hap is loss, our hope but sad despair, | our 2.03. 9
the widow likes it not, for she looks very sad. 3.02.110
told the sad story of my father's death, | and R3 1.02.160
in that sad time | my manly eyes did scorn an 1.02.163
that it may please you leave these sad designs 1.02.210
like /two children in their deaths' sad story. 4.03. 8
york's wife, and queen of sad mischance, | these 4.04.114
thou drown the sad remembrance of those wrongs 4.04.252
my lord of surrey, why look you so sad? 5.03. 2
sad, high, and working, full of state and woe: H8 pr 3
of the town, | be sad, as we would make ye. pr 25
in trust) of him | things to strike honor sad. 1.02.126
and when you would say something that is sad, 2.01.135
private, | full of sad thoughts and troubles. 2.02. 15
from these sad thoughts that work too much upon 2.02. 57
how sad he looks! sure he is much afflicted. 2.02. 62
lute, wench, my soul grows sad with troubles. 3.01. 1
cause the musicians play me that sad note | i 4.02. 78
and to make a sweet lady sad is a sour offense. TRO 3.01. 72 P
tell these sad women | 'tis fond to wail COR 4.01. 25
my lovely aaron, wherefore look'st thou sad, TIT 2.03. 10
heart's deep languor, and my soul's sad tears: 3.01. 13
thus, in this strange and sad habiliment, | i 5.02. 1
the door | that so my sad decrees may fly away, 5.02. 11
know, thou sad man, i am not tamora; 5.02. 28
'tis sad titus calls. 5.02.121
to love–sick dido's sad attending ear | the 5.03. 82
you sad andronici, have done with woes. 5.03.176
ay me, sad hours seem long. ROM 1.01.161
sweet nurse — o lord, why lookest thou sad? 2.05. 21
though news be sad, yet tell them merrily; 2.05. 22
our wedding cheer to a sad burial feast; 4.05. 87
go hence to have more talk of these sad things; 5.03.307
(prithee be not sad, | thou art true and honest; TIM 2.02.220
hath chanc'd to–day | that caesar looks so sad. JC 1.02.218
and after that, he came thus sad away? 1.02.276
are the ruddy drops | that visit my sad heart. 2.01.290
to thee, | all the charactery of my sad brows. 2.01.308
shade, and there | weep our sad bosoms empty. MAC 4.03. 2
and decay, | have follow'd your sad steps — LR 5.03.290
the weight of this sad time we must obey, 5.03.324
if you find him sad, | say i am dancing; ANT 1.03. 3
what, was he sad, or merry? 1.05. 50
of hot and cold, he was nor sad nor merry. 1.05. 52
he was not sad, for he would shine on those 1.05. 55
be'st thou sad or merry, | the violence of 1.05. 59
caesar is sad, and lepidus, | since pompey's 3.02. 4
pray you look not sad, | nor make replies of 3.11. 17
call to me | all my sad captains, fill our bowls 3.13.183
look you sad, friends? 5.01. 26
i never saw him sad. CYM 1.06. 63
live here, fidele, | i'll sweeten thy sad grave. 4.02.220
what's thy interest | in this sad wrack? 4.02.366
the sad companion, dull–ey'd melancholy, | /be PER 1.02. 2
e'er dull'd sleep | did mock sad fools withal. 5.01.162
sad lady, rise. TNK 1.01. 35
come all sad and solemn shows, | that are 1.05. 7

and yet his songs are sad ones. 2.04. 20
narcissus was a sad boy, but a heavenly. 4.02. 32
so mingled as if mirth did make him sad, | and 5.03. 52
so she at these sad signs draws up her breath, VEN 929
which strook her sad, and then it faster rock'd, LUC 262
sad pause and deep regard beseems the sage; 277
her sad behavior feeds his vulture folly, | a 556
and solemn night with slow sad gait descended 1081
annoy, | sad souls are slain in merry company, 1110
make thy sad grove in my dishevell'd hair; 1129
so i at each sad strain will strain a tear, 1131
stern, sad tunes to change their kinds; 1147
that he may vow, in that sad hour of mine, 1179
and sorts a sad look to her lady's sorrow | (for 1221
to see sad sights moves more than hear them told 1324
that one might see those far–off eyes look sad. 1386
on this sad shadow lucrece spends her eyes, 1457
sad tales doth tell | to pencill'd pensiveness 1496
saw, | amazedly in her sad face he stares: 1591
with sad attention long to hear her words. 1610
begins the sad dirge of her certain ending: 1612
with sad set eyes, and wretched arms across, 1662
but she, that yet her sad task hath not said, 1699
sole arabian tree, | herald sad and trumpet be, PHT 3
o'er | the sad account of fore–bemoaned moan, SON 30.11
i send them back again and straight grow sad. 45.14
let this sad int'rim like the ocean be | which 56. 9
but like a sad slave stay and think of nought 57.11
sea, | but sad mortality o'ersways their power, 65. 2
and the sad augurs mock their own presage, 107. 6
and thither hied, a sad distemper'd guest; 153.12
o, that sad breath his spungy lungs bestowed, LC 326

SAD–BEHOLDING 1 FR 0.0001 REL FR 1 V 0 P
which when her sad–beholding husband saw, LUC 1590

SADDER 3 FR 0.0003 REL FR 1 V 2 P
are you sadder than you were before? TGV 4.02. 54 P
so say i, methinks you are sadder. ADO 3.02. 16 P
come, | now sadder, that you come so unprovided.
SHR 3.02. 99

SADDEST 2 FR 0.0002 REL FR 2 V 0 P
the wisest aunt, telling the saddest tale, MND 2.01. 51
the saddest spectacle that e'er i view'd. 3H6 2.01. 67

SADDLE 10 FR 0.0011 REL FR 5 V 5 P
with an old mothy saddle and stirrups of no SHR 3.02. 49 P
saddle my horse. R2 5.02. 74
give me my boots, i say, saddle my horse. 5.02. 77
tom, beat cut's saddle, put a few flocks in the 1H4 2.01. 5 P
(saving your manhoods) to buy a saddle, and he 2H4 2.01. 27 P
saddle my horse. 5.03.122 P
or by vauting into my saddle with my armor on my
H5 5.02.137 P
saddle white surrey for the field to–morrow. R3 5.03. 64
saddle my horses; LR 1.04.253
prince, i shall not then | freeze in my saddle. TNK 2.05. 48

SADDLE–BOW 1 FR 0.0001 REL FR 1 V 0 P
and rein his proud head to the saddle–bow; VEN 14

SADDLER 2 FR 0.0002 REL FR 2 V 0 P
to pay the saddler for my mistress' crupper? ERR 1.02. 56
the saddler had it, sir, i kept it not. 1.02. 57

SADDLES 1 FR 0.0001 REL FR 0 V 1 P
out of their saddles into the dirt, and thereby SHR 4.01. 57 P

SAD–EY'D 1 FR 0.0001 REL FR 1 V 0 P
the sad–ey'd justice, with his surly hum, H5 1.02.202

SAD–FAC'D 1 FR 0.0001 REL FR 1 V 0 P
you sad–fac'd men, people and sons of rome, | by TIT 5.03. 67

SAD–HEARTED 1 FR 0.0001 REL FR 1 V 0 P
sad–hearted men, much overgone with care, | here
3H6 2.05.123

SADLY 24 FR 0.0027 REL FR 20 V 4 P
float | bound sadly home for naples, | supposing TMP 1.02.235
when you look'd sadly, it was for want of money: TGV 2.01. 29 P
the conference was sadly borne; ADO 2.03.221 P
wheresoe'er she is, | her heart weighs sadly. AWW 3.05. 67
why dost thou look so sadly on my son? JN 3.01. 20
march sadly after, grace my mournings here, | in R2. 5.06. 51
and with his spirits sadly i survive, | to mock 2H4 5.02.125
so part we sadly in this troublous world, | to 3H6 5.05. 7
heaven | that frowns on me looks sadly upon him. R3 5.03.287
groan? why, no; | but sadly tell me, who? ROM 1.01.201
to borrow of your masters, they approach sadly, TIM 2.02.100 P
my master's house merrily, and go away sadly. 2.02.102 P
but look where sadly the poor wretch comes HAM 2.02.168
touching the turkish loss, yet he looks sadly, OTH 2.01. 32
why so sadly | greet you our victory? CYM 5.05. 23
amongst the rar'st of good ones), sitting sadly, 5.05.160
a day or two | let us look sadly, and give grace TNK 5.04.125
this dismal cry rings sadly in her ear, VEN 889
and here she meets another sadly scowling, | to 917
her pity–pleading eyes are sadly fixed | in the LUC 561
he like a thievish dog creeps sadly thence, 736
this plot of death when sadly she had laid, 1212
music to hear, why hear'st thou music sadly? SON 8. 1
found yet moe letters sadly penn'd in blood, LC 47

SADNESS 26 FR 0.0029 REL FR 16 V 10 P
in good sadness, sir, i am sorry that for my WIV 3.05.123 P
ay, in good sadness, is he, and talks of the 4.02. 91 P
breeds, therefore the sadness is without limit. ADO 1.03. 4 P
why, sadness is one and the self–same thing, LLL 1.02. 4 P
how canst thou part sadness and melancholy, my 1.02. 7 P
and such a want–wit sadness makes of me, | that MV 1.01. 6
so full of unmannerly sadness in his youth. 1.02. 50 P
and there begins my sadness. AYL 1.01. 5 P
rumination wraps me in a most humorous sadness. 4.01. 20 P
seeing too much sadness hath congeal'd your SHR in.2. 132
now, in good sadness, son petruchio, | i think 5.02. 63
in good sadness, i do not know. AWW 4.03.203 P
made | will give her sadness very little cure. JN 2.01.546
brothers, you /mix your sadness with some fear: 2H4 5.02. 46
accords not with the sadness of my suit. 3H6 3.02. 77
is like that mirth fate turns to sudden sadness. TRO 1.01. 40
it was. what sadness lengthens romeo's hours? ROM 1.01.163
tell me in sadness, who is that you love? 1.01.199
/bid a sick man in sadness /make his will — | a 1.01.202
in sadness, cousin, i do love a woman. 1.01.204
fell into a sadness, then into a fast, | thence HAM 2.02.147
he did incline to sadness, and oft–times | not CYM 1.06. 62
which are often the sadness of parting, as the 5.04.159 P
but palamon's sadness is a kind of mirth, | so TNK 5.03. 51

if mirth did make him sad, | and sadness merry; 5.03. 53
green, | therefore, in sadness, now i will away; VEN 807

SAD–TUN'D 1 FR 0.0001 REL FR 1 V 0 P
and down i laid to list the sad–tun'd tale, LC 4

SAF'D 1 FR 0.0001 REL FR 1 V 0 P
best you saf'd the bringer | out of the host; ANT 4.06. 25

/SAFE 1 FR 0.0001 REL FR 1 V 0 P
/hap /more //to–night, /safe /scape /the /king! LR 3.06.114

SAFE 81 FR 0.0091 REL FR 74 V 7 P
but are they, ariel, safe? TMP 1.02.217
yourself, | he's safe for these three hours. 3.01. 21
but the doors be lock'd and the keys kept safe, TGV 3.01.111
nor do i think the man of safe discretion | that MM 1.01. 71
heaven keep your honor safe! 2.02.157
by this lord angelo perceives he's safe; 5.01.494
me, | and soon, and safe, arrived where i was. ERR 1.01. 48
in what safe place you have bestow'd my money; 1.02. 78
i greatly fear my money is not safe. 1.02.105
gave to dromio is laid up | safe at the centaur, 2.02. 2
see him safe convey'd | home to my house. 4.04.122
i long that we were safe and sound aboard. 4.04.150
duke's pleasure is that you keep costard safe, LLL 1.02.128 P
thing | so sore, as keeping safe nerissa's ring. MV 5.01.307
baptista is safe, talking with the deceiving SHR 4.04. 82 P
whilst thou li'st warm at home, secure and safe; 5.02.151
life, | but hold himself safe in his prisonment. JN 3.04.161
out, | and keep it safe for our remembrance. 5.02. 2
and with uplifted arms is safe arriv'd | at R2 2.02. 50
all souls that will be safe, fly from my side, 3.02. 80
villain, i'll make thee safe. 5.03. 41
impawn'd | some surety for a safe return again, 1H4 4.03.109
convey them with safe conduct. H5 1.02.297
and thence to france shall we convey you safe, 2.pr. 37
is the duke of exeter safe? 3.06. 5 P
and where they would be safe, they perish. 4.01.173 P
he that outlives this day, and comes safe home, 4.03. 41
heavens keep old bedford safe! 1H6 3.02.100
set this diamond safe | in golden palaces, as it 5.03.169
of the realm, | and yet shalt thou be safe? 3H6 1.01.241
not montague that of itself | england is safe, 4.01. 40
which if they do, yet will i keep thee safe, 4.01. 81
by what safe means the crown may be recover'd. 4.07. 52
we are not safe, clarence, we are not safe. R3 1.01. 70
we are not safe, clarence, we are not safe. 1.01. 70
that think themselves as safe | as thou and i, 3.02. 66
you sleeping safe, they bring to you unrest; 5.03.320
he is, my lord, and safe in leicester town, 5.05. 10
a sure and safe one, though thy master miss'd it H8 3.02.438
receive him, | and see him safe i' th' tower. 5.02.132
if the dull brainless ajax come safe off, TRO 1.03.380
and thy life shall be as safe | as priam is in 4.04.115
and keep your honors safe! COR 1.02. 37
it, and rome | sits safe and still without him. 4.06. 37
and gratulate his safe return to rome, | the TIT 1.01.221
and with my sword i'll keep this door safe. 1.01.288
safe out of fortune's shot, and sits aloft, 2.01. 2
their mother's bedchamber should not be safe 4.01.108
this maugre all the world will i keep safe, | or 4.02.110
save thou the child, so we may all be safe. 4.02.131
then is all safe, the anchor in the port. 4.04. 38
that i hope i may use with a safe conscience, JC 1.01. 13 P
safe, antony, brutus is safe enough. 5.04. 20
safe, antony, brutus is safe enough. 5.04. 20
keep this man safe, | give him all kindness; 5.04. 27
every thing | safe toward your love and honor. MAC 1.04. 27
but banquo's safe? 3.04. 24
safe in a ditch he bides, | with twenty trenched 3.04. 25
are near at hand | that chambers will be safe. 5.04. 2
i would the friends we miss were safe arriv'd. 5.09. 1
nor stands it safe with us | to let his madness HAM 3.03. 1
to keep those many many bodies safe | that live 3.03. 9
to have found a safe redress, but now grow LR 1.04.206
'tis politic and safe to let him keep | at point 1.04.323
what safe and nicely i might well delay | by 5.03.145
he looks sadly, | and /prays the moor be safe; OTH 2.01. 33
o world, | to be direct and honest is not safe. 3.03.378
are his wits safe? is he not light of brain? 4.01.269
that which most with you should safe my going, ANT 1.03. 55
that thou depart'st hence safe | does pay thy 4.14. 36
i am safe: 4.15. 26
whom in constancy you think stands so safe. CYM 1.04.127 P
being strange, | to have them in safe stowage. 1.06.192
send your trunk to me, it shall safe be kept, 1.06.209
safe mayst thou wander, safe return again! 3.05.105
safe mayst thou wander, safe return again! 3.05.105
my horse is tied up safe; 4.01. 22 P
but in all safe reason | he must have some 4.02.131
but in our orbs /we'll live so round and safe, PER 1.02.122
should house him safe is wrack'd and split, 2.ch. 32
i sav'd her, | and set her safe to land; TNK 4.01. 96

SAFE–CONDUCT 2 FR 0.0002 REL FR 0 V 2 P
and to procure safe–conduct for his person of TRO 3.03.276 P
and to procure safe–conduct from agamemnon. 3.03.287 P

SAFE–CONDUCTING 1 FR 0.0001 REL FR 1 V 0 P
safe–conducting the rebels from their ships? R3 4.04.482

SAFEGUARD 7 FR 0.0008 REL FR 7 V 0 P
consenting to the safeguard of your honor, | i MM 5.01.419
to safeguard thine own life | the best way is to R2 1.02. 35
since we have locks to safeguard necessaries, H5 1.02.176
and doves will peck in safeguard of their brood. 3H6 2.02. 18
if you do fight in safeguard of your wives, R3 5.03.259
on safeguard he came to me, and did curse COR 3.01. 9
for the inheritance of their loves and safeguard 3.02. 68

SAFELY 27 FR 0.0030 REL FR 24 V 3 P
art | so safely ordered that there is no soul — TMP 1.02. 29
safely in harbor | is the king's ship, in the 1.02.226
so, king, go safely on to seek thy son. 2.01.327
that we have safely found | our king and company 5.01.221
i, costard, running out, that was safely within, LLL 3.01.116
certain that my ships | are safely come to road. MV 5.01.288
till then i'll keep him dark and safely lock'd. AWW 4.01. 94
with what manners i might safely be admitted. 4.05. 89 P
to keep him safely till his day of trial. R2 4.01.153
god, and not we, hath safely fought to–day. 2H4 4.02.121
had all your quarters been as safely kept | as 1H6 2.01. 63
see them guarded | and safely brought to dover, 5.01. 49
i charge thee waft me safely cross the channel. 2H6 4.01.115
for how can tyrants safely govern home, | unless 3H6 3.03. 69

god safely quit her of her burthen, and | with H8 5.01. 70
of my authority | might go one way, and safely; 5.02. 71
in manacles, | then reason safely with you. COR 1.09. 58
the wars, and safely home | loaden with honor. 5.03.163
vouchsafe that antony | may safely come to him, JC 3.01.131
to be thus is nothing, | but to be safely thus. MAC 3.01. 48
safely stow'd. HAM 4.02. 1 P
it, gave't th' impression, plac'd it safely, 5.02. 52
letting go safely by | the divine desdemona. OTH 2.01. 72
safely, i think; CYM 1.04. 54 P
and might so safely, had it | been all the worth 5.05.190
gods | would safely deliver me from this place! PER 4.06.180
and safely presently | into your bush again, sir TNK 3.06.110
SAFER 20 FR 0.0022 REL FR 18 V 2 P
eye, | safer than mine own two, more dear. AWW 2.01.109
but i am sure 'tis safer to | avoid what's grown WT 1.02.432
nor shall you be safer | than one condemn'd by 1.02.444
paw, | a fasting tiger safer by the tooth, JN 3.01.260
safer shall he be upon the sandy plains | than 2H6 1.04. 36
safer shall he be upon the sandy plains | than 1.04. 68
but the safer when 'tis back'd with france. 3H6 4.01. 41
finds safer footing than blind reason stumbling TRO 3.02. 72 P
and on a safer judgment all revoke | your COR 2.03.218
but safer triumph is this funeral pomp, | that TIT 1.01.176
good for their meat, and safer for their lives. TIM 1.02. 45
fortune | shall keep us both the safer. MAC 2.03.139
'tis safer to be that which we destroy | than by 3.02. 6
safer than trust too far. LR 1.04.328
the safer sense will ne'er accommodate | his 4.06. 81
of effects, throws a more safer voice on you. OTH 1.03.226 P
my blood begins my safer guides to rule, | and 2.03.205
the sharded beetle in a safer hold | than is the CYM 3.03. 20
lives, invent a way | safer than banishment. TNK 3.06.218
forgiven | is safer wars than ever you can make, STM II.C 112
SAFE'S 1 FR 0.0001 REL FR 0 V 1 P
brother arthur watchins sergeant safe's yeoman. STM II.C 43 P
/SAFEST 1 FR 0.0001 REL FR 1 V 0 P
/to /take /the /safest /occasion /by /the /front OTH 3.01. 49
SAFEST 7 FR 0.0008 REL FR 7 V 0 P
mistress, dispatch you with your safest haste, AYL 1.03. 41
devise the fittest time and safest way | to hide 1.03.135
and, parolles, live | safest in shame! AWW 4.03.338
here is the best and safest passage in? 1H6 3.02. 22
her life is safest only in her birth. R3 4.04.214
and our safest way | is to avoid the aim. MAC 2.03.142
with safest distance i mine honor shielded. LC 151
SAFETIES 1 FR 0.0001 REL FR 1 V 0 P
be your dishonors, | but mine own safeties. MAC 4.03. 30
SAFETY 75 FR 0.0084 REL FR 65 V 10 P
you take your rest, | and watch your safety. TMP 2.01.198
the heavens give safety to your purposes! MM 1.01. 73
you shall find | your safety manifested. 4.03. 90
true, | let me in safety raise me from my knees, 5.01.231
the sailors sought for safety by our boat, | and ERR 1.01. 76
owner of it blest | ever shall in safety rest. MND 5.01.420
than with safety of a pure blush thou mayst in AYL 1.02. 28 P
for your own sake to embrace your own safety, 1.02.179 P
is running away, when fear proposes the safety. AWW 1.01.203 P
which with as much safety you might answer him; TN 3.04.250 P
pursue with any safety this sport /t' the upshot 4.02. 70 P
i must have done no less with wit and safety. 5.01.211
counsel and aid them, for their better safety, WT 3.02. 20 P
and my wife's, in safety | here, where we are. 5.01.167
humorous ladyship is by | to teach thee safety! JN 3.01.120
her highness is in safety, fear you not. 3.02. 8
i remember to be holy) | for your fair safety; 3.03. 16
for he that steeps his safety in true blood 3.04.147
in true blood | shall find but bloody safety, 3.04.148
your safety, for the which myself and them 4.02. 50
deliver him to safety, and return, | for i must 4.02.158
it is our safety, and we must embrace | this 4.03. 12
to seek sweet safety out | in vaults and prisons 5.02.142
tend'ring the precious safety of my prince, R2 1.01. 32
nettle, danger, we pluck this flower, safety. 1H4 2.03. 10 P
and shake the peace and safety of our throne. 3.02.117
drove us to seek out | this head of safety, and 4.03.103
nimble wing | we were enforc'd, for safety sake, 5.01. 65
what i have done my safety urg'd me to; 5.05. 11
under the smile of safety wounds the world; 2H4 in 10
than did our soldiers, aiming at their safety, 1.01.124
man | the aptest way for safety and revenge. 1.01.213
to this monstrous form | to hold our safety up. 4.02. 35
in heat of day, | that scald'st with safety. 4.05. 31
that guards the peace and safety of your person? 5.02. 88
but we our kingdom's safety must so tender, H5 2.02.175
give all my fame for a pot of ale and safety. 3.02. 13 P
to view the field in safety, and dispose | of 4.07. 82
and for his safety there i'll best devise. 1H6 1.01.172
i tender so the safety of my liege. 2H6 3.01.277
i know our safety is to follow them, | for, as i 5.03. 23
such safety finds | the trembling lamb environed 3H6 1.01.241
or than for strength and safety of our country. 3.03.211
in them, and in ourselves, our safety lies. 4.01. 46
and shut the gates for safety of ourselves; 4.07. 18
hath pass'd in safety through the narrow seas, 4.08. 3
tend'ring my person's safety, hath appointed R3 1.01. 44
the peace of england, and our persons' safety, 3.05. 45
and only in that safety died her brothers. 4.04.215
wishes towards you | honor and plenteous safety) H8 1.01.104
now, and provide | for thine own future safety. 3.02.421
in her days every man shall eat in safety 5.04. 33
farewell, the gods with safety stand about thee! TRO 5.03. 94
th' honor'd gods | keep rome in safety, and the COR 3.03. 34
now talk at pleasure of your safety. TIT 4.02.134
and if he stand /on hostage for his safety, 4.04.105
hold him in safety till the prince come hither. ROM 5.03.183
hold, no reason | can sound his state in safety. TIM 2.01. 13
all thy safety were remotion and thy defense 4.03.342 P
rome, | no rome of safety for octavius yet; JC 3.01.289
that doth guide his valor | to act in safety. MAC 3.01. 53
the safety and health of this whole state, | and HAM 1.03. 21
be wary then, best safety lies in fear: 1.03. 43
on such regards of safety and allowance | as 2.02. 79
hamlet, this deed, for thine especial safety — 4.03. 40
as by your safety, greatness, wisdom, all things 4.07. 8
/fear'd to lose it, | thy safety being motive. LR 1.01.157
as we shall find their merits and our safety 5.03. 44
cannot with safety cast him, for he's embark'd OTH 1.01.149
in night, and on the court and guard of safety? 2.03.216
yes, something you can deny for your own safety: ANT 2.06. 92 P
of caesar seek your honor, with your safety. 4.15. 46
the worthy leonatus is in safety | and greets CYM 1.06. 12
and pawn mine honor for their safety. 1.06.194
love and beyond reason, | or wit, or safety. TNK 2.06. 12
SAFFRON 4 FR 0.0004 REL FR 2 V 2 P
who with thy saffron wings upon my flow'rs TMP 4.01. 78
did this companion with the saffron face | revel ERR 4.04. 61
whose villainous saffron would have made all the AWW 4.05. 2 P
i must have saffron to color the warden pies; WT 4.03. 45 P
SAG 1 FR 0.0001 REL FR 1 V 0 P
shall never sag with doubt, nor shake with fear. MAC 5.03. 10
SAGE 7 FR 0.0008 REL FR 5 V 2 P
whisper o'er a couplet or two of most sage saws. TN 3.04.378 P
all you sage counsellors, hence! 2H4 4.05.120
to deceive de most sage demoiselle dat is en H5 5.02.219 P
cousin of buckingham, and sage grave men, R3 3.07.227
how's this? how's this? some more, be sage. PER 4.06. 95
this blur to youth, this sorrow to the sage, LUC 222
sad pause and deep regard beseems the sage; 277
SAGITTARY 3 FR 0.0003 REL FR 3 V 0 P
the dreadful sagittary | appalls our numbers. TRO 5.05. 14
him, | lead to the sagittary the raised search; OTH 1.01.158
you, | send for the lady to the sagittary, | and 1.03.115
SAID *(also sain)*
/SAID 3 FR 0.0003 REL FR 2 V 1 P
/the /accompt /of /chance /before /you /said, 2H4 1.01.167
/look /what /i /have /said, | i will avouch't in R3 1.03.113
/as /'tis /said, /the /bastard /son /of LR 4.07. 88 P
SAID 421 FR 0.0475 REL FR 266 V 155 P
of virtue, and | she said thou wast my daughter; TMP 1.02. 57
what if he had said "widower aeneas" too? 2.01. 80 P
"widow dido," said you? 2.01. 82 P
for it hath been said, "as proper a man as ever 2.02. 60 P
and it shall be said so again while stephano 2.02. 62 P
why, i said nothing. 3.02. 50 P
honest lord, | thou hast said well; 3.03. 35
time, my lord, | you said our work should cease. 5.01. 5
but what said she? TGV 1.01.110 P
what said she? 1.01.128 P
what said she? 1.01.131 P
what said she? nothing? 1.01.142 P
for all these exercises | he said that proteus, 1.03. 12
you have said, sir. 2.04. 29 P
if not, to hide what i have said to thee, | that 4.03. 35
dog, and a fair dog — can there be more said? WIV 1.01. 97 P
said i well, bully hector? 1.03. 11 P
shalt have egress and regress — said i well? 2.01.218 P
said i well? 2.03. 89 P
said i well? 2.03. 95 P
by gar, 'tis good; vell said. 2.03. 96 P
"nay," said i, "will you cast away your child on 3.04. 95 P
well said, brazen–face! 4.02.135 P
ere she sleep, has thrice her prayers said, 5.05. 50
well said, fairy hugh. 5.05.131 P
i think thou never wast where grace was said. MM 1.02. 19 P
and longing (as i said) for pruins; 2.01. 99 P
and having but two in the dish (as i said), 2.01.100 P
very man, having eaten the rest (as i said) and 2.01.101 P
ay, well said. 2.02. 89
that's well said. 2.02.109
say that i said so. 3.02.184 P
upon a wrong'd — i would fain have said a maid! 5.01. 21
a gentlewoman denies all that you have said. 5.01.282 P
and do you remember what you said of the duke? 5.01.331 P
thou art said to have a stubborn soul | that 5.01.480
your highness said even now i made you a duke; 5.01.515 P
and you said no. ERR 3.01. 55
and what said he? 4.02. 11
this (though i cannot be said to be a flattering ADO 1.03. 31 P
lessen god's sending that way, for it is said, 2.01. 22 P
well, this was signior benedick that said so. 2.01.131 P
when i said i would die a bachelor, i did not 2.03.243 P
well said, i' faith, neighbor verges. 3.05. 35 P
i might have said, "no part of it is mine; 4.01.134
this man said, sir, that don john, the prince's 4.02. 39 P
i said thou hadst a fine wit. 5.01.160 P
"true," said she, "a fine little one." 5.01.161 P
"no," said i, "a great wit." 5.01.161 P
"nay," said i, "a good wit." 5.01.163 P
"just," said she, "it hurts nobody." 5.01.163 P
"nay," said i, "the gentleman is wise." 5.01.164 P
"certain," said she, "a wise gentleman." 5.01.165 P
"nay," said i, "he hath the tongues." 5.01.166 P
"that i believe," said she, "for he swore a 5.01.167 P
which she wept heartily and said she car'd not. 5.01.174 P
flout at me for what i have said against it; 5.04.107 P
i said the deer was not a haud credo, 'twas a LLL 4.02. 20 P
for so they say the fool said, and so say i, and 4.03. 5 P
'twas treason, he said. 4.03.192
lord longaville said i came o'er his heart, 5.02.278
well said, old mocker. 5.02.549
and therefore is love said to be a child, MND 1.01.238
then how can it be said i am alone, | when all 2.01.225
such separation as may well be said | becomes a 2.02. 58
this is he, my master said, | despised the 2.02. 72
methoughts you said you neither lend nor borrow MV 1.03. 69
and well said too; 2.09. 37
well said — that was laid on with a trowel. AYL 1.02.106 P
but what said jaques? 2.01. 43
giving her them again, said with weeping tears, 2.04. 53 P
well said! 2.06. 14 P
you have said; 3.02.121 P
what said he? 3.02.221 P
in poetry may be said as lovers they do feign. 3.03. 21 P
it is said, "many a man knows no end of his 3.03. 52 P
he said mine eyes were black and my hair black, 3.05.130
it may be said of him that cupid hath clapp'd 4.01. 47 P
me word, if i said his beard was not cut well, 5.04. 71 P
of an if, as, "if you said so, then i said so"; 5.04.101 P
of an if, as, "if you said so, then i said so" 5.04.101 P
well said, master, mum, and gaze your fill. SHR 1.01. 73
that i may soon make good | what i have said, 1.01. 75
so said, so done, is well. 1.02.185
what will be said? 3.02. 4
what said the wench when he rose again? 3.02.166
sir, to satisfy you in what i have said, | stand 4.02. 4
the note lies in 's throat if he say i said so. 4.03.132 P
master, if ever i said loose–bodied gown, sew me 4.03.135 P
i said a gown. 4.03.137 P
there's little can be said in't, 'tis against AWW 1.01.135 P
fortune, she said, was no goddess, that had put 1.03.111 P
when i said "a mother," | methought you saw a 1.03.140
just, you say well; so would i have said. 2.03. 19 P
that's it i would have said, the very same. 2.03. 25 P
i would have said it; 2.03. 39 P
what should be said? 2.03.141
you should have said, sir, "before a knave th' 2.04. 29 P
"five or six thousand horse," i said — i will 4.03.148 P
methought you said | you saw one here in court 5.03.199
i did go between them, as i said, but more than 5.03.259 P
what is to be said to him, lady? TN 1.05.144 P
doctrine, and much may be said of it. 1.05.222 P
sir, though it was said she much resembled me, 2.01. 25 P
you have said, sir. 3.01. 11 P
or unsafe circumstance — what can be said? 3.04. 81 P
i have said too much unto a heart of stone, 3.04.201
but to be said an honest man and a good 4.02. 8 P
very wittily said to a niece of king gorboduc, 4.02. 13 P
well said, master parson. 4.02. 27 P
thou hast said to me a thousand times | thou 5.01.267
you shall see, as i have said, great difference WT 1.01. 3 P
well said, hermione. 1.02. 33
have i twice said well? 1.02. 90
when you have said she's goodly, come between 2.01. 75
i have said | she's an adultress, i have said 2.01. 87
she's an adultress, i have said with whom: 2.01. 88
last — o lords, | when i have said, cry "woe!" 3.02.200
to me for help and said his name was antigonus, 3.03. 96 P
for i have heard it said, | there is an art 4.04. 86
how often said my dignity would last | but till 4.04.475
so 'tis said, sir — about his son, that should 4.04.766 P
for has not the divine apollo said, | is't not 5.01. 37
you yourself | have said and writ so, but your 5.01. 99
in vain, said many | a prayer upon her grave. 5.03.140
son, have i not ever said | how that ambitious JN 1.01. 31
if thou hadst said him nay, it had been sin. 1.01.275
when i have said, make answer to us both. 2.01.235
o, let it not be said! 5.01. 59
or if he do, let it at least be said, | they saw 5.01. 75
no, no, on my soul, it never shall be said. 5.02.108
who was he that said | king john did fly an hour 5.05. 16
what said our cousin when you parted with him? R2 1.04. 10
nay, nothing, all is said. 2.01.148
thou hast said enough. 3.02.203
comprising all that may be sworn or said, | his 3.03.111
and will maintain what thou hast said is false 4.01. 27
then, as i said, the duke, great bullingbrook, 5.02. 7
walls | with painted imagery had said at once, 5.02. 16
and what said the gallant? 5.03. 15
for more is to be said and to be done | than out 1H4 1.01.106
why, that's well said. 1.02.144 P
my lord, | i answered indirectly, as i said, 1.03. 66
what e'er lord harry percy then had said | to 1.03. 71
wrong or any way impeach | what then he said, so 1.03. 76
he said he would not ransom mortimer, | forbade 1.03.219
ay, ay, he said four. 2.04.199 P
and said he would swear truth out of england but 2.04.305 P
my lord, and i said i heard your grace say so; 3.03.105 P
man as he is, and said he would cudgel you. 3.03.107 P
and said this other day you ought him a thousand 3.03.133 P
call'd you jack, and said he would cudgel you. 3.03.138 P
indeed, sir john, you said so. 3.03.141 P
yea, if he said my ring was copper. 3.03.142 P
well said, my noble scot! 4.01. 1
that ever said i heark'ned for your death. 5.04. 52
well said, hal! 5.04. 75 P
said he young harry percy's spur was cold? 2H4 1.01. 49
he said, sir, the water itself was a good 1.02. 3 P
what said master dommelton about the satin for 1.02. 29 P
he said, sir, you should procure him better 1.02. 31 P
aside, i had lied in my throat if i had said so. 1.02. 82 P
faith, you said so before. 2.01.137 P
but i never said so. 2.02.141 P
putting off his hat, said, "i will now take my 2.04. 7 P
why, that's well said; 2.04. 31 P
and, as he said to me — 'twas no longer ago 2.04. 86 P
civil, for," said he, "you are in an ill name." 2.04. 90 P
now 'a said so, i can tell whereupon. 2.04. 91 P
you would bless you to hear what he said. 2.04. 95 P
it is well said, in faith, sir, and it is well 3.02. 68 P
in faith, sir, and it is well said indeed too. 3.02. 68 P
singular good, in faith, well said, sir john, 3.02.109 P
in faith, well said, sir john, very well said. 3.02.109 P
well said, good woman's tailor! 3.02.158 P
well said, courageous feeble! 3.02.158 P
ha, sir john, said i well? 3.02.212 P
well said, th' art a good fellow. 3.02.239 P
well said, i' faith, wart, th' art a good scab. 3.02.275 P
well said, davy. 5.03. 9 P
well said, master silence. 5.03. 49 P
which salique, as i said, 'twixt /elbe and sala, H5 1.02. 52
'a did, and said they were dev'ls incarnate. 2.03. 31 P
'a said once, the dev'l would have him about 2.03. 35 P
and 'a said it was a black soul burning in hell? 2.03. 41 P
himself, and he said he car'd not who knew it. 3.07.107 P
"ill will never said well." 3.07.113 P
ay, he said so, to make us fight cheerfully; 4.01.192 P
they have said their prayers, and they stay for 4.02. 56
i said so, dear katherine, and i must not blush 5.02.113 P
here, said they, is the terror of the french, 1H6 1.04. 42
and i have heard it said, unbidden guests | are 2.02. 55
that shall maintain what i have said is true, 2.04. 73
lest it be said, "speak, sirrah, when you should 3.01. 62
i do remember how my father said | a stouter 3.04. 18
once i encount'red him, and thus i said: 4.07. 37
'tis said the stout parisians do revolt, | and 5.02. 2
that the said henry shall espouse the lady 2H6 1.01. 46 P
my master said that he was, and that the king 1.03. 31 P
i never said nor thought any such matter. 1.03.187 P
well said, my masters, and welcome all. 1.04. 13 P
ask what thou wilt. that i had said, and done! 1.04. 28
by good saint albon, who said, "simon, come; 2.01. 89
why, that's well said. what color is my gown of? 2.01.109
why, that's well said. 3.02. 8

had i but said, i would have kept my word; 3.02.293
and yet it is said, labor in thy vocation; 4.02. 16 P
nay, it shall ne'er be said, while england 4.10. 42
you said so much before, and yet you fled. 3H6 2.02.106
'tis better said than done, my gracious lord. 3.02. 90
but what said lady bona to my marriage? 4.01. 97
but what said henry's queen? 4.01.102
but what said warwick to these injuries? 4.01.107
thought, at least, he would have said the king, 5.01. 29
and said, "commend me to my valiant brother." 5.02. 42
and more he would have said, and more he spoke, 5.02. 43
you, | imagine i have said farewell already. R3 1.02.224
and said, "dear brother, live, and be a king"? 2.01.114
you said that idle weeds are fast in growth: 3.01.103
'tis said, my liege, in yorkshire are in arms. 4.04.519
more than i have said, loving countrymen, | the 5.03.237
what said northumberland as touching richmond? 5.03.271
he said the truth, and what said surrey then? 5.03.273
he said the truth, and what said surrey then? 5.03.273
he smil'd and said, "the better for our purpose. 5.03.274
'twas said they saw but one, and no discerner H8 1.01. 32
it's long, and't may be said | it reaches far, 1.01.110
as the duke said, | the will of heaven be done, 1.01.214
presently the duke | said, 'twas the fear indeed 1.02.158
well said, lord sands, | your colt's tooth is 1.03. 47
he had a black mouth that said other of him. 1.03. 58
well said, my lord. 1.04. 30
you have said well. 3.02.149
'tis well said again, | and 'tis a kind of good 3.02.152
he said he did, and with his deed did crown 3.02.155
better | have burnt that tongue than said so. 3.02.254
so said her woman, and that her suff'rance made 5.01. 68
i have said. 5.01. 86
i fear nothing | what can be said against me. 5.01.126
said i for this, the girl was like to him? 5.01.174
who said he came hurt home to-day? TRO 1.02.214 P
paris and troilus, you have both said well, 2.02.163
i have said my prayers, and devil envy say amen. 2.03. 20 P
'tis said he holds you well, and will be led 2.03.180
well said, my lord! well, you say so in fits. 3.01. 57 P
when th' have said as false | as air, as water, 3.02.191
i said, "good morrow, ajax"; 3.03.260 P
that i have said to some my standers-by, | "lo 4.05.190
well said, adversity! 5.01. 12 P
thou art said to be achilles' male varlot. 5.01. 15 P
now she sharpens. well said, whetstone! 5.02. 75 P
unless she said, "my mind is now turn'd whore." 5.02.114
they said they were an-hungry; COR 1.01.205
said to be something imperfect in favoring the 2.01. 49 P
he said he had wounds, which he could show in 2.03.166
you should have said | that as his worthy deeds 2.03.185
thus to have said, | as you were fore-advis'd, 2.03.190
h'as said enough. 3.01.161
let what is meet be said it must be meet, | and 3.01.169
well said, noble woman! 3.02. 31
as thou hast said | my praises made thee first a 3.02.107
there's no more to be said, but he is banish'd 3.03.117
i have heard it said, the fittest time to 4.03. 32 P
in some sort, may be said to be a ravisher, so 4.05.228 P
when i said banish him, i said 'twas pity. 4.06.140
when i said banish him, i said 'twas pity. 4.06.140
i ever said we were i' th' wrong when we 4.06.154 P
you hear what he hath said | which was sometime 5.01. 1
he said 'twas folly, | for one poor grain or two 5.01. 26
'twas very faintly he said, "rise"; 5.01. 66
i say to you, as i was said to, "away!" 5.02.108 P
you have said you will not grant us any thing; 5.03. 87
to wait, said i? TIT 2.01. 21
say | that to her brother which i said to thee: 3.01.145
go to the empress, tell her this i said. 4.02.145
o, well said, lucius! 4.03. 64
but saying o'er what i have said before: ROM 1.02. 7
but, as i said, | on lammas-eve at night shall 1.03. 20
nay, i do bear a brain — but, as i said, | when 1.03. 29
the pretty wretch left crying and said, "ay." 1.03. 44
and, pretty fool, it stinted and said, "ay." 1.03. 48
it stinted and said, "ay." 1.03. 57
well said, my hearts! 1.05. 86
by my troth, it is well said; 2.04.117 P
why followed not, when she said, "tybalt's dead, 3.02.118
mass, and well said, a merry whoreson, ha! 4.04. 20
with music straight, | for so he said he would. 4.04. 23
noting this penury, to myself i said, | "an' if 5.01. 49
what said my man, when my betossed soul | did 5.03. 76
said he not so? 5.03. 79
heavens, have i said, the bounty of this lord! TIM 2.02.164
as you have said, my lord. 2.02.194 P
true, as you said, timon is shrunk indeed, | and 3.02. 61
'tis said he gave unto | his steward a mighty 5.01. 7
so it is said, my noble lord, but therefore 5.01. 78
caesar said to me, "dar'st thou, cassius, now JC 1.02.102
what you have said | i will consider; 1.02.167
what said he when he came unto himself? 1.02.262
when he came to himself again, he said, if he 1.02.269 P
he said, if he had done or said any thing amiss, 1.02.270 P
it shall be said his judgment rul'd our hands; 2.01.147
but all remember | what you have said, and show 2.01.223
what said popilius lena? 3.01. 15
i said an elder soldier, not a better. 4.03. 56
you said the enemy would not come down, | but 5.01. 2
much drink may be said to be an equivocator with MAC 2.03. 31 P
'tis said, they eat each other. 2.04. 18
yet it was said | it should not stand in thy 3.01. 3
as it is said | mark antony's was by caesar. 3.01. 55
this is the air-drawn dagger which you said 3.04. 61
i have said. 4.03.213
and remember well | what i have said to you. HAM 1.03. 85
what is't, ophelia, he hath said to you? 1.03. 88
well said, old mole, canst work i' th' earth so 1.05.162
marry, well said, very well said. 2.01. 6
marry, well said, very well said. 2.01. 6
what said he? 2.01. 83
that i have positively said, "'tis so," | when 2.02.154
me not at first, 'a said i was a fishmonger. 2.02.188 P
why did ye laugh then, when i said, "man 2.02.313 P
i remember one said there were no sallets in the 2.02.441 P
you need not tell us what lord hamlet said, | we 3.01.179
"by and by" is easily said. 3.02.387
and, as you said, and wisely was it said, | 'tis 3.03. 30
and, as you said, and wisely was it said, | 'tis 3.03. 30
no life to breathe | what thou hast said to me. 3.04.199
that justly think'st and hast most rightly said! LR 1.01.183
remember what i have said. 1.03. 21
have you nothing said | upon his party 'gainst 2.01. 25
would he deny his letter, said he? 2.01. 78
regan, said you so? 2.04.254
he said it would be thus, poor banish'd man. 3.04.164
thou shouldst have said, "good porter, turn the 3.07. 64
to say "ay" and "no" to every thing that i said! 4.06. 99 P
what said she to you? OTH 1.01.166
fled from her wish, and yet said, "now i may"; 2.01.151
ay, well said, whisper. 2.01.168 P
by me that's said or done amiss this night, 2.03.201
if i had said i had seen him do you wrong? 4.01. 24
hath he said any thing? 4.01. 29
what hath he said? 4.01. 31
go to, well said, well said. 4.01.114
go to, well said, well said. 4.01.114
such as she said my lord did say i was. 4.02.119
you have said now. 4.02.201 P
and said nothing but what i protest intendment 4.02.202 P
but what said he then? 4.03. 55
i have heard it said so. 4.03. 60
o, that's well said: 5.01. 98
she said so; i must needs report the truth. 5.02.128
a /damned slave, | what shall be said to thee? 5.02.293
i have said. ANT 1.02. 57
cold in blood, | to say as i said then! 1.05. 75
well said. 2.05. 46
ten times as much | as i have said you did. 2.06. 78
y' have said, sir. 2.06.107 P
caesar, and (as i said before) that which is the 2.06.128 P
i have said. 3.02. 34
and 'tis said in rome | that photinus an eunuch 3.07. 13
well said, come on. 4.02. 8
this way — well said. 4.04. 28
'tis said, man, and farewell. 4.14. 92
if you but said so, 'twere as deep with me. CYM 2.03. 91
ay, i said so, sir; 2.03.150
she gave it me, and said | she priz'd it once. 2.04.103
and, as i said, there is no moe such caesars. 3.01. 36 P
she said upon a time (the bitterness of it i now 3.05.133 P
for 'tis said a woman's fitness comes by fits. 4.01. 5 P
he said he was gentle, but unfortunate; 4.02. 39
yet said hereafter | i might know more. 4.02. 41
which he said was precious | and cordial to me, 4.02.326
and on it said a century of prayers | (such as i 4.02.391
"if pisanio | have," said she, "given his 5.05.246
said not i as much when i saw the porpas how he PER 2.01. 23 P
hark you, my friend. you said you could not beg? 2.01. 85 P
well said, well said. 3.02. 87
well said, well said. 3.02. 87
and it is said | for certain in our story, she 4.ch. 18
remember what i have said. 4.01. 46
i said, my lord, if you did know my parentage, 5.01. 99
some such thing | i said, and said no more but 5.01.133
and said no more but what my thoughts | did 5.01.133
you said you would believe me, | but, not to be 5.01.150
as in the rest you said | thou hast been godlike 5.01.205
is't said this war's afoot? TNK 1.02.104
the one of th' other may be said to water 1.03. 58
you | have said enough to shake me from the arm 1.03. 92
my father said so; 2.05. 6
have i said, "thus let be," and "there let be," 3.05. 9
the one said it was an owl, | the other he said 3.05. 68
one said it was an owl, | the other he said nay, 3.05. 69
he said nay, | the third he said it was a hawk, 3.05. 70
and i could wish i had not said i lov'd her, 3.06. 40
that's well said. 3.06. 49
i have said they die; 3.06.224
was nothing said of me | concerning the escape 4.01. 1
they said that palamon had arcite's body 5.03. 79
but that your wills have said it must be so, 5.03.140
can that be, when | venus i have said is false? 5.04. 45
this said, impatience chokes her pleading tongue VEN 217
so of concealed sorrow may be said, | free vent 333
and would say after her, if she said "no." 852
this said, she hasteth to a myrtle grove, 865
this said, his guilty hand pluck'd up the latch, LUC 358
this said, he shakes aloft his roman blade, 505
this said, he sets his foot upon the light, 673
as well to hear as grant what he hath said. 915
this said, from her betumbled couch she starteth 1037
she would have said, "can lurk in such a look"; 1535
but she, that yet her sad task hath not said, 1699
that no man could distinguish what he said. 1785
this said, he strook his hand upon his breast, 1842
have you not heard it said full oft, | a woman's PP 18.41
yet will she blush, here be it said, | to hear 18.53
and yet it may be said i lov'd her dearly; SON 42. 2
be it not said | thy edge should blunter be than 56. 1
even those that said i could not love you dearer 115. 2
breath'd forth the sound that said "i hate" | to 145. 2
this said, in top of rage the lines she rents, LC 55
that's to ye sworn to none was ever said, | for 180
"this said, his wat'ry eyes he did dismount, 281

SAIDST 4 FR 0.0004 REL FR 3 V 1 P
what, four? thou saidst but two even now. 1H4 2.04.197 P
that saidst i begg'd the empire at thy hands. TIT 1.01.307
thou saidst (o, it comes o'er my memory, | as OTH 4.01. 20
i think thou saidst | thou hadst been toss'd PER 5.01.129

/SAIL 1 FR 0.0001 REL FR 1 V 0 P
the steerage of my course | direct my /sail! ROM 1.04.113

SAIL 47 FR 0.0053 REL FR 42 V 5 P
nor tackle, sail, nor mast, the very rats TMP 1.02.147
and sail so expeditious, that shall catch | your 5.01.316
sail like my pinnace to these golden shores. WIV 1.03. 80
had not their /bark been very slow of sail; ERR 1.01.116
had hoisted sail and put to sea to-day. 5.01. 21
the ship is under sail, and here she comes amain LLL 5.02.546
when the false troyan under sail was seen, | by MND 1.01.174
and sail upon the land | to fetch me trifles, 2.01.132
there where your argosies with portly sail MV 1.01. 9
desire no more delight | than to be under sail, 2.06. 68
why, man, i saw bassanio under sail, | with him 2.08. 1
he came too late, the ship was under sail, | but 2.08. 6
will you hoist sail, sir? here lies your way. TN 1.05.202 P
a whole armado of convicted sail | is scattered JN 3.04. 2
and, like a shifted wind unto a sail, | it makes 4.02. 23
all the shrouds wherewith my life should sail 5.07. 53
that must strike sail to spirits of vile sort! 2H4 5.02. 18
and show my sail of greatness | when i do rouse H5 1.02.274
as doth a sail, fill'd with a fretting gust, 3H6 2.06. 35
must strike her sail and learn a while to serve 3.03. 5
than bear so low a sail to strike to thee. 5.01. 52
sail how thou canst, have wind and tide thy 5.01. 53
hois'd sail, and made his course again for R3 4.04.527
how many shallow bauble boats dare sail | upon TRO 1.03. 35
light boats sail swift, though greater hulks 2.03.266
as weeds before | a vessel under sail, so men COR 2.02.106
here's goodly gear! a sail, a sail! ROM 2.04.102 P
here's goodly gear! a sail, a sail! 2.04.102 P
but in a sieve i'll thither sail, | and, like a MAC 1.03. 8
the wind sits in the shoulder of your sail, HAM 1.03. 56
finding ourselves too slow of sail, we put on a 4.06. 17 P
but yaw neither, in respect of his quick sail. 5.02.115 P
of thirty sail; OTH 1.03. 37
'twixt the heaven and the main, | descry a sail. 2.01. 4
stand ranks of people, and they cry, "a sail!" 2.01. 54
and swell his sail with thine own pow'rful 2.01. 78
a sail. 2.01. 93
my butt | and very sea-mark of my utmost sail. 5.02.268
o' th' haven, | and questionedst every sail. CYM 1.03. 2
shore, | a portly sail of ships make hitherward. PER 1.04. 61
diligence | that horse and sail and high expense 3.ch. 20
sail seas in cockles, have and wish but for't, 4.04. 2
of their ladies, | like tall ships under sail; TNK 2.02. 12
and sail | by east and north-east to the king of 3.04. 14
is) | the humble as the proudest sail doth bear, SON 80. 6
was it the proud full sail of his great verse, 86. 1
that i have hoisted sail to all the winds 117. 7

SAIL'D 3 FR 0.0003 REL FR 2 V 1 P
a league from epidamium had we sail'd | before ERR 1.01. 62
off, and you are now sail'd into the north of my TN 3.02. 26 P
could best express how slow his soul sail'd on, CYM 1.03. 13

SAILING 3 FR 0.0003 REL FR 2 V 1 P
turk, there's no more sailing by the star. ADO 3.04. 58 P
and this sailing pandar | our doubtful hope, our TRO 1.01.103
bark thy body is, | sailing in this salt flood; ROM 3.05.134

SAILMAKER 1 FR 0.0001 REL FR 0 V 1 P
o villain, he is a sailmaker in bergamo. SHR 5.01. 77 P

SAILOR 4 FR 0.0004 REL FR 2 V 2 P
with a tang, | would cry to a sailor, 'go hang!' TMP 2.02. 51
grand-jurymen since before noah was a sailor. TN 3.02. 17 P
looks | lives like a drunken sailor on a mast, R3 3.04. 99
with his fist, as a sailor breaks a biscuit. TRO 2.01. 40 P

SAILOR'S 2 FR 0.0002 REL FR 2 V 0 P
every day some sailor's wife, | the masters of TMP 2.01. 4
a sailor's wife had chestnuts in her lap, | and MAC 1.03. 4

SAILORS 11 FR 0.0012 REL FR 8 V 3 P
with child, | and here was left by th' sailors. TMP 1.02.270
of sack which the sailors heav'd o'erboard — by 2.02.121 P
the sailors sought for safety by our boat, | and ERR 1.01. 76
but ships are but boards, sailors but men; MV 1.03. 22 P
with some of the sailors that escap'd the wrack. 3.01.104 P
he is not drown'd — what think you, sailors? TN 1.02. 5
i'll drown more sailors than the mermaid shall, 3H6 3.02.186
and half our sailors swallow'd in the flood? 5.04. 5
sailors, my lord, they say, i saw them not. HAM 4.07. 39
to commix | with winds that sailors rail at. CYM 4.02. 56
to the sailors, galling | his kingly hands PER 4.01. 53

SAILS 20 FR 0.0022 REL FR 20 V 0 P
gentle breath of yours my sails | must fill, or TMP ep 11
clap on more sails, pursue; WIV 2.02.136
when we have laugh'd to see the sails conceive MND 2.01.128
with over-weather'd ribs and ragged sails, MV 2.06. 18
we see the wind sit sore upon our sails, | and R2 2.01.265
behold the threaden sails, | borne with th' H5 3.pr. 10
like a poor bark of sails and tackling reft, R3 4.04.234
your breath with full consent bellied his sails; TRO 2.02. 74
clouds, | and sails upon the bosom of the air. ROM 2.02. 32
my boat sails freely, both with wind and stream. OTH 2.03. 63
purple the sails, and so perfumed that | the ANT 2.02.193
thou canst not fear us, pompey, with thy sails; 2.06. 24
i have sixty sails, caesar none better. 3.07. 49
like a cow in /june — | hoists sails and flies. 3.10. 15
o my lord, my lord, | forgive my fearful sails! 3.11. 55
have built | in cleopatra's sails their nests. 4.12. 4
and winds of all the corners kiss'd your sails, CYM 2.04. 28
toward ephesus | turn our blown sails; PER 5.01.255
in feather'd briefness sails are fill'd, | and 5.02. 15
we | the sails that must these vessels port even TNK 5.01. 29

SAIN *(also said)*

SAIN 1 FR 0.0001 REL FR 1 V 0 P
obscure precedence that hath tofore been sain. LLL 3.01. 82

SAINT 117 FR 0.0132 REL FR 89 V 28 P
even she; and is she not a heavenly saint? TGV 2.04.145
there — and saint nicholas be thy speed! 3.01.300 P
at saint gregory's well. 4.02. 84
the sisterhood, the votarists of saint clare. MM 1.04. 5
be talk'd with in sincerity, | as with a saint. 1.04. 37
o cunning enemy, that, to catch a saint, | with 2.02.179
i will presently to saint luke's; 3.01.264 P
and good fortune, by the saint whom i profess, i 4.02.179 P
they would swear down each particular saint, 5.01.243
teach sin the carriage of a holy saint; ERR 3.02. 14
deliver i up my apes, and away to saint peter. ADO 2.01. 47 P
saint cupid, then! and, soldiers, to the field! LLL 4.03.363
saint denis to saint cupid! 5.02. 87
saint denis to saint cupid! 5.02. 87
saint george's half-cheek in a brooch. 5.02.616 P
saint valentine is past; MND 4.01.139
the condition of a saint and the complexion of a MV 1.02.130 P
kiss this shrine, this mortal breathing saint. 2.07. 40
go by, saint jeronimy! SHR in.1. 9 P
yes, by saint anne, do i. 1.01.250 P
now, by saint george, i am too young for you. 2.01.236
for such an injury would vex a very saint, 3.02. 28
nay, by saint jamy, | i hold you a penny, | a 3.02. 82
the old priest of saint luke's church is at your 4.04. 88 P
appointed me to go to saint luke's to bid the 4.04.103 P
"i am saint jaques' pilgrim, thither gone. AWW 3.04. 4
to saint jaques le grand. 3.05. 34

at the saint francis here beside the port. 3.05. 36
four or five, to great saint jaques bound, 3.05. 95
is a pilgrimage to saint jaques le grand; 4.03. 48 P
yes, by saint anne, and ginger shall be hot i' TN 2.03.117 P
tripping measure, or the bells of saint bennet, 5.01. 39 P
saint george, that swing'd the dragon, and e'er JN 2.01.288
for at saint mary's chapel presently | the rites 2.01.538
call'd, | canonized and worshipp'd as a saint, 3.01.177
lords, i will meet him at saint edmundsbury. 4.03. 11
with me, | upon the altar at saint edmundsbury, 5.04. 18
it, | at coventry upon saint lambert's day. R2 1.01.199
mine innocence and saint george to thrive! 1.03. 84
and art indeed able to corrupt a saint. 1H4 1.02. 91 P
if they meet not with saint nicholas' clerks, 2.01. 61 P
know thou worshippest saint nicholas as truly as 2.01. 64 P
for they pray continually to their saint, the 2.01. 80 P
stol'n from my host at saint albons, or the 4.02. 46 P
as the way between saint albons and london. 2H4 2.02.168 P
night in the windmill in saint george's field? 3.02.195 P
cry, "god for harry, england, and saint george!" H5 3.01. 34
his leek about his pate | upon saint davy's day. 4.01. 55
and say, "to-morrow is saint crispian." 4.03. 46
that fought with us upon saint crispin's day. 4.03. 67
no scorn to wear the leek upon saint tavy's day. 4.07.103 P
saint davy's day is past. 5.01. 2 P
saint denis be my speed! 5.02.183 P
and i, between saint denis and saint george, 5.02.207 P
between saint denis and saint george, compound a 5.02.207 P
to keep our great saint george's feast withal. 1H6 1.01.154
at touraine, in saint katherine's churchyard, 1.02.100
expect saint martin's summer, halcyons' days, 1.02.131
nor yet saint philip's daughters, were like thee 1.02.143
no longer on saint denis will we cry, | but joan 1.06. 28
but joan de pucelle shall be france's saint. 1.06. 29
saint denis bless this happy stratagem! 3.02. 18
and have thee reverenc'd like a blessed saint. 3.03. 15
god and saint george, talbot and england's right 4.02. 55
saint george and victory! 4.06. 1
knight of the noble order of saint george, 4.07. 68
worthy saint michael, and the golden fleece, 4.07. 69
you do prepare to ride unto saint albons, 2H6 1.02. 57
when from saint albons we do make return, 1.02. 83
king is now in progress towards saint albons, 1.04. 72
forsooth, a blind man at saint albon's shrine, 2.01. 61
by good saint albon, who said, "simon, come; 2.01. 89
clear as day, i thank god and saint albon. 2.01.106 P
my lords, saint albon here hath done a miracle; 2.01.129
my masters of saint albons, have you not 2.01.133
down saint magnus' corner! 4.08. 1 P
meet me to-morrow in saint george's field, | you 5.01. 46
the castle in saint albons, somerset | hath made 5.02. 68
saint albons battle won by famous york | shall 5.03. 30
march'd toward saint albons to intercept the 3H6 2.01.114
short tale to make, we at saint albons met, 2.01.120
god and saint george for us! 2.01.204
cry "saint george!" 2.02. 80
when you and i met at saint albons last, | your 2.02.103
at saint albons field | this lady's husband, sir 3.02. 1
warwick and his friends, god and saint george! 4.02. 29
saint george and victory! 5.01.113
now, by saint john, that news is bad indeed! R3 1.01.138
villains, set down the corse, or, by saint paul, 1.02. 36
or, by saint paul, i'll strike thee to my foot, 1.02. 41
sweet saint, for charity, be not so curst. 1.02. 49
in margaret's battle at saint albons slain? 1.03.129
and seem a saint, when most i play the devil. 1.03.337
now by saint paul i swear | i will not dine 3.04. 76
and that dear saint which then i weeping 4.01. 69
god and saint george! 5.03.270
this, and saint george to /boot! 5.03.301
our ancient word of courage, fair saint george, 5.03.349
within the parish | saint lawrence poultney, did H8 1.02.153
god and saint steven give you god-den. TIT 4.04. 42 P
o then, dear saint, let lips do what hands do, ROM 1.05.103
my name, dear saint, is hateful to myself, 2.02. 55
holy saint francis, what a change is here! 2.03. 65
a /damned saint, an honorable villain! 3.02. 79
the county paris, at saint peter's church, 3.05.114
now, by saint peter's church and peter too, | he 3.05.116
to go with paris to saint peter's church, | or i 3.05.154
saint francis be my speed! 5.03.121
till he disbursed at saint colme's inch | ten MAC 1.02. 61
yes, by saint patrick, but there is, horatio, HAM 1.05.136
"to-morrow is saint valentine's day, | all in 4.05. 48
"by gis, and by saint charity, | alack, and fie 4.05. 58
that have the office opposite to saint peter, OTH 4.02. 91
this earthly saint, adored by this devil, LUC 85
and would corrupt my saint to be a devil, PP 2. 7
with men, | to sin and never for to saint: 18.44
and would corrupt my saint to be a devil, SON 144. 7

SAINTED 4 FR 0.0004 REL FR 4 V 0 P
i hold you as a thing enskied, and sainted, | by MM 1.04. 34
with sainted vow my faults to have amended. AWW 3.04. 7
would make her sainted spirit | again possess WT 5.01. 57
thy royal father | was a most sainted king; MAC 4.03.109

SAINT-LIKE 4 FR 0.0004 REL FR 4 V 0 P
and have perform'd | a saint-like sorrow. WT 5.01. 2
thy meekness saint-like, wife-like government, H8 2.04.139
and saint-like | cast her fair eyes to heaven, 4.01. 83
blot with hell-born sin such saint-like forms. LUC 1519

SAINTS 14 FR 0.0015 REL FR 14 V 0 P
great men may jest with saints; MM 2.02.127
catch a saint, | with saints dost bait thy hook! 2.02.180
i conjure thee by all the saints in heaven! ERR 4.04. 57
she call'd the saints to surety | that she would AWW 5.03.108
my subjects for a pair of carved saints, | and R2 3.03.152
loves | are brazen images of canonized saints. 2H6 1.03. 60
gapes, hell burns, fiends roar, saints pray, R3 4.04. 75
the prayers of holy saints and wronged souls, 5.03.241
must die, | she must, the saints must have her; H8 5.04. 60
for saints have hands that pilgrims' hands do ROM 1.05. 99
have not saints lips, and holy palmers too? 1.05.101
saints do not move, though grant for prayers' 1.05.105
and thy saints for aye | be crown'd with plagues TIM 5.01. 52
saints in your injuries, devils being offended, OTH 2.01.111

SAINT-SEDUCING 1 FR 0.0001 REL FR 1 V 0 P
eyes, | nor ope her lap to saint-seducing gold. ROM 1.01.214

SAITH 12 FR 0.0013 REL FR 8 V 4 P
robert shallow, esquire, saith he is wrong'd. WIV 1.01.107 P
and, as a certain father saith — LLL 4.02.148 P
for society, saith the text, is the happiness of 4.02.161 P
death, as the psalmist saith, is certain to all, 2H4 3.02. 37 P
"thus saith the duke, thus hath the duke R3 3.07. 32
and as he saith, so say we all with him. TIT 5.01. 17
saith that the world hath ending with thy life. VEN 12
he saith she is immodest, blames her miss; 53
"fondling," she saith, "since i have hemm'd thee 229
"give me my hand," saith he, "why dost thou feel 373
"give me my heart," saith she, "and thou shalt 374
or whether shall i say mine eye saith true, SON 114. 3

SAKE 190 FR 0.0214 REL FR 156 V 34 P
and for your sake | am i this patient log-man. TMP 3.01. 66
and when it's writ, for my sake read it over, TGV 2.01.130
keep this remembrance for thy julia's sake. 2.02. 5
day | wherein i sigh not, julia, for thy sake, 2.02. 10
thus, for my duty's sake, i rather chose | to 3.01. 17
and, for your friend's sake, will be glad of you 3.02. 63
ay, silvia — for your sake. 4.02. 23
i give thee this | for thy sweet mistress' sake, 4.04.177
i'll use thee kindly for thy mistress' sake 4.04.202
for whose dear sake thou didst then rend thy 5.04. 47
but count the world a stranger for thy sake. 5.04. 70
i now beseech you (for your daughter's sake) 5.04.149
would i were young for your sake, mistress anne! WIV 1.01.260 P
/god pless you from his mercy sake, all of you! 3.01. 42 P
am sorry that for my sake you have suffer'd all 3.05.124 P
lamentation, which she yet wears for his sake; MM 3.01.229 P
in our trade, and are now "for the lord's sake." 4.03. 19 P
honor, you must pardon | for mariana's sake; 5.01.403
your brother, for his sake | is he pardon'd, and 5.01.490
is he pardon'd, and, for your lovely sake, 5.01.491
and, for the sake of them thou sorrowest for, ERR 1.01.121
for god sake hold your hands! 1.02. 93
for god's sake send some other messenger. 2.01. 77
hold, sir, for god's sake! 2.02. 24
can you tell for whose sake? 3.01. 57
then for her wealth's sake use her with more 3.02. 6
hold, hurt him not for god sake! 5.01. 33
for god's sake take a house! 5.01. 36
so would not i for your own sake, for i have ADO 2.01.101 P
o that i were a man for his sake! 4.01.317 P
i had any friend would be a man for my sake! 4.01.318 P
and will lend nothing for god's sake. 5.01.312 P
if you spite it for my sake, i will spite it for 5.02. 69 P
you give him for my sake but one loving kiss. LLL 2.01.249
when, for fame's sake, for praise, an outward 4.01. 32
that self-sovereignty | only for praise' sake, 4.01. 37
did never sonnet for her sake compile, | nor 4.03.132
for wisdom's sake, a word that all men love, 4.03.354
or for love's sake, a word that loves all men, 4.03.355
or for men's sake, the /authors of these women, 4.03.356
or women's sake, by whom we men are men, | /let 4.03.357
die, | and for her sake do i rear up her boy; MND 2.01.136
and for her sake i will not part with him. 2.01.137
love and languish for his sake. 2.02. 29
for my sake, my dear, | lie further off yet; 2.02. 43
and run through fire i will for thy sweet sake. 2.02.103
tell true, even for my sake! 3.02. 68
make | to have it of my trust, or for my sake. MV 1.01.185
it will be for his gentle daughter's sake, | and 2.04. 34
/slubber not business for my sake, bassanio, 2.08. 39
a halter gratis — nothing else, for god sake. 4.01.379
me your gloves, i'll wear them for your sake, 4.01.426
pray you for your own sake to embrace your own AYL 1.02.178 P
and pity her for her good father's sake; 1.02.281
no, faith, hate him not, for my sake. 1.03. 35 P
ay, celia, we stay'd her for your sake, | else 1.03. 67
with weeping tears, "wear these for my sake." 2.04. 54 P
and wish, for her sake more than for mine own, 2.04. 76
for my sake be comfortable, hold death a while 2.06. 9 P
but yet, for fashion sake, i thank you too for 3.02.255 P
for god's sake, a pot of small ale. SHR in.2. 1 P
but, sirrah, not for my sake, but your master's, 1.01.241
y' are welcome, sir, and he, for your good sake. 2.01. 61
i know him well; you are welcome for his sake. 2.01. 70
litio, | all for my master's sake, lucentio. 3.02.148
this favor will i do you for his sake; 4.02.104
sweet kate, embrace her for her beauty's sake. 4.05. 34
then pardon him, sweet father, for my sake. 5.01.130
would for the king's sake he were living! AWW 1.01. 22 P
i love him for his sake, | and yet i know him a 1.01. 99
and i hope to have friends for my wive's sake. 1.03. 40 P
i'll never do you wrong for your own sake. 2.03. 90
i would it were hell-pains for thy sake, and my 2.03.232 P
and for the contents' sake are sorry for our 3.02. 63
we'll strive to bear it for your worthy sake 3.03. 5
which for traffic's sake | most of our city did. TN 3.03. 34
sir, he will fight with you for 's oath sake. 3.04.297 P
the gentleman will, for his honor's sake, have 3.04.306 P
for his sake | did i expose myself (pure for his 5.01. 82
even for your son's sake, and thereby for WT 1.02.337
and for that england's sake | with burden of our JN 2.01. 91
for heaven sake, hubert, let me not be bound! 4.01. 77
uncle, for god's sake speak comfortable words. R2 2.02. 76
for god's sake fairly let her be entreated. 3.01. 37
for god's sake let us sit upon the ground | and 3.02.155
what ho, my liege! for god's sake let me in. 5.03. 74
that the true prince may (for recreation sake) 1H4 1.02.155 P
and for his sake wear the detested blot | of 1.03.162
the which for sport sake are content to do the 2.01. 70 P
into) for their own credit sake make all whole. 2.01. 72 P
for god's sake, lords, convey my /tristful queen 2.04.393
for god's sake, cousin, stay till all come in. 4.03. 29
nimble wing | we were enforc'd, for safety sake, 5.01. 65
for god's sake come. 5.04. 16
o yet, for god's sake, go not to these wars! 2H4 2.03. 9
for god's sake be quiet. 2.04.178 P
for god's sake thrust him down stairs. 2.04.188 P
yea, for my sake, even to the eyes of richard 3.01. 64
master corporal captain, for my old dame's sake, 3.02.230 P
me to verses, or to dance for your sake, kate, H5 5.02.133 P
and, for their sake, | in your fair minds let ep 13
therefore, good uncle, for my father's sake, 1H6 2.05. 51
and for alliance sake, declare the cause | my 2.05. 53
that will not trust thee but for profit's sake? 3.03. 63
for god's sake let him have /'em; 4.07. 89
and for thy sake have i shed many a tear. 5.04. 19
had been a little ratsbane for thy sake! 5.04. 29
for god's sake pity my case. 2H6 1.03.213 P
me, that, for his father's sake, henry the fift 4.02.157 P
thou hast one son, for his sake pity me, | lest 3H6 1.03. 40
that is my office, for my father's sake. 1.04.109
for god's sake, lords, give signal to the fight. 2.02.100
i wear the willow garland for his sake. 3.03.228
i'll wear the willow garland for his sake." 4.01.100
for god's sake, take away this captive scold. 5.05. 29
foul devil, for god's sake hence, and trouble us R3 1.02. 50
would it were mortal poison for thy sake! 1.02.145
therefore for god's sake entertain good comfort, 1.03. 4
for edward's sake, and see how he requites me! 1.04. 68
for whose sake did i that ill deed? 1.04.211
for edward, for my brother, for his sake. 1.04.212
for god sake let not us two stay at home; 2.02.147
he for his father's sake so loves the prince 3.01.165
her uncle rivers, ay (and for her sake!), 4.04.282
arm, fight, and conquer for fair england's sake! 5.03.158
therefore, for goodness sake, and as you are H8 pr 23
you speak truth, for their poor mistress' sake; 3.01. 47
for her sake that i have been — for i feel 3.01. 77
take heed, for heaven's sake take heed, lest at 3.01.110
for goodness sake, consider what you do, | how 3.01.159
justice | for truth's sake and his conscience, 3.02.397
to love her for her mother's sake that lov'd him 4.02.137
but for your health and your disgestion sake, TRO 2.03.111
small as nothing, for request's sake only, | he 2.03.169
why then, for venus' sake, give me a kiss | when 4.05. 49
for my wounds' sake to give their suffrage. COR 2.02.138
for conscience' sake to help to get thee a wife. 2.03. 33 P
thee, | take this along, i writ it for thy sake, 5.02. 90
marcus, for thy sake and thy brother's here, TIT 1.01.482
for my father's sake, | that gave thee life when 2.03.158
offended me, | even for his sake am i pitiless. 2.03.162
and for our father's sake, and mother's care, 3.01.181
will hold thee dearly for thy mother's sake." 5.01. 36
do not move, though grant for prayers' sake. ROM 1.05.105
for juliet's sake, for her sake, rise and stand; 3.03. 89
for juliet's sake, for her sake, rise and stand; 3.03. 89
for whose dear sake thou wast but lately dead: 3.03.136
h'ad sent to me first, but for my mind's sake; TIM 3.03. 23
meet, for timon's sake | let's yet be fellows. 4.02. 24
against your city, | in part for his sake mov'd. 5.02. 13
and, for my sake, stay here with antony. JC 3.02. 56
for brutus' sake, i am beholding to you. 3.02. 65
for brutus' sake | he finds himself beholding to 3.02. 66
did not great julius bleed for justice' sake? 4.03. 19
who committed treason enough for god's sake, yet MAC 2.03. 10 P
if for my sake | thou wilt o'ertake us hence a LR 4.01. 41
the one the other poison'd for my sake, | and 5.03.241
for your sake, jewel, | i am glad at soul i have OTH 1.03.195
would they were clyster-pipes for your sake! 2.01.177 P
that he desires you, for love's sake, to make no 3.01. 13 P
here, here! for heaven sake, help me! 5.01. 50
if for the sake of merit thou wilt hear me, ANT 2.07. 55
for my sake wear this: CYM 1.01.121
though light, take pieces for the figure's sake; 5.04. 25
and for his sake i wish the having of it; PER 2.01.139
for the sake of it | be manly, and take comfort. 3.01. 21
for pity's sake and true gentility's, | hear and TNK 1.01. 25
for your mother's sake, | and as you wish your 1.01. 26
your bed, and for the sake | of clear virginity, 1.01. 30
what man to man may do for our sake more: 1.04. 39
for honor's sake, and safely presently | into 3.06.110
for heaven's sake save their lives, and banish 3.06.251
must open | and bleed to death for my sake else. 4.02. 2
so neither for my sake should fall untimely. 4.02. 69
and for my sake hath learn'd to sport and dance, VEN 105
"then for thy husband and thy children's sake, LUC 533
husband is thy friend, for his sake spare me; 582
thyself art mighty, for thine own sake leave me; 583
and for my sake serve thou false tarquin so. 1197
"and for my sake when i might charm thee so, 1681
for adon's sake, a youngster proud and wild, PP 9. 4
and for my sake even so doth she abuse me, SON 42. 7
suff'ring my friend for my sake to approve her. 42. 8
and both for my sake lay on me this cross. 42.12
to play the watchman ever for thy sake. 61.12
o, for my sake do you /with fortune chide, | the 111. 1
use, | and sue a friend came debtor for my sake, 134.11
"i hate" | to me that languish'd for her sake; 145. 3
forgot | am of myself, all tyrant for thy sake? 149. 4
make | what i should do again for such a sake. LC 322

SAKES 3 FR 0.0003 REL FR 2 V 1 P
i have suffer'd more for their sakes — more WIV 4.05.108 P
for your fair sakes have we neglected time, LLL 5.02.755
for both our sakes, i would that word were true. SHR 5.02. 15

SALA 3 FR 0.0003 REL FR 3 V 0 P
between the floods of sala and of /elbe; H5 1.02. 45
which salique, as i said, 'twixt /elbe and sala, 1.02. 52
and did seat the french | beyond the river sala, 1.02. 63

SALAD *(also sallet*, etc.)*

SALAD 1 FR 0.0001 REL FR 1 V 0 P
my salad days, | when i was green in judgment, ANT 1.05. 73

SALAMANDER 1 FR 0.0001 REL FR 0 V 1 P
maintain'd that salamander of yours with fire 1H4 3.03. 47 P

/SALARY 1 FR 0.0001 REL FR 1 V 0 P
why, this is /hire /and /salary, not revenge. HAM 3.03. 79

SALE 10 FR 0.0011 REL FR 8 V 2 P
not utt'red by base sale of chapmen's tongues. LLL 2.01. 16
to things of sale a seller's praise belongs: 4.03.236
and bounds of feed | are now on sale, and at our AYL 2.04. 84
who in that sale sells pardon from himself; JN 3.01.167
thy sale of offices and towns in france, | if 2H6 1.03.135
now, | whose sale is present death in mantua, ROM 5.01. 51
"i saw him enter such a house of sale," HAM 2.01. 58
the other is not a thing for sale, and only the CYM 1.04. 85 P
dwell in proclaims you to be a creature of sale. PER 4.06. 78 P
her well, | and set her person forth to sale. PP 18.12

SALERIO 5 FR 0.0005 REL FR 5 V 0 P
what, and my old venetian friend salerio? MV 3.02.219
lorenzo and salerio, welcome hither, | if that 3.02.220
you here, | but meeting with salerio by the way, 3.02.228
your hand, salerio. 3.02.238
but is it true, salerio? 3.02.266

SALE WORK 1 FR 0.0001 REL FR 1 V 0 P
than in the ordinary | of nature's sale-work. AYL 3.05. 43
SALICAM 1 FR 0.0001 REL FR 1 V 0 P
"in terram salicam mulieres ne /succedant," H5 1.02. 38
SALIQUE 9 FR 0.0010 REL FR 9 V 0 P
and religiously unfold | why the law salique, H5 1.02. 11
"no woman shall succeed in salique land"; 1.02. 39
which salique land the french unjustly gloze 1.02. 40
affirm | that the land salique is in germany, 1.02. 44
female | should be inheritrix in salique land; 1.02. 51
which salique, as i said, 'twixt /elbe and sala, 1.02. 52
then doth it well appear the salique law | was 1.02. 54
nor did the french possess the salique land 1.02. 56
they would hold up this salique law | to bar 1.02. 91
SALISBURY 47 FR 0.0053 REL FR 47 V 0 P
stay yet, lord salisbury, i'll go with thee, JN 4.02. 96
besides, i met lord bigot and lord salisbury, 4.02.162
stand back, lord salisbury, stand back, i say; 4.03. 81
thou wert better gall the devil, salisbury. 4.03. 95
defense | cries out upon the name of salisbury! 5.02. 19
lift up thy brow, renowned salisbury, | and with 5.02. 54
my lord of salisbury, we have stay'd ten days, R2 2.04. 1
and salisbury | is gone to meet the king, who 3.03. 2
with him are the lord aumerle, lord salisbury, 3.03. 27
i have to london sent | the heads of salisbury, 5.06. 8
farewell, good salisbury, and good luck go with H5 4.03. 11
warwick and talbot, salisbury and gloucester, 4.03. 54
the earl of salisbury craveth supply, | and 1H6 1.01.159
remaineth none but mad-brain'd salisbury, | and 1.02. 15
salisbury is a desperate homicide, | he fighteth 1.02. 25
speak, salisbury; 1.04. 73
in thirteen battles salisbury o'ercame; 1.04. 78
yet liv'st thou, salisbury? 1.04. 82
alive, | if salisbury wants mercy at thy hands! 1.04. 86
salisbury, cheer thy spirit with this comfort, 1.04. 90
hear, hear how dying salisbury doth groan! 1.04.104
frenchmen, i'll be a salisbury to you. 1.04.106
convey me salisbury into his tent, | and then 1.04.110
help salisbury to make his testament. 1.05. 17
o, would i were to die with salisbury! 1.05. 38
now, salisbury, for thee, and for the right | of 2.01. 35
bring forth the body of old salisbury, | and 2.02. 4
buckingham, somerset, | salisbury, and warwick; 2H6 1.01. 70
brave york, salisbury, and victorious warwick, 1.01. 86
salisbury and warwick are no simple peers. 1.03. 74
invite my lords of salisbury and warwick | to 1.04. 79
now, my good lords of salisbury and warwick, 2.02. 1
then, father salisbury, kneel we together, | and 2.02. 59
stay, salisbury, | with the rude multitude till 3.02.134
an answer from the king, my lord of salisbury! 3.02.270
but all the honor salisbury hath won | is, that 3.02.275
go, salisbury, and tell them all from me, | i 3.02.279
bid salisbury and warwick come to me. 5.01.147
old salisbury, shame to thy silver hair, | thou 5.01.162
of salisbury, who can report of him, | that 5.03. 1
have we won one foot, | if salisbury be lost. 5.03. 7
post to salisbury; R3 4.04.444
can make, | and meet me suddenly at salisbury. 4.04.451
may it please you, shall i do at salisbury? 4.04.453
away towards salisbury! 4.04.535
take order buckingham be brought | to salisbury, 4.04.538
th' usurper richard, who, being at salisbury, H8 1.02.196
SALISBURY'S 1 FR 0.0001 REL FR 1 V 0 P
you all consented unto salisbury's death, | for 1H6 1.05. 34
SALL *(also s'*, shall)*
SALL 6 FR 0.0006 REL FR 0 V 6 P
it sall be vary gud, gud feith, gud captens bath H5 3.02.102 P
captens bath, and i sall quit you with gud leve, 3.02.103 P
that sall i, marry. 3.02.104 P
as valorously as i may, that sall i suerly do, 3.02.117 P
the maps of the orld, i warrant you sall find, 4.07. 24 P
den it sall also content me. 5.02.250 P
SALLET* *(also salad)*
SALLET* 5 FR 0.0005 REL FR 0 V 5 P
she was the sweet marjorom of the sallet, or AWW 4.05. 17 P
i can eat grass, or pick a sallet another while, 2H6 4.10. 8 P
and i think this word "sallet" was born to do me 4.10. 10 P
for many a time, but for a sallet, my brain-pan 4.10. 11 P
and now the word "sallet" must serve me to feed 4.10. 15 P
SALLETS 3 FR 0.0003 REL FR 0 V 3 P
may pick a thousand sallets ere we light on such AWW 4.05. 14 P
said there were no sallets in the lines to make HAM 2.02.441 P
the foul fiend rages, eats cow-dung for sallets; LR 3.04.132 P
SALLIED *(also sullied, etc.)*
SALLIED 1 FR 0.0001 REL FR 1 V 0 P
o, that this too too sallied flesh would melt, HAM 1.02.129
SALLIES* 2 FR 0.0002 REL FR 2 V 0 P
and thou hast talk'd | of sallies and retires, 1H4 2.03. 51
you laying these slight sallies on my son, | as HAM 2.01. 39
SALLOW 1 FR 0.0001 REL FR 1 V 0 P
hath wash'd thy sallow cheeks for rosaline! ROM 2.03. 70
SALLY 3 FR 0.0003 REL FR 2 V 1 P
when you sally upon him, speak what terrible AWW 4.01. 2 P
force | might with a sally of the very town | be 1H6 4.04. 4
no notes of sally, for the heavens, sweet TRO 5.03. 14
SALMON 1 FR 0.0001 REL FR 0 V 1 P
before one salmon, you shall take a number of TNK 2.01. 4 P
SALMON'S 1 FR 0.0001 REL FR 1 V 0 P
to change the cod's head for the salmon's tail; OTH 2.01.155
SALMONS 1 FR 0.0001 REL FR 0 V 1 P
is to my fingers, and there is salmons in both. H5 4.07. 31 P
SALOMON 2 FR 0.0002 REL FR 1 V 1 P
yet was salomon so seduced, and he had a very LLL 1.02.174 P
a gig, | and profound salomon to tune a jig, 4.03.166
/SALT* 1 FR 0.0001 REL FR 1 V 0 P
/and /yet /salt /water /blinds /them /not /so R2 4.01.245
SALT* 44 FR 0.0049 REL FR 32 V 12 P
when i have deck'd the sea with drops full salt, TMP 1.02.155
it much to tread the ooze | of the salt deep, 1.02.253
rather new dy'd than stain'd with salt water. 2.01. 65 P
the cover of the salt hides the salt, and TGV 3.01.360 P
the cover of the salt hides the salt, and 3.01.360 P
salt, and therefore it is more than the salt; 3.01.361 P
is the fresh fish, the salt fish is an old coat. WIV 1.01. 22 P
page, we have some salt of our youth in us, we 2.03. 48 P
whose salt imagination yet hath wrong'd | your MM 5.01.401
by the salt rheum that ran between france and it ERR 3.02.128 P
and salt too little which may season give | to ADO 4.01.142
now, by the salt /wave of the mediterraneum, a LLL 5.01. 58 P
not with salt tears; MND 2.02. 92
turns into yellow gold his salt green streams. 3.02.393
/loneliness, and find | your salt tears' head. AWW 1.03.172
sir, with salt water, though i seem to drown her TN 2.01. 30 P
tempests are kind and salt waves fresh in love. 3.04.384
the salt in them is hot. JN 5.07. 45
as many fresh streams meet in one salt sea; H5 1.02.209
and prings me pread and salt yesterday, look you 5.01. 9 P
our isle be made a nourish of salt tears, | and 1H6 1.01. 50
me drown'd on shore | with tears as salt as sea, 2H6 3.02. 96
to drain | upon his face an ocean of salt tears, 3.02.143
eyes of thine from mine have drawn salt tears, R3 1.02.153
such-like, the spice and salt that season a man? TRO 1.02.255 P
than in the pride and salt scorn of his eyes, 1.03.370
kiss, | distasted with the salt of broken tears. 4.04. 48
for certain drops of salt, your city rome, | i COR 5.06. 92
how much salt water thrown away in waste, | to ROM 2.03. 71
bark thy body is, | sailing in this salt flood; 3.05.134
make use of thy salt hours, season the slaves TIM 4.03. 86
surge resolves | the moon into salt tears; 4.03.440
upon the beached verge of the salt flood, | who 5.01.216
ere yet the salt of most unrighteous tears | had HAM 1.02.154
neptune's salt wash and tellus' orbed ground, 3.02.156
tears seven times salt | burn out the sense and 4.05.155
why, this would make a man a man of salt, | to LR 4.06.195
better compass of his salt and most hidden loose OTH 2.01.240 P
as salt as wolves in pride, and fools as gross 3.03.404
i have a salt and sorry rheum offends me; 3.04. 51
her salt tears fell from her, and soft'ned the 4.03. 46
of love, | salt cleopatra, soften thy wan'd lip! ANT 2.01. 21
my sighs are blown away, my salt tears gone, VEN 1071
that pay a daily debt | to their salt sovereign, LUC 650
SALT-BUTTER 1 FR 0.0001 REL FR 0 V 1 P
hang him, mechanical salt-butter rogue! WIV 2.02.278 P
SALTER 1 FR 0.0001 REL FR 1 V 0 P
thy tears are salter than a younger man's, | and COR 4.01. 22
SALT-FISH 1 FR 0.0001 REL FR 1 V 0 P
your diver | did hang a salt-fish on his hook, ANT 2.05. 17
SALTIERS 1 FR 0.0001 REL FR 0 V 1 P
they call themselves saltiers, and they have a WT 4.04.327 P
SALTNESS 1 FR 0.0001 REL FR 0 V 1 P
some relish of the saltness of time in you, and 2H4 1.02. 98 P
SALTPETRE 1 FR 0.0001 REL FR 1 V 0 P
this villainous saltpetre should be digg'd | out 1H4 1.03. 60
SALT-SEA 1 FR 0.0001 REL FR 1 V 0 P
maw and gulf | of the ravin'd salt-sea shark, MAC 4.01. 24
SALT-WATER 2 FR 0.0002 REL FR 1 V 1 P
notable pirate, thou salt-water thief! TN 5.01. 69
you shall find us in our salt-water girdle. CYM 3.01. 80 P
SALT-WAV'D 1 FR 0.0001 REL FR 1 V 0 P
who in a salt-wav'd ocean quench their light, LUC 1231
SALUTATION 7 FR 0.0008 REL FR 4 V 3 P
most military sir, salutation. LLL 5.01. 35 P
salutation and greeting to you all! AYL 5.04. 39 P
cock | hath twice done salutation to the morn, R3 5.03.210
there's a french salutation to your french slop. ROM 2.04. 44 P
is come | to do you salutation from his master. JC 4.02. 5
that speak my salutation in their minds; MAC 5.09. 23
eyes | give salutation to my sportive blood? SON 121. 6
SALUTATIONS 2 FR 0.0002 REL FR 2 V 0 P
loud shouts and salutations from their mouths, 1H4 3.02. 53
forth | from goneril his mistress salutations; LR 2.04. 32
SALUTE 17 FR 0.0019 REL FR 16 V 1 P
esteem | are journeying to salute the emperor, TGV 1.03. 41
there's not a man i meet but doth salute me | as ERR 4.03. 1
you told me you salute not at the court but you AYL 3.02. 48 P
corner of the west | salute thee for her king; JN 2.01. 30
when his fair angels would salute my palm, | but 2.01.590
dear earth, i do salute thee with my hand, R2 3.02. 6
we do salute you, duke of burgundy, | and, H5 5.02. 7
you english princes all, i do salute you. 5.02. 22
makes me the bolder to salute my king | with 2H6 1.01. 29
first | that shall salute our rightful sovereign 2.02. 61
then i salute you with this royal title — R3 3.07.239
and i'll salute your grace of york as mother 4.01. 29
was then present, saw them salute on horseback, H8 1.01. 8
i had no being | if this salute my blood a jot; 2.03.103
my lord, i scarce have leisure to salute you, TRO 4.02. 59
our general doth salute you with a kiss. 4.05. 19
but if the prince do live, let us salute him, PER 2.04. 27
SALUTED 1 FR 0.0001 REL FR 0 V 1 P
these weird sisters saluted me, and referr'd me MAC 1.05. 8 P
SALUTES 6 FR 0.0006 REL FR 6 V 0 P
general welcome from his grace | salutes ye all; H8 1.04. 2
salutes each other with each other's form; TRO 3.03.108
as when the golden sun salutes the morn, | and, TIT 2.01. 5
lord of his fortunes he salutes thee, and ANT 3.12. 11
he bows his noble body, then salutes me thus: TNK 2.04. 23
venus salutes him with this fair good morrow: VEN 859
SALUTETH 2 FR 0.0002 REL FR 1 V 1 P
a soul feminine saluteth us. LLL 4.02. 81 P
what early tongue so sweet saluteth me? ROM 2.03. 32
SALVAGES *(also savages)*
SALVAGES 1 FR 0.0001 REL FR 0 V 1 P
tricks upon 's with salvages and men of inde? TMP 2.02. 58 P
SALVATION 6 FR 0.0006 REL FR 2 V 4 P
it were pity but they should suffer salvation, ADO 3.03. 3 P
of justice, none of us | should see salvation. MV 4.01.200
he will sell the fee-simple of his salvation, AWW 4.03.279 P
they take it already upon their salvation, that 1H4 2.04. 9 P
act | that has no relish of salvation in't — HAM 3.03. 92
when she willfully seeks her own salvation? 5.01. 2 P
SALV'D 1 FR 0.0001 REL FR 1 V 0 P
i would have salv'd it with a longer treatise. ADO 1.01.315
SALVE* 13 FR 0.0014 REL FR 9 V 4 P
riddle, no l'envoy, no salve in the mail, sir. LLL 3.01. 72 P
no l'envoy, no l'envoy, no salve, sir, but a 3.01. 74 P
doth the inconsiderate take salve for l'envoy, 3.01. 78 P
for l'envoy, and the word "l'envoy" for a salve? 3.01. 79 P
is not l'envoy a salve? 3.01. 80
some salve for perjury. 4.03.285
i do beseech your majesty may salve | the 1H4 3.02.155
provide | a salve for any sore that may betide. 3H6 4.06. 88
you may salve so, | not what is dangerous COR 3.02. 70
earth's sovereign salve, to do a goddess good. VEN 28
to see the salve doth make the wound ache more, LUC 1116
for no man well of such a salve can speak | that SON 34. 7
the humble salve which wounded bosoms fits! 120.12
SALVING 1 FR 0.0001 REL FR 1 V 0 P
compare, | myself corrupting, salving thy amiss, SON 35. 7
/SAME 1 FR 0.0001 REL FR 1 V 0 P
/for /that /same /word, /rebellion, /did /divide 2H4 1.01.194
SAME 219 FR 0.0247 REL FR 164 V 55 P
yond same black cloud, yond huge one, looks like TMP 2.02. 20 P
yond same cloud cannot choose but fall by 2.02. 23 P
what is this same? 3.02.125 P
in the same fashion as you gave in charge, 5.01. 8
nay, would i were so ang'red with the same. TGV 1.02.101
what letter is this same? 3.01.137
why, this is the very same: WIV 2.01. 82 P
together to be revenge on this same scall, 3.01.120 P
i would all of the same strain were in the same 3.03.186 P
of the same strain were in the same distress. 3.03.186 P
says that the very same man that beguil'd master 4.05. 36 P
that same knave ford, her husband, hath the 5.01. 17 P
admonition, and still forfeit in the same kind! MM 3.02.194 P
call that same isabel here once again, i would 5.01.269 P
clock | i shall receive the money for the same: ERR 4.01. 11
and for the same he promis'd me a chain: 4.03. 84
o, if thou be'st the same egeon, speak, | and 5.01.345
egeon, speak, | and speak unto the same aemilia! 5.01.346
yea, the same. ADO 2.01.184 P
let there be the same net spread for her, and 2.03.213 P
and got a calf in that same noble feat | much 5.04. 50
this same is she, and i do give you her. 5.04. 54
give me the paper, let me read the same, | and LLL 1.01.116
i will praise an eel with the same praise. 1.02. 26 P
for still her cheeks possess the same | which 1.02.105
sir, i pray you a word. what lady is that same? 2.01.194
this same shall go. 4.03. 57
that same berowne i'll torture ere i go. 5.02. 60
in that same place thou hast appointed me MND 1.01.177
and this same progeny of evils comes | from our 2.01.115
through, saying thus, or to the same defect: 3.01. 39 P
that same cowardly, giant-like ox-beef hath 3.01.192 P
stand close; this is the same athenian. 3.02. 41
and that same dew, which sometime on the buds 4.01. 53
their unbreathed memories | with this same play, 5.01. 75
in this same enterlude it doth befall | that i, 5.01.155
this stone doth show | that i am that same wall; 5.01.162
i must be one of these same dumb wise men, | for MV 1.01.106
tell me now what lady is the same | to whom you 1.01.119
miseries were in the same abundance as your good 1.02. 4 P
fed with the same food, hurt with the same 3.01. 61 P
with the same food, hurt with the same weapons, 3.01. 61 P
the same weapons, subject to the same diseases, 3.01. 62 P
to the same diseases, heal'd by the same means, 3.01. 62 P
warm'd and cool'd by the same winter and summer, 3.01. 63 P
servants, and this same myself | are yours — my 3.02.170
are some shrowd contents in yond same paper 3.02.243
of any thing | that this same paper brings you. 3.02.250
take this same letter, | and use thou all th' 3.04. 47
and that same prayer doth teach us all to render 4.01.201
and many an error by the same example | will 4.01.221
a pound of that same merchant's flesh is thine, 4.01.299
by heaven, it is the same i gave the doctor! 5.01.257
for that same scrubbed boy, the doctor's clerk, 5.01.261
but the same tradition takes not away my blood, AYL 1.01. 47 P
that same wicked bastard of venus that was begot 4.01.211 P
o, i have heard him speak of that same brother, 4.03.121
that's it i would have said, the very same. AWW 2.03. 25 P
yond's that same knave | that leads him to these 3.05. 82
by this same coxcomb that we have i' th' wind, 3.06.114
e'en a crow a' th' same nest; 4.03.286 P
sir, much like | the same upon your finger. 5.03.226
run after that same peevish messenger, | the TN 1.05.300
get thee to yond same sovereign cruelty. 2.04. 80
if i think so, i think the same of you. 3.01.140
with the same havior that your passion bears 3.04.206
ay, my lord, this same. | now, malvolio? 5.01.327
let me pass | the same i am, ere ancient'st WT 4.01. 10
wrack'd the same instant of their master's death 5.02. 69 P
and put the same into young arthur's hand, | thy JN 1.01. 14
the son and heir to that same faulconbridge. 1.01. 56
when this same lusty gentleman was got. 1.01.108
colbrand the giant, that same mighty man? 1.01.225
what cracker is this same that deafs our ears 2.01.147
our colors do return in those same hands | that 2.01.319
in the ear | with that same purpose-changer, 2.01.567
and this same bias, this commodity, | this bawd, 2.01.581
if this same were a churchyard where we stand, 3.03. 40
with this same very iron to burn them out. 4.01.124
with that same weak wind which enkindled it. 5.02. 87
and these same thoughts people this little world R2 5.05. 9
lies that this same fat rogue will tell us when 1H4 1.02.187 P
and that same greatness too which our own hands 1.03. 12
those same noble scots | that are your prisoners 1.03.212
and that same sword-and-buckler prince of wales, 1.03.230
creep | of that same noble prelate well belov'd, 1.03.267
that same mad fellow of the north, percy, and he 2.04.335 P
owen, owen, the same; 2.04.341 P
at the same season if your mother's cat had 3.01. 18
than one of these same metre ballet-mongers. 3.01.128
that this same child of honor and renown, | this 3.02.139
did give him that same royalty he wears, | and 4.03. 55
is fall'n into this same whoreson apoplexy. 2H4 1.02.108 P
foretelling this same time's condition | and the 3.01. 78
and that same word even now cries out on us. 3.01. 94
the same sir john, the very same. 3.02. 29 P
the same sir john, the very same. 3.02. 29 P
and the very same day did i fight with one 3.02. 31 P
and this same half-fac'd fellow, shadow, give me 3.02.264 P
this same starv'd justice hath done nothing but 3.02.304 P
i promis'd you redress of these same grievances 4.02.113
this same young sober-blooded boy doth not love 4.03. 87 P
that you use the same | with the like bold, just 5.02.115
grey of northumberland, this same is yours: H5 2.02. 68
if that same demon that hath gull'd thee thus 2.02.121
out of doubt, be of the same relish as ours are; 4.01.109 P
discuss the same in french unto him. 4.04. 29 P
but hark, what new alarum is this same? 4.06. 35
in your behalf still will i wear the same. 1H6 2.04.130
teach, | but prove a chief offender in the same? 3.01.130
face, | until thy head be circled with the same. 2H6 1.02. 10

whip him till he leap over that same stool. 2.01.145 P
as willingly do i the same resign | as ere thy 2.03. 33
attracts the same for aidance 'gainst the enemy, 3.02.165
relent, | that were unworthy to behold the same? 4.04. 18
up, | and with the same to act controlling laws. 5.01.103
and on the gates of york | they set the same, 3H6 2.01. 66
we'll quickly rouse the traitors in the same. 5.01. 65
and that same vengeance doth he hurl on thee R3 1.04.201
hold | in him that did object the same to thee: 2.04. 17
news, | that this same very day your enemies, 3.02. 49
i swear | i will not dine until i see the same. 3.04. 77
that you might well have signified the same 3.05. 59
the same; H8 2.01. 23
this same cranmer's | a worthy fellow, and hath 3.02. 71
'tis the same: high steward. 4.01. 41
and with the same full state pac'd back again 4.01. 93
madam, the same; your servant. 4.02.111
their practices | must bear the same proportion, 5.01.129
by the same token, you are a bawd. TRO 1.02.281 P
success in a bad cause, | can qualify the same? 2.02.118
to their benumbed wills, resist the same, 2.02.179
what troyan is that same that looks so heavy? 4.05. 95
that same diomed's a false–hearted rogue, a most 5.01. 88 P
has got that same scurvy doting foolish /young 5.04. 3 P
see them meet, that that same young troyan ass, 5.04. 5 P
cheese, nestor, and that same dog–fox, ulysses, 5.04. 11 P
may these same instruments, which you profane, COR 1.09. 41
of the same house publius and quintus were, 2.03.241
in your wars to seem | the same you are not, 3.02. 47
the same, sir. 4.03. 7 P
peace | even with the same austerity and garb 4.07. 44
to infringe my vow | in the same time 'tis made? 5.03. 21
these eyes are not the same i wore in rome. 5.03. 38
if you do hold the same intent wherein | you 5.06. 12
which overshades the mouth of that same pit TIT 2.03.273
he for the same | will send thee hither both thy 3.01.154
i know from whence this same device proceeds. 4.04. 52
therefore thou shalt vow | by that same god, 5.01. 82
at this same ancient feast of capulet's | sups ROM 1.02. 82
why, that same pale hard–hearted wench, that 2.04. 4
that same villain romeo. 3.05. 80
where that same banish'd runagate doth live, 3.05. 89
or to dispraise my lord with that same tongue 3.05.237
thou shall be borne to that same ancient vault 4.01.111
since this same wayward girl is so reclaim'd. 4.02. 47
what a pestilent knave is this same! 4.05.144 P
o, this same thought did but forerun my need, 5.01. 53
need, | and this same needy man must sell it me. 5.01. 54
this same should be the voice of friar john. 5.02. 2
for all this same, i'll hide me hereabout, | his 5.03. 43
post he came from mantua | to this same place, 5.03.274
to this same place, to this same monument. 5.03.274
soul, and just of the same piece | is every TIM 3.02. 64
him | his friend that dips in the same dish? 3.02. 66
at all times alike | men are not still the same; 5.01.122
and that same eye whose bend doth awe the world JC 1.02.123
as that same ague which hath made you lean. 2.02.113
that every like is not the same, o caesar, | the 2.02.128
speak | in the same pulpit whereto i am going, 3.01.250
good of rome, i have the same dagger for myself, 3.02. 46 P
but this same day | must end that work the ides 5.01.112
to be the same in thine own act and valor | as MAC 1.07. 40
when yond same star that's westward from the HAM 1.01. 36
in the same figure, like the king that's dead. 1.01. 41
why this same strict and most observant watch 1.01. 71
by the same comart | and carriage of the article 1.01. 93
the same, my lord, and your poor servant ever. 1.02.162
do they hold the same estimation they did when i 2.02.334 P
sole son, do this same villain send | to heaven. 3.03. 77
for this same lord, | i do repent; 3.04.172
the very same. 4.07. 92
this same skull, sir, was, sir, yorick's skull, 5.01.180 P
and many more of the same breed that i know the 5.02.188 P
but let this same be presently perform'd | even 5.02.393
i'll talk a word with this same learned theban. LR 3.04.157
when shall i come to th' top of that same hill? 4.06. 1
my reason all the same, and they are ready 5.03. 52
i am old now, | and these same crosses spoil me. 5.03.279
the same: 5.03.283
but this same cassio, though he speak of comfort OTH 2.01. 31
you give me now | for that same handkerchief? 3.03.306
did you mean by that same handkerchief you gave 4.01.149 P
excellent good. what trumpet is that same? 4.01.213
prithee shroud me | in one of these same sheets. 4.03. 25
the same indeed, a very valiant fellow. 5.01. 52
i'll after that same villain, | for 'tis a 5.02.242
i know by that same eye there's some good news. ANT 1.03. 19
both as the same, or rather ours the elder — 3.10. 13
these same whoreson devils do the gods great 5.02.275 P
how far it is | to this same blessed milford. CYM 3.02. 59
the same suit he wore when he took leave of my 3.05.125 P
thou dost approve thyself the very same; 4.02.380
the same dead thing alive. 5.05.123
the same. TNK 3.03. 2
and with the same breath smil'd, and kiss'd her 4.01. 93
the same, my lord. | are they not sweet ones? 4.02.120
present stood unfeignedly on the same terms. 4.03. 69 P
and those same hands | that you like rebels lift STM II.C 108
thou art not what thou seem'st, and if the same, LUC 600
the same disgrace which they themselves behold; 751
to push grief on, and back the same grief draw. 1673
thus appalled, | that the self was not the same; PHT 38
dwell | will play the tyrants to the very same, SON 5. 3
for that same groan doth put this in my mind: 50.13
they, | or whether revolution be the same. 59.12
but those same tongues that give thee so thine 69. 6
why write i still all one, ever the same, | and 76. 5
i must each day say o'er the very same, 108. 6
SAMINGO 1 FR 0.0001 REL FR 1 V 0 P
"do me right, | and dub me knight, | samingo." 2H4 5.03. 75
SAMPIRE 1 FR 0.0001 REL FR 1 V 0 P
half way down | hangs one that gathers sampire, LR 4.06. 15
SAMPLE 1 FR 0.0001 REL FR 1 V 0 P
a sample to the youngest, to th' more mature | a CYM 1.01. 48
SAMPLER 2 FR 0.0002 REL FR 2 V 0 P
both on one sampler, sitting on one cushion, MND 3.02.205
and in a tedious sampler sew'd her mind; TIT 2.04. 39
SAMPSON 6 FR 0.0006 REL FR 1 V 5 P
sampson, master; LLL 1.02. 70 P
o well–knit sampson! 1.02. 73 P
strong–jointed sampson! 1.02. 73 P
color, methinks sampson had small reason for it. 1.02. 87 P
yet was sampson so tempted, and he had an 1.02.173 P
i am not sampson, nor sir guy, nor colbrand, H8 5.03. 22
SAMPSON'S 1 FR 0.0001 REL FR 0 V 1 P
who was sampson's love, my dear moth? LLL 1.02. 76 P
SAMSON 1 FR 0.0001 REL FR 0 V 1 P
same day did i fight with one samson stockfish, 2H4 3.02. 32 P
SAMSONS 1 FR 0.0001 REL FR 1 V 0 P
for none but samsons and goliases | it sendeth 1H6 1.02. 33
SANCTA 1 FR 0.0001 REL FR 1 V 0 P
ah, sancta majestas! 2H6 5.01. 5
SANCTIFIED 7 FR 0.0008 REL FR 6 V 1 P
are sanctified and holy traitors to you. AYL 2.03. 13
buried in highways out of all sanctified limit, AWW 1.01.140 P
shall for my legacy be sanctified | by th' 1.03.245
and draw no swords but what are sanctified. 2H4 4.04. 4
breathing like sanctified and pious bonds, | the HAM 1.03.130
so help me every spirit sanctified, | as i have OTH 3.04.126
or sister sanctified, of holiest note, | which LC 233
SANCTIFIES 1 FR 0.0001 REL FR 0 V 1 P
of him, sanctifies himself with 's hand, and COR 4.05.195 P
SANCTIFY 4 FR 0.0004 REL FR 4 V 0 P
idolatrous fancy | must sanctify his reliques. AWW 1.01. 98
far | his name with zealous fervor sanctify. 3.04. 11
hearse | be drops of balm to sanctify thy head; 2H4 4.05.114
crown up the verse, | and sanctify the numbers. TRO 3.02.183
SANCTIMONIES 1 FR 0.0001 REL FR 1 V 0 P
if souls guide vows, if vows be sanctimonies, TRO 5.02.139
SANCTIMONIOUS 2 FR 0.0002 REL FR 1 V 1 P
before | all sanctimonious ceremonies may | with TMP 4.01. 16
thou conclud'st like the sanctimonious pirate, MM 1.02. 7 P
SANCTIMONY 3 FR 0.0003 REL FR 1 V 2 P
with most austere sanctimony she accomplish'd; AWW 4.03. 50 P
if sanctimony be the gods' delight, | if there TRO 5.02.140
if sanctimony and a frail vow betwixt an erring OTH 1.03.355 P
SANCTITIES 1 FR 0.0001 REL FR 1 V 0 P
between the grace, the sanctities of heaven, 2H4 4.02. 21
SANCTITY 6 FR 0.0006 REL FR 4 V 2 P
is as full of sanctity as the touch of holy AYL 3.04. 13 P
which way is he, in the name of sanctity? TN 3.04. 84 P
reliev'd him with such sanctity of love, | and 3.04.361
like very sanctity, she did approach | my cabin WT 3.03. 23
such sanctity hath heaven given his hand, | they MAC 4.03.144
of mine, my sanctity | will to my sense bend no PER 5.03. 29
SANCTUARIZE 1 FR 0.0001 REL FR 1 V 0 P
no place indeed should murther sanctuarize, HAM 4.07.127
SANCTUARY 15 FR 0.0017 REL FR 14 V 1 P
shall we desire to raze the sanctuary | and MM 2.02.170
he took this place for sanctuary, | and it shall ERR 5.01. 94
man may live as quiet in hell as in a sanctuary, ADO 2.01.258 P
i'll hence forthwith unto the sanctuary, | to 3H6 4.04. 31
come, come, my boy, we will to sanctuary. R3 2.04. 66
go, i'll conduct you to the sanctuary. 2.04. 73
and your brother york | have taken sanctuary. 3.01. 28
the holy privilege | of blessed sanctuary! 3.01. 42
age, | you break not sanctuary in seizing him. 3.01. 47
oft have i heard of sanctuary men, | but 3.01. 55
men, | but sanctuary children never till now. 3.01. 56
go thou to sanctuary, and good thoughts possess 4.01. 93
nor sleep nor sanctuary, | being naked, sick, COR 1.10. 19
let's think this prison holy sanctuary | to keep TNK 2.02. 71
should break out, though i' th' sanctuary. 3.01. 62
SAND 7 FR 0.0008 REL FR 6 V 1 P
as twenty seas, if all their sand were pearl, TGV 2.04.170
and see my wealthy andrew /dock'd in sand, MV 1.01. 27
hearts are all as false | as stairs of sand, 3.02. 84
even as men wrack'd upon a sand, that look to be H5 4.01. 97 P
here shall they make their ransom on the sand, 2H6 4.01. 10
tread on the sand, why, there you quickly sink; 3H6 5.04. 30
one sand another | not more resembles that sweet CYM 5.05.120
SANDAL* 2 FR 0.0002 REL FR 2 V 0 P
you are come to sandal in a happy hour; 3H6 1.02. 63
cockle hat and staff, | and his sandal shoon." HAM 4.05. 26
SAND-BLIND 2 FR 0.0002 REL FR 0 V 2 P
father, who, being more than sand–blind, high MV 2.02. 36 P
alack, sir, i am sand–blind, i know you not. 2.02. 74 P
SANDED 1 FR 0.0001 REL FR 1 V 0 P
so flew'd, so sanded; MND 4.01.120
SANDS 24 FR 0.0027 REL FR 23 V 1 P
come unto these yellow sands, | and then take TMP 1.02.375
and ye that on the sands with printless foot 5.01. 34
forsake unsounded deeps to dance on sands. TGV 3.02. 80
heart | as full of sorrows as the sea of sands, 4.03. 33
and sat with me on neptune's yellow sands, MND 2.01.126
are wrack'd three nights ago on goodwin sands; JN 5.03. 11
are cast away, and sunk on goodwin sands. 5.05. 13
is numb'ring sands and drinking oceans dry; R2 2.02.146
turn the sands into eloquent tongues, and my H5 3.07. 34 P
splitting rocks cow'r'd in the sinking sands, 2H6 3.02. 97
the sands are numb'red that makes up my life, 3H6 1.04. 25
than with ruthless waves, with sands and rocks. 5.04. 36
well said, lord sands, | your colt's tooth is H8 1.03. 47
my lord sands, you are one will keep 'em waking; 1.04. 23
my lord sands, | i am beholding to you; 1.04. 40
you are a merry gamester, | my lord sands. 1.04. 46
will blow these sands like sibyl's leaves abroad TIT 4.01.105
here, in the sands, | thee i'll rake up, the LR 4.06.273
the gutter'd rocks and congregated sands, OTH 2.01. 69
with sands that will not bear your enemies' CYM 3.01. 21
where horses have been nimbler than the sands 3.02. 72
now our sands are almost run, | more a little, PER 5.02. 1
dance on the sands, and yet no footing seen. VEN 148
high winds, strong pirates, shelves and sands, LUC 335
SANDY 6 FR 0.0006 REL FR 6 V 0 P
i should not see the sandy hour–glass run | but MV 1.01. 25
to run, | finish the process of his sandy hour, 1H6 4.02. 36
safer shall he be upon the sandy plains | than 2H6 1.04. 36
safer shall he be upon the sandy plains | than 1.04. 68
false | as air, as water, wind, or sandy earth, TRO 3.02.192
this sandy plot is plain; TIT 4.01. 69
SANDY-BOTTOM'D 1 FR 0.0001 REL FR 1 V 0 P
wye | and sandy–bottom'd severn have i sent him 1H4 3.01. 65
SANDYS *(see sands)*
SANG 1 FR 0.0001 REL FR 1 V 0 P
/ruin'd choirs, where late the sweet birds sang. SON 73. 4
SANGUINE 4 FR 0.0004 REL FR 3 V 1 P
this sanguine coward, this bed–presser, this 1H4 2.04.242 P
saying the sanguine color of the leaves | did 1H6 4.01. 92
what, what, ye sanguine, shallow–hearted boys! TIT 4.02. 97
had | upon his neck a mole, a sanguine star, CYM 5.05.364
SANGUIS 1 FR 0.0001 REL FR 0 V 1 P
the deer was, as you know, sanguis, in blood, LLL 4.02. 3 P
/SANITY 1 FR 0.0001 REL FR 0 V 1 P
hits on, which reason and /sanity could not so HAM 2.02.210 P
SANS 16 FR 0.0018 REL FR 15 V 1 P
had indeed no limit, | a confidence sans bound. TMP 1.02. 97
sans fable, she herself revil'd you there. ERR 4.04. 73
i do, sans question. LLL 5.01. 86 P
my love to thee is sound, sans crack or flaw. 5.02.415
sans "sans," i pray you. 5.02.416
sans "sans," i pray you. 5.02.416
and i did laugh sans intermission | an hour by AYL 2.07. 32
sans teeth, sans eyes, sans taste, sans every 2.07.166
sans teeth, sans eyes, sans taste, sans every 2.07.166
teeth, sans eyes, sans taste, sans every thing. 2.07.166
teeth, sans eyes, sans taste, sans every thing. 2.07.166
come, come; sans compliment, what news abroad? JN 5.06. 16
of a king, | sans check, to good and bad. TRO 1.03. 94
throat shall cut, | and mince it sans remorse. TIM 4.03.123
ears without hands or eyes, smelling sans all, HAM 3.04. 79
or lame of sense), | sans witchcraft could not. OTH 1.03. 64
SANTRAILLES 1 FR 0.0001 REL FR 1 V 0 P
call'd the brave lord ponton de santrailles, 1H6 1.04. 28
/SAP 1 FR 0.0001 REL FR 1 V 0 P
/and /disbranch | /from /her /material /sap, LR 4.02. 35
SAP 14 FR 0.0015 REL FR 14 V 0 P
with intrusion | infect thy sap, and live on thy ERR 2.02.180
i am bound to you. | there is some sap in this. WT 4.04.565
lest, being over–proud in sap and blood, | with R2 3.04. 59
why wither not the leaves that want their sap? R3 2.02. 42
the purple sap from her sweet brother's body, 4.04.277
if with the sap of reason you would quench, | or H8 1.01.148
root, thus hack'd, | the air will drink the sap. 1.02. 98
as knots, by the conflux of meeting sap, TRO 1.03. 7
come on, my queen, | there's sap in't yet. ANT 3.13.191
and in the breach appears | green–dropping sap, VEN 1176
to dry the old oak's sap and cherish springs, LUC 950
his leaves will wither and his sap decay; 1168
sap check'd with frost and lusty leaves quite SON 5. 7
vaunt in their youthful sap, at height decrease, 15. 7
SAP-CONSUMING 1 FR 0.0001 REL FR 1 V 0 P
hid | in sap–consuming winter's drizzled snow, ERR 5.01.313
SAPEGO *(also suppeago)*
SAPEGO 1 FR 0.0001 REL FR 1 V 0 P
do curse the gout, sapego, and the rheum | for MM 3.01. 31
/SAPIENT 1 FR 0.0001 REL FR 1 V 0 P
/thou, /sapient /sir, /sit /here. LR 3.06. 22
/SAPIT 1 FR 0.0001 REL FR 0 V 1 P
but vir /sapit qui pauca loquitur. LLL 4.02. 80 P
SAPLESS 2 FR 0.0002 REL FR 2 V 0 P
that droops his sapless branches to the ground. 1H6 2.05. 12
when sapless age and weak unable limbs | should 4.05. 4
/SAPLING 1 FR 0.0001 REL FR 1 V 0 P
/peace, /tender /sapling, /thou /art /made /of TIT 3.02. 50
SAPLING 2 FR 0.0002 REL FR 1 V 1 P
mine arm | is like a blasted sapling, wither'd R3 3.04. 69
you're a young foolish sapling, and must be PER 4.02. 88 P
SAPPHIRE 2 FR 0.0002 REL FR 2 V 0 P
like sapphire, pearl, and rich embroidery, WIV 5.05. 71
the heaven–hu'd sapphire and the opal blend LC 215
SAPPHIRES 1 FR 0.0001 REL FR 0 V 1 P
carbuncles, sapphires, declining their rich ERR 3.02.135 P
SAPPY 1 FR 0.0001 REL FR 1 V 0 P
herbs for their smell, and sappy plants to bear: VEN 165
SARACENS 1 FR 0.0001 REL FR 1 V 0 P
against black pagans, turks, and saracens, | and R2 4.01. 95
SARCENET 2 FR 0.0002 REL FR 1 V 1 P
and givest such sarcenet surety for thy oaths 1H4 3.01.251
thou green sarcenet flap for a sore eye, thou TRO 5.01. 31 P
SARDIANS 1 FR 0.0001 REL FR 1 V 0 P
pella | for taking bribes here of the sardians; JC 4.03. 3
SARDINIA 1 FR 0.0001 REL FR 1 V 0 P
you have made me offer | of sicily, sardinia; ANT 2.06. 35
SARDIS 3 FR 0.0003 REL FR 3 V 0 P
they mean this night in sardis to be quarter'd. JC 4.02. 28
coming from sardis, on our former ensign | two 5.01. 79
at sardis once, | and, this last night, here in 5.05. 18
SARSENET *(see sarcenet)*
SARUM 1 FR 0.0001 REL FR 1 V 0 P
goose, /and i had you upon sarum plain, | i'ld LR 2.02. 83
SAT *(also sate*)*
SAT 24 FR 0.0027 REL FR 20 V 4 P
i have sat in the stocks for puddings he hath TGV 4.04. 30 P
sing madrigals — | when as i sat in pabylon — WIV 3.01. 24
i have sat here all day. MM 4.01. 19 P
o me, with what strict patience have i sat, | to LLL 4.03.163
land, | and in the shape of corin sat all day, MND 2.01. 66
and sat with me on neptune's yellow sands, 2.01.126
since once i sat upon a promontory, | and heard 2.01.149
away, | and you sat smiling at his cruel prey. 2.02.150
or if thou hast not sat as i do now, | wearing AYL 2.04. 37
church, | if ever sat at any good man's feast, 2.07.115
and sat at good men's feasts, and wip'd our eyes 2.07.122
him forth, h'as sat i' th' stocks all night, AWW 4.03.101 P
she sat like patience on a monument, | smiling TN 2.04.114
long, sat in the council–house | early and late, 2H6 1.01. 90
methought i sat in seat of majesty | in the 1.02. 36
wherein my grandsire and my father sat? 3H6 1.01.125
i sat me down, | devis'd a new commission, wrote HAM 5.02. 31
pillicock sat on pillicock–hill, alow! LR 3.04. 76 P
"the poor soul sat /sighing by a sycamore tree, OTH 4.03. 40
the barge she sat in, like a burnish'd throne, ANT 2.02.191
at the feet sat | caesarion, whom they call my 3.06. 5
the place | was knee–deep where she sat; TNK 4.01. 83
now was she just before him as he sat, | and VEN 349
when he again desires her, being sat, | her LC 66
SATAN *(see sathan)*
SATCHEL 1 FR 0.0001 REL FR 1 V 0 P
with his satchel | and shining morning face, AYL 2.07.145
SATE* *(also sat)*
/SATE* 1 FR 0.0001 REL FR 1 V 0 P

will /sate itself in a celestial bed | and prey HAM 1.05. 56
SATE* 8 FR 0.0009 REL FR 7 V 1 P
how he would woo, | as if she sate in 's heart. AWW 4.02. 70
well | how troublesome it sate upon my head. 2H4 4.05.186
as if allegiance in their bosoms sate | crowned H5 2.02. 4
while her grace sate down | to rest a while, H8 4.01. 65
within thine eyes sate twenty thousand deaths, COR 3.03. 70
i have sate too long. 5.03.131
arms, and there have sate | the livelong day, JC 1.01. 40
the crowner hath sate on her, and finds it HAM 5.01. 4 P
SATED 1 FR 0.0001 REL FR 0 V 1 P
when she is sated with his body, she will find OTH 1.03.350 P
SATHAN 8 FR 0.0009 REL FR 2 V 6 P
and one that is as slanderous as sathan? WIV 5.05.155 P
sathan, avoid! i charge thee tempt me not. ERR 4.03. 48
master, is this mistress sathan? 4.03. 49 P
i charge thee, sathan, hous'd within this man, 4.04. 54
and talk'd of sathan and of limbo and of furies AWW 5.03.260 P
for gravity to play at cherry–pit with sathan. TN 3.04.116 P
fie, thou dishonest sathan! 4.02. 31 P
youth, falstaff, that old white–bearded sathan. 1H4 2.04.463 P
SATIATE 1 FR 0.0001 REL FR 1 V 0 P
that satiate yet unsatisfied desire, that tub CYM 1.06. 48
SATIETY *(also saciety)*
SATIETY 1 FR 0.0001 REL FR 0 V 1 P
inflame it and to give satiety a fresh appetite, OTH 2.01.228 P
SATIN 4 FR 0.0004 REL FR 1 V 3 P
for some four suits of peach–color'd satin, MM 4.03. 11 P
dommelton about the satin for my short cloak and
2H4 1.02. 29 P
have sent me two and twenty yards of satin (as i 1.02. 44 P
and bid nicander | bring me the satin coffin. PER 3.01. 67
SATIRE 4 FR 0.0004 REL FR 3 V 1 P
thou think i care for a satire or an epigram? ADO 5.04.102 P
that is some satire, keen and critical, | not MND 5.01. 54
a satire against the softness of prosperity, TIM 5.01. 35
if any, be a satire to decay, | and make time's SON 100.11
SATIRICAL 1 FR 0.0001 REL FR 0 V 1 P
for the satirical rogue says here that old men HAM 2.02.196 P
SATIS 1 FR 0.0001 REL FR 0 V 1 P
satis quid sufficit. LLL 5.01. 1 P
SATISFACTION 33 FR 0.0037 REL FR 20 V 13 P
no promise of satisfaction at her hands? WIV 2.02.209 P
and we may soon our satisfaction have | touching MM 1.01. 82
the satisfaction i would require is likewise 3.01.155 P
to his bed, give him promise of satisfaction. 3.01.263 P
for my better satisfaction, let me have 4.02.122 P
therefore make present satisfaction, | or i'll ERR 4.01. 5
to give me ample satisfaction | for these deep 5.01.253
company, | and we shall make full satisfaction. 5.01.400
so much to find the thief, and no satisfaction, MV 3.01. 94 P
ceas'd | in heavy satisfaction and would never AWW 5.03.100
that satisfaction can be none but by pangs of TN 3.04.239 P
this satisfaction | the by–gone day proclaim'd. WT 1.02. 31
conscience will make any possible satisfaction, 2H4 ep 21 P
king lewis his satisfaction, all appear | to H5 1.02. 88
and partly for the satisfaction, look you, of my 3.02. 99 P
our feet but a weak and worthless satisfaction. 3.06.133 P
how canst thou make me satisfaction? 4.08. 45
nor other satisfaction do i crave, | but only, 1H6 2.03. 77
what satisfaction canst thou make | for bearing 3H6 5.05. 14
o worthy satisfaction! TRO 2.03. 4 P
any scath, | let him make treble satisfaction. TIT 5.01. 8
what satisfaction canst thou have to–night? ROM 2.02.126
but for your private satisfaction, | because i JC 2.02. 73
all that we call ours, | to you in satisfaction; HAM 4.05.210
an auricular assurance have your satisfaction, LR 1.02. 92 P
in /me defunct) and proper satisfaction; OTH 1.03.264
but for a satisfaction of my thought, | no 3.03. 97
where's satisfaction? 3.03.401
the door of truth | will give you satisfaction, 3.03.408
assure yourself i will seek satisfaction of you. 4.02.199 P
i gave him satisfaction! CYM 2.01. 14 P
the satisfaction of her knowledge only | in 5.05.251
"nor gives it satisfaction to our blood | that LC 162
SATISFICE 1 FR 0.0001 REL FR 1 V 0 P
no, let them satisfice their lust on thee. TIT 2.03.180
/SATISFIED 2 FR 0.0002 REL FR 2 V 0 P
/the /commons /will /not /then /be /satisfied. R2 4.01.272
/they /shall /be /satisfied. 4.01.273
SATISFIED 48 FR 0.0054 REL FR 45 V 3 P
who by repentance is not satisfied | is nor of TGV 5.04. 79
i cannot be thus satisfied. WIV 2.01.188 P
be satisfied; MM 2.02.104
breast, | and go well satisfied to france again. LLL 2.01.152
he is well paid that is well satisfied, | and i, MV 4.01.415
and i, delivering you, am satisfied, | and 4.01.416
and yet i am sure you are not satisfied | of 5.01.296
i will satisfy you, if ever i satisfied man, and AYL 5.02.115 P
as you shall well be satisfied with all. SHR 3.02.109
though i am satisfied and need no more | than WT 2.01.189
i will be satisfied, let me see the writing. R2 5.02. 59
i will be satisfied, let me see it, i say. 5.02. 71
but gladly would be better satisfied | how in 2H4 1.03. 6
france, till satisfied | that fair queen isabel, H5 1.02. 80
my soul shall then be satisfied. 1H6 2.05. 21
yet so my fancy may be satisfied, | and peace 5.03. 91
ay, and old york, and yet not satisfied. 3H6 2.02. 99
death | take on with me, and ne'er be satisfied! 2.05.104
shed seas of tears, and ne'er be satisfied! 2.05.106
misthink the king, and not be satisfied! 2.05.108
be satisfied, dear god, with our true blood, R3 3.03. 22
so, i am satisfied. 5.03. 72
not there | at once and fully satisfied), H8 2.04.149
yourself to say | how far you satisfied me. 2.04.212
which | have satisfied the king for his divorce, 3.02. 65
in second voice we'll not be satisfied, | we TRO 2.03.140
speak but one rhyme, and i am satisfied; ROM 2.01. 9
let me be satisfied, is't good or bad? 2.05. 37
tender | as dearly as mine own — be satisfied. 3.01. 72
and then i hope thou wilt be satisfied. 3.05. 92
indeed i never shall be satisfied | with romeo, 3.05. 93
wrong, nor without cause | will he be satisfied. JC 3.01. 48
come unto this place, | he shall be satisfied; 3.01.141
the son of caesar, | you should be satisfied. 3.01.226
we will be satisfied! let us be satisfied! 3.02. 1
we will be satisfied! let us be satisfied! 3.02. 1
but if he be at hand | i shall be satisfied. 4.02. 10
i will be satisfied. MAC 4.01.104
i am satisfied in nature, | whose motive, in HAM 5.02.244
how may the duke be therewith satisfied, | whose OTH 1.02. 88
would i were satisfied! 3.03.390
you would be satisfied? 3.03.393
how satisfied, my lord? 3.03.394
and you shall be satisfied. 4.02.245 P
iago in the /nick | came in and satisfied him. 5.02.318
i am satisfied. ANT 3.13.167
if further yet you will be satisfied | why (as PER 1.03. 15
prey, | sharp hunger by the conquest satisfied, LUC 422
SATISFIES 1 FR 0.0001 REL FR 1 V 0 P
but she makes hungry | where most she satisfies; ANT 2.02.237
SATISFY 28 FR 0.0031 REL FR 20 V 8 P
satisfy me once more, once more search with me. WIV 4.02.164 P
do not satisfy your resolution with hopes that MM 3.01.168 P
and satisfy the deputy with the visage | of 4.03. 75
nor i, | and yet, to satisfy this good old man, ADO 5.01.276
satisfy me so. LLL 2.01.162
i will satisfy you, if ever i satisfied man, and AYL 5.02.115 P
sir, to satisfy you in what i have said, | stand SHR 4.02. 4
let it satisfy you, you are too old. AWW 2.03.196 P
i pray you let us satisfy our eyes | with the TN 3.03. 22
to satisfy your highness and the entreaties | of WT 1.02.232
satisfy? 1.02.233
satisfy? 1.02.234
shall satisfy your father. 4.04.622
yet in some measure satisfy her so | that we JN 2.01.557
of your reputation, and satisfy the poor woman. 2H4 2.01.130 P
partly to satisfy my opinion, and partly for the H5 3.02. 99 P
in this close walk to satisfy myself | in 2H6 2.02. 3
york and young rutland could not satisfy. 3H6 2.06. 84
and what your pleasure is shall satisfy me. 3.02. 20
that is enough to satisfy the senate. JC 2.02. 72
to satisfy my remembrance the more strongly. MAC 5.01. 33 P
straight satisfy yourself. OTH 1.01.137
of this my letters | before did satisfy you. ANT 2.02. 52
will this description satisfy him? 2.07. 50 P
satisfy me home, | what is become of her? CYM 3.05. 92
to satisfy, | if of my freedom 'tis the main 5.04. 15
to satisfy my lady. PER 4.01. 71
eye, | which having all, all could not satisfy; LUC 96
SATISFYING 3 FR 0.0003 REL FR 3 V 0 P
and yet he hath given me satisfying reasons. OTH 5.01. 9
if you seek | for further satisfying, under her CYM 2.04.134
time nothing becoming you, | nor satisfying us. 4.04. 16
SATURDAY 1 FR 0.0001 REL FR 1 V 0 P
/on saturday we will return to france. LLL 4.01. 6
SATURDAYS 1 FR 0.0001 REL FR 0 V 1 P
faith, will i, fridays and saturdays and all. AYL 4.01.116 P
/SATURN 1 FR 0.0001 REL FR 1 V 0 P
"to /saturn," caius, not to saturnine: TIT 4.03. 57
SATURN 6 FR 0.0006 REL FR 4 V 2 P
as thou say'st thou art, born under saturn) ADO 1.03. 11 P
saturn and venus this year in conjunction! 2H4 2.04.263 P
your desires, | saturn is dominator over mine: TIT 2.03. 31
view on't | might well have warm'd old saturn; CYM 2.05. 12
cold as old saturn, and like him possess'd TNK 5.04. 62
that heavy saturn laugh'd and leapt with him. SON 98. 4
SATURNINE 16 FR 0.0018 REL FR 16 V 0 P
proud saturnine, interrupter of the good | that TIT 1.01.208
lord saturnine, whose virtues will, i hope, 1.01.225
and say, "long live our emperor saturnine!" 1.01.233
grace, | and here in sight of rome to saturnine, 1.01.246
none in rome to make a stale | but saturnine? 1.01.305
if saturnine advance the queen of goths, | she 1.01.330
sent by the heavens for prince saturnine, 1.01.335
receive him then to favor, saturnine, | that 1.01.421
judge, | how i have lov'd and honored saturnine! 1.01.427
this siren that will charm rome's saturnine, 2.01. 23
and make proud saturnine and his emperess | beg 3.01.297
a pow'r, | to be reveng'd on rome and saturnine. 3.01.300
or slunk not saturnine, as tarquin erst, | that 4.01. 63
and vengeance on the traitor saturnine. 4.03. 35
"to /saturn," caius, not to saturnine: 4.03. 57
my gracious lord, my lovely saturnine, | lord of 4.04. 27
SATURNINUS' 1 FR 0.0001 REL FR 1 V 0 P
know that justice lives | in saturninus' health, TIT 4.04. 24
SATURNINUS 4 FR 0.0004 REL FR 4 V 0 P
patience, prince saturninus. TIT 1.01.203
them not | till saturninus be rome's emperor. 1.01.205
create | lord saturninus rome's great emperor, 1.01.232
ay, and as good as saturninus may. 2.01. 90
SATYR 1 FR 0.0001 REL FR 1 V 0 P
hyperion to a satyr, so loving to my mother HAM 1.02.140
SAUC'D 4 FR 0.0004 REL FR 3 V 1 P
say'st his meat was sauc'd with thy upbraidings: ERR 5.01. 73
into folly, his folly sauc'd with discretion. TRO 1.02. 23 P
should be dieted | in praises sauc'd with lies. COR 1.09. 53
and sauc'd our broths, as juno had been sick CYM 4.02. 50
SAUCE 17 FR 0.0019 REL FR 6 V 11 P
i'll sauce them. WIV 4.03. 9 P
i'll sauce them, come. 4.03. 11 P
with no sauce that can be devis'd to it. ADO 4.01.279 P
to beauty is to have honey a sauce to sugar. AYL 3.03. 31 P
looks, i'll sauce her with bitter words. 3.05. 69 P
item, sauce ... 4d.. 1H4 2.04.536 P
is as arrant a villain and a jack sauce, as ever H5 4.07.141 P
come, there is sauce for it. 5.01. 34 P
will you have some more sauce to your leek? 5.01. 50 P
very bitter sweeting, it is a most sharp sauce. ROM 2.04. 80 P
sauce his palate | with thy most operant poison! TIM 4.03. 24
to sauce thy dishes. 4.03.299 P
this rudeness is a sauce to his good wit, JC 1.02.300
from thence, the sauce to meat is ceremony, MAC 3.04. 35
and my more–having would be as a sauce | to make 4.03. 81
sharpen with cloyless sauce his appetite, | that ANT 2.01. 25
your hunger needs no sauce, i see. TNK 3.03. 25
SAUCERS 1 FR 0.0001 REL FR 1 V 0 P
then incision | would let her out in saucers. LLL 4.03. 96
SAUCES 1 FR 0.0001 REL FR 1 V 0 P
to bitter sauces did i frame my feeding, | and, SON 118. 6
SAUCILY 3 FR 0.0003 REL FR 2 V 1 P
knave came something saucily to the world before
LR 1.01. 21 P
display'd so saucily against your highness — 2.04. 41
while others saucily | promise more speed, but LUC 1348
SAUCINESS 6 FR 0.0006 REL FR 3 V 3 P
you, | your sauciness will jest upon my love, ERR 2.02. 28
which he thinks is a patent for his sauciness, AWW 4.05. 66 P
this /unhair'd sauciness and boyish troops, JN 5.02.133
with such more than impudent sauciness from you,
2H4 2.01.113 P
you call honorable boldness impudent sauciness; 2.01.123 P
that my noble lord be rated | for sauciness. TIT 2.03. 82
SAUCY 35 FR 0.0039 REL FR 29 V 6 P
you, minion, are too saucy. TGV 1.02. 89
their saucy sweetness that do coin heaven's MM 2.04. 45
a saucy friar, | a very scurvy fellow. 5.01.135
that will not be deep search'd with saucy looks; LLL 1.01. 85
tongue | of saucy and audacious eloquence. MND 5.01.103
i will speak to him like a saucy lackey, and AYL 3.02.296 P
you are more saucy with lords and honorable AWW 2.03.260 P
when saucy trusting of the cozen'd thoughts 4.04. 23
i heard you were saucy at my gates, and allow'd TN 1.05.197 P
is't so saucy? 3.04.145 P
as we will ours, against these saucy walls, JN 2.01.404
chaps, and you play the saucy cuttle with me. 2H4 2.04.130 P
am i not protector, saucy priest? 1H6 3.01. 45
the envious barking of your saucy tongue 3.04. 33
but thou wilt brave me with these saucy terms? 2H6 4.10. 36
you are a saucy fellow, | deserve we no more H8 4.02.100
where's then the saucy boat | whose weak TRO 1.03. 42
saucy controller of my private steps! TIT 2.03. 60
go to, go to, | you are a saucy boy. ROM 1.05. 83
sir, what saucy merchant was this, that was so 2.04.145 P
mend me, thou saucy fellow? JC 1.01. 18
or else the world, too saucy with the gods, 1.03. 12
get you hence, sirrah; saucy fellow, hence! 4.03.134
confin'd, bound in | to saucy doubts and fears. MAC 3.04. 24
saucy and overbold, how did you dare | to trade 3.05. 3
doth affect | a saucy roughness, and constrains LR 2.02. 97
we then have done you bold and saucy wrongs; OTH 1.01.128
them | so saucy with the hand of she here — ANT 3.13. 98
hence, saucy eunuch, peace! 4.14. 25
saucy lictors | will catch at us like strumpets, 5.02.214
it fit | a saucy stranger in his court to mart CYM 1.06.151
quick–answer'd, saucy, and | as quarrellous as 3.04.158
i am too blunt and saucy: 5.05.325
my saucy bark (inferior far to his) | on your SON 80. 7
since saucy jacks so happy are in this, | give 128.13
SAUF 5 FR 0.0005 REL FR 0 V 5 P
sauf votre honneur, en verite, vous prononcez H5 3.04. 37 P
sauf votre honneur, d' elbow. 3.04. 48 P
oui, vraiment, sauf votre grace, ainsi dit–il. 5.02.112 P
sauf votre honneur, me understand well. 5.02.131 P
sauf votre honneur, le francois que vous parlez, 5.02.188 P
SAUNDER 2 FR 0.0002 REL FR 2 V 0 P
saunder simpcox, and if it please you, master. 2H6 2.01.122
then, saunder, sit there, the lying'st knave 2.01.123
SAVAGE 33 FR 0.0037 REL FR 29 V 4 P
when thou didst not, savage, | know thine own TMP 1.02.355
"in time the savage bull doth bear the yoke." ADO 1.01.261
the savage bull may, but if ever the sensible 1.01.262 P
animals | that rage in savage sensuality. 4.01. 61
when shall we set the savage bull's horns on the 5.01.181 P
i think he thinks upon the savage bull. 5.04. 43
that, like a rude and savage man of inde, | at LLL 4.03.218
o, then his lines would ravish savage ears | and 4.03.345
their savage eyes turn'd to a modest gaze, | by MV 5.01. 78
if this uncouth forest yield any thing savage, i AYL 2.06. 7 P
i thought that all things had been savage here, 2.07.107
(a savage jealousy | that sometime savors nobly) TN 5.01.119
a savage clamor! WT 3.03. 56
up, | and tame the savage spirit of wild war, JN 5.02. 74
ingrateful, savage, and inhuman creature? H5 2.02. 95
our scions, put in wild and savage stock, 3.05. 7
savage islanders | pompey the great; 2H6 4.01.137
than have made that savage duke thine heir, 3H6 1.01.224
not to relent is beastly, savage, devilish. R3 1.04.262
even where his raging eye or savage heart, 3.05. 83
here tend the savage strangeness he puts on, TRO 2.03.126
fie, savage, fie! 5.03. 49
who, like a boar too savage, doth root up | his TIM 5.01.165
or else were this a savage spectacle. JC 3.01.223
to fright you thus methinks i am too savage; MAC 4.02. 70
most savage and unnatural! LR 3.03. 7 P
and by and by | breaks out to savage madness. OTH 4.01. 55
for i have savage cause, | and to proclaim it ANT 3.13.128
'tis some savage hold. CYM 3.06. 18
if savage, | take or lend. 3.06. 23
our courtiers say all's savage but at court. 4.02. 33
as she should have been, | by savage cleon. PER 5.01.216
savage, extreme, rude, cruel, not to trust, SON 129. 4
SAVAGELY 1 FR 0.0001 REL FR 1 V 0 P
your wife, and babes, | savagely slaughter'd. MAC 4.03.205
SAVAGENESS 3 FR 0.0003 REL FR 2 V 1 P
casting their savageness aside, have done | like WT 2.03.188
fiery mind, | a savageness in unreclaimed blood, HAM 2.01. 34
o, she will sing the savageness out of a bear. OTH 4.01.189 P
SAVAGERY 2 FR 0.0002 REL FR 2 V 0 P
the wildest savagery, the vildest stroke, | that JN 4.03. 48
rusts | that should deracinate such savagery; H5 5.02. 47
SAVAGES *(also salvages)*
SAVAGES 3 FR 0.0003 REL FR 3 V 0 P
face, | that we (like savages) may worship it. LLL 5.02.202
but grow like savages — as soldiers will | that H5 5.02. 59
with patience more | than savages could suffer. ANT 1.04. 61
SAVAGE–WILD 1 FR 0.0001 REL FR 1 V 0 P
the time and my intents are savage–wild, | more ROM 5.03. 37
SAV'D 39 FR 0.0044 REL FR 22 V 17 P
one that i sav'd from drowning, when three or TGV 4.04. 3 P
here, by this is your brother sav'd, your honor MM 3.01.253 P
this is another prisoner that i sav'd, | who 5.01.487
and then there's a partridge wing sav'd, for the ADO 2.01.149 P
see, see, my beauty will be sav'd by merit. LLL 4.01. 21
i shall be sav'd by my husband, he hath made me MV 3.05. 19 P
the thrifty hire i sav'd under your father, AYL 2.03. 39
his youthful hose, well sav'd, a world too wide 2.07.160
if your life be sav'd, will you undertake to AWW 4.03.292 P
you might have sav'd me my pains, to have taken TN 2.02. 6 P
that means to be sav'd by believing rightly can 3.02. 71 P
deny, | that honor, sav'd, may upon asking give? 3.04.212
thou hast not sav'd one drop of blood | in this JN 2.01.341
o, if men were to be sav'd by merit, what hole 1H4 1.02.107 P
thou hast sav'd me a thousand marks in links and 3.03. 42 P

and sav'd the treacherous labor of your son. 5.04. 57
in the which better part i have sav'd my life. 5.04.121 P
be ransom'd, and a many poor men's lives sav'd. H5 4.01.123 P
part of thy father may be sav'd in thee. 1H6 4.05. 38
all these are sav'd if thou wilt fly away. 4.06. 41
which industry and courage might have sav'd? 3H6 5.04. 11
i would he knew that i had sav'd his brother! R3 1.04.276
a labor sav'd! TRO 3.03.241
done, and sav'd | your husband so much sweat. COR 4.01. 18
you have well sav'd me a day's journey. 4.03. 12 P
sir, you have sav'd my longing, and i feed TIM 1.01.252
led him, begg'd for him, sav'd him from despair; LR 5.03.192
i might have sav'd her, now she's gone for ever! 5.03.271
and there be souls must be sav'd, and there be OTH 2.03.103 P
be sav'd, and there be souls must not be sav'd. 2.03.104 P
nor any man of quality — i hope to be sav'd. 2.03.107 P
lieutenant is to be sav'd before the ancient. 2.03.110 P
no, as i shall be sav'd. 4.02. 86
say, shall never be sav'd by half that they do. ANT 5.02.256 P
their honors | to have sav'd their carcasses! CYM 5.03. 67
this brace — | "for that it sav'd me, keep it. PER 2.01.128
sav'd too, | speaking it truly? TNK 1.02. 48
i sav'd her, | and set her safe to land; 4.01. 95
threw, | and sav'd my life, saying "not you." SON 145.14
'SAVE 13 FR 0.0014 REL FR 7 V 6 P
'save his majesty! TMP 2.01.169
i will be king and queen — 'save our graces! 3.02.107 P
sir proteus! 'save you! saw you my master? TGV 1.01. 70
'save your honor! MM 2.02. 25
'save your honor! 2.02.161
'save you, fair queen! AWW 1.01.106 P
'save you, good madam. 3.02. 45
'save thee, friend, and thy music! TN 3.01. 1 P
'save you, gentleman. 3.01. 69 P
'save you, sir. COR 4.04. 6
'save thee, timon. TIM 4.03.411 P
'save thee, curan. LR 2.01. 1 P
'save you, friend cassio! OTH 3.04.169
SAVE* *(also sa')*
/SAVE* 4 FR 0.0004 REL FR 3 V 1 P
/god /save you, sir! WIV 2.02.154 P
/god /save /the /king! R2 4.01.172
/god /save /the /king! 4.01.174
/god /save /king /henry, /unking'd /richard 4.01.220
SAVE* 214 FR 0.0242 REL FR 169 V 45 P
(save for the son that /she did litter here, | a TMP 1.02.282
true — save means to live. 2.01. 51 P
face remember, | save, from my glass, mine own; 3.01. 50
go, go, be gone, to save your ship from wrack, TGV 1.01.148
save the fall is in the ord "dissolutely." WIV 1.01.253 P
by gar, he has save his soul, dat he is no come; 2.03. 6 P
/god save you, master doctor caius! 2.03. 19 P
/god save you, good sir hugh! 3.01. 41 P
save that we do the denunciation lack | of MM 1.02.148
whom i would save, had a most noble father! 2.01. 7
a charity in sin | to save this brother's life? 2.04. 64
admit no other way to save his life | (as i 2.04. 88
that there were | no earthly mean to save him, 2.04. 95
none, but such remedy as, to save a head, | to 3.01. 61
what sin you do to save a brother's life, 3.01.133
prayers for thy death, | no word to save thee. 3.01.146
this substitute, and to save your brother? 3.01.188 P
to save me from the danger that might come | if 4.03. 85
save that his riotous youth with dangerous sense 4.04. 29
laboring to save his life, and would not rather 5.01.391
and, knowing whom it was their hap to save, ERR 1.01.113
to save the money that he spends in /tiring; 2.02. 97 P
that labor may you save; see where he comes. 4.01. 14
o mistress, mistress, shift and save yourself! 5.01.168
wars, and took | deep scars to save thy life; 5.01.193
haply i see a friend will save my life, | and 5.01.284
things | save in the office and affairs of love; ADO 2.01.176
my lord and brother, god save you! 3.02. 80 P
save this of hers, fram'd by thy villainy! 5.01. 71
god save the foundation! 5.01.318 P
great persuasion, and partly to save your life, 5.04. 96 P
won, | save base authority from others' books. LLL 1.01. 87
now god save thy life! 2.01.191
thus will i save my credit in the shoot: 4.01. 26
sir, god save your life! 4.02.144 P
fair sir, god save you! where's the princess? 5.02.310
god save you, madam! 5.02.716
save that, in love unto demetrius, | i told him MND 3.02.309
save of joy | express'd and not express'd. MV 3.02.182
that 'scuse serves many men to save their gifts, 4.01.444
god save you, brother. AYL 5.02. 17 P
your fellow tranio here, to save my life, | puts SHR 1.01.228
while i make way from hence to save my life. 1.01.234
grumio, mum! god save you, signior gremio. 1.02.162
gentlemen, god save you. 1.02.218
god save you, gentlemen! 2.01. 40 P
god save you, sir! 4.02. 72
to save your life in this extremity, | this 4.02.103
that is virtuous — save what thou dislik'st, AWW 2.03.122
god save you, captain. 2.05. 31 P
had it, save that he comes not along with her. 3.02. 2 P
god save you, pilgrim! 3.05. 32 P
thou mayst inform | something to save thy life. 4.01. 83
little harm, save to his bed–clothes about him; 4.03.256 P
god save you, noble captain. 4.03.316 P
god save you, sir. 5.01. 8
save your word. 5.02. 38 P
save in the constant image of the creature TN 2.04. 19
a thousand thousand sighs to save, | lay me, o, 2.04. 63
none | shall mistress be of it, save i alone. 3.01.160
gentleman, god save thee! 3.04.218 P
to save both, | farewell, our brother. WT 1.02. 26
fees | when you depart, and save your thanks. 1.02. 54
to save this bastard's life — for 'tis a 2.03.161
will you adventure | to save this brat's life? 2.03.163
which i have left | to save the innocent — any 2.03.167
save him from danger, do him love and honor, 4.04.510
to save unscratch'd your city's threat'ned JN 2.01.225
save in aspect, hath all offense seal'd up; 2.01.250
save what is opposite to england's love. 3.01.254
o, save me, hubert, save me! 4.01. 72
o, save me, hubert, save me! 4.01. 72
save back to england, all the world's my way. R2 1.03.207
save bidding farewell to so sweet a guest | as 2.02. 8
god save your majesty! 2.02. 41
your husband, he is gone to save far off, 2.02. 80
sign, | save men's opinions and my living blood, 3.01. 26
save our deposed bodies to the ground? 3.02.150
whilst all tongues cried, "god save /thee, 5.02. 11
no man cried "god save him!" 5.02. 28
god save your grace! 5.03. 26
as, god save thy grace — majesty i should say, 1H4 1.02. 17 P
guns, and drums, and wounds, god save the mark! 1.03. 56
no, if a scot would save his soul, he shall not! 1.03.215
save how to gall and pinch this bullingbrook, 1.03.229
speed, | to save our heads by raising of a head, 1.03.284
save mine, which hath desir'd to see thee more, 3.02. 89
and will, to save the blood on either side, 5.01. 99
give me life, which if i can save, so; 5.03. 60 P
i am loath to pawn my plate, so god save me law! 2H4 2.01.155 P
god save your grace! 2.02. 73 P
god save you, sir john! 2.04.110 P
good morrow, and god save your majesty! 5.02. 43
sir john, god save you! 5.03. 84 P
god save thy grace, king hal! my royal hal! 5.05. 41
god save thee, my sweet boy! 5.05. 43
save that there was not time enough to hear, H5 1.01. 84
save those to god, that run before our business. 1.02.303
have blowed up the town, so chrish save me law, 3.02. 92 P
it is no time to discourse, so chrish save me. 3.02.105 P
so chrish save me, i will cut off your head. 3.02.133 P
not too, | save ceremony, save general ceremony? 4.01.239
not too, | save ceremony, save general ceremony? 4.01.239
herald, save thou thy labor. 4.03.121
he prays you to save his life. 4.04. 44 P
save the phrase is a little variations. 4.07. 17 P
god save your majesty! 5.02.281 P
woman, do what thou canst to save our honors; 1H6 1.02.147
to save myself by flight. 3.02.105
all the talbots in the world, to save my life. 3.02.108
are glad and fain by flight to save themselves. 3.02.114
god save king henry, of that name the sixt! 4.01. 2
so should we save a valiant gentleman | by 4.03. 26
to save a paltry life and slay bright fame, 4.06. 45
so doth the swan her downy cygnets save, 5.03. 56
to save your subjects from such massacre | and 5.04.160
if you mean to save yourself from whipping, leap 2H6 2.01.139 P
the king will labor still to save his life, 3.01.239
the commons haply rise, to save his life; 3.01.240
any | save to the god of heaven and to my king; 4.01.126
god save your majesty! 4.02. 71 P
and therefore yet relent, and save my life. 4.07.117
up his cap, and say, "god save his majesty!" 4.08. 15
god save the king! god save the king! 4.08. 19 P
god save the king! god save the king! 4.08. 19 P
god save the king! god save the king! 4.09. 22 P
god save the king! god save the king! 4.09. 22 P
to save, at least, the heir of edward's right; 3H6 4.04. 32
fly, lords, and save yourselves, | for warwick 5.02. 48
relent, and save your souls. R3 1.04.256
their country's good | cry, "god save richard, 3.07. 22
some ten voices cried, "god save king richard!" 3.07. 36
save that, for reverence to some alive, | i give 3.07.193
and die ere men can say, "god save the queen!" 4.01. 62
and kneels, and says, "god save the queen"? 4.04. 94
to save her life, i'll say she is not so. 4.04.213
save for a night of groans | endur'd of her, for 4.04.303
hold my thanks, | and save me so much talking. H8 1.04. 40
o, god save ye! 2.01. 1
i'll save you | that labor, sir. 2.01. 3
this cannot save you. 3.02.302
god save you, sir! where have you been broiling? 4.01. 56
and that i would not for a cow, god save her! 5.03. 27
save such as doth revolve | and ruminate himself TRO 2.03.187
save these men's looks, who do methinks find out 3.03. 90
please you, save the thanks this prince expects. 4.04.117
'tis not to save labor, nor that i want love. COR 1.03. 81 P
god save your good worships! 2.01.144 P
amen, amen. god save thee, noble consul! 2.03.136 P
not one amongst us, save yourself, but says | he 2.03.162
(mistake me not) to save my life, for if | i had 4.05. 80
that our request did tend | to save the romans, 5.03.133
sir, if you'ld save your life, fly to your house 5.04. 35
vain | to save your brother from the sacrifice, TIT 2.03.164
therefore mine shall save my brothers' lives. 3.01.166
save thou the child, so we may all be safe. 4.02.131
save the child | and bear it from me to the 5.01. 53
to save my boy, to nourish and bring him up, 5.01. 84
good thou, save me a piece of marchpane, and, as ROM 1.05. 7 P
save what thou must combine | by holy marriage. 2.03. 60
i saw it with mine eyes — | god save the mark! 3.02. 53
hope, now all are fled, | save only the gods. TIM 3.03. 36
but all, save thee, | i fell with curses. 4.03.500
and land, | in every place, save here in italy. JC 1.03. 88
depart, | save i alone, till antony have spoke. 3.02. 61
all the conspirators, save only he, | did that 5.05. 69
god save the king! MAC 1.02. 47
god save you, sir! HAM 2.02.221 P
and how his audit stands who knows save heaven? 3.03. 82
save me, and hover o'er me with your wings, 3.04.103
save yourself, my lord! 4.05. 99
can save the thing from death | that is but 4.07.145
save what beats there — filial ingratitude! LR 3.04. 14
couldst thou save nothing? 3.04. 64
save him, save him! 5.03.152
save him, save him! 5.03.152
(save that they say the wars must make example OTH 3.03. 65
/god save /thee, worthy general! 4.01.216
will denote him so | that i may save my speech. 4.01.280
for you, mistress, | save you your labor. 5.01.101
save when command to your dismission tends, CYM 2.03. 52
and words, | save that euriphile must be fidele. 4.02.238
horse, save one that had | a rider like myself, 4.04. 38
away, boy, from the troops, and save thyself; 5.02. 14
and may save | but to look back in frown. 5.03. 27
save him, sir, | and spare no blood beside. 5.05. 91
him hence, | the whole world shall not save him. 5.05.321
all o'erjoy'd, | save these in bonds. 5.05.402
that without covering, save yon field of stars, PER 1.01. 37
what courage, sir? god save you! 3.01. 38 P
you between, | and save poor me, the weaker. 4.01. 90
shall tack about | and something do to save us. TNK pr 27
our crowned heads we have no roof | save this, 1.01. 53
save when my lids scour'd off their /brine. 3.02. 28
all offices are done | save what i fail in. 3.02. 37
for heaven's sake save their lives, and banish 3.06.251
without appetite, save often drinking, dreaming 4.03. 4 P
lost what's dearest to me | save what is bought, 5.03.113
lack, | save a proud rider on so proud a back. VEN 300
save sometime too much wonder of his eye, LUC 95
save thieves, and cares, and troubled minds that 126
save of their lord no bearing yoke they knew, 409
yet save that labor, for i have them here. 1290
was left unseen, save to the eye of mind: 1426
did banish moan, | save the nightingale alone. PP 20. 8
tyrant wing, | save the eagle, feath'red king; PHT 11
time's scythe can make defense | save breed, to SON 12.14
save that my soul's imaginary sight | presents 27. 9
save where thou art not, though i feel thou art, 48.10
save where you are how happy you make those. 57.12
gone, | save that to die, i leave my love alone. 66.14
save what is had or must from you be took. 75.12
save thou, my rose, in it thou art my all. 109.14
in nothing art thou black save in thy deeds, 131.13
SAVED 3 FR 0.0003 REL FR 3 V 0 P
it is perchance that you yourself were saved. TN 1.02. 6
when you, and those poor number saved with you, 1.02. 10
so had you saved | the noble imogen to repent, CYM 5.01. 9
SAVES 6 FR 0.0006 REL FR 5 V 1 P
and the cure of it not only saves your brother, MM 3.01.236 P
he saves my labor by his own approach. AYL 2.07. 8
slay | in common sense, sense saves another way. AWW 2.01.178
chaplain, away, thy priesthood saves thy life. 3H6 1.03. 3
makes the true man kill'd and saves the thief; CYM 2.03. 71
of what is in her chamber nothing saves | the 2.04. 94
SAVING* 15 FR 0.0017 REL FR 6 V 9 P
and longing (saving your honors' reverence) for MM 2.01. 90 P
saving your merry humor, here's the note | how ERR 4.01. 27
you would have me say, "saving your reverence, a ADO 3.04. 32 P
who, saving your reverence, is the devil himself MV 2.02. 26 P
master and he (saving your worship's reverence) 2.02.130 P
saving your tale, petruchio, i pray | let us SHR 2.01. 71
would, | saving in dialogue of compliment, | and JN 1.01.201
it, but that he is, saving your reverence, a 1H4 2.04.469 P
to pie–corner (saving your manhoods) to buy a 2H4 2.01. 27 P
majesty hear now, saving your majesty's manhood, H5 4.08. 33 P
as i have a saving faith within me tells me thou 5.02.204 P
and which gifts | (saving your mincing) the H8 2.03. 31
every flaw, | and saving those that eye thee! COR 5.03. 75
and then i swore thee, saving of thy life, JC 5.03. 38
the rather (saving reverence of the word) for CYM 4.01. 5 P
SAVIOUR'S 1 FR 0.0001 REL FR 1 V 0 P
wherein our saviour's birth is celebrated, HAM 1.01.159
/SAVOR 1 FR 0.0001 REL FR 1 V 0 P
/seem /vild, | /filths /savor /but /themselves. LR 4.02. 39
SAVOR 9 FR 0.0010 REL FR 9 V 0 P
she lov'd not the savor of tar nor of pitch, TMP 2.02. 52
to | a savor that may strike the dullest nostril WT 1.02.421
keep | seeming and savor all the winter long. 4.04. 75
says that you savor too much of your youth, H5 1.02.250
his jest will savor but of shallow wit, | when 1.02.295
is much o' th' savor | of other your new pranks. LR 1.04.237
to me | the very doors and windows savor vilely. PER 4.06.110
both favor, savor, hue, and qualities, | whereat VEN 747
for compound sweet forgoing simple savor, SON 125. 7
SAVORING 1 FR 0.0001 REL FR 0 V 1 P
be very unlearned, neither savoring of poetry, LLL 4.02.159 P
SAVORS 8 FR 0.0009 REL FR 8 V 0 P
favors, | in those freckles live their savors. MND 2.01. 13
"thisby, the flowers of odious savors sweet" — 3.01. 82
"odors savors sweet; 3.01. 84
i smell sweet savors, and i feel soft things. SHR in.2. 71
(a savage jealousy | that sometime savors nobly) TN 5.01.120
this savors not much of distraction. 5.01.314
fancy) something savors | of tyranny, and will WT 2.03.119
th' uncleanly savors of a slaughter–house, | for JN 4.03.112
SAVORY 3 FR 0.0003 REL FR 2 V 1 P
hot lavender, mints, savory, marjorum, | the WT 4.04.104
sallets in the lines to make the matter savory, HAM 2.02.442 P
our stomachs | will make what's homely savory; CYM 3.06. 33
SAVOY 1 FR 0.0001 REL FR 0 V 1 P
now go some and pull down the savoy; 2H6 4.07. 2 P
/SAW* 6 FR 0.0006 REL FR 4 V 2 P
videlicet, he came, /saw, and overcame: LLL 4.01. 69 P
/saw, two; 4.01. 70 P
my lord, | was i betrothed ere i /saw hermia; MND 4.01.172
/not /live /long /after /i /saw /richmond. R3 4.02.107
/saw you my lord? ANT 1.02. 80
but we /saw him dead. CYM 5.05.126
SAW* 286 FR 0.0323 REL FR 225 V 61 P
i have suffered | with those that i saw suffer. TMP 1.02. 6
supposing that they saw the king's ship wrack'd, 1.02.236
for nothing natural | i ever saw so noble. 1.02.420
this | is the third man that e'er i saw; 1.02.446
i saw him beat the surges under him, | and ride 2.01.115
mine eyes open'd, | i saw their weapons drawn. 2.01.320
the very instant that i saw you, did | my heart 3.01. 64
i never saw a woman | but only sycorax my dam 3.02.100
if i should say i saw such /islanders | (for, 3.03. 29
till this day | saw i him touch'd with anger, so 4.01.145
and, since i saw thee, | th' affliction of my 5.01.114
i have heard renown, | but never saw before; 5.01.194
such a pickle since i saw you last that i fear 5.01.282 P
sir proteus! 'save you! saw you my master? TGV 1.01. 70
you never saw her since she was deform'd. 2.01. 63 P
i have lov'd her ever since i saw her, and still 2.01. 66 P
which of you saw eglamour of late? 5.02. 32
saw you my daughter? 5.02. 33
o that my husband saw this letter! WIV 2.01.100 P
sir, that you might avoid him if you saw him. 2.02.277 P
his own gravity and patience that ever you saw. 3.01. 55 P
for i never saw him so gross in his jealousy 3.03.188 P
i saw him arrested; MM 1.02. 67 P
saw him carried away; 1.02. 68 P
she and that friar, | i saw them at the prison. 5.01.135
of five years | i never spake with her, saw her, 5.01.223

weeping before for what she saw must come, | and ERR 1.01. 71
i, sir? i never saw her till this time. 2.02.162
faith, i saw it not; 3.02.131 P
ring — | the ring i saw upon his finger now — 4.04.139
you saw they speak us fair, give us gold: 4.04.152 P
the chain, | which, god he knows, i saw not; 5.01.229
these people saw the chain about his neck. 5.01.259
i never saw the chain, so help me heaven; 5.01.268
i never saw you in my life till now. 5.01.297
grief hath chang'd me since you saw me last, 5.01.298
i never saw my father in my life. 5.01.320
i ne'er saw syracusa in my life. 5.01.326
during which time he ne'er saw syracusa: 5.01.329
i saw him not. ADO 2.01. 2 P
i never yet saw man, | how wise, how noble, 3.01. 59
john, saw afar off in the orchard this amiable 3.03.151 P
shame her with what he saw o'ernight, and send 3.03.162 P
i saw the duchess of milan's gown that they 3.04. 15 P
god saw him when he was hid in the garden. 5.01.179 P
into the orchard and saw me court margaret in 5.01.237 P
solemnized | in normandy, saw i this longaville, LLL 2.01. 43
i saw him at the duke alanson's once, | and much 2.01. 61
and much too little of that good i saw | is my 2.01. 62
a woman sometimes, and you saw her in the light. 2.01.198
that all eyes saw his eyes enchanted with gazes. 2.01.247
what saw he? 4.01. 73 P
saw sighs reek from you, noted well your passion 4.03.138
of you, my lord berowne, | before i saw you; 5.02.842
and coughing drowns the parson's saw | and birds 5.02.922
that very time i saw (but thou couldst not) MND 2.01.155
which, when i saw rehears'd, i must confess, 5.01. 68
very best at a beast, my lord, that e'er i saw. 5.01.230 P
than i have of my face when i /last saw him. MV 2.02. 98 P
why, man, i saw bassanio under sail, | with him 2.08. 1
i saw bassanio and antonio part: 2.08. 36
you saw the mistress, i beheld the maid; 3.02.198
dew, | and saw the lion's shadow ere himself, 5.01. 8
it away before ever he saw those pancakes or AYL 1.02. 79 P
if you saw yourself with your eyes, or knew 1.02.175 P
can it be possible that no man saw them? 2.02. 1
saw her a–bed, and in the morning early | they 2.02. 6
that young swain that you saw here but erewhile, 2.04. 89
love, | who you saw sitting by me on the turf, 3.04. 49
dead shepherd, now i find thy saw of might, 3.05. 81
i saw her hand, she has a leathern hand, | a 4.03. 24
and caesar's thrasonical brag of "i came, saw, 5.02. 32 P
the first time that i ever saw him | methought 5.04. 28
these, | which never were, nor no man ever saw. SHR in.2. 96
o yes, i saw sweet beauty in her face, | such as 1.01.167
saw you no more? 1.01.171
tranio, i saw her coral lips to move, | and with 1.01.174
sacred and sweet was all i saw in her. 1.01.176
as if they saw some wondrous monument, | some 3.02. 95
i never saw a better fashion'd gown, | more 4.03.101
you saw my master wink and laugh upon you? 4.04. 75 P
you, for i never saw you before in all my life. 5.01. 51 P
said "a mother," | methought you saw a serpent. AWW 1.03.141
her leave at court, | i saw upon her finger. 5.03. 80
i am sure i saw her wear it. 5.03. 91
you are deceiv'd, my lord, she never saw it. 5.03. 92
she never saw it. 5.03.112
you saw one here in court could witness it. 5.03.200
i saw the man to–day, if man he be. 5.03.203
hung on our driving boat, i saw your brother, TN 1.02. 11
i saw him hold acquaintance with the waves | so 1.02. 16
who saw cesario, ho? 1.04. 10
i saw him put down the other day with an 1.05. 84 P
be the lady of the house, for i never saw her. 1.05.172 P
i saw thee late at the count orsino's. 3.01. 37 P
i think i saw your wisdom there. 3.01. 41 P
i saw your niece do more favors to the count's 3.02. 5 P
hermit of prague, that never saw pen and ink, 4.02. 13 P
yet, when i saw it last, it was besmear'd | as 5.01. 52
and saw myself unbreech'd | in my green velvet WT 1.02.155
i saw his heart in 's face. 1.02.447
never | saw i men scour so on their way. 2.01. 35
i never saw a vessel of like sorrow, | so fill'd 3.03. 21
i never saw | the heavens so dim by day. 3.03. 55
i have not wink'd since i saw these sights. 3.03.104 P
it is fifteen years since i saw my country; 4.02. 4 P
sir, it is three days since i saw the prince. 4.02. 29 P
by which means i saw whose purse was best in 4.04.603 P
whose purse was best in picture, and what i saw, 4.04.604 P
never saw i | wretches so quake: 5.01.198
but we saw not | that which my daughter came to 5.03. 12
for i saw her, | as i thought, dead; 5.03.139
i saw a smith stand with his hammer, thus, | the JN 4.02.193
be said, | they saw we had a purpose of defense. 5.01. 76
eyes | that never saw the giant world enrag'd, 5.02. 57
my lord, some two days since i saw the prince, R2 5.03. 13
we two saw you four set on four and bound them, 1H4 2.04.253 P
faith, i ran when i saw others run. 2.04.302 P
i saw young harry with his beaver on, | his 4.01.104
i saw him hold lord percy at the point, | with 5.04. 21
i did, i saw him dead, | breathless and bleeding 5.04.133
why, percy i kill'd myself, and saw thee dead. 5.04.144
when he saw | the fortune of the day quite 5.05. 17
saw you the field? 2H4 1.01. 24
but these mine eyes saw him in bloody state, 1.01.107
i'll be sworn 'a ne'er saw him but once in the 3.02.322 P
i saw it, and told john a' gaunt he beat his own 3.02.324 P
he saw me, and yielded, that i may justly say, 4.03. 40 P
"there, cousin, i came, saw, and overcame." 4.03. 42 P
who saw the duke of clarence? 4.05. 7
for after i saw him fumble with the sheets, and H5 2.03. 13 P
'a saw a flea stick upon bardolph's nose, and 'i 2.03. 40 P
saw his heroical seed, and smil'd to see him, 2.04. 59
the armor that i saw in your tent to–night, are 3.07. 69 P
never anybody saw it but his lackey. 3.07.110 P
thrice within this hour | i saw him down; 4.06. 5
who ever saw the like? 1H6 1.02. 22
because till now we never saw your face. 3.04. 24
i never saw but humphrey duke of gloucester 2H6 1.01.183
i saw not better sport these seven years' day; 2.01. 2
a man that ne'er saw in his life before. 2.01. 63
i never saw a fellow worse bestead, | or more 2.03. 56
oft have i struck | those that i never saw, and 4.07. 82
i saw him in the battle range about, | and 3H6 2.01. 11
but when we saw our sunshine made thy spring, 2.02.163
queen margaret saw | thy murd'rous falchion R3 1.02. 93
saw you the king to–day, my lord of derby? 1.03. 30
methoughts i saw a thousand fearful wracks; 1.04. 24
i hope he is much grown since last i saw him. 2.04. 5
i saw good strawberries in your garden there. 3.04. 32
which when i saw, i reprehended them, | and 3.07. 27
who saw the sun to–day? 5.03.277
how have ye done | since last we saw in france? H8 1.01. 2
since a fresh admirer | of what i saw there. 1.01. 4
was then present, saw them salute on horseback, 1.01. 8
'twas said they saw but one, and no discerner 1.01. 32
for, with all the care i had, i saw well chosen, 2.02. 2 P
glad, or sorry | as i saw it inclin'd. 2.04. 27
were tried by ev'ry tongue, ev'ry eye saw 'em, 3.01. 35
now, my lords, | saw you the cardinal? 3.02.111
you saw | the ceremony? 4.01. 59
such joy | i never saw before. 4.01. 76
saw ye none enter since i slept? 4.02. 86
saw you not even now a blessed troop | invite me 4.02. 87
i think your highness saw this many a day. 5.02. 21
yesternight fairer than ever i saw her look, or TRO 1.01. 33 P
ay, if i ever saw him before and knew him. 1.02. 65 P
he never saw three and twenty. 1.02.235 P
we saw him at the opening of his tent, | he is 2.03. 84
still lock'd in steel, | i never saw till now. 4.05.196
dead | since first i saw yourself and diomed 4.05.215
i saw him run after a gilded butterfly, and when COR 1.03. 60 P
i saw our party to their trenches driven, | and 1.06. 12
i saw him prisoner; 1.09. 84
i never saw the like. 2.01.268
whom with all praise i point at, saw him fight, 2.02. 90
no, no; no man saw 'em. 2.03.165
saw you aufidius? 3.01. 8
you had more beard when i last saw you, but your 4.03. 8 P
heart | than when i first my wedded mistress saw 4.05.117
the dismall'st day is this that e'er i saw, | to TIT 1.01.384
how many women saw this child of his? 4.02.135
but say again, how many saw the child? 4.02.140
saw you him to–day? ROM 1.01.116
ne'er saw her match since first the world begun. 1.02. 93
tut, you saw her fair, none else being by, 1.02. 94
for i ne'er saw true beauty till this night. 1.05. 53
i would not for the world they saw thee here. 2.02. 74
i saw no man use you at his pleasure; 2.04.157 P
i saw the wound, i saw it with mine eyes — 3.02. 52
i saw the wound, i saw it with mine eyes — 3.02. 52
most miserable hour that e'er time saw | in 4.05. 44
i saw her laid low in her kindred's vault, | and 5.01. 20
i saw them speak together. TIM 1.01. 62
and when you saw his chariot but appear, | have JC 1.01. 43
i saw mark antony offer him a crown — yet 'twas 1.02.236 P
why, saw you any thing more wonderful? 1.03. 14
with their fear, who swore they saw | men, all 1.03. 24
she dreamt to–night she saw my statue, | which, 2.02. 76
for when the noble caesar saw him stab, 3.02.184
ay. saw you any thing? 4.03.304
no, my lord, i saw nothing. 4.03.305
but i have spoke | with one that saw him die; MAC 1.04. 4
if i stand here, i saw him. 3.04. 73
saw you the weird sisters? 4.01.136
for that i saw the tyrant's power afoot. 4.03.185
lord, | i should report that which i say i saw, 5.05. 30
i saw him once, 'a was a goodly king. HAM 1.02.186
my lord, i think i saw him yesternight. 1.02.189
saw, who? 1.02.190
then saw you not his face? 1.02.229
wherein we saw thee quietly interr'd, | hath 1.04. 49
i saw him yesterday, or th' other day, | or then 2.01. 54
"i saw him enter such a house of sale," 2.01. 58
why, thy face is valanc'd since i saw thee last; 2.02.423 P
is nearer to heaven than when i saw you last, by 2.02.426 P
when she saw pyrrhus make malicious sport | in 2.02.513
nor do not saw the air too much with your hand, 3.02. 4 P
sailors, my lord, they say, i saw them not. 4.07. 39
/come, /come, when saw you my father last? LR 1.02.152 P
and when he saw my best alarum'd spirits, | bold 2.01. 53
good king, that must approve the common saw, 2.02.160
i stumbled when i saw. 4.01. 19
i' th' last night's storm i such a fellow saw, 4.01. 32
i saw othello's visage in his mind, | and to his OTH 1.03.252
i nev'r saw this before. 3.04.100
but then i saw no harm, and then i heard | each 4.02. 4
by heaven, i saw my handkerchief in 's hand. 5.02. 62
i saw the handkerchief. 5.02. 66
i saw it in his hand; 5.02.215
yet at the first | i saw the treasons planted. ANT 1.03. 26
i saw her once | hop forty paces through the 2.02.228
ghosted, | there saw you laboring for him. 2.06. 14
since i saw you last, | there's a change upon 2.06. 52
and saw her led | between her brother and mark 3.03. 9
i never saw an action of such shame; 3.10. 21
for when she saw | (which never shall be found) 4.14.121
i never saw him sad. CYM 1.06. 63
never saw i figures | so likely to report 2.04. 82
but made not here his brag | of "came, and saw, 3.01. 24
i saw him not these many years, and yet | i know 4.02. 66
long is it since i saw him, | but time hath 4.02.103
i saw jove's bird, the roman eagle, wing'd 4.02.348
done aught but well, | whose face i never saw? 5.04. 36
beget young gibbets, i never saw one so prone. 5.04.199 P
i never saw | such noble fury in so poor a thing 5.05. 7
said not i as much when i saw the porpas how he PER 2.01. 24 P
i never saw so huge a billow, sir, | as toss'd 3.02. 58
i saw you lately | when you caught hurt in 4.01. 86
by th' helm of mars, i saw them in the war, TNK 1.04. 17
i never saw 'em. 2.01. 45 P
i saw her first. 2.02.160
i saw her too. 2.02.161
i, that first saw her; 2.02.167
and such as you never saw. 2.03. 65
first, i saw him: 2.04. 7
i never saw such valor. 3.06. 74
when i saw you charge first, | methought i heard 3.06. 82
by the fishermen, | i saw it was your daughter. 4.01. 65
she saw me, and straight sought the flood. 4.01. 95
three or four | i saw from far off cross her — 4.01.100
who saw 'em? 4.02. 70
judge by the outside) | i never saw nor read of. 4.02. 75
you never saw him dance? 5.02. 47
half–sights saw | that arcite was no babe. 5.03. 95
lady | did lie in you, for you first saw her, 5.04.117
his eyes saw her eyes as they had not seen them, VEN 357
but when he saw his love, his youth's fair fee, 393
as those poor birds that helpless berries saw. 604
ne'er saw the beauteous livery that he wore — 1107
who fears a sentence or an old man's saw | shall LUC 244
the more she saw the blood his cheeks replenish, 1357
one would swear he saw them quake and tremble. 1393
which when her sad–beholding husband saw, 1590
even so his sighs, his sorrows, make a saw, | to 1672
she showed hers, he saw more wounds than one, PP 9.13
that the turtle saw his right | flaming in the PHT 34
itself confounded, | saw division grow together, 42
i never saw that you did painting need, | and SON 83. 1
since first i saw you fresh, which yet are green 104. 8
fears, | still losing when i saw myself to win? 119. 4
i grant i never saw a goddess go — | my 130.11
but when she saw my woeful state, | straight in 145. 4
whereon the thought might think sometime it saw LC 10
each eye that saw him did enchant the mind, 89
saw how deceits were gilded in his smiling, 172

SAW'D 1 FR 0.0001 REL FR 0 V 1 P
if i were saw'd into quantities, i should make 2H4 5.01. 62 P

SAWEST 3 FR 0.0003 REL FR 2 V 1 P
ago, jack, since thou sawest thine own knee? 1H4 2.04.328 P
cut her hands, and trimm'd her as thou sawest. TIT 5.01. 93
sawest thou not signs of fear lurk in mine eye? VEN 644

SAWN 1 FR 0.0001 REL FR 1 V 0 P
what largeness thinks in paradise was sawn. LC 91

SAWPIT 1 FR 0.0001 REL FR 1 V 0 P
let them from forth a sawpit rush at once | with WIV 4.04. 54

SAWS 4 FR 0.0004 REL FR 3 V 1 P
cut, | full of wise saws and modern instances; AYL 2.07.156
whisper o'er a couplet or two of most sage saws. TN 3.04.378 P
his weapons holy saws of sacred writ, | his 2H6 1.03. 58
all saws of books, all forms, all pressures past HAM 1.05.100

SAW'ST 10 FR 0.0011 REL FR 5 V 5 P
which thou heardst cry, which thou saw'st sink. TMP 1.02. 32
saw'st thou him enter at the abbey here? ERR 5.01.279
wast at court, thou never saw'st good manners; AYL 3.02. 41 P
if thou never saw'st good manners, then thy 3.02. 41 P
what did he when thou saw'st him? 3.02.220 P
saw'st thou not, boy, how silver made it good SHR in.1. 19
say to me, when saw'st thou the prince florizel, WT 4.02. 25 P
saw'st thou the melancholy lord northumberland? R3 5.03. 68
boy, wink at me, and say thou saw'st me not. TIM 3.01. 44 P
thou saw'st them, when i had prosperity. 4.03. 78

SAW'T 6 FR 0.0006 REL FR 4 V 2 P
i saw't i' th' orchard. TN 3.02. 7 P
yes certain, there's a letter for you, i saw't. COR 2.01.113 P
not when i saw't. HAM 1.02.239
i saw't not, thought it not; OTH 3.03.339
in venice, | though i should swear i saw't. 4.01.243
i do think | i saw't this morning; CYM 2.03.145

SAXONS 2 FR 0.0002 REL FR 2 V 0 P
charles the great, having subdu'd the saxons, H5 1.02. 46
and charles the great | subdu'd the saxons, and 1.02. 62

SAXONY'S 1 FR 0.0001 REL FR 0 V 1 P
the young german, the duke of saxony's nephew? MV 1.02. 85 P

/SAY* 13 FR 0.0014 REL FR 9 V 4 P
wind were but long enough /to /say /my /prayers, WIV 4.05.103 P
/will /no /man /say /amen? R2 4.01.172
/say /that /again. 4.01.293
if he be slain, /say /so; 2H4 1.01. 96
/yet /did /you /say, "/go /forth!" 1.01.175
/and /you /shall /say, /indeed, /it /is /the 4.01.103
scars, | /and /say, "/these /wounds /i /had /on H5 4.03. 48
/i /pray /god /he /be /not, /i /say. R3 3.04. 58
/will /they /not /say /afterwards, /if /they HAM 2.02.348 P
/man's /life's /no /more /than /to /say "/one." 5.02. 74
/they /say /edgar, /his /banish'd /son, /is LR 4.07. 89 P
/what /say /you? OTH 1.03.377 P
didst thou not /say, when i did push thee back PER 5.01.126

SAY* 1756 FR 0.1985 REL FR 1206 V 550 P
out of our way, i say. TMP 1.01. 27 P
created | the creatures that were mine, i say, 1.02. 82
the mariners, say how thou hast dispos'd, | and 1.02.225
dull thing, i say so; 1.02.285
say what? 1.02.300
come forth, i say, there's other business for 1.02.315
eye advance | and say what thou seest yond. 1.02.410
what, i say, | my foot my tutor? 1.02.469
pockets could speak, would it not say he lies? 2.01. 67 P
what is it thou didst say? 2.01.212
prithee say on. 2.01.228
how say you? 2.01.254
say this were death | that now hath seiz'd them, 2.01.260
to any business that | we say befits the hour. 2.01.290
o my father, | i have broke your hest to say so! 3.01. 37
they say there's but five upon this isle: 3.02. 5 P
lie like dogs, and yet say nothing neither. 3.02. 20 P
i say by sorcery he got this isle; 3.02. 52
didst thou not say he lied? 3.02. 74 P
i say, to–night. no more. 3.03. 17
if i should say i saw such /islanders | (for, 3.03. 29
thou nothing bated | in what thou hadst to say; 3.03. 86
before you can say "come" and "go," | and 4.01. 44
say again, where didst thou leave these varlots? 4.01.170
your fairy, which you say is a harmless fairy, 4.01.196 P
i did say so, | when first i rais'd the tempest. 5.01. 5
say, my spirit, | how fares the king and 's 5.01. 6
arise, and say how thou cam'st here. 5.01.181
i say amen, gonzalo! 5.01.204
say, how came you hither? 5.01.228
these men, my lords, | then say if they be true. 5.01.268
yet writers say: TGV 1.01. 42
and writers say: 1.01. 45
i say, she did nod; 1.01.113 P
and you ask me if she did nod, and i say, "ay." 1.01.114 P
but say, lucetta, now we are alone, | wouldst 1.02. 1
"to julia" — say, from whom? 1.02. 35

say, say; who gave it thee? 1.02. 37
say, say; who gave it thee? 1.02. 37
say "no" to that | which they would have the 1.02. 55
ay, madam, you may say what sights you see; 1.02.135
by a letter, i should say. 2.01.150 P
what say you to a letter from your friends | of 2.04. 51
they say that love hath not an eye at all. 2.04. 96
shot be paid and the hostess say "welcome." 2.05. 7 P
if he say ay, it will; 2.05. 35 P
if he say no, it will; 2.05. 36 P
if he shake his tail and say nothing, it will. 2.05. 36 P
and, may i say to thee, this pride of hers, 3.01. 72
take no repulse, what ever she doth say; 3.01.100
ne'er so black, say they have angels' faces. 3.01.103
that man that hath a tongue, i say is no man, 3.01.104
sirrah, i say, forbear. 3.01.205
that's as much as to say, "can she so?" 3.01.307 P
that's as much as to say "bastard virtues," that 3.01.318 P
but say this weed her love from valentine, | it 3.02. 49
say that upon the altar of her beauty | you 3.02. 72
say "ay" and be the captain of us all: 4.01. 63
that you shall say my cunning drift excels. 4.02. 83
say that she be; 4.02.108
and i have heard thee say | no grief did ever 4.03. 18
taught him, even as one would say precisely, 4.04. 5 P
i would have (as one should say) one that takes 4.04. 11 P
away, i say! 4.04. 61
for i have heard him say a thousand times | his 4.04.134
now i dare not say | i have one friend alive; 5.04. 65
forbear, forbear, i say; 5.04.122
i heard say he was outrun on cotsall. WIV 1.01. 90 P
slice, i say! 1.01.132 P
i will say "marry trap" with you, if you run the 1.01.167 P
what say you, scarlet and john? 1.01.173 P
i say the gentleman had drunk himself out of his 1.01.174 P
and being fap, sir, was, as they say, cashier'd; 1.01.178 P
but if you say, "marry her," i will marry her; 1.01.250 P
and "to her, boy," say i. 1.03. 55 P
peter simple, you say your name is? 1.04. 15 P
how say you? 1.04. 28 P
what, john, i say! 1.04. 40 P
i will not say, pity me — 'tis not a 2.01. 12 P
'tis not a soldier–like phrase — but i say, 2.01. 13 P
what should i say to him? 2.01. 27 P
yet i say i could show you to the contrary. 2.01. 40 P
the horn, i say. 2.01.121
cavaleiro justice, i say! 2.01.194 P
well, on. mistress ford, you say — 2.02. 47 P
(in any such sort, as they say) but in the way 2.02. 73 P
why, you say well. 2.02. 94 P
do what she will, say what she will, take all, 2.02.118 P
have discretion, as they say, and know the world 2.02.130 P
let them say 'tis grossly done, so it be fairly 2.02.142 P
for they say, if money go before, all ways do 2.02.168 P
rate, and that hath taught me to say this: 2.02.206 P
some say that, though she appear honest to me, 2.02.221 P
what say you to't, sir john? 2.02.251 P
i say you shall. 2.02.257 P
i say i shall be with her between ten and eleven 2.02.264 P
they say the jealous wittolly knave hath masses 2.02.272 P
peace, i say, gallia and gaul, french and welsh, 3.01. 97 P
peace, i say! 3.01.100 P
what say you to young master fenton? 3.02. 66 P
i warrant. what, robin, i say! 3.03. 4 P
/by /the /lord, thou art a tyrant to say so. 3.03. 61 P
i cannot cog and say thou art this and that, 3.03. 70 P
thou mightst as well say i love to walk by the 3.03. 77 P
bardolph, i say! 3.05. 1 P
had been one number more, because they say, 4.01. 24 P
what, wife, i say! 4.02.119 P
so say i too, sir. 4.02.128 P
empty the basket, i say! 4.02.143 P
let them say of me, "as jealous as ford, that 4.02.163 P
down, you witch, you hag you, come down, i say! 4.02.179 P
you say he has been thrown in the rivers, and 4.04. 20 P
knock, i say. 4.05. 10 P
say the woman told me so. 4.05. 51 P
may i be bold to say so, sir? 4.05. 53 P
meet the duke, villain, do not say they be fled. 4.05. 72 P
here is a letter will say somewhat. 4.05.123 P
they say there is divinity in odd numbers, 5.01. 3 P
away, i say, time wears, hold up your head and 5.01. 7 P
call hither, | i say, bid come before us angelo. MM 1.01. 15
nay, not, as one would say, healthy; 1.02. 55 P
and yet, to say the truth, i had as lief have 1.02.133 P
was (as they say) pluck'd down in the suburbs; 2.01. 65 P
i say, sir, i will detest myself also, as well 2.01. 75 P
as i say, this mistress elbow, being (as i say) 2.01. 97 P
mistress elbow, being (as i say) with child, and 2.01. 98 P
and (as i say) paying for them very honestly; 2.01.102 P
sir, sitting (as i say) in a lower chair, sir — 2.01.128 P
what say you to it? 2.01.160 P
see this come to pass, say pompey told you so. 2.01.243 P
you say seven years together? 2.01.262 P
to him, i say! 2.02. 47
say you so? 2.04. 51
how say you? 2.04. 58
for i can speak | against the thing i say. 2.04. 60
as for you, | say what you can: 2.04.170
say to thyself, | from their abominable and 3.02. 23
go say i sent thee thither. 3.02. 64 P
some say he is with the emperor of russia; 3.02. 88 P
they say this angelo was not made by man and 3.02.104 P
the duke (i say to thee again) would eat mutton 3.02.181 P
yet (and i say to thee) he would mouth with a 3.02.182 P
say that i said so. 3.02.184 P
little have you to say | when you depart from 4.01. 67
painting, sir, i have heard say, is a mystery; 4.02. 36 P
what say you to this, sir? 4.02.127 P
and say it was the desire of the penitent to be 4.02.175 P
if you have any thing to say to me, come to my 4.03. 62 P
mark what i say, which you shall find | by every 4.03.125
say, by this token, i desire his company | at 4.03.139
but they say the duke will be here to–morrow. 4.03.155 P
i would say the truth, but to accuse him so, 4.06. 2
what would you say? 5.01. 68
and say by whose advice | thou cam'st here to 5.01.113
no? you say your husband. 5.01.201
did not you say you knew that friar lodowick to 5.01.260 P
say you? 5.01.274 P
say: 5.01.375
hold up your hands, say nothing; 5.01.438
they say best men are moulded out of faults, 5.01.439
stand up, i say. 5.01.455
give me your hand and say you will be mine, | he 5.01.492
say in brief the cause | why thou departedst ERR 1.01. 28
but ere they came — o, let me say no more! 1.01. 94
they say this town is full of cozenage: 1.02. 97
say, is your tardy master now at hand? 2.01. 44
say, didst thou speak with him? 2.01. 47
but say, i prithee, is he coming home? 2.01. 55
for they say, every why hath a wherefore. 2.02. 43 P
but say, sir, is it dinner–time? 2.02. 54 P
say he dines forth, and let no creature enter. 2.02.210
i'll say as they say, and persever so, | and in 2.02.215
i'll say as they say, and persever so, | and in 2.02.215
say that i linger'd with you at your shop | to 3.01. 3
say what you will, sir, but i know what i know: 3.01. 11
you would say so, master, if your garments were 3.01. 70
may not speak of without he say "sir–reverence." 3.02. 91 P
good sir, say whe'r you'll answer me or no: 4.01. 60
you gave me none, you wrong me much to say so. 4.01. 66
ah, but i think him better than i say, | and yet 4.02. 25
have you not heard men say, | that time comes 4.02. 59
and thereof comes that the wenches say, "god 4.03. 53 P
"god damn me," that's as much as to say, "god make 4.03. 54 P
how say you now? is not your husband mad? 4.04. 45
sir, sooth to say, you did not dine at home. 4.04. 69
say, wherefore didst thou lock me forth to–day? 4.04. 95
say now, whose suit is he arrested at? 4.04.131
say, how grows it due? 4.04.134
a grievous fault! say, woman, didst thou so? 5.01.206
my liege, i am advised what i say, | neither 5.01.214
you say he din'd at home; 5.01.274
sirrah, what say you? 5.01.275
no, i say nay to that. 5.01.372
an old cuckold with horns on his head, and say, ADO 2.01. 45 P
it is my cousin's duty to make cur'sy and say, 2.01. 53 P
or else make another cur'sy and say, "father, as 2.01. 55 P
and look sweetly, and say nothing, i am yours 2.01. 89 P
i may say so when i please. 2.01. 92 P
and when please you to say so? 2.01. 93 P
i say my prayers aloud. 2.01.104 P
know the gentleman, i'll tell him what you say. 2.01.145 P
your saying, by my faith you say honestly. 2.01.235 P
your grace may well say i have lost it. 2.01.281 P
made the match, and all grace say amen to it. 2.01.304 P
were but little happy, if i could say how much! 2.01.307 P
for i have heard my daughter say, she hath often 2.01.345 P
tell benedick of it, and hear what 'a will say. 2.03.171 P
the managing of quarrels you may say he is wise, 2.03.190 P
they say i will bear myself proudly, if i 2.03.225 P
they say too that she will rather die than give 2.03.226 P
they say the lady is fair; 2.03.230 P
pains to thank me" — that's as much as to say, 2.03.261 P
say that thou overheardst us, | and bid her 3.01. 6
yet tell her of it, hear what she will say. 3.01. 81
for others say thou dost deserve, and i 3.01.115
so say i, methinks you are sadder. 3.02. 16 P
yet say i, he is in love. 3.02. 30 P
that's as much as to say, the sweet youth's in 3.02. 52 P
for the which i hear what they say of him. 3.02. 58 P
i could say she were worse; 3.02.110 P
so will you say when you have seen the sequel. 3.02.134 P
you may say they are not the men you took them 3.03. 47 P
conrade, i say! 3.03. 97 P
tush, i may as well say the fool's the fool. 3.03.123 P
seest thou not, i say, what a deformed thief 3.03.130 P
so good, and i warrant your cousin will say so. 3.04. 10 P
o, that exceeds, they say. 3.04. 17 P
i think you would have me say, "saving your 3.04. 32 P
it pleases your worship to say so, but we are 3.05. 19 P
i would fain know what you have to say. 3.05. 29 P
as they say, "when the age is in, the wit is out 3.05. 34 P
i know what you would say. 4.01. 48
you will say, she did embrace me as a husband, 4.01. 49
so attir'd in wonder, | i know not what to say. 4.01.145
as possible for me to say i lov'd nothing so 4.01.270 P
i must say she is dead; 4.01.335 P
marry, sir, we say we are none. 4.02. 24 P
i say to you, it is thought you are false knaves 4.02. 27 P
sir, i say to you, we are none. 4.02. 29 P
what heard you him say else? 4.02. 46 P
i say thou hast belied mine innocent child! 5.01. 67
thine, claudio, thine, i say. 5.01. 72
you say not right, old man. 5.01. 73
not carve most curiously, say my knife's naught. 5.01.156 P
did he not say my brother was fled? 5.01.204 P
they say he wears a key in his ear and a lock 5.01.308 P
any purpose that the world can say against it, 5.04.106 P
i can but say their protestation over: LLL 1.01. 33
let me say no, my liege, and if you please: 1.01. 50
swear me to this, and i will ne'er say no. 1.01. 69
well, say i am, why should proud summer boast 1.01.102
than for that angel knowledge you can say, | yet 1.01.113
what say you, lords? why, this was quite forgot. 1.01.141
but if he say it is so, he is, in telling true 1.01.224 P
but with this i passion to say wherewith" — 1.01.261 P
but, sirrah, what say you to this? 1.01.282 P
i do say thou art quick in answers; 1.02. 29 P
i say, sing. 1.02.125 P
so i heard you say. 1.02.142 P
their words, and therefore i will say nothing. 1.02.164 P
they say so most that most his humors know. 2.01. 53
but say that he, or we, as neither have, 2.01.132
i say lead is slow. 3.01. 61
you are too swift, sir, to say so. 3.01. 61
i will add the l'envoy. say the moral again. 3.01. 87 P
first praise me, and again say no? 4.01. 14
and he it was that might rightly say, veni, vidi 4.01. 67 P
but omne bene, say i, being of an old father's 4.02. 32
i say, th' allusion holds in the exchange. 4.02. 44 P
and i say, the pollution holds in the exchange, 4.02. 46 P
and i say beside that, 'twas a pricket that the 4.02. 48 P
some say a sore, but not a sore, till now made 4.02. 57
i do invite you too, you shall not say me nay: 4.02.165 P
for so they say the fool said, and so say i, and 4.03. 4 P
for so they say the fool said, and so say i, and 4.03. 5 P
stoop, i say, | her shoulder is with child. 4.03. 87
what will berowne say when that he shall hear 4.03.143
say, can you fast? 4.03.290
speak "dout," fine, when he should say "doubt"; 5.01. 20 P
ad dunghill, at the fingers' ends, as they say. 5.01. 78 P
i say none so fit as to present the nine 5.01.122 P
say, scout, say. 5.02. 88
say, scout, say. 5.02. 88
what would they, say they? 5.02.180
say to her we have measur'd many miles, | to 5.02.184
they say that they have measur'd many a mile 5.02.186
say you so? 5.02.239
i am, as /they say, but to parfect one man in 5.02.501 P
i say they shall not come. 5.02.514
but we will put it, as they say, to fortuna de 5.02.530 P
if your ladyship would say, "thanks, pompey," i 5.02.556
prepare, i say. 5.02.729
o, shall i say, i thank you, gentle wife? 5.02.826
i'll mark no words that smooth–fac'd wooers say. 5.02.828
what say you, hermia? MND 1.01. 46
and ere a man hath power to say "behold!" 1.01.147
good peter quince, say what the play treats on; 1.02. 8 P
that i will make the duke say, "let him roar 1.02. 72 P
pride, | if hermia meant to say lysander lied. 2.02. 55
amen, amen, to that fair prayer, say i — | and 2.02. 62
do not say so, lysander, say not so. 2.02.108
do not say so, lysander, say not so. 2.02.108
the prologue seem to say we will do no harm with 3.01. 18 P
and a lantern, and say he comes to disfigure, or 3.01. 60 P
what say you, bottom? 3.01. 65 P
doth move me | on the first view to say, to 3.01.141
and yet, to say the truth, reason and love keep 3.01.143 P
i say i love thee more than he can do. 3.02.254
if thou say so, withdraw, and prove it too. 3.02.255
in earnest, shall i say? 3.02.277
i am amaz'd, and know not what to say. 3.02.344
or say, sweet love, what thou desirest to eat. 4.01. 30
dispatch, i say, and find the forester. 4.01.108
i swear, | i cannot truly say how i came here. 4.01.148
past the wit of man to say what dream it was. 4.01.206 P
if he will offer to say what methought i had. 4.01.210 P
you must say "paragon." 4.02. 13 P
and i do not doubt but to hear them say, it is a 4.02. 44 P
say, what abridgment have you for this evening? 5.01. 39
all that i have to say is to tell you that the 5.01.257 P
it wearies me, you say it wearies you; MV 1.01. 2
then let us say you are sad | because you are 1.01. 47
and say you are merry | because you are not sad. 1.01. 49
say, when? 1.01. 66
as who should say, "i am sir oracle, | and when 1.01. 93
then do but say to me what i should do | that in 1.01.158
he doth nothing but frown, as who should say, 1.02. 47 P
how say you by the french lord, monsieur le /bon 1.02. 54 P
what say you then to falconbridge, the young 1.02. 66 P
you know i say nothing to him, for he 1.02. 68 P
no, not take interest, not, as you would say, 1.03. 76
go to then, you come to me, and you say, 1.03.115
"shylock, we would have moneys," you say so — 1.03.116
what should i say to you? 1.03.120
should i not say, | "hath a dog money? 1.03.120
breath and whisp'ring humbleness, | say this: 1.03.125
and say there is much kindness in the jew. 1.03.153
i say, | to buy his favor, i extend this 1.03.167
"conscience," say i, "you counsel well." 2.02. 21 P
"fiend," say i, "you counsel well." 2.02. 22 P
or, as you would say in plain terms, gone to 2.02. 64 P
infection, sir, as one would say, to serve — 2.02.126 P
old man, and, though i say it, though old man, 2.02.139 P
eyes | thus with my hat, and sigh and say amen, 2.02.194
and rend apparel out — | why, jessica, i say! 2.05. 6
i will not say you shall see a masque, but if 2.05. 23 P
go you before me, sirrah, | say i will come. 2.05. 39
thou wilt say anon he is some kin to thee, 2.09. 97
of many a tall ship lie buried, as they say, if 3.01. 6 P
let me say amen betimes, lest the devil cross my 3.01. 19 P
i say, my daughter is my flesh and my blood. 3.01. 37 P
the other half yours — | mine own, i would say; 3.02. 17
o, then be bold to say bassanio's dead! 3.02.185
i'll tell my husband, launcelot, what you say. 3.05. 27 P
and now, good sweet, say thy opinion, | how dost 3.05. 71
but say it is my humor, is it answer'd? 4.01. 43
shall i say to you, | "let them be free! 4.01. 93
you, merchant, have you any thing to say? 4.01.263
say how i lov'd you, speak me fair in death; 4.01.275
a daniel, still say i, a second daniel! 4.01.340
in which predicament i say thou stand'st; 4.01.357
art thou contented, jew? what dost thou say? 4.01.393
what should i say, sweet lady? 5.01.215
let me go, i say. AYL 1.01. 65 P
they say he is already in the forest of arden, 1.01.114 P
they say many young gentlemen flock to him every 1.01.117 P
can i not say, i thank you? 1.02.249
say what thou canst, i'll go along with thee. 1.03.105
even till i shrink with cold, i smile and say, 2.01. 9
peace, i say. good even to /you, friend. 2.04. 69
when that i say the city–woman bears | the cost 2.07. 75
who can come in and say that i mean her, | when 2.07. 77
but forbear, i say, | he dies that touches any 2.07. 97
a better instance, i say; 3.02. 58 P
to say ay and no to these particulars is more 3.02.227 P
sweet, say on. 3.02.250 P
but — wind away, | be gone, i say, | i will not 3.03.104
and you shall say | i'll prove a busy actor in 3.04. 58
say that you love me not, but say not so | in 3.05. 2
you love me not, but say not so | in bitterness. 3.05. 2
lie not, to say mine eyes are murtherers! 3.05. 19
they say you are a melancholy fellow. 4.01. 3 P
why, 'tis good to be sad and say nothing. 4.01. 8 P
what would you say to me now, and i were your 4.01. 70 P
i take some joy to say you are, because i would 4.01. 89 P
well, in her person, i say i will not have you. 4.01. 91 P
what do you say, sister? 4.01.126 P
i cannot say the words. 4.01.128 P
then you must say, "i take thee, rosalind, for 4.01.135 P
say "a day," without the "ever." 4.01.146 P
that had a wife with such a wit, he might say, 4.01.166 P

marry, to say she came to seek you there. 4.01.171 P
how say you now? 4.03. 1 P
i say she never did invent this letter, | this 4.03. 28
made thee a tame snake) and say this to her: 4.03. 70 P
it is no boast, being ask'd, to say we are. 4.03. 90
but say with me, i love aliena; 5.02. 7 P
say with her that she loves me; 5.02. 8 P
of my knowledge, insomuch i say i know you are; 5.02. 55 P
i tender dearly, though i say i am a magician. 5.02. 71 P
you say, if i bring in your rosalind, | you will 5.04. 6
and you say you will have her, when i bring her. 5.04. 9
you say you'll marry me, if i be willing? 5.04. 11
you say that you'll have phebe, if she will? 5.04. 16
again, it was not well cut, he would say i lie: 5.04. 80 P
and how oft did you say his beard was not well 5.04. 83 P
and with a low submissive reverence | say, "what SHR in.1. 54
and say, "will't please your lordship cool your in.1. 58
and when he says he is, say that he dreams, in.1. 64
he is no less than what we say he is. in.1. 71
and say, "what is't your honor will command, in.1. 115
if she say i am not fourteen pence on the score in.2. 22 P
say thou wilt walk; in.2. 40
say thou wilt course, thy greyhounds are as in.2. 47
yet would you say ye were beaten out of door, in.2. 85
and say you would present her at the leet, in.2. 87
they say that i have dream'd | and slept above in.2. 112
i say, a husband. 1.01.122 P
i say, a devil. 1.01.123 P
faith, as you say, there's small choice in 1.01.134 P
how say you, signior gremio? 1.01.141 P
here, sirrah grumio, knock, i say. 1.02. 5
villain, i say, knock me here soundly. 1.02. 8
villain, i say, knock me at this gate, | and rap 1.02. 11
con tutto /il core, ben trovato, may i say. 1.02. 24
sir, you say well, and well you do conceive, 1.02.269
say that she rail, why then i'll tell her plain 2.01.170
say that she frown, i'll say she looks as clear 2.01.172
i'll say she looks as clear | as morning roses 2.01.172
say she be mute, and will not speak a word, 2.01.174
and say she uttereth piercing eloquence; 2.01.176
i know not what to say, but give me your hands. 2.01.318
amen, say we. we will be witnesses. 2.01.320
say, signior gremio, what can you assure her? 2.01.345
and say, "lo, there is mad petruchio's wife, 3.02. 19
but say, what to thine old news? 3.02. 42 P
didst thou not say he comes? 3.02. 76 P
sir, i say his horse comes, with him on his back 3.02. 79 P
which once perform'd, let all the world say no, 3.02.141
a bridegroom, say you? 3.02.152
why, when, i say? 4.01.143
he is my father, sir, and, sooth to say, | in 4.02. 99
as who should say, if i should sleep or eat, 4.03. 13
what say you to a neat's foot? 4.03. 17
how say you to a fat tripe finely broil'd? 4.03. 20
what say you to a piece of beef and mustard? 4.03. 23
go get thee gone, i say. 4.03. 35
your betters have endur'd me say my mind, | and 4.03. 75
i say unto thee, i bid thy master cut out the 4.03.126 P
the note lies in 's throat if he say i said so. 4.03.132 P
this is true that i say; 4.03.149 P
hortensio, say thou wilt see the tailor paid. 4.03.164
go take it hence, be gone, and say no more. 4.03.165
away, i say, commend me to thy master. 4.03.168
i do, | it shall be what a' clock i say it is. 4.03.195
sir, pardon me in what i have to say — | your 4.04. 38
and therefore, if you say no more than this, 4.04. 43
be not that you look for, i have no more to say, 4.04. 96
i say it is the moon that shines so bright. 4.05. 4
say as he says, or we shall never go. 4.05. 11
i say it is the moon. 4.05. 16
but sun it is not, when you say it is not; 4.05. 19
i say he shall go to prison. 5.01. 96 P
then thou wert best say that i am not lucentio. 5.01.103 P
would say your head and butt were head and horn. 5.02. 41
well, i say no; 5.02. 65
your mistress, | say i command her come to me. 5.02. 96
away, i say, and bring them hither straight. 5.02.105
come on, i say, and first begin with her. 5.02.133
i say she shall, and first begin with her. 5.02.135
when thou hast leisure, say thy prayers; AWW 1.01.213 P
he would always say — | methinks i hear him now 1.02. 52
what say you of this gentlewoman? 1.03. 1 P
for they say barnes are blessings. 1.03. 25 P
i say i am your mother, | and put you in the 1.03.142
does it curd thy blood | to say i am thy mother? 1.03.150
i say i am your mother. 1.03.154
of thy passion, | to say thou dost not: 1.03.175
i say farewell. 2.01. 17
they say our french lack language to deny | if 2.01. 20
say to him i live, and observe his reports for 2.01. 45 P
this is his majesty, say your mind to him. 2.01. 95
i say we must not | so stain our judgment, or 2.01.119
kiss his hand, and say nothing, has neither leg, 2.02. 11 P
and indeed such a fellow, to say precisely, were 2.02. 12 P
have you, i say, an answer of such fitness for 2.02. 28 P
they say miracles are past, and we have our 2.03. 1 P
so i say, both of galen and paracelsus. 2.03. 11 P
right, so i say. 2.03. 13 P
why, there 'tis, so say i too. 2.03. 15 P
just, you say well; so would i have said. 2.03. 19 P
i may truly say it is a novelty to the world. 2.03. 20 P
ay, so i say. 2.03. 32 P
you say well. 2.03. 39 P
i dare not say i take you, but i give | me and 2.03.102
my knowledge, that i may say in the default, "he 2.03.229 P
and i her money, i would she did as you say. 2.04. 21 P
why, i say nothing. 2.04. 22 P
to say nothing, to do nothing, to know nothing, 2.04. 25 P
sir, i can nothing say, | but that i am your 2.05. 71
well, what would you say? 2.05. 78
of the wealth i owe, | nor dare i say 'tis mine; 2.05. 80
therefore dare not | say what i think of it, 3.01. 14
so say i, madam, if he run away, as i hear he 3.02. 40 P
do not say so. 3.02. 47
they say the french count has done most 3.05. 3 P
but you say she's honest. 3.06.111
what shall i say i have done? 4.01. 25 P
some hurts, and say i got them in exploit. 4.01. 37 P
they will say, "came you off with so little?" 4.01. 39 P
of my beard, and to say it was in stratagem. 4.01. 49 P
or to drown my clothes, and say i was stripp'd. 4.01. 52 P
say thou art mine, and ever | my love, as it 4.02. 36
which could not be her office to say is come, 4.03. 58 P
he can say nothing of me. 4.03.116 P
what will you say without 'em? 4.03.121 P
if ye pinch me like a pasty, i can say no more. 4.03.123 P
what say you to that? 4.03.130 P
i said — i will say true — "or thereabouts," 4.03.149 P
"poor rogues," i pray you say. 4.03.154 P
what say you to that? 4.03.159 P
what say you to this? 4.03.180 P
a dumb innocent, that could not say him nay. 4.03.188 P
and say a soldier, dian, told thee this: 4.03.227
i have but little more to say, sir, of his 4.03.258 P
what say you to his expertness in war? 4.03.265 P
this i must say — | but first i beg my pardon 5.03. 11
me when his wife was dead, i blush to say it, he 5.03.141 P
already, unless thou canst say they are married. 5.03.268 P
this ring you say was yours? 5.03.270
they say, she hath abjur'd the /company | and TN 1.02. 40
fie, that you'll say so! 1.03. 25 P
scoundrels and substractors that say so of him. 1.03. 35 P
say i do speak with her, my lord, what then? 1.04. 23
thy happy years, | that say thou art a man. 1.04. 31
and that may you be bold to say in your foolery. 1.05. 12 P
bade take away the fool, therefore i say again, 1.05. 53 P
that's as much to say as i wear not motley in my 1.05. 56 P
how say you to that, malvolio? 1.05. 82 P
give me faith, say i. 1.05.129 P
i can say little more than i have studied, and 1.05.178 P
have you no more to say? 1.05.229 P
faith, so they say, but i think it rather 2.03. 11 P
marian, i say! 2.03. 14 P
say that some lady, as perhaps there is, | hath 2.04. 89
we men may say more, swear more, but indeed 2.04.116
say | my love can give no place, bide no denay. 2.04.123
peace, i say! 2.05. 34 P
excellent wench, say i. 2.05.109 P
did not i say he would work it out? 2.05.127 P
i say, remember. 2.05.154 P
nay, but say true, does it work upon him? 2.05.195 P
so thou mayst say, the /king lies by a beggar, 3.01. 8 P
are out of my welkin — i might say "element," 3.01. 58 P
do you know what you say? 3.04. 99 P
lady would not lose him for more than i'll say. 3.04.105 P
get him to say his prayers, good sir toby, get 3.04.118 P
they say he has been fencer to the sophy. 3.04.278 P
o, say so, and so be! 4.01. 65
goes as fairly as to say a careful man and a 4.02. 9 P
what ho, i say! peace in this prison! 4.02. 18 P
mad, sir topas, i say to you this house is dark. 4.02. 40 P
i say there is no darkness but ignorance, in 4.02. 42 P
i say this house is as dark as ignorance, though 4.02. 45 P
and i say there was never man thus abus'd. 4.02. 46 P
fool, i say! 4.02. 78 P
advise you what you say; 4.02. 94 P
fool, fool, fool, i say! 4.02.102 P
what say you, sir? 4.02.103 P
what do you say? 4.03. 31
but, as you say, sir, let your bounty take a nap 5.01. 48 P
what do you say, cesario? good my lord — 5.01.106
and say, "thrice welcome, drowned viola!" 5.01.241
they say, poor gentleman, he's much distract. 5.01.280
or say 'tis not your seal, not your invention. 5.01.333
you can say none of this. 5.01.334
in so rare — i know not what to say — we will WT 1.01. 13 P
no sneaping winds at home, to make us say, 1.02. 13
say this to him, | he's beat from his best ward. 1.02. 32
but let him say so then, and let him go; 1.02. 35
with oaths, | should yet say, "sir, no going." 1.02. 49
how say you? 1.02. 54
lest you say | your queen and i are devils. 1.02. 81
they say it is a copy out of mine. 1.02.122
yet they say we are | almost as like as eggs; 1.02.129
women say so — | that will say any thing. 1.02.130
women say so — | that will say any thing. 1.02.131
yet were it true | to say this boy were like me. 1.02.135
i am like you, /they say. 1.02.208
say. 1.02.228
thought, then say | my wife's a /hobby–horse, 1.02.275
say it be, 'tis true. 1.02.298
i say thou liest, camillo, and i hate thee, 1.02.300
know, you must, | and cannot say you dare not. 1.02.380
yet black brows, they say, | become some women 2.01. 8
but i'ld say he had not; 2.01. 62
be but about | to say she is a goodly lady, and 2.01. 66
come between | ere you can say she's honest: 2.01. 76
should a villain say so, | the most replenish'd 2.01. 78
me throughly, then, to say | you did mistake. 2.01. 99
i can hook to me — say that she were gone, 2.03. 7
i say, i come | from your good queen. 2.03. 57
queen, my lord, good queen, i say good queen, 2.03. 60
take up the bastard, | take't up, i say; 2.03. 77
and wilt encounter with my wrath, say so; 2.03.139
wolves and bears, they say, | casting their 2.03.187
since what i am to say must be but that | which 3.02. 22
it shall scarce boot me | to say "not guilty." 3.02. 26
i say she's dead; 3.02.203
say no more. 3.02.216
your patience to you, | and i'll say nothing. 3.02.232
but i am not to say it is a sea, for it is now 3.03. 84 P
if never, yet that time himself doth say, | he 4.01. 31
say to me, when saw'st thou the prince florizel, 4.02. 25 P
a man, they say, that from very nothing, and 4.02. 38 P
his vices, you would say; 4.03. 91 P
vices, i would say, sir. 4.03. 94 P
what would he say? 4.04. 22
i am most constant, | though destiny say no. 4.04. 46
say there be; 4.04. 88
over that art | which you say adds to nature, is 4.04. 91
would wish | this youth should say 'twere well, 4.04.102
say, whither? 4.04.308
dance which the wenches say is a gallimaufry of 4.04.328 P
but, my daughter, | say you the like to him? 4.04.380
you forth at every sitting | what you must say; 4.04.562
say you so? 4.04.577
i cannot say 'tis pity | she lacks instructions, 4.04.581
who, i may say, is no honest man, neither to his 4.04.700 P
say you have none. 4.04.743 P
some say he shall be ston'd; 4.04.778 P
but that death is too soft for him, say i. 4.04.779 P
we are bless'd in this man, as i may say, even 4.04.827 P
but thou strik'st me | sorely, to say i did. 5.01. 18
now, good now, | say so but seldom. 5.01. 20
his princess, say you, with him? 5.01. 93
shrewdly ebb'd, | to say you have seen a better. 5.01.103
whom he loves | (he bade me say so) more than 5.01.146
methought, i heard the shepherd say, he found 5.02. 7 P
could not say if th' importance were joy or 5.02. 17 P
i would fain say, bleed tears; 5.02. 88 P
hermione that they say one would speak to her 5.02.101 P
say you see them not and think me still no 5.02.130 P
you were best say these robes are not gentlemen 5.02.132 P
you may say it, but not swear it. 5.02.158 P
let boors and franklins say it, i'll swear it. 5.02.160 P
behold, and say 'tis well. 5.03. 20
that i may say indeed | thou art hermione; 5.03. 24
and do not say 'tis superstition, that | i kneel 5.03. 43
now say, chatillion, what would france with us? JN 1.01. 1
who, as you say, took pains to get this son, 1.01.121
i durst not stick a rose | lest men should say, 1.01.143
who lives and dares but say thou didst not well 1.01.271
and they shall say, when richard me begot, | if 1.01.274
who says it was, he lies, i say 'twas not. 1.01.276
what england says, say briefly, gentle lord, 2.01. 52
i have but this to say, | that he is not only 2.01.183
say, shall the current of our right roam on? 2.01.335
let it be so. say, where will you assault? 2.01.408
if not complete of, say he is not she, | and she 2.01.434
what say you? 2.01.483
what say these young ones? 2.01.521
what say you, my niece? 2.01.521
do | what you in wisdom still vouchsafe to say. 2.01.523
rail, | and say there is no sin but to be rich; 2.01.594
shall be | to say there is no vice but beggary. 2.01.596
it cannot be, thou dost but say 'tis so. 3.01. 6
thou dar'st not say so, villain, for thy life. 3.01.132
what should he say, but as the cardinal? 3.01.203
i am perplex'd, and know not what to say. 3.01.221
what canst thou say but will perplex thee more, 3.01.222
i had a thing to say, | but i will fit it with 3.03. 25
to say what good respect i have of thee. 3.03. 28
good friend, thou hast no cause to say so yet, 3.03. 30
i had a thing to say, but let it go. 3.03. 33
well, i'll not say what i intend for thee. 3.03. 68
i have heard you say | that we shall see and 3.04. 76
if you say ay, the king will not say no. 3.04.183
if you say ay, the king will not say no. 3.04.183
i have to say with you. 4.01. 8
give me the iron, i say, and bind him here. 4.01. 74
which (as they say) attend | the steps of wrong, 4.02. 56
whom they say is kill'd to–night | on your 4.02.165
my lord, they say five moons were seen to–night; 4.02.182
stand back, lord salisbury, stand back, i say; 4.03. 81
keep the peace, i say. 4.03. 93
prophet | say that before ascension–day at noon 5.01. 26
they say king john, sore sick, hath left the 5.04. 6
i say again, if lewis do win the day, | he is 5.04. 30
as to be hush'd and nought at all to say. R2 1.01. 53
besides i say, and will in battle prove, | or 1.01. 92
further i say, and further will maintain | upon 1.01. 98
our doctors say this is no month to bleed. 1.01.157
what shall i say? 1.02. 35
say who thou art | and why thou comest thus 1.03. 11
i look'd when some of you should say | i was too 1.03.243
go, say i sent thee forth to purchase honor, 1.03.282
and say, what store of parting tears were shed? 1.04. 5
but they say the tongues of dying men | enforce 2.01. 5
he that no more must say is listened more | than 2.01. 9
right, you say true: 2.01.145
now, afore god — god forbid i say true! 2.01.200
but i dare not say | how near the tidings of our 2.01.271
sister — cousin, i would say — pray pardon me. 2.02.105
tongue, | before i make reply to aught you say. 2.03. 73
castle, which they say is held | by bushy, bagot 2.03.164
uncle, you say the queen is at your house, | for 3.01. 36
say, is my kingdom lost? 3.02. 95
thus, | how can you say to me i am a king? 3.02.177
say, scroop, where lies our uncle with his power 3.02.192
my tongue hath but a heavier tale to say. 3.02.197
what say you now? 3.02.206
the lord northumberland | to say king richard. 3.03. 8
northumberland, say thus the king returns: 3.03.121
then i must not say no. 3.03.209
why dost thou say king richard is depos'd? 3.04. 77
say, where, when, and how, | /cam'st thou by 3.04. 79
to breathe this news, yet what i say is true: 3.04. 82
i heard you say, "is not my arm of length, 4.01. 11
i heard you say that you had rather refuse | the 4.01. 15
i say thou liest, | and will maintain what thou 4.01. 26
i heard thee say, and vauntingly thou spak'st it 4.01. 36
and spit upon him whilst i say he lies, | and 4.01. 75
i heard the banished norfolk say | that thou, 4.01. 80
once more, adieu, the rest let sorrow say. 5.01.102
i will be satisfied, let me see it, i say. 5.02. 71
give me my boots, i say, saddle my horse. 5.02. 77
give me my boots, i say. 5.02. 87
for there, they say, he daily doth frequent, 5.03. 6
even such, they say, as stand in narrow lanes 5.03. 8
nay, do not say "stand up"; 5.03.111
say "pardon" first, and afterwards "stand up." 5.03.112
say "pardon," king, let pity teach thee how. 5.03.116
speak it in french, king, say "pardonne moy." 5.03.119
he wishtly look'd on me | as who should say, "i 5.04. 8
my tongue dares not, that my heart shall say. 5.05. 97
god save thy grace — majesty i should say, for 1H4 1.02. 17 P
and let men say we be men of good government, 1.02. 27 P
therefore i say — 1.03.187
peace, cousin, say no more. 1.03.187
you say true. 1.03.250
happy man be his dole, say i, every man to his 2.02. 76 P
say you so, say you so? 2.03. 14 P
say you so, say you so? 2.03. 14 P
i say unto you again, you are a shallow, 2.03. 14 P

a plague of all cowards, i say, and a vengeance 2.04.114 P
a bad world, i say. 2.04.132 P
a plague of all cowards, i say still. 2.04.134 P
a plague of all cowards, still say i. 2.04.156 P
as thou hast done, and then say it was in fight! 2.04.262 P
but to say i know more harm in him than in 2.04.466 P
than in myself, were to say more than i know. 2.04.467 P
play, i have much to say in the behalf of that 2.04.485 P
i say the earth did shake when i was born. 3.01. 20
and i say the earth was not of my mind, | if you 3.01. 21
who shall say me nay? 3.01.116
others would say, "where, which is bullingbrook? 3.02. 49
and what say you to this? 3.02.118
would cudgel him like a dog if he would say so. 3.03. 87 P
my lord, and i said i heard your grace say so; 3.03.106 P
say, what thing? what thing? 3.03.116 P
aside, thou art a beast to say otherwise. 3.03.123 P
say, what beast, thou knave, thou? 3.03.124 P
i say 'tis copper. 3.03.143 P
what say you to it? 4.01. 41
and the shirt, to say the truth, stol'n from my 4.02. 45 P
why say you so? looks he not for supply? 4.03. 3
to–night, say i. 4.03. 15
what say you to it? 5.01. 15
say thy prayers, and farewell. 5.01.124 P
deliver what you will, i'll say 'tis so. 5.02. 26
i'll follow, as they say, for reward. 5.04.162 P
what shall i say you are? 2H4 1.01. 2
say, morton, didst thou come from shrewsbury? 1.01. 64
this thou wouldst say, "your son did thus and 1.01. 76
yet, for all this, say not that percy's dead. 1.01. 93
yet he will not stick to say his face is a face 1.02. 22 P
why, sir, did i say you were an honest man? 1.02. 80 P
in your throat if you say i am any other than an 1.02. 85 P
i heard say your lordship was sick, i hope your 1.02. 95 P
the disease, for you hear not what i say to you. 1.02.119 P
if i did say of wax, my growth would approve the 1.02.159 P
if ye will needs say i am an old man, you should 1.02.216 P
and first, lord marshal, what say you to it? 1.03. 4
if a man will make curtsy and say nothing, he is 2.01.124 P
i say to you, i do desire deliverance from these 2.01.126 P
but the midwives say the children are not in the 2.02. 25 P
the worst that they can say of me is that i am a 2.02. 66 P
for they never prick their finger but they say, 2.02.113 P
which is as much as to say, as thou usest him, 2.02.132 P
wine, and it perfumes the blood ere one can say, 2.04. 28 P
you, you are the weaker vessel, as they say, the 2.04. 60 P
hold hook and line, say i. 2.04.158 P
come, atropos, i say! 2.04.199
they say poins has a good wit. 2.04.239 P
they say the bishop and northumberland | are 3.01. 95
i dare say my cousin william is become a good 3.02. 9 P
and i may say to you, we knew where the bona 3.02. 23 P
is, when a man is, as they say, accommodated, or 3.02. 78 P
she would always say she could not abide master 3.02.202 P
tah, tah," would 'a say, "bounce," would 'a say, 3.02.284 P
"bounce," would 'a say, and away again would 'a 3.02.284 P
say on, my lord of westmerland, in peace, | what 4.01. 29
i say, if damn'd commotion so /appear'd | in his 4.01. 36
say you not then our offer is compell'd. 4.01.156
since sudden sorrow | serves to say thus, some 4.02. 84
me, and yielded, that i may justly say, with the 4.03. 40 P
say it did so a little time before | that our 4.04.127
what, davy, i say! 5.01. 2 P
go to, i say, he shall have no wrong. 5.01. 52 P
no prince nor peer shall have just cause to say, 5.02.144
why then say an old man can do somewhat. 5.03. 78 P
say they. 5.03.140
for what i have to say is of mine own making, ep 4 P
own making, and what indeed (i should say) will ep 5 P
you would say it hath been all in all his study; H5 1.01. 42
besides, their writers say, | king pepin, which 1.02. 64
i say little; 2.01. 5 P
at that time, and some say knives have edges. 2.01. 22 P
hear me, hear me what i say. 2.01. 63 P
o, | what shall i say to thee, lord scroop, thou 2.02. 94
they say he cried out of sack. 2.03. 27 P
and that's but unwholesome food, they say. 2.03. 57 P
therefore, i say, 'tis meet we all go forth | to 2.04. 21
say: 2.04.127
and therefore he scorns to say his prayers, lest 3.02. 38 P
i say gud day, captain fluellen. 3.02. 83 P
what say you? 3.03. 42
at us, and plainly say | our mettle is bred out, 3.05. 28
and let him say to england that we send | to 3.05. 62
say thou to harry of england, though we seem'd 3.06.118 P
for, to say the sooth, | though 'tis no wisdom 3.06.142
nor, as we are, we say we will not shun it. 3.06.165
i will not say so, for fear i should be fac'd 3.07. 82 P
you may as well say, that's a valiant flea that 3.07.145 P
since i may say, "now lie i like a king." 4.01. 17
i dare say you love him not so ill to wish him 4.01.124 P
i myself heard the king say he would not be 4.01.190 P
if ever thou come to me and say, after to–morrow 4.01.214 P
what's to say? 4.02. 32
and say, "to–morrow is saint crispian." 4.03. 46
you say very true, scald knave, when god's will 5.01. 32 P
i say, i will make him eat some part of my leek, 5.01. 40 P
it in love, but directly to say "i love you"* 5.02.127 P
urge me farther than to say "do you in faith?" 5.02.128 P
how say you, lady? 5.02.130 P
if not, to say to thee that i shall die, is true 5.02.150 P
take me by the hand, and say, "harry of england, 5.02.237 P
to kiss before they are married, would she say? 5.02.266 P
what should i say? 1H6 1.01. 15
why, no, i say. 1.02.126
as who should say, "when i am dead and gone, 1.04. 93
a maid, they say. 2.01. 21
how say you, madam? 2.03. 61
then say at once if i maintain'd the truth; 2.04. 5
and say withal, i think he held the right. 2.04. 38
or durst not for his craven heart say thus. 2.04. 87
look to it well, and say you are well warn'd. 2.04.103
i dare say | this quarrel will drink blood 2.04.132
why didst thou say, of late thou wert despis'd? 2.05. 42
stay, stay, i say! 3.01.103
and if you love me, as you say you do, | let me 3.01.104
to say the truth, this fact was infamous | and 4.01. 30
how say you, my lord? 4.01. 70
say, gentlemen, what makes you thus exclaim? 4.01. 83
the world will say, he is not talbot's blood, 4.05. 16
but, if i bow, they'll say it was for fear. 4.05. 29
boy, he smiles, methinks, as who should say, 4.07. 27
say, that i may honor thee. 5.03. 50
say, earl of suffolk — if thy name be so — 5.03. 72
lady, vouchsafe to listen what i say. 5.03.103
say, gentle princess, would you not suppose 5.03.110
how say you, madam, are ye so content? 5.03.126
a maid, | a virgin, and his servant, say to him. 5.03.178
to say the truth, it is your policy | to save 5.04.159
be gone, i say, for, till you do return, | i 5.05. 94
lordings, farewell, and say, when i am gone, | i 2H6 1.01.145
i dare not say from the rich cardinal | and from 1.02. 94
they say, "a crafty knave does need no broker," 1.02.100
did the duke of york say he was rightful heir to 1.03. 29 P
my lord of suffolk, say, is this the guise, | is 1.03. 42
i say, my sovereign, york is meetest man | to be 1.03.160
say, man, were these thy words? 1.03.186
uncle, what shall we say to this in law? 1.03.203
sometime i'll say, i am duke humphrey's wife, 2.04. 42
i will subscribe, and say i wrong'd the duke. 3.01. 38
it serves you well, my lord, to say so much. 3.01.119
i say no more than truth, so help me god! 3.01.120
and 'twixt each groan | say, "who's a traitor, 3.01.222
say as you think, and speak it from your souls: 3.01.247
say but the word, and i will be his priest. 3.01.272
say you consent, and censure well the deed, 3.01.275
and so say i. 3.01.279
say he be taken, rack'd, and tortured, | i know 3.01.376
will make him say i mov'd him to those arms. 3.01.378
say that he thrive, as 'tis great like he will, 3.01.379
say we intend to try his grace to–day, | if he 3.02. 16
forbear, i say! 3.02. 46
but well forewarning wind | did seem to say, 3.02. 86
say, if thou dar'st, proud lord of warwickshire, 3.02.201
madam, be still — with reverence may i say — 3.02.207
and say it was thy mother that thou meant'st, 3.02.222
they say, by him the good duke humphrey died; 3.02.248
they say, in him they fear your highness' death; 3.02.249
they say, in care of your most royal person, 3.02.254
worth, | they say is shamefully bereft of life. 3.02.269
no more, i say! 3.02.291
well, i say, it was never merry world in england 4.02. 8 P
which is as much to say as, let the magistrates 4.02. 17 P
some say the bee stings, but i say, 'tis the 4.02. 81 P
some say the bee stings, but i say, 'tis the 4.02. 82 P
away with him, i say! 4.02.109 P
but i say, 'tis true. 4.02.141
i tell you that that lord say hath gelded the 4.02.165 P
lord say, jack cade hath sworn to have thy head. 4.04. 19
lord say, the traitors hateth thee, | therefore 4.04. 43
here's the lord say, which sold the towns in 4.07. 21 P
ah, thou say, thou serge, nay, thou buckram lord 4.07. 25 P
what say you of kent? 4.07. 55 P
he nods at us, as who should say, i'll be even 4.07. 94 P
take him away, i say, and strike off his head 4.07.109 P
what say ye, countrymen? 4.08. 11
fling up his cap, and say, "god save his majesty 4.08. 15
to say if that the bastard boys of york | shall 5.01.115
say, what news with thee? 5.01.125
clifford, i say, come forth and fight with me. 5.02. 5
i know not what to say, my title's weak. 3H6 1.01.134
tears, | and say, "alas, it was a piteous deed!" 1.04.163
say how he died, for i will hear it all. 2.01. 49
for chair and dukedom, throne and kingdom say, 2.01. 93
if for the last, say ay, and to it, lords. 2.01.165
fault, | and long hereafter say unto his child, 2.02. 36
say, henry, shall i have my right, or no? 2.02.126
and he nor sees nor hears us what we say. 2.06. 63
for wise men say it is the wisest course. 3.01. 25
say, what art thou talk'st of kings and queens? 3.01. 55
ay, if thou wilt say ay to my request; 3.02. 79
no, if thou dost say no to my demand. 3.02. 80
say that king edward take thee for his queen? 3.02. 89
it, | and so, i say, i'll cut the causes off, 3.02.142
well, say there is no kingdom then for richard; 3.02.146
why, say, fair queen, whence springs this deep 3.03. 12
myself have often heard him say, and swear, 3.03.123
i hear, yet say not much, but think the more. 4.01. 83
she could say little less; 4.01.101
but say, is warwick friends with margaret? 4.01.115
i say not, slaughter him, | for i intend but 4.02. 24
but say, i pray, what nobleman is that | that 4.03. 9
ay, say you so? the gates shall then be opened. 4.07. 29
say, somervile, what says my loving son? 5.01. 7
say warwick was our anchor; 5.04. 13
keep our course (though the rough wind say no) 5.04. 22
say you can swim, alas, 'tis but a while; 5.04. 29
gentlemen, what i should say | my tears gainsay; 5.04. 73
away, i say, i charge ye bear her hence. 5.05. 81
my good lord — my lord, i should say rather. 5.06. 2
down to hell, and say i sent thee thither — | i 5.06. 67
for i have often heard my mother say | i came 5.06. 70
to say the truth, so judas kiss'd his master, 5.07. 33
you may partake of any thing we say: R3 1.01. 89
we say the king | is wise and virtuous, and his 1.01. 90
we say that shore's wife hath a pretty foot, | a 1.01. 93
how say you, sir? 1.01. 96
say that i slew them not? 1.02. 89
then say they were not slain. 1.02. 89
say then my peace is made. 1.02.197
to your good prayer will scarcely say amen. 1.03. 21
what doth she say, my lord of buckingham? 1.03.294
and say poor margaret was a prophetess! 1.03.300
no, he'll say 'twas done cowardly when he wakes. 1.04.101 P
why, then he'll say we stabb'd him sleeping. 1.04.105 P
take thou the fee and tell him what i say, | for 1.04.277
then say at once what is it thou requests. 2.01. 99
therefore i say with noble buckingham, | that it 2.02.138
and so say i. 2.02.140
they say my son of york | has almost overta'en 2.04. 6
marry (they say) my uncle grew so fast | that he 2.04. 27
say, uncle gloucester, if our brother come, 3.01. 61
but say, my lord, it were not regist'red, 3.01. 75
so wise so young, they say do never live long. 3.01. 79
what say you, uncle? 3.01. 80
i say, without characters fame lives long. 3.01. 81
o my fair cousin, i must not say so. 3.01.106
in weightier things you'll say a beggar nay. 3.01.119
so it appears by that i have to say: 3.02. 7
i'll go, my lord, and tell him what you say. 3.02. 34
pray god, i say, i prove a needless coward! 3.02. 88
i say, my lord, they have deserved death. 3.04. 66
how now, how now, what say the citizens? 3.07. 1
lord, | the citizens are mum, say not a word. 3.07. 3
for them | as i can say nay to thee for myself, 3.07. 53
marry, god defend his grace should say us nay! 3.07. 81
you say that edward is your brother's son: 3.07.177
so say we too, but not by edward's wife; 3.07.178
god bless your grace! we see it and will say it. 3.07.237
in saying so you shall but say the truth. 3.07.238
and die ere men can say, "god save the queen!" 4.01. 62
o, when, i say, i look'd on richard's face, 4.01. 70
say on, my loving lord. 4.02. 11
why, buckingham, i say i would be king. 4.02. 12
say, have i thy consent that they shall die? 4.02. 23
i say again, give out | that anne, my queen, is 4.02. 56
say it is done, | and i will love thee and 4.02. 80
but where (to say the truth) i do not know. 4.03. 30
say that right for right | hath dimm'd your 4.04. 15
that i may live to say, "the dog is dead." 4.04. 78
strike, i say! 4.04.151
i say amen to her. 4.04.198
to save her life, i'll say she is not so. 4.04.213
which, say to her, did drain | the purple sap 4.04.276
say that i did all this for love of her. 4.04.288
what were i best to say? 4.04.337
or shall i say her uncle? 4.04.338
say she shall be a high and mighty queen. 4.04.347
say i will love her everlastingly. 4.04.349
say i, her sovereign, am her subject low. 4.04.355
withal say that the queen hath heartily 4.05. 7
leave me, i say. 5.03. 78
what shall i say more than i have inferr'd? 5.03.314
great god of heaven, say amen to all! 5.05. 8
that she may long live here, god say amen! 5.05. 41
i'll say | a man may weep upon his wedding–day. H8 pr 31
men might say | till this time pomp was single, 1.01. 14
i say again, there is no english soul | more 1.01.146
say not treasonous. 1.01.156
they say | they are devis'd by you, or else you 1.02. 50
doing, let me say | 'tis but the fate of place, 1.02. 74
i say, take heed; 1.02.175
canst thou say further? 1.02.187
say, lord chamberlain, | they have done my poor 1.04. 72
what say they? 1.04. 82
hear what i say, and then go home and lose me. 2.01. 57
had my trial, | and must needs say a noble one; 2.01.119
and when you would say something that is sad, 2.01.135
who's there, i say? 2.02. 64
they will not stick to say you envied him, | and 2.02.126
which, to say sooth, are blessings; 2.03. 30
i'll to the king, | and say i spoke with you. 2.03. 80
say, | are you not stronger than you were? 2.03. 99
say, henry king of england, come into the court. 2.04. 6 P
say, katherine queen of england, come into the 2.04. 10 P
therefore i say again, | i utterly abhor, yea, 2.04. 80
unthink your speaking | and to say so no more. 2.04.105
that's to say, | i meant to rectify my 2.04.203
long, be pleas'd yourself to say | how far you 2.04.211
i say, set on. 2.04.242
they will'd me say so, madam. 3.01. 18
but say i warn'd ye; 3.01.109
a woman (i dare say without vainglory) | never 3.01.127
and 'tis a kind of good deed to say well, | and 3.02.153
confess it, say withal | if you are bound to us, 3.02.164
what say you? 3.02.165
of me more must be heard of, say i taught thee; 3.02.434
say wolsey, that once trod the ways of glory, 3.02.435
their coronets say so. these are stars indeed. 4.01. 54
no man living | could say, "this is my wife" 4.01. 80
i' th' presence | he would say untruths, and be 4.02. 38
say his long trouble now is passing | out of 4.02.162
affairs that walk | (as they say spirits do) at 5.01. 14
they say in great extremity, and fear'd | she'll 5.01. 19
of late | heard many grievous — i do say, my 5.01. 98
say ay, and of a boy. 5.01.163
i could say more, | but reverence to your 5.02.103
you may worst | of all this table say so. 5.02.114
not sound, i say. 5.02.117
good my lords, | i have a little yet to say. 5.02.133
i will say thus much for him, if a prince | may 5.02.190
so, 'tis clear, | they'll say 'tis naught; ep 5
and say 'twill do, i know within a while | all ep 12
as true thou tell'st me, when i say i love her, TRO 1.01. 60
say i she is not fair? 1.01. 79
they say he is a very man per se and stands 1.02. 15 P
they say he yesterday cop'd hector in the battle 1.02. 33 P
well, i say troilus is troilus. 1.02. 66 P
then you say as i say, for i am sure he is not 1.02. 67 P
then you say as i say, for i am sure he is not 1.02. 67 P
faith, to say truth, brown and not brown. 1.02. 96 P
to say the truth, true and not true. 1.02. 97 P
laying on, take't off who will, as they say. 1.02.207 P
say one of your watches. 1.02.265 P
if none, he'll say in troy when he retires, 1.03.281
and those biles did run — say so — did not the 2.01. 5 P
i say, the proclamation! 2.01. 31 P
in his head, /i'll tell you what i say of him. 2.01. 74 P
i say, this ajax — 2.01. 76 P
hector, what say you to't? 2.02. 7
then i say, | well may we fight for her whom, we 2.02.160
i have said my prayers, and devil envy say amen. 2.03. 21 P
i shall say so to him. 2.03. 83
achilles bids me say, he is much sorry | if any 2.03.107
not sin | if you do say we think him over–proud 2.03.123
will you subscribe his thought, and say he is? 2.03.147 P
what should i say? 2.03.176
and say in thunder, "achilles go to him." 2.03.199
well said, my lord! well, you say so in fits. 3.01. 57 P
why should you say cressida? 3.01. 91 P
they say all lovers swear more performance than 3.02. 84 P
as what envy can say worst shall be a mock for 3.02. 96 P
son, | yea, let them say, to stick the heart of 3.02.195

say, amen. 3.02.204 P
which you say live to come in my behalf. 3.03. 16
as who should say there were wit in this head, 3.03.255 P
what say you to't? 3.03.292 P
let her say what. 4.02. 27 P
is he here, say you? 4.02. 51 P
some say the genius /so | cries "/come" to him 4.04. 50
but "be thou true," say i, to fashion in | my 4.04. 65
but that you say "be't so," | i speak it in my 4.04.134
greek and troyan so | that thou couldst say, 4.05.125
they say he keeps a troyan drab, and uses the 5.01. 96 P
no more, i say. 5.03. 7
be gone, i say, the gods have heard me swear. 5.03. 15
hold you still, i say; 5.03. 25
troilus, i say, where's troilus? 5.06. 2
troilus, i say, what, troilus! 5.06. 5
fate, hear me what i say! 5.06. 25
about me, you my myrmidons, | mark what i say. 5.07. 2
i say, at once, let your brief plagues be mercy, 5.10. 8
aye be call'd | go in to troy and say /there, 5.10. 17
there is no more to say. 5.10. 22
i say unto you, what he hath done famously, he COR 1.01. 36 P
men can be content to say it was for his country 1.01. 38 P
you must in no way say he is covetous. 1.01. 42 P
they say poor suitors have strong breaths; 1.01. 59 P
what say you to't? 1.01.146
whereof they say | the city is well stor'd. 1.01.189
they say? 1.01.190
they say there's grain enough? 1.01.196
yet, they say, all the yarn she spun in ulysses' 1.03. 83 P
say, has our general met the enemy? 1.04. 3
shall say against their hearts, "we thank the 1.09. 8
no more, i say! 1.09. 47
i /cannot say your worships have deliver'd the 2.01. 57 P
bear with those that say you are reverend grave 2.01. 60 P
this, as you say, suggested | at some time when 2.01.253
three, they say; 2.02. 3 P
to heal again | than hear say how i got them. 2.02. 70
this last, | before and in corioles, let me say, 2.02.102
no matter, the greater part carries it, i say. 2.03. 37 P
what must i say? 2.03. 49
your good voice, sir, what say you? 2.03. 78 P
say you chose him | more after our commandment 2.03.229
say we read lectures to you, | how youngly he 2.03.235
say you ne'er had done't | (harp on that still) 2.03.251
i say again, | in soothing them we nourish 3.01. 68
to say he'll turn your current in a ditch, | and 3.01. 96
i say they nourish'd disobedience, fed | the 3.01.117
rather say, i play | the man i am. 3.02. 15
i have heard you say | honor and policy, like 3.02. 41
or say to them, | thou art their soldier, and, 3.02. 80
prithee now, say you will, and go about it. 3.02. 98
and when they hear me say, "it shall be so | i' 3.03. 13
then let them, | if i say fine, cry "fine!" 3.03. 16
list to your tribunes. audience! peace, i say! 3.03. 40
well, say. peace ho! 3.03. 41
but, as i say, such as become a soldier | rather 3.03. 56
say then; 'tis true, i ought so. 3.03. 62
i would say | "thou liest" unto thee with a 3.03. 72
i' th' people's name, | i say it shall be so. 3.03.105
to say extremities was the trier of spirits, 4.01. 4
resume that spirit when you were wont to say, 4.01. 16
say their great enemy is gone, and they | stand 4.02. 6
they say she's mad. 4.02. 9
would i had the power | to say so to my husband. 4.02. 16
have you an army ready, say you? 4.03. 42 P
say, what's thy name? 4.05. 59
and say "'tis true," i'd not believe them more 4.05.105
to those that shall | say yea to thy desires. 4.05.145
look you, one cannot tell how to say that. 4.05.169 P
why do you say, "thwack our general"? 4.05.180 P
i do not say, "thwack our general," but he was 4.05.181 P
i have heard him say so himself. 4.05.184 P
hard for him, directly to say the troth on't, 4.05.185 P
let me have war, say i, it exceeds peace as far 4.05.221 P
if they | should say, "be good to rome," they 4.06.112
i have not the face | to say, "beseech you cease 4.06.117
say not we brought it. 4.06.120
and, to say the truth, so did very many of us. 4.06.142 P
very well. | could he say less? 5.01. 22
well, and say that martius | return me, as 5.01. 41
you have been his liar, as you say you have, i 5.02. 32 P
true under him, must say you cannot pass. 5.02. 33 P
back, i say, go; 5.02. 56 P
i'll say an arrant for you. 5.02. 60 P
i say to you, as i was said to, "away!" 5.02.107 P
but do not say | for that, "forgive our romans." 5.03. 43
while the volsces | may say, "this mercy we have 5.03.137
say my request's unjust, | and spurn me back; 5.03.164
but i say there is no hope in't; 5.04. 7 P
or move the people | with what he would say, let 5.06. 55
say no more. | here come the lords. 5.06. 58
i say "your city," to his wife and mother, 5.06. 93
crown him and say, "long live our emperor!" TIT 1.01.229
and say, "long live our emperor saturnine!" 1.01.233
i say no more, | nor wish no less, and so i take 1.01.401
away, i say! 2.01. 60
lavinia, how say you? 2.02. 16
i say, no; 2.02. 16
had i the pow'r that some say dian had, | thy 2.03. 61
some say that ravens foster forlorn children 2.03.153
o, be to me, though thy hard heart say no, 2.03.155
say, who art thou that lately didst descend 2.03.248
shall i say 'tis so? 2.04. 33
and let me say (that never wept before) | my 3.01. 25
o, say thou for her, who hath done this deed? 3.01. 87
now would she say | that to her brother which i 3.01.144
and that you'll say ere half an hour pass. 3.01.191
say i account of them | as jewels purchas'd at 3.01.197
for i have heard my grandsire say full oft, 4.01. 18
boy, what say you? 4.01.106
i say, my lord, that if i were a man, | their 4.01.107
youth, | the hope of rome, for so he bid me say; 4.02. 13
here lacks but your mother for to say amen. 4.02. 44
as who should say, "old lad, i am thine own." 4.02.121
aaron, what shall i say unto the empress? 4.02.128
but say again, how many saw the child? 4.02.140
sir, i could never say grace in all my life. 4.03.100 P
as who would say, in rome no justice were. 4.04. 20
myself hath often heard them say, | when i have 4.04. 74
say that the emperor requests a parley | of 4.04.101
and as he saith, so say we all with him. 5.01. 17
say, wall-ey'd slave, whither wouldst thou 5.01. 44
say on, and if it please me which thou speak'st, 5.01. 59
tell on thy mind, i say thy child shall live. 5.01. 69
what, canst thou say all this and never blush? 5.01.121
and say i am revenge, sent from below | to join 5.02. 3
where they say he keeps | to ruminate strange 5.02. 5
what say you, boys, will you abide with him, 5.02.137
what would you say if i should let you speak? 5.02.178
now have you heard the truth, what say you, 5.03.128
speak, romans, speak, and if you say we shall, 5.03.135
is the law of our side if i say ay? ROM 1.01. 48 P
say "better," here comes one of my master's 1.01. 58 P
my sword, i say! 1.01. 77
is to himself (i will not say how true) | but to 1.01.148
but now, my lord, what say you to my suit? 1.02. 6
whose names are written there, and to them say, 1.02. 36
ye say honestly, rest you merry! 1.02. 62 P
laugh | to think it should leave crying and say, 1.03. 51
and stint thou too, i pray thee, nurse, say i. 1.03. 58
i would say thou hadst suck'd wisdom from thy 1.03. 68
what say you? 1.03. 79
and, to say truth, verona brags of him | to be a 1.05. 67
i say he shall, go to! 1.05. 77
i know thou wilt say "ay," | and i will take thy 2.02. 90
at lovers' perjuries, | they say, jove laughs. 2.02. 93
i'll frown and be perverse, and say thee nay, 2.02. 96
doth cease to be | ere one can say it lightens. 2.02.120
that i shall say good night till it be morrow. 2.02.185
that's as much as to say, such a case as yours 2.04. 52 P
you say well. 2.04.124 P
what she bid me say, i will keep to myself. 2.04.164 P
lead her in a fool's paradise, as they say, it 2.04.166 P
were a very gross kind of behavior, as they say; 2.04.167 P
go to, i say you shall. 2.04.184 P
did you ne'er hear say, | "two may keep counsel, 2.04.196
i'll warrant you, when i say so, she looks as 2.04.205 P
to say to me that thou art out of breath? 2.05. 32
say either, and i'll stay the circumstance. 2.05. 36
say thou but ay, | and that bare vowel i shall 3.02. 45
ay, | if he be slain, say ay, or if not, no. 3.02. 50
be merciful, say "death"; 3.03. 12
do not say "banishment"! 3.03. 14
but what say you to thursday? 3.04. 28
i'll say yon grey is not the morning's eye, 3.05. 19
some say the lark makes sweet division; 3.05. 29
some say the lark and loathed toad change eyes; 3.05. 31
stuff'd, as they say, with honorable parts, 3.05.181
you say you do not know the lady's mind? 4.01. 4
ay, marry, go, i say, and fetch him hither. 4.02. 30
fest'ring in his shroud, where, as they say, 4.03. 43
what, nurse, i say! 4.04. 24
he is come already, | make haste, i say. 4.04. 28
why, love, i say! 4.05. 3
what say you, simon catling? 4.05.130 P
/pretty! what say you, hugh rebeck? 4.05.133 P
i say, "silver sound," because musicians sound 4.05.134 P
/pretty too! what say you, james soundpost? 4.05.136 P
faith, i know not what to say. 4.05.138 P
i will say for you; 4.05.140 P
and hereafter say | a madman's mercy bid thee 5.03. 66
then say at once what thou dost know in this. 5.03.228
what can he say to this? 5.03.271
i will say of it, | it tutors nature. TIM 1.01. 36
imprison'd is he, say you? 1.01. 94
none | can truly say he gives if he receives. 1.02. 11
they say, my lords, "ira furor brevis est," 1.02. 28
i have one word | to say to you. 1.02.168
caphis, i say! 2.01. 14
off, | and say you /found them in mine honesty. 2.02.135
and i am proud, say, that my occasions have 2.02.191 P
boy, wink at me, and say thou saw'st me not. 3.01. 44 P
i am not able to do (the more beast, i say!) 3.02. 49 P
i count it one of my greatest afflictions, say, 3.02. 56 P
why, /i say, my lords, h'as done fair service, 3.05. 62
alack, my fellows, what should i say to you? 4.02. 3
let's shake our heads, and say, | as 'twere a 4.02. 25
in purity of manhood stand upright | and say, 4.03. 15
i flatter not, but say thou art a caitiff. 4.03.235
i'll say th' hast gold; 4.03.393
what i shall say i have provided for him. 5.01. 33
e'en so, sir, as i say. 5.01. 83
i must needs say you have a little fault; 5.01. 87
come not to me again, but say to athens, | timon 5.01.214
heart before, | to say thou't enter friendly. 5.04. 49
workman, i am but, as you would say, a cobbler. JC 1.01. 11 P
for our elders say, | the barren, touched in 1.02. 7
when could they say, till now, that talk'd of 1.02.154
you and i have heard our fathers say | there was 1.02.158
what you have to say | i will with patience hear 1.02.168
did cicero say any thing? 1.02.278
do so conjointly meet, let not men say, | "these 1.03. 29
indeed, they say, the senators to-morrow | mean 1.03. 85
lucius, i say! 2.01. 3
awake, i say! 2.01. 5
what say the augurers? 2.02. 37
and he shall say you are not well to-day. 2.02. 53
mark antony shall say i am not well, | and, for 2.02. 55
say he is sick. 2.02. 65
i have, when you have heard what i can say; 2.02. 92
mock | apt to be render'd, for some one to say, 2.02. 97
and commend me to my lord, | say i am merry. 2.04. 45
and bring me word what he doth say to thee. 2.04. 46
and, being prostrate, thus he bade me say: 3.01.125
say, i love brutus, and i honor him; 3.01.128
say, i fear'd caesar, honor'd him, and lov'd him 3.01.129
gentlemen all — alas, what shall i say? 3.01.190
the enemies of caesar shall say this: 3.01.212
of caesar, | and say you do't by our permission; 3.01.247
and bid me say to you by word of mouth — | o 3.01.280
any dear friend of caesar's, to him i say, that 3.02. 19 P
what does he say of brutus? 3.02. 66
peace, let us hear what antony can say. 3.02. 71
i heard him say, brutus and cassius | are rid 3.02.268
wisely i say, i am a bachelor. 3.03. 16 P
that's as much as to say, they are fools that 3.03. 17 P
i say you are not. 4.03. 34
you say you are a better soldier: 4.03. 51
did i say "better"? 4.03. 57
there is no more to say? 4.03.229
i may say "thrusting" it; 5.03. 75
might stand up | and say to all the world, "this 5.05. 75
say to the king the knowledge of the broil | as MAC 1.02. 6
if i say sooth, i must report they were | as 1.02. 36
and say which grain will grow, and which will 1.03. 59
say from whence | you owe this strange 1.03. 75
only i have left to say, | more is thy due than 1.04. 20
thou'rt mad to say it! 1.05. 31
a foolish thought, to say a sorry sight. 2.02. 19
but they did say their prayers, and address'd 2.02. 22
list'ning their fear, i could not say "amen," 2.02. 26
say "amen," | when they did say "god bless us!" 2.02. 27
our chimneys were blown down, and, as they say, 2.03. 55
some say, the earth | was feverous, and did 2.03. 60
what is't you say — the life? 2.03. 69
contradict thyself, | and say, it is not so. 2.03. 90
to half a soul and to a notion craz'd | say, 3.01. 83
say to the king, i would attend his leisure 3.02. 3
well, let's away, and say how much is done. 3.03. 22
thou canst not say i did it; 3.04. 49
how say you? 3.04. 68
it will have blood, they say; 3.04.121
only i say | things have been strangely borne. 3.06. 2
whom you may say (if't please you) fleance 3.06. 6
so that, i say, | he has borne all things well, 3.06. 16
and hums, as who should say, "you'll rue the 3.06. 42
say, if th' hadst rather hear it from our mouths 4.01. 62
hear his speech, but say thou nought. 4.01. 70
that this great king may kindly say | our duties 4.01.131
womanly defense, | to say i have done no harm? 4.02. 79
did you say all? 4.03.217
what, at any time, have you heard her say? 5.01. 13 P
out, i say! 5.01. 35 P
some say he's mad; 5.02. 13
sick at heart | when i behold — seyton, i say! 5.03. 20
pull't off, i say. 5.03. 54
make us know | what we shall say we have, and 5.04. 18
lord, | i should report that which i say i saw, 5.05. 30
well, say, sir. 5.05. 31
i say, a moving grove. 5.05. 37
they say he parted well, and paid his score, 5.09. 18
say — | what, is horatio there? HAM 1.01. 18
for which, they say, your spirits oft walk in 1.01.138
some say that ever 'gainst that season comes 1.01.158
and then they say no spirit dare stir abroad, 1.01.161
i would not hear your enemy say so, | nor shall 1.02.170
arm'd, say you? 1.02.226
men, | carrying, i say, the stamp of one defect, 1.04. 31
say why is this? 1.04. 57
i say, away! 1.04. 86
how say you then, would heart of man once think 1.05.121
in part him — but," you may say, "not well. 2.01. 17
'a this — 'a does — what was i about to say? 2.01. 49
by the mass, i was about to say something. 2.01. 50
or then, with such or such, and, as you say, 2.01. 55
say, voltemand, what from our brother norway? 2.02. 59
or rather say, the cause of this defect, | for 2.02.102
how say you by that? 2.02.187 P
what should we say, my lord? 2.02.277 P
what say you? 2.02.289 P
though by your smiling you seem to say so. 2.02.310 P
/sere, and the lady shall say her mind freely, 2.02.324 P
them, for they say an old man is twice a child. 2.02.385 P
you say right, sir, a' monday morning, 'twas 2.02.387 P
prithee say on, he's for a jig or a tale of 2.02.500 P
say on, come to hecuba. 2.02.501 P
unpregnant of my cause, | and can say nothing; 2.02.569
and by a sleep to say we end | the heart-ache 3.01. 60
i say we will have no moe marriage. 3.01.147 P
and, as i may say, whirlwind of your passion, 3.02. 6 P
you play'd once i' th' university, you say? 3.02. 99 P
command, or, rather, as you say, my mother. 3.02.323 P
my mother, you say — 3.02.325 P
i will say so. 3.02.386 P
o, say! 3.04.109
i do not know | why yet i live to say, "this 4.04. 44
say you? 4.05. 28 P
they say the owl was a baker's daughter. 4.05. 42 P
when they ask you what it means, say you this: 4.05. 47 P
they say 'a made a good end — "for bonny sweet 4.05.185 P
they say they have letters for you. 4.06. 2 P
sailors, my lord, they say, i saw them not. 4.07. 39
for a quality | wherein, they say, you shine. 4.07. 73
her custom holds, | let shame say what it will; 4.07.188
now thou dost ill to say the gallows is built 5.01. 47 P
ask'd this question next, say "a grave-maker": 5.01. 58 P
or of a courtier, which could say, "good morrow, 5.01. 82 P
dost lie in't, to be in't and say it is thine. 5.01.125 P
very strangely, they say. 5.01.157 P
but, as i say, spacious in the possession of 5.02. 87 P
their repair hither, and say you are not fit. 5.02.218 P
what say you? 5.02.285
say you so? come on. 5.02.300
which of you shall we say doth love us most, LR 1.01. 51
what can you say to draw | a third more opulent 1.01. 85
husbands, if they say | they love you all? 1.01. 99
my lord of burgundy, | what say you to the lady? 1.01.238
is not little i have to say of what most nearly 1.01.283 P
and, as i say, retire with me to my lodging, 1.02.168 P
say i am sick. 1.03. 8
so your face bids me, though you say nothing. 1.04.196 P
oswald, i say! 1.04.327
brother, i say! 2.01. 19
how fell you out? say that. 2.02. 86
no, i say. 2.04. 17
i say yea. 2.04. 18
say? how is that? 2.04.140
say you have wrong'd her. 2.04.152
give me your hand. have you no more to say? 3.01. 51
pattern of all patience, | i will say nothing. 3.02. 38
say you nothing. 3.03. 8 P
you will say they are persian, but let them be 3.06. 80 P
bind him, i say. 3.07. 32

thee in my touch, | i'ld say i had eyes again. 4.01. 24
who is't can say, "i am at the worst"? 4.01. 25
the worst is not | so long as we can say, "this 4.01. 28
often 'twould say, | "the fiend, the fiend!" 4.06. 78
to say "ay" and "no" to every thing that i said! 4.06. 99 P
does offend, none, i say none, i'll able 'em. 4.06.168
(wife, so i would say) affectionate servant, 4.06.269 P
i know not what to say. 4.07. 53
either say thou'lt do't, | or thrive by other 5.03. 33
mark, i say instantly, and carry it so | as i 5.03. 36
say thou "no," | this sword, this arm, and my 5.03.139
that thy tongue some say of breeding breathes, 5.03.144
say if i do, the laws are mine, not thine; 5.03.159
on, | you look as you had something more to say. 5.03.202
my master calls me, i must not say no. 5.03.323
speak what we feel, not what we ought to say: 5.03.325
arise, i say! OTH 1.01. 92
in honest plainness thou hast heard me say | my 1.01. 97
i say again, hath made a gross revolt, | tying 1.01.134
light, i say, light! 1.01.144
my letters say a hundred and seven galleys. 1.03. 3
how say you by this change? 1.03. 17
what, in your own part, can you say to this? 1.03. 74
say it, othello. 1.03.127
ere i would say i would drown myself for the 1.03.314 P
i say put money in thy purse. 1.03.341 P
you have little cause to say so. 2.01.108
how say you, cassio? 2.01.163 P
you say true, 'tis so indeed. 2.01.171 P
(as they say base men being in love have then a 2.01.215 P
it were an honest action to say | so to the moor 2.03.141
away, i say; 2.03.157
which till to–night | i ne'er might say before. 2.03.236
now the general — i may say so in this respect, 2.03.315 P
away, i say, thou shalt know more hereafter. 2.03.381
but (as they say) to hear music the general does 3.01. 16 P
what dost thou say? 3.03. 35
(save that they say the wars must make example 3.03. 65
what dost thou say, iago? 3.03. 93
i heard thee say even now, thou lik'st not that, 3.03.109
why, say they are vild and false, | as where's 3.03.136
to make me jealious | to say my wife is fair, 3.03.184
dost thou say so? 3.03.205
i did say so. 3.03.329
what shall i say? 3.03.401
but yet, i say, | if imputation and strong 3.03.405
in sleep i heard him say, "sweet desdemona, 3.03.419
patience, i say; your mind /perhaps may change. 3.03.452
within these three days let me hear thee say 3.03.472
i dare not say he lies any where. 3.04. 3 P
a soldier, and for me to say a soldier lies, 3.04. 5 P
for me to devise a lodging and say he lies here, 3.04. 12 P
you may, indeed, say so; 3.04. 44
say you? 3.04. 82
i say, it is not lost. 3.04. 85
and say if i shall see you soon at night. 3.04.198
or heard him say — as knaves be such abroad, 4.01. 25
we say lie on her, when they belie her. 4.01. 35 P
my lord, i say! 4.01. 48
i say, but mark his gesture. 4.01. 87
or i shall say y' are all in all in spleen, 4.01. 88
prithee say true. 4.01.124 P
go to; say no more. 4.01.169 P
hang her, i do but say what she is. 4.01.187 P
and she's obedient, as you say, obedient; 4.01.255
she's a simple bawd | that cannot say as much. 4.02. 21
such as she said my lord did say i was. 4.02.119
i cannot say "whore." 4.02.161
say that they slack their duties, | and pour our 4.03. 87
or say they strike us, | or scant our former 4.03. 90
if you say /so, i hope you will not kill me. 5.02. 35
i say, amen. 5.02. 57
he will not say so. 5.02. 71
but while i say one prayer! 5.02. 83
you /heard her say herself, it was not i. 5.02.127
thou art rash as fire to say | that she was 5.02.134
i say thy husband. 5.02.150
my husband say she was false? 5.02.152
i say thy husband; 5.02.153
if he say so, may his pernicious soul | rot half 5.02.155
did you say with cassio? 5.02.182
and say besides, that in aleppo once, | where a 5.02.352
caesar's, i would say — both? ANT 1.01. 28
which, you say, must change his horns with 1.02. 4 P
antony, thou wouldst say — 1.02.104
say our pleasure, | to such whose places under 1.02.194
if you find him sad, | say i am dancing; 1.03. 4
let her not say 'tis i that keep you here, | i 1.03. 22
to me, and say the tears | belong to egypt. 1.03. 77
say this becomes him | (as his composure must be 1.04. 21
"say the firm roman to great egypt sends | this 1.05. 43
the east, | say thou, shall call her mistress." 1.05. 47
say "the brave antony." 1.05. 69
cold in blood, | to say as i said then! 1.05. 75
i | should say myself offended, and with you 2.02. 32
for that you must | but say i could not help it. 2.02. 71
say not /so, agrippa. 2.02.120
if i would say, "agrippa, be it so," | to make 2.02.141
say to me, whose fortunes shall rise higher, 2.03. 16
i say again, thy spirit | is all afraid to 2.03. 29
say to ventidius i would speak with him. 2.03. 32
them every one an antony, | and say, "ah, ha! 2.05. 15
if thou say so, villain, | thou kill'st thy 2.05. 26
sirrah, mark, we use | to say the dead are well. 2.05. 33
yet, if thou say antony lives, 'tis well, | or 2.05. 43
what say you? 2.05. 62
say 'tis not so, a province i will give thee, 2.05. 68
thee worser than i do, | if thou again say yes. 2.05. 91
say in mine ear, what is't. 2.07. 37
what's else to say? 2.07. 58
would you praise caesar, say "caesar," go no 3.02. 13
then does he say he lent me | some shipping 3.06. 26
do not say so, my lord. 3.06. 62
what is't you say? 3.07. 9
they say, one taurus. 3.07. 78
fall not a tear, i say, one of them rates | all 3.11. 69
none but friends: say boldly. 3.13. 47
shall i say to caesar | what you require of him? 3.13. 65
say to great caesar this in /deputation: 3.13. 74
that will take rewards | and say "god quit you!" 3.13.124
look thou say | he makes me angry with him; 3.13.140
peace, i say. | what should this mean? 4.03. 14
from caesar's camp | say "i am none of thine." 4.05. 9
say that i wish he never find more cause | to 4.05. 15
and they say we shall embattle | by th' second 4.09. 3
the auguries | say they know not, they cannot 4.12. 5
say that the last i spoke was "antony," | and 4.13. 8
let me say, | before i strike this bloody stroke 4.14. 90
i say, o caesar, antony is dead. 5.01. 13
go and say | we purpose her no shame. 5.01. 61
say, i would die. 5.02. 70
say, good caesar, | that i some lady trifles 5.02.164
and say | some nobler token i have kept apart 5.02.167
but he that will believe all that they say, 5.02.256 P
that i may say | the gods themselves do weep! 5.02.299
of him, but had | most pretty things to say. CYM 1.03. 26
judgment (if i offend /not to say it is mended) 1.04. 47 P
will my lord say so? 1.06. 73
that others do | (i was about to say) enjoy your 1.06. 91
i may say, | the credit that thy lady hath of 1.06.156
why, so i say. 2.01. 31 P
they say it will penetrate. 2.03. 12 P
but that you shall not say i yield being silent, 2.03. 94
now say, what would augustus caesar with us? 3.01. 1
i do not say i am one; 3.01. 41 P
we do say then to caesar, | our ancestor was 3.01. 53
for mine's beyond beyond — say, and speak thick 3.02. 56
a sickness, say | she'll home to her father; 3.02. 74
there's no more to say: 3.02. 81
say, "thus mine enemy fell, | and thus i set my 3.03. 91
son, i say, follow the king. 3.05. 53
(which, as i say, to vex her i will execute in 3.05.142 P
if it be sin to say so, sir, i yoke me | in my 4.02. 19
i love this youth, and i have heard you say, 4.02. 21
who is't shall die, i'ld say | "my father, not 4.02. 23
our courtiers say all's savage but at court. 4.02. 33
say what thou art; 4.02. 79
good time with him, | you say he is so fell. 4.02.109
say, where shall 's lay him? 4.02.233
go fetch him, | we'll say our song whilst. 4.02.254
say his name, good friend. 4.02.376
say you, sir? 4.02.379
i will not say | thou shalt be so well master'd, 4.02.382
so say i, amen. 4.04. 47
prithee say. 5.05. 36
that it was folly in me, thou mayst say, | and 5.05. 67
i know not why, wherefore, | to say "live, boy." 5.05. 96
upon your finger, say | how came it yours? 5.05.137
the good posthumus | (what should i say? 5.05.158
never say hereafter | but i am truest speaker. 5.05.375
all syria — | i tell you what mine authors say. PER 1.ch. 20
and if jove stray, who dares say jove doth ill? 1.01.104
say, is it done? 1.01.158
unless thou say prince pericles is dead. 1.01.164
nor boots it me to say i honor /him, | if he 1.02. 20
who wanteth food and will not say he wants it, 1.04. 11
what, patch–breech, i say! 2.01. 14 P
what say you, master? 2.01. 15 P
they say they're half fish, half flesh. 2.01. 24 P
to say you're welcome were superfluous. 2.03. 2
say we drink this standing–bowl of wine to him. 2.03. 65
sir, say if you had, who takes offense | at that 2.05. 71
thee, whiles i say | a priestly farewell to her. 3.01. 68
i thank thee. mariner, say, what coast is this? 3.01. 72
o, you say well. 3.02. 20
by the holy gods | i cannot rightly say. 3.04. 8
come say your prayers. 4.01. 65
you say she's a virgin? 4.02. 40 P
therefore say what a paragon she is, and thou 4.02.140 P
what canst thou say | when noble pericles shall 4.03. 12
i'll say so. 4.03. 16
and as for pericles, | what should he say? 4.03. 41
do the deeds of darkness, thou wouldst say. 4.06. 30 P
your honor knows what 'tis to say well enough. 4.06. 31 P
i hear say you're of honorable parts, and are 4.06. 80 P
come your ways, i say. 4.06.130 P
what say you? 5.01. 98
than | to say my mother's name was thaisa? 5.01.210
you have heard me say, when i did fly from tyre, 5.03. 50
for, to say truth, it were an endless thing, TNK pr 22
poor lady, say no more. 1.01.101
pray you say nothing, pray you. 1.01.119
they themselves, some say, | groan under such a 1.01.230
reason has no manners | to say it is not you. 1.03. 49
and this high–speeded pace is but to say | that 1.03. 83
boldly to gaze against bright arms, and say, 2.02. 35
they must not, say they could; 2.02. 67
shall i say more? 2.02.111
i say again, i love, and, in loving her, 2.02.178
but say that one | had rather combat me? 2.02.196
let that one say so, | and use thy freedom; 2.02.197
say i ventur'd | to set him free? 2.04. 30
that knew me | would say it was my best piece; 2.05. 14
seen so young a man so noble | (if he say true) 2.05. 19
and because you say | you are a horseman, i must 2.05. 44
thy hand, and do but say | that emily is thine, 3.01. 75
when you shall stretch yourself, and say but, 3.01. 87
i say again, | that sigh was breath'd for emily. 3.03. 43
i'll say never a word. 3.04. 18
but i say, where's their women? 3.05. 25
and, to say verity, and not to fable, | we are a 3.05.105
say "ay," and all shall presently advance. 3.05.134
and a down, | say the schoolmaster's no clown. 3.05.141
'tis the duke's, | and, to say true, i stole it. 3.06. 55
and me my love! is there aught else to say? 3.06. 93
if i fall, curse me, and say i was a coward, 3.06.104
scorn us, | and say we had a noble difference, 3.06.116
decider of all injuries, | say, "fight again!" 3.06.154
me | a thing as soon to die as thee to say it, 3.06.159
man calls me traitor, | let me say thus much: 3.06.161
and if she say "traitor," | i am a villain fit 3.06.170
for, to say true, your cousin | has ten times 3.06.180
say i felt | compassion to 'em both, how would 3.06.212
say, emilia, | if one of them were dead, as one 3.06.272
as ever you heard, but say nothing. 4.01.135
his face a prince | (his very looks so say him), 4.02. 78
say you come to eat with her and to commune of 4.03. 77 P
the huntress | all moist and cold, some say, 5.01. 93
white, which some will say | weakens his price, 5.04. 51
made (for, as they say, from iron | came music's 5.04. 60
but, as it is with schoolboys, cannot say; ep 2
now what say ye? ep 10
i dare say, many a better, to prolong | your old ep 16
what say you to the mercy of the king? STM II.C 17
how say you now, /prentices? II.C 22 P
peace i say, peace! II.C 35 P
alas, alas, say now the king, | as he is clement II.C 122
what shall she say? VEN 253
as who should say, "lo thus my strength is tried 280
his flattering "holla," or his "stand, i say"? 284
for lovers say, the heart hath treble wrong 329
"say that the sense of feeling were bereft me, 439
may say, the plague is banish'd by thy breath. 510
say for non–payment that the debt should double, 521
"now let me say 'good night,' and so say you; 535
"now let me say 'good night,' and so say you; 535
if you will say so, you shall have a kiss." 536
say, shall we, shall we? 586
"more i could tell, but more i dare not say, 805
and would say after her, if she said "no." 852
as who should say, "this glove to wanton tricks LUC 320
when pattern'd by thy fault foul sin may say 629
we have no good that we can say is ours, | but 873
not, faint heart, but stoutly say, 'so be it'; 1209
what should i say? 1291
"then be this all the task it hath to say: 1618
with this they all at once began to say, | her 1709
interest, let no mourner say | he weeps for her, 1797
and wherefore say not i that i am old? PP 1.10
halt — | but plainly say thou lov'st her well, 18.11
strength, | and ban and brawl, and say thee nay; 18.32
when craft hath taught her thus to say: 18.34
to say within thine own deep–sunken eyes | were SON 2. 7
know | you had a father, let your son say so. 13.14
wind, | or say with princes if it shall go well, 14. 7
the age to come would say, "this poet lies, 17. 7
let them say more that like of hearsay well, | i 21.13
forget to say | the perfect ceremony of love's 23. 5
how would (i say) mine eyes be blessed made | by 43. 9
doth teach that ease and that repose to say, 50. 3
that i might see what the old world could say 59. 9
o, if (i say) you look upon this verse, | when i 71. 9
then thank him not for that which he doth say, 79.13
which can say more | than this rich praise, that 84. 1
hearing you prais'd, i say, "'tis so, 'tis true, 85. 9
say that thou didst forsake me for some fault, 89. 1
some say thy fault is youth, some wantonness, 96. 1
some say thy grace is youth and gentle sport; 96. 2
wilt thou not haply say, | "truth needs no color 101. 5
i must each day say o'er the very same, 108. 6
o, never say that i was false of heart, | though 109. 1
or whether shall i say mine eye saith true, 114. 3
might i not then say, "now i love you best," 115.10
love is a babe, then might i not say so, | to 115.13
yet in good faith some say that thee behold, 131. 5
to say they err i dare not be so bold, 131. 7
or mine eyes seeing this, say this is not, | to 137.11
and wherefore say not i that i am old? 138.10
what means the world to say it is not so? 148. 6
canst thou, o cruel, say i love thee not, | when 149. 1
"well could he ride, and often men would say, LC 106
and dialogu'd for him what he would say, | ask'd 132
"for further i could say, 'this man's untrue,' 169

'SAY'D *(also assay'd)*

'SAY'D 2 FR 0.0002 REL FR 2 V 0 P
of all 'say'd yet, mayst thou prove prosperous! PER 1.01. 59
of all 'say'd yet, i wish thee happiness! 1.01. 60

SAYEST 17 FR 0.0019 REL FR 5 V 12 P
din'd at home? thou villain, what sayest thou? ERR 4.04. 68
ha, ha? what sayest thou? LLL 3.01. 53 P
what sayest thou, bully bottom? MND 3.01. 8 P
ha, what sayest thou? MV 3.01. 16 P
by my troth, thou sayest true; AYL 1.02. 88 P
what sayest thou? 4.01.120 P
thou, now a–dying, sayest thou flatterest me. R2 2.01. 90
thou sayest well, and it holds well too, for the 1H4 1.02. 30 P
what sayest thou to a hare, or the melancholy of 1.02. 77 P
what sayest thou to this? 2.04.233 P
lad, thou sayest true, it is like we shall have 2.04.364 P
and sayest thou yet that exile is not death? ROM 3.03. 43
thou sayest the king grows mad, i'll tell thee, LR 3.04.165
what sayest thou? ANT 4.05. 9
sayest thou? CYM 2.01. 25 P
thou sayest true, there's two unwholesome, a' PER 4.02. 21 P
thou sayest true, i' faith, so they must: 4.02.126 P

SAYING 59 FR 0.0066 REL FR 35 V 24 P
and the old saying is, | black men are pearls in TGV 5.02. 11
what mean you by that saying? 5.04.167
the goldsmith here | denies that saying. ERR 5.01.275
is, | saying i lik'd her ere i went to wars. ADO 1.01.305
if their singing answer your saying, by my faith 2.01.234 P
a proper saying! 4.01.310 P
i pretty, and my saying apt? LLL 1.02. 20 P
or i apt, and my saying pretty? 1.02. 20 P
by saying that a costard was broken in a shin. 3.01.106
shall i come upon thee with an old saying, that 4.01.119 P
and he himself must speak through, saying thus, MND 3.01. 38 P
only are reputed wise | for saying nothing; MV 1.01. 97
my meaning in saying he is a good man is to have 1.03. 15 P
is at mine elbow and tempts me, saying to me, 2.02. 3 P
nay more, while grace is saying, hood mine eyes 2.02.193
let's see once more this saying grav'd in gold: 2.07. 36
the ancient saying is no heresy, | hanging and 2.09. 82
way, | he did entreat me, past all saying nay, 3.02.229
other had pull'd out thy tongue for saying so. AYL 1.01. 61 P
good enough, for all the old gentleman's saying. 5.01. 4 P
i do now remember a saying, "the fool doth think 5.01. 31 P
hawking or spitting or saying we are hoarse, 5.03. 12 P
for saying so, there's gold. TN 1.02. 18
i can tell thee where that saying was born, of 1.05. 10 P
saying, "cousin toby, my fortunes, having cast 2.05. 69 P
is a good play, and the old saying is, the third 5.01. 37 P
and i'll be sworn you would believe my saying, WT 2.01. 63
though 'tis a saying, sir, not due to me. 3.02. 58

that give you cause to prove my saying true. JN 3.01. 28
up the heavy time, | saying, "what lack you?" 4.01. 48
twice saying "pardon" doth not pardon twain, R2 5.03.134
thou art an unjust man in saying so. 1H4 3.03.129 P
saying that ere long they should call me madam? 2H4 2.01.100 P
but there's a saying very old and true, | "if H5 1.02.166
saying our grace is only in our heels, | and 3.05. 34
come, 'tis a foolish saying. 4.01.202 P
but the saying is true, "the empty vessel makes 4.04. 68 P
saying the sanguine color of the leaves | did 1H6 4.01. 92
for saying that the duke of york was rightful 2H6 1.03. 26 P
saying, he'll lade it dry to have his way: 3H6 3.02.139
the saying did not hold | in him that did object R3 2.04. 16
citizen | only for saying he would make his son 3.05. 77
in saying so you shall but say the truth. 3.07.238
you cause) my doing well | with my well saying! H8 3.02.152
but, saying thus, in stead of oil and balm, TRO 1.01. 61
cudgelling that he raves in saying nothing. 3.03.249 P
"o heart," as the goodly saying is, "o heart, 4.04. 15 P
yet you must be saying martius is proud; COR 2.01. 90 P
can give, | to have't with saying "good morrow." 3.03. 93
ay, like a black dog, as the saying is. TIT 5.01.122
but saying o'er what i have said before: ROM 1.02. 7
people | the deed of saying is quite out of use. TIM 5.01. 26
that thou hast prov'd lucilius' saying true. JC 5.05. 59
my father is not dead, for all your saying. MAC 4.02. 37
act and place | may give his saying deed, which HAM 1.03. 27
i will not have excuse with saying this | loud PER 2.03. 96
as cold as a snowball, saying his prayers too. 4.06.140 P
saying, some shape in sinon's was abus'd: LUC 1529
threw, | and sav'd my life, saying "not you." SON 145.14

SAYINGS 5 FR 0.0005 REL FR 4 V 1 P

why do you put these sayings upon me? MM 2.02.133
to fates and destinies, and such odd sayings, MV 2.02. 63 P
on every tree, | that shall civil sayings show: AYL 3.02.128
and all those sayings will i over swear, | and TN 5.01.269
methinks there is much reason in his sayings. JC 3.02.108

SAY'S 1 FR 0.0001 REL FR 0 V 1 P

we'll have the lord say's head for selling the 2H6 4.02.160 P

/SAYS 5 FR 0.0005 REL FR 4 V 1 P

/save /king /henry, /unking'd /richard /says, R2 4.01.220
/hark, /marcus, /what /she /says; TIT 3.02. 35
/she /says, /she /drinks /no /other /drink /but 3.02. 37
/the /scripture /says /adam /digg'd; HAM 5.01. 36 P
our thing of learning /says so — | where he TNK 2.03. 51

SAYS 251 FR 0.0283 REL FR 161 V 90 P

and says such baseness | had never like executor TMP 3.01. 12
loss, and patience | says, it is past her cure. 5.01.141
i'll die on him that says so but yourself. TGV 2.04.114
"out with the dog," says one. 4.04. 20 P
says another. 4.04. 21 P
"whip him out," says the third. 4.04. 21 P
"hang him up," says the duke. 4.04. 22 P
and what says she to my little jewel? 4.04. 47 P
marry, she says your dog was a cur, and tells 4.04. 48 P
sir proteus, what says silvia to my suit? 5.02. 1
what says she to my face? 5.02. 8
she says it is a fair one. 5.02. 9
what says she to my valor? 5.02. 19
what says she to my birth? 5.02. 22
nay, i will do as my cousin shallow says. WIV 1.01.217 P
what says my bully-rook? 1.03. 2 P
your worship says very true. 2.02. 48 P
but what says she to me? 2.02. 79 P
then you may come and see the picture, she says, 2.02. 87 P
who says this is improvident jealousy? 2.02.289 P
what says my aesculapius? 2.03. 28 P
for a gentleman that he says is here now in the 3.03.108 P
my husband says my son profits nothing in the 4.01. 14 P
and what says she, i pray, sir? 4.05. 35 P
she says that the very same man that beguil'd 4.05. 36 P
what says my brother? MM 3.01.115
to do it, | he says, to veil full purpose. 4.06. 4
carnally, she says. 5.01.214
that thinks a man always going to bed and says, ERR 4.03. 32 P
"fly pride," says the peacock: 4.03. 80
the one is too like an image and says nothing, ADO 2.01. 8 P
'tis true indeed, so your daughter says. 2.03.127 P
"shall i," says she, "that have so oft 2.03.128 P
this says she now when she is beginning to write 2.03.130 P
"i measure him," says she, "by my own spirit, 2.03.143 P
she doth indeed, my daughter says so; 2.03.150 P
for she says she will die if he love her not, 2.03.174 P
so says the prince and my new-trothed lord. 3.01. 38
i will make him eat it that says i love not you. 4.01.277 P
"right," says she, "a great gross one." 5.01.162 P
my physic says ay. LLL 2.01.188
a mark, says my lady! 4.01.131
or rather, as horace says in his — what, my 4.02.102 P
says one, "o jove!" 4.03.139
she says, you have it, and you may be gone. 5.02.183
your nose says, no, you are not; 5.02.565
what says maria? 5.02.833
and reason says you are the worthier maid. MND 2.02.116
for pyramus and thisby (says the story) did talk 3.01. 63 P
to prove him false that says i love thee not. 3.02.253
he says they can do nothing in this kind. 5.01. 88
my conscience says, "no; MV 2.02. 7 P
says the fiend; 2.02. 11 P
says the fiend; 2.02. 11 P
rouse up a brave mind," says the fiend, "and run 2.02. 12 P
the neck of my heart, says very wisely to me, 2.02. 14 P
taste — well, my conscience says, "launcelot, 2.02. 19 P
"bouge," says the fiend. 2.02. 19 P
"bouge not," says my conscience. 2.02. 20 P
what says that fool of hagar's offspring, ha? 2.05. 44
what says this leaden casket? 2.07. 15
what says the silver with her virgin hue? 2.07. 22
what says the golden chest? 2.09. 23
and he says you are no good member of the 3.05. 34 P
ay, so he says. 4.01.181
so says the bond, doth it not, noble judge? 4.01.253
thrice a villain that says such a father begot AYL 1.01. 58 P
eye, | says very wisely, "it is ten a' clock. 2.07. 22
and says, if ladies be but young and fair, 2.07. 37
that says his bravery is not on my cost, 2.07. 80
she says i am not fair, that i lack manners; 4.03. 15
and when he says he is, say that he dreams, SHR in.1. 64
she says she'll see thee hang'd first. 2.01.300
what says lucentio to this shame of ours? 3.02. 7
he says so, tranio. 4.02. 53
she says your worship means to make a puppet of 4.03.105 P
say as he says, or we shall never go. 4.05. 11
sir, so his mother says, if i may believe her. 5.01. 33 P
my widow says, thus she conceives her tale. 5.02. 24
she says you have some goodly jest in hand. 5.02. 91
lustick, as the dutchman says. AWW 2.03. 41 P
he says he has a stratagem for't. 3.06. 35 P
she says all men | have the like oaths. 4.02. 70
the general says, you that have so traitorously 4.03.304 P
displeasure, and, as he says, is muddied withal. 5.02. 21 P
what says he to your daughter? have you spoke? 5.03. 28
this it says: 5.03.311
for what says quinapalus? TN 1.05. 35 P
and he says he'll stand at your door like a 1.05.147 P
he says he'll come. 3.04. 1
"cast thy humble slough," says she; 3.04. 68 P
says, "my poor prisoner, | i am innocent as you. WT 2.02. 26
he says he loves my daughter. 4.04.171
and remain, as he says, your pawn till it be 4.04.822 P
"o sir," says answer, "at your best command, JN 1.01.197
"no, sir," says question, "i, sweet sir, at 1.01.199
who says it was, he lies, i say 'twas not. 1.01.276
what england says, say briefly, gentle lord, 2.01. 52
what says the world | to your proceedings? 4.02.132
whereon he says | i shall yield up my crown, let 4.02.156
he flatly says he'll not lay down his arms. 5.02.126
that ever fury breath'd, | the youth says well. 5.02.128
what says he? R2 2.01.148
northumberland, | what says king bullingbrook? 3.03.173
you make a leg, and bullingbrook says ay. 3.03.175
what says his majesty? 3.03.184
says that this deed is chronicled in hell. 5.05.116
what says monsieur remorse? 1H4 1.02.112 P
what says sir john sack and sugar? 1.02.113 P
were, as he says, not with such strength denied 1.03. 25
washes his hands, and says to his wife, "fie 2.04.104 P
"o my sweet harry," says she, "how many hast 2.04.105 P
"give my roan horse a drench," says he, and 2.04.107 P
says the drunkard. 2.04.111 P
he says he comes from your father. 2.04.288 P
dead, | not he which says the dead is not alive. 2H4 1.01. 99
you giant, what says the doctor to my water? 1.02. 1 P
soul, and she says up and down the town that her 2.01.104 P
says he, that takes upon him not to conceive. 2.02.114 P
"neighbor quickly," says he — master dumbe, our 2.04. 87 P
"neighbor quickly," says he, "receive those that 2.04. 89 P
"for," says he, "you are an honest woman, and 2.04. 91 P
receive," says he, "no swaggering companions." 2.04. 94 P
i am the worse when one says swagger. 2.04.105 P
what says th' almanac to that? 2.04.264 P
what says your grace? 2.04.349 P
his grace says that which his flesh rebels 2.04.350 P
says that you savor too much of your youth, H5 1.02.250
thus says my king: 2.04.120
thus says my king: 3.06.118 P
he says his name is master fer. 4.04. 27 P
and, with a feeble gripe, says, "dear my lord, 4.06. 22
your majesty says very true. 4.07. 97 P
what says she, fair one? 5.02.117 P
madam my interpreter, what says she? 5.02.260 P
what she says i'll confirm. we'll fight it out. 1H6 1.02.128
when gloucester says the word, king henry goes, 3.01.183
my hand would free her, but my heart says no. 5.03. 61
and so says york — for he hath greatest cause. 2H6 1.01.207
his sons, he says, shall give their words for 5.01.137
what says lord warwick? 5.03. 27
if that be right which warwick says is right, 3H6 2.02.131
she weeps, and says her henry is depos'd; 3.01. 45
he smiles, and says his edward is install'd; 3.01. 46
and says that once more i shall interchange | my 4.07. 3
say, somervile, what says my loving son? 5.01. 7
which says that g | of edward's heirs the R3 1.01. 39
and says a wizard told him that by g | his issue 1.01. 56
besides, he says there are two councils kept; 3.02. 12
yet who/'s so bold but says he sees it not? 3.06. 12
now, catesby, what says your lord to my request? 3.07. 58
now, catesby, what says his grace? 3.07. 83
what says your highness to my just request? 4.02. 94
and kneels, and says, "god save the queen"? 4.04. 94
what says lord stanley? 5.03.342
what traitor hears me, and says not amen? 5.05. 22
spoke by a holy monk "that oft," says he, H8 1.02.160
amen, and yet my conscience says | she's a good 5.01. 24
is verified | of thee, which says thus, "do my 5.02.210
so he says here. TRO 1.02. 54 P
who, as ulysses says, opinion crowns | with an 1.03.186
what says ulysses? 1.03.311
thus once again says nestor from the greeks: 2.02. 2
that lays thee out says thou art a fair corse, 2.03. 32 P
what says my sweet queen, my very very sweet 3.01. 79 P
what says my sweet queen? 3.01. 84 P
what says achilles? would he aught with us? 3.03. 57
thus says aeneas, one that knows the youth 4.05.110
what says she there? 5.03.106 P
my good friends, this says the belly, mark me. COR 1.01.141
but i beseech you, | what says the other troop? 1.01.204
save yourself, but says | he us'd us scornfully. 2.03.162
it in scorn, | "i would be consul," says he; 2.03.168
lo, citizens, he says he is content. 3.03. 48
he'll go, he says, and sowl the porter of rome 4.05.200 P
what says jupiter? TIT 4.03. 80
he says that he hath taken them down again, for 4.03. 81 P
but what says jupiter, i ask thee? 4.03. 84
knock at my door, and tell me what he says. 4.03.119
what says our general? 5.01.162
what says andronicus to this device? 5.02.120
she speaks, yet she says nothing; ROM 2.02. 12
what says he of our marriage? 2.05. 47
sweet, sweet nurse, tell me, what says my love? 2.05. 54
your love says, like an honest gentleman, | an' 2.05. 55
"your love says, like an honest gentleman, 2.05. 60
here's such a coil! come, what says romeo? 2.05. 65
claps me his sword upon the table, and says, 3.01. 7 P
and what says | my conceal'd lady to our 3.03. 97
o, she says nothing, sir, but weeps and weeps, 3.03. 99
what says romeo? 5.02. 3
"nothing doubting," says he? TIM 3.01. 21 P
when caesar says, "do this," it is perform'd. JC 1.02. 10
tell him he hates flatterers | he says he does, 2.01.208
so says my master antony. 3.01.137
he says, for brutus' sake | he finds himself 3.02. 66
but brutus says he was ambitious, | and brutus 3.02. 86
yet brutus says he was ambitious, | and brutus 3.02. 93
yet brutus says he was ambitious, | and sure he 3.02. 98
what says my general? 5.01. 70
what says my lord? 5.05. 16
horatio says 'tis but our fantasy, | and will HAM 1.01. 23
what says polonius? 1.02. 57
then, if he says he loves you, | it fits your 1.03. 24
the satirical rogue says here that old men have 2.02.196 P
then thus she says: 3.02.326 P
says she hears | there's tricks i' th' world, 4.05. 4
and in a postscript here, he says, "alone." 4.07. 52
what says our second daughter, | our dearest LR 1.01. 67
converse with him that is wise and says little, 1.04. 16 P
what says the fellow there? 1.04. 46 P
he says, my lord, your /daughter is not well. 1.04. 50 P
a spirit, a spirit! he says his name's poor tom. 3.04. 42 P
says suum, mun, nonny. 3.04. 99 P
he knows not what he says, and vain is it | that 5.03.294
for, "certes," says he, | "i have already chose OTH 1.01. 16
and what's he then that says i play the villain? 2.03.336
she says enough; 4.02. 20
he says he will return incontinent, | and hath 4.03. 12
he says thou toldst him that his wife was false. 5.02.173
what, says the married woman you may go? ANT 1.03. 20
auguring hope | says it will come to th' full. 2.01. 11
hoo, says 'a. there's my cap. 2.07.134
since pompey's feast, as menas says, is troubled 3.02. 5
he says so. 3.13. 16
we'll hear him what he says. 5.01. 51
and with your speediest bring us what she says, 5.01. 67
says to 'em, if king pericles | come not home in PER 3.ch. 30
my father, as nurse says, did never fear, | but 4.01. 52
says one, "wolt out?" 4.01. 61
chances | into an honest house, our story says. 5.ch. 2
what says the law then? TNK 2.04. 31
a learned poet says, unless by th' tail | and 3.05. 49
songs of love as she says palamon hath sung in 4.03. 82 P
what e'er her father says, if you perceive | her 5.02. 33
faith, 'a says true. STM II.C 141 P
and, ere he says "adieu," | the honey fee of VEN 537
"sweet boy," she says, "this night i'll waste in 583
"fie, fie," he says, "you crush me, let me go, 611
she says, "'tis so," they answer all, "'tis so," 851
and says, within her bosom it shall dwell, 1173
she says, her subjects with foul insurrection LUC 722
"he, he," she says, | but more than "he" her 1717
the father says, "she's mine." 1795
but wherefore says my love that she is young? PP 1. 9
and says in him /thy fair appearance lies. SON 46. 8
who is it that says most, which can say more 84. 1
since my appeal says i did strive to prove | the 117.13
that every tongue says beauty should look so. 127.14
but wherefore says she not she is unjust? 138. 9
"father," she says, "though in me you behold LC 71

SAY'ST 68 FR 0.0076 REL FR 41 V 27 P

by foul play (as thou say'st) were we heav'd TMP 1.02. 62
what thou say'st? TGV 2.05. 28 P
how say'st thou that my master is become a 2.05. 42 P
what say'st thou? 4.01. 62
what say'st thou? 4.04.139
what say'st thou, my bully-rook? WIV 2.01.205 P
say'st thou so, old jack? 2.02.138 P
do so. between nine and ten, say'st thou? 3.05. 53 P
what say'st thou to this tune, matter, and MM 3.02. 48 P
what say'st thou, trot? 3.02. 49 P
thou say'st his meat was sauc'd with thy ERR 5.01. 73
thou say'st his sports were hind'red by thy 5.01. 77
thou (being, as thou say'st thou art, born under ADO 1.03. 11 P
crowns, and, as thou say'st, charg'd my brother, AYL 1.01. 3 P
hah! what say'st thou, silvius? 3.05. 83
why, thou say'st well. 5.01. 30 P
no, say'st me so, friend? what countryman? SHR 1.02.189
why, thou say'st true, it is /a paltry cap, | a 4.03. 81
what say'st thou, biondello? 4.04. 74 P
and not a maiden, as thou say'st he is. 4.05. 44
what say'st thou to her? AWW 5.03.187
what say'st thou? TN 3.04. 44 P
say'st thou that house is dark? 4.02. 33 P
what say'st thou, boy? look in the lady's face. JN 2.01.495
philip, what say'st thou to the cardinal? 3.01.202
thomas of norfolk, what say'st thou to this? R2 1.01.110
by the lord, thou say'st true, lad. 1H4 1.02. 39 P
what say'st thou, my lady? 2.03. 74
what say'st thou, kate? 2.03. 95
what say'st thou to me? 2.04.286 P
what say'st thou, mistress quickly? 3.03. 92 P
what say'st thou, jack? 3.03. 96 P
thou say'st true, hostess, and he slanders thee 3.03.131 P
mass, thou say'st true. 2H4 2.04. 4 P
thou't set me a-weeping and thou say'st so. 2.04.279 P
say'st thou me so? H5 4.04. 22
and what say'st thou then to my love? 5.02.167 P
what say'st thou, my fair flower-de-luce? 5.02.210 P
what say'st thou, man, before dead henry's corse 1H6 1.01. 62
what say'st thou, charles? 3.03. 39
how say'st thou, charles? 5.04.165
what say'st thou? majesty? i am but grace. 2H6 1.02. 71
what say'st thou, man? 1.02. 74
what say'st thou? 1.03. 28 P
say'st thou me so? what color is this cloak of? 2.01.107
what say'st thou, henry, wilt thou yield the 3H6 2.02.101
huntsman, what say'st thou? wilt thou go along? 4.05. 25
what say'st thou now? R3 4.02. 20
what say'st? H8 1.02.202
what say'st thou? 5.01. 66
what say'st thou, my dear nurse? ROM 2.04.195
what say'st thou? 3.05.211
what say'st thou to me now? speak once again. JC 1.02. 22
how say'st thou, that macduff denies his person MAC 3.04.127
ha, ha, boy, say'st thou so? HAM 1.05.150
why, there thou say'st, and the more pity that 5.01. 26 P

ha? say'st thou so? LR 1.04. 63 P
himself; what say'st thou to him? 5.03.126
what is't thou say'st? 5.03.273
with the moor, say'st thou? OTH 1.01.164
what say'st thou, noble heart? 1.03.302 P
in state of health thou say'st, and thou say'st ANT 2.05. 56
of health thou say'st, and thou say'st free. 2.05. 56
what say'st thou? 2.07. 61
being in these wars, | and say'st it is not fit. 3.07. 4
what is't thou say'st? 5.01. 12
weeps she still, say'st thou? CYM 1.05. 46
thou say'st true. PER 4.02. 13 P

SAY'T 5 FR 0.0005 REL FR 4 V 1 P
his father, though i say't, is an honest MV 2.02. 52 P
say't and justify't. WT 1.02.278
to th' king i'll say't, and make my vouch as H8 1.01.157
say't be so? COR 5.01. 45
file, | not i' th' worst rank of manhood, say't, MAC 3.01.102

/'SBLOOD 1 FR 0.0001 REL FR 1 V 0 P
/'sblood, but you'll not hear me. OTH 1.01. 4

'SBLOOD 10 FR 0.0011 REL FR 1 V 9 P
'sblood, i am as melancholy as a gib cat or a 1H4 1.02. 73 P
king of smiles, this bullingbrook — | 'sblood! 1.03.247
'sblood, i'll not bear my own flesh so far afoot 2.02. 35 P
'sblood, you starveling, you /eel–skin, you 2.04.244 P
'sblood, my lord, they are false. 2.04.443 P
'sblood, i would my face were in your belly! 3.03. 49 P
'sblood, and he were here, i would cudgel him 3.03. 86 P
'sblood, 'twas time to counterfeit, or that hot 5.04.113 P
'sblood, there is something in this more than HAM 2.02.366 P
'sblood, do you think i am easier to be play'd 3.02.369 P

'SBLUD 1 FR 0.0001 REL FR 0 V 1 P
'sblud, an arrant traitor as any's in the H5 4.08. 9 P

SCAB 4 FR 0.0004 REL FR 0 V 4 P
i thought there would a scab follow. ADO 3.03.100 P
out, scab! TN 2.05. 74 P
well said, i' faith, wart, th' art a good scab. 2H4 3.02.276 P
would make thee the loathsomest scab in greece. TRO 2.01. 29 P

SCABBARD 4 FR 0.0004 REL FR 2 V 2 P
it is in my scabbard, shall i draw it? ADO 5.01.125 P
had a pass with him, rapier, scabbard, and all; TN 3.04.275 P
here in my scabbard, meditating that | shall dye 1H6 2.04. 60
we'll no defense, | obedient as the scabbard. CYM 3.04. 80

SCABS 1 FR 0.0001 REL FR 1 V 0 P
itch of your opinion | make yourselves scabs? COR 1.01.166

SCAFFOLAGE 1 FR 0.0001 REL FR 1 V 0 P
'twixt his stretch'd footing and the scaffolage, TRO 1.03.156

SCAFFOLD 2 FR 0.0002 REL FR 2 V 0 P
dar'd | on this unworthy scaffold to bring forth H5 pr 10
up to some scaffold, there to lose their heads. R3 4.04.243

SCAL'D* 2 FR 0.0002 REL FR 1 V 1 P
advantag'd, and the corrupt deputy scal'd. MM 3.01.255 P
and made | a cestern for scal'd snakes! ANT 2.05. 95

SCALD* *(also scall)*

SCALD* 8 FR 0.0009 REL FR 3 V 5 P
the rascally, scald, beggarly, lousy, pragging H5 5.01. 5 P
will you be so good, scald knave, as eat it? 5.01. 30 P
you say very true, scald knave, when god's will 5.01. 32 P
much good do you, scald knave, heartily. 5.01. 53 P
setting on water to scald such chickens as you TIM 2.02. 69 P
may these add to the number that may scald thee! 3.01. 51
that mine own tears | do scald like molten lead. LR 4.07. 47
and scald rhymers | ballad 's out a' tune. ANT 5.02.215

SCALDED 1 FR 0.0001 REL FR 1 V 0 P
i am scalded with my violent motion | and spleen JN 5.07. 49

SCALDING 2 FR 0.0002 REL FR 2 V 0 P
went all afoot in summer's scalding heat, | that 3H6 5.07. 18
there is the sulphurous pit, burning, scalding, LR 4.06.128

SCALD'ST 1 FR 0.0001 REL FR 1 V 0 P
in heat of day, | that scald'st with safety. 2H4 4.05. 31

SCALE* 15 FR 0.0017 REL FR 12 V 3 P
would serve to scale another hero's tow'r, | so TGV 3.01.119
a feather will turn the scale. MM 4.02. 31 P
if the scale do turn | but in the estimation of MV 4.01.330
dream | we, poising us in her defective scale, AWW 2.03.154
in your lord's scale is nothing but himself, R2 3.04. 85
let us resolve to scale their flinty bulwarks. 1H6 2.01. 27
dread father's, in a scale | of common ounces? TRO 2.02. 27
swear in both the scales against either scale, MAC 2.03. 9 P
scale of dragon, tooth of wolf, | witch's mummy, 4.01. 22
in equal scale weighing delight and dole, HAM 1.02. 13
with weight | /till our scale turn the beam. 4.05.158
our lives had not one scale of reason to poise OTH 1.03.327 P
ranks of blue veins, as his hand did scale, LUC 440
under that color am i come to scale | thy 481
white weighs down the airy scale of praise, LC 226

SCALES* 8 FR 0.0009 REL FR 6 V 2 P
your vows to her and me, put in two scales, MND 3.02.132
weight of a hair will turn scales between their 2H4 2.04.254 P
and lord scales with him, and lord hungerford. 1H6 1.01.146
and poise the cause in justice' equal scales, 2H6 2.01.200
to give the heir and daughter of lord scales 3H6 4.01. 52
but in that crystal scales let there be weigh'd ROM 1.02. 96
swear in both the scales against either scale, MAC 2.03. 9 P
o' th' nile | by certain scales i' th' pyramid; ANT 2.07. 18

SCALING* 2 FR 0.0002 REL FR 2 V 0 P
like scaling sculls | before the belching whale; TRO 5.05. 22
scaling his present bearing with his past, COR 2.03.249

SCALL *(also scald*)*

SCALL 1 FR 0.0001 REL FR 0 V 1 P
together to be revenge on this same scall, WIV 3.01.120 P

SCALP 2 FR 0.0002 REL FR 2 V 0 P
by the bare scalp of robin hood's fat friar, TGV 4.01. 36
take this transformed scalp | from off the head MND 4.01. 64

SCALPS 2 FR 0.0002 REL FR 2 V 0 P
have arm'd their thin and hairless scalps R2 3.02.112
the scalps of many, almost hid behind, | to jump LUC 1413

SCALY 1 FR 0.0001 REL FR 1 V 0 P
a scaly gauntlet now with joints of steel | must 2H4 1.01.146

SCAMBLE 1 FR 0.0001 REL FR 1 V 0 P
and england now is left | to tug and scamble, JN 4.03.146

SCAMBLING 3 FR 0.0003 REL FR 2 V 1 P
scambling, outfacing, fashion–monging boys, ADO 5.01. 94
but that the scambling and unquiet time | did H5 1.01. 4
tells me thou shalt, i get thee with scambling, 5.02.205 P

SCAMELS 1 FR 0.0001 REL FR 1 V 0 P
i'll get thee | young scamels from the rock. TMP 2.02.172

SCAN 2 FR 0.0002 REL FR 2 V 0 P
your honor | to scan this thing no farther; OTH 3.03.245
that makes us scan | the outward habit by the PER 2.02. 56

SCANDAL 21 FR 0.0023 REL FR 21 V 0 P
that no particular scandal once can touch | but MM 4.04. 27
and, not without some scandal to yourself, ERR 5.01. 15
o, in a tomb where never scandal slept, | save ADO 5.01. 70
your wrongs do set a scandal on my sex. MND 2.01.240
give scandal to the blood o' th' prince my son WT 1.02.330
ah, would the scandal vanish with my life, | how R2 2.01. 67
o, what a scandal is it to our crown | that two 1H6 3.01. 69
why, yet thy scandal were not wip'd away, | but 2H6 2.04. 65
but ne'er till now his scandal of retire. 3H6 2.01.150
nor now my scandal, richard, dost thou hear; 2.01.151
but if black scandal or foul–fac'd reproach R3 3.07.231
men and hug them hard, | and after scandal them; JC 1.02. 76
noble substance of a doubt | to his own scandal. HAM 1.04. 38
you must not put another scandal on him, | that 2.01. 29
sinon's weeping | did scandal many a holy tear, CYM 3.04. 60
i should pluck | all ladies' scandal on me. TNK 1.01.192
tail without offense | or scandal to the ladies; 3.05. 35
"yea, though i die, the scandal will survive, LUC 204
thou plantest scandal and displacest laud. 887
for greatest scandal waits on greatest state. 1006
which vulgar scandal stamp'd upon my brow, | for SON 112. 2

SCANDALIZ'D 2 FR 0.0002 REL FR 2 V 0 P
i fear me, it will make me scandaliz'd. TGV 2.07. 61
mouth | live scandaliz'd and foully spoken of. 1H4 1.03.154

SCANDALL'D 2 FR 0.0002 REL FR 2 V 0 P
her and her blind boy's scandall'd company | i TMP 4.01. 90
scandall'd the suppliants for the people, call'd COR 3.01. 44

SCANDALOUS 2 FR 0.0002 REL FR 2 V 0 P
a blasting and a scandalous breath to fall | on MM 5.01.122
make you, | yea, scandalous to the world. WT 2.03.121

SCANN'D 3 FR 0.0003 REL FR 3 V 0 P
who, every word by all my wit being scann'd, ERR 2.02.150
which must be acted ere they may be scann'd. MAC 3.04.139
that would be scann'd: HAM 3.03. 75

SCANT 10 FR 0.0011 REL FR 10 V 0 P
in measure rain thy joy, scant this excess! MV 3.02.112
therefore i scant this breathing courtesy. 5.01.141
and she shall scant show well that now seems ROM 1.02. 99
he's fat, and scant of breath. HAM 5.02.287
value her desert | than she to scant her duty. LR 2.04.140
to bandy hasty words, to scant my sizes, | and 2.04.175
i will your serious and great business scant OTH 1.03.267
us, | or scant our former having in despite: 4.03. 91
scant not my cups, and make as much of me | as ANT 4.02. 21
but if store of crowns be scant, | no man will PP 20.35

SCANTED 5 FR 0.0005 REL FR 4 V 1 P
and what he hath scanted /men in hair he hath ERR 2.02. 80 P
but if my father had not scanted me, | and MV 2.01. 17
you have obedience scanted, | and well are worth LR 1.01.278
in) return, and force | their scanted courtesy. 3.02. 67
that i have scanted all | wherein i should your SON 117. 1

SCANTER 1 FR 0.0001 REL FR 1 V 0 P
be something scanter of your maiden presence, HAM 1.03.121

SCANTING 1 FR 0.0001 REL FR 1 V 0 P
doth like a miser spoil his coat with scanting H5 2.04. 47

SCANTLING 1 FR 0.0001 REL FR 1 V 0 P
shall give a scantling | of good or bad unto the TRO 1.03.341

SCANTLY 1 FR 0.0001 REL FR 1 V 0 P
spoke scantly of me; ANT 3.04. 6

SCANTS 1 FR 0.0001 REL FR 1 V 0 P
and scants us with a single famish'd kiss, TRO 4.04. 47

SCAP'D 15 FR 0.0017 REL FR 10 V 5 P
i have not scap'd drowning to be afeard now of TMP 2.02. 59 P
o stephano, two neapolitans scap'd! 2.02.113 P
have /i scap'd love–letters in the holiday–time WIV 2.01. 1 P
he could not have scap'd sixpence a day. MND 4.02. 21 P
i have scap'd by miracle. 1H4 2.04.165 P
unready? ay, and glad we scap'd so well. 1H6 2.01. 40
like to a ship that, having scap'd a tempest, 2H6 4.09. 32
i wonder how our princely father scap'd; 3H6 2.01. 1
or whether he be scap'd away or no | from 2.01. 2
or had he scap'd, methinks we should have heard 2.01. 6
how scap'd i killing when i cross'd you so? JC 4.03.150
most royal sir, fleance is scap'd. MAC 3.04. 19
dark | by roderigo and fellows that are scap'd. OTH 5.01.113
he scap'd the land to perish at the sea. PER 1.03. 28
do not, when my heart hath scap'd this sorrow, SON 90. 5

SCAPE *(also escape, etc.)*

/SCAPE 2 FR 0.0002 REL FR 2 V 0 P
/justicer, /why /hast /thou /let /her /scape? LR 3.06. 56
/hap /more //to–night, /safe /scape /the /king! 3.06.114

SCAPE 39 FR 0.0044 REL FR 25 V 14 P
scape being drunk, for want of wine. TMP 2.01.147
how didst thou scape? 2.02.119 P
fled — | the thicket is beset, he cannot scape. TGV 5.03. 11
it was a miracle to scape suffocation. WIV 3.05.117 P
he cannot scape me; 3.05.145 P
nor greatness in mortality | can censure scape; MM 3.02.186
or other shall scape a predestinate scratch'd ADO 1.01.134 P
luck | now to scape the serpent's tongue, | we MND 5.01.433
and then to scape drowning thrice, and to be in MV 2.02.163 P
and not one vessel scape the dreadful touch | of 3.02.270
i cannot see else how thou shouldst scape. AYL 3.02. 85 P
nay, hear you, kate. in sooth you scape not so. SHR 2.01.240
sure some scape. WT 3.03. 72 P
yet i can read waiting–gentlewoman in the scape. 3.03. 73 P
should scape the true acquaintance of mine ear. JN 5.06. 15
this, if i scape hanging for killing that rogue. 1H4 2.02. 14 P
if they scape from your encounter, then they 2.02. 61 P
though i could scape shot–free at london, i fear 5.03. 30 P
good master snare, let him not scape. 2H4 2.01. 26 P
sky, | in thy despite shall scape mortality. 1H6 4.07. 22
but if we haply scape | (as well we may, if not 2H6 5.02. 79
ah, whither shall i fly to scape their hands? 3H6 1.03. 1
of his eyes, | should he scape hector fair. TRO 1.03.371
progeny | thou shouldst not scape me here. COR 1.08. 13
and if we meet we shall not scape a brawl, | for ROM 3.01. 3
that cop'st with death himself to scape from it; 4.01. 75
your blood to froth, | and so scape hanging. TIM 4.03.431
if he scape, | heaven forgive him too! MAC 4.03.234
after his desert, and who shall scape whipping? HAM 2.02.530 P
and scape /detecting, i will pay the theft. 3.02. 89
the fault | would not scape censure, nor the LR 1.04.210
all ports i'll bar, the villain shall not scape; 2.01. 80
whiles i may scape | i will preserve myself, and 2.03. 5
some innocents scape not the thunderbolt. ANT 2.05. 77
turn craver too, and so i shall scape whipping. PER 2.01. 89 P
fault | to scape his hands where i was to die. 4.02. 75
i one question | of your name or his scape. TNK 4.01. 16
or fear of my miscarrying on his scape, | or 4.01. 50
could scape the hail of his all–hurting aim, LC 310

SCAPES 8 FR 0.0009 REL FR 7 V 1 P
edge of a feather–bed, here are simple scapes. MV 2.02.165 P
to smile at scapes and perils overblown. SHR 5.02. 3
how scapes he agues, in the devil's name? 1H4 3.01. 68
who scapes the lurking serpent's mortal sting? 3H6 2.02. 15
virtue itself scapes not calumnious strokes. HAM 1.03. 38
of hair–breadth scapes i' th' imminent deadly OTH 1.03.136
marina thus the brothel scapes, and chances PER 5.ch. 1
day," quoth she, "night's scapes doth open lay, LUC 747

SCAPETH 1 FR 0.0001 REL FR 1 V 0 P
the scars of battle scapeth by the flight, | and LC 244

SCAR 12 FR 0.0013 REL FR 9 V 3 P
never mole, hare–lip, nor scar, | nor mark MND 5.01.411
with a pin, and there remains | some scar of it; AYL 3.05. 22
whence honor but of danger wins a scar, | as oft AWW 3.02.121
whether there be a scar under't or no, the 4.05. 95 P
a scar nobly got, or a noble scar, is a good 4.05. 99 P
a scar nobly got, or a noble scar, is a good 4.05. 99 P
show me one scar character'd on thy skin: 2H6 3.01.300
let paris bleed, 'tis but a scar to scorn; TRO 1.01.111
nor scar that whiter skin of hers than snow, OTH 5.02. 4
than a band of clotens | had ever scar for. CYM 5.05.305
the scar that will despite of cure remain, LUC 732
o unfelt sore, crest–wounding private scar! 828

/SCARCE 1 FR 0.0001 REL FR 0 V 1 P
/and /dare /scarce /come /thither. HAM 2.02.344 P

SCARCE 78 FR 0.0088 REL FR 55 V 23 P
and scarce think | their eyes do offices of TMP 5.01.155
i fear me, he will scarce be pleas'd withal. TGV 2.07. 67
so long that going will scarce serve the turn. 3.01.379 P
disease will scarce obey this medicine. WIV 3.03.192 P
scarce confesses | that his blood flows; MM 1.03. 51
there is scarce truth enough alive to make 3.02.226 P
beshrew his hand, i scarce could understand it. ERR 2.01. 49
doubtfully, that i could scarce understand them. 2.01. 54 P
full of welcome makes scarce one dainty dish. 3.01. 23
i would scarce trust myself, though i had sworn ADO 1.01.195 P
she (an attending star) scarce seen a light. LLL 4.03.227
scarce show a harvest of their heavy toil; 4.03.323
the face of an old roman coin, scarce seen. 5.02.613 P
where phoebus' fire scarce thaws the icicles, MV 2.01. 5
worship's reverence) are scarce cater–cousins — 2.02.131 P
who dare scarce show his head on the rialto; 3.01. 45 P
that she makes fair she scarce makes honest, and AYL 1.02. 38 P
i scarce can speak to thank you for myself. 2.07.170
or i will scarce think you have swam in a 4.01. 37 P
but taking up, and that thou'rt scarce worth. AWW 2.03.208 P
something, and scarce so much; 2.05. 83
great oaths would scarce make that be believ'd. 4.01. 59 P
think his mother's milk were scarce out of him. TN 1.05.161 P
were i ta'en here, it would scarce be answer'd. 3.03. 28
fabian can scarce hold him yonder. 3.04.282 P
he finds that now scarce to be worth talking of; 3.04.299 P
you scarce can right me throughly, then, to say WT 2.01. 99
it shall scarce boot me | to say "not guilty." 3.02. 25
there's scarce a maid westward but she sings it. 4.04.290 P
scarce any joy | did ever so long live; 5.03. 51
where words are scarce, they are seldom spent in R2 2.01. 7
thy lips are scarce wip'd since thou drunk'st 1H4 2.04.153 P
scarce blood enough in all their sickly veins H5 4.02. 20
having full scarce six thousand in his troop, 1H6 1.01.112
and humphrey duke of gloucester scarce himself, 2H6 2.03. 40
scarce can i speak, my choler is so great. 5.01. 23
scarce serves to quench my furnace–burning heart 3H6 2.01. 80
for scarce i can refrain | the execution of my 2.02.110
into this breathing world, scarce half made up, R3 1.01. 21
cannot be quiet scarce a breathing while | but 1.03. 60
that scarce some two days since were worth a 1.03. 81
your fire–new stamp of honor is scarce current. 1.03.255
when scarce the blood was well wash'd from his 4.01. 67
you have scarce time | to steal from spiritual H8 3.02.139
(whom, if he live, will scarce be gentlemen), 3.02.292
ignorance itself knows is so abundant scarce, it TRO 2.03. 15 P
my lord, i scarce have leisure to salute you, 4.02. 59
can scarce entreat you to be odd with him. 4.05.265
things as you, i can scarce think there's any, COR 5.02.103 P
we scarce thought us blest | that god had lent ROM 3.05.164
i scarce know how. TIM 1.02.180
and birth | scarce is dividant, touch them with 4.03. 5
man's knell | is there scarce ask'd for who, and MAC 4.03.171
corses, that will scarce hold the laying in — HAM 5.01.166 P
i am scarce in breath, my lord. LR 2.02. 52 P
i can scarce speak to thee; 2.04.136
for many miles about | there's scarce a bush. 2.04.302
malady is fix'd, | the lesser is scarce felt. 3.04. 9
yet my mind | was then scarce friends with him. 4.01. 35
midway air | show scarce so gross as beetles. 4.06. 14
he's scarce awake, let him alone a while. 4.07. 50
which at the first are scarce found to distaste, OTH 3.03.327
i scarce did know you, uncle; 5.02.201
and his sword | grants scarce distinction. ANT 3.01. 29
am poor of thanks, | and scarce can spare them. CYM 2.03. 90
she can scarce be there yet. 3.05.150 P
no wonder, | when rich ones scarce tell true. 3.06. 12
being scarce made up, | i mean, to man, he had 4.02.109
did see scarce man die, scarce ever look'd on blood, 4.04. 36
is that we scarce are men and you are gods. 5.02. 10
have scarce strength left to give them burial. PER 1.04. 49
well–a–day, we could scarce help ourselves. 2.01. 22 P
she stay'd, | and fell, scarce to be got away. TNK 4.01.102
and scarce hath eyes his treasure to behold, LUC 857
and yet the duteous vassal scarce is gone; 1360
scarce had the sun dried up the dewy morn, | and PP 6. 1
and scarce the herd gone to the hedge for shade, 6. 2
complain, | scarce i could from tears refrain; 20.16

SCARCE–BEARDED 1 FR 0.0001 REL FR 1 V 0 P
if the scarce–bearded caesar have not sent | his ANT 1.01. 21

SCARCE–COLD 2 FR 0.0002 REL FR 2 V 0 P
the conquest of our scarce–cold conqueror, 1H6 4.03. 50
ere the stroke | of yet this scarce–cold battle, CYM 5.05.469

/SCARCELY 1 FR 0.0001 REL FR 1 V 0 P
/we /scarcely /think /our /miseries /our /foes. LR 3.06.103
SCARCELY 18 FR 0.0020 REL FR 15 V 3 P
they will scarcely believe this without trial. ADO 2.02. 40 P
west of this forest, scarcely off a mile, | in 2H4 4.01. 19
as black and white, my eye will scarcely see it. H5 2.02.104
to your good prayer will scarcely say amen. R3 1.03. 21
you scarcely have the hearts to tell me so, 1.04.175
i promise you, i scarcely know myself. 2.03. 2
put mine armor on, | which i can scarcely bear. COR 3.02. 35
had scarcely more | than would make up his MAC 1.05. 36
scarcely have coveted what was mine own, | at no 4.03.127
scarcely hears | of this his nephew's purpose — HAM 1.02. 29
of his lands will scarcely lie in this box, and 5.01.111 P
mischief of your person it would scarcely allay. LR 1.02.163 P
wear'st, | which scarcely keeps thee warm. 2.04.270
for they yet glance by and scarcely bruise, 5.03.149
the sword like me, he'll scarcely look on't. CYM 3.06. 26
straight | must cast thee, scarcely coffin'd, in PER 3.01. 60
nor scarcely | could i persuade him to become a TNK 2.06. 23
and scarcely greet me with that sun, thine eye, SON 49. 6
SCARCITY 4 FR 0.0004 REL FR 4 V 0 P
scarcity and want shall shun you, | ceres' TMP 4.01.116
now heavens forfend such scarcity of /youth! TRO 1.03.302
poor, | imprison'd, and in scarcity of friends, TIM 2.02.225
that on the earth would breed a scarcity | and VEN 753
SCAR'D 6 FR 0.0006 REL FR 2 V 4 P
spirit of wantonness is sure scar'd out of him. WIV 4.02.210 P
hath scar'd thy husband from the use of wits. ERR 5.01. 86
they have scar'd away two of my best sheep, WT 3.03. 65 P
son, and scar'd my choughs from the chaff, i had 4.04.617 P
am sure i scar'd the dolphin and his trull, 1H6 2.02. 28
poor tom hath been scar'd out of his good wits. LR 4.01. 57 P
SCARE 4 FR 0.0004 REL FR 4 V 0 P
night, | did scare away, or rather did affright; MND 5.01.141
noise of thy cross–bow | will scare the herd, 3H6 3.01. 7
and, in a word, | scare troy out of itself. TRO 5.10. 21
but then a noise did scare me from the tomb, ROM 5.03.262
SCARECROW 2 FR 0.0002 REL FR 2 V 0 P
we must not make a scarecrow of the law, MM 2.01. 1
the scarecrow that affrights our children so. 1H6 1.04. 43
SCARECROWS 1 FR 0.0001 REL FR 0 V 1 P
no eye hath seen such scarecrows. 1H4 4.02. 38 P
SCARF 9 FR 0.0010 REL FR 4 V 5 P
rich scarf to my proud earth — why hath thy TMP 4.01. 82
or under your arm, like a lieutenant's scarf? ADO 2.01.190 P
the beauteous scarf | veiling an indian beauty; MV 3.02. 98
me to see thee wear thy heart in a scarf! AYL 5.02. 20 P
ever thou be'st bound in thy scarf and beaten, AWW 2.03.226 P
whole theoric of war in the knot of his scarf, 4.03.143 P
you are undone, captain, all but your scarf; 4.03.324 P
we'll have no cupid hoodwink'd with a scarf, ROM 1.04. 4
night, | scarf up the tender eye of pitiful day, MAC 3.02. 47
SCARF'D 1 FR 0.0001 REL FR 1 V 0 P
my sea–gown scarf'd about me, in the dark HAM 5.02. 13
SCARFED 1 FR 0.0001 REL FR 1 V 0 P
the scarfed bark puts from her native bay, MV 2.06. 15
SCARFS 5 FR 0.0005 REL FR 2 V 3 P
with scarfs and fans, and double change of SHR 4.03. 57
yet the scarfs and the bannerets about thee did AWW 2.03.203 P
that jack–an–apes with scarfs. 3.05. 85 P
ladies and maids their scarfs and handkerchers, COR 2.01.264
flavius, for pulling scarfs off caesar's images, JC 1.02.285 P
SCARING 1 FR 0.0001 REL FR 1 V 0 P
lath, | scaring the ladies like a crow–keeper, ROM 1.04. 6
SCARLET 14 FR 0.0015 REL FR 11 V 3 P
what say you, scarlet and john? WIV 1.01.173 P
a velvet hose, a scarlet cloak, and a copatain SHR 5.01. 67 P
of her maid–pale peace | to scarlet indignation, R2 3.03. 99
they call drinking deep, dyeing scarlet, and 1H4 2.04. 15 P
"and robin hood, scarlet, and john." 2H4 5.03.103
thy scarlet robes as a child's bearing–cloth 1H6 1.03. 42
out, scarlet hypocrite! 1.03. 56
thou scarlet sin, robb'd this bewailing land H8 3.02.255
to be thus jaded by a piece of scarlet, 3.02.280
by her high forehead and her scarlet lip, | by ROM 2.01. 18
they'll be in scarlet straight at any news. 2.05. 71
the oaks bear mast, the briers scarlet heps; TIM 4.03.419
his scarlet lust came evidence to swear | that LUC 1650
that have profan'd their scarlet ornaments, SON 142. 6
SCARR'D 3 FR 0.0003 REL FR 3 V 0 P
england hath long been mad and scarr'd herself: R3 5.05. 23
broke, | and scarr'd the moon with splinters. COR 4.05.109
hath pierc'd him deep and scarr'd his heart, TIT 4.04. 31
SCARRE 1 FR 0.0001 REL FR 1 V 0 P
i see that men make rope's in such a scarre AWW 4.02. 38
/SCARS 1 FR 0.0001 REL FR 1 V 0 P
/flesh /was /capable | /of /wounds /and /scars; 2H4 1.01.173
SCARS 16 FR 0.0018 REL FR 16 V 0 P
wars, and took | deep scars to save thy life; ERR 5.01.193
will he strip his sleeve and show his scars, H5 4.03. 47
patches will i get unto these cudgell'd scars, 5.01. 88
receiv'd deep scars in france and normandy? 2H6 1.01. 87
/her face defac'd with scars of infamy, | /her R3 3.07.126
to such as boasting show their scars | a mock is TRO 4.05.290
them th' unaching scars which i should hide, COR 2.02.148
with briers, | scars to move laughter only. 3.03. 52
that hath more scars of sorrow in his heart TIT 4.01.126
my scars can witness, dumb although they are, 5.03.114
he jests at scars that never felt a wound. ROM 2.02. 1
the scars upon your honor, therefore, he | does ANT 3.13. 58
i'll force | the wine peep through their scars. 3.13.190
thou and those thy scars had once prevail'd | to 4.05. 2
scars and bare weeds | the gain o' th' TNK 1.02. 15
the scars of battle scapeth by the flight, | and LC 244
SCATH 3 FR 0.0003 REL FR 3 V 0 P
to pray for them that have done scath to us. R3 1.03.316
and wherein rome hath done you any scath, | let TIT 5.01. 7
this trick may chance to scath you. ROM 1.05. 84
SCATHE 2 FR 0.0002 REL FR 2 V 0 P
tide | to do offense and scathe in christendom. JN 2.01. 75
all these could not procure me any scathe | so 2H6 2.04. 62
SCATHFUL 1 FR 0.0001 REL FR 1 V 0 P
with which such scathful grapple did he make TN 5.01. 56
SCATTER 6 FR 0.0006 REL FR 5 V 1 P
would scatter all her spices on the stream, MV 1.01. 33
that want their leader, scatter up and down, 2H6 3.02.126
to scatter 'em, as 'tis to make 'em sleep | on H8 5.03. 14
hand, | to scatter and disperse the giddy goths, TIT 5.02. 78
in our shadow, to scatter his crowns in the sun. PER 4.02.112 P
they scatter and unloose it from their bond, LUC 136
SCATTER'D 9 FR 0.0010 REL FR 8 V 1 P
his plausive words | he scatter'd not in ears, AWW 1.02. 54
the troops are all scatter'd, and the commanders 4.03.132 P
the french have reinforc'd their scatter'd men. H5 4.06. 36
to gather our soldiers, scatter'd and dispers'd, 1H6 2.01. 76
buckingham's army is dispers'd and scatter'd, R3 4.04.511
have plough'd for, sow'd, and scatter'd, | by COR 3.01. 71
scatter'd by winds and high tempestuous gusts, TIT 5.03. 69
having bound things scatter'd, we will post | to TNK 1.04. 48
sir, they call | the scatter'd to the banket. 3.01.109
/SCATTERED 1 FR 0.0001 REL FR 1 V 0 P
/a /power | /into /this /scattered /kingdom, LR 3.01. 31
SCATTERED 5 FR 0.0005 REL FR 5 V 0 P
whose sons lie scattered on the bleeding ground. JN 2.01.304
is scattered and disjoin'd from fellowship. 3.04. 3
the thieves are all scattered and possess'd with 1H4 2.02.105
this scattered corn into one mutual sheaf, TIT 5.03. 71
and old cakes of roses | were thinly scattered, ROM 5.01. 48
SCATTERING 1 FR 0.0001 REL FR 1 V 0 P
out of his scattering and unsure observance. OTH 3.03.151
SCATTERS 3 FR 0.0003 REL FR 3 V 0 P
such wind as scatters young men through the SHR 1.02. 50
the king's soul, and there scatters | dangers, H8 2.02. 26
upon the slime and ooze scatters his grain, ANT 2.07. 22
SCATT'RED 5 FR 0.0005 REL FR 5 V 0 P
loose now and then | a scatt'red smile, and that AYL 3.05.104
strike up our drums, pursue the scatt'red stray; 2H4 4.02.120
the scatt'red foe that hopes to rise again; 3H6 2.06. 93
all scatt'red in the bottom of the sea: R3 1.04. 28
and mock'd the dead bones that lay scatt'red by. 1.04. 33
SCELERA 1 FR 0.0001 REL FR 1 V 0 P
dominator poli, | tam lentus audis scelera? TIT 4.01. 82
SCELERISQUE 1 FR 0.0001 REL FR 1 V 0 P
"integer vitae, scelerisque purus, | non eget TIT 4.02. 20
/SCENE 2 FR 0.0002 REL FR 2 V 0 P
/in /troy, /there /lies /the /scene. TRO pr 1
while our /scene must play | his daughter's woe PER 4.04. 48
SCENE 35 FR 0.0039 REL FR 33 V 2 P
fat falstaff | hath a great scene; WIV 4.06. 17
that's the scene that i would see, which will be ADO 2.03.217 P
o, what a scene of fool'ry have i seen, | of LLL 4.03.161
worthies, away! the scene begins to cloud. 5.02.721
forsook his scene, and ent'red in a brake; MND 3.02. 15
"a tedious brief scene of young pyramus | and 5.01. 56
presents more woeful pageants than the scene AYL 2.07.138
last scene of all, | that ends this strange 2.07.163
and give my scene such growing | as you had WT 4.01. 16
appointed, as if | the scene you play were mine. 4.04.593
pomp, | allowing him a breath, a little scene, R2 3.02.164
our scene is alt'red from a serious thing, | and 5.03. 79
set | on bloody courses, the rude scene may end, 2H4 1.01.159
for all my reign hath been but as a scene 4.05.197
and monarchs to behold the swelling scene! H5 pr 4
from london, and the scene | is now transported, 2.pr. 34
then, | unto southampton do we shift our scene. 2.pr. 42
thus with imagin'd wing our swift scene flies 3.pr. 1
and so our scene must to the battle fly; 4.pr. 48
what scene of death hath roscius now to act? 3H6 5.06. 10
what means this scene of rude impatience? R3 2.02. 38
woe's scene, world's shame, grave's due by life 4.04. 27
a queen in jest, only to fill the scene. 4.04. 91
defects of age | must be the scene of mirth; TRO 1.03.173
when he might act the woman in the scene, | he COR 2.02. 96
down, and this unnatural scene | they laugh at. 5.03.184
in fair verona, where we lay our scene, | from ROM pr 2
my dismal scene i needs must act alone. 4.03. 19
shall this our lofty scene be acted over | in JC 3.01.112
scene individable, or poem unlimited; HAM 2.02.399 P
have by the very cunning of the scene | been 2.02.590
one scene of it comes near the circumstance 3.02. 76
now, play one scene | of excellent dissembling, ANT 1.03. 78
whom our fast–growing scene must find | at PER 4.ch. 6
of love, | as chorus to their tragic scene. PHT 52
SCENE'S 1 FR 0.0001 REL FR 1 V 0 P
the scene's not for our seeing, go we hence, TNK 5.03.134
SCENES 6 FR 0.0006 REL FR 5 V 1 P
at your industrious scenes and acts of death. JN 2.01.376
such noble scenes as draw the eye to flow, | we H8 pr 4
well digested in the scenes, set down with as HAM 2.02.440 P
several clime | where our scenes seems to live. PER 4.04. 7
(whose modest scenes blush on his marriage–day, TNK pr 4
you shall hear | scenes, though below his art, pr 28
SCENT 3 FR 0.0003 REL FR 2 V 1 P
and twice to–day pick'd out the dullest scent. SHR in.1. 24
o ay, make up that. he is now at a cold scent. TN 2.05.122 P
but soft, methinks i scent the morning air, HAM 1.05. 58
SCENT–SNUFFING 1 FR 0.0001 REL FR 1 V 0 P
the hot scent–snuffing hounds are driven to VEN 692
/SCEPTRE 1 FR 0.0001 REL FR 1 V 0 P
/and /this /unwieldy /sceptre /from /my /hand, R2 4.01.205
SCEPTRE 28 FR 0.0031 REL FR 26 V 2 P
his sceptre shows the force of temporal power, MV 4.01.190
ay, by my sceptre and my hopes of /heaven. AWW 2.01.192
a sceptre snatch'd with an unruly hand | must be JN 3.04.135
can gripe the sacred handle of our sceptre, R2 3.03. 80
wood, | my sceptre for a palmer's walking–staff, 3.03.151
and his high sceptre yields | to the possession 4.01.109
chair shall be my state, this dagger my sceptre, 1H4 2.04.379 P
thy golden sceptre for a leaden dagger, and thy 2.04.381 P
now, by my sceptre and my soul to boot, | he 3.02. 97
king'd, | her sceptre so fantastically borne, H5 2.04. 27
and i know | 'tis not the balm, the sceptre, and 4.01.260
queen, | to put a golden sceptre in thy hand, 1H6 5.03.118
nor hold the sceptre in his childish fist, | nor 2H6 1.01.245
words, | except a sword or sceptre balance it. 5.01. 9
a sceptre shall it have, have i a soul, | on 5.01. 10
and not to grace an aweful princely sceptre. 5.01. 98
here is a hand to hold a sceptre up, | and with 5.01.102
a sceptre, or an earthly sepulchre!" 3H6 1.04. 17
and wring the aweful sceptre from his fist, 2.01.154
place is fill'd, thy sceptre wrung from thee, 3.01. 16
his hand to wield a sceptre, and himself 4.06. 73
he'll carry it so | to make the sceptre his. H8 1.02.135
who's that that bears the sceptre? 4.01. 38
age, | but not a sceptre to control the world. TIT 1.01.199
crown, | and put a barren sceptre in my gripe, MAC 3.01. 61
me | to throw my sceptre at the injurious gods, ANT 4.15. 76
the sceptre, learning, physic, must | all follow CYM 4.02.268
would with the sceptre straight be strooken down LUC 217
SCEPTRED 3 FR 0.0003 REL FR 3 V 0 P
but mercy is above this sceptred sway, | it is MV 4.01.193
this royal throne of kings, this sceptred isle, R2 2.01. 40
the sceptred office of your ancestors, | your R3 3.07.119
SCEPTRE'S 3 FR 0.0003 REL FR 3 V 0 P
thou, a sceptre's heir, | that thus affects a WT 4.04.419
son, | now by /my sceptre's awe i make a vow, R2 1.01.118
wipe off the dust that hides our sceptre's gilt, 2.01.294
SCEPTRES 5 FR 0.0005 REL FR 5 V 0 P
(he bade me say so) more than all the sceptres, WT 5.01.146
much, when sceptres are in children's hands; 1H6 4.01.192
prerogative of age, crowns, sceptres, laurels, TRO 1.03.107
that twofold balls and treble sceptres carry. MAC 4.01.121
lycaonia, | with a more larger list of sceptres. ANT 3.06. 76
SCHEDULE 5 FR 0.0005 REL FR 5 V 0 P
that are recorded in this schedule here. LLL 1.01. 18
of a blinking idiot, | presenting me a schedule! MV 2.09. 55
take, my lord of westmerland, this schedule, 2H4 4.01.166
hail, caesar! read this schedule. JC 3.01. 3
by this short schedule collatine may know | her LUC 1312
SCHEDULES 2 FR 0.0002 REL FR 1 V 1 P
i will give out divers schedules of my beauty. TN 1.05.245 P
of folded schedules had she many a one, | which LC 43
'SCHEW *(also eschew'd)*
/'SCHEW 1 FR 0.0001 REL FR 1 V 0 P
will /'schew no course to keep them from the PER 1.01.136
SCHOLAR 19 FR 0.0021 REL FR 8 V 11 P
sir, i hear you are a scholar (i will be brief WIV 2.02.180 P
he is a better scholar than i thought he was. 4.01. 80 P
and he shall appear to the envious a scholar, a MM 3.02.146 P
i would to god some scholar would conjure her, ADO 2.01.256 P
are sweetly varied, like a scholar at the least; LLL 4.02. 9 P
a venetian, a scholar and a soldier, that came MV 1.02.113 P
words | than you — unless you were a scholar, SHR 1.02.158
freely give unto /you this young scholar, that 2.01. 79 P
i am no breeching scholar in the schools, | i'll 3.01. 18
th' art a scholar; TN 2.03. 13 P
as to say a careful man and a great scholar. 4.02. 10 P
say my cousin william is become a good scholar. 2H4 3.02. 10 P
never was such a sudden scholar made; H5 1.01. 32
from his cradle | he was a scholar, and a ripe H8 4.02. 51
thou art a scholar, speak to it, horatio. HAM 1.01. 42
him more in the soldier than in the scholar. OTH 2.01.166 P
and, eros, | thy master dies thy scholar: ANT 4.14.102
to exceed, | and you are her labor'd scholar. PER 2.03. 17
be her master, | and she will be your scholar; 2.05. 39
SCHOLARLY 1 FR 0.0001 REL FR 0 V 1 P
speak scholarly and wisely. WIV 1.03. 2 P
SCHOLAR'S 2 FR 0.0002 REL FR 1 V 1 P
i have neither the scholar's melancholy, which AYL 4.01. 10 P
the courtier's, soldier's, scholar's, eye, HAM 3.01.151
SCHOLARS 6 FR 0.0006 REL FR 6 V 0 P
my fellow scholars, and to keep those statutes LLL 1.01. 17
all scholars, lawyers, courtiers, gentlemen, 2H6 4.04. 36
scholars allow'd freely to argue for her. H8 2.02.112
as you are friends, scholars, and soldiers, HAM 1.05.141
the worst of all her scholars, my good lord. PER 2.05. 31
this populous city will | yield many scholars. 4.06.187
SCHOOL 27 FR 0.0030 REL FR 19 V 8 P
i'll but bring my young man here to school. WIV 4.01. 8 P
how now, sir hugh, no school to–day? 4.01. 10 P
for "school," "fool," a babbling rhyme: ADO 5.02. 39 P
a patch set on learning, to see him in a school: LLL 4.02. 31
the hue of dungeons, and the school of night; 4.03.251
hath wisdom's warrant and the help of school, 5.02. 71
she was a vixen when she went to school; MND 3.02.324
that men shall swear i have discontinued school MV 3.04. 75
my brother jaques he keeps at school, and report AYL 1.01. 6 P
creeping like snail | unwillingly to school. 2.07.147
as willingly as e'er i came from school. SHR 3.02.150
like a pedant that keeps a school i' th' church. TN 3.02. 76 P
west, north, south, or, like a school broke up, 2H4 4.02.104
i have a whole school of tongues in this belly 4.03. 18 P
youth of the realm in erecting a grammar school; 2H6 4.07. 34 P
and set the murtherous machevil to school. 3H6 3.02.193
love from love, toward school with heavy looks. ROM 2.02.157
he was quick mettle when he went to school. JC 1.02.296
know'st that we two went to school together; 5.05. 26
my dearest coz, | i pray you school yourself. MAC 4.02. 15
intent | in going back to school in wittenberg, HAM 1.02.113
we'll set thee to school to an ant, to teach LR 2.04. 67 P
his bed shall seem a school, his board a shrift, OTH 3.03. 24
since first we went to school, may we perceive TNK 1.02. 14
for princes are the glass, the school, the book, LUC 615
wilt thou be the school where lust shall learn? 617
now set thy long–experienc'd wit to school. 1820
SCHOOLBOY 5 FR 0.0005 REL FR 3 V 2 P
to sigh, like a schoolboy that had lost his abc; TGV 2.01. 22 P
the flat transgression of a schoolboy, who, ADO 2.01.222 P
then the whining schoolboy, with his satchel AYL 2.07.145
prince, | whom like a schoolboy you may overawe. 1H6 1.01. 36
a peevish schoolboy, worthless of such honor, JC 5.01. 61
SCHOOLBOY'S 2 FR 0.0002 REL FR 2 V 0 P
nor to the motion of a schoolboy's tongue, | nor LLL 5.02.403
is not big enough to bear | a schoolboy's top. WT 2.01.103
SCHOOLBOYS' 1 FR 0.0001 REL FR 1 V 0 P
and schoolboys' tears take up | the glasses of COR 3.02.116
SCHOOLBOYS 3 FR 0.0003 REL FR 3 V 0 P
goes toward love as schoolboys from their books, ROM 2.02.156
fitter for girls and schoolboys) will be seen, TNK 3.06. 34
but, as it is with schoolboys, cannot say; ep 2
SCHOOL'D 4 FR 0.0004 REL FR 3 V 1 P
yet he's gentle, never school'd and yet learned, AYL 1.01.166 P
'twere good he were school'd. SHR 4.04. 9
well, i am school'd: 1H4 3.01.188
sword, and is ill school'd | in bolted language; COR 3.01.319
SCHOOL–DAYS 3 FR 0.0003 REL FR 3 V 0 P
all school–days friendship, childhood innocence? MND 3.02.202
in my school–days, when i had lost one shaft, MV 1.01.140
thy school–days frightful, desp'rate, wild, and R3 4.04.170
SCHOOL–DOING 1 FR 0.0001 REL FR 1 V 0 P
forgets school–doing, being therein train'd TNK 5.04. 68
SCHOOLFELLOWS 1 FR 0.0001 REL FR 1 V 0 P

letters seal'd, and my two schoolfellows, | whom HAM 3.04.202
SCHOOLING 1 FR 0.0001 REL FR 1 V 0 P
i have some private schooling for you both. MND 1.01.116
SCHOOL–MAIDS 1 FR 0.0001 REL FR 1 V 0 P
as school–maids change their names | by vain MM 1.04. 47
SCHOOLMASTER 15 FR 0.0017 REL FR 10 V 5 P
and here | have i, thy schoolmaster, made thee TMP 1.02.172
marry, master schoolmaster, he that is likel'est LLL 4.02. 85 P
the schoolmaster is exceeding fantastical, too 5.02.528 P
you will be schoolmaster, | and undertake the SHR 1.01.191
to old baptista as a schoolmaster | well seen in 1.02.133
about a schoolmaster for the fair bianca, | and 1.02.166
were it not that my fellow schoolmaster | doth 3.02.138
and hear a drum than look upon his schoolmaster. COR 1.03. 56 P
keep a schoolmaster that can teach thy fool to LR 1.04.179 P
we sent our schoolmaster, | is 'a come back? ANT 3.11. 71
caesar, 'tis his schoolmaster, | an argument 3.12. 2
i am unworthy for her schoolmaster. PER 2.05. 40
but will the dainty domine, the schoolmaster, TNK 2.03. 40
schoolmaster, i thank you. 3.05.151
worse man than giraldo, emilia's schoolmaster. 4.03. 13 P
SCHOOLMASTER'S 1 FR 0.0001 REL FR 1 V 0 P
and a down, | say the schoolmaster's no clown. TNK 3.05.141
SCHOOLMASTERS 3 FR 0.0003 REL FR 3 V 0 P
schoolmasters will i keep within my house, | fit SHR 1.01. 94
get her cunning schoolmasters to instruct her? 1.01.187
procure | must be their schoolmasters. LR 2.04.304
SCHOOLS 5 FR 0.0005 REL FR 5 V 0 P
i am no breeching scholar in the schools, | i'll SHR 3.01. 18
a poor unlearned virgin, when the schools, AWW 1.03.240
degrees in schools, and brotherhoods in cities, TRO 1.03.104
and schools should fall | for private faults in TIM 5.04. 25
busy yourselves in skill–contending schools, LUC 1018
SCIATICA 2 FR 0.0002 REL FR 1 V 1 P
of your hips has the most profound sciatica? MM 1.02. 59 P
thou cold sciatica, | cripple our senators, that TIM 4.01. 23
SCIATICAS 1 FR 0.0001 REL FR 0 V 1 P
lungs, bladders full of imposthume, sciaticas, TRO 5.01. 21 P
SCIENCE 2 FR 0.0002 REL FR 2 V 0 P
since i am put to know that your own science MM 1.01. 5
hath not in nature's mystery more science | than AWW 5.03.103
SCIENCES 2 FR 0.0002 REL FR 2 V 0 P
to instruct her fully in those sciences, SHR 2.01. 57
the sciences that should become our country, H5 5.02. 58
SCIMITAR 2 FR 0.0002 REL FR 2 V 0 P
by this scimitar | that slew the sophy and a MV 2.01. 24
which with my scimitar i'll cool to–morrow. TRO 5.01. 2
SCIMITAR'S 1 FR 0.0001 REL FR 1 V 0 P
got, | he dies upon my scimitar's sharp point, TIT 4.02. 91
SCION 2 FR 0.0002 REL FR 1 V 1 P
we marry | a gentler scion to the wildest stock, WT 4.04. 93
this that you call love to be a sect or scion. OTH 1.03.332 P
SCIONS 1 FR 0.0001 REL FR 1 V 0 P
our scions, put in wild and savage stock, H5 3.05. 7
SCISSOR'D 1 FR 0.0001 REL FR 1 V 0 P
too, for 'tis not scissor'd just | to such a TNK 1.02. 54
SCISSORS 1 FR 0.0001 REL FR 1 V 0 P
his man with scissors nicks him like a fool; ERR 5.01.175
SCOFF 2 FR 0.0002 REL FR 2 V 0 P
by heaven, all dry–beaten with pure scoff! LLL 5.02.263
scoff on, vile fiend and shameless courtezan! 1H6 3.02. 45
SCOFFER 1 FR 0.0001 REL FR 1 V 0 P
foul is most foul, being foul to be a scoffer. AYL 3.05. 62
SCOFFING 1 FR 0.0001 REL FR 1 V 0 P
scoffing his state and grinning at his pomp, R2 3.02.163
SCOFFS 3 FR 0.0003 REL FR 3 V 0 P
with scoffs and scorns and contumelious taunts. 1H6 1.04. 39
they that of late were daring with their scoffs 3.02.113
your blunt upbraidings and your bitter scoffs. R3 1.03.103
SCOGGIN'S 1 FR 0.0001 REL FR 0 V 1 P
i see him break scoggin's head at the court–gate 2H4 3.02. 30 P
SCOLD 8 FR 0.0009 REL FR 6 V 2 P
i had rather hear them scold than fight. WIV 2.01.232 P
visor began to assume life and scold with her. ADO 2.01.242 P
began to scold and raise up such a storm | that SHR 1.01.172
i know she is an irksome brawling scold. 1.02.187
thou unadvised scold, i can produce | a will JN 2.01.191
for god's sake, take away this captive scold. 3H6 5.05. 29
i will have more or scold it out of him. H8 5.01.173
first time that ever | i was forc'd to scold. COR 5.06.105
SCOLDING 6 FR 0.0006 REL FR 4 V 2 P
renown'd in padua for her scolding tongue. SHR 1.02.100
she would think scolding would do little good 1.02.109 P
the one as famous for a scolding tongue, | as is 1.02.252
horn, as a scolding quean to a wrangling knave, AWW 2.02. 25 P
nay, take away this scolding crook–back, rather. 3H6 5.05. 30
i have seen tempests when the scolding winds JC 1.03. 5
/SCOLDS 1 FR 0.0001 REL FR 1 V 0 P
that /scolds against the quality of flesh | and TIM 4.03.156
SCOLDS 1 FR 0.0001 REL FR 1 V 0 P
pays shame | when shrill–tongu'd fulvia scolds. ANT 1.01. 32
SCONCE* 7 FR 0.0008 REL FR 3 V 4 P
or i shall break that merry sconce of yours ERR 1.02. 79
or i will beat this method in your sconce. 2.02. 34
sconce call you it? 2.02. 35 P
blows long, i must get a sconce for my head, and 2.02. 37 P
services were done — at such and such a sconce, H5 3.06. 72 P
must i go show them my unbarb'd sconce? COR 3.02. 99
knock him about the sconce with a dirty shovel, HAM 5.01.102 P
SCONE 3 FR 0.0003 REL FR 3 V 0 P
nam'd, and gone to scone | to be invested. MAC 2.04. 31
will you to scone? 2.04. 35
whom we invite to see us crown'd at scone. 5.09. 41
SCOPE 29 FR 0.0032 REL FR 29 V 0 P
your scope is as mine own, | so to enforce or MM 1.01. 64
so every scope by the immoderate use | turns to 1.02.127
sith 'twas my fault to give the people scope, 1.03. 35
vastidity you had, | to a determin'd scope. 3.01. 69
now, good my lord, give me the scope of justice, 5.01.234
the fated sky | gives us free scope, only doth AWW 1.01.218
no scope of nature, no distemper'd day, | no JN 3.04.154
i do know the scope | and warrant limited unto 5.02.122
his coming hither hath no further scope | than R2 3.03.112
i'll give thee scope to beat, | since foes have 3.03.140
since foes have scope to beat both thee and me. 3.03.141
and curbs himself even of his natural scope 1H4 3.01.169
but, being moody, give him time and scope, 2H4 4.04. 39
at, | and the offender granted scope of speech, 2H6 3.01.176
that my pent heart may have some scope to beat, R3 4.01. 34
orators of miseries, | let them have scope! 4.04.130
within her scope of choice | lies my consent and ROM 1.02. 18
'tis conceiv'd to scope. TIM 1.01. 72
making your wills | the scope of justice; 5.04. 5
be angry when you will, it shall have scope; JC 4.03.108
but, in the gross and scope of mine opinion, HAM 1.01. 68
more than the scope | of these delated articles 1.02. 37
/an anchor's cheer in prison be my scope! 3.02.219
but let his disposition have that scope | as LR 1.04.292
desiring this man's art, and that man's scope, SON 29. 7
blessed are you, whose worthiness gives scope, 52.13
in me, | the scope and tenure of thy jealousy? 61. 8
that, having such a scope to show her pride, 103. 2
themes in one, which wondrous scope affords. 105.12
SCORCH* 5 FR 0.0005 REL FR 4 V 1 P
of her eye did seem to scorch me up like a WIV 1.03. 67 P
to scorch your face, and to disfigure you. ERR 5.01.183
bid him that we, whom flaming war doth scorch, TNK 1.01. 91
the heavenly fires | did scorch his mortal son, 5.01. 92
his hot heart, which fond desire doth scorch, LUC 314
SCORCH'D* 2 FR 0.0002 REL FR 2 V 0 P
thy burning car never had scorch'd the earth. 3H6 2.06. 13
we have scorch'd the snake, not kill'd it; MAC 3.02. 13
SCORCHED 1 FR 0.0001 REL FR 1 V 0 P
within the scorched veins of one new burn'd. JN 3.01.278
SCOR'D 1 FR 0.0001 REL FR 0 V 1 P
have you scor'd me? well. OTH 4.01.126 P
/SCORE 2 FR 0.0002 REL FR 2 V 0 P
for she will /score your fault upon my pate: ERR 1.02. 65
how many /score of miles may we well rid CYM 3.02. 67
SCORE 25 FR 0.0028 REL FR 11 V 14 P
yes, for a score of kingdoms you should wrangle, TMP 5.01.174
as a cannon will shoot point–blank twelve score. WIV 3.02. 34 P
not fourteen pence on the score for sheer ale, SHR in.2. 23 P
sheer ale, score me up for the lying'st knave in in.2. 24 P
may perhaps call him half a score knaves or so. 1.02.110 P
six score fat oxen standing in my stalls, | and 2.01.358
after he scores, he never pays the score. AWW 4.03.224
amongst three or four score hogsheads. 1H4 2.04. 5 P
score a pint of bastard in the half–moon," or so 2.04. 27 P
know his death will be a march of twelve score. 2.04.547 P
you, he's an infinitive thing upon my score. 2H4 2.01. 24 P
would have clapp'd i' th' clout at twelve score, 3.02. 46 P
how a score of ewes now? 3.02. 49 P
a score of good ewes may be worth ten pounds. 3.02. 50 P
all shall eat and drink on my score, and i will 2H6 4.02. 73 P
had no other books but the score and the tally, 4.07. 35 P
and entertain a score or two of tailors | to R3 1.02.256
a hare that is hoar | is too much for a score, ROM 2.04.138
of twenty be without a score of villains. TIM 3.06. 77 P
they say he parted well, and paid his score, MAC 5.09. 18
thou shalt have more | than two tens to a score. LR 1.04.127
time, | strike off this score of absence. OTH 3.04.179
let us score their backs, | and snatch 'em up, ANT 4.07. 12
one score 'twixt sun and sun, | madam, 's enough CYM 3.02. 68
nor need i tallies thy dear love to score; SON 122.10
SCORES 2 FR 0.0002 REL FR 2 V 0 P
after he scores, he never pays the score. AWW 4.03.224
strikes some scores away | from the great compt; 5.03. 56
SCORING 1 FR 0.0001 REL FR 0 V 1 P
shot here, here's no scoring but upon the pate. 1H4 5.03. 31 P
SCORN 109 FR 0.0123 REL FR 95 V 14 P
be in love — where scorn is bought with groans; TGV 1.01. 29
but she did scorn a present that i sent her. 3.01. 92
for scorn at first makes after–love the more. 3.01. 95
but if thou scorn our courtesy, thou diest. 4.01. 66
whilst man and master laughs my woes to scorn. ERR 2.02.205
case, | if he should scorn me so apparently. 4.01. 78
not her kitchen maid rail, taunt, and scorn me? 4.04. 74
pack | to make a loathsome abject scorn of me; 4.04.103
argument of his own scorn by falling in love — ADO 2.03. 11 P
"that have so oft encount'red him with scorn, 2.03.129 P
'tis very possible he'll scorn it, for the man 2.03.179 P
disdain and scorn ride sparkling in her eyes, 3.01. 51
stand i condemn'd for pride and scorn so much? 3.01.108
i scorn that with my heels. 3.04. 50 P
for "scorn," "horn," a hard rhyme; 5.02. 38 P
these oaths and laws will prove an idle scorn. LLL 1.01.309
i think scorn to sigh; 1.02. 63 P
how will he scorn! 4.03.145
bruise me with scorn, confound me with a flout, 5.02.397
when at your hands did i deserve this scorn? MND 2.02.124
why should you think that i should woo in scorn? 3.02.122
scorn and derision never come in tears. 3.02.123
how can these things in me seem scorn to you, 3.02.126
i scorn you not; 3.02.221
it seems that you scorn me. 3.02.221
have you not set lysander, as in scorn, | to 3.02.222
sweet, do not scorn her so. 3.02.247
by moonshine did these lovers think no scorn 5.01.137
do not run, scorn running with thy heels." MV 2.02. 9 P
that is the way to make her scorn you still. AYL 2.04. 22
and the red glow of scorn and proud disdain, 3.04. 54
sweet phebe, do not scorn me, do not, phebe; 3.05. 1
take thou no scorn to wear the horn, | it was a 4.02. 13
lusty horn | is not a thing to laugh to scorn. 4.02. 18
"if the scorn of your bright eyne | have power 4.03. 50
but one that scorn to live in this disguise SHR 4.02. 18
till their own scorn return to them unnoted AWW 1.02. 34
that is honor's scorn, | which challenges itself 2.03.133
good beauties, let me sustain no scorn; TN 1.05.175 P
o, what a deal of scorn looks beautiful | in the 3.01.145
what means this scorn, thou most untoward knave? JN 1.01.243
i scorn you, scurvy companion. 2H4 2.04.123 P
how? you fat fool, i scorn you. 2.04.296 P
which hath been with scorn shov'd from the court 4.02. 37
shall have cause to curse the dolphin's scorn. H5 1.02.288
now by /gadslugs i swear i scorn the term; 2.01. 30
scorn and defiance, slight regard, contempt, 2.04.117
your majesty takes no scorn to wear the leek 4.07.102 P
o'ertake me if thou canst, i scorn thy strength. 1H6 1.05. 15
i scorn thee and thy fashion, peevish boy. 2.04. 76
proud pole, i will, and scorn both him and thee. 2.04. 78
and take foul scorn to fawn on him by sending. 4.04. 35
to be shame's scorn and subject of mischance! 4.06. 49
antic death, which laugh'st us here to scorn, 4.07. 18
but with a proud majestical high scorn | he 4.07. 39
poor, | and our nobility will scorn the match. 5.03. 96
the nobility think scorn to go in leather aprons 2H6 4.02. 12 P
clifford, how i scorn his worthless threats! 3H6 1.01.101
dare he presume to scorn us in this manner? 3.03.178
time | my manly eyes did scorn an humble tear; R3 1.02.164
teach not thy lip such scorn; 1.02.171
what, dost thou scorn me for my gentle counsel? 1.03.296
there were crept | (as 'twere in scorn of eyes) 1.04. 31
you do him injury to scorn his corse. 2.01. 81
to mitigate the scorn he gives his uncle, | he 3.01.133
to taunt and scorn you thus opprobriously? 3.01.153
helms, | and i did scorn it and disdain to fly. 3.04. 83
let paris bleed, 'tis but a scar to scorn; TRO 1.01.111
than in the pride and salt scorn of his eyes, 1.03.370
but his evasion, wing'd thus swift with scorn, 2.03.114
what, does the cuckold scorn me? 3.03. 64
and with his hat, thus waving it in scorn, | "i COR 2.03.167
and therefore law shall scorn him further trial 3.01.267
thou com'st not to be made a scorn in rome; TIT 1.01.265
here's thy hand, in scorn to thee sent back — 3.01.237
who, nothing hurt withal, hiss'd him in scorn. ROM 1.01.112
face, | to fleer and scorn at our solemnity? 1.05. 57
in spite | to scorn at our solemnity this night. 1.05. 63
which too untimely here did scorn the earth. 3.01.118
and, with a martial scorn, with one hand beats 3.01.161
i scorn thy meat, 'twould choke me; TIM 1.02. 38 P
he shall spurn fate, scorn death, and bear | his MAC 3.05. 30
laugh to scorn | the pow'r of man; 4.01. 79
castle's strength | will laugh a siege to scorn; 5.05. 3
but swords i smile at, weapons laugh to scorn, 5.07. 12
to show virtue her feature, scorn her own image, HAM 3.02. 23 P
me | the fixed figure for the time of scorn | to OTH 4.02. 54
let nobody blame him, his scorn i approve" — 4.03. 52
we scorn her most when most she offers blows. ANT 3.11. 74
their blood thinks scorn | till it fly out and CYM 4.04. 53
borne | as i wear mine, are titles but of scorn. 5.02. 7
and to become the geck and scorn | o' th' 5.04. 67
but (o scorn!) 5.04.125
scorn now their hand should give them burial. PER 2.04. 12
you scorn. 5.01.166
then all the world will scorn us, | and say we TNK 3.06.115
me, | till i am nothing but the scorn of women. 3.06.250
and make him, to the scorn of his hoarse throat, 5.01. 88
hunting he lov'd, but love he laugh'd to scorn. VEN 4
to love a cheek that smiles at thee in scorn! 252
the sun doth scorn you and the wind doth hiss 1084
for in my death i murther shameful scorn: LUC 1189
in scorn of nature, art gave liveless life: 1374
so mild that patience seem'd to scorn his woes. 1505
in scorn or friendship, nill i conster whether. PP 14. 8
in black mourn i, all fears scorn i, | love hath 17.13
it be day, | that which with scorn she put away. 18.30
that then i scorn to change my state with kings. SON 29.14
light, | and place my merit in the eye of scorn, 88. 2
SCORN'D 16 FR 0.0018 REL FR 14 V 2 P
certes she did, the kitchen vestal scorn'd you. ERR 4.04. 75
that hath slander'd, scorn'd, dishonor'd my ADO 4.01.302 P
mock'd at my gains, scorn'd my nation, thwarted MV 3.01. 56 P
and, now i am rememb'red, scorn'd at me. AYL 3.05.131
dear perfection hearts that scorn'd to serve AWW 5.03. 18
scorn'd a fair color, or express'd it stol'n, 5.03. 50
disdaining, scorn'd, and craved death | rather 1H6 1.04. 32
to be so baited, scorn'd, and stormed at. R3 1.03.108
for she that scorn'd at me, now scorn'd of me; 4.04.102
for she that scorn'd at me, now scorn'd of me; 4.04.102
a woman lost among ye, laugh'd at, scorn'd? H8 3.01.107
humble weed, | how in his suit he scorn'd you; COR 2.03.222
and scorn'd his spirit | that could be mov'd to JC 1.02.206
all poverty was scorn'd, and pride so great, PER 1.04. 30
then shall offer | to mars's so scorn'd altar? TNK 1.02. 20
be scorn'd, like old men of less truth than SON 17.10
SCORN'DST 1 FR 0.0001 REL FR 1 V 0 P
scorn'dst our brains' flow, and those our TIM 5.04. 76
SCORNFUL 11 FR 0.0012 REL FR 11 V 0 P
about him, fairies, sing a scornful rhyme, | and WIV 5.05. 91
scornful lysander, true, he hath my love; MND 1.01. 95
and dart not scornful glances from those eyes, SHR 5.02.137
proud scornful boy, unworthy this good gift, AWW 2.03.151
contempt his scornful perspective did lend me, 5.03. 48
your blinding flames | into her scornful eyes! LR 2.04.166
thou scornful page, | there lie thy part. CYM 5.05.228
this is that scornful piece, that scurvy hilding TNK 3.05. 42
but he is like his master, coy and scornful. 5.02. 63
hath taught them scornful tricks, and such VEN 501
remain | the scornful mark of every open eye; LUC 520
SCORNFULLY 4 FR 0.0004 REL FR 4 V 0 P
and our air shakes them passing scornfully. H5 4.02. 42
save yourself, but says | he us'd us scornfully. COR 2.03.163
his eye, which scornfully glisters like fire, VEN 275
then looking scornfully, he doth despise | his LUC 187
SCORNING 7 FR 0.0008 REL FR 7 V 0 P
to join with men in scorning your poor friend? MND 3.02.216
scorning what e'er you can afflict me with. 3H6 1.04. 38
scorning the base degrees | by which he did JC 2.01. 26
scorning advice, read the conclusion then; PER 1.01. 56
for scorning thy edict, duke, ask that lady TNK 3.06.168
scorning his churlish drum and ensign red, VEN 107
as scorning it should pass | to wash the foul 982
SCORNS 23 FR 0.0026 REL FR 22 V 1 P
a woman sometime scorns what best contents her. TGV 3.01. 93
will hear your idle scorns, continue then, | and LLL 5.02.865
in her behalf that scorns your services. MND 3.02.331
voice, | which scorns a modern invocation. JN 3.04. 42
scorns to unsay what once it hath delivered. R2 4.01. 9
had his great name profaned with their scorns, 1H4 3.02. 64
men, and therefore he scorns to say his prayers, H5 3.02. 37 P
with scoffs and scorns and contumelious taunts. 1H6 1.04. 39
turn not thy scorns this way, plantagenet. 2.04. 77
back, | and in her heart she scorns our poverty. 2H6 1.03. 81
and after many scorns, many foul taunts, | they 3H6 2.01. 64
setting your scorns and your mislike aside, 4.01. 24
and with thy scorns drew'st rivers from his eyes R3 1.03.175
and dallies with the wind and scorns the sun. 1.03.264
this troyan scorns us, or the men of troy | are TRO 1.03.233
o deadly gall, and theme of all our scorns, 4.05. 30

hue, | in that it scorns to bear another hue; TIT 4.02.100
fortunes, | the greater scorns the lesser. TIM 4.03. 6
for who would bear the whips and scorns of time, HAM 3.01. 69
and notable scorns | that dwell in every region OTH 4.01. 82
the boy disdains me, | he leaves me, scorns me. CYM 5.05.106
truly pertains (without obbraidings, scorns, TNK 3.06. 32
at his love, and scorns the heat he feels, VEN 311
SCORN'ST 1 FR 0.0001 REL FR 1 V 0 P
why scorn'st thou at sir robert? JN 1.01.228
SCORPION 1 FR 0.0001 REL FR 1 V 0 P
did confess | was as a scorpion to her sight, CYM 5.05. 45
SCORPION'S 1 FR 0.0001 REL FR 1 V 0 P
did seem to say, "seek not a scorpion's nest, 2H6 3.02. 86
SCORPIONS 1 FR 0.0001 REL FR 1 V 0 P
o, full of scorpions is my mind, dear wife! MAC 3.02. 36
SCOT* 17 FR 0.0019 REL FR 14 V 3 P
that ever–valiant and approved scot, | at 1H4 1.01. 54
by god, he shall not have a scot of them, | no, 1.03.214
no, if a scot would save his soul, he shall not! 1.03.215
and that sprightly scot of scots, douglas, that 2.04.343 P
well said, my noble scot! 4.01. 1
you, my lord, or any scot that this day lives. 4.03. 12
i was not born a yielder, thou proud scot, | and 5.03. 11
thus, | i never had triumph'd upon a scot. 5.03. 15
hold up thy head, vile scot, or thou art like 5.04. 39
or that hot termagant scot had paid me scot and 5.04.114 P
hot termagant scot had paid me scot and lot too. 5.04.114 P
the noble scot, lord douglas, when he saw | the 5.05. 17
so soon ta'en prisoner, and that furious scot, 2H4 1.01.126
our proportions to defend | against the scot, H5 1.02.138
but fear the main intendment of the scot, | who 1.02.144
but that the scot on his unfurnish'd kingdom 1.02.148
prey, | to her unguarded nest the weasel (scot) 1.02.170
SCOTCH 2 FR 0.0002 REL FR 0 V 2 P
and repenting, is as a scotch jig, a measure, ADO 2.01. 74 P
first suit is hot and hasty, like a scotch jig, 2.01. 75 P
SCOTCH'D 1 FR 0.0001 REL FR 0 V 1 P
he scotch'd him and notch'd him like a carbinado COR 4.05.186 P
SCOTCHES 1 FR 0.0001 REL FR 1 V 0 P
i have yet | room for six scotches more. ANT 4.07. 10
SCOTLAND 28 FR 0.0031 REL FR 27 V 1 P
where scotland? ERR 3.02.119 P
son your only mean | for powers in scotland, 1H4 1.03.262
your son in scotland being thus employed, 1.03.265
and then the power of scotland, and of york, 1.03.280
that chides the banks of england, scotland, 3.01. 44
lord mortimer of scotland hath sent word | that 3.02.164
spoke of in scotland as this term of fear. 4.01. 85
o, fly to scotland, | till that the nobles and 2H4 2.03. 50
i will resolve for scotland; 2.03. 67
to scotland, and concludes in hearty prayers 4.01. 14
france win, | then with scotland first begin." H5 1.02.168
from scotland am i stol'n, even of pure love, 3H6 3.01. 13
man, | and forc'd to live in scotland a forlorn; 3.03. 26
scotland hath will to help, but cannot help; 3.03. 34
henry now lives in scotland at his ease; 3.03.151
laid open all your victories in scotland, | your R3 3.07. 15
mark, king of scotland, mark! MAC 1.02. 28
that it resounds | as if it felt with scotland, 4.03. 7
scotland hath foisons to fill up your will | of 4.03. 88
o scotland, scotland! 4.03.100
o scotland, scotland! 4.03.100
upon thyself | hath banish'd me from scotland. 4.03.113
stands scotland where it did? 4.03.164
your eye in scotland | would create soldiers, 4.03.186
bring thou this fiend of scotland and myself; 4.03.233
hail, king of scotland! 5.09. 25
hail, king of scotland! 5.09. 25
the first that ever scotland | in such an honor 5.09. 29
SCOTS 8 FR 0.0009 REL FR 5 V 3 P
ten thousand bold scots, two and twenty knights, 1H4 1.01. 68
those same noble scots | that are your prisoners 1.03.212
some six or seven dozen of scots at a breakfast, 2.04.103 P
and that sprightly scot of scots, douglas, that 2.04.343 P
with a great power of english and of scots, 2H4 4.04. 98
and impounded as a stray | the king of scots; H5 1.02.161
here 'a comes, and the scots captain, captain 3.02. 74 P
because, forsooth, the king of scots is crown'd. 1H6 4.01.157
SCOTTISH 3 FR 0.0003 REL FR 2 V 1 P
what think you of the scottish lord, his MV 1.02. 77 P
then once more to your scottish prisoners: 1H4 1.03.259
to meet your father and the scottish power, | as 3.01. 84
SCOUNDRELS 1 FR 0.0001 REL FR 0 V 1 P
they are scoundrels and substractors that say so TN 1.03. 34 P
SCOUR* 8 FR 0.0009 REL FR 5 V 3 P
"item, she can wash and scour." TGV 3.01.311 P
brew, bake, scour, dress meat and drink, make WIV 1.04. 96 P
the several chairs of order look you scour 5.05. 61
never | saw i men scour so on their way. WT 2.01. 35
wash'd away, shall scour my shame with it. 1H4 3.02.137
pistol, i will scour you with my rapier, as i H5 2.01. 56 P
drug, | would scour these english hence? MAC 5.03. 56
rust | until this day, to scour it in the dust. PER 2.02. 55
SCOUR'D 3 FR 0.0003 REL FR 1 V 2 P
for then she need not be wash'd and scour'd. TGV 3.01.313 P
with a rust than to be scour'd to nothing with 2H4 1.02.220 P
save when my lids scour'd off their /brine. TNK 3.02. 28
SCOURED 1 FR 0.0001 REL FR 1 V 0 P
that shall be scoured in his rancorous heart 2H6 3.02.199
SCOURG'D 2 FR 0.0002 REL FR 1 V 1 P
look you, i am /whipt and scourg'd with rods, 1H4 1.03.239
yet nature finds itself scourg'd by the sequent LR 1.02.106 P
SCOURGE 16 FR 0.0018 REL FR 15 V 1 P
the scourge of greatness to be us'd on it, | and 1H4 1.03. 11
he'll breed revengement and a scourge for me; 3.02. 7
and will scourge | with haughty arms this 5.02. 39
and with them scourge the bad revolting stars 1H6 1.01. 4
assign'd am i to be the english scourge. 1.02.129
is this the scourge of france? 2.03. 15
memory, | to scourge you for this apprehension. 2.04.102
our nation's terror and their bloody scourge! 4.02. 16
is talbot slain, the frenchmen's only scourge, 4.07. 77
outcast of naples, england's bloody scourge! 2H6 5.01.118
aloud, "what scourge for perjury | can this dark R3 1.04. 50
you have been a scourge to her enemies, you have
COR 2.03. 91 P
see what a scourge is laid upon your hate, ROM 5.03.292
me, | that i must be their scourge and minister. HAM 3.04.175
'tis so, th' offender's scourge is weigh'd, 4.03. 6
to scourge th' ingratitude that despiteful rome ANT 2.06. 22
SCOURING* 3 FR 0.0003 REL FR 2 V 1 P
with such a heady currance, scouring faults; H5 1.01. 34
as we were scouring my lord of york's armor. 2H6 1.03.192 P
and fearful scouring | doth choke the air with TIM 5.02. 15
/SCOUT* 1 FR 0.0001 REL FR 1 V 0 P
"flout 'em and /scout 'em, | and scout 'em and TMP 3.02.121
SCOUT* 3 FR 0.0003 REL FR 2 V 1 P
and /scout 'em, | and scout 'em and flout 'em! TMP 3.02.122
say, scout, say. LLL 5.02. 88
scout me for him at the corner of the orchard TN 3.04.176 P
SCOUTS 5 FR 0.0005 REL FR 5 V 0 P
are not the speedy scouts return'd again | that 1H6 4.03. 1
what tidings send our scouts? i prithee speak. 5.02. 10
for by my scouts i was advertised | that she was 3H6 2.01.116
our scouts have found the adventure very easy; 4.02. 18
where slept our scouts, or how are they seduc'd, 5.01. 19
SCOWL 2 FR 0.0002 REL FR 2 V 0 P
men's eyes | did scowl on gentle richard. R2 5.02. 28
that is not | glad at the thing they scowl at. CYM 1.01. 15
SCOWLING 1 FR 0.0001 REL FR 1 V 0 P
and here she meets another sadly scowling, | to VEN 917
SCOWLS 1 FR 0.0001 REL FR 1 V 0 P
he scowls and hates himself for his offense, LUC 738
SCRAMBLE *(see scamble, etc.)*
/SCRAP'D 1 FR 0.0001 REL FR 1 V 0 P
/king /richard, /scrap'd /from /pomfret /stones; 2H4 1.01.205
SCRAP'D 2 FR 0.0002 REL FR 0 V 2 P
commandements, but scrap'd one out of the table.
MM 1.02. 9 P
you will be scrap'd out of the painted cloth for LLL 5.02.575 P
SCRAPE 3 FR 0.0003 REL FR 1 V 2 P
nor scrape trenchering, nor wash dish. TMP 2.02.183
if it be but to scrape the figures out of your WIV 4.02.216 P
he scrape a trencher? ROM 1.05. 2 P
SCRAPING 1 FR 0.0001 REL FR 1 V 0 P
as thriftless sons their scraping fathers' gold. R2 5.03. 69
SCRAPS 5 FR 0.0005 REL FR 4 V 1 P
great feast of languages, and stol'n the scraps. LLL 5.01. 37 P
those scraps are good deeds past, which are TRO 3.03.148
the fragments, scraps, the bits and greasy 5.02.159
with scraps o' th' court, it is no contract, CYM 2.03.115
live | disdain to him disdained scraps to give. LUC 987
SCRATCH 19 FR 0.0021 REL FR 11 V 8 P
yet a tailor might scratch her where e'er she TMP 2.02. 53
babe, will scratch the nurse | and presently, TGV 1.02. 58
scratch my head, peaseblossom. MND 4.01. 7 P
but to help cavalery cobweb to scratch. 4.01. 23 P
if my hair do but tickle me, i must scratch. 4.01. 26 P
scratch thee but with a pin, and there remains AYL 3.05. 21
knave with fortune that she should scratch you, AWW 5.02. 30 P
in this farthel will make him scratch his beard. WT 4.04.708 P
and god forbid a shallow scratch should drive 1H4 5.04. 11
i'll scratch your heads; H8 5.03. 9 P
my bright hair and scratch my praised cheeks, TRO 4.02.107
i had rather have one scratch my head i' th' sun COR 2.02. 75
ay, ay, a scratch, a scratch, marry, 'tis enough ROM 3.01. 93
ay, a scratch, a scratch, marry, 'tis enough. 3.01. 93
rat, a mouse, a cat, to scratch a man to death! 3.01.101 P
prognostication, i cannot scratch mine ear. ANT 1.02. 53 P
each envious brier his weary legs do scratch, VEN 705
and wast afeard to scratch her wicked foe, LUC 1035
and with my knife scratch out the angry eyes 1469
SCRATCH'D 8 FR 0.0009 REL FR 5 V 3 P
i should have scratch'd out your unseeing eyes, TGV 4.04.204
other shall scape a predestinate scratch'd face. ADO 1.01.135 P
/bone /for /bene, priscian a little scratch'd, LLL 5.01. 29 P
i am a man whom fortune hath cruelly scratch'd. AWW 5.02. 27 P
have thy beauty scratch'd with briers and made WT 4.04.425
then you scratch'd your head, | and too JC 2.01.243
thing from death | that is but scratch'd withal. HAM 4.07.146
shaking their scratch'd ears, bleeding as they VEN 924
SCRATCHES 1 FR 0.0001 REL FR 1 V 0 P
scratches with briers, | scars to move laughter COR 3.03. 51
SCRATCHING 3 FR 0.0003 REL FR 1 V 2 P
scratching could not make it worse, and 'twere ADO 1.01.136 P
scratching her legs that one shall swear she SHR in.2. 58
and i had the scratching of thee, i would make TRO 2.01. 28 P
SCRAWL *(see scrowl)*
SCREAM 1 FR 0.0001 REL FR 1 V 0 P
i heard the owl scream and the crickets cry. MAC 2.02. 15
SCREAMS 1 FR 0.0001 REL FR 1 V 0 P
strange screams of death, | and prophesying, MAC 2.03. 56
SCREECHING 1 FR 0.0001 REL FR 1 V 0 P
glow, | whilst the screech–owl, screeching loud, MND 5.01.376
SCREECH–OWL *(also scritch–owl)*
SCREECH–OWL 3 FR 0.0003 REL FR 3 V 0 P
whilst the screech–owl, screeching loud, | puts MND 5.01.376
bring forth that fatal screech–owl to our house 3H6 2.06. 56
chirp, the screech–owl | calls in the dawn! TNK 3.02. 35
SCREECH–OWLS 2 FR 0.0002 REL FR 2 V 0 P
the time when screech–owls cry and ban–dogs howl
2H6 1.04. 18
and boding screech–owls make the consort full! 3.02.327
SCREEN 1 FR 0.0001 REL FR 1 V 0 P
to have no screen between this part he play'd TMP 1.02.107
SCREEN'D 1 FR 0.0001 REL FR 1 V 0 P
that your grace hath screen'd and stood between HAM 3.04. 3
SCREENS 1 FR 0.0001 REL FR 1 V 0 P
your leavy screens throw down, | and show like MAC 5.06. 1
SCREW 1 FR 0.0001 REL FR 1 V 0 P
but screw your courage to the sticking place, MAC 1.07. 60
SCREW'D 2 FR 0.0002 REL FR 2 V 0 P
down, that's riveted, | screw'd to my memory? CYM 2.02. 44
aged cramp | had screw'd his square foot round, TNK 5.01.111
SCREWS 1 FR 0.0001 REL FR 1 V 0 P
that screws me from my true place in your favor, TN 5.01.123
SCRIBBLED 2 FR 0.0002 REL FR 1 V 1 P
i am a scribbled form, drawn with a pen | upon a JN 5.07. 32
that parchment, being scribbled o'er, should 2H6 4.02. 81 P
SCRIBE 2 FR 0.0002 REL FR 2 V 0 P
that my master, being scribe, to himself should TGV 2.01.140
and if thy stumps will let thee play the scribe. TIT 2.04. 4
SCRIBES 1 FR 0.0001 REL FR 1 V 0 P
tongues, /figures, scribes, bards, poets, cannot ANT 3.02. 16
SCRIMERS 1 FR 0.0001 REL FR 1 V 0 P
the scrimers of their nation | he swore had HAM 4.07.100
SCRIP* 2 FR 0.0002 REL FR 0 V 2 P
generally, man by man, according to the scrip. MND 1.02. 3 P
bag and baggage, yet with scrip and scrippage. AYL 3.02.162 P
SCRIPPAGE 1 FR 0.0001 REL FR 0 V 1 P
bag and baggage, yet with scrip and scrippage. AYL 3.02.162 P
/SCRIPTURE 2 FR 0.0002 REL FR 0 V 2 P
/how /dost /thou /understand /the /scripture? HAM 5.01. 36 P
/the /scripture /says /adam /digg'd; 5.01. 36 P
SCRIPTURE 2 FR 0.0002 REL FR 2 V 0 P
the devil can cite scripture for his purpose. MV 1.03. 98
but then i sigh, and, with a piece of scripture, R3 1.03.333
SCRIPTURES 1 FR 0.0001 REL FR 1 V 0 P
the scriptures of the loyal leonatus, | all CYM 3.04. 81
SCRITCH–OWL *(also screech–owl)*
SCRITCH–OWL 1 FR 0.0001 REL FR 1 V 0 P
let him that will a scritch–owl aye be call'd TRO 5.10. 16
SCRIVENER 1 FR 0.0001 REL FR 1 V 0 P
my boy shall fetch the scrivener presently. SHR 4.04. 59
SCROLL 12 FR 0.0013 REL FR 9 V 3 P
here is the scroll of every man's name, which is MND 1.02. 4 P
quince, call forth your actors by the scroll. 1.02. 15 P
whose empty eye | there is a written scroll! MV 2.07. 64
here's the scroll, | the continent and summary 3.02.129
a gentle scroll. 3.02.139
gracing the scroll that tells of this war's loss JN 2.01.348
you set down your name in the scroll of youth, 2H4 1.02.178 P
accept this scroll, most gracious sovereign, 1H6 3.01.148
and give the king this fatal–plotted scroll. TIT 2.03. 47
a scroll, and written round about. 4.02. 18
do not exceed | the prescript of this scroll. ANT 3.08. 5
eye | receives the scroll without or yea or no, LUC 1340
SCROLLS 1 FR 0.0001 REL FR 1 V 0 P
sweet scrolls to fly about the streets of rome! TIT 4.04. 16
SCROOP 11 FR 0.0012 REL FR 10 V 1 P
say, scroop, where lies our uncle with his power R2 3.02.192
sir stephen scroop, besides a clergyman | of 3.03. 28
his brother's death at bristow, the lord scroop. 1H4 1.03.271
this to my cousin scroop, and all the rest | to 4.04. 3
to meet northumberland and the prelate scroop, 5.05. 37
mowbray, the bishop scroop, hastings, and all, 2H4 4.04. 84
henry lord scroop of masham, and the third, H5 2.pr. 24
though cambridge, scroop, and grey, in their 2.02. 58
there yours, lord scroop of masham; 2.02. 67
o, | what shall i say to thee, lord scroop, thou 2.02. 94
by the name of /henry lord scroop of masham. 2.02.148 P
SCROWL 1 FR 0.0001 REL FR 1 V 0 P
see how with signs and tokens she can scrowl. TIT 2.04. 5
SCROYLES 1 FR 0.0001 REL FR 1 V 0 P
by heaven, these scroyles of angiers flout you, JN 2.01.373
SCRUBBED 2 FR 0.0002 REL FR 2 V 0 P
a youth, | a kind of boy, a little scrubbed boy, MV 5.01.162
for that same scrubbed boy, the doctor's clerk, 5.01.261
SCRUPLE 23 FR 0.0026 REL FR 15 V 8 P
have given ourselves without scruple to hell, WIV 5.05.149 P
lends | the smallest scruple of her excellence, MM 1.01. 37
on mine honor, have to do | with any scruple. 1.01. 64
what they weigh, even to the utmost scruple — ADO 5.01. 93
of the twentieth part | of one poor scruple, nay, MV 4.01.330
dram of it, and i will not bate thee a scruple. AWW 2.03.222 P
if i lose a scruple of this sport, let me be TN 2.05. 2 P
adheres together, that no dram of a scruple, no 3.04. 79 P
no dram of a scruple, no scruple of a scruple, 3.04. 79 P
no dram of a scruple, no scruple of a scruple, 3.04. 79 P
our former scruple in our strong–barr'd gates, JN 2.01.370
the wise may make some dram of a scruple, or 2H4 1.02.130 P
dram of a scruple, or indeed a scruple itself. 1.02.131 P
but there remains a scruple in that too; 1H6 5.03. 93
to the good queen possess'd him with a scruple H8 2.01.158
your scruple to the voice of christendom. 2.02. 87
or | laid any scruple in your way which might 2.04.151
scruple, and prick, on certain speeches utter'd 2.04.172
not appearance and | the king's late scruple, by 4.01. 31
seek her, | not making any scruple of her soil, TRO 4.01. 57
for every scruple | of her contaminated carrion 4.01. 71
or some craven scruple | of thinking too HAM 4.04. 40
made scruple of his praise, and wager'd with him CYM 5.05.182
SCRUPLES 5 FR 0.0005 REL FR 5 V 0 P
uncleanly scruples! JN 4.01. 7
with scruples and do set the word itself R2 5.05. 13
fears and scruples shake us. MAC 2.03.129
hath from my soul | wip'd the black scruples, 4.03.116
he made such scruples of the wrong he did | to TNK 2.06. 25
SCRUPULOUS 2 FR 0.0002 REL FR 2 V 0 P
away with scrupulous wit! now arms must rule. 3H6 4.07. 61
two domestic powers | breed scrupulous faction; ANT 1.03. 48
SCUDS 1 FR 0.0001 REL FR 1 V 0 P
sometime he scuds far off, and there he stares, VEN 301
SCUFFLES 1 FR 0.0001 REL FR 1 V 0 P
which in the scuffles of great fights hath burst ANT 1.01. 7
SCULLION 1 FR 0.0001 REL FR 0 V 1 P
away, you scullion! 2H4 2.01. 59 P
SCULLS 1 FR 0.0001 REL FR 1 V 0 P
like scaling sculls | before the belching whale; TRO 5.05. 22
SCUM 4 FR 0.0004 REL FR 4 V 0 P
froth and scum, thou liest! WIV 1.01.164
now, neighbor confines, purge you of your scum! 2H4 4.05.123
rebellious hinds, the filth and scum of kent, 2H6 4.02.122
a scum of britains and base lackey peasants, R3 5.03.317
SCURRIL 2 FR 0.0002 REL FR 2 V 0 P
bed the livelong day | breaks scurril jests, TRO 1.03.148
thine ear | (which nev'r heard scurril term, TNK 5.01.147
SCURRILITY *(also squirility)*
SCURRILITY 1 FR 0.0001 REL FR 0 V 1 P
pleasant without scurrility, witty without LLL 5.01. 4 P
SCURRILOUS 1 FR 0.0001 REL FR 0 V 1 P
him that he use no scurrilous words in 's tunes. WT 4.04.213 P
SCURVY 29 FR 0.0032 REL FR 8 V 21 P
this is a very scurvy tune to sing at a man's TMP 2.02. 44 P
this is a scurvy tune too; 2.02. 55 P
a most scurvy monster! 2.02.155 P
thou scurvy patch! 3.02. 63
and i will teach a scurvy jack–a–nape priest to WIV 1.04.109 P
scurvy jack–dog priest! 2.03. 63 P
to be revenge on this same scall, scurvy, 3.01.120 P
a saucy friar, | a very scurvy fellow. MM 5.01.136
not scurvy, nor a temporary meddler, | as he's 5.01.145
a son shall take this disgrace off me, scurvy, AWW 2.03.236 P
off me, scurvy, old, filthy, scurvy lord! 2.03.236 P

let thy curtsies alone, they are scurvy ones. 5.03.324 P
thou art, thou art but a scurvy fellow." TN 3.04.148 P
i scorn you, scurvy companion. 2H4 2.04.123 P
than i love e'er a scurvy young boy of them all. 2.04.272 P
you scurvy, lousy knave, god pless you! H5 5.01. 18 P
i peseech you heartily, scurvy, lousy knave, at 5.01. 22 P
you scurvy valiant ass! TRO 2.01. 45 P
you scurvy lord! 2.01. 51 P
has got that same scurvy doting foolish /young 5.04. 3 P
i am a rascal, a scurvy railing knave, a very 5.04. 28 P
scurvy knave, i am none of his flirt–gills, i am ROM 2.04.153 P
scurvy knave! 2.04.162 P
and, like a scurvy politician, seem | to see the LR 4.06.171
and spoke such scurvy and provoking terms OTH 1.02. 7
some base notorious knave, some scurvy fellow. 4.02.140
/by /this /hand, i think it is scurvy, and begin 4.02.193 P
bring'st such pelting scurvy news continually, TNK 2.02.266
is that scornful piece, that scurvy hilding, 3.05. 42
'SCUSE *(also excuse, etc.)*
'SCUSE 1 FR 0.0001 REL FR 1 V 0 P
that 'scuse serves many men to save their gifts, MV 4.01.444
'SCUSES 1 FR 0.0001 REL FR 1 V 0 P
away, | and laid good 'scuses upon your ecstasy; OTH 4.01. 79
SCUT 1 FR 0.0001 REL FR 0 V 1 P
my doe with the black scut? WIV 5.05. 18 P
SCUTCHEON 2 FR 0.0002 REL FR 1 V 1 P
my scutcheon plain declares that i am alisander" LLL 5.02.564
i'll none of it, honor is a mere scutcheon. 1H4 5.01.140 P
SCUTCHEONS 1 FR 0.0001 REL FR 1 V 0 P
your scutcheons and your signs of conquest, ANT 5.02.135
SCYLLA 1 FR 0.0001 REL FR 0 V 1 P
thus when i shun scylla, your father, i fall MV 3.05. 16 P
SCYTHE 6 FR 0.0006 REL FR 6 V 0 P
wanting the scythe withal, uncorrected, rank, H5 5.02. 50
i will contend | even with his pestilent scythe. ANT 3.13.193
nothing 'gainst time's scythe can make defense SON 12.13
and nothing stands but for his scythe to mow: 60.12
so thou prevent'st his scythe and crooked knife. 100.14
i will be true, despite thy scythe and thee. 123.14
SCYTHED 1 FR 0.0001 REL FR 1 V 0 P
time had not scythed all that youth begun, | nor LC 12
SCYTHE'S 1 FR 0.0001 REL FR 1 V 0 P
honor which shall bate his scythe's keen edge, LLL 1.01. 6
SCYTHE–TUSK'D 1 FR 0.0001 REL FR 1 V 0 P
that hast slain | the scythe–tusk'd boar; TNK 1.01. 79
SCYTHIA 2 FR 0.0002 REL FR 2 V 0 P
was never scythia half so barbarous. TIT 1.01.131
oppose not scythia to ambitious rome; 1.01.132
SCYTHIAN 2 FR 0.0002 REL FR 2 V 0 P
exploit | as scythian tomyris by cyrus' death. 1H6 2.03. 6
the barbarous scythian, | or he that makes his LR 1.01.116
'SDEATH 1 FR 0.0001 REL FR 1 V 0 P
sicinius velutus, and i know not — 'sdeath, COR 1.01.217
/SE 1 FR 0.0001 REL FR 0 V 1 P
it must be /se /offendendo, it cannot be else. HAM 5.01. 9 P
SE 1 FR 0.0001 REL FR 0 V 1 P
say he is a very man per se and stands alone. TRO 1.02. 15 P
SEA 231 FR 0.0261 REL FR 199 V 32 P
when the sea is. TMP 1.01. 16 P
set her two courses off to sea again! 1.01. 50 P
a thousand furlongs of sea for an acre of barren 1.01. 65 P
but that the sea, mounting to th' welkin's cheek 1.02. 4
have sunk the sea within the earth or ere | it 1.02. 11
bore us some leagues to sea, where they prepared 1.02.145
us, | to cry to th' sea, that roar'd to us; 1.02.149
when i have deck'd the sea with drops full salt, 1.02.155
go make thyself like a nymph o' th' sea; 1.02.301
being, as they were, drench'd in the sea, hold 2.01. 63 P
sowing the kernels of it in the sea, bring forth 2.01. 93 P
"i shall no more to sea, to sea, | here shall i 2.02. 42
"i shall no more to sea, to sea, | here shall i 2.02. 42
then to sea, boys, and let her go hang!" 2.02. 54
for my part, the sea cannot drown me; 3.02. 13 P
and the sea mocks | our frustrate search on land 3.03. 9
the never–surfeited sea | hath caus'd to belch 3.03. 55
expos'd unto the sea (which hath requit it) 3.03. 71
and 'twixt the green sea and the azur'd vault 5.01. 43
rigg'd as when | we first put out to sea. 5.01.225
rock, | and throw it thence into the raging sea. TGV 1.02.119
and drench'd me in the sea, where i am drown'd. 1.03. 79
a sea of melting pearl, which some call tears; 3.01.226
with my /master's /ship? why, it is at sea. 3.01.283 P
heart | as full of sorrows as the sea of sands, 4.03. 33
come under my hatches, i'll never to sea again. WIV 2.01. 93 P
that went to sea with the ten commandements, but MM 1.02. 8 P
the great soldier who miscarried at sea? 3.01.210 P
her brother frederick was wrack'd at sea, having 3.01.217 P
eye | but hath his bound in earth, in sea, in ERR 2.01. 17
for he is bound to sea, and stays but for it. 4.01. 33
had hoisted sail and put to sea to–day. 5.01. 21
hath he not lost much wealth by wrack of sea? 5.01. 49
besides her urging of her wrack at sea — 5.01.360
ever, | one foot in sea and one on shore, | to ADO 2.03. 64
that the wide sea | hath drops too few to wash 4.01.140
the sea will ebb and flow, heaven show his face; LLL 4.03.212
brook, | or in the beached margent of the sea, MND 2.01. 85
have suck'd up from the sea | contagious fogs; 2.01. 89
that the rude sea grew civil at her song, | and 2.01.152
or, as it were, the pageants of the sea, | do MV 1.01. 11
what harm a wind too great might do at sea. 1.01. 24
thou know'st that all my fortunes are at sea, 1.01.177
whether antonio have had any loss at sea or no? 3.01. 43 P
but the guiled shore | to a most dangerous sea; 3.02. 98
doth it not flow as hugely as the sea, | till AYL 2.07. 72
have i not heard the sea, puff'd up with winds, SHR 1.02.201
body | to painful labor, both by sea and land; 5.02.149
thy capacity | receiveth as the sea, nought TN 1.01. 11
to a strong mast that liv'd upon the sea; 1.02. 14
from the breach of the sea was my sister drown'd 2.01. 22 P
i would have men of such constancy put to sea, 2.04. 76 P
revolt, | but mine is all as hungry as the sea, 2.04.100
as well | forbid the sea for to obey the moon WT 1.02.427
i have seen two such sights, by sea and by land! 3.03. 83 P
but i am not to say it is a sea, for it is now 3.03. 84 P
the ship, to see how the sea flap–dragon'd it; 3.03. 98 P
the poor souls roar'd, and the sea mock'd them; 3.03. 99 P
both roaring louder than the sea or weather. 3.03.101 P
i wish you | a wave o' th' sea, that you might 4.04.141
i am put to sea | with her who here i cannot 4.04.498
match, | the sea enraged is not half so deaf, JN 2.01.451
and all that we upon this side the sea | (except 2.01.488
ire, | in rage, deaf as the sea, hasty as fire. R2 1.01. 19
this precious stone set in the silver sea, 2.01. 46
england, bound in with the triumphant sea, 2.01. 61
not all the water in the rough rude sea | can 3.02. 54
being govern'd, as the sea is, by our noble and 1H4 1.02. 28 P
the moon's men doth ebb and flow like the sea, 1.02. 32 P
sea, being govern'd, as the sea is, by the moon. 1.02. 32 P
clipt in with the sea | that chides the banks of 3.01. 43
melt itself | into the sea, and other times to 2H4 3.01. 49
now doth it turn and ebb back to the sea, 5.02.131
there roar'd the sea, and trumpet–clangor sounds 5.05. 40
as is the ooze and bottom of the sea | with H5 1.02.164
as many fresh streams meet in one salt sea; 1.02.209
cheerly to sea! 2.02.192
draw the huge bottoms through the furrowed sea, 3.pr. 12
it is a theme as fluent as the sea; 3.07. 34 P
merchandise do sinfully miscarry upon the sea, 4.01.148 P
upon your winged thoughts | athwart the sea. 5.pr. 9
shouts and claps out–voice the deep–mouth'd sea, 5.pr. 11
now, sir, to you, that were so hot at sea, 1H6 3.04. 28
crossing the sea from england into france, 4.01. 89
and in that sea of blood my boy did drench | his 4.07. 14
commit them to the fortune of the sea. 5.01. 50
was i for this nigh wrack'd upon the sea, | and 2H6 3.02. 82
the pretty vaulting sea refus'd to drown me, 3.02. 94
me drown'd on shore | with tears as salt as sea, 3.02. 96
the sea receiv'd it, | and so i wish'd thy body 3.02.108
day | is crept into the bosom of the sea; 4.01. 2
and i unto the sea, from whence i came. 3H6 1.01.209
(as if a channel should be call'd the sea), 2.02.141
like a mighty sea | forc'd by the tide to combat 2.05. 5
like the self–same sea | forc'd to retire by 2.05. 7
from whence shall warwick cut the sea to france, 2.06. 89
and then to brittany i'll cross the sea | to 2.06. 97
and chides the sea that sunders him from thence, 3.02.138
stops thy spring, my sea shall suck them dry, 4.08. 55
lad, | with tearful eyes add water to the sea, 5.04. 8
and what is edward but a ruthless sea? 5.04. 25
the sea | whose envious gulf did swallow up his 5.06. 24
all scatt'red in the bottom of the sea: R3 1.04. 28
bulk, | who almost burst to belch it in the sea. 1.04. 41
being a bark to brook no mighty sea — | than in 3.07.162
thus hulling in | the wild sea of my conscience, H8 2.04.201
heard him play, | even the billows of the sea, 3.01. 10
bladders, | this many summers in a sea of glory, 3.02.360
as the shrouds make at sea in a stiff tempest, 4.01. 72
the sea being smooth, | how many shallow bauble TRO 1.03. 34
what raging of the sea! 1.03. 97
which you priz'd | richer than sea and land? 2.02. 92
age | man–ent'red thus, he waxed like a sea, COR 2.02. 99
that when the sea was calm all boats alike 4.01. 6
of tribunes, such as you, | a sea and land full. 5.04. 55
what fool hath added water to the sea? TIT 3.01. 68
a rock, | environ'd with a wilderness of sea, 3.01. 94
if the winds rage, doth not the sea wax mad, 3.01.222
i am the sea; 3.01.225
then must my sea be moved with her sighs; 3.01.227
happily you may catch her in the sea; 4.03. 8
the east, | until his very downfall in the sea; 5.02. 57
being vex'd, a sea nourish'd with loving tears. ROM 1.01.192
the fish lives in the sea, and 'tis much pride 1.03. 89
that vast shore /wash'd with the farthest sea, 2.02. 83
my bounty is as boundless as the sea, | my love 2.02.133
little body | thou counterfeits a bark, a sea, a 3.05.131
for still thy eyes, which i may call the sea, 3.05.132
far | than empty tigers or the roaring sea. 5.03. 39
but moves itself | in a wide sea of wax. TIM 1.01. 47
we must all part | into this sea of air. 4.02. 22
lie where the light foam of the sea may beat 4.03.378
with his great attraction | robs the vast sea; 4.03.437
dead, | entomb'd upon the very hem o' th' sea, 5.04. 66
and he shall wear his crown by sea and land, JC 1.03. 87
on such a full sea are we now afloat, | and we 4.03.222
hand in hand, | posters of the sea and land, MAC 1.03. 33
but float upon a wild and violent sea | each way 4.02. 21
whether in sea or fire, in earth or air, | th' HAM 1.01.153
cliff | that beetles o'er his base into the sea, 1.04. 71
that looks so many fadoms to the sea | and hears 1.04. 77
or to take arms against a sea of troubles, | and 3.01. 58
mad as the sea and wind, when both contend 4.01. 7
ere we were two days old at sea, a pirate of 4.06. 16 P
bids the wind blow the earth into the sea, | or LR 3.01. 5
but if /thy flight lay toward the roaring sea, 3.04. 10
the sea, with such a storm as his bare head | in 3.07. 59
he was met even now | as mad as the vex'd sea, 4.04. 2
horrible steep. | hark, do you hear the sea? 4.06. 4
horns welk'd and waved like the /enridged sea. 4.06. 71
what from the cape can you discern at sea? OTH 2.01. 1
if it hath ruffian'd so upon the sea, | what 2.01. 7
the moor himself at sea, | and is in full 2.01. 28
for i have lost him on a dangerous sea. 2.01. 46
on the brow o' th' sea | stand ranks of people, 2.01. 53
the great contention of /the sea and skies 2.01. 92
like to the pontic sea, | whose icy current and 3.03.453
more fell than anguish, hunger, or the sea! 5.02.362
to caesar, and commands | the empire of the sea. ANT 1.02.185
pompey is strong at sea, | and it appears he is 1.04. 36
makes the sea serve them, which they ear and 1.04. 49
both what by sea and land i can be able | to 1.04. 78
the people love me, and the sea is mine; 2.01. 9
but by sea | he is an absolute master. 2.02.162
we'll speak with thee at sea. 2.06. 25
and i must | rid all the sea of pirates; 2.06. 36
at sea, i think. 2.06. 84 P
you have been a great thief by sea. 2.06. 92 P
we should have met you | by sea and land, 3.06. 54
he could so quickly cut the ionian sea, | and 3.07. 22
canidius, we | will fight with him by sea. 3.07. 28
by sea, what else? 3.07. 28
shall fall you for refusing him at sea, | being 3.07. 39
by sea, by sea. 3.07. 40
by sea, by sea. 3.07. 40
i'll fight at sea. 3.07. 48
o noble emperor, do not fight by sea, | trust 3.07. 61
justeius, | publicola, and caelius, are for sea; 3.07. 73
provoke not battle | till we have done at sea. 3.08. 4
our fortune on the sea is out of breath, | and 3.10. 24
morn–dew on the myrtle leaf | to his grand sea. 3.12. 10
soldier, | by sea and land i'll fight; 4.02. 5
their preparation is to–day by sea, | we please 4.10. 1
shall stay with us — order for sea is given, 4.10. 6
arch and the rich crop | of sea and land, which CYM 1.06. 34
if you are sick at sea, | or stomach–qualm'd at 3.04.189
creek | behind our rock, and let it to the sea, 4.02.152
after your will, have cross'd the sea, attending 4.02.334
with language that would make me spurn the sea 5.05.294
he scap'd the land to perish at the sea. PER 1.03. 28
earth, sea, and air | were all too little to 1.04. 34
master, i marvel how the fishes live in the sea. 2.01. 27 P
how from the /finny subject of the sea | these 2.01. 48
may see the sea hath cast upon your coast — 2.01. 56
a drunken knave was the sea to cast thee in our 2.01. 57 P
and, spite of all the /rapture of the sea, 2.01.155
her nurse, she takes, | and so to sea. 3.ch. 44
the sea works high, the wind is loud, and will 3.01. 47 P
with us at sea it hath been still observ'd, and 3.01. 51 P
our lodgings, standing bleak upon the sea, 3.02. 14
did the sea toss up upon our shore this chest. 3.02. 50
did the sea cast it up? 3.02. 57
they were too rough | that threw her in the sea. 3.02. 80
i rage and roar | as doth the sea she lies in, 3.03. 11
for she was born at sea, i have nam'd so, here 3.03. 13
that i was shipp'd at sea i well remember, 3.04. 5
come | give me your flowers, ere the sea mar it. 4.01. 26
endur'd a sea | that almost burst the deck. 4.01. 55
swear she's dead, | and thrown into the sea. 4.01. 99
he /puts on sackcloth, and to sea. 4.04. 29
she would serve after a long voyage at sea. 4.06. 45 P
thoughts again, | where we left him, on the sea. 5.ch. 13
call'd marina | for i was born at sea. 5.01.156
at sea! what mother? 5.01.156
lest this great sea of joys rushing upon me 5.01.192
thou that wast born at sea, buried at tharsus, 5.01.196
buried at tharsus, | and found at sea again! 5.01.197
reveal how thou at sea didst lose thy wife. 5.01.244
at sea in child–bed died she, but brought forth 5.03. 5
thy burden at the sea, and call'd marina | for 5.03. 47
when our friends don their helms, or put to sea, TNK 1.03. 19
yonder's the sea, and there's a ship. 3.04. 5
the sea hath bounds, but deep desire hath none, VEN 389
"thou art," quoth she, "a sea, a sovereign king, LUC 652
thy sea within a puddle's womb is hearsed, | and 657
and not the puddle in thy sea dispersed. 658
so she, deep drenched in a sea of care, | holds 1100
for nimble thought can jump both sea and land SON 44. 7
brass, nor stone, nor earth, nor boundless sea, 65. 1
the mountain or the sea, the day or night, | the 113.11
the sea, all water, yet receives rain still, 135. 9
SEA–BANK 1 FR 0.0001 REL FR 0 V 1 P
other day talking on the sea–bank with certain OTH 4.01.133 P
SEA–BANKS 1 FR 0.0001 REL FR 1 V 0 P
a willow in her hand | upon the wild sea–banks, MV 5.01. 11
//SEA–BOY 1 FR 0.0001 REL FR 1 V 0 P
to the wet //sea–boy in an hour so rude, | and 2H4 3.01. 27
SEA–CAP 1 FR 0.0001 REL FR 1 V 0 P
though now you have no sea–cap on your head. TN 3.04.330
SEA–CHANGE 1 FR 0.0001 REL FR 1 V 0 P
but doth suffer a sea–change | into something TMP 1.02.401
SEA–COAL 2 FR 0.0002 REL FR 0 V 2 P
in faith, at the latter end of a sea–coal fire. WIV 1.04. 9 P
at the round table by a sea–coal fire, upon 2H4 2.01. 88 P
SEACOLE 3 FR 0.0003 REL FR 0 V 3 P
sir, or george seacole, for they can write and ADO 3.03. 11 P
come hither, neighbor seacole. 3.03. 13 P
go, get you to francis seacole, bid him bring 3.05. 58 P
SEA–FARER 1 FR 0.0001 REL FR 1 V 0 P
of this poor infant, this fresh new sea–farer, PER 3.01. 41
SEA–FARING 2 FR 0.0002 REL FR 1 V 1 P
such as sea–faring men provide for storms; ERR 1.01. 80
sea–faring men, sir. HAM 4.06. 2 P
SEA–FIGHT 2 FR 0.0002 REL FR 2 V 0 P
once in a sea–fight 'gainst the count his TN 3.03. 26
the next day | was our sea–fight, and what to HAM 5.02. 54
SEA–GOWN 1 FR 0.0001 REL FR 1 V 0 P
my sea–gown scarf'd about me, in the dark HAM 5.02. 13
SEAL 71 FR 0.0080 REL FR 62 V 9 P
to seal our happiness with their consents! TGV 1.03. 49
and seal the bargain with a holy kiss. 2.02. 7
i'll be so bold to break the seal for once. 3.01.139
you, sir, here is the hand and seal of the duke; MM 4.02.192 P
which with experimental seal doth warrant | the ADO 4.01.166
which i had rather seal with my death than 5.01.240 P
all, | that he was fain to seal on cupid's name. LLL 5.02. 9
this princess of pure white, this seal of bliss! MND 3.02.144
to a notary, seal me there | your single bond; MV 1.03.144
content, in faith, i'll seal to such a bond, 1.03.152
you shall not seal to such a bond for me, | i'll 1.03.154
yes, shylock, i will seal unto this bond. 1.03.171
pigeons fly | to seal love's bonds new made, 2.06. 6
till thou canst rail the seal from off my bond, 4.01.139
and by him seal up thy mind, | whether that thy AYL 4.03. 58
bride | and seal the title with a lovely kiss! SHR 3.02.123
it is the show and seal of nature's truth, AWW 1.03.132
her lucrece, with which she uses to seal. TN 2.05. 93 P
or say 'tis not your seal, not your invention. 5.01.333
you have not dar'd to break the holy seal | nor WT 3.02.129
kiss | as seal to this indenture of my love: JN 2.01. 20
here is your hand and seal for what i did. 4.02.215
then shall this hand and seal | witness against 4.02.217
there is my gage, the manual seal of death, R2 4.01. 25
what seal is that, that hangs without thy bosom? 5.02. 56
by this our book is drawn, we'll but seal, | and 1H4 3.01.265
and giddy /mast | seal up the ship–boy's eyes, 2H4 3.01. 19
that you should seal this lawless bloody book 4.01. 91
book | of forg'd rebellion with a seal divine. 4.01. 92
and my thumb, and shortly will i seal with him. 4.03.131 P
seal up your lips, and give no words but mum; 2H6 1.02. 89
that thou mightst think upon these by the seal, 3.02.344
for i did but seal once to a thing, and i was 4.02. 82 P
and thus i seal my truth, and bid adieu. 3H6 4.08. 29
i seal upon the lips of this sweet babe. 5.07. 29
and with my hand i seal my true heart's love. R3 2.01. 10

seal thou this league | with thy embracements to 2.01. 29
i'll resign unto your grace | the seal i keep, 2.04. 71
whom after under the /confession's seal | he H8 1.02.164
i now seal it; 2.01.105
to render up the great seal presently | into our 3.02.229
that seal | you ask with such a violence, the 3.02.245
bold | to carry into flanders the great seal. 3.02.319
about the giving–back the great seal to us, 3.02.347
go to, a bargain made, seal it, seal it, i'll be TRO 3.02.197 P
made, seal it, seal it, i'll be the witness. 3.02.197 P
to shame the seal of my petition to thee | in 4.04.122
i will not seal your knowledge with showing them COR 2.03.108 P
both divine and human, | seal what i end withal! 3.01.142
together with the seal a' th' senate, what | we 5.06. 82
the empress sends it thee, thy stamp, thy seal, TIT 4.02. 69
side, | although my seal be stamped in his face. 4.02.127
seal with a righteous kiss | a dateless bargain ROM 5.03.114
seal up the mouth of outrage for a while, | till 5.03.216
but here's a parchment with the seal of caesar, JC 3.02.128
here is the will, and under caesar's seal: 3.02.240
read it, afterwards seal it, and again return to MAC 5.01. 7 P
where every god did seem to set his seal | to HAM 3.04. 61
now must your conscience my acquittance seal, 4.07. 1
which was the model of that danish seal; 5.02. 50
who have the power | to seal th' accuser's lips. LR 4.06.170
this kingly seal | and plighter of high hearts! ANT 3.13.125
seal then, and all is done. 4.14. 49
seal it with feasts. CYM 5.05.483
nay, come, your hands and lips must seal it too; PER 2.05. 85
who is at hand to seal | the promise of his TNK 1.02. 92
beauty, | thus let me seal my vow'd faith. 2.05. 39
when he frowns | to seal his will with. 4.02. 87
slips, | set thy seal manual on my wax–red lips. VEN 516
to stamp the seal of time in aged things, | to LUC 941
she carv'd thee for her seal, and meant thereby SON 11.13
SEAL'D 31 FR 0.0035 REL FR 30 V 1 P
seals of love, but seal'd in vain, seal'd in MM 4.01. 6
of love, but seal'd in vain, seal'd in vain. 4.01. 6
worth and credit | that's seal'd in approbation? 5.01.245
have seal'd his rigorous statutes with their ERR 1.01. 9
became his surety and seal'd under for another. MV 1.02. 82 P
she brought stone jugs and no seal'd quarts. SHR in.2. 88
of this compact | seal'd in my function, by my TN 5.01.161
(thus by apollo's great divine seal'd up) WT 3.01. 19
save in aspect, hath all offense seal'd up; JN 2.01.250
my death | thou hast seal'd up my expectation. 2H4 4.05.103
to death, with blood he seal'd | a testament of H5 4.06. 26
here had the conquest fully been seal'd up, | if 1H6 1.01.130
fly, | now thou art seal'd the son of chivalry? 4.06. 29
thou that wast seal'd in thy nativity | the R3 1.03.228
and ere this hand, by thee to romeo's seal'd, ROM 4.01. 56
seal'd up the doors and would not let us forth, 5.02. 11
our town till we | have seal'd thy full desire. TIM 5.04. 54
i found | this paper, thus seal'd up, and i am JC 2.01. 37
by a seal'd compact | well ratified by law and HAM 1.01. 86
last | upon his will i seal'd my hard consent. 1.02. 60
sh' hath seal'd thee for herself, for thou hast 3.02. 65
there's letters seal'd, and my two schoolfellows 3.04.202
for every thing is seal'd and done | that else 4.03. 56
how was this seal'd? 5.02. 47
may be written | and seal'd between us. ANT 2.06. 59
virtue | which their own conscience seal'd them, CYM 3.06. 84
his seal'd commission, left in trust with me, PER 1.03. 12
the belief | both seal'd with eye and ear. TNK 5.03. 15
her letter now is seal'd, and on it writ, | "at LUC 1331
and seal'd false bonds of love as oft as mine, SON 142. 7
enswath'd, and seal'd to curious secrecy. LC 49
SEAL'D -UP 2 FR 0.0002 REL FR 2 V 0 P
see thou do commend | this seal'd–up counsel. LLL 3.01.169
thence have brought | this seal'd–up oracle, by WT 3.02.127
SEALED 5 FR 0.0005 REL FR 5 V 0 P
than stamps in gold, or sums in sealed bags; WIV 3.04. 16
a sealed bag, two sealed bags of ducats, | of MV 2.08. 18
a sealed bag, two sealed bags of ducats, | of 2.08. 18
which being sealed interchangeably | (a business 1H4 3.01. 80
bear this sealed brief | with winged haste to 4.04. 1
SEA -LIKE 1 FR 0.0001 REL FR 1 V 0 P
again, and fleet, threat'ning most sea–like. ANT 3.13.171
SEALING 3 FR 0.0003 REL FR 3 V 0 P
and thereby for sealing | the injury of tongues WT 1.02.337
the other three are sealing. ANT 3.02. 3
what bargains may i make, still to be sealing? VEN 512
SEALING -DAY 1 FR 0.0001 REL FR 1 V 0 P
the sealing–day betwixt my love and me | for MND 1.01. 84
SEAL–RING 2 FR 0.0002 REL FR 0 V 2 P
i have lost a seal–ring of my grandfather's 1H4 3.03. 82 P
a–piece, and a seal–ring of my grandfather's. 3.03.102 P
SEALS 11 FR 0.0012 REL FR 10 V 1 P
seals of love, but seal'd in vain, seal'd in MM 4.01. 6
break up the seals, and read. WT 3.02.131
this covenant makes, my hand thus seals it. R2 2.03. 50
virgins with the broken seals of perjury; H5 4.01.164 P
the match is made, she seals it with a cur'sy. 3H6 3.02. 57
consent proceeded | under your hands and seals. H8 2.04.223
seals a commission to a blank of danger, | and TRO 3.03.231
to give them seals never my soul consent! HAM 3.02.399
all seals and symbols of redeemed sin, | his OTH 2.03.344
lips, sweet seals in my soft lips imprinted, VEN 511
death's second self, that seals up all in rest. SON 73. 8
SEAM 1 FR 0.0001 REL FR 1 V 0 P
that bastes his arrogance with his own seam, TRO 2.03.185
SEA -MAID 1 FR 0.0001 REL FR 0 V 1 P
some report a sea–maid spawn'd him; MM 3.02.108 P
SEA -MAID'S 1 FR 0.0001 REL FR 1 V 0 P
their spheres, | to hear the sea–maid's music? MND 2.01.154
SEAMAN 1 FR 0.0001 REL FR 1 V 0 P
that ever yet betoken'd | wrack to the seaman, VEN 454
SEAMAN'S 1 FR 0.0001 REL FR 1 V 0 P
the seaman's whistle | is as a whisper in the PER 3.01. 8
SEA -MARGE 1 FR 0.0001 REL FR 1 V 0 P
and thy sea–marge, sterile and rocky–hard, TMP 4.01. 69
SEA -MARK 2 FR 0.0002 REL FR 2 V 0 P
and stick i' th' wars | like a great sea–mark, COR 5.03. 74
my butt | and very sea–mark of my utmost sail. OTH 5.02.268
SEAMEN 2 FR 0.0002 REL FR 2 V 0 P
but on this day let seamen fear no wrack; JN 3.01. 92
says, did never fear, | but cried "good seamen!" PER 4.01. 53
SEA–MONSTER 2 FR 0.0002 REL FR 2 V 0 P
paid by howling troy | to the sea–monster. MV 3.02. 57
show'st thee in a child | than the sea–monster. LR 1.04.261
SEAMS 1 FR 0.0001 REL FR 0 V 1 P
garment through the rough seams of the waters. PER 2.01.149 P
SEAMSTER'S *(see sempster's)*
SEAMY 1 FR 0.0001 REL FR 1 V 0 P
that turn'd your wit the seamy side without, OTH 4.02.146
SEA–NYMPHS 1 FR 0.0001 REL FR 1 V 0 P
sea–nymphs hourly ring his knell: TMP 1.02.403
SEAR *(also sere*)*
SEAR 4 FR 0.0004 REL FR 4 V 0 P
does, for calumny will sear | virtue itself), WT 2.01. 73
were red–hot steel, to sear me to the brains! R3 4.01. 60
thy crown does sear mine eyeballs. MAC 4.01.113
my way of life | is fall'n into the sear, the 5.03. 23
SEARCH 51 FR 0.0057 REL FR 29 V 22 P
and let's make further search | for my poor son. TMP 2.01.323
the sea mocks | our frustrate search on land. 3.03. 10
and thus i search it with a sovereign kiss. TGV 1.02.113
and my assurance bids me search — there i shall WIV 3.02. 46 P
to search for a gentleman that he says is here 3.03.107 P
windsor at his heels, to search for such a one. 3.03.115 P
ascend my chambers, search, seek, find out. 3.03.163 P
him, gentlemen, see the issue of his search. 3.03.175 P
to search his house for his wive's love. 3.05. 77 P
and did he search for you, and could not find 3.05. 81 P
well, on went he for a search, and away went i 3.05.106 P
should aid him, i will search impossible places. 3.05.148 P
help to search my house this one time. 4.02.160 P
satisfy me once more, once more search with me. 4.02.165 P
search windsor castle, elves, within and out. 5.05. 56
you have them, they are not worth the search. MV 1.01.118 P
who went with him to search bassanio's ship. 2.08. 5
so — and i know not what's spent in the search. 3.01. 92 P
in that it is a thing of his own search, and AYL 1.01.135 P
and let not search and inquisition quail | to 2.02. 20
that seeks not to find that her search implies, AWW 1.03.216
the search, sir, was profitable, and much fool 2.04. 35 P
marry, we'll search. 4.03.202 P
if zealous love should go in search of virtue, JN 2.01.428
at the door, they are come to search the house. 1H4 2.04.490 P
search his pockets. 2.04.530 P
search out thy wit for secret policies, | and we 1H6 3.03. 12
to search the secret treasons of the world. 3H6 5.02. 18
now to the bottom dost thou search my wound; TIT 2.03.262
mist–like infold me from the search of eyes. ROM 3.03. 73
ground is bloody, search about the churchyard. 5.03.172
some others search. 5.03.178
search, seek, and know how this foul murder 5.03.198
ran through caesar's bowels, search this bosom. JC 5.03. 42
if aught of woe or wonder, cease your search. HAM 5.02.363
search every acre in the high–grown field, | and LR 4.04. 7
him, | lead to the sagittary the raised search; OTH 1.01.158
about three several quests | to search you out. 1.02. 47
so slackly guarded, and the search so slow, CYM 1.01. 64
my woman | search for a jewel that too casually 2.03.141
i hope so; go and search. 2.03.149
name of fame and honor which dies i' th' search, 3.03. 51
you and my brother search | what companies are 4.02. 68
be a day fits you, search out of the calendar, PER 2.01. 54 P
go search like nobles, like noble subjects, 2.04. 50
and in your search spend your adventurous worth; 2.04. 51
painful perch, | of pericles the careful search, 3.ch. 16
search the market narrowly, meteline is full of 4.02. 3 P
but shall i search the market? 4.02. 17 P
but i'll go search the market. 4.02. 25 P
for mirth doth search the bottom of annoy, | sad LUC 1109
SEARCH'D 7 FR 0.0008 REL FR 3 V 4 P
lest the lunatic knave would have search'd it; WIV 3.05.104 P
carried out, the last time he search'd for him, 4.02. 32 P
that search'd a hollow walnut for his wive's 4.02.163 P
that will not be deep search'd with saucy looks; LLL 1.01. 85
who, inward search'd, have livers white as milk, MV 3.02. 86
i have search'd, i have inquir'd, so has my 1H4 3.03. 56 P
he hath been search'd among the dead and living; CYM 5.05. 11
SEARCHERS 1 FR 0.0001 REL FR 1 V 0 P
and finding him, the searchers of the town, ROM 5.02. 8
SEARCHES 1 FR 0.0001 REL FR 1 V 0 P
the tent that searches | to th' bottom of the TRO 2.02. 16
SEARCHING 6 FR 0.0006 REL FR 5 V 1 P
searching of /thy /wound, | i have by hard AYL 2.04. 44
that when the searching eye of heaven is hid R2 3.02. 37
and that's a marvellous searching wine, and it 2H4 2.04. 27 P
i would invent as bitter searching terms, | as 2H6 3.02.311
my own searching eyes | shall find him by his TRO 4.05.161
searching the window for a flint, i found | this JC 2.01. 36
SEAR'D 3 FR 0.0003 REL FR 3 V 0 P
my maiden's name | sear'd otherwise; AWW 2.01.173
the sun that sear'd the wings of my sweet boy, 3H6 5.06. 23
beauty peep'd through lettice of sear'd age. LC 14
SEA–ROOM 1 FR 0.0001 REL FR 0 V 1 P
but sea–room, and the brine and cloudy billow PER 3.01. 45 P
SEA'S 5 FR 0.0005 REL FR 5 V 0 P
from the rude sea's enrag'd and foamy mouth TN 5.01. 78
the sea's a thief, whose liquid surge resolves TIM 4.03.439
and confine | for the sea's worth. OTH 1.02. 28
if the sea's stomach be o'ercharg'd with gold, PER 3.02. 54
sun and moon, with earth and sea's rich gems, SON 21. 6
SEAS 53 FR 0.0060 REL FR 51 V 2 P
have | incens'd the seas and shores — yea, all TMP 3.03. 74
though the seas threaten, they are merciful, | i 5.01.178
and promise you calm seas, auspicious gales, 5.01.315
as rich in having such a jewel | as twenty seas, TGV 2.04.170
of his wished light | the seas wax'd calm, and ERR 1.01. 91
lord of the wide world and wild wat'ry seas, 2.01. 21
in the narrow seas that part | the french and MV 2.08. 28
ship of rich lading wrack'd on the narrow seas; 3.01. 4 P
is as rough | as are the swelling adriatic seas, SHR 1.02. 74
'twill bring you gain, or perish on the seas. 2.01.329
and great seas have dried | when miracles have AWW 2.01.140
or the profound seas hides | in unknown fadoms, WT 4.04.490
large lengths of seas and shores | between my JN 1.01.105
spits forth death and mountains, rocks and seas, 2.01.458
after your late tossing on the breaking seas? R2 3.02. 3
knew that we ventured on such dangerous seas 2H4 1.01.181
charming the narrow seas | to give you gentle H5 2.pr. 38
to cross the seas and to be crown'd in france. 1H6 3.01.179
repeat their semblance often on the seas, | that 5.03.193
to cross the seas to england and be crown'd 5.05. 90
the dolphin hath prevail'd beyond the seas, 2H6 1.03.125
should make a start o'er seas and vanquish you? 4.08. 43
stern falconbridge commands the narrow seas, 3H6 1.01.239
for slaughter of my son | shed seas of tears, 2.05.106
shall cross the seas and bid false edward battle 3.03.235
let us be back'd with god, and with the seas, 4.01. 43
well have we pass'd and now repass'd the seas, 4.07. 5
hath pass'd in safety through the narrow seas, 4.08. 3
if thou wilt outstrip death, go cross the seas, R3 4.01. 41
richmond is on the seas. 4.04.462
there let him sink, and be the seas on him! 4.04.463
then tell me, what makes he upon the seas? 4.04.473
let's whip these stragglers o'er the seas again; 5.03.327
the seas and winds, old wranglers, took a truce, TRO 2.02. 75
but our undertakings, when we vow to weep seas, 3.02. 78 P
rather | the multitudinous seas incarnadine, MAC 2.02. 59
haply the seas and countries different | with HAM 3.01.171
tempests themselves, high seas, and howling OTH 2.01. 68
and let the laboring bark climb hills of seas 2.01.187
i cross'd the seas on purpose and on promise CYM 1.06.202
on our terrible seas, | like egg–shells mov'd 3.01. 27
th' imperious seas breeds monsters; 4.02. 35
since he's gone, the king's seas must please: PER 1.03. 27
he, doing so, put forth to seas, | where when 2.ch. 27
alas, the seas hath cast me on the rocks, 2.01. 5
till the rough seas, that spares not any man, 2.01.131
was by the rough seas reft of ships and men, 2.03. 84
who only by misfortune of the seas | bereft of 2.03. 88
take i your wish, i leap into the seas, 2.04. 43
sail seas in cockles, have and wish but for't, 4.04. 2
is now again thwarting /the wayward seas, 4.04. 10
our fiery horses | like proud seas under us! TNK 2.02. 20
none here, nor the seas | swallow their youth. 2.02. 87
//SEA–SALT 1 FR 0.0001 REL FR 1 V 0 P
/the /lamenting /fool /in //sea–salt /tears. TIT 3.02. 20
SEA–SICK 3 FR 0.0003 REL FR 2 V 1 P
sea–sick, i think, coming from muscovy. LLL 5.02.393
be), who began to be much sea–sick, and himself WT 5.02.119 P
on | the dashing rocks thy sea–sick weary bark! ROM 5.03.118
SEA–SIDE 7 FR 0.0008 REL FR 4 V 3 P
my cellar is in a rock by th' sea–side, where my TMP 2.02.135 P
if any where i have them, 'tis by the sea–side, WT 3.03. 68 P
thus we set on, camillo, to th' sea–side. 4.04.668
walk before toward the sea–side, go on the right 4.04.825 P
carriages he hath dispatch'd | to the sea–side, JN 5.07. 91
let's to the sea–side, ho! OTH 2.01. 36
to the sea–side straightway; ANT 3.11. 20
SEASON* 46 FR 0.0052 REL FR 40 V 6 P
past the mid season. TMP 1.02.239
buck, and of the season too, it shall appear. WIV 3.03.159 P
for our kitchens | we kill the fowl of season. MM 2.02. 85
as the flow'r, | corrupt with virtuous season. 2.02.167
dromio, come, these jests are out of season, ERR 1.02. 68
there ever any man thus beaten out of season, 2.02. 47
and owes more than he's worth to season. 4.02. 58
that you frame the season for your own harvest. ADO 1.03. 25 P
and salt too little which may season give | to 4.01.142
but like of each thing that in season grows. LLL 1.01.107
and wait the season, and observe the times, 5.02. 63
things growing are not ripe until their season, MND 2.02.117
how many things by season season'd are | to MV 5.01.107
best brine a maiden can season her praise in. AWW 1.01. 48 P
i am not a day of season, | for thou mayst see a 5.03. 32
all this to season | a brother's dead love, TN 1.01. 29
the fairest flow'rs o' th' season | are our WT 4.04. 81
at the same season if your mother's cat had 1H4 3.01. 18
you wish me health in very happy season, | for i 2H4 4.02. 79
and for a season after | could not believe but R3 1.04. 61
in brief — for so the season bids us be — 5.03. 87
such–like, the spice and salt that season a man? TRO 1.02.255 P
insisture, course, proportion, season, form, 1.03. 87
to season love, that of it doth not taste! ROM 2.03. 72
not that, if money and the season can yield it. TIM 3.06. 50 P
hours, season the slaves | for tubs and baths, 4.03. 86
weighing the youthful season of the year. JC 2.01.108
you lack the season of all natures, sleep. MAC 3.04.140
and best knows | the fits o' th' season. 4.02. 17
some say that ever 'gainst that season comes HAM 1.01.158
season your admiration for a while | with an 1.02.192
farewell, my blessing season this in thee! 1.03. 81
it then draws near the season | wherein the 1.04. 5
faith, as you may season it in the charge: 2.01. 28
/confederate season, else no creature seeing, 3.02.256
thus out of season, threading dark–ey'd night: LR 2.01.119
but i will tell you at some meeter season. ANT 5.01. 49
and be friended | with aptness of the season; CYM 2.03. 48
you can borrow | from youth of such a season) 3.04.172
we'll slip you for a season, but our jealousy 4.03. 22
did relieve me | to see this gracious season. 5.05.401
you, at such a season | as now it is with me, i TNK 1.01. 60
as sweet flowers as the season is mistress of, 4.03. 83 P
and now the happy season once more fits | that VEN 327
now serves the season that they may surprise LUC 166
plots the sin, thou 'point'st the season; 879
SEASON'D 8 FR 0.0009 REL FR 8 V 0 P
but, being season'd with a gracious voice, MV 3.02. 76
their palates | be season'd with such viands"? 4.01. 97
how many things by season season'd are | to 5.01.107
so season'd with your faithful love to me, R3 3.07.149
to take | from rome all season'd office, and to COR 3.03. 64
when he is fit and season'd for his passage? HAM 3.03. 86
has more ground, is more maturely season'd, TNK 1.03. 56
to my petition, | season'd with holy fear. 5.01.149
SEASONED 1 FR 0.0001 REL FR 1 V 0 P
brine | that seasoned woe had pelleted in tears, LC 18
SEASONING 1 FR 0.0001 REL FR 1 V 0 P
seasoning the earth with show'rs of silver brine LUC 796
SEASON'S 1 FR 0.0001 REL FR 1 V 0 P
as not a soldier of this season's stamp | should 1H4 4.01. 4
SEASONS' 2 FR 0.0002 REL FR 2 V 0 P
the seasons' difference, as the icy fang | and AYL 2.01. 6
of plagues, of dearths, or seasons' quality; SON 14. 4
SEASONS* 10 FR 0.0011 REL FR 10 V 0 P
this distemperature we see | the seasons alter: MND 2.01.107
show likest god's | when mercy seasons justice. MV 4.01.197
the seasons change their manners, as the year 2H4 4.04.123

so cares and joys abound, as seasons fleet. 2H6 2.04. 4
sorrow breaks seasons and reposing hours, R3 1.04. 76
doth try, | directly seasons him his enemy. HAM 3.02.209
defend you | from seasons such as these? LR 3.04. 32
their honest wills, | which seasons comfort. CYM 1.06. 9
make glad and sorry seasons as thou fleet'st, SON 19. 5
turn'd | in process of the seasons have i seen, 104. 6
SEA-SORROW 1 FR 0.0001 REL FR 1 V 0 P
sit still, and hear the last of our sea–sorrow: TMP 1.02.170
SEA-STORM 1 FR 0.0001 REL FR 1 V 0 P
mind, your reason | for raising this sea–storm? TMP 1.02.177
SEAS-TOSS'D 1 FR 0.0001 REL FR 1 V 0 P
the seas–toss'd pericles appears to speak. PER 3.ch. 60
SEA-SWALLOW'D 1 FR 0.0001 REL FR 1 V 0 P
she that from whom | we all were sea–swallow'd, TMP 2.01.251
/SEAT 1 FR 0.0001 REL FR 1 V 0 P
/thou /live /in /richard's /seat /to /sit, R2 4.01.218
SEAT 56 FR 0.0063 REL FR 56 V 0 P
who, newly in the seat, that it may know | he MM 1.02.161
let love forbid | sleep his seat on thy eyelid. MND 2.02. 81
which makes her seat of belmont colchis' strond, MV 1.01.171
it gives a very echo to the seat | where love is TN 2.04. 21
this earth of majesty, this seat of mars, | this R2 2.01. 41
manage rusty bills | against thy seat: 3.02.119
and in this seat of peace tumultuous wars 4.01.140
thy seat is up on high, | whilst my gross flesh 5.05.111
betwixt that holmedon and this seat of ours; 1H4 1.01. 65
and vaulted with such ease into his seat | as if 4.01.107
the seat of gaunt, dukedom of lancaster. 5.01. 45
and strook me in my very seat of judgment; 2H4 5.02. 80
willfulness | so soon did lose his seat (and all H5 1.01. 36
and generally to the crown and seat of france, 1.01. 88
and did seat the french | beyond the river sala, 1.02. 62
we never valu'd this poor seat of england, | and 1.02.269
upon the valleys whose low vassal seat | the 3.05. 51
we'll quickly hoise duke humphrey from his seat. 2H6 1.01.169
methought i sat in seat of majesty | in the 1.02. 36
the rightful heir to england's royal seat. 5.01.178
of the fearful king, | and this the regal seat. 3H6 1.01. 26
for in thy shoulder do i build my seat, | and 2.06.100
where i must take like seat unto my fortune, 3.03. 10
fortune, | and to my humble seat conform myself. 3.03. 11
york, | usurps the regal title and the seat | of 3.03. 28
and force the tyrant from his seat by war. 3.03.206
have shaken edward from the regal seat, | and 4.06. 2
thus have we swept suspicion from our seat, 5.07. 13
thy honor, state, and seat is due to me. R3 1.03.111
duke | in the seat royal of this famous isle? 3.01.164
and, for more slander to thy dismal seat, | we 3.03. 13
your fault that you resign | the supreme seat, 3.07.118
of time, | will well become the seat of majesty, 3.07.169
a grave | as thou canst yield a melancholy seat! 4.04. 32
with due observance of /thy godlike seat, TRO 1.03. 31
the court, the heart, to th' seat o' th' brain, COR 1.01.136
not dishonor to approach | the imperial seat, to TIT 1.01. 14
he's flung in rage from this ingrateful seat TIM 4.02. 45
and after this let caesar seat him sure, | for JC 1.02.321
metellus cimber throws before thy seat | an 3.01. 34
this castle hath a pleasant seat, the air MAC 1.06. 1
pray you keep seat. 3.04. 53
whiles memory holds a seat | in this distracted HAM 1.05. 96
had witchcraft in't, he grew unto his seat, 4.07. 85
the lusty moor | hath leap'd into my seat; OTH 2.01.296
forsake thy seat, i do beseech thee, captain, ANT 2.07. 38
whilst the wheel'd seat | of fortunate caesar, 4.14. 75
have made my throne | a seat for baseness. CYM 1.01.142
and thrown | from leonati seat, and cast | from 5.04. 60
built up this city for his chiefest seat, | the PER 1.ch. 18
place | to seat something i would confound. TNK 5.01. 28
they would glance their eyes | toward my seat, 5.03. 62
that oft they interchange each other's seat. LUC 70
and in the self–same seat sits collatine. 289
ay me, but yet thou mightst my seat forbear, SON 41. 9
which three till now never kept seat in one. 105.14
SEATED 12 FR 0.0013 REL FR 11 V 1 P
happiness, therefore, to be seated in the mean: MV 1.02. 8 P
before i see thee seated in that throne | which 3H6 1.01. 22
to henry, | if he were seated as king edward is. 3.01. 96
and see him seated in the regal throne. 4.03. 64
now am i seated as my soul delights, | having my 5.07. 35
and being seated, and domestic broils | clean R3 2.04. 60
and thy assistance, is king richard seated; 4.02. 4
so now y' are fairly seated. H8 1.04. 31
and make my seated heart knock at my ribs, MAC 1.03.136
see what a grace was seated on this brow: HAM 3.04. 55
glory, | when he was seated in a chariot | of an PER 2.04. 7
some dark deep desert, seated from the way, LUC 1144
SEAT'S 1 FR 0.0001 REL FR 1 V 0 P
now, by my seat's right royal majesty, | wert R2 2.01.120
/SEATS 1 FR 0.0001 REL FR 1 V 0 P
/mounted /and /both /roused /in /their /seats, 2H4 4.01.116
SEATS 4 FR 0.0004 REL FR 4 V 0 P
give us some seats. MM 5.01.165
for your great seats now quit you of great H5 3.05. 47
the nature of our seats and make the rabble COR 3.01.136
for this from stiller seats we came, | our CYM 5.04. 69
SEA-WALLED 1 FR 0.0001 REL FR 1 V 0 P
when our sea–walled garden, the whole land, | is R2 3.04. 43
SEA-WATER 2 FR 0.0002 REL FR 1 V 1 P
sea–water shalt thou drink; TMP 1.02.463
of the sea–water green, sir. LLL 1.02. 82 P
SEA-WING 1 FR 0.0001 REL FR 1 V 0 P
claps on his sea–wing, and (like a doting ANT 3.10. 19
SEBASTIAN 17 FR 0.0019 REL FR 14 V 3 P
my lord sebastian, | the truth you speak doth TMP 2.01.137
might, | worthy sebastian, o, what might — ? 2.01.205
noble sebastian, | thou let'st thy fortune sleep 2.01.215
keep in tunis, | and let sebastian wake." 2.01.260
thou art pinch'd for't now, sebastian. 5.01. 74
whom, with sebastian | (whose inward pinches 5.01. 76
sebastian is thy name? TGV 4.04. 40
sebastian, i have entertained thee, | partly 4.04. 63
sebastian, so many; AWW 4.03.162 P
antonio, my name is sebastian, which i call'd TN 2.01. 16 P
my father was that sebastian of messaline, whom 2.01. 17 P
thou hast, sebastian, done good feature shame. 3.04.366
he nam'd sebastian. 3.04.379
sebastian are you? 5.01.221
which is sebastian? 5.01.224
sebastian was my father — | such a sebastian 5.01.232
father — | such a sebastian was my brother too; 5.01.233
/SECOND 1 FR 0.0001 REL FR 1 V 0 P
/second /to /none, /unseconded /by /you, | /to 2H4 2.03. 34
SECOND 103 FR 0.0116 REL FR 84 V 19 P
i'll be thy second. TMP 3.03.103
of whom i have | receiv'd a second life; 5.01.195
and second father | this lady makes him to me. 5.01.195
i second thee; WIV 1.03.104 P
and these are of the second edition. 2.01. 76 P
pardon is still the nurse of second woe. MM 2.01.284
for urging it the second time to me. ERR 2.02. 46
second to none that lives here in the city: 5.01. 7
and 'tis not wisdom thus to second grief ADO 5.01. 2
the first and second cause will not serve my LLL 1.02.178 P
the second, silver, which this promise carries, MV 2.07. 6
often known | to be the dowry of a second head, 3.02. 95
a second daniel! 4.01.333
a daniel, still say i, a second daniel! 4.01.340
so he serv'd the second, and so the third. AYL 1.02.129 P
you shall not entreat him to a second, that have 1.02.206 P
is second childishness and mere oblivion, | sans 2.07.165
the second, the quip modest; 5.04. 93 P
i am the second son of old sir rowland, | that 5.04.152
for patience she will prove a second grissel, SHR 2.01.295
my son from me, i bury a second husband. AWW 1.01. 2 P
a second time receive | the confirmation of my 2.03. 49
stay | to see our widower's second marriage–day. 5.03. 70
heat makes him a fool, the second mads him, and TN 1.05.132 P
the second and the third, nine, and some five; WT 2.01.145
nay, rather, good my lords, be second to me. 2.03. 27
my second joy | and first–fruits of my body, 3.02. 96
being but the second generation | removed from JN 2.01.181
second a villain and a murtherer? 4.03.102
thee | to make a second fall of cursed man? R2 3.04. 76
being the agents or base second means, | the 1H4 1.03.165
never shall | a second time do such a courtesy. 5.02.100
can say of me is that i am a second brother, and 2H4 2.02. 67 P
down, | we have supplies to second our attempt; 4.02. 45
if they miscarry, theirs shall second them, 4.02. 46
the second property of your excellent sherris is 4.03.102 P
and mock your workings in a second body? 5.02. 90
one, richard earl of cambridge, and the second, H5 2.pr. 23
your mock | in second accent of his ordinance. 2.04.126
break out into a second course of mischief, 4.03.106
a second hector, for his grim aspect | and large 1H6 2.03. 20
art thou not second woman in the realm? 2H6 1.02. 43
the second, william of hatfield; 2.02. 12
and now is york in arms to second him. 4.09. 35
ay, now begins a second storm to rise, | for 3H6 3.03. 47
richard the second here was hack'd to death; R3 3.03. 12
and by the second hour in the morning | desire 5.03. 31
agent of our cardinal, | to second all his plot. H8 3.02. 60
his second marriage shall be publish'd, and 3.02. 68
in second voice we'll not be satisfied, | we TRO 2.03.140
and on him erect | a second hope, as fairly 4.05.109
i will the second time, | as i would buy thee, 4.05.237
been too violent for | a second course of fight. COR 1.05. 16
of threepence to a second day of audience. 2.01. 72 P
the second name of men, obeys his points | as if 4.06.125
when she, poor hen, fond of no second brood, 5.03.162
let him feel your sword, | which we will second. 5.06. 56
very first house, of the first and second cause. ROM 2.04. 25 P
the operation of the second cup draws him on the 3.01. 8 P
i think you are happy in this second match, 3.05.222
the second cock hath crowed, | the curfew–bell 4.04. 3
mean | to rid her from this second marriage, 5.03.241
for many so arrive at second masters, | upon TIM 4.03.505
what was the second noise for? JC 1.02.224
he is address'd; press near and second him. 3.01. 29
night | we shall try fortune in a second fight. 5.03.110
hark! who lies i' th' second chamber? MAC 2.02. 17
of hurt minds, great nature's second course, 2.02. 36
sir, we were carousing till the second cock; 2.03. 24 P
which is now | our point of second meeting. 3.01. 85
grace, | occasion smiles upon a second leave. HAM 1.03. 54
happily he is the second time come to them, for 2.02.384 P
in second husband let me be accurs'd! 3.02.179
none wed the second but who kill'd the first. 3.02.180
the instances that second marriage move | are 3.02.182
a second time i kill my husband dead, | when 3.02.184
dead, | when second husband kisses me in bed. 3.02.185
so think thou wilt no second husband wed, | but 3.02.214
this project | should have a back or second, 4.07.153
if hamlet give the first or second hit, | or 5.02.268
what says our second daughter, | our dearest LR 1.01. 67
where each second | stood heir to th' first. OTH 1.01. 37
her in it and compel her to some second choice. 2.01.235 P
should hazard such a place as his own second 2.03.139
this is his second fit; 4.01. 51
i will be near to second your attempt, and he 4.02.238 P
shall embattle | by th' second hour i' th' morn. ANT 4.09. 4
where's dolabella, | to second proculeius? 5.01. 70
than the opportunity of a second conference, and CYM 1.04.130 P
a second night of such sweet shortness which 2.04. 44
that is the second thing that i have commanded 3.05.152 P
you some permit | to second ills with ills, each 5.01. 14
who is the second that presents himself? PER 2.02. 23
and curs'd be he that will not second it. 2.04. 20
be buried | a second time within these arms. 5.03. 44
off | this great adventure to a second trial. TNK 3.06.119
and to second them, | that truly noble prince 4.01. 12
dead at first, what needs a second striking? VEN 250
a second fear through all her sinews spread, 903
amiss | the second burthen of a former child! SON 59. 4
away, | to live a second life on second head; 68. 7
away, | to live a second life on second head; 68. 7
death's second self, that seals up all in rest. 73. 8
SECONDARILY 1 FR 0.0001 REL FR 0 V 1 P
secondarily, they are slanders; ADO 5.01.216 P
SECONDARY 2 FR 0.0002 REL FR 2 V 0 P
though first in question, is thy secondary. MM 1.01. 46
be propertied, | to be a secondary at control, JN 5.02. 80
SECONDED 3 FR 0.0003 REL FR 2 V 1 P
a man's good wit seconded with the forward child AYL 3.03. 13 P
wolf | (so doubly seconded with will and power), TRO 1.03.122
the slave's report is seconded, and more, | more COR 4.06. 63
SECONDS 5 FR 0.0005 REL FR 5 V 0 P
now prove good seconds: COR 1.04. 43
you have sham'd me | in your condemned seconds. 1.08. 15
no seconds? LR 4.06.194
drooping here, if seconds | had answer'd him. CYM 5.03. 90
which is not mix'd with seconds, knows no art, SON 125.11
SECRECIES 1 FR 0.0001 REL FR 1 V 0 P
nor read the subtle shining secrecies | writ in LUC 101
SECRECY *(also secrety)*
SECRECY 15 FR 0.0017 REL FR 11 V 4 P
this secrecy of thine shall be a tailor to thee WIV 3.03. 33 P
thanks, provost, for thy care and secrecy, | we MM 5.01.530
and to be so still requires nothing but secrecy. WT 3.03.126 P
you are, | but yet a woman, and for secrecy, 1H4 2.03.109
the business asketh silent secrecy. 2H6 1.02. 90
perform'd, | but with advice and silent secrecy. 2.02. 68
whom the king hath in secrecy long married, H8 3.02.403
to defend my wiles, upon my secrecy, to defend TRO 1.02.261 P
to me | in dreadful secrecy impart they did, HAM 1.02.207
and your secrecy to the king and queen moult no 2.02.294 P
no, in despite of sense and secrecy, | unpeg the 3.04.192
in nature's infinite book of secrecy | a little ANT 1.02. 10
partakes her private actions | to your secrecy; PER 1.01.153
her spite | against the unseen secrecy of night: LUC 763
enswath'd, and seal'd to curious secrecy. LC 49
/SECRET 1 FR 0.0001 REL FR 1 V 0 P
/have /secret /feet | /in /some /of /our /best LR 3.01. 32
SECRET 70 FR 0.0079 REL FR 61 V 9 P
being transported | and rapt in secret studies. TMP 1.02. 77
me, i have writ your letter | unto the secret, TGV 2.01.105
never get such a secret from me but by a parable 2.05. 39 P
that touch me near, wherein thou must be secret. 3.01. 60
why i desire thee | to give me secret harbor, MM 1.03. 4
'tis a secret must be lock'd within the teeth 3.02.134 P
put them in secret holds, both barnardine and 4.03. 87
what secret hath held you here, that you ADO 1.01.204 P
count claudio, i can be secret as a dumb man; 1.01.209 P
they have had | a thousand times in secret. 4.01. 94
one word in secret. LLL 5.02.236
same | to whom you swore a secret pilgrimage, MV 1.01.120
i have toward heaven breath'd a secret vow | to 3.04. 27
a secret and villainous contriver against me his AYL 1.01.144 P
that art to me as secret and as dear | as anna SHR 1.01.153
to thee the book even of my secret soul. TN 1.04. 14
and what i would, are as secret as maidenhead: 1.05.216 P
things you found about her, those secret things, WT 4.04.696 P
will have fulfill'd their secret purposes; 5.01. 36
for had i been the finder–out of this secret, it 5.02.122 P
that takes away by any secret course | thy JN 3.01.178
so, | stay, and be secret, and myself will go. R2 2.01.298
choose out some secret place, some reverent room 5.06. 25
and now i will unclasp a secret book, | and to 1H4 1.03.188
that, in his secret doom, out of my blood 3.02. 6
the secret whispers of each other's watch. H5 4.pr. 7
/wont through a secret grate of iron bars | in 1H6 1.04. 10
search out thy wit for secret policies, | and we 3.03. 12
madam, i have a secret to reveal. 5.03.100
hast thou by secret means | us'd intercession to 5.04.147
from treason's secret knife and traitors' rage 2H6 3.01.174
god's secret judgment. 3.02. 31
will i stay | and live alone as secret as i may. 4.04. 48
i have advertis'd him by secret means | that if 3H6 4.05. 9
if secret powers | suggest but truth to my 4.06. 68
him | in secret ambush on the forest side, | and 4.06. 83
to search the secret treasons of the world. 5.02. 18
for love | as for another secret close intent R3 1.01.158
the secret mischiefs that i set abroach | i lay 1.03.324
the history of all her secret thoughts. 3.05. 28
this secret is so weighty, 'twill require | a H8 2.01.144
worth to know | the secret of your conference? 2.03. 51
made me put this main secret in the packet | i 3.02.215
and durst commend a secret to your ear | much 5.01. 17
drag hence her husband to some secret hole, TIT 2.03.129
true) | but to himself so secret and so close, ROM 1.01.149
give leave a while, | we must talk in secret. 1.03. 8
my joy | must be my convoy in the secret night. 2.04.191
is your man secret? 2.04.196
what other bond | than secret romans, that have JC 2.01.125
this were true, then should i know this secret. 2.01.291
how now, you secret, black, and midnight hags? MAC 4.01. 48
his secret murthers sticking on his hands; 5.02. 17
but you'll be secret? HAM 1.05.122
in the secret parts of fortune? 2.02.235 P
counsellor | is now most still, most secret, and 3.04.214
her brother is in secret come from france, 4.05. 88
it sin | to rush into the secret house of death ANT 4.15. 81
this secret | will force him think i have pick'd CYM 2.02. 40
i'll have this secret from thy heart, or rip 3.05. 86
some marks | of secret on her person, that he 5.05.206
if by which time our secret be undone, | this PER 1.01.117
through which secret art, | by turning o'er 3.02. 32
nev'r reveal'd secret, for i knew none — would TNK 5.01. 99
birds never lim'd no secret bushes fear: LUC 88
"but if thou yield, i rest thy secret friend: 526
"thy secret pleasure turns to open shame, | thy 890
"nor shall he smile at thee in secret thought, 1065
and therein so ensconc'd his secret evil, | that 1515
whereon the stars in secret influence comment; SON 15. 4
SECRETARY 5 FR 0.0005 REL FR 5 V 0 P
prithee call gardiner to me, my new secretary. H8 2.02.115
newly preferr'd from the king's secretary, | the 4.01.102
master | o' th' rolls, and the king's secretary; 5.01. 35
speak to the business, master secretary. 5.02. 36
good master secretary, | i cry your honor mercy; 5.02.112
SECRET-FALSE 1 FR 0.0001 REL FR 1 V 0 P
be secret–false: ERR 3.02. 15
SECRETLY 12 FR 0.0013 REL FR 8 V 4 P
what duke should that be comes so secretly? WIV 4.03. 4 P
for dead, | let her awhile be secretly kept in, ADO 4.01.203
in this | as secretly and justly as your soul 4.01.248
john is this morning secretly stol'n away. 4.02. 61 P
and thisby, | did whisper often, very secretly. MND 5.01.160
give him this letter, do it secretly, | and so MV 2.03. 7
secretly to understand that your younger brother AYL 1.01.123 P
confesses that she secretly o'erheard | your 2.02. 11
shall secretly into the bosom creep | of that 1H4 1.03.266
one) | were best to do it secretly alone. R3 1.01.100
a juggling trick — to be secretly open. TRO 5.02. 24 P

and secretly to greet the empress' friends. TIT 4.02.174
SECRETS 28 FR 0.0031 REL FR 21 V 7 P
a while, | we have some secrets to confer about. TGV 3.01. 2
slave, that will thrust himself into secrets. 3.01.384 P
— of other men's secrets, i beseech you. LLL 1.01.230 P
in faith, secrets! 4.03. 24 P
and wretched fools' secrets heedfully o'er–eye. 4.03. 78
and all the secrets of our camp i'll show, AWW 4.01. 84
discover'd the secrets of your army and made 4.03.305 P
break the holy seal | nor read the secrets in't. WT 3.02.130
to whistle /off these secrets, but you must be 4.04.245 P
oath full well, | thou to me thy secrets tell. 4.04.301
there lies such secrets in this farthel and box, 4.04.756 P
asleep, | to pry into the secrets of the state, 2H6 1.01.250
as to him | the secrets of his overcharged soul; 3.02.376
death | to gaze upon these secrets of the deep? R3 1.04. 35
the secrets of neighbor pandar | have not more TRO 4.02. 72
see thou wilt not trust the air | with secrets. TIT 4.02.170
is it excepted i should know no secrets | that JC 2.01.281
with patience, | and not my husband's secrets? 2.01.302
bosom shall partake | the secrets of my heart. 2.01.306
their deaf pillows will discharge their secrets. MAC 5.01. 73
forbid | to tell the secrets of my prison–house, HAM 1.05. 14
all blest secrets, | all you unpublish'd virtues LR 4.04. 15
a closet lock and key of villainous secrets; OTH 4.02. 22
the secrets of the grave | this viperous slander CYM 3.04. 38
king, desir'd he might know none of his secrets. PER 1.03. 6 P
hail, sovereign queen of secrets, who hast power TNK 5.01. 77
meed | a thousand honey secrets shalt thou know. VEN 16
be it said, | to hear her secrets so bewray'd. PP 18.54
SECRET'ST 1 FR 0.0001 REL FR 1 V 0 P
brought forth | the secret'st man of blood. MAC 3.04.125
SECRETY *(also secrecy)*
SECRETY 1 FR 0.0001 REL FR 0 V 1 P
sweet heart, i do implore secrety — that the LLL 5.01.110 P
SECT 4 FR 0.0004 REL FR 2 V 2 P
would she begin a sect, might quench the zeal WT 5.01.107
so is all her sect; 2H4 2.04. 37 P
not i know you for a favorer | of this new sect? H8 5.02.116
this that you call love to be a sect or scion. OTH 1.03.332 P
/SECTARY 1 FR 0.0001 REL FR 0 V 1 P
/have /you /been /a /sectary /astronomical? LR 1.02.150 P
SECTARY 1 FR 0.0001 REL FR 1 V 0 P
my lord, my lord, you are a sectary, | that's H8 5.02.105
SECTS 3 FR 0.0003 REL FR 3 V 0 P
all sects, all ages smack of this vice, and he MM 2.02. 5
world | when sects and factions were newly born. TIM 3.05. 30
a wall'd prison, packs and sects of great ones, LR 5.03. 18
SECUNDO 1 FR 0.0001 REL FR 0 V 1 P
primo, secundo, tertio, is a good play, and the TN 5.01. 36 P
SECURE 33 FR 0.0037 REL FR 28 V 5 P
though page be a secure fool, and stands so WIV 2.01.233 P
page is an ass, a secure ass; 2.02.300 P
page himself for a secure and willful actaeon; 3.02. 43 P
truth enough alive to make societies secure, but MM 3.02.227 P
whilst thou li'st warm at home, secure and safe; SHR 5.02.151
still secure | and confident from foreign JN 2.01. 27
child, sleep doubtless and secure | that hubert, 4.01.129
open the door, secure, foolhardy king! R2 5.03. 43
we may do it as secure as sleep. 1H4 1.02.131 P
proud of their numbers and secure in soul, | the H5 4.pr. 17
in iron walls they deem'd me not secure; 1H6 1.04. 49
us, | this happy night the frenchmen are secure, 2.01. 11
mine was secure. 2.01. 66
and once again we'll sleep secure in roan. 3.02. 19
enemy way, and to secure us | by what we can, 2H6 5.02. 76
shade, | all which secure and sweetly he enjoys, 3H6 2.05. 50
there shall i rest secure from force and fraud. 4.04. 33
i think there is no man /is secure | but the R3 1.01. 71
think you, but that i know our state secure, | i 3.02. 81
and i myself secure, in grace and favor. 3.04. 91
/surety secure, but modest doubt is call'd | the TRO 2.02. 15
rest, | secure from worldly chances and mishaps! TIT 1.01.152
secure of thunder's crack or lightning flash, 2.01. 3
secure thy heart; TIM 2.02.176
upon my secure hour thy uncle stole, | with HAM 1.05. 61
heavens secure him! 1.05.113
our means secure us, and our mere defects LR 4.01. 20
i do not so secure me in the error | but the OTH 1.03. 10
wear your eyes thus, not jealious nor secure. 3.03.198
arch–mock, | to lip a wanton in a secure couch, 4.01. 71
we'll higher to the mountains, there secure us. CYM 4.04. 8
he's more secure to keep it shut than shown; PER 1.01. 95
now he's secure, | not dreams we stand before TNK 1.01.154
SECURELY 7 FR 0.0008 REL FR 6 V 1 P
she dwells so securely on the excellency of her WIV 2.02.243 P
and stand securely on their battlements | as in JN 2.01.374
securely i espy | virtue with valor couched in R2 1.03. 97
and yet we strike not, but securely perish. 2.01.266
but securely done, | a little proudly, and great TRO 4.05. 73
in dangerous wars whilst you securely slept; TIT 3.01. 3
so guiltless she securely gives good cheer | and LUC 89
SECURING 1 FR 0.0001 REL FR 1 V 0 P
whiles we stood here securing your repose, TMP 2.01.310
SECURITY 16 FR 0.0018 REL FR 7 V 9 P
but security enough to make fellowships accurs'd MM 3.02.227 P
whilst bullingbrook, through our security, R2 3.02. 34
his band and yours, he lik'd not the security. 2H4 1.02. 33 P
gentleman in hand, and then stand upon security! 1.02. 37 P
taking up, then they must stand upon security. 1.02. 41 P
in my mouth as offer to stop it with security. 1.02. 43 P
i am a true knight), and he sends me security! 1.02. 45 P
well, he may sleep in security, for he hath the 1.02. 45 P
that's mercy, but too much security. H5 2.02. 44
our seat, | and made our footstool of security. 3H6 5.07. 14
fair leave and large security. TRO 1.03.223
upon bare friendship without security. TIM 3.01. 43 P
for i know your reverend ages love | security, 3.05. 80
security gives way to conspiracy. JC 2.03. 7 P
all know, security | is mortals' chiefest enemy. MAC 3.05. 32
to chance and hazard, | from firm security. ANT 3.07. 48
SEDG'D 1 FR 0.0001 REL FR 1 V 0 P
with your sedg'd crowns and ever–harmless looks, TMP 4.01.129
SEDGE 1 FR 0.0001 REL FR 1 V 0 P
giving a gentle kiss to every sedge | he TGV 2.07. 29
SEDGES 4 FR 0.0004 REL FR 3 V 1 P
now will he creep into sedges. ADO 2.01.203 P
running brook, | and cytherea all in sedges hid, SHR in.2. 51
even as the waving sedges play with wind. in.2. 53
the far shore, thick set with reeds and sedges, TNK 4.01. 54
SEDGY 1 FR 0.0001 REL FR 1 V 0 P
took, | when on the gentle severn's sedgy bank, 1H4 1.03. 98
SEDITION 3 FR 0.0003 REL FR 3 V 0 P
while the vulture of sedition | feeds in the 1H6 4.03. 47
and heap'd sedition on his crown at home. 3H6 2.02.158
the cockle of rebellion, insolence, sedition, COR 3.01. 70
SEDITIOUS 2 FR 0.0002 REL FR 2 V 0 P
jars | 'twixt thy seditious countrymen and us, ERR 1.01. 12
king, | seditious to his grace and to the state. 2H6 5.01. 37
SEDUC'D 6 FR 0.0006 REL FR 5 V 1 P
many a maid hath been seduc'd by them, and the AWW 3.05. 21 P
by long and vehement suit i was seduc'd | to JN 1.01.254
i have seduc'd a headstrong kentishman, | john 2H6 3.01.356
where slept our scouts, or how are they seduc'd, 3H6 5.01. 19
seduc'd the pitch and height of his degree | to R3 3.07.188
for who so firm that cannot be seduc'd? JC 1.02.312
SEDUCE 3 FR 0.0003 REL FR 3 V 0 P
for me, the gold of france did not seduce, H5 2.02.155
the doubt is that he will seduce the rest. 3H6 4.08. 37
and gifts that have the power | so to seduce! HAM 1.05. 45
SEDUCED 2 FR 0.0002 REL FR 1 V 1 P
so conceitless, | to be seduced by thy flattery, TGV 4.02. 97
yet was salomon so seduced, and he had a very LLL 1.02.175 P
SEDUCER 1 FR 0.0001 REL FR 0 V 1 P
otherwise a seducer flourishes, and a poor maid AWW 5.03.146 P
SEDUCING 2 FR 0.0002 REL FR 2 V 0 P
with dews of flattery, | seducing so my friends; COR 5.06. 23
appeal, | not to seducing lust, thy rash relier. LUC 639
/SEE* 16 FR 0.0018 REL FR 16 V 0 P
of gracious order, late come from the /see, | in MM 3.02.219
/eyes /are /full /of /tears, /i /cannot /see; R2 4.01.244
/but /they /can /see /a /sort /of /traitors 4.01.246
/when /i /do /see /the /very /book /indeed 4.01.274
/ha, /let's /see. 4.01.294
/early /spring | /we /see /th' /appearing /buds, 2H4 1.03. 39
/and /when /we /see /the /figure /of /the /house 1.03. 43
/we /see /which /way /the /stream /of /time 4.01. 70
/mov'd, | /doth /weep /to /see /his /grandsire's TIT 3.02. 49
/i /see /thou /art /not /for /my /company. 3.02. 58
i think it was to see my mother's wedding. HAM 1.02.178
do you /see this, o god? 4.05.202
/for /by /the /image /of /my /cause /i /see 5.02. 77
/i'll /see /their /trial /first, /bring /in LR 3.06. 35
/we /our /betters /see /bearing /our /woes, 3.06.102
/means | /will /yield /to /see /his /daughter. 4.03. 41
SEE* 1533 FR 0.1732 REL FR 1139 V 394 P
would i might | but ever see that man! TMP 1.02.169
it goes on, i see, | as my soul prompts it. 1.02.420
i have no ambition | to see a goodlier man. 1.02.484
italy removed | i ne'er again shall see her. 2.01.112
more — | and yet methinks i see it in thy face, 2.01.206
they will lay out ten to see a dead indian. 2.02. 33 P
i would i could see this taborer; 3.02.151 P
where i have hope to see the nuptial | of these 5.01.309
to see the wonders of the world abroad, | than TGV 1.01. 6
expects my coming, there to see me shipp'd. 1.01. 54
lord, lord! to see what folly reigns in us! 1.02. 15
see it be return'd, | or else return no more 1.02. 46
let's see your song. how now, minion? 1.02. 85
i see you have a month's mind to them. 1.02.134
ay, madam, you may say what sights you see; 1.02.135
i see things too, although you judge i wink. 1.02.136
lend me the letter; let me see what news. 1.03. 55
let me see; 2.01. 3
since i saw her, and still i see her beautiful. 2.01. 67 P
if you love her, you cannot see her. 2.01. 68 P
what should i see then? 2.01. 74 P
being in love, could not see to garter his hose; 2.01. 76 P
being in love, cannot see to put on your hose. 2.01. 77 P
last morning you could not see to wipe my shoes. 2.01. 80 P
but see how i lay the dust with my tears. 2.03. 31 P
how could he see his way to seek out you? 2.04. 94
to see such lovers, thurio, as yourself: 2.04. 97
then let me see thy cloak — | i'll get me one 3.01.132
here if thou stay, thou canst not see thy love; 3.01.246
fellows, stand fast; i see a passenger. 4.01. 1
shall hear music and see the gentleman that you 4.02. 31 P
when didst thou see me heave up my leg and make 4.04. 37 P
didst thou ever see me do such a trick? 4.04. 39 P
let me see; 4.04.184
see where she comes. 5.01. 7
i see, and hear — | love, lend me patience to 5.04. 26
let me see. 5.04. 92
well, let us see honest master page. WIV 1.01. 66 P
i am glad to see your worships well. 1.01. 79 P
master page, i am glad to see you. 1.01. 81 P
i am glad to see you, good master slender. 1.01. 88 P
you are afraid if you see the bear loose, are 1.01.292 P
let me see thee froth and /lime. 1.03. 14 P
the casement, and see if you can see my master, 1.04. 2 P
the casement, and see if you can see my master, 1.04. 2 P
i shall see her to–day. 1.04.155 P
let me see. 2.01. 3 P
you are come to see my daughter anne? 2.01.162 P
go in with us and see. 2.01.166 P
and then you may come and see the picture, she 2.02. 87 P
see the hell of having a false woman! 2.02.291 P
to see thee fight, to see thee foin, to see thee 2.03. 24 P
to see thee fight, to see thee foin, to see thee 2.03. 24 P
to see thee foin, to see thee traverse, to see 2.03. 24 P
to see thee traverse, to see thee here, to see 2.03. 25 P
to see thee here, to see thee there, to see thee 2.03. 25 P
to see thee there, to see thee pass thy puncto, 2.03. 26 P
be old and of the peace, if i see a sword out, 2.03. 45 P
see what humor he is in; 2.03. 77 P
flattering boy, now i see you'll be a courtier. 3.02. 8 P
truly, sir, to see your wife. is she at home? 3.02. 11 P
by your leave, sir. i am sick till i see her. 3.02. 29 P
have with you to see this monster. 3.02. 92 P
i see how thine eye would emulate the diamond. 3.03. 55 P
i see what thou wert, if fortune thy foe were 3.03. 64 P
she shall not see me, i will ensconce me behind 3.03. 89 P
up, gentlemen, you shall see sport anon. 3.03.169 P
him, gentlemen, see the issue of his search. 3.03.174 P
by gar, i see 'tis an honest woman. 3.03.222 P
i see i cannot get thy father's love, 3.04. 1
it, that it would yearn your heart to see it. 3.05. 44 P
'tis a playing–day, i see. 4.01. 10 P
i see you are obsequious in your love, and i 4.02. 2 P
now he shall see his own foolery. 4.02. 37 P
see but the issue of my jealousy. 4.02.196 P
that you cannot see a white spot about her. 4.05.113 P
at herne's oak, and you shall see wonders. 5.01. 12 P
master /brook, as you see, like a poor old man, 5.01. 15 P
i' th' castle–ditch till we see the light of our 5.02. 2 P
when you see your time, take her by the hand, 5.03. 2 P
more fertile–fresh than all the field to see; 5.05. 68
see you these, husband? 5.05.107
see now how wit may be made a jack–a–lent, when 5.05.126 P
hence shall we see, | if power change purpose, MM 1.03. 53
i'll see what i can do. 1.04. 84
find, we stoop and take't, | because we see it; 2.01. 25
but what we do not see | we tread upon, and 2.01. 25
see that claudio | be executed by nine to–morrow 2.01. 33
doth your honor see any harm in his face? 2.01.153 P
if you live to see this come to pass, say pompey 2.01.242 P
see you the fornicatress be remov'd. 2.02. 23
do me the common right | to let me see them, and 2.03. 6
and see how he goes about to abuse me! 3.02.202 P
rather rejoicing to see another merry, than 3.02.235 P
yet since i see you fearful, that neither my 4.02.189 P
see this be done, | and sent according to 4.03. 79
am pale at mine heart to see thine eyes so red; 4.03.152 P
old and faithful friend, we are glad to see you. 5.01. 2
and let the subject see, to make them know 5.01. 14
this is a strange abuse. let's see thy face. 5.01.205
to question, you shall see how i'll handle her. 5.01.271 P
methinks i see a quick'ning in his eye. 5.01.495
prison, | and see our pleasure herein executed. 5.01.521
whom whilst i labored of a love to see, | i ERR 1.01.130
time is their master, and when they see time, 2.01. 8
but, if thou live to see like right bereft, 2.01. 40
i see the jewel best enamelled | will lose his 2.01.109
see, here he comes. 2.02. 6
i did not see you since you sent me hence | home 2.02. 15
i am glad to see you in this merry vein. 2.02. 20
i know thou canst, and therefore see thou do it. 2.02.139
your shop | to see the making of her carcanet, 3.01. 4
knock elsewhere, to see if they'll disdain me. 3.01.121
for fear you ne'er see chain nor money more. 3.02.177
i see a man here needs not live by shifts, 3.02.182
that labor may you save; see where he comes. 4.01. 14
but soft, i see the goldsmith. 4.01. 19
i pray you see him presently discharg'd, | for 4.01. 32
i pray you let me see it. 4.01. 58
i see, sir, you have found the goldsmith now. 4.03. 46
hast thou delight to see a wretched man | do 4.04.115
see him safe convey'd | home to my house. 4.04.122
it may be so, but i did never see it. 4.04.141
i see these witches are afraid of swords. 4.04.147
to see a reverent syracusian merchant, | who put 5.01.124
see where they come, we will behold his death. 5.01.128
i have not breath'd almost since i did see it. 5.01.181
me dote, | i see my son antipholus and dromio. 5.01.196
as sure, my liege, as i do see your grace. 5.01.280
haply i see a friend will save my life, | and 5.01.284
i see thy age and dangers make thee dote. 5.01.330
i see two husbands, or mine eyes deceive me. 5.01.332
i to this fortune that you see me in. 5.01.356
good, | if this be not a dream i see and hear. 5.01.377
i see we still did meet each other's man, | and 5.01.387
i see by you i am a sweet–fac'd youth. 5.01.419
will you walk in to see their gossiping? 5.01.420
i see, lady, the gentleman is not in your books. ADO 1.01. 78 P
i can see yet without spectacles, and i see no 1.01.189 P
without spectacles, and i see no such matter. 1.01.189 P
shall i never see a bachelor of threescore again 1.01.199 P
i shall see thee, ere i die, look pale with love 1.01.247 P
"here you may see benedick the married man." 1.01.267 P
and thou shalt see how apt it is to learn | any 1.01.292
i never can see him but i am heart–burn'd an 2.01. 4 P
i hope to see you one day fitted with a husband. 2.01. 57 P
good eye, uncle, i can see a church by daylight. 2.01. 82 P
did you see him? 2.01.212 P
likelihood than to see me at her chamber–window, 2.02. 42 P
and bring them to see this the very night before 2.02. 45 P
have walk'd ten mile afoot to see a good armor, 2.03. 16 P
may i be so converted and see with these eyes? 2.03. 22 P
see you where benedick hath hid himself? 2.03. 40
to see how much he is unworthy so good a lady. 2.03.208 P
that's the scene that i would see, which will be 2.03.217 P
the pleasant'st angling is to see the fish | cut 3.01. 26
you shall see her chamber–window ent'red, even 3.02.113 P
if you dare not trust that you see, confess not 3.02.119 P
if i see any thing to–night why i should not 3.02.123 P
for i cannot see how sleeping should offend; 3.03. 40 P
all this i see, and i see that the fashion wears 3.03.139 P
i see, and i see that the fashion wears out more 3.03.139 P
enough, you'll see he shall lack no barns. 3.04. 48 P
pray you, for you see it is a busy time with me. 3.05. 4 P
god help us, it is a world to see! 3.05. 35 P
all you that see her, that she were a maid, | by 4.01. 39
and this grieved count | did see her, hear her, 4.01. 90
see, see, here comes the man we went to seek. 5.01.110
see, see, here comes the man we went to seek. 5.01.110
let me see his eyes, | that when i note another 5.01.259
sweet, let me see your face. 5.04. 55
as, not to see a woman in that term, | which i LLL 1.01. 37
not to see ladies, study, fast, not sleep. 1.01. 48
let's see the penalty. 1.01.123 P
but i would see his own person in flesh and 1.01.184 P
there did i see that low–spirited swain, that 1.01.247 P
my lord berowne, see him delivered o'er, | and 1.01.305
if ever i do see the merry days of desolation 1.02.159 P
of desolation that i have seen, some shall see. 1.02.160 P
what shall some see? 1.02.161 P
my commendations — i would be glad to see it. 2.01.182 P
his tongue, all impatient to speak and not see. 2.01.238
what then, do you see? 2.01.257
let me see: 3.01.104
and to her white hand see thou do commend | this 3.01.168
see, see, my beauty will be sav'd by merit. 4.01. 21
see, see, my beauty will be sav'd by merit. 4.01. 21

to see. 4.01. 72 P
why did he see? 4.01. 72 P
to see him walk before a lady and to bear her 4.01.145
to see him kiss his hand! 4.01.146
a patch set on learning, to see him in a school: 4.02. 31
for all the wealth that ever i did see, | i 4.03.147
you found his mote, the king your mote did see; 4.03.159
i sat, | to see a king transformed to a gnat! 4.03.164
to see great hercules whipping a gig, | and 4.03.165
when shall you see me write a thing in rhyme, 4.03.179
look, here's thy love; my foot and her face see. 4.03.273
the street should see as she walk'd overhead. 4.03.277
to fast, to study, and to see no woman — | flat 4.03.288
then when ourselves we see in ladies' eyes, 4.03.312
do we not likewise see our learning there? 4.03.314
"for," quoth the king, "an angel shalt thou see; 5.02.103
grace, | despite of suit, to see a lady's face. 5.02.129
see where it comes! 5.02.337
soft, let us see — | write "lord have mercy on 5.02.418
free, | for the lord's tokens on you do i see. 5.02.423
i see the trick an't; 5.02.460
alas, you see how 'tis — a little o'erparted. 5.02.584 P
do you not see pompey is uncasing for the combat 5.02.701 P
he no more shall see my face; MND 1.01.202
before the time i did lysander see, | seem'd 1.01.204
a proper man as one shall see in a summer's day; 1.02. 87 P
be, | in their gold coats spots you see: 2.01. 11
and thorough this distemperature we see | the 2.01.106
when we have laugh'd to see the sails conceive 2.01.128
in our round | and see our moonlight revels, go 2.01.141
but i might see young cupid's fiery shaft 2.01.161
that | it is not night when i do see your face, 2.01.221
i see no blood, no wound. 2.02.101
that through thy bosom makes me see thy heart. 2.02.105
auditor, | an actor too perhaps, if i see cause. 3.01. 80
he goes but to see a noise that he heard, and is 3.01. 91 P
what do i see on thee? 3.01.115 P
what do you see? 3.01.116 P
you see an ass–head of your own, do you? 3.01.116 P
i see their knavery. 3.01.120 P
a privilege never to see me more. 3.02. 79
see me no more, whether he be dead or no. 3.02. 81
by some illusion see thou bring her here. 3.02. 98
shall we their fond pageant see? 3.02.114
i see you all are bent | to set against me for 3.02.145
and never did desire to see thee more. 3.02.278
you see how simple and how fond i am. 3.02.317
this dear, | if ever i thy face by daylight see. 3.02.427
see as thou wast wont to see. 4.01. 72
see as thou wast wont to see. 4.01. 72
methinks i see these things with parted eye, 4.01.189
choice of which your highness will see first. 5.01. 43
i love not to see wretchedness o'ercharg'd, 5.01. 85
why, gentle sweet, you shall see no such thing. 5.01. 87
but what see i? 5.01.179
no thisby do i see. 5.01.179
o wicked wall, through whom i see no bliss! 5.01.180
you shall see it will fall pat as i told you. 5.01.186 P
i see a voice! 5.01.192
for, you see, it is already in snuff. 5.01.250 P
eyes, do you see? 5.01.279
will it please you to see the epilogue, or to 5.01.353 P
i should not see the sandy hour–glass run | but MV 1.01. 25
and see my wealthy andrew /dock'd in sand, 1.01. 27
to church | and see the holy edifice of stone, 1.01. 30
and yet, for aught i see, they are as sick that 1.02. 5 P
and let me see — but hear you, | methoughts you 1.03. 68
then, let me see, the rate — 1.03.104
see to my house, left in the fearful guard | of 1.03.175
see these letters deliver'd, put the liveries to 2.02.116 P
see it done. 2.02.155
well, we shall see your bearing. 2.02.198
soon at supper shalt thou see | lorenzo, who is 2.03. 5
not have my father | see me in talk with thee. 2.03. 9
well, thou shalt see, thy eyes shall be thy 2.05. 1
i will not say you shall see a masque, but if 2.05. 23 P
and lovers cannot see | the pretty follies that 2.06. 36
blush | to see me thus transformed to a boy. 2.06. 39
let me see, | i will survey th' inscriptions 2.07. 13
let's see once more this saying grav'd in gold: 2.07. 36
they come | as o'er a brook to see fair portia. 2.07. 47
let me see: 2.09. 23
for i long to see | quick cupid's post that 2.09. 99
i shall never see my gold again. 3.01.111 P
and you shall see 'tis purchas'd by the weight, 3.02. 89
but her eyes — | how could he see to do them? 3.02.124
so, | as doubtful whether what i see be true, 3.02.147
you see me, lord bassanio, where i stand, | such 3.02.149
you shall see | how much i was a braggart: 3.02.257
you and i, if i might but see you at my death. 3.02.320 P
pray god bassanio come | to see me pay his debt, 3.03. 36
see thou render this | into my /cousin's hands, 3.04. 49
we'll see our husbands | before they think of us 3.04. 58
shall they see us? 3.04. 59
of justice, none of us | should see salvation. 4.01.200
thyself shalt see the act; 4.01.314
that thou shalt see the difference of our spirit 4.01.368
i see, sir, you are liberal in offers. 4.01.438
i'll see if i can get my husband's ring, | which 4.02. 13
did you see master lorenzo? 5.01. 41 P
that light we see is burning in my hall. 5.01. 89
when the moon shone, we did not see the candle. 5.01. 92
nothing is good, i see, without respect; 5.01. 99
but you see my finger | hath not the ring upon 5.01.187
ne'er come in your bed | until i see the ring! 5.01.191
nor i in yours | till i again see mine! 5.01.192
thine own fair eyes, | wherein i see myself — 5.01.243
i hope i shall see an end of him; AYL 1.01.164 P
herein i see thou lov'st me not with the full 1.02. 8 P
let me see — what think you of falling in love? 1.02. 25 P
it please your ladyships, you may see the end, 1.02.114 P
any else longs to see this broken music in his 1.02.141 P
shall we see this wrastling, cousin? 1.02.143 P
let us now stay and see it. 1.02.148 P
are you crept hither to see the wrastling? 1.02.156 P
speak to him, ladies, see if you can move him. 1.02.162 P
i cannot hear of any that did see her. 2.02. 4
but what is, come see, | and in my voice most 2.04. 86
here shall he see | no enemy | but winter and 2.05. 6
here shall he see | /no /enemy | /but /winter 2.05. 43
here shall he see | gross fools as he, | and if 2.05. 55
thus we may see," quoth he, "how the world wags. 2.07. 23
let me see wherein | my tongue hath wrong'd him; 2.07. 83
not see him since? 3.01. 1
shall see thy virtue witness'd every where. 3.02. 8
of my pride is to see my ewes graze and my lambs 3.02. 76 P
i cannot see else how thou shouldst scape. 3.02. 85 P
and when shalt thou see him again? 3.02.224 P
though it be pity to see such a sight, it well 3.02.242 P
look but in, and you shall see him. 3.02.288 P
there i shall see mine own figure. 3.02.289 P
as the cony that you see dwell where she is 3.02.339 P
i would fain see this meeting. 3.03. 46 P
i am very glad to see you. 3.03. 76 P
if you will see a pageant truly play'd | between 3.04. 52
i see no more in you | than without candle may 3.05. 38
i see no more in you than in the ordinary | of 3.05. 42
though all the world could see, | none could be 3.05. 78
you have sold your own lands to see other men's; 4.01. 23 P
her (for i see love hath made thee a tame snake) 4.03. 69 P
it is meat and drink to me to see a clown. 5.01. 10 P
how it grieves me to see thee wear thy heart in 5.02. 20 P
to see no pastime i. 5.04.195
is not the fashion to see the lady the epilogue; ep 1 P
unhandsome than to see the lord the prologue. ep 3 P
see, doth he breathe? SHR in.1. 31
sirrah, go see what trumpet 'tis that sounds. in.1. 74
and see him dress'd in all suits like a lady; in.1. 106
to see her noble lord restor'd to health, | who in.1. 121
see this dispatch'd with all the haste thou in.1. 129
i see, i hear, i speak; in.2. 70
o how we joy to see your wit restor'd! in.2. 77
for the great desire i had | to see fair padua, 1.01. 2
but in the other's silence do i see | maid's 1.01. 70
but see, while idly i stood looking on, | i 1.01.150
i take my leave | to see my friends in padua, 1.02. 2
being perhaps (for aught i see) two and thirty, 1.02. 33 P
home, | and so am come abroad to see the world. 1.02. 58
i will not sleep, hortensio, till i see her, 1.02.103
have no more eyes to see withal than a cat. 1.02.115 P
see, to beguile the old folks, how the young 1.02.138 P
all books of love, see that at any hand — | and 1.02.146
and see you read no other lectures to her. 1.02.147
me, | and i do hope good days and long to see. 1.02.192
you, | did you yet ever see baptista's daughter? 1.02.250
see thou dissemble not. 2.01. 9
nay, now i see | she is your treasure, she must 2.01. 31
i see you do not mean to part with her, | or 2.01. 64
you shall go see your pupils presently. 2.01.107
it is my fashion when i see a crab. 2.01.229
o, let me see thee walk. 2.01.256
for by this light whereby i see thy beauty, 2.01.273
i'll see thee hang'd on sunday first. 2.01.299
she says she'll see thee hang'd first. 2.01.300
'tis a world to see | how tame, when men and 2.01.311
i see no reason but suppos'd lucentio | must get 2.01.407
now let me see if i can conster it: 3.01. 41
see not your bride in these unreverent robes, 3.02.112
i'll after him, and see the event of this. 3.02.127
i see a woman may be made a fool, | if she had 3.02.220
peter, didst ever see the like? 4.01.179 P
see how they kiss and court! 4.02. 27
see how beastly she doth court him! 4.02. 34
come, tailor, let us see these ornaments; 4.03. 61
i see she's like to have neither cap nor gown. 4.03. 93
hortensio, say thou wilt see the tailor paid. 4.03.164
let's see, i think 'tis now some seven a' clock, 4.03.187
and wander we to see thy honest son, | who will 4.05. 69
come go along and see the truth hereof, | for 4.05. 75
faith, i'll see the church a' your back, and 5.01. 4 P
didst thou never see thy /master's father, 5.01. 53 P
sir — see where he looks out of the window. 5.01. 55 P
kate, let's stand aside and see the end of this 5.01. 61 P
i charge you see that he be forthcoming. 5.01. 93 P
let's follow, to see the end of this ado. 5.01.142
see where she comes, and brings your froward 5.02.119
but now i see our lances are but straws, | our 5.02.173
to see him every hour, to sit and draw | his AWW 1.01. 93
withal, full oft we see | cold wisdom waiting on 1.01.104
let me see. 1.01.152 P
that makes me see, and cannot feed mine eye? 1.01.221
for our gentlemen that mean to see | the tuscan 1.02. 13
now i see | the myst'ry of your /loneliness, and 1.03.170
eyes | see it so grossly shown in thy behaviors 1.03.178
monarchy) see that you come | not to woo honor, 2.01. 14
i'll see thee to stand up. 2.01. 62
there's one arriv'd, | if you will see her. 2.01. 80
will you see her — | for that is her demand — 2.01. 85
i see things may serve long, but not serve ever. 2.02. 58 P
make choice and see, | who shuns thy love shuns 2.03. 72
'twill be two days ere i shall see you, so | i 2.05. 70
let me see what he writes, and when he means to 3.02. 10 P
i will entreat you, when you see my son, | to 3.02. 92
here you shall see a countryman of yours | that 3.05. 47
emboss'd him, you shall see his fall to–night; 3.06. 99 P
find him, which you shall see this very night. 3.06.105 P
will you go see her? 3.06.117
now i see | the bottom of your purpose. 3.07. 28
you see it lawful then. 3.07. 30
i see that men make rope's in such a scarre 4.02. 38
treasons, we still see them reveal themselves, 4.03. 22 P
would gladly have him see his company anatomiz'd 4.03. 32 P
let me see: 4.03.161 P
we'll see what may be done, so you confess 4.03.246 P
lord, sir, let me live, or let me see my death! 4.03.309 P
me, that i hope i shall see him ere i die. 4.05. 84 P
let us go see your son, i pray you. 4.05.102 P
since you are like to see the king before me, 5.01. 30
for thou mayst see a sunshine and a hail | in me 5.03. 33
our own love waking cries to see what's done, 5.03. 65
stay | to see our widower's second marriage–day. 5.03. 70
now pray you let me see it; 5.03. 81
win me to believe, | more than to see this ring. 5.03.120
is't real that i see? 5.03.306
lord, | 'tis but the shadow of a wife you see, 5.03.307
o my dear mother, do i see you living? 5.03.319
o, when mine eyes did see olivia first, TN 1.01. 18
with the waves | so long as i could see. 1.02. 17
my tongue blabs, then let mine eyes not see. 1.02. 63
when did i see thee so put down? 1.03. 81 P
i think, unless you see canary put me down. 1.03. 82 P
and i hope to see a huswife take thee between 1.03.103 P
let me see thee caper. 1.03.140 P
he shall see none to fear. 1.05. 8 P
now you see, sir, how your fooling grows old, 1.05.110 P
good madam, let me see your face. 1.05.230 P
i see you what you are, you are too proud; 1.05.250
else would i very shortly see thee there. 2.01. 46
i see thou art a wickedness | wherein the 2.02. 27
did you never see the picture of "we three"? 2.03. 16 P
nay, but first, let me see, let me see, let me 2.05.111 P
but first, let me see, let me see, let me see. 2.05.111 P
but first, let me see, let me see, let me see. 2.05.111 P
you might see more detraction at your heels than 2.05.137 P
and wish'd to see thee ever cross–garter'd: 2.05.154 P
if not, let me see thee a steward still, the 2.05.156 P
if you will then see the fruits of the sport, 2.05.197 P
if you will see it, follow me. 2.05.204 P
to see this age! 3.01. 11 P
did she see /thee the while, old boy? 3.02. 8 P
as plain as i see you now. 3.02. 10 P
and not all love to see you (though so much | as 3.03. 6
shall we go see the reliques of this town? 3.03. 19
to–morrow, sir. best first go see your lodging. 3.03. 20
"and wish'd to see thee cross–garter'd." 3.04. 50 P
"if not, let me see thee a servant still." 3.04. 55 P
do you not see you move him? 3.04.109 P
but see, but see. 3.04.141 P
but see, but see. 3.04.141 P
give ground if you see him furious. 3.04.304 P
this youth that you see here | i snatch'd one 3.04.359
come, let's see the event. 3.04.395 P
ne'er believe a madman till i see his brains. 4.02.116 P
now, as thou lov'st me, let me see his letter. 5.01. 1 P
do not desire to see this letter. 5.01. 5 P
sot, didst see dick surgeon, sot? 5.01.197 P
and let me see thee in thy woman's weeds. 5.01.273
see him deliver'd, fabian, bring him hither. 5.01.315
my services are now on foot, you shall see, as i WT 1.01. 3 P
was born desire yet their life to see him a man. 1.01. 40 P
to tell he longs to see his son were strong; 1.02. 34
canst with thine eyes at once see good and evil, 1.02.303
eyes | to see alike mine honor as their profits 1.02.310
who mayst see | plainly as heaven sees earth and 1.02.314
be with me, for you see | my plight requires it. 2.01.117
i never wish'd to see you sorry, now | i trust i 2.01.123
than when i feel and see her no farther trust 2.01.136
fourteen they shall not see | to bring false 2.01.147
and see withal | the instruments that feel. 2.01.153
is't lawful, pray you, to see her women? 2.02. 11
to see his nobleness, | conceiving the dishonor 2.03. 12
go, | see how he fares. 2.03. 18
and see it instantly consum'd with fire. 2.03.134
shall i live on to see this bastard kneel | and 2.03.155
that he did but see | the flatness of my misery, 3.02.121
look down | and see what death is doing. 3.02.149
if word nor oath | prevail not, go and see. 3.02.204
thou ne'er shalt see | thy wife paulina more." 3.03. 35
if thou'lt see a thing to talk on when thou art 3.03. 80 P
i would you did but see how it chafes, how it 3.03. 88 P
sometimes to see 'em, and not to see 'em; 3.03. 91 P
sometimes to see 'em, and not to see 'em; 3.03. 91 P
to see how the bear tore out his shoulder–bone, 3.03. 95 P
the ship, to see how the sea flap–dragon'd it; 3.03. 98 P
so, let's see — it was told me i should be rich 3.03.117 P
i'll go see if the bear be gone from the 3.03.129 P
let me see: 4.03. 32 P
let me see: 4.03. 36 P
i should blush | to see you so attir'd — sworn, 4.04. 13
how would he look to see his work, so noble, 4.04. 21
see, your guests approach, | address yourself to 4.04. 52
you see, sweet maid, we marry | a gentler scion 4.04. 92
and let's first see moe ballads. 4.04.273 P
pray let's see these four threes of herdsmen. 4.04.336 P
sigh | that thou no more shalt see this knack 4.04.428
i mean not | to see him any more) cast your good 4.04.495
king, my master, whom | i so much thirst to see. 4.04.513
enjoy your mistress — from the whom, i see, 4.04.528
your fair princess | (for so i see she must be) 4.04.545
methinks i see | leontes opening his free arms 4.04.547
i see the play so lies | that i must bear a part 4.04.655
i see this is the time that the unjust man doth 4.04.673 P
see, see; 4.04.687 P
see, see; 4.04.687 P
to be honest, i see fortune would not suffer me: 4.04.831 P
it should take joy | to see her in your arms. 5.01. 81
sure | when i shall see this gentleman, thy 5.01.121
the stars, i see, will kiss the valleys first; 5.01.206
that "once," i see, by your good father's speed, 5.01.210
that which you hear you'll swear you see, there 5.02. 32 P
did you see the meeting of the two kings? 5.02. 39 P
see you these clothes? 5.02.130 P
say you see them not and think me still no 5.02.130 P
kindred, are going to see the queen's picture. 5.02.173 P
but we came | to see the statue of our queen. 5.03. 10
to see the life as lively mock'd as ever | still 5.03. 19
see, my lord, | would you not deem it breath'd? 5.03. 63
do not shun her | until you see her die again, 5.03.106
being, have preserv'd | myself to see the issue. 5.03.128
i see a yielding in the looks of france; JN 2.01.474
if he see aught in you that makes him like, 2.01.511
my lord, | that all i see in you is worthy love, 2.01.517
that nothing do i see in you, | though churlish 2.01.518
day about | shall never see it but a holy day. 3.01. 82
archbishop | of canterbury, from that holy see? 3.01.144
now shall i see thy love. 3.01.313
and ere our coming see thou shake the bags | of 3.03. 7
or if that thou couldst see me without eyes, 3.03. 48
lo! now! now see the issue of your peace. 3.04. 21
that we shall see and know our friends in heaven 3.04. 77
if that be true, i shall see my boy again; 3.04. 78
methinks i see this hurly all on foot; 3.04.169
see else yourself, | there is no malice in this 4.01.107
well, see to live; 4.01.121

out of my sight, and never see me more! 4.02.242
or do you almost think, although you see, | that 4.03. 43
think, although you see, | that you do see? 4.03. 44
let not the world see fear and sad distrust 5.01. 46
/were born to see so sad an hour as this, 5.02. 26
church, | the great metropolis and see of rome; 5.02. 72
for i do see the cruel pangs of death | right in 5.04. 59
and spleen of speed to see your majesty! 5.07. 50
you, we shall see | justice design the victor's R2 1.01.202
who, when they see the hour's ripe on earth, 1.02. 7
and what shall good old york there see | but 1.02. 67
glasses of thine eyes | i see thy grieved heart. 1.03.209
and blindfold death not let me see my son. 1.03.224
whether our kinsman come to see his friends. 1.04. 22
i am in health, i breathe, and see thee ill. 2.01. 92
now he that made me knows i see thee ill, | ill 2.01. 93
ill in myself to see, and in thee, seeing ill. 2.01. 94
to us to ely house | to see this business. 2.01.217
we see the wind sit sore upon our sails, | and 2.01.265
we see the very wrack that we must suffer, | and 2.01.267
for methinks in you | i see old gaunt alive. 2.03.118
and let him never see joy that breaks that oath! 2.03.151
well, well, i see the issue of these arms. 2.03.152
mind | i see thy glory like a shooting star 2.04. 19
see them delivered over | to execution and the 3.01. 29
my lord northumberland, see them dispatch'd. 3.01. 35
shall see us rising in our throne, the east, 3.02. 50
sweet love, i see, changing his property, 3.02.135
see, see, king richard doth himself appear, | as 3.03. 62
see, see, king richard doth himself appear, | as 3.03. 62
well, i see | i talk but idlely, and you laugh 3.03.170
love | than my unpleased eye see your courtesy. 3.03.193
thou dar'st not, coward, live to see that day. 4.01. 41
i see your brows are full of discontent, | your 4.01.331
but soft, but see, or rather do not see, | my 5.01. 7
but soft, but see, or rather do not see, | my 5.01. 7
let me see the writing. 5.02. 57
no matter then who see it. 5.02. 58
i will be satisfied, let me see the writing. 5.02. 59
which for some reasons, sir, i mean to see. 5.02. 63
boy, let me see the writing. 5.02. 69
i will be satisfied, let me see it, i say. 5.02. 71
'tis full three months since i did see him last. 5.03. 2
through both | i see some sparks of better hope, 5.03. 21
knees, | and never see day that the happy sees, 5.03. 94
did sir walter see | on holmedon's plains. 1H4 1.01. 69
see riot and dishonor stain the brow | of my 1.01. 85
i see no reason why thou shouldst be so 1.02. 10 P
i see a good amendment of life in thee, from 1.02.102 P
our horses they shall not see — i'll tie them 1.02.177 P
for i do see | danger and disobedience in thine 1.03. 15
to see him shine so brisk and smell so sweet, 1.03. 54
and see already how he doth begin | to make us 1.03.289
me thy lantern, to see my gelding in the stable. 2.01. 34 P
marry, i'll see thee hang'd first. 2.01. 40 P
let me see some more. 2.03. 6 P
you shall see now in very sincerity of fear and 2.03. 30 P
such as we see when men restrain their breath 2.03. 61
come, wilt thou see me ride? 2.03.100
let me see — about michaelmas next i shall be 2.04. 54 P
didst thou never see titan kiss a dish of butter 2.04.120 P
i'll see thee damn'd ere i call thee coward, but 2.04.146 P
dark, hal, that thou couldest not see thy hand. 2.04.224 P
it was so dark thou couldst not see thy hand? 2.04.232 P
my lord, do you see these meteors? 2.04.319 P
one of these harlotry players as ever i see! 2.04.396 P
for, harry, i see virtue in his looks. 2.04.427 P
let's see what they be. read them. 2.04.534 P
then the earth shook to see the heavens on fire, 3.01. 24
see how this river comes me cranking in, | and 3.01. 97
not wind? it shall, it must, you see it doth. 3.01.105
save mine, which hath desir'd to see thee more, 3.02. 89
i never see thy face but i think upon hell–fire 3.03. 31 P
on, | to see how fortune is dispos'd to us, 4.01. 38
i did never see such pitiful rascals. 4.02. 64 P
if thou see me down in the battle and bestride 5.01.121 P
why then i see | a very valiant rebel of the 5.04. 61
embowell'd will i see thee by and by, | till 5.04.109
to see what friends are living, who are dead. 5.04.161
see what a ready tongue suspicion hath! 2H4 1.01. 84
i see a strange confession in thine eye. 1.01. 94
and yet cannot he see, though he have his own 1.02. 47 P
wait close, i will not see him. 1.02. 57 P
i am glad to see your lordship abroad. 1.02. 94 P
how might we see falstaff bestow himself 2.02.169 P
threw many a northward look to see his father 2.03. 13
and see if thou canst find out sneak's noise. 2.04. 10 P
i'll see if i can find out sneak. 2.04. 21 P
and whether i shall ever see thee again or no, 2.04. 67 P
i'll see her damn'd first, to pluto's damned 2.04.156 P
see now whether pure fear and entire cowardice 2.04.325 P
you see, my good wenches, how men of merit are 2.04.374 P
sent away post, i will see you again ere i go. 2.04.378 P
and see the revolution of the times | make 3.01. 46
and other times to see | the beachy girdle of 3.01. 49
i see him break scoggin's head at the court–gate 3.02. 29 P
and to see how many of my old acquaintance are 3.02. 34 P
it would have done a man's heart good to see. 3.02. 49 P
i am glad to see you well, good master robert 3.02. 85 P
let me see them, i beseech you. 3.02. 95 P
let me see, let me see, let me see. 3.02. 97 P
let me see, let me see, let me see. 3.02. 97 P
let me see, let me see, let me see. 3.02. 97 P
let me see, where is mouldy? 3.02.100 P
for th' other, sir john, let me see: 3.02.120 P
yea, marry, let's see bullcalf. 3.02.173 P
i am glad to see you, by my troth, master 3.02.192 P
wart, you see what a ragged appearance it is. 3.02.260 P
i shall ne'er see such a fellow. 3.02.286 P
i do see the bottom of justice shallow. 3.02.302 P
i see no reason in the law of nature but i may 3.02.331 P
whose see is by a civil peace maintain'd, 4.01. 42
text | /than now to see you here an iron man, 4.02. 8
lead him hence, and see you guard him sure. 4.03. 75
let me see him. 4.05. 53
see, sons, what things you are! 4.05. 64
davy, davy, davy, let me see, davy, let me see, 5.01. 9 P
let me see, davy, let me see, davy, let me see. 5.01. 10 P
let me see, davy, let me see, davy, let me see. 5.01. 10 P
i am glad to see your worship. 5.01. 56 P
a wonderful thing to see the semblable coherence 5.01. 65 P
you shall see him laugh till his face be like a 5.01. 84 P
and never shall you see that i will beg | a 5.02. 37
see your most dreadful laws so loosely slighted, 5.02. 94
till you do live to see a son of mine | offend 5.02.105
nay, you shall see my orchard, where, in an 5.03. 1 P
i hope to see london once ere i die. 5.03. 60 P
and i might see you there, davy! 5.03. 61 P
this doth infer the zeal i had to see him. 5.05. 14 P
and sweating with desire to see him, thinking of 5.05. 25 P
were nothing else to be done but to see him. 5.05. 27 P
lord, | to see perform'd the tenure of my word. 5.05. 71
that you see them | printing their proud hoofs H5 pr 26
but see, thy fault france hath in thee found out 2.pr. 20
now, we shall see willful adultery and murther 2.01. 37 P
what see you in those papers that you lose | so 2.02. 72
see you, my princes and my noble peers, | these 2.02. 84
as black and white, my eye will scarcely see it. 2.02.104
saw his heroical seed, and smil'd to see him, 2.04. 59
you see this chase is hotly followed, friends. 2.04. 68
work your thoughts, and therein see a siege; 3.pr. 25
i see you stand like greyhounds in the slips, 3.01. 31
in a moment look to see | the blind and bloody 3.03. 33
for i am sure, when he shall see our army, 3.05. 58
world, but i did see him do as gallant service. 3.06. 15 P
the pridge as you shall see in a summer's day. 3.06. 64 P
shall repent his folly, see his weakness, and 3.06.124 P
but, let me see, by ten | we shall have each a 3.07.156
yet sit and see, | minding true things by what 4.pr. 52
we see yonder the beginning of the day, but i 4.01. 89 P
but i think we shall never see the end of it. 4.01. 90 P
him outlive that day to see his greatness and to 4.01.184 P
if i live to see it, i will never trust his word 4.01.195 P
if ever i live to see it, i will challenge it. 4.01.217 P
he that shall see this day, and live old age, 4.03. 44
or if i can see my glove in his cap, which he 4.07.128 P
if he be perjur'd, see you now, his reputation 4.07.140 P
i would fain see the man, that hath but two legs 4.07.161 P
but i would fain see it once, and please god of 4.07.163 P
and please god of his grace that i might see. 4.07.164 P
follow, and see there be no harm between them. 4.07.182
land, | and solemnly see him set on to london. 5.pr. 14
to wear it in my cap till i see him once again, 5.01. 12 P
quiet thy cudgel, thou dost see i eat. 5.01. 52 P
when you take occasions to see leeks hereafter, 5.01. 56 P
best | shall see advantageable for our dignity, 5.02. 88
vous avez le possession de moi — let me see, 5.02.182 P
my lord, when they see not what they do. 5.02.303 P
who cannot see many a fair french city for one 5.02.317 P
yes, my lord, you see them perspectively: 5.02.320 P
that beauty am i blest with which you may see. 1H6 1.02. 86
see the coast clear'd, and then we will depart. 1.03. 89
three days have i watch'd | if i could see them. 1.04. 17
for aught i see, this city must be famish'd, 1.04. 68
then i see our wars | will turn unto a peaceful 2.02. 44
i see report is fabulous and false. 2.03. 18
i laugh to see your ladyship so fond | to think 2.03. 45
for what you see is but the smallest part | and 2.03. 52
taste of your wine and see what cates you have, 2.03. 79
will see his burial better than his life. 2.05.121
plantagenet, i see, must hold his tongue, | lest 3.01. 61
you see what mischief, and what murther too, 3.01.115
or i would see his heart out ere the priest 3.01.120
see here, my friends and loving countrymen, 3.01.137
and i will see what physic the tavern affords. 3.01.147
see, noble charles, the beacon of our friend, 3.02. 29
but see his exequies fulfill'd in roan. 3.02.133
and see the cities and the towns defac'd | by 3.03. 45
eyes, | see, see the pining malady of france! 3.03. 49
eyes, | see, see the pining malady of france! 3.03. 49
see then, thou fight'st against thy countrymen 3.03. 74
when thou shalt see | i'll meet thee to thy cost. 3.04. 43
i see no reason, if i wear this rose, | that any 4.01.152
these eyes, that see thee now well colored, 4.02. 37
shall see thee withered, bloody, pale, and dead. 4.02. 38
this seven years did not talbot see his son, 4.03. 37
see where he lies inhearsed in the arms | of the 4.07. 45
see them guarded | and safely brought to dover, 5.01. 48
see, they forsake me! 5.03. 24
see how the ugly witch doth bend her brows, | as 5.03. 34
see, reignier, see, thy daughter prisoner! 5.03.131
see, reignier, see, thy daughter prisoner! 5.03.131
provide | to see her coronation be perform'd. 2H6 1.01. 74
proud prelate, in thy face | i see thy fury. 1.01.143
we'll see these things effected to the full. 1.02. 84
let me see them. 1.03. 14 P
come, somerset, we'll see thee sent away. 1.03.220 P
see you well guerdon'd for these good deserts. 1.04. 46
we'll see your trinkets here all forthcoming. 1.04. 53
now pray, my lord, let's see the devil's writ. 1.04. 57
to see how god in all his creatures works! 2.01. 7
protector, see to't well, protect yourself. 2.01. 52
let me see thine eyes. 2.01.103
and yet, i think, jet did he never see. 2.01.112
it made me laugh to see the villain run. 2.01.152
gloucester, see here the tainture of thy nest, 2.01.184
i see no reason why a king of years | should be 2.03. 28
left i the court, to see this quarrel tried. 2.03. 53
a' god's name see the lists and all things fit; 2.03. 54
thump? then see thou thump thy master well. 2.03. 84 P
my tear–stain'd eyes to see her miseries. 2.04. 16
come you, my lord, to see my open shame? 2.04. 19
see how the giddy multitude do point | and nod 2.04. 21
to see my tears and hear my deep–fet groans. 2.04. 33
go, lead the way, i long to see my prison. 2.04.110
can you not see? 3.01. 4
thou shalt not see me blush | nor change my 3.01. 98
humphrey, in thy face i see | the map of honor, 3.01.202
a charge, lord york, that i will see perform'd. 3.01.321
i'll see it truly done, my lord of york. 3.01.330
that is to see how deep my grave is made, | for 3.02.150
for, seeing him, i see my life in death. 3.02.152
see how the blood is settled in his face. 3.02.160
but see, his face is black and full of blood, 3.02.168
on the sheets his hair, you see, is sticking, 3.02.174
see how the pangs of death do make him grin! 3.03. 24
i see them, i see them! 4.02. 21 P
i see them, i see them! 4.02. 21 P
i'll see if his head will stand steadier on a 4.07. 95 P
broil | i see them lording it in london streets, 4.08. 45
i see them lay their heads together to surprise 4.08. 58 P
into this garden, to see if i can eat grass, or 4.10. 7 P
see if thou canst outface me with thy looks. 4.10. 46
see, buckingham, somerset comes with th' queen. 5.01. 83
see where they come, i'll warrant they'll make 5.01.122
we then should see the bottom | of all our 5.02. 78
and we will live | to see their day, and them 5.02. 89
before i see thee seated in that throne | which 3H6 1.01. 22
will follow mine, if once they see them spread; 1.01.252
victory /from the field | i'll see your grace; 1.01.262
thou wouldst be fee'd, i see, to make me sport: 1.04. 92
see, ruthless queen, a hapless father's tears! 1.04.156
him, | to see how inly sorrow gripes his soul. 1.04.171
see how the morning opes her golden gates, | and 2.01. 21
dazzle mine eyes, or do i see three suns? 2.01. 25
see, see, they join, embrace, and seem to kiss, 2.01. 29
see, see, they join, embrace, and seem to kiss, 2.01. 29
again, | never, o never, shall i see more joy! 2.01. 78
ne'er may he live to see a sunshine day | that 2.01.187
to see this sight, it irks my very soul. 2.02. 6
thereby to see the minutes how they run: 2.05. 25
but let me see: 2.05. 82
see, see what show'rs arise, | blown with the 2.05. 85
see, see what show'rs arise, | blown with the 2.05. 85
see who it is. 2.06. 44
first will i see the coronation, | and then to 2.06. 96
to london | to see these honors in possession. 2.06.110
with remorse | to hear and see her plaints, her 3.01. 41
i see the lady hath a thing to grant, | before 3.02. 12
see that he be convey'd unto the tower; 3.02.120
and see where comes the breeder of my sorrow! 3.03. 43
but most himself if he could see his shame. 3.03.185
but see where somerset and clarence comes! 4.02. 3
this is his tent, and see where stand his guard. 4.03. 23
nay, then i see that edward needs must down. 4.03. 42
see that forthwith duke edward be convey'd 4.03. 52
and see him seated in the regal throne. 4.03. 64
this way, man, see where the huntsmen stand. 4.05. 15
for, till i see them here, by doubtful fear | my 4.06. 62
see how the surly warwick mans the wall! 5.01. 17
o cheerful colors! see where oxford comes! 5.01. 58
this cheers my heart, to see your forwardness. 5.04. 65
i speak, | ye see i drink the water of my eye. 5.04. 75
and see our gentle queen how well she fares. 5.05. 89
see how my sword weeps for the poor king's death 5.06. 63
unless to see my shadow in the sun | and descant R3 1.01. 26
o gentlemen, see, see dead henry's wounds | open 1.02. 55
see dead henry's wounds | open their congeal'd 1.02. 55
tears) | i will with all expedient duty see you. 1.02.216
me too, | to see you are become so penitent. 1.02.220
a glass, | that i may see my shadow as i pass. 1.02.263
northumberland, then present, wept to see it. 1.03.186
and see another, as i see thee now, | deck'd in 1.03.204
death, | and see another, as i see thee now, 1.03.204
for edward's sake, and see how he requites me! 1.04. 68
let him see our commission, and talk no more. 1.04. 90 P
that came too lag to see him buried. 2.01. 91
that grieves me when i see my shame in him. 2.02. 54
i do cry you mercy, | i did not see your grace. 2.02.105
then, masters, look to see a troublous world. 2.03. 9
as by proof we see | the water swell before a 2.03. 43
i long with all my heart to see the prince. 2.04. 4
i see the ruin of my house: 2.04. 49
i see (as in a map) the end of all. 2.04. 54
then i see you will part but with light gifts! 3.01.118
where he shall see the boar will use us kindly. 3.02. 33
before i'll see the crown so foul misplac'd. 3.02. 44
but yet you see how soon the day o'ercast. 3.02. 86
well met, my lord, i am glad to see your honor. 3.02.108
i swear | i will not dine until i see the same. 3.04. 77
make a short shrift, he longs to see your head. 3.04. 95
he is, and see, he brings the mayor along. 3.05. 13
die | until your lordship came to see his end, 3.05. 53
so gross | that cannot see this palpable device? 3.06. 11
see where his grace stands, 'tween two clergymen 3.07. 95
and see, a book of prayer in his hand — | true 3.07. 98
for god doth know, and you may partly see, | how 3.07.235
god bless your grace! we see it and will say it. 3.07.237
i am their father's mother, i will see them. 4.01. 22
the king is angry, see, he gnaws his lip. 4.02. 27
but didst thou see them dead? 4.03. 27
decline all this, and see what now thou art: 4.04. 97
we have many goodly days to see: 4.04.320
morning | desire the earl to see me in my tent. 5.03. 32
to see if any mean to shrink from me. 5.03.222
those that come to see | only a show or two, and H8 pr 9
i'll undertake may see away their shilling pr 12
or to see a fellow | in a long motley coat pr 15
think ye see | the very persons of our noble pr 25
think you see them great, | and follow'd with pr 27
see | how soon this mightiness meets misery; pr 29
but i can see his pride | peep through each part 1.01. 68
in july when | we see each grain of gravel, i do 1.01.155
under pretense to see the queen his aunt | (for 1.01.177
to see you ta'en from liberty, to look on | the 1.01.205
yet see, | when these so noble benefits shall 1.02.114
as far as i see, all the good our english | have 1.03. 5
it, | that never see 'em pace before, the spavin 1.03. 12
courtier may be wise | and never see the louvre. 1.03. 23
let me see then, | by all your good leaves, 1.04. 84
and see the noble ruin'd man you speak of. 2.01. 54
see the barge be ready; 2.01. 98
look into these affairs see this main end, | the 2.02. 40
my wolsey, see it furnish'd. 2.02.140
see, see, | i have been begging sixteen years in 2.03. 81
see, see, | i have been begging sixteen years in 2.03. 81
and we shall see him | for it an archbishop. 3.02. 73
in the evening, | and no man see me more. 3.02.227
i blush, | it is to see a nobleman want manners. 3.02.308
my heart weeps to see him | so little of his 3.02.335
a gentleman, sent from the king, to see you. 4.02.106
but this fellow | let me ne'er see again. 4.02.108
and this morning see | you do appear before them 5.01.144
i see your end, | 'tis my undoing. 5.02. 96

receive him, | and see him safe i' th' tower. 5.02.132
now let me see the proudest | he, that dares 5.02.165
there's some of ye, i see, | more out of malice 5.02.179
the common voice, i see, is verified | of thee, 5.02.209
of four foot | (you see the poor remainder) 5.03. 20
let me ne'er hope to see a chine again, | and 5.03. 26
when i might see from far some forty 5.03. 51 P
our children's children | shall see this, and 5.04. 55
many days shall see her, | and yet no day 5.04. 57
i shall desire | to see what this child does, 5.04. 68
ye must all see the queen, and she must thank ye 5.04. 73
and so i'll tell her the next time i see her. TRO 1.01. 82 P
as subject all the vale, | to see the battle. 1.02. 4
do you know a man if you see him? 1.02. 64 P
shall we stand up here and see them as they pass 1.02.178 P
excellent place, here we may see most bravely. 1.02.182 P
you shall see anon. 1.02.188 P
if he see me, you shall see him nod at me. 1.02.194 P
if he see me, you shall see him nod at me. 1.02.194 P
you shall see. 1.02.197 P
look you yonder, do you see? 1.02.206 P
would i could see troilus now! 1.02.216 P
you shall see troilus anon. 1.02.217 P
but more in troilus thousandfold i see | than in 1.02.284
i see them not with my old eyes, what are they? 1.03.365
i see none now. 2.01. 9 P
you see him there? do you? 2.01. 57 P
i will see you hang'd like clatpoles ere i come 2.01.117 P
devils, but i'll see some issue of my spiteful 2.03. 6 P
you see he is his argument that has his argument 2.03. 96 P
draw this curtain and let's see your picture. 3.02. 47 P
make devils of cherubins, they never see truly. 3.02. 70 P
see, we fools! 3.02.123
see, see, your silence, | /cunning in dumbness, 3.02.131
see, see, your silence, | /cunning in dumbness, 3.02.131
is /mirror'd there | where it may see itself. 3.03.111
now shall we see to–morrow — | an act that very 3.03.130
to see these grecian lords! 3.03.138
i see my reputation is at stake, | my fame is 3.03.227
lords after the combat | to see us here unarm'd. 3.03.237
to see great hector in his weeds of peace, | to 3.03.239
you shall see the pageant of ajax. 3.03.272 P
and i myself see not the bottom of it. 3.03.309
see, ho! who is that there? 4.01. 1
good uncle, go and see. 4.02. 35
we see it, we see it. 4.04. 23 P
we see it, we see it. 4.04. 23 P
when shall we see again? 4.04. 57
be thou true, | and i will see thee. 4.04. 67
and you this glove. when shall i see you? 4.04. 71
doth long to see unarm'd the valiant hector. 4.05.153
i will go eat with thee and see your knights. 4.05.158
next | to feast with me and see me at my tent. 4.05.229
i pray you let us see you in the field; 4.05.266
yonder 'tis, | there where we see the lights. 5.01. 68
i will rather leave to see hector than not to 5.01. 95 P
but with my heart the other eye doth see. 5.02.108
i would fain see them meet, that that same young 5.04. 5 P
now do i see thee, ha! have at thee, hector! 5.06. 13
be sent | to pray achilles see us at our tent. 5.09. 8
let me see: 5.10. 40 P
where th' other instruments | did see and hear, COR 1.01.102
once cannot | see what i do deliver out to each, 1.01.143
see, our best elders. 1.01.226
shalt see me once more strike at tullus' face. 1.01.240
see him pluck aufidius down by th' hair; 1.03. 30
methinks i see him stamp thus, and call thus: 1.03. 32
i am glad to see your ladyship. 1.03. 50 P
he had rather see the swords and hear a drum 1.03. 55 P
see, they have shut him in. 1.04. 47
see here these movers that do prize their hours 1.05. 4
love this painting | wherein you see me smear'd; 1.06. 69
if you see this in the map of my microcosm, 2.01. 62 P
coffin'd home, | that weep'st to see me triumph? 2.01.177
on 's heart, | that is not glad to see thee! 2.01.186
i have lived | to see inherited my very wishes 2.01.199
the bleared sights | are spectacled to see him. 2.01.206
all agreeing | in earnestness to see him. 2.01.213
i have seen the dumb men throng to see him, and 2.01.262
when you now see | he had rather venture all his 2.02. 79
you see how he intends to use the people. 2.02.155
that we shall hardly in our ages see | their 3.01. 7
go see him out at gates, and follow him, | as he 3.03.138
come, come, let's see him out at gates, come. 3.03.142
vexed, whom we see have sided | in his behalf. 4.02. 2
this lady's husband here — this (do you see?) 4.02. 41
but that i see thee here, | thou noble thing, 4.05.115
but when they shall see, sir, his crest up again 4.05.210 P
i hope to see romans as cheap as volscians. 4.05.232 P
than see | our tradesmen singing in their shops, 4.06. 7
go see this rumorer whipt. 4.06. 48
to see your wives dishonor'd to your noses — 4.06. 83
you'll see your rome embrac'd with fire before 5.02. 7
'tis a spell, you see, of much power. 5.02. 96 P
wife, and child to see | the son, the husband, 5.03.101
requires nor child nor woman's face to see. 5.03.130
see you yond coign a' th' capitol, yond 5.04. 1 P
see, lord and father, how we have perform'd TIT 1.01.142
o titus, see! 1.01.341
o, see what thou hast done! 1.01.341
and see his shipwrack and his commonweal's. 2.01. 24
madam, now shall ye see | our roman hunting. 2.02. 19
to see the general hunting in this forest? 2.03. 59
a barren detested vale you see it is; 2.03. 93
let it be your glory | to see her tears, but be 2.03.140
farewell, my sons, see that you make her sure. 2.03.187
my heart suspects more than mine eye can see. 2.03.213
and see a fearful sight of blood and death. 2.03.216
i'll see what hole is here, | and what he is 2.03.246
you see it is apparent. 2.03.292
thou shalt not bail them, see thou follow me. 2.03.299
see how with signs and tokens she can scrowl. 2.04. 5
and for these bitter tears which now you see 3.01. 6
will it consume me? let me see it then. 3.01. 62
see how my wretched sister sobs and weeps. 3.01.137
see thy two sons' heads, | thy warlike hand, thy 3.01.254
come let me see what task i have to do. 3.01.275
good uncle marcus, see how swift she comes. 4.01. 3
see, lucius, see, how much she makes of thee; 4.01. 10
see, lucius, see, how much she makes of thee; 4.01. 10
some book there is that she desires to see. 4.01. 31
see, brother, see, note how she cotes the leaves 4.01. 50
brother, see, note how she cotes the leaves. 4.01. 50
see, see! 4.01. 54
see, see! 4.01. 54
and see their blood or die with this reproach. 4.01. 94
let's see: 4.02. 19
but me more good to see so great a lord | basely 4.02. 37
o, tell me, did you see aaron the moor? 4.02. 52
hark ye, lords, you see i have given her physic, 4.02.162
this done, see that you take no longer days, 4.02.165
i see thou wilt not trust the air | with secrets 4.02.169
sir boy, let me see your archery. 4.03. 2
case, | to see thy noble uncle thus distract? 4.03. 26
see, see, thou hast shot off one of taurus' 4.03. 70
see, see, thou hast shot off one of taurus' 4.03. 70
i'll be at hand, sir, see you do it bravely. 4.03.112 P
come let me see it. 4.03.115
see, here's to jove, and this to mercury, | this 4.04. 14
hang the child, that he may see it sprawl — | a 5.01. 51
child shall live, and i will see it nourish'd. 5.01. 60
do | see here in bloody lines i have set down: 5.02. 14
see here he comes, and i must ply my theme. 5.02. 80
and see them ready against their mother comes. 5.02.205
and see the ambush of our friends be strong, | i 5.03. 9
some stay to see him fast'ned in the earth. 5.03.183
side, | so early walking did i see your son. ROM 1.01.123
see where he comes! 1.01.156
should, without eyes, see pathways to his will! 1.01.172
hear all, all see; 1.02. 30
but, i pray, can you read any thing you see? 1.02. 60 P
to see it techy and fall out wi' th' dug! 1.03. 32
to see now how a jest shall come about! 1.03. 45
and i might live to see thee married once, | i 1.03. 61
and see how one another lends content; 1.03. 84
o then i see queen mab hath been with you. 1.04. 53
see how she leans her cheek upon her hand! 2.02. 23
if they do see thee, they will murther thee. 2.02. 70
man, if i see occasion in a good quarrel, and 2.04.159 P
good soul, had as lieve see a toad, a very toad, 2.04.203 P
as lieve see a toad, a very toad, as see him. 2.04.203 P
do you not see that i am out of breath? 2.05. 30
therefore farewell, i see thou knowest me not. 3.01. 65
lovers can see to do their amorous rites | by 3.02. 8
that ever i should live to see thee dead! 3.02. 63
o, then i see that /madmen have no ears. 3.03. 61
methinks i see thee now, thou art so low, | as 3.05. 55
and see how he will take it at your hands. 3.05.125
child, | but now i see this one is one too much, 3.05.166
see where she comes from shrift with merry look. 4.02. 15
let me see the county; 4.02. 29
methinks i see my cousin's ghost | seeking out 4.03. 55
hah, let me see her. 4.05. 25
have i thought /long to see this morning's face, 4.05. 41
let's see for means. 5.01. 35
i see that thou art poor. 5.01. 58
see thou deliver it to my lord and father. 5.03. 24
poison, i see, hath been his timeless end. 5.03.162
we see the ground whereon these woes do lie, 5.03.179
up | to see thy son and heir now /early down. 5.03.209
look and thou shalt see. 5.03.213
see what a scourge is laid upon your hate, 5.03.292
see, | magic of bounty! TIM 1.01. 5
let's see your piece. 1.01. 28
you see this confluence, this great flood of 1.01. 42
you see how all conditions, how all minds, | as 1.01. 52
ay, to see meat fill knaves, and wine heat fools 1.01.261
it grieves me to see so many dip their meat in 1.02. 41 P
you see, my lord, how ample y' are belov'd. 1.02.130
do so, my friends. see them well entertain'd. 2.02. 44
would we could see you at corinth! 2.02. 70 P
now i see thou art a fool, and fit for thy 3.01. 49 P
see, by good hap, yonder's my lord; 3.02. 25 P
i have sweat to see his honor. 3.02. 26 P
see the monstrousness of man | when he looks out 3.02. 72
i see no sense for't, | but his occasions might 3.03. 14
push, did you see my cap? 3.06.109 P
did you see my jewel? 3.06.113 P
did you see my cap? 3.06.115 P
wear timon's livery, | that see i by our faces; 4.02. 18
i see them now, then was a blessed time. 4.03. 79
if i hope well, i'll never see thee more. 4.03.171
i know not what else to do, i'll see thee again. 4.03.354 P
i swound to see thee. 4.03.368
let us first see peace in athens. 4.03.456 P
ne'er see thou man, and let me ne'er see thee. 4.03.536
ne'er see thou man, and let me ne'er see thee. 4.03.536
you shall see him a palm in athens again, and 5.01. 10
have i once liv'd to see two honest men? 5.01. 56
ay, and you hear him cog, see him dissemble, 5.01. 95
sir, we make holiday to see caesar, and to JC 1.01. 31 P
to see great pompey pass the streets of rome; 1.01. 42
see whe'er their basest metal be not mov'd; 1.01. 61
set him before me, let me see his face. 1.02. 20
will you go see the order of the course? 1.02. 25
tell me, good brutus, can you see your face? 1.02. 51
into your eye, | that you might see your shadow. 1.02. 58
and since you know you cannot see yourself | so 1.02. 67
yet i see | thy honorable mettle may be wrought 1.02.308
and, thus unbraced, casca, as you see, | have 1.03. 48
to see the strange impatience of the heavens; 1.03. 61
i will yet, ere day, | see brutus at his house. 1.03.154
awake, and see thyself! 2.01. 46
at the door, | who doth desire to see you. 2.01. 71
when they shall see | the face of caesar, they 2.02. 11
see, antony, that revels long a–nights, | is 2.02.116
my stand, | to see him pass on to the capitol. 2.04. 26
hands and this our present act | you see we do, 3.01.167
act | you see we do, yet see you but our hands, 3.01.167
our hearts you see not, they are pitiful; 3.01.169
thy death, | to see thy antony making his peace, 3.01.197
passion, i see, is catching, /for mine eyes, 3.01.283
you all did see that on the lupercal | i thrice 3.02. 95
see what a rent the envious casca made; 3.02.175
is himself, marr'd as you see with traitors. 3.02.197
a friendly eye could never see such faults. 4.03. 90
let me go in to see the generals. 4.03.124
let me see, let me see; 4.03.273
let me see, let me see; 4.03.273
to tell thee thou shalt see me at philippi. 4.03.283
well; then i shall see thee again? 4.03.284
why, i will see thee at philippi then. 4.03.286
yes, that thou didst. didst thou see any thing? 4.03.297
to see my best friend ta'en before my face! 5.03. 35
apace, | and see how i regarded caius cassius. 5.03. 88
to this dead man than you shall see me pay. 5.03.102
go on, | and see whe'er brutus be alive or dead, 5.04. 30
i'll see it done. MAC 1.02. 66
let not light see my black and deep desires; 1.04. 51
which the eye fears, when it is done, to see. 1.04. 53
that my keen knife see not the wound it makes, 1.05. 52
o, never | shall sun that morrow see! 1.05. 61
see, see, our honor'd hostess! 1.06. 10
see, see, our honor'd hostess! 1.06. 10
is this a dagger which i see before me, | the 2.01. 33
i have thee not, and yet i see thee still. 2.01. 35
i see thee yet, in form as palpable | as this 2.01. 40
i see thee still; 2.01. 45
see, and then speak yourselves. 2.03. 73
up, up, and see | the great doom's image! 2.03. 77
why, see you not? 2.04. 21
well, may you see things well done there: 2.04. 37
see, they encounter thee with their hearts' 3.04. 9
prithee see there! 3.04. 67
my little spirit, see, | sits in a foggy cloud, 3.05. 34
call 'em; let me see 'em. 4.01. 63
i'll see no more. 4.01.118
and some i see | that twofold balls and treble 4.01.120
now i see 'tis true, | for the blood–bolter'd 4.01.122
when shalt thou see thy wholesome days again, 4.03.105
see who comes here. 4.03.159
you see her eyes are open. 5.01. 24 P
within this three mile may you see it coming; 5.05. 36
whiles i see lives, the gashes | do better upon 5.08. 2
and underwrit, | "here may you see the tyrant." 5.08. 27
and yet, by these i see, | so great a day as 5.09. 2
i see thee compass'd with thy kingdom's pearl, 5.09. 22
whom we invite to see us crown'd at scone. 5.09. 41
see, it stalks away! HAM 1.01. 50
i am glad to see you well. 1.02.160
i am very glad to see you. 1.02.167
my lord, i came to see your father's funeral. 1.02.176
my father — methinks i see my father. 1.02.184
see you now, | your bait of falsehood take this 2.01. 59
moreover that we much did long to see you, | the 2.02. 2
that great baby you see there is not yet out of 2.02.383 P
i am glad to see thee well. 2.02.422 P
/french falc'ners — fly at any thing we see; 2.02.430 P
begin at this line — let me see, let me see: 2.02.449 P
begin at this line — let me see, let me see: 2.02.449 P
but, as we often see, against some storm, | a 2.02.483
but if the gods themselves did see her then, 2.02.512
my lord, will you see the players well bestow'd? 2.02.522 P
your majesties | to hear and see the matter. 3.01. 23
now see /that noble and most sovereign reason, 3.01.157
t' have seen what i have seen, see what i see! 3.01.161
t' have seen what i have seen, see what i see! 3.01.161
you shall see anon. 3.02.240 P
your love, if i could see the puppets dallying. 3.02.247 P
you shall see anon how the murtherer gets the 3.02.263 P
let me see one. 3.02.345 P
do you see yonder cloud that's almost in shape 3.02.376 P
where you may see the /inmost part of you. 3.04. 20
see what a grace was seated on this brow: 3.04. 55
and there i see such black and /grained spots 3.04. 90
do you see nothing there? 3.04.131
nothing at all, yet all that is i see. 3.04.132
in heaven, send thither to see; 4.03. 33 P
i see a cherub that sees them. 4.03. 48 P
while to my shame i see | the imminent death of 4.04. 59
shall i beg leave to see your kingly eyes, when 4.07. 45 P
and that i see, in passages of proof, | time 4.07.112
soft, let me see. 4.07.154
an hour of quiet /shortly shall we see, | till 5.01.298
for this, sir, now shall you see the other — 5.02. 1
continent of what part a gentleman would see. 5.02.111 P
this is too heavy; let me see another. 5.02.264
she sounds to see them bleed. 5.02.308
what is it you would see? 5.02.362
see better, lear, and let me still remain | the LR 1.01.158
nor shall ever see | that face of hers again. 1.01.263
you see how full of changes his age is; 1.01.288 P
let's see. 1.02. 34 P
let's see, let's see. 1.02. 43 P
let's see, let's see. 1.02. 43 P
i see the business. 1.02.182
shalt see thy other daughter will use thee 1.05. 14 P
and receiv'd | this hurt you see, striving to 2.01.108
than stands on any shoulder that i see | before 2.02. 94
that bear bags | shall see their children kind. 2.04. 51
i am glad to see your highness. 2.04.128
we'll no more meet, no more see one another. 2.04.220
you see me here, you gods, a poor old man, | as 2.04.272
if you shall see cordelia | (as fear not but you 3.01. 46
blanch, and sweetheart, see, they bark at me. 3.06. 63
see what breeds about her heart. 3.06. 76 P
because i would not see thy cruel nails | pluck 3.07. 56
but i shall see | the winged vengeance overtake 3.07. 65
if you see vengeance — 3.07. 72
have one eye left | to see some mischief on him. 3.07. 82
lest it see more, prevent it. 3.07. 83
you cannot see your way. 4.01. 17
might i but live to see thee in my touch, | i'ld 4.01. 23
that will not see | because he does not feel, 4.01. 68
see thyself, devil! 4.02. 59
soon may i hear and see him! 4.04. 29
when i do stare, see how the subject quakes. 4.06.108
were all thy letters suns, i could not see. 4.06.140
in a light, yet you see how this world goes. 4.06.147 P
i see it feelingly. 4.06.149
a man may see how this world goes with no eyes. 4.06.150 P
see how yond justice rails upon yond simple 4.06.151 P
seem | to see the things thou dost not. 4.06.172
let's see these pockets; 4.06.256

et us see. 4.06.258
hould ev'n die with pity | to see another thus. 4.07. 53
et's see, | i feel this pin prick. 4.07. 54
ou see, is kill'd in him, /and /yet /it /is 4.07. 78
vithin our power, | shall never see his pardon; 5.01. 68
hall we not see these daughters and these 5.03. 7
ve'll see 'em starv'd first. 5.03. 25
ll see that straight. 5.03.288
, see, see! 5.03.305
, see, see! 5.03.305
o you see this? 5.03.311
ve that are young | shall never see so much, nor 5.03.327
ow, roderigo, | where didst thou see her? OTH 1.01.163
aughters' minds | by what you see them act. 1.01.171
did not see you; 1.03. 50
ook to her, moor, if thou hast eyes to see; 1.03.292
nd thou shalt see an answerable sequestration 1.03.345 P
et me see now: 1.03.392
et's see — | after some time, to abuse 1.03.394
s well to see the vessel that's come in | as to 2.01. 37
ee for the news. 2.01. 95
ee suitors following, and not look behind: 2.01.157
reat as my content | to see you here before me. 2.01.184
idst thou not see her paddle with the palm of 2.01.254 P
ou see this fellow that is gone before: 2.03.121
nd do but see his vice, | 'tis to his virtue a 2.03.123
o, iago, | i'll see before i doubt; 3.03.190
n venice they do let /god see the pranks | they 3.03.202
see this hath a little dash'd your spirits. 3.03.214
ut i do see y' are mov'd. 3.03.217
vorthy friend — | my lord, i see y' are mov'd. 3.03.224
vhereto we see in all things nature tends — 3.03.231
see, /sir, you are eaten up with passion; 3.03.391
f ever mortal eyes do see them bolster | more 3.03.399
t is impossible you should see this, | were 3.03.402
et we see nothing done; 3.03.432
lid i to–day | see cassio wipe his beard with. 3.03.439
ow do i see 'tis true. 3.03.444
or my wish, | to have him see me woman'd. 3.04.195
nd say if i shall see you soon at night. 3.04.198
ut i'll see you soon. 3.04.200
, i see that nose of yours, but not that dog i 4.01.142 P
vell, i may chance to see you; 4.01.166 P
nd did you see the handkerchief? 4.01.173 P
nd to see how he prizes the foolish woman your 4.01.175 P
ee, your wife's with him. 4.01.215
am very glad to see you, signior; 4.01.220
am glad to see you mad. 4.01.239
et me see your eyes; | look in my face. 4.02. 25
vhy, now i see there's mettle in thee, and even 4.02.204 P
hey see, and smell, | and have their palates 4.03. 94
am glad to see you. 5.01. 95
o you see, gentlemen? 5.01.109
entlemen, let's go see poor cassio dress'd. 5.01.124
e not afraid though you do see me weapon'd; 5.02.266
nd you shall see in him | the triple pillar of ANT 1.01. 11
ehold and see. 1.01. 13
s it is a heart–breaking to see a handsome man 1.02. 71 P
ve see how mortal an unkindness is to them; 1.02.133 P
did not see him since. 1.03. 1
ee where he is, who's with him, what he does. 1.03. 2
he last, best, | see when and where she died. 1.03. 62
ow i see, i see, | in fulvia's death, how mine 1.03. 64
ow i see, i see, | in fulvia's death, how mine 1.03. 64
ou may see, lepidus, and henceforth know, | it 1.04. 1
'er–picturing that venus where we see | the 2.02.200
see it in my motion, have it not in my tongue; 2.03. 14
ill i shall see you in your soldier's dress, 2.04. 4
et's part, | you see we have burnt our cheeks. 2.07.122
'll see you by and by. 3.11. 24
ee you here, sir? 3.11. 30
ee | how i convey my shame out of thine eyes 3.11. 51
see men's judgments are | a parcel of their 3.13. 31
ee, my women, | against the blown rose may they 3.13. 38
ill like a boy you see him cringe his face, 3.13.100
nd i see still | a diminution in our captain's 3.13.196
ee it done, | and feast the army; 4.01. 14
aply you shall not see me more, or if, | a 4.02. 26
et's see if other watchmen | do hear what we do 4.03. 17
et's see how it will give off. 4.03. 22
hat thou couldst see my wars to–day, and 4.04. 16
ccupation, thou shouldst see | a workman in't. 4.04. 17
efore the sun shall see 's, we'll spill the 4.08. 3
 sun, thy uprise shall i see no more, | fortune 4.12. 18
ometime we see a cloud that's dragonish, | a 4.14. 2
vhen i should see behind me | th' inevitable 4.14. 64
nd see | thy master thus with pleach'd arms, 4.14. 72
, see, my women: 4.15. 62
et before him, | he needs must see himself. 5.01. 35
vhere you shall see | how hardly i was drawn 5.01. 73
go with me, and see | what i can show in this. 5.01. 76
ou see how easily she may be surpris'd. 5.02. 35
et the world see | his nobleness well acted, 5.02. 44
leep, that i might see | but such another man! 5.02. 77
ee, caesar! 5.02.150
nd i shall see | some squeaking cleopatra boy 5.02.219
 see him rouse himself | to praise my noble act 5.02.284
lost thou not see my baby at my breast, | that 5.02.309
to see perform'd the dreaded act which thou | so 5.02.331
i do not see them bleed. 5.02.338
see | high order in this great solemnity. 5.02.365
this jewel in the world | that i may see again. CYM 1.01. 92
o the gods! | when shall we see again? 1.01.124
you shall, at least, | go see my lord aboard. 1.01.178
but i see you have some religion in you, that 1.04.136 P
to see this vaulted arch and the rich crop | of 1.06. 33
on purpose and on promise | to see your grace. 1.06.203
come, i'll go see this italian. 2.01. 48 P
to see th' enclosed lights, now canopied | under 2.02. 21
see! jachimo! 2.04. 26
see! 2.04. 96
i see her yet: 2.04.101
pisanio, | who long'st like me to see thy lord; 3.02. 53
i see before me, man; 3.02. 78
thus | draws us a profit from all things we see; 3.03. 18
ne'er long'd my mother so | to see me first, as 3.04. 3
i see into thy end and am almost | a man already 3.04.166
there shall she see my valor, which will then be 3.05.139 P
i see a man's life is a tedious one, | i have 3.06. 1
i see you're angry. 3.06. 55
but see, thy brother. 4.02.112
stark, as you see; 4.02.209
great griefs, i see, med'cine the less; 4.02.243
let's see the boy's face. 4.02.359
though cloten then but young, you see, not wore 4.04. 23
what thing is't that i never | did see man die, 4.04. 36
best use of eyes to see the way of blindness! 5.04.189 P
i see a thing | bitter to me as death; 5.05.103
peace, peace, see further. 5.05.124
be silent; let's see further. 5.05.127
whereupon — | methinks i see him now — 5.05.209
see, | posthumus anchors upon imogen; 5.05.392
did relieve me | to see this gracious season. 5.05.401
see where she comes, apparelled like the spring, PER 1.01. 12
as sick men do | who know the world, see heaven, 1.01. 48
and the sore eyes see clear | to stop the air 1.01. 99
now do i see he had some reason for't; 1.03. 6 P
see if 'twill teach us to forget our own? 1.04. 3
but see what heaven can do by this our change: 1.04. 33
yet those which see them fall | have scarce 1.04. 48
pray you see the sea hath cast upon your coast — 2.01. 56
for that i am a man, pray you see me buried. 2.01. 77
i pray you let me see it. 2.01.120
shall make the gazer joy to see him tread. 2.01.159
whom nature gat | for men to see, and seeing 2.02. 7
whereby i see that time's the king of men, 2.03. 45
see, not a man in private conference | or 2.04. 17
it pleaseth me so well that i will see you wed, 2.05. 92
see how she gins | to blow into life's flower 3.02. 94
my wedded lord, i ne'er shall see again, | a 3.04. 9
but i'll see further: 4.01. 99
i have gone through for this piece you see. 4.02. 44 P
at it, and swore he would see her to–morrow. 4.02.109 P
to see his daughter, all his live's delight. 4.04. 12
like motes and shadows see them move a while, 4.04. 21
see how belief may suffer by foul show! 4.04. 23
i am glad to see your honor in good health. 4.06. 22 P
white and red, you shall see a rose, and she 4.06. 35 P
my authority shall not see thee, or else look 4.06. 89 P
well, i will see what i can do for thee. 4.06.192 P
may we not see him? 5.01. 31
recount it to you, | but see, i am prevented. 5.01. 64
see, she will speak to him. 5.01. 81
of your melancholy state, | did come to see you. 5.01.221
at ephesus the temple see, | our king and all 5.02. 17
may we see them? 5.03. 25
who cannot feel nor see the rain, being in't, TNK 1.01.120
set you forward, | for i will see you gone. 1.01.218
if | you stay to see of us such spinsters, we 1.03. 23
never see | the hardy youths strive for the 2.02. 9
no figures of ourselves shall we ev'r see | to 2.02. 33
till she for shame see what a wrong she has done 2.02. 39
the vine shall grow, but we shall never see it; 2.02. 43
i see two comforts rising, two mere blessings, 2.02. 58
the wills of men to vanity | i see through now, 2.02.102
we'll see how near art can come near their 2.02.149
out, | and leap the garden, when i see her next, 2.02.216
once more | i would but see this fair one. 2.02.232
he shall see thebes again and call to arms | the 2.02.248
may i see the garden? 2.02.268
thou shalt stay and see | her bright eyes break 2.03. 8
i'll see her and be near her, or no more. 2.03. 23
and you shall see her | take a new lesson out, 2.03. 34
and she must see the duke, and she must dance 2.03. 45
we'll see the sports, then every man to 's 2.03. 55
by any means | before the ladies see us, and do 2.03. 57
much, | and me as much to see his misery. 2.04. 28
i'll see you furnish'd, and because you say 2.05. 44
your hunger needs no sauce, i see. 3.03. 25
couple then, | and see what's wanting. 3.05. 33
one see 'em all rewarded. 3.05.152
and thou shalt see me, theseus, | do such a 3.06.154
o sir, when did you see her? 4.01. 33
to bury you, | and see the house made handsome. 4.01. 79
for, if she see him once, she's gone — she's 4.01.124
in | quickly, by any means, i long to see 'em. 4.02. 65
now, as i have a soul, i long to see 'em. 4.02.142
lady, you shall see men fight now. 4.02.143
for in the next world will dido see palamon, and 4.03. 15 P
see what our general of ebbs and flows | out 5.01.163
pray bring her in | and let's see how she is. 5.02. 25
did you nev'r see the horse he gave me? 5.02. 45
i had rather see a wren hawk at a fly | than 5.03. 2
she shall see deeds of honor in their kind 5.03. 12
i see one eye of yours conceives a tear, | the 5.03.137
then it goes hard, i see. ep 5
'tis in vain, i see, to stay ye; ep 9
he that will not see a red herring at a harry STM II.C 1 P
imagine that you see the wretched strangers, II.C 74
"thou canst not see one wrinkle in my brow, VEN 139
being proud, as females are, to see him woo her, 309
though neither eyes nor ears to hear nor see, 437
and that i could not see, nor hear, nor touch, 440
"then shalt thou see the dew–bedabbled wretch 703
o yes, it may, thou hast no eyes to see, | but 939
those eyes that taught all other eyes to see? 952
"to see his face the lion walk'd along | behind 1093
if he did see his face, why then i know | he 1109
night–wand'ring weasels shriek to see him there; LUC 307
what could he see but mightily he noted? 414
"i see what crosses my attempt will bring, | i 491
that thou shalt see thy state, and pity mine." 644
receipt | ere he can see his own abomination. 704
"they think not but that every eye can see | the 750
and time to see one that by alms doth live 986
"let him have time to see his friends his foes, 988
but cloudy lucrece shames herself to see, | and 1084
to see the salve doth make the wound ache more, 1116
how was i overseen that thou shalt see it! 1206
(if ever, love, thy lucrece thou wilt see) 1306
to see sad sights moves more than hear them told 1324
for lucrece thought he blush'd to see her shame, 1344
there might you see the laboring pioner 1380
that one might see those far–off eyes look sad. 1386
there pleading might you see grave nestor stand, 1401
to see their youthful sons bright weapons wield, 1432
to see those borrowed tears that sinon sheeds! 1549
and they that watch see time how slow it creeps. 1575
glass, | that i no more can see what once i was! 1764
lucrece, live again and see | thy father die, 1770
"did i see a fair sweet youth | here in these PP 9. 9
see, in my thigh," quoth she, "here was the sore 9.12
an englishman, the fairest that eye could see, 15. 3
for now i see inconstancy | more in women than 17.11
in howling wise, to see my doleful plight. 17.22
other help for him i see that there is none. 17.36
and see the shepherds feed their flocks, | by 19. 6
and see thy blood warm when thou feel'st it cold SON 2.14
so thou through windows of thine age shalt see, 3.11
and see the brave day sunk in hideous night; 12. 2
when lofty trees i see barren of leaves, | which 12. 5
and die as fast as they see others grow, | and 12.12
so long as men can breathe or eyes can see, | so 18.13
for through the painter must you see his skill 24. 5
now see what good turns eyes for eyes have done: 24. 9
they draw but what they see, know not the heart. 24.14
looking on darkness which the blind do see; 27. 8
to see his active child do deeds of youth, | so 37. 2
when most i wink, then do mine eyes best see, 43. 1
all days are nights to see till i see thee, 43.13
all days are nights to see till i see thee, 43.13
when i shall see thee frown on my defects, 49. 2
to–morrow see again, and do not kill | the 56. 7
that, when they see | return of love, more blest 56.11
that i might see what the old world could say 59. 9
when sometime lofty towers i see down rased, 64. 3
better'd that the world may see my pleasure; 75. 8
i see a better state to me belongs | than that 92. 7
and all things turns to fair that eyes can see! 95.12
yet i none could see | but sweet or color it had 99.14
time | i see descriptions of the fairest wights, 106. 2
i see their antique pen would have express'd 106. 7
for if it see the rud'st or gentlest sight, 113. 9
for thy records and what we see doth lie, | made 123.11
white, | but no such roses see i in her cheeks, 130. 6
that they behold and see not what they see? 137. 2
that they behold and see not what they see? 137. 2
they know what beauty is, see where it lies, 137. 3
that censures falsely what they see aright? 148. 4
those that can see thou lov'st, and i am blind. 149.14
the more i hear and see just cause of hate? 150.10
or made them swear against the thing they see; 152.12
a storm | as oft 'twixt may and april is to see, LC 102
"'all my offenses that abroad you see | are 183

SEED 6 FR 0.0006 REL FR 5 V 1 P
they shall stand for seed. MM 1.02. 99 P
then be gleaned | from the true seed of honor? MV 2.09. 47
would of that seed grow to a greater falseness, 2H4 3.01. 90
saw his heroical seed, and smil'd to see him, H5 2.04. 59
son, | a cousin–german to great priam's seed; TRO 4.05.121
'tis an unweeded garden | that grows to seed, HAM 1.02.136

SEEDED 2 FR 0.0002 REL FR 2 V 0 P
the seeded pride | that hath to this maturity TRO 1.03.316
"how will thy shame be seeded in thine age, LUC 603

SEEDNESS 1 FR 0.0001 REL FR 1 V 0 P
that from the seedness the bare fallow brings MM 1.04. 42

SEEDS 10 FR 0.0011 REL FR 9 V 1 P
breeds | a native slip to us from foreign seeds. AWW 1.03.146
th' earth together, | and mar the seeds within! WT 4.04.479
who in their seeds | and weak beginning lie 2H4 3.01. 84
green earthen pots, bladders, and musty seeds, ROM 5.01. 46
if you can look into the seeds of time, | and MAC 1.03. 58
to make them kings — the seeds of banquo kings! 3.01. 69
she that sets seeds and roots of shame and PER 4.06. 85 P
expels the seeds of fear and th' apprehension TNK 5.01. 36
seeds spring from seeds and beauty breedeth VEN 167
seeds spring from seeds and beauty breedeth 167

SEEDSMAN 1 FR 0.0001 REL FR 1 V 0 P
the seedsman | upon the slime and ooze scatters ANT 2.07. 21

SEEING 58 FR 0.0065 REL FR 50 V 8 P
seeing you are beautified | with goodly shape, TGV 4.01. 53
sent to her, seeing her go through the streets, WIV 4.05. 31 P
seeing how much another man is a fool when he ADO 2.03. 8 P
it adds a precious seeing to the eye: LLL 4.03.330
with eyes best seeing, heaven's fiery eye, | by 5.02.375
wherein it doth impair the seeing sense, | it MND 3.02.179
seeing orlando, it unlink'd itself, | and with AYL 4.03.111
that but seeing, you should love her? 5.02. 2 P
seeing too much sadness hath congeal'd your SHR in.2. 132
and i, seeing this, came thence for very shame, 3.02.180
nought for approbation | but only seeing, all WT 2.01.178
that knew no more but seeing, could not say if 5.02. 17 P
ill in myself to see, and in thee, seeing ill. R2 2.01. 94
but, seeing thou fall'st on me so luckily, | i 1H4 5.04. 33
of a naked blind boy in her naked seeing self? H5 5.02.297 P
in france, | not seeing what is likely to ensue. 1H6 3.01.187
my tongue, | seeing the deed is meritorious, 2H6 3.01.270
for, seeing him, i see my life in death. 3.02.152
well, seeing gentle words will not prevail, 4.02.174
and seeing ignorance is the curse of god, 4.07. 73
seeing thou hast prov'd so unnatural a father! 3H6 1.01.218
and seeing thou dost, i here divorce myself 1.01.247
then, seeing 'twas he that made you to depose, 1.02. 26
well worth the seeing. H8 4.01. 61
you must be seeing christenings? 5.03. 10 P
blind fear, that seeing reason leads, finds TRO 3.02. 71 P
than now in first seeing he had prov'd himself a COR 1.03. 17 P
or, seeing it, of such childish friendliness 2.03.175
and, seeing me, dost not | think me for the man 4.05. 55
now, seeing she is advanc'd | above the clouds, ROM 4.05. 73
ill | that you run mad, seeing that she is well. 4.05. 76
seeing his reputation touch'd to death, | he did TIM 3.05. 19
seeing that death, a necessary end, | will come JC 2.02. 36
seeing those beads of sorrow stand in thine, 3.01.284
that you, at such times seeing me, never shall, HAM 1.05.173
we'll so bestow ourselves that, seeing unseen, 3.01. 32
/confederate season, else no creature seeing, 3.02.256
seeing how loathly opposite i stood | to his LR 2.01. 49
the griefs are ended | by seeing the worst, OTH 1.03.203
steal away so guilty–like, | seeing your coming. 3.03. 40
the seeing these effects will be | both noisome CYM 1.05. 25
gat | for men to see, and seeing wonder at. PER 2.02. 7
seeing this goodly vessel ride before us, | i 5.01. 18
licentious ear, | but curb it, spite of seeing. 5.03. 31

i, seeing, thought he was a goodly man; TNK 2.04. 8
(if there be a right in seeing | and first 3.06.147
the scene's not for our seeing, go we hence, 5.03.134
"what should i do, seeing thee so indeed, | that VEN 667
seeing his beauty, thou shouldst strike at it: 938
swearing i slew him, seeing thee embrace him. LUC 518
side, | seeing such emulation in their woe, 1808
and steal dead seeing of his living hue? SON 67. 6
by seeing farther than the eye hath shown. 69. 8
blind, | seems seeing, but effectually is out; 113. 4
o, 'tis the first, 'tis flatt'ry in my seeing, 114. 9
not by our feeling, but by others' seeing. 121. 4
or mine eyes seeing this, say this is not, | to 137.11
lest eyes well seeing thy foul faults should 148.14

SEEK 249 FR 0.0281 REL FR 207 V 42 P

till thou didst seek to violate | the honor of TMP 1.02.347
so, king, go safely on to seek thy son. 2.01.327
i'll seek him deeper than e'er plummet sounded, 3.03.101
i'll be wise hereafter, | and seek for grace. 5.01.296
but i seek my master, and my master seeks not me TGV 1.01. 87 P
put forth their sons to seek preferment out: 1.03. 7
how could he see his way to seek out you? 2.04. 94
as seek to quench the fire of love with words. 2.07. 20
i do not seek to quench your love's hot fire, 2.07. 21
run, boy, run, run, and seek him out. 3.01.188 P
gone to seek his dog, which to-morrow, by his 4.02. 78 P
seek shelter, pack! WIV 1.03. 82
i will seek out falstaff. 2.01.140 P
ascend my chambers, search, seek, find out. 3.03.163 P
expense, | i seek to heal it only by his wealth. 3.04. 6
yet seek my father's love, still seek it, sir. 3.04. 19
yet seek my father's love, still seek it, sir. 3.04. 19
i mean it not, i seek you a better husband. 3.04. 84
he will seek there, on my word. 4.02. 60 P
well, he's not here i seek for. 4.02.158 P
if i find not what i seek, show no color for my 4.02.161 P
doth he so seek his life? MM 1.04. 72
to sue to live, i find i seek to die, | and, 3.01. 42
duke, | you bid me seek redemption of the devil. 5.01. 29
come you to seek the lamb here of the fox, 5.01.298
forc'd me to seek delays for them and me. ERR 1.01. 74
day | to seek thy /health by beneficial help. 1.01.151
i'll to the centaur to go seek this slave; 1.02.104
that in such haste i sent to seek his master? 2.01. 2
is wand'red forth, in care to seek me out. 2.02. 3
or else i shall seek my wit in my shoulders. 2.02. 38 P
and he not coming thither, | i went to seek him. 5.01.225
look, don pedro is return'd to seek you. ADO 1.01.203 P
let me be that i am, and seek not to alter me. 1.03. 37 P
brought count claudio, whom you sent me to seek. 2.01.287 P
shall we go seek benedick, and tell him of her 2.03.199 P
see, see, here comes the man we went to seek. 5.01.110
i came to seek you both. 5.01.121 P
we have been up and down to seek thee, for we 5.01.122 P
pore upon a book | to seek the light of truth, LLL 1.01. 75
court, | than seek a dispensation for his oath, 2.01. 87
i love, i sue, i seek a wife — | a woman, that 3.01.189
as i for praise alone now seek to spill | the 4.01. 34
where nothing wants that want itself doth seek. 4.03.233
how i would make him fawn, and beg, and seek, 5.02. 62
our states are forfeit, seek not to undo us. 5.02.425
rest, | but seek the weary beds of people sick. 5.02.822
to seek new friends and /stranger /companies. MND 1.01.219
i must go seek some dewdrops here, | and hang a 2.01. 14
thou shalt fly him and he shall seek thy love. 2.01.246
thou some of it, and seek through this grove: 2.01.259
thou seest these lovers seek a place to fight; 3.02.354
i have a venturous fairy that shall seek | the 4.01. 35
you shall seek all day ere you find them, and MV 1.01.117 P
the four strangers seek for you, madam, to take 1.02.123 P
i have sent twenty out to seek for you. 2.06. 66
we have been up and down to seek him. 3.01. 76 P
falls to you, | be content, and seek no new. 3.02.134
as seek to soften that — than which what's 4.01. 79
attempts | he seek the life of any citizen, 4.01.351
no, let my father seek another heir. AYL 1.03. 99
and do not seek to take your change upon you, 1.03.102
to seek my uncle in the forest of arden. 1.03.107
at seventeen years many their fortunes seek, 2.03. 73
and i'll go seek the duke, his banket is 2.05. 62 P
go seek him, tell him i would speak with him. 2.07. 7
i should not seek an absent argument | of my 3.01. 3
seek him with candle; 3.01. 6
no more | to seek a living in our territory. 3.01. 8
do lack a hind, | let him seek out rosalind. 3.02.102
marry, to say she came to seek you there. 4.01.171 P
to seek their fortunes farther than at home, SHR 1.02. 51
the gain i seek is, quiet /in the match. 2.01.330
or seek for rule, supremacy, and sway, | when 5.02.163
find what you seek, | that fame may cry you loud AWW 2.01. 16
with true observance seek to eke out that 2.05. 74
seek these suitors. 5.03.151
of) | that he did seek the love of fair olivia. TN 1.02. 34
go thou and seek the crowner, and let him sit o' 1.05.134 P
seek him out, and play the tune the while. 2.04. 14
that he did range the town to seek me out. 4.03. 7
though you would seek t' unsphere the stars with WT 1.02. 48
if you would seek us, | we are yours i' th' 1.02.177
which if you seek to prove, | i dare not stand 1.02.443
the bug which you would fright me with, i seek. 3.02. 92
i'll not seek far | (for him, i partly know his 5.03.141
is it sir robert's son that you seek so? JN 1.01.226
to seek the beauteous eye of heaven to garnish, 4.02. 15
do not seek to stuff | my head with more ill 4.02.133
more, going to seek the grave | of arthur, whom 4.02.164
i will seek them out. 4.02.169
what, shall they seek the lion in his den, | and 5.01. 57
should seek a plaster by contemn'd revolt, | and 5.02. 13
to seek sweet safety out | in vaults and prisons 5.02.142
seek out king john and fall before his feet; 5.04. 13
straight let us seek, or straight we shall be 5.07. 79
to seek out sorrow that dwells every where. R2 1.02. 72
since thou dost seek to kill my name in me, | i 2.01. 86
seek you to seize and gripe into your hands 2.01.189
sing, | yet seek no shelter to avoid the storm; 2.01.264
and i am come to seek that name in england, 2.03. 71
up to the top of the hill, i'll go seek him. 1H4 2.02. 9 P
and in conclusion drove us to seek out | this 4.03.102
what honor dost thou seek | upon my head? 5.03. 2
boys | seek percy and thyself about the field, 5.04. 32
there, | or it will seek me in another place, 2H4 2.03. 49
go seek him out. 4.05. 59
policy | seek to divert the english purposes. H5 2.pr. 15
touching our person seek we no revenge, | but we 2.02.174
i must leave them, and seek some better service. 3.02. 51 P
back, | and tell thy king i do not seek him now, 3.06.140
we would not seek a battle as we are, | nor, as 3.06.164
ay, or more than we should seek after; 4.01.130 P
absence, | seek through your camp to find you. 4.01.286
pray thee go seek him, and bring him to my tent. 4.07.167 P
or how haps it i seek not to advance | or raise 1H6 3.01. 31
powers, | and seek how we may prejudice the foe. 3.03. 91
and not to seek a queen to make him rich: 5.05. 52
for that's the golden mark i seek to hit. 2H6 1.01.243
'tis that they seek; 2.02. 75
snar'd, | nor never seek prevention of thy foes. 2.04. 57
do seek subversion of thy harmless life? 3.01.208
did seem to say, "seek not a scorpion's nest, 3.02. 86
whom have i injur'd that ye seek my death? 4.07.101
i seek not to wax great by others' /waning, | or 4.10. 20
and seek for sorrow with thy spectacles? 5.01.165
seek thee out some other chase, | for i myself 5.02. 14
in cruelty will i seek out my fame. 5.02. 60
unless he seek to thrust you out perforce. 3H6 1.01. 34
they seek revenge, and therefore will not yield. 1.01.190
to seek to put me down and reign thyself. 1.01.200
more, | but that i seek occasion how to rise, 1.02. 45
flies through these wounds to seek out thee. 1.04.178
why, therefore warwick came to seek you out, 2.01.166
misery, | but seek revenge on edward's mockery. 3.03.265
too, | unless they seek for hatred at my hands; 4.01. 80
now, montague, sit fast, i seek for thee, | that 5.02. 3
but cheerly seek how to redress their harms. 5.04. 2
and seek their ruin that usurp'd our right? 5.06. 73
and never seek for aid out of himself. H8 1.02.114
if your business | seek me out, and that way i 3.01. 38
seek the king! 3.02.414
men's prayers then would seek you, not their 5.02.118
let not virtue seek | remuneration for the thing TRO 3.03.169
he merits well to have her that doth seek her, 4.01. 56
half hector comes to seek | this blended knight, 4.05. 85
i'll seek them. 5.04. 35 P
till when, go seek thy fortune. 5.06. 19
strike, fellows, strike, this is the man i seek. 5.08. 10
till then i'll sweat and seek about for eases, 5.10. 55
pleas'd to let him seek danger where he was like COR 1.03. 12 P
i wish i had a cause to seek him there, | to 3.01. 19
send | o'er the vast world to seek a single man, 4.01. 42
grace to both parts | than seek the end of one, 5.03.122
now will i hence to seek my lovely moor, | and TIT 2.03.190
thou shalt not stir one foot to seek a foe. ROM 1.01. 80
go, girl, seek happy nights to happy days. 1.03.105
to seek him here that means not to be found. 2.01. 42
search, seek, and know how this foul murder 5.03.198
and seek to thrive | by that which has undone TIM 4.03.210
why dost thou seek me out? 4.03.236
nay, let's seek him: 5.01. 40
seek not my name: 5.04. 71
that you would have me seek into myself | for JC 1.02. 64
and he's gone | to seek you at your house. 1.03.150
seek none, conspiracy! 2.01. 81
that's all i seek, | and am, moreover, suitor 3.01.226
seek! 3.02.204 P
away then, come, seek the conspirators. 3.02.232
'tis better that the enemy seek us; 4.03.199
seek him, titinius, whilst i go to meet | the 5.03. 73
and i will seek for pindarus the while. 5.03. 79
seek to hide themselves | in drops of sorrow. MAC 1.04. 34
seek to know no more. 4.01.103
let us seek out some desolate shade, and there 4.03. 1
lids | seek for thy noble father in the dust. HAM 1.02. 71
i will go seek the king. 2.01. 98
you go to seek the lord hamlet, there he is. 2.02.220 P
go seek him out, speak fair, and bring the body 4.01. 36
i have sent to seek him, and to find the body. 4.03. 1
not there, seek him i' th' other place yourself. 4.03. 34 P
go seek him there. 4.03. 38 P
and calves which seek out assurance in that. 5.01.116 P
seek it out. 5.02.312
why so earnestly seek you to put up that letter? LR 1.02. 28
go, sirrah, seek him; 1.02. 77 P
edmund, seek him out; 1.02. 97 P
i will seek him, sir, presently; 1.02.101 P
and potential spirits | to make thee seek it." 2.01. 77
what, did my father's godson seek your life? 2.01. 91
i will go seek the king. 3.01. 50
prithee go in thyself, seek thine own ease. 3.04. 23
who's there? what is't you seek? 3.04.127
you, | yet have i ventured to come seek you out, 3.04.152
his daughters seek his death. 3.04.163
evil disposition made him seek his death; 3.05. 6 P
seek out where thy father is, that he may be 3.05. 18 P
seek out the traitor gloucester. 3.07. 3 P
go seek the traitor gloucester, | pinion him 3.07. 22
seek, seek for him, | lest his ungovern'd rage 4.04. 18
seek, seek for him, | lest his ungovern'd rage 4.04. 18
seek him out | upon the english party. 4.06.249
here comes another troop to seek for you. OTH 1.02. 54
seek thou rather to be hang'd in compassing thy 1.03.359 P
seek him, bid him come hither. 3.04. 18 P
i will go seek him. 3.04.165
suit | and seek to effect it to my uttermost. 3.04.167
assure yourself i will seek satisfaction of you. 4.02.199 P
i have been to seek you. 5.01. 81
seek him, and bring him hither. where's alexas? ANT 1.02. 85
nay, pray you, seek no color for your going, 1.03. 32
i will seek | some way to leave him. 3.13.199
no, i will go seek | some ditch wherein to die; 4.06. 36
of caesar seek your honor, with your safety. 4.15. 46
but if you seek | to lay on me a cruelty, by 5.02.128
to seek through the regions of the earth | for CYM 1.01. 20
if you seek | for further satisfying, under her 2.04.133
honor, | which he to seek of me again, perforce, 3.01. 71
if you seek us afterwards in other terms, you 3.01. 78 P
a pain that only seems to seek out danger | i' 3.03. 50
would seek us through | and put us to our answer 4.02.160
nor seek for danger | where there's no profit. 4.02.162
to seek her on the mountains near to milford, 5.05.281
thither frame | to seek her as a bedfellow, | in PER 1.ch. 33
if in the world he live, we'll seek him out; 2.04. 29
o, seek not to entrap me, gracious lord, | a 2.05. 45
not o'erboard thrown me | for to seek my mother! 4.02. 67
with his wicked wife, | did seek to murther me; 5.01.172
no surfeits seek us; TNK 2.02. 86
take manhood to her, | and seek to ravish me. 2.02.259
what made you seek this place, sir? 2.05. 25
which will seek of me | some news from earth, 3.01. 79
and i'll go seek him through the world that is 3.04. 23
by night | that seek out silent hanging. 3.05.127
we seek not | thy breath of mercy, theseus. 3.06.157
thy brave soul seek elysium! 5.04. 95
although we grant you get the thing you seek? STM II.C 69
doubt, but mercy may be found if you so seek it. II.C 147
before i know myself, seek not to know me, | no VEN 525
"what win i if i gain the thing i seek? LUC 211
who seek to stain the ocean of thy blood. 655
being so bad, such numbers seek for thee? 896
mad, | himself himself seek every hour to kill! 998
and seek in vain | some happy mean to end a 1044
yet for the self-same purpose seek a knife; 1047
when what i seek (my weary travel's end) | doth SON 50. 2
why should poor beauty indirectly seek | roses 67. 7
and therefore art enforc'd to seek anew | some 82. 7
if thou dost seek to have what thou dost hide, 142.13

SEEKING 23 FR 0.0026 REL FR 20 V 3 P

i seek to die, | and, seeking death, find life. MM 3.01. 43
light, seeking light, doth light of light LLL 1.01. 77
seeking sweet favors for this hateful fool, | i MND 4.01. 49
to live i' th' sun, | seeking the food he eats, AYL 2.05. 40
seeking the bubble reputation | even in the 2.07.152
i was seeking for a fool when i found you. 3.02.285 P
this comes with seeking you; TN 3.04.332
lords, i am hot with haste in seeking you. JN 4.03. 74
and they in seeking that | shall find their 2H6 2.02. 75
seeking a way, and straying from the way, | not 3H6 3.02.176
seeking for richmond in the throat of death. R3 5.04. 5
in seeking tales and informations | against this H8 5.02.145
i have been seeking you this hour, my lord. TRO 5.02.182
what's their seeking? COR 1.01.188
seeking means | to pluck away their power, as 3.03. 95
seeking to hide herself, as doth the deer | that TIT 3.01. 89
i see my cousin's ghost | seeking out romeo, ROM 4.03. 56
so i lose none | in seeking to augment it, but MAC 2.01. 27
seeking to give | losses their remedies." LR 2.02.169
there wants no diligence in seeking him, | and CYM 4.03. 20
to himself unknown, without seeking find, and be 5.04.139 P
to himself unknown, without seeking find, and be 5.05.436 P
seeking that beauteous roof to ruinate, | which SON 10. 7

/SEEKS 2 FR 0.0002 REL FR 2 V 0 P

and /seeks his praise more than he fears his TRO 1.03.267
life | /seeks to take off by treason's knife, PER 4.ch. 14

SEEKS 30 FR 0.0034 REL FR 25 V 5 P

and all the more it seeks to hide itself, | the TMP 3.01. 80
the shepherd seeks the sheep, and not the sheep TGV 1.01. 86 P
i seek my master, and my master seeks not me: 1.01. 88 P
water, | that in the ocean seeks another drop, ERR 1.02. 36
he seeks my life; MV 3.03. 21
our master and mistress seeks you. AYL 5.01. 60 P
and with saciety seeks to quench his thirst. SHR 1.01. 24
that seeks not to find that her search implies, AWW 1.03.216
that seeks to overthrow religion | because he is 1H6 1.03. 65
accurs'd be he that seeks to make them foes! 3H6 1.01.205
is this th' alliance that he seeks with france? 3.03.177
than the business | that seeks dispatch by day. H8 5.01. 16
but he seeks their hate with greater devotion COR 2.02. 18 P
the valiant paris seeks you for his love. ROM 1.03. 74
who seeks for better of thee, sauce his palate TIM 4.03. 24
and he whose pious breath seeks to convert you, 4.03.141
hellish pyrrhus | old grandsire priam seeks." HAM 2.02.464
when she willfully seeks her own salvation? 5.01. 2 P
that sir which serves and seeks for gain, | and LR 2.04. 78
presently be sought, | or else he seeks out us. ANT 2.02.159
who seeks, and will not take when once 'tis 2.07. 83
your best love draw to that point which seeks 3.04. 21
withdraw, | and meet the time as it seeks us. CYM 4.03. 33
your lady seeks my life, come you between, | and PER 4.01. 89
seeks all foul means | of boist'rous and rough TNK 5.04. 71
to fan and blow them dry again she seeks. VEN 52
a thousand ways he seeks | to mend the hurt that 477
she seeks to kindle with continual kissing. 606
but with a pure appeal seeks to the heart, LUC 293
know, | which he by dumb demeanor seeks to show; 474

SEEK'ST 6 FR 0.0006 REL FR 6 V 0 P

why seek'st thou then to cover with excuse ADO 4.01.174
why seek'st thou me? MND 3.02.189
why seek'st thou to possess me with these fears? JN 4.02.203
thou seek'st the greatness that will overwhelm 2H4 4.05. 97
but tell me whom thou seek'st. 1H6 4.07. 59
not | for such an end thou seek'st — as base as CYM 1.06.144

SEEK'T 1 FR 0.0001 REL FR 1 V 0 P

if none, | let him not seek't of us. H8 1.02.213

SEEL 4 FR 0.0004 REL FR 4 V 0 P

of feather'd cupid seel with wanton dullness OTH 1.03.269
such a seeming | to seel her father's eyes up, 3.03.210
the wise gods seel our eyes, | in our own filth ANT 3.13.112
i had rather seel my lips than to my peril 5.02.146

SEELING 1 FR 0.0001 REL FR 1 V 0 P

come, seeling night, | scarf up the tender eye MAC 3.02. 46

SEELY *(also silly)*

SEELY 4 FR 0.0004 REL FR 4 V 0 P

not be the last — like seely beggars | who, R2 5.05. 25
the heads of brocas and sir bennet seely, | two 5.06. 14
when, seely groom, god wot, it was defect | of LUC 1345
so | as seely jeering idiots are with kings, 1812

/SEEM 3 FR 0.0003 REL FR 3 V 0 P

/perfection /to /abuse | /to /seem /like /him; 2H4 2.03. 28
/of /hotspur's /name | /did /seem /defensible: 2.03. 38
/and /goodness /to /the /vild /seem /vild, LR 4.02. 38

SEEM 191 FR 0.0216 REL FR 159 V 32 P

the most mighty neptune | seem to besiege, and TMP 1.02.205
though this island seem to be desert — 2.01. 35 P
that our garments seem now as fresh as when we 2.01. 97 P
resolve you | (which to you shall seem probable) 5.01.249

deed, madam, i seem so. TGV 2.04. 9 P
em you that you are not? 2.04. 10 P
hat seem i that i am not? 2.04. 14 P
f her eye did seem to scorch me up like a WIV 1.03. 67 P
ould seem in me t' affect speech and discourse, MM 1.01. 4
miliar sin | with maids to seem the lapwing, 1.04. 32
ther you are ignorant, | or seem so /craftily; 2.04. 75
at we were all, as some would seem to be, 3.02. 38
ay seem as shy, as grave, as just, as absolute 5.01. 54
ut lest my liking might too sudden seem, | i ADO 1.01.314
ey seem to pity the lady. 2.03.222 P
must not seem proud; 2.03.229 P
ou seem to me as dian in her orb, | as chaste 4.01. 57
ean time let wonder seem familiar, | and to the 5.04. 70
ut i believe, although i seem so loath, | i am LLL 1.01.159
ise things seem foolish and rich things but 5.02.378
nd let the prologue seem to say we will do no MND 3.01. 17 P
ow can these things in me seem scorn to you, 3.02.126
e'll | seem to break loose — take on as you 3.02.258
hall seem a dream and fruitless vision, | and 3.02.371
very region near | seem all one mutual cry. 4.01.117
ese things seem small and undistinguishable, 4.01.187
yself the man i' th' moon do seem to be. 5.01.245
should seem then that dobbin's tail grows MV 2.02. 96 P
ou to break up this, it shall seem to signify. 2.04. 11 P
n the balls of mine, | seem they in motion? 3.02.118
ilt show more bright and seem more virtuous AYL 1.03. 81
e smart, | /not /to seem senseless of the bob; 2.07. 55
prey on nothing that doth seem as dead. 4.03.118
udy | to seem despiteful and ungentle to you. 5.02. 80
would seem strange unto him when he wak'd. SHR in.1. 43
hich seem to move and wanton with her breath, in.2. 52
m not litio, | nor a musician, as i seem to be, 4.02. 17
y tale, | i'll make him glad to seem vincentio, 4.02. 68
ou seem a sober ancient gentleman by your habit 5.01. 73 P
nd would seem | to have us make denial. AWW 1.02. 8
hall seem expedient on the now–born brief, 2.03.179
r my respects are better than they seem, | and 2.05. 66
buy his will, it would not seem too dear, 3.07. 27
r we must not seem to understand him, unless 4.01. 4 P
we seem to know, is to know straight our 4.01. 18 P
ou, interpreter, you must seem very politic. 4.01. 21 P
nly to seem to deserve well, and to beguile the 4.03.299 P
hough time seem so adverse and means unfit. 5.01. 26
hough i seem to know their remembrance again TN 2.01. 31 P
o adore thee so | that danger shall seem sport, 2.01. 48
hore soon | than love that would seem hid: 3.01.148
ot have, | wherein olivia may seem serviceable? 5.01.102
our young prince as we | do seem to be of ours? WT 1.02.165
will seem friendly, as thou hast advis'd me. 1.02.350
our evils, | than such as most seem yours. 2.03. 57
est know | (/who least will seem to do so) my 3.02. 33
pollo, a poor humble swain, | as i seem now. 4.04. 31
efore this ancient sir, whom, it should seem, 4.04.361
ell me (for you seem to be honest plain men) 4.04.793 P
muse your majesty doth seem so cold, | when JN 3.01.317
our vild intent must needs seem horrible. 4.01. 95
, makes it seem | like rivers of remorse and 4.03.109
he uglier seem the clouds that in it fly. R2 1.01. 42
hall i seem crestfallen in my father's sight? 1.01.188
ow he did seem to dive into their hearts | with 1.04. 25
veary lords | shall make their way seem short, 2.03. 17
nists | of vapors that did seem to strangle him. 1H4 1.02.203
r nothing can seem foul to those that win. 5.01. 8
nd my pension shall seem the more reasonable. 2H4 1.02.247 P
hat even our corn shall seem as light as chaff, 4.01.193
ook you, he must seem thus to the world. 5.05. 78 P
ow did this offer seem receiv'd, my lord? H5 1.01. 82
eem they grave and learned? 2.02.128
eem they religious? 2.02.130
uch and so finely bolted didst thou seem. 2.02.137
heir mouths when what they seem to threaten 2.04. 70
uick blood, spirited with wine, | seem frosty? 3.05. 22
or though he seem with forged quaint conceit 1H6 4.01.102
ut well forewarning wind | did seem to say, 2H6 3.02. 86
y, every joint should seem to curse and ban; 3.02.319
tis government that makes them seem divine, 3H6 1.04.132
ee, see, they join, embrace, and seem to kiss, 2.01. 29
nd, for the time shall not seem tedious, | i'll 3.01. 9
nore than i seem, and less than i was born to; 3.01. 56
nd now may seem as wise as virtuous | by spying 4.06. 27
hat | of whom you seem to have so tender care? 4.06. 66
nd seem a saint, when most i play the devil. R3 1.03.337
an make seem pleasing to her tender years? 4.04.342
noble troop of strangers, | for so they seem. H8 1.04. 54
he hard and soft, seem all affin'd and kin; TRO 1.03. 25
oaring typhon dropp'd, | would seem hyperboles. 1.03.161
ut when they would seem soldiers, they have 1.03.237
t should seem, fellow, thou hast not seen the 3.01. 37 P
hard to seem won; 3.02.117
hy stained name, | and they'll seem glorious. 5.02.180
which yet seem shut, we have but pinn'd with COR 1.04. 18
op of praises vouch'd, | would seem but modest; 1.09. 25
o seem to affect the malice and displeasure of 2.02. 21 P
nd this shall seem, as partly 'tis, their own, 2.03.262
e that you seem, truly your country's friend, 3.01.217
hat seem like prudent helps, are very poisonous 3.01.220
f it be honor in your wars to seem | the same 3.02. 46
et us seem humbler after it is done | than when 4.02. 4
o have | this true which they so seem to fear. 4.06.151
e would not seem to know me. 5.01. 8
f such a decay'd dotant as you seem to be? 5.02. 45 P
ell me not | wherein i seem unnatural; 5.03. 84
eceive my tears, and seem to weep with me, TIT 3.01. 42
or these two heads do seem to speak to me, 3.01.271
ay me, sad hours seem long. ROM 1.01.161
and it should seem by th' sum | your master's TIM 3.04. 30
with him as he made it seem in the trial of his 3.06. 6 P
our course will seem too bloody, caius cassius, JC 2.01.162
an act of rage, | and after seem to chide 'em. 2.01.177
how foolish do your fears seem now, calphurnia! 2.02.105
did this in caesar seem ambitious? 3.02. 90
their shadows seem | a canopy most fatal, under 5.01. 86
you seem to understand me, | by each at once her MAC 1.03. 43
and seem to fear | things that do sound so fair? 1.03. 51
which fate and metaphysical aid doth seem | to 1.05. 29
grooms withal, | for it must seem their guilt. 2.02. 54
black macbeth | will seem as pure as snow, and 4.03. 53
and yet seem cold, the time you may so hoodwink. 4.03. 72
action with her, to seem thus washing her hands. 5.01. 28 P
these indeed seem, | for they are actions that a HAM 1.02. 83
seem to me all the uses of this world! 1.02.134
that they may seem the taints of liberty, | the 2.01. 32
as it did seem to shatter all his bulk | and end 2.01. 92
though by your smiling you seem to say so. 2.02.310 P
and there did seem in him a kind of joy | to 3.01. 18
play upon me, you would seem to know my stops, 3.02.365 P
where every god did seem to set his seal | to 3.04. 61
even, | this sudden sending him away must seem 4.03. 8
which may to you, perhaps, seem much unsinow'd, 4.07. 10
it did always seem so to us; LR 1.01. 3 P
i do profess to be no less than i seem, to serve 1.04. 13 P
draw, seem to defend yourself; 2.01. 30
i pray you, father, being weak, seem so. 2.04.201
servants, who seem no less, | which are to 3.01. 23
seem | to see the things thou dost not. 4.06.171
wretched though i seem, | i can produce a 5.01. 42
that thinks men honest that but seem to be so, OTH 1.03.400
pleasure and action make the hours seem short. 2.03.379
stir hither, i shall seem to notify unto her. 3.01. 29 P
his bed shall seem a school, his board a shrift, 3.03. 24
men should be what they seem, | or those that be 3.03.126
those that be not, would they might seem none! 3.03.127
certain, men should be what they seem. 3.03.128
i'll seem the fool i am not. ANT 1.01. 42
his faults, in him, seem as the spots of heaven, 1.04. 12
all little jealousies, which now seem great, 2.02.131
whose wind did seem | to /glow the delicate 2.02.203
the least cause | for what you seem to fear. 3.02. 36
that antony may seem to spend his fury | upon 4.06. 9
our courtiers' | still seem as does the king's. CYM 1.01. 3
you do seem to know | something of me, or what 1.06. 93
so seem as if | you were inspir'd to do those 2.03. 49
how look i | that i should seem to lack humanity 3.02. 16
citizen a wanton as | to seem to die ere sick. 4.02. 9
that we the horrider may seem to those | which 4.02.331
of her departure and | dost seem so ignorant, 4.03. 11
how courtesy would seem to cover sin, | when PER 1.01.121
all viands that i eat do seem unsavory, 2.03. 31
the very principals did seem to rend, | and all 3.02. 16
fate, fair creature, | rare as you seem to be. 3.02.104
you must seem to do that fearfully which you 4.02.117 P
it would seem | like lies disdain'd in the 5.01.118
thy relation | to points that seem impossible, 5.01.124
any nymph, | that makes the stream seem flowers!
TNK 3.01. 9
the light may rather seem to steal in than be 4.03. 75 P
a summer's day will seem an hour but short, VEN 23
and i will wink, so shall the day seem night. 122
would in thy palm dissolve, or seem to melt. 144
incorporate then they seem, face grows to face. 540
that cedar tops and hills seem burnish'd gold. 858
her sight dazzling makes the wound seem three, 1064
this guilt would seem death–worthy in thy LUC 635
poor lucrece' cheeks unto her maid seem so | as 1217
truth may seem, but cannot be, | beauty brag, PHT 62
and in mine own love's strength seem to decay, SON 23. 7
which wit so poor as mine | may make seem bare, 26. 6
doth nightly make grief's length seem stronger. 28.14
find, | when swift extremity can seem but slow? 51. 6
o, how much more doth beauty beauteous seem | by 54. 1
o, lest your true love may seem false in this, 72. 9
and other strains of woe, which now seem woe, 90.13
compar'd with loss of thee will not seem so. 90.14
so love's face | may still seem love to me, 93. 3
i teach thee how | to make him seem long hence, 101.14
so suited, and they mourners seem | at such who, 127.10
shall will in others seem right gracious, | and 135. 7
/SEEM'D 4 FR 0.0004 REL FR 4 V 0 P
/their /weapons /only | /seem'd /on /our /side; 2H4 1.01.198
/it /seem'd /she /was /a /queen | /over /her LR 4.03. 13
/on /her /ripe /lip /seem'd /not /to /know 4.03. 20
/this /would /have /seem'd /a /period | /to 5.03.205
SEEM'D 51 FR 0.0057 REL FR 45 V 6 P
madness i ever yet beheld seem'd but tameness, WIV 4.02. 27 P
and it in you more dreadful would have seem'd MM 1.03. 33
you seem'd of late to make the law a tyrant, 2.04.114
in all outward behaviors seem'd ever to abhor. ADO 2.03. 97 P
and seem'd i ever otherwise to you? 4.01. 55
and what in us hath seem'd ridiculous — | as LLL 5.02.759
see, | seem'd athens as a paradise to me; MND 1.01.205
and seem'd to ask him sops as he was drinking. SHR 3.02.176
embassies, that they have seem'd to be together, WT 1.01. 29 P
they seem'd almost, with staring on one another, 5.02. 11 P
such manner that it seem'd sorrow wept to take 5.02. 45 P
that words seem'd buried in my sorrow's grave. R2 1.04. 15
that seem'd in eating him to hold him up, | are 3.04. 51
which his aspiring rider seem'd to know, | with 5.02. 9
seem'd it in contempt? 1H4 5.02. 50
so | he seem'd in running to devour the way, 2H4 1.01. 47
it seem'd in me | but as an honor snatch'd with 4.05.190
wildness, mortified in him, | seem'd to die too; H5 1.01. 27
thou to harry of england, though we seem'd dead, 3.06.119 P
in the hatching, | it seem'd, appear'd to rome. COR 1.02. 22
till at the last | i seem'd his follower, not 5.06. 38
and when the cross blue lightning seem'd to open JC 1.03. 50
impatience | which seem'd too much enkindled; 2.01.249
from that spring whence comfort seem'd to come MAC 1.02. 27
and what seem'd corporal melted, | as breath 1.03. 81
those of his chamber, as it seem'd, had done't. 2.03.101
he seem'd to find his way without his eyes, HAM 2.01. 95
of reverent priam, seem'd i' th' air to stick. 2.02.479
and when she seem'd to shake and fear your looks
OTH 3.03.207
which seem'd to tell them his remembrance lay ANT 1.05. 57
yet my mother seem'd | the dian of that time. CYM 2.05. 6
the sinful father | seem'd not to strike, but PER 1.02. 78
who seem'd my good protector, and, being here, 1.02. 82
trod thy ground, | a falser nev'r seem'd friend. TNK 3.06.142
that what was life | in him seem'd torture. 5.01.115
his head, | seem'd with strange art to hang. 5.04. 79
stole his blood and seem'd with him to bleed. VEN 1056
that nothing in him seem'd inordinate, | save LUC 94
as heaven (it seem'd) to kiss the turrets bow'd. 1372
many a dry drop seem'd a weeping tear, | shed 1375
in speech it seem'd his beard, all silver white, 1405
which seem'd to swallow up his sound advice, 1409
to jump up higher seem'd, to mock the mind. 1414
it seem'd they would debate with angry swords. 1421
so mild that patience seem'd to scorn his woes. 1505
a brow unbent, that seem'd to welcome woe, 1509
yet this abundant issue seem'd to me | but hope SON 97. 9
yet seem'd it winter still, and, you away, | as 98.13
though absence seem'd my flame to qualify! 109. 2
ink would have seem'd more black and damned here
LC 54
whose bare outbragg'd the web it seem'd to wear; 95
SEEMED 2 FR 0.0002 REL FR 2 V 0 P
the gods for murder seemed so content | to PER 5.03. 99
that through their light joy seemed to appear LUC 1434
SEEMERS 1 FR 0.0001 REL FR 1 V 0 P
if power change purpose, what our seemers be. MM 1.03. 54
SEEMEST 2 FR 0.0002 REL FR 1 V 1 P
thou picture of what thou seemest, and idol of TRO 5.01. 6 P
and thou seemest a /palace | for the crown'd PER 5.01.121
SEEMETH 12 FR 0.0013 REL FR 12 V 0 P
therefore to 's seemeth it a needful course, LLL 2.01. 25
so sensible | seemeth their conference, their 5.02.260
quoniam he seemeth in minority, | ergo i come 5.02.592
sun, | that every thing i look on seemeth green; SHR 4.05. 47
for sorrow ends not when it seemeth done. R2 1.02. 61
me seemeth then it is no policy, | respecting 2H6 3.01. 23
my lords, what to your wisdoms seemeth best, 3.01.195
me seemeth good that, with some little train, R3 2.02.120
as seemeth by his plight, of the revolt | the MAC 1.02. 2
so, | that every present sorrow seemeth chief, VEN 970
who is but drunken when she seemeth drown'd. 984
"how true a twain | seemeth this concordant one! PHT 46
SEEMING 63 FR 0.0071 REL FR 55 V 8 P
and tie the wiser souls | to thy false seeming! MM 2.04. 15
seeming, seeming! 2.04.150
seeming, seeming! 2.04.150
from our faults, as faults from seeming, free! 3.02. 39
and show'd him a seeming warrant for it; 4.02.151 P
seeming as burdened | with lesser weight, but ERR 1.01.107
there shall appear such seeming truth of hero's ADO 2.02. 48 P
out on thee seeming! 4.01. 56
like to a double cherry, seeming parted, | but MND 3.02.209
so, with two seeming bodies but one heart, | two 3.02.212
the seeming truth which cunning times put on MV 3.02.100
are, every one fault seeming monstrous till his AYL 3.02.355 P
yourself, than seeming the lover of any other. 3.02.383 P
times remov'd (bear your body more seeming, 5.04. 69 P
that seeming to be most which we indeed least SHR 5.02.175
ensconcing ourselves into seeming knowledge, AWW 2.03. 4 P
or stupefied | or seeming so in skill — cannot, WT 2.01.166
keep | seeming and savor all the winter long. 4.04. 75
disliken | the truth of your own seeming, that 4.04.653
on the way | the father of this seeming lady and 5.01.191
thou art essentially made, without seeming so. 1H4 2.04.493 P
this seeming brow of justice, did he win | the 4.03. 83
the seeming sufferances that you had borne, 5.01. 51
there is no seeming mercy in the king. 5.02. 34
grace | by seeming cold or careless of his will, 2H4 4.04. 29
you borrow not that face | of seeming sorrow, it 5.02. 29
who hath writ me down | after my seeming. 5.02.129
run o'er | in seeming to augment it wastes it? H8 1.01.145
sign your place and calling, in full seeming, 2.04.108
but sorrow that is couch'd in seeming gladness TRO 1.01. 39
such to–be–pitied and o'er–wrested seeming | he 1.03.157
now seeming sweet, convert to bitt'rest gall. ROM 1.05. 92
unseemly woman in a seeming man, | and 3.03.112
man, | and ill–beseeming beast in seeming both, 3.03.113
the will of my most seeming virtuous queen. HAM 1.05. 46
seeming to feel this blow, with flaming top 2.02.475
our judgments join | in censure of his seeming. 3.02. 87
if aught within that little seeming substance, LR 1.01.198
that under covert and convenient seeming | has 3.02. 56
and duty, | but seeming so, for my peculiar end; OTH 1.01. 60
of modern seeming do prefer against him. 1.03.109
beguile | the thing i am by seeming otherwise. 2.01.123
on the mere form of civil and humane seeming, 2.01.240 P
she that so young could give out such a seeming 3.03.209
but now he spake | (after long seeming dead) 5.02.328
at the helm | a seeming mermaid steers; ANT 2.02.209
and we punish it | seeming to bear it lightly. 4.14.138
sets him off, | more than a mortal seeming. CYM 1.06.171
all good seeming, | by thy revolt, o husband, 3.04. 54
not seeming | so worthy as thy birth. 4.02. 93
my heart, | that thought her like her seeming. 5.05. 65
this hath some seeming. 5.05.452
where ev'ry seeming good's | a certain evil; TNK 1.02. 39
arcite, by his seeming | should be a stout man, 4.02. 76
but of a tough soul, seeming | as great as any. 4.02.117
grave, | seeming to bury that posterity, | which VEN 758
all the neighbor caves, as seeming troubled, 830
lovers' hours are long, though seeming short. 842
devil, | he entertain'd a show so seeming just, LUC 1514
whose speechless song, being many, seeming one, SON 8.13
is strength'ned, though more weak in seeming, 102. 1
o, love's best habit is in seeming trust, | and 138.11
o, all that borrowed motion seeming owed, LC 327
SEEMINGLY 1 FR 0.0001 REL FR 1 V 0 P
her mother's plot | she, seemingly obedient, WIV 4.06. 33
SEEMLY 2 FR 0.0002 REL FR 2 V 0 P
wit | to make a seemly answer to such persons. H8 3.01.178
thee | is but the seemly raiment of my heart, SON 22. 6
/SEEMS 2 FR 0.0002 REL FR 2 V 0 P
/past /and /to /come /seems /best; 2H4 1.03.108
/light /and /portable /my /pain /seems /now, LR 3.06.108
SEEMS 132 FR 0.0149 REL FR 114 V 18 P
the sky, it seems, would pour down stinking TMP 1.02. 3
a space whose ev'ry cubit | seems to cry out, 2.01.258
it seems you lov'd not her, /to leave her token: TGV 4.04. 74
for the which his wife seems to me well–favor'd. WIV 2.02.273 P
qualify the laws | as to your soul seems good. MM 1.01. 66
so then it seems your most offenseful act | was 2.03. 26
in't, | which seems a little fouler than it is, 2.04.146
how seems he to be touch'd? 4.02.141 P
not impossible | that which but seems unlike; 5.01. 52
to make the truth appear where it seems hid, 5.01. 66
it seems hid, | and hide the false seems true. 5.01. 67
do with your injuries as seems you best, | in 5.01.256
it seems he hath great care to please his wife. ERR 2.01. 56

it seems thou want'st breaking, out upon thee, 3.01. 77
it seems his sleeps were hind'red by thy railing 5.01. 71
god, howsoever it seems not in him by some large ADO 2.03.197 P
it seems her affections have their full bent. 2.03.223 P
highly that to her | all matter else seems weak. 3.01. 54
where his codpiece seems as massy as his club? 3.03.137 P
but that, it seems, he little purposeth: LLL 2.01.141
it seems that you scorn me. MND 3.02.221
seems to me now | as the remembrance of an idle 4.01.166
parted eye, | when every thing seems double. 4.01.190
it seems to me | that yet we sleep, we dream. 4.01.193
gave me his countenance seems to take from me. AYL 1.01. 18 P
is so hard that it seems the length of seven 3.02.316 P
for he seems to have the quotidian of love upon 3.02.365 P
ay, and the time seems thirty unto me, | being SHR in.2. 114
thou, it seems, that calls for company to 4.01.102 P
holy seems the quarrel | upon your grace's part; AWW 3.01. 4
that so confidently seems to undertake this 3.06. 87 P
but that your daughter, ere she seems as won, 3.07. 31
all yet seems well, and if it end so meet, | the 5.03.333
he seems to have a foreknowledge of that too, TN 1.05.143 P
and she (mistaken) seems to dote on me. 2.02. 35
if this be so, as yet the glass seems true, | i 5.01.265
he something seems unsettled. WT 1.02.147
integrity, deceiv'd | in that which seems so. 1.02.241
of this present, as my tale | now seems to it. 4.01. 15
nothing she does, or seems, | but smacks of 4.04.157
how prettily th' young swain seems to wash | the 4.04.366
for she seems a mistress | to most that teach. 4.04.582
he seems to be the more noble in being 4.04.751 P
he seems to be of great authority. 4.04.800 P
whiles he was hast'ning (in the chase, it seems, 5.01.189
has not only his innocence (which seems much) to 5.02. 65 P
much wrinkled, nothing | so aged as this seems. 5.03. 29
the very life seems warm upon her lip. 5.03. 66
you came not of one mother then, it seems. JN 1.01. 58
it seems you know not then so much as we. 5.07. 81
in me it seems it will make wise men mad. R2 5.05. 63
it seems then that the tidings of this broil 1H4 1.01. 47
present want | seems more than we shall find it. 4.01. 45
seems to weep | over his /country's wrongs, and 4.03. 81
he seems indifferent; H5 1.01. 72
to weigh | the enemy more mighty than he seems, 2.04. 44
big mars seems bankrout in their beggar'd host, 4.02. 43
'fore the king | seems to prepare his way. 5.pr. 13
attire, | and every thing that seems unnatural. 5.02. 62
so seems this gorgeous beauty to mine eyes. 1H6 5.03. 64
what though i be enthrall'd, he seems a knight, 5.03.101
gazing on that which seems to dim thy sight? 2H6 1.02. 6
seems he a dove? 3.01. 75
such it seems | as may beseem a monarch like 3H6 3.03.121
where it seems best unto your royal self. R3 3.01. 63
that seems disgracious in the city's eye, | and 3.07.112
it seems the marriage with his brother's wife H8 2.02. 16
expense by th' hour | seems to flow from him! 3.02.109
it seems you are in haste. 5.01. 11
yet that which seems the wound to kill, | doth TRO 3.01.122
whose double bosoms seems to wear one heart, COR 4.04. 13
although it seems, | and so he thinks, and is no 4.07. 19
why then it seems some certain snatch or so TIT 2.01. 95
a very fatal place it seems to me. 2.03.202
she shall scant show well that now seems best. ROM 1.02. 99
it seems she hangs upon the cheek of night | as 1.05. 45
me, | but, as it seems, did violence on herself. 5.03.264
her weeping, | or a dog that seems a–sleeping, TIM 1.02. 67
it seems to me most strange that men should fear JC 2.02. 35
he look | that seems to speak things strange. MAC 1.02. 47
and of royal hope, | that he seems rapt withal; 1.03. 57
now o'er the one half world | nature seems dead, 2.01. 50
where violent sorrow seems | a modern ecstasy. 4.03.169
clatter, one of greatest note | seems bruited. 5.07. 22
it be, | why seems it so particular with thee? HAM 1.02. 75
seems, madam? 1.02. 76
nay, it is, i know not "seems." 1.02. 76
the earth, seems to me a sterile promontory; 2.02.299 P
each toy seems prologue to some great amiss, 4.05. 18
this seems a fair deserving, and must draw me LR 3.03. 23
most he should dislike seems pleasant to him; 4.02. 10
methinks he seems no bigger than his head. 4.06. 16
it seems not meet, nor wholesome to my place, OTH 1.01.145
is the man — this moor, whom now, it seems, 1.03. 71
the chidden billow seems to pelt the clouds, 2.01. 12
mane, | seems to cast water on the burning bear, 2.01. 14
and rather, as it seems to me now, keep'st from 4.02.176 P
and this, it seems, | roderigo meant t' have 5.02.315
me for what you make me do | seems much unequal. ANT 2.05.101
find the band that seems to tie their friendship 2.06.121 P
for he seems | proud and disdainful, harping on 3.13.141
one | an eminent monsieur that, it seems, much CYM 1.06. 65
a pain that only seems to seek out danger | i' 3.03. 50
th' world's volume | our britain seems as of it, 3.04.138
those clothes, | which, as it seems, make thee. 4.02. 83
for it seems | they crave to be demanded. 4.02.361
the time seems long, their blood thinks scorn 4.04. 53
though you, it seems, come from the fliers? 5.03. 2
whose arm seems far too short to hit me here. PER 1.02. 8
'tis time to fear when tyrants seems to kiss. 1.02. 79
he seems to be a stranger; 2.02. 42
to me he seems like diamond to glass. 2.03. 36
several clime | where our scenes seems to live. 4.04. 7
o'er, point by point, for yet he seems to dote, 5.01.225
for it seems | you have been noble towards her. 5.01.262
it seems to me they have no more sense of their TNK 2.01. 37 P
is grav'd, and seems to bury what it frowns on, 5.03. 46
she puts on outward strangeness, seems unkind: VEN 310
o hard–believing love, how strange it seems! 985
his face seems twain, each several limb is 1067
and most deceiving when it seems most just; 1156
who, therefore angry, seems to part in sunder, LUC 388
and seems to point her out where she sits 1087
another, smother'd, seems to pelt and swear, 1418
short time seems long in sorrow's sharp 1573
which seems to weep upon the tainted place, 1746
thine eye jove's lightning seems, thy voice his PP 5.11
to spite me now, each minute seems /a /moon, 14.27
play'd, | plays not at all, but seems afraid; 17.20
your eye i ey'd, | such seems your beauty still. SON 104. 3
blind, | seems seeing, but effectually is out; 113. 4
to be forbod the sweets that seems so good | for LC 164

SEEM'ST 7 FR 0.0008 REL FR 7 V 0 P

that in civility thou seem'st so empty? AYL 2.07. 93
why at our justice seem'st thou then to low'r? R2 1.03.235
thou art not what thou seem'st. 1H4 5.04.137
just opposite to what thou justly seem'st, | a ROM 3.02. 78
a better cause, | but now thou seem'st a coward. CYM 3.04. 73
thou art not what thou seem'st, and if the same, LUC 600
thou seem'st not what thou art, a god, a king; 601

/SEEN 3 FR 0.0003 REL FR 3 V 0 P

/as /flatteries, /when /they /are /seen /abus'd. LR 1.03. 20
/you /have /seen | /sunshine /and /rain /at 4.03. 17
/who, /having /seen /me /in /my /worst /estate, 5.03.210

SEEN 289 FR 0.0326 REL FR 232 V 57 P

shapes as he, | having seen but him and caliban. TMP 1.02.480
i have seen thee in her, and i do adore thee. 2.02.140
nor have i seen | more that i may call men than 3.01. 50
a jew would have wept to have seen our parting; TGV 2.03. 12 P
this love of theirs myself have often seen, 3.01. 24
what light is light, if silvia be not seen? 3.01.174
i have seen sackerson loose twenty times, and WIV 1.01.295 P
i have seen the time, with my long sword i would 2.01.227 P
threepence — your honors have seen such dishes; MM 2.01. 93 P
under your good correction, i have seen | when, 2.02. 10
angelo hath seen them both, and will discover 4.02.172 P
where i have seen corruption boil and bubble, 5.01.318
more, if any born at ephesus be seen | at any ERR 1.01. 16
hath any man seen him at the barber's? ADO 3.02. 43 P
but the barber's man hath been seen with him, 3.02. 46 P
show you enough, and when you have seen more, 3.02.121 P
so will you say when you have seen the sequel. 3.02.134 P
it is not seen enough, you should wear it in 3.04. 71 P
and not be seen to wink of all the day — | when LLL 1.01. 43
if any man be seen to talk with a woman within 1.01.129 P
i was seen with her in the manor–house, sitting 1.01.206 P
the merry days of desolation that i have seen, 1.02.160 P
o, what a scene of fool'ry have i seen, | of 4.03.161
she (an attending star) scarce seen a light. 4.03.227
a man of travel, that hath seen the world; 5.01.108 P
cutting a smaller hair than may be seen; 5.02.258
the face of an old roman coin, scarce seen. 5.02.613 P
i have seen the day of wrong through the little 5.02.723 P
when the false troyan under sail was seen, | by MND 1.01.174
double tongue, | thorny hedgehogs, be not seen, 2.02. 10
half his face must be seen through the lion's 3.01. 37 P
my oberon, what visions have i seen! 4.01. 76
the ear of man hath not seen, man's hand is not 4.01.212 P
where i have seen them shiver and look pale, 5.01. 95
that in a gondilo were seen together | lorenzo MV 2.08. 8
yet i have not seen | so likely an embassador of 2.09. 91
that have stood by and seen our wishes prosper, 3.02.187
my purpose was not to have seen you here, | but 3.02.227
you have seen cruel proof of this man's strength AYL 1.02.174 P
true is it that we have seen better days, | and 2.07.120
is not so keen, | because thou art not seen, 2.07.178
then, to have seen much, and to have nothing, is 4.01. 23 P
this seen, orlando did approach the man | and 4.03.119
we have not yet been seen in any house, | nor SHR 1.01.199
baptista as a schoolmaster | well seen in music, 1.02.134
would katherine had never seen him though! 3.02. 26
a son of mine, which long i have not seen. 4.05. 57
i have seen them in the church together, god 5.01. 41 P
'tis often seen | adoption strives with nature, AWW 1.03.144
most admirable! i have seen those wars. 2.01. 26
i have seen a medicine | that's able to breathe 2.01. 72
sir, i have seen you in the court of france. 5.01. 10
i have seen her wear it, and she reckon'd it 5.03. 90
your niece will not be seen, or if she be, it's TN 1.03.106 P
you have not seen such a thing as 'tis. 3.02. 80 P
a very devil, i have not seen such a firago. 3.04.274 P
i'd have seen him damn'd ere i'd have challeng'd 3.04.284 P
but when in other habits you are seen, 5.01.387
ha' not you seen, camillo | (but that's past WT 1.02.267
i have seen a lady's nose | that has been blue, 2.01. 14
i have drunk, and seen the spider. 2.01. 45
i have seen two such sights, by sea and by land! 3.03. 83 P
horseman's coat, it hath seen very hot service. 4.03. 68 P
methinks i play as i have seen them do | in 4.04.133
so must thy grave | give way to what's seen now! 5.01. 98
shrewdly ebb'd, | to say you have seen a better. 5.01.103
jewel of children, seen this hour, he had pair'd 5.01.116
then have you lost a sight which was to be seen, 5.02. 43 P
that i have seen inhabit in those cheeks? JN 4.02.107
my lord, they say five moons were seen to–night; 4.02.182
than had i seen the vaulty top of heaven 5.02. 52
on some apparent danger seen in him | aim'd at R2 1.01. 13
seen how his son's son should destroy his sons, 2.01.105
lord's departure weep not — more is not seen, 2.02. 25
rue, even for ruth, here shortly shall be seen, 3.04.106
that honorable day shall never be seen. 4.01. 91
hear, | although apparent guilt be seen in them, 4.01.124
which for some reasons i would not have seen. 5.02. 62
high sparks of honor in thee have i seen. 5.06. 29
ornament, | a virtue that was never seen in you. 1H4 3.01.124
by being seldom seen, i could not stir | but 3.02. 46
ne'er seen but wond'red at, and so my state, 3.02. 57
so when he had occasion to be seen, | he was but 3.02. 74
seen, but with such eyes | as, sick and blunted 3.02. 76
no eye hath seen such scarecrows. 4.02. 38 P
let it be seen to–morrow in the battle | which 4.03. 13
that which i would to god i had not seen, | but 2H4 1.01.106
in his true colors, and not ourselves be seen? 2.02.170 P
you have not seen a hulk better stuff'd in the 2.04. 64 P
we have seen the seven stars. 2.04.187 P
o, if this were seen, | the happiest youth, 3.01. 53
that thou hadst seen that that this knight and i 3.02.211 P
seen that that this knight and i have seen! 3.02.212 P
jesus, the days that we have seen! 3.02.219 P
which was never seen in such an assembly. ep 25 P
suppose that you have seen | the well–appointed H5 3.pr. 3
there seen, | heave him away upon your winged 5.pr. 7
i have seen you gleeking and galling at this 5.01. 73 P
i know thee well, though never seen before. 1H6 1.02. 67
i thought i should have seen some hercules, | a 2.03. 19
where false plantagenet dare not be seen. 2.04. 74
for i have seen our enemies' overthrow. 3.02.111
i fear we should have seen decipher'd there 4.01.184
and ruthless slaughters as are daily seen | by 5.04.161
spirit | (more than in women commonly is seen) 5.05. 71
oft have i seen the haughty cardinal, | more 2H6 1.01.185
well hath your highness seen into this duke; 3.01. 42
in ireland have i seen this stubborn cade 3.01.360
i have seen | him caper upright like a wild 3.01.364
oft have i seen a timely–parted ghost, | of ashy 3.02.161
friend, | and 'tis well seen he found an enemy. 3.02.185
were there a serpent seen, with forked tongue, 3.02.259
where death's approach is seen so terrible! 3.03. 6
for i have seen him whipt three market–days 4.02. 57 P
oft have i seen a hot o'erweening cur | run back 5.01.151
would i had died a maid | and never seen thee, 3H6 1.01.217
as i have seen a swan | with bootless labor swim 1.04. 19
and yet be seen to wear a woman's face? 1.04.140
who hath not seen them, even with those wings 2.02. 29
diamonds and indian stones, | nor to be seen. 3.01. 64
when clouds are seen, wise men put on their R3 2.03. 32
words shall serve | as well as i had seen, and 3.05. 63
when such ill dealing must be seen in thought. 3.06. 14
eighty odd years of sorrow have i seen, | and 4.01. 95
lest, being seen, thy brother, tender george, 5.03. 95
the sun will not be seen to–day, | the sky doth 5.03.282
being now seen possible enough, got credit, H8 1.01. 37
strange postures | we have seen him set himself. 3.02.119
a loyal breast, | for you have seen him open't. 3.02.201
there is seen | the baby figure of the giant TRO 1.03.344
fellow, thou hast not seen the lady cressid. 3.01. 37 P
have you seen my cousin? 3.02. 7 P
i would not for half troy have you seen here. 4.02. 41
i have, thou gallant troyan, seen thee oft, 4.05.183
ranks of greekish youth, and i have seen thee, 4.05.185
and i have seen thee pause and take thy breath, 4.05.192
this have i seen, | but this thy countenance, 4.05.194
i have seen the time. 4.05.210
that you may be abhorr'd | farther than seen, COR 1.04. 33
martius, and i have | before–time seen him thus. 1.06. 24
i have seen the dumb men throng to see him, and 2.01.262
battles thrice six | i have seen, and heard of; 2.03.129
come, try upon yourselves what you have seen me. 3.01.224
what you have seen him do, and heard him speak, 3.03. 77
i have seen thee stern, and thou hast oft beheld 4.01. 24
makes fear'd and talk'd of more than seen — 4.01. 31
those maims | of shame seen through thy country, 4.05. 87
had the monster seen those lily hands | tremble TIT 2.04. 44
had i but seen thy picture in this plight, | it 3.01.103
was ever seen | an emperor in rome thus 4.04. 1
which i have seen thee careful to observe, 5.01. 77
many a morning hath he there been seen, | with ROM 1.01.131
she hath not seen the change of fourteen years; 1.02. 9
i have seen the day | that i have worn a visor 1.05. 21
too early seen unknown, and known too late! 1.05.139
never was seen so black a day as this. 4.05. 53
yet put it out, for i would not be seen. 5.03. 2
i have not seen you long, how goes the world? TIM 1.01. 2
to show lord timon that mean eyes have seen 1.01. 93
is not my lord seen yet? 3.04. 9
master's fortunes, | "we have seen better days." 4.02. 27
what you are | make them best seen and known. 5.01. 69
it will be seen to–morrow. 5.01.186
fiery eyes | as we have seen him in the capitol, JC 1.02.187
i have seen tempests when the scolding winds 1.03. 5
and i have seen | th' ambitious ocean swell, and 1.03. 6
two or three of us have seen strange sights. 1.03.138
besides the things that we have heard and seen, 2.02. 15
recounts most horrid sights seen by the watch. 2.02. 16
when beggars die there are no comets seen; 2.02. 30
octavius, i have seen more days than you, | and 4.01. 18
for i have seen more years, i'm sure, than ye. 4.03.132
so foul and fair a day i have not seen. MAC 1.03. 38
as they had seen me with these hangman's hands. 2.02. 25
within the volume of which time i have seen 2.04. 2
my here–remain in england, | i have seen him do. 4.03.149
but who knows nothing, is once seen to smile; 4.03.167
the field, i have seen her rise from her bed, 5.01. 5 P
i have seen nothing. HAM 1.01. 22
touching this dreaded sight, twice seen of us; 1.01. 25
our story, | what we have two nights seen. 1.01. 33
let us impart what we have seen to–night | unto 1.01.169
foe in heaven | or ever i had seen that day, 1.02.183
it was, as i have seen it in his life, | a sable 1.02.240
never make known what you have seen to–night. 1.05.144
never to speak of this that you have seen, 1.05.153
having ever seen in the prenominate crimes | the 2.01. 43
when i had seen this hot love on the wing — 2.02.132
"but who, ah woe, had seen the mobled queen" — 2.02.502
who this had seen, with tongue in venom steep'd, 2.02.510
the spirit that i have seen | may be a /dev'l, 2.02.598
t' have seen what i have seen, see what i see! 3.01.161
t' have seen what i have seen, see what i see! 3.01.161
o, there be players that i have seen play — and 3.02. 29 P
it is a damned ghost that we have seen, | and my 3.02. 82
and oft 'tis seen the wicked prize itself | buys 3.03. 59
ah, mine own lord, what have i seen to–night! 4.01. 5
i have seen myself, and serv'd against, the 4.07. 83
'twill not be seen in him there, there the men 5.01.154 P
i do not fear it, i have seen you both; 5.02.262
we have seen the best of our time. LR 1.02.112 P
i have told you what i have seen and heard; 1.02.174 P
i have not seen him this two days. 1.04. 72 P
i have seen drunkards | do more than this in 2.01. 34
i have seen better faces in my time | than 2.02. 93
what hath been seen, | either in snuffs and 3.01. 25
full oft 'tis seen, | our means secure us, and 4.01. 19
lark so far | cannot be seen or heard. 4.06. 59
thou hast seen a farmer's dog bark at a beggar? 4.06.154 P
i have seen the day, with my good biting 5.03.277
of whom his eyes had seen the proof | at rhodes, OTH 1.01. 28
hath seen a grievous wrack and sufferance | on 2.01. 23
knavery's plain face is never seen till us'd. 2.01.312
much will be seen in that. 3.03.252
have you not sometimes seen a handkerchief 3.03.434
i have seen the cannon | when it hath blown his 3.04.134
her honor is an essence that's not seen; 4.01. 16
if i had said i had seen him do you wrong? 4.01. 24
in me to speak | what i have seen and known. 4.01.278

you have seen nothing then? 4.02. 1
yes, you have seen cassio and she together. 4.02. 3
i have seen her do't. 4.02. 23
i would you had never seen him! 4.03. 18
i have seen the day | that, with this little arm 5.02.261
you have seen and prov'd a fairer former fortune ANT 1.02. 33
i have seen her die twenty times upon far poorer 1.02.141 P
would i had never seen her! 1.02.152
peep forth, but 'tis as soon | taken as seen; 1.04. 54
i have seen thee fight, | when i have envied thy 2.06. 74
a huge sphere, and not to be seen to move in't, 2.07. 15 P
the man hath seen some majesty, and should know. 3.03. 42
hath he seen majesty? 3.03. 43
thou hast seen these signs, | they are black 4.14. 7
but i have seen small reflection of her wit. CYM 1.02. 31 P
believe it, sir, i have seen him in britain. 1.04. 1 P
i have seen him in france. 1.04. 11 P
if she went before others i have seen, as that 1.04. 73 P
but i have not seen the most precious diamond 1.04. 75 P
let it be granted you have seen all this (and 2.04. 92
we have seen nothing. 3.03. 39
not seen of late? 3.05. 52
old servant, | i have not seen these two days. 3.05. 55
honor untaught, | civility not seen from other; 4.02.179
time into a crutch, | than have seen this. 4.02.201
and but the backs of britains seen, all flying 5.03. 6
i have not seen him so pictur'd. 5.04.179 P
i have surely seen him; 5.05. 92
are but felt, and seen with mischief's eyes, PER 1.04. 8
tyre, | and seen the desolation of your streets; 1.04. 89
when — the which i hope shall ne'er be seen — 1.04.105
here have you seen a mighty king | his child, i 2.ch. 1
of her lips i may | melt, and no more be seen. 5.03. 43
in pericles, his queen and daughter, seen, 5.03. 87
when that shall be seen, i tender my consent. TNK 2.01. 14 P
i have not seen, | since hercules, a man of 2.05. 1
i have not seen so young a man so noble | (if he 2.05. 18
y'ave seen me use my sword | against th' advice 3.01. 59
i have seen you move in such a place, which well 3.01. 63
the sun has seen my folly. 3.04. 3
fitter for girls and schoolboys) will be seen, 3.06. 34
if you be seen, you perish instantly | for 3.06.113
speak, | you that have seen them, what they are. 4.02. 72
i have seen it approv'd, how many times i know 4.03. 96 P
lose the noblest sight | that ev'r was seen. 5.02.100
dance on the sands, and yet no footing seen. VEN 148
his eyes saw her eyes as they had not seen them, 357
shone like the moon in water seen by night. 492
but for thy piteous lips no more had seen. 504
till the wild waves will have him seen no more, 819
her eye seen in the tears, tears in her eye, 962
which seen, her eyes /as murd'red with the view, 1031
means to immure herself, and not be seen. 1194
this heraldry in lucrece' face was seen, LUC 64
that had narcissus seen her as she stood, 265
then had they seen the period of their ill! 380
distance and no space was seen | 'twixt this PHT 30
full many a glorious morning have i seen SON 33. 1
his beauty shall in these black lines be seen, 63.13
when i have seen by time's fell hand defaced 64. 1
when i have seen the hungry ocean gain 64. 5
when i have seen such interchange of state, | or 64. 9
in him those holy antique hours are seen, 68. 9
so are those errors that in thee are seen | to 96. 7
what freezings have i felt, what dark days seen! 97. 3
turn'd | in process of the seasons have i seen, 104. 6
have i not seen dwellers on form and favor 125. 5
i have seen roses damask'd, red and white, | but 130. 5
advice is often seen | by blunting us to make LC 160
"'among the many that mine eyes have seen, | not 190

SEEN'T 3 FR 0.0003 REL FR 2 V 1 P
as he had seen't or been an instrument | to vice WT 1.02.415
if all the world could have seen't, the woe had 5.02. 92 P
then would to /god that i had never seen't! OTH 3.04. 77

SEES 56 FR 0.0063 REL FR 44 V 12 P
my strong imagination sees a crown | dropping TMP 2.01.208
my sweet mistress | weeps when she sees me work, 3.01. 12
that not an eye that sees you but is a physician TGV 2.01. 40 P
when slender sees his time | to take her by the WIV 4.06. 36
that soul that sees thee without wonder; LLL 4.02.113
who sees the heavenly rosaline, | that, like a 4.03.217
dote | upon the next live creature that it sees. MND 2.01.172
she sees not hermia. 2.02.135
one sees more devils than vast hell can hold; 5.01. 9
sees helen's beauty in a brow of egypt. 5.01. 11
in both my eyes he doubly sees himself, | in MV 5.01.244
and out of you she sees herself more proper AYL 3.05. 55
when he stands where i am and sees you there. SHR 3.02. 40 P
when your lordship sees the bottom of /his AWW 3.06. 36 P
without thy beard and gown, he sees thee not. TN 4.02. 65 P
plainly as heaven sees earth and earth sees WT 1.02.315
as heaven sees earth and earth sees heaven, 1.02.315
may | be thereat gleaned, for all the sun sees, 4.04.489
that any thing he sees, which moves his liking, JN 2.01.512
he will the rather do it when he sees 5.07. 87
knees, | and never see day that the happy sees, R2 5.03. 94
if he fight longer than he sees reason, i'll 1H4 1.02.185 P
the shoulders, you care not who sees your back. 2.04.149 P
confutes me but eyes, and nobody sees me. 5.04.127 P
each battle sees the other's umber'd face. H5 4.pr. 9
therefore, when he sees reason of fears, as we 4.01.108 P
never sees horrid night, the child of hell; 4.01.271
his glass for love of any thing he sees there, 5.02.148 P
me, | when he sees me go back one foot or fly. 1H6 1.02. 21
no simple man that sees | this jarring discord 4.01.187
fresh, | and sees fast by a butcher with an axe, 2H6 3.02.189
and he nor sees nor hears us what we say. 3H6 2.06. 63
yet who/'s so bold but says he sees it not? R3 3.06. 12
clouds, | that sees into the bottom of my grief? ROM 3.05.197
a number of men eats timon, and he sees 'em not!
TIM 1.02. 40 P
for the eye sees not itself | but by reflection, JC 1.02. 52
but that he sees the romans are but sheep; 1.03.105
i see a cherub that sees them. HAM 4.03. 48 P
nothing almost sees miracles | but misery. LR 2.02.165
he's a mad yeoman that sees his son a gentleman 3.06. 13 P
perhaps he sees it not, or his good nature OTH 2.03.133
sees and knows more, much more, than he unfolds. 3.03.243
for wisdom sees those men | blush not in actions PER 1.01.134
because another | first sees the enemy, shall i TNK 2.02.194
her help she sees, but help she cannot get, VEN 93
he sees his love, and nothing else he sees, 287
he sees his love, and nothing else he sees, 287
he sees her coming, and begins to glow, | even 337
"who sees his true-love in her naked bed, 397
"in night," quoth she, "desire sees best of all. 720
who sees the lurking serpent steps aside; LUC 362
thus cavils she with every thing she sees: 1093
many she sees where cares have carved some, 1445
at last she sees a wretched image bound, | that 1501
that soul that sees the without wonder, | which PP 5. 9
the sun itself sees not till heaven clears. SON 148.12

SEESE *(also cheese)*

SEESE 2 FR 0.0002 REL FR 0 V 2 P
seese is not good to give putter; WIV 5.05.140 P
"seese" and "putter"! 5.05.142 P

SEEST 55 FR 0.0062 REL FR 42 V 13 P
what seest thou else | in the dark backward and TMP 1.02. 49
eye advance | and say what thou seest yond. 1.02.410
this gallant which thou seest | was in the wrack 1.02.414
seest thou here, | this is the mouth o' th' cell 4.01.215
seest | some rare noteworthy object in thy TGV 1.01. 12
thee, | because thou seest me dote upon my love. 2.04.173
what seest thou? 3.01.190 P
i pray thee, launce, and if thou seest my boy, 3.01.259
if thou seest her before me, commend me. WIV 1.04.157 P
thou seest, thou wicked varlet, now, what's come MM 2.01.190 P
but seest thou not what a deformed thief this ADO 3.03.124 P
seest thou not, i say, what a deformed thief 3.03.130 P
thou seest that all the grace that she hath left 4.01.171
thou viewest, beholdest, surveyest, or seest. LLL 1.01.244 P
what thou seest when thou dost wake, | do it for MND 2.02. 27
thou seest these lovers seek a place to fight; 3.02.354
seest thou this sweet sight? 4.01. 46
thou seest we are not all alone unhappy: AYL 2.07.136
thou seest how diligent i am | to dress thy meat SHR 4.03. 39
for thou seest it will not /curl /by nature. TN 1.03. 98 P
so soon as ever thou seest him, draw, and, as 3.04.178 P
or else a fool | that seest a game play'd home, WT 1.02.248
mark and perform it — seest thou? 2.03.170
seest thou not the air of the court in these 4.04.731 P
and then all this thou seest is but a clod | and JN 5.07. 57
in that thou seest thy wretched brother die, R2 1.02. 27
thou seest i have more flesh than another man, 1H4 3.03.166 P
thou seest i am pacified still. 3.03.173 P
fears | thou seest with peril i have answered; 2H4 4.05.196
and thou seest that i no issue have, | and that 1H6 2.05. 94
what seest thou there? 2H6 1.02. 7
in my opinion yet thou seest not well. 2.01.104
o god, seest thou this, and bearest so long? 2.01.151
eleanor, the law, thou seest, hath judged thee; 2.03. 15
what seest thou in me, york? 5.02. 19
and, as thou seest, ourselves in heavy plight. 3H6 3.03. 37
thou seest what's pass'd, go fear thy king 3.03.226
o god that seest it, do not suffer it! R3 1.03.270
not my blood | wherein thou seest me mask'd; COR 1.08. 10
seest thou this letter? TIT 2.03. 46
this is dear mercy, and thou seest it not. ROM 3.03. 28
what e'er thou hearest or seest, stand all aloof 5.03. 26
that seest not thy loss in transformation! TIM 4.03.345 P
thou seest the world, volumnius, how it goes; JC 5.05. 22
thou seest the heavens, as troubled with man's MAC 2.04. 5
i prithee, when thou seest that act afoot, HAM 3.02. 78
seest thou this object, kent? LR 5.03.239
seest not? ANT 2.07. 91 P
seest thou, my good fellow? 4.04. 9
when thou seest him, | a little witness my CYM 3.04. 65
what seest thou in our looks? PER 1.02. 51
what seest thou in the ground? VEN 118
thou seest our mistress' ornaments are chaste." LUC 322
in me thou seest the twilight of such day | as SON 73. 5
in me thou seest the glowing of such fire | that 73. 9

SEE'T 23 FR 0.0026 REL FR 17 V 6 P
let me see't, let me see't, o, let me see't! WIV 3.03.136 P
let me see't, let me see't, o, let me see't! 3.03.137 P
let me see't, let me see't, o, let me see't! 3.03.137 P
well, we'll see't. SHR in.2. 142 P
come, tailor, let us see't. 4.03. 86
this pearl she gave me, i do feel't and see't, TN 4.03. 2
but i do see't, and feel't, | as you feel doing WT 2.01.152
his noble carelessness lets them plainly see't. COR 2.02. 15 P
why either were you ignorant to see't, | or, 2.03.174
o, pray let's see't. for the lord timon, sir? TIM 1.01. 13
let it go naked, men may see't the better. 5.01. 67
fine revolution, and we had the trick to see't. HAM 5.01. 91 P
then comes the time, who lives to see't, | that LR 3.02. 93
see't shalt thou never. 3.07. 67
this fortification, gentlemen, shall we see't? OTH 3.02. 5
make me to see't; 3.03.364
fetch't, let me see't. 3.04. 85
to see't mine eyes are blasted. ANT 3.10. 4
i would not see't. 4.14. 77
i'll never see't! 5.02.223
let's see't. CYM 3.05.100
if you deserve well, sir, i shall soon see't. TNK 2.05. 42
you'll see't done now for ever. 5.04. 25

SEETHE 1 FR 0.0001 REL FR 1 V 0 P
till the high fever seethe your blood to froth, TIM 4.03.430

SEETHES 1 FR 0.0001 REL FR 0 V 1 P
assault upon him, for my business seethes. TRO 3.01. 40 P

SEETHING 2 FR 0.0002 REL FR 2 V 0 P
lovers and madmen have such seething brains, MND 5.01. 4
and grew a seething bath, which yet men prove SON 153. 7

SEGREGATION 1 FR 0.0001 REL FR 1 V 0 P
a segregation of the turkish fleet: OTH 2.01. 10

SEIGNEUR *(also signieur)*

SEIGNEUR 9 FR 0.0010 REL FR 1 V 8 P
o seigneur dieu, je m'en oublie d' elbow. H5 3.04. 31 P
o seigneur dieu! 3.04. 52 P
o seigneur dieu! 4.04. 6 P
et tres /distingue seigneur d'angleterre. 4.04. 57 P
valorous, and thrice-worthy seigneur of england. 4.04. 62 P
o seigneur! le jour est perdu, tout est perdu! 4.05. 2
laissez, mon seigneur, laissez, laissez! 5.02.253 P
en baisant la main d'une (notre seigneur!) 5.02.255 P
je vous supplie, mon tres puissant seigneur. 5.02.256 P

SEIGNEURS 1 FR 0.0001 REL FR 0 V 1 P
ces mots devant les seigneurs de france pour H5 3.04. 55 P

SEIZ'D 17 FR 0.0019 REL FR 16 V 1 P
say this were death | that now hath seiz'd them, TMP 2.01.261
brain him, | having first seiz'd his books; 3.02. 89
at length, another ship had seiz'd on us, | and, ERR 1.01.112
hath something seiz'd | his wish'd ability, he WT 5.01.142
john hath seiz'd arthur, and it cannot be | that JN 3.04.131
bullingbrook | hath seiz'd the wasteful king. R2 3.04. 55
seiz'd on the realm, depos'd the rightful king, 2H6 2.02. 24
and seiz'd upon their towns and provinces. 3H6 1.01.109
his land then seiz'd on by the conqueror. 3.02. 3
our treasure seiz'd, our soldiers put to flight, 3.03. 36
the tiger now hath seiz'd the gentle hind; R3 2.04. 50
a horse, thou wouldst be seiz'd by the leopard; TIM 4.03.339 P
all /those his lands | which he stood seiz'd of, HAM 1.01. 89
sleep hath seiz'd me wholly. CYM 2.02. 7
haply despair hath seiz'd her; 3.05. 60
pirate valdes, | and they have seiz'd marina. PER 4.01. 97
the wolf hath seiz'd his prey, the poor lamb LUC 677

/SEIZE 1 FR 0.0001 REL FR 1 V 0 P
/here, /cousin, /seize /the /crown; R2 4.01.181

SEIZE 33 FR 0.0037 REL FR 32 V 1 P
which is the lady i must seize upon? ADO 5.04. 53
doth contrive | shall seize one half his goods; MV 4.01.353
worth seizure do we seize into our hands, | till AYL 3.01. 10
eyes on every stale, | seize thee that list. SHR 3.01. 91
(and by good testimony) or i'll seize thy life, WT 2.03.137
towards our assistance we do seize to us | the R2 2.01.160
seek you to seize and gripe into your hands 2.01.189
if you do wrongfully seize herford's rights, 2.01.201
you will, we seize into our hands | his plate, 2.01.209
seize it, if thou dar'st. 4.01. 48
let vultures vile seize on his lungs also! 2H4 5.03.139
lord of the soil come to seize me for a stray, 2H6 4.10. 25 P
let's seize upon him. 3H6 3.01. 23
beat down edward's guard, | and seize himself; 4.02. 24
seize on the shame-fac'd henry, bear him hence, 4.08. 52
seize on him, furies, take him unto torment!" R3 1.04. 57
seize him, aediles! COR 3.01.182
aediles, seize him! 3.01.213
rape call you it, my lord, to seize my own, | my TIT 1.01.405
shall seize this prey out of his father's hands. 4.02. 96
they may seize | on the white wonder of dear ROM 3.03. 35
hid in an auger-hole, may rush and seize us? MAC 2.03.122
seize upon fife, give to th' edge o' th' sword 4.01.151
thee and thy virtues here i seize upon, | be it LR 1.01.252
you we first seize on. 2.01.116
devils themselves | should fear to seize thee; OTH 4.02. 37
and seize upon the fortunes of the moor, | for 5.02.366
her head's declin'd, and death will seize her, ANT 3.11. 47
yet death | will seize the doctor too. CYM 5.05. 30
face, | seize with thine eagle's talents. PER 4.03. 48
joy seize on you again! TNK 1.05. 12
can thy right hand seize love upon thy left? VEN 158
sits sin, to seize the souls that wander by him. LUC 882

SEIZED 2 FR 0.0002 REL FR 2 V 0 P
had i been seized by a hungry lion, | i would TGV 5.04. 33
quoth she, "he seized on my lips," | and with PP 11. 9

SEIZES 2 FR 0.0002 REL FR 1 V 1 P
open made to justice, | that justice seizes. MM 2.01. 22
upon his own appeal, seizes him. ANT 3.05. 11 P

SEIZETH 2 FR 0.0002 REL FR 2 V 0 P
this prince in justice seizeth but his own. TIT 1.01.281
with this she seizeth on his sweating palm, VEN 25

SEIZING 1 FR 0.0001 REL FR 1 V 0 P
age, | you break not sanctuary in seizing him. R3 3.01. 47

SEIZURE 4 FR 0.0004 REL FR 4 V 0 P
worth seizure do we seize into our hands, | till AYL 3.01. 10
unyoke this seizure and this kind regreet? JN 3.01.241
to whose soft seizure | the cygnet's down is TRO 1.01. 57
and with her lips on his did act the seizure: PP 11.10

SELD 2 FR 0.0002 REL FR 2 V 0 P
as seld i have the chance — i would desire | my TRO 4.05.150
and as goods lost are seld or never found, | as PP 13. 7

SELDOM 35 FR 0.0039 REL FR 28 V 7 P
it seldom visits sorrow; TMP 2.01.195
worship that her husband is seldom from home, WIV 2.02.101 P
seldom when | the steeled jailer is the friend MM 4.02. 86
if my observation (which very seldom lies), | by LLL 2.01.228
but such traitors | his majesty seldom fears. AWW 2.01. 97
the merit of service is seldom attributed to the 3.06. 61 P
that in such intelligence hath seldom fail'd. 4.05. 83 P
that he is seldom from the house of a most WT 4.02. 37 P
now, good now, | say so but seldom. 5.01. 20
words are scarce, they are seldom spent in vain, R2 2.01. 7
but when they seldom come, they wish'd for come,
1H4 1.02.206
by being seldom seen, i could not stir | but 3.02. 46
seldom but sumptuous, show'd like a feast, | and 3.02. 58
when it shines seldom in admiring eyes; 3.02. 80
'tis seldom when the bee doth leave her comb 2H4 4.04. 79
for things are often spoke and seldom meant; 2H6 3.01.268
men's flesh preserv'd so whole do seldom win. 3.01.301
a crown it is that seldom kings enjoy. 3H6 3.01. 65
yet hasty marriage seldom proveth well. 4.01. 18
ill news, by'r lady — seldom comes the better. R3 2.03. 4
knows, | seldom or never jumpeth with the heart. 3.01. 11
thou art a soldier, therefore seldom rich, | it TIM 1.02.222
i did endure | not seldom, nor no slight checks, 2.02.140
blood is cak'd, 'tis cold, it seldom flows; 2.02.216
body, which doth seldom | play the recanter, 5.01.145
seldom he smiles, and smiles in such a sort | as JC 1.02.205
that do die of it do seldom or never recover. ANT 5.02.247 P
where when men been, there's seldom ease, | for PER 2.ch. 28
seldom but that pity begets you a good opinion, 4.02.120 P
it be for great ones, yet they seldom come: TNK 2.01. 3 P
for unstain'd thoughts do seldom dream on evil; LUC 87
men's faults do seldom to themselves appear, 633
though woe be heavy, yet it seldom sleeps, | and 1574
for blunting the fine point of seldom pleasure. SON 52. 4
since, seldom coming, in the long year set, 52. 6

SELD-SHOWN 1 FR 0.0001 REL FR 1 V 0 P
seld-shown flamens | do press among the popular COR 2.01.213

SELECT 2 FR 0.0002 REL FR 2 V 0 P
(though thanks to all) must i select from all; COR 1.06. 81
/are of a most select and generous chief in that HAM 1.03. 74

SELEUCUS 4 FR 0.0004 REL FR 4 V 0 P

where's seleucus? ANT 5.02.140
speak the truth, seleucus. 5.02.144
the ingratitude of this seleucus does | even 5.02.153
forbear, seleucus. 5.02.175
/SELF 1 FR 0.0001 REL FR 1 V 0 P
/else /one /self /mate /and /make /could /not LR 4.03. 34
SELF 79 FR 0.0089 REL FR 75 V 4 P
purpose hurried thence | me and thy crying self. TMP 1.02.132
banish'd from her | is self from self, a deadly TGV 3.01.173
banish'd from her | is self from self, a deadly 3.01.173
with them, upon her knees, her humble self, 3.01.228
for since the substance of your perfect self 4.02.123
for my poor self, | i am combined by a sacred MM 4.03.143
and that self chain about his neck, | which he ERR 5.01. 10
turn'd over and over as my poor self in love. ADO 5.02. 35 P
your fair self should make | a yielding 'gainst LLL 2.01.150
the curate and your sweet self are good at such 5.01.114 P
shut | my woeful self up in a mourning house, 5.02.808
to shoot another arrow that self way | which you MV 1.01.148
that comes to hazard for my worthless self. 2.09. 18
swear by your double self, | and there's an oath 5.01.245
to dissever so | our great self and our credit, AWW 2.01.123
your mother was | when your sweet self was got. 4.02. 10
her sweet perfections with one self king! TN 1.01. 38
your precious self had then not cross'd the eyes WT 1.02. 79
your high self, | the gracious mark o' th' land, 4.04. 7
which is | your gracious self, embrace but my 4.04.523
and happily may your sweet self put on | the JN 5.07.101
that mettle, that self mould, that fashioned R2 1.02. 23
infusing him with self and vain conceit, | as if 3.02.166
that i have turn'd away my former self; 2H4 5.05. 58
that self bill is urg'd | which in th' eleventh H5 1.01. 1
of a naked blind boy in her naked seeing self? 5.02.298 P
in this self place where now we mean to stand. 3H6 3.01. 11
by circumstance /t' /accuse thy cursed self. R3 1.02. 80
outlive thy glory like my wretched self! 1.03.202
my other self, my counsel's consistory, | my 2.02.151
to brother, | blood to blood, self against self. 2.04. 63
to brother, | blood to blood, self against self. 2.04. 63
where it seems best unto your royal self. 3.01. 63
first, he commends him to your noble self. 3.02. 8
your gracious self to take on you the charge 3.07.131
take to your royal self | this proffer'd benefit 3.07.195
some life, | which action's self was tongue to. H8 1.01. 42
invited by your noble self, hath sent | one 2.02. 94
weeps to see him | so little of his great self. 3.02.336
his royal self in judgment comes to hear | the 5.02.155
i have a kind of self resides with you; TRO 3.02.148
but an unkind self, that itself will leave | to 3.02.149
tarquin's self he met, | and struck him on his COR 2.02. 94
of that self blood that first gave life to you, TIT 4.02.123
be found, | being one too many by my weary self, ROM 1.01.128
or, if thou wilt, swear by thy gracious self, 2.02.113
and his poor self, | a dedicated beggar to the TIM 4.02. 12
and make thine own self the conquest of thy fury 4.03.337 P
but, for my single self, | i had as lief not be JC 1.02. 94
which you thought had been | our innocent self? MAC 3.01. 78
by self and violent hands | took off her life; 5.09. 36
to thine own self be true, | and it must follow, HAM 1.03. 78
i am made of that self metal as my sister, | and LR 1.01. 69
and your noble self | i am sure is sent for. OTH 1.02. 92
the heaviest club, | subdue my worthiest self. ANT 4.12. 47
but that self hand | which writ his honor in the 5.01. 21
as i my poor self did exchange for you, | to CYM 1.01.119
with tomboys hir'd with that self exhibition 1.06.122
woman it pretty self) into a waggish courage, 3.04.157
from so fair a tree | as your fair self, doth PER 1.01.115
a roof | soon fall to ruin — your noble self, 2.04. 37
out together where death's self was lodg'd; TNK 1.03. 40
with self–same hand, self reasons, and self STM II.C 85
self–same hand, self reasons, and self right, II.C 85
"mine enemy was strong, my poor self weak | (and LUC 1646
let my unsounded self, suppos'd a fool, | now 1819
thus appalled, | that the self was not the same; PHT 38
thyself thy foe, to thy sweet self too cruel. SON 1. 8
thou of thyself thy sweet self dost deceive, 4.10
make thee another self for love of me, | that 10.13
what can mine own praise to mine own self bring? 39. 3
if thou this self deceivest | by willful taste 40. 7
self so self–loving were iniquity. 62.12
death's second self, that seals up all in rest. 73. 8
such cherubins as your sweet self resemble, 114. 6
thy lovers withering as thy sweet self grow'st; 126. 4
and my next self thou harder hast engrossed: 133. 6
lest guilty of my faults thy sweet self prove: 151. 4
my woeful self, that did in freedom stand | and LC 143
SELF–ABUSE 1 FR 0.0001 REL FR 1 V 0 P
my strange and self–abuse | is the initiate fear MAC 3.04.141
SELF–ADMISSION 1 FR 0.0001 REL FR 1 V 0 P
any, | in will peculiar and in self–admission. TRO 2.03.166
SELF–AFFAIRS 1 FR 0.0001 REL FR 1 V 0 P
but, being over–full of self–affairs, | my mind MND 1.01.113
SELF–AFFECTED 1 FR 0.0001 REL FR 1 V 0 P
or strange, or self–affected! TRO 2.03.239
SELF–AFFRIGHTED 1 FR 0.0001 REL FR 1 V 0 P
day, | but, self–affrighted, tremble at his sin. R2 3.02. 53
SELF–APPLIED 1 FR 0.0001 REL FR 1 V 0 P
myself, if i had self–applied | love to myself, LC 76
SELF–ASSUMPTION 1 FR 0.0001 REL FR 1 V 0 P
in self–assumption greater | than in the note of TRO 2.03.124
SELF–BORN 1 FR 0.0001 REL FR 1 V 0 P
law, and in one self–born hour | to plant and WT 4.01. 8
SELF–BORNE 1 FR 0.0001 REL FR 1 V 0 P
fright our native peace with self–borne arms. R2 2.03. 80
SELF–BOUNTY 1 FR 0.0001 REL FR 1 V 0 P
noble nature, | out of self–bounty, be abus'd; OTH 3.03.200
SELF–BREATH 1 FR 0.0001 REL FR 1 V 0 P
but with a pride | that quarrels at self–breath. TRO 2.03.172
SELF–CHARITY 1 FR 0.0001 REL FR 1 V 0 P
unless self–charity be sometimes a vice, | and OTH 2.03.202
SELF–COMPARISONS 1 FR 0.0001 REL FR 1 V 0 P
proof, | confronted him with self–comparisons, MAC 1.02. 55
//SELF–COVER'D 1 FR 0.0001 REL FR 1 V 0 P
/thou /changed /and //self–cover'd /thing, /for LR 4.02. 62
SELF–DANGER 1 FR 0.0001 REL FR 1 V 0 P
must not yet be | but by self–danger, you should CYM 3.04.146
SELF–DOING 1 FR 0.0001 REL FR 1 V 0 P
belong | yourself to pardon of self–doing crime. SON 58.12
SELF DRAWING 1 FR 0.0001 REL FR 1 V 0 P
but spider–like | out of his self–drawing web, H8 1.01. 63
SELF–ENDEARED 1 FR 0.0001 REL FR 1 V 0 P
project of affection, | she is so self–endeared. ADO 3.01. 56
SELF–EXAMPLE 1 FR 0.0001 REL FR 1 V 0 P
hide, | by self–example mayst thou be denied. SON 142.14
SELF–EXPLICATION 1 FR 0.0001 REL FR 1 V 0 P
a thing perplex'd | beyond self–explication. CYM 3.04. 8
SELF–FIGUR'D 1 FR 0.0001 REL FR 1 V 0 P
but brats and beggary) in self–figur'd knot, CYM 2.03.119
SELF–GLORIOUS 1 FR 0.0001 REL FR 1 V 0 P
free from vainness and self–glorious pride; H5 5.pr. 20
SELF–GRACIOUS 1 FR 0.0001 REL FR 0 V 1 P
his majesty, out of a self–gracious remembrance, AWW 4.05. 73 P
SELF–HARMING 1 FR 0.0001 REL FR 1 V 0 P
self–harming jealousy — fie, beat it hence! ERR 2.01.102
SELF–KILL'D 1 FR 0.0001 REL FR 1 V 0 P
with beauty's treasure ere it be self–kill'd. SON 6. 4
SELF–LOVE 8 FR 0.0009 REL FR 6 V 2 P
idle, made of self–love, which is the most AWW 1.01.144 P
o, you are sick of self–love, malvolio, and TN 1.05. 90 P
self–love, my liege, is not so vile a sin | as H5 2.04. 74
is truly dedicate to war | hath no self–love; 2H6 5.02. 38
self–love had never drown'd him in the flood. LUC 266
the tomb, | of his self–love, to stop posterity? SON 3. 8
sin of self–love possesseth all mine eye, | and 62. 1
mine own self–love quite contrary i read; 62.11
SELF–LOVING 3 FR 0.0003 REL FR 3 V 0 P
ambitious past all thinking, | self–loving — COR 4.06. 32
love–lacking vestals and self–loving nuns, VEN 752
self so self–loving were iniquity. SON 62.12
SELF–METTLE 1 FR 0.0001 REL FR 1 V 0 P
being allow'd his way, | self–mettle tires him. H8 1.01.134
SELF–MISUS'D 1 FR 0.0001 REL FR 1 V 0 P
thyself is self–misus'd. R3 4.04.374
SELF–NEGLECTING 1 FR 0.0001 REL FR 1 V 0 P
is not so vile a sin | as self–neglecting. H5 2.04. 75
SELF–OFFENSES 1 FR 0.0001 REL FR 1 V 0 P
others paying | than by self–offenses weighing. MM 3.02.266
SELF–REPROVING 1 FR 0.0001 REL FR 1 V 0 P
he's full of alteration | and self–reproving — LR 5.01. 4
SELF'S 2 FR 0.0002 REL FR 2 V 0 P
am better than thy dear self's better part. ERR 2.02.123
it is thyself, mine own self's better part: 3.02. 61
SELF–SAME 28 FR 0.0031 REL FR 27 V 1 P
that bear in them one and the self–same tongue, MM 2.04.173
in self–same manner doth accuse my husband, 5.01.196
that very hour, and in the self–same inn, | a ERR 1.01. 53
sadness is one and the self–same thing, dear imp LLL 1.02. 4 P
i shot his fellow of the self–same flight | the MV 1.01.141
the self–same way with more advised watch | to 1.01.142
while i with self–same kindness welcome thine. SHR 5.02. 5
the self–same sun that shines upon his court WT 4.04.444
for self–same wind that i should speak withal 3H6 2.01. 82
like the self–same sea | forc'd to retire by 2.05. 7
for both of you are birds of self–same feather. 3.03.161
whilst i propose the self–same words to thee, 5.05. 20
stabb'd by the self–same hand that made these R3 1.02. 11
the self–same name, but one of better nature. 1.02.143
for the self–same heaven | that frowns on me 5.03.286
and with an accent tun'd in self–same key TRO 1.03. 53
the self–same gods that arm'd the queen of troy TIT 1.01.136
whose self–same mettle, | whereof thy proud TIM 4.03.179
myself have letters of the self–same tenure. JC 4.03.171
to th' self–same tune and words. who's here? MAC 1.03. 88
in viewing o'er the rest o' th' self–same day, 1.03. 94
this is a fellow of the self–same color | our LR 2.02.138
and i' th' self–same place | to seat something i TNK 5.01. 27
i' th' self–same state | stands many a father 5.04. 2
with self–same hand, self reasons, and self STM II.C 85
and in the self–same seat sits collatine. LUC 289
yet for the self–same purpose seek a knife; 1047
cheered and check'd even by the self–same sky, SON 15. 6
/SELF–SLAUGHTER 1 FR 0.0001 REL FR 1 V 0 P
not fix'd | his canon 'gainst /self–slaughter! HAM 1.02.132
SELF–SLAUGHTER 1 FR 0.0001 REL FR 1 V 0 P
against self–slaughter | there is a prohibition CYM 3.04. 76
SELF–SLAUGHT'RED 1 FR 0.0001 REL FR 1 V 0 P
himself on her self–slaught'red body threw, LUC 1733
SELF–SOVEREIGNTY 1 FR 0.0001 REL FR 1 V 0 P
do not curst wives hold that self–sovereignty LLL 4.01. 36
SELF–SUBDUED 1 FR 0.0001 REL FR 1 V 0 P
king | for him attempting who was self–subdued, LR 2.02.122
SELF–SUBSTANTIAL 1 FR 0.0001 REL FR 1 V 0 P
thy light's flame with self–substantial fuel, SON 1. 6
SELF–TRUST 1 FR 0.0001 REL FR 1 V 0 P
then where is truth, if there be no self–trust? LUC 158
SELF–UNABLE 1 FR 0.0001 REL FR 1 V 0 P
of a council frames | by self–unable motion; AWW 3.01. 13
SELF–WILL 1 FR 0.0001 REL FR 1 V 0 P
till, like a jade, self–will himself doth tire. LUC 707
SELF/–WILL'D 1 FR 0.0001 REL FR 1 V 0 P
a peevish self/–will'd harlotry it is. ROM 4.02. 14
SELF–WILL'D 3 FR 0.0003 REL FR 3 V 0 P
desperate here, a peevish self–will'd harlotry, 1H4 3.01.196
ajax is grown self–will'd, and bears his head TRO 1.03.188
be not self–will'd, for thou art much too fair SON 6.13
SELF–WRONG 1 FR 0.0001 REL FR 1 V 0 P
but, lest myself be guilty to self–wrong, | i'll ERR 3.02.163
SELL 41 FR 0.0046 REL FR 34 V 7 P
you will needs buy and sell men and women like MM 3.02. 2 P
so they sell bullocks. ADO 2.01.195 P
to sell a bargain well is as cunning as fast and LLL 3.01.103
i will never buy and sell out of this word. 3.01.142 P
and we that sell by gross, the lord doth know, 5.02.319
i will buy with you, sell with you, talk with MV 1.03. 35 P
she made me vow | that i should neither sell, 4.01.443
sell when you can, you are not for all markets. AYL 3.05. 60
a cardecue he will sell the fee–simple of his AWW 4.03.278 P
when you sing, | i'ld have you buy and sell so; WT 4.04.138
yet sell your face for five pence and 'tis dear. JN 1.01.153
they sell the pasture now to buy the horse, H5 2.pr. 5
so sell | his sovereign's life to death and 2.02. 10
unfought withal, but i will sell my dukedom, 3.05. 12
bid them achieve me, and then sell my bones. 4.03. 91
the man that once did sell the lion's skin 4.03. 93
poor market folks that come to sell their corn. 1H6 3.02. 15
sell every man his life as dear as mine, | and 4.02. 53
long, | or sell my title for a glorious grave. 2H6 3.01. 92
therefore, when merchant–like i sell revenge, 4.01. 41
does buy and sell his honor as he pleases, | and H8 1.01.192
foul wares, | and think perchance they'll sell; TRO 1.03.359
we'll not commend what we intend to sell. 4.01. 79
must poorly sell ourselves | with the rude 4.04. 40
a mother should not sell him an hour from her COR 1.03. 9 P
no, i'll nor sell nor give him; 1.04. 6
things created | to buy and sell with groats, to 3.02. 10
here lives a caitiff wretch would sell it him." ROM 5.01. 52
need, | and this same needy man must sell it me. 5.01. 54
these poor compounds that thou mayest not sell. 5.01. 82
i sell thee poison, thou hast sold me none. 5.01. 83
'tis rated | as those which sell would give; TIM 1.01.169
if i would sell my horse and buy twenty moe 2.01. 7
to sell and mart your offices for gold | to JC 4.03. 11
and sell the mighty space of our large honors 4.03. 25
then you'll buy 'em to sell again. MAC 4.02. 41
i'll sell all my land. OTH 1.03.382 P
is gold for you, | sell me your good report. CYM 2.03. 83
to sell myself i can be well contented, | so VEN 513
lucrece to their sight | must sell her joy, her LUC 385
i will not praise that purpose not to sell. SON 21.14
SELLER'S 1 FR 0.0001 REL FR 1 V 0 P
to things of sale a seller's praise belongs: LLL 4.03.236
SELLING 3 FR 0.0003 REL FR 2 V 1 P
lord say's head for selling the dukedom of maine 2H6 4.02.161 P
a huswife that by selling her desires | buys OTH 4.01. 94
buy terms divine in selling hours of dross; SON 146.11
SELLINGLY 1 FR 0.0001 REL FR 0 V 1 P
indeed, to speak sellingly of him, he is the HAM 5.02.109 P
SELLS 2 FR 0.0002 REL FR 2 V 0 P
who in that sale sells pardon from himself; JN 3.01.167
or sells eternity to get a toy? LUC 214
SELVES 6 FR 0.0006 REL FR 5 V 1 P
valor men hang and drown | their proper selves. TMP 3.03. 60
than we do minister | to our gross selves? MM 2.02. 87
between our kingdoms and our royal selves, | and JN 3.01.232
spicery they will breed | selves of themselves, R3 4.04.425
to our own selves bend we our needful talk. TRO 4.04.139
make but an interior survey of your good selves! COR 2.01. 40 P
SEMBLABLE 5 FR 0.0005 REL FR 2 V 3 P
thing to see the semblable coherence of his 2H4 5.01. 65 P
que dit–il? que je suis semblable a les anges? H5 5.02.111 P
his semblable, yea, himself, timon disdains; TIM 4.03. 22
diction of him, his semblable is his mirror, and HAM 5.02.118 P
and thousands more | of semblable import — but ANT 3.04. 3
SEMBLABLY 1 FR 0.0001 REL FR 1 V 0 P
semblably furnish'd like the king himself. 1H4 5.03. 21
SEMBLANCE 26 FR 0.0029 REL FR 22 V 4 P
if you go out in your own semblance, you die, WIV 4.02. 66 P
then another fault in the semblance of a fowl — 5.05. 10 P
and these two dromios, one in semblance — ERR 5.01.359
to be cozen'd with the semblance of a maid — ADO 2.02. 39 P
she's but the sign and semblance of her honor. 4.01. 33
in the rare semblance that i lov'd it first. 5.01.252
in purchasing the semblance of my soul, | from MV 3.04. 20
that induc'd me to the semblance i put on; TN 5.01.307 P
this ship–boy's semblance hath disguis'd me JN 4.03. 4
with cheerful semblance and sweet majesty; H5 4.pr. 40
repeat their semblance often on the seas, | that 1H6 5.03.193
of ashy semblance, meagre, pale, and bloodless, 2H6 3.02.162
but now two mirrors of his princely semblance R3 2.02. 51
if granted | (as he made semblance of his duty) H8 1.02.198
an ill–beseeming semblance for a feast. ROM 1.05. 74
for if thou path, thy native semblance on, | not JC 2.01. 83
t' assume a semblance | that very dogs disdain'd LR 5.03.188
truth, where semblance; CYM 2.04.109
with speechless tongues and semblance pale, PER 1.01. 36
for, by the semblance | of their white flags 1.04. 71
under whose simple semblance he hath fed | upon VEN 795
when with like semblance it is sympathiz'd. LUC 1113
wherein is stamp'd the semblance of a devil. 1246
of what she was, no semblance did remain. 1453
in thy sweet semblance my old age new born, 1759
and your sweet semblance to some other give. SON 13. 4
SEMBLANCES 2 FR 0.0002 REL FR 2 V 0 P
have | that do outface it with their semblances. AYL 1.03.122
fetch'd | from glist'ring semblances of piety; H5 2.02.117
SEMBLATIVE 1 FR 0.0001 REL FR 1 V 0 P
sound, | and all is semblative a woman's part. TN 1.04. 34
SEMICIRCLE 1 FR 0.0001 REL FR 1 V 0 P
not | too much hair there, but in a semicircle, WT 2.01. 10
SEMICIRCLED 1 FR 0.0001 REL FR 0 V 1 P
motion to thy gait in a semicircled farthingale. WIV 3.03. 64 P
SEMIRAMIS 3 FR 0.0003 REL FR 3 V 0 P
bed | on purpose trimm'd up for semiramis. SHR in.2. 39
this goddess, this semiramis, this nymph, | this TIT 2.01. 22
ay, come, semiramis, nay, barbarous tamora, 2.03.118
SEMPER 1 FR 0.0001 REL FR 0 V 1 P
'tis "semper idem," for "obsque hoc nihil est." 2H4 5.05. 28 P
SEMPRONIUS 3 FR 0.0003 REL FR 2 V 1 P
no, publius and sempronius, you must do it, TIT 4.03. 10
you to sempronius. TIM 2.02.190 P
lucius, lucullus, and sempronius — all. 3.04.111
SEMPSTER'S 1 FR 0.0001 REL FR 1 V 0 P
would | be here, cicely the sempster's daughter. TNK 3.05. 44
SENATE 29 FR 0.0032 REL FR 26 V 3 P
our business is not unknown to th' senate; COR 1.01. 57 P
of the city | you cry against the noble senate, 1.01.186
is the senate possess'd of this? 2.01.132 P
the senate has letters from the general, wherein 2.01.134 P
the senate, coriolanus, are well pleas'd | to 2.02.132
marks invested, you | anon do meet the senate. 2.03.141
in soothing them we nourish 'gainst our senate 3.01. 69
which they have often made against the senate, 3.01.128
in time | break ope the locks a' th' senate, and 3.01.138
you are sent for to the senate. 4.06. 74
together with the seal a' th' senate, what | we 5.06. 82
it your honors | to call me to your senate, i'll 5.06.139
he by the senate is accited home | from weary TIT 1.01. 27
what's this but libelling against the senate, 4.04. 17
there are certain nobles of the senate | newly TIM 1.02.174
honor, health, and compassion to the senate! 3.05. 5
banish usury, | that makes the senate ugly! 3.05. 99
is this the balsom that the usuring senate 3.05.109
pluck the grave wrinkled senate from the bench, 4.01. 5

by two of their most reverend senate, greet thee 5.01.129
that is enough to satisfy the senate. JC 2.02. 72
the senate have concluded | to give this day a 2.02. 93
say, | "break up the senate till another time, 2.02. 98
amiss | that caesar and his senate must redress? 3.01. 32
the senate hath sent about three several quests OTH 1.02. 46
pilot, | and by him do my duties to the senate. 3.02. 2
is this the noble moor whom our full senate 4.01.264
the senate hath stirr'd up the confiners | and CYM 4.02.337
supply | of roman gentlemen, by the senate sent. 4.03. 26
SENATE–HOUSE 7 FR 0.0008 REL FR 7 V 0 P
where? at the senate–house? COR 2.03.145
myself again, | repair to th' senate–house. 2.03.148
earnestness are going | all to the senate–house; 4.06. 59
we'll send mark antony to the senate–house, JC 2.02. 52
i come to fetch you to the senate–house. 2.02. 59
i prithee, boy, run to the senate–house; 2.04. 1
the senate–house of planets all did sit, | to PER 1.01. 10
SENATE'S 2 FR 0.0002 REL FR 2 V 0 P
bosom multiplied digest | the senate's courtesy? COR 3.01.132
and in the capitol and senate's right, | whom TIT 1.01. 41
/SENATOR 1 FR 0.0001 REL FR 1 V 0 P
the /senator shall bear contempt hereditary, TIM 4.03. 10
SENATOR 2 FR 0.0002 REL FR 1 V 1 P
i heard a senator speak it. COR 1.03. 95 P
you are a senator. OTH 1.01.118
SENATORS 31 FR 0.0035 REL FR 28 V 3 P
like to the senators of th' antique rome, | with H5 5.pr. 26
most fitly | as you malign our senators for that COR 1.01.113
the senators of rome are this good belly, | and 1.01.148
where senators shall mingle tears with smiles; 1.09. 3
you grave but reakless senators, have you thus 3.01. 92
you are plebeians, | if they be senators; 3.01.102
your wife, your son, these senators, the nobles; 3.02. 65
with old menenius and those senators | that 3.03. 7
the people against the senators, patricians, and 4.03. 14 P
and take our friendly senators by th' hands, 4.05.132
him by any of the senators but they stand bald 4.05.193 P
the senators and patricians love him too; 4.07. 30
this volumnia | is worth of consuls, senators, 5.04. 53
the senators of athens, happy men! TIM 1.01. 40
go you, sir, to the senators — | of whom, even 2.02.196
o gods — the senators of athens, together with 3.06. 80 P
cripple our senators, that their limbs may halt 4.01. 24
and approbation | with senators on the bench. 4.03. 38
the senators of athens greet thee, timon. 5.01.136
the senators with one consent of love | entreat 5.01.140
and i'll beweep these comforts, worthy senators. 5.01.158
being cross'd in conference by some senators. JC 1.02.188
say, the senators to–morrow | mean to establish 1.03. 85
time | to bear my greeting to the senators, 2.02. 61
of senators, of praetors, common suitors, | will 2.04. 35
people and senators, be not affrighted; 3.01. 82
lepidus | have put to death an hundred senators. 4.03.175
mine speak of seventy senators that died | by 4.03.177
the tyrant custom, most grave senators, | hath OTH 1.03.229
the duke and the senators of venice greet you. 4.01.217
three, | the senators alone of this great world, ANT 2.06. 9
/SEND 2 FR 0.0002 REL FR 2 V 0 P
/and /send /him /many /years /of /sunshine /days R2 4.01.221
/send /quickly /down /to /tame /these /vild LR 4.02. 47
SEND 258 FR 0.0291 REL FR 212 V 46 P
i must go send some better messenger: TGV 1.01.151
then tell me, whither were i best to send him? 1.03. 24
i will send him hither to you presently. 2.04. 86
send her another; 3.01. 94
and slaves they are to me that send them flying: 3.01.141
send to me in the morning, and i'll send it; 4.02.131
send to me in the morning, and i'll send it; 4.02.131
well, heaven send anne page no worse fortune! WIV 1.04. 32 P
would desire you to send her your little page, 2.02.113 P
you must send her your page, no remedy. 2.02.121 P
send him by your two men to datchet–mead. 3.03.132 P
shall we send that foolish carrion, mistress 3.03.193 P
now heaven send thee good fortune! 3.04.101 P
what honest clothes you send forth to bleaching! 4.02.121 P
and did he send you both these letters at an 4.04. 3 P
to send him word they'll meet him in the park at 4.04. 17 P
go, send to falstaff straight. 4.04. 75
send quickly to sir john, to know his mind. 4.04. 83
send me a cool rut–time, jove, or who can blame 5.05. 13 P
i would send for certain of my creditors; MM 1.02.132 P
send after the duke and appeal to him. 1.02.174 P
i'll send him certain word of my success. 1.04. 89
quick, dispatch, and send the head to angelo. 4.03. 92
but send me flavius first. 4.05. 10
for god's sake send some other messenger. ERR 2.01. 77
either send the chain, or send me by some token. 4.01. 56
either send the chain, or send me by some token. 4.01. 56
let her send it. 4.01.105
will you send him, mistress, redemption, the 4.02. 46
nor send him forth, that we may bear him hence. 5.01.158
and sure (unless you send some present help) 5.01.176
i will send for him, and question him yourself. ADO 1.02. 18 P
by being too curst, god will send you no horns. 2.01. 25 P
just, if he send me no husband, for the which 2.01. 27 P
the antipodes that you can devise to send me on; 2.01.265 P
let us send her to call him in to dinner. 2.03.218 P
and send her home again without a husband. 3.03.163 P
i, but god send every one their heart's desire! 3.04. 60 P
and when i send for you, come hither masked. 5.04. 12
and send you many lovers! LLL 2.01.125
sir, you must send the ass upon the horse, for 3.01. 54 P
by whom shall i send this? — company? stay. 4.03. 75
this will i send and something else more plain 4.03.119
did he not send you twain? 5.02. 48
honor, | how true a gentleman you send relief, MV 3.04. 6
send the deed after me, | and i will sign it. 4.01.396
i was enforc'd to send it after him, | i was 5.01.216
send to his brother; AYL 2.02. 17
why, god will send more, if the man will be 3.02.209 P
cut, he would send me word he cut it to please 5.04. 74 P
us, | or shall i send my daughter kate to you? SHR 2.01.167
god send you joy, petruchio! 2.01.319
send for your daughter by your servant here; 4.04. 58
the church together, god send 'em good shipping! 5.01. 42 P
assurance | let's each one send unto his wife, 5.02. 66
to come at first when he doth send for her, 5.02. 68
pray god, sir, your wife send you not a worse. 5.02. 84
what is your will, sir, that you send for me? 5.02.100
i know not what he shall — god send him well! AWW 1.01.176
fair maid, send forth thine eye. 2.03. 52
them whipt, or i would send them to th' turk, to 2.03. 87 P
i'll send her to my house, | acquaint my mother 2.03.286
i'll send her straight away. 2.03.295
not in heaven, whither god send her quickly! 2.04. 12 P
in earth, from whence god send her quickly! 2.04. 13 P
thither they send one another. 3.05. 31 P
send forth your amorous token for fair maudlin. 5.03. 68
send for your ring, i will return it home, | and 5.03.223
god send you, sir, a speedy infirmity, for the TN 1.05. 78 P
let him send no more — | unless, perchance, you 1.05.280
thou hadst need send for more money. 2.03.183 P
send for money, knight; 2.03.186 P
his next commodity of hair, send thee a beard! 3.01. 45 P
i did send, | after the last enchantment you did 3.01.111
keep me in darkness, send ministers to me, asses 4.02. 92 P
send one presently to sir toby. 5.01.172 P
madam, if't please the queen to send the babe, WT 2.02. 54
jove send her | a better guiding spirit! 2.03.126
that a king, at friend, | can send his brother; 5.01.141
when i was got, i'll send his soul to hell. JN 1.01.272
we from the west will send destruction | into 2.01.409
i'll send those powers o'er to your majesty. 3.03. 70
send fair–play orders and make compremise, 5.01. 67
and send him word by me which way you go. 5.03. 7
gold, | and send them after to supply our wants, R2 1.04. 51
bid her send me presently a thousand pound. 2.02. 91
tell her i send to her my kind commends; 3.01. 38
through brazen trumpet send the breath of parley 3.03. 33
and send | defiance to the traitor, and so die? 3.03.129
didst send two of thy men | to execute the noble 4.01. 81
and send the hearers weeping to their beds. 5.01. 45
banish us both, and send the king with me. 5.01. 83
your use and counsel, we shall send for you. 1H4 1.03. 21
send me your prisoners with the speediest means, 1.03.120
send us your prisoners, or you will hear of it. 1.03.124
come and roar for them, | i will not send them. 1.03.126
send danger from the east unto the west, | so 1.03.195
divers reasons | which i shall send you written, 1.03.263
royal man, and send him back again to my mother. 2.04.291 P
faith, and i'll send him packing. 2.04.297 P
to–morrow dinner–time | send him to answer thee, 2.04.516
a shorter time shall send me to you, lords, 3.01. 90
ill–spirited worcester, did not we send grace, 5.05. 2
and send you back again to your master for a 2H4 1.02. 18 P
well, god send the prince a better companion! 1.02.199 P
god send the companion a better prince! 1.02.201 P
god send the wench no worse fortune! 2.02.140 P
god send us peace! 3.02.293 P
and send discoverers forth | to know the numbers 4.01. 3
send colevile with his confederates | to york, 4.03. 73
and roughly send to prison | th' immediate heir 5.02. 70
send for him, good uncle. H5 1.02. 2
whom she did send to france | to fill king 1.02.161
as send precepts to the leviathan | to come 3.03. 26
and let him say to england that we send | to 3.05. 62
shall we go send them dinners and fresh suits, 4.02. 57
the king from eltam i intend to send, | and sit 1H6 1.01.176
shall send between the red rose and the white 2.04.126
o, send some succor to the distress'd lord! 4.03. 30
it is too late, i cannot send them now. 4.04. 1
talbot, i did send for thee | to tutor thee in 4.05. 1
what tidings send our scouts? i prithee speak. 5.02. 10
never yet taint with love, i send the king. 5.03.183
presume | to send such peevish tokens to a king. 5.03.186
in, and send for his master with a pursuivant 2H6 1.03. 34 P
then send for one presently. 2.01.136
send succors, lords, and stop the rage betime, 3.01.285
done, | to send me packing with an host of men: 3.01.342
give thee thy hire and send thy soul to hell, 3.02.225
dread lord, the commons send you word by me, 3.02.243
could send such message to their sovereign. 3.02.272
i'll send some holy bishop to entreat; 4.04. 9
and thither i will send you matthew goffe. 4.05. 10
tell him i'll send duke edmund to the tower; 4.09. 38
i'll send them all as willing as i live. 5.01. 51
i send thee, warwick, such a messenger | as 3H6 1.01. 99
answer | lewis and the lady bona send to him. 4.03. 56
forthwith we'll send him hence to brittany, 4.06. 97
our dukedom till god please to send the rest. 4.07. 47
that made him send lord hastings to the tower, R3 1.01. 68
that i will shortly send thy soul to heaven, 1.01.119
let him thank me that holp to send him thither; 1.02.107
makes him to send, that he may learn the ground. 1.03. 68
and i will send you to my brother gloucester, 1.04.229
may send forth plenteous tears to drown the 2.02. 70
send straight for him, | let him be crown'd, in 2.02. 97
persuade the queen to send the duke of york 3.01. 33
i'll send some packing that yet think not on't. 3.02. 61
i do beseech you send for some of them. 3.04. 33
factor to buy souls | and send them thither; 4.04. 73
send to her by the man that slew her brothers 4.04.271
to love, | send her a letter of thy noble deeds: 4.04.280
send out a pursuivant–at–arms | to stanley's 5.03. 59
where this is question'd send our letters, with H8 1.02. 99
from thy endless goodness send prosperous life, 5.04. 1 P
send thy brass voice through all these lazy TRO 1.03.257
to send their smiles before them to achilles, 3.03. 72
i'll send the fool to ajax and desire him | t' 3.03.235
might send that greekish whoremasterly villain 5.04. 6 P
i send it through the rivers of your blood, COR 1.01.135
if i do send, dispatch | those centuries to our 1.07. 2
send us to rome | the best, with whom we may 1.09. 76
of the volsces and | to send for titus lartius, 2.02. 38
we shall not send | o'er the vast world to seek 4.01. 41
their latest refuge | was to send him; 5.03. 12
send thee by me, their tribune and their trust, TIT 1.01.181
chop off your hand | and send it to the king; 3.01.154
will send thee hither both thy sons alive, | and 3.01.155
with all my heart i'll send the emperor my hand. 3.01.160
sons | presents that i intend to send them both. 4.01.116
a lord | basely insinuate and send us gifts. 4.02. 38
days, | but send the midwife presently to me. 4.02.166
to send down justice for to wreak our wrongs. 4.03. 52
i'll make him send for lucius his son; 5.02. 75
to send for lucius, thy thrice–valiant son, 5.02.112
thy purpose marriage, send me word to–morrow, ROM 2.02.144
to–morrow will i send. 2.02.153
what a' clock to–morrow | shall i send to thee? 2.02.168
the clock strook nine when i did send the nurse; 2.05. 1
send thy man away. 2.05. 19
table, and says, "god send me no need of thee!" 3.01. 7 P
wilt not keep him long, | but send him back. 3.05. 64
i'll send to one in mantua, | where that same 3.05. 88
unless that husband send it me from heaven | by 3.05.207
i'll send a friar with speed | to mantua, with 4.01.123
send for the county, go tell him of this. 4.02. 23
i could not send it — here it is again — | nor 5.02. 14
cell, | till i conveniently could send to romeo. 5.03.256
i will send his ransom, | and being enfranchis'd TIM 1.01.105
bid 'em send o' th' instant | a thousand talents 2.02.198
lucullus denied him, | and does he send to me? 3.03. 9
wear rich jewels | and send for money for 'em. 3.04. 24
where wouldst thou send it? 4.03.298 P
thank them, and would send them back the plague, 5.01.137
and send forth us to make their sorrowed render, 5.01.149
so thou wilt send thy gentle heart before, | to 5.04. 48
the gods, | incenses them to send destruction. JC 1.03. 13
send word to you he would be there to–morrow. 1.03. 38
when the most mighty gods by tokens send | such 1.03. 55
send him but hither, and i'll fashion him. 2.01.220
we'll send mark antony to the senate–house, 2.02. 52
shall caesar send a lie? 2.02. 65
if you shall send them word you will not come, 2.02. 95
i did send to you | for certain sums of gold, 4.03. 69
i did send | to you for gold to pay my legions, 4.03. 75
why didst thou send me forth, brave cassius? 5.03. 80
come therefore, and to /thasos send his body; 5.03.104
if charnel–houses and our graves must send MAC 3.04. 70
did you send to him, sir? 3.04.128
but i will send. 3.04.129
i'll send my prayers with him. 3.06. 49
send out moe horses, skirr the country round, 5.03. 35
seyton, send out. 5.03. 49
to england send him, or confine him where | your HAM 3.01.186
sole son, do this same villain send | to heaven. 3.03. 77
in heaven, send thither to see; 4.03. 33 P
must send thee hence | /with /fiery /quickness; 4.03. 42
his picture | i will send far and near, that all LR 2.01. 82
from home, | and not send back my /messenger. 2.04. 2
send down, and take my part. 2.04.192
a /century send forth; 4.04. 6
it fit | to send the old and miserable king | to 5.03. 46
quickly send | (be brief in it) to th' castle, 5.03.245
nay, send in time. 5.03.248
send | thy token of reprieve. 5.03.249
you, | send for the lady to the sagittary, | and OTH 1.03.115
have made bold, iago, | to send in to your wife. 3.01. 34
i'll send her to you presently; 3.01. 36
i'll send for you anon. 4.01.259
nor send you out o' th' way? 4.02. 7
/god me such uses send, | not to pick bad from 4.03.104
send for the man, and ask him. 5.02. 50
send for him hither; 5.02. 67
i did not send you. ANT 1.03. 3
why do you send so thick? 1.05. 63
born that day | when i forget to send to antony, 1.05. 64
then, to send | measures of wheat to rome. 2.06. 36
i must | to the young man send humble treaties, 3.11. 62
to the boy caesar send this grizzled head, | and 3.13. 17
teeth, | and send to darkness all that stop me. 3.13.181
go, eros, send his treasure after; 4.05. 12
lock yourself, and send him word you are dead. 4.13. 4
when did she send thee? 4.14.119
and i send him | the greatness he has got. 5.02. 29
you with your children will he send before. 5.02.202
with mine eyes i'll drink the words you send, CYM 1.01.100
service, doctor, | until i send for thee. 1.05. 45
i will make bold | to send them to you, only for 1.06.198
send your trunk to me, it shall safe be kept, 1.06.209
he'll grant the tribute, send th' arrearages, 2.04. 13
may be she pluck'd it off | to send it me. 2.04.105
are dead, and send him | some bloody sign of it; 3.04.124
thou, king, send out | for torturers ingenious; 5.05.214
god | for every graff would send a caterpillar, PER 5.01. 60
your spirit | to send him hence forgiven. TNK 5.04.120
again | as from a furnace, vapors doth he send; VEN 274
to thee i send this written ambassage | to SON 26. 3
i send them back again and straight grow sad. 45.14
SEND–A 1 FR 0.0001 REL FR 0 V 1 P
sir hugh send–a you? WIV 1.04. 87 P
SENDER 4 FR 0.0004 REL FR 4 V 0 P
to the great sender turns a sour offense, AWW 5.03. 59
we hope to make the sender blush at it. H5 1.02.299
that may not misbecome | the mighty sender, doth 2.04.119
him | according to the honor of his sender, CYM 2.03. 58
SENDETH 1 FR 0.0001 REL FR 1 V 0 P
and goliases | it sendeth forth to skirmish. 1H6 1.02. 34
SENDING 11 FR 0.0012 REL FR 8 V 3 P
i shall lessen god's sending that way, for it is ADO 2.01. 22 P
do as she has done | by sending me a letter? AWW 3.04. 3
your highness, lately sending into france, | did H5 1.02.246
and take foul scorn to fawn on him by sending. 1H6 4.04. 35
that lewis of france is sending over masquers 3H6 3.03.224
that lewis of france is sending over masquers 4.01. 94
beshrew your heart for sending me about | to ROM 2.05. 51
he's ever sending. TIM 3.02. 32 P
i was sending to use lord timon myself, these 3.02. 50 P
have to use you did provoke | our hasty sending. HAM 2.02. 4
even, | this sudden sending him away must seem 4.03. 8
/SENDS 3 FR 0.0003 REL FR 2 V 1 P
/that /she /sends /you /to /prison /hither? HAM 2.02.241 P
/it /sends /some /precious /instance /of /itself 4.05.163
desire, | /sends /word /of all that haps in tyre: PER 2.ch. 22
SENDS 38 FR 0.0043 REL FR 33 V 5 P
are in, and sends me forth | (for else his TMP 2.01.298
o, he sends you for a picture? TGV 4.04.115
madam, he sends your ladyship this ring. 4.04.132
the more shame for him that he sends it me; 4.04.133
he sends a warrant | for my poor brother's head. MM 5.01.102
is said, "god sends a curst cow short horns" — ADO 2.01. 22 P
horns" — but to a cow too curst he sends none. 2.01. 24 P
consider who the king your father sends, | to LLL 2.01. 2

to whom he sends, and what's his embassy: 2.01. 3
his rosalind | he sends this bloody napkin. AYL 4.03. 93
my mistress sends you word | that she is busy, SHR 5.02. 80
she sends him on purpose, that i may appear TN 3.04. 66 P
and sends allegiance and true faith of heart R2 3.03. 37
keeps, and sends me word | i shall have none but 1H4 1.01. 94
i am a true knight), and he sends me security! 2H4 1.02. 45 P
he therefore sends you, meeter for your spirit, H5 1.02.254
rak'd, | he sends you this most memorable line, 2.04. 88
and sends the poor well pleased from my gate. 2H6 4.10. 23
the duke of norfolk sends you word by me | the 3H6 2.01.206
his, | sends me a paper to persuade me patience? 3.03.176
'tis not the king that sends you to the tower; R3 1.01. 63
he sends you not to murther me for this, | for 1.04.213
'tis he that sends us to destroy you here. 1.04.243
therefore he sends to know your lordship's 3.02. 15
and thereupon he sends you this good news, 3.02. 48
by me | sends you his princely commendations, H8 4.02.118
this challenge that the gallant hector sends, TRO 1.03.321
my lord the emperor | sends thee this word — TIT 3.01.151
and sends them weapons wrapp'd about with lines 4.02. 27
the empress sends it thee, thy stamp, thy seal, 4.02. 69
no, my good lord, but pluto sends you word, | if 4.03. 38
and with the other sends | it back to tybalt, ROM 3.01.162
your lord sends now for money. TIM 3.04. 18
in hand, sends out arrests | on fortinbras, HAM 2.02. 67
he sends to know if your pleasure hold to play 5.02.197 P
"say the firm roman to great egypt sends | this ANT 1.05. 43
hither | he sends so poor a pinion of his wing, 3.12. 4
caesar sends greeting to the queen of egypt, 5.02. 9
SEND'ST 1 FR 0.0001 REL FR 1 V 0 P
is it thy spirit that thou send'st from thee SON 61. 5
SENECA 1 FR 0.0001 REL FR 0 V 1 P
seneca cannot be too heavy, nor plautus too HAM 2.02.400 P
SENIOR 1 FR 0.0001 REL FR 1 V 0 P
we'll draw cuts for the senior, till then, lead ERR 5.01.423
SENIOR/–JUNIOR 1 FR 0.0001 REL FR 1 V 0 P
this senior/–junior, giant–dwarf, dan cupid, LLL 3.01.180
SENIORY 1 FR 0.0001 REL FR 1 V 0 P
reverent, | give mine the benefit of seniory, R3 4.04. 36
SENIS 3 FR 0.0003 REL FR 1 V 2 P
hic steterat priami regia celsa senis." SHR 3.01. 29
bearing my port, "celsa senis," that we might 3.01. 36 P
presume not, "celsa senis," despair not. 3.01. 45 P
SE'NNIGHT *(also sevennight, sev'nnight, etc.)*
SE'NNIGHT 1 FR 0.0001 REL FR 0 V 1 P
if the interim be but a se'nnight, time's pace AYL 3.02.315 P
SE'NNIGHT'S 1 FR 0.0001 REL FR 1 V 0 P
anticipates our thoughts | a se'nnight's speed. OTH 2.01. 77
SENNOIS 1 FR 0.0001 REL FR 1 V 0 P
and sennois, | and rycas, and three better lads TNK 2.03. 37
SENOYS 1 FR 0.0001 REL FR 1 V 0 P
the florentines and senoys are by th' ears, AWW 1.02. 1
/SENSE 2 FR 0.0002 REL FR 2 V 0 P
ear, | to set his /sense on /the attentive bent, TRO 1.03.252
aid, hath /sense withal | of it own fall, TIM 5.01.147
SENSE 139 FR 0.0157 REL FR 125 V 14 P
mine ears against | the stomach of my sense. TMP 2.01.108
and, were there sense in his idolatry, | my TGV 4.04.200
believe it, page, he speaks sense. WIV 2.01.125
the wanton stings and motions of the sense; MM 1.04. 59
under whose heavy sense your brother's life 1.04. 65
in the beastliest sense you are pompey the great 2.01.218 P
'tis | such sense that my sense breeds with it. 2.02.142
'tis | such sense that my sense breeds with it. 2.02.142
that modesty may more betray our sense | than 2.02.168
nay, but hear me, | your sense pursues not mine. 2.04. 74
the sense of death is most in apprehension, 3.01. 77
save that his riotous youth with dangerous sense 4.04. 29
she speaks this in th' infirmity of sense. 5.01. 47
her madness hath the oddest frame of sense, 5.01. 61
as there is sense in truth, and truth in virtue, 5.01.226
against all sense you do importune her. 5.01.433
indu'd with intellectual sense and souls, | of ERR 2.01. 22
establish him in his true sense again, | and i 4.04. 48
hast frighted the word out of his right sense, ADO 5.02. 56 P
hid and barr'd, you mean, from common sense. LLL 1.01. 57
when mistresses from common sense are hid; 1.01. 64
all senses to that sense did make their repair, 2.01.240
child, make passionate my sense of hearing. 3.01. 1 P
above the sense of sense, so sensible | seemeth 5.02.259
above the sense of sense, so sensible | seemeth 5.02.259
royalty, bestow on me the sense of hearing. 5.02.664 P
o, take the sense, sweet, of my innocence! MND 2.02. 45
their sense thus weak, lost with their fears 3.02. 27
wherein it doth impair the seeing sense, | it 3.02.179
than common sleep of all these /five the sense. 4.01. 82
you should in all sense be much bound to him, MV 5.01.136
he, | although i think 'twas in another sense — SHR 1.01.215
are very sensible, and yet you miss my sense: 5.02. 18
fair buds, | and in no sense is meet or amiable. 5.02.141
to those | that weigh their pains in sense, and AWW 1.01.225
for her, they touch'd not any stranger sense. 1.03.110 P
now to all sense 'tis gross: 1.03.172
a senseless help when help past sense we deem. 2.01.124
what impossibility would slay | in common sense, 2.01.178
slay | in common sense, sense saves another way. 2.01.178
hand, whose banish'd sense | thou hast repeal'd, 2.03. 48
i have no skill in sense | to make distinction. 3.04. 39
lack'd the sense to know | her estimation home. 5.03. 3
life, | in your denial i would find no sense. TN 1.05.266
very brief, and to exceeding good sense — less. 3.04.158 P
let fancy still my sense in lethe steep; 4.01. 62
for though my soul disputes well with my sense, 4.03. 9
you smell this business with a sense as cold WT 2.01.151
kin to jove's thunder, so surpris'd my sense, 3.01. 10
hair, | any annoyance in that precious sense! JN 4.01. 93
nor with thy sweets comfort his ravenous sense, R2 3.02. 13
the time misord'red doth, in common sense, 2H4 4.02. 33
were, | i spake unto this crown as having sense, 4.05.157
of every fool whose sense no more can feel | but H5 4.01.235
take from them now | the sense of reck'ning, /if 4.01.291
he'll wrest the sense and hold us here all day. 2H6 3.01.186
ay, but, i fear me, in another sense. 3H6 3.02. 60
the cygnet's down is harsh and spirit of sense TRO 1.01. 58
our project's life this shape of sense assumes: 1.03.384
dost thou think i have no sense, thou strikest 2.01. 22 P
more spungy to suck in the sense of fear, | more 2.02. 12
relish is so sweet | that it enchants my sense; 3.02. 20
that most pure spirit of sense, behold itself, 3.03.106
and violenteth in a sense as strong | as that 4.04. 4
a woman of quick sense. 4.05. 54
by the din of war gan pierce | his ready sense; COR 2.02.116
maidenheads, take it in what sense thou wilt. ROM 1.01. 26 P
they must take it /in sense that feel it. 1.01. 27 P
your worship in that sense may call him man. 3.01. 59
i see no sense for't, | but his occasions might TIM 3.03. 14
ay, but their sense are shut. MAC 5.01. 25 P
that palter with us in a double sense, | that 5.08. 20
common | as any the most vulgar thing to sense, HAM 1.02. 99
so | that it be proof and bulwark against sense. 3.04. 38
sense sure you have, | else could you not have 3.04. 71
have motion, but sure that sense | is apoplex'd, 3.04. 72
nor sense to ecstasy was ne'er so thrall'd | but 3.04. 74
or but a sickly part of one true sense | could 3.04. 80
that monster custom, who all sense doth eat, 3.04.161
no, in despite of sense and secrecy, | unpeg the 3.04.192
as my great power thereof may give thee sense, 4.03. 59
things in doubt | that carry but half sense. 4.05. 7
burn out the sense and virtue of mine eye! 4.05.156
of little employment hath the daintier sense. 5.01. 70 P
whose wicked deed thy most ingenious sense 5.01.248
the most precious square of sense /possesses, LR 1.01. 74
father's curse | pierce every sense about thee! 1.04.301
wisdom | in the restoring his bereaved sense? 4.04. 9
the safer sense will ne'er accommodate | his 4.06. 81
how stiff is my vild sense | that i stand up, 4.06.279
believe | that, from the sense of all civility, OTH 1.01.131
her, | for i'll refer me to all things of sense, 1.02. 64
judge me the world, if 'tis not gross in sense, 1.02. 72
main article i do approve | in fearful sense. 1.03. 12
(being not deficient, blind, or lame of sense), 1.03. 63
in the bitter letter | after your own sense; 1.03. 69
as having sense of beauty, do omit | their 2.01. 71
have you forgot all place of sense and duty? 2.03.167
there is more sense in that than in reputation. 2.03.267 P
what sense had i in her stol'n hours of lust? 3.03.338
or sense? 3.03.374
our other healthful members even to a sense | of 3.04.147
so sweet | that the sense aches at thee, would 4.02. 69
or any sense | delighted them /in any other form 4.02.154
know | their wives have sense like them; 4.03. 94
have rubb'd this young quat almost to the sense, 5.01. 11
that hast such noble sense of thy friend's wrong 5.01. 32
for, in my sense, 'tis happiness to die. 5.02.290
a strange invisible perfume hits the sense | of ANT 2.02.212
that the conquering wine hath steep'd our sense 2.07.107
you take me in too dolorous a sense, | for i 4.02. 39
remain thou here, | while sense can keep it on. CYM 1.01.118
has | will stupefy and dull the sense awhile, 1.05. 37
and man's o'erlabor'd sense | repairs itself by 2.02. 11
upon her, | and be her sense but as a monument, 2.02. 32
to th' smothering of the sense), how far it is 3.02. 58
or a speaking such | as sense cannot untie. 5.04.148
whose containing | is so from sense in hardness, 5.05.431
you are a fair viol, and your sense the strings; PER 1.01. 81
it smells most sweetly in my sense. 3.02. 60
will to my sense bend no licentious ear, | but 5.03. 30
and bridegroom's feet, | blessing their sense! TNK 1.01. 15
to me they have no more sense of their captivity 2.01. 37 P
have in them | a sense to know a man unarm'd, 3.02. 16
let not my sense unsettle | lest i should drown, 3.02. 29
she sung much, but no sense; 4.01. 66
odors which are grateful to the sense. 4.03. 85 P
that the sense | could not be judge between 'em. 5.03.127
"say that the sense of feeling were bereft me, VEN 439
urging the worser sense for vantage still; LUC 249
he in the worst sense consters their denial: 324
"it cannot be" she in that sense forsook, | and 1538
touch | upon the lute doth ravish human sense; PP 8. 6
doth cite each moving sense from idle rest, 14.15
for to thy sensual fault i bring in sense — SON 35. 9
that my steel'd sense or changes right or wrong. 112. 8
voices, that my adder's sense | to critic and to 112.10
of woe might have rememb'red | my deepest sense, 120.10
'gainst rule, 'gainst sense, 'gainst shame, LC 271
/SENSELESS 1 FR 0.0001 REL FR 1 V 0 P
/then /senseless /ilium, | seeming to feel this HAM 2.02.474
SENSELESS 28 FR 0.0031 REL FR 24 V 4 P
himself would lodge where, senseless, they are TGV 3.01.143
o thou senseless form, | thou shalt be 4.04.198
thou whoreson, senseless villain! ERR 4.04. 24 P
i would i were senseless, sir, that i might not 4.04. 25 P
here to be the most senseless and fit man for ADO 3.03. 23 P
made senseless things begin to do them wrong, MND 3.02. 28
he smart, | /not /to seem senseless of the bob; AYL 2.07. 55
a senseless villain! SHR 1.02. 36
a senseless help when help past sense we deem. AWW 2.01.124
might have pinch'd a placket, it was senseless; WT 4.04.610 P
mock not my senseless conjuration, lords, | this R2 3.02. 23
the senseless brands will sympathize | the heavy 5.01. 46
against the senseless winds shall grin in vain, 2H6 4.01. 77
who sensibly outdares his senseless sword | and, COR 1.04. 53
tickle the senseless rushes with their heels. ROM 1.04. 36
no care, no stop, so senseless of expense, TIM 2.02. 1
you stones, you worse than senseless things! JC 1.01. 35
the ears are senseless that should give us HAM 5.02.369
your vexation, | i am senseless of your wrath; CYM 1.01.135
senseless linen, happier therein than i! 1.03. 7
tends, | and therein you are senseless. 2.03. 53
senseless? not so. 2.03. 53
senseless bauble, | art thou a feodary for this 3.02. 20
or senseless speaking, or a speaking such | as 5.04.147
liveless picture, cold and senseless stone, VEN 211
"let my good name, that senseless reputation, LUC 820
she tears the senseless sinon with her nails, 1564
senseless trees they cannot hear thee, PP 20.21
SENSELESS–OBSTINATE 1 FR 0.0001 REL FR 1 V 0 P
you are too senseless–obstinate, my lord, | too R3 3.01. 44
SENSES 39 FR 0.0044 REL FR 29 V 10 P
it eats and sleeps and hath such senses | as we TMP 1.02.413
my charms i'll break, their senses i'll restore, 5.01. 31
to work mine end upon their senses that | this 5.01. 53
so their rising senses | begin to chase the 5.01. 66
you have | been justled from your senses, know 5.01.158
it is his five senses. WIV 1.01.176 P
be not amaz'd, call all your senses to you, 3.03.118 P
all senses to that sense did make their repair, LLL 2.01.240
methought all his senses were lock'd in his eye, 2.01.242
organs, dimensions, senses, affections, passions MV 3.01. 60 P
whose apprehensive senses | all but new things AWW 1.02. 60
have i the benefit of my senses as well as your TN 5.01.305 P
we will give you sleepy drinks, that your senses WT 1.01. 14 P
if not, my senses, better pleas'd with madness, 4.04.484
to me that all their other senses stuck in ears. 4.04.609 P
also, to smell out work for th' other senses. 4.04.673 P
no settled senses of the world can match | the 5.03. 72
down, | and steep my senses in forgetfulness? 2H4 3.01. 8
let senses rule; H5 2.03. 49
all his senses have but human conditions. 4.01.104 P
the tongue and makes the senses rough. 1H6 5.03. 71
and give as soft attachment to thy senses | as TRO 4.02. 5
being tasted, stays all senses with the heart. ROM 2.03. 26
the five best senses | acknowledge thee their TIM 1.02.123
me in your wisdom, and awake your senses, that JC 3.02. 17 P
recommends itself | unto our gentle senses. MAC 1.06. 3
eyes are made the fools o' th' other senses, 2.01. 44
blame | his pester'd senses to recoil and start, 5.02. 23
been, my senses would have cool'd | to hear a 5.05. 10
doth from my senses take all feeling else, LR 3.04. 13
why then your other senses grow imperfect | by 4.06. 5
th' untun'd and jarring senses, o, wind up | of 4.07. 15
fear, ere wildness | vanquish my staider senses. CYM 3.04. 10
have i not found it | murd'rous to th' senses? 4.02.328
and make /my senses credit thy relation | to PER 5.01.123
of her eye hath distemper'd the other senses. TNK 4.03. 71 P
appalls her senses and her spirit confounds. VEN 882
till, cheering up her senses all dismay'd, | she 896
but my five wits nor my five senses can SON 141. 9
SENSIBLE 24 FR 0.0027 REL FR 13 V 11 P
who are of such sensible and nimble lungs that TMP 2.01.174 P
'twas a good sensible fellow — well. WIV 2.01.147 P
this sensible warm motion to become | a kneaded MM 3.01.119
thou art sensible in nothing but blows, and so ERR 4.04. 27 P
may, but if ever the sensible benedick bear it, ADO 1.01.262 P
bull's horns on the sensible benedick's head? 5.01.182 P
an animal, only sensible in the duller parts; LLL 4.02. 27 P
love's feeling is more soft and sensible | than 4.03.334
sense, so sensible | seemeth their conference, 5.02.259
methinks, being sensible, should curse again. MND 5.01.182 P
and with affection wondrous sensible | he wrung MV 2.08. 48
lord, | from whom he bringeth sensible regreets: 2.09. 89
and therefore 'tis call'd a sensible tale; SHR 4.01. 64 P
you are very sensible, and yet you miss my sense 5.02. 18
for, being not mad, but sensible of grief, | my JN 3.04. 53
if thou wert sensible of courtesy, | i should 1H4 5.04. 94
prince, and you took it like a sensible lord. 2H4 1.02.196 P
would your cambric were sensible as your finger, COR 1.03. 85 P
not sensible of fire, remain'd unscorch'd. JC 1.03. 18
fatal vision, sensible | to feeling as to sight? MAC 2.01. 36
believe | without the sensible and true avouch HAM 1.01. 57
to be now a sensible man, by and by a fool, and OTH 2.03.306 P
move | each part in me that were but sensible: VEN 436
my woe too sensible thy passion maketh | more LUC 1678
SENSIBLY 4 FR 0.0004 REL FR 3 V 1 P
i will tell you sensibly. LLL 3.01.113 P
who sensibly outdares his senseless sword | and, COR 1.04. 53
sensibly fed | of that self blood that first TIT 4.02.122
death, | and am most sensibly in grief for it, HAM 4.05.151
SENSUAL 4 FR 0.0004 REL FR 4 V 0 P
and now i give my sensual race the rein. MM 2.04.160
as sensual as the brutish sting itself, | and AYL 2.07. 66
for to thy sensual fault i bring in sense — SON 35. 9
invited | to any sensual feast with thee alone; 141. 8
SENSUALITY 2 FR 0.0002 REL FR 1 V 1 P
animals | that rage in savage sensuality. ADO 4.01. 61
scale of reason to poise another of sensuality, OTH 1.03.328 P
SENSUALLY 1 FR 0.0001 REL FR 1 V 0 P
do, being sensually subdu'd | we lose our human TNK 1.01.232
/SENT 3 FR 0.0003 REL FR 3 V 0 P
/why /am /i /sent /for /to /a /king | /before /i R2 4.01.162
/do /what /service /am /i /sent /for /hither? 4.01.176
/to /the /port /of /athens /sent /their /ships TRO pr 3
SENT 270 FR 0.0305 REL FR 198 V 72 P
be here confin'd by you, | or sent to naples. TMP ep 5
and sent, i think, from proteus. TGV 1.02. 38
good, i think, your lordship sent him thither: 1.03. 29
or two | of commendations sent from valentine, 1.03. 53
look what thou want'st shall be sent after thee. 1.03. 74
come; come away, man — i was sent to call thee. 2.03. 55 P
his tears pure messengers sent from his heart, 2.07. 77
but she did scorn a present that i sent her. 3.01. 92
i curse myself, for they are sent by me, | that 3.01.148
i was sent to deliver him as a present to 4.04. 6 P
to hear me speak the message i am sent on. 4.04.112
this is the ring you sent to silvia. 5.04. 95
and hath sent your worship a morning's draught WIV 2.02.146 P
my wife hath sent to him, the hour is fix'd, the 2.02.290 P
let him be sent for to–morrow, eight a' clock, 3.03.197 P
he sent me word to stay within. 3.05. 58 P
my master slender, sent to her, seeing her go 4.05. 30 P
picklock, which we have sent to the deputy. MM 3.02. 17 P
go say i sent thee thither. 3.02. 64 P
my lord hath sent you this note, and by me this 4.02.102 P
let me have claudio's head sent me by five. 4.02.123 P
done, | and sent according to command, whiles i 4.03. 80
hath yet the deputy sent my brother's pardon? 4.03.114
the world, | his head is off and sent to angelo. 4.03.116
'tis that he sent me of the duke's return. 4.03.138
of a sisterhood) | was sent to by my brother; 5.01. 73
friar that set them on, | let him be sent for. 5.01.249
that in such haste i sent to seek his master? ERR 2.01. 2
since at first | i sent him from the mart! 2.02. 6
your mistress sent to have me home to dinner? 2.02. 10
i did not see you since you sent me hence | home 2.02. 15
she sent for you by dromio home to dinner. 2.02.154
spain, who sent whole armadoes of carrects to be 3.02.136 P
a ship you sent me to, to hire waftage. 4.01. 95
thou drunken slave, i sent thee for a rope, 4.01. 96
you sent me for a rope's end as soon: 4.01. 98
you sent me to the bay, sir, for a bark. 4.01. 99
master, here's the gold you sent me for. 4.03. 12 P
are the angels that you sent for to deliver you. 4.03. 40 P

have you that i sent you for? 4.04. 9
alas, i sent you money to redeem you, | by 4.04. 83
that i was sent for nothing but a rope! 4.04. 91
once did i get him bound, and sent him home, 5.01.145
and sent my peasant home | for certain ducats; 5.01.231
i sent you money, sir, to be your bail, | by 5.01.382
brought count claudio, whom you sent me to seek. ADO 2.01.287 P
against my will i am sent to bid you come in to 2.03.247 P
"against my will i am sent to bid you come in to 2.03.257 P
these gloves the count sent me — they are an 3.04. 62 P
duty pricks me on) have sent to thee, to receive LLL 1.01.266 P
me by costard, and sent me from don armado. 4.02. 91 P
the clown bore it, the fool sent it, and the 4.03. 16 P
who sent it? 5.02. 31
what was sent to you from fair dumaine? 5.02. 47
this, and these /pearls, to me sent longaville. 5.02. 53
and her fairy sent | to bear him to my bower in MND 4.01. 60
have you sent to bottom's house? 4.02. 1 P
i am sent with broom before, | to sweep the dust 5.01.389
i have sent twenty out to seek for you. MV 2.06. 66
whom i have sent for to determine this, | come 4.01.106
upon more advice | hath sent you here this ring, 4.02. 7
hath not fortune sent in this fool to cut off AYL 1.02. 46 P
/and hath sent this natural for our whetstone; 1.02. 54 P
me not fool till heaven hath sent me fortune." 2.07. 19
he sent me hither, stranger as i am, | to tell 4.03.152
he sent me word, if i said his beard was not cut 5.04. 70 P
if i sent him word again, it was not well cut, 5.04. 73 P
wife, | and sent you hither so unlike yourself? SHR 3.02.104
i am sent before to make a fire, and they are 4.01. 4 P
where is the foolish knave i sent before? 4.01.127
nose, that would have sent me to the jail. 5.01.132 P
"i have sent you a daughter–in–law; AWW 3.02. 19 P
juno, sent him forth | from courtly friends, 3.04. 13
and found her wondrous cold, but i sent to her, 3.06.113
i have letters sent me | that sets him high in 5.03. 30
come, or sent it us | upon her great disaster. 5.03.111
the jeweller that owes the ring is sent for, 5.03.296
were you sent hither to praise me? TN 1.05.249 P
why, he sent her none. 2.02. 24
i sent thee sixpence for thy leman; 2.03. 25 P
i have sent after him; 3.04. 1
i sent for thee upon a sad occasion. 3.04. 18 P
you make me believe that i am not sent for you? 4.01. 1 P
know you, nor i am not sent to you by my lady, 4.01. 6 P
from those you sent to th' oracle are come | an WT 2.03.194
my master, hath sent for me, to whose feeling 4.02. 7 P
sent by the king your father | to greet him and 4.04.556
arthur doth live, the king hath sent for you. JN 4.03. 75
what munition sent, | to underprop this action? 5.02. 98
i am sent to speak: 5.02.119
go, say i sent thee forth to purchase honor, R2 1.03.282
and hath sent post–haste | to entreat your 1.04. 55
sent from my brother worcester, whencesoever. 2.03. 22
and sent me over by berkeley, to discover | what 2.03. 33
sent back like hollowmas or short'st of day. 5.01. 80
i have to london sent | the heads of salisbury, 5.06. 7
i have from oxford sent to london | the heads of 5.06. 13
but i have sent for him to answer this; 1H4 1.01.100
and hath sent for you | to line his enterprise, 2.03. 82
wye | and sandy–bottom'd severn have i sent him 3.01. 65
lord mortimer of scotland hath sent word | that 3.02.164
the king hath sent to know | the nature of your 4.03. 41
sir nicholas gawsey hath for succor sent, | and 5.04. 45
who i sent | on tuesday last to listen after 2H4 1.01. 28
and hath sent out | a speedy power to encounter 1.01.132
i look'd 'a should have sent me two and twenty 1.02. 43 P
john, i sent for you before your expedition to 1.02.101 P
you would not come when i sent for you. 1.02.106 P
i sent for you, when there were matters against 1.02.132 P
good wenches, if i be not sent away post, i will 2.04.377 P
have you read o'er the /letters that i sent you? 3.01. 36
the powers that you already have sent forth 3.01.100
we have sent forth already. 4.01. 5
i sent your grace | the parcels and particulars 4.02. 35
fondly brought here and foolishly sent hence. 4.02.119
dead, | and tell him who hath sent me after him. 5.02. 41
at this, i shall be sent for in private to him. 5.05. 77 P
i shall be sent for soon at night. 5.05. 89 P
call in the messengers sent from the dolphin. H5 1.02.221
sweeten the bitter mock you sent his majesty, 2.04.122
that is by his father sent about merchandise do 4.01.147 P
should be impos'd upon his father that sent him; 4.01.150 P
who hath sent thee now? 4.03. 88
is this the king we sent to for his ransom? 4.05. 9
hundreds he sent to hell, and none durst stand 1H6 1.01.123
which by a vision sent to her from heaven 1.02. 52
and sent our sons and husbands captivate. 2.03. 42
we sent unto the temple, unto his chamber, | and 2.05. 19
letter | sent from our uncle duke of burgundy. 4.01. 49
how now, sir william, whither were you sent? 4.04. 12
york set him on, york should have sent him aid. 4.04. 29
he might have sent, and had the horse. 4.04. 33
on what submissive message art thou sent? 4.07. 53
and she sent over of the king of england's own 2H6 1.01. 60 P
come, somerset, we'll see thee sent away. 1.03.220 P
sent his poor queen to france, from whence she 2.02. 25
for soldiers' pay in france, and never sent it, 3.01. 62
that somerset be sent as regent thither: 3.01.290
sent from a sort of tinkers to the king. 3.02.277
and i am sent to tell his majesty | that even 3.02.377
and sent the ragged soldiers wounded home. 4.01. 90
the king hath sent him sure; 5.01. 13
he was lately sent | from your kind aunt, 3H6 2.01.145
sent from your brother, marquess montague. 3.03.164
your queen and my son edward | be sent for, to 4.06. 61
down to hell, and say i sent thee thither — | i 5.06. 67
and hither have they sent it for her ransom. 5.07. 40
sent before my time | into this breathing world, R3 1.01. 20
and sent to warn them to his royal presence. 1.03. 39
i dare adventure to be sent to th' tow'r. 1.03.115
who sent you hither? 1.04.171
marry, we were sent for to the justices. 2.03. 46
lord rivers and lord grey are sent to pomfret, 2.04. 42
i have sent for these strawberries. 3.04. 47
lord mayor, the reason we have sent — 3.05. 18
for yesternight by catesby was it sent me; 3.06. 6
come, madam, come, i in all haste was sent. 4.01. 56
richmond in dorsetshire sent out a boat | unto 4.04.522
have been commissions | sent down among 'em, H8 1.02. 21
"hath sent to me, wishing me to permit | john de 1.02.161
earl surrey was sent thither, and in haste too, 2.01. 43
he sent command to the lord mayor straight | to 2.01.151
the horses your lordship sent for, with all the 2.02. 1 P
excuse me, | the king has sent me otherwhere. 2.02. 59
self, hath sent | one general tongue unto us: 2.02. 94
they have sent me such a man i would have wish'd 2.02.100
who had been hither sent on the debating | /a 2.04.174
morning | papers of state he sent me to peruse, 3.02.121
main secret in the packet | i sent the king? 3.02.216
you sent me deputy for ireland, | far from his 3.02.260
you sent a large commission | to gregory de 3.02.320
then, that you have sent innumerable substance 3.02.326
is staying | a gentleman, sent from the king, to 4.02.106
that letter | i caus'd you write yet sent away? 4.02.128
me, but by her woman | i sent your message, who 5.01. 64
do desire to know | wherefore i sent for you. 5.01. 90
that was sent to me from the council pray'd me 5.02. 2
i have a roisting challenge sent amongst | the TRO 2.02.208
let him be sent, great princes, | and he shall 3.03. 27
i was sent for to the king, but why, i know not. 4.01. 36
let one be sent | to pray achilles see us at our 5.09. 7
that the gods sent not | corn for the rich men COR 1.01.207
to a cruel war i sent him, from whence he 1.03. 14 P
you are sent for to the capitol. 2.01.260
you are sent for to the senate. 4.06. 74
what he would do | he sent in writing after me; 5.01. 68
writ it for thy sake, | and would have sent it. 5.02. 91
whom with a crack'd heart i have sent to rome, 5.03. 9
sent by the heavens for prince saturnine, TIT 1.01.335
down so many enemies, | shall not be sent. 3.01.164
here's thy hand, in scorn to thee sent back — 3.01.237
hath sent by me | the goodliest weapons of his 4.02. 10
what hath he sent her? 4.02. 63
sent from below | to join with him and right his 5.02. 3
sent from th' infernal kingdom | to ease the 5.02. 30
and art thou sent to me, | to be a torment to 5.02. 41
a rape, | and i am sent to be reveng'd on him. 5.02. 95
out, | and sent her enemies unto the grave. 5.03.103
but i am sent to find those persons whose names ROM 1.02. 41 P
hath sent a letter to his father's house. 2.04. 7
and has sent your honor two brace of greyhounds. TIM 1.02.188 P
and i am sent expressly to your lordship. 2.02. 32
hath sent to your lordship to furnish him, 3.01. 19 P
yet, had he mistook him and sent to me, i should 3.02. 23 P
may it please your honor, my lord hath sent — 3.02. 30 P
what has he sent? 3.02. 31 P
and what has he sent now? 3.02. 33 P
h'as only sent his present occasion now, my lord 3.02. 34 P
worth of thrice the sum | h'ad sent to me first, 3.03. 23
he hath sent me an earnest inviting, which many 3.06. 9 P
i am sorry, when he sent to borrow of me, that 3.06. 15 P
he sent to me, sir — here he comes. 3.06. 24 P
when your lordship this other day sent to me, i 3.06. 42 P
if you had sent but two hours before — 3.06. 45 P
gods out of my misery | has sent thee treasure. 4.03.525
fear, | we sent to thee to give thy rages balm, 5.04. 16
unmeritable man, | meet to be sent on errands; JC 4.01. 13
we are sent | to give thee from our royal master MAC 1.03.100
and | sent forth great largess to your offices. 2.01. 14
whom we, to gain our peace, have sent to peace, 3.02. 20
sent he to macduff? 3.06. 39
made, but sent to my account | with all my HAM 1.05. 78
he sent out to suppress | his nephew's levies, 2.02. 61
were you not sent for? 2.02.274 P
you were sent for, and there is a kind of 2.02.278 P
know the good king and queen have sent for you. 2.02.281 P
direct with me, whether you were sent for or no! 2.02.288 P
my lord, we were sent for. 2.02.292 P
for we have closely sent for hamlet hither, 3.01. 29
great affliction of spirit, hath sent me to you. 3.02.312 P
i have sent to seek him, and to find the body. 4.03. 1
let the king have the letters i have sent, and 4.06. 23 P
born — he that is mad, and sent into england. 5.01.148 P
ay, marry, why was he sent into england? 5.01.149 P
saucily to the world before he was sent for, yet LR 1.01. 22 P
king, | on whose employment i was sent to you. 2.02.129
to whose hands you have sent the lunatic king — 3.07. 46
where hast thou sent the king? 3.07. 50
with him i sent the queen, | my reason all the 5.03. 51
galleys | have sent a dozen sequent messengers OTH 1.02. 41
the senate hath sent about three several quests 1.02. 46
and your noble self | i am sure is sent for. 1.02. 93
good grace shall think | to be sent after me. 1.03.287
i have sent to bid cassio come speak with you. 3.04. 50
roderigo meant t' have sent this damned villain; 5.02.316
if the scarce–bearded caesar have not sent | his ANT 1.01. 21
upon her landing, antony sent to her, | invited 2.02.219
have we | our written purposes before us sent, 2.06. 4
how you take | the offers we have sent you. 2.06. 31
we sent our schoolmaster, | is 'a come back? 3.11. 71
antony | hath after thee sent all thy treasure, 4.06. 20
lord, | my mistress cleopatra sent me to thee. 4.14.118
not be purg'd, she sent you word she was dead; 4.14.124
work, hath sent | me to proclaim the truth, and 4.14.125
caesar knows, | and he hath sent for thee. 5.02. 66
caesar hath sent — 5.02.321
there's dolabella sent from caesar; call him. 5.02.324
the letter | that i have sent her, by her own CYM 3.02. 18
i have sent cloten's clotpole down the stream 4.02.184
sent by a consul to me, should not sooner | than 4.02.385
supply | of roman gentlemen, by the senate sent. 4.03. 26
and she sent him away as cold as a snowball, PER 4.06.139 P
o, here's | the lady that i sent for. 5.01. 65
and thou by some incensed god sent hither | to 5.01.143
appalls) hath sent | deadly defiance to him, and TNK 1.02. 90
why is he sent for? 2.02.225
i have sent him where a cedar, | higher than all 2.06. 4
that forc'd him on so fast | (in rage sent out, LUC 1671
here what tributes wounded fancies sent me, | of LC 197
"'lo this device was sent me from a nun, | or 232

SENTENC'D 6 FR 0.0006 REL FR 3 V 3 P
he's sentenc'd; 'tis too late. MM 2.02. 55
is with child, | and he that got it, sentenc'd; 2.03. 13
if he chance to fail, he hath sentenc'd himself. 3.02.257 P
to the law than angelo who hath sentenc'd him. 4.02.159 P
he's sentenc'd; no more hearing. COR 3.03.109
our throats are sentenc'd, and stay upon 5.04. 7 P

SENTENCE 42 FR 0.0047 REL FR 40 V 2 P
you must be the first that gives this sentence, MM 2.02.106
under your sentence? 2.04. 37
pronounce a sentence on your brother's life; 2.04. 62
were not you then as cruel as the sentence 2.04.109
immediate sentence then, and sequent death, | is 5.01.373
and passed sentence may not be recall'd | but to ERR 1.01.147
sir, i will pronounce your sentence: LLL 1.01.300 P
must needs give sentence 'gainst the merchant MV 4.01.205
i pray thee pursue sentence. 4.01.298
most learned judge! a sentence! come, prepare! 4.01.304
pronounce that sentence then on me, my liege, AYL 1.03. 85
the fairest boughs, | or at every sentence end, 3.02.136
as she stood, | and gave this sentence then: AWW 1.03. 76
this is a dreadful sentence. 3.02. 61
a sentence is but a chev'ril glove to a good wit TN 3.01. 11 P
a heavy sentence, my most sovereign liege, | and R2 1.03.154
what is thy sentence /then but speechless death, 1.03.172
after our sentence plaining comes too late. 1.03.175
and in the sentence my own life destroyed. 1.03.242
that laid the sentence of dread banishment | on 3.03.134
what subject can give sentence on his king? 4.01.121
thy kingly doom and sentence of his pride. 5.06. 23
after this cold considerance, sentence me, | and 2H4 5.02. 98
hear your sentence. H5 2.02.166
receive the sentence of the law for /sins | such 2H6 2.03. 3
write in the dust this sentence with thy blood: 3H6 5.01. 56
the bitter sentence of poor clarence' death? R3 1.04.186
execution | of what we chance to sentence. COR 3.03. 22
give sentence on this execrable wretch | that TIT 5.03.177
and hear the sentence of your moved prince. ROM 1.01. 88
pronounce this sentence then: 2.03. 79
to die | in our black sentence and proscription. JC 4.01. 17
to come betwixt our sentence and our power, LR 1.01.170
but let your sentence | even fall upon my life. OTH 1.03.119
let me speak like yourself, and lay a sentence, 1.03.199
he bears the sentence well that nothing bears 1.03.212
but he bears both the sentence and the sorrow 1.03.214
you lean'd unto his sentence with what patience CYM 1.01. 78
should from my lips | pluck a hard sentence. 5.05.289
either expound now, or receive your sentence. PER 1.01. 90
who fears a sentence or an old man's saw | shall LUC 244
and midst the sentence so her accent breaks, 566

SENTENCES 6 FR 0.0006 REL FR 3 V 3 P
had drunk himself out of his five sentences. WIV 1.01.175 P
shall quips and sentences and these paper ADO 2.03.240 P
pale, | make periods in the midst of sentences, MND 5.01. 96
good sentences, and well pronounc'd. MV 1.02. 10 P
ears | to steal his sweet and honeyed sentences; H5 1.01. 50
these sentences, to sugar or to gall, | being OTH 1.03.216

SENTENCING 1 FR 0.0001 REL FR 1 V 0 P
force, | or sentencing for aye their vigor dumb, TNK 1.01.195

SENTENTIOUS 3 FR 0.0003 REL FR 0 V 3 P
at dinner have been sharp and sententious: LLL 5.01. 3 P
by my faith, he is very swift and sententious. AYL 5.04. 62 P
and she hath the prettiest sententious of it, of ROM 2.04.211 P

SENTINEL 4 FR 0.0004 REL FR 4 V 0 P
one aloof stand sentinel. MND 2.02. 26
alarum'd by his sentinel, the wolf, | whose MAC 2.01. 53
doth call himself affection's sentinel, | gives VEN 650
to wake the morn and sentinel the night, | to LUC 942

/SENTINELS 1 FR 0.0001 REL FR 1 V 0 P
use careful watch, choose trusty /sentinels. R3 5.03. 54

SENTINELS 3 FR 0.0003 REL FR 3 V 0 P
that the fix'd sentinels almost receive | the H5 4.pr. 6
to and fro, | about relieving of the sentinels. 1H6 2.01. 70
i will corrupt the grecian sentinels, | to give TRO 4.04. 72

SENTRY *(see century*)*

SENT'ST 1 FR 0.0001 REL FR 1 V 0 P
for that good hand thou sent'st the emperor. TIT 3.01.235

SEPARABLE 1 FR 0.0001 REL FR 1 V 0 P
though in our lives a separable spite, | which SON 36. 6

SEPARATE 3 FR 0.0003 REL FR 1 V 2 P
holiness | to separate the husband and the wife. ERR 5.01.111
if you can separate yourself and your TN 2.03. 98 P
a man can no more separate age and covetousness 2H4 1.02.229 P

SEPARATED 4 FR 0.0004 REL FR 4 V 0 P
sun, | not separated with the racking clouds, 3H6 2.01. 27
lord, | bid him not fear the separated council: R3 3.02. 20
life and these lips have long been separated. ROM 4.05. 27
our separated fortune | shall keep us both the MAC 2.03.138

SEPARATES 1 FR 0.0001 REL FR 1 V 0 P
and, stickler–like, the armies separates. TRO 5.08. 18

SEPARATION 5 FR 0.0005 REL FR 4 V 1 P
such separation as may well be said | becomes a MND 2.02. 58
necessities made separation of their society, WT 1.01. 26 P
of late days hear | a buzzing of a separation H8 2.01.148
our separation so abides and flies, | that thou, ANT 1.03.102
that by this separation i may give | that due to SON 39. 7

SEPTENTRION 1 FR 0.0001 REL FR 1 V 0 P
unto us, | or as the south to the septentrion. 3H6 1.04.136

SEPULCHER'D 1 FR 0.0001 REL FR 1 V 0 P
made | may likewise be sepulcher'd in thy shade. LUC 805

SEPULCHRE 12 FR 0.0013 REL FR 11 V 1 P
or, at the least, in hers sepulchre thine. TGV 4.02.117
the skull that bred them in the sepulchre. MV 3.02. 96
can be none but by pangs of death and sepulchre. TN 3.04.240 P
banish'd this frail sepulchre of our flesh | as R2 1.03.196
as is the sepulchre in stubborn jewry | of the 2.01. 55
as far as to the sepulchre of christ — | whose 1H4 1.01. 19
crown, | what is it, but to make thy sepulchre, 3H6 1.01.236
a sceptre, or an earthly sepulchre!" 1.04. 17
my heart, sweet boy, shall be thy sepulchre, 2.05.115
stains | the stony entrance of this sepulchre? ROM 5.03.141
a bell | that warns my old age to a sepulchre. 5.03.207
why the sepulchre, | wherein we saw thee quietly HAM 1.04. 48

SEPULCHRES 4 FR 0.0004 REL FR 4 V 0 P
blood, | were lik'ned oft to kingly sepulchres; 3H6 5.02. 20
his snout digs sepulchres where e'er he goes; VEN 622
the right of sepulchres, were shorn away, | to SON 68. 6
bidding them find their sepulchres in mud, LC 46

SEPULCHRING 1 FR 0.0001 REL FR 1 V 0 P
thy /mother's tomb, | sepulchring an adult'ress. LR 2.04.132

SEQUEL 10 FR 0.0011 REL FR 6 V 4 P
well — i guess the sequel; TGV 2.01.116
but mark the sequel, master /brook. WIV 3.05.107 P
gather the sequel by that went before. ERR 1.01. 95
so will you say when you have seen the sequel. ADO 3.02.134 P
like the sequel, i. signior costard, adieu. LLL 3.01.134
but then there is no consonancy in the sequel; TN 2.05.130 P
and in sequel, all, | according to their firm H5 5.02.333
and mark how well the sequel hangs together: R3 3.06. 4
reproach | attend the sequel of your imposition, 3.07.232
but is there no sequel at the heels of this HAM 3.02.329 P
SEQUENCE 4 FR 0.0004 REL FR 4 V 0 P
king, | cut off the sequence of posterity, JN 2.01. 96
a king | but by fair sequence and succession? R2 2.01.199
why lifts she up her arms in sequence thus? TIT 4.01. 37
tell athens, in the sequence of degree, | from TIM 5.01.208
SEQUENT 10 FR 0.0011 REL FR 7 V 3 P
immediate sentence then, and sequent death, | is MM 5.01.373
framed a letter to a sequent of the stranger LLL 4.02.138 P
is very sequent to your whipping; AWW 2.02. 54 P
conferr'd by testament to th' sequent issue, 5.03.197
say i, to fashion in | my sequent protestation: TRO 4.04. 66
and what to this was sequent | thou knowest HAM 5.02. 54
finds itself scourg'd by the sequent effects. LR 1.02.106 P
galleys | have sent a dozen sequent messengers OTH 1.02. 41
or i am none | that draw i' th' sequent trace. TNK 1.02. 60
in sequent toil all forwards do contend. SON 60. 4
SEQUESTER 1 FR 0.0001 REL FR 1 V 0 P
of yours requires | a sequester from liberty: OTH 3.04. 40
SEQUESTRATION 3 FR 0.0003 REL FR 2 V 1 P
any sequestration | from open haunts and H5 1.01. 58
arms, | this loathsome sequestration have i had; 1H6 2.05. 25
thou shalt see an answerable sequestration — OTH 1.03.345 P
SEQUEST'RED 2 FR 0.0002 REL FR 2 V 0 P
to the which place a poor sequest'red stag, AYL 2.01. 33
why are you sequest'red from all your train, TIT 2.03. 75
SEQUEST'RING 1 FR 0.0001 REL FR 1 V 0 P
fortunes, sequest'ring from me all | that time, TRO 3.03. 8
SERE* *(also sear)*
/SERE* 2 FR 0.0002 REL FR 1 V 1 P
being often read, | grown /sere and tedious; MM 2.04. 9
/whose /lungs /are /tickle /a' /th' /sere, and HAM 2.02.324 P
SERE* 1 FR 0.0001 REL FR 1 V 0 P
he is deformed, crooked, old, and sere, ERR 4.02. 19
SERENISSIMA 1 FR 0.0001 REL FR 0 V 1 P
erga te mentis integritas, regina serenissima — H8 3.01. 41 P
SERGE 1 FR 0.0001 REL FR 0 V 1 P
ah, thou say, thou serge, nay, thou buckram lord 2H6 4.07. 25 P
SERGEANT 9 FR 0.0010 REL FR 6 V 3 P
if any hour meet a sergeant, 'a turns back for ERR 4.02. 56
be in debt and theft, and a sergeant in the way, 4.02. 61
ay, sir, the sergeant of the band: 4.03. 30 P
you hind'red by the sergeant to tarry for the 4.03. 39 P
sergeant, you shall. 1H6 2.01. 5
your office, sergeant; execute it. H8 1.01.198
this is the sergeant, | who like a good and MAC 1.02. 3
had i but time — as this fell sergeant, death, HAM 5.02.336
brother arthur watchins sergeant safe's yeoman. STM II.C 43 P
SERIOUS 25 FR 0.0028 REL FR 20 V 5 P
i am more serious than my custom; TMP 2.01.219
love, | and make a common of my serious hours. ERR 2.02. 29
on serious business craving quick dispatch, LLL 2.01. 31
other /importunate and most serious designs, and 5.01.100 P
a very serious business calls on him. AWW 2.04. 40
make trivial price of serious things we have, 5.03. 61
a servant grafted in my serious trust | and WT 1.02.246
if thou be'st capable of things serious, thou 4.04.764 P
our scene is alt'red from a serious thing, | and R2 5.03. 79
i'll hence to london on a serious matter. 3H6 5.05. 47
now | that bear a weighty and a serious brow, H8 pr 2
he view'd, | he did it with a serious mind; 3.02. 80
the moon, not worth | his serious considering. 3.02.135
o heavy lightness, serious vanity, | misshapen ROM 1.01.178
and so, intending other serious matters, | after TIM 2.02.210
instant, | there's nothing serious in mortality: MAC 2.03. 93
but lend thy serious hearing | to what i shall HAM 1.05. 5
edmund, what serious contemplation are you in? LR 1.02.138 P
faith, he is posted hence on serious matter. 4.05. 8
i will your serious and great business scant OTH 1.03.267
with what else more serious | importeth thee to ANT 1.02.120
have cause to use thee with a serious industry, CYM 3.05.111 P
words with that | which is so serious. 4.02.231
and so stand /aloof for more serious wooing. PER 4.06. 88 P
/wear) i followed | for my most serious decking. TNK 1.03. 74
SERIOUSLY 5 FR 0.0005 REL FR 4 V 1 P
juno and ceres whisper seriously; TMP 4.01.125
if seriously i may convey my thoughts | in this AWW 2.01. 81
at all of this that so seriously he does address 3.06. 95 P
dost thou speak seriously, servilius? TIM 3.02. 42
to hear | would desdemona seriously incline; OTH 1.03.146
SERIOUSNESS 1 FR 0.0001 REL FR 1 V 0 P
though craving seriousness and skill, pass'd TNK 1.03. 28
SERMON 2 FR 0.0002 REL FR 1 V 1 P
chamber, making a sermon of continency to her, SHR 4.01.182 P
come, sermon me no further. TIM 2.02.172
SERMONS 1 FR 0.0001 REL FR 1 V 0 P
sermons in stones, and good in every thing. AYL 2.01. 17
SERPENT 25 FR 0.0028 REL FR 22 V 3 P
indeed | as i dare take a serpent by the tongue. ADO 5.01. 90
to pluck this crawling serpent from my breast! MND 2.02.146
methought a serpent eat my heart away, | and you 2.02.149
with doubler tongue | than thine, thou serpent, 3.02. 73
or i will shake thee from me like a serpent! 3.02.261
wouldst thou have a serpent sting thee twice? MV 4.01. 69
said "a mother," | methought you saw a serpent. AWW 1.03.141
france, thou mayst hold a serpent by the tongue, JN 3.01.258
my friend, | he is a very serpent in my way, 3.03. 61
what eve, what serpent, hath suggested thee | to R2 3.04. 75
a serpent that will sting thee to the heart. 5.03. 58
were there a serpent seen, with forked tongue, 2H6 3.02.259
he leers than i will a serpent when he hisses. TRO 5.01. 90 P
not afric owns a serpent i abhor | more than thy COR 1.08. 3
o serpent heart, hid with a flow'ring face! ROM 3.02. 73
innocent flower, | but be the serpent under't. MAC 1.05. 66
there the grown serpent lies; 3.04. 28
a serpent stung me, so the whole ear of denmark HAM 1.05. 36
the serpent that did sting thy father's life 1.05. 39
and, in thy /attaint, | this gilded serpent. LR 5.03. 84
or murmuring, "where's my serpent of old nile?" ANT 1.05. 25
your serpent of egypt is bred now of your mud by 2.07. 26 P
'tis a strange serpent. 2.07. 48 P
here come and sit, where never serpent hisses, VEN 17
who sees the lurking serpent steps aside; LUC 362
SERPENTINE 1 FR 0.0001 REL FR 0 V 1 P
lose all the serpentine craft of thy caduceus, TRO 2.03. 12 P
SERPENT–LIKE 1 FR 0.0001 REL FR 1 V 0 P
most serpent–like, upon the very heart. LR 2.04.161
SERPENT'S 8 FR 0.0009 REL FR 8 V 0 P
luck | now to scape the serpent's tongue, | we MND 5.01.433
their touch affrights me as a serpent's sting. 2H6 3.02. 47
their music frightful as the serpent's hiss, 3.02.326
who scapes the lurking serpent's mortal sting? 3H6 2.02. 15
and therefore think him as a serpent's egg, JC 2.01. 32
how sharper than a serpent's tooth it is | to LR 1.04.288
let heaven requite it with the serpent's curse! OTH 4.02. 16
hath yet but life, | and not a serpent's poison. ANT 1.02.194
SERPENTS' 1 FR 0.0001 REL FR 1 V 0 P
the more do thou in serpents' natures think them STM III 17
SERPENTS 7 FR 0.0008 REL FR 6 V 1 P
thus did he strangle serpents in his manus. LLL 5.02.591
from such fell serpents as false suffolk is; 2H6 3.02.266
ways, or bid me lurk | where serpents are; ROM 4.01. 80
and kindly creatures | turn all to serpents! ANT 2.05. 79
y' have strange serpents there? 2.07. 24 P
if knife, drugs, serpents have | edge, sting, or 4.15. 25
and both like serpents are, who though they feed PER 1.01.132
SERPIGO *(see sapego, suppeago)*
SERVANT 118 FR 0.0133 REL FR 97 V 21 P
come away, servant, come; TMP 1.02.187
as thou report'st thyself, was then her servant, 1.02.271
you may deny me, but i'll be your servant, 3.01. 85
my industrious servant, ariel! 4.01. 33
sir valentine and servant! to you two thousand. TGV 2.01.100 P
i thank you, gentle servant — 'tis very clerkly 2.01.108
and so, good morrow, servant. 2.01.134
servant! 2.04. 1 P
servant, you are sad. 2.04. 8 P
who is that, servant? 2.04. 36 P
too low a mistress for so high a servant. 2.04.106
but too mean a servant | to have a look of such 2.04.107
sweet lady, entertain him for your servant. 2.04.110
servant, you are welcome to a worthless mistress 2.04.113
once more, new servant, welcome; 2.04.118
sir proteus, gentle lady, and your servant. 4.02. 91
your servant and your friend; 4.03. 4
when a man's servant shall play the cur with him 4.04. 1 P
how many masters would do this for his servant? 4.04. 30 P
but cannot be true servant to my master, 4.04.104
(though you respect not aught your servant doth) 5.04. 20
kind fellow as ever servant shall come in house WIV 1.04. 11 P
/brook, i shall be glad to be your servant. 2.02.179 P
him know | i have a servant comes with me along, MM 4.01. 45
my servant straight was mute. LLL 5.02.277
your servant, and costard. 5.02.571 P
fear not, my lord! your servant shall do so. MND 2.01.268
all this i give you, let me be your servant. AYL 2.03. 46
my trusty servant, well approv'd in all, | here SHR 1.01. 7
was it fit for a servant to use his master so, 1.02. 32 P
your ancient, trusty, pleasant servant grumio. 1.02. 47
send for your daughter by your servant here; 4.04. 58
sir, what are you that offer to beat my servant? 5.01. 64 P
at home, my son and my servant spend all at the 5.01. 69 P
and i | his servant live, and will his vassal AWW 1.03.159
say, | but that i am your most obedient servant. 2.05. 72
a servant only, and a gentleman | which i have 3.02. 84
you never had a servant to whose trust | your 4.04. 15
murther me for my love, let me be your servant. TN 2.01. 36 P
my servant, sir? 3.01. 98
y' are servant to the count orsino, youth. 3.01.100
your servant's servant is your servant, madam. 3.01.102
your servant's servant is your servant, madam. 3.01.102
so did i abuse | myself, my servant, and, i fear 3.01.114
and suits well for a servant with my fortunes. 3.04. 6
"if not, let me see thee a servant still." 3.04. 55 P
counted | a servant grafted in my serious trust WT 1.02.246
beverage, | account me not your servant. 1.02.347
who professes | myself your loyal servant, your 2.03. 54
i knew him once a servant of the prince. 4.03. 87 P
pantler, butler, cook, | both dame and servant; 4.04. 57
as it on earth hath been thy servant still. JN 5.07. 73
endure | the moody frontier of a servant brow. 1H4 1.03. 19
man by man, boy by boy, servant by servant. 3.03. 57 P
man by man, boy by boy, servant by servant. 3.03. 57 P
here comes my servant travers, who i sent | on 2H4 1.01. 28
or if a servant, under his master's command H5 4.01.151 P
of his son, nor the master of his servant; 4.01.157 P
so, | let me thy servant and not sovereign be. 1H6 1.02.111
thy humble servant vows obedience | and humble 3.01.166
this is my servant, hear him, noble prince. 4.01. 80
servant in arms to harry king of england, | and 4.02. 4
a maid, | a virgin, and his servant, say to him. 5.03.178
the servant of this armorer, my lords. 2H6 2.03. 58
and if thy poor devoted servant may | but beg R3 1.02.206
i had rather be a country servant maid | than a 1.03.106
of such a time, being my sworn servant, | the H8 1.02.191
flying for succor to his servant banister, 2.01.109
york, are join'd with me their servant | in the 2.02.105
my learn'd and well–beloved servant, cranmer, 2.04.239
which you brought the king | to be your servant. 3.02.316
madam, the same; your servant. 4.02.111
many good–nights, my lord! i rest your servant. 5.01. 55
'twill make us proud to be his servant, paris! TRO 3.01.155
as thou unworthy to be call'd her servant. 4.04.125
go, go, my servant, take thou troilus' horse, 5.05. 1
i had rather be their servant in my way | than COR 2.01.203
power, | but was a petty servant to the state, 2.03.178
first he was | a noble servant to them, but he 4.07. 36
i'll deliver | myself your loyal servant, or 5.06.140
thou hast a servant nam'd lucilius. TIM 1.01.111
one varro's servant, my good lord — 2.02. 27
i think no usurer but has a fool to his servant; 2.02. 98 P
an honest poor servant of yours. 4.03.475
our will became the servant to defect, | which MAC 2.01. 18
them but in his house | i keep a servant fee'd. 3.04.131
the same, my lord, and your poor servant ever. HAM 1.02.162
give me my servant forth. LR 2.04.115
who stock'd my servant? 2.04.188
this trusty servant | shall pass between us. 4.02. 18
slain by his servant, going to put out | the 4.02. 71
a servant that he bred, thrill'd with remorse, 4.02. 73
so i would say) affectionate servant, goneril." 4.06.269 P
your servant kent. 5.03.284
where is your servant caius? 5.03.284
he's never any thing but your true servant. OTH 3.03. 9
i go from hence | thy soldier, servant, making ANT 1.03. 70
that mine own servant should | parcel the sum of 5.02.162
i your servant. 5.02.205
here is your servant. CYM 1.01.159
this hath been | your faithful servant. 1.01.174
thy hand, thou art | no servant of thy master's. 3.04. 76
that man of hers, pisanio, her old servant, | i 3.05. 54
cadwal and i | will play the cook and servant, 3.06. 30
your highness, | hold me your loyal servant. 4.03. 16
every good servant does not all commands; 5.01. 6
your servant, princes. 5.05.425
helps, | as i am son and servant to your will, PER 1.01. 23
fit counsellor and servant for a prince, | who 1.02. 63
who by thy wisdom makes a prince thy servant, 1.02. 64
you, | i'll not bereave you of your servant. 4.01. 31
who is a servant for | the tenor of /thy speech; TNK 1.01. 89
when your servant | (your most unworthy creature 2.05. 39
beshrew my heart, you have a servant | that, if 2.05. 62
whose servant (if there be a right in seeing 3.06.147
poor servant, thou hast lost. 5.03. 72
"why hath thy servant opportunity | betray'd the LUC 932
when you have bid your servant once adieu. SON 57. 8
SERVANTED 1 FR 0.0001 REL FR 1 V 0 P
my affairs | are servanted to others; COR 5.02. 83
SERVANT–MONSTER 3 FR 0.0003 REL FR 0 V 3 P
servant–monster, drink to me. TMP 3.02. 3 P
servant–monster? 3.02. 4 P
drink, servant–monster, when i bid thee. 3.02. 8 P
SERVANT'S 6 FR 0.0006 REL FR 5 V 1 P
cesario is your servant's name, fair princess. TN 3.01. 97
your servant's servant is your servant, madam. 3.01.102
master the author of the servant's damnation. H5 4.01.154 P
for he hath witness of his servant's malice. 2H6 1.03.209
the forfeit, sovereign, of my servant's life, R3 2.01.100
then, soul, live thou upon thy servant's loss, SON 146. 9
SERVANTS' 1 FR 0.0001 REL FR 1 V 0 P
because myself do want my servants' fortune. TGV 3.01.147
/SERVANTS 1 FR 0.0001 REL FR 0 V 1 P
/sort /you /with /the /rest /of /my /servants; HAM 2.02.268 P
SERVANTS 43 FR 0.0048 REL FR 36 V 7 P
my brother's servants | were then my fellows, TMP 2.01.273
all these are servants to deceitful men. TGV 2.07. 72
/god bless them and make them his servants! WIV 2.02. 53 P
dromio, go bid the servants spread for dinner. ERR 2.02.187
for servants must their masters' minds fulfill. 4.01.113
then let your servants bring my husband forth. 5.01. 93
of this fair mansion, master of my servants, MV 3.02.168
this house, these servants, and this same myself 3.02.170
give order to my servants that they take | no 5.01.119
o, this is it that makes your servants droop! SHR in.2. 27
look how thy servants do attend on thee, | each in.2. 33
servants, leave me and her alone. in.2. 116
keep house and port and servants, as i should. 1.01.203
pitchers have ears, and i have many servants; 4.04. 52
be forg'd in your thoughts be servants to you! AWW 1.01. 75
do other servants so? 2.03.251 P
be opposite with a kinsman, surly with servants; TN 2.05.150 P
thee a steward still, the fellow of servants, 2.05.157 P
opposite with a kinsman, surly with servants; 3.04. 69 P
if i | had servants true about me, that bare WT 1.02.309
and all the household servants fled with him R2 2.02. 60
love thy husband, look to thy servants, cherish 1H4 3.03.171 P
that no man could better command his servants. 2H4 5.01. 75 P
which stretch'd unto their servants, daughters, R3 3.05. 82
both | fell by our servants, by those men we H8 2.01.122
we profess, peacemakers, friends, and servants. 3.01.167
that were the servants to this chosen infant, 5.04. 48
here were the servants of your adversary, | and ROM 1.01.106
present grace to present slaves and servants TIM 1.01. 71
bound servants, steal; 4.01. 10
lug your priests and servants from your sides, 4.03. 32
do, | stir up their servants to an act of rage, JC 2.01.176
to your throne and state, children and servants; MAC 1.04. 25
your servants ever | have theirs, themselves, 1.06. 25
children, servants, all | that could be found. 4.03.211
this time invests you, go, your servants tend. HAM 1.03. 83
rabble make servants of their betters. LR 1.04.256
from those that she calls servants or from mine? 2.04.244
servants, who seem no less, | which are to 3.01. 23
the servants of the /duke? OTH 1.02. 34
call forth my household servants, let's to–night ANT 4.02. 9
that hath moe kings his servants than | thyself CYM 3.01. 63
"out, idle words, servants to shallow fools! LUC 1016
SERV'D 53 FR 0.0060 REL FR 33 V 20 P
serv'd | without or grudge or grumblings. TMP 1.02.248
i remember the trick you serv'd me, when i took TGV 4.04. 35 P
well, /and i be serv'd such another trick, i'll WIV 3.05. 6 P
we tell our husbands how we have serv'd him? 4.02.214 P
i have serv'd him from the hour of my nativity ERR 4.04. 30 P
long since thy husband serv'd me in my wars, 5.01.161
you think the prince would have serv'd you thus? ADO 2.01.196 P
if your leisure serv'd, i would speak with you. 3.02. 82 P
this was a venture, sir, that jacob serv'd for, MV 1.03. 91
for the table, sir, it shall be serv'd in; 3.05. 61 P
so he serv'd the second, and so the third. AYL 1.02.128 P
nor shalt not, till necessity be serv'd. 2.07. 89
thy will by my performance shall be serv'd. AWW 2.01.202
o that i serv'd that lady, | and might not be TN 1.02. 41
we have always truly serv'd you, and beseech' WT 2.03.148
i have serv'd prince florizel, and in my time 4.03. 13 P
welcom'd all, serv'd all; 4.04. 57
men, and i would have you serv'd with the best. 2H4 3.02.256 P
those precepts cannot be serv'd; 5.01. 14 P
i have serv'd your worship truly, sir, this 5.01. 47 P
it hath serv'd me instead of a quart pot to 2H6 4.10. 14 P
were you well serv'd, you would be taught your R3 1.03.249
his master would be serv'd before a subject, if H8 2.02. 7 P
had i but serv'd my god with half the zeal | i 3.02.455
my god with half the zeal | i serv'd my king, he 3.02.456
why hast thou not serv'd thyself in to my table TRO 2.03. 42 P

but since he hath | serv'd well for rome — COR 3.03. 83
serv'd his designments | in mine own person; 5.06. 34
up, | and they have serv'd me to effectless use. TIT 3.01. 76
the guests are come, supper serv'd up, you ROM 1.03.100 P
is it not then well serv'd in to a sweet goose? 2.04. 81 P
this gentleman of mine hath serv'd me long; TIM 1.01.142
ay, would they serv'd us! 2.02. 93 P
as good a trick as ever hangman serv'd thief. 2.02. 95 P
what touches us ourself shall be last serv'd. JC 3.01. 8
all that serv'd brutus, i will entertain them. 5.05. 60
and let the angel whom thou still hast serv'd MAC 5.08. 14
i have seen myself, and serv'd against, the HAM 4.07. 83
serv'd the lust of my mistress' heart and did LR 3.04. 86 P
i have serv'd you ever since i was a child; 3.07. 73
for i have serv'd him, and the man commands OTH 2.01. 35
thou hast serv'd me with much faith; ANT 2.07. 58
of those that serv'd mark antony but late, 4.01. 13
you have serv'd me well, | and kings have been 4.02. 12
and have fought | not as you serv'd the cause, 4.08. 6
mark antony i serv'd, who best was worthy | best 5.01. 6
serv'd, who best was worthy | best to be serv'd. 5.01. 7
whom | he serv'd with glory and admir'd success: CYM 1.01. 32
britain harm, | though he have serv'd a roman. 5.05. 91
she is serv'd | as i would serve a rat." 5.05.247
as i have serv'd her truest, worthiest, | as i TNK 3.06.165
when nought serv'd, | when neither curb would 5.04. 73
hath serv'd a dumb arrest upon his tongue, | who LUC 1780

/SERVE 1 FR 0.0001 REL FR 1 V 0 P
/all /our /griefs | (/when /time /shall /serve) 2H4 4.01. 74

SERVE 193 FR 0.0218 REL FR 112 V 81 P
a plague upon the tyrant that i serve! TMP 2.02.162
the mistress which i serve quickens what's dead, 3.01. 6
i'll not serve him, he is not valiant. 3.02. 24 P
thou shalt be lord of it, and i'll serve thee. 3.02. 57
than a pound shall serve me for carrying your TGV 1.01.105 P
would serve to scale another hero's tow'r, | so 3.01.119
a cloak as long as thine will serve the turn? 3.01.131
why, any cloak will serve the turn, my lord. 3.01.134
so long that going will scarce serve the turn. 3.01.379 P
i have a sonnet that will serve the turn | to 3.02. 92
on my word, it will serve him; WIV 4.02. 77 P
sure, one of you does not serve heaven well, 4.05.125 P
will none but herne the hunter serve your turn? 5.05.104
sir john falstaff, serve got, and leave your 5.05.129 P
not men in your ward sufficient to serve it? MM 2.01.267 P
shall we serve heaven | with less respect than 2.02. 85
sir, i will serve him; 4.02. 49 P
but let your reason serve | to make the truth 5.01. 65
look when i serve him so, he takes it /ill. ERR 2.01. 12
how many fond fools serve mad jealousy? 2.01.116
i'll serve you, sir, five hundred at the rate. 4.04. 14
look what will serve is fit: ADO 1.01.318
will it serve for any model to build mischief on 1.03. 46 P
masters, do you serve god? 4.02. 16 P
write down, that they hope they serve god; 4.02. 18 P
when time and place shall serve, that i am an 5.01.256 P
serve god, love me, and mend. 5.02. 93 P
this maid will not serve your turn, sir. LLL 1.01.298 P
this maid will serve my turn, sir. 1.01.299 P
it would neither serve for the writing nor the 1.02.113 P
first and second cause will not serve my turn; 1.02.178 P
i am bound to serve. 4.01. 56
priscian a little scratch'd, 'twill serve. 5.01. 29 P
doth this man serve god? 5.02.524 P
i'll serve thee true and faithfully till then. 5.02.831
and i serve the fairy queen, | to dew her orbs MND 2.01. 8
one turf shall serve as pillow for us both, 2.02. 41
this wood, i have enough to serve mine owe turn. 3.01.150 P
my conscience will serve me to run from this jew MV 2.02. 1 P
if i serve not him, i will run as far as god has 2.02.110 P
for i am a jew if i serve the jew any longer. 2.02.112 P
infection, sir, as one would say, to serve — 2.02.126 P
the short and the long is, i serve the jew, and 2.02.127 P
serve you, sir. 2.02.142 P
bid them cover the table, serve in the meat, and 3.05. 59 P
no, pray thee, let it serve for table–talk; 3.05. 88
of men | their graces serve them but as enemies? AYL 2.03. 11
and you serve me such another trick, never come 4.01. 40 P
to–morrow i cannot serve your turn for rosalind? 5.02. 48 P
it shall become to serve all hopes conceiv'd, SHR 1.01. 15
and while i pause, serve in your harmony. 3.01. 14
and serve it thus to me that love it not? 4.01.164
coming down the hill, | will serve the turn. 4.02. 62
when they are bound to serve, love, and obey. 5.02.164
my instruction shall serve to naturalize thee, AWW 1.01.208 P
it well may serve | a nursery to our gentry, who 1.02. 15
would god would serve the world so all the year! 1.03. 83 P
health, at your bidding, serve your majesty! 2.01. 18
beware of being captives | before you serve. 2.01. 22
but for me, i have an answer will serve all men. 2.02. 13 P
will your answer serve fit to all questions? 2.02. 20 P
i see things may serve long, but not serve ever. 2.02. 58 P
i see things may serve long, but not serve ever. 2.02. 58 P
whom i serve above is my master. 2.03.246 P
madam, he's gone to serve the duke of florence. 3.02. 52
we serve you, madam, | in that and all your 3.02. 95
the cutting of my garments would serve the turn, 4.01. 47 P
hardly serve. 4.01. 54 P
ay, so you serve us | till we serve you; 4.02. 17
ay, so you serve us | till we serve you; 4.02. 18
held, can serve the world for no honest use; 4.03.306 P
sir, if i cannot serve you, i can serve as great 4.05. 36 P
you, i can serve as great a prince as you are. 4.05. 36 P
serve him still. 4.05. 46 P
dear perfection hearts that scorn'd to serve 5.03. 18
i'll serve this duke; TN 1.02. 55
if that this simple syllogism will serve, so; 1.05. 50 P
i serve her, she is my lady. 2.05.116 P
i was preserv'd to serve this noble count. 5.01.256
let him be, | until a time may serve. WT 2.03. 22
within, i'll serve you | as i would do the gods. 3.02.206
if | his going i could frame to serve my turn, 4.04.509
from her womb | will serve to strangle thee; JN 4.03.129
must i not serve a long apprenticehood | to R2 1.03.271
york | hath power enough to serve our turn. 3.02. 90
if he serve god, | we'll serve him too, and be 3.02. 98
we'll serve him too, and be his fellow so. 3.02. 99
to serve me last that i may longest keep | thy 3.04. 95
not so much as will serve to be prologue to an 1H4 1.02. 20 P
how long hast thou to serve, francis? 2.04. 41 P
the powers of us may serve so great a day. 4.01.132
and made her serve your uses both in purse and 2H4 2.01.115 P
it shall serve among wits of no higher breeding 2.02. 35 P
for to serve bravely is to come halting off, you 2.04. 49 P
shadow will serve for summer, prick him, for we 3.02.133 P
no man's too good to serve 's prince, and let it 3.02.237 P
there is no excuse shall serve, you shall not be 5.01. 6 P
but when time shall serve, there shall be smiles H5 2.01. 6 P
and do serve you | with hearts create of duty 2.02. 30
but all they three, though they would serve me, 3.02. 30 P
that is well, i warrant you, when time is serve. 3.06. 66 P
under what captain serve you? 4.01. 93 P
moy shall not serve, i will have forty moys, 4.04. 13
for you, and i pray you to serve god, and keep 4.08. 64 P
i can tell you it will serve you to mend your 4.08. 69 P
for soldiers' stomachs always serve them well. 1H6 2.03. 80
then, york, be still awhile, till time do serve. 2H6 1.01.248
a subtile knave, but yet it shall not serve. 2.01.102
now the word "sallet" must serve me to feed on. 4.10. 15 P
ay, noble father, if our words will serve. 5.01.139
must strike her sail and learn a while to serve 3H6 3.03. 5
again, | i came to serve a king and not a duke. 4.07. 49
if fortune serve me, i'll requite this kindness. 4.07. 78
to serve me well, you all should do me duty, R3 1.03.250
o, serve me well, and teach yourselves that duty 1.03.252
your grace's words shall serve | as well as i 3.05. 62
when they should serve their sovereign in the 4.04.485
serve your will as't please | yourself pronounce H8 2.04.114
serve the king, and — prithee lead me in. 3.02.450
i serve thee not. TRO 2.01. 92 P
i serve here voluntary. 2.01. 94 P
thersites is a fool to serve such a fool, and 2.03. 64 P
nay, that shall not serve your turn, that shall 3.01. 74 P
will the time serve to tell? COR 1.06. 46
the rest will serve | for a short holding. 1.07. 3
no better thought of, a little help will serve; 2.03. 15 P
how youngly he began to serve his country, | how 2.03.236
i think 'twill serve, if he | can thereto frame 3.02. 96
no, i serve not thy master. 4.05. 45 P
serve with thy trencher. 4.05. 48 P
straight | and make my misery serve thy turn. 4.05. 88
thereby to destroy | the volsces whom you serve, 5.03.134
i am as able and as fit as thou | to serve, and TIT 2.01. 34
certain snatch or so | would serve your turns. 2.01. 96
there serve your lust, shadowed from heaven's 2.01.130
my hand will serve the turn. 3.01.164
let it serve | to ransom my two nephews from 3.01.171
at such a bay, by turn to serve our lust. 4.02. 42
is as fit as can be to serve for your oration, 4.03. 95 P
i serve as good a man as you. ROM 1.01. 54 P
what doth her beauty serve but as a note | where 1.01.235
go thy ways, wench, serve god. 2.05. 45 P
as a church–door, but 'tis enough, 'twill serve. 3.01. 97 P
not, and all these woes shall serve | for sweet 3.05. 52
our bridal flowers serve for a buried corse; 4.05. 89
i must serve my turn | out of mine own. TIM 2.01. 20
you three serve three usurers? 2.02. 91 P
ay, but this answer will not serve. 3.04. 57
if 'twill not serve, 'tis not so base as you, 3.04. 58
'tis not so base as you, | for you serve knaves. 3.04. 59
i'll ever serve his mind with my best will; 4.02. 49
and, as my lord, | still serve him with my life. 4.03.471
kept were knaves, to serve in meat to villains. 4.03.478
i must serve him so too: 5.01. 20
you serve octavius caesar, do you not? JC 3.01.276
yet when we can entreat an hour to serve, | we MAC 2.01. 22
and none serve with him but constrained things, 5.04. 13
but, o, what form of prayer | can serve my turn? HAM 3.03. 52
of choice, | to serve in such a difference. 3.04. 76
i do serve you in this business. LR 1.02.178 P
if thou canst serve where thou dost stand 1.04. 5
to serve him truly that will put me in trust, to 1.04. 14 P
who wouldst thou serve? 1.04. 24 P
follow me, thou shalt serve me. 1.04. 40 P
i shall serve you, sir, | truly, however else. 2.01.116
i serve you, madam. 2.01.128
call not your stocks for me, i serve the king, 2.02.128
when time shall serve, let but the herald cry, 5.01. 48
i follow him to serve my turn upon him. OTH 1.01. 42
you are one of those that will not serve god, if 1.01.109 P
you shall outlive the lady whom you serve. ANT 1.02. 31
makes the sea serve them, which they ear and 1.04. 49
and make the hearts of romans serve your ends! 3.02. 37
if we should serve with horse and mares together 3.07. 7
which serve not for his vantage, he shakes off, 3.07. 33
to–morrow | you'll serve another master. 4.02. 28
wilt thou serve me? CYM 3.05.117 P
wilt thou serve me? 3.05.121 P
how fit his garments serve me! 4.01. 3 P
serve truly; 4.02.373
she is serv'd | as i would serve a rat." 5.05.248
and when came you to serve our roman captive? 5.05.385
nor place | will serve our long interrogatories. 5.05.392
these roguing thieves serve the great pirate PER 4.01. 96
she would serve after a long voyage at sea. 4.06. 44 P
where a man may serve seven years for the loss 4.06.171 P
serve by indenture to the common hangman: 4.06.176
if you serve faithfully, i dare assure you TNK 2.05. 56
worn a lighter, | but i shall make it serve. 3.06. 57
and for my sake serve thou false tarquin so. LUC 1197
serve always with assured trust, | and in thy PP 18.19
when time shall serve, be thou not slack | to 18.23
that did his picture get | to serve their eyes, LC 135

SERVED 3 FR 0.0003 REL FR 3 V 0 P
which served me as fit, by all men's judgments, TGV 4.04.162
ay, so the turn were served. TIT 2.01. 96
he is justly served, | it is a poison temper'd HAM 5.02.327

SERVE'S 1 FR 0.0001 REL FR 1 V 0 P
too high a fame when him we serve's away. ANT 3.01. 15

SERVES 39 FR 0.0044 REL FR 34 V 5 P
wood, and serves in offices | that profit us. TMP 1.02.312
the time now serves not to expostulate: TGV 3.01.253
she is her master's maid, and serves for wages. 3.01.271 P
one that serves a bad woman; MM 2.01. 64 P
i am sorry that your leisure serves you not. MV 4.01.405
that 'scuse serves many men to save their gifts, 4.01.444
to them as you find your stomach serves you: SHR 1.01. 38
o lord, sir! — why, there't serves well again. AWW 2.02. 62 P
there is a gentleman that serves the count 3.05. 56
hope, | whereto thy speech serves for authority, TN 1.02. 20
sea, | which serves it in the office of a wall, R2 2.01. 47
which serves as paste and cover to our bones. 3.02.154
yet time serves wherein you may redeem | your 1H4 1.03.180
since sudden sorrow | serves to say thus, some 2H4 4.02. 84
this davy serves you for good uses, he is your 5.03. 10 P
the cry of talbot serves me for a sword, | for i 1H6 2.01. 79
although you break it when your pleasure serves. 5.04.164
it serves you well, my lord, to say so much. 2H6 3.01.119
scarce serves to quench my furnace–burning heart 3H6 2.01. 80
and, as occasion serves, this noble queen | and 3.03.236
shame serves thy life and doth thy death attend. R3 4.04.196
all in uproar, | and danger serves among them. H8 1.02. 37
is not, serves | as stuff for these two to make TRO 1.03.183
but, since it serves my purpose, i will venture COR 1.01. 91
the day serves well for them now. 4.03. 31 P
my leisure serves me, pensive daughter, now. ROM 4.01. 39
that time serves still. TIM 1.01.258
when the day serves, before black–corner'd night 5.01. 44
when it serves | for the base matter to JC 1.03.109
and we must take the current when it serves, 4.03.223
whereto serves mercy | but to confront the HAM 3.03. 46
our indiscretion sometime serves us well | when 5.02. 8
that sir which serves and seeks for gain, | and LR 2.04. 78
in heaven | but what serves for the thunder? OTH 5.02.235
serves for the matter that is then born in't. ANT 2.02. 10
and our advantage serves | for a fair victory. 4.07. 11
day serves not light more faithful than i'll be. PER 1.02.110
now serves the season that they may surprise LUC 166
debate where leisure serves with dull debaters; 1019

SERVETH 1 FR 0.0001 REL FR 1 V 0 P
this token serveth for a flag of truce | betwixt 1H6 3.01.138

/SERVICE 2 FR 0.0002 REL FR 2 V 0 P
/to /do /what /service /am /i /sent /for /hither R2 4.01.176
/and /did /him /service | /improper /for /a LR 5.03.221

SERVICE 228 FR 0.0257 REL FR 171 V 57 P
remember i have done thee worthy service, | told TMP 1.02.247
he, that caliban | whom now i keep in service. 1.02.286
riches, poverty, | and use of service, none; 2.01.152
you, did | my heart fly to your service, there 3.01. 65
thou and thy meaner fellows your last service 4.01. 35
for a little | follow, and do me service. 4.01.266
all this service | have i done since i went. 5.01.225
and to commend their service to his will. TGV 1.03. 42
in losing thy master, lose thy service, and, in 2.03. 44 P
and, in losing thy service — why dost thou stop 2.03. 44 P
and the master, and the service, and the tied! 2.03. 51 P
nor to his service no such joy on earth: 2.04.139
at thy service. 2.05. 59 P
love | will creep in service where it cannot go. 4.02. 20
i am thus early come to know what service | it 4.03. 9
and will employ thee in some service presently. 4.04. 41
madam, this service i have done for you 5.04. 19
men — very rogues, now they be out of service. WIV 2.01.176 P
it hath done meritorious service. 4.02.205 P
have worn your eyes almost out in the service, MM 1.02.110 P
i prithee, lucio, do me this kind service: 1.02.176
he knew the service, and that instructed him to 3.02.120 P
habit, i am still | attorney'd at your service. 5.01.385
i'll lend you all my life to do you service. 5.01.432
if i last in this service, you must case me in ERR 2.01. 85
nothing at his hands for my service but blows. 4.04. 32 P
even for the service that long since i did thee, 5.01.191
he hath done good service, lady, in these wars. ADO 1.01. 48 P
grace command me any service to the world's end? 2.01.263 P
and shape his service wholly to my device, | and LLL 5.02. 65
dumaine was at my service, and his sword: 5.02.276
and longaville was for my service born. 5.02.284
majesty | command me any service to her thither? 5.02.312
impose some service on me for thy love. 5.02.840
and conn'd with cruel pain, | to do you service. MND 5.01. 81
and duty in his service perishing. 5.01. 86
i am famish'd in his service; MV 2.02.106 P
be preferment | to leave a rich jew's service, 2.02.147
i cannot get a service, no; 2.02.156 P
above, | in love and service to you evermore. 4.01.414
most true, i have lost my teeth in your service. AYL 1.01. 83 P
turning these jests out of service, let us talk 1.03. 26 P
when service should in my old limbs lie lame, 2.03. 41
i'll do the service of a younger man | in all 2.03. 54
the constant service of the antique world, 2.03. 57
when service sweat for duty, not for meed! 2.03. 58
and having that do choke their service up | even 2.03. 61
it is to be all made of faith and service, | and 5.02. 89
players | that offer service to your lordship. SHR in.1. 78
not a lawful cause for me to leave his service, 1.02. 30 P
pray accept his service. 2.01. 83 P
the poorest service is repaid with thanks, | and 4.03. 45
gentlemen that mean to see | the tuscan service, AWW 1.02. 14
he did look far | into the service of the time, 1.02. 27
service is no heritage, and i think i shall 1.03. 23 P
but i give | me and my service, ever whilst i 2.03.103
french count has done most honorable service. 3.05. 4 P
of yours | that has done worthy service. 3.05. 48
not to be blam'd in the command of the service; 3.06. 52 P
that the merit of service is seldom attributed 3.06. 61 P
will for ever | do thee all rights of service. 4.02. 17
sir, at a woman's service, and a knave at a 4.05. 24 P
cozen the man of his wife and do his service. 4.05. 28 P
so you were a knave at his service indeed. 4.05. 29 P
give his wife my bauble, sir, to do her service. 4.05. 31 P
at your service. 4.05. 34 P
that will allow me very worth his service. TN 1.02. 59
here, madam, at your service. 1.05.299
my duty, madam, and most humble service. 3.01. 95
the count his galleys | i did some service, of 3.03. 27
his counsel now might do me golden service, 4.03. 8
and for your service done him, | so much against 5.01.321
i'll put | my fortunes to your service, which WT 1.02.440
i have eyes under my service which look upon his 4.02. 35 P
wore three–pile, but now i am out of service. 4.03. 14 P
horseman's coat, it hath seen very hot service. 4.03. 68 P
commend them and condemn them to her service, 4.04.377
at your employment, at your service, sir." JN 1.01.198

but you at your sick service had a prince. 4.01. 52
well, | upon your oath of service to the pope, 5.01. 23
but are gone | to offer service to your enemy; 5.01. 34
home, | for christian service and true chivalry, R2 2.01. 54
to offer service to the duke of herford, | and 2.03. 32
my gracious lord, i tender you my service, 2.03. 41
confirm | to more approved service and desert. 2.03. 44
his heart | to faithful service of your majesty. 3.03.118
as my true service shall deserve your love. 3.03.199
so | for some displeasing service i have done, 1H4 3.02. 5
put thee into my service for any other reason 2H4 1.02. 13 P
he hath since done good service at shrewsbury, 1.02. 62 P
your day's service at shrewsbury hath a little 1.02.148 P
mouldy, stay at home till you are past service; 3.02.251 P
the service that i truly did his life | hath 5.02. 7
so service shall with steeled sinews toil, | and H5 2.02. 36
that's all the riches i got in his service. 2.03. 44 P
by that piece of service the men would carry 3.02. 46 P
i must leave them, and seek some better service. 3.02. 52 P
themselves to slomber, ay'll de gud service, or 3.02.115 P
world, but i did see him do as gallant service. 3.06. 16 P
hark how our steeds for present service neigh! 4.02. 8
soldiers' heads | and turn them out of service. 4.03.119
my lord, | commend my service to my sovereign." 4.06. 23
the welshmen did good service in a garden where 4.07. 99 P
this hour is an honorable badge of the service; 4.07.101 P
and humble service till the point of death. 1H6 3.01.167
your faithful service, and your toil in war; 3.04. 21
and do some service to duke humphrey's ghost. 2H6 3.02.231
he were created knight for his good service. 5.01. 77
and such a piece of service will you do, | if 5.01.155
your legs did better service than your hands. 3H6 2.02.104
so shall you bind me to your highness' service. 3.02. 43
what service wilt thou do me if i give them? 3.02. 44
i'll do thee service for so good a gift. 5.01. 33
which i will purchase with my duteous service; R3 2.01. 64
a boon, my sovereign, for my service done! 2.01. 96
ghastly looks | are at my service, like enforced 3.05. 9
me, | who, earnest in the service of my god, 3.07.106
repays he my deep service | with such contempt? 4.02.119
a most unnatural and faithless service. H8 2.01.123
breed | (and service to his majesty and you) 3.01. 52
a sign of peace, | his service and his counsel. 3.01. 67
to use our utmost studies in your service. 3.01.174
pray do my service to his majesty; 3.01.179
weary and old with service, to the mercy | of a 3.02.363
not to let | thy hopeful service perish too. 3.02.419
the king shall have my service; 3.02.426
first, mine own service to your grace, the next, 4.02.115
i | am for his love and service so to him. 5.02.192
of bombards, when | ye should do service. 5.03. 82
your last service was suff'rance, 'twas not TRO 2.01. 95 P
to make the service greater than the god, | and 2.02. 57
wranglers, took a truce, | and did him service; 2.02. 76
now, princes, for the service i have done, | th' 3.03. 1
and here, to do you service, am become | as new 3.03. 11
shall quite strike off all service i have done, 3.03. 29
high birth, vigor of bone, desert in service, 3.03.172
fellow, commend my service to her beauty; 5.05. 3
to gratify his noble service that | hath thus COR 2.02. 40
i got them in my country's service, when | some 2.03. 52
well assur'd | they ne'er did service for't; 3.01.122
this kind of service | did not deserve corn 3.01.124
the service of the foot | being once gangren'd, 3.01.304
the warlike service he has done, consider; 3.03. 49
what do you prate of service? 3.03. 83
he give me way, | i'll do his country service. 4.04. 26
what service is here? 4.05. 1 P
'tis an honester service than to meddle with thy 4.05. 47 P
the painful service, | the extreme dangers, and 4.05. 68
to thy shame, unless | it be to do thee service. 4.05.101
that in your country's service drew your swords, TIT 1.01.175
in right and service of their noble country. 1.01.197
now all the service i require of them | is that 3.01. 77
for hands to do rome service is but vain. 3.01. 80
can do no service on her sorrowful cheeks. 3.01.147
do me some service ere i come to thee. 5.02. 44
here, at your lordship's service. TIM 1.01.115
doubled with thanks and service, from whose help 1.02. 7
my heart is ever at your service, my lord. 1.02. 75 P
his service done | at lacedaemon and byzantium 3.05. 59
why, /i say, my lords, h'as done fair service, 3.05. 62
thou mightst have sooner got another service; 4.03.504
we are hither come to offer you our service. 5.01. 72
what we can do, we'll do, to do you service. 5.01. 75
that did the latest service to my master. JC 5.05. 67
the service and the loyalty i owe, | in doing it MAC 1.04. 22
all our service | in every point twice done, and 1.06. 14
so bold to call, | for 'tis my limited service. 2.03. 52
the inward service of the mind and soul | grows HAM 1.03. 13
bent, | to lay our service freely at your feet, 2.02. 31
and hither are they coming to offer you service. 2.02.318 P
here, sweet lord, at your service. 3.02. 53
officers do the king best service in the end: 4.02. 17 P
and your lean beggar is but variable service, 4.03. 24 P
we should profane the service of the dead | to 5.01.236
but, sir, now | it did me yeman's service. 5.02. 36
service. LR 1.04. 23 P
i thank thee, there's earnest of thy service. 1.04. 94 P
that wouldst be a bawd in way of good service, 2.02. 20 P
his daughter speak, commands, tends service. 2.04.102
but better service have i never done you | than 3.07. 74
and of the loyal service of his son, | when i 4.02. 7
'tis the curse of service; OTH 1.01. 35
throwing but shows of service on their lords, 1.01. 52
we come to do you service and you think we are 1.01.110 P
i lack iniquity | sometime to do me service. 1.02. 4
my general will forget my love and service. 3.03. 18
hands, heart, | to wrong'd othello's service! 3.03.467
of such mortal kind | that nor my service past, 3.04.116
i have done the state some service, and they 5.02.339
here, at your service. my lord approaches. ANT 1.02. 86
there i deny my land service. 2.06. 94 P
that will do me no service as a partisan i could 2.07. 13 P
villainy, | in thee't had been good service. 2.07. 75
prevail | under the service of a child as soon 3.13. 24
that i might do you service | so good as you 4.02. 18
like a master | married to your good service, 4.02. 31
how wouldst thou have paid | my better service, 4.06. 32
'tis the last service that i shall command you. 4.14.132
doctor, your service for this time is ended, CYM 1.05. 30
no further service, doctor, | until i send for 1.05. 44
let me my service tender on your lips. 1.06.140
cannot choose but take this service i have done 2.03. 35 P
if it be so to do good service, never | let me 3.02. 14
this service is not service, so being done, 3.03. 16
this service is not service, so being done, 3.03. 16
lucius | present yourself, desire his service, 3.04.173
not be a villain, but do me true service, 3.05.109 P
the first service thou dost me, fetch that suit 3.05.127 P
let it be thy first service, go. 3.05.128 P
willing spirits | that promise noble service; 4.02.339
from east to occident, cry out for service, 4.02.372
and leaving so his service, follow you, | so 4.02.393
hath not deserv'd my service nor your loves, 4.04. 25
he brags his service | as if he were of note. 5.03. 93
the service that you three have done is more 5.05.353
my good master, | i will yet do you service. 5.05.404
and heavy well–a–day | in her unholy service. PER 4.04. 50
cleon, but i am | for other service first. 5.01.254
this is a service, whereto i am going, | greater TNK 1.01.171
i freely lend | to do these poor queens service. 1.01.199
commands men service, | and what they win in't, 1.02. 69
and do my ablest service | to such a well–found 2.05. 26
i shall give you | to a most noble service — to 2.05. 34
call a wolf, | and do him but that service. 3.02. 11
treason | in service of so excellent a beauty, 3.06.162
and must needs be by | to give the service pay. 5.03. 32
we, and all our might, | rest at your service. ep 18
that is so proud thy service to despise, | when SON 149.10
SERVICEABLE 5 FR 0.0005 REL FR 5 V 0 P
should be full–fraught with serviceable vows. TGV 3.02. 70
"be serviceable to my son," quoth he, | although SHR 1.01.214
not have, | wherein olivia may seem serviceable? TN 5.01.102
a serviceable villain, | as duteous to the vices LR 4.06.252
service, never | let me be counted serviceable. CYM 3.02. 15
SERVICES 35 FR 0.0039 REL FR 21 V 14 P
in her behalf that scorns your services. MND 3.02.331
she that would alter services with thee, the TN 2.05.158 P
occasion whereon my services are now on foot, WT 1.01. 2 P
present our services to a fine new prince | one 2.01. 17
(as recompense of our dear services | past and 2.03.150
out the rest of thy services by leaving me now. 4.02. 11 P
away with thee the very services thou hast done; 4.02. 16 P
i think | you have heard of my poor services, i' 4.04.516
all my services | you have paid home; 5.03. 3
i do bequeath my faithful services | and true JN 5.07.104
heads, and they have bought out their services; 1H4 4.02. 23 P
rooms of them as have bought out their services, 4.02. 33 P
lives, and services | to this imperial throne. H5 1.02. 34
with hope | to do your grace incessant services. 2.02. 38
is very excellent services committed at the 3.06. 3 P
learn you by rote where services were done — at 3.06. 71 P
their death when they purpose their services. 4.01.158 P
consider you what services he has done for his COR 1.01. 30 P
i do owe them still | my life and services. 2.02.134
thinking upon his services, took from you | th' 2.03.223
i am a roman, and my services are, as you are, 4.03. 4 P
it | that my revengeful services may prove | as 4.05. 89
tender down | their services to lord timon. TIM 1.01. 55
my services to your lordship. LR 1.01. 29 P
my goddess, to thy law | my services are bound. 1.02. 2
if you come slack of former services, | you 1.03. 9
what services canst do? 1.04. 31 P
to thee a woman's services are due, | /a fool 4.02. 27
my services which i have done the signiory OTH 1.02. 18
of time commands | our services awhile; ANT 1.03. 43
once, | or thy precedent services are all | but 4.14. 83
make denials | increase your services; CYM 2.03. 49
alike conversant in general services, and more 4.01. 13 P
our services stand now for thebes, not creon. TNK 1.02. 99
spend, | nor services to do, till you require. SON 57. 4
SERVILE 11 FR 0.0012 REL FR 11 V 0 P
thou art, | servile to all the skyey influences, MM 3.01. 9
where fearing dying pays death servile breath. R2 3.02.185
yet, if this servile usage once offend, | go, 1H6 5.03. 58
forth thunder | upon these paltry, servile, 2H6 4.01.105
away with slavish weeds and servile thoughts! TIT 2.01. 18
trot like a servile footman all day long, | even 5.02. 55
men, | and keep us all in servile fearfulness. JC 1.01. 75
but yet i call you servile ministers, | that LR 3.02. 21
obeyed, | yet was he servile to my coy disdain. VEN 112
sire, | subject and servile to all discontents, 1161
and therein heartens up his servile powers, LUC 295
SERVILELY 1 FR 0.0001 REL FR 1 V 0 P
tree, | servilely master'd with a leathern rein! VEN 392
SERVILITY 1 FR 0.0001 REL FR 1 V 0 P
more vile | than is a slave in base servility; 1H6 5.03.113
SERVILIUS 8 FR 0.0009 REL FR 4 V 4 P
servilius! TIM 2.02.185
servilius? 3.02. 27 P
dost thou speak seriously, servilius? 3.02. 42
servilius, now before the gods, i am not able to 3.02. 48 P
good servilius, will you befriend me so far as 3.02. 57 P
i'll look you out a good turn, servilius. 3.02. 60
o, here's servilius; 3.04. 66 P
servilius, help! my lord, my lord! 3.04. 78
SERVING 6 FR 0.0006 REL FR 6 V 0 P
serving of becks and jutting–out of bums! TIM 1.02.231
we are fellows still, | serving alike in sorrow. 4.02. 19
and serving you so long! ANT 3.03. 44
would you in their serving | (and with what CYM 3.04.170
sight, | serving with looks his sacred majesty, SON 7. 4
dissuade one foolish heart from serving thee, 141.10
SERVING–CREATURE
1 FR 0.0001 REL FR 0 V 1 P
then will i give you the serving–creature. ROM 4.05.116 P
SERVING–CREATURE'S
1 FR 0.0001 REL FR 0 V 1 P
will i lay the serving–creature's dagger on your ROM 4.05.117 P
SERVINGMAN 8 FR 0.0009 REL FR 2 V 6 P
a wither'd servingman a fresh tapster. WIV 1.03. 18 P
good master slender's servingman, and friend 3.01. 2 P
to the count's servingman than ever she bestow'd TN 3.02. 6 P
or useful servingman and instrument | to any JN 5.02. 81
them, is turn'd into a justice–like servingman. 2H4 5.01. 68 P
uses, he is your servingman and your husband. 5.03. 11 P
a servingman! LR 3.04. 85 P
the chambermaid and servingman, by night | that TNK 3.05.126
SERVINGMEN 2 FR 0.0002 REL FR 0 V 2 P
swept, the servingmen in their new fustian, SHR 4.01. 47 P
but discarded unjust servingmen, younger sons to 1H4 4.02. 28 P
SERVITEUR 2 FR 0.0002 REL FR 0 V 2 P
et vous aussi; votre serviteur. TN 3.01. 72 P
indigne serviteur. H5 5.02.255 P
SERVITOR 3 FR 0.0003 REL FR 3 V 0 P
pass, | and henceforth i am thy true servitor. 3H6 3.03.196
commenting | is leaden servitor to dull delay; R3 4.03. 52
your trusty and most valiant servitor, | with OTH 1.03. 40
SERVITORS 3 FR 0.0003 REL FR 3 V 0 P
thus are poor servitors, | when others sleep 1H6 2.01. 5
here none but soldiers and rome's servitors TIT 1.01.352
both which, as servitors to the unjust, | so LUC 285
SERVITUDE 4 FR 0.0004 REL FR 3 V 1 P
this servitude makes you to keep unwed. ERR 2.01. 26
me, begins to mutiny against this servitude. AYL 1.01. 24 P
his princes and his peers to servitude, | his H5 2.02.171
and awkward casualties | bound me in servitude. PER 5.01. 94
SERV'ST 3 FR 0.0003 REL FR 1 V 2 P
who serv'st thou under? H5 4.07.147 P
straightway give thy soul to him thou serv'st. 1H6 1.05. 7
thou serv'st me, and i'll love thee. LR 1.04. 87 P
SESSA 3 FR 0.0003 REL FR 0 V 3 P
sessa! SHR in.1. 6 P
dolphin my boy, boy, sessa! LR 3.04.100 P
sessa! 3.06. 74 P
SESSION 7 FR 0.0008 REL FR 6 V 1 P
prince, | no longer session hold upon my shame, MM 5.01.371
summon a session, that we may arraign | our most
WT 2.03.202
every shop, church, session, hanging, yields a 4.04.685 P
madam, | it's fit this royal session do proceed, H8 2.04. 66
t' appear | where you shall hold your session. LR 5.03. 54
of law and course of direct session | call thee OTH 1.02. 86
from this session interdict | every fowl of PHT 9
SESSIONS 4 FR 0.0004 REL FR 4 V 0 P
this sessions (to our great grief we pronounce) WT 3.02. 1
the sessions shall proceed; 3.02.141
keep leets and law–days and in sessions sit OTH 3.03.140
when to the sessions of sweet silent thought | i SON 30. 1
SESTOS 1 FR 0.0001 REL FR 0 V 1 P
of that age found it was — hero of sestos. AYL 4.01.106 P
/SET* 4 FR 0.0004 REL FR 3 V 1 P
shall we /set about some revels? TN 1.03.135 P
/your /cares /set /up /do /not /pluck /my /cares R2 4.01.195
/a /kingdom /down | /and /set /another /up), 2H4 1.03. 50
/prayers /and /love | /were /set /on /herford, 4.01.136
SET* 484 FR 0.0547 REL FR 380 V 104 P
set her two courses off to sea again! TMP 1.01. 49 P
set all hearts i' th' state | to what tune 1.02. 84
nor set | a mark so bloody on the business; 1.02.141
delicate ariel, | i'll set thee free for this. 1.02.443
but | for every trifle are they set upon me, 2.02. 8
pray set it down, and rest you. 3.01. 18
the sun will set before i shall discharge | what 3.01. 22
chiefly that i might set it in my prayers — 3.01. 35
thy eyes are almost set in thy head. 3.02. 9 P
where should they be set else? 3.02. 10 P
monster indeed if they were set in his tail. 3.02. 11 P
sea and the azur'd vault | set roaring war; 5.01. 44
and set it down | with gold on lasting pillars: 5.01.207
set caliban and his companions free; 5.01.252
pardon'd be, | let your indulgence set me free. ep 20
war with good counsel, set the world at nought; TGV 1.01. 68
and that set together is "noddy." 1.01.115 P
now you have taken the pains to set it together, 1.01.116 P
give me a note, your ladyship can set. 1.02. 78
i would you were set, so your affection would 2.01. 85 P
then may i set the world on wheels, when she can 3.01.315 P
o villain, that set this down among her vices! 3.01.333 P
here, set it down. WIV 3.03. 6 P
alas, i had rather be set quick i' th' earth, 3.04. 86
if he bid you set it down, obey him. 4.02.110 P
set down the basket, villain! 4.02.115 P
and set spurs and away, like three german devils 4.05. 68 P
the knave constable had set me i' th' stocks, i' 4.05.119 P
a bull for thy europa, love set on thy horns. 5.05. 4 P
the oil that's in me should set hell on fire; 5.05. 35 P
yourselves in order set; 5.05. 77
'tis set down so in heaven, but not in earth. MM 2.04. 50
make with speed, | to–morrow you set on. 3.01. 60
one fruitful meal would set me to't. 4.03.154 P
in brief, to set the needless process by — 5.01. 92
some one hath set you on; 5.01.112
and to set on this wretched woman here | against 5.01.132
there is another friar that set them on, | let 5.01.248
hath set the women on to this complaint. 5.01.251
sir, did you set these women on to slander lord 5.01.288 P
town, | dies ere the weary sun set in the west. ERR 1.02. 7
you with a proverb — shall i set in my staff? 3.01. 51
he set up his bills here in messina, and ADO 1.01. 39 P
the bull's horns and set them in my forehead, 1.01.264 P
and lac'd with silver, set with pearls, down 3.04. 20 P
only get the learned writer to set down our 3.05. 63 P
but when shall we set the savage bull's horns on 5.01.181 P
but did my brother set thee on to this? 5.01.247
i give thee thy liberty, set thee from durance, LLL 3.01.128 P
king cophetua set eye upon the pernicious and 4.01. 65 P
and such barren plants are set before us, that 4.02. 28
so were there a patch set on learning, to see 4.02. 31
well, "set thee down, sorrow!" 4.03. 4 P
well bandied both, a set of wit well played. 5.02. 29
you, nick bottom, are set down for pyramus. MND 1.02. 20 P
of sweet summer buds | is, as in mockery, set; 2.01.111
set your heart at rest; 2.01.121
your wrongs do set a scandal on my sex. 2.01.240
who would set his wit to so foolish a bird? 3.01.134 P
are bent | to set against me for your merriment. 3.02.146
have you not set lysander, as in scorn, | to 3.02.222
worn, | our purpos'd hunting shall be set aside. 4.01.183
i pray thee set a deep glass of rhenish wine on MV 1.02. 96 P
own part, as i have set up my rest to run away, 2.02.103 P
so rich a gem | was set in worse than gold. 2.07. 55
well, i'll set you forth. 3.05. 90

padua, | and it is meet i presently set forth. 4.01.404
here | shall witness i set forth as soon as you, 5.01.271
in good set terms, and yet a motley fool. AYL 2.07. 17
set down your venerable burthen, | and let him 2.07.167
and i set him every day to woo me. 3.02.408 P
it would do well to set the deer's horns upon 4.02. 4 P
to you, to set her before your eyes to–morrow, 5.02. 66 P
or, if not so, until the sun be set. SHR in.2. 120
to a husband we set his youngest free for a 1.01.138 P
elder, set the younger free | for our access — 1.02.266
take you the lute, and you the set of books. 2.01.106
in his waning age | set foot under thy table. 2.01.402
letters for her name fairly set down in studs, 3.02. 62 P
set your countenance, sir. 4.04. 18
if knowledge could be set up against mortality. AWW 1.01. 31 P
rest, | there is a remedy, approv'd, set down, 1.03.228
since you set up your rest 'gainst remedy. 2.01.135
thou wert best set thy lower part where thy nose 2.03.252 P
whoever shoots at him, i set him there; 3.02.112
me, | whom i myself embrace to set him free." 3.04. 17
though little he do feel it, set down sharply. 3.04. 33
so curiously he had set this counterfeit. 4.03. 34 P
shall i set down your answer so? 4.03.135 P
well, that's set down. 4.03.147 P
"or thereabouts," set down, for i'll speak truth 4.03.149 P
well, that's set down. 4.03.155 P
well, that's set down. 4.03.174 P
men that crow so at these set kind of fools no TN 1.05. 89 P
in women's waxen hearts to set their forms! 2.02. 30
wilt thou set thy foot o' my neck? 2.05.188 P
have you not set mine honor at the stake, | and 3.01.118
for the bed of ware in england, set 'em down. 3.02. 48 P
arguments of fear, | set forth in your pursuit. 3.03. 13
set upon aguecheek a notable report of valor, 3.04.191 P
and convey what i will set down to my lady. 4.02.110 P
that i did, i was set on to do't by sir toby. 5.01.185 P
i think you set nothing by a bloody coxcomb. 5.01.191 P
his eyes were set at eight i' th' morning. 5.01.199 P
toby | set this device against malvolio here, 5.01.360
me | even so as i mine own course have set down. WT 1.02.340
thou, traitor, hast set on thy wife to this. 2.03.131
ay, my lord, even so | as it is here set down. 3.02.139
doth set my pugging tooth an edge, | for a quart 4.03. 7
the dibble in earth to set one slip of them; 4.04.100
if it be doleful matter merrily set down, or a 4.04.189 P
thus we set on, camillo, to th' sea–side. 4.04.668
with honey, set on the head of a wasp's nest; 4.04.784 P
shall he be set against a brick–wall, the sun 4.04.788 P
i would set an ox–head to your lion's hide, JN 2.01.292
where we'll set forth | in best appointment all 2.01.295
when the rich blood of kings is set on fire! 2.01.351
that it in golden letters should be set | among 3.01. 85
set armed discord 'twixt these perjur'd kings! 3.01.111
all reverence set apart | to him and his usurp'd 3.01.159
abbots, imprisoned angels | set at liberty. 3.03. 9
as patches set upon a little breach | discredit 4.02. 32
like heralds 'twixt two dreadful battles set: 4.02. 78
there is no sure foundation set on blood; 4.02.104
be mercury, set feathers to thy heels, | and fly 4.02.174
or rather then set forward, for 'twill be | two 4.03. 19
till i have set a glory to this hand, | by 4.03. 71
and on our actions set the name of right | with 5.02. 67
and shall i now give o'er the yielded set? 5.02.107
set on toward swinstead. 5.03. 16
the sun of heaven, methought, was loath to set, 5.05. 1
you are born | to set a form upon that indigest 5.07. 26
o cousin, thou art come to set mine eye. 5.07. 51
where ever englishman durst set his foot. R2 1.01. 66
and dares him to set forward to the fight. 1.03.109
sound, trumpets, and set forward, combatants. 1.03.117
envy, set on you | to wake our peace, which in 1.03.131
esteem as foil wherein thou art to set | the 1.03.266
this precious stone set in the silver sea, 2.01. 46
who strongly hath set footing in this land: 2.02. 48
side, | for time hath set a blot upon my pride. 3.02. 81
i'll give my jewels for a set of beads, | my 3.03.147
set on towards london, cousin, is it so? 3.03.208
old adam's likeness, set to dress this garden, 3.04. 73
here in this place | i'll set a bank of rue, 3.04.105
then set before my face the lord aumerle. 4.01. 6
from whence set forth in pomp | she came adorned 5.01. 78
and interchangeably set down their hands, | to 5.02. 98
it was, villain, ere thy hand did set it down. 5.03. 54
thine eye begins to speak, set thy tongue there; 5.03.125
with scruples and do set the word itself 5.05. 13
and many limits of the charge set down | but 1H4 1.01. 35
now shall we know if gadshill have set a match. 1.02.106 P
why, we will set forth before or after them and 1.02.169 P
have no sooner achiev'd but we'll set upon them. 1.02.173 P
than that which hath no foil to set it off. 1.02.215
did set forth | upon his irish expedition; 1.03.149
you, that set the crown | upon the head of this 1.03.160
i know | is ruminated, plotted, and set down, 1.03.274
are they not some of them set forward already? 2.03. 28 P
i will set forward to–night. 2.03. 35 P
to–day will i set forth, to–morrow you. 2.03.116
we four set upon some dozen — 2.04.174 P
some six or seven fresh men set upon us — 2.04.181 P
we two saw you four set on four and bound them, 2.04.253 P
then did we two set on you four, and, with a 2.04.256 P
well, here i am set. 2.04.438 P
i | and my good lord of worcester will set forth 3.01. 83
and that would set my teeth nothing an edge, 3.01.131
when i from france set foot at ravenspurgh, 3.02. 95
the earl of westmerland set forth to–day, | with 3.02.170
on wednesday next, harry, you shall set forward, 3.02.173
he did, my lord, four days ere i set forth, 4.01. 22
good | to set the exact wealth of all our states 4.01. 46
to set so rich a main | on the nice hazard of 4.01. 47
the king himself in person is set forth, | or 4.01. 91
this present enterprise set off his head, | i do 5.01. 88
for, on their answer, will we set on them, | and 5.01.119
can honor set to a leg? 5.01.131 P
and set on. 5.02. 96
that, each heart being set | on bloody courses, 2H4 1.01.158
service for any other reason than to set me off, 1.02. 13 P
then set your knighthood and your soldiership 1.02. 83 P
do you set down your name in the scroll of youth 1.02.178 P
shall we go draw our numbers and set on? 1.03.109
come, come, i know thou wast set on to this. 2.01.152 P
the prince once set a dish of apple–johns before 2.04. 5 P
why then cover and set them down, and see if 2.04. 10 P
thou't set me a–weeping and thou say'st so. 2.04.278 P
every thing set off | that might so much as 4.01.143
grace of york, in god's name then set forward. 4.01.225
what mischiefs might he set abroach | in shadow 4.02. 14
set me the crown upon my pillow here. 4.05. 5
to have a son set your decrees at nought? 5.02. 85
set on. 5.05. 72
play a set | shall strike his father's crown H5 1.02.262
the king is set from london, and the scene | is 2.pr. 34
it was excess of wine that set him on, | and on 2.02. 42
now set the teeth and stretch the nostril wide, 3.01. 15
but like a lackey, from the rise to set, 4.01.272
the french are bravely in their battles set, 4.03. 69
land, | and solemnly see him set on to london. 5.pr. 14
french | was round encompassed, and set upon. 1H6 1.01.114
he wanted pikes to set before his archers; 1.01.116
some odd gimmors or device | their arms are set, 1.02. 42
after that things are set in order here, | we'll 2.02. 32
which obloquy set bars before my tongue, | else 2.05. 49
broil, | and set this unaccustom'd fight aside. 3.01. 93
stoop then and set your knee against my foot, 3.01.168
out of hand, | and set upon our boasting enemy. 3.02.103
we'll set thy statue in some holy place, | and 3.03. 14
when talbot hath set footing once in france 3.03. 64
they set him free without his ransom paid, | in 3.03. 72
lord bishop, set the crown upon his head. 4.01. 1
conceit | to set a gloss upon his bold intent, 4.01.103
york set him on to fight and die in shame, 4.04. 8
set from our o'ermatch'd forces forth for aid. 4.04. 11
york set him on, york should have sent him aid. 4.04. 29
hand, | and set a precious crown upon thy head, 5.03.119
set this diamond safe | in golden palaces, as it 5.03.169
to me, | and on my head did set the diadem. 2H6 1.02. 40
and set the triple crown upon his head — | that 1.03. 63
i could set my ten commandements in your face. 1.03.142
the time of night when troy was set on fire, 1.04. 17
an empty eagle were set | to guard the chicken 3.01.248
nor set no footing on this unkind shore"? 3.02. 87
of bury, | set all upon me, mighty sovereign. 3.02.241
like lime–twigs set to catch my winged soul. 3.03. 16
and as for these whose ransom we have set, | it 4.01.139
and turn it, and set a new nap upon it. 4.02. 5 P
but first go and set london bridge on fire, and, 4.06. 14 P
set ope thy everlasting gates | to entertain my 4.09. 13
set limb to limb, and thou art far the lesser; 4.10. 47
but that my heart's on future mischief set, | i 5.02. 84
sweet father, do so, set it on your head. 3H6 1.01.115
proud, | can set the duke up in despite of me. 1.01.158
let's set our men in order, | and issue forth 1.02. 69
hold you his hands whilest i do set it on. 1.04. 95
off with his head, and set it on york gates, 1.04.179
and on the gates of york | they set the same, 2.01. 66
for grace, | and set thy diadem upon my head, 2.02. 82
increase, | we set the axe to thy usurping root; 2.02.165
but set his murth'ring knife unto the root 2.06. 49
and set the murtherous machevil to school. 3.02.193
all dissembling set aside, | tell me for truth 3.03.119
the king by this is set him down to sleep. 4.03. 2
to set the crown once more on henry's head. 4.04. 27
and men | to set him free from his captivity. 4.05. 13
confess who set thee up and pluck'd thee down, 5.01. 26
so other foes may set upon our backs. 5.01. 61
the stones together, | and set up lancaster. 5.01. 85
to set my brother clarence and the king | in R3 1.01. 34
set down, set down your honorable load — | if 1.02. 1
set down, set down your honorable load — | if 1.02. 1
stay, you that bear the corse, and set it down. 1.02. 33
villains, set down the corse, or, by saint paul, 1.02. 36
but 'twas thy heavenly face that set me on. 1.02.182
death, and hell have set their marks on him, 1.03.292
the secret mischiefs that i set abroach | i lay 1.03.324
they that set you on | to do this deed will hate 1.04.254
wit, | his wit set down to make his valure live. 3.01. 86
we have not yet set down this day of triumph. 3.04. 42
which in a set hand fairly is engross'd | that 3.06. 2
hath he set bounds between their love and me? 4.01. 20
the weary sun hath made a golden set, | and by 5.03. 19
set it down. 5.03. 75
of england's chair, where he is falsely set; 5.03.251
advance our standards, set upon our foes. 5.03.348
slave, i have set my life upon a cast, | and i 5.04. 9
who set the body and the limbs | of this great H8 1.01. 46
most liberal, | they are set here for examples. 1.03. 62
when they were ready to set out for london, a 2.02. 5 P
i say, set on. 2.04.242
'em, | envy and base opinion set against 'em, 3.01. 36
i was set at work | among my maids, full little, 3.01. 74
that little thought, when she set footing here, 3.01.183
strange postures | we have seen him set himself. 3.02.119
that sun, i pray, may never set! 3.02.415
patience, be near me still, and set me lower; 4.02. 76
what grief hath set these jaundies o'er your TRO 1.03. 2
ear, | to set his /sense on /the attentive bent, 1.03.252
will you set your wit to a fool's? 2.01. 86 P
if he do set | the very wings of reason to his 2.02. 43
should once set footing in your generous bosoms? 2.02.155
but her brain to set down her reckoning; 3.03.253 P
set them down | for sluttish spoils of 4.05. 61
they set me up, in policy, that mongril cur, 5.04. 12 P
look, hector, how the sun begins to set, | how 5.08. 5
how earnestly are you set a–work, and how ill 5.10. 38 P
in the flesh, set this in your painted cloths: 5.10. 45 P
if they set down before 's, for the remove COR 1.02. 28
how 'twas, he did so set his teeth and tear it. 1.03. 64 P
and titus lartius are set down before their city 1.03. 98 P
set me against aufidius and his antiates, | and 1.06. 59
keep your duties, | as i have set them down. 1.07. 2
set up the bloody flag against all patience, and 2.01. 75 P
and that's as easy | as to set dogs on sheep — 2.01.257
in his person wrought | to be set high in place, 2.03.247
have you not set them on? 3.01. 37
the people are abus'd, set on. 3.01. 58
that we have procur'd | set down by th' pole? 3.03. 10
i think, that shall set them in present action. 4.03. 47 P
th' one half of my commission, and set down — 4.05.138
finger and his thumb as one would set up a top. 4.05.153 P
set at upper end o' th' table; 4.05.192 P
to my request, | and then i'll set upon him. 5.01. 58
the walls of rome to–morrow | set down our host. 5.03. 2
i am glad thou hast set thy mercy and thy honor 5.03.200
on, | and help to set a head on headless rome. TIT 1.01.186
life, | and set abroad new business for you all? 1.01.192
ransomless here we set our prisoners free. 1.01.274
mother, | as sure a card as ever won the set; 5.01.100
myself, | set deadly enmity between two friends, 5.01.131
set fire on barns and haystalks in the night, 5.01.133
and set them upright at their dear friends' door 5.01.136
do | see here in bloody lines i have set down: 5.02. 14
set him breast–deep in earth and famish him, 5.03.179
who set this ancient quarrel new abroach? ROM 1.01.104
you will set cock–a–hoop! 1.05. 81
then plainly know my heart's dear love is set 2.03. 57
as mine on hers, so hers is set on mine, | and 2.03. 59
flask, | is set afire by thine own ignorance, 3.03.133
but look thou stay not till the watch be set, 3.03.148
either be gone before the watch be set, | or by 3.03.167
the county paris hath set up his rest | that you 4.05. 6
o, here | will i set up my everlasting rest, 5.03.110
there shall no figure at such rate be set | as 5.03.301
at first | to set a gloss on faint deeds, hollow TIM 1.02. 16
set a fair fashion on our entertainment, | which 1.02.147
exactest auditors, | and set me on the proof. 2.02.157
to a wasteful cock | and set mine eyes at flow. 2.02.163
end, the villainies of man will set him clear. 3.03. 30 P
hot ardent zeal would set whole realms on fire; 3.03. 33 P
and set quarrelling | upon the head of valor; 3.05. 27
writ, | but set them down horrible traitors. 4.03.119
by thy virtue | set them into confounding odds, 4.03.391
for he is set so only to himself, | that nothing 5.01.117
before proud athens he's set down by this, 5.03. 9
set but thy foot | against our rampir'd gates 5.04. 46
whom you yourselves shall set out for reproof 5.04. 57
set on, and leave no ceremony out. JC 1.02. 11
set him before me, let me see his face. 1.02. 20
set honor in one eye and death i' th' other, 1.02. 86
and i will set this foot of mine as far | as who 1.03.119
set this up with wax | upon old brutus' statue. 1.03.145
set on your foot, | and with a heart new–fir'd i 2.01.331
set a huge mountain 'tween my heart and tongue! 2.04. 7
set in a note–book, learn'd, and conn'd by rote, 4.03. 98
bid him set on his pow'rs betimes before, | and 4.03.307
am i compell'd to set | upon one battle all our 5.01. 74
let them set on at once; 5.02. 3
so in his red blood cassius' day is set! 5.03. 62
the sun of rome is set. 5.03. 63
labio and flavio, set our battles on. 5.03.108
that will be ere the set of sun. MAC 1.01. 5
pardon, and set forth | a deep repentance. 1.04. 6
be my oracles as well, | and set me up in hope? 3.01. 10
that i would set my life on any chance, | to 3.01.112
poor birds they are not set for. 4.02. 36
within my sword's length set him; 4.03.234
i will set down what comes from her, to satisfy 5.01. 32 P
set your entreatments at a higher rate | than a HAM 1.03.122
i do not set my life at a pin's fee, | and for 1.04. 65
meet it is i set it down | that one may smile, 1.05.107
spite, | that ever i was born to set it right! 1.05.189
safety and allowance | as therein are set down. 2.02. 80
i hold it not honesty to have it thus set down, 2.02.202 P
set down with as much modesty as cunning. 2.02.440 P
lines, which i would set down and insert in't, 2.02.542 P
have in quick determination | thus set it down: 3.01.169
clowns speak no more than is set down for them, 3.02. 39 P
will themselves laugh to set on some quantity of 3.02. 41 P
nay, then i'll set those to you that can speak. 3.04. 17
you go not till i set you up a glass | where you 3.04. 19
where every god did seem to set his seal | to 3.04. 61
this man shall set me packing; 3.04.211
us — thou mayst not coldly set | our sovereign 4.03. 62
you shall know i am set naked on your kingdom. 4.07. 43 P
and set a double varnish on the fame | the 4.07.132
that were wont to set the table on a roar? 5.01.191 P
good gertrude, set some watch over your son. 5.01.296
set me the stoups of wine upon that table. 5.02.267
i'll play this bout first, set it by a while. 5.02.284
and thought to set my rest | on her kind nursery LR 1.01.123
thou trowest, | set less than thou throwest; 1.04.123
my father hath set guard to take my brother, 2.01. 16
where may we set our horses? 2.02. 4 P
so much thy place mistook | to set thee here? 2.04. 13
and thou hadst been set i' th' stocks for that 2.04. 64 P
we'll set thee to school to an ant, to teach 2.04. 67 P
i set him there, sir; 2.04.199
that their great stars | thron'd and set high? 3.01. 23
in his pew, set ratsbane by his porridge, made 3.04. 55 P
spouse, set not thy sweet heart on proud array. 3.04. 82 P
set a–work by a reprovable badness in himself. 3.05. 7 P
i have a letter guessingly set down, | which 3.07. 47
upon these eyes of thine i'll set my foot. 3.07. 68
but are my brother's pow'rs set forth? 4.05. 1
our troops set forth to–morrow, stay with us; 4.05. 16
set me where you stand. 4.06. 24
and carry it so | as i have set it down. 5.03. 37
wife), | that never set a squadron in the field, OTH 1.01. 22
or sow lettuce, set hyssop and weed up /tine, 1.03.322 P
but i'll set down the pegs that make this music, 2.01.200
platform, masters, come, let's set the watch. 2.03.120
he'll watch the horologe a double set | if drink 2.03.130
who set it on; 2.03.210
cassio to her mistress — | i'l set her on — 2.03.384
set on thy wife to observe. 3.03.240
thou hast set me on the rack. 3.03.335
cassio hath here been set on in the dark | by 5.01.112
and your reports have set the murder on. 5.02.187
seeming dead) iago hurt him, | iago set him on. 5.02.329
extenuate, | nor set down aught in malice. 5.02.343
set you down this: 5.02.351
i'll set a bourn how far to be belov'd. ANT 1.01. 16
i'll set thee in a shower of gold, and hail 2.05. 45
shall set thee on triumphant chariots, and | put 3.01. 10
let not the piece of virtue which is set 3.02. 28
set we our squadrons on yond side o' th' hill, 3.09. 1

but now i'll set my teeth, | and send to 3.13.180
fetch thee up, | and set thee by jove's side. 4.15. 36
when such a spacious mirror's set before him, 5.01. 34
give him that parting kiss which i had set CYM 1.03. 34
we will have these things set down by lawful 1.04.165 P
that set thee on to this desert, am bound | to 1.05. 73
and thus i set my foot on 's neck," even then 3.03. 92
that didst set up my disobedience 'gainst the 3.04. 88
and on the gates of lud's–town set your heads. 4.02. 99
they grow, | and set them on lud's–town. 4.02.123
no single soul | can we set eye on; 4.02.131
life is yours, | i humbly set it at your will; 4.03. 13
i, since of your lives you set | so slight a 4.04. 48
upon me, set | the dogs o' th' street to bay me; 5.05.222
set we forward. 5.05.479
set on there! 5.05.484
and on set purpose let his armor rust | until PER 2.02. 54
of tyrus on the head | of helicanus would set on 3.ch. 27
would set me free from this unhallowed place, 4.06.100
book of trespasses | all you are set down there. TNK 1.01. 34
o, my petition was | set down in ice, which, by 1.01.107
set you forward, | for i will see you gone. 1.01.217
'hath set a mark which nature could not reach to 1.04. 43
and life, must he set foot | upon this kingdom. 2.02.246
say i ventur'd | to set him free? 2.04. 31
i'll set it down | he's torn to pieces. 3.02. 17
for, ere the sun set, both shall sleep for ever. 3.06.184
maim your honor | (for now i am set a–begging, 3.06.238
half his own heart, set in too, that i hope 4.01. 14
the far shore, thick set with reeds and sedges, 4.01. 54
i sav'd her, | and set her safe to land; 4.01. 96
set it to th' north. 4.01.143
another wanton ganymede | set /jove afire with, 4.02. 16
snatch up the goodly boy and set him by him, | a 4.02. 17
tough and nimble set, | which shows an active 4.02.125
many a murther | set off whereto she's guilty. 5.03. 28
set both thine ears to th' business. 5.03. 92
let me set up before your thoughts, good friends STM II.C 90
and being set, i'll smother thee with kisses. VEN 18
else, suffer'd, it will set the heart on fire: 388
slips, | set thy seal manual on my wax–red lips. 516
"on his bow–back he hath a battle set | of 619
his breath and beauty set | gloss on the rose, 935
and set dissension 'twixt the son and sire, 1160
happ'ly that name of "chaste" unhapp'ly set LUC 8
made | to set forth that which is so singular? 32
may set at noon and make perpetual night. 784
but as the earth doth weep, the sun being set, 1226
of those fair suns set in her mistress' sky, 1230
once set on ringing, with his own weight goes; 1494
so lucrece, set a–work, sad tales doth tell | to 1496
and then against my heart he set his sword, 1640
with sad set eyes, and wretched arms across, 1662
now set thy long–experienc'd wit to school. 1820
her well, | and set her person forth to sale. PP 18.12
since, seldom coming, in the long year set, SON 52. 6
on helen's cheek all art of beauty set, | and 53. 7
time doth transfix the flourish set on youth, 60. 9
and therefore to your fair no painting set; 83. 2
when thou shalt be dispos'd to set me light, 88. 1
upon thy part i can set down a story | of faults 88. 6
so ill, | to set a form upon desired change, 89. 6
threw, | upon whose weeping margent she was set,
LC 39
like fools that in th' imagination set | the 136
SETEBOS 2 FR 0.0002 REL FR 2 V 0 P
pow'r, | it would control my dam's god, setebos, TMP 1.02.373
o setebos, these be brave spirits indeed! 5.01.261
/SETS 2 FR 0.0002 REL FR 2 V 0 P
and their labor | delight in them /sets off; TMP 3.01. 2
/sets /all /on /hazard — /and /hither /am /i TRO pr 22
SETS 32 FR 0.0036 REL FR 26 V 6 P
some more mightier member | that sets them on. MM 5.01.238
he that sets up his rest to do more exploits ERR 4.03. 27 P
letters sent me | that sets him high in fame. AWW 5.03. 31
and consequently sets down the manner how: TN 3.04. 72 P
the heaven sets spies upon us, will not have WT 5.01.203
the man that mocks at it and sets it light. R2 1.03.293
thy sun sets weeping in the lowly west, 2.04. 21
who sets me else? 4.01. 57
that sets the word itself against the word! 5.03.122
nothing without sack (for that sets it a–work) 2H4 4.03.114 P
sack commences it and sets it in act and use. 4.03.116 P
not he that sets his foot upon her back. 3H6 2.02. 16
when the sun sets, who doth not look for night? R3 2.03. 34
of war, | bold as an oracle, and sets thersites, TRO 1.03.192
that cause sets up, with and against itself, 5.02.143
the public power, | which he so sets at nought. COR 3.01.269
when the sun sets, the earth doth drizzle dew, ROM 3.05.126
it sets him on, and it takes him off; MAC 2.03. 32 P
pause, | a roused vengeance sets him new a–work,
HAM 2.02.488
of an innocent love | and sets a blister there, 3.04. 44
gross crime or other | that sets us all at odds. LR 1.03. 5
caesar sets down in alexandria, where | i will ANT 3.13.168
he hath a kind of honor sets him off, | more CYM 1.06.170
that it is place which lessens and sets off, 3.03. 13
our wonder, and sets up | your fame for ever. PER 3.02. 96
she that sets seeds and roots of shame and 4.06. 85 P
whose grim aspect sets every joint a–shaking; LUC 452
this said, he sets his foot upon the light, 673
thou sets the wolf where he the lamb may get; 878
what wit sets down is blotted straight with will 1299
sets you most rich in youth before my sight, SON 15.10
sets down her babe and makes all swift dispatch 143. 3
SET'ST 3 FR 0.0003 REL FR 3 V 0 P
it to the fire, | for thou set'st on thy wife. WT 2.03.142
and like a civil war set'st oath to oath, | thy JN 3.01.264
but, warwick, after god, thou set'st me free, 3H6 4.06. 16
SET'T 1 FR 0.0001 REL FR 1 V 0 P
set't down, let's look upon't. PER 3.02. 51
SETTER 1 FR 0.0001 REL FR 0 V 1 P
o, 'tis our setter, i know his voice. 1H4 2.02. 51 P
SETTER-UP 2 FR 0.0002 REL FR 2 V 0 P
thou setter–up and plucker–down of kings, 3H6 2.03. 37
proud setter–up and puller–down of kings! 3.03.157
SETTING 24 FR 0.0027 REL FR 14 V 10 P
the setting of thine eye and cheek proclaim | a TMP 2.01.229
setting the attraction of my good parts aside, i WIV 2.02.105 P
law, | setting it up to fear the birds of prey, MM 2.01. 2
my sweet soul, i mean setting thee at liberty, LLL 3.01.123 P
but by your setting on, by your consent? MND 3.02.231
and therefore, setting all this chat aside, SHR 2.01.268
man, setting down before you, will undermine you
AWW 1.01.118 P
instant disaster of his setting i' th' stocks; 4.03.110 P
setting aside his high blood's royalty, | and R2 1.01. 58
the setting sun, and music at the close, | as 2.01. 12
how shall we part with them in setting forth? 1H4 1.02.167 P
and, setting thy knighthood aside, thou art a 3.03.120 P
setting thy womanhood aside, thou art a beast to 3.03.122 P
setting my knighthood and my soldiership aside, 2H4 1.02. 81 P
setting endeavor in continual motion; H5 1.02.185
we took him setting of boys' copies. 2H6 4.02. 88 P
setting your scorns and your mislike aside, 3H6 4.01. 24
of my glory, | i haste now to my setting. H8 3.02.225
men shut their doors against a setting sun. TIM 1.02.145
she's e'en setting on water to scald such 2.02. 69 P
he is a man (setting his fate aside) | of comely 3.05. 14
o setting sun, | as in thy red rays thou dost JC 5.03. 60
men | already at a point, was setting forth. MAC 4.03.135
and will endure | our setting down before't. 5.04. 10
SETTLE 5 FR 0.0005 REL FR 4 V 1 P
that can fly from us | shall on them settle. AWW 3.01. 21
then, till the fury of his highness settle, WT 4.04.471
modesty, can settle | the heart of antony, ANT 2.02.240
when ye return, who wins i'll settle here; TNK 3.06.307
they may return and settle again to execute 4.03. 72 P
SETTLED 19 FR 0.0021 REL FR 17 V 2 P
whose settled visage and deliberate word | nips MM 3.01. 89
we'll light upon some settled low content. AYL 2.03. 68
knavish professions, he settled only in rogue. WT 4.03. 99 P
if your more ponderous and settled project | may 4.04.524
no settled senses of the world can match | the 5.03. 72
the swelling difference of your settled hate. R2 1.01.201
which before (cold and settled) left the liver 2H4 4.03.104 P
there left behind and settled certain french; H5 1.02. 47
with long continuance in a settled place. 1H6 2.05.106
do breed love's settled passions in my heart, 5.05. 4
see how the blood is settled in his face. 2H6 3.02.160
no, he's settled | (not to come off) in his H8 3.02. 22
her blood is settled, and her joints are stiff; ROM 4.05. 26
i am settled, and bend up | each corporal agent MAC 1.07. 79
than settled age his sables and his weeds, HAM 4.07. 80
tyre, | welcom'd and settled to his own desire. PER 4.ch. 2
and when he's angry, then a settled valor | (not TNK 4.02.100
ne'er settled equally, but high or low, | that VEN 1139
was | shall reasons find of settled gravity — SON 49. 8
SETTLEST 1 FR 0.0001 REL FR 1 V 0 P
foam, | settlest admired reverence in a slave. TIM 5.01. 51
SETTLING 1 FR 0.0001 REL FR 1 V 0 P
in, trouble him no more | till further settling. LR 4.07. 81
SEVEN 71 FR 0.0080 REL FR 37 V 34 P
by seven a' clock i'll get you such a ladder. TGV 3.01.126
will desire, and seven hundred pounds of moneys,
WIV 1.01. 50 P
did her grandsire leave her seven hundred pound? 1.01. 58 P
seven hundred pounds, and possibilities, is goot 1.01. 64 P
again else, of seven groats in mill–sixpences, 1.01.155 P
you bear witness that me have stay six or seven, 2.03. 36 P
seven year and a half, sir. MM 2.01.260 P
you say seven years together? 2.01.262 P
you bring me in the names of some six or seven, 2.01.273 P
and six or seven winters more respect | than a 3.01. 75
sin, | or of the deadly seven it is the least. 3.01.110
splitted my poor tongue | in seven short years, ERR 5.01.310
but seven years since, in syracusa, boy, | thou 5.01.321
'a has been a vile thief this seven year; ADO 3.03.126 P
from athens is her house remote seven leagues; MND 1.01.159
"the fire seven times tried this: MV 2.09. 63
seven times tried that judgment is, | that did 2.09. 64
plays many parts, | his acts being seven ages. AYL 2.07.143
i was seven of the nine days out of the wonder 3.02.174 P
so hard that it seems the length of seven year. 3.02.317 P
upon a lie seven times remov'd (bear your body 5.04. 68 P
i knew when seven justices could not take up a 5.04. 98 P
who for this seven years hath esteemed him | no SHR in.1. 122
let's see, i think 'tis now some seven a' clock, 4.03.187
it shall be seven ere i go to horse. 4.03.191
the element itself, till seven years' heat, TN 1.01. 25
seven of my people, with an obedient start, make 2.05. 58 P
nutmegs, seven; WT 4.03. 47 P
not at your father's house these seven years 4.04.578
edward's seven sons, whereof thyself art one, R2 1.02. 11
one, | were as seven vials of his sacred blood, 1.02. 12
or seven fair branches springing from one root. 1.02. 13
some of those seven are dried by nature's course 1.02. 14
and every thing is left at six and seven. 2.02.122
take purses go by the moon and the seven stars, 1H4 1.02. 14 P
kills me some six or seven dozen of scots at a 2.04.103 P
some six or seven fresh men set upon us — 2.04.180 P
but took all their seven points in my target, 2.04.202 P
seven? why, there were but four even now. 2.04.203 P
seven, by these hilts, or i am a villain else. 2.04.206 P
and with a thought seven of the eleven i paid. 2.04.217 P
i did that i did not this seven year before, i 2.04.312 P
swore little, dic'd not above seven times — a 3.03. 16 P
the earl of westmerland, seven thousand strong, 4.01. 88
seven groats and two pence. 2H4 1.02.235 P
we have seen the seven stars. 2.04.187 P
cities, and seven walled towns of strength, 1H6 3.04. 7
this seven years did not talbot see his son, 4.03. 37
seven earls, twelve barons, and twenty reverend 2H6 1.01. 8
i saw not better sport these seven years' day; 2.01. 2
edward the third, my lords, had seven sons: 2.02. 10
shall be in england seven halfpenny loaves sold 4.02. 65 P
six or seven thousand is their utmost power. R3 5.03. 10
that after seven years' siege yet troy walls TRO 1.03. 12
it gives me an estate of seven years' health, in COR 2.01.114 P
the repulse of tarquin seven hurts i' th' body. 2.01.150 P
if i could shake off but one seven years | from 4.01. 55
i wonder on't, he was wont to shine at seven. TIM 3.04. 10
for here have been | some six or seven, who did JC 2.01.277
he lies to–night within seven leagues of rome. 3.01.286
man be master of his time | till seven at night. MAC 3.01. 41
tears seven times salt | burn out the sense and HAM 4.05.155
the reason why the seven stars are no moe than LR 1.05. 35 P
stars are no moe than seven is a pretty reason. 1.05. 35 P
have been tom's food for seven long year. 3.04.139
my letters say a hundred and seven galleys. OTH 1.03. 3
since these arms of mine had seven years' pith, 1.03. 83
upon the world for four times seven years, and 1.03.312 P
seven days and nights? 3.04.173
were you a gamester at five, or at seven? PER 4.06. 75 P
where a man may serve seven years for the loss 4.06.171 P
SEVENFOLD 2 FR 0.0002 REL FR 2 V 0 P
no meed but he repays | sevenfold above itself; TIM 1.01.278
the sevenfold shield of ajax cannot keep | the ANT 4.14. 38
SEVENNIGHT *(also se'nnight, etc., sev'nnight, etc.)*
SEVENNIGHT 1 FR 0.0001 REL FR 0 V 1 P
which is hence a just sevennight, and a time too ADO 2.01.360 P
/SEVENTEEN 1 FR 0.0001 REL FR 1 V 0 P
from /seventeen years till now almost fourscore AYL 2.03. 71
SEVENTEEN 5 FR 0.0005 REL FR 2 V 3 P
she is able to overtake seventeen years old. WIV 1.01. 53 P
and old ginger, ninescore and seventeen pounds, MM 4.03. 6 P
at seventeen years many their fortunes seek, AYL 2.03. 73
faith, for seventeen poniards are at thy bosom. AWW 4.01. 76 P
and in the brunt of seventeen battles since | he COR 2.02.100
SEVENTH 9 FR 0.0010 REL FR 4 V 5 P
seventh sweet, adieu. LLL 5.02.234
found the quarrel was upon the seventh cause. AYL 5.04. 50 P
how seventh cause? 5.04. 51 P
but for the seventh cause — how did you find 5.04. 66 P
did you find the quarrel on the seventh cause? 5.04. 67 P
the seventh, the lie direct. 5.04. 96 P
william of windsor was the seventh and last. 2H6 2.02. 17
henry the seventh succeeding, truly pitying | my H8 2.01.112
a seventh? MAC 4.01.118
SEVENTY 3 FR 0.0003 REL FR 3 V 0 P
we would muster all | from twelve to seventy, COR 4.05.129
mine speak of seventy senators that died | by JC 4.03.177
thy flame — at seventy thou canst catch, | and TNK 5.01. 87
SEVENTY-FIVE 1 FR 0.0001 REL FR 1 V 0 P
to every several man, seventy–five drachmaes. JC 3.02.242
SEVER 3 FR 0.0003 REL FR 3 V 0 P
the law, | and who can sever love from charity? LLL 4.03.362
sever themselves and madly sweep the sky, | so, MND 3.02. 23
chances, | were we from hence, would sever us. TNK 2.02. 95
SEVERAL 74 FR 0.0083 REL FR 70 V 4 P
for several virtues | have i lik'd several women TMP 3.01. 42
several virtues | have i lik'd several women, 3.01. 43
ministers | their several kinds have done. 3.03. 88
with strange and several noises | of roaring, 5.01.232
i'll kiss each several paper for amends. TGV 1.02.105
that i have wept a hundred several times. 4.04.145
i suffer'd the pangs of three several deaths: WIV 3.05.108 P
the several chairs of order look you scour 5.05. 61
think, i think and pray | to several subjects. MM 2.04. 2
good morrow, masters — each his several way. ADO 5.03. 29
my lips are no common, though several they be. LLL 2.01.223
where several worthies make one dignity, | where 4.03.232
will advance | unto his several mistress, which 5.02.124
know | by favors several which they did bestow. 5.02.125
their several counsels they unbosom shall | to 5.02.141
take his gait, | and each several chamber bless, MND 5.01.417
the several caskets to this noble prince. MV 2.07. 2
have worn me out | with several applications. AWW 1.02. 74
and will by twos and threes at several posterns WT 1.02.438
he sings several tunes faster than you'll tell 4.04.184 P
which sways usurpingly these several titles, JN 1.01. 13
and loving farewell of our several friends. R2 1.03. 51
uncle, help to order several powers | to oxford, 5.03.140
in reckoning up the several devils' names | that 1H4 3.01.155
he should draw his several strengths together, 2H4 1.03. 76
each several article herein redress'd, | all 4.01.168
your powers unto their several counties, | as we 4.02. 61
as many arrows loosed several ways | come to one
H5 1.02.207
that here you maintain several factions; 1H6 1.01. 71
name, to repair to your several dwelling–places, 1.03. 77 P
that we do make our entrance several ways; 2.01. 30
your several suits | have been consider'd and 5.01. 34
as thus | to name the several colors we do wear. 2H6 2.01.126
with every several pleasure in the world; 3.02.363
i do dismiss you to your several countries. 4.09. 21
rood, | i do not like these several councils, i. R3 3.02. 76
limit each leader to his several charge, | and 5.03. 25
my conscience hath a thousand several tongues, 5.03.193
and every tongue brings in a several tale, | and 5.03.194
all several sins, all us'd in each degree, 5.03.198
importing | the several parcels of his plate, H8 3.02.125
which hath our several honors all engag'd | to TRO 2.02.124
upon our joint and several dignities. 2.02.193
that in these several places of the city | you COR 1.01.185
thou hast beat me out | twelve several times, 4.05.122
reports the volsces with two several powers 4.06. 39
i take all and your several visitations | so TIM 1.02.218
it seem in the trial of his several friends. 3.06. 6 P
is dividant, touch them with several fortunes, 4.03. 5
in several hands, in at his windows throw, | as JC 1.02.316
throw, | as if they came from several citizens, 1.02.317
nobly bears, | is guilty of a several bastardy, 2.01.138
to every several man, seventy–five drachmaes. 3.02.242
appear'd to me | two several times by night; 5.05. 18
abound | in the division of each several crime, MAC 4.03. 96
time | before we reckon with your several loves, 5.09. 27
larded with many several sorts of reasons, HAM 5.02. 20
will to publish | our daughters' several dowers, LR 1.01. 44
the several messengers | from hence attend 2.01.124
the senate hath sent about three several quests OTH 1.02. 46
ay, madam, twenty several messengers. ANT 1.05. 62
he shall have every day a several greeting, | or 1.05. 77
war, whose several ranges | frighted each other? 3.13. 5
them gather | their several virtues and effects. CYM 1.05. 23
then discourse our woes, felt several years, PER 1.04. 18
these knights unto their several lodgings! 2.03.109
to use one language in each several clime 4.04. 6
each took | a several land. TNK 3.01. 2
thousand fresh water–flowers of several colors, 4.01. 85
face seems twain, each several limb is doubled, VEN 1067
all jointly list'ning, but with several graces, LUC 1410
why should my heart think that a several plot, SON 137. 9
i have receiv'd from many a several fair, LC 206

each several stone, | with wit well blazon'd, 216
SEVERALLY 4 FR 0.0004 REL FR 3 V 1 P
shall | concur together, severally entreat him. TRO 4.05.274
i will dispatch you severally: TIM 2.02.187 P
reasons, | when severally we hear them rendered. JC 3.02. 10
the counterchange | is severally in all. CYM 5.05.397
SEVERALS 3 FR 0.0003 REL FR 3 V 0 P
by some severals | of head-piece extraordinary? WT 1.02.226
the severals and unhidden passages | of his true H5 1.01. 86
shapes, | severals and generals of grace exact, TRO 1.03.180
SEVER'D 10 FR 0.0011 REL FR 8 V 2 P
is she the goddess that hath sever'd us, | and TMP 5.01.187
thus have you heard me sever'd from my bliss, ERR 1.01.118
here are sever'd lips, | parted with sugar MV 3.02.118
howsome'er their hearts are sever'd in religion, AWW 1.03. 53 P
well, the king hath sever'd you. 2H4 1.02.203 P
but sever'd in a pale clear-shining sky. 3H6 2.01. 28
god forbid that i should wish them sever'd 4.01. 21
rome, | by uproars sever'd, as a flight of fowl TIT 5.03. 68
so should my thoughts be sever'd from my griefs, LR 4.06.282
our sever'd navy too | have knit again, and ANT 3.13.170
SEVERE 9 FR 0.0010 REL FR 7 V 2 P
lord angelo is severe. MM 2.01.282
o just but severe law! 2.02. 41
but my brother-justice have i found so severe, 3.02.253 P
heaven will bear | should be as holy as severe; 3.02.262
with eyes severe and beard of formal cut, | full AYL 2.07.155
shall be with such strict and severe covenants 1H6 5.04.114
come, you are too severe a moraler. OTH 2.03.299 P
which knows no pity, but is still severe; VEN 1000
it shall be merciful, and too severe, | and most 1155
SEVERED 1 FR 0.0001 REL FR 1 V 0 P
no more can i be severed from your side | than 1H6 4.05. 48
SEVERELY 2 FR 0.0002 REL FR 2 V 0 P
worth, | and kept severely from resort of men, TGV 3.01.108
that will the king severely prosecute | 'gainst R2 2.01.244
SEVEREST 1 FR 0.0001 REL FR 1 V 0 P
his time, | unto the rigor of severest law. ROM 5.03.269
SEVERING 2 FR 0.0002 REL FR 2 V 0 P
panging | as soul and body's severing. H8 2.03. 16
do lace the severing clouds in yonder east. ROM 3.05. 8
SEVERITY 4 FR 0.0004 REL FR 3 V 1 P
too general a vice, and severity must cure it. MM 3.02. 99 P
shadow | whereon to practice your severity. 1H6 2.03. 47
trial | than the severity of the public power, COR 3.01.268
for beauty starv'd with her severity | cuts ROM 1.01.219
SEVERN 4 FR 0.0004 REL FR 4 V 0 P
wye | and sandy-bottom'd severn have i sent him 1H4 3.01. 65
england, from trent and severn hitherto, | by 3.01. 73
all westward, wales beyond the severn shore, 3.01. 75
my lords, | till he have cross'd the severn. CYM 3.05. 17
SEVERN'S 2 FR 0.0002 REL FR 2 V 0 P
took, | when on the gentle severn's sedgy bank, 1H4 1.03. 98
upon agreement, of swift severn's flood, | who 1.03.103
SEVERS 1 FR 0.0001 REL FR 1 V 0 P
continent the fire | that severs day from night. TN 5.01.272
SEV'NNIGHT *(also se'nnight, etc., sevennight)*
SEV'NNIGHT 1 FR 0.0001 REL FR 1 V 0 P
one sev'nnight longer. WT 1.02. 17
SEV'NNIGHTS 1 FR 0.0001 REL FR 1 V 0 P
weary sev'nnights, nine times nine, | shall he MAC 1.03. 22
SEV'RAL 1 FR 0.0001 REL FR 1 V 0 P
each fair installment, coat, and sev'ral crest, WIV 5.05. 63
SEW 4 FR 0.0004 REL FR 1 V 3 P
"item, she can sew." TGV 3.01.306 P
loose-bodied gown, sew me in the skirts of it, SHR 4.03.136 P
i lead this life long, i'll sew nether-stocks, 1H4 2.04.116 P
proclaim that i can sing, weave, sew, and dance, PER 4.06.183
SEW'D 4 FR 0.0004 REL FR 3 V 1 P
sleeves should be cut out, and sew'd up again, SHR 4.03.146 P
and in a tedious sampler sew'd her mind; TIT 2.04. 39
that could have better sew'd than philomel. 2.04. 43
in her prophetic fury sew'd the work; OTH 3.04. 72
SEWER *(also shores*)*
SEWER 1 FR 0.0001 REL FR 0 V 1 P
sweet sink, sweet sewer. TRO 5.01. 76 P
SEWING 2 FR 0.0002 REL FR 1 V 1 P
what are you sewing here? COR 1.03. 52 P
my lord, as i was sewing in my closet, | lord HAM 2.01. 74
SEX 22 FR 0.0024 REL FR 19 V 3 P
i do not know | one of my sex; TMP 3.01. 49
and from this testimony of your own sex | (since MM 2.04.131
as being a profess'd tyrant to their sex? ADO 1.01.169 P
your wrongs do set a scandal on my sex. MND 2.01.240
our sex, as well as i, may chide you for it, 3.02.218
he hath generally tax'd their whole sex withal. AYL 3.02.350 P
have simply misus'd our sex in your love-prate. 4.01.201 P
i have spoke | with one that, in her sex, her AWW 2.01. 83
him, | so much against the mettle of your sex, TN 5.01.322
not prone to weeping, as our sex | commonly are, WT 2.01.108
and thou shalt find that i exceed my sex. 1H6 1.02. 90
how ill-beseeming is it in thy sex | to triumph 3H6 1.04.113
ah, poor our sex! TRO 5.02.109
to square the general sex | by cressid's rule. 5.02.132
think you i am no stronger than my sex, | being JC 2.01.296
like the greatest spot | of all thy sex; ANT 4.12. 36
which before | have often sham'd our sex. 5.02.124
i'ld change my sex to be companion with them, CYM 3.06. 87
wast near to make the male | to thy sex captive, TNK 1.01. 81
but alas, | being a natural sister of our sex, 1.01.125
and maid may be | more than in sex /dividual. 1.03. 82
their gentle sex to weep are often willing, LUC 1237
SEXES 1 FR 0.0001 REL FR 1 V 0 P
of young, of old, and sexes both enchanted, | to LC 128
SEXTON 7 FR 0.0008 REL FR 1 V 6 P
o, a stool and a cushion for the sexton. ADO 4.02. 2 P
god's my life, where's the sexton? 4.02. 70 P
by this time our sexton hath reform'd signior 5.01.254 P
master signior leonato, and the sexton too. 5.01.258 P
time the clock-setter, that bald sexton time! JN 3.01.324
i have been sexton here, man and boy, thirty HAM 5.01.161 P
master, if i had been the sexton, i would have PER 2.01. 36 P
SEXTON'S 2 FR 0.0002 REL FR 1 V 1 P
and threw the sops all in the sexton's face, SHR 3.02.173
about the /mazzard with a sexton's spade. HAM 5.01. 90 P
SEXTUS 3 FR 0.0003 REL FR 3 V 0 P
sextus pompeius | /hath given the dare to caesar ANT 1.02.183
sextus pompeius | makes his approaches to the 1.03. 45
having in sicily | sextus pompeius spoil'd, we 3.06. 25
SEYMOUR 1 FR 0.0001 REL FR 1 V 0 P
it are the lords of york, berkeley, and seymour, R2 2.03. 55
SEYTON 4 FR 0.0004 REL FR 4 V 0 P
seyton! MAC 5.03. 19
i am sick at heart | when i behold — seyton, i 5.03. 20
seyton! 5.03. 29
seyton, send out. 5.03. 49
'SFOOT 1 FR 0.0001 REL FR 0 V 1 P
'sfoot, i'll learn to conjure and raise devils, TRO 2.03. 5 P
SH' *(also she)*
SH' 2 FR 0.0002 REL FR 2 V 0 P
sh' adulterates hourly with thine uncle john, JN 3.01. 56
sh' hath seal'd thee for herself, for thou hast HAM 3.02. 65
SHACKLE 1 FR 0.0001 REL FR 1 V 0 P
that dost in vile misprision shackle up | my AWW 2.03.152
SHACKLES 6 FR 0.0006 REL FR 5 V 1 P
bolts and shackles! TN 2.05. 56 P
which shackles accidents and bolts up change, ANT 5.02. 6
now i feel my shackles. TNK 2.02.157
live | to knock thy brains out with my shackles. 2.02.219
i'll prove it in my shackles, with these hands 3.01. 39
"his shackles will betray him, he'll be taken, 4.01. 70
SHADE 33 FR 0.0037 REL FR 32 V 1 P
sweet leaves, shade folly. LLL 4.03. 42
under the cool shade of a sycamore | i thought 5.02. 89
toward that shade i might behold address'd | the 5.02. 92
in silence sad | trip we after night's shade. MND 4.01. 96
and thisby, tarrying in mulberry shade, | his 5.01.148
under the shade of melancholy boughs, | lose and AYL 2.07.111
a bush, under which bush's shade | a lioness, 4.03.113
us be diana's foresters, gentlemen of the shade, 1H4 1.02. 26 P
under the sweet shade of your government. H5 2.02. 28
but darkness and the gloomy shade of death 1H6 5.04. 89
for in the shade of death i shall find joy; 2H6 3.02. 54
their sweetest shade a grove of cypress trees! 3.02.323
gives not the hawthorn bush a sweeter shade | to 3H6 2.05. 42
his wonted sleep under a fresh tree's shade, 2.05. 49
under whose shade the ramping lion slept, 5.02. 13
and turns the sun to shade — alas, alas! R3 1.03.265
witness my son, now in the shade of death, 1.03.266
and shade thy person | under their blessed wings H8 5.01.160
and flies fled under shade, why then the thing TRO 1.03. 51
ere in our own house i do shade my head, | the COR 2.01.195
under their sweet shade, aaron, let us sit, TIT 2.03. 16
let us seek out some desolate shade, and there MAC 4.03. 1
to some shade, | and fit you to your manhood. CYM 3.04.191
and there, all smoth'red up, in shade doth sit, VEN 1035
coucheth the fowl below with his wings' shade, LUC 507
made | may likewise be sepulcher'd in thy shade. 805
and scarce the herd gone to the hedge for shade, PP 6. 2
by her, | under a myrtle shade began to woo him. 11. 2
month of may, | sitting in a pleasant shade, 20. 3
shall death brag thou wand'rest in his shade, SON 18.11
when to unseeing eyes thy shade shines so! 43. 8
when in dead night /thy fair imperfect shade 43.11
since every one hath, every one, one shade, 53. 3
SHADED 1 FR 0.0001 REL FR 1 V 0 P
bright orient pearl, alack, too timely shaded! PP 10. 3
SHADES 4 FR 0.0004 REL FR 4 V 0 P
you moonshine revellers, and shades of night, WIV 5.05. 38
to dwell in solemn shades of endless night. R2 1.03.177
with cain go wander thorough shades of night, 5.06. 43
and brave souls in shades, | that have died TNK 3.01. 78
/SHADOW 6 FR 0.0006 REL FR 3 V 3 P
/the /shadow /of /your /sorrow /hath /destroy'd R2 4.01.292
/hath /destroy'd | /the /shadow /of /your /face. 4.01.293
/the /shadow /of /my /sorrow! 4.01.294
/is /merely /the /shadow /of /a /dream. HAM 2.02.258 P
/a /dream /itself /is /but /a /shadow. 2.02.260 P
/that /it /is /but /a /shadow's /shadow. 2.02.262 P
SHADOW 84 FR 0.0095 REL FR 66 V 18 P
whose shadow the dismissed bachelor loves, TMP 4.01. 67
is by, | and feed upon the shadow of perfection. TGV 3.01.177
self | is else devoted, i am but a shadow; 4.02.124
and to your shadow will i make true love. 4.02.125
deceive it, | and make it but a shadow, as i am. 4.02.127
would better fit his chamber than this shadow. 4.04.120
come, shadow, come, and take this shadow up, 4.04.197
come, shadow, come, and take this shadow up, 4.04.197
"love like a shadow flies when substance love WIV 2.02.207
the time may have all shadow and silence in it; MM 3.01.247 P
swift as a shadow, short as any dream, | brief MND 1.01.144
he will fence with his own shadow. MV 1.02. 62 P
substance of my praise doth wrong this shadow 3.02.127
it, so far this shadow | doth limp behind the 3.02.128
dew, | and saw the lion's shadow ere himself, 5.01. 8
i'll go find a shadow, and sigh till he come. AYL 4.01.217 P
lord, | 'tis but the shadow of a wife you see, AWW 5.03.307
behavior to his own shadow this half hour. TN 2.05. 17 P
the shadow of myself form'd in her eye, | which, JN 2.01.498
eye, | which, being but the shadow of your son, 2.01.499
becomes a sun and makes your son a shadow. 2.01.500
let's step into the shadow of these trees. R2 3.04. 25
the state | than thou the shadow of succession. 1H4 3.02. 99
i am your shadow, my lord, i'll follow you. 2H4 2.02.159 P
simon shadow! 3.02.121 P
where's shadow? 3.02.124 P
shadow, whose son art thou? 3.02.126 P
like enough, and thy father's shadow. 3.02.129 P
the son of the female is the shadow of the male. 3.02.129 P
shadow will serve for summer, prick him, for we 3.02.133 P
then, mouldy, bullcalf, feeble, and shadow. 3.02.249 P
and this same half-fac'd fellow, shadow, give me 3.02.265 P
he set abroach | in shadow of such greatness? 4.02. 15
long time thy shadow hath been thrall to me, 1H6 2.03. 36
to think that you have aught but talbot's shadow 2.03. 46
no, no, i am but shadow of myself. 2.03. 50
that talbot is but shadow of himself? 2.03. 62
must he be then as shadow of himself? 5.04.133
of that great shadow i did represent: 2H6 1.01. 14
arms, | yet parted but the shadow with his hand. 3H6 1.04. 69
and be true king indeed, thou but the shadow. 4.03. 50
we'll yoke together like a double shadow | to 4.06. 49
unless to see my shadow in the sun | and descant R3 1.01. 26
a glass, | that i may see my shadow as i pass. 1.02.263
then came wand'ring by | a shadow like an angel, 1.04. 53
i call'd thee then poor shadow, painted queen, 4.04. 83
i am the shadow of poor buckingham, | whose H8 1.01.224
disdains the shadow | which he treads on at noon COR 1.01.260
and make a checker'd shadow on the ground. TIT 2.03. 15
knowing that with the shadow of his wings | he 4.04. 85
dost dialogue with thy shadow? TIM 2.02. 51 P
as slept within the shadow of your power | have 5.04. 6
into your eye, | that you might see your shadow. JC 1.02. 58
hence, horrible shadow! MAC 3.04.105
thereby shall we shadow | the numbers of our 5.04. 5
life's but a walking shadow, a poor player, 5.05. 24
lear's shadow. LR 1.04.231 P
bridges, to course his own shadow for a traitor. 3.04. 57 P
take the shadow of this tree | for your good 5.02. 1
and discourse fustian with one's own shadow? OTH 2.03.281 P
not see me more, or if, | a mangled shadow. ANT 4.02. 27
i know he will come in our shadow, to scatter PER 4.02.112 P
under the shadow of his sword may cool us; TNK 1.01. 92
humane grace | affords them dust and shadow. 1.01.145
to tell the world 'tis but a gaudy shadow | that 2.02.103
by him, like a shadow, | i'll ever dwell. 2.06. 34
is but his foil, to him, a mere dull shadow; 4.02. 26
and died to kiss his shadow in the brook. VEN 162
for where they lay the shadow had forsook them, 176
i'll make a shadow for thee of my hairs; 191
cool shadow to his melting buttock lent; 315
and coal-black clouds that shadow heaven's light 533
each shadow makes him stop, each murmur stay, 706
then, gentle shadow (truth i must confess), | i 1001
"when he beheld his shadow in the brook, | the 1099
at his own shadow let the thief run mad, LUC 997
on this sad shadow lucrece spends her eyes, 1457
presents /thy shadow to my sightless view, SON 27.10
whilst that this shadow doth such substance give 37.10
thou, whose shadow shadows doth make bright, 43. 5
and you, but one, can every shadow lend: 53. 4
year, | the one doth shadow of your beauty show, 53.10
poor beauty indirectly seek | roses of shadow, 67. 8
as with your shadow i with these did play. 98.14
SHADOWED 3 FR 0.0003 REL FR 3 V 0 P
the shadowed livery of the burnish'd sun, | to MV 2.01. 2
serve your lust, shadowed from heaven's eye, TIT 2.01.130
his nose being shadowed by his neighbor's ear; LUC 1416
SHADOWING 2 FR 0.0002 REL FR 1 V 1 P
shadowing their right under your wings of war. JN 2.01. 14
herself in such shadowing passion without some OTH 4.01. 40 P
/SHADOW'S 1 FR 0.0001 REL FR 0 V 1 P
/that /it /is /but /a /shadow's /shadow. HAM 2.02.262 P
SHADOW'S 2 FR 0.0002 REL FR 2 V 0 P
shadows kiss, | such have but a shadow's bliss. MV 2.09. 67
how would thy shadow's form form happy show | to SON 43. 6
/SHADOWS 4 FR 0.0004 REL FR 3 V 1 P
/are /merely /shadows /to /the /unseen /grief R2 4.01.297
/but /shadows /and /the /shows /of /men, /to 2H4 1.01.193
/him, | /he /takes /false /shadows /for /true TIT 3.02. 80
/outstretch'd /heroes /the /beggars' /shadows. HAM 2.02.264 P
SHADOWS 29 FR 0.0032 REL FR 27 V 2 P
to worship shadows and adore false shapes, TGV 4.02.130
believe me, king of shadows, i mistook. MND 3.02.347
the best in this kind are but shadows; 5.01.211 P
if we shadows have offended, | think but this, 5.01.423
some there be that shadows kiss, | such have but MV 2.09. 66
that creep like shadows by him and do sigh | at WT 2.03. 34
each substance of a grief hath twenty shadows, R2 2.02. 14
is, is nought but shadows | of what it is not; 2.02. 23
at heart | so many of his shadows thou hast met 1H4 5.04. 30
him, for we have a number of shadows fill up the 2H4 3.02.134 P
nay, good my lord, be not afraid of shadows. R3 5.03.215
shadows to-night | have strook more terror to 5.03.216
bones, | that so the shadows be not unappeas'd, TIT 1.01.100
t' appease their groaning shadows that are gone. 1.01.126
whose circling shadows kings have sought to 2.04. 19
driving back shadows over low'ring hills; ROM 2.05. 6
when but love's shadows are so rich in joy! 5.01. 11
their shadows seem | a canopy most fatal, under JC 5.01. 86
come like shadows, so depart. MAC 4.01.111
piece 'gainst fancy, | condemning shadows quite. ANT 5.02.100
poor shadows of elysium, hence, and rest | upon CYM 5.04. 97
like motes and shadows see them move a while, PER 4.04. 21
thrives not in the heart that shadows dreadeth, LUC 270
such shadows are the weak brain's forgeries, 460
let ghastly shadows his lewd eyes affright, 971
"wander," a word for shadows like myself, | as PP 14.11
thou, whose shadow shadows doth make bright, SON 43. 5
that millions of strange shadows on you tend? 53. 2
while shadows like to thee do mock my sight? 61. 4
SHADOWY 3 FR 0.0003 REL FR 3 V 0 P
this shadowy desert, unfrequented woods, | i TGV 5.04. 2
with shadowy forests and with champains rich'd, LR 1.01. 64
o sacred, shadowy, cold, and constant queen, TNK 5.01.137
SHADY 4 FR 0.0004 REL FR 4 V 0 P
a nun, | for aye to be in shady cloister mew'd, MND 1.01. 71
to draw | the shady curtains from aurora's bed, ROM 1.01.136
and in thy shady cell, where none may spy him, LUC 881
thou by thy dial's shady stealth mayst know SON 77. 7
SHAFALUS 2 FR 0.0002 REL FR 2 V 0 P
not shafalus to procrus was so true. MND 5.01.198
as shafalus to procrus, i to you. 5.01.199
/SHAFT 1 FR 0.0001 REL FR 1 V 0 P
the /shaft /confounds | not that it wounds, TRO 3.01.118
SHAFT 9 FR 0.0010 REL FR 7 V 2 P
i'll make a shaft or a bolt on't. WIV 3.04. 24 P
but i might see young cupid's fiery shaft MND 2.01.161
in my school-days, when i had lost one shaft, MV 1.01.140
how will she love when the rich golden shaft TN 1.01. 34
you a forehand shaft a fourteen and fourteen and 2H4 3.02. 47 P
i am too sore enpierced with his shaft | to soar ROM 1.04. 19
this murtherous shaft that's shot | hath not yet MAC 2.03.141
the bow is bent and drawn, make from the shaft. LR 1.01.143
greatness was no guard | to bar heaven's shaft, PER 2.04. 15
SHAFTS 1 FR 0.0001 REL FR 1 V 0 P
kinsmen, shoot all your shafts into the court, TIT 4.03. 62
SHAG 1 FR 0.0001 REL FR 1 V 0 P
short-jointed, fetlocks shag and long, | broad VEN 295
SHAG-EAR'D 1 FR 0.0001 REL FR 1 V 0 P
thou li'st, thou shag-ear'd villain! MAC 4.02. 83
SHAG-HAIR'D 1 FR 0.0001 REL FR 1 V 0 P
full often, like a shag-hair'd crafty kern, 2H6 3.01.367

SHAK'D 5 FR 0.0005 REL FR 4 V 1 P
i shak'd you, sir, and cried. TMP 2.01.319
foundation of the earth | shak'd like a coward. 1H4 3.01. 17
he is so shak'd of a burning quotidian tertian, H5 2.01.118 P
o, when degree is shak'd, | which is the ladder TRO 1.03.101
a sly and constant knave, | not to be shak'd; CYM 1.05. 76
/SHAKE 1 FR 0.0001 REL FR 1 V 0 P
that /shake not, though they blow perpetually. SHR 2.01.141
SHAKE 110 FR 0.0124 REL FR 98 V 12 P
waves tremble, | yea, his dread trident shake. TMP 1.02.206
shake it off. 1.02.307
keep a care, | shake off slumber, and beware. 2.01.304
this will shake your shaking, i can tell you, 2.02. 84 P
the strong–bas'd promontory | have i made shake, 5.01. 47
if he shake his tail and say nothing, it will. TGV 2.05. 36 P
no stronger | than faults may shake our frames), MM 2.04.133
the devil will shake her chain, and fright us ERR 4.03. 76
come, you shake the head at so long a breathing, ADO 2.01.362 P
might shake off fifty, looking in her eye: LLL 4.03.239
or i will shake thee from me like a serpent! MND 3.02.261
a soft and dull–ey'd fool | to shake the head, MV 3.03. 15
and thou shalt hear how he will shake me up. AYL 1.01. 28 P
i could shake them off my coat; 1.03. 16 P
thy fame, as whirlwinds shake fair buds, | and SHR 5.02.140
whilst i can shake my sword or hear the drum. AWW 2.05. 91
of the which dare not shake the snow from off 4.03.168 P
cassocks, lest they shake themselves to pieces. 4.03.169 P
and shall do till the pangs of death shake him. TN 1.05. 75 P
go shake your ears. 2.03.125 P
be pleas'd that i shake off these names you give 5.01. 73
as or by oath remove or counsel shake | the WT 1.02.428
you, | but as you shake off one to take another; 4.04.569
so heavy as thou shalt not shake them off, | but JN 3.01.296
and ere our coming see thou shake the bags | of 3.03. 7
then with a passion would i shake the world, 3.04. 39
when they talk of him, they shake their heads, 4.02.188
and to thrill and shake | even at the crying of 5.02.143
if then we shall shake off our slavish yoke, R2 2.01.291
i say the earth did shake when i was born. 1H4 3.01. 20
and shake the peace and safety of our throne. 3.02.117
feel, masters, how i shake, look you, i warrant 2H4 2.04.105 P
enemy, | he doth unfasten so and shake a friend, 4.01.207
and you withal shall make all gallia shake. H5 1.02.216
shake in their fear, and with pale policy | seek 2.pr. 14
he'll make your paris louvre shake for it, 2.04.132
roan, i'll shake thy bulwarks to the ground. 1H6 3.02. 17
quake, | shake he his weapon at us and pass by. 2H6 4.08. 18
thus do i hope to shake king henry's head. 3H6 1.01. 20
dares stir a wing if warwick shake his bells. 1.01. 47
that stand high have many blasts to shake them, R3 1.03.258
why do you look on us, and shake your head, 2.02. 5
would shake the press | and make 'em reel before H8 4.01. 78
her foes shake like a field of beaten corn, 5.04. 31
on his gorget, | shake in and out the rivet; TRO 1.03.175
which shall shake him more | than if not look'd 3.03. 53
you shake, my lord, at something; 5.02. 50
thou mad'st thine enemies shake, as if the world COR 1.04. 60
or i shall shake thy bones | out of thy garments 3.01.178
let every feeble rumor shake your hearts! 3.03.125
if i could shake off but one seven years | from 4.01. 55
he'll shake | your rome about your ears. 4.06. 98
as hercules | did shake down mellow fruit. 4.06.100
them weep and shake with fear and sorrow, 5.03.100
shake, quoth the dove–house; ROM 1.03. 33
and shake the yoke of inauspicious stars | from 5.03.111
i am not of that feather to shake off | my TIM 1.01.100
but they do shake their heads, and i am here 2.02.202
let's shake our heads, and say, | as 'twere a 4.02. 25
holy chase, | shake off their sterile curse. JC 1.02. 9
him, i did mark | how he did shake — 'tis true, 1.02.121
he did shake — 'tis true, this god did shake; 1.02.121
for we will shake him, or worse days endure. 1.02.322
that i do bear | i can shake off at pleasure. 1.03.100
first, marcus brutus, will i shake with you; 3.01.185
ass) to shake his ears | and graze in commons. 4.01. 26
visitings of nature | shake my fell purpose, nor MAC 1.05. 46
say, the earth | was feverous, and did shake. 2.03. 61
shake off this downy sleep, death's counterfeit, 2.03. 76
fears and scruples shake us. 2.03.129
these terrible dreams | that shake us nightly. 3.02. 19
never shake | thy gory locks at me. 3.04. 49
shall never sag with doubt, nor shake with fear. 5.03. 10
of nature | so horridly to shake our disposition HAM 1.04. 55
i hold it fit that we shake hands and part, 1.05.128
to shake all cares and business from our age, LR 1.01. 39
in your own honor and shake in pieces the heart 1.02. 85 P
that thou hast power to shake my manhood thus, 1.04.297
caitiff, to pieces shake, | that under covert 3.02. 55
that thou mayst shake the superflux to them, 3.04. 35
upon your chin, | i'ld shake it on this quarrel. 3.07. 77
shake patiently my great affliction off. 4.06. 36
and does shake the head | to hear of pleasure's 4.06.120
time of his infirmity, | will shake this island. OTH 2.03.128
when she seem'd to shake and fear your looks, 3.03.207
this the nature | whom passion could not shake? 4.01.266
will (though he do shake me off | to beggarly 4.02.157
what, do you shake at that? 5.01.118
supp'd at my house, but i therefore shake not. 5.01.119
(though you in swearing shake the throned gods), ANT 1.03. 28
let me shake thy hand, | i never hated thee. 2.06. 73
dare but what it can, | no chance may shake it. 3.13. 81
of a lady fever thee, | shake thou to look on't. 3.13.139
antony part here, even here | do we shake hands. 4.12. 20
but when he meant to quail and shake the orb, 5.02. 85
which to shake off | becomes a warlike people, CYM 3.01. 51
hours | shake off the golden slumber of repose. PER 3.02. 23
and shake to lose his honor) is like her | that, TNK pr 5
how will it shake the bones of that good man, pr 17
small winds shake him. | but what's the matter? 1.02. 88
you | have said enough to shake me from the arm 1.03. 92
no more shake | our pointed javelins, whilst the 2.02. 48
i'll shake 'em so, ye shall not sleep, | i'll 2.02.272
come shake hands again then, | and take heed, as 3.06.302
it is our infection will make the city shake, STM II.C 14 P
fear whereof doth make him shake and shudder; VEN 880
not my tongue be mute, my frail joints shake? LUC 227
rough winds do shake the darling buds of may, SON 18. 3
do in consent shake hands to torture me, | the 28. 6
upon those boughs which shake against the cold, 73. 3
SHAKEN 5 FR 0.0005 REL FR 5 V 0 P
so shaken as we are, so wan with care, | find we 1H4 1.01. 1
have shaken edward from the regal seat, | and 3H6 4.06. 2
shaken with sorrows in ungrateful rome. TIT 1.03. 17
that looks on tempests and is never shaken; SON 116. 6
for if you were by my unkindness shaken | as i 120. 5
SHAKER 1 FR 0.0001 REL FR 1 V 0 P
shaker of o'er–rank states, thou grand decider TNK 5.01. 63
SHAKES 22 FR 0.0024 REL FR 20 V 2 P
and shakes a chain | in a most hideous and WIV 4.04. 33
for many a man's tongue shakes out his master's AWW 2.04. 24 P
that shakes the rotten carcass of old death JN 2.01.456
shakes the old beldame earth, and topples down 1H4 3.01. 31
and our air shakes them passing scornfully. H5 4.02. 42
and shakes his head, and trembling stands aloof, 2H6 1.01.227
that slightly shakes his parting guest by th' TRO 3.03.166
than his that shakes for age and feebleness. TIT 1.01.188
and shakes his threat'ning sword | against the TIM 5.01.166
the sway of earth | shakes like a thing unfirm? JC 1.03. 4
shakes so my single state of man that function MAC 1.03.140
it is not words that shakes me thus. OTH 4.01. 41 P
some bloody passion shakes your very frame. 5.02. 44
which serve not for his vantage, he shakes off, ANT 3.07. 33
of the north | shakes all our buds from growing. CYM 1.03. 37
their vessel shakes | on neptune's billow; PER 3.ch. 44
your shakes of fortune, though they haunt you 3.03. 6
sometime she shakes her head, and then his hand,
VEN 223
like an earthquake, shakes thee on my breast. 648
for passage, earth's foundation shakes, | which 1047
beating her bulk, that his hand shakes withal. LUC 467
this said, he shakes aloft his roman blade, 505
SHAKING 12 FR 0.0013 REL FR 10 V 2 P
this will shake your shaking, i can tell you, TMP 2.02. 84 P
laid upon him for shaking off so good a wife and AWW 4.03. 7 P
fire, | to make a shaking fever in your walls, JN 2.01.228
what dost thou mean by shaking of thy head? 3.01. 19
shaking the bloody darts as he his bells. 2H6 3.01.366
that with the very shaking of their chains 5.01.145
shaking of earth! TRO 1.03. 97
peace, | shaking the bloody fingers of thy foes, JC 3.01.198
macbeth | is ripe for shaking, and the pow'rs MAC 4.03.238
at last, a little shaking of mine arm, | and HAM 2.01. 89
shaking her wings, devouring all in haste, VEN 57
shaking their scratch'd ears, bleeding as they 924
SHAK'ST 2 FR 0.0002 REL FR 1 V 1 P
why shak'st thou so? WT 4.04.628 P
thou shak'st thy head, and hold'st it fear or 2H4 1.01. 95
SHALES 1 FR 0.0001 REL FR 1 V 0 P
leaving them but the shales and husks of men. H5 4.02. 18
'SHALL 1 FR 0.0001 REL FR 1 V 0 P
'shall not be long but i'll be here again. MAC 4.02. 23
SHALL *(also s'*, sall)*
/SHALL 21 FR 0.0023 REL FR 18 V 3 P
SHALL 3849 FR 0.4350 REL FR 2983 V 866 P
SHALLENGE *(also challenge)*
SHALLENGE 1 FR 0.0001 REL FR 0 V 1 P
by gar, it is a shallenge. WIV 1.04.108 P
SHALLOW 96 FR 0.0108 REL FR 34 V 62 P
this good light, this is a very shallow monster! TMP 2.02.144 P
that's on some shallow story of deep love, | how TGV 1.01. 21
my mind | according to my shallow simple skill. 1.02. 8
think'st thou i am so shallow, so conceitless, 4.02. 96
he shall not abuse robert shallow, esquire. WIV 1.01. 3 P
and your friend, and justice shallow, and here 1.01. 76 P
i thank you for my venison, master shallow. 1.01. 80 P
believe me, robert shallow, esquire, saith he is 1.01.106 P
now, master shallow, you'll complain of me to 1.01.109 P
nay, i will do as my cousin shallow says. 1.01.217 P
you are my man, go wait upon my cousin shallow. 1.01.272 P
master shallow, you have yourself been a great 2.03. 42 P
'tis true, master shallow. 2.03. 50 P
"to shallow rivers, to whose falls | melodious 3.01. 17
to shallow —" | mercy on me! 3.01. 21
to shallow, etc." 3.01. 26
"to shallow rivers, to whose falls —" | heaven 3.01. 29
there comes my master, master shallow, and 3.01. 32 P
good master shallow, let him woo for himself. 3.04. 50 P
come, master shallow; 3.04. 75
but that the shore was shelvy and shallow — a 3.05. 15 P
smoth'red in errors, feeble, shallow, weak, ERR 3.02. 35
hath laugh'd at such shallow follies in others, ADO 2.03. 10 P
these shallow fools have brought to light, who 5.01.233 P
"that shallow vassal" — LLL 1.01.253 P
their shallow shows and prologue vildly penn'd, 5.02.305
which shallow laughing hearers give to fools. 5.02.860
let not the sound of shallow fopp'ry enter | my MV 2.05. 35
shallow, shallow. AYL 3.02. 57 P
shallow, shallow. 3.02. 57 P
shallow again. 3.02. 61 P
most shallow man! 3.02. 65 P
god help thee, shallow man! 3.02. 72 P
fantastical, apish, shallow, inconstant, full of 3.02.412 P
a shallow plash to plunge him in the deep, | and SHR 1.01. 23
y' are shallow, madam — in great friends, for AWW 1.03. 42 P
you are idle shallow things, i am not of your TN 3.04.123 P
of, | for shallow draught and bulk unprizable, 5.01. 55
i say unto you again, you are a shallow, 1H4 2.03. 15 P
with shallow jesters, and rash bavin wits, 3.02. 61
and god forbid a shallow scratch should drive 5.04. 11
a good shallow young fellow. 2H4 2.04.237 P
good morrow, good cousin shallow. 3.02. 4 P
alas, a black woosel, cousin shallow! 3.02. 8 P
where i think they will talk of mad shallow yet. 3.02. 15 P
you were call'd lusty shallow then, cousin. 3.02. 16 P
i beseech you, which is justice shallow? 3.02. 56 P
i am robert shallow, sir, a poor esquire of this 3.02. 57 P
to see you well, good master robert shallow. 3.02. 86 P
well, master shallow, deep, master shallow. 3.02.161 P
well, master shallow, deep, master shallow. 3.02.162 P
am glad to see you, by my troth, master shallow. 3.02.193 P
no more of that, master shallow, /no /more /of 3.02.196 P
she lives, master shallow. 3.02.200 P
always say she could not abide master shallow. 3.02.203 P
old, old, master shallow. 3.02.206 P
heard the chimes at midnight, master shallow. 3.02.215 P
will you tell me, master shallow, how to choose 3.02.257 P
give me the spirit, master shallow. 3.02.260 P
these fellows woll do well, master shallow. 3.02.287 P
i do see the bottom of justice shallow. 3.02.302 P
you are too shallow, hastings, much too shallow, 4.02. 50
you are too shallow, hastings, much too shallow, 4.02. 50
and there will i visit master robert shallow, 4.03.129 P
you must excuse me, master robert shallow. 5.01. 3 P
i'll follow you, good master robert shallow. 5.01. 60 P
such bearded hermits' staves as master shallow. 5.01. 64 P
if i had a suit to master shallow, i would humor 5.01. 71 P
curry with master shallow that no man could 5.01. 74 P
enough out of this shallow to keep prince harry 5.01. 78 P
i come, master shallow, i come, master shallow. 5.01. 87 P
i come, master shallow, i come, master shallow. 5.01. 88 P
master robert shallow, choose what office thou 5.03.123 P
master shallow, my lord shallow — be what thou 5.03.129 P
master shallow, my lord shallow — be what thou 5.03.130 P
boot, boot, master shallow! 5.03.135 P
stand here by me, master shallow, i will make 5.05. 5 P
master shallow, i owe you a thousand pound. 5.05. 73 P
that can hardly be, master shallow. 5.05. 76 P
his companies unletter'd, rude, and shallow, H5 1.01. 55
his jest will savor but of shallow wit, | when 1.02.295
by a vain, giddy, shallow, humorous youth, 2.04. 28
i have perhaps some shallow spirit of judgment; 1H6 2.04. 16
which being shallow, you shall give me leave 3H6 4.01. 62
incapable and shallow innocents, | you cannot R3 2.02. 18
tell him his fears are shallow, without instance 3.02. 25
your reasons are too shallow and too quick. 4.04.361
relenting fool, and shallow, changing woman! 4.04.431
armed in proof and led by shallow richmond. 5.03.219
how many shallow bauble boats dare sail | upon TRO 1.03. 35
a base, proud, shallow, beggarly, three–suited, LR 2.02. 16 P
thinks he that her husband's shallow tongue — LUC 78
"out, idle words, servants to shallow fools! 1016
sounds make lesser noise than shallow fords, 1329
but now he throws that shallow habit by, 1814
by shallow rivers, by whose falls | melodious PP 19. 7
SHALLOWEST 2 FR 0.0002 REL FR 2 V 0 P
the shallowest thick–skin of that barren sort, MND 3.02. 13
your shallowest help will hold me up afloat, SON 80. 9
SHALLOW–HEARTED 1 FR 0.0001 REL FR 1 V 0 P
what, what, ye sanguine, shallow–hearted boys! TIT 4.02. 97
SHALLOWLY 1 FR 0.0001 REL FR 1 V 0 P
most shallowly did you these arms commence, 2H4 4.02.118
SHALLOW–ROOTED 1 FR 0.0001 REL FR 1 V 0 P
'tis the spring, and weeds are shallow–rooted; 2H6 3.01. 31
SHALLOWS 2 FR 0.0002 REL FR 2 V 0 P
but i should think of shallows and of flats, MV 1.01. 26
life | is bound in shallows and in miseries. JC 4.03.221
SHALL'T 3 FR 0.0003 REL FR 3 V 0 P
merry, or sad, shall't be? WT 2.01. 23
but shall't be shortly? OTH 3.03. 56
shall't be to–night at supper? 3.03. 57
/SHALT 2 FR 0.0002 REL FR 2 V 0 P
/thou /shalt /not /sigh, /nor /hold /thy /stumps TIT 3.02. 42
/and /thou /shalt /read /when /mine /begin /to 3.02. 85
SHALT 314 FR 0.0355 REL FR 254 V 60 P
this, be sure, to–night thou shalt have cramps, TMP 1.02.325
thou shalt be pinch'd | as thick as honeycomb, 1.02.328
sea–water shalt thou drink; 1.02.463
hark what thou else shalt do me. 1.02.496
thou shalt be as free | as mountain winds; 1.02.499
by this light, thou shalt be my lieutenant, 3.02. 15 P
thou shalt be lord of it, and i'll serve thee. 3.02. 57
for thou shalt find she will outstrip all praise 4.01. 10
end, and thou | shalt have the air at freedom. 4.01.265
quickly, spirit, | thou shalt ere long be free. 5.01. 87
miss thee, | but yet thou shalt have freedom. 5.01. 96
there shalt thou find the mariners asleep 5.01. 98
bravely, my diligence. thou shalt be free. 5.01.241
i am resolv'd that thou shalt spend some time TGV 1.03. 66
like exhibition thou shalt have from me. 1.03. 69
pence, thou shalt have five thousand welcomes. 2.05. 10 P
thou shalt never get such a secret from me but 2.05. 39 P
thou shalt not live to brag what we have offer'd 4.01. 67
where thou shalt find me sad and solitary. 4.04. 89
thou shalt be worshipp'd, kiss'd, lov'd, and 4.04.199
tester i'll have in pouch when thou shalt lack, WIV 1.03. 87
thou shalt have egress and regress — said i 2.01.217 P
thou shalt know i will predominate over the 2.02.281 P
the peasant, and thou shalt lie with his wife. 2.02.282 P
master /brook, shalt know him for knave, and 2.02.285 P
and thou shalt woo her. 2.03. 88 P
cricket, to windsor chimneys shalt thou leap; 5.05. 43
thou shalt eat a posset to–night at my house, 5.05.170 P
"thou shalt not steal"? MM 1.02. 10 P
thou shalt not do't. 3.01.102
upon mine honor, thou shalt marry her. 5.01.518
be quiet and depart, thou shalt not have him. ERR 5.01.112
discover how, and thou shalt find me just. 5.01.203
and thou shalt see how apt it is to learn | any ADO 1.01.292
and with her father, | and thou shalt have her. 1.01.310
there shalt thou find my cousin beatrice 3.01. 2
if thou kill'st me, boy, thou shalt kill a man. 5.01. 79
thou shalt fast for thy offenses ere thou be LLL 1.02.146 P
thou shalt be heavily punished. 1.02.150 P
thou shalt to prison. 1.02.158 P
thou shalt know her, fellow, by the rest that 4.01. 44 P
what shalt thou exchange for rags? 4.01. 82 P
"for," quoth the king, "an angel shalt thou see; 5.02.103
hold, rosaline, this favor thou shalt wear, 5.02.130
thou shalt die. 5.02.679 P
thou shalt not from this grove | till i torment MND 2.01.146
thou shalt fly him and he shall seek thy love. 2.01.246
thou shalt know the man | by the athenian 2.01.263
thou shalt remain here, whether thou wilt or no. 3.01.153
so, | that thou shalt like an aery spirit go. 3.01.161
little show of love to her, | thou shalt aby it. 3.02.335
thou shalt buy this dear, | if ever i thy face 3.02.426
thou shalt not know the sound of thine own MV 1.01.109
soon at supper shalt thou see | lorenzo, who is 2.03. 5
well, thou shalt see, thy eyes shall be thy 2.05. 1
thou shalt not gurmandize, | as thou hast done 2.05. 3
how shalt thou hope for mercy, rend'ring none? 4.01. 88
ere thou shalt lose for me one drop of blood. 4.01.113
thyself shalt see the act; 4.01.314
thou shalt have justice more than thou desir'st. 4.01.316

thou shalt have nothing but the forfeiture, | to 4.01.343
that thou shalt see the difference of our spirit 4.01.368
in christ'ning shalt thou have two godfathers: 4.01.398
and thou shalt hear how he will shake me up. AYL 1.01. 27 P
which thou shalt find i will most kindly requite 1.01.138 P
and truly, when he dies, thou shalt be his heir; 1.02. 19 P
and thou shalt have to pay for it of us. 2.04. 93
and thou shalt not die for lack of a dinner if 2.06. 16 P
thou shalt have one. 2.07. 44
nor shalt not, till necessity be serv'd. 2.07. 89
and when shalt thou see him again? 3.02.224 P
very taunting letter, | and thou shalt bear it; 3.05.135
i thank thee, thou shalt not lose by it. SHR in.2. 99
thou shalt be master, tranio, in my stead; 1.01.202
(she being now at hand) thou shalt soon feel, to 4.01. 31 P
as thou shalt think on prating whilst thou 4.03.113
well, go thy ways, old lad, for thou shalt ha't. 5.02.181
why, helen, thou shalt have my leave and love, AWW 1.03.251
what i can help thee to thou shalt not miss. 1.03.256
then shalt thou give me with thy kingly hand 2.01.193
thou shalt have none, rossillion, none in france 3.02.101
thou shalt present me as an eunuch to him, | it TN 1.02. 56
and thou shalt live as freely as thy lord, | to 1.04. 39
if ever thou shalt love, | in the sweet pangs of 2.04. 15
thou shalt not choose but go; 4.01. 57
thou shalt hold th' opinion of pythagoras ere i 4.02. 58 P
thou shalt not be the worse for me, there's gold 5.01. 27 P
thou shalt be both the plaintiff and the judge 5.01.354
thee than it), so thou | shalt feel our justice; WT 3.02. 90
thou ne'er shalt see | thy wife paulina more." 3.03. 35
thou shalt accompany us to the place, where we 4.02. 47 P
not thou, man, thou shalt lose nothing here. 4.04.255 P
if thou'lt bear a part, thou shalt hear; 4.04.293 P
sigh | that thou no more shalt see this knack 4.04.428
see this knack (as never | i mean thou shalt), 4.04.429
for thou shalt hear that i, | knowing by paulina 5.03.125
for by this knot thou shalt so surely tie | thy JN 2.01.470
thou shalt be punish'd for thus frighting me, 3.01. 11
thou mayst, thou shalt, i will not go with thee. 3.01. 67
thou shalt stand curs'd and excommunicate, | and 3.01.173
so heavy as thou shalt not shake them off, | but 3.01.296
thou shalt not need. 3.01.320
thou shalt rue this hour within this hour. 3.01.323
burn thee up, and thou shalt turn | to ashes, 3.01.344
no cause to say so yet, | but thou shalt have; 3.03. 31
me mad, | and thou shalt be canoniz'd, cardinal; 3.04. 52
yet so ugly a fiend of hell | as thou shalt be, 4.03.124
for thou shalt thrust thy hand as deep | into 5.02. 60
and thou shalt find it, dolphin, do not doubt. 5.02.180
my life thou shalt command, but not my shame: R2 1.01.166
to dark dishonor's use thou shalt not have. 1.01.169
and thou shalt have twelve thousand fighting men 3.02. 70
bagot, forbear, thou shalt not take it up. 4.01. 30
thou shalt think, | though he divide the realm 5.01. 59
and thou shalt know | the treason that my haste 5.03. 49
no, thou shalt. 1H4 1.02. 63 P
i mean thou shalt have the hanging of the 1.02. 67 P
thou shalt have a share in our purchase, as i am 2.01. 91 P
thou need'st him, there thou shalt find him. 2.02. 71 P
ask me when thou wilt, and thou shalt have it. 2.04. 62 P
not quite out of thee, now shalt thou be mov'd. 2.04.384 P
thou shalt have charge and sovereign trust 3.02.161
thou shalt find me tractable to any honest 3.03.172 P
there shalt thou know thy charge, and there 3.03.201
and thou shalt find a king that will revenge 5.03. 12
money a' thursday, shalt have a cap to–morrow. 2H4 2.04.275 P
come, thou shalt go to the wars in a gown. 3.02.184 P
and thou shalt prove a shelter to thy friends, 4.04. 42
approach me, and thou shalt be as thou wast, 5.05. 61
a noble shalt thou have, and present pay, | and H5 2.01.107
thou never shalt hear herald any more. 4.03.127
or mangled shalt thou be by this my sword. 4.04. 39
base troyan, thou shalt die. 5.01. 31
a saving faith within me tells me thou shalt, i 5.02.204 P
and thou shalt wear me, if thou wear me, better 5.02.232 P
which word thou shalt no sooner bless mine ear 5.02.238 P
thou shalt find the best king of good fellows. 5.02.242 P
and thou shalt find that i exceed my sex. 1H6 1.02. 90
thou shalt be fortunate | if thou receive me for 1.02. 91
in single combat thou shalt buckle with me; 1.02. 95
but now thou shalt not. 1.04. 5
and thou shalt find me at the governor's. 1.04. 20
this comfort, | thou shalt not die whiles — 1.04. 91
ah, thou shalt find us ready for thee still; 2.04.104
thou shalt rue this treason with thy tears, | if 3.02. 36
when thou shalt see i'll meet thee to thy cost. 3.04. 43
and i'll direct thee how thou shalt escape | by 4.05. 10
thou shalt well perceive | that neither in birth 5.01. 58
thou shalt be plac'd as viceroy under him, | and 5.04.131
till thou speak, thou shalt not pass from hence. 2H6 1.04. 27
and, will, thou shalt have my hammer; 2.03. 75 P
thou shalt not see me blush | nor change my 3.01. 98
thou shalt be waking while i shed thy blood, 3.02.227
and therefore to revenge it shalt thou die, 4.01. 26
rate me at what thou wilt, thou shalt be paid. 4.01. 30
but jove was never slain, as thou shalt be. 4.01. 49
thou shalt have cause to fear before i leave 4.01.118
is, and thou shalt have a license to kill for a 4.03. 7 P
it a lordship, thou shalt have it for that word. 4.07. 4 P
but thou shalt wear it as a herald's coat, | to 4.10. 70
thou shalt rule no more | o'er him whom heaven 5.01.104
prove it, henry, and thou shalt be king. 3H6 1.01.131
and thou shalt reign in quiet while thou liv'st. 1.01.173
as thou shalt reign but by their sufferance. 1.01.234
of the realm, | and yet shalt thou be safe? 1.01.241
brother, thou shalt to london presently, | and 1.02. 36
thou, richard, shalt to the duke of norfolk, 1.02. 38
for thou shalt know this strong right hand of 2.01.152
for king of england shalt thou be proclaim'd 2.01.194
so shalt thou sinow both these lands together, 2.06. 91
thou shalt not dread | the scatt'red foe that 2.06. 92
why then thou shalt not have thy husband's lands 3.02. 71
answer no more, for thou shalt be my queen. 3.02.106
shalt stir up in suffolk, norfolk, and in kent, 4.08. 12
shalt find | men well inclin'd to hear what thou 4.08. 15
in oxfordshire shalt muster up thy friends. 4.08. 18
and thou shalt still remain the duke of york. 5.01. 28
and thou shalt be the third, /and this sword 5.01. 75
and of our labors thou shalt reap the gain. 5.07. 20
go tread the path that thou shalt ne'er return: R3 1.01.117
and by despairing shalt thou stand excused | for 1.02. 86
he is in heaven, where thou shalt never come. 1.02.106
to both their deaths shalt thou be accessary. 1.02.191
that shalt thou know hereafter. 1.02.198
stay, dog, for thou shalt hear me. 1.03.215
the day will come that thou shalt wish for me 1.03.244
law commanded | that thou shalt do no murther. 1.04.197
wherein thyself shalt highly be employ'd. 3.01.180
to–day shalt thou behold a subject die | for 3.03. 3
when thou shalt tell the process of their death. 4.03. 32
that thou shalt know, troyan, he is awake, | he TRO 1.03.255
come, thou shalt bear a letter to him straight. 3.03.305
and thou shalt hunt a lion that will fly | with 4.01. 20
farewell, | thou never shalt mock diomed again. 5.02. 99
ay, but thou shalt not go. 5.03. 70
now, | but thou anon shalt hear of me again; 5.06. 18
shalt see me once more strike at tullus' face. COR 1.01.240
devise with thee | where thou shalt rest, that 4.01. 39
nay, but thou shalt stay too. 4.02. 23
one, thou shalt no sooner | march to assault thy 5.03.122
(trust to't, thou shalt not) on thy mother's 5.03.124
which thou shalt thereby reap is such a name 5.03.143
titus, thou shalt obtain and ask the empery. TIT 1.01.201
a valiant son–in–law thou shalt enjoy, | one fit 1.01.311
full well shalt thou perceive how much i dare. 2.01. 44
thou shalt not bail them, see thou follow me. 2.03.299
and, lavinia, thou shalt be employ'd; 3.01.281
by me thou shalt have justice at his hands. 4.03.104
therefore thou shalt vow | by that same god, 5.01. 81
to that which thou shalt hear of me anon. 5.01. 90
well shalt thou know her by thine own proportion 5.02.106
and on them shalt thou ease thy angry heart. 5.02.119
thou shalt inquire him out among the goths: 5.02.123
thou shalt not stir one foot to seek a foe. ROM 1.01. 80
till thou shalt know the reason of my love, 3.01. 70
didst consort him here, | shalt with him hence. 3.01.131
where thou shalt live till we can find a time 3.03.150
death | thou shalt continue two and forty hours, 4.01.105
in the mean time, against thou shalt awake, 4.01.113
thou shalt be logger–head. 4.04. 21
digging up of graves, | but thou shalt hear it. 5.03. 7
so shalt thou show me friendship. 5.03. 41
look and thou shalt see. 5.03.213
thou wilt not hear me now, thou shalt not then. TIM 1.02.247 P
a dog, and thou shalt famish a dog's death. 2.02. 86 P
notwithstanding, thou shalt be no less esteem'd. 2.02.106 P
o, thou shalt find — 4.03.232
nothing living but thee, thou shalt be welcome. 4.03.356 P
thou shalt build from men; 4.03.526
the captainship, thou shalt be met with thanks, 5.01.161
thou rather shalt enforce it with thy smile 5.04. 45
thou shalt not back till i have borne this corse JC 3.01.291
according to the which thou shalt discourse | to 3.01.295
it was well done, and thou shalt sleep again; 4.03.264
to tell thee thou shalt see me at philippi. 4.03.283
all hail, macbeth, that shalt be king hereafter! MAC 1.03. 50
thou shalt get kings, though thou be none. 1.03. 67
on of time with 'hail, king that shalt be!' 1.05. 10 P
cawdor, and shalt be | what thou art promis'd. 1.05. 15
thou shalt not live, | that i may tell 4.01. 84
when shalt thou see thy wholesome days again, 4.03.105
so art thou to revenge, when thou shalt hear. HAM 1.05. 7
as pure as snow, thou shalt not escape calumny. 3.01.136 P
and thou shalt live in this fair world behind, 3.02.175
haply one as kind | for husband shalt thou — 3.02.177
"horatio, when thou shalt have overlook'd this, 4.06. 13 P
follow me, thou shalt serve me. LR 1.04. 40 P
and thou shalt have more | than two tens to a 1.04.126
thou shalt find | that i'll resume the shape 1.04.308
shalt see thy other daughter will use thee 1.05. 14 P
thou shalt have as many dolors for thy daughters 2.04. 54 P
no, regan, thou shalt never have my curse. 2.04.170
and thou shalt find a /dearer father in my love. 3.05. 24 P
friend, where thou shalt meet | both welcome and 3.06. 91
villain, thou shalt find — 3.07. 34
see't shalt thou never. 3.07. 67
thou shalt not die. 4.06.111
this thou shalt answer; i know thee, roderigo. OTH 1.01.119
and thou shalt see an answerable sequestration 1.03.345 P
and all the tribe of hell, thou shalt enjoy her; 1.03.357 P
away, i say, thou shalt know more hereafter. 2.03.381
shalt thou have report | how 'tis abroad. ANT 1.04. 35
thou shalt be whipt with wire, and stew'd in 2.05. 65
thou shalt bring him to me | where i will write. 3.03. 46
our nineteen legions thou shalt hold by land, 3.07. 58
thou shalt | go back, i warrant thee; 5.02.155
when thou shalt bring me word she loves my son, CYM 1.05. 49
what shalt thou expect | to be depender on a 1.05. 57
thou shalt not damn my hand. 3.04. 74
shalt hereafter find | it is no act of common 3.04. 90
when thou shalt be disedg'd by her | that now 3.04. 93
and shalt be ever. 4.02. 46
thou shalt know | i am son to th' queen. 4.02. 92
thou shalt not lack | the flower that's like thy 4.02.220
i will not say | thou shalt be so well master'd, 4.02.383
thou shalt be then freer than a jailer; 5.04.196 P
and thou shalt die for't. 5.05.310
as these before thee, thou thyself shalt bleed. PER 1.01. 58
come, thou shalt go home, and we'll have flesh 2.01. 81 P
and flap–jacks, and thou shalt be welcome. 2.01. 83 P
thou shalt have my best gown to make thee a pair 2.01.162 P
when thou shalt kneel, and justify in knowledge 5.01.217
and | thou shalt remember nothing more than what TNK 1.01.185
thou shalt stay and see | her bright eyes break 2.03. 8
thou shalt feed | upon the sweetness of a noble 2.03. 10
thou shalt know, palamon, i dare as well | die 3.06.128
and thou shalt see me, theseus, | do such a 3.06.154
thou shalt have pity of us both, o theseus, | if 3.06.172
meed | a thousand honey secrets shalt thou know. VEN 16
begg'd for that which thou unask'd shalt have. 102
i'll be a park, and thou shalt be my deer: 231
my heart," saith she, "and thou shalt have it. 374
"then shalt thou see the dew–bedabbled wretch 703
nay, do not struggle, for thou shalt not rise. 710
when thou shalt charge me with so black a deed? LUC 226
shalt have thy trespass cited up in rhymes, 524
that thou shalt see thy state, and pity mine." 644
thou shalt not know | the stained taste of 1058
but thou shalt know thy int'rest was not bought 1067
"thou, collatine, shalt oversee this will; 1205
how was i overseen that thou shalt see it! 1206
the help that thou shalt lend me | comes all too 1685
tak'st, | 'mongst our mourners shalt thou go. PHT 20
so thou through windows of thine age shalt see, SON 3.11
if thou issueless shalt hap to die, | the world 9. 3
as fast as thou shalt wane, so fast thou grow'st 11. 1
and shalt by fortune once more re–survey | these 32. 3
that time when thou shalt strangely pass, | and 49. 5
and thou shalt find | those children nurs'd, 77.10
when thou shalt be dispos'd to set me light, 88. 1
and thou in this shalt find thy monument, | when 107.13
time, thou shalt not boast that i do change: 123. 1
and thou shalt find it merits not reproving, 142. 4
so shalt thou feed on death, that feeds on men, 146.13

SHAMBLES 2 FR 0.0002 REL FR 2 V 0 P
to make a shambles of the parliament house! 3H6 1.01. 71
o, ay, as summer flies are in the shambles, OTH 4.02. 66

SHAM'D 17 FR 0.0019 REL FR 10 V 7 P
you're sham'd, y' are overthrown, y' are undone WIV 3.03. 95 P
why then you are utterly sham'd, and he's but a 4.02. 42 P
now shall the devil be sham'd. 4.02.119 P
i'll warrant they'll have him publicly sham'd, 4.02.221 P
to the jest, should he not be publicly sham'd. 4.02.222 P
there is but one sham'd that was never gracious; AYL 1.02.187 P
dies, | or my sham'd life in his dishonor lies: R2 5.03. 71
sham'd their aspects with store of childish R3 1.02.154
you have sham'd me | in your condemned seconds. COR 1.08. 14
by this our mother is for ever sham'd. TIT 4.02.112
age, thou art sham'd! JC 1.02.150
reserv'd a blanket, else we had been all sham'd. LR 3.04. 66 P
which before | have often sham'd our sex. ANT 5.02.124
whose rags sham'd gilded arms, whose naked CYM 5.05. 4
that my posterity, sham'd with the note, | shall LUC 208
when life is sham'd and death reproach's debtor. 1155
for i am sham'd by that which i bring forth, SON 72.13

/SHAME 5 FR 0.0005 REL FR 5 V 0 P
/would /it /not /shame /thee /in /so /fair /a R2 4.01.231
/for /shame | /bemonster /not /thy /feature. LR 4.02. 62
/shame /of /ladies! 4.03. 27
/a /sovereign /shame /so /elbows /him: 4.03. 42
/that /burning /shame | /detains /him /from 4.03. 46

SHAME 344 FR 0.0388 REL FR 309 V 35 P
dear madam, 'tis a passing shame | that i TGV 1.02. 17
it were a shame to call her back again, | and 1.02. 51
a slave, that still an end turns me to shame! 4.04. 62
the more shame for him that he sends it me; 4.04.133
my shame and guilt confounds me. 5.04. 73
if shame live | in a disguise of love! 5.04.106
i fear not mine own shame so much as his peril. WIV 3.03.122 P
for shame, never stand "you had rather" and "you 3.03.125 P
for shame, oman. 4.01. 64 P
better shame than murther. 4.02. 44 P
i do; and bear the shame most patiently. MM 2.03. 20
as that the sin hath brought you to this shame, 2.03. 31
as it is an evil, | and take the shame with joy. 2.03. 36
sick for, ere i'ld yield | my body up to shame. 2.04.104
why give you me this shame? 3.01. 80
to take life | from thine own sister's shame? 3.01.139
shame to him whose cruel striking | kills for 3.02.267
twice treble shame on angelo, | to weed my vice 3.02.269
but that her tender shame | will not proclaim 4.04. 23
a dishonor'd life | with ransom of such shame. 4.04. 32
i now begin with grief and shame to utter. 5.01. 96
prince, | no longer session hold upon my shame, 5.01.371
by falsehood and corruption doth it shame. ERR 2.01.113
shame hath a bastard fame, well managed; 3.02. 19
to your notorious shame, i doubt it not. 4.01. 84
free from these slanders and this open shame! 4.04. 67
it is no shame; 4.04. 80
that you would put me to this shame and trouble, 5.01. 14
beside the charge, the shame, imprisonment, 5.01. 18
accusation, and my cunning shall not shame me. ADO 2.02. 55 P
where i should wed, there will i shame her. 3.02.125 P
shame her with what he saw o'ernight, and send 3.03.162 P
death is the fairest cover for her shame | that 4.01.116
not every earthly thing | cry shame upon her? 4.01.121
this shame derives itself from unknown loins"? 4.01.135
seal with my death than repeat over to my shame. 5.01.241 P
so the life that died with shame | lives in 5.03. 7
how well this yielding rescues thee from shame! LLL 1.01.118
endure such public shame as the rest of the 1.01.131 P
degree | stands in attainder of eternal shame. 1.01.157
one for herself, to desire that were a shame. 2.01.200
in love, i hope — sweet fellowship in shame. 4.03. 47
you were born to do me shame. 4.03.200
and they, well mock'd, depart away with shame. 5.02.156
here, | unseen, unvisited, much to our shame. 5.02.358
berowne, they will shame us; 5.02.511
run away for shame, alisander. 5.02.579 P
the more shame for you, judas. 5.02.602 P
how canst thou thus for shame, titania, | glance MND 2.01. 74
have you no modesty, no maiden shame, | no touch 3.02.285
must yield to such inevitable shame | as to MV 4.01. 57
i will not shame myself to give you this. 4.01.431
him, | i was beset with shame and courtesy, | my 5.01.217
or if thou canst not, o, for shame, for shame, AYL 3.05. 18
or if thou canst not, o, for shame, for shame, 3.05. 18
some of my shame, if you will know of me | what 4.03. 95
i do not shame | to tell you what i was, since 4.03.135
for shame, thou hilding of a devilish spirit, SHR 2.01. 26
what says lucentio to this shame of ours? 3.02. 7
no shame but mine. 3.02. 8
fie, doff this habit, shame to your estate, | an 3.02.100
and i, seeing this, came thence for very shame, 3.02.180
if thou accountedst it shame, lay it on me, 4.03.181
a strumpet's boldness, a divulged shame, AWW 2.01.171
at home be encount'red with a shame as ample. 4.03. 70 P
but women were that had receiv'd so much shame, 4.03.327 P
and, parolles, live | safest in shame! 4.03.338
rascally sheep–biter come by some notable shame? TN 2.05. 6 P
thou hast, sebastian, done good feature shame. 3.04.366

in the streets, desperate of shame and state, 5.01. 64
but to do myself much right, or you much shame. 5.01.308 P
wherein our entertainment shall shame us: WT 1.01. 8 P
knows | what she should shame to know herself 2.01. 91
fasten'd and fix'd the shame on't in himself, 2.03. 15
as you were past all shame | (those of your fact 3.02. 84
their death appear (unto | our shame perpetual). 3.02.238
more, which will shame you to give him again. 4.04.240 P
that title and what shame else belongs to't. 4.04.840 P
on thee, rude man, thou dost shame thy mother, JN 1.01. 64
where how he did prevail i shame to speak. 1.01.104
now shame upon you, whe'er she does or no! 2.01.167
week, | this day of shame, oppression, perjury. 3.01. 88
thou dost shame | that bloody spoil. 3.01.114
doff it for shame, | and hang a calve's–skin on 3.01.128
so we could find some pattern of our shame. 3.04. 16
and bitter shame hath spoil'd the sweet word's 3.04.110
that it yields nought but shame and bitterness. 3.04.111
blush | and glow with shame of your proceedings, 4.01.113
it is apparent foul play and 'tis shame | that 4.02. 93
quoted, and sign'd to do a deed of shame, | this 4.02.222
deep shame had struck me dumb, made me break off 4.02.235
this is the bloodiest shame, | the wildest 4.03. 47
or teach thy hasty spleen to do me shame, | i'll 4.03. 97
of your dear mother england, blush for shame; 5.02.153
thou and endless night | have done me shame. 5.06. 13
to push destruction and perpetual shame | out of 5.07. 77
my life thou shalt command, but not my shame: R2 1.01.166
take but my shame, | and i resign my gage. 1.01.175
where shame doth harbor, even in mowbray's face. 1.01.195
of wat'ry neptune, is now bound in with shame, 2.01. 63
forth thy reach he would have laid thy shame, 2.01.106
it were a shame to let this land by lease; 2.01.110
is it not more than shame to shame it so? 2.01.112
is it not more than shame to shame it so? 2.01.112
live in thy shame, but die not shame with thee! 2.01.135
live in thy shame, but die not shame with thee! 2.01.135
god, 'tis shame such wrongs are borne | in him, 2.01.238
an' he shall spend mine honor with his shame, 5.03. 68
who, sitting in the stocks, refuge their shame, 5.05. 26
not be | without much shame retold or spoken of. 1H4 1.01. 46
shall it for shame be spoken in these days, | or 1.03.170
and shall it in more shame be further spoken, 1.03.177
to hide thee from this open and apparent shame? 2.04.264 P
coz, to shame the devil | by telling truth: 3.01. 57
tell truth and shame the devil. 3.01. 58
i'll be sworn i have power to shame him hence. 3.01. 60
while you live, tell truth and shame the devil! 3.01. 61
i am too perfect in, and, but for shame, | in 3.01.200
wash'd away, shall scour my shame with it. 3.02.137
for my part, i may speak it to my shame, | i 5.01. 93
gan vail his stomach and did grace the shame 2H4 1.01.129
though it be a shame to be on any side but one, 1.02. 75 P
it is worse shame to beg than to be on the worst 1.02. 76 P
that day, that it is a shame to be thought on. 2.01. 36 P
that argues but the shame of your offense: 4.01.158
you must not dare, for shame, to talk of mercy, H5 2.02. 81
witness our too much memorable shame | when 2.04. 53
'tis shame for us all. 3.02.110 P
so god sa' me, 'tis shame to stand still, it is 3.02.110 P
'tis shame to stand still, it is shame, by my 3.02.111 P
reproach and everlasting shame | sits mocking in 4.05. 4
o perdurable shame! 4.05. 7
shame and eternal shame, nothing but shame! 4.05. 10
shame and eternal shame, nothing but shame! 4.05. 10
shame and eternal shame, nothing but shame! 4.05. 10
let life be short, else shame will be too long. 4.05. 23
ground | to hurl at the beholders of my shame. 1H6 1.04. 46
the shame hereof will make me hide my head. 1.05. 39
blush for pure shame to counterfeit our roses, 2.04. 66
for shame, my lord of winchester, relent! 3.01.132
or else let talbot perish with this shame. 3.02. 57
shame to the duke of burgundy and thee! 4.01. 13
york set him on to fight and die in shame, 4.04. 8
his fame lives in the world, his shame in you. 4.04. 46
ay, rather than i'll shame my mother's womb. 4.05. 35
no part of him but will be shame in me. 4.05. 39
my age was never tainted with such shame. 4.05. 46
on that advantage, bought with such a shame, 4.06. 44
and give her as a prey to law and shame, | that 2H6 2.01.194
with envious looks laughing at thy shame, | that 2.04. 12
come you, my lord, to see my open shame? 2.04. 19
and, in thy closet pent up, rue my shame, | and 2.04. 24
mail'd up in shame, with papers on my back, 2.04. 31
but be thou mild, and blush not at my shame, 2.04. 48
although thou hast been conduct of my shame. 2.04.101
my shame will not be shifted with my sheet. 2.04.107
nay, then a shame take all! 3.01.307
and, in the number, thee that wishest shame! 3.01.308
were't not a shame that, whilst you live at jar, 4.08. 41
old salisbury, shame to thy silver hair, | thou 5.01.162
war, | and shame thine honorable age with blood? 5.01.170
for shame, in duty bend thy knee to me | that 5.01.173
charity, for shame! 5.01.213
shame and confusion! 5.02. 31
away, my lord! you are slow, for shame, away! 5.02. 72
for shame, come down. he made thee duke of york. 3H6 1.01. 77
i shame to hear thee speak. 1.01.231
were shame enough to shame thee, wert thou not 1.04.120
were shame enough to shame thee, wert thou not 1.04.120
for shame, my liege, make them your president! 2.02. 33
ah, what a shame were this! 2.02. 39
for shame, leave henry, and call edward king. 3.03.100
but most himself if he could see his shame. 3.03.185
and am i guerdon'd at the last with shame? 3.03.191
shame on himself! 3.03.192
ah, what a shame, ah, what a fault were this! 5.04. 12
why, 'twere perpetual shame. 5.04. 51
hie thee to hell for shame, and leave this world R3 1.03.142
foul shame upon you, you have all mov'd mine. 1.03.248
peace, peace, for shame! if not, for charity. 1.03.272
urge neither charity nor shame to me. 1.03.273
my charity is outrage, life my shame, | and in 1.03.276
and in that shame still live my sorrow's rage! 1.03.277
he is my son — ay, and therein my shame, | yet 2.02. 29
that grieves me when i see my shame in him. 2.02. 54
woe's scene, world's shame, grave's due by life 4.04. 27
shame serves thy life and doth thy death attend. 4.04.196
come lead me, officers, to the block of shame; 5.01. 28
and weigh thee down to ruin, shame, and death! 5.03.148
and in record left them the heirs of shame. 5.03.335
the more shame for ye! H8 3.01.102
mend 'em for shame, my lords! 3.01.105
they would shame to make me | wait else at door, 5.02. 16
this is too much. | forbear for shame, my lords. 5.02.121
why, what a shame was this? 5.02.176
be friends, for shame, my lords! 5.02.194
the disdain and shame whereof hath ever since TRO 1.02. 34 P
peace, for shame, peace! 1.02.230 P
for both our honor and our shame in this | are 1.03.363
no, i warrant you, the fool's will shame it. 2.01. 87 P
fie, for godly shame! 2.02. 32
disgrace to your great worths, and shame to me, 2.02.151
to shame the seal of my petition to thee | in 4.04.122
let me not shame respect, but give me leave | to 5.03. 73
and bid the snail–pac'd ajax arm for shame. 5.05. 18
ignominy, shame | pursue thy life, and live aye 5.10. 33
never shame to hear | what you have nobly done. COR 2.02. 67
ay, fool, is that a shame? 4.02. 17
those maims | of shame seen through thy country, 4.05. 87
and cannot live but to thy shame, unless | it be 4.05.100
the tribunes cannot do't for shame; 4.06.109
that thou mayst prove | to shame unvulnerable, 5.03. 73
let us shame him with our knees. 5.03.169
to the antiates | than shame to th' romans; 5.06. 80
which was your shame, by this unholy braggart, 5.06.118
for shame, put up. TIT 2.01. 53
for shame, be friends, and join for that you jar 2.01.103
were it not for shame, | well could i leave our 2.03.196
ah, now thou turn'st away thy face for shame! 2.04. 28
sons' sweet blood will make it shame and blush. 3.01. 15
our empress' shame, and stately rome's disgrace! 4.02. 60
villains, for shame you could not beg for grace. 5.02.179
because the girl should not survive her shame, 5.03. 41
die, die, lavinia, and thy shame with thee, 5.03. 46
and with thy shame thy father's sorrow die! 5.03. 47
why, uncle, 'tis a shame. ROM 1.05. 82
for shame, | i'll make you quiet. 1.05. 87
brightness of her cheek would shame those stars, 2.02. 19
gentlemen, for shame, forbear this outrage! 3.01. 87
shame come to romeo! 3.02. 90
he was not born to shame: 3.02. 91
upon his brow shame is asham'd to sit; 3.02. 92
a thing like death to chide away this shame, 4.01. 74
this shall free thee from this present shame, 4.01.118
for shame, bring juliet forth, her lord is come. 4.05. 22
peace ho, for shame! 4.05. 65
and here is come to do some villainous shame 5.03. 52
honorable lord, i am e'en sick of shame that, TIM 3.06. 42 P
shame not these woods | by putting on the 4.03.208
shame, that they wanted cunning in excess, 5.04. 28
the gods do this in shame of cowardice; JC 2.02. 41
for shame, you generals! 4.03.130
the gods defend him from so great a shame! 5.04. 23
but i shame | to wear a heart so white. MAC 2.02. 61
is't night's predominance, or the day's shame, 2.04. 8
shame itself, | why do you make such faces? 3.04. 65
fie, for shame! 3.04. 73
aboard, aboard, for shame! HAM 1.03. 55
show, he'll not shame to tell you what it means. 3.02.145 P
o shame, where is thy blush? 3.04. 81
proclaim no shame | when the compulsive ardure 3.04. 85
while to my shame i see | the imminent death of 4.04. 59
by saint charity, | alack, and fie for shame! 4.05. 59
her custom holds, | let shame say what it will; 4.07.188
will gain nothing but my shame and the odd hits. 5.02.177 P
who covers faults, at last with shame derides. LR 1.01.281
which else were shame, that then necessity 1.04.213
the shame itself doth speak | for instant remedy 1.04.246
o lady, lady, shame would have it hid! 2.01. 93
ha? | mak'st thou this shame thy pastime? 2.04. 6
worth | the shame which here it suffers. 2.04. 45
let shame come when it will, i do not call it. 2.04.226
for shame, put on your gown; OTH 1.01. 86
i confess it is my shame to be so fond, but it 1.03.317 P
hold, for shame! 2.03.168
for christian shame, put by this barbarous brawl 2.03.172
that she with cassio hath the act of shame | a 5.02.211
all, all, cry shame against me, yet i'll speak. 5.02.222
else so thy cheek pays shame | when ANT 1.01. 31
i never saw an action of such shame; 3.10. 21
speak to him, | he's unqualited with very shame. 3.11. 44
see | how i convey my shame out of thine eyes 3.11. 52
'twas a shame no less | than was his loss, to 3.13. 10
for shame, | transform us not to women. 4.02. 35
his face subdu'd | to penetrative shame, whilst 4.14. 75
go and say | we purpose her no shame. 5.01. 62
o caesar, what a wounding shame is this, | that 5.02.159
with shame | (the first that ever touch'd him) CYM 3.01. 24
to shame the guise o' th' world, i will begin 5.01. 32
cowards living | to die with length'ned shame. 5.03. 13
than those for preservation cas'd, or shame), 5.03. 22
part shame, part spirit renew'd, that some, 5.03. 35
sin, | ay, and the targets to put off the shame; PER 1.01.140
is it a shame to get when we are old? 4.02. 28 P
goes to that with shame which is her way to go 4.02.127 P
i do shame | to think of what a noble strain you 4.03. 23
that sets seeds and roots of shame and iniquity. 4.06. 86 P
and here to keep in abstinence we shame | as in TNK 1.02. 6
till she for shame see what a wrong she has done 2.02. 39
that were a shame, sir, | while i have horses. 2.05. 53
he that faints now, shame take him! 3.06.121
fire, | he red for shame, but frosty in desire. VEN 36
he burns with bashful shame, she with her tears 49
pure shame and aw'd resistance made him fret, 69
'twixt crimson shame and anger ashy–pale. 76
"for shame," he cries, "let go, and let me go, 379
cynthia for shame obscures her silver shine, 728
to shame the sun by day and her by night. 732
my face is full of shame, my heart of teen, 808
virtue bragg'd, beauty would blush for shame; LUC 54
when shame assail'd, the red should fence the 63
"o shame to knighthood and to shining arms! 197
sage, | this dying virtue, this surviving shame, 223
the shame and fault finds no excuse nor end. 238
covers the shame that follows sweet delight." 357
that dazzleth them, or else some shame supposed, 377
what wrong, what shame, what sorrow i shall 499
the shame that from them no device can take, 535
hast thou put on his shape to do him shame? 597
"how will thy shame be seeded in thine age, 603
must he in thee read lectures of such shame? 618
black lust, dishonor, shame, misgoverning, | who 654
thou loathed in their shame, they in thy pride. 662
shame folded up in blind concealing night, 675
upon my cheeks what helpless shame i feel." 756
dim register and notary of shame! 765
will couple my reproach to tarquin's shame; 816
"o unseen shame, invisible disgrace! 827
"thy secret pleasure turns to open shame, | thy 890
king, | to shame his hope with deeds degenerate; 1003
honor thyself to rid me of this shame, | for if 1031
my shame so dead, mine honor is new born. 1190
my shame be his that did my fame confound; 1202
to those that live and think no shame of me. 1204
make weak–made women tenants to their shame. 1260
and shame that might ensue | by that her death, 1263
for lucrece thought he blush'd to see her shame, 1344
else lasting shame | on thee and thine this 1629
so should my shame still rest upon record, | and 1643
till manly shame bids him possess his breath, 1777
own deep–sunken eyes | were an all–eating shame, SON 2. 8
that on himself such murd'rous shame commits. 9.14
for shame deny that thou bear'st love to any, 10. 1
nor can thy shame give physic to my grief, 34. 9
lest my bewailed guilt should do thee shame, 36.10
is, | and live no more to shame nor me nor you. 72.12
how sweet and lovely dost thou make the shame 95. 1
/one blushing shame, another white despair; 99. 9
and beauty slander'd with a bastard shame, | for 127. 4
th' expense of spirit in a waste of shame | is 129. 1
they sought their shame that so their shame did LC 187
sought their shame that so their shame did find, 187
and so much less of shame in me remains | by how 188
'gainst rule, 'gainst sense, 'gainst shame, 271

SHAMED 1 FR 0.0001 REL FR 1 V 0 P
and shamed life a hateful. MM 3.01.116

SHAME–FAC'D 2 FR 0.0002 REL FR 1 V 1 P
seize on the shame–fac'd henry, bear him hence, 3H6 4.08. 52
'tis a blushing shame–fac'd spirit that mutinies R3 1.04.138 P

SHAMEFUL 19 FR 0.0021 REL FR 19 V 0 P
that would behold in me this shameful sport. ERR 4.04.105
while shameful hate sleeps out the afternoon. AWW 5.03. 66
to force that on you in a shameful cunning TN 3.01.116
it is the shameful work of hubert's hand, | the JN 4.03. 62
hath made a shameful conquest of itself. R2 2.01. 66
o peers of england, shameful is this league, 2H6 1.01. 98
ah, humphrey, can i bear this shameful yoke? 2.04. 37
crown | by shameful murther of a guiltless king 4.01. 95
you do me shameful injury | falsely to draw me R3 1.03. 87
sort, dragg'd through the shameful field. TRO 5.10. 5
and make two pasties of your shameful heads, TIT 5.02.189
castaway, | do shameful execution on herself, 5.03. 76
won to his shameful lust | the will of my most HAM 1.05. 45
eyes, not to behold | this shameful lodging. LR 2.02.172
rebukable | and worthy shameful check it were, ANT 4.04. 31
"shameful it is: LUC 239
to be thy partner in this shameful doom." 672
alas, how many bear such shameful blows, | which 832
for in my death i murther shameful scorn: 1189

SHAMEFULLY 5 FR 0.0005 REL FR 5 V 0 P
you would have married her most shamefully, WIV 5.05.221
we had not been thus shamefully surpris'd. 1H6 2.01. 65
worth, | they say is shamefully bereft of life. 2H6 3.02.269
and shamefully my hopes, by you, are butcher'd. R3 1.03.275
and gilded honor shamefully misplac'd, | and SON 66. 5

SHAMELESS 7 FR 0.0008 REL FR 7 V 0 P
that she this day hath shameless thrown on me. ERR 5.01.202
misuse, | such beastly shameless transformation, 1H4 1.01. 44
scoff on, vile fiend and shameless courtezan! 1H6 3.02. 45
enough to shame thee, wert thou not shameless. 3H6 1.04.120
to make this shameless callet know herself. 2.02.145
peace, impudent and shameless warwick, | proud 3.03.156
his strange absence, | grew shameless desperate; CYM 5.05. 58

SHAME–PROOF 1 FR 0.0001 REL FR 1 V 0 P
we are shame–proof, my lord; LLL 5.02.512

SHAME'S 5 FR 0.0005 REL FR 4 V 1 P
be not thy tongue thy own shame's orator: ERR 3.02. 10
to be shame's scorn and subject of mischance! 1H6 4.06. 49
shame's a baby. TRO 3.02. 40 P
forgetting shame's pure blush and honor's wrack. VEN 558
so of shame's ashes shall my fame be bred, | for LUC 1188

SHAMES 20 FR 0.0022 REL FR 20 V 0 P
for these deep shames and great indignities. ERR 5.01.254
i thy spirits were stronger than thy shames, ADO 4.01.125
a thousand innocent shames | in angel whiteness 4.01.160
for fear lest day should look their shames upon, MND 3.02.385
forget the shames that you have stain'd me with, MV 1.03.139
what, must i hold a candle to my shames? 2.06. 41
his mother shames him so, poor boy, he weeps. JN 2.01.166
grandame's wrongs, and not his mother's shames, 2.01.168
off | by him for whom these shames ye underwent? 1H4 1.03.179
and on my head | my shames redoubled! 3.02.144
your great seats now quit you of great shames. H5 3.05. 47
quitting thee thereby of ten thousand shames, 2H6 3.02.218
and call them shames which are indeed nought TRO 1.03. 19
of the south light on you, | you shames of rome! COR 1.04. 31
all kind of sores and shames on my bare head, OTH 4.02. 49
let his shames quickly | drive him to rome. ANT 1.04. 72
i think the echoes of his shames have deaf'd TNK 1.02. 80
but cloudy lucrece shames herself to see, | and LUC 1084
pry, | to find out shames and idle hours in me, SON 61. 7
to know my shames and praises from your tongue; 112. 6

SHAMEST 2 FR 0.0002 REL FR 2 V 0 P
good, thou shamest the music of sweet news | by ROM 2.05. 23
fie, fie, thou shamest thy shape, thy love, thy 3.03.122

SHAMING 2 FR 0.0002 REL FR 2 V 0 P
sore shaming | those rich–left heirs that let CYM 4.02.225
day, | as shaming any eye should thee behold, LUC 1143

SHAM'ST 3 FR 0.0003 REL FR 3 V 0 P
son, | thou sham'st to acknowledge me in misery. ERR 5.01.323

sham'st thou not, knowing whence thou art 3H6 2.02.142
sham'st thou to show thy dang'rous brow by night JC 2.01. 78
SHANK 1 FR 0.0001 REL FR 1 V 0 P
a world too wide | for his shrunk shank, and his AYL 2.07.161
SHANKS 3 FR 0.0003 REL FR 2 V 1 P
with reeky shanks and yellow /chapless skulls; ROM 4.01. 83
you rogue, or i'll so carbonado your shanks! LR 2.02. 38 P
art fetter'd | more than my shanks and wrists. CYM 5.04. 9
SHAP'D 6 FR 0.0006 REL FR 5 V 1 P
then, since the heavens have shap'd my body so, 3H6 5.06. 78
but i, that am not shap'd for sportive tricks, R3 1.01. 14
shap'd out a man | whom this beneath world doth TIM 1.01. 43
it is shap'd, sir, like itself, and it is as ANT 2.07. 42 P
the more it shap'd | unto my end of stealing CYM 5.05.346
fitted and shap'd just to that strength of STM III 4
/SHAPE 1 FR 0.0001 REL FR 1 V 0 P
/a /woman's /shape /doth /shield /thee. LR 4.02. 67
SHAPE 93 FR 0.0105 REL FR 82 V 11 P
hag–born) not honor'd with | a human shape. TMP 1.02.284
go take this shape | and hither come in't. 1.02.303
nor can imagination form a shape, | besides 3.01. 56
who, though they are of monstrous shape, yet, 3.03. 31
thy shape invisible retain thou still. 4.01.185
in his manners | as in his shape. 5.01.292
seeing you are beautified | with goodly shape, TGV 4.01. 54
i would my husband would meet him in this shape. WIV 4.02. 85 P
come, to the forge with it, then shape it. 4.02.223 P
and in this shape when you have brought him 4.04. 45
paths he dares to tread | in shape profane. 4.04. 61
he beat me grievously, in the shape of a woman; 5.01. 20 P
for in the shape of man, master /brook, i fear 5.01. 21 P
and let it keep one shape, till custom make it MM 2.01. 3
nay, master, both in mind and in my shape. ERR 2.02.197
nor take no shape nor project of affection, ADO 3.01. 55
for shape, for bearing, argument, and valor, 3.01. 96
or in the shape of two countries at once, as a 3.02. 34 P
will fashion the event in better shape | than i 4.01.235
in every lineament, branch, shape, and form; 5.01. 14
for he hath wit to make an ill shape good, | and LLL 2.01. 59
and shape to win grace though he had no wit. 2.01. 60
the shape of love's tyburn that hangs up 4.03. 52
such as the shortness of the time can shape, 4.03.375
and shape his service wholly to my device, | and 5.02. 65
either i mistake your shape and making quite, MND 2.01. 32
land, | and in the shape of corin sat all day, 2.01. 66
so is mine eye enthralled to thy shape; 3.01.139
a creature that did bear the shape of man | so MV 3.02.275
if sight and shape be true, | why then my love AYL 5.04.120
succeed thy father | in manners, as in shape! AWW 1.01. 62
commit, | only shape thou thy silence to my wit. TN 1.02. 61
and in dimension and the shape of nature | a 1.05.261
by the color of his beard, the shape of his leg, 2.03.156 P
and if my brother had my shape | and i had his, JN 1.01.138
and, to his shape, were heir to all this land, 1.01.144
what, is my richard both in shape and mind R2 5.01. 26
and shape of likelihood the news was told; 1H4 1.01. 58
let time shape, and there an end. 2H4 3.02.332 P
in his true, native, and most proper shape, 4.01. 37
the blood weeps from my heart when i do shape, 4.04. 58
what your highness suffer'd under that shape, i H5 4.08. 53 P
and more than may be gathered by thy shape. 1H6 2.03. 69
as if, with circe, she would change my shape! 5.03. 35
chang'd to a worser shape thou canst not be. 5.03. 36
no shape but his can please your dainty eye. 5.03. 38
who cannot steal a shape that means deceit? 2H6 3.01. 79
lump, | as crooked in thy manners as thy shape! 5.01.158
to shape my legs of an unequal size, | to 3H6 3.02.159
that deceit should steal such gentle shape, R3 2.02. 27
unless thou couldst put on some other shape 4.04.286
i do pronounce him in that very shape | he shall H8 1.01.196
is not birth, beauty, good shape, discourse, TRO 1.02.253 P
of the thought | that gave't surmised shape. 1.03. 17
be you my time to bring it to some shape. 1.03.313
our project's life this shape of sense assumes: 1.03.384
hair, | nor age nor honor shall shape privilege; TIT 4.04. 57
comes | in shape no bigger than an agot–stone ROM 1.04. 55
fie, fie, thou shamest thy shape, thy love, thy 3.03.122
true use indeed | which should bedeck thy shape, 3.03.125
thy noble shape is but a form of wax, 3.03.126
thy wit, that ornament to shape and love, 3.03.130
man | when he looks out in an ungrateful shape! TIM 3.02. 73
and could it work so much upon your shape | as JC 2.01.253
take any shape but that, and my firm nerves MAC 3.04.101
thou com'st in such a questionable shape | that HAM 1.04. 43
though lewdness court it in a shape of heaven, 1.05. 54
/dev'l hath power | t' assume a pleasing shape, 2.02.600
imagination to give them shape, or time to act 3.01.126 P
yonder cloud that's almost in shape of a camel? 3.02.377 P
of time and means | may fit us to our shape. 4.07.150
he'll shape his old course in a country new. LR 1.01.187
my mind as generous, and my shape as true, | as 1.02. 8
that i'll resume the shape which thou dost think 1.04.309
to take the basest and most poorest shape | that 2.03. 7
my hopes do shape him for the governor. OTH 2.01. 55
of mankind, had | destroyed in such a shape. ANT 4.08. 26
yet cannot hold this visible shape, my knave. 4.14. 14
move the king | to any shape of thy preferment, CYM 1.05. 71
i know the shape of 's leg; 4.02.309
her neele composes | nature's own shape of bud, PER 5.ch. 6
another shape shall make me, | or end my TNK 2.03. 21
you shall perceive how horrible a shape | your STM II.C 92
in shape, in courage, color, pace, and bone. VEN 294
hast thou put on his shape to do him shame? LUC 597
shape every bush a hideous shapeless devil. 973
saying, some shape in sinon's was abus'd: 1529
but tarquin's shape came in her mind the while, 1536
by children's eyes, her husband's shape in mind. SON 9. 8
mine eye have drawn thy shape, and thine for me 24.10
and you in every blessed shape we know. 53.12
no shape so true, no truth of such account, 62. 6
bird, of flow'r, or shape, which it doth /latch, 113. 6
SHAPELESS 6 FR 0.0006 REL FR 6 V 0 P
wear out thy youth with shapeless idleness. TGV 1.01. 8
ill–fac'd, worse bodied, shapeless every where; ERR 4.02. 20
disguis'd like muscovites, in shapeless gear; LLL 5.02.303
which he hath left so shapeless and so rude. JN 5.07. 27
"who wears a garment shapeless and unfinish'd? VEN 415
shape every bush a hideous shapeless devil. LUC 973
/SHAPES 1 FR 0.0001 REL FR 1 V 0 P
with all forms, moods, /shapes of grief, | that HAM 1.02. 82
SHAPES 29 FR 0.0032 REL FR 25 V 4 P
think'st there is no more such shapes as he, TMP 1.02.479
i cannot too much muse | such shapes, such 3.03. 37
to worship shadows and adore false shapes, TGV 4.02.130
to change their shapes than men their minds. 5.04.109
full of forms, figures, shapes, objects, ideas, LLL 4.02. 67 P
they will again be here | in their own shapes; 5.02.288
do, | if they return in their own shapes to woo? 5.02.299
full of straying shapes, of habits, and of forms 5.02.763
turns them to shapes and gives to aery nothing MND 5.01. 16
so full of shapes is fancy | that it alone is TN 1.01. 14
have taken | the shapes of beasts upon them. WT 4.04. 27
find shapes of grief, more than himself, to wail R2 2.02. 22
the front of heaven was full of fiery shapes 1H4 3.01. 14
the front of heaven was full of fiery shapes, 3.01. 37
as the malice of /this age shapes /them, /are 2H4 1.02.172 P
of nimble, fiery, and delectable shapes, which, 4.03.100 P
change shapes with proteus for advantages, | and 3H6 3.02.192
all our abilities, gifts, natures, shapes, TRO 1.03.179
nothing been but shapes and forms of slaughter. 5.03. 12
that bear the shapes of men, how have you run COR 1.04. 35
deity than nature, | that shapes man better; 4.06. 92
in all shapes that man goes up and down in from TIM 2.02.112 P
profess'd, that you work not | in holier shapes; 4.03.427
eyes | that shapes this monstrous apparition. JC 4.03.277
that i, in forgery of shapes and tricks, | come HAM 4.07. 89
us | there's a divinity that shapes our ends, 5.02. 10
/oft my jealousy | shapes faults that are not), OTH 3.03.148
and shapes her sorrow to the beldame's woes, LUC 1458
crow or dove, it shapes them to your feature. SON 113.12
SHAPING 1 FR 0.0001 REL FR 1 V 0 P
such shaping fantasies, that apprehend | more MND 5.01. 5
SHAR'D 3 FR 0.0003 REL FR 3 V 0 P
is all the counsel that we two have shar'd, MND 3.02.198
while all is shar'd and all is borne away, 2H6 1.01.228
on your love, | shar'd dangers with you — OTH 3.04. 95
SHARD–BORNE 1 FR 0.0001 REL FR 1 V 0 P
the shard–borne beetle with his drowsy hums MAC 3.02. 42
SHARDED 1 FR 0.0001 REL FR 1 V 0 P
we find | the sharded beetle in a safer hold CYM 3.03. 20
/SHARDS* 1 FR 0.0001 REL FR 1 V 0 P
/shards, flints, and pebbles should be thrown on HAM 5.01.231
SHARDS* 1 FR 0.0001 REL FR 1 V 0 P
they are his shards, and he their beetle, so. ANT 3.02. 20
SHARE 32 FR 0.0036 REL FR 28 V 4 P
didst not thou share? WIV 2.02. 14
and our revolted wives share damnation together. 3.02. 39 P
such gifts that heaven shall share with you. MM 2.02.147
shall share the good of our returned fortune, AYL 5.04.174
out of hope of all but my share of the feast. SHR 5.01.141
and thy goodness | share with thy birthright! AWW 1.01. 64
share the advice betwixt you. 2.01. 3
my part of death, no one so true | did share it. TN 2.04. 58
i shall have share in this most happy wrack. 5.01.266
nay, let us share thy thoughts, as thou dost R2 2.01.273
thou shalt have a share in our purchase, as i am 1H4 2.01. 91 P
my masters, let us share, and then to horse 2.02. 98 P
percy, | to share with me in glory any more. 5.04. 64
the fewer men, the greater share of honor. H5 4.03. 22
as one man more methinks would share from me, 4.03. 32
the other, walter whitmore, is thy share. 2H6 4.01. 14
but god he knows thy share thereof is small. 3H6 1.04.129
the least of you shall share his part thereof. R3 5.03.268
were he not proud, we all should share with him. TRO 1.03.367
untent his person and share th' air with us? 2.03.168
that book in many's eyes doth share the glory, ROM 1.03. 91
so shall you share all that he doth possess, 1.03. 93
we'll share a bounteous time | in different TIM 1.01.254
the latest of my wealth i'll share amongst you. 4.02. 23
he should stand | one of the three to share it? JC 4.01. 15
pains, | and every one shall share i' th' gains. MAC 4.01. 40
half a share. HAM 3.02.279 P
that we may nothing share | of his loud infamy; TNK 1.02. 75
the marshal's sister | had her share too, as i 3.03. 37
their single share, | their nobleness peculiar 5.03. 86
ah, neither be my share! PP 14. 1
and in his thoughts of love doth share a part. SON 47. 8
SHARES 4 FR 0.0004 REL FR 3 V 1 P
there is an art which in their piedness shares WT 4.04. 87
what glory our achilles shares from hector, TRO 1.03.366
'a would have ten shares. 2.03.220 P
mind that's honest | but in it shares some woe, MAC 4.03.198
SHARING 3 FR 0.0003 REL FR 2 V 1 P
as we were sharing, some six or seven fresh men 1H4 2.04.180 P
in sharing that which you have pill'd from me! R3 1.03.158
sharing joy | to see their youthful sons bright LUC 1431
SHARK 2 FR 0.0002 REL FR 2 V 0 P
maw and gulf | of the ravin'd salt–sea shark, MAC 4.01. 24
would shark on you, and men like ravenous fishes STM II.C 86
SHARK'D 1 FR 0.0001 REL FR 1 V 0 P
there | shark'd up a list of lawless resolutes, HAM 1.01. 98
SHARP 82 FR 0.0092 REL FR 76 V 6 P
deep, | to run upon the sharp wind of the north, TMP 1.02.254
follow'd through | tooth'd briers, sharp furzes, 4.01.180
(how sharp the point of this remembrance is!) 5.01.138
no, madam, 'tis too sharp. TGV 1.02. 88
but you, sir thurio, are not sharp enough: 3.02. 67
and what he gets more of her than sharp words, WIV 2.01.183 P
thou rather with thy sharp and sulphurous bolt MM 2.02.115
fit thy consent to my sharp appetite, | lay by 2.04.161
if voluble and sharp discourse be marr'd, ERR 2.01. 92
alas, how fiery, and how sharp, he looks! 4.04. 50
a good sharp fellow. ADO 1.02. 18 P
is a sharp wit match'd with too blunt a will, LLL 2.01. 49
at dinner have been sharp and sententious: 5.01. 3 P
look how you butt yourself in these sharp mocks! 5.02.251
thrust thy sharp wit quite through my ignorance, 5.02.398
and to that place the sharp athenian law MND 1.01.162
axe, bear half the keenness | of thy sharp envy. MV 4.01.126
thy sting is not so sharp | as friend rememb'red AYL 2.07.188
my falcon now is sharp and passing empty, | and SHR 4.01.190
he roar'd | with sharp constraint of hunger; AWW 3.02.118
ah, what sharp stings are in her mildest words! 3.04. 18
as well as thorns, | and be as sweet as sharp. 4.04. 33
and therefore, goaded with most sharp occasions, 5.01. 14
more sharp than filed steel, did spur me forth, TN 3.03. 5
by heaven, i think my sword's as sharp as yours. JN 3.03. 82
shall feel this day as sharp to them as thorn. R2 4.01.323
for his nose was as sharp as a pen, and 'a H5 2.03. 16 P
let him greet england with our sharp defiance. 3.05. 37
in stead whereof sharp stakes pluck'd out of 1H6 1.01.117
but in these nice sharp quillets of the law, 2.04. 17
ay, sharp and piercing, to maintain his truth, 2.04. 70
i feel such sharp dissension in my breast, 5.05. 84
sharp buckingham unburthens with his tongue 2H6 3.01.156
you put sharp weapons in a madman's hands. 3.01.347
woes will make them sharp and pierce like mine. R3 4.04.125
peace | by this one bloody trial of sharp war. 5.02. 16
and i know his sword | hath a sharp edge; H8 1.01.110
alleged | many sharp reasons to defeat the law. 2.01. 14
but the sharp thorny points | of my alleged 2.04.225
sharp enough, | lord, for thy justice! 3.02. 92
are a little, | by your good favor, too sharp; 5.02.109
no marvel though you bite so sharp /at reasons, TRO 2.02. 33
tun'd too sharp in sweetness | for the capacity 3.02. 24
troy is ours, and our sharp wars are ended. 5.09. 10
of troy | with opportunity of sharp revenge TIT 1.01.137
but if we live we'll be as sharp with you. 1.01.410
got, | he dies upon my scimitar's sharp point, 4.02. 91
true, 'tis true, witness my knive's sharp point. 5.03. 63
very bitter sweeting, it is a most sharp sauce. ROM 2.04. 80 P
looks, | sharp misery had worn him to the bones; 5.01. 41
hollow bones of man, strike their sharp shins, TIM 4.03.152
and his great love, sharp as his spur, hath holp MAC 1.06. 23
i not, | though inclination be as sharp as will. HAM 3.03. 39
here stood he in the dark, his sharp sword out, LR 2.01. 38
the wolf and owl — | necessity's sharp pinch. 2.04.211
"through the sharp hawthorn blow the /cold winds 3.04. 47 P
do not please sharp fate | to grace it with your ANT 4.14.135
with thy sharp teeth this knot intrinsicate | of 5.02.304
be a pinch in death | more sharp than this is. CYM 1.01.131
of space had pointed him sharp as my needle; 1.03. 19
your majesty, | forbear sharp speeches to her. 3.05. 39
we'll enforce it from thee | by a sharp torture. 4.03. 12
sharp physic is the last. PER 1.01. 72
so sharp are hunger's teeth, that man and wife 1.04. 45
or when she would with sharp needle wound | the 4.ch. 23
if fires be hot, knives sharp, or waters deep, 4.02.146
roses, their sharp spines being gone, | not TNK 1.01. 1
sharp | to spy advantages, and where he finds 4.02.132
bent, or a sharp weapon | in a soft sheath; 5.03. 42
pig–like he whines | at the sharp rowel, which 5.04. 70
gay skins with thought of their sharp state, STM III 18
even as an empty eagle, sharp by fast, | tires VEN 55
under whose sharp fangs on his back doth lie 663
sun and sharp air | lurk'd like two thieves, to 1085
he ran upon the boar with his sharp spear, | who 1112
prey, | sharp hunger by the conquest satisfied, LUC 422
like a white hind under the gripe's sharp claws, 543
thy part | to keep thy sharp woes waking, 1136
will fix a sharp knife to affright mine eye, 1138
time seems long in sorrow's sharp sustaining; 1573
kill'd too soon by death's sharp sting! PP 10. 4
more sharp to me than spurring to his side, SON 50.12
SHARPEN 1 FR 0.0001 REL FR 1 V 0 P
sharpen with cloyless sauce his appetite, | that ANT 2.01. 25
SHARPENS 3 FR 0.0003 REL FR 2 V 1 P
now she sharpens. well said, whetstone! TRO 5.02. 75 P
and it pierces and sharpens the stomach. PER 4.01. 28
extremity, that sharpens sundry wits, | makes me TNK 1.01.118
SHARPER 6 FR 0.0006 REL FR 6 V 0 P
whose sting is sharper than the sword's, and WT 2.03. 87
finds brotherhood in thee no sharper spur? R2 1.02. 9
of honor edged | more sharper than your swords, H5 3.05. 39
feel | how sharper than a serpent's tooth it is LR 1.04.288
sweeter to you | that have a sharper known; CYM 3.03. 31
whose edge is sharper than the sword, whose 3.04. 34
SHARPEST 3 FR 0.0003 REL FR 2 V 1 P
all deaths are too few, the sharpest too easy. WT 4.04.780 P
your sharpest deeds of malice on this town. JN 2.01.380
or death, | i wait the sharpest blow, antiochus. PER 1.01. 55
SHARP–GROUND 1 FR 0.0001 REL FR 1 V 0 P
thou no poison mix'd, no sharp–ground knife, ROM 3.03. 44
SHARP–LOOKING 1 FR 0.0001 REL FR 1 V 0 P
a needy, hollow–ey'd, sharp–looking wretch, | a ERR 5.01.241
SHARPLY 5 FR 0.0005 REL FR 4 V 1 P
that relish all as sharply | passion as they, be TMP 5.01. 23
though little he do feel it, set down sharply. AWW 3.04. 33
with a swaggering accent sharply twang'd off, TN 3.04.180 P
that are betray'd | do feel the treason sharply, CYM 3.04. 86
for sharply he did think to reprehend her, VEN 470
SHARP'NED 1 FR 0.0001 REL FR 1 V 0 P
to–morrow sharp'ned in his former might. SON 56. 4
/SHARPNESS 1 FR 0.0001 REL FR 1 V 0 P
/by /those /that /feel /their /sharpness. LR 5.03. 57
SHARPNESS 3 FR 0.0003 REL FR 3 V 0 P
nor bitterness | were in his pride or sharpness; AWW 1.02. 37
thou must not take my former sharpness ill. ANT 3.03. 35
of all this sprightly sharpness, not a smile. TNK 4.02. 30
SHARP–POINTED 1 FR 0.0001 REL FR 1 V 0 P
lo here i lend thee this sharp–pointed sword, R3 1.02.174
SHARP–PROVIDED 1 FR 0.0001 REL FR 1 V 0 P
with what a sharp–provided wit he reasons! R3 3.01.132
SHARP–QUILL'D 1 FR 0.0001 REL FR 1 V 0 P
were almost like a sharp–quill'd porpentine; 2H6 3.01.363
SHARPS 1 FR 0.0001 REL FR 1 V 0 P
straining harsh discords and unpleasing sharps. ROM 3.05. 28
SHARP'ST 2 FR 0.0002 REL FR 2 V 0 P
so give me up | to the sharp'st kind of justice. H8 2.04. 44
tan sacred beauty, blunt the sharp'st intents, SON 115. 7
SHARP–TOOTH'D 1 FR 0.0001 REL FR 1 V 0 P
she hath tied | sharp–tooth'd unkindness, like a LR 2.04.135
SHATTER 1 FR 0.0001 REL FR 1 V 0 P
as it did seem to shatter all his bulk | and end HAM 2.01. 92
SHAV'D 1 FR 0.0001 REL FR 0 V 1 P
bardolph was shav'd and lost many a hair, and 1H4 3.03. 59 P
SHAVE 2 FR 0.0002 REL FR 1 V 1 P
shave the head, and tie the beard, and say it MM 4.02.175 P
mother, priest, i'll shave your crown for this, 2H6 2.01. 50
SHAVEN 1 FR 0.0001 REL FR 0 V 1 P
sometime like the shaven hercules in the ADO 3.03.136 P

SHAVE'T 1 FR 0.0001 REL FR 1 V 0 P
antonio's beard, | i would not shave't to–day. ANT 2.02. 8
SHAW 1 FR 0.0001 REL FR 1 V 0 P
go, lovel, with all speed to doctor shaw; R3 3.05.103
SHE *(also sh')*
/SHE 25 FR 0.0028 REL FR 19 V 6 P
(save for the son that /she did litter here, | a TMP 1.02.282
that /she would have follow'd her exile, or have AYL 1.01.109 P
she was belov'd, /she /lov'd; TRO 4.05.292
/violent /hands /can /she /lay /on /her /life? TIT 3.02. 25
/hark, /marcus, /what /she /says; 3.02. 35
/she /says, /she /drinks /no /other /drink /but 3.02. 37
/she /drinks /no /other /drink /but /tears, 3.02. 37
like niobe, all tears — why, she, /even /she — HAM 1.02.149
/that /she /sends /you /to /prison /hither? 2.02.241 P
/and /she /must /not /speak | /why /she /dares LR 3.06. 27
/why /she /dares /not /come /over /to /thee." 3.06. 28
/she /kick'd /the /poor /king /her /father. 3.06. 47 P
/she /cannot /deny /it. 3.06. 51
/if /she /live /long, | /and /in /the /end /meet 3.07.100
/she /that /herself /will /sliver /and 4.02. 34
/ay, /sir, /she /took /them, /read /them /in /my 4.03. 11
/it /seem'd /she /was /a /queen | /over /her 4.03. 13
/made /she /no /verbal /question? 4.03. 24
/once /or /twice /she /heav'd /the /name /of 4.03. 25
/there /she /shook | /the /holy /water /from 4.03. 29
/then /away /she /started | /to /deal /with 4.03. 31
/she /must /have /change, /she /must; OTH 1.03.351 P
/she /must /have /change, /she /must; 1.03.352 P
/she makes our profession as it were to stink PER 4.06.135 P
will sourly leave her till /she have prevailed? SON 41. 8
SHE 2686 FR 0.3036 REL FR 2033 V 653 P
of virtue, and | she said thou wast my daughter; TMP 1.02. 57
thou hast. where was she born? speak. tell me. 1.02.260
o, was she so? 1.02.261
for one thing she did | they would not take her 1.02.266
refusing her grand hests, she did confine thee, 1.02.274
within which space she died, | and left thee 1.02.279
she was of carthage, not of tunis. 2.01. 83 P
my son is lost and (in my rate) she too, | who 2.01.110
where she, at least, is banish'd from your eye, 2.01.127
if she would continue in it five weeks without 2.01.183 P
she that is queen of tunis; 2.01.246
she that dwells | ten leagues beyond man's life; 2.01.246
she that from naples | can have no note, unless 2.01.247
she that from whom | we all were sea–swallow'd, 2.01.250
's queen of tunis, | so is she heir of naples; 2.01.256
for she had a tongue with a tang, | would cry to 2.02. 50
she lov'd not the savor of tar nor of pitch, 2.02. 52
might scratch her where e'er she did itch. 2.02. 53
she is | ten times more gentle than her father's 3.01. 7
my sweet mistress | weeps when she sees me work, 3.01. 12
did quarrel with the noblest grace she ow'd, 3.01. 45
saw a woman | but only sycorax my dam and she; 3.02.101
but she as far surpasseth sycorax | as great'st 3.02.102
ay, lord, she will become thy bed, i warrant, 3.02.104
for thou shalt find she will outstrip all praise 4.01. 10
sit then and talk with her, she is thine own. 4.01. 32
is she the goddess that hath sever'd us, | and 5.01.187
sir, she is mortal; 5.01.188
she | is daughter to this famous duke of milan, 5.01.191
(a lac'd mutton), and she (a lac'd mutton) gave TGV 1.01. 97 P
but what said she? 1.01.110 P
i say, she did nod; 1.01.113 P
and you ask me if she did nod, and i say, "ay." 1.01.114 P
what said she? 1.01.128 P
what said she? 1.01.132 P
what said she? nothing? 1.01.142 P
what 'fool is she, that knows i am a maid, | and 1.02. 53
she makes it strange, but she would be best 1.02. 99
but she would be best pleas'd | to be so ang'red 1.02. 99
she is not within hearing, sir. 2.01. 8 P
she that your worship loves? 2.01. 16 P
she that you gaze on so as she sits at supper? 2.01. 43 P
she that you gaze on so as she sits at supper? 2.01. 43 P
hast thou observ'd that? even she, i mean. 2.01. 44 P
is she not hard–favor'd, sir? 2.01. 48 P
that she is not so fair as (of you) well favor'd 2.01. 52 P
you never saw her since she was deform'd. 2.01. 63 P
how long hath she been deform'd? 2.01. 64 P
last night she enjoin'd me to write some lines 2.01. 87 P
me to write some lines to one she loves. 2.01. 88 P
peace, here she comes. 2.01. 93 P
should give her interest, and she gives it him. 2.01.103 P
and she hath taught her suitor, | he being her 2.01.137
to yourself; why, she woos you by a figure. 2.01.148 P
why, she hath not writ to me? 2.01.151 P
what need she, when she hath made you write to 2.01.152 P
she, when she hath made you write to yourself? 2.01.152 P
she gave me none, except an angry word. 2.01.158 P
why, she hath given you a letter. 2.01.159 P
and that letter hath she deliver'd, and there an 2.01.161 P
and she, in modesty, | or else for want of idle 2.01.165
she is as white as a lily and as small as a wand 2.03. 20 P
o, that she could speak now like a /wood woman! 2.03. 27 P
mark the moan she makes. 2.03. 30 P
belike that now she hath enfranchis'd them 2.04. 90
sure, i think she holds them prisoners still. 2.04. 92
even she; and is she not a heavenly saint? 2.04.145
even she; and is she not a heavenly saint? 2.04.145
no; but she is an earthly paragon. 2.04.146
she shall be dignified with this high honor — 2.04.158
she is alone. 2.04.167
why, man, she is mine own, | and i as rich in 2.04.168
but she loves you? 2.04.178
she is fair; 2.04.199
but shall she marry him? 2.05. 14 P
much less shall she that hath love's wings to 2.07. 11
and should she thus be stol'n away from you, 3.01. 15
and thence she cannot be convey'd away. 3.01. 37
no, trust me, she is peevish, sullen, froward, 3.01. 68
duty, | neither regarding that she is my child, 3.01. 70
for me and my possessions she esteems not. 3.01. 79
but she is nice and coy, | and nought esteems my 3.01. 82
win her with gifts, if she respect not words: 3.01. 89
but she did scorn a present that i sent her. 3.01. 92
if she do frown, 'tis not in hate of you, | but 3.01. 96
if she do chide, 'tis not to have you gone, 3.01. 98
take no repulse, what ever she doth say; 3.01.100
for "get you gone," she doth not mean "away!" 3.01.101
but she i mean is promis'd by her friends | unto 3.01.106
unless it be to think that she is by, | and feed 3.01.176
she is my essence, and i leave to be, | if i be 3.01.182
hath she forsworn me? 3.01.213
and she hath offered to the doom | (which, 3.01.224
at her father's churlish feet she tender'd, 3.01.227
him so, | when she for thy repeal was suppliant, 3.01.236
yet 'tis not a maid, for she hath had gossips; 3.01.270 P
yet 'tis a maid, for she is her master's maid, 3.01.271 P
she hath more qualities than a water–spaniel, 3.01.272 P
"inprimis, she can fetch and carry." 3.01.275 P
only carry, therefore is she better than a jade. 3.01.277 P
"item, she can milk." 3.01.278 P
"inprimis, she can milk." 3.01.301 P
ay, that she can. 3.01.302 P
"item, she brews good ale." 3.01.303 P
"item, she can sew." 3.01.306 P
that's as much as to say, "can she so?" 3.01.307 P
"item, she can knit." 3.01.308 P
with a wench, when she can knit him a stock? 3.01.310 P
"item, she can wash and scour." 3.01.311 P
for then she need not be wash'd and scour'd. 3.01.312 P
"item, she can spin." 3.01.314 P
on wheels, when she can spin for her living. 3.01.316 P
"item, she hath many nameless virtues." 3.01.317 P
"item, she is not to be /kiss'd fasting, in 3.01.323 P
"item, she hath a sweet mouth." 3.01.327 P
"item, she doth talk in her sleep." 3.01.329 P
matter for that, so she sleep not in her talk. 3.01.330 P
"item, she is slow in words." 3.01.332 P
"item, she is proud." 3.01.337 P
"item, she hath no teeth." 3.01.340 P
"item, she is curst." 3.01.343 P
well, the best is, she hath no teeth to bite. 3.01.344 P
"item, she will often praise her liquor." 3.01.345 P
if her liquor be good, she shall; 3.01.346 P
if she will not, i will; 3.01.346 P
"item, she is too liberal." 3.01.348 P
of her tongue she cannot, for that's writ down 3.01.349 P
she cannot, for that's writ down she is slow of; 3.01.350 P
of her purse she shall not, for that i'll keep 3.01.350 P
now, of another thing she may, and that cannot i 3.01.351 P
"item, she hath more hair than wit, and more 3.01.353 P
she was mine and not mine twice or thrice in 3.01.355 P
"item, she hath more hair than wit" — 3.01.358 P
fear not but that she will love you | now 3.02. 1
since his exile she hath despis'd me most, 3.02. 3
ignorant | how she opposes her against my will? 3.02. 26
she did, my lord, when valentine was here. 3.02. 27
ay, and perversely she persevers so. 3.02. 28
by one whom she esteemeth as his friend. 3.02. 37
she shall not long continue love to him. 3.02. 48
it follows not that she will love sir thurio. 3.02. 50
for she is lumpish, heavy, melancholy, | and, 3.02. 62
she twits me with my falsehood to my friend; 4.02. 8
she bids me think how i have been forsworn | in 4.02. 10
yet, spaniel–like, the more she spurns my love, 4.02. 14
what is she, | that all our swains commend her? 4.02. 39
holy, fair, and wise is she; 4.02. 41
grace did lend her, | that she might admired be. 4.02. 43
is she kind as she is fair? 4.02. 44
is she kind as she is fair? 4.02. 44
she excels each mortal thing | upon the dull 4.02. 51
but she is dead. 4.02.106
for i am sure she is not buried. 4.02.107
say that she be; 4.02.108
and what says she to my little jewel? 4.04. 47 P
marry, she says your dog was a cur, and tells 4.04. 48 P
but she receiv'd my dog? 4.04. 51 P
no indeed did she not; 4.04. 52 P
she lov'd me well deliver'd it to me. 4.04. 73
she is dead, belike? 4.04. 75
not so; i think she lives. 4.04. 75
because methinks that she lov'd you as well | as 4.04. 79
she dreams on him that has forgot her love; 4.04. 81
what would you with her, if that i be she? 4.04.110
if you be she, i do entreat your patience | to 4.04.111
she thanks you. 4.04.138
belike she thinks that proteus hath forsook her? 4.04.146
i think she doth; 4.04.147
is she not passing fair? 4.04.148
she hath been fairer, madam, than she is: 4.04.149
she hath been fairer, madam, than she is: 4.04.149
when she did think my master lov'd her well, 4.04.150
well, | she, in my judgment, was as fair as you; 4.04.151
but since she did neglect her looking–glass, 4.04.152
face, | that now she is become as black as i. 4.04.156
how tall was she? 4.04.157
therefore i know she is about my height. 4.04.164
she is beholding to thee, gentle youth. 4.04.173
and she shall thank you for't, if e'er you know 4.04.179
since she respects my mistress' love so much. 4.04.182
she will not fail, for lovers break not hours, 5.01. 4
see where she comes. 5.01. 7
o, sir, i find her milder than she was, | and 5.02. 2
and yet she takes exceptions at your person. 5.02. 3
what says she to my face? 5.02. 8
she says it is a fair one. 5.02. 9
how likes she my discourse? 5.02. 15
what says she to my valor? 5.02. 19
o, sir, she makes no doubt of that. 5.02. 20
she needs not, when she knows it cowardice. 5.02. 21
she needs not, when she knows it cowardice. 5.02. 21
what says she to my birth? 5.02. 22
considers she my possessions? 5.02. 25
him he knew well, and guess'd that it was she, 5.02. 39
she did intend confession | at patrick's cell 5.02. 41
patrick's cell this even, and there she was not. 5.02. 42
here she stands: 5.04.129
i claim her not, and therefore she is thine. 5.04.135
she has brown hair, and speaks small like a WIV 1.01. 47 P
when she is able to overtake seventeen years old 1.01. 53 P
know the young gentlewoman, she has good gifts. 1.01. 62 P
she discourses, she carves, she gives the leer 1.03. 45 P
she discourses, she carves, she gives the leer 1.03. 45 P
she carves, she gives the leer of invitation. 1.03. 45 P
now, the report goes she has all the rule of her 1.03. 52 P
she did so course o'er my exteriors with such a 1.03. 65 P
she bears the purse too; 1.03. 68 P
she is a region in guiana, all gold and bounty. 1.03. 70 P
in truth, sir, and she is pretty, and honest, 1.04.139 P
fenton, i'll be sworn on a book she loves you. 1.04.146 P
she is given too much to allicholy and musing; 1.04.153 P
she shall be our messenger to this paltry knight 2.01.158 P
she was in his company at page's house; 2.01.235 P
if she be otherwise, 'tis labor well bestow'd. 2.01.239 P
but what says she to me? 2.02. 79 P
marry, she hath receiv'd your letter — for the 2.02. 81 P
for the which she thanks you a thousand times — 2.02. 82 P
and she gives you to notify that her husband 2.02. 83 P
then you may come and see the picture, she says, 2.02. 87 P
she leads a very frampold life with him, good 2.02. 90 P
and she bade me tell your worship that her 2.02.100 P
from home, but she hopes there will come a time. 2.02.102 P
in windsor leads a better life than she does: 2.02.117 P
do what she will, say what she will, take all, 2.02.118 P
do what she will, say what she will, take all, 2.02.118 P
pay all, go to bed when she list, rise when she 2.02.119 P
go to bed when she list, rise when she list, all 2.02.119 P
list, rise when she list, all is as she will; 2.02.120 P
and truly she deserves it, for if there be a 2.02.120 P
if there be a kind woman in windsor, she is one. 2.02.121 P
she is my prize, or ocean whelm them all! 2.02.137
to many to know what she would have given; 2.02.200 P
some say that, though she appear honest to me, 2.02.221 P
yet in other places she enlargeth her mirth so 2.02.222 P
she dwells so securely on the excellency of her 2.02.242 P
she is too bright to be look'd against. 2.02.244 P
then she plots, then she ruminates, then she 2.02.306 P
then she plots, then she ruminates, then she 2.02.306 P
she plots, then she ruminates, then she devises; 2.02.306 P
truly, sir, to see your wife. is she at home? 3.02. 11 P
ay, and as idle as she may hang together, for 3.02. 13 P
indeed she is. 3.02. 27 P
she shall not see me, i will ensconce me behind 3.03. 89 P
no, she shall not dismay me. 3.04. 27 P
she calls you, coz. 3.04. 53 P
she is no match for you. 3.04. 73
my daughter will i question how she loves you, 3.04. 90
she must needs go in, | her father will be angry 3.04. 92
she does so take on with her men; 3.05. 39 P
well, she laments, sir, for it, that it would 3.05. 43 P
she desires you once more to come to her, 3.05. 45 P
i was at her house the hour she appointed me. 3.05. 65 P
how so, sir? did she change her determination? 3.05. 68 P
never name her, child, if she be a whore. 4.01. 63 P
she comes of errands, does she? 4.02.173 P
she comes of errands, does she? 4.02.174 P
she works by charms, by spells, by th' figure, 4.02.176 P
as falstaff, she, and i are newly met, | let 4.04. 53
be so bold as stay, sir, till she come down. 4.05. 13 P
and what says she, i pray, sir? 4.05. 35 P
she says that the very same man that beguil'd 4.05. 36 P
she hath consented. 4.06. 25
to this her mother's plot | she, seemingly 4.06. 33
her father means she shall be all in white; 4.06. 35
hand and bid her go, | she shall go with him. 4.06. 38
that quaint in green she shall be loose enrob'd, 4.06. 41
which means she to deceive, father or mother? 4.06. 46
she cries "budget"; 5.02. 6 P
and where you find a maid | that, ere she sleep, 5.05. 50
sleep she as sound as careless infancy; 5.05. 52
if anne page be my daughter, she is, by this, 5.05.175 P
/white and cried "mum," and she cried "budget," 5.05.198 P
and indeed she is now with the doctor at the 5.05.202 P
the truth is, she and i (long since contracted) 5.05.223
th' offense is holy that she hath committed, 5.05.225
since therein she doth evitate and shun | a 5.05.228
she determines | herself the glory of a creditor MM 1.01. 38
she is fast my wife, | save that we do the 1.02.147
shoulders that a milkmaid, if she be in love, 1.02.173 P
that she make friends | to the strict deputy; 1.02.180
she hath prosperous art | when she will play 1.02.184
when she will play with reason and discourse, 1.02.185
and discourse, | and well she can persuade. 1.02.186
i pray she may; 1.02.187 P
is she your cousin? 1.04. 46
she it is. 1.04. 48
and now she professes a hot–house; 2.01. 65 P
i will detest myself also, as well as she, that 2.01. 76 P
who, if she had been a woman cardinally given, 2.01. 79 P
but as she spit in his face, so she defied him. 2.01. 84 P
but as she spit in his face, so she defied him. 2.01. 84 P
sir, she came in great with child; 2.01. 89 P
is yet to come that she was ever respected with 2.01.168 P
she was respected with him before he married 2.01.170 P
ever i was respected with her, or she with me, 2.01.176 P
hath she had any more than one husband? 2.01.201 P
pray heaven she win him! 2.02.125
she speaks, and 'tis | such sense that my sense 2.02.141
not she; 2.02.164
nor doth she tempt; 2.02.164
she is with child, | and he that got it, 2.03. 12
sweet uncleanness | as she that he hath stain'd? 2.04. 55
she (having the truth of honor in her) hath made 3.01.164 P
she should this angelo have married; 3.01.213 P
there she lost a noble and renown'd brother, in 3.01.219 P
lamentation, which she yet wears for his sake; 3.01.228 P
but how out of this can she avail? 3.01.234 P
procures she still? 3.02. 55 P
sir, she hath eaten up all her beef, and she is 3.02. 56 P
up all her beef, and she is herself in the tub. 3.02. 57 P
beggar, though she smelt brown bread and garlic. 3.02.183 P
with this maid, | she comes to do you good. 4.01. 51
her maiden loss, | how might she tongue me! 4.04. 25
she hath been a suitor to me for her brother, 5.01. 34
and she will speak most bitterly and strange. 5.01. 36
she speaks this in th' infirmity of sense. 5.01. 47
if she be mad — as i believe no other — | her 5.01. 60
but yesternight, my lord, she and that friar, 5.01.134
touch or soil with her | as she from one ungot. 5.01.142
know you that friar lodowick that she speaks of? 5.01.143
to her eyes, | till she herself confess it. 5.01.162
my lord, she may be a punk; 5.01.179 P

she that accuses him of fornication, | in 5.01.195
charges she moe than me? 5.01.200
carnally, she says. 5.01.214
handled her privately, she would sooner confess; 5.01.276 P
should she kneel down in mercy of this fact, 5.01.434
she, claudio, that you wrong'd, look you restore 5.01.525
there had she not been long but she became | a ERR 1.01. 49
there had she not been long but she became | a 1.01. 49
weeping before for what she saw must come, | and 1.01. 71
she is so hot, because the meat is cold: 1.02. 47
for she will /score your fault upon my pate: 1.02. 65
she that doth fast till you come home to dinner; 1.02. 89
no marvel though she pause — | they can be meek 2.01. 32
she sent for you by dromio home to dinner. 2.02.154
how can she thus then call us by our names, 2.02.166
to me she speaks, she moves me for her theme: 2.02.181
to me she speaks, she moves me for her theme: 2.02.181
'tis true she rides me and i long for grass. 2.02.200
but i should know her as well as she knows me. 2.02.202
but she will well excuse | why at this time the 3.01. 92
what need she be acquainted? 3.02. 15
let love, being light, be drowned if she sink! 3.02. 52
what claim lays she to thee? 3.02. 84 P
to your horse, and she would have me as a beast; 3.02. 86 P
i being a beast, she would have me, but that she 3.02. 87 P
she would have me, but that she, being a very 3.02. 87 P
what is she? 3.02. 89 P
match, and yet is she a wondrous fat marriage. 3.02. 92 P
if she lives till doomsday, she'll burn a week 3.02. 99 P
what complexion is she of? 3.02.101 P
she sweats, a man may go over shoes in the grime 3.02.103 P
then she bears some breadth? 3.02.112 P
she is spherical, like a globe; 3.02.114 P
she had transform'd me to a curtal dog, and made 3.02.146
she that doth call me husband, even my soul 3.02.158
comes aboard, | and then, sir, she bears away. 4.01. 87
she is too big, i hope, for me to compass. 4.01.111
nay, she is worse, she is the devil's dam, and 4.03. 51 P
she is worse, she is the devil's dam, and here 4.03. 51 P
and here she comes in the habit of a light wench 4.03. 52 P
but she, more covetous, would have a chain. 4.03. 74
and did not she herself revile me there? 4.04. 72
sans fable, she herself revil'd you there. 4.04. 73
certes she did, the kitchen vestal scorn'd you. 4.04. 75
and i am witness with her that she did. 4.04. 89
she that would be your wife now ran from you. 4.04.148
she never reprehended him but mildly, | when he 5.01. 87
she did betray me to my own reproof. 5.01. 90
she is a virtuous and a reverend lady: 5.01.134
it cannot be that she hath done thee wrong. 5.01.135
she whom thou gav'st to me to be my wife; 5.01.198
that she this day hath shameless thrown on me. 5.01.202
day, great duke, she shut the doors upon me, 5.01.204
while she with harlots feasted in my house. 5.01.205
but she tells to your highness simple truth! 5.01.211
if thou art she, tell me, where is that son 5.01.348
and so do i, yet did she call me so; 5.01.373
she now shall be my sister, not my wife. 5.01.417
she would not have his head on her shoulders for ADO 1.01.113 P
for all messina, as like him as she is. 1.01.115 P
should die while she hath such meet food to feed 1.01.120 P
is she not a modest young lady? 1.01.165 P
can afford her, that were she other than she is, 1.01.174 P
her, that were she other than she is, she were 1.01.174 P
were she other than she is, she were unhandsome, 1.01.174 P
and being no other but as she is, i do not like 1.01.175 P
in mine eye.she is the sweetest lady that ever i 1.01.187 P
cousin, and she were not possess'd with a fury, 1.01.190 P
that she is worthy, i know. 1.01.229 P
i neither feel how she should be lov'd nor know 1.01.230 P
be lov'd nor know how she should be worthy, is 1.01.231 P
that she brought me up, i likewise give her most 1.01.239 P
and the conclusion is, she shall be thine. 1.01.327
that she may be the better prepar'd for an 1.02. 22 P
him from her, she is no equal for his birth. 2.01.165 P
with her told her she is much wrong'd by you. 2.01.238 P
o, she misus'd me past the endurance of a block; 2.01.239 P
she told me, not thinking i had been myself, 2.01.242 P
she speaks poniards, and every word stabs. 2.01.247 P
near her, she would infect to the north star. 2.01.250 P
though she were endow'd with all that adam had 2.01.251 P
she would have made hercules have turn'd spit, 2.01.253 P
for certainly, while she is here, a man may live 2.01.257 P
look here she comes. 2.01.262 P
and so she doth, cousin. 2.01.317 P
she is never sad but when she sleeps, and not 2.01.343 P
she is never sad but when she sleeps, and not 2.01.343 P
she hath often dreamt of unhappiness and wak'd 2.01.345 P
she cannot endure to hear tell of a husband. 2.01.347 P
no means, she mocks all her wooers out of suit. 2.01.349 P
she were an excellent wife for benedick. 2.01.351 P
that she shall fall in love with benedick, and i 2.01.381 P
rich she shall be, that's certain; 2.03. 30 P
but most wonderful that she should so dote on 2.03. 96 P
whom she hath in all outward behaviors seem'd 2.03. 96 P
to think of it but that she loves him with an 2.03.100 P
may be she doth but counterfeit. 2.03.102 P
so near the life of passion as she discovers it. 2.03.106 P
why, what effects of passion shows she? 2.03.107 P
she will sit you — you heard my daughter tell 2.03.110 P
she did indeed. 2.03.112 P
hath she made her affection known to benedick? 2.03.123 P
no, and swears she never will. 2.03.125 P
"shall i," says she, "that have so oft 2.03.128 P
this says she now when she is beginning to write 2.03.130 P
this says she now when she is beginning to write 2.03.130 P
and there will she sit in her smock till she 2.03.132 P
sit in her smock till she have writ a sheet of 2.03.132 P
o, when she had writ it, and was reading it over 2.03.136 P
she found "benedick" and "beatrice" between the 2.03.137 P
she tore the letter into a thousand halfpence; 2.03.140 P
that she should be so immodest to write to one 2.03.141 P
to write to one that she knew would flout her. 2.03.142 P
"i measure him," says she, "by my own spirit, 2.03.143 P
then down upon her knees she falls, weeps, sobs, 2.03.146 P
she doth indeed, my daughter says so; 2.03.150 P
is sometime afeard she will do a desperate 2.03.152 P
it by some other, if she will not discover it. 2.03.155 P

and (out of all suspicion) she is virtuous. 2.03.160 P
and she is exceeding wise. 2.03.161 P
i would she had bestow'd this dotage on me, i 2.03.168 P
hero thinks surely she will die, for she says 2.03.173 P
for she says she will die if he love her not, 2.03.173 P
for she says she will die if he love her not, 2.03.174 P
and she will die ere she make her love known, 2.03.174 P
and she will die ere she make her love known, 2.03.175 P
her love known, and she will die if he woo her, 2.03.175 P
her, rather than she will bate one breath of her 2.03.176 P
she doth well. 2.03.178 P
if she should make tender of her love, 'tis very 2.03.178 P
impossible, she may wear her heart out first. 2.03.203 P
they say too that she will rather die than give 2.03.227 P
there will she hide her, | to listen our propose 3.01. 11
no, truly, ursula, she is too disdainful, | i 3.01. 34
she cannot love, | nor take no shape nor project 3.01. 54
project of affection, | she is so self–endeared. 3.01. 56
certainly it were not good | she knew his love, 3.01. 58
featur'd, | but she would spell him backward. 3.01. 61
she would swear the gentleman should be her 3.01. 62
so turns she every man the wrong side out, | and 3.01. 68
if i should speak, | she would mock me into air; 3.01. 75
o, she would laugh me | out of myself, press me 3.01. 75
yet tell her of it, hear what she will say. 3.01. 81
she cannot be so much without true judgment — 3.01. 88
excellent a wit | as she is priz'd to have — as 3.01. 90
she shall be buried with her face upwards. 3.02. 68 P
(for she has been too long a–talking of), the 3.02.103 P
even she — leonato's hero, your hero, every 3.02.106 P
i could say she were worse; 3.02.110 P
she leans me out at her mistress' chamber–window 3.03.146 P
but the devil my master knew she was margaret; 3.03.155 P
ask my lady beatrice else, here she comes. 3.04. 38 P
behold how like a maid she blushes here! 4.01. 34
all you that see her, that she were a maid, | by 4.01. 39
but she is none: 4.01. 40
she knows the heat of a luxurious bed; 4.01. 41
you will say, she did embrace me as a husband, 4.01. 49
yea, wherefore should she not? 4.01.119
could she here deny | the story that is printed 4.01.121
valuing of her — why, she, o, she is fall'n 4.01.139
o, she is fall'n | into a pit of ink, that the 4.01.139
thou seest that all the grace that she hath left 4.01.171
left | is that she will not add to her damnation 4.01.172
she not denies it. 4.01.173
in, | and publish it that she is dead indeed. 4.01.204
she dying, as it must be so maintain'd, | upon 4.01.214
upon the instant that she was accus'd, | shall 4.01.215
when he shall hear she died upon his words, 4.01.223
of his soul, | than when she liv'd indeed. 4.01.230
sweet hero, she is wrong'd, she is sland'red, 4.01.312 P
she is wrong'd, she is sland'red, she is undone. 4.01.312 P
she is wrong'd, she is sland'red, she is undone. 4.01.313 P
i must say she is dead; 4.01.335 P
and she lies buried with her ancestors — | o, 5.01. 69
and she is dead, slander'd to death by villains, 5.01. 88
she was charg'd with nothing | but what was true 5.01.104
"true," said she, "a fine little one." 5.01.161 P
"right," says she, "a great gross one." 5.01.162 P
"just," said she, "it hurts nobody." 5.01.164 P
"certain," said she, "a wise gentleman." 5.01.165 P
"that i believe," said she, "for he swore a 5.01.167 P
thus did she an hour together trans–shape thy 5.01.170 P
virtues, yet at last she concluded with a sigh, 5.01.171 P
for the which she wept heartily and said she 5.01.174 P
which she wept heartily and said she car'd not. 5.01.175 P
yea, that she did, but yet, for all that, and if 5.01.176 P
all that, and if she did not hate him deadly, 5.01.177 P
not hate him deadly, she would love him dearly. 5.01.177 P
you, she shall ne'er weigh more reasons in her 5.01.207 P
people in messina here | how innocent she died, 5.01.282
dead, | and she alone is heir to both of us. 5.01.290
no, by my soul, she was not, | nor knew not what 5.01.300
nor knew not what she did when she spoke to me, 5.01.301
nor knew not what she did when she spoke to me, 5.01.301
did i not tell you she was innocent? 5.04. 1
i'll hold my mind were she an ethiope. 5.04. 38
this same is she, and i do give you her. 5.04. 54
she died, my lord, but whiles her slander liv'd. 5.04. 66
decree, | she must lie here on mere necessity. LLL 1.01.148
was no damsel neither, sir, she was a virgin. 1.01.292 P
it was so, sir, for she had a green wit. 1.02. 89 P
if she be made of white and red, | her faults 1.02. 99
then if she fear, or be to blame, | by this you 1.02.103
possess the same | which native she doth owe. 1.02.106
she deserves well. 1.02.118 P
she is allow'd for the dey–woman. 1.02.131 P
when she did starve the general world beside 2.01. 11
i beseech you a word. what is she in the white? 2.01.197
she hath but one for herself, to desire that 2.01.200
not offended, | she is an heir of falconbridge. 2.01.205
she is a most sweet lady. 2.01.207
is she wedded or no? 2.01.211
why, she that bears the bow. | finely put off! 4.01.109
with her, boyet, and she strikes at the brow. 4.01.117
but she herself is hit lower. 4.01.118
then will she get the upshoot by cleaving the 4.01.136
well, she hath one a' my sonnets already: 4.03. 14 P
how shall she know my griefs? 4.03. 41
by earth, she is not, corporal, there you lie. 4.03. 84
she | reigns in my blood and will rememb'red be. 4.03. 93
she (an attending star) scarce seen a light. 4.03.227
o, she needs it not. 4.03.235
she passes praise, then praise too short doth 4.03.237
if that she learn not of her eye to look: 4.03.248
and therefore is she born to make black fair. 4.03.257
no devil will fright thee then so much as she. 4.03.271
then, as she goes, what upward lies | the street 4.03.276
the street should see as she walk'd overhead. 4.03.277
melancholy, sad, and heavy, | and so she died. 5.02. 15
had she been light, like you, | of such a merry, 5.02. 15
she might 'a' been /a grandam ere she died. 5.02. 17
she might 'a' been /a grandam ere she died. 5.02. 17
i should have fear'd her had she been a devil." 5.02.106
she says, you have it, and you may be gone. 5.02.183
she hears herself. 5.02.195
yet still she is the moon, and i the man. 5.02.215

that she vouchsafe me audience for one word. 5.02.313
i will, and so will she, i know, my lord. 5.02.314
when she shall challenge this, you will reject 5.02.438
pardon me, sir, this jewel did she wear, | and 5.02.456
following the signs, woo'd but the sign of she. 5.02.469
ship is under sail, and here she comes amain. 5.02.546
fellow hector, she is gone; 5.02.672 P
she is two months on her way. 5.02.672 P
she lingers my desires, | like to a step–dame, MND 1.01. 4
be it so she will not here before your grace 1.01. 39
as she is mine, i may dispose of her; 1.01. 42
and she is mine, and all my right of her | i do 1.01. 97
and she, sweet lady, dotes, | devoutly dotes, 1.01.108
of great revenue, and she hath no child. 1.01.158
and she respects me as her only son. 1.01.160
through athens i am thought as fair as she. 1.01.227
because that she as her attendant hath | a 2.01. 21
she never had so sweet a changeling. 2.01. 23
but she perforce withholds the loved boy, 2.01. 26
and when she drinks, against her lips i bob, 2.01. 49
then slip i from her bum, down topples she, 2.01. 53
full often hath she gossip'd by my side, | and 2.01.125
which she with pretty and with swimming gait 2.01.130
but she, being mortal, of that boy did die, 2.01.135
juice, | i'll watch titania when she is asleep, 2.01.177
the next thing then she waking looks upon | (be 2.01.179
she shall pursue it with the soul of love. 2.01.182
prove | more fond on her than she upon her love; 2.01.266
soul, she durst not lie | near this lack–love, 2.02. 76
happy is hermia, wheresoe'er she lies, | for she 2.02. 90
for she hath blessed and attractive eyes. 2.02. 91
she sees not hermia. 2.02.135
and when she weeps, weeps every little flower, 3.01.199
her eye, | which she must dote on in extremity. 3.02. 3
while she was in her dull and sleeping hour, | a 3.02. 8
that, when he wak'd, of force she must be ey'd. 3.02. 40
all fancy–sick she is and pale of cheer | with 3.02. 96
i'll charm his eyes against she do appear. 3.02. 99
when thou wak'st, if she be by, | beg of her for 3.02.108
she is one of this confederacy. 3.02.192
if she cannot entreat, i can compel. 3.02.248
thou canst compel no more than she entreat. 3.02.249
now i perceive that she hath made compare 3.02.290
she hath urg'd her height, | and with her 3.02.291
height, forsooth, she hath prevail'd with him. 3.02.293
because she is something lower than myself, 3.02.304
be not afraid; she shall not harm thee, helena. 3.02.321
she shall not, though you take her part. 3.02.322
o, when she is angry, she is keen and shrewd! 3.02.323
o, when she is angry, she is keen and shrewd! 3.02.323
she was a vixen when she went to school; 3.02.324
she was a vixen when she went to school; 3.02.324
and though she be but little, she is fierce. 3.02.325
and though she be but little, she is fierce. 3.02.325
now she holds me not; 3.02.335
here she comes, curst and sad. 3.02.439
for she his hairy temples then had rounded 4.01. 51
her, | and she in mild terms begg'd my patience, 4.01. 58
which straight she gave me, and her fairy sent 4.01. 60
of my consent that she should be your wife. 4.01.159
and, as she fled, her mantle she did fall, 5.01.142
and, as she fled, her mantle she did fall, 5.01.142
she is to enter now, and i am to spy her through 5.01.185 P
yonder she comes. 5.01.187 P
she will find him by starlight. 5.01.314 P
here she comes, and her passion ends the play. 5.01.314 P
methinks she should not use a long one for such 5.01.316 P
i hope she will be brief. 5.01.317 P
she for a woman, god bless us. 5.01.320 P
she hath spied him already with those sweet eyes 5.01.321 P
and thus she means, videlicet — 5.01.323 P
and she is fair and, fairer than that word, | of MV 1.01.162
she hath directed | how i shall take her from 2.04. 29
what gold and jewels she is furnish'd with, 2.04. 31
with, | what page's suit she hath in readiness. 2.04. 32
her foot, | unless she do it under this excuse, 2.04. 36
excuse, | that she is issue to a faithless jew. 2.04. 37
how like the prodigal doth she return, | with 2.06. 17
for she is wise, if i can judge of her, | and 2.06. 53
and fair she is, if that mine eyes be true, 2.06. 54
and true she is, as she hath prov'd herself; 2.06. 55
and true she is, as she hath prov'd herself; 2.06. 55
true, | shall she be placed in my constant soul. 2.06. 57
she hath the stones upon her, and the ducats." 2.08. 22
i would she were as lying a gossip in that as 3.01. 8 P
her neighbors believe she wept for the death of 3.01. 10 P
the tailor that made the wings she flew withal. 3.01. 27 P
she is damn'd for it. 3.01. 31 P
would she were hears'd at my foot, and the 3.01. 89 P
this, she is not yet so old | but she may learn; 3.02.160
this, she is not yet so old | but she may learn; 3.02.161
she is not bred so dull but she can learn; 3.02.162
she is not bred so dull but she can learn; 3.02.162
but if she be less than an honest woman, she is 3.05. 41 P
woman, she is indeed more than i took her for. 3.05. 42 P
husband | hast thou of me as she is for /a wife. 3.05. 84
penance | of such misery doth she cut me off. 4.01.272
if she were by to hear you make the offer. 4.01.289
i would she were in heaven, so she could 4.01.291
so she could | entreat some power to change this 4.01.291
and when she put it on, she made me vow | that i 4.01.442
she made me vow | that i should neither sell, 4.01.442
she would not hold out enemy for ever | for 4.01.447
she doth stray about | by holy crosses, where 5.01. 30
where she kneels and prays | for happy wedlock 5.01. 31
the nightingale, if she should sing by day, 5.01.104
a paltry ring | that she did give me, whose posy 5.01.148
whether till the next night she had rather stay, 5.01.302
she is at the court, and no less belov'd of her AYL 1.01.110 P
for those that she makes fair she scarce makes 1.02. 37 P
that she makes fair she scarce makes honest, and 1.02. 37 P
and those that she makes honest she makes very 1.02. 38 P
and those that she makes honest she makes very 1.02. 39 P
may she not by fortune fall into the fire? 1.02. 44 P
i cannot speak to her, yet she urg'd conference. 1.02.258
else had she with her father rang'd along. 1.03. 68
if she be a traitor, | why so am i. 1.03. 72
she is too subtile for thee, and her smoothness, 1.03. 77

she robs thee of thy name, | and thou wilt show 1.03. 80
and seem more virtuous | when she is gone. 1.03. 82
she is banish'd. 1.03. 84
confesses that she secretly o'erheard | your 2.02. 11
and she believes, where ever they are gone, 2.02. 15
when such a one as she, such is her neighbor? 2.07. 78
the fair, the chaste, and unexpressive she. 3.02. 10
heaven would that she these gifts should have, 3.02.153
thought of pleasing you when she was christen'd. 3.02.267 P
what stature is she of? 3.02.268 P
cony that you see dwell where she is kindled. 3.02.339 P
it, which i warrant she is apter to do than to 3.02.388 P
she is apter to do than to confess she does. 3.02.389 P
truly, she must be given, or the marriage is not 3.03. 69 P
life, | i think she means to tangle my eyes too! 3.05. 44
times a properer man | than she a woman. 3.05. 52
and out of you she sees herself more proper 3.05. 55
as fast as she answers thee with frowning looks, 3.05. 68 P
then she puts you to entreaty, and there begins 4.01. 79 P
why now, as fast as she can marry us. 4.01.134 P
by my life, she will do as i do. 4.01.158 P
o, but she is wise. 4.01.159 P
or else she could not have the wit to do this; 4.01.160 P
marry, to say she came to seek you there. 4.01.171 P
herself, for she will breed it like a fool! 4.01.176 P
which she did use as she was writing of it, | it 4.03. 10
which she did use as she was writing of it, | it 4.03. 10
she says i am not fair, that i lack manners; 4.03. 15
she calls me proud, and that she could not love 4.03. 16
and that she could not love me | were man as 4.03. 16
why writes she so to me? 4.03. 19
i saw her hand, she has a leathern hand, | a 4.03. 24
she has a huswive's hand — but that's no matter 4.03. 27
i say she never did invent this letter, | this 4.03. 28
why, she defies me, | like turk to christian. 4.03. 32
she phebes me. 4.03. 39
that if she love me, i charge her to love thee; 4.03. 71 P
if she will not, i will never have her unless 4.03. 71 P
and wooing, she should grant? 5.02. 3 P
say with her that she loves me; 5.02. 8 P
know into what straits of fortune she is driven, 5.02. 65 P
her before your eyes to–morrow, human as she is, 5.02. 67 P
you say that you'll have phebe, if she will? 5.04. 16
that you'll marry her | if she refuse me; 5.04. 24
nor ne'er wed woman, if you be not she. 5.04.124
the fat ale–wife of wincot, if she know me not. SHR in.2. 22 P
if she say i am not fourteen pence on the score in.2. 22 P
we'll show thee io as she was a maid, | and how in.2. 54
maid, | and how she was beguiled and surpris'd, in.2. 55
her legs that one shall swear she bleeds, | and in.2. 58
and till the tears that she hath shed for thee in.2. 64
she was the fairest creature in the world, | and in.2. 66
in the world, | and yet she is inferior to none. in.2. 67
because she brought stone jugs and no seal'd in.2. 88
best | put finger in the eye, and she knew why. 1.01. 79
and for i know she taketh most delight | in 1.01. 92
fit man to teach her that wherein she delights, 1.01.111 P
and with her breath she did perfume the air. 1.01.175
because she will not be annoy'd with suitors. 1.01.184
and yet i'll promise thee she shall be rich, 1.02. 62
be she as foul as was florentius' love, | as old 1.02. 69
she moves me not, or not removes, at least, 1.02. 72
/whe'er she is as rough | as are the swelling 1.02. 73
though she have as many diseases as two and 1.02. 80 P
is that she is intolerable curst | and shrowd 1.02. 89
though she chide as loud | as thunder when the 1.02. 95
a' my word, and she knew him as well as i do, 1.02.108 P
she would think scolding would do little good 1.02.109 P
she may perhaps call him half a score knaves or 1.02.110 P
sir, and she stand him but a little, he will 1.02.113 P
that she shall have no more eyes to see withal 1.02.114 P
for she is sweeter than perfume itself | to whom 1.02.152
i know she is an irksome brawling scold. 1.02.187
but so is not she. 1.02.232
and were his daughter fairer than she is, | she 1.02.240
is, | she may more suitors have, and me for one. 1.02.241
and so she shall. 1.02.244
poor girl, she weeps. 2.01. 24
when did she cross thee with a bitter word? 2.01. 28
now i see | she is your treasure, she must have 2.01. 32
she is your treasure, she must have a husband; 2.01. 32
sciences, | whereof i know she is not ignorant. 2.01. 58
she is not for your turn, the more my grief. 2.01. 63
of | her widowhood, be it that she survive me, 2.01.124
i am as peremptory as she proud–minded; 2.01.131
so i to her, and so she yields to me, | for i am 2.01.136
why no, for she hath broke the lute to me. 2.01.148
i did but tell her she mistook her frets, | and 2.01.149
quoth she, "i'll fume with them." 2.01.152
and with that word she strook me on the head, 2.01.153
while she did call me rascal fiddler | and 2.01.157
terms, | as had she studied to misuse me so. 2.01.159
and woo her with some spirit when she comes. 2.01.169
say that she rail, why then i'll tell her plain 2.01.170
plain | she sings as sweetly as a nightingale; 2.01.171
say that she frown, i'll say she looks as clear 2.01.172
i'll say she looks as clear | as morning roses 2.01.172
say she be mute, and will not speak a word, 2.01.174
and say she uttereth piercing eloquence; 2.01.176
if she do bid me pack, i'll give her thanks, 2.01.177
as though she bid me stay by her a week; 2.01.178
if she deny to wed, i'll crave the day | when i 2.01.179
but here she comes, and now, petruchio, speak. 2.01.181
if she be curst, it is for policy, | for she's 2.01.292
she is not hot, but temperate as the morn; 2.01.294
for patience she will prove a second grissel, 2.01.295
she says she'll see thee hang'd first. 2.01.300
if she and i be pleas'd, what's that to you? 2.01.303
that she shall still be curst in company. 2.01.305
incredible to believe | how much she loves me. 2.01.307
she hung about my neck, and kiss on kiss | she 2.01.308
and kiss on kiss | she vied so fast, protesting 2.01.309
oath, | that in a twink she won me to her love. 2.01.310
hers, | if whilst i live she will be only mine. 2.01.362
that she shall have, besides an argosy | that 2.01.374
and she can have no more than all i have; 2.01.382
if you like me, she shall have me and mine. 2.01.383
she is your own, else you must pardon me; 2.01.388
could i repair what she will wear in me, | as i 3.02.118
curster than she? why, 'tis impossible. 3.02.154
a fool, | if she had not a spirit to resist. 3.02.221
but for my bonny kate, she must with me. 3.02.227
she is my goods, my chattels, she is my house, 3.02.230
she is my goods, my chattels, she is my house, 3.02.230
and here she stands, touch her whoever dare, 3.02.233
she shall, lucentio. come, gentlemen, let's go. 3.02.252
is she so hot a shrew as she's reported? 4.01. 21 P
she was, good curtis, before this frost; 4.01. 22 P
whose hand (she being now at hand) thou shalt 4.01. 30 P
how her horse fell and she under her horse; 4.01. 74 P
heard in how miry a place, how she was bemoil'd, 4.01. 75 P
how she waded through the dirt to pluck him off 4.01. 78 P
swore, how she pray'd that never pray'd before; 4.01. 79 P
by this reck'ning he is more shrew than she. 4.01. 86 P
why, she hath a face of her own. 4.01.100 P
why, she comes to borrow nothing of them. 4.01.105 P
and swears, and rates, that she, poor soul, 4.01.184
and till she stoop, she must not be full–gorg'd, 4.01.191
and till she stoop, she must not be full–gorg'd, 4.01.191
for then she never looks upon her lure. 4.01.192
she eat no meat to–day, nor none shall eat; 4.01.197
last night she slept not, nor to–night she shall 4.01.198
night she slept not, nor to–night she shall not; 4.01.198
and, in conclusion, she shall watch all night, 4.01.205
and if she chance to nod i'll rail and brawl, 4.01.206
i tell you, sir, she bears me fair in hand. 4.02. 3
to marry with her though she would entreat. 4.02. 33
see how beastly she doth court him! 4.02. 34
she says your worship means to make a puppet of 4.03.105 P
he beareth to your daughter | and she to him, to 4.04. 30
doth love my daughter, and she loveth him, | or 4.04. 41
i pray the gods she may with all my heart! 4.04. 67
in an afternoon as she went to the garden for 4.04.100 P
i may and will, if she be so contented. 4.04.105
she will be pleas'd, then wherefore should i 4.04.106
she is of good esteem, | her dowry wealthy, and 4.05. 64
and if she /be froward, | then hast thou taught 4.05. 78
my widow says, thus she conceives her tale. 5.02. 24
she hath prevented me. 5.02. 49
my mistress sends you word | that she is busy, 5.02. 81
word | that she is busy, and she cannot come. 5.02. 81
she is busy, and she cannot come! 5.02. 82
she is busy, and she cannot come! 5.02. 82
nay then she must needs come. 5.02. 88
she says you have some goodly jest in hand. 5.02. 91
she will not come; 5.02. 92
she bids you come to her. 5.02. 92
she will not come! 5.02. 93
she will not. 5.02. 97
for she is chang'd, as she had never been. 5.02.115
for she is chang'd, as she had never been. 5.02.115
see where she comes, and brings your froward 5.02.119
she shall not. 5.02.134
i say she shall, and first begin with her. 5.02.135
and when she is froward, peevish, sullen, sour, 5.02.157
will, | what is she but a foul contending rebel, 5.02.159
a wonder, by your leave, she will be tam'd so. 5.02.189
her dispositions she inherits, which makes fair AWW 1.01. 40 P
she derives her honesty and achieves her 1.01. 44 P
"was this fair face the cause," quoth she, 1.03. 70
with that she sighed as she stood, | with that 1.03. 74
with that she sighed as she stood, | with that 1.03. 74
she stood, | with that she sighed as she stood, 1.03. 75
she stood, | with that she sighed as she stood, 1.03. 75
father bequeath'd her to me, and she herself, 1.03.102 P
make title to as much love as she finds. 1.03.103 P
late more near her than i think she wish'd me. 1.03.107 P
alone she was, and did communicate to herself 1.03.107 P
she thought, i dare vow for her, they touch'd 1.03.109 P
her matter was, she lov'd your son. 1.03.110 P
fortune, she said, was no goddess, that had put 1.03.111 P
this she deliver'd in the most bitter touch of 1.03.116 P
but lend and give where she is sure to lose; 1.03.215
but riddle–like lives sweetly where she dies! 1.03.217
why, doctor she! 2.01. 79
thou not, bertram, | what she has done for me? 2.03.109
thou know'st she has rais'd me from my sickly 2.03.111
she had her breeding at my father's charge — 2.03.114
if she be | all that is virtuous — save what 2.03.121
she is young, wise, fair, | in these to nature 2.03.131
virtue and she | is her own dower; 2.03.143
honor | flies where you bid it, i find that she, 2.03.170
her by the hand, | and tell her she is thine; 2.03.174
i'll to the wars, she to her single sorrow. 2.03.296
my mother greets me kindly. is she well? 2.04. 1 P
she is not well, but yet she has her health. 2.04. 2 P
she is not well, but yet she has her health. 2.04. 2 P
she's very merry, but yet she is not well; 2.04. 3 P
but yet she is not well. 2.04. 5 P
if she be very well, what does she ail that 2.04. 6 P
what does she ail that she's not very well? 2.04. 6 P
and i her money, i would she did as you say. 2.04. 21 P
is she gone to the king? 2.05. 20 P
she is. 2.05. 21 P
will she away to–night? 2.05. 22 P
she hath recover'd the king, and undone me. 3.02. 20 P
here that is too good for him | but only she, 3.02. 81
and she deserves a lord | that twenty such rude 3.02. 81
might you not know she would do as she has done 3.04. 2
might you not know she would do as she has done 3.04. 2
her intents, | which thus she hath prevented. 3.04. 22
at overnight, | she might have been o'erta'en; 3.04. 24
and yet she writes, | pursuit would be but vain. 3.04. 24
when haply he shall hear that she is gone, | he 3.04. 35
gone, | he will return, and hope i may that she, 3.04. 36
i know she will lie at my house; 3.05. 31 P
she is too mean | to have her name repeated. 3.05. 60
i /warr'nt, good creature, wheresoe'er she is, 3.05. 66
might do her | a shrewd turn, if she pleas'd. 3.05. 68
but she is arm'd for him and keeps her guard 3.05. 73
tokens and letters which she did re–send, | and 3.06.115
if you misdoubt me that i am not she, | i know 3.07. 1
but that your daughter, ere she seems as won, 3.07. 31
instruct my daughter how she shall persever, 3.07. 37
she then was honest. 4.02. 11
how he would woo, | as if she sate in 's heart. 4.02. 70
she says all men | have the like oaths. 4.02. 70
with most austere sanctimony she accomplish'd; 4.03. 50 P
of her last breath, and now she sings in heaven. 4.03. 53 P
if she had partaken of my flesh, and cost me the 4.05. 10 P
sir, she was the sweet marjorom of the sallet, 4.05. 16 P
knave with fortune that she should scratch you, 5.02. 30 P
that she whom all men prais'd and whom myself, 5.03. 53
of my daughter, | that she may quickly come. 5.03. 76
it, and she reckon'd it | at her live's rate. 5.03. 90
you are deceiv'd, my lord, she never saw it. 5.03. 92
noble she was, and thought | i stood engag'd; 5.03. 95
course of honor | as she had made the overture, 5.03. 99
she ceas'd | in heavy satisfaction and would 5.03. 99
she call'd the saints to surety | that she would 5.03.108
that she would never put it from her finger, 5.03.109
finger, | unless she gave it to yourself in bed, 5.03.110
she never saw it. 5.03.112
and she is dead, which nothing but to close 5.03.118
her bed in florence, | where yet she never was. 5.03.127
her | with an importing visage, and she told me, 5.03.136
that she which marries you must marry me, 5.03.174
she hath that ring of yours. 5.03.209
i think she has. 5.03.210
she knew her distance and did angle for me, 5.03.212
she got the ring, | and i had that which any 5.03.217
glove, my lord, she goes off and on at pleasure. 5.03.277 P
she does abuse our ears. to prison with her! 5.03.294
dead though she be, she feels her young one kick 5.03.302
though she be, she feels her young one kick. 5.03.302
if she, my liege, can make me know this clearly, 5.03.315
methought she purg'd the air of pestilence! TN 1.01. 19
but like a cloistress she will veiled walk, 1.01. 27
which she would keep fresh | and lasting in her 1.01. 30
o, she that hath a heart of that fine frame | to 1.01. 32
how will she love when the rich golden shaft 1.01. 34
what's she? 1.02. 35
she hath abjur'd the /company | and /sight of 1.02. 40
because she will admit no kind of suit, | no, 1.02. 45
your niece will not be seen, or if she be, it's 1.03.106 P
if she be so abandon'd to her sorrow | as it is 1.04. 19
as it is spoke, she never will admit me. 1.04. 20
she will attend it better in thy youth | than in 1.04. 27
the honorable lady of the house, which is she? 1.05.167 P
most certain, if you are she, you do usurp 1.05.187 P
you are the cruell'st she alive | if you will 1.05.241
sir, though it was said she much resembled me, 2.01. 25 P
she bore a mind that envy could not but call 2.01. 29 P
she is drown'd already, sir, with salt water, 2.01. 30 P
she returns this ring to you, sir. 2.02. 5 P
she adds, moreover, that you should put your 2.02. 7 P
into a desperate assurance she will none of him. 2.02. 8 P
she took the ring of me, i'll none of it. 2.02. 12 P
she made good view of me; 2.02. 19
for she did speak in starts distractedly. 2.02. 21
she loves me sure, the cunning of her passion 2.02. 22
'tis, | poor lady, she were better love a dream. 2.02. 26
and she (mistaken) seems to dote on me. 2.02. 35
you that, though she harbors you as her kinsman, 2.03. 96 P
of her, she is very willing to bid you farewell. 2.03.100 P
she shall know of it, by this hand. 2.03.123 P
to–day with my lady, she is much out of quiet. 2.03.133 P
she is not worth thee then. 2.04. 27
an elder than herself, so wears she to him; 2.04. 30
so sways she level in her husband's heart. 2.04. 31
but if she cannot love you, sir? 2.04. 87
must she not then be answer'd? 2.04. 92
she never told her love, | but let concealment, 2.04.110
she pin'd in thought, | and with a green and 2.04.112
she sat like patience on a monument, | smiling 2.04.114
maria once told me she did affect me, and i have 2.05. 24 P
that, should she fancy, it should be one of my 2.05. 25 P
she uses me with a more exalted respect than any 2.05. 26 P
and her t's, and thus makes she her great p's. 2.05. 87 P
her lucrece, with which she uses to seal. 2.05. 93 P
what dish a' poison has she dress'd him! 2.05.112 P
why, she may command me: 2.05.115 P
i serve her, she is my lady. 2.05.116 P
she thus advises thee that sighs for thee. 2.05.152 P
she that would alter services with thee, the 2.05.158 P
she did commend my yellow stockings of late, she 2.05.166 P
she did praise my leg being cross–garter'd, and 2.05.166 P
and in this she manifests herself to my love, 2.05.168 P
yellow stockings, and 'tis a color she abhors, 2.05.199 P
and cross–garter'd, a fashion she detests; 2.05.200 P
being addicted to a melancholy as she is, that 2.05.203 P
she will keep no fool, sir, till she be married, 3.01. 33 P
sir, till she be married, and fools are as like 3.01. 33 P
i mean, she is the list of my voyage. 3.01. 76 P
servingman than ever she bestow'd upon me. 3.02. 6 P
did she see /thee the while, old boy? 3.02. 8 P
she did show favor to the youth in your sight 3.02. 18 P
if she do, he'll smile, and take't for a great 3.02. 82 P
she sends him on purpose, that i may appear 3.04. 66 P
for she incites me to that in the letter. 3.04. 67 P
"cast thy humble slough," says she; 3.04. 68 P
and when she went away now, "let this fellow be 3.04. 75 P
ah ha, does she so? 3.04. 94 P
olivia, and in my sight she uses thee kindly. 3.04.156 P
"alas, why is she so?" 4.02. 77
"she loves another" — who calls, ha? 4.02. 79 P
this pearl she gave me, i do feel't and see't, 4.03. 2
so, | she could not sway her house, command her 4.03. 17
and stable bearing | as i perceive she does. 4.03. 20
a sister! you are she. 5.01.326
me, it was she | first told me thou wast mad. 5.01.348
o' th' clock behind | what lady she her lord. WT 1.02. 44
how she holds up the neb! 1.02.183
that little thinks she has been sluic'd in 's 1.02.194
she would not live | the running of one glass. 1.02.305
she is spread of late | into a goodly bulk. 2.01. 19
be but about | to say she is a goodly lady, and 2.01. 66
knows | what she should shame to know herself 2.01. 91
dram of woman's flesh is false, | if she be. 2.01.139
be she honor–flaw'd, | i have three daughters: 2.01.143
from our free person she should be confin'd, 2.01.194
she is, something before her time, deliver'd. 2.02. 23
if she dares trust me with her little babe, 2.02. 35
minister of honor, | lest she should be denied. 2.02. 49

ing — part o' th' cause, | she the adultress; 2.03. 4
t she | i can hook to me — say that she were 2.03. 6
an hook to me — say that she were gone, 2.03. 7
ach them, nor | shall she, within my pow'r. 2.03. 26
harg'd thee that she should not come about me 2.03. 43
new she would. 2.03. 44
ril and on mine, | she should not visit you. 2.03. 46
hen she will take the rein i let her run, | but 2.03. 51
e good queen | (for she is good) hath brought 2.03. 66
colors | no yellow in't, lest she suspect, 2.03.107
at makes the fire, | not she which burns in't. 2.03.116
e durst not call me so, | if she did know me 2.03.123
rst not call me so, | if she did know me one. 2.03.124
r, as she hath | been publicly accus'd, so 2.03.203
shall she have | a just and open trial. 2.03.204
hile she lives | my heart will be a burthen to 2.03.205
e will recover. 3.02.150
e did approach | my cabin where i lay; 3.03. 23
d so, with shrieks, | she melted into air. 3.03. 37
r mistress of the feast, and she lays it on. 4.03. 40 P
e hath made me four and twenty nosegays for 4.03. 41 P
on | this day she was both pantler, butler, 4.04. 56
d the thing she took to quench it | she would 4.04. 61
ok to quench it | she would to each one sip. 4.04. 62
thing she does, or seems, | but smacks of 4.04.157
oth, she is | the queen of curds and cream. 4.04.160
e dances featly. 4.04.176
she does any thing, though i report it | that 4.04.177
e shall bring him that | which he not dreams 4.04.179
d how she long'd to eat adders' heads, and 4.04.264 P
was thought she was a woman and was turn'd 4.04.278 P
o a cold fish for she would not exchange 4.04.279 P
ere's scarce a maid westward but she sings it. 4.04.290 P
u do, i was wont | to load my she with knacks. 4.04.349
ow | she prizes not such trifles as these are. 4.04.357
e gifts she looks from me are pack'd and 4.04.358
ur fair princess | (for so i see she must be) 4.04.545
e shall be habited as it becomes | the partner 4.04.546
r breeding as | she is i' th' rear 'our birth. 4.04.581
annot say 'tis pity | she lacks instructions, 4.04.582
r she seems a mistress | to most that teach. 4.04.582
e being none of your flesh and blood, your 4.04.693 P
cret things, all but what she has with her. 4.04.697 P
e drops booties in my mouth. 4.04.832 P
oman, she you kill'd | would be unparallel'd. 5.01. 15
e i kill'd? 5.01. 17
d she such power, | she had just cause. 5.01. 60
d she such power, | she had just cause. 5.01. 61
e had, and would incense me | to murther her i 5.01. 61
e shall not be so young | as was your former, 5.01. 78
was your former, but she shall be such | as, 5.01. 79
incess (she | the fairest i have yet beheld), 5.01. 86
colder than that theme, "she had not been, 5.01.100
e other, when she has obtain'd your eye, 5.01.105
ould she begin a sect, might quench the zeal 5.01.107
ake proselytes | of who she but bid follow. 5.01.109
at she is a woman | more worth than any man; 5.01.110
en, that she is | the rarest of all women. 5.01.111
r she did print your royal father off, 5.01.125
od my lord, | she came from libya. 5.01.157
e is, | when once she is my wife. 5.01.208
e is, | when once she is my wife. 5.01.209
w'r no jot | hath she to change our loves. 5.01.218
e was more worth such gazes | than what you 5.01.226
e had one eye declin'd for the loss of her 5.02. 74 P
e lifted the princess from the earth, and so 5.02. 76 P
nbracing, as if she would pin her to her heart, 5.02. 77 P
at she might no more be in danger of losing. 5.02. 78 P
ath (with the manner how she came to't bravely 5.02. 85 P
om one sign of dolor to another, she did (with 5.02. 88 P
hought she had some great matter there in 5.02.104 P
r she hath privately twice or thrice a day, 5.02.105 P
she liv'd peerless, | so her dead likeness, i 5.03. 14
rather, thou art she | in thy not chiding; 5.03. 25
r she was as tender | as infancy and grace. 5.03. 26
xteen years, and makes her | as she liv'd now. 5.03. 32
now she might have done, | so much to my good 5.03. 32
thus she stood, | even with such life of 5.03. 34
u perceive she stirs. 5.03.103
hen she was young, you woo'd her; 5.03.108
w, in age, | is she become the suitor? 5.03.109
e embraces him. 5.03.111
e hangs about his neck. 5.03.112
she pertain to life let her speak too. 5.03.113
, and make it manifest where she has liv'd, 5.03.114
at she is living, | were it but told you, 5.03.115
it it appears she lives, | though yet she speak 5.03.117
pears she lives, | though yet she speak not. 5.03.118
ould not cease | till she had kindled france, JN 1.01. 33
d if she did play false, the fault was hers, 1.01.118
ath she no husband | that will take pains to 1.01.218
w shame upon you, whe'er she does or no! 2.01.167
whom in favor she shall give the day, | and 2.01.393
ich as she is, in beauty, virtue, birth, | is 2.01.432
not complete of, say he is not she, | and she 2.01.434
nd she again wants nothing, to name want, | if 2.01.435
ant, | if want it be not that she is not he. 2.01.436
an, | left to be finished by such as she, | and 2.01.438
she, | and she a fair divided excellence, 2.01.439
she in beauty, education, blood, | holds hand 2.01.493
at she is bound in honor still to do | what 2.01.522
know she is not, for this match made up | her 2.01.541
here is she and her son? 2.01.543
e is sad and passionate at your highness' tent 2.01.544
e is corrupted, chang'd, and won from thee; 3.01. 55
e looks upon them with a threat'ning eye. 3.04.120
e drawn in france, | and she not hear of it? 4.02.119
ere did she fall a tear, here in this place R2 3.04.104
omp | she came adorned hither like sweet may, 5.01. 79
know she is come to pray for your foul sin. 5.03. 82
ill she hold out water in foul way? 1H4 2.01. 84 P
e will, she will, justice hath liquor'd her. 2.01. 85 P
e will, she will, justice hath liquor'd her. 2.01. 85 P
o my sweet harry," says she, "how many hast 2.04.106 P
n mad, | so much she doteth on her mortimer. 3.01.144
ll her that she and my aunt percy | shall 3.01.194
e is desperate here, a peevish self-will'd 3.01.196
ay, if you melt, then will she run mad. 3.01.209

she bids you on the wanton rushes lay you down, 3.01.211
and she will sing the song that pleaseth you, 3.01.213
peace, she sings. 3.01.244 P
telling us she had a good dish of prawns, 2H4 2.01. 96 P
didst thou not, when she was gone down stairs, 2.01. 98 P
soul, and she says up and down the town that her 2.01.104 P
she hath been in good case, and the truth is, 2.01.106 P
althaea dreamt she was deliver'd of a fire-brand 2.02. 89 P
she is pistol-proof, sir; 2.04.116 P
and so she is, by my troth. 2.04.304 P
is she of the wicked? 2.04.327 P
her money, and whether she be damn'd for that, i 2.04.340 P
she comes blubber'd. 2.04.390 P
she lives, master shallow. 3.02.200 P
she never could away with me. 3.02.201 P
she would always say she could not abide master 3.02.202 P
she would always say she could not abide master 3.02.202 P
she was then a bona roba. 3.02.205 P
doth she hold her own well? 3.02.205 P
nay, she must be old, she cannot choose but be 3.02.207 P
she must be old, she cannot choose but be old, 3.02.207 P
she has nobody to do any thing about her when i 3.02.230 P
thing about her when i am gone, and she is old, 3.02.231 P
she either gives a stomach and no food — | such 4.04.105
over to me, and she shall have whipping cheer, i 5.04. 5 P
come, come, you she knight-arrant, come. 5.04. 22 P
she hath been then more fear'd than harm'd, my H5 1.02.155
and she a mourning widow of her nobles, | she 1.02.158
she hath herself not only well defended | but 1.02.159
whom she did send to france | to fill king 1.02.161
cat, | to 'tame and havoc more than she can eat. 1.02.173
nell quickly, and certainly she did you wrong, 2.01. 18 P
patience be a tir'd /mare, yet she will plod — 2.01. 24 P
doll tearsheet she by name, and her espouse. 2.01. 77
hold, the quondam quickly | for the only she; 2.01. 79
for, my good liege, she is so idly king'd, | her 2.04. 26
harflew | till in her ashes she lies buried. 3.03. 9
and she is painted also with a wheel, to signify 3.06. 32 P
which is the moral of it, that she is turning, 3.06. 34 P
o then belike she was old and gentle, and you 3.07. 52 P
by her foot, that she may tread out the oath. 3.07. 95 P
alas, she hath from france too long been chas'd, 5.02. 38
she is our capital demand, compris'd | within 5.02. 96
she hath good leave. 5.02. 98
what says she, fair one? 5.02.117 P
madam my interpreter, what says she? 5.02.260 P
to kiss before they are married, would she say? 5.02.266 P
is she not apt? 5.02.285 P
if she deny the appearance of a naked blind boy 5.02.296 P
in the latter end, and she must be blind too. 5.02.314 P
thy wife is proud, she holdeth thee in awe, 1H6 1.01. 39
the spirit of deep prophecy she hath, 1.02. 55
what's past and what's to come she can descry. 1.02. 57
this means shall we sound what skill she hath. 1.02. 63
she takes upon her bravely at first dash. 1.02. 71
her aid she promis'd, and assur'd success; 1.02. 82
in complete glory she reveal'd herself; 1.02. 83
with those clear rays which she infus'd on me 1.02. 85
what she says i'll confirm. we'll fight it out. 1.02.128
no prophet will i trust, if she prove false. 1.02.150
here, here she comes. 1.05. 4
back our troops and conquers as she lists: 1.05. 22
in memory of her when she is dead, | her ashes, 1.06. 23
pray god she prove not masculine ere long, | if 2.01. 22
the french | she carry armor as she hath begun. 2.01. 24
the french | she carry armor as she hath begun. 2.01. 24
to visit her poor castle where she lies, | that 2.02. 41
that she may boast she hath beheld the man 2.02. 42
that she may boast she hath beheld the man 2.02. 42
now she is there, how will she specify | here is 3.02. 21
how will she specify | here is the best and 3.02. 21
no way to that, for weakness, which she ent'red. 3.02. 25
either she hath bewitch'd me with her words, 3.03. 58
he doth intend she shall be england's queen. 5.01. 45
as if, with circe, she would change my shape! 5.03. 35
is she not here? 5.03. 68
how canst thou tell she will deny thy suit, 5.03. 75
she is a woman; 5.03. 79
she was the first fruit of my bach'lorship. 5.04. 13
take her away, for she hath liv'd too long, | to 5.04. 34
because she is a maid, | spare for no faggots, 5.04. 55
she and the dolphin have been juggling. 5.04. 68
i think she knows not well | (there were so many 5.04. 80
well | (there were so many) whom she may accuse. 5.04. 81
it's sign she hath been liberal and free. 5.04. 82
and yet, forsooth, she is a virgin pure. 5.04. 83
and, which is more, she is not so divine, | so 5.05. 16
mind | she is content to be at your command — 5.05. 19
us | in our opinions she should be preferr'd. 5.05. 61
that margaret shall be queen, and none but she. 5.05. 78
and she sent over of the king of england's own 2H6 1.01. 60 P
she should have stay'd in france, and starv'd in 1.01.135
gold cannot come amiss, were she a devil. 1.02. 92
she sweeps it through the court with troops of 1.03. 77
she bears a duke's revenues on her back, | and 1.03. 80
back, | and in her heart she scorns our poverty. 1.03. 81
contemptuous base-born callot as she is, | she 1.03. 83
she vaunted 'mongst her minions t' other day, 1.03. 84
that she will light to listen to the lays, | and 1.03. 90
she shall not strike dame eleanor unreveng'd. 1.03.147
and what a pitch she flew above the rest! 2.01. 6
noble she is; 2.01.190
but if she have forgot | honor and virtue, and 2.01.190
his poor queen to france, from whence she came, 2.02. 25
she was heir | to roger earl of march, who was 2.02. 47
uneath may she endure the flinty streets, | to 2.04. 8
but soft, i think she comes, and i'll prepare 2.04. 15
as if she had suborned some to swear | false 3.01.180
i knew her well, she was a midwife. 4.02. 43 P
she was indeed a pedlar's daughter, and sold 4.02. 45 P
her furr'd pack, she washes bucks here at home. 4.02. 48 P
but she shall pay to me her maidenhead ere they 4.07.122 P
tell kent from me, she hath lost her best man, 4.10. 73 P
reveng'd may she be on that hateful duke, 3H6 1.01.266
she is hard by with twenty thousand men; 1.02. 51
she shall not need, we'll meet her in the field. 1.02. 65
ah, would she break from hence, that this my 2.01. 75
that she was coming with a full intent | to dash 2.01.117

the tiger will be mild whiles she doth mourn; 3.01. 39
she, on his left side, craving aid for henry; 3.01. 43
she weeps, and says her henry is depos'd; 3.01. 45
that she, poor wretch, for grief can speak no 3.01. 47
i fear her not, unless she chance to fall. 3.02. 24
the match is made, she seals it with a cur'sy. 3.02. 57
the widow likes him not, she knits her brows. 3.02. 82
one way or other, she is for a king, | and she 3.02. 87
and she shall be my love or else my queen. 3.02. 88
the widow likes it not, for she looks very sad. 3.02.110
she did corrupt frail nature with some bribe, 3.02.155
and thou no more art prince than she is queen. 3.03. 80
son edward, she is fair and virtuous, 3.03.245
yes, i accept her, for she well deserves it, 3.03.249
she better would have fitted me or clarence; 4.01. 54
she could say little less; 4.01.101
she had the wrong. 4.01.102
for i have heard that she was there in place. 4.01.103
"tell him," quoth she, "my mourning weeds are 4.01.104
belike she minds to play the amazon. 4.01.106
if she have time to breathe, be well assur'd 5.03. 16
why should she live, to fill the world with 5.05. 44
doth she swoun? 5.05. 45
and see our gentle queen how well she fares. 5.05. 89
by this, i hope, she hath a son for me. 5.05. 90
'tis she | that /tempers him to this extremity. R3 1.01. 64
was it not she, and that good man of worship, 1.01. 66
hath she forgot already that brave prince, 1.02.239
and will she yet abase her eyes on me, | that 1.02.246
upon my life, she finds (although i cannot) 1.02.253
or, if she be accus'd of true report, | bear 1.03. 27
she may, my lord, for — 1.03. 91
she may, lord rivers! 1.03. 92
she may do more, sir, than denying that: 1.03. 93
she may help you to many fair preferments, | and 1.03. 94
what may she not, she may, ay, marry, may she. 1.03. 97
what may she not, she may, ay, marry, may she. 1.03. 97
what may she not, she may, ay, marry, may she. 1.03. 97
what, marry, may she? 1.03. 98
what, marry, may she? 1.03. 99
thereof, | for i am she, and altogether joyless. 1.03.155
dispute not with her, she is lunatic. 1.03.253
what doth she say, my lord of buckingham? 1.03.294
she hath had too much wrong, and i repent | my 1.03.306
she for an edward weeps, and so do i; 2.02. 82
i for a clarence /weep, so doth not she; 2.02. 83
his nurse? why, she was dead ere thou wast born. 2.04. 33
if 'twere not she, i cannot tell who told me. 2.04. 34
if she deny, lord hastings, go with him, | and 3.01. 35
but if she be obdurate | to mild entreaties, god 3.01. 39
when she exclaim'd on hastings, you, and i, 3.03. 16
then curs'd she richard, then curs'd she 3.03. 18
curs'd she richard, then curs'd she buckingham, 3.03. 18
she buckingham, | then curs'd she hastings. 3.03. 19
if she convey | letters to richmond, you shall 4.02. 92
that from the prime creation e'er she framed." 4.03. 19
for she that scorn'd at me, now scorn'd of me; 4.04.102
for she being fear'd of all, now fearing one; 4.04.103
for she commanding all, obey'd of none. 4.04.104
o, she that might have intercepted thee, | by 4.04.137
and must she die for this? 4.04.206
so she may live unscarr'd of bleeding slaughter, 4.04.210
i will confess she was not edward's daughter. 4.04.211
wrong not her birth, she is a royal princess. 4.04.212
to save her life, i'll say she is not so. 4.04.213
then haply will she weep. 4.04.273
nay then indeed she cannot choose but hate thee, 4.04.289
and she shall be sole victoress, caesar's caesar 4.04.336
which she shall purchase with still-lasting war. 4.04.344
say she shall be a high and mighty queen. 4.04.347
but she, your subject, loathes such sovereignty. 4.04.356
"when he," quoth she, "shall split thy heart 5.01. 26
that she may long live here, god say amen! 5.05. 41
by heaven, she is a dainty one. H8 1.04. 94
cruel | that she should feel the smart of this? 2.01.166
will have his will, and she must fall. 2.01.167
ay, and the best she shall have; 2.02.113
and she | so good a lady that no tongue could 2.03. 2
she never knew harm-doing — o, now after | so 2.03. 5
will, much better | she ne'er had known pomp! 2.03. 13
that would not be a queen, that would she not, 2.03. 91
and like her true nobility she has | carried 2.04.143
back her appeal | she intends unto his holiness. 2.04.236
believe me, she has had much wrong. 3.01. 48
and to that woman (when she has done most) | yet 3.01.136
she now begs | that little thought, when she set 3.01.182
that little thought, when she set footing here, 3.01.183
she should have bought her dignities so dear. 3.01.184
she is a gallant creature, and complete | in 3.02. 49
cause, that she should lie i' th' bosom of | our 3.02.100
to which | she was often cited by them, but 4.01. 29
of all these learned men she was divorc'd, | and 4.01. 32
since which she was remov'd to kimmalton, 4.01. 34
to kimmalton, | where she remains now sick. 4.01. 35
sir, as i have a soul, she is an angel; 4.01. 44
it, she that carries up the train | is that old 4.01. 51
she is the goodliest woman | that ever lay by 4.01. 69
paces | came to the altar, where she kneel'd, 4.01. 83
she had all the royal makings of a queen, | as 4.01. 87
so she parted, | and with the same full state 4.01. 92
she is asleep. 4.02. 81
how pale she looks, | and of an earthy cold! 4.02. 97
she is going, wench. pray, pray. 4.02. 99
knowing she will not lose her wonted greatness, 4.02.102
she is young, and of a noble modest nature, | i 4.02.135
i hope she will deserve well — and a little 4.02.136
the fruit she goes with | i pray for heartily, 5.01. 20
her two hands, and she | sleep in their graves. 5.01. 31
what, is she crying out? 5.01. 67
he or she, cuckold or cuckold-maker, | let me 5.03. 25
the hope o' th' strond, where she was quarter'd. 5.03. 53 P
shall this lady, | when she has so much english. 5.04. 14
she shall be | (but few now living can behold 5.04. 20
she shall be lov'd and fear'd: 5.04. 30
so shall she leave her blessedness to one 5.04. 43
star-like rise as great in fame as she was, 5.04. 46
she shall be, to the happiness of england, | an 5.04. 56
but she must die, | she must, the saints must 5.04. 59

must die, | she must, the saints must have her; 5.04. 60
a most unspotted lily shall she pass | to th' 5.04. 61
must all see the queen, and she must thank ye, 5.04. 73
and she must thank ye, | she will be sick else. 5.04. 74
patience herself, what goddess e'er she be, TRO 1.01. 27
so, traitor, then she comes when she is thence. 1.01. 31
so, traitor, then she comes when she is thence. 1.01. 31
she look'd yesternight fairer than ever i saw 1.01. 32 P
but, for my part, she is my kinswoman; 1.01. 43 P
thou answer'st she is fair, | pourest in the 1.01. 52
i'll not meddle in it, let her be as she is; 1.01. 66 P
if she be fair, 'tis better for her; 1.01. 67 P
and she be not, she has the mends in her own 1.01. 67 P
she be not, she has the mends in her own hands. 1.01. 68 P
and she were /not kin to me, she would be as 1.01. 75 P
she would be as fair a' friday as helen is on 1.01. 75 P
i care not and she were a blackamoor, 'tis all 1.01. 77 P
say i she is not fair? 1.01. 79
as she is stubborn–chaste against all suit. 1.01. 97
her bed is india, there she lies, a pearl; 1.01.100
between our ilium and where she /resides, | let 1.01.101
helen was not up, was she? 1.02. 49 P
she prais'd his complexion above paris. 1.02. 98 P
if she prais'd him above, his complexion is 1.02.101 P
nay, i am sure she does. 1.02.110 P
she came to him th' other day into the compass'd 1.02.110 P
she came and puts me her white hand to his 1.02.118 P
but laugh to think how she tickled his chin. 1.02.135 P
indeed she has a marvell's white hand, i must 1.02.136 P
and she takes upon her to spy a white hair on 1.02.139 P
quoth she, "here's but two and fifty hairs on 1.02.157 P
"jupiter," quoth she, "which of these hairs is 1.02.163 P
that she belov'd knows nought that knows not 1.02.288
that she was never yet that ever knew | love got 1.02.290
modest as morning when she coldly eyes | the 1.03.229
she is not worth what she doth cost | the 2.02. 51
she is not worth what she doth cost | the 2.02. 51
is she worth keeping? 2.02. 81
why, she is a pearl, | whose price hath launch'd 2.02. 81
as it is known she is, these moral laws | of 2.02.184
hector, | she is a theme of honor and renown, 2.02.199
then if she that lays thee out says thou art a 2.03. 31 P
be sworn and sworn upon't she never shrouded any 2.03. 33 P
him that gat thee, she that gave thee suck; 2.03.241
she shall have it, my lord, if it be not my lord 3.01. 99 P
she does so blush, and fetches her wind so short 3.02. 31 P
so short, as if she were fray'd with a spirit. 3.02. 32 P
she fetches her breath as short as a new–ta'en 3.02. 33 P
here she is now, swear the oaths now to her that 3.02. 41 P
too, if she call your activity in question. 3.02. 56 P
since she could speak, | she hath not given so 4.01. 73
she hath not given so many good words breath 4.01. 74
with venomous wights she stays | as tediously as 4.02. 12
crown of falsehood, | if ever she leave troilus! 4.02.101
troilus, | tell you the lady what she is to do, 4.03. 4
bid them have patience, she shall come anon. 4.04. 52
hand, | and by the way possess thee what she is. 4.04.112
she is as far high–soaring o'er thy praises | as 4.04.124
to her own worth | she shall be priz'd; 4.04.134
even she. 4.05. 17
'twere better she were kiss'd in general. 4.05. 21
had she no lover there | that wails her absence? 4.05.288
she was belov'd, /she /lov'd; 4.05.292
she is, and doth: 4.05.292
she comes to you. 5.02. 4
she will sing any man at first sight. 5.02. 9
what shall she remember? 5.02. 16
she strokes his cheek! 5.02. 51
now she sharpens. well said, whetstone! 5.02. 75 P
a proof of strength she could not publish more, 5.02.113
unless she said, "my mind is now turn'd whore." 5.02.114
she was not, sure. 5.02.126
most sure she was. 5.02.126
what hath she done, prince, that can /soil our 5.02.134
nothing at all, unless that this were she. 5.02.135
this she? 5.02.137
if beauty have a soul, this is not she; 5.02.138
be rule in unity itself, | this was not she. 5.02.142
what says she there? 5.03.107 P
my love with words and errors still she feeds, 5.03.111
when she did suckle hector, look'd not lovelier COR 1.03. 41
she shall, she shall. 1.03. 73 P
she shall, she shall. 1.03. 73 P
all the yarn she spun in ulysses' absence did 1.03. 83 P
as she is now, she will but disease our better 1.03.104 P
is now, she will but disease our better mirth. 1.03.104 P
in troth, i think she would. 1.03.106 P
friend no less | than those she placeth highest! 1.05. 24
her blood, | when she does praise me grieves me. 1.09. 15
and the moon, were she earthly, no nobler — 2.01. 98 P
rapture lets her baby cry | while she chats him; 2.01.208
even as she speaks, why, their hearts were yours 3.02. 87
when she, poor hen, fond of no second brood, 5.03.162
from whence at first she weigh'd her anchorage, TIT 1.01. 73
goths, | she will a handmaid be to his desires, 1.01.331
is she not then beholding to the man | that 1.01.396
i care not, i, knew she and all the world, | i 2.01. 71
she is a woman, therefore may be woo'd, | she is 2.01. 82
she is a woman, therefore may be won, | she is 2.01. 83
won, | she is lavinia, therefore must be lov'd. 2.01. 84
and she shall file our engines with advice, 2.01.123
even as an adder when she doth unroll | to do 2.03. 35
and shall she carry this unto her grave? 2.03.127
and if she do, i would i were an eunuch. 2.03.128
o, do not learn her wrath — she taught it thee; 2.03.143
see how with signs and tokens she can scrowl. 2.04. 5
she hath no tongue to call, nor hands to wash, 2.04. 7
fair philomela, why, she but lost her tongue, 2.04. 38
why, marcus, so she is. 3.01. 63
perchance she weeps because they kill'd her 3.01.114
perchance because she knows them innocent. 3.01.115
had she a tongue to speak, now would she say 3.01.144
now would she say | that to her brother which i 3.01.144
she is the weeping welkin, i the earth: 3.01.226
good uncle marcus, see how swift she comes. 4.01. 3
she loves thee, boy, too well to do thee harm. 4.01. 6
ay, when my father was in rome she did. 4.01. 7
fear her not, lucius, somewhat doth she mean. 4.01. 9
see, lucius, see, how much she makes of thee; 4.01. 10
somewhither would she have thee go with her. 4.01. 11
read to her sons than she hath read to thee 4.01. 13
thou not guess wherefore she plies thee thus? 4.01. 15
some book there is that she desires to see. 4.01. 31
why lifts she up her arms in sequence thus? 4.01. 37
i think she means that there were more than one 4.01. 38
or else to heaven she heaves them for revenge. 4.01. 40
lucius, what book is that she tosseth so? 4.01. 41
perhaps, she cull'd it from among the rest. 4.01. 44
soft, so busily she turns the leaves! 4.01. 45
what would she find? 4.01. 46
brother, see, note how she cotes the leaves. 4.01. 50
o, do ye read, my lord, what she hath writ? 4.01. 77
the dam will wake and if she wind ye once; 4.01. 97
and lulls him whilst she playeth on her back, 4.01. 99
and when he sleeps will she do what she list. 4.01.100
and when he sleeps will she do what she list. 4.01.100
afoot, | she would applaud andronicus' conceit, 4.02. 30
and that would she for twenty thousand more. 4.02. 45
she is delivered, lords, she is delivered. 4.02. 61
she is delivered, lords, she is delivered. 4.02. 61
i mean she is brought a–bed. 4.02. 62
why, then she is the devil's dam: 4.02. 65
although she lave them hourly in the flood. 4.02.103
age | to keep mine own, excuse it how she can. 4.02.105
shall she live to betray this guilt of ours, | a 4.02.149
marry, for justice, she is so employ'd, | he 4.03. 40
she laugh'd, and told the moor he should not 4.03. 75
why, she was wash'd, and cut, and trimm'd, and 5.01. 95
sport, | she sounded almost at my pleasing tale, 5.01.119
she is thy enemy, and i thy friend. 5.02. 29
for up and down she doth resemble thee. 5.02.107
to, | and this the banket she shall surfeit on, 5.02.193
hand, | because she was enforc'd, stain'd, and 5.03. 38
what, was she ravish'd? tell who did the deed. 5.03. 53
eating the flesh that she herself hath bred. 5.03. 62
and she whom mighty kingdoms cur'sy to, | like a 5.03. 74
hit | with cupid's arrow, she hath dian's wit; ROM 1.01.209
love's weak childish bow she lives uncharm'd. 1.01.211
she will not stay the siege of loving terms, 1.01.212
o, she is rich in beauty, only poor | that, when 1.01.215
only poor | that, when she dies, with beauty 1.01.216
then she hath sworn that she will still live 1.01.217
she hath sworn that she will still live chaste? 1.01.217
she hath, and in that sparing /makes huge waste; 1.01.218
she is too fair, too wise, wisely too fair, | to 1.01.221
she hath forsworn to love, and in that vow | do 1.01.223
she hath not seen the change of fourteen years; 1.02. 9
younger than she are happy mothers made. 1.02. 12
earth hath swallowed all my hopes but she; 1.02. 14
and, she agreed, within her scope of choice 1.02. 18
and she shall scant show well that now seems 1.02. 99
come lammas–eve at night shall she be fourteen. 1.03. 17
susan and she — god rest all christian souls! 1.03. 18
susan is with god, | she was too good for me. 1.03. 20
on lammas–eve at night shall she be fourteen, 1.03. 21
that shall she, marry, i remember it well. 1.03. 22
and she was wean'd — i never shall forget it — 1.03. 24
years, | for then she could stand high–lone; 1.03. 36
she could have run and waddled all about; 1.03. 37
for even the day before, she broke her brow, 1.03. 38
she is the fairies' midwife, and she comes | in 1.04. 54
and she comes | in shape no bigger than an 1.04. 54
and in this state she gallops night by night 1.04. 70
sometime she gallops o'er a courtier's nose, 1.04. 77
and sometime comes she with a tithe–pig's tail 1.04. 79
sometime she driveth o'er a soldier's neck, 1.04. 82
this is she — 1.04. 95
she that makes dainty, | she i'll swear hath 1.05. 19
that makes dainty, | she i'll swear hath corns. 1.05. 20
o, she doth teach the torches to burn bright! 1.05. 44
it seems she hangs upon the cheek of night | as 1.05. 45
is she a capulet? 1.05.117
and she steal love's sweet bait from fearful 2.pr. 8
and she as much in love, her means much less 2.pr. 11
till she had laid it and conjur'd it down. 2.01. 26
o, romeo, that she were, o that she were | an 2.01. 37
that she were, o that she were | an open/–arse, 2.01. 37
that thou, her maid, art far more fair than she. 2.02. 6
be not her maid, since she is envious; 2.02. 7
o that she knew she were! 2.02. 11
o that she knew she were! 2.02. 11
she speaks, yet she says nothing; 2.02. 12
she speaks, yet she says nothing; 2.02. 12
i am too bold, 'tis not to me she speaks. 2.02. 14
see how she leans her cheek upon her hand! 2.02. 23
she speaks! 2.02. 25
she knew well | thy love did read by rote that 2.03. 87
(marry, she had a better love to berhyme her), 2.04. 40 P
she will indite him to some supper. 2.04.129 P
what she bid me say, i will keep to myself. 2.04.164 P
lord, lord, she will be a joyful woman. 2.04.174 P
and there she shall at friar lawrence' cell | be 2.04.181
this afternoon, sir? well, she shall be there. 2.04.185 P
but she, good soul, had as lieve see a toad, a 2.04.202 P
so, she looks as pale as any clout in the versal 2.04.205 P
and she hath the prettiest sententious of it, of 2.04.211 P
in half an hour she promised to return. 2.05. 2
perchance she cannot meet him — that's not so. 2.05. 3
o, she is lame! 2.05. 4
is /three long hours, yet she is not come. 2.05. 11
had she affections and warm youthful blood, 2.05. 12
she would be as swift in motion as a ball; 2.05. 13
o god, she comes! 2.05. 18
why, she is within, | where should she be? 2.05. 58
why, she is within, | where should she be? 2.05. 59
o, here comes my nurse, | and she brings news; 3.02. 32
why followed not, when she said, "tybalt's dead, 3.02.118
even so lies she, | blubb'ring and weeping, 3.03. 86
doth not she think me an old murtherer, | now i 3.03. 94
where is she? 3.03. 97
and how doth she? 3.03. 97
o, she says nothing, sir, but weeps and weeps, 3.03. 99
here, sir, a ring she bid me give you, sir. 3.03.163
look you, she lov'd her kinsman tybalt dearly, 3.04. 3
i think she will /be rul'd | in all respects by 3.04. 13
her, | she shall be married to this noble earl. 3.04. 21
nightly she sings on yond pomegranate tree. 3.05. 4
this doth not so, for she divideth us. 3.05. 30
is she not down so late, or up so early? 3.05. 66
sir, but she will none, she /gives you thanks. 3.05.139
sir, but she will none, she /gives you thanks. 3.05.139
how, will she none? 3.05.142
doth she not give us thanks? 3.05.142
is she not proud? 3.05.143
doth she not count her blest, | unworthy as she 3.05.143
unworthy as she is, that we have wrought | so 3.05.144
which she hath prais'd him with above compare 3.05.238
immoderately she weeps for tybalt's death, | and 4.01. 6
that she do give her sorrow so much sway; 4.01. 10
see where she comes from shrift with merry look. 4.02. 15
what should she do here? 4.03. 18
fast, i warrant her, she. 4.05. 1
how sound is she asleep! 4.05. 8
there she lies, | flower as she was, deflowered 4.05. 36
lies, | flower as she was, deflowered by him. 4.05. 37
for 'twas your heaven she should be advanc'd, 4.05. 72
now, seeing she is advanc'd | above the clouds, 4.05. 73
ill | that you run mad, seeing that she is well. 4.05. 76
again, | for nothing can be ill if she be well. 5.01. 16
then she is well and nothing can be ill: 5.01. 17
she will beshrew me much that romeo | hath had 5.02. 26
and she, there dead, /that romeo's faithful wife 5.03.232
then comes she to me, | and with wild looks bid 5.03.239
or in my cell there would she kill herself. 5.03.242
she wakes, and i entreated her come forth | and 5.03.260
and she, too desperate, would not go with me, 5.03.263
does she love him? TIM 1.01.131
she is young and apt. 1.01.132
ay, my good lord, and she accepts of it. 1.01.135
how shall she be endowed, | if she be mated with 1.01.139
if she be mated with an equal husband? 1.01.140
lord, | pawn me to this your honor, she is his. 1.01.147
what's she, if i be a dog? 1.01.202
she, whom the spittle–house and ulcerous sores 4.03. 40
and her pale fire she snatches from the sun; 4.03.438
she dreamt to–night she saw my statue, | which, JC 2.02. 76
she dreamt to–night she saw my statue, | which, 2.02. 76
and these does she apply for warnings and 2.02. 80
she is dead. 4.03.149
with this she fell distract, | and, her 4.03.155
for certain she is dead, and by strange manner. 4.03.189
with meditating that she must die once, | i have 4.03.191
and she goes down at twelve. MAC 2.01. 3
my drink is ready, | she strike upon the bell. 2.01. 32
than on her feet, | died every day she liv'd. 4.03.111
when was it she last walk'd? 5.01. 2
lo you, here she comes! 5.01. 19
how came she by that light? 5.01. 21
she has light by her continually, 'tis her 5.01. 22
what is it she does now? 5.01. 26
look how she rubs her hands. 5.01. 26
hark, she speaks. 5.01. 32
where is she now? 5.01. 43
she has spoke what she should not, i am sure of 5.01. 48
she has spoke what she should not, i am sure of 5.01. 48
heaven knows what she has known. 5.01. 49
will she go now to bed? 5.01. 69
more needs she the divine than the physician. 5.01. 74
my mind she has mated, and amaz'd my sight. 5.01. 78
as she is troubled with thick–coming fancies, 5.03. 38
she should have died hereafter; 5.05. 17
why, she should hang on him | as if increase of HAM 1.02.143
with which she followed my poor father's body, 1.02.148
like niobe, all tears — why, she, /even /she — 1.02.149
the flushing in her galled eyes, | she married. 1.02.156
enough | if she unmask her beauty to the moon. 1.03. 37
i have a daughter — have while she is mine — 2.02.106
but how hath she | receiv'd his love? 2.02.128
that she should lock herself from /his resort, 2.02.143
which done, she took the fruits of my advice; 2.02.145
o, most true, she is a strumpet. 2.02.236
when she saw pyrrhus make malicious sport | in 2.02.513
the instant burst of clamor that she made, 2.02.515
if she find him not, | to england send him, or 3.01.185
finger | to sound what stop she please. 3.02. 71
if she should break it now! 3.02.224
then thus she says: 3.02.326
she desires to speak with you in her closet ere 3.02.331
we shall obey, were she ten times our mother. 3.02.333
how in my words somever she be shent, | to give 3.02.398
she is importunate, indeed distract. 4.05. 2
what would she have? 4.05. 3
she speaks much of her father, says she hears 4.05. 4
says she hears | there's tricks i' th' world, 4.05. 4
'twere good she were spoken with, for she may 4.05. 14
for she may strew | dangerous conjectures in 4.05. 14
"quoth she, 'before you tumbled me, | you 4.05. 62
how long hath she been thus? 4.05. 67
itself, | she turns to favor and to prettiness. 4.05.189
she is so /conjunctive to my life and soul, 4.07. 14
therewith fantastic garlands did she make | of 4.07.168
which time she chaunted snatches of old lauds, 4.07.177
alas, then she is drown'd? 4.07.183
is she to be buried in christian burial when she 5.01. 1
in christian burial when she willfully seeks her 5.01. 2
i tell thee she is, therefore make her grave 5.01. 3
unless she drown'd herself in her own defense? 5.01. 6
/argal, she drown'd herself wittingly. 5.01. 12
she should have been buried out a' christian 5.01. 24
an inch thick, to this favor she must come. 5.01.194
she should in ground unsanctified been lodg'd 5.01.229
yet here she is allow'd her virgin crants, | her 5.01.232
she well instructs me. 5.02.208
she sounds to see them bleed. 5.02.308
whereupon she grew round–womb'd, and had indeed, LR 1.01. 14
son for her cradle ere she had a husband for her 1.01. 15
heart | i find she names my very deed of love; 1.01. 71
only she comes too short, that i profess 1.01. 72
let pride, which she calls plainness, marry her. 1.01.129
when she was dear to us, we did hold her so, 1.01.196
sir, there she stands: 1.01.197
your grace, | she's there, and she is yours. 1.01.201
will you, with those infirmities she owes, 1.01.202

at she, whom even but now was your /best 1.01.214
e is herself a dowry. 1.01.241
her, that else will take the thing she begs, 1.04.248
she must teem, | create her child of spleen, 1.04.281
at she may feel | how sharper than a serpent's 1.04.287
hen she shall hear this of thee, with her nails 1.04.307
she sustain him and his hundred knights, 1.04.332
e will taste as like this as a crab does to a 1.05. 18 P
e that's a maid now, and laughs at my 1.05. 51
is both he and she, | your son and daughter. 2.04. 13
d to the eels when she put 'em i' th' paste 2.04.123 P
e knapp'd 'em o' th' coxcombs with a stick, 2.04.123 P
gan, she hath tied | sharp–tooth'd unkindness, 2.04.134
lue her desert | than she to scant her duty. 2.04.140
e have restrain'd the riots of your followers, 2.04.143
e hath abated me of half my train; 2.04.159
er letter, | that she would soon be here. 2.04.184
d, and so — | but she knows what she does. 2.04.236
d, and so — | but she knows what she does. 2.04.236
om those that she calls servants or from mine? 2.04.244
d she will tell you who that fellow is | that 3.01. 48
t fair woman but she made mouths in a glass. 3.02. 35 P
hy should she write to edmund? 4.05. 19
e gave strange eliads and most speaking looks 4.05. 25
ar /me not. | she and the duke her husband! 5.01. 17
s she is sub–contracted to this lord, | and i 5.03. 86
e is not well, convey her to my tent. 5.03.106
e confesses it. 5.03.228
on her own despair, | that she fordid herself. 5.03.256
ist or stain the stone, | why then she lives. 5.03.264
is feather stirs, she lives! 5.03.266
fortune brag of two she lov'd and hated, 5.03.281
she be in her chamber or your house, | let OTH 1.01.138
ne she is; 1.01.160
w didst thou know 'twas she? 1.01.165
she deceives me | past thought! 1.01.165
hat said she to you? 1.01.166
w got she out? 1.01.169
she in chains of magic were not bound, 1.02. 65
opposite to marriage that she shunn'd | the 1.02. 67
e is abus'd, stol'n from me, and corrupted 1.03. 60
d she, in spite of nature, | of years, of 1.03. 96
fall in love with what she fear'd to look on! 1.03. 98
d, /till she come, as truly as to heaven | i 1.03.122
this fair lady's love, | and she in mine. 1.03.126
ich ever as she could with haste dispatch, 1.03.148
hereof by parcels she had something heard, 1.03.154
e gave me for my pains a world of /sighs; 1.03.159
e swore, in faith 'twas strange, 'twas passing 1.03.160
e wish'd she had not heard it, yet she wish'd 1.03.162
e wish'd she had not heard it, yet she wish'd 1.03.162
t she wish'd | that heaven had made her such a 1.03.162
e thank'd me, | and bade me, if i had a friend 1.03.163
e lov'd me for the dangers i had pass'd, | and 1.03.167
d i lov'd her that she did pity them. 1.03.168
she confess that she was half the wooer, 1.03.176
she confess that she was half the wooer, 1.03.176
d great business scant | /for she is with me. 1.03.268
e has deceiv'd her father, and may thee. 1.03.293
e must change for youth; 1.03.349 P
en she is sated with his body, she will find 1.03.350 P
dy, she will find the /error of her choice. 1.03.350 P
at is she? 2.01. 73
e that i spake of, our great captain's captain 2.01. 74
uld she give you so much of her lips | as of 2.01.100
s | as of her tongue she oft bestows on me, 2.01.101
as! she has no speech. 2.01.102
e puts her tongue a little in her heart, | and 2.01.106
t my muse labors, | and thus she is deliver'd: 2.01.128
she be fair and wise, fairness and wit, | the 2.01.129
ell prais'd! how if she be black and witty? 2.01.131
she be black, and thereto have a wit, 2.01.132
e never yet was foolish that was fair, | for 2.01.136
e that was ever fair, and never proud, | had 2.01.148
e that being ang'red, her revenge being nigh, 2.01.152
e that in wisdom never was so frail | to 2.01.154
e that could think, and nev'r disclose her 2.01.156
e was a wight (if ever such /wight were) — 2.01.158
e with what violence she first lov'd the moor, 2.01.222 P
d what delight shall she have to look on the 2.01.226 P
e wine she drinks is made of grapes. 2.01.251 P
she had been bless'd, she would never have 2.01.252 P
ess'd, she would never have lov'd the moor. 2.01.252 P
at she loves him, 'tis apt and of great credit 2.01.287
d she is sport for jove. 2.03. 17 P
at an eye she has! 2.03. 22 P
d when she speaks, is it not an alarum to love 2.03. 26 P
e is indeed perfection. 2.03. 28 P
e is of so free, so kind, so apt, so bless'd a 2.03.319 P
e holds it a vice in her goodness not to do 2.03.321 P
odness not to do more than she is requested. 2.03.322 P
at she may make, unmake, do what she list, 2.03.346
at she may make, unmake, do what she list, 2.03.346
d she for him pleads strongly to the moor, 2.03.355
at she repeals him for her body's lust, | and 2.03.357
d by how much she strives to do him good, 2.03.358
od, | she shall undo her credit with the moor. 2.03.359
e is stirring, sir. 3.01. 28 P
she will stir hither, i shall seem to notify 3.01. 28 P
her | is that she will to virtuous desdemona 3.01. 35
king of it, | and she speaks for you stoutly. 3.01. 44
her revolt, | for she had eyes, and chose me. 3.03.189
e did deceive her father, marrying you, | and 3.03.206
d when she seem'd to shake and fear your looks 3.03.207
d fear your looks, | she lov'd them most. 3.03.208
d so she did. 3.03.208
e that so young could give out such a seeming 3.03.209
ng live she so! and long live you to think so! 3.03.226
ok where she comes: 3.03.277
she be false, /o, /then heaven /mocks itself! 3.03.278
t she so loves the token | (for he conjur'd 3.03.293
r he conjur'd her she should ever keep it) 3.03.294
at she reserves it evermore about her | to 3.03.295
e let it drop by negligence, | and, to th' 3.03.311
dy, she'll run mad | when she shall lack it. 3.03.318
hink my wife be honest, and think she is not; 3.03.384
e may be honest yet. 3.03.433
e was a charmer, and could almost read | the 3.04. 57

she told her, while she kept it, | 'twould make 3.04. 58
she told her, while she kept it, | 'twould make 3.04. 58
but if she lost it, | or made a gift of it, my 3.04. 60
she, dying, gave it me, | and bid me, when my 3.04. 63
'tis she must do't; 3.04.107
hers, | she may, i think, bestow't on any man. 4.01. 13
she is protectress of her honor too; 4.01. 14
may she give that? 4.01. 15
and knowing what i am, i know what she shall be. 4.01. 73
poor rogue, i think, /i' /faith, she loves me. 4.01.111
she gives it out that you shall marry her. 4.01.115
she is persuaded i will marry her, out of her 4.01.127 P
she was here even now; 4.01.132 P
she haunts me in every place. 4.01.132 P
now he tells how she pluck'd him to my chamber. 4.01.141 P
before me! look where she comes. 4.01.145 P
she gave it him, and he hath giv'n it his whore. 4.01.176 P
and be damn'd to–night, for she shall not live. 4.01.182 P
she might lie by an emperor's side and command 4.01.184 P
hang her, i do but say what she is. 4.01.187 P
o, she will sing the savageness out of a bear. 4.01.188 P
in her bed, even the bed she hath contaminated. 4.01.208 P
she weeps. 4.01.244
each drop she falls would prove a crocodile. 4.01.246
sir, she can turn, and turn; 4.01.253
and she can weep, sir, weep; 4.01.254
yes, you have seen cassio and she together. 4.02. 3
i durst, my lord, to wager she is honest; 4.02. 12
for, if she be not honest, chaste, and true, 4.02. 17
she says enough; 4.02. 20
such as she said my lord did say i was. 4.02.119
hath she forsook so many noble matches? 4.02.125
you have told me she hath receiv'd them and 4.02.188 P
if she will return me my jewels, i will give 4.02.197 P
she was in love, and he she lov'd prov'd mad, 4.03. 27
she was in love, and he she lov'd prov'd mad, 4.03. 27
she had a song of "willow," | an old thing 'twas 4.03. 28
her fortune, | and she died singing it. 4.03. 30
yet she must die, else she'll betray more men. 5.02. 6
she wakes. 5.02. 22
'tis like she comes to speak of cassio's death; 5.02. 92
shall she come in? 5.02. 94
i think she stirs again. 5.02. 95
if she come in, she'll sure speak to my wife. 5.02. 96
she comes more nearer earth than she was wont, 5.02.110
she comes more nearer earth than she was wont, 5.02.110
why, how should she be murd'red? 5.02.126
she said so; i must needs report the truth. 5.02.128
o, the more angel she, | and you the blacker 5.02.130
she turn'd to folly, and she was a whore. 5.02.132
she turn'd to folly, and she was a whore. 5.02.132
she was false as water. 5.02.134
art rash as fire to say | that she was false. 5.02.135
o, she was heavenly true! 5.02.135
that she was false to wedlock? 5.02.142
/nay, had she been true, | if heaven would make 5.02.143
my husband say she was false? 5.02.152
she was too fond of her most filthy bargain. 5.02.157
but did you ever tell him she was false? 5.02.178
she false with cassio? 5.02.182
o, she was foul! 5.02.200
that she with cassio hath the act of shame | a 5.02.211
and she did gratify his amorous works | with 5.02.213
she give it cassio? 5.02.230
moor, she was chaste; 5.02.249
she lov'd thee, cruel moor; 5.02.249
am i not an inch of fortune better than she? ANT 1.02. 58 P
name cleopatra as she is call'd in rome. 1.02.106
where died she? 1.02.118
act upon her, she hath such a celerity in dying. 1.02.144 P
she is cunning past man's thought. 1.02.145
be, she makes a show'r of rain as well as jove. 1.02.150 P
the business she hath broached in the state 1.02.171
would she had never given you leave to come! 1.03. 21
leisure read | the garboils she awak'd: 1.03. 61
the last, best, | see when and where she died. 1.03. 62
when she first met mark antony, she purs'd up 2.02.186 P
she purs'd up his heart upon the river of cydnus 2.02.186 P
there she appear'd indeed; 2.02.188 P
the barge she sat in, like a burnish'd throne, 2.02.191
she did lie | in her pavilion — cloth of gold, 2.02.198
she replied, | it should be better he became her 2.02.220
which she entreated. 2.02.222
she made great caesar lay his sword to bed; 2.02.227
he ploughed her, and she cropp'd. 2.02.228
and having lost her breath, she spoke, and 2.02.230
panted, | that she did make defect perfection, 2.02.231
but she makes hungry | where most she satisfies; 2.02.236
but she makes hungry | where most she satisfies; 2.02.237
holy priests | bless her when she is riggish. 2.02.239
bid you alexas | bring me word how tall she is. 2.05.118
my face, | but in my bosom shall she never come, 2.06. 55
true, sir, she was the wife of caius marcellus. 2.06.110 P
but she is now the wife of marcus antonius. 2.06.112 P
is she as tall as me? 3.03. 11
she is not, madam. 3.03. 11
is she shrill–tongu'd or low? 3.03. 12
madam, i heard her speak; she is low–voic'd. 3.03. 13
she creeps; 3.03. 18
she shows a body rather than a life, | a statue, 3.03. 20
madam, | she was a widow — 3.03. 27
and her forehead | as low as she would wish it. 3.03. 34
she | in th' abiliments of the goddess isis 3.06. 16
tell of her approach, | long ere she did appear; 3.06. 46
she once being loof'd, | the noble ruin of her 3.10. 17
we scorn her most when most she offers blows. 3.11. 74
so she | from egypt drive her all–disgraced 3.12. 21
this if she perform, | she shall not sue unheard 3.12. 23
if she perform, | she shall not sue unheard. 3.12. 24
promise, | and in our name, what she requires; 3.12. 28
then have courtesy, so she | will yield us up. 3.13. 15
them | so saucy with the hand of she here — 3.13. 98
what's her name, | since she was cleopatra? 3.13. 99
to the young roman boy she hath sold me, and i 4.12. 48
she dies for't. 4.12. 49
whose heart i thought i had, for she had mine — 4.14. 16
(now lost) — she, eros, has | pack'd cards with 4.14. 18
she has robb'd me of my sword. 4.14. 23

she hath betray'd me, and shall die the death. 4.14. 26
be paid but once, | and that she has discharg'd. 4.14. 28
the last she spake | was "antony, most noble 4.14. 29
she rend'red life, | thy name so buried in her. 4.14. 33
than she which by her death our caesar tells, 4.14. 61
when did she send thee? 4.14.119
where is she? 4.14.119
she had a prophesying fear | of what hath come 4.14.120
for when she saw | (which never shall be found) 4.14.121
you did suspect | she had dispos'd with caesar, 4.14.123
not be purg'd, she sent you word she was dead; 4.14.124
not be purg'd, she sent you word she was dead; 4.14.124
confin'd in all she has, her monument, | of thy 5.01. 53
that she preparedly may frame herself | to th' 5.01. 55
she soon shall know of us, by some of ours, 5.01. 57
by some mortal stroke | she do defeat us; 5.01. 65
and with your speediest bring us what she says, 5.01. 67
you see how easily she may be surpris'd. 5.02. 35
of honesty — how she died of the biting of it, 5.02.253 P
died of the biting of it, what pain she felt. 5.02.254 P
truly, she makes a very good report o' th' worm; 5.02.254 P
if she first meet the curled antony, | he'll 5.02.301
she levell'd at our purposes, and, being royal, 5.02.336
charmian liv'd but now, she stood and spake. 5.02.341
tremblingly she stood, | and on the sudden 5.02.343
but she looks like sleep, | as she would catch 5.02.346
as she would catch another antony | in her 5.02.347
most probable | that so she died; 5.02.354
tells me | she hath pursu'd conclusions infinite 5.02.355
she shall be buried by her antony; 5.02.358
wedded, | her husband banish'd, she imprison'd: CYM 1.01. 8
her own price | proclaims how she esteem'd him; 1.01. 52
you tell me, | is she sole child to th' king? 1.01. 56
fine this tyrant | can tickle where she wounds! 1.01. 85
and that she should love this fellow, and refuse 1.02. 25 P
be a sin to make a true election, she is damn'd. 1.02. 28 P
she shines not upon fools, lest the reflection 1.02. 32 P
she holds her virtue still, and i my mind. 1.04. 64 P
if she went before others i have seen, as that 1.04. 72 P
i could not /but believe she excell'd many. 1.04. 74 P
such honor as you have trust in, she your jewel, 1.04.153 P
she is not worth our debate. 1.04.160 P
if she remain unseduc'd, you not making it 1.04.160 P
she doth think she has | strange ling'ring 1.05. 33
she doth think she has | strange ling'ring 1.05. 33
those she has | will stupefy and dull the sense 1.05. 36
she is fool'd | with a most false effect; 1.05. 42
weeps she still, say'st thou? 1.05. 46
dost thou think in time | she will not quench, 1.05. 47
when thou shalt bring me word she loves my son, 1.05. 49
and which she after, | except she bend her humor 1.05. 80
except she bend her humor, shall be assur'd | to 1.05. 81
if she be furnish'd with a mind so rare, | she 1.06. 16
she is alone th' arabian bird, and i | have lost 1.06. 17
yea, what she cannot choose | but must be, will 1.06. 71
or she that bore you was no queen, and you 1.06.127
she hath been reading late | the tale of tereus; 2.02. 44
will she not forth? 2.03. 38
her with musics, but she vouchsafes no notice. 2.03. 39 P
is too new, | she hath not yet forgot him. 2.03. 42
if she be up, i'll speak with her; 2.03. 64
your lady's person. is she ready? 2.03. 81
story | proud cleopatra, when she met her roman, 2.04. 70
she stripp'd it from her arm. 2.04.101
she gave it me, and said | she priz'd it once. 2.04.103
she gave it me, and said | she priz'd it once. 2.04.104
may be she pluck'd it off | to send it me. 2.04.104
she writes so to you? doth she? 2.04.105
she writes so to you? doth she? 2.04.105
it may be probable she lost it; 2.04.115
i am sure | she would not lose it. 2.04.124
she hath bought the name of whore thus dearly. 2.04.128
never talk on't: | she hath been colted by him. 2.04.133
me of my lawful pleasure she restrain'd, | and 2.05. 9
but what he look'd for should oppose and she 2.05. 18
lo here she comes. 3.02. 22
she hath my letter for the purpose; 3.04. 29 P
she hath not appear'd | before the roman, nor to 3.05. 30
she /looks us like | a thing more made of malice 3.05. 32
where is she, sir? 3.05. 41
she pray'd me to excuse her keeping close, 3.05. 46
she should that duty leave unpaid to you | which 3.05. 48
to you | which daily she was bound to proffer. 3.05. 49
this | she wish'd me to make known; 3.05. 50
but for her, | where is she gone? 3.05. 60
gone she is | to death or to dishonor, and my 3.05. 62
she being down, | i have the placing of the 3.05. 64
'tis certain she is fled. 3.05. 66
and that she hath all courtly parts more 3.05. 71
from every one | the best she hath, and she, of 3.05. 73
from every one | the best she hath, and she, of 3.05. 73
is she with posthumus? 3.05. 87
alas, my lord, | how can she be with him? 3.05. 90
when was she miss'd? 3.05. 90
where is she, sir? 3.05. 91
she said upon a time (the bitterness of it i now 3.05.133 P
that she held the very garment of posthumus in 3.05.134 P
there shall she see my valor, which will then be 3.05.139 P
will execute in the clothes that she so prais'd) 3.05.143 P
she hath despis'd me rejoicingly, and i'll be 3.05.144 P
how long is't since she went to milford–haven? 3.05.148 P
she can scarce be there yet. 3.05.150 P
i nothing know where she remains, why gone, 4.03. 14
why gone, | nor when she purposes return. 4.03. 15
the day that she was missing he was here; 4.03. 17
brain of britain, | by whom, i grant, she lives. 5.05. 15
how ended she? 5.05. 30
what she confess'd | i will report, so please 5.05. 33
wet cheeks | were present when she finish'd. 5.05. 36
first, she confess'd she never lov'd you; 5.05. 37
first, she confess'd she never lov'd you; 5.05. 37
she alone knew this; 5.05. 40
and, but she spoke it dying, i would not 5.05. 41
whom she bore in hand to love | with such 5.05. 43
she did confess | was as a scorpion to her sight 5.05. 44
prevented it, she had | ta'en off by poison. 5.05. 46
she did confess she had | for you a mortal 5.05. 49
she did confess she had | for you a mortal 5.05. 49

in which time she purpos'd, | by watching, 5.05. 52
time | (when she had fitted you with her craft), 5.05. 55
the evils she hatch'd were not effected; 5.05. 60
eyes | were not in fault, for she was beautiful; 5.05. 63
since she is living, let the time run on | to 5.05.128
dian had hot dreams, | and she alone were cold; 5.05.181
the temple | of virtue was she; 5.05.221
yea, and she herself. 5.05.221
"if pisanio | have," said she, "given his 5.05.246
she is serv'd | as i would serve a rat." 5.05.247
o, she was naught; 5.05.271
if i discover'd not which way she was gone, | it 5.05.277
by the queen's dram she swallow'd. 5.05.381
and she (like harmless lightning) throws her eye 5.05.394
see where she comes, apparelled like the spring, PER 1.01. 12
and she an eater of her mother's flesh | by the 1.01.130
she hath so strictly tied | her to her chamber, 2.05. 8
this by the eye of cynthia hath she vowed, | and 2.05. 11
she tells me here, she'll wed the stranger 2.05. 16
and she is fair too, is she not? 2.05. 35
and she is fair too, is she not? 2.05. 35
be her master, | and she will be your scholar; 2.05. 39
she thinks not so; peruse this writing else. 2.05. 41
a letter that she loves the knight of tyre! 2.05. 43
here comes my daughter, she can witness it. 2.05. 66
lychorida, her nurse, she takes, | and so to sea 3.ch. 43
yield 'er, for she must overboard straight. 3.01. 53 P
here she lies, sir. 3.01. 55
her burying, | she was the daughter of a king. 3.02. 73
to-night, | for look how fresh she looks! 3.02. 79
she hath not been | entranc'd above five hours. 3.02. 93
see how she gins | to blow into life's flower 3.02. 94
she is alive; 3.02. 97
i rage and roar | as doth the sea she lies in, 3.03. 11
for she was born at sea, i have nam'd so, here 3.03. 13
that she may be | manner'd as she is born. 3.03. 16
that she may be | manner'd as she is born. 3.03. 17
till she be married, madam, | by bright diana, 3.03. 27
in our story, she | would ever with marina be: 4.ch. 19
or when she would with sharp needle wound | the 4.ch. 23
which she made more sound | by hurting it; 4.ch. 24
or when to th' lute | she sung, and made the 4.ch. 26
or when | she would with rich and constant pen 4.ch. 28
i will do't, but yet she is a goodly creature. 4.01. 9
here she comes weeping for her only mistress' 4.01. 11
why would she have me kill'd now? 4.01. 72
there's no hope she will return. 4.01. 98
if she remain, | whom they have ravish'd must by 4.01.101
ay, she quickly poop'd him, she made him 4.02. 24 P
poop'd him, she made him roast-meat for worms. 4.02. 24 P
boult, has she any qualities? 4.02. 46 P
she has a good face, speaks well, and has 4.02. 47 P
take her in, instruct her what she has to do, 4.02. 55 P
that she may not be raw in her entertainment. 4.02. 55 P
fram'd this piece, she meant thee a good turn; 4.02.139 P
therefore say what a paragon she is, and thou 4.02.140 P
that she is dead. 4.03. 14
she died at night; 4.03. 16
attribute cry out, | "she died by foul play." 4.03. 19
yet none does know but you how she came dead, 4.03. 29
she did /distain my child, and stood between 4.03. 31
she was of tyrus the king's daughter, | on whom 4.04. 36
marina was she call'd, and at her birth, 4.04. 38
wherefore she does, and swears she'll never 4.04. 42
do in such a place as this, she being once gone. 4.05. 3 P
twice the worth of her she had ne'er come here. 4.06. 2 P
when she should do for clients her fitment, and 4.06. 5 P
of our profession, she has me her quirks, her 4.06. 7 P
that she would make a puritan of the devil, if 4.06. 9 P
sir, if she would — but there never came her 4.06. 27 P
shall see a rose, and she were a rose indeed, if 4.06. 35 P
and she were a rose indeed, if she had but — 4.06. 35 P
is she not a fair creature? 4.06. 43 P
she would serve after a long voyage at sea. 4.06. 44 P
she that sets seeds and roots of shame and 4.06. 85 P
she has here spoken holy words to the lord 4.06.132 P
and she sent him away as cold as a snowball, 4.06.139 P
and if she were a thornier piece of ground than 4.06.144 P
she were a thornier piece of ground than she is, 4.06.145 P
of ground than she is, she shall be plough'd. 4.06.145 P
she conjures, away with her! 4.06.147 P
would she had never come within my doors. 4.06.147 P
she sings like one immortal, and she dances | as 5.ch. 3
and she dances | as goddess-like to her admired 5.ch. 3
deep clerks she dumbs, and with her neele 5.ch. 5
that pupils lacks she none of noble race, | who 5.ch. 9
and her gain | she gives the cursed bawd. 5.ch. 11
she questionless with her sweet harmony, | and 5.01. 45
she is all happy as the fairest of all, | and, 5.01. 49
see, she will speak to him. 5.01. 81
she speaks, | my lord, that, may be, hath 5.01. 86
who starves the ears she feeds, and makes them 5.01.112
them hungry, | the more she gives them speech. 5.01.113
she never would tell | her parentage; 5.01.187
demanded that, | she would sit still and weep. 5.01.189
she is not dead at tharsus, as she should have 5.01.215
is not dead at tharsus, as she should have been, 5.01.215
she shall tell thee all; 5.01.216
justify in knowledge | she is thy very princess. 5.01.218
at sea in child-bed died she, but brought forth 5.03. 5
she at tharsus | was nurs'd with cleon, who at 5.03. 7
she | made known herself my daughter. 5.03. 12
what means the /nun? she dies, help, gentlemen! 5.03. 15
and call'd marina | for she was yielded there. 5.03. 48
how she came plac'd here in the temple; 5.03. 67
which | she makes it in, from henceforth i'll TNK 1.01.203
to her | what i shall be advis'd she likes. 1.03. 16
you were at wars when she the grave enrich'd, 1.03. 51
of love, but i | and she (i sigh and spoke of) 1.03. 60
what she lik'd | was then of me approv'd, what 1.03. 64
she would long | till she had such another, and 1.03. 68
she would long | till she had such another, and 1.03. 69
i have, sir. here she comes. 2.01. 15 P
till she for shame see what a wrong she has done 2.02. 39
till she for shame see what a wrong she has done 2.02. 39
by heaven, she is a goddess! 2.02.134
do reverence; | she is a goddess, arcite! 2.02.135
how modestly she blows, and paints the sun 2.02.139
she locks her beauties in her bud again, | and 2.02.142
her modesty will blow so far she falls for't. 2.02.144
a maid, if she have any honor, would be loath 2.02.145
she is wondrous fair! 2.02.147
she is all the beauty extant! 2.02.147
her | as she is heavenly and a blessed goddess; 2.02.163
still as she tasted, should be doubled on her, 2.02.240
and if she be not heavenly, i would make her 2.02.241
and then i am sure she would love me. 2.02.243
her, | and, if she be as gentle as she's fair, 2.03. 15
and she must see the duke, and she must dance 2.03. 45
she must see the duke, and she must dance too. 2.03. 45
she takes strong note of me, | hath made me near 3.01. 17
upon my mistress, | for note you, mine she is — 3.01.118
she lov'd a black-hair'd man. 3.03. 31
she did so; well, sir? 3.03. 31
she met him in an arbor: 3.03. 33
what did she there, coz? 3.03. 34
something she did, sir. 3.03. 35
that gave her promise faithfully she would | be 3.05. 43
nay, and she fail me once — you can tell, arcas 3.05. 46
she swore by wine and bread she would not break. 3.05. 47
she swore by wine and bread she would not break. 3.05. 47
a fire ill take her! does she flinch now? 3.05. 52
ask that lady | why she is fair, and why her 3.06.169
and if she say "traitor," | i am a villain fit 3.06.170
he that she refuses | must die then. 3.06.280
if she refuse me, yet my grave will wed me, 3.06.284
was she well? 4.01. 34
was she in health? 4.01. 34
sir, when did she sleep? 4.01. 35
i do not think she was very well, for, now | you 4.01. 36
and she answered me | so far from what she was, 4.01. 38
and she answered me | so far from what she was, 4.01. 39
childishly, | so sillily, as if she were a fool, 4.01. 40
no, sir, not well: | 'tis too true, she is mad. 4.01. 46
me down | and list'ned to the words she sung, 4.01. 63
she sung much, but no sense; 4.01. 66
then she talk'd of you, sir — | that you must 4.01. 76
and she must gather flowers to bury you, | and 4.01. 78
then she sung | nothing but "willow, willow, 4.01. 79
the place | was knee-deep where she sat; 4.01. 83
that methought she appear'd like the fair nymph 4.01. 86
rings she made | of rushes that grew by, and to 4.01. 88
and then she wept, and sung again, and sigh'd, 4.01. 92
she saw me, and straight sought the flood. 4.01. 95
when presently | she slipp'd away, and to the 4.01. 97
that, believe me, | she left me far behind her. 4.01. 99
where she stay'd, | and fell, scarce to be got 4.01.101
she is then distemper'd | /far worse than now 4.01.119
distemper'd | /far worse than now she shows. 4.01.120
but she shall never have him, tell her so, | for 4.01.122
for, if she see him once, she's gone — she's 4.01.124
does she know him? 4.01.141
no, would she did! 4.01.142
she sows into the births of noble bodies, | were 4.02. 9
yet doubtless | she would run mad for this man. 4.02. 12
as if she ever meant to /crown his valor. 4.02.109
she is continually in a harmless distemper, 4.03. 3 P
lards it, that she farces ev'ry business withal, 4.03. 7 P
look where she comes, you shall perceive her 4.03. 9 P
and then will she be out of love with aeneas. 4.03. 15 P
how she continues this fancy! 4.03. 48 P
i think she has a perturb'd mind, which i cannot 4.03. 59 P
understand you she ever affected any man ere she 4.03. 62 P
ever affected any man ere she beheld palamon? 4.03. 63 P
in great hope she had fix'd her liking on this 4.03. 64 P
my state that both she and i at this present 4.03. 68 P
green songs of love as she says palamon hath 4.03. 81 P
it is a falsehood she is in, which is with 4.03. 93 P
on, where she sticks | the queen of flowers. 5.01. 44
goddess of it grant, she gives | victory too. 5.01. 71
i | believ'd it was his, for she swore it was, 5.01.117
within this half hour she came smiling to me 5.02. 4
then she told me | she would watch with me 5.02. 8
she told me | she would watch with me to-night, 5.02. 9
for well she knew | what hour my fit would take 5.02. 9
she would have me sing. 5.02. 12
if she entreat again, do any thing, | lie with 5.02. 17
do any thing, | lie with her, if she ask you. 5.02. 18
then if she will be honest, | she has the path 5.02. 22
will be honest, | she has the path before her. 5.02. 23
pray bring her in | and let's see how she is. 5.02. 25
why, do you think she is not honest, sir? 5.02. 30
how old is she? 5.02. 31
she may be, | but that's all one, 'tis nothing 5.02. 31
you'll find it so. she comes. pray /humor her. 5.02. 40
she is horribly in love with him, poor beast, 5.02. 62
what dowry has she? 5.02. 64
what stuff she utters! 5.02. 68
o, she must. 5.03. 11
she shall see deeds of honor in their kind 5.03. 12
pray, how does she? 5.04. 25
i heard she was not well; 5.04. 26
"thrice fairer than myself," thus she began, VEN 7
with this she seizeth on his sweating palm, 25
she red and hot as coals of glowing fire, | he 35
bridle on a ragged bough | nimbly she fastens (o 38
even now | to tie the rider she begins to prove. 40
backward she push'd him, as she would be thrust, 41
backward she push'd him, as she would be thrust, 41
so soon was she along as he was down, | each 43
now doth she stroke his cheek, now doth he frown 45
and gins to chide, but soon she stops his lips, 46
she with her tears | doth quench the maiden 49
to fan and blow them dry again she seeks. 52
he saith she is immodest, blames her miss; 53
what follows more, she murthers with a kiss. 54
even so she kiss'd his brow, his cheek, his chin 59
chin, | and where she ends, she doth anew begin. 60
chin, | and where she ends, she doth anew begin. 60
she feedeth on the steam as on a prey, | and 63
still she entreats, and prettily entreats, | for 73
for to a pretty ear she tunes her tale. 74
being red, she loves him best, and being white, 77
look how he can, she cannot choose but love, 79
and by her fair immortal hand she swears | from 80
so offers he to give what she did crave, | but 88
thirst for drink than she for this good turn. 92
her help she sees, but help she cannot get, 93
her help she sees, but help she cannot get, 93
she bathes in water, yet her fire must burn. 94
"o, pity," gan she cry, "flint-hearted boy, 95
she had not brought forth thee, but died unkind. 204
being judge in love, she cannot right her cause. 220
and now she weeps, and now she fain would speak, 221
and now she weeps, and now she fain would speak, 221
sometime she shakes her head, and then his hand, 223
now gazeth she on him, now on the ground; 224
she would, he will not in her arms be bound; 226
gone, | she locks her lily fingers one in one. 228
"fondling," she saith, "since i have hemm'd thee 229
being mad before, how doth she now for wits? 249
now which way shall she turn? 253
what shall she say? 253
"pity," she cries, "some favor, some remorse!" 257
and forth she rushes, snorts, and neighs aloud. 262
her, | she answers him, as if she knew his mind; 308
her, | she answers him, as if she knew his mind; 308
she puts on outward strangeness, seems unkind: 310
mind, | taking no notice that she is so nigh, 341
view | how she came stealing to the wayward boy! 344
now was she just before him as he sat, | and 349
sat, | and like a lowly lover down she kneels; 350
with one fair hand she heaveth up his hat, | her 351
full gently now she takes him by the hand, | a 361
"give me my heart," saith she, "and thou shalt 374
thus she replies: 385
quoth she, "hast thou a tongue? 427
this ill presage advisedly she marketh: 457
and at his look she flatly falleth down, | for 463
the silly boy, believing she is dead, | claps 467
for on the grass she lies as she were slain, 473
for on the grass she lies as she were slain, 473
her, and she by her good will | will never rise, 479
her two blue windows faintly she upheaveth, 482
quoth she, "in earth or heaven, | or in the 493
"good night," quoth she, and, ere he says "adieu 537
with her plenty press'd, she faint with dearth, 545
and glutton-like she feeds, yet never filleth; 548
that she will draw his lips' rich treasure dry. 552
with blindfold fury she begins to forage; 554
while she takes all she can, not all she listeth 564
while she takes all she can, not all she listeth 564
she takes all she can, not all she listeth. 564
when he did frown, o, had she then gave over, 571
such nectar from his lips she had not suck'd. 572
for pity now she can no more detain him; 577
she is resolv'd no longer to restrain him, 579
the which, by cupid's bow she doth protest, | he 581
"sweet boy," she says, "this night i'll waste in 583
quoth she, whereat a sudden pale, | like lawn 589
she trembles at his tale, | and on his neck her 591
and on his neck her yoking arms she throws. 592
she sinketh down, still hanging by his neck, 593
neck, | he on her belly falls, she on her back. 594
now is she in the very lists of love, | her 595
all is imaginary she doth prove, | he will not 597
even so she languisheth in her mishaps, | as 603
the warm effects which she in him finds missing 605
she seeks to kindle with continual kissing. 606
she hath assay'd as much as may be prov'd. 608
she's love, she loves, and yet she is not lov'd. 610
she's love, she loves, and yet she is not lov'd. 610
"thou hadst been gone," quoth she, "sweet boy, 613
quoth she. 717
"in night," quoth she, "desire sees best of all. 720
lest she should steal a kiss and die forsworn. 726
wherein she fram'd thee in high heaven's despite 731
"and therefore hath she brib'd the destinies 733
which after him she darts, as one on shore 817
wood, | even so confounded in the dark she lay, 827
and now she beats her heart, whereat it groans, 829
she cries, and twenty times, "woe, woe!" 833
she, marking them, begins a wailing note, | and 835
for who hath she to spend the night withal, 847
she says, "'tis so," they answer all, "'tis so," 851
and would say after her, if she said "no." 852
this said, she hasteth to a myrtle grove, 865
and yet she hears no tidings of her love. 867
she hearkens for his hounds and for his horn; 868
anon she hears them chaunt it lustily, | and all 869
and all in haste she coasteth to the cry. 870
and as she runs, the bushes in the way, | some 871
she wildly breaketh from their strict embrace, 874
by this she hears the hounds are at a bay, 877
whereat she starts like one that spies an adder 878
for now she knows it is no gentle chase, | but 883
thus stands she in a trembling ecstasy, | till, 895
she tells them 'tis a causeless fantasy | and 897
and with that word she spied the hunted boar, 900
which madly hurries her she knows not whither: 904
this way she runs, and now she will no further, 905
this way she runs, and now she will no further, 905
she treads the path that she untreads again; 908
she treads the path that she untreads again; 908
here kennell'd in a brake she finds a hound, 913
and here she meets another sadly scowling, | to 917
to whom she speaks, and he replies with howling. 918
so she at these sad signs draws up her breath, 929
divorce of love" — thus chides she death — 932
she vail'd her eyelids, who like sluices stopp'd 956
this, far off, she hears some huntsman hallow; 973
the dire imagination she did follow | this sound 975
who is but drunken when she seemeth drown'd. 984
now she unweaves the web that she hath wrought: 991
now she unweaves the web that she hath wrought: 991
it was not she that call'd him all to naught: 993
now she adds honors to his hateful name; 994
she clepes him king of graves and grave for 995
"no, no," quoth she, "sweet death, i did but 997
is alive, | her rash suspect she doth extenuate, 1010
thrive, | with death she humbly doth insinuate; 1012
"o jove," quoth she, "how much a fool was i | to 1015
even at this word she hears a merry horn, 1025
whereat she leaps, that was but late forlorn. 1026

as falcons to the lure, away she flies, | the 1027
the grass stoops not, she treads on it so light, 1028
over one shoulder doth she hang her head; 1058
dumbly she passions, franticly she doteth, | she 1059
dumbly she passions, franticly she doteth, | she 1059
she thinks he could not die, he is not dead; 1060
upon his hurt she looks so steadfastly, | that 1063
and then she reprehends her mangling eye, | that 1065
and yet," quoth she, "behold two adons dead! 1070
with this she falleth in the place she stood, 1121
with this she falleth in the place she stood, 1121
she looks upon his lips, and they are pale, 1123
she takes him by the hand, and that is cold, 1124
cold, | she whispers in his ears a heavy tale, 1125
as if they heard the woeful words she told; 1126
she lifts the coffer–lids that close his eyes, 1127
"wonder of time," quoth she, "this is my spite, 1133
she bows her head, the new–sprung flow'r to 1171
she crops the stalk, and in the breach appears 1175
green–dropping sap, which she compares to tears. 1176
"poor flow'r," quoth she, "this was thy father's 1177
thus weary of the world, away she hies, | and 1189
so guiltless she securely gives good cheer | and LUC 89
but she, that never cop'd with stranger eyes, 99
she touch'd no unknown baits, nor fear'd no 103
nor could she moralize his wanton sight, | more 104
her joy with heav'd–up hand she doth express, 111
but she is not her own; 241
quoth he, "she took me kindly by the hand, | and 253
until her husband's welfare she did hear; 263
whereat she smiled with so sweet a cheer | that 264
that had narcissus seen her as she stood, 265
but she, sound sleeping, fearing no such thing, 363
whether it is that she reflects so bright | that 376
where like a virtuous monument she lies, | to be 391
lies, | do tell her she is dreadfully beset, 444
she much amaz'd breaks ope her lock'd–up eyes, 446
that thinks she hath beheld some ghastly sprite, 451
but she in worser taking, | from sleep disturbed 453
like to a new–kill'd bird she trembling lies; 457
she dares not look, yet, winking, there appears 458
but she with vehement prayers urgeth still 475
while she, the picture of pure piety, | like a 542
she puts the period often from his place, | and 565
that twice she doth begin ere once she speaks. 567
that twice she doth begin ere once she speaks. 567
she conjures him by high almighty jove, | by 568
quoth she, "reward not hospitality | with such 575
"thou art," quoth she, "a sea, a sovereign king, 652
for with the nightly linen that she wears | he 680
but she hath lost a dearer thing than life, 687
to ask the spotted princess how she fares. 721
she says, her subjects with foul insurrection 722
which in her prescience she controlled still, 727
she bears the load of lust he left behind, | and 734
she like a wearied lamb lies panting there; 737
she, desperate, with her nails her flesh doth 739
she stays, exclaiming on the direful night, | he 741
she there remains a hopeless castaway; 744
light, | she prays she never may behold the day: 746
light, | she prays she never may behold the day: 746
"for day," quoth she, "night's scapes doth open 747
here she exclaims against repose and rest, | and 757
she wakes her heart by beating on her breast, 759
with grief thus breathes she forth her spite 762
said, from her betumbled couch she starteth, 1037
"in vain," quoth she, "i live, and seek in vain 1044
seems to point her out where she sits weeping, 1087
she sits weeping, | to whom she sobbing speaks: 1088
thus cavils she with every thing she sees: 1093
thus cavils she with every thing she sees: 1093
so she, deep drenched in a sea of care, | holds 1100
holds disputation with each thing she views, 1101
"you mocking birds," quoth she, "your tunes 1121
out readily, | so with herself is she in mutiny, 1153
"to kill myself," quoth she, "alack, what were 1156
this plot of death when sadly she had laid, 1212
with untun'd tongue she hoarsely calls her maid, 1214
her mistress she doth give demure good morrow, 1219
"my girl," quoth she, "on what occasion break 1221
(and there she stay'd | till after a deep groan) 1275
she would request to know your heaviness." 1283
her maid is gone, and she prepares to write, 1296
at last she thus begins: 1303
here folds she up the tenure of her woe, | her 1310
she dares not thereof make discovery, | lest he 1314
ere she with blood had stain'd her stain'd 1316
life and feeling of her passion | she hoards, to 1318
she would not blot the letter | with words, till 1322
the post attends, and she delivers it, 1333
more than speed but dull and slow she deems: 1336
she thought he blush'd, as knowing tarquin's 1354
the more she saw the blood his cheeks replenish, 1357
the more she thought he spied in her some 1358
but long she thinks till he return again, | and 1359
the weary time she cannot entertain, | for now 1361
that she her plaints a little while doth stay, 1364
at last she calls to mind where hangs a piece 1366
many she sees where cares have carved some, 1445
dwell'd, | till she despairing hecuba beheld, 1447
of what she was, no semblance did remain. 1453
"poor instrument," quoth she, "without a sound, 1464
here feelingly she weeps troy's painted woes, 1492
she lends them words, and she their looks doth 1498
them words, and she their looks doth borrow. 1498
she throws her eyes about the painting round, 1499
and who she finds forlorn she doth lament. 1500
and who she finds forlorn she doth lament. 1500
at last she sees a wretched image bound, | that 1501
this picture she advisedly perus'd, | and chid 1527
and still on him she gaz'd, and gazing still, 1531
such signs of truth in his plain face she spied, 1532
that she concludes the picture was belied. 1533
"it cannot be," quoth she, "that so much guile" 1534
she would have said, "can lurk in such a look"; 1535
"it cannot be" she in that sense forsook, | and 1538
she tears the senseless sinon with her nails, 1564
at last she smilingly with this gives o'er; 1567
fool," quoth she, "his wounds will not be sore." 1568
she looks for night, and then she longs for 1571
looks for night, and then she longs for morrow, 1571
and both she thinks too long with her remaining. 1572
that she with painted images hath spent, | being 1577
he hath no power to ask her how she fares. 1594
three times with sighs she gives her sorrow fire 1604
ere once she can discharge one word of woe; 1605
she modestly prepares to let them know | her 1607
"few words," quoth she, "shall fit the trespass 1613
which speechless woe of his poor she attendeth, 1674
for she that was thy lucrece, now attend me: 1682
you fair lords," quoth she | (speaking to those 1688
but she, that yet her sad task hath not said, 1699
"o, speak," quoth she, | "how may this forced 1700
while with a joyless smile she turns away | the 1711
no," quoth she, "no dame hereafter living | by 1714
would break, | she throws forth tarquin's name: 1717
"he, he," she says, | but more than "he" her 1717
she utters this, "he, he, fair lords, 'tis he, 1721
even here she sheathed in her harmless breast 1723
"o, mine she is," | replies her husband, "do not 1795
say | he weeps for her, for she was only mine, 1798
which she too early and too late hath spill'd." 1801
"woe, woe," quoth collatine, "she was my wife, 1802
i owed her, and 'tis mine that she hath kill'd." 1803
when my love swears that she is made of truth, PP 1. 1
i do believe her (though i know she lies) | that 1. 2
that she might think me some untutor'd youth, 1. 3
thus vainly thinking that she thinks me young, 1. 5
but wherefore says my love that she is young? 1. 9
she told him stories to delight his /ear; 4. 5
she show'd him favors to allure his eye; 4. 6
to win his heart she touch'd him here and there 4. 7
then fell she on her back, fair queen, and 4.13
she hotter that did look | for his approach that 6. 7
"o jove," quoth she, "why was not i a flood?" 6.14
her lips to mine how often hath she joined, 7. 7
how many tales to please me hath she coined, 7. 9
she burnt with love, as straw with fire flameth, 7.13
she burnt out love, as soon as straw out–burneth 7.14
she fram'd the love, and yet she foil'd the 7.15
fram'd the love, and yet she foil'd the framing, 7.15
she bade love last, and yet she fell a–turning. 7.16
she bade love last, and yet she fell a–turning. 7.16
her stand she takes upon a steep–up hill. 9. 5
she, silly queen, with more than love's good 9. 7
"once," quoth she, "did i see a fair sweet youth 9. 9
in my thigh," quoth she, "here was the sore." 9.12
she showed hers, he saw more wounds than one, 9.13
she told the youngling how god mars did try her, 11. 3
her, | and as he fell to her, she fell to him. 11. 4
"even thus," quoth she, "the warlike god 11. 5
me," | and then she clipt adonis in her arms; 11. 6
"even thus," quoth she, "the warlike god unlac'd 11. 7
"even thus," quoth she, "he seized on my lips," 11. 9
and as she fetched breath, away he skips, | and 11.11
she bade good night that kept my rest away, 14. 2
"farewell," quoth she, "and come again to–morrow 14. 5
yet at my parting sweetly did she smile, | in 14. 7
't may be she joy'd to jest at my exile, | 't 14. 9
for she doth welcome daylight with her ditty, 14.19
for why, she sight, and bade me come to–morrow. 14.24
alas, she could not help it! 15.12
talk, | lest she some subtile practice smell — 18. 9
slack | to proffer, though she put thee back. 18.24
and then too late she will repent | that thus 18.27
it be day, | that which with scorn she put away. 18.30
what though she strive to try her strength, 18.31
she will not stick to round me on th' ear, | to 18.51
yet will she blush, here be it said, | to hear 18.53
she, poor bird, as all forlorn, | lean'd her 20. 9
"fie, fie, fie," now would she cry, | "tereu, 20.13
but cannot be, | beauty brag, but 'tis not she, PHT 63
for where is she so fair whose unear'd womb SON 3. 5
and she in thee | calls back the lovely april of 3. 9
and being frank she lends to those are free: 4. 4
look whom she best endow'd she gave the more; 11.11
look whom she best endow'd she gave the more; 11.11
she carv'd thee for her seal, and meant thereby 11.13
till nature, as she wrought thee, fell a–doting, 20.10
but since she prick'd thee out for women's 20.13
that she hath thee, is of my wailing chief, | a 42. 3
and for my sake even so doth she abuse me, 42. 7
then she loves but me alone. 42.14
veins, | for she hath no exchequer now but his, 67.11
o, him she stores, to show what wealth she had 67.13
to show what wealth she had | in days long since 67.13
she keeps thee to this purpose, that her skill 126. 7
she may detain, but not still keep, her treasure 126.10
my mistress when she walks treads on the ground. 130.12
as rare | as any she belied with false compare. 130.14
when my love swears that she is made of truth, 138. 1
i do believe her, though i know she lies, | that 138. 2
that she might think me some untutor'd youth, 138. 3
thus vainly thinking that she thinks me young, 138. 5
although she knows my days are past the best, 138. 6
but wherefore says she not she is unjust? 138. 9
but wherefore says she not she is unjust? 138. 9
therefore i lie with her, and she with me, | and 138.13
and therefore from me her face she turns my foes, 139.11
that she that makes me sin awards me pain. 141.14
in pursuit of the thing she would have stay; 143. 4
but when she saw my woeful state, | straight in 145. 4
"i hate" she alter'd with an end | that follow'd 145. 9
"i hate" from hate away she threw, | and sav'd 145.13
this brand she quenched in a cool well by, 154. 9
oft did she heave her napkin to her eyne, LC 15
a thousand favors from a maund she drew, | of 36
jet, | which one by one she in a river threw, 38
threw, | upon whose weeping margent she was set, 39
of folded schedules had she many a one, | which 43
which she perus'd, sigh'd, tore, and gave the 44
these often bath'd she in her fluxive eyes, 50
this said, in top of rage the lines she rents, 55
"father," she says, "though in me you behold 71
and when in his fair parts she did abide, | she 83
abide, | she was new lodg'd and newly deified. 84
the destin'd ill she must herself assay? 156
for she was sought by spirits of richest coat, 236
she that her fame so to herself contrives, | the 243
and now she would the caged cloister fly: 249
not to be tempted would she be enur'd, | and now 251
SHEAF 2 FR 0.0002 REL FR 2 V 0 P
they that reap must sheaf and bind, | then to AYL 3.02.107
this scattered corn into one mutual sheaf, TIT 5.03. 71
SHEAL'D *(also shell)*
SHEAL'D 1 FR 0.0001 REL FR 0 V 1 P
that's a sheal'd peascod. LR 1.04.200 P
SHE–ANGEL 1 FR 0.0001 REL FR 0 V 1 P
you would think a smock were a she–angel, he so WT 4.04.209 P
SHEAR 2 FR 0.0002 REL FR 2 V 0 P
and do not shear the fleeces that i graze. AYL 2.04. 79
so many years ere i shall shear the fleece: 3H6 2.05. 37
SHEARERS 2 FR 0.0002 REL FR 0 V 2 P
me four and twenty nosegays for the shearers WT 4.03. 42 P
bring out another, and the shearers prove sheep, 4.03.121 P
SHEARING 1 FR 0.0001 REL FR 1 V 0 P
be to you both, | and welcome to our shearing! WT 4.04. 77
SHEARMAN 1 FR 0.0001 REL FR 1 V 0 P
and thou thyself a shearman, art thou not? 2H6 4.02.133
SHEARS 4 FR 0.0004 REL FR 3 V 1 P
there went but a pair of shears between us. MM 1.02. 27 P
you have shore | with shears his thread of silk. MND 5.01.341
think you i bear the shears of destiny? JN 4.02. 91
who, with his shears and measure in his hand, 4.02.196
SHEATH 5 FR 0.0005 REL FR 3 V 2 P
you tailor's yard, you sheath, you bowcase, you 1H4 2.04.247 P
in chines of beef ere thou sleep in thy sheath, 2H6 4.10. 58 P
have your lath glued within your sheath, | till TIT 2.01. 41
o happy dagger, | this is thy sheath; ROM 5.03.170
bent, or a sharp weapon | in a soft sheath; TNK 5.03. 43
SHEATH'D 5 FR 0.0005 REL FR 5 V 0 P
and sheath'd their swords for lack of argument. H5 3.01. 21
till i have sheath'd | my rapier in his bosom, TIT 2.01. 53
whose tushes never sheath'd he whetteth still, VEN 617
sheath'd unaware the tusk in his soft groin. 1116
eyes like marigolds had sheath'd their light, LUC 397
SHEATHE 9 FR 0.0010 REL FR 8 V 1 P
/but /first sheathe thy impatience, throw cold WIV 2.03. 84 P
not till i sheathe it in a murtherer's skin. JN 4.03. 80
draw out, | and sheathe for lack of sport. H5 4.02. 23
here sheathe thy sword, i'll pardon thee my 3H6 5.05. 70
his period, | to sheathe his knife in us. H8 1.02.210
goths have given me leave to sheathe my sword. TIT 1.01. 85
and sheathe them not | till saturninus be rome'i 1.01.204
sheathe your dagger. JC 4.03.107
an unbattered edge | i sheathe again undeeded. MAC 5.07. 20
SHEATHED 1 FR 0.0001 REL FR 1 V 0 P
even here she sheathed in her harmless breast LUC 1723
SHEATHING 2 FR 0.0002 REL FR 2 V 0 P
and walter's dagger was not come from sheathing; SHR 4.01.135
sheathing the steel in my advent'rous body. TIT 5.03.112
SHEAV'D 1 FR 0.0001 REL FR 1 V 0 P
for some, untuck'd, descended her sheav'd hat, LC 31
SHEAVES 1 FR 0.0001 REL FR 1 V 0 P
and summer's green all girded up in sheaves SON 12. 7
SHEBA *(see saba)*
SHE–BEAR 1 FR 0.0001 REL FR 1 V 0 P
pluck the young sucking cubs from the she–bear, MV 2.01. 29
SHE–BEGGAR 1 FR 0.0001 REL FR 1 V 0 P
stuff | to some she–beggar and compounded thee TIM 4.03.273
SHE'D 1 FR 0.0001 REL FR 0 V 1 P
if she'd do the deeds of darkness, thou wouldst PER 4.06. 29 P
/SHED 1 FR 0.0001 REL FR 1 V 0 P
/dear /blood /shed /for /our /grievous /sins, R3 1.04.190
SHED 54 FR 0.0061 REL FR 49 V 5 P
like a foul bumbard that would shed his liquor. TMP 2.02. 21 P
did not this cruel–hearted cur shed one tear. TGV 2.03. 9 P
tears | the passion of loud laughter never shed. MND 5.01. 70
if thou dost shed | one drop of christian blood, MV 4.01.309
shed thou no blood, nor cut thou less nor more 4.01.325
bid him shed tears, as being overjoyed | to see SHR in.1. 120
and till the tears that she hath shed for thee in.2. 64
remembrance more | than those i shed for him. AWW 1.01. 81
he weeps like a wench that had shed her milk. 4.03.107 P
would have shed water out of fire ere done't; WT 3.02.193
and tears shed there | shall be my recreation. 3.02.239
first gentleman–like tears that ever we shed. 5.02.145 P
we may live, son, to shed many more. 5.02.146 P
blood | that hot rash haste so indirectly shed. JN 2.01. 49
farewell, my blood, which if to–day thou shed, R2 1.03. 57
and say, what store of parting tears were shed? 1.04. 5
and shed my dear blood drop by drop in the dust, 1H4 1.03.134
for there will be a world of water shed | upon 3.01. 93
and interchanging blows i quickly shed | some of 1H6 4.06. 19
and for thy sake have i shed many a tear. 5.04. 19
my sword should shed hot blood, mine eyes no 2H6 1.01.118
thou shalt be waking while i shed thy blood, 3.02.227
must not be shed by such a jaded groom. 4.01. 52
upon my soul, the hearers will shed tears; 3H6 1.04.161
yea, even my foes will shed fast–falling tears, 1.04.162
for slaughter of my son | shed seas of tears, 2.05.106
they that stabb'd caesar shed no blood at all, 5.05. 53
may such purple tears be alway shed | from those 5.06. 64
these eyes, which never shed remorseful tear — R3 1.02.155
the liquid drops of tears that you have shed 4.04.321
the brother blindly shed the brother's blood, 5.05. 24
i did not think to shed a tear | in all my H8 3.02.428
by th' blood we have shed together, by th' vows COR 1.06. 57
as for my country i have shed my blood, | not 3.01. 76
shed for my thankless country are requited | but 4.05. 70
and bear the palm for having bravely shed | thy 5.03.117
victorious titus, rue the tears i shed, | a TIT 1.01.105
joy | shed on this earth for thy return to rome. 1.01.162
no man shed tears for noble mutius, | he lives 1.01.389
i beg this boon, with tears not lightly shed, 2.03.289
for all my blood in rome's great quarrel shed, 3.01. 4
why, i have not another tear to shed. 3.01.266
near | to shed obsequious tears upon this trunk. 5.03.152
for blood of ours, shed blood of montague. ROM 3.01.149
o god, did romeo's hand shed tybalt's blood? 3.02. 71
woe to the hand that shed this costly blood! JC 3.01.258
if you have tears, prepare to shed them now. 3.02.169
blood hath been shed ere now, i' th' olden time, MAC 3.04. 74

yet i'll not shed her blood, | nor scar that OTH 5.02. 3
how many worthy princes' bloods were shed | to PER 1.02. 88
and that blood we desire to shed is mutual — TNK 3.06. 95
whose blood upon the fresh flowers being shed VEN 665
tears | that ever modest eyes with sorrow shed. LUC 683
shed for the slaught'red husband by the wife; 1376
SHEDDING 3 FR 0.0003 REL FR 2 V 1 P
a' my breathing, no tears but a' my shedding. MV 3.01. 96 P
and make some pretty match with shedding tears? R2 3.03.165
achilles must or now be cropp'd | or, shedding, TRO 1.03.319
SHEDS 2 FR 0.0002 REL FR 1 V 1 P
now the dog all this while sheds not a tear, nor TGV 2.03. 31 P
for he to–day that sheds his blood with me H5 4.03. 61
SHEEDS 2 FR 0.0002 REL FR 2 V 0 P
to see those borrowed tears that sinon sheeds! LUC 1549
but those tears are pearl which thy love sheeds, SON 34.13
SHEEN 2 FR 0.0002 REL FR 2 V 0 P
by fountain clear, or spangled starlight sheen, MND 2.01. 29
and thirty dozen moons with borrowed sheen HAM 3.02.157
/SHEEP 2 FR 0.0002 REL FR 2 V 0 P
/thy /sheep /be /in /the /corn, | /and /for /one LR 3.06. 42
/mouth, | /thy /sheep /shall /take /no /harm." 3.06. 44
SHEEP 42 FR 0.0047 REL FR 19 V 23 P
thy turfy mountains, where live nibbling sheep, TMP 4.01. 62
and i have play'd the sheep in losing him. TGV 1.01. 73
indeed a sheep doth very often stray, | and if 1.01. 74
my master is a shepherd then, and i /a sheep? 1.01. 77 P
a silly answer, and fitting well a sheep. 1.01. 81 P
this proves me still a sheep. 1.01. 82 P
the shepherd seeks the sheep, and not the sheep 1.01. 86 P
seeks the shepherd, and not the sheep the shepherd; 1.01. 87 P
therefore i am no sheep. 1.01. 88 P
the sheep for fodder follow the shepherd, the 1.01. 89 P
the shepherd for food follows not the sheep; 1.01. 90 P
therefore thou art a sheep. 1.01. 92 P
why, thou peevish sheep, | what ship of ERR 4.01. 93
no sheep, sweet lamb, unless we feed on your LLL 2.01.220
you sheep, and i pasture: 2.01.221
it kills sheep; 4.03. 7 P
it kills me, i a sheep: 4.03. 7 P
ba, most silly sheep, with a horn. 5.01. 50 P
the sheep: the other two concludes it — o,u. 5.01. 56 P
when jacob graz'd his uncle laban's sheep — MV 1.03. 71
that good pasture makes fat sheep; AYL 3.02. 27 P
often tarr'd over with the surgery of our sheep; 3.02. 63 P
they have scar'd away two of my best sheep, WT 3.03. 66 P
let my sheep go. 3.03.126 P
and the shearers prove sheep, let me be unroll'd 4.03.121 P
so i were out of prison and kept sheep, | i JN 4.01. 17
renounce your soil, give sheep in lions' stead: 1H6 1.05. 29
sheep run not half so treacherous from the wolf, 1.05. 30
as market men for oxen, sheep, or horse. 5.05. 54
being burnt i' th' hand for stealing of sheep. 2H6 4.02. 63 P
they fell before thee like sheep and oxen, and 4.03. 3 P
on sheep or oxen could i spend my fury. 5.01. 27
to shepherds looking on their silly sheep | than 3H6 2.05. 43
so first the harmless sheep doth yield his 5.06. 8
rather be a tick in a sheep than such a valiant TRO 3.03.312 P
and that's as easy | as to set dogs on sheep — COR 2.01.257
than baits to fish, or honey–stalks to sheep, TIT 4.04. 91
but that he sees the romans are but sheep; JC 1.03.105
they are sheep and calves which seek out HAM 5.01.116 P
the beast no hide, the sheep no wool, the cat no LR 3.04.104 P
the sheep are gone to fold, birds to their nest, VEN 532
"sometime he runs among a flock of sheep, | to 685
SHEEP–BITER 1 FR 0.0001 REL FR 0 V 1 P
the niggardly rascally sheep–biter come by some TN 2.05. 5 P
SHEEP–BITING 1 FR 0.0001 REL FR 0 V 1 P
show your sheep–biting face, and be hang'd an MM 5.01.354 P
SHEEP–COTE 3 FR 0.0003 REL FR 2 V 1 P
are now on sale, and at our sheep–cote now, | by AYL 2.04. 84
a sheep–cote fenc'd about with olive–trees? 4.03. 77
draw our throne into a sheep–cote! WT 4.04.779 P
SHEEP–COTES 1 FR 0.0001 REL FR 1 V 0 P
poor pelting villages, sheep–cotes, and mills, LR 2.03. 18
SHEEP–HOOK 1 FR 0.0001 REL FR 1 V 0 P
heir, | that thus affects a sheep–hook! WT 4.04.420
SHEEP'S 4 FR 0.0004 REL FR 1 V 3 P
is it not strange that sheep's guts should hale ADO 2.03. 59 P
your liver as clean as a sound sheep's heart, AYL 3.02.423 P
bit and a head–stall of sheep's leather which, SHR 3.02. 57 P
i'll chase hence, thou wolf in sheep's array. 1H6 1.03. 55
SHEEPS 1 FR 0.0001 REL FR 1 V 0 P
two hot sheeps, marry. LLL 2.01.219
SHEEP–SHEARING 5 FR 0.0005 REL FR 2 V 3 P
what am i to buy for our sheep–shearing feast? WT 4.03. 37 P
i must go buy spices for our sheep–shearing. 4.03.117 P
i'll be with you at your sheep–shearing too. 4.03.120 P
this your sheep–shearing | is as a meeting of 4.04. 3
on, | and bid us welcome to your sheep–shearing, 4.04. 69
SHEEP–SKINS 1 FR 0.0001 REL FR 0 V 1 P
is not parchment made of sheep–skins? HAM 5.01.114 P
SHEEP–WHISTLING 1 FR 0.0001 REL FR 0 V 1 P
an old sheep–whistling rogue, a ram–tender, to WT 4.04.776 P
SHEER 2 FR 0.0002 REL FR 1 V 1 P
not fourteen pence on the score for sheer ale, SHR in.2. 23 P
thou sheer, immaculate, and silver fountain, R2 5.03. 61
SHEET 12 FR 0.0013 REL FR 7 V 5 P
her smock till she have writ a sheet of paper. ADO 2.03.133 P
now you talk of a sheet of paper, i remember a 2.03.134 P
"benedick" and "beatrice" between the sheet? 2.03.138 P
as would be cramm'd up in a sheet of paper, LLL 5.02. 7
as many lies as will lie in thy sheet of paper, TN 3.02. 46 P
although the sheet were big enough for the bed 3.02. 47 P
the white sheet bleaching on the hedge, | with WT 4.03. 5
madam, your penance done, throw off this sheet, 2H6 2.04.105
my shame will not be shifted with my sheet. 2.04.107
tybalt, liest thou there in thy bloody sheet? ROM 5.03. 97
a spade, a spade, | for and a shrouding sheet: HAM 5.01. 95
who o'er the white sheet peers her whiter chin, LUC 472
SHEETED 1 FR 0.0001 REL FR 1 V 0 P
graves stood /tenantless and the sheeted dead HAM 1.01.115
SHEETS 19 FR 0.0021 REL FR 13 V 6 P
this way the coverlet, another way the sheets. SHR 4.01.202
sully | the purity and whiteness of my sheets WT 1.02.327
my traffic is sheets; 4.03. 23 P
i'll canvass thee between a pair of sheets. 2H4 2.04.225 P
put thy face between his sheets, and do the H5 2.01. 84 P
for after i saw him fumble with the sheets, and 2.03. 14 P
look, on the sheets his hair, you see, is 2H6 3.02.174
post | with such dexterity to incestious sheets! HAM 1.02.157
such sheets of fire, such bursts of horrid LR 3.02. 46
my daughters | got 'tween the lawful sheets. 4.06.116
and it is thought abroad that 'twixt my sheets OTH 1.03.387
well — happiness to their sheets! 2.03. 29 P
i have laid those sheets you bade me on the bed. 4.03. 22
prithee shroud me | in one of these same sheets. 4.03. 25
you think none but your sheets are privy to your ANT 1.02. 41 P
like the stag, when snow the pasture sheets, 1.04. 65
live, like diana's priest, betwixt cold sheets, CYM 1.06.133
fresh lily, | and whiter than the sheets! 2.02. 16
teaching the sheets a whiter hue than white, VEN 398
SHEFFIELD 1 FR 0.0001 REL FR 1 V 0 P
of wingfield, lord furnival of sheffield, | the 1H6 4.07. 66
//SHE–FOXES 1 FR 0.0001 REL FR 1 V 0 P
/now, /you //she–foxes — LR 3.06. 22
SHEKELS *(see sicles)*
SHE–LAMB 1 FR 0.0001 REL FR 0 V 1 P
and to betray a she–lamb of a twelvemonth to a AYL 3.02. 81 P
SHE'LD 2 FR 0.0002 REL FR 2 V 0 P
there's some great matter she'ld employ me in. TGV 4.03. 3
she'ld come again, and with a greedy ear OTH 1.03.149
SHELF 1 FR 0.0001 REL FR 1 V 0 P
that from a shelf the precious diadem stole, HAM 3.04.100
SHE'LL 48 FR 0.0054 REL FR 31 V 17 P
i fear she'll prove as hard to you in telling TGV 1.01.139 P
ay, but she'll think that it is spoke in hate. 3.02. 34
trust me, i thought on her. she'll fit it. WIV 2.01.161 P
she'll make you amends, i warrant you. 3.05. 47 P
she'll take the enterprise upon her, father, MM 4.01. 65
perchance, publicly, she'll be asham'd. 5.01.277 P
she'll burn a week longer than the whole world. ERR 3.02. 99 P
for she'll be up twenty times a night, and there ADO 2.03.131 P
she knew his love, lest she'll make sport at it. 3.01. 58
foulness, and she'll fall in love with my anger. AYL 3.05. 67 P
i think she'll sooner prove a soldier, | iron SHR 2.01.145
she says she'll see thee hang'd first. 2.01.300
and more shall be paid her than she'll demand. AWW 1.03.105 P
blood will nought deny | that she'll demand. 3.07. 22
if she be, it's four to one she'll none of me. TN 1.03.107 P
she'll none o' th' count. 1.03.109 P
she'll not match above her degree, neither in 1.03.109 P
rein i let her run, | but she'll not stumble. WT 2.03. 52
my daughter weeps, she'll not part with you, 1H4 3.01.192
she'll be a soldier too, she'll to the wars. 3.01.193
she'll be a soldier too, she'll to the wars. 3.01.193
she'll hamper thee, and dandle thee like a baby. 2H6 1.03.145
she'll gallop far enough to her destruction. 1.03.151
and fear'd | she'll with the labor end. H8 5.01. 20
he? no! she'll none of him. they two are twain. TRO 3.01.101 P
she's making her ready, she'll come straight. 3.02. 30 P
but she'll bereave you a' th' deeds too, if she 3.02. 56 P
she'll not be hit | with cupid's arrow, she hath ROM 1.01.208
'tis very late, she'll not come down to–night. 3.04. 5
she'll close and be herself, whilest our poor MAC 3.02. 14
let's make haste, she'll soon be back again. 3.05. 36
o, but she'll keep her word. HAM 3.02.231 P
i'll warrant she'll tax him home, | and, as you 3.03. 29
with her nails | she'll flea thy wolvish visage. LR 1.04.308
she'll find a white that shall her blackness OTH 2.01.133
lady, she'll run mad | when she shall lack it. 3.03.317
/faith, i must, she'll rail in the streets else. 4.01.163 P
and yet she'll kneel and pray; 4.02. 23
yet she must die, else she'll betray more men. 5.02. 6
if she come in, she'll sure speak to my wife. 5.02. 96
first, perchance, she'll prove on cats and dogs, CYM 1.05. 38
a sickness, say | she'll home to her father; 3.02. 75
that for this twelvemonth she'll not undertake PER 2.05. 3
twelve moons more she'll wear diana's livery; 2.05. 10
tells me here, she'll wed the stranger knight, 2.05. 16
she does, and swears she'll never stint, | make 4.04. 42
or she'll disfurnish us of all our cavalleria, 4.06. 11 P
i warrant her, she'll do the rarest gambols. TNK 3.05. 75
SHELL *(also sheal'd)*
SHELL 4 FR 0.0004 REL FR 1 V 3 P
idle head, you would eat chickens i' th' shell. TRO 1.02.134 P
grow mischievous, | and kill him in the shell. JC 2.01. 34
lapwing runs away with the shell on his head. HAM 5.02.185 P
canst tell how an oyster makes his shell? LR 1.05. 25 P
SHELLS 1 FR 0.0001 REL FR 1 V 0 P
thy corpse, | lying with simple shells. PER 3.01. 64
SHELLY 1 FR 0.0001 REL FR 1 V 0 P
shrinks backward in his shelly cave with pain, VEN 1034
SHELTER 15 FR 0.0017 REL FR 9 V 6 P
there is no other shelter hereabout. TMP 2.02. 39 P
seek shelter, pack! WIV 1.03. 82
oaths, under the shelter of your honor! 2.02. 28 P
tempest of provocation, i will shelter me here. 5.05. 21 P
i will bear thee to some shelter, and thou shalt AYL 2.06. 16 P
sing, | yet seek no shelter to avoid the storm; R2 2.01.264
which his broad–spreading leaves did shelter, 3.04. 50
come, shelter, shelter! 1H4 2.02. 1 P
come, shelter, shelter! 2.02. 1 P
and thou shalt prove a shelter to thy friends, 2H4 4.04. 42
whose arms gave shelter to the princely eagle, 3H6 5.02. 12
shall be no shelter to these outrages, | but he TIT 4.04. 22
the gods to their dear shelter take thee, maid, LR 1.01.182
now upon | the leavy shelter that abuts against PER 5.01. 51
to shelter thee from tempest and from rain: VEN 238
SHELTERS 1 FR 0.0001 REL FR 1 V 0 P
and the shelters whither | the routed fly; ANT 3.01. 8
SHELT'RED 1 FR 0.0001 REL FR 1 V 0 P
he was the covert'st shelt'red traitor | that R3 3.05. 33
SHELVES 3 FR 0.0003 REL FR 3 V 0 P
from shelves and rocks that threaten us with 3H6 5.04. 23
and about his shelves | a beggarly account of ROM 5.01. 44
high winds, strong pirates, shelves and sands, LUC 335
SHELVING 1 FR 0.0001 REL FR 1 V 0 P
and built so shelving that one cannot climb it TGV 3.01.115
SHELVY 1 FR 0.0001 REL FR 0 V 1 P
but that the shore was shelvy and shallow — a WIV 3.05. 15 P
SHE–MERCURY 1 FR 0.0001 REL FR 0 V 1 P
be brief, my good she–mercury. WIV 2.02. 80 P
/SHENT 1 FR 0.0001 REL FR 1 V 0 P
he /shent our messengers, and we lay by | our TRO 2.03. 79
SHENT 4 FR 0.0004 REL FR 1 V 3 P
we shall all be shent. WIV 1.04. 37 P
i am shent for speaking to you. TN 4.02.104 P
do you hear how we are shent for keeping your COR 5.02. 98 P
how in my words somever she be shent, | to give HAM 3.02.398
/SHEPHERD 1 FR 0.0001 REL FR 1 V 0 P
"/sleepest /or /wakest /thou, /jolly /shepherd? LR 3.06. 41
SHEPHERD 54 FR 0.0061 REL FR 32 V 22 P
stray, | and if the shepherd be awhile away. TGV 1.01. 75
you conclude that my master is a shepherd then, 1.01. 76 P
true; and thy master a shepherd. 1.01. 83 P
the shepherd seeks the sheep, and not the sheep 1.01. 86 P
seeks the shepherd, and not the sheep the shepherd; 1.01. 87 P
the sheep for fodder follow the shepherd, the 1.01. 89 P
the shepherd for food follows not the sheep; 1.01. 90 P
a fox to be the shepherd of thy lambs. 4.04. 92
look, th' unfolding star calls up the shepherd. MM 4.02.203 P
the wall | and dick the shepherd blows his nail LLL 5.02.913
the skillful shepherd pill'd me certain wands, MV 1.03. 84
alas, poor shepherd! AYL 2.04. 44
i prithee, shepherd, if that love or gold | can 2.04. 71
but i am shepherd to another man, | and do not 2.04. 78
truly, shepherd, in respect of itself, it is a 3.02. 13 P
hast any philosophy in thee, shepherd? 3.02. 22 P
wast ever in court, shepherd? 3.02. 33 P
thou art in a parlous state, shepherd. 3.02. 44 P
mend the instance, shepherd. 3.02. 69 P
shepherd, go off a little. 3.02.158 P
come, shepherd, let us make an honorable retreat 3.02.160 P
after the shepherd that complain'd of love, 3.04. 48
you foolish shepherd, wherefore do you follow 3.05. 49
so take her to thee, shepherd. 3.05. 63
shepherd, ply her hard. 3.05. 76
dead shepherd, now i find thy saw of might, 3.05. 81
well, shepherd, well, | this is a letter of your 4.03. 19
"art thou god to shepherd turn'd, | that a 4.03. 40
alas, poor shepherd! 4.03. 65
unto the shepherd youth | that he in sport doth 4.03.155
upon you, and here live and die a shepherd. 5.02. 12 P
you are there followed by a faithful shepherd — 5.02. 81
good shepherd, tell this youth what 'tis to love 5.02. 83
give yourself to this most faithful shepherd? 5.04. 14
or else, refusing me, to wed this shepherd; 5.04. 22
i do remember in this shepherd boy | some lively 5.04. 26
seldom from the house of a most homely shepherd, WT 4.02. 38 P
we are) have some question with the shepherd; 4.02. 49 P
do plainly give you out an unstain'd shepherd, 4.04.149
pray, good shepherd, what fair swain is this 4.04.166
how now, fair shepherd? 4.04.345
if that shepherd be not in hand–fast, let him 4.04.768 P
heard the old shepherd deliver the manner how he 5.02. 4 P
methought, i heard the shepherd say, he found 5.02. 7 P
now he thanks the old shepherd, which stands by 5.02. 55 P
master's death and in the view of the shepherd; 5.02. 70 P
not me begotten of a shepherd swain, | but 1H6 5.04. 37
till they have snar'd the shepherd of the flock, 2H6 2.02. 73
thus is the shepherd beaten from thy side, | and 3.01.191
what time the shepherd, blowing of his nails, 3H6 2.05. 3
so flies the reakless shepherd from the wolf; 5.06. 7
the shepherd knows not thunder from a tabor COR 1.06. 25
like a shepherd, | approach the fold and cull TIM 5.04. 42
o, sweet shepherd, hie thee, | for methinks thou PP 12.11
SHEPHERDESS 5 FR 0.0005 REL FR 4 V 1 P
with this shepherdess, my sister; AYL 3.02.335 P
praising the proud disdainful shepherdess | that 3.04. 50
shepherdess, look on him better, | and be not 3.05. 77
no shepherdess, but flora, | peering in april's WT 4.04. 2
shepherdess | (a fair one are you!), 4.04. 77
SHEPHERD'S 16 FR 0.0018 REL FR 10 V 6 P
more tuneable than lark to shepherd's ear | when MND 1.01.184
this shepherd's passion | is much upon my AYL 2.04. 60
and how like you this shepherd's life, master 3.02. 11 P
but in respect that it is a shepherd's life, it 3.02. 14 P
the shepherd's note since we have left our WT 1.02. 2
a shepherd's daughter, | and what to her adheres 4.01. 27
that should have married a shepherd's daughter. 4.04.767 P
o, that's the case of the shepherd's son. 4.04.816 P
his hopes, and with | a shepherd's daughter. 5.01.185
this avouches the shepherd's son, who has not 5.02. 64 P
that time, overfond of the shepherd's daughter 5.02.117 P
dolphin, i am by birth a shepherd's daughter, 1H6 1.02. 72
and to conclude, the shepherd's homely curds, 3H6 2.05. 47
and my leonatus | our neighbor shepherd's son! CYM 1.01.150
my shepherd's pipe can sound no deal, | my PP 17.17
young, | and truth in every shepherd's tongue, 19.18
SHEPHERDS 10 FR 0.0011 REL FR 7 V 3 P
when shepherds pipe on oaten straws | and merry LLL 5.02.903
would be uncleanly if courtiers were shepherds. AYL 3.02. 50 P
this, the devil himself will have no shepherds. 3.02. 84 P
there is three carters, three shepherds, three WT 4.04.324 P
to shepherds looking on their silly sheep | than 3H6 2.05. 43
pity of him as the wolf | does of the shepherds. COR 4.06.111
that liberal shepherds give a grosser name, HAM 4.07.170
sorrow to shepherds, woe unto the birds, | gusts VEN 455
that piteous looks to phrygian shepherds lent; LUC 1502
and see the shepherds feed their flocks, | by PP 19. 6
SHERIFF *(also shrieve, etc.)*
SHERIFF 10 FR 0.0011 REL FR 6 V 4 P
butler brought those horses from the sheriff? 1H4 2.03. 67
the sheriff with a most monstrous watch is at 2.04.482 P
the sheriff and all the watch are at the door, 2.04.489 P
if you will deny the sheriff, so, if not, let 2.04.496 P
call in the sheriff. 2.04.505 P
now, master sheriff, what is your will with me? 2.04.506
and, sheriff, i will engage my word to thee 2.04.514
your grace, we'll take her from the sheriff. 2H6 2.04. 17
and, master sheriff, | let not her penance 2.04. 74
sheriff, farewell, and better than i fare, 2.04.100
SHERIFF'S 1 FR 0.0001 REL FR 0 V 1 P
he'll stand at your door like a sheriff's post, TN 1.05.148 P
SHERRIS 4 FR 0.0004 REL FR 0 V 4 P
of your excellent sherris is the warming of the 2H4 4.03.103 P
but the sherris warms it, and makes it course 4.03.106 P
and this valor comes of sherris. 4.03.113 P
drinking good and good store of fertile sherris, 4.03.121 P
SHERRIS–SACK 1 FR 0.0001 REL FR 0 V 1 P
a good sherris–sack hath a twofold operation in 2H4 4.03. 96 P

SHE'S 173 FR 0.0195 REL FR 118 V 55 P
the still–vex'd bermoothes, there she's hid; TMP 1.02.229
but by immortal providence she's mine. 5.01.189
no token but stones, for she's as hard as steel. TGV 1.01.140 P
then | she's fled unto that peasant valentine; 5.02. 35
why, sir, she's a good creature. WIV 2.02. 55 P
your ear, she's as fartuous a civil modest wife, 2.02. 97 P
and now she's going to my wife, and falstaff's 3.02. 36 P
pray you do so, she's a very tattling woman. 3.03. 91 P
she's coming; 3.04. 36 P
she's as big as he is. 4.02. 77 P
he swears she's a witch, forbade her my house, 4.02. 86 P
old fat woman even now with me, but she's gone. 4.05. 25 P
anne page, and she's a great lubberly boy. 5.05.184 P
she's very near her hour. MM 2.02. 16
she's come to know | if yet her brother's pardon 4.03.107
sir, she's the kitchen wench and all grease, and ERR 3.02. 95 P
faith, methinks she's too low for a high praise, ADO 1.01.171 P
no child but hero, she's his only heir. 1.01.295
in faith, she's too curst. 2.01. 20 P
she's an excellent sweet lady, and (out of all 2.03.159 P
she's a fair lady. 2.03.245 P
she's limed, i warrant you. 3.01.104
she's but the sign and semblance of her honor. 4.01. 33
why then she's mine. 5.04. 55
she's too hard for you at pricks, sir, challenge LLL 4.01.138
took the moon at full, but now she's changed. 5.02.214
to make my lady laugh when she's dispos'd, 5.02.466
she's quick, the child brags in her belly 5.02.676 P
be a woman, she's a good wench for this gear. MV 2.02.166 P
or shall i think in silver she's immur'd, 2.07. 52
she's too rough for me. SHR 1.01. 55
that she's the choice love of signior gremio. 1.02.234
that she's the chosen of signior hortensio. 1.02.235
she's apt to learn and thankful for good turns. 2.01.165
for she's not froward, but modest as the dove; 2.01.293
to me she's married, not unto my clothes. 3.02.117
why, she's a devil, a devil, the devil's dam. 3.02.156
tut, she's a lamb, a dove, a fool to him! 3.02.157
that, being mad herself, she's madly mated. 3.02.244
is she so hot a shrew as she's reported? 4.01. 21 P
i see she's like to have neither cap nor gown. 4.03. 93
and how she's like to be lucentio's wife. 4.04. 66
then, young bertram, take her, she's thy wife. AWW 2.03.105
fair, | in these to nature she's immediate heir; 2.03.132
she's very merry, but yet she is not well; 2.04. 3 P
but thanks be given, she's very well, and wants 2.04. 4 P
what does she ail that she's not very well? 2.04. 7 P
truly, she's very well indeed, but for two 2.04. 8 P
one, that she's not in heaven, whither god send 2.04. 11 P
the other, that she's in earth, from whence god 2.04. 12 P
but you say she's honest. 3.06.111
she's a fair creature; 3.06.116
she's none of mine, my lord. 5.03.169
she's impudent, my lord, | and was a common 5.03.187
kinsman, she's nothing allied to your disorders. TN 2.03. 97 P
from my niece, and that she's in love with him. 2.03.165 P
before me, she's a good wench. 2.03.178 P
she's a beagle, true–bred, and one that adores 2.03.179 P
as she's rare, | must it be great; WT 1.02.452
her sport herself | with that she's big with, 2.01. 61
will thereto add | 'tis pity she's not honest — 2.01. 68
when you have said she's goodly, come between 2.01. 75
come between | ere you can say she's honest: 2.01. 76
to grieve it should be) | she's an adultress. 2.01. 78
i have said | she's an adultress, i have said 2.01. 88
more — she's a traitor, and camillo is | a 2.01. 89
vild principal — that she's | a bed–swerver, 2.01. 92
if it prove | she's otherwise, i'll keep my 2.01.134
i say she's dead; 3.02.203
she's as forward of her breeding as | she is i' 4.04.580
way but to tell the king she's a changeling, and 4.04.688 P
o, she's warm! 5.03.109
she's neither fish nor flesh, a man knows not 1H4 3.03.127 P
for one of them, she's in hell already, and 2H4 2.04.338 P
she cannot choose but be old, certain she's old, 3.02.208 P
marry, for that she's in a wrong belief, | i go 1H6 2.03. 31
she's beautiful; 5.03. 78
she's tickled now; 2H6 1.03.150
win him, | for she's a woman to be pitied much. 3H6 3.01. 36
ay, but she's come to beg; 3.01. 42
notwithstanding she's your wife | and loves not R3 1.03. 22
and so doth mine. i muse why she's at liberty. 1.03.304
now, for my life, she's wand'ring to the tower, 4.01. 3
alas, poor lady! | she's a stranger now again. H8 2.03. 17
she's going away. 2.04.124
she's noble born; 2.04.142
yet my conscience says | she's a good creature, 5.01. 25
because she's kin to me, therefore she's not so TRO 1.01. 74 P
kin to me, therefore she's not so fair as helen. 1.01. 74 P
she's a fool to stay behind her father, let her 1.01. 80 P
then she's a merry greek indeed. 1.02.109 P
she's making her ready, she'll come straight. 3.02. 30 P
she's bitter to her country. 4.01. 69
she's well, but bade me not commend her to you. 4.05.180
name her not now, sir, she's a deadly theme. 4.05.181
she's noted. 5.02. 11 P
they say she's mad. COR 4.02. 9
a man's wife is when she's fall'n out with her 4.03. 33 P
she's with the lion deeply still in league, TIT 4.01. 98
you rememb'red, marcus, she's gone, she's fled. 4.03. 5
you rememb'red, marcus, she's gone, she's fled. 4.03. 5
a right good mark–man! and she's fair i love. ROM 1.01.206
she's the hopeful lady of my earth. 1.02. 15
she's not fourteen. 1.03. 12
spoken, i have but four — | she's not fourteen. 1.03. 14
to–night she's mewed up to her heaviness. 3.04. 11
she's dead, deceas'd, she's dead, alack the day! 4.05. 23
she's dead, deceas'd, she's dead, alack the day! 4.05. 23
alack the day, she's dead, she's dead, she's 4.05. 24
the day, she's dead, she's dead, she's dead! 4.05. 24
the day, she's dead, she's dead, she's dead! 4.05. 24
out, alas, she's cold, | her blood is settled, 4.05. 25
she's not well married that lives married long, 4.05. 77
but she's best married that dies married young. 4.05. 78
she's e'en setting on water to scald such TIM 2.02. 69 P
a woman, sir, but, rest her soul, she's dead. HAM 5.01.136 P
your grace, | she's there, and she is yours. LR 1.01.201
for though she's as like this as a crab's like 1.05. 15 P
go after her; she's desperate, govern her. 5.03.162
it came even from the heart of — o, she's dead! 5.03.225
she's gone for ever! 5.03.260
she's dead as earth. 5.03.262
i might have sav'd her, now she's gone for ever! 5.03.271
in her, she's full of most bless'd condition. OTH 2.01.249 P
she's a most exquisite lady. 2.03. 18 P
indeed she's a most fresh and delicate creature. 2.03. 20 P
she's fram'd as fruitful | as the free elements. 2.03.341
of years (yet that's not much), | she's gone. 3.03.267
give me a living reason she's disloyal. 3.03.409
she's the worse for all this. 4.01.191 P
and she's obedient, as you say, obedient; 4.01.255
yet she's a simple bawd | that cannot say as 4.02. 20
she's dead. 5.02. 91
she's like a liar gone to burning hell: 5.02.129
she's good, being gone; ANT 1.02.126
she's dead, my queen. 1.03. 59
she's a most triumphant lady, if report be 2.02.184 P
and i do think she's thirty. 3.03. 28
she's dead too, our sovereign. 4.15. 69
may frame herself | to th' way she's forc'd to. 5.01. 56
she's wedded, | her husband banish'd, she CYM 1.01. 7
she's a good sign, but i have seen small 1.02. 30 P
is dead, or she's outpriz'd by a trifle. 1.04. 81 P
of his remembrance on't, | and then she's yours. 2.03. 44
she's my good lady, and will conceive, i hope, 2.03.153
she's punish'd for her truth, and undergoes, 3.02. 7
she's a lady | so tender of rebukes that words 3.05. 39
love, she's flown | to her desir'd posthumus. 3.05. 61
for she's fair and royal, | and that she hath 3.05. 70
she's fair enough, and what he learns by this 3.05.102
i'll write to my lord she's dead. 3.05.104
nay, how absolute she's in't, | not minding PER 2.05. 19
i'll swear she's dead, | and thrown into the sea 4.01. 98
you say she's a virgin? 4.02. 41 P
upon her, she's able to freeze the god priapus, 4.06. 3 P
my lord, she's not pac'd yet, you must take some 4.06. 63 P
she's born to undo us. 4.06.149 P
she's a gallant lady. 5.01. 66
she's such a one that, were i well assur'd 5.01. 67
o, she's but overjoy'd. 5.03. 21
her, | and, if she be as gentle as she's fair, TNK 2.03. 15
be as gentle as she's fair, | i know she's his; 2.03. 16
if she see him once, she's gone — she's done, 4.01.124
if she see him once, she's gone — she's done, 4.01.124
she's lost | past all cure. 4.01.139
what broken piece of matter soe'er she's about, 4.03. 6 P
how prettily she's amiss! 4.03. 28 P
i hope she's pleas'd, | her signs were gracious. 5.01.172
she's eighteen. 5.02. 31
many a murther | set off whereto she's guilty. 5.03. 28
sir, she's well restor'd, | and to be married 5.04. 27
she's love, she loves, and yet she is not lov'd. VEN 610
the father says, "she's mine." LUC 1795
SHES 2 FR 0.0002 REL FR 2 V 0 P
him swear | the shes of italy should not betray CYM 1.03. 29
'twixt two such shes would chatter this way, and 1.06. 40
SHEW *(also show)*
SHEW 1 FR 0.0001 REL FR 1 V 0 P
'tis charity to shew. SHR 4.01.211
SHE–WOLF 1 FR 0.0001 REL FR 1 V 0 P
she–wolf of france, but worse than wolves of 3H6 1.04.111
/SHIELD 1 FR 0.0001 REL FR 1 V 0 P
/a /woman's /shape /doth /shield /thee. LR 4.02. 67
SHIELD 26 FR 0.0029 REL FR 24 V 2 P
heaven shield my mother play'd my father fair! MM 3.01.140
heaven shield your grace from woe, | as i, thus 5.01.118
field with targe and shield did make my foe to LLL 5.02.553
with /yourselves, to bring in (god shield us!) MND 3.01. 30 P
heavens shield lysander, if they mean a fray! 3.02.447
jove shield thee well for this! 5.01.178
god shield you mean it not! AWW 1.03.168
and sword and shield, | in bloody field, | doth H5 3.02. 9
shield thee from warwick's frown, | and pray 3H6 4.05. 28
my counsel is my shield; R3 4.03. 56
master — | whose honor heaven shield from soil! H8 1.02. 26
the great aufidius | a shield as hard as his. COR 1.06. 80
given your enemy your shield, think to front his 5.02. 41 P
jove shield your husband from his hounds to–day! TIT 2.03. 70
than foemen's marks upon his batt'red shield, 4.01.127
god shield i should disturb devotion! ROM 4.01. 41
before my body | i throw my warlike shield. MAC 5.08. 33
to shield thee from disasters of the world, LR 1.01.174
o, he's more mad | than telamon for his shield; ANT 4.13. 2
the sevenfold shield of ajax cannot keep | the 4.14. 38
it hath been a shield | 'twixt me and death" — PER 2.01.126
and the device he bears upon his shield | is a 2.02. 19
and the device he bears upon his shield | is an 2.02. 25
and hang | your shield afore your heart, about TNK 1.01.197
his batt'red shield, his uncontrolled crest, VEN 104
silver cheeks, and call'd it then their shield, LUC 61
SHIELDED 2 FR 0.0002 REL FR 2 V 0 P
and shielded him | from this earth–vexing smart. CYM 5.04. 41
with safest distance i mine honor shielded. LC 151
SHIELDS 2 FR 0.0002 REL FR 2 V 0 P
now put your shields before your hearts, and COR 1.04. 24
and fight | with hearts more proof than shields. 1.04. 25
/SHIFT 1 FR 0.0001 REL FR 0 V 1 P
/have /made /a /shift /to eat up thy holland. 2H4 2.02. 22 P
SHIFT 27 FR 0.0030 REL FR 14 V 13 P
every man shift for all the rest, and let no man TMP 5.01.256 P
i must cony–catch, i must shift. WIV 1.03. 34 P
o mistress, mistress, shift and save yourself! ERR 5.01.168
no, faith, thou sing'st well enough for a shift. ADO 2.03. 78 P
i hope i shall make shift to go without him. MV 1.02. 90 P
matter, the cleanliest shift is to kiss. AYL 4.01. 77 P
tears, | an onion will do well for such a shift, SHR in.1. 126
i mean to shift my bush, | and then pursue me as 5.02. 46
you have made shift to run into't, boots and AWW 2.05. 36 P
let it alone, i'll make other shift. 2H4 2.01.156 P
to remember, not to have patience to shift me — 5.05. 22 P
then, | unto southampton do we shift our scene. H5 2.pr. 42
and now there rests no other shift but this, 1H6 2.01. 75
for me, i will make shift for one; 2H6 4.08. 31 P
when he was made a shriver, 'twas for shift. 3H6 3.02.108
be that heart that forc'd us to this shift! TIT 4.01. 72
he shift a trencher? ROM 1.05. 2 P
when fortune in her shift and change of mood TIM 1.01. 84
legs sometime, yet i made a shift to cast him. MAC 2.03. 41 P
not be dainty of leave–taking, | but shift away. 2.03.145
then we'll shift our ground. HAM 1.05.156
taught me to shift | into a madman's rags, t' LR 5.03.187
and, should we shift estates, yours would be ANT 5.02.152
sir, i would advise you to shift a shirt; CYM 1.02. 1 P
if my shirt were bloody, then to shift it. 1.02. 5 P
to shift his being | is to exchange one misery 1.05. 54
guilty of treason, forgery, and shift, | guilty LUC 920
SHIFTED 4 FR 0.0004 REL FR 3 V 1 P
too, that thou hast shifted out of thy tale into ADO 3.03.142 P
and, like a shifted wind unto a sail, | it makes JN 4.02. 23
my shame will not be shifted with my sheet. 2H6 2.04.107
i shifted him away, | and laid good 'scuses upon OTH 4.01. 78
SHIFTING 3 FR 0.0003 REL FR 3 V 0 P
thou run'st before me, shifting every place, MND 3.02.423
o, hear me then, injurious, shifting time! LUC 930
but not acquainted | with shifting change, as is SON 20. 4
SHIFTS 9 FR 0.0010 REL FR 9 V 0 P
for thy complexion shifts to strange effects, MM 3.01. 24
i see a man here needs not live by shifts, ERR 3.02.182
the sixt age shifts | into the lean and AYL 2.07.157
i'll find a thousand shifts to get away. JN 4.03. 7
for it is you that puts us to our shifts. TIT 4.02.176
dodge | and palter in the shifts of lowness, who ANT 3.11. 63
danger deviseth shifts, wit waits on fear. VEN 690
and as one shifts, another straight ensues: LUC 1104
in the world doth spend | shifts but his place, SON 9.10
SHILLING *(also silling)*
SHILLING 5 FR 0.0005 REL FR 1 V 4 P
that cost me two shilling and two pence a–piece WIV 1.01.156 P
tods, every tod yields pound and odd shilling; WT 4.03. 33 P
him down, bardolph, like a shove–groat shilling. 2H4 2.04.193 P
twenty fifteens, and one shilling to the pound, 2H6 4.07. 22 P
i'll undertake may see away their shilling H8 pr 12
/SHILLINGS 1 FR 0.0001 REL FR 0 V 1 P
/have /my /eight /shillings /i /won /from /you H5 2.01.105 P
SHILLINGS 10 FR 0.0011 REL FR 0 V 10 P
had rather than forty shillings i had my book of WIV 1.01.198 P
five shillings to one on't, with any man that ADO 3.03. 78 P
rather than forty shillings i had such a leg, TN 2.03. 20 P
if thou darest not stand for ten shillings. 1H4 1.02.141 P
in his life than "eight shillings and sixpence," 2.04. 25 P
a true woman, holland of eight shillings an ell. 3.03. 72 P
kiss me, and bid me fetch thee thirty shillings? 2H4 2.01.102 P
four harry ten shillings in french crowns for 3.02.221 P
pay me the eight shillings i won of you at H5 2.01. 94 P
a pound, meal at nine shillings a bushel, and STM II.C 2 P
SHIN 7 FR 0.0008 REL FR 4 V 3 P
i bruis'd my shin th' other day with playing at WIV 1.01.283 P
here's a costard broken in a shin. LLL 3.01. 70
by saying that a costard was broken in a shin. 3.01.106
me, how was there a costard broken in a shin? 3.01.112 P
fell over the threshold, and broke my shin. 3.01.117
till there be more matter in the shin. 3.01.119 P
for your broken shin. ROM 1.02. 52
SHINE 54 FR 0.0061 REL FR 46 V 8 P
you, and shine through you like the water in an TGV 2.01. 39 P
thou reach stars, because they shine on thee? 3.01.156
then did the sun on dunghill shine. WIV 1.03. 63 P
thou, fair sun, which on my earth dost shine, LLL 4.03. 67
ay, as some days, but then no sun must shine. 4.03. 89
o, 'tis the sun that maketh all things shine! 4.03.242
and these thy stars, to shine | (those clouds 5.02.205
and phibbus' car | shall shine from far, | and MND 1.02. 36
doth the moon shine that night we play our play? 3.01. 51 P
yes; it doth shine that night. 3.01. 55 P
open, and the moon may shine in at the casement. 3.01. 58 P
let her shine as gloriously | as the venus of 3.02.106
shine, comforts, from the east, | that i may 3.02.432
my stars shine darkly over me. TN 2.01. 3 P
and heavens so shine | that they may fairly note 4.03. 34
that sun that warms you here shall shine on me, R2 1.03.145
to see him shine so brisk and smell so sweet, 1H4 1.03. 54
let it shine, then. 2H4 4.03. 57 P
thine's too thick to shine. 4.03. 58 P
late did he shine upon the english side; 1H6 1.02. 3
it pleas'd | to shine on my contemptible estate. 1.02. 75
now shine it like a comet of revenge, | a 3.02. 31
advance our half–fac'd sun, striving to shine, 2H6 4.01. 98
shine out, fair sun, till i have bought a glass, R3 1.02.262
then he disdains to shine, for by the book | he 5.03.278
not shine to–day? 5.03.285
of beauty | shall shine at full upon them. H8 1.04. 60
where ever the bright sun of heaven shall shine, 5.04. 50
but let desert in pure election shine, | and, TIT 1.01. 16
i will be bright, and shine in pearl and gold, 2.01. 19
doth shine upon the dead man's earthy cheeks, 2.03.229
so pale did shine the moon on /pyramus | when he 2.03.231
i wonder on't, he was wont to shine at seven. TIM 3.04. 10
if after two days' shine athens contain thee, 3.05.100
whereon hyperion's quick'ning fire doth shine: 4.03.184
they are all fire, and every one doth shine; JC 3.01. 64
like stars, shall shine | on all deservers. MAC 1.04. 41
as upon thee, macbeth, their speeches shine — 3.01. 7
your spirits shine through you. 3.01.127
for a quality | wherein, they say, you shine. HAM 4.07. 73
for he would shine on those | that make their ANT 1.05. 55
thou show'dst a subject's shine, | a true PER 1.02.124
still blossom | as her bright eyes shine on ye, TNK 2.02.234
i' th' night, and you | the only star to shine. 5.03. 20
as if from thence they borrowed all their shine. VEN 488
eyes like glow–worms shine when he doth fret, 621
cynthia for shame obscures her silver shine, 728
thou, fair sun, that on this earth doth shine, PP 3.10
yet not for me, shine sun to succor flowers! 14.28
so between them love did shine, | that the PHT 33
even so my sun one early morn did shine | with SON 33. 9
but you shall shine more bright in these 55. 3
in black ink my love may still shine bright. 65.14
and in my will no fair acceptance shine? 135. 8
SHINES 31 FR 0.0035 REL FR 25 V 6 P
when the sun shines, let foolish gnats make ERR 2.02. 30
nor shines the silver moon one half so bright LLL 4.03. 29
fast, | and yonder shines aurora's harbinger, MND 3.02.380

truly, the moon shines with a good grace. 5.01.267 P
the moon shines bright. MV 5.01. 1
so shines a good deed in a naughty world. 5.01. 91
a substitute shines brightly as a king | until a 5.01. 94
lord, how bright and goodly shines the moon! SHR 4.05. 2
i say it is the moon that shines so bright. 4.05. 4
i know it is the sun that shines so bright. 4.05. 5
the orb like the sun, it shines every where. TN 3.01. 39 P
the pale moon shines by night; WT 4.03. 16
the self–same sun that shines upon his court 4.04.444
the moon shines fair, you may away by night. 1H4 3.01.140
when it shines seldom in admiring eyes; 3.02. 80
and the lightness of his wife shines through it; 2H4 1.02. 47 P
for it shines bright and never changes, but H5 5.02.163 P
and who shines now but henry's enemies? 3H6 2.06. 10
the sun shines hot, and, if we use delay, | cold 4.08. 60
here never shines the sun, here nothing breeds, TIT 2.03. 96
for though it be night, yet the moon shines; LR 2.02. 31 P
our italy | shines o'er with civil swords; ANT 1.03. 45
thy lustre thickens | when he shines by. 2.03. 29
she shines not upon fools, lest the reflection CYM 1.02. 32 P
hath britain all the sun that shines? 3.04.136
by this sun that shines, | i'll thither. 4.04. 34
cymbeline, | which shines here in the west. 5.05.476
"the sun that shines from heaven shines but warm VEN 193
sun that shines from heaven shines but warm, 193
sometime too hot the eye of heaven shines, | and SON 18. 5
when to unseeing eyes thy shade shines so! 43. 8

/SHINETH 1 FR 0.0001 REL FR 1 V 0 P
/a /brittle /glory /shineth /in /this /face, R2 4.01.287

SHINING 17 FR 0.0019 REL FR 17 V 0 P
have no more profit of their shining nights LLL 1.01. 90
i thank thee, moon, for shining now so bright; MND 5.01.273
with his satchel | and shining morning face, AYL 2.07.146
so clear, so shining, and so evident, | that it 1H6 2.04. 23
with shining checker'd slough, doth sting a 2H6 3.01.229
i bear | upon my target three fair shining suns. 3H6 2.01. 40
cause | to wail the dimming of our shining star; R3 2.02.102
that i will show you shining at this feast, ROM 1.02. 98
will cry | to th' shining synod of the rest CYM 5.04. 89
and set him by him, | a shining constellation. TNK 4.02. 18
him, black and shining | like ravens' wings; 4.02. 83
from whom each lamp and shining star doth borrow VEN 861
nor read the subtle shining secrecies | writ in LUC 101
"o shame to knighthood and to shining arms! 197
words like wildfire burnt the shining glory | of 1523
with shining falchion in my chamber came | a 1626
good, | a shining gloss that vadeth suddenly, PP 13. 2

SHINS 4 FR 0.0004 REL FR 3 V 1 P
and thorns, | which ent'red their frail shins. TMP 4.01.181
arms, legs, backs, shoulders, sides, and shins. WIV 5.05. 54
mine own wit till i break my shins against it. AYL 2.04. 59 P
hollow bones of man, strike their sharp shins, TIM 4.03.152

SHIN'ST 1 FR 0.0001 REL FR 1 V 0 P
thou shin'st in every tear that i do weep, | no LLL 4.03. 32

SHINY 1 FR 0.0001 REL FR 1 V 0 P
the night | is shiny, and they say we shall ANT 4.09. 3

/SHIP 1 FR 0.0001 REL FR 0 V 1 P
with my /master's /ship? why, it is at sea. TGV 3.01.282 P

SHIP 54 FR 0.0061 REL FR 44 V 10 P
though the ship were no stronger than a nutshell TMP 1.01. 47 P
it should the good ship so have swallow'd and 1.02. 12
i boarded the king's ship; 1.02.196
of the king's ship, | the mariners, say how thou 1.02.224
safely in harbor | is the king's ship, in the 1.02.227
supposing that they saw the king's ship wrack'd, 1.02.236
to the king's ship, invisible as thou art; 5.01. 97
the next, our ship — | which, but three glasses 5.01.222
beheld | our royal, good, and gallant ship; 5.01.237
and in the morn | i'll bring you to your ship, 5.01.308
go, go, be gone, to save your ship from wrack, TGV 1.01.148
and left the ship, then sinking–ripe, to us. ERR 1.01. 77
our helpful ship was splitted in the midst; 1.01.103
at length, another ship had seiz'd on us, | and, 1.01.112
if any ship put out, then straight away. 3.02.185
the ship is in her trim, the merry wind | blows 4.01. 90
sheep, | what ship of epidamium stays for me? 4.01. 94
a ship you sent me to, to hire waftage. 4.01. 95
the ship is under sail, and here she comes amain LLL 5.02.546
and in their ship i am sure lorenzo is not. MV 2.08. 3
who went with him to search bassanio's ship. 2.08. 5
he came too late, the ship was under sail, | but 2.08. 6
duke | they were not with bassanio in his ship. 2.08. 11
that antonio hath a ship of rich lading wrack'd 3.01. 3 P
the carcasses of many a tall ship lie buried, as 3.01. 6 P
why, the end is, he hath lost a ship. 3.01. 17 P
assure yourself, after our ship did split, TN 1.02. 9
our ship hath touch'd upon | the deserts of WT 3.03. 1
now the ship boring the moon with her mainmast, 3.03. 92 P
but to make an end of the ship, to see how the 3.03. 98 P
i would you had been by the ship side, to have 3.03.109 P
he is gone aboard a new ship to purge melancholy 4.04.763 P
their promises, | ere he take ship for france; H5 2.pr. 30
now am i like that proud insulting ship | which 1H6 1.02.138
for there i'll ship them all for ireland. 2H6 3.01.329
like to a ship that, having scap'd a tempest, 4.09. 32
in his moan, the ship splits on the rock, 3H6 5.04. 10
but we will ship him hence, and this vile deed HAM 4.01. 30
on the instant they got clear of our ship, so i 4.06. 19 P
a noble ship of venice | hath seen a grievous OTH 2.01. 22
the ship is here put in. 2.01. 25
that he may bless this bay with his tall ship, 2.01. 79
the riches of the ship is come on shore! 2.01. 83
we'll to our ship, | away, my thetis! ANT 3.07. 59
i have a ship | laden with gold, take that, 3.11. 4
i will possess you of that ship and treasure. 3.11. 21
slow his soul sail'd on, | how swift his ship. CYM 1.03. 14
that the ship | should house him safe is wrack'd PER 2.ch. 31
dives, | so up and down the poor ship drives. 3.ch. 50
in your imagination hold | this stage the ship, 3.ch. 59
and will not lie till the ship be clear'd of the 3.01. 49 P
from whence | lysimachus our tyrian ship espies, 5.ch. 18
yonder's the sea, and there's a ship. TNK 3.04. 5
you are master of a ship? 4.01.142

SHIPBOARD 2 FR 0.0002 REL FR 2 V 0 P
master, shall i fetch your stuff from shipboard? ERR 5.01.409
fear eyes over) to shipboard | get undescried. WT 4.04.654

SHIP–BOY'S 2 FR 0.0002 REL FR 2 V 0 P
this ship–boy's semblance hath disguis'd me JN 4.03. 4
and giddy /mast | seal up the ship–boy's eyes, 2H4 3.01. 19

SHIP–BOYS 1 FR 0.0001 REL FR 1 V 0 P
upon the hempen tackle ship–boys climbing; H5 3.pr. 8

SHIPMAN'S 2 FR 0.0002 REL FR 2 V 0 P
quarters that they know | i' th' shipman's card. MAC 1.03. 17
so puts himself unto the shipman's toil, | with PER 1.03. 23

SHIPMEN 1 FR 0.0001 REL FR 1 V 0 P
spout | which shipmen do the hurricano call, TRO 5.02.172

SHIPP'D 11 FR 0.0012 REL FR 10 V 1 P
expects my coming, there to see me shipp'd. TGV 1.01. 54
twenty to one then he is shipp'd already, | and 1.01. 72
thy master is shipp'd, and thou art to post 2.03. 34 P
i hope the king is not yet shipp'd for ireland. R2 2.02. 42
then wherefore dost thou hope he is not shipp'd? 2.02. 45
and safely brought to dover, wherein shipp'd, 1H6 5.01. 49
lord — | and shipp'd from thence to flanders? 3H6 4.05. 21
andronicus, would thou were shipp'd to hell, TIT 1.01.206
this wicked emperor may have shipp'd her hence, 4.03. 23
is he well shipp'd? OTH 2.01. 47
that i was shipp'd at sea i well remember, PER 3.04. 5

SHIPPED 1 FR 0.0001 REL FR 1 V 0 P
his clutch, | and hath shipped me into the land, HAM 5.01. 73

SHIPPING 6 FR 0.0006 REL FR 5 V 1 P
the church together, god send 'em good shipping! SHR 5.01. 42 P
take therefore shipping, post, my lord, to 1H6 5.05. 87
he say he lent me | some shipping unrestor'd. ANT 3.06. 27
our overplus of shipping will we burn, | and, 3.07. 50
and his shipping | (poor ignorant baubles!) CYM 3.01. 26
what shipping and what lading's in our haven, PER 1.02. 49

/SHIPS 1 FR 0.0001 REL FR 1 V 0 P
/to /the /port /of /athens /sent /their /ships TRO pr 3

SHIPS 30 FR 0.0034 REL FR 27 V 3 P
and we discovered | two ships from far, making ERR 1.01. 92
ere the ships could meet by twice five leagues, 1.01.100
is there any ships puts forth to–night? 4.03. 35 P
and wherefore not ships? LLL 2.01.219
but ships are but boards, sailors but men; MV 1.03. 22 P
my ships come home a month before the day. 1.03.181
"sweet bassanio, my ships have all miscarried, 3.02.315 P
for here i read for certain that my ships | are 5.01.287
your ships are stay'd at venice, and the duke, SHR 4.02. 83
my ships are ready, and | my people did expect WT 1.02.449
i ey'd them | even to their ships. 2.01. 36
by the duke of britain | with eight tall ships, R2 2.01.286
your ships already are in readiness. 1H6 3.01.185
turn back and fly, like ships before the wind, 3H6 1.04. 4
safe–conducting the rebels from their ships? R3 4.04.482
price hath launch'd above a thousand ships, TRO 2.02. 82
your ships are not well mann'd, | your mariners ANT 3.07. 34
their ships are yare, yours heavy. 3.07. 38
place | we may the number of the ships behold, 3.09. 3
his coin, ships, legions, | may be a coward's, 3.13. 22
green neptune's back | with ships made cities, 4.14. 59
you here at milford–haven with your ships. CYM 4.02.335
shore, | a portly sail of ships make hitherward. PER 1.04. 61
let not our ships and number of our men | be 1.04. 86
and these our ships, you happily may think | are 1.04. 92
and harborage for ourself, our ships, and men. 1.04.100
was by the rough seas reft of ships and men, 2.03. 84
of the seas | bereft of ships and men, cast on 2.03. 89
well–sailing ships and bounteous winds have 4.04. 17
of their ladies, | like tall ships under sail; TNK 2.02. 12

SHIP–TIRE 1 FR 0.0001 REL FR 0 V 1 P
beauty of the brow that becomes the ship–tire, WIV 3.03. 57 P

SHIPWRACK 4 FR 0.0004 REL FR 4 V 0 P
either to suffer shipwrack, or arrive | where i 1H6 5.05. 8
and see his shipwrack and his commonweal's. TIT 2.01. 24
my shipwrack now's no ill, | since i have here PER 2.01.133
and after shipwrack driven upon this shore. 2.03. 85

SHIPWRACK'D 2 FR 0.0002 REL FR 2 V 0 P
healthful welcome to their shipwrack'd guests, ERR 1.01.114
shipwrack'd upon a kingdom, where no pity, | no H8 3.01.149

SHIPWRACKING 1 FR 0.0001 REL FR 1 V 0 P
shipwracking storms and direful thunders /break, MAC 1.02. 26

SHIPWRIGHT 2 FR 0.0002 REL FR 0 V 2 P
stronger than either the mason, the shipwright, HAM 5.01. 42 P
who builds stronger than a mason, a shipwright, 5.01. 50 P

SHIPWRIGHTS 1 FR 0.0001 REL FR 1 V 0 P
why such impress of shipwrights, whose sore task HAM 1.01. 75

SHIRE 1 FR 0.0001 REL FR 1 V 0 P
let there be letters writ to every shire, | of H8 1.02.103

SHIRLEY 1 FR 0.0001 REL FR 1 V 0 P
the spirits | of valiant shirley, stafford, 1H4 5.04. 41

SHIRT 15 FR 0.0017 REL FR 5 V 10 P
i'll do it in my shirt. LLL 5.02.698 P
pardon me, i will not combat in my shirt. 5.02.705 P
the naked truth of it is, i have no shirt; 5.02.710 P
there's not a shirt and a half in all my company 1H4 4.02. 42 P
and the half shirt is two napkins tack'd 4.02. 43 P
and the shirt, to say the truth, stol'n from my 4.02. 45 P
and work in their shirt too, as myself, for 2H6 4.07. 52 P
two, two: a shirt and a smock. ROM 2.04.103 P
chamberlain, | will put thy shirt on warm? TIM 4.03.223
pale as his shirt, his knees knocking each other HAM 2.01. 78
here's one comes in his shirt, with light and OTH 5.01. 47
i'll bind it with my shirt. 5.01. 73
the shirt of nessus is upon me; ANT 4.12. 43
sir, i would advise you to shift a shirt; CYM 1.02. 1 P
if my shirt were bloody, then to shift it. 1.02. 5 P

SHIRTS 6 FR 0.0006 REL FR 1 V 5 P
ramm'd me in with foul shirts and smocks, socks, WIV 3.05. 90 P
i bought you a dozen of shirts to your back. 1H4 3.03. 68 P
by the lord, i take but two shirts out with me, 2H4 1.02.209 P
or to bear the inventory of thy shirts, as, one 2.02. 17 P
suits to his back, six shirts to his body — LR 3.04.136 P
things needful — files and shirts and perfumes. TNK 3.03. 48

SHIVE 1 FR 0.0001 REL FR 1 V 0 P
and easy it is | of a cut loaf to steal a shive, TIT 2.01. 87

SHIVER 1 FR 0.0001 REL FR 1 V 0 P
where i have seen them shiver and look pale, MND 5.01. 95

SHIVER'D 2 FR 0.0002 REL FR 2 V 0 P
precipitating), | thou'dst shiver'd like an egg: LR 4.06. 51
torn, | and shiver'd all the beauty of my glass, LUC 1763

SHIVERING* 2 FR 0.0002 REL FR 2 V 0 P
"the raging rocks | and shivering shocks | shall MND 1.02. 32
where shivering cold and sickness pines the R2 5.01. 77

/SHIVERS 1 FR 0.0001 REL FR 1 V 0 P
/it /is, /crack'd /in /an /hundred /shivers. R2 4.01.289

SHIVERS 1 FR 0.0001 REL FR 0 V 1 P
he would pun thee into shivers with his fist, as TRO 2.01. 39 P

/SHOAL 1 FR 0.0001 REL FR 1 V 0 P
but here, upon this bank and /shoal of time, MAC 1.07. 6

SHOALS 1 FR 0.0001 REL FR 1 V 0 P
and sounded all the depths and shoals of honor, H8 3.02.436

SHOCK 6 FR 0.0006 REL FR 6 V 0 P
of the world in arms, | and we shall shock them. JN 5.07.117
bray, | and grating shock of wrathful iron arms, R2 1.03.136
when their thund'ring shock | at meeting tears 3.03. 56
did lately meet in the intestine shock | and 1H4 1.01. 12
but in plain shock and even play of battle, H5 4.08.109
and aid thee in this doubtful shock of arms; R3 5.03. 93

SHOCKS 3 FR 0.0003 REL FR 3 V 0 P
"the raging rocks | and shivering shocks | shall MND 1.02. 32
the heart–ache and the thousand natural shocks HAM 3.01. 61
the aloes of all forces, shocks, and fears. LC 273

SHOE 14 FR 0.0015 REL FR 2 V 12 P
let me lick thy shoe. TMP 3.02. 23 P
this shoe is my father; TGV 2.03. 14 P
no, this left shoe is my father; 2.03. 15 P
no, no, this left shoe is my mother; 2.03. 16 P
this shoe, with the hole in it, is my mother, 2.03. 17 P
now should not the shoe speak a word for weeping 2.03. 25 P
swart, like my shoe, but her face nothing like ERR 3.02.102 P
(which is base) where her shoe (which is baser) LLL 1.02.168 P
his own good parts that he can shoe him himself. MV 1.02. 42 P
your sleeve unbutton'd, your shoe untied, and AYL 3.02.380 P
i kiss his dirty shoe, and from heart–string | i H5 4.01. 47
as ever his black shoe trod upon god's ground 4.07.142 P
nor the soles of her shoe? HAM 2.02.230 P
stratagem, to shoe | a troop of horse with felt. LR 4.06.184

SHOEING 1 FR 0.0001 REL FR 0 V 1 P
the smith's note for shoeing and plough–irons. 2H4 5.01. 19 P

SHOEING–HORN 1 FR 0.0001 REL FR 0 V 1 P
of cuckolds, a thrifty shoeing–horn in a chain, TRO 5.01. 55 P

SHOEMAKER 1 FR 0.0001 REL FR 0 V 1 P
is written that the shoemaker should meddle with ROM 1.02. 39 P

SHOES *(also shoon)*

SHOES 20 FR 0.0022 REL FR 7 V 13 P
love, | for he was more than over shoes in love. TGV 1.01. 24
last morning you could not see to wipe my shoes. 2.01. 80 P
a man may go over shoes in the grime of it. ERR 3.02.104 P
being o'er shoes in blood, plunge in the deep, MND 3.02. 48
than legs, nor no more shoes than feet — nay, SHR in.2. 10 P
sometime more feet than shoes, or such shoes as in.2. 11 P
shoes, or such shoes as my toes look through the in.2. 11 P
smock, | creaking my shoes on the plain masonry, AWW 2.01. 31
do now wear nothing but high shoes, and bunches 2H4 1.02. 38 P
tell you it will serve you to mend your shoes. H5 4.08. 69 P
your shoes is not so good. 4.08. 70 P
life | felt so much cold as over shoes in snow? R3 5.03.326
not in their liking | below their cobbled shoes. COR 1.01.196
you have dancing shoes | with nimble soles, i ROM 1.04. 14
another for tying his new shoes with old riband? 3.01. 29 P
withal i am indeed, sir, a surgeon to old shoes; JC 1.01. 24 P
sir, to wear out their shoes, to get myself into 1.01. 29 P
or ere those shoes were old | with which she HAM 1.02.147
with /two provincial roses on my raz'd shoes, 3.02.277 P
not the creaking of shoes nor the rustling of LR 3.04. 94 P

SHOE–TIE 2 FR 0.0002 REL FR 0 V 2 P
and brave master shoe–tie the great traveller, MM 4.03. 17 P
tape, glove, shoe–tie, bracelet, horn–ring, to WT 4.04.599 P

SHOG 2 FR 0.0002 REL FR 0 V 2 P
will you shog off? i would have you solus. H5 2.01. 45 P
shall we shog? 2.03. 45 P

SHONE 6 FR 0.0006 REL FR 5 V 1 P
well shone, moon. MND 5.01.267 P
when the moon shone, we did not see the candle. MV 5.01. 92
i think, | that e'er the sun shone bright on. WT 5.01. 95
like heathen gods, | shone down the english; H8 1.01. 20
that shone so brightly when this boy was got, TIT 4.02. 90
shone like the moon in water seen by night. VEN 492

/SHOOK 2 FR 0.0002 REL FR 2 V 0 P
/king | /before /i /have /shook /off /the /regal R2 4.01.163
/there /she /shook | /the /holy /water /from LR 4.03. 29

SHOOK 30 FR 0.0034 REL FR 25 V 5 P
and they shook hands and swore brothers. AYL 5.04.102 P
trembled and shook; SHR 3.02.167
shook hands, as over a vast; WT 1.01. 30 P
hadst thou but shook thy head or made a pause JN 4.02.231
which with such gentle sorrow he shook off, R2 5.02. 31
and shook off | by him for whom these shames ye 1H4 1.03.178
mind, | if you suppose as fearing you it shook. 3.01. 22
then the earth shook to see the heavens on fire, 3.01. 24
having this distemp'rature, | in passion shook. 3.01. 34
hath shook and trembled at th' ill neighborhood. H5 1.02.154
your mistress shrewdly shook your back. 3.07. 49 P
her husband's neck, hardly to be shook off. 5.02.181 P
and thought thee happy when i shook my head? 2H6 4.01. 55
till our king henry had shook hands with death. 3H6 1.04.102
howl'd, and hideous tempest shook down trees; 5.06. 46
black–fac'd clifford shook his sword at him; R3 1.02.158
this respite shook | the bosom of my conscience, H8 2.04.182
dewdrop from the lion's mane, | be shook to air. TRO 3.03.225
bid me | return so much, i have shook my head, TIM 2.02.137
smil'd at one another, and shook their heads; JC 1.02.283 P
which nev'r shook hands, nor bade farewell to MAC 1.02. 21
that we can let our beard be shook with danger HAM 4.07. 32
a fuller blast ne'er shook our battlements. OTH 2.01. 6
from euphrates | his conquering banner shook, ANT 1.02.102
should have shook lions into civil streets, 5.01. 16
shook down my mellow hangings, nay, my leaves, CYM 3.03. 63
upon the sea, | shook as the earth did quake; PER 3.02. 15
that shook the aged forest with their echoes, TNK 2.02. 47
have from the forests shook three summers' pride SON 104. 4
shook off my sober guards and civil fears; LC 298

SHOON *(also shoes)*

SHOON 2 FR 0.0002 REL FR 2 V 0 P
spare none but such as go in clouted shoon, 2H6 4.02.185
cockle hat and staff, | and his sandal shoon." HAM 4.05. 26

SHOOT 29 FR 0.0032 REL FR 25 V 4 P
swears he will shoot no more, but play with TMP 4.01.100

asy as a cannon will shoot point–blank twelve WIV 3.02. 33 P
ang me in a bottle like a cat, and shoot at me, ADO 1.01.258 P
nd the little hangman dare not shoot at him. 3.02. 11 P
shoot thee at the swain. LLL 3.01. 65
stand where you may make the fairest shoot. 4.01. 10
thank my beauty, i am fair that shoot, | and 4.01. 11
nd thereupon thou speak'st the fairest shoot. 4.01. 12
hus will i save my credit in the shoot: 4.01. 26
ndeed 'a must shoot nearer, or he'll ne'er hit 4.01.134
lease | to shoot another arrow that self way MV 1.01.148
hat self way | which you did shoot the first, i 1.01.149
ent upon him | and watch'd the time to shoot. AWW 5.03. 11
hey shoot but calm words folded up in smoke, JN 2.01.229
ustria and france shoot in each other's mouth. 2.01.414
peak quickly, or i shoot. 5.06. 1
a shot a fine shoot. 2H4 3.02. 44 P
ed, | ready they were to shoot me to the heart. 1H6 1.04. 56
hat i in rage might shoot them at your faces! 4.07. 80
od, to shoot forth thunder | upon these paltry, 2H6 4.01.104
ll stay above the hill, so both may shoot. 3H6 3.01. 5
ill scare the herd, and so my shoot is lost. 3.01. 7
ou were as good to shoot against the wind. TIT 4.03. 58
insmen, shoot all your shafts into the court, 4.03. 62
o bid the soldiers shoot. HAM 5.02.403
do not bid the thunder–bearer shoot, | nor LR 2.04.227
nd thy ill aim before thy shoot be ended; LUC 579
in, and shoot their foam at simois' banks. 1442
ut shoot not at me in your wakened hate: SON 117.12
HOOTER 3 FR 0.0003 REL FR 3 V 0 P
ho is the shooter? who is the shooter? LLL 4.01.108
ho is the shooter? who is the shooter? 4.01.108
ell then i am the shooter. 4.01.114
HOOTETH 1 FR 0.0001 REL FR 1 V 0 P
ok how a bright star shooteth from the sky, VEN 815
HOOTING 4 FR 0.0004 REL FR 3 V 1 P
an at a mark, with a whole army shooting at me. ADO 2.01.247 P
ll, | and shooting well is then accounted ill. LLL 4.01. 25
ot a sore, till now made sore with shooting. 4.02. 57
see thy glory like a shooting star | fall to R2 2.04. 19
HOOTS 6 FR 0.0006 REL FR 5 V 1 P
e presentation of that he shoots his wit. AYL 5.04.107 P
hoever shoots at him, i set him there; AWW 3.02.112
ant'st a rough pash and the shoots that i have, WT 1.02.128
r, o, love's bow | shoots buck and doe. TRO 3.01.117
hat a mental power | this eye shoots forth! TIM 1.01. 32
s one of those odd tricks which sorrow shoots ANT 4.02. 14
HOP 14 FR 0.0015 REL FR 12 V 2 P
and like the forfeits in a barber's shop, | as MM 5.01.321
y that i linger'd with you at your shop | to ERR 3.01. 3
all the metal in your shop will answer. 4.01. 82
en now a tailor call'd me in his shop, | and 4.03. 7
at penthouse–like o'er the shop of your eyes; LLL 3.01. 18 P
sfigure not his shop. 4.03. 57
ash, | like to a censer in a barber's shop. SHR 4.03. 91
ery lane's end, every shop, church, session, WT 4.04.685 P
ecause i am the store–house and the shop | of COR 1.01.133
d in his needy shop a tortoise hung, | an ROM 5.01. 42
ing holiday, the beggar's shop is shut. 5.01. 56
at wherefore art not in thy shop to–day? JC 1.01. 27
shop of all the qualities that man | loves CYM 5.05.166
hich in my bosom's shop is hanging still, SON 24. 7
HOPS 3 FR 0.0003 REL FR 3 V 0 P
d we, for fear, compell'd to shut our shops. 1H6 3.01. 85
an see | our tradesmen singing in their shops, COR 4.06. 8
athens go, | break open shops; TIM 4.03.447
HORE* *(also shorn)*
HORE* 70 FR 0.0079 REL FR 64 V 6 P
dy) hath mine enemies | brought to this shore; TMP 1.02.180
at was not this nigh shore? 1.02.216
s good arms in lusty stroke | to th' shore, 2.01.121
e i could recover the shore, five and thirty 3.02. 14 P
urs since | were wrack'd upon this shore; 5.01.137
o most strangely | upon this shore (where you 5.01.161
ear'st grace o'erboard, not an oath on shore? 5.01.219
ing destin'd to a drier death on shore. TGV 1.01.150
t that the shore was shelvy and shallow — a WIV 3.05. 15 P
ntleman to the extremest shore of my modesty, MM 3.02.252 P
ad, | and if the wind blow any way from shore, ERR 3.02.148
er, | one foot in sea and one on shore, | to ADO 2.03. 64
ce you have shore | with shears his thread of MND 5.01.340
s ornament is but the guiled shore | to a MV 3.02. 97
captain that did bring me first on shore TN 5.01.274
afes, how it rages, how it takes up the shore! WT 3.03. 89 P
a | with her who hence i cannot hold on shore; 4.04.499
he think it fit to shore them again, and that 4.04.837 P
gether with that pale, that white–fac'd shore, JN 2.01. 23
yself, | and /gripple thee unto a pagan shore, 5.02. 36
ose rocky shore beats back the envious siege R2 2.01. 62
d shortly mean to touch our northern shore. 2.01.288
westward, wales beyond the severn shore, 1H4 3.01. 75
me, | my father gave him welcome to the shore; 4.03. 59
s poor, | upon the naked shore at ravenspurgh, 4.03. 77
at beats upon the high shore of this world — H5 4.01.265
r set no footing on this unkind shore"? 2H6 3.02. 87
d them blow towards england's blessed shore, 3.02. 90
at thou wouldst have me drown'd on shore 3.02. 95
en from thy shore the tempest beat us back, 3.02.102
with their blood stain this discolored shore. 4.01. 11
d spies a far–off shore where he would tread, 3H6 3.02.136
at trudge betwixt the king and mistress shore. R3 1.01. 73
ught to do with mistress shore? 1.01. 98
e mistress shore one gentle kiss the more. 3.01.185
nsorted with that harlot, strumpet shore, 3.04. 71
er he once fell in with mistress shore. 3.05. 51
they not now upon the western shore, 4.04.481
dorsetshire sent out a boat | unto the shore, 4.04.523
d make my vouch as strong | as shore of rock. H8 1.01.158
ale, a shore, confines | /thy spacious and TRO 2.03.249
, | to hover on the dreadful shore of styx? TIT 1.01. 88
that vast shore /wash'd with the farthest sea ROM 2.02. 83
do but stand upon the foaming shore, | the OTH 2.01. 11
the warlike moor othello, | is come on shore; 2.01. 28
riches of the ship is come on shore! 2.01. 83
d pure grief | shore his old thread in twain. 5.02.206
try you on the shore. ANT 2.07.126
nas, i'll not on shore. 2.07.130
rkling stand | the varying shore o' th' world! 4.15. 11

we have descried, upon our neighboring shore, PER 1.04. 60
wash'd me from shore to shore, and left /me 2.01. 6
wash'd me from shore to shore, and left /me 2.01. 6
how far is his court distant from this shore? 2.01.106 P
and after shipwrack driven upon this shore. 2.03. 85
bereft of ships and men, cast on this shore. 2.03. 89
did the sea toss up upon our shore this chest. 3.02. 50
huge a billow, sir, | as toss'd it upon shore. 3.02. 59
bring your grace e'en to the edge a' th' shore, 3.03. 35
being on shore, honoring of neptune's triumphs, 5.01. 17
shall we refresh us, sir, upon your shore, | and 5.01.256
her to meteline, 'gainst whose shore | riding, 5.03. 10
morn this lady was | thrown upon this shore. 5.03. 23
from the far shore, thick set with reeds and TNK 4.01. 54
as one on shore | gazing upon a late embarked VEN 817
'tis double death to drown in ken of shore, | he LUC 1114
ranks began | to break upon the galled shore, 1440
which parts the shore where two contracted new SON 56.10
as the waves make towards the pibbled shore, 60. 1
gain | advantage on the kingdom of the shore, 64. 6
SHORE'S 2 FR 0.0002 REL FR 2 V 0 P
we say that shore's wife hath a pretty foot, | a R3 1.01. 93
i mean, his conversation with shore's wife — 3.05. 31
SHORES* *(also sewer)*
/SHORES* 4 FR 0.0004 REL FR 4 V 0 P
will shortly fill the reasonable /shores | that TMP 5.01. 81
two traded pilots 'twixt the dangerous /shores TRO 2.02. 64
here of these /shores? PER 5.01.103
no, nor of any /shores, | yet i was mortally 5.01.103
SHORES* 19 FR 0.0021 REL FR 19 V 0 P
have | incens'd the seas and shores — yea, all TMP 3.03. 74
sail like my pinnace to these golden shores. WIV 1.03. 80
to unpath'd waters, undream'd shores, most WT 4.04.567
i have from your sicilian shores dismiss'd; 5.01.164
large lengths of seas and shores | between my JN 1.01.105
with course disturb'd even thy confining shores, 2.01.338
and two such shores to two such streams made one 2.01.443
which makes the silver rivers drown their shores R2 3.02.107
whose very shores look pale | with envy of each H5 5.02.350
to our shores | throng many doubtful R3 4.04.434
peaceful commerce from dividable shores, | the TRO 1.03.105
should lift their bosoms higher than the shores, 1.03.112
of your sounds | made in her concave shores? JC 1.01. 47
stream | do kiss the most exalted shores of all. 1.01. 60
the troubled tiber chafing with her shores, 1.02.101
would thou grew'st unto the shores o' th' haven, CYM 1.03. 1
make raging battery upon shores of flint." PER 4.04. 43
empty | old receptacles, or common shores, of 4.06.175
upon me | o'erbear the shores of my mortality, 5.01.193
SHORN *(also shore*)*
SHORN 2 FR 0.0002 REL FR 1 V 1 P
fifteen hundred shorn, what comes the wool to? WT 4.03. 34 P
the right of sepulchres, were shorn away, | to SON 68. 6
/SHORT 1 FR 0.0001 REL FR 1 V 0 P
/it /will /be /short; HAM 5.02. 73
SHORT 105 FR 0.0118 REL FR 87 V 18 P
there's the short and the long. WIV 2.01.132 P
go — a short knife and a throng! 2.02. 18 P
marry, this is the short and the long of it: 2.02. 59 P
brief, short, quick, snap. 4.05. 2 P
proportions | came short of composition, but in MM 5.01.220
splitted my poor tongue | in seven short years, ERR 5.01.310
mark how short his answer is: ADO 1.01.213 P
with hero, leonato's short daughter. 1.01.214 P
"god sends a curst cow short horns" — but to a 2.01. 23 P
indeed, neighbor, he comes too short of you. 3.05. 41 P
and so to study three years is but short. LLL 1.01.180
the way is but short, away! 3.01. 56 P
passes praise, then praise too short doth blot. 4.03.237
the chain were longer and the letter short? 5.02. 56
coming too short of thanks | for my great suit 5.02.738
a time methinks too short | to make a 5.02.788
sound, | swift as a shadow, short as any dream, MND 1.01.144
for the short and the long is, our play is 4.02. 38 P
indeed the short and the long is, i serve the MV 2.02.127 P
i will be bitter with him and passing short. AYL 3.05.138
and, to be short, what not, that's sweet and SHR 5.02.110
who hath for four or five removes come short AWW 5.03.131
your reputation comes too short for my daughter, 5.03.176 P
he makes a july's day short as december, | and WT 1.02.169
hours | and added years to his short banishment, R2 1.04. 17
if that come short, | our substitutes at home 1.04. 47
show'rs last long, but sudden storms are short; 2.01. 35
be merry, for our time of stay is short. 2.01.223
weary lords | shall make their way seem short, 2.03. 17
for one step i'll groan, the way being short, 5.01. 91
the word is short, but not so short as sweet, 5.03.117
the word is short, but not so short as sweet, 5.03.117
o, let the hours be short, | till fields, and 1H4 1.03.301
in short time after, he depos'd the king, | soon 4.03. 90
but in short space | it rain'd down fortune 5.01. 46
and that no man might draw short breath to–day 5.02. 48
o gentlemen, the time of life is short! 5.02. 81
about the satin for my short cloak and my slops? 2H4 1.02. 30 P
is not your voice broken, your wind short, your 1.02.183 P
for women are shrows, both short and tall; 5.03. 33
take up the english short, and let them know H5 2.04. 72
let life be short, else shame will be too long. 4.05. 23
what, is't too short? 2H6 1.02. 12
hangs on the cutting short that fraudful man. 3.01. 81
rather than bloody war shall cut them short, 4.04. 12
short tale to make, we at saint albons met, 3H6 2.01.120
short summers lightly have a forward spring. R3 3.01. 94
make a short shrift, he longs to see your head. 3.04. 95
away their shilling | richly in two short hours. H8 pr 13
short blist'red breeches, and those types of 1.03. 31
have ever come too short of my desires, | yet 3.02.170
and, to be short, for not appearance and | the 4.01. 30
of more moment, | we will be short with you. 5.02. 87
to us | that we come short of our suppose so far TRO 1.03. 11
and fetches her wind so short, as if she were 3.02. 32 P
she fetches her breath as short as a new–ta'en 3.02. 34 P
the rest will serve | for a short holding. COR 1.07. 4
is't possible that so short a time can alter the 5.04. 9 P
'tis good, sir, you are very short with us; TIT 1.01.409
not having that which, having, makes them short. ROM 1.01.164
i would have made it short, for i was come to 2.04. 99 P
that one short minute gives me in her sight. 2.06. 5

come, come with me, and we will make short work, 2.06. 35
on thursday, sir? the time is very short. 4.01. 1
we shall be short in our provision, | 'tis now 4.02. 38
for my short date of breath | is not so long as 5.03.229
his means most short, his creditors most strait. TIM 1.01. 96
gentle heavens, | cut short all intermission. MAC 4.03.232
and he repell'd, a short tale to make, | fell HAM 2.02.146
he finds him | striking too short at greeks. 2.02.469
us, whose providence | should have kept short, 4.01. 18
shapes and tricks, | come short of what he did. 4.07. 90
only she comes too short, that i profess LR 1.01. 72
all vengeance comes too short | which can pursue 2.01. 88
my life will be too short, | and every measure 4.07. 2
and rogues forlorn | in short and musty straw? 4.07. 39
pleasure and action make the hours seem short. OTH 2.03.379
he comes too short of that great property ANT 1.01. 58
good will is show'd, though't come too short, 2.05. 8
or i shall short my word | by length'ning my CYM 1.06.200
well, madam, we must take a short farewell, 3.04.185
but in short time | all offices of nature should 5.05.256
whose arm seems far too short to hit me here. PER 1.02. 8
thus time we waste, and long leagues make short; 4.04. 1
yet a great deal short, | methinks, of him TNK 4.02. 89
by my short life, | i am most glad on't. 5.04. 28
and let my life be now as short | as my 5.04. 37
part is play'd, and, though it were too short, 5.04.102
so much come too short of your great trespass STM II.C 124
ten kisses short as one, one long as twenty: VEN 22
a summer's day will seem an hour but short, 23
high crest, short ears, straight legs and 297
his short thick neck cannot be easily harmed; 627
lovers' hours are long, though seeming short. 842
as palmers' chat makes short their pilgrimage. LUC 791
and how swift and short | his time of folly and 991
by this short schedule collatine may know | her 1312
short time seems long in sorrow's sharp 1573
untimely breathings, sick and short assays, 1720
youth is full of sport, age's breath is short, PP 12. 5
short night to–night, and length thyself 14.30
and summer's lease hath all too short a date; SON 18. 4
how far a modern quill doth come too short, 83. 7
which proves more short than waste or ruining? 125. 4
why so large cost, having so short a lease, 146. 5
SHORT–ARM'D 1 FR 0.0001 REL FR 0 V 1 P
which short–arm'd ignorance itself knows is so TRO 2.03. 14 P
SHORTCAKE 1 FR 0.0001 REL FR 0 V 1 P
lend it to alice shortcake upon all–hallowmas WIV 1.01.204 P
SHORTEN 5 FR 0.0005 REL FR 5 V 0 P
shorten up their sinews | with aged cramps, and TMP 4.01.259
thee i can | but shorten thy life one week. WT 4.04.422
shorten my days thou canst with sullen sorrow, R2 1.03.227
have been so brief /with /you to shorten you, 3.03. 13
say, | god shorten harry's happy life one day! 2H4 5.02.145
SHORTENED 1 FR 0.0001 REL FR 1 V 0 P
stake, | that so her torture may be shortened. 1H6 5.04. 58
SHORTENS 3 FR 0.0003 REL FR 2 V 1 P
me | he shortens four years of my son's exile, R2 1.03.217
of his own death shortens not his own life. HAM 5.01. 20 P
yet to be known shortens my made intent. LR 4.07. 9
SHORTER 6 FR 0.0006 REL FR 5 V 1 P
longer or shorter, he may be so fitted | that MM 2.04. 40
a shorter time shall send me to you, lords, 1H4 3.01. 90
ay, but the days are wax'd shorter with him. TIM 3.04. 11
be a maid long, unless things be cut shorter. LR 1.05. 52
so shall you have a shorter journey to your OTH 2.01.277 P
your way is shorter, | my purposes do draw me ANT 2.04. 7
SHORT–GRASS'D 1 FR 0.0001 REL FR 1 V 0 P
summon'd me hither, to this short–grass'd green? TMP 4.01. 83
SHORT–JOINTED 1 FR 0.0001 REL FR 1 V 0 P
round–hoof'd, short–jointed, fetlocks shag and VEN 295
SHORT–LEGG'D 1 FR 0.0001 REL FR 0 V 1 P
davy, a couple of short–legg'd hens, a joint of 2H4 5.01. 27 P
SHORT–LIV'D 2 FR 0.0002 REL FR 2 V 0 P
such short–liv'd wits do wither as they grow. LLL 2.01. 54
o short–liv'd pride! 4.01. 15
/SHORTLY 2 FR 0.0002 REL FR 2 V 0 P
an hour of quiet /shortly shall we see, | till HAM 5.01.298
/it /must /be /shortly /known /to /him /from 5.02. 71
SHORTLY 46 FR 0.0052 REL FR 32 V 14 P
shortly shall all my labors end, and thou TMP 4.01.264
tide | will shortly fill the reasonable /shores 5.01. 81
which shall be shortly, single i'll resolve you 5.01.248
maid, | and to be shortly of a sisterhood, | if MM 2.02. 21
if my passion change not shortly, god forbid it ADO 1.01.219 P
in venice, thou wilt quake for this shortly. 1.01.272 P
and it will go near to be thought so shortly. 4.02. 22 P
and either i must shortly hear from him, or i 5.02. 58 P
we shall not shortly have a rasher on the coals MV 3.05. 25 P
i shall grow jealious of you shortly, launcelot, 3.05. 29 P
grace of wit will shortly turn into silence, and 3.05. 44 P
we shall have shortly discord in the spheres. AYL 2.07. 6
his son, her brother, | who shortly also died; TN 1.02. 39
else would i very shortly see thee there. 2.01. 46
and shortly mean to touch our northern shore. R2 2.01.288
rue, even for ruth, here shortly shall be seen, 3.04.106
return | to be depos'd, and shortly murdered. 1H4 1.03.152
i shall be out of heart shortly, and then i 3.03. 6 P
'a must then to the inns a' court shortly. 2H4 3.02. 13 P
and my thumb, and shortly will i seal with him. 4.03.131 P
open the gates, or i'll shut thee out shortly. 1H6 1.03. 26
death | hang over thee, as sure it shortly will; 2H6 2.04. 50
tell him, in hope he'll prove a widower shortly, 3H6 3.03.227
and to that end i shortly mind to leave you. 4.01. 64
him, in hope he'll prove a widower shortly, 4.01. 99
that i will shortly send thy soul to heaven, R3 1.01.119
they smile at me who shortly shall be dead. 3.04.107
and will, no doubt, shortly be rid of me. 4.01. 86
write to me very shortly, | and you shall 4.04.428
or shortly after | this world had air'd them. H8 2.04.193
shortly, i believe, | his second marriage shall 3.02. 67
then shortly art thou mine. COR 4.07. 57
we should have none shortly, for one would kill ROM 3.01. 16 P
thou wilt give away thyself in paper shortly. TIM 1.02.242 P
thou wilt be throng'd to shortly. 4.03.394
me to cut down, | and shortly must i fell it. 5.01.207
faith, i must leave thee, love, and shortly too; HAM 3.02.173
you shortly shall hear more. 4.07. 33
as the wind sits, thou'lt catch cold shortly. LR 1.04.101 P

i have a journey, sir, shortly to go: 5.03.322
shall be to him shortly as /acerb as /the OTH 1.03.349 P
but that he's well and will be shortly here. 2.01. 90
but shall't be shortly? 3.03. 56
his grain, | and shortly comes to harvest. ANT 2.07. 23
daughters, | and shortly you may keep yourself. TNK 2.06. 39
well restor'd, | and to be married shortly. 5.04. 28
SHORT'NED 2 FR 0.0002 REL FR 1 V 1 P
and, circumstances short'ned (for she has been ADO 3.02.103 P
discovery | we shall be short'ned in our aim, COR 1.02. 23
SHORTNESS 5 FR 0.0005 REL FR 5 V 0 P
such as the shortness of the time can shape, LLL 4.03.375
plainness and your shortness please me well. SHR 4.04. 39
to spend that shortness basely were too long 1H4 5.02. 82
a second night of such sweet shortness which CYM 2.04. 44
the prejudice of disparity, value's shortness, TNK 5.03. 88
SHORT'NING 1 FR 0.0001 REL FR 1 V 0 P
'tis but the short'ning of my life one day. 1H6 4.06. 37
SHORT-NUMB'RED 1 FR 0.0001 REL FR 1 V 0 P
which works on leases of short-numb'red hours, SON 124.10
SHORT'ST 1 FR 0.0001 REL FR 1 V 0 P
sent back like hollowmas or short'st of day. R2 5.01. 80
SHORT-WINDED 2 FR 0.0002 REL FR 1 V 1 P
and breathe short-winded accents of new broils 1H4 1.01. 3
he sure means brevity in breath, short-winded. 2H4 2.02.124 P
SHOT 44 FR 0.0049 REL FR 30 V 14 P
of words, gentlemen, and quickly shot off. TGV 2.04. 34 P
till some certain shot be paid and the hostess 2.05. 6 P
where, for one shot of five pence, thou shalt 2.05. 9 P
a mark marvellous well shot, for they both did LLL 4.01.130
shot, by heaven! 4.03. 22 P
and certain stars shot madly from their spheres, MND 2.01.153
i shot his fellow of the self-same flight | the MV 1.01.141
therefore a health to all that shot and miss'd. SHR 5.02. 51
of wonder that hath shot out in our latter times AWW 2.03. 8 P
where thou | wast shot at with fair eyes, to be 3.02.107
near or far off, well won is still well shot, JN 1.01.174
off, | when with a volley of our needless shot, 5.05. 5
scape shot-free at london, i fear the shot here, 1H4 5.03. 31 P
'a shot a fine shoot. 2H4 3.02. 44 P
always a little, lean, old, chopp'd, bald shot. 3.02.275 P
who came off bravely, who was shot, who H5 3.06. 74 P
by how much "a fool's bolt is soon shot." 3.07.122 P
you have shot over. 3.07.123 P
that's a perilous shot out of an elder-gun, that 4.01.197 P
father, i know, and oft have shot at them, 1H6 1.04. 3
they may vex us with shot or with assault. 1.04. 13
wherefore a guard of chosen shot i had | that 1.04. 53
i am your butt, and i abide your shot. 3H6 1.04. 29
flag | to be the aim of every dangerous shot; R3 4.04. 89
suddenly a file of boys behind 'em, loose shot, H8 5.03. 56 P
safe out of fortune's shot, and sits aloft, TIT 2.01. 2
see, thou hast shot off one of taurus' horns. 4.03. 70
when publius shot, | the bull, being gall'd, 4.03. 71
young abraham cupid, he that shot so /trim, ROM 2.01. 13
name, | shot from the deadly level of a gun, 3.03.103
this murtherous shaft that's shot | hath not yet MAC 2.03.141
out of the shot and danger of desire. HAM 1.03. 35
transports his pois'ned shot, may miss our name, 4.01. 43
that i have shot my arrow o'er the house | and 5.02.243
cell, | that thou so many princes at a shot | so 5.02.366
they do discharge their shot of courtesy; OTH 2.01. 56
virtue | the shot of accident nor dart of chance 4.01.267
and shot their fires | into th' abysm of hell. ANT 3.13.146
and i shall here abide the hourly shot | of CYM 1.01. 89
'twas but a bolt of nothing, shot at nothing, 4.02.300
to the spectators, the dish pays the shot. 5.04.156 P
and like an arrow shot | from a well-experienc'd PER 1.01.161
with sighs shot through and biggest tears 4.04. 26
and little stars shot from their fixed places, LUC 1525
SHOT-FREE 1 FR 0.0001 REL FR 0 V 1 P
though i could scape shot-free at london, i fear 1H4 5.03. 30 P
SHOTTEN 1 FR 0.0001 REL FR 0 V 1 P
face of the earth, then am i a shotten herring. 1H4 2.04.130 P
SHOUGHS 1 FR 0.0001 REL FR 1 V 0 P
shoughs, water-rugs, and demi-wolves are clipt MAC 3.01. 93
SHOULD *(also sould)*
/SHOULD 13 FR 0.0014 REL FR 12 V 1 P
/of /aids /incertain /should /not /be /admitted. 2H4 1.03. 24
/should /we /survey | /the /plot /of /situation 1.03. 50
/that /you /should /have /an /inch /of /any 4.01.107
/me, /i /being /by, /that /i /should /kill /him? R3 4.02.101
/i /should /not /live /long /after /i /saw 4.02.107
who /should /be /else? 4.04.266
/marcus, /no /man /should /be /mad /but /i. TIT 3.02. 24
/as /if /we /should /forget /we /had /no /hands, 3.02. 32
/if /they /should /grow /themselves /to /common HAM 2.02.348 P
/i /should /be /false /persuaded | /i /had LR 1.04.233
what /i /should deny | (as this i would, /ay, 2.01. 70
/strove | /who /should /express /her /goodliest. 4.03. 17
/that /sister | /should /loosen /him /and /me. 5.01. 19
SHOULD 1691 FR 0.1911 REL FR 1314 V 377 P
it should the good ship so have swallow'd and TMP 1.02. 12
'tis time | i should inform thee farther. 1.02. 23
me — that a brother should | be so perfidious! 1.02. 67
i should sin | to think but nobly of my 1.02.118
should presently extirpate me and mine | out of 1.02.125
stomach, to bear up | against what should ensue. 1.02.158
where should this music be? 1.02.388
have taken it wiselier than i meant you should. 2.01. 22 P
at | which end o' th' beam should bow. 2.01.132
the sore, | when you should bring the plaster. 2.01.140
letters should not be known; 2.01.151
all things in common nature should produce 2.01.160
but nature should bring forth, | of it own kind, 2.01.163
prudence, who | should not upbraid our course. 2.01.287
if it should thunder as it did before, i know 2.02. 22 P
where the devil should he learn our language? 2.02. 67 P
i should know that voice; 2.02. 87 P
it should be — but he is drown'd; 2.02. 87 P
back, | than you should such dishonor undergo, 3.01. 27
and i should do it | with much more ease, for my 3.01. 29
where should they be set else? 3.02. 10 P
that a monster should be such a natural! 3.02. 32 P
if in naples | i should report this now, would 3.03. 28
if i should say i saw such /islanders | (for, 3.03. 29
if i should take a displeasure against you, look 4.01.201 P
time, my lord, | you said our work should cease. 5.01. 5
but how should prospero | be living, and be here 5.01.119
yes, for a score of kingdoms you should wrangle, 5.01.174
have inly wept, | or should have spoke ere this. 5.01.201
that his issue | should become kings of naples? 5.01.206
where should they | find this grand liquor that 5.01.279
i should have been a sore one then. 5.01.289 P
methinks should not be chronicled for wise. TGV 1.01. 41
but, were i you, he never should be mine. 1.02. 11
i am) | should censure thus on lovely gentlemen. 1.02. 19
lest he should take exceptions to my love, | and 1.03. 81
what should i see then? 2.01. 74 P
he should give her interest, and she gives it 2.01.102 P
scribe, to himself should write the letter? 2.01.140
by a letter, i should say. 2.01.150 P
that tide will stay me longer than i should. 2.02. 15
ay, so true love should do: 2.02. 17
now should not the shoe speak a word for weeping 2.03. 24 P
now should i kiss my father; 2.03. 25 P
where should i lose my tongue? 2.03. 47 P
should i have wish'd a thing, it had been he. 2.04. 82
nay then he should be blind, and, being blind, 2.04. 93
should from her vesture chance to steal a kiss, 2.04.160
but there i leave to love where i should love. 2.06. 18
lest it should burn above the bounds of reason. 2.07. 23
else, no worldly good should draw from me. 3.01. 9
and should she thus be stol'n away from you, 3.01. 15
should have been cherish'd by her child-like 3.01. 75
that they should harbor where their lord should 3.01.149
they should harbor where their lord should be." 3.01.149
for good things should be prais'd. 3.01.347 P
him, | lest it should ravel and be good to none, 3.02. 52
should be full-fraught with serviceable vows. 3.02. 70
of which if you should here disfurnish me, | you 4.01. 14
'twere false, if i should speak it; 4.02.106
i would have (as one should say) one that takes 4.04. 11 P
'tis pity love should be so contrary; 4.04. 83
deliver'd you a paper that i should not: 4.04.123
what should it be that he respects in her, | but 4.04.194
my substance should be statue in thy stead. 4.04.201
i should have scratch'd out your unseeing eyes, 4.04.204
silvia at friar patrick's cell should meet me. 5.01. 3
that such an ass should owe them. 5.02. 28
who should be trusted, when one's right hand 5.04. 67
all foes that a friend should be the worst! 5.04. 72
pity two such friends should be long foes. 5.04.118
if i were young again, the sword should end it. WIV 1.01. 41 P
o, i should remember him. 1.04. 28 P
mov'd, you should have heard him so loud and so 1.04. 90 P
what should i say to him? 2.01. 27 P
i should have borne the humor'd letter to her; 2.01.130 P
if he should intend this voyage toward my wife, 2.01.181 P
sir, you should lay my countenance to pawn. 2.02. 6 P
good that children should know any wickedness. 2.02.129 P
that i should win what you would enjoy? 2.02.239 P
if you should fight, you go against the hair of 2.03. 40 P
warrant you, he's the man should fight with him. 3.01. 68 P
alas, i should be a pitiful lady! 3.03. 52 P
i should love thee but as a property. 3.04. 10
the bottom were as deep as hell, i should down. 3.05. 14 P
and what a thing should i have been when i had 3.05. 17 P
i should have been a mountain of mummy. 3.05. 17 P
but fate (ordaining he should be a cuckold) held 3.05.105 P
'tis impossible he should; 3.05.146 P
lest the devil that guides him should aid him, i 3.05.148 P
which way should he go? 4.02. 46 P
how should i bestow him? 4.02. 47 P
to the jest, should he not be publicly sham'd. 4.02.222 P
what duke should that be comes so secretly? 4.03. 4 P
methinks there should be terrors in him that he 4.04. 22 P
be terrors in him that he should not come; 4.04. 22 P
and 'tis not convenient you should be cozen'd. 4.05. 81 P
if it should come to the ear of the court, how i 4.05. 94 P
what should this be? 5.05. 32 P
the oil that's in me should set hell on fire; 5.05. 35 P
of money, to whom you should have been a pander. 5.05.167 P
have swing'd him, or he should have swing'd me. 5.05.186 P
i tell you how you should know my daughter by 5.05.195 P
this day my sister should the cloister enter, MM 1.02.177
who i would be sorry should be thus foolishly 1.02.190 P
he should receive his punishment in thanks: 1.04. 28
and most desire should meet the blow of justice; 2.02. 30
if you should need a pin, | you could not with 2.02. 45
should it then be thus? 2.02. 68
of judgment, should | but judge you as you are? 2.02. 76
or my son, | it should be thus with him: 2.02. 82
and so stop the air | by which he should revive; 2.04. 26
sister, by redeeming him, | should die for ever. 2.04.108
to whom should i complain? 2.04.171
before his sister should her body stoop | to 2.04.182
time | that i should do what i abhor to name, 3.01.101
what should i think? 3.01.139
reprieve thee from thy fate, it should proceed. 3.01.144
for his falling, i should wonder at angelo. 3.01.187 P
the law than my son should be unlawfully born. 3.01.190 P
she should this angelo have married; 3.01.213 P
(that in all reason should have quench'd her 3.01.241 P
how should he be made then? 3.02.107 P
why should he die, sir? 3.02.171 P
by my pity, it should not be so with him. 3.02.210 P
heaven will bear | should be as holy as severe; 3.02.262
but what mystery there should be in hanging, if 4.02. 39 P
should be in hanging, if i should be hang'd, i 4.02. 40 P
into amazement how these things should be; 4.02.205 P
and why should we proclaim it in an hour before 4.04. 8 P
they should exhibit their petitions in the 4.04. 10 P
he should have liv'd, | save that his riotous 4.04. 28
i should not think it strange, for 'tis a physic 4.06. 7
and i should wrong it | to lock it in the wards 5.01. 9
that with such vehemency he should pursue 5.01.109
'tis he should hear me speak. 5.01.294
lord, | i should be guiltier than my guiltiness, 5.01.367
should she kneel down in mercy of this fact, 5.01.434
that should by private order else have died, | i 5.01.466
should slip so grossly, both in the heat of 5.01.472
who should have died when claudio lost his head 5.01.488
yet behind, that/'s meet you all should know. 5.01.539
my soul should sue as advocate for thee: ERR 1.01.145
your maw, like mine, should be your /clock, 1.02. 66
if i should pay your worship those again, 1.02. 85
why should their liberty than ours be more? 2.01. 10
as much, or more, we should ourselves complain: 2.01. 37
that at dinner they should not drop in his 2.02. 98
thee, | by ruffian lust should be contaminate? 2.02.133
but i should know her as well as she knows me. 2.02.202
i should kick, being kick'd, and, being at that 3.01. 17
gaze when you should, and that will clear your 3.02. 57
all this my sister is, or else should be. 3.02. 65
what i should think of this, i cannot tell: 3.02.179
i should have chid you for not bringing it, 4.01. 50
i answer you? what should i answer you? 4.01. 62
case, | if he should scorn me so apparently. 4.01. 78
/that he, unknown to me, should be in debt. 4.02. 48
that i should be attach'd in ephesus; 4.04. 6
you should for that have reprehended him. 5.01. 57
for trouble being gone, comfort should remain; ADO 1.01.101
is it possible disdain should die while she hath 1.01.120
do you question me, as an honest man should do, 1.01.167
not so, but indeed, god forbid it should be so." 1.01.217
not shortly, god forbid it should be otherwise. 1.01.220
i neither feel how she should be lov'd nor know 1.01.230
be lov'd nor know how she should be worthy, is 1.01.231
if this should ever happen, thou wouldst be 1.01.269
you should hear reason. 1.03. 5
it is impossible you should take true root but 1.03. 23
upon that the prince should woo hero for himself 1.03. 62
what should i do with him? 2.01. 34
for god defend the lute should be like the case! 2.01. 95
why then your visor should be thatch'd. 2.01. 98
but that my lady beatrice should know me, and 2.01.203
so i would not he should do me, my lord, lest i 2.01.285
lord, lest i should prove the mother of fools. 2.01.286
that sheep's guts should hale souls out of men's 2.03. 59
he had been a dog that should have howl'd thus, 2.03. 79
wonderful that she should so dote on signior 2.03. 96
i should think this a gull, but that the 2.03.118
that she should be so immodest to write to one 2.03.141
"by my own spirit, for i should flout him, if he 2.03.144
writ to me, yea, though i love him, i should." 2.03.145
and he should, it were an alms to hang him. 2.03.158
if she should make tender of her love, 'tis very 2.03.178
i did not think i should live till i were 2.03.244
would swear the gentleman should be her sister; 3.01. 62
if i should speak, | she would mock me into air; 3.01. 74
what should that bode? 3.02. 42
any thing to-night why i should not marry her, 3.02.123
in the congregation, where i should wed, there 3.02.125
it were pity but they should suffer salvation, 3.03. 2
if they should have any allegiance in them, 3.03. 5
for i cannot see how sleeping should offend; 3.03. 41
it possible that any villainy should be so dear? 3.03.110
it were possible any villainy should be so rich; 3.03.113
vildly, i should first tell thee how the prince, 3.03.148
not seen enough, you should wear it in your cap. 3.04. 71
impediment why you should not be conjoin'd, i 4.01. 13
what should i speak? 4.01. 63
yea, wherefore should she not? 4.01.119
and justly as your soul | should with your body. 4.01.249
for god defend but god should go before such 4.02. 19
when he should groan, | patch grief with 5.01. 16
if it should give your age such cause of fear. 5.01. 56
i doubt we should have been too young for them. 5.01.118
how you disgrac'd her when you should marry her. 5.01.239
her the right you should have giv'n her cousin, 5.01.291
why, that to know which else we should not know.
LLL 1.01. 56
why should proud summer boast | before the birds 1.01.102
why should i joy in any abortive birth? 1.01.104
it doth forget to do the thing it should; 1.01.144
methinks i should outswear cupid. 1.02. 64
it should none spare that come within his power. 2.01. 51
the hour that fools should ask. 2.01.122
your fair self should make | a yielding 'gainst 2.01.150
maids' girdles for your waist should be fit. 4.01. 50
are set before us, that we thankful should be — 4.02. 28
and if one should be pierc'd, which is the one? 4.02. 84
you may look pale, but i should blush, i know, 4.03.127
hair | should ravish doters with a false aspect: 4.03.256
for fear their colors should be wash'd away. 4.03.267
the street should see as she walk'd overhead. 4.03.277
speak "dout," fine, when he should say "doubt"; 5.01. 20
"det," when he should pronounce "debt" — 5.01. 21
that he should be my fool and i his fate. 5.02. 68
i should have fear'd her had she been a devil." 5.02.106
but your legs should do it. 5.02.217
should be presented at our tent to us. 5.02.307
vice you should have spoke, | for virtue's 5.02.349
a world of torments though i should endure, | i 5.02.353
sir, it were pity you should get your living by 5.02.496
it should have followed in the end of our show. 5.02.887
to you your father should be as a god; MND 1.01. 47
why should not i then prosecute my right? 1.01.105
my ear should catch your voice, my eye your eye, 1.01.188
my tongue should catch your tongue's sweet 1.01.189
and you should do it too terribly, you would 1.02. 74
if you should fright the ladies out of their 1.02. 79
why should titania cross her oberon? 2.01.119
as it should pierce a hundred thousand hearts; 2.01.160
we should be woo'd, and were not made to woo. 2.01.242
should of another therefore be abus'd! 2.02.134
you should have little reason for that. 3.01.142
but i should use thee worse, | for thou, i fear, 3.02. 45
so should a murtherer look — so dead, so grim. 3.02. 57
so should the murthered look, and so should i, 3.02. 58
so should the murthered look, and so should i, 3.02. 58
and if i could, what should i get therefore? 3.02. 78
why should you think that i should woo in scorn? 3.02.122
why should you think that i should woo in scorn? 3.02.122
why should he stay, whom love doth press to go? 3.02.184
this you should pity rather than despise. 3.02.235
should i hurt her, strike her, kill her dead? 3.02.269
did not you tell me i should know the man | by 3.02.348
for fear lest day should look their shames upon, 3.02.385
known, | that every man should take his own, 3.02.459
that hermia should give answer of her choice? 4.01.136
of my consent that she should be your wife. 4.01.159
that you should think, we come not to offend, 5.01.109

hat you should here repent you, | the actors 5.01.115
nethinks, being sensible, should curse again. 5.01.182 P
o, in truth, sir, he should not. 5.01.184 P
i should as lion come in strife | into this 5.01.225
e should have worn the horns on his head. 5.01.240 P
he man should be put into the lanthorn. 5.01.247 P
hy, all these should be in the lanthorn; 5.01.260 P
nethinks she should not use a long one for such 5.01.316 P
should be still | plucking the grass to know MV 1.01. 17
should not see the sandy hour-glass run | but 1.01. 25
ut i should think of shallows and of flats, 1.01. 26
hould i go to church | and see the holy edifice 1.01. 29
hy should a man, whose blood is warm within, 1.01. 83
s who should say, "i am sir oracle, | and when 1.01. 93
they should speak, would almost damn those 1.01. 98
nen do but say to me what i should do | that in 1.01.158
nat i should questionless be fortunate! 1.01.176
e doth nothing but frown, as who should say, 1.02. 46 P
i should marry him, i should marry twenty 1.02. 62 P
arry him, i should marry twenty husbands. 1.02. 62 P
he should offer to choose, and choose the 1.02. 92 P
ou should refuse to perform your father's will, 1.02. 93 P
ill, if you should refuse to accept him. 1.02. 94 P
ur farewell, i should be glad of his approach. 1.02.128 P
had rather he should shrive me than wive me. 1.02.131 P
reak'd and pied | should fall as jacob's hire, 1.03. 80
hat should i say to you? 1.03.120
hould i not say, | "hath a dog money? 1.03.120
he should break his day, what should i gain 1.03.163
ay, what should i gain | by the exaction of the 1.03.163
should stay with the jew my master, who, god 2.02. 23 P
om the jew, i should be rul'd by the fiend, 2.02. 25 P
should seem then that dobbin's tail grows 2.02. 96 P
ut wherefore should i go? 2.05. 12
discovery, love, | and i should be obscur'd. 2.06. 44
ow many then should cover that stand bare? 2.09. 44
w, what should his sufferance be by christian 3.01. 70 P
ut lest you should not understand me well — 3.02. 7
weet a bar | should sunder such sweet friends. 3.02.120
ethinks it should have power to steal both his 3.02.125
should then have told you | that i was worse 3.02.259
esides, it should appear, that if he had | the 3.02.272
paying it, it is impossible i should live, 3.02.318 P
e sins of my mother should be visited upon me. 3.05. 14 P
uch that the moor should be more than reason; 3.05. 40 P
| in reason he should never come to heaven! 3.05. 78
two gods should play some heavenly match, 3.05. 79
justice, none of us | should see salvation. 4.01.200
u teach me how a beggar should be answer'd. 4.01.440
e made me vow | that i should neither sell, 4.01.443
hy should we go in? 5.01. 50
e nightingale, if she should sing by day, 5.01.104
should hold day with the antipodes, | if you 5.01.127
u should in all sense be much bound to him, 5.01.136
d that it should lie with you in your grave. 5.01.154
u should have been respective and have kept it 5.01.156
d 'twere to me i should be mad at it. 5.01.176
hat should i say, sweet lady? 5.01.215
hould wish it dark | till i were couching 5.01.304
ve i spent, that i should come to such penury? AYL 1.01. 39 P
ntle condition of blood you should so know me. 1.01. 45 P
t should i anatomize him to thee as he is, i 1.01.156 P
u should not have mock'd me before. 1.02.208 P
mine eye, i can tell who should down. 1.02.215 P
hould have given him tears unto entreaties, 1.02.238
treaties, | ere he should thus have ventur'd. 1.02.239
nen the one should be lam'd with reasons and 1.03. 8 P
u should fall into so strong a liking with old 1.03. 27 P
sue that you should love his son dearly? 1.03. 31 P
this kind of chase, i should hate him, for my 1.03. 32 P
y should i not? doth he not deserve well? 1.03. 36 P
ould in their own confines with forked heads 2.01. 24
nen service should in my old limbs lie lame, 2.03. 41
t i should bear no cross if i did bear you, 2.04. 12 P
at fools should be so deep contemplative; 2.07. 31
what kind should this cock come of? 2.07. 90
hould not seek an absent argument | of my 3.01. 3
hy should this /a desert be? 3.02.125
ture charg'd | that one body should be fill'd 3.02.142
aven would that she these gifts should have, 3.02.153
w thy name should be hang'd and carv'd upon 3.02.173 P
u should ask me what time o' day; 3.02.300 P
venue — then your hose should be ungarter'd, 3.02.378 P
ould be called tyrants, butchers, murtherers! 3.05. 14
rry, that should you if i were your mistress, 4.01. 83 P
i should think my honesty ranker than my wit. 4.01. 84 P
n should i know you by description — | such 4.03. 84
tch, | when that the sleeping man should stir; 4.03.116
aith, i should have been a woman by right. 4.03.175 P
so little acquaintance you should like her? 5.02. 2 P
at but seeing, you should love her? 5.02. 2 P
d wooing, she should grant? 5.02. 3 P
t this that you should bear a good opinion of 5.02. 54 P
at will i, should i die the hour after. 5.04. 12
s, | if you should smile, he grows impatient. SHR in.1. 99
ould be infused with so foul a spirit! in.2. 16
men should call me "lord"; in.2. 105
t i should yet absent me from your bed. in.2. 123
ubt not her care should be | to comb your 1.01. 63
t love should of a sudden take such hold? 1.01.147
p house and port and servants, as i should. 1.01.203
om should i knock? 1.02. 6 P
i, sir, that i should knock you here, sir? 1.02. 10 P
hould knock you first, | and then i know 1.02. 13
d yet as heavy as my weight should be. 2.01.205
uld be! should — buzz! 2.01.206
uld be! should — buzz! 2.01.206
were impossible i should speed amiss. 2.01.283
ou should die before him, where's her dower? 2.01.389
hould be arguing still upon that doubt. 3.01. 55
t katherine and petruchio should be married, 3.02. 2
e it better i should rush in thus: 3.02. 91
en i should bid good morrow to my bride | and 3.02.122
uld ask if katherine should be his wife, 3.02.159
uld ask if katherine should be his wife, 3.02.159
y not quickly, i should die with laughing. 3.02.241
ly, ere i should come by a fire to thaw me. 4.01. 8 P
k that you take upon you as you should; 4.02.109
nor never needed that i should entreat, | am 4.03. 8
as who should say, if i should sleep or eat, 4.03. 13
as who should say, if i should sleep or eat, 4.03. 13
grumio gave order how it should be done. 4.03.117
but how did you desire it should be made? 4.03.119
i commanded the sleeves should be cut out, and 4.03.146 P
will be pleas'd, then wherefore should i doubt? 4.04.106
thus the bowl should run, | and not unluckily 4.05. 24
to offer war where they should kneel for peace, 5.02.162
should well agree with our external parts? 5.02.168
and death should have play for lack of work. AWW 1.01. 21 P
that i should love a bright particular star 1.01. 86
and should be buried in highways out of all 1.01.139 P
that man should be at woman's command, and yet 1.03. 92 P
thy tongue, | that truth should be suspected. 1.03.181
him, | yet never know how that desert should be. 1.03.200
helen, | if you should tender your supposed aid, 1.03.236
more should i question thee, and more i must — 2.01.205
faith, if the learned should speak truth of it. 2.02. 35 P
when we should submit ourselves to an unknown 2.03. 5 P
which should indeed give us a further use to be 2.03. 35 P
be not afraid that i your hand should take, 2.03. 89
but never hope to know why i should marry her. 2.03.110
the property by what /it is should go, | not by 2.03.130
what should be said? 2.03.141
general offense, and every man should beat thee. 2.03.255 P
which should sustain the bound and high curvet 2.03.282
you should have said, sir, "before a knave th' 2.04. 29 P
when i should take possession of the bride, 2.05. 26
with, should be once heard and thrice beaten. 2.05. 30 P
why should he be kill'd? 3.02. 39 P
i should believe you, | for you have show'd me 3.07. 12
what the devil should move me to undertake the 4.01. 34 P
is it possible he should know what he is, and be 4.01. 44 P
dead, you should be such a one | as you are now; 4.02. 7
and now you should be as your mother was | when 4.02. 9
so should you be. 4.02. 11
if i should swear by jove's great attributes | i 4.02. 25
sir, so should i be a great deal of his act. 4.03. 45 P
every thing that an honest man should not have; 4.03.260 P
what an honest man should have, he has nothing. 4.03.260 P
knave with fortune that she should scratch you, 5.02. 30 P
and inform him | so 'tis our will he should. 5.03. 27
to reave her | of what should stead her most? 5.03. 87
if it should prove | that thou art so inhuman — 5.03.115
and what should i do in illyria? TN 1.02. 3
my very walk should be a jig. 1.03.129 P
madonna, as if thy eldest son should be a fool; 1.05.113 P
o, you should not rest | between the elements of 1.05.274
of air and earth, | but you should pity me! 1.05.276
that you should put your lord into a desperate 2.02. 7 P
and her will is, it should be so return'd. 2.02. 14 P
so please your lordship, that should sing it. 2.04. 9 P
were i a woman, | i should your lordship. 2.04.109
that, should she fancy, it should be one of my 2.05. 25 P
she fancy, it should be one of my complexion. 2.05. 25 P
what should i think on't? 2.05. 28 P
my place as i would they should do theirs — to 2.05. 54 P
to whom should this be? 2.05. 94 P
if this should be thee, malvolio? 2.05.101 P
what should that alphabetical position portend? 2.05.118 P
a should follow, but o does. 2.05.130 P
but the fool should be as oft with your master 3.01. 40 P
my niece is desirous you should enter, if your 3.01. 75 P
if one should be a prey, how much the better 3.01.128
you should then have accosted her, and with some 3.02. 21 P
you should have bang'd the youth into dumbness. 3.02. 23 P
firm, | you should find better dealing. 3.03. 18
why should i not (had i the heart to do it), 5.01.117
i should my tears let fall upon your cheek, 5.01.240
i should have given't you to-day morning. 5.01.286 P
no other excuse why they should desire to live. WT 1.01. 44 P
and yet we should, for perpetuity, | go hence in 1.02. 5
so it should now, | were there necessity in your 1.02. 21
with oaths, | should yet say, "sir, no going." 1.02. 49
to be your prisoner should import offending, 1.02. 57
blood, we should have answer'd heaven | boldly, 1.02. 73
dagger muzzled | lest it should bite its master, 1.02.157
should all despair | that have revolted wives, 1.02.198
"good" should be pertinent, | but so it is, it 1.02.221
would do that | which should undo more doing; 1.02.312
but with a ling'ring dram that should not work 1.02.320
how should this grow? 1.02.431
him that has most cause to grieve it should be) 2.01. 77
should a villain say so, | the most replenish'd 2.01. 78
should a like language use to all degrees, | and 2.01. 85
knows | what she should shame to know herself 2.01. 91
than they | should not produce fair issue. 2.01.150
from our free person she should be confin'd, 2.01.194
minister of honor, | lest she should be denied. 2.02. 49
they should not laugh if i could reach them, nor 2.03. 25
to-night, commanded | none should come at him. 2.03. 32
charg'd thee that she should not come about me: 2.03. 43
peril and on mine, | she should not visit you. 2.03. 46
habits | (methinks i so should term them) and 3.01. 5
i have here alive, | that i should fear to die? 3.02.108
and what's past help | should be past grief. 3.02.223
have minded you | of what you should forget. 3.02.226
of king polixenes) it should here be laid, 3.03. 44
it was told me i should be rich by the fairies. 3.03.117 P
he should be a footman by the garments he has 4.03. 66 P
i should blush | to see you so attir'd — sworn, 4.04. 12
accident, | should pass this way as you did. 4.04. 20
or how | should i, in these my borrowed flaunts, 4.04. 23
it is my father's will i should take on me | the 4.04. 71
would wish | this youth should say 'twere well, 4.04.102
i should leave grazing, were i of your flock, 4.04.109
though i report it | that should be silent. 4.04.178
plackets where they should bear their faces? 4.04.243 P
why should i carry lies abroad? 4.04.271 P
if your lass | interpretation should abuse, and 4.04.353
before this ancient sir, whom, it should seem, 4.04.361
reason my son | should choose himself a wife, 4.04.407
should hold some counsel | in such a business. 4.04.409
they throng who should buy first, as if my 4.04.601 P
should i now meet my father, | he would not call 4.04.657
that should have married a shepherd's daughter. 4.04.766 P
my lord should to the heavens be contrary, 5.01. 45
i should so: 5.01. 62
that even your ears | should rift to hear me, 5.01. 66
words that follow'd | should be "remember mine." 5.01. 67
it should take joy | to see her in your arms. 5.01. 80
'tis strange | he thus should steal upon us. 5.01.115
(his very air) that i should call you brother, 5.01.128
should chase us with my father, pow'r no jot 5.01.217
you, should be hooted at | like an old tale; 5.03.116
i durst not stick a rose | lest men should say, JN 1.01.143
this toil of ours should be a work of thine; 2.01. 93
if lusty love should go in quest of beauty, 2.01.426
where should he find it fairer than in blanch? 2.01.427
if zealous love should go in search of virtue, 2.01.428
where should he find it purer than in blanch? 2.01.429
there should be | in such a love so vile a lout 2.01.508
thoughts themselves should be your judge, | that 2.01.519
judge, | that i can find should merit any hate. 2.01.520
be content, | for then i should not love thee; 3.01. 49
that it in golden letters should be set | among 3.01. 85
o, that a man should speak those words to me! 3.01.130
what should he say, but as the cardinal? 3.01.203
else what a mockery should it be to swear! 3.01.285
for then 'tis like i should forget myself. 3.04. 49
o, if i could, what grief should i forget! 3.04. 50
if i were mad, i should forget my son, | or 3.04. 57
the misplac'd john should entertain an hour, 3.04.133
methinks nobody should be sad but i: 4.01. 13
i should be as merry as the day is long; 4.01. 18
and if an angel should have come to me | and 4.01. 68
and told me hubert should put out mine eyes, | i 4.01. 69
all things that you should use to do me wrong 4.01.117
should move you to mew up | your tender kinsman, 4.02. 57
this is the man should do the bloody deed; 4.02. 69
that greatness should so grossly offer it. 4.02. 94
for when you should be told they do prepare, 4.02.114
your highness should deliver up your crown. 4.02.152
at noon | my crown i should give off? 5.01. 27
i did suppose it should be on constraint, | but, 5.01. 28
should seek a plaster by contemn'd revolt, | and 5.02. 13
brought in matter that should feed this fire; 5.02. 85
he is prepar'd, and reason too he should — 5.02.130
what in the world should make me now deceive, 5.04. 26
why should i then be false, since it is true 5.04. 28
should scape the true acquaintance of mine ear. 5.06. 15
'tis strange that death should sing. 5.07. 20
all the shrouds wherewith my life should sail 5.07. 53
malice, | or worthily, as a good subject should, R2 1.01. 10
should nothing privilege him nor partialize 1.01.120
obedience bids i should not bid again. 1.01.163
(which god defend a knight should violate!) 1.03. 18
that our kingdom's earth should not be soil'd 1.03.125
smooth his fault i should have been more mild. 1.03.240
i look'd when some of you should say | i was too 1.03.243
when the tongue's office should be prodigal | to 1.03.256
that my tongue | should so profane the word, 1.04. 13
he should have had a volume of farewells; 1.04. 18
should dying men flatter with those that live? 2.01. 88
seen how his son's son should destroy his sons, 2.01.105
head | should run thy head from thy unreverent 2.01.123
why i should welcome such a guest as grief, 2.02. 7
should i do so, i should belie my thoughts. 2.02. 77
should i do so, i should belie my thoughts. 2.02. 77
i should to plashy too, | but time will not 2.02.120
o, then how quickly should this arm of mine, 2.03.103
he should have found his uncle gaunt a father 2.03.127
when such a sacred king should hide his head! 3.03. 9
mistake not, uncle, further than you should. 3.03. 15
take not, good cousin, further than you should, 3.03. 16
such crimson tempest should bedrench | the fresh 3.03. 46
methinks king richard and myself should meet 3.03. 54
that any harm should stain so fair a show! 3.03. 71
the king | should so with civil and uncivil arms 3.03.102
on yon proud man should take it off again | with 3.03.135
shriek where mounting larks should sing. 3.03.183
why should we in the compass of a pale | keep 3.04. 40
should grace the triumph of great bullingbrook? 3.04. 99
climate souls refin'd | should show so heinous, 4.01.131
why should hard-favor'd grief be lodg'd in thee, 5.01. 14
what should you fear? 5.02. 64
"pardon" should be the first word of thy speech. 5.03.114
he wishtly look'd on me | as who should say, "i 5.04. 8
that blood should sprinkle me to make me grow. 5.06. 46
should be the father to so blest a son — | a 1H4 1.01. 80
god save thy grace — majesty i should say, for 1.02. 17 P
and now am i, if a man should speak truly, 1.02. 94 P
he should, or he should not — for he made me 1.03. 53
he should, or he should not — for he made me 1.03. 53
this villainous saltpetre should be digg'd | out 1.03. 60
but not the form of what he should attend. 1.03.210
that would (if matters should be look'd into) 2.01. 72 P
now cannot i strike him, if i should be hang'd. 2.02. 73 P
were't not for laughing, i should pity him. 2.02.110
ever this fellow should have fewer words than a 2.04. 98 P
should i turn upon the true prince? 2.04.269 P
if that man should be lewdly given, he deceiveth 2.04.426 P
shame, | in such a parley should i answer thee. 3.01.201
then should you be nothing but musical, for you 3.01.232 P
my oath should be "by this fire, that/'s god's 3.03. 34 P
so should i be sure to be heart-burnt. 3.03. 50 P
o, if it should, how would thy guts fall about 3.03.152 P
and what should poor jack falstaff do in the 3.03.165 P
such attribution should the douglas have | as 4.01. 3
should go so general current through the world. 4.01. 5
that with our small conjunction we should on, 4.01. 37
for therein should we read | the very bottom and 4.01. 49
faith, and so we should, | where now remains a 4.01. 52
and god defend but still i should stand so, | so 4.03. 38
that you and i should meet upon such terms | as 5.01. 10
the king should keep his word in loving us. 5.02. 5
unless a brother should a brother dare | to 5.02. 53
and god forbid a shallow scratch should drive 5.04. 11
i should not make so dear a show of zeal; 5.04. 95
i should have a heavy miss of thee | if i were 5.04.105
how if he should counterfeit too and rise? 5.04.122 P
let them that should reward valor bear the sin 5.04.149 P
sack, and live cleanly as a nobleman should do. 5.04.165 P
now | should be the father of some stratagem. 2H4 1.01. 8
why should that gentleman that rode by travers 1.01. 55

i am sorry i should force you to believe | that 1.01.105
you should procure him better assurance than 1.02. 31 P
i look'd 'a should have sent me two and twenty 1.02. 43 P
but how i should be your patient to follow your 1.02.129 P
hair in your face but should have his effect of 1.02.161 P
say i am an old man, you should give me rest. 1.02.217 P
how in our means we should advance ourselves 1.03. 7
my judgment is we should not step too far 1.03. 20
should be still–born, and that we now possess'd 1.03. 64
that he should draw his several strengths 1.03. 76
if he should do so, | /to french and welsh he 1.03. 78
who is it like should lead his forces hither? 1.03. 81
unless a woman should be made an ass and a beast 2.01. 37 P
you should have been well on your way to york. 2.01. 67
saying that ere long they should call me madam? 2.01.101 P
a prince should not be so loosely studied as to 2.02. 7 P
have labor'd so hard, you should talk so idlely! 2.02. 29 P
i tell thee it is not meet that i should be sad, 2.02. 40 P
what wouldst thou think of me if i should weep? 2.02. 52 P
this doll tearsheet should be some road. 2.02.166 P
strange that desire should so many years outlive 2.04.260 P
which should not find a ground to root upon 3.01. 91
it well befits you should be of the peace. 3.02. 89 P
that you should seal this lawless bloody book 4.01. 91
then reason will our hearts should be as good. 4.01.155
peruse the men | we should have cop'd withal. 4.02. 95
would be sorry, my lord, but it should be thus. 4.03. 30 P
you should have won them dearer than you have. 4.03. 67
and cowards, which some of us should be too, but 4.03. 95 P
humane principle i would teach them should be, 4.03.124 P
and wherefore should these good news make me 4.04.102
i should rejoice now at this happy news, | and 4.04.109
hath wrought the mure that should confine it in 4.04.119
let all the tears that should bedew my hearse 4.05.113
many years, | i should not die but in jerusalem, 4.05.237
but a knave should have some countenance at his 5.01. 44 P
i should make four dozen of such bearded 5.01. 63 P
how many nobles then should hold their places, 5.02. 17
o god, that right should thus overcome might! 5.04. 24 P
own making, and what indeed (i should say) will ep 5 P
then should the warlike harry, like himself, H5 pr 5
(leash'd in, like hounds) should famine, sword, pr 7
which is a wonder how his grace should glean it, 1.01. 53
or should, or should not, bar us in our claim; 1.02. 12
or should, or should not, bar us in our claim; 1.02. 12
that you should fashion, wrest, or bow your 1.02. 14
female | should be inheritrix in salique land; 1.02. 51
do all expect that you should rouse yourself, 1.02.123
why the devil should we keep knives to cut one 2.01. 91 P
that he should, for a foreign purse, so sell 2.02. 10
should with his lion gait walk the whole world, 2.02.122
comfort him, bid him 'a should not think of god; 2.03. 20 P
for peace itself should not so dull a kingdom 2.04. 16
should be maintain'd, assembled, and collected, 2.04. 19
with me, | my purpose should not fail with me, 3.02. 16
his prayers, lest 'a should be thought a coward; 3.02. 38 P
if i should take from another's pocket to put 3.02. 49 P
so, for fear i should be fac'd out of my way. 3.07. 82 P
the greater therefore should our courage be. 4.01. 2
that we should dress us fairly for our end. 4.01. 10
meet, think you, that we should also, look you, 4.01. 78 P
nor it is not meet he should. 4.01.100 P
no man should possess him with any appearance of 4.01.110 P
he, by showing it, should dishearten his army. 4.01.111 P
so should he be sure to be ransom'd, and a many 4.01.121 P
ay, or more than we should seek after; 4.01.130 P
should be impos'd upon his father that sent him; 4.01.149 P
therefore should every soldier in the wars do as 4.01.178 P
and to teach others how they should prepare. 4.01.185 P
i do not desire he should answer for me, and yet 4.01.188 P
something too round, i should be angry with you, 4.01.204 P
god, why should they mock poor fellows thus? 4.03. 92
o signieur dew should be a gentleman. 4.04. 7
'tis the gage of one that i should fight withal, 4.07.123 P
i by bargain should | wear it myself. 4.07.174
come, wherefore should you be so pashful? 4.08. 70 P
should not in this best garden of the world, 5.02. 36
rusts | that should deracinate such savagery; 5.02. 47
the sciences that should become our country, 5.02. 58
peace | should not expel these inconveniences, 5.02. 66
be it spoken, i should quickly leap into a wife. 5.02.139 P
it is not possible you should love the enemy of 5.02.171 P
loving me, you should love the friend of france; 5.02.172 P
and they should sooner persuade harry of england 5.02.278 P
what should i say? 1H6 1.01. 15
and whilst a field should be dispatch'd and 1.01. 72
thus contumeliously should break the peace! 1.03. 58
god, these nobles should such stomachs bear! 1.03. 90
as who should say, "when i am dead and gone, 1.04. 93
how, or which way, should they first break in? 2.01. 71
i thought i should have seen some hercules, | a 2.03. 19
should strike such terror to his enemies. 2.03. 24
it is because no one should sway but he, | no 3.01. 37
he, | no one, but he, should be about the king; 3.01. 38
methinks my lord should be religious, | and know 3.01. 54
methinks his lordship should be humbler, | it 3.01. 56
it be said, "speak, sirrah, when you should; 3.01. 62
that two such noble peers as ye should jar! 3.01. 70
who should be pitiful, if you be not? 3.01.109
or who should study to prefer a peace, | if holy 3.01.110
priest | should ever get that privilege of me. 3.01.121
that henry born at monmouth should win all, 3.01.197
methinks i should revive the soldiers' hearts, 3.02. 97
nor should that nation boast it so with us, 3.03. 23
for ever should they be expuls'd from france, 3.03. 25
should grieve thee more than streams of foreign 3.03. 55
or else this blow should broach thy dearest 3.04. 40
and should (if i were worthy to be judge) | be 4.01. 42
there should be found such false dissembling 4.01. 63
i should have begg'd i might have been employ'd. 4.01. 72
that any one should therefore be suspicious | i 4.01.153
i fear we should have seen decipher'd there 4.01.184
so should we save a valiant gentleman | by 4.03. 26
the levied succors that should lend him aid, 4.04. 23
york set him on, york should have sent him aid. 4.04. 29
should bring thy father to his drooping chair. 4.05. 5
your loss is great, so your regard should be; 4.05. 22
boy, he smiles, methinks, as who should say, 4.07. 27
in, | we should have found a bloody day of this. 4.07. 34
should reign among professors of one faith. 5.01. 14
i promised | should be delivered to his holiness 5.01. 53
for princes should be free. 5.03.114
so should i give consent to flatter sin. 5.05. 25
that he should be so abject, base, and poor, 5.05. 49
us | in our opinions she should be preferr'd. 5.05. 61
whom should we match with henry, being a king, 5.05. 66
but now it is impossible we should. 2H6 1.01.108
my sword should shed hot blood, mine eyes no 1.01.118
france should have torn and rent my very heart 1.01.126
that suffolk should demand a whole fifteenth 1.01.133
she should have stay'd in france, and starv'd in 1.01.135
there's reason he should be displeas'd at it. 1.01.155
why should he then protect our sovereign, | he 1.01.165
why somerset should be preferr'd in this. 1.03.114
image of pride, why should i hold my peace? 1.03.176
the issue of the next son should have reign'd. 2.02. 32
till lionel's issue fails, his should not reign. 2.02. 56
years | should be to be protected like a child. 2.03. 29
land, | methinks i should not thus be led along, 2.04. 30
and should you fall, he is the next will mount. 3.01. 22
that he should come about your royal person, 3.01. 26
i think i should have told your grace's tale. 3.01. 44
for i should melt at an offender's tears, | and 3.01.126
this gloucester should be quickly rid the world, 3.01.233
that he should die is worthy policy, | but yet 3.01.235
so the poor chicken should be sure of death. 3.01.251
his guilt should be but idly posted over, 3.01.255
god forbid any malice should prevail, | that 3.02. 23
why, warwick, who should do the duke to death? 3.02.179
and i should rob the deathsman of his fee, 3.02.217
that if your highness should intend to sleep, 3.02.255
and charge that no man should disturb your rest 3.02.256
wherefore should i curse them? 3.02.309
my tongue should stumble in mine earnest words, 3.02.316
mine eyes should sparkle like the beaten flint, 3.02.317
ay, every joint should seem to curse and ban; 3.02.319
heart would break, | should i not curse them. 3.02.321
where, from thy sight, i should be raging mad, 3.02.394
soul, | or i should breathe it so into thy body, 3.02.398
where should he die? 3.03. 9
and so should these, if i might have my will. 4.01. 27
birth | and told me that by water i should die: 4.01. 35
it is impossible that i should die | by such a 4.01.110
far be it we should honor such as these | with 4.01.123
and therefore should we be magistrates. 4.02. 18 P
but methinks he should stand in fear of fire, 4.02. 62 P
of an innocent lamb should be made parchment? 4.02. 80 P
being scribbled o'er, should undo a man? 4.02. 81 P
but where's the body that i should embrace? 4.04. 6
many simple souls | should perish by the sword! 4.04. 11
my love, i should not mourn, but die for thee. 4.04. 25
he nods at us, as who should say, i'll be even 4.07. 94 P
god should be so obdurate as yourselves, | how 4.07.115
that you should leave me at the white hart in 4.08. 24 P
should make a start o'er seas and vanquish you? 4.08. 43
than you should stoop unto a frenchman's mercy. 4.08. 48
i know thee not, why then should i betray thee? 4.10. 32
should raise so great a power without his leave, 5.01. 21
with thy brave bearing should i be in love, 5.02. 20
nor should thy prowess want praise and esteem, 5.02. 22
and disorder wounds | where it should guard. 5.02. 33
we then should see the bottom | of all our 5.02. 78
whom should he follow but his natural king? 3H6 1.01. 82
but that the next heir should succeed and reign. 1.01.146
why should you sigh, my lord? 1.01.191
if you be king, why should not i succeed? 1.01.227
the soldiers should have toss'd me on their 1.01.244
i took an oath that he should quietly reign. 1.02. 15
no; god forbid your grace should be forsworn. 1.02. 18
what should we fear? 1.02. 68
why should i not now have the like success? 1.02. 75
the passage where thy words should enter. 1.03. 22
deadly, | i should lament thy miserable state. 1.04. 85
you should not be king | till our king henry had 1.04.101
i should not for my life but weep with him, | to 1.04.170
he been ta'en, we should have heard the news; 2.01. 4
he been slain, we should have heard the news; 2.01. 5
methinks we should have heard | the happy 2.01. 6
should not notwithstanding join our lights together, 2.01. 37
for self–same wind that i should speak withal 2.01. 82
if we should recompt | our baleful news, and at 2.01. 96
should lose his birthright by his father's fault 2.02. 35
i am his king, and he should bow his knee. 2.02. 87
who should succeed the father but the son? 2.02. 94
(as if a channel should be call'd the sea), 2.02.141
that winter should cut off our spring–time so. 2.03. 47
for i have murthered where i should not kill. 2.05.122
that phaeton should check thy fiery steeds, 2.06. 12
henry, hadst thou sway'd as kings should do, 2.06. 14
no, 'tis impossible he should escape; 2.06. 38
rail at him, | this hand should chop it off; 2.06. 82
a man at least, for less i should not be; 3.01. 57
'twere pity they should lose their father's 3.02. 31
your grace my sons should call you father. 3.02.100
you'ld think it strange if i should marry her. 3.02.111
and, for i should not deal in her soft laws, 3.02.154
these peers of france should smile at that. 3.03. 91
god forbid that i should wish them sever'd 4.01. 21
should not become my wife and england's queen. 4.01. 26
alas, how should you govern any kingdom, | that 4.03. 35
in field | should not be able to encounter mine. 4.08. 36
then why should they love edward more than me? 4.08. 47
who should that be? belike unlook'd–for friends. 5.01. 14
is't meet that he | should leave the helm and, 5.04. 7
a woman of this valiant spirit | should, if a 5.04. 40
man, | he should have leave to go away betimes, 5.04. 45
gentlemen, what i should say | my tears gainsay; 5.04. 73
why should she live, to fill the world with 5.05. 44
my good lord — my lord, i should say rather. 5.06. 2
which plainly signified | that i should snarl, 5.06. 77
this day should clarence closely be mew'd up R3 1.01. 38
he should for that commit your godfathers. 1.01. 48
that you should be new christ'ned in the tower. 1.01. 50
that by g | his issue disinherited should be; 1.01. 57
more pity that the eagles should be mew'd, 1.01.132
by such despair i should accuse myself. 1.02. 85
these nails should rent that beauty from my 1.02.126
you should not blemish it, if i stood by: 1.02.128
so should we you, if you should be our king. 1.03.147
so should we you, if you should be our king. 1.03.147
if i should be? 1.03.148
as you suppose | you should enjoy, were you this 1.03.151
should all but answer for that peevish brat? 1.03.193
to serve me well, you all should do me duty, 1.03.250
that deceit should steal such gentle shape, 2.02. 27
the new–heal'd wound of malice should break out, 2.02.125
it should be put | to no apparent likelihood of 2.02.135
that it is meet so few should fetch the prince. 2.02.139
if his rule were true, he should be gracious. 2.04. 20
forbid | we should infringe the holy privilege 3.01. 41
methinks the truth should live from age to age, 3.01. 76
ape, | he thinks that you should bear me on your 3.01.131
why, what should you fear? 3.01.143
grace, we think, should soonest know his mind. 3.04. 9
yet had we not determin'd he should die | until 3.05. 52
marry, god defend his grace should say us nay! 3.07. 81
sorry i am my noble cousin should | suspect me 3.07. 88
which god defend that i should wring from him! 3.07.173
that edward still should live true noble prince! 4.02. 16
did prophesy that richmond should be king, 4.02. 96
that i should wish for thee to help me curse 4.04. 80
why should calamity be full of words? 4.04.126
with a golden crown | where should be branded, 4.04.141
my tongue should to thy ears not name my boys 4.04.231
your highness told me i should post before. 4.04.455
when they should serve their sovereign in the 4.04.485
he should espouse elizabeth her daughter. 4.05. 8
so long sund'red friends should dwell upon. 5.03.100
when i should mount with wings of victory. 5.03.106
and wherefore should they, since that i myself 5.03.202
he should have brav'd the east an hour ago. 5.03.279
th' king) t' appoint | who should attend on him? H8 1.01. 75
we should take root here where we sit, or sit 1.02. 87
that if the king | should without issue die, 1.02.134
to no creature living but | to me should utter, 1.02.167
thomas lovell's heads | should have gone off. 1.02.186
is't possible the spells of france should juggle 1.03. 1
men of his way should be most liberal, | they 1.03. 61
some of these | should find a running banket, 1.04. 12
i would i were, | they should find easy penance. 1.04. 17
there should be one amongst 'em, by his person 1.04. 78
you, cardinal, | i should judge now unhappily. 1.04. 89
in haste too, | lest he should help his father. 2.01. 44
cruel | that she should feel the smart of this? 2.01.166
what kind of my obedience i should tender. 2.03. 66
that thus you should proceed to put me off, 2.04. 21
should | do no more offices of life to't than 2.04.190
th' world) should not | be gladded in't by me. 2.04.196
they should be good men, their affairs as 3.01. 22
i am sorry my integrity should breed | (and 3.01. 51
why should we, good lady, | upon what cause, 3.01.155
she should have bought her dignities so dear. 3.01.184
i should be glad to hear such news as this 3.02. 24
cause, that she should lie i' th' bosom of | our 3.02.100
object, he should still | dwell in his musings, 3.02.132
what should this mean? 3.02.160
should, notwithstanding that your bond of duty, 3.02.188
all the world should crack their duty to you 3.02.193
should the approach of this wild river break, 3.02.198
what should this mean? 3.02.203
i should tell you | you have as little honesty 3.02.270
thy spirit wonder | a great man should decline? 3.02.375
i should have been beholding to your paper. 4.01. 21
that should be | the duke of suffolk. 4.01. 40
which he himself | foretold should be his last, 4.02. 27
you should be lord ambassador from the emperor, 4.02.109
one, i dare avow | (and now i should not lie), 4.02.143
these should be hours for necessities, | not for 5.01. 2
i should have ta'en some pains to bring together 5.01.119
want of wisdom, you, that best should teach us, 5.02. 48
yet should find respect | for what they have 5.02.110
what should you do, but knock 'em down by th' 5.03. 32
the door, he should be a brazier by his face, 5.03. 40
of bombards, when | ye should do service. 5.03. 82
why should i war without the walls of troy, TRO 1.01. 2
lest hector or my father should perceive me, | i 1.01. 36
but how should this man, that makes me smile, 1.02. 3[illegible]
then troilus should have too much: 1.02.10[illegible]
been a green hair, i should have laugh'd too. 1.02.15[illegible]
a daughter a goddess, he should take his choice. 1.02.23[illegible]
and the minds of all | should be shut up, hear 1.03. 58
hand of greece | should hold up high in brass, 1.03. 6[illegible]
should with a bond of air, strong as the 1.03. 66
should lift their bosoms higher than the shores, 1.03.11[illegible]
strength should be lord of imbecility, | and the 1.03.11[illegible]
and the rude son should strike his father dead; 1.03.11[illegible]
force should be right, or rather, right and 1.03.11[illegible]
should lose their names, and so should justice 1.03.11[illegible]
lose their names, and so should justice too! 1.03.11[illegible]
were he not proud, we all should share with him. 1.03.36[illegible]
of his eyes, | should he scape hector fair. 1.03.37[illegible]
should not our father | bear the great sway of 2.02. 3[illegible]
manhood and honor | should have hare hearts, 2.02. 4[illegible]
paris should do some vengeance on the greeks. 2.02. 7[illegible]
and jove forbid there should be done amongst us 2.02.12[illegible]
paris should ne'er retract what he hath done, 2.02.14[illegible]
should once set footing in your generous bosoms? 2.02.15[illegible]
why should a man be proud? 2.03.15[illegible]
what should i say? 2.03.17[illegible]
be the physician that should be the patient. 2.03.21[illegible]
'a should not bear it so, 'a should eat swords 2.03.21[illegible]
not bear it so, 'a should eat swords first. 2.03.21[illegible]
wherefore should you so? 2.03.23[illegible]
you should not have the eminence of him, | but 2.03.25[illegible]
it should seem, fellow, thou hast not seen the 3.01. 3[illegible]
why should you say cressida? 3.01. 9[illegible]
what should they grant? 3.02. 6[illegible]
fool slides o'er the ice that you should break. 3.03.21[illegible]
as who should say there were wit in this head, 3.03.25[illegible]
business | should rob my bed–mate of my company. 4.01. [illegible]
here, what should he do here? 4.02. 4[illegible]
what should he do here? 4.02. 5[illegible]
aunt, should by my mortal sword | be drained! 4.05.13[illegible]
should wit larded with malice and malice fac'd 5.01. 5[illegible]

lest your displeasure should enlarge itself | to 5.02. 37
it on thy horn, | it should be challeng'd. 5.02. 96
by vulcan's skill, | my sword should bite it. 5.02.171
who should withhold me? 5.03. 51
oppos'd to hinder me, should stop my way, | /but 5.03. 57
bite another, and wherefore should one bastard? 5.07. 19 P
why should our endeavor be so lov'd and the 5.10. 38 P
it should be now, but that my fear is this, 5.10. 53
should by the cormorant belly be restrain'd, COR 1.01.121
where he should find you lions, finds you hares; 1.01.171
the rabble should have first /unroof'd the city 1.01.218
ere (almost) rome | should know we were afoot. 1.02. 25
i should freelier rejoice in that absence 1.03. 3 P
entreaties a mother should not sell him an hour 1.03. 8 P
then his good report should have been my son; 1.03. 20 P
if i should tell thee o'er this thy day's work, 1.09. 1
should they not, | well might they fester 1.09. 29
as if i lov'd my little should be dieted | in 1.09. 52
of my son, he should | be free as is the wind. 1.09. 88
dries, 'tis time | it should be look'd to. 1.09. 94
think, should we encounter | as often as we eat. 1.10. 9
why then you should discover a brace of 2.01. 43 P
/you are three | that rome should dote on; 2.01.187
his honors | from where he should begin and end, 2.01.225
of coriolanus | should not be utter'd feebly. 2.02. 83
them th' unaching scars which i should hide, 2.02.148
what he requested | should be in them to give. 2.02.158
should bring ourselves to be monstrous members. 2.03. 12 P
of one direct way should be at once to all the 2.03. 23 P
you should account me the more virtuous that i 2.03. 94 P
why in this woolvish /toge should i stand here 2.03.115
what custom wills, in all things should we do't, 2.03.118
he should have show'd us | his marks of merit, 2.03.163
if he should still malignantly remain | fast foe 2.03.183
you should have said | that as his worthy deeds 2.03.185
you should have ta'en th' advantage of his 2.03.198
what you rather must do | than what you should, 2.03.233
why then should i be consul? 3.01. 50
measles | which we disdain should tetter us, yet 3.01. 79
state | of that integrity which should become't; 3.01.159
what should the people do with these bald 3.01.164
do not cry havoc where you should but hunt 3.01.273
an unnatural dam | should now eat up her own! 3.01.292
before he should thus stoop to th' /herd, but 3.02. 32
at stake requir'd | i should do so in honor. 3.02. 64
they to dust should grind it | and throw't 3.02.103
if that i could for weeping, you should hear — 4.02. 13
should from yond cloud speak divine things, 4.05.104
we should by this, to all our lamentation, | if 4.06. 34
if martius should be join'd /wi' /th' volscians 4.06. 89
if they | should say, "be good to rome," they 4.06.112
as those should do that had deserv'd his hate, 4.06.113
to my house the brand | that should consume it, 4.06.116
what should i do? 5.01. 39
words in your own, you should not pass here; 5.02. 26 P
then you should hate rome, as he does. 5.02. 38 P
bows, | as if olympus to a molehill should | in 5.03. 30
should we be silent and not speak, our raiment 5.03. 94
which should | make our eyes flow with joy, 5.03. 98
though we had | our wish, which side should win; 5.03.113
with a bolt | that should but rive an oak. 5.03.153
dismiss your followers, and, as suitors should, TIT 1.01. 44
what should i don this robe and trouble you? 1.01.189
'forfend | i should be author to dishonor you! 1.01.435
and should the empress know | this discord's 2.01. 69
then why should he despair that knows to court 2.01. 91
then should not we be tir'd with this ado. 2.01. 98
t offend you then | that both should speed? 2.01.101
thy temples should be planted presently | with 2.03. 62
should drive upon thy new–transformed limbs, 2.03. 64
tis pity they should take him for a stag. 2.03. 71
body hearing it | should straight fall mad, or 2.03.104
so should i rob my sweet sons of their fee. 2.03.179
that should have murthered bassianus here. 2.03.279
death, | that end upon them should be executed. 2.03.303
and 'twere my cause, i should go hang myself. 2.04. 9
ah, that this sight should make so deep a wound, 3.01.246
that ever death should let life bear his name, 3.01.248
o, why should nature build so foul a den, 4.01. 59
their mother's bedchamber should not be safe 4.01.108
as who should say, "old lad, i am thine own." 4.02.121
and who should find them but the empress' 4.03. 74
and told the moor he should not choose | but 4.03. 75
god forbid i should be so bold to press to 4.03. 91 P
in hope thyself should govern rome and me. 4.04. 60
why should you fear? is not your city strong? 4.04. 78
yet should both ear and heart obey my tongue. 4.04. 99
who should i swear by? 5.01. 71
what would you say if i should let you speak? 5.02.178
because the girl should not survive her shame, 5.03. 41
time | when it should move ye to attend me most, 5.03. 92
o, were the sum of these that i should pay 5.03.158
ah, why should wrath be mute and fury dumb? 5.03.184
prayers | i should repent the evils i have done. 5.03.186
no, for then we should be colliers. ROM 1.01. 2 P
sun | should in the farthest east begin to draw 1.01.135
should be so tyrannous and rough in proof! 1.01.170
should, without eyes, see pathways to his will! 1.01.172
o, teach me how i should forget to think. 1.01.226
that the shoemaker should meddle with his yard 1.02. 39 P
whither should they come? 1.02. 71
indeed i should have ask'd /thee that before. 1.02. 77
warrant, and i should live a thousand years, 1.03. 46
a thousand years, | i never should forget it: 1.03. 47
laugh | to think it should leave crying and say, 1.03. 51
and, to sink in it, should you burthen love — 1.04. 23
this, by his voice, should be a montague. 1.05. 54
sea, | i should adventure for such merchandise. 2.02. 84
should have been more strange, i must confess, 2.02.102
yet i should kill thee with much cherishing. 2.02.183
where the dev'l should this romeo be? 2.04. 1
that we should be thus afflicted with these 2.04. 32 P
had, my weapon should quickly have been out. 2.04.158 P
ye, if ye should lead her in a fool's paradise, 2.04.165 P
therefore, if you should deal double with her, 2.04.168 P
love's heralds should be thoughts, | which ten 2.05. 4
why, she is within, | where should she be? 2.05. 59
were two such, we should have none shortly, for 3.01. 15 P

any man should buy the fee–simple of my life for 3.01. 32 P
his fault concludes but what the law should end, 3.01.185
this torture should be roar'd in dismal hell. 3.02. 44
that ever i should live to see thee dead! 3.02. 63
o that deceit should dwell | in such a gorgeous 3.02. 84
how should they when that wise men have no eyes? 3.03. 62
why should you fall into so deep an o? 3.03. 90
true use indeed | which should bedeck thy shape, 3.03.125
that romeo should, upon receipt thereof, | soon 3.05. 98
ere he that should be husband comes to woo. 3.05.119
that heaven should practice stratagems | upon so 3.05.209
i would i knew not why it should be slowed. 4.01. 16
to answer that, i should confess to you. 4.01. 23
god shield i should disturb devotion! 4.01. 41
this is as't should be. 4.02. 29
what should she do here? 4.03. 18
lest in this marriage he should be dishonor'd 4.03. 26
i fear it is, and yet methinks it should not, 4.03. 28
for 'twas your heaven she should be advanc'd, 4.05. 72
as i remember, this should be the house. 5.01. 55
this same should be the voice of friar john. 5.02. 2
he told me paris should have married juliet. 5.03. 78
i do remember well where i should be, | and 5.03.149
what should it be that is so /shrik'd abroad? 5.03.190
that he should hither come as this dire night 5.03.247
being the time the potion's force should cease. 5.03.249
if i should pay you for't as 'tis extoll'd, | it TIM 1.01.167
that there should be small love amongest these 1.01.249
for i should ne'er flatter thee. 1.02. 39 P
methinks they should invite them without knives: 1.02. 44
a huge man, i should fear to drink at meals, 1.02. 49 P
lest they should spy my windpipe's dangerous 1.02. 51
great men should drink with harness on their 1.02. 52
freedom, | or my friends, if i should need 'em. 1.02. 69
we should think ourselves for ever perfect. 1.02. 86 P
friends, if we should ne'er have need of 'em? 1.02. 96 P
living, should we ne'er have use for 'em; 1.02. 97 P
i should fear those that dance before me now 1.02.143
else i should tell him well (i' faith, i should) 1.02.161
i should tell him well (i' faith, i should), 1.02.161
false hearts should never have sound legs. 1.02.234
for if i should be brib'd too, there would be 1.02.238 P
o, that men's ears should be | to counsel deaf, 1.02.249
is't possible the world should so much differ, 3.01. 46
why should it thrive and turn to nutriment 3.01. 58
i should ne'er have denied his occasion so many 3.02. 23 P
i should not urge it half so faithfully. 3.02. 41
it happ'ned that i should purchase the day 3.02. 47 P
and the best half should have return'd to him, 3.02. 84
timon in this should pay more than he owes; 3.04. 22
and e'en as if your lord should wear rich jewels 3.04. 23
and it should seem by th' sum | your master's 3.04. 30
some other hour, i should derive much from't; 3.04. 69 P
methinks he should the sooner pay his debts, 3.04. 75
what if it should be so? 3.04.106
'tis necessary he should die. 3.05. 2
it could not else be i should prove so base | to 3.05. 93
soldiers should brook as little wrongs as gods. 3.05.116
it should not be, by the persuasion of his new 3.06. 7 P
i should think so. 3.06. 9 P
alack, my fellows, what should i say to you? 4.02. 3
then what should war be? 4.03. 62
sick of man's unkindness | should yet be hungry! 4.03.177
thou wealth again, | rascals should have't. 4.03.218
i'll beat thee, but i should infect my hands. 4.03.364
where should he have this gold? 4.03.398 P
why should you want? 4.03.417
you should have fear'd false times when you did 4.03.513
by all description this should be the place. 5.03. 1
and schools should fall | for private faults in 5.04. 25
a man of such a feeble temper should | so get JC 1.02.129
what should be in that "caesar"? 1.02.142
why should that name be sounded more than yours? 1.02.143
i do not know the man i should avoid | so soon 1.02.200
i should not then ask casca what had chanc'd. 1.02.220
and he were cassius, | he should not humor me. 1.02.315
of life | that should be in a roman you do want, 1.03. 58
and why should caesar be a tyrant then? 1.03.103
well belov'd of caesar, | should outlive caesar. 2.01.157
and that were much he should, for he is given 2.01.188
your condition, | i should not know you brutus. 2.01.255
i should not need, if you were gentle brutus. 2.01.279
is it excepted i should know no secrets | that 2.01.281
this were true, then should i know this secret. 2.01.291
seems to me most strange that men should fear, 2.02. 35
caesar should be a beast without a heart | if he 2.02. 42
if he should stay at home to–day for fear. 2.02. 43
madam, what should i do? 2.04. 10
that i was constant cimber should be banish'd, 3.01. 72
lest some friend of caesar's | should chance — 3.01. 88
rushing on us, should do your age some mischief. 3.01. 93
the son of caesar, | you should be satisfied. 3.01.226
ambition should be made of sterner stuff: 3.02. 92
i should do brutus wrong, and cassius wrong, 3.02.123
for if you should, o, what would come of it? 3.02.146
that should move | the stones of rome to rise 3.02.229
he should stand | one of the three to share it? 4.01. 14
and took his voice who should be prick'd to die 4.01. 16
but when they should endure the bloody spur, 4.02. 25
and if not so, how should i wrong a brother? 4.02. 39
(which should perceive nothing but love from us) 4.02. 44
that every nice offense should bear his comment. 4.03. 8
you have done that you should be sorry for. 4.03. 65
should i have answer'd caius cassius so? 4.03. 78
a friend should bear his friend's infirmities; 4.03. 86
love, and be friends, as two such men should be, 4.03.131
what should the wars do with these jigging fools 4.03.137
even so great men great losses should endure. 4.03.193
i should not urge thy duty past thy might; 4.03.261
that ever rome | should breed thy fellow. 5.03.101
so brutus should be found. 5.05. 58
so should he look | that seems to speak things MAC 1.02. 46
you should be women, | and yet your beards 1.03. 45
do contend | which should be thine or his. 1.03. 93
which do but what they should, by doing every 1.04. 26
but without | the illness should attend it. 1.05. 20
dost fear to do | than wishest should be undone. 1.05. 25
who should against his murtherer shut the door, 1.07. 15

if we should fail? 1.07. 59
for thy undaunted mettle should compose 1.07. 73
defect, | which else should free have wrought. 2.01. 19
hell gate, he should have old turning the key. 2.03. 2 P
what should be spoken here, where our fate, 2.03.121
entomb, | when living light should kiss it? 2.04. 10
was said | it should not stand in thy posterity, 3.01. 4
but that myself should be the root and father 3.01. 5
we should have else desir'd your good advice 3.01. 20
those thoughts which should indeed have died 3.02. 10
without all remedy | should be without regard: 3.02. 12
stepp'd in so far that, should i wade no more, 3.04.136
they should find | what 'twere to kill a father; 3.06. 19
so should fleance. 3.06. 20
and hums, as who should say, "you'll rue the 3.06. 42
i am so much a fool, should i stay longer, | it 4.02. 28
why should i, mother? 4.02. 36
a good sign that i should quickly have a new 4.02. 62 P
whither should i fly? 4.02. 73
what should he be? 4.03. 49
i should cut off the nobles for their lands, 4.03. 79
that i should forge | quarrels unjust against 4.03. 82
i should | pour the sweet milk of concord into 4.03. 97
air, | where hearing should not latch them. 4.03.195
you may to me, and 'tis most meet you should. 5.01. 16 P
you have known what you should not. 5.01. 47 P
she has spoke what she should not, i am sure of 5.01. 48 P
leaf, | and that which should accompany old age, 5.03. 24
to the very echo, | that should applaud again. 5.03. 54
profit again should hardly draw me here. 5.03. 62
they not forc'd with those that should be ours, 5.05. 5
she should have died hereafter; 5.05. 17
lord, | i should report that which i say i saw, 5.05. 30
why should i play the roman fool, and die | on 5.08. 1
why should we in our peevish opposition | take HAM 1.02.100
that it should come /to /this! 1.02.137
why, she should hang on him | as if increase of 1.02.143
though hell itself should gape | and bid me hold 1.02.244
i do not know, my lord, what i should think. 1.03.104
what should we do? 1.04. 57
why, what should be the fear? 1.04. 64
wherefore should you do this? 2.01. 36
what it should be, | more than his father's 2.02. 7
to expostulate | what majesty should be, what 2.02. 87
that she should lock herself from /his resort, 2.02.143
what should we say, my lord? 2.02.277 P
should more appear like entertainment than yours 2.02.374 P
or he to /hecuba, | that he should weep for her? 2.02.560
hah, 'swounds, i should take it; 2.02.576
this | i should 'a' fatted all the region kites 2.02.579
/your /honesty should admit no discourse to your 3.01.107 P
you should not have believ'd me, for virtue 3.01.116 P
what should such fellows as i do crawling 3.01.126 P
why should the poor be flatter'd? 3.02. 59
what should a man do but be merry, for look you 3.02.125 P
that even our loves should with our fortunes 3.02.201
if she should break it now! 3.02.224 P
your wisdom should show itself more richer to 3.02.304 P
them partial, should o'erhear | the speech, of 3.03. 32
us, whose providence | should have kept short, 4.01. 18
what replication should be made by the son of a 4.02. 13 P
pole | a ranker rate, should it be sold in fee. 4.04. 22
"how should i your true–love know | from another 4.05. 23
should be as mortal as /an /old man's life? 4.05.161
what part of the world | i should be greeted, if 4.06. 6
what should this mean? 4.07. 49
it be so, laertes — | as how should it be so? 4.07. 58
that we would do, | we should do when we would; 4.07.119
and then this "should" is like a spendthrift's 4.07.122
no place indeed should murther sanctuarize, 4.07.127
sanctuarize, | revenge should have no bounds. 4.07.128
if this should fail, | and that our drift look 4.07.150
this project | should have a back or second, 4.07.153
she should have been buried out a' christian 5.01. 24 P
pity that great folk should have count'nance in 5.01. 27 P
should patch a wall t' expel the /winter's flaw! 5.01.216
she should in ground unsanctified been lodg'd 5.01.229
flints, and pebbles should be thrown on her. 5.01.231
we should profane the service of the dead | to 5.01.236
and that should learn us | there's a divinity 5.02. 9
of the axe, | my head should be strook off. 5.02. 25
as peace should still her wheaten garland wear 5.02. 41
he should those bearers put to sudden death, 5.02. 46
i should impart a thing to you from his majesty. 5.02. 90 P
lest i should compare with him in excellence, 5.02.138 P
this case, should stir me most | to my revenge, 5.02.245
ears are senseless that should give us hearing, 5.02.369
where should we have our thanks? 5.02.372
should in this trice of time | commit a thing so LR 1.01.216
without miracle | should never plant in me. 1.01.223
my love should kindle to inflam'd respect. 1.01.255
wherefore should i | stand in the plague of 1.02. 2
him, you should enjoy half his revenue for ever, 1.02. 53 P
i wake him, you should enjoy half his revenue." 1.02. 56 P
the father should be as ward to the son, and the 1.02. 73 P
of his intent, you should run a certain course; 1.02. 82 P
/fut, i should have been that i am, had the 1.02.131 P
other day, what should follow these eclipses. 1.02.141 P
sung, | that such a king should play bo–peep, 1.04.177
which if you should, the fault | would not scape 1.04.209
as you are old and reverend, should be wise. 1.04.240
from me perforce, | should make thee worth them. 1.04.299
such a daughter, | should sure to the slaughter, 1.04.319
that such a slave as this should wear a sword, 2.02. 72
though i should win your displeasure to entreat 2.02.112 P
your father's dog, | you should not use me so. 2.02.137
messenger, | should have him thus restrained. 2.02.147
strange that they should so depart from home, 2.04. 1
wherefore | should he sit here? 2.04.113
you should be rul'd and led | by some discretion 2.04.148
what should you need of more? 2.04.238
house | should many people under two commands 2.04.241
makes his toe | what he his heart should make 3.02. 32
is it not as this mouth should tear this hand 3.04. 15
should have thus little mercy on their flesh? 3.04. 73
hospitable favors | you should not ruffle thus. 3.07. 41
how should this be? 4.01. 37
so distribution should undo excess, | and each 4.01. 70

what most he should dislike seems pleasant to 4.02. 10
why should she write to edmund? 4.05. 19
i should show | what party i do follow. 4.05. 39
my snuff and loathed part of nature should 4.06. 39
so should my thoughts be sever'd from my griefs, 4.06.282
should have stood that night | against my fire, 4.07. 36
i should ev'n die with pity | to see another 4.07. 52
methinks i should know you, and know this man, 4.07. 63
that were the most, if he should husband you. 5.03. 70
well, else i should answer | from a full–flowing 5.03. 73
in wisdom i should ask thy name, | but, since 5.03.142
use them so | that heaven's vault should crack. 5.03.260
why should a dog, a horse, a rat, have life, 5.03.307
i should have known it | without a prompter. OTH 1.02. 83
practices of cunning hell | why this should be. 1.03.103
i should but teach him how to tell my story, 1.03.165
what should i do? 1.03.317 P
long that desdemona should continue her love to 1.03.342 P
for i mine own gain'd knowledge should profane 1.03.384
but that our loves and comforts should increase 2.01.194
dull with the act of sport, there should be, 2.01.227 P
so much was his pleasure should be proclaim'd. 2.02. 8 P
should hazard such a place as his own second 2.03.139
than it should do offense to michael cassio; 2.03.222
that men should put an enemy in their mouths to 2.03.290 P
that we should, with joy, pleasance, revel, and 2.03.291 P
soul | what you would ask me that i should deny, 3.03. 69
'tis as i should entreat you wear your gloves, 3.03. 77
men should be what they seem, | or those that be 3.03.126
certain, men should be what they seem. 3.03.128
should you do so, my lord, | my speech should 3.03.221
my speech should fall into such vild success 3.03.222
(for he conjur'd her she should ever keep it) 3.03.294
i should be wise — for honesty's a fool | and 3.03.382
it is impossible you should see this, | were 3.03.402
where should i lose the handkerchief, emilia? 3.04. 23
my father's eye | should hold her loathed, and 3.04. 62
and his spirits should hunt | after new fancies. 3.04. 62
nor should i know him | were he in favor as in 3.04.124
bianca's /pow'r, | how quickly should you speed! 4.01.108
work, that you should find it in your chamber, 4.01.151 P
by heaven, that should be my handkerchief! 4.01.158 P
in venice, | though i should swear i saw't. 4.01.243
devils themselves | should fear to seize thee; 4.02. 37
i should have found in some place of my soul | a 4.02. 52
i should make very forges of my cheeks, | that 4.02. 74
have i none | but what should go by water. 4.02.104
'tis meet i should be us'd so, very meet. 4.02.107
why should he call her whore? 4.02.137
/by /my troth, i think i should, and undo't when 4.03. 71 P
i should venture purgatory for't. 4.03. 77 P
who they should be that have thus mangled you? 5.01. 79
thy former light restore, | should i repent me; 5.02. 10
why i should fear i know not, | since guiltiness 5.02. 38
methinks it should be now a huge eclipse | of 5.02. 99
why, how should she be murd'red? 5.02.126
what should such a fool | do with so good a wife 5.02.233
but why should honor outlive honesty? 5.02.245
where should othello go? 5.02.271
there's not a minute of our lives should stretch ANT 1.01. 46
property | which still should go with antony. 1.01. 59
a great cause, they should be esteem'd nothing. 1.02.139 P
live in an onion that should water this sorrow. 1.02.169 P
what should i do, i do not? 1.03. 8
why should i think you can be mine, and true 1.03. 27
that which most with you should safe my going, 1.03. 55
i should take you | for idleness itself. 1.03. 92
i should have known no less: 1.04. 40
'twere pregnant they should square between 2.01. 45
our armies, and to fight, | i should do thus. 2.02. 27
i | should say myself offended, and with you 2.02. 32
at, that i should | once name you derogately, 2.02. 33
that truth should be silent i had almost forgot. 2.02.108 P
what hoop should hold us staunch from edge to 2.02.115
noble antony, | not sickness should detain me. 2.02.170
it should be better he became her guest; 2.02.221
should i lie, madam? 2.05. 93
o, that his fault should make a knave of thee, 2.05.102
wherefore my father should revengers want, 2.06. 11
in't, are the holes where eyes should be, which 2.07. 15 P
i am not so well as i should be; 2.07. 30 P
how should that be? 2.07. 63
i should have found it afterwards well done, 2.07. 79
in his offense | should my performance perish. 3.01. 27
the man hath seen some majesty, and should know. 3.03. 42
twain would be | as if the world should cleave, 3.04. 31
and that slain men | should solder up the rift. 3.04. 32
lepidus of the triumpherate | should be depos'd; 3.06. 29
sir, this should be answer'd. 3.06. 30
that ever i should call thee castaway! 3.06. 40
of antony | should have an army for an usher, 3.06. 44
the trees by th' way | should have borne men, 3.06. 47
should have ascended to the roof of heaven, 3.06. 49
we should have met you | by sea and land, 3.06. 53
us, why should not we | be there in person? 3.07. 5
if we should serve with horse and mares together 3.07. 7
from 's time, | what should not then be spar'd. 3.07. 12
his vantage, he shakes off, | and so should you. 3.07. 34
impossible | strange that his power should be. 3.07. 57
why should he follow? 3.13. 6
the itch of his affection should not then | have 3.13. 7
from which the world should note | something 3.13. 21
that he should dream, | knowing all measures, 3.13. 34
that of his fortunes you should make a staff 3.13. 68
should i find them | so saucy with the hand of 3.13. 97
though you can guess what temperance should be, 3.13.121
why should he not? 4.02. 2
peace, i say. | what should this mean? 4.03. 15
that when the exigent should come, which now 4.14. 63
when i should see behind me | th' inevitable 4.14. 64
eros, what | i should, and thou couldst not. 4.14. 97
so it should be, that none but antony | should 4.15. 16
that none but antony | should conquer antony, 4.15. 17
the strong–wing'd mercury should fetch thee up, 4.15. 35
the breaking of so great a thing should make | a 5.01. 14
should have shook lions into civil streets, 5.01. 16
should divide | our equalness to this. 5.01. 47
and, should we shift estates, yours would be 5.02.152

that mine own servant should | parcel the sum of 5.02.162
me, that i should not | be noble to myself. 5.02.191
be the party that should desire you to touch him 5.02.246 P
lie, as a woman should not do but in the way of 5.02.253 P
what should i stay — 5.02.313
something failing | in him that should compare. CYM 1.01. 22
that a king's children should be so convey'd, 1.01. 63
hath charg'd you should not speak together. 1.01. 83
should we be taking leave | as long a term as 1.01.106
notes | of what commands i should be subject to, 1.01.172
and that she should love this fellow, and refuse 1.02. 25 P
upon fools, lest the reflection should hurt her. 1.02. 33 P
if he should write | and i not have it, 'twere a 1.03. 2
him swear | the shes of italy should not betray 1.03. 29
it had been pity you should have been put 1.04. 40 P
i should get ground of your fair mistress; 1.04.104 P
lest the bargain should catch cold and starve. 1.04.166 P
oppos'd, | should make desire vomit emptiness, 1.06. 45
should i (damn'd then) | slaver with lips as 1.06.104
that all the plagues of hell should at one time 1.06.111
how should i be reveng'd? 1.06.129
if it be true, | how should i be reveng'd? 1.06.132
should he make me | live, like diana's priest, 1.06.132
is not fit /your lordship should undertake every 2.01. 26 P
but it is fit i should commit offense to my 2.01. 28 P
is his mother | should yield the world this ass! 2.01. 53
why should i write this down, that's riveted, 2.02. 43
this foolish imogen, i should have gold enough. 2.03. 8 P
one of your great knowing | should learn, being 2.03. 98
i should have lost the worth of it in gold. 2.04. 42
but what he look'd for should oppose and she 2.05. 18
oppose and she | should from encounter guard. 2.05. 19
why should we pay tribute? 3.01. 42 P
that i should murther her, | upon the love and 3.02. 11
how look i | that i should seem to lack humanity 3.02. 16
wrath, should he take me in his dominion, could 3.02. 40 P
(love's counsellor should fill the bores of 3.02. 57
why should excuse be born or e'er begot? 3.02. 65
what should we speak of | when we are old as you 3.03. 35
for 'tis commanded | i should do so. 3.04.126
you should tread a course | pretty and full of 3.04.146
report should render him hourly to your ear | as 3.04.150
she should that duty leave unpaid to you | which 3.05. 48
wherein i should have cause to use thee with a 3.05.110 P
i should be sick, | but that my resolution helps 3.06. 3
such, i mean, | where they should be reliev'd. 3.06. 8
victuals, i should think | here were a fairy. 3.06. 40
fault, i should | have died had i not made it. 3.06. 56
i should woo hard, but be your groom in honesty: 3.06. 69
i am near to th' place where they should meet, 4.01. 1 P
why should his mistress, who was made by him 4.01. 3 P
so man and man should be, | but clay and clay 4.02. 3
yet who this should be | doth miracle itself, 4.02. 28
why i should yield to thee. 4.02. 80
then why should we be tender | to let an 4.02.126
that an invisible instinct should frame them 4.02.177
solemn things | should answer solemn accidents. 4.02.192
how should this be? 4.02.323
should not sooner | than thine own worth prefer 4.02.385
should reserve | my crack'd one to more care. 4.04. 49
if each of you should take this course, how many 5.01. 3
you | should have ta'en vengeance on my faults, 5.01. 8
that a man should have the best use of eyes to 5.04.189 P
so should i, if i were one. 5.04.202 P
should by the minute feed on life, and ling'ring 5.05. 51
we should not, when the blood was cool, have 5.05. 77
the good posthumus | (what should i say? 5.05.158
all offices of nature should again | do their 5.05.257
i would not thy good deeds should from my lips 5.05.288
branches, which | distinction should be rich in. 5.05.384
i know not how much more, should be demanded, 5.05.389
should again unite | his favor with the radiant 5.05.474
entice his own | to evil should be done by none. PER 1.ch. 28
for death remembered should be like a mirror, 1.01. 45
and all good men, as every prince should do; 1.01. 51
why should this change of thoughts, | the sad 1.02. 1
the tomb where grief should sleep, can breed me 1.02. 5
that kings should let their ears hear their 1.02. 62
and should he /doubt't, as no doubt he doth, 1.02. 86
that i should open to the list'ning air | how 1.02. 87
but should he wrong my liberties in my absence? 1.02.112
be quiet then, as men should be, | till he hath 2.ch. 5
should house him safe is wrack'd and split, 2.ch. 32
because he should have swallow'd me too, and 2.01. 39 P
that he should never have left till he cast 2.01. 41 P
it's fit it should be so, for princes are | a 2.02. 10
princes in this should live like gods above, 2.03. 59
scorn now their hand should give them burial. 2.04. 12
you, should at these early hours | shake off the 3.02. 22
nature should be so conversant with pain, 3.02. 25
if neglection | should therein make me vile, the 3.03. 21
the fitter then the gods should have her. 4.01. 10
he should have strook, not spoke; 4.02. 65
traveller, we should lodge them with this sign. 4.02.114 P
who should deny it? 4.02.133 P
and as for pericles, | what should he say? 4.03. 41
when she should do for clients her fitment, and 4.06. 6 P
the devil, if he should cheapen a kiss of her. 4.06. 9 P
we should have both lord and lown, if the 4.06. 18 P
a courtesy | which if we should deny, the most 5.01. 59
if i should tell my history, it would seem 5.01.118
is not dead at tharsus, as she should have been, 5.01.215
the day | that he should marry you, at such a TNK 1.01. 60
much unlike | you should be so transported, as 1.01.187
as much sorry | i should be such a suitor; 1.01.188
i should pluck | all ladies' scandal on me. 1.01.191
as we are men | thus should we do, being 1.01.232
us to an eddy | where we should turn or drown; 1.02. 11
blood we venture | should be as for our health, 1.02.110
spinsters, we | should hold you here for ever. 1.03. 24
than a gap | should be in their dear rites, we 1.04. 9
in prison, and 'twere pity they should be out. 2.01. 22 P
where you should never know it, and so perish 2.02. 92
possible our friendship | should ever leave us. 2.02.115
i think i should not, madam. 2.02.124
why should a friend be treacherous? 2.02.229
still as she tasted, should be doubled on her, 2.02.240
near the gods in nature, they should fear her; 2.02.242

blushing virgin, should take manhood to her, 2.02.258
hold? | what should ail us? 2.03. 37
why should i love this gentleman? 2.04. 1
what should i do to make him know i love him, 2.04. 29
but your silence | should break out, though i' 3.01. 62
if he not answer'd, i should call a wolf, | and 3.02. 10
i would not, | should i try death by dozens. 3.02. 25
let not my sense unsettle | lest i should drown, 3.02. 30
i should be near the place. ho, cousin palamon! 3.03. 1
stop no more holes but what you should. 3.05. 83
too | and have done as good boys should do, 3.05.143
stood staggering whether he should follow | his 4.01. 10
why, as it should be: 4.01. 26
should clap their wings and sing | to all the 4.02. 23
so neither for my sake should fall untimely. 4.02. 69
by his seeming | should be a stout man, by his 4.02. 77
'tis pity love should be so tyrannous. 4.02.146
then from this gather | how i should tender you. 5.01. 25
out of two i should | choose one, and pray for 5.01.152
that which perish'd should | go to't unsentenc'd 5.01.156
you should observe her ev'ry way. 5.02. 14
and we should give her physic till we find that 5.02. 29
his race | should show i' th' world too godlike. 5.03.118
than all women, | i should and would die too. 5.03.144
that four such eyes should be so fix'd on one 5.03.145
that we should things desire which do cost us 5.04.110
how insolence and strong hand should prevail, STM II.C 81
how /order should be quell'd, and by this II.C 82
not /one of you should live an aged man, | for II.C 83
should so much come too short of your great II.C 124
nature of your error | should give you harbor? II.C 127
should step as 'twere up to my country's head III 7
beauty within itself should not be wasted. VEN 130
be | that thou should think it heavy unto thee? 156
as who should say, "lo thus my strength is tried 280
as if the dead the living should exceed; 292
look what a horse should have he did not lack, 299
"thy palfrey, as he should, | welcomes the warm 385
see, | yet should i be in love by touching thee. 438
should by his stealing in disturb the feast?" 450
say for non–payment that the debt should double, 521
that if i love thee, i thy death should fear. 660
"what should i do, seeing thee so indeed, | that 667
lest she should steal a kiss and die forsworn. 726
"lest the deceiving harmony should run | into 781
love's golden arrow at him should have fled, 947
as striving who should best become her grief; 968
as scorning it should pass | to wash the foul 982
makes more gashes where no breach should be. 1066
would strive who first should dry his tears. 1092
with kissing him i should have kill'd him first, 1118
thou being dead, the day should yet be light. 1134
it shall not fear where it should most mistrust, 1154
of that rich jewel he should keep unknown | from LUC 34
that meaner men should vaunt | that golden hap 41
which of them both should underprop her fame. 53
shame assail'd, the red should fence the white. 63
lest between them both it should be kill'd, 74
true valor still a true respect should have; 201
as who should say, "this glove to wanton tricks 320
as if the heavens should countenance his sin. 343
for kings like gods should govern every thing. 602
the lesser thing should not the greater hide: 663
o that prone lust should stain so pure a bed! 684
her tears should drop on them perpetually. 686
night's black bosom should not peep again. 788
so should i have co–partners in my pain, | and 789
"why should the worm intrude the maiden bud? 848
wretched hands such wretched blood should spill; 999
day, | as shaming any eye should thee behold, 1143
peace," quoth lucrece, "if it should be told, 1284
what should i say? 1291
lest he should hold it her own gross abuse, 1315
"why should the private pleasure of some one 1478
for one's offense why should so many fall, | to 1483
false creeping craft and perjury should thrust 1517
but such a face should bear a wicked mind. 1540
i should not live to speak another word; 1642
so should my shame still rest upon record, | and 1643
their oaths, should right poor ladies' harms." 1694
if they surcease to be that should survive. 1766
who, mad that sorrow should his use control, 1781
weep with equal strife | who should weep most, 1792
to slay herself, that should have slain her foe. 1827
forbade the boy he should not pass those grounds PP 9. 8
falls, through wind, before the fall should be. 10. 6
as if the boy should use like loving charms; 11. 8
die, | but as the riper should by time decease, SON 1. 3
now is the time that face should form another, 3. 2
which to repair should be thy chief desire. 10. 8
if all were minded so, the times should cease, 11. 7
against this coming end you should prepare, 13. 3
so should that beauty which you hold in lease 13. 5
your sweet issue your sweet form should bear. 13. 8
so should the lines of life that life repair 16. 9
so should my papers (yellowed with their age) 17. 9
you should live twice, in it and in my rhyme. 17.14
then look i death my days should expiate. 22. 4
lest my bewailed guilt should do thee shame, 36.10
injurious distance should not stop my way, | for 44. 2
where thou art, why should i haste me thence? 51. 3
then should i spur though mounted on the wind, 51. 7
said | thy edge should blunter be than appetite, 56. 2
what should i do but tend | upon the hours and 57. 1
i should in thought control your times of 58. 2
is it thy will thy image should keep open | my 61. 1
dost thou desire my slumbers should be broken 61. 3
ah, wherefore with infection should he live, 67. 1
that sin by him advantage should achieve, | and 67. 3
why should false painting imitate his cheek, 67. 5
why should poor beauty indirectly seek | roses 67. 7
why should he live, now nature bankrout is, 67. 9
if thinking on me then should make you woe. 71. 8
lest the wise world should look into your moan, 71.13
lest the world should task you to recite | what 72. 1
what merit liv'd in me that you should love 72. 2
and so should you, to love things nothing worth. 72.14
which should example where your equal grew? 84. 4

lest i (too much profane) should do it wrong, 89.11
that in thy face sweet love should ever dwell; 93.10
thy looks should nothing thence but sweetness 93.12
why | my most full flame should afterwards burn 115. 4
all | wherein i should your great deserts repay, 117. 2
which should transport me farthest from your 117. 8
for why should others' false adulterate eyes 121. 5
that every tongue says beauty should look so. 127.14
my poor lips, which should that harvest reap, 128. 7
why should my heart think that a several plot, 137. 9
for if i should despair, i should grow mad, 140. 9
for if i should despair, i should grow mad, 140. 9
eyes well seeing thy foul faults should find. 148.14
make | what i should do again for such a sake. LC 322
SHOULDER 26 FR 0.0029 REL FR 17 V 9 P
as, the mark of my shoulder, the mole in my neck ERR 3.02.143 P
let him be clapp'd on the shoulder, and call'd ADO 1.01.259 P
stoop, i say, | her shoulder is with child. LLL 4.03. 88
sometime to lean upon my poor shoulder, and with 5.01.103 P
all laugh'd, and clapp'd him on the shoulder, 5.02.107
him that cupid hath clapp'd him o' th' shoulder, AYL 4.01. 48 P
mayst slide from my shoulder to my heel with no SHR 4.01. 15 P
on his shoulder, and his; WT 4.04. 60
i have it on my shoulder. JN 1.01.245
which gently laid my knighthood on my shoulder, R2 1.01. 79
god's light, with two points on your shoulder? 2H4 2.04.133 P
you have hurt him, sir, i' th' shoulder. 2.04.214 P
thou hast drawn my shoulder out of joint. 5.04. 3 P
lord warwick, on thy shoulder will i lean, | and 3H6 2.01.189
for in thy shoulder do i build my seat, | and 2.06.100
this shoulder was ordain'd so thick to heave, 5.07. 23
from cupid's shoulder pluck his painted wings, TRO 3.02. 14
they clap the lubber ajax on the shoulder, | as 3.03.139
i' th' shoulder and i' th' left arm. COR 2.01.147 P
did from the flames of troy upon his shoulder JC 1.02.113
the wind sits in the shoulder of your sail, HAM 1.03. 56
and, with his head over his shoulder turn'd, 2.01. 94
than stands on any shoulder that i see | before LR 2.02. 94
hind that shall | once touch my shoulder. CYM 5.03. 78
far sweeter, | smoother than pelops' shoulder! TNK 4.02. 21
over one shoulder doth she hang her head; VEN 1058
SHOULDER–BLADE 1 FR 0.0001 REL FR 0 V 1 P
i fear, sir, my shoulder–blade is out. WT 4.03. 73 P
SHOULDER–BONE 1 FR 0.0001 REL FR 0 V 1 P
to see how the bear tore out his shoulder–bone, WT 3.03. 95 P
SHOULDER–CLAPPER 1 FR 0.0001 REL FR 1 V 0 P
a back–friend, a shoulder–clapper, one that ERR 4.02. 37
SHOULDERING 1 FR 0.0001 REL FR 1 V 0 P
this shouldering of each other in the court, 1H6 4.01.189
SHOULDER–PIECE 1 FR 0.0001 REL FR 1 V 0 P
to the shoulder–piece | gently they swell, like TNK 4.02.127
SHOULDERS 33 FR 0.0037 REL FR 16 V 17 P
staggering) take this basket on your shoulders. WIV 3.03. 13 P
they took me on their shoulders; 3.05.100 P
sirs, take the basket again on your shoulders. 4.02.109 P
my shoulders for the fellow of this walk — and 5.05. 25 P
arms, legs, backs, shoulders, sides, and shins. 5.05. 54
out of our hearts by the head and shoulders, and 5.05.148 P
so tickle on thy shoulders that a milkmaid, if MM 1.02.173 P
some of my mistress' marks upon my shoulders: ERR 1.02. 83
i thank him, i bare home upon my shoulders: 2.01. 73
or else i shall seek my wit in my shoulders. 2.02. 39 P
nay, i bear it on my shoulders, as a beggar wont 4.04. 37 P
have his head on her shoulders for all messina, ADO 1.01.114 P
luck stirring but what lights a' my shoulders, MV 3.01. 95 P
the cost of princes on unworthy shoulders? AYL 2.07. 76
or lay on that shall make your shoulders crack. JN 2.01.146
run thy head from thy unreverent shoulders. R2 2.01.123
rob them, cut this head off from my shoulders. 1H4 1.02.166 P
you are straight enough in the shoulders, you 2.04.149 P
and thrown over the shoulders like a herald's 4.02. 44 P
fellow that never had the ache in his shoulders! 2H4 5.01. 84 P
beat us, for they bear them on their shoulders; H5 4.01.227 P
and from my shoulders crack my arms asunder, 1H6 1.05. 11
weak shoulders, overborne with burthening grief, 2.05. 10
realm shall not wear a head on his shoulders, 2H6 4.07.120 P
bear, | so bear i thee upon my manly shoulders; 5.02. 63
laid their guilt upon my guiltless shoulders. R3 1.02. 98
that you should bear me on your shoulders. 3.01.131
have this crown of mine cut from my shoulders 3.02. 43
and from these shoulders, | these ruin'd pillars H8 3.02.381
whose heads | /do /grow beneath their shoulders. OTH 1.03.145
cowards | to run and show their shoulders. ANT 3.11. 8
which now is growing upon thy shoulders, shall CYM 4.01. 16 P
his shoulders broad and strong, | arm'd long and TNK 4.02. 84
SHOULDER–SHOTTEN 1 FR 0.0001 REL FR 0 V 1 P
bots, /sway'd in the back and shoulder–shotten, SHR 3.02. 56 P
SHOULD'RED 1 FR 0.0001 REL FR 1 V 0 P
and almost should'red in the swallowing gulf R3 3.07.128
/SHOULDST 1 FR 0.0001 REL FR 1 V 0 P
/there /shouldst /thou /find /one /heinous R2 4.01.233
SHOULDST 79 FR 0.0089 REL FR 61 V 18 P
i see it in thy face, | what thou shouldst be. TMP 2.01.207
for fear thou shouldst lose thy tongue. TGV 2.03. 46 P
wherefore shouldst thou pity her? 4.04. 78
and so thou shouldst not alter the article of WIV 2.01. 52 P
lest thou a feverous life shouldst entertain, MM 3.01. 74
shouldst thou but hear i were licentious, | and ERR 2.02.131
thou shouldst rather ask if it were possible any ADO 3.03.112 P
to whom shouldst thou give it? LLL 4.01.102
world, thou shouldst have it to buy gingerbread. 5.01. 72 P
i been judge, thou shouldst have had ten more, MV 4.01.399
thou shouldst have better pleas'd me with this AYL 1.02.227
i cannot see else how thou shouldst scape. 3.02. 85 P
thou shouldst have heard how her horse fell and SHR 4.01. 73 P
thou shouldst have heard in how miry a place, 4.01. 74 P
had thee in place where, thou shouldst know it. 4.03.150 P
me, | "we blush that thou shouldst choose; AWW 2.03. 70
thyself, if thou shouldst strive to choose. 2.03.146
thou never shouldst love woman like to me. TN 5.01.268
with mopsa, thou shouldst take no money of me, WT 4.04.232 P
thou shouldst a husband take by my consent, | as 5.03.136
for thine own gain shouldst defend mine honor? JN 1.01.242
but thou shouldst please me better wouldst thou R2 3.04. 20
no reason why thou shouldst be so superfluous to 1H4 1.02. 11 P
to thank god on, i would thou shouldst know it. 3.03.119 P
thee no instance why thou shouldst do treason, H5 2.02.119
or thou shouldst find thou hast dishonor'd me. 1H6 3.01. 9
so shouldst thou either turn my flying soul, 2H6 3.02.397
thou shouldst be mad; 3H6 1.04. 89
and birth that thou shouldst stand while lewis 3.03. 3
harry, that prophesied thou shouldst be king, R3 5.03.129
thou shouldst feel | my sword i' th' life–blood H8 5.02. 88 P
thou shouldst strike him. TRO 2.01. 37 P
thou shouldst not bear from me a greekish member 4.05.130
fly not, for shouldst thou take the river styx, 5.04. 19
general, thou shouldst have my office | ere that 5.06. 4
progeny | thou shouldst not scape me here. COR 1.08. 13
and displeasure | which thou shouldst bear me. 4.05. 73
and, lest thou shouldst detect /him, cut thy TIT 2.04. 27
and thou shouldst, thou'dst anger ladies. TIM 1.01.205 P
shouldst have kept one to thyself, for i mean to 1.01.265 P
thou shouldst desire to die, being miserable. 4.03.248
why shouldst thou hate men? 4.03.269
thou shouldst have lov'd thyself better now. 4.03.310 P
and oft thou shouldst hazard thy life for thy 4.03.335 P
ere i can tell thee what thou shouldst do there. JC 2.04. 5
i did bid thee do, | thou shouldst attempt it. 5.03. 40
there thou shouldst be; MAC 5.07. 20
and duller shouldst thou be than the fat weed HAM 1.05. 32
i hop'd thou shouldst have been my hamlet's wife 5.01.244
thou shouldst not have been old till thou hadst LR 1.05. 44 P
if thou shouldst not be glad, | i would divorce 2.04.130
if thou shouldst dally half an hour, his life, 3.06. 93
thou shouldst have said, "good porter, turn the 3.07. 64
the strings were thine, shouldst know of this. OTH 1.01. 3
wouldst write of me, if thou shouldst praise me? 2.01.117
nay, stay. thou shouldst be honest. 3.03.381
thou shouldst know | there were a heart in egypt ANT 1.03. 40
where be the sacred vials thou shouldst fill 1.03. 63
thou shouldst come like a fury crown'd with 2.05. 40
ah, this thou shouldst have done, | and not have 2.07. 73
th' strings, | and thou shouldst /tow me after. 3.11. 58
occupation, thou shouldst see | a workman in't. 4.04. 17
that shouldst repair my youth, thou heap'st | a CYM 1.01.132
thou shouldst have made him | as little as a 1.03. 14
thou shouldst neither want my means for thy 3.05.114 P
for i wish'd | thou shouldst be color'd thus. 5.01. 2
thou shouldst have been, and shielded him | from 5.04. 41
i had rather thou shouldst live while nature 5.05.151
thou shouldst perceive my passion, if these TNK 3.01. 31
the earth's increase why shouldst thou feed, VEN 169
"what am i, that thou shouldst contemn me this? 205
seeing his beauty, thou shouldst strike at it: 938
and stall'd the deer that thou shouldst strike, PP 18. 2
what could death do if thou shouldst depart, SON 6.11
in singleness the parts that thou shouldst bear. 8. 8
bounteous gift thou shouldst in bounty cherish. 11.12
and meant thereby | thou shouldst print more, 11.14
then thou alone kingdoms of hearts shouldst owe. 70.14
with others thou shouldst not abhor my state: 150.12
/SHOUT 2 FR 0.0002 REL FR 2 V 0 P
hark, hark, what /shout is this? TRO 5.09. 1
done — | you /shout me forth | in acclamations COR 1.09. 50
SHOUT 8 FR 0.0009 REL FR 8 V 0 P
eyes, | hearing applause and universal shout, MV 3.02.143
have i not heard these islanders shout out JN 5.02.103
hark how they shout! 2H4 4.02. 87
i, | "this general applause and cheerful shout R3 3.07. 39
what shout is this? COR 5.03. 19
appear, | have you not made an universal shout, JC 1.01. 44
another general shout! 1.02.132
and hark, they shout for joy. 5.03. 32
SHOUTED 2 FR 0.0002 REL FR 1 V 1 P
they shouted thrice; what was the last cry for? JC 1.02.226
every putting–by mine honest neighbors shouted. 1.02.231 P
/SHOUTING 1 FR 0.0001 REL FR 1 V 0 P
horns a' th' moon, | /shouting their emulation. COR 1.01.214
SHOUTING 4 FR 0.0004 REL FR 4 V 0 P
tabors and cymbals, and the shouting romans, COR 5.04. 50
what means this shouting? JC 1.02. 79
and hoist thee up to the shouting plebeians! ANT 4.12. 34
up, | and show me to the shouting varlotry | of 5.02. 56
SHOUTS 7 FR 0.0008 REL FR 6 V 1 P
loud shouts and salutations from their mouths, 1H4 3.02. 53
and boys, | whose shouts and claps out–voice the H5 5.pr. 11
hark, hark, my lord, what shouts are these? 3H6 4.08. 51
what shouts are these? COR 1.01. 46 P
a shower and thunder with their caps and shouts. 2.01.267
him to his house | with shouts and clamors. JC 3.02. 53
didst thou not hear their shouts? 5.03. 83
SHOV'D 2 FR 0.0002 REL FR 2 V 0 P
hath been with scorn shov'd from the court, 2H4 4.02. 37
hand could pluck her back that shov'd her on. ANT 1.02.127
/SHOVE 1 FR 0.0001 REL FR 1 V 0 P
offense's gilded hand may /shove by justice, HAM 3.03. 58
SHOVE–GROAT 1 FR 0.0001 REL FR 0 V 1 P
him down, bardolph, like a shove–groat shilling. 2H4 2.04.192 P
SHOVEL 1 FR 0.0001 REL FR 0 V 1 P
knock him about the sconce with a dirty shovel, HAM 5.01.102 P
SHOVEL–BOARDS 1 FR 0.0001 REL FR 0 V 1 P
in mill–sixpences, and two edward shovel–boards, WIV 1.01.156 P
SHOVELS 1 FR 0.0001 REL FR 1 V 0 P
and lay me | where no priest shovels in dust. WT 4.04.458
SHOW *(also shew)*
/SHOW 4 FR 0.0004 REL FR 4 V 0 P
/that /it /may /show /me /what /a /face /i /have R2 4.01.266
/but /rather /show /a /while /like /fearful /war 2H4 4.01. 63
/time /shall /serve) /to /show /in /articles; 4.01. 74
/at /point | /to /show /their /open /banner. LR 3.01. 34
SHOW 442 FR 0.0499 REL FR 350 V 92 P
who mak'st a show but dar'st not strike, thy TMP 1.02.471
i'll show thee every fertile inch o' th' island; 2.02.148
i'll show thee the best springs; 2.02.160
show thee a jay's nest, and instruct thee how 2.02.169
for i'll not show him | where the quick freshes 3.02. 66
thou beest a man, show thyself in thy likeness. 3.02.128 P
the clouds methought would open and show riches 3.02.141
mine eyes, ev'n sociable to the show of thine, 5.01. 63
i'll show my mind | according to my shallow TGV 1.02. 7
they do not love that do not show their love. 1.02. 31
that the contents will show. 1.02. 36
i fear'd to show my father julia's letter, 1.03. 80
nay, i'll show you the manner of it. 2.03. 14 P
youth | of greater time than i shall show to be. 2.07. 48
and show thee all the treasure we have got; 4.01. 73
worn to pieces with age to show himself a young WIV 2.01. 22 P
i have to show to the contrary. 2.01. 38 P
yet i say i could show you to the contrary. 2.01. 41 P
meeting, give him a show of comfort in his suit, 2.01. 94 P
he is not show his face. 2.03. 32 P
i will show you a monster. 3.02. 81 P
let the court of france show me such another. 3.03. 54 P
show me now, william, some declensions of your 4.01. 74 P
not what i seek, show no color for my extremity; 4.02.161 P
can be manifested, | without the show of both. 4.06. 16
image of the jest | i'll show you here at large. 4.06. 18
fellow, why dost thou show me thus to th' world? MM 1.02.116
then, if you speak, you must not show your face, 1.04. 12
or, if you show your face, you must not speak. 1.04. 13
yet show some pity. 2.02. 99
i show it most of all when i show justice; 2.02.100
i show it most of all when i show justice; 2.02.100
by all external warrants), show it now, | by 2.04.137
show me how, good father. 3.01.238 P
of precept, he did show me | the way twice o'er. 4.01. 39
show your wisdom, daughter, in your close 4.03.118
his actions show much like to madness, pray 4.04. 4 P
first, let her show /her face, and after speak. 5.01.168
i will not show my face | until my husband bid 5.01.169
show your knave's visage, with a pox to you! 5.01.353 P
show your sheep–biting face, and be hang'd an 5.01.354 P
palace, where we'll show | what's yet behind, 5.01.538
beat me at the mart, i have your hand to show; ERR 3.01. 12
your false love with some show of blindness: 3.02. 8
though others have the arm, show us the sleeve: 3.02. 23
in your knowledge and your grace you show not 3.02. 31
that joy could not show itself modest enough ADO 1.01. 22 P
they show well outward. 1.02. 8 P
not make the full show of this till you may do 1.03. 19 P
show me briefly how. 2.02. 11 P
he doth indeed show some sparks that are like 2.03.186 P
i would see, which will be merely a dumb show. 2.03.218 P
in, | i'll show thee some attires, and have thy 3.01.102
of your marriage as to show a child his new coat 3.02. 6 P
if you will follow me, i will show you enough, 3.02.121 P
till midnight, and let the issue show itself. 3.02.130 P
is to let him show himself what he is and steal 3.03. 59 P
what authority and show of truth | can cunning 4.01. 35
the virtue that possession would not show us 4.01.221
is there any way to show such friendship? 4.01.263 P
i will go before and show him their examination. 4.02. 65 P
go anticly, and show outward hideousness, | and 5.01. 96
marry, i cannot show it in rhyme; 5.02. 36 P
if wounding, then it was to show my skill, LLL 4.01. 28
or rather ostentare, to show, as it were, his 4.02. 16 P
and they thy glory through my grief will show. 4.03. 36
the sea will ebb and flow, heaven show his face; 4.03.212
did these rent lines show some love of thine? 4.03.216
scarce show a harvest of their heavy toil; 4.03.323
that show, contain, and nourish all the world, 4.03.350
with some delightful ostentation, or show, or 5.01.112 P
of time, some show in the posterior of this day, 5.01.119 P
vouchsafe to show the sunshine of your face, 5.02.201
or ever but in vizards show their faces? 5.02.271
have not the grace to grace it with such show. 5.02.320
to show his teeth as white as whale's bone; 5.02.332
sir, will show whereuntil it doth amount. 5.02.500 P
to have one show worse than the king's and his 5.02.513
these four worthies in their first show thrive, 5.02.538
there is five in the first show. 5.02.540
it should have followed in the end of our show. 5.02.888 P
o, how ripe in show | thy lips, those kissing MND 3.02.139
if you were men, as men you are in show, | you 3.02.151
intend | never so little show of love to her, 3.02.334
for if but once thou show me thy grey light, 3.02.419
to show our simple skill, | that is the true 5.01.110
and, by their show, | you shall know all, that 5.01.116
gentles, perchance you wonder at this show; 5.01.127
and this stone doth show | that i am that same 5.01.161
show me thy chink, to blink through with mine 5.01.177
that they'll not show their teeth in way of MV 1.01. 55
but, alas, who can converse with a dumb show? 1.02. 73 P
this kindness will i show. 1.03.143
why, there they show | something too liberal. 2.02.184
by the fool multitude, that choose by show, 2.09. 26
sweet, | to show how costly summer was at hand, 2.09. 94
who dare scarce show his head on the rialto; 3.01. 45 P
a gracious voice, | obscures the show of evil? 3.02. 77
his letter there | will show you his estate. 3.02.236
bid your friends welcome, show a merry cheer — 3.02.312
but if you knew to whom you show this honor, 3.04. 5
wilt thou show the whole wealth of thy wit in an 3.05. 56 P
thou'lt show thy mercy and remorse more strange 4.01. 20
and earthly power doth then show likest god's 4.01.196
i pray you show my youth old shylock's house. 4.02. 11
come, good sir, will you show me to this house? 4.02. 19
i show more mirth than i am mistress of, and AYL 1.02. 3 P
foolery that wise men have makes a great show. 1.02. 90 P
and thou wilt show more bright and seem more 1.03. 81
show me the place. 2.01. 66
and hose ought to show itself courageous to 2.04. 7 P
of bare distress hath ta'en from me the show 2.07. 95
on every tree, | that shall civil sayings show: 3.02.128
of every sprite | heaven would in little show. 3.02.140
go with me to it and i'll show it you; 3.02.430 P
now show the wound mine eye hath made in thee. 3.05. 20
than any of her lineaments can show her. 3.05. 56
and show the world what the bird hath done to 4.01.203 P
to show the letter that i writ to you. 5.02. 78
may show her duty and make known her love?" SHR in.1. 117
we'll show thee io as she was a maid, | and how in.2. 54
master, some show to welcome us to town. 1.01. 47
am bold to show myself a forward guest | within 2.01. 51
then show it me. 2.01.232
e la mi, show pity, or i die." 3.01. 78
but your words show you a madman. 5.01. 74 P
yet, | and show more sign of her obedience, 5.02.117
and show what we alone must think, which never AWW 1.01.185
who ever strove | to show her merit, that did 1.01.227
it is the show and seal of nature's truth, 1.03.132

i will show myself highly fed and lowly taught. 2.02. 3 P
and show me a child begotten of thy body that i 3.02. 58 P
the house, and show you | the lass i spoke of. 3.06.110
and all the secrets of our camp i'll show, 4.01. 84
and then show you the heart of my message. TN 1.05.190 P
will draw the curtain and show you the picture. 1.05.233 P
fate, show thy force: 1.05.310
"his eyes do show his days are almost done." 2.03.104
she did show favor to the youth in your sight 3.02. 18 P
thee so, for i will show thee no reason for't." 3.04.151 P
stand here, make a good show on't; 3.04.289 P
sicilia cannot show himself overkind to bohemia. WT 1.01. 21 P
thou lov'st us, show in our brother's welcome; 1.02.174
that did but show thee, of a fool, inconstant 3.02.186
sworn, i think, | to show myself a glass. 4.04. 14
show those things you found about her, those 4.04.695 P
show the inside of your purse to the outside of 4.04.803 P
must to the king, and show our strange sights. 4.04.819 P
come, lady, i will show thee to my kin, | and JN 1.01.273
and i shall show you peace and fair–fac'd league 2.01.417
on their departure most of all show evil. 3.04.115
/doth show the mood of a much troubled breast, 4.02. 73
show boldness and aspiring confidence. 5.01. 56
a noble temper dost thou show in this, | and 5.02. 40
peace, | and be no further harmful than in show. 5.02. 77
show me the very wound of this ill news; 5.06. 21
show now your mended faiths, | and instantly 5.07. 75
know, | from where you do remain let paper show.
R2 1.03.250
rightly gaz'd upon | show nothing but confusion; 2.02. 19
show me thy humble heart, and not thy knee, 2.03. 83
blood, | to show the world i am a gentleman. 3.01. 27
land, | my stooping duty tenderly shall show. 3.03. 48
that any harm should stain so fair a show! 3.03. 71
show us the hand of god | that hath dismiss'd us 3.03. 77
all apart, | and show fair duty to his majesty. 3.03.188
tears show their love, but want their remedies. 3.03.203
climate souls refin'd | should show so heinous, 4.01.131
i'll lay | a plot shall show us all a merry day. 4.01.334
i do beseech you pardon me, i may not show it. 5.02. 70
the treason that my haste forbids me show. 5.03. 50
and tears, and groans | show minutes, times, and 5.05. 58
and never show thy head by day nor light. 5.06. 44
shall show more goodly and attract more eyes 1H4 1.02.214
so low | to show the line and the predicament 1.03.168
step aside, and i'll show thee a /president. 2.04. 33 P
and show it a fair pair of heels and run from it 2.04. 48 P
it, yea, and can show it you here in the house; 2.04.257 P
and all the courses of my life do show | i am 3.01. 41
though sometimes it show greatness, courage, 3.01.179
frowns, | to show how much thou art degenerate. 3.02.128
i should not make so dear a show of zeal; 5.04. 95
doth it not show vildly in me to desire small 2H4 2.02. 6 P
feathers turn back in any show of resistance. 2.04.100 P
'a has, that show a weak mind and an able body, 2.04.251 P
i was then sir dagonet in arthur's show — there 3.02.281 P
this will i show the general. 4.01.176
to ye | shall show itself more openly hereafter. 4.02. 76
if you do not all show like gilt twopences to me 4.03. 50 P
the element (which show like pins' heads to her) 4.03. 53 P
and never live to show th' incredulous world 4.05.153
but 'tis no matter, this poor show doth better, 5.05. 13 P
or shall we sparingly show you far off | the H5 1.02.239
and show my sail of greatness | when i do rouse 1.02.274
good corporal nym, show thy valor, and put up 2.01. 43 P
sir, | you show great mercy if you give him life 2.02. 50
show men dutiful? 2.02.127
and let us do it with no show of fear, | no, 2.04. 23
show us here | the mettle of your pasture; 3.01. 26
he would gladly make show to the world he is. 3.06. 83 P
he may show what outward courage he will; 4.01.113 P
o ceremony, show me but thy worth! 4.01.244
and your fair show shall suck away their souls, 4.02. 17
will he strip his sleeve and show his scars, 4.03. 47
as i suck blood, i will some mercy show. 4.04. 64
way for my wish shall show me the way to my will 5.02.328 P
that will i show you presently. 1H6 2.03. 60
and make a show of love to proud duke humphrey,
2H6 1.01.241
to show your highness | a spirit rais'd from 1.02. 78
peace, son, and show some reason, buckingham, 1.03.113
give me leave | to show some reason, of no 1.03.163
robes, | and show itself, attire me how i can. 2.04.109
and in his simple show he harbors treason. 3.01. 54
and gloucester's show | beguiles him as the 3.01.225
show me one scar character'd on thy skin: 3.01.300
to show how quaint an orator you are; 3.02.274
then show me where he is, | i'll give a thousand 3.03. 12
come, soldiers, show what cruelty ye can, | that 4.01.132
now show yourselves men, 'tis for liberty. 4.02.183
will you we show our title to the crown? 3H6 1.01.102
show thy descent by gazing 'gainst the sun; 2.01. 92
her words doth show her wit incomparable, | all 3.02. 85
distinguish of a man | than of his outward show, R3 3.01. 10
so smooth he daub'd his vice with show of virtue 3.05. 29
those that come to see | only a show or two, and H8 pr 10
to rank our chosen truth with such a show | as pr 18
only to show his pomp as well in france | as 1.01.163
sparing would show a worse sin than ill doctrine 1.03. 60
you cannot show me. 1.04. 48
cardinal, | you'll show a little honesty. 3.02.306
i'll show your grace the strangest sight — 5.02. 20
man, those joyful tears show thy true /heart. 5.02.208
i'll show you troilus anon. TRO 1.02.193 P
so | doth valor's show and valor's worth divide 1.03. 46
let us, like merchants, first show foul wares, 1.03.358
let him show us a cause. 2.03. 88 P
perchance, my lord, i show more craft than love, 3.02.153
whereupon i will show you a chamber, which bed, 3.02.207 P
hath no other glass | to show itself but pride; 3.03. 48
show not their mealy wings but to the summer, 3.03. 79
a flint, which will not show without knocking. 3.03.257 P
to such as boasting show their scars | a mock is 4.05.290
come, come, thou boy–queller, show thy face, 5.05. 45
troilus, thou coward troilus, show thy head! 5.06. 1
intend to do, which now we'll show 'em in deeds. COR 1.01. 59 P
till when | they needs must show themselves, 1.02. 21
of his bed where he would show most love. 1.03. 5 P
will be large cicatrices to show the people, 2.01.148 P
show them th' unaching scars which i should hide 2.02.148
for if he show us his wounds and tell us his 2.03. 5 P
i have wounds to show you, which shall be yours 2.03. 77 P
he had wounds, which he could show in private; 2.03.166
you show too much of that | for which the people 3.01. 52
groats, to show bare heads | in congregations, 3.02. 10
and you will rather show our general louts | how 3.02. 66
must i go show them my unbarb'd sconce? 3.02. 99
which show | like graves i' th' holy churchyard. 3.03. 50
and can show /for rome | her enemies' marks upon 3.03.110
which not to cut would show thee but a fool, 4.05. 97
(look you, sir) show themselves (as we term it) 4.05.207 P
go home, | and show no sign of fear. 4.06.152
of thy deep duty more impression show | than 5.03. 51
show duty as mistaken all this while | between 5.03. 55
of full time | may show like all yourself. 5.03. 70
rather to show a noble grace to both parts 5.03.121
this for me, struck home to show my strength. TIT 2.03.117
do thou entreat her show a woman's pity. 2.03.147
now let me show a brother's love to thee. 3.01.182
if thou do this, i'll show thee wondrous things, 5.01. 55
show me a murtherer, i'll deal with him. 5.02. 93
show me a villain that hath done a rape, | and i 5.02. 94
show me a thousand that hath done thee wrong, 5.02. 96
the trumpets show the emperor is at hand. 5.03. 16
have we done aught amiss, show us wherein, | and 5.03.129
i will show myself a tyrant: ROM 1.01. 21 P
show me a mistress that is passing fair, | what 1.01.234
compare her face with some that i shall show, 1.02. 86
that i will show you shining at this feast, 1.02. 98
and she shall scant show well that now seems 1.02. 99
show a fair presence and put off these frowns, 1.05. 73
despised substance of divinest show! 3.02. 77
call peter, he will show thee where they are. 4.04. 17
were thinly scattered, to make up a show. 5.01. 48
so shalt thou show me friendship. 5.03. 41
the sun, for sorrow, will not show his head. 5.03.306
a thousand moral paintings i can show | that TIM 1.01. 90
to show lord timon that mean eyes have seen 1.01. 93
when dinner's done, | show me this piece. 1.01.246
let's be provided to show them entertainment. 1.02.179
this, | to show him what a beggar his heart is, 1.02.195
i'll show you how t' observe a strange event. 3.04. 17
now | (like all mankind) show me an iron heart? 3.04. 83
that which i show, heaven knows, is merely love, 4.03.515
hate all, curse all, show charity to none, | but 4.03.527
it will show honestly in us, | and is very 5.01. 13
and show of love as i was wont to have. JC 1.02. 34
struck but thus much show of fire from brutus. 1.02.177
our yoke and sufferance show us womanish. 1.03. 84
sham'st thou to show thy dang'rous brow by night 2.01. 78
you have said, and show yourselves true romans. 2.01.223
let me a little show it, even in this — | that 3.01. 71
and show the reason of our caesar's death. 3.01.237
and let me show you him that made the will. 3.02.159
show you sweet caesar's wounds, poor, poor, dumb 3.02.225
make gallant show and promise of their mettle; 4.02. 24
go show your slaves how choleric you are, | and 4.03. 43
the enemy comes on in gallant show; 5.01. 13
why dost thou show to the apt thoughts of men 5.03. 68
show me, show me. MAC 1.03. 27
show me, show me. 1.03. 27
or that indeed | which outwardly ye show? 1.03. 54
away, and mock the time with fairest show: 1.07. 81
occasion call us | and show us to be watchers. 2.02. 68
to show an unfelt sorrow is an office | which 2.03.136
to bear my part, | or show the glory of our art? 3.05. 9
thyself and office deftly show! 4.01. 68
show! 4.01.107
show! 4.01.108
show! 4.01.109
show his eyes, and grieve his heart; 4.01.110
filthy hags, | why do you show me this? 4.01.116
sprites, | and show the best of our delights. 4.01.128
throw down, | and show like those you are. 5.06. 2
tyrant, show thy face! 5.07. 14
and live to be the show and gaze o' th' time! 5.08. 24
majestical, | to offer it the show of violence, HAM 1.01.144
in that, and all things, will we show our duty. 1.02. 40
to denmark | to show my duty in your coronation, 1.02. 53
but i have that within which passes show, 1.02. 85
show me the steep and thorny way to heaven, 1.03. 48
not of that dye which their investments show, 1.03.128
you | to show us so much gentry and good will 2.02. 22
i tell you, must show fairly outwards, should 2.02.374 P
row of the pious chanson will show you more, for 2.02.419 P
that show of such an exercise may color | your 3.01. 44
all alone entreat him | to show his grief. 3.01.183
to show virtue her feature, scorn her own image, 3.02. 22 P
belike this show imports the argument of the 3.02.139 P
will 'a tell us what this show meant? 3.02.143 P
ay, or any show that you will show him. 3.02.144 P
ay, or any show that you will show him. 3.02.144 P
be not you asham'd to show, he'll not shame to 3.02.145 P
your wisdom should show itself more richer to 3.02.304 P
nothing but to show you how a king may go a 4.03. 30 P
to show yourself indeed your father's son | more 4.07.125
'swounds, show me what thou't do. 5.01.274
fault, | how ugly didst thou in cordelia show! LR 1.04.267
show too bold malice | against the grace and 2.02.130
(as fear not but you shall), show her this ring, 3.01. 47
to them, | and show the heavens more just. 3.04. 36
to my lord your husband, show him this letter. 3.07. 2 P
i should show | what party i do follow. 4.05. 39
midway air | show scarce so gross as beetles. 4.06. 14
life, | i must show out a flag and sign of love, OTH 1.01.156
that gives me this bold show of courtesy. 2.01. 99
if thou dost love me, | show me thy thought. 3.03.116
to show the love and duty that i bear you | with 3.03.194
the pranks | they dare not show their husbands; 3.03.203
courage, and valor), this night show it. 4.02.214 P
i will show you such a necessity in his death 4.02.240 P
show him your hand. ANT 1.02. 11
time we twain | did show ourselves i' th' field, 1.04. 74
show 's the way, sir. 2.06. 81
show me which way. 2.07. 69
six kings already | show me the way of yielding. 3.10. 34
cowards | to run and show their shoulders. 3.11. 8
unstate his happiness and be stag'd to th' show 3.13. 30
not th' imperious show | of the full–fortun'd 4.15. 23
go with me, and see | what i can show in this. 5.01. 77
up, | and show me to the shouting varlotry | of 5.02. 56
or i shall show the cinders of my spirits 5.02.173
show me, my women, like a queen; 5.02.227
army shall | in solemn show attend this funeral, 5.02.364
is | no danger in what show of death it makes, CYM 1.05. 40
which not to read would show the britains cold. 3.01. 75
ourself | to show less sovereignty than they, 3.05. 6
to show what coast thy sluggish /crare | mightst 4.02.205
till it fly out and show them princes born. 4.04. 54
men know | more valor in me than my habits show. 5.01. 30
show | thy spite on mortal flies: 5.04. 30
kissing, to | o'ercome you with her show, and, 5.05. 54
let him show | his skill in the construction. 5.05.432
to show his sorrow, he'd correct himself; PER 1.03. 22
who makes the fairest show means most deceit. 1.04. 75
i'll show you those in troubles reign, | losing 2.ch. 7
i'll show the virtue i have borne in arms. 2.01.145
he had need mean better than his outward show 2.02. 48
since every worth in show commends itself. 2.03. 6
had not a show might countervail his worth. 2.03. 56
what's dumb in show i'll plain with speech. 3.ch. 14
hair of mine remain, | though i show /ill in't. 3.03. 30
see how belief may suffer by foul show! 4.04. 23
if you were born to honor, show it now; 4.06. 92
pleas'd | to show in generous terms your griefs, TNK 3.01. 54
and you show | more than a mistress to me; 3.06. 25
o theseus, | if unto neither thou show mercy. 3.06.173
the circles of his eyes show /fire within him, 4.02. 81
for his show | has all the ornament of honor 4.02. 92
they show | great and fine art in nature. 4.02.122
they would show | bravely about the titles of 4.02.144
were there aught in me which strove to show 5.01. 20
honor in their kind | which sometime show well, 5.03. 13
his race | should show i' th' world too godlike. 5.03.118
the gods will show their glory in a life | that 5.04. 43
a young handsome wench then, show his face — ep 6
but we will show no mercy upon the strangers. STM II.C 19 P
which far exceeds his barren skill to show. LUC 81
no cloudy show of stormy blust'ring weather 115
who, flatt'red by their leader's jocund show, 296
know, | which he by dumb demeanor seeks to show; 474
the light will show, character'd in my brow, 807
"to show the beldame daughters of her daughter, 953
red blood reek'd, to show the painter's strife, 1377
"show me the strumpet that began this stir, 1471
and give the harmless show | an humble gait, 1507
devil, | he entertain'd a show so seeming just, 1514
burying in lucrece' wound his folly's show. 1810
to show her bleeding body thorough rome, | and 1851
women work, | dissembled with an outward show, PP 18.38
leese but their show, their substance still SON 5.14
ambassage | to witness duty, not to show my wit; 26. 4
may make seem bare, in wanting words to show it, 26. 6
to show me worthy of /thy sweet respect: 26.12
not show my head where thou mayst prove me. 26.14
how would thy shadow's form form happy show | to 43. 6
nights bright days when dreams do show thee me. 43.14
year, | the one doth shadow of your beauty show, 53.10
but, for their virtue only is their show, | they 54. 9
sun, | show me your image in some antique book, 59. 7
to show what wealth she had | in days long since 67.13
to show false art what beauty was of yore. 68.14
but why thy odor matcheth not thy show, | the 69.13
if some suspect of ill mask'd not thy show, 70.13
thy glass will show thee how thy beauties /wear, 77. 1
the wrinkles which thy glass will truly show, 77. 5
well might show | how far a modern quill doth 83. 6
grow, | if thy sweet virtue answer not thy show! 93.14
that do not do the thing they most do show, 94. 2
i love not less, though less the show appear; 102. 2
that, having such a scope to show her pride, 103. 2
idolatry, | nor my beloved as an idol show, 105. 2
where time and outward form would show it dead. 108.14
"small show of man was yet upon his chin, | his LC 92

/SHOW'D 1 FR 0.0001 REL FR 1 V 0 F
/mayor /in /courtesy /show'd /me /the /castle, R3 4.02.104

SHOW'D 61 FR 0.0069 REL FR 54 V 7 P
and show'd thee all the qualities o' th' isle, TMP 1.02.337
my mistress show'd me thee, and thy dog, and thy 2.02.141
you have show'd yourself a wise physician, and WIV 2.03. 53 P
and show'd him a seeming warrant for it; MM 4.02.151 P
and show'd me silks that he had bought for me, ERR 4.03. 8
show'd | bashful sincerity and comely love. ADO 4.01. 53
whoe'er 'a was, 'a show'd a mounting mind. LLL 4.01. 4
what wert thou | till this madman show'd thee? 5.02.338
that hid the worse and show'd the better face. 5.02.388
our letters, madam, show'd much more than jest. 5.02.785
one of them show'd me a ring that he had of your MV 3.01.118 P
to sound when he show'd me your handkercher? AYL 5.02. 26 P
you | you have show'd a tender fatherly regard, SHR 2.01.286
for you have show'd me that which well approves AWW 3.07. 13
for the fair kindness you have show'd me here, TN 3.04.342
i have show'd too much | the rashness of a woman
WT 3.02.220
the stone is mine), | i'ld not have show'd it. 5.03. 59
he show'd his warrant to a friend of mine. JN 4.02. 70
show'd like a stubble–land at harvest–home. 1H4 1.03. 35
of all humors that have show'd themselves humors 2.04. 92 P
seldom but sumptuous, show'd like a feast, | and 3.02. 58
tell me, tell me, | how show'd his tasking? 5.02. 50
and show'd thou mak'st some tender of my life 5.04. 49
it better show'd with you | when that your flock 2H4 4.02. 4
and show'd how well you love your prince and 2H6 4.09. 16
with downright payment show'd unto my father. 3H6 1.04. 32
choosing for yourself, you show'd your judgment; 4.01. 61
his face | by any livelihood he show'd to–day? R3 3.04. 55
every man that stood | show'd like a mine. H8 1.01. 22
the o'er–great cardinal | hath show'd him gold; 1.01.223
in all the rest show'd a most noble patience. 2.01. 36
of good women, | for such a one we show'd 'em. ep 11
he should have show'd us | his marks of merit, COR 2.03.163
and revolts, wherein they show'd | most valor, 3.01.126
you had not show'd them how ye were dispos'd 3.02. 22
all boats alike | show'd mastership in floating; 4.01. 7

his hate, | and therein show'd like enemies. 4.06.114
love i have | (though i show'd sourly to him) 5.03. 13
volsces | may say, "this mercy we have show'd"; 5.03.137
thy life | show'd thy dear mother any courtesy, 5.03.161
and when they show'd me this abhorred pit, TIT 2.03. 98
for't, and show'd what necessity belong'd to't, TIM 3.02. 13 P
there was very little honor show'd in't. 3.02. 19 P
you show'd your /teeth like apes, and fawn'd JC 5.01. 41
statilius show'd the torchlight, but, my lord, 5.05. 2
/quarrel smiling, | show'd like a rebel's whore. MAC 1.02. 15
to you they have show'd some truth. 2.01. 21
when i have show'd th' unfitness — how now, LR 1.04.333
sir, you have show'd to–day your valiant strain, 5.03. 40
and so much duty as my mother show'd | to you, OTH 1.03.186
and when good will is show'd, though't come too ANT 2.05. 8
they show'd his back above | the element they 5.02. 89
when from the mountain top pisanio show'd thee, CYM 3.06. 5
last night the very gods show'd me a vision | (i 4.02.346
good sooth, it show'd well in you. PER 4.01. 88
me language such | as thou hast show'd me feat! TNK 3.01. 45
so the deities | have show'd due justice. 5.04.109
white | show'd like an april daisy on the grass, LUC 395
fed, | show'd life imprison'd in a body dead. 1456
face, though full of cares, yet show'd content; 1503
she show'd him favors to allure his eye; PP 4. 6

SHOW'DST 2 FR 0.0002 REL FR 2 V 0 P
thank thee for the love thou show'dst the king, LR 4.02. 95
thou show'dst a subject's shine, i a true PER 1.02.124

SHOWED 6 FR 0.0006 REL FR 6 V 0 P
the herb i showed thee once. MND 2.01.169
ere i was risen from the place that showed | my LR 2.04. 29
showed like two silver doves that sit a–billing. VEN 366
showed deep regard and smiling government. LUC 1400
she showed hers, he saw more wounds than one, PP 9.13
yet showed his visage by that cost more dear, LC 96

SHOWER 3 FR 0.0003 REL FR 3 V 0 P
gift | to rain a shower of commanded tears, | an SHR in.1. 125
a shower and thunder with their caps and shouts. COR 2.01.267
i'll set thee in a shower of gold, and hail ANT 2.05. 45

SHOWERS 7 FR 0.0008 REL FR 7 V 0 P
for raging wind blows up incessant showers, 3H6 1.04.145
as sun and showers | there had made a lasting H8 3.01. 7
come, and learn of us | to melt in showers; TIT 5.03.161
the ground did not go | with true–love showers." HAM 4.05. 40
spring, | and these the showers to bring it on. ANT 3.02. 44
so they were dew'd with such distilling showers. VEN 66
or as sweet–season'd showers are to the ground; SON 75. 2

SHOWEST 2 FR 0.0002 REL FR 2 V 0 P
thou showest the naked pathway to thy life, R2 1.02. 31
have more than thou showest, | speak less than LR 1.04.118

/SHOWING 1 FR 0.0001 REL FR 1 V 0 P
/showing /an /outward /pity, /yet /you /pilates R2 4.01.240

SHOWING 15 FR 0.0017 REL FR 10 V 5 P
showing we would not spare heaven as we love it, MM 2.03. 33
by something showing a more swelling port | than MV 1.01.124
if you will have it in showing, you shall read AWW 2.03. 21 P
"a showing of a heavenly effect in an earthly 2.03. 23 P
showing as in a model our firm estate, | when R2 3.04. 42
lest he, by showing it, should dishearten his H5 4.01.111 P
shall exceed | by showing the worse first. TRO 1.03.361
nor, showing (as the manner is) his wounds | to COR 2.01.235
will not seal your knowledge with showing them. 2.03.108 P
heart, | for showing me again the eyes of man! TIM 4.03. 51
of very soft society, and great showing; HAM 5.02.108 P
showing the sun his teeth, grinning at the moon, TNK 1.01.100
showing life's triumph in the map of death, LUC 402
showing their birth and where they did proceed? SON 76. 8
showing fair nature is both kind and tame; LC 311

SHOWN 34 FR 0.0038 REL FR 32 V 2 P
(for thou hast shown some sign of good desert) TGV 3.02. 18
and sir hugh hath shown himself a wise and WIV 2.03. 54 P
faults are bred | and fears by pale white shown: LLL 1.02.102
dismask'd, their damask sweet commixture shown, 5.02.296
take his own, | in your waking shall be shown. MND 3.02.460
eyes | see it so grossly shown in thy behaviors AWW 1.03.178
so holy writ in babes hath judgment shown, 2.01.138
to one of your receiving | enough is shown; TN 3.01.121
his valors shown upon our crests to–day | have 1H4 5.05. 29
which oft our stage hath shown; H5 ep 13
but that 'tis shown ignobly and in treason. 2H6 5.02. 23
as thou hast shown it flintly by thy deeds, | i 3H6 2.01.202
for, were he, he had shown it in his looks. R3 3.04. 57
i am sure have shown at full their royal minds H8 4.01. 8
now we have shown our power, | let us seem COR 4.02. 3
this love that thou hast shown | doth add more ROM 1.01.188
i'll go along no such sight to be shown, | but 1.02.100
recanting goodness, sorry ere 'tis shown; TIM 1.02. 17
time, when i might ha' shown myself honorable! 3.02. 46 P
with an entreaty, herein further shown, | that HAM 2.02. 76
this in obedience hath my daughter shown me, 2.02.125
i hear that you have shown your father | a LR 2.01.105
in thy thought | too hideous to be shown. OTH 3.03.108
you have shown all hectors. ANT 4.08. 7
be shown | for poor'st diminutives, for dolts, 4.12. 36
this sword but shown to caesar, with this 4.14.112
have shown to thee such a declining day, | or 5.01. 38
puppet, shall be shown | in rome as well as i. 5.02.208
he's more secure to keep it shut than shown; PER 1.01. 95
through whom the gods have shown their power; 5.03. 60
where shall be shown you all was found with her; 5.03. 66
for her griefs, so lively shown, | made me think PP 20.17
by seeing farther than the eye hath shown. SON 69. 8
their rank thoughts my deeds must not be shown, 121.12

SHOW–PLACE 1 FR 0.0001 REL FR 1 V 0 P
i' th' common show–place, where they exercise. ANT 3.06. 12

SHOW'R 7 FR 0.0008 REL FR 4 V 3 P
a man may hear this show'r sing in the wind. WIV 3.02. 37 P
this show'r, blown up by tempest of the soul, JN 5.02. 50
even then that sunshine brew'd a show'r for him, 3H6 2.02.156
and once more | i show'r a welcome on ye. H8 1.04. 63
loose shot, deliver'd such a show'r of pibbles, 5.03. 56 P
travail'd in the great show'r of your gifts, TIM 5.01. 70
be, she makes a show'r of rain as well as jove. ANT 1.02.150 P

SHOW'R'D 1 FR 0.0001 REL FR 1 V 0 P
show'r'd on me daily have been more than could H8 3.02.167

SHOW'RING 2 FR 0.0002 REL FR 2 V 0 P
it rain'd down fortune show'ring on your head, 1H4 5.01. 47
evermore show'ring? ROM 3.05.130

SHOW'RS 10 FR 0.0011 REL FR 10 V 0 P
diffusest honey–drops, refreshing show'rs, | and TMP 4.01. 79
so he dissolv'd, and show'rs of oaths did melt. MND 1.01.245
small show'rs last long, but sudden storms are R2 2.01. 35
and lay the summer's dust with show'rs of blood 3.03. 43
faster than spring–time show'rs comes thought on 2H6 3.01.337
see, see what show'rs arise, | blown with the 3H6 2.05. 85
than youthful april shall with all his show'rs. TIT 3.01. 18
one cloud of winter show'rs, | these flies are TIM 2.02.171
the earth with show'rs of silver brine, LUC 796
it nor grows with heat nor drowns with show'rs. SON 124.12

/SHOWS 4 FR 0.0004 REL FR 4 V 0 P
of him | as great alcides' /shows upon an ass. JN 2.01.144
/but /shadows /and /the /shows /of /men, /to 2H4 1.01.193
/free /things /and /happy /shows /behind, | /but LR 3.06.105
proper deformity /shows not in the fiend | so 4.02. 60

SHOWS 113 FR 0.0127 REL FR 98 V 15 P
this visitation shows it. TMP 3.01. 32
to hide itself, | the bigger bulk it shows. 3.01. 81
his little speaking shows his love but small. TGV 1.02. 29
which now shows all the beauty of the sun, | and 1.03. 86
her fair) | shows julia but a swarthy ethiope. 2.06. 26
this discipline shows thou hast been in love. 3.02. 87
looks in a glass that shows what future evils, MM 2.02. 95
he shows his reason for that: 4.04. 11 P
heavens, he shows me where the bachelors sit, ADO 2.01. 48 P
finding a bird's nest, shows it his companion, 2.01.224 P
why, what effects of passion shows she? 2.03.107 P
that shows thou art unconfirm'd. 3.03.117 P
that she were a maid, | by these exterior shows? 4.01. 40
than wish a snow in may's new–fangled shows; LLL 1.01.106
their shallow shows and prologue vildly penn'd, 5.02.305
transparent helena, nature shows art, | that MND 2.02.104
a golden mind stoops not to shows of dross. MV 2.07. 20
so may the outward shows be least themselves — 3.02. 73
his sceptre shows the force of temporal power, 4.01.190
for herein fortune shows herself more kind 4.01.267
as 'tis with us that square our guess by shows; AWW 2.01.150
greater than shows itself at the first view | to 2.05. 68
example, that so terrible shows in the wrack of 3.05. 22 P
more, but indeed | our shows are more than will; TN 2.04.117
for folly that he wisely shows is fit, | but 3.01. 67
a murd'rous guilt shows not itself more soon 3.01.147
me a mirror | which shows me mine chang'd too; WT 1.02.382
this shows a sound affection. 4.04.379
happy be you! | all that you speak shows fair. 4.04.623
nobleness which nature shows above her breeding; 5.02. 37 P
silence, it the more shows off | your wonder; 5.03. 21
which shows like grief itself, but is not so; R2 2.02. 15
that fair sun which shows me where thou stand'st 4.01. 35
the truth of what we are | shows us but this. 5.01. 20
he shows in this, he loves his own barn better 1H4 2.03. 5 P
curtain | that shows the ignorant a kind of fear 4.01. 74
it shows my earnestness of affection — 2H4 5.05. 16 P
to /fine his title with some shows of truth, H5 1.02. 72
the element shows to him as it doth to me; 4.01.103 P
in life so liveless as it shows itself. 4.02. 55
once discern'd, shows that her meaning is, | no 1H6 3.02. 24
day, | he knits his brow and shows an angry eye, 2H6 3.01. 15
more than mistrust, that shows him worthy death. 3.01.242
as on a mountain top the cedar shows | that 5.01.205
my mangled body shows, | my blood, my want of 3H6 5.02. 7
blood, my want of strength, my sick heart shows, 5.02. 8
with stately triumphs, mirthful comic shows, 5.07. 43
that in your outward action shows itself R3 1.03. 66
forward | in celebration of this day with shows, H8 4.01. 10
th' unworthiest shows as fairly in the mask. TRO 1.03. 84
for what he has he gives, what thinks he shows, 4.05.101
if these shows be not outward, which of you COR 1.06. 77
our large temples with the shows of peace, | and 3.03. 36
and shows good husbandry for the volscian state, 4.07. 22
and shows the ragged entrails of this pit: TIT 2.03.230
and in dumb shows | pass the remainder of our 3.01.131
that shows thee a weak slave, for the weakest ROM 1.01. 13 P
so shows a snowy dove trooping with crows, | as 1.05. 48
crows, | as yonder lady o'er her fellows shows. 1.05. 49
much, | which mannerly devotion shows in this: 1.05. 98
some grief shows much of love, | but much of 3.05. 72
but much of grief shows still some want of wit. 3.05. 73
fire i' th' flint | shows not till it be strook; TIM 1.01. 23
as this pomp shows to a little oil and root. 1.02.135
it shows but little love or judgment in him. 3.03. 10
mark how strange it shows, | timon in this 3.04. 21
war, | forgets the shows of love to other men. JC 1.02. 47
fire, | who, much enforced, shows a hasty spark, 4.03.112
who bears a glass | which shows me many more; MAC 4.01.120
it shows a will most incorrect to heaven, | a HAM 1.02. 95
the glow–worm shows the matin to be near, | and 1.05. 89
nothing but inexplicable dumb shows and noise. 3.02. 12 P
and shows a most pitiful ambition in the fool 3.02. 44 P
a mineral of metals base, | shows itself pure: 4.01. 27
and shows no cause without | why the man dies. 4.04. 28
that shows his hoary leaves in the glassy stream 4.07.167
becomes the field, but here shows much amiss. 5.02.402
with their manners, | shows like a riotous inn. LR 1.04.244
this shows you are above, | you /justicers, that 4.02. 78
throwing but shows of service on their lords, OTH 1.01. 52
one unperfectness shows me another, to make me 2.03.297 P
they do suggest at first with heavenly shows, 2.03.352
'tis not a year or two shows us a man: 3.04.103
i know this act shows horrible and grim. 5.02.203
him, it shows to man the tailors of the earth; ANT 1.02.163 P
(to this good purpose, that so fairly shows) 2.02.144
she shows a body rather than a life, | a statue, 3.03. 20
strikes life into my speech and shows much more CYM 3.03. 97
with other spritely shows | of mine own kindred. 5.05.428
this mercy shows we'll joy in such a son; PER 1.01.118
which shows that beauty hath his power and will, 2.02. 34
what pageantry, what feats, what shows, | what 5.02. 6
come all sad and solemn shows, | that are TNK 1.05. 7
distemper'd | /far worse than now she shows. 4.01.120
which shows him hardy, fearless, proud of 4.02. 80
fear he cannot, | he shows no such soft temper. 4.02.103
and nimble set, | which shows an active soul; 4.02.126
and when he smiles | he shows a lover, when he 4.02.136
there is but envy in that light which shows 5.03. 21
upon thy tempting lip | shows thee unripe; VEN 128
shows his hot courage and his high desire. 276
perverse it shall be where it shows most toward, 1157
that what is vile shows like a virtuous deed. LUC 252
losing her woes in shows of discontent. 1580
woes, | corrupted blood some watery token shows, 1748
shows me a bare–bon'd death by time outworn. 1761
that this huge stage presenteth nought but shows SON 15. 3
hides your life, and shows not half your parts. 17. 4
lascivious grace, in whom all ill well shows, 40.13
but when my glass shows me myself indeed, 62. 9
to make him seem long hence, as he shows now. 101.14
your own glass shows you when you look in it. 103.14
or to turn white and sound at tragic shows; LC 308

SHOW'ST 3 FR 0.0003 REL FR 3 V 0 P
tackle's torn, | thou show'st a noble vessel. COR 4.05. 62
more hideous when thou show'st thee in a child LR 1.04.260
and therein show'st | thy lovers withering as SON 126. 3

SHOW'T 1 FR 0.0001 REL FR 1 V 0 P
i'll show't the king, and undertake to be | her WT 2.02. 36

SHREDS 2 FR 0.0002 REL FR 2 V 0 P
with these shreds | they vented their COR 1.01.208
a king of shreds and patches — | save me, and HAM 3.04.102

'SHREW *(also beshrew, beshrow)*

'SHREW 1 FR 0.0001 REL FR 1 V 0 P
'shrew my heart, | you never spoke what did WT 1.02.281

SHREW *(also shrow, etc.)*

SHREW 11 FR 0.0012 REL FR 8 V 3 P
but, like a shrew, you first begin to brawl. ERR 4.01. 51
a meacock wretch can make the curstest shrew. SHR 2.01.313
much more a shrew of /thy impatient humor. 3.02. 29
is she so hot a shrew as she's reported? 4.01. 21 P
by this reck'ning he is more shrew than she. 4.01. 85 P
he that knows better how to tame a shrew, | now 4.01.210
to tame a shrew and charm her chattering tongue. 4.02. 58
your husband, being troubled with a shrew, 5.02. 28
i think thou hast the veriest shrew of all. 5.02. 64
bless you, fair shrew. TN 1.03. 47 P
shrew me, | if i would lose it for a revenue CYM 2.03.142

SHREWD *(also shrowd, etc.)*

SHREWD 21 FR 0.0023 REL FR 16 V 5 P
so far that there is shrewd construction made of WIV 2.02.223 P
to your tent, and prove a shrewd caesar to you; MM 2.01.249 P
a husband, if thou be so shrewd of thy tongue. ADO 2.01. 19 P
or else you are that shrewd and knavish sprite MND 2.01. 33
o, when she is angry, she is keen and shrewd! 3.02.323
that have endur'd shrewd days and nights with us AYL 5.04.173
her elder sister is so curst and shrewd | that SHR 1.01.180
and wish thee to a shrewd ill–favor'd wife? 1.02. 60
this young maid might do her | a shrewd turn, if AWW 3.05. 68
a shrewd knave and an unhappy. 4.05. 63 P
ah, foul shrewd news! JN 5.05. 14
to lift shrewd steel against our golden crown, R2 3.02. 59
methought 'a made a shrewd thrust at your belly. 2H4 2.04.211 P
these women are shrewd tempters with their 1H6 1.02.123
scarce himself, | that bears so shrewd a maim: 2H6 2.03. 41
a parlous boy! go to, you are too shrewd. R3 2.04. 35
or two o' th' face — but they are shrewd ones, H8 1.03. 7
"do my lord of canterbury | a shrewd turn, and 5.02.211
we shall find of him | a shrewd contriver; JC 2.01.158
'tis a shrewd doubt, though it be but a dream, OTH 3.03.429
this last day was | a shrewd one to 's. ANT 4.09. 5

SHREWDLY 7 FR 0.0008 REL FR 4 V 3 P
cousin, you apprehend passing shrewdly. ADO 2.01. 81 P
he's shrewdly vex'd at something. AWW 3.05. 89 P
you boggle shrewdly, every feather starts you. 5.03.232
practice hath most shrewdly pass'd upon thee; TN 5.01.352
'tis shrewdly ebb'd, | to say you have seen a WT 5.01.102
your mistress shrewdly shook your back. H5 3.07. 49 P
misgiving still | falls shrewdly to the purpose. JC 3.01.146

SHREWISH 1 FR 0.0001 REL FR 1 V 0 P
my wife is shrewish when i keep not hours: ERR 3.01. 2

SHREWISHLY 1 FR 0.0001 REL FR 0 V 1 P
very well–favor'd and he speaks very shrewishly. TN 1.05.160 P

SHREWISHNESS 1 FR 0.0001 REL FR 1 V 0 P
i have no gift at all in shrewishness; MND 3.02.301

/SHREWSBURY 1 FR 0.0001 REL FR 0 V 1 P
shrewsbury, /shrewsbury! STM II.C 38 P

SHREWSBURY 21 FR 0.0023 REL FR 13 V 8 P
power, | as is appointed us, at shrewsbury. 1H4 3.01. 85
met | the eleventh of this month at shrewsbury. 3.02.166
your honor had already been at shrewsbury. 4.02. 53 P
for, sir, at shrewsbury, | as i am truly given 4.04. 10
and fought a long hour by shrewsbury clock. 5.04.148 P
who in a bloody field by shrewsbury | hath 2H4 in 24
between that royal field of shrewsbury | and in 34
i bring you certain news from shrewsbury. 1.01. 12
came you from shrewsbury? 1.01. 24
of him | i did demand what news from shrewsbury. 1.01. 40
say, morton, didst thou come from shrewsbury? 1.01. 64
i ran from shrewsbury, my noble lord, | where 1.01. 65
he hath since done good service at shrewsbury, 1.02. 62 P
for you before your expedition to shrewsbury. 1.02.102 P
day's service at shrewsbury hath a little gilded 1.02.148 P
it was young hotspur's cause at shrewsbury. 1.03. 26
deserts | we here create you earl of shrewsbury, 1H6 3.04. 26
valiant lord talbot, earl of shrewsbury, 4.07. 61
the noble earl of shrewsbury, let's hear him. STM II.C 30 P
the earl of shrewsbury. II.C 32 P
shrewsbury, /shrewsbury! II.C 38 P

SHRIEK *(also shrike, etc.)*

SHRIEK 4 FR 0.0004 REL FR 4 V 0 P
then i'ld shriek, that even your ears | should WT 5.01. 65
for night–owls shriek where mounting larks R2 3.03.183
and ghosts did shriek and squeal about the JC 2.02. 24
night–wand'ring weasels shriek to see him there; LUC 307

SHRIEK'D 4 FR 0.0004 REL FR 3 V 1 P
the women have so cried and shriek'd at it, that WIV 1.01.297 P
the owl shriek'd at thy birth, an evil sign; 3H6 5.06. 44
dabbled in blood, and he shriek'd out aloud, R3 1.04. 54
it was the owl that shriek'd, the fatal bellman, MAC 2.02. 3

SHRIEKING 2 FR 0.0002 REL FR 2 V 0 P
and several noises | of roaring, shrieking, TMP 5.01.233
upon the market–place, | howting and shrieking. JC 1.03. 28

SHRIEKS 4 FR 0.0004 REL FR 4 V 0 P
and so, with shrieks, | she melted into air. WT 3.03. 36
and shrieks that rent the air | are made, not MAC 4.03.168
the lady shrieks, and well–a–near | does fall in PER 3.ch. 51

owl (night's herald) shrieks, 'tis very late; VEN 531
SHRIEVALTRY 1 FR 0.0001 REL FR 0 V 1 P
'a keeps a plentiful shrievaltry, and 'a made my STM II.C 42 P
SHRIEVE *(also sheriff, etc.)*
SHRIEVE 6 FR 0.0006 REL FR 1 V 5 P
are by the shrieve of yorkshire overthrown. 2H4 4.04. 99
shrieve more speaks. STM II.C 41 P
shall we hear shrieve more speak? II.C 41 P
let's hear shrieve more. II.C 44 P
shrieve more, more, more, shrieve more! II.C 45 P
shrieve more, more, more, shrieve more! II.C 45 P
SHRIEVE'S 1 FR 0.0001 REL FR 0 V 1 P
whipt for getting the shrieve's fool with child, AWW 4.03.187 P
SHRIFT 9 FR 0.0010 REL FR 8 V 1 P
give him a present shrift and advise him for a MM 4.02.207 P
the ghostly father now hath done his shrift. 3H6 3.02.107
make a short shrift, he longs to see your head. R3 3.04. 95
wert so happy by thy stay | to hear true shrift. ROM 1.01.159
riddling confession finds but riddling shrift. 2.03. 56
some means to come to shrift this afternoon, 2.04.180
have you got leave to go to shrift to–day? 2.05. 66
see where she comes from shrift with merry look. 4.02. 15
his bed shall seem a school, his board a shrift, OTH 3.03. 24
/SHRIK'D 1 FR 0.0001 REL FR 1 V 0 P
what should it be that is so /shrik'd abroad? ROM 5.03.190
SHRIKE *(also shriek, etc.)*
SHRIKE 2 FR 0.0002 REL FR 1 V 1 P
duchess and the ladies, that they would shrike; MND 1.02. 76 P
what noise? what shrike is this? TRO 2.02. 97
SHRIKES 1 FR 0.0001 REL FR 1 V 0 P
and shrikes like mandrakes' torn out of the ROM 4.03. 47
SHRIKING 3 FR 0.0003 REL FR 3 V 0 P
brave hector's breast | and great troy shriking. TRO 3.03.141
but thou shriking harbinger, | foul precurrer of PHT 5
as often shriking undistinguish'd woe, | in LC 20
SHRILL 6 FR 0.0006 REL FR 5 V 1 P
and fetch shrill echoes from the hollow earth. SHR in.2. 46
is as the maiden's organ, shrill and sound, TN 1.04. 33
"you are welcome," with this shrill addition, 1H4 2.04. 26 P
hear the shrill whistle which doth order give H5 3.pr. 9
the neighing steed and the shrill trump, | the OTH 3.03.351
sport, | i heard a voice, a shrill one; TNK 4.01. 56
SHRILLER 1 FR 0.0001 REL FR 1 V 0 P
i hear a tongue shriller than all the music JC 1.02. 16
SHRILL–GORG'D 1 FR 0.0001 REL FR 1 V 0 P
the shrill–gorg'd lark so far | cannot be seen LR 4.06. 58
SHRILLS 1 FR 0.0001 REL FR 1 V 0 P
how poor andromache shrills her dolors forth! TRO 5.03. 84
SHRILL–SHRIKING 1 FR 0.0001 REL FR 1 V 0 P
the locks of your shrill–shriking daughters; H5 3.03. 35
SHRILL–SOUNDING 1 FR 0.0001 REL FR 1 V 0 P
doth with his lofty and shrill–sounding throat HAM 1.01.151
SHRILL–TONGU'D 3 FR 0.0003 REL FR 3 V 0 P
pays shame | when shrill–tongu'd fulvia scolds. ANT 1.01. 32
is she shrill–tongu'd or low? 3.03. 12
like shrill–tongu'd tapsters answering every VEN 849
SHRILL/–VOIC'D 1 FR 0.0001 REL FR 1 V 0 P
what shrill/–voic'd suppliant makes this eager R2 5.03. 75
SHRILLY 2 FR 0.0002 REL FR 2 V 0 P
replying shrilly to the well–tun'd horns, | as TIT 2.03. 18
title plead, | nor sound his quillets shrilly; TIM 4.03.155
SHRIMP 2 FR 0.0002 REL FR 2 V 0 P
and when he was a babe, a child, a shrimp, LLL 5.02.590
it cannot be this weak and writhled shrimp 1H6 2.03. 23
SHRINE 7 FR 0.0008 REL FR 7 V 0 P
of the earth they come | to kiss this shrine, MV 2.07. 40
forsooth, a blind man at saint albon's shrine, 2H6 2.01. 61
by chance | or of devotion, to this holy shrine? 2.01. 86
come offer at my shrine, and i will help thee." 2.01. 90
with my unworthiest hand | this holy shrine, the ROM 1.05. 94
the shrine of venus or straight–pight minerva, CYM 5.05.164
offer pure incense to so pure a shrine: LUC 194
SHRINK 11 FR 0.0012 REL FR 11 V 0 P
if there be ten, shrink not, but down with 'em. TGV 4.01. 2
upon my body | even till i shrink with cold, i AYL 2.01. 9
and against this fire | do i shrink up. JN 5.07. 34
makes me with heavy nothing faint and shrink. R2 2.02. 32
arm | that he shall shrink under my courtesy. 1H4 5.02. 74
stay, | if the first hour i shrink and run away. 1H6 4.05. 31
when he perceiv'd me shrink and on my knee, 4.07. 5
to shrink mine arm up like a wither'd shrub, 3H6 3.02.156
to see if any mean to shrink from me. R3 5.03.222
will find a friend will not shrink from him. H8 4.01.107
and yet detested life not shrink thereat! TIT 3.01.247
SHRINKING 2 FR 0.0002 REL FR 2 V 0 P
not fearing death, nor shrinking for distress, 1H6 4.01. 37
tanlings and | the shrinking slaves of winter. CYM 4.04. 30
SHRINKS 4 FR 0.0004 REL FR 2 V 2 P
to wed it, when | the bravest questant shrinks. AWW 2.01. 16
and the ground shrinks before his treading. COR 5.04. 19 P
done and past, and his estate shrinks from him. TIM 3.02. 7 P
shrinks backward in his shelly cave with pain, VEN 1034
SHRIV'D 1 FR 0.0001 REL FR 1 V 0 P
friar lawrence' cell | be shriv'd and married. ROM 2.04.182
SHRIVE 2 FR 0.0002 REL FR 1 V 1 P
and shrive you of a thousand idle pranks. ERR 2.02.208
i had rather he should shrive me than wive me. MV 1.02.131 P
SHRIVELL'D 1 FR 0.0001 REL FR 1 V 0 P
him, | a fire from heaven came and shrivell'd up PER 2.04. 9
SHRIVER 1 FR 0.0001 REL FR 1 V 0 P
when he was made a shriver, 'twas for shift. 3H6 3.02.108
SHRIVES 1 FR 0.0001 REL FR 1 V 0 P
doubtless he shrives this woman to her smock, 1H6 1.02.119
SHRIVING 2 FR 0.0002 REL FR 2 V 0 P
your honor hath no shriving work in hand. R3 3.02.115
to sudden death, | not shriving time allow'd. HAM 5.02. 47
/SHROUD 1 FR 0.0001 REL FR 1 V 0 P
and hide me with a dead man in his /shroud — ROM 4.01. 85
SHROUD 12 FR 0.0013 REL FR 11 V 1 P
i will here shroud till the dregs of the storm TMP 2.02. 40 P
die when you will, a smock shall be your shroud. LLL 5.02.479
that lies in woe | in remembrance of a shroud. MND 5.01.378
my shroud of white, stuck all with yew, | o, TN 2.04. 55
some hangman must put on my shroud and lay me WT 4.04.457
this thick–grown brake we'll shroud ourselves, 3H6 3.01. 1
nor how to shroud yourself from enemies? 4.03. 40
lies fest'ring in his shroud, where, as they say ROM 4.03. 43
and pluck the mangled tybalt from his shroud, 4.03. 52
"white his shroud as the mountain snow" — HAM 4.05. 36
prithee shroud me | in one of these same sheets. OTH 4.03. 24
antony, | and put yourself under his shroud, ANT 3.13. 71
SHROUDED 4 FR 0.0004 REL FR 3 V 1 P
i have been closely shrouded in this bush | and LLL 4.03.135
if honor may be shrouded in a hearse — | whilst R3 1.02. 2
sworn upon't she never shrouded any but lazars. TRO 2.03. 33 P
shrouded in cloth of state, balm'd and PER 3.02. 65
SHROUDING 1 FR 0.0001 REL FR 1 V 0 P
a spade, a spade, | for and a shrouding sheet: HAM 5.01. 95
SHROUDS 3 FR 0.0003 REL FR 3 V 0 P
and all the shrouds wherewith my life should JN 5.07. 53
the friends of france our shrouds and tacklings? 3H6 5.04. 18
as the shrouds make at sea in a stiff tempest, H8 4.01. 72
SHROVE 1 FR 0.0001 REL FR 0 V 1 P
forefinger, as a pancake for shrove tuesday, a AWW 2.02. 24 P
SHROVE–TIDE 1 FR 0.0001 REL FR 1 V 0 P
wags all, | and welcome merry shrove–tide. 2H4 5.03. 35
SHROW *(also shrew)*
SHROW 2 FR 0.0002 REL FR 2 V 0 P
night | did pretty jessica (like a little shrow) MV 5.01. 21
now go thy ways, thou hast tam'd a curst shrow. SHR 5.02.188
SHROWD *(also shrewd, etc.)*
SHROWD 7 FR 0.0008 REL FR 5 V 2 P
ay, and a shrowd unhappy gallows too. LLL 5.02. 12
there are some shrowd contents in yond same MV 3.02.243
and as curst and shrowd | as socrates' xantippe, SHR 1.02. 70
is intolerable curst | and shrowd and froward, 1.02. 90
he has a shrowd wit, i can tell you, and he's TRO 1.02.190 P
o, they have shrowd measure! TNK 4.03. 34 P
thy eyes' shrowd tutor, that hard heart of thine VEN 500
SHROWDLY 3 FR 0.0003 REL FR 2 V 1 P
ay, but these english are shrowdly out of beef. H5 3.07.152 P
is at stake, | my fame is shrowdly gor'd. TRO 3.03.228
the air bites shrowdly, it is very cold. HAM 1.04. 1
SHROWDNESS 1 FR 0.0001 REL FR 1 V 0 P
which not wanted | shrowdness of policy too — i ANT 2.02. 69
SHROWS 2 FR 0.0002 REL FR 2 V 0 P
and i beshrow all shrows, | but, katherine, what LLL 5.02. 46
for women are shrows, both short and tall; 2H4 5.03. 33
SHRUB 2 FR 0.0002 REL FR 1 V 1 P
neither bush nor shrub to bear off any weather TMP 2.02. 18 P
to shrink mine arm up like a wither'd shrub, 3H6 3.02.156
SHRUB'S 1 FR 0.0001 REL FR 1 V 0 P
the cedar stoops not to the base shrub's foot, LUC 664
SHRUBS 3 FR 0.0003 REL FR 3 V 0 P
and kept low shrubs from winter's pow'rful wind. 3H6 5.02. 15
marcus, we are but shrubs, no cedars we, | no TIT 4.03. 46
but low shrubs wither at the cedar's root. LUC 665
SHRUG 3 FR 0.0003 REL FR 3 V 0 P
still have i borne it with a patient shrug, MV 1.03.109
speech) and straight | the shrug, the hum or ha WT 2.01. 71
where great patricians shall attend and shrug, COR 1.09. 4
SHRUGS 1 FR 0.0001 REL FR 1 V 0 P
itself), these shrugs, these hums and ha's, WT 2.01. 74
SHRUG'ST 1 FR 0.0001 REL FR 1 V 0 P
shrug'st thou, malice? TMP 1.02.367
SHRUNK 9 FR 0.0010 REL FR 8 V 1 P
a world too wide | for his shrunk shank, and his AYL 2.07.161
then one of you will prove a shrunk panel, and 3.03. 88 P
ill–weav'd ambition, how much art thou shrunk! 1H4 5.04. 88
and in this borrowed likeness of shrunk death ROM 4.01.104
true, as you said, timon is shrunk indeed, | and TIM 3.02. 61
spoils, | shrunk to this little measure? JC 3.01.150
and at the sound it shrunk in haste away | and HAM 1.02.219
it in — shrunk thee into | the bound thou wast TNK 1.01. 83
the spring that those shrunk pipes have fed, LUC 1455
SHUDDER 1 FR 0.0001 REL FR 1 V 0 P
fear whereof doth make him shake and shudder; VEN 880
SHUDDERS 1 FR 0.0001 REL FR 1 V 0 P
into strong shudders and to heavenly agues | th' TIM 4.03.138
SHUDD'RING 1 FR 0.0001 REL FR 1 V 0 P
and shudd'ring fear, and green–eyed jealousy! MV 3.02.110
SHUFFLE 3 FR 0.0003 REL FR 2 V 1 P
mine honor in my necessity, am fain to shuffle, WIV 2.02. 25 P
that he shall likewise shuffle her away, | while 4.06. 29
life, good master, | must shuffle for itself. CYM 5.05.105
SHUFFLED 2 FR 0.0002 REL FR 2 V 0 P
are shuffled off with such uncurrent pay; TN 3.03. 16
when we have shuffled off this mortal coil, HAM 3.01. 66
SHUFFLING 3 FR 0.0003 REL FR 3 V 0 P
'tis like the forc'd gait of a shuffling nag. 1H4 3.01.133
there is no shuffling, there the action lies HAM 3.03. 61
or with a little shuffling, you may choose | a 4.07.137
SHUN 25 FR 0.0028 REL FR 24 V 1 P
scarcity and want shall shun you, | ceres' TMP 4.01.116
since therein she doth evitate and shun | a WIV 5.05.228
for him thou labor'st by thy flight to shun, MM 3.01. 12
if not, shun me, and i will spare your haunts. MND 2.01.142
thus when i shun scylla, your father, i fall MV 3.05. 16 P
who doth ambition shun, | and loves to live i' AYL 2.05. 38
do not shun her | until you see her die again, WT 5.03.105
nor, as we are, we say we will not shun it. H5 3.06.165
let him shun castles. 2H6 1.04. 35
"let him shun castles; 1.04. 67
and were i strong, i would not shun their fury. 3H6 1.04. 24
and weak we are and cannot shun pursuit. 2.03. 13
to shun the danger that his soul divines. R3 3.02. 18
you cannot shun yourself. TRO 3.02.146
thou'dst shun a bear, | but if /thy flight lay LR 3.04. 9
o, that way madness lies, let me shun that! 3.04. 21
you that | like beasts which you shun beastly, CYM 5.03. 27
by flight i'll shun the danger which i fear. PER 1.01.142
court mine eyes, and mine eyes shun them, | and 1.02. 6
taint mine eye | with dread sights it may shun. TNK 5.03. 10
i could prevent this storm, and shun thy wrack! LUC 966
to shun this blot, she would not blot the letter 1322
we sicken to shun sickness when we purge; SON 118. 4
to shun the heaven that leads men to this hell. 129.14
which late her noble suit in court did shun, LC 234
SHUNLESS 1 FR 0.0001 REL FR 1 V 0 P
city, which he painted | with shunless destiny; COR 2.02.112
/SHUNN'D 1 FR 0.0001 REL FR 1 V 0 P
/shunn'd /my /abhorr'd /society, /but /then, LR 5.03.211
SHUNN'D 8 FR 0.0009 REL FR 7 V 1 P
thus have i shunn'd the fire for fear of burning TGV 1.03. 78
man | (a rashness that i ever yet have shunn'd), 3.01. 30
where i arrive, and my approach be shunn'd, WT 1.02.422
the mouse ne'er shunn'd the cat as they did COR 1.06. 44
and gladly shunn'd who gladly fled from me. ROM 1.01.130
so opposite to marriage that she shunn'd | the OTH 1.02. 67
rather shunn'd to go even with what i heard than CYM 1.04. 44 P
who ever shunn'd by precedent | the destin'd ill LC 155
SHUNNING 2 FR 0.0002 REL FR 2 V 0 P
comes that rock | that i advise your shunning. H8 1.01.114
children from a bear, the volsces shunning him. COR 1.03. 31
SHUNS 5 FR 0.0005 REL FR 5 V 0 P
comes it that your kindred shuns your house, SHR in.2. 28
who shuns thy love shuns all his love in me. AWW 2.03. 73
who shuns thy love shuns all his love in me. 2.03. 73
my desert | unmeritable shuns your high request. R3 3.07.155
who shuns not to break one will crack /them both PER 1.02.121
/SHUT 1 FR 0.0001 REL FR 1 V 0 P
or those eyes /shut, that makes thee answer ay, ROM 3.02. 49
SHUT 56 FR 0.0063 REL FR 48 V 8 P
would, with themselves, shut up my thoughts. TMP 2.01.192
purse she shall not, for that i'll keep shut. TGV 3.01.351 P
his own doors being shut against his entrance. ERR 4.03. 89
on purpose shut the doors against his way. 4.03. 91
whilst upon me the guilty doors were shut, | and 4.04. 63
were not my doors lock'd up, and i shut out? 4.04. 70
your doors were lock'd, and you shut out. 4.04. 71
day, great duke, she shut the doors upon me, 5.01.204
take away this villain, shut him up. LLL 1.02.153 P
and till that /instant shut | my woeful self up 5.02.807
whiles we shut the gate upon one wooer, another MV 1.02.133
do as i bid you, shut doors after you; 2.05. 53
who shut their coward gates on atomies, | should AYL 3.05. 13
shut that, and 'twill out at the key–hole; 4.01.163 P
whose baser stars do shut us up in wishes, AWW 1.01.183
would in so just a business shut his bosom 3.01. 8
to come into me, | which i would fain shut out. 5.03.115
let the garden door be shut, and leave me to my TN 3.01. 92 P
'gainst knaves and thieves men shut their gate, 5.01.395
shut the door, there comes no swaggerers here; 2H4 2.04. 76 P
shut the door, i pray you. 2.04. 78 P
would shut the book, and sit him down and die. 3.01. 56
the gates of mercy shall be all shut up, | and H5 3.03. 10
open the gates, or i'll shut thee out shortly. 1H6 1.03. 26
priest, dost thou command me to be shut out? 1.03. 30
and we, for fear, compell'd to shut our shops. 3.01. 85
is all thy comfort shut in gloucester's tomb? 2H6 3.02. 78
unless our halberds did shut up his passage. 3H6 4.03. 20
and shut the gates for safety of ourselves; 4.07. 18
these gates must not be shut | but in the night 4.07. 35
let the foul'st contempt | shut door upon me, H8 2.04. 43
and the minds of all | should be shut up, hear TRO 1.03. 58
of reason, | /let's shut our gates and sleep. 2.02. 47
which yet seem shut, we have but pinn'd with COR 1.04. 18
see, they have shut him in. 1.04. 47
and shut your gates upon 's. 1.07. 6
the gates shut on me, and turn'd weeping out TIT 5.03.105
shut up in prison, kept without my food, | whipt ROM 1.02. 55
o, shut the door, and when thou hast done so, 4.01. 44
being holiday, the beggar's shop is shut. 5.01. 56
letter he desires | to those have shut him up, TIM 1.01. 98
men shut their doors against a setting sun. 1.02.145
were all the wealth i have shut up in thee, 4.03.279
who should against his murtherer shut the door, MAC 1.07. 15
hostess, and shut up | in measureless content. 2.01. 16
ay, but their sense are shut. 5.01. 25 P
let the doors be shut upon him, that he may play HAM 3.01.131 P
shut up your doors. LR 2.04.304
shut up your doors, my lord, 'tis a wild night, 2.04.308
in such a night | to shut me out? 3.04. 18
shut your mouth, dame, | or with this paper 5.03.155
as if thou then hadst shut up in thy brain OTH 3.03.114
and shut myself up in some other course, | to 3.04.121
leave procreants alone, and shut the door; 4.02. 28
to th' trunk again, and shut the spring of it. CYM 2.02. 47
he's more secure to keep it shut than shown; PER 1.01. 95
SHUTS 6 FR 0.0006 REL FR 6 V 0 P
and here the abbess shuts the gates on us, | and ERR 5.01.156
and sleep, that sometimes shuts up sorrow's eye, MND 3.02.435
so grieving | that he shuts up himself — WT 4.01. 19
shuts up his windows, locks fair daylight out, ROM 1.01.139
like death when he shuts up the day of life; 4.01.101
that shuts him from the heaven of his thought, LUC 338
SHUTTLE 1 FR 0.0001 REL FR 0 V 1 P
beam, because i know also life is a shuttle. WIV 5.01. 23 P
SHY 2 FR 0.0002 REL FR 1 V 1 P
a shy fellow was the duke, and i believe i know MM 3.02.130 P
may seem as shy, as grave, as just, as absolute 5.01. 54
SHYLOCK 17 FR 0.0019 REL FR 14 V 3 P
shylock, do you hear? MV 1.03. 52
shylock, albeit i neither lend nor borrow | by 1.03. 61
well, shylock, shall we be beholding to you? 1.03.105
"shylock, we would have moneys," you say so — 1.03.116
yes, shylock, i will seal unto this bond. 1.03.171
shylock thy master spoke with me this day, | and 2.02.145
well parted between my master shylock and you, 2.02.150 P
the difference of old shylock and bassanio. 2.05. 2
how now, shylock, what news among the merchants? 3.01. 22 P
and shylock, for his own part, knew the bird was 3.01. 28 P
hear me yet, good shylock. 3.03. 3
shylock, the world thinks, and i think so too, 4.01. 17
antonio and old shylock, both stand forth. 4.01.175
is your name shylock? 4.01.176
shylock is my name. 4.01.176
shylock, there's thrice thy money off'red thee. 4.01.227
have by some surgeon, shylock, on your charge, 4.01.257
SHYLOCK'S 1 FR 0.0001 REL FR 1 V 0 P
i pray you show my youth old shylock's house. MV 4.02. 11
SI 3 FR 0.0003 REL FR 2 V 1 P
"si fortune me tormente, sperato me contento." 2H4 2.04.181
si fortuna me tormenta, spero contenta. 5.05. 96
ecoutez, dites–moi si je parle bien: H5 3.04. 17 P
SIB 1 FR 0.0001 REL FR 1 V 0 P
the blood of mine that's sib to him be suck'd TNK 1.02. 72
SIBYL 2 FR 0.0002 REL FR 2 V 0 P
as old as sibyl, and as curst and shrowd | as SHR 1.02. 70
a sibyl, that had numb'red in the world | the OTH 3.04. 70
SIBYLLA 1 FR 0.0001 REL FR 0 V 1 P
if i live to be as old as sibylla, i will die as MV 1.02.106 P

SIBYL'S 1 FR 0.0001 REL FR 1 V 0 P
blow these sands like sibyl's leaves abroad, TIT 4.01.105
SIBYLS 1 FR 0.0001 REL FR 1 V 0 P
hath, | exceeding the nine sibyls of old rome: 1H6 1.02. 56
SIC 1 FR 0.0001 REL FR 1 V 0 P
"sic spectanda fides." PER 2.02. 38
SICIL 1 FR 0.0001 REL FR 1 V 0 P
in presence of the kings of france and sicil, 2H6 1.01. 6
SICILIA 14 FR 0.0015 REL FR 7 V 7 P
difference betwixt our bohemia and your sicilia. WT 1.01. 4 P
the king of sicilia means to pay bohemia the 1.01. 6 P
sicilia cannot show himself overkind to bohemia. 1.01. 21 P
what means sicilia? 1.02.146
"sicilia is a so–forth." 1.02.218
queen to the worthy leontes, king of sicilia, 3.02. 13 P
of that fatal country sicilia, prithee speak no 4.02. 20 P
business, and lay aside the thoughts of sicilia. 4.02. 52 P
purchase the sight again of dear sicilia | and 4.04.511
make for sicilia, | and there present yourself 4.04.543
bohemia's son, | nor shall appear in sicilia. 4.04.589
in whose company | i shall re–view sicilia, for 4.04.666
by his command | have i here touch'd sicilia, 5.01.139
daughter unto reignier king of naples, sicilia, 2H6 1.01. 48 P
SICILIAN 1 FR 0.0001 REL FR 1 V 0 P
i have from your sicilian shores dismiss'd; WT 5.01.164
SICILIUS' 1 FR 0.0001 REL FR 1 V 0 P
praise o' th' world, | as great sicilius' heir. CYM 5.04. 51
SICILIUS 1 FR 0.0001 REL FR 1 V 0 P
his father | was call'd sicilius, who did join CYM 1.01. 29
SICILS 2 FR 0.0002 REL FR 2 V 0 P
of naples, | of both the sicils and jerusalem, 3H6 1.04.122
france | hath pawn'd the sicils and jerusalem, 5.07. 39
SICILY 6 FR 0.0006 REL FR 6 V 0 P
let what is dear in sicily be cheap. WT 1.02.175
now let hot aetna cool in sicily, | and be my TIT 3.01.241
and carry back to sicily much tall youth | that ANT 2.06. 7
you have made me offer | of sicily, sardinia; 2.06. 35
your mother came to sicily and did find | her 2.06. 45
having in sicily | sextus pompeius spoil'd, we 3.06. 24
SICINIUS 3 FR 0.0003 REL FR 3 V 0 P
sicinius velutus, and i know not — 'sdeath, COR 1.01.217
sicinius! 3.01.186
speak, good sicinius. 3.01.191
/SICK 2 FR 0.0002 REL FR 2 V 0 P
/commonwealth /is /sick /of /their /own /choice, 2H4 1.03. 87
/to /diet /rank /minds /sick /of /happiness, 4.01. 64
SICK 166 FR 0.0187 REL FR 134 V 32 P
wit with musing weak, heart sick with thought. TGV 1.01. 69
when i was sick, you gave me bitter pills, | and 2.04.149
by your leave, sir. i am sick till i see her. WIV 3.02. 28 P
longing, have been sick for, ere i'ld yield | my MM 2.04.103
but at this instant he is sick, my lord, | of a 5.01.151
how then? sick? ADO 2.01.291 P
the count is neither sad, nor sick, nor merry, 2.01.293 P
i am sick in displeasure to him, and whatsoever 2.02. 5 P
be how benedick | is sick in love with beatrice. 3.01. 21
why, how now? do you speak in the sick tune? 3.04. 42 P
by my troth, i am sick. 3.04. 72 P
art thou sick, or angry? 5.01.131 P
they swore that you were almost sick for me. 5.04. 80
up of aquitaine | to her decrepit, sick, and LLL 1.01.138
is the fool sick? 2.01.184
sick at the heart. 2.01.185
that the lover, sick to death, | /wish'd himself 4.03.105
bear with me, i am sick; 5.02.417
rest, | but seek the weary beds of people sick. 5.02.822
visit the speechless sick and still converse 5.02.851
spirit, | for i am sick when i do look on thee. MND 2.01.212
and i am sick when i look not on you. 2.01.213
they are as sick that surfeit with too much as MV 1.02. 6 P
not sick, my lord, unless it be in mind, | nor 3.02.234
which i denying, they fell sick and died. 3.04. 71
at the receipt of your letter i am very sick, 4.01.151 P
this night methinks is but the daylight sick, 5.01.124
cast away my physic but on those that are sick. AYL 3.02.359 P
who are sick | for breathing and exploit. AWW 1.02. 16
her eye is sick on't; 1.03.136
off, | but give thyself unto my sick desires, 4.02. 35
o, you are sick of self–love, malvolio, and TN 1.05. 90 P
if it be a suit from the count, i am sick, or 1.05.108 P
i told him you were sick; 1.05.140 P
i'll tell thee, i am almost sick for one — 3.01. 46 P
me, | for i am sick and capable of fears, JN 3.01. 12
are you sick, hubert? 4.01. 28
in sooth, i would you were a little sick, | that 4.01. 29
but you at your sick service had a prince. 4.01. 52
makes sound opinion sick, and truth suspected, 4.02. 26
was | before the child himself felt he was sick. 4.02. 88
for the present time's so sick, | that present 5.01. 14
o, my heart is sick! 5.03. 4
they say king john, sore sick, hath left the 5.04. 6
not sick, although i have to do with death, R2 1.03. 65
old john of gaunt is grievous sick, my lord, 1.04. 54
can sick men play so nicely with their names? 2.01. 84
land, | wherein thou liest in reputation sick, 2.01. 96
now comes the sick hour that his surfeit made, 2.02. 84
yet am i sick for fear, speak it again, | twice 5.03.133
such eyes | as, sick and blunted with community, 1H4 3.02. 77
he cannot come, my lord, he is grievous sick. 4.01. 16
how has he the leisure to be sick | in such a 4.01. 17
sick now? 4.01. 28
sick in the world's regard, wretched and low, 4.03. 57
having been well, that would have made me sick, 2H4 1.01.138
being sick, have (in some measure) made me well. 1.01.139
i heard say your lordship was sick, i hope your 1.02. 95 P
fathers being so sick as yours at this time is. 2.02. 31 P
that i should be sad, now my father is sick, 2.02. 40 P
heart bleeds inwardly that my father is so sick, 2.02. 48 P
though that be sick, it dies not. 2.02.105 P
sick of a calm, yea, good faith. 2.04. 36 P
and they be once in a calm, they are sick. 2.04. 38 P
lords, | i hear the king my father is sore sick. 4.03. 77
wherefore should these good news make me sick? 4.04.102
if he be sick with joy, he'll recover without 4.05. 14 P
o my poor kingdom, sick with civil blows! 4.05.133
i know the young king is sick for me. 5.03.135 P
he is very sick, and would to bed. H5 2.01. 82 P
to view the sick and feeble parts of france; 2.04. 22
his soldiers sick and famish'd in their march; 3.05. 57
in the wars do as every sick man in his bed, 4.01.179 P
o, be sick, great greatness, | and bid thy 4.01.251
that stout pendragon in his litter sick | came 1H6 3.02. 95
as i am sick with working of my thoughts. 5.05. 86
i would be blind with weeping, sick with groans, 2H6 3.02. 62
blood, my want of strength, my sick heart shows, 3H6 5.02. 8
that anne, my wife, is very grievous sick; R3 4.02. 51
that anne, my queen, is sick and like to die. 4.02. 57
by sick interpreters (once weak ones) is | not H8 1.02. 82
i would not be so sick though for his place. 2.02. 82
which | i then did feel full sick, and yet not 2.04.205
put my sick cause into his hands that hates me? 3.01.118
to kimmalton, | where she remains now sick. 4.01. 35
o griffith, sick to death! 4.02. 1
he fell sick suddenly and grew so ill | he could 4.02. 15
and she must thank ye, | she will be sick else. 5.04. 74
unless th' are drunk, sick, or have no legs. TRO 1.02. 17 P
of all high designs, | the enterprise is sick! 1.03.103
exampled by the first pace that is sick | of his 1.03.132
the fever whereof all our power is sick. 1.03.139
at the opening of his tent, | he is not sick. 2.03. 85
yes, lion–sick, sick of proud heart. 2.03. 86 P
come, your disposer is sick. 3.01. 89 P
no, your /poor disposer's sick. 3.01. 92 P
longing, | an appetite that i am sick withal, 3.03.238
and your affections are | a sick man's appetite, COR 1.01.178
being naked, sick, nor fane nor capitol, | the 1.10. 20
of lead, bright smoke, cold fire, sick health, ROM 1.01.180
/bid a sick man in sadness /make his will — | a 1.01.202
who is already sick and pale with grief | that 2.02. 5
her vestal livery is but sick and green, | and 2.02. 8
you'll be sick to–morrow | for this night's 4.04. 7
all night for lesser cause, and ne'er been sick. 4.04. 10
me, | here in this city visiting the sick, | and 5.02. 7
and, when he's sick to death, let not that part TIM 3.01. 61
many do keep their chambers are not sick; 3.04. 73
i am sick of that grief too, as i understand how 3.06. 17 P
honorable lord, i am e'en sick of shame that, 3.06. 41 P
city hang his poison | in the sick air. 4.03.111
that nature being sick of man's unkindness 4.03.176
i am sick of this false world, and will love 4.03.375
me some drink, titinius," | as a sick girl. JC 1.02.128
is brutus sick? 2.01.261
what, is brutus sick? 2.01.263
you have some sick offense within your mind, 2.01.268
here is a sick man that would speak with you. 2.01.310
would you were not sick! 2.01.315
i am not sick, if brutus have in hand | any 2.01.316
a piece of work that will make sick men whole. 2.01.327
but are not some whole that we must make sick? 2.01.328
say he is sick. 2.02. 65
o cassius, i am sick of many griefs. 4.03.144
i am sick at heart | when i behold — seyton, i MAC 5.03. 19
not so sick, my lord, | as she is troubled with 5.03. 37
'tis bitter cold, | and i am sick at heart. HAM 1.01. 9
was sick almost to doomsday with eclipse. 1.01.120
but woe is me, you are so sick of late, | so far 3.02.163
to my sick soul, as sin's true nature is, | each 4.05. 17
the world, that when we are sick in fortune — LR 1.02.119 P
say i am sick. 1.03. 8
they are sick? 2.04. 88
sick, o, sick! 5.03. 95
sick, o, sick! 5.03. 95
now, my sick fool roderigo, | whom love hath OTH 2.03. 51
if in mirth, report | that i am sudden sick. ANT 1.03. 5
i am sick and sullen. 1.03. 13
and quietness, grown sick of rest, would purge 1.03. 53
my heart | with pity that doth make me sick. CYM 1.06.119
if you are sick at sea, | or stomach–qualm'd at 3.04.189
i should be sick, | but that my resolution helps 3.06. 3
i am very sick. 4.02. 5
so sick i am not, yet i am not well; 4.02. 7
citizen a wanton as | to seem to die ere sick. 4.02. 9
i am not very sick, | since i can reason of it. 4.02. 13
i am sick still, heart–sick. 4.02. 37
pray, be not sick, | for you must be our huswife 4.02. 44
as juno had been sick | and he her dieter. 4.02. 50
poor sick fidele! 4.02.166
am i better | than one that's sick o' th' gout, 5.04. 5
and, as sick men do | who know the world, see PER 1.01. 47
i am persuaded this question, sick between 's, TNK 3.01.113
heal'st with blood | the earth when it is sick, 5.01. 65
for my sick heart commands mine eyes to watch. VEN 584
to one sore sick that hears the passing bell. 702
let their exhal'd unwholesome breaths make sick LUC 779
give physic to the sick, ease to the pained? 901
untimely breathings, sick and short assays, 1720
passage find, | that the lover, sick to death, PP 16. 7
and my sick muse doth give another place. SON 79. 4
i was not sick of any fear from thence: 86.12
and, sick of welfare, found a kind of meetness 118. 7
drugs poison him that so fell sick of you. 118.14
as testy sick men, when their deaths be near, 140. 7
i, sick withal, the help of bath desired, | and 153.11
SICK'D 1 FR 0.0001 REL FR 1 V 0 P
our great–grandsire, edward, sick'd and died. 2H4 4.04.128
SICKEN 8 FR 0.0009 REL FR 8 V 0 P
he may be so fitted | that his soul sicken not. MM 2.04. 41
the appetite may sicken, and so die. TN 1.01. 3
when love begins to sicken and decay | it useth JC 4.02. 20
all together, | even till destruction sicken; MAC 4.01. 60
in their caps, | dying or e'er they sicken. 4.03.173
mine eyes did sicken at the sight and could not ANT 3.10. 16
i might sicken, cousin, | where you should never TNK 2.02. 91
we sicken to shun sickness when we purge; SON 118. 4
SICKEN'D 1 FR 0.0001 REL FR 1 V 0 P
that have | by this so sicken'd their estates, H8 1.01. 82
SICKENS 2 FR 0.0002 REL FR 1 V 1 P
i know the more one sickens the worse at ease he AYL 3.02. 24 P
whose nature sickens but to speak a truth. AWW 5.03.207
SICKER 1 FR 0.0001 REL FR 1 V 0 P
o no, thou diest, though i the sicker be. R2 2.01. 91
SICK–FALL'N 1 FR 0.0001 REL FR 1 V 0 P
waits, | as doth a raven on a sick–fall'n beast, JN 4.03.153
SICKLE 1 FR 0.0001 REL FR 1 V 0 P
dost hold time's fickle glass, his sickle, hour; SON 126. 2
SICKLEMEN 1 FR 0.0001 REL FR 1 V 0 P
you sunburn'd sicklemen, of august weary, | come TMP 4.01.134
SICKLE'S 1 FR 0.0001 REL FR 1 V 0 P
within his bending sickle's compass come, | love SON 116.10
SICKLIED 1 FR 0.0001 REL FR 1 V 0 P
is sicklied o'er with the pale cast of thought, HAM 3.01. 84
SICKLINESS 1 FR 0.0001 REL FR 1 V 0 P
words | to wayward sickliness and age in him. R2 2.01.142
SICKLY 20 FR 0.0022 REL FR 19 V 1 P
i am not such a sickly creature, i give heaven WIV 3.04. 59 P
then, if sickly ears, | deaf'd with the clamors LLL 5.02.863
know'st she has rais'd me from my sickly bed. AWW 2.03.111
and hence, thou sickly coif! 2H4 1.01.147
my army but a weak and sickly guard; H5 3.06.155
scarce blood enough in all their sickly veins 4.02. 20
the king is sickly, weak, and melancholy, | and R3 1.01.136
is this thy vow unto my sickly heart. 2.01. 42
rule, | this sickly land might solace as before. 2.03. 30
thy lord look well, | for he went sickly forth; JC 2.04. 14
downward look on us | as we were sickly prey. 5.01. 86
who wear our health but sickly in his life, MAC 3.01.106
meet we the med'cine of the sickly weal, | and 5.02. 27
this physic but prolongs thy sickly days. HAM 3.03. 96
or but a sickly part of one true sense | could 3.04. 80
to take the indispos'd and sickly fit | for the LR 2.04.111
of honor, cold and sickly | he vented /them, ANT 3.04. 7
thyself) | than i will trust a sickly appetite, TNK 1.03. 89
ill, | th' uncertain sickly appetite to please. SON 147. 4
weak sights their sickly radiance do amend; LC 214
SICKNESS 53 FR 0.0060 REL FR 51 V 2 P
diet his sickness, for it is my office, | and ERR 5.01. 99
with anger, with sickness, or with hunger, my ADO 1.01.249 P
go, sickness as thou art! LLL 5.02.280
war, death, or sickness did lay siege to it, MND 1.01.142
sickness is catching; 1.01.186
but like a sickness did i loathe this food; 4.01.173
'twere deadly sickness or else present death. SHR 4.03. 14
nature and sickness | debate it at their leisure AWW 1.02. 74
health shall live free, and sickness freely die. 2.01.168
there is a sickness | which puts some of us in WT 1.02.384
a sickness caught of me, and yet i well? 1.02.398
'tis hop'd his sickness is discharg'd. 2.03. 11
'tis a sickness denying thee any thing; 4.02. 2 P
indeed we fear'd his sickness was past cure. JN 4.02. 86
o vanity of sickness! 5.07. 13
join with the present sickness that i have, R2 2.01.132
shivering cold and sickness pines the clime; 5.01. 77
whole | ere he by sickness had been visited, 1H4 4.01. 26
this sickness doth infect | the very life–blood 4.01. 28
he writes me here, that inward sickness — | and 4.01. 31
your father's sickness is a maim to us. 4.01. 42
what with the sickness of northumberland, 4.04. 14
hours perforce must add | unto your sickness. 2H4 3.01.106
till his friend sickness /have determin'd me? 4.05. 81
on, and sickness growing | upon our soldiers, we H5 3.03. 55
my people are with sickness much enfeebled, | my 3.06.145
place, | fitter for sickness and for crazy age. 1H6 3.02. 89
for suddenly a grievous sickness took him, 2H6 3.02.370
hath made me full of sickness and diseases. 4.07. 89
from wayward sickness and no grounded malice. R3 1.03. 29
i do lament the sickness of the king, | as loath 2.02. 9
that, had the king in his last sickness fail'd, H8 1.02.184
where eagerly his sickness | pursu'd him still, 4.02. 24
to one man's honor, this contagious sickness, 5.02. 61
the nature of the sickness found, ulysses, TRO 1.03.140
be of any power | to expel sickness, but prolong TIM 3.01. 63
which argues a great sickness in his judgment 5.01. 29
my long sickness | of health and living now 5.01.186
'tis very like, he hath the falling sickness. JC 1.02.254
and honest casca, we have the falling sickness. 1.02.256
and unpurged air | to add unto his sickness? 2.01.267
romans bow before, | i here discard my sickness! 2.01.321
upon what sickness? 4.03.152
that so his sickness, age, and impotence | was HAM 2.02. 66
it warms the very sickness in my heart | that i 4.07. 55
my sickness grows upon me. LR 5.03.105
her length of sickness, with what else more ANT 1.02.120
noble antony, | not sickness should detain me. 2.02.170
bid my woman feign a sickness, say | she'll home CYM 3.02. 74
the boy fidele's sickness | did make my way long 4.02.148
sickness in will | /o'er–wrastling strength in TNK 1.04. 44
the marrow–eating sickness, whose attaint VEN 741
we sicken to shun sickness when we purge; SON 118. 4
SICK–THOUGHTED 1 FR 0.0001 REL FR 1 V 0 P
sick–thoughted venus makes amain unto him, | and VEN 5
SICLES 1 FR 0.0001 REL FR 1 V 0 P
not with fond sicles of the tested gold, | or MM 2.02.149
SICYON 3 FR 0.0003 REL FR 3 V 0 P
from sicyon how the news? speak there! ANT 1.02.113
the man from sicyon — is there such an one? 1.02.114
in sicyon: 1.02.119
/SIDE* 6 FR 0.0006 REL FR 6 V 0 P
/on /this /side /my /hand, /and /on /that /side R2 4.01.183
/side /my /hand, /and /on /that /side /thine. 4.01.183
/their /weapons /only | /seem'd /on /our /side; 2H4 1.01.198
/on /one /and /other /side, /troyan /and /greek, TRO pr 21
/of /equity, | /bench /by /his /side. LR 3.06. 38
evil | tempteth my better angel from my /side, SON 144. 6
SIDE* 165 FR 0.0186 REL FR 139 V 26 P
of troy become, | and by my side wear steel? WIV 1.03. 76
it in the muddy ditch close by the thames side. 3.03. 16 P
him hide, | though angel on the outward side! MM 3.02.272
whose western side is with a vineyard back'd; 4.01. 29
he speak against me on the adverse side, | i 4.06. 6
poor fool, it keeps on the windy side of care. ADO 2.01.315 P
so turns she every man the wrong side out, | and 3.01. 68
pearls, down sleeves, side sleeves, and skirts, 3.04. 20 P
dost thou wear thy wit by thy side? 5.01.126 P
on whose side? LLL 4.01. 75 P
on whose side? 4.01. 76 P
on whose side? 4.01. 77 P
armado /a' /th' /one side — o, a most dainty 4.01.144
and his page a' t'other side, that handful of 4.01.147
well prov'd again a' my side! 4.03. 8 P
this side is hiems, winter; 5.02.891 P
full often hath she gossip'd by my side, | and MND 2.01.125
then by your side no bed–room me deny; 2.02. 51
too — | and the athenian woman by his side; 3.02. 39

what love could press lysander from my side? 3.02.185
which, touching but my gentle vessel's side, MV 1.01. 32
for never shall you lie by portia's side | with 3.02.305
with spectacles on nose and pouch on side, | his AYL 2.07.159
damn'd, like an ill–roasted egg all on one side. 3.02. 38 P
that spurs his horse but on one side, breaks his 3.04. 44 P
madam wife, sit by my side, and let the world SHR in.2. 143 P
sit, my preserver, by thy patient's side, | and AWW 2.03. 47
how quickly the wrong side may be turn'd outward TN 3.01. 13 P
still you keep o' th' windy side of the law; 3.04.164 P
he did me kindness, sir, drew on my side, | but 5.01. 66
that most ingrateful boy there by your side 5.01. 77
against this cruelty fight on thy side, | poor WT 2.03.191
sometimes her head on one side, some another — 3.03. 20
i would you had been by the ship side, to have 3.03.109 P
though the pennyworth on his side be the worst, 4.04.636 P
brother by th' mother's side, give me your hand; JN 1.01.163
cull forth | out of one side her happy minion, 2.01.392
and all that we upon this side the sea | (except 2.01.488
thou ever strong upon the stronger side! 3.01.117
hast thou not spoke like thunder on my side? 3.01.124
which is the side that i must go withal? 3.01.327
whoever wins, on that side shall i lose; 3.01.335
to train ten thousand english to their side, 3.04.175
that i must draw this metal from my side | to be 5.02. 16
as far as land will let me, by your side. R2 1.03.252
and will, i fear, revolt on herford's side. 2.02. 89
where one on his side fights, thousands will fly 2.02.147
all souls that will be safe, fly from my side, 3.02. 80
he, from the one side to the other turning, 5.02. 18
thou hadst fire and sword on thy side, and yet 1H4 2.04.317 P
me up | with like advantage on the other side, 3.01.108
much | as on the other side it takes from you. 3.01.110
and on this north side win this cape of land, 3.01.112
for well you know we of the off'ring side | must 4.01. 69
and will, to save the blood on either side, 5.01. 99
though it be a shame to be on any side but one, 2H4 1.02. 75 P
worse shame to beg than to be on the worst side, 1.02. 76 P
and by his bloody side | (yoke–fellow to his H5 4.06. 8
the duke of alanson flieth to his side. 1H6 1.01. 95
late did he shine upon the english side; 1.02. 3
deck'd with /five flower–de–luces on each side, 1.02. 99
one of thy eyes and thy cheek's side struck off! 1.04. 75
the truth appears so naked on my side | that any 2.04. 20
and on my side it is so well apparell'd, | so 2.04. 22
till you conclude that he upon whose side | the 2.04. 40
giving my verdict on the white rose side. 2.04. 48
red, | and fall on my side so against your will. 2.04. 51
and keep me on the side where still i am. 2.04. 54
fear, as witnessing | the truth on our side. 2.04. 64
no more can i be severed from your side | than 4.05. 48
come, side by side, together live and die, | and 4.05. 54
come, side by side, together live and die, | and 4.05. 54
if thou wilt fight, fight by thy father's side, 4.06. 56
suddenly made him from my side to start | into 4.07. 12
blood, | and stablish quietness on every side. 5.01. 10
peace, | and lay them gently on thy tender side. 5.03. 49
this evening, on the east side of the grove. 2H6 2.01. 42
are ye advis'd? the east side of the grove. 2.01. 47
thus is the shepherd beaten from thy side, | and 3.01.191
as if duke humphrey's ghost | were by his side; 3.02.374
and on our longboat's side | strike off his head 4.01. 68
god on our side, doubt not of victory. 4.08. 52
and full as oft came edward to my side | with 3H6 1.04. 11
she, on his left side, craving aid for henry; 3.01. 43
still like thyself, | and sit thee by our side. 3.03. 16
him | in secret ambush on the forest side, | and 4.06. 83
come thou on my side, and entreat for me, | as R3 1.04.265
but that i'll give my voice on richard's side 3.02. 53
speak and look back, and pry on every side, 3.05. 6
then, on the other side, i check'd my friends. 3.07.150
but on thy side i may not be too forward, | lest 5.03. 94
god and good angels fight on richmond's side, 5.03.175
god and our good cause fight upon our side; 5.03.240
whose puissance on either side | shall be well 5.03.299
what men of name are slain on either side? 5.05. 12
place you that side, i'll take the charge of H8 1.04. 20
to th' water side i must conduct your grace; 2.01. 95
were those that went on each side of the queen? 4.01.100
a' th' t' other side, the policy of those crafty TRO 5.04. 9 P
the other side a' th' city is risen; COR 1.01. 47 P
point of battle, | the one side must have bale. 1.01.163
side factions, and give out | conjectural 1.01.193
know you on which side | they have plac'd their 1.06. 51
these are a side that would be glad to have 4.06.150
though we had | our wish, which side should win; 5.03.113
and each in either side | give the all–hail to 5.03.138
gave you a dancing–rapier by your side, | are TIT 2.01. 39
upon the north side of this pleasant chase; 2.03.255
nay, he is your brother by the surer side, 4.02.126
tree, | and by his side his fruit of bastardy. 5.01. 48
lo by thy side where rape and murder stands; 5.02. 45
is the law of our side if i say ay? ROM 1.01. 47 P
that westward rooteth from this city side, | so 1.01.122
turning his side to the dew–dropping south. 1.04.103
in a good quarrel, and the law on my side. 2.04.160 P
my back a' t' other side — ah, my back, my back 2.05. 50
as he was coming from this churchyard's side. 5.03.186
o constancy, be strong upon my side, | set a JC 2.04. 6
with ate by his side come hot from hell, | shall 3.01.271
and new–planted orchards, | on this side tiber; 3.02.249
wherein my letters, praying on his side, 4.03. 4
bills | unto the legions on the other side. 5.02. 2
(for so this side of our known world esteem'd HAM 1.01. 85
your grace has laid the odds a' th' weaker side. 5.02.261
to keep one's eyes of either side 's nose, that LR 1.05. 22 P
one side will mock another; th' other too. 3.07. 71
and told me i had turn'd the wrong side out. 4.02. 9
goneril, | and hardly shall i carry out my side, 5.01. 61
more, | to pluck the common bosom on his side, 5.03. 49
whose messengers are here about my side, | upon OTH 1.02. 89
whom love hath turn'd almost the wrong side out, 2.03. 52
lie by an emperor's side and command him tasks. 4.01.185 P
that turn'd your wit the seamy side without, 4.02.146
but to go hang my head all at one side | and 4.03. 32
yea, curse his better angel from his side, | and 5.02.208
ay, ay! o, lay me by my mistress' side. 5.02.237
thou hast a sister by the mother's side, ANT 2.02.118
on each side her | stood pretty dimpled boys, 2.02.201
therefore, o antony, stay not by his side. 2.03. 19
set we our squadrons on yond side o' th' hill, 3.09. 1
on our side like the token'd pestilence, | where 3.10. 9
look out o' th' other side your monument, | his 4.15. 8
fetch thee up, | and set thee by jove's side. 4.15. 36
of his endowments had been tabled by his side, CYM 1.04. 6 P
on either side i come to spend my breath; 5.03. 81
stand by my side, you whom the gods have made 5.05. 1
come, stand thou by our side, | make thy demand 5.05.129
shelter that abuts against | the island's side. PER 5.01. 52
into twain and doing | each side like justice, TNK 1.03. 47
upon my right side still i wore thy picture, 5.03. 73
on the sinister side the heart lies; 5.03. 76
so he were like him, and by venus' side. VEN 180
by this the boy that by her side lay kill'd 1165
then collatine again by lucrece' side | in his LUC 381
swelling on either side to want his bliss; 389
not suppress'd, for standing by her side, | his 425
blood | circles her body in on every side, | who 1739
who pluck'd the knife from lucrece' side, 1807
evil | tempteth my better angel from my side; PP 2. 6
more sharp to me than spurring to his side, SON 50.12
upon thy side against myself i'll fight, | and 88. 3
be, | to stand in thy affairs, fall by thy side. 151.12
laid by his side his heart–inflaming brand, 154. 2
bat, | and comely distant sits he by her side; LC 65
"but quickly on this side the verdict went: 113
SIDED 1 FR 0.0001 REL FR 1 V 0 P
vexed, whom we see have sided | in his behalf. COR 4.02. 2
SIDE–PIERCING 1 FR 0.0001 REL FR 1 V 0 P
o thou side–piercing sight! LR 4.06. 85
/SIDES 1 FR 0.0001 REL FR 0 V 1 P
/has /been /much /to /do /on /both /sides, /and HAM 2.02.353 P
SIDES 44 FR 0.0049 REL FR 36 V 8 P
i will keep my sides to myself, my shoulders for WIV 5.05. 25 P
arms, legs, backs, shoulders, sides, and shins. 5.05. 54
writ a' both sides the leaf, margent and all, LLL 5.02. 8
as if our hands, our sides, voices, and minds MND 3.02.207
longs to see this broken music in his sides? AYL 1.02.142 P
our cake's dough on both sides. SHR 1.01.109 P
taurus? that/'s sides and heart. TN 1.03.139 P
there is no woman's sides | can bide the beating 2.04. 93
justly weigh'd | that have on both sides pass'd. 5.01.368
he hath drunk, he cracks his gorge, his sides, WT 2.01. 44
let nature crush the sides o' th' earth together 4.04.478
upon our sides it never shall be broken. JN 5.02. 8
against the panting sides of his poor jade | up 2H4 1.01. 45
and would not dash me with their ragged sides, 2H6 3.02. 98
battles join'd, and both sides fiercely fought; 3H6 2.01.121
such which breaks | the sides of loyalty, and H8 1.02. 28
read, | and on all sides th' authority allow'd; 2.04. 4
fools on both sides, helen must needs be fair, TRO 1.01. 90
boat | whose weak untimber'd sides but even now 1.03. 43
a man may wear it on both sides, like a leather 3.03.264 P
there is expectance here from both the sides, 4.05.146
on both sides more respect. COR 3.01.180
let us take the law of our sides, let them begin ROM 1.01. 38 P
it is the paster lards the brother's sides, TIM 4.03. 12
lug your priests and servants from your sides, 4.03. 32
hack'd one another in the sides of caesar. JC 5.01. 40
have no spur | to prick the sides of my intent, MAC 1.07. 26
both sides are even; 3.04. 10
the tyrant's people on both sides do fight, 5.07. 25
matter, if we could carry a cannon by our sides; HAM 5.02.159 P
they bleed on both sides. how is it, my lord? 5.02.304
thou hast par'd thy wit o' both sides, and left LR 1.04.187 P
o sides, you are too tough! 2.04.197
how shall your houseless heads and unfed sides, 3.04. 30
being strong on both sides, are equivocal. OTH 1.03.217
going on, | the sides o' th' world may danger. ANT 1.02.192
long, the sides of nature | will not sustain it. 1.03. 16
/bear as loud | as his strong sides can volley. 2.07.112
o, cleave, my sides! 4.14. 39
can my sides hold, to think that man, who knows CYM 1.06. 69
it did almost stretch | the sides o' th' world, 3.01. 50
/ravish'd our sides, like age, must run to rust, TNK 2.02. 22
"his brawny sides, with hairy bristles armed, VEN 625
on both sides thus is simple truth suppress'd. SON 138. 8
SIDE–STITCHES 1 FR 0.0001 REL FR 1 V 0 P
side–stitches, that shall pen thy breath up; TMP 1.02.326
SIEGE 33 FR 0.0037 REL FR 30 V 3 P
cam'st thou to be the siege of this moon–calf? TMP 2.02.106 P
it, as to lay an amiable siege to the honesty of WIV 2.02.234 P
upon the very siege of justice | lord angelo MM 4.02. 98
war, death, or sickness did lay siege to it, MND 1.01.142
lays down his wanton siege before her beauty, AWW 3.07. 18
then turn your forces from this paltry siege, JN 2.01. 54
all preparation for a bloody siege | and 2.01.213
and his siege is now | against the /mind, the 5.07. 16
whose rocky shore beats back the envious siege R2 2.01. 62
girding with grievous siege castles and towns; H5 1.02.152
work your thoughts, and therein see a siege; 3.pr. 25
to whom the order of the siege is given, is 3.02. 66 P
are yet not ready | to raise so great a siege. 3.03. 47
lord, | retiring from the siege of orleance, 1H6 1.01.111
let's raise the siege; 1.02. 13
walls they'll tear down than forsake the siege. 1.02. 40
ordained is to raise this tedious siege, | and 1.02. 53
this night the siege assuredly i'll raise: 1.02.130
leave off delays, and let us raise the siege. 1.02.146
is come with a great power to raise the siege. 1.04.103
of horsemen, that were levied for this siege! 4.03. 11
that lays strong siege unto this wretch's soul, 2H6 3.03. 22
after seven years' siege yet troy walls stand, TRO 1.03. 12
she will not stay the siege of loving terms, ROM 1.01.212
you, to remove that siege of grief from her, 5.03.237
(to whom all sores lay siege) can bear great TIM 4.03. 7
castle's strength | will laugh a siege to scorn; MAC 5.05. 3
that, in my regard, | of the unworthiest siege. HAM 4.07. 76
my life and being | from men of royal siege, and OTH 1.02. 22
hath been to me | as fearful as a siege. CYM 3.04.134
remove your siege from my unyielding heart, | to VEN 423
this siege that hath engirt his marriage, | this LUC 221
against the wrackful siege of batt'ring days, SON 65. 6
SIEGES 1 FR 0.0001 REL FR 1 V 0 P
year to year — the /battles, sieges, /fortunes, OTH 1.03.130
SIENNA'S 1 FR 0.0001 REL FR 1 V 0 P
the conduct of bold jachimo, | sienna's brother. CYM 4.02.341
SIENNESE *(see senoys)*
SIEVE 4 FR 0.0004 REL FR 4 V 0 P
mine ears as profitless | as water in a sieve. ADO 5.01. 5
yet in this captious and intenible sieve | i AWW 1.03.202
viands | we do not throw in unrespective sieve, TRO 2.02. 71
but in a sieve i'll thither sail, | and, like a MAC 1.03. 8
SIFT 3 FR 0.0003 REL FR 3 V 0 P
we'll sift this matter further. AWW 5.03.124
as near as i could sift him on that argument, R2 1.01. 12
well, we shall sift him. HAM 2.02. 58
SIFTED 1 FR 0.0001 REL FR 1 V 0 P
beside, i fear me, if thy thoughts were sifted, 1H6 3.01. 24
/SIGEIA 3 FR 0.0003 REL FR 1 V 2 P
hic est /sigeia tellus; SHR 3.01. 28
son unto vincentio of pisa, "/sigeia tellus," 3.01. 33 P
i know you not, "hic est /sigeia tellus," i 3.01. 42 P
/SIGH 1 FR 0.0001 REL FR 1 V 0 P
/thou /shalt /not /sigh, /nor /hold /thy /stumps TIT 3.02. 42
SIGH 60 FR 0.0067 REL FR 45 V 15 P
to sigh | to th' winds, whose pity, sighing back TMP 1.02.149
to sigh, like a schoolboy that had lost his abc; TGV 2.01. 22 P
o'erslips me in the day | wherein i sigh not, 2.02. 10
to that i'll speak, to that i'll sigh and weep; 4.02.122
a milkmaid, if she be in love, may sigh it off. MM 1.02.174 P
wear the print of it, and sigh away sundays. ADO 1.01.201 P
sigh no more, ladies, sigh no more, | men were 2.03. 62
sigh no more, ladies, sigh no more, | men were 2.03. 62
then sigh not so, but let them go, | and be you 2.03. 66
then sigh not so, etc. 2.03. 74
what? sigh for the toothache? 3.02. 26 P
yet at last she concluded with a sigh, thou wast 5.01.172 P
assist our moan, | help us to sigh and groan, 5.03. 17
i think scorn to sigh; LLL 1.02. 63 P
up your eyelids, sigh a note and sing a note, 3.01. 13 P
favor, sweet welkin, i must sigh in thy face: 3.01. 67
love's whip, | a very beadle to a humorous sigh, 3.01.175
and i to sigh for her, to watch for her, | to 3.01.200
well, i will love, write, sigh, pray, sue, groan 3.01.204
eyes | thus with my hat, and sigh and say amen, MV 2.02.194
head, relent, and sigh, and yield | to christian 3.03. 15
i'll go find a shadow, and sigh till he come. AYL 4.01.217 P
lord, let me never have a cause to sigh, | till SHR 5.02.123
and then to sigh, as 'twere | the mort o' th' WT 1.02.117
stopping the career | of laughter with a sigh (a 1.02.287
that creep like shadows by him and do sigh | at 2.03. 34
if i may ever know thou dost but sigh | that 4.04.427
my heart will sigh when i miscall it so, | which R2 1.03.263
with | a rising sigh he wisheth you in heaven. 1H4 3.01. 10
thou hast a sigh to blow away this praise, 2H4 1.01. 80
why should you sigh, my lord? 3H6 1.01.191
and many an old man's sigh and many a widow's, 5.06. 39
but then i sigh, and, with a piece of scripture, R3 1.03.333
would insinuate with thee but to make thee sigh. 1.04.149 P
as wedged with a sigh, would rive in twain, TRO 1.01. 35
buried this sigh in wrinkle of a smile, | but 1.01. 38
why sigh you so profoundly? 4.02. 80 P
appear thou in the likeness of a sigh! ROM 2.01. 8
what a sigh is there! MAC 5.01. 53 P
he rais'd a sigh so piteous and profound | as it HAM 2.01. 91
and target, the lover shall not sigh gratis, the 2.02.322 P
never alone | did the king sigh, but /with a 3.03. 23
then this "should" is like a spendthrift's sigh, 4.07.122
melancholy, with a sigh like tom o' bedlam. LR 1.02.135 P
wherefore breaks that sigh | from th' inward of CYM 3.04. 5
nobly he yokes | a smiling with a sigh, as if 4.02. 52
as if the sigh | was that it was for not being 4.02. 52
the smile mocking the sigh, that it would fly 4.02. 54
(such as i can) twice o'er, i'll weep and sigh, 4.02.392
love, but i | and she (i sigh and spoke of) were TNK 1.03. 60
yet sometime a divided sigh, martyr'd as 'twere 2.01. 41 P
that i could wish myself a sigh to be so chid, 2.01. 44 P
i say again, | that sigh was breath'd for emily. 3.03. 44
say, began to throw | her bow away, and sigh. 5.01. 94
and vow that lover never yet made sigh | truer 5.01.125
i'll sigh celestial breath, whose gentle wind VEN 189
for now 'tis stale to sigh, to weep, and groan. LUC 1362
here with a sigh, as if her heart would break, 1716
for these dead birds sigh a prayer. PHT 67
i sigh the lack of many a thing i sought, | and SON 30. 3
SIGH'D *(also sight*)*
/SIGH'D 1 FR 0.0001 REL FR 1 V 0 P
laid his leg | /over my thigh, and /sigh'd, and OTH 3.03.425
SIGH'D 10 FR 0.0011 REL FR 8 V 2 P
the first | that e'er i sigh'd for. TMP 1.02.447
and sigh'd his soul toward the grecian tents, MV 5.01. 5
a lover | as ever sigh'd upon a midnight pillow. AYL 2.04. 27
no sooner lov'd but they sigh'd; 5.02. 34 P
no sooner sigh'd but they ask'd one another the 5.02. 35 P
and sigh'd my english breath in foreign clouds, R2 3.01. 20
sigh'd forth proverbs — | that hunger broke COR 1.01.205
never man | sigh'd truer breath; 4.05.115
and then she wept, and sung again, and sigh'd, TNK 4.01. 92
which she perus'd, sigh'd, tore, and gave the LC 44
SIGHED 2 FR 0.0002 REL FR 2 V 0 P
with that she sighed as she stood, | with that AWW 1.03. 74
she stood, | with that she sighed as she stood, 1.03. 75
SIGHER 1 FR 0.0001 REL FR 0 V 1 P
so chid, or at least a sigher to be comforted. TNK 2.01. 44 P
/SIGHING 3 FR 0.0003 REL FR 3 V 0 P
/through /proud /london /he /came /sighing /on 2H4 1.03.104
/wound /it /with /sighing, /girl, /kill /it TIT 3.02. 15
"the poor soul sat /sighing by a sycamore tree, OTH 4.03. 40
SIGHING 8 FR 0.0009 REL FR 6 V 2 P
to th' winds, whose pity, sighing back again, TMP 1.02.150
sighing like furnace, with a woeful ballad AYL 2.07.148
else sighing every minute and groaning every 3.02.303 P
a plague of sighing and grief, it blows a man up 1H4 2.04.332 P
my sighing breast shall be thy funeral bell; 3H6 2.05.117
ever smiles, | and farewell goes out sighing. TRO 3.03.169
musing and sighing, with your arms across; JC 2.01.240
and sighing it again, exclaims on death. VEN 930
/SIGHS 1 FR 0.0001 REL FR 1 V 0 P
she gave me for my pains a world of /sighs; OTH 1.03.159
SIGHS 66 FR 0.0074 REL FR 60 V 6 P
whom i left cooling of the air with sighs, | in TMP 1.02.222
coy looks with heart–sore sighs; TGV 1.01. 30

were down, i could drive the boat with my sighs. 2.03. 54 P
with nightly tears, and daily heart–sore sighs, 2.04.132
sad sighs, deep groans, nor silver–shedding 3.01.232
beauty | you sacrifice your tears, your sighs, 3.02. 73
fire, | consume away in sighs, waste inwardly. ADO 3.01. 78
th' anointed sovereign of sighs and groans, LLL 3.01.182
saw sighs reek from you, noted well your passion 4.03.138
of sighs, of groans, of sorrow, and of teen! 4.03.162
until his ink were temp'red with love's sighs: 4.03.344
as due to love as thoughts and dreams and sighs, MND 1.01.154
she is and pale of cheer | with sighs of love, 3.02. 97
a' my shoulders, no sighs but a' my breathing, MV 3.01. 95 P
it is to be all made of sighs and tears, | and AYL 5.02. 84
love, that god most high, | do my sighs stream. AWW 2.03. 76
groans that thunder love, with sighs of fire. TN 1.05.256
what thriftless sighs shall poor olivia breathe? 2.02. 39
a thousand thousand sighs to save, | lay me, o, 2.04. 63
she thus advises thee that sighs for thee. 2.05.152 P
our sighs and they shall lodge the summer corn, R2 3.03.162
go count thy way with sighs, i mine with groans. 5.01. 89
and with sighs they jar | their watches on unto 5.05. 51
so sighs, and tears, and groans | show minutes, 5.05. 57
behold | my sighs and tears, and will not once 1H6 3.01.108
or blood–consuming sighs recall his life, | i 2H6 3.02. 61
look pale as primrose with blood–drinking sighs, 3.02. 63
whom a thousand sighs are breath'd for thee! 3.02.345
her sighs will make a batt'ry in his breast, 3H6 3.01. 37
and stop the rising of blood–sucking sighs, 4.04. 22
lest with my sighs or tears i blast or drown 4.04. 23
that with so many thousand sighs | did buy each TRO 4.04. 39
thinking on his bed | of thee and me, and sighs, 5.02. 79
i have been blown out of your gates with sighs, COR 5.02. 75 P
or with our sighs we'll breathe the welkin dim, TIT 3.01.211
hark how her sighs doth /blow! 3.01.225
then must my sea be moved with her sighs; 3.01.227
to clouds more clouds with his deep sighs, | but ROM 1.01.133
love is a smoke made with the fume of sighs, 1.01.190
the sun not yet thy sighs from heaven clears, 2.03. 73
the winds, thy sighs, | who, raging with thy 3.05.134
is a friar, that trembles, sighs, and weeps. 5.03.184
where sighs, and groans, and shrieks that rent MAC 4.03.168
there's matter in these sighs, these profound HAM 4.01. 1
call her winds and waters sighs and tears; ANT 1.02.148 P
then shall the sighs of octavia blow the fire up 2.06.127 P
he furnaces | the thick sighs from him, whiles CYM 1.06. 67
with sighs shot through and biggest tears PER 4.04. 26
bring away, | vapors, sighs, darken the day; TNK 1.05. 2
then with her windy sighs and golden hairs | to VEN 51
being steel'd, soft sighs can never grave it. 376
sorrow that friendly sighs sought still to dry; 964
sighs dry her cheeks, tears make them wet again. 966
my sighs are blown away, my salt tears gone, 1071
her modest eloquence with sighs is mixed, LUC 563
my sighs like whirlwinds labor hence to heave 586
be moved with my tears, my sighs, my groans. 588
when sighs and groans and tears may grace the 1319
three times with sighs she gives her sorrow fire 1604
even so his sighs, his sorrows, make a saw, | to 1672
her contrite sighs unto the clouds bequeathed 1727
with sighs so deep procures to weep, | in PP 17.21
how sighs resound through heartless ground, 17.23
or heart in love with sighs himself doth smother SON 47. 4
/hallowed with sighs that burning lungs did LC 228
and supplicant their sighs to you extend | to 276

SIGH'ST 1 FR 0.0001 REL FR 1 V 0 P
heart, | why sigh'st thou without breaking?" TRO 4.04. 17

SIGHT* *(also sigh'd)*

/SIGHT* 2 FR 0.0002 REL FR 2 V 0 P
hath abjur'd the /company | and /sight of men. TN 1.02. 41
/and /go /with /me, /thy /sight /is /young, TIT 3.02. 84

SIGHT* 225 FR 0.0254 REL FR 206 V 19 P
be subject | to no sight but thine and mine, TMP 1.02.302
at the first sight | they have chang'd eyes. 1.02.441
which i wear in my head, here's a goodly sight. 5.01.260 P
or else return no more into my sight. TGV 1.02. 47
you | now valentine is banish'd from her sight. 3.02. 2
again, | or ne'er return again into my sight. 4.04. 60
that could but niggardly give me sight of her; WIV 2.02.198 P
upon their sight, | we two in great amazedness 4.04. 55
only to stick it in their children's sight | for MM 1.03. 25
stead me | as bring me to the sight of isabella, 1.04. 18
you shall not be admitted to his sight. 4.03.120
and in our sight they three were taken up | by ERR 1.01.110
when you should, and that will clear your sight. 3.02. 57
keep him out of my sight when the dance is done! ADO 2.01.109 P
the sight whereof i think you had from me, 5.04. 25
to–morrow you shall have a sight of them. LLL 2.01.165
come on then, wear the favors most in sight. 5.02.136
we must starve our sight | from lovers' food MND 1.01.222
to have his sight thither and back again. 1.01.251
take heed the queen come not within his sight; 2.01. 19
and ere i take this charm from off her sight 2.01.183
sky, | so, at his sight, away his fellows fly; 3.02. 24
laid the love–juice on some true–love's sight. 3.02. 89
and make his eyeballs roll with wonted sight. 3.02.369
thou tak'st | true delight | in the sight | of 3.02.456
seest thou this sweet sight? 4.01. 46
i trust to take of truest thisby sight. 5.01.275
wrastling, which you have lost the sight of. AYL 1.02.111 P
though it be pity to see such a sight, it well 3.02.242 P
the sight of lovers feedeth those in love. 3.04. 57
bring us to this sight, and you shall say | i'll 3.04. 58
heart th' accustom'd sight of death makes hard, 3.05. 4
see, | none could be so abus'd in sight as he. 3.05. 79
"who ever lov'd that lov'd not at first sight?" 3.05. 82
such another trick, never come in my sight more. 4.01. 41 P
and you be so tardy, come no more in my sight. 4.01. 52 P
aliena, i cannot be out of the sight of orlando. 4.01.216 P
if there be truth in sight, you are my daughter. 5.04.118
if there be truth in sight, you are my rosalind. 5.04.119
if sight and shape be true, | why then my love 5.04.120
and at that sight shall sad apollo weep, | so SHR in.2. 59
well, bring our lady hither to our sight, | and in.2. 74
whose sudden sight hath thrall'd my wounded eye. 1.01.220
what, in my sight? bianca, get thee in. 2.01. 30
approach the city, we shall lose all the sight. AWW 3.05. 2 P
to the youth in your sight only to exasperate TN 3.02. 18 P
olivia, and in my sight she uses thee kindly. 3.04.156 P
out of my sight! 4.01. 49
that lack'd sight only, nought for approbation WT 2.01.177
how he may soften at the sight o' th' child: 2.02. 38
here's a sight for thee; 3.03.115 P
of him what he is, fetch me to th' sight of him. 3.03.135 P
as hardly | will he endure your sight as yet, i 4.04.470
purchase the sight again of dear sicilia | and 4.04.511
for whose sight | i have a woman's longing. 4.04.666
then have you lost a sight which was to be seen, 5.02. 42 P
if i had thought the sight of my poor image 5.03. 57
but on the sight of us, your lawful king, | who JN 2.01.222
i cannot brook thy sight, | this news hath made 3.01. 36
how oft the sight of means to do ill deeds 4.02.219
out of my sight, and never see me more! 4.02.242
shall i seem crestfallen in my father's sight? R2 1.01.188
substitute, | his deputy anointed in his sight, 1.02. 38
as mine hath done | by sight of what i have, 2.03. 18
his face, | not able to endure the sight of day, 3.02. 52
never more come in my sight. 5.02. 86
not an eye | but is a–weary of thy common sight, 1H4 3.02. 88
even our love durst not come near your sight 5.01. 63
out of your sight and raise this present head, 5.01. 66
dimensions to any thick sight were /invisible. 2H4 3.02.313 P
in sight of both our battles we may meet, | /and 4.01.177
and now my sight fails, and my brain is giddy. 4.04.110
upon thy sight | my worldly business makes a 4.05.229
they do offend our sight. H5 4.07. 59
day | so dreadful will not be as was his sight. 1H6 1.01. 30
us look in, the sight will much delight thee. 1.04. 62
wilt thou be daunted at a woman's sight? 5.03. 69
voice, | by sight of these our baleful enemies. 5.04.122
in sight of england and her lordly peers, 2H6 1.01. 11
her sight did ravish, but her grace in speech, 1.01. 32
gazing on that which seems to dim thy sight? 1.02. 6
and never more abase our sight so low | as to 1.02. 15
within this half hour, hath receiv'd his sight, 2.01. 62
although by his sight his sin be multiplied. 2.01. 69
sight may distinguish colors; 2.01.127
in sight of god and us, your guilt is great; 2.03. 2
go, take hence that traitor from our sight, 2.03.100
thou baleful messenger, out of my sight! 3.02. 48
and kill the innocent gazer with thy sight; 3.02. 53
my earnest–gaping sight of thy land's view, | i 3.02.105
and in thy sight to die, what were it else | but 3.02.389
where, from thy sight, i should be raging mad, 3.02.394
may, even in their wives' and children's sight, 4.02.179
the sight of me is odious in their eyes; 4.04. 46
shall i endure the sight of somerset? 5.01. 90
even at this sight | my heart is turn'd to stone 5.02. 49
the sight of any of the house of york | is as a 3H6 1.03. 30
to see this sight, it irks my very soul. 2.02. 6
having the fearful flying hare in sight, | with 2.05.130
to greet mine own land with my wishful sight. 3.01. 14
king lewis, i here protest in sight of heaven, 3.03.181
out of my sight, thou dost infect mine eyes! R3 1.02.148
wrinkled witch, what mak'st thou in my sight? 1.03.163
to draw the brats of clarence out of sight, 3.05.107
dead life, blind sight, poor mortal–living ghost 4.04. 26
george, | be executed in his father's sight. 5.03. 96
if my sight fail not, | you should be lord H8 4.02.108
i'll show your grace the strangest sight — 5.02. 20
use, or purblind argus, all eyes and no sight. TRO 1.02. 30 P
through the sight i bear in things to /come, | i 3.03. 4
she will sing any man at first sight. 5.02. 9
might down stretch | below the beam of sight, COR 3.02. 5
tears take up | the glasses of my sight! 3.02.117
since that thy sight, which should | make our 5.03. 98
grace, | and here in sight of rome to saturnine, TIT 1.01.246
and here in sight of heaven to rome i swear, 1.01.329
my sight is very dull, what e'er it bodes. 2.03.195
that ever eye with sight made heart lament! 2.03.205
and see a fearful sight of blood and death. 2.03.216
for such a sight will blind a father's eye. 2.04. 53
hath made thee handless in thy father's sight? 3.01. 67
ah, that this sight should make so deep a wound, 3.01.246
thy other banish'd son with this dear sight 3.01.256
and be this dismal sight | the closing up of our 3.01.261
as for thee, boy, go get thee from my sight; 3.01.283
and how desirous of our sight they are. 5.01. 4
a sight to vex the father's soul withal. 5.01. 52
i'll go along no such sight to be shown, | but ROM 1.02.100
forswear it, sight! 1.05. 52
that one short minute gives me in her sight. 2.06. 5
i sounded at the sight. 3.02. 56
and doth it give me such a sight as this? 4.05. 42
and cruel death hath catch'd it from my sight! 4.05. 48
pitiful sight! 5.03.174
this sight of death is as a bell | that warns my 5.03.206
and i feed | most hungerly on your sight. TIM 1.01.253
nor sight of priests in holy vestments bleeding, 4.03.126
a common slave — you know him well by sight — JC 1.03. 15
o most bloody sight! 3.02.202 P
my sight was ever thick; 5.03. 21
the ears of brutus | as tidings of this sight. 5.03. 78
thanks, | only to herald thee into his sight, MAC 1.03.102
fatal vision, sensible | to feeling as to sight? 2.01. 37
this is a sorry sight. 2.02. 18
a foolish thought, to say a sorry sight. 2.02. 19
and destroy your sight | with a new gorgon. 2.03. 71
with barefac'd power sweep him from my sight, 3.01.118
avaunt, and quit my sight! 3.04. 92
horrible sight! 4.01.122
my mind she has mated, and amaz'd my sight. 5.01. 78
take hold of him | touching this dreaded sight, HAM 1.01. 25
in haste away | and vanish'd from our sight. 1.02.220
if you have hitherto conceal'd this sight, | let 1.02.246
or look'd upon this love with idle sight, | what 2.02.138
eyes without feeling, feeling without sight, 3.04. 78
that he cried out 'twould be a sight indeed | if 4.07. 99
where is this sight? 5.02.362
the sight is dismal, | and our affairs from 5.02.367
such a sight as this | becomes the field, but 5.02.401
hence, and avoid my sight! LR 1.01.124
out of my sight! 1.01.157
out, varlet, from my sight! 2.04.187
her cock, a buoy | almost too small for sight. 4.06. 20
and the deficient sight | topple down headlong. 4.06. 23
o thou side–piercing sight! 4.06. 85
the small gilded fly | does lecher in my sight. 4.06.113
a sight most pitiful in the meanest wretch, 4.06.204
with this ungracious paper strike the sight | of 4.06.276
this is a dull sight. are you not kent? 5.03.283
out of my sight! OTH 4.01.247
this sight would make him do a desperate turn, 5.02.207
from the possession of this heavenly sight! 5.02.278
the object poisons sight, | let it be hid. 5.02.364
mine eyes did sicken at the sight and could not ANT 3.10. 16
a heavy sight! 4.15. 40
thou basest thing, avoid hence, from my sight! CYM 1.01.125
did confess | was as a scorpion to her sight, 5.05. 45
o, get thee from my sight, | thou gav'st me 5.05.236
the which is good in nothing but in sight! PER 1.01.123
tables were stor'd full, to glad the sight, 1.04. 28
in your supposing once more put your sight: 5.ch. 21
you may, | but bootless is your sight; 5.01. 33
more of the maid to sight than husband's pains. TNK pr 8
out of their sight! 2.01. 52 P
do you think me | unworthy of her sight? 2.02.192
no; but unjust | if thou pursue that sight. 2.02.193
place | where i may ever dwell in sight of her? 2.03. 82
the blessed spirits — as there's a sight now! 4.01. 22 P
you'll lose the noblest sight | that ev'r was 5.02. 99
will you lose this sight? 5.03. 1
be bold to play, our sport is not in sight; VEN 124
his low'ring brows o'erwhelming his fair sight, 183
for nothing else with his proud sight agrees. 288
o, what a sight it was, wistly to view | how she 343
fold in the object that did feed her sight. 822
that her sight dazzling makes the wound seem 1064
he fed them with his sight, they him with 1104
with sweets that shall the truest sight beguile; 1144
kill'd | was melted like a vapor from her sight, 1166
nor could she moralize his wanton sight, | more LUC 104
rushing from forth a cloud, bereaves our sight, 373
and holy–thoughted lucrece to their sight | must 384
the sight which makes supposed terror true. 455
that it beguil'd attention, charm'd the sight. 1404
hath his hope, and eyes their wished sight: PP 14.22
for why, she sight, and bade me come to–morrow. 14.24
saw his right | flaming in the phoenix' sight; PHT 35
eye | doth homage to his new–appearing sight, SON 7. 3
sets you most rich in youth before my sight, 15.10
save that my soul's imaginary sight | presents 27. 9
and moan th' expense of many a vanish'd sight; 30. 8
in me | worthy perusal stand against thy sight, 38. 6
war, | how to divide the conquest of thy sight: 46. 2
eye my heart /thy picture's sight would bar, 46. 3
thy picture in my sight | awakes my heart to 47.13
while shadows like to thee do mock my sight? 61. 4
king | are vanishing, or vanish'd out of sight, 63. 7
sometime all full with feasting on your sight, 75. 9
for if it see the rud'st or gentlest sight, 113. 9
should transport me farthest from your sight. 117. 8
they are but dressings of a former sight. 123. 4
tell me thou lov'st elsewhere, but in my sight, 139. 5
which have no correspondence with true sight, 148. 2
to make me give the lie to my true sight, | and 150. 3
the mind and sight distractedly commix'd. LC 28

SIGHTED 1 FR 0.0001 REL FR 1 V 0 P
make me not sighted like the basilisk. WT 1.02.388

SIGHT–HOLES 1 FR 0.0001 REL FR 1 V 0 P
and stop all sight–holes, every loop from whence 1H4 4.01. 71

SIGHTLESS 6 FR 0.0006 REL FR 6 V 0 P
full of unpleasing blots and sightless stains, JN 3.01. 45
wherever in your sightless substances | you wait MAC 1.05. 49
hors'd | upon the sightless couriers of the air, 1.07. 23
poor grooms are sightless night, kings glorious LUC 1013
presents /thy shadow to my sightless view, SON 27.10
through heavy sleep on sightless eyes doth stay! 43.12

SIGHTLY 1 FR 0.0001 REL FR 1 V 0 P
it lies as sightly on the back of him | as great JN 2.01.143

SIGHT–OUTRUNNING 1 FR 0.0001 REL FR 1 V 0 P
more momentary | and sight–outrunning were not; TMP 1.02.203

/SIGHTS 2 FR 0.0002 REL FR 2 V 0 P
/you /will, /so /i /were /from /your /sights. R2 4.01.315
/fire /sparkling /through /sights /of /steel, 2H4 4.01.119

SIGHTS 22 FR 0.0024 REL FR 19 V 3 P
ay, madam, you may say what sights you see; TGV 1.02.135
i have seen two such sights, by sea and by land! WT 3.03. 83 P
i have not wink'd since i saw these sights. 3.03.105 P
must to the king, and show our strange sights. 4.04.819 P
so full of fearful dreams, of ugly sights, R3 1.04. 3
what sights of ugly death within /my eyes! 1.04. 23
then bring me to their sights. 4.01. 24
day with shows, | pageants, and sights of honor. H8 4.01. 11
and the bleared sights | are spectacled to see COR 2.01.205
i am joyful of your sights. TIM 1.01.246
two or three of us have seen strange sights. JC 1.03.138
recounts most horrid sights seen by the watch. 2.02. 16
when now i think you can behold such sights, MAC 3.04.113
what sights, my lord? 3.04.115
but no more sights! 4.01.155
and in your sights | shake patiently my great LR 4.06. 35
why cloud they not their sights perpetually, PER 1.01. 74
taint mine eye | with dread sights it may shun. TNK 5.03. 10
darkness daunts them with more dreadful sights. LUC 462
to see sad sights moves more than hear them told 1324
weak sights their sickly radiance do amend; LC 214
whose sights till then were levell'd on my face, 282

/SIGN 1 FR 0.0001 REL FR 1 V 0 P
/nor /nod, /nor /kneel, /nor /make /a /sign, TIT 3.02. 43

SIGN 52 FR 0.0058 REL FR 41 V 11 P
(for thou hast shown some sign of good desert) TGV 3.02. 18
sign me a present pardon for my brother, | or MM 2.04.152
of a brothel–house for the sign of blind cupid. ADO 1.01.254 P
let them signify under my sign, "here you may 1.01.267 P
will rather die than give any sign of affection. 2.03.227 P
she's but the sign and semblance of her honor. 4.01. 33
what sign is it when a man of great spirit grows LLL 1.02. 1 P
a great sign, sir, that he will look sad. 1.02. 3 P
following the signs, woo'd but the sign of she. 5.02.469
send the deed after me, | and i will sign it. MV 4.01.397
out, give him this deed, | and let him sign it. 4.02. 2

in sign whereof, | please ye we may contrive SHR 1.02.273
yet, | and show more sign of her obedience, 5.02.117
till, from one sign of dolor to another, she did WT 5.02. 87 P
ras'd out my imprese, leaving me no sign, | save R2 3.01. 25
for 'tis a sign of love; 5.05. 65
very smooth, like unto the sign of the leg, and 2H4 2.04.249 P
by some apparent sign | let us have knowledge at 1H6 2.01. 3
in sign whereof i pluck a white rose too. 2.04. 58
i'll by a sign give notice to our friends, 3.02. 8
in sign whereof, this arm, that hath reclaim'd 3.04. 5
give thee her hand, for sign of plighted faith. 5.03.162
it's sign she hath been liberal and free. 5.04. 82
i can express no kinder sign of love | than this 2H6 1.01. 18
it, | and make my image but an alehouse sign. 3.02. 81
ah, what a sign it is of evil life, | where 3.03. 5
he dies, and makes no sign. 3.03. 29
for there's no better sign of a brave mind than 4.02. 19 P
for underneath an alehouse' paltry sign, | the 5.02. 67
hath pawn'd an open hand in sign of love; 3H6 4.02. 9
in sign of truth, i kiss your highness' hand. 4.08. 26
the owl shriek'd at thy birth, an evil sign; 5.06. 44
hand | in sign of league and amity with thee. R3 1.03.280
which by the sign thereof was termed so. 3.05. 79
a sign of dignity, a breath, a bubble; 4.04. 90
you sign your place and calling, in full seeming H8 2.04.108
too far), | offers, as i do, in a sign of peace, 3.01. 66
in sign of what you are, not to reward | what COR 1.09. 26
go home, | and show no sign of fear. 4.06.152
or make some sign how i may do thee ease. TIT 3.01.121
upon a laboring day without the sign | of your JC 1.01. 4
of your hand | gave sign for me to leave you. 2.01.247
their bloody sign of battle is hung out, | and 5.01. 14
mark antony, shall we give sign of battle? 5.01. 23
it were a good sign that i should quickly have a MAC 4.02. 62 P
life, | i must show out a flag and sign of love, OTH 1.01.156
and sign of love, | which is indeed but sign. 1.01.157
she's a good sign, but i have seen small CYM 1.02. 30 P
render to me some corporal sign about her, 2.04.119
are dead, and send him | some bloody sign of it; 3.04.125
traveller, we should lodge them with this sign. PER 4.02.114 P
and bless me with a sign | of thy great pleasure TNK 5.01.128
SIGNAL 10 FR 0.0011 REL FR 10 V 0 P
or shall we give the signal to our rage, | and JN 2.01.265
desire, | attending but the signal to begin. R2 1.03.116
giving full trophy, signal, and ostent | quite H5 5.pr. 21
mean time, in signal of my love to thee, 1H6 2.04.121
hold up thy hand, make signal of thy hope. 2H6 3.03. 28
for god's sake, lords, give signal to the fight. 3H6 2.02.100
give signal to the fight, and to it, lords! 5.04. 72
be valiant, and give signal to the fight. 5.04. 82
as signal that thou hearest something approach. ROM 5.03. 8
stir not until the signal. JC 5.01. 26
SIGN'D 3 FR 0.0003 REL FR 3 V 0 P
until confirm'd, sign'd, ratified by you. MV 3.02.148
quoted, and sign'd to do a deed of shame, | this JN 4.02.222
sign'd in thy spoil, and crimson'd in thy lethe. JC 3.01.206
SIGNET 3 FR 0.0003 REL FR 2 V 1 P
doubt not, and the signet is not strange to you. MM 4.02.193 P
way) | to them to use your signet and your name, TIM 2.02.201
i had my father's signet in my purse, | which HAM 5.02. 49
SIGNIEUR *(also seigneur)*
SIGNIEUR 4 FR 0.0004 REL FR 4 V 0 P
o signieur dew should be a gentleman. H5 4.04. 7
perpend my words, o signieur dew, and mark: 4.04. 8
o signieur dew, thou diest on point of fox, 4.04. 9
of fox, | except, o signieur, thou do give to me 4.04. 10
SIGNIFICANT 1 FR 0.0001 REL FR 0 V 1 P
bear this significant to the country maid LLL 3.01.130 P
SIGNIFICANTS 1 FR 0.0001 REL FR 1 V 0 P
in dumb significants proclaim your thoughts: 1H6 2.04. 26
SIGNIFIED 3 FR 0.0003 REL FR 3 V 0 P
which plainly signified | that i should snarl, 3H6 5.06. 76
that you might well have signified the same R3 3.05. 59
this by calphurnia's dream is signified. JC 2.02. 90
SIGNIFIES 4 FR 0.0004 REL FR 3 V 1 P
is a familiar beast to man, and signifies love. WIV 1.01. 21 P
what signifies my deadly–standing eye, | my TIT 2.03. 32
rome | which signifies what hate they bear their 5.01. 3
signifies that from you great rome shall suck JC 2.02. 87
SIGNIFY 25 FR 0.0028 REL FR 15 V 10 P
the tenure of them doth but signify | my health TGV 3.01. 56
fox and lambskins too, to signify that craft, MM 3.02. 9 P
horse to hire," let them signify under my sign, ADO 1.01.266 P
haste, signify so much, while we attend, | like LLL 2.01. 33
or some rough–cast about him, to signify wall; MND 3.01. 69 P
you to break up this, it shall seem to signify. MV 2.04. 11 P
before | to signify th' approaching of his lord, 2.09. 88
my friend /stephano, signify, i pray you, 5.01. 51
a messenger before, | to signify their coming. 5.01.118
bend, to signify | not only my success in libya, WT 5.01.165
go signify as much, while here we march | upon R2 3.03. 49
eyes, to signify to you that fortune is blind; H5 3.06. 31 P
is painted also with a wheel, to signify to you, 3.06. 33 P
to signify that rebels there are up | and put 2H6 3.01.283
to signify unto his majesty | that cardinal 3.02.368
to signify thou cam'st to bite the world; 3H6 5.06. 54
i'll to the king and signify to him | that thus R3 1.04. 96
i'll signify so much unto him straight. 3.07. 70
me, | and signify this loving interview | to the TRO 4.05.155
and he shall signify from time to time | every ROM 3.03.170
bears that office to signify their pleasures. TIM 1.02.120 P
we attend his lordship; pray signify so much. 3.04. 37 P
more richer to signify this to the doctor, for, HAM 3.02.305 P
his majesty bade me signify to you that 'a has 5.02.102 P
i'll humbly signify what in his name, | that ANT 3.01. 30
SIGNIFYING 1 FR 0.0001 REL FR 1 V 0 P
full of sound and fury, | signifying nothing. MAC 5.05. 28
SIGNIOR 136 FR 0.0153 REL FR 71 V 65 P
how now, signior launce? TGV 3.01.280 P
marry, sir, that's claudio, signior claudio. MM 1.02. 64 P
here comes signior claudio, led by the provost 1.02.114 P
look, signior, here's your sister. 3.01. 49
signior lucio, did not you say you knew that 5.01.260 P
what can you vouch | against him, signior lucio? 5.01.324
good signior angelo, you must excuse us all, ERR 3.01. 1
y' are sad, signior balthazar, pray god our 3.01. 19
o, signior balthazar, either at flesh or fish, 3.01. 22
good signior, take the stranger to my house, 4.01. 36
signior antipholus, i wonder much | that you 5.01. 13
is signior mountanto return'd from the wars or ADO 1.01. 30 P
my cousin means signior benedick of padua. 1.01. 35 P
niece, you tax signior benedick too much, but 1.01. 46 P
of merry war betwixt signior benedick and her; 1.01. 62 P
good signior leonato, are you come to meet your 1.01. 96 P
signior benedick, no, for then were you a child. 1.01.107 P
if signior leonato be her father, she would not 1.01.113 P
you will still be talking, signior benedick, 1.01.117 P
such meet food to feed it as signior benedick? 1.01.121 P
signior claudio and signior benedick — my dear 1.01.147 P
signior claudio and signior benedick — my dear 1.01.147 P
didst thou note the daughter of signior leonato? 1.01.163 P
in the mean time, good signior benedick, repair 1.01.275 P
then half signior benedick's tongue in count 2.01. 11 P
john's melancholy in signior benedick's face — 2.01. 13 P
i know you well enough, you are signior antonio. 2.01.112 P
well, this was signior benedick that said so. 2.01.131 P
are not you signior benedick? 2.01.161 P
signior, you are very near my brother in his 2.01.163 P
now, signior, where's the count? 2.01.211 P
you have lost the heart of signior benedick. 2.01.277 P
to bring signior benedick and the lady beatrice 2.01.366 P
signior? 2.03. 2 P
beatrice was in love with signior benedick? 2.03. 91 P
that she should so dote on signior benedick, 2.03. 96 P
you have no stomach, signior, fare you well. 2.03.256 P
so rare a gentleman as signior benedick. 3.01. 91
signior benedick, | for shape, for bearing, 3.01. 95
old signior, walk aside with me, i have studied 3.02. 71 P
i pray you watch about signior leonato's door, 3.03. 92 P
prince, the count, signior benedick, don john, 3.04. 96 P
signior benedick! 4.01.114
signior leonato, let the friar advise you, | and 4.01.244
now, signior, what news? 5.01.111 P
welcome, signior, you are almost come to part 5.01.113 P
our sexton hath reform'd signior leonato of the 5.01.254 P
here, here comes master signior leonato, and the 5.01.257 P
yea, signior, and depart when you bid me. 5.02. 44 P
will you go hear this news, signior? 5.02.101 P
to do what, signior? 5.04. 19
signior leonato, truth it is, good signior, 5.04. 21
signior leonato, truth it is, good signior, 5.04. 21
signior arme — arme — commends you. LLL 1.01.187 P
demonstration of the working, my tough signior. 1.02. 10 P
why tough signior? why tough signior? 1.02. 11 P
why tough signior? why tough signior? 1.02. 11 P
and i tough signior as an appertinent title to 1.02. 16 P
like the sequel, i. signior costard, adieu. 3.01.134
have you overflowen with a honey–bag, signior. MND 4.01. 16 P
you look not well, signior antonio, | you have MV 1.01. 73
this is signior antonio. 1.03. 40 P
rest you fair, good signior, | your worship was 1.03. 59
but note me, signior. 1.03. 97
signior antonio, many a time and oft | in the 1.03.106
signior bassanio! 2.02.175
signior bassanio, hear me: 2.02.189
signior antonio! 2.06. 61
signior antonio | commends him to you. 3.02.231
farewell, good signior love. AYL 3.02.292 P
signior baptista, will you be so strange? SHR 1.01. 85
signior baptista, for this fiend of hell, | and 1.01. 88
or, signior gremio, you, know any such, | prefer 1.01. 96
so will i, signior gremio. 1.01.113 P
how say you, signior gremio? 1.01.141 P
signior hortensio, come you to part the fray? 1.02. 23
signior hortensio, thus it stands with me: 1.02. 53
signior hortensio, 'twixt such friends as we 1.02. 65
over and beside | signior baptista's liberality, 1.02.149
grumio, mum! god save you, signior gremio. 1.02.162
and you are well met, signior hortensio. 1.02.163
way | to the house of signior baptista minola? 1.02.220
that she's the choice love of signior gremio. 1.02.234
that she's the chosen of signior hortensio. 1.02.235
you wrong me, signior gremio, give me leave. 2.01. 46
pardon me, signior gremio, i would fain be doing 2.01. 74
a thousand thanks, signior gremio. 2.01. 84 P
signior baptista, my business asketh haste, 2.01.114
signior petruchio, will you go with us, | or 2.01.166
now, signior petruchio, how speed you with my 2.01.281
say, signior gremio, what can you assure her? 2.01.345
as any one | old signior gremio has in padua, 2.01.368
what, have i pinch'd you, signior gremio? 2.01.371
if not, to signior gremio. 2.01.397
signior lucentio, this is the 'pointed day, 3.02. 1
signior gremio, came you from the church? 3.02.149
signior hortensio, i have often heard | of your 4.02. 22
signior lucentio, | here is my hand, and here i 4.02. 27
and so farewell, signior lucentio. 4.02. 40
signior petruchio, fie, you are to blame. 4.03. 48
signior baptista may remember me | near twenty 4.04. 3
signior baptista, you are happily met. 4.04. 19
you, | signior baptista, of whom i hear so well. 4.04. 37
signior baptista, shall i lead the way? 4.04. 69
is signior lucentio within, sir? 5.01. 18 P
i pray you tell signior lucentio that his father 5.01. 27 P
help, son! help, signior baptista! 5.01. 60 P
and heir to the lands of me, signior vincentio. 5.01. 86 P
talk not, signior gremio; 5.01. 96 P
take heed, signior baptista, lest you be 5.01. 98 P
yes, i know thee to be signior lucentio. 5.01.105 P
here, signior tranio, | this bird you aim'd at, 5.02. 49
come thy ways, signior fabian. TN 2.05. 1 P
signior fabian, stay you by this gentleman till 3.04.257 P
signior, no. 1H6 3.02. 67
signior, hang! 3.02. 68
"signior martino and his wife and daughters; ROM 1.02. 64 P
signior placentio and his lovely nieces; 1.02. 66 P
signior valentio and his cousin tybalt; 1.02. 69 P
signior romeo, bon jour! 2.04. 43 P
what ho! brabantio, signior brabantio, ho! OTH 1.01. 78
signior, is all your family within? 1.01. 84
most reverend signior, do you know my voice? 1.01. 93
signior, it is the moor. 1.02. 57
good signior, you shall more command with years 1.02. 60
'tis true, most worthy signior; 1.02. 91
report here to the state | by signior angelo. 1.03. 16
signior montano, | your trusty and most valiant 1.03. 39
welcome, gentle signior, | we lack'd your 1.03. 50
and, noble signior, | if virtue no delighted 1.03.288
i am very glad to see you, signior; 4.01.220
signior lodovico? 5.01. 67
signior gratiano? 5.01. 93
this worthy signior, i thank him, makes no CYM 1.04.100 P
signior jachimo will not from it. 1.04.171 P
when signior sooth here does proclaim peace, PER 1.02. 44
SIGNIORS 3 FR 0.0003 REL FR 3 V 0 P
like signiors and rich burghers on the flood, MV 1.01. 10
good signiors both, when shall we laugh? 1.01. 66
most potent, grave, and reverend signiors, | my OTH 1.03. 76
SIGNIORY 1 FR 0.0001 REL FR 1 V 0 P
my services which i have done the signiory OTH 1.02. 18
SIGNOR 1 FR 0.0001 REL FR 0 V 1 P
ben venuto, molto honorato signor mio petruchio. SHR 1.02. 26 P
/SIGNORIES 1 FR 0.0001 REL FR 1 V 0 P
/to /all /the /duke /of /norfolk's /signories, 2H4 4.01.109
SIGNORIES 3 FR 0.0003 REL FR 3 V 0 P
through all the signories it was the first, TMP 1.02. 71
whilst you have fed upon my signories, R2 3.01. 22
restor'd again | to all his lands and signories. 4.01. 89
/SIGNS 2 FR 0.0002 REL FR 2 V 0 P
/of /woe, /that /thus /dost /talk /in /signs! TIT 3.02. 12
/i /can /interpret /all /her /martyr'd /signs: 3.02. 36
SIGNS 38 FR 0.0043 REL FR 35 V 3 P
some woman, there is no believing old signs. ADO 3.02. 41 P
following the signs, woo'd but the sign of she. LLL 5.02.469
there stay until the twelve celestial signs 5.02.797
the meaning or moral of his signs and tokens. SHR 4.04. 79 P
though he does bear some signs of me, yet you WT 2.01. 57
be these sad signs confirmers of thy words? JN 3.01. 24
and call them meteors, prodigies, and signs, 3.04.157
but thou didst understand me by my signs, | and 4.02.237
and didst in signs again parley with sin, | yea, 4.02.238
with signs of war about his aged neck. R2 2.02. 74
these signs forerun the death or fall of kings. 2.04. 15
of bawds, and dials the signs of leaping–houses, 1H4 1.02. 8 P
these signs have mark'd me extraordinary, | and 3.01. 40
the signs of war advance! H5 2.02.192
me | and give me signs of future accidents. 1H6 5.03. 4
the least of all these signs were probable. 2H6 3.02.178
teeth, | with full as many signs of deadly hate, 3.02.314
no, madam, these are no venereal signs. TIT 2.03. 37
see how with signs and tokens she can scrowl. 2.04. 5
i understand her signs. 3.01.143
what means my niece lavinia by these signs? 4.01. 8
give signs, sweet girl, for here are none but 4.01. 61
ye alehouse painted signs! 4.02. 98
but if my frosty signs and chaps of age, | grave 5.03. 77
but signs of nobleness, like stars, shall shine MAC 1.04. 41
it signs well, does it not? ANT 4.03. 14
thou hast seen these signs, | they are black 4.14. 7
your scutcheons and your signs of conquest, 5.02.135
if these signs | of prisonment were off me and TNK 3.01. 31
i do take | thy signs auspiciously, and in thy 5.01. 67
i hope she's pleas'd, | her signs were gracious. 5.01.173
sawest thou not signs of fear lurk in mine eye? VEN 644
poor people are amazed | at apparitions, signs, 926
so she at these sad signs draws up her breath, 929
and in their rage such signs of rage they bear, LUC 1419
such signs of truth in his plain face she spied, 1532
these are certain signs to know | faithful PP 20.55
before these bastard signs of fair were born, SON 68. 3
SIGNUM 1 FR 0.0001 REL FR 0 V 1 P
my sword hack'd like a hand–saw — ecce signum! 1H4 2.04.169 P
SILENC'D 6 FR 0.0006 REL FR 5 V 1 P
the little wit that fools have was silenc'd, the AYL 1.02. 89 P
is it therefore | th' ambassador is silenc'd? H8 1.01. 97
have made them mules, silenc'd their pleaders, COR 2.01.247
nor then silenc'd when | "commend me to your TIM 2.01. 17
silenc'd with that, | in viewing o'er the rest MAC 1.03. 93
authority quite silenc'd by your brawl, | and STM II.C 78
/SILENCE 1 FR 0.0001 REL FR 1 V 0 P
/that /swells /with /silence /in /the /tortur'd R2 4.01.298
SILENCE 88 FR 0.0099 REL FR 61 V 27 P
silence! TMP 1.01. 17 P
if you can command these elements to silence, 1.01. 22 P
silence! 1.02.476
sweet now, silence! 4.01.124
then in dumb silence will i bury mine, | for TGV 3.01.208
the night's dead silence | will well become such 3.02. 84
silence, you aery toys! WIV 5.05. 42
the time may have all shadow and silence in it; MM 3.01.247 P
silence that fellow. 5.01.181
for the benefit of silence, would thou wert so 5.01.190 P
silence is the perfectest heralt of joy; ADO 2.01.306 P
your silence most offends me, and to be merry 2.01.331 P
night and silence — who is here? MND 2.02. 70
silence a while. 4.01. 80
in silence sad | trip we after night's shade. 4.01. 95
out of this silence yet i pick'd a welcome; 5.01.100
pyramus draws near the wall. silence! 5.01.169 P
but silence! 5.01.261 P
for silence is only commendable | in a neat's MV 1.01.111
and wish'd in silence that it were not his. 2.08. 32
grace of wit will shortly turn into silence, and 3.05. 45 P
who comes so fast in silence of the night? 5.01. 25
silence bestows that virtue on it, madam. 5.01.101
her very silence, and her patience | speak to AYL 1.03. 78
but in the other's silence do i see | maid's SHR 1.01. 70
her silence flouts me, and i'll be reveng'd. 2.01. 29
and therefore be not — cock's passion, silence! 4.01.118 P
be check'd for silence, | but never tax'd for AWW 1.01. 67
commit, | only shape thou thy silence to my wit. TN 1.02. 61
though our silence be drawn from us with cars, 2.05. 63 P
but silence, like a lucrece knife, | with 2.05.105
the silence often of pure innocence | persuades WT 2.02. 39
silence! 3.02. 10
i like your silence, it the more shows off 5.03. 21
silence, good mother, hear the embassy. JN 1.01. 6
silence, no more. 4.01.132
heart is great, but it must break with silence, R2 2.01.228
there's for your silence. 2H4 2.02.162 P
and how doth my good cousin silence? 3.02. 3 P
sir john, it is my cousin silence, in commission 3.02. 87 P

good master silence, it well befits you should 3.02. 89 P
ha, cousin silence, that thou hadst seen that 3.02.211 P
god keep you, master silence, i will not use 3.02.288 P
come, cousin silence — and then to bed. 5.03. 4 P
good master silence, i'll give you a health for 5.03. 23 P
i did not think master silence had been a man of 5.03. 37 P
well said, master silence. 5.03. 49 P
health and long life to you, master silence. 5.03. 52 P
carry master silence to bed. 5.03.129 P
lords and gentlemen, what means this silence? 1H6 2.04. 1
if i have fewest, i subscribe in silence. 2.04. 44
with silence, nephew, be thou politic. 2.05.101
o, hold me not with silence over–long! 5.03. 13
down kings and princes — command silence. 2H6 4.02. 37 P
silence! 4.02. 38 P
silence! 3H6 3.02. 15
ask'd the mayor what meant this willful silence. R3 3.07. 28
i cannot tell if to depart in silence, | or 3.07.141
then we shall have 'em | talk us to silence. H8 1.04. 45
from rome is read, | let silence be commanded. 2.04. 2
carry gentle peace | to silence envious tongues. 3.02.446
and how his silence drinks up his applause! TRO 2.03.201
see, see, your silence, | /cunning in dumbness, 3.02.131
but we in silence hold this virtue well — 4.01. 78
hide your doings, and to silence that | which, COR 1.09. 23
my gracious silence, hail! 2.01.175
there greet in silence, as the dead are wont, TIT 1.01. 90
no noise, but silence and eternal sleep. 1.01.155
my silence, an' my cloudy melancholy, | my 2.03. 33
cold–moving nods, | they froze me into silence. TIM 2.02.213
scarfs off caesar's images, are put to silence. JC 1.02.286 P
the noble brutus is ascended; silence! 3.02. 11
peace, silence! brutus speaks. 3.02. 54
let it be tenable in your silence still, | and HAM 1.02.247
a silence in the heavens, the rack stand still, 2.02.484
i'll silence me even here; 3.04. 4
are disclosed, | his silence will sit drooping. 5.01.288
which have solicited — the rest is silence. 5.02.358
silence that dreadful bell, it frights the isle OTH 2.03.175
town, | and silence those whom this vild brawl 2.03.256
speak, or thy silence on the instant is | thy CYM 3.05. 97
o imogen, | i'll speak to thee in silence. 5.04. 29
think me speaking, though i swear to silence; PER 1.02. 19
me doubted, but your silence | should break out, TNK 3.01. 61
peace, peace, silence, peace! STM II.C 50 P
this silence for my sin you did impute, | which SON 83. 9
as victors of my silence cannot boast; 86.11
excuse not silence so, for't lies in thee | to 101.10
SILENCING 1 FR 0.0001 REL FR 1 V 0 P
and in your power soft silencing your son. 2H4 5.02. 97
/SILENT 1 FR 0.0001 REL FR 1 V 0 P
/mark, /silent /king, /the /moral /of /this R2 4.01.290
SILENT 36 FR 0.0040 REL FR 29 V 7 P
be silent. TMP 4.01. 59
dumb jewels often in their silent kind | more TGV 3.01. 90
if silent, why, a block moved with mine. ADO 3.01. 67
a little, | for i have only been silent so long, 4.01.156
for prisoners to be too silent in their words, LLL 1.02.163 P
years, | no woman may approach his silent court; 2.01. 24
you had only in your silent judgment tried it, WT 2.01.171
though i report it | that should be silent. 4.04.178
the business asketh silent secrecy. 2H6 1.02. 90
deep night, dark night, the silent of the night, 1.04. 16
perform'd, | but with advice and silent secrecy. 2.02. 68
lords, | and be you silent and attentive too, 3H6 1.01.122
why then, let's on our way in silent sort. 4.02. 28
with the sweet silent hours of marriage joys; R3 4.04.330
the silent hours steal on, | and flaky darkness 5.03. 85
but 'tis before his face, | i will be silent. TRO 2.03.230
prithee be silent, /boy, i profit not by thy 5.01. 14 P
their tongues to be silent and not confess so COR 2.02. 30 P
i would you rather had been silent. 2.02. 61
should we be silent and not speak, our raiment 5.03. 94
and so let's leave her to her silent walks. TIT 2.04. 8
a stone is silent, and offendeth not, | and 3.01. 46
prithee let my meat make thee silent. TIM 1.02. 37 P
hear me for my cause, and be silent, that you JC 3.02. 14 P
why are you silent? MAC 4.03.137
what shall cordelia speak? love, and be silent. LR 1.01. 62
for my duty cannot be silent when i think your 1.04. 65 P
how silent is this town! OTH 5.01. 64
that truth should be silent i had almost forgot. ANT 2.02.108 P
but that you shall not say i yield being silent, CYM 2.03. 94
be silent; let's see further. 5.05.127
by night | that seek out silent hanging. TNK 3.05.127
this silent war of lilies and of roses, | which LUC 71
in silent wonder of still–gazing eyes. 84
o, learn to read what silent love hath writ: SON 23.13
when to the sessions of sweet silent thought | i 30. 1
SILENTLY 1 FR 0.0001 REL FR 1 V 0 P
tie up my lover's tongue, bring him silently. MND 3.01.201
SILIUS 3 FR 0.0003 REL FR 3 V 0 P
o silius, silius, | i have done enough; ANT 3.01. 11
o silius, silius, | i have done enough; 3.01. 11
for learn this, silius: 3.01. 13
SILK 20 FR 0.0022 REL FR 14 V 6 P
i warrant you, in silk and gold, and in such WIV 2.02. 67 P
that silk will i go buy. 4.04. 73
o, why then three–farthing worth of silk. LLL 3.01.149 P
you have shore | with shears his thread of silk. MND 5.01.341
'tis not your inky brows, your black silk hair, AYL 3.05. 46
any silk, any thread, | any toys for your head WT 4.04.318
and sackcloth, but in new silk and old sack. 2H4 1.02.198 P
note how many pair of silk stockings thou hast, 2.02. 15 P
when steel grows soft as the parasite's silk, COR 1.09. 45
and resolution like | a twist of rotten silk, 5.06. 95
the very butcher of a silk button, a duellist, a ROM 2.04. 23 P
thy flatterers yet wear silk, drink wine, lie TIM 4.03.206
thou ow'st the worm no silk, the beast no hide, LR 3.04.104 P
the worms were hallowed that did breed the silk, OTH 3.04. 73
was hang'd | with tapestry of silk and silver; CYM 2.04. 69
prouder than rustling in unpaid–for silk: 3.03. 24
be't when they weav'd the sleided silk | with PER 4.ch. 21
her inkle, silk, /twin with the rubied cherry, 5.ch. 8
canst not thou work such flowers in silk, wench? TNK 2.02.127
blood, | with sleided silk feat and affectedly LC 48
SILKEN 18 FR 0.0020 REL FR 17 V 1 P
no, girl, i'll knit it up in silken strings, TGV 2.07. 45
fetter strong madness in a silken thread, ADO 5.01. 25
taffata phrases, silken terms precise, LLL 5.02.406
with silken coats and caps, and golden rings, SHR 4.03. 55
cap, | a custard–coffin, a bauble, a silken pie. 4.03. 82
a silken doublet, a velvet hose, a scarlet cloak 5.01. 66 P
the pedlar's silken treasury and have pour'd it WT 4.04.350
a cock'red silken wanton, brave our fields, JN 5.01. 70
honor, for a silken point | i'll give my barony. 2H4 1.01. 53
and silken dalliance in the wardrobe lies; H5 2.pr. 2
with silken streamers the young phoebus /fanning 3.pr. 6
his simple truth must be abus'd | with silken, R3 1.03. 53
and make the silken strings delight to kiss them TIT 2.04. 46
and with a silken thread plucks it back again, ROM 2.02.180
the silken tackle | swell with the touches of ANT 2.02.209
honor, | or tie my pleasure up in silken bags, PER 3.02. 41
laund'ring the silken figures in the brine LC 17
wind | upon his lips their silken parcels hurls. 87
SILKEN–COATED 1 FR 0.0001 REL FR 1 V 0 P
as for these silken–coated slaves, i pass not, 2H6 4.02.128
SILK–MAN 1 FR 0.0001 REL FR 0 V 1 P
lumbert street, to master smooth's the silk–man. 2H4 2.01. 29 P
SILKS 4 FR 0.0004 REL FR 3 V 1 P
and show'd me silks that he had bought for me, ERR 4.03. 8
enrobe the roaring waters with my silks, | and, MV 1.01. 34
we turn not back the silks upon the merchant, TRO 2.02. 69
nor the rustling of silks betray thy poor heart LR 3.04. 95 P
SILLIEST 1 FR 0.0001 REL FR 0 V 1 P
this is the silliest stuff that ever i heard. MND 5.01.210 P
SILLILY 1 FR 0.0001 REL FR 1 V 0 P
so sillily, as if she were a fool, | an innocent TNK 4.01. 40
SILLINESS 1 FR 0.0001 REL FR 0 V 1 P
it is silliness to live, when to live is torment OTH 1.03.308 P
SILLING *(also shilling)*
SILLING 1 FR 0.0001 REL FR 0 V 1 P
'tis a good silling, i warrant you, or i will H5 4.08. 71 P
SILLY *(also seely)*
SILLY 23 FR 0.0026 REL FR 18 V 5 P
a silly answer, and fitting well a sheep. TGV 1.01. 81 P
no outrages | on silly women or poor passengers. 4.01. 70
thou enforcest laughter — thy silly thought, my LLL 3.01. 76 P
ba, most silly sheep, with a horn. 5.01. 50 P
sigh, | till i be brought to such a silly pass! SHR 5.02.124
it is silly sooth, | and dallies with the TN 2.04. 46
caparison, and my revenue is the silly cheat. WT 4.03. 28 P
alas, this is a child, a silly dwarf! 1H6 2.03. 22
here's a silly stately style indeed! 4.07. 72
while as the silly owner of the goods | weeps 2H6 1.01.225
had i been there, which am a silly woman, | the 3H6 1.01.243
to shepherds looking on their silly sheep | than 2.05. 43
a silly time | to make prescription for a 3.03. 93
why, thou silly gentleman? OTH 1.03.307 P
there was a fourth man, in a silly habit, | that CYM 5.03. 86
the silly boy, believing she is dead, | claps VEN 467
was i | to be of such a weak and silly mind, 1016
and never fright the silly lamb that day. 1098
it shall be raging mad and silly mild, | make 1151
season that they may surprise | the silly lambs: LUC 167
she, silly queen, with more than love's good PP 9. 7
alas, it was a spite | unto the silly damsel! 15. 8
one silly cross wrought all my loss, | o 17. 9
SILLY–DUCKING 1 FR 0.0001 REL FR 1 V 0 P
ends | than twenty silly–ducking observants LR 2.02.103
SILVER 74 FR 0.0083 REL FR 60 V 14 P
fool there but would give a piece of silver. TMP 2.02. 30 P
silver! there it goes, silver! 4.01.256
silver! there it goes, silver! 4.01.256
and gold, and silver, is her grandsire upon his WIV 1.01. 51 P
spread o'er the silver waves thy golden hairs, ERR 3.02. 48
cut with her golden oars the silver stream, ADO 3.01. 27
cloth a' gold and cuts, and lac'd with silver, 3.04. 20 P
nor shines the silver moon one half so bright LLL 4.03. 29
like to a silver bow | /new bent in heaven, MND 1.01. 9
behold | her silver visage in the wat'ry glass, 1.01.210
devis'd in these three chests of gold, silver, MV 1.02. 30 P
or is your gold and silver ewes and rams? 1.03. 95
the second, silver, which this promise carries, 2.07. 6
what says the silver with her virgin hue? 2.07. 22
or shall i think in silver she's immur'd, 2.07. 52
gold, silver, and base lead. 2.09. 20
why then to thee, thou silver treasure house! 2.09. 34
how silver made it good | at the hedge–corner, SHR in.1. 19
let one attend him with a silver basin | full of in.1. 55
unless thou let his silver water keep | a JN 2.01.339
o, two such silver currents when they join | do 2.01.441
when gold and silver becks me to come on. 3.03. 13
where but by chance a silver drop hath fall'n, 3.04. 63
this precious stone set in the silver sea, R2 2.01. 46
which makes the silver rivers drown their shores 3.02.107
thou sheer, immaculate, and silver fountain, 5.03. 61
and here the smug and silver trent shall run 1H4 3.01.101
but i will inset you neither in gold nor silver, 2H4 1.02. 17 P
whose beard the silver hand of peace hath 4.01. 43
your fathers taken by the silver beards, | and H5 3.03. 36
troubles the silver spring where england drinks. 2H6 4.01. 72
old salisbury, shame to thy silver hair, | thou 5.01.162
to achieve | the silver livery of advised age, 5.02. 47
again | as venerable nestor, hatch'd in silver, TRO 1.03. 65
me | i'll hide my silver beard in a gold beaver, 1.03.296
a murrain on't! i took this for silver. COR 1.05. 3 P
rent off thy silver hair, thy other hand TIT 3.01.260
that tips with silver all these fruit–tree tops ROM 2.02.108
/oppress, | then music with her silver sound" — 4.05.128
with her silver sound" — | why "silver sound"? 4.05.129 P
why "music with her silver sound"? 4.05.129 P
marry, sir, because silver hath a sweet sound. 4.05.131 P
i say, "silver sound," because musicians sound 4.05.134 P
sound," because musicians sound for silver. 4.05.135 P
it is "music with her silver sound," because 4.05.140 P
"then music with her silver sound | with speedy 4.05.142
you | four milk–white horses, trapp'd in silver. TIM 1.02.183
i dreamt of a silver basin and ew'r to–night. 3.01. 6 P
drinks | but timon's silver treads upon his lip, 3.02. 71
for his silver hairs | will purchase us a good JC 2.01.144
his silver skin lac'd with his golden blood, MAC 2.03.112
the oars were silver, | which to the tune of ANT 2.02.194
was hang'd | with tapestry of silk and silver; CYM 2.04. 69
were two winking cupids | of silver, each on one 2.04. 90
all gold and silver rather turn to dirt, | as 3.06. 53
do't, and happy, by my silver bow! PER 5.01.248
whom, o goddess, | wears yet thy silver livery. 5.03. 7
more famous yet 'twixt po and silver trent. TNK pr 12
he bears a charging–staff emboss'd with silver. 4.02.140
must bring a piece of silver on the tip of your 4.03. 20 P
and, sacred silver mistress, lend thine ear 5.01.146
showed like two silver doves that sit a–billing. VEN 366
cynthia for shame obscures her silver shine, 728
from whose silver breast | the sun ariseth in 855
through the flood–gates breaks the silver rain, 959
and yokes her silver doves, by whose swift aid 1190
as is the morning's silver melting dew | against LUC 24
virtue would stain that o'er with silver white. 56
the golden age to gild | their silver cheeks, 61
to draw the cloud that hides the silver moon. 371
the earth with show'rs of silver brine, 796
the stain upon his silver down will stay. 1012
in speech it seem'd his beard, all silver white, 1405
roses have thorns, and silver fountains mud, SON 35. 2
SILVER–BRIGHT 1 FR 0.0001 REL FR 1 V 0 P
armors, that march'd hence so silver–bright, JN 2.01.315
SILVER'D 4 FR 0.0004 REL FR 4 V 0 P
alive, iwis, | silver'd o'er, and so was this. MV 2.09. 69
i have seen it in his life, | a sable silver'd. HAM 1.02.241
i' th' market–place, on a tribunal silver'd, ANT 3.06. 3
and sable curls /all silver'd o'er with white; SON 12. 4
SILVERLY 1 FR 0.0001 REL FR 1 V 0 P
that silverly doth progress on thy cheeks. JN 5.02. 46
SILVER–SHEDDING 1 FR 0.0001 REL FR 1 V 0 P
nor silver–shedding tears | could penetrate her TGV 3.01.232
SILVER–SHINING 1 FR 0.0001 REL FR 1 V 0 P
the silver–shining queen he would distain; LUC 786
SILVER–SWEET 1 FR 0.0001 REL FR 1 V 0 P
how silver–sweet sound lovers' tongues by night, ROM 2.02.165
SILVER–VOIC'D 1 FR 0.0001 REL FR 1 V 0 P
as silver–voic'd, her eyes as jewel–like | and PER 5.01.110
SILVER–WHITE 1 FR 0.0001 REL FR 1 V 0 P
blue | and lady–smocks all silver–white | and LLL 5.02.895
SILVIA 53 FR 0.0060 REL FR 44 V 9 P
decks a thing divine — | ah, silvia, silvia! TGV 2.01. 5
decks a thing divine — | ah, silvia, silvia! 2.01. 5
madam silvia! madam silvia! 2.01. 6 P
madam silvia! madam silvia! 2.01. 6 P
go to, sir; tell me, do you know madam silvia? 2.01. 15 P
but tell me: dost thou know my lady silvia? 2.01. 42 P
to be a spokesman from madam silvia. 2.01.146 P
now, daughter silvia, you are hard beset. 2.04. 49
silvia, i speak to you, and you, sir thurio; 2.04. 84
to love fair silvia, shall i be forsworn; 2.06. 2
for julia, silvia. 2.06. 22
and silvia (witness heaven, that made her fair) 2.06. 25
enemy, | aiming at silvia as a sweeter friend. 2.06. 30
"to silvia"? 3.01.137
"my thoughts do harbor with my silvia nightly, 3.01.140
"silvia, this night i will enfranchise thee." 3.01.151
be banish'd from myself, | and silvia is myself: 3.01.172
what light is light, if silvia be not seen? 3.01.174
what joy is joy, if silvia be not by? 3.01.175
except i be by silvia in the night, | there is 3.01.178
unless i look on silvia in the day, | there is 3.01.180
is silvia dead? 3.01.210
no valentine indeed, for sacred silvia. 3.01.212
no valentine, if silvia have forsworn me. 3.01.215
from hence, from silvia, and from me thy friend. 3.01.220
doth silvia know that i am banished? 3.01.223
as thou lov'st silvia (though not for thyself) 3.01.257
o my dear silvia! hapless valentine! 3.01.262
where you with silvia may confer at large — 3.02. 61
but silvia is too fair, too true, too holy, | to 4.02. 5
who? silvia? 4.02. 23
ay, silvia — for your sake. 4.02. 23
who is silvia? 4.02. 39
then to silvia let us sing, | that silvia is 4.02. 49
silvia let us sing, | that silvia is excelling; 4.02. 50
this is the hour that madam silvia | entreated 4.03. 1
as a present to mistress silvia from my master; 4.04. 7 P
serv'd me, when i took my leave of madam silvia. 4.04. 36 P
i carried mistress silvia the dog you bade me. 4.04. 45 P
ring with thee, | deliver it to madam silvia — 4.04. 72
you as well | as you do love your lady silvia: 4.04. 80
to bring me where to speak with madam silvia. 4.04.109
that silvia at friar patrick's cell should meet 5.01. 3
sir proteus, what says silvia to my suit? 5.02. 1
eglamour | than for the love of reckless silvia. 5.02. 52
more to cross that love | than hate for silvia, 5.02. 56
repair me with thy presence, silvia; 5.04. 11
free, | all that was mine in silvia i give thee. 5.04. 83
charg'd me to deliver a ring to madam silvia, 5.04. 89 P
this is the ring you sent to silvia. 5.04. 95
yonder is silvia; and silvia's mine. 5.04.125
do not name silvia thine; 5.04.128
take thou thy silvia, for thou hast deserv'd her 5.04.147
SILVIA'S 4 FR 0.0004 REL FR 4 V 0 P
to climb celestial silvia's chamber–window, TGV 2.06. 34
more for silvia's love | than hate of eglamour 5.02. 53
what is in silvia's face, but i may spy | more 5.04.114
yonder is silvia; and silvia's mine. 5.04.125
SILVIUS 8 FR 0.0009 REL FR 8 V 0 P
hah! what say'st thou, silvius? AYL 3.05. 83
why, i am sorry for thee, gentle silvius. 3.05. 85
silvius, the time was that i hated thee; 3.05. 92
there be some women, silvius, had they mark'd 3.05.124
wilt thou, silvius? 3.05.135
go with me, silvius. 3.05.139
keep your word, silvius, that you'll marry her 5.04. 23
from silvius, sir. ANT 2.01. 18
SIMILE 1 FR 0.0001 REL FR 1 V 0 P
a good swift simile, but something currish. SHR 5.02. 54
/SIMILES 2 FR 0.0002 REL FR 0 V 2 P
his distress in my /similes of comfort and leave AWW 5.02. 25 P
the most unsavory /similes and art indeed the 1H4 1.02. 79 P
SIMILES 3 FR 0.0003 REL FR 3 V 0 P
o yes, into a thousand similes. AYL 2.01. 45
wants similes, truth tir'd with iteration, | as TRO 3.02.176
take all these similes to your own command, LC 227
SIMOIS' 2 FR 0.0002 REL FR 2 V 0 P
to simois' reedy banks the red blood ran, LUC 1437
join, and shoot their foam at simois' banks. 1442

SIMOIS 3 FR 0.0003 REL FR 1 V 2 P
"hic ibat simois; SHR 3.01. 28
as i told you before, "simois," i am lucentio, 3.01. 31 P
"hic ibat simois," i know you not, "hic est 3.01. 42 P
SIMON 3 FR 0.0003 REL FR 1 V 2 P
simon shadow! 2H4 3.02.121 P
by good saint albon, who said, "simon, come; 2H6 2.01. 89
what say you, simon catling? ROM 4.05.130 P
SIMONIDES 8 FR 0.0009 REL FR 6 V 2 P
if the good king simonides were of my mind — PER 2.01. 43 P
simonides? 2.01. 45
pentapolis, and our king the good simonides. 2.01.100 P
the good simonides, do you call him? 2.01.101
we are honor'd much by good simonides. 2.03. 20
good morrow to the good simonides! 2.05. 1
all fortune to the good simonides! 2.05. 24
to th' court of king simonides | are letters 3.ch. 23
SIMONY 1 FR 0.0001 REL FR 1 V 0 P
simony was fair play; H8 4.02. 36
SIMPCOX 1 FR 0.0001 REL FR 1 V 0 P
saunder simpcox, and if it please you, master. 2H6 2.01.122
SIMPLE 77 FR 0.0087 REL FR 47 V 30 P
my mind | according to my shallow simple skill. TGV 1.02. 8
without you were so simple, none else would: 2.01. 37 P
skirts for yourself, in my simple conjectures. WIV 1.01. 30 P
where's simple, my man? can you tell, cousin? 1.01.134 P
how now, simple, where have you been? 1.01.200 P
in his country, simple though i stand here. 1.01.219 P
peter simple, you say your name is? 1.04. 15 P
servingman, and friend simple by your name, 3.01. 2 P
and smell like bucklersbury in simple time — i 3.03. 73 P
simple of itself; 3.05. 31 P
mistress ford, in the simple office of love, but 4.02. 4 P
we are simple men, we do not know what's brought 4.02.174 P
what simple thief brags of his own /attaint? ERR 3.02. 16
but she tells to your highness simple truth! 5.01.211
man should do, for my simple true judgment? ADO 1.01.167 P
as modest evidence | to witness simple virtue? 4.01. 38
by my soul, a swain, a most simple clown! LLL 4.01.140
this is a gift that i have, simple; 4.02. 65 P
simple, a foolish extravagant spirit, full of 4.02. 65 P
farewell, mad wenches, you have simple wits. 5.02.264
you see how simple and how fond i am. MND 3.02.317
to show our simple skill, | that is the true 5.01.110
go to, here's a simple line of life! MV 2.02.160 P
and nine maids is a simple coming–in for one man 2.02.163 P
edge of a feather–bed, here are simple scapes. 2.02.165 P
there is no /vice so simple but assumes | some 3.02. 81
that is another simple sin in you, to bring the AYL 3.02. 78 P
doth my simple feature content you? 3.03. 3 P
when they do homage to this simple peasant. SHR in.1. 135
daughters, | i here bestow a simple instrument, 2.01. 99
i am asham'd that women are so simple | to offer 5.02.161
whose simple touch | is powerful to araise king AWW 2.01. 75
great floods have flown | from simple sources; 2.01.140
there's a simple putting off. 2.02. 41 P
i am a simple maid, and therein wealthiest 2.03. 66
if that this simple syllogism will serve, so; TN 1.05. 50 P
he's simple, and tells much. WT 4.04.345
his sworn brother, a very simple gentleman! 4.04.596 P
how blessed are we that are not simple men! 4.04.745
it is a simple one, but what though? H5 2.01. 8 P
no simple man that sees | this jarring discord 1H6 4.01.187
salisbury and warwick are no simple peers. 2H6 1.03. 74
our simple supper ended, give me leave | in this 2.02. 2
and in his simple show he harbors treason. 3.01. 54
for god forbid so many simple souls | should 4.04. 10
and trust not simple henry nor his oaths. 3H6 1.02. 59
ah, simple men, you know not what you swear! 3.01. 83
about, | and but attended by a simple guard, 4.02. 16
simple plain clarence, i do love thee so | that R3 1.01.118
but thus his simple truth must be abus'd | with 1.03. 52
darkness, | i do beweep to many simple gulls — 1.03.327
i wonder he's so simple | to trust the mock'ry 3.02. 26
i am a simple woman, much too weak | t' oppose H8 2.04.106
well, you have made a simple choice, you know ROM 2.05. 38 P
the fee–simple! o simple! 3.01. 34 P
bold, | think true love acted simple modesty. 3.02. 16
there are no tricks in plain and simple faith; JC 4.02. 22
an understanding simple and unschool'd: HAM 1.02. 97
how yond justice rails upon yond simple thief. LR 4.06.152 P
in simple and pure soul i come to you. OTH 1.01.107
yet she's a simple bawd | that cannot say as 4.02. 20
not think i am so simple but i know the devil ANT 5.02.272 P
a simple countryman, that brought her figs. 5.02.339
in simple and low things to prince it much CYM 3.03. 85
ado | with that harsh, noble, simple nothing, 3.04.132
thy corpse, | lying with simple shells. PER 3.01. 64
prentices simple, down with him! STM II.C 22 P
prentices simple, prentices simple! II.C 23 P
prentices simple, prentices simple! II.C 23 P
slain, | he might be buried in a tomb so simple, VEN 244
under whose simple semblance he hath fed | upon 795
the poisonous simple sometime is compacted | in LUC 530
neither, | simple were so well compounded: PHT 44
skill, | and simple truth miscall'd simplicity, SON 66.11
for compound sweet forgoing simple savor, 125. 7
on both sides thus is simple truth suppress'd. 138. 8
who, young and simple, would not be so lover'd? LC 320
SIMPLE–ANSWER'D 1 FR 0.0001 REL FR 1 V 0 P
be simple–answer'd, for we know the truth. LR 3.07. 43
SIMPLENESS 5 FR 0.0005 REL FR 4 V 1 P
that | which simpleness and merit purchaseth. ADO 3.01. 70
be amiss, | when simpleness and duty tender it. MND 5.01. 83
in her they are the better for their simpleness; AWW 1.01. 44 P
god's will, | what simpleness is this? ROM 3.03. 77
charter in your voice | t' assist my simpleness. OTH 1.03.246
SIMPLER 2 FR 0.0002 REL FR 2 V 0 P
and simpler than the infancy of truth. TRO 3.02.170
but in the plainer and simpler kind of people TIM 5.01. 25
SIMPLES 5 FR 0.0005 REL FR 3 V 2 P
dere is some simples in my closet, dat i vill WIV 1.04. 63 P
of mine own, compounded of many simples, AYL 4.01. 16 P
with overwhelming brows, | culling of simples; ROM 5.01. 40
collected from all simples that have virtue HAM 4.07.144
are many simples operative, whose power | will LR 4.04. 14
SIMPLEST 1 FR 0.0001 REL FR 1 V 0 P
you are the simplest things that ever stood in STM II.C 21

SIMPLICITY 14 FR 0.0015 REL FR 10 V 4 P
you are a very simplicity oman; WIV 4.01. 30 P
such is the simplicity of man to hearken after LLL 1.01.217 P
twice sod simplicity, bis coctus! 4.02. 22 P
shape of love's tyburn that hangs up simplicity. 4.03. 52
vildly compiled, profound simplicity. 5.02. 52
apply | to prove, by wit, worth in simplicity. 5.02. 78
head, | by the simplicity of venus' doves, | by MND 1.01.171
and tongue–tied simplicity | in least speak most 5.01.104
for that in low simplicity | he lends out money MV 1.03. 43
from whose simplicity i think it not uneasy to WT 4.02. 49 P
but alas, | i am as true as truth's simplicity, TRO 3.02.169
i with great truth catch mere simplicity; 4.04.104
truth, and rarity, | grace in all simplicity, PHT 54
skill, | and simple truth miscall'd simplicity, SON 66.11
SIMPLY 12 FR 0.0013 REL FR 4 V 8 P
if he take her, let him take her simply. WIV 3.02. 76 P
he hath simply the best wit of any handicraft MND 4.02. 9 P
for simply your having in beard is a younger AYL 3.02.377 P
you have simply misus'd our sex in your 4.01.201 P
wealthiest | that i protest i simply am a maid. AWW 2.03. 67
simply the thing i am | shall make me live. 4.03.333
have the back–trick simply as strong as any man TN 1.03.123 P
i were simply the most active fellow in europe. 2H4 4.03. 21 P
he is simply the most active gentleman of france H5 3.07. 97 P
summer, | and not a man, for being simply man, TRO 3.03. 80
he is simply the rarest man i' th' world. COR 4.05.160 P
simply i credit her false–speaking tongue; SON 138. 7
SIMP'RING 3 FR 0.0003 REL FR 2 V 1 P
(as i perceive by your simp'ring, none of you AYL ep 16 P
behold yond simp'ring dame, | whose face between LR 4.06.118
but have blush'd | at simp'ring sirs that did. TNK 5.01.104
SIMULAR 2 FR 0.0002 REL FR 2 V 0 P
and thou simular of virtue | that art incestuous LR 3.02. 54
that i return'd with simular proof enough | to CYM 5.05.200
SIMULATION 1 FR 0.0001 REL FR 0 V 1 P
m.o.a.i. this simulation is not as the former; TN 2.05.139 P
SIN* *(also chin)*
/SIN* 3 FR 0.0003 REL FR 2 V 1 P
/and /water /cannot /wash /away /your /sin. R2 4.01.242
/nation /holds /it /no /sin /to /tarre /them /to HAM 2.02.353 P
/plate /sin with gold, | and the strong lance of LR 4.06.165
SIN* 179 FR 0.0202 REL FR 156 V 23 P
i should sin | to think but nobly of my TMP 1.02.118
you are three men of sin, whom destiny, | that 3.03. 53
now shall i sin in my wish: WIV 3.03. 49 P
though 'tis my familiar sin | with maids to seem MM 1.04. 31
some rise by sin, and some by virtue fall; 2.01. 38
that doth goad us on | to sin in loving virtue. 2.02.182
repent you, fair one, of the sin you carry? 2.03. 19
then was your sin of heavier kind than his. 2.03. 28
as that the sin hath brought you to this shame, 2.03. 31
might there not be a charity in sin | to save 2.04. 63
to my soul, | it is no sin at all, but charity. 2.04. 66
soul, | were equal poise of sin and charity. 2.04. 68
that i do beg his life, if it be sin, | heaven 2.04. 69
if that be sin, i'll make it my morn–prayer | to 2.04. 71
sure it is no sin, | or of the deadly seven it 3.01.109
what sin you do to save a brother's life, 3.01.133
if the devil have given thee proofs for sin, 3.02. 30
to bring you thus together 'tis no sin, | sith 4.01. 72
purchas'd by such sin | for which the pardoner 4.02.108
and many such–like liberties of sin: ERR 1.02.102
teach sin the carriage of a holy saint; 3.02. 14
love — | a sin prevailing much in youthful men, 5.01. 52
and truly i hold it a sin to match in my kinred. ADO 2.01. 64 P
as in a sanctuary, and people sin upon purpose, 2.01.259 P
of truth | can cunning sin cover itself withal! 4.01. 36
a husband, | and so extenuate the 'forehand sin. 4.01. 50
not add to her damnation | a sin of perjury; 4.01.173
penance your invention | can lay upon my sin; 5.01.274
'tis deadly sin to keep that oath, my lord, LLL 2.01.105
keep that oath, my lord, | and sin to break it. 2.01.106
do not call it sin in me, | that i am forsworn 4.03.113
i that hold it sin | to break the vow i am 4.03.175
and even that falsehood, in itself a sin, | thus 5.02.775
in truth, i know it is a sin to be a mocker, but MV 1.02. 57 P
what heinous sin is it in me | to be ashamed to 2.03. 16
me, | but if you do, you'll make me wish a sin, 3.02. 13
most mischievous foul sin, in chiding sin: AYL 2.07. 64
most mischievous foul sin, in chiding sin: 2.07. 64
manners must be wicked, and wickedness is sin, 3.02. 43 P
and wickedness is sin, and sin is damnation. 3.02. 43 P
that is another simple sin in you, to bring the 3.02. 78 P
which is the most inhibited sin in the canon. AWW 1.01.145 P
only sin | and hellish obstinacy tie thy tongue, 1.03.179
where both not sin, and yet a sinful fact. 3.07. 47
only in this disguise i think't no sin | to 4.02. 75
that transgresses is but patch'd with sin, and TN 1.05. 49 P
and sin that amends is but patch'd with virtue. 1.05. 49 P
my desire of having is the sin of covetousness; 5.01. 47 P
which to reiterate were sin | as deep as that, WT 1.02.283
person | (so sacred as it is) i have done sin, 5.01.172
if thou hadst said him nay, it had been sin. JN 1.01.275
say, | that he is not only plagued for her sin, 2.01.184
but god hath made her sin and her the plague 2.01.185
plagued for her | and with her plague, her sin; 2.01.187
injury | her injury, the beadle to her sin — 2.01.188
then god forgive the sin of all those souls 2.01.283
rail, | and say there is no sin but to be rich; 2.01.594
and didst in signs again parley with sin, | yea, 4.02.238
a purity, | to the yet unbegotten sin of times; 4.03. 54
for i am stifled with this smell of sin. 4.03.113
or sin of thought | be guilty of the stealing 4.03.135
o, god defend my soul from such deep sin! R2 1.01.187
day, | but, self–affrighted, tremble at his sin. 3.02. 53
ere foul sin gathering head | shall break into 5.01. 58
i know she is come to pray for your foul sin. 5.03. 82
me sad, and mak'st me sin | in envy that my lord 1H4 1.01. 78
'tis no sin for a man to labor in his vocation. 1.02.104 P
i'll be no longer guilty of this sin. 2.04.241 P
if to be old and merry be a sin, then many an 2.04.471 P
reward valor bear the sin upon their own heads. 5.04.150 P
and hold'st it fear or sin | to speak a truth. 2H4 1.01. 95
and he doth sin that doth belie the dead, | not 1.01. 98
"the time will come, that foul sin, gathering 3.01. 76
conscience wash'd | as pure as sin with baptism. H5 1.02. 32

the sin upon my head, dread sovereign! 1.02. 97
is not so vile a sin | as self–neglecting. 2.04. 74
de sin. le col, de nick; le menton, de sin. 3.04. 36 P
de sin. le col, de nick; le menton, de sin. 3.04. 36 P
d' elbow, de nick, et de sin. 3.04. 49 P
d' elbow, de nick, de sin, de foot, le count. 3.04. 59 P
him that escapes, it were not sin to think that, 4.01.183 P
but if it be a sin to covet honor, | i am the 4.03. 28
thou that giv'st whores indulgences to sin. 1H6 1.03. 35
that malice was a great and grievous sin; 3.01.128
so should i give consent to flatter sin. 5.05. 25
although by his sight his sin be multiplied. 2H6 2.01. 69
murther indeed, that bloody sin, i tortur'd 3.01.131
then is sin struck down like an ox, and 4.02. 26 P
it is great sin to swear unto a sin, | but 5.01.182
it is great sin to swear unto a sin, | but 5.01.182
a sin, | but greater sin to keep a sinful oath. 5.01.183
for of that sin | my mild entreaty shall not 3H6 3.01. 90
'twas sin before, but now 'tis charity. 5.05. 76
'tis sin to flatter, "good" was little better: 5.06. 3
sin, death, and hell have set their marks on him R3 1.03.292
for this, | for in that sin he is as deep as i. 1.04.214
this land | would i be guilty of so deep a sin. 3.01. 43
in | so far in blood that sin will pluck on sin. 4.02. 64
in | so far in blood that sin will pluck on sin. 4.02. 64
would show a worse sin than ill doctrine. H8 1.03. 60
the willing'st sin i ever yet committed | may be 3.01. 49
thou scarlet sin, robb'd this bewailing land 3.02.255
by that sin fell the angels; 3.02.441
were unsatisfied in getting | (which was a sin), 4.02. 56
and you shall not sin | if you do say we think TRO 2.03.122
(which i beseech you call a virtuous sin) 4.04. 81
i sin in envying his nobility; COR 1.01.230
if any such be here | (as it were sin to doubt) 1.06. 68
which rome reputes to be a heinous sin, | yield TIT 1.01.448
that left the camp to sin in lucrece' bed? 4.01. 64
kin, | to strike him dead i hold it not a sin. ROM 1.05. 59
hand | this holy shrine, the gentle sin is this: 1.05. 94
thus from my lips, by thine, my sin is purg'd. 1.05.107
then have my lips the sin that they have took. 1.05.108
sin from my lips? 1.05.109
give me my sin again. 1.05.110
god pardon sin! wast thou with rosaline? 2.03. 44
o deadly sin! 3.03. 24
still blush, as thinking their own kisses sin; 3.03. 39
is it more sin to wish me thus forsworn, | or to 3.05.236
where i have learnt me to repent the sin | of 4.02. 17
well thou knowest, is cross and full of sin. 4.03. 5
thee, youth, | put not another sin upon my head, 5.03. 62
rich men sin, and i eat root. TIM 1.02. 71
upon thee, and then thou wouldst sin the faster. 1.02.240 P
nothing emboldens sin so much as mercy. 3.05. 3
he has a sin that often | drowns him and takes 3.05. 67
when man's worst sin is, he does too much good! 4.02. 39
then do we sin against our own estate, | when we 5.01. 41
the sin of my ingratitude even now | was heavy MAC 1.04. 15
smacking of every sin | that has a name; 4.03. 59
cut off even in the blossoms of my sin, HAM 1.05. 76
i stand accomptant for as great a sin), | but OTH 2.01.293
and to defend ourselves it be a sin | when 2.03.203
all seals and symbols of redeemed sin, | his 2.03.344
alas, what ignorant sin have i committed? 4.02. 70
therefore confess thee freely of thy sin; 5.02. 53
then is it sin | to rush into the secret house ANT 4.15. 80
if it be a sin to make a true election, she is CYM 1.02. 27 P
to leave you in your madness, 'twere my sin; 2.03. 99
you sin against | obedience, which you owe your 2.03.111
if it be sin to say so, sir, i yoke me | in my 4.02. 19
turn'd coward | but by example (o, a sin in war, 5.03. 36
did begin | was with long use account'd no sin. PER 1.ch. 30
perfections wait | that, knowing sin within, 1.01. 80
how courtesy would seem to cover sin, | when 1.01.121
one sin, i know, another doth provoke: 1.01.137
poison and treason are the hands of sin, | ay, 1.01.139
nor tell the world antiochus doth sin | in such 1.01.146
him, | for flattery is the bellows blows up sin, 1.02. 39
how thaliard came full bent with sin | and hid 2.ch. 23
to bar heaven's shaft, but sin had his reward. 2.04. 15
where sin is justice, lust and ignorance | the TNK 2.02.106
'tis a sin | which oft th' apostle did forewarn STM II.C 93
estate, | hiding base sin in pleats of majesty; LUC 93
and hold it for no sin | to wish that i their 209
as if the heavens should countenance his sin. 343
the blackest sin is clear'd with absolution; 354
wherein it shall discern | authority for sin, 620
when pattern'd by thy fault foul sin may say 629
thy fault foul sin may say | he learn'd to sin, 630
o, deeper sin than bottomless conceit | can 701
be, | to have their unseen sin remain untold; 753
whoever plots the sin, thou 'point'st the season 879
sits sin, to seize the souls that wander by him. 882
they buy thy help, but sin ne'er gives a fee, 913
my sable ground of sin i will not paint, | to 1074
let sin, alone committed, light alone | upon his 1480
many fall, | to plague a private sin in general? 1484
or blot with hell–born sin such saint–like forms 1519
with men, | to sin and never for to saint: PP 18.44
sin of self–love possesseth all mine eye, | and SON 62. 1
and for this sin there is no remedy, | it is so 62. 3
that sin by him advantage should achieve, | and 67. 3
this silence for my sin you did impute, | which 83. 9
'tis the lesser sin | that mine eye loves it and 114.13
that she that makes me sin awards me pain. 141.14
love is my sin, and thy dear virtue hate, | hate 142. 1
hate of my sin, grounded on sinful loving: 142. 2
SIN–ABSOLVER 1 FR 0.0001 REL FR 1 V 0 P
a sin–absolver, and my friend profess'd, | to ROM 3.03. 50
SINCE *(also sith, sithence)*
/SINCE 7 FR 0.0008 REL FR 5 V 2 P
/since /it /is /bankrout /of /his /majesty. R2 4.01.267
/have /since /miscarried /under /bullingbrook. 2H4 4.01.127
therefore, /since brevity is the soul of wit, HAM 2.02. 90
/who /since /possesses /chambermaids /and LR 4.01. 62 P
/which /since /his /coming /forth /is /thought 4.03. 4 P
/you /spoke /not /with /her /since? 4.03. 35
/no, /since. 4.03. 37
SINCE 478 FR 0.0540 REL FR 396 V 82 P
twelve year since, miranda, twelve year since, TMP 1.02. 53

twelve year since, miranda, twelve year since, 1.02. 53
necessaries, | which since have steaded much; 1.02.165
since thou dost give me pains, | let me remember 1.02.242
who with mine eyes (never since at ebb) beheld 1.02.436
not since widow dido's time. 2.01. 77 P
with mine own hands since i was cast ashore. 2.02.123 P
since | they have left their viands behind; 3.03. 40
no matter, since i feel | the best is past. 3.03. 50
since they did plot | the means that dusky dis 4.01. 88
and, since i saw thee, | th' affliction of my 5.01.114
whom three hours since | were wrack'd upon this 5.01.136
my dukedom since you have given me again, | i 5.01.168
which, but three glasses since, we gave out 5.01.223
all this service | have i done since i went. 5.01.226
been in such a pickle since i saw you last that 5.01.282 P
accidents gone by | since i came to this isle. 5.01.307
let me not, | since i have my dukedom got, | and ep 6
but since thou lov'st, love still, and thrive TGV 1.01. 9
since maids, in modesty, say "no" to that 1.02. 55
you never saw her since she was deform'd. 2.01. 63 P
ever since you lov'd her. 2.01. 65 P
i have lov'd her ever since i saw her, and still 2.01. 66 P
writ, | but (since unwillingly) take them again. 2.01.123
since his exile she hath despis'd me most, 3.02. 3
for since the substance of your perfect self 4.02.123
but since your falsehood shall become you well 4.02.129
which since i know they virtuously are plac'd, 4.03. 38
but since she did neglect her looking–glass, 4.04.152
since she respects my mistress' love so much. 4.04.182
i cannot abide the smell of hot meat since. WIV 1.01.286 P
i never prosper'd since i forswore myself at 4.05.101 P
since i pluck'd geese, play'd truant, and whipt 5.01. 24 P
the truth is, she and i (long since contracted) 5.05.223
since therein she doth evitate and shun | a 5.05.228
since i am put to know that your own science MM 1.01. 5
he promis'd to meet me two hours since, and he 1.02. 75 P
(since i suppose we are made to be no stronger 2.04.132
'twas never merry world since, of two usuries, 3.02. 5 P
believe that, since you know not what you speak. 3.02.153 P
none since the curfew rung. 4.02. 75
yet since i see you fearful, that neither my 4.02.188 P
and five years since there was some speech of 5.01.217
since which time of five years | i never spake 5.01.222
since it is so, | let him not die. 5.01.447
for since the mortal and intestine jars | 'twixt ERR 1.01. 11
since that my beauty cannot please his eye, 2.01.114
i could not speak with dromio since at first | i 2.02. 5
even now, even here, not half an hour since. 2.02. 14
i did not see you since you sent me hence | home 2.02. 15
since mine own doors refuse to entertain me, 3.01.120
you know since pentecost the sum is due, | and 4.01. 1
due, | and since i have not much importun'd you, 4.01. 2
you know i gave it you half an hour since. 4.01. 65
you word an hour since that the bark expedition 4.03. 38 P
that since have felt the vigor of his rage. 4.04. 78
long since thy husband serv'd me in my wars, 5.01.161
i have not breath'd almost since i did see it. 5.01.181
even for the service that long since i did thee, 5.01.191
grief hath chang'd me since you saw me last, 5.01.298
but seven years since, in syracusa, boy, | thou 5.01.321
i think i told your lordship a year since, how ADO 2.02. 12 P
since many a wooer doth commence his suit | to 2.03. 50
men was ever so, | since summer first was leavy. 2.03. 73
ever since you left it. 3.04. 69 P
and since you could not be my son–in–law, | be 5.01.287
in brief, since i do purpose to marry, i will 5.04.105 P
guilty of such a ballet some three ages since, LLL 1.02.112 P
and since her time are colliers counted bright. 4.03.263
since all the power thereof it doth apply | to 5.02. 77
since you are strangers and come here by chance, 5.02.218
since you can cog, i'll play no more with you. 5.02.235
since when, i'll be sworn, he wore none but a 5.02.713 P
yet, since love's argument was first on foot, 5.02.747
since to wail friends lost | is not by much so 5.02.749
and never, since the middle summer's spring, MND 2.01. 82
since once i sat upon a promontory, | and heard 2.01.149
since night you lov'd me; 3.02.275
yet since night you left me: 3.02.275
and since we have the vaward of the day, | my 4.01.105
since lion vild hath here deflow'r'd my dear; 5.01.292
since you have shore | with shears his thread of 5.01.340
my lord bassanio, since you have found antonio, MV 1.01. 69
since this fortune falls to you, | be content, 3.02.133
since you are dear bought, i will love you dear. 3.02.313
and since in paying it, it is impossible i 3.02.317 P
since i have your good leave to go away, | i 3.02.324
cause, | but, since i am a dog, beware my fangs. 3.03. 7
since that the trade and profit of the city 3.03. 30
but since he stands obdurate, | and that no 4.01. 8
since nought so stockish, hard, and full of rage 5.01. 81
since you do take it, love, so much at heart. 5.01.145
since he hath got the jewel that i loved, | and 5.01.224
for since the little wit that fools have was AYL 1.02. 88 P
since the youth will not be entreated, his own 1.02.149 P
'tis but an hour ago since it was nine, | and 2.07. 24
not see him since? 3.01. 1
i was never so berhym'd since pythagoras' time, 3.02.176 P
but since that thou canst talk of love so well, 3.05. 94
i was, since my conversion | so sweetly tastes, 4.03.136
i have, since i was three year old, convers'd 5.02. 60 P
since once he play'd a farmer's eldest son. SHR in.1. 84
since for the great desire i had | to see fair 1.01. 1
come, since this bar in law makes us friends, it 1.01.135 P
for in a quarrel since i came ashore | i kill'd 1.01.231
petruchio, since we are stepp'd thus far in, | i 1.02. 83
and since you do profess to be a suitor, | you 1.02.270
since, of ourselves, ourselves are choleric, 4.01.174
and since mine eyes are witness of her lightness 4.02. 24
forward, i pray, since we have come so far, 4.05. 12
brought him up ever since he was three years old 5.01. 82 P
nay, that you shall not, since you have begun; 5.02. 44
cost me /a hundred crowns since supper–time. 5.02.128
too, | since i nor wax nor honey can bring home, AWW 1.02. 65
since the physician at your father's died? 1.02. 70
some six months since, my lord. 1.02. 71
since you set up your rest 'gainst remedy. 2.01.135
since i cannot yet find in my heart to repent. 2.05. 12 P
it, since i have found | myself in my incertain 3.01. 14

i have no mind to isbel since i was at court. 3.02. 12 P
five descents | since the first father wore it. 3.07. 25
since frenchmen are so braid, | marry that will, 4.02. 73
i have deliv'red it an hour since. 4.03. 3 P
wife some two months since fled from his house. 4.03. 47 P
since i heard of the good lady's death and that 4.05. 69 P
but since you have made the days and nights as 5.01. 3
since you are like to see the king before me, 5.01. 30
since i have lost, have lov'd, was in mine eye 5.03. 54
i pray you yet | (since you lack virtue, i will 5.03.222
fell and cruel hounds, | e'er since pursue me. TN 1.01. 22
of a count | that died some twelvemonth since, 1.02. 37
a moderate pace i have since arriv'd but hither. 2.02. 4 P
dear heart, since i must needs be gone." 2.03.102
since the youth of the count's was to–day with 2.03.132 P
are very rascals since bonds disgrac'd them. 3.01. 21 P
since lowly feigning was call'd compliment. 3.01. 99
have been grand–jurymen since before noah was a 3.02. 16 P
but since you make your pleasure of your pains, 3.03. 2
it might have since been answer'd in repaying 3.03. 33
since you to non–regardance cast my faith, | and 5.01.121
since when, my watch hath told me, toward my 5.01.162
and tortur'd me, | since i have lost thee! 5.01.220
all the occurrence of my fortune since | hath 5.01.257
and since you call'd me master for so long, 5.01.324
since their more mature dignities and royal WT 1.01. 24 P
the shepherd's note since we have left our 1.02. 2
by this we gather | you have tripp'd since. 1.02. 76
temptations have since then been born to 's: 1.02. 77
but since | nor brass nor stone nor parchment 1.02.359
since i am charg'd in honor and by him | that i 1.02.407
you sent to th' oracle are come | an hour since. 2.03.195
since we so openly | proceed in justice, which 3.02. 5
since what i am to say must be but that | which 3.02. 22
since he came, | with what encounter so 3.02. 48
even since it could speak, from an infant, 3.02. 70
and that since then | you have not dar'd to 3.02.128
since fate (against thy better disposition) 3.03. 28
i have not wink'd since i saw these sights. 3.03.104 P
gap, since it is in my pow'r | to o'erthrow law, 4.01. 7
it is fifteen years since i saw my country; 4.02. 4 P
sir, it is three days since i saw the prince. 4.02. 29 P
he hath been since an ape–bearer, then a 4.03. 95 P
since my desires | run not before mine honor, 4.04. 33
since these good men are pleas'd, let them come 4.04.340 P
remember since you ow'd no more to time | than i 5.01.219
thrice a day, ever since the death of hermione, 5.02.106 P
perform'd in this wide gap of time since first 5.03.154
and e'er since | sits on 's horseback at mine JN 2.01.288
since i first call'd my brother's father dad. 2.01.467
since kings break faith upon commodity, | gain, 2.01.597
therefore, since law itself is perfect wrong, 3.01.189
what since thou swor'st is sworn against thyself 3.01.268
for since the birth of cain, the first male 3.04. 79
since all and every part of what we would | doth 4.02. 38
'tis not an hour since i left him well. 4.03.104
but since you are a gentle convertite, | my 5.01. 19
since i must lose the use of all deceit? 5.04. 27
since it is true | that i must die here and live 5.04. 28
who half an hour since came from the dolphin, 5.07. 83
since it hath been beforehand with our griefs. 5.07.111
since the more fair and crystal is the sky, R2 1.01. 41
since last i went to france to fetch his queen. 1.01.131
which since we cannot do to make you friends, 1.01.197
since we cannot atone you, we shall see 1.01.202
but since correction lieth in those hands 1.02. 4
since thou hast far to go, bear not along | the 1.03.199
but since it would not, he had none of me. 1.04. 19
since thou dost seek to kill my name in me, | i 2.01. 86
but since i cannot, be it known unto you | i do 2.03.158
since presently your souls must part your bodies 3.01. 3
to fear the foe, since fear oppresseth strength, 3.02.180
since foes have scope to beat both thee and me. 3.03.141
since, wedding it, there is such length in grief 5.01. 94
'tis full three months since i did see him last. 5.03. 2
my lord, some two days since i saw the prince, 5.03. 13
since pride must have a fall, and break the neck 5.05. 88
since thou, created to be aw'd by man, | wast 5.05. 91
is turn'd upside down since robin ostler died. 1H4 2.01. 10 P
fellow never joy'd since the price of oats rose, 2.01. 12 P
bit than i have been since the first cock. 2.01. 17 P
well, do not then, for since you love me not, 2.03. 97
themselves humors since the old days of goodman 2.04. 93 P
lips are scarce wip'd since thou drunk'st last. 2.04.153 P
i never dealt better since i was a man; 2.04.169 P
and ever since thou hast blush'd extempore. 2.04.316 P
ago, jack, since thou sawest thine own knee? 2.04.327 P
and since your coming hither have done enough 3.01.176
i not fall'n away vilely since this last action? 3.03. 1 P
since not to be avoided it falls on me. 5.05. 13
day, | and since this business so fair is done, 5.05. 43
to dignify the times, | since caesar's fortunes. 2H4 1.01. 23
and since we are o'erset, venture again. 1.01.185
if he had writ man ever since his father was a 1.02. 27 P
my lord, but he hath since done good service at 1.02. 61 P
but since all is well, keep it so, wake not a 1.02.153 P
have weekly sworn to marry since i perceiv'd the 1.02.241 P
since my exion is ent'red and my case so openly 2.01. 30 P
since when, i pray you, sir? 2.04.132 P
years gone | since richard and northumberland, 3.01. 58
it is but eight years since | this percy was the 3.01. 60
do you remember since we lay all night in the 3.02.194 P
coz, since sudden sorrow | serves to say thus, 4.02. 83
art not firm enough, since griefs are green, 4.05.203
since a crooked figure may | attest in little H5 pr 15
it, | since his addiction was to courses vain, 1.01. 54
since we have locks to safeguard necessaries, 1.02.176
since we are well persuaded | we carry not a 2.02. 20
since god so graciously hath brought to light 2.02.185
since i may say, "now lie i like a king." 4.01. 17
since that my penitence comes after all, 4.01.304
i was not angry since i came to france | until 4.07. 55
since then my office hath so far prevail'd, 5.02. 29
since arms avail not now that henry's dead. 1H6 1.01. 47
since they, so few, watch such a multitude. 1.01.161
shall we disturb him, since he keeps no mean? 1.02.121
days, | since i have entered into these wars. 1.02.132
since henry's death, i fear, there is conveyance 1.03. 2

of all exploits since first i follow'd arms, 2.01. 43
well then, alone (since there's no remedy) | i 2.02. 57
but since your ladyship is not at leisure, 2.03. 26
since you are tongue–tied and so loath to speak, 2.04. 25
since henry monmouth first began to reign, 2.05. 23
and even since then hath richard been obscur'd, 2.05. 26
long since we were resolved of your truth, 3.04. 20
who two hours since | i met in travel toward his 4.03. 35
since thou dost deign to woo her little worth 5.03.151
live, | especially since charles must father it. 5.04. 71
since, lords of england, it is thus agreed 5.04.116
and therefore, lords, since he affects her most, 5.05. 59
since thou wert king — as who is king but thou? 2H6 1.03.123
we know the time since he was mild and affable, 3.01. 9
merry world in england since gentlemen came up. 4.02. 8 P
to a thing, and i was never mine own man since. 4.02. 83 P
cade, | who since i heard to be discomfited. 5.01. 63
since when, his oath is broke; 3H6 2.02. 89
yet know thou, since we have begun to strike, 2.02.167
since thou deniedst the gentle king to speak. 2.02.172
since this earth affords no joy to me | but to 3.02.165
and fled (as he hears since) to burgundy. 4.06. 79
then, since the heavens have shap'd my body so, 5.06. 78
since i cannot prove a lover | to entertain R3 1.01. 28
since that our brother dubb'd them gentlewomen, 1.01. 82
but since you teach me how to flatter you, 1.02.223
her lord, whom i, some three months since, 1.02.240
since i am crept in favor with myself, | i will 1.02.258
since every jack became a gentleman, | there's 1.03. 71
scarce some two days since were worth a noble. 1.03. 81
since i have made my friends at peace on earth. 2.01. 6
yet, since it is but green, it should be put 2.02.135
i hope he is much grown since last i saw him. 2.04. 5
and since, methinks i would not grow so fast, 2.04. 14
which, since, succeeding ages have re–edified. 3.01. 71
which since you come too late of our intent, 3.05. 69
men, | since you will buckle fortune on my back, 3.07.228
march on, march on, since we are up in arms, 4.04.528
since that i myself | find in myself no pity to 5.03.202
a drowsy head | have i since your departure had, 5.03.229
how have ye done | since last we saw in france? H8 1.01. 2
and ever since a fresh admirer | of what i saw 1.01. 3
i am not such a truant since my coming, | as not 3.01. 43
since virtue finds no friends) a wife, a true 3.01.126
since i had my office, | i have kept you next my 3.02.156
since you provoke me, shall be most notorious. 3.02.288
which, since they are of you, and odious, | i 3.02.331
since which she was remov'd to kimmalton, 4.01. 34
for since the cardinal fell that title's lost. 4.01. 96
saw ye none enter since i slept? 4.02. 86
strangely | with me since first you knew me. 4.02.113
whereof hath ever since kept hector fasting and TRO 1.02. 35 P
since the first sword was drawn about this 2.02. 18
since i have taken such pain to bring you 3.02.199 P
since things in motion sooner catch the eye 3.03.183
since she could speak, | she hath not given so 4.01. 73
dead | since first i saw yourself and diomed 4.05.215
we have had pelting wars since you refus'd | the 4.05.267
but, since it serves my purpose, i will venture COR 1.01. 91
'tis not four days gone | since i heard thence; 1.02. 7
how long is't since? 1.06. 14
i, sir, | half an hour since brought my report. 1.06. 21
is worth all your predecessors since deucalion, 2.01. 91 P
and in the brunt of seventeen battles since | he 2.02.100
and since the wisdom of their choice is rather 2.03. 98 P
bred i' th' wars | since 'a could draw a sword, 3.01.319
since that to both | it stands in like request? 3.02. 50
but since he hath | serv'd well for rome — 3.03. 82
since i have ever followed thee with hate, 4.05. 98
and i have nightly since | dreamt of encounters 4.05.122
since thou know'st | thy country's strength and 4.05.139
and my true lip | hath virgin'd it e'er since. 5.03. 48
bewray what life | we have led since thy exile. 5.03. 96
since that thy sight, which should | make our 5.03. 98
ten years are spent since first he undertook TIT 1.01. 31
'tis not an hour since i left them there. 2.03.256
since 'tis my father's mind | that i repair to 5.03. 1
ne'er saw her match since first the world begun. ROM 1.02. 93
'tis since the earthquake now aleven years, 1.03. 23
and since that time it is aleven years, | for 1.03. 35
how long is't now since last yourself and i 1.05. 32
'tis since the nuptial of lucentio, | come 1.05. 35
be not her maid, since she is envious; 2.02. 7
since birth, and heaven, and earth, all three do 3.03.120
since arm from arm that voice doth us affray, 3.05. 33
then, since the case so stands as now it doth, 3.05.216
since this same wayward girl is so reclaim'd. 4.02. 47
since you did leave it for my office, sir. 5.01. 23
for since dishonor traffics with man's nature, TIM 1.01.158
and the detention of long since due debts, 2.02. 38
since riches point to misery and contempt? 4.02. 32
do, /villains, do, since you protest to do't. 4.03.434
and since you know you cannot see yourself | so JC 1.02. 67
when went there by an age since the great flood 1.02.152
besides — i ha' not since put up my sword — 1.03. 19
and since the quarrel | will bear no color for 2.01. 28
since cassius first did whet me against caesar, 2.01. 61
but since the affairs of men rests still 5.01. 95
hath it slept since? MAC 1.07. 36
our mistrust, since he delivers | our offices, 3.03. 2
ay, and since too, murthers have been perform'd 3.04. 76
since that the truest issue of thy throne | by 4.03.106
which often, since my here–remain in england, 4.03.148
since his majesty went into the field, i have 5.01. 4 P
guilty | (since nature cannot choose his origin) HAM 1.04. 26
why, thy face is valanc'd since i saw thee last; 2.02.423 P
since my dear soul was mistress of her choice 3.02. 63
since love our hearts and hymen did our hands 3.02.159
since nature makes them partial, should o'erhear 3.03. 32
since i am still possess'd | of those effects 3.03. 53
since frost itself as actively doth burn, | and 3.04. 87
since yet thy cicatrice looks raw and red 4.03. 60
you have been talk'd of since your travel much, 4.07. 71
two months since | here was a gentleman of 4.07. 81
how long is that since? 5.01.145 P
since he went into france i have been in 5.02.210 P
since no man, of aught he leaves, knows what 5.02.223 P
but since he is /better'd, we have therefore 5.02.263

but since, so jump upon this bloody question, 5.02.375
(since now we will divest us both of rule, LR 1.01. 49
since i am sure my love's | more ponderous than 1.01. 77
and purpose not, since what i /well intend, 1.01.225
since that /respects /of /fortune are his love, 1.01.248
since my young lady's going into france, sir, 1.04. 73 P
e'er since thou mad'st thy daughters thy mothers 1.04.172 P
since i came hither | (which i can call but now) 2.01. 86
is it two days since i tripp'd up thy heels, and 2.02. 29 P
but knaves follow it, since a fool gives it. 2.04. 77 P
since i was man, | such sheets of fire, such 3.02. 45
i have serv'd you ever since i was a child; 3.07. 73
i have heard more since. 4.01. 35
but not without that harmful stroke which since 4.02. 77
or whether since he is advis'd by aught | to 5.01. 2
since thy outside looks so fair and warlike, 5.03.143
for since these arms of mine had seven years' OTH 1.03. 83
and since i could distinguish betwixt a benefit 1.03.312 P
but since it is as it is, mend it for your own 2.03.302 P
fear i know not, | since guiltiness i know not; 5.02. 39
i did not see him since. ANT 1.03. 1
since my becomings kill me when they do not 1.03. 96
since he went from egypt, 'tis | a space for 2.01. 30
since i myself | have given myself the cause. 2.05. 83
having a son and friends, since julius caesar, 2.06. 12
but since the cuckoo builds not for himself, 2.06. 28
since i saw you last, | there's a change upon 2.06. 52
since pompey's feast, as menas says, is troubled 3.02. 5
their lust | since then hath made between them. 3.06. 8
what's her name, | since she was cleopatra? 3.13. 99
since | thou hast been whipt for following him. 3.13.136
but since my lord | is antony again, i will be 3.13.185
since the torch is out, | lie down and stray no 4.14. 46
since cleopatra died | i have liv'd in such 4.14. 55
but, fearing since how it might work, hath sent 4.14.125
to prove so worthy as since he hath been allow'd CYM 1.04. 3 P
since when i have been debtor to you for 1.04. 36 P
since doubting things go ill often hurts more 1.06. 95
since | my lord hath interest in them, i will 1.06.194
wrought, | since the true life on't was — 2.04. 76
since i receiv'd command to do this business | i 3.04. 99
since the exile of posthumus, most retir'd 3.05. 36
for since patiently and constantly thou hast 3.05.117 P
how long is't since she went to milford–haven? 3.05.148 P
be companion with them, | since leonatus' false. 3.06. 88
that since the common men are now in action 3.07. 2
i am not very sick, | since i can reason of it. 4.02. 14
long is it since i saw him, | but time hath 4.02.103
since death of my dear'st mother | i did not 4.02.190
i heard no letter from my master since | i wrote 4.03. 36
i, since of your lives you set | so slight a 4.04. 48
since he had rather | groan so in perpetuity 5.04. 5
since, jupiter, our son is good, | take off his 5.04. 85
but since the gods | will have it thus, that 5.05. 78
since she is living, let the time run on | to 5.05.128
since he's so great can make his will his act, PER 1.02. 18
my lord, since you have given me leave to speak, 1.02.101
but since he's gone, the king's seas must please 1.03. 27
but since my landing i have understood | your 1.03. 33
since he gains from his subjects the name of 2.01.104 P
since i have here my father gave in his will. 2.01.134
since every worth in show commends itself. 2.03. 6
since men take women's gifts for impudence. 2.03. 69
since they love men in arms as well as beds. 2.03. 98
and since lord helicane enjoineth us, | we with 2.04. 55
but since king pericles, | my wedded lord, i 3.04. 8
e'er since i can remember. 4.06. 73 P
have plac'd me in this sty, where, since i came, 4.06. 97
since they do better thee in their command. 4.06.162
but since my master and mistress hath bought you 4.06.196 P
but since your kindness | we have stretch'd thus 5.01. 54
since that our theme is haste, | i stamp this TNK 1.01.215
since first we went to school, may we perceive 1.02. 14
since in our terrene state petitions are not 1.03. 14
since his depart, his sports, | though craving 1.03. 27
observ'd him | since our great lord departed? 1.03. 34
since i have known frights, fury, friends' 1.04. 40
seen, | since hercules, a man of tougher sinews. 2.05. 2
since that | your question's with your equal, 3.01. 54
in me, | since thy best props are warp'd! 3.02. 32
since i know | their lives but pinch 'em. 5.03.132
but one hour since, i was as dearly sorry | as 5.04.129
then why not lips on lips, since eyes in eyes? VEN 120
"since i have hemm'd thee here | within the 229
then be my deer, since i am such a park, | no 239
since sweating lust on earth usurp'd his name, 794
since her best work is ruin'd with thy rigor." 954
what canst thou boast | of things long since, or 1078
"since thou art dead, lo here i prophesy, 1135
since he himself is reft from her by death. 1174
since thou art guilty of my cureless crime, LUC 772
be guilty of my death, since of my crime. 931
since that my case is past the help of law. 1022
since thou couldst not defend thy loyal dame, 1034
since men prove beasts, let beasts bear gentle 1148
and ever since, as pitying lucrece' woes, 1747
(since rome herself in them doth stand disgraced 1833
since that our faults in love thus smother'd be. PP 1.14
since sweets and beauties do themselves forsake, SON 12.11
but since she prick'd thee out for women's 20.13
and weep afresh love's long since cancell'd woe, 30. 7
but since he died and poets better prove, 32.13
laws, | since why to love i can allege no cause. 49.14
since from thee going he went willful–slow, 51.13
since, seldom coming, in the long year set, 52. 6
since every one hath, every one, one shade, 53. 3
since mind at first in character was done! 59. 8
since brass, nor stone, nor earth, nor boundless 65. 1
seek | roses of shadow, since his rose is true? 67. 8
show what wealth she had | in days long since, 67.14
since what he owes thee thou thyself dost pay. 79.14
but since your worth (wide as the ocean is) 80. 5
since that my life on thy revolt doth lie; 92.10
since first i saw you fresh, which yet are green 104. 8
since all alike my songs and praises be | to one 105. 3
since, spite of him, i'll live in this poor 107.11
since i left you, mine eye is in my mind, | and 113. 1
since my appeal says i did strive to prove | the 117.13
for since each hand hath put on nature's power, 127. 5
since saucy jacks so happy are in this, | give 128.13
to mourn for me, since mourning doth thee grace, 132.11
yet do not so, but since i am near slain, | kill 139.13
be, | since i their altar, you enpatron me. LC 224

/SINCERE 1 FR 0.0001 REL FR 1 V 0 P
/suppos'd /sincere /and /holy /in /his /thoughts 2H4 1.01.202

SINCERE 3 FR 0.0003 REL FR 3 V 0 P
his love sincere, his thoughts immaculate, | his TGV 2.07. 76
but | from sincere motions, by intelligence, H8 1.01.153
sir, in good faith, in sincere verity, | under LR 2.02.105

SINCERELY 3 FR 0.0003 REL FR 1 V 2 P
most sincerely. ADO 5.01.198 P
perceive i speak sincerely, and high note's H8 2.03. 59
hear me profess sincerely: COR 1.03. 22 P

SINCERITY 6 FR 0.0006 REL FR 4 V 2 P
spirit, | and to be talk'd with in sincerity, MM 1.04. 36
think | a due sincerity governed his deeds, 5.01.446
show'd | bashful sincerity and comely love. ADO 4.01. 54
a riot on the gentle brow | of true sincerity? JN 3.01.248
see now in very sincerity of fear and cold heart 1H4 2.03. 30 P
in the sincerity of love and honest kindness. OTH 2.03.327 P

SIN–CONCEALING 1 FR 0.0001 REL FR 1 V 0 P
vast sin–concealing chaos! LUC 767

SIN–CONCEIVING 1 FR 0.0001 REL FR 1 V 0 P
removed from thy sin–conceiving womb. JN 2.01.182

SINEL'S 1 FR 0.0001 REL FR 1 V 0 P
by sinel's death i know i am thane of glamis, MAC 1.03. 71

SINEW *(also sinow, etc.)*

SINEW 2 FR 0.0002 REL FR 1 V 1 P
with him, the portion and sinew of her fortune, MM 3.01.221 P
thence, | who with them was a rated sinew too, 1H4 4.04. 17

SINEWED 1 FR 0.0001 REL FR 1 V 0 P
he sees | ourselves well sinewed to our defense. JN 5.07. 88

/SINEWS 1 FR 0.0001 REL FR 1 V 0 P
/might /yet /have /balm'd /thy /broken /sinews, LR 3.06. 98

SINEWS 25 FR 0.0028 REL FR 22 V 3 P
i had rather crack my sinews, break my back, TMP 3.01. 26
shorten up their sinews | with aged cramps, and 4.01.259
for orpheus' lute was strung with poets' sinews, TGV 3.02. 77
patience, or we break the sinews of our plot! TN 2.05. 75 P
that knit your sinews to the strength of mine. JN 5.02. 63
help | and yours, the noble sinews of our power, H5 1.02.223
so service shall with steeled sinews toil, | and 2.02. 36
stiffen the sinews, /conjure up the blood, 3.01. 7
these are his substance, sinews, arms, and 1H6 2.03. 63
till bones and flesh and sinews fall away, | so 3.01.192
robb'd my strong–knit sinews of their strength, 3H6 2.03. 4
that keeps troy on foot, | not her own sinews. TRO 1.03.136
too, lies in your sinews, or else there be liars 2.01. 99 P
the edge of steel | or force of greekish sinews. 3.01.153
apollo get his sinews to make catlings on. 3.03.304 P
the sinews of this leg | all greek, and this all 4.05.126
let grow thy sinews till their knots be strong, 5.03. 33
here lies thy heart, thy sinews, and thy bone. 5.08. 12
for which my sinews shall be stretch'd upon him COR 5.06. 44
and we did buffet it | with lusty sinews, JC 1.02.108
steel, | be soft as sinews of the new–born babe! HAM 3.03. 71
his /nemean hide, | and swore his sinews thaw'd. TNK 1.01. 69
seen, | since hercules, a man of tougher sinews. 2.05. 2
his arms are brawny, | lin'd with strong sinews; 4.02.127
a second fear through all her sinews spread, VEN 903

SINEWY 1 FR 0.0001 REL FR 0 V 1 P
fellows, and like to prove most sinewy swordmen. AWW 2.01. 60 P

SINFUL 13 FR 0.0014 REL FR 12 V 1 P
fie on sinful fantasy! WIV 5.05. 93
o sinful thought! MV 2.07. 54
where both not sin, and yet a sinful fact. AWW 3.07. 47
you have in manner with your sinful hours | made R2 3.01. 11
why, thou globe of sinful continents, what a 2H4 2.04.285 P
a sin, | but greater sin to keep a sinful oath. 2H6 5.01.183
ope | and give sweet passage to my sinful soul! 3H6 2.03. 41
sinful macduff, | they were all strook for thee! MAC 4.03.224
the beauty of this sinful dame | made many PER 1.ch. 31
found, the sinful father | seem'd not to strike, 1.02. 77
were it not sinful then, striving to mend, | to SON 103. 9
hate of my sin, grounded on sinful loving: 142. 2
poor soul, the centre of my sinful earth, | /... 146. 1

SINFULLY 2 FR 0.0002 REL FR 1 V 1 P
merchandise do sinfully miscarry upon the sea, H5 4.01.148 P
my remembrance brutish wrath | sinfully pluck'd, R3 2.01.120

/SING 1 FR 0.0001 REL FR 0 V 1 P
/quality /no /longer /than /they /can /sing? HAM 2.02.347 P

SING 161 FR 0.0182 REL FR 116 V 45 P
storm brewing, i hear it sing i' th' wind. TMP 2.02. 20 P
a very scurvy tune to sing at a man's funeral. 2.02. 44 P
come on, trinculo, let us sing. 3.02.120 P
the winds did sing it to me, and the thunder, 3.03. 97
that i might sing it, madam, to a tune: TGV 1.02. 77
best sing it to the tune of "light o' love." 1.02. 80
ay; and melodious were it, would you sing it. 1.02. 83
keep tune there still, so you will sing it out. 1.02. 86
then to silvia let us sing, | that silvia is 4.02. 49
vat is you sing? WIV 1.04. 44 P
heed, ere summer comes or cuckoo–birds do sing. 2.01.123
"melodious birds sing madrigals — | when as i 3.01. 23
a man may hear this show'r sing in the wind. 3.02. 37 P
and nightly, meadow–fairies, look you sing, 5.05. 65
about him, fairies, sing a scornful rhyme, | and 5.05. 91
sing, siren, for thyself, and i will dote; ERR 3.02. 47
therefore i have decreed not to sing in my cage. ADO 1.03. 34 P
i will but teach them to sing, and restore them 2.01.232 P
i pray thee sing, and let me woo no more. 2.03. 48
because you talk of wooing, i will sing, | since 2.03. 49
sing no more ditties, sing no moe, | of dumps so 2.03. 70
sing no more ditties, sing no moe, | of dumps so 2.03. 70
do you sing it, and i'll dance it. 3.04. 45 P
and sing it to her bones, sing it to–night. 5.01.285
and sing it to her bones, sing it to–night. 5.01.285
now, music, sound, and sing your solemn hymn. 5.03. 11
boast | before the birds have any cause to sing? LLL 1.01.103
sing, boy, my spirit grows heavy in love. 1.02.122 P
i say, sing. 1.02.125 P
up your eyelids, sigh a note and sing a note, 3.01. 14 P
nay, he can sing | a mean most meanly and in 5.02.327
sing me now asleep; MND 2.02. 7
with melody | sing in our sweet lullaby, | lulla 2.02. 14
i will walk up and down here, and i will sing, 3.01.123 P
i pray thee, gentle mortal, sing again. 3.01.137
and sing while thou on pressed flowers dost 3.01.159
and i will sing it in the latter end of a play, 4.01.217 P
the more gracious, i shall sing it at her death. 4.01.219 P
after me, | sing, and dance it trippingly. 5.01.396
grace, | will we sing, and bless this place. 5.01.400
if a throstle sing, he falls straight a–cap'ring MV 1.02. 61 P
the crow doth sing as sweetly as the lark | when 5.01.102
the nightingale, if she should sing by day, 5.01.104
you to please me, i do desire you to sing. AYL 2.05. 18 P
will you sing? 2.05. 22 P
come, sing; 2.05. 29 P
and i'll sing it. 2.05. 48 P
give us some music, and, good cousin, sing. 2.07.173
heigh–ho, sing heigh–ho! 2.07.180
heigh–ho, sing, etc. 2.07.190
i would sing my song without a burthen; 3.02.247 P
sing it. 4.02. 8 P
then sing him home. 4.02. 12
when birds do sing, hey ding a ding, ding, 5.03. 20
whiles a wedlock–hymn we sing, | feed yourselves 5.04.137
plays, | and twenty caged nightingales do sing. SHR in.2. 36
i'll try how you can sol, fa, and sing it. 1.02. 17
he will look upon his boot and sing, mend the AWW 3.02. 6 P
upon his boot and sing, mend the ruff and sing, 3.02. 7 P
mend the ruff and sing, ask questions and sing, 3.02. 7 P
ask questions and sing, pick his teeth and sing. 3.02. 8 P
even tun'd his bounty to sing happiness to him. 4.03. 10 P
for i can sing | and speak to him in many sorts TN 1.02. 57
and sing them loud even in the dead of night; 1.05.271
and so sweet a breath to sing, as the fool has. 2.03. 21 P
coming, | that can sing both high and low. 2.03. 41
so please your lordship, that should sing it. 2.04. 9 P
ay, prithee sing. 2.04. 50
with hey, the sweet birds, o, how they sing! WT 4.03. 6
would sing her song and dance her turn; 4.04. 58
when you sing, | i'ld have you buy and sell so; 4.04.137
the ord'ring your affairs, | to sing them too. 4.04.140
we can both sing it. 4.04.292 P
'tis strange that death should sing. JN 5.07. 20
but, lords, we hear this fearful tempest sing, R2 2.01.263
shriek where mounting larks should sing. 3.03.183
madam, i'll sing. 3.04. 19
and i could sing, would weeping do me good, 3.04. 22
i would i were a weaver, i could sing psalms, or 1H4 2.04.133 P
and she will sing the song that pleaseth you, 3.01.213
with all my heart i'll sit and hear her sing. 3.01.220
ye thief, and hear the lady sing in welsh. 3.01.234 P
come sing. 3.01.257 P
i will not sing. 3.01.258 P
come sing me a bawdy song, make me merry. 3.03. 13 P
i heard a bird so sing, | whose music, to my 2H4 5.05.107
but not as truly, | as bird doth sing on bough." H5 3.02. 19
solemn priests | sing still for richard's soul. 4.01.302
shall in procession sing her endless praise. 1H6 1.06. 20
came he right now to sing a raven's note, 2H6 3.02. 40
rave, and fret, that i may sing and dance. 3H6 1.04. 91
sing, and disperse 'em if thou canst. H8 3.01. 2
that freeze, | bow themselves when he did sing. 3.01. 5
and sing | the merry songs of peace to all his 5.04. 34
shall not hedge us out, we'll hear you sing, TRO 3.01. 61 P
hear no more of this, i'll sing you a song now. 3.01.106 P
and all the greekish girls shall tripping sing, 3.03.211
i cannot sing, | nor heel the high lavolt, nor 4.04. 85
she will sing any man at first sight. 5.02. 9
and any man may sing her, if he can take her 5.02. 10 P
full merrily the humble–bee doth sing, | till he 5.10. 41
daughter, sing, or express yourself in a more COR 1.03. 1 P
did ever raven sing so like a lark | that gives TIT 3.01.158
the eagle suffers little birds to sing, | and is 4.04. 83
that birds would sing and think it were not ROM 2.02. 22
he fights as you sing prick–song, keeps time, 2.04. 21 P
and now about the cauldron sing, | like elves MAC 4.01. 41
you must sing, "a–down, a–down," and you call HAM 4.05.171 P
skull had a tongue in it, and could sing once. 5.01. 75 P
dead | to sing a requiem and such rest to her 5.01.237
and flights of angels sing thee to thy rest! 5.02.360
we two alone will sing like birds i' th' cage; LR 5.03. 9
and pray, and sing, and tell old tales, and 5.03. 12
o, she will sing the savageness out of a bear. OTH 4.01.189 P
all at one side | and sing it like poor barbary. 4.03. 33
by a sycamore tree, | sing all a green willow; 4.03. 41
head on her knee, | sing willow, willow, willow. 4.03. 43
her moans, | sing willow, willow, willow; 4.03. 45
her, and soft'ned the stones, | sing willow" — 4.03. 47
"sing all a green willow must be my garland. 4.03. 51
sing willow, willow, willow; 4.03. 56
not now to hear thee sing. ANT 1.05. 9
most gracious pardon, | i sing but after you. 1.05. 73
while i'll place you, then the boy shall sing. 2.07.110
think, speak, cast, write, sing, number, hoo! 3.02. 17
the crickets sing, and man's o'erlabor'd sense CYM 2.02. 11
prison'd bird, | and sing our bondage freely. 3.03. 44
got the mannish crack, sing him to th' ground, 4.02.236
cadwal, | i cannot sing. 4.02.240
to sing a song that old was sung, | from ashes PER 1.ch. 1
and that to hear an old man sing | may to your 1.ch. 13
and /crickets sing at the oven's mouth, | are 3.ch. 7
shall 's go hear the vestals sing? 4.05. 7 P
proclaim that i can sing, weave, sew, and dance, 4.06.183
pie, | may on our bridehouse perch or sing, | or TNK 1.01. 22
(rather dwell on) | and sing it in her slumbers. 1.03. 78
to hear him | sing in an evening, what a heaven 2.04. 19
some honest–hearted maids, will sing my dirge, 2.06. 15
will wed me, | and soldiers sing my epitaph. 3.06.285
i can sing twenty more. 4.01.106
i can sing "the broom," | and "bonny robin." 4.01.107
for musicians, | and sing the wars of theseus. 4.01.134
should clap their wings and sing | to all the 4.02. 23
sing to her such green songs of love as she says 4.03. 81 P
this shall become palamon, for palamon can sing, 4.03. 86 P
she would have me sing. 5.02. 12
that some would sing, some other in their bills VEN 1102
and give the sneaped birds more cause to sing. LUC 333
the adder hisses where the sweet birds sing, 871
to sing heaven's praise with such an earthly PP 5.14
clear wells spring not, sweet birds sing not, 17.25

by whose falls | melodious birds sing madrigals. 19. 8
made, | beasts did leap and birds did sing, 20. 5
all thy fellow birds do sing, | careless of thy 20.25
who all in one, one pleasing note do sing: SON 8.12
o, how thy worth with manners may i sing, | when 39. 1
eyes, that taught the dumb on high to sing, 78. 5
or, if they sing, 'tis with so dull a cheer 97.13
sing to the ear that doth thy lays esteem, | and 100. 7
lays, | as philomel in summer's front doth sing, 102. 7
they had not still enough your worth to sing: 106.12
SING'D 2 FR 0.0002 REL FR 2 V 0 P
beard they have sing'd off with brands of fire, ERR 5.01.171
thus hath the candle sing'd the moth. MV 2.09. 79
SINGE 2 FR 0.0002 REL FR 2 V 0 P
for your foe so hot | that it do singe yourself. H8 1.01.141
thunderbolts, | singe my white head! LR 3.02. 6
SINGEING 1 FR 0.0001 REL FR 1 V 0 P
singeing his pate against the burning zone, HAM 5.01.282
SINGER 4 FR 0.0004 REL FR 1 V 3 P
his filching was like an unskillful singer, he WIV 1.03. 26 P
and an ill singer, my lord. ADO 2.03. 76 P
tearing the thracian singer in their rage." MND 5.01. 49
o, i cry you mercy, you are the singer; ROM 4.05.139 P
SINGETH 1 FR 0.0001 REL FR 1 V 0 P
this bird of dawning singeth all night long, HAM 1.01.160
SINGING 13 FR 0.0014 REL FR 6 V 7 P
if their singing answer your saying, by my faith ADO 2.01.234 P
how pitiful i deserve" — | i mean in singing; 5.02. 30 P
/as if you swallow'd love with singing love, LLL 3.01. 15 P
no pains, sir, i take pleasure in singing, sir. TN 2.04. 68 P
bring him in, and let him approach singing. WT 4.04.212 P
suppose the singing birds musicians, | the grass R2 1.03.288
lost it with hallowing and singing of anthems. 2H4 1.02.190 P
the singing masons building roofs of gold, | the H5 1.02.198
than see | our tradesmen singing in their shops, COR 4.06. 8
to love a woman for singing, nor so old to dote LR 1.04. 37 P
now | as mad as the vex'd sea, singing aloud, 4.04. 2
her fortune, | and she died singing it. OTH 4.03. 30
drown'd | when as himself to singing he betakes. PP 8.12
SINGING-MAN 1 FR 0.0001 REL FR 0 V 1 P
liking his father to a singing–man of windsor, 2H4 2.01. 90 P
/SINGLE 1 FR 0.0001 REL FR 1 V 0 P
/on /his /fair /worth /and /single /chivalry. TRO 4.04.148
SINGLE 59 FR 0.0066 REL FR 48 V 11 P
a single thing, as i am now, that wonders | to TMP 1.02.433
which shall be shortly, single i'll resolve you 5.01.248
use for it, a double heart for his single one. ADO 2.01.279 P
have cudgell'd thee out of thy single life, to 5.04.114 P
we single you | as our best–moving fair LLL 2.01. 28
grows, lives, and dies in single blessedness. MND 1.01. 78
to protest | for aye austerity and single life. 1.01. 90
to death, or to a vow of single life. 1.01.121
oath, | so then two bosoms and a single troth. 2.02. 50
to a notary, seal me there | your single bond; MV 1.03.145
is the single man therefore bless'd? AYL 3.03. 58 P
i'll to the wars, she to her single sorrow. AWW 2.03.296
but the plain single vow that is vow'd true. 4.02. 22
i beseech your honor to hear me one single word. 5.02. 35 P
you beg a single penny more. 5.02. 37 P
sedgy bank, | in single opposition hand to hand, 1H4 1.03. 99
side, | try fortune with him in a single fight. 5.01.100
and, nephew, challeng'd you to single fight. 5.02. 46
your chin double, your wit single, and every 2H4 1.02.183 P
in single combat thou shalt buckle with me; 1H6 1.02. 95
them | for single combat in convenient place, 2H6 1.03.208
nay, warwick, single out some other chase, | for 3H6 2.04. 12
by this i challenge him to single fight. 4.07. 75
but, whiles he thought to steal the single ten, 5.01. 43
men might say | till this time pomp was single, H8 1.01. 15
i know but of a single part in aught | pertains 1.02. 41
further gone in this than by | a single voice, 1.02. 70
there living | (i speak it with a single heart, 5.02. 73
for what, alas, can these my single arms? TRO 2.02.135
and scants us with a single famish'd kiss, 4.04. 47
or else your actions would grow wondrous single; COR 2.01. 37 P
wherein every one of us has a single honor, in 2.03. 44 P
yet, were there but this single plot to lose, 3.02.102
send | o'er the vast world to seek a single man, 4.01. 42
single you thither then this dainty doe, | and TIT 2.01.117
that, when the single sole of it is worn, the ROM 2.04. 62 P
no, thou stand'st single, th' art not on him yet TIM 2.02. 56 P
perchance some single vantages you took, | when 2.02.129
each man apart, all single and alone, | yet an 5.01.107
but, for my single self, | i had as lief not be JC 1.02. 94
shakes so my single state of man that function MAC 1.03.140
were poor and single business to contend 1.06. 16
is it a fee–grief | due to some single breast? 4.03.197
the single and peculiar life is bound | with all HAM 3.03. 11
when sorrows come, they come not single spies, 4.05. 78
trust to thy single virtue, for thy soldiers, LR 5.03.103
so hath my lord dar'd him to single fight. ANT 3.07. 30
determine this great war in single fight! 4.04. 37
the death of antony | is not a single doom, in 5.01. 18
and more remarkable in single oppositions; CYM 4.01. 13 P
with his own single hand he'ld take us in, 4.02.121
no single soul | can we set eye on; 4.02.130
to equal any single crown a' th' earth | i' th' PER 4.03. 8
their single share, | their nobleness peculiar TNK 5.03. 86
single nature's double name | neither two nor PHT 39
die single, and thine image dies with thee. SON 3.14
"thou single wilt prove none." 8.14
that thou consum'st thyself in single life? 9. 2
and our dear love lose name of single one, 39. 6
SINGLED *(also singuled)*
SINGLED 4 FR 0.0004 REL FR 4 V 0 P
and watch'd him how he singled clifford forth. 3H6 2.01. 12
now, clifford, i have singled thee alone: 2.04. 1
you | are singled forth to try thy experiments. TIT 2.03. 69
their clamorous cry till they have singled VEN 693
SINGLENESS 2 FR 0.0002 REL FR 1 V 1 P
jest, soly singular for the singleness! ROM 2.04. 66 P
in singleness the parts that thou shouldst bear. SON 8. 8
SINGLE-SOL'D 1 FR 0.0001 REL FR 0 V 1 P
o single–sol'd jest, soly singular for the ROM 2.04. 65 P
SINGLY 5 FR 0.0005 REL FR 3 V 2 P
that neither, singly, can be manifested, WIV 4.06. 15
demand them singly. AWW 4.03.183 P
he must fight singly to–morrow with hector, and TRO 3.03.247 P

cannot in the world | be singly counterpois'd. COR 2.02. 87
thou singly honest man, | here, take; TIM 4.03.523
SINGS 35 FR 0.0039 REL FR 27 V 8 P
juno sings her blessings on you. TMP 4.01.109
whose falls | melodious birds sings madrigals; WIV 3.01. 18
that sings heaven's praise with such an earthly LLL 4.02.118
for thus sings he, | "cuckoo; 5.02.899
for thus sings he, | "cuckoo; 5.02.908
be /foul, | then nightly sings the staring owl, 5.02.917
the bowl, | then nightly sings the staring owl, 5.02.926
and others, when the bagpipe sings i' th' nose, MV 4.01. 49
but in his motion like an angel sings, | still 5.01. 61
plain | she sings as sweetly as a nightingale; SHR 2.01.171
comes by destiny, | your cuckoo sings by kind. AWW 1.03. 63
still–peering air | that sings with piercing, do 3.02.111
of her last breath, and now she sings in heaven. 4.03. 53 P
amongst them, and he sings psalms to hornpipes. WT 4.03. 44 P
he sings several tunes faster than you'll tell 4.04.183 P
he sings 'em over as they were gods or goddesses 4.04.208 P
there's scarce a maid westward but she sings it. 4.04.290 P
and from the organ–pipe of frailty sings | his JN 5.07. 23
peace, she sings. 1H4 3.01.244 P
which ever in the haunch of winter sings | the 2H4 4.04. 92
the earth sings when he touches it; H5 3.07. 16 P
bell, | sings heavy music to thy timorous soul, 1H6 4.02. 40
nightly she sings on yond pomegranate tree. ROM 3.05. 4
it is the lark that sings so out of tune, 3.05. 27
that happy verse | which aptly sings the good." TIM 1.01. 17
'a sings in grave–making. HAM 5.01. 66 P
is free of speech, sings, plays, and dances OTH 3.03.185
hark, hark, the lark at heaven's gate sings, CYM 2.03. 20
how angel–like he sings! 4.02. 48
she sings like one immortal, and she dances | as PER 5.ch. 3
through his mane and tail the high wind sings, VEN 305
note, | and sings extemporally a woeful ditty, 836
while philomela sits and sings, i sit and mark, PP 14.17
being many, seeming one, | sings this to thee: SON 8.14
from sullen earth) sings hymns at heaven's gate, 29.12
SING'ST 4 FR 0.0004 REL FR 3 V 1 P
no, faith, thou sing'st well enough for a shift. ADO 2.03. 77 P
thou sing'st sweet music. R3 4.02. 78
"come, philomele, that sing'st of ravishment, LUC 1128
for, poor bird, thou sing'st not in the day, 1142
SINGULAR 8 FR 0.0009 REL FR 4 V 4 P
a most singular and choice epithet. LLL 5.01. 15 P
your doing | (so singular in each particular) WT 4.04.144
very singular good, in faith, well said, sir 2H4 3.02.108 P
men | of singular integrity and learning, | yea, H8 2.04. 59
may remain, after the wearing, soly singular. ROM 2.04. 64 P
jest, soly singular for the singleness! 2.04. 65 P
ay, and singular in his art, hath done you both CYM 3.04.121
made | to set forth that which is so singular? LUC 32
SINGULARITER 1 FR 0.0001 REL FR 0 V 1 P
and be thus declin'd, singulariter, nominativo, WIV 4.01. 41 P
SINGULARITIES 1 FR 0.0001 REL FR 1 V 0 P
without much content | in many singularities; WT 5.03. 12
SINGULARITY 3 FR 0.0003 REL FR 1 V 2 P
put thyself into the trick of singularity. TN 2.05.152 P
put thyself into the trick of singularity"; 3.04. 71 P
more than his singularity, he goes | upon this COR 1.01.278
SINGULED *(also singled)*
SINGULED 1 FR 0.0001 REL FR 0 V 1 P
we will be singuled from the barbarous. LLL 5.01. 81 P
SINISTER 7 FR 0.0008 REL FR 4 V 3 P
to have receiv'd no sinister measure from his MM 3.02.242 P
and this the cranny is, right and sinister, MND 5.01.163
an emblem of war, here on his sinister cheek; AWW 2.01. 44 P
comptible, even to the least sinister usage. TN 1.05.176 P
know | 'tis no sinister nor no awkward claim, H5 2.04. 85
and this sinister | bounds in my father's"; TRO 4.05.128
on the sinister side the heart lies; TNK 5.03. 76
/SINK 1 FR 0.0001 REL FR 1 V 0 P
/eyes /let /fall | /may /run /into /that /sink, TIT 3.02. 19
SINK 38 FR 0.0043 REL FR 35 V 3 P
have you a mind to sink? TMP 1.01. 39 P
let's all sink wi' th' king. 1.01. 63
which thou heardst cry, which thou saw'st sink. 1.02. 32
why | doth it not then our eyelids sink? 2.01.201
let love, being light, be drowned if she sink! ERR 3.02. 52
faster and faster, till he sink into his grave. ADO 2.01. 79 P
why, how now, cousin, wherefore sink you down? 4.01.110
cupid's archery, | sink in apple of his eye. MND 3.02.104
than for to think that i would sink it here. AWW 5.03.181
if he fall in, good night, or sink or swim. 1H4 1.03.194
he'll drop his heart into the sink of fear, H5 3.05. 59
puddle, sink, whose filth and dirt | troubles 2H6 4.01. 71
tread on the sand, why, there you quickly sink; 3H6 5.04. 30
blood of lancaster | sink in the ground? 5.06. 62
there let him sink, and be the seas on him! R3 4.04.463
and if i have a conscience, let it sink me, H8 2.01. 60
found again | but where they mean to sink ye. 2.01.131
out of pity taken | a load would sink a navy — 3.02.383
sweet sink, sweet sewer. TRO 5.01. 76 P
come, troy, sink down! 5.08. 11
be restrain'd, | who is the sink a' th' body — COR 1.01.122
sink, my knee, i' th' earth; 5.03. 50
under love's heavy burthen do i sink. ROM 1.04. 22
and, to sink in it, should you burthen love — 1.04. 23
timon's fortunes 'mong his friends can sink. TIM 2.02.231
sink, athens! 3.06.104
caesar cried, "help me, cassius, or i sink!" JC 1.02.111
and like deceitful jades | sink in the trial. 4.02. 27
as in thy red rays thou dost sink to–night, | so 5.03. 61
arm, the best of you | shall sink in my rebuke. OTH 2.03.209
lepidus, | keep off them, for you sink. ANT 2.07. 60
sink rome, and their tongues rot | that speak 3.07. 15
even before, i was | at point to sink for food. CYM 3.06. 17
here many sink, yet those which see them fall PER 1.04. 48
doth prop it, | would sink and overwhelm you. 4.06.120
i' th' aid o' th' current were almost to sink, TNK 1.02. 8
so they grow together, | will never sink; 2.02. 67
not gross to sink, but light, and will aspire. VEN 150
SINK-A-PACE *(also cinquepace)*
SINK-A-PACE 1 FR 0.0001 REL FR 0 V 1 P
not so much as make water but in a sink–a–pace. TN 1.03.130 P
SINKETH 1 FR 0.0001 REL FR 1 V 0 P
she sinketh down, still hanging by his neck, VEN 593
SINKING 5 FR 0.0005 REL FR 4 V 1 P

size that i have a kind of alacrity in sinking; WIV 3.05. 13 P
splitting rocks cow'r'd in the sinking sands, 2H6 3.02. 97
and sore blows | for sinking under them. COR 2.01.253
leaky | that we must leave thee to thy sinking, ANT 3.13. 64
then who fears sinking where such treasure lies? LUC 280
SINKING-RIPE 1 FR 0.0001 REL FR 1 V 0 P
and left the ship, then sinking–ripe, to us. ERR 1.01. 77
SINKS 6 FR 0.0006 REL FR 6 V 0 P
whilst my gross flesh sinks downward, here to R2 5.05.112
why sinks that cauldron? MAC 4.01.106
i think our country sinks beneath the yoke: 4.03. 39
is out of breath, | and sinks most lamentably. ANT 3.10. 25
but now my heavy conscience sinks my knee, | as CYM 5.05.413
with two alone | sinks down to death, oppress'd SON 45. 8
SINN'D 6 FR 0.0006 REL FR 5 V 1 P
o sweet–suggesting love, if thou hast sinn'd, TGV 2.06. 7
yet sinn'd i not, | but in mistaking. ADO 5.01.274
i have then sinn'd against his experience and AWW 2.05. 10 P
if you first sinn'd with us, and that with us WT 1.02. 84
i am a man | more sinn'd against than sinning. LR 3.02. 60
and doubting lest he had err'd or sinn'd, | to PER 1.03. 21
SINNER 4 FR 0.0004 REL FR 3 V 1 P
made such a sinner of his memory | to credit his TMP 1.02.101
i cross me for a sinner. ERR 2.02.188
i will be so much a sinner to be a double–dealer TN 5.01. 34 P
here's that which is too weak to be a sinner, TIM 1.02. 58
SINNERS' 1 FR 0.0001 REL FR 1 V 0 P
like damned guilty deeds to sinners' minds: ROM 3.02.111
SINNERS 3 FR 0.0003 REL FR 2 V 1 P
o lord, have mercy on us, wretched sinners! 1H6 1.04. 70
forbear to judge, for we are sinners all. 2H6 3.03. 31
why wouldst thou be a breeder of sinners? HAM 3.01.121 P
SINNING 1 FR 0.0001 REL FR 1 V 0 P
i am a man | more sinn'd against than sinning. LR 3.02. 60
SINON 7 FR 0.0008 REL FR 7 V 0 P
could, | and, like a sinon, take another troy. 3H6 3.02.190
tell us what sinon hath bewitch'd our ears, | or TIT 5.03. 85
this mild image drew | for perjur'd sinon, whose LUC 1521
"for even as subtile sinon here is painted, | so 1541
to see those borrowed tears that sinon sheeds! 1549
for sinon in his fire doth quake with cold, 1556
she tears the senseless sinon with her nails, 1564
SINON'S 3 FR 0.0003 REL FR 3 V 0 P
and sinon's weeping | did scandal many a holy CYM 3.04. 59
saying, some shape in sinon's was abus'd: LUC 1529
priam's trust false sinon's tears doth flatter, 1560
SINOW *(also sinew, etc.)*
SINOW 2 FR 0.0002 REL FR 2 V 0 P
so shalt thou sinow both these lands together, 3H6 2.06. 91
crowns | the sinow and the forehand of our host, TRO 1.03.143
SINOWS 1 FR 0.0001 REL FR 1 V 0 P
and you, my sinows, grow not instant old, | but HAM 1.05. 94
SINOWY 4 FR 0.0004 REL FR 4 V 0 P
tires | the sinowy vigor of the traveller. LLL 4.03.304
that did but lately foil the sinowy charles, AYL 2.02. 14
milo his addition yield | to sinowy ajax. TRO 2.03.248
whose sinowy neck in battle ne'er did bow, | who VEN 99
SIN'S 5 FR 0.0005 REL FR 5 V 0 P
thy sin's not accidental, but a trade. MM 3.01.148
days, | to sin's rebuke and my creator's praise. 3H6 4.06. 44
to kill, i grant, is sin's extremest gust, | but TIM 3.05. 54
to my sick soul, as sin's true nature is, | each HAM 4.05. 17
base watch of woes, sin's pack–horse, virtue's LUC 928
/SINS 3 FR 0.0003 REL FR 3 V 0 P
/indeed | /where /all /my /sins /are /writ, /and R2 4.01.275
receive the sentence of the law for /sins | such 2H6 2.03. 3
/dear /blood /shed /for /our /grievous /sins, R3 1.04.190
SINS 38 FR 0.0043 REL FR 31 V 7 P
o, forgive me my sins! TMP 3.02.130 P
makes him run through all th' sins: TGV 5.04.112
heaven forgive my sins at the day of judgment! WIV 3.03.212 P
heaven forgive our sins! 5.05. 31 P
but those as sleep and think not on their sins, 5.05. 53
the tempter, or the tempted, who sins most, ha? MM 2.02.163
our compell'd sins | stand more for number than 2.04. 57
doth warrant, | let all my sins lack mercy! ADO 4.01.180
you must be purged too, your sins are rack'd, LLL 5.02.818
the sins of the father are to be laid upon the MV 3.05. 1 P
so the sins of my mother should be visited upon 3.05. 14 P
if the sins of your youth are forgiven you, WT 3.03.120 P
some sins do bear their privilege on earth, JN 1.01.261
thy sins are visited in this poor child, | the 2.01.179
be mowbray's sins so heavy in his bosom | that R2 1.02. 50
then murthers, treasons, and detested sins, 3.02. 44
more sins for this forgiveness prosper may. 5.03. 84
the oldest sins the newest kind of ways? 2H4 4.05.126
our children, and our sins lay on the king! H5 4.01.232
o, god forgive my sins, and pardon thee! 3H6 5.06. 60
o, let them keep it till thy sins be ripe, | and R3 1.03.218
all several sins, all us'd in each degree, 5.03.198
but cardinal sins and hollow hearts i fear ye. H8 3.01.104
produce the grand sum of his sins, the articles 3.02.293
you cannot make gross sins look clear; TIM 3.05. 38
in thy orisons | be all my sins rememb'red. HAM 3.01. 89
/god forgive us our sins! OTH 2.03.112 P
when devils will the blackest sins put on, 2.03.351
think on thy sins. 5.02. 40
portends | (unless my sins abuse my divination) CYM 4.02.351
few love to hear the sins they love to act; PER 1.01. 92
wicked, all my sins | could never pluck upon me. TNK 2.03. 6
what sins have i committed, chaste diana, | that 4.02. 58
wins | loses a noble cousin for thy sins. 4.02.156
by thine inclination | to all sins past, and all LUC 923
excusing /thy sins more than /thy sins are; SON 35. 8
excusing /thy sins more than /thy sins are; 35. 8
o, in what sweets dost thou thy sins enclose! 95. 4
SIP 3 FR 0.0003 REL FR 2 V 1 P
never get her so much as sip on a cup with the WIV 2.02. 75 P
will deign to sip or touch one drop of it. SHR 5.02.145
took to quench it | she would to each one sip. WT 4.04. 62
SIPP'D 1 FR 0.0001 REL FR 1 V 0 P
i none these two days — | sipp'd some water. TNK 3.02. 27
SIPPING 1 FR 0.0001 REL FR 1 V 0 P
a chalice for the nonce, whereon but sipping, HAM 4.07.160
SIR *(also zir)*
/SIR 22 FR 0.0024 REL FR 17 V 5 P
/sir, this is the house, please it you that i SHR 4.04. 1
/pardon /me, /sir, /it /was /a /black TIT 3.02. 66

/but /there /is, /sir, /an /aery /of /children, HAM 2.02.339 P
have reform'd that indifferently with us, /sir. 3.02. 37 P
/sir, /in /this /audience, | let my disclaiming 5.02.240
/o, /sir, /are /you /come? LR 1.04.257
/thou, /sapient /sir, /sit /here. 3.06. 22
/how /do /you, /sir? 3.06. 33
/ay, /sir, /she /took /them, /read /them /in /my 4.03. 11
/well, /sir, /the /poor /distressed /lear's /i' 4.03. 38
/why, /good /sir? 4.03. 41
/well, /sir, /i'll /bring /you /to /our /master 4.03. 50
/good /sir — 4.06.197
/no, /sir, you must not kneel. 4.07. 58
/holds /it /true, /sir, /that /the /duke /of 4.07. 84 P
/most /certain, /sir. 4.07. 86 P
/fare /you /well, /sir. 4.07. 94 P
/sir, /you /speak /nobly. 5.01. 28
/kent, /sir, /the /banish'd /kent, /who /in 5.03.220
lieutenant — sir — montano — /sir — | help, OTH 2.03.159
i see, /sir, you are eaten up with passion; 3.03.391
why, so i can, /sir, but i will not now. 3.04. 86

SIR 2591 FR 0.2928 REL FR 1278 V 1313 P

certainly, sir, i can. TMP 1.02. 41
sir, are not you my father? 1.02. 55
sir, most heedfully. 1.02. 78
o, good sir, i do. 1.02. 88
your tale, sir, would cure deafness. 1.02.106
and now i pray you, sir, | for still 'tis 1.02.175
all hail, great master, grave sir, hail! 1.02.189
i do not, sir. 1.02.256
no, sir. 1.02.260
sir, in argier. 1.02.261
ay, sir. 1.02.268
'tis a villain, sir, | i do not love to look on. 1.02.309
believe me, sir, | it carries a brave form. 1.02.411
no wonder, sir, | but certainly a maid. 1.02.428
a word, good sir, | i fear you have done 1.02.443
soft, sir, one word more. 1.02.450
sir, have pity, | i'll be his surety. 1.02.475
comfort, | my father's of a better nature, sir, 1.02.497
beseech you, sir, be merry; 2.01. 1
then wisely, good sir, weigh | our sorrow with 2.01. 8
sir — 2.01. 14
this tunis, sir, was carthage. 2.01. 84 P
sir, we were talking that our garments seem now 2.01. 97 P
is not, sir, my doublet as fresh as the first 2.01.103 P
sir, he may live. 2.01.114
sir, you may thank yourself for this great loss, 2.01.124
it is foul weather in us all, good sir, | when 2.01.142
i would with such perfection govern, sir, | t' 2.01.168
and — do you mark me, sir? 2.01.170
please you, sir, | do not omit the heavy offer 2.01.193
thus, sir: 2.01.231
ay, sir; 2.01.276
put | this ancient morsel, this sir prudence, 2.01.286
upon mine honor, sir, i heard a humming | (and 2.01.317
i shak'd you, sir, and cried. 2.01.319
by'r lakin, i can go no further, sir, | my old 3.03. 1
faith, sir, you need not fear. 3.03. 43
i' th' name of something holy, sir, why stand 3.03. 94
i warrant you, sir, | the white cold virgin snow 4.01. 54
be cheerful, sir. 4.01.147
sir, i am vex'd; 4.01.158
i told you, sir, they were red–hot with drinking 4.01.171
all prisoners, sir, | in the line–grove which 5.01. 9
but chiefly | him that you term'd, sir, "the 5.01. 15
mine would, sir, were i human. 5.01. 20
i'll fetch them, sir. 5.01. 32
and a loyal sir | to him thou follow'st! 5.01. 69
behold, sir king, | the wronged duke of milan, 5.01.106
for you, most wicked sir, whom to call brother 5.01.130
i am woe for't, sir. 5.01.139
welcome, sir; 5.01.165
sir, she is mortal; 5.01.188
there, sir, stop. 5.01.198
o, look, sir, look, sir, here is more of us. 5.01.216
o, look, sir, look, sir, here is more of us. 5.01.216
sir, all this service | have i done since i went 5.01.225
if i did think, sir, i were well awake, | i'ld 5.01.229
sir, my liege, | do not infest your mind with 5.01.245
how fares my gracious sir? 5.01.253
sir, i invite your highness and your train | to 5.01.301
sir proteus! 'save you! saw you my master? TGV 1.01. 70
ay, sir; 1.01. 96 P
nay, sir, less than a pound shall serve me for 1.01.105 P
you mistook, sir: 1.01.113 P
why, sir, how do you bear with me? 1.01.122 P
marry, sir, the letter, very orderly, having 1.01.123 P
well, sir, here is for your pains. 1.01.131 P
truly, sir, i think you'll hardly win her. 1.01.133 P
sir, i could perceive nothing at all from her; 1.01.136 P
and so, sir, i'll commend you to my master. 1.01.146 P
what think'st thou of the fair sir eglamour? 1.02. 9
sir valentine's page; 1.02. 38
sir proteus, your /father calls for you: 1.03. 88
sir, your glove. 2.01. 1
she is not within hearing, sir. 2.01. 8 P
why, sir, who bade you call her? 2.01. 9 P
your worship, sir, or else i mistook. 2.01. 10 P
go to, sir; tell me, do you know madam silvia? 2.01. 14 P
you have learn'd, like sir proteus, to wreathe 2.01. 19 P
why, sir, i know her not. 2.01. 45 P
is she not hard–favor'd, sir? 2.01. 48 P
sir, i know that well enough. 2.01. 50 P
marry, sir, so painted to make her fair, that no 2.01. 59 P
to have when you chid at sir proteus for going 2.01. 72 P
true, sir; 2.01. 81 P
sir valentine and servant! to you two thousand. 2.01.100 P
you writ them, sir, at my request, | but i will 2.01.126
how now, sir? 2.01.141 P
no believing you indeed, sir: 2.01.156 P
why muse you, sir? 2.01.170 P
ay, but hearken, sir; 2.01.172 P
sir proteus, you are stay'd for. 2.02. 19
and am going with sir proteus to the imperial's 2.03. 4 P
now, sir, this staff is my sister, for, look you 2.03. 19 P
sir — call me what thou dar'st. 2.03. 57 P
master, sir thurio frowns on you. 2.04. 3 P
what, angry, sir thurio? do you change color? 2.04. 23 P
you have said, sir. 2.04. 29 P
ay, sir, and done too — for this time. 2.04. 30 P
i know it well, sir; 2.04. 31 P
sir thurio borrows his wit from your ladyship's 2.04. 38 P
sir, if you spend word for word with me, i shall 2.04. 41 P
i know it well, sir; 2.04. 43 P
sir valentine, your father is in good health: 2.04. 50
yet hath sir proteus (for that's his name) 2.04. 67
beshrew me, sir, but if he make this good, | he 2.04. 75
well, sir — this gentleman is come to me | with 2.04. 78
silvia, i speak to you, and you, sir thurio; 2.04. 84
come, sir thurio, | go with me. 2.04.117
of such divine perfection, as sir proteus. 2.07. 13
sir thurio, give us leave, i pray, a while, | we 3.01. 1
know, worthy prince, sir valentine, my friend, 3.01. 10
forbid | sir valentine her company and my court; 3.01. 27
adieu, my lord, sir valentine is coming. 3.01. 50
sir valentine, whither away so fast? 3.01. 51
to match my friend sir thurio to my daughter. 3.01. 62
when would you use it? pray, sir, tell me that. 3.01.123
why, sir, i'll strike nothing. i pray you — 3.01.203 P
sir, there is a proclamation that you are 3.01.217 P
sir thurio, fear not but that she will love you 3.02. 1
how now, sir proteus? 3.02. 11
the match between sir thurio and my daughter? 3.02. 23
the love of valentine, and love sir thurio? 3.02. 30
it follows not that she will love sir thurio. 3.02. 50
much | as you in worth dispraise sir valentine. 3.02. 55
but you, sir thurio, are not sharp enough: 3.02. 67
stand, sir, and throw us that you have about ye. 4.01. 3
sir, we are undone; 4.01. 5
that's not so, sir; we are your enemies. 4.01. 8
how now, sir proteus, are you crept before us? 4.02. 18
ay, but i hope, sir, that you love not here. 4.02. 21
sir, but i do; or else i would be hence. 4.02. 22
doth this sir proteus that we talk on | often 4.02. 73
sir thurio, fear not you, i will so plead, 4.02. 82
sir proteus, as i take it. 4.02. 90
sir proteus, gentle lady, and your servant. 4.02. 91
i am very loath to be your idol, sir; 4.02.128
pray you, where lies sir proteus? 4.02.136 P
sir eglamour, a thousand times good morrow. 4.03. 6
sir eglamour, i would to valentine, | to mantua, 4.03. 22
good morrow, kind sir eglamour. 4.03. 46
marry, sir, i carried mistress silvia the dog 4.04. 45 P
ay, sir, the other squirrel was stol'n from me 4.04. 55 P
from my master, sir proteus, madam. 4.04.114
sir proteus, what says silvia to my suit? 5.02. 1
o, sir, i find her milder than she was, | and 5.02. 2
o, sir, she makes no doubt of that. 5.02. 20
how now, sir proteus? 5.02. 31
o good sir, my master charg'd me to deliver a 5.04. 88 P
o, cry you mercy, sir, i have mistook; 5.04. 94
sir valentine! 5.04.124
sir valentine, i care not for her, i; 5.04.132
sir valentine, | thou art a gentleman and well 5.04.145
sir hugh, persuade me not; WIV 1.01. 1 P
if he were twenty sir john falstaffs, he shall 1.01. 2 P
if sir john falstaff have committed 1.01. 31 P
the knight sir john is there, and i beseech you 1.01. 70 P
sir, i thank you. 1.01. 86 P
sir, i thank you; by yea and no, i do. 1.01. 87 P
how does your fallow greyhound, sir? 1.01. 89 P
it could not be judg'd, sir. 1.01. 91 P
a cur, sir. 1.01. 95 P
sir! 1.01. 96 P
is sir john falstaff here? 1.01. 97 P
sir, he is within; 1.01. 99 P
sir, he doth in some sort confess it. 1.01.103 P
here comes sir john. 1.01.108 P
pauca verba; sir john, good worts. 1.01.120 P
marry, sir, i have matter in my head against you 1.01.123 P
sir john, and master mine, | i combat challenge 1.01.161
be avis'd, sir, and pass good humors. 1.01.166 P
why, sir, for my part, i say the gentleman had 1.01.174 P
and being fap, sir, was, as they say, cashier'd; 1.01.178 P
kind of tender, made afar off by sir hugh here. 1.01.209 P
ay, sir, you shall find me reasonable. 1.01.210 P
so i do, sir. 1.01.213 P
ay, there's the point, sir. 1.01.222 P
i hope, sir, i will do as it shall become one 1.01.233 P
i will marry her, sir, at your request; 1.01.245 P
will't please your worship to come in, sir? 1.01.266 P
the dinner attends you, sir. 1.01.269 P
i pray you, sir, walk in. 1.01.281 P
i think there are, sir, i heard them talk'd of. 1.01.288 P
ay indeed, sir. 1.01.293 P
i'll eat nothing, i thank you, sir. 1.01.302 P
by cock and pie, you shall not choose, sir! 1.01.303 P
come on, sir. 1.01.306 P
not i, sir, pray you keep on. 1.01.308 P
i pray you, sir. 1.01.311 P
well, sir. 1.02. 6 P
rightly) is, "i am sir john falstaff's." 1.03. 48 P
shall i sir pandarus of troy become, | and by my 1.03. 75
is it this, sir? 1.04. 53 P
here, sir! 1.04. 57 P
'tis ready, sir, here in the porch. 1.04. 61 P
sir hugh send–a you? 1.04. 87 P
you jack'nape, give–a this letter to sir hugh. 1.04.107 P
sir, the maid loves you, and all shall be well. 1.04.120 P
in truth, sir, and she is pretty, and honest, 1.04.139 P
troth, sir, all is in his hands above. 1.04.144 P
sir alice ford! 2.01. 51 P
sir john affects thy wife. 2.01.111
why, sir, my wife is not young. 2.01.112 P
or go thou | like sir actaeon he, with ringwood 2.01.118
what name, sir? 2.01.120 P
away, sir corporal nym! 2.01.124
sir, there is a fray to be fought between sir 2.01.200 P
to be fought between sir hugh the welsh priest 2.01.200 P
tut, sir; 2.01.224 P
i have been content, sir, you should lay my 2.02. 5 P
sir, here's a woman would speak with you. 2.02. 31 P
there is one mistress ford, sir — i pray come a 2.02. 44 P
why, sir, she's a good creature. 2.02. 55 P
sir john, there's one master /brook below would 2.02.144 P
ay, sir. 2.02.149 P
/god /save you, sir! 2.02.154 P
and you, sir! would you speak with me? 2.02.155 P
sir, i am a gentleman that have spent much. 2.02.160 P
good sir john, i sue for yours — not to charge 2.02.164 P
money is a good soldier, sir, and will on. 2.02.170 P
if you will help to bear it, sir john, take all, 2.02.172 P
sir, i know not how i may deserve to be your 2.02.174 P
i will tell you, sir, if you will give me the 2.02.176 P
sir, i hear you are a scholar (i will be brief 2.02.180 P
but, good sir john, as you have one eye upon my 2.02.185 P
very well, sir, proceed. 2.02.190 P
well, sir. 2.02.193 P
now, sir john, here is the heart of my purpose: 2.02.224 P
o sir! 2.02.230 P
what say you to't, sir john? 2.02.251 P
o good sir! 2.02.256 P
want no money, sir john, you shall want none. 2.02.258 P
do you know ford, sir? 2.02.269 P
i would you knew ford, sir, that you might avoid 2.02.276 P
sir? 2.03. 2 P
'tis past the hour, sir, that sir hugh promis'd 2.03. 4 P
the hour, sir, that sir hugh promis'd to meet. 2.03. 4 P
he is wise, sir; 2.03. 10 P
alas, sir, i cannot fence. 2.03. 15 P
give you good morrow, sir. 2.03. 21 P
and sir hugh hath shown himself a wise and 2.03. 54 P
sir hugh is there, is he? 2.03. 76 P
marry, sir, the pittie–ward, the park–ward — 3.01. 5 P
i will, sir. 3.01. 10 P
yonder he is coming, this way, sir hugh. 3.01. 27 P
no weapons, sir. 3.01. 31 P
good morrow, good sir hugh. 3.01. 37 P
/god save you, good sir hugh! 3.01. 41 P
my sir hugh? 3.01.104 P
truly, sir, to see your wife. is she at home? 3.02. 11 P
sir john falstaff. 3.02. 22 P
sir john falstaff! 3.02. 23 P
by your leave, sir. i am sick till i see her. 3.02. 28 P
and so must i, sir. 3.02. 54 P
so shall you, master page, and you, sir hugh. 3.02. 83 P
my master, sir john, is come in at your back 3.03. 24 P
o sweet sir john! 3.03. 47 P
i your lady, sir john? 3.03. 52 P
a plain kerchief, sir john. 3.03. 59 P
do not betray me, sir. 3.03. 75 P
what, sir john falstaff! 3.03.139 P
that my husband is deceiv'd, or sir john. 3.03.179 P
yet seek my father's love, still seek it, sir. 3.04. 19
you wrong me, sir, thus still to haunt my house. 3.04. 69
i told you, sir, my daughter is dispos'd of. 3.04. 70
sir, will you hear me? 3.04. 74
till then farewell, sir; 3.04. 92
of another errand to sir john falstaff from my 3.04.110 P
here, sir. 3.05. 2 P
here's mistress quickly, sir, to speak with you. 3.05. 19 P
with eggs, sir? 3.05. 30 P
marry, sir, i come to your worship from mistress 3.05. 33 P
well, she laments, sir, for it, that it would 3.05. 43 P
eight and nine, sir. 3.05. 54 P
peace be with you, sir. 3.05. 56 P
bless you, sir! 3.05. 60 P
that indeed, sir john, is my business. 3.05. 63 P
and sped you, sir? 3.05. 66 P
how so, sir? did she change her determination? 3.05. 68 P
in good sadness, sir, i am sorry that for my 3.05.123 P
'tis past eight already, sir. 3.05.132 P
how now, sir hugh, no school to–day? 4.01. 10 P
sir hugh, my husband says my son profits nothing 4.01. 14 P
adieu, good sir hugh. 4.01. 84 P
he's a–birding, sweet sir john. 4.02. 8 P
step into th' chamber, sir john. 4.02. 11 P
you die, sir john — unless you go out disguis'd 4.02. 67 P
run up, sir john. 4.02. 79 P
go, go, sweet sir john. 4.02. 80 P
so say i too, sir. 4.02.128 P
sir, the /germans /desire to have three of your 4.03. 1 P
ay, sir; i'll call /them to you. 4.03. 7 P
send quickly to sir john, to know his mind. 4.04. 83
marry, sir, i come to speak with sir john 4.05. 4 P
sir, i come to speak with sir john falstaff from 4.05. 4 P
i'll be so bold as stay, sir, till she come down 4.05. 12 P
bully sir john! 4.05. 16 P
pray you, sir, was't not the wise woman of 4.05. 26 P
my master, sir, my master slender, sent to her, 4.05. 30 P
the streets, to know, sir, whether one nym, sir, 4.05. 32 P
whether one nym, sir, that beguil'd him of a 4.05. 32 P
and what says she, i pray, sir? 4.05. 35 P
i may not conceal them, sir. 4.05. 44 P
why, sir, they were nothing but about mistress 4.05. 46 P
what, sir? 4.05. 50 P
may i be bold to say so, sir? 4.05. 53 P
ay, sir; like who more bold? 4.05. 54 P
thou /art clerkly, thou art clerkly, sir john. 4.05. 57 P
out, alas, sir, cozenage! mere cozenage. 4.05. 63 P
what is the matter, sir? 4.05. 74 P
sir — let me speak with you in your chamber. 4.05.121 P
now, sir, | her mother (even strong against that 4.06. 26
went you not to her yesterday, sir, as you told 5.01. 13 P
fare you well, sir. 5.03. 6 P
sir john? art thou there, my deer? my male deer? 5.05. 16 P
now, good sir john, how like you windsor wives? 5.05.106
now, sir, who's a cuckold now? 5.05.109 P
sir john, we have had ill luck; 5.05.116 P
sir john falstaff, serve got, and leave your 5.05.129 P
why, sir john, do you think, though we would 5.05.146 P
marry, sir, we'll bring you to windsor, to one 5.05.165 P
o'er by a country fire — | sir john and all. 5.05.243
let it be so, sir john, | to master /brook you 5.05.243
i shall desire you, sir, to give me leave | to MM 1.01. 76
marry, sir, that's claudio, signior claudio. 1.02. 64 P
away, sir, you must go. 1.02.141
my holy sir, none better knows than you | how i 1.03. 7
now, pious sir, | you will demand of me why i do 1.03. 16
sir, make me not your story. 1.04. 30
good sir, adieu. 1.04. 90
sir, he must die. 2.01. 31
how now, sir, what's your name? 2.01. 45 P
i do lean upon justice, sir, and do bring in 2.01. 49 P

he cannot, sir; he's out at elbow.		2.01. 61 P
what are you, sir?		2.01. 62 P
he, sir!		2.01. 63 P
a tapster, sir;		2.01. 63 P
whose house, sir, was (as they say) pluck'd down		2.01. 64 P
my wife, sir, whom i detest before heaven and		2.01. 69 P
ay, sir; whom i thank heaven is an honest woman.		2.01. 72 P
i say, sir, i will detest myself also, as well		2.01. 75 P
marry, sir, by my wife, who, if she had been a		2.01. 79 P
ay, sir, by mistress overdone's means;		2.01. 83 P
sir, if it please your honor, this is not so.		2.01. 85 P
sir, she came in great with child;		2.01. 89 P
sir, we had but two in the house, which at that		2.01. 91 P
go to, go to; no matter for the dish, sir.		2.01. 95 P
no indeed, sir, not of a pin;		2.01. 96 P
sir, your honor cannot come to that yet.		2.01.119 P
no, sir, nor i mean it not.		2.01.120 P
sir, but you shall come to it, by your honor's		2.01.121 P
i beseech you, look into master froth here, sir;		2.01.123 P
he, sir, sitting (as i say) in a lower chair,		2.01.128 P
in a lower chair, sir — 'twas in the bunch of		2.01.128 P
now, sir, come on.		2.01.139 P
once, sir? there was nothing done to her once.		2.01.141 P
i beseech you, sir, ask him what this man did to		2.01.143 P
well, sir, what did this gentleman to her?		2.01.146 P
i beseech you, sir, look in this gentleman's		2.01.147 P
ay, sir, very well.		2.01.150 P
by this hand, sir, his wife is a more respected		2.01.165 P
sir, she was respected with him before he		2.01.170 P
here in vienna, sir.		2.01.194 P
yes, and't please you, sir.		2.01.196 P
so. what trade are you of, sir?		2.01.197 P
nine, sir; overdone by the last.		2.01.202 P
bum, sir.		2.01.216 P
truly, sir, i am a poor fellow that would live.		2.01.223 P
if the law would allow it, sir.		2.01.227 P
truly, sir, in my poor opinion, they will to't		2.01.233 P
seven year and a half, sir.		2.01.260 P
and a half, sir.		2.01.264 P
faith, sir, few of any wit in such matters.		2.01.268 P
to your worship's house, sir?		2.01.274 P
eleven, sir.		2.01.277 P
come, sir.		2.01.286
what shall be done, sir, with the groaning		2.02. 15
sir, believe this, | i had rather give my body		2.04. 55
dear sir, ere long i'll visit you again.		3.01. 46
most holy sir, i thank you.		3.01. 47
come your way, sir.		3.02. 11 P
what offense hath this man made you, sir?		3.02. 14 P
marry, sir, he hath offended the law;		3.02. 15 P
and, sir, we take him to be a thief too, sir,		3.02. 15 P
we take him to be a thief too, sir, for we have		3.02. 16 P
sir, for we have found upon him, sir, a strange		3.02. 17 P
indeed, it does stink in some sort, sir;		3.02. 28 P
but yet, sir, i would prove —		3.02. 29 P
he must before the deputy, sir, he has given him		3.02. 34 P
his neck will come to your waist — a cord, sir.		3.02. 40 P
troth, sir, she hath eaten up all her beef, and		3.02. 56 P
yes, faith, sir.		3.02. 62 P
i hope, sir, your good worship will be my bail.		3.02. 72 P
come your ways, sir, come.		3.02. 80 P
you will not bail me then, sir?		3.02. 81 P
come your ways, sir, come.		3.02. 84 P
you are pleasant, sir, and speak apace.		3.02.113 P
o, sir, you are deceiv'd.		3.02.123 P
sir, i was an inward of his.		3.02.130 P
sir, i know him, and i love him.		3.02.149 P
come, sir, i know what i know.		3.02.152 P
sir, my name is lucio, well known to the duke.		3.02.159 P
he shall know you better, sir, if i may live to		3.02.161 P
why should he die, sir?		3.02.171 P
i pray you, sir, of what disposition was the		3.02.230 P
i cry you mercy, sir, and well could wish | you		4.01. 10
if the man be a bachelor, sir, i can;		4.02. 3 P
come, sir, leave me your snatches, and yield me		4.02. 6 P
sir, i have been an unlawful bawd time out of		4.02. 15 P
do you call, sir?		4.02. 21 P
a bawd, sir?		4.02. 28 P
go to, sir, you weigh equally;		4.02. 30 P
pray, sir, by your good favor — for surely, sir		4.02. 32 P
favor — for surely, sir, a good favor you have,		4.02. 33 P
do you call, sir, your occupation a mystery?		4.02. 34 P
ay, sir, a mystery.		4.02. 35 P
painting, sir, i have heard say, is a mystery;		4.02. 36 P
and your whores, sir, being members of my		4.02. 37 P
sir, it is a mystery.		4.02. 41 P
sir, i will serve him;		4.02. 49 P
i do desire to learn, sir;		4.02. 56 P
for truly, sir, for your kindness, i owe you a		4.02. 58 P
none, sir, none.		4.02. 93
now, sir, what news?		4.02.114 P
what say you to this, sir?		4.02.127 P
pray, sir, in what?		4.02.163 P
look you, sir, here is the hand and seal of the		4.02.192 P
your friends, sir — the hangman.		4.03. 26 P
you must be so good, sir, to rise and be put to		4.03. 27 P
he is coming, sir, he is coming.		4.03. 35 P
very ready, sir.		4.03. 38 P
truly, sir, i would desire you to clap into your		4.03. 41 P
o, the better, sir;		4.03. 45 P
look you, sir, here comes your ghostly father.		4.03. 48 P
sir, induc'd by my charity, and hearing how		4.03. 50 P
o sir, you must;		4.03. 57
now, sir, how do you find the prisoner?		4.03. 66
not within, sir.		4.03.150 P
sir, the duke is marvellous little beholding to		4.03.159 P
you have told me too many of him already, sir,		4.03.168 P
sir, your company is fairer than honest.		4.03.175 P
i shall, sir. fare you well.		4.04. 18 P
marry, sir, i think, if you handled her		5.01.275 P
come, sir, did you set these women on to slander		5.01.288 P
i remember you, sir, by the sound of your voice;		5.01.327 P
most notedly, sir.		5.01.332 P
do you so, sir?		5.01.333 P
you must, sir, change persons with me, ere you		5.01.336 P
stay, sir, stay a while.		5.01.349 P
come, sir, come, sir, come, sir;		5.01.351 P
come, sir, come, sir, come, sir;		5.01.351 P
come, sir, come, sir, come, sir;		5.01.351 P
foh, sir, why, you bald-pated, lying rascal, you		5.01.351 P
sneak not away, sir, for the friar and you		5.01.358
sir, by your leave.		5.01.362
now, sir, to you.		5.01.429
most bounteous sir:		5.01.443
whipt first, sir, and hang'd after.		5.01.507
a trusty villain, sir, that very oft, | when i	ERR	1.02. 19
i am invited, sir, to certain merchants, | of		1.02. 24
sir, i commend you to your own content.		1.02. 32
stop in your wind, sir;		1.02. 53
the saddler had it, sir, i kept it not.		1.02. 57
i pray you jest, sir, as you sit at dinner.		1.02. 62
to me, sir? why, you gave no gold to me.		1.02. 71
come on, sir knave, have done your foolishness,		1.02. 72
home to your house, the phoenix, sir, to dinner;		1.02. 75
there, take you that, sir knave.		1.02. 92
what mean you, sir?		1.02. 93
nay, and you will not, sir, i'll take my heels.		1.02. 94
"my mistress, sir," quoth i:		2.01. 67
how now, sir, is your merry humor alter'd?		2.02. 7
what answer, sir? when spake i such a word?		2.02. 13
hold, sir, for god's sake!		2.02. 24
but i pray, sir, why am i beaten?		2.02. 39 P
nothing, sir, but that i am beaten.		2.02. 41 P
ay, sir, and wherefore;		2.02. 43 P
well, sir, i thank you.		2.02. 49 P
thank me, sir, for what?		2.02. 50 P
marry, sir, for this something that you gave me		2.02. 51 P
but say, sir, is it dinner-time?		2.02. 54 P
no, sir, i think the meat wants that i have.		2.02. 55 P
in good time, sir: what's that?		2.02. 57 P
well, sir, then 'twill be dry.		2.02. 59 P
if it be, sir, i pray you eat none of it.		2.02. 60 P
well, sir, learn to jest in good time — there's		2.02. 64 P
by what rule, sir?		2.02. 68 P
marry, sir, by a rule as plain as the plain bald		2.02. 69 P
marry, and did, sir:		2.02.102 P
did you converse, sir, with this gentlewoman?		2.02.160
i, sir? i never saw her till this time.		2.02.162
come, sir, to dinner.		2.02.206
say what you will, sir, but i know what i know:		3.01. 11
i hold your dainties cheap, sir, and your		3.01. 21
good meat, sir, is common;		3.01. 24
right, sir, i'll tell you when, and you'll tell		3.01. 39
the porter for this time, sir, and my name is		3.01. 43
your wife, sir knave! go get you from the door.		3.01. 64
here is neither cheer, sir, nor welcome:		3.01. 66
a man may break a word with /you, sir, and words		3.01. 75
have patience, sir, o, let it not be so!		3.01. 85
and doubt not, sir, but she will well excuse		3.01. 92
good sir, make haste.		3.01.119
o, soft, sir, hold you still;		3.02. 69
do you know me, sir?		3.02. 73 P
marry, sir, besides myself, i am due to a woman:		3.02. 81 P
marry, sir, such claim as you would lay to your		3.02. 85 P
marry, sir, she's the kitchen wench and all		3.02. 95 P
no, sir, 'tis in grain, noah's flood could not		3.02.106 P
nell, sir;		3.02.109 P
marry, sir, in her buttocks, i found it out by		3.02.117 P
o, sir, upon her nose, all o'er embellish'd with		3.02.134 P
o, sir, i did not look so low.		3.02.139 P
i know it well, sir.		3.02.166
what please yourself, sir;		3.02.170
made it for me, sir! i bespoke it not.		3.02.171
i pray you, sir, receive the money now, | for		3.02.176
you are a merry man, sir, fare you well.		3.02.178
well, sir, i will. have you the chain about you?		4.01. 42
and if i have not, sir, i hope you have:		4.01. 43
nay, come, i pray you, sir, give me the chain:		4.01. 45
the hour steals on, i pray you, sir, dispatch.		4.01. 52
good sir, say whe'r you'll answer me or no:		4.01. 60
you wrong me more, sir, in denying it.		4.01. 67
i do arrest you, sir: you hear the suit.		4.01. 79
sir, sir, i shall have law in ephesus, | to your		4.01. 83
sir, sir, i shall have law in ephesus, | to your		4.01. 83
comes aboard, | and then, sir, she bears away.		4.01. 87
our fraughtage, sir, | i have convey'd aboard,		4.01. 87
you sent me to the bay, sir, for a bark.		4.01. 99
he that came behind you, sir, like an evil angel		4.03. 20 P
the man, sir, that, when gentlemen are tir'd,		4.03. 24 P
he, sir, that takes pity on decay'd men and		4.03. 26 P
ay, sir, the sergeant of the band:		4.03. 30 P
well, sir, there rest in your foolery.		4.03. 34 P
why, sir, i brought you word an hour since that		4.03. 37 P
i see, sir, you have found the goldsmith now.		4.03. 46
your man and you are marvellous merry, sir.		4.03. 58
and i'll be gone, sir, and not trouble you.		4.03. 70
i pray you, sir, my ring, or else the chain;		4.03. 77
how now, sir?		4.04. 9
why, sir, i gave the money for the rope.		4.04. 12
i'll serve you, sir, five hundred at the rate.		4.04. 14
to a rope's end, sir, and to that end am i		4.04. 16
and to that end, sir, i will welcome you.		4.04. 17
good sir, be patient.		4.04. 18
i would i were senseless, sir, that i might not		4.04. 25 P
sir, sooth to say, you did not dine at home.		4.04. 69
but i confess, sir, that we were lock'd out.		4.04. 99
i am sorry, sir, that i have hind'red you, | but		5.01. 1
of very reverent reputation, sir, | of credit		5.01. 5
good sir, draw near to me, i'll speak to him.		5.01. 12
yes, that you did, sir, and forswore it too.		5.01. 24
sir, he din'd with her there, at the porpentine.		5.01.276
is not your name, sir, call'd antipholus?		5.01.287
within this hour i was his bondman, sir, | but		5.01.289
ourselves we do remember, sir, by you;		5.01.293
you are not pinch's patient, are you, sir?		5.01.295
no, trust me, sir, nor i.		5.01.303
ay, sir, but i am sure i do not — and		5.01.305 P
i, sir, am dromio, command him away.		5.01.336
i, sir, am dromio, pray let me stay.		5.01.337
no, sir, not i, i came from syracuse.		5.01.364
that is the chain, sir, which you had of me.		5.01.378
i think it be, sir, i deny it not.		5.01.379
and you, sir, for this chain arrested me.		5.01.380
i think i did, sir, i deny it not.		5.01.381
i sent you money, sir, to be your bail, | by		5.01.382
sir, i must have that diamond from you.		5.01.392
your goods that lay at host, sir, in the centaur		5.01.411
not i, sir, you are my elder.		5.01.421
you must not, sir, mistake my niece.	ADO	1.01. 61 P
were you in doubt, sir, that you ask'd her?		1.01.106 P
o god, sir, here's a dish i love not, i cannot		2.01.274 P
i am here already, sir.		2.03. 5 P
hugh oatcake, sir, or george seacole, for they		3.03. 11 P
well, for your favor, sir, why, give god thanks,		3.03. 19 P
well, sir.		3.03. 49 P
marry, sir, i would have some confidence with		3.05. 2 P
marry, this it is, sir.		3.05. 6 P
yes, in truth it is, sir.		3.05. 7 P
goodman verges, sir, speaks a little /off the		3.05. 9 P
an old man, sir, and his wits are not so blunt		3.05. 10 P
marry, sir, our watch to-night, excepting your		3.05. 30 P
a good old man, sir, he will be talking;		3.05. 33 P
honest soul, i' faith, sir, by my troth he is,		3.05. 38 P
one word, sir.		3.05. 45 P
our watch, sir, have indeed comprehended two		3.05. 45 P
sir, they are spoken, and these things are true.		4.01. 67
sir, sir, be patient.		4.01.143
sir, sir, be patient.		4.01.143
i am a gentleman, sir, and my name is conrade.		4.02. 13 P
yea, sir, we hope.		4.02. 17 P
marry, sir, we say we are none.		4.02. 24 P
a word in your ear, sir.		4.02. 27 P
sir, i say to you, we are none.		4.02. 29 P
this man said, sir, that don john, the prince's		4.02. 39 P
come, sir boy, come follow me.		5.01. 83
sir boy, i'll whip you from your foining fence,		5.01. 84
sir, i shall meet your wit in the career, and		5.01.135 P
sir, your wit ambles well, it goes easily.		5.01.158 P
come you, sir.		5.01.206 P
marry, sir, they have committed false report;		5.01.215 P
o noble sir!		5.01.292
moreover, sir, which indeed is not under white		5.01.304 P
your answer, sir, is enigmatical, | but, for my		5.04. 27
bull jove, sir, had an amiable low, | and some		5.04. 48
by yea and nay, sir, then i swore in jest.	LLL	1.01. 54
sir, the contempts thereof are as touching me.		1.01.190 P
to hear meekly, sir, and to laugh moderately;		1.01.197 P
well, sir, be it as the style shall give us		1.01.199 P
the matter is to me, sir, as concerning		1.01.201 P
in manner and form following, sir, all those		1.01.205 P
now, sir, for the manner — it is the manner of		1.01.209 P
for the following, sir?		1.01.212 P
sir, i confess the wench.		1.01.283 P
i was taken with none, sir, i was taken with a		1.01.289 P
this was no damsel neither, sir, she was a		1.01.292 P
this maid will not serve your turn, sir.		1.01.298 P
this maid will serve my turn, sir.		1.01.299 P
sir, i will pronounce your sentence:		1.01.300 P
i suffer for the truth, sir;		1.01.311 P
a great sign, sir, that he will look sad.		1.02. 3 P
no, no, o lord, sir, no.		1.02. 6 P
how mean you, sir?		1.02. 19 P
i am answer'd, sir.		1.02. 31 P
you may do it in an hour, sir.		1.02. 37 P
you are a gentleman and a gamester, sir.		1.02. 42 P
why, sir, is this such a piece of study?		1.02. 50 P
of the sea-water green, sir.		1.02. 82 P
as i have read, sir, and the best of them too.		1.02. 84 P
it was so, sir, for she had a green wit.		1.02. 89 P
sir, the duke's pleasure is that you keep		1.02.127 P
well, sir, i hope when i do it i shall do it on		1.02.148 P
let me not be pent up, sir;		1.02.155 P
no, sir, that were fast and loose;		1.02.157 P
sir, i pray you a word. what lady is that same?		2.01.194
pray you, sir, whose daughter?		2.01.201
good sir, be not offended, | she is an heir of		2.01.204
not unlike, sir, that may be.		2.01.208
to her will, sir, or so.		2.01.212
o, you are welcome, sir, adieu.		2.01.213
farewell to me, sir, and welcome to you.		2.01.214
marry, sir, you must send the ass upon the horse		3.01. 54 P
as swift as lead, sir.		3.01. 57 P
you are too swift, sir, to say so.		3.01. 61
riddle, no l'envoy, no salve in the mail, sir.		3.01. 73 P
o sir, plantan, a plain plantan:		3.01. 73 P
no l'envoy, no salve, sir, but a plantan!		3.01. 74 P
sir, your pennyworth is good, and your goose be		3.01.102
pray you, sir, how much carnation ribbon may a		3.01.145 P
marry, sir, halfpenny farthing.		3.01.148 P
when would you have it done, sir?		3.01.154 P
well, i will do it, sir; fare you well.		3.01.156 P
i shall know, sir, when i have done it.		3.01.158 P
i will do it, sir, in print.		3.01.172 P
what's your will, sir? what's your will?		4.01. 52
she's too hard for you at pricks, sir, challenge		4.01.138
but, sir, i assure ye it was a buck of the first		4.02. 9 P
sir nathaniel, haud credo.		4.02. 11 P
sir, he hath never fed of the dainties that are		4.02. 24
sir nathaniel, will you hear an extemporal		4.02. 50 P
sir, i praise the lord for you, and so may my		4.02. 73 P
under pardon, sir, what are the contents?		4.02.101 P
ay, sir, and very learned.		4.02.103 P
ay, sir, from one monsieur berowne, one of the		4.02.129 P
sir /nathaniel, this berowne is one of the		4.02.136 P
sir, god save your life!		4.02.144 P
sir, you have done this in the fear of god, very		4.02.147 P
sir, tell not me of the father, i do fear		4.02.149 P
did they please you, sir nathaniel?		4.02.151 P
sir, i do invite you too, you shall not say me		4.02.164 P
come, sir, you blush;		4.03.129
nay, it makes nothing, sir.		4.03.189
for, sir, to tell you plain, | i'll find a		4.03.268
i praise god for you, sir.		5.01. 2 P
most military sir, salutation.		5.01. 35 P
sir, it is the king's most sweet pleasure and		5.01. 87 P
the posterior of the day, most generous sir, is		5.01. 91 P
and apt, i do assure you, sir, i do assure.		5.01. 94 P
sir, the king is a noble gentleman, and my		5.01. 95 P
sir, you shall present before her the nine		5.01.117 P
sir /nathaniel, as concerning some entertainment		5.01.118 P
pardon, sir, error:		5.01.130 P
nor understood none neither, sir.		5.01.151 P
o for your reason! quickly, sir — i long!		5.02.244
fair sir, god save you! where's the princess?		5.02.310

but take it, sir, again. 5.02.453
pardon me, sir, this jewel did she wear, | and 5.02.456
and stand between her back, sir, and the fire, 5.02.476
o lord, sir, they would know | whether the three 5.02.485
no, sir, but it is vara fine, | for every one 5.02.487
not so, sir, under correction, sir, i hope it is 5.02.489
sir, under correction, sir, i hope it is not so. 5.02.489
you cannot beg us, sir, i can assure you, sir, 5.02.490
i can assure you, sir, we know what we know. 5.02.490
i hope, sir, three times thrice, sir — 5.02.491
i hope, sir, three times thrice, sir — 5.02.491
under correction, sir, we know whereuntil it 5.02.493 P
o lord, sir, it were pity you should get your 5.02.496 P
you should get your living by reck'ning, sir. 5.02.497 P
o lord, sir, the parties themselves, the actors, 5.02.499 P
the actors, sir, will show whereuntil it doth 5.02.500 P
one man in one poor man, pompion the great, sir. 5.02.503 P
we will turn it finely off, sir; 5.02.510
it is "great," sir. 5.02.552
o, sir, you have overthrown alisander the 5.02.574 P
not iscariot, sir. 5.02.597 P
what mean you, sir? 5.02.603 P
begin, sir, you are my elder. 5.02.605 P
come, sir, it wants a twelvemonth an' a day, 5.02.877
lysander, if you live, good sir, awake. MND 2.02.102
your name, i beseech you, sir? 3.01.189 P
no, sir; 3.02.322
no, in truth, sir, he should not. 5.01.184 P
believe me, sir, had i such venture forth, | the MV 1.01. 15
conceit, | as who should say, "i am sir oracle, 1.01. 93
ay, sir, for three months. 1.03. 2 P
this was a venture, sir, that jacob serv'd for, 1.03. 91
"fair sir, you spet on me on wednesday last, 1.03.126
no master, sir, but a poor man's son. 2.02. 51 P
your worship's friend and launcelot, sir. 2.02. 56 P
alack, sir, i am sand–blind, i know you not. 2.02. 74 P
pray you, sir, stand up. 2.02. 81 P
here's my son, sir, a poor boy — 2.02.122 P
not a poor boy, sir, but the rich jew's man, 2.02.123 P
that would, sir, as my father shall specify — 2.02.124 P
he hath a great infection, sir, as one would say 2.02.125 P
serve you, sir. 2.02.142 P
that is the very defect of the matter, sir. 2.02.143 P
parted between my master shylock and you, sir: 2.02.150 P
you have the grace of god, sir, and he hath 2.02.151 P
yonder, sir, he walks. 2.02.174
by your leave, sir. 2.04. 15 P
marry, sir, to bid my old master the jew to sup 2.04. 17 P
i beseech you, sir, go. 2.05. 19 P
i will go before, sir. 2.05. 40 P
that is done, sir, they have all stomachs! 3.05. 48 P
that is done too, sir, only "cover" is the word. 3.05. 51 P
will you cover then, sir? 3.05. 53 P
not so, sir, neither, i know my duty. 3.05. 54 P
for the table, sir, it shall be serv'd in; 3.05. 61 P
for the meat, sir, it shall be cover'd; 3.05. 62 P
for your coming in to dinner, sir, why, let it 3.05. 63 P
sir, i entreat you home with me to dinner. 4.01.401
dear sir, of force i must attempt you further. 4.01.421
this ring, good sir, alas, it is a trifle! 4.01.430
i see, sir, you are liberal in offers. 4.01.438
good sir, this ring was given me by my wife, 4.01.441
fair sir, you are well o'erta'en. 4.02. 5
sir, i would speak with you. 4.02. 12
come, good sir, will you show me to this house? 4.02. 19
sir, you are very welcome to our house. 5.01.139
sir, grieve not you, you are welcome 5.01.239
now, sir, what make you here? AYL 1.01. 29 P
what mar you then, sir? 1.01. 31 P
marry, sir, i am helping you to mar that which 1.01. 32 P
marry, sir, be better employ'd and be naught a 1.01. 35 P
know you where you are, sir? 1.01. 40 P
o, sir, very well; here in your orchard. 1.01. 41 P
know you before whom, sir? 1.01. 42 P
i am the youngest son of sir rowland de boys. 1.01. 57 P
well, sir, get you in. 1.01. 76 P
there's no news at the court, sir, but the old 1.01. 98 P
marry, do i, sir; 1.01.122 P
i am given, sir, secretly to understand that 1.01.123 P
to–morrow, sir, i wrastle for my credit, and he 1.01.126 P
do, young sir, your reputation shall not 1.02.180 P
ready, sir, but his will hath in it a more 1.02.202 P
liege, the youngest son of sir rowland de boys. 1.02.222 P
i am more proud to be sir rowland's son, | his 1.02.232
my father lov'd sir rowland as his soul, | and 1.02.235
sir, you have well deserv'd. 1.02.242
did you call, sir? 1.02.253
sir, you have wrastled well, and overthrown 1.02.254
good sir, i do in friendship counsel you | to 1.02.261
i thank you, sir; 1.02.268
sir, fare you well. 1.02.283
a liking with old sir rowland's youngest son? 1.03. 28 P
o you memory | of old sir rowland! 2.03. 4
your betters, sir. 2.04. 68
and to you, gentle sir, and to you all. 2.04. 70
fair sir, i pity her, | and wish, for her sake 2.04. 75
"no, sir," quoth he, | "call me not fool till 2.07. 18
and why, sir, must they so? 2.07. 51
if that you were the good sir rowland's son, 2.07.191
sir, sir, that cannot be. 3.01. 1
sir, sir, that cannot be. 3.01. 1
sir, i am a true laborer: 3.02. 73 P
by no means, sir. 3.02.308 P
to that end i have been with sir oliver martext, 3.03. 43 P
here comes sir oliver. 3.03. 64 P
sir oliver martext, you are well met. 3.03. 64 P
how do you, sir? 3.03. 74 P
even a toy in hand here, sir. 3.03. 76 P
as the ox hath his bow, sir, the horse his curb, 3.03. 79 P
sir, it was i. 4.02. 2 P
yes, sir. 4.02. 7 P
good sir, go with us. 4.03.178 P
a most wicked sir oliver, audrey, a most vile 5.01. 5 P
and good ev'n to you, sir. 5.01. 15 P
five and twenty, sir. 5.01. 19 P
william, sir. 5.01. 21 P
ay, sir, i thank god. 5.01. 24 P
faith, sir, so, so. 5.01. 26 P
ay, sir, i have a pretty wit. 5.01. 29 P
i do, sir. 5.01. 37 P
no, sir. 5.01. 39 P
which he, sir? 5.01. 45 P
he, sir, that must marry this woman. 5.01. 46 P
god rest you merry, sir. 5.01. 59 P
revenue that was old sir rowland's will i estate 5.02. 11 P
you are deceiv'd, sir, we kept time, we lost not 5.03. 37 P
god 'ild you, sir, i desire you of the like. 5.04. 54 P
i press in here, sir, amongst the rest of the 5.04. 55 P
a poor virgin, sir, an ill–favor'd thing, sir, 5.04. 57 P
sir, an ill–favor'd thing, sir, but mine own; 5.04. 58 P
a poor humor of mine, sir, to take that that no 5.04. 59 P
rich honesty dwells like a miser, sir, in a poor 5.04. 60 P
according to the fool's bolt, sir, and such 5.04. 64 P
your body more seeming, audrey), as thus, sir. 5.04. 69 P
o sir, we quarrel in print, by the book — as 5.04. 90 P
i am the second son of old sir rowland, | that 5.04.152
sir, by your patience. 5.04.180
why, sir, you know no house nor no such maid, SHR in.2. 91
in brief, sir, study what you most affect. 1.01. 40
i pray you, sir, is it your will | to make a 1.01. 57
i' faith, sir, you shall never need to fear. 1.01. 61
sir, to your pleasure humbly i subscribe; 1.01. 81
marry, sir, to get a husband for her sister. 1.01.120 P
i pray, sir, tell me, is it possible | that love 1.01.146
i pray, awake, sir; 1.01.178
ay, marry, am i, sir; and now 'tis plotted. 1.01.188
in brief, sir, sith it your pleasure is, | and i 1.01.211
ay, sir! — ne'er a whit. 1.01.235
knock, sir? 1.02. 6 P
knock you here, sir? 1.02. 9 P
why, sir, what am i, sir, that i should knock 1.02. 9 P
what am i, sir, that i should knock you here, 1.02. 10 P
am i, sir, that i should knock you here, sir? 1.02. 10 P
'tis no matter, sir, what he 'leges in latin. 1.02. 28 P
for me to leave his service, look you, sir. 1.02. 30 P
he bid me knock him and rap him soundly, sir. 1.02. 31 P
look you, sir, he tells you flatly what his mind 1.02. 77 P
i pray you, sir, let him go while the humor 1.02.107 P
i'll tell you what, sir, and she stand him but a 1.02.113 P
you know him not, sir. 1.02.116 P
hark you, sir, i'll have them very fairly bound 1.02.145
than you — unless you were a scholar, sir. 1.02.158
o sir, such a life, with such a wife, were 1.02.193
hark you, sir, you mean not her to — 1.02.223
perhaps him and her, sir; what have you to do? 1.02.224
not her that chides, sir, at any hand, i pray. 1.02.225
i love no chiders, sir. biondello, let's away. 1.02.226
sir, a word ere you go. 1.02.227
and if i be, sir, is it any offense? 1.02.229
why, sir, i pray, are not the streets as free 1.02.231
sir, give him head, i know he'll prove a jade. 1.02.247
sir, let me be so bold as ask you, | did you yet 1.02.249
no, sir, but hear i do that he hath two: 1.02.251
sir, sir, the first's for me! let her go by. 1.02.254
sir, sir, the first's for me! let her go by. 1.02.254
sir, understand you this of me, in sooth: 1.02.257
if it be so, sir, that you are the man | must 1.02.263
sir, you say well, and well you do conceive, 1.02.269
sir, i shall not be slack; 1.02.273
and you, good sir! 2.01. 42
i have a daughter, sir, call'd katherina. 2.01. 44
i am a gentleman of verona, sir, | that, hearing 2.01. 47
y' are welcome, sir, and he, for your good sake. 2.01. 61
whence are you, sir? 2.01. 67
i doubt it not, sir; 2.01. 75
but, gentle sir, methinks you walk like a 2.01. 86 P
pardon me, sir, the boldness is mine own, | that 2.01. 88
of pisa, sir, son to vincentio. 2.01.103
you are very welcome, sir. 2.01.105
how but well, sir? 2.01.282
sir, list to me: 2.01.363
fiddler, forbear, you grow too forward, sir. 3.01. 1
are you so formal, sir? 3.01. 61
why, no, sir. 3.02. 36 P
o, sir, his lackey, for all the world 3.02. 65 P
why, sir, he comes not. 3.02. 75 P
no, sir, i say his horse comes, with him on his 3.02. 79 P
you are welcome, sir. 3.02. 88
why, sir, you know this is your wedding–day. 3.02. 97
but, sir, love concerneth us to add | her 3.02.128
i'll tell you, sir lucentio: 3.02.158
ay, sir, they be ready; 3.02.205 P
the door is open, sir, there lies your way; 3.02.210
ay, marry, sir, now it begins to work. 3.02.218
here, here, sir, here, sir. 4.01.123 P
here, here, sir, here, sir. 4.01.123 P
here, sir! 4.01.124
here, sir! 4.01.124
here, sir! 4.01.124
here, sir! 4.01.124
here, sir — as foolish as i was before. 4.01.128
nathaniel's coat, sir, was not fully made, | and 4.01.132
i tell you, sir, she bears me fair in hand. 4.02. 3
sir, to satisfy you in what i have said, | stand 4.02. 4
and may you prove, sir, master of your art! 4.02. 9
know, sir, that i am call'd hortensio. 4.02. 21
god save you, sir! 4.02. 72
and you, sir! 4.02. 72
sir, at the farthest for a week or two, | but 4.02. 74
of mantua, sir? 4.02. 78
my life, sir? how, i pray? for that goes hard. 4.02. 80
alas, sir, it is worse for me than so! 4.02. 88
well, sir, to do you courtesy, | this will i do, 4.02. 91
ay, sir, in pisa have i often been, | pisa 4.02. 94
he is my father, sir, and, sooth to say, | in 4.02. 99
fortunes | that you are like to sir vincentio. 4.02.106
you understand me, sir? 4.02.110
if this be court'sy, sir, accept of it. 4.02.112
o sir, i do, and will repute you ever | the 4.02.113
i thank you, sir. 4.03. 47
what news with you, sir? 4.03. 62
why, sir, i trust i may have leave to speak, 4.03. 73
for you shall hop without my custom, sir. 4.03. 99
marry, sir, with needle and thread. 4.03.120
error i' th' bill, sir, error i' th' bill! 4.03.145 P
well, sir, in brief, the gown is not for me. 4.03.155
you are i' th' right, sir, 'tis for my mistress. 4.03.156 P
why, sir, what's your conceit in that? 4.03.160
o, sir, the conceit is deeper than you think for 4.03.161
i dare assure you, sir, 'tis almost two, | and 4.03.189
but, sir, here comes your boy; 4.04. 8
set your countenance, sir. 4.04. 18
sir, this is the gentleman i told you of. 4.04. 20
sir, by your leave, having come to padua | to 4.04. 24
sir, pardon me in what i have to say — | your 4.04. 38
i thank you, sir. 4.04. 48
come, sir, we will better it in pisa. 4.04. 71
parsley to stuff a rabbit, and so may you, sir. 4.04.101 P
and so adieu, sir; 4.04.102 P
fair sir, and you my merry mistress, | that with 4.05. 53
lucentio, gentle sir. 4.05. 58
softly and swiftly, sir, for the priest is ready 5.01. 1 P
sir, here's the door, this is lucentio's house. 5.01. 8
thither must i, and here i leave you, sir. 5.01. 10
is signior lucentio within, sir? 5.01. 18 P
he's within, sir, but not to be spoken withal. 5.01. 19 P
do you hear, sir? 5.01. 26 P
ay, sir, so his mother says, if i may believe 5.01. 33 P
i hope i may choose, sir. 5.01. 47 P
no, sir. 5.01. 50 P
yes, marry, sir — see where he looks out of the 5.01. 55 P
sir, what are you that offer to beat my servant? 5.01. 63 P
what am i, sir? 5.01. 65 P
nay, what are you, sir? 5.01. 65 P
sir, you seem a sober ancient gentleman by your 5.01. 73 P
why, sir, what 'cerns it you if i wear pearl and 5.01. 75 P
you mistake, sir, you mistake, sir. 5.01. 79 P
you mistake, sir, you mistake, sir. 5.01. 79 P
but do you hear, sir? 5.01.133 P
no, sir, god forbid, but asham'd to kiss. 5.01.146
believe me, sir, they butt together well. 5.02. 39
o, sir, lucentio slipp'd me like his greyhound, 5.02. 52
'tis well, sir, that you hunted for yourself; 5.02. 55
sir, my mistress sends you word | that she is 5.02. 80
pray god, sir, your wife send you not a worse. 5.02. 84
i am afraid, sir, | do what you can, yours will 5.02. 88
what is your will, sir, that you send for me? 5.02.100
you, sir, a father. AWW 1.01. 7 P
he was famous, sir, in his profession, and it 1.01. 26 P
how might one do, sir, to lose it to her own 1.01.150 P
so 'tis reported, sir. 1.02. 3
his good remembrance, sir, | lies richer in your 1.02. 48
you're loved, sir; 1.02. 67
well, sir. 1.03. 15 P
get you gone, sir, i'll talk with you more anon. 1.03. 64 P
you'll be gone, sir knave, and do as i command 1.03. 90 P
'tis our hope, sir, | after well–ent'red 2.01. 5
dear sir, to my endeavors give consent, | of 2.01.153
come on, sir, i shall now put you to the height 2.02. 1 P
i pray you, sir, are you a courtier? 2.02. 40 P
o lord, sir! 2.02. 41 P
sir, i am a poor friend of yours that loves you. 2.02. 43 P
o lord, sir! — thick, thick, spare not me. 2.02. 45 P
i think, sir, you can eat none of this homely 2.02. 46 P
o lord, sir! — nay, put me to't, i warrant you. 2.02. 48 P
you were lately whipt, sir, as i think. 2.02. 50 P
o lord, sir! — spare not me. 2.02. 51 P
do you cry, "o lord, sir!" 2.02. 52 P
indeed your "o lord, sir!" 2.02. 53 P
had worse luck in my life in my "o lord, sir!" 2.02. 58 P
o lord, sir! — why, there't serves well again. 2.02. 62 P
/an end, sir, to your business! 2.02. 63
sir, will you hear my suit? 2.03. 76
thanks, sir; all the rest is mute. 2.03. 77
the honor, sir, that flames in your fair eyes, 2.03. 80
your pleasure, sir? 2.03.185 P
you are too old, sir; 2.03.196 P
ay, sir. 2.03.248 P
go to, sir, you were beaten in italy for picking 2.03.258 P
i hope, sir, i have your good will to have mine 2.04. 15 P
you should have said, sir, "before a knave th' 2.04. 29 P
this had been truth, sir. 2.04. 31 P
did you find me in yourself, sir, or were you 2.04. 33 P
the search, sir, was profitable, and much fool 2.04. 35 P
these things shall be done, sir. 2.05. 15 P
pray you, sir, who's his tailor? 2.05. 16 P
sir? 2.05. 17 P
o, i know him well, i, sir, he, sir, 's a good 2.05. 18 P
i, sir, he, sir, 's a good workman, a very good 2.05. 18 P
i have, sir, as i was commanded from you, 2.05. 54
sir, i can nothing say, | but that i am your 2.05. 71
pray, sir, your pardon. 2.05. 78
sir, it is | a charge too heavy for my strength, 3.03. 3
no, sir, i warrant you. 4.01. 10 P
kerelybonto, sir, betake thee to thy faith, for 4.01. 75 P
so i will, sir. 4.01. 93
let it be forbid, sir, so should i be a great 4.03. 45 P
sir, his wife some two months since fled from 4.03. 47 P
he met the duke in the street, sir, of whom he 4.03. 76 P
i humbly thank you, sir. 4.03.156 P
by my troth, sir, if i were to live this present 4.03.160 P
that is not the duke's letter, sir; 4.03.212 P
i pray you, sir, put it up again. 4.03.216 P
this is your devoted friend, sir, the manifold 4.03.235 P
i perceive, sir, by /the general's looks, we 4.03.239 P
my life, sir, in any case! 4.03.241 P
let me live, sir, in a dungeon, i' th' stocks, 4.03.244 P
he will steal, sir, an egg out of a cloister. 4.03.250 P
he will lie, sir, with such volubility, that you 4.03.253 P
i have but little more to say, sir, of his 4.03.258 P
faith, sir, h'as led the drum before the english 4.03.266 P
sir, for a cardecue he will sell the fee–simple 4.03.278 P
there is no remedy, sir, but you must die. 4.03.303 P
o lord, sir, let me live, or let me see my death 4.03.309 P
fare ye well, sir, i am for france too. 4.03.328 P
indeed, sir, she was the sweet marjorom of the 4.05. 16 P
i am no great nebuchadnezzar, sir, i have not 4.05. 20 P
a fool, sir, at a woman's service, and a knave 4.05. 24 P
and i would give his wife my bauble, sir, to do 4.05. 30 P
why, sir, if i cannot serve you, i can serve as 4.05. 36 P
faith, sir, 'a has an english /name, but his 4.05. 39 P
the black prince, sir, alias the prince of 4.05. 42 P
i am a woodland fellow, sir, that always lov'd a 4.05. 47 P
if i put any tricks upon 'em, sir, they shall be 4.05. 60 P

god save you, sir. 5.01. 8
sir, i have seen you in the court of france. 5.01. 10
i do presume, sir, that you are not fall'n 5.01. 12
not here, sir? 5.01. 22
i do beseech you, sir, | since you are like to 5.01. 29
i have ere now, sir, been better known to you, 5.02. 2 P
but i am now, sir, muddied in fortune's mood, 5.02. 4 P
nay, you need not to stop your nose, sir; 5.02. 10 P
indeed, sir, if your metaphor stink, i will stop 5.02. 12 P
pray you, sir, deliver me this paper. 5.02. 15 P
here is a purr of fortune's, sir, or of 5.02. 19 P
pray you, sir, use the carp as you may, for he 5.02. 22 P
i wonder, sir, /sith wives are monsters to you, 5.03.155
i am her mother, sir, whose age and honor | both 5.03.162
sir, for my thoughts, you have them ill to 5.03.182
sir, much like | the same upon your finger. 5.03.225
faith, sir, he did love her, but how? 5.03.243 P
he did love her, sir, as a gentleman loves a 5.03.245 P
he lov'd her, sir, and lov'd her not. 5.03.248 P
stay, royal sir. 5.03.295
by my troth, sir toby, you must come in earlier TN 1.03. 4 P
who, sir andrew aguecheek? 1.03. 18 P
for here comes sir andrew agueface. 1.03. 43 P
sir toby belch! how now, sir toby belch? 1.03. 44 P
sir toby belch! how now, sir toby belch? 1.03. 44 P
sweet sir andrew! 1.03. 46 P
and you too, sir. 1.03. 48 P
accost, sir andrew, accost. 1.03. 49 P
my name is mary, sir. 1.03. 54 P
and thou let part so, sir andrew, would thou 1.03. 61 P
sir, i have not you by th'.hand. 1.03. 66 P
now, sir, thought is free. 1.03. 69 P
it's dry, sir. 1.03. 73 P
a dry jest, sir. 1.03. 76 P
ay, sir, i have them at my fingers' ends. 1.03. 78 P
i'll ride home to–morrow, sir toby. 1.03. 89 P
faith, i'll home to–morrow, sir toby. 1.03.105 P
no, sir, it is legs and thighs. 1.03.140 P
is he inconstant, sir, in his favors? 1.04. 7 P
go thy way, if sir toby would leave drinking, 1.05. 27 P
sir, i bade them take away you. 1.05. 54 P
well, sir, for want of other idleness, i'll bide 1.05. 64 P
god send you, sir, a speedy infirmity, for the 1.05. 78 P
sir toby will be sworn that i am no fox, but he 1.05. 79 P
sir toby, madam, your kinsman. 1.05.105 P
now you see, sir, how your fooling grows old, 1.05.110 P
good sir toby! 1.05.122 P
whence came you, sir? 1.05.177 P
will you hoist sail, sir? here lies your way. 1.05.202 P
now, sir, what is your text? 1.05.219 P
look you, sir, such a one i was this present. 1.05.234 P
is in grain, sir, 'twill endure wind and 1.05.237 P
, sir, i will not be so hard–hearted; 1.05.244 P
no, sooth, sir; 2.01. 11 P
but you, sir, alter'd that, for some hour before 2.01. 21 P
lady, sir, though it was said she much 2.01. 25 P
he is drown'd already, sir, with salt water, 2.01. 30 P
pardon me, sir, your bad entertainment. 2.01. 33 P
even now, sir — on a moderate pace i have since 2.02. 3 P
he returns this ring to you, sir. 2.02. 5 P
ome, sir, you peevishly threw it to her; 2.02. 13 P
pproach, sir andrew. 2.03. 1 P
y'r lady, sir, and some dogs will catch well. 2.03. 62 P
e did keep time, sir, in our catches. sneck up! 2.03. 93 P
r toby, i must be round with you. 2.03. 95 P
ay, good sir toby. 2.03.103 P
r toby, there you lie. 2.03.107
ut o' tune, sir! 2.03.113 P
o, sir, rub your chain with crumbs. 2.03.119 P
weet sir toby, be patient for to–night. 2.03.131 P
arry, sir, sometimes he is a kind of puritan. 2.03.140 P
re you ready, sir? 2.04. 49 P
o pains, sir, i take pleasure in singing, sir. 2.04. 68 P
o pains, sir, i take pleasure in singing, sir. 2.04. 68 P
uly, sir, and pleasure will be paid, one time 2.04. 70 P
ut if she cannot love you, sir? 2.04. 87
r, shall i to this lady? 2.04.122
m black and blue, shall we not, sir andrew? 2.05. 11 P
one sir andrew" — 2.05. 80 P
ad politic authors, i will baffle sir toby, i 2.05.162 P
o, sir, i live by the church. 3.01. 3 P
o such matter, sir. 3.01. 5 P
ou have said, sir. 3.01. 11 P
ould therefore my sister had had no name, sir. 3.01. 17 P
ny, sir, her name's a word, and to dally with 3.01. 19 P
oth, sir, i can yield you none without words, 3.01. 23 P
ot so, sir, i do care for something; 3.01. 28 P
ut in my conscience, sir, i do not care for you 3.01. 29 P
that be to care for nothing, sir, i would it 3.01. 30 P
o, indeed, sir, the lady olivia has no folly. 3.01. 32 P
e will keep no fool, sir, till she be married, 3.01. 33 P
olery, sir, does walk about the orb like the 3.01. 38 P
would be sorry, sir, but the fool should be as 3.01. 39 P
ould not a pair of these have bred, sir? 3.01. 49 P
would play lord pandarus of phrygia, sir, to 3.01. 51 P
nderstand you, sir. 'tis well begg'd. 3.01. 53 P
pe, is not great, sir — begging but a beggar: 3.01. 54 P
y lady is within, sir. 3.01. 56 P
d you, sir. 3.01. 70 P
ope, sir, you are, and i am yours. 3.01. 73 P
m bound to your niece, sir; 3.01. 76 P
ste your legs, sir, put them to motion. 3.01. 78 P
y legs do better understand me, sir, than i 3.01. 79 P
nean, to go, sir, to enter. 3.01. 81 P
ve me your hand, sir. 3.01. 94 P
y servant, sir? 3.01. 98
u must needs yield your reason, sir andrew. 3.02. 3 P
will prove it legitimate, sir, upon the oaths 3.02. 14 P
ere is no way but this, sir andrew. 3.02. 39 P
s is a dear manikin to you, sir toby. 3.02. 53 P
–morrow, sir. best first go see your lodging. 3.03. 20
ld, sir, here's my purse. 3.03. 38
re | i think is not for idle markets, sir. 3.03. 46
worse man than sir toby to look to me! 3.04. 65 P
low tongue, in the habit of some sir of note, 3.04. 73 P
re he is, here he is. how is't with you, sir? 3.04. 87 P
toby, my lady prays you to have a care of 3.04. 92 P
! 3.04.114 P

get him to say his prayers, good sir toby, get 3.04.118 P
go, sir andrew, scout me for him at the corner 3.04.176 P
but, sir, i will deliver his challenge by word 3.04.190 P
and you, sir. 3.04.219 P
you mistake, sir, i am sure; 3.04.226 P
i pray you, sir, what is he? 3.04.234 P
sir, no; 3.04.246 P
pray you, sir, do you know of this matter? 3.04.259 P
he is indeed, sir, the most skillful, bloody, 3.04.266 P
had rather go with sir priest than sir knight. 3.04.271 P
had rather go with sir priest than sir knight. 3.04.271 P
there's no remedy, sir, he will fight with you 3.04.296 P
come, sir andrew, there's no remedy, the 3.04.305 P
you, sir? why, what are you? 3.04.315 P
one, sir, that for his love dares yet do more 3.04.316
o good sir toby, hold! here come the officers. 3.04.319 P
pray, sir, put your sword up, if you please. 3.04.321 P
marry, will i, sir; 3.04.322 P
you do mistake me, sir. 3.04.328
no, sir, no jot. 3.04.329
come, sir, away. 3.04.339
what money, sir? 3.04.341
come, sir, i pray you go. 3.04.358
come, come, sir. 3.04.371
now, sir, have i met you again? there's for you. 4.01. 24 P
hold, sir, or i'll throw your dagger o'er the 4.01. 28 P
come on, sir, hold! 4.01. 32 P
come, sir, i will not let you go. 4.01. 38 P
make him believe thou art sir topas the curate, 4.02. 2 P
i'll call sir toby the whilst. 4.02. 3 P
bonos dies, sir toby: 4.02. 12 P
to him, sir topas. 4.02. 17 P
sir topas the curate, who comes to visit 4.02. 21 P
sir topas, sir topas, good sir topas, go to my 4.02. 23 P
sir topas, sir topas, good sir topas, go to my 4.02. 23 P
topas, sir topas, good sir topas, go to my lady. 4.02. 23 P
sir topas, never was man thus wrong'd. 4.02. 28 P
good sir topas, do not think i am mad; 4.02. 29 P
as hell, sir topas. 4.02. 35 P
i am not mad, sir topas, i say to you this house 4.02. 40 P
sir topas, sir topas! 4.02. 61 P
sir topas, sir topas! 4.02. 61 P
my most exquisite sir topas! 4.02. 62 P
alas, sir, how fell you besides your five wits? 4.02. 86 P
sir topas! 4.02. 98 P
who, i, sir? 4.02.100 P
not i, sir. 4.02.100 P
god buy you, good sir topas. 4.02.100 P
i will, sir, i will. 4.02.101 P
alas, sir, be patient. 4.02.103 P
what say you, sir? 4.02.103 P
well–a–day that you were, sir! 4.02.108 P
i am gone, sir, | and anon, sir, | i'll be with 4.02.120
i am gone, sir, | and anon, sir, | i'll be with 4.02.121
ay, sir, we are some of her trappings. 5.01. 9 P
truly, sir, the better for my foes and the worse 5.01. 12 P
no, sir, the worse. 5.01. 15 P
marry, sir, they praise me and make an ass of me 5.01. 17 P
so that by my foes, sir, i profit in the 5.01. 19 P
by my troth, sir, no; 5.01. 25 P
but that it would be double–dealing, sir, i 5.01. 29 P
put your grace in your pocket, sir, for this 5.01. 32 P
the triplex, sir, is a good tripping measure, or 5.01. 38 P
or the bells of saint bennet, sir, may put you 5.01. 39 P
marry, sir, lullaby to your bounty till i come 5.01. 45 P
i go, sir, but i would not have you to think 5.01. 46 P
as you say, sir, let your bounty take a nap, i 5.01. 48 P
here comes the man, sir, that did rescue me. 5.01. 50
he did me kindness, sir, drew on my side, | but 5.01. 66
orsino, noble sir, | be pleas'd that i shake off 5.01. 72
send one presently to sir toby. 5.01.173 P
across and has given sir toby a bloody coxcomb 5.01.176 P
who has done this, sir andrew? 5.01.179 P
that i did, i was set on to do't by sir toby. 5.01.186 P
here comes sir toby halting — you shall hear 5.01.192 P
o, he's drunk, sir toby, an hour agone; 5.01.198 P
i'll help you, sir toby, because we'll be 5.01.204 P
to frown | upon sir toby and the lighter people; 5.01.339
the letter at sir toby's great importance, | in 5.01.363
i was one, sir, in this enterlude — one sir 5.01.372 P
sir, in this enterlude — one sir topas, sir, 5.01.372 P
one sir topas, sir, but that's all one. 5.01.373 P
sir, that's to–morrow. WT 1.02. 10
i had thought, sir, to have held my peace until 1.02. 28
you, sir, | charge him too coldly. 1.02. 29
with oaths, | should yet say, "sir, no going." 1.02. 49
come, sir page, | look on me with your welkin 1.02.135
if at home, sir, | he's all my exercise, my 1.02.165
next neighbor — by | sir smile, his neighbor. 1.02.196
camillo, this great sir will yet stay longer. 1.02.212
sir, my lord, | i could do this, and that with 1.02.318
i must believe you, sir. 1.02.333
hail, most royal sir! 1.02.366
sir, i will tell you, | since i am charg'd in 1.02.406
come, sir, away. 1.02.465
come, sir, now | i am for you again. 2.01. 21
let's have that, good sir. 2.01. 26
be certain what you do, sir, lest your justice 2.01.127
i dare my life lay down — and will do't, sir, 2.01.130
now, good sir, | you know me, do you not? 2.02. 4
you need not fear it, sir. 2.02. 56
not so hot, good sir, | i come to bring him 2.03. 32
i did not, sir. 2.03.142
you, sir, come you hither: 2.03.158
sir, be prosperous | in more than this deed does 2.03.189
so please you, sir, their speed | hath been 2.03.197
i appeal | to your own conscience, sir, before 3.02. 46
though 'tis a saying, sir, not due to me. 3.02. 58
sir, | you speak a language that i understand 3.02. 79
sir, spare your threats. 3.02. 91
o sir, i shall be hated to report it! 3.02.143
sir, royal sir, forgive a foolish woman. 3.02.227
sir, royal sir, forgive a foolish woman. 3.02.227
sir, it is three days since i saw the prince. 4.02. 29 P
i have heard, sir, of such a man, who hath a 4.02. 41 P
o sir, the loathsomeness of them offend me more 4.03. 56 P
i am robb'd, sir, and beaten; 4.03. 61 P
a footman, sweet sir, a footman. 4.03. 65 P

o good sir, tenderly, o! 4.03. 70 P
o good sir, softly, good sir! 4.03. 72 P
o good sir, softly, good sir! 4.03. 72 P
i fear, sir, my shoulder–blade is out. 4.03. 72 P
softly, dear sir; 4.03. 75 P
good sir, softly. 4.03. 75 P
no, good sweet sir; 4.03. 79 P
no, i beseech you, sir. 4.03. 79 P
a fellow, sir, that i have known to go about 4.03. 86 P
i cannot tell, good sir, for which of his 4.03. 88 P
vices, i would say, sir. 4.03. 94 P
very true, sir; 4.03.103 P
he, sir, he. 4.03.103 P
i must confess to you, sir, i am no fighter. 4.03.107 P
sweet sir, much better than i was: 4.03.111 P
no, good–fac'd sir, no, sweet sir. 4.03.115 P
no, good–fac'd sir, no, sweet sir. 4.03.115 P
prosper you, sweet sir! 4.03.118 P
sir, my gracious lord, | to chide at your 4.04. 5
o, but, sir, | your resolution cannot hold when 4.04. 35
sir, welcome. 4.04. 70
you're welcome, sir. 4.04. 72
sir, the year growing ancient, | not yet on 4.04. 79
and indeed, sir, there are cozeners abroad, 4.04.253 P
i hope so, sir, for i have about me many parcels 4.04.257 P
i know, sir, we weary you. 4.04.333 P
by their own report, sir, hath danc'd before the 4.04.337 P
why, they stay at door, sir. 4.04.342 P
old sir, i know | she prizes not such trifles as 4.04.356
me breathe my life | before this ancient sir, 4.04.361
no, good sir; 4.04.402
but for some other reasons, my grave sir, 4.04.411
mark your divorce, young sir, | whom son i dare 4.04.417
will't please you, sir, be gone? 4.04.446
o sir, | you have undone a man of fourscore 4.04.452
this is desperate, sir. 4.04.485
sir, i think | you have heard of my poor 4.04.515
sir, | the manner of your bearing towards him, 4.04.557
your pardon, sir; 4.04.583
for instance, sir, | that you may know you shall 4.04.593
i am a poor fellow, sir. 4.04.630 P
i am a poor fellow, sir. i know ye well enough. 4.04.638 P
are you in earnest, sir? i smell the trick on't. 4.04.642 P
adieu, sir. 4.04.659
we are but plain fellows, sir. 4.04.721 P
are you a courtier, and't like you, sir? 4.04.729 P
my business, sir, is to the king. 4.04.739 P
none, sir; i have no pheasant cock, nor hen. 4.04.744 P
sir, there lies such secrets in this farthel and 4.04.756 P
why, sir? 4.04.761 P
so 'tis said, sir — about his son, that should 4.04.766 P
think you so, sir? 4.04.771 P
has the old man e'er a son, sir, do you hear, 4.04.781 P
a son, sir, do you hear, and't like you, sir? 4.04.782 P
and't please you, sir, to undertake the business 4.04.806 P
ay, sir. 4.04.811 P
in some sort, sir; 4.04.814 P
sir, i will give you as much as this old man 4.04.821 P
sir, you have done enough, and have perform'd 5.01. 1
yet, if my lord will marry — if you will, sir, 5.01. 76
sir, you yourself | have said and writ so, but 5.01. 98
most royal sir, from thence; 5.01.159
to signify | not only my success in libya, sir, 5.01.166
most noble sir, | that which i shall report will 5.01.178
please you, great sir, | bohemia greets you from 5.01.180
camillo, sir; 5.01.197
we are not, sir, nor are we like to be. 5.01.205
beseech you, sir, | remember since you ow'd no 5.01.218
sir, my liege, | your eye hath too much youth 5.01.224
beseech you, sir, were you present at this 5.02. 1 P
how goes it now, sir? 5.02. 27 P
you are well met, sir. 5.02.128 P
i know you are now, sir, a gentleman born. 5.02.135 P
i humbly beseech you, sir, to pardon me all the 5.02.149 P
i will prove so, sir, to my power. 5.02.169 P
what, sovereign sir, | i did not well, i meant 5.03. 2
i am sorry, sir, i have thus far stirr'd you; 5.03. 74
if old sir robert did beget us both, | and were JN 1.01. 80
o old sir robert, father, on my knee | i give 1.01. 82
well, sir, by this you cannot get my land; 1.01. 97
of no more force to dispossess me, sir, | than 1.01.132
had my shape | and i had his, sir robert's his, 1.01.139
it would not be sir nob in any case. 1.01.147
philip, good old sir robert's wive's eldest son. 1.01.159
great, | arise sir richard, and plantagenet. 1.01.162
or day | when i was got, sir robert was away! 1.01.166
"good den, sir richard!" 1.01.185
"my dear sir," | thus, leaning on mine elbow, i 1.01.193
"o sir," says answer, "at your best command, 1.01.197
at your employment, at your service, sir." 1.01.198
"no, sir," says question, "i, sweet sir, at 1.01.199
sir," says question, "i, sweet sir, at yours"; 1.01.199
my brother robert, old sir robert's son? 1.01.224
is it sir robert's son that you seek so? 1.01.226
sir robert's son! 1.01.227
ay, thou unreverend boy, | sir robert's son! 1.01.228
why scorn'st thou at sir robert? 1.01.228
he is sir robert's son, and so art thou. 1.01.229
madam, i was not old sir robert's son; 1.01.233
sir robert might have eat his part in me | upon 1.01.234
sir robert could do well — marry, to confess — 1.01.236
sir robert could not do it; 1.01.237
sir robert never holp to make this leg. 1.01.240
but, mother, i am not sir robert's son, | i have 1.01.246
son, | i have disclaim'd sir robert and my land, 1.01.247
one that will play the devil, sir, with you, 2.01.135
o holy sir, | my reverend father, let it not be 3.01.248
o sir, when he shall hear of your approach, | if 3.04.162
sir, sir, impatience hath his privilege. 4.03. 32
sir, sir, impatience hath his privilege. 4.03. 32
sir richard, what think you? 4.03. 41
your sword is bright, sir, put it up again. 4.03. 79
do but hear me, sir. 4.03.119
o my sweet sir, news fitting to the night, 5.06. 19
sir thomas erpingham, sir john ramston, | sir R2 2.01.283
sir thomas erpingham, sir john ramston, | sir 2.01.283
sir john norbery, sir robert waterton, and 2.01.284
sir john norbery, sir robert waterton, and 2.01.284

sir stephen scroop, besides a clergyman | of		3.03. 28
well have you argued, sir, and, for your pains,		4.01.150
which for some reasons, sir, i mean to see.		5.02. 63
now, sir, the sound that tells what hour it is		5.05. 55
sir pierce of exton, who | lately came from the		5.05.100
the heads of brocas and sir bennet seely, | two		5.06. 14
sir walter blunt, new lighted from his horse,	1H4	1.01. 63
did sir walter see | on holmedon's plains.		1.01. 69
me the other day in the street about you, sir,		1.02. 85 P
what says sir john sack and sugar?		1.02.113 P
sir john stands to his word, the devil shall		1.02.117 P
sir john, i prithee leave the prince and me		1.02.149 P
o, sir, your presence is too bold and peremptory		1.03. 17
for if i hang, old sir john hangs with me, and		2.01. 68 P
what, a coward, sir john paunch?		2.02. 66 P
with this shrill addition, "anon, anon, sir!		2.04. 27 P
anon, anon, sir.		2.04. 37 P
anon, anon, sir.		2.04. 44 P
o lord, sir, i'll be sworn upon all the books in		2.04. 49 P
anon, sir.		2.04. 52 P
anon, sir. pray stay a little, my lord.		2.04. 57 P
o lord, sir, who do you mean?		2.04. 72 P
in barbary, sir, it cannot come to so much.		2.04. 75 P
what, sir?		2.04. 76 P
old sir john with half a dozen more are at the		2.04. 82 P
anon, anon, sir.		2.04. 86 P
anon, anon, sir.		2.04. 97 P
here was sir john bracy from your father;		2.04.334 P
sir john, you are so fretful you cannot live		3.03. 11 P
you are so fat, sir john, that you must needs be		3.03. 21 P
out of all reasonable compass, sir john.		3.03. 23 P
why, sir john, my face does you no harm.		3.03. 28 P
why, sir john, what do you think, sir john?		3.03. 54 P
why, sir john, what do you think, sir john?		3.03. 54 P
no, sir john, you do not know me, sir john.		3.03. 65 P
no, sir john, you do not know me, sir john.		3.03. 65 P
i know you, sir john, you owe me money, sir john		3.03. 66 P
you owe me money, sir john, and now you pick a		3.03. 66 P
you owe money here besides, sir john, for your		3.03. 72 P
an otter, sir john, why an otter?		3.03.126 P
indeed, sir john, you said so.		3.03.141 P
faith, sir john, 'tis more than time that i were		4.02. 54 P
but, sir john, methinks they are exceeding poor		4.02. 68 P
he is, sir john. i fear we shall stay too long.		4.02. 77 P
welcome, sir walter blunt;		4.03. 32
not so, sir walter;		4.03.107
hie, good sir michael, bear this sealed brief		4.04. 1
to–morrow, good sir michael, is a day | wherein		4.04. 8
for, sir, at shrewsbury, | as i am truly given		4.04. 10
and i fear, sir michael, | what with the		4.04. 13
and, to prevent the worst, sir michael, speed;		4.04. 35
to other friends, and so farewell, sir michael.		4.04. 41
o no, my nephew must not know, sir richard,		5.02. 1
sir walter blunt.		5.03. 32 P
like not such grinning honor as sir walter hath.		5.03. 59 P
sir nicholas gawsey hath for succor sent, | and		5.04. 45
make up to clifton, i'll to sir nicholas gawsey.		5.04. 58
and harry monmouth's brawn, the hulk sir john,	2H4	1.01. 19
sir john umfrevile turn'd me back | with joyful		1.01. 34
he said, sir, the water itself was a good		1.02. 3 P
he said, sir, you should procure him better		1.02. 31 P
sir, here comes the nobleman that committed the		1.02. 55 P
sir john falstaff!		1.02. 65 P
sir john!		1.02. 71 P
you mistake me, sir.		1.02. 79 P
why, sir, did i say you were an honest man?		1.02. 80 P
i pray you, sir, then set your knighthood and		1.02. 83 P
sir, my lord would speak with you.		1.02. 91 P
sir john falstaff, a word with you.		1.02. 92 P
sir john, i sent for you before your expedition		1.02.101 P
the truth is, sir john, you live in great infamy		1.02.136 P
fie, fie, fie, sir john!		1.02.186 P
sir?		1.02.233 P
snare, we must arrest sir john falstaff.		2.01. 8 P
how now, sir john?		2.01. 65
how comes this, sir john?		2.01. 80 P
sir john, sir john, i am well acquainted with		2.01.109 P
sir john, sir john, i am well acquainted with		2.01.109 P
pray thee, sir john, let it be but twenty nobles		2.01.153 P
my good lord here, i thank you, good sir john.		2.01.185 P
sir john, you loiter here too long, being you		2.01.186 P
master taught you these manners, sir john?		2.01.190 P
in bodily health, sir.		2.02.103 P
cap, "i am the king's poor cousin, sir."		2.02.116 P
"sir john falstaff, knight, to the son of the		2.02.119 P
and sisters, and sir john with all europe."		2.02.134 P
a proper gentlewoman, sir, and a kinswoman of my		2.02.155 P
i have no tongue, sir.		2.02.163 P
and for mine, sir, i will govern it.		2.02.164 P
thou knowest sir john cannot endure an		2.04. 2 P
and told him there were five more sir johns, and		2.04. 6 P
and aprons, and sir john must not know of it.		2.04. 17 P
lo here comes sir john.		2.04. 32 P
sir, ancient pistol's below, and would speak		2.04. 69 P
pray ye pacify yourself, sir john.		2.04. 80 P
tilly–fally, sir john, ne'er tell me;		2.04. 83 P
god save you, sir john!		2.04.110 P
i will discharge upon her, sir john, with two		2.04.114 P
she is pistol–proof, sir;		2.04.116 P
since when, i pray you, sir?		2.04.132 P
yea, sir.		2.04.213 P
you have hurt him, sir, i' th' shoulder.		2.04.214 P
the music is come, sir.		2.04.226 P
anon, anon, sir.		2.04.282 P
very true, sir, and i come to draw you out by		2.04.289 P
and asking every one for sir john falstaff.		2.04.360
you must away to court, sir, presently, | a		2.04.371
on, give me your hand, sir, give me your hand,		3.02. 2 P
give me your hand, sir, give me your hand, sir.		3.02. 2 P
by yea and no, sir.		3.02. 9 P
indeed, sir, to my cost.		3.02. 12 P
then was jack falstaff, now sir john, a boy, and		3.02. 25 P
this sir john, cousin, that comes hither anon		3.02. 27 P
the same sir john, the very same.		3.02. 29 P
dead, sir.		3.02. 42 P
here come two of sir john falstaff's men, as i		3.02. 53 P
i am robert shallow, sir, a poor esquire of this		3.02. 57 P
my captain, sir, commends him to you, my captain		3.02. 60 P
my captain, sir john falstaff, a tall gentleman,		3.02. 61 P
he greets me well, sir.		3.02. 63 P
sir, pardon, a soldier is better /accommodated		3.02. 66 P
in faith, sir, and it is well said indeed too.		3.02. 68 P
pardon, sir, i have heard the word.		3.02. 73 P
look, here comes good sir john.		3.02. 81 P
welcome, good sir john.		3.02. 84 P
no, sir john, it is my cousin silence, in		3.02. 87 P
marry, have we, sir. will you sit?		3.02. 94 P
yea, marry, sir.		3.02. 98 P
what think you, sir john?		3.02.102 P
in faith, well said, sir john, very well said.		3.02.109 P
for th' other, sir john, let me see:		3.02.120 P
here, sir.		3.02.125 P
my mother's son, sir.		3.02.127 P
do you like him, sir john?		3.02.132 P
here, sir.		3.02.138 P
yea, sir.		3.02.140 P
shall i prick him, sir john?		3.02.142 P
you can do it, sir, you can do it, i commend you		3.02.146 P
here, sir.		3.02.148 P
a woman's tailor, sir.		3.02.150 P
shall i prick him, sir?		3.02.151 P
i will do my good will, sir, you can have no		3.02.156 P
i would wart might have gone, sir.		3.02.163 P
it shall suffice, sir.		3.02.169 P
here, sir.		3.02.174 P
o lord, sir, i am a diseas'd man.		3.02.179 P
a whoreson cold, sir, a cough, sir, which i		3.02.181 P
a cough, sir, which i caught with ringing in the		3.02.181 P
the king's affairs upon his coronation–day, sir.		3.02.183 P
your number, you must have but four here, sir.		3.02.189 P
o sir john, do you remember since we lay all		3.02.194 P
ha, sir john, said i well?		3.02.212 P
have, that we have, in faith, sir john, we have.		3.02.217 P
in very truth, sir, i had as live be hang'd, sir		3.02.222 P
sir, i had as live be hang'd, sir, as go, and		3.02.223 P
and yet, for mine own part, sir, i do not care,		3.02.223 P
stay with my friends, else, sir, i did not care,		3.02.226 P
you shall have forty, sir.		3.02.232 P
come, sir, which men shall i have?		3.02.241 P
sir, a word with you.		3.02.243 P
come, sir john, which four will you have?		3.02.246 P
sir john, sir john, do not yourself wrong.		3.02.254 P
sir john, sir john, do not yourself wrong.		3.02.254 P
i was then sir dagonet in arthur's show — there		3.02.280 P
sir john, the lord bless you!		3.02.292 P
what's your name, sir?		4.03. 1 P
i am a knight, sir, and my name is colevile of		4.03. 3 P
are not you sir john falstaff?		4.03. 10 P
as good a man as he, sir, whoe'er i am.		4.03. 11 P
do ye yield, sir?		4.03. 12 P
i think you are sir john falstaff, and in that		4.03. 16 P
valor, taken sir john colevile of the dale, a		4.03. 38 P
by cock and pie, sir, you shall not away		5.01. 1 P
here, sir.		5.01. 8 P
sir john, you shall not be excus'd.		5.01. 11 P
marry, sir, thus;		5.01. 13 P
and again, sir, shall we sow the hade land with		5.01. 14 P
yes, sir.		5.01. 18 P
sir john, you shall not be excus'd.		5.01. 20 P
now, sir, a new link to the bucket must needs be		5.01. 22 P
and, sir, do you mean to stop any of william's		5.01. 23 P
doth the man of war stay all night, sir?		5.01. 29 P
no worse than they are backbitten, sir, for they		5.01. 34 P
i beseech you, sir, to countenance william visor		5.01. 38 P
i grant your worship that he is a knave, sir;		5.01. 43 P
god forbid, sir, but a knave should have some		5.01. 44 P
an honest man, sir, is able to speak for himself		5.01. 46 P
i have serv'd your worship truly, sir, this		5.01. 47 P
the knave is mine honest friend, sir, therefore		5.01. 50 P
where are you, sir john?		5.01. 53 P
come, sir john.		5.01. 59 P
sir john!		5.01. 86 P
well, you must now speak sir john falstaff fair,		5.02. 33
barren, beggars all, beggars all, sir john!		5.03. 8 P
a good varlet, a very good varlet, sir john.		5.03. 13 P
sweet sir, sit, i'll be with you anon, most		5.03. 26 P
sit, i'll be with you anon, most sweet sir, sit.		5.03. 27 P
a cup of wine, sir?		5.03. 45 P
yea, sir, in a pottle–pot.		5.03. 64 P
and i'll stick by him, sir.		5.03. 68 P
sir john, god save you!		5.03. 84 P
sir john, i am thy pistol and thy friend, | and		5.03. 93
give me pardon, sir.		5.03.109 P
if, sir, you come with news from the court, i		5.03.109 P
i am, sir, under the king, in some authority.		5.03.111 P
sir john, thy tender lambkin now is king;		5.03.116
o the lord, that sir john were come!		5.04. 11 P
marry, sir john, which i beseech you to let me		5.05. 74 P
i beseech you, good sir john, let me have five		5.05. 83 P
sir, i will be as good as my word.		5.05. 85 P
a color that i fear you will die in, sir john.		5.05. 87 P
go carry sir john falstaff to the fleet.		5.05. 91
will continue the story, with sir john in it,		ep 28 P
sir thomas grey, knight, of northumberland,	H5	2.pr. 25
you come of women, come in quickly to sir john.		2.01.118 P
sir, | you show great mercy if you give him life		2.02. 49
and, sir knight, | grey of northumberland, this		2.02. 67
"how now, sir john?"		2.03. 17 P
by my faith, sir, but it is;		3.07.110 P
good morrow, old sir thomas erpingham.		4.01. 13
lend me thy cloak, sir thomas.		4.01. 24
under sir /thomas erpingham.		4.01. 94 P
sir john falstaff.		4.07. 51 P
sir, know you this glove?		4.08. 6 P
how now, sir? you villain!		4.08. 11 P
of france, the brave sir guichard dolphin,		4.08. 95
suffolk, | sir richard ketly, davy gam, esquire;		4.08.104
if sir john falstaff had not play'd the coward.	1H6	1.01.131
sir thomas gargrave, and sir william glansdale,		1.04. 63
sir thomas gargrave, and sir william glansdale,		1.04. 63
sir thomas gargrave, hast thou any life?		1.04. 88
ay, lordly sir;		3.01. 43
are ye so hot, sir?		3.02. 58
whither away, sir john falstaff, in such haste?		3.02.104
now, sir, to you, that were so hot at sea,		3.04. 28
yes, sir, as well as you dare patronage | the		3.04. 32
here is sir william lucy, who with me | set from		4.04. 10
how now, sir william, whither were you sent?		4.04. 12
sir john!	2H6	1.02. 68
but how now, sir john hume?		1.02. 88
how now, sir knave?		1.03. 22 P
alas, sir, i am but a poor petitioner of our		1.03. 23 P
no malice, sir, no more than well becomes | so		2.01. 27
well, sir, we must have you find your legs.		2.01.144 P
alas, sir, we did it for pure need.		2.01.154
with sir john stanley, in the isle of man.		2.03. 13
give up your staff, sir, and the king his realm.		2.03. 31
and sir john stanley is appointed now | to take		2.04. 77
must you, sir john, protect my lady here?		2.04. 79
and so, sir john, farewell!		2.04. 84
and we, i hope, sir, are no murtherers.		3.02.181
i'll give it, sir, and therefore spare my life.		4.01. 23
sir poole!		4.01. 70
sir, i thank god, i have been so well brought up		4.02.105 P
sir humphrey stafford and his brother are hard		4.02.113 P
rise up sir john mortimer.		4.02.120 P
ay, sir.		4.02.138
sir, he made a chimney in my father's house, and		4.02.148 P
here, sir.		4.03. 2 P
sir humphrey stafford and his brother's death		4.04. 34
into his son–in–law's house, sir james cromer,		4.07.111 P
sir john and sir hugh mortimer, mine uncles,	3H6	1.02. 62
sir john and sir hugh mortimer, mine uncles,		1.02. 62
ay, marry, sir, now looks he like a king!		1.04. 96
field | this lady's husband, sir richard grey,		3.02. 2
now, my lord hastings and sir william stanley,		4.05. 1
brother, this is sir john montgomery, | our		4.07. 40
welcome, sir john! but why come you in arms?		4.07. 42
nay, stay, sir john, a while, and we'll debate		4.07. 51
is not a dukedom, sir, a goodly gift?		5.01. 31
how say you, sir?	R3	1.01. 96
she may do more, sir, than denying that:		1.03. 93
'tis better, sir, than to be tedious.		1.04. 89
you may, sir, 'tis a point of wisdom.		1.04. 98
here comes sir richard ratcliffe and the duke.		2.01. 46
give you good morrow, sir.		2.03. 6
ay, sir, it is too true, god help the while!		2.03. 8
and with them sir thomas vaughan, prisoners.		2.04. 43
i thank thee, good sir john, with all my heart.		3.02.109
sir richard ratcliffe, let me tell thee this:		3.03. 2
sir edward courtney and the haughty prelate,		4.04.500
sir thomas lovel and lord marquess dorset,		4.04.518
sir christopher, tell richmond this from me:		4.05. 1
sir walter herbert, a renowned soldier, | sir		4.05. 12
sir gilbert talbot, sir william stanley,		4.05. 13
sir gilbert talbot, sir william stanley,		4.05. 13
oxford, redoubted pembroke, sir james blunt,		4.05. 14
sir william brandon, you shall bear my standard.		5.03. 22
my lord of oxford — you, sir william brandon —		5.03. 27
and /you, sir walter herbert — stay with me.		5.03. 28
sir robert brakenbury, and sir william brandon.		5.05. 14
sir robert brakenbury, and sir william brandon.		5.05. 14
surely, sir, | there's in him stuff that puts	H8	1.01. 57
sir, | i am thankful to you, and i'll go along		1.01.149
pray give me favor, sir:		1.01.168
sir, | my lord the duke of buckingham and earl		1.01.198
please you, sir, | i know but of a single part		1.02. 40
sir, a chartreux friar, | his confessor, who fed		1.02.148
the cardinal's and sir thomas lovell's heads		1.02.185
reprov'd the duke | about sir william /bulmer —		1.02.190
what news, sir thomas lovell?		1.03. 16
sir thomas, | whither were you a–going?		1.03. 49
come, good sir thomas, | we shall be late else,		1.03. 64
to, with sir henry guilford | this night to be		1.03. 66
you are young, sir harry guilford.		1.04. 9
sir thomas lovell, had the cardinal | but half		1.04. 10
sir harry, | place you that side, i'll take the		1.04. 19
was he mad, sir?		1.04. 27
your grace, sir thomas bullen's daughter —		1.04. 92
sir thomas lovell, is the banket ready | i' th'		1.04. 98
i'll save you | that labor, sir.		2.01. 4
sir gilbert /perk his chancellor, and john car,		2.01. 20
stay there, sir, | and see the noble ruin'd man		2.01. 53
sir thomas lovell, i as free forgive you | as i		2.01. 82
then give my charge up to sir nicholas vaux,		2.01. 96
nay, sir nicholas, | let it alone;		2.01.100
sir, it calls, | i fear, too many curses on		2.01.137
you do not doubt my faith, sir?		2.01.143
you shall, sir.		2.01.147
but that slander, sir, | is found a truth now;		2.01.153
before the king, which stopp'd our mouths, sir."		2.02. 9
most learned reverend sir, into our kingdom,		2.02. 76
sir, you cannot.		2.02. 78
sir, i desire you do me right and justice, | and		2.04. 13
alas, sir!		2.04. 18
sir, call to mind | that i have been your wife		2.04. 34
please you, sir, | the king, your father, was		2.04. 44
wherefore i humbly | beseech you, sir, to spare		2.04. 54
sir, | i am about to weep;		2.04. 69
most gracious sir, | in humblest manner i		2.04.144
how, sir?		3.01. 92
sir, | i should be glad to hear such news as		3.02. 23
sir, | for holy offices i have a time;		3.02.143
speak on, sir, | i dare your worst objections.		3.02.306
i have no power to speak, sir.		3.02.373
that sir thomas more is chosen | lord chancellor		3.02.393
good sir, have patience.		3.02.458
nor, i'll assure you, better taken, sir.		4.01. 12
i thank you, sir;		4.01. 20
sir, as i have a soul, she is an angel;		4.01. 44
god save you, sir! where have you been broiling?		4.01. 56
good sir, speak it to us.		4.01. 61
believe me, sir, she is the goodliest woman		4.01. 69
sir, | you must no more call it york–place,		4.01. 94
you may command us, sir.		4.01.117
sir, i most humbly pray you to deliver | this to		4.02.129
good hour of night, sir thomas!		5.01. 5
i did, sir thomas, and left him at primero		5.01. 7
not yet, sir thomas lovell.		5.01. 10
but for the stock, sir thomas, | i wish it		5.01. 22
but, sir, sir, | hear me, sir thomas, y' are a		5.01. 26
but, sir, sir, | hear me, sir thomas, y' are a		5.01. 26
hear me, sir thomas, y' are a gentleman | of		5.01. 27
'twill not, sir thomas lovell, take't of me —		5.01. 30

now, sir, you speak of two | the most remark'd 5.01. 32
further, sir, | stands in the gap and trade of 5.01. 35
yes, yes, sir thomas, | there are that dare, and 5.01. 39
day, | sir (i may tell it you), i think i have 5.01. 42
he's a rank weed, sir thomas, | and we must root 5.01. 52
good night, sir thomas. 5.01. 54
sir, i did never win of you before. 5.01. 58
charles, good night. | well, sir, what follows? 5.01. 79
sir, i have brought my lord the archbishop, | as 5.01. 80
sir, your queen | desires your visitation, and 5.01.166
sir? 5.01.169
no, sir, it does not please me. 5.02.169
pray, sir, be patient; 5.03. 12
could distribute, | i made no spare, sir. 5.03. 21
you did nothing, sir. 5.03. 21
i am not sampson, nor sir guy, nor colbrand, 5.03. 22
the spoons will be the bigger, sir. 5.03. 39 P
let me speak, sir, | for heaven now bids me; 5.04. 14
sir, my lord would instantly speak with you. TRO 1.02.272 P
and at this sport | sir valor dies; 1.03.176
sir, you of troy, call you yourself aeneas? 1.03.245
sir, pardon, 'tis for agamemnon's ears. 1.03.248
to our pavilion shall i lead you, sir. 1.03.305
this, sir, is proclaim'd through all our host: 2.01.121
sir, i propose not merely to myself | the 2.02.146
ay, sir, when he goes before me. 3.01. 3 P
sir, i do depend upon the lord. 3.01. 5 P
faith, sir, superficially. 3.01. 10 P
i do but partly know, sir, it is music in parts. 3.01. 18 P
wholly, sir. 3.01. 20 P
to the hearers, sir. 3.01. 22 P
at mine, sir, and theirs that love music. 3.01. 24 P
who shall i command, sir? 3.01. 26 P
that's to't indeed, sir. 3.01. 30 P
marry, sir, at the request of paris my lord, who 3.01. 30 P
no, sir, helen. 3.01. 35 P
o sir — 3.01. 55 P
no, sir, /he stays for you to conduct him 3.02. 3 P
sir, mine own company. 3.02.145
your answer, sir. 3.03.294 P
your answer, sir. 3.03.298 P
health to you, valiant sir, | during all 4.01. 11
welcome, sir diomed! 4.04.109
i'll have my kiss, sir. lady, by your leave. 4.05. 35
if not achilles, sir, | what is your name? 4.05. 75
here is sir diomed. 4.05. 88
name her not now, sir, she's a deadly theme. 4.05.181
ah, sir, there's many a greek and troyan dead 4.05.214
sir, i foretold you then what would ensue. 4.05.217
you shall command me, sir. 4.05.286
o, sir, to such as boasting show their scars | a 4.05.290
sweet sir, you honor me. 5.01. 86
you know me dutiful, therefore, dear sir, | let 5.03. 72
we cannot, sir, we are undone already. COR 1.01. 64
well, i'll hear it, sir; 1.01. 93 P
well, sir, what answer made the belly? 1.01.106
sir, i shall tell you. 1.01.107
ay, sir, well, well. 1.01.142
the news is, sir, the volsces are in arms. 1.01.224
sir, it is, | and i am constant. 1.01.238
slain, sir, doubtless. 1.04. 48
look, sir. 1.04. 61
worthy sir, thou bleed'st, | thy exercise hath 1.05. 14
sir, praise me not; 1.05. 16
three or four miles about, else had i, sir, 1.06. 20
fear not our care, sir. 1.07. 5
i shall, sir. 1.10. 33
well, sir. 2.01. 15 P
well, well, sir, well. 2.01. 27 P
we do it not alone, sir. 2.01. 34 P
what then, sir? 2.01. 42 P
come, sir, come, we know you well enough. 2.01. 66 P
look, sir, your mother! 2.01.169
sir, i hope | my words disbench'd you not? 2.02. 70
no, sir; 2.02. 71
sir, the people | must have their voices; 2.02.139
we may, sir, if we will. 2.03. 3 P
o sir, you are not right. 2.03. 48
"i pray, sir" — plague upon't! 2.03. 50
"look, sir, my wounds! 2.03. 51
you know the cause, sir, of my standing here. 2.03. 62
we do, sir, tell us what hath brought you to't. 2.03. 63 P
no, sir, 'twas never my desire yet to trouble 2.03. 69 P
kindly, sir, i pray let me ha't. 2.03. 76 P
your good voice, sir, what say you? 2.03. 78 P
you shall ha't, worthy sir. 2.03. 79 P
a match, sir. 2.03. 80 P
i will, sir, flatter my sworn brother, the 2.03. 95 P
that is, sir, i will counterfeit the bewitchment 2.03.101 P
the gods give you joy, sir, heartily! 2.03.111 P
you may, sir. 2.03.146
he has our voices, sir. 2.03.156
amen, sir. 2.03.158
not in this heat, sir, now. 3.01. 63
ag'd sir, hands off. 3.01.177
sir, those cold ways, | that seem like prudent 3.01.219
come, sir, along with us. 3.01.236
sir, sir — 3.01.271
sir, sir — 3.01.271
sir, how comes't that you | have holp to make 3.01.274
o, sir, sir, sir, | i would have had you put 3.02. 16
o, sir, sir, sir, | i would have had you put 3.02. 16
o, sir, sir, sir, | i would have had you put 3.02. 16
and, sir, 'tis fit | you make strong party, or 3.02. 93
now, pray, sir, get you gone; 4.02. 37
i know you well, sir, and you know me. 4.03. 1 P
it is so, sir. truly, i have forgot you. 4.03. 3 P
the same, sir. 4.03. 7 P
banish'd, sir. 4.03. 28 P
so, sir, heartily well met, and most glad of 4.03. 48 P
you take my part from me, sir, i have the most 4.03. 50 P
'save you, sir. 4.04. 6
thank you, sir, farewell. 4.04. 11
whence are you, sir? 4.05. 11 P
how, sir? do you meddle with my master? 4.05. 46 P
here, sir. 4.05. 51 P
therefore, most absolute sir, if thou wilt have 4.05.136
he had, sir, a kind of face, methought — i 4.05.155 P
for look you, sir, he has as many friends as 4.05.205 P
which friends, sir, as it were, durst not (look 4.05.206 P
durst not (look you, sir) show themselves (as we 4.05.207 P
but when they shall see, sir, his crest up again 4.05.210 P
hail, sir! 4.06. 12
yes, worthy sir, | the slave's report is 4.06. 62
but is this true, sir? 4.06.101
and you are dark'ned in this action, sir, | even 4.07. 5
yet i wish, sir | (i mean for your particular), 4.07. 12
sir, i beseech you, think you he'll carry rome? 4.07. 27
faith, sir, if you had told as many lies in his 5.02. 24 P
now, sir, is your name menenius? 5.02. 95 P
and, sir, it is no little thing to make | mine 5.03.195
but, good sir, | what peace you'll make, advise 5.03.196
sir, if you'ld save your life, fly to your house 5.04. 35
sir, we have all | great cause to give great 5.04. 59
most noble sir, | if you do hold the same intent 5.06. 11
sir, i cannot tell, | we must proceed as we do 5.06. 14
sir, his stoutness | when he did stand for 5.06. 26
how, sir? are you in earnest then, my lord? TIT 1.01.277
god give you joy, sir, of your gallant bride! 1.01.400
'tis good, sir, you are very short with us; 1.01.409
mean while, sir, with the little skill i have, 2.01. 43
ay, marry, will we, sir, and we'll be waited on. 4.01.122
o lord, sir, 'tis a deed of policy. 4.02.148
sir boy, let me see your archery. 4.03. 2
alas, sir, i know not jubiter, i never drank 4.03. 85 P
ay, of my pigeons, sir, nothing else. 4.03. 88 P
alas, sir, i never came there. 4.03. 90 P
why, sir, that is as fit as can be to serve for 4.03. 95 P
truly, sir, i could never say grace in all my 4.03.100 P
ay, sir. 4.03.108 P
i'll be at hand, sir, see you do it bravely. 4.03.112 P
i warrant you, sir, let me alone. 4.03.114 P
god be with you, sir, i will. 4.03.120 P
do you bite your thumb at us, sir? ROM 1.01. 44 P
i do bite my thumb, sir. 1.01. 45 P
do you bite your thumb at us, sir? 1.01. 46 P
no, sir, i do not bite my thumb at you, sir, but 1.01. 50 P
i do not bite my thumb at you, sir, but i bite 1.01. 50 P
my thumb at you, sir, but i bite my thumb, sir. 1.01. 51 P
do you quarrel, sir? 1.01. 52 P
quarrel, sir? no, sir. 1.01. 53 P
quarrel, sir? no, sir. 1.01. 53 P
but if you do, sir, i am for you. 1.01. 54 P
well, sir. 1.01. 57 P
yes, better, sir. 1.01. 60 P
god gi' god–den. i pray, sir, can you read? 1.02. 57 P
i mean, sir, in delay | we waste our lights in 1.04. 44
his son is elder, sir; 1.05. 38
i know not, sir. 1.05. 43
the slip, sir, the slip, can you not conceive? 2.04. 48 P
if you be he, sir, i desire some confidence with 2.04.127 P
no hare, sir, unless a hare, sir, in a lenten 2.04.132 P
sir, unless a hare, sir, in a lenten pie, that 2.04.132 P
i pray you, sir, what saucy merchant was this, 2.04.145 P
pray you, sir, a word: 2.04.162 P
i will tell her, sir, that you do protest, which 2.04.177 P
no, truly, sir, not a penny. 2.04.183 P
this afternoon, sir? well, she shall be there. 2.04.185 P
now god in heaven bless thee! hark you, sir. 2.04.194
well, sir, my mistress is the sweetest lady — 2.04.199 P
you shall find me apt enough to that, sir, and 3.01. 41 P
well, peace be with you, sir, here comes my man. 3.01. 56
but i'll be hang'd, sir, if he wear your livery. 3.01. 57
come, sir, your passado. 3.01. 85 P
up, sir, go with me; 3.01.139
ah sir, ah sir, death's the end of all! 3.03. 92
ah sir, ah sir, death's the end of all! 3.03. 92
o, she says nothing, sir, but weeps and weeps, 3.03. 99
here, sir, a ring she bid me give you, sir. 3.03.163
here, sir, a ring she bid me give you, sir. 3.03.163
things have fall'n out, sir, so unluckily | that 3.04. 1
sir paris, i will make a desperate tender | of 3.04. 12
ay, sir, but she will none, she /gives you 3.05.139
on thursday, sir? the time is very short. 4.01. 1
now, sir, her father counts it dangerous | that 4.01. 9
look, sir, here comes the lady toward my cell. 4.01. 17
that may be, sir, when i may be a wife. 4.01. 19
that is no slander, sir, which is a truth, | and 4.01. 33
you shall have none ill, sir, for i'll try if 4.02. 3 P
marry, sir, 'tis an ill cook that cannot lick 4.02. 6 P
things for the cook, sir, but i know not what. 4.04. 15
i have a head, sir, that will find out logs, 4.04. 18
sir, go you in, and, madam, go with him; 4.05. 91
and go, sir paris. 4.05. 92
marry, sir, because silver hath a sweet sound. 4.05.131 P
since you did leave it for my office, sir. 5.01. 23
i do beseech you, sir, have patience. 5.01. 27
i will be gone, sir, and not trouble ye. 5.03. 40
it doth so, holy sir, and there's my master, 5.03.128
i dare not, sir. 5.03.131
good day, sir. TIM 1.01. 1
it wears, sir, as it grows. 1.01. 3
o, pray let's see't. for the lord timon, sir? 1.01. 13
you are rapt, sir, in some work, some dedication 1.01. 19
a picture, sir. when comes your book forth? 1.01. 26
upon the heels of my presentment, sir. 1.01. 27
sir, i have upon a high and pleasant hill 1.01. 63
nay, sir, but hear me on: 1.01. 77
sir, your jewel | hath suffered under praise. 1.01.164
most welcome, sir! 1.01.247
sir, you have sav'd my longing, and i feed 1.01.252
right welcome, sir! 1.01.253
here, sir, what is your pleasure? 2.01. 14
i go, sir. 2.01. 33
ay, go, sir; 2.01. 34
i will, sir. 2.01. 35
go you, sir, to the senators — | of whom, even 2.02.196
i thank you, sir. 3.01. 3 P
you are very respectively welcome, sir. 3.01. 8 P
his health is well, sir. 3.01. 12 P
i am right glad that his health is well, sir; 3.01. 13 P
faith, nothing but an empty box, sir, which, in 3.01. 16 P
you are kindly met, sir. 3.02. 27 P
upon my soul, 'tis true, sir. 3.02. 43
yes, sir, i shall. 3.02. 59 P
and, sir, philotus too! 3.04. 6
sir, a word. 3.04. 34 P
do you hear, sir? 3.04. 43
by your leave, sir — 3.04. 44
we wait for certain money here, sir. 3.04. 46
we cannot take this for answer, sir. 3.04. 77
the good time of day to you, sir. 3.06. 1 P
he sent to me, sir — here he comes. 3.06. 24 P
o, sir, let it not trouble you. 3.06. 38 P
think not on't, sir. 3.06. 44 P
have you forgot me, sir? 4.03.472
sir, | having often of your open bounty tasted, 5.01. 57
e'en so, sir, as i say. 5.01. 83
well, sir, i will; 5.01.168
therefore i will, sir, thus: 5.01.168
why, sir, a carpenter. JC 1.01. 6 P
you, sir, what trade are you? 1.01. 9
truly, sir, in respect of a fine workman, i am 1.01. 10 P
a trade, sir, that i hope i may use with a safe 1.01. 13 P
which is indeed, sir, a mender of bad soles. 1.01. 14 P
nay, i beseech you, sir, be not out with me; 1.01. 16 P
yet if you be out, sir, i can mend you. 1.01. 17 P
why, sir, cobble you. 1.01. 19 P
truly, sir, all that i live by is with the awl: 1.01. 21 P
but withal i am indeed, sir, a surgeon to old 1.01. 23 P
truly, sir, to wear out their shoes, to get 1.01. 29 P
but indeed, sir, we make holiday to see caesar, 1.01. 30 P
the taper burneth in your closet, sir. 2.01. 35
i know not, sir. 2.01. 41
i will, sir. 2.01. 43
sir, march is wasted fifteen days. 2.01. 59
sir, 'tis your brother cassius at the door, 2.01. 70
no, sir, there are moe with him. 2.01. 72
no, sir, their hats are pluck'd about their ears 2.01. 73
o, pardon, sir, it doth; 2.01.103
sir, octavius is already come to rome. 3.02.262
your name, sir, truly. 3.03. 26 P
it is my duty, sir. 4.03.260
good sir, why do you start, and seem to fear MAC 1.03. 51
i take't, 'tis later, sir. 2.01. 3
what, sir, not yet at rest? 2.01. 12
thanks, sir; the like to you! 2.01. 30
faith, sir, we were carousing till the second 2.03. 24 P
and drink, sir, is a great provoker of three 2.03. 25 P
marry, sir, nose–painting, sleep, and urine. 2.03. 28 P
lechery, sir, it provokes, and unprovokes: 2.03. 29 P
that it did, sir, i' the very throat on me; 2.03. 38 P
good morrow, noble sir. 2.03. 44
how goes the world, sir, now? 2.04. 21
to–night we hold a solemn supper, sir, | and 3.01. 14
pronounce it for me, sir, to all our friends, 3.04. 7
most royal sir, fleance is scap'd. 3.04. 19
his absence, sir, | lays blame upon his promise. 3.04. 42
here is a place reserv'd, sir. 3.04. 45
did you send to him, sir? 3.04.128
sir, can you tell | where he bestows himself? 3.06. 23
and with an absolute "sir, not i," | the cloudy 3.06. 40
ay, sir, all this is so. 4.01.125
ay, sir; 4.03.141
sir, amen. 4.03.163
that, sir, which i will not report after her. 5.01. 14 P
pray god it be, sir. 5.01. 58 P
for certain, sir, he is not; 5.02. 8
soldiers, sir. 5.03. 13
come, sir, dispatch. 5.03. 50
well, say, sir. 5.05. 31
enter, sir, the castle. 5.07. 29
now, sir, young fortinbras, | of unimproved HAM 1.01. 95
sir, my good friend — i'll change that name 1.02.163
good even, sir. 1.02.167
look you, sir, | inquire me first what danskers 2.01. 6
but, sir, such wanton, wild, and usual slips 2.01. 22
marry, sir, here's my drift, | and i believe it 2.01. 37
"good sir," or so, or "friend," or "gentleman," 2.01. 46
and then, sir, does 'a this — 'a does — what 2.01. 49
ay, sir, to be honest, as this world goes, is to 2.02.178 P
slanders, sir; 2.02.196 P
all which, sir, though i most powerfully and 2.02.200 P
down, for yourself, sir, shall grow old as i am, 2.02.203 P
god save you, sir! 2.02.221 P
you say right, sir, a' monday morning, 'twas 2.02.387 P
would not this, sir, and a forest of feathers — 3.02.275 P
sir, a whole history. 3.02.298 P
the king, sir — 3.02.299 P
ay, sir, what of him? 3.02.300 P
with drink, sir? 3.02.302 P
i am tame, sir. pronounce. 3.02.310 P
sir, i cannot. 3.02.319 P
but, sir, such answer as i can make, you shall 3.02.322 P
sir, i lack advancement. 3.02.340 P
ay, sir, but "while the grass grows" — the 3.02.343 P
god bless you, sir. 3.02.373 P
come, sir, to draw toward an end with you. 3.04.216
ay, sir, that soaks up the king's countenance, 4.02. 15 P
good sir, whose powers are these? 4.04. 9
they are of norway, sir. 4.04. 10
how purpos'd, sir, i pray you? 4.04. 11
who commands them, sir? 4.04. 13
goes it against the main of poland, sir, | or 4.04. 15
i humbly thank you, sir. 4.04. 29
god buy you, sir. 4.04. 30
sea–faring men, sir. 4.06. 2 P
god bless you, sir. 4.06. 7 P
'a shall, sir, and/'t please him. 4.06. 9 P
there's a letter for you, sir — it came from 4.06. 10 P
sir, this report of his | did hamlet so envenom 4.07.102
mine, sir. 5.01.119 P
you lie out on't, sir, and therefore 'tis not 5.01.123 P
'tis a quick lie, sir, 'twill away again from me 5.01.128 P
for no man, sir. 5.01.131 P
one that was a woman, sir, but, rest her soul, 5.01.135 P
why, sir, his hide is so tann'd with his trade 5.01.170 P
this same skull, sir, was, sir, yorick's skull, 5.01.181 P
sir, was, sir, yorick's skull, the king's jester 5.01.181 P
hear you, sir, | what is the reason that you use 5.01.288
so much for this, sir, now shall you see the 5.02. 1
sir, in my heart there was a kind of fighting 5.02. 4
but, sir, now | it did me yeman's service. 5.02. 35
i humbly thank you, sir. 5.02. 82

i will receive it, sir, with all diligence of 5.02. 91 P
sir, this is the matter — 5.02.103 P
sir, here is newly come to court laertes, 5.02.106 P
sir, his definement suffers no perdition in you, 5.02.112 P
the concernancy, sir? 5.02.122 P
sir? 5.02.124 P
you will to't, sir, really. 5.02.126 P
of him, sir. 5.02.132 P
i would you did, sir, yet, in faith, if you did, 5.02.134 P
well, sir? 5.02.135 P
i mean, sir, for /his weapon, but in the 5.02.141 P
the king, sir, hath wager'd with him six barbary 5.02.147 P
the /carriages, sir, are the hangers. 5.02.157 P
the king, sir, hath laid, sir, that in a dozen 5.02.165 P
hath laid, sir, that in a dozen passes between 5.02.165 P
sir, i will walk here in the hall. 5.02.173 P
to this effect, sir — after what flourish your 5.02.180 P
'a did /comply, sir, with his dug before 'a 5.02.187 P
give me your pardon, sir. 5.02.226
you mock me, sir. 5.02.257
come on, sir. 5.02.280
his breeding, sir, hath been at my charge. LR 1.01. 9 P
sir, this young fellow's mother could; 1.01. 13 P
and had indeed, sir, a son for her cradle ere 1.01. 15 P
but i have a son, sir, by order of law, some 1.01. 19 P
sir, i shall study deserving. 1.01. 31 P
sir, i love you more than /words can wield the 1.01. 55
dear sir, forbear. 1.01.162
sir, there she stands: 1.01.197
pardon me, royal sir, | election makes not up in 1.01.205
then leave her, sir, for, by the pow'r that made 1.01.207
i beseech you, sir, pardon me. 1.02. 36 P
give me the letter, sir. 1.02. 40 P
i will seek him, sir, presently; 1.02.101 P
a man, sir. 1.04. 10 P
no, sir, but you have that in your countenance 1.04. 27 P
not so young, sir, to love a woman for singing, 1.04. 37 P
sir, he answer'd me in the roundest manner, he 1.04. 54 P
since my young lady's going into france, sir, 1.04. 74 P
o, you, sir, you, come you hither, sir. 1.04. 78 P
o, you, sir, you, come you hither, sir. 1.04. 78 P
who am i, sir? 1.04. 78 P
come, sir, arise, away! 1.04. 89 P
not only, sir, this your all–licens'd fool, 1.04.201
sir, | i had thought, by making this well known 1.04.204
this admiration, sir, is much o' th' savor | of 1.04.237
speak, sir. 1.04.258
pray, sir, be patient. 1.04.261
what's the matter, sir? 1.04.295
you, sir, more knave than fool, after your 1.04.314
and /you, sir. 2.01. 2 P
you may do then in time. fare you well, sir. 2.01. 13 P
o sir, fly this place, | intelligence is given 2.01. 20
look, sir, i bleed. 2.01. 41
fled this way, sir, when by no means he could — 2.01. 42
sir, in fine, | seeing how loathly opposite i 2.01. 48
it was my duty, sir. 2.01.106
i shall serve you, sir, | truly, however else. 2.01.116
a tailor, sir. 2.02. 58 P
this ancient ruffian, sir, whose life i have 2.02. 62 P
yes, sir, but anger hath a privilege. 2.02. 70
sir, 'tis my occupation to be plain: 2.02. 92
sir, in good faith, in sincere verity, | under 2.02.105
i know, sir, i am no flatterer. 2.02.110 P
sir, i am too old to learn. 2.02.127
sir, being his knave, i will. 2.02.137
pray do not, sir. 2.02.155
with the earl, sir, here within. 2.04. 59
that sir which serves and seeks for gain, | and 2.04. 78
i pray you, sir, take patience. 2.04.138
if, sir, perchance | she have restrain'd the 2.04.142
o, sir, you are old, | nature in you stands on 2.04.146
good sir, no more; 2.04.157
fie, sir, fie! 2.04.164
good sir, to th' purpose. 2.04.181
why not by th' hand, sir? 2.04.195
i set him there, sir; 2.04.199
at your choice, sir. 2.04.217
give ear, sir, to my sister, | for those that 2.04.233
i dare avouch it, sir. 2.04.237
o sir, to willful men, | the injuries that they 2.04.302
sir, i do know you, | and dare upon the warrant 3.01. 17
alas, sir, are you here? 3.02. 42
he hath no daughters, sir. 3.04. 69
o, cry you mercy, sir. 3.04.171
sir, where is the patience now | that you so oft 3.06. 58
you, sir, i entertain for one of my hundred; 3.06. 78 P
here, sir, but trouble him not — his wits are 3.06. 87
come, sir, what letters had you late from france 3.07. 42
alack, sir, he is mad. 4.01. 45
come on, sir, here's the place; 4.06. 11
now fare ye well, good sir. 4.06. 32
gone, sir; 4.06. 41
ho, you, sir! 4.06. 46
hear you, sir! 4.06. 46
what are you, sir? 4.06. 48
ay, sir. 4.06.156
sir, | your most dear daughter — 4.06.188
hail, gentle sir. 4.06.208
sir, speed you: what's your will? 4.06.208
do you hear aught, sir, of a battle toward? 4.06.209
i thank you, sir, that's all. 4.06.214
i thank you, sir. 4.06.216
now, good sir, what are you? 4.06.220
sir, do you know me? 4.07. 47
o, look upon me, sir, | and hold your hand in 4.07. 56
in your own kingdom, sir. 4.07. 75
sir, this i heard: 5.01. 21
grace go with you, sir! 5.02. 4
no further, sir, a man may rot even here. 5.02. 8
sir, you have show'd to–day your valiant strain, 5.03. 40
sir, i thought it fit | to send the old and 5.03. 45
sir, by your patience, | i hold you but a 5.03. 59
hold, sir. 5.03.156
your lady, sir, your lady; 5.03.227
thank you, sir. 5.03.310
i have a journey, sir, shortly to go: 5.03.322
but he, sir, had th' election; OTH 1.01. 27

now, sir, be judge yourself | whether i in any 1.01. 38
o, sir, content you; 1.01. 41
for, sir, | it is as sure as you are roderigo, 1.01. 55
/'zounds, sir, y' are robb'd! 1.01. 86
sir, sir, sir — 1.01.102
sir, sir, sir — 1.01.102
sir, sir, sir — 1.01.102
patience, good sir. 1.01.104
/'zounds, sir, you are one of those that will 1.01.108 P
i am one, sir, that comes to tell you your 1.01.115 P
sir, i will answer any thing. 1.01.120
yes, sir, i have indeed. 1.01.174
but i pray you, sir, | are you fast married? 1.02. 10
you, roderigo! come, sir, i am for you. 1.02. 58
i pray you, sir, go forth, | and give us truth 2.01. 57
sir, would she give you so much of her lips | as 2.01.100
now again you are most apt to play the sir in. 2.01.174 P
now, sir, this granted (as it is a most pregnant 2.01.235 P
but, sir, be you rul'd by me. 2.01.263 P
sir, he's rash and very sudden in choler, and 2.01.272 P
i pray you, sir, hold your hand. 2.03.151 P
let me go, sir, or i'll knock you o'er the 2.03.153 P
lieutenant — sir — montano — /sir — | help, 2.03.159
lieutenant — sir — montano — gentlemen — 2.03.166
sir, this gentleman | steps in to cassio and 2.03.228
sir, for your hurts, | myself will be your 2.03.253
i have well approv'd it, sir. i drunk! 2.03.312 P
how, sir? how? 3.01. 5 P
ay, marry, are they, sir. 3.01. 7 P
whereby hangs a tale, sir? 3.01. 9 P
marry, sir, by many a wind instrument that i 3.01. 10 P
well, sir, we will not. 3.01. 14 P
we have none such, sir. 3.01. 18 P
she is stirring, sir. 3.01. 28 P
and then, sir, would he gripe and wring my hand; 3.03.421
good sir, be a man; 4.01. 65
with all my heart, sir. 4.01.216
lives, sir. 4.01.223
what would you with her, sir? 4.01.250
sir, she can turn, and turn; 4.01.253
and she can weep, sir, weep; 4.01.254
concerning this, sir — o well–painted passion! 4.01.257
sir, i obey the mandate, | and will return to 4.01.259
and, sir, to–night | i do entreat that we may 4.01.261
you are welcome, sir, to cyprus. 4.01.263
sir, there is especial commission come from 4.02.220 P
i do beseech you, sir, trouble yourself no 4.03. 1
will you walk, sir? | o, desdemona! 4.03. 4
he, sir. 5.01. 68
even he, sir; did you know him? 5.01. 92
i bleed, sir, but not kill'd. 5.02.288
sir, you shall understand what hath befall'n, 5.02.307
sir, sometimes when he is not antony, | he comes ANT 1.01. 57
is't you, sir, that know things? 1.02. 8 P
good sir, give me good fortune. 1.02. 14 P
what's your pleasure, sir? 1.02.131 P
alack, sir, no, her passions are made of nothing 1.02.146 P
o, sir, you had then left unseen a wonderful 1.02.153 P
sir? 1.02.157 P
why, sir, give the gods a thankful sacrifice. 1.02.161 P
sir, you and i must part, but that's not it; 1.03. 87
sir, you and i have lov'd, but there's not it; 1.03. 88
but, sir, forgive me, | since my becomings kill 1.03. 95
of stirs abroad, i shall beseech you, sir, | to 1.04. 82
doubt not, sir, | i knew it for my bond. 1.04. 83
from silvius, sir. 2.01. 18
sit, sir. 2.02. 28
sir, | he fell upon me, ere admitted, then; 2.02. 74
welcome from egypt, sir. 2.02.171 P
ay, sir, we did sleep day out of countenance, 2.02.177 P
humbly, sir, i thank you. 2.02.244
good night, sir. 2.03. 4
good night, sir. 2.03. 8
sir, mark antony | will e'en but kiss octavia, 2.04. 2
sir, good success! 2.04. 9
come, you'll play with me, sir? 2.05. 6
come hither, sir. 2.05. 84
i did not think, sir, to have met you here. 2.06. 49
i have fair /meanings, sir. 2.06. 66
sir, | i never lov'd you much, but i ha' prais'd 2.06. 75
show 's the way, sir. 2.06. 81
you and i have known, sir. 2.06. 83 P
we have, sir. 2.06. 85 P
y' have said, sir. 2.06.107 P
true, sir, she was the wife of caius marcellus. 2.06.110 P
pray ye, sir? 2.06.113 P
come, sir, will you aboard? 2.06.132 P
i shall take it, sir; 2.06.134 P
thus do they, sir: 2.07. 17
it is shap'd, sir, like itself, and it is as 2.07. 42 P
go hang, sir, hang! 2.07. 53
and shall, sir, give 's your hand. 2.07.127
no further, sir. 3.02. 23
sir, look well to my husband's house; and — 3.02. 45
come, sir, come, | i'll wrastle with you in my 3.02. 61
go to, go to. come hither, sir. 3.03. 2
there's strange news come, sir. 3.05. 2 P
come, sir. 3.05. 24
sir, this should be answer'd. 3.06. 30
is it so, sir? 3.06. 96
most worthy sir, you therein throw away | the 3.07. 41
see you here, sir? 3.11. 30
sir, sir! 3.11. 34
sir, sir! 3.11. 34
most noble sir, arise, the queen approaches. 3.11. 46
sir, the queen. 3.11. 50
admit him, sir. 3.13. 40
he needs as many, sir, as caesar has, | or needs 3.13. 49
sir, sir, thou art so leaky | that we must leave 3.13. 63
sir, sir, thou art so leaky | that we must leave 3.13. 63
what mean you, sir, | to give them this 4.02. 33
well, sir, good night. 4.03. 6
briefly, sir. 4.04. 10
a thousand, sir, | early though't be, have on 4.04. 21
sir, | he is with caesar. 4.05. 9
sir, his chests and treasure | he has not with 4.05. 10
they are beaten, sir, and our advantage serves 4.07. 11
awake, sir, awake, speak to us. 4.09. 28

hear you, sir? 4.09. 28
o, sir, pardon me! 4.14. 80
woe are we, sir, you may not live to wear | all 4.14.133
sir, i will eat no meat, i'll not drink, sir; 5.02. 49
sir, i will eat no meat, i'll not drink, sir; 5.02. 49
know, sir, that i | will not wait pinion'd at 5.02. 52
no matter, sir, what i have heard or known. 5.02. 73
i thank you, sir. 5.02.105
nay, pray you, sir. 5.02.108
sir, the gods | will have it thus, my master and 5.02.115
sole sir o' th' world, | i cannot project mine 5.02.120
behold, sir. 5.02.197
o, sir, you are too sure an augurer; 5.02.334
i do extend him, sir, within himself, | crush CYM 1.01. 25
may well be laugh'd at, | yet is it true, sir. 1.01. 67
i beseech you, sir, | harm not yourself with 1.01.133
sir, | it is your fault that i have lov'd 1.01.143
almost, sir: 1.01.148
how now, sir? 1.01.159
o brave sir! 1.01.166
sir, i would advise you to shift a shirt; 1.02. 1 P
sir, as i told you always: 1.02. 29 P
believe it, sir, i have seen him in britain. 1.04. 1 P
sir, we have known together in orleance. 1.04. 35 P
sir, you o'errate my poor kindness, i was glad i 1.04. 38 P
by your pardon, sir, i was then a young 1.04. 43 P
sir, with all my heart. 1.04.100 P
thanks, good sir, | you're kindly welcome. 1.06. 13
you are as welcome, worthy sir, as i | have 1.06. 29
what, dear sir, | thus raps you? are you well? 1.06. 50
beseech you, sir, | desire my man's abode where 1.06. 52
i was going, sir, | to give him welcome. 1.06. 54
what do you pity, sir? 1.06. 82
am i one, sir? 1.06. 83
i pray you, sir, | deliver with more openness 1.06. 87
a lady to the worthiest sir that ever | country 1.06.160
judgment | in the election of a sir so rare, 1.06.175
all's well, sir. 1.06.179
so like you, sir, ambassadors from rome; 2.03. 54
good morrow, sir. 2.03. 87
i am much sorry, sir, | you put me to forget a 2.03.104
ay, i said so, sir; 2.03.150
so i leave /you, sir, | to th' worst of 2.03.154
fear it not, sir. 2.04. 1
welcome, sir. 2.04. 29
make /not, sir, | your loss your sport. 2.04. 47
good sir, we must, | if you keep covenant. 2.04. 49
sir, my circumstances, | being so near the truth 2.04. 61
sir (i thank her), that. 2.04.100
have patience, sir, | and take your ring again, 2.04.113
sir, be patient. 2.04.130
remember, sir, my liege, | the kings your 3.01. 16
else, sir, no more tribute, pray you now. 3.01. 45 P
so, sir. 3.01. 83
thanks, royal sir. 3.05. 1
our subjects, sir, | will not endure his yoke; 3.05. 4
so, sir. 3.05. 7
sir, the event | is yet to name the winner. 3.05. 14
royal sir, | since the exile of posthumus, most 3.05. 35
where is she, sir? 3.05. 41
please you, sir, | her chambers are all lock'd, 3.05. 42
where is she, sir? 3.05. 91
then, sir: 3.05. 98
sir, as i think. 3.05.107 P
sir, i will. 3.05.122 P
what's the matter, sir? 3.06. 41
fidele, sir. 3.06. 60
thanks, sir. 3.06. 94
if it be sin to say so, sir, i yoke me | in my 4.02. 19
you health. so please you, sir. 4.02. 31
yes, sir, to milford–haven, which is the way? 4.02.291
now, sir, | what have you dream'd of late of 4.02.344
say you, sir? 4.02.379
fidele, sir. 4.02.379
i'll follow, sir. 4.02.387
sir, my life is yours, | i humbly set it at your 4.03. 12
what pleasure, sir, /find /we in life, to lock 4.04. 2
this is, sir, a doubt | in such a time nothing 4.04. 14
pray, sir, to th' army. 4.04. 31
if you will bless me, sir, and give me leave, 4.04. 44
no blame be to you, sir, for all was lost | but 5.03. 3
nay, be not angry, sir. 5.03. 59
come, sir, are you ready for death? 5.04.151 P
hanging is the word, sir. 5.04.153 P
a heavy reckoning for you, sir. 5.04.157 P
your neck, sir, is pen, book, and counters; 5.04.169 P
indeed, sir, he that sleeps feels not the 5.04.172 P
look you, sir, you know not which way you shall 5.04.175 P
sir, | in cambria are we born, and gentlemen. 5.05. 16
more, sir, and worse. 5.05. 49
consider, sir, the chance of war, the day | was 5.05. 75
save him, sir, | and spare no blood beside. 5.05. 91
i'll tell you, sir, in private, if you please 5.05.115
fidele, sir. 5.05.118
sir, step you forth; 5.05.130
a nobler sir ne'er liv'd | 'twixt sky and ground 5.05.145
well may you, sir, | remember me at court, where 5.05.192
the queen, sir, very oft importun'd me | to 5.05.249
your blessing, sir. 5.05.266
stay, sir king. 5.05.301
mighty sir, | these two young gentlemen, that 5.05.327
my breeding was, sir, as | your highness knows. 5.05.339
but, gracious sir, | here are your sons again, 5.05.347
he, sir, was lapp'd | in a most curious mantle, 5.05.360
i am, sir, | the soldier that did company these 5.05.407
you holp us, sir, | as you did mean indeed to be 5.05.422
alas, sir! PER 1.02. 95
i'll do my best, sir. 1.04. 20
i thank you, sir. 2.01. 84
hark you, sir; do you know where ye are? 2.01. 96 P
ay, sir, and he deserves so to be call'd for his 2.01.102 P
marry, sir, half a day's journey. 2.01.107 P
o, sir, things must be as they may; 2.01.113 P
what mean you, sir? 2.01.135 P
i hope, sir, if you thrive, you'll remember from 2.01.151 P
sir, yonder is your place. 2.03. 23
contend not, sir, for we are gentlemen | have 2.03. 24
sit, sir, sit. 2.03. 27

the king my father, sir, has drunk to you — 2.03. 75
come, sir, here's a lady that wants breathing 2.03.100
yours, sir, | we have given order be next our 2.03.109
sir, i am beholding to you | for your sweet 2.05. 25
sir, you are music's master. 2.05. 30
what do you think of my daughter, sir? 2.05. 33
sir, my daughter thinks very well of you, | ay, 2.05. 37
why, sir, say if you had, who takes offense | at 2.05. 71
your will to mine — and you, sir, hear you — 2.05. 82
yes, if you love me, sir. 2.05. 88
patience, good sir, do not assist the storm. 3.01. 19
patience, good sir, | even for this charge. 3.01. 26
what courage, sir? god save you! 3.01. 38 P
sir, your queen must overboard. 3.01. 47 P
pardon us, sir; 3.01. 51 P
here she lies, sir. 3.01. 55
sir, we have a chest beneath the hatches, 3.01. 70 P
sir, | our lodgings, standing bleak upon the sea 3.02. 13
sir, even now | did the sea toss up upon our 3.02. 49
tis like a coffin, sir. 3.02. 52
never saw so huge a billow, sir, | as toss'd 3.02. 58
most likely, sir. 3.02. 78
sir? 4.02. 2 P
o, sir, we doubt it not. 4.02. 42 P
now, sir, hast thou cried her through the market 4.02. 93 P
we have here one, sir, if she would — but there 4.06. 27 P
for flesh and blood, sir, white and red, you 4.06. 34 P
o, sir, i can be modest. 4.06. 38 P
what trade, sir? 4.06. 68 P
earlier too, sir, if now i be one. 4.06. 76 P
sir, there is a barge put off from meteline, 5.01. 3
sir, | this is the man that can, in aught you 5.01. 11
hail, reverent sir! the gods preserve you! 5.01. 14
sir, | our vessel is of tyre, in it the king, 5.01. 22
sir king, all hail! 5.01. 39
hail, royal sir! 5.01. 40
sir, | we have a maid in meteline, i durst wager 5.01. 42
sir, a courtesy | which if we should deny, the 5.01. 58
it, sir, i will recount it to you, | but see, i 5.01. 63
sir, i will use | my utmost skill in his 5.01. 75
hail, sir! my lord, lend ear. 5.01. 82
patience, good sir! | or here i'll cease. 5.01.144
but, good sir, | whither will you have me? 5.01.175
not, but | here's the regent, sir, of meteline 5.01.186
helicanus, strike me, honored sir, | give me a 5.01.190
first, sir, i pray, | what is your title? 5.01.202
sir, 'tis the governor of meteline, | who, 5.01.219
sir? 5.01.251
shall we refresh us, sir, upon your shore, | and 5.01.256
sir, | with all my heart, and, when you come 5.01.259
sir, lend me your arm. 5.01.263
noble sir, | if you have told diana's altar true 5.03. 16
great sir, they shall be brought you to my house 5.03. 26
reverent sir, | the gods can have no mortal 5.03. 61
lord cerimon hath letters of good credit, sir, 5.03. 77
sir, lead 's the way. 5.03. 84
therefore, sir, | as i shall here make trial of TNK 1.01.192
sir, | i'll follow you at heels; 1.01.220
sir, farewell. 1.03. 1
thanks, sir. 1.03. 11
sir, i demand no more than your own offer, and i 2.01. 10 P
have, sir. here she comes. 2.01. 15 P
no, sir, no, that's palamon. 2.01. 49 P
how do you, sir? 2.02. 1
speak on, sir. 2.02.117
cousin, cousin! how do you, sir? why, palamon! 2.02.131
ne, sir! 2.02.203
not far, sir. | are there such games to-day? 2.03. 63
not yet, sir. 2.03. 68
well, sir, | take your own time. come, boys. 2.03. 68
is youngest, sir. 2.05. 8
what made you seek this place, sir? 2.05. 25
sir, we are much indebted to your travel, | nor 2.05. 30
kiss her fair hand, sir. 2.05. 37
sir, y' are a noble giver. 2.05. 38
you deserve well, sir, i shall soon see't. 2.05. 42
wait well, sir, | upon your mistress. 2.05. 51
that were a shame, sir, | while i have horses. 2.05. 53
hope too wise for that, sir. 2.05. 64
sir, | i have seen you move in such a place, 3.01. 62
or | your offer do't i only, sir; 3.01. 94
hark, sir, they call | the scatter'd to the 3.01.108
sir, your attendance | cannot please heaven, and 3.01.110
here, sir, drink — | i know you are faint — 3.03. 6
well, sir, i'll pledge you. 3.03. 16
he did so; well, sir? 3.03. 31
something she did, sir. 3.03. 35
let us alone, sir. 3.05. 31
yes, sir. 3.05. 37
what | shall we determine, sir? 3.05. 53
some country sport, upon my life, sir. 3.05. 97
well, sir, go forward, we will edify. 3.05. 98
never so pleas'd, sir. 3.05.149
i have put you | to too much pains, sir. 3.06. 18
would you were so in all, sir! 3.06. 20
will't please you arm, sir? 3.06. 35
choose you, sir. 3.06. 45
now to you, sir. 3.06. 69
safely presently | into your bush again, sir. 3.06.111
for i gave him | more mercy than you found, sir, 3.06.182
sir, by our tie of marriage — 3.06.195
by all our friendship, sir, by all our dangers, 3.06.202
first let me entreat, sir. 3.06.210
for now i am set a-begging, sir, i am deaf | to 3.06.238
let it not fall again, sir. 3.06.272
i cannot, sir, they are both too excellent: 3.06.286
yes, i must, sir, | else both miscarry. 3.06.301
good sir, remember. 4.01. 3
alas, sir, where's your daughter? 4.01. 32
sir, when did you see her? 4.01. 33
sir, when did she sleep? 4.01. 35
but what of her, sir? 4.01. 42
well, sir? 4.01. 44
no, sir, not well: | 'tis too true, she is mad. 4.01. 45
but why all this haste, sir? 4.01. 51
pray go on, sir. 4.01. 65
then she talk'd of you, sir — | that you must 4.01. 76
how now, sir? 4.02. 55

from whence come you, sir? 4.02. 71
i will, sir, | and truly what i think. 4.02. 72
yes, sir. 4.02.151
what think you of her, sir? 4.03. 58 P
i was once, sir, in great hope she had fix'd her 4.03. 64 P
take upon you, young sir her friend, the name of 4.03. 76 P
sir, they enter. 5.01. 7
farewell, sir! 5.01. 33
i have no voice, sir, to confirm her that way! 5.02. 15
why, do you think she is not honest, sir? 5.02. 30
yet very well, sir. 5.02. 36
o, sir, you would fain be nibbling. 5.02. 87
sir, my good lord, | your sister will no further 5.03. 10
sir, pardon me, | the title of a kingdom may be 5.03. 32
sir, she's well restor'd, | and to be married 5.04. 27
arise, great sir, and give the tidings ear 5.04. 46

/SIRE 2 FR 0.0002 REL FR 2 V 0 P
for thine own bowels, which do call thee /sire, MM 3.01. 29
dear divorce | 'twixt natural /son and /sire! TIM 4.03.382

SIRE 22 FR 0.0024 REL FR 22 V 0 P
could penetrate her uncompassionate sire; TGV 3.01.233
a child shall get a sire, if i fail not of my SHR 2.01.411
as honor's born, | and is not like the sire. AWW 2.03.135
that could conceive a gross and foolish sire WT 3.02.197
which like unruly children make their sire R2 3.04. 30
whiles that his mountain sire, on mountain H5 2.04. 57
then follow thou thy desp'rate sire of crete, 1H6 4.06. 54
king, | and raise his issue like a loving sire; 3H6 2.02. 22
but thou art neither like thy sire nor dam, 2.02.135
and grac'd thy poor sire with his bridal day, 2.02.155
these hands that slew thy sire and brother | to 2.04. 9
the son, compell'd, been butcher to the sire. R3 5.05. 26
too like the sire for ever being good. TIT 5.01. 50
the lin'd crutch from thy old limping sire, TIM 4.01. 14
father cowards and base things sire base: CYM 4.02. 26
your father | sure is a happy sire then. TNK 2.05. 9
or butcher sire that reaves his son of life: VEN 766
and set dissension 'twixt the son and sire, 1160
sweet issue of a more sweet-smelling sire — 1178
"had collatinus kill'd my son or sire, | or lain LUC 232
the sire, the son, the dame, and daughter die. 1477
resembling sire, and child, and happy mother, SON 8.11

SIREN 3 FR 0.0003 REL FR 3 V 0 P
sing, siren, for thyself, and i will dote; ERR 3.02. 47
this siren that will charm rome's saturnine, TIT 2.01. 23
what potions have i drunk of siren tears SON 119. 1

/SIRE'S 1 FR 0.0001 REL FR 1 V 0 P
hence will i to my ghostly /sire's close cell, ROM 2.02.188

SIRRAH *(also chirrah)*

/SIRRAH 1 FR 0.0001 REL FR 1 V 0 P
/ah, /sirrah! TIT 3.02. 75

SIRRAH 149 FR 0.0168 REL FR 79 V 70 P
you'ld be king o' the isle, sirrah? TMP 5.01.288 P
go, sirrah, to my cell; 5.01.292
how now, sirrah? TGV 2.01. 7 P
but, sirrah, how did thy master part with madam 2.05. 11 P
sirrah, i say, forbear. 3.01.205
go, sirrah, find him out. come, valentine. 3.01.261
go, sirrah, for all you are my man, go wait upon WIV 1.01.271 P
hold, sirrah, bear you these letters tightly; 1.03. 79
what do you call your knight's name, sirrah? 3.02. 21 P
come on, sirrah; 4.01. 19 P
come forth, sirrah! 4.02.136 P
fie, sirrah, a bawd, a wicked bawd! MM 3.02. 19
come hither, sirrah; 4.02. 1 P
sirrah, here's a fellow will help you to-morrow 4.02. 22 P
you, sirrah, provide your block and your axe 4.02. 52 P
sirrah, bring barnardine hither. 4.03. 20 P
is the axe upon the block, sirrah? 4.03. 37 P
sirrah, no more! 5.01.214
sirrah, thou art said to have a stubborn soul 5.01.480
you, sirrah, that knew me for a fool, a coward, 5.01.500
sirrah, if any ask you for your master, | say he ERR 2.02.209
if a crow help us in, sirrah, we'll pluck a crow 3.01. 83
but, sirrah, you shall buy this sport as dear 4.01. 81
sirrah, what say you? 5.01.275
pray write down borachio. yours, sirrah? ADO 4.02. 12 P
come you hither, sirrah; 4.02. 27 P
but, sirrah, what say you to this? LLL 1.01.281 P
sirrah, come on. 1.01.310 P
sirrah costard, i will enfranchise thee. 3.01.120 P
/quare chirrah, not sirrah? 5.01. 33 P
sirrah, go before. MV 1.02.132
go you before me, sirrah, | say i will come. 2.05. 38
go in, sirrah, bid them prepare for dinner. 3.05. 46 P
go with him, sirrah. AYL 3.02.159 P
ah, sirrah, a body would think this was well 4.03.165 P
sirrah, go see what trumpet 'tis that sounds. SHR in.1. 74
go, sirrah, take them to the buttery, | and give in.1. 102
sirrah, go you to barthol'mew my page, | and see in.1. 105
sirrah, where have you been? 1.01.221
sirrah, come hither, 'tis no time to jest, | and 1.01.226
but, sirrah, not for my sake, but your master's, 1.01.241
here, sirrah grumio, knock, i say. 1.02. 5
faith, sirrah, and you'll not knock, i'll ring 1.02. 16
now, knock when i bid you, sirrah villain! 1.02. 19
spake you not these words plain, "sirrah, knock 1.02. 40 P
sirrah, be gone, or talk not, i advise you. 1.02. 44
peace, sirrah! 1.02.161
sirrah, lead these gentlemen | to my daughters, 2.01.108
sirrah, young gamester, your father were a fool 2.01.400
sirrah, i will not bear these braves of thine. 3.01. 15
sirrah, get you hence, | and bid my cousin 4.01.150
sirrah biondello, | now do your duty throughly, 4.04. 10
come, sirrah, let's away. 5.01.147
sirrah biondello, go and entreat my wife | to 5.02. 86
sirrah grumio, go to your mistress, | say i 5.02. 95
get you gone, sirrah. AWW 1.03. 9 P
sirrah, tell my gentlewoman i would speak with 1.03. 68 P
you corrupt the song, sirrah. 1.03. 81 P
i must tell thee, sirrah, i write man; 2.03.198 P
sirrah, your lord and master's married, there's 2.03.242 P
i pray you. come, sirrah. 2.04. 55
sirrah, inquire further after me. 5.02. 52 P
tell me, sirrah — but tell me true, i charge 5.03.234
her husband, sirrah? TN 5.01.145
how does he, sirrah? 5.01.283 P
read it you, sirrah. 5.01.301 P

sirrah, speak, | what doth move you to claim JN 1.01. 90
sirrah, your brother is legitimate, | your 1.01.116
sirrah, look to't, i' faith i will, i' faith. 2.01.140
sirrah, were i at home, | at your den, sirrah, 2.01.290
at your den, sirrah, with your lioness, | i 2.01.291
sirrah, get thee to plashy, to my sister R2 2.02. 90
and, sirrah, i have cases of buckrom for the 1H4 1.02.179 P
but, sirrah, henceforth | let me not hear you 1.03.118
sirrah carrier, what time do you mean to come to 2.01. 41 P
sirrah, if they meet not with saint nicholas' 2.01. 61 P
sirrah jack, thy horse stands behind the hedge; 2.02. 70 P
sirrah, i am sworn brother to a leash of drawers 2.04. 6 P
sirrah, falstaff and the rest of the thieves are 2.04. 87 P
sirrah, do i owe you a thousand pound? 3.03.135 P
but, sirrah, there's no room for faith, truth, 3.03.153 P
but, sirrah, make haste, percy is already in the 4.02. 74 P
therefore, sirrah, with a new wound in your 5.04.127 P
sirrah, you giant, what says the doctor to my 2H4 1.02. 1 P
sirrah! where's snare? 2.01. 5 P
sirrah, you boy, and bardolph, no word to your 2.02.160 P
sirrah, here will be the prince and master poins 2.04. 15 P
sirrah, what humor's the prince of? 2.04.236 P
pay the musicians, sirrah. 2.04.373 P
ah, sirrah, quoth 'a, we shall "do nothing but 5.03. 16 P
then keep thy vow, sirrah, when thou meet'st the H5 4.07.144 P
sirrah, thou know'st how orleance is besieg'd, 1H6 1.04. 1
it be said, "speak, sirrah, when you should; 3.01. 62
sirrah, thy lord i honor as he is. 3.04. 35
sirrah, or you must fight, or else be hang'd. 2H6 1.03.217
tell me, sirrah, what's my name? 2.01.115
sirrah, go fetch the beadle hither straight. 2.01.137
now, sirrah, if you mean to save yourself from 2.01.139 P
sirrah beadle, whip him till he leap over that 2.01.145 P
come on, sirrah, off with your doublet quickly. 2.01.147 P
sirrah, what's thy name? 2.03. 80 P
come hither, sirrah, i must examine thee. 4.02. 97 P
go to, sirrah, tell the king from me, that, for 4.02.156 P
sirrah, call in my /sons to be my bail. 5.01.111
sirrah, leave us to ourselves, we must confer. 3H6 5.06. 6
how now, sirrah? R3 3.02. 96
keep the door close, sirrah. H8 5.03. 30 P
sirrah, walk off. TRO 3.02. 6
sirrah, if thy captain knew i were here, he COR 5.02. 51 P
your knee, sirrah. 5.03. 75
sirrah, what tidings? TIT 4.03. 79
sirrah, come hither, make no more ado, | but 4.03.102
sirrah, can you with a grace deliver up a 4.03.106 P
sirrah, hast thou a knife? 4.03.115
come, sirrah, you must be hang'd. 4.04. 47
go, sirrah, trudge about | through fair verona, ROM 1.02. 34
ah, sirrah, this unlook'd-for sport comes well. 1.05. 29
ah, sirrah, by my fay, it waxes late, | i'll to 1.05.126
sirrah, go hire me twenty cunning cooks. 4.02. 2
sirrah, fetch drier logs. 4.04. 16
sirrah, what made your master in this place? 5.03.280
get you gone, sirrah. TIM 3.01. 38 P
sirrah, give place. JC 3.01. 10
get you hence, sirrah; saucy fellow, hence! 4.03.134
sirrah claudio! 4.03.299
sirrah, what news? 5.03. 25
come hither, sirrah. 5.03. 36
sirrah, a word with you. MAC 3.01. 44
sirrah, your father's dead, | and what will you 4.02. 30
whose grave's this, sirrah? HAM 5.01.118 P
go, sirrah, seek him; LR 1.02. 77 P
you, you, sirrah, where's my daughter? 1.04. 44 P
sirrah, you were best take my coxcomb. 1.04. 97 P
take heed, sirrah — the whip. 1.04.110 P
sirrah, i'll teach thee a speech. 1.04.115 P
were you wont to be so full of songs, sirrah? 1.04.171 P
and you lie, sirrah, we'll have you whipt. 1.04.181 P
peace, sirrah! 2.02. 68
sirrah, come on; go along with us. 3.04.179 P
sirrah, naked fellow — 4.01. 51
do you know, sirrah, where lieutenant cassio OTH 3.04. 1 P
now, sirrah; you do wish yourself in egypt? ANT 2.03. 10
but, sirrah, mark, we use | to say the dead are 2.05. 32
sirrah iras, go. 5.02.229
what, are you packing, sirrah? CYM 3.05. 80
sirrah, is this letter true? 3.05.106 P
sirrah, if thou wouldst not be a villain, but do 3.05.108 P
sirrah — TNK 3.03. 52
sirrah tinker, | stop no more holes but what you 3.05. 82

/SIR-REVERENCE 1 FR 0.0001 REL FR 1 V 0 P
from the mire | /of /this /sir-reverence love, ROM 1.04. 42

SIR-REVERENCE 1 FR 0.0001 REL FR 0 V 1 P
may not speak of without he say "sir-reverence." ERR 3.02. 91 P

SIR'S 1 FR 0.0001 REL FR 0 V 1 P
no feeling, but my sir's song, and admiring the WT 4.04.612 P

/SIRS 1 FR 0.0001 REL FR 1 V 0 P
/sirs, /take /up /the /corse. R3 1.02.225

SIRS 42 FR 0.0047 REL FR 33 V 9 P
we'll have him. sirs, a word. TGV 4.01. 38
well, sirs, i am almost out at heels. WIV 1.03. 31 P
go, sirs, take the basket again on your 4.02.108 P
hence, sirs, away! LLL 4.03.208
sirs, cover the while; AYL 2.05. 31 P
sirs, i will practice on this drunken man. SHR in.1. 36
this do, and do it kindly, gentle sirs; in.1. 66
for i tell you, sirs, | if you should smile, he in.1. 98
sirs, let't alone, | i will not go to-day, and 4.03.193
reverend sirs, | for you there's rosemary and WT 4.04. 73
sirs, you four shall front them in the narrow 1H4 2.02. 60 P
speak, sirs, how was it? 2.04.173 P
now, sirs, by'r lady, you fought fair, so did 2.04.298 P
play, sirs. 2H4 2.04.227 P
sirs, take your places and be vigilant. 1H6 2.01. 1
somewhat too sudden, sirs, the warning is, | but 5.02. 14
and hark ye, sirs: 5.04. 55
sirs, what's a' clock? 2H6 2.04. 5
sirs, take away the duke, and guard him sure. 3.01.188
now, sirs, have you dispatch'd this thing? 3.02. 6
sirs, stand apart, the king shall know your mind 3.02.242
so, sirs. 4.07. 1 P
but, sirs, be sudden in the execution, | withal R3 1.03.345
o, sirs, consider, they that set you on | to do 1.04.254
follow me, sirs, and my proceedings eye, | it is TRO 5.07. 7
believe me, sirs, | we shall be charg'd again. COR 1.06. 3

look, sirs, if you can find the huntsman out, TIT 2.03.278
sirs, drag them from the pit unto the prison, 2.03.283
sirs, strive no more: 3.01.177
sirs, take you to your tools. 4.03. 6
sirs, stop his mouth, and let him speak no more. 5.01.151
sirs, stop their mouths, let them not speak to 5.02.167
sirs, help our uncle to convey him in. 5.03. 15
i pray you, sirs, lie in my tent and sleep; JC 4.03.246
lie down, good sirs, | it may be i shall 4.03.250
sirs, awake! 4.03.289
why did you so cry out, sirs, in your sleep? 4.03.303
indeed, /indeed, sirs. HAM 1.02.224
come, sirs. 2.02.534 P
where is this king? sirs, stand you all without. 4.05.113
good sirs, take heart, | we'll bury him; ANT 4.15. 85
but have blush'd | at simp'ring sirs that did. TNK 5.01.104

/SISTER 2 FR 0.0002 REL FR 2 V 0 P
/rather /lose /the /battle /than /that /sister LR 5.01. 18
for your claim, fair /sister, | i bar it in the 5.03. 84

SISTER 201 FR 0.0227 REL FR 169 V 32 P
how does my bounteous sister? TMP 4.01.103
my father wailing, my sister crying, our maid TGV 2.03. 7 P
now, sir, this staff is my sister, for, look you 2.03. 20 P
now come i to my sister; 2.03. 29 P
this day my sister should the cloister enter, MM 1.02.177
and the fair sister | to her unhappy brother 1.04. 19
you know | i am that isabella and his sister. 1.04. 23
here is the sister of the man condemn'd 2.02. 18
hath he a sister? 2.02. 19
one isabel, a sister, desires access to you. 2.04. 18
in the loss of question), that you, his sister, 2.04. 90
than that a sister, by redeeming him, | should 2.04.107
before his sister should her body stoop | to 2.04.182
look, signior, here's your sister. 3.01. 49
now, sister, what's the comfort? 3.01. 54
sweet sister, let me live. 3.01.132
vouchsafe a word, young sister, but one word. 3.01.151
what hath pass'd between you and your sister. 3.01.161 P
let me ask my sister pardon. 3.01.171 P
heard speak of mariana, the sister of frederick, 3.01.209 P
in that perish'd vessel the dowry of his sister. 3.01.218 P
i am the sister of one claudio, | condemn'd upon 5.01. 69
my mistress and her sister stays for you. ERR 1.02. 76
good sister, let us dine, and never fret; 2.01. 6
if so, be patient, sister. 2.01. 9
sister, you know he promis'd me a chain; 2.01.106
when were you wont to use my sister thus? 2.02.153
come, sister. 2.02.211
if you did wed my sister for her wealth, | then 3.02. 5
let not my sister read it in your eye; 3.02. 9
comfort my sister, cheer her, call her /wife: 3.02. 26
i know | your weeping sister is no wife of mine, 3.02. 42
why call you me love? call my sister so. 3.02. 59
thy sister's sister. 3.02. 60
that's my sister. 3.02. 60
all this my sister is, or else should be. 3.02. 65
call thyself sister, sweet, for i am thee: 3.02. 66
i'll fetch my sister to get her good will. 3.02. 70
but her fair sister, | possess'd with such a 3.02.159
go fetch it, sister. 4.02. 47
come, sister, i am press'd down with conceit — 4.02. 65
sister, go you with me. 4.04.130
he, and my sister | to–day did dine together: 5.01.207
by th' way we met | my wife, her sister, and a 5.01.236
and this fair gentlewoman, her sister here, 5.01.374
she now shall be my sister, not my wife. 5.01.417
would swear the gentleman should be her sister; ADO 3.01. 62
as a brother to his sister, show'd | bashful 4.01. 53
be friends with him, 'a kill'd your sister. LLL 5.02. 13
mew'd, | to live a barren sister all your life, MND 1.01. 72
here comes my sister reading, stand aside. AYL 3.02.124
with this shepherdess, my sister; 3.02.335 P
come, sister, will you go? 3.02.435 P
will you go, sister? 3.05. 76
come, sister. 3.05. 77
come, sister, you shall be the priest, and marry 4.01.124 P
what do you say, sister? 4.01.126 P
favor, and bestows himself | like a ripe sister; 4.03. 87
and you, fair sister. 5.02. 18 P
for your brother and my sister no sooner met but 5.02. 33 P
sister, content you in my discontent. SHR 1.01. 80
marry, sir, to get a husband for her sister. 1.01.120 P
mark'd you not how her sister | began to scold 1.01.171
her elder sister is so curst and shrewd | that 1.01.180
any man, | until the elder sister first be wed. 1.02.261
good sister, wrong me not, nor wrong yourself, 2.01. 1
believe me, sister, of all the men alive | i 2.01. 10
if you affect him, sister, here i swear | i'll 2.01. 14
i prithee, sister kate, untie my hands. 2.01. 21
to me, | in the preferment of the eldest sister. 2.01. 93
her sister katherine welcom'd you withal? 3.01. 3
mistress, what's your opinion of your sister? 3.02.243
the sister to my wife, this gentlewoman, | thy 4.05. 62
brother petruchio, sister katherina, | and thou, 5.02. 6
where is your sister, and hortensio's wife? 5.02.101
i do for heaven, | so i were not his sister. AWW 1.03.165
he left behind him myself and a sister, both TN 2.01. 19 P
the breach of the sea was my sister drown'd. 2.01. 22 P
but died thy sister of her love, my boy? 2.04.119
i would therefore my sister had had no name, sir 3.01. 16 P
with that word might make my sister wanton. 3.01. 20 P
i had a sister, | whom the blind waves and 5.01.228
that day that made my sister thirteen years. 5.01.248
on, | to think me as well a sister as a wife, 5.01.317
a sister! you are she. 5.01.326
mean time, sweet sister, | we will not part from 5.01.384
it has an elder sister, | or i mistake you. WT 1.02. 98
what will this sister of mine do with rice? 4.03. 39 P
have more in them than you'ld think, sister. 4.04.216 P
know 'tis none of your daughter nor my sister; 4.04.820 P
and the princess, my sister, call'd my father 5.02.143 P
sister, farewell, i must to coventry. R2 1.02. 56
get thee to plashy, to my sister gloucester, 2.02. 90
come, sister — cousin, i would say — pray 2.02.105
he swears thou art to marry his sister nell. 2H4 2.02.129 P
must i marry your sister? 2.02.139 P
unto our brother france, and to our sister, H5 5.02. 2
will you, fair sister, | go with the princes, or 5.02. 90
york, | marrying my sister that thy mother was, 1H6 2.05. 86
his eldest sister, anne, | my mother, being heir 2H6 2.02. 43
thither gone to crave the french king's sister 3H6 3.01. 30
her | with promise of his sister and what else, 3.01. 51
that virtuous lady bona, thy fair sister, | to 3.03. 56
the measure of his love | unto our sister bona. 3.03.121
now, sister, let us hear your firm resolve. 3.03.129
our sister shall be edward's. 3.03.134
were it to call king edward's widow sister, | i R3 1.01.109
sister, have comfort. 2.02.101
and you, my sister, will you go | to give your 2.02.143
and for my sister and her princely sons, | be 3.03. 21
to bona, sister to the king of france. 3.07.182
as much to you, good sister! whither away? 4.01. 7
kind sister, thanks, we'll enter all together. 4.01. 11
see this main end, | the french king's sister. H8 2.02. 41
duchess of alanson, | the french king's sister; 3.02. 86
will not dispraise your sister cassandra's wit, TRO 1.01. 46 P
had i a sister were a grace, or a daughter a 1.02.236 P
'tis our mad sister, i do know her voice. 2.02. 98
peace, sister, peace! 2.02.103
of divination in our sister work | some touches 2.02.114
sing, | "great hector's sister did achilles win, 3.03.212
here, sister, arm'd, and bloody in intent. 5.03. 8
the noble sister of publicola, | the moon of COR 5.03. 64
speak, gentle sister, who hath marr'red thee? TIT 3.01. 81
witness the sorrow that their sister makes. 3.01.119
see how my wretched sister sobs and weeps. 3.01.137
farewell, lavinia, my noble sister, | o, would 3.01.292
and they it were that ravished our sister. 5.03. 99
where hast thou been, sister? MAC 1.03. 1
sister, where thou? 1.03. 3
therefore our sometime sister, now our queen, HAM 1.02. 8
and, sister, as the winds give benefit | and 1.03. 2
fear it, ophelia, fear it, my dear sister, | and 1.03. 33
dear maid, kind sister, sweet ophelia! 4.05.159
lost, | a sister driven into desp'rate terms, 4.07. 26
a minist'ring angel shall my sister be | when 5.01.241
i am made of that self metal as my sister, | and LR 1.01. 69
and like a sister am most loath to call | your 1.01.270
sister, it is not little i have to say of what 1.01.283 P
he always lov'd our sister most, and with what 1.01.290 P
if he distaste it, let him to my sister, | whose 1.03. 14
i'll write straight to my sister | to hold my 1.03. 25
what he hath utter'd i have writ my sister; 1.04.331
what, have you writ that letter to my sister? 1.04.334
i have this present evening from my sister 2.01.101
our father he hath writ, so hath our sister, 2.01.122
the messengers from our sister and the king. 2.02. 50 P
of the self–same color | our sister speaks of. 2.02.139
my sister may receive it much more worse | to 2.02.148
i cannot think my sister in the least | would 2.04.141
you | that to our sister you do make return. 2.04.151
return you to my sister. 2.04.158
you will return and sojourn with my sister, 2.04.203
give ear, sir, to my sister, | for those that 2.04.233
edmund, keep you our sister company; 3.07. 7 P
farewell, dear sister, farewell, my lord of 3.07. 12 P
farewell, sweet lord, and sister. 3.07. 21
nor thy fierce sister | in his anointed flesh 3.07. 57
'tis from your sister. 4.02. 83
your sister is the better soldier. 4.05. 3
speak the truth, | do you not love my sister? 5.01. 9
our very loving sister, well bemet. 5.01. 20
sister, you'll go with us? 5.01. 34
exasperates, makes mad her sister goneril, | and 5.01. 60
and her sister | by her is poison'd; 5.03.227
thou hast a sister by the mother's side, ANT 2.02.118
a sister i bequeath you, whom no brother | did 2.02.149
caesar's sister is call'd octavia. 2.06.109 P
sister, prove such a wife | as my thoughts make 3.02. 25
farewell, my dearest sister, fare thee well! 3.02. 39
you come not | like caesar's sister. 3.06. 43
no, my most wronged sister, cleopatra | hath 3.06. 65
sister, welcome. 3.06. 97
my dear'st sister! 3.06. 98
good morrow, fairest: sister, your sweet hand. CYM 2.03. 86
call'd me brother, | when i was but your sister; 5.05.377
but alas, | being a natural sister of our sex, TNK 1.01.125
if you grant not | my sister her petition, in 1.01.201
farewell, my beauteous sister. 1.01.219
now, alack, weak sister, | i must no more 1.03. 86
but sure, my sister, | if i were ripe for your 1.03. 90
sister, beshrew my heart, you have a servant 2.05. 62
the marshal's sister | had her share too, as i 3.03. 36
against /thy own edict, follows thy sister, 3.06.145
now or never, sister, | speak, not to be denied. 3.06.185
in my face, dear sister, | i find no anger to 3.06.188
help me, dear sister, in a deed so virtuous 3.06.193
you are a right woman, sister, you have pity, 3.06.215
what is it, sister? 3.06.233
are you content, sister? 3.06.301
o, is he so? you have a sister? 4.01.121
now if my sister — more for palamon. 4.02. 49
ask me now, sweet sister — | i may go look! 4.02. 51
now, my fair sister, | you must love one of them 4.02. 67
o my soft–hearted sister, what think you? 4.02.147
my good lord, | your sister will no further. 5.03. 11
farewell, sister, | i am like to know your 5.03. 36
lo where our sister is in expectation, | yet 5.03.105
o loved sister, | he speaks now of as brave a 5.03.114
as they must needs (the sister and the brother), PP 8. 2
or sister sanctified, of holiest note, | which LC 233

SISTERHOOD 5 FR 0.0005 REL FR 4 V 1 P
a more strict restraint | upon the sisterhood, MM 1.04. 5
maid, | and to be shortly of a sisterhood, | if 2.02. 21
i (in probation of a sisterhood) | was sent to 5.01. 72
a nun of winter's sisterhood kisses not more AYL 3.04. 16 P
of thee | among a sisterhood of holy nuns. ROM 5.03.157

SISTERLY 1 FR 0.0001 REL FR 1 V 0 P
my sisterly remorse confutes mine honor, | and i MM 5.01.100

/SISTER'S 1 FR 0.0001 REL FR 1 V 0 P
to drown me in thy /sister's flood of tears. ERR 3.02. 46

SISTER'S 15 FR 0.0017 REL FR 15 V 0 P
to take life | from thine own sister's shame? MM 3.01.139
thy sister's sister. ERR 3.02. 60
and help to dress your sister's chamber up. SHR 3.01. 83
place, | and let bianca take her sister's room. 3.02.250
thou art, great lord, my father's sister's son, TRO 4.05.120
tend'ring our sister's honor and our own. TIT 1.01.476
they cut thy sister's tongue, and ravish'd her, 5.01. 92
below thy sister's orb | infect the air! TIM 4.03. 2
live, | who is your sister's son, mark antony. JC 4.01. 5
your sister's drown'd, laertes. HAM 4.07.164
beloved regan, | thy sister's naught. LR 2.04.134
i know't, my sister's. 2.04.183
what might import my sister's letter to him? 4.05. 6
our sister's man is certainly miscarried. 5.01. 5
and do invite you to my sister's view, | whither ANT 2.02.167

SISTERS' 3 FR 0.0003 REL FR 3 V 0 P
the sisters' vows, the hours that we have spent, MND 3.02.199
draw | a third more opulent than your sisters'? LR 1.01. 86
have told 's | they are sisters' children, TNK 1.04. 16

/SISTERS 4 FR 0.0004 REL FR 4 V 0 P
/cried, "/sisters, /sisters! LR 4.03. 27
/cried, "/sisters, /sisters! 4.03. 27
/sisters! 4.03. 27
/sisters! 4.03. 28

SISTERS 23 FR 0.0026 REL FR 18 V 5 P
of his blind brothers and sisters went to it. TGV 4.04. 4 P
o sisters three, | come, come to me, | with MND 5.01.336
and such odd sayings, the sisters three, and MV 2.02. 63 P
are dearer than the natural bond of sisters. AYL 1.02.276
john with my brothers and sisters, and sir john 2H4 2.02.134 P
gaping wounds | untwind the sisters three! 2.04.199
brethren and sisters of the hold–door trade, TRO 5.10. 51
county anselme and his beauteous sisters; ROM 1.02. 65 P
the weird sisters, hand in hand, | posters of MAC 1.03. 32
before, these weird sisters saluted me, and 1.05. 8 P
i dreamt last night of the three weird sisters: 2.01. 20
he chid the sisters | when first they put the 3.01. 56
(and betimes i will) to the weird sisters. 3.04.132
come, sisters, cheer we up his sprites, | and 4.01.127
saw you the weird sisters? 4.01.136
why have my sisters husbands, if they say | they LR 1.01. 99
sure i shall never marry like my sisters, | /to 1.01.103
bid farewell to your sisters. 1.01.267
repair those violent harms that my two sisters 4.07. 27
know you do not love me, for your sisters | have 4.07. 72
to both these sisters have i sworn my love; 5.01. 55
we not see these daughters and these sisters? 5.03. 7
that even her art sisters the natural roses; PER 5.ch. 7

SIST'RING 1 FR 0.0001 REL FR 1 V 0 P
a plaintful story from a sist'ring vale, | my LC 2

/SIT* 7 FR 0.0008 REL FR 7 V 0 P
o, /sit my husband's wrongs on herford's spear, R2 1.02. 47
/thou /live /in /richard's /seat /to /sit, 4.01.218
that many have and others must /sit there; 5.05. 27
/so, /now /sit, /and /look /you /eat /no /more TIT 3.02. 1
/come /sit /thou /here, /most /learned /justicer LR 3.06. 21
/thou, /sapient /sir, /sit /here. 3.06. 22
/are /o' /th' /commission, | /sit /you /too. 3.06. 39

SIT* 218 FR 0.0246 REL FR 182 V 36 P
sit down, | for thou must now know farther. TMP 1.02. 32
sit still, and hear the last of our sea–sorrow: 1.02.170
and look how well my garments sit upon me, 2.01.272
if you'll sit down, | i'll bear your logs the 3.01. 23
such dishonor undergo, | while i sit lazy by. 3.01. 28
sit down, and rest. 3.03. 6
sit then and talk with her, she is thine own. 4.01. 32
if not, we'll make you sit, and rifle you. TGV 4.01. 4
here can i sit alone, unseen of any, | and to 5.04. 4
they will not sit till you come. WIV 1.01.278
i sit at ten pounds a week. 1.03. 8
where indeed you have a delight to sit, have you MM 2.01.130
you, lord escalus, | sit with my cousin; 5.01.246
sit you down, | we'll borrow place of him. 5.01.361
i pray you jest, sir, as you sit at dinner. ERR 1.02. 62
thee from the door, or sit down at the hatch: 3.01. 33
rais'd with it when i sit, driven out of doors 4.04. 35
he shows me where the bachelors sit, and there ADO 2.01. 49
i may sit in a corner and cry "heigh–ho for a 2.01.320
she will sit you — you heard my daughter tell 2.03.110
and there will she sit in her smock till she 2.03.132
let us go sit here upon the church–bench till 3.03. 89
well, sit you out; go home, berowne; adieu. LLL 1.01.110
and men sit down to that nourishment which is 1.01.237
again, and till then, sit thee down, sorrow! 1.01.315
like a demigod here sit i in the sky, | and 4.03. 77
saw | and birds sit brooding in the snow | and 5.02.923
come, sit down, every mother's son, and rehearse MND 3.01. 72
come sit thee down upon this flow'ry bed, 4.01. 1
sit like his grandsire cut in alablaster? MV 1.01. 84
wherein doth sit the dread and fear of kings; 4.01.192
here will we sit, and let the sounds of music 5.01. 55
sit, jessica. 5.01. 58
let us sit and mock the good huswife fortune AYL 1.02. 31
sit down and feed, and welcome to our table. 2.07.105
and therefore sit you down in gentleness | and 2.07.124
will you sit down with me? 3.02.277
come, sit, sit, and a song. 5.03. 8
come, sit, sit, and a song. 5.03. 8
we are for you, sit i' th' middle. 5.03. 10
madam wife, sit by my side, and let the world SHR in.2. 142
talk not to me, i will go sit and weep, | till i 2.01. 35
thou hast hit it; come sit on me. 2.01.198
and to cut off all strife, here sit we down: 3.01. 21
are those" — | sit down, kate, and welcome. 4.01.142
come, kate, sit down, i know you have a stomach. 4.01.158
pray you sit down, | for now we sit to chat as 5.02. 10
down, | for now we sit to chat as well as eat. 5.02. 11
nothing but sit and sit, and eat and eat! 5.02. 12
nothing but sit and sit, and eat and eat! 5.02. 12
they sit conferring by the parlor fire. 5.02.102
every hour, to sit and draw | his arched brows, AWW 1.01. 93
yet these fix'd evils sit so fit in him, | that 1.01.102
sit, my preserver, by thy patient's side, | and 2.03. 47
let the white death sit on thy cheek for ever, 2.03. 71
and seek the crowner, and let him sit o' my coz; TN 1.05.134
under your hard construction must i sit, | to 3.01.115
pray you sit by us, | and tell 's a tale. WT 2.01. 22
come on, sit down, come on, and do your best 2.01. 27
nay, come sit down; then on. 2.01. 29
here i and sorrows sit; JN 3.01. 73
that i might sit all night and watch with you. 4.01. 30
men away, | and i will sit as quiet as a lamb; 4.01. 79

ere once again we sit; 4.02. 1
voe doth the heavier sit | where it perceives it R2 1.03.280
thousand flatterers sit within thy crown, 2.01.100
ve see the wind sit sore upon our sails, | and 2.01.265
is treasons will sit blushing in his face, 3.02. 51
or god's sake let us sit upon the ground | and 3.02.155
ny lord, wise men ne'er sit and wail their woes, 3.02.178
n winter's tedious nights sit by the fire 5.01. 40
nd cousin glendower, | will you sit down? 1H4 3.01. 4
it, cousin percy, sit, good cousin hotspur, 3.01. 7
it, cousin percy, sit, good cousin hotspur, 3.01. 7
vith all my heart i'll sit and hear her sing. 3.01.220
t and attend. 3.01.225
he mailed mars shall on his /altar sit | up to 4.01.116
pirits of the wise sit in the clouds and mock 2H4 2.02.143 P
t on my knee, doll. 2.04.227 P
vould shut the book, and sit him down and die. 3.01. 56
narry, have we, sir. will you sit? 3.02. 94 P
narry, let me have him to sit under, he's like 3.02.122 P
o, i will sit and watch here by the king. 4.05. 20
hou dost sit | like a rich armor worn in heat 4.05. 29
ege, | who undertook to sit and watch by you. 4.05. 52
ome hither, harry, sit thou by my bed, | and 4.05.181
ow sit down, now sit down. 5.03. 14 P
ow sit down, now sit down. 5.03. 14 P
weet sir, sit, i'll be with you anon, most 5.03. 26 P
t, i'll be with you anon, most sweet sir, sit. 5.03. 27 P
aster page, good master page, sit. 5.03. 27 P
ou are their heir, you sit upon their throne; H5 1.02.117
r there we'll sit, | ruling in large and ample 1.02.225
here is the playhouse now, there must you sit, 2.pr. 36
atchful fires | sit patiently and inly ruminate 4.pr. 24
et sit and see, | minding true things by what 4.pr. 52
e horsemen sit like fixed candlesticks, | with 4.02. 45
ouncil presently | to sit with us once more, 5.02. 80
n like a butcher and sit like a jack-an-apes, 5.02.141 P
nd sit at chiefest stern of public weal. 1H6 1.01.177
ere will i sit before the walls of roan | and 3.02. 91
york must sit, and fret, and bite his tongue, 2H6 1.01.230
adam, sit you and fear not. 1.04. 21
under, sit there, the lying'st knave | in 2.01.123
sit and /witch me, as ascanius did | when he 3.02.116
e durst not sit there, had your father liv'd. 3H6 1.01. 63
nd shall i stand, and thou sit in my throne? 1.01. 84
ii faciant laudis summa sit ista tuae! 1.03. 48
ere on this molehill will i sit me down. 2.05. 14
sit upon a hill, as i do now, | to carve out 2.05. 23
f england, worthy margaret, | sit down with us. 3.03. 2
at thou shouldst stand while lewis doth sit. 3.03. 3
ill like thyself, | and sit thee by our side. 3.03. 16
ow, brother king, farewell, and sit you fast, 4.01.119
ow, montague, sit fast, i seek for thee, | that 5.02. 3
rds, wise men ne'er sit and wail their loss, 5.04. 1
e will not from the helm to sit and weep, | but 5.04. 21
nce more we sit in england's royal throne, 5.07. 1
eeper, i prithee sit by me awhile. R3 1.04. 73
andam, one night as we did sit at supper, | my 2.04. 10
the tower | to sit about the coronation. 3.01.173
ortune and victory sit on thy helm! 5.03. 79
t me sit heavy on thy soul to-morrow! 5.03.118
t me sit heavy in thy soul to-morrow, | i that 5.03.131
t me sit heavy in thy soul to-morrow, | rivers 5.03.139
e should take root here where we sit, or sit H8 1.02. 87
ere where we sit, or sit | state-statues only. 1.02. 87
t by us, you shall hear | (this was his 1.02.124
weet ladies, will it please you sit? 1.04. 19
ray sit between these ladies. 1.04. 24
nd grew so ill | he could not sit his mule. 4.02. 16
hilst i sit meditating | on that celestial 4.02. 79
t's sit down quiet | for fear we wake her; 4.02. 81
m very sorry | to sit here at this present, 5.02. 44
ood man, sit down. 5.02.165
priam's royal table do i sit, | and when fair TRO 1.01. 29
ven then when they sit idly in the sun. 3.03.233
t, gods, upon your thrones, and smile at troy! 5.10. 7
ey'll sit by th' fire, and presume to know COR 1.01.191
t, coriolanus; 2.02. 67
ray now, sit down. 2.02. 74
hen the alarum were struck than idly sit | to 2.02. 76
ell you, he does sit in gold, his eye | red 5.01. 63
e glorious gods sit in hourly synod about thy 5.02. 68 P
t fas aut nefas, till i find the stream | to TIT 2.01.133
nder their sweet shade, aaron, let us sit, 2.03. 16
t us sit down and mark their yellowing noise; 2.03. 20
nd thou, and i, sit round about some fountain, 3.01.123
t down, sweet niece; 4.01. 65
rother, sit down by me. 4.01. 65
en sit we down and let us all consult. 4.02.132
ay, sit, nay, sit, good cousin capulet, | for ROM 1.05. 30
ay, sit, nay, sit, good cousin capulet, | for 1.05. 30
ow will he sit under a medlar tree, | and wish 2.01. 34
here upon thy cheek the stain doth sit | of 2.03. 75
at they cannot sit at ease on the old bench? 2.04. 34 P
oon his brow shame is asham'd to sit; 3.02. 92
nd let the nurse this night sit up with you, 4.03. 10
ray sit, more welcome are ye to my fortunes TIM 1.02. 19
t, sit. 3.06. 68 P
t, sit. 3.06. 68 P
there sit twelve women at the table, let a 3.06. 78 P
all sit and pant in your great chairs of ease, 5.04. 11
nd yesterday the bird of night did sit | even JC 1.03. 26
nd let us presently go sit in council, | how 4.01. 45
ow sit we close about this taper here, | and 4.03.164
t thee down, clitus; 5.05. 4
st our old robes sit easier than our new! MAC 2.04. 38
ou know your own degrees, sit down. 3.04. 1
ere i'll sit i' th' midst. 3.04. 10
ay't please your highness sit. 3.04. 38
t, worthy friends; 3.04. 52
ve and health to all, | then i'll sit down. 3.04. 87
ray you sit still. 3.04.107
t down a while, | and let us once again assail HAM 1.01. 30
ell, sit we down, | and let us hear barnardo 1.01. 33
ood now, sit down, and tell me, he that knows, 1.01. 70
l then sit still, my soul. 1.02.256
ome hither, my dear hamlet, sit by me. 3.02.108 P
ome, and sit you down, you shall not boudge; 3.04. 18
t you down, | and let me wring your heart, for 3.04. 34

are disclosed, | his silence will sit drooping. 5.01.288
life and honor, | there shall he sit till noon. LR 2.02.134
wherefore | should he sit here? 2.04.113
sit you down, father; 4.06.255
keep leets and law-days and in sessions sit OTH 3.03.140
upon your sword | sit laurel victory, and smooth ANT 1.03.100
to sit | and keep the turn of tippling with a 1.04. 18
sit. 2.02. 28
sit, sir. 2.02. 28
enthron'd i' th' market-place, did sit alone, 2.02.215
sit — and some wine! a health to lepidus! 2.07. 29 P
let me sit down. o juno! 3.11. 28
when on my three-foot stool i sit and tell | the CYM 3.03. 89
the senate-house of planets all did sit, | to PER 1.01. 10
sit down. 1.02. 60
sit, sir, sit. 2.03. 27
sit, sir, sit. 2.03. 27
had princes sit like stars about his throne, 2.03. 39
awhile, | yon knight doth sit too melancholy, 2.03. 54
come, gentlemen, we sit too long on trifles, 2.03. 92
you shall like diamonds sit about his crown. 2.04. 53
shall be discover'd, please you sit and hark. 5.ch. 24
sit, sir, i will recount it to you, | but see, i 5.01. 63
come sit by me. 5.01.141
demanded that, | she would sit still and weep. 5.01.189
sit down, and, good now, | no more of these vain TNK 3.03. 9
pray sit down then, and let me entreat you | by 3.03. 13
ladies, sit down, we'll stay it. 3.05. 99
and that you sit as kings in your desires, STM II.C 77
here come and sit, where never serpent hisses, VEN 17
showed like two silver doves that sit a-billing. 366
and there, all smoth'red up, in shade doth sit, 1035
infamy, | but i alone, alone must sit and pine, LUC 795
while philomela sits and sings, i sit and mark, PP 14.17
there will we sit upon the rocks, | and see the 19. 5
more, | entitled in /thy parts do crowned sit, SON 37. 7
and more, much more than in my verse can sit, 103.13

SITH *(also since, sithence)*

/SITH 1 FR 0.0001 REL FR 1 V 0 P
i wonder, sir, /sith wives are monsters to you, AWW 5.03.155

SITH 23 FR 0.0026 REL FR 22 V 1 P
not, sith so prettily | he couples it to his TGV 1.02.123
sith you yourself know how easy it is to be such WIV 2.02.188 P
sith 'twas my fault to give the people scope, MM 1.03. 35
sith that the justice of your title to him 4.01. 73
in brief, sir, sith it your pleasure is, | and i SHR 1.01.211
talk not of france, sith thou hast lost it all. 3H6 1.01.110
me, | lest in revenge thereof, sith god is just, 1.03. 41
i come to tell you things sith then befall'n. 2.01.106
sith /every action that hath gone before, TRO 1.03. 13
sith yet there is a credence in my heart, | an 5.02.120
sith true nobility | warrants these words in TIT 1.01.271
gods, | sith priest and holy water are so near, 1.01.323
and, sith there's no justice in earth nor hell, 4.03. 50
it, | sith nor th' exterior nor the inward man HAM 2.02. 6
and sith so neighbored to his youth and havior, 2.02. 12
thing's to do," | sith i have cause, and will, 4.04. 45
sith you have heard, and with a knowing ear, 4.07. 3
sith thus thou wilt appear, | freedom lives LR 1.01.180
sith that both charge and danger | speak 'gainst 2.04.239
love no friend, sith love breeds such offense. OTH 3.03.380
but, sith i am ent'red in this cause so far 3.03.411
sith in thy pride so fair a hope is slain. VEN 762
sith in his prime death doth my love destroy, 1163

SITHENCE 2 FR 0.0002 REL FR 1 V 1 P
duty speedily to acquaint you withal, sithence, AWW 1.03.119 P
have you inform'd them sithence? COR 3.01. 47

/SITS 1 FR 0.0001 REL FR 1 V 0 P
/a /moral /fool, /sits /still /and /cries, LR 4.02. 58

SITS 61 FR 0.0069 REL FR 55 V 6 P
she that you gaze on so as she sits at supper? TGV 2.01. 43 P
your brother's death i know sits at your heart; MM 5.01.389
o, ay, stalk on, stalk on, the fowl sits. ADO 2.03. 93 P
is't possible? sits the wind in that corner? 2.03. 98 P
"the god of love, | that sits above, | and knows 5.02. 27
plucking the grass to know where sits the wind, MV 1.01. 18
with that keen appetite that he sits down? 2.06. 9
speak, | and sits as one new risen from a dream. SHR 4.01.186
where he sits crowned in his master's spite. TN 5.01.128
sits on 's horseback at mine hostess' door, JN 2.01.289
and in his forehead sits | a bare-ribb'd death, 5.02.176
the wind sits fair for news to go for ireland, R2 2.02.123
keeps death his court, and there the antic sits, 3.02.162
and who sits here that is not richard's subject? 4.01.122
that man that sits within a monarch's heart 2H4 4.02. 11
lo where it sits, | which god shall guard; 4.05. 43
majesty, | sits not so easy on me as you think. 5.02. 45
for now sits expectation in the air, | and hides H5 2.pr. 8
now sits the wind fair, and we will aboard. 2.02. 12
that sits in heart-grief and uneasiness | under 2.02. 27
the throne he sits on, nor the tide of pomp 4.01.264
everlasting shame | sits mocking in our plumes. 4.05. 5
murderous tyranny | sits in grim majesty, to 2H6 3.02. 50
my lords, look where the sturdy rebel sits, 3H6 1.01. 50
and over the chair of state, where now he sits, 1.01.168
here sits a king more woeful than you are. 2.05.124
my back, | where sits deformity to mock my body; 3.02.158
victory sits on our helms. R3 5.03.351
there sits a judge | that no king can corrupt. H8 3.01.100
it, and rome | sits safe and still without him. COR 4.06. 37
all places yields to him ere he sits down, | and 4.07. 28
he sits in his state, as a thing made for 5.04. 22 P
safe out of fortune's shot, and sits aloft, TIT 2.01. 2
empress i am, but yonder sits the emperor. 4.04. 41
for our judgment sits | five times in that ere ROM 1.04. 46
my bosom's lord sits lightly in his throne, 5.01. 3
the fellow that sits next him, now parts bread TIM 1.02. 46 P
to dispense, | for policy sits above conscience. 3.02. 87
o, he sits high in all the people's hearts; JC 1.03.157
see, | sits in a foggy cloud, and stays for me. MAC 3.05. 35
accord of hamlet | sits smiling to my heart, in HAM 1.02.124
the wind sits in the shoulder of your sail, 1.03. 56
soul | o'er which his melancholy sits on brood, 3.01.165
but look, amazement on thy mother sits, | o, 3.04.112
nay, and thou canst not smile as the wind sits, LR 1.04.100 P
stands he, or sits he? ANT 1.05. 19
mark antony | in egypt sits at dinner, and will 2.01. 12
though my reason | sits in the wind against me. 3.10. 36

he sits 'mongst men like a /descended god; CYM 1.06.169
sits here like beauty's child, whom nature gat PER 2.02. 6
here love himself sits smiling. TNK 4.02. 14
and in his rolling eyes sits victory, | as if 4.02.108
all swoll'n with chafing, down adonis sits, VEN 325
within his thought her heavenly image sits, LUC 288
and in the self-same seat sits collatine. 289
but like still-pining tantalus he sits, | and 858
sits sin, to seize the souls that wander by him. 882
seems to point her out where she sits weeping, 1087
while philomela sits and sings, i sit and mark, PP 14.17
no love toward others in that bosom sits | that SON 9.13
bat, | and comely distant sits he by her side; LC 65

SIT'ST 1 FR 0.0001 REL FR 1 V 0 P
and start so often when thou sit'st alone? 1H4 2.03. 43

SITTING 22 FR 0.0024 REL FR 15 V 7 P
in an odd angle of the isle, and sitting, | his TMP 1.02.223
sitting on a bank, | weeping again the king my 1.02.390
he, sir, sitting (as i say) in a lower chair, MM 2.01.128 P
the manor-house, sitting with her upon the form, LLL 1.01.206 P
holds his poll-axe sitting on a close-stool, 5.02.577 P
both on one sampler, sitting on one cushion, MND 3.02.205
fourscore ducats at a sitting! MV 3.01.111 P
love, | who you saw sitting by me on the turf, AYL 3.04. 49
months married to her, sitting in my state — TN 2.05. 45 P
the which shall point you forth at every sitting WT 4.04.561
like seely beggars | who, sitting in the stocks, R2 5.05. 26
for every honor sitting on his helm | would they 1H4 3.02.142
goblet, sitting in my dolphin chamber, at the 2H4 2.01. 87 P
and here, sitting upon london stone, i charge 2H6 4.06. 2 P
long sitting to determine poor men's causes 4.07. 88
sitting in the sun under the dove-house wall. ROM 1.03. 27
is there no pity sitting in the clouds, | that 3.05.196
that guilty creatures sitting at a play | have HAM 2.02.589
amongst the rar'st of good ones), sitting sadly, CYM 5.05.160
sitting by a brook | with young adonis, lovely, PP 4. 1
venus, with adonis sitting by her, | under a 11. 1
month of may, | sitting in a pleasant shade, 20. 3

SITUATE 2 FR 0.0002 REL FR 1 V 1 P
there's nothing situate under heaven's eye | but ERR 2.01. 16
i know where it is situate. LLL 1.02.137 P

/SITUATION 1 FR 0.0001 REL FR 1 V 0 P
/the /plot /of /situation /and /the /model, 2H4 1.03. 51

SITUATION 1 FR 0.0001 REL FR 1 V 0 P
state | and situation with those dancing chips, SON 128.10

SITUATIONS 1 FR 0.0001 REL FR 0 V 1 P
macedon and monmouth, that the situations, look H5 4.07. 25 P

SIWARD 4 FR 0.0004 REL FR 4 V 0 P
aid | to wake northumberland and warlike siward, MAC 3.06. 31
old siward, with ten thousand warlike men 4.03.134
gracious england hath | lent us good siward, and 4.03.190
his uncle siward, and the good macduff. 5.02. 2

SIWARD'S 1 FR 0.0001 REL FR 1 V 0 P
there is siward's son, | and many unrough youths MAC 5.02. 9

SIX 58 FR 0.0065 REL FR 39 V 19 P
the time 'twixt six and now | must by us both be TMP 1.02.240
you bear witness that me have stay six or seven, WIV 2.03. 36 P
you bring me in the names of some six or seven, MM 2.01.272 P
and six or seven winters more respect | than a 3.01. 75
from whom my absence was not six months old ERR 1.01. 44
and it shall be written in eight and six. MND 3.01. 24 P
black monday last at six a' clock i' th' morning MV 2.05. 25 P
pay him six thousand, and deface the bond; 3.02.299
double six thousand, and then treble that, 3.02.300
for thy three thousand ducats here is six. 4.01. 84
if every ducat in six thousand ducats | were in 4.01. 85
in six thousand ducats | were in six parts, and 4.01. 86
the poor world is almost six thousand years old, AYL 4.01. 95 P
six score fat oxen standing in my stalls, | and SHR 2.01.358
one girth six times piec'd, and a woman's 3.02. 60 P
some six months since, my lord. AWW 1.02. 71
five or six thousand, but very weak and 4.03.131 P
"five or six thousand horse," i said — i will 4.03.148 P
of six preceding ancestors, that gem, 5.03.196
and five or six honest wives that were present. WT 4.04.270 P
six frozen winters spent, | return with welcome R2 1.03.211
ere the six years that he hath to spend | can 1.03.219
six years we banish him, and he shall go. 1.03.248
what is six winters? they are quickly gone. 1.03.260
and every thing is left at six and seven. 2.02.122
he that kills me some six or seven dozen of 1H4 2.04.103 P
some six or seven fresh men set upon us — 2.04.180 P
and when he was not six and twenty strong, 4.03. 56
"i will now take my leave of these six dry, 2H4 2.04. 7 P
laughter the wearing out of six fashions, which 5.01. 80 P
six thousand and two hundred good esquires; H5 1.01. 14
having full scarce six thousand in his troop, 1H6 1.01.112
i was six thousand strong | and that the french 4.01. 20
within six hours they will be at his aid. 4.04. 41
some six miles off the duke is with the soldiers 3H6 2.01.144
whom thou obey'dst thirty and six years, | and 3.03. 96
six or seven thousand is their utmost power. R3 5.03. 10
i think there be six richmonds in the field; 5.04. 11
at dunstable — six miles off | from ampthill, H8 4.01. 27
battles thrice six | i have seen, and heard of; COR 2.03.128
six of his labors you'ld have done, and sav'd 4.01. 18
worth six on him. 4.05.166 P
with six aufidiuses, or more, his tribe, | to 5.06.128
on forfeiture, my lord, six weeks | and past. TIM 2.02. 30
yet may your pains six months | be quite 4.03.144
for here have been | some six or seven, who did JC 2.01.277
sir, hath wager'd with him six barbary horses, HAM 5.02.147 P
as i take it, six french rapiers and poniards, 5.02.149 P
six barb'ry horses against six french swords, 5.02.160 P
six barb'ry horses against six french swords, 5.02.161 P
suits to his back, six shirts to his body — LR 3.04.136 P
some five or six and thirty of his knights, 3.07. 16
six kings already | show me the way of yielding. ANT 3.10. 33
i have yet | room for six scotches more. 4.07. 10
can it be six mile yet? CYM 4.02.293
pericles | come not home in twice six moons, PER 3.ch. 31
six braver spirits | than these they have TNK 4.02. 73
his age some six and thirty. 4.02.139

//SIX-GATED 1 FR 0.0001 REL FR 1 V 0 P
/priam's //six-gated /city, | /dardan /and TRO pr 15

SIX-OR-SEVEN-TIMES-HONOR'D 1 FR 0.0001 REL FR 0 V 1 P

six–or–seven–times–honor'd captain–general of TRO 3.03.277 P
SIXPENCE 12 FR 0.0013 REL FR 2 V 10 P
sixpence that i had a' we'nsday last | to pay ERR 1.02. 55
i will even take sixpence in earnest of the ADO 2.01. 40 P
thus hath he lost sixpence a day during his life MND 4.02. 20 P
he could not have scap'd sixpence a day. 4.02. 21 P
had not given him sixpence a day for playing 4.02. 22 P
sixpence a day in pyramus, or nothing. 4.02. 23 P
i sent thee sixpence for thy leman; TN 2.03. 25 P
come on, there is sixpence for you. 2.03. 31 P
in his life than "eight shillings and sixpence," 1H4 2.04. 25 P
a barber shall never earn sixpence out of it; 2H4 1.02. 25 P
well, there is sixpence to preserve thee. 2.02. 95 P
he held them sixpence all too dear, | with that OTH 2.03. 91
SIXPENNY 1 FR 0.0001 REL FR 0 V 1 P
land–rakers, no long–staff sixpenny strikers, 1H4 2.01. 74 P
SIXT 21 FR 0.0023 REL FR 16 V 5 P
on the sixt hour, at which time, my lord, | you TMP 5.01. 4
the sixt of july. your loving friend, benedick. ADO 1.01.283 P
sixt and lastly, they have belied a lady; 5.01.217 P
sixt and lastly, why they are committed; 5.01.221 P
about the sixt hour; LLL 1.01.235 P
the sixt age shifts | into the lean and AYL 2.07.157
the sixt, the lie with circumstance; 5.04. 95 P
henry the sixt, in infant bands crown'd king H5 ep 9
god save king henry, of that name the sixt! 1H6 4.01. 2
great marshal to henry the sixt | of all his 4.07. 70
the sixt was thomas of woodstock, duke of 2H6 2.02. 16
you told not how henry the sixt hath lost | all 3H6 3.03. 89
so stood the state when henry the sixt | was R3 2.03. 16
me, henry the sixt | did prophesy that richmond 4.02. 95
harry the sixt bids thee despair and die. 5.03.127
from each | the sixt part of his substance, to H8 1.02. 58
sixt part of each? 1.02. 94
and on the sixt to turn thy hated back | upon LR 1.01.175
at the sixt hour of morn, at noon, at midnight, CYM 1.03. 31
a sixt, a tenth, letting them thrive again | on 5.04. 20
and what's | the sixt and last, the which the PER 2.02. 40
SIXTEEN 12 FR 0.0013 REL FR 9 V 3 P
some sixteen months, and longer might have TGV 4.01. 21
i have to–night dispatch'd sixteen businesses, a AWW 4.03. 85 P
o'er sixteen years and leave the growth untried WT 4.01. 6
which lets go by some sixteen years, and makes 5.03. 31
on, | which sixteen winters cannot blow away, 5.03. 50
sixteen at least, my lord. 1H4 2.04.175 P
there are but sixteen hundred mercenaries; H5 4.08. 88
i have been begging sixteen years in court | (am H8 2.03. 82
at sixteen years, | when tarquin made a head for COR 2.02. 87
/son of sixteen, | pluck the lin'd crutch from TIM 4.01. 13
a speech of some dozen lines, or sixteen lines, HAM 2.02.541 P
have skipp'd from sixteen years of age to sixty, CYM 4.02.199
SIXTH *(see sixt)*
/SIXTY 1 FR 0.0001 REL FR 1 V 0 P
/sixty /and /nine, /that /wore | /their TRO pr 5
SIXTY 3 FR 0.0003 REL FR 3 V 0 P
i have sixty sails, caesar none better. ANT 3.07. 49
with all their sixty, fly and turn the rudder. 3.10. 3
have skipp'd from sixteen years of age to sixty, CYM 4.02.199
SIZ'D 1 FR 0.0001 REL FR 1 V 0 P
know, | and as my love is siz'd, my fear is so. HAM 3.02.170
SIZE 12 FR 0.0013 REL FR 9 V 3 P
you may know by my size that i have a kind of WIV 3.05. 12 P
word too great for any mouth of this age's size. AYL 3.02.227 P
of most monstrous size that must fit all demands AWW 2.02. 33 P
to shape my legs of an unequal size, | to 3H6 3.02.159
oppos'd, and with a malice | of as great size. H8 5.01.135
shall find him by his large and portly size. TRO 4.05.162
with all the size that verity | would without COR 5.02. 18
no big–bon'd men fram'd of the cyclops' size, TIT 4.03. 47
of this ingratitude | with any size of words. TIM 5.01. 66
our size of sorrow, | proportion'd to our cause, ANT 4.15. 4
were one such, | it's past the size of dreaming. 5.02. 97
in clamors of all size, both high and low. LC 21
SIZES 2 FR 0.0002 REL FR 1 V 1 P
he hath songs for man or woman, of all sizes; WT 4.04.192 P
to bandy hasty words, to scant my sizes, | and LR 2.04.175
SKAINS–MATES 1 FR 0.0001 REL FR 0 V 1 P
his flirt–gills, i am none of his skains–mates. ROM 2.04.154 P
SKEIN 2 FR 0.0002 REL FR 1 V 1 P
brav'd in mine own house with a skein of thread? SHR 4.03.110
thou idle immaterial skein of sleave–silk, thou TRO 5.01. 31 P
SKIES 12 FR 0.0013 REL FR 11 V 1 P
the skies, the fountains, every region near MND 4.01.116
and heaven's artillery thunder in the skies? SHR 1.02.204
the skies look grimly | and threaten present WT 3.03. 3
the skies are painted with unnumb'red sparks, JC 3.01. 63
the wrathful skies | gallow the very wanderers LR 3.02. 43
thy uncover'd body this extremity of the skies. 3.04.102 P
the great contention of /the sea and skies OTH 2.01. 92
as if another chase were in the skies. VEN 696
their mistress mounted through the empty skies, 1191
which, like a falcon tow'ring in the skies, LUC 506
my soul and body to the skies and ground, | my 1199
of rich–built ilion, that the skies were sorry, 1524
SKIFF'D 1 FR 0.0001 REL FR 1 V 0 P
they have skiff'd | torrents whose roaring TNK 1.03. 37
SKILL 61 FR 0.0069 REL FR 50 V 11 P
my mind | according to my shallow simple skill. TGV 1.02. 8
if not, to compass her i'll use my skill. 2.04.214
the frenchman hath good skill in his rapier. WIV 2.01.223 P
read it not truly, my ancient skill beguiles me; MM 4.02.155 P
go you with me, and i will use your skill. ADO 1.02. 26 P
if wounding, then it was to show my skill, LLL 4.01. 28
here stand i, lady, dart thy skill at me, 5.02.396
your frowns would teach my smiles such skill! MND 1.01.195
and touching now the point of human skill, 2.02.119
to show our simple skill, | that is the true 5.01.110
and by how much defense is better than no skill, AYL 3.03. 62 P
whose skill was almost as great as his honesty; AWW 1.01. 18 P
something in't | more than my father's skill, 1.03.243
skill infinite or monstrous desperate. 2.01.184
i have no skill in sense | to make distinction. 3.04. 39
sir, i have not much skill in /grass. 4.05. 21 P
into a most hideous opinion of his rage, skill, TN 3.04.194 P
strength, skill, and wrath can furnish man 3.04.232 P
or stupefied | or seeming so in skill — cannot, WT 2.01.166
have | as little skill to fear as i have purpose 4.04.152
they do confound their skill in covetousness, JN 4.02. 29
i would my skill were subject to thy curse. R2 3.04.103
i'll so offend, to make offense a skill, 1H4 1.02.216
honor hath no skill in surgery then? 5.01.133 P
so that skill in the weapon is nothing without 2H4 4.03.113 P
but first, to try her skill, | reignier, stand 1H6 1.02. 60
this means shall we sound what skill she hath. 1.02. 63
dame | (had i sufficient skill to utter them) 5.05. 13
fierce to their skill, and to their fierceness TRO 1.01. 8
were it a casque compos'd by vulcan's skill, 5.02.170
mean while, sir, with the little skill i have, TIT 2.01. 43
mine, and that thy skill be more | to blazon it, ROM 2.06. 25
our captain hath in every figure skill, | an TIM 5.03. 7
i have not the skill. HAM 3.02.362 P
we must with all our majesty and skill | both 4.01. 31
in mine ignorance | your skill shall, like a 5.02.256
and all the skill i have | remembers not these LR 4.07. 65
julius caesar | smil'd at their lack of skill, CYM 2.04. 22
yet 'tis greater skill | in a true hate, to pray 2.05. 33
let him show | his skill in the construction. 5.05.433
this philoten contends in skill | with absolute PER 4.ch. 30
i will use | my utmost skill in his recovery, 5.01. 76
though craving seriousness and skill, pass'd TNK 1.03. 28
mercy, all our best | their best skill tender! 1.04. 47
i then left my angle | to his own skill, came 4.01. 60
instruct this day | with military skill, that to 5.01. 58
the best hobby–horse | (if i have any skill) in 5.02. 53
which far exceeds his barren skill to show. LUC 81
with too much labor drowns for want of skill. 1099
while thou on tereus descants better skill. 1134
is form'd in them by force, by fraud, or skill. 1243
in him the painter labor'd with his skill | to 1506
and chid the painter for his wondrous skill, 1528
and you must live drawn by your own sweet skill. SON 16.14
for through the painter must you see his skill 24. 5
and folly (doctor–like) controlling skill, | and 66.10
some glory in their birth, some in their skill, 91. 1
and gives thy pen both skill and argument. 100. 8
that her skill | may time disgrace and wretched 126. 7
there is such strength and warrantise of skill 150. 7
weep, | he had the dialect and different skill, LC 125
SKILL–CONTENDING 1 FR 0.0001 REL FR 1 V 0 P
busy yourselves in skill–contending schools, LUC 1018
SKILL'D 3 FR 0.0003 REL FR 3 V 0 P
to sort some gentlemen well skill'd in music. TGV 3.02. 91
o thou well skill'd in curses, stay awhile, R3 4.04.116
but thou art deeper read, and better skill'd; TIT 4.01. 33
SKILLESS 4 FR 0.0004 REL FR 4 V 0 P
how features are abroad | i am skilless of; TMP 3.01. 53
your travel, | being skilless in these parts; TN 3.03. 9
night, | and skilless as unpractic'd infancy. TRO 1.01. 12
like powder in a skilless soldier's flask, | is ROM 3.03.132
SKILLET 1 FR 0.0001 REL FR 1 V 0 P
let housewives make a skillet of my helm, | and OTH 1.03.272
SKILLFUL 8 FR 0.0009 REL FR 5 V 3 P
the skillful shepherd pill'd me certain wands, MV 1.03. 84
he was skillful enough to have liv'd still, if AWW 1.01. 30 P
for thy assailant is quick, skillful, and deadly TN 3.04.225 P
he is indeed, sir, the most skillful, bloody, 3.04.266 P
for once allow'd the skillful pilot's charge? 3H6 5.04. 20
are strong, and skillful to their strength, TRO 1.01. 7
and it was dy'd in mummy which the skillful OTH 3.04. 74
mind where hangs a piece | of skillful painting, LUC 1367
SKILLFULLY 1 FR 0.0001 REL FR 1 V 0 P
art an old love–monger and speakest skillfully. LLL 2.01.254
SKILLS 3 FR 0.0003 REL FR 2 V 1 P
it skills not much, we'll fit him to our turn — SHR 3.02.132
so it skills not much when they are deliver'd. TN 5.01.288 P
it skills not greatly who impugns our doom. 2H6 3.01.281
SKIM 1 FR 0.0001 REL FR 1 V 0 P
skim milk, and sometimes labor in the quern, MND 2.01. 36
SKIMBLE–SKAMBLE 1 FR 0.0001 REL FR 1 V 0 P
and such a deal of skimble–skamble stuff | as 1H4 3.01.152
SKIM–MILK 1 FR 0.0001 REL FR 0 V 1 P
such a dish of skim–milk with so honorable an 1H4 2.03. 33 P
SKIN 21 FR 0.0023 REL FR 16 V 5 P
and tear the stain'd skin off my harlot brow, ERR 2.02.136
if the skin were parchment, and the blows you 3.01. 13
in faith, honest as the skin between his brows. ADO 3.05. 12 P
and there the snake throws her enamell'd skin, MND 2.01.255
his leather skin and horns to wear. AYL 4.02. 11
because his painted skin contents the eye? SHR 4.03.178
friar's mouth, nay, as the pudding to his skin. AWW 2.02. 27 P
not till i sheathe it in a murtherer's skin. JN 4.03. 80
do wound the bark, the skin of our fruit–trees, R2 3.04. 58
my skin hangs about me like an old lady's loose 1H4 3.03. 3 P
the man that once did sell the lion's skin H5 4.03. 93
away, the skin is good for your broken coxcomb. 5.01. 54 P
his skin is surely lent him, | for he's inclin'd 2H6 3.01. 77
show me one scar character'd on thy skin: 3.01.300
that of the skin of an innocent lamb should be 4.02. 79 P
his silver skin lac'd with his golden blood, MAC 2.03.112
it will but skin and film the ulcerous place, HAM 3.04.147
this contentious storm | invades us to the skin; LR 3.04. 7
nor scar that whiter skin of hers than snow, OTH 5.02. 4
admired | her azure veins, her alablaster skin, LUC 419
like unshorn velvet on that termless skin, LC 94
SKIN–COAT 1 FR 0.0001 REL FR 1 V 0 P
i'll smoke your skin–coat and i catch you right. JN 2.01.139
SKINNY 1 FR 0.0001 REL FR 1 V 0 P
her choppy finger laying | upon her skinny lips. MAC 1.03. 45
SKIN'S 1 FR 0.0001 REL FR 1 V 0 P
ay, here's a deer whose skin's a keeper's fee: 3H6 3.01. 22
SKINS 7 FR 0.0008 REL FR 5 V 2 P
toe to crown he'll fill our skins with pinches, TMP 4.01.233
your hearts are mighty, your skins are whole, WIV 3.01.109 P
in itself, | that skins the vice o' th' top. MM 2.02.136
he shall have the skins of our enemies, to make 2H6 4.02. 23 P
and on their skins, as on the bark of trees, TIT 5.01.138
stuff'd, and other skins | of ill–shap'd fishes, ROM 5.01. 43
fear their gay skins with thought of their sharp STM III 18
SKIP 8 FR 0.0009 REL FR 6 V 2 P
have made you four tall fellows skip like rats. WIV 2.01.229 P
/fairies, skip hence — | i have forsworn his MND 2.01. 61
to skip o'er the meshes of good counsel the MV 1.02. 20 P
let not thy sword skip one. TIM 4.03.111
thy heels | and skip when thou point'st out? 4.03.225
biting falchion | i would have made /them skip. LR 5.03.278
and with a dropping industry they skip | from PER 4.01. 62
howsoev'r | you skip them in me, and with them, TNK 3.01. 52
SKIPP'D 2 FR 0.0002 REL FR 2 V 0 P
have skipp'd from sixteen years of age to sixty, CYM 4.02.199
have skipp'd thy flame — at seventy thou canst TNK 5.01. 87
SKIPPER 1 FR 0.0001 REL FR 1 V 0 P
skipper, stand back! SHR 2.01.339
SKIPPING 5 FR 0.0005 REL FR 4 V 1 P
all wanton as a child, skipping and vain, LLL 5.02.761
cold drops of modesty | thy skipping spirit, MV 2.02.187
with me to make one in so skipping a dialogue. TN 1.05.201 P
the skipping king, he ambled up and down, | with 1H4 3.02. 60
compell'd these skipping kerns to trust their MAC 1.02. 30
SKIPS 1 FR 0.0001 REL FR 1 V 0 P
and as she fetched breath, away he skips, | and PP 11.11
SKIRMISH 2 FR 0.0002 REL FR 1 V 1 P
meet but there's a skirmish of wit between them. ADO 1.01. 63 P
and goliases | it sendeth forth to skirmish. 1H6 1.02. 34
SKIRMISHES 1 FR 0.0001 REL FR 1 V 0 P
famish'd, | or with light skirmishes enfeebled. 1H6 1.04. 69
SKIRR 2 FR 0.0002 REL FR 2 V 0 P
and make them skirr away, as swift as stones H5 4.07. 61
send out moe horses, skirr the country round, MAC 5.03. 35
SKIRT 1 FR 0.0001 REL FR 1 V 0 P
will't not do | rarely upon a skirt, wench? TNK 2.02.130
SKIRTED 1 FR 0.0001 REL FR 1 V 0 P
thrift, you rogues — myself and skirted page. WIV 1.03. 84
SKIRTS 6 FR 0.0006 REL FR 2 V 4 P
coat, there is but three skirts for yourself, in WIV 1.01. 29 P
side sleeves, and skirts, round underborne with ADO 3.04. 21 P
here in the skirts of the forest, like fringe AYL 3.02.336 P
and to the skirts of this wild wood he came; 5.04.159
loose–bodied gown, sew me in the skirts of it, SHR 4.03.136 P
hath in the skirts of norway here and there HAM 1.01. 97
/SKITTISH 1 FR 0.0001 REL FR 1 V 0 P
/now /expectation, /tickling /skittish /spirits, TRO pr 20
SKITTISH 2 FR 0.0002 REL FR 2 V 0 P
are, | unstaid and skittish in all motions else, TN 2.04. 18
how some men creep in skittish fortune's hall, TRO 3.03.134
SKOGAN'S *(see scoggin's)*
SKULKING 1 FR 0.0001 REL FR 1 V 0 P
skulking in corners? WT 1.02.289
SKULL 11 FR 0.0012 REL FR 4 V 7 P
or with a log | batter his skull, or paunch him TMP 3.02. 90
brains, | now useless, /boil'd within thy skull! 5.01. 60
the skull that bred them in the sepulchre. MV 3.02. 96
whose skull jove cram with brains! TN 1.05.113 P
lie | in earth as quiet as thy father's skull; R2 4.01. 69
if all our wits were to issue out of one skull, COR 2.03. 22 P
that skull had a tongue in it, and could sing HAM 5.01. 75 P
why may not that be the skull of a lawyer? 5.01. 99 P
here's a skull now hath lien you i' th' earth 5.01.173 P
this same skull, sir, was, sir, yorick's skull, 5.01.181 P
was, sir, yorick's skull, the king's jester. 5.01.181
SKULLS 5 FR 0.0005 REL FR 5 V 0
the field of golgotha and dead men's skulls. R2 4.01.144
some lay in dead men's skulls, and, in the holes R3 1.04. 29
with reeky shanks and yellow /chapless skulls; ROM 4.01. 83
lends his light | to grubs and eyeless skulls? 5.03.126
havoc in vast field | unearthed skulls proclaim, TNK 5.01. 52
SKY 48 FR 0.0054 REL FR 42 V 6
the sky, it seems, would pour down stinking TMP 1.02. 3
thou thyself dost air — the queen o' th' sky, 4.01. 70
the sun begins to gild the western sky, | and TGV 5.01. 1
let the sky rain potatoes; WIV 5.05. 18
but hath his bound in earth, in sea, in sky. ERR 2.01. 17
like a jewel in the ear of caelo, the sky, the LLL 4.02. 5
like a demigod here sit i in the sky, | and 4.03. 77
sever themselves and madly sweep the sky, | so, MND 3.02. 23
shine as gloriously | as the venus of the sky. 3.02.107
my soul is in the sky. 5.01.303
freeze, freeze, thou bitter sky, | that dost not AYL 2.07.184
maids, but the sky changes when they are wives. 4.01.149
the fated sky | gives us free scope, only doth AWW 1.01.217
you'll be found, | be you beneath the sky. WT 1.02.180
the covering sky is nothing, bohemia nothing, 1.02.294
not to say it is a sea, for it is now the sky — 3.03. 85
now, by the sky that hangs above our heads, | i JN 2.01.397
some airy devil hovers in the sky | and pours 3.02. 2
no natural exhalation in the sky, | no scope of 3.04.153
so foul a sky clears not without a storm, | pour 4.02.108
since the more fair and crystal is the sky, R2 1.01. 41
men judge by the complexion of the sky | the 3.02.194
and i in the clear sky of fame o'ershine you as 2H4 4.03. 51
and yet my sky shall not want. H5 3.07. 73
brandish your crystal tresses in the sky, | and 1H6 1.01. 3
two talbots, winged through the lither sky, | in 4.07. 21
and when the dusky sky began to rob | my 2H6 3.02.104
but sever'd in a pale clear–shining sky. 3H6 2.01. 28
i will not think but they ascend the sky, | and R3 1.03.286
the sky doth frown and low'r upon our army. 5.03.283
divides more wider than the sky and earth, | and TRO 5.02.149
whose smoke like incense doth perfume the sky. TIT 1.01.145
now, by the burning tapers of the sky, | that 4.02. 89
this disturbed sky | is not to walk in. JC 1.03. 39
where the norweyan banners flout the sky | and MAC 1.02. 49
outface | the winds and persecutions of the sky. LR 2.03. 12
what e'er the ocean pales, or sky inclips, | is ANT 2.07. 68
nobler sir ne'er liv'd | 'twixt sky and ground. CYM 5.05.146
strengthless doves will draw me through the sky, VEN 153
like misty vapors when they blot the sky, 184
flash'd forth fire, as lightning from the sky, 348
and as the bright sun glorifies the sky, | so is 485
look how a bright star shooteth from the sky, 815
which triumph'd in that sky of his delight; LUC 12
of those fair suns set in her mistress' sky, 1230
thin winding breath, which purl'd up to the sky. 1407
blue circles stream'd, like rainbows in the sky. 1587
cheered and check'd even by the self–same sky, SON 15. 6
SKY–ASPIRING 1 FR 0.0001 REL FR 1 V 0
pride | of sky–aspiring and ambitious thoughts, R2 1.03.130
SKYEY 1 FR 0.0001 REL FR 1 V 0
thou art, | servile to all the skyey influences, MM 3.01. 9
SKYISH 1 FR 0.0001 REL FR 1 V 0
pelion, or the skyish head | of blue olympus. HAM 5.01.253
SKY–PLANTED 1 FR 0.0001 REL FR 1 V 0
sky–planted, batters all rebelling coasts? CYM 5.04. 96
SLAB 1 FR 0.0001 REL FR 1 V 0
by a drab, | make the gruel thick and slab. MAC 4.01. 32

SLACK 13 FR 0.0014 REL FR 11 V 2 P
what a beast am i to slack it! WIV 3.04.111 P
sir, i shall not be slack; SHR 1.02.273
bedford, if thou be slack, i'll fight it out. 1H6 1.01. 99
woman, i will not be slack | to play my part in 2H6 1.02. 66
the duke shall know how slack you have been! R3 1.04.275
that their negotiations all must slack, TRO 3.03. 24
so, | and i am nothing slow to slack his haste. ROM 4.01. 3
if you come slack of former services, | you LR 1.03. 9
if then they chanc'd to slack ye, | we could 2.04.245
say that they slack their duties, | and pour our OTH 4.03. 87
slack the bolins there! PER 3.01. 43 P
alack that leonine was so slack, so slow! 4.02. 64
shall serve, be thou not slack | to proffer, PP 18.23
SLACKLY 2 FR 0.0002 REL FR 2 V 0 P
so slackly guarded, and the search so slow, CYM 1.01. 64
though slackly braided in loose negligence. LC 35
SLACKNESS 2 FR 0.0002 REL FR 2 V 0 P
as interpreters | of my behind–hand slackness. WT 5.01.151
the best of men, | to taunt at slackness. ANT 3.07. 27
/SLAIN 1 FR 0.0001 REL FR 0 V 1 P
/that /the /duke /of /cornwall /was /so /slain? LR 4.07. 85 P
SLAIN 136 FR 0.0153 REL FR 133 V 3 P
if thou hast slain lysander in his sleep, MND 3.02. 47
hast thou slain him then? 3.02. 66
and finds his trusty thisby's mantle slain; 5.01.145
away, breath, | i am slain by a fair cruel maid. TN 2.04. 54
divers dear friends slain? JN 3.04. 7
he count melune is slain; 5.05. 10
and breathest, | yet art thou slain in him. R2 1.02. 25
now some have been depos'd, some slain in war, 3.02.157
fear, and be slain — no worse can come to fight 3.02.183
but whether they be ta'en or slain we hear not. 5.06. 4
of prisoners' ransom, and of soldiers slain, 1H4 2.03. 54
three knights upon our party slain to–day, | a 5.05. 6
the noble percy slain, and all his men | upon 5.05. 19
prince harry slain outright, and both the blunts 2H4 1.01. 16
f he be slain, /say /so; 1.01. 96
had three times slain th' appearance of the king 1.01.128
thousand french | that in the field lie slain; H5 4.08. 81
s talbot slain then? 1H6 1.01.141
years | wasted our country, slain our citizens, 2.03. 41
too late comes rescue, he is ta'en or slain; 4.04. 42
fly, to revenge my death, if i be slain. 4.05. 18
you cannot witness for me, being slain. 4.05. 43
s talbot slain, the frenchmen's only scourge, 4.07. 77
all will be ours, now bloody talbot's slain. 4.07. 96
which i will win from france, or else be slain. 2H6 1.01.213
but jove was never slain, as thou shalt be. 4.01. 49
ord, and picardy | hath slain their governors, 4.01. 89
how now? is jack cade slain? 4.05. 1
no, my lord, nor likely to be slain; 4.05. 2 P
o, i am slain! 4.10. 60 P
famine and no other hath slain me. 4.10. 60 P
s't cade that i have slain, that monstrous 4.10. 66
were by the swords of common soldiers slain. 3H6 1.01. 9
s either slain or wounded dangerous; 1.01. 11
but when the duke is slain, they'll quickly fly. 1.01. 69
god is just, | he be as miserably slain as i. 1.03. 42
my uncles both are slain in rescuing me; 1.04. 2
had he been slain, we should have heard the news 2.01. 5
when as the noble duke of york was slain, | your 2.01. 46
of sweet young rutland, by rough clifford slain. 2.01. 63
thou hast slain | the flow'r of europe for his 2.01. 70
o valiant lord, the duke of york is slain! 2.01.100
lady's husband, sir richard grey, was slain, 3.02. 2
then is my sovereign slain? 4.04. 6
ay, almost slain, for he is taken prisoner, 4.04. 7
his realm a slaughter–house, his subjects slain, 5.04. 78
then say they were not slain. R3 1.02. 89
nay, he is dead, and slain by edward's hands. 1.02. 92
in margaret's battle at saint albons slain? 1.03.129
say, | for i repent me that the duke is slain. 1.04.278
you speak as if that i had slain my cousins! 4.04.222
you sleep in peace, the tyrant being slain; 5.03.256
his horse is slain, and all on foot he fights, 5.04. 4
we have i slain to–day in stead of him. 5.04. 12
what men of name are slain on either side? 5.05. 12
carrion weight, | a troyan hath been slain. TRO 4.01. 73
polyxenes is slain, | amphimachus and thoas 5.05. 11
patroclus ta'en or slain, and palamedes | sore 5.05. 13
'achilles hath the mighty hector slain!" 5.08. 14
achilles! achilles! hector's slain! achilles! 5.09. 3
the bruit is, hector's slain, and by achilles. 5.09. 4
starve we out the night — | hector is slain. 5.10. 3
slain, sir, doubtless. COR 1.04. 48
alms empoison'd, | and with his charity slain. 5.06. 11
whose children he hath slain, their base throats 5.06. 52
sleep in peace, slain in your country's wars! TIT 1.01. 91
and for their brethren slain | religiously they 1.01.123
knighted in field, slain manfully in arms, | in 1.01.196
in wrongful quarrel you have slain your son. 1.01.293
in a bad quarrel slain a virtuous son. 1.01.342
none basely slain in brawls. 1.01.353
thee life when well he might have slain thee, 2.03.159
so long, | poor i was slain when bassianus died. 2.03.171
why hast thou slain thine only daughter thus? 5.03. 55
he /gone in triumph, and mercutio slain! ROM 3.01.122
the citizens are up, and tybalt slain. 3.01.133
there lies the man, slain by young romeo, | that 3.01.144
tybalt, here slain, whom romeo's hand did slay! 3.01.152
could draw to part them, was stout tybalt slain; 3.01.173
hath romeo slain himself? 3.02. 45
ay, | if he be slain, say ay, or if not, no. 3.02. 50
my husband lives that tybalt would have slain, 3.02.105
tybalt's dead that would have slain my husband. 3.02.106
'banished," | hath slain ten thousand tybalts. 3.02.114
tybalt, romeo, juliet, | all slain, all dead: 3.02.124
hast thou slain tybalt? 3.03.116
two, | for hark you, tybalt being slain so late, 3.04. 24
beguil'd, divorced, wronged, spited, slain! 4.05. 55
o, i am slain! 5.03. 72
here lies the county slain, | and juliet 5.03.174
sovereign, here lies the county paris slain, 5.03.195
and slain in fight many of your enemies. TIM 3.05. 63
he is slain. JC 5.03. 93
he is or ta'en or slain. 5.05. 3
those that macbeth hath slain. MAC 2.04. 23
and it hath been | the sword of our slain kings. 4.03. 87
if thou beest slain and with no stroke of mine, 5.07. 15
o, i am slain. HAM 3.04. 25
hamlet in madness hath polonius slain, | and 4.01. 34
tomb enough and continent | to hide the slain? 4.04. 65
first, her father slain; 4.05. 79
that he which hath your noble father slain 4.07. 4
/hamlet, thou art slain. 5.02.313
o, i am slain! LR 3.07. 81
slain by his servant, going to put out | the 4.02. 71
slave, thou hast slain me. 4.06.246
though in the trade of war i have slain men, OTH 1.02. 1
o, i am slain. 5.01. 26
he that lies slain here, cassio, | was my dear 5.01.101
he's almost slain, and roderigo quite dead. 5.01.114
found in the pocket of the slain roderigo, | and 5.02.309
wept | when at philippi he found brutus slain. ANT 3.02. 56
and that slain men | should solder up the rift. 3.04. 31
mardian, go tell him i have slain myself; 4.13. 7
when i have slain thee with my proper hand, CYM 4.02. 97
a good, | that here by mountaineers lies slain. 4.02.370
my master since | i wrote him imogen was slain. 4.03. 37
how they wound | some slain before, some dying, 5.03. 47
country's cause | fell bravely and were slain, 5.04. 72
here they stand martyrs, slain in cupid's wars; PER 1.01. 38
whom they have ravish'd must by me be slain. 4.01.102
the winds | with stench of our slain lords. TNK 1.01. 47
that hast slain | the scythe–tusk'd boar; 1.01. 78
duke, think | what beds our slain kings have! 1.01.140
in me hath grief slain fear, and, but for one 3.02. 5
love made those hollows, if himself were slain, VEN 243
for on the grass she lies as she were slain, 473
sith in thy pride so fair a hope is slain. 762
for he being dead, with him is beauty slain, 1019
"'tis true, 'tis true, thus was adonis slain: 1111
i fear'd by tarquin's falchion to be slain, LUC 1046
annoy, | sad souls are slain in merry company, 1110
to slay herself, that should have slain her foe. 1827
number there in love was slain. PHT 28
presume not on thy heart when mine is slain, SON 22.13
yet do not so, but since i am near slain, | kill 139.13
SLAK'D *(also yslacked)*
SLAK'D 1 FR 0.0001 REL FR 1 V 0 P
slak'd, not suppress'd, for standing by her side LUC 425
SLAKE 1 FR 0.0001 REL FR 1 V 0 P
it could not slake mine ire nor ease my heart. 3H6 1.03. 29
SLAKETH 1 FR 0.0001 REL FR 1 V 0 P
no flood by raining slaketh. LUC 1677
SLANDER 47 FR 0.0053 REL FR 39 V 8 P
the best way is to slander valentine | with TGV 3.02. 31
then you must undertake to slander him. 3.02. 38
him, | your slander never can endamage him; 3.02. 43
my nature never in the fight | to do in slander. MM 1.03. 43
ear, you might have your action of slander too. 2.01.181 P
you set these women on to slander lord angelo? 5.01.289 P
slander to th' state! | away with him to prison. 5.01.322
for slander lives upon succession, | for ever ERR 3.01.105
a voice | to slander music any more than once. ADO 2.03. 45
did confirm any slander that don john had made, 3.03.158 P
shall on her behalf | change slander to remorse; 4.01.211
then, with public accusation, uncover'd slander, 4.01.305 P
thy slander hath gone through and through her 5.01. 68
that lie and cog and flout, deprave and slander, 5.01. 95
brother incens'd me to slander the lady hero, 5.01.236 P
she died, my lord, but whiles her slander liv'd. 5.04. 66
slander her love, and he forgave it her. MV 5.01. 22
fortune, and prevents the slander of his wife. AYL 4.01. 61 P
there is no slander in an allow'd fool, though TN 1.05. 94 P
hopeful son's, his babe's, betrays to slander, WT 2.03. 86
till i have told this slander of his blood | how R2 1.01.113
a partial slander sought i to avoid, | and in 1.03.241
wrought | a deed of slander with thy fatal hand 5.06. 35
do me no slander, douglas. 1H4 4.03. 8
his behalf | is slander to your royal dignity. 2H6 3.02.209
thou slander of thy heavy mother's womb! R3 1.03.230
o, do not slander him, for he is kind. 1.04.241
and, for more slander to thy dismal seat, | we 3.03. 13
slander myself as false to edward's bed, | throw 4.04.208
but that slander, sir, | is found a truth now; H8 2.01.153
you, and you slander | the helms o' th' state, COR 1.01. 76
my reputation stain'd | with tybalt's slander — ROM 3.01.112
that is no slander, sir, which is a truth, | and 4.01. 33
have you so slander any moment leisure | as to HAM 1.03.133
if thou dost slander her and torture me, | never OTH 3.03.368
the purest of their wives | is foul as slander. 4.02. 19
some office, | have not devis'd this slander. 4.02.133
no slander, they steal hearts. ANT 2.06.101 P
after the slander of most stepmothers, CYM 1.01. 71
no, 'tis slander, | whose edge is sharper than 3.04. 33
of the grave | this viperous slander enters. 3.04. 39
the leaf of eglantine, whom not to slander, 4.02.223
fear not slander, censure rash. 4.02.272
i did but act, he's author of thy slander. VEN 1006
my blood shall wash the slander of mine ill; LUC 1207
good, slander doth but approve | /thy worth the SON 70. 5
and thence this slander, as i think, proceeds. 131.14
SLANDER'D 6 FR 0.0006 REL FR 5 V 1 P
as the sentence | that you have slander'd so? MM 2.04.110
in the height a villain, that hath slander'd, ADO 4.01.302 P
and she is dead, slander'd to death by villains, 5.01. 88
but once he slander'd me with bastardy. JN 1.01. 74
and you have slander'd nature in my form, 4.02.256
and beauty slander'd with a bastard shame, | for SON 127. 4
SLANDERED 1 FR 0.0001 REL FR 1 V 0 P
then let not him be slandered with revolt. 1H4 1.03.112
SLANDERER 4 FR 0.0004 REL FR 4 V 0 P
thou monstrous slanderer of heaven and earth! JN 2.01.173
of heaven and earth, | call not me slanderer! 2.01.175
which, slanderer, he imitation calls, | he TRO 1.03.150
o, fie upon thee, slanderer! OTH 2.01.113
SLANDERERS 2 FR 0.0002 REL FR 2 V 0 P
have well determin'd | upon these slanderers. MM 5.01.259
bad, | mad slanderers by mad ears believed be. SON 140.12
SLANDERING 1 FR 0.0001 REL FR 1 V 0 P
slandering a prince deserves it. MM 5.01.524
SLANDEROUS 5 FR 0.0005 REL FR 4 V 1 P
and one that is as slanderous as sathan? WIV 5.05.155 P
can tie the gall up in the slanderous tongue? MM 3.02.188
"done to death by slanderous tongues | was the ADO 5.03. 3
call him a slanderous coward, and a villain, R2 1.01. 61
with the attainder of his slanderous lips. 4.01. 24
SLANDER'S 4 FR 0.0004 REL FR 4 V 0 P
to the soul with slander's venom'd spear, | the R2 1.01.171
shall my name with slander's tongue be wounded, 2H6 3.02. 68
i give | a badge of fame to slander's livery, LUC 1054
for slander's mark was ever yet the fair; SON 70. 2
SLANDERS 16 FR 0.0018 REL FR 11 V 5 P
thy slanders i forgive, and therewithal | remit MM 5.01.519
free from these slanders and this open shame! ERR 4.04. 67
his gift is in devising impossible slanders. ADO 2.01.138 P
and truly i'll devise some honest slanders | to 3.01. 84
secondarily, they are slanders; 5.01.217 P
hostess, and he slanders thee most grossly. 1H4 3.03.131 P
upon my tongues continual slanders ride, | the 2H4 in 6
you must learn to know such slanders of the age, H5 3.06. 80 P
that slanders me with murther's crimson badge. 2H6 3.02.200
that slanders him with cowardice | whose frown 3H6 1.04. 47
the envious slanders of her false accusers; R3 1.03. 26
a slave whose gall coins slanders like a mint, TRO 1.03.193
slanders, sir; HAM 2.02.196 P
when slanders do not live in tongues; LR 3.02. 89
nice longing, slanders, mutability, | all faults CYM 2.05. 26
on | the low posthumus slanders so her judgment 3.05. 76
SLAND'RED 2 FR 0.0002 REL FR 1 V 1 P
she is wrong'd, she is sland'red, she is undone. ADO 4.01.312 P
thy face is mine, and thou hast sland'red it. ROM 4.01. 35
SLAND'RING 1 FR 0.0001 REL FR 1 V 0 P
lack, | sland'ring creation with a false esteem: SON 127.12
SLAND'ROUS 8 FR 0.0009 REL FR 8 V 0 P
o sland'rous world! SHR 2.01.253
ugly, and sland'rous to thy mother's womb, JN 3.01. 44
i was provoked by her sland'rous tongue, | that R3 1.02. 97
to ease ourselves of divers sland'rous loads, JC 4.01. 20
and hath as oft a sland'rous epitaph | as record CYM 3.03. 52
the crow, the sland'rous cuckoo, nor | the TNK 1.01. 19
to sland'rous tongues and wretched hateful days? LUC 161
as sland'rous deathsman to so base a slave? 1001
SLASH 2 FR 0.0002 REL FR 1 V 1 P
i'll slash, i'll do it by the sword. LLL 5.02.695 P
here's snip and nip and cut and slish and slash, SHR 4.03. 90
SLAUGHTER 31 FR 0.0035 REL FR 29 V 2 P
a wolf, who, hang'd for human slaughter, | even MV 4.01.134
dy'd in the dying slaughter of their foes. JN 2.01.323
with slaughter coupled to the name of kings. 2.01.349
you would have sold your king to slaughter, H5 2.02.170
ran from the battle ha' done this slaughter. 4.07. 7 P
of loss, of slaughter, and discomfiture: 1H6 1.01. 59
after the slaughter of so many peers, | so many 5.04.103
will suspect 'twas he that made the slaughter? 2H6 3.02.190
i wear no knife to slaughter sleeping men, | but 3.02.197
how will my wife for slaughter of my son | shed 3H6 2.05.105
i say not, slaughter him, | for i intend but 4.02. 24
ay, and for much more slaughter after this. 5.06. 59
that didst unworthy slaughter upon others. R3 1.02. 88
provoke us hither now to slaughter thee. 1.04.225
waiting vassals | have done a drunken slaughter, 2.01.123
the slaughter of the prince that ow'd that crown 4.04.142
sons of the royal blood | for thee to slaughter. 4.04.201
so she may live unscarr'd of bleeding slaughter, 4.04.210
nothing been but shapes and forms of slaughter. TRO 5.03. 12
have added slaughter to the sword of traitors. JC 5.01. 55
but for mine, | fell slaughter on their souls. MAC 4.03.227
especially when he speaks of priam's slaughter. HAM 2.02.448 P
such a daughter, | should sure to the slaughter, LR 1.04.319
the country base than to commit such slaughter, CYM 5.03. 20
great the slaughter is | here made by th' roman; 5.03. 78
their good souls may be appeas'd with slaughter 5.05. 72
might stand peerless by this slaughter. PER 4.ch. 40
such a piece of slaughter | the sun and moon 4.03. 2
on whom foul death hath made this slaughter. 4.04. 37
to slay the tiger that doth live by slaughter, LUC 955
murther straight, and then i'll slaughter thee, 1634
/SLAUGHTER'D 1 FR 0.0001 REL FR 1 V 0 P
here is a friar, and /slaughter'd romeo's man, ROM 5.03.199
SLAUGHTER'D 6 FR 0.0006 REL FR 6 V 0 P
most of the rest slaughter'd or took likewise. 1H6 1.01.147
live whose fathers thou hast slaughter'd, R3 4.04.391
the father rashly slaughter'd his own son, | the 5.05. 25
as that the villain lives which slaughter'd him. ROM 3.05. 79
upon his body that hath slaughter'd him! 3.05.102
your wife, and babes, | savagely slaughter'd. MAC 4.03.205
SLAUGHTERED 5 FR 0.0005 REL FR 5 V 0 P
shall our feast be kept with slaughtered men? JN 3.01.302
from the wounds of slaughtered englishmen, | the R2 3.03. 44
and slaughtered those that were the means to R3 5.03.249
but must my sons be slaughtered in the streets TIT 1.01.112
all on a heap, like to a slaughtered lamb, | in 2.03.223
SLAUGHTERER 1 FR 0.0001 REL FR 1 V 0 P
me, as that slaughterer doth | which giveth many 1H6 2.05.109
SLAUGHTER–HOUSE 7 FR 0.0008 REL FR 6 V 1 P
th' uncleanly savors of a slaughter–house, | for JN 4.03.112
bearing it to the bloody slaughter–house, | even 2H6 3.01.212
if thou hadst been in thine own slaughter–house; 4.03. 5 P
his realm a slaughter–house, his subjects slain, 3H6 5.04. 78
as loath to bear me to the slaughter–house. R3 3.04. 86
go hie thee, hie thee from this slaughter–house, 4.01. 43
but this no slaughter–house no tool imparteth, LUC 1039
SLAUGHTER–MAN 3 FR 0.0003 REL FR 3 V 0 P
had he been slaughter–man to all my kin, | i 3H6 1.04.169
for this proud mock i'll be thy slaughter–man, TIT 4.04. 58
are now each one the slaughter–man of twenty. CYM 5.03. 49
SLAUGHTER–MEN 2 FR 0.0002 REL FR 2 V 0 P
jewry | at herod's bloody–hunting slaughter–men. H5 3.03. 41
and join'st with them will be thy slaughter–men. 1H6 3.03. 75
SLAUGHTEROUS 1 FR 0.0001 REL FR 1 V 0 P
direness, familiar to my slaughterous thoughts, MAC 5.05. 14
SLAUGHTER'S 1 FR 0.0001 REL FR 1 V 0 P
and over–stain'd | with slaughter's pencil — JN 3.01.237
SLAUGHTERS 4 FR 0.0004 REL FR 4 V 0 P
slaughters a thousand waiting upon that. WT 1.02. 93
and ruthless slaughters as are daily seen | by 1H6 5.04.161
from all the slaughters, wretch, that thou hast R3 4.04.139
of accidental judgments, casual slaughters, | of HAM 5.02.382
SLAUGHT'RED 9 FR 0.0010 REL FR 9 V 0 P
in suff'ring thus thy brother to be slaught'red, R2 1.02. 30

here is the number of the slaught'red french. H5 4.08. 74
and have our bodies slaught'red by thy foes. 1H6 3.01.101
but only slaught'red by the ireful arm | of 3H6 2.01. 57
our slaught'red friends the tackles; 5.04. 15
wife to thy edward, to thy slaught'red son, R3 1.02. 10
is romeo slaught'red? ROM 3.02. 65
a lanthorn, slaught'red youth; 5.03. 84
shed for the slaught'red husband by the wife; LUC 1376
SLAUGHT'RING 3 FR 0.0003 REL FR 3 V 0 P
to hold your slaught'ring hands and keep the 1H6 3.01. 87
to be /adjudg'd some direful slaught'ring death, TIT 5.03.144
lolling the tongue with slaught'ring — having CYM 5.03. 8
/SLAVE 2 FR 0.0002 REL FR 2 V 0 P
/made /glory /base, /and /sovereignty /a /slave; R2 4.01.251
/did /him /service | /improper /for /a /slave. LR 5.03.222
SLAVE 131 FR 0.0148 REL FR 112 V 19 P
thou, my slave, | as thou report'st thyself, was TMP 1.02.270
we'll visit caliban my slave, who never | yields 1.02.308
slave! 1.02.313
thou poisonous slave, got by the devil himself 1.02.319
thou most lying slave, | whom stripes may move, 1.02.344
abhorred slave, | which any print of goodness 1.02.351
so, slave, hence! 1.02.374
to make me slave to it, and for your sake | am i 3.01. 66
overweening slave! TGV 3.01.157
for reading my letter — an unmannerly slave, 3.01.383 P
a slave, that still an end turns me to shame! 4.04. 62
what mistress, slave, hast thou? ERR 1.02. 87
i'll to the centaur to go seek this slave; 1.02.104
neither my husband nor the slave return'd, 2.01. 1
go back again, thou slave, and fetch him home. 2.01. 75
back, slave, or i will break thy pate across. 2.01. 78
and the heedful slave | is wand'red forth, in 2.02. 2
to counterfeit thus grossly with your slave, 2.02.169
thou drunken slave, i sent thee for a rope, 4.01. 96
hie thee, slave, be gone! 4.01.107
this pernicious slave, | forsooth, took on him 5.01.242
art thou the slave that with thy breath hast ADO 5.01.263
come, you transgressing slave, away. LLL 1.02.154 P
o, stay, slave; 3.01.151 P
hark, slave, it is but this: 3.01.162 P
you have among you many a purchas'd slave, MV 4.01. 90
should have, | and i to live and die her slave." AYL 3.02.154
and let me be a slave, t' achieve that maid SHR 1.01.219
to make a bondmaid and a slave of me — | that i 2.01. 2
go get thee gone, thou false deluding slave, 4.03. 31
the mere word's a slave | debosh'd on every tomb AWW 2.03.137
what a past–saving slave is this! 4.03.138 P
he's quoted for a most perfidious slave, | with 5.03.205
pronounce thee a gross lout, a mindless slave, WT 1.02.301
where is that slave, thy brother? JN 1.01.222
thou slave, thou wretch, thou coward! 3.01.115
thou cold–blooded slave, | hast thou not spoke 3.01.123
am i rome's slave? 5.02. 97
a king, woe's slave, shall kingly woe obey. R2 3.02.210
villain, traitor, slave! 5.02. 72
what a slave art thou to hack thy sword as thou 1H4 2.04.261 P
you slave, for what? 2H4 2.04.144 P
ah, rascally slave! 2.04.222 P
a rascal bragging slave! 2.04.228 P
base is the slave that pays. H5 2.01. 96
can sleep so soundly as the wretched slave; 4.01.268
the slave, a member of the country's peace, 4.01.281
ask me this slave in french | what is his name. 4.04. 23
hold the chamber–door | whilst /by /a slave, no 4.05. 15
name | to make a bastard and a slave of me! 1H6 4.05. 15
more vile | than is a slave in base servility; 5.03.113
base slave, thy words are blunt and so art thou. 2H6 4.01. 67
a roman sworder and bandetto slave | murder'd 4.01.135
but dead they are, and, devilish slave, by thee. R3 1.02. 90
the slave of nature and the son of hell! 1.03.229
and shall that tongue give pardon to a slave? 2.01.104
slave, i have set my life upon a cast, | and i 5.04. 9
this tractable obedience is a slave | to each H8 1.02. 64
a slave whose gall coins slanders like a mint, TRO 1.03.193
among those of any wit, like a barbarian slave. 2.01. 47 P
is boundless and the act a slave to limit. 3.02. 83 P
turn, slave, and fight. 5.07. 13 P
where is that slave | which told me they had COR 1.06. 39
let the first budger die the other's slave, 1.08. 5
there is a slave, whom we have put in prison, 4.06. 38
'tis this slave — | go whip him 'fore the 4.06. 60
o slave! 5.06.103
look how the black slave smiles upon the father, TIT 4.02.120
come on, you thick–lipp'd slave, i'll bear you 4.02.175
"peace, tawny slave, half me and half thy dame. 5.01. 27
say, wall–ey'd slave, whither wouldst thou 5.01. 44
away, inhuman dog, unhallowed slave! 5.03. 14
that shows thee a weak slave, for the weakest ROM 1.01. 13 P
what dares the slave | come hither, cover'd with 1.05. 55
and let mischance be slave to patience. 5.03.221
this slave | unto his honor has my lord's meat TIM 3.01. 56
this yellow slave | will knit and break 4.03. 34
thou art a slave, whom fortune's tender arm 4.03.250
slave! 4.03.372
think thy slave man rebels, and by thy virtue 4.03.390
foam, | settlest admired reverence in a slave. 5.01. 51
a common slave — you know him well by sight — JC 1.03. 15
out his passage | till he fac'd the slave; MAC 1.02. 20
o slave! 3.03. 18
liar and slave! 5.05. 34
o, what a rogue and peasant slave am i! HAM 2.02.550
give me that man | that is not passion's slave, 3.02. 72
purpose is but the slave to memory, | of violent 3.02.188
a slave that is not twentith part the /tithe 3.04. 97
why came not the slave back to me when i call'd LR 1.04. 52 P
you whoreson dog, you slave, you cur! 1.04. 81 P
one–trunk–inheriting slave; 2.02. 19 P
strike, you slave! 2.02. 41 P
stand, rogue, stand, you neat slave! 2.02. 42 P
that such a slave as this should wear a sword, 2.02. 72
this is a slave whose easy–borrowed pride 2.04.185
persuade me rather to be slave and sumpter | to 2.04.216
here i stand your slave, | a poor, infirm, weak, 3.02. 19
throw this slave | upon the dunghill. 3.07. 96
let go, slave, or thou di'st! 4.06.236
slave, thou hast slain me. 4.06.246
i kill'd the slave that was a–hanging thee. 5.03.275
mine, 'tis his, and has been slave to thousands; OTH 3.03.158
o, that the slave had forty thousand lives! 3.03.442
some cogging, cozening slave, to get some office 4.02.132
o murd'rous slave! o villain! 5.01. 61
that same villain, | for 'tis a damned slave. 5.02.243
o cursed, cursed slave! 5.02.276
fall'n in the practice of a /damned slave, 5.02.292
for this slave, | if there be any cunning 5.02.332
and keep the turn of tippling with a slave, | to ANT 1.04. 19
call the slave again, | though i am mad, i will 2.05. 79
o slave, of no more trust | than love that's 5.02.154
slave, soulless villain, dog! 5.02.157
every jack slave hath his bellyful of fighting, CYM 2.01. 20 P
the precious note of it with a base slave, | a 2.03.122
what slave art thou? 4.02. 72
ne'er than answering | a slave without a knock. 4.02. 74
yet hath he been my captive, and my slave, | and VEN 101
a martial man to be soft fancy's slave! LUC 200
done, some worthless slave of thine i'll slay, 515
these slaves be king, and thou their slave; 659
eater of youth, false slave to false delight, 927
let him have time to live a loathed slave, | let 984
as sland'rous deathsman to so base a slave? 1001
being your slave, what should i do but tend SON 57. 1
but like a sad slave stay and think of nought 57.11
that god forbid, that made me first your slave, 58. 1
rased, | and brass eternal slave to mortal rage; 64. 4
but slave to slavery my sweet'st friend must be? 133. 4
thy proud heart's slave and vassal wretch to be: 141.12
SLAVE–LIKE 1 FR 0.0001 REL FR 1 V 0 P
this slave–like habit? TIM 4.03.205
SLAVER 1 FR 0.0001 REL FR 1 V 0 P
slaver with lips as common as the stairs | that CYM 1.06.105
SLAVERY 5 FR 0.0005 REL FR 4 V 1 P
more endure | this wooden slavery than to suffer TMP 3.01. 62
and delight to live in slavery to the nobility. 2H6 4.08. 28 P
and free us from his slavery. H8 2.02. 43
taken by the insolent foe | and sold to slavery, OTH 1.03.138
but slave to slavery my sweet'st friend must be? SON 133. 4
SLAVE'S 2 FR 0.0002 REL FR 2 V 0 P
the slave's report is seconded, and more, | more COR 4.06. 63
all the region kites | with this slave's offal. HAM 2.02.580
SLAVES 38 FR 0.0043 REL FR 32 V 6 P
and slaves they are to me that send them flying: TGV 3.01.141
hang 'em, slaves! WIV 2.01.173 P
he throws upon the gross world's baser slaves; LLL 1.01. 30
you will answer, | "the slaves are ours." MV 4.01. 98
you heedless joltheads and unmanner'd slaves! SHR 4.01.166
profess | ourselves to be the slaves of chance, WT 4.04.540
by slaves that take their humors for a warrant JN 4.02.209
what reverence he did throw away on slaves, R2 1.04. 27
that they are not the first of fortune's slaves, 5.05. 24
such a commodity of warm slaves, as had as lieve 1H4 4.02. 18 P
slaves as ragged as lazarus in the painted cloth 4.02. 25 P
but thoughts, the slaves of life, and life, 5.04. 81
this town, for they are hare–brain'd slaves, 1H6 1.02. 37
as you fly from your oft–subdued slaves. 1.05. 32
as for these silken–coated slaves, i pass not, 2H6 4.02.128
ye rude slaves, leave your gaping. H8 5.03. 2 P
with thousands of these quarter'd slaves, as COR 1.01.199
have you run | from slaves that apes would beat! 1.04. 36
with those that wore them, these base slaves, 1.05. 7
and suffer'd me by th' voice of slaves to be 4.05. 77
o slaves, i can tell you news — news, you 4.05.172 P
present grace to present slaves and servants TIM 1.01. 71
how many prodigal bits have slaves and peasants 2.02.165
have e'en put my breath from me, the slaves. 3.04.103
cap–and–knee slaves, vapors, and minute–jacks! 3.06. 97
slaves and fools, | pluck the grave wrinkled 4.01. 4
hours, season the slaves | for tubs and baths, 4.03. 86
you came for gold, ye slaves. 5.01.112
rather caesar were living, and die all slaves, JC 3.02. 23 P
go show your slaves how choleric you are, | and 4.03. 43
that were the slaves of drink and thralls of MAC 3.06. 13
that slaves your ordinance, that will not see LR 4.01. 68
i am not bound to that all slaves are free /to. OTH 3.03.135
mechanic slaves | with greasy aprons, rules, and ANT 5.02.209
tanlings and | the shrinking slaves of winter. CYM 4.04. 30
slaves, | the strides /they victors made: 5.03. 42
like straggling slaves for pillage fighting, LUC 428
"so shall these slaves be king, and thou their 659
SLAVISH 7 FR 0.0008 REL FR 7 V 0 P
mules, | you use in abject and in slavish parts, MV 4.01. 92
tear | the slavish motive of recanting fear, R2 1.01.193
if then we shall shake off our slavish yoke, 2.01.291
away with slavish weeds and servile thoughts! TIT 2.01. 18
thing | more slavish did i ne'er than answering CYM 4.02. 73
paying more slavish tribute than they owe. LUC 299
worse than a slavish wipe or birth–hour's blot; 537
/SLAY 1 FR 0.0001 REL FR 1 V 0 P
thou hast the strength of will to /slay thyself, ROM 4.01. 72
SLAY 32 FR 0.0036 REL FR 31 V 1 P
the one i'll slay; MND 2.01.190
and what impossibility would slay | in common AWW 2.01.177
i will slay myself | for living idly here in 1H6 1.01.141
cain, | to slay thy brother abel, if thou wilt. 1.03. 40
i will not slay thee, but i'll drive thee back. 1.03. 41
to slay your sovereign and destroy the realm. 3.01.114
to save a paltry life and slay bright fame, 4.06. 45
and do not stand on quillets how to slay him; 2H6 3.01.261
i never did thee harm; why wilt thou slay me? 3H6 1.03. 38
i'll slay more gazers than the basilisk, | i'll 3.02.187
o, 'twas the foulest deed to slay that babe, R3 1.03.182
among a world of men | to slay the innocent? 1.04.182
and boys with stones | in puny battle slay me. COR 4.04. 6
if he slay me, | he does fair justice; 4.04. 24
with his own hand did slay his youngest son, TIT 1.01.418
to slay his daughter with his own right hand, 5.03. 37
tybalt, here slain, whom romeo's hand did slay! ROM 3.01.152
wilt thou slay thyself, | and slay thy lady that 3.03.116
and slay thy lady that in thy life /lives, | by 3.03.117
turn to another, this shall slay them both. 4.01. 59
never shall turn back, | for i will slay myself. JC 3.01. 22
slay! 3.02.205 P
did slay this fortinbras, who, by a seal'd HAM 1.01. 86
must or for britains slay us or receive us | for CYM 4.04. 5
revolts | during their use, and slay us after. 4.04. 7
and whom he strikes his crooked tushes slay. VEN 624
theirs whose desperate hands themselves do slay, 765
done, some worthless slave of thine i'll slay, LUC 515
to slay the tiger that doth live by slaughter, 955
one, | will slay the other and be nurse to none. 1162
to slay herself, that should have slain her foe. 1827
use power with power and slay me not by art. SON 139. 4
SLAYETH 1 FR 0.0001 REL FR 1 V 0 P
the other slayeth me. MND 2.01.190
SLAYING 1 FR 0.0001 REL FR 1 V 0 P
slaying is the word, | it is a deed in fashion. JC 5.05. 4
SLAYS 1 FR 0.0001 REL FR 1 V 0 P
are poison, and he slays | moe than you rob. TIM 4.03.432
SLEAVE 1 FR 0.0001 REL FR 1 V 0 P
sleep that knits up the ravell'd sleave of care, MAC 2.02. 34
SLEAVE–SILK 1 FR 0.0001 REL FR 0 V 1 P
thou idle immaterial skein of sleave–silk, thou TRO 5.01. 31 P
SLEDDED 1 FR 0.0001 REL FR 1 V 0 P
he smote the sledded /polacks on the ice. HAM 1.01. 63
SLEEK 3 FR 0.0003 REL FR 3 V 0 P
and stick musk–roses in thy sleek smooth head, MND 4.01. 3
and how sleek and wanton | ye appear in every H8 3.02.241
gentle my lord, sleek o'er your rugged looks, MAC 3.02. 27
SLEEK–HEADED 1 FR 0.0001 REL FR 1 V 0 P
sleek–headed men and such as sleep a–nights. JC 1.02.193
/SLEEP 1 FR 0.0001 REL FR 1 V 0 P
for debt that bankrout /sleep doth sorrow owe; MND 3.02. 85
SLEEP 275 FR 0.0310 REL FR 229 V 46 P
thou art inclin'd to sleep; TMP 1.02.185
go sleep, and hear us. 2.01.190 P
i find not | myself dispos'd to sleep. 2.01.202
language, and thou speak'st | out of thy sleep. 2.01.212
thou let'st thy fortune sleep — die, rather; 2.01.216
what a sleep were this | for your advancement! 2.01.267
a custom with him | i' th' afternoon to sleep. 3.02. 88
that, if i then had wak'd after long sleep, 3.02.139
after long sleep, | will make me sleep again; 3.02.140
and our little life | is rounded with a sleep. 4.01.158
we were dead of sleep, | and (how we know not) 5.01.230
my horns are his horns, whether i wake or sleep. TGV 1.01. 80 P
love hath chas'd sleep from my enthralled eyes, 2.04.134
now can i break my fast, dine, sup, and sleep, 2.04.141
"item, she doth talk in her sleep." 3.01.329 P
matter for that, so she sleep not in her talk. 3.01.330 P
sure they sleep, he hath no use of them. WIV 3.02. 31 P
do i sleep? 3.05.140 P
and where you find a maid | that, ere she sleep, 5.05. 50
sleep she as sound as careless infancy; 5.05. 52
but those as sleep and think not on their sins, 5.05. 53
thy best of rest is sleep, | and that thou oft MM 3.01. 17
age, | but as it were an after–dinner's sleep, 3.01. 33
as fast lock'd up in sleep as guiltless labor 4.02. 66
death no more dreadfully but as a drunken sleep, 4.02.143 P
till you are executed, and sleep afterwards. 4.03. 33 P
morning, may sleep the sounder all the next day. 4.03. 46 P
and then return and sleep within mine inn, | for ERR 1.02. 14
or sleep i now and think i hear all this? 2.02.183
i am wak'd with it when i sleep, rais'd with it 4.04. 34 P
ne'er may i look on day, nor sleep on night, 5.01.210
sleep when i am drowsy, and tend on no man's ADO 1.03. 16 P
we will rather sleep than talk, we know what 3.03. 37 P
and then, to sleep but three hours in the night, LLL 1.01. 42
not to see ladies, study, fast, not sleep. 1.01. 48
sleep give thee all his rest! MND 2.02. 64
let love forbid | sleep his seat on thy eyelid. 2.02. 81
hermia, sleep thou there, | and never mayst thou 2.02.135
sing while thou on pressed flowers dost sleep. 3.01.159
if thou hast slain lysander in his sleep, 3.02. 47
till o'er their brows death–counterfeiting sleep 3.02.364
and sleep, that sometimes shuts up sorrow's eye, 3.02.435
on the ground | sleep sound; 3.02.449
i have an exposition of sleep come upon me. 4.01. 39 P
sleep thou, and i will wind thee in my arms. 4.01. 40
than common sleep of all these /five the sense. 4.01. 82
music, ho, music, such as charmeth sleep! 4.01. 83
jealousy | to sleep by hate and fear no enmity? 4.01.145
shall reply amazedly, | half sleep, half waking; 4.01.147
it seems to me | that yet we sleep, we dream. 4.01.194
sleep when he wakes? MV 1.01. 85
and sleep and snore, and rend apparel out — 2.05. 5
i'll go sleep, if i can; AYL 2.05. 60 P
for they sleep between term and term, and then 3.02.331 P
hyen, and that when thou art inclin'd to sleep. 4.01.156 P
and i'll sleep. 4.01.218 P
bow and arrows and is gone forth — to sleep. 4.03. 5 P
this were a bed but cold to sleep so soundly. SHR in.1. 33
or wilt thou sleep? in.2. 37
i do not sleep: in.2. 70
i will not sleep, hortensio, till i see her, 1.02.103
am starv'd for meat, giddy for lack of sleep, 4.03. 9
as who should say, if i should sleep or eat, 4.03. 13
but not frighted me, therefore i'll sleep again. 5.02. 43
to beguile two hours in a sleep, and then to AWW 4.01. 22 P
and in his sleep he does little harm, save to 4.03.256 P
and drink, and sleep as soft | as captain shall. 4.03.332
if it be thus to dream, still let me sleep! TN 4.01. 63
endeavor thyself to sleep, and leave thy vain 4.02. 96 P
of my sheets | (which to preserve is sleeping, WT 1.02.328
threw off his spirit, his appetite, his sleep, 2.03. 16
so hot, good sir, | i come to bring him sleep. 2.03. 33
him of that humor | that presses him from sleep. 2.03. 39
or that youth would sleep out the rest; 3.03. 60 P
the life to come, i sleep out the thought of it. 4.03. 30 P
mock'd as ever | still sleep mock'd death. 5.03. 20
and rouse from sleep that fell anatomy | which JN 3.04. 40
child, sleep doubtless and secure | that hubert, 4.01.129
draws the sweet infant breath of gentle sleep; R2 1.03.133
peace shall go sleep with turks and infidels, 4.01.139
we may do it as secure as sleep. 1H4 1.02.131 P
'tis dangerous to take a cold, to sleep, to 2.03. 8 P
thy stomach, pleasure, and thy golden sleep? 2.03. 41
and thus hath so bestirr'd thee in thy sleep, 2.03. 57
there let him sleep till day. 2.04.543 P
and on your eyelids crown the god of sleep, 3.01.214
making such difference 'twixt wake and sleep 3.01.216
thy ignominy sleep with thee in the grave, | but 5.04.100
well, he may sleep in security, for he hath the 2H4 1.02. 45 P
the undeserver may sleep when the man of action 2.04.376 P

o sleep! 3.01. 5
o gentle sleep! 3.01. 5
why rather, sleep, liest thou in smoky cribs, 3.01. 9
canst thou, o partial sleep, give /then repose 3.01. 26
the king your father is dispos'd to sleep. 4.05. 17
so many a watchful night, sleep with it now! 4.05. 25
this sleep is sound indeed, this is a sleep 4.05. 35
this is a sleep | that from this golden rigol 4.05. 35
hasty that he doth suppose | my sleep my death? 4.05. 61
fathers | have broke their sleep with thoughts, 4.05. 68
men may sleep, and they may have their throats H5 2.01. 21 P
though we seem'd dead, we did but sleep; 3.06.119 P
can sleep so soundly as the wretched slave; 4.01.268
up days with toil, and nights with sleep, | had 4.01.279
when others sleep upon their quiet beds, 1H6 2.01. 6
and once again we'll sleep secure in roan. 3.02. 19
that thus we die, while remiss traitors sleep. 4.03. 29
a hundred times and oft'ner, in my sleep, | by 2H6 2.01. 88
that if your highness should intend to sleep, 3.02.255
the mortal worm might make the sleep eternal. 3.02.263
they have the more need to sleep now then. 4.02. 3 P
in chines of beef ere thou sleep in thy sheath, 4.10. 58 P
his wonted sleep under a fresh tree's shade, 3H6 2.05. 49
the king by this is set him down to sleep. 4.03. 2
that did haunt me in my sleep | to undertake the R3 1.02.122
no sleep close up that deadly eye of thine, 1.03.224
my soul is heavy, and i fain would sleep. 1.04. 74
shall not sleep in quiet at the tower. 3.01.142
shall we hear from you, catesby, ere we sleep? 3.01.188
my lord stanley sleep these tedious nights? 3.02. 6
his bed | did i enjoy the golden dew of sleep, 4.01. 83
the sons of edward sleep in abraham's bosom, 4.03. 38
when didst thou sleep when such a deed was done? 4.04. 24
forbear to sleep the /nights, and fast the /days 4.04.118
the king, | doth comfort thee in thy sleep. 5.03.130
sleep, richmond, sleep in peace and wake in joy. 5.03.150
sleep, richmond, sleep in peace and wake in joy. 5.03.150
thee, | now fills thy sleep with perturbations. 5.03.161
thou quiet soul, sleep thou a quiet sleep, 5.03.164
thou quiet soul, sleep thou a quiet sleep, 5.03.164
the sweetest sleep and fairest-boding dreams 5.03.227
you sleep in peace, the tyrant being slain; 5.03.256
and sleep in dull cold marble where no mention H8 3.02.433
her two hands, and she | sleep in their graves. 5.01. 32
as 'tis to make 'em sleep | on may-day morning, 5.03. 14
nor shall this peace sleep with her; 5.04. 39
to take their ease, | and sleep an act or two; ep 3
tamer than sleep, fonder than ignorance, | less TRO 1.01. 10
of reason, | /let's shut our gates and sleep. 2.02. 47
let achilles sleep: 2.03.265
sleep kill those pretty eyes, | and give as soft 4.02. 4
would he not, a naughty man, let it sleep? 4.02. 33 P
nor sleep nor sanctuary, | being naked, sick, COR 1.10. 19
our office may, | during his power, go sleep. 2.01.223
were i as patient as the midnight sleep, | by 3.01. 85
passions and whose plots have broke their sleep 4.04. 19
we have been down together in my sleep, 4.05.124
and sleep in peace, slain in your country's wars TIT 1.01. 91
no noise, but silence and eternal sleep. 1.01.155
you that survive, and you that sleep in fame! 1.01.173
have been troubled in my sleep this night, 2.02. 9
well could i leave our sport to sleep a while. 2.03.197
me down, | that i may slumber an eternal sleep! 2.04. 15
circling shadows kings have sought to sleep in, 2.04. 19
in saturninus' health, whom, if he sleep, 4.04. 24
still-waking sleep, that is not what it is! ROM 1.01.181
this field-bed is too cold for me to sleep. 2.01. 40
sleep dwell upon thine eyes, peace in thy breast 2.02.186
would i were sleep and peace, so sweet to rest! 2.02.187
and where care lodges, sleep will never lie; 2.03. 36
couch his limbs, there golden sleep doth reign. 2.03. 38
upon receipt thereof, | soon sleep in quiet. 3.05. 99
and then awake as from a pleasant sleep. 4.01.106
sleep for a week, for the next night, i warrant, 4.05. 5
if i may trust the flattering truth of sleep, 5.01. 1
as i did sleep under this /yew tree here, | i 5.03.137
nest | of death, contagion, and unnatural sleep. 5.03.152
sleep upon't, | and let the foes quietly cut TIM 3.05. 43
sleek-headed men and such as sleep a-nights. JC 1.02.193
would it were my fault to sleep so soundly. 2.01. 4
i will not let you eat, nor talk, nor sleep; 2.01.252
thrice hath calphurnia in her sleep cried out, 2.02. 2
i'll have them sleep on cushions in my tent. 4.03.243
i pray you, sirs, lie in my tent and sleep; 4.03.246
it was well done, and thou shalt sleep again; 4.03.264
sleep again, lucius. 4.03.299
why did you so cry out, sirs, in your sleep? 4.03.303
sleep shall neither night nor day | hang upon MAC 1.03. 19
when in swinish sleep | their drenched natures 1.07. 67
like lead upon me, | and yet i would not sleep. 2.01. 7
and wicked dreams abuse | the curtain'd sleep; 2.01. 51
there's one did laugh in 's sleep, and one cried 2.02. 20
prayers, and address'd them | again to sleep. 2.02. 23
methought i heard a voice cry, "sleep no more! 2.02. 32
macbeth does murther sleep" — the innocent 2.02. 33
does murther sleep" — the innocent sleep, 2.02. 33
sleep that knits up the ravell'd sleave of care, 2.02. 34
still it cried, "sleep no more!" 2.02. 38
glamis hath murther'd sleep, and therefore 2.02. 39
and therefore cawdor | shall sleep no more — 2.02. 40
sleep no more — macbeth shall sleep no more." 2.02. 40
marry, sir, nose-painting, sleep, and urine. 2.03. 28 P
in conclusion, equivocates him in a sleep, and, 2.03. 35 P
shake off this downy sleep, death's counterfeit, 2.03. 76
and sleep | in the affliction of these terrible 3.02. 17
you lack the season of all natures, sleep. 3.04.140
come, we'll to sleep. 3.04.141
were the slaves of drink and thralls of sleep? 3.06. 13
give to our tables meat, sleep to our nights; 3.06. 34
tear it lies, | and sleep in spite of thunder. 4.01. 86
yet all this while in a most fast sleep. 5.01. 8 P
once the benefit of sleep and do the effects of 5.01. 10 P
have walk'd in their sleep who have died holily 5.01. 60 P
and convey /is assistant, do not sleep, | but HAM 1.03. 3
to die, to sleep, | no more, and by a sleep to 3.01. 59
and by a sleep to say we end | the heart-ache 3.01. 60
to die, to sleep, | to sleep, perchance to dream 3.01. 63
tie, to sleep, | to sleep, perchance to dream! 3.01. 64
for in that sleep of death what dreams may come, 3.01. 65
i would beguile | the tedious day with sleep. 3.02.227
sleep rock thy brain, | and never come mischance 3.02.227
for some must watch, while some must sleep, 3.02.273
market of his time | be but to sleep and feed? 4.04. 35
and let all sleep, while to my shame i see | the 4.04. 59
kind of fighting | that would not let me sleep. 5.02. 5
if our father would sleep till i wak'd him, you LR 1.02. 52 P
"sleep till i wake him, you should enjoy half 1.02. 55 P
not scape censure, nor the redresses sleep, 1.04.210
i will not sleep, my lord, till i have deliver'd 1.05. 6 P
some time i shall sleep out, the rest i'll 2.02.156
i'll beat the drum | till it cry sleep to death. 2.04.119
of a corn cry woe, | and turn his sleep to wake. 3.02. 34
i'll pray, and then i'll sleep. 3.04. 27
in the heaviness of sleep | we put fresh 4.07. 20
why, go to bed and sleep. OTH 1.03.304 P
i find it still, when i have /list to sleep. 2.01.104
'tis evermore /the prologue to his sleep. 2.03.129
shall ever medicine thee to that sweet sleep 3.03.332
with a raging tooth, | i could not sleep. 3.03.415
in sleep i heard him say, "sweet desdemona, 3.03.419
that i might sleep out this great gap of time ANT 1.05. 5
that sleep and feeding may prorogue his honor 2.01. 26
sir, we did sleep day out of countenance, and 2.02.177 P
sleep a little. 4.04. 1
bad a prayer as his | was never yet for sleep. 4.09. 27
long day's task is done, | and we must sleep. 4.14. 36
once be necessary, | i'll not sleep neither. 5.02. 51
o, such another sleep, that i might see | but 5.02. 77
feed, and sleep. 5.02.187
but she looks like sleep, | as she would catch 5.02.346
sleep hath seiz'd me wholly. CYM 2.02. 7
o sleep, thou ape of death, lie dull upon her, 2.02. 31
if sleep charge nature, | to break it with a 3.04. 42
faith, i'll lie down and sleep. 4.02.294
bed | with the defunct, or sleep upon the dead. 4.02.358
sleep, thou hast been a grandsire and begot | a 5.04.123
but a man that were to sleep your sleep, and a 5.04.173 P
but a man that were to sleep your sleep, and a 5.04.173 P
the tomb where grief should sleep, can breed me PER 1.02. 5
drew sleep out of mine eyes, blood from my 1.02. 96
now sleep yslacked hath the rout, | no din but 3.ch. 1
this is the rarest dream that e'er dull'd sleep 5.01.161
enough, | though doubts did ever sleep. 5.01.202
to his bones sweet sleep! TNK pr 29
peace sleep with him! 1.05. 12
i'll shake 'em so, ye shall not sleep, | i'll 2.02.272
i shall sleep like a top else. 3.04. 26
a place prepar'd for those that sleep in honor, 3.06. 99
i dare as well | die as discourse or sleep. 3.06.129
for, ere the sun set, both shall sleep for ever. 3.06.184
this quarrel | sleep till the hour prefix'd, and 3.06.304
sir, when did she sleep? 4.01. 35
this may bring her to eat, to sleep, and reduce 4.03. 95 P
and then we'll sleep together? 5.02.110
when heavy sleep had clos'd up mortal eyes. LUC 163
each in her sleep themselves so beautify, | as 404
from forth dull sleep by dreadful fancy waking, 450
from sleep disturbed, heedfully doth view | the 454
cave-keeping evils that obscurely sleep. 1250
if thou wake, he cannot sleep; PP 20.52
but when i sleep, in dreams they look on thee, SON 43. 3
through heavy sleep on sightless eyes doth stay! 43.12
or, if they sleep, thy picture in my sight 47.13
in sleep a king, but waking no such matter. 87.14
for his advantage still did wake and sleep. LC 123

SLEEPER 1 FR 0.0001 REL FR 1 V 0 P
i have been long a sleeper; R3 3.04. 23

SLEEPERS 4 FR 0.0004 REL FR 4 V 0 P
at my command | have wak'd their sleepers, op'd, TMP 5.01. 49
and rock the ground whereon these sleepers be. MND 4.01. 86
calls to parley | the sleepers of the house? MAC 2.03. 83
hark, the drums | demurely wake the sleepers. ANT 4.09. 30

/SLEEPEST 1 FR 0.0001 REL FR 1 V 0 P
"/sleepest /or /wakest /thou, /jolly /shepherd? LR 3.06. 41

SLEEPEST 1 FR 0.0001 REL FR 1 V 0 P
thou sleepest. R2 3.02. 84

SLEEPING 52 FR 0.0058 REL FR 46 V 6 P
sleeping or waking, mad or well-advis'd? ERR 2.02.213
for i cannot see how sleeping should offend; ADO 3.03. 40 P
the juice of it on sleeping eyelids laid | will MND 2.01.170
and here the maiden, sleeping sound, | on the 2.02. 74
to fan the moonbeams from his sleeping eyes. 3.01.173
while she was in her dull and sleeping hour, | a 3.02. 8
i took him sleeping — that is finish'd too — 3.02. 38
he have stolen away | from sleeping hermia? 3.02. 52
and hast thou kill'd him sleeping? 3.02. 70
came this night | that i sleeping here was found 4.01.101
o'ergrown with hair, | lay sleeping on his back; AYL 4.03.107
watch, | when that the sleeping man should stir; 4.03.116
a day-bed, where i have left olivia sleeping — TN 2.05. 49 P
(all proofs sleeping else | but what your WT 3.02.112
and but for our approach those sleeping stones, JN 2.01.216
awak'd the sleeping rheum, and so by chance R2 1.04. 8
for sleeping england long time have i watch'd, 2.01. 77
poisoned by their wives, some sleeping kill'd, 3.02.159
supper, and sleeping upon benches after noon, 1H4 1.02. 3 P
your lordship, a kind of sleeping in the blood, 2H4 1.02.112 P
is well, keep it so, wake not a sleeping wolf. 1.02.154 P
upon, | when i am sleeping with my ancestors. 4.04. 61
how you awake our sleeping sword of war — | we H5 1.02. 22
sleeping or waking, must i still prevail, | or 1H6 2.01. 56
sleeping neglection doth betray to loss | the 4.03. 49
by bloody hands, in sleeping on your beds! 5.03. 41
sleeping, or waking, 'tis no matter how, | so he 2H6 3.01.263
i wear no knife to slaughter sleeping men, | but 3.02.197
hell, | pernicious blood-sucker of sleeping men! 3.02.226
why, then he'll say we stabb'd him sleeping. R3 1.04.105 P
not sleeping, to engross his idle body, | but 3.07. 76
sleeping and waking, o, defend me still! 5.03.117
you sleeping safe, they bring to you unrest; 5.03.320
have wish'd the sleeping of this business, never H8 2.04.164
the wind, | it is not agamemnon's sleeping hour. TRO 1.03.254
we do allowance give | before a sleeping giant. 2.03.138
a sleeping potion, which so took effect | as i ROM 5.03.244
pity's sleeping: TIM 4.03.485
the sleeping and the dead | are but as pictures; MAC 2.02. 50
has thirty-one | swelt'red venom sleeping got, 4.01. 8
'tis given out that, sleeping in my orchard, | a HAM 1.05. 35
sleeping within my orchard, | my custom always 1.05. 59
thus was i, sleeping, by a brother's hand | of 1.05. 74
and, as the sleeping soldiers in th' alarm, 3.04.120
or dead, or sleeping on him? CYM 4.02.356
a willing man dies sleeping, and all's done. TNK 2.02. 68
why hast thou cast into eternal sleeping | those VEN 951
but she, sound sleeping, fearing no such thing, LUC 363
so o'er this sleeping soul doth tarquin stay, 423
with thy tickling beams eyes that are sleeping; 1090
herds stands weeping, flocks all sleeping, PP 17.27
desire | was sleeping by a virgin hand disarm'd. SON 154. 8

SLEEPING-HOURS 1 FR 0.0001 REL FR 0 V 1 P
dinners and suppers and sleeping-hours excepted. AYL 3.02. 97 P

SLEEP'S 1 FR 0.0001 REL FR 1 V 0 P
foes to my rest and my sweet sleep's disturbers, R3 4.02. 73

/SLEEPS 2 FR 0.0002 REL FR 2 V 0 P
/with /wanton /paris /sleeps — /and /that's TRO pr 10
/oppressed /nature /sleeps. LR 3.06. 97

SLEEPS 34 FR 0.0038 REL FR 27 V 7 P
it eats and sleeps and hath such senses | as we TMP 1.02.413
he's undrown'd, | as he that sleeps here swims. 2.01.238
can rule naples | as well as he that sleeps; 2.01.263
it seems his sleeps were hind'red by thy railing ERR 5.01. 71
she is never sad but when she sleeps, and not ADO 2.01.343 P
there sleeps titania sometime of the night, MND 2.01.253
and he sleeps by day | more than the wild-cat. MV 2.05. 47
how sweet the moonlight sleeps upon this bank! 5.01. 54
the moon sleeps with endymion | and would not be 5.01.109
for the one sleeps easily because he cannot AYL 3.02.320 P
while shameful hate sleeps out the afternoon. AWW 5.03. 66
of phoebus, and all night | sleeps in elysium; H5 4.01.274
what, shall /i stab him as he sleeps? R3 1.04.100 P
he has run his course and sleeps in blessings, H8 3.02.398
and when he sleeps will she do what she list. TIT 4.01.100
swears a prayer or two, | and sleeps again. ROM 1.04. 88
her body sleeps in capel's monument, | and her 5.01. 18
for here it sleeps, and does no hired harm. TIM 4.03.291
after life's fitful fever he sleeps well. MAC 3.02. 23
for a jig or a tale of bawdry, or he sleeps. HAM 2.02.501 P
of it, a knavish speech sleeps in a foolish ear. 4.02. 23 P
break not your sleeps for that. 4.07. 30
madam, sleeps still. LR 4.07. 13
that in their sleeps will mutter their affairs; OTH 3.03.417
let's do so. but he sleeps. ANT 4.09. 25
which sleeps, and never palates more the dung, 5.02. 7
why, he but sleeps! CYM 4.02.215
sir, he that sleeps feels not the toothache; 5.04.172 P
in a harmless distemper, sleeps little, TNK 4.03. 4 P
but soundly sleeps, while now it sleeps alone. VEN 786
but soundly sleeps, while now it sleeps alone. 786
the dove sleeps fast that this night-owl will LUC 360
"the patient dies while the physician sleeps, 904
though woe be heavy, yet it seldom sleeps, | and 1574

SLEEP'ST 4 FR 0.0004 REL FR 4 V 0 P
hector, thou sleep'st, | awake thee! TRO 4.05.114
"brutus, thou sleep'st; JC 2.01. 46
"brutus, thou sleep'st; 2.01. 48
therefore thou sleep'st so sound. 2.01.233

/SLEEPY 1 FR 0.0001 REL FR 0 V 1 P
mull'd, deaf, /sleepy, insensible, a getter of COR 4.05.224 P

SLEEPY 9 FR 0.0010 REL FR 7 V 2 P
and surely | it is a sleepy language, and thou TMP 2.01.211
away, you rogue, away! i am sleepy. MM 4.03. 29 P
moist hesperus hath quench'd her sleepy lamp, AWW 2.01.164
what to say — we will give you sleepy drinks, WT 1.01. 14 P
whiles, in the mildness of your sleepy thoughts, R3 3.07.123
this is a sleepy tune. JC 4.03.267
when we have mark'd with blood those sleepy two MAC 1.07. 75
them, and smear | the sleepy grooms with blood. 2.02. 47
'tis not sleepy business, | but must be look'd CYM 3.05. 26

SLEEVE 20 FR 0.0022 REL FR 13 V 7 P
come, i will fasten on this sleeve of thine: ERR 2.02.173
though others have the arm, show us the sleeve: 3.02. 23
this gallant pins the wenches on his sleeve; LLL 5.02.321
i knew her by this jewel on her sleeve. 5.02.455
your bonnet unbanded, your sleeve unbutton'd, AYL 3.02.379 P
a sleeve? SHR 4.03. 88
"with a trunk sleeve" — 4.03.141 P
will he strip his sleeve and show his scars, H5 4.03. 47
wear this sleeve. TRO 4.04. 70
here, diomed, keep this sleeve. 5.02. 66
you look upon that sleeve, behold it well. 5.02. 69
that sleeve is mine that he'll bear on his helm. 5.02.169
i come to lose my arm, or win my sleeve. 5.03. 96
/young knave's sleeve of troy there in his helm. 5.04. 4 P
villain with the sleeve back to the dissembling 5.04. 7 P
soft, here comes sleeve and t' other. 5.04. 18 P
now the sleeve, now the sleeve! 5.04. 25 P
now the sleeve, now the sleeve! 5.04. 25 P
as they pass by, pluck casca by the sleeve, JC 1.02.179
but i will wear my heart upon my sleeve | for OTH 1.01. 64

SLEEVE-HAND 1 FR 0.0001 REL FR 0 V 1 P
so chaunts to the sleeve-hand and the work about WT 4.04.210 P

SLEEVELESS 1 FR 0.0001 REL FR 0 V 1 P
luxurious drab, of a sleeveless arrant. TRO 5.04. 8 P

SLEEVES 8 FR 0.0009 REL FR 1 V 7 P
set with pearls, down sleeves, side sleeves, and ADO 3.04. 20 P
pearls, down sleeves, side sleeves, and skirts, 3.04. 21 P
some sleeves, some hats, from yielders all MND 3.02. 30
i confess two sleeves. SHR 4.03.142 P
"the sleeves curiously cut." 4.03.143 P
i commanded the sleeves should be cut out, and 4.03.146 P
dost make hose of thy sleeves? AWW 2.03.251 P
shoulders like a herald's coat without sleeves; 1H4 4.02. 45 P

SLEIDED 2 FR 0.0002 REL FR 2 V 0 P
be't when they weav'd the sleided silk | with PER 4.ch. 21
blood, | with sleided silk feat and affectedly LC 48

SLEIGHT 1 FR 0.0001 REL FR 1 V 0 P
with sleight and manhood stole to rhesus' tents 3H6 4.02. 20

SLEIGHTS 1 FR 0.0001 REL FR 1 V 0 P
and that, distill'd by magic sleights, | shall MAC 3.05. 26

/SLENDER 1 FR 0.0001 REL FR 1 V 0 P
/would /he /hang /his /slender /gilded /wings TIT 3.02. 61

SLENDER 36 FR 0.0040 REL FR 13 V 23 P
home, | while other men, of slender reputation, TGV 1.03. 6
ay, cousin slender, and custa–lorum. WIV 1.01. 7 P
shallow, and here young master slender, that 1.01. 76 P
i am glad to see you, good master slender. 1.01. 88 P
slender, i broke your head; 1.01.121 P
master slender, i will description the matter to 1.01.214 P
cousin abraham slender, can you love her? 1.01.232 P
come, gentle master slender, come; 1.01.300 P
and master page, and eke cavaleiro slender, go 2.03. 74 P
a match between anne page and my cousin slender, 3.02. 58 P
you have, master slender, i stand wholly for you 3.02. 61 P
ye, master slender would speak a word with you. 3.04. 29 P
now, master slender — 3.04. 54 P
i mean, master slender, what would you with me? 3.04. 60 P
now, master slender. 3.04. 67
come, son slender, in. 3.04. 75
or i would master slender had her; 3.04.105 P
master slender is let the boys leave to play. 4.01. 11 P
time | shall master slender steal my nan away, 4.04. 74
that slender, though well landed, is an idiot; 4.04. 86
with sir john falstaff from master slender. 4.05. 5 P
my master, sir, my master slender, sent to her, 4.05. 30 P
man that beguil'd master slender of his chain 4.05. 37 P
hath commanded her to slip | away with slender, 4.06. 24
when slender sees his time | to take her by the 4.06. 36
remember, son slender, my /daughter. 5.02. 3 P
tell her master slender hath married her 5.05.173 P
how chance you went not with master slender? 5.05.218 P
your waist, mistress, were as slender as my wit, LLL 4.01. 49
must be lin'd, | so must slender rosalind. AYL 3.02.106
like the hazel–twig | is straight and slender, SHR 2.01.254
the worst is this, that, at so slender warning, 4.04. 60
are like to have a thin and slender pittance. 4.04. 61
your means are very slender, and your waste is 2H4 1.02.140 P
fragment, some slender ort of his remainder. TIM 4.03.399 P
grief /joys, joy grieves, on slender accident. HAM 3.02.199
/SLENDERER 1 FR 0.0001 REL FR 0 V 1 P
my means were greater and my waist /slenderer. 2H4 1.02.143 P
SLENDERLY 1 FR 0.0001 REL FR 0 V 1 P
yet he hath ever but slenderly known himself. LR 1.01.294 P
SLENDER'S 3 FR 0.0003 REL FR 0 V 3 P
pistol, did you pick master slender's purse? WIV 1.01.151 P
and master slender's your master? 1.04. 18 P
pray you now, good master slender's servingman, 3.01. 1 P
SLEPT 37 FR 0.0041 REL FR 34 V 3 P
thou hast slept well, | awake! TMP 1.02.305
law hath not been dead, though it hath slept. MM 2.02. 90
in bed he slept not for my urging it; ERR 5.01. 63
o, in a tomb where never scandal slept, | save ADO 5.01. 70
we still have slept together, | rose at an AYL 1.03. 73
or when you wak'd, so wak'd as if you slept. SHR in.2. 80
and slept above some fifteen year or more. in.2. 113
last night she slept not, nor to–night she shall 4.01.198
madam — he hath not slept to–night, commanded
WT 2.03. 31
scene such growing | as you had slept between. 4.01. 17
where hath it slept? JN 4.02.117
slept in his face and rend'red such aspect | as 1H4 3.02. 82
hadst thou been meek, our title still had slept, 3H6 2.02.160
where slept our scouts, or how are they seduc'd, 5.01. 19
under whose shade the ramping lion slept, 5.02. 13
wife, | that never slept a quiet hour with thee, R3 5.03.160
how have you slept, my lord? 5.03.226
that so long have slept upon | this bold bad man H8 2.02. 42
his blessed part to heaven, and slept in peace. 4.02. 30
saw ye none enter since i slept? 4.02. 86
i was advertis'd their great general slept, TRO 2.02.211
hast not slept to–night? 4.02. 32 P
in dangerous wars whilst you securely slept; TIT 3.01. 3
such | as slept within the shadow of your power TIM 5.04. 6
did whet me against caesar, | i have not slept. JC 2.01. 62
i have slept, my lord, already. 4.03.263
hath it slept since? MAC 1.07. 36
had he not resembled | my father as he slept, i 2.02. 13
one that slept in the contriving of lust, and LR 3.04. 89 P
he hath slept long. 4.07. 17
i slept the next night well, fed well, was free OTH 3.03.340
not till you have slept; ANT 2.07. 32 P
her bedchamber | (where i confess i slept not, CYM 2.04. 67
to do this business | i have not slept one wink. 3.04.100
i thought he slept, and put | my clouted brogues 4.02.213
as i slept, methought | great jupiter, upon his 5.05.426
and therefore have i slept in your report, SON 83. 5
SLEW 39 FR 0.0044 REL FR 36 V 3 P
repent, | but yet i slew him manfully in fight, TGV 4.01. 28
the night, | those that slew thy virgin knight, ADO 5.03. 13
that slew the sophy and a persian prince | that MV 2.01. 25
with his own hand he slew the duke's brother. AWW 3.05. 6 P
belike you slew great number of his people? TN 3.03. 29
death, | i slew him not, but to my own disgrace R2 1.01.133
here, there, and every where, enrag'd he slew. 1H6 1.01.124
head, | the head of cade, whom i in combat slew. 2H6 5.01. 67
me, my friend, art thou the man that slew him? 5.01. 71
the deadly–handed clifford slew my steed; 5.02. 9
earl of northumberland, he slew thy father, 3H6 1.01. 54
and slew your fathers, and with colors spread 1.01. 91
where i shall kneel to him that slew my father! 1.01.162
whose father slew my father, he shall die. 1.03. 5
thy father slew my father; 1.03. 47
i slew thy father, call'st thou him a child? 2.02.113
and this the hand that slew thy brother rutland, 2.04. 7
these hands that slew thy sire and brother | to 2.04. 9
this man whom hand to hand i slew in fight | may 2.05. 56
say that i slew them not? R3 1.02. 89
who slew to–day a riotous gentleman | lately 2.01.101
were, | and he that slew them fouler than he is. 4.04.121
send to her by the man that slew her brothers 4.04.271
or he that slew her brothers and her uncles? 4.04.339
and i' th' consul's view | slew three opposers. COR 2.02. 94
upon advice did bury ajax | that slew himself; TIT 1.01.380
romeo, | that slew thy kinsman, brave mercutio. ROM 3.01.145
romeo slew tybalt, romeo must not live. 3.01.181
romeo slew him, he slew mercutio; 3.01.182
romeo slew him, he slew mercutio; 3.01.182
another fought, | and that my master slew him. 5.03.139
but, as he was ambitious, i slew him. JC 3.02. 27 P
as i slew my best lover for the good of rome, i 3.02. 45 P
i slew the coward, and did take it from him. 5.03. 4
poison'd for my sake, | and after slew herself. LR 5.03.242
let me end the story: | i slew him there. CYM 5.05.287
this man is better than the man he slew, | as 5.05.302
swearing i slew him, seeing thee embrace him. LUC 518
story | the credulous old priam after slew; 1522
SLEWEST 1 FR 0.0001 REL FR 1 V 0 P
would kill thee, | but thou slewest tybalt: ROM 3.03.138
SLEW'ST 1 FR 0.0001 REL FR 1 V 0 P
modena, where thou slew'st | hirtius and pansa, ANT 1.04. 57
SLICE 2 FR 0.0002 REL FR 0 V 2 P
slice, i say! WIV 1.01.132 P
slice! 1.01.132 P
SLICKLY 1 FR 0.0001 REL FR 0 V 1 P
let their heads be slickly comb'd, their blue SHR 4.01. 91 P
'SLID 2 FR 0.0002 REL FR 0 V 2 P
'slid, 'tis but venturing. WIV 3.04. 24 P
'slid, i'll after him again and beat him. TN 3.04.391 P
SLIDE 5 FR 0.0005 REL FR 3 V 2 P
therefore paucas pallabris, let the world slide. SHR in.1. 6 P
it, thou mayst slide from my shoulder to my heel 4.01. 15 P
that i slide | o'er sixteen years and leave the WT 4.01. 5
but let the famish'd flesh slide from the bone TIM 4.03.528
these present–absent with swift motion slide. SON 45. 4
SLIDES 2 FR 0.0002 REL FR 2 V 0 P
the fool slides o'er the ice that you should TRO 3.03.215
so slides he down upon his grained bat, | and LC 64
SLIDING 1 FR 0.0001 REL FR 1 V 0 P
and rather prov'd the sliding of your brother MM 2.04.115
'SLIGHT 2 FR 0.0002 REL FR 0 V 2 P
'slight, i could so beat the rogue! TN 2.05. 33 P
'slight! will you make an ass o' me? 3.02. 13 P
SLIGHT 31 FR 0.0035 REL FR 22 V 9 P
done, | and leave her on such slight conditions. TGV 5.04.138
fee'd every slight occasion that could but WIV 2.02.197 P
carry–tale, some please–man, some slight zany, LLL 5.02.463
which now in some slight measure it will pay, MND 3.02. 86
for if thou dost him any slight disgrace, or if AYL 1.01.148 P
yet slight ones will not carry it. AWW 4.01. 38 P
cardinal, devise a name | so slight, unworthy, JN 3.01.150
and for thy walls, a pretty slight drollery, or 2H4 2.01.144 P
i muse you make so slight a question. 4.01.165
that every slight and false–derived cause, | yea 4.01.188
that a lie with a slight oath and a jest with a 5.01. 82 P
scorn and defiance, slight regard, contempt, H5 2.04.117
when for so slight and frivolous a cause | such 1H6 4.01.112
no quarrel, but a slight contention. 3H6 1.02. 6
can scarce think there's any, y' are so slight. COR 5.02.104 P
to make | what cannot be, slight work. 5.03. 62
my moneys, be not ceas'd | with slight denial; TIM 2.01. 17
i did endure | not seldom, nor no slight checks, 2.02.140
this is a slight unmeritable man, | meet to be JC 4.01. 12
away, slight man! 4.03. 37
you laying these slight sallies on my son, | as HAM 2.01. 39
to deceive so good a commander with so slight, OTH 2.03.278 P
is caesar with antonius priz'd so slight? ANT 1.01. 56
importance of so slight and trivial a nature. CYM 1.04. 42 P
is mended) my quarrel was not altogether slight. 1.04. 48 P
us, for | we have been too slight in sufferance. 3.05. 35
of your lives you set | so slight a valuation, 4.04. 49
did you suffer jachimo, | slight thing of italy, 5.04. 64
these poor slight sores | need not a plantin; TNK 1.02. 60
if my slight muse do please these curious days, SON 38.13
the other two, slight air and purging fire, 45. 1
SLIGHTED 3 FR 0.0003 REL FR 2 V 1 P
the rogues slighted me into the river with as WIV 3.05. 9 P
see your most dreadful laws so loosely slighted, 2H4 5.02. 94
because i knew the man, was slighted off. JC 4.03. 5
SLIGHTEST 3 FR 0.0003 REL FR 2 V 1 P
i will go on the slightest arrand now to the ADO 2.01.264 P
if thou rememb'rest not the slightest folly AYL 2.04. 34
yea, even the slightest worship of his time, 1H4 3.02.151
SLIGHTLY 10 FR 0.0011 REL FR 9 V 1 P
the guards are but slightly basted on neither. ADO 1.01.287 P
to part so slightly with your wive's first gift, MV 5.01.167
untouch'd or slightly handled in discourse. R3 3.07. 19
gone slightly o'er low steps and now are mounted H8 2.04.112
that slightly shakes his parting guest by th' TRO 3.03.166
too slightly timber'd for so /loud /a /wind, HAM 4.07. 22
this contagion, that, if i gall him slightly, 4.07.147
that he, so slightly valued in his messenger, LR 2.02.146
down | some mortally, some slightly touch'd, CYM 5.03. 10
skill, pass'd slightly | his careless execution, TNK 1.03. 28
SLIGHTNESS 1 FR 0.0001 REL FR 1 V 0 P
and give way the while | to unstable slightness. COR 3.01.148
SLIGHTS 1 FR 0.0001 REL FR 0 V 1 P
man" — puts him off, slights him, with "whoop, WT 4.04.199 P
SLILY 6 FR 0.0006 REL FR 6 V 0 P
that slily glided towards your majesty, | it 2H6 3.02.260
north, | he slily stole away and left his men; 3H6 1.01. 3
nestor, | deceive more slily than ulysses could, 3.02.189
the king was slily finger'd from the deck! 5.01. 44
here in these confines slily have i lurk'd, | to R3 4.04. 3
him | were slily crept into his human powers, COR 2.01.220
SLIME 5 FR 0.0005 REL FR 5 V 0 P
dry, | with miry slime left on them by a flood? TIT 3.01.126
is, and hates the slime | that sticks on filthy OTH 5.02.148
by the fire | that quickens nilus' slime, i go ANT 1.03. 69
upon the slime and ooze scatters his grain, 2.07. 22
and these fig leaves | have slime upon them, 5.02.352
SLIMY 2 FR 0.0002 REL FR 2 V 0 P
gems, | that woo'd the slimy bottom of the deep, R3 1.04. 32
my bended hook shall pierce | their slimy jaws; ANT 2.05. 13
SLINGS 2 FR 0.0002 REL FR 2 V 0 P
stones | enforced from the old assyrian slings; H5 4.07. 62
the slings and arrows of outrageous fortune, HAM 3.01. 57
SLINK 3 FR 0.0003 REL FR 2 V 1 P
nay, we will slink away in supper–time, MV 2.04. 1
'tis he. slink by, and note him. AYL 3.02.252 P
to his buried fortunes | slink all away, leave TIM 4.02. 11
/SLIP* 1 FR 0.0001 REL FR 1 V 0 P
on their knees and /hands, let him /slip down, TIM 1.01. 87
SLIP* 24 FR 0.0027 REL FR 19 V 5 P
otherwise you might slip away ere he came. WIV 4.02. 53 P
her father hath commanded her to slip | away 4.06. 23
which for this fourteen years we have let slip, MM 1.03. 21
for such a warped slip of wilderness | ne'er 3.01.141
should slip so grossly, both in the heat of 5.01.472
then slip i from her bum, down topples she, MND 2.01. 53
and with indented glides did slip away | into a AYL 4.03.112
sit by my side, and let the world slip, we shall SHR in.2. 143 P
breeds | a native slip to us from foreign seeds. AWW 1.03.146
let him let the matter slip, and i'll give him TN 3.04.286 P
the dibble in earth to set one slip of them; WT 4.04.100
before the game is afoot thou still let'st slip. 1H4 1.03.278
and noble stock | was graft with crab–tree slip, 2H6 3.02.214
from which even here i slip my /weary head, R3 4.04.112
in the leash, | to let him slip at will. COR 1.06. 39
brave slip, sprung from the great andronicus, TIT 5.01. 9
the slip, sir, the slip, can you not conceive? ROM 2.04. 48 P
the slip, sir, the slip, can you not conceive? 2.04. 48 P
cry "havoc," and let slip the dogs of war, JC 3.01.273
if they do nothing, 'tis a venial slip; OTH 4.01. 9
we'll slip you for a season, but our jealousy CYM 4.03. 22
him | and the tanner's daughter to let slip now; TNK 2.03. 44
of law in lyam | to slip him like a hound; STM II.C 122
make use of time, let not advantage slip, VEN 129
SLIPP'D 9 FR 0.0010 REL FR 8 V 1 P
you would have slipp'd like him, but he, like MM 2.02. 65
o, sir, lucentio slipp'd me like his greyhound, SHR 5.02. 52
and that you slipp'd not | with any but with us. WT 1.02. 85
king, | had slipp'd our claim until another age. 3H6 2.02.162
thou /wouldst not have slipp'd out of my TRO 2.03. 26 P
the bonds of heaven are slipp'd, dissolv'd, and 5.02.156
a thing slipp'd idlely from me. TIM 1.01. 20
timely on him, | i have almost slipp'd the hour. MAC 2.03. 47
when presently | she slipp'd away, and to the TNK 4.01. 97
SLIPPER* 3 FR 0.0003 REL FR 1 V 2 P
'twere a kibe, | 'twould put me to my slipper; TMP 2.01.277
i do adore thy sweet grace's slipper. LLL 5.02.667 P
none, why, none — a slipper and subtle knave, a OTH 2.01.242 P
SLIPPER'D 1 FR 0.0001 REL FR 1 V 0 P
shifts | into the lean and slipper'd pantaloon, AYL 2.07.158
SLIPPERS 2 FR 0.0002 REL FR 2 V 0 P
where are my slippers? SHR 4.01.153
standing on slippers, which his nimble haste JN 4.02.197
SLIPPERY 8 FR 0.0009 REL FR 8 V 0 P
man that does not think) | my wife is slippery? WT 1.02.273
with deafing clamor in the slippery clouds, 2H4 3.01. 24
when they fall, as being slippery standers, TRO 3.03. 84
the love that lean'd on them as slippery too, 3.03. 85
o world, thy slippery turns! COR 4.04. 12
my credit now stands on such slippery ground JC 3.01.191
our slippery people, | whose love is never ANT 1.02.185
as slippery as the gordian knot was hard! CYM 2.02. 34
SLIPP'RY 3 FR 0.0003 REL FR 3 V 0 P
and he that stands upon a slipp'ry place | makes JN 3.04.137
as well of glib and slipp'ry creatures as | of TIM 1.01. 53
or so slipp'ry that | the fear's as bad as CYM 3.03. 48
SLIPS* 9 FR 0.0010 REL FR 8 V 1 P
without any slips of prolixity or crossing the MV 3.01. 11 P
barren, and i care not | to get slips of them. WT 4.04. 85
i see you stand like greyhounds in the slips, H5 3.01. 31
and in thy sons, fair slips of such a stock. 2H6 2.02. 58
ay, for these slips have made him noted long, TIT 2.03. 86
mind, | that from it all consideration slips — TIM 4.03.196
goat, and slips of yew | sliver'd in the moon's MAC 4.01. 27
and usual slips | as are companions noted and HAM 2.01. 22
which purchase if thou make, for fear of slips, VEN 515
SLIP–SHOD 1 FR 0.0001 REL FR 0 V 1 P
be merry, thy wit shall not go slip–shod. LR 1.05. 12 P
SLISH 1 FR 0.0001 REL FR 1 V 0 P
here's snip and nip and cut and slish and slash, SHR 4.03. 90
SLIT 1 FR 0.0001 REL FR 0 V 1 P
i'll slit the villain's nose, that would have SHR 5.01.131 P
/SLIVER 1 FR 0.0001 REL FR 1 V 0 P
/that /herself /will /sliver /and /disbranch LR 4.02. 34
SLIVER 1 FR 0.0001 REL FR 1 V 0 P
clamb'ring to hang, an envious sliver broke, HAM 4.07.173
SLIVER'D 1 FR 0.0001 REL FR 1 V 0 P
slips of yew | sliver'd in the moon's eclipse, MAC 4.01. 28
SLOBB'RY 1 FR 0.0001 REL FR 1 V 0 P
to buy a slobb'ry and a dirty farm | in that H5 3.05. 13
SLOMBER *(also slumber)*
SLOMBER 1 FR 0.0001 REL FR 0 V 1 P
theise eyes of mine take themselves to slomber, H5 3.02.115 P
SLOP 1 FR 0.0001 REL FR 0 V 1 P
there's a french salutation to your french slop. ROM 2.04. 45 P
SLOPE 1 FR 0.0001 REL FR 1 V 0 P
though palaces and pyramids do slope | their MAC 4.01. 57
SLOPS 2 FR 0.0002 REL FR 0 V 2 P
as a german from the waist downward, all slops, ADO 3.02. 36 P
about the satin for my short cloak and my slops? 2H4 1.02. 30 P
SLOTH 7 FR 0.0008 REL FR 6 V 1 P
do so. to ebb | hereditary sloth instructs me. TMP 2.01.223
the bottom run | by their own fear or sloth. 2.01.228
let not sloth dim your honors new begot. 1H6 1.01. 79
abhor | this dilatory sloth and tricks of rome. H8 2.04.238
hog in sloth, fox in stealth, wolf in greediness LR 3.04. 93 P
when resty sloth | finds the down pillow hard. CYM 3.06. 34
and his army full | of bread and sloth. TNK 1.01.159
SLOTHFUL 1 FR 0.0001 REL FR 1 V 0 P
and that we find the slothful watch but weak, 1H6 3.02. 7
SLOUGH* 5 FR 0.0005 REL FR 2 V 3 P
from behind one of them, in a slough of mire; WIV 4.05. 68 P
to be, cast thy humble slough and appear fresh. TN 2.05.149 P
"cast thy humble slough," says she; 3.04. 68 P
move | with casted slough and fresh legerity. H5 4.01. 23
with shining checker'd slough, doth sting a 2H6 3.01.229
SLOVENLY 1 FR 0.0001 REL FR 1 V 0 P
to bring a slovenly unhandsome corse | betwixt 1H4 1.03. 44
SLOVENRY 1 FR 0.0001 REL FR 1 V 0 P
fly — | and time hath worn us into slovenry. H5 4.03.114
SLOW 58 FR 0.0065 REL FR 46 V 12 P
the man i' th' moon's too slow — till new–born TMP 2.01.249
and yet it cannot overtake your slow purse. TGV 1.01.126 P
and yet i was last chidden for being too slow. 2.01. 13 P
"item, she is slow in words." 3.01.332 P
to be slow in words is a woman's only virtue. 3.01.334 P
she cannot, for that's writ down she is slow of; 3.01.350 P
it makes me have a slow heart. 4.02. 65 P
had not their /bark been very slow of sail; ERR 1.01.116
is not lead a metal heavy, dull, and slow? LLL 3.01. 59
i say lead is slow. 3.01. 61
is that lead slow which is fir'd from a gun? 3.01. 62
other slow arts entirely keep the brain; 4.03.321

, methinks, how slow | this old moon /wanes! MND 1.01. 3
 it be, give it me, for i am slow of study. 1.02. 67 P
low in pursuit; 4.01.123
ut slow in speech, yet sweet as spring–time SHR 2.01.246
old comfort, for being slow in thy hot office? 4.01. 31 P
ur slow designs when we ourselves are dull. AWW 1.01.219
 reverend carriage, a slow tongue, in the habit TN 3.04. 73 P
nd creep time ne'er so slow, | yet it shall JN 3.03. 31
low hours shall not determinate | the dateless R2 1.03.150
ith slow but stately pace kept on his course, 5.02. 10
ou are as slow | as hot lord percy is on fire 1H4 3.01.263
who with their drowsy, slow, and flagging wings 2H6 4.01. 5
way, my lord! you are slow, for shame, away! 5.02. 72
or posted off their suits with slow delays; 3H6 4.08. 40
weet flow'rs are slow and weeds make haste. R3 2.04. 15
limb steep hills | requires slow pace at first. H8 1.01.132
hurlish as the bear, slow as the elephant; TRO 1.02. 21 P
ncursions, thou strikest as slow as another. 2.01. 30 P
isely and slow, they stumble that run fast. ROM 2.03. 94
ead, | unwieldy, slow, heavy, and pale as lead. 2.05. 17
o swift arrives as tardy as too slow. 2.06. 15
, | and i am nothing slow to slack his haste. 4.01. 3
hat swiftest wing of recompense is slow | to MAC 1.04. 17
alued file | distinguishes the swift, the slow, 3.01. 95
rd, wrung from me my slow leave | by laborsome
HAM 1.02. 58
olemn march | goes slow and stately by them. 1.02.202
nding ourselves too slow of sail, we put on a 4.06. 17 P
corn | to point his slow /unmoving finger at! OTH 4.02. 55
o slow a messenger. ANT 5.02.321
 slackly guarded, and the search so slow, CYM 1.01. 64
ould best express how slow his soul sail'd on, 1.03. 13
 languishing death, | but though slow, deadly. 1.05. 10
 's execution, man, | could never go so slow. 3.02. 71
ou art too slow to do thy master's bidding 3.04. 97
ack that leonine was so slack, so slow! PER 4.02. 64
ake slow pursuit, or altogether balk | the prey LUC 696
t him have time to mark how slow time goes 990
nd solemn night with slow sad gait descended 1081
ith soft slow tongue, true mark of modesty, 1220
ore than speed but dull and slow she deems: 1336
nd they that watch see time how slow it creeps. 1575
 doth divide | in two slow rivers, that the 1738
eceiving /nought by elements so slow | but SON 44.13
us can my love excuse the slow offense | of my 51. 1
nd, | when swift extremity can seem but slow? 51. 6
one, | unmoved, cold, and to temptation slow, 94. 4
LOWED 1 FR 0.0001 REL FR 1 V 0 P
would i knew not why it should be slowed. ROM 4.01. 16
LOWER 3 FR 0.0003 REL FR 2 V 1 P
hich i did think with slower foot came on, MM 5.01.395
its | and fall something into a slower method: R3 1.02.116
ll the speed of his rage goes slower; LR 1.02.167 P
LOW–GAITED 1 FR 0.0001 REL FR 0 V 1 P
s upon the horse, for he is very slow–gaited. LLL 3.01. 55 P
LOWLY 5 FR 0.0005 REL FR 4 V 1 P
nd to torment me | for bringing wood in slowly. TMP 2.02. 16
r though he comes slowly, he carries his house AYL 4.01. 54 P
te, | like a remorseful pardon slowly carried, AWW 5.03. 58
ood father's speed, | will come on very slowly. WT 5.01.211
conjure thee but slowly; JN 4.02.269
LOWNESS 2 FR 0.0002 REL FR 1 V 1 P
s my slowness that i do not, for i know you AWW 1.03. 10 P
is fool's speed | be cross'd with slowness; CYM 3.05.162
LOW–WING'D 1 FR 0.0001 REL FR 1 V 0 P
 slow–wing'd turtle, shall a buzzard take thee? SHR 2.01.207
SLUBBER 1 FR 0.0001 REL FR 1 V 0 P
lubber not business for my sake, bassanio, MV 2.08. 39
LUBBER 1 FR 0.0001 REL FR 0 V 1 P
 content to slubber the gloss of your new OTH 1.03.227 P
LUG 2 FR 0.0002 REL FR 2 V 0 P
ou /drumble, thou snail, thou slug, thou sot! ERR 2.02.194
, what a slug is hastings, that he comes not R3 3.01. 22
LUG–A–BED 1 FR 0.0001 REL FR 1 V 0 P
, you slug–a–bed! ROM 4.05. 2
LUGGARD 2 FR 0.0002 REL FR 2 V 0 P
at you have ta'en a tardy sluggard here. R3 5.03.225
he more to blame my sluggard negligence. LUC 1278
LUGGARDIZ'D 1 FR 0.0001 REL FR 1 V 0 P
an (living dully sluggardiz'd at home) | wear TGV 1.01. 7
LUGGISH 1 FR 0.0001 REL FR 1 V 0 P
 show what coast thy sluggish /crare | mightst CYM 4.02.205
LUIC'D 2 FR 0.0002 REL FR 2 V 0 P
inks she has been sluic'd in 's absence, | and WT 1.02.194
uic'd out his innocent soul through streams of R2 1.01.103
LUICES 2 FR 0.0002 REL FR 2 V 0 P
ho like sluices stopp'd | the crystal tide that VEN 956
ongue shall utter all, mine eyes like sluices, LUC 1076
LUMBER *(also slomber)*
LUMBER 21 FR 0.0023 REL FR 20 V 1 P
eep a care, | shake off slumber, and beware. TMP 2.01.304
urtling | from miserable slumber i awaked. AYL 4.03.132
ut you must not now slumber in it. AWW 3.06. 73 P
nd thought | this was so, and no slumber. WT 3.03. 39
ush'd with buzzing night–flies to thy slumber, 2H4 3.01. 11
at keep'st the ports of slumber open wide | to 4.05. 24
st, being suffer'd in that harmful slumber, 2H6 3.02.262
se | but like a pleasant slumber in thy lap? 3.02.390
st leaden slumber peize me down to–morrow, R3 5.03.105
erefore best | not wake him in his slumber. H8 1.01.122
ur pastimes done), possess a golden slumber, TIT 2.03. 26
 down, | that i may slumber an eternal sleep! 2.04. 15
hen will this fearful slumber have an end? 3.01.252
ou dost not slumber; 3.01.254
atter, | enjoy the honey–heavy dew of slumber. JC 2.01.230
 murd'rous slumber! 4.03.267
us smiling, as some fly had tickled slumber, CYM 4.02.210
 heaven slumber while their creatures want, PER 1.04. 16
ours | shake off the golden slumber of repose. 3.02. 23
nd thick slumber | hangs upon mine eyes. 5.01.234
w leaden slumber with live's strength doth LUC 124
LUMBERS 6 FR 0.0006 REL FR 6 V 0 P
 thy faint slumbers i by thee have watch'd, 1H4 2.03. 47
 trust the mock'ry of unquiet slumbers. R3 3.02. 27
u are for dreams and slumbers, brother priest, TRO 2.02. 37
 have their balmy slumbers wak'd with strife. OTH 2.03.258
ather dwell on) | and sing it in her slumbers. TNK 1.03. 78
ost thou desire my slumbers should be broken SON 61. 3

SLUMB'RED 1 FR 0.0001 REL FR 1 V 0 P
that you have but slumb'red here | while these MND 5.01.425
SLUMB'RY 1 FR 0.0001 REL FR 0 V 1 P
in this slumb'ry agitation, besides her walking MAC 5.01. 11 P
SLUNK 1 FR 0.0001 REL FR 1 V 0 P
or slunk not saturnine, as tarquin erst, | that TIT 4.01. 63
SLUT 2 FR 0.0002 REL FR 0 V 2 P
honesty upon a foul slut were to put good meat AYL 3.03. 36 P
i am not a slut, though i thank the gods i am 3.03. 38 P
SLUTS 2 FR 0.0002 REL FR 2 V 0 P
our radiant queen hates sluts and sluttery. WIV 5.05. 46
hold up, you sluts, | your aprons mountant. TIM 4.03.135
SLUTTERY 2 FR 0.0002 REL FR 2 V 0 P
our radiant queen hates sluts and sluttery. WIV 5.05. 46
sluttery, to such neat excellence oppos'd, CYM 1.06. 44
SLUTTISH 5 FR 0.0005 REL FR 4 V 1 P
displeasure is but sluttish if it smell so AWW 5.02. 6 P
them down | for sluttish spoils of opportunity, TRO 4.05. 62
and bakes the /elf–locks in foul sluttish hairs, ROM 1.04. 90
to wash the foul face of the sluttish ground, VEN 983
unswept stone, besmear'd with sluttish time. SON 55. 4
SLUTTISHNESS 1 FR 0.0001 REL FR 0 V 1 P
sluttishness may come hereafter. AYL 3.03. 41 P
SLY 14 FR 0.0015 REL FR 12 V 2 P
by some sly trick blunt thurio's dull proceeding TGV 2.06. 41
i am christophero sly, call not me honor nor SHR in.2. 5 P
am not i christopher sly, old sly's son of in.2. 18 P
indeed | and not a tinker nor christopher sly. in.2. 73
as stephen sly, and old john naps of greece, in.2. 93
with that same purpose–changer, that sly devil, JN 2.01.567
the sly, slow hours shall not determinate | the R2 1.03.150
thy sly conveyance and thy lord's false love, 3H6 3.03.160
simple truth must be abus'd | with silken, sly, R3 1.03. 53
age confirm'd, proud, subtle, sly, and bloody, 4.04.172
the sly whoresons | have got a speeding trick to H8 1.03. 39
sly frantic wretch, that holp'st to make me TIT 4.04. 59
a sly and constant knave, | not to be shak'd; CYM 1.05. 75
but the mild glance that sly ulysses lent LUC 1399
SLYLY *(see slily)*
SLY'S 1 FR 0.0001 REL FR 0 V 1 P
christopher sly, old sly's son of burton–heath, SHR in.2. 18 P
SLYS 1 FR 0.0001 REL FR 0 V 1 P
y' are a baggage, the slys are no rogues. SHR in.1. 3 P
SMACK* *(also smatch)*
/SMACK* 1 FR 0.0001 REL FR 1 V 0 P
time | that doth not /smack of observation — JN 1.01.208
SMACK* 8 FR 0.0009 REL FR 4 V 4 P
all sects, all ages smack of this vice, and he MM 2.02. 5
son, for indeed my father did something smack, MV 2.02. 17 P
and kiss'd her lips with such a clamorous smack SHR 3.02.178
thou hast to pull at a smack a' th' contrary. AWW 2.03.225 P
now he hath a smack of all neighboring languages 4.01. 16 P
and so am i, whether i smack or no; JN 1.01.209
youth, have yet some smack of an ague in you, 2H4 1.02. 97 P
thee as thy wounds, | they smack of honor both. MAC 1.02. 44
SMACKING 1 FR 0.0001 REL FR 1 V 0 P
smacking of every sin | that has a name; MAC 4.03. 59
SMACKS 2 FR 0.0002 REL FR 2 V 0 P
but smacks of something greater than herself, WT 4.04.158
smacks it not something of the policy? JN 2.01.396
/SMALL 1 FR 0.0001 REL FR 1 V 0 P
tatter'd clothes /small vices do appear; LR 4.06.164
SMALL 97 FR 0.0109 REL FR 76 V 21 P
here's too small a pasture for such store of TGV 1.01. 99 P
his little speaking shows his love but small. 1.02. 29
is as white as a lily and as small as a wand. 2.03. 21 P
but were you banish'd for so small a fault? 4.01. 31
has brown hair, and speaks small like a woman. WIV 1.01. 48 P
had fast'ned him unto a small spare mast, | such ERR 1.01. 79
small cheer and great welcome makes a merry 3.01. 26
small have continual plodders ever won, | save LLL 1.01. 86
color, methinks sampson had small reason for it. 1.02. 87 P
no, he is best indu'd in the small. 5.02.641 P
a mask, and you may speak as small as you will. MND 1.02. 50 P
leathren wings | to make my small elves coats, 2.02. 5
these things seem small and undistinguishable, 4.01.187
it appears, by his small light of discretion, 5.01.253 P
here's a small trifle of wives! MV 2.02.161 P
and after some small space, being strong at AYL 4.03.151
the poverty of her, the small acquaintance, my 5.02. 6 P
for god's sake, a pot of small ale. SHR in.2. 1 P
you say, there's small choice in rotten apples. 1.01.134 P
than at home, | where small experience grows. 1.02. 52
and this small packet of greek and latin books. 2.01.100
"with a small compass'd cape" — 4.03.139 P
thy small pipe | is as the maiden's organ, TN 1.04. 32
that none so small advantage shall step forth JN 3.04.151
then feeling what small things are boisterous 4.01. 94
small show'rs last long, but sudden storms are R2 2.01. 35
head, | and yet, /incaged in so small a verge, 2.01.102
and that small model of the barren earth | which 3.02.153
i play the torturer by small and small | to 3.02.198
i play the torturer by small and small | to 3.02.198
it is a matter of small consequence, | which for 5.02. 61
to thread the postern of a small needle's eye." 5.05. 17
that with our small conjunction we should on, 1H4 4.01. 37
a kingdom for it was too small a bound, | but 5.04. 90
it not show vildly in me to desire small beer? 2H4 2.02. 6 P
i do now remember the poor creature, small beer. 2.02. 11 P
a night is but small breath, and little pause, H5 2.04.145
small time, but in that small most greatly lived ep 5
but in that small most greatly lived | this star ep 5
to hazard all our lives in one small boat! 1H6 4.06. 33
small curs are not regarded when they grin, 2H6 3.01. 18
devise strange deaths for small offenses done? 3.01. 59
small things make base men proud. 4.01.106
and i will make it felony to drink small beer. 4.02. 68 P
this small inheritance my father left me 4.10. 18
but god he knows thy share thereof is small. 3H6 1.04.129
are the fount that makes small brooks to flow; 4.08. 54
if not, the city being but of small defense, 5.01. 64
small joy have i in being england's queen. R3 1.03.109
and less'ned be that small, god i beseech him! 1.03.110
"small herbs have grace, great weeds do grow 2.04. 13
within so small a time, my woman's heart 4.01. 78
and part in just proportion our small power. 5.03. 26
your enemies are many, and not small; H8 5.01.128
was a haberdasher's wife of small wit near him, 5.03. 47 P

and between, but small thanks for my labor. TRO 1.01. 72 P
(although small pricks | to their subsequent 1.03.343
things small as nothing, for request's sake only 2.03.169
if you'll bestow a small (of what you have COR 1.01.125
the strongest nerves and small inferior veins 1.01.138
into a pipe | small as an eunuch, or the virgin 3.02.114
but a small thing would make it flame again; 4.03. 20 P
let me go grind their bones to powder small, TIT 5.02.198
film, | her waggoner a small grey–coated gnat, ROM 1.04. 67
the tears have got small victory by that, | for 4.01. 30
that there should be small love amongest these TIM 1.01.249
i have receiv'd some small kindnesses from him, 3.02. 21 P
each small annexment, petty consequence, HAM 3.03. 21
o most small fault, | how ugly didst thou in LR 1.04.266
you shall do small respects, show too bold 2.02.130
chance the king comes with so small a number? 2.04. 63
were like an old lecher's heart, a small spark, 3.04.112 P
but mice and rats, and such small deer, | have 3.04.138
her cock, a buoy | almost too small for sight. 4.06. 20
and the small gilded fly | does lecher in my 4.06.112
to suckle fools and chronicle small beer. OTH 2.01.160
and thou by that small hurt /hast cashier'd 2.03.375
it is a great price | for a small vice. 4.03. 70
but small to greater matters must give way. ANT 2.02. 11
not if the small come first. 2.02. 12
but i have seen small reflection of her wit. CYM 1.02. 31 P
t' entreat your grace but in a small request, 1.06.181
yet left in heaven as small a drop of pity | as 4.02.304
my good will is great, though the gift small. PER 3.04. 18
the sleided silk | with fingers long, small, 4.ch. 22
small winds shake him. | but what's the matter? TNK 1.02. 88
the birch upon the breeches of the small ones, 3.05.111
the body of our sport, of no small study, | i 3.05.121
through a small glade cut by the fishermen, | i 4.01. 64
'fore yourself | by some small start of time. 5.03. 38
breast, full eye, small head, and nostril wide, VEN 296
small lights are soon blown out, huge fires LUC 647
know, gentle wench, it small avails my mood; 1273
will be a totter'd weed, of small worth held: SON 2. 4
that to his subject lends not some small glory, 84. 6
"small show of man was yet upon his chin, | his LC 92
lies | in the small orb of one particular tear! 289
/SMALLER 1 FR 0.0001 REL FR 1 V 0 P
but yet indeed the /smaller is his daughter. AYL 1.02.272
SMALLER 3 FR 0.0003 REL FR 3 V 0 P
a smaller boon than this i cannot beg, | and TGV 5.04. 24
cutting a smaller hair than may be seen; LLL 5.02.258
much smaller than the smallest of his thoughts, 2H4 1.03. 30
SMALLEST 17 FR 0.0019 REL FR 15 V 2 P
lends | the smallest scruple of her excellence, MM 1.01. 37
you swerve not from the smallest article of it, 4.02.104 P
as claudio's, to cross this in the smallest. 4.02.168 P
flow in grief, | the smallest twine may lead me. ADO 4.01.250
down | that violates the smallest branch herein. LLL 1.01. 21
the smallest monstrous mouse that creeps on MND 5.01.220
there's not the smallest orb which thou MV 5.01. 60
and once again a pot o' th' smallest ale. SHR in.2. 75
the smallest thread | that ever spider twisted JN 4.03.127
ere break the smallest parcel of this vow. 1H4 3.02.159
much smaller than the smallest of his thoughts, 2H4 1.03. 30
for what you see is but the smallest part | and 1H6 2.03. 52
the smallest worm will turn, being trodden on, 3H6 2.02. 17
her traces of the smallest spider web, | her ROM 1.04. 64
if he do break the smallest particle | of any JC 2.01.139
draw | the smallest fear or doubt of her revolt, OTH 3.03.188
or my affection put to th' smallest teen, | or LC 192
SMALL–KNOWING 1 FR 0.0001 REL FR 0 V 1 P
"that unlettered small–knowing soul" — LLL 1.01.250 P
SMALLNESS 2 FR 0.0002 REL FR 2 V 0 P
melted from | the smallness of a gnat to air, CYM 1.03. 21
one that sung, and, by the smallness of it, | a TNK 4.01. 58
SMALL'ST 1 FR 0.0001 REL FR 1 V 0 P
stick | the small'st opinion on my least misuse? OTH 4.02.109
SMALUS 1 FR 0.0001 REL FR 1 V 0 P
where the warlike smalus, | that noble honor'd WT 5.01.157
SMART 9 FR 0.0010 REL FR 9 V 0 P
and shall, or some of us will smart for it. ADO 5.01.109
hit | doth very foolishly, although he smart, AYL 2.07. 54
the sword of orleance hath not made me smart; 1H6 4.06. 42
their softest touch as smart as lizards' stings! 2H6 3.02.325
cruel | that she should feel the smart of this? H8 2.01.166
"because thou canst not ease thy smart | by TRO 4.04. 19
and they smart | to hear themselves rememb'red. COR 1.09. 28
how smart a lash that speech doth give my HAM 3.01. 49
and shielded him | from this earth–vexing smart. CYM 5.04. 42
SMARTING 2 FR 0.0002 REL FR 2 V 0 P
i then, all smarting with my wounds being cold, 1H4 1.03. 49
stew'd in brine, | smarting in ling'ring pickle. ANT 2.05. 66
SMARTLY 1 FR 0.0001 REL FR 1 V 0 P
and loos'd his love–shaft smartly from his bow, MND 2.01.159
SMARTS 1 FR 0.0001 REL FR 1 V 0 P
grieving themselves to guess at others' smarts, LUC 1238
SMATCH *(also smack*)*
SMATCH 1 FR 0.0001 REL FR 1 V 0 P
thy life hath had some smatch of honor in it. JC 5.05. 46
SMATTER 1 FR 0.0001 REL FR 1 V 0 P
good prudence, smatter with your gossips, go. ROM 3.05.171
SMEAR 2 FR 0.0002 REL FR 2 V 0 P
them, and smear | the sleepy grooms with blood. MAC 2.02. 46
and smear with dust their glitt'ring golden LUC 945
SMEAR'D 5 FR 0.0005 REL FR 5 V 0 P
triumphant death, smear'd with captivity, 1H6 4.07. 3
lo, now my glory smear'd in dust and blood! 3H6 5.02. 23
love this painting | wherein you see me smear'd; COR 1.06. 69
hath now this dread and black complexion smear'd
HAM 2.02.455
like to a pair of lions smear'd with prey, TNK 1.04. 18
SMEARED 1 FR 0.0001 REL FR 1 V 0 P
begrim'd with sweat, and smeared all with dust, LUC 1381
SMELL 56 FR 0.0063 REL FR 34 V 22 P
a very ancient and fish–like smell; TMP 2.02. 26 P
monster, i do smell all horse–piss, at which my 4.01.199 P
i, having been acquainted with the smell before, TGV 4.04. 23 P
i cannot abide the smell of hot meat since. WIV 1.01.286 P
and smell like bucklersbury in simple time — i 3.03. 72 P
of villainous smell that ever offended nostril. 3.05. 92 P
but stay, i smell a man of middle–earth. 5.05. 80
in your own report, | and smell of calumny. MM 2.04.159

can you smell him out by that? ADO 3.02. 51 P
i am stuff'd, cousin, i cannot smell. 3.04. 64 P
i smell some l'envoy, some goose, in this. LLL 3.01.121 P
o, i smell false latin, "dunghill" for unguem. 5.01. 79 P
yes, to smell pork, to eat of the habitation MV 1.03. 33 P
thou losest thy old smell. AYL 1.02.108 P
i smell sweet savors, and i feel soft things. SHR in.2. 71
mood, and smell somewhat strong of her strong AWW 5.02. 5 P
is but sluttish if it smell so strongly as thou 5.02. 7 P
mine eyes smell onions, i shall weep anon. 5.03.320
excellent! i smell a device. TN 2.03.162 P
you smell this business with a sense as cold WT 2.01.151
are you in earnest, sir? i smell the trick on't. 4.04.642 P
also, to smell out work for th' other senses. 4.04.673 P
for i am stifled with this smell of sin. JN 4.03.113
to see him shine so brisk and smell so sweet, 1H4 1.03. 54
i smell it. upon my life, it will do well. 1.03.277
to wake a wolf is as bad as smell a fox. 2H4 1.02.155 P
the smell whereof shall breed a plague in france H5 4.03.103
i am qualmish at the smell of leek. 5.01. 21
with whose sweet smell the air shall be perfum'd 2H6 1.01.255
a rose | by any other word would smell as sweet; ROM 2.02. 44
that this foul deed shall smell above the earth JC 3.01.274
here's the smell of the blood still. MAC 5.01. 50 P
do you smell a fault? LR 1.01. 16 P
that what a man cannot smell out, he may spy 1.05. 23 P
among twenty but can smell him that's stinking. 2.04. 71 P
and fum, | i smell the blood of a british man.'" 3.04.184
at gates, and let him smell | his way to dover. 3.07. 93
the first time that we smell the air | we wawl 4.06.179
foh, one may smell in such, a will most rank, OTH 3.03.232
they see, and smell, | and have their palates 4.03. 94
i'll smell thee on the tree. 5.02. 15
his celestial breath | was sulphurous to smell; CYM 5.04.115
and | perfumes to kill the smell o' th' prison; TNK 3.01. 86
unarm'd, and can | smell where resistance is. 3.02. 17
herbs for their smell, and sappy plants to bear: VEN 165
and nothing but the very smell were left me, 441
to make the cunning hounds mistake their smell, 686
"for there his smell with others being mingled, 691
set | gloss on the rose, smell to the violet. 936
bows her head, the new-sprung flow'r to smell, 1171
unapt for tender smell, or speedy flight, | make LUC 695
talk, | lest she some subtile practice smell — PP 18. 9
to thy fair flower add the rank smell of weeds: SON 69.12
lilies that fester smell far worse than weeds. 94.14
nor the sweet smell | of different flowers in 98. 5
nor taste, nor smell, desire to be invited | to 141. 7
SMELL'D 1 FR 0.0001 REL FR 0 V 1 P
to have smell'd like a fool. CYM 2.01. 16 P
SMELLING 6 FR 0.0006 REL FR 3 V 3 P
smelling so sweetly, all musk, and so rushling, WIV 2.02. 66 P
as if you snuff'd up love by smelling love; LLL 3.01. 17 P
but for smelling out the odoriferous flowers of 4.02.124 P
and then dreams he of smelling out a suit; ROM 1.04. 78
ears without hands or eyes, smelling sans all, HAM 3.04. 79
breath perfum'd, that breedeth love by smelling. VEN 444
SMELL-LESS 1 FR 0.0001 REL FR 1 V 0 P
daisies smell-less, yet most quaint, | and sweet TNK 1.01. 5
SMELLS 15 FR 0.0017 REL FR 12 V 3 P
a fish, he smells like a fish; TMP 2.02. 25 P
he speaks holiday, he smells april and may — he WIV 3.02. 68 P
your nose smells "no" in /this, most LLL 5.02.566
the violet smells to him as it doth to me; H5 4.01.102 P
the feast smells well, but i | appear not like a COR 4.05. 5
thy counsel, lad, smells of no cowardice. TIT 2.01.132
so early waking — what with loathsome smells, ROM 4.03. 46
to foresee, | smells from the general weal. TIM 4.03.160
that the heaven's breath | smells wooingly here; MAC 1.06. 6
o, my offense is rank, it smells to heaven, | it HAM 3.03. 36
let me wipe it first, it smells of mortality. LR 4.06.133
the buffet | with knaves that smells of sweat: ANT 1.04. 21
it smells most sweetly in my sense. PER 3.02. 60
being gone, | not royal in their smells alone, TNK 1.01. 2
whence didst thou steal thy sweet that smells, SON 99. 2
SMELL'ST 1 FR 0.0001 REL FR 1 V 0 P
who art so lovely fair and smell'st so sweet OTH 4.02. 68
SMELL'T 1 FR 0.0001 REL FR 1 V 0 P
upon't, i think — i smell't — o villainy! OTH 5.02.191
SMELT 7 FR 0.0008 REL FR 3 V 4 P
lifted up their noses | as they smelt music. TMP 4.01.178
a pissing-while, but all the chamber smelt him. TGV 4.04. 20 P
beggar, though she smelt brown bread and garlic. MM 3.02.183 P
musty chaff, and you are smelt | above the moon. COR 5.01. 31
for this, being smelt, with that part cheers ROM 2.03. 25
and smelt so? pah! HAM 5.01.200 P
there i found 'em, there i smelt 'em out. LR 4.06.103 P
/SMIL'D 1 FR 0.0001 REL FR 1 V 0 P
/on /whom /fortune /would /then /have /smil'd? 2H4 4.01.131
SMIL'D 12 FR 0.0013 REL FR 10 V 2 P
when men were fond, i smil'd and wond'red how. MM 2.02.186
whose miseries are to be smil'd at, their WT 4.04.792 P
it in snuff — and still he smil'd and talk'd: 1H4 1.03. 41
saw his heroical seed, and smil'd to see him, H5 2.04. 59
he smil'd me in the face, raught me his hand, 4.06. 21
he smil'd and said, "the better for our purpose. R3 5.03.274
those that understood him smil'd at one another, JC 1.02.282 P
he smil'd at it. LR 4.02. 5
julius caesar | smil'd at their lack of skill, CYM 2.04. 22
and with the same breath smil'd, and kiss'd her TNK 4.01. 93
whilst as fickle fortune smil'd, | thou and i PP 20.27
wit well blazon'd, smil'd or made some moan. LC 217
SMIL'DST 1 FR 0.0001 REL FR 1 V 0 P
and thou that smil'dst at good duke humphrey's 2H6 4.01. 76
SMILE 87 FR 0.0098 REL FR 71 V 16 P
thou didst smile, | infused with a fortitude TMP 1.02.153
do not smile at me that i boast her /off, | for 4.01. 9
when inward joy enforc'd my heart to smile! TGV 1.02. 63
with our discourse to make your grace to smile. 5.04.163
you do not smile at this, lord angelo? MM 5.01.163
i did but smile till now. 5.01.233
when i have cause, and smile at no man's jests; ADO 1.03. 14 P
if such a one will smile and stroke his beard, 5.01. 15
affliction may one day smile again, and till LLL 1.01.314 P
wit | to enforce the pained impotent to smile. 5.02.854
i jest to oberon and make him smile | when i a MND 2.01. 44
they'll not show their teeth in way of smile MV 1.01. 55
even till i shrink with cold, i smile and say, AYL 2.01. 9
him take that for coming a-night to jane smile; 2.04. 48 P
loose now and then | a scatt'red smile, and that 3.05.104
sirs, | if you should smile, he grows impatient. SHR in.1. 99
to smile at scapes and perils overblown. 5.02. 3
favor of the king | smile upon this contract, AWW 2.03.178
quenching my familiar smile with an austere TN 2.05. 66 P
therefore in my presence still smile, dear my 2.05.177 P
i will smile, i will do every thing that thou 2.05.178 P
and he will smile upon her, which will now be so 2.05.201 P
why then methinks 'tis time to smile again. 3.01.126
he does smile his face into more lines than is 3.02. 78 P
if she do, he'll smile, and take't for a great 3.02. 82 P
no, madam, he does nothing but smile. 3.04. 11 P
why dost thou smile so, and kiss thy hand so oft 3.04. 32 P
up, that thou thereby | mayst smile at this. 4.01. 57
and you smile not, he's gagg'd." 5.01.375 P
next neighbor — by | sir smile, his neighbor. WT 1.02.196
the king doth smile at, and is well prepar'd JN 5.02.134
under the smile of safety wounds the world; 2H4 in 10
with flowers, and smile upon his finger's end, i H5 2.03. 15 P
bids them good morrow with a modest smile, | and 4.pr. 33
young talbot's valor makes me smile at thee. 1H6 4.07. 4
whose smile and frown, like to achilles' spear, 2H6 5.01.100
smile, gentle heaven! 3H6 2.03. 6
why, i can smile, and murther whiles i smile, 3.02.182
why, i can smile, and murther whiles i smile, 3.02.182
these peers of france should smile at that. 3.03. 91
and who durst smile when warwick bent his brow? 5.02. 22
smile in men's faces, smooth, deceive, and cog, R3 1.03. 48
they smile at me who shortly shall be dead. 3.04.107
english woes shall make me smile in france. 4.04.115
smile heaven upon this fair conjunction, | that 5.05. 20
methought | i stood not in the smile of heaven, H8 2.04.188
there is, betwixt that smile we would aspire to, 3.02.368
if they smile, | and say 'twill do, i know ep 11
buried this sigh in wrinkle of a smile, | but TRO 1.01. 38
but how should this man, that makes me smile, 1.02. 32 P
you smile and mock me, as if i meant naughtily. 4.02. 37
sit, gods, upon your thrones, and smile at troy! 5.10. 7
with a kind of smile, | which ne'er came from COR 1.01.107
i may make the belly smile | as well as speak — 1.01.109
when i am forth, | bid me farewell, and smile. 4.01. 50
so smile the heavens upon this holy act, | that ROM 2.06. 1
to move the heavens to smile upon my state, 4.03. 4
then they could smile, and fawn upon his debts, TIM 3.04. 51
thou rather shalt enforce it with thy smile 5.04. 45
that could be mov'd to smile at any thing. JC 1.02.207
that mothers shall but smile when they behold 3.01.267
and some that smile have in their hearts, i fear 4.01. 50
if we do meet again, why, we shall smile; 5.01.117
if we do meet again, we'll smile indeed; 5.01.120
but who knows nothing, is once seen to smile; MAC 4.03.167
but swords i smile at, weapons laugh to scorn, 5.07. 12
meet it is i set it down | that one may smile, HAM 1.05.108
i set it down | that one may smile, and smile, 1.05.108
nay, and thou canst not smile as the wind sits, LR 1.04.100 P
smile you my speeches, as i were a fool? 2.02. 82
smile once more, turn thy wheel! 2.02.173
we lose it not, so long as we can smile. OTH 1.03.211
ay, smile upon her, do; 2.01.169 P
as he shall smile, othello shall go mad; 4.01.100
if't be summer news, | smile to't before; CYM 3.04. 13
was that it was for not being such a smile; 4.02. 53
the smile mocking the sigh, that it would fly 4.02. 54
until our stars that frown lend us a smile. PER 1.04.108
of all this sprightly sharpness, not a smile. TNK 4.02. 30
we'll put on | and smile with palamon; 5.04.128
no man smile? ep 4
to toy, to wanton, dally, smile, and jest, VEN 106
a smile recures the wounding of a frown. 465
"nor shall he smile at thee in secret thought, LUC 1065
while with a joyless smile she turns away | the 1711
but smile and jest at every gentle offer. PP 4.12
yet at my parting sweetly did she smile, | in 14. 7
SMILED 1 FR 0.0001 REL FR 1 V 0 P
whereat she smiled with so sweet a cheer | that LUC 264
/SMILES 1 FR 0.0001 REL FR 1 V 0 P
/her /smiles /and /tears | /were /like /a LR 4.03. 18
SMILES 47 FR 0.0053 REL FR 42 V 5 P
bestow thy fawning smiles on equal mates, | and TGV 3.01.158
this is the flow'r that smiles on every one, LLL 5.02.331
that smiles his cheek in years and knows the 5.02.465
your frowns would teach my smiles such skill! MND 1.01.195
he hears merry tales and smiles not. MV 1.02. 48 P
inconstant, full of tears, full of smiles; AYL 3.02.412 P
thy smiles become thee well. TN 2.05.176 P
as now they are, and making practic'd smiles, WT 1.02.116
dimples of his chin and cheek, his smiles, | the 2.03.102
wooing poor craftsmen with the craft of smiles R2 1.04. 28
fondly with her tears and smiles in meeting, 3.02. 9
his face still combating with tears and smiles, 5.02. 32
first bow'd my knee | unto this king of smiles, 1H4 1.03.246
when time shall serve, there shall be smiles — H5 2.01. 6 P
now we are victors, upon us he smiles. 1H6 1.02. 4
he beckons with his hand and smiles on me, | as 1.04. 92
we mourn, france smiles; 4.03. 32
poor boy, he smiles, methinks, as who should say 4.07. 27
he smiles, and says his edward is install'd; 3H6 3.01. 46
fair queen and mistress | smiles at her news, 3.03.168
looks | are at my service, like enforced smiles; R3 3.05. 9
the noble troops that waited | upon my smiles. H8 3.02.412
o, he smiles valiantly. TRO 1.02.124 P
as smiles upon the forehead of this action | for 2.02.205
to send their smiles before them to achilles, 3.03. 72
the welcome ever smiles, | and farewell goes out 3.03.168
where senators shall mingle tears with smiles; COR 1.09. 3
the smiles of knaves | tent in my cheeks, and 3.02.115
in pleasing smiles such murderous tyranny. TIT 2.03.267
look how the black slave smiles upon the father, 4.02.120
the grey-ey'd morn smiles on the frowning night, ROM 2.03. 1
for venus smiles not in a house of tears. 4.01. 8
but rather one that smiles and still invites TIM 2.01. 11
whose dimpled smiles from fools exhaust their 4.03.120
seldom he smiles, and smiles in such a sort | as JC 1.02.205
and smiles in such a sort | as if he mock'd 1.02.205
hide it in smiles and affability; 2.01. 82
for look he smiles, and caesar doth not change. 3.01. 24
where we are, | there's daggers in men's smiles; MAC 2.03.140
for the blood-bolter'd banquo smiles upon me, 4.01.123
grace, | occasion smiles upon a second leave. HAM 1.03. 54
the robb'd that smiles steals something from the OTH 1.03.208
jealousy must /conster | poor cassio's smiles, 4.01.102
fortune at you | dimpled her cheek with smiles. TNK 1.01. 66
and when he smiles | he shows a lover, when he 4.02.135
at this adonis smiles as in disdain, | that in VEN 241
to love a cheek that smiles at thee in scorn! 252
SMILEST 1 FR 0.0001 REL FR 1 V 0
and smilest upon the stroke that murders me. ROM 3.03. 23
/SMILETS 1 FR 0.0001 REL FR 1 V 0
/those /happy /smilets | /that /play'd /on /her LR 4.03. 19
SMILING 36 FR 0.0040 REL FR 32 V 4
of my lungs provokes me to ridiculous smiling — LLL 3.01. 77
of progeny | forbid the smiling courtesy of love 5.02.745
away, | and you sat smiling at his cruel prey. MND 2.02.150
is like a villain with a smiling cheek, | a MV 1.03.100
like patience on a monument, | smiling at grief. TN 2.04.115
my love, let it appear in thy smiling; 2.05.176
bade me come smiling and cross-garter'd to you, 5.01.337
then cam'st in smiling, | and in such forms 5.01.349
of smiling peace to march a bloody host, | and JN 3.01.246
so weeping, smiling, greet i thee, my earth, R2 3.02. 10
by smiling pick-thanks and base newsmongers, | i 1H4 3.02. 25
hill | stood smiling to behold his lion's whelp H5 1.02.109
thou smiling while he knit his angry brows: 3H6 2.02. 20
with smiling plenty, and fair prosperous days! R3 5.05. 34
i think his smiling becomes him better than any TRO 1.02.122
our powers, with smiling fronts encount'ring, COR 1.06. 8
most smiling, smooth, detested parasites, TIM 3.06. 94
came smiling and did bathe their hands in it. JC 2.02. 79
pipes, | in which so many smiling romans bath'd, 2.02. 86
and fortune, on his damned /quarrel smiling, MAC 1.02. 14
i would, while it was smiling in my face, | have 1.07. 56
accord of hamlet | sits smiling to my heart, in HAM 1.02.124
o villain, villain, smiling, damned villain! 1.05.106
though by your smiling you seem to say so. 2.02.310
such smiling rogues as these, | like rats, oft LR 2.02. 73
stood pretty dimpled boys, like smiling cupids, ANT 2.02.202
com'st thou smiling from | the world's great 4.08. 17
nobly he yokes | a smiling with a sigh, as if CYM 4.02. 52
thus smiling, as some fly had tickled slumber, 4.02.210
graves, and smiling | extremity out of act. PER 5.01.138
here love himself sits smiling. TNK 4.02. 14
within this half hour she came smiling to me 5.02. 4
showed deep regard and smiling government. LUC 1400
it smiling credit her false-speaking tongue, PP 1. 7
it suffers not in smiling pomp, nor falls SON 124. 6
saw how deceits were gilded in his smiling, LC 172
SMILINGLY 3 FR 0.0003 REL FR 3 V 0
all the regions | do smilingly revolt, and who COR 4.06.103
of passion, joy and grief, | burst smilingly. LR 5.03.200
at last she smilingly with this gives o'er; LUC 1567
SMIL'ST 2 FR 0.0002 REL FR 1 V 1
smil'st thou? TN 3.04. 18
come, grin on me, and i will think thou smil'st, JN 3.04. 34
SMIRCH 1 FR 0.0001 REL FR 1 V 0
and with a kind of umber smirch my face; AYL 1.03.112
SMIRCH'D 2 FR 0.0002 REL FR 1 V 1
hercules in the smirch'd worm-eaten tapestry, ADO 3.03.136
do with his smirch'd complexion all fell feats H5 3.03. 17
SMIRCHED 1 FR 0.0001 REL FR 1 V 0
who smirched thus and mir'd with infamy, | i ADO 4.01.133
SMIT *(also smote)*
SMIT 1 FR 0.0001 REL FR 1 V 0
on his fracted dates | have smit my credit. TIM 2.01. 23
/SMITE 1 FR 0.0001 REL FR 1 V 0
the next caesarion /smite, | till by degrees the ANT 3.13.162
SMITE 1 FR 0.0001 REL FR 0 V 1
well, i will smite his noddles. pray you follow. WIV 3.01.125
/SMITES 1 FR 0.0001 REL FR 1 V 0
a grief that /smites | my very heart at root. ANT 5.02.104
SMITES 1 FR 0.0001 REL FR 1 V 0
it smites me | beneath the fall i have. ANT 5.02.171
SMITETH 1 FR 0.0001 REL FR 1 V 0
his falchion on a flint he softly smiteth, LUC 176
SMITH 3 FR 0.0003 REL FR 1 V 2
my lady his mother play'd false with a smith. MV 1.02. 44
i saw a smith stand with his hammer, thus, | the JN 4.02.193
and smith the weaver — 2H6 4.02. 28
SMITHFIELD 5 FR 0.0005 REL FR 2 V 3
he's gone /into smithfield to buy your worship a 2H4 1.02. 50
paul's, and he'll buy me a horse in smithfield; 1.02. 53
the witch in smithfield shall be burnt to ashes, 2H6 2.03. 7
but get you to smithfield and gather head, | and 4.05. 9
there's an army gather'd together in smithfield. 4.06. 12
SMITH'S 1 FR 0.0001 REL FR 0 V 1
here is now the smith's note for shoeing and 2H4 5.01. 18
SMOCK 8 FR 0.0009 REL FR 4 V 4
will she sit in her smock till she have writ a ADO 2.03.132
die when you will, a smock shall be your shroud. LLL 5.02.479
i shall stay here the forehorse to a smock, AWW 2.01. 30
you would think a smock were a she-angel, he so WT 4.04.209
doubtless he shrives this woman to her smock, 1H6 1.02.119
two, two: a shirt and a smock. ROM 2.04.103
o ill-starr'd wench, | pale as thy smock! OTH 5.02.273
your old smock brings forth a new petticoat, and ANT 1.02.168
SMOCKS 3 FR 0.0003 REL FR 2 V 1
ramm'd me in with foul shirts and smocks, socks, WIV 3.05. 90
daws, | and maidens bleach their summer smocks, LLL 5.02.906
but this poor petticoat and two coarse smocks. TNK 5.02. 84
SMOK'D 2 FR 0.0002 REL FR 1 V 1
he was first smok'd by the old lord lafew. AWW 3.06.103
steel, | which smok'd with bloody execution, MAC 1.02. 18
SMOKE 27 FR 0.0030 REL FR 24 V 3
sweet smoke of rhetoric! LLL 3.01. 63
thus must i from the smoke into the smother, AYL 1.02.287
'twill fly with the smoke out at the chimney. 4.01.164
they begin to smoke me, and disgraces have of AWW 4.01. 27
as black as vulcan in the smoke of war. TN 5.01. 53
i'll smoke your skin-coat and i catch you right. JN 2.01.139
they shoot but calm words folded up in smoke, 2.01.229
he speaks plain cannon-fire, and smoke, and 2.01.462
so bees with smoke and doves with noisome stench 1H6 1.05. 23
for smoke and dusky vapors of the night, | am 2.02. 27
whose smoke like incense doth perfume the sky. TIT 1.01.145
or some of you shall smoke for it in rome. 4.02.111

feather of lead, bright smoke, cold fire, sick ROM 1.01.180
love is a smoke made with the fume of sighs, 1.01.190
smoke and lukewarm water | is your perfection. TIM 3.06. 89
up, | let your close fire predominate his smoke, 4.03.143
whilst your purpled hands do reek and smoke, JC 3.01.158
and pall thee in the dunnest smoke of hell, MAC 1.05. 51
and smoke the temple with our sacrifices. CYM 5.05.398
murther's as near to lust as flame to smoke; PER 1.01.138
one cries, "o, this smoke!" TNK 4.03. 53 P
her face doth reek and smoke, her blood doth VEN 555
stay, | and blows the smoke of it into his face, LUC 312
"o night, thou furnace of foul reeking smoke! 799
this helpless smoke of words doth me no right. 1027
so vanisheth | as smoke from aetna, that in air 1042
way, | hiding thy brav'ry in their rotten smoke? SON 34. 4
SMOKES 3 FR 0.0003 REL FR 3 V 0 P
breath | already smokes about the burning crest JN 5.04. 34
'tis hot, it smokes, | it came even from the LR 5.03.224
and let our crooked smokes climb to their CYM 5.05.477
SMOKING 5 FR 0.0005 REL FR 4 V 1 P
for a perfumer, as i was smoking a musty room, ADO 1.03. 59 P
stain'd their fetlocks in his smoking blood, 3H6 2.03. 21
thy murd'rous falchion smoking in his blood; R3 1.02. 94
that we with smoking swords may march from hence
COR 1.04. 11
smoking with pride, march'd on, to make his LUC 438
SMOKY 6 FR 0.0006 REL FR 6 V 0 P
fair eyes, to be the mark | of smoky muskets? AWW 3.02.108
a railing wife, | worse than a smoky house. 1H4 3.01.159
and to the fire–ey'd maid of smoky war | all hot 4.01.114
why rather, sleep, liest thou in smoky cribs, 2H4 3.01. 9
base and illustrious as the smoky light | that's CYM 1.06.109
that in their smoky ranks his smoth'red light LUC 783
SMOOTH 41 FR 0.0046 REL FR 38 V 3 P
the course of true love never did run smooth; MND 1.01.134
and stick musk–roses in thy sleek smooth head, 4.01. 3
ta'en from me the show | of smooth civility; AYL 2.07. 96
politic with my friend, smooth with mine enemy, 5.04. 45 P
why are our bodies soft, and weak, and smooth, SHR 5.02.165
diana's lip | is not more smooth and rubious; TN 1.04. 32
affairs and their dispatch | with such a smooth, 4.03. 19
to smooth the ice, or add another hue | unto the JN 4.02. 13
to smooth his fault i should have been more mild R2 1.03.240
and he hath brought us smooth and welcome news.
1H4 1.01. 66
which hath been smooth as oil, soft as young 1.03. 7
tongues | they bring smooth comforts false, 2H4 in 40
and wears his boots very smooth, like unto the 2.04.249 P
how smooth and even they do bear themselves! H5 2.02. 3
is rough, coz, and my condition is not smooth; 5.02.287 P
and smooth my way upon their headless necks; 2H6 1.02. 65
smooth runs the water where the brook is deep, 3.01. 53
will bring to light in smooth duke humphrey. 3.01. 65
and smooth the frowns of war with peaceful looks
3H6 2.06. 32
how haps it in this smooth discourse | you told 3.03. 88
smile in men's faces, smooth, deceive, and cog, R3 1.03. 48
grace looks cheerfully and smooth this morning; 3.04. 48
so smooth he daub'd his vice with show of virtue 3.05. 29
the sea being smooth, | how many shallow bauble TRO 1.03. 34
for i can smooth and fill his aged ears | with TIT 4.04. 96
yield to his humor, smooth and speak him fair, 5.02.140
to smooth that rough touch with a tender kiss. ROM 1.05. 96
poor my lord, what tongue shall smooth thy name, 3.02. 98
most smiling, smooth, detested parasites, TIM 3.06. 94
thy verse swells with stuff so fine and smooth 5.01. 84
vile and loathsome crust, | all my smooth body. HAM 1.05. 73
to bear all smooth and even, | this sudden 4.03. 7
smooth every passion | that in the natures of LR 2.02. 75
he hath a person and a smooth dispose | to be OTH 1.03.397
snow, | and smooth as monumental alablaster. 5.02. 5
and smooth success | be strew'd before your feet ANT 1.03.100
father | seem'd not to strike, but smooth. PER 1.02. 78
place | to give the smooth and dexter way to me STM III 11
my smooth moist hand, were it with thy hand felt VEN 143
the path is smooth that leadeth on to danger. 788
tell, | smooth not thy tongue with filed talk, PP 18. 8
SMOOTH'D 2 FR 0.0002 REL FR 2 V 0 P
war hath smooth'd his wrinkled front; R3 1.01. 9
grize of fortune | is smooth'd by that below. TIM 4.03. 17
SMOOTHED 2 FR 0.0002 REL FR 2 V 0 P
not now | but every rub is smoothed on our way. H5 2.02.188
fury, | as by his smoothed brows it doth appear. 1H6 3.01.124
SMOOTHER 1 FR 0.0001 REL FR 1 V 0 P
far sweeter, | smoother than pelops' shoulder! TNK 4.02. 21
SMOOTH–FAC'D 3 FR 0.0003 REL FR 3 V 0 P
i'll mark no words that smooth–fac'd wooers say. LLL 5.02.828
that smooth–fac'd gentleman, tickling commodity,
JN 2.01.573
enrich the time to come with smooth–fac'd peace,
R3 5.05. 33
SMOOTHING 3 FR 0.0003 REL FR 3 V 0 P
let not his smoothing words | bewitch your 2H6 1.01.156
tongue could never learn sweet smoothing word; R3 1.02.168
fast, | thy smoothing titles to a ragged name, LUC 892
SMOOTHLY 2 FR 0.0002 REL FR 1 V 1 P
whose names yet run smoothly in the even road of
ADO 5.02. 33 P
when it comes so smoothly off, so obscenely as LLL 4.01.143
SMOOTHNESS 3 FR 0.0003 REL FR 2 V 1 P
she is too subtile for thee, and her smoothness, AYL 1.03. 77
beget a temperance that may give it smoothness. HAM 3.02. 8 P
their smoothness, like a goodly champaign plain, LUC 1247
SMOOTH'S 1 FR 0.0001 REL FR 0 V 1 P
turnbert street, to master smooth's the silk–man. 2H4 2.01. 29 P
SMOOTHS 1 FR 0.0001 REL FR 1 V 0 P
warwick tells his title, smooths the wrong, 3H6 3.01. 48
SMOOTH'ST 1 FR 0.0001 REL FR 1 V 0 P
that smooth'st it so with king and commonweal! 2H6 2.01. 22
SMOOTH–TONGUE 1 FR 0.0001 REL FR 0 V 1 P
caddis–garter, smooth–tongue, spanish–pouch — 1H4 2.04. 71 P
SMOOTHY–PATES 1 FR 0.0001 REL FR 0 V 1 P
the whoreson smoothy–pates do now wear nothing
2H4 1.02. 38 P
SMOTE (*also smit*)
SMOTE 5 FR 0.0005 REL FR 5 V 0 P
so full of valor that they smote the air | for TMP 4.01.172
when their fresh rays have smote | the night of LLL 4.03. 27
our aediles smote, ourselves resisted? COR 3.01.317
he smote the sledded /polacks on the ice. HAM 1.01. 63
the circumcised dog, | and smote him — thus. OTH 5.02.356
SMOTHER 10 FR 0.0011 REL FR 10 V 0 P
come thus to light, | smother her spirits up. ADO 4.01.112
thus must i from the smoke into the smother, AYL 1.02.287
to smother up his beauty from the world, | that, 1H4 1.02.199
to smother up the english in our throngs, | if H5 4.05. 20
out, | though ne'er so cunningly you smother it. 1H6 4.01.110
and in the breath of bitter words let's smother R3 4.04.133
being more known grows worse, to smother it. PER 1.01.106
and being set, i'll smother thee with kisses. VEN 18
their own transgressions partially they smother: LUC 634
heart in love with sighs himself doth smother, SON 47. 4
SMOTHER'D 7 FR 0.0008 REL FR 7 V 0 P
air, | but smother'd it within my panting bulk, R3 1.04. 40
be hid | and in the vapor of my glory smother'd. 3.07.164
my damned son that thy two sweet sons smother'd. 4.04.134
are smother'd up, leads fill'd, and ridges COR 2.01.211
of man that function | is smother'd in surmise, MAC 1.03.141
another, smother'd, seems to pelt and swear, LUC 1418
since that our faults in love thus smother'd be. PP 1.14
SMOTHERED 2 FR 0.0002 REL FR 2 V 0 P
"we smothered | the most replenished sweet work
R3 4.03. 17
dream on thy cousins smothered in the tower. 5.03.146
SMOTHERING 1 FR 0.0001 REL FR 1 V 0 P
to th' smothering of the sense), how far it is CYM 3.02. 58
SMOTHER'ST 1 FR 0.0001 REL FR 1 V 0 P
thou smother'st honesty, thou murth'rest troth, LUC 885
SMOTH'RED 4 FR 0.0004 REL FR 4 V 0 P
smoth'red in errors, feeble, shallow, weak, ERR 3.02. 35
untimely smoth'red in their dusky graves. R3 4.04. 70
and there, all smoth'red up, in shade doth sit, VEN 1035
that in their smoky ranks his smoth'red light LUC 783
SMUG 3 FR 0.0003 REL FR 2 V 1 P
that was us'd to come so smug upon the mart: MV 3.01. 46 P
and here the smug and silver trent shall run 1H4 3.01.101
i will die bravely, like a smug bridegroom. LR 4.06.198
SMULKIN 1 FR 0.0001 REL FR 0 V 1 P
peace, smulkin, peace, thou fiend! LR 3.04.140 P
SMUTCH'D 1 FR 0.0001 REL FR 1 V 0 P
/hast smutch'd thy nose? WT 1.02.121
SNAFFLE 1 FR 0.0001 REL FR 1 V 0 P
yours, which with a snaffle | you may pace easy, ANT 2.02. 63
SNAIL 8 FR 0.0009 REL FR 4 V 4 P
dromio, thou /drumble, thou snail, thou slug, ERR 2.02.194
worm nor snail, do no offense. MND 2.02. 23
creeping like snail | unwillingly to school. AYL 2.07.146
i had as lief be woo'd of a snail. 4.01. 52 P
of a snail? 4.01. 53 P
ay, of a snail; 4.01. 54 P
but i can tell why a snail has a house. LR 1.05. 27 P
or as the snail, whose tender horns being hit, VEN 1033
SNAIL–PAC'D 2 FR 0.0002 REL FR 2 V 0 P
delay /leads impotent and snail–pac'd beggary. R3 4.03. 53
and bid the snail–pac'd ajax arm for shame. TRO 5.05. 18
SNAILS 2 FR 0.0002 REL FR 2 V 0 P
than are the tender horns of cockled snails. LLL 4.03.335
to go on, i mean, | else wish we to be snails. TNK 5.01. 42
SNAIL–SLOW 1 FR 0.0001 REL FR 1 V 0 P
snail–slow in profit, and he sleeps by day MV 2.05. 47
/SNAKE 1 FR 0.0001 REL FR 1 V 0 P
the /snake lies rolled in the cheerful sun, TIT 2.03. 13
SNAKE 11 FR 0.0012 REL FR 8 V 3 P
his enter and exit shall be strangling a snake; LLL 5.01.135 P
done, hercules, now thou crushest the snake!" 5.01.139 P
and there the snake throws her enamell'd skin, MND 2.01.255
(for i see love hath made thee a tame snake) and AYL 4.03. 70 P
a green and gilded snake had wreath'd itself, 4.03.108
revenge from ebon den with fell alecto's snake, 2H4 5.05. 37
or as the snake roll'd in a flow'ring bank, 2H6 3.01.228
i fear me you but warm the starved snake, | who, 3.01.343
as frozen water to a starved snake. TIT 3.01.251
we have scorch'd the snake, not kill'd it; MAC 3.02. 13
fillet of a fenny snake, | in the cauldron boil 4.01. 12
SNAKES 5 FR 0.0005 REL FR 5 V 0 P
you spotted snakes with double tongue, | thorny MND 2.02. 9
snakes, in my heart–blood warm'd, that sting my R2 3.02.131
a thousand fiends, a thousand hissing snakes, TIT 2.03.100
shouldst come like a fury crown'd with snakes, ANT 2.05. 40
and made | a cestern for scal'd snakes! 2.05. 95
SNAKY 1 FR 0.0001 REL FR 1 V 0 P
so are those crisped snaky golden locks, | which MV 3.02. 92
SNAP 3 FR 0.0003 REL FR 0 V 3 P
brief, short, quick, snap. WIV 4.05. 3 P
venue of wit — snip, snap, quick and home. LLL 5.01. 60 P
in the law of nature but i may snap at him: 2H4 3.02.332 P
SNAPP'D 1 FR 0.0001 REL FR 0 V 1 P
had our two noses snapp'd off with two old men ADO 5.01.116 P
SNAPPER–UP 1 FR 0.0001 REL FR 0 V 1 P
was likewise a snapper–up of unconsider'd WT 4.03. 26 P
SNAR'D 2 FR 0.0002 REL FR 2 V 0 P
till they have snar'd the shepherd of the flock, 2H6 2.02. 73
but fear not thou, until thy foot be snar'd, 2.04. 56
SNARE 10 FR 0.0011 REL FR 4 V 6 P
thee how | to snare the nimble marmazet. TMP 2.02.170
sirrah! where's snare? 2H4 2.01. 5 P
o lord, ay! good master snare. 2.01. 6 P
snare, we must arrest sir john falstaff. 2.01. 8 P
yea, good master snare, i have ent'red him and 2.01. 9 P
good master snare, let him not scape. 2.01. 25 P
offices, master fang and master snare, do me, do 2.01. 41 P
ours is the fall, i fear, our foes the snare. TIM 5.02. 17
smiling from | the world's great snare uncaught? ANT 4.08. 18
watch of woes, sin's pack–horse, virtue's snare! LUC 928
SNARES 5 FR 0.0005 REL FR 5 V 0 P
stands with the snares of war to tangle thee. 1H6 4.02. 22
with sorrow snares relenting passengers; 2H6 3.01.227
be it by gins, by snares, by subtlety, 3.01.262
weaves tedious snares to trap mine enemies. 3.01.340
that fled the snares of watchful tyranny, MAC 5.09. 33
SNARL 1 FR 0.0001 REL FR 1 V 0 P
which plainly signified | that i should snarl, 3H6 5.06. 77
SNARLETH 1 FR 0.0001 REL FR 1 V 0 P
and snarleth in the gentle eyes of peace; JN 4.03.150
SNARLING 1 FR 0.0001 REL FR 1 V 0 P
were you snarling all before i came, | ready to R3 1.03.187
SNATCH 11 FR 0.0012 REL FR 11 V 0 P
it were a fault to snatch words from my tongue. LLL 5.02.382
for briers and thorns at their apparel snatch; MND 3.02. 29
as now again to snatch our palm from palm, JN 3.01.244
snatch at his master that doth tarre him on. 4.01.116
nay, do not snatch it from me. TRO 5.02. 81
why then it seems some certain snatch or so TIT 2.01. 95
from heaven, | and fiends will snatch at it. OTH 5.02.275
and snatch 'em up, as we take hares, behind: ANT 4.07. 13
you snatch some hence for little faults; CYM 5.01. 12
goodly gifts | and snatch them straight away? PER 3.01. 24
snatch up the goodly boy and set him by him, | a TNK 4.02. 17
SNATCH'D 7 FR 0.0008 REL FR 6 V 1 P
he did, and from my finger snatch'd that ring. ERR 5.01.277
the life of helen, lady, | was foully snatch'd. AWW 5.03.154
i snatch'd one half out of the jaws of death, TN 3.04.360
a sceptre snatch'd with an unruly hand | must be JN 3.04.135
most resolutely snatch'd on monday night and 1H4 1.02. 34 P
but as an honor snatch'd with boist'rous hand, 2H4 4.05.191
but death hath snatch'd my husband from my arms,
R3 2.02. 57
SNATCHERS 1 FR 0.0001 REL FR 1 V 0 P
we do not mean the coursing snatchers only, H5 1.02.143
SNATCHES 4 FR 0.0004 REL FR 3 V 1 P
sir, leave me your snatches, and yield me a MM 4.02. 6 P
and her pale fire she snatches from the sun; TIM 4.03.438
which time she chaunted snatches of old lauds, HAM 4.07.177
the snatches in his voice, | and burst of CYM 4.02.105
/SNATCHING 1 FR 0.0001 REL FR 0 V 1 P
/the /fool /to /myself, /they'll /be /snatching. LR 1.04.155 P
SNEAK 2 FR 0.0002 REL FR 1 V 1 P
sneak not away, sir, for the friar and you MM 5.01.358
i'll see if i can find out sneak. 2H4 2.04. 21 P
SNEAKING 3 FR 0.0003 REL FR 2 V 1 P
and low, | a poor unminded outlaw sneaking home,
1H4 4.03. 58
comes sneaking, and so sucks her princely eggs, H5 1.02.171
what sneaking fellow comes yonder? TRO 1.02.226 P
SNEAK'S 1 FR 0.0001 REL FR 0 V 1 P
and see if thou canst find out sneak's noise. 2H4 2.04. 11 P
SNEAK–UP 1 FR 0.0001 REL FR 0 V 1 P
the prince is a jack, a sneak–up. 1H4 3.03. 85 P
SNEAP 1 FR 0.0001 REL FR 0 V 1 P
i will not undergo this sneap without reply. 2H4 2.01.122 P
SNEAPED 1 FR 0.0001 REL FR 1 V 0 P
and give the sneaped birds more cause to sing. LUC 333
SNEAPING 2 FR 0.0002 REL FR 2 V 0 P
berowne is like an envious sneaping frost | that LLL 1.01.100
that may blow | no sneaping winds at home, to WT 1.02. 13
SNECK 1 FR 0.0001 REL FR 0 V 1 P
we did keep time, sir, in our catches. sneck up! TN 2.03. 94 P
SNIP 3 FR 0.0003 REL FR 1 V 2 P
not too long in one tune, but a snip and away: LLL 3.01. 22 P
sweet touch, a quick venue of wit — snip, snap, 5.01. 59 P
here's snip and nip and cut and slish and slash, SHR 4.03. 90
SNIPE 1 FR 0.0001 REL FR 1 V 0 P
if i would time expend with such /a snipe | but OTH 1.03.385
SNIPT–TAFFATA 1 FR 0.0001 REL FR 0 V 1 P
was misled with a snipt–taffata fellow there, AWW 4.05. 1 P
SNORE 3 FR 0.0003 REL FR 3 V 0 P
thou dost snore distinctly, | there's meaning in TMP 2.01.217
and sleep and snore, and rend apparel out — MV 2.05. 5
weariness | can snore upon the flint, when resty CYM 3.06. 34
SNORES 5 FR 0.0005 REL FR 5 V 0 P
distinctly, | there's meaning in thy snores. TMP 2.01.218
whilst the heavy ploughman snores, | all with MND 5.01.373
biggen bound | snores out the watch of night. 2H4 4.05. 28
grooms | do mock their charge with snores. MAC 2.02. 6
rout, | no din but snores /the /house /about, PER 3.ch. 2
SNORING 1 FR 0.0001 REL FR 1 V 0 P
while you here do snoring lie, | open–ey'd TMP 2.01.300
SNORTING 2 FR 0.0002 REL FR 1 V 1 P
behind the arras, and snorting like a horse. 1H4 2.04.529 P
awake the snorting citizens with the bell, | or OTH 1.01. 90
SNORTS 1 FR 0.0001 REL FR 1 V 0 P
and forth she rushes, snorts, and neighs aloud. VEN 262
/SNOUT 1 FR 0.0001 REL FR 1 V 0 P
it doth befall | that i, one /snout by name, MND 5.01.156
SNOUT 3 FR 0.0003 REL FR 1 V 2 P
tom snout, the tinker. MND 1.02. 61 P
snout, the tinker! 4.01.203 P
his snout digs sepulchres where e'er he goes; VEN 622
/SNOW 1 FR 0.0001 REL FR 1 V 0 P
/o, /that /i /were /a /mockery /king /of /snow, R2 4.01.260
SNOW 39 FR 0.0044 REL FR 36 V 3 P
sir, | the white cold virgin snow upon my heart TMP 4.01. 55
thou wouldst as soon go kindle fire with snow TGV 2.07. 19
hail kissing–comfits, and snow eringoes; WIV 5.05. 20 P
hid | in sap–consuming winter's drizzled snow, ERR 5.01.313
than wish a snow in may's new–fangled shows; LLL 1.01.106
saw | and birds sit brooding in the snow | and 5.02.923
that pure congealed white, high taurus' snow, MND 3.02.141
my love to hermia | (melted as the snow) seems 4.01.166
that is hot ice and wondrous strange snow. 5.01. 59
well be amity and life | 'tween snow and fire, MV 3.02. 31
dare not shake the snow from off their cassocks, AWW 4.03.168 P
lawn as white as driven snow, | cypress black as WT 4.04.218
tooth, or the fann'd snow that's bolted | by th' 4.04.364
or as a little snow, tumbled about, | anon JN 3.04.176
or wallow naked in december snow | by thinking R2 1.03.298
as doth the melted snow | upon the valleys whose H5 3.05. 50
lords, cold snow melts with the sun's hot beams: 2H6 3.01.223
right, as snow in harvest. R3 1.04.242
life | felt so much cold as over shoes in snow? 5.03.326
that's curdied by the frost from purest snow COR 5.03. 66
in winter with warm tears i'll melt the snow, TIT 3.01. 20
whiter than new snow upon a raven's back. ROM 3.02. 19
whose blush doth thaw the consecrated snow TIM 4.03.385
black macbeth | will seem as pure as snow, and MAC 4.03. 53
be thou as chaste as ice, as pure as snow, thou HAM 3.01.136 P
in the sweet heavens | to wash it white as snow? 3.03. 46
"white his shroud as the mountain snow" — 4.05. 36
"his beard was as white as snow, | /all flaxen 4.05.195
being oil to fire, snow to the colder moods; LR 2.02. 77
whose face between her forks presages snow; 4.06.119
nor scar that whiter skin of hers than snow, OTH 5.02. 4
like the stag, when snow the pasture sheets, ANT 1.04. 65
that i thought her | as chaste as unsunn'd snow. CYM 2.05. 13

and pure | as wind–fann'd snow, who to thy TNK 5.01.140
as apt as new–fall'n snow takes any dint. VEN 354
the hand, | a lily prison'd in a jail of snow, 362
as mountain snow melts with the midday sun. 750
as winter meads when sun doth melt their snow. LUC 1218
if snow be white, why then her breasts are dun; SON 130. 3
SNOWBALL 1 FR 0.0001 REL FR 0 V 1 P
and she sent him away as cold as a snowball, PER 4.06.140 P
SNOWBALLS 1 FR 0.0001 REL FR 0 V 1 P
if i had swallow'd snowballs for pills to cool WIV 3.05. 23 P
SNOW–BROTH 1 FR 0.0001 REL FR 1 V 0 P
angelo, a man whose blood | is very snow–broth; MM 1.04. 58
SNOW–WHITE 6 FR 0.0006 REL FR 4 V 2 P
draweth from my snow–white pen the ebon–colored
LLL 1.01.242 P
"to the snow–white hand of the most beauteous 4.02.132 P
dismounted from your snow–white goodly steed, TIT 2.03. 76
spots and stains love's modest snow–white weed. LUC 196
her coral lips, her snow–white dimpled chin. 420
but if the like the snow–white swan desire, 1011
SNOWY 1 FR 0.0001 REL FR 1 V 0 P
so shows a snowy dove trooping with crows, | as ROM 1.05. 48
SNUFF 8 FR 0.0009 REL FR 7 V 1 P
you'll mar the light by taking it in snuff; LLL 5.02. 22
for, you see, it is already in snuff. MND 5.01.250 P
lacks oil, to be the snuff | of younger spirits, AWW 1.02. 59
took it in snuff — and still he smil'd and 1H4 1.03. 41
candle burns not clear, 'tis i must snuff it, H8 3.02. 96
a kind of week or snuff that will abate it, HAM 4.07.115
my snuff and loathed part of nature should LR 4.06. 39
sun, and solace | i' th' dungeon by a snuff! CYM 1.06. 87
SNUFF'D 1 FR 0.0001 REL FR 0 V 1 P
as if you snuff'd up love by smelling love; LLL 3.01. 16 P
SNUFFS 1 FR 0.0001 REL FR 1 V 0 P
either in snuffs and packings of the dukes, | or LR 3.01. 26
SNUG 3 FR 0.0003 REL FR 1 V 2 P
snug, the joiner, you the lion's part. MND 1.02. 64 P
and tell them plainly he is snug the joiner. 3.01. 45 P
then know that i as snug the joiner am | a lion 5.01.223
SO *(also s'*, zo)*
/SO 53 FR 0.0060 REL FR 41 V 12 P
SO 5410 FR 0.6115 REL FR 4293 V 1117 P
SOAK'D 1 FR 0.0001 REL FR 1 V 0 P
lie drown'd and soak'd in mercenary blood; H5 4.07. 76
/SOAKING 1 FR 0.0001 REL FR 1 V 0 P
/may /run /into /that /sink, /and /soaking /in, TIT 3.02. 19
SOAKING 1 FR 0.0001 REL FR 1 V 0 P
for thy conceit is soaking, will draw in | more WT 1.02.224
SOAKS 1 FR 0.0001 REL FR 0 V 1 P
sir, that soaks up the king's countenance, his HAM 4.02. 15 P
SOAR 7 FR 0.0008 REL FR 6 V 1 P
thou hast hawks will soar | above the morning SHR in.2. 43
when i bestride him, i soar, i am a hawk; H5 3.07. 15 P
that mounts no higher than a bird can soar. 2H6 2.01. 14
although the kite soar with unbloodied beak? 3.02.193
and soar with them above a common bound. ROM 1.04. 18
his shaft | to soar with his light feathers, and 1.04. 20
who else would soar above the view of men, | and JC 1.01. 74
SOARING 2 FR 0.0002 REL FR 2 V 0 P
at some time when his soaring insolence | shall COR 2.01.254
from south to west on wing soaring aloft, CYM 5.05.471
SOARS 1 FR 0.0001 REL FR 1 V 0 P
how high a pitch his resolution soars! R2 1.01.109
SOB 2 FR 0.0002 REL FR 1 V 1 P
are tir'd, gives them a sob and 'rests them; ERR 4.03. 25 P
and twenty times made pause to sob and weep, R3 1.02.161
SOBBING 2 FR 0.0002 REL FR 2 V 0 P
weeping and commenting | upon the sobbing deer.
AYL 2.01. 66
she sits weeping, | to whom she sobbing speaks: LUC 1088
SOBER 18 FR 0.0020 REL FR 13 V 5 P
her sober virtue, years, and modesty, | plead on ERR 3.01. 90
no, i pray thee speak in sober judgment. ADO 1.01.170 P
why then let them alone till they are sober. 3.03. 46 P
very vildly in the morning, when he is sober, MV 1.02. 86 P
if i do not put on a sober habit, | talk with 2.02.190
sound of shallow fopp'ry enter | my sober house. 2.05. 36
what damned error but some sober brow | will 3.02. 78
speak'st thou in sober meanings? AYL 5.02. 69 P
and offer me disguis'd in sober robes | to old SHR 1.02.132
you seem a sober ancient gentleman by your habit 5.01. 73 P
him, | and we with sober speed will follow you. 2H4 4.03. 80
and with such sober and unnoted passion | he did TIM 3.05. 21
brutus, this sober form of yours hides wrongs, JC 4.02. 40
for who, that's but a queen, fair, sober, wise, HAM 3.04.189
nor once be chastis'd with the sober eye | of ANT 5.02. 54
fight, | making such sober action with his hand, LUC 1403
even | doth half that glory to the sober west, SON 132. 8
shook off my sober guards and civil fears; LC 298
SOBER–BLOODED 1 FR 0.0001 REL FR 0 V 1 P
this same young sober–blooded boy doth not love
2H4 4.03. 87 P
SOBERLY 1 FR 0.0001 REL FR 1 V 0 P
and soberly did mount an arm–gaunt steed, | who ANT 1.05. 48
SOBER–SAD 1 FR 0.0001 REL FR 1 V 0 P
so sober–sad, so weary, and so mild | (as if LUC 1542
SOBER–SUITED 1 FR 0.0001 REL FR 1 V 0 P
night, | thou sober–suited matron all in black, ROM 3.02. 11
SOBRIETY 2 FR 0.0002 REL FR 1 V 1 P
do i see | maid's mild behavior and sobriety. SHR 1.01. 71
and the forms of it, and the sobriety of it, and H5 4.01. 73 P
SOBS 5 FR 0.0005 REL FR 4 V 1 P
knees she falls, weeps, sobs, beats her heart, ADO 2.03.147 P
and swore with sobs | that he would labor my R3 1.04.245
my clear voice with sobs and break my heart TRO 4.02.108
see how my wretched sister sobs and weeps. TIT 3.01.137
and now her sobs do her intendments break. VEN 222
SOCIABLE 6 FR 0.0006 REL FR 4 V 2 P
mine eyes, ev'n sociable to the show of thine, TMP 5.01. 63
'tis too respective and too sociable | for your JN 1.01.188
/friends | do glue themselves in sociable grief, 3.04. 65
can he not be sociable? TRO 2.03.210 P
now art thou sociable, now art thou romeo; ROM 2.04. 89 P
society is no comfort | to one not sociable. CYM 4.02. 13
SOCIETIES 4 FR 0.0004 REL FR 3 V 1 P
before me, | my riots past, my wild societies, WIV 3.04. 8
truth enough alive to make societies secure, but MM 3.02.227 P
therefore be abhorr'd | all feasts, societies, TIM 4.03. 21
witch | that he enchants societies into him; CYM 1.06.167
/SOCIETY 1 FR 0.0001 REL FR 1 V 0 P
/shunn'd /my /abhorr'd /society, /but /then, LR 5.03.211
SOCIETY 26 FR 0.0029 REL FR 16 V 10 P
of her society | be not afraid. TMP 4.01. 91
i beseech your society. LLL 4.02.160 P
for society, saith the text, is the happiness of 4.02.161 P
the triumphery, the corner–cap of society, | the 4.03. 51
that in love's grief desir'st society: 4.03.126
or to abjure | for ever the society of men. MND 1.01. 66
fashion sake, i thank you too for your society. AYL 3.02.256 P
which is in the vulgar leave — the society — 5.01. 48 P
together is, abandon the society of this female, 5.01. 50 P
necessities made separation of their society, WT 1.01. 26 P
then i lost | (all mine own folly) the society, 5.01.135
but this is worshipful society, | and fits the JN 1.01.205
attempts, | such barren pleasures, rude society, 1H4 3.02. 14
the participation of society that they flock 2H4 5.01. 70 P
if sorrow can admit society, | /tell /over /your R3 4.04. 38
life, | they are a sweet society of fair ones. H8 1.04. 14
herself alone, | may be put from her by society. ROM 4.01. 14
nay, and you begin to rail on society once, i am TIM 1.02.244 P
sprinkle our society with thankfulness. 3.06. 70 P
that their society (as their friendship) may 4.01. 31
to make society | the sweeter welcome, we will MAC 3.01. 41
ourself will mingle with society, | and play the 3.04. 3
excellent differences, of very soft society, and HAM 5.02.108 P
society is no comfort | to one not sociable. CYM 4.02. 12
grief best is pleas'd with grief's society; LUC 1111
achieve, | and lace itself with his society? SON 67. 4
SOCKS 1 FR 0.0001 REL FR 0 V 1 P
ramm'd me in with foul shirts and smocks, socks, WIV 3.05. 90 P
SOCRATES' 1 FR 0.0001 REL FR 1 V 0 P
and as curst and shrowd | as socrates' xantippe, SHR 1.02. 71
SOD 3 FR 0.0003 REL FR 2 V 1 P
twice sod simplicity, bis coctus! LLL 4.02. 22 P
or women | that have sod their infants in (and TNK 1.03. 21
her eyes, though sod in tears, look'd red and LUC 1592
SODDEN 3 FR 0.0003 REL FR 1 V 2 P
can sodden water, | a drench for sur–rein'd H5 3.05. 18
sodden business! there's a stew'd phrase indeed! TRO 3.01. 41 P
blow it to pieces, they are so pitifully sodden. PER 4.02. 20 P
SODDEN–WITTED 1 FR 0.0001 REL FR 0 V 1 P
thou sodden–witted lord! TRO 2.01. 43 P
SOE'ER 6 FR 0.0006 REL FR 4 V 2 P
there, | of what validity and pitch soe'er, TN 1.01. 12
whose tongue soe'er speaks false, | not truly JN 4.03. 91
what god soe'er it be | that thou adorest and TIT 5.01. 82
how mean soe'er, that have their honest wills, CYM 1.06. 8
that is, what villainy soe'er i bid thee do, to 3.05.112 P
what broken piece of matter soe'er she's about, TNK 4.03. 6 P
SOEVER 5 FR 0.0005 REL FR 3 V 2 P
all eve's daughters, of what complexion soever; WIV 4.02. 25 P
how low soever the matter, i hope in god for LLL 1.01.192 P
private conference | (of what degree soever) R3 1.01. 87
whose hand soever lanch'd their tender hearts, 4.04.225
how rank soever rounded in with danger. TRO 1.03.196
SO–FORTH 1 FR 0.0001 REL FR 1 V 0 P
"sicilia is a so–forth." WT 1.02.218
SOFT 136 FR 0.0153 REL FR 123 V 13 P
soft, sir, one word more. TMP 1.02.450
of whose soft grace | for the like loss i have 5.01.142
his gold will hold, | and his soft couch defile. WIV 1.03. 99
and gnarled oak | than the soft myrtle; MM 2.02.117
frail, | for we are soft as our complexions are, 2.04.129
for thou dost fear the soft and tender fork | of 3.01. 16
when you depart from him, but, soft and low, 4.01. 68
but soft, who wafts us yonder? ERR 2.02.109 P
but soft, my door is lock'd; 3.01. 30
o, soft, sir, hold you still; 3.02. 69
but soft, i see the goldsmith. 4.01. 19
come thronging soft and delicate desires, | all ADO 1.01.303
but soft you, let me be. 5.01.203 P
soft and fair, friar. which is beatrice? 5.04. 72
soft, whither away so fast? LLL 4.03.184
love's feeling is more soft and sensible | than 4.03.334
soft, let us see — | write "lord have mercy on 5.02.418
but soft! MND 4.01.127
but soft, how many months | do you desire? MV 1.03. 58
i'll not be made a soft and dull–ey'd fool | to 3.03. 14
let their beds | be made as soft as yours, and 4.01. 96
soft, | the jew shall have all justice. 4.01.320
soft, no haste. 4.01.321
soft stillness and the night | become the 5.01. 56
you bring me out. soft, comes he not here? AYL 3.02.251 P
do, | with soft low tongue and lowly courtesy, SHR in.1. 114
i smell sweet savors, and i feel soft things. in.2. 71
with gentle conference, soft, and affable. 2.01.251
soft, son! 4.04. 23
but soft, company is coming here. 4.05. 26
why are our bodies soft, and weak, and smooth, 5.02.165
but that our soft conditions and our hearts 5.02.167
and drink, and sleep as soft | as captain shall. AWW 4.03.332
soft, soft! TN 1.05.293
soft, soft! 1.05.293
soft! 2.05. 92 P
soft, here follows prose. 2.05.142 P
so far beneath your soft and tender breeding, 5.01.323
's | with one soft kiss a thousand furlongs ere WT 1.02. 95
as soft as dove's down and as white as it, | or 4.04.363
soft, swain, awhile, beseech you. 4.04.391
but that death is too soft for him, say i. 4.04.779 P
melted by the windy breath | of soft petitions, JN 2.01.478
rage | presented to the tears of soft remorse. 4.03. 50
but soft, but see, or rather do not see, | my R2 5.01. 7
hath been smooth as oil, soft as young down, 1H4 1.03. 7
but soft, i pray you, did king richard then 1.03.155
by god, soft, i know a trick worth two of that, 2.01. 36 P
soft, who are you? 5.03. 32 P
but soft, whom have we here? 5.04.131
nature's soft nurse, how have i frighted thee, 2H4 3.01. 6
and in your power soft silencing your son. 5.02. 97
touch her soft mouth, and march. H5 2.03. 58
we yield our town and lives to thy soft mercy. 3.03. 48
a good soft pillow for that good white head 4.01. 14
but soft, i think she comes, and i'll prepare 2H6 2.04. 15
women are soft, mild, pitiful, and flexible; 3H6 1.04.141
and this soft courage makes your followers faint 2.02. 57
and, for i should not deal in her soft laws, 3.02.154
or edward's soft and pitiful, like mine: R3 1.03.140
but soft, here come my executioners. 1.03.338
soft, he wakes. 1.04.158 P
soft, i did but dream. 5.03.178
of your soft cheveril conscience would receive H8 2.03. 32
to whose soft seizure | the cygnet's down is TRO 1.01. 57
the hard and soft, seem all affin'd and kin; 1.03. 25
soft infancy, that nothing canst but cry, | add 2.02.105
and give as soft attachment to thy senses | as 4.02. 5
yet soft! 5.03. 89
soft, here comes sleeve and t' other. 5.04. 18 P
soft, who comes here? COR 1.01. 50 P
when steel grows soft as the parasite's silk, 1.09. 45
hast not the soft way which, thou dost confess, 3.02. 82
a stone is soft as wax, tribunes more hard than TIT 3.01. 45
soft, so busily she turns the leaves! 4.01. 45
soft, who comes here? 4.02. 51
but soft, methinks i do digress too much, 5.03.116
soft, i will go along; ROM 1.01.195
but soft, what light through yonder window 2.02. 2
we'nsday next — | but soft, what day is this? 3.04. 18
soft, take me with you, take me with you, wife. 3.05.141
stratagems | upon so soft a subject as myself! 3.05.210
soft, take thy physic first — thou too — and TIM 3.06.100
virgin's cheek | make soft thy trenchant sword; 4.03.116
flatterers yet wear silk, drink wine, lie soft, 4.03.206
whose soft impression | interprets for my poor 5.04. 68
but soft, i pray you; what, did caesar swound? JC 1.02.251
soft, who comes here? a friend of antony's. 3.01.122
but soft, behold! HAM 1.01.126
but soft, methinks i scent the morning air, 1.05. 58
soft you now, | the fair ophelia. 3.01. 87
soft, now to my mother. 3.02.392
steel, | be soft as sinews of the new–born babe! 3.03. 71
but soft, what noise? 4.02. 3 P
soft, let me see. 4.07.154
but soft, but soft awhile! 5.01.217
but soft, but soft awhile! 5.01.217
excellent differences, of very soft society, and 5.02.108 P
her voice was ever soft, | gentle, and low, an LR 5.03.273
little bless'd with the soft phrase of peace; OTH 1.03. 82
and have not those soft parts of conversation 3.03.264
soft, by and by, let me the curtains draw. 5.02.104
soft you; 5.02.338
now for the love of love, and her soft hours, ANT 1.01. 44
your captain | to soft and gentle speech. 2.02. 3
soft, caesar! 2.02. 83
the beds i' th' east are soft, and thanks to you 2.06. 50
steep'd our sense | in soft and delicate lethe. 2.07.108
as sweet as balm, as soft as air, as gentle — 5.02.311
soft, soft, we'll no defense, | obedient as the CYM 3.04. 79
soft, soft, we'll no defense, | obedient as the 3.04. 79
soft, what are you | that fly me thus? 4.02. 70
but soft! 4.02.295
soft ho, what trunk is here? 4.02.353
strange he hides him in fresh cups, soft beds, 5.03. 71
soft, here he comes, i must dissemble it. PER 2.05. 23
soft! 3.02. 60
villainy | so well as soft and tender flattery. 4.04. 45
fear he cannot, | he shows no such soft temper. TNK 4.02.103
o, then, most soft sweet goddess, | give me the 5.01.126
bent, or a sharp weapon | in a soft sheath; 5.03. 43
she swears | from his soft bosom never to remove VEN 81
my flesh is soft and plump, my marrow burning, 142
tend'rer cheek receives her soft hand's print, 353
being steel'd, soft sighs can never grave it. 376
lips, sweet seals in my soft lips imprinted, 511
nor thy soft hands, sweet lips, and crystal eyne 633
that the boar had trench'd | in his soft flank, 1053
sheath'd unaware the tusk in his soft groin. 1116
a martial man to be soft fancy's slave! LUC 200
soft pity enters at an iron gate. 595
with soft slow tongue, true mark of modesty, 1220
touches so soft still conquer chastity. PP 4. 8
but soft, enough — too much, i fear — | lest 18.49
which on thy soft cheek for complexion dwells SON 99. 4
lending soft audience to my sweet design, | and LC 278
SOFT–CONSCIENC'D 1 FR 0.0001 REL FR 0 V 1 P
though soft–conscienc'd men can be content to COR 1.01. 37 P
SOFTEN 6 FR 0.0006 REL FR 6 V 0 P
golden touch could soften steel and stones, TGV 3.02. 78
grace by your fair prayer | to soften angelo. MM 1.04. 70
as seek to soften that — than which what's MV 4.01. 79
how he may soften at the sight o' th' child: WT 2.02. 38
of love, | salt cleopatra, soften thy wan'd lip! ANT 2.01. 21
to soften it with their continual motion; LUC 591
SOFTENS 1 FR 0.0001 REL FR 1 V 0 P
oft have i heard that grief softens the mind, 2H6 4.04. 1
SOFTER 4 FR 0.0004 REL FR 4 V 0 P
softer and sweeter than the lustful bed | on SHR in.2. 38
priam, | there is no lady of more softer bowels, TRO 2.02. 11
whilst with no softer cushion than the flint | i COR 5.03. 53
softer than wax, and yet as iron rusty: PP 7. 4
SOFTEST 3 FR 0.0003 REL FR 3 V 0 P
eyes, that are the frail'st and softest things, AYL 3.05. 12
their softest touch as smart as lizards' stings! 2H6 3.02.325
night, | like softest music to attending ears! ROM 2.02.166
SOFT–HEARTED 3 FR 0.0003 REL FR 3 V 0 P
fie, coward woman and soft–hearted wretch! 2H6 3.02.307
why stand we like soft–hearted women here, 3H6 2.03. 25
o my soft–hearted sister, what think you? TNK 4.02.147
/SOFTLY 1 FR 0.0001 REL FR 1 V 0 P
/softly, /pray. 2H4 4.04.132
SOFTLY 24 FR 0.0027 REL FR 16 V 8 P
pray you tread softly, that the blind mole may TMP 4.01.194
therefore speak softly, | all's hush'd as 4.01.206
speak softly, yonder, as i think, he walks. ERR 5.01. 9
so you walk softly, and look sweetly, and say ADO 2.01. 88 P
bleat softly then, the butcher hears you cry. LLL 5.02.255
for though he go as softly as foot can fall, he AYL 3.02.328 P
softly, my masters! SHR 1.02.236
softly and swiftly, sir, for the priest is ready 5.01. 1 P
softly! TN 2.05.120 P
i will tell it softly, | yond crickets shall not WT 2.01. 30
o good sir, softly, good sir! 4.03. 72 P
softly, dear sir; 4.03. 75 P
good sir, softly. 4.03. 76 P

f you, and pace softly towards my kinsman's. 4.03.113 P
peak softly, or the loss of those great towns 1H6 1.01. 63
oftly, gentle patience. H8 4.02. 82
assius, be content, | speak your griefs softly; JC 4.02. 42
ead your battle softly on | upon the left hand 5.01. 16
o softly on. HAM 4.04. 8
peak softly, wake her not. ANT 5.02.320
id softly press the rushes ere he waken'd | the CYM 2.02. 13
ray walk softly, do not heat your blood. PER 4.01. 48
is falchion on a flint he softly smiteth, LUC 176
nd softly cried, 'awake, thou roman dame, | and 1628
OFTLY–SPRIGHTED 1 FR 0.0001 REL FR 0 V 1 P
softly–sprighted man, is he not? WIV 1.04. 24 P
OFT'NED 2 FR 0.0002 REL FR 2 V 0 P
nd in my temper soft'ned valor's steel! ROM 3.01.115
ears fell from her, and soft'ned the stones, OTH 4.03. 46
OFTNESS 1 FR 0.0001 REL FR 1 V 0 P
satire against the softness of prosperity, TIM 5.01. 35
OHO 2 FR 0.0002 REL FR 0 V 2 P
oho, soho! TGV 3.01.189 P
oho, soho! 3.01.189 P
SOIL* 2 FR 0.0002 REL FR 2 V 0 P
ne done, prince, that can /soil our mothers? TRO 5.02.134
ne /soil is this, that thou dost common grow. SON 69.14
OIL* 24 FR 0.0027 REL FR 21 V 3 P
ho is as free from touch or soil with her | as MM 5.01.141
ould be as great a soil in the new gloss of ADO 3.02. 5 P
e only soil of his fair virtue's gloss, | if LLL 2.01. 47
virtue's gloss will stain with any soil, | is 2.01. 48
ke a crab on the face of terra, the soil, the 4.02. 7 P
you like upon report | the soil, the profit, AYL 2.04. 98
nd flesh his spirit in a warlike soil, JN 5.01. 71
ngland's ground, farewell, sweet soil, adieu; R2 1.03.306
o more the thirsty entrance of this soil 1H4 1.01. 5
orse, | stain'd with the variation of each soil 1.01. 64
ost subject is the fattest soil to weeds, | and 2H4 4.04. 54
or all the soil of the achievement goes | with 4.05.189
enounce your soil, give sheep in lions' stead: 1H6 1.05. 29
ven as i have of fertile england's soil. 2H6 1.01.238
e lord of the soil come to seize me for a 4.10. 24 P
oul | leads discontented steps in foreign soil, R3 4.04.312
aster — | whose honor heaven shield from soil! H8 1.02. 26
, | but i would have the soil of her fair rape TRO 2.02.148
ek her, | not making any scruple of her soil, 4.01. 57
or did he soil the fact with cowardice | (/an TIM 3.05. 16
hich give some soil, perhaps, to my behaviors; JC 1.02. 42
nd now no soil nor cautel doth besmirch | the HAM 1.03. 15
nd with swinish phrase | soil our addition, and 1.04. 20
nd the firm soil win of the wat'ry main, SON 64. 7
OIL'D 5 FR 0.0005 REL FR 5 V 0 P
at our kingdom's earth should not be soil'd R2 1.03.125
r have mine honor soil'd | with the attainder 4.01. 23
hen we have soil'd them, nor the remainder TRO 2.02. 70
thing a little soil'd /wi' /th' working, HAM 2.01. 40
at my unspotted youth must now be soil'd TNK 4.02. 59
OILED 1 FR 0.0001 REL FR 1 V 0 P
e fitchew nor the soiled horse goes to't LR 4.06.122
OIL'S 1 FR 0.0001 REL FR 1 V 0 P
e soil's fertility from wholesome flowers. R2 3.04. 39
OIT 1 FR 0.0001 REL FR 1 V 0 P
nd "honi soit qui mal y pense" write | in WIV 5.05. 69
OJOURN 7 FR 0.0008 REL FR 6 V 1 P
here shall we sojourn till our coronation? R3 3.01. 62
ojourn in mantua. ROM 3.03.169
our court have made their amorous sojourn, LR 1.01. 47
at if they come to sojourn at my house, | i'll 2.01.103
ou will return and sojourn with my sister, 2.04.203
ut how comes it he is to sojourn with you? CYM 1.04. 24 P
as a note | whereon her spirits would sojourn TNK 1.03. 77
OJOURN'D 3 FR 0.0003 REL FR 3 V 0 P
ave you long sojourn'd there? TGV 4.01. 20
y heart to her but as guest–wise sojourn'd, MND 3.02.171
nd in the mean time sojourn'd at my father's; JN 1.01.103
OJOURNER 1 FR 0.0001 REL FR 0 V 1 P
port what a sojourner we have; PER 4.02.138 P
OL* 5 FR 0.0005 REL FR 3 V 2 P
, re, sol, la, mi, fa. LLL 4.02.100 P
l try how you can sol, fa, and sing it. SHR 1.02. 17
sol re, one cliff, two notes have i; 3.01. 77
nd therefore is the glorious planet sol | in TRO 1.03. 89
, sol, la, mi. LR 1.02.137 P
OLA 10 FR 0.0011 REL FR 2 V 8 P
la, sola! LLL 4.01.149
la, sola! 4.01.149
la, sola! wo ha, ho! sola, sola! MV 5.01. 39 P
la, sola! wo ha, ho! sola, sola! 5.01. 39 P
la, sola! wo ha, ho! sola, sola! 5.01. 39 P
la, sola! wo ha, ho! sola, sola! 5.01. 39 P
la! 5.01. 41 P
aster lorenzo, sola, sola! 5.01. 42 P
aster lorenzo, sola, sola! 5.01. 42 P
la! where, where? 5.01. 44 P
OLACE 9 FR 0.0010 REL FR 9 V 0 P
e will with some strange pastime solace them, LLL 4.03.374
rrow would solace, and mine age would ease. 2H6 2.03. 21
r with his soul fled all my worldly solace; 3.02.151
le, | this sickly land might solace as before. R3 2.03. 30
ell | my hazards still have been your solace, COR 4.01. 28
ild, | but one thing to rejoice and solace in, ROM 4.05. 47
n, and solace | i' th' dungeon by a snuff! CYM 1.06. 86
rrow chang'd to solace, and solace mix'd with PP 14.23
ang'd to solace, and solace mix'd with sorrow; 14.23
SOLD 1 FR 0.0001 REL FR 0 V 1 P
ick of melancholy /sold a goodly manor for a AWW 3.02. 9 P
OLD 40 FR 0.0045 REL FR 30 V 10 P
oney buys lands, and wives are sold by fate. WIV 5.05.233
man mad as a buck to be so bought and sold. ERR 3.01. 72
e boy hath sold him a bargain, a goose, that's LLL 3.01.101
any a man his life hath sold | but my outside MV 2.07. 67
suredly the thing is to be sold. AYL 2.04. 96
ear you have sold your own lands to see other 4.01. 22 P
ave sold all my trompery; WT 4.04.597 P
ave sold their fortunes at their native homes, JN 2.01. 69
y, noble english, you are bought and sold! 5.04. 10
y father's goods are all distrain'd and sold, R2 2.03.131
know not how they sold themselves, but thou, 2H4 4.03. 68 P
u would have sold your king to slaughter, H5 2.02.170
elve leagues, and sold it for three halfpence. 3.02. 43 P

wouldst think i had sold my farm to buy my crown 5.02.125 P
from bought and sold lord talbot, | who, ring'd 1H6 4.04. 13
and sold their bodies for their country's 5.04.106
while his own lands are bargain'd for and sold. 2H6 1.01.231
by thee anjou and maine were sold to france. 4.01. 86
indeed a pedlar's daughter, and sold many laces. 4.02. 46 P
england seven halfpenny loaves sold for a penny; 4.02. 66 P
the lord say, which sold the towns in france; 4.07. 21 P
i sold not maine, i lost not normandy, | yet to 4.07. 65
have sold their lives unto the house of york, 3H6 5.01. 74
for dickon thy master is bought and sold." R3 5.03.305
thou art bought and sold among those of any wit, TRO 2.01. 46 P
lies, he sold the blood and labor | of our great COR 5.06. 46
but not possess'd it, and, though i am sold, ROM 3.02. 27
i sell thee poison, thou hast sold me none. 5.01. 83
let all my land be sold. TIM 2.02.145
the feast is sold | that is not often vouch'd, MAC 3.04. 32
pole | a ranker rate, should it be sold in fee. HAM 4.04. 22
taken by the insolent foe | and sold to slavery, OTH 1.03.138
chrysolite, | i'ld not have sold her for it. 5.02.146
'tis thou | hast sold me to this novice, and my ANT 4.12. 14
to the young roman boy she hath sold me, and i 4.12. 48
prize with you | of things that merchants sold. 5.02.184
the one may be sold or given, or if there were CYM 1.04. 82 P
diseases have been sold dearer than physic — PER 4.06. 98
laid down, | you have sold 'em too too cheap. TNK 5.04. 15
mine own thoughts, sold cheap what is most dear, SON 110. 3
SOLDAT 1 FR 0.0001 REL FR 0 V 1 P
car ce soldat ici est dispose tout /a /cette H5 4.04. 35 P
SOLDER 1 FR 0.0001 REL FR 1 V 0 P
and that slain men | should solder up the rift. ANT 3.04. 32
SOLDEST 1 FR 0.0001 REL FR 0 V 1 P
thy soul that thou soldest him on good friday 1H4 1.02.115 P
/SOLDIER 1 FR 0.0001 REL FR 1 V 0 P
o, farewell, honest /soldier. HAM 1.01. 16
SOLDIER 143 FR 0.0161 REL FR 97 V 46 P
i'll woo you like a soldier, at arms' end, | and TGV 5.04. 57
least, if the love of a soldier can suffice — WIV 2.01. 11 P
money is a good soldier, sir, and will on. 2.02.170 P
there's not a soldier of us all, that, in the MM 1.02. 14 P
i never heard any soldier dislike it. 1.02. 17 P
word, | which in the soldier is flat blasphemy. 2.02.131
the great soldier who miscarried at sea? 3.01.210 P
envious a scholar, a statesman, and a soldier. 3.02.146 P
and a good soldier too, lady. ADO 1.01. 53 P
and a good soldier to a lady, but what is he to 1.01. 54 P
the purpose (like an honest man and a soldier), 2.03. 19 P
and as it is base for a soldier to love, so am i LLL 1.02. 58 P
his greatness to impart to armado, a soldier, a 5.01.107 P
and i will right myself like a soldier. 5.02.725 P
a venetian, a scholar and a soldier, that came MV 1.02.113 P
then a soldier, | full of strange oaths, and AYL 2.07.149
i think she'll sooner prove a soldier, | iron SHR 2.01.145
you have some stain of soldier in you; AWW 1.01.111 P
i hope your lordship thinks not him a soldier. 2.05. 2 P
and to be a soldier? 3.02. 69
by the hand of a soldier, i will undertake it. 3.06. 72 P
this dialogue between the fool and the soldier? 4.03. 98 P
and say a soldier, dian, told thee this: 4.03.227
manifold linguist and the armipotent soldier. 4.03.236 P
i long to talk with the young noble soldier. 4.05.103 P
as he is a gentleman and a soldier, he will not TN 3.04.308 P
come, my young soldier, put up your iron; 4.01. 39 P
my parasite, my soldier, statesman, all. WT 1.02.168
a soldier, by the honor–giving hand | of JN 1.01. 53
i am a soldier, and now bound to france. 1.01.150
brought to the field | as god's own soldier, 2.01.566
been sworn my soldier, bidding me depend | upon 3.01.125
brave soldier, pardon me | that any accent 5.06. 13
whose soldier now, under whose blessed cross 1H4 1.01. 20
guns | he would himself have been a soldier. 1.03. 64
she'll be a soldier too, she'll to the wars. 3.01.193
have | as not a soldier of this season's stamp 4.01. 4
a soldier is better /accommodated than with a 2H4 3.02. 66 P
to sit under, he's like to be a cold soldier. 3.02.123 P
put him to a private soldier that is the leader 3.02.166 P
and, my little soldier there, be merry. 5.03. 31 P
i'll run him up to the hilts, as i am a soldier. H5 2.01. 65 P
for, as i am a soldier, | a name that in my 3.03. 5
and the flesh'd soldier, rough and hard of heart 3.03. 11
the blind and bloody soldier with foul hand 3.03. 34
bardolph, a soldier firm and sound of heart, 3.06. 25
return into london under the form of a soldier. 3.06. 69 P
advantage is a better soldier than rashness. 3.06.120 P
should every soldier in the wars do as every 4.01.178 P
in which array, brave soldier, doth he lie, 4.06. 7
then every soldier kill his prisoners, | give 4.06. 37
hath caus'd every soldier to cut his prisoner's 4.07. 9 P
soldier, you must come to the king. 4.07.119 P
soldier, why wear'st thou that glove in thy cap? 4.07.120 P
which he swore, as he was a soldier, he would 4.07.129 P
is it fit this soldier keep his oath? 4.07.132 P
call him hither to me, soldier. 4.07.151 P
if that the soldier strike him, as i judge | by 4.07.176
give me thy glove, soldier. 4.08. 39 P
will you vouchsafe to teach a soldier terms, 5.02. 99
i speak to thee plain soldier. 5.02.149 P
and take me, take a soldier; 5.02.166 P
take a soldier, take a king. 5.02.166 P
if any noise or soldier you perceive | near to 1H6 2.01. 2
a braver soldier never couched lance, | a 3.02.134
i am a soldier and unapt to weep | or to exclaim 5.03.133
more like a soldier than a man o' th' church, 2H6 1.01.186
let no soldier fly. 5.02. 36
come, fellow soldier, make thou proclamation. 3H6 4.07. 70
for well i wot that henry is no soldier. 4.07. 83
again, | or die a soldier as i liv'd a king. R3 3.01. 93
sir walter herbert, a renowned soldier, | sir 4.05. 12
and may that soldier a mere recreant prove, TRO 1.03.287
he was a soldier good, | but, by great mars, the 4.05.197
that this great soldier may his welcome know. 4.05.276
the counsellor heart, the arm our soldier, | our COR 1.01.116
thou wast a soldier | even to /cato's wish, not 1.04. 56
thank the gods | our rome hath such a soldier." 1.09. 9
nay, my good soldier, up; 2.01.171
thou art their soldier, and, being bred in 3.02. 81
said | my praises made thee first a soldier, so, 3.02.108

like a citizen, | you find him like a soldier; 3.03. 54
such as become a soldier | rather than envy you. 3.03. 56
but a greater soldier than he, you wot one. 4.05.162 P
but i take him to be the greater soldier. 4.05.168 P
i am return'd your soldier; 5.06. 70
rome, i have been thy soldier forty years, | and TIT 1.01.193
thou art a soldier, therefore seldom rich, | it TIM 1.02.222
but he's a tried and valiant soldier. JC 4.01. 28
i am a soldier, i, | older in practice, abler 4.03. 30
you say you are a better soldier: 4.03. 51
i said an elder soldier, not a better. 4.03. 56
lie, | most like a soldier, ordered honorably. 5.05. 79
who like a good and hardy soldier fought MAC 1.02. 4
an older and a better soldier none | that 4.03.191
fie, my lord, fie, a soldier, and afeard? 5.01. 37 P
let every soldier hew him down a bough, | and 5.04. 4
why then, god's soldier be he! 5.09. 13
let four captains | bear hamlet, like a soldier, HAM 5.02.396
your sister is the better soldier. LR 4.05. 3
him, and the man commands | like a full soldier. OTH 2.01. 36
him more in the soldier than in the scholar. 2.01.166 P
not past a pint, as i am a soldier. 2.03. 67 P
why then let a soldier drink." 2.03. 73
he's a soldier fit to stand by caesar | and give 2.03.122
more or less than truth, | thou art no soldier. 2.03.220
he's a soldier, and for me to say a soldier lies 3.04. 5 P
and for me to say a soldier lies, 'tis stabbing. 3.04. 5 P
and life, stands up | for the main soldier; ANT 1.02.191
or thou, the greatest soldier of the world, 1.03. 38
slime, i go from hence | thy soldier, servant, 1.03. 70
was borne so like a soldier, that thy cheek | so 1.04. 70
thou art a soldier only, speak no more. 2.02.107
i know thee now: how far'st thou, soldier? 2.06. 71
let's ha't, good soldier. 2.07.105
that | without the which a soldier and his sword 3.01. 28
good fortune, worthy soldier, and farewell. 3.02. 22
the mares would bear | a soldier and his horse. 3.07. 9
how now, worthy soldier? 3.07. 60
soldier, thou art; 3.07. 68
to–morrow, soldier, | by sea and land i'll fight 4.02. 4
and the soldier | that has this morning left 4.05. 4
no more a soldier. 4.14. 42
ah, soldier! 5.02.328
and when a soldier was the theme, my name | was CYM 3.03. 59
this attempt | i am soldier to, and will abide 3.04.183
which gave advantage to an ancient soldier | (an 5.03. 15
that the poor soldier that so richly fought, 5.05. 3
why, old soldier: 5.05.306
the forlorn soldier, that /so nobly fought, | he 5.05.405
the soldier that did company these three | in 5.05.408
melt thee, but be | a soldier to thy purpose. PER 4.01. 8
use them | and pray for me, your soldier. TNK 1.01. 76
queens, | follow your soldier. 1.01.211
fit of jealousy | to get the soldier work, that 1.02. 23
meet you no ruin but the soldier in | the cranks 1.02. 27
your pity, | but th' unconsider'd soldier? 1.02. 31
and greatest, | i would be thought a soldier. 2.05. 15
if he fail, | he's neither man nor soldier. 3.06. 4
like a swine, to fight, | and not a soldier: 3.06. 13
you are deceived, for, as i am a soldier, | i 3.06. 48
he shows a lover, when he frowns, a soldier. 4.02.136
take to thy grace | me thy vow'd soldier, who do 5.01. 95
SOLDIER–BREEDER 1 FR 0.0001 REL FR 0 V 1 P
therefore needs prove a good soldier–breeder. H5 5.02.206 P
SOLDIERESS 1 FR 0.0001 REL FR 1 V 0 P
soldieress | that equally canst poise sternness TNK 1.01. 85
SOLDIER–LIKE 2 FR 0.0002 REL FR 0 V 2 P
pity me — 'tis not a soldier–like phrase — but WIV 2.01. 13 P
word with my sword to be a soldier–like word, 2H4 3.02. 75 P
SOLDIER'S 17 FR 0.0019 REL FR 16 V 1 P
i look'd upon her with a soldier's eye, | that ADO 1.01.298
nor the soldier's, which is ambitious; AYL 4.01. 13 P
i will embrace him with a soldier's arm | that 1H4 5.02. 73
it is the soldier's; H5 4.07.174
and not a hair upon a soldier's head | which COR 4.06.133
sometime she driveth o'er a soldier's neck, ROM 1.04. 82
like powder in a skilless soldier's flask, | is 3.03.132
your son, my lord, has paid a soldier's debt. MAC 5.09. 5
the courtier's, soldier's, scholar's, eye, HAM 3.01.151
a soldier's a man; OTH 2.03. 71
did itself sustain | upon a soldier's thigh. 5.02.261
till i shall see you in your soldier's dress, ANT 2.04. 4
and ambition | (the soldier's virtue) rather 3.01. 23
this is a soldier's kiss; 4.04. 30
of the war, | the soldier's pole is fall'n! 4.15. 65
address'd, | i will well become a soldier's dance. PER 2.03. 95
o' my conscience, | was never soldier's friend. TNK 4.02. 88
SOLDIERS' 10 FR 0.0011 REL FR 10 V 0 P
o god of battles, steel my soldiers' hearts, H5 4.01.289
gay new coats o'er the french soldiers' heads 4.03.118
for soldiers' stomachs always serve them well. 1H6 2.03. 80
methinks i should revive the soldiers' hearts, 3.02. 97
through the realm | for soldiers' pay in france, 2H6 3.01. 62
and, being protector, stay'd the soldiers' pay, 3.01.105
our soldiers', like the night–owl's lazy flight, 3H6 2.01.130
gorging and feeding from our soldiers' hands, JC 5.01. 81
the soldiers' music and the rite of war | speak HAM 5.02.399
'tis the soldiers' life | to have their balmy OTH 2.03.257
SOLDIERS 112 FR 0.0126 REL FR 93 V 19 P
you were good soldiers and tall fellows; WIV 2.02. 11 P
them like pharaoh's soldiers in the reechy ADO 3.03.134 P
saint cupid, then! and, soldiers, to the field! LLL 4.03.363
gentlemen and soldiers, pardon me, i will not 5.02.704 P
after well–ent'red soldiers, to return | and AWW 2.01. 6
within between two soldiers and my young lady! 3.02. 34 P
our own wings, and to rend our own soldiers! 3.06. 50 P
and they often give us soldiers the lie, but we WT 4.04.724 P
his forces strong, his soldiers confident. JN 2.01. 61
the swords of soldiers are his teeth, his fangs, 2.01.353
in name of lendings for your highness' soldiers, R2 1.01. 89
disburs'd i duly to his highness' soldiers; 1.01.127
to deck our soldiers for these irish wars. 1.04. 62
and these stones | prove armed soldiers, ere her 3.02. 25
and as the soldiers bore dead bodies by, | he 1H4 1.03. 42
of prisoners' ransom, and of soldiers slain, 2.03. 54
holds from all soldiers chief majority | and 3.02.109
our soldiers shall march through; 4.02. 2 P
if i be not asham'd of my soldiers, i am a 4.02. 11 P

in exchange of a hundred and fifty soldiers, 4.02. 14 P
and such as indeed were never soldiers, but 4.02. 27 P
and, fellows, soldiers, friends, | better 5.02. 75
our soldiers stand full fairly for the day. 5.03. 29
toward their aim | than did our soldiers, aiming 2H4 1.01.124
do not the rebels need soldiers? 1.02. 74 P
you are to take soldiers up in counties as you 2.01.187 P
cousin, that comes hither anon about soldiers? 3.02. 28 P
bardolph, give the soldiers coats. 3.02.291 P
others, like soldiers, armed in their stings, H5 1.02.193
upon th' enraged soldiers in their spoil, | as 3.03. 25
whiles yet my soldiers are in my command, 3.03. 29
on, and sickness growing | upon our soldiers, we 3.03. 56
his soldiers sick and famish'd in their march; 3.05. 57
answer the particular endings of his soldiers, 4.01.156 P
can try it out with all unspotted soldiers. 4.01.161 P
and my poor soldiers tell me, yet ere night, 4.03.116
now, soldiers, march away, | and how thou 4.03.132
as soldiers will | that nothing do but meditate 5.02. 59
amongst the soldiers this is muttered, | that 1H6 1.01. 70
his soldiers, spying his undaunted spirit, | "a 1.01.127
ten thousand soldiers with me i will take, 1.01.155
improvident soldiers, had your watch been good, 2.01. 58
to gather our soldiers, scatter'd and dispers'd, 2.01. 76
will ye, like soldiers, come and fight it out? 3.02. 66
fight, soldiers, fight! 4.06. 1
soldiers, adieu! 4.07. 31
so many captains, gentlemen, and soldiers, 5.04.104
i never robb'd the soldiers of their pay, | nor 2H6 3.01.108
provide me soldiers, lords, | whiles i take 3.01.319
fourteen days | at bristow i expect my soldiers, 3.01.328
therefore bring forth the soldiers of our prize, 4.01. 8
and sent the ragged soldiers wounded home. 4.01. 90
come, soldiers, show what cruelty ye can, | that 4.01.132
soldiers, defer the spoil of the city until 4.07.133 P
follow me, soldiers, we'll devise a mean | to 4.08. 68
soldiers, this day have you redeem'd your lives, 4.09. 15
soldiers, i thank you all; 5.01. 45
were by the swords of common soldiers slain. 3H6 1.01. 9
and, soldiers, stay and lodge by me this night. 1.01. 32
and they have troops of soldiers at their beck? 1.01. 68
and i'll keep london with my soldiers. 1.01.207
the soldiers should have toss'd me on their 1.01.244
in them i trust, for they are soldiers, | witty, 1.02. 42
soldiers, away with him! 1.03. 7
muster'd my soldiers, gathered flocks of friends 2.01.112
that robb'd my soldiers of their heated spleen; 2.01.124
six miles off the duke is with the soldiers, 2.01.144
with aid of soldiers to this needful war. 2.01.147
our treasure seiz'd, our soldiers put to flight, 3.03. 36
us | with some few bands of chosen soldiers, 3.03.204
these soldiers shall be levied, | and thou, lord 3.03.251
his soldiers lurking in the town about, | and 4.02. 15
to do | but march to london with our soldiers? 4.03. 61
come on, brave soldiers; 4.07. 87
went through the army, cheering up the soldiers. R3 5.03. 71
than can the substance of ten thousand soldiers 5.03.218
god will in justice ward you as his soldiers; 5.03.254
i will lead forth my soldiers to the plain, 5.03.291
proclaim a pardon to the soldiers fled | that in 5.05. 16
but when they would seem soldiers, they have TRO 1.03.237
but we are soldiers, | and may that soldier a 1.03.286
your soldiers use him as the grace 'fore meat, COR 4.07. 3
the tribunes are no soldiers, and their people 4.07. 31
the god of soldiers, | with the consent of 5.03. 70
do not bid me | dismiss my soldiers, or 5.03. 82
help, three a' th' chiefest soldiers; 5.06.148
here none but soldiers and rome's servitors TIT 1.01.352
a halter, soldiers! 5.01. 47
bid him encamp his soldiers where they are. 5.02.126
soldiers should brook as little wrongs as gods. TIM 3.05.116
there's gold to pay thy soldiers, | make large 4.03.127
soldiers, not thieves. 4.03.413 P
likewise enrich'd poor straggling soldiers with 5.01. 6
so shall he waste his means, weary his soldiers, JC 4.03.200
his soldiers fell to spoil, | whilst we by 5.03. 7
your eye in scotland | would create soldiers, MAC 4.03.187
soldiers, sir. 5.03. 13
what soldiers, patch? 5.03. 15
what soldiers, whey-face? 5.03. 17
as you are friends, scholars, and soldiers, HAM 1.05.141
and his commission to employ those soldiers, 2.02. 74
and, as the sleeping soldiers in th' alarm, 3.04.120
go bid the soldiers shoot. 5.02.403
to't, luxury, pell-mell, for i lack soldiers. LR 4.06.117
take thou my soldiers, prisoners, patrimony; 5.03. 75
trust to thy single virtue, for thy soldiers, 5.03.103
soldiers, have careful watch. ANT 4.03. 7
his father and i were soldiers together, to whom CYM 1.04. 26 P
us, and he shall be interr'd | as soldiers can. 4.02.402
we have been soldiers, and we cannot weep | when TNK 1.03. 18
will wed me, | and soldiers sing my epitaph. 3.06.285
like soldiers when their captain once doth yield VEN 893

SOLDIERSHIP 9 FR 0.0010 REL FR 5 V 4 P
in friendship | first tried our soldiership! AWW 1.02. 26
possibility of thy soldiership will subscribe 3.06. 83 P
not, and more of his soldiership i know not, 4.03.268 P
setting my knighthood and my soldiership aside, 2H4 1.02. 81 P
set your knighthood and your soldiership aside, 1.02. 84 P
event, and put we on | industrious soldiership. MAC 5.04. 16
without practice, | is all his soldiership. OTH 1.01. 27
his soldiership | is twice the other twain; ANT 2.01. 34
the absolute soldiership you have by land, 3.07. 42

SOLD'REST 1 FR 0.0001 REL FR 1 V 0 P
god, | that sold'rest close impossibilities, TIM 4.03.387

SOLE* 29 FR 0.0032 REL FR 24 V 5 P
the sole drift of my purpose doth extend | not a TMP 5.01. 29
it is so, it is so — it hath the worser sole. TGV 2.03. 17 P
my sole earth's heaven, and my heaven's claim. ERR 3.02. 64
the crown of his head to the sole of his foot, ADO 3.02. 9 P
vicegerent, and sole dominator of navarre, my LLL 1.01.220 P
to parley with the sole inheritor | of all 2.01. 5
sole imperator and great general | of trotting 3.01.185
not on thy sole, but on thy soul, harsh jew, MV 4.01.123
his sole child, my lord, and bequeath'd to my AWW 1.01. 38 P
and this, so sole and unmatchable, | shall give JN 4.03. 52
sole heir male | of the true line and stock of H5 1.02. 70
tenth, | who was sole heir to the usurper capet, 1.02. 78
sole daughter unto lionel duke of clarence; 2H6 2.02. 50
lewis, | that henry, sole possessor of my love, 3H6 3.03. 24
and she shall be sole victoress, caesar's caesar R3 4.04.336
fame blows, that praise, sole pure, transcends. TRO 1.03.244
and affecting one sole throne, | without COR 4.06. 32
that, when the single sole of it is worn, the ROM 2.04. 62 P
crown'd | sole monarch of the universal earth. 3.02. 94
tyrant, whose sole name blisters our tongues, MAC 4.03. 12
and for that | i, his sole son, do this same HAM 3.03. 77
sole sir o' th' world, | i cannot project mine ANT 5.02.120
(whom | he purpos'd to his wive's sole son — a CYM 1.01. 5
you tell me, | is she sole child to th' king? 1.01. 56
that mightst have had the sole son of my queen! 1.01.138
of kindness | perform'd to your sole daughter. PER 4.03. 39
blest a /place | with thy sole presence. TNK 3.01. 11
bird of loudest lay, | on the sole arabian tree, PHT 2
which though it alter not love's sole effect, SON 36. 7

SOLELY *(also soly)*

SOLELY 3 FR 0.0003 REL FR 3 V 0 P
leave me solely. WT 2.03. 17
reigns solely in the breast of every man. H5 2.pr. 4
come | give solely sovereign sway and masterdom. MAC 1.05. 70

SOLEMN 40 FR 0.0045 REL FR 38 V 2 P
the solemn temples, the great globe itself, TMP 4.01.153
that rejoice | to hear the solemn curfew: 5.01. 40
a solemn air, and the best comforter | to an 5.01. 58
and us, | it hath in solemn synods been decreed, ERR 1.01. 13
now, music, sound, and sing your solemn hymn. ADO 5.03. 11
to check their folly, passion's solemn tears. LLL 5.02.118
here, a young man and an old in solemn talk. AYL 2.04. 20 P
estate, | an eye-sore to our solemn festival! SHR 3.02.101
the solemn feast | shall more attend upon the AWW 2.03.180
although before the solemn priest i have sworn, 2.03.269
sir, of whom he hath taken a solemn leave. 4.03. 77 P
a solemn combination shall be made | of our dear TN 5.01.383
how ceremonious, solemn, and unearthly | it was WT 3.01. 7
why do you bend such solemn brows on me? JN 4.02. 90
to dwell in solemn shades of endless night. R2 1.03.177
not flesh and blood | with solemn reverence, 3.02.172
where the sad and solemn priests | sing still H5 4.01.301
still, | for here we entertain a solemn peace. 1H6 5.04.175
a dreadful oath, sworn with a solemn tongue! 2H6 3.02.158
who can be bound by any solemn vow | to do a 5.01.184
wrong | but that he was bound by a solemn oath? 5.01.190
is crown'd so soon, and broke his solemn oath? 3H6 1.04.100
for he hath made a solemn vow | never to lie and 4.03. 4
my lords, a solemn hunting is in hand, | there TIT 2.01.112
when he is here, even at thy solemn feast, | i 5.02.115
when with his solemn tongue he did discourse 5.03. 81
our solemn hymns to sullen dirges change; ROM 4.05. 88
to-night we hold a solemn supper, sir, | and MAC 3.01. 14
mother, | nor customary suits of solemn black, HAM 1.02. 78
and with solemn march | goes slow and stately by 1.02.201
we'll make a solemn wager on your cunnings — 4.07.155
for often, with a solemn earnestness | (more OTH 5.02.227
army shall | in solemn show attend this funeral, ANT 5.02.364
all solemn things | should answer solemn CYM 4.02.191
solemn things | should answer solemn accidents. 4.02.192
come all sad and solemn shows, | that are TNK 1.05. 7
this is a solemn rite | they owe bloom'd may, 3.01. 2
this solemn sympathy poor venus noteth, | over VEN 1057
and solemn night with slow sad gait descended LUC 1081
therefore are feasts so solemn and so rare, SON 52. 5

SOLEMNITIES 1 FR 0.0001 REL FR 1 V 0 P
shall behold the night | of our solemnities. MND 1.01. 11

SOLEMNITY 13 FR 0.0014 REL FR 11 V 2 P
jars | with triumphs, mirth, and rare solemnity. TGV 5.04.161
time of the contract and limit of the solemnity, MM 3.01.216 P
intent, | came here in grace of our solemnity. MND 4.01.134
three, | we'll hold a feast in great solemnity. 4.01.185
a fortnight hold we this solemnity, | in nightly 5.01.369
messenger bid her repair | to our solemnity. JN 2.01.555
a feast, | and wan by rareness such solemnity. 1H4 3.02. 59
face, | to fleer and scorn at our solemnity? ROM 1.05. 57
in spite | to scorn at our solemnity this night. 1.05. 63
thou now | to murther, murther our solemnity? 4.05. 61
see | high order in this great solemnity. ANT 5.02.366
the feast's solemnity | shall want till your TNK 1.01.221
talk more of this when the solemnity is past. 2.01. 12 P

SOLEMNIZ'D 4 FR 0.0004 REL FR 3 V 1 P
straight shall our nuptial rites be solemniz'd; MV 2.09. 6
of her marriage and the day it is solemniz'd. AYL 3.02.315 P
the rites of marriage shall be solemniz'd. JN 2.01.539
news, | and make this marriage to be solemniz'd. 1H6 5.03.168

SOLEMNIZE 2 FR 0.0002 REL FR 2 V 0 P
and when your honors mean to solemnize | the MV 3.02.192
to solemnize this day the glorious sun | stays JN 3.01. 77

SOLEMNIZED 2 FR 0.0002 REL FR 2 V 0 P
nuptial | of these our dear-belov'd solemnized, TMP 5.01.310
jaques falconbridge, solemnized | in normandy, LLL 2.01. 42

SOLEMNLY 6 FR 0.0006 REL FR 6 V 0 P
and will to-morrow midnight solemnly | dance in MND 4.01. 88
on wednesday next we solemnly proclaim | our R2 4.01.319
all studies here i solemnly defy, | save how to 1H4 1.03.228
land, | and solemnly see him set on to london. H5 5.pr. 14
(after i have solemnly interr'd | at chertsey R3 1.02.213
seal | he solemnly had sworn that what he spoke H8 1.02.165

SOLEMNNESS 1 FR 0.0001 REL FR 0 V 1 P
virgilia, turn thy solemnness out a' door, and COR 1.03.108 P

SOLES 3 FR 0.0003 REL FR 1 V 2 P
you have dancing shoes | with nimble soles, i ROM 1.04. 15
which is indeed, sir, a mender of bad soles. JC 1.01. 14 P
nor the soles of her shoe? HAM 2.02.230 P

SOLICIT 13 FR 0.0014 REL FR 11 V 2 P
therefore be gone, solicit me no more. TGV 5.04. 40
and require her to solicit your master's desires WIV 1.02. 10 P
if the prince do solicit you in that kind, you ADO 2.01. 67 P
i had rather hear you to solicit that | than TN 3.01.109
blood | doth more solicit me than your exclaims R2 1.02. 2
solicit henry with her wondrous praise; 1H6 5.03.190
we heartily solicit | your gracious self to take R3 3.07.130
perceive | he did solicit you in free contempt COR 2.03.200
mean to solicit him | for mercy to his country. 5.01. 72
we will solicit heaven and move the gods | to TIT 4.03. 51
to heaven and grace, | solicit for it straight. OTH 5.02. 28
angry father if my tongue | did e'er solicit, or PER 2.05. 69
whose speed | the great bellona i'll solicit; TNK 1.03. 13

SOLICITATION 2 FR 0.0002 REL FR 1 V 1 P
my suit and repent my unlawful solicitation; OTH 4.02.199 P
can, fitt'st time | for best solicitation? TNK 1.01.170

SOLICITED 4 FR 0.0004 REL FR 3 V 1 P
how you have been solicited by a gentleman his AWW 3.05. 15 P
i am solicited, not by a few, | and those of H8 1.02. 18
which have solicited — the rest is silence. HAM 5.02.358
having solicited th' eternal power | that his LUC 345

SOLICITING 2 FR 0.0002 REL FR 2 V 0 P
this supernatural soliciting | cannot be ill; MAC 1.03.130
when he may cassio find | soliciting his wife. OTH 2.03.387

SOLICITINGS 1 FR 0.0001 REL FR 1 V 0 P
me, | and more /above, hath his solicitings, HAM 2.02.126

SOLICITOR 2 FR 0.0002 REL FR 2 V 0 P
single you | as our best-moving fair solicitor. LLL 2.01. 29
for thy solicitor shall rather die | than give OTH 3.03. 27

/SOLICITS 1 FR 0.0001 REL FR 1 V 0 P
frame yourself | to orderly /solicits, and be CYM 2.03. 47

SOLICITS 3 FR 0.0003 REL FR 3 V 0 P
may be the amorous count solicits her | in the AWW 3.05. 69
how he solicits heaven, | himself best knows; MAC 4.03.149
and | solicits here a lady that disdains | thee CYM 1.06.147

SOLID 3 FR 0.0003 REL FR 3 V 0 P
weary of solid firmness, melt itself | into the 2H4 3.01. 48
and make a sop of all this solid globe; TRO 1.03.113
whose solid virtue | the shot of accident nor OTH 4.01.266

SOLIDARES 1 FR 0.0001 REL FR 0 V 1 P
here's three solidares for thee; TIM 3.01. 43 P

SOLIDITY 1 FR 0.0001 REL FR 1 V 0 P
glow | o'er this solidity and compound mass, HAM 3.04. 49

SOLINUS 1 FR 0.0001 REL FR 1 V 0 P
proceed, solinus, to procure my fall, | and by ERR 1.01. 1

SOLITARY 3 FR 0.0003 REL FR 2 V 1 P
where thou shalt find me sad and solitary. TGV 4.04. 89
in respect that it is solitary, i like it very AYL 3.02. 15 P
sweet, solitary, white as chaste, and pure | as TNK 5.01.139

SOLOMON *(see salomon)*

SOLON'S 1 FR 0.0001 REL FR 1 V 0 P
pomp, | that hath aspir'd to solon's happiness, TIT 1.01.177

SOLUM 1 FR 0.0001 REL FR 0 V 1 P
of her, cum privilegio ad imprimendum solum; SHR 4.04. 93 P

SOLUS 5 FR 0.0005 REL FR 4 V 1 P
will you shog off? i would have you solus. H5 2.01. 45 P
"solus," egregious dog? 2.01. 46
the "solus" in thy most mervailous face, | the 2.01. 47
the "solus" in thy teeth, and in thy throat, 2.01. 48
i do retort the "solus" in thy bowels, | for i 2.01. 51

SOLY *(also solely)*

SOLY 6 FR 0.0006 REL FR 4 V 2 P
in terms of choice i am not soly led | by nice MV 2.01. 13
me, | left soly heir to all his lands and goods, SHR 2.01.117
think him a great way fool, soly a coward; AWW 1.01.101
of yourself, or else | to him had left it soly. COR 4.07. 16
may remain, after the wearing, soly singular. ROM 2.04. 63 P
jest, soly singular for the singleness! 2.04. 65 P

SOLYMAN 1 FR 0.0001 REL FR 1 V 0 P
that won three fields of sultan solyman, | i MV 2.01. 26

/SOME 13 FR 0.0014 REL FR 13 V 0 P
to /some kind of men | their graces serve them AYL 2.03. 10
/though /some /of /you, /with /pilate, /wash R2 4.01.239
/go /some /of /you, /and /fetch /a 4.01.268
/go /some /of /you, /convey /him /to /the /tower 4.01.316
/or /get /some /little /knife /between /thy TIT 3.02. 16
/my /aunt /merry /with /some /pleasing /tale. 3.02. 47
/it /sends /some /precious /instance /of /itself HAM 4.05.163
/secret /feet | /in /some /of /our /best /ports, LR 3.01. 33
/shall /find | /some /that /will /thank /you, 3.01. 37
/and, /from /some /knowledge /and /assurance, 3.01. 41
/i'll /fetch /some /flax /and /whites /of /eggs 3.07.106
/some /dear /cause | /will /in /concealment 4.03. 51
so pure | /but /some uncleanly apprehensions OTH 3.03.139

SOME 1405 FR 0.1588 REL FR 1079 V 326 P
(who had, no doubt, some noble creature in her) TMP 1.02. 7
bore us some leagues to sea, where they prepared 1.02.145
some food we had, and some fresh water, that | a 1.02.160
some food we had, and some fresh water, that | a 1.02.160
mad, and play'd | some tricks of desperation. 1.02.210
and sure it waits upon | some god o' th' island. 1.02.390
and that you will some good instruction give 1.02.425
sir, | i fear you have done yourself some wrong; 1.02.444
every day some sailor's wife, | the masters of 2.01. 4
the masters of some merchant, and the merchant 2.01. 5
the truth you speak doth lack some gentleness, 2.01.138
all were sea-swallow'd, though some cast again, 2.01.251
'twixt which regions | there is some space. 2.01.257
this is some monster of the isle with four legs, 2.02. 65
i will give him some relief, if it be but for 2.02. 67
i will pour some in thy other mouth. 2.02. 94
there be some sports are painful, and their 3.01. 1
some kinds of baseness | are nobly undergone; 3.01. 2
i must remove | some thousands of these logs, 3.01. 10
with so full soul but some defect in her | did 3.01. 44
this hand, i will supplant some of your teeth. 3.02. 49
for some of you there present | are worse than 3.03. 35
of this young couple | some vanity of mine art. 4.01. 41
and some donation freely to estate | on the 4.01. 85
done | some wanton charm upon this man and maid, 4.01. 95
your father's in some passion | that works him 4.01.143
monster, come put some lime upon your fingers, 4.01.245
and when i have requir'd | some heavenly music 5.01. 52
some heavenly power guide us | out of this 5.01.105
or some enchanted trifle to abuse me | (as late 5.01.112
you do yet taste | some subtleties o' th' isle, 5.01.124
some oracle | must rectify our knowledge. 5.01.244
company | some few odd lads you remember not. 5.01.255
some rare noteworthy object in thy travel. TGV 1.01. 13
upon some book i love i'll pray for thee. 1.01. 20
that's on some shallow story of deep love, | how 1.01. 21
i must go send some better messenger: 1.01.151
some love of yours hath writ to you in rhyme. 1.02. 76
heavy? belike it hath some burden then? 1.02. 82
that, some whirlwind bear | unto a ragged, 1.02.117
some to the wars, to try their fortune there; 1.03. 8
some to discover islands far away; 1.03. 9
some to the studious universities. 1.03. 10
i am resolv'd that thou shalt spend some time 1.03. 66
enjoin'd me to write some lines to one she loves 2.01. 87

fearing else some messenger, that might her 2.01.167
e next ensuing hour some foul mischance 2.02. 11
em | upon some other pawn for fealty. 2.04. 91
nfirm his welcome with some special favor. 2.04.101
me necessaries that i needs must use, | and 2.04.188
a place till some certain shot be paid and 2.05. 6 P
thout some treachery us'd to valentine. 2.06. 32
some sly trick blunt thurio's dull proceeding 2.06. 41
lesson me and tell me some good mean | how 2.07. 5
eeds | as may beseem some well–reputed page. 2.07. 43
while, | we have some secrets to confer about. 3.01. 2
m to break with thee of some affairs | that 3.01. 59
sea of melting pearl, which some call tears; 3.01.226
ve some malignant power upon my life; 3.01.240
r thou hast shown some sign of good desert) 3.02. 18
d frame some feeling line | that may discover 3.02. 75
dy's chamber–window | with some sweet consort; 3.02. 83
sort some gentlemen well skill'd in music. 3.02. 91
me sixteen months, and longer might have 4.01. 21
ow, then, that some of us are gentlemen, 4.01. 42
d give some evening music to her ear. 4.02. 17
ere's some great matter she'ld employ me in. 4.03. 3
d will employ thee in some service presently. 4.04. 41
at can with some discretion do my business — 4.04. 65
ear i am attended by some spies. 5.01. 10
v, | have some unhappy passenger in chase. 5.04. 15
, he doth in some sort confess it. WIV 1.01.103 P
st, i must turn away some of my followers. 1.03. 4 P
re is some simples in my closet, dat i vill 1.04. 63 P
gby, /baillez me some paper. 1.04. 88 P
nistress page, give me some counsel! 2.01. 42 P
less he know some strain in me that i know not 2.01. 87 P
pe is a curtal dog in some affairs. 2.01.110
hath wrong'd me in some humors. 2.01.129 P
th, thou hast some crotchets in thy head now. 2.01.154 P
me say that, though she appear honest to me, 2.02.221 P
ge, we have some salt of our youth in us, we 2.03. 47 P
like having receiv'd wrong by some person, is 3.01. 53 P
artily, some of you go home with me to dinner. 3.02. 79 P
re at hand, bethink you of some conveyance. 3.03.127 P
nk my husband hath some special suspicion of 3.03.187 P
me pour in some sack to the thames water; 3.05. 21 P
ay you ask him some questions in his 4.01. 16 P
w, william, some declensions of your pronouns. 4.01. 74 P
ge and i will look some linen for your head. 4.02. 81 P
awpit rush at once | with some diffused song. 4.04. 55
e, that in some respects makes a beast a man; 5.05. 4 P
some other, a man a beast. 5.05. 5 P
there be some more test made of my mettle MM 1.01. 48
ne one with child by him? my cousin juliet? 1.04. 45
ne rise by sin, and some by virtue fall; 2.01. 38
ne rise by sin, and some by virtue fall; 2.01. 38
ne run from brakes of ice and answer none, 2.01. 39
ne, | and some condemned for a fault alone. 2.01. 40
a fruit–dish, a dish of some threepence — 2.01. 93 P
cause he hath some offenses in him that thou 2.01.185 P
office, you had continu'd in it some time. 2.01.262 P
o it for some piece of money, and go through 2.01.270 P
a bring me in the names of some six or seven, 2.01.272 P
pose of her | to some more fitter place; 2.02. 17
show some pity. 2.02. 99
ould by and by have some speech with you. 3.01.154 P
eed, it does stink in some sort, sir; 3.02. 28 P
t we were all, as some would seem to be, 3.02. 38
ne say he is with the emperor of russia; 3.02. 88 P
er some, he is in rome; 3.02. 89 P
ne report a sea–maid spawn'd him; 3.02.108 P
ne, that he was begot between two stock–fishes 3.02.108 P
had some feeling of the sport; 3.02.119 P
on you anon for some advantage to yourself. 4.01. 23 P
glad to receive some instruction from my 4.02. 17 P
ope it is some pardon or reprieve | for the 4.02. 71
re's some in hope. 4.02. 78
chance entering into some monastery, but, by 4.02.202 P
some four suits of peach–color'd satin, 4.03. 10 P
ne one hath set you on; 5.01.112
e us some seats. 5.01.165
ould he had some cause | to prattle for 5.01.181
rs since there was some speech of marriage 5.01.217
instruments of some more mightier member 5.01.237
ave some marks of yours upon my pate: ERR 1.02. 82
ne of my mistress' marks upon my shoulders: 1.02. 83
, by some device or other | the villain is 1.02. 95
haps some merchant hath invited him, | and 2.01. 4
, were you wedded, you would bear some sway. 2.01. 28
v if your husband start some other where? 2.01. 30
god's sake send some other messenger. 2.01. 77
ne other mistress hath thy sweet aspects: 2.02.111
ad on /her part some cause to you unknown; 3.01. 91
meet you at that place some hour hence. 3.01.122
so. this jest shall cost me some expense. 3.01.123
ar false love with some show of blindness: 3.02. 8
n she bears some breadth? 3.02.112 P
ides, i have some business in the town. 4.01. 35
er send the chain, or send me by some token. 4.01. 56
ne tender money to me, some invite me; 4.03. 4
ne tender money to me, some invite me; 4.03. 4
ne other give me thanks for kindnesses; 4.03. 5
ne offer me commodities to buy. 4.03. 6
e blessed power deliver us from hence! 4.03. 44
e devils ask but the parings of one's nail, 4.03. 71
y must be bound and laid in some dark room. 4.04. 94
, not without some scandal to yourself, 5.01. 15
e get within him, take his sword away: 5.01. 34
is some priory, in, or we are spoil'd! 5.01. 37
ed some dear friend? 5.01. 50
nely, some love that drew him oft from home. 5.01. 56
some of you, knock at the abbey–gate, | and 5.01.165
sure (unless you send some present help) 5.01.176
| yet hath my night of life some memory, 5.01.315
wasting lamps some fading glimmer left, | my 5.01.316
ome gentleman or other shall scape a ADO 1.01.134 P
he heartily prays some occasion may detain 1.01.150 P
ll assume thy part in some disguise, | and 1.01.321
till god make men of some other mettle than 2.01. 59 P
ould to god some scholar would conjure her, 2.01.256 P
ay thee get us some excellent music; 2.03. 85 P
d that benedick knew of it by some other, if 2.03.155 P

he doth indeed show some sparks that are like 2.03.186 P
it seems not in him by some large jests he will 2.03.197 P
i may chance have some odd quirks and remnants 2.03.236 P
i do spy some marks of love in her. 2.03.245 P
and truly i'll devise some honest slanders | to 3.01. 84
in, | i'll show thee some attires, and have thy 3.01.102
some cupid kills with arrows, some with traps. 3.01.106
some cupid kills with arrows, some with traps. 3.01.106
if he be not in love with some woman, there is 3.02. 40 P
some treason, masters; yet stand close. 3.03.106 P
get you some of this distill'd carduus 3.04. 73 P
you have some moral in this benedictus. 3.04. 78 P
sir, i would have some confidence with you that 3.05. 2 P
drink some wine ere you go; fare you well. 3.05. 53 P
that shall drive some of them to a non–come; 3.05. 62 P
why then, some be of laughing, as, ah, ha, he! 4.01. 21 P
not guiltless here | under some biting error. 4.01.170
there is some strange misprision in the princes. 4.01.185
that is some good. 4.01.211
in some reclusive and religious life, | out of 4.01.242
use it for my love some other way than swearing 4.01.326 P
we have some haste, leonato. 5.01. 47
some haste, my lord! 5.01. 48
with quarrelling, | some of us would lie low. 5.01. 52
and shall, or some of us will smart for it. 5.01.109
but margaret was in some fault for this, 5.04. 4
and some such strange bull leapt your father's 5.04. 49
or study where to meet some mistress fine, LLL 1.01. 63
for the form — in some form. 1.01.211 P
guilty of such a ballet some three ages since, 1.02.112 P
example my digression by some mighty president. 1.02.116 P
of desolation that i have seen, some shall see. 1.02.160 P
what shall some see? 1.02.161 P
assist me, some extemporal god of rhyme, for i 1.02.183 P
some merry mocking lord belike, is't so? 2.01. 52
a yielding 'gainst some reason in my breast, 2.01.151
as jewels in crystal for some prince to buy, 2.01.243
some enigma, some riddle — come, thy l'envoy — 3.01. 71
some enigma, some riddle — come, thy l'envoy — 3.01. 71
some obscure precedence that hath tofore been 3.01. 82
i smell some l'envoy, some goose, in this. 3.01.121 P
i smell some l'envoy, some goose, in this. 3.01.122 P
some men must love my lady, and some joan. 3.01.205
some men must love my lady, and some joan. 3.01.205
some say a sore, but not a sore, till now made 4.02. 57
which is to me some praise that i thy parts 4.02.114
ay, as some days, but then no sun must shine. 4.03. 89
some certain treason. 4.03.188
did these rent lines show some love of thine? 4.03.216
ay marry, there — some flattery for this evil. 4.03.282
o, some authority how to proceed; 4.03.283
some tricks, some quillets, how to cheat the 4.03.284
some tricks, some quillets, how to cheat the 4.03.284
some salve for perjury. 4.03.285
some entertainment for them in their tents. 4.03.370
we will with some strange pastime solace them, 4.03.374
some certain special honors it pleaseth his 5.01.106 P
(sweet chuck) with some delightful ostentation, 5.01.111 P
as concerning some entertainment of time, some 5.01.118 P
of time, some show in the posterior of this day, 5.01.119 P
some thousand verses of a faithful lover. 5.02. 50
i thought to close mine eyes some half an hour; 5.02. 90
that some plain man recount their purposes. 5.02.177
the music plays, vouchsafe some motion to it. 5.02.216
for our rude transgression | some fair excuse. 5.02.432
some carry–tale, some please–man, some slight 5.02.463
some carry–tale, some please–man, some slight 5.02.463
carry–tale, some please–man, some slight zany, 5.02.463
some mumble–news, some trencher–knight, some 5.02.464
some mumble–news, some trencher–knight, some 5.02.464
mumble–news, some trencher–knight, some dick, 5.02.464
we will take some care. 5.02.510
and 'tis some policy | to have one show worse 5.02.512
will speak their mind in some other sort. 5.02.585 P
keep some state in thy exit, and vanish. 5.02.594 P
speed | to some forlorn and naked hermitage, 5.02.795
then, if i have much love, i'll give you some. 5.02.830
impose some service on me for thy love. 5.02.840
i have some private schooling for you both. MND 1.01.116
i must employ you in some business | against our 1.01.124
how happy some o'er other some can be! 1.01.226
how happy some o'er other some can be! 1.01.226
and when this hail some heat from hermia felt, 1.01.244
that will ask some tears in the true performing 1.02. 25 P
i will condole in some measure. 1.02. 27 P
some of your french crowns have no hair at all; 1.02. 97 P
i must go seek some dewdrops here, | and hang a 2.01. 14
take thou some of it, and seek through this 2.01.259
effect it with some care, that he may prove 2.01.265
some to kill cankers in the musk–rose buds, 2.02. 3
some war with rere–mice for their leathren wings 2.02. 4
coats, and some keep back | the clamorous owl, 2.02. 5
wake when some vile thing is near. 2.02. 34
some man or other must present wall; 3.01. 67 P
and let him have some plaster, or some loam, or 3.01. 68 P
and let him have some plaster, or some loam, or 3.01. 68 P
or some loam, or some rough–cast about him, to 3.01. 68 P
more the pity that some honest neighbors will 3.01.145 P
flower, | lamenting some enforced chastity. 3.01.200
some sleeves, some hats, from yielders all 3.02. 30
some sleeves, some hats, from yielders all 3.02. 30
which now in some slight measure it will pay, 3.02. 86
pay, | if for his tender here i make some stay. 3.02. 87
laid the love–juice on some true–love's sight. 3.02. 89
must perforce ensue | some true love turn'd, and 3.02. 91
by some illusion see thou bring her here. 3.02. 98
in some bush? 3.02.406
what, wilt thou hear some music, my sweet love? 4.01. 27
not by what power | (but by some power it is), 4.01.165
that, if it would but apprehend some joy, | it 5.01. 19
joy, | it comprehends some bringer of that joy; 5.01. 20
or in the night, imagining some fear, | how easy 5.01. 21
the lazy time, if not with some delight? 5.01. 41
that is some satire, keen and critical, | not 5.01. 54
a play there is, my lord, some ten words long, 5.01. 61
some that will evermore peep through their eyes, MV 1.01. 52
you may be won by some other sort than your 1.02.104 P
so i will not rest till i have run some ground. 2.02.104 P

pain | to allay with some cold drops of modesty 2.02.186
but fare you well, | i have some business. 2.02.204
didst rob it of some taste of tediousness. 2.03. 3
at gratiano's lodging some hour hence. 2.04. 26
there is some ill a–brewing towards my rest, 2.05. 17
and gild myself | with some moe ducats, and be 2.06. 50
some god direct my judgment! 2.07. 13
bassanio told him he would make some speed | of 2.08. 37
embraced heaviness | with some delight or other. 2.08. 53
some there be that shadows kiss, | such have but 2.09. 66
thou wilt say anon he is some kin to thee, 2.09. 97
i spoke with some of the sailors that escap'd 3.01.104 P
i would detain you here some month or two 3.02. 9
what damned error but some sober brow | will 3.02. 78
some mark of virtue on his outward parts. 3.02. 82
after some oration fairly spoke | by a beloved 3.02.178
there are some shrowd contents in yond same 3.02.243
some dear friend dead, else nothing in the world 3.02.245
the which my love and some necessity | now lays 3.04. 34
if two gods should play some heavenly match, 3.05. 79
some men there are love not a gaping pig; 4.01. 47
some that are mad if they behold a cat; 4.01. 48
some three or four of you | go give him 4.01.147
have by some surgeon, shylock, on your charge, 4.01.257
entreat some power to change this currish jew. 4.01.292
take some remembrance of us, as a tribute, | not 4.01.422
some welcome for the mistress of the house. 5.01. 38
that took some pains in writing, he begg'd mine, 5.01.182
i'll die for't but some woman had the ring! 5.01.208
my clerk hath some good comforts too for you. 5.01.289
you shall have some part of your will. AYL 1.01. 77 P
escapes me without some broken limb shall acquit 1.01.127 P
poison, entrap thee by some treacherous device, 1.01.151 P
ta'en thy life by some indirect means or other; 1.01.152 P
i would thou hadst been son to some man else: 1.02.224
cast away upon curs, throw some of them at me. 1.03. 5 P
no, some of it is for my child's father. 1.03. 11 P
some villains of my court | are of consent and 2.02. 2
we'll light upon some settled low content. 2.03. 68
come, i will bear thee to some shelter, and thou 2.06. 16 P
yet am i inland bred | and know some nurture. 2.07. 97
give us some music, and, good cousin, sing. 2.07.173
some, how brief the life of man | runs his 3.02.129
some, of violated vows | 'twixt the souls of 3.02.133
for some of them had in them more feet than the 3.02.165 P
i prithee recount some of them. 3.02.357 P
i would give him some good counsel, for he seems 3.02.364 P
a poet, i might have some hope thou didst feign. 3.03. 27 P
with a pin, and there remains | some scar of it; 3.05. 22
capable impressure | thy palm some moment keeps; 3.05. 24
you meet in some fresh cheek the power of fancy, 3.05. 29
there be some women, silvius, had they mark'd 3.05.124
i take some joy to say you are, because i would 4.01. 89 P
some of my shame, if you will know of me | what 4.03. 95
his arm | the lioness had torn some flesh away, 4.03.147
and after some small space, being strong at 4.03.151
of me then (for now i speak to some purpose) 5.02. 52 P
esteem than may in some little measure draw a 5.02. 57 P
some lively touches of my daughter's favor. 5.04. 27
after some question with him, was converted 5.04.161
some one be ready with a costly suit, | and ask SHR in.1. 59
belike some noble gentleman that means in.1. 75
gentleman that means | (travelling some journey) in.1. 76
the rather for i have some sport in hand, in.1. 91
you break into some merry passion | and so in.1. 97
and slept above some fifteen year or more. in.2. 113
master, some show to welcome us to town. 1.01. 47
husht, master, here's some good pastime toward; 1.01. 68
advis'd, he took some care | to get her cunning 1.01.186
i will some other be, some florentine, | some 1.01.204
i will some other be, some florentine, | some 1.01.204
some neapolitan, or meaner man of pisa. 1.01.205
but be thou arm'd for some unhappy words. 2.01.139
o, how i long to have some chat with her! 2.01.162
and woo her with some spirit when she comes. 2.01.169
'tis some odd humor pricks him to this fashion; 3.02. 72
as if they saw some wondrous monument, | some 3.02. 95
monument, | some comet or unusual prodigy? 3.02. 96
word, | though in some part enforced to digress, 3.02.107
he hath some meaning in his mad attire. 3.02.124
some water here! 4.01.149
shall i have some water? 4.01.153
some undeserved fault | i'll find about the 4.01.199
i prithee go, and get me some repast; 4.03. 15
let's see, i think 'tis now some seven a' clock, 4.03.187
having come to padua | to gather in some debts, 4.04. 25
i, upon some agreement | me shall you find ready 4.04. 33
clerk, and some sufficient honest witnesses. 4.04. 94 P
and by all likelihood some cheer is toward. 5.01. 13
she says you have some goodly jest in hand. 5.02. 91
you have some stain of soldier in you; AWW 1.01.111 P
unfold to us some warlike resistance. 1.01.116 P
from my hive, | to give some laborers room. 1.02. 67
some six months since, my lord. 1.02. 71
you know my father left me some prescriptions 1.03.221
methinks in thee some blessed spirit doth speak 2.01.175
give me some help here ho! 2.01.209
your lordship to make some reservation of your 2.03.245 P
only he desires | some private speech with you. 2.05. 57
nay, there is some comfort in the news, some 3.02. 36 P
there is some comfort in the news, some comfort. 3.02. 36 P
and, after some dispatch in hand at court, 3.02. 54
i will bestow some precepts of this virgin 3.05.100
he might at some great and trusty business in a 3.06. 15 P
some dishonor we had in the loss of that drum, 3.06. 56 P
we'll make you some sport with the fox ere we 3.06.102 P
some four or five descents | since the first 3.07. 24
to understand him, unless some one among us, 4.01. 5 P
he must think us some band of strangers i' th' 4.01. 14 P
i must give myself some hurts, and say i got 4.01. 37 P
his wife some two months since fled from his 4.03. 47 P
and how mightily some other times we drown our 4.03. 67 P
some that humble themselves may, but the many 4.05. 52 P
my lord, to bring me in some grace, for you did 5.02. 46 P
strikes some scores away | from the great compt; 5.03. 56
i think thee now some common customer. 5.03.286
of a count | that died some twelvemonth since, TN 1.02. 37
shall we /set about some revels? 1.03.136 P

some four or five attend him — | all, if you 1.04. 36
some mollification for your giant, sweet lady. 1.05.204 P
sure you have some hideous matter to deliver, 1.05.206 P
for some hour before you took me from the breach 2.01. 21 P
by'r lady, sir, and some dogs will catch well. 2.03. 62 P
i will drop in his way some obscure epistles of 2.03.155 P
come, i'll go burn some sack, 'tis too late to 2.03.190 P
give me some music. 2.04. 1
eye | hath stay'd upon some favor that it loves. 2.04. 24
say that some lady, as perhaps there is, | hath 2.04. 89
rascally sheep–biter come by some notable shame? 2.05. 5 P
up my watch, or play with my — some rich jewel. 2.05. 60 P
some are /born great, some /achieve greatness, 2.05.145 P
some are /born great, some /achieve greatness, 2.05.145 P
and some have greatness thrust upon 'em. 2.05.146 P
accosted her, and with some excellent jests, 3.02. 22 P
you do redeem it by some laudable attempt either 3.02. 28 P
if thou thou'st him some thrice, it shall not be 3.02. 45 P
to him, lad, some two thousand strong, or so. 3.02. 54 P
the count his galleys | i did some service, of 3.03. 27
haply your eye shall light upon some toy | you 3.03. 44
ladyship were best to have some guard about you, 3.04. 12 P
this does make some obstruction in the blood, 3.04. 21 P
"some are born great" — 3.04. 41 P
"some achieve greatness" — 3.04. 43 P
"and some have greatness thrust upon them." 3.04. 45 P
let some of my people have a special care of him 3.04. 62 P
a slow tongue, in the habit of some sir of note, 3.04. 73 P
he is now in some commerce with my lady, and 3.04.174 P
the while upon some horrid message for a 3.04.199 P
the house and desire some conduct of the lady. 3.04.242 P
i have heard of some kind of men that put 3.04.243 P
i must entreat of you some of that money. 3.04.340
he has heard that word of some great man and now 4.01. 13 P
i would not be in some of your coats for 4.01. 31 P
good fool, help me to some light and some paper. 4.02.105 P
good fool, help me to some light and some paper. 4.02.105 P
good fool, some ink, paper, and light; 4.02.109 P
that this may be some error, but no madness, 4.03. 10
ay, sir, we are some of her trappings. 5.01. 9 P
he upon some action | is now in durance, at 5.01.275
upon some stubborn and uncourteous parts | we 5.01.361
why, "some are born great, some achieve 5.01.370 P
"some are born great, some achieve greatness, 5.01.370 P
and some have greatness thrown upon them." 5.01.371 P
WT th' other for some while a friend. 1.02.108
why, that's some comfort. | what? camillo there? 1.02.208
by some severals | of head–piece extraordinary? 1.02.226
as he had lost some province and a region 1.02.369
a sickness | which puts some of us in distemper, 1.02.385
become some women best, so that there be not 2.01. 9
though he does bear some signs of me, yet you 2.01. 57
there's some ill planet reigns; 2.01.105
and by some putter–on | that will be damn'c 2.01.141
the second and the third, nine, and some five; 2.01.145
about some gossips for your highness. 2.03. 41
so bloody, must | lead on to some foul issue. 2.03.153
it | to some remote and desert place quite out 2.03.176
that thou commend it strangely to some place 2.03.182
some powerful spirit instruct the kites and 2.03.186
tenderly apply to her | some remedies for life. 3.02.153
sometimes her head on one side, some another — 3.03. 20
and, gasping to begin some speech, her eyes 3.03. 25
sure some scape. 3.03. 72 P
this has been some stair–work, some trunk–work, 3.03. 74 P
this has been some stair–work, some trunk–work, 3.03. 74 P
some trunk–work, some behind–door–work. 3.03. 74 P
this is some changeling; 3.03.118 P
i, that please some, try all, both joy and 4.01. 1
to whose feeling sorrows i might be some allay 4.02. 8 P
camillo, and with some care, so far that i have 4.02. 35 P
we are) have some question with the shepherd; 4.02. 48 P
some call him autolycus. 4.03.100 P
to think your father, by some accident, | should 4.04. 19
gillyvors, | which some call nature's bastards. 4.04. 83
i would i had some flow'rs o' th' spring that 4.04.113
and where some stretch–mouth'd rascal would, as 4.04.196 P
pray now buy some. 4.04.260 P
let's have some merry ones. 4.04.287 P
be not too rough for some that know little but 4.04.330 P
should hold some counsel | in such a business. 4.04.409
but for some other reasons, my grave sir, 4.04.411
some hangman must put on my shroud and lay me 4.04.457
i am bound to you. | there is some sap in this. 4.04.565
be the worst, yet hold thee, there's some boot. 4.04.637 P
you must retire yourself | into some covert. 4.04.650
some say he shall be ston'd; 4.04.778 P
with aqua–vitae or some other hot infusion; 4.04.787 P
in some sort, sir; 4.04.814 P
some swounded, all sorrow'd. 5.02. 90 P
i thought she had some great matter there in 5.02.104 P
every wink of an eye some new grace will be born 5.02.110 P
which lets go by some sixteen years, and makes 5.03. 31
will wing me to some wither'd bough and there 5.03.133
JN do you not read some tokens of my son | in the 1.01. 87
some proper man, i hope. 1.01.250
some sins do bear their privilege on earth, 1.01.261
some trumpet summon hither to the walls | these 2.01.198
some bastards too. 2.01.279
at mine hostess' door, | teach us some fence! 2.01.290
be by some certain king purg'd and depos'd. 2.01.372
some speedy messenger bid her repair | to our 2.01.554
yet in some measure satisfy her so | that we 2.01.557
impose | some gentle order, and then we shall be 3.01.251
some aery devil hovers in the sky | and pours 3.02. 2
say, | but i will fit it with some better /time. 3.03. 26
so we could find some pattern of our shame. 3.04. 16
preach some philosophy to make me mad, | and 3.04. 51
i fear some outrage, and i'll follow her. 3.04.106
some reasons of this double coronation | i have 4.02. 40
need | some messenger betwixt me and the peers, 4.02.179
by some damn'd hand was robb'd and ta'en away. 5.01. 41
brain | (which some suppose the soul's frail 5.07. 3
o that there were some virtue in my tears, 5.07. 44
R2 on some known ground of treachery in him? 1.01. 11
on some apparent danger seen in him | aim'd at 1.01. 13
some of those seven are dried by nature's course 1.02. 14
some of those branches by the destinies cut; 1.02. 15
in some large measure to thy father's death, 1.02. 26
which i with some unwillingness pronounce: 1.03.149
i look'd when some of you should say | i was too 1.03.243
the pleasure that some fathers feed upon | is my 2.01. 79
and, for these great affairs do ask some charge, 2.01.159
yet again methinks | some unborn sorrow, ripe in 2.02. 10
at some thing it grieves, | more than with 2.02. 12
is still deriv'd | from some forefather grief; 2.02. 35
go, fellow, get thee home, provide some carts, 2.02.106
men | i will unfold some causes of your deaths: 3.01. 7
how some have been depos'd, some slain in war, 3.02.157
how some have been depos'd, some slain in war, 3.02.157
some haunted by the ghosts they have deposed, 3.02.158
some poisoned by their wives, some sleeping 3.02.159
poisoned by their wives, some sleeping kill'd, 3.02.159
to ear the land that hath some hope to grow, 3.02.212
with some few private friends upon this coast. 3.03. 4
some way of common trade, where subjects' feet 3.03.156
and make some pretty match with shedding tears? 3.03.165
therefore no dancing, girl, some other sport. 3.04. 9
give some supportance to the bending twigs. 3.04. 32
and some few vanities that make him light; 3.04. 86
some honest christian trust me with a gage — 4.01. 83
and cloister thee in some religious house. 5.01. 23
and some will mourn in ashes, some coal–black, 5.01. 49
and some will mourn in ashes, some coal–black, 5.01. 49
that were some love, but little policy. 5.01. 84
that had not god, for some strong purpose, 5.02. 34
which for some reasons i would not have seen. 5.02. 62
which for some reasons, sir, i mean to see. 5.02. 63
'tis nothing but some band that he is ent'red 5.02. 65
my lord, some two days since i saw the prince, 5.03. 13
through both | i see some sparks of better hope, 5.03. 21
to have some conference with your grace alone. 5.03. 27
choose out some secret place, some reverent room 5.06. 25
out some secret place, some reverent room, 5.06. 25
1H4 that some night–tripping fairy had exchang'd 1.01. 87
and in some sort it jumps with my humor as well 1.02. 69 P
imagination of some great exploit | drives him 1.03.199
and would be glad he met with some mischance, 1.03.232
are content to do the profession some grace, 2.01. 71 P
some eight or ten. 2.02. 64 P
let me see some more. 2.03. 6 P
and are they not some of them set forward 2.03. 28 P
their breath | on some great sudden hest. 2.03. 62
some heavy business hath my lord in hand, | and 2.03. 63
i prithee do thou stand in some by–room, while i 2.04. 29 P
he that kills me some six or seven dozen of 2.04.102 P
he, and answers, "some fourteen," an hour after; 2.04.107 P
we four set upon some dozen — 2.04.174 P
some six or seven fresh men set upon us — 2.04.180 P
pray god you have not murd'red some of them. 2.04.189 P
a whit, i' faith, i lack some of thy instinct. 2.04.371 P
and, as i think, his age some fifty, or, by'r 2.04.424 P
wales and i | must have some private conference, 3.02. 2
so | for some displeasing service i have done, 3.02. 5
i may for some things true, wherein my youth 3.02. 26
and in the closing of some glorious day | be 3.02.133
some twelve days hence | our general forces at 3.02.177
and that suddenly, while i am in some liking. 3.03. 5 P
a trifle, some eight–penny matter. 3.03.104 P
thought | by some that know not why he is away 4.01. 63
some of us love you well, and even those some 4.03. 34
and even those some | envy your great deservings 4.03. 34
some certain edicts and some strait decrees 4.03. 79
some certain edicts and some strait decrees 4.03. 79
impawn'd | some surety for a safe return again, 4.03.109
with some fine color that may please the eye 5.01. 75
some of us never shall | a second time do such a 5.02. 99
because some tell me that thou art a king. 5.03. 5
and show'd thou mak'st some tender of my life 5.04. 49
2H4 the big year, swoll'n with some other grief, in 13
now | should be the father of some stratagem. 1.01. 8
he was some hilding fellow that had stol'n | the 1.01. 57
being sick, have (in some measure) made me well. 1.01.139
is now going with some charge to the lord john 1.02. 63 P
youth, have yet some smack of an ague in you, 1.02. 97 P
you, some relish of the saltness of time in you, 1.02. 98 P
is return'd with some discomfort from wales. 1.02.104 P
the wise may make some dram of a scruple, or 1.02.130 P
and yet in some respects i grant i cannot go. 1.02.167 P
it may chance cost some of us our lives, for he 2.01. 11 P
it is more than for some, my lord, it is for all 2.01. 73 P
of his, but i will have some of it out again, or 2.01. 76 P
whereby thou didst desire to eat some, whereby i 2.01. 97 P
say, "there's some of the king's blood spilt." 2.02.113 P
this doll tearsheet should be some road. 2.02.166 P
mistress tearsheet would fain hear some music. 2.04. 12 P
you two never meet but you fall to some discord. 2.04. 56 P
come give 's some sack. 2.04.180 P
give me some sack, and, sweet heart, lie thou 2.04.183
some sack, francis. 2.04.281 P
and some about him have too lavishly | wrested 4.02. 57
to say thus, some good thing comes to–morrow. 4.02. 84
some guard /these /traitors to the block of 4.02.122
one time or other break some gallows' back. 4.03. 29
and cowards, which some of us should be too, but 4.03. 95 P
had found some months asleep and leapt them over 4.04.124
up, and bear me hence | into some other chamber. 4.04.132
unless some dull and favorable hand | will 4.05. 2
thou hast stol'n that which after some few hours 4.05.101
some pigeons, davy, a couple of short–legg'd 5.01. 26 P
but a knave should have some countenance at his 5.01. 44 P
brothers, you /mix your sadness with some fear: 5.02. 46
give master bardolph some wine, davy. 5.03. 25 P
i am, sir, under the king, in some authority. 5.03.112 P
bate me some, and i will pay you some, and (as ep 14 P
bate me some, and i will pay you some, and (as ep 15 P
H5 of his true titles to some certain dukedoms, 1.01. 87
him, of some things of weight | that task our 1.02. 5
for some dishonest manners of their life, 1.02. 49
to /fine his title with some shows of truth, 1.02. 72
where some, like magistrates, correct at home; 1.02.191
did claim some certain dukedoms, in the right 1.02.247
and some are yet ungotten and unborn | that 1.02.287
at that time, and some say knives have edges. 2.01. 22 P
he passes some humors and careers. 2.01.126 P
man and best indued | with some suspicion. 2.02.140
'a did in some sort, indeed, handle women; 2.03. 3
dowry, | some petty and unprofitable dukedoms. 3.pr. 3
i must leave them, and seek some better service. 3.02. 5
i wad full fain heard some question 'tween you 3.02.11
god, and i have merited some love at his hands. 3.06. 2
some of them will fall to–morrow, i hope. 3.07. 7
and 'twere more honor some were away. 3.07. 7
as well, were some of your brags dismounted. 3.07. 7
there is some soul of goodness in things evil, 4.01.
"we died at such a place" — some swearing, some 4.01.13
some swearing, some crying for a surgeon, some 4.01.13
some upon their wives left poor behind them, 4.01.13
poor behind them, some upon the debts they owe, 4.01.14
they owe, some upon their children rawly left. 4.01.14
some, peradventure, have on them the guilt of 4.01.16
some, of beguiling virgins with the broken seals 4.01.16
some, making the wars their bulwark, that have 4.01.16
as i suck blood, i will some mercy show. 4.04. 6
word, | some sudden mischief may arise of it; 4.07.17
i say, i will make him eat some part of my leek, 5.01. 4
will you have some more sauce to your leek? 5.01. 4
to appoint some of your council presently | to 5.02. 7
happily a woman's voice may do some good, | when 5.02. 9
and you may, some of you, thank love for my 5.02.31
1H6 quite, | except some petty towns of no import. 1.01. 9
i think by some odd gimmors or device | their 1.02. 4
by some apparent sign | let us have knowledge at 2.01.
'tis sure they found some place | but weakly 2.01. 7
i thought i should have seen some hercules, | a 2.03. 1
i'll sort some other time to visit you. 2.03. 2
i have perhaps some shallow spirit of judgment; 2.04. 1
some words there grew 'twixt somerset and me; 2.05. 4
would some part of my young years | might but 2.05.10
lord, | we will bestow you in some better place, 3.02. 8
now will we take some order in the town, 3.02.12
town, | placing therein some expert officers, 3.02.12
we'll set thy statue in some holy place, | and 3.03. 1
pretend some alteration in good will? 4.01. 5
after some respite, will return to callice; 4.01.17
but that it doth presage some ill event. 4.01.19
out, some light horsemen, and peruse their wings 4.02. 4
o, send some succor to the distress'd lord! 4.03. 3
i quickly shed | some of his bastard blood, and 4.06. 2
he talks of wood; it is some carpenter. 5.03. 9
i wish some ravenous wolf had eaten thee! 5.04. 3
approacheth, to confer about some matter. 5.04.10
2H6 some sudden qualm hath struck me at the heart, 1.01. 5
that's some wrong indeed. 1.03. 1
peace, son, and show some reason, buckingham, 1.03.11
give me leave | to show some reason, of no 1.03.16
alas, good master, my wife desired some damsons, 2.01.10
as if she had suborned some to swear | false 3.01.18
collected choicely, from each county some, | and 3.01.31
i will stir up in england some black storm 3.01.34
some violent hands were laid on humphrey's life! 3.02.13
mother took into her blameful bed | some stern, 3.02.21
and do some service to duke humphrey's ghost. 3.02.23
give me some drink, and bid the apothecary 3.03. 1
some say the bee stings, but i say, 'tis the 4.02. 8
i'll send some holy bishop to entreat; 4.04.
now go some and pull down the savoy; 4.07.
the giving up of some more towns in france. 4.07.13
go some, and follow him, | and he that brings 4.08. 6
seek thee out some other chase, | for i myself 5.02. 1
3H6 kiss, | as if they vow'd some league inviolable. 2.01. 3
in this the heaven figures some event. 2.01. 3
some dreadful story hanging on thy tongue? 2.01. 4
some six miles off the duke is with the soldiers 2.01.14
nay, warwick, single out some other chase, | for 2.04. 1
may be possessed with some store of crowns, 2.05. 5
yield both my life and them | to some man else, 2.05. 6
some troops pursue the bloody–minded queen, 2.06. 3
and come some other time to know our mind. 3.02. 1
to do them good i would sustain some harm. 3.02. 3
thou art a widow, and thou hast some children, 3.02.10
i, being but a bachelor, | have other some. 3.02.10
she did corrupt frail nature with some bribe, 3.02.15
warwick, this is some post to us or thee. 3.03.16
us | with some few bands of chosen soldiers, 3.03.20
tell me some reason why the lady grey | should 4.01. 2
give me assurance with some friendly vow, | that 4.01.14
loss of some pitch'd battle against warwick? 4.04.
and do expect him here some two hours hence. 5.01.
if case some one of you would fly from us, 5.04.
ere ye come there, be sure to hear some news. 5.05.
and heave it shall some weight, or break my back 5.07.
R3 belike his majesty hath some intent | that you 1.01. 4
no beast so fierce but knows some touch of pity. 1.02. 7
me have | some patient leisure to excuse myself. 1.02. 8
some dungeon. 1.02.1
her lord, whom i, some three months since, 1.02.2
i will maintain it with some little cost. 1.02.2
that scarce some two days since were worth a 1.03.
age, | but by some unlook'd accident cut off! 1.03.2
unless it be while some tormenting dream 1.03.2
some lay in dead men's skulls, and, in the holes 1.04.
some certain dregs of conscience are yet within 1.04.1
my friend, i spy some pity in thy looks. 1.04.2
i'll go hide the body in some hole | till that 1.04.2
some tardy cripple bare the countermand, | that 2.01.
god grant that some, less noble and less loyal, 2.01.
me seemeth good that, with some little train, 2.02.1
why with some little train, my lord of 2.02.1
some day or two | your highness shall repose you 3.01.
we may digest our complots in some form. 3.01.2
i'll send some packing that yet think not on't. 3.02.
and so 'twill do | with some men else, that 3.02.
than some that have accus'd them wear their hats 3.02.
i do beseech you send for some of them. 3.04.
there's some conceit or other likes him well, 3.04.
now will i go to take some privy order | to draw 3.05.1
when he had done, some followers of mine own, 3.07.
and some ten voices cried, "god save king 3.07.
intend some fear, | be not you spoke with but by 3.07.
are come to have some conference with his grace. 3.07.
i do suspect i have done some offense | that 3.07.1
save that, for reverence to some alive, | i give 3.07.1
but we will plant some other in the throne, | to 3.07.2

t my pent heart may have some scope to beat, 4.01. 34
e me some little breath, some pause, dear 4.02. 24
e me some little breath, some pause, dear 4.02. 24
uire me out some mean poor gentleman, | whom 4.02. 53
to some scaffold, there to lose their heads. 4.04.243
ess thou couldst put on some other shape 4.04.286
ne light–foot friend post to the duke of 4.04.440
ne one take order buckingham be brought | to 4.04.537
for some men of sound direction: 5.03. 16
e me some ink and paper in my tent; 5.03. 23
nt, make some good means to speak with him, 5.03. 40
e me some ink and paper. 5.03. 49
uld by a good discourser lose some life, H8 1.01. 41
— let some graver eye | pierce into that — 1.01. 67
his instant | he bores me with some trick. 1.01.128
ough their amity | breed him some prejudice; 1.01.182
ır | to hear from him a matter of some moment; 1.02.163
, until | it forg'd him some design, which, 1.02.181
ne of these | should find a running banket, 1.04. 11
k out there, some of ye. 1.04. 50
ne attend him. 1.04. 60
some about him near, have out of malice | to 2.01.157
with some other business put the king | from 2.02. 56
some of these | the queen is put in anger. 2.04.161
e are some will thank you, | if you speak 3.01. 46
may be left | to some ears unrecounted. 3.02. 48
m her | will fall some blessing to this land, 3.02. 51
ne strange commotion | is in his brain; 3.02.112
ne spirit put this paper in the packet, | to 3.02.129
t remember | some of these articles, and out 3.02.304
ne little memory of me will stir him | (i know 3.02.417
vn | to rest a while, some half an hour or so, 4.01. 66
t his noble grace would have some pity | upon 4.02.139
r friend | some touch of your late business. 5.01. 13
ould have ta'en some pains to bring together 5.01.119
is of purpose laid by some that hate me 5.02. 14
some o' th' guard be ready there. 5.02.130
thought i had had men of some understanding 5.02.170
re's some of ye, i see, | more out of malice 5.02.179
have we some strange indian with the great 5.03. 34 P
ight see from far some forty truncheoners 5.03. 51 P
ve some of 'em in limbo patrum, and there 5.03. 64 P
ne come to take their ease, | and sleep an act ep 2
n an attaint but he carries some stain of it. TRO 1.02. 26 P
nor hector is not troilus in some degrees. 1.02. 69 P
rd, | as he being dress'd to some oration." 1.03.166
you my time to bring it to some shape. 1.03.313
n would come some matter from him; 2.01. 8 P
morrow morning call some knight to arms 2.01.124
hout some image of th' affected merit. 2.02. 60
is should do some vengeance on the greeks. 2.02. 73
ur sister work | some touches of remorse? 2.02.115
ils, but i'll see some issue of my spiteful 2.03. 6 P
nding destruction, or some joy too fine, 3.02. 23
ne thing not worth in me such rich beholding 3.03. 91
eavens, what some men do, | while some men 3.03.132
at some men do, | while some men leave to do! 3.03.133
v some men creep in skittish fortune's hall, 3.03.134
ne say the genius /so | cries "/come" to him 4.04. 50
lst some with cunning gild their copper 4.04.105
t i have said to some my standers–by, | "lo 4.05.190
prodigious, there will come some change; 5.01. 93 P
e me some token for the surety of it. 5.02. 60
f you cannot weep, yet give some groans, 5.10. 49
ne two months hence my will shall here be made 5.10. 52
ne galled goose of winchester would hiss. 5.10. 54
un, | lead'st first to win some vantage. COR 1.01.160
ne parcels of their power are forth already, 1.02. 32
demning some to death, and some to exile; 1.06. 35
demning some to death, and some to exile; 1.06. 35
ll bear the business in some other fight, 1.06. 82
ve some wounds upon me, and they smart | to 1.09. 28
e that bled, or foil'd some debile wretch — 1.09. 48
e sword to sword, i'll potch at him some way, 1.10. 15
ugh peradventure some of the best of 'em were 2.01. 92 P
have some old crab–trees here at home that 2.01.188
some time when his soaring insolence | shall 2.01.254
that our heads are some brown, some black, 2.03. 19 P
that our heads are some brown, some black, 2.03. 19 P
ne brown, some black, some abram, some bald, 2.03. 19 P
ne abram, some bald, but that our wits are so 2.03. 20 P
en | some certain of your brethren roar'd, and 2.03. 53
nterfeit the bewitchment of some popular man, 2.03.101 P
r voices have | done many things, some less, 2.03.130
e | done many things, some less, some more. 2.03.130
re's some among you have beheld me fighting; 3.01.223
possess me | some harlot's spirit! 3.02.112
as most | abated captives to some nation 3.03.132
ermine on some course | more than a wild 4.01. 35
uld hear — | nay, and you shall hear some. 4.02. 14
ake the one the other, by some chance, 4.04. 20
ne trick not worth an egg, shall grow dear 4.04. 21
, poor gentleman, take up some other station; 4.05. 29 P
as wars, in some sort, may be said to be a 4.05.227 P
ne news is coming | that turns their 4.06. 59
ing | made by some other deity than nature, 4.06. 91
of some death more long in spectatorship and 5.02. 65 P
ger, there is some hope the ladies of rome, 5.04. 5 P
took some pride | to do myself this wrong; 5.06. 36
rn thou to make some meaner choice, | lavinia TIT 2.01. 73
y then it seems some certain snatch or so 2.01. 95
doth unroll | to do some fatal execution? 2.03. 36
i the pow'r that some say dian had, | thy 2.03. 61
g hence her husband to some secret hole, 2.03.129
ne say that ravens foster forlorn children 2.03.153
, | and tumble me into some loathsome pit, 2.03.176
e, | which, like a taper in some monument, 2.03.228
ne never–heard–of tortering pain for them. 2.03.285
ne bring the murthered body, some the 2.03.300
g the murthered body, some the murtherers. 2.03.300
do wake, some planet strike me down, | that 2.04. 14
sure some tereus hath deflow'red thee, | and 2.04. 26
in some sort they are better than the 3.01. 39
r | that hath receiv'd some unrecuring wound. 3.01. 90
ecting ever when some envious surge | will in 3.01. 96
make some sign how i may do thee ease. 3.01.121
thou, and i, sit round about some fountain, 3.01.123
gues | plot some device of further misery, 3.01.134

to weep with them that weep doth ease some deal, 3.01.244
unless some fit or frenzy do possess her; 4.01. 17
some book there is that she desires to see. 4.01. 31
of lucius, | he hath some message to deliver us. 4.02. 2
ay, some mad message from his mad grandfather. 4.02. 3
or some of you shall smoke for it in rome. 4.02.111
we may, | till time beget some careful remedy. 4.03. 30
thinks, with jove in heaven, or some where else, 4.03. 41
curse — | wherein i did not some notorious ill: 5.01.127
accuse some innocent, and forswear myself, | set 5.01.130
do me some service ere i come to thee. 5.02. 44
now give some surance that thou art revenge — 5.02. 46
i'll find some cunning practice out of hand, 5.02. 77
i pray thee do on them some violent death, 5.02.108
him | some of the chiefest princes of the goths. 5.02.125
some devil whisper curses in my ear, | and 5.03. 11
to be /adjudg'd some direful slaught'ring death, 5.03.144
some stay to see him fast'ned in the earth. 5.03.183
some loving friends convey the emperor hence, 5.03.191
this is not romeo, he's some other where. ROM 1.01.198
take thou some new infection to thy eye, | and 1.02. 49
compare her face with some that i shall show, 1.02. 86
your lady's love against some other maid | that 1.02. 97
some consequence yet hanging in the stars 1.04.107
breast | by some vile forfeit of untimely death. 1.04.111
some five and twenty years, and then we mask'd. 1.05. 37
of some strange nature, letting it there stand 2.01. 25
that were some spite. 2.01. 27
having some business, /do entreat her eyes | to 2.02. 16
o, be some other name! 2.02. 42
i hear some noise within; 2.02.136
none but for some, and yet all different. 2.03. 14
but to the earth some special good doth give; 2.03. 18
thou art up–rous'd with some distemp'rature; 2.03. 40
be he, sir, i desire some confidence with you. 2.04.127 P
she will indite him to some supper. 2.04.129 P
some means to come to shrift this afternoon, 2.04.180
i know it begins with some other letter — and 2.04.210 P
could you not take some occasion without giving? 3.01. 43 P
either withdraw unto some private place, | or 3.01. 51
help me into some house, benvolio, | or i shall 3.01.105
some twenty of them fought in this black strife, 3.01.178
as is the night before some festival | to an 3.02. 29
give me some aqua–vitae; 3.02. 88
some word there was, worser than tybalt's death, 3.02.108
therefore we'll have some half a dozen friends, 3.04. 27
it is some meteor that the sun /exhal'd | to be 3.05. 13
some say the lark makes sweet division; 3.05. 29
some say the lark and loathed toad change eyes; 3.05. 31
some grief shows much of love, | but much of 3.05. 72
but much of grief shows still some want of wit. 3.05. 73
some comfort, nurse. 3.05.212
give me some present counsel, or, behold, 4.01. 61
well, he may chance to do some good on her. 4.02. 13
at some hours in the night spirits resort — 4.03. 44
in this rage, with some great kinsman's bone, 4.03. 53
some aqua–vitae ho! 4.05. 16
the heavens do low'r upon you for some ill; 4.05. 94
o, play me some merry dump to comfort me. 4.05.107 P
my dreams presage some joyful news at hand. 5.01. 2
and wild, and do import | some misadventure. 5.01. 29
and here is come to do some villainous shame 5.03. 52
o, much i fear some ill unthrifty thing. 5.03.136
i hear some noise, lady. 5.03.151
lips, | haply some poison yet doth hang on them, 5.03.165
go, some of you, whoe'er you find attach. 5.03.173
some others search. 5.03.178
cry "romeo," | some "juliet," and some "paris," 5.03.192
some "juliet," and some "paris," and all run 5.03.192
and with wild looks bid me devise some mean | to 5.03.240
some minute ere the time | of her awakening, 5.03.257
life | be sacrific'd some hour before his time, 5.03.268
some shall be pardon'd, and some punished: 5.03.308
some shall be pardon'd, and some punished: 5.03.308
sir, in some work, some dedication | to the TIM 1.01. 19
some work, some dedication | to the great lord. 1.01. 19
some better than his value — on the moment 1.01. 79
'tis alcibiades, and some twenty horse, | all of 1.01.241
whereby we might express some part of our zeals, 1.02. 86 P
with apemantus, let's ha' some sport with 'em. 2.02. 47 P
perchance some single vantages you took, | when 2.02.129
when, for some trifling present, you have bid me 2.02.136
'tis all engag'd, some forfeited and gone, | and 2.02.146
and in some sort these wants of mine are crown'd 2.02.181
bid him suppose some good necessity | touches 2.02.227
fill me some wine. 3.01. 8 P
i have receiv'd some small kindnesses from him, 3.02. 20 P
now we shall know some answer. 3.04. 66 P
gentlemen, to repair some other hour, i should 3.04. 69 P
let each take some; 4.02. 27
i have heard in some sort of thy miseries. 4.03. 77
here is some gold for thee. 4.03.101
will o'er some high–vic'd city hang his poison 4.03.110
give us some gold, good timon; hast thou more? 4.03.133
burthens of the dead — some that were hang'd, 4.03.146
of the war | derive some pain from you. 4.03.162
that never knew but better, is some burthen: 4.03.267
stuff | to some she–beggar and compounded thee 4.03.273
thou hadst some means to keep a dog. 4.03.316 P
it is some poor fragment, some slender ort of 4.03.398 P
fragment, some slender ort of his remainder. 4.03.399 P
confound them by some course, and come to me, 5.01.103
uncertain voyage, i will some kindness do them: 5.01.202
some beast read this; 5.03. 4
i do lack some part | of that quick spirit that JC 1.02. 28
i am | of late with passions of some difference, 1.02. 40
which give some soil, perhaps, to my behaviors; 1.02. 42
but by reflection, by some other things. 1.02. 53
alas, it cried, "give me some drink, titinius," 1.02.127
for some new honors that are heap'd on caesar. 1.02.134
men at some time are masters of their fates; 1.02.139
what you would work me to, i have some aim. 1.02.163
being cross'd in conference by some senators. 1.02.188
of fear and warning | unto some monstrous state. 1.03. 71
some certain of the noblest–minded romans | to 1.03.122
some two months hence, up higher toward the 2.01.109
you have some sick offense within your mind, 2.01.268
for here have been | some six or seven, who did 2.01.277

but are not some whole that we must make sick? 2.01.328
most mighty caesar, let me know some cause, 2.02. 69
mock | apt to be render'd, for some one to say, 2.02. 97
friends, go in, and taste some wine with me, 2.02.126
thou hast some suit to caesar, hast thou not? 2.04. 27
some to the common pulpits, and cry out, 3.01. 80
lest some friend of caesar's | should chance — 3.01. 87
rushing on us, should do your age some mischief. 3.01. 93
if it be found so, some will dear abide it. 3.02.114
belike they had some notice of the people, | how 3.02.270
some to decius' house, and some to casca's; 3.03. 36 P
some to decius' house, and some to casca's; 3.03. 37 P
some to ligarius'. 3.03. 37 P
how to cut off some charge in legacies. 4.01. 9
and, in some taste, is lepidus but so: 4.01. 34
and some that smile have in their hearts, i fear 4.01. 50
hath given me some worthy cause to wish | things 4.02. 8
there is some grudge between 'em; 4.03.125
call claudio and some other of my men, | i'll 4.03.242
art thou some god, some angel, or some devil, 4.03.279
art thou some god, some angel, or some devil, 4.03.279
art thou some god, some angel, or some devil, 4.03.279
make forth, the generals would have some words. 5.01. 25
to stay the providence of some high powers 5.01.106
early, | who, having some advantage on octavius, 5.03. 6
now some light. 5.03. 31
thy life hath had some smatch of honor in it. 5.05. 46
to you they have show'd some truth. MAC 2.01. 21
we would spend it in some words upon that 2.01. 23
go get some water, | and wash this filthy 2.02. 43
to have let in some of all professions that go 2.03. 18 P
some say, the earth | was feverous, and did 2.03. 60
the west yet glimmers with some streaks of day; 3.03. 5
give me some wine, fill full. 3.04. 87
king that he | prepares for some attempt of war. 3.06. 39
some holy angel | fly to the court of england, 3.06. 45
and some i see | that twofold balls and treble 4.01.120
i doubt some danger does approach you nearly. 4.02. 67
let us seek out some desolate shade, and there 4.03. 1
is it a fee–grief | due to some single breast? 4.03.197
mind that's honest | but in it shares some woe, 4.03.198
some say he's mad; 5.02. 13
and with some sweet oblivious antidote | cleanse 5.03. 43
some must go off; 5.09. 2
this bodes some strange eruption to our state. HAM 1.01. 69
to some enterprise | that hath a stomach in't, 1.01. 99
some say that ever 'gainst that season comes 1.01.158
you told us of some suit, what is't, laertes? 1.02. 43
in filial obligation for some term | to do 1.02. 91
all is not well, | i doubt some foul play. 1.02.255
do not, as some ungracious pastors do, | show me 1.03. 47
that for some vicious mole of nature in them, 1.04. 24
by their o'ergrowth of some complexion | oft 1.04. 27
or by some habit, that too much o'er–leavens 1.04. 29
as if it some impartment did desire | to you 1.04. 59
and there assume some other horrible form, 1.04. 72
or by pronouncing of some doubtful phrase, | as 1.05.175
you, as 'twere, some distant knowledge of him, 2.01. 13
your rest here in our court | some little time, 2.02. 14
go some of you, | and bring these gentlemen 2.02. 36
but, as we often see, against some storm, | a 2.02.483
for need, study a speech of some dozen lines, or 2.02.541 P
when we would bring him on to some confession 3.01. 9
hatch and the disclose | will be some danger: 3.01.167
that i have thought some of nature's journeymen 3.02. 33 P
laugh to set on some quantity of barren 3.02. 41 P
in the mean time some necessary question of the 3.02. 42 P
give me some light. away! 3.02.269 P
for some must watch, while some must sleep, 3.02.273
for some must watch, while some must sleep, 3.02.273
come, some music! 3.02.291 P
come, some music! 3.02.295 P
put your discourse into some frame, and /start 3.02.308 P
'tis meet that some more audience than a mother, 3.03. 31
or about some act | that has no relish of 3.03. 91
thou find'st to be too busy is some danger. 3.04. 33
but it reserv'd some quantity of choice, | to 3.04. 75
like some ore | among a mineral of metals base, 4.01. 25
friends both, go join you with some further aid: 4.01. 33
against some part of poland. 4.04. 12
the main of poland, sir, | or for some frontier? 4.04. 16
or some craven scruple | of thinking too 4.04. 40
each toy seems prologue to some great amiss, 4.05. 18
there's rue for you, and here's some for me; 4.05.182 P
i would give you some violets, but they wither'd 4.05.184 P
this, give these fellows some means to the king, 4.06. 14 P
or is it some abuse, and no such thing? 4.07. 50
'a will last you some eight year or nine year. 5.01.167 P
'twas of some estate. 5.01.221
good gertrude, set some watch over your son. 5.01.296
desires you to use some gentle entertainment to 5.02.206 P
till by some elder masters of known honor | i 5.02.248
here's yet some liquor left. 5.02.342
i have some rights, of memory in this kingdom, 5.02.389
by order of law, some year elder than this, who LR 1.01. 19 P
for that i am some twelve or fourteen moonshines 1.02. 5
forbear his presence until some little time hath 1.02.161 P
some villain hath done me wrong. 1.02.165 P
/nor crumb, | weary of all, shall want some. 1.04.199
take you some company, and away to horse. 1.04.336
some blood drawn on me would beget opinion | of 2.01. 33
occasions, noble gloucester, of some prize, 2.01.120
this is some fellow | who, having been prais'd 2.02. 95
some time i shall sleep out, the rest i'll 2.02.156
some other time for that. 2.04.133
by some discretion that discerns your state 2.04.149
being the worst | stands in some rank of praise. 2.04.258
some friendship will it lend you 'gainst the 3.02. 62
do poor tom some charity, whom the foul fiend 3.04. 60 P
that will to some provision | give thee quick 3.06. 96
some five or six and thirty of his knights, 3.07. 16
who, with some other of the lord's dependants, 3.07. 18
to live till he be old, | give me some help! 3.07. 70
have one eye left | to see some mischief on him. 3.07. 82
he has some reason, else he could not beg. 4.01. 31
and bring some covering for this naked soul, 4.01. 44
belike | some things — i know not what. 4.05. 21
'twas yet some comfort, | when misery could 4.06. 62

it was some fiend; 4.06. 72
me your hand, | i'll lead you to some biding. 4.06.224
you have some cause, they have not. 4.07. 74
some officers take them away. 5.03. 1
king | to some retention /and /appointed /guard, 5.03. 47
and that thy tongue some say of breeding 5.03.144
until some half hour past, when i was arm'd. 5.03.194
some good i mean to do, | despite of mine own 5.03.244
these fellows have some soul, | and such a one OTH 1.01. 54
of vexation on't, | as it may lose some color. 1.01. 73
(how ever this may gall him with some check) 1.01.148
you not read, roderigo, | of some such thing? 1.01.174
some one way, some another. 1.01.176
some one way, some another. 1.01.176
and raise some special officers of /night. 1.01.182
it is a business of some heat. 1.02. 40
side, | upon some present business of the state, 1.02. 90
till now some nine moons wasted, they have us'd 1.03. 84
that with some mixtures pow'rful o'er the blood, 1.03.104
or with some dram, conjur'd to this effect, | he 1.03.105
when i did speak of some distressful stroke 1.03.157
othello, leave some officer behind, | and he 1.03.280
after some time, to abuse othello's /ear | that 1.03.395
her in it and compel her to some second choice. 2.01.235 P
do you find some occasion to anger cassio, 2.01.267 P
some to dance, some to make bonfires, each man 2.02. 4 P
some to dance, some to make bonfires, each man 2.02. 4 P
wish courtesy would invent some other custom of 2.03. 35 P
am i to put our cassio in some action | that may 2.03. 60
some wine ho! 2.03. 68 P
some wine, boys! 2.03. 74 P
some wine ho! 2.03. 97 P
him in, | on some odd time of his infirmity, 2.03.127
but now | (as if some planet had unwitted men), 2.03.182
though cassio did some little wrong to him, | as 2.03.242
from him that fled some strange indignity 2.03.245
had thought you had receiv'd some bodily wound; 2.03.267 P
to virtuous desdemona | procure me some access. 3.01. 36
give me advantage of some brief discourse | with 3.01. 52
not now, sweet desdemon, some other time. 3.03. 55
as if there were some monster in thy thought 3.03.107
shut up in thy brain | some horrible conceit. 3.03.115
if it be not for some purpose of import, 3.03.316
i'll have some proof. 3.03.386
to furnish me with some swift means of death 3.03.478
sure, there's some wonder in this handkerchief; 3.04.101
and shut myself up in some other course, | to 3.04.121
or some unhatch'd practice | made demonstrable 3.04.141
this is some token from a newer friend; 3.04.181
jealious now | that this is from some mistress, 3.04.186
this is from some mistress, some remembrance; 3.04.186
suit, | or voluntary dotage of some mistress, 4.01. 27
such shadowing passion without some instruction. 4.01. 41 P
prithee bear some charity to my wit, do not 4.01.120 P
this is some minx's token, and i must take out 4.01.153 P
get me some poison, iago, this night. 4.01.204 P
some of your function, mistress; 4.02. 27
i should have found in some place of my soul | a 4.02. 52
i will be hang'd if some eternal villain, | some 4.02.130
villain, | some busy and insinuating rogue, 4.02.131
some cogging, cozening slave, to get some office 4.02.132
cogging, cozening slave, to get some office, 4.02.132
the moor's abus'd by some most villainous knave, 4.02.139
some base notorious knave, some scurvy fellow. 4.02.140
some base notorious knave, some scurvy fellow. 4.02.140
some such squire he was | that turn'd your wit 4.02.145
every day thou daff'st me with some device, iago 4.02.175 P
his abode be ling'red here by some accident; 4.02.226 P
there be some such, no question. 4.03. 63
and though we have some grace, | yet have we 4.03. 92
we have some grace, | yet have we some revenge. 4.03. 93
'tis some mischance, the voice is very direful. 5.01. 38
give me some help. 5.01. 55
come in, and give some help. 5.01. 59
some good man bear him carefully from hence, 5.01. 99
some bloody passion shakes your very frame. 5.02. 44
i have done the state some service, and they 5.02.339
should stretch | without some pleasure now. ANT 1.01. 47
good now, some excellent fortune! 1.02. 26 P
death, which commits some loving act upon her, 1.02.143 P
i know by that same eye there's some good news. 1.03. 19
strange flesh, | which some did die to look on; 1.04. 68
and have my learning from some true reports 2.02. 47
give me some music; 2.05. 1
to bring forth | some monstrous malefactor. 2.05. 53
some innocents scape not the thunderbolt. 2.05. 77
but mark antony | put me to some impatience. 2.06. 42
some o' their plants are ill rooted already, the 2.07. 1 P
sit — and some wine! a health to lepidus! 2.07. 29 P
the man hath seen some majesty, and should know. 3.03. 42
he say he lent me | some shipping unrestor'd. 3.06. 27
with labor, and throes forth | each minute some. 3.07. 81
have letters from me to some friends that will 3.11. 16
some wine, within there, and our viands! 3.11. 73
i will seek | some way to leave him. 3.13.200
no, i will go seek | some ditch wherein to die; 4.06. 37
give me some wine, and let me speak a little. 4.15. 42
gods will give us | some faults to make us men. 5.01. 33
but i will tell you at some meeter season. 5.01. 49
she soon shall know of us, by some of ours, 5.01. 57
by some mortal stroke | she do defeat us; 5.01. 64
that i some lady trifles have reserv'd, 5.02.165
and say | some nobler token i have kept apart 5.02.168
see | some squeaking cleopatra boy my greatness 5.02.220
some twenty years. CYM 1.01. 62
and make yourself some comfort | out of your 1.01.155
about some half hour hence, | pray you speak 1.01.176
he added to your having, gave you some ground. 1.02. 18 P
would there had been some hurt done! 1.02. 35 P
but i see you have some religion in you, that 1.04.136 P
but heavens know | some men are much to blame. 1.06. 77
some dozen romans of us and your lord | (the 1.06.185
ah, but some natural notes about her body, 2.02. 28
some more time | must wear the print of his 2.03. 42
that's more | than some, whose tailors are as 2.03. 79
have heard of here, by me, | or by some other. 2.04. 78
render to me some corporal sign about her, 2.04.119
some coiner with his tools | made me a 2.05. 5
such assaults | as would take in some virtue. 3.02. 9
some griefs are med'cinable, that is one of them 3.02. 33
outcraftied him, | and he's at some hard point. 3.04. 16
thy tongue | may take off some extremity, which 3.04. 17
some jay of italy | (whose mother was her 3.04. 49
some villain, | ay, and singular in his art, 3.04.120
some roman courtezan? 3.04.123
are dead, and send him | some bloody sign of it; 3.04.125
to some shade, | and fit you to your manhood. 3.04.191
'tis some savage hold. 3.06. 18
he wrings at some distress. 3.06. 78
i fear some ambush. 4.02. 65
some villain mountainers? 4.02. 71
thou art some fool, | i am loath to beat thee. 4.02. 85
all safe reason | he must have some attendants. 4.02.132
and in time | may make some stronger head, the 4.02.139
thus smiling, as some fly had tickled slumber, 4.02.210
some falls are means the happier to arise. 4.02.403
fortune brings in some boats that are not 4.03. 46
you snatch some hence for little faults; 5.01. 12
you some permit | to second ills with ills, each 5.01. 13
strook down | some mortally, some slightly 5.03. 10
down | some mortally, some slightly touch'd, 5.03. 10
touch'd, some falling | merely through fear, 5.03. 10
part spirit renew'd, that some, turn'd coward 5.03. 35
how they wound | some slain before, some dying, 5.03. 47
how they wound | some slain before, some dying, 5.03. 47
some their friends | o'erborne i' th' former 5.03. 47
again, | but end it by some means for imogen. 5.03. 83
either be directed by some that take upon them 5.04.180 P
and there be some of them too that die against 5.04.201 P
nay, some marks | of secret on her person, that 5.05.205
or knife, or poison, | some upright justicer! 5.05.214
this hath some seeming. 5.05.452
now do i see he had some reason for't; PER 1.03. 7 P
he would depart, i'll give some light unto you. 1.03. 17
took some displeasure at him, at least he judg'k 1.03. 20
and so in ours, some neighboring nation, 1.04. 65
to make some good, but others to exceed, | and 2.03. 16
some other is more fit. 2.03. 23
'tis of some wrack. 3.02. 51
this letter and some certain jewels | lay with 3.04. 1
as i think, i have brought up some eleven — 4.02. 14 P
our youths we could pick up some pretty estate, 4.02. 32 P
must be quench'd with some present practice. 4.02.124 P
faith, some do, and some do not. 4.02.129 P
faith, some do, and some do not. 4.02.129 P
i'll bring home some to–night. 4.02.144 P
being proud, swallowed some part a' th' earth. 4.04. 39
you must take some pains to work her to your 4.06. 64 P
come bring me to some private place. 4.06. 90 P
how's this? how's this? some more, be sage. 4.06. 95
that he have his. call up some gentlemen. 5.01. 6
there is some of worth would come aboard; 5.01. 9
i durst wager, | would win some words of him. 5.01. 44
some such thing | i said, and said no more but 5.01.132
and thou by some incensed god sent hither | to 5.01.143
name | was given me by one that had some power, 5.01.148
take some note | that for our crowned heads we TNK 1.01. 51
o, i hope some god, | some god hath put his 1.01. 71
some god hath put his mercy in your manhood, 1.01. 72
you were | the ground–piece of some painter, i 1.01.122
my brother's heart, and warm it to some pity, 1.01.128
which to do | must make some work with creon. 1.01.150
either presuming them to have some force, | or 1.01.194
they themselves, some say, | groan under such a 1.01.230
or it shall be, | on fail of some condition? 1.02.105
had mine ear | stol'n some new air, or at 1.03. 75
some of thebes have told 's | they are sisters' 1.04. 15
could not reach to | without some imposition, 1.04. 44
venture, | and in some poor disguise be there. 2.03. 79
me, and then condemn me for't, some wenches, 2.06. 14
some honest–hearted maids, will sing my dirge, 2.06. 15
come between, | and chop on some cold thought! 3.01. 13
which will seek of me | some news from earth, 3.01. 80
i none these two days — | sipp'd some water. 3.02. 27
and i have heard some call him arcite, and — 3.03. 32
i'll come again some two hours hence and bring 3.03. 49
give me some meditation, | and mark your cue. 3.05. 93
some country sport, upon my life, sir. 3.05. 97
his age some five and twenty. 4.02.116
his age some six and thirty. 4.02.139
is more at some time of the moon than at other 4.03. 1 P
at some time of the moon than at other some, is 4.03. 2 P
make an addition of some other compounded odors 4.03. 84 P
me, great mars, | some token of thy pleasure. 5.01. 61
the huntress | all moist and cold, some say, 5.01. 93
some two hundred bottles, | and twenty strike of 5.02. 64
some blind priest for the purpose that will 5.02. 78
get herself | some part of a good name, and many 5.03. 27
'fore yourself | by some small start of time. 5.03. 38
go we hence, | right joyful, with some sorrow. 5.03.135
some comfort | we have by so considering: 5.04. 3
her kind of ill | gave me some sorrow. 5.04. 27
white, which some will say | weakens his price, 5.04. 51
he much desires | to have some speech with you. 5.04. 85
are sorry, still | are children in some kind. 5.04.134
"pity," she cries, "some favor, some remorse!" VEN 257
"pity," she cries, "some favor, some remorse!" 257
their light blown out in some mistrustful wood, 826
some catch her by the neck, some kiss her face, 872
some catch her by the neck, some kiss her face, 872
some twin'd about her thigh to make her stay. 873
hasting to feed her fawn hid in some brake. 876
this, far off, she hears some huntsman hallow; 973
face the lion walk'd along | behind some hedge, 1094
that some would sing, some other in their bills 1102
some other in their bills | would bring him 1102
but some untimely thought did instigate | his LUC 43
some loathsome dash the herald will contrive, 206
fearing some hard news from the warlike band 255
which drives the creeping thief to some regard; 305
that dazzleth them, or else some shame supposed, 377
that thinks she hath beheld some ghastly sprite, 451
done, some worthless slave of thine i'll slay, 515
earth's dark womb some gentle gust doth get, 549
thee | unto the base bed of some rascal groom, 671
find | some purer chest to close so pure a mind. 761
absolute, | that some impurity doth not pollute. 854
with some mischance cross tarquin in his flight. 968
to find some desp'rate instrument of death, 1038
in vain | some happy mean to end a hapless life. 1045
some dark deep desert, seated from the way, 1144
if in this blemish'd fort i make some hole 1175
see) | some present speed to come and visit me. 1307
more she thought he spied in her some blemish. 1358
pausing for means to mourn some newer way. 1365
as if some mermaid did their ears entice, | some 1411
some high, some low, the painter was so nice; 1412
some high, some low, the painter was so nice; 1412
many she sees where cares have carved some, 1445
"why should the private pleasure of some one 1478
saying, some shape in sinon's was abus'd: 1529
it easeth some, though none it ever cured, | to 1581
"'for some hard–favor'd groom of thine,' quoth 1632
some of her blood still pure and red remain'd, 1742
and some look'd black, and that false tarquin 1743
woes, | corrupted blood some watery token shows, 1748
that she might think me some untutor'd youth, PP 1. 3
which is to me some praise, that i thy parts 5.10
take counsel of some wiser head, | neither too 18. 5
talk, | lest she some subtile practice smell — 18. 9
dost beguile the world, unbless some mother. SON 3. 4
make sweet some vial; 6. 3
treasure thou some place | with beauty's 6. 3
and your sweet semblance to some other give. 13. 4
but were some child of yours alive that time, 17.13
or some fierce thing replete with too much rage, 23. 3
but that i hope some good conceit of thine | in 26. 7
as if by some instinct the wretch did know | his 50. 7
to make some special instant special blest, | by 52.11
in all external grace you have some part, | but 53.13
sun, | show me your image in some antique book, 59. 7
if some suspect of ill mask'd not thy show, 70.13
unless you would devise some virtuous lie, | to 72. 5
away, | my life hath in this line some interest, 74. 3
some fresher stamp of the time–bettering days. 82. 8
that to his subject lends not some small glory, 84. 6
say that thou didst forsake me for some fault, 89. 1
some glory in their birth, some in their skill, 91. 1
some glory in their birth, some in their skill, 91. 1
some in their wealth, some in their body's force 91. 2
in their wealth, some in their body's force, 91. 2
some in their garments, though new–fangled ill, 91. 3
some in their hawks and hounds, some in their 91. 4
in their hawks and hounds, some in their horse; 91. 4
some say thy fault is youth, some wantonness, 96. 1
some say thy fault is youth, some wantonness, 96. 1
some say thy grace is youth and gentle sport; 96. 2
spend'st thou thy fury on some worthless song, 100. 3
and in some perfumes is there more delight 130. 7
yet in good faith some say that thee behold, 131. 5
that she might think me some untutor'd youth, 138. 3
some beauty peep'd through lettice of sear'd age LC 14
for some, untuck'd, descended her sheav'd hat, 31
some in her threaden fillet still did bide, 33
lets not bounty fall | where want cries some, 42
"yet did i not, as some my equals did, | demand 148
have of my suffering youth some feeling pity 178
wit well blazon'd, smil'd or made some moan. 217

SOMEBODY 8 FR 0.0009 REL FR 3 V 5

somebody call my wife. WIV 4.02.116
didst thou not hear somebody? ADO 3.03.128
'a means to cozen somebody in this city under my SHR 5.01. 39
i would make this a bloody day to somebody. 2H4 5.04. 12
i was too hot to do somebody good | that is too R3 1.03.310
a black day will it be to somebody. 5.03.280
her, but i would somebody had heard her talk TRO 1.01. 45
go to the gate, somebody knocks. JC 2.01. 60

SOME'ER *(also somever)*

SOME'ER 1 FR 0.0001 REL FR 1 V 0

how strange or odd some'er i bear myself — | as HAM 1.05.170

SOMERSET 65 FR 0.0073 REL FR 64 V 1

or else was wrangling somerset in th' error? 1H6 2.04. 6
i pluck this red rose with young somerset, | and 2.04. 37
now, somerset, where is your argument? 2.04. 59
hath not thy rose a canker, somerset? 2.04. 68
now, by god's will, thou wrong'st him, somerset; 2.04. 82
and that i'll prove on better men than somerset, 2.04. 98
thee, | against proud somerset and william pole, 2.04.122
some words there grew 'twixt somerset and me; 2.05. 46
which somerset hath offer'd to my house, | i 2.05.125
tongue | against my lord the duke of somerset. 3.04. 34
will not this malice, somerset, be left? 4.01.108
good cousins both, of york and somerset, | quiet 4.01.114
there is my pledge, accept it, somerset. 4.01.120
i more incline to somerset than york: 4.01.154
and, good my lord of somerset, unite | your 4.01.164
not, | in that he wears the badge of somerset. 4.01.177
a plague upon that villain somerset, | that thus 4.03. 9
o god, that somerset, who in proud heart | doth 4.03. 24
all long of this vile traitor somerset. 4.03. 33
won away, | long all of somerset and his delay. 4.03. 46
cries out for noble york and somerset | to beat 4.04. 15
had york and somerset brought rescue in, | we 4.07. 33
gloucester, york, buckingham, somerset, 2H6 1.01. 69
have you yourselves, somerset, buckingham, 1.01. 85
cousin of somerset, join you with me, | and all 1.01.167
or thou or i, somerset, will be /protector, 1.01.178
plac'd the heads of edmund duke of somerset, 1.02. 29
we beauford | the imperious churchman, somerset, 1.03. 69
which, | or somerset or york, all's one to me. 1.03.102
if somerset be unworthy of the place, | let york 1.03.105
why somerset should be preferr'd in this. 1.03.114
my lord of somerset will keep me here | without 1.03.168
let somerset be regent o'er the french, 1.03.205
come, somerset, we'll see thee sent away. 1.03.220
"what shall /betide the duke of somerset?" 1.04. 34
"what shall betide the duke of somerset?" 1.04. 66
welcome, lord somerset. what news from france? 3.01. 83
cold news, lord somerset; 3.01. 86
that somerset be sent as regent thither: 3.01.290
sweet somerset, be still. 3.01.304
only to remove from thee | the duke of somerset, 4.09. 30
and, somerset, we will commit thee thither, 4.09. 39

is to remove proud somerset from the king, 5.01. 36
the duke of somerset is in the tower. 5.01. 41
i have | is his to use, so somerset may die. 5.01. 53
to heave the traitor somerset from hence, | and 5.01. 61
see, buckingham, somerset comes with th' queen. 5.01. 83
is somerset at liberty? 5.01. 87
shall i endure the sight of somerset? 5.01. 90
somerset | hath made the wizard famous in his 5.02. 68
but is your grace dead, my lord of somerset? 3H6 1.01. 18
and you too, somerset and montague, | speak 4.01. 27
clarence and somerset both gone to warwick? 4.01.127
but see where somerset and clarence comes! 4.02. 3
welcome unto warwick, | and welcome, somerset! 4.02. 7
my lord of somerset, at my request, | see that 4.03. 51
my lord of somerset, what youth is that | of 4.06. 65
somerset, somerset, for lancaster! 5.01. 72
somerset, somerset, for lancaster! 5.01. 72
two of thy name, both dukes of somerset, | have 5.01. 73
and somerset, with oxford, fled to her; 5.03. 15
and somerset another goodly mast? 5.04. 17
thanks, gentle somerset, sweet oxford, thanks. 5.04. 58
for somerset, off with his guilty head. 5.05. 3
three dukes of somerset, threefold /renown'd 5.07. 5

SOMERSET'S 2 FR 0.0002 REL FR 2 V 0 P
with somerset's and buckingham's ambition; 2H6 1.01.202
at beauford's pride, at somerset's ambition, 2.02. 71

SOMERVILE 1 FR 0.0001 REL FR 1 V 0 P
say, somervile, what says my loving son? 3H6 5.01. 7

/SOMETHING 1 FR 0.0001 REL FR 0 V 1 P
/something /he /left /imperfect /in /the /state, LR 4.03. 3 P

SOMETHING 188 FR 0.0212 REL FR 136 V 52 P
a sea–change | into something rich and strange. TMP 1.02.402
and, but he's something stain'd | with grief 1.02.415
but i prattle | something too wildly, and my 3.01. 58
i' th' name of something holy, sir, why stand 3.03. 94
there's something else to do. 4.01.126
my will is something sorted with his wish: TGV 1.03. 63
he is something peevish that way; WIV 1.04. 13 P
the which hath something embold'ned me to this 2.02.167 P
thee there's something extraordinary in thee. 3.03. 69 P
good hearts, devise something; 4.02. 73 P
while other jests are something rank on foot, 4.06. 22
that we may bring you something on the way. MM 1.01. 61
it draws something near to the speech we had to 1.02. 77 P
something do excuse the thing i hate, | for 2.04.119
something too crabbed that way, friar. 3.02. 98 P
happily | you something know, yet i believe 4.02. 96
for this something that you gave me for nothing. ERR 2.02. 51 P
amends next, to give you nothing for something. 2.02. 54 P
there is something in the wind, that we cannot 3.01. 69
go fetch me something: i'll break ope the gate. 3.01. 73
and something of that jealous complexion. ADO 2.01.295 P
something then in rhyme. LLL 1.01. 99
will something affect the letter, for it 4.02. 55
his will i send and something else more plain 4.03.119
of something nearly that concerns yourselves. MND 1.01.126
because she is something lower than myself, 3.02.304
and, for the morning now is something worn, 4.01.182
and grows to something of great constancy; 5.01. 26
by something showing a more swelling port | than MV 1.01.124
debts | wherein my time something too prodigal 1.01.129
son, for indeed my father did something smack, 2.02. 17 P
father did something smack, something grow to, 2.02. 17 P
why, there they show | something too liberal. 2.02.185
foolish drops do something drown my manly spirit 2.03. 13 P
there's something tells me (but it is not love) 3.02. 4
but the full sum of me | is sum of something; 3.02.158
where every something, being blent together, 3.02.181
there must be something else | pawn'd with the 3.05. 81
tarry a little, there is something else. 4.01.305
gives me, the something that nature gave me his AYL 1.01. 17 P
or charles, or something weaker, masters thee. 1.02.260
something that hath a reference to my state: 1.03.127
and mine, but it grows something stale with me. 2.04. 62 P
and if i bring thee not something to eat, i will 2.06. 11 P
your accent is something finer than you could 3.02.341 P
for every passion something and for no passion 3.02.413 P
something browner than judas's. 3.04. 8 P
shall devise something; 4.03.181 P
have you heard, but something hard of hearing: SHR 2.01.183
a good swift simile, but something currish. 5.02. 54
happen, it concerns you something to know it. AWW 1.03.120 P
there's something in't | more than my father's 1.03.242
a good traveller is something at the latter end 2.05. 28 P
something, and scarce so much; 2.05. 83
he's shrewdly vex'd at something. 3.05. 89 P
thou mayst inform | something to save thy life. 4.01. 83
there is something in't that stings his nature; 4.03. 4 P
yet must suffer | something in my behalf. 4.04. 28
as, possess us, tell us something of him. TN 2.03.138 P
if i could make that resemble something in me! 2.05.120 P
not so, sir, i do care for something; 3.01. 28 P
there's something in me that reproves my fault; 3.04.203
it is something of my negligence, nothing of my 3.04.255 P
mean and low ability | i'll lend you something. 3.04.345
there's something in't | that is deceivable. 4.03. 20
credent | thou mayst co–join with something, and WT 1.02.143
he something seems unsettled. 1.02.147
he is, something before her time, deliver'd. 2.02. 23
please you, come something nearer. 2.02. 53
fancy) something savors | of tyranny, and will 2.03.119
something rare | even then will rush to 3.01. 20
but smacks of something greater than herself, 4.04.158
he tells her something | that makes her blood 4.04.159
your heart is full of something that does take 4.04.346
if this be so, a wrong | something unfilial. 4.04.406
that i may call thee something more than man 4.04.535
who wants but something to be a reasonable man) 4.04.605 P
being something gently consider'd, i'll bring 4.04.795 P
took something good | to make a perfect woman, 5.01. 14
and speak of something wildly | by us perform'd 5.01.129
hath something seiz'd | his wish'd ability, he 5.01.142
comes it not something near? 5.03. 23
something about, a little from the right, | in JN 1.01.170
smacks it not something of the policy? 2.01.396
so, | for nothing hath begot my something grief, R2 2.02. 36
or something hath the nothing that i grieve — 2.02. 37
with a white head and something a round belly. 2H4 1.02.188 P
season, | for i am on the sudden something ill. 4.02. 80
let it do something, my good lord, that may do 4.03. 59 P
and withal devise something to do thyself good. 5.03.134 P
your reproof is something too round, i should be H5 4.01.203 P
and something lean to cutpurse of quick hand. 5.01. 86
town, | something i must do to procure me grace. 1H6 1.04. 7
though the edge hath something hit ourselves, 3H6 2.02.166
wits | and fall something into a slower method: R3 1.02.116
something we will determine. 3.01.193
something against our meanings, have prevented; 3.05. 55
if something thou wouldst swear to be believ'd, 4.04.372
swear then by something that thou hast not 4.04.373
could wish he were | something mistaken in't. H8 1.01.195
there's something more would out of thee; 1.02.202
and something spoke in choler, ill, and hasty. 2.01. 34
and when you would say something that is sad, 2.01.135
he's vex'd at something. 3.02.104
i would 'twere something that would fret the 3.02.105
something i can command. 4.01.116
'em, | and something over to remember me by. 4.02.151
he hangs the lip at something. TRO 3.01.139 P
but something may be done that we will not, 4.04. 94
you shake, my lord, at something; 5.02. 50
i'll give you something else. 5.02. 86
said to be something imperfect in favoring the COR 2.01. 49 P
but this is something odd. 2.03. 82 P
you have been too rough, something too rough; 3.02. 25
by his face that there was something in him. 4.05.155 P
your enemies and his find something in him. 4.06.106
no, | nothing so kind, but something pitiful! TIT 2.03.156
that is something stale and hoar ere it be spent ROM 2.04.133 P
couple it with something, make it a word and a 3.01. 40 P
as signal that thou hearest something approach. 5.03. 8
the boy gives warning, something doth approach. 5.03. 18
a fool in good clothes, and something like thee. TIM 2.02.108 P
something hath been amiss — a noble nature 2.02.208
wert a dog, | that i might love thee something. 4.03. 56
forth of doors, | yet something leads me forth. JC 3.03. 4
out, | and something to be done immediately. 5.01. 15
done to–night, | and something from the palace; MAC 3.01.131
of my thumbs, | something wicked this way comes. 4.01. 45
but something | you may discern of him through 4.03. 14
royal preparation | makes us hear something. 5.03. 58
is not this something more than fantasy? HAM 1.01. 54
please you, something touching the lord hamlet. 1.03. 89
be something scanter of your maiden presence, 1.03.121
something is rotten in the state of denmark. 1.04. 90
by the mass, i was about to say something. 2.01. 50
something have you heard | of hamlet's 2.02. 4
there is something in this more than natural, if 2.02.367 P
play something like the murther of my father 2.02.595
but that the dread of something after death, 3.01. 77
there's something in his soul | o'er which his 3.01.164
something too much of this. 3.02. 74
grass grows" — the proverb is something musty. 3.02.344 P
fit, | behind the arras hearing something stir, 4.01. 9
rash, | yet have i in me something dangerous, 5.01.262
this knave came something saucily to the world LR 1.01. 21 P
we must do something, and i' th' heat. 1.01.308 P
that's something yet: 2.03. 21
or something deeper, | whereof, perchance, these 3.01. 28
way to loyalty, something fears me to think of. 3.05. 3 P
thou dost bear | with something rich about me. 4.01. 77
on, | you look as you had something more to say. 5.03.202
something from cyprus, as i may divine; OTH 1.02. 39
whereof by parcels she had something heard, 1.03.154
that smiles steals something from the thief; 1.03.208
spare speech, which something now offends me — 2.03.199
something that's brief; 3.01. 2
thou dost mean something. 3.03.108
'tis something, nothing; 3.03.157
this may do something. 3.03.324
something of moment then. 3.04.138
something sure of state, | either from venice, 3.04.140
i warrant, something from venice. 4.01.214
something it is i would — | o, my oblivion is a ANT 1.03. 89
yes, something you can deny for your own safety: 2.06. 91 P
the world should note | something particular. 3.13. 22
do something mingle with our younger brown, yet 4.08. 20
very honest woman — but something given to lie, 5.02.252 P
there is a vent of blood, and something blown; 5.02.349
there would be something failing | in him that CYM 1.01. 21
i something fear my father's wrath, but nothing 1.01. 86
had been something too fair and too good for any 1.04. 71 P
which in my opinion o'ervalues it something. 1.04.110 P
you do seem to know | something of me, or what 1.06. 94
and i am something curious, being strange, | to 1.06.191
i'll do something — 2.04.149
being born your vassal, | am something nearer. 5.05.114
i think i shall have something to do with you. PER 4.02. 87 P
o, you have heard something of my power, and so 4.06. 87 P
but there is something glows upon my cheek, 5.01. 95
you're like something that — what 5.01.102
shall tack about | and something do to save us. TNK pr 27
something i may cast to you, not much. 2.01. 1 P
something she did, sir. 3.03. 35
and here's something | to paint your pole withal 3.05.152
place | to seat something i would confound. 5.01. 28
wit, | make something nothing by augmenting it. LUC 154
and to the most of praise add something more, SON 85.10
please thee hold | that nothing me, a something, 136.12

SOMETHING'S 1 FR 0.0001 REL FR 1 V 0 P
something's /afore't. CYM 3.04. 79

SOMETHING–SETTLED 1 FR 0.0001 REL FR 1 V 0 P
this something–settled matter in his heart, HAM 3.01.173

/SOMETIME 2 FR 0.0002 REL FR 2 V 0 P
/jove /sometime /went /disguis'd, /and /why /not 2H6 4.01. 48
/town, | /who /sometime, /in /his /better /tune, LR 4.03. 39

SOMETIME 97 FR 0.0109 REL FR 81 V 16 P
sometime i'ld divide, | and burn in many places; TMP 1.02.198
sometime like apes that mow and chatter at me, 2.02. 9
sometime am i | all wound with adders, who with 2.02. 12
will hum about mine ears, and sometime voices, 3.02.138
and myself present | as i was sometime milan. 5.01. 86
a woman sometime scorns what best contents her. TGV 3.01. 93
a justice of peace sometime may be beholding to WIV 1.01.273 P
(sometime a keeper here in windsor forest) 4.04. 29
whether you had not sometime in your life MM 2.01. 14
be sometime honor'd for his burning throne! 5.01.293
body of your discourse is sometime guarded with ADO 1.01.286 P
that my daughter is sometime afeard she will do 2.03.152 P
sometime like god bel's priests in the old 3.03.134 P
sometime like the shaven hercules in the 3.03.135 P
and sing a note, sometime through the throat, LLL 3.01. 14 P
with singing love, sometime through /the nose, 3.01. 16 P
world) sometime to lean upon my poor shoulder, 5.01.102 P
and sometime make the drink to bear no barm, MND 2.01. 38
and sometime lurk i in a gossip's bowl, | in 2.01. 47
sometime for three–foot stool mistaketh me; 2.01. 52
there sleeps titania sometime of the night, 2.01.253
sometime a horse i'll be, sometime a hound, | a 3.01.108
sometime a horse i'll be, sometime a hound, | a 3.01.108
a hog, a headless bear, sometime a fire, | and 3.01.109
like to lysander sometime frame thy tongue; 3.02.360
and sometime rail thou like demetrius; 3.02.362
which sometime on the buds | was wont to swell 4.01. 53
nay, sometime more feet than shoes, or such SHR in.2. 11 P
and a gentleman | which i have sometime known. AWW 3.02. 85
creature, | whom sometime i have laugh'd with. 5.03.179
(a savage jealousy | that sometime savors nobly) TN 5.01.120
doings of the world, | sometime puts forth. WT 1.02.254
whom, it should seem, | hath sometime lov'd! 4.04.362
sometime he angers me | with telling me of the 1H4 3.01.146
verified | henry the fift did sometime prophesy: 1H6 5.01. 31
sometime i'll say, i am duke humphrey's wife, 2H6 2.04. 42
sometime he talks as if duke humphrey's ghost 3.02.373
sometime he calls the king, | and whispers to 3.02.374
which sometime they have us'd with fearful 3H6 2.02. 30
sometime the flood prevails, and then the wind; 2.05. 9
sometime, great agamemnon, | thy topless TRO 1.03.151
i sometime lay here in corioles | at a poor COR 1.09. 82
gratis, as 'twas us'd | sometime in greece — 3.01.115
my sometime general, | i have seen thee stern, 4.01. 23
he hath said | which was sometime his general, 5.01. 2
as sometime clouds | when they do hug him in TIT 3.01.212
sometime she gallops o'er a courtier's nose, ROM 1.04. 77
and sometime comes she with a tithe–pig's tail 1.04. 79
sometime she driveth o'er a soldier's neck, 1.04. 82
and vice sometime by action dignified. 2.03. 22
appears like a lord, sometime like a lawyer, TIM 2.02.110 P
like a lawyer, sometime like a philosopher, with 2.02.110 P
sometime the philosopher. 2.02.122 P
which sometime hath his hour with every man. JC 2.01.251
love that follows us sometime is our trouble, MAC 1.06. 11
though he took up my legs sometime, yet i made a 2.03. 40 P
to do good sometime | accounted dangerous folly. 4.02. 76
therefore our sometime sister, now our queen, HAM 1.02. 8
this was sometime a paradox, but now the time 3.01.113 P
know | our indiscretion sometime serves us well 5.02. 8
and reliev'd, | as thou my sometime daughter. LR 1.01.120
with lunatic bans, sometime with prayers, 2.03. 19
i lack iniquity | sometime to do me service. OTH 1.02. 4
sometime we see a cloud that's dragonish, | a ANT 4.14. 2
a vapor sometime like a bear or lion, | a 4.14. 3
nay, sometime hangs both thief and true man. CYM 2.03. 72
the ruin speaks that sometime | it was a worthy 4.02.354
am that belarius whom you sometime banish'd. 5.05.333
worth, | for it was sometime target to a king; PER 2.01.137
yet sometime a divided sigh, martyr'd as 'twere TNK 2.01. 40 P
sometime we go to barley–break, we of the 4.03. 30 P
honor in their kind | which sometime show well, 5.03. 13
yet sometime 'tis not so, but alters to | the 5.03. 47
sometime she shakes her head, and then his hand, VEN 223
sometime her arms infold him like a band: 225
sometime he trots, as if he told the steps, 277
sometime he scuds far off, and there he stares, 301
that sometime true news, sometime false doth 658
sometime true news, sometime false doth bring, 658
"sometime he runs among a flock of sheep, | to 685
and sometime where earth–delving conies keep, 687
and sometime sorteth with a herd of deer: 689
save sometime too much wonder of his eye, LUC 95
little frosts that sometime threat the spring, 331
the poisonous simple sometime is compacted | in 530
sometime her grief is dumb and hath no words, 1105
sometime 'tis mad and too much talk affords. 1106
yet sometime "tarquin" was pronounced plain, 1786
sometime too hot the eye of heaven shines, | and SON 18. 5
and every fair from fair sometime declines, | by 18. 7
when i am sometime absent from thy heart, | thy 41. 2
when sometime lofty towers i see down rased, 64. 3
sometime all full with feasting on your sight, 75. 9
therefore, like her, i sometime hold my tongue, 102.13
whereon the thought might think sometime it saw LC 10
sometime diverted their poor balls are tied | to 24
sometime a blusterer that the ruffle knew | of 58

/SOMETIMES 1 FR 0.0001 REL FR 1 V 0 P
/did /they /not /sometimes /cry "/all /hail!" R2 4.01.169

SOMETIMES 60 FR 0.0067 REL FR 45 V 15 P
and sometimes i'll get thee | young scamels from TMP 2.02.171
sometimes a thousand twangling instruments 3.02.137
sometimes the beam of her view gilded my foot, WIV 1.03. 61 P
view gilded my foot, sometimes my portly belly. 1.03. 62 P
i, i myself sometimes, leaving the fear of /god 2.02. 23 P
though sometimes you do blench from this to that MM 4.05. 5
because that i familiarly sometimes | do use you ERR 2.02. 26
sometimes fashioning them like pharaoh's ADO 3.03.133 P
a woman sometimes, and you saw her in the light. LLL 2.01.198
and, out of question, so it is sometimes: 4.01. 30
skim milk, and sometimes labor in the quern, MND 2.01. 36
and sleep, that sometimes shuts up sorrow's eye, 3.02.435
sometimes from her eyes | i did receive fair MV 1.01.163
i sometimes do believe, and sometimes do not, AYL 5.04. 3
i sometimes do believe, and sometimes do not, 5.04. 3
sometimes you would call out for cicely hacket. SHR in.2. 89
and bonny kate, and sometimes kate the curst; 2.01.186
how mightily sometimes we make us comforts of AWW 4.03. 65 P
i have been sometimes there. 5.01. 11
methinks sometimes i have no more wit than a TN 1.03. 83 P
in masques and revels sometimes altogether. 1.03.114 P

marry, sir, sometimes he is a kind of puritan.- 2.03.140 P
how sometimes nature will betray its folly! WT 1.02.151
sometimes her head on one side, some another — 3.03. 20
sometimes to see 'em, and not to see 'em; 3.03. 91 P
naturally honest, i am so sometimes by chance. 4.04.713 P
thy sometimes brother's wife | with her R2 1.02. 54
good sometimes queen, prepare thee hence for 5.01. 37
sometimes am i king; 5.05. 32
to look upon my sometimes royal master's face. 5.05. 75
though sometimes it show greatness, courage, 1H4 3.01.179
coal of fire, sometimes plue and sometimes red, H5 3.06.104 P
sometimes plue and sometimes red, but his nose 3.06.105 P
thus sometimes hath the brightest day a cloud, 2H6 2.04. 1
as sometimes margaret | did to thy father, R3 4.04.274
men shall deal unadvisedly sometimes, | which 4.04.292
the dowager, | sometimes our brother's wife. H8 2.04.182
and sometimes falling ones. 4.01. 55
not, | and sometimes we are devils to ourselves, TRO 4.04. 95
nay, sometimes, | like to a bowl upon a subtle COR 5.02. 19
i anger her sometimes and tell her that paris is ROM 2.04.204 P
comfort your bed, | and talk to you sometimes? JC 2.01.285
majesty of buried denmark | did sometimes march? HAM 1.01. 49
you know sometimes he walks four hours together 2.02.160
how pregnant sometimes his replies are! 2.02.209 P
and sometimes i am whipt for holding my peace. LR 1.04.184 P
sometimes with lunatic bans, sometime with 2.03. 19
unless self–charity be sometimes a vice, | and OTH 2.03.202
the best sometimes forget. 2.03.241
whereinto foul things | sometimes intrude not? 3.03.138
have you not sometimes seen a handkerchief 3.03.434
sir, sometimes when he is not antony, | he comes ANT 1.01. 57
the world and my great office will sometimes 2.03. 1
very eyes | are sometimes like our judgments, CYM 4.02.302
yon sometimes famous princes, like thyself, PER 1.01. 34
sometimes her modesty will blow so far she falls TNK 2.02.144
yet sometimes falls an orient drop beside, VEN 981
on | that sometimes anger thrusts into his hide, SON 50.10
sometimes her levell'd eyes their carriage ride, LC 22
sometimes they do extend | their view right on; 25

SOMETIME'T 1 FR 0.0001 REL FR 0 V 1 P
sometime't appears like a lord, sometime like a TIM 2.02.109 P

SOMEVER *(also some'er)*

SOMEVER 1 FR 0.0001 REL FR 1 V 0 P
how in my words somever she be shent, | to give HAM 3.02.398

SOMEWHAT 18 FR 0.0020 REL FR 13 V 5 P
i'll wear a boot, to make it somewhat rounder. TGV 5.02. 6
here is a letter will say somewhat. WIV 4.05.123 P
this gentleman told somewhat of my tale — MM 5.01. 84
that's somewhat madly spoken. 5.01. 89
in count'nance somewhat doth resemble you. SHR 4.02.100
mood, and smell somewhat strong of her strong AWW 5.02. 5 P
and liberal largess, are grown somewhat light, R2 1.04. 44
well, somewhat we must do. 2.02.116
why then say an old man can do somewhat. 2H4 5.03. 79 P
somewhat too sudden, sirs, the warning is, | but 1H6 5.02. 14
that's somewhat sudden; H8 3.02.394
there is a fellow somewhat near the door, he 5.03. 40 P
her hair were not somewhat darker than helen's TRO 1.01. 41 P
somewhat too early for new–married ladies. TIT 2.02. 15
fear her not, lucius, somewhat doth she mean. 4.01. 9
thou givest me somewhat to repair myself; PER 2.01.122
and somewhat better than your rank i'll use you. TNK 2.05. 43
he's somewhat bigger than the knight he spoke of 4.02. 94

SOMEWHERE 2 FR 0.0002 REL FR 2 V 0 P
and from the mart he's somewhere gone to dinner. ERR 2.01. 5
i prithee vent thy folly somewhere else, | thou TN 4.01. 10

SOMEWHITHER 1 FR 0.0001 REL FR 1 V 0 P
somewhither would she have thee go with her. TIT 4.01. 11

SOMME 1 FR 0.0001 REL FR 1 V 0 P
'tis certain he hath pass'd the river somme. H5 3.05. 1

/SON* 10 FR 0.0011 REL FR 8 V 2 P
/son /and /heir /to /th' /earl /of /arundel, R2 2.01.280
/the /dole /of /blows /your /son /might /drop. 2H4 1.01.169
/my /lord /your /son /had /only /but /the 1.01.192
/o /my /son, | god put /it in thy mind to take 4.05.177
langley, edward the third's fift /son, son. 2H6 2.02. 46
/son of sixteen, | pluck the lin'd crutch from TIM 4.01. 13
dear divorce | 'twixt natural /son and /sire! 4.03.382
the /son of duncan | (from whom this tyrant MAC 3.06. 24
/'tis /said, /the /bastard /son /of /gloucester. LR 4.07. 88 P
/they /say /edgar, /his /banish'd /son, /is 4.07. 89 P

SON* 617 FR 0.0697 REL FR 499 V 118 P
then all afire with me, the king's son, TMP 1.02.212
the king's son have i landed by himself, | whom 1.02.221
(save for the son that /she did litter here, | a 1.02.282
yes — caliban her son. 1.02.284
duke of milan | and his brave son being twain. 1.02.439
in his pocket, and give it his son for an apple. 2.01. 92 P
my son is lost and (in my rate) she too, | who 2.01.110
we have lost your son, | i fear for ever. 2.01.132
and let's make further search | for my poor son. 2.01.324
so, king, go safely on to seek thy son. 2.01.327
thee of thy son, alonso, | they have bereft; 3.03. 75
therefore my son i' th' ooze is bedded; 3.03.100
if venus or her son, as thou dost know, | do now 4.01. 87
and her son | dove–drawn with her. 4.01. 93
her waspish–headed son has broke his arrows, 4.01. 99
you do look, my son, in a mov'd sort, | as if 4.01.146
my dear son ferdinand. 5.01.139
mudded in that oozy bed | where my son lies. 5.01.152
the island, one dear son | shall i twice lose. 5.01.176
'twas of his nephew proteus, your son. TGV 1.03. 3
exercises | he said that proteus, your son, was 1.03. 12
receiv'd my proportion, like the prodigious son, 2.03. 4 P
hath he not a son? 2.04. 58
a son that well deserves | the honor and regard 2.04. 59
why, phaeton (for thou art merops' son), | wilt 3.01.153
marry, the son of my grandfather. 3.01.295 P
it was the son of thy grandmother. 3.01.296 P
come, son slender, in. WIV 3.04. 75
my husband says my son profits nothing in the 4.01. 14 P
nan page (my daughter) and my little son, | and 4.04. 48
remember, son slender, my /daughter. 5.02. 2 P
son? how now? how now, son? have you dispatch'd? 5.05.178 P
son? how now? how now, son? have you dispatch'd? 5.05.178 P
of what, son? 5.05.182 P
were he my kinsman, brother, or my son, | it MM 2.02. 81
son, i have overheard what hath pass'd between 3.01.160 P
die by the law than my son should be unlawfully 3.01.190 P
me dote, | i see my son antipholus and dromio. ERR 5.01.196
that here my only son | knows not my feeble key 5.01.310
err — | tell me thou art my son antipholus. 5.01.319
thou know'st we parted, but perhaps, my son, 5.01.322
where is that son | that floated with thee on 5.01.348
by force took dromio and my son from them, | and 5.01.353
hath leonato any son, my lord? ADO 1.01.294
how now, brother, where is my cousin, your son? 1.02. 2 P
and the other too like my lady's eldest son, 2.01. 9 P
not till monday, my dear son, which is hence a 2.01.359 P
as freely, son, as god did give her me. 4.01. 26
and she respects me as her only son. MND 1.01.160
that would hang us, every mother's son. 1.02. 78 P
sit down, every mother's son, and rehearse your 3.01. 73 P
being an honest man's son" — or rather an MV 2.02. 16 P
or rather an honest woman's son, for indeed my 2.02. 16 P
no master, sir, but a poor man's son. 2.02. 51 P
well, old man, i will tell you news of your son. 2.02. 78 P
a man's son may, but in the end truth will out. 2.02. 80 P
your boy that was, your son that is, your child 2.02. 85 P
i cannot think you are my son. 2.02. 87 P
here's my son, sir, a poor boy — 2.02.122 P
go, father, with thy son. 2.02.152
unto his son lorenzo and his daughter. 4.01.390
i am the youngest son of sir rowland de boys. AYL 1.01. 56 P
liege, the youngest son of sir rowland de boys. 1.02.222 P
i would thou hadst been son to some man else: 1.02.224
i am more proud to be sir rowland's son, | his 1.02.232
his youngest son — and would not change that 1.02.233
had i before known this young man his son, | i 1.02.237
a liking with old sir rowland's youngest son? 1.03. 28 P
ensue that you should love his son dearly? 1.03. 32 P
no, no brother, yet the son | (yet not the son, 2.03. 19
yet the son | (yet not the son, i will not call 2.03. 20
son | (yet not the son, i will not call him son) 2.03. 20
if that you were the good sir rowland's son, 2.07.191
i am the second son of old sir rowland, | that 5.04.152
since once he play'd a farmer's eldest son. SHR in.1. 84
christopher sly, old sly's son of burton–heath, in.2. 18 P
vincentio's son, brought up in florence, | it 1.01. 14
part, | and be in padua here vincentio's son, 1.01.195
"be serviceable to my son," quoth he, | although 1.01.214
born in verona, old /antonio's son. 1.02.190
petruchio is my name, antonio's son, | a man 2.01. 68
of pisa, sir, son to vincentio. 2.01.103
a witty mother! witless else her son. 2.01.264
i am my father's heir and only son. 2.01.364
"hic est," son unto vincentio of pisa, "/sigeia 3.01. 32 P
soft, son! 4.04. 23
my son lucentio | made me acquainted with a 4.04. 25
your son lucentio here | doth love my daughter, 4.04. 40
your son shall have my daughter with consent. 4.04. 47
with the deceiving father of a deceitful son. 4.04. 83 P
now, by my mother's son, and that's myself, | it 4.05. 6
there to visit | a son of mine, which long i 4.05. 57
happily met, the happier for thy son. 4.05. 59
gentlewoman, | thy son by this hath married. 4.05. 63
and wander we to see thy honest son, | who will 4.05. 69
i told you your son was well belov'd in padua. 5.01. 25 P
help, son! help, signior baptista! 5.01. 60 P
at home, my son and my servant spend all at the 5.01. 69 P
his name is lucentio, and he is mine only son, 5.01. 85 P
o, my son, my son! 5.01. 89 P
o, my son, my son! 5.01. 89 P
tell me, thou villain, where is my son lucentio? 5.01. 90 P
lives my sweet son? 5.01.112
lucentio, | right son to the right vincentio, 5.01.115
padua affords this kindness, son petruchio. 5.02. 13
now, in good sadness, son petruchio, | i think 5.02. 63
son, i'll be your half, bianca comes. 5.02. 78
in delivering my son from me, i bury a second AWW 1.01. 1 P
her matter was, she lov'd your son. 1.03.111 P
so that my lord your son were not my brother — 1.03.162
you love my son. 1.03.173
do you love my son? 1.03.186
love you my son? 1.03.187
and next unto high heaven, | i love your son. 1.03.194
my lord your son made me to think of this; 1.03.232
commend me to my kinsmen and my son. 2.02. 65
good, | to make yourself a son out of my blood. 2.03. 97
thou hast a son shall take this disgrace off me, 2.03.235 P
your unfortunate son, bertram." 3.02. 26 P
your son will not be kill'd so soon as i thought 3.02. 37 P
for my part, i only hear your son was run away. 3.02. 44 P
where is my son, i pray you? 3.02. 51
he was my son, | but i do wash his name out of 3.02. 66
my son corrupts a well–derived nature | with his 3.02. 88
i will entreat you, when you see my son, | to 3.02. 92
of war | my dearest master, your dear son, may 3.04. 9
that is antonio, the duke's eldest son, | that, 3.05. 76
hath succeeded in his house | from son to son, 3.07. 24
hath succeeded in his house | from son to son, 3.07. 24
your son was misled with a snipt–taffata fellow 4.05. 1 P
alive at this hour, and your son here at home, 4.05. 5 P
and that my lord your son was upon his return 4.05. 70 P
displeasure he hath conceiv'd against your son, 4.05. 76 P
i have letters that my son will be here to–night 4.05. 85 P
yonder's my lord your son with a patch of velvet 4.05. 94 P
let us go see your son, i pray you. 4.05.102 P
but your son, | as mad in folly, lack'd the 5.03. 2
come on, my son, in whom my house's name | must 5.03. 73
son, on my life, | i have seen her wear it, and 5.03. 89
then leaving her | in the protection of his son, TN 1.02. 38
madonna, as if thy eldest son should be a fool; 1.05.113 P
meeting, | every wise man's son doth know." 2.03. 44
if the king had no son, they would desire to WT 1.01. 45 P
to tell he longs to see his son were strong; 1.02. 34
give scandal to the blood o' th' prince my son 1.02.330
ones suffer, | yourself, your queen, your son. 2.01.129
the prince your son, with mere conceit and fear 3.02.144
me | to the dead bodies of my queen and son. 3.02.235
up for pity — yet i'll tarry till my son come; 3.03. 77 P
i mentioned a son o' th' king's, which florizel 4.01. 22
when saw'st thou the prince florizel, my son? 4.02. 26 P
i fear, the angle that plucks our son thither. 4.02. 46 P
then he compass'd a motion of the prodigal son, 4.03. 97 P
is at the nuptial of his son a guest | that best 4.04.395
reason my son | should choose himself a wife, 4.04.406
let him, my son. 4.04.415
divorce, young sir, | whom son i dare not call. 4.04.418
asks thee there, son, forgiveness, | as 'twere 4.04.549
we are not furnish'd like bohemia's son, | nor 4.04.588
whoobub against his daughter and the king's son, 4.04.616 P
now meet my father, | he would not call me son. 4.04.658
sir — about his son, that should have married a 4.04.766 P
has the old man e'er a son, sir, do you hear, 4.04.781 P
he has a son, who shall be flay'd alive; 4.04.783 P
o, that's the case of the shepherd's son. 4.04.816 P
son of polixenes, with his princess (she | the 5.01. 86
might i a son and daughter now have look'd on, 5.01.177
desires you to attach his son, who has | (his 5.01.182
this avouches the shepherd's son, who has not 5.02. 64 P
the old man and his son aboard the prince; 5.02.115 P
for the king's son took me by the hand, and 5.02.140 P
we may live, son, to shed many more. 5.02.146 P
prithee, son, do; 5.02.152 P
how if it be false, son? 5.02.161 P
and son unto the king, whom heavens directing, 5.03.150
behalf | of thy deceased brother geffrey's son, JN 1.01. 8
what now, my son, have i not ever said | how 1.01. 31
world, | upon the right and party of her son? 1.01. 34
born in northamptonshire, and eldest son, | as i 1.01. 51
the son and heir to that same faulconbridge. 1.01. 56
and were our father, and this son like him, | o 1.01. 81
do you not read some tokens of my son | in the 1.01. 87
that this my mother's son was none of his; 1.01.111
who, as you say, took pains to get this son, 1.01.121
had of your father claim'd this son for his? 1.01.122
my mother's son did get your father's heir; 1.01.128
or the reputed son of cordelion, | lord of thy 1.01.136
philip, good old sir robert's wive's eldest son. 1.01.159
my brother robert, old sir robert's son? 1.01.224
is it sir robert's son that you seek so? 1.01.226
sir robert's son! 1.01.227
ay, thou unreverend boy, | sir robert's son! 1.01.228
he is sir robert's son, and so art thou. 1.01.229
madam, i was not old sir robert's son; 1.01.233
but, mother, i am not sir robert's son, | i have 1.01.246
was thy elder brother born, | and this his son; 2.01.105
let me make answer: thy usurping son. 2.01.121
my bed was ever to thy son as true | as thine 2.01.124
this is thy eldest son's son, | infortunate in 2.01.177
produce | a will that bars the title of thy son. 2.01.192
son to the elder brother of this man, | and king 2.01.239
son, list to this conjunction, make this match, 2.01.468
if that the dolphin there, thy princely son, 2.01.484
eye, | which, being but the shadow of your son, 2.01.499
becomes a sun and makes your son a shadow. 2.01.500
command thy son and daughter to join hands. 2.01.532
where is she and her son? 2.01.543
why dost thou look so sadly on my son? 3.01. 20
curse, | a mother's curse, on her revolting son. 3.01.257
wife, | young arthur is my son, and he is lost. 3.04. 47
if i were mad, i should forget my son, | or 3.04. 57
"o that these hands could so redeem my son | as 3.04. 71
he talks to me that never had a son. 3.04. 91
o lord, my boy, my arthur, my fair son! 3.04.103
is it my fault that i was geffrey's son? 4.01. 22
and i would to heaven | i were your son, so you 4.01. 24
many a poor man's son would have lien still, 4.01. 50
brought hither henry herford thy bold son, R2 1.01. 3
heir, | as he is but my father's brother's son, 1.01.117
we'll calm the duke of norfolk, you your son. 1.01.159
throw down, my son, the duke of norfolk's gage. 1.01.161
a' gaunt, | even in the lusty havior of his son. 1.03. 77
and blindfold death not let me see my son. 1.03.224
thy son is banish'd upon good advice, | whereto 1.03.233
come, come, my son, i'll bring thee on thy way; 1.03.304
of the world's ransom, blessed mary's son; 2.01. 56
seen how his son's son should destroy his sons, 2.01.105
wert thou not brother to great edward's son, 2.01.121
o, spare me not, my /brother edward's son, | for 2.01.124
son, | for that i was his father edward's son, 2.01.125
is not his heir a well–deserving son? 2.01.194
and living too, for now his son is duke. 2.01.225
lord northumberland, his son young harry percy, 2.02. 53
my lord, your son was gone before i came. 2.02. 86
it is my son, young harry percy, | sent from my 2.03. 21
you have a son, aumerle, my noble cousin, | had 2.03.125
here comes my son aumerle. 5.02. 41
welcome, my son! 5.02. 46
and wilt thou pluck my fair son from mine age, 5.02. 92
away, fond woman, were he twenty times my son, 5.02.101
bed, | and that he is a bastard, not thy son. 5.02.106
can no man tell me of my unthrifty son? 5.03. 1
o loyal father of a treacherous son! 5.03. 60
excuse | this deadly blot in thy digressing son. 5.03. 66
come, my old son, i pray god make thee new. 5.03.146
mordake earl of fife and eldest son | to beaten 1H4 1.01. 71
should be the father to so blest a son — | a 1.01. 80
a son who is the theme of honor's tongue, 1.01. 81
be damn'd for never a king's son in christendom. 1.02. 97
is guilty of this fault, and not my son. 1.03. 28
we license your departure with your son. 1.03.123
and make the douglas' son your only mean | for 1.03.261
your son in scotland being thus employed, 1.03.265
help me to my horse, good king's son. 2.02. 41
words than a parrot, and yet the son of a woman! 2.04. 99
a king's son! 2.04.136
that thou art my son i have partly thy mother's 2.04.402
if then thou be son to me, here lies the point: 2.04.406
why, being son to me, art thou so pointed at? 2.04.406
shall the son of england prove a thief and take 2.04.409
and bring him out that is but woman's son | can 3.01. 46
day | be bold to tell you that i am your son, 3.02.134
with him my son, lord john of lancaster, | for 3.02.171
light in thy face, the son of utter darkness. 3.03. 37
where is his son, | the nimble–footed madcap 4.01. 94
and sav'd the treacherous labor of your son. 5.04. 57
you, son john, and my cousin westmerland 5.05. 35
myself and you, son harry, will towards wales, 5.05. 39
and, in the fortune of my lord your son, 2H4 1.01. 15

ne hulk sir john, | is prisoner to your son. 1.01. 20
my young lord your son have not the day, 1.01. 52
ow doth my son and brother? 1.01. 67
hou wouldst say, "your son did thus and thus; 1.01. 76
nding with "brother, son, and all are dead." 1.01. 81
our brother yet, | but, for my lord your son — 1.01. 83
cannot think, my lord, your son is dead. 1.01.104
own the town that her eldest son is like you. 2.01.105 P
the son of the king nearest his father, harry 2.02.119 P
did your son, | he was so suff'red; 2.03. 56
bastard son of the king's? 2.04.283 P
nadow, whose son art thou? 3.02.126 P
y mother's son, sir. 3.02.127 P
ny mother's son! 3.02.128 P
the son of the female is the shadow of the 3.02.129 P
ourt, | whereon this hydra son of war is born, 4.02. 38
umphrey, my son of gloucester, | where is the 4.04. 12
rince john your son doth kiss your grace's hand 4.04. 83
od knows, my son, | by what by–paths and 4.05.183
hou bring'st me happiness and peace, son john, 4.05.227
have a son set your decrees at nought? 5.02. 85
e now the father and propose a son, | hear your 5.02. 92
ehold yourself so by a son disdained; 5.02. 95
nd in your power soft silencing your son. 5.02. 97
ll you do live to see a son of mine | offend 5.02.105
old, | that dares do justice on my proper son; 5.02.109
aving such a son | that would deliver up his 5.02.110
ho was the son | to lewis the emperor, and H5 1.02. 75
nd lewis the son | of charles the great. 1.02. 76
s sont les mots de son mauvais, corruptible, 3.04. 53 P
le chien est retourne a son propre vomissement, 3.07. 64 P
, if a son that is by his father sent about 4.01.147 P
ndings of his soldiers, the father of his son, 4.01.157 P
is story shall the good man teach his son; 4.03. 56
u'il est contre son jurement de pardonner aucun 4.04. 50 P
ake her, fair son, and from her blood raise up 5.02.348
nd of it left his son imperial lord. ep 8
hird son to the third edward, king of england. 1H6 2.04. 84
epos'd his nephew richard, edward's son, | the 2.05. 64
larence, third son | to king edward the third; 2.05. 75
nd on his son young john, who two hours since 4.03. 35
is seven years did not talbot see his son, 4.03. 37
bid his young son welcome to his grave? 4.03. 40
nd am i your son? 4.05. 12
nen here i take my leave of thee, fair son, 4.05. 52
, twice my father, twice am i thy son! 4.06. 6
y, | now thou art seal'd the son of chivalry? 4.06. 29
ave won, | and if i fly, i am not talbot's son. 4.06. 51
son to talbot, die at talbot's foot. 4.06. 53
my dear lord, lo where your son is borne! 4.07. 17
or henry, son unto a conqueror, | is likely to 5.05. 73
ut wherefore weeps warwick, my valiant son? 2H6 1.01.115
arwick, my son, the comfort of my age, | thy 1.01.190
eace, son, and show some reason, buckingham, 1.03.113
nd left behind him richard, his only son, | who 2.02. 19
ne eldest son and heir of john of gaunt, 2.02. 22
ne issue of the next son should have reign'd. 2.02. 32
ne third son, duke of clarence, from whose line 2.02. 34
angley, edward the third's fift /son, son. 2.02. 46
f march, who was the son | of edmund mortimer, 2.02. 48
the issue of the elder son | succeed before 2.02. 51
he fourth son, york claims it from the third; 2.02. 55
ere's best's son, the tanner of wingham — 4.02. 21 P
is son am i, deny it if you can. 4.02.146
cade the son of henry the fift, | that thus 4.08. 34
ommand my eldest son, nay, all my sons, | as 5.01. 49
hou mad misleader of thy brain–sick son! 5.01.163
war, thou son of hell, | whom angry heavens do 5.02. 33
am the son of henry the fift, | who made the 3H6 1.01.107
hat wrong is this unto the prince your son! 1.01.176
ot for myself, lord warwick, but my son, | whom 1.01.192
nd never seen thee, never borne thee son, 1.01.217
hine heir, | and disinherited thine only son. 1.01.225
ardon me, margaret, pardon me, sweet son, | the 1.01.228
hou hast undone thyself, thy son, and me, | and 1.01.232
e repeal'd | whereby my son is disinherited. 1.01.250
ome, son, let's away. 1.01.255
entle son edward, thou wilt stay /with me? 1.01.259
ome, son, away, we may not linger thus. 1.01.263
ow love to me and to her son | hath made her 1.01.264
agle | tire on the flesh of me and of my son! 1.01.269
hou canst not, son; it is impossible. 1.02. 21
hou hast one son, for his sake pity me, | lest 1.03. 40
nethinks 'tis prize enough to be his son. 2.01. 20
e, but a duke, would have his son a king, | and 2.02. 21
hou, being a king, blest with a goodly son, 2.02. 23
nd happy always was it for that son | whose 2.02. 47
'll leave my son my virtuous deeds behind, 2.02. 49
ou promis'd knighthood to our forward son, 2.02. 58
o blot out me, and put his own son in. 2.02. 92
ho should succeed the father but the son? 2.02. 94
h, no, no, no, it is mine only son! 2.05. 83
ow will my wife for slaughter of my son | shed 2.05.105
as ever son so ru'd a father's death? 2.05.109
as ever father so bemoan'd his son? 2.05.110
hou didst love york, and i am son to york. 2.06. 73
ny queen and son are gone to france for aid; 3.01. 28
oor queen and son, your labor is but lost; 3.01. 32
clarence, henry, and his son young edward, 3.02.130
ith this my son, prince edward, henry's heir, 3.03. 31
et here prince edward stands, king henry's son. 3.03. 73
on edward, she is fair and virtuous, 3.03.245
f the lord bonville on your new wive's son, 4.01. 57
hat margaret your queen and my son edward | be 4.06. 60
nd thou, son clarence, | shalt stir up in 4.08. 11
ay, somervile, what says my loving son? 5.01. 7
y this, i hope, she hath a son for me. 5.05. 90
hat taught his son the office of a fowl! 5.06. 19
hy son i kill'd for his presumption. 5.06. 34
hou hadst not liv'd to kill a son of mine. 5.06. 36
ing henry and the prince his son are gone; 5.06. 89
wo cliffords, as the father and the son, | and 5.07. 7
made glorious summer by this son of york; R3 1.01. 2
wife to thy edward, to thy slaught'red son, 1.02. 10
he heavens have blest you with a goodly son 1.03. 9
ower, | and edward, my poor son, at tewksbury. 1.03.119
a husband and a son thou ow'st to me — | and 1.03.169
dward thy son, that now is prince of wales, 1.03.198
for edward our son, that was prince of wales, 1.03.199
when my son | was stabb'd with bloody daggers: 1.03.210
the slave of nature and the son of hell! 1.03.229
witness my son, now in the shade of death, 1.03.266
unrip'st the bowels of thy sov'reign's son. 1.04.207
which of you, if you were a prince's son, 1.04.257
nor you, son dorset; 2.01. 19
and cry, "o clarence, my unhappy son!"? 2.02. 4
he is my son — ay, and therein my shame, | yet 2.02. 29
edward, my lord, thy son, our king, is dead! 2.02. 40
a careful mother | of the young prince your son. 2.02. 97
king, | we are to reap the harvest of his son. 2.02.116
no, no, by god's good grace his son shall reign. 2.03. 10
they say my son of york | has almost overta'en 2.04. 6
for standing by when richard stabb'd her son. 3.03. 17
only for saying he would make his son | heir to 3.05. 77
you say that edward is your brother's son: 3.07.177
loath to depose the child, your brother's son; 3.07.209
your brother's son shall never reign our king, 3.07.215
how doth the prince and my young son of york? 4.01. 14
you shall have letters from me to my son | in 4.01. 49
stanley, he is your wive's son: 4.02. 87
the son of clarence have i pent up close, | his 4.03. 36
when holy harry died, and my sweet son. 4.04. 25
my damned son that thy two sweet sons smother'd. 4.04.134
and little ned plantagenet, his son? 4.04.146
art thou my son? 4.04.155
the loss you have is but a son being king, | and 4.04.307
dorset your son, that with a fearful soul 4.04.311
but leave behind | your son, george stanley. 4.04.495
my son george stanley is frank'd up in hold; 4.05. 3
holy king henry and thy fair son edward, 5.01. 4
lest his son george fall | into the blind cave 5.03. 61
off with his son george's head! 5.03.344
the father rashly slaughter'd his own son, | the 5.05. 25
the son, compell'd, been butcher to the sire. 5.05. 26
now his son, | henry the eight, life, honor, H8 2.01.115
blind priest, like the eldest son of fortune, 2.02. 20
which perforce | i, her frail son, amongst my 3.02.148
and the rude son should strike his father dead; TRO 1.03.115
thou bitch–wolf's son, canst thou not hear? 2.01. 10 P
ay, my good son. 2.03.257
pard to the hind, or step–dame to her son, | yea 3.02.194
give us a prince of blood, a son of priam, | in 3.03. 26
now, great thetis' son! 3.03. 94
the youngest son of priam, a true knight, | not 4.05. 96
thou art, great lord, my father's sister's son, 4.05.120
a bastard son of priam's. 5.07. 15 P
if the son of a whore fight for a whore, he 5.07. 21 P
if my son were my husband, i should freelier COR 1.03. 2 P
but tender–bodied and the only son of my womb; 1.03. 6 P
then his good report should have been my son; 1.03. 21 P
how does your little son? 1.03. 53 P
a' my word, the father's son. 1.03. 57 P
were he the butcher of my son, he should | be 1.09. 88
wherein he gives my son the whole name of the 2.01.135 P
that ancus martius, numa's daughter's son, | who 2.03.239
i am in this | your wife, your son, these 3.02. 65
i prithee now, my son, | go to them, with this 3.02. 72
i prithee now, sweet son, as thou hast said | my 3.02.107
your son | will or exceed the common or be 4.01. 31
my first son, | whither /wilt thou go? 4.01. 33
i would my son | were in arabia, and thy tribe 4.02. 23
the meanest house in rome, so far my son, | this 4.02. 40
here within as if he were son and heir to mars; 4.05.192 P
cannot office me from my son coriolanus. 5.02. 63 P
o my son, my son! 5.02. 71 P
o my son, my son! 5.02. 71 P
to your corrected son? 5.03. 57
wife, and child to see | the son, the husband, 5.03.102
for myself, son, | i purpose not to wait on 5.03.118
thou know'st, great son, | the end of war's 5.03.140
speak to me, son. 5.03.148
but, for your son, believe it — o, believe it 5.03.187
he kill'd my son! 5.06.121 P
i am his first–born son, that was the last TIT 1.01. 5
of my right, | if ever bassianus, caesar's son, 1.01. 10
the eldest son of this distressed queen. 1.01.103
shed, | a mother's tears in passion for her son; 1.01.106
to thee, | o, think my son to be as dear to me! 1.01.108
thrice–noble titus, spare my first–born son! 1.01.120
to this your son is mark'd, and die he must, 1.01.125
that you create our emperor's eldest son, | lord 1.01.224
in wrongful quarrel you have slain your son. 1.01.293
in a bad quarrel slain a virtuous son. 1.01.342
no son of mine, | nor thou, nor these, 1.01.343
and wise laertes' son | did graciously plead for 1.01.380
with his own hand did slay his youngest son, 1.01.418
this is a witness that i am thy son. 2.03.116
here stands my other son, a banish'd man, | and 3.01. 99
ah, son lucius, look on her! 3.01.110
sweet father, if i shall be thought thy son, 3.01.179
thy other banish'd son with this dear sight 3.01.256
demetrius, here's the son of lucius, | he hath 4.02. 1
belike for joy the emperor hath a son. 4.02. 50
that touches this my first–born son and heir! 4.02. 92
my son and i will have the wind of you; 4.02.133
conduct | of lucius, son to old andronicus, 4.04. 66
but he will not entreat his son for us. 4.04. 94
i'll make him send for lucius his son; 5.02. 75
to send for lucius, thy thrice–valiant son, 5.02.112
face, | the last true duties of thy noble son! 5.03.155
side, | so early walking did i see your son. ROM 1.01.123
bed, | away from light steals home my heavy son, 1.01.137
his son is elder, sir; 1.05. 38
his son is thirty. 1.05. 39
his son was but a ward two years ago. 1.05. 40
the son and heir of old tiberio. 1.05.129
a montague, | the only son of your great enemy. 1.05.137
one nickname for her purblind son and /heir, 2.01. 12
young son, it argues a distempered head | so 2.03. 33
that's my good son, but where hast thou been 2.03. 47
be plain, good son, and homely in thy drift, 2.03. 55
is my dear son with such sour company! 3.03. 7
bed, | acquaint her here of my son paris' love, 3.04. 16
but for the sunset of my brother's son | it 3.05.127
o son, the night before thy wedding–day | hath 4.05. 35
up | to see thy son and heir now /early down. 5.03.209
than to repute himself a son of rome | under JC 1.02.173
brave son, deriv'd from honorable loins! 2.01.322
that were you, antony, the son of caesar, | you 3.01.225
live, | who is your sister's son, mark antony. 4.01. 5
i am the son of marcus cato, ho! 5.04. 4
i am the son of marcus cato, ho! 5.04. 6
and mayst be honor'd, being cato's son. 5.04. 11
an unlineal hand, | no son of mine succeeding. MAC 3.01. 63
fleance his son, that keeps him company, | whose 3.01.134
there's but one down; the son is fled. 3.03. 20
you have done | hath been but for a wayward son, 3.05. 11
there is siward's son, | and many unrough youths 5.02. 9
shall with my cousin, your right noble son, 5.06. 3
macduff is missing, and your noble son. 5.09. 4
your son, my lord, has paid a soldier's debt. 5.09. 5
but now, my cousin hamlet, and my son — HAM 1.02. 64
than that which dearest father bears his son 1.02.111
our chiefest courtier, cousin, and our son. 1.02.117
drift of question | that they do know my son, 2.01. 11
you laying these slight sallies on my son, | as 2.01. 39
former lecture and advice, | shall you my son. 2.01. 65
instantly to visit | my too much changed son. 2.02. 36
your noble son is mad: 2.02. 92
that i, the son of a dear /father murthered, 2.02.583
o wonderful son, that can so stonish a mother! 3.02.328 P
and for that | i, his sole son, do this same 3.03. 77
do you not come your tardy son to chide, | that, 3.04.106
o gentle son, | upon the heat and flame of thy 3.04.122
where is your son? 4.01. 3
replication should be made by the son of a king? 4.02. 13 P
next, your son gone, and he most violent author 4.05. 80
to show yourself indeed your father's son | more 4.07.125
o my son, what theme? 5.01.268
good gertrude, set some watch over your son. 5.01.296
our son shall win. 5.02.287
is not this your son, my lord? LR 1.01. 8 P
a son for her cradle ere she had a husband for 1.01. 15 P
but i have a son, sir, by order of law, some 1.01. 19 P
our son of cornwall, | and you, our no less 1.01. 41
and you, our no less loving son of albany, | we 1.01. 42
my son edgar! 1.02. 56 P
the father should be as ward to the son, and the 1.02. 73 P
ward to the son, and the son manage his revenue. 1.02. 74 P
and the bond crack'd 'twixt son and father. 1.02.109 P
there's son against father: 1.02.110 P
pandar, and the son and heir of a mungril bitch; 2.02. 22 P
it is both he and she, | your son and daughter. 2.04. 14
your son and daughter found this trespass worth 2.04. 44
i had a son, | now outlaw'd from my blood; 3.04.166
i lov'd him, friend, | no father his son dearer; 3.04.169
he's a yeoman that has a gentleman to his son; 3.06. 13 P
yeoman that sees his son a gentleman before him. 3.06. 13 P
where's my son edmund? 3.07. 85
o dear son edgar, | the food of thy abused 4.01. 21
my son | came then into my mind, and yet my mind 4.01. 33
bless thee, good man's son, from the foul fiend! 4.01. 58 P
and of the loyal service of his son, | when i 4.02. 7
where was his son when they did take his eyes? 4.02. 88
for gloucester's bastard son | was kinder to his 4.06.114
my name is edgar, and thy father's son. 5.03.170
though our proper son | stood in your action. OTH 1.03. 69
the great and all his dignities | upon his son, ANT 1.02.189
having a son and friends, since julius caesar, 2.06. 12
sat | caesarion, whom they call my father's son, 3.06. 6
please | to give me conquer'd egypt for my son, 5.02. 19
(whom | he purpos'd to his wive's sole son — a CYM 1.01. 5
that mightst have had the sole son of my queen! 1.01.138
and my leonatus | our neighbor shepherd's son! 1.01.150
my lord your son drew on my master. 1.01.160
he's for his master, | and enemy to my son. 1.05. 29
when thou shalt bring me word she loves my son, 1.05. 49
to boot, my son, | who shall take notice of thee 1.05. 69
and this her son | cannot take two from twenty, 2.01. 54
our dear son, | when you have given good morning 2.03. 60
yes, and a gentlewoman's son. 2.03. 78
wert thou the son of jupiter, and no more | but 2.03.125
son, let your mother end. 3.01. 39
son, i say, follow the king. 3.05. 53
how now, my son? 3.05. 66
know him, 'tis | cloten, the son o' th' queen. 4.02. 65
thou shalt know | i am son to th' queen. 4.02. 93
son to the queen (after his own report), | who 4.02.119
and tell the fishes he's the queen's son, cloten 4.02.153
he was a queen's son, boys, | and though he came 4.02.244
a fever with the absence of her son; 4.03. 2
her son gone, | so needful for this present! 4.03. 7
now for the counsel of my son and queen! 4.03. 27
since, jupiter, our son is good, | take off his 5.04. 85
your low–laid son our godhead will uplift. 5.04.103
work | her son into th' adoption of the crown; 5.05. 56
but her son | is gone, we know not how, nor 5.05.272
cadwal, arviragus, | your younger princely son. 5.05.360
helps, | as i am son and servant to your will, PER 1.01. 23
that would be son to great antiochus. 1.01. 26
he's father, son, and husband mild; 1.01. 68
this mercy shows we'll joy in such a son; 1.01.118
where now /you're both a father and a son | by 1.01.127
our son and daughter shall in tyrus reign. 5.03. 82
any palamon or any living | that is a man's son. TNK 2.02.182
thou art mine aunt's son, | and that blood we 3.06. 94
the heavenly fires | did scorch his mortal son, 5.01. 92
art thou a woman's son and canst not feel | what VEN 201
or butcher sire that reaves his son of life: 766
there lives a son that suck'd an earthly mother, 863
and set dissension 'twixt the son and sire, 1160
"had collatinus kill'd my son or sire, | or lain LUC 232
the sire, the son, the dame, and daughter die. 1477
then son and father weep with equal strife | who 1791
noon, | unlook'd on diest unless thou get a son. SON 7.14
know | you had a father, let your son say so. 13.14
what woman's son | will sourly leave her till 41. 7

SONANCE 1 FR 0.0001 REL FR 1 V 0 P
the tucket sonance and the note to mount; H5 4.02. 35

SONG 59 FR 0.0066 REL FR 35 V 24 P
let's see your song. how now, minion? TGV 1.02. 85
there wanteth but a mean to fill your song. 1.02. 92
a sawpit rush at once | with some diffused song. WIV 4.04. 55
break off thy song, and haste thee quick away. MM 4.01. 7

i'll stop mine ears against the mermaid's song. ERR 3.02.164
what key shall a man take you to go in the song? ADO 1.01.186 P
come, balthasar, we'll hear that song again. 2.03. 43
by my troth, a good song. 2.03. 75 P
nor woo in rhyme, like a blind harper's song! LLL 5.02.405
that the rude sea grew civil at her song, | and MND 2.01.152
come, now a roundel and a fairy song; 2.02. 1
both warbling of one song, both in one key, | as 3.02.206
first, rehearse your song by rote, | to each 5.01.397
i can suck melancholy out of a song, as a weasel AYL 2.05. 13 P
well, i'll end the song. 2.05. 31 P
here was he merry, hearing of a song. 2.07. 4
i would sing my song without a burthen; 3.02.247 P
have you no song, forester, for this purpose? 4.02. 6 P
come, sit, sit, and a song. 5.03. 9 P
it but time lost to hear such a foolish song. 5.03. 40 P
you corrupt the song, sirrah. AWW 1.03. 81 P
in ten, madam, which is a purifying a' th' song. 1.03. 83 P
of melancholy /sold a goodly manor for a song. 3.02. 9 P
now a song. TN 2.03. 30 P
let's have a song. 2.03. 32 P
you have a love–song, or a song of good life? 2.03. 35 P
now, good cesario, but that piece of song, 2.04. 2
that old and antique song we heard last night; 2.04. 3
o fellow, come, the song we had last night. 2.04. 42
would sing her song and dance her turn; WT 4.04. 58
we'll have this song out anon by ourselves. 4.04.309 P
grew so in love with the wenches' song, that he 4.04.606 P
no feeling, but my sir's song, and admiring the 4.04.613 P
and she will sing the song that pleaseth you, 1H4 3.01.213
come, kate, i'll have your song too. 3.01.245 P
come sing me a bawdy song, make me merry. 3.03. 13 P
a merry song! 2H4 2.04.276 P
a french song and a fiddle has no fellow. H8 1.03. 41
hear no more of this, i'll sing you a song now. TRO 3.01.106 P
let thy song be love. 3.01.110 P
be unto us as is a nurse's song | of lullaby to TIT 2.03. 28
alas, sweet lady, what imports this song? HAM 4.05. 27
'fore /god, an excellent song. OTH 2.03. 75 P
this is a more exquisite song than the other. 2.03. 98 P
she had a song of "willow," | an old thing 'twas 4.03. 28
that song to–night | will not go from my mind; 4.03. 30
what did thy song bode, lady? 5.02.246
go fetch him, | we'll say our song whilst. CYM 4.02.254
to sing a song that old was sung, | from ashes PER 1.ch. 1
is not this a fine song? TNK 4.01.105
her song was tedious and outwore the night, VEN 841
a nurse's song ne'er pleas'd her babe so well. 974
to recreate himself when he hath song, | the 1095
got the lady gay, | for now my song is ended. PP 15.16
i fear — | lest that my mistress hear my song; 18.50
whose speechless song, being many, seeming one, SON 8.13
rage, | and stretched metre of an antique song: 17.12
spend'st thou thy fury on some worthless song, 100. 3
because i would not dull you with my song. 102.14
SONG–MEN 1 FR 0.0001 REL FR 0 V 1 P
for the shearers (three–man song–men all, and WT 4.03. 42 P
SONGS 17 FR 0.0019 REL FR 11 V 6 P
i had my book of songs and sonnets here. WIV 1.01.199 P
knight, | for the which, with songs of woe, ADO 5.03. 14
of mercury are harsh after the songs of apollo. LLL 5.02.931 P
sorts, and songs compos'd | to her unworthiness. AWW 3.07. 40
are summer songs for me and my aunts, | while we WT 4.03. 11
he hath songs for man or woman, of all sizes; 4.04.191 P
nothing but songs of death? R3 4.04.507
the merry songs of peace to all his neighbors. H8 5.04. 35
if with too credent ear you list his songs, | or HAM 1.03. 30
now, your gambols, your songs, your flashes of 5.01.190 P
when were you wont to be so full of songs, LR 1.04.170 P
and in their songs curse ever–blinded fortune TNK 2.02. 38
and yet his songs are sad ones. 2.04. 20
and in their funeral songs for these two cousins 3.06.248
sing to her such green songs of love as she says 4.03. 81 P
bewitching like the wanton mermaids' songs, VEN 777
since all alike my songs and praises be | to one SON 105. 3
SON–IN–LAW 11 FR 0.0012 REL FR 8 V 3 P
and since you could not be my son–in–law, | be ADO 5.01.287
and yet we hear not of our son–in–law. SHR 3.02. 3
i will buy me a son–in–law in a fair, and toll AWW 5.03.148 P
then embraces his son–in–law; WT 5.02. 53 P
this your son–in–law, | and son unto the king, 5.03.149
and his son–in–law mortimer, and old 1H4 2.04.341 P
words | i've heard him utter to his son–in–law, H8 1.02.136
a valiant son–in–law thou shalt enjoy, | one fit TIT 1.01.311
death is my son–in–law, death is my heir, | my ROM 4.05. 38
your son–in–law is far more fair than black. OTH 1.03.290
we'll learn our freeness of a son–in–law: CYM 5.05.421
SON–IN–LAW'S 1 FR 0.0001 REL FR 0 V 1 P
and then break into his son–in–law's house, sir 2H6 4.07.110 P
SON–IN–LAWS 1 FR 0.0001 REL FR 1 V 0 P
and when i have stol'n upon these son–in–laws, LR 4.06.186
SONNET 9 FR 0.0010 REL FR 3 V 6 P
i have a sonnet that will serve the turn | to TGV 3.02. 92
will you then write me a sonnet in praise of my ADO 5.02. 4 P
hand, | a halting sonnet of his own pure brain, 5.04. 87
god of rhyme, for i am sure i shall turn sonnet. LLL 1.02.184 P
did never sonnet for her sake compile, | nor 4.03.132
me a copy of the sonnet you writ to diana in AWW 4.03.320 P
one, it is with me as the very true sonnet is, TN 3.04. 23 P
i once writ a sonnet in his praise and began H5 3.07. 39 P
i have heard a sonnet begin so to one's mistress 3.07. 41 P
SONNETING 1 FR 0.0001 REL FR 1 V 0 P
tush, none but minstrels like of sonneting! LLL 4.03.156
SONNETS 4 FR 0.0004 REL FR 2 V 2 P
lime to tangle her desires | by wailful sonnets, TGV 3.02. 69
i had my book of songs and sonnets here. WIV 1.01.199 P
well, she hath one a' my sonnets already: LLL 4.03. 15 P
and deep–brain'd sonnets that did amplify | each LC 209
/SON'S 1 FR 0.0001 REL FR 1 V 0 P
where now his /son's like a glow–worm in the PER 2.03. 43
SON'S 19 FR 0.0021 REL FR 17 V 2 P
professes to persuade) the king his son's alive, TMP 2.01.236
welcome, count, | my son's no dearer. AWW 1.02. 76
even for your son's sake, and thereby for WT 1.02.337
his hopeful son's, his babe's, betrays to 2.03. 86
to get the cause of my son's resort thither. 4.02. 50 P
all, every word, yea, and his son's pranks too; 4.04.700 P
this is thy eldest son's son, | infortunate in JN 2.01.177
me | he shortens four years of my son's exile, R2 1.03.217
seen how his son's son should destroy his sons, 2.01.105
were two honors lost, yours and your son's: 2H4 2.03. 16
for richard, the first son's heir, being dead, 2H6 2.02. 31
and this thy son's blood cleaving to my blade 3H6 1.03. 50
sons, | to whom i sued for my dear son's life; TIT 1.01.453
can the son's eye behold his father bleed? 5.03. 65
grief of my son's exile hath stopp'd her breath. ROM 5.03.211
the head and source of all your son's distemper. HAM 2.02. 55
bear the king's son's body | before our army. ANT 3.01. 3
your son's my father's friend, he takes his part CYM 1.01.165
had doting priam check'd his son's desire, LUC 1490
SONS' 4 FR 0.0004 REL FR 4 V 0 P
my sons' sweet blood will make it shame and TIT 3.01. 15
so thou refuse to drink my dear sons' blood. 3.01. 22
see thy two sons' heads, | thy warlike hand, thy 3.01.254
when, for his hand, he had his two sons' heads, 5.01.115
/SONS 2 FR 0.0002 REL FR 2 V 0 P
sirrah, call in my /sons to be my bail. 2H6 5.01.111
/bolts | /sperr /up /the /sons /of /troy. TRO pr 19
SONS 149 FR 0.0168 REL FR 134 V 15 P
good wombs have borne bad sons. TMP 1.02.120
put forth their sons to seek preferment out: TGV 1.03. 7
of our youth in us, we are the sons of women, WIV 2.03. 48 P
she became | a joyful mother of two goodly sons: ERR 1.01. 50
i bought, and brought up to attend my sons. 1.01. 57
that bore thee at a burthen two fair sons. 5.01.344
have i but gone in travail | of you, my sons, 5.01.402
adam's sons are my brethren, and truly i hold it ADO 2.01. 63 P
for their sons are well tutor'd by you, and LLL 4.02. 74 P
mehercle, if their sons be /ingenious, they 4.02. 78 P
there comes an old man and his three sons — AYL 1.02.119 P
or die, be you the sons | of worthy frenchmen. AWW 2.01. 11
and they were sons of mine, i'd have them whipt, 2.03. 86 P
but thy sons and daughters will be all gentlemen WT 5.02.127 P
whose sons lie scattered on the bleeding ground. JN 2.01.304
that we, the sons and children of this isle, 5.02. 25
edward's seven sons, whereof thyself art one, R2 1.02. 11
seen how his son's son should destroy his sons, 2.01.105
i am the last of noble edward's sons, | of whom 2.01.171
ten thousand bloody crowns of mothers' sons 3.03. 96
have we more sons? 5.02. 90
as thriftless sons their scraping fathers' gold. 5.03. 69
they are villains and the sons of darkness. 1H4 2.04.172 P
me none but good householders, /yeomen's sons, 4.02. 15 P
servingmen, younger sons to younger brothers, 4.02. 28 P
if i had a thousand sons, the first humane 2H4 4.03.123 P
see, sons, what things you are! 4.05. 64
their sons with arts and martial exercises; 4.05. 73
mock mothers from their sons, mock castles down; H5 1.02.286
and sent our sons and husbands captivate. 1H6 2.03. 42
like true subjects, sons of your progenitors, 4.01.166
edward the third, my lords, had seven sons: 2H6 2.02. 10
and in thy sons, fair slips of such a stock. 2.02. 58
command my eldest son, nay, all my sons, | as 5.01. 49
the sons of york, thy betters in their birth, 5.01.119
his sons, he says, shall give their words for 5.01.137
will you not, sons? 5.01.138
richard hath best deserv'd of all my sons. 3H6 1.01. 17
you both have vow'd revenge | on him, his sons, 1.01. 56
plantagenet, of thee and these thy sons, | thy 1.01. 95
sons, peace! 1.01.119
and long live thou, and these thy forward sons! 1.01.203
why, how now, sons and brother, at a strife? 1.02. 4
my sons, god knows what hath bechanced them; 1.04. 6
where are your mess of sons to back you now, 1.04. 73
field, | that we, the sons of brave plantagenet, 2.01. 35
more, | as priam was for all his valiant sons. 2.05.120
grieve your grace my sons should call you father 3.02.100
a happy thing | to be the father unto many sons. 3.02.105
men for their sons, wives for their husbands, 5.06. 41
blest his three sons with his victorious arm, R3 1.04.236
and the queen's sons and brothers haught and 2.03. 28
and often up and down my sons were toss'd | for 2.04. 58
and for my sister and her princely sons, | be 3.03. 21
a care–craz'd mother to a many sons, | a 3.07.184
the sons of edward sleep in abraham's bosom, 4.03. 38
where be thy two sons? 4.04. 93
my damned son that thy two sweet sons smother'd. 4.04.134
and the dire death of my poor sons and brothers? 4.04.143
i have no moe sons of the royal blood | for thee 4.04.200
if i did take the kingdom from your sons, | to 4.04.294
edward's unhappy sons do bid thee flourish. 5.03.153
is my father, and all the rest are his sons." TRO 1.02.162 P
and achilles' horse | makes many thetis' sons. 1.03.212
i am no more touch'd than all priam's sons; 2.02.126
for emulation hath a thousand sons | that one by 3.03.156
had i a dozen sons, each in my love alike, and COR 1.03. 22 P
in corioles wear, | and mothers that lack sons. 2.01.179
more impression show | than that of common sons. 5.03. 52
that with his sons, a terror to our foes, | hath TIT 1.01. 29
bearing his valiant sons | in coffins from the 1.01. 34
thine, | thy noble brother titus and his sons, 1.01. 50
romans, of five and twenty valiant sons, | half 1.01. 79
why suffer'st thou thy sons, unburied yet, | to 1.01. 87
how many sons hast thou of mine in store, | that 1.01. 94
and if thy sons were ever dear to thee, | o, 1.01.107
but must my sons be slaughtered in the streets 1.01.112
in peace and honor rest you here, my sons, 1.01.150
in peace and honor rest you here, my sons! 1.01.156
with these our late–deceased emperor's sons. 1.01.184
and buried one and twenty valiant sons, 1.01.195
nor thou, nor he, are any sons of mine, | my 1.01.294
of mine, | my sons would never so dishonor me. 1.01.295
thee never, nor thy traitorous haughty sons, 1.01.302
enjoy, | one fit to bandy with thy lawless sons, 1.01.312
unworthy brother, and unworthy sons! 1.01.346
i saw, | to be dishonored by my sons in rome! 1.01.385
the cruel father and his traitorous sons, | to 1.01.452
sons, let it be your charge, as it is ours, | to 2.02. 7
to–day, | thy sons make pillage of her chastity, 2.03. 44
him, and i'll go fetch thy sons | to back thy 2.03. 53
yet every mother breeds not sons alike — | do 2.03.146
so should i rob my sweet sons of their fee. 2.03.179
farewell, my sons, see that you make her sure. 2.03.187
and let my spleenful sons this trull deflow'r. 2.03.191
the unhappy sons of old andronicus, | brought 2.03.250
that this fell fault of my accursed sons — 2.03.290
fear not thy sons, they shall do well enough. 2.03.305
in my cheeks, | be pitiful to my condemned sons, 3.01. 8
for two and twenty sons i never wept, | because 3.01. 10
unbind my sons, reverse the doom of death, | and 3.01. 24
this way to death my wretched sons are gone, 3.01. 98
thee this word — that, if thou love thy sons, 3.01.151
will send thee hither both thy sons alive, | and 3.01.155
as for my sons, say i account of them | as 3.01.197
look by and by to have thy sons with thee. 3.01.201
here are the heads of thy two noble sons, | and 3.01.236
read to her sons than she hath read to thee 4.01. 13
the lustful sons of tamora | performers of this 4.01. 79
boy | shall carry from me to the empress' sons 4.01.115
against the willful sons | of old andronicus. 4.04. 8
th' effects of sorrow for his valiant sons, 4.04. 30
may this be borne as if his traitorous sons, 4.04. 53
'twas her two sons that murdered bassianus; 5.01. 91
confederate with the queen and her two sons; 5.01.108
good lord, how like the empress' sons they are! 5.02. 64
how like the empress and her sons you are! 5.02. 84
i will bring in the empress and her sons, | the 5.02.116
the empress' sons, take them, chiron, demetrius 5.02.154
villains, forbear, we are the empress' sons. 5.02.162
you sad–fac'd men, people and sons of rome, | by 5.03. 67
yield him who all the human sons do hate, | from TIM 4.03.185
both too, and women's sons. 4.03.414 P
sons, kinsmen, thanes, | and you whose places MAC 1.04. 35
malcolm and donalbain, the king's two sons, 2.04. 25
think | that, had he duncan's sons under his key 3.06. 18
had i as many sons as i have hairs, | i would 5.09. 14
with blood of fathers, mothers, daughters, sons, HAM 2.02.458
beloved sons, be yours, which to confirm, | this LR 1.01.138
that, sons at perfect age and fathers declin'd, 1.02. 72 P
his sons /he /there proclaim'd the /kings of ANT 3.06. 13
two other sons, who in the wars o' th' time CYM 1.01. 35
he had two sons (if this be worth your hearing, 1.01. 57
boys know little they are sons to th' king, 3.03. 80
that they | had been my father's sons, then had 3.06. 76
sons, | we'll higher to the mountains, there 4.04. 7
thought the old man and his sons were angels. 5.03. 85
my sons, i must | for mine own part unfold a 5.05.312
first pay me for the nursing of thy sons, | and 5.05.322
nursing of my sons? 5.05.324
ere i arise, i will prefer my sons; 5.05.326
call me father | and think they are my sons, are 5.05.329
here are your sons again, and i must lose | two 5.05.348
know not how to wish | a pair of worthier sons. 5.05.356
thy lopp'd branches point | thy two sons forth; 5.05.455
following the dead–cold ashes of their sons, TNK 4.02. 5
they are all the sons of honor. 4.02.141
and barren dearth of daughters and of sons, | be VEN 754
to see their youthful sons bright weapons wield, LUC 1432
SONT 3 FR 0.0003 REL FR 0 V 3 P
je pense qu'ils sont appeles de fingres, oui, de H5 3.04. 11 P
ils sont les mots de son mauvais, corruptible, 3.04. 53 P
langues des hommes sont pleines de tromperies. 5.02.115 P
SONTIES 1 FR 0.0001 REL FR 0 V 1 P
be god's sonties, 'twill be a hard way to hit. MV 2.02. 45 P
/SOON 3 FR 0.0003 REL FR 3 V 0 P
/and /soon /lie /richard /in /an /earthy /pit! R2 4.01.219
/how /soon /my /sorrow /hath /destroy'd /my 4.01.291
/but /my /deeds /shall /stay /thy /fury /soon. 2H6 4.01.113
SOON 160 FR 0.0180 REL FR 132 V 28 P
what, all so soon asleep! TMP 2.01.191
my lord, i cannot be so soon provided: TGV 1.03. 72
thou wouldst as soon go kindle fire with snow 2.07. 19
knowing that tender youth is soon suggested, | i 3.01. 34
and cannot soon revolt and change your mind. 3.02. 59
but i shall as soon quarrel at it as any man in WIV 1.01.290 P
and we'll have a posset for't soon at night, in 1.04. 8 P
if any man may, you may as soon as any. 2.02.237 P
come to me soon at night. 2.02.283 P
come to me soon at night. 2.02.286 P
three hours too soon than a minute too late. 2.02.312 P
for so soon as i came beyond eton, they threw me 4.05. 66 P
and we may soon our satisfaction have | touching MM 1.01. 82
soon at night | i'll send him certain word of my 1.04. 88
me, | and soon, and safe, arrived where i was. ERR 1.01. 48
too soon | we came aboard. 1.01. 60
lest that your goods too soon be confiscate: 1.02. 2
soon at five a' clock, | please you, i'll meet 1.02. 26
how chance thou art return'd so soon? 1.02. 42
return'd so soon! 1.02. 43
fair | a sunny look of his would soon repair. 2.01. 99
and soon at supper–time i'll visit you, | and 3.02.174
perchance i will be there as soon as you. 4.01. 39
you sent me for a rope's end as soon: 4.01. 98
'twill be heavier soon by the weight of a man. ADO 3.04. 26 P
nay, you must do it soon. LLL 5.02.211
man, an honest man, look you, and soon dash'd. 5.02.582 P
i'll believe as soon | this whole earth may be MND 3.02. 52
which death, or absence, soon shall remedy. 3.02.244
we the globe can compass soon, | swifter than 4.01. 97
soon at supper shalt thou see | lorenzo, who is MV 2.03. 5
here | shall witness i set forth as soon as you, 5.01.271
unseal this letter soon; 5.01.275
foot can fall, he thinks himself too soon there. AYL 3.02.329 P
you may as soon make her that you love believe 3.02.387 P
that i may soon make good | what i have said, SHR 1.01. 74
have you so soon forgot the entertainment | her 3.01. 2
were not i a little pot and soon hot, my very 4.01. 6 P
(she being now at hand) thou shalt soon feel, to 4.01. 31 P
then come back to my /master's as soon as i can. 5.01. 5 P
to the grief, the excess makes it soon mortal. AWW 1.01. 58 P
ev'n as soon as thou canst, for thou hast to 2.03.224 P
will not be kill'd so soon as i thought he would 3.02. 37 P
a murd'rous guilt shows not itself more soon TN 3.01.147
so soon as ever thou seest him, draw, and, as 3.04.177 P
i' th' world, | so soon as yours could win me. WT 1.02. 21
this means being there | so soon as you arrive, 4.04.620
him time | to land his legions all as soon as i; JN 2.01. 59
my life as soon. 2.01.155
the day shall not be up so soon as i, | to try 5.05. 21
and all too soon, i fear, the king shall rue. R2 1.03.205
for violent fires soon burn out themselves; 2.01. 34
consuming means, soon preys upon itself. 2.01. 39

ope i shall as soon be strangled with a 1H4 2.04.498 P
on kindled and soon burnt, carded his state, 3.02. 62
on kindled and soon burnt, carded his state, 3.02. 62
deputation could not | so soon be drawn, nor 4.01. 33
on after that, depriv'd him of his life, | and 4.03. 91
at noble worcester | so soon ta'en prisoner, 2H4 1.01.126
lord northumberland will soon be cool'd. 3.01. 44
ubt not but your majesty | shall soon enjoy. 4.04. 12
hall be sent for soon at night. 5.05. 90 P
annot now speak, i will hear you soon. 5.05. 94
llfulness | so soon did lose his seat (and all H5 1.01. 36
oportions for these wars | be soon collected, 1.02.305
u shall be soon dispatch'd, with fair 2.04.144
how much "a fool's bolt is soon shot." 3.07.122 P
all — my ransom then | will soon be levied. 4.03.121
thread of life had not so soon decay'd. 1H6 1.01. 34
ll, miscreant, i'll be there as soon as you, 3.04. 44
thy first fight, i soon encountered, | and 4.06. 18
oucester, know that thou art come too soon, 2H6 3.01. 95
ese kentish rebels would be soon appeas'd! 4.04. 42
that great plantagenet | is crown'd so soon, 3H6 1.04.100
father gave thee life too soon, | and hath 2.05. 92
d lewis a prince soon won with moving words. 3.01. 34
at's soon perform'd, because i am a subject. 3.02. 54
'll soon find means to make the body follow. 4.07. 26
wise stout captain, and soon persuaded! 4.07. 30
out we shall soon persuade | both him and all 4.07. 33
ittle gale will soon disperse that cloud, 5.03. 10
ll soon recover his accustom'd health. R3 1.03. 2
t yet you see how soon the day o'ercast. 3.02. 86
d soon i'll rid you from the fear of them. 4.02. 77
me to me, tyrrel, soon, /at after–supper, 4.03. 31
at thou wouldst as soon afford a grave | as 4.04. 31
e | how soon this mightiness meets misery; H8 pr 30
the king know | (as soon he shall by me) 1.01.191
ithmetic may soon bring his particulars TRO 1.02.113 P
| he shall as soon read in the eyes of others 3.03. 77
st as they are made, forgot as soon | as done. 3.03.149
ot soon provok'd, nor being provok'd soon 4.05. 99
on provok'd, nor being provok'd soon calm'd; 4.05. 99
our wit will not so soon out as another man's COR 2.03. 27 P
ow soon confusion | may enter 'twixt the gap of 3.01.110
ad does achieve as soon | as draw his sword; 4.07. 23
llow, my lord, and i'll soon bring her back. TIT 1.01.289
ve it me, my sword shall soon dispatch it. 4.02. 86
hen soon i heard | the crying babe controll'd 5.01. 25
is will i do, and soon return again. 5.02.131
it all so soon as the all–cheering sun | should ROM 1.01.134
ad too soon marr'd are those so early made. 1.02. 13
ll soon the canker death eats up that plant. 2.03. 30
ad | so soon to bid good morrow to thy bed. 2.03. 34
ou didst love so dear, | so soon forsaken? 2.03. 67
arrant you, i dare draw as soon as another man, 2.04.159 P
ust climb a bird's nest soon when it is dark. 2.05. 74
it you shall bear the burthen soon at night. 2.05. 76
any in italy, and as soon mov'd to be moody, 3.01. 12 P
be moody, and as soon moody to be mov'd. 3.01. 13 P
ell, we'nsday is too soon, | a' thursday let it 3.04. 19
ram | that he shall soon keep tybalt company; 3.05. 91
on receipt thereof, | soon sleep in quiet. 3.05. 99
soon as dinner's done, we'll forth again, TIM 2.02. 14
soon we shall drive back | of alcibiades th' 5.01.163
ill start a spirit as soon as "caesar." JC 1.02.147
should avoid | so soon as that spare cassius. 1.02.201
error, soon conceiv'd, | thou never com'st 5.03. 69
their newest gloss, | not cast aside so soon. MAC 1.07. 35
t's make haste, she'll soon be back again. 3.05. 36
ay soon return to this our suffering country 3.06. 48
l have thee speak out the rest of this soon. HAM 2.02.522 P
er letter, | that she would soon be here. LR 2.04.184
on may i hear and see him! 4.04. 29
nd say if i shall see you soon at night. OTH 3.04.198
ut i'll see you soon. 3.04.200
ut soon that war had end, and the time's state ANT 1.02. 91
eep forth, but 'tis as soon | taken as seen; 1.04. 53
hich soon he granted, | being an abstract 3.06. 60
nder the service of a child as soon | as i' th' 3.13. 24
he soon shall know of us, by some of ours, 5.01. 57
soon as i can win th' offended king, | i will CYM 1.01. 75
ath in gallia | will soon be drawn to head, 3.05. 25
would have left it on the board so soon | as i 3.06. 50
ey went hence so soon as they were born. 5.04.126
ll too soon i shall, | unless thou wouldst 5.05.169
onfiscate all, so soon | as i have receiv'd it. 5.05.323
eft without a roof | soon fall to ruin — your PER 2.04. 37
hou canst not do a thing in the world so soon 4.01. 3
hat he can hither come so soon | is by your 5.02. 19
oon as they /move, as aspray do the fish, TNK 1.01.138
soon as the court hurry is over, we will have 2.01. 18 P
you deserve well, sir, i shall soon see't. 2.05. 42
e | a thing as soon to die as thee to say it, 3.06.159
soon was she along as he was down, | each VEN 43
nd gins to chide, but soon she stops his lips, 46
which the hot tyrant stains, and soon bereaves, 797
nd, if possess'd, as soon decay'd and done, LUC 23
which gives the watch–word to his hand full soon 370
mall lights are soon blown out, huge fires 647
ause craves haste, and it will soon be writ." 1295
win me soon to hell, my female evil PP 2. 5
urnt out love, as soon as straw out–burneth; 7.14
ose, fair flower, untimely pluck'd, soon vaded, 10. 1
ill'd too soon by death's sharp sting! 10. 4
were i with her, the night would post too soon, 14.25
mell — | a cripple soon can find a halt — 18.10
s soon as think the place where he would be. SON 44. 8
nd soon to you, as you to me then, tend'red 120.11
win me soon to hell, my female evil 144. 5

SOON–BELIEVING 1 FR 0.0001 REL FR 1 V 0 P
leath, | suggest his soon–believing adversaries, R2 1.01.101

SOONER 64 FR 0.0072 REL FR 35 V 29 P
f you turn not, you will return the sooner. TGV 2.02. 4
why didst not tell me sooner? 3.01.380 P
nd i came no sooner into the dining–chamber but 4.04. 8 P
nd the rheum | for ending thee no sooner. MM 3.01. 32
andled her privately, she would sooner confess; 5.01.276 P
it prove so, i will be gone the sooner. ERR 1.02.103
he plainer dealer, the sooner lost; 2.02. 88 P
e is sooner caught than the pestilence, and the ADO 1.01. 87 P
you will the sooner, that i were away, | for LLL 2.01.112
superfluity comes sooner by white hairs, but MV 1.02. 8 P
beauty provoketh thieves sooner than gold. AYL 1.03.110
your lips will feel them the sooner. 3.02. 60 P
and my sister no sooner met but they look'd; 5.02. 33 P
no sooner look'd but they lov'd; 5.02. 33 P
no sooner lov'd but they sigh'd; 5.02. 34 P
no sooner sigh'd but they ask'd one another the 5.02. 35 P
no sooner knew the reason but they sought the 5.02. 36 P
i think she'll sooner prove a soldier, | iron SHR 2.01.145
thy marriage, sooner than thy wickedness. AWW 1.03. 38 P
more longing, wavering, sooner lost and worn, TN 2.04. 34
i fear the wolf will sooner find than the master WT 3.03. 66 P
no sorrow | but kill'd itself much sooner. 5.03. 53
they shall have no sooner achiev'd but we'll set 1H4 1.02.173 P
such as will strike sooner than speak, and speak 2.01. 77 P
sooner than speak, and speak sooner than drink, 2.01. 78 P
sooner than drink, and drink sooner than pray; 2.01. 78 P
the more it is wasted, the sooner it wears. 2.04.402 P
i will sooner have a beard grow in the palm of 2H4 1.02. 20 P
the breath no sooner left his father's body, H5 1.01. 25
sooner than quittance of desert and merit, 2.02. 34
a motive | the sooner to effect what i intended. 2.02.157
word thou shalt no sooner bless mine ear withal, 5.02.238 P
and they should sooner persuade harry of england 5.02.278 P
and after meet you, sooner than you would. 1H6 3.04. 45
the sooner to effect | and surer bind this knot 5.01. 15
where reignier sooner will receive than give. 5.05. 47
to this gear, the sooner the better. 2H6 1.04. 14 P
and sooner dance upon a bloody pole | than stand 4.01.127
no sooner was i crept out of my cradle | but i 4.09. 3
his nose | will make this sting the sooner. H8 3.02. 56
i shall sooner rail thee into wit and holiness, TRO 2.01. 16 P
but i think thy horse will sooner con an oration 2.01. 17 P
and 'twere dark you'd close sooner. 3.02. 49 P
since things in motion sooner catch the eye 3.03.183
no sooner got but lost? 4.02. 74 P
one, thou shalt no sooner | march to assault thy COR 5.03.122
no sooner had they told this hellish tale, | but TIT 2.03.105
sooner this sword shall plough thy bowels up. 4.02. 87
come knock and enter, and no sooner in, | but ROM 1.04. 33
methinks he should the sooner pay his debts, TIM 3.04. 75
and th' hadst hated meddlers sooner, thou 4.03.309 P
thou mightst have sooner got another service; 4.03.504
no sooner justice had, with valor arm'd, MAC 1.02. 29
the which no sooner had his prowess confirm'd 5.09. 7
power of beauty will sooner transform honesty HAM 3.01.111 P
the sun no sooner shall the mountains touch, 4.01. 29
the sooner, sweet, for you. OTH 3.03. 56
the legion now in gallia sooner landed | in our CYM 2.04. 18
or adder, spider, | 'twould move me sooner. 4.02. 91
should not sooner | than thine own worth prefer 4.02.385
the sooner her vile thoughts to stead, PER 4.ch. 41
sure shall please the gods | sooner than such, TNK 5.04. 12
enjoy'd no sooner but despised straight, | past SON 129. 5
past reason hunted, and no sooner had, | past 129. 6

SOONEST 6 FR 0.0006 REL FR 5 V 1 P
devils soonest tempt, resembling spirits of LLL 4.03.253
the gentler gamester is the soonest winner. H5 3.06.113 P
and fearless minds climb soonest unto crowns. 3H6 4.07. 62
grace, we think, should soonest know his mind. R3 3.04. 9
a right fair mark, fair coz, is soonest hit. ROM 1.01.207
make your soonest haste; ANT 3.04. 27

SOON–SPEEDING 1 FR 0.0001 REL FR 1 V 0 P
such soon–speeding gear | as will disperse ROM 5.01. 60

SOOTH 43 FR 0.0048 REL FR 30 V 13 P
well drawn, monster, in good sooth! TMP 2.02.147 P
or, in sooth, i would master fenton had her. WIV 3.04.106 P
yes, in good sooth, the vice is of a great MM 3.02.101 P
sir, sooth to say, you did not dine at home. ERR 4.04. 69
good troth, you do me wrong (good sooth, you do) MND 2.02.129
3.02.265
yes, sooth; and so do you.
in sooth, i know not why i am so sad; MV 1.01. 1
they in themselves, good sooth, are too too 2.06. 42
but, in good sooth, are you he that hangs the AYL 3.02.391 P
sir, understand you this of me, in sooth: SHR 1.02.257
nay, hear you, kate. in sooth you scape not so. 2.01.240
good sooth, even thus; 3.02.116
he is my father, sir, and, sooth to say, | in 4.02. 99
was i, in sooth? AWW 5.02. 44 P
no, sooth, sir; TN 2.01. 11 P
in sooth, thou wast in very gracious fooling 2.03. 22 P
it is silly sooth, | and dallies with the 2.04. 46
sooth, but you must. 2.04. 88
very sooth, to–morrow. WT 1.02. 17
good sooth, she is | the queen of curds and 4.04.160
he looks like sooth. 4.04.171
sooth, when i was young, | and handed love as 4.04.347
in sooth, good friend, your father might have JN 1.01.123
in sooth he might; 1.01.125
in sooth, i would you were a little sick, | that 4.01. 29
no, in good sooth; 4.01.105
should take it off again | with words of sooth! R2 3.03.136
not mine, in good sooth. 1H4 3.01.246 P
not yours, in good sooth! 3.01.247 P
"not you, in good sooth," and "as true as i live 3.01.248 P
a good mouth–filling oath, and leave "in sooth," 3.01.254
for, to say the sooth, | though 'tis no wisdom H5 3.06.142
which, to say sooth, are blessings; H8 2.03. 30
yes, good sooth. to achilles, to ajax, to — TRO 2.01.109 P
rude, in sooth, in good sooth, very rude. 3.01. 56 P
rude, in sooth, in good sooth, very rude. 3.01. 56 P
sooth, madam, i hear nothing. JC 2.04. 20
if i say sooth, i must report they were | as MAC 1.02. 36
if thy speech be sooth, | i care not if thou 5.05. 39
sooth law, i'll help. thus it must be. ANT 4.04. 8
good sooth, i care not for you. PER 1.01. 86
when signior sooth here does proclaim peace, 1.02. 44
good sooth, it show'd well in you. 4.01. 88

SOOTH'D 1 FR 0.0001 REL FR 1 V 0 P
you sooth'd not, therefore hurt not; COR 2.02. 73

SOOTHE 4 FR 0.0004 REL FR 4 V 0 P
is't good to soothe him in these contraries? ERR 4.04. 79
and now, to soothe your forgery and his, | sends 3H6 3.03.175
and soothe the devil that i warn thee from? R3 1.03.297
good my lord, soothe him; LR 3.04.177

SOOTHERS 1 FR 0.0001 REL FR 1 V 0 P
i do defy | the tongues of soothers, but a 1H4 4.01. 7

SOOTHING 4 FR 0.0004 REL FR 4 V 0 P
cities be | made all of false–fac'd soothing! COR 1.09. 44
in soothing them we nourish 'gainst our senate 3.01. 69
call, | soothing the humor of fantastic wits? VEN 850
o, love's best habit's in a soothing tongue, PP 1.11

SOOTHSAY 1 FR 0.0001 REL FR 0 V 1 P
go, you wild bedfellow, you cannot soothsay. ANT 1.02. 51 P

SOOTHSAYER 4 FR 0.0004 REL FR 2 V 2 P
a soothsayer bids you beware the ides of march. JC 1.02. 19
where's the soothsayer that you prais'd so to ANT 1.02. 3 P
soothsayer! 1.02. 6 P
my lord of rome, | call forth your soothsayer. CYM 5.05.426

SOOTH'ST 1 FR 0.0001 REL FR 1 V 0 P
art perjur'd too, | and sooth'st up greatness. JN 3.01.121

SOOTY 1 FR 0.0001 REL FR 1 V 0 P
run from her guardage to the sooty bosom | of OTH 1.02. 70

SOP 3 FR 0.0003 REL FR 1 V 2 P
o excellent device! and make a sop of him. R3 1.04.157 P
and make a sop of all this solid globe; TRO 1.03.113
i'll make a sop o' th' moonshine of you, you LR 2.02. 32 P

SOPHISTER 1 FR 0.0001 REL FR 1 V 0 P
a subtle traitor needs no sophister. 2H6 5.01.191

SOPHISTICATED 1 FR 0.0001 REL FR 0 V 1 P
here's three on 's are sophisticated. LR 3.04.106 P

SOPHY 3 FR 0.0003 REL FR 1 V 2 P
that slew the sophy and a persian prince | that MV 2.01. 25
pension of thousands to be paid from the sophy. TN 2.05.181 P
they say he has been fencer to the sophy. 3.04.279 P

SOPS 2 FR 0.0002 REL FR 2 V 0 P
and threw the sops all in the sexton's face, SHR 3.02.173
and seem'd to ask him sops as he was drinking. 3.02.176

SORCERER 1 FR 0.0001 REL FR 1 V 0 P
a sorcerer, that by his cunning hath | cheated TMP 3.02. 43

SORCERERS 3 FR 0.0003 REL FR 3 V 0 P
dark–working sorcerers that change the mind, ERR 1.02. 99
wiles, | and lapland sorcerers inhabit here. 4.03. 11
subtile–witted french | conjurers and sorcerers, 1H6 1.01. 26

SORCERESS 3 FR 0.0003 REL FR 3 V 0 P
thou art, as you are all, a sorceress: ERR 4.03. 66
pucelle, that witch, that damned sorceress, 1H6 3.02. 38
bring forth that sorceress condemn'd to burn. 5.04. 1

SORCERIES 1 FR 0.0001 REL FR 1 V 0 P
for mischiefs manifold and sorceries terrible TMP 1.02.264

SORCERY 2 FR 0.0002 REL FR 2 V 0 P
i say by sorcery he got this isle; TMP 3.02. 52
deceit | contriv'd by art and baleful sorcery. 1H6 2.01. 15

SORE* 49 FR 0.0055 REL FR 40 V 9 P
you rub the sore, | when you should bring the TMP 2.01.139
and pile them up, | upon a sore injunction. 3.01. 11
i should have been a sore one then. 5.01.289 P
went in pain, master, this knave would go sore. ERR 3.01. 65
some say a sore, but not a sore, till now made LLL 4.02. 57
some say a sore, but not a sore, till now made 4.02. 57
not a sore, till now made sore with shooting. 4.02. 57
put l to sore, then sorel jumps from thicket, 4.02. 58
from thicket, | or pricket sore, or else sorel; 4.02. 59
if sore be sore, then l to sore makes fifty 4.02. 60
if sore be sore, then l to sore makes fifty 4.02. 60
sore, then l to sore makes fifty sores o' sorel: 4.02. 60
of one sore i an hundred make by adding but one 4.02. 61
while i live i'll fear no other thing | so sore, MV 5.01.307
my lord, your sorrow was too sore laid on, WT 5.03. 49
i am not glad that such a sore of time | should JN 5.02. 12
they say king john, sore sick, hath left the 5.04. 6
than when he bites, but lanceth not the sore. R2 1.03.303
we see the wind sit sore upon our sails, | and 2.01.265
lords, | i hear the king my father is sore sick. 2H4 4.03. 77
drops | are every one a woe, a sore complaint, H5 1.02. 26
soul | shall stand sore charged for the wasteful 1.02.283
mass, 'twill be sore law then, for he was thrust 2H6 4.07. 8 P
provide | a salve for any sore that may betide. 3H6 4.06. 88
awak'd you not in this sore agony? R3 1.04. 42
that it wounds, | but tickles still the sore. TRO 3.01.120
thou green sarcenet flap for a sore eye, thou 5.01. 32 P
or slain, and palamedes | sore hurt and bruised. 5.05. 14
and sore blows | for sinking under them. COR 2.01.252
for 'tis a sore upon us | you cannot tent 3.01.234
i am too sore enpierced with his shaft | to soar ROM 1.04. 19
the death of each day's life, sore labor's bath, MAC 2.02. 35
but this sore night | hath trifled former 2.04. 3
whose sore task | does not divide the sunday HAM 1.01. 75
while, and your water is a sore decayer of your 5.01.172 P
how i am punish'd | with a sore distraction. 5.02.230
the conflict be sore between that and my blood. LR 3.05. 22 P
my arm is sore, best play with mardian. ANT 2.05. 4
out, sword, and to a sore purpose! CYM 4.01. 23 P
sore shaming | those rich–left heirs that let 4.02.225
and the sore eyes see clear | to stop the air PER 1.01. 99
the sore terms we stand upon with the gods will 4.02. 34 P
'tis a sore life they have i' th' tother place, TNK 4.03. 31 P
they breed sore eyes and 'tis enough to infect STM II.C 10 P
sweet music, and heart's deep sore wounding. VEN 432
to one sore sick that hears the passing bell. 702
o unfelt sore, crest–wounding private scar! LUC 828
fool," quoth she, "his wounds will not be sore." 1568
in my thigh," quoth she, "here was the sore." PP 9.12

SOREL 3 FR 0.0003 REL FR 3 V 0 P
put l to sore, then sorel jumps from thicket, LLL 4.02. 58
from thicket, | or pricket sore, or else sorel; 4.02. 59
sore, then l to sore makes fifty sores o' sorel: 4.02. 60

SORELY 6 FR 0.0006 REL FR 4 V 2 P
this drum sticks sorely in your disposition. AWW 3.06. 44 P
but thou strik'st me | sorely, to say i did. WT 5.01. 18
as a man sorely tainted, to his answer, | he H8 4.02. 14
the heart is sorely charg'd. MAC 5.01. 53 P
on, and the /bleak winds | do sorely ruffle; LR 2.04.301
of which i do accuse myself so sorely | that i ANT 4.06. 18

SORER 1 FR 0.0001 REL FR 1 V 0 P
in fullness | is sorer than to lie for need; CYM 3.06. 13

SORES* 9 FR 0.0010 REL FR 8 V 1 P
for to strange sores strangely they strain the ADO 4.01.252
sore, then l to sore makes fifty sores o' sorel: LLL 4.02. 60
and all th' embossed sores and headed evils, AYL 2.07. 67
where the glutton's dogs lick'd his sores, and 1H4 4.02. 26 P
not nature | (to whom all sores lay siege) can TIM 4.03. 7
she, whom the spittle–house and ulcerous sores 4.03. 40
all kind of sores and shames on my bare head, OTH 4.02. 49

these poor slight sores | need not a plantin; TNK 1.02. 60
'gainst venom'd sores the only sovereign plaster VEN 916

SORREL *(see sorel)*

SORRIER 1 FR 0.0001 REL FR 1 V 0 P
i am the sorrier, would 'twere otherwise! 2H4 5.02. 32

SORRIEST 1 FR 0.0001 REL FR 1 V 0 P
of sorriest fancies your companions making, MAC 3.02. 9

/SORROW 11 FR 0.0012 REL FR 11 V 0 P
/give /sorrow /leave /a /while /to /tutor /me R2 4.01.166
/hath /sorrow /struck | /so /many /blows /upon 4.01.277
/how /soon /my /sorrow /hath /destroy'd /my 4.01.291
/the /shadow /of /your /sorrow /hath /destroy'd 4.01.292
/the /shadow /of /my /sorrow! 4.01.294
/has /sorrow /made /thee /dote /already? TIT 3.02. 23
/brew'd /with /her /sorrow, /mesh'd /upon /her 3.02. 38
/of /how /unnatural /and /bemadding /sorrow LR 3.01. 38
/patience /and /sorrow /strove | /who /should 4.03. 16
/sorrow /would /be /a /rarity /most /beloved, 4.03. 23
/a /period | /to /such /as /love /not /sorrow, 5.03.206

SORROW 215 FR 0.0243 REL FR 202 V 13 P
good sir, weigh | our sorrow with our comfort. TMP 2.01. 9
it seldom visits sorrow; 2.01.195
your heads — is nothing but heart's sorrow, 3.03. 81
over them, | brimful of sorrow and dismay; 5.01. 14
let grief and sorrow still embrace his heart 5.01.214
made them watchers of mine own heart's sorrow. TGV 2.04.135
and that's her cause of sorrow. 4.04.147
dead | if i in thought felt not her very sorrow. 4.04.172
if hearty sorrow | be a sufficient ransom for 5.04. 74
ford, your sorrow hath eaten up my sufferance. WIV 4.02. 1 P
which sorrow is always toward ourselves, not MM 2.03. 32
i am sorry that such sorrow i procure, | and so 5.01.474
i'll utter what my sorrow gives me leave. ERR 1.01. 35
alike | what to delight in, what to sorrow for. 1.01.106
me, sorrow abides and happiness takes his leave. ADO 1.01.102 P
stroke his beard, | and, sorrow wag, cry "hem!" 5.01. 16
to those that wring under the load of sorrow, 5.01. 28
again, and till then, sit thee down, sorrow! LLL 1.01.315 P
well, "set thee down, sorrow!" 4.03. 4 P
of sighs, of groans, of sorrow, and of teen! 4.03.162
let not the cloud of sorrow justle it | from 5.02.748
for debt that bankrout /sleep doth sorrow owe; MND 3.02. 85
where ever sorrow is, relief would be. AYL 3.05. 86
if you do sorrow at my grief in love, | by 3.05. 87
your sorrow and my grief | were both extermin'd. 3.05. 88
sorrow on thee and all the pack of you | that SHR 4.03. 33
measures my husband's sorrow by his woe: 5.02. 29
thought you affect a sorrow than to have — AWW 1.01. 53 P
i do affect a sorrow indeed, but i have it too. 1.01. 54 P
most bitter touch of sorrow that e'er i heard 1.03.117 P
i'll to the wars, she to her single sorrow. 2.03.296
would have tears, and sorrow bids me speak. 3.04. 42
if she be so abandon'd to her sorrow | as it is TN 1.04. 19
make their pastime at my sorrow: WT 2.03. 24
i never saw a vessel of like sorrow, | so fill'd 3.03. 21
and have perform'd | a saint-like sorrow. 5.01. 2
not say if th' importance were joy or sorrow; 5.02. 18 P
that it seem'd sorrow wept to take leave of them 5.02. 45 P
that 'twixt joy and sorrow was fought in paulina 5.02. 73 P
my lord, your sorrow was too sore laid on, 5.03. 49
no sorrow | but kill'd itself much sooner. 5.03. 52
o, if thou teach me to believe this sorrow, JN 3.01. 29
teach thou this sorrow how to make me die, | and 3.01. 30
lady, you utter madness, and not sorrow. 3.04. 43
for sorrow ends not when it seemeth done. R2 1.02. 61
to seek out sorrow that dwells every where. 1.02. 72
shorten my days thou canst with sullen sorrow, 1.03.227
for gnarling sorrow hath less power to bite 1.03.292
yet again methinks | some unborn sorrow, ripe in 2.02. 10
have woe to woe, sorrow to sorrow join'd. 2.02. 66
have woe to woe, sorrow to sorrow join'd. 2.02. 66
eyes | write sorrow on the bosom of the earth. 3.02.147
sorrow and grief of heart | makes him speak 3.03.184
of sorrow or of /joy? 3.04. 11
it doth remember me the more of sorrow; 3.04. 14
had, | it adds more sorrow to my want of joy; 3.04. 16
i may longest keep | thy sorrow in my breast. 3.04. 96
your hearts of sorrow, and your eyes of tears. 4.01.332
come, come, in wooing sorrow let's be brief, 5.01. 93
once more, adieu, the rest let sorrow say. 5.01.102
which with such gentle sorrow he shook off, 5.02. 31
reason taken from me all ostentation of sorrow. 2H4 2.02. 50 P
coz, since sudden sorrow | serves to say thus, 4.02. 83
with such a deep demeanor in great sorrow | that 4.05. 84
you borrow not that face | of seeming sorrow, it 5.02. 29
sorrow so royally in you appears | that i will 5.02. 51
mourn not, except thou sorrow for my good, 1H6 2.05.111
sorrow and grief have vanquish'd all my powers; 2H6 2.01.179
will bring thy head with sorrow to the ground! 2.03. 19
sorrow would solace, and mine age would ease. 2.03. 21
with sorrow snares relenting passengers; 3.01.227
what were it but to make my sorrow greater? 3.02.148
mischance and sorrow go along with you! 3.02.300
and seek for sorrow with thy spectacles? 5.01.165
and now in england to our heart's great sorrow, 3H6 1.01.128
and i with grief and sorrow to the court. 1.01.210
him, | to see how inly sorrow gripes his soul. 1.04.171
much is your sorrow; 2.05.112
o, but impatience waiteth on true sorrow. 3.03. 42
and see where comes the breeder of my sorrow! 3.03. 43
mine full of sorrow and heart's discontent. 3.03.173
then none but i shall turn his jest to sorrow. 3.03.261
doth cloud my joys with danger and with sorrow. 4.01. 74
what danger or what sorrow can befall thee | so 4.01. 76
this sorrow that i have, by right is yours, R3 1.03.171
when he shall split thy very heart with sorrow, 1.03.299
sorrow breaks seasons and reposing hours, 1.04. 76
i prithee peace, my soul is full of sorrow. 2.01. 97
it were lost sorrow to wail one that's lost. 2.02. 11
so much interest have /i in thy sorrow | as i 2.02. 47
drown desperate sorrow in dead edward's grave, 2.02. 99
and, when thou wed'st, let sorrow haunt thy bed; 4.01. 73
eighty odd years of sorrow have i seen, | and 4.01. 95
if ancient sorrow be most reverent, | give mine 4.04. 35
if sorrow can admit society, | /tell /over /your 4.04. 38
not | usurp the just proportion of my sorrow? 4.04.110
flatter my sorrow with report of it; 4.04.246
endur'd of her, for whom you bid like sorrow. 4.04.304
quoth she, "shall split thy heart with sorrow, 5.01. 26
a glist'ring grief | and wear a golden sorrow. H8 2.03. 22
nor to betray you any way to sorrow — | you 3.01. 56
with what a sorrow cromwell leaves his lord. 3.02.425
but that time offer'd sorrow, | this, general 4.01. 6
beaten corn, | and hang their heads with sorrow. 5.04. 32
but sorrow that is couch'd in seeming gladness TRO 1.01. 39
the sorrow that delivers us thus chang'd | makes COR 5.03. 39
them weep and shake with fear and sorrow, 5.03.100
my rage is gone, | and i am struck with sorrow. 5.06.147
sorrow concealed, like an oven stopp'd, | doth TIT 2.04. 36
i bring consuming sorrow to thine age. 3.01. 61
witness the sorrow that their sister makes. 3.01.119
is not my sorrow deep, having no bottom? 3.01.216
deal, | but sorrow flouted at is double death. 3.01.245
besides, this sorrow is an enemy, | and would 3.01.267
read that hecuba of troy | ran mad for sorrow. 4.01. 21
and so beguile thy sorrow, till the heavens 4.01. 35
that hath more scars of sorrow in his heart 4.01.126
th' effects of sorrow for his valiant sons, 4.04. 30
"let not your sorrow die, though i am dead." 5.01.140
witness all sorrow, that i know thee well | for 5.02. 25
and with thy shame thy father's sorrow die! 5.03. 47
parting is such sweet sorrow, | that i shall say ROM 2.02.184
that after-hours with sorrow chide us not! 2.06. 2
but come what sorrow can, | it cannot 2.06. 3
what sorrow craves acquaintance at my hand, 3.03. 5
bed, | which heavy sorrow makes them apt unto. 3.03.157
dry sorrow drinks our blood. 3.05. 59
that she do give her sorrow so much sway; 4.01. 10
the sun, for sorrow, will not show his head. 5.03.306
we are fellows still, | serving alike in sorrow. TIM 4.02. 19
thus part we rich in sorrow, parting poor. 4.02. 29
seeing those beads of sorrow stand in thine, JC 3.01.284
no man bears sorrow better. portia is dead. 4.03.147
seek to hide themselves | in drops of sorrow. MAC 1.04. 35
nor our strong sorrow | upon the foot of motion. 2.03.124
to show an unfelt sorrow is an office | which 2.03.136
where violent sorrow seems | a modern ecstasy. 4.03.169
give sorrow words. 4.03.209
pluck from the memory a rooted sorrow, | raze 5.03. 41
your cause of sorrow | must not be measur'd by 5.09. 10
he's worth more sorrow, | and that i'll spend 5.09. 16
nature | that we with wisest sorrow think on him HAM 1.02. 6
for some term | to do obsequious sorrow. 1.02. 92
a countenance more | in sorrow than in anger. 1.02.232
or are you like the painting of a sorrow, | a 4.07.108
whose phrase of sorrow | conjures the wand'ring 5.01.255
for me, with sorrow i embrace my fortune. 5.02.388
sudden joy did weep, | and i for sorrow sung, LR 1.04.176
/hysterica passio, down, thou climbing sorrow, 2.04. 57
bad is the trade that must play fool to sorrow, 4.01. 38
let sorrow split my heart, if ever i | did hate 5.03.178
but he bears both the sentence and the sorrow OTH 1.03.214
it /yet hath felt no age nor known no sorrow. 3.04. 37
so it is a deadly sorrow to behold a foul knave ANT 1.02. 72 P
live in an onion that should water this sorrow. 1.02.170 P
'tis one of those odd tricks which sorrow shoots 4.02. 14
thus i do escape the sorrow | of antony's death. 4.14. 94
our size of sorrow, | proportion'd to our cause, 4.15. 4
change now at my end | lament nor sorrow at; 4.15. 52
all | is outward sorrow, though i think the king CYM 1.01. 9
of issue, took such sorrow | that he quit being, 1.01. 37
for notes of sorrow out of tune are worse | than 4.02.241
i am sorrow for thee; 5.05.297
as from thence | sorrow were ever ras'd, and PER 1.01. 17
to show his sorrow, he'd correct himself; 1.03. 22
one sorrow never comes but brings an heir | that 1.04. 63
nor come we to add sorrow to your tears, | but 1.04. 90
and pericles, in sorrow all devour'd, | with 4.04. 25
know at large the cause | of your king's sorrow. 5.01. 63
so sorrow, wanting form, | is press'd with TNK 1.01.108
your sorrow beats so ardently upon me | that it 1.01.126
lady, | if ever thou hast felt what sorrow was, 2.02.276
go we hence, | right joyful, with some sorrow. 5.03.135
her kind of ill | gave me some sorrow. 5.04. 27
so of concealed sorrow may be said, | free vent VEN 333
sorrow to shepherds, woe unto the birds, | gusts 455
the night of sorrow now is turn'd to day: 481
she says, "this night i'll waste in sorrow, 583
i prophesy thy death, my living sorrow, | if 671
crystals, where they view'd each other's sorrow, 963
sorrow that friendly sighs sought still to dry; 964
so, | that every present sorrow seemeth chief, 970
sorrow on love hereafter shall attend; 1136
what following sorrow may on this arise. LUC 186
this blur to youth, this sorrow to the sage, 222
wrong, what shame, what sorrow i shall breed, 499
tears | that ever modest eyes with sorrow shed. 683
to mark how slow time goes | in time of sorrow, 991
the well-tun'd warble of her nightly sorrow, 1080
views, | and to herself all sorrow doth compare; 1102
true sorrow then is feelingly suffic'd | when 1112
and sorts a sad look to her lady's sorrow | (for 1221
her woe, | her certain sorrow writ uncertainly. 1311
'tis but a part of sorrow that we hear: 1328
and sorrow ebbs, being blown with wind of words. 1330
and shapes her sorrow to the beldame's woes, 1458
for sorrow, like a heavy hanging bell, | once 1493
to pencill'd pensiveness and color'd sorrow; 1497
thus ebbs and flows the current of her sorrow, 1569
times with sighs she gives her sorrow fire, 1604
thy sorrow to my sorrow lendeth | another power; 1676
thy sorrow to my sorrow lendeth | another power; 1676
and bids lucretius give his sorrow place, | and 1773
who, mad that sorrow should his use control, 1781
paler for sorrow than her milk-white dove, | for PP 9. 3
fare well i could not, for i supp'd with sorrow. 14. 6
sorrow chang'd to solace, and solace mix'd with 14.23
chang'd to solace, and solace mix'd with sorrow; 14.23
if thou sorrow, he will weep; 20.51
th' offender's sorrow lends but weak relief | to SON 34.11
do not, when my heart hath scap'd this sorrow, 90. 5
now, | and for that sorrow which i then did feel 120. 2
my deepest sense, how hard true sorrow hits, 120.10
lest sorrow lend me words, and words express 140. 3
old, | not age, but sorrow, over me hath power; LC 74

SORROW'D 1 FR 0.0001 REL FR 0 V 1 P
some swounded, all sorrow'd. WT 5.02. 91

SORROWED 1 FR 0.0001 REL FR 1 V 0
and send forth us to make their sorrowed render, TIM 5.01.149

SORROWEST 1 FR 0.0001 REL FR 1 V 0
and, for the sake of them thou sorrowest for, ERR 1.01.121

SORROWFUL 5 FR 0.0005 REL FR 5 V 0
can do no service on her sorrowful cheeks. TIT 3.01.147
a joyless, dismal, black, and sorrowful issue! 4.02. 66
go, go into old titus' sorrowful house, | and 5.03.142
these sorrowful drops upon thy blood/-stain'd 5.03.154
vials thou shouldst fill | with sorrowful water? ANT 1.03. 64

SORROWING 2 FR 0.0002 REL FR 2 V 0
do not | consume your blood with sorrowing; PER 4.01. 23
birds do sing, | careless of thy sorrowing. PP 20.26

SORROW'S 15 FR 0.0017 REL FR 15 V 0
so sorrow's heaviness doth heavier grow | for MND 3.02. 84
and sleep, that sometimes shuts up sorrow's eye, 3.02.435
fell sorrow's tooth doth never rankle more R2 1.03.302
that words seem'd buried in my sorrow's grave. 1.04. 15
for sorrow's eyes, glazed with blinding tears, 2.02. 16
or if it be, 'tis with false sorrow's eye, 2.02. 26
woe, | and bullingbrook my sorrow's dismal heir. 2.02. 63
and in that shame still live my sorrow's rage! R3 1.03.277
i am your sorrow's nurse, | and i will pamper it 2.02. 87
this sorrow's heavenly, | it strikes where it OTH 5.02. 21
(for why her face wore sorrow's livery), | but LUC 1222
time seems long in sorrow's sharp sustaining; 1573
held back his sorrow's tide, to make it more; 1789
"do not take away | my sorrow's interest, let no 1797
storming her world with sorrow's wind and rain. LC 7

SORROWS' 1 FR 0.0001 REL FR 1 V 0
my widow-comfort, and my sorrows' cure! JN 3.04.105

SORROWS 45 FR 0.0050 REL FR 43 V 2
a pack of sorrows which would press you down, TGV 3.01. 20
heart | as full of sorrows as the sea of sands, 4.03. 33
which of these sorrows is he subject to? ERR 5.01. 54
for, by this heaven, now at our sorrows pale, AYL 1.03.104
the tyranny of her sorrows takes all livelihood AWW 1.01. 50
come, and lead me | to these sorrows. WT 3.02.243
to whose feeling sorrows i might be some allay 4.02. 8
i will instruct my sorrows to be proud, | for JN 3.01. 68
here i and sorrows sit; 3.01. 73
this will break out | to all our sorrows, and 4.02.102
me | is tears and heavy sorrows of the blood, 2H4 4.05. 38
for the earth's increase, mine for my sorrows? 2H6 3.02.385
and give my tongue-tied sorrows leave to speak. 3H6 3.03. 22
my fear to hope, my sorrows unto joys, | at our 4.06. 4
and what these sorrows could not thence exhale, R3 1.02.165
so foolish sorrows bids your stones farewell. 4.01.103
our mistress' sorrows we were pitying. H8 2.03. 53
once | the burthen of my sorrows fall upon ye. 3.01.111
we are to cure such sorrows, not to sow 'em. 3.01.158
continual meditations, tears, and sorrows, | he 4.02. 28
by, | and you recount your sorrows to a stone. TIT 3.01. 29
therefore i tell my sorrows to the stones, | who 3.01. 37
heaven guide thy pen to print thy sorrows plain, 4.01. 75
shaken with sorrows in ungrateful rome. 4.03. 17
kinsmen, his sorrows are past remedy, | but /... 4.03. 31
if | his sorrows have so overwhelm'd his wits? 4.04. 10
ay, now begins our sorrows to approach. 4.04. 72
even when their sorrows almost was forgot, | and 5.01.137
and by her presence still renew his sorrows. 5.03. 42
could we but learn from whence his sorrows grow, ROM 1.01.154
griefs, these woes, these sorrows make me old. 3.02. 89
cry, new sorrows | strike heaven on the face, MAC 4.03. 5
when sorrows come, they come not single spies, HAM 4.05. 78
who, by the art of known and feeling sorrows, LR 4.06.222
and have ingenious feeling | of my huge sorrows! 4.06.281
it is a chance which does redeem all sorrows 5.03.267
that it engluts and swallows other sorrows, OTH 1.03. 57
that nor my service past, nor present sorrows, 3.04.116
sharp fate | to grace it with your sorrows. ANT 4.14.136
our tongues and sorrows to sound deep our woes PER 1.04. 13
speak out thy sorrows which /thou bring'st in 1.04. 58
old woes, not infant sorrows, bear them mild; LUC 1096
even so his sighs, his sorrows, make a saw, | to 1672
but day doth daily draw my sorrows longer, | and SON 28.13
all losses are restor'd, and sorrows end. 30.14

//SORROW-WREATHEN 1 FR 0.0001 REL FR 1 V 0
/marcus, /unknit /that //sorrow-wreathen /knot; TIT 3.02. 4

/SORRY 1 FR 0.0001 REL FR 1 V 0
/but /i /am /very /sorry, /good /horatio, HAM 5.02. 75

SORRY 97 FR 0.0109 REL FR 82 V 15
i am sorry i beat thee; TMP 3.02.111
i am sorry i must never trust thee more, | but TGV 5.04. 69
i am sorry that for my sake you have suffer'd WIV 3.05.123
who i would be sorry should be thus foolishly MM 1.02.190
i am sorry, one so learned and so wise | as you, 5.01.470
i am sorry that such sorrow i procure, | and so 5.01.474
i am sorry, sir, that i have hind'red you, | but ERR 5.01. 1
i am sorry now that i did draw on him. 5.01. 43
vale, | the place of /death and sorry execution, 5.01.121
i am sorry for her, as i have just cause, being ADO 2.03.165
well, i am sorry for your niece. 2.03.198
leonato, | i am sorry you must hear. 4.01. 88
lady, | i am sorry for thy much misgovernment. 4.01. 99
i am sorry for my cousin. 4.01.272
my heart is sorry for your daughter's death; 5.01.103
i am sorry, madam, for the news i bring | is LLL 5.02.718
i am sorry thou wilt leave my father so. MV 2.03. 1
i am sorry for thee. 4.01. 3
i am sorry that your leisure serves you not. 4.01.405
why, i am sorry for thee, gentle silvius. AYL 3.05. 85
sorry am i that our good will effects | bianca's SHR 1.01. 86
for the contents' sake are sorry for our pains. AWW 3.02. 63
i am heartily sorry that he'll be glad of this. 4.03. 63
i would be sorry, sir, but the fool should be as TN 3.01. 39
i am sorry, madam, i have hurt your kinsman, 5.01.209
i never wish'd to see you sorry, now | i trust i WT 2.01.123
i am sorry for't. 3.02.218
i am sorry that by hanging thee i can | but 4.04.421
i am but sorry, not afeard; 4.04.463
i am sorry, | most sorry, you have broken from 5.01.211
most sorry, you have broken from his liking, 5.01.212
and as sorry | your choice is not so rich in 5.01.213
i am sorry, sir, i have thus far stirr'd you; 5.03. 74

am sorry i should force you to believe | that 2H4 1.01.105
would be sorry, my lord, but it should be thus 4.03. 30 P
orry am i his numbers are so few, | his H5 3.05. 56
or i am sorry that with reverence | i did not 1H6 2.03. 71
sorry breakfast for my lord protector. 2H6 1.04. 75
orry i am to hear what i have heard. 2.01.189
am sorry for't. 4.02. 95 P
am so sorry for my trespass made | that, to 3H6 5.01. 92
orry i am my noble cousin should | suspect me R3 3.07. 88
am sorry | to hear this of him; H8 1.01.193
am sorry, | to see you ta'en from liberty, to 1.01.204
am sorry that the duke of buckingham | is run 1.02.109
am sorry for't. 2.01. 9
ad, or sorry | as i saw it inclin'd. 2.04. 26
am sorry my integrity should breed | (and 3.01. 51
nd am right sorry to repeat what follows. 5.01. 96
m very sorry | to sit here at this present, 5.02. 43
e is much sorry | if any thing more than your TRO 2.03.107
rt thou not sorry for these heinous deeds? TIT 5.01.123
faith, i am sorry that thou art not well. ROM 2.05. 53
canting goodness, sorry ere 'tis shown; TIM 1.02. 17
annot | do what they would, are sorry; 2.02.206
am sorry, when he sent to borrow of me, that 3.06. 15 P
am sorry i shall lose a stone by thee. 4.03.370
hat we are sorry for ourselves in thee. 5.01.139
y love, | i may do that i shall be sorry for. JC 4.03. 64
ou have done that you should be sorry for. 4.03. 65
is is a sorry sight. MAC 2.02. 18
foolish thought, to say a sorry sight. 2.02. 19
am sorry they offend you, heartily, | yes, HAM 1.05.134
am sorry — | what, have you given him any 2.01.103
am sorry that with better heed and judgment 2.01.108
am sorry then you have so lost a father | that LR 1.01.246
am sorry for thee, friend, 'tis the /duke's 2.02.152
art in my heart | that's sorry yet for thee. 3.02. 73
am only sorry | he had no other deathsman. 4.06.257
e are very sorry for't. OTH 1.03. 73
am sorry | for your displeasure; 3.01. 41
am very sorry that you are not well. 3.03.289
am sorry to hear this. 3.03.344
have a salt and sorry rheum offends me; 3.04. 51
am sorry that i am deceiv'd in him. 4.01.282
am sorry to find you thus; 5.01. 81
am not sorry neither, i'ld have thee live; 5.02.289
am full sorry | that he approves the common ANT 1.01. 59
am sorry to give breathing to my purpose — 1.03. 14
y part, i am sorry it is turn'd to a drinking. 2.06.103 P
d be thou sorry | to follow caesar in his 3.13.135
am much sorry, sir, | you put me to forget a CYM 2.03.104
am sorry, cymbeline, | that i am to pronounce 3.01. 61
d am right sorry that i must report ye | my 3.05. 3
am sorry for't; 4.02. 93
t enough i am sorry? 5.04. 11
rry that you have paid too much, and sorry 5.04.162 P
o much, and sorry that you are paid too much; 5.04.162 P
am sorry for't, my lord. 5.05.270
much sorry | i should be such a suitor; TNK 1.01.187
would be sorry else. | give me your hand. 3.05. 77
was as dearly sorry | as glad of arcite; 5.04.129
d am now as glad | as for him sorry. 5.04.131
r what we have are sorry, still | are children 5.04.133
r what's a sorry parsnip to a good heart? STM II.C 9 P
rich–built ilion, that the skies were sorry, LUC 1524
ake glad and sorry seasons as thou fleet'st, SON 19. 5

ORT* 2 FR 0.0002 REL FR 1 V 1 P
hey /can /see /a /sort /of /traitors /here. R2 4.01.246
/will /not /sort /you /with /the /rest /of HAM 2.02.267 P

ORT* 69 FR 0.0078 REL FR 51 V 18 P
nean, in a sort. TMP 2.01.104 P
at "sort" was well fish'd for. 2.01.105 P
u do look, my son, in a mov'd sort, | as if 4.01.146
sort some gentlemen well skill'd in music. TGV 3.02. 91
, he doth in some sort confess it. WIV 1.01.103 P
t i defy all angels (in any such sort, as they 2.02. 73 P
deed, it does stink in some sort, sir; MM 3.02. 28 P
tice to such men of sort and suit as are to 4.04. 17 P
t few of any sort, and none of name. ADO 1.01. 7 P
ere was none such in the army of any sort. 1.01. 33 P
d if it sort not well, you may conceal her, 4.01.240
ll speak their mind in some other sort. LLL 5.02.586 P
e shallowest thick–skin of that barren sort, MND 3.02. 13
e, | or russet–pated choughs, many in sort, 3.02. 21
ne of noble sort | would so offend a virgin 3.02.159
d so far am i glad it so did sort, | as this 3.02.352
t we are spirits of another sort. 3.02.388
ere are a sort of men whose visages | do cream MV 1.01. 88
ay be won by some other sort than your father's 1.02.104 P
bassanio so for me — | but god sort all! 5.01.132
, | to teach you gamouth in a briefer sort, SHR 3.01. 67
some sort, sir; WT 4.04.814 P
e better sort, | as thoughts of things divine, R2 5.05. 11
d in some sort it jumps with my humor as well 1H4 1.02. 69 P
ls upon thee in a more fairer sort; 2H4 4.05.200
at must strike sail to spirits of vile sort! 5.02. 18
did in some sort, indeed, handle women; H5 2.03. 37 P
sort our nobles from our common men. 4.07. 74
ay be his enemy is a gentleman of great sort, 4.07.136 P
at prisoners of good sort are taken, uncle? 4.08. 75
e mayor and all his brethren in best sort, 5.pr. 25
sort some other time to visit you. 1H6 2.03. 27
ok'd with ambition of the meaner sort; 2.05.123
k like the vulgar sort of market men | that 3.02. 4
then, that is not furnish'd in this sort, 4.01. 39
t how it will, i shall have gold for all. 2H6 1.02.107
ort of naughty persons, lewdly bent, | under 2.01.163
ay thee sort thy heart to patience, | these 2.04. 68
t from a sort of tinkers to the king. 3.02.277
e, | or any he the proudest of thy sort. 3H6 2.02. 97
y then, let's on our way in silent sort. 4.02. 28
charge the common sort | with pay and thanks, 5.05. 87
t, | but i will sort a pitchy day for thee; 5.06. 85
by the way, i'll sort occasion, | as index R3 2.02.148
if god sort it so, | 'tis more than we 2.03. 36
rt of vagabonds, rascals, and runaways, | a 5.03.316
draw | the sort to fight with hector; TRO 1.03.375
an alive can love in such a sort | the thing 4.01. 24
cle — yet, in a sort, lechery eats itself. 5.04. 35 P
astly sort, dragg'd through the shameful 5.10. 5

or express yourself in a more comfortable sort. COR 1.03. 2 P
and as wars, in some sort, may be said to be a 4.05.227 P
rais'd only that the weaker sort may wish | good 4.06. 70
with voices and applause of every sort, TIT 1.01.230
yet in some sort they are better than the 3.01. 39
but i'll deceive you in another sort, | and that 3.01.190
closet | to help me sort such needful ornaments ROM 4.02. 34
and in some sort these wants of mine are crown'd TIM 2.02.181
i have heard in some sort of thy miseries. 4.03. 77
fault | assemble all the poor men of your sort; JC 1.01. 57
and smiles in such a sort | as if he mock'd 1.02.205
but, as it were, in sort or limitation, | to 2.01.283
well may it sort that this portentous figure HAM 1.01.109
as it is common for the younger sort | to lack 2.01.113
of the people, especially of the younger sort? PER 4.02. 97 P
a man so noble | (if he say true) of his sort. TNK 2.05. 19
when wilt thou sort an hour great strifes to end LUC 899
but do not so, i love thee in such sort, | as SON 36.13
but do not so, i love thee in such sort, | as 96.13

SORTANCE 1 FR 0.0001 REL FR 1 V 0 P
as might hold sortance with his quality, | the 2H4 4.01. 11

SORTED 5 FR 0.0005 REL FR 3 V 2 P
my will is something sorted with his wish: TGV 1.03. 63
"sorted and consorted, contrary to thy LLL 1.01.258 P
and all my pains is sorted to no proof. SHR 4.03. 43
an excellent good word before it was ill sorted; 2H4 2.04.150 P
hath sorted out a sudden day of joy, | that thou ROM 3.05.109

SORTETH 1 FR 0.0001 REL FR 1 V 0 P
and sometime sorteth with a herd of deer: VEN 689

SORTING 1 FR 0.0001 REL FR 1 V 0 P
critical, | not sorting with a nuptial ceremony. MND 5.01. 55

SORTS 16 FR 0.0018 REL FR 12 V 4 P
night–dogs run, all sorts of deer are chas'd. WIV 5.05.238
well, i am glad that all things sorts so well. ADO 5.04. 7
noble device, of all sorts enchantingly belov'd, AYL 1.01.167 P
every night he comes | with musics of all sorts, AWW 3.07. 40
and speak to him in many sorts of music | that TN 1.02. 58
men of all sorts take a pride to gird at me. 2H4 1.02. 6 P
they have a king, and officers of sorts, | where H5 1.02.190
it sorts well with your fierceness. 4.01. 63 P
why then it sorts, brave warriors. let's away. 3H6 2.01.209
his currish riddles sorts not with this place. 5.05. 26
this woman's answer sorts, | for womanish it is TRO 1.01.106
to his love and tendance | all sorts of hearts; TIM 1.01. 58
golden opinions from all sorts of people, MAC 1.07. 33
larded with many several sorts of reasons, HAM 5.02. 20
come, other sorts offend as well as we. PER 4.02. 36 P
and sorts a sad look to her lady's sorrow | (for LUC 1221

SO'S 1 FR 0.0001 REL FR 1 V 0 P
my friends were poor, but honest, so's my love. AWW 1.03.195

SO–SEEMING 1 FR 0.0001 REL FR 0 V 1 P
of modesty from the so–seeming mistress page, WIV 3.02. 42 P

SOSSIUS 1 FR 0.0001 REL FR 1 V 0 P
sossius, | one of my place in syria, his ANT 3.01. 17

SOT 7 FR 0.0008 REL FR 3 V 4 P
for without them | he's but a sot, as i am; TMP 3.02. 93
have you make–a de sot of us, ha, ha? WIV 3.01.116 P
thou /drumble, thou snail, thou slug, thou sot! ERR 2.02.194
how now, sot? TN 1.05.121 P
sot, didst see dick surgeon, sot? 5.01.197 P
sot, didst see dick surgeon, sot? 5.01.197 P
when i inform'd him, then he call'd me sot, LR 4.02. 8

SOTO 1 FR 0.0001 REL FR 1 V 0 P
i think 'twas soto that your honor means. SHR in.1. 88

SOTS 1 FR 0.0001 REL FR 1 V 0 P
or his description | prov'd us unspeaking sots. CYM 5.05.178

SOTTED 1 FR 0.0001 REL FR 1 V 0 P
i am sotted, | utterly lost. TNK 4.02. 45

SOTTISH 1 FR 0.0001 REL FR 1 V 0 P
patience is sottish, and impatience does ANT 4.15. 79

SOUD 4 FR 0.0004 REL FR 4 V 0 P
soud, soud, soud, soud! SHR 4.01.142
soud, soud, soud, soud! 4.01.142
soud, soud, soud, soud! 4.01.142
soud, soud, soud, soud! 4.01.142

/SOUGHT 1 FR 0.0001 REL FR 1 V 0 P
/sought /to /be /king /o'er /her. LR 4.03. 15

SOUGHT 45 FR 0.0050 REL FR 41 V 4 P
i rather think | you have not sought her help, TMP 5.01.142
'tis not unknown to thee that i have sought | to TGV 3.01. 61
the sailors sought for safety by our boat, | and ERR 1.01. 76
lies, | how honorable ladies sought my love, MV 3.04. 70
knew the reason but they sought the remedy: AYL 5.02. 36 P
love sought is good, but given unsought is TN 3.01.156
if love ambitious sought a match of birth, JN 2.01.430
let us seek, or straight we shall be sought; 5.07. 79
a partial slander sought i to avoid, | and in R2 1.03.241
that sought at oxford thy dire overthrow. 5.06. 16
sought to entrap me by intelligence, | rated 1H4 4.03. 98
i have not sought the day of this dislike. 5.01. 26
you have not sought it, how comes it then? 5.01. 27
good wenches, how men of merit are sought after. 2H4 2.04.375 P
whose ruin you /have sought, that to her laws H5 2.02.176
have i sought every country far and near, | and, 1H6 5.04. 3
that sought to be encompass'd with your crown. 3H6 2.02. 3
but those that sought it i could wish more H8 2.01. 64
but to those men that sought him, sweet as 4.02. 54
i never sought their malice) | to quench mine 5.02. 15
us, yet sought | the very way to catch them. COR 3.01. 79
circling shadows kings have sought to sleep in, TIT 2.04. 19
which then most sought where most might not be ROM 1.01.127
for and call'd for, ask'd for and sought for, in 1.05. 13 P
have found him than he was when you sought him. 2.04.122 P
the most you sought was her promotion, | for 4.05. 71
look, lucius, here's the book i sought for so; JC 4.03.252
by many of these trains hath sought to win me MAC 4.03.118
that thou hast sought to make us break our /vow LR 1.01.168
he sought my life, | but lately, very late. 3.04.167
of us must pompey presently be sought, | or else ANT 2.02.158
i sought a husband, in which labor | i found PER 1.01. 66
i sought the purchase of a glorious beauty, 1.02. 72
who at fourteen years | he sought to murder, but 5.03. 9
she saw me, and straight sought the flood. TNK 4.01. 95
at great feasts | sought to betray a beauty, but 5.01.103
sorrow that friendly sighs sought still to dry; VEN 964
barr'd him from the blessed thing he sought. LUC 340
which i to conquer sought with all my might; 488
"o, that is gone for which i sought to live, 1051
whose waves to imitate the battle sought | with 1438
i sigh the lack of many a thing i sought, | and SON 30. 3
they sought their shame that so their shame did LC 187
for she was sought by spirits of richest coat, 236
against the thing he sought he would exclaim: 313

SOUGHT'ST 1 FR 0.0001 REL FR 1 V 0 P
dreaded act which thou | so sought'st to hinder. ANT 5.02.332

/SOUL 2 FR 0.0002 REL FR 2 V 0 P
/swells /with /silence /in /the /tortur'd /soul. R2 4.01.298
/us /from /his /soul /to /love /each /other, R3 1.04.237

SOUL 466 FR 0.0526 REL FR 422 V 44 P
art | so safely ordered that there is no soul — TMP 1.02. 29
not a soul | but felt a fever of the mad, and 1.02.208
it goes on, i see, | as my soul prompts it. 1.02.421
us, and the fair soul herself | weigh'd between 2.01.130
any | with so full soul but some defect in her 3.01. 44
hear my soul speak: 3.01. 63
much turmoil | a blessed soul doth in elysium. TGV 2.07. 38
marry | vain thurio, whom my very soul /abhors. 4.03. 17
whose life's as tender to me as my soul! 5.04. 37
think'st thou i'll endanger my soul gratis? WIV 2.02. 16 P
that the folly of my soul dares not present 2.02.244 P
by gar, he has save his soul, dat he is no come; 2.03. 6 P
/jeshu pless my soul! 3.01. 11 P
pless my soul! 3.01. 16 P
we have with special soul | elected him our MM 1.01. 17
qualify the laws | as to your soul seems good. 1.01. 66
he may be so fitted | that his soul sicken not. 2.04. 41
this, | i had rather give my body than my soul. 2.04. 56
i talk not of your soul; 2.04. 57
to do't, | i'll take it as a peril to my soul, 2.04. 65
pleas'd you to do't at peril of your soul, 2.04. 67
but grace, being the soul of your complexion, 3.01.183 P
that our soul | cannot but yield you forth to 5.01. 6
poor soul, | she speaks this in th' infirmity of 5.01. 46
thou art said to have a stubborn soul | that 5.01.480
her part, poor soul! ERR 1.01.107
my soul should sue as advocate for thee: 1.01.145
a wretched soul, bruis'd with adversity, | we 2.01. 34
husband, even my soul | doth for a wife abhor. 3.02.158
o that thou wert not, poor distressed soul! 4.04. 59
so befall my soul | as this is false he burthens 5.01.208
now is his soul ravish'd! ADO 2.03. 58 P
but they should suffer salvation, body and soul. 3.03. 3 P
an honest soul, i' faith, sir, by my troth he is 3.05. 38 P
will you with free and unconstrained soul | give 4.01. 24
not to knit my soul to an approved wanton. 4.01. 44
o, on my soul, my cousin is belied! 4.01.146
life, | into the eye and prospect of his soul, 4.01.229
as secretly and justly as your soul | should 4.01.248
think you in your soul the count claudio hath 4.01.328 P
yea, as sure as i have a thought or a soul. 4.01.330 P
my soul doth tell me hero is belied, | and that 5.01. 42
by my soul, nor i, | and yet, to satisfy this 5.01.275
no, by my soul, she was not, | nor knew not what 5.01.300
"that unlettered small–knowing soul" — LLL 1.01.251 P
by my sweet soul, i mean setting thee at liberty 3.01.123 P
but if thou strive, poor soul, what art thou 4.01. 92
by my soul, a swain, a most simple clown! 4.01.140
a soul feminine saluteth us. 4.02. 81 P
as horace says in his — what, my soul, verses? 4.02.102 P
all ignorant that soul that sees thee without 4.02.113
out of a new–sad soul, that you vouchsafe | in 5.02.731
mirth cannot move a soul in agony. 5.02.857
yoke | my soul consents not to give sovereignty. MND 1.01. 82
to nedar's daughter, helena, | and won her soul; 1.01.108
she shall pursue it with the soul of love. 2.01.182
pretty soul, she durst not lie | near this 2.02. 76
deny your love (so rich within his soul) | and 3.02.229
my love, my life, my soul, fair helena! 3.02.246
my soul is in the sky. 5.01.303
an evil soul producing holy witness | is like a MV 1.03. 99
me, is my boy, god rest his soul, alive or dead? 2.02. 72 P
true, | shall she be placed in my constant soul. 2.06. 57
you lie by portia's side | with an unquiet soul. 3.02.306
in purchasing the semblance of my soul, | from 3.04. 20
not on thy sole, but on thy soul, harsh jew, 4.01.123
even from the gallows did his fell soul fleet, 4.01.135
shall i lay perjury upon my soul? 4.01.229
by my soul i swear | there is no power in the 4.01.240
and sigh'd his soul toward the grecian tents, 5.01. 5
stealing her soul with many vows of faith, | and 5.01. 19
sweet soul, let's in, and there expect their 5.01. 49
no, by my honor, madam, by my soul, | no woman 5.01.209
and by my soul i swear | i never more will break 5.01.247
my soul upon the forfeit, that your lord | will 5.01.252
for my soul (yet i know not why) hates nothing AYL 1.01.165 P
my father lov'd sir rowland as his soul, | and 1.02.235
and swears, and rates, that she, poor soul, SHR 4.01.184
the soul of this man is his clothes. AWW 2.05. 43 P
with the divine forfeit of his soul upon oath, 3.06. 32 P
but, fair soul, | in your fine frame hath love 4.02. 3
to thee the book even of my secret soul. TN 1.04. 14
i think his soul is in hell, madonna. 1.05. 68 P
i know his soul is in heaven, fool. 1.05. 69 P
mourn for your brother's soul being in heaven. 1.05. 71 P
gate, | and call upon my soul within the house; 1.05.269
that nature pranks her in attracts my soul. 2.04. 86
a fiend like thee might bear my soul to hell. 3.04.217
beshrew his soul for me, | he started one poor 4.01. 58
that the soul of our grandam might happily 4.02. 52 P
i think nobly of the soul, and no way approve 4.02. 55 P
lest thou dispossess the soul of thy grandam. 4.02. 60 P
for though my soul disputes well with my sense, 4.03. 9
that my most jealious and too doubtful soul 4.03. 27
my soul the faithfull'st off'rings have breath'd 5.01.114
o, that record is lively in my soul! 5.01.246
and all those swearings keep as true in soul 5.01.270
a gracious innocent soul, | more free than he is WT 2.03. 29
alack, poor soul, thou hast need of more rags to 4.03. 54 P
alas, poor soul! 4.03. 71 P
good comfort as it is | now piercing to my soul. 5.03. 34
when i was got, i'll send his soul to hell. JN 1.01.272
by my soul, i think | his father never was so 2.01.129
and, by disjoining hands, hell lose a soul. 3.01.197
there is a soul counts thee her creditor, | and 3.03. 21
a grave unto a soul, | holding th' eternal 3.04. 17

i'll make a peace between your soul and you. 4.02.250
heaven take my soul, and england keep my bones! 4.03. 10
from whose obedience i forbid my soul, 4.03. 64
upon my soul — 4.03.125
swearing allegiance and the love of soul | to 5.01. 10
so, on my soul, he did, for aught he knew. 5.01. 43
o, it grieves my soul, | that i must draw this 5.02. 15
this show'r, blown up by tempest of the soul, 5.02. 50
no, no, on my soul, it never shall be said. 5.02.108
in peace, and part this body and my soul | with 5.04. 47
and beshrew my soul | but i do love the favor 5.04. 49
sings | his soul and body to their lasting rest. 5.07. 24
ay, marry, now my soul hath elbow–room; 5.07. 28
and then my soul shall wait on thee to heaven, 5.07. 72
i have a kind soul that would give thanks, | and 5.07.108
earth, | or my divine soul answer it in heaven. R2 1.01. 38
out his innocent soul through streams of blood, 1.01.103
the unstooping firmness of my upright soul. 1.01.121
a trespass that doth vex my grieved soul; 1.01.138
pierc'd to the soul with slander's venom'd spear 1.01.171
o, god defend my soul from such deep sin! 1.01.187
more than my dancing soul doth celebrate | this 1.03. 91
along | the clogging burthen of a guilty soul. 1.03.200
look what thy soul holds dear, imagine it | to 1.03.286
my brother gloucester, plain well–meaning soul, 2.01.128
me, and my inward soul | with nothing trembles; 2.02. 11
but yet my inward soul | persuades me it is 2.02. 28
now hath my soul brought forth her prodigy, 2.02. 64
as in a soul rememb'ring my good friends, | and, 2.03. 47
now, by my soul, i would it were this hour. 4.01. 42
and his pure soul unto his captain christ, 4.01. 99
sweet peace conduct his sweet soul to the bosom 4.01.103
who with willing soul | adopts /thee heir, and 4.01.108
learn, good soul, | to think our former state a 5.01. 17
we pray with heart and soul, and all beside; 5.03.104
my brain i'll prove the female to my soul, | my 5.05. 6
my soul the father, and these two beget | a 5.05. 7
mount, mount, my soul! 5.05.111
i protest my soul is full of woe | that blood 5.06. 45
and thee about thy soul that thou soldest him on 1H4 1.02.115 P
which the proud soul ne'er pays but to the proud 1.03. 9
who, on my soul, hath willfully betray'd | the 1.03. 81
and let my soul | want mercy if i do not join 1.03.131
no, if a scot would save his soul, he shall not! 1.03.215
and the soul of every man | prophetically do 3.02. 37
now, by my sceptre and my soul to boot, | he 3.02. 97
and dear a trust | on any soul remov'd, but on 4.01. 35
we read | the very bottom and the soul of hope, 4.01. 50
my cousin vernon, welcome, by my soul! 4.01. 86
in both your armies there is many a soul | shall 5.01. 83
no, by my soul, i never in my life | did hear a 5.02. 51
/a fool go with thy soul, whither it goes! 5.03. 22
john, | but now i do respect thee as my soul. 5.04. 20
my lord, this is a poor /mad soul, and she says 2H4 2.01.104 P
since | this percy was the man nearest my soul, 3.01. 61
upon my soul, my lord, | the powers that you 3.01. 99
with speed redress'd, | upon my soul they shall. 4.02. 60
led by th' impartial conduct of my soul; 5.02. 36
or nicely charge your understanding soul | with H5 1.02. 15
and his soul | shall stand sore charged for the 1.02.282
that knew'st the very bottom of my soul, | that 2.02. 97
win | a soul so easy as that englishman's." 2.02.125
and 'a said it was a black soul burning in hell? 2.03. 41 P
by my hand i swear, and my father's soul, the 3.02. 90 P
and a man that i love and honor with my soul, 3.06. 8 P
proud of their numbers and secure in soul, | the 4.pr. 17
there is some soul of goodness in things evil, 4.01. 4
the king's, but every subject's soul is his own. 4.01.177 P
what is thy soul of /adoration? 4.01.245
solemn priests | sing still for richard's soul. 4.01.302
honor, | i am the most offending soul alive. 4.03. 29
my soul shall thine keep company to heaven; 4.06. 16
tarry, sweet soul, for mine, then fly abreast, 4.06. 17
a far more glorious star thy soul will make 1H6 1.01. 55
straightway give thy soul to him thou serv'st. 1.05. 7
now have i paid my vow unto his soul; 2.02. 7
and, by my soul, this pale and angry rose, | as 2.04.107
my soul shall then be satisfied. 2.05. 21
and peace, no war, befall thy parting soul! 2.05.115
o, how this discord doth afflict my soul! 3.01.106
now, quiet soul, depart when heaven please, 3.02.110
upon no christian soul but english talbot. 4.02. 30
bell, | sings heavy music to thy timorous soul, 4.02. 40
then god take mercy on brave talbot's soul, 4.03. 34
and soul with soul from france to heaven fly. 4.05. 55
and soul with soul from france to heaven fly. 4.05. 55
then take my soul — my body, soul, and all, 5.03. 22
then take my soul — my body, soul, and all, 5.03. 22
face | a world of earthly blessings to my soul, 2H6 1.01. 22
but god in mercy so deal with my soul | as i in 1.03.157
poor soul, god's goodness hath been great to 2.01. 82
my thoughts that labor to persuade my soul 3.02.137
for with his soul fled all my worldly solace; 3.02.151
as surely as my soul intends to live | with that 3.02.153
give thee thy hire and send thy soul to hell, 3.02.225
as to him | the secrets of his overcharged soul; 3.02.376
here could i breathe my soul into the air, | as 3.02.391
so shouldst thou either turn my flying soul, 3.02.397
like lime–twigs set to catch my winged soul. 3.03. 16
that lays strong siege unto this wretch's soul, 3.03. 22
peace to his soul, if god's good pleasure be! 3.03. 26
because the unconquer'd soul of cade is fled. 4.10. 65 P
so wish i, i might thrust thy soul to hell. 4.10. 79
a sceptre shall it have, have i a soul, | on 5.01. 10
it grieves my soul to leave thee unassail'd. 5.02. 18
my soul and body on the action both! 5.02. 26
peace with his soul, heaven, if it be thy will! 5.02. 30
and, by his soul, thou and thy house shall rue 3H6 1.01. 94
house of york | is as a fury to torment my soul; 1.03. 31
upon my soul, the hearers will shed tears; 1.04.161
my soul to heaven, my blood upon your heads! 1.04.168
him, | to see how inly sorrow gripes his soul. 1.04.171
my soul flies through these wounds to seek out 1.04.178
to see this sight, it irks my very soul. 2.02. 6
and in this vow do chain my soul to thine! 2.03. 34
ope | and give sweet passage to my sinful soul! 2.03. 41
more than my body's parting with my soul. 2.06. 4
whose soul is that which takes her heavy leave? 2.06. 42

i know by that he's dead, and, by my soul, | if 2.06. 79
o margaret, thus 'twill be, and thou, poor soul, 3.01. 53
i speak no more than what my soul intends, | and 3.02. 94
and with thy lips keep in my soul a while. 5.02. 35
sweet rest his soul! 5.02. 48
now am i seated as my soul delights, | having my 5.07. 35
thoughts, down to my soul — here clarence comes R3 1.01. 41
that i will shortly send thy soul to heaven, 1.01.119
his mortal body, | his soul thou canst not have. 1.02. 48
and let the soul forth that adoreth thee, | i 1.02.176
from bitterness of soul | denounc'd against thee 1.03.178
the worm of conscience still begnaw thy soul! 1.03.221
still the envious flood | stopp'd in my soul, 1.04. 38
o, then began the tempest to my soul! 1.04. 44
the first that there did greet my stranger soul 1.04. 48
(that now give evidence against my soul) | for 1.04. 67
my soul is heavy, and i fain would sleep. 1.04. 74
and more /in peace my soul shall part to heaven, 2.01. 5
by heaven, my soul is purg'd from grudging hate, 2.01. 9
alive | with whom my soul is any jot at odds 2.01. 71
i prithee peace, my soul is full of sorrow. 2.01. 97
who told me how the poor soul did forsake | the 2.01.110
speak unto myself | for him, poor soul. 2.01.129
i'll join with black despair against my soul, 2.02. 36
to shun the danger that his soul divines. 3.02. 18
wherein my soul recorded | the history of all 3.05. 27
but praying, to enrich his watchful soul. 3.07. 77
albeit against my conscience and my soul. 3.07.226
go, go, poor soul, i envy not thy glory, | to 4.01. 63
no more than with my soul i mourn for yours. 4.01. 88
adieu, poor soul, that tak'st thy leave of it! 4.01. 90
so in the lethe of thy angry soul | thou drown 4.04.251
then know that from my soul i love thy daughter. 4.04.256
my daughter's mother thinks it with her soul. 4.04.257
that thou dost love my daughter from thy soul; 4.04.259
i mean that with my soul i love thy daughter, 4.04.263
that with a fearful soul | leads discontented 4.04.311
herself, the land, and many a christian soul, 4.04.408
this, this all–souls' day to my fearful soul, 5.01. 18
to thee i do commend my watchful soul | ere i 5.03.115
let me sit heavy on thy soul to–morrow! 5.03.118
let me sit heavy in thy soul to–morrow, | i that 5.03.131
let me sit heavy in thy soul to–morrow, | rivers 5.03.139
think upon grey, and let thy soul despair! 5.03.141
quiet untroubled soul, awake, awake! 5.03.157
thou quiet soul, sleep thou a quiet sleep, 5.03.164
loves me, | and if i die no soul will pity me. 5.03.201
have strook more terror to the soul of richard 5.03.217
my soul is very jocund | in the remembrance of 5.03.232
there is no english soul | more stronger to H8 1.01.146
a noble person | and spoil your nobler soul; 1.02.175
on my soul, i'll speak but truth. 1.02.177
sweet sacrifice, | and lift my soul to heaven. 2.01. 78
and, till my soul forsake, | shall cry for 2.01. 89
he dives into the king's soul, and there 2.02. 26
panging | as soul and body's severing. 2.03. 16
yea, from my soul | refuse you for my judge, 2.04. 81
lute, wench, my soul grows sad with troubles. 3.01. 1
could speak this with as free a soul as i do! 3.01. 32
upon my soul, two reverend cardinal virtues; 3.01.103
noble temper, | a soul as even as a calm; 3.01.166
duty to you | and throw it from their soul, 3.02.194
by my soul, | your long coat, priest, protects 3.02.275
methinks | (out of a fortitude of soul i feel), 3.02.388
sir, as i have a soul, she is an angel; 4.01. 44
for virtue and true beauty of the soul, | for 4.02.144
and a soul | none better in my kingdom. 5.01.154
and fair virtue | than this pure soul shall be. 5.04. 25
won are done, joy's soul lies in the doing. TRO 1.02.287
soul and only sprite | in whom the tempers and 1.03. 56
if none of them have soul in such a kind, | we 1.03.285
every tithe soul, 'mongst many thousand dismes, 2.02. 19
heart–blood of beauty, love's invisible soul. 3.01. 33 P
like to a strange soul upon the stygian banks 3.02. 9
my weakness draws | my very soul of counsel! 3.02.133
durst never meddle) in the soul of state, 3.03.202
true, | even in soul of sound good–fellowship — 4.01. 53
no soul so near me | as the sweet troilus. 4.02. 98
entreat her fair, and, by my soul, fair greek, 4.04.113
and with private soul | did in great ilion thus 4.05.111
to make a recordation to my soul | of every 5.02.116
if beauty have a soul, this is not she; 5.02.138
within my soul there doth conduce a fight | of 5.02.147
man fancy | with so eternal and so fix'd a soul. 5.02.166
of no more soul nor fitness for the world | than COR 2.01.250
and my soul aches | to know, when two 3.01.108
renowmed titus, more than half my soul — TIT 1.01.373
dear father, soul and substance of us all — 1.01.374
hark, tamora, the empress of my soul, | which 2.03. 40
for, by my soul, were there worse end than death 2.03.302
but that which gives my soul the greatest spurn 3.01.101
spurn | is dear lavinia, dearer than my soul. 3.01.102
aaron will have his soul black like his face. 3.01.205
and swear unto my soul to right your wrongs. 3.01.278
a sight to vex the father's soul withal. 5.01. 52
'twill vex thy soul to hear what i shall speak: 5.01. 62
life i did, | i do repent it from my very soul. 5.03.190
and then my husband — god be with his soul! ROM 1.03. 39
i have a soul of lead | so stakes me to the 1.04. 15
god shall mend my soul, | you'll make a mutiny 1.05. 79
so thrive my soul — 2.02.153
it is my soul that calls upon my name. 2.02.164
but she, good soul, had as lieve see a toad, a 2.04.202 P
for mercutio's soul | is but a little way above 3.01.126
how is't, my soul? 3.05. 25
o god, i have an ill–divining soul! 3.05. 54
for, by my soul, i'll ne'er acknowledge thee, 3.05.193
and from my soul too, else beshrew them both. 3.05.227
poor soul, thy face is much abus'd with tears. 4.01. 29
my soul, and not my child! 4.05. 62
when my betossed soul | did not attend him as we 5.03. 76
o, he's the very soul of bounty! TIM 1.02.209
upon my soul, 'tis true, sir. 3.02. 43
why, this is the world's soul, and just of the 3.02. 64
for, take't of my soul, my lord leans wondrously 3.04. 70 P
you only speak from your distracted soul; 3.04.113
lies a wretched corse, of wretched soul bereft; 5.04. 70

where i stood, cried, "alas, good soul!" JC 1.02.272
soul of rome! 2.01.321
poor soul, his eyes are red as fire with weeping 3.02.115
might | to half a soul and to a notion craz'd MAC 3.01. 82
hath from my soul | wip'd the black scruples, 4.03.115
death of thy soul! 5.03. 16
my soul is too much charg'd | with blood of 5.08. 5
till then sit still, my soul. HAM 1.02.256
the inward service of the mind and soul | grows 1.03. 13
grapple them unto thy soul with hoops of steel, 1.03. 63
how prodigal the soul | lends the tongue vows. 1.03.116
and for my soul, what can it do to that, | being 1.04. 66
whose lightest word | would harrow up thy soul, 1.05. 16
o my prophetic soul! | my uncle? 1.05. 40
nor let thy soul contrive | against thy mother 1.05. 85
good liege | i hold my duty as i hold my soul, 2.02. 44
therefore, /since brevity is the soul of wit, 2.02. 90
could force his soul so to his own conceit 2.02.553
of the scene | been strook so to the soul, that 2.02.591
there's something in his soul | o'er which his 3.01.164
it offends me to the soul to hear a robustious 3.02. 8
since my dear soul was mistress of her choice 3.02. 63
even with the very comment of thy soul | observe 3.02. 79
ever | the soul of nero enter this firm bosom, 3.02.394
my tongue and soul in this be hypocrites — 3.02.397
to give them seals never my soul consent! 3.02.399
o limed soul, that, struggling to be free, | art 3.03. 68
to take him in the purging of his soul, | when 3.03. 85
and that his soul may be as damn'd and black 3.03. 94
the body of contraction plucks | the very soul, 3.04. 47
thou turn'st my /eyes into my /very soul, | and 3.04. 89
o, step between her and her fighting soul, 3.04.113
lay not that flattering unction to your soul, 3.04.145
my soul is full of discord and dismay. 4.01. 45
to my sick soul, as sin's true nature is, | each 4.05. 17
we cast away moan, | god 'a' mercy on his soul!" 4.05.199
and we shall jointly labor with your soul | to 4.05.212
she is so /conjunctive to my life and soul, 4.07. 14
a woman, sir, but, rest her soul, she's dead. 5.01.136
the devil take thy soul! 5.01.259
i take him to be a soul of great article, and 5.02.116
and bring some covering for this naked soul, LR 4.01. 44
thou art a soul in bliss, but i am bound | upon 4.07. 45
friends of my soul, you twain | rule in this 5.03.320
these fellows have some soul, | and such a one OTH 1.01. 54
heart is burst, you have lost half your soul; 1.01. 87
in simple and pure soul i come to you. 1.01.107
and my perfect soul | shall manifest me rightly. 1.02. 31
such fair question | as soul to soul affordeth? 1.03.114
such fair question | as soul to soul affordeth? 1.03.114
i am glad at soul i have no other child, | for 1.03.196
parts | did i my soul and fortunes consecrate. 1.03.254
i fear | my soul hath her content so absolute 2.01.191
and let thy soul be instructed. 2.01.221
and nothing can or shall content my soul | till 2.01.298
carve for his own rage | holds his soul light; 2.03.174
sin, | his soul is so enfetter'd to her love, 2.03.345
i wonder in my soul | what you would ask me that 3.03. 68
perdition catch my soul, | but i do love thee! 3.03. 90
when i shall turn the business of my soul | to 3.03.181
proof, | or, by the worth of mine eternal soul, 3.03.361
have you a soul? 3.03.374
there are a kind of men, so loose of soul, 3.03.416
i am) | arraigning his unkindness with my soul; 3.04.152
lay down my soul at stake. 4.02. 13
i should have found in some place of my soul | a 4.02. 52
"the poor soul sat /sighing by a sycamore tree, 4.03. 40
it is the cause, it is the cause, my soul. 5.02. 1
i would not kill thy soul. 5.02. 32
no, by my life and soul! 5.02. 49
sweet soul, take heed, | take heed of perjury, 5.02. 50
may his pernicious soul | rot half a grain a day 5.02.155
upon my soul, a lie, a wicked lie. 5.02.181
so come my soul to bliss, as i speak true; 5.02.250
look of thine will hurl my soul from heaven, 5.02.274
why he hath thus ensnar'd my soul and body? 5.02.302
o this false soul of egypt! ANT 4.12. 25
the soul and body rive not more in parting 4.13. 5
could best express how slow his soul sail'd on, CYM 1.03. 13
would force the feeler's soul | to th' oath of 1.06.101
o dearest soul! 1.06.118
no single soul | can we set eye on; 4.02.130
hang there like fruit, my soul, | till the tree 5.05.263
with a soul | embold'ned with the glory of her PER 1.01. 3
so bad | as with foul incest to abuse your soul; 1.01.126
makes both my body pine and soul to languish, 1.02. 32
get, he may lawfully deal for his wive's soul. 2.01.115
i love her with my soul; TNK 2.02.176
not i | part of /your blood, part of your soul? 2.02.185
and, as i have a soul, i'll nail thy life to't! 2.02.213
upon my soul, a proper man! 2.05. 16
i wish his weary soul that falls may win it. 3.06.100
seeing | and first bequeathing of the soul to) 3.06.148
as thou art valiant, for thy cousin's soul, 3.06.175
that i may tell my soul he shall not have her. 3.06.179
to crown all this, by your most noble soul, 3.06.208
pretty soul! 4.01. 69
a little man, but of a tough soul, seeming | as 4.02.117
and nimble set, | which shows an active soul; 4.02.126
now, as i have a soul, i long to see 'em. 4.02.142
what stuff's here? poor soul! 4.03. 17
pretty soul, | how do ye? 5.02. 69
thy brave soul seek elysium! 5.04. 95
so o'er this sleeping soul doth tarquin stay, LUC 423
"i have debated, even in my soul, | what wrong, 498
or free that soul which wretchedness hath 90
"my body or my soul, which was the dearer, 116
so must my soul, her bark being pill'd away. 116
through which i may convey this troubled soul. 117
my soul and body to the skies and ground, | my 119
harmful knife, that thence her soul unsheathed; 172
the deep vexation of his inward soul | hath 177
and by chaste lucrece' soul that late complained 183
all ignorant that soul that sees thee without PP 5.
eye, | and all my soul, and all my every part; SON 62.
nor the prophetic soul | of the wide world, 107.
might i from myself depart | as from my soul, 109.
a true soul | when most impeach'd stands least 125.

if thy soul check thee that i come so near, 136. 1
swear to thy blind soul that i was thy will, 136. 2
and will, thy soul knows, is admitted there; 136. 3
poor soul, the centre of my sinful earth, | /... 146. 1
then, soul, live thou upon thy servant's loss, 146. 9
my soul doth tell my body that he may | triumph 151. 7
and credent soul to that strong-bonded oath LC 279
SOUL-CONFIRMING 1 FR 0.0001 REL FR 1 V 0 P
with twenty thousand soul-confirming oaths. TGV 2.06. 16
SOUL-CURER 1 FR 0.0001 REL FR 0 V 1 P
french and welsh, soul-curer and body-curer! WIV 3.01. 98 P
SOULD *(also should)*
SOULD 1 FR 0.0001 REL FR 0 V 1 P
is it possible dat i sould love de enemy of H5 5.02.169 P
SOUL-FEARING 1 FR 0.0001 REL FR 1 V 0 P
till their soul-fearing clamors have brawl'd JN 2.01.383
SOUL-KILLING 1 FR 0.0001 REL FR 1 V 0 P
soul-killing witches that deform the body, ERR 1.02.100
SOULLESS 1 FR 0.0001 REL FR 1 V 0 P
slave, soulless villain, dog! ANT 5.02.157
/SOUL'S 1 FR 0.0001 REL FR 1 V 0 P
/for /i /have /given /here /my /soul's /consent R2 4.01.249
SOUL'S 22 FR 0.0024 REL FR 20 V 2 P
know'st thou not his looks are my soul's food? TGV 2.07. 15
and fit his mind to death, for his soul's rest. MM 2.04.187
against my soul's pure truth, why labor you, ERR 3.02. 37
dominator of navarre, my soul's earth's god, and LLL 1.01.220 P
a virgin and extort | a poor soul's patience, MND 3.02.161
on thy soul's peril and thy body's torture, WT 2.03.181
some suppose the soul's frail dwelling-house) JN 5.07. 3
omitting suffolk's exile, my soul's treasure? 2H6 3.02.382
now my soul's palace is become a prison; 3H6 2.01. 74
which held thee dearly as his soul's redemption, 2.01.102
and yet, between my soul's desire and me — 3.02.128
and prov'd the subject of mine own soul's curse, R3 4.01. 80
so from thy soul's love didst thou love her 4.04.260
there is the man of my soul's hate, aufidius, COR 1.05. 10
heart's deep languor, and my soul's sad tears: TIT 3.01. 13
banquo, thy soul's flight, | if it find heaven, MAC 3.01.140
"to the celestial and my soul's idol, the most HAM 2.02.109 P
o my soul's joy! OTH 2.01.184
besides, his soul's fair temple is defaced, | to LUC 719
it, | but with my body my poor soul's pollution? 1157
good conceit of thine | in thy soul's thought SON 26. 8
save that my soul's imaginary sight | presents 27. 9
/SOULS 3 FR 0.0003 REL FR 3 V 0 P
/the /souls /of /men | /may /deem /that /you R2 4.01.226
/action /of /their /bodies /from /their /souls, 2H4 1.01.195
/but, /for /their /spirits /and /souls, | /this 1.01.198
SOULS 119 FR 0.0134 REL FR 104 V 15 P
poor souls, they perish'd. TMP 1.02. 9
swallow'd and | the fraughting souls within her. 1.02. 13
he is a curer of souls, and you a curer of WIV 2.03. 39 P
why, all the souls that were were forfeit once, MM 2.02. 73
ere sun-rise, prayers from preserved souls, 2.02.153
wrench awe from fools and tie the wiser souls 2.04. 14
but o, poor souls, | come you to seek the lamb 5.01.297
ndu'd with intellectual sense and souls, | of ERR 2.01. 22
before the judgment carries poor souls to hell. 4.02. 40
god help, poor souls, how idlely do they talk! 4.04.129
guts should hale souls out of men's bodies? ADO 2.03. 59 P
charge you on your souls to utter it. 4.01. 14 P
by that which knitteth souls and prospers loves, MND 1.01.172
do, | but you must join in souls to mock me too? 3.02.150
and through wall's chink, poor souls, they are 5.01.133
whose souls do bear an egall yoke of love, MV 3.04. 13
that souls of animals infuse themselves | into 4.01.132
such harmony is in immortal souls, | but whilst 5.01. 63
vows | 'twixt the souls of friend and friend; AYL 3.02.134
that will draw three souls out of one weaver? TN 2.03. 59 P
well, and god have mercy upon one of our souls! 3.04.167 P
souls and bodies hath he divorc'd three, and his 3.04.237 P
this shall end without the perdition of souls. 3.04.290 P
combination shall be made | of our dear souls. 5.01.384
, the most piteous cry of the poor souls! WT 3.03. 90 P
first, how the poor souls roar'd, and the sea 3.03. 99 P
then god forgive the sin of all those souls JN 2.01.283
urge them while their souls | are capable of 2.01.475
knit, | and the conjunction of our inward souls 3.01.227
now that their souls are topful of offense. 3.04.180
our souls religiously confirm thy words. 4.03. 73
all you whose souls abhor | th' uncleanly savors 4.03.111
as, | one of our souls had wand'red in the air, R2 1.03.195
this land of such dear souls, this dear dear 2.01. 57
whom fair befall in heaven 'mongst happy souls, 2.01.129
pushy and green, i will not vex your souls — 3.01. 2
since presently your souls must part your bodies 3.01. 3
my comfort is, that heaven will take our souls, 3.01. 33
all souls that will be safe, fly from my side, 3.02. 80
make war upon their spotted souls for this! 3.02.134
again uncurse their souls, their peace is made 3.02.137
have torn their souls by turning them from us, 3.03. 83
od, | that in a christian climate souls refin'd 4.01.130
he's in hell already, and burns poor souls; 2H4 2.04.339 P
of indigent faint souls past corporal toil, | a H5 1.01. 16
on the poor souls for whom this hungry war 2.04.104
et us our lives, our souls, | our debts, our 4.01.230
and your fair show shall suck away their souls, 4.02. 17
that their souls | may make a peaceful and a 4.03. 85
thousand souls to death and deadly night. 1H6 2.04.127
at to believing souls | gives light in 2H6 2.01. 64
ay as you think, and speak it from your souls: 3.01.247
shall blow ten thousand souls to heaven or hell; 3.01.350
or god forbid so many simple souls | should 4.04. 10
ow would it fare with your departed souls? 4.07.116
fright the souls of fearful adversaries, | he R3 1.01. 11
ve you that holy feeling in your souls | to 1.04.250
d are you yet to your own souls so blind 1.04.252
ent, and save your souls. 1.04.256
at our swift-winged souls may catch the king's 2.02. 44
et your gentle souls fly in the air | and be 4.04. 11
at reigns in galled eyes of weeping souls, 4.04. 53
y reserv'd their factor to buy souls | and 4.04. 72
there the little souls of edward's children 4.04.192
hat your moody discontented souls | do 5.01. 7
the wronged souls | of butchered princes 5.03.121
nephews' souls bid thee despair and die! 5.03.149
hought the souls of all that i had murther'd 5.03.204

methought their souls whose bodies richard 5.03.230
the prayers of holy saints and wronged souls, 5.03.241
let not our babbling dreams affright our souls; 5.03.308
as you wish christian peace to souls departed, H8 4.02.156
win straying souls with modesty again, | cast 5.02. 99
or those that with the fineness of their souls TRO 1.03.209
and choice (being mutual act of all our souls) 1.03.348
if souls guide vows, if vows be sanctimonies, 5.02.139
you souls of geese, | that bear the shapes of COR 1.04. 34
we have suppler souls | than in our priest-like 5.01. 55
make this his latest farewell to their souls. TIT 1.01.149
whose souls is not corrupted as 'tis thought. 3.01. 9
and on the ragged stones beat forth our souls, 5.03.133
susan and she — god rest all christian souls! ROM 1.03. 18
there is thy gold, worse poison to men's souls, 5.01. 80
the sufferance of our souls, the time's abuse — JC 2.01.115
and such suffering souls | that welcome wrongs; 2.01.130
kind souls, what weep you when you but behold 3.02.195
never come such division 'tween our souls! 4.03.235
and all unfortunate souls | that trace him in MAC 4.01.152
there are a crew of wretched souls | that stay 4.03.141
but for mine, | fell slaughter on their souls. 4.03.227
with thoughts beyond the reaches of our souls? HAM 1.04. 56
your majesty and we that have free souls, it 3.02.242 P
two thousand souls and twenty thousand ducats 4.04. 25
and of all christians' souls, /i /pray /god. 4.05.200 P
and such rest to her | as to peace-parted souls. 5.01.238
even now stands in act) that, for their souls, OTH 1.01.151
and heaven defend your good souls, that you 1.03.266
and there be souls must be sav'd, and there be 2.03.103 P
be sav'd, and there be souls must not be sav'd. 2.03.103 P
lord, | is the immediate jewel of their souls. 3.03.156
the souls of all my tribe defend | from jealousy 3.03.175
but jealious souls will not be answer'd so; 3.04.159
where souls do couch on flowers, we'll hand in ANT 4.14. 51
to knit their souls | (on whom there is no more CYM 2.03.117
to darkness fleet souls that fly backwards. 5.03. 25
that their good souls may be appeas'd with 5.05. 72
alas, poor souls, it griev'd my heart to hear PER 2.01. 20 P
operance, our souls | did so to one another. TNK 1.03. 63
most true, two souls | put in two noble bodies, 2.02. 64
and brave souls in shades, | that have died 3.01. 78
with all our souls. 3.06.280
blessed souls be with thee! 5.04. 96
what do you to your souls | in doing this, o STM II.C 106
sits sin, to seize the souls that wander by him. LUC 882
annoy, | sad souls are slain in merry company, 1110
let guiltless souls be freed from guilty woe: 1482
and leave the falt'ring feeble souls alive? 1768
steals men's eyes and women's souls amazeth. SON 20. 8
all tongues (the voice of souls) give thee that 69. 3
SOUL-VEX'D 1 FR 0.0001 REL FR 1 V 0 P
(where we offenders now) appear soul-vex'd, WT 5.01. 59
SOUND* *(also swoon, swoonds, swoun, swound, etc.)*
/SOUND* 3 FR 0.0003 REL FR 3 V 0 P
/nothing /but /the /sound /of /hotspur's /name 2H4 2.03. 37
/sound, /trumpet! LR 5.03.109
/sound! 5.03.115
SOUND* 190 FR 0.0214 REL FR 163 V 27 P
business, nor no sound | that the earth owes. TMP 1.02.407
o heaven, o earth, bear witness to this sound, 3.01. 68
the sound is going away. 3.02.148 P
shapes, such gesture, and such sound expressing 3.03. 37
and deeper than did ever plummet sound | i'll 5.01. 56
o, how oddly will it sound that i | must ask my 5.01.197
into't, and i have a disguise to sound falstaff. WIV 2.01.238 P
let the supposed fairies pinch him sound, | and 4.04. 62
sleep she as sound as careless infancy; 5.05. 52
but thou art full of error — i am sound. MM 1.02. 54 P
but so sound as things that are hollow. 1.02. 56 P
let it not sound a thought upon your tongue 2.02.140
and try your penitence, if it be sound, | or 2.03. 22
i remember you, sir, by the sound of your voice; 5.01.327 P
for two — and sound ones too. ERR 2.02. 91 P
nay, not sound, i pray you. 2.02. 92 P
i tell you, 'twill sound harshly in her ears. 4.04. 7
i long that we were safe and sound aboard. 4.04.150
he hath a heart as sound as a bell, and his ADO 3.02. 12 P
now, music, sound, and sing your solemn hymn. 5.03. 11
a lover's ear will hear the lowest sound, | when LLL 4.03.332
he'll sound! 5.02.392
my love to thee is sound, sans crack or flaw. 5.02.415
siege to it, | making it momentany as a sound, MND 1.01.143
and here the maiden, sleeping sound, | on the 2.02. 74
no sound, no word? 2.02.152
mine ear, i thank it, brought me to thy sound. 3.02.182
on the ground | sleep sound; 3.02.449
sound, music! 4.01. 85
prologue like a child on a recorder — a sound, 5.01.123 P
shalt not know the sound of thine own tongue. MV 1.01.109
let not the sound of shallow fopp'ry enter | my 2.05. 35
let music sound while he doth make his choice; 3.02. 43
the law, your exposition | hath been most sound. 4.01.238
if they but hear perchance a trumpet sound, | or 5.01. 75
treble, pipes | and whistles in his sound. AYL 2.07.163
your liver as clean as a sound sheep's heart, 3.02.423 P
i counterfeited to sound when he show'd me your 5.02. 26 P
wakes, | to make a dulcet and a heavenly sound; SHR in.1. 51
the rest will comfort, for thy counsel 's sound. 1.01.164
and i, to sound the depth of this knavery. 5.01.137 P
what is infirm from your sound parts shall fly, AWW 2.01.167
speak | his powerful sound within an organ weak; 2.01.176
so that the muster-file, rotten and sound, upon 4.03.166 P
it came o'er my ear like the sweet sound | that TN 1.01. 5
is as the maiden's organ, shrill and sound, 1.04. 33
is rotten | as ever oak or stone was sound. WT 2.03. 91
this shows a sound affection. 4.04.379
the latest breath that gave the sound of words JN 3.01.230
mouth | sound on into the drowsy race of night; 3.03. 39
eyes, ears, and harmful sound of words — | then 3.03. 51
sound rottenness! 3.04. 26
makes sound opinion sick, and truth suspected, 4.02. 26
to sound the purposes of all their hearts, 4.02. 48
sound but another, and another shall | (as loud 5.02.171
or sound so base a parley, my teeth shall tear R2 1.01.192
sound, trumpets, and set forward, combatants. 1.03.117
us, and let the trumpets sound | while we return 1.03.121
to whose venom sound | the open ear of youth 2.01. 19

thy harsh rude tongue sound this unpleasing news 3.04. 74
fest'red joint cut off, the rest rest sound, 5.03. 85
sir, the sound that tells what hour it is | are 5.05. 55
this music mads me, let it sound no more, | for 5.05. 61
ay, by my faith, that bears a frosty sound. 1H4 4.01.128
sound all the lofty instruments of war, | and by 5.02. 97
and his coffers sound | with hollow poverty and 2H4 1.03. 74
and lull'd with sound of sweetest melody? 3.01. 14
to sound the bottom of the after-times. 4.02. 51
yet not so sound, and half so deeply sweet, | as 4.05. 26
this sleep is sound indeed, this is a sleep 4.05. 35
my voice shall sound as you do prompt mine ear, 5.02.119
ish give over, the trompet sound the retreat. H5 3.02. 89 P
bardolph, a soldier firm and sound of heart, 3.06. 25
then let the trumpets sound | the tucket sonance 4.02. 34
"the empty vessel makes the greatest sound." 4.04. 69 P
sound, sound alarum! 1H6 1.02. 18
sound, sound alarum! 1.02. 18
this means shall we sound what skill she hath. 1.02. 63
whilst any trump did sound, or drum struck up, 1.04. 80
here sound retreat, and cease our hot pursuit. 2.02. 3
by the sound of drum you may perceive | their 3.03. 29
sound, trumpets, alarum to the combatants! 2H6 2.03. 92
can chase away the first-conceived sound? 3.02. 44
thy name affrights me, in whose sound is death. 4.01. 33
any be so bold to sound retreat or parley when i 4.08. 4 P
sound drum and trumpets, and to london all, 5.03. 32
sound drums and trumpets, and the king will fly. 3H6 1.01.118
but sound the trumpets, and about our task. 2.01.200
sound trumpets! 2.02.173
death shall stop his dismal threat'ning sound, 2.06. 58
sound trumpet, edward shall be here proclaim'd. 4.07. 69
go, trumpet, to the walls, and sound a parle. 5.01. 16
spurr'd their coursers at the trumpet's sound; 5.07. 9
sound drums and trumpets! 5.07. 45
sound thou lord hastings | how he doth stand R3 3.01.170
the late request that you did sound me in. 4.02. 84
call for some men of sound direction: 5.03. 16
look that my staves be sound, and not too heavy. 5.03. 65
sound drums and trumpets boldly and cheerfully. 5.03.269
the trumpets sound; H8 4.01. 36
pray heaven he sound not my disgrace! 5.02. 13
ye are not sound. 5.02.116
not sound? 5.02.116
not sound, i say. 5.02.117
as much as one sound cudgel of four foot | (you 5.03. 19
hark, the trumpets sound; 5.03. 82
infects the sound pine and diverts his grain TRO 1.03. 8
to hear the wooden dialogue and sound | 'twixt 1.03.155
when fame shall in our islands sound her trump, 3.03.210
true, | even in soul of sound good-fellowship — 4.01. 53
ho! bid my trumpet sound! 5.03. 13
the troyans' trumpet sound the like, my lord. 5.08. 16
go sound thy trumpet in the market-place; COR 1.05. 26
more than i know the sound of martius' tongue 1.06. 26
me clip ye | in arms as sound as when i woo'd, 1.06. 30
which you profane, | never sound more! 1.09. 42
i'll have five hundred voices of that sound. 2.03.211
volscians' ears, | and harsh in sound to thine. 4.05. 59
here's no sound jest! TIT 4.02. 26
shall | go sound the ocean, and cast your nets; 4.03. 7
of thy tongue's uttering, yet i know the sound. ROM 2.02. 59
how silver-sweet sound lovers' tongues by night, 2.02.165
then, dreadful trumpet, sound the general doom, 3.02. 67
that word's death, no words can that woe sound. 3.02.126
how sound is she asleep! 4.05. 8
/oppress, | then music with her silver sound" — 4.05.128
with her silver sound" — | why "silver sound"? 4.05.129 P
why "music with her silver sound"? 4.05.130 P
marry, sir, because silver hath a sweet sound. 4.05.132 P
i say, "silver sound," because musicians sound 4.05.134 P
sound," because musicians sound for silver. 4.05.135 P
it is "music with her silver sound," because 4.05.140 P
"then music with her silver sound | with speedy 4.05.142
false hearts should never have sound legs. TIM 1.02.234
hold, no reason | can sound his state in safety. 2.01. 13
will fare so harshly o' th' trumpet's sound; 3.06. 35 P
title plead, | nor sound his quillets shrilly; 4.03.155
sound to this coward and lascivious town | our 5.04. 1
sound them, it doth become the mouth as well; JC 1.02.145
shall we sound him? 2.01.141
therefore thou sleep'st so sound. 2.01.233
to sound more sweetly in great caesar's ear 3.01. 50
and seem to fear | things that do sound so fair? MAC 1.03. 52
i'll charm the air to give a sound, | while you 4.01.129
which shall possess them with the heaviest sound 4.03.202
and purge it to a sound and pristine health, | i 5.03. 52
tale | told by an idiot, full of sound and fury, 5.05. 27
if thou hast any sound, or use of voice, | speak HAM 1.01.128
and at the sound it shrunk in haste away | and 1.02.219
your party in converse, him you would sound, 2.01. 42
finger | to sound what stop she please. 3.02. 71
you would sound me from my lowest note to /the 3.02.366 P
indispos'd and sickly fit | for the sound man. LR 2.04.112
substance, bleed'st not, speak'st, art sound. 4.06. 52
one hears that, | which can distinguish sound. 4.06.211
let the trumpet sound | for him that brought it. 5.01. 41
art armed, gloucester, let the trumpet sound. 5.03. 90
let the trumpet sound, | and read out this. 5.03.107
him appear by the third sound of the trumpet. 5.03.113 P
when to sound your name | it not concern'd me. ANT 2.02. 34
sound and be hang'd, sound out! 2.07.133
sound and be hang'd, sound out! 2.07.133
who ever yet could sound thy bottom? CYM 4.02.204
our tongues and sorrows to sound deep our woes PER 1.04. 13
which make a sound, but kill'd are wond'red at. 2.03. 63
round, | and every one with claps can sound, 3.ch. 36
that we have, | cause it to sound, beseech you. 3.02. 89
which she made more sound | by hurting it; 4.ch. 24
you that your resorters stand upon sound legs. 4.06. 24 P
much money gi'n, | if they stand sound and well; TNK pr 3
and the first sound this child hear be a hiss, pr 16
in their morning state | (sound and at liberty), 1.04. 35
there's a leak sprung, a sound one. 3.04. 8
but yet perceiv'd not | who made the sound, the 4.01. 61
into whose port | ne'er ent'red wanton sound) to 5.01.148
nay, now the sound is "arcite." 5.03. 90
nay, this' a sound fellow i tell you, let's mark STM II.C 89 P

or how can well that proclamation sound | when II.C 117
and will not let a false sound enter there, VEN 780
follow | this sound of hope doth labor to expel, 976
but she, sound sleeping, fearing no such thing, LUC 363
begin | to sound a parley to his heartless foe, 471
which seem'd to swallow up his sound advice, 1409
"poor instrument," quoth she, "without a sound, 1464
thou lov'st to hear the sweet melodious sound PP 8. 9
my shepherd's pipe can sound no deal, | my 17.17
trumpet be, | to whose sound chaste wings obey. PHT 4
that music hath a far more pleasing sound; SON 130.10
breath'd forth the sound that said "i hate" | to 145. 2
or to turn white and sound at tragic shows; LC 308
SOUND–A 1 FR 0.0001 REL FR 1 V 0 P
have your company | till /i come to the sound–a! TNK 3.05. 66
/SOUNDED* 1 FR 0.0001 REL FR 1 V 0 P
/twice /then /the /trumpets /sounded, | /and LR 5.03.218
SOUNDED* 17 FR 0.0019 REL FR 13 V 4 P
i'll seek him deeper than e'er plummet sounded, TMP 3.03.101
twice have the trumpets sounded; MM 4.06. 12
but it cannot be sounded; AYL 4.01.207 P
thy virtues spoke of, and thy beauty sounded, SHR 2.01.192
tell me, moreover, hast thou sounded him, | if R2 1.01. 8
i have sounded the very base–string of humility. 1H4 2.04. 5 P
the trumpets have sounded twice. 2H4 5.05. 2 P
thy name is gualtier, being rightly sounded. 2H6 4.01. 37
spoke, | which sounded like a cannon in a vault, 3H6 5.02. 44
i have not sounded him, nor he deliver'd | his R3 3.04. 16
catesby hath sounded hastings in our business, 3.04. 36
and sounded all the depths and shoals of honor, H8 3.02.436
sport, | she sounded almost at my pleasing tale, TIT 5.01.119
i sounded at the sight. ROM 3.02. 56
why should that name be sounded more than yours? JC 1.02.143
nor do we find him forward to be sounded, | but HAM 3.01. 7
has he never before sounded you in this business LR 1.02. 69 P
SOUNDER 3 FR 0.0003 REL FR 1 V 2 P
morning, may sleep the sounder all the next day. MM 4.03. 47 P
a more sounder instance, come. AYL 3.02. 61 P
dare mate a sounder man than surrey can be, H8 3.02.274
SOUNDEST 2 FR 0.0002 REL FR 0 V 2 P
he's one o' th' soundest judgments in troy, TRO 1.02.192 P
the best and soundest of his time hath been but LR 1.01.295 P
SOUNDING* 6 FR 0.0006 REL FR 5 V 1 P
sounding destruction, or some joy too fine, TRO 3.02. 23
sobs and break my heart | with sounding troilus. 4.02.109
so close, | so far from sounding and discovery, ROM 1.01.150
because musicians have no gold for sounding: 4.05.141 P
melodious discord, heavenly tune harsh sounding, VEN 431
or of weeping water, | or sounding paleness; LC 305
SOUNDLESS* 2 FR 0.0002 REL FR 2 V 0 P
o yes, and soundless too; JC 5.01. 36
whilst he upon your soundless deep doth ride, SON 80.10
SOUNDLY 24 FR 0.0027 REL FR 14 V 10 P
pay for him that hath him, and that soundly. TMP 2.02. 78 P
your shaking, i can tell you, and that soundly. 2.02. 85 P
let them be hunted soundly. 4.01.262
in your retirement, i had swing'd him soundly. MM 5.01.130
this were a bed but cold to sleep so soundly. SHR in.1. 33
villain, i say, knock me here soundly. 1.02. 8
he bid me knock him and rap him soundly, sir. 1.02. 31 P
knock me well, and knock me soundly"? 1.02. 42 P
swinge me them soundly forth unto their husbands 5.02.104
do, cuff him soundly, but never draw thy sword. TN 3.04.392 P
i will have you as soundly swing'd for this — 2H4 5.04. 19 P
can sleep so soundly as the wretched slave; H5 4.01.268
wear if alive, i will strike it out soundly. 4.07.130 P
if you will love me soundly with your french 5.02.105 P
i mean to tug it and to cuff you soundly. 1H6 1.03. 48
good catesby, go effect this business soundly. R3 3.01.186
has he disciplin'd aufidius soundly? COR 2.01.126 P
i have it, | and soundly too. ROM 3.01.108
i will then give it you soundly. 4.05.112 P
i would it were my fault to sleep so soundly. JC 2.01. 4
his day's hard journey | soundly invite him), MAC 1.07. 63
soundly, my lord. ANT 3.13.132
justice of affection, | i'll pay thee soundly. TNK 3.06. 52
but soundly sleeps, while now it sleeps alone. VEN 786
SOUNDNESS 1 FR 0.0001 REL FR 1 V 0 P
i would i had that corporal soundness now | as AWW 1.02. 24
SOUNDPOST 1 FR 0.0001 REL FR 0 V 1 P
/pretty too! what say you, james soundpost? ROM 4.05.136 P
SOUNDS* 42 FR 0.0047 REL FR 38 V 4 P
it sounds no more; TMP 1.02.389
sounds, and sweet airs, that give delight and 3.02.136
and moe diversity of sounds, all horrible, | we 5.01.234
amaimon sounds well; WIV 2.02.297 P
converting all your sounds of woe | into hey ADO 2.03. 68
the trumpet sounds, be mask'd; the maskers come. LLL 5.02.157
is | as are those dulcet sounds in break of day MV 3.02. 51
and let the sounds of music | creep in our ears. 5.01. 55
nor is not moved with concord of sweet sounds, 5.01. 84
methinks it sounds much sweeter than by day. 5.01.100
sirrah, go see what trumpet 'tis that sounds. SHR in.1. 74
no, it is stopp'd with other flattering sounds, R2 2.01. 17
the trumpet sounds retrait, the day is our. 1H4 5.04.159
his tongue | sounds ever after as a sullen bell, 2H4 1.01.102
roar'd the sea, and trumpet–clangor sounds. 5.05. 40
which doth order give | to sounds confus'd; H5 3.pr. 10
the town sounds a parley. 3.02.137 P
night, | the hum of either army stilly sounds, 4.pr. 5
now, when the angry trumpet sounds alarum, | and 2H6 5.02. 3
particularities and petty sounds | to cease! 5.02. 44
the trumpet sounds, be copious in exclaims. R3 4.04.135
peace, rude sounds! TRO 1.01. 89
and | the thunder–like percussion of thy sounds, COR 1.04. 59
his rougher /accents for malicious sounds, | but 3.03. 55
brief sounds determine my weal or woe. ROM 3.02. 51
in cases that keeps their sounds to themselves. TIM 1.02. 99 P
to hear the replication of your sounds | made in JC 1.01. 46
she sounds to see them bleed. HAM 5.02.308
nor are those empty–hearted whose low sounds LR 1.01.153
methinks it sounds a parley to provocation. OTH 2.03. 22 P
and earth may strike their sounds together, ANT 4.08. 38
instrument | (hark, polydore), it sounds! CYM 4.02.187

rarest sounds! do ye not hear? PER 5.01.231
he speaks, his tongue | sounds like a trumpet. TNK 4.02.113
falls, and sounds more like | a bell than blade. 5.03. 5
withal, | but idle sounds resembling parasits, VEN 848
for now against himself he sounds this doom, LUC 717
unprofitable sounds, weak arbitrators! 1017
deep sounds make lesser noise than shallow fords 1329
here manly hector faints, here troilus sounds, 1486
if the true concord of well–tuned sounds, | by SON 8. 5
upon that blessed wood whose motion sounds 128. 2
/SOUR 1 FR 0.0001 REL FR 1 V 0 P
/have /here /deliver'd /me /to /my /sour /cross, R2 4.01.241
SOUR 35 FR 0.0039 REL FR 32 V 3 P
by moonshine do the green sour ringlets make, TMP 5.01. 37
that makes amends for her sour breath. TGV 3.01.328 P
this week he hath been heavy, sour, sad, | and ERR 5.01. 45
therefore welcome the sour cup of prosperity! LLL 1.01.313 P
you must not look so sour. SHR 2.01.228
here's no crab, and therefore look not sour. 2.01.230
and when she is froward, peevish, sullen, sour, 5.02.157
to the great sender turns a sour offense, AWW 5.03. 59
things sweet to taste prove in digestion sour. R2 1.03.236
have ever made me sour my patient cheek, | or 2.01.169
speak sweetly, man, although thy looks be sour. 3.02.193
i'll set a bank of rue, sour herb of grace. 3.04.105
ah, my sour husband, my hard–hearted lord, 5.03.121
how sour sweet music is | when time is broke, 5.05. 42
with clog of conscience and sour melancholy 5.06. 20
heart's discontent and sour affliction | be 2H6 3.02.301
let me embrace /thee, sour /adversities, | for 3H6 3.01. 24
farewell sour annoy! 5.07. 45
with that sour ferryman which poets write of, R3 1.04. 46
lofty and sour to them that lov'd him not, | but H8 4.02. 53
and to make a sweet lady sad is a sour offense. TRO 3.01. 72 P
nor with sour looks afflict his gentle heart. TIT 1.01.441
news | by playing it to me with so sour a face. ROM 2.05. 24
if sour woe delights in fellowship | and needly 3.02.116
is my dear son with such sour company! 3.03. 7
one writ with me in sour misfortune's book! 5.03. 82
if thou didst put this sour cold habit on | to TIM 4.03.239
and he will (after his sour fashion) tell you JC 1.02.180
and have their palates both for sweet and sour, OTH 4.03. 95
to sour your happiness, i must report | the CYM 5.05. 26
lest jealousy, that sour unwelcome guest, VEN 449
fast, | or being early pluck'd is sour to taste. 528
"this sour informer, this bate–breeding spy, 655
were it not thy sour leisure gave sweet leave SON 39.10
you, | nor think the bitterness of absence sour, 57. 7
SOURCE 6 FR 0.0006 REL FR 6 V 0 P
and blow it to the source from whence it came; 3H6 5.03. 11
defeat and quell | the source of all erection. TIM 4.03.164
is stopp'd, the very source of it is stopp'd. MAC 2.03. 99
the source of this our watch, and the chief head HAM 1.01.106
the head and source of all your son's distemper. 2.02. 55
and poison it in the source, and the first stone ANT 3.13.160
SOURCES 1 FR 0.0001 REL FR 1 V 0 P
great floods have flown | from simple sources; AWW 2.01.140
SOUR'D 1 FR 0.0001 REL FR 1 V 0 P
crabbed months had sour'd themselves to death, WT 1.02.102
SOUREST 4 FR 0.0004 REL FR 4 V 0 P
sweetest nut hath sourest rind, | such a nut is AYL 3.02.109
turns to the sourest and most deadly hate. R2 3.02.136
touch you the sourest points with sweetest terms ANT 2.02. 24
for sweetest things turn sourest by their deeds; SON 94.13
SOUREST–NATUR'D 1 FR 0.0001 REL FR 0 V 1 P
my dog be the sourest–natur'd dog that lives: TGV 2.03. 6 P
SOUR–EY'D 1 FR 0.0001 REL FR 1 V 0 P
sour–ey'd disdain, and discord shall bestrew TMP 4.01. 20
SOUR–FAC'D 1 FR 0.0001 REL FR 1 V 0 P
charging the sour–fac'd groom to hie as fast LUC 1334
SOURING 2 FR 0.0002 REL FR 2 V 0 P
souring his cheeks, cries, "fie, no more of love VEN 185
his taste delicious, in digestion souring, LUC 699
SOURLY 3 FR 0.0003 REL FR 3 V 0 P
love i have | (though i show'd sourly to him) COR 5.03. 13
to that sweet thief which sourly robs from me. SON 35.14
will sourly leave her till /she have prevailed? 41. 8
SOURS 2 FR 0.0002 REL FR 1 V 1 P
the tartness of his face sours ripe grapes. COR 5.04. 18 P
the sweets we wish for turn to loathed sours LUC 867
SOUS'D 1 FR 0.0001 REL FR 0 V 1 P
asham'd of my soldiers, i am a sous'd gurnet. 1H4 4.02. 12 P
SOUSE 1 FR 0.0001 REL FR 1 V 0 P
to souse annoyance that comes near his nest; JN 5.02.150
SOUTH 24 FR 0.0027 REL FR 21 V 3 P
north, and south, i spread my conquering might. LLL 5.02.563
like foggy south, puffing with wind and rain? AYL 3.05. 50
in the south suburbs at the elephant | is best TN 3.03. 39
toward the south north are as lustrous as ebony; 4.02. 37 P
think it — | from east, west, north, and south. WT 1.02.203
our thunder from the south | shall rain their JN 2.01.411
from north to south — | austria and france 2.01.413
so honor cross it from the north to south, | and 1H4 1.03.196
by south and east is to my part assign'd; 3.01. 74
like the south | borne with black vapor, doth 2H4 2.04.363
west, north, south, or, like a school broke up, 4.02.104
unto us, | or as the south to the septentrion. 3H6 1.04.136
least | south from the mighty power of the king. R3 5.03. 38
now the rotten diseases of the south, the TRO 5.01. 18 P
all the contagion of the south light on you, COR 1.04. 30
i pray you | ('tis south the city mills) bring 1.10. 31
north, south, and their consent of one direct 2.03. 22 P
turning his side to the dew–dropping south. ROM 1.04.103
which is a great way growing on the south, JC 2.01.107
i hear a knocking | at the south entry. MAC 2.02. 63
the chimney | is south the chamber, and the CYM 2.04. 81
from the spungy south to this part of the west, 4.02.349
from south to west on wing soaring aloft, 5.05.471
"the george alow came from the south, | from the TNK 3.05. 59
SOUTHAM 2 FR 0.0002 REL FR 2 V 0 P
at southam i did leave him with his forces, 3H6 5.01. 9
it is not his, my lord, here southam lies; 5.01. 12
SOUTHAMPTON 4 FR 0.0004 REL FR 3 V 1 P
and in southampton. H5 2.pr. 30
is now transported, gentles, to southampton; 2.pr. 35
then, | unto southampton do we shift our scene. 2.pr. 42
the king will be gone from southampton. 2.03. 46 P
SOUTHERLY 1 FR 0.0001 REL FR 0 V 1 P

when the wind is southerly i know a hawk from a HAM 2.02.379
SOUTHERN 3 FR 0.0003 REL FR 3 V 0
and all your southern gentlemen in arms | upon R2 3.02.202
and with the southern clouds contend in tears, 2H6 3.02.384
'tis not thy southern power | of essex, norfolk, 3H6 1.01.155
SOUTH–FOG 1 FR 0.0001 REL FR 1 V 0
the south–fog rot him! CYM 2.03.131
SOUTHREN 1 FR 0.0001 REL FR 1 V 0
the southren wind | doth play the trumpet to his 1H4 5.01. 3
SOUTH–SEA 1 FR 0.0001 REL FR 0 V 1
inch of delay more is a south–sea of discovery. AYL 3.02.197
SOUTHWARD 2 FR 0.0002 REL FR 0 V 2
the sun looking with a southward eye upon him, WT 4.04.789
if it were at liberty, 'twould sure southward. COR 2.03. 29
SOUTHWARK 2 FR 0.0002 REL FR 1 V 1
the rebels are in southwark; 2H6 4.04. 27
should leave me at the white hart in southwark? 4.08. 25
SOUTHWELL 1 FR 0.0001 REL FR 0 V 1
john southwell, read you; 2H6 1.04. 12
SOUTH–WEST 2 FR 0.0002 REL FR 2 V 0
a south–west blow on ye, | and blister you all TMP 1.02.323
south–west. PER 4.01. 50
SOUTH–WIND 1 FR 0.0001 REL FR 1 V 0
thence | (a prosperous south–wind friendly) we WT 5.01.161
SOUVIENDRAI 1 FR 0.0001 REL FR 0 V 1
j'oublie les doigts, mais je me souviendrai. H5 3.04. 10
/SOVEREIGN 1 FR 0.0001 REL FR 1 V 0
/a /sovereign /shame /so /elbows /him: LR 4.03. 42
SOVEREIGN 150 FR 0.0169 REL FR 145 V 5
thee leave these, and with her sovereign grace, TMP 4.01. 72
for the like loss i have her sovereign aid, 5.01.143
and thus i search it with a sovereign kiss. TGV 1.02.113
sovereign to all the creatures on the earth. 2.04.153
possess'd with such a gentle sovereign grace, ERR 3.02.160
a man of sovereign /parts, /peerless esteem'd, LLL 2.01. 44
th' anointed sovereign of sighs and groans, 3.01.182
dear sovereign, hear me speak. AYL 1.03. 66
thy life, thy keeper, | thy head, thy sovereign; SHR 5.02.147
an enemy, | a guide, a goddess, and a sovereign, AWW 1.01.169
o'er whom both sovereign power and father's 2.03. 54
blames, | dear sovereign, pardon to me. 5.03. 37
my gracious sovereign, | howe'er it pleases you 5.03. 87
gracious sovereign, | whether i have been to 5.03.128
these sovereign thrones, are all supplied, and TN 1.01. 37
get thee to yond same sovereign cruelty. 2.04. 80
to hear | my sovereign mistress clouded so, WT 1.02.280
away the life of our sovereign lord the king, 3.02. 16
the remembrance | of his most sovereign name; 5.01. 26
what, sovereign sir, | i did not well, i meant 5.03. 2
hand, | thy nephew and right royal sovereign. JN 1.01. 15
pope, | your sovereign greatness and authority. 5.01. 4
to any sovereign state throughout the world. 5.02. 82
of happy days befall | my gracious sovereign, my R2 1.01. 21
and wish (so please my sovereign) ere i move, 1.01. 45
o, let my sovereign turn away his face, | and 1.01.111
for that my sovereign liege was in my debt, 1.01.129
myself i throw, dread sovereign, at thy foot, 1.01.165
and derby | stands here for god, his sovereign, 1.03.105
to god, his sovereign, and to him disloyal, 1.03.114
a heavy sentence, my most sovereign liege, | and 1.03.154
t' one is my sovereign, whom both my oath | and 2.02.112
time, | in braving arms against thy sovereign. 2.03.112
stoop | unto the sovereign mercy of the king; 2.03.157
our house, my sovereign liege, little deserves 1H4 1.03. 10
he never did fall off, my sovereign liege, | but 1.03. 94
shalt have charge and sovereign trust herein. 3.02.161
health to my sovereign, and new happiness 2H4 4.04. 81
my sovereign lord, cheer up yourself, look up. 4.04.113
then hear me, gracious sovereign, and you peers, H5 1.02. 33
the sin upon my head, dread sovereign! 1.02. 97
they of those marches, gracious sovereign, 1.02.140
let him be punish'd, sovereign, lest example 2.02. 45
and i, my royal sovereign. 2.02. 65
my fault, but not my body, pardon, sovereign. 2.02.165
good my sovereign, | take up the english short, 2.04. 71
'tis a subject for a sovereign to reason on, and 3.07. 36
on, and for a sovereign's sovereign to ride on; 3.07. 36
my sovereign lord, bestow yourself with speed. 4.03. 68
my lord, | commend my service to my sovereign." 4.06. 23
that here i kiss her as my sovereign queen. 5.02.358
so, | let me thy servant and not sovereign be. 1H6 1.02.111
whom henry, our late sovereign, ne'er could 1.03. 24
the king, thy sovereign, is not quite exempt 3.01. 25
to slay your sovereign and destroy the realm. 3.01.114
accept this scroll, most gracious sovereign, 3.01.148
unto my wars, | to do my duty to my sovereign; 3.04. 4
my gracious sovereign, as i rode from callice, 4.01. 9
hath he forgot he is his sovereign? 4.01. 52
grant me the combat, gracious sovereign. 4.01. 78
be humble to us, call my sovereign yours, | and 4.02. 6
beads, | with you, mine alder–liefest sovereign, 2H6 1.01. 28
between our sovereign and the french king 1.01. 41
why should he then protect our sovereign, | he 1.01.165
when thou wert regent for our sovereign, | have 1.01.197
i say, my sovereign, york is meetest man | to be 1.03.160
that shall salute our rightful sovereign | with 2.02. 61
long live our sovereign richard, england's king! 2.02. 63
no, no, my sovereign, gloucester is a man 3.01. 56
all health unto my gracious sovereign! 3.01. 82
as i am clear from treason to my sovereign. 3.01.102
and you, my sovereign lady, with the rest, 3.01.161
hath he not twit our sovereign lady here | with 3.01.178
and to preserve my sovereign from his foe, | say 3.01.271
comfort, my sovereign! gracious henry, comfort! 3.02. 38
it is reported, mighty sovereign, | that good 3.02.122
come hither, gracious sovereign, view this body. 3.02.149
of bury, | set all upon me, mighty sovereign. 3.02.241
could send such message to their sovereign. 3.02.272
speak, beauford, to thy sovereign. 3.03. 1
beauford, it is thy sovereign speaks to thee. 3.03. 7
and let my sovereign, virtuous henry, | command 5.01. 49
we are thy sovereign, clifford, kneel again; 5.01.12[illegible]
i am thy sovereign. 3H6 1.01. 7[illegible]
he rose against him, being his sovereign, | and 1.01.14[illegible]
i live | to honor me as thy king and sovereign, 1.01.19[illegible]
before thy sovereign and thy lawful king? 2.02. 8[illegible]
jest withal, | but far unfit to be a sovereign. 3.02. 9[illegible]
my lord and sovereign and thy vowed friend, | i 3.03. [illegible]

and their true sovereign whom they must obey? 4.01. 78
my sovereign liege, no letters, and few words, 4.01. 86
ay, gracious sovereign, they are so link'd in 4.01.116
then is my sovereign slain? 4.04. 6
it shall be done, my sovereign, with all speed. 4.06. 64
but let us hence, my sovereign, to provide | a 4.06. 87
ay, now my sovereign speaketh like himself, 4.07. 67
my sovereign, with the loving citizens, | like 4.08. 19
farewell, my sovereign. 4.08. 24
henry, your sovereign, | is prisoner to the foe, 5.04. 76
we follow'd then our lord, our sovereign king. R3 1.03.146
good morrow to my sovereign king and queen, 2.01. 47
a blessed labor, my most sovereign lord. 2.01. 53
my sovereign lord, i do beseech your highness 2.01. 76
a boon, my sovereign, for my service done! 2.01. 96
the forfeit, sovereign, of my servant's life, 2.01.100
welcome, dear cousin, my thoughts' sovereign, 3.01. 2
he may command me as my sovereign, | but you 3.01.108
my gracious sovereign? 4.02. 2
all health, my sovereign lord! 4.03. 23
say i, her sovereign, am her subject low. 4.04.355
most mighty sovereign, on the western coast 4.04.433
i know not, mighty sovereign, but by guess. 4.04.465
they should serve their sovereign in the west? 4.04.485
most mighty sovereign, | you have no cause to 4.04.491
my gracious sovereign, now in devonshire, | as i 4.04.498
a good direction, warlike sovereign. 5.03.302
in the name | of our most sovereign king. H8 1.01.202
(whereof my sovereign would have note), they are 1.02. 48
and thy parts | sovereign and pious else, could 2.04.141
my sovereign, i confess your royal graces 3.02.166
dread sovereign, how much are we bound to heaven 5.02.149
my most dread sovereign, may it like your grace 5.02.183
the most sovereign prescription in galen is but COR 2.01.116 P
how now, dear sovereign and our gracious mother? TIT 2.03. 89
sovereign, here lies the county paris slain, ROM 5.03.195
whose eyes are on this sovereign lady fix'd, TIM 1.01. 68
come | give solely sovereign sway and masterdom. MAC 1.05. 70
to dew the sovereign flower and drown the weeds. 5.02. 30
might, by the sovereign power you have of us, HAM 2.02. 27
now see /that noble and most sovereign reason, 3.01.157
mayst not coldly set | our sovereign process, 4.03. 63
yet opinion, a sovereign mistress of effects, OTH 1.03.225 P
and at thy sovereign leisure read | the garboils ANT 1.03. 60
sovereign of egypt, hail! 1.05. 34
o sovereign mistress of true melancholy, | the 4.09. 12
she's dead too, our sovereign. 4.15. 69
with tears as sovereign as the blood of hearts, 5.01. 41
most sovereign creature — 5.02. 81
sweet sovereign, | leave us to ourselves, and CYM 1.01.154
reign, | we thus submit unto — our sovereign. PER 2.04. 39
lady fortune | (next after emily my sovereign), TNK 3.01. 16
hail, sovereign queen of secrets, who hast power 5.01. 77
earth's sovereign salve, to do a goddess good. VEN 28
venom'd sores the only sovereign plaster; 916
that pay a daily debt | to their salt sovereign, LUC 650
"thou art," quoth she, "a sea, a sovereign king, 652
flatter the mountain tops with sovereign eye, SON 33. 2
whilst i, my sovereign, watch the clock for you, 57. 6
if nature (sovereign mistress over wrack), | as 126. 5
against strange maladies a sovereign cure. 153. 8
SOVEREIGNEST 1 FR 0.0001 REL FR 1 V 0 P
and telling me the sovereignest thing on earth 1H4 1.03. 57
SOVEREIGNLY 1 FR 0.0001 REL FR 1 V 0 P
mistress | (so sovereignly being honorable). WT 1.02.323
SOVEREIGN'S 12 FR 0.0013 REL FR 11 V 1 P
let me kiss my sovereign's hand | and bow my R2 1.03. 46
or bend one wrinkle on my sovereign's face. 2.01.170
feed not thy sovereign's foe, my gentle earth, 3.02. 12
throw death upon thy sovereign's enemies. 3.02. 22
may hourly trample on their sovereign's head; 3.03.157
his sovereign's life to death and treachery. H5 2.02. 11
on, and for a sovereign's sovereign to ride on; 3.07. 36 P
by wicked means to frame our sovereign's fall. 2H6 3.01. 52
and that my sovereign's presence makes me mild, 3.02.219
to tell the passion of my sovereign's heart, 3H6 3.03. 62
what answers clarence to his sovereign's will? 4.06. 45
that you'd guide me to your sovereign's court, PER 2.01.140
SOVEREIGNS 1 FR 0.0001 REL FR 1 V 0 P
whose sovereigns fell before | the wrath of TNK 1.01. 39
/SOVEREIGNTY 2 FR 0.0002 REL FR 2 V 0 P
/made /glory /base, /and /sovereignty /a /slave; R2 4.01.251
/that, /for /by /the /marks /of /sovereignty, LR 1.04.232
SOVEREIGNTY 23 FR 0.0026 REL FR 23 V 0 P
no sovereignty — TMP 2.01.157
whose sovereignty so oft thou hast preferr'd TGV 2.06. 15
employ'd and pain'd | your unknown sovereignty! MM 5.01.387
of all complexions the cull'd sovereignty | do LLL 4.03.230
yoke | my soul consents not to give sovereignty. MND 1.01. 82
had collected | for general sovereignty; AWW 1.03.224
to tread down fair respect of sovereignty, | and JN 3.01. 58
place, | my person, or my liege's sovereignty. 2H4 5.02.101
realm | have been as bondmen to thy sovereignty. 2H6 1.03.127
all her perfections challenge sovereignty: 3H6 3.02. 86
why then i do but dream on sovereignty, | like 3.02.134
take on his grace the sovereignty thereof, | but R3 3.07. 79
to bear the golden yoke of sovereignty, | which 3.07.146
th' aspiring flame | of golden sovereignty; 4.04.329
but she, your subject, loathes such sovereignty. 4.04.356
him every minute | with words of sovereignty. H8 1.02.150
yet | affected eminence, wealth, sovereignty; 2.03. 29
fish, who takes it | by sovereignty of nature. COR 4.07. 35
like | the sovereignty will fall upon macbeth. MAC 2.04. 30
baby-brow the round | and top of sovereignty? 4.01. 89
which might deprive your sovereignty of reason, HAM 1.04. 73
ourself | to show less sovereignty than they, CYM 3.05. 6
the sovereignty of either being so great | that LUC 69
SOV'REIGN'S 1 FR 0.0001 REL FR 1 V 0 P
unrip'st the bowels of thy sov'reign's son. R3 1.04.207
SOV'REIGNS 1 FR 0.0001 REL FR 1 V 0 P
may challenge nothing of their sov'reigns, | but 3H6 4.06. 6
SOV'REIGNTY 1 FR 0.0001 REL FR 1 V 0 P
perchance his boast of lucrece' sov'reignty LUC 36
SOW* 9 FR 0.0010 REL FR 5 V 4 P
our corn's to reap, for yet our tithe's to sow. MM 4.01. 75
before thee like a sow that hath overwhelm'd all 2H4 1.02. 11 P
sir, shall we sow the hade land with wheat? 5.01. 14 P
a boast as that, if i had a sow to my mistress. H5 3.07. 63 P
we are to cure such sorrows, not to sow 'em. H8 3.01.158
sow all th' athenian bosoms, and their crop | be TIM 4.01. 29
consumptions sow | in hollow bones of man, 4.03.151
so that if we will plant nettles or sow lettuce, OTH 1.03.322 P
methought alcides was | to him a sow of lead. TNK 5.03.120
SOW'D 5 FR 0.0005 REL FR 5 V 0 P
sow'd cockle reap'd no corn, | and justice LLL 4.03.380
be | when time hath sow'd a grizzle on thy case? TN 5.01.165
and reap the harvest which that rascal sow'd. 2H6 3.01.381
which we ourselves have plough'd for, sow'd, and COR 3.01. 71
but yields a crop | as if it had been sow'd. CYM 4.02.181
SOWING 1 FR 0.0001 REL FR 0 V 1 P
and, sowing the kernels of it in the sea, bring TMP 2.01. 93 P
SOWL 1 FR 0.0001 REL FR 0 V 1 P
and sowl the porter of rome gates by th' ears. COR 4.05.200 P
SOW'S 1 FR 0.0001 REL FR 1 V 0 P
pour in sow's blood, that hath eaten | her nine MAC 4.01. 64
SOWS 1 FR 0.0001 REL FR 1 V 0 P
she sows into the births of noble bodies, | were TNK 4.02. 9
SOW-SKIN 1 FR 0.0001 REL FR 1 V 0 P
leave to live, | and bear the sow-skin bouget, WT 4.03. 20
SOW'T 1 FR 0.0001 REL FR 1 V 0 P
he'd sow't with nettle-seed. TMP 2.01.145
SOWTER 1 FR 0.0001 REL FR 0 V 1 P
sowter will cry upon't for all this, though it TN 2.05.123 P
/SPACE 1 FR 0.0001 REL FR 0 V 1 P
/count /myself /a /king /of /infinite /space — HAM 2.02.255 P
SPACE 32 FR 0.0036 REL FR 31 V 1 P
within which space she died, | and left thee TMP 1.02.279
space enough | have i in such a prison. 1.02.493
'twixt which regions | there is some space. 2.01.257
a space whose ev'ry cubit | seems to cry out, 2.01.257
writ with blank space for different names (sure, WIV 2.01. 75 P
stay here in your court for three years' space. LLL 1.01. 52
thousand times within this three years' space; 1.01.150
and after some small space, being strong at AYL 4.03.151
the mightiest space in fortune nature brings AWW 1.01.222
within what space | hop'st thou my cure? 2.01.159
feast | shall more attend upon the coming space, 2.03.181
come on, thou /art granted space. 4.01. 88
within that space you may have drawn together 1H4 3.01. 88
but in short space | it rain'd down fortune 5.01. 46
if after three days' space thou here be'st found 2H6 3.02.295
no space of earth shall sunder our two hates. TRO 5.10. 27
and sell the mighty space of our large honors JC 4.03. 25
for the whole space that's in the tyrant's grasp MAC 4.03. 36
dearer than eyesight, space, and liberty, LR 1.01. 56
no less in space, validity, and pleasure, | than 1.01. 81
o indistinguish'd space of woman's will! 4.06.271
they are ready | to-morrow, or at further space, 5.03. 53
here is my space, | kingdoms are clay; ANT 1.01. 34
from egypt, 'tis | a space for farther travel. 2.01. 31
therefore | make space enough between you. 2.03. 24
of space had pointed him sharp as my needle; CYM 1.03. 19
if you require a little space for prayer, | i PER 4.01. 67
so it far'd | good space between these kinsmen; TNK 5.03.129
and counterfeits to die with her a space, | till LUC 1776
distance and no space was seen | 'twixt this PHT 30
for then, despite of space, i would be brought, SON 44. 3
vow, bond, nor space, | in thee hath neither LC 264
SPACES 1 FR 0.0001 REL FR 1 V 0 P
the world's large spaces cannot parallel. TRO 2.02.162
SPACIOUS 14 FR 0.0015 REL FR 12 V 2 P
use a more spacious ceremony to the noble lords; AWW 2.01. 50 P
here, | it is of such a spacious lofty pitch, 1H6 2.03. 55
the spacious world cannot again afford. R3 1.02.245
confines | /thy spacious and dilated parts. TRO 2.03.250
and yet the spacious breadth of this division 5.02.150
and vows revenge as spacious as between | the COR 4.06. 68
the forest walks are wide and spacious, | and TIT 2.01.114
'tis in few words, but spacious in effect: TIM 3.05. 96
convey your pleasures in a spacious plenty, MAC 4.03. 71
as i say, spacious in the possession of dirt. HAM 5.02. 87 P
when such a spacious mirror's set before him, ANT 5.01. 34
were i chief lord of all this spacious world, PER 4.03. 5
of what a spacious majesty, he carries, | arch'd TNK 4.02. 19
wilt thou, whose will is large and spacious, SON 135. 5
SPADE 7 FR 0.0008 REL FR 5 V 2 P
'tis you must dig with mattock and with spade, TIT 4.03. 11
we took this mattock and this spade from him, ROM 5.03.185
why this spade? TIM 4.03.204
come, my spade. HAM 5.01. 29 P
about the /mazzard with a sexton's spade. 5.01. 90 P
"a pickaxe and a spade, a spade, | for and a 5.01. 94
"a pickaxe and a spade, a spade, | for and a 5.01. 94
SPAIN 13 FR 0.0014 REL FR 11 V 2 P
where spain? ERR 3.02.130 P
their rich aspect to the hot breath of spain, 3.02.136 P
is haunted | with a refined traveller of spain, LLL 1.01.163
the worth of many a knight | from tawny spain, 1.01.173
with her her niece, the lady blanch of spain; JN 2.01. 64
that daughter there of spain, the lady blanch, 2.01.423
the fig of spain. H5 3.06. 59
all which did subdue the greatest part of spain; 3H6 3.03. 82
my father, king of spain, was reckon'd one | the H8 2.04. 48
till i may | be by my friends in spain advis'd, 2.04. 55
he had a fever when he was in spain, | and when JC 1.02.119
it was a sword of spain, the ice-brook's temper OTH 5.02.253
to any german province, spain or portigal, | nay STM II.C 128
SPAKE *(also spoke, etc.)*
/SPAKE 1 FR 0.0001 REL FR 1 V 0 P
but nothing /spake in warrant from himself. R3 3.07. 33
SPAKE 51 FR 0.0057 REL FR 41 V 10 P
who is that that spake? TGV 4.02. 87
ay, you spake in latin then too: WIV 1.01.180 P
i spake with the old woman about it. 4.05. 34 P
there spake my brother; MM 3.01. 85
for certain words he spake against your grace 5.01.129
time of five years | i never spake with her, saw 5.01.223
spake he so doubtfully, thou couldst not feel ERR 2.01. 50 P
what answer, sir? when spake i such a word? 2.02. 13
unless i spake, or look'd, or touch'd, or carv'd 2.02.118
i never spake with her in all my life. 2.02.165
not well cut, he would answer i spake not true: AYL 5.04. 78 P
spake you not these words plain, "sirrah, knock SHR 1.02. 39 P
i spake but by a metaphor. AWW 5.02. 11 P
i spake with him; WT 5.01.197
a pause | when i spake darkly what i purposed, JN 4.02.232
and even there, methinks an angel spake. 5.02. 64
was not so resolv'd when last we spake together. R2 2.03. 29
you would have thought the very windows spake, 5.02. 12
thou not mark the king, what words he spake? 5.04. 1
he spake it twice, | and urg'd it twice together 5.04. 4
one that never spake other english in his life 1H4 2.04. 24 P
i spake with one, my lord, that came from thence 2H4 1.01. 25
were, | i spake unto this crown as having sense, 4.05.157
my lord, hang me if ever i spake the words. 2H6 1.03.197 P
who spake aloud, "what scourge for perjury | can R3 1.04. 50
o, now i need the priest that spake to me! 3.04. 87
no, so god help me, they spake not a word, | but 3.07. 24
spake one the least word that might | be to the H8 2.04.154
this is about that which the bishop spake. 5.01. 84
ever spake against | your liberties and the COR 2.03.179
what villain was it spake that word? TIT 1.01.359
and what i spake, i spake it to my face. ROM 4.01. 34
and what i spake, i spake it to my face. 4.01. 34
caius ligarius, that metellus spake of. JC 2.01.311
nor what he spake, though it lack'd form a HAM 3.01.163
spake you with him? LR 1.02.154 P
swore as many oaths as i spake words, and broke 3.04. 88 P
lord edmund spake not with your lord at home? 4.05. 4
upon this hint i spake: OTH 1.03.166
she that i spake of, our great captain's captain 2.01. 74
and even but now he spake | (after long seeming 5.02.327
spake you of caesar? how, the nonpareil! ANT 3.02. 11
for i spake to you for your comfort, did desire 4.02. 40
the last she spake | was "antony, most noble 4.14. 29
charmian liv'd but now, she stood and spake. 5.02.341
what was the last | that he spake to thee? CYM 1.03. 5
he spake of her, as dian had hot dreams, | and 5.05.180
in that he spake too far. 5.05.309
i never spake bad word, nor did ill turn | to PER 4.01. 75
like him you spake, | like him you are! 5.03. 32
i spake of thebes, | how dangerous, if we will TNK 1.02. 36
SPAKEST 1 FR 0.0001 REL FR 1 V 0 P
spakest thou of juliet? ROM 3.03. 93
SPAK'ST 2 FR 0.0002 REL FR 2 V 0 P
heard thee say, and vauntingly thou spak'st it, R2 4.01. 36
thou maintain the former words thou spak'st? 1H6 3.04. 31
SPAN 4 FR 0.0004 REL FR 4 V 0 P
that the stretching of a span | buckles in his AYL 3.02.131
to steal from spiritual leisure a brief span H8 3.02.140
"timon is dead, who hath outstretch'd his span: TIM 5.03. 3
o, man's life's but a span; OTH 2.03. 72
SPAN-COUNTER 1 FR 0.0001 REL FR 0 V 1 P
time boys went to span-counter for french crowns 2H6 4.02.158 P
SPANGLE 1 FR 0.0001 REL FR 1 V 0 P
what stars do spangle heaven with such beauty, SHR 4.05. 31
SPANGLED 2 FR 0.0002 REL FR 2 V 0 P
by fountain clear, or spangled starlight sheen, MND 2.01. 29
who, stuck and spangled /with /your flatteries, TIM 3.06. 91
SPANIARD 4 FR 0.0004 REL FR 3 V 1 P
all slops, and a spaniard from the hip upward, ADO 3.02. 36 P
this armado is a spaniard that keeps here in LLL 4.01. 98
this, and fig me like | the bragging spaniard. 2H4 5.03.119
the spaniard, tied by blood and favor to her, H8 2.02. 89
SPANIARD'S 2 FR 0.0002 REL FR 0 V 2 P
therefore too much odds for a spaniard's rapier. LLL 1.02.177 P
there was a spaniard's mouth wat'red, and he PER 4.02.100 P
SPANIEL 7 FR 0.0008 REL FR 6 V 1 P
i am your spaniel; MND 2.01.203
use me but as your spaniel; 2.01.205
where's my spaniel troilus? SHR 4.01.150
to me you cannot reach you play the spaniel, H8 5.02.161
low-crooked curtsies, and base spaniel fawning. JC 3.01. 43
hound or spaniel, brach or /lym, | or bobtail LR 3.06. 69
household, let me be gelded like a spaniel. PER 4.06.125 P
SPANIEL'D *(see spannell'd)*
SPANIEL-LIKE 1 FR 0.0001 REL FR 1 V 0 P
yet, spaniel-like, the more she spurns my love, TGV 4.02. 14
SPANIELS 1 FR 0.0001 REL FR 1 V 0 P
hounds and greyhounds, mungrels, spaniels, curs, MAC 3.01. 92
SPANISH 3 FR 0.0003 REL FR 2 V 1 P
the turn, or the breaking of my spanish sword. AWW 4.01. 47 P
of breaches, ambuscadoes, spanish blades, | of ROM 1.04. 84
the motto thus, in spanish: PER 2.02. 27
SPANISH-POUCH 1 FR 0.0001 REL FR 0 V 1 P
caddis-garter, smooth-tongue, spanish-pouch — 1H4 2.04. 71 P
SPANN'D 1 FR 0.0001 REL FR 1 V 0 P
my life is spann'd already. H8 1.01.223
/SPANNELL'D 1 FR 0.0001 REL FR 1 V 0 P
the hearts | that /spannell'd me at heels, to ANT 4.12. 21
SPANS 1 FR 0.0001 REL FR 1 V 0 P
fathomless | with spans and inches so diminutive TRO 2.02. 31
SPAR *(see sperr)*
SPAR'D 7 FR 0.0008 REL FR 6 V 1 P
up your place, | and you shall well be spar'd. MM 2.02. 14
with other princes that may best be spar'd, JN 5.07. 97
i could have better spar'd a better man. 1H4 5.04.104
but if i spar'd any | that had a head to hit, H8 5.03. 23
whose life i have spar'd at suit of his grey LR 2.02. 63 P
from 's time, | what should not then be spar'd. ANT 3.07. 12
day discourse you into health, | as i am spar'd. TNK 3.06. 39
/SPARE 1 FR 0.0001 REL FR 1 V 0 P
/tell /him, /and /spare /not. R3 1.03.113
SPARE 65 FR 0.0073 REL FR 54 V 11 P
i prithee spare. TMP 2.01. 25
spare him, spare him! MM 2.02. 83
spare him, spare him! 2.02. 83
showing we would not spare heaven as we love it, 2.03. 33
had fast'ned him unto a small spare mast, | such ERR 1.01. 79
i would not spare my brother in this case, | if 4.01. 77
spare not to tell him that he hath wrong'd his ADO 2.02. 22 P
we will spare for no wit, i warrant you. 3.05. 61 P
it should none spare that come within his power. LLL 2.01. 51
if not, shun me, and i will spare your haunts. MND 2.01.142
me | that i shall hardly spare a pound of flesh MV 3.03. 33
as it is a spare life, look you, it fits my AYL 3.02. 19 P
bill, give me thy mete-yard, and spare not me. SHR 4.03.152 P
the rather will i spare my praises towards him, AWW 2.01.103
o lord, sir! — thick, thick, spare not me. 2.02. 45 P
o lord, sir! — spare not me. 2.02. 51 P
at your whipping, and "spare not me"? 2.02. 53 P

the general is content to spare thee yet, | and, 4.01. 80
"shall i bid him go, and spare not?" TN 2.03.111
it | as i weigh grief, which i would spare; WT 3.02. 43
sir, spare your threats. 3.02. 91
o, spare mine eyes, | though to no use but still JN 4.01.101
o, spare me not, my /brother edward's son, | for R2 2.01.124
foin like any devil, he will spare neither man, 2H4 2.01. 16 P
o, give me the spare men, and spare me the great 3.02.269 P
me the spare men, and spare me the great ones. 3.02.269 P
or are they spare in diet, | free from gross H5 2.02.131
maid, | spare for no faggots, let there be enow. 1H6 5.04. 56
i'll give it, sir, and therefore spare my life. 2H6 4.01. 23
spare none but such as go in clouted shoon, 4.02.185
such aid as i can spare you shall command, | but 4.05. 6
spare england, for it is your native coast. 4.08. 50
when clifford cannot spare his friends an oath. 3H6 2.06. 78
o, spare my guiltless wife and my poor children! R3 1.04. 72
you may then spare that time. H8 2.04. 5
sir, to spare me, till i may | be by my friends 2.04. 54
come, come, my lord, you'd spare your spoons. 5.02.201
could distribute, | i made no spare, sir. 5.03. 21
being mov'd, he will not spare to gird the gods. COR 1.01.256
ay, spare us not. 2.03.235
thrice-noble titus, spare my first-born son! TIT 1.01.120
my youth can better spare my blood than you, 3.01.165
agree between you, i will spare my hand. 3.01.183
meats, good angelica, | spare not for cost. ROM 4.04. 6
he'll spare none. TIM 1.01.177
spare not the babe, | whose dimpled smiles from 4.03.119
spare your oaths; 4.03.139
spare thy athenian cradle and those kin | which 5.04. 40
i should avoid | so soon as that spare cassius. JC 1.02.201
spare my grey beard, you wagtail? LR 2.02. 67 P
spare speech. 4.02. 21
while i spare speech, which something now OTH 2.03.199
am poor of thanks, | and scarce can spare them. CYM 2.03. 90
i pray you spare me. 2.03. 95
give me leave to spare when you shall find | you 2.04. 65
spare your arithmetic, never count the turns. 2.04.142
save him, sir, | and spare no blood beside. 5.05. 92
then spare not the old father. 5.05.327
the pow'r that i have on you is to spare you; 5.05.418
spare it not, | the duke has more, coz. eat now. TNK 3.03. 19
all, or dost thou do it | to make me spare thee? 3.06. 47
for, as i am a soldier, | i will not spare you. 3.06. 49
do, and spare not. 3.06. 68
husband is thy friend, for his sake spare me; LUC 582
spare not to spend, and chiefly there | where PP 18.14

SPARES 4 FR 0.0004 REL FR 3 V 1 P
he that ears my land spares my team and gives me AWW 1.03. 44 P
york not our old men spares; 2H6 5.02. 51
must feel war's blow, who spares not innocence: PER 1.02. 93
till the rough seas, that spares not any man, 2.01.131

SPARING 6 FR 0.0006 REL FR 6 V 0 P
ay, to a niggardly host and more sparing guest: ERR 3.01. 27
alive, | i give a sparing limit to my tongue. R3 3.07.194
sparing would show a worse sin than ill doctrine H8 1.03. 60
she hath, and in that sparing /makes huge waste; ROM 1.01.218
"it shall be sparing, and too full of riot, VEN 1147
die, | for sparing justice feeds iniquity. LUC 1687

SPARINGLY 2 FR 0.0002 REL FR 2 V 0 P
or shall we sparingly show you far off | the H5 1.02.239
yet touch this sparingly, as 'twere far off, R3 3.05. 93

SPARK 11 FR 0.0012 REL FR 10 V 1 P
'tis not his fault, the spark. AWW 2.01. 25
could out of thee extract one spark of evil H5 2.02.101
nay then, this spark will prove a raging fire, 2H6 3.01.302
in whose cold blood no spark of honor bides. 3H6 1.01.184
if any spark of life be yet remaining, | down, 5.06. 66
a noble man that hath no spark of fire | to TRO 1.03.294
fire, | who, much enforced, shows a hasty spark, JC 4.03.112
time qualifies the spark and fire of it. HAM 4.07.113
were like an old lecher's heart, a small spark, LR 3.04.112 P
but a spark | to which that /blast gives heat PER 1.02. 40
with fire malevolent, darted a spark, | or what TNK 5.04. 63

SPARKLE 5 FR 0.0005 REL FR 5 V 0 P
they sparkle still the right promethean fire; LLL 4.03.348
you | to sparkle in the spirits of my daughter, AWW 5.03. 75
nay, it perchance will sparkle in your eyes; JN 4.01.114
mine eyes should sparkle like the beaten flint, 2H6 3.02.317
of what a fiery sparkle and quick sweetness, TNK 4.02. 13

SPARKLES 1 FR 0.0001 REL FR 1 V 0 P
sparkles this stone as it was wont, or is't not CYM 2.04. 40

/SPARKLING 1 FR 0.0001 REL FR 1 V 0 P
/eyes /of /fire /sparkling /through /sights /of 2H4 4.01.119

SPARKLING 7 FR 0.0008 REL FR 7 V 0 P
disdain and scorn ride sparkling in her eyes, ADO 3.01. 51
his sparkling eyes, replete with wrathful fire, 1H6 1.01. 12
beauford's red sparkling eyes blab his heart's 2H6 3.01.154
his viands sparkling in a golden cup, | his body 3H6 2.05. 52
with fiery eyes sparkling for very wrath, | and 2.05.131
being purg'd, a fire sparkling in lovers' eyes, ROM 1.01.191
when sparkling stars twire not, thou /gild'st SON 28.12

SPARKS 10 FR 0.0011 REL FR 8 V 2 P
doth indeed show some sparks that are like wit. ADO 2.03.186 P
good sparks and lustrous, a word, good metals: AWW 2.01. 41 P
through both | i see some sparks of better hope, R2 5.03. 21
high sparks of honor in thee have i seen. 5.06. 29
my drops of tears | i'll turn to sparks of fire. H8 2.04. 73
and those sparks of life | that should be in a JC 1.03. 57
the skies are painted with unnumb'red sparks, 3.01. 63
edmund, enkindle all the sparks of nature, | to LR 3.07. 86
how hard it is to hide the sparks of nature! CYM 3.03. 79
that from the cold stone sparks of fire do fly, LUC 177

SPARROW 9 FR 0.0010 REL FR 4 V 5 P
the finch, the sparrow, and the lark, | the MND 3.01.130
feed, | yea, providently caters for the sparrow, AYL 2.03. 44
sparrow! JN 1.01.231
and with his pistol kills a sparrow flying. 1H4 2.04.346 P
so did he never the sparrow. 2.04.348 P
gull, the cuckoo's bird, | useth the sparrow; 5.01. 61
mater is not worth the ninth part of a sparrow. TRO 2.01. 72 P
her breath as short as a new-ta'en sparrow. 3.02. 34 P
is special providence in the fall of a sparrow. HAM 5.02.220 P

SPARROWS' 1 FR 0.0001 REL FR 1 V 0 P
or hateful cuckoos hatch in sparrows' nests? LUC 849

SPARROWS 4 FR 0.0004 REL FR 2 V 2 P
he will shoot no more, but play with sparrows, TMP 4.01.100
sparrows must not build in his house-eaves, MM 3.02.175 P
/i will buy nine sparrows for a penny, and his TRO 2.01. 71 P
yes, | as sparrows eagles; MAC 1.02. 35

SPARTA 3 FR 0.0003 REL FR 3 V 0 P
they bay'd the bear | with hounds of sparta. MND 4.01.114
horn, | in crete, in sparta, nor in thessaly. 4.01.126
a knight of sparta, my renowned father, | and PER 2.02. 18

SPARTAN 3 FR 0.0003 REL FR 2 V 1 P
my hounds are bred out of the spartan kind; MND 4.01.119
now my double-henn'd spartan! TRO 5.07. 11 P
o spartan dog, | more fell than anguish, hunger, OTH 5.02.361

SPARTA'S 1 FR 0.0001 REL FR 1 V 0 P
if helen then be wife to sparta's king, | as it TRO 2.02.183

SPAVIN 1 FR 0.0001 REL FR 1 V 0 P
the spavin | /and springhalt reign'd among 'em. H8 1.03. 12

SPAVINS 1 FR 0.0001 REL FR 0 V 1 P
full of windgalls, sped with spavins, ray'd with SHR 3.02. 53 P

SPAWN 1 FR 0.0001 REL FR 1 V 0 P
your multiplying spawn how can he flatter — COR 2.02. 78

SPAWN'D 1 FR 0.0001 REL FR 0 V 1 P
some report a sea-maid spawn'd him; MM 3.02.108 P

SPAY *(see splay)*

SPE 1 FR 0.0001 REL FR 1 V 0 P
"in hac spe vivo." PER 2.02. 44

SPEAK *(also speken)*

/SPEAK 8 FR 0.0009 REL FR 7 V 1 P
/those /that /could /speak /low /and /tardily 2H4 2.03. 26
/you /speak, /lord /mowbray, /now /you /know 4.01.128
/speak, /prince /of /ithaca, /and /be't /of TRO 1.03. 70
/to /speak /to /you /like /an /honest /man, /i HAM 2.02.268 P
/speak. LR 1.01. 68
/and /i /shall, | /that /i /may /speak. 1.03. 25
/and /she /must /not /speak | /why /she /dares 3.06. 27
/sir, /you /speak /nobly. 5.01. 28

SPEAK 1199 FR 0.1355 REL FR 928 V 271 P
speak to th' mariners. TMP 1.01. 3 P
thou hast. where was she born? speak. tell me. 1.02.260
speak. 1.02.314
took pains to make thee speak, taught thee each 1.02.354
i am the best of them that speak this speech, 1.02.430
that wonders | to hear thee speak of naples. 1.02.434
speak not you for him; 1.02.461
come, follow. speak not for him. 1.02.502
few in millions | can speak like us. 2.01. 8
if but one of his pockets could speak, would it 2.01. 66 P
the truth you speak doth lack some gentleness, 2.01.138
lack some gentleness, | and time to speak it in. 2.01.139
do you not hear me speak? 2.01.210
voice now is to speak well of his friend; 2.02. 90 P
thou beest stephano, touch me, and speak to me; 2.02.101 P
hear my soul speak: 3.01. 63
i profess with kind event | if i speak true! 3.01. 70
moon-calf, speak once in thy life, if thou beest 3.02. 21 P
therefore speak softly, | all's hush'd as 4.01.206
that a living prince | does now speak to thee, i 5.01.109
to speak puling, like a beggar at hallowmas. TGV 2.01. 25 P
all this i speak in print, for in print i found 2.01.169 P
it cannot speak, | for truth hath better deeds 2.02. 17
should not the shoe speak a word for weeping; 2.03. 25 P
o, that she could speak now like a /wood woman! 2.03. 27 P
silvia, i speak to you, and you, sir thurio; 2.04. 84
madam, my lord your father would speak with you. 2.04.116
then speak the truth by her; 2.04.151
can nothing speak? master, shall i strike? 3.01.199 P
it | by aught that i can speak in his dispraise, 3.02. 47
but shall i hear him speak? 4.02. 33 P
'twere false, if i should speak it; 4.02.106
to that i'll speak, to that i'll sigh and weep; 4.02.122
to bring me where to speak with madam silvia. 4.04.109
to hear me speak the message i am sent on. 4.04.112
speak. 5.04. 87 P
it is spoke as a christians ought to speak. WIV 1.01.101 P
you must speak possitable, if you can carry her 1.01.236 P
speak scholarly and wisely. 1.03. 2 P
do intend vat i speak? 1.04. 46 P
to speak a good word to mistress anne page for 1.04. 83 P
i speak and i avouch; 2.01.133 P
sir, here's a woman would speak with you. 2.02. 31 P
master /brook below would fain speak with you, 2.02.145 P
and you, sir! would you speak with me? 2.02.155 P
speak, good master /brook, i shall be glad to be 2.02.178 P
for he speak for a jack-an-ape to anne page. 2.03. 82 P
i pray you let-a me speak a word with your ear. 3.01. 79 P
with her for more money than i'll speak of. 3.02. 56 P
i'll speak it before the best lord, i would make 3.03. 50 P
and would needs speak with you presently. 3.03. 87 P
quickly, my kinsman shall speak for himself. 3.04. 23 P
ye, master slender would speak a word with you. 3.04. 29 P
speak to mistress page. 3.04. 77 P
here's mistress quickly, sir, to speak with you. 3.05. 19 P
no, certainly. speak louder. 4.02. 16 P
let me speak with the gentlemen; 4.03. 5 P
they speak english? 4.03. 6 P
speak, breathe, discuss; 4.05. 2 P
sir, i come to speak with sir john falstaff from 4.05. 4 P
he'll speak like an anthropophaginian unto thee. 4.05. 9 P
i come to speak with her indeed. 4.05. 13 P
speak from thy lungs military. 4.05. 16 P
speak well of them, varletto. 4.05. 64 P
sir — let me speak with you in your chamber. 4.05.121 P
yet hear me speak. 4.06. 3
speak i like herne the hunter? 5.05. 27 P
do i speak feelingly now? MM 1.02. 34 P
if i could speak so wisely under an arrest, i 1.02.131 P
what (but to speak of) would offend again. 1.02.136
may your grace speak of it? 1.03. 6
i speak not as desiring more, | but rather 1.04. 3
vow'd, you must not speak with men | but in the 1.04. 10
then, if you speak, you must not show your face, 1.04. 12
or, if you show your face, you must not speak. 1.04. 13
why dost thou not speak, elbow? 2.01. 59 P
i, that do speak a word, | may call it again. 2.02. 57
her, | that i desire to hear her speak again? 2.02.177
for i can speak | against the thing i say. 2.04. 59
to be received plain, i'll speak more gross: 2.04. 82
what we would have, we speak not what we mean. 2.04.118
let me entreat you speak the former language. 2.04.140
bring /me to hear /them speak, where i may be 3.01. 52 P
if ever he return, and i can speak to him, i 3.01.192 P
let me hear you speak farther. 3.01.205 P
have you not heard speak of mariana, the sister 3.01.209 P
you are pleasant, sir, and speak apace. 3.02.113 P
therefore you speak unskillfully; 3.02.147 P
believe that, since you know not what you speak. 3.02.154 P
to speak so indirectly i am loath. 4.06. 1
he speak against me on the adverse side, | i 4.06. 6
speak loud and kneel before him. 5.01. 19
for that which i must speak | must either punish 5.01. 30
and she will speak most bitterly and strange. 5.01. 36
but yet most truly will i speak: 5.01. 37
you were not bid to speak. 5.01. 78
are i' the wrong | to speak before your time. 5.01. 87
to speak, as from his mouth, what he doth know 5.01.155
first, let her show /her face, and after speak. 5.01.168
isabel here once again, i would speak with her. 5.01.270 P
speak not you to him till we call upon you. 5.01.285 P
'tis he should hear me speak. 5.01.294
and we will hear you speak. 5.01.295
look you speak justly. 5.01.296
let him speak no more. 5.01.347 P
i'll speak all. 5.01.438
impos'd | than i to speak my griefs unspeakable: ERR 1.01. 32
say, didst thou speak with him? 2.01. 47
i could not speak with dromio since at first | i 2.02. 5
look sweet, speak fair, become disloyalty; 3.02. 11
teach me, dear creature, how to think and speak: 3.02. 33
a one as a man may not speak of without he say 3.02. 91 P
didst speak him fair? 4.02. 16
you saw they speak us fair, give us gold: 4.04.152 P
speak softly, yonder, as i think, he walks. 5.01. 9
good sir, draw near to me, i'll speak to him. 5.01. 12
most mighty duke, vouchsafe me speak a word: 5.01.283
speak freely, syracusian, what thou wilt. 5.01.286
speak, old egeon, if thou be'st the man | that 5.01.342
o, if thou be'st the same egeon, speak, | and 5.01.345
egeon, speak, | and speak unto the same aemilia! 5.01.346
or would you have me speak after my custom, as ADO 1.01.168 P
no, i pray thee speak in sober judgment. 1.01.170 P
but speak you this with a sad brow? 1.01.182 P
you speak this to fetch me in, my lord. 1.01.223 P
by my troth, i speak my thought. 1.01.224 P
speak low if you speak love. 2.01. 99 P
speak low if you speak love. 2.01. 99 P
speak, count, 'tis your cue. 2.01.305 P
speak, cousin, or, if you cannot, stop his mouth 2.01.310 P
with a kiss, and let not him speak neither. 2.01.311 P
me, i was born to speak all mirth and no matter. 2.01.330 P
he was wont to speak plain and to the purpose 2.03. 18 P
why, you speak truth. 3.01. 59
if i should speak, | she would mock me into air; 3.01. 74
eight or nine wise words to speak to you, which 3.02. 72 P
if your leisure serv'd, i would speak with you. 3.02. 82 P
hear, for what i would speak of concerns him. 3.02. 86 P
why, you speak like an ancient and most quiet 3.03. 39 P
never speak, we charge you; 3.03.175 P
why, how now? do you speak in the sick tune? 3.04. 41 P
is my lord well, that he doth speak so wide? 4.01. 62
sweet prince, why speak not you? 4.01. 63
what should i speak? 4.01. 63
if they speak but truth of her, | these hands 4.01.190
like mine, | and bid him speak of patience; 5.01. 10
can counsel and speak comfort to that grief 5.01. 21
no, 'tis all men's office to speak patience | to 5.01. 27
i speak not like a dotard nor a fool, | as under 5.01. 59
and speak /off half a dozen dang'rous words, 5.01. 97
shall i speak a word in your ear? 5.01.143 P
how to pray your patience, | yet i must speak. 5.01.272
french king's daughter with yourself to speak — LLL 1.01.135
if i break faith, this word shall speak for me: 1.01.153
it is the manner of a man to speak to a woman; 1.01.210 P
speak you this in my praise, master? 1.02. 24 P
his tongue, all impatient to speak and not see, 2.01.238
but to speak that in words which his eye hath 2.01.251
i will speak that l'envoy: 3.01.115 P
when tongues speak sweetly, then they name her 3.01.166
i may speak of thee as the traveller doth of 4.02. 95 P
such rackers of ortography, as to speak "dout," 5.01. 20 P
"thus must thou speak," and "thus thy body bear" 5.02.100
yet fear not thou, but speak audaciously." 5.02.104
if they do speak our language, 'tis our will 5.02.176
how blow? how blow? speak to be understood. 5.02.294
madam, speak true. 5.02.364
speak for yourselves, my wit is at an end. 5.02.430
a conqueror, and afeard to speak! 5.02.579 P
a-coming will speak their mind in some other 5.02.585 P
speak, brave hector, we are much delighted. 5.02.665 P
a mask, and you may speak as small as you will. MND 1.02. 50 P
i'll speak in a monstrous little voice, "thisne! 1.02. 52 P
do i speak you fair? 2.01.199
and to speak troth, i have forgot our way. 2.02. 36
speak, and if you hear; 2.02.153
speak, of all loves! 2.02.154
lion's neck, and he himself must speak through, 3.01. 38 P
speak, pyramus. thisby, stand forth. 3.01. 81 P
must i speak now? 3.01. 89 P
why, you must not speak that yet! 3.01. 99 P
you speak all your part at once, cues and all. 3.01.100 P
you speak not as you think. it cannot be. 3.02.191
speak! 3.02.296
speak not of helena, | take not her part. 3.02.332
where art thou, proud demetrius? speak thou now. 3.02.401
lysander, speak again! 3.02.404
speak! 3.02.406
but speak, egeus, is not this the day | that 4.01.135
but, as i think — for truly would i speak, 4.01.149
strange, my theseus, that these lovers speak of. 5.01. 1
tongue-tied simplicity | in least speak most, to 5.01.105
it is not enough to speak, but to speak true. 5.01.121 P
it is not enough to speak, but to speak true. 5.01.121 P
i wonder if the lion be to speak. 5.01.152 P
would you desire lime and hair to speak better? 5.01.165 P
speak, speak! 5.01.327
speak, speak! 5.01.327
if they should speak, would almost damn those MV 1.01. 98
wise men, | for gratiano never lets me speak. 1.01.107

therefore speak. 1.01.160
may i speak with antonio? 1.03. 30 P
choose wrong | never to speak to lady afterward 2.01. 41
one speak for both. what would you? 2.02.141 P
speak it privately. 2.04. 20
at his house and desires to speak with you both. 3.01. 75 P
speak too long, but 'tis to peize the time, 3.02. 22
ay, but i fear you speak upon the rack, | where 3.02. 32
rack, | where men enforced do speak any thing. 3.02. 33
'll have my bond, speak not against my bond, 3.03. 4
pray thee hear me speak. 3.03. 11
will not hear thee speak. 3.03. 12
'll have my bond, and therefore speak no more. 3.03. 13
madam, although i speak it in your presence, 3.04. 1
and speak between the change of man and boy 3.04. 66
and speak of frays | like a fine bragging youth, 3.04. 68
and so now i speak my agitation of the matter; 3.05. 4 P
thou but offend'st thy lungs to speak so loud. 4.01.140
say how i lov'd you, speak me fair in death; 4.01.275
sir, i would speak with you. 4.02. 12
speak not so grossly, you are all amaz'd. 5.01.266
or, to speak more properly, stays me here at AYL 1.01. 8 P
he duke's wrastler, here to speak with me? 1.01. 90 P
and almost with tears i speak it) there is not 1.01.154 P
speak but brotherly of him, but should i 1.01.155 P
speak no more of him, you'll be whipt for 1.02. 84 P
hat fools may not speak wisely what wise men do 1.02. 86 P
why, this that i speak of. 1.02.136 P
peak to him, ladies, see if you can move him. 1.02.161 P
e cannot speak, my lord. 1.02.220
cannot speak to her, yet she urg'd conference. 1.02.258
more suits you to conceive than i to speak of. 1.02.267
dear sovereign, hear me speak. 1.03. 66
and her patience | speak to the people, and they 1.03. 79
go seek him, tell him i would speak with him. 2.07. 7
give me leave | to speak my mind, and i will 2.07. 59
peak you so gently? 2.07.106
scarce can speak to thank you for myself. 2.07.170
ell me who is it quickly, and speak apace. 3.02.198 P
peak sad brow and true maid. 3.02.214 P
when i think, i must speak. 3.02.250 P
will speak to him like a saucy lackey, and 3.02.295 P
old religious uncle of mine taught me to speak, 3.02.344 P
re you so much in love as your rhymes speak? 3.02.397 P
nay, you were better speak first, and when you 4.01. 73 P
, i have heard him speak of that same brother, 4.03.121
of me then (for now i speak to some purpose) 5.02. 52 P
speak not this that you should bear a good 5.02. 54 P
why do you speak too, "why blame you me to love 5.02.106 P
and if he chance to speak, be ready straight, SHR in.1. 52
see, i hear, i speak; in.2. 70
ap, | but did i never speak of all that time? in.2. 82
ark, tranio, thou mayst hear minerva speak. 1.01. 84
sten to me, and if you speak me fair, | i'll 1.02.179
mistake me not, i speak but as i find. 2.01. 66
et us that are poor petitioners speak too. 2.01. 72
ay she be mute, and will not speak a word, 2.01.174
but here she comes, and now, petruchio, speak. 2.01.181
o speak the ceremonial rites of marriage? 3.02. 6
nows not which way to stand, to look, to speak, 4.01.185
etter how to tame a shrew, | now let him speak; 4.01.211
why, sir, i trust i may have leave to speak, 4.03. 73
may have leave to speak, | and speak i will. 4.03. 74
ook what i speak, or do, or think to do, | you 4.03.192
isa, and is here at the door to speak with him. 5.01. 29 P
now call'd you the man you speak of, madam? AWW 1.01. 24 P
o speak on the part of virginity is to accuse 1.01.136 P
he true minute when | exception bid him speak, 1.02. 40
, madam, and i speak the truth the next way: 1.03. 58 P
f her i am to speak. 1.03. 67 P
ell my gentlewoman i would speak with her — 1.03. 68 P
will speak with you further anon. 1.03.127 P
ehaviors | that in their kind they speak it. 1.03.179
peak, is't so? 1.03.181
ad you not lately an intent — speak truly — 1.03.218
this was your motive | for paris, was it? speak. 1.03.231
at, speak, and move under the influence of the 2.01. 54 P
methinks in thee some blessed spirit doth speak 2.01.175
aith, if the learned should speak truth of it. 2.02. 35 P
fore me, i speak in respect — 2.03. 27 P
efore i speak, too threat'ningly replies. 2.03. 81
peak, thine answer. 2.03.166
y; is it not a language i speak? 2.03.189 P
o the king | that which i durst not speak. 2.03.289
would have tears, and sorrow bids me speak. 3.04. 42
any malice, but to speak of him as my kinsman, 3.06. 8 P
well in it, the duke shall both speak of it, and 3.06. 69 P
upon him, speak what terrible language you will. 4.01. 2 P
linsey-woolsey hast thou to speak to us again? 4.01. 12 P
e'en such as you speak to me. 4.01. 13 P
ancy, not to know what we speak one to another; 4.01. 18 P
talian, or french, let him speak to me, | i'll 4.01. 72
understand thee, and can speak thy tongue. 4.01. 75 P
nay, i'll speak that | which you will wonder at. 4.01. 85
emain there but an hour, nor speak to me. 4.02. 58
hereabouts," set down, for i'll speak truth. 4.03.149 P
we shall speak of you there. 4.03.329 P
than by that red-tail'd humble-bee i speak of. 4.05. 7 P
and the master i speak of ever keeps a good fire 4.05. 48 P
he king my master to speak in the behalf of my 4.05. 71 P
whose nature sickens but to speak a truth. 5.03.207
what he'll utter, | that will speak any thing? 5.03.209
s this the man you speak of? 5.03.233
aith, i know more than i'll speak. 5.03.256 P
but wilt thou not speak all thou know'st? 5.03.257 P
which would derive me ill will to speak of; 5.03.265 P
therefore i will not speak what i know. 5.03.266 P
sing | and speak to him in many sorts of music TN 1.02. 58
say i do speak with her, my lord, what then? 1.04. 23
young gentleman much desires to speak with you. 1.05.100 P
yond young fellow swears he will speak with you. 1.05.140 P
so much, and therefore comes to speak with you. 1.05.142 P
that too, and therefore comes to speak with you. 1.05.144 P
tell him he shall not speak with me. 1.05.146 P
supporter to a bench, but he'll speak with you. 1.05.149 P
he'll speak with you, will you or no. 1.05.153 P
speak to me, i shall answer for her. your will? 1.05.168 P
speak your office. 1.05.207 P
for she did speak in starts distractedly. 2.02. 21
thou dost speak masterly. 2.04. 22
i bade you never speak again of him; 3.01.107
so, let me hear you speak. 3.01.122
i speak too loud. 3.04. 4
himself possess'd him, yet i'll speak to him. 3.04. 86 P
la you, and you speak ill of the devil, how he 3.04.100 P
let me speak a little. 3.04.359
you by my lady, to bid you come speak with her, 4.01. 7 P
let your lady know i am here to speak with her, 5.01. 43 P
my lord would speak, my duty hushes me. 5.01.107
why do you speak to me? 5.01.187
little unthought of, and speak out of my injury. 5.01.310 P
good madam, hear me speak, | and let no quarrel 5.01.355
i speak it in the freedom of my knowledge: WT 1.01. 11 P
i speak as my understanding instructs me and as 1.01. 19 P
tongue-tied our queen? speak you. 1.02. 27
now, while i speak this) holds his wife by th' 1.02.193
not speak? 1.02.365
you'll kiss me hard and speak to me as if | i 2.01. 5
he who shall speak for her is afar off guilty 2.01.104
it is for you we speak, not for ourselves. 2.01.140
come follow us, | we are to speak in public; 2.01.197
even since it could speak, from an infant, 3.02. 70
you speak a language that i understand not. 3.02. 80
thou canst not speak too much, i have deserv'd 3.02.215
i'll speak of her no more, nor of your children; 3.02.229
thou didst speak but well | when most the truth; 3.02.232
and with speed so pace | to speak of perdita, 4.01. 24
fatal country sicilia, prithee speak no more, 4.02. 21 P
which then will speak, that you must change this 4.04. 39
when you speak, sweet, | i'ld have you do it 4.04.136
i cannot speak | so well, nothing so well; 4.04.380
can he speak? 4.04.399
for once or twice | i was about to speak, and 4.04.443
why, how now, father? | speak ere thou diest. 4.04.451
i cannot speak, nor think, | nor dare to know 4.04.451
it is my father's music | to speak your deeds; 4.04.519
bosom there, | and speak his very heart. 4.04.564
happy be you! | all that you speak shows fair. 4.04.623
and speak of something wildly | by us perform'd 5.01.129
where's bohemia? speak. 5.01.185
i speak amazedly, and it becomes | my marvel and 5.01.187
forswear themselves as often as they speak. 5.01.200
they say one would speak to her and stand in 5.02.101 P
but yet speak. 5.03. 22
what to speak, | i am content to hear; 5.03. 92
for 'tis as easy | to make her speak as move. 5.03. 94
if she pertain to life let her speak too. 5.03.113
appears she lives, | though yet she speak not. 5.03.118
sirrah, speak, | what doth move you to claim JN 1.01. 90
where how he did prevail i shame to speak. 1.01.104
lay, | as i have heard my father speak himself, 1.01.107
chatillion, speak. 2.01. 53
let us hear them speak | whose title they admit, 2.01.199
speak, citizens, for england. who's your king? 2.01.362
speak on with favor, we are bent to hear. 2.01.422
speak england first, that hath been forward 2.01.482
been forward first | to speak unto this city: 2.01.483
or if you will, to speak more properly, | i will 2.01.514
speak then, prince dolphin, can you love this 2.01.524
then speak again, not all thy former tale, | but 3.01. 25
is | as it makes harmful all that speak of it. 3.01. 41
o, that a man should speak those words to me! 3.01.130
now hear me speak with a prophetic spirit; 3.04.126
for even the breath of what i mean to speak 3.04.127
i will not stir, nor winch, nor speak a word, 4.01. 80
to any tongue, speak it of what it will. 4.02.140
i am sent to speak: 5.02.119
king, | for thus his royalty doth speak in me: 5.02.129
give me leave to speak. 5.02.162
no, i will speak. 5.02.163
speak ho! 5.06. 1
speak quickly, or i shoot. 5.06. 1
his highness yet doth speak, and holds belief 5.07. 6
hear | the accuser and the accused freely speak. R2 1.01. 17
for what i speak | my body shall make good upon 1.01. 36
look what i speak, my life shall prove it true: 1.01. 87
speak truly on thy knighthood and thy oath, | as 1.03. 14
speak like a true knight, so defend thee heaven! 1.03. 34
nay, speak thy mind, and let him ne'er speak 2.01.230
and let him ne'er speak more | that speaks thy 2.01.230
that thou wouldst speak to the duke of herford? 2.01.232
be confident to speak, northumberland: 2.01.274
uncle, for god's sake speak comfortable words. 2.02. 76
and bids me speak of nothing but despair. 3.02. 66
strive to speak big, and clap their female 3.02.114
no matter where — of comfort no man speak: 3.02.144
speak sweetly, man, although thy looks be sour. 3.02.193
let no man speak again | to alter this, for 3.02.213
speak to his gentle hearing kind commends. 3.03.126
not, | to look so poorly and to speak so fair? 3.03.128
base court he doth attend | to speak with you, 3.03.177
makes him speak fondly like a frantic man, | yet 3.03.185
speak, thou wretch. 3.04. 80
so, | i speak no more than every one doth know. 3.04. 91
now, bagot, freely speak thy mind, | what thou 4.01. 2
worst in this royal presence may i speak, | yet 4.01.115
yet best beseeming me to speak the truth. 4.01.116
i speak to subjects, and a subject speaks, 4.01.132
my lord, | before i freely speak my mind herein, 4.01.327
my mouth, | unless a pardon ere i rise or speak. 5.03. 32
shall i for love speak treason to thy face? 5.03. 44
speak, | recover breath, tell us how near is 5.03. 46
speak with me, pity me, open the door! 5.03. 77
speak it in french, king, say "pardonne moy." 5.03.119
speak "pardon" as 'tis current in our land, 5.03.123
thine eye begins to speak, set thy tongue there; 5.03.125
yet am i sick for fear, speak it again, | twice 5.03.133
and now am i, if a man should speak truly, 1H4 1.02. 94 P
you were about to speak. 1.03. 22
let me not hear you speak of mortimer. 1.03.119
speak of mortimer! 1.03.130
'zounds, i will speak of him, and let my soul 1.03.131
forbade my tongue to speak of mortimer, | but i 1.03.220
i'll have a starling shall be taught to speak 1.03.224
i speak not this in estimation, | as what i 1.03.272
such as will strike sooner than speak, and speak 2.01. 78 P
sooner than speak, and speak sooner than drink, 2.01. 78 P
speak terms of manage to thy bounding steed, 2.03. 49
nay, tell me if you speak in jest or no. 2.03. 99
let them speak; 2.04.171 P
if they speak more or less than truth, they are 2.04.171 P
speak, sirs, how was it? 2.04.173 P
in base comparisons, hear me speak but this — 2.04.251 P
of the court at door would speak with you. 2.04.288 P
i have wept, for i must speak in passion, and i 2.04.386 P
now i do not speak to thee in drink but in tears 2.04.415 P
then, peremptorily i speak it, there is virtue 2.04.430 P
dost thou speak like a king? 2.04.433 P
name as oft as lancaster | doth speak of you, 3.01. 9
let me understand you then, | speak it in welsh. 3.01.118
i can speak english, lord, as well as you, | for 3.01.119
my wife can speak no english, i no welsh. 3.01.191
so hath the business that i come to speak of. 3.02.163
well, | you speak it out of fear and cold heart. 4.03. 7
for my part, i may speak it to my shame, | i 5.01. 93
i prithee speak, we will not trust our eyes 5.04.136
i speak of peace, while covert enmity | under 2H4 in 9
but what mean i | to speak so true at first? in 28
yet speak, morton, | tell thou an earl his 1.01. 87
and hold'st it fear or sin | to speak a truth. 1.01. 96
i hear for certain and dare speak the truth, 1.01.188
i knew of this before, but, to speak truth, 1.01.210
you must speak louder, my master is deaf. 1.02. 67 P
pluck him by the elbow, i must speak with him. 1.02. 69 P
sir, my lord would speak with you. 1.02. 91 P
i pray you let me speak with you. 1.02.110 P
you for your life, to come speak with me. 1.02.133 P
all | speak plainly your opinions of our hopes. 1.03. 3
you speak as having power to do wrong, but 2.01.129 P
i have given over, i will speak no more; 2.03. 5
pistol's below, and would speak with you. 2.04. 70 P
and 'a do nothing but speak nothing, 'a shall be 2.04.193 P
good doll, do not speak like a death's-head, do 2.04.234 P
how vildly did you speak of me /even now before 2.04.301 P
i cannot speak. 2.04.379 P
did speak these words, now prov'd a prophecy? 3.01. 69
will not go off until they hear you speak. 4.02.100
shall better speak of you than you deserve. 4.03. 85
speak lower, princes, for the king recovers. 4.04.129
sweet prince, speak low, | the king your father 4.05. 16
i never thought to hear you speak again. 4.05. 91
sir, is able to speak for himself, when a knave 5.01. 46 P
we meet like men that had forgot to speak. 5.02. 22
well, you must now speak sir john falstaff fair, 5.02. 33
speak in your state | what i have done that 5.02. 99
so shall i live to speak my father's words: 5.02.107
i speak of africa and golden joys. 5.03.100
under which king, besonian? speak, or die. 5.03.113
i speak the truth. 5.03.117
as nail in door. the things i speak are just. 5.03.121
my lord chief justice, speak to that vain man. 5.05. 44
know you what 'tis you speak? 5.05. 45
my king! my jove! i speak to thee, my heart! 5.05. 46
i cannot now speak, i will hear you soon. 5.05. 94
before the frenchman speak a word of it. H5 1.01. 97
under this conjuration speak, my lord; 1.02. 29
that what you speak is in your conscience wash'd 1.02. 31
with full mouth | speak freely of our acts, or 1.02.231
the duke of gloucester would speak with you. 3.02. 55 P
therefore go speak, the duke will hear thy voice 3.06. 46
speak, captain, for his life, and i will thee 3.06. 49
and i must speak with him from the pridge. 3.06. 86 P
now we speak upon our cue, and our voice is 3.06.123 P
in the name of jesu christ, speak fewer. 4.01. 65 P
i will speak lower. 4.01. 81 P
for, though i speak it to you, i think the king 4.01.101 P
troth, i will speak my conscience of the king: 4.01.118 P
howsoever you speak this to feel other men's 4.01.125 P
let me speak proudly: 4.03.108
i speak but in the figures and comparisons of it 4.07. 44 P
because he could not speak english in the native 5.01. 75 P
shall mock at me, i cannot speak your england. 5.02.103 P
i am glad thou canst speak no better english, 5.02.123 P
i speak to thee plain soldier. 5.02.149 P
speak, my fair, and fairly, i pray thee. 5.02.167 P
the kingdom as to speak so much more french. 5.02.185 P
who, though i speak it before his face, if he be 5.02.241 P
god speak this amen! 5.02.368
speak softly, or the loss of those great towns 1H6 1.01. 63
speak, shall i call her in? 1.02. 58
speak, salisbury; 1.04. 73
at least, if thou canst, speak. 1.04. 73
speak unto talbot, nay, look up to him. 1.04. 89
here is the talbot, who would speak with him? 2.02. 37
since you are tongue-tied and so loath to speak, 2.04. 25
lest it be said, "speak, sirrah, when you should 3.01. 62
i speak not to that railing hecate, | but unto 3.02. 64
speak, pucelle, and enchant him with thy words. 3.03. 40
stay, let thy humble handmaid speak to thee. 3.03. 42
speak on, but be not over-tedious. 3.03. 43
be patient, lords, and give them leave to speak. 4.01. 82
speak, thy father's care: 4.06. 26
speak to thy father ere thou yield thy breath! 4.07. 24
what tidings send our scouts? i prithee speak. 5.02. 10
fain would i woo her, yet i dare not speak: 5.03. 65
speak, winchester, for boiling choler chokes 5.04.120
ambitious warwick, let thy betters speak. 2H6 1.03.109
he did speak them to me in the garret one night, 1.03.191 P
for, till thou speak, thou shalt not pass from 1.04. 27
witness my tears, i cannot stay to speak. 2.04. 86
and, had i first been put to speak my mind, | i 3.01. 43
but shall i speak my conscience, | our kinsman 3.01. 68
and well such losers may have leave to speak. 3.01.185
say as you think, and speak it from your souls: 3.01.247
the duke was dumb and could not speak a word. 3.02. 32
for every word you speak in his behalf | is 3.02.208
go, speak not to me; 3.02.352
speak, beauford, to thy sovereign. 3.03. 1
speak, captain, shall i stab the forlorn swain? 4.01. 65
my gracious lord, entreat him, speak him fair. 4.01.120
not, | it is to you, good people, that i speak, 4.02.129
and more than that, he can speak french, and 4.02.166 P
and, to speak truth, thou deserv'st no less. 4.03. 10 P
hear me but speak, and bear me where you will. 4.07. 59

speak. 4.07. 98
scarce can i speak, my choler is so great. 5.01. 23
speak not in spite, | for you shall sup with 5.01.213
set, | i would speak blasphemy ere bid you fly. 5.02. 85
speak thou for me and tell them what i did. 3H6 1.01. 16
peace thou! and give king henry leave to speak. 1.01.120
plantagenet shall speak first. 1.01.121
i shame to hear thee speak. 1.01.231
stay, gentle margaret, and hear me speak. 1.01.257
prove the contrary, if you'll hear me speak. 1.02. 20
sweet clifford, hear me speak before i die: 1.03. 18
speak thou, northumberland. 1.04. 53
york cannot speak unless he wear a crown. 1.04. 93
by your leave i speak it, | you love the breeder 2.01. 41
o, speak no more, for i have heard too much. 2.01. 48
for self-same wind that i should speak withal 2.01. 82
'tis love i bear thy glories make me speak. 2.01.158
ay, now methinks i hear great warwick speak. 2.01.186
are you there, butcher? o, i cannot speak! 2.02. 95
how now, long-tongu'd warwick, dare you speak? 2.02.102
done with words, my lords, and hear me speak. 2.02.117
tongue, | i am a king, and privileg'd to speak. 2.02.120
since thou deniedst the gentle king to speak. 2.02.172
for (though before his face i speak the words) 2.06. 39
and his ill-boding tongue no more shall speak. 2.06. 59
speak, clifford, dost thou know who speaks to 2.06. 61
no humble suitors press to speak for right, | no 3.01. 19
she, poor wretch, for grief can speak no more; 3.01. 47
i speak no more than what my soul intends, | and 3.02. 94
and give my tongue-tied sorrows leave to speak. 3.03. 22
bona, hear me speak | before you answer warwick. 3.03. 65
warwick, canst thou speak against thy liege, 3.03. 95
and montague, | speak freely what you think. 4.01. 28
speak suddenly, my lords, are we all friends? 4.02. 4
hence with him to the tower, let him not speak. 4.08. 57
speak gentle words and humbly bend thy knee, 5.01. 22
that glues my lips and will not let me speak. 5.02. 38
as good to chide the waves as speak them fair. 5.04. 24
this speak i, lords, to let you understand, | if 5.04. 33
should, if a coward heard her speak these words, 5.04. 40
i speak not this as doubting any here; 5.04. 43
for every word i speak, | ye see i drink the 5.04. 74
go bear them hence, i will not hear them speak. 5.05. 4
bring forth the gallant, let us hear him speak. 5.05. 12
speak like a subject, proud ambitious york! 5.05. 17
o ned, sweet ned, speak to thy mother, boy! 5.05. 51
canst thou not speak? 5.05. 52
no, no, my heart will burst and if i speak, 5.05. 59
and i will speak, that so my heart may burst. 5.05. 60
we speak no treason, man. R3 1.01. 90
heart sues, and prompts my tongue to speak. 1.02.170
speak it again, and even with the word | this 1.02.188
'tis time to speak, my pains are quite forgot. 1.03.116
i would speak with clarence, and i came hither 1.04. 86 P
how darkly and how deadly dost thou speak! 1.04.169
but for my brother not a man would speak, | nor 2.01.127
i, ungracious, speak unto myself | for him, poor 2.01.128
in god's name speak, when is the royal day? 3.04. 3
speak and look back, and pry on every side, 3.05. 6
i would have had you heard | the traitor speak, 3.05. 57
as well as i had seen, and heard him speak; 3.05. 63
would they not speak? 3.07. 42
silence, | or bitterly to speak in your reproof, 3.07.142
therefore — to speak, and to avoid the first, 3.07.151
o dorset, speak not to me, get thee gone! 4.01. 38
think now what i would speak. 4.02. 10
speak suddenly, be brief. 4.02. 20
dear lord, | before i positively speak in this. 4.02. 25
conscience and remorse | they could not speak; 4.03. 21
o, let me speak! 4.04.160
i prithee hear me speak. 4.04.180
you speak too bitterly. 4.04.181
for i shall never speak to thee again. 4.04.182
you speak as if that i had slain my cousins! 4.04.222
will not king richard let me speak with him? 5.01. 1
blunt, make some good means to speak with him, 5.03. 40
fool, of thyself speak well; 5.03.192
speak freely. H8 1.02.131
speak on. 1.02.143
hast thou heard him | at any time speak aught? 1.02.146
on my soul, i'll speak but truth. 1.02.177
you can speak the french tongue; 1.04. 57
because they speak no english, thus they pray'd 1.04. 65
pray speak what has happen'd. 2.01. 6
and see the noble ruin'd man you speak of. 2.01. 54
and, if he speak of buckingham, pray tell him 2.01. 87
say something that is sad, | speak how i fell. 2.01.136
not to speak of. 2.02. 81
perceive i speak sincerely, and high note's 2.03. 59
vouchsafe to speak my thanks and my obedience, 2.03. 71
lord cardinal, | to you i speak. 2.04. 69
i do profess | you speak not like yourself, who 2.04. 85
the which before | his highness shall speak in, 2.04.103
sovereign and pious else, could speak thee out) 2.04.141
i speak my good lord card'nal to this point, 2.04.167
would they speak with me? 3.01. 17
speak it here; 3.01. 29
could speak this with as free a soul as i do! 3.01. 32
pray speak in english. 3.01. 46
if you speak truth, for their poor mistress' 3.01. 47
ye speak like honest men (pray god ye prove so!) 3.01. 69
have i liv'd thus long (let me speak myself, 3.01.125
my lords, you speak your pleasures. 3.02. 13
speak on, sir, | i dare your worst objections. 3.02.306
i have no power to speak, sir. 3.02.373
good sir, speak it to us. 4.01. 61
thus far, griffith, give me leave to speak him, 4.02. 32
your highness | to hear me speak his good now? 4.02. 47
that christendom shall ever speak his virtue. 4.02. 63
sir, you speak of two | the most remark'd i' th' 5.01. 32
and who dare speak | one syllable against him? 5.01. 38
myself have ventur'd | to speak my mind of him; 5.01. 41
ah, my good lord, i grieve at what i speak, 5.01. 95
speak to the business, master secretary. 5.02. 36
there living | (i speak it with a single heart, 5.02. 73
let me speak, sir, | for heaven now bids me; 5.04. 14
i speak no more than truth. TRO 1.01. 64 P
thou dost not speak so much. 1.01. 65
pray you speak no more to me, i will leave all 1.01. 87 P
speak not so loud. 1.02.185 P
sir, my lord would instantly speak with you. 1.02.272 P
thou great, and wise, to hear ulysses speak. 1.03. 69
on /the attentive bent, | and then to speak. 1.03.253
speak frankly as the wind, | it is not 1.03.253
me take a trumpet, | and to this purpose speak: 1.03.264
speak then, thou /whinid'st leaven, speak; 2.01. 14 P
speak then, thou /whinid'st leaven, speak; 2.01. 14 P
i shall speak as much as thou afterwards. 2.01.111 P
you speak | like one besotted on your sweet 2.02.142
of nature and of nations speak aloud | to have 2.02.185
come, patroclus, i'll speak with nobody. 2.03. 69 P
go and tell him | we come to speak with him, and 2.03.122
not be satisfied, | we come to speak with him. 2.03.141
i come to speak with paris from the prince 3.01. 38 P
you speak your fair pleasure, sweet queen. 3.01. 48 P
why do you not speak to her? 3.02. 46 P
and what truth can speak truest not truer than 3.02. 97 P
for in this rapture i shall surely speak | the 3.02.130
i know not what i speak. 3.02.151
know they what they speak that speak so wisely. 3.02.152
know they what they speak that speak so wisely. 3.02.152
bed, because it shall not speak of your pretty 3.02.208 P
what comes the general to speak with me? 3.03. 55
i as your lover speak: 3.03.214
since she could speak, | she hath not given so 4.01. 73
it doth import him much to speak with me. 4.02. 50
i speak not "be thou true" as fearing thee, 4.04. 62
hear why i speak it, love. 4.04. 75
so," | i speak it in my spirit and honor, "no." 4.04.135
what, are you up here, ho? speak! 5.02. 1
all hell's torments, | i will not speak a word! 5.02. 44
by jove, i will not speak a word. 5.02. 52
one cannot speak a word | but it straight starts 5.02.100
i do not speak of flight, of fear, of death, 5.10. 12
before we proceed any further, hear me speak. COR 1.01. 2 P
speak, speak. 1.01. 3 P
speak, speak. 1.01. 3 P
for the gods know i speak this in hunger for 1.01. 24 P
nay, but speak not maliciously. 1.01. 35 P
speak, i pray you. 1.01. 56
i may make the belly smile | as well as speak — 1.01.110
o, doubt not that, | i speak from certainties. 1.02. 31
i heard a senator speak it. 1.03. 95 P
when you speak best unto the purpose, it is not 2.01. 86 P
all tongues speak of him, and the bleared sights 2.01.205
to see him, and | the blind to hear him speak. 2.01.263
speak, good cominius: 2.02. 48
please you | to hear cominius speak? 2.02. 62
worthy cominius, speak. 2.02. 66
the man i speak of cannot in the world | be 2.02. 86
corioles, let me say, | i cannot speak him home. 2.02.103
then remains | that you do speak to the people. 2.02.135
tongues into those wounds and speak for them; 2.03. 7 P
you must not speak of that. 2.03. 55
pray you speak to 'em, i pray you, | in 2.03. 59
you speak a' th' people | as if you were a god, 3.01. 80
of breath, | confusion's near, i cannot speak. 3.01.189
speak, good sicinius. 3.01.191
speak, speak, speak! 3.01.192
speak, speak, speak! 3.01.192
speak, speak, speak! 3.01.192
the vengeance, | could he not speak 'em fair? 3.01.262
hear me speak! 3.01.275
speak briefly then, | for we are peremptory to 3.01.283
ordinance stood up | to speak of peace or war. 3.02. 13
be too noble, | but when extremities speak. 3.02. 41
because that now it lies you on to speak | to 3.02. 52
come, go with us, speak fair. 3.02. 70
first hear me speak. 3.03. 41
what you have seen him do, and heard him speak, 3.03. 77
let me speak. 3.03.109
then if i would | speak that — 3.03.116
we know your drift. speak what? 3.03.116
speak, man: 4.05. 54
should from yond cloud speak divine things, 4.05.104
if he coy'd | to hear cominius speak, i'll keep 5.01. 7
of state, and come | to speak with coriolanus. 5.02. 4
with fire before | you'll speak with coriolanus. 5.02. 8
for i would not speak with him till after dinner 5.02. 35 P
word, menenius, | i will not hear thee speak. 5.02. 92
should we be silent and not speak, our raiment 5.03. 94
speak to me, son. 5.03.148
why dost not speak? 5.03.153
daughter, speak you; 5.03.155
speak thou, boy; 5.03.156
city be afire, | and then i'll speak a little. 5.03.182
peace both, | and hear me speak. 5.06.110
my noble masters, hear me speak. 5.06.131
beat thou the drum, that it speak mournfully; 5.06.149
speak, queen of goths, dost thou applaud my TIT 1.01.321
father, and in that name doth nature speak — 1.01.371
speak thou no more, if all the rest will speed. 1.01.372
then hear me speak indifferently for all; 1.01.430
there speak, and strike, brave boys, and take 2.01.129
i will not her speak, away with her! 2.03.137
speak, brother, hast thou hurt thee with the 2.03.203
let them not speak a word, the guilt is plain, 2.03.301
so now go tell, and if thy tongue can speak, 2.04. 1
speak, gentle niece: 2.04. 16
why dost not speak to me? 2.04. 21
shall i speak for thee? 2.04. 33
my gracious lord, no tribune hears you speak. 3.01. 32
speak, lavinia, what accursed hand | hath made 3.01. 66
speak, gentle sister, who hath mart'red thee? 3.01. 81
had she a tongue to speak, now would she say 3.01.144
o brother, speak with possibility, | and do not 3.01.214
for these two heads do seem to speak to me, 3.01.271
now, good fellow, wouldst thou speak with us? 4.04. 39
why dost not speak? 5.01. 46
i'll speak no more but "vengeance rot you all!" 5.01. 58
'twill vex thy soul to hear what i shall speak: 5.01. 62
sirs, stop his mouth, and let him speak no more. 5.01.151
yield to his humor, smooth and speak him fair, 5.02.140
close their mouths, let them not speak a word. 5.02.164
stop their mouths, let them not speak to me, 5.02.167
what would you say if i should let you speak? 5.02.178
speak, rome's dear friend, as erst our ancestor, 5.03. 80
while i stand by and weep to hear him speak. 5.03. 95
now is my turn to speak. 5.03.119
speak, romans, speak, and if you say we shall, 5.03.135
speak, romans, speak, and if you say we shall, 5.03.135
o lord, i cannot speak to him for weeping, | my 5.03.174
speak, nephew, were you by when it began? ROM 1.01.105
speak briefly, can you like of paris' love? 1.03. 96
speak but one rhyme, and i am satisfied; 2.01. 9
speak to my gossip venus one fair word, | one 2.01. 11
o, speak again, bright angel, for thou art | as 2.02. 26
shall i hear more, or shall i speak at this? 2.02. 37
that which thou hast heard me speak to-night. 2.02. 87
bondage is hoarse, and may not speak aloud, 2.02.160
and will speak more in a minute than he will 2.04.148 P
and 'a speak any thing against me, i'll take him 2.04.150 P
nay, come, i pray thee speak, good, good nurse, 2.05. 28
i pray thee speak, good, good nurse, speak. 2.05. 28
follow me close, for i will speak to them. 3.01. 37
will you speak well of him that kill'd your 3.02. 96
shall i speak ill of him that is my husband? 3.02. 97
"romeo is banished," to speak that word, | is 3.02.122
/thou fond mad man, hear me a little speak. 3.03. 52
o, thou wilt speak again of banishment. 3.03. 53
thou canst not speak of that thou dost not feel. 3.03. 64
then mightst thou speak, then mightst thou tear 3.03. 68
hear me with patience but to speak a word. 3.05.159
speak not, reply not, do not answer me! 3.05.163
i speak no treason. 3.05.172
may not one speak? 3.05.173
talk not to me, for i'll not speak a word. 3.05.202
be not so long to speak, i long to die, | if 4.01. 66
if what thou speak'st speak not of remedy. 4.01. 67
ties up my tongue and will not let me speak. 4.05. 32
i saw them speak together. TIM 1.01. 62
lord timon, hear me speak. 1.01.110
common tongue | which all men speak with him. 1.01.175
you can with modesty speak in your own behalf; 1.02. 94 P
i speak not to thee. 2.02. 52 P
speak to 'em, fool. 2.02. 65 P
pray you walk near, i'll speak with you anon. 2.02.123
could i frankly use | as i can bid thee speak. 2.02.180
ingeniously i speak, | no blame belongs to thee. 2.02.221
nev'r speak or think | that timon's fortunes 2.02.230
dost thou speak seriously, servilius? 3.02. 42
who can speak broader than he that has no house 3.04. 63 P
you only speak from your distracted soul; 3.04.113
favor, pardon me | if i speak like a captain. 3.05. 41
what art thou there? speak. 4.03. 49
speak not, be gone. 4.03.129
speak truth, y' are honest men. 5.01. 77
it is vain that you would speak with timon; 5.01.116
promise to th' athenians | to speak with timon. 5.01.121
timon, | look out and speak to friends. 5.01.128
speak to them, noble timon. 5.01.130
speak and be hang'd. 5.01.131
we speak in vain. 5.01.190
force, | and made us speak like friends. 5.02. 9
speak ho! 5.03. 2
speak, what trade art thou? JC 1.01. 5
speak, caesar is turn'd to hear. 1.02. 17
what say'st thou to me now? speak once again. 1.02. 22
pull'd me by the cloak, would you speak with me? 1.02.216 P
to-morrow, if you please to speak with me, | i 1.02.304
perhaps, speak this | before a willing bondman; 1.03.112
you speak to casca, and to such a man | that is 1.03.116
and to speak truth of caesar, | i have not known 2.01. 19
speak, strike, redress!" 2.01. 47
"speak, strike, redress!" 2.01. 55
am i entreated | to speak and strike? 2.01. 56
here is a sick man that would speak with you. 2.01.310
there | speak to great caesar as he comes along. 2.04. 38
speak hands for me! 3.01. 76
a friend, | speak in the order of his funeral. 3.01.230
not consent | that antony speak in his funeral. 3.01.233
what antony shall speak, i will protest | he 3.01.238
but speak all good you can devise of caesar, 3.01.246
and you shall speak | in the same pulpit whereto 3.01.249
those that will hear me speak, let 'em stay here 3.02. 5
i will hear brutus speak. 3.02. 8
if any, speak, for him have i offended. 3.02. 30 P
if any, speak, for him have i offended. 3.02. 32 P
if any, speak, for him have i offended. 3.02. 33 P
'twere best he speak no harm of brutus here! 3.02. 68
men), | come i to speak in caesar's funeral. 3.02. 84
i speak not to disprove what brutus spoke, | but 3.02.100
spoke, | but here i am to speak what i do know. 3.02.101
now mark him, he begins again to speak. 3.02.117
that gave me public leave to speak of him. 3.02.220
i only speak right on. 3.02.223
poor, dumb mouths, | and bid them speak for me. 3.02.226
yet hear me, countrymen, yet hear me speak. 3.02.233
stand ho! speak the word along. 4.02. 33
cassius, be content, | speak your griefs softly; 4.02. 42
hear me, for i will speak. 4.03. 38
speak no more of her. 4.03.158
mine speak of seventy senators that died | by 4.03.177
speak to me what thou art. 4.03.281
the very last time we shall speak together: 5.01. 98
he look | that seems to speak things strange. MAC 1.02. 47
speak, if you can: what are you? 1.03. 47
to me you speak not. 1.03. 57
speak then to me, who neither beg nor fear 1.03. 60
speak, i charge you. 1.03. 78
were such things here as we do speak about? 1.03. 83
what, can the devil speak true? 1.03.107
let us speak | our free hearts each to other. 1.03.154
we will speak further. 1.05. 71
did not you speak? 2.02. 16
do not bid me speak; 2.03. 72
see, and then speak yourselves. 2.03. 73
speak, speak! 2.03. 83
speak, speak! 2.03. 83
'tis not for you to hear what i can speak: 2.03. 84
of king upon me, | and bade them speak to him; 3.01. 58
if thou canst nod, speak too. 3.04. 69
i pray you speak not. 3.04.116
have been known to move and trees to speak; 3.04.122

more shall they speak; 3.04.133
speak. 4.01. 61
listen, but speak not to't. 4.01. 89
i dare not speak much further, | but cruel are 4.02. 17
i speak not as in absolute fear of you. 4.03. 38
if such a one be fit to govern, speak. 4.03.101
about his throne | that speak him full of grace. 4.03.159
the grief that does not speak | whispers the 4.03.209
i think, but dare not speak. 5.01. 79
make all our trumpets speak, give them all 5.06. 9
that speak my salutation in their minds; 5.09. 23
come, | he may approve our eyes and speak to it. HAM 1.01. 29
down, | and let us hear barnardo speak of this. 1.01. 34
thou art a scholar, speak to it, horatio. 1.01. 42
speak to it, horatio. 1.01. 45
by heaven i charge thee speak! 1.01. 49
stay! speak, speak, i charge thee speak! 1.01. 51
stay! speak, speak, i charge thee speak! 1.01. 51
stay! speak, speak, i charge thee speak! 1.01. 51
hast any sound, or use of voice, | speak to me. 1.01.129
to thee do ease, and grace to me, | speak to me. 1.01.132
happily, foreknowing may avoid, | o speak! 1.01.135
your spirits oft walk in death, | speak of it; 1.01.139
stay, and speak! 1.01.139
it was about to speak, when the cock crew. 1.01.147
this spirit, dumb to us, will speak to him. 1.01.171
you cannot speak of reason to the dane | and 1.02. 44
act of fear, | stand dumb and speak not to him. 1.02.206
did you not speak to it? 1.02.214
itself to motion, like as it would speak; 1.02.217
i'll speak to it, though hell itself should gape 1.02.244
you speak like a green girl, | unsifted in such 1.03.101
questionable shape | that i will speak to thee. 1.04. 44
it will not speak, then i will follow it. 1.04. 63
speak, i'll go no further. 1.05. 1
speak, i am bound to hear. 1.05. 6
never to speak of this that you have seen, 1.05.153
never to speak of this that you have heard. 1.05.160
or "if we list to speak," or "there be, and if 1.05.177
been loosed out of hell | to speak of horrors — 2.01. 81
o, speak of that, that do i long to hear. 2.02. 50
i'll speak to him again. 2.02.191 P
come, come — nay, speak. 2.02.276 P
i heard thee speak me a speech once, but it was 2.02.434 P
i'll have thee speak out the rest of this soon. 2.02.521 P
tongue, will speak | with most miraculous organ. 2.02.593
but from what cause 'a will by no means speak. 3.01. 6
speak the speech, i pray you, as i pronounc'd it 3.02. 1 P
and that highly — not to speak it profanely, 3.02. 30 P
that play your clowns speak no more than is set 3.02. 39 P
i do believe you think what now you speak, | but 3.02.186
she desires to speak with you in her closet ere 3.02.331 P
this little organ, yet cannot you make it speak. 3.02.369 P
my lord, the queen would speak with you, and 3.02.374 P
i will speak /daggers to her, but use none. 3.02.396
nay, then i'll set those to you that can speak. 3.04. 17
o hamlet, speak no more! 3.04. 88
o, speak to me no more! 3.04. 94
bodies strongest works, | speak to her, hamlet. 3.04.115
to whom do you speak this? 3.04.131
go seek him out, speak fair, and bring the body 4.01. 36
truly to speak, and with no addition, | we go to 4.04. 17
i will not speak with her. 4.05. 1
speak, man. 4.05.128
now you speak | like a good child and a true 4.05.148
what are they that would speak with me? 4.06. 1 P
i have words to speak in thine ear will make 4.06. 25 P
i will speak to this fellow. 5.01.117 P
we must speak by the card, or equivocation will 5.01.137 P
indeed, to speak sellingly of him, he is the 5.02.109 P
cups, | and let the kettle to the trumpet speak, 5.02.275
and let me speak to /th' yet unknowing world 5.02.379
of that i shall have also cause to speak, | and 5.02.391
and the rite of war | speak loudly for him. 5.02.400
goneril, | our eldest–born, speak first. LR 1.01. 54
what shall cordelia speak? love, and be silent. 1.01. 62
speak. 1.01. 86
nothing will come of nothing, speak again. 1.01. 90
thou that duty shall have dread to speak | when 1.01.147
glib and oily art | to speak and purpose not, 1.01.225
i'll do't before i speak — that you make known 1.01.226
come to me, that of this i may speak more. 1.02. 52 P
will fitly bring you to hear my lord speak. 1.02.169 P
from hunting, | i will not speak with him; 1.03. 8
you and tell my daughter i would speak with her. 1.04. 76 P
thou showest, | speak less than thou knowest, 1.04.119
if i speak like myself in this, let him be whipt 1.04.164 P
speak thus? 1.04.227
the shame itself doth speak | for instant remedy 1.04.246
speak, sir. 1.04.258
what is your difference? speak. 2.02. 51 P
speak yet, how grew your quarrel? 2.02. 61 P
an honest mind and plain, he must speak truth! 2.02. 99
made you no more offense but what you speak of? 2.04. 61
deny to speak with me? 2.04. 88
'ld speak with the duke of cornwall and his 2.04. 97
the king would speak with cornwall, the dear 2.04.101
the dear father | would with his daughter speak, 2.04.102
the duke, and 's wife, i'ld speak with them — 2.04.116
can scarce speak to thee; 2.04.136
and danger | speak 'gainst so great a number? 2.04.240
i'll speak a prophecy ere i go: 3.02. 80 P
perpetual displeasure neither to speak of him, 3.03. 5 P
hands you have sent the lunatic king — | speak. 3.07. 47
this kiss, if it durst speak, | would stretch 4.02. 22
speak in understanding: 4.05. 28
speak! 4.06. 46
speak yet again. 4.06. 55
that thing you speak of, | i took it for a man; 4.06. 77
he wakes, speak to him. 4.07. 41
tell me but truly, but then speak the truth, 5.01. 8
overtake you. — speak. 5.01. 39
nt | to prove upon thy heart, whereto i speak, 5.03.141
trumpets, speak! 5.03.151
t speak you on, | you look as you had 5.03.201
ak, man. 5.03.223
o dead? speak, man. 5.03.226
ak, edmund, where's the king? 5.03.238
speak what we feel, not what we ought to say: 5.03.325
siege, and my demerits | may speak, unbonneted, OTH 1.02. 23
and little of this great world can i speak 1.03. 86
but, othello, speak. 1.03.110
and let her speak of me before her father. 1.03.116
it was my hint to speak — such was my process 1.03.142
when i did speak of some distressful stroke 1.03.157
i pray you hear her speak. 1.03.175
let me speak like yourself, and lay a sentence, 1.03.199
though he speak of comfort | touching the 2.01. 31
i cannot speak enough of this content, | it 2.01.196
can stand well enough, and i speak well enough. 2.03.116 P
iago, that looks dead with grieving, | speak: 2.03.178
i cannot speak | any beginning to this peevish 2.03.184
i pray you pardon me, i cannot speak. 2.03.189
to speak the truth | shall nothing wrong him. 2.03.223
and speak parrot? 2.03.279 P
in naples, that they speak i' th' nose thus? 3.01. 4 P
shall have time | to speak your bosom freely. 3.01. 55
why, stay, and hear me speak. 3.03. 31
i prithee speak to me as to thy thinkings, | as 3.03.131
i speak not yet of proof. 3.03.196
i do not in position | distinctly speak of her, 3.03.235
why do you speak so faintly? | are you not well? 3.03.282
i cannot speak of this. come now, your promise. 3.04. 48
i have sent to bid cassio come speak with you. 3.04. 50
why do you speak so startingly and rash? 3.04. 79
speak, is't out o' th' way? 3.04. 80
i would on great occasion speak with you. 4.01. 58
bade him anon return and here speak with me, 4.01. 80
for i would very fain speak with you. 4.01.167 P
it is not honesty in me to speak | what i have 4.01.277
burn up modesty, | did i but speak thy deeds. 4.02. 76
speak within door. 4.02.144
it does abhor me now i speak the word; 4.02.162
nay, guiltiness will speak, | though tongues 5.01.109
o, good my lord, i would speak a word with you! 5.02. 90
'tis like she comes to speak of cassio's death; 5.02. 92
if she come in, she'll sure speak to my wife. 5.02. 96
i do beseech you | that i may speak with you. 5.02.102
o lady, speak again! 5.02.120
sweet desdemona, o sweet mistress, speak! 5.02.121
speak, for my heart is full. 5.02.175
i am bound to speak. 5.02.184
good gentlemen, let me have leave to speak. 5.02.195
no, i will speak as liberal as the north: 5.02.220
all, all, cry shame against me, yet i'll speak. 5.02.222
so come my soul to bliss, as i speak true; 5.02.250
look in upon me then and speak with me, | or, 5.02.257
from this time forth i never will speak word. 5.02.304
unlucky deeds relate, | speak of me as i am; 5.02.342
then must you speak | of one that lov'd not 5.02.343
speak not to us. ANT 1.01. 55
speak to me home, mince not the general tongue; 1.02.105
from sicyon how the news? speak there! 1.02.113
more urgent touches, | do strongly speak to us; 1.02.181
(it wounds thine honor that i speak it now) 1.04. 69
over caesar's head | and speak as loud as mars. 2.02. 6
no, lepidus, let him speak. 2.02. 84
thou art a soldier only, speak no more. 2.02.107
wrong this presence, therefore speak no more. 2.02.109
speak, agrippa. 2.02.117
let me hear agrippa further speak. 2.02.123
whose virtue and whose general graces speak 2.02.129
will caesar speak? 2.02.138
whom ne'er the word of "no" woman heard speak, 2.02.223
speak this no more. 2.03. 24
say to ventidius i would speak with him. 2.03. 32
pity me, charmian, | but do not speak to me. 2.05.119
we'll speak with thee at sea. 2.06. 25
thee, captain, | and hear me speak a word. 2.07. 39
poets, cannot | think, speak, cast, write, sing, 3.02. 17
didst hear her speak? 3.03. 12
madam, i heard her speak; she is low–voic'd. 3.03. 13
and their tongues rot | that speak against us! 3.07. 16
speak not against it, | i will not stay behind. 3.07. 18
go to him, madam, speak to him, | he's 3.11. 43
approach and speak. 3.12. 6
do so, we'll speak to them, and to–night i'll 3.13.189
let's speak to him. 4.09. 23
awake, sir, awake, speak to us. 4.09. 28
grimly, | and dare not speak their knowledge. 4.12. 6
give me some wine, and let me speak a little. 4.15. 42
no, let me speak, and let me rail so high, 4.15. 43
to caesar i will speak what you shall please, 5.02. 69
this is my treasurer, let him speak, my lord, 5.02.142
speak the truth, seleucus. 5.02.144
lips than to my peril | speak that which is not. 5.02.147
o, couldst thou speak, | that i might hear thee 5.02.306
speak softly, wake her not. 5.02.320
you speak him far. CYM 1.01. 24
hath charg'd you should not speak together. 1.01. 83
some half hour hence, | pray you speak with me. 1.01.177
you speak of him when he was less furnish'd than 1.04. 8 P
the gods to venge it, | not mine to speak on't. 1.06. 93
if she be up, i'll speak with her; 2.03. 64
say i yield being silent, | i would not speak. 2.03. 95
let proof speak. 3.01. 76
say, and speak thick | (love's counsellor should 3.02. 56
prithee speak, | how many /score of miles may we 3.02. 66
out of your proof you speak; 3.03. 27
what should we speak of | when we are old as you 3.03. 35
how you speak! 3.03. 44
speak, man, thy tongue | may take off some 3.04. 16
i speak not out of weak surmises, but from proof 3.04. 23 P
talk thy tongue weary, speak. 3.04.112
but speak. 3.04.115
speak, or thy silence on the instant is | thy 3.05. 97
if any thing that's civil, speak; 3.06. 23
of thy story, | so far as thou wilt speak it. 3.06. 92
i dare speak it to myself, for it is not 4.01. 7 P
of my dear'st mother | it did not speak before. 4.02.191
we'll speak it then. 4.02.242
o imogen, | i'll speak to thee in silence. 5.04. 29
i speak against my present profit, but my wish 5.04.205 P
speak, | wilt have him live? 5.05.110
speak freely. 5.05.119
/on, speak to him. 5.05.134
strive, man, and speak. 5.05.152
swell'd boast | of him that best could speak; 5.05.163
wilt thou not speak to me? 5.05.266
lord, | now fear is from me, i'll speak troth. 5.05.274
that i was he, | speak, jachimo. 5.05.411
my lord, since you have given me leave to speak, PER 1.02.101
given me leave to speak, | freely will i speak. 1.02.102
does speak sufficiently he's gone to travel. 1.03. 13
and, wanting breath to speak, help me with tears 1.04. 19
speak out thy sorrows which /thou bring'st in 1.04. 58
what need speak i? 2.ch. 16
show | can any way speak in his just commend; 2.02. 49
the seas–toss'd pericles appears to speak. 3.ch. 60
and can speak of the disturbances | that nature 3.02. 37
madam, if this you purpose as ye speak, 3.04. 12
what thou professest, a baboon, could he speak, 4.06.178
but can you teach all this you speak of? 4.06.188 P
he will not speak | to any. 5.01. 33
it is in vain, he will not speak to you. 5.01. 41
see, she will speak to him. 5.01. 81
whispers in mine ear, "go not till he speak." 5.01. 96
prithee speak. 5.01.119
well, speak on. 5.01.154
i'll speak anon. TNK 1.01.106
'tis not this | i did begin to speak of. 1.02. 35
speak on, sir. 2.02.117
speak truly: 2.02.191
twenty to one, he'll come to speak to her, | and 2.03. 14
you might as well | speak this, and act it in 3.01. 70
to speak, before thy noble grace, this tenner; 3.05.123
none here speak for 'em, | for, ere the sun set, 3.06.183
now or never, sister, | speak, not to be denied. 3.06.186
pray speak, | you that have seen them, what they 4.02. 71
pray speak him, friend. 4.02. 91
you speak well. 5.01. 30
to me deserving | than i can quite or speak of. 5.04. 35
shall we hear shrieve more speak? STM II.C 41 P
good masters, hear me speak. II.C 57
speak, fair, but speak fair words, or else be VEN 208
fair, but speak fair words, or else be mute. 208
and now she weeps, and now she fain would speak, 221
the wise dumb, and teach the fool to speak. 1146
mild patience bid fair lucrece speak | to the LUC 1268
i should not live to speak another word; 1642
my bloody judge forbod my tongue to speak, | no 1648
"o, speak," quoth she, | "how may this forced 1700
more than "he" her poor tongue could not speak, 1718
for no man well of such a salve can speak | that SON 34. 7
speak of the spring and foison of the year, 53. 9
that you for love speak well of me untrue, | my 72.10
speak of my lameness, and i straight will halt, 89. 3
to speak of that which gives thee all thy might? 100. 2
what's new to speak, what now to register, 108. 3
i love to hear her speak, yet well i know | that 130. 9
and in my madness might speak ill of thee; 140.10

SPEAK–A 1 FR 0.0001 REL FR 0 V 1 P
peace–a your tongue. — speak–a your tale. WIV 1.04. 81 P

SPEAKER 9 FR 0.0010 REL FR 7 V 2 P
to us the speaker in his parliament, | to us th' 2H4 4.02. 18
a speaker is but a prater, a rhyme is but a H5 5.02.158 P
who shall be the speaker? 1H6 3.02. 60
gentleman is learn'd, and a most rare speaker, H8 1.02.111
no other speaker of my living actions | to keep 4.02. 70
by my place and message, | to be a speaker free. TRO 4.04.131
that of an hour's age doth hiss the speaker; MAC 4.03.175
never say hereafter | but i am truest speaker. CYM 5.05.376
it can appear to me report is a true speaker. TNK 2.01. 6 P

SPEAKER'S 1 FR 0.0001 REL FR 1 V 0 P
that contempt will kill the speaker's heart, LLL 5.02.149

SPEAKERS 1 FR 0.0001 REL FR 1 V 0 P
stay, you imperfect speakers, tell me more: MAC 1.03. 70

SPEAKEST 5 FR 0.0005 REL FR 4 V 1 P
art an old love–monger and speakest skillfully. LLL 2.01.254
thou speakest aright; MND 2.01. 42
that what thou speakest may move and what he 1H4 1.02.153 P
thou speakest wonders. H8 5.04. 55
though thou speakest truth, | methinks thou COR 1.06. 13

SPEAKETH 1 FR 0.0001 REL FR 1 V 0 P
ay, now my sovereign speaketh like himself, 3H6 4.07. 67

/SPEAKING 1 FR 0.0001 REL FR 1 V 0 P
/and /speaking /thick (/which /nature /made /his 2H4 2.03. 24

SPEAKING 46 FR 0.0052 REL FR 38 V 8 P
eyes wide open — standing, speaking, moving — TMP 2.01.214
his little speaking shows his love but small. TGV 1.02. 29
if speaking, why, a vane blown with all winds; ADO 3.01. 66
not angry with me, madam, | speaking my fancy: 3.01. 95
of speaking honorably? 3.04. 29 P
and bad thinking do not wrest true speaking, 3.04. 34 P
lov'd her so, that, speaking of her foulness, 4.01.153
i'll have no speaking, i will have my bond. MV 3.03. 17
while i was speaking, oft was fasten'd to't. AWW 5.03. 82
i am sent for speaking to you. TN 4.02.104 P
pure innocence | persuades when speaking fails. WT 2.02. 40
we three are but thyself, and, speaking so, R2 2.01.275
i am press'd to death through want of speaking! 3.04. 72
and speaking it, he wishtly look'd on me | as 5.04. 7
if speaking truth | in this fine age were not 1H4 4.01. 1
but thy speaking of my tongue, and i thine, most H5 5.02.190 P
brave death by speaking, whether he will or no; 1H6 4.07. 25
and then, in speaking, not to incur the last — R3 3.07.152
to unthink your speaking | and to say so no more H8 2.04.104
nought be trusted | for speaking false in that. 2.04.137
women had men's privilege | of speaking first. TRO 3.02.129
speaking is for beggars; 3.03.269 P
ease thy smart | by friendship nor by speaking." 4.04. 20
speaking /in deeds, and deedless in his tongue, 4.05. 98
if thou couldst please me with speaking to me, TIM 4.03.346 P
o' th' tongue, | consuming it with speaking! 5.01.134
speaking of brutus | and groaning underneath JC 1.02. 60
who rated him for speaking well of pompey; 2.01.216
my first false speaking | was this upon myself. MAC 4.03.130
they'll have me whipt for speaking true; LR 1.04.183 P
she gave strange eliads and most speaking looks 4.05. 25
meanest wretch, | past speaking of in a king! 4.06.205
shall i grace my cause | in speaking for myself. OTH 1.03. 89
to anger cassio, either by speaking too loud, or 2.01.267 P
so speaking as i think, alas, i die. 5.02.251
he's speaking now, | or murmuring, "where's my ANT 1.05. 24

his voice, | and burst of speaking, were as his. CYM 4.02.106
or senseless speaking, or a speaking such | as 5.04.147
or a speaking such | as sense cannot untie. 5.04.147
act, | will think me speaking, though i swear to PER 1.02. 19
sav'd too, | speaking it truly? TNK 1.02. 49
(speaking to those that came with collatine), LUC 1689
and dumb presagers of my speaking breast, | who SON 23.10
to make me tongue–tied, speaking of your fame. 80. 4
speaking of worth, what worth in you doth grow. 83. 8
me for my dumb thoughts, speaking in effect. 85.14
SPEAKS 129 FR 0.0145 REL FR 97 V 32 P
why speaks my father so ungently? TMP 1.02.445
th' occasion speaks thee, and | my strong 2.01.207
the devil speaks in him. 5.01.129
this while sheds not a tear, nor speaks a word; TGV 2.03. 31 P
has brown hair, and speaks small like a woman. WIV 1.01. 48 P
alas! he speaks but for his friend. 1.04.114 P
believe it, page, he speaks sense. 2.01.125
he writes verses, he speaks holiday, he smells 3.02. 68 P
are fairies, he that speaks to them shall die. 5.05. 47
she speaks, and 'tis | such sense that my sense MM 2.02.141
o, your desert speaks loud, and i should wrong 5.01. 9
she speaks this in th' infirmity of sense. 5.01. 47
know you that friar lodowick that she speaks of? 5.01.143
to me she speaks, she moves me for her theme: ERR 2.02.181
he speaks to me. 5.01.412
she speaks poniards, and every word stabs. ADO 2.01.247 P
why, these are very crotchets that he speaks — 2.03. 56
but that the white–bearded fellow speaks it. 2.03.119 P
for what his heart thinks, his tongue speaks. 3.02. 14 P
verges, sir, speaks a little /off the matter; 3.05. 9 P
your worship speaks like a most thankful and 5.01.315 P
he speaks the mere contrary, crosses love not LLL 1.02. 33 P
and when love speaks, the voice of all the gods 4.03.341
'a speaks not like a man of god his making. 5.02.526 P
wherefore speaks he this | to her he hates? MND 3.02.227
i love thee, and 'tis my love that speaks — MV 1.01. 87
gratiano speaks an infinite deal of nothing, 1.01.114 P
only my blood speaks to you in my veins, | and 3.02.176
and report speaks goldenly of his profit. AYL 1.01. 6 P
he writes brave verses, speaks brave words, 3.04. 41 P
when he that speaks them pleases those that hear 3.05.112
and speaks three or four languages word for word
TN 1.03. 26 P
off, i pray you, he speaks nothing but madman; 1.05.106 P
very well–favor'd and he speaks very shrewishly. 1.05.160 P
lo, how hollow the fiend speaks within him! 3.04. 91 P
for her is afar off guilty | but that he speaks. WT 2.01.105
speaks the king of france | in my behavior to JN 1.01. 2
he speaks plain cannon–fire, and smoke, and 2.01.462
the lady constance speaks not from her faith, 3.01.210
and he that speaks doth gripe the hearer's wrist 4.02.190
whose tongue soe'er speaks false, | not truly 4.03. 91
tongue soe'er speaks false, | not truly speaks; 4.03. 92
who speaks not truly, lies. 4.03. 92
the king | yet speaks, and peradventure may 5.06. 31
what my tongue speaks, my right drawn sword may
R2 1.01. 46
that speaks thy words again to do thee harm! 2.01.231
i speak to subjects, and a subject speaks, 4.01.132
i think there's no man speaks better welsh. 1H4 3.01. 49
my lord, he speaks most vilely of you, like a 3.03.106 P
the vent of hearing when loud rumor speaks? 2H4 in 2
a tongue of them all speaks any other word but 4.03. 19 P
pistol speaks nought but truth. 5.05. 38
that, when he speaks, | the air, a charter'd H5 1.01. 47
this the dolphin speaks. 1.02.257
and hold their manhoods cheap whiles any speaks 4.03. 66
he speaks with such a proud commanding spirit. 1H6 4.07. 88
speaks suffolk as he thinks? 5.03.141
beauford, it is thy sovereign speaks to thee. 2H6 3.03. 7
drudge's words, | that speaks he knows not what? 4.02.152
can he that speaks with the tongue of an enemy 4.02.171 P
away with him, away with him! he speaks latin. 4.07. 57 P
under his tongue, he speaks not a' god's name. 4.07.108 P
clifford, dost thou know who speaks to thee? 3H6 2.06. 61
madam, good hope, his grace speaks cheerfully. R3 1.03. 34
to who in all this presence speaks your grace? 1.03. 54
every tongue speaks 'em, | and every true heart H8 2.02. 38
should be shut up, hear what ulysses speaks. TRO 1.03. 58
and when he speaks, | 'tis like a chime 1.03.158
and speaks not to himself but with a pride 2.03.171
eye, her cheek, her lip, | nay, her foot speaks; 4.05. 56
'fore me, this fellow speaks! COR 1.01.120
people give | one that speaks thus their voice? 3.01.119
even as she speaks, why, their hearts were yours 3.02. 87
then he speaks | what's in his heart, and that 3.03. 28
that when he speaks not like a citizen, | you 3.03. 53
how fair the tribune speaks to calm my thoughts! TIT 1.01. 46
whose fury not dissembled speaks his griefs. 1.01.438
she speaks, yet she says nothing; ROM 2.02. 12
i am too bold, 'tis not to me she speaks. 2.02. 14
she speaks! 2.02. 25
affection makes him false, he speaks not true. 3.01.177
and every tongue that speaks | but romeo's name 3.02. 32
but romeo's name speaks heavenly eloquence. 3.02. 33
how this grace | speaks his own standing! TIM 1.01. 31
he speaks the common tongue | which all men 1.01.174
his state | that what he speaks is all in debt: 1.02.198
your lordship speaks your pleasure. 3.01. 33 P
then let him know, and tell him timon speaks it, 5.01.175
peace ho, caesar speaks. JC 1.02. 1
popilius lena speaks not of our purposes, | for 3.01. 23
protest | he speaks by leave and by permission; 3.01.239
peace, silence! brutus speaks. 3.02. 54
you know that you are brutus that speaks this, 4.03. 13
friends, | for my heart speaks they are welcome. MAC 3.04. 8
hark, she speaks. 5.01. 32 P
especially when he speaks of priam's slaughter. HAM 2.02.447 P
that not your trespass, but my madness speaks; 3.04.146
she speaks much of her father, says she hears 4.05. 4
speaks things in doubt | that carry but half 4.05. 6
your lordship speaks most infallibly of him. 5.02.121 P
if his fitness speaks, mine is ready; 5.02.201 P
of the self–same color | our sister speaks of. LR 2.02.139
the letters that he speaks of | may be my 4.06.256
what's he that speaks for edmund earl of 5.03.125
he speaks home, madam. OTH 2.01.165 P
and when she speaks, is it not an alarum to love 2.03. 26 P
the general speaks to you; 2.03.168
talking of it, | and she speaks for you stoutly. 3.01. 44
it speaks against her with the other proofs. 3.03.441
he speaks well. 4.03. 37
common liar, who | thus speaks of him at rome; ANT 1.01. 61
that drums him from his sport and speaks as loud 1.04. 29
that the present need | speaks to atone you. 2.02.102
and mine own tongue | spleets what it speaks; 2.07.124
and what thou think'st his very action speaks 3.12. 35
for the things he speaks | may concern caesar. 4.09. 24
the ruin speaks that sometime | it was a worthy CYM 4.02.354
she has a good face, speaks well, and has PER 4.02. 47 P
she speaks, | my lord, that, may be, hath 5.01. 86
regent, sir, of meteline | speaks nobly of her. 5.01.187
when he speaks, his tongue | sounds like a TNK 4.02.112
which speaks him prone to labor, never fainting 4.02.129
he speaks now of as brave a knight as e'er | did 5.03.115
shrieve more speaks. STM II.C 41 P
and kissing speaks, with lustful language broken VEN 47
to whom she speaks, and he replies with howling. 918
and to the flame thus speaks advisedly: LUC 180
that twice she doth begin ere once she speaks. 567
she sits weeping, | to whom she sobbing speaks: 1088
SPEAK'ST 36 FR 0.0040 REL FR 32 V 4 P
language, and thou speak'st | out of thy sleep. TMP 2.01.211
unless the next word that thou speak'st | have TGV 3.01.239
wretch, thou know'st not what thou speak'st, MM 5.01.105
villain, thou speak'st false in both. ERR 4.04.100
there thou speak'st reason; ADO 5.01. 41
and thereupon thou speak'st the fairest shoot. LLL 4.01. 12
thou speak'st it well. MV 2.02.152
then, howsome'er thou speak'st, 'mong other 3.05. 89
thou speak'st wiser than thou art ware of. AYL 2.04. 57 P
speak'st thou in sober meanings? 5.02. 69 P
if it smell so strongly as thou speak'st of. AWW 5.02. 7 P
thou speak'st it falsely, as i love mine honor, 5.03.113
with leasing, for thou speak'st well of fools! TN 1.05. 98 P
thou speak'st truth: WT 5.01. 55
thou speak'st as if i would deny my name. 1H4 5.04. 60
thou speak'st cheerfully. H5 4.01. 34
why speak'st thou not? what ransom must i pay? 1H6 5.03. 77
in vain thou speak'st, poor boy; 3H6 1.03. 21
truth, | methinks thou speak'st not well. COR 1.06. 14
why speak'st not? 4.05. 54
say on, and if it please me which thou speak'st, TIT 5.01. 59
speak'st thou from thy heart? ROM 3.05.226
if what thou speak'st speak not of remedy. 4.01. 67
there is no leprosy but what thou speak'st. TIM 4.03.362
that speak'st with every tongue | to every 4.03.388
what, thou speak'st drowsily? JC 4.03.240
thou speak'st with all thy wit, and yet, i' MAC 4.02. 42
if thou speak'st false, | upon the next tree 5.05. 37
my sword | i'll prove the lie thou speak'st. 5.07. 11
and thou speak'st | in better phrase and matter LR 4.06. 7
substance, bleed'st not, speak'st, art sound. 4.06. 52
that handkerchief thou speak'st of | i found by OTH 5.02.225
i have a mind to strike thee ere thou speak'st; ANT 2.05. 42
thou weep'st, and speak'st. CYM 5.05.352
thou speak'st like a physician, helicanus, PER 1.02. 67
thou speak'st like /him's untutor'd to repeat: 1.04. 74
SPEAK'T 3 FR 0.0003 REL FR 3 V 0 P
this was my speech, and i will speak't again — COR 3.01. 62
and speak't again, my lord, no more with me. LR 2.04.255
speak't in a woman's key — like such a woman TNK 1.01. 94
SPEAR 9 FR 0.0010 REL FR 8 V 1 P
to the soul with slander's venom'd spear, | the R2 1.01.171
o, /sit my husband's wrongs on herford's spear, 1.02. 47
for me, if i be gor'd with mowbray's spear. 1.03. 60
loud | on the unsteadfast footing of a spear. 1H4 1.03.193
thrust talbot with a spear into the back, | whom 1H6 1.01.138
for he was thrust in the mouth with a spear, and 2H6 4.07. 9 P
whose smile and frown, like to achilles' spear, 5.01.100
he ran upon the boar with his sharp spear, | who VEN 1112
that for achilles' image stood his spear, LUC 1424
SPEARGRASS 1 FR 0.0001 REL FR 0 V 1 P
our noses with speargrass to make them bleed, 1H4 2.04.309 P
SPEAR'S 1 FR 0.0001 REL FR 1 V 0 P
better proof than thy spear's point can enter; VEN 626
SPEARS 1 FR 0.0001 REL FR 1 V 0 P
let them lay by their helmets and their spears, R2 1.03.119
SPECIAL 38 FR 0.0043 REL FR 29 V 9 P
marry, by these special marks: TGV 2.01. 18 P
confirm his welcome with some special favor. 2.04.101
a special virtue; 3.01.312 P
think my husband hath some special suspicion of WIV 3.03.187 P
you have ta'en a special stand to strike at me, 5.05.234 P
we have with special soul | elected him our MM 1.01. 17
but from lord angelo by special charge. 1.02.119
/see, | in special business from his holiness. 3.02.220
and hold you ever to our special drift, | though 4.05. 4
had you a special warrant for the deed? 5.01.459
not by might mast'red, but by special grace. LLL 1.01.152
for such a sum from special officers | of 2.01.161
some certain special honors it pleaseth his 5.01.106 P
from the rich jew, a special deed of gift, MV 5.01.292
i never yet beheld that special face | which i SHR 2.01. 11
ay, when the special thing is well obtain'd, 2.01.128
thus he his special nothing ever prologues. AWW 2.01. 92
what place make you special, when you put off 2.02. 6 P
some of my people have a special care of him. TN 3.04. 62 P
take special care my greetings be delivered. R2 3.01. 39
the special head of all the land together: 1H4 4.04. 28
king is, | being ordain'd his special governor, 1H6 1.01.171
the special watchmen of our english weal, | i 3.01. 66
'tis my special hope | that you will clear 2H6 3.01.139
but such as i (without your special pardon) 3H6 4.01. 87
for whom we stand | a special party, have by TIT 1.01. 21
but to the earth some special good doth give; ROM 2.03. 18
who have thought | on special dignities, which TIM 5.01.142
a summer's cloud, | without our special wonder? MAC 3.04.111
to the action, with this special observance, HAM 3.02. 18 P
o, for two special reasons, | which may to you, 4.07. 9
there is special providence in the fall of a 5.02.219 P
though that the queen on special cause is here, LR 4.06.215
and raise some special officers of /night. OTH 1.01.182
your special mandate for the state affairs 1.03. 72
that there he dropp'd it for a special purpose 5.02.322
to make some special instant special blest, | by SON 52.11
to make some special instant special blest, | by 52.11
SPECIALLY 2 FR 0.0002 REL FR 1 V 1 P
happiness | by virtue specially to be achiev'd. SHR 1.01. 20
love, to labor and effect one thing specially. 1.01.118 P
SPECIALTIES 2 FR 0.0002 REL FR 2 V 0 P
where that and other specialties are bound: LLL 2.01.164
let specialties be therefore drawn between us, SHR 2.01.126
SPECIALTY 1 FR 0.0001 REL FR 1 V 0 P
the specialty of rule hath been neglected, | and TRO 1.03. 78
SPECIFY 4 FR 0.0004 REL FR 1 V 3 P
masters, do not forget to specify, when time and ADO 5.01.255 P
that would, sir, as my father shall specify — MV 2.02.124 P
and have a desire, as my father shall specify — 2.02.128 P
how will she specify | here is the best and 1H6 3.02. 21
SPECIOUSLY 2 FR 0.0002 REL FR 0 V 2 P
as my word, but speciously for master fenton. WIV 3.04.108 P
speciously one of them. 4.05.111 P
SPECTACLE 11 FR 0.0012 REL FR 10 V 1 P
the direful spectacle of the wrack, which TMP 1.02. 26
did he not moralize this spectacle? AYL 2.01. 44
a jest, | exampled by this heinous spectacle. JN 4.03. 56
they me | to be a public spectacle to all: 1H6 1.04. 41
o barbarous and bloody spectacle! 2H6 4.01.144
the saddest spectacle that e'er i view'd. 3H6 2.01. 67
o piteous spectacle! 2.05. 73
or else were this a savage spectacle. JC 3.01.223
o piteous spectacle! 3.02.198 P
"think but how vile a spectacle it were | to LUC 631
boar, | deep in the thigh, a spectacle of ruth! PP 9.11
SPECTACLED 1 FR 0.0001 REL FR 1 V 0
the bleared sights | are spectacled to see him. COR 2.01.206
SPECTACLES 8 FR 0.0009 REL FR 5 V 3
i can see yet without spectacles, and i see no ADO 1.01.189
with spectacles on nose and pouch on side, | his AYL 2.07.159
and call'd them blind and dusky spectacles, 2H6 3.02.112
and seek for sorrow with thy spectacles? 5.01.165
what a pair of spectacles is here! TRO 4.04. 14
hast oft beheld | heart–hard'ning spectacles; COR 4.01. 25
if it be nothing, i shall not need spectacles. LR 1.02. 35
not | partition make with spectacles so precious CYM 1.06. 37
SPECTANDA 1 FR 0.0001 REL FR 1 V 0
"sic spectanda fides." PER 2.02. 38
SPECTATORS 4 FR 0.0004 REL FR 2 V 2
though devis'd | and play'd to take spectators. WT 3.02. 37
gentle spectators, that i now may be | in fair 4.01. 20
some quantity of barren spectators to laugh too, HAM 3.02. 41
if i prove a good repast to the spectators, the CYM 5.04.155
SPECTATORSHIP 1 FR 0.0001 REL FR 0 V 1
death more long in spectatorship and crueller in COR 5.02. 66
SPECULATION 3 FR 0.0003 REL FR 3 V 0
basis by | took stand for idle speculation — H5 4.02. 31
for speculation turns not to itself, | till it TRO 3.03.109
thou hast no speculation in those eyes | which MAC 3.04. 94
SPECULATIONS 1 FR 0.0001 REL FR 1 V 0
which are to france the spies and speculations LR 3.01. 24
SPECULATIVE 2 FR 0.0002 REL FR 2 V 0
thoughts speculative their unsure hopes relate, MAC 5.04. 19
my speculative and offic'd /instruments, | that OTH 1.03.270
SPED 10 FR 0.0011 REL FR 7 V 3
and sped you, sir? WIV 3.05. 66
so be gone, you are sped." MV 2.09. 72
full of windgalls, sped with spavins, ray'd with SHR 3.02. 52
we three are married, but you two are sped. 5.02.185
who have sped the better | by my regard, but WT 1.02.389
how i have sped among the clergymen | the sums i
JN 4.02.141
here cometh charles, i marvel how he sped. 1H6 2.01. 48
not long before your highness sped to france, H8 1.02.151
i long to hear how they sped to–day. TRO 3.01.142
i am sped. ROM 3.01. 91
/SPEECH 1 FR 0.0001 REL FR 1 V 0
/so /that /in /speech, /in /gait, | /in /diet, 2H4 2.03. 28
SPEECH 136 FR 0.0153 REL FR 108 V 28
i am the best of them that speak this speech, TMP 1.02.430
better nature, sir, | than he appears by speech. 1.02.498
would seem in me t' affect speech and discourse, MM 1.01. 4
but i do bend my speech | to one that can my 1.01. 40
to give me leave | to have free speech with you; 1.01. 77
indeed with most painful feeling of thy speech. 1.02. 37
near to the speech we had to such a purpose. 1.02. 78
i would by and by have some speech with you. 3.01.154
years since there was some speech of marriage 5.01.217
first he did praise my beauty, then my speech. ERR 4.02. 15
runs not this speech like iron through your ADO 5.01.245
hands by helping me to the speech of beatrice. 5.02. 2
swore | a better speech was never spoke before. LLL 5.02.110
nor to their penn'd speech render we no grace, 5.02.147
when you have spoken your speech, enter into MND 3.01. 75
his speech was like a tangled chain; 5.01.125
but if you fail, without more speech, my lord, MV 2.09. 7
suits | his folly to the mettle of my speech? AYL 2.07. 82
but slow in speech, yet sweet as spring–time SHR 2.01.246
where did you study all this goodly speech? 2.01.262
for silence, | but never tax'd for speech. AWW 1.01. 68
lives not his epitaph | as in your royal speech. 1.02. 51
and common speech | gives him a worthy pass. 2.05. 52
only he desires | some private speech with you. 2.05. 57
vanquish'd thereto by the fair grace and speech 5.03.133
hope, | whereto thy speech serves for authority, TN 1.02. 20
i would be loath to cast away my speech; 1.05.173
of the house, that i may proceed in my speech. 1.05.181
i will on with my speech in your praise, and 1.05.190
niece, give me this prerogative of speech" — 2.05. 71
but in conclusion put strange speech upon me. 5.01. 67
(which on my faith deserves high speech) and WT 2.01. 70
made fault | i' th' boldness of your speech. 3.02.218
gasping to begin some speech, her eyes | became 3.03. 25
at this time | he will allow no speech (which i 4.04.468
this hour, if i may come to th' speech of him. 4.04.75
there was speech in their dumbness, language in 5.02. 1
first, heaven be the record to my speech, | in R2 1.01. 3
from giving reins and spurs to my free speech, 1.01. 5
free speech and fearless i to thee allow. 1.01.12
"pardon" should be the first word of thy speech. 5.03.11
and here is my speech. stand aside, nobility. 1H4 2.04.3
i in chief address | the substance of my speech. 2H4 4.01. 3
out of the speech of peace that bears such grace 4.01. 4

s, | the moist impediments unto my speech, 4.05.139
strength of speech is utterly denied me. 4.05.217
my fear, then my cur'sy, last my speech. ep 1 P
duty, and my speech, to beg your pardons. ep 3 P
u look for a good speech now, you undo me, ep 4 P
my speech entreats | that i may know the let H5 5.02. 64
leeds exceed all speech: 1H6 1.01. 15
ne'er could he so long protract his speech. 1.02.120
gh thy speech doth fail, | one eye thou hast 1.04. 82
with sudden and extemporal speech | purpose 3.01. 6
sight did ravish, but her grace in speech, 2H6 1.01. 32
thy head for this thy traitor's speech. 1.03.194
and the offender granted scope of speech, 3.01.176
ce, in gait, in speech, he doth resemble. 3.01.373
e thee beg pardon for thy passed speech, 3.02.221
is my sword report what speech forbears. 4.10. 54
his one speech lord hastings well deserves 3H6 4.01. 47
prophet, in thy speech: 5.06. 57
d not find | his hour of speech a minute — H8 1.02.121
y day | it would infect his speech — that 1.02.133
and | what was the speech among the londoners 1.02.154
ements to the field, or speech for truce, TRO 1.03.182
pardon to my speech: 1.03.356
use your speech hath none that tell him so? 2.02. 36
ess the process of your speech, wherein 4.01. 9
tis his kind of speech, he did not mock us. COR 2.03.161
was my speech, and i will speak't again — 3.01. 62
fair speech. 3.02. 96
, shall this speech be spoke for our excuse? ROM 1.04. 1
shall not in your funeral speech blame us, JC 3.01.245
eto i am going, | after my speech is ended. 3.01.251
grace his speech | tending to caesar's 3.02. 57
he power of speech | to stir men's blood; 3.02.222
e gods, this speech were else your last. 4.03. 14
his speech, but say thou nought. MAC 4.01. 70
ot a niggard of your speech; how goes't? 4.03.180
one, having no witness to confirm my speech. 5.01. 18 P
speech be sooth, | i care not if thou 5.05. 39
hath given countenance to his speech, my HAM 1.03.113
have a speech straight. 2.02.431 P
ur quality, come, a passionate speech. 2.02.432 P
speech, my good lord? 2.02.433 P
rd thee speak me a speech once, but it was 2.02.434 P
speech in't i chiefly lov'd, 'twas aeneas' 2.02.445 P
eed, study a speech of some dozen lines, or 2.02.541 P
cleave the general ear with horrid speech, 2.02.563
t a lash that speech doth give my conscience 3.01. 49
k the speech, i pray you, as i pronounc'd it 3.02. 1 P
| do not itself unkennel in one speech, 3.02. 81
d o'erhear | the speech, of vantage. 3.03. 33
a knavish speech sleeps in a foolish ear. 4.02. 23 P
peech is nothing, | yet the unshaped use of 4.05. 7
e a speech a' fire that fain would blaze, 4.07.190
patience in our last night's speech, 5.01.294
that makes breath poor, and speech unable: LR 1.01. 60
your speech a little, | lest you may mar 1.01. 94
can my speech defuse, my good intent | may 1.04. 2
, i'll teach thee a speech. 1.04.115 P
curst speech | i threaten'd to discover him 2.01. 65
speech. 4.02. 21
r your grace had speech with man so poor, 5.01. 38
if my speech offend a noble heart, | thy 5.03.127
peech of yours hath mov'd me, | and shall 5.03.200
am i in my speech, | and little bless'd OTH 1.03. 81
she has no speech. 2.01.102
earliest | let me have speech with you. 2.03. 8
i spare speech, which something now 2.03.199
ano and myself being in speech, | there 2.03.225
entreats her a little favor of speech. 3.01. 26 P
e of speech, sings, plays, and dances 3.03.185
to pray you not to strain my speech | to 3.03.218
peech should fall into such vild success 3.03.222
of his displeasure | for my free speech! 3.04.129
enote him so | that i may save my speech. 4.01.280
my knee, what doth your speech import? 4.02. 31
peech sticks in my heart. ANT 1.05. 41
captain | to soft and gentle speech. 2.02. 3
speech is passion; 2.02. 12
atter, but | the manner of his speech; 2.02.112
mislike | my speech and what is done, tell 3.13.148
s life into my speech and shows much more CYM 3.03. 97
peech of insultment ended on his dead body, 3.05.140 P
ine own part unfold a dangerous speech, 5.05.313
s dumb in show i'll plain with speech. PER 3.ch. 14
rupted mind, | thy speech had altered it. 4.06.105
hungry, | the more she gives them speech. 5.01.113
transported with your speech, and suffer'd TNK 1.01. 55
s a servant for | the tenor of /thy speech; 1.01. 90
be fond upon | another's way of speech, 1.02. 47
uch desires | to have some speech with you. 5.04. 85
to his speech did honey passage yield, VEN 452
eech it seem'd his beard, all silver white, LUC 1405

ECHES 22 FR 0.0024 REL FR 18 V 4 P
is to utter foul speeches and to detract. TMP 2.02. 92 P
spoke most villainous speeches of the duke. MM 5.01.264 P
pluck thee by the nose for thy speeches? 5.01.340 P
er my speeches better, if you may. LLL 5.02.341
ver will i trust to speeches penn'd, | nor 5.02.402
eeches | will bring me to consider that WT 5.01.121
ot my speeches that you do mislike, | but 2H6 1.01.140
rtain speeches utter'd | by th' bishop of H8 2.04.172
to both your speeches, which were such TRO 1.03. 62
so many hours, lives, speeches spent, 2.02. 1
reproachful speeches down his throat, TIT 2.01. 55
u uphold and maintain in your speeches, 5.02. 72
him, and write his speeches in their books, JC 1.02.126
on thee, macbeth, their speeches shine — MAC 3.01. 7
now | have you consider'd of my speeches? 3.01. 75
rmer speeches have but hit your thoughts, 3.06. 1
pestilent speeches of his father's death, HAM 4.05. 91
our large speeches may your deeds approve, LR 1.01.184
you my speeches, as i were a fool? 2.02. 82
he master of my speeches, and would CYM 1.04.140 P
majesty, | forbear sharp speeches to her. 3.05. 39
ash at speeches rank, to weep at woes, | or LC 307

ECHLESS 1 FR 0.0001 REL FR 1 V 0 P
chless /complainant, /i /will /learn /thy TIT 3.02. 39

SPEECHLESS 14 FR 0.0015 REL FR 13 V 1 P
youth | there is a prone and speechless dialect, MM 1.02.183
and would afford my speechless vizard half. LLL 5.02.246
visit the speechless sick and still converse 5.02.851
eyes | i did receive fair speechless messages. MV 1.01.164
i left him almost speechless, and broke out | to JN 5.06. 24
what is thy sentence /then but speechless death, R2 1.03.172
dismiss'd me | thus, with his speechless hand. COR 5.01. 67
and foam'd at mouth, and was speechless. JC 1.02.253 P
the bold winds speechless, and the orb below HAM 2.02.485
for | his fortunes all lie speechless, and his CYM 1.05. 52
with speechless tongues and semblance pale, PER 1.01. 36
which speechless woe of his poor she attendeth, LUC 1674
whose speechless song, being many, seeming one, SON 8.13
he insults o'er dull and speechless tribes: 107.12

/SPEED 1 FR 0.0001 REL FR 1 V 0 P
/so /far | /to /make /your /speed /to /dover, LR 3.01. 36

SPEED 127 FR 0.0143 REL FR 116 V 11 P
as thou lov'st thy life, make speed from hence. TGV 3.01.169
there — and saint nicholas be thy speed! 3.01.300 P
as, heaven it knows, i would not have him speed. 4.04.107
you to me at night, you shall know how i speed. WIV 2.02.267 P
no, heaven so speed me in my time to come! 3.04. 12
leisure, and you shall know how i speed; 3.05.135 P
and that with speed. MM 2.02. 17
therefore your best appointment make with speed, 3.01. 59
i'll make all speed. 4.03.105
was carried with more speed before the wind, ERR 1.01.109
i would my horse had the speed of your tongue, ADO 1.01.141 P
and hymen now with luckier issue speed 's | than 5.03. 32
forms | all causes to the purpose of his speed, LLL 5.02.741
but go with speed | to some forlorn and naked 5.02.794
god speed fair helena! whither away? MND 1.01.180
mild hind | makes speed to catch the tiger — 2.01.233
speed to catch the tiger — bootless speed, 2.01.233
bassanio told him he would make some speed | of MV 2.08. 37
all th' endeavor of a man | in speed to /padua. 3.04. 49
bring them i pray thee with imagin'd speed 3.04. 52
madam, i go with all convenient speed. 3.04. 56
which speed, we hope, the better for our words. 5.01.115
now hercules be thy speed, young man! AYL 1.02.210 P
one, | though paris came in hope to speed alone. SHR 1.02.245
well mayst thou woo, and happy be thy speed! 2.01.138
petruchio, how speed you with my daughter? 2.01.281
it were impossible i should speed amiss. 2.01.283
ay, madam, with the swiftest wing of speed. AWW 3.02. 73
that ride upon the violent speed of fire, | fly 3.02.109
hearing so much, will speed her foot again, 3.04. 37
if you speed well in it, the duke shall both 3.06. 68 P
let us assay our plot, which, if it speed, | is 3.07. 44
i will come after you with what good speed | our 5.01. 34
sir, their speed | hath been beyond accompt. WT 2.03.197
'tis good speed; 2.03.199
mere conceit and fear | of the queen's speed, is 3.02.145
blossom, speed thee well! 3.03. 46
and with speed so pace | to speak of perdita, 4.01. 23
fortune speed us! 4.04.667
the swifter speed the better. 4.04.669
that "once," i see, by your good father's speed, 5.01.210
richard, we must speed | for france, for france, JN 1.01.178
forewearied in this action of swift speed, 2.01.233
speed then to take advantage of the field. 2.01.297
so hot a speed with such advice dispos'd, | such 3.04. 11
the copy of your speed is learn'd by them; 4.02.113
withhold thy speed, dreadful occasion! 4.02.125
the spirit of the time shall teach me speed. 4.02.176
away that child, | and follow me with speed. 4.03.157
and spleen of speed to see your majesty! 5.07. 50
with all good speed at plashy visit me. R2 1.02. 66
a brace of draymen bid god speed him well, | and 1.04. 32
with all swift speed you must away to france. 5.01. 54
but come yourself with speed to us again, | for 1H4 1.01.105
and 'tis no little reason bids us speed, | to 1.03.283
he that rides at high speed and with his pistol 2.04.345 P
good manners be your speed! 3.01.188
thy looks are full of speed. 3.02.162
and with all speed | you shall have your desires 4.03. 48
and, to prevent the worst, sir michael, speed; 4.04. 35
arm, arm with speed! 5.02. 75
york shall bend you with your dearest speed, 5.05. 36
hard | a gentleman, almost forespent with speed, 2H4 1.01. 37
upon enforcement flies with greatest speed, | so 1.01.120
and letters, and make friends with speed — 1.01.214
make good speed. 3.01. 3
these griefs shall be with speedy redress'd, 4.02. 59
him, | and we with sober speed will follow you. 4.03. 80
dispatch us with all speed, lest that our king H5 2.04.141
speed him hence, | let him greet england with 3.05. 36
my sovereign lord, bestow yourself with speed. 4.03. 68
saint denis be my speed! 5.02.183 P
god speed the parliament! 1H6 3.01. 60
us in, and with all speed provide | to see her 2H6 1.01. 73
nay, stay not to expostulate, make speed, | or 3H6 2.05.135
and leave your brothers to go speed elsewhere. 4.01. 58
be sent for, to return from france with speed; 4.06. 61
it shall be done, my sovereign, with all speed. 4.06. 64
neighbors, god speed! R3 2.03. 6
and with all speed post with him toward the 3.02. 17
go, lovel, with all speed to doctor shaw; 3.05.103
be valiant, and speed well! 5.03.102
the devil speed him! H8 1.01. 52
dry enough), will, with great speed of judgment, TRO 1.03.329
on, you heavens, effect your rage with speed! 5.10. 6
speed thee straight | and make my misery serve COR 4.05. 87
good faith, i'll prove him, | speed how it will. 5.01. 61
speak thou no more, if all the rest will speed. TIT 1.01.372
it offend you then | that both should speed? 2.01.101
i'll send a friar with speed | to mantua, with ROM 4.01.123
so that my speed to mantua there was stay'd. 5.02. 12
saint francis be my speed! 5.03.121
and he that's once denied will hardly speed. TIM 3.02. 62
forget not, in your speed, antonio, | to touch JC 1.02. 6
for let the gods so speed me as i love | the 1.02. 88
the heavens speed thee in thine enterprise! 2.04. 41
post back with speed, and tell him what hath 3.01.287
one of my fellows had the speed of him, | who, MAC 1.05. 35
o, most wicked speed! HAM 1.02.156
he shall with speed to england | for the demand 3.01.169
follow him at foot, tempt him with speed aboard. 4.03. 54
to me with as much speed as thou wouldest fly 4.06. 24 P
if this letter speed | and my invention thrive, LR 1.02. 19
forbearance till the speed of his rage goes 1.02.167 P
sir, speed you: what's your will? 4.06.208
affair cries haste, | and speed must answer it. OTH 1.03.277
h'as had most favorable and happy speed: 2.01. 67
anticipates our thoughts | a se'nnight's speed. 2.01. 77
bianca's /pow'r, | how quickly should you speed! 4.01.108
this speed of caesar's | carries beyond belief. ANT 3.07. 74
this fool's speed | be cross'd with slowness; CYM 3.05.161
and how you shall speed in your journey's end, i 5.04.183 P
speed to him, | store never hurts good governors TNK 1.03. 5
for whose speed | the great bellona i'll solicit 1.03. 12
yea, the speed also — to go on, i mean, | else 5.01. 41
did instigate | his all too timeless speed, if LUC 44
or stop the headlong fury of his speed. 501
he in his speed looks for the morning light, 745
bid him with speed prepare to carry it, | the 1294
see) | some present speed to come and visit me. 1307
speed more than speed but dull and slow she 1336
speed more than speed but dull and slow she 1336
while others saucily | promise more speed, but 1349
breed not, | my rams speed not, all is amiss; PP 17. 2
the wretch did know | his rider lov'd not speed, SON 50. 8
of my dull bearer, when from thee i speed: 51. 2
wind, | in winged speed no motion shall i know. 51. 8

SPEEDED 2 FR 0.0002 REL FR 1 V 1 P
it shall be speeded well. MM 4.05. 10
i have speeded hither with the very extremest 2H4 4.03. 34 P

SPEEDIER 2 FR 0.0002 REL FR 2 V 0 P
a speedier course /than ling'ring languishment TIT 2.01.110
and do't the speedier, that you may direct me HAM 4.06. 33

SPEEDIEST 3 FR 0.0003 REL FR 3 V 0 P
even with the speediest expedition | i will TGV 1.03. 37
send me your prisoners with the speediest means, 1H4 1.03.120
and with your speediest bring us what she says, ANT 5.01. 67

SPEEDILY 13 FR 0.0014 REL FR 10 V 3 P
but speedily. MM 1.04. 84
haste you speedily to angelo; 3.01.262 P
i held my duty speedily to acquaint you withal, AWW 1.03.119 P
go speedily and bring again the count. 5.03.152
percy | shall follow in your conduct speedily. 1H4 3.01.195
set forth, | or hitherwards intended speedily, 4.01. 92
come let us take a muster speedily. 4.01.133
come therefore, let's about it speedily. 3H6 4.06.102
speedily i wish | to hear from rome. H8 3.02. 89
post speedily to my lord your husband, show him LR 3.07. 1 P
these our nether crimes | so speedily can venge! 4.02. 80
but must be look'd to speedily and strongly. CYM 3.05. 27
bear 'em speedily | from our kind air, to them TNK 1.04. 37

SPEEDINESS 1 FR 0.0001 REL FR 1 V 0 P
answer made | the speediness of your return. CYM 2.04. 31

SPEEDING 4 FR 0.0004 REL FR 4 V 0 P
is this your speeding? SHR 2.01.301
have got a speeding trick to lay down ladies. H8 1.03. 40
to-morrow all for speeding do their best. PER 2.03.115
o cruel speeding, fraughted with gall. PP 17.16

SPEEDS 4 FR 0.0004 REL FR 4 V 0 P
your wit's too hot, it speeds too fast, 'twill LLL 2.01.119
a lip of much contempt, speeds from me, and | so WT 1.02.373
an honest tale speeds best being plainly told. R3 4.04.358
if we draw lots, he speeds; ANT 2.03. 36

SPEEDY 21 FR 0.0023 REL FR 18 V 3 P
the florentine will move us | for speedy aid; AWW 1.02. 7
you, sir, a speedy infirmity, for the better TN 1.05. 78 P
as it hath been to us rare, pleasant, speedy, WT 3.01. 13
some speedy messenger bid her repair | to our JN 2.01.554
which would have been as speedy in your end | as 1H4 5.04. 55
hath sent out | a speedy power to encounter you, 2H4 1.01.133
are not the speedy scouts return'd again | that 1H6 4.03. 1
you speedy helpers, that are substitutes | under 5.03. 5
this speedy and quick appearance argues proof 5.03. 8
and craves your company for speedy counsel. 3H6 2.01.208
good lords, make all the speedy haste you may. R3 3.01. 60
i will wish her speedy strength, and visit her COR 1.03. 78 P
sound | with speedy help doth lend redress." ROM 4.05.143
he humbly prays your speedy payment. TIM 2.02. 28
arm you, i pray you, to this speedy viage, | for HAM 3.03. 24
if your diligence be not speedy, i shall be LR 1.05. 4 P
this letter, madam, craves a speedy answer; 4.02. 82
near and on speedy foot; 4.06.213
be rid of him devise | his speedy taking off. 5.01. 65
unapt for tender smell, or speedy flight, | make LUC 695
which being done with speedy diligence, | the 1853

SPEKEN *(also speak)*

/SPEKEN 1 FR 0.0001 REL FR 1 V 0 P
each man | thinks all is writ he /speken can; PER 2.ch. 12

SPELL* 10 FR 0.0011 REL FR 9 V 1 P
hush and be mute, | or else our spell is marr'd. TMP 4.01.127
untie the spell. 5.01.253
dwell | in this bare island by your spell, | but ep 8
featur'd, | but she would spell him backward. ADO 3.01. 61
nor spell, nor charm, | come our lovely lady MND 2.02. 17
shall be holy, as | you hear my spell is lawful. WT 5.03.105
o, fear him not, | his spell in that is out. H8 3.02. 20
'tis a spell, you see, of much power. COR 5.02. 96 P
thy love did read by rote that could not spell. ROM 2.03. 88
ah, thou spell! ANT 4.12. 30

SPELL'D 1 FR 0.0001 REL FR 0 V 1 P
what is a,b, spell'd backward, with the horn on LLL 5.01. 47 P

SPELLING 1 FR 0.0001 REL FR 1 V 0 P
unchain your spirits now with spelling charms, 1H6 5.03. 31

SPELLS 5 FR 0.0005 REL FR 4 V 1 P
she works by charms, by spells, by th' figure, WIV 4.02.177 P
now help, ye charming spells and periapts, | and 1H6 5.03. 2
is't possible the spells of france should juggle H8 1.03. 1
your vessels and your spells provide, | your MAC 3.05. 18
by spells and medicines bought of mountebanks; OTH 1.03. 61

SPELL-STOPP'D 1 FR 0.0001 REL FR 1 V 0 P
there stand, | for you are spell-stopp'd. TMP 5.01. 61

/SPENCER 1 FR 0.0001 REL FR 1 V 0 P
london sent | the heads of salisbury, /spencer, R2 5.06. 8

SPEND 74 FR 0.0083 REL FR 63 V 11 P
would suffer him to spend his youth at home, TGV 1.03. 5
you | to let him spend his time no more at home, 1.03. 14
i am resolv'd that thou shalt spend some time 1.03. 66
sir, if you spend word for word with me, i shall 2.04. 41 P

and here he means to spend his time a while. 2.04. 80
even for this time i spend in talking to thee. 4.02.104
there is money, spend it, spend it; WIV 2.02.232 P
there is money, spend it, spend it; 2.02.232 P
spend more; 2.02.232 P
spend all i have; 2.02.232 P
how will he spend his wit! LLL 4.03.145
joan, or spend a minute's time | in pruning me? 4.03.180
and spend his prodigal wits in bootless rhymes, 5.02. 64
we number nothing that we spend for you; 5.02.198
a twelvemonth shall you spend, and never rest, 5.02.821
you spend your passion on a mispris'd mood. MND 3.02. 74
and herein spend but time | to wind about my MV 1.01.153
at home, my son and my servant spend all at the SHR 5.01. 69 P
that we with thee | may spend our wonder too, or AWW 2.01. 89
majesty's ear, | if he would spend his power. 5.01. 8
spend this for me. TN 1.05.283
league, | and not to spend it so unneighborly! JN 5.02. 39
ere the six years that he hath to spend | can R2 1.03.219
his noble hand | did win what he did spend, and 2.01.180
an' he shall spend mine honor with his shame, 5.03. 68
where they did spend a sad and bloody hour, | as 1H4 1.01. 56
we may boldly spend upon the hope of what | /is 4.01. 54
to spend that shortness basely were too long 5.02. 82
most spend their mouths when what they seem to H5 2.04. 70
we may as bootless spend our vain command | upon 3.03. 24
and he may well in fretting spend his gall — 1H6 1.02. 16
neck, | and in his bosom spend my latter gasp. 2.05. 38
did my brother henry spend his youth, | his 2H6 1.01. 78
on sheep or oxen could i spend my fury. 5.01. 27
and spend her strength with overmatching waves. 3H6 1.04. 21
life, | and in devotion spend my latter days, 4.06. 43
and men ne'er spend their fury on a child. 5.05. 57
and now what rests but that we spend the time 5.07. 42
i would not spend another such a night | though R3 1.04. 5
he will spend his mouth and promise, like TRO 5.01. 91 P
i utter, and spend my malice in my breath. COR 2.01. 53 P
and is content | to spend the time to end it. 2.02.129
than spend a fawn upon 'em | for the inheritance 3.02. 67
and spend our flatteries to drink those men TIM 1.02.137
supper to him of purpose to have him spend less, 3.01. 25 P
i have no more to reckon, he to spend. 3.04. 56
we would spend it in some words upon that MAC 2.01. 23
this night i'll spend | unto a dismal and a 3.05. 20
more sorrow, | and that i'll spend for him. 5.09. 17
we shall not spend a large expense of time 5.09. 26
and thy best graces spend it at thy will! HAM 1.02. 63
i will but spend a word here in the house, | and OTH 1.02. 48
matter and direction, | to spend with thee. 1.03.300
and spend your rich opinion for the name | of a 2.03.195
that antony may seem to spend his fury | upon ANT 4.06. 9
and i wore my life | to spend upon his haters. 5.01. 9
and spend that kiss | which is my heaven to have 5.02.302
of him and might not spend them at my pleasure. CYM 2.01. 5 P
on either side i come to spend my breath; 5.03. 81
and in your search spend your adventurous worth;
PER 2.04. 51
boult, spend thou that in the town. 4.02.137 P
will in that kingdom spend our following days. 5.03. 81
then do they spend their mouths: VEN 695
for who hath she to spend the night withal, 847
bred, | not spend the dowry of a lawful bed. LUC 938
she hoards, to spend when he is by to hear her, 1318
spare not to spend, and chiefly there | where PP 18.14
friend, | whilst thou hast wherewith to spend; 20.34
why dost thou spend | upon thyself thy beauty's SON 4. 1
look what an unthrift in the world doth spend 9. 9
i have no precious time at all to spend, | nor 57. 3
dost thou upon thy fading mansion spend? 146. 6
on me, do i not spend | revenge upon myself with 149. 7
remove | to spend her living in eternal love. LC 238
SPENDEST 1 FR 0.0001 REL FR 0 V 1 P
do not only marvel where thou spendest thy time,
1H4 2.04.398 P
SPENDING 3 FR 0.0003 REL FR 3 V 0 P
in spending your wit in the praise of mine. LLL 2.01. 19
home, | spending his manly marrow in her arms, AWW 2.03.281
new, | spending again what is already spent: SON 76.12
SPENDS 5 FR 0.0005 REL FR 3 V 2 P
looks, and spends what he borrows kindly in your TGV 2.04. 39 P
to save the money that he spends in /tiring; ERR 2.02. 97 P
he robs himself that spends a bootless grief. OTH 1.03.209
on this sad shadow lucrece spends her eyes, LUC 1457
and in the praise thereof spends all his might, SON 80. 3
SPEND'ST 2 FR 0.0002 REL FR 2 V 0 P
thou spend'st such high-day wit in praising him. MV 2.09. 98
spend'st thou thy fury on some worthless song, SON 100. 3
SPENDTHRIFT 1 FR 0.0001 REL FR 1 V 0 P
fie, what a spendthrift is he of his tongue! TMP 2.01. 24
SPENDTHRIFT'S 1 FR 0.0001 REL FR 1 V 0 P
then this "should" is like a spendthrift's sigh, HAM 4.07.122
SPENSER 1 FR 0.0001 REL FR 1 V 0 P
spenser to me, whose deep conceit is such | as, PP 8. 7
SPENT 77 FR 0.0087 REL FR 62 V 15 P
now | must by us both be spent most preciously. TMP 1.02.241
we have convers'd and spent our hours together, TGV 2.04. 63
sir, i am a gentleman that have spent much. WIV 2.02.160 P
five summers have i spent in farthest greece, ERR 1.01.132
if cupid have not spent all his quiver in venice ADO 1.01.271 P
surely suit ill spent and labor ill bestow'd. 3.02. 99 P
mirth, | i never spent an hour's talk withal. LLL 2.01. 68
the tedious minutes i with her have spent. MND 2.02.112
the sisters' vows, the hours that we have spent, 3.02.199
so — and i know not what's spent in the search. MV 3.01. 91 P
your daughter spent in genoa, as i heard, one 3.01.108 P
what prodigal portion have i spent, that i AYL 1.01. 38 P
beg, when that is spent? 1.01. 76 P
and ere we have thy youthful wages spent, 2.03. 67
and when in music we have spent an hour, | your SHR 3.01. 7
the fury spent, anon | did this break from her: WT 3.03. 26
if ever you have spent time worse ere now; 4.01. 30
our cannons' malice vainly shall be spent JN 2.01.251
we hold our time too precious to be spent | with 5.02.161
this arm shall do it, or this life be spent. R2 1.01.108
six frozen winters spent, | return with welcome 1.03.211
words are scarce, they are seldom spent in vain, 2.01. 7
words, life, and all, old lancaster hath spent. 2.01.150
his time is spent, our pilgrimage must be. 2.01.154
spend, and spent not that | which his triumphant 2.01.180
more hath he spent in peace than they in wars. 2.01.255
and most dissolutely spent on tuesday morning; 1H4 1.02. 35 P
"lay by," and spent with crying "bring in"; 1.02. 36 P
jesu, jesu, the mad days that i have spent! 2H4 3.02. 33 P
mouldy, it is time you were spent. 3.02.117 P
spent? 3.02.118 P
eyes, like lamps whose wasting oil is spent, 1H6 2.05. 8
in prison hast thou spent a pilgrimage, | and 2.05.116
and so break off, the day is almost spent; 2H6 3.01.325
and think it but a minute spent in sport. 3.02.338
his statutes cancell'd, and his treasure spent; 3H6 5.04. 79
to royalize his blood i spent mine own. R3 1.03.124
happy indeed, as we have spent the day. 2.01. 49
though we have spent our harvest of this king, 2.02.115
the day is spent. 3.02. 89
eleven hours i have spent to write it over, 3.06. 5
after so many hours, lives, speeches spent, TRO 2.02. 1
of troyan blood | spent more in her defense. 2.02.198
how have we spent this morning! 4.04.140
this night in banqueting must all be spent. 5.01. 46
ten years are spent since first he undertook TIT 1.01. 31
whose youth was spent | in dangerous wars whilst 3.01. 2
is something stale and hoar ere it be spent. ROM 2.04.133 P
for a score, | when it hoars ere it be spent. 2.04.139
mine shall be spent, | when theirs are dry, for 3.02.130
when all's spent, he'ld be cross'd then, and he TIM 1.02.162
i know my lord hath spent of timon's wealth, 3.04. 26
he did behoove his anger, ere 'twas spent, | as 3.05. 22
and, thy fury spent, | confounded be thyself! 4.03.128
as two spent swimmers that do cling together MAC 1.02. 8
nought's had, all's spent, | where our desire is 3.02. 4
all 's golden words are spent. HAM 5.02.131 P
my money is almost spent; OTH 2.03.365 P
look | our lamp is spent, it's out. ANT 4.15. 85
my youth i spent | much under him; CYM 3.01. 69
to whom being going, almost spent with hunger, 3.06. 62
his comforts thrive, his trials well are spent. 5.04.104
and time that is so briefly spent | with your PER 3.ch. 12
be as for our health, which were not spent, TNK 1.02.110
the time is spent, her object will away, | and VEN 255
the night is spent." 717
which by him tainted shall for him be spent, LUC 1182
that she with painted images hath spent, | being 1577
foretell new storms to those already spent; 1589
love, what spite hath thy fair color spent? 1600
new, | spending again what is already spent: SON 76.12
redeem | in gentle numbers time so idly spent; 100. 6
and in this change is my invention spent, 105.11
tyrants' crests and tombs of brass are spent. 107.14
and gain by ills thrice more than i have spent. 119.14
pitiful thrivers, in their gazing spent? 125. 8
it saw | the carcass of a beauty spent and done. LC 11
SPERATO 1 FR 0.0001 REL FR 1 V 0 P
"si fortune me tormente, sperato me contento." 2H4 2.04.181
SPERMACETI *(see parmaciti)*
SPERO 1 FR 0.0001 REL FR 1 V 0 P
si fortuna me tormenta, spero contenta. 2H4 5.05. 96
/SPERR 1 FR 0.0001 REL FR 1 V 0 P
/bolts | /sperr /up /the /sons /of /troy. TRO pr 19
SPET *(also spit*, etc.)*
SPET 4 FR 0.0004 REL FR 4 V 0 P
dog, | and spet upon my jewish gaberdine, | and MV 1.03.112
"fair sir, you spet on me on wednesday last, 1.03.126
to spet on thee again, to spurn thee too. 1.03.131
storm, venomously | wilt thou spet all thyself? PER 3.01. 8
SPETS 1 FR 0.0001 REL FR 1 V 0 P
ambitious head | spets in the face of heaven, is MV 2.07. 45
SPHER'D 1 FR 0.0001 REL FR 1 V 0 P
in noble eminence enthron'd and spher'd | amidst TRO 1.03. 90
SPHERE 10 FR 0.0011 REL FR 8 V 2 P
you would lift the moon out of her sphere, if TMP 2.01.183 P
every where, | swifter than the moon's sphere; MND 2.01. 7
as yonder venus in her glimmering sphere. 3.02. 61
with thy chaste eye, from thy pale sphere above, AYL 3.02. 3
light | must i be comforted, not in his sphere. AWW 1.01. 89
two stars keep not their motion in one sphere, 1H4 5.04. 65
that labor on the bosom of this sphere | to TIM 1.01. 66
that, as the star moves not but in his sphere, HAM 4.07. 15
to be call'd into a huge sphere, and not to be ANT 2.07. 14 P
o sun, | burn the great sphere thou mov'st in! 4.15. 10
SPHERED 1 FR 0.0001 REL FR 1 V 0 P
till thy sphered bias cheek | outswell the colic TRO 4.05. 8
SPHERES 11 FR 0.0012 REL FR 11 V 0 P
and certain stars shot madly from their spheres, MND 2.01.153
we shall have shortly discord in the spheres. AYL 2.07. 6
to solicit that | than music from the spheres. TN 3.01.110
now, you stars that move in your right spheres, JN 5.07. 74
to twinkle in their spheres till they return. ROM 2.02. 17
two eyes, like stars, start from their spheres, HAM 1.05. 17
voice was propertied | as all the tuned spheres, ANT 5.02. 84
the music of the spheres! PER 5.01.229
his globy eyes | had almost drawn their spheres, TNK 5.01.114
have mine eyes out of their spheres been fitted SON 119. 7
as they did batt'ry to the spheres intend; LC 23
SPHERICAL 3 FR 0.0003 REL FR 0 V 3 P
she is spherical, like a globe; ERR 3.02.114 P
look you, is fixed upon a spherical stone, which H5 3.06. 36 P
and treachers by spherical predominance; LR 1.02.123 P
SPHERY 1 FR 0.0001 REL FR 1 V 0 P
made me compare with hermia's sphery eyne! MND 2.02. 99
SPHINX 1 FR 0.0001 REL FR 1 V 0 P
subtile as sphinx, as sweet and musical | as LLL 4.03.339
SPICE 3 FR 0.0003 REL FR 1 V 2 P
purse is not hot enough to purchase your spice. WT 4.03.119 P
you | for all this spice of your hypocrisy. H8 2.03. 26
such-like, the spice and salt that season a man? TRO 1.02.255 P
SPICED 1 FR 0.0001 REL FR 1 V 0 P
and, in the spiced indian air, by night, | full MND 2.01.124
SPICERY 1 FR 0.0001 REL FR 1 V 0 P
where in that nest of spicery they will breed R3 4.04.424
SPICES 8 FR 0.0009 REL FR 7 V 1 P
would scatter all her spices on the stream, MV 1.01. 33
thy by-gone fooleries were but spices of it. WT 3.02.184
i must go buy spices for our sheep-shearing. 4.03.116 P
as he hath spices of them all — not all, | for COR 4.07. 46
take these keys and fetch more spices, nurse. ROM 4.04. 1
this embalms and spices | to th' april day again TIM 4.03. 41
bid nestor bring me spices, ink and /paper, | my PER 3.01. 65
and entreasur'd | with full bags of spices! 3.02. 66
SPIDER 10 FR 0.0011 REL FR 9 V 1
in her hairs | the painter plays the spider, and MV 3.02.121
there may be in the cup | a spider steep'd, and WT 2.01. 40
i have drunk, and seen the spider. 2.01. 45
thread | that ever spider twisted from her womb JN 4.03.128
my brain, more busy than the laboring spider, 2H6 3.01.339
why strew'st thou sugar on that bottled spider R3 1.03.241
for thee to help me curse | that bottled spider, 4.04. 81
in circumvention deliver a fly from a spider, TRO 2.03. 16
her traces of the smallest spider web, | her ROM 1.04. 64
were it toad, or adder, spider, | 'twould move CYM 4.02. 90
SPIDER-LIKE 1 FR 0.0001 REL FR 1 V 0
but spider-like | out of his self-drawing web, H8 1.01. 62
SPIDERS' 1 FR 0.0001 REL FR 1 V 0
to draw with idle spiders' strings | most MM 3.02.275
SPIDERS 3 FR 0.0003 REL FR 3 V 0
weaving spiders, come not here; MND 2.02. 20
but let thy spiders, that suck up thy venom, R2 3.02. 14
thee | than i can wish to wolves — to spiders, R3 1.02. 19
SPIED 11 FR 0.0012 REL FR 7 V 4
spied a blossom passing fair | playing in the LLL 4.03.101
she hath spied him already with those sweet eyes MND 5.01.321
but at last i spied | an ancient angel coming SHR 4.02. 60
look, he has spied us. AWW 3.05. 90
at last i spied his eyes, and methought he had 2H4 2.02. 81
white hair that helen spied on troilus' chin. TRO 1.02.150
the fire | is spied in populous cities. OTH 1.01. 77
and with that word she spied the hunted boar, VEN 900
more she thought he spied in her some blemish. LUC 1358
such signs of truth in his plain face she spied, 1532
was ever may, | spied a blossom passing fair, PP 16. 3
SPIES 16 FR 0.0018 REL FR 15 V 1
if these be true spies which i wear in my head, TMP 5.01.259
i fear i am attended by some spies. TGV 5.01. 10
and when the doctor spies his vantage ripe, | to WIV 4.06. 43
the heaven sets spies upon us, will not have WT 5.01.203
i'll fill these dogged spies with false reports; JN 4.01.128
and spies a far-off shore where he would tread, 3H6 3.02.136
spies of the volsces | held me in chase, that i COR 1.06. 18
when sorrows come, they come not single spies, HAM 4.05. 78
which are to france the spies and speculations LR 3.01. 24
mystery of things | as if we were god's spies; 5.03. 17
in such distractions as | beguil'd all spies. ANT 3.07. 77
whereat she starts like one that spies an adder VEN 878
and in her haste unfortunately spies | the foul 1029
by the light he spies | lucretia's glove, LUC 316
revealing day through every cranny spies, | and 1086
or on my frailties why are frailer spies, SON 121. 7
SPIGOT 1 FR 0.0001 REL FR 0 V 1
wilt thou the spigot wield? WIV 1.03. 21
SPILL 6 FR 0.0006 REL FR 6 V 0
as i for praise alone now seek to spill | the LLL 4.01. 34
you came in arms to spill mine enemies' blood, JN 3.01.102
base, | and misbegotten blood i spill of thine, 1H6 4.06. 22
moulds, all germains spill at once | that makes LR 3.02. 8
we'll spill the blood | that has to-day escap'd. ANT 4.08. 3
wretched hands such wretched blood should spill; LUC 999
SPILL'D 4 FR 0.0004 REL FR 4 V 0
both have i spill'd; R2 5.05.114
o, the blood is spill'd | of my dear kinsman! ROM 3.01.147
and in his blood that on the ground lay spill'd, VEN 1167
which she too early and too late hath spill'd." LUC 1801
SPILLING 2 FR 0.0002 REL FR 2 V 0
thou respect'st not spilling edward's blood. R2 2.01.131
no cause, but company, of her drops spilling. LUC 1236
SPILLS 2 FR 0.0002 REL FR 2 V 0
he forfeits his own blood that spills another. TIM 3.05. 87
it spills itself in fearing to be spilt. HAM 4.05. 20
SPILT 4 FR 0.0004 REL FR 3 V 1
is crack'd, and all the precious liquor spilt, R2 1.02. 19
say, "there's some of the king's blood spilt." 2H4 2.02.113
which, as thou know'st, unjustly must be spilt. R3 3.03. 23
it spills itself in fearing to be spilt. HAM 4.05. 20
SPILTH 1 FR 0.0001 REL FR 1 V 0
vaults have wept | with drunken spilth of wine, TIM 2.02.160
SPIN 4 FR 0.0004 REL FR 1 V 3
"item, she can spin." TGV 3.01.314
on wheels, when she can spin for her living. 3.01.316
take thee between her legs, and spin it off. TN 1.03.104
that their hot blood may spin in english eyes, H5 4.02. 10
SPINES 1 FR 0.0001 REL FR 1 V
roses, their sharp spines being gone, | not TNK 1.01.
SPINII 1 FR 0.0001 REL FR 0 V
the regiment of the spinii one captain spurio, AWW 2.01. 4
SPINNERS' 1 FR 0.0001 REL FR 1 V
her waggon-spokes made of long spinners' legs, ROM 1.04. 6
SPINNERS 1 FR 0.0001 REL FR 1 V
hence, you long-legg'd spinners, hence! MND 2.02. 2
SPINSTER 1 FR 0.0001 REL FR 1 V
of a battle knows | more than a spinster — OTH 1.01. 2
SPINSTERS 3 FR 0.0003 REL FR 3 V
the spinsters and the knitters in the sun, | and TN 2.04. 4
'longing, have put off | the spinsters, carders, H8 1.02. 3
if | you stay to see of us such spinsters, we TNK 1.03. 2
SPIRE 1 FR 0.0001 REL FR 1 V
which, to the spire and top of praises vouch'd, COR 1.09. 2
/SPIRIT 1 FR 0.0001 REL FR 1 V
/and /that /his /forward /spirit | /would /lift 2H4 1.01.17
SPIRIT 259 FR 0.0292 REL FR 219 V 4
hast thou, spirit, | perform'd to point the TMP 1.02.19
my brave spirit! 1.02.20
why, that's my spirit! 1.02.21
for thou wast a spirit too delicate | to act her 1.02.27
what, is't a spirit? 1.02.41
but 'tis a spirit. 1.02.41
spirit, fine spirit, i'll free thee | within two 1.02.42
spirit, fine spirit, i'll free thee | within two 1.02.42
if the ill spirit have so fair a house, | good 1.02.45
persuaded | (for he's a spirit of persuasion, 2.01.23
here comes a spirit of his, and to torment me 2.02. 1
the spirit torments me! o! 2.02. 6
nor hath not | one spirit to command: 3.02. 9
bring a corollary, | rather than want a spirit. 4.01. 5
spirit, | we must prepare to meet with caliban. 4.01.16
say, my spirit, | how fares the king and 's 5.01.
dost thou think so, spirit? 5.01.

quickly, spirit, | thou shalt ere long be free. 5.01. 86
my tricksy spirit! 5.01.226
come hither, spirit. 5.01.251
who then? his spirit? TGV 3.01.195 P
if the gentle spirit of moving words | can no 5.04. 55
i do applaud thy spirit, valentine, | and think 5.04.140
what spirit, what devil suggests this WIV 3.03.215 P
the spirit of wantonness is sure scar'd out of 4.02.209 P
you have heard of such a spirit, and well you 4.04. 35
dis–horn the spirit, | and mock him home to 4.04. 64
as i am a true spirit, welcome! 5.05. 29 P
by your renouncement an immortal spirit, | and MM 1.04. 35
and the delighted spirit | to bathe in fiery 3.01.120
i have spirit to do any thing that appears not 3.01.205 P
that appears not foul in the truth of my spirit. 3.01.207 P
is the natural man, | and which the spirit? ERR 5.01.335
have thought her spirit had been invincible ADO 2.03.114 P
says she, "by my own spirit, for i should flout 2.03.143 P
(as you know all) hath a contemptible spirit. 2.03.181 P
nay, but his jesting spirit, which is now crept 3.02. 59 P
it when a man of great spirit grows melancholy? LLL 1.02. 2 P
reck'ning, it fitteth the spirit of a tapster. 1.02. 40 P
sing, boy, my spirit grows heavy in love. 1.02.122 P
a foolish extravagant spirit, full of forms, 4.02. 66 P
you, | of such a merry, nimble, stirring spirit, 5.02. 16
why, that's the way to choke a gibing spirit, 5.02.858
but if they will not, throw away that spirit, 5.02.867
awake the pert and nimble spirit of mirth, MND 1.01. 13
how now, spirit, whither wander you? 2.01. 1
tempt not too much the hatred of my spirit, 2.01.211
i am a spirit of no common rate; 3.01.154
so, | that thou shalt like an aery spirit go. 3.01.161
how now, mad spirit? 3.02. 4
cold drops of modesty | thy skipping spirit, MV 2.02.187
drops do something drown my manly spirit. 2.03. 14 P
are, | are with more spirit chased than enjoy'd. 2.06. 13
giddy in spirit, still gazing in a doubt 3.02.144
is that her gentle spirit | commits itself to 3.02.163
the best–condition'd and unwearied spirit | in 3.02.293
of lineaments, of manners, and of spirit; 3.04. 15
arm'd | to suffer, with a quietness of spirit, 4.01. 12
thy currish spirit | govern'd a wolf, who, 4.01.133
thou shalt see the difference of our spirit, | i 4.01.368
the motions of his spirit are dull as night, 5.01. 86
that grieves me, and the spirit of my father, AYL 1.01. 22 P
the spirit of my father grows strong in me, and 1.01. 70 P
an unquestionable spirit, which you have not; 3.02.375 P
should be infused with so foul a spirit! SHR in.2. 16
for shame, thou hilding of a devilish spirit, 2.01. 26
when, with a most impatient devilish spirit, 2.01.151
and woo her with some spirit when she comes. 2.01.169
a fool, | if she had not a spirit to resist. 3.02.221
methinks in thee some blessed spirit doth speak AWW 2.01.175
he's of a most facinerious spirit that will not 2.03. 30 P
o spirit of love, how quick and fresh art thou, TN 1.01. 9
and spirit | do give thee fivefold blazon. 1.05.292
and the spirit of humors intimate reading aloud 2.05. 84 P
hands, let thy blood and spirit embrace them, 2.05.147 P
a spirit i am indeed, | but am in that dimension 5.01.236
threw off his spirit, his appetite, his sleep, WT 2.03. 16
jove send her | a better guiding spirit! 2.03.127
some powerful spirit instruct the kites and 2.03.186
i would your spirit were easier for advice, | or 4.04.505
would make her sainted spirit | again possess 5.01. 57
never, paulina, so be bless'd my spirit! 5.01. 71
the very spirit of plantagenet! JN 1.01.167
and fits the mounting spirit like myself; 1.01.206
or if that surly spirit, melancholy, | had bak'd 3.03. 42
holding th' eternal spirit, against her will, 3.04. 18
now hear me speak with a prophetic spirit; 3.04.126
the breath of heaven hath blown his spirit out, 4.01.109
the spirit of the time shall teach me speed. 4.02.176
o me, my uncle's spirit is in these stones. 4.03. 9
and put on | the dauntless spirit of resolution. 5.01. 53
and flesh his spirit in a warlike soil, 5.01. 71
himself to rome, his spirit is come in, | that 5.02. 70
up, | and tame the savage spirit of wild war, 5.02. 74
put spirit in the french; 5.04. 2
chest | is a bold spirit in a loyal breast. R2 1.01.181
whose youthful spirit, in me regenerate, | doth 1.03. 70
god give thee the spirit of persuasion and him 1H4 1.02.152 P
as full of peril and adventerous spirit | as to 1.03.191
thy spirit within thee hath been so at war, 2.03. 56
again as that fiend douglas, that spirit percy, 2.04.368 P
images, | as full of spirit as the month of may, 4.01.101
as if he mast'red there a double spirit | of 5.02. 63
i did not think thee lord of such a spirit. 5.04. 18
when that this body did contain a spirit, | a 5.04. 89
your spirit is too true, your fears too certain. 2H4 1.01. 92
whose spirit lent a fire | even to the dullest 1.01.112
but let one spirit of the first–born cain 1.01.157
upon the easy–yielding spirit of this woman, and 2.01.115 P
give me the spirit, master shallow. 3.02.260 P
the dove, and very blessed spirit of peace, 4.01. 46
believe me, i am passing light in spirit. 4.02. 85
hand | will whisper music to my weary spirit. 4.05. 3
which my most inward true and duteous spirit 4.05.147
if any rebel or vain spirit of mine | did with 4.05.171
and impartial spirit | as you have done 'gainst 5.02.116
invoke his warlike spirit, | and your H5 1.02.104
he therefore sends you, meeter for your spirit, 1.02.254
constant in spirit, not swerving with the blood, 2.02.133
and bend up every spirit | to his full height. 3.01. 16
follow your spirit; 3.01. 33
with spirit of honor edged | more sharper than 3.05. 38
so the spirit is eased; 4.01. 19
o brave spirit! 4.02. 3
cannot so conjure up the spirit of love in her, 5.02.289 P
his soldiers, spying his undaunted spirit, | "a 1H6 1.01.127
the spirit of deep prophecy she hath, 1.02. 55
salisbury, cheer thy spirit with this comfort, 1.04. 90
i have perhaps some shallow spirit of judgment; 2.04. 16
undaunted spirit in a dying breast! 3.02. 99
man, | of an invincible unconquer'd spirit! 4.02. 32
my boy did drench | his overmounting spirit; 4.07. 15
my spirit can no longer bear these harms. 4.07. 30
he speaks with such a proud commanding spirit. 4.07. 88
her valiant courage and undaunted spirit | (more 5.05. 70

a spirit rais'd from depth of under ground, 2H6 1.02. 79
reported to be a woman of an invincible spirit; 1.04. 7 P
he dares not calm his contumelious spirit, | nor 3.02.204
hast thou not spirit to curse thine enemy? 3.02.308
inspir'd with the spirit of putting down kings 4.02. 36 P
whose haughty spirit, winged with desire, | will 3H6 1.01.267
witty, courteous, liberal, full of spirit. 1.02. 43
methinks a woman of this valiant spirit | should 5.04. 39
and make him of like spirit to himself. 5.04. 47
a blushing shame–fac'd spirit that mutinies in a R3 1.04.138 P
when that he bids good morrow with such spirit. 3.04. 50
of birth, | yet so much is my poverty of spirit, 3.07.159
whose humble means match not his haughty spirit. 4.02. 37
yet much less spirit to curse | abides in me; 4.04.197
i have not that alacrity of spirit | nor cheer 5.03. 73
forth, and with bold spirit relate what you, H8 1.02.129
a noble spirit | as yours was put into you, ever 3.01.169
some spirit put this paper in the packet, | to 3.02.129
can thy spirit wonder | a great man should 3.02.374
the cygnet's down is harsh and spirit of sense TRO 1.01. 58
there's not the meanest spirit on our party 2.02.156
so short, as if she were fray'd with a spirit. 3.02. 32 P
that most pure spirit of sense, behold itself, 3.03.106
so," | i speak it in my spirit and honor, "no." 4.04.135
that spirit of his | in aspiration lifts him 4.05. 15
breach whereout | hector's great spirit flew. 4.05.246
and grieve his spirit that dares not challenge 5.02. 94
with those that have the spirit, will haste | to COR 1.05. 13
death, that dark spirit, in 's nervy arm doth 2.01.160
then straight his doubled spirit | requick'ned 2.02.116
had touch'd his spirit | and tried his 2.03.191
which you are out of, with a gentler spirit, 3.01. 55
wants not spirit | to say he'll turn your 3.01. 95
serve, if he | can thereto frame his spirit. 3.02. 97
and possess me | some harlot's spirit! 3.02.112
resume that spirit when you were wont to say, 4.01. 16
then cheer thy spirit, for know thou, emperor, TIT 4.04. 88
that codding spirit had they from their mother, 5.01. 99
him | to raise a spirit in his mistress' circle, ROM 2.01. 24
that gallant spirit hath aspir'd the clouds, 3.01.117
when thou didst bower the spirit of a fiend | in 3.02. 81
and all this day an unaccustom'd spirit | lifts 5.01. 4
a noble spirit! TIM 1.02. 14
'tis a spirit; 2.02.109 P
fourscore to thirteen, this spirit walks in. 2.02.114 P
thee always for a towardly prompt spirit — give 3.01. 35 P
fault), | but with a noble fury and fair spirit, 3.05. 18
and, not to swell our spirit, | he shall be 3.05.101
part | of that quick spirit that is in antony. JC 1.02. 29
will start a spirit as soon as "caesar." 1.02.147
and scorn'd his spirit | that could be mov'd to 1.02.206
can be retentive to the strength of spirit; 1.03. 95
we all stand up against the spirit of caesar, 2.01.167
and in the spirit of men there is no blood; 2.01.168
o, that we then could come by caesar's spirit, 2.01.169
hast conjur'd up | my mortified spirit. 2.01.324
if then thy spirit look upon us now, | shall it 3.01.195
and caesar's spirit, ranging for revenge, | with 3.01.270
on, | his corporal motion govern'd by my spirit; 4.01. 33
o, i could weep | my spirit from mine eyes! 4.03.100
thy evil spirit, brutus. 4.03.282
ill spirit, i would hold more talk with thee. 4.03.288
for i am fresh of spirit, and resolv'd | to meet 5.01. 90
thy spirit walks abroad, and turns our swords 5.03. 95
arm 'gainst arm, | curbing his lavish spirit; MAC 1.02. 57
my little spirit, see, | sits in a foggy cloud, 3.05. 34
thou art too like the spirit of banquo; 4.01.112
th' extravagant and erring spirit hies | to his HAM 1.01.154
and then they say no spirit dare stir abroad, 1.01.161
this spirit, dumb to us, will speak to him. 1.01.171
my father's spirit — in arms! 1.02.254
wherein the spirit held his wont to walk. 1.04. 6
be thou a spirit of health, or goblin damn'd, 1.04. 40
i am thy father's spirit, | doom'd for a certain 1.05. 9
rest, rest, perturbed spirit! 1.05.182
the spirit that i have seen | may be a /dev'l, 2.02.598
in most great affliction of spirit, hath sent me 3.02.312 P
that spirit upon whose weal depends and rests 3.03. 14
whose spirit with divine ambition puff'd | makes 4.04. 49
receive it, sir, with all diligence of spirit. 5.02. 92 P
the potent poison quite o'er–crows my spirit. 5.02.353
come not in here, nuncle, here's a spirit. LR 3.04. 39 P
a spirit, a spirit! he says his name's poor tom. 3.04. 42 P
a spirit, a spirit! he says his name's poor tom. 3.04. 42 P
it is the cowish terror of his spirit | that 4.02. 12
let not my worser spirit tempt me again | to die 4.06.218
you are a spirit, i know; /when did you die? 4.07. 48
of spirit so still and quiet that her motion OTH 1.03. 95
o thou invisible spirit of wine, if thou hast no 2.03.281 P
and duty that i bear you | with franker spirit; 3.03.195
and knows all /qualities, with a learned spirit, 3.03.259
so help me every spirit sanctified, | as i have 3.04.126
cyprus to him, | hath puddled his clear spirit; 3.04.143
i would not kill thy unprepared spirit, | no, 5.02. 31
there's a great spirit gone! ANT 1.02.122
i would you had her spirit in such another; 2.02. 62
thy daemon, that thy spirit which keeps thee, is 2.03. 20
thy spirit | is all afraid to govern thee near 2.03. 29
o'er my spirit | /thy full supremacy thou 3.11. 58
like the spirit of a youth | that means to be of 4.04. 26
now my spirit is going, | i can no more. 4.15. 58
this case of that huge spirit now is cold. 4.15. 89
a rarer spirit never | did steer humanity; 5.01. 31
i do know her spirit, | and will not trust one CYM 1.05. 34
part shame, part spirit renew'd, that some, 5.03. 35
strain you are, | and of how coward a spirit. PER 4.03. 25
whose spirit in you | expels the seeds of fear TNK 5.01. 35
hark how yon spurs to spirit do incite | the 5.03. 56
and costliness of spirit look'd through him, it 5.03. 97
and desir'd your spirit | to send him hence 5.04.119
love is a spirit all compact of fire, | not VEN 149
appalls her senses and her spirit confounds. 882
god wot, it was defect | of spirit, life, and LUC 1346
fair), | my worser spirit a woman (color'd ill). PP 2. 4
the spirit of love with a perpetual dullness: SON 56. 8
is it thy spirit that thou send'st from thee 61. 5
my spirit is thine, the better part of me. 74. 8
knowing a better spirit doth use your name, 80. 2

to every hymn that able spirit affords | in 85. 7
was it his spirit, by spirits taught to write 86. 5
hath put a spirit of youth in every thing, 98. 3
which hath not figur'd to thee my true spirit? 108. 2
th' expense of spirit in a waste of shame | is 129. 1
fair, | the worser spirit a woman color'd ill. 144. 4

SPIRITED 1 FR 0.0001 REL FR 1 V 0 P
and shall our quick blood, spirited with wine, H5 3.05. 21

SPIRITLESS 1 FR 0.0001 REL FR 1 V 0 P
even such a man, so faint, so spiritless, | so 2H4 1.01. 70

SPIRIT'S 1 FR 0.0001 REL FR 1 V 0 P
that spirit's possess'd with haste | that wounds MM 4.02. 88

/SPIRITS 3 FR 0.0003 REL FR 3 V 0 P
/but, /for /their /spirits /and /souls, | /this 2H4 1.01.198
/now /expectation, /tickling /skittish /spirits, TRO pr 20
/the /heavens /do /not /their /visible /spirits LR 4.02. 46

SPIRITS 132 FR 0.0149 REL FR 123 V 9 P
my spirits, as in a dream, are all bound up. TMP 1.02.487
nor i, my spirits are nimble. 2.01.202
his spirits hear me, | and yet i needs must 2.02. 3
with weariness | to th' dulling of my spirits. 3.03. 6
time after) | now gins to bite the spirits. 3.03.106
may i be bold | to think these spirits? 4.01.120
spirits, which by mine art | i have from their 4.01.120
(as i foretold you) were all spirits, and | are 4.01.149
my spirits obey; 5.01. 2
o setebos, these be brave spirits indeed! 5.01.261
now i want | spirits to enforce, art to enchant, ep 14
is dark, light and spirits will become it well. WIV 5.02. 11 P
spirits are not finely touch'd | but to fine MM 1.01. 35
i come to visit the afflicted spirits | here in 2.03. 4
heaven give your spirits comfort! 4.02. 70
the best and wholesom'st spirits of the night 4.02. 73
i know her spirits are as coy and wild | as ADO 3.01. 35
come thus to light, | smother her spirits up. 4.01.112
thought i thy spirits were stronger than thy 4.01.125
whose spirits toil in frame of villainies. 4.01.189
now, madam, summon up your dearest spirits; LLL 2.01. 1
soonest tempt, resembling spirits of light. 4.03.253
poisons up | the nimble spirits in the arteries, 4.03.302
"out of your favors, heavenly spirits, vouchsafe 5.02.166
or hide | the liberal opposition of our spirits, 5.02.733
farewell, thou lob of spirits; MND 2.01. 16
hoots and wonders | at our quaint spirits. 2.02. 7
damned spirits all, | that in crossways and 3.02.382
but we are spirits of another sort. 3.02.388
is no bar | to stop the foreign spirits, but MV 2.07. 46
because i will not jump with common spirits, 2.09. 32
the reason is, your spirits are attentive; 5.01. 70
your spirits are too bold for your years. AYL 1.02.173 P
o jupiter, how /weary are my spirits! 2.04. 1 P
i care not for my spirits, if my legs were not 2.04. 2 P
that can entame my spirits to your worship. 3.05. 48
pluck up thy spirits, look cheerfully upon me. SHR 4.03. 38
oil, to be the snuff | of younger spirits, whose AWW 1.02. 60
day and night | must wear your spirits low; 5.01. 2
you | to sparkle in the spirits of my daughter, 5.03. 75
if spirits can assume both form and suit, | you TN 5.01.235
and our weak spirits ne'er been higher rear'd WT 1.02. 72
the spirits o' th' dead | may walk again. 3.03. 16
from thy admiring daughter took the spirits, 5.03. 41
a braver choice of dauntless spirits | than now JN 2.01. 72
let us in — your king, whose labor'd spirits, 2.01.232
you equal potents, fiery kindled spirits! 2.01.358
with my vex'd spirits i cannot take a truce, 3.01. 17
and cull'd these fiery spirits from the world, 5.02.114
i have a thousand spirits in one breast, | to R2 4.01. 58
i can call spirits from the vasty deep. 1H4 3.01. 52
the spirits | of valiant shirley, stafford, 5.04. 40
and the spirits of the wise sit in the clouds 2H4 2.02.143 P
you do draw my spirits from me | with new 2.03. 46
and inland petty spirits muster me all to their 4.03.110 P
coherence of his men's spirits and his. 5.01. 65 P
their spirits are so married in conjunction with 5.01. 68 P
that must strike sail to spirits of vile sort! 5.02. 18
and with his spirits sadly i survive, | to mock 5.02.125
the flat unraised spirits that hath dar'd | on H5 pr 9
t' envelop and contain celestial spirits. 1.01. 31
thy spirits are most tall. 2.01. 68
let them practice and converse with spirits. 1H6 2.01. 25
news, my lords, may cheer our drooping spirits: 5.02. 1
and ye choice spirits that admonish me | and 5.03. 3
now, ye familiar spirits, that are cull'd | out 5.03. 10
unchain your spirits now with spelling charms, 5.03. 31
i never had to do with wicked spirits. 5.04. 42
and spirits walk, and ghosts break up their 2H6 1.04. 19
raising up wicked spirits from under ground, 2.01.170
unless you be possess'd with devilish spirits 4.07. 75
my lord, cheer up your spirits, our foes are 3H6 2.02. 56
children | whisper the spirits of thine enemies R3 4.04.193
heralds challeng'd | the noble spirits to arms, H8 1.01. 35
but to stubborn spirits | they swell and grow, 3.01.163
spirits of peace, where are ye? 4.02. 83
affairs that walk | (as they say spirits do) at 5.01. 14
will /strike amazement to their drowsy spirits. TRO 2.02.210
her wanton spirits look out | at every joint and 4.05. 56
to say extremities was the trier of spirits, COR 4.01. 4
at some hours in the night spirits resort — ROM 4.03. 44
all these spirits thy power | hath conjur'd to TIM 1.01. 6
whose thankless natures (o abhorred spirits!) 5.01. 60
these well express in thee thy latter spirits: 5.04. 74
heaven hath infus'd them with these spirits, JC 1.03. 69
and we are govern'd with our mothers' spirits; 1.03. 83
steel with valor | the melting spirits of women, 2.01.122
nor th' insuppressive mettle of our spirits, 2.01.134
do, | with untir'd spirits and formal constancy. 2.01.227
the choice and master spirits of this age. 3.01.163
were an antony | would ruffle up your spirits, 3.02.228
that i may pour my spirits in thine ear, | and MAC 1.05. 26
you spirits | that tend on mortal thoughts, 1.05. 40
your spirits shine through you. 3.01.127
the spirits that know | all mortal consequences 5.03. 4
which, they say, your spirits oft walk in death, HAM 1.01.138
as he is very potent with such spirits, | abuses 2.02.602
that no revenue hast but thy good spirits | to 3.02. 58
my spirits grow dull, and fain i would beguile 3.02.226
forth at your eyes your spirits wildly peep, 3.04.119
and when he saw my best alarum'd spirits, | bold LR 2.01. 53

were very pregnant and potential spirits | to 2.01. 76
would stretch thy spirits up into the air. 4.02. 23
and my best spirits are bent | to prove upon thy 5.03.140
my spirits and my place have in their power | to OTH 1.01.103
give renew'd fire to our extincted spirits, 2.01. 81
noble swelling spirits | that hold their honors 2.03. 55
i see this hath a little dash'd your spirits. 3.03.214
and his spirits should hunt | after new fancies. 3.04. 62
to thee, and make | thy spirits all of comfort. ANT 3.02. 41
but it would warm his spirits | to hear from me 3.13. 69
or i shall show the cinders of my spirits 5.02.173
more than the locking up the spirits a time, CYM 1.05. 41
have done, his spirits fly out | into my story; 3.03. 90
italy, most willing spirits | that promise noble 4.02.338
no more, you petty spirits of region low, 5.04. 93
and my false spirits | quail to remember — give 5.05.148
yet neither pleasure's art can joy my spirits, PER 1.02. 9
of life kindle again | the o'erpress'd spirits. 3.02. 84
was a note | whereon her spirits would sojourn TNK 1.03. 77
the poison of pure spirits, might, like women, 2.02. 75
and after death our spirits shall be led | to 2.02.116
six braver spirits | than these they have 4.02. 73
your chance to come where the blessed spirits — 4.03. 22 P
me your aid | and bend your spirits towards him. 5.01. 48
then blend your spirits with mine, | you whose 5.01. 72
with 'em, | for we are more clear spirits. 5.04. 13
that like two spirits do suggest me still: PP 2. 2
by spirits taught to write | above a mortal SON 86. 5
which like two spirits do suggest me still: 144. 2
my spirits t' attend this double voice accorded, LC 3
for she was sought by spirits of richest coat, 236
SPIRIT–STIRRING 1 FR 0.0001 REL FR 1 V 0 P
the spirit–stirring drum, th' ear–piercing fife, OTH 3.03.352
SPIRITUAL 6 FR 0.0006 REL FR 6 V 0 P
will bring all, whose spiritual counsel had, WT 2.01.186
upon our spiritual convocation | and in regard H5 1.01. 76
art reverent | touching thy spiritual function, 1H6 3.01. 50
honor than | your high profession spiritual; H8 2.04.117
and fix'd on spiritual object, he should still 3.02.132
to steal from spiritual leisure a brief span 3.02.140
SPIRITUALTY 1 FR 0.0001 REL FR 1 V 0 P
in aid whereof we of the spiritualty | will H5 1.02.132
SPIRT 1 FR 0.0001 REL FR 1 V 0 P
spirt up so suddenly into the clouds | and H5 3.05. 8
SPIT* *(also spet, etc.)*
SPIT* 26 FR 0.0029 REL FR 17 V 9 P
but as she spit in his face, so she defied him. MM 2.01. 84 P
the capon burns, the pig falls from the spit; ERR 1.02. 44
wouldst thou not spit at me, and spurn at me, 2.02.134
she would have made hercules have turn'd spit, ADO 2.01.253 P
thin/–bellied doublet like a rabbit on a spit; LLL 3.01. 19 P
now weep for him, then spit at him; AYL 3.02.417 P
when they are out, they will spit, and for 4.01. 76 P
spit in the hole, man, and tune again. SHR 3.01. 40
if you had but look'd big and spit at him, he'ld WT 4.03.106 P
and ready mounted are they to spit forth | their JN 2.01.211
to my liege, | i do defy him, and i spit at him, R2 1.01. 60
and spit it bleeding in his high disgrace, 1.01.194
and spit upon him whilst i say he lies, | and 4.01. 75
if i tell thee a lie, spit in my face, call me 1H4 2.04.194 P
bottle, i would i might never spit white again. 2H4 1.02.212 P
the alps doth spit and void his rheum upon. H5 3.05. 52
here. why dost thou spit at me? R3 1.02.144
tongues spit their duties out, and cold hearts H8 1.02. 61
to cough and spit, | and, with a palsy fumbling TRO 1.03.173
than hector's forehead when it spit forth blood COR 1.03. 42
so cries a pig prepared to the spit. TIT 4.02.146
that did spit his body | upon a rapier's point. ROM 4.03. 56
would thou wert clean enough to spit upon! TIM 4.03.359
spit, fire! LR 3.02. 14
spit, and throw stones, cast mire upon me, set CYM 5.05.222
thou mayst cut a morsel off the spit. PER 4.02.131 P
SPITAL *(see spittle, etc.)*
SPITE 68 FR 0.0076 REL FR 63 V 5 P
ay; that change is the spite. TGV 4.02. 69 P
o spite of spites! ERR 2.02.189
(be it for nothing but to spite my wife) | upon 3.01.118
he meant he did me none: the more my spite. 4.02. 8
in spite of your heart, i think. ADO 5.02. 68 P
poor heart, if you spite it for my sake, i will 5.02. 69 P
spite it for my sake, i will spite it for yours, 5.02. 69 P
when, spite of cormorant devouring time, | th' LLL 1.01. 4
o spite! too old to be engag'd to young. MND 1.01.138
o spite! 3.02.145
to fashion this false sport, in spite of me. 3.02.194
i'll find demetrius and revenge this spite. 3.02.420
o spite! 5.01.276
the more my wrong, the more his spite appears. SHR 4.03. 2
where he sits crowned in his master's spite. TN 5.01.128
love, | to spite a raven's heart within a dove. 5.01.131
o'erbearing interruption, spite of france? JN 3.04. 9
in spite of spite, alone upholds the day. 5.04. 5
in spite of spite, alone upholds the day. 5.04. 5
hath power to keep you king in spite of all. R2 3.02. 28
this is the deadly spite that angers me: 1H4 3.01.190
ragged'st hour that time and spite dare bring 2H4 1.01.151
in spite of pope or dignities of church, | here 1H6 1.03. 50
is ent'red into orleance | in spite of us, or 1.05. 37
these my friends in spite of thee shall wear. 2.04.106
in spite of burgundy and all his friends. 3.03. 73
seen decipher'd there | more rancorous spite, 4.01.185
the spite of man prevaileth against me. 2H6 1.03.214 P
climbing my walls in spite of me the owner, 4.10. 35
that keeps his leaves in spite of any storm, 5.01.206
speak not in spite, | for you shall sup with 5.01.213
and spite of spite needs must i rest awhile. 3H6 2.03. 5
and spite of spite needs must i rest awhile. 2.03. 5
that i may conquer fortune's spite | by living 4.06. 19
o unbid spite, is sportful edward come? 5.01. 18
in spite of fortune | will bring me off again. H8 3.02.219
as if that /luck, in very spite of cunning, TRO 5.05. 41
but in mere spite, | to be full quit of those my COR 4.05. 82
come, | and flourishes his blade in spite of me. ROM 1.01. 78
a villain that is hither come in spite | to 1.05. 62
that were some spite. 2.01. 27
for it was bad enough before their spite. 4.01. 31
it up again | with poisonous spite and envy. TIM 1.02.139
whose naked natures live in all the spite | of 4.03.228
who in spite put stuff | to some she–beggar and 4.03.272
i am reckless what | i do to spite the world. MAC 3.01.110
fear it lies, | and sleep in spite of thunder. 4.01. 86
the time is out of joint — o cursed spite, HAM 1.05.188
deliver'd letters, spite of intermission, LR 2.04. 33
let him do his spite; OTH 1.02. 17
and she, in spite of nature, | of years, of 1.03. 96
o, 'tis the spite of hell, the fiend's arch–mock 4.01. 70
show | thy spite on mortal flies: CYM 5.04. 31
and, spite of all the /rapture of the sea, PER 2.01.155
licentious ear, | but curb it, spite of seeing. 5.03. 31
and so in spite of death thou dost survive, | in VEN 173
"wonder of time," quoth she, "this is my spite, 1133
with grief thus breathes she forth her spite LUC 762
love, what spite hath thy fair color spent? 1600
in spite of physic, painting, pain, and cost. PP 13.12
to spite me now, each minute seems /a /moon, 14.27
alas, it was a spite | unto the silly damsel! 15. 7
though in our lives a separable spite, | which SON 36. 6
so i, made lame by fortune's dearest spite, 37. 3
join with the spite of fortune, make me bow, 90. 3
when other petty griefs have done their spite, 90.10
since, spite of him, i'll live in this poor 107.11
all quit, but, spite of heaven's fell rage, LC 13
SPITED 1 FR 0.0001 REL FR 1 V 0 P
beguil'd, divorced, wronged, spited, slain! ROM 4.05. 55
SPITEFUL 3 FR 0.0003 REL FR 2 V 1 P
as for your spiteful false objections, | prove 2H6 1.03.155
i'll see some issue of my spiteful execrations. TRO 2.03. 7 P
son, | spiteful and wrathful, who (as others do) MAC 3.05. 12
SPITES 3 FR 0.0003 REL FR 3 V 0 P
o spite of spites! ERR 2.02.189
and that which spites me more than all these SHR 4.03. 11
kill me with spites, yet we must not be foes. SON 40.14
SPITS* 3 FR 0.0003 REL FR 3 V 0 P
that spits forth death and mountains, rocks and JN 2.01.458
that thy wives with spits and boys with stones COR 4.04. 5
to have a thousand with red burning spits | come LR 3.06. 15
SPITTED 1 FR 0.0001 REL FR 1 V 0 P
your naked infants spitted upon pikes, | whiles H5 3.03. 38
SPITTING* 2 FR 0.0002 REL FR 1 V 1 P
without hawking or spitting or saying we are AYL 5.03. 12 P
yea, with a spitting power, and made to tremble H8 2.04.184
SPITTLE 2 FR 0.0002 REL FR 2 V 0 P
no, to the spittle go, | and from the H5 2.01. 74
news have i that my doll is dead i' th' spittle 5.01. 81
SPITTLE–HOUSE 1 FR 0.0001 REL FR 1 V 0 P
she, whom the spittle–house and ulcerous sores TIM 4.03. 40
SPLAY 1 FR 0.0001 REL FR 0 V 1 P
mean to geld and splay all the youth of the city MM 2.01.230 P
SPLEEN 29 FR 0.0032 REL FR 26 V 3 P
laughter — thy silly thought, my spleen; LLL 3.01. 76 P
that in this spleen ridiculous appears, | to 5.02.117
that, in a spleen, unfolds both heaven and earth MND 1.01.146
that was begot of thought, conceiv'd of spleen, AYL 4.01.212 P
presence | may well abate the over–merry spleen, SHR in.1. 137
heart | unto a mad–brain rudesby full of spleen, 3.02. 10
if you desire the spleen, and will laugh TN 3.02. 68 P
with swifter spleen than powder can enforce, JN 2.01.448
or teach thy hasty spleen to do me shame, | i'll 4.03. 97
and spleen of speed to see your majesty! 5.07. 50
a weasel hath not such a deal of spleen | as you 1H4 2.03. 78
base inclination, and the start of spleen, | to 3.02.125
a hare–brain'd hotspur, govern'd by a spleen. 5.02. 19
quicken'd with youthful spleen and warlike rage, 1H6 4.06. 13
that robb'd my soldiers of their heated spleen; 3H6 2.01.124
and frantic outrage, end thy damned spleen, | or R3 2.04. 64
inspire us with the spleen of fiery dragons! 5.03.350
you charge not in your spleen a noble person H8 1.02.174
i have no spleen against you, nor injustice 2.04. 89
your heart | is cramm'd with arrogancy, spleen, 2.04.110
i shall split all | in pleasure of my spleen." TRO 1.03.178
such things as might offend the weakest spleen 2.02.128
against my cank'red country with the spleen | of COR 4.05. 91
could not take truce with the unruly spleen | of ROM 3.01.157
it is a cause worthy my spleen and fury, | that TIM 3.05.112
you shall digest the venom of your spleen JC 4.03. 47
create her child of spleen, that it may live LR 1.04.282
or i shall say y' are all in all in spleen, OTH 4.01. 88
a brook where adon us'd to cool his spleen. PP 6. 6
SPLEENFUL 2 FR 0.0002 REL FR 2 V 0 P
myself have calm'd their spleenful mutiny, 2H6 3.02.128
and let my spleenful sons this trull deflow'r. TIT 2.03.191
SPLEENS 4 FR 0.0004 REL FR 4 V 0 P
who, with our spleens, | would all themselves MM 2.02.122
with ladies' faces and fierce dragons' spleens, JN 2.01. 68
than the performance of our heaving spleens, | i TRO 2.02.196
a thousand spleens bear her a thousand ways, VEN 907
SPLEENY 1 FR 0.0001 REL FR 1 V 0 P
yet i know her for | a spleeny lutheran, and not H8 3.02. 99
SPLEET *(also split, etc.)*
SPLEET 1 FR 0.0001 REL FR 0 V 1 P
rags, to spleet the ears of the groundlings, who HAM 3.02. 10 P
SPLEETS 1 FR 0.0001 REL FR 1 V 0 P
and mine own tongue | spleets what it speaks; ANT 2.07.124
SPLENATIVE *(see splenitive)*
SPLENDOR 4 FR 0.0004 REL FR 4 V 0 P
turning with splendor of his precious eye | the JN 3.01. 79
shown, | but to rejoice in splendor of mine own. ROM 1.02.101
dew | against the golden splendor of the sun! LUC 25
shine | with all–triumphant splendor on my brow, SON 33.10
SPLENITIVE 1 FR 0.0001 REL FR 1 V 0 P
for though i am not splenitive /and rash, | yet HAM 5.01.261
SPLINTER 2 FR 0.0002 REL FR 1 V 1 P
and not worth | the splinter of a lance. TRO 1.03.283
you and her husband entreat her to splinter; OTH 2.03.323 P
SPLINTER'D 1 FR 0.0001 REL FR 1 V 0 P
but lately splinter'd, knit, and join'd together R3 2.02.118
SPLINTERS 1 FR 0.0001 REL FR 1 V 0 P
broke, | and scarr'd the moon with splinters. COR 4.05.109
SPLIT *(also spleet, etc.)*
SPLIT 17 FR 0.0019 REL FR 15 V 2 P
"we split, we split!" TMP 1.01. 61
"we split, we split!" 1.01. 61
"we split, we split, we split!" 1.01. 62
"we split, we split, we split!" 1.01. 62
"we split, we split, we split!" 1.01. 62
but three glasses since, we gave out split — 5.01.223
or a part to tear a cat in, to make all split. MND 1.02. 30 P
assure yourself, after our ship did split, TN 1.02. 9
i stabb'd your fathers' bosoms, split my breast. 3H6 2.06. 30
when he shall split thy very heart with sorrow, R3 1.03.299
quoth she, "shall split thy heart with sorrow, 5.01. 26
i shall split all | in pleasure of my spleen." TRO 1.03.177
now crack thy lungs, and split thy brazen pipe. 4.05. 7
venom of your spleen | though it do split you; JC 4.03. 48
let sorrow split my heart, if ever i | did hate LR 5.03.178
should house him safe is wrack'd and split, PER 2.ch. 32
blow, and split thyself. 3.01. 44 P
SPLITS 2 FR 0.0002 REL FR 2 V 0 P
bolt | splits the unwedgeable and gnarled oak MM 2.02.116
in his moan, the ship splits on the rock, 3H6 5.04. 10
SPLIT'ST 1 FR 0.0001 REL FR 1 V 0 P
do't not, thou split'st thine own. WT 1.02.349
SPLITTED 4 FR 0.0004 REL FR 4 V 0 P
our helpful ship was splitted in the midst; ERR 1.01.103
hast thou so crack'd and splitted my poor tongue 5.01.309
even as a splitted bark, so sunder we; 2H6 3.02.411
the heart did lend it, | splitted the heart. ANT 5.01. 24
SPLITTING 3 FR 0.0003 REL FR 3 V 0 P
the splitting rocks cow'r'd in the sinking sands 2H6 3.02. 97
but when the splitting wind | makes flexible the TRO 1.03. 49
but he returns | splitting the air with noise. COR 5.06. 51
SPOIL 28 FR 0.0031 REL FR 24 V 4 P
he fleshes his will in the spoil of her honor. AWW 4.03. 16 P
thou dost shame | that bloody spoil. JN 3.01.115
and is not this an honorable spoil? 1H4 1.01. 74
villainous company, hath been the spoil of me. 3.03. 10 P
doth like a miser spoil his coat with scanting H5 2.04. 47
upon th' enraged soldiers in their spoil, | as 3.03. 25
contagious clouds | of headly murther, spoil, 3.03. 32
of beauty, can do no more spoil upon my face. 5.02.231 P
but death doth front thee with apparent spoil, 1H6 4.02. 26
swear | to spoil the city and your royal court. 2H6 4.04. 53
defer the spoil of the city until night; 4.07.134 P
nor knows he how to live but by the spoil, 4.08. 39
and yonder is the wolf that makes this spoil. 3H6 5.04. 80
having bought love with such a bloody spoil. R3 4.04.290
a noble person | and spoil your nobler soul; H8 1.02.175
their nicely gawded cheeks to th' wanton spoil COR 2.01.217
lives of men, as if | 'twere a perpetual spoil; 2.02.120
and that the spoil got on the antiates | was 3.03. 4
that we look'd | for no less spoil than glory — 5.06. 43
power | of high–resolved men, bent to the spoil, TIT 4.04. 64
sign'd in thy spoil, and crimson'd in thy lethe. JC 3.01.206
his soldiers fell to spoil, | whilst we by 5.03. 7
i am old now, | and these same crosses spoil me. LR 5.03.279
and having felt the sweetness of the spoil, VEN 553
leaving his spoil perplex'd in greater pain. LUC 733
to spoil antiquities of hammer'd steel, | and 951
or who his spoil /of beauty can forbid? SON 65.12
of this false jewel, and his amorous spoil. LC 154
SPOIL'D 9 FR 0.0010 REL FR 7 V 2 P
this is some priory, in, or we are spoil'd! ERR 5.01. 37
of the fives, stark spoil'd with the staggers, SHR 3.02. 54 P
o, we are spoil'd and — yonder he is. 5.01.110 P
bitter shame hath spoil'd the sweet word's taste JN 3.04.110
disorder, that hath spoil'd us, friend us now! H5 4.05. 17
that spoil'd your summer fields and fruitful R3 5.02. 8
o, i am spoil'd, undone by villains! OTH 5.01. 54
having in sicily | sextus pompeius spoil'd, we ANT 3.06. 25
her sacred temple spotted, spoil'd, corrupted, LUC 1172
SPOILING 1 FR 0.0001 REL FR 1 V 0 P
wound arcite to | the spoiling of his figure. TNK 5.03. 59
SPOILS 10 FR 0.0011 REL FR 10 V 0 P
is fit for treasons, stratagems, and spoils; MV 5.01. 85
sword, | for i have loaden me with many spoils, 1H6 2.01. 80
not his that spoils her young before her face. 3H6 2.02. 14
them down | for sluttish spoils of opportunity, TRO 4.05. 62
our spoils he kick'd at, | and look'd upon COR 2.02.124
our spoils we have brought home | doth more than 5.06. 76
and now at last, laden with honor's spoils, TIT 1.01. 36
all thy conquests, glories, triumphs, spoils, JC 3.01.149
only it spoils the pleasure of the time. MAC 3.04. 97
and make time's spoils despised every where. SON 100.12
SPOKE *(also spake, etc.)*
/SPOKE 2 FR 0.0002 REL FR 2 V 0 P
/faintly /spoke | /after /the /prompter, /for ROM 1.04. 7
/you /spoke /not /with /her /since? LR 4.03. 35
SPOKE 157 FR 0.0177 REL FR 128 V 29 P
methought the billows spoke, and told me of it; TMP 3.03. 96
fairly spoke. 4.01. 31
have inly wept, | or should have spoke ere this. 5.01.201
ay, but she'll think that it is spoke in hate. TGV 3.02. 34
it is spoke as a christians ought to speak. WIV 1.01.101 P
i have spoke; 1.03. 13 P
as it were, spoke the prologue of our comedy; 3.05. 74 P
there is no better way than that they spoke of. 4.04. 16
forsooth, i have spoke with her, and we have a 5.02. 4 P
if it be honest you have spoke, you have courage MM 3.02.157 P
and one that hath spoke most villainous speeches 5.01.263 P
here comes the rascal i spoke of, here with the 5.01.283 P
this is the rascal; this is he i spoke of. 5.01.304
you indeed spoke so of him, and much more, much 5.01.337 P
what you have spoke i pardon. 5.01.361
my lord, i spoke it but according to the trick. 5.01.504 P
and in faith, my lord, i spoke mine. ADO 1.01.225 P
my two faiths and troths, my lord, i spoke mine. 1.01.227 P
not to be named, my lord, | not to be spoke of; 4.01. 96
nor knew not what she did when she spoke to me, 5.01.301
and though i have for barbarism spoke more LLL 1.01.112
i spoke it tender juvenal as a congruent 1.02. 13 P
swore | a better speech was never spoke before. 5.02.110
but while 'tis spoke each turn away /her face. 5.02.148
vice you should have spoke, | for virtue's 5.02.349
with demetrius thought to have spoke thereof; MND 1.01.112
broke | (in number more than ever women spoke), 1.01.176
shylock thy master spoke with me this day, | and MV 2.02.145
we have not spoke us yet of torch–bearers. 2.04. 5
i spoke with some of the sailors that escap'd 3.01.104 P
after some oration fairly spoke | by a beloved 3.02.178
i have spoke thus much | to mitigate the justice 4.01.202
he would not have spoke such a word. AYL 1.01. 84 P
thou the youth that spoke to me yerwhile? 3.05.105
i would kiss before i spoke. 4.01. 72 P
thy virtues spoke of, and thy beauty sounded, SHR 2.01.192

spoke like an officer. ha' to thee, lad! 5.02. 37
the king very lately spoke of him admiringly and AWW 1.01. 29 P
light deliverance, i have spoke | with one that, 2.01. 82
time, or flinch in property | of what i spoke, 2.01.188
spoke with the king, and have procur'd his leave 2.05. 55
had i spoke with her, | i could have well 3.04. 20
the house, and show you | the lass i spoke of. 3.06.111
i spoke with her but once | and found her 3.06.112
what says he to your daughter? have you spoke? 5.03. 28
i have spoke the truth. 5.03.230
be so abandon'd to her sorrow | as it is spoke, TN 1.04. 20
thou hast spoke for us, madonna, as if thy 1.05.112 P
but once before i spoke to th' purpose? WT 1.02.100
i have spoke to th' purpose twice: 1.02.106
you never spoke what did become you less | than 1.02.282
and toward your friend, whose love had spoke, 3.02. 69
but spoke the harm that is by others done? JN 3.01. 39
hast thou not spoke like thunder on my side? 3.01.124
and ne'er have spoke a loving word to you; 4.01. 51
spoke like a sprightful noble gentleman. 4.02.177
whoever spoke it, it is true, my lord. 5.05. 19
what i have spoke, or thou canst worse devise. R2 1.01. 77
as oft as he hears | owen glendower spoke of. 1H4 3.01. 12
spoke of in scotland as this term of fear. 4.01. 85
spoke your deservings like a chronicle, | making 5.02. 57
rode on, and, upon my life, | spoke at a venter. 2H4 1.01. 59
by this light, i am well spoke on, i can hear it 2.02. 65 P
and spoke it on purpose to try my patience. 2.04.308 P
go to, i have spoke at a word. god keep you! 3.02.297 P
ere you with grief had spoke and i had heard 4.05.141
why, there spoke a king. 5.03. 69 P
nym, thou hast spoke the right. H5 2.01.123
what he has spoke to me, that is well, i warrant 3.06. 65 P
far truer spoke than meant. 2H6 3.01.183
thrice–noble suffolk, 'tis resolutely spoke. 3.01.266
for things are often spoke and seldom meant; 3.01.268
and now we three have spoke it, | it skills not 3.01.280
thou hast spoke too much already; get thee gone. 3H6 1.01.258
and more he would have said, and more he spoke, 5.02. 43
spoke like a tall man that respects thy R3 1.04.152 P
who spoke of brotherhood? 2.01.109
who spoke of love? 2.01.109
not used | to be spoke to but by the recorder. 3.07. 30
be not you spoke with but by mighty suit; 3.07. 46
i think the duke will not be spoke withal. 3.07. 57
certain words | spoke by a holy monk "that oft," H8 1.02.160
he solemnly had sworn that what he spoke | my 1.02.165
for i was spoke to, with sir henry guilford 1.03. 66
much | he spoke, and learnedly, for life; 2.01. 28
and something spoke in choler, ill, and hasty. 2.01. 34
i'll to the king, | and say i spoke with you. 2.03. 80
i have spoke long, be pleas'd yourself to say 2.04.211
what troy means fairly shall be spoke aloud. TRO 1.03.259
my soul | of every syllable that here was spoke. 5.02.117
they lie in view, but have not spoke as yet. COR 1.04. 4
in troth, there's wondrous things spoke of him. 2.01.137 P
spoke he of me? 3.01. 12
they show'd | most valor, spoke not for them. 3.01.127
repent what you have spoke. 3.02. 37
each word thou hast spoke hath weeded from my 4.05.102
it is spoke freely out of many mouths — | how 4.06. 65
that i would have spoke of: 5.06. 28
what, shall this speech be spoke for our excuse? ROM 1.04. 1
fain deny | what i have spoke, but farewell 2.02. 89
not to his father's, i spoke with his man. 2.04. 3
romeo that spoke him fair, bid him bethink | how 3.01.153
being spoke behind your back, than to your face. 4.01. 28
him her resort, | myself have spoke in vain. TIM 1.01.128
that's well spoke. 5.01.193
i have spoke the least. 5.02. 2
ay, he spoke greek. JC 1.02.279 P
that have spoke the word | and will not palter? 2.01.125
depart, | save i alone, till antony have spoke. 3.02. 61
i speak not to disprove what brutus spoke, | but 3.02.100
when i spoke that, i was ill–temper'd too. 4.03.116
but i have spoke | with one that saw him die; MAC 1.04. 3
was it not yesterday we spoke together? 3.01. 73
what you have spoke, it may be so perchance. 4.03. 11
she has spoke what she should not, i am sure of 5.01. 48 P
it would be spoke to. HAM 1.01. 45
do, i had as live the town–crier spoke my lines. 3.02. 4 P
by what yourself too late have spoke and done, LR 1.04.207
spoke, with how manifold and strong a bond | the 2.01. 47
this is the letter which he spoke of, which 3.05. 10 P
have been demanded | ere you had spoke so far. 5.03. 63
and spoke such scurvy and provoking terms OTH 1.02. 7
wherein i spoke of most disastrous chances: 1.03.134
methinks the wind hath spoke aloud at land, | a 2.01. 5
time, | when i have spoke of you dispraisingly, 3.03. 72
i hope you will consider what is spoke | comes 3.03.216
all that is spoke is marr'd. 5.02.357
who neigh'd so high that what i would have spoke ANT 1.05. 49
pardon what i have spoke, | for 'tis a studied, 2.02.136
antony is touch'd | with what is spoke already. 2.02.140
would we had spoke together! 2.02.164
and having lost her breath, she spoke, and 2.02.230
shouldst have done, | and not have spoke on't! 2.07. 74
spoke scantly of me; 3.04. 6
say that the last i spoke was "antony," | and 4.13. 8
whilst he stood up and spoke, | he was my master 5.01. 7
i have spoke already, and it is provided; 5.02.195
on th' approbation of what i have spoke! CYM 1.04.124 P
i have spoke this to know if your affiance 1.06.163
likewise reap, | being, as it is, much spoke of. 2.04. 87
perchance he spoke not, but, | like a 2.05. 15
with those legions | which i have spoke of, 3.07. 13
i have spoke it; 4.02. 16
and, but she spoke it dying, i would not 5.05. 41
he, i am sure | he would have spoke to us. 5.05.126
me to leave unspoken that | which, to be spoke, 5.05.140
i have spoke it, and i did it. 5.05.290
he should have strook, not spoke; PER 4.02. 65
did not think | thou couldst have spoke so well, 4.06.103
love, but i | and she (i sigh and spoke of) were TNK 1.03. 60
eyes, and as noble | as ever fame yet spoke of. 3.06.277
by, and to 'em spoke | the prettiest posies — 4.01. 89
somewhat bigger than the knight he spoke of, 4.02. 94
her mood inclining that way that i spoke of, 5.02. 34
each part of him to th' all i have spoke, your 5.03.121
"hadst thou but bid beware, then he had spoke, VEN 943
if he had spoke, the wolf would leave his prey, 1097

SPOKEN 56 FR 0.0063 REL FR 38 V 18 P
this speech, | were i but where 'tis spoken. TMP 1.02.431
you have spoken truer than you purpos'd. 2.01. 19 P
therefore it must with circumstance be spoken TGV 3.02. 36
i would i could have spoken with the woman WIV 4.05. 39 P
other things to have spoken with her too from 4.05. 40 P
that's somewhat madly spoken. MM 5.01. 89
why, that's spoken like an honest drovier; ADO 2.01.194 P
are these things spoken, or do i but dream? 4.01. 66
sir, they are spoken, and these things are true. 4.01. 67
moreover, they have spoken untruths; 5.01.216 P
"then" is spoken; 5.02. 46 P
thou hast spoken no word all this while. LLL 5.01.149 P
when you have spoken your speech, enter into MND 3.01. 74 P
he's within, sir, but not to be spoken withal. SHR 5.01. 19 P
i have spoken better of you than you have or AWW 2.05. 47 P
and what to your sworn counsel i have spoken 3.07. 9
when you have spoken it, 'tis dead, and i am the 4.03. 12 P
thou hast spoken all already, unless thou canst 5.03.267 P
you might have spoken a thousand things that WT 5.01. 21
sight which was to be seen, cannot be spoken of. 5.02. 43 P
to lengthen out the worst that must be spoken: R2 3.02.199
not be | without much shame retold or spoken of. 1H4 1.01. 46
mouth | live scandaliz'd and foully spoken of. 1.03.154
shall it for shame be spoken in these days, | or 1.03.170
and shall it in more shame be further spoken, 1.03.177
who hath not heard it spoken | how deep you were 2H4 4.02. 16
under the correction of bragging be it spoken, i H5 5.02.139 P
well hast thou spoken, cousin, be it so. 3H6 1.01. 66
why, that is spoken like a toward prince. 2.02. 66
his grace | hath spoken well and justly; H8 2.04. 65
'tis nobly spoken. 3.02.199
h'as spoken like a traitor, and shall answer COR 3.01.162
blows for rome | than thou hast spoken words? 4.02. 20
and yet, to my teen be it spoken, i have but ROM 1.03. 13
'tis most nobly spoken. TIM 5.04. 63
what should be spoken here, where our fate, MAC 2.03.121
i am as i have spoken. 4.03.102
put on with holy prayers, and 'tis spoken, | to 4.03.154
my lord, well spoken, with good accent and good HAM 2.02.466 P
'twere good she were spoken with, for she may 4.05. 14
have you not spoken 'gainst the duke of cornwall LR 2.01. 23
is this well spoken? 2.04.236
this night — 'tis dangerous to be spoken; 3.03. 11 P
methinks y' are better spoken. 4.06. 10
th' hast spoken right, 'tis true. 5.03.174
as i have spoken for you all my best, | and OTH 3.04.127
'tis spoken well. ANT 2.02. 25
'tis noble spoken. 2.02. 98
worthily spoken, maecenas. 2.02.102
be it art or hap, | he hath spoken true. 2.03. 34
and would undergo what's spoken, i swear. CYM 1.04.141 P
she has here spoken holy words to the lord PER 4.06.133 P
a man who for this three months hath not spoken 5.01. 24
fairer spoken | was never gentleman. TNK 2.04. 20
plainly spoken! 3.01.105
as thou art spoken, great and virtuous, | the 3.06.152

SPOKES 2 FR 0.0002 REL FR 2 V 0 P
break all the spokes and /fellies from her wheel HAM 2.02.495
to whose /huge spokes ten thousand lesser things 3.03. 19

SPOKESMAN 1 FR 0.0001 REL FR 0 V 1 P
to be a spokesman from madam silvia. TGV 2.01.146 P

SPOK'ST 3 FR 0.0003 REL FR 2 V 1 P
last night, when thou spok'st of pigrogromitus, TN 2.03. 23 P
dearest, thou never spok'st | to better purpose. WT 1.02. 88
yes, thou spok'st well of me. TIM 4.03.173

SPONGE *(see spunge, etc.)*

SPOON 4 FR 0.0004 REL FR 1 V 3 P
i will leave him, i have no long spoon. TMP 2.02. 99 P
do, expect spoon–meat, or bespeak a long spoon. ERR 4.03. 61 P
he must have a long spoon that must eat with the 4.03. 63 P
thyself, | put but a little water in a spoon, JN 4.03.131

SPOON–MEAT 1 FR 0.0001 REL FR 0 V 1 P
if /you do, expect spoon–meat, or bespeak a long ERR 4.03. 60 P

SPOONS 3 FR 0.0003 REL FR 2 V 1 P
come, come, my lord, you'd spare your spoons. H8 5.02.201
the spoons will be the bigger, sir. 5.03. 39 P
cushions, leaden spoons, | irons of a doit, COR 1.05. 5

/SPORT 1 FR 0.0001 REL FR 1 V 0 P
/silent /king, /the /moral /of /this /sport, R2 4.01.290

SPORT 134 FR 0.0151 REL FR 95 V 39 P
in this very place, | to come and sport. TMP 4.01. 74
strays | with willing sport to the wild ocean. TGV 2.07. 32
i love the sport well, but i shall as soon WIV 1.01.290 P
we have sport in hand. 2.01.197 P
hark, i will tell you what our sport shall be. 2.01.210 P
besides your cheer, you shall have sport; 3.02. 81 P
without cause, why then make sport at me, then 3.03.150 P
up, gentlemen, you shall see sport anon. 3.03.169 P
and the rest of their company from their sport, 4.02. 35 P
wives | yet once again (to make us public sport) 4.04. 13
heaven prosper our sport! 5.02. 12 P
and laugh this sport o'er by a country fire — 5.05.242
he had some feeling of the sport; MM 3.02.119 P
the sun shines, let foolish gnats make sport, ERR 2.02. 30
'tis holy sport to be a little vain, | when the 3.02. 27
you shall buy this sport as dear | as all the 4.01. 81
that would behold in me this shameful sport. 4.04.105
in food, in sport, and life–preserving rest | to 5.01. 83
thou thinkest i am in sport. ADO 1.01.177 P
he would make but a sport of it, and torment the 2.03.156 P
the sport will be, when they hold one an opinion 2.03.215 P
she knew his love, lest she'll make sport at it. 3.01. 58
costard the swain and he shall be our sport, LLL 1.01.179
and one that makes sport | to the prince and his 4.01. 99
very reverent sport, truly, and done in the 4.02. 1 P
most dull, honest dull! to our sport; away! 5.01.155
there's no such sport as sport by sport 5.02.153
no such sport as sport by sport o'erthrown, | to 5.02.153
no such sport as sport by sport o'erthrown, | to 5.02.153
and might not you | forestall our sport, to make 5.02.473
that sport best pleases that doth /least know 5.02.516
a right description of our sport, my lord. 5.02.521
might well have made our sport a comedy. 5.02.876
with thy brawls thou hast disturb'd our sport. MND 2.01. 87
sort, | who pyramus presented, in their sport, 3.02. 14
that must needs be sport alone. 3.02.119
a poor soul's patience, all to make you sport. 3.02.161
all three | to fashion this false sport, in 3.02.194
this sport, well carried, shall be chronicled. 3.02.240
sort, | as this their jangling i esteem a sport. 3.02.353
i with the morning's love have oft made sport, 3.02.389
if our sport had gone forward, we had all been 4.02. 17 P
unless you can find sport in their intents, 5.01. 79
our sport shall be to take what they mistake; 5.01. 90
and, in a merry sport, | if you repay me not on MV 1.03.145
we shall ne'er win at that sport, and stake down 3.02.216 P
marry, i prithee do, to make sport withal. AYL 1.02. 26 P
no man in good earnest, nor no further in sport, 1.02. 28 P
what shall be our sport then? 1.02. 30 P
fair princess, you have lost much good sport. 1.02.100 P
sport! of what color? 1.02.101 P
but what is the sport, monsieur, that the ladies 1.02.134 P
i heard breaking of ribs was sport for ladies. 1.02.139 P
youth | that he in sport doth call his rosalind. 4.03.156
the rather for i have some sport in hand, SHR in.1. 91
to feast and sport us at thy father's house. 4.03.183
we'll make you some sport with the fox ere we AWW 3.06.102 P
that's gone made himself much sport out of him. 4.05. 65 P
wait on me home, i'll make sport with thee. 5.03.323 P
do adore thee so | that danger shall seem sport, TN 2.01. 48
sport royal, i warrant you. 2.03.172 P
if i lose a scruple of this sport, let me be 2.05. 3 P
not give my part of this sport for a pension of 2.05.180 P
if you will then see the fruits of the sport, 2.05.197 P
with any safety this sport /t' the upshot. 4.02. 71 P
what is this? sport? WT 2.01. 58
and let her sport herself | with that she's big 2.01. 60
whom he hath us'd rather for sport than need) JN 5.02.175
no, misery makes sport to mock itself: R2 2.01. 85
what sport shall we devise here in this garden 3.04. 1
therefore no dancing, girl, some other sport. 3.04. 9
to sport would be as tedious as to work; 1H4 1.02.205
fields, and blows, and groans applaud our sport! 1.03.302
the which for sport sake are content to do the 2.01. 70 P
o jesu, this is excellent sport, i' faith! 2.04.390 P
draw out, | and sheathe for lack of sport. H5 4.02. 23
wars | will turn unto a peaceful comic sport, 1H6 2.02. 45
i saw not better sport these seven years' day; 2H6 2.01. 2
the fowl so suddenly, | we had had more sport. 2.01. 45
and think it but a minute spent in sport. 3.02.338
thou wouldst be fee'd, i see, to make me sport: 3H6 1.04. 92
so many hours must i sport myself, | so many 2.05. 34
and the limbs | of this great sport together, as H8 1.01. 47
hark what good sport is out of town to–day. TRO 1.01.113
but to the sport abroad — are you bound thither 1.01.115
and at this sport | sir valor dies; 1.03.175
if any thing more than your sport and pleasure 2.03.108
o, like a book of sport thou'lt read me o'er; 4.05.239
made the coward | turn terror into sport; COR 2.02.105
and chariots let us have, | and to our sport. TIT 2.02. 19
and, being intercepted in your sport, | great 2.03. 80
well could i leave our sport to sleep a while. 2.03.197
this was the sport, my lord. 4.03. 71
trim sport for them which had the doing of it. 5.01. 96
and when i told the empress of this sport, | she 5.01.118
ah, sirrah, this unlook'd–for sport comes well. ROM 1.05. 29
away, be gone, the sport is at the best. 1.05.119
with apemantus, let's ha' some sport with 'em. TIM 2.02. 47 P
of the same piece | is every flatterer's sport. 3.02. 65
how many times shall caesar bleed in sport, JC 3.01.114
when she saw pyrrhus make malicious sport | in HAM 2.02.513
sport and repose lock from me day and night, 3.02.217
for 'tis the sport to have the enginer | hoist 3.04.206
mother fair, there was good sport at his making, LR 1.01. 23 P
seen drunkards | do more than this in sport. 2.01. 35
we to th' gods, | they kill us for their sport. 4.01. 37
him, thou dost thyself a pleasure, me a sport. OTH 1.03.369 P
such /a snipe | but for my sport and profit. 1.03.386
the blood is made dull with the act of sport, 2.01.227 P
each man to what sport and revels his /addiction 2.02. 5 P
and she is sport for jove. 2.03. 17 P
is it sport? 4.03. 97
desires for sport, and frailty, as men have? 4.03.101
what sport to–night? ANT 1.01. 47
that drums him from his sport and speaks as loud 1.04. 29
'tis sport to maul a runner. 4.07. 14
here's sport indeed! 4.15. 32
make /not, sir, | your loss your sport. CYM 2.04. 48
now for our mountain sport: 3.03. 10
i wish ye sport. 4.02. 31
some country sport, upon my life, sir. TNK 3.05. 97
the body of our sport, of no small study, | i 3.05.121
sedges, | as patiently i was attending sport, 4.01. 55
i were a beast and i'ld call it good sport. 4.03. 53 P
being wasted in such time–beguiling sport." VEN 24
and for my sake hath learn'd to sport and dance, 105
be bold to play, our sport is not in sight; 124
morn till night, even where i list to sport me. 154
in such–like circumstance, with such–like sport: 844
short | his time of folly and his time of sport; LUC 992
youth is full of sport, age's breath is short, PP 12. 5
plains, | all our evening sport from us is fled, 17.31
days | (making lascivious comments on thy sport) SON 95. 6
some say thy grace is youth and gentle sport; 96. 2

SPORTFUL 4 FR 0.0004 REL FR 4 V 0 P
and then let kate be chaste and dian sportful! SHR 2.01.261
how with a sportful malice it was follow'd | may TN 5.01.365
o unbid spite, is sportful edward come? 3H6 5.01. 18
though't be a sportful combat, | yet in the TRO 1.03.335

SPORTING 1 FR 0.0001 REL FR 1 V 0 P
advice is sporting while infection breeds. LUC 907

SPORTING–PLACE 1 FR 0.0001 REL FR 1 V 0 P
each hurries toward his home and sporting–place. 2H4 4.02.105

SPORTIVE 5 FR 0.0005 REL FR 5 V 0 P
i am not in a sportive humor now: ERR 1.02. 58
it i | that drive thee from the sportive court, AWW 3.02.106
but i, that am not shap'd for sportive tricks, R3 1.01. 14
for sportive words and utt'ring foolish things. LUC 1813
eyes | give salutation to my sportive blood? SON 121. 6

SPORTS 15 FR 0.0017 REL FR 14 V 1 P
there be some sports are painful, and their TMP 3.01. 1
while other sports are tasking of their minds, WIV 4.06. 30
thou say'st his sports were hind'red by thy ERR 5.01. 77
there is a brief how many sports are ripe. MND 5.01. 42
from henceforth i will, coz, and devise sports. AYL 1.02. 25 P
hours fill'd up with riots, banquets, sports; H5 1.01. 56
to thee sent back — | thy grief their sports! TIT 3.01.238
for he is given | to sports, to wildness, and JC 2.01.189
and in our sports my better cunning faints ANT 2.03. 35
kindness | makes my past miseries sports. PER 5.03. 41
since his depart, his sports, | though craving TNK 1.03. 27
we'll see the sports, then every man to 's 2.03. 55
the sports | once ended, we'll perform. 2.03. 58
now to our sports again. 3.05.153
playing patient sports in unconstrained gyves? LC 242
SPOT 12 FR 0.0013 REL FR 7 V 5 P
that you cannot see a white spot about her. WIV 4.05.113 P
that there shall not be one spot of love in't. AYL 3.02.424 P
weep | upon the spot of this enforced cause — JN 5.02. 30
we make, | to rest without a spot for evermore. 5.07.107
a fine spot, in good faith. COR 1.03. 52 P
the angry spot doth glow on caesar's brow, | and JC 1.02.183
look, with a spot i damn him. 4.01. 6
yet here's a spot. MAC 5.01. 31 P
out, damn'd spot! 5.01. 35 P
like the greatest spot | of all thy sex; ANT 4.12. 35
to clear this spot by death, at least, i give LUC 1053
doth spot the beauty of thy budding name! SON 95. 3
SPOTLESS 9 FR 0.0010 REL FR 8 V 1 P
that the queen is spotless | i' th' eyes of WT 2.01.131
mortal times afford | is spotless reputation; R2 1.01.178
be his cause never so spotless, if it come to H5 4.01.159 P
a man, | to force a spotless virgin's chastity, 2H6 5.01.186
fairer | and spotless shall mine innocence arise H8 3.02.301
this palliament of white and spotless hue, | and TIT 1.01.182
than hands or tongue, her spotless chastity, 5.02.176
by your own spotless honor — TNK 3.06.196
abuse, | immaculate and spotless is my mind; LUC 1656
SPOTS 11 FR 0.0012 REL FR 10 V 1 P
dapples the drowsy east with spots of grey. ADO 5.03. 27
be, | in their gold coats spots you see: MND 2.01. 11
with all the spots a' th' world tax'd and AWW 5.03.206
not painted with the crimson spots of blood. JN 4.02.253
yea, but not change his spots. R2 1.01.175
and wash away thy country's stained spots. 1H6 3.03. 57
and the spots of thy kindred were jurors on thy TIM 4.03.341 P
and there i see such black and /grained spots HAM 3.04. 90
his faults, in him, seem as the spots of heaven, ANT 1.04. 12
that spots and stains love's modest snow–white LUC 196
the spots whereof could weeping purify, | her 685
SPOTTED 13 FR 0.0014 REL FR 13 V 0 P
upon this spotted and inconstant man. MND 1.01.110
you spotted snakes with double tongue, | thorny 2.02. 9
is sleep, which being spotted | is goads, thorns WT 1.02.328
make war upon their spotted souls for this! R2 3.02.134
thy garments are not spotted with our blood; R3 1.03.282
abhorr'd | than spotted livers in the sacrifice. TRO 5.03. 18
body's hue, | spotted, detested, and abominable. TIT 2.03. 74
and by the hazard of the spotted die | let die TIM 5.04. 34
hazard of the spotted die | let die the spotted. 5.04. 35
spotted with strawberries in your wive's hand? OTH 3.03.435
shall with lust's blood be spotted. 5.01. 36
to ask the spotted princess how she fares. LUC 721
her sacred temple spotted, spoil'd, corrupted, 1172
SPOUSAL 2 FR 0.0002 REL FR 2 V 0 P
so be there 'twixt your kingdoms such a spousal, H5 5.02.362
there shall we consummate our spousal rites. TIT 1.01.337
SPOUSE 5 FR 0.0005 REL FR 4 V 1 P
drew me from kind embracements of my spouse; ERR 1.01. 43
may beseem | the spouse of any noble gentleman. SHR 4.05. 67
hound of crete, think'st thou my spouse to get? H5 2.01. 73
commit not with man's sworn spouse, set not thy LR 3.04. 82 P
then mine host | and his fat spouse, that TNK 3.05.128
SPOUT 5 FR 0.0005 REL FR 5 V 0 P
which here we came to spout against your town, JN 2.01.256
stretch thy chest, and let thy eyes spout blood; TRO 4.05. 10
not the dreadful spout | which shipmen do the 5.02.171
spout | till you have drench'd our steeples, LR 3.02. 2
spout, rain! 3.02. 14
SPOUTING 1 FR 0.0001 REL FR 1 V 0 P
your statue spouting blood in many pipes, | in JC 2.02. 85
SPOUTS 3 FR 0.0003 REL FR 3 V 0 P
begin some speech, her eyes | became two spouts; WT 3.03. 26
as from a conduit with /three issuing spouts, TIT 2.04. 30
which, like a fountain with an hundred spouts, JC 2.02. 77
SPRAG 1 FR 0.0001 REL FR 0 V 1 P
he is a good sprag memory. WIV 4.01. 82 P
SPRANG 1 FR 0.0001 REL FR 0 V 1 P
i sprang not more in joy at first hearing he was COR 1.03. 15 P
SPRANG'ST 1 FR 0.0001 REL FR 1 V 0 P
that i love the tree from whence thou sprang'st, 3H6 5.07. 31
SPRAT 1 FR 0.0001 REL FR 0 V 1 P
parted, tell me what a sprat you shall find him, AWW 3.06.105 P
SPRAWL 1 FR 0.0001 REL FR 1 V 0 P
hang the child, that he may see it sprawl — | a TIT 5.01. 51
SPRAWL'ST 1 FR 0.0001 REL FR 1 V 0 P
sprawl'st thou? take that, to end thy agony. 3H6 5.05. 39
SPRAY 1 FR 0.0001 REL FR 1 V 0 P
whence that tender spray did sweetly spring, | i 3H6 2.06. 50
SPRAYS 3 FR 0.0003 REL FR 3 V 0 P
cut off the heads of /too fast growing sprays, R2 3.04. 34
shall a few sprays of us, | the emptying of our H5 3.05. 5
droops this lofty pine and hangs his sprays, 2H6 2.03. 45
SPREAD 34 FR 0.0038 REL FR 30 V 4 P
dromio, go bid the servants spread for dinner. ERR 2.02.187
spread o'er the silver waves thy golden hairs, 3.02. 48
let there be the same net spread for her, and ADO 2.03.214 P
north, and south, i spread my conquering might. LLL 5.02.563
masters, spread yourselves. MND 1.02. 15 P
she is spread of late | into a goodly bulk. WT 2.01. 19
hither is he come | to spread his colors, boy, JN 2.01. 8
mocking the air with colors idlely spread, | and 5.01. 72
spread, davy, spread, davy. 2H4 5.03. 8 P
spread, davy, spread, davy. 5.03. 8 P
his arms spread wider than a dragon's wings; 1H6 1.01. 11
great fear of my name 'mongst them were spread 1.04. 50
there goes the talbot, with his colors spread, 3.03. 31
and with colors spread | march'd through the 3H6 1.01. 91
will follow mine, if once they see them spread; 1.01.252
and spread they shall be, to thy foul disgrace, 1.01.253
another spread on 's breast, mounting his eyes, H8 1.02.205
believe me, there's an ill opinion spread then, 2.02.124
sends, | however it is spread in general name, TRO 1.03.322
being of catching nature, | spread further. COR 3.01.309
ere he can spread his sweet leaves to the air ROM 1.01.152
spread thy close curtain, love–performing night, 3.02. 5
lord, | into our city with thy banners spread; TIM 5.04. 30
and do not spread the compost on the weeds | to HAM 3.04.151
her clothes spread wide, | and, mermaid–like, 4.07.175
blows dust in others' eyes, to spread itself; PER 1.01. 97
when fame | had spread his cursed deed, the 5.03. 96
your tresses, | nor in more bounty spread her. TNK 1.01. 64
how i would spread, and fling my wanton arms 2.02.237
like lawn being spread upon the blushing rose, VEN 590
a second fear through all her sinews spread, 903
the fishes spread on it their golden gills; 1100
that dying fear through all her body spread, LUC 1266
princes' favorites their fair leaves spread SON 25. 5
SPREADING 3 FR 0.0003 REL FR 3 V 0 P
till by broad spreading it disperse to nought. 1H6 1.02.135
top–branch overpeer'd jove's spreading tree, 3H6 5.02. 14
i might as yet have been a spreading flower, LC 75
/SPREADS 1 FR 0.0001 REL FR 1 V 0 P
/france /spreads /his /banners /in /our LR 4.02. 56
SPREADS 1 FR 0.0001 REL FR 1 V 0 P
rest, spreads like a plane | fast by a brook, TNK 2.06. 5
SPRIGHTFUL *(also sprite, etc.)*
SPRIGHTFUL 1 FR 0.0001 REL FR 1 V 0 P
spoke like a sprightful noble gentleman. JN 4.02.177
SPRIGHTFULLY 1 FR 0.0001 REL FR 1 V 0 P
the duke of norfolk, sprightfully and bold, R2 1.03. 3
SPRIGHTLY 7 FR 0.0008 REL FR 5 V 2 P
address yourself to entertain them sprightly, WT 4.04. 53
and that sprightly scot of scots, douglas, that 1H4 2.04.342 P
it's sprightly, /waking, audible, and full of COR 4.05.222 P
reward thee | once for thy sprightly comfort, ANT 4.07. 15
and with our sprightly port make the ghosts gaze 4.14. 52
be sprightly, for you fall 'mongst friends. CYM 3.06. 74
of all this sprightly sharpness, not a smile. TNK 4.02. 30
SPRIGS 1 FR 0.0001 REL FR 1 V 0 P
pins, wooden pricks, nails, sprigs of rosemary; LR 2.03. 16
/SPRING 1 FR 0.0001 REL FR 1 V 0 P
/as /in /an /early /spring | /we /see /th' 2H4 1.03. 38
SPRING 74 FR 0.0083 REL FR 71 V 3 P
spring come to you at the farthest | in the very TMP 4.01.114
o, how this spring of love resembleth | the TGV 1.03. 84
even in the spring of love, thy love–springs rot ERR 3.02. 3
the spring is near when green geese are LLL 1.01. 97
that bites the first–born infants of the spring. 1.01.101
from whence doth spring the true promethean fire 4.03.300
this ver, the spring; 5.02.891 P
and never, since the middle summer's spring, MND 2.01. 82
the spring, the summer, | the childing autumn, 2.01.111
in spring time, the only pretty /ring time, AYL 5.03. 19
a ding, ding, | sweet lovers love the spring. 5.03. 21
country folks would lie, | in spring time, etc. 5.03. 25
a life was but a flower, | in spring time, etc. 5.03. 29
crowned with the prime, | in spring time, etc. 5.03. 33
cesario, by the roses of the spring, | by TN 3.01.149
i had some flow'rs o' th' spring that might WT 4.04.113
welcome hither, | as is the spring to th' earth. 5.01.152
from false mowbray their first head and spring. R2 1.01. 97
currents that spring from one most gracious head 3.03.108
he that hath suffered this disordered spring 3.04. 48
that strew the green lap of the new–come spring? 5.02. 47
well, bear you well in this new spring of time, 5.02. 50
farewell, the latter spring! 1H4 1.02.158 P
we, as the spring of all, shall pay for all. 5.02. 23
as flaws congealed in the spring of day. 2H4 4.04. 35
that shall first spring and be most delicate. H5 2.04. 40
spring crestless yeomen from so deep a root? 1H6 2.04. 85
from whence you spring by lineal descent. 3.01.165
now 'tis the spring, and weeds are 2H6 3.01. 31
the purest spring is not so free from mud | as i 3.01.101
troubles the silver spring where england drinks. 4.01. 72
but when we saw our sunshine made thy spring, 3H6 2.02.163
whence that tender spray did sweetly spring, | i 2.06. 50
from his loins no hopeful branch may spring, 3.02.126
now stops thy spring, my sea shall suck them dry 4.08. 55
short summers lightly have a forward spring. R3 3.01. 94
and showers | there had made a lasting spring. H8 3.01. 8
and i'll spring up in his tears an' 'twere a TRO 1.02.175 P
here stands the spring whom you have stain'd TIT 5.02.170
back, foolish tears, back to your native spring, ROM 3.02.102
and know their spring, their head, their true 5.03.218
so from that spring whence comfort seem'd to MAC 1.02. 27
the spring, the head, the fountain of your blood 2.03. 98
the canker galls the infants of the spring | too HAM 1.03. 39
work like the spring that turneth wood to stone, 4.07. 20
fair and unpolluted flesh | may violets spring! 5.01.240
that good effects may spring from words of love. LR 1.01.185
and from her derogate body never spring | a babe 1.04.280
virtues of the earth, | spring with my tears! 4.04. 17
the april's in her eyes, it is love's spring, ANT 3.02. 43
minist'red, | and in 's spring became a harvest; CYM 1.01. 46
to th' trunk again, and shut the spring of it. 2.02. 47
see where she comes, apparelled like the spring, PER 1.01. 12
lies here, | who withered in her spring of year. 4.04. 35
youths must wither | like a too–timely spring. TNK 2.02. 28
"the tender spring upon thy tempting lip | shows VEN 127
my beauty as the spring doth yearly grow, | my 141
seeds spring from seeds and beauty breedeth 167
this canker that eats up love's tender spring, 656
love's gentle spring doth always fresh remain, 801
thy hasty spring still blasts and ne'er grows LUC 49
little frosts that sometime threat the spring, 331
when thus thy vices bud before thy spring? 604
"unruly blasts wait on the tender spring, 869
as from a mountain spring that feeds a dale, 1077
wanting the spring that those shrunk pipes had 1455
pluck'd in the bud, and vaded in the spring! PP 10. 2
clear wells spring not, sweet birds sing not, 17.25
sing, | trees did grow and plants did spring; 20. 6
ornament, | and only herald to the gaudy spring, SON 1.10
speak of the spring and foison of the year, 53. 9
stealing away the treasure of his spring; 63. 8
from you have i been absent in the spring, 98. 1
our love was new, and then but in the spring, 102. 5
SPRINGE 2 FR 0.0002 REL FR 1 V 1 P
if the springe hold, the cock's mine. WT 4.03. 35 P
why, as a woodcock to mine own springe, osric: HAM 5.02.306
SPRINGES 1 FR 0.0001 REL FR 1 V 0 P
ay, springes to catch woodcocks. HAM 1.03.115
SPRINGETH 1 FR 0.0001 REL FR 1 V 0 P
it is a fault that springeth from your eye. ERR 3.02. 55
SPRINGHALT 1 FR 0.0001 REL FR 1 V 0 P
the spavin | /and springhalt reign'd among 'em. H8 1.03. 13
SPRINGING 2 FR 0.0002 REL FR 2 V 0 P
or seven fair branches springing from one root. R2 1.02. 13
if springing things be any jot diminish'd, VEN 417
SPRINGS 16 FR 0.0018 REL FR 16 V 0 P
the fresh springs, brine–pits, barren place and TMP 1.02.338
i'll show thee the best springs; 2.02.160
four lagging winters and four wanton springs R2 1.03.214
and as my duty springs, so perish they | that 1H6 3.01.174
fair queen, whence springs this deep despair? 3H6 3.03. 12
springs not from edward's well–meant honest love 3.03. 67
all springs reduce their currents to mine eyes, R3 2.02. 68
straight | springs out into fast gait, then H8 3.02.116
long continued, and what stock he springs of — COR 2.03.237
within this mile break forth a hundred springs; TIM 4.03.418
it springs | all from her father's death — and HAM 4.05. 75
his steeds to water at those springs | on CYM 2.03. 22
but the main grief springs from the loss | of a PER 5.01. 29
away he springs, and hasteth to his horse. VEN 258
to dry the old oak's sap and cherish springs, LUC 950
three beauteous springs to yellow autumn turn'd SON 104. 5
SPRING–TIME 4 FR 0.0004 REL FR 4 V 0 P
in speech, yet sweet as spring–time flowers. SHR 2.01.246
faster than spring–time show'rs comes thought on
2H6 3.01.337
that winter should cut off our spring–time so. 3H6 2.03. 47
and keep eternal spring–time /on /thy face, | so TIT 3.01. 21
SPRING–TIME'S 1 FR 0.0001 REL FR 1 V 0 P
child of ver, | merry spring–time's harbinger, TNK 1.01. 8
SPRINKLE 3 FR 0.0003 REL FR 2 V 1 P
that blood should sprinkle me to make me grow. R2 5.06. 46
sprinkle our society with thankfulness. TIM 3.06. 70 P
flame of thy distemper | sprinkle cool patience. HAM 3.04.124
SPRINKLES 1 FR 0.0001 REL FR 1 V 0 P
off, and sprinkles in your faces | your reeking TIM 3.06. 92
SPRITE *(also sprightful, etc.)*
SPRITE 9 FR 0.0010 REL FR 9 V 0 P
or else you are that shrewd and knavish sprite MND 2.01. 33
gaping wide, | every one lets forth his sprite, 5.01.381
every elf and fairy sprite | hop as light as 5.01.393
the quintessence of every sprite | heaven would AYL 3.02.139
soul and only sprite | in whom the tempers and TRO 1.03. 56
and now adonis, with a lazy sprite, | and with a VEN 181
bed, | intending weariness with heavy sprite; LUC 121
that thinks she hath beheld some ghastly sprite, 451
unto the clouds bequeathed | her winged sprite, 1728
SPRITED 1 FR 0.0001 REL FR 1 V 0 P
i am sprited with a fool, | frighted, and CYM 2.03.139
SPRITELY 3 FR 0.0003 REL FR 3 V 0 P
dance canary | with spritely fire and motion, AWW 2.01. 75
my spritely brethren, i propend to you | in TRO 2.02.190
with other spritely shows | of mine own kindred. CYM 5.05.428
SPRITES 9 FR 0.0010 REL FR 8 V 1 P
and, sweet sprites, /the /burthen /bear. TMP 1.02.380
be fine things, and if they be not sprites. 2.02.116
we talk with goblins, owls, and sprites; ERR 2.02.190
i have one | of sprites and goblins. WT 2.01. 26
do your best | to fright me with your sprites; 2.01. 28
sprites and fires! TRO 5.01. 66 P
from your graves rise up, and walk like sprites, MAC 2.03. 79
shall raise such artificial sprites | as by the 3.05. 27
come, sisters, cheer we up his sprites, | and 4.01.127
SPRITING 1 FR 0.0001 REL FR 1 V 0 P
to command | and do my spriting gently. TMP 1.02.298
SPROUT 1 FR 0.0001 REL FR 1 V 0 P
that it may grow and sprout as high as heaven, 2H4 2.03. 60
SPRUCE 3 FR 0.0003 REL FR 1 V 2 P
he is too picked, too spruce, too affected, too LLL 5.01. 13 P
three–pil'd hyperboles, spruce affection, 5.02.407
now, my spruce companions, is all ready, and all SHR 4.01.113 P
SPRUNG 12 FR 0.0013 REL FR 12 V 0 P
sprung from the rancorous outrage of your duke ERR 1.01. 6
from whence with life he never more sprung up. 2H4 1.01.111
they never then had sprung like summer flies; 3H6 2.06. 17
to his music plants and flowers | ever sprung, H8 3.01. 7
again, there is sprung up | an heretic, an 3.02.101
brave slip, sprung from the great andronicus, TIT 5.01. 9
my only love sprung from my only hate! ROM 1.05.138
and at that instant like a babe sprung up. TIM 1.02.111
a poor unmanly melancholy sprung | from change 4.03.203
of his grief | sprung from neglected love. HAM 3.01.178
there's a leak sprung, a sound one. TNK 3.04. 8
a purple flow'r sprung up, check'red with white, VEN 1168
SPUN 3 FR 0.0003 REL FR 1 V 2 P
argo, their thread of life is spun. 2H6 4.02. 29 P
all the yarn she spun in ulysses' absence did COR 1.03. 83 P
is, when the thread of hazard is once spun, | a STM III 20
SPUNGE 4 FR 0.0004 REL FR 0 V 4 P
nerissa, ere i will be married to a spunge. MV 1.02. 99 P
to be demanded of a spunge, what replication HAM 4.02. 12 P
take you me for a spunge, my lord? 4.02. 14 P
you, and, spunge, you shall be dry again. 4.02. 20 P
SPUNGY 5 FR 0.0005 REL FR 5 V 0 P
brims, | which spungy april at thy hest betrims, TMP 4.01. 65
more spungy to suck in the sense of fear, | more TRO 2.02. 12
what not put upon | his spungy officers, who MAC 1.07. 71
from the spungy south to this part of the west, CYM 4.02.349
o, that sad breath his spungy lungs bestowed, LC 326
/SPUR 1 FR 0.0001 REL FR 1 V 0 P
/neighing /coursers /daring /of /the /spur, 2H4 4.01.117
SPUR 36 FR 0.0040 REL FR 34 V 2 P
time, | so much they spur their expedition. TGV 5.01. 6
he can command, lets it straight feel the spur; MM 1.02.162
'tis long of you that spur me with such LLL 2.01.118
more sharp than filed steel, did spur me forth, TN 3.03. 5
furlongs ere | with spur we heat an acre. WT 1.02. 96
spiritual counsel had, | shall stop or spur me. 2.01.187

so), which is another spur to my departure. 4.02. 9 P
finds brotherhood in thee no sharper spur? R2 1.02. 9
and spur thee on with full as many lies | as may 4.01. 53
how fondly dost thou spur a forward horse! 4.01. 72
spur post, and get before him to the king, | and 5.02.112
and that young harry percy's spur was cold. 2H4 1.01. 42
said he young harry percy's spur was cold? 1.01. 49
from helmet to the spur all blood he was. H5 4.06. 6
spur to the rescue of the noble talbot, | who 1H6 4.03. 19
spur your proud horses hard, and ride in blood; R3 5.03.340
their mouths with stubborn bits and spur 'em H8 5.02. 58
a spur to valiant and magnanimous deeds, | whose TRO 2.02.200
as hot as perseus, spur thy phrygian steed, 4.05.186
spur them to ruthful work, rein them from ruth. 5.03. 48
to the pace of it | i may spur on my journey. COR 1.10. 33
with that spur as he would to the lip of his TIM 3.06. 65 P
what need we any spur but our own cause | to JC 2.01.123
but when they should endure the bloody spur, 4.02. 25
with horsemen, that make to him on the spur, 5.03. 29
and his great love, sharp as his spur, hath holp MAC 1.06. 23
i have no spur | to prick the sides of my intent 1.07. 25
inform against me, | and spur my dull revenge! HAM 4.04. 33
spur through media, | mesopotamia, and the ANT 3.01. 7
discover to me | what both you spur and stop. CYM 1.06. 99
but if to that my nature need a spur, | the gods PER 3.03. 23
when i spur | my horse, i chide him /not; TNK 3.01.106
brave a knight as e'er | did spur a noble steed. 5.03.116
what cares he now for curb or pricking spur, VEN 285
the bloody spur cannot provoke him on | that SON 50. 9
then should i spur though mounted on the wind, 51. 7

SPURIO 2 FR 0.0002 REL FR 0 V 2 P
the regiment of the spinii one captain spurio, AWW 2.01. 43 P
spurio, a hundred and fifty; 4.03.161 P

SPURN 29 FR 0.0032 REL FR 27 V 2 P
me, | that like a football you do spurn me thus? ERR 2.01. 83
you spurn me hence, and he will spurn me hither: 2.01. 84
you spurn me hence, and he will spurn me hither: 2.01. 84
wouldst thou not spit at me, and spurn at me, 2.02.134
spurn me, strike me, | neglect me, lose me; MND 2.01.205
(who even but now did spurn me with his foot), 3.02.225
and threat'ned me | to strike me, spurn me, nay, 3.02.313
beard | and foot me as you spurn a stranger cur MV 1.03.118
to spet on thee again, to spurn thee too. 1.03.131
our holy mother, | so willfully dost spurn; JN 3.01.142
nay more, to spurn at your most royal image, 2H4 5.02. 89
steel, | and spurn in pieces posts of adamant; 1H6 1.04. 52
when he might spurn him with his foot away? 3H6 1.04. 58
and spurn upon thee, beggar, for thy boldness. R3 1.02. 42
will you then | spurn at his edict, and fulfill 1.04.198
say my request's unjust, | and spurn me back; COR 5.03.165
but that which gives my soul the greatest spurn TIT 3.01.101
away, unpeaceable dog, or i'll spurn thee hence! TIM 1.01.270 P
dies that bears not one spurn to their graves 1.02.141
i know no personal cause to spurn at him, | but JC 2.01. 11
him, | i spurn thee like a cur out of my way. 3.01. 46
he shall spurn fate, scorn death, and bear | his MAC 3.05. 30
by rule of knighthood, i disdain and spurn. LR 5.03.146
or i'll spurn thine eyes | like balls before me; ANT 2.05. 63
and all this done, spurn her home to her father, CYM 4.01. 19 P
with language that would make me spurn the sea 5.05.294
being able | to make mars spurn his drum. TNK 1.01.182
spurn you like dogs, and like as if that god STM II.C 135
in vain i spurn at my confirm'd despite: LUC 1026

SPURN'D 1 FR 0.0001 REL FR 1 V 0 P
you spurn'd me such a day, another time | you MV 1.03.127

SPURNS 7 FR 0.0008 REL FR 7 V 0 P
yet, spaniel-like, the more she spurns my love, TGV 4.02. 14
whose foot spurns back the ocean's roaring tides JN 2.01. 24
change of mood | spurns down her late beloved, TIM 1.01. 85
and the spurns | that patient merit of th' HAM 3.01. 72
spurns enviously at straws, speaks things in 4.05. 6
and spurns | the rush that lies before him; ANT 3.05. 16
spurns at his love, and scorns the heat he feels VEN 311

SPURN'ST 1 FR 0.0001 REL FR 1 V 0 P
'tis thou that spurn'st at right, at law, at LUC 880

SPURR'D 5 FR 0.0005 REL FR 5 V 0 P
but love will not be spurr'd to what it loathes. TGV 5.02. 7
was that the king that spurr'd his horse so hard LLL 4.01. 1
an ass, | spurr'd, gall'd, and tir'd by jauncing R2 5.05. 94
ne'er spurr'd their coursers at the trumpet's 3H6 5.07. 9
i spurr'd hard to come up, and under me | i had TNK 3.06. 76

SPURRING 4 FR 0.0004 REL FR 4 V 0 P
bloody with spurring, fiery-red with haste. R2 2.03. 58
after him came spurring hard | a gentleman, 2H4 1.01. 36
their sharp shins, | and mar men's spurring. TIM 4.03.153
more sharp to me than spurring to his side, SON 50.12

SPURS 16 FR 0.0018 REL FR 10 V 6 P
and by the spurs pluck'd up | the pine and cedar TMP 5.01. 47
and set spurs and away, like three german devils WIV 4.05. 68 P
that in himself which he spurs on his pow'r | to MM 4.02. 82
tilter, that spurs his horse but on one side, AYL 3.04. 43 P
shift to run into't, boots and spurs and all, AWW 2.05. 37 P
have deserv'd it, in usurping his spurs so long. 4.03.104 P
from giving reins and spurs to my free speech, R2 1.01. 55
he tires betimes that spurs too fast betimes; 2.01. 36
her fume needs no spurs, | she'll gallop far 2H6 1.03.150
swits and spurs, swits and spurs, or i'll cry a ROM 2.04. 69 P
swits and spurs, swits and spurs, or i'll cry a 2.04. 69 P
and hide thy spurs in him | till he have brought JC 5.03. 15
that make to him on the spur, | yet he spurs on. 5.03. 30
now spurs the lated traveller apace | to gain MAC 3.03. 6
in them both, | mingle their spurs together. CYM 4.02. 58
hark how yon spurs to spirit do incite | the TNK 5.03. 56

SPY 28 FR 0.0031 REL FR 17 V 11 P
hast put thyself | upon this island as a spy, to TMP 1.02.456
but i may spy | more fresh in julia's with a TGV 5.04.114
i spy entertainment in her. WIV 1.03. 44 P
i spy a great peard under his muffler. 4.02.194 P
i spy comfort, i cry bail. MM 3.02. 41 P
i do spy some marks of love in her. ADO 2.03.245 P
when they him spy, | as wild geese that the MND 3.02. 19
enter now, and i am to spy her through the wall. 5.01.186 P
chink, | to spy and i can hear my thisby's face. 5.01.193
the hollow eyes of death | i spy life peering, R2 2.01.271
i'll never trouble you, if i may spy them. 1H6 1.04. 22
and, when i spy advantage, claim the crown, 2H6 1.01.242
i spy a black, suspicious, threat'ning cloud, 3H6 5.03. 4
my friend, i spy some pity in thy looks. R3 1.04.263
she takes upon her to spy a white hair on his TRO 1.02.139 P
i spy. 3.01. 93 P
you spy? 3.01. 94 P
what do you spy? 3.01. 94 P
but such an eye would spy out such a quarrel? ROM 3.01. 21 P
i do spy a kind of hope, | which craves as 4.01. 68
lest they should spy my windpipe's dangerous TIM 1.02. 51
acquaint you with the perfect spy o' th' time, MAC 3.01.129
what a man cannot smell out, he may spy into. LR 1.05. 23 P
you will come to me | (for now i spy a danger), 2.04.247
it is my nature's plague | to spy into abuses, OTH 3.03.147
sharp | to spy advantages, and where he finds TNK 4.02.133
"this sour informer, this bate-breeding spy, VEN 655
and in thy shady cell, where none may spy him, LUC 881

SPYING 3 FR 0.0003 REL FR 3 V 0 P
his soldiers, spying his undaunted spirit, | "a 1H6 1.01.127
by spying and avoiding fortune's malice, | for 3H6 4.06. 28
he spying her, bounc'd in, whereas he stood; PP 6.13

SPY'ST 1 FR 0.0001 REL FR 1 V 0 P
if thou spy'st any, run and bring me word, | and 1H6 1.04. 19

SQUABBLE 1 FR 0.0001 REL FR 0 V 1 P
and squabble? OTH 2.03.280 P

SQUADRON 1 FR 0.0001 REL FR 1 V 0 P
wife), | that never set a squadron in the field, OTH 1.01. 22

SQUADRONS 3 FR 0.0003 REL FR 3 V 0 P
on either hand thee there are squadrons pitch'd, 1H6 4.02. 23
in ranks and squadrons and right form of war, JC 2.02. 20
set we our squadrons on yond side o' th' hill, ANT 3.09. 1

SQUAND'RED 1 FR 0.0001 REL FR 0 V 1 P
and other ventures he hath, squand'red abroad. MV 1.03. 21 P

SQUAND'RING 1 FR 0.0001 REL FR 1 V 0 P
even by the squand'ring glances of the fool. AYL 2.07. 57

SQUAR'D 2 FR 0.0002 REL FR 2 V 0 P
superstitiously, | i will be squar'd by this. WT 3.03. 41
o that ever i | had squar'd me to thy counsel! 5.01. 52

SQUARE *(also squier)*

/SQUARE 1 FR 0.0001 REL FR 1 V 0 P
/fie, /how /franticly /i /square /my /talk, TIT 3.02. 31

SQUARE 15 FR 0.0017 REL FR 12 V 3 P
but they do square, that all their elves for MND 2.01. 30
as 'tis with us that square our guess by shows; AWW 2.01.150
sleeve-hand and the work about the square on't. WT 4.04.210 P
to square the general sex | by cressid's rule. TRO 5.02.132
ye, and are you such fools | to square for this? TIT 2.01.100
that will not suffer you to square yourselves, 2.01.124
it is not square to take | on those that are, TIM 5.04. 36
the most precious square of sense /possesses, LR 1.01. 74
pregnant they should square between themselves, ANT 2.01. 45
triumphant lady, if report be square to her. 2.02.185 P
i have not kept my square, but that to come 2.03. 6
mine honesty and i begin to square. 3.13. 41
my queen's square brows, | her stature to an PER 5.01.108
what's now out of square in her into their TNK 4.03. 95 P
aged cramp | had screw'd his square foot round, 5.01.111

SQUARER 1 FR 0.0001 REL FR 0 V 1 P
is there no young squarer now that will make a ADO 1.01. 82 P

SQUARES 2 FR 0.0002 REL FR 2 V 0 P
action swarm | about our squares of battle, were H5 4.02. 28
no practice had | in the brave squares of war; ANT 3.11. 40

SQUAR'ST 1 FR 0.0001 REL FR 1 V 0 P
this world, | and squar'st thy life according. MM 5.01.482

SQUASH 3 FR 0.0003 REL FR 1 V 2 P
i pray you commend me to mistress squash, your MND 3.01.186 P
as a squash is before 'tis a peascod, or a TN 1.05.157 P
to this kernel, | this squash, this gentleman. WT 1.02.160

SQUEAK 2 FR 0.0002 REL FR 1 V 1 P
that ye squeak out your coziers' catches without TN 2.03. 89 P
did squeak and gibber in the roman streets. HAM 1.01.116

SQUEAKING 1 FR 0.0001 REL FR 1 V 0 P
see | some squeaking cleopatra boy my greatness ANT 5.02.220

SQUEAL 1 FR 0.0001 REL FR 1 V 0 P
ghosts did shriek and squeal about the streets. JC 2.02. 24

SQUEALING 1 FR 0.0001 REL FR 1 V 0 P
and the vile squealing of the wry-neck'd fife, MV 2.05. 30

SQUEEZING 1 FR 0.0001 REL FR 0 V 1 P
what you have glean'd, it is but squeezing you, HAM 4.02. 20 P

SQUELE 1 FR 0.0001 REL FR 0 V 1 P
and francis pickbone, and will squele, a cotsole 2H4 3.02. 21 P

SQUIER *(also square)*

SQUIER 3 FR 0.0003 REL FR 1 V 2 P
do not you know my lady's foot by th' squier, LLL 5.02.474
but jumps twelve foot and a half by th' squier. WT 4.04.339 P
but four foot by the squier further afoot, i 1H4 2.02. 12 P

/SQUINIES 1 FR 0.0001 REL FR 0 V 1 P
he gives the web and the pin, /squinies the eye, LR 3.04.117 P

SQUINY 1 FR 0.0001 REL FR 0 V 1 P
dost thou squiny at me? LR 4.06.137 P

SQUIRE 11 FR 0.0012 REL FR 7 V 4 P
cut and long-tail, under the degree of a squire. WIV 3.04. 47 P
a proper squire! ADO 1.03. 52 P
(her womb then rich with my young squire) MND 2.01.131
so stands this squire | offic'd with me. WT 1.02.171
a landless knight makes thee a landed squire. JN 1.01.177
and now is this vice's dagger become a squire, 2H4 3.02.320 P
i will make you to-day a squire of low degree. H5 5.01. 36 P
given, | like to a trusty squire did run away; 1H6 4.01. 23
no squire in debt, nor no poor knight; LR 3.02. 88
some such squire he was | that turn'd your wit OTH 4.02.145
and my queen's a squire | more tight at this ANT 4.04. 14

SQUIRE-LIKE 1 FR 0.0001 REL FR 1 V 0 P
and, squire-like, pension beg | to keep base LR 2.04.214

SQUIRE'S 2 FR 0.0002 REL FR 1 V 1 P
look thee, a bearing-cloth for a squire's child! WT 3.03.115 P
a hilding for a livery, a squire's cloth, | a CYM 2.03.123

SQUIRES 4 FR 0.0004 REL FR 3 V 1 P
let not us that are squires of the night's body 1H4 1.02. 24 P
of other lords and barons, knights and squires, H5 4.08. 78
are princes, barons, lords, knights, squires, 4.08. 89
here do you keep a hundred knights and squires, LR 1.04.241

SQUIRILITY *(also scurrility)*

SQUIRILITY 1 FR 0.0001 REL FR 0 V 1 P
so it shall please you to abrogate squirility. LLL 4.02. 54 P

SQUIRREL 2 FR 0.0002 REL FR 1 V 1 P
the other squirrel was stol'n from me by the TGV 4.04. 55 P
made by the joiner squirrel or old grub, | time ROM 1.04. 60

SQUIRREL'S 1 FR 0.0001 REL FR 1 V 0 P
fairy that shall seek | the squirrel's hoard, MND 4.01. 36

STAB 16 FR 0.0018 REL FR 13 V 3 P
ye call me coward, by the lord, i'll stab thee. 1H4 2.04.145 P
cost some of us our lives, for he will stab. 2H4 2.01. 12 P
heart | to stab at half an hour of my life. 4.05.108
let's stab ourselves. H5 4.05. 7
speak, captain, shall i stab the forlorn swain? 2H6 4.01. 65
first let my words stab him, as he hath me. 4.01. 66
stab poniards in our flesh till all were told, 3H6 2.01. 98
what, shall /i stab him as he sleeps? R3 1.04.100 P
this sudden stab of rancor i misdoubt; 3.02. 87
stab them, or tear them on thy chariot-wheels, TIT 5.02. 47
good murther, stab him, he's a murtherer. 5.02.100
thee, | good rapine, stab him, he is a ravisher. 5.02.103
hang them, or stab them, drown them in a draught TIM 5.01.102
for when the noble caesar saw him stab, JC 3.02.184
his body, that did stab | and not for justice? 4.03. 20
sense unsettle | lest i should drown, or stab, TNK 3.02. 30

/STABB'D 1 FR 0.0001 REL FR 1 V 0 P
o, i am /stabb'd with laughter! LLL 5.02. 80

STABB'D 19 FR 0.0021 REL FR 14 V 5 P
who, in my mood, i stabb'd unto the heart. TGV 4.01. 49
and wild half-can that stabb'd pots, and i think MM 4.03. 18 P
he stabb'd me in mine own house, most beastly, 2H4 2.01. 13 P
brutus' bastard hand | stabb'd julius caesar; 2H6 4.01.137
this is the hand that stabb'd thy father york, 3H6 2.04. 6
i stabb'd your fathers' bosoms, split my breast. 2.06. 30
they that stabb'd caesar shed no blood at all, 5.05. 53
stabb'd by the self-same hand that made these R3 1.02. 11
'twas i that stabb'd young edward — | but 'twas 1.02.181
since, | stabb'd in my angry mood at tewksbury? 1.02.241
when my son | was stabb'd with bloody daggers: 1.03.211
that stabb'd me in the field by tewksbury: 1.04. 56
why, then he'll say we stabb'd him sleeping. 1.04.105 P
for standing by when richard stabb'd her son. 3.03. 17
thy clarence he is dead that stabb'd my edward, 4.04. 67
dead, stabb'd with a white wench's black eye, ROM 2.04. 14 P
if caesar had stabb'd their mothers, they would JC 1.02.274 P
men | whose daggers have stabb'd caesar; 3.02.152
through this the well-beloved brutus stabb'd, 3.02.176

STABBING 2 FR 0.0002 REL FR 0 V 2 P
for it with stamped coin, not stabbing steel, WT 4.04.725 P
and for me to say a soldier lies, 'tis stabbing. OTH 3.04. 6 P

STABLE* 6 FR 0.0006 REL FR 4 V 2 P
france is a stable, we that dwell in't jades, AWW 2.03.284
and stable bearing | as i perceive she does. TN 4.03. 19
to crouch in litter of your stable planks, | to JN 5.02.140
i was a poor groom of thy stable, king, | when R2 5.05. 72
me thy lantern, to see my gelding in the stable. 1H4 2.01. 35 P
the ostler bring my gelding out of the stable. 2.01. 96 P

STABLENESS 1 FR 0.0001 REL FR 1 V 0 P
as justice, verity, temp'rance, stableness, MAC 4.03. 92

STABLES 3 FR 0.0003 REL FR 2 V 1 P
if your husband have stables enough, you'll see ADO 3.04. 48 P
i'll keep my stables where | i lodge my wife; WT 2.01.134
his barbed steeds to stables, and his heart | to R2 3.03.117

STABLISH *(also establish, etc.)*

STABLISH 1 FR 0.0001 REL FR 1 V 0 P
blood, | and stablish quietness on every side. 1H6 5.01. 10

STABLISHMENT 1 FR 0.0001 REL FR 1 V 0 P
unto her | he gave the stablishment of egypt, ANT 3.06. 9

STABS 4 FR 0.0004 REL FR 3 V 1 P
loud winds, or with bemock'd-at stabs | kill the TMP 3.03. 63
she speaks poniards, and every word stabs. ADO 2.01.248 P
thy intention stabs the centre. WT 1.02.138
and his gash'd stabs look'd like a breach in MAC 2.03.113

STAB'ST 1 FR 0.0001 REL FR 1 V 0 P
think how thou stab'st me in my prime of youth R3 5.03.119

STAFF *(also stave's)*

/STAFF 1 FR 0.0001 REL FR 1 V 0 P
/own /life /hung /upon /the /staff /he /threw), 2H4 4.01.124

STAFF 34 FR 0.0038 REL FR 25 V 9 P
this airy charm is for, i'll break my staff, TMP 5.01. 54
now, sir, this staff is my sister, for, look you TGV 2.03. 19 P
my staff understands me. 2.05. 27 P
i'll but lean, and my staff understands me. 2.05. 30 P
hope is a lover's staff; 3.01.248
you with a proverb — shall i set in my staff? ERR 3.01. 51
nay then give him another staff, this last was ADO 5.01.138 P
there is no staff more reverent than one tipp'd 5.04.123 P
let me hear a staff, a stanze, a verse; LLL 4.02.104
the boy was the very staff of my age, my very MV 2.02. 67 P
i look like a cudgel or a hovel-post, a staff, 2.02. 69 P
by jacob's staff i swear | i have no mind of 2.05. 36
one side, breaks his staff like a noble goose. AYL 3.04. 44 P
crest | that is removed by a staff of france; JN 2.01.318
the earl of worcester | hath broken his staff, R2 2.02. 59
broken his staff of office, and dispers'd | the 2.03. 27
for you my staff of office did i break | in 1H4 5.01. 34
methought this staff, mine office-badge in court 2H6 1.02. 25
ere thou go, | give up thy staff. 2.03. 23
give up your staff, sir, and the king his realm. 2.03. 31
my staff? 2.03. 32
here, noble henry, is my staff. 2.03. 32
this staff of honor raught, there let it stand, 2.03. 43
"a staff is quickly found to beat a dog." 3.01.171
main'd, and fain to go with a staff, but that my 4.02.163 P
thy hand is made to grasp a palmer's staff | and 5.01. 97
the rampant bear chain'd to the ragged staff, 5.01.203
now thou art gone we have no staff, no stay. 3H6 2.01. 69
give me a staff of honor for mine age, | but not TIT 1.01.198
give me my staff. MAC 5.03. 48
by his cockle hat and staff, | and his sandal HAM 4.05. 25
that of his fortunes you should make a staff ANT 3.13. 68
knights have done, | h'as broken a staff or so; PER 2.03. 35
he wears a well-steel'd axe, the staff of gold. TNK 4.02.115

STAFFORD 9 FR 0.0010 REL FR 8 V 1 P
the lord of stafford dear to-day hath bought 1H4 5.03. 7
the spirits | of valiant shirley, stafford, 5.04. 41
and westmerland and stafford fled the field; 2H4 1.01. 18
stafford, take her to thee. 2H6 1.04. 52
sir humphrey stafford and his brother are hard 4.02.113 P
sir humphrey stafford and his brother's death 4.04. 34
lord clifford, and lord stafford, all abreast, 3H6 1.01. 7
pembroke and stafford, you in our behalf | go 4.01.130
of buckingham and earl | of /herford, stafford, H8 1.01.200

STAFFORD'S 2 FR 0.0002 REL FR 2 V 0 P
king that will revenge | lord stafford's death. 1H4 5.03. 13

lord stafford's father, duke of buckingham, | is 3H6 1.01. 10
STAFFORDSHIRE 1 FR 0.0001 REL FR 0 V 1 P
and little john doit of staffordshire, and black 2H4 3.02. 19 P
STAG 6 FR 0.0006 REL FR 5 V 1 P
for me, i am here a windsor stag, and the WIV 5.05. 13 P
to the which place a poor sequest'red stag, AYL 2.01. 33
'tis pity they should take him for a stag. TIT 2.03. 71
yea, like the stag, when snow the pasture sheets ANT 1.04. 65
this way the stag took. TNK 3.05. 95
may the stag thou hunt'st stand long, | and thy 3.05.154
STAG'D 1 FR 0.0001 REL FR 1 V 0 P
unstate his happiness and be stag'd to th' show ANT 3.13. 30
STAGE 25 FR 0.0028 REL FR 23 V 2 P
but do not like to stage me to their eyes; MM 1.01. 68
this green plot shall be our stage, this MND 3.01. 4 P
a stage, where every man must play a part, | and MV 1.01. 78
all the world's a stage, | and all the men and AYL 2.07.139
if this were play'd upon a stage now, i could TN 3.04.127 P
again possess her corpse, and on this stage WT 5.01. 58
after a well-graced actor leaves the stage, R2 5.02. 24
and let this world no longer be a stage | to 2H4 1.01.155
a kingdom for a stage, princes to act, | and H5 pr 3
which oft our stage hath shown; ep 13
is now the two hours' traffic of our stage; ROM pr 12
with man's act, | threatens his bloody stage. MAC 2.04. 6
that struts and frets his hour upon the stage, 5.05. 25
he would drown the stage with tears, | and HAM 2.02.562
bodies | high on a stage be placed to the view, 5.02.378
bear hamlet, like a soldier, to the stage, | for 5.02.396
that we are come | to this great stage of fools. LR 4.06.183
land, supplying every stage | with an augmented ANT 3.06. 54
quick comedians | extemporally will stage us, 5.02.217
in your imagination hold | this stage the ship, PER 3.ch. 59
and call your lovers from the stage of death, TNK 5.04.123
part is youth, and beats these from the stage. LUC 278
black stage for tragedies and murthers fell! 766
that this huge stage presenteth nought but shows SON 15. 3
as an unperfect actor on the stage, | who with 23. 1
/STAGES 1 FR 0.0001 REL FR 0 V 1 P
/and /so /berattle /the /common /stages — /so HAM 2.02.342 P
STAGES 1 FR 0.0001 REL FR 1 V 0 P
gaps to teach you, | the stages of our story. PER 4.04. 9
STAGGER 3 FR 0.0003 REL FR 2 V 1 P
i stagger in — but this new governor | awakes MM 1.02.165
of a fearful heart, stagger in this attempt; AYL 3.03. 49 P
the question did at first so stagger me, H8 2.04.213
STAGGERING 2 FR 0.0002 REL FR 1 V 1 P
and (without any pause or staggering) take this WIV 3.03. 12 P
methought stood staggering whether he should TNK 4.01. 10
STAGGERS 4 FR 0.0004 REL FR 3 V 1 P
stark spoil'd with the staggers, begnawn with SHR 3.02. 54 P
ever | into the staggers and the careless lapse AWW 2.03.163
fire | that staggers thus my person. R2 5.05.109
how comes these staggers on me? CYM 5.05.233
STAGS 2 FR 0.0002 REL FR 2 V 0 P
thy greyhounds are as swift | as breathed stags; SHR in.2. 48
and, desperate stags, | turn on the bloody 1H6 4.02. 50
STAIDER 1 FR 0.0001 REL FR 1 V 0 P
fear, ere wildness | vanquish my staider senses. CYM 3.04. 10
STAIN 48 FR 0.0054 REL FR 45 V 3 P
do no stain to your own gracious person; MM 3.01.202 P
some honest slanders | to stain my cousin with. ADO 3.01. 85
if virtue's gloss will stain with any soil, | is LLL 2.01. 48
which lion vile with bloody mouth did stain. MND 5.01.143
you have some stain of soldier in you; AWW 1.01.111 P
i say we must not | so stain our judgment, or 2.01.120
here's such ado to make no stain a stain | as WT 2.02. 17
here's such ado to make no stain a stain | as 2.02. 17
stain your own | with oily painting. 5.03. 82
lest unadvis'd you stain your swords with blood. JN 2.01. 45
to dim his glory and to stain the track | of his R2 3.03. 66
that any harm should stain so fair a show! 3.03. 71
base | to stain the temper of my knightly sword. 4.01. 29
see riot and dishonor stain the brow | of my 1H4 1.01. 85
loseth men's hearts and leaves behind a stain 3.01.185
blood, | and stain my favors in a bloody mask, 3.02.136
whose temper i intend to stain | with the best 5.02. 93
veins | to give each naked curtle-axe a stain, H5 4.02. 21
stain to thy countrymen, thou hear'st thy doom! 1H6 4.01. 45
flight cannot stain the honor you have won, 4.05. 26
charge shall clear thee from that stain. 4.05. 42
or with their blood stain this discolored shore. 2H6 4.01. 11
and i'll corrupt her manners, stain her beauty, R3 4.04.207
man an attaint but he carries some stain of it. TRO 1.02. 26 P
poison'd | with only suff'ring stain by him; COR 1.10. 18
men and lads, | stain all your edges on me. 5.06.112
andronicus, stain not thy tomb with blood! TIT 1.01.116
and stain the sun with fog, as sometime clouds 3.01.212
lo here upon thy cheek the stain doth sit | of ROM 2.03. 75
giving our holy virgins to the stain | of TIM 5.01.173
but do not stain | the even virtue of our JC 2.01.132
weapons, water-drops, | stain my man's cheeks! LR 2.04.278
if that her breath will mist or stain the stone, 5.03.263
preparation of a war | shall stain your brother. ANT 3.04. 27
you do remember | this stain upon her? CYM 2.04.139
and it doth confirm | another stain, as big as 2.04.140
stain to all nymphs, more lovely than a man, VEN 9
virtue would stain that o'er with silver white. LUC 56
while lust and murder wakes to stain and kill. 168
who seek to stain the ocean of thy blood. 655
o that prone lust should stain so pure a bed! 684
the stain upon his silver down will stay. 1012
"how may this forced stain be wip'd from me? 1701
and why not i from this compelled stain?" 1708
her body's stain her mind untainted clears, 1710
suns of the world may stain when heaven's sun SON 33.14
clouds and eclipses stain both moon and sun, 35. 3
so that myself bring water for my stain. 109. 8
STAIN'D 32 FR 0.0036 REL FR 30 V 2 P
and, but he's something stain'd | with grief TMP 1.02.415
rather new dy'd than stain'd with salt water. 2.01. 64 P
sweet uncleanness | as she that he hath stain'd? MM 2.04. 55
and tear the stain'd skin off my harlot brow, ERR 2.02.136
thy mantle good, | what, stain'd with blood? MND 5.01.283
forget the shames that you have stain'd me with, MV 1.03.139
why, and where | this handkercher was stain'd. AYL 4.03. 97
and stain'd the beauty of a fair queen's cheeks R2 3.01. 14
the king's blood stain'd the king's own land. 5.05.110
horse, | stain'd with the variation of each soil 1H4 1.01. 64
this, | where stain'd nobility lies trodden on, 5.04. 13
but to stand stain'd with travel, and sweating 2H4 5.05. 24 P
stain'd with the guiltless blood of innocents, 1H6 5.04. 44
and that my sword be stain'd | with heart-blood 2H6 2.02. 65
before his chaps be stain'd with crimson blood, 3.01.259
i stain'd this napkin with the blood | that 3H6 1.04. 79
have touch'd, would not have stain'd with blood; 1.04.153
that stain'd their fetlocks in his smoking blood 2.03. 21
how they are stain'd like meadows yet not dry, TIT 3.01.125
the spring whom you have stain'd with mud, 5.02.170
hand, | because she was enforc'd, stain'd, and 5.03. 38
my reputation stain'd | with tybalt's slander — ROM 3.01.111
now i have stain'd the childhood of our joy 3.03. 95
that have a father kill'd, a mother stain'd, HAM 4.04. 57
behold it stain'd | with his most noble blood. ANT 5.01. 25
an image like thyself, all stain'd with gore, VEN 664
she with blood had stain'd her stain'd excuse. LUC 1316
she with blood had stain'd her stain'd excuse. 1316
seemed to appear | (like bright things stain'd) 1435
my gross blood be stain'd with this abuse, 1655
look'd black, and that false tarquin stain'd. 1743
that it could so preposterously be stain'd, | to SON 109.11
STAINED 7 FR 0.0008 REL FR 7 V 0 P
back to the stained field, | you equal potents, JN 2.01.357
the faiths of men ne'er stained with revolt; 4.02. 6
and wash away thy country's stained spots. 1H6 3.03. 57
let all untruths stand by thy stained name, TRO 5.02.179
not know | the stained taste of violated troth; LUC 1059
my stained blood to tarquin i'll bequeath, 1181
and by this chaste blood so unjustly stained, 1836
STAINES 1 FR 0.0001 REL FR 0 V 1 P
husband, let me bring thee to staines. H5 2.03. 2 P
STAINETH 2 FR 0.0002 REL FR 2 V 0 P
or as the berry breaks before it staineth, | or VEN 460
the world may stain when heaven's sun staineth. SON 33.14
STAINING 1 FR 0.0001 REL FR 1 V 0 P
not put my reputation now | in any staining act. AWW 3.07. 7
STAINLESS 2 FR 0.0002 REL FR 2 V 0 P
of great estate, of fresh and stainless youth; TN 1.05.259
play'd for a pair of stainless maidenhoods. ROM 3.02. 13
STAINS 9 FR 0.0010 REL FR 9 V 0 P
to look into the blots and stains of right. JN 2.01.114
full of unpleasing blots and sightless stains, 3.01. 45
from all the impure blots and stains thereof; R3 3.07.234
this, which stains | the stony entrance of this ROM 5.03.140
it stains the glory in that happy verse | which TIM 1.01. 16
great men shall press | for tinctures, stains, JC 2.02. 89
which the hot tyrant stains, and soon bereaves, VEN 797
and stains her face with his congealed blood. 1122
that spots and stains love's modest snow-white LUC 196
STAIR 1 FR 0.0001 REL FR 1 V 0 P
and bring thee cords made like a tackled stair, ROM 2.04.189
STAIRS 13 FR 0.0014 REL FR 3 V 10 P
why, shall i always keep below stairs? ADO 5.02. 10 P
the stairs, as he treads on them, kiss his feet. LLL 5.02.330
hearts are all as false | as stairs of sand, MV 3.02. 84
have they made a pair of stairs to marriage, AYL 5.02. 38 P
his industry is up stairs and down stairs, his 1H4 2.04.100 P
his industry is up stairs and down stairs, his 2.04.100 P
when she was gone down stairs, desire me to be 2H4 2.01. 99 P
for god's sake thrust him down stairs. 2.04.188 P
thrust him down stairs! 2.04.190 P
come, get you down stairs. 2.04.195 P
get you down stairs. 2.04.203 P
nose him as you go up the stairs into the lobby. HAM 4.03. 37 P
slaver with lips as common as the stairs | that CYM 1.06.105
STAIR-WORK 1 FR 0.0001 REL FR 0 V 1 P
this has been some stair-work, some trunk-work,
WT 3.03. 74 P
STAKE* 18 FR 0.0020 REL FR 15 V 3 P
batter his skull, or paunch him with a stake, TMP 3.02. 90
i will die in it at the stake. ADO 1.01.233 P
what, and stake down? MV 3.02.215 P
shall ne'er win at that sport, and stake down. 3.02.217 P
my honor's at the stake, which to defeat, | i AWW 2.03.149
have you not set mine honor at the stake, | and TN 3.01.118
seest a game play'd home, the rich stake drawn, WT 1.02.248
curse, miscreant, when thou com'st to the stake. 1H6 5.03. 44
place barrels of pitch upon the fatal stake, 5.04. 57
call hither to the stake my two brave bears, 2H6 5.01.144
i see my reputation is at stake, | my fame is TRO 3.03.227
my fortunes and my friends at stake requir'd | i COR 3.02. 63
for we are at the stake, | and bay'd about with JC 4.01. 48
they have tied me to a stake; MAC 5.07. 1
quarrel in a straw | when honor's at the stake. HAM 4.04. 56
bringing the murderous coward to the stake; LR 2.01. 62
i am tied to th' stake, and i must stand the 3.07. 54
lay down my soul at stake. OTH 4.02. 13
STAKES* 3 FR 0.0003 REL FR 3 V 0 P
stead whereof sharp stakes pluck'd out of hedges 1H6 1.01.117
lead | so stakes me to the ground i cannot move. ROM 1.04. 16
than i did truly find her, stakes this ring, CYM 5.05.188
STAL'D 1 FR 0.0001 REL FR 1 V 0 P
which, out of use and stal'd by other men, JC 4.01. 38
/STALE* 1 FR 0.0001 REL FR 1 V 0 P
valiant lord | shall not so /stale his palm, TRO 2.03.191
STALE* 26 FR 0.0029 REL FR 21 V 5 P
it hither, | for stale to catch these thieves. TMP 4.01.187
poor i am but his stale. ERR 2.01.101
you mightily hold up — to a contaminated stale, ADO 2.02. 25 P
to link my dear friend to a common stale. 4.01. 65
find — | a proverb never stale in thrifty mind. MV 2.05. 55
and mine, but it grows something stale with me. AYL 2.04. 62 P
to make a stale of me amongst these mates? SHR 1.01. 58
to cast thy wand'ring eyes on every stale, 3.01. 90
and make stale | the glistering of this present, WT 4.01. 13
patience is stale, and i am weary of it. R2 5.05.103
of men, | so stale and cheap to vulgar company, 1H4 3.02. 41
you basket-hilt stale juggler, you! 2H4 2.04.131 P
had he none else to make a stale but me? 3H6 3.03.260
rascals, that stale old mouse-eaten dry cheese, TRO 5.04. 10 P
was none in rome to make a stale | but saturnine TIT 1.01.304
that is something stale and hoar ere it be spent ROM 2.04.133 P
did use | to stale with ordinary oaths my love JC 1.02. 73
how /weary, stale, flat, and unprofitable | seem HAM 1.02.133
than doth, within a dull, stale, tired bed, | go LR 1.02. 13
the stale of horses and the gilded puddle ANT 1.04. 62
her, nor custom stale | her infinite variety. 2.02.234
poor i am stale, a garment out of fashion, | and CYM 3.04. 51
vassal, and induce | stale gravity to dance; TNK 5.01. 85
not halting under crimes | many and stale. 5.04. 11
for now 'tis stale to sigh, to weep, and groan. LUC 1362
what are precepts worth | of stale example? LC 268
STALENESS 1 FR 0.0001 REL FR 1 V 0 P
for want, | but weary for the staleness. PER 5.01. 58
/STALE'T 1 FR 0.0001 REL FR 1 V 0 P
i will venture | to /stale't a little more. COR 1.01. 92
STALK* 9 FR 0.0010 REL FR 6 V 3 P
o, ay, stalk on, stalk on, the fowl sits. ADO 2.03. 92 P
o, ay, stalk on, stalk on, the fowl sits. 2.03. 92 P
rage, | and stalk in blood to our possession? JN 2.01.266
their lips were four red roses on a stalk, R3 4.03. 12
no, pandarus, i stalk about her door, | like to TRO 3.02. 8
with martial stalk hath he gone by our watch. HAM 1.01. 66
here comes that which grows to the stalk, never PER 4.06. 41 P
she crops the stalk, and in the breach appears VEN 1175
reserv'd the stalk and gave him all my flower. LC 147
STALKING-HORSE 1 FR 0.0001 REL FR 0 V 1 P
he uses his folly like a stalking-horse, and AYL 5.04.106 P
STALKS 3 FR 0.0003 REL FR 2 V 1 P
why, 'a stalks up and down like a peacock — a TRO 3.03.251 P
see, it stalks away! HAM 1.01. 50
into the chamber wickedly he stalks, | and LUC 365
STALL 3 FR 0.0003 REL FR 2 V 1 P
stall this in your bosom, and i thank you for AWW 1.03.126 P
looks, | and we shall feed like oxen at a stall, 1H4 5.02. 14
we could not stall together | in the whole world ANT 5.01. 39
STALL'D *(also install'd)*
STALL'D 2 FR 0.0002 REL FR 2 V 0 P
in thy rights as thou art stall'd in mine! R3 1.03.205
and stall'd the deer that thou shouldst strike, PP 18. 2
STALLED 1 FR 0.0001 REL FR 1 V 0 P
the steed is stalled up, and even now | to tie VEN 39
STALLING 1 FR 0.0001 REL FR 0 V 1 P
that differs not from the stalling of an ox? AYL 1.01. 10 P
STALLION 1 FR 0.0001 REL FR 1 V 0 P
fall a-cursing, like a very drab, | a stallion. HAM 2.02.587
STALLS 4 FR 0.0004 REL FR 4 V 0 P
that work for bread upon athenian stalls, | were MND 3.02. 10
six score fat oxen standing in my stalls, | and SHR 2.01.358
stalls, bulks, windows, | are smother'd up, COR 2.01.210
turn'd wild in nature, broke their stalls, flung MAC 2.04. 16
/STAMFORD 1 FR 0.0001 REL FR 0 V 1 P
how a good yoke of bullocks at /stamford fair? 2H4 3.02. 38 P
STAMMER 1 FR 0.0001 REL FR 0 V 1 P
i would thou couldst stammer, that thou mightst AYL 3.02.199 P
STAMMERS 1 FR 0.0001 REL FR 0 V 1 P
by my troth, i think fame but stammers 'em, they TNK 2.01. 27 P
STAMP 25 FR 0.0028 REL FR 24 V 1 P
and, at our stamp, here o'er and o'er one falls; MND 3.02. 25
and be honorable | without the stamp of merit? MV 2.09. 39
nay, look not big, nor stamp, nor stare, nor SHR 3.02.228
to brag and stamp and swear | upon my party! JN 3.01.122
as not a soldier of this season's stamp | should 1H4 4.01. 4
under my feet i stamp thy cardinal's hat; 1H6 1.03. 49
your hearts i'll stamp out with my horse's heels 1.04.108
stamp, rave, and fret, that i may sing and dance 3H6 1.04. 91
your fire-new stamp of honor is scarce current. R3 1.03.255
he regard | the stamp of nobleness in any person H8 3.02. 12
methinks i see him stamp thus, and call thus: COR 1.03. 32
gods, | he has the stamp of martius, and i have 1.06. 23
his sword, death's stamp, | where it did mark, 2.02.107
the empress sends it thee, thy stamp, thy seal, TIT 4.02. 69
before me now | would one day stamp upon me. TIM 1.02.144
hanging a golden stamp about their necks, | put MAC 4.03.153
men, | carrying, i say, the stamp of one defect, HAM 1.04. 31
for use almost can change the stamp of nature, 3.04.168
let it stamp wrinkles in her brow of youth, LR 1.04.284
that /has an eye can stamp and counterfeit OTH 2.01.243 P
'tween man and man they weigh not every stamp;
CYM 5.04. 24
who hath upon him still that natural stamp. 5.05.366
haste, | i stamp this kiss upon thy currant lip. TNK 1.01.216
to stamp the seal of time in aged things, | to LUC 941
some fresher stamp of the time-bettering days. SON 82. 8
STAMP'D 11 FR 0.0012 REL FR 11 V 0 P
and so great a figure | be stamp'd upon it. MM 1.01. 50
bears the figure of an angel | stamp'd in gold, MV 2.07. 57
he stamp'd and swore | as if the vicar meant to SHR 3.02.167
i, that am rudely stamp'd, and want love's R3 1.01. 16
your holy hat to be stamp'd on the king's coin. H8 3.02.325
his praise | have (almost) stamp'd the leasing. COR 5.02. 22
and too impatiently stamp'd with your foot. JC 2.01.244
was i know not where | when i was stamp'd. CYM 2.05. 5
reproach is stamp'd in collatinus' face, | and LUC 829
wherein is stamp'd the semblance of a devil. 1246
which vulgar scandal stamp'd upon my brow, | for SON 112. 2
STAMPED 2 FR 0.0002 REL FR 1 V 1 P
but we pay them for it with stamped coin, not WT 4.04.725 P
side, | although my seal be stamped in his face. TIT 4.02.127
STAMPS 5 FR 0.0005 REL FR 4 V 1 P
found thee of more value | than stamps in gold, WIV 3.04. 16
coin heaven's image | in stamps that are forbid. MM 2.04. 46
as the /event stamps them, but they have a good ADO 1.02. 7 P
nay, mark how lewis stamps as he were nettled. 3H6 3.03.169
he stamps, and bites the poor flies in his fume. VEN 316
STANCH *(see staunch)*
STANCHLESS 1 FR 0.0001 REL FR 1 V 0 P
affection such | a stanchless avarice that, were MAC 4.03. 78
/STAND 6 FR 0.0006 REL FR 6 V 0 P
/all /of /you /that /stand /and /look /upon /me R2 4.01.237
/stand thou when i command. R3 1.02. 39
/here /by /me, | /do /thou /for /him /stand. LR 1.04.143
/stand /you /not /so /amaz'd. 3.06. 33
/will /not /allow, | /stand /in /hard /cure. 3.06.100
/to /stand /against /the /deep //dread-bolted 4.07. 32
STAND 583 FR 0.0659 REL FR 468 V 115 P
stand fast, good fate, to his hanging, make the TMP 1.01. 30 P
that stand 'twixt me and milan, candied be they, 2.01.279
'tis best we stand upon our guard, | or that we 2.01.321
i will stand, and so shall trinculo. 3.02. 40 P
prithee stand further off. 3.02. 83 P
stand farther. — come, proceed. 3.02. 86
i will stand to, and feed, | although my last, 3.03. 49
my lord the duke, | stand to, and do as we. 3.03. 52

sir, why stand you | in this strange stare? 3.03. 94
there stand, | for you are spell–stopp'd. 5.01. 60
and how stand you affected to his wish? TGV 1.03. 60
in conclusion, i stand affected to her. 2.01. 84 P
to take a note of what i stand in need of, | to 2.07. 84
fellows, stand fast; i see a passenger. 4.01. 1
stand, sir, and throw us that you have about ye. 4.01. 3
peace, stand aside, the company parts. 4.02. 81
therefore i pray you stand not to discourse, 5.02. 44
in his country, simple though i stand here. WIV 1.01.219 P
in these times you stand on distance: 2.01.225 P
you stand upon your honor! 2.02. 20 P
but stand under the adoption of abominable terms 2.02.295 P
have, master slender, i stand wholly for you; 3.02. 61 P
never stand "you had rather" and "you had rather 3.03.125 P
now doth thy honor stand, | in him that was of 4.04. 8
that it may stand till the perpetual doom | in 5.05. 58
have i liv'd to stand at the taunt of one that 5.05.142 P
stand not amaz'd; 5.05.231
you have ta'en a special stand to strike at me, 5.05.235 P
they shall stand for seed. MM 1.02. 99 P
which else would stand under grievous imposition 1.02.188 P
as we love it, | but as we stand in fear — 2.03. 34
sins | stand more for number than for accompt. 2.04. 58
to know, | grace to stand, and virtue go; 3.02.264
shall then have no power to stand against us. 4.04. 13 P
come, i have found you out a stand most fit, 4.06. 10
stand like the forfeits in a barber's shop, | as 5.01.321
stand up, i say. 5.01.455
they stand at the door, master, bid them welcome ERR 3.01. 68
you stand here in the cold. 3.01. 71
more | than i stand debted to this gentleman. 4.01. 31
against thee presently, if thou dar'st stand. 5.01. 31
come, stand by me, fear nothing. 5.01.185
stay, stand apart, i know not which is which. 5.01.365
stand i condemn'd for pride and scorn so much? ADO 3.01.108
you are to bid any man stand, in the prince's 3.03. 26 P
how if 'a will not stand? 3.03. 27 P
if he will not stand when he is bidden, he is 3.03. 31 P
stand thee close then under this penthouse, for 3.03.103 P
some treason, masters; yet stand close. 3.03.107 P
we charge you, in the prince's name, stand! 3.03.165 P
stand thee by, friar. 4.01. 23
i stand dishonor'd, that have gone about | to 4.01. 64
leonato, stand i here? 4.01. 69
well, stand aside. 4.02. 30 P
here stand a pair of honorable men, | a third is 5.01.266
my will is your good will | may stand with ours, 5.04. 29
our late edict shall strongly stand in force: LLL 1.01. 11
that we must stand and play the murtherer in? 4.01. 8
a stand where you may make the fairest shoot. 4.01. 10
stand aside, good bearer. 4.01. 55
muster your wits, stand in your own defense, 5.02. 85
here stand i, lady, dart thy skill at me, 5.02.396
that you stand forfeit, being those that sue? 5.02.427
and stand between her back, sir, and the fire, 5.02.476
degree of the worthy, but i am to stand for him. 5.02.507 P
stand aside, good pompey. 5.02.587 P
stand forth, demetrius. MND 1.01. 24
stand forth, lysander. 1.01. 26
one aloof stand sentinel. 2.02. 26
speak, pyramus. thisby, stand forth. 3.01. 81 P
stand close; this is the same athenian. 3.02. 41
stand aside. 3.02.116
and dar'st not stand, nor look me in the face. 3.02.424
i pray you all, stand up. 4.01.141
this fellow doth not stand upon points. 5.01.118 P
nature's hand | shall not in their issue stand; 5.01.410
it, | and if it stand, as you yourself still do, MV 1.01.136
pray you, sir, stand up. 2.02. 81 P
under which lorenzo | desir'd us to make stand. 2.06. 2
behold, there stand the caskets, noble prince. 2.09. 4
how many then should cover that stand bare? 2.09. 44
nerissa and the rest, stand all aloof. 3.02. 42
that the comparison | may stand more proper, my 3.02. 46
i stand for sacrifice; 3.02. 57
or no, | so, thrice–fair lady, stand i, even so, 3.02.146
you see me, lord bassanio, where i stand, | such 3.02.149
rich, | that only to stand high in your account, 3.02.155
madam, it is, so you stand pleas'd withal. 3.02.209
know | a many fools, that stand in better place, 3.05. 68
make room, and let him stand before our face. 4.01. 16
you may as well go stand upon the beach | and 4.01. 71
i stand for judgment! 4.01.103
i stand here for law. 4.01.142
antonio and old shylock, both stand forth. 4.01.175
you stand within his danger, do you not? 4.01.180
and stand indebted, over and above, | in love 4.01.413
you shall perceive them make a mutual stand, 5.01. 77
now i'll stand to it, the pancakes were naught AYL 1.02. 65 P
stand you both forth now. 1.02. 71 P
i pray thee, if it stand with honesty, | buy 2.04. 91
here comes my sister reading, stand aside. 3.02.124
sir, and she stand him but a little, he will SHR 1.02.113 P
petruchio, stand by a while. 1.02.142
you | as for my patron, stand you so assur'd, 1.02.155
bianca, stand aside. 2.01. 24
skipper, stand back! 2.01.339
knows not which way to stand, to look, to speak, 4.01.185
stand by and mark the manner of his teaching. 4.02. 5
i pray you let it stand. 4.03. 44
i pray you stand good father to me now, | give 4.04. 21
as shall with either part's agreement stand? 4.04. 50
kate, let's stand aside and see the end of this 5.01. 61 P
i will stand for't a little, though therefore i AWW 1.01.133 P
have they leave | to stand on either part. 1.02. 15
and thy mind stand to't, boy, steal away bravely 2.01. 29
i'll see thee to stand up. 2.01. 62
and that at my bidding you could so stand up. 2.01. 65
of noble bachelors stand at my bestowing, | o'er 2.03. 53
stand no more off, | but give thyself unto my 4.02. 34
foh, prithee stand away. 5.02. 16 P
distracted clouds give way, so stand thou forth; 5.03. 35
too fine in thy evidence, therefore stand aside. 5.03.269 P
stand you awhile aloof. TN 1.04. 12
her, | be not denied access, stand at her doors, 1.04. 16
and he says he'll stand at your door like a 1.05.147 P
my house, and my house doth stand by the church. 3.01. 6 P
by thy tabor, if thy tabor stand by the church. 3.01. 10 P
stand here, make a good show on't; 3.04.288 P
you stand amaz'd, | but be of comfort. 3.04.337
do i stand there? 5.01.226
but, for me, | what case stand i in? WT 1.02.352
if you seek to prove, | i dare not stand by; 1.02.444
honor, i | will stand betwixt you and danger. 2.02. 64
from me to mine, | and only that i stand for. 3.02. 45
how now? canst stand? 4.03. 74 P
i can stand and walk. 4.03.111 P
o lady fortune, | stand you auspicious! 4.04. 52
not a word, a word, we stand upon our manners. 4.04.164
upon the water as he'll stand and read | as 4.04.173
but o, the thorns we stand upon! 4.04.585
then stand till he be three quarters and a dram 4.04.785 P
would speak to her and stand in hope of answer. 5.02.102 P
so long could i | stand by, a looker–on. 5.03. 85
then, all stand still; 5.03. 95
stand in his face to contradict his claim. JN 2.01.280
at the other hill | command the rest to stand. 2.01.299
why stand these royal fronts amazed thus? 2.01.356
and stand securely on their battlements | as in 2.01.374
or, if it must stand still, let wives with child 3.01. 89
thou shalt stand curs'd and excommunicate, | and 3.01.173
o lewis, stand fast! 3.01.208
more, | if thou stand excommunicate and curs'd? 3.01.223
if this same were a churchyard where we stand, 3.03. 40
that john may stand, then arthur needs must fall 3.04.139
hot, and look thou stand | within the arras. 4.01. 1
i will not struggle, i will stand stone–still. 4.01. 76
go stand within; let me alone with him. 4.01. 84
doth make a stand at what your highness will. 4.02. 39
i saw a smith stand with his hammer, thus, | the 4.02.193
all murthers past do stand excus'd in this; 4.03. 51
stand back, lord salisbury, stand back, i say; 4.03. 81
stand back, lord salisbury, stand back, i say; 4.03. 81
stand by, or i shall gall you, faulconbridge. 4.03. 94
i, who ready here do stand in arms | to prove by R2 1.03. 36
now for the rebels which stand out in ireland, 1.04. 38
whereof our uncle gaunt did stand possess'd. 2.01.162
will you permit that i shall stand condemn'd | a 2.03.119
for joy | to stand upon my kingdom once again. 3.02. 5
stand bare and naked, trembling at themselves? 3.02. 46
stand all apart, | and show fair duty to his 3.03.187
cousin, stand forth, and look upon that man. 4.01. 7
if that thy valure stand on sympathy, | there is 4.01. 33
ah, thou, the model where old troy did stand, 5.01. 11
as stand in narrow lanes | and beat our watch 5.03. 8
good aunt, stand up. 5.03.111
nay, do not say "stand up"; 5.03.111
say "pardon" first, and afterwards "stand up." 5.03.112
good aunt, stand up. 5.03.129
i do not sue to stand; 5.03.129
while i stand fooling here, his jack of the 5.05. 60
most omnipotent villain that ever cried "stand!" 1H4 1.02.109 P
if thou darest not stand for ten shillings. 1.02.141 P
stand close. 2.02. 3 P
stand. 2.02. 48 P
farewell, and stand fast. 2.02. 72 P
here, hard by. stand close. 2.02. 75 P
stand! 2.02. 81 P
stand close, i hear them coming. 2.02. 97 P
come, i prithee do thou stand in some by–room, 2.04. 29 P
do thou stand for my father and examine me upon 2.04.376 P
and here is my speech. stand aside, nobility. 2.04.389 P
do thou stand for me, and i'll play my father. 2.04.433 P
and here i stand. judge, my masters. 2.04.439 P
and stand the push | of every beardless vain 3.02. 66
and yet you will stand to it, you will not 3.03.162 P
quality, | but stand against us like an enemy. 4.03. 37
and god defend but still i should stand so, | so 4.03. 38
true rule | you stand against anointed majesty. 4.03. 40
whereby we stand opposed by such means | as you 5.01. 67
our soldiers stand full fairly for the day. 5.03. 29
gentleman in hand, and then stand upon security! 2H4 1.02. 37 P
taking up, then they must stand upon security. 1.02. 41 P
will 'a stand to't? 2.01. 4 P
i beseech you stand to me. 2.01. 64 P
stand from him, fellow, wherefore hang'st thou 2.01. 68
i stand the push of your one thing that you will 2.02. 37 P
peace, stand aside, know you where you are? 3.02.119 P
good master corporate bardolph, stand my friend, 3.02.220 P
go to, stand aside. 3.02.228 P
for my old dame's sake, stand my friend. 3.02.230 P
go to, stand aside. 3.02.233 P
here stand, my lords, and send discoverers forth 4.01. 3
of what conditions we shall stand upon? 4.01.163
me | that no conditions of our peace can stand. 4.01.182
our peace shall stand as firm as rocky mountains 4.01.186
the leaders, having charge from you to stand, 4.02. 99
court, stand my good lord in your good report. 4.03. 83 P
and, when they stand against you, may they fall 4.04. 95
stand from him, give him air, he'll straight be 4.04.116
to find, | you stand in coldest expectation. 5.02. 31
stand here by me, master shallow, i will make 5.05. 5 P
come here, pistol, stand behind me. 5.05. 10 P
but to stand stain'd with travel, and sweating 5.05. 24 P
stand for your own, unwind your bloody flag, H5 1.02.101
and let another half stand laughing by, | all 1.02.113
soul | shall stand sore charged for the wasteful 1.02.283
but he that temper'd thee, bade thee stand up, 2.02.118
for the dolphin, | i stand here for him. 2.04.116
but think | you stand upon the rivage and behold 3.pr. 14
i see you stand like greyhounds in the slips, 3.01. 31
so god sa' me, 'tis shame to stand still, it is 3.02.110 P
and such another neighbor | stand in our way. 3.06.158
basis by | took stand for idle speculation — 4.02. 31
will stand a' tiptoe when this day is named, 4.03. 42
stand away, captain gower, i will give treason 4.08. 13 P
he sent to hell, and none durst stand him; 1H6 1.01.123
reignier, stand thou as dolphin in my place; 1.02. 61
stand back, you lords, and give us leave a while 1.02. 70
stand back, thou manifest conspirator, | thou 1.03. 33
nay, stand thou back, i will not budge a foot: 1.03. 38
therefore stand up, and for these good deserts 3.04. 25
and make the cowards stand aloof at bay. 4.02. 52
shall our condition stand? 5.04.165
my masters, let's stand close. 2H6 1.03. 1 P
sandy plains | than where castles mounted stand. 1.04. 37
plains | than where castles mounted stand." 1.04. 69
stand by, my masters. 2.01. 70
alas, master, i am not able to stand alone; 2.01.142
i am not able to stand. 2.01.150 P
stand forth, dame eleanor cobham, gloucester's 2.03. 1
this staff of honor raught, there let it stand, 2.03. 43
and do not stand on quillets how to slay him; 3.01.261
sirs, stand apart, the king shall know your mind 3.02.242
pole | than stand uncover'd to the vulgar groom. 4.01.128
but methinks he should stand in fear of fire, 4.02. 62 P
stand, villain, stand, or i'll fell thee down. 4.02.115 P
stand, villain, stand, or i'll fell thee down. 4.02.115 P
see if his head will stand steadier on a pole, 4.07. 95 P
but boldly stand and front him to his face. 5.01. 86
and shall i stand, and thou sit in my throne? 3H6 1.01. 84
fight it out, and not stand cavilling thus. 1.01.117
come make him stand upon this molehill here 1.04. 67
cry, | the rest stand all aloof and bark at him. 2.01. 17
ay, crook–back, here i stand to answer thee, 2.02. 96
why stand we like soft–hearted women here, 2.03. 25
i'll never pause again, never stand still, 2.03. 30
and call them pillars that will stand to us; 2.03. 51
and in this covert will we make our stand, 3.01. 3
here stand we both and aim we at the best; 3.01. 8
in this self place where now we mean to stand. 3.01. 11
for many lives stand between me and home; 3.02.173
that thou shouldst stand while lewis doth sit. 3.03. 3
vouchsafe, at our request, to stand aside, 3.03.110
that you stand pensive as half malecontent? 4.01. 10
and for this once my will shall stand for law. 4.01. 50
now, brother richard, will you stand by us? 4.01.145
come on, my masters, each man take his stand, 4.03. 1
this is his tent, and see where stand his guard. 4.03. 23
this way, man, see where the huntsmen stand. 4.05. 15
stand you thus close to steal the bishop's deer? 4.05. 17
why, master mayor, why stand you in a doubt? 4.07. 27
brother, wherefore stand you on nice points? 4.07. 58
fair lords, take leave and stand not to reply. 4.08. 23
stand we in good array; 5.01. 62
resign thy chair, and where i stand kneel thou, 5.05. 19
my lord, stand back, and let the coffin pass. R3 1.02. 38
and by despairing shalt thou stand excused | for 1.02. 86
they that stand high have many blasts to shake 1.03.258
my hair doth stand an end to hear her curses. 1.03.303
tut, tut, my lord, we will not stand to prate; 1.03.349
how he doth stand affected to our purpose, | and 3.01.171
and i believe will never stand upright | till 3.02. 39
and stand between two churchmen, good my lord — 3.07. 48
stand all apart. cousin of buckingham — 4.02. 1
cold fearful drops stand on my trembling flesh. 5.03.181
high–rear'd bulwarks, stand before our faces. 5.03.242
cast, | and i will stand the hazard of the die. 5.04. 10
if we shall stand still, | in fear our motion H8 1.02. 85
stand forth, and with bold spirit relate what 1.02.129
let's stand close and behold him. 2.01. 55
as i am made without him, so i'll stand, | if 2.02. 51
how you stand minded in the weighty difference 3.01. 58
the cardinal | cannot stand under them. 3.02. 3
wild river break, | and stand unshaken yours. 3.02.199
you come to take your stand here, and behold 4.01. 2
stand close, the queen is coming. 4.01. 36
stand these poor people's friend, and urge the 4.02.157
stand up, good canterbury! 5.01.113
give me thy hand, stand up; 5.01.115
the good i stand on is my truth and honesty. 5.01.122
present, and behold | that chair stand empty; 5.02. 45
be what they will, may stand forth face to face, 5.02. 82
all that stand about him are under the line, 5.03. 42 P
stand close up, or i'll make your head ache. 5.03. 88
stand up, lord. 5.04. 9
great in fame as she was, | and so stand fix'd. 5.04. 47
troilus will stand to the proof, if you'll prove TRO 1.02.129 P
shall we stand up here and see them as they pass 1.02.178 P
after seven years' siege yet troy walls stand, 1.03. 12
and look how many grecian tents do stand 1.03. 79
but by degree, stand in authentic place? 1.03.108
to blench from this and to stand firm by honor. 2.02. 68
troy must not be, nor goodly ilion stand. 2.02.109
valor | to stand the push and enmity of those 2.02.137
it, the walls will stand till they fall of 2.03. 9 P
we must with all our main of power stand fast; 2.03.262
i stand condemn'd for this. 3.03.219
and down like a peacock — a stride and a stand; 3.03.252 P
if e'er thou stand at mercy of my sword, | name 4.04.114
go, gentle knight, | stand by our ajax. 4.05. 89
there they stand yet, and modestly i think | the 4.05.222
stand fair, i pray thee, let me look on thee. 4.05.235
stand again. 4.05.248
stand where the torch may not discover us. 5.02. 5
let all untruths stand by thy stained name, 5.02.179
stand fast, and wear a castle on thy head! 5.02.187
i'll stand to–day for thee and me and troy. 5.03. 36
and i do stand engag'd to many greeks, | even in 5.03. 68
farewell, the gods with safety stand about thee! 5.03. 94
i'll fight with him alone. stand, diomed. 5.06. 9
stand, stand, thou greek, thou art a goodly mark 5.06. 27
stand, stand, thou greek, thou art a goodly mark 5.06. 27
stand ho! yet are we masters of the field. 5.10. 1
and feebling such as stand not in their liking COR 1.01.195
if you'll stand fast, we'll beat them to their 1.04. 41
and stand upon my common part with those | that 1.09. 39
the people, when he shall stand for his place. 2.01.149 P
doubt not | the commoners, for whom we stand, 2.01.227
were he to stand for consul, never would he 2.01.232
how many stand for consulships? 2.02. 2 P
for i cannot | put on the gown, stand naked, and 2.02.137
do not stand upon't. 2.02.150
if it may stand with the tune of your voices 2.03. 85 P
why in this woolvish /toge should i stand here 2.03.115
so then the volsces stand but as at first, 3.01. 4
or let us stand to our authority, | or let us 3.01.207
stand fast, | we have as many friends as enemies 3.01.230
and they | stand in their ancient strength. 4.02. 7
let me but stand, i will not hurt your hearth. 4.05. 24 P
those my banishers, | stand i before thee here. 4.05. 84
of the senators but they stand bald before him. 4.05.194 P
the commonwealth doth stand, and so would do, 4.06. 14

stand, and go back. 5.02. 1
but stand | as if a man were author of himself, 5.03. 35
o, stand up blest! 5.03. 52
you, and pray you | stand to me in this cause. 5.03.199
his stoutness | when he did stand for consul, 5.06. 27
stand, aufidius, | and trouble not the peace. 5.06.126
of rome, for whom we stand | a special party, TIT 1.01. 20
stand gracious to the rites that we intend! 1.01. 78
madam, stand resolv'd, but hope withal | the 1.01.135
every thing | in readiness for hymenaeus stand, 1.01.325
stand up. 1.01.485
this way, or not at all, stand you in hope. 2.01.119
for now i stand as one upon a rock, | environ'd 3.01. 93
stand by me, lucius, do not fear thine aunt. 4.01. 5
and if he stand /on hostage for his safety, 4.04.105
while i stand by and weep to hear him speak. 5.03. 95
stand all aloof, but, uncle, draw you near | to 5.03.151
there let him stand and rave and cry for food. 5.03.180
move is to stir, and to be valiant is to stand; ROM 1.01. 10 P
a dog of that house shall move me to stand! 1.01. 11 P
me they shall feel while i am able to stand, and 1.01. 28 P
may stand in number, though in reck'ning none. 1.02. 33
years, | for then she could stand high-lone; 1.03. 36
the measure done, i'll watch her place of stand, 1.05. 50
ready stand | to smooth that rough touch with a 1.05. 95
letting it there stand | till she had laid it 2.01. 25
let me stand here till thou remember it. 2.02.171
i shall forget, to have thee still stand there, 2.02.172
o, let us hence, i stand on sudden haste. 2.03. 93
/pardon-me's, who stand so much on the new form, 2.04. 34 P
in a minute than he will stand to in a month. 2.04.149 P
and thou must stand by too and suffer every 2.04.155 P
stand not amazed, the prince will doom thee 3.01.134
stand up; 3.03. 75
stand up, stand up, stand, and you be a man. 3.03. 88
stand up, stand up, stand, and you be a man. 3.03. 88
stand up, stand up, stand, and you be a man. 3.03. 88
for juliet's sake, for her sake, rise and stand; 3.03. 89
why, i am glad on't, this is well, stand up. 4.02. 28
hence, and stand aloof. 5.03. 1
i am almost afraid to stand alone | here in the 5.03. 10
e'er thou hearest or seest, stand all aloof, 5.03. 26
and here i stand both to impeach and purge 5.03.226
grave, | and bid me stand aloof, and so i did. 5.03.282
and we, poor mates, stand on the dying deck, TIM 4.02. 20
in purity of manhood stand upright | and say, 4.03. 14
when gouty keepers of thee cannot stand. 4.03. 47
all villains that do stand by thee are pure. 4.03.361
needs | stand for a villain in thine own work? 5.01. 38
we stand much hazard if they bring not timon. 5.02. 5
stand you directly in antonio's way | when he JC 1.02. 3
stand close a while, for here comes one in haste 1.03.131
shall rome stand under one man's awe? 2.01. 52
i think he will stand very strong with us. 2.01.142
we all stand up against the spirit of caesar, 2.01.167
boy, stand aside. 2.01.312
here will i stand till caesar pass along, | and 2.03. 11
i go to take my stand, | to see him pass on to 2.04. 25
fly not, stand still; 3.01. 83
stand fast together, lest some friend of 3.01. 87
and drawing days out, that men stand upon. 3.01.100
didst thou fall, and here thy hunters stand, 3.01.205
seeing those beads of sorrow stand in thine, 3.01.284
a ring, stand round. 3.02.164 P
stand from the hearse, stand from the body. 3.02.165 P
stand from the hearse, stand from the body. 3.02.165 P
nay, press not so upon me, stand far off. 3.02.167
stand back; room, bear back! 3.02.168 P
he should stand | one of the three to share it? 4.01. 14
stand ho! 4.02. 1
give the word ho! and stand. 4.02. 2
stand ho! 4.02. 32
stand ho! speak the word along. 4.02. 33
stand! 4.02. 34
stand! 4.02. 35
stand! 4.02. 36
must i stand and crouch | under your testy humor 4.03. 45
ground | do stand but in a forc'd affection, 4.03.205
you, we will stand and watch your pleasure. 4.03.249
they stand, and would have parley. 5.01. 21
stand fast, titinius; we must out and talk. 5.01. 22
the gods to-day stand friendly, that we may, 5.01. 93
stand not to answer; 5.03. 43
so mix'd in him that nature might stand up | and 5.05. 74
makes him stand to, and not stand to; MAC 2.03. 34 P
makes him stand to, and not stand to; 2.03. 34 P
in the great hand of god i stand, and thence 2.03.130
was said | it should not stand in thy posterity, 3.01. 4
then stand with us. 3.03. 4
stand to't. 3.03. 15
if i stand here, i saw him. 3.04. 73
stand not upon the order of your going, | but go 3.04.118
hour | stand aye accursed in the calendar! 4.01.134
observe her, stand close. 5.01. 20 P
as i did stand my watch upon the hill, | i 5.05. 32
nay, answer me. stand and unfold yourself. HAM 1.01. 2
i think i hear them. stand ho! who is there? 1.01. 14
do, if it will not stand. 1.01.141
act of fear, | stand dumb and speak not to him. 1.02.206
and each particular hair to stand an end, | like 1.05. 19
a silence in the heavens, the rack stand still, 2.02.484
i stand in pause where i shall first begin, 3.03. 42
life in excrements, | start up and stand an end. 3.04.122
how stand i then, | that have a father kill'd, a 4.04. 56
where is this king? sirs, stand you all without. 4.05.113
to this point i stand, | that both the worlds i 4.05.134
the wand'ring stars and makes them stand | like 5.01.256
wear | and stand a comma 'tween their amities, 5.02. 42
does it not, think thee, stand me now upon — 5.02. 63
and his crib shall stand at the king's mess. 5.02. 86 P
but in my terms of honor | i stand aloof, and 5.02.247
should i | stand in the plague of custom, and LR 1.02. 3
now, gods, stand up for bastards! 1.02. 22
canst serve where thou dost stand condemn'd, 1.04. 5
the lady brach may stand by th' fire and stink. 1.04.112 P
the moon | to stand /'s auspicious mistress. 2.01. 40
if i would stand against thee, would the reposal 2.01. 68
stand, rogue, stand, you neat slave! 2.02. 41 P
stand, rogue, stand, you neat slave! 2.02. 41 P
here i stand your slave, | a poor, infirm, weak, 3.02. 19
offer to defend him, | stand in assured loss. 3.06. 95
tied to th' stake, and i must stand the course. 3.07. 54
give me thy sword. a peasant stand up thus? 3.07. 80
stand still. 4.06. 11
set me where you stand. 4.06. 24
you stand. 4.06. 65
how stiff is my vild sense | that i stand up, 4.06.280
person, | the which immediacy may well stand up, 5.03. 65
holla, stand there! OTH 1.02. 56
for do but stand upon the foaming shore, | the 2.01. 11
(not surfeited to death) | stand in bold cure. 2.01. 51
on the brow o' th' sea | stand ranks of people, 2.01. 54
i stand accomptant for as great a sin), | but 2.01.293
for his quick hunting, stand the putting on, 2.01.304
i can stand well enough, and i speak well enough 2.03.115 P
he's a soldier fit to stand by caesar | and give 2.03.122
he shall in strangeness stand no farther off 3.03. 12
that i should deny, | or stand so mamm'ring on. 3.03. 70
stand you a while apart, | confine yourself but 4.01. 74
come, stand not amaz'd at it, but go along with 4.02.239 P
here, stand behind this /bulk, straight will he 5.01. 1
here, at thy hand; be bold, and take thy stand. 5.01. 7
there stand i in much peril. 5.01. 21
the world to weet | we stand up peerless. ANT 1.01. 40
pray you stand farther from me. 1.03. 18
and stand the buffet | with knaves that smells 1.04. 20
would stand and make his eyes grow in my brow; 1.05. 32
were't not that we stand up against them all, 2.01. 44
ah, stand by. 3.11. 41
an absolute hope | our landmen will stand up. 4.03. 11
it were, to stand | on more mechanic compliment. 4.04. 31
stand close, and list him. 4.09. 6
where yond pine does stand | i shall discover 4.12. 1
darkling stand | the varying shore o' th' world! 4.15. 10
the villain would not stand me. CYM 1.02. 14 P
stand you? 1.02. 17 P
that thou mayst stand | t' enjoy thy banish'd 2.01. 64
up | their deer to th' stand o' th' stealer; 2.03. 70
to be unbent when thou hast ta'en thy stand, 3.04.108
stand, stand! 5.02. 11
stand, stand! 5.02. 11
stand, stand, and fight! 5.02. 13
stand, stand, and fight! 5.02. 13
cam'st thou from where they made the stand? 5.03. 1
stand, | or we are romans and will give you that 5.03. 25
stand, stand!" 5.03. 28
stand, stand!" 5.03. 28
the rest do nothing — with this word "stand, 5.03. 31
do nothing — with this word "stand, stand!" 5.03. 31
who dares not stand his foe, i'll be his friend; 5.03. 60
stand! 5.03. 88
where was he | that could stand up his parallel, 5.04. 54
stand by my side, you whom the gods have made 5.05. 1
come, stand thou by our side, | make thy demand 5.05.129
i stand on fire: | come to the matter. 5.05.168
here they stand martyrs, slain in cupid's wars; PER 1.01. 38
might stand peerless by this slaughter. 4.ch. 40
the sore terms we stand upon with the gods will 4.02. 34 P
of me, who stand /i' /th' gaps to teach you, 4.04. 8
you that your resorters stand upon sound legs. 4.06. 24 P
and so stand /aloof for more serious wooing. 4.06. 87 P
much money gi'n, | if they stand sound and well; TNK pr 3
stand up. 1.01. 35
pray stand up, | your grief is written in your 1.01.109
not dreams we stand before your puissance, 1.01.155
pray stand up. 1.01.205
our services stand now for thebes, not creon. 1.02. 99
must | with him stand to the mercy of our fate, 1.02.102
they stand a grise above the reach of report. 2.01. 28 P
first sees the enemy, shall i stand still, | and 2.02.194
how stand i then? 3.02. 20
for why, here stand i; 3.05. 12
may the stag thou hunt'st stand long, | and thy 3.05.154
stand off then. 3.06. 89
if such vows | stand for express will, all the 3.06.229
if your vow stand, shall curse me and my beauty, 3.06.247
stand both together: 4.02. 50
they shall stand in fire up to the nav'l, and in 4.03. 42 P
horror, who does stand accurs'd | of many mortal 5.03. 23
if you'll stand our friend to procure our pardon STM II.C 142 P
upon his compass'd crest now stand on end, | his VEN 272
his flattering "holla," or his "stand, i say"? 284
and they would stand auspicious to the hour, LUC 347
on, to make his stand | on her bare breast, the 438
a pretty while these pretty creatures stand, 1233
there pleading might you see grave nestor stand, 1401
thee befall'n, that thou dost trembling stand? 1599
rome herself in them doth stand disgraced) | by 1833
her stand she takes upon a steep-up hill. PP 9. 5
full oft, | a woman's nay doth stand for nought? 18.42
now stand you on the top of happy hours, | and SON 16. 5
in me | worthy perusal stand against thy sight, 38. 6
no matter then although my foot did stand | upon 44. 5
and yet to times in hope my verse shall stand, 60.13
the roses fearfully on thorns did stand, | /one 99. 8
your sweet hue, which methinks still doth stand, 104.11
at the wood's boldness by thee blushing stand. 128. 8
be, | to stand in thy affairs, fall by thy side. 151.12
self, that did in freedom stand | and was my own LC 143
o appetite, from judgment stand aloof! 166
how coldly those impediments stand forth | of 269

STANDARD 5 FR 0.0005 REL FR 3 V 2 P
shalt be my lieutenant, monster, or my standard. TMP 3.02. 16 P
your lieutenant if you list, he's no standard. 3.02. 17 P
if underneath the standard of the french | she 1H6 2.01. 23
and in my standard bear the arms of york, | to 2H6 1.01.256
sir william brandon, you shall bear my standard. R3 5.03. 22

STANDARDS 3 FR 0.0003 REL FR 3 V 0 P
advance your standards, and upon them, lords; LLL 4.03.364
advance your standards, draw your willing swords R3 5.03.264
advance our standards, set upon our foes. 5.03.348

STANDER-BY 1 FR 0.0001 REL FR 1 V 0 P
i would not be a stander-by to hear | my WT 1.02.279

STANDERS 1 FR 0.0001 REL FR 1 V 0 P
when they fall, as being slippery standers, TRO 3.03. 84

STANDERS-BY 4 FR 0.0004 REL FR 3 V 1 P
that all the standers-by had wet their cheeks R3 1.02.162
rivers and dorset, you were standers-by, | and 1.03.209
that i have said to some my standers-by, | "lo TRO 4.05.190
it is not for any standers-by to curtal his CYM 2.01. 11 P

STANDEST 2 FR 0.0002 REL FR 2 V 0 P
thee, thou lamb, that standest as his prey; LLL 4.01. 89
and in that very line, harry, standest thou, 1H4 3.02. 85

STANDETH 3 FR 0.0003 REL FR 2 V 1 P
it standeth north-north-east and by east from LLL 1.01.245 P
here standeth thomas mowbray, duke of norfolk, R2 1.03.110
the question then, lord hastings, standeth thus: 2H4 1.03. 15

/STANDING 1 FR 0.0001 REL FR 1 V 0 P
/standing /before /the /sun /of /bullingbrook, R2 4.01.261

STANDING 32 FR 0.0036 REL FR 27 V 5 P
to be asleep | with eyes wide open — standing, TMP 2.01.214
well — i am standing water. 2.01.221
of hills, brooks, standing lakes, and groves, 5.01. 33
do cream and mantle like a standing pond, | and MV 1.01. 89
six score fat oxen standing in my stalls, | and SHR 2.01.358
the danger is in standing to't. AWW 3.02. 41 P
'tis with him in standing water, between boy and TN 1.05.159 P
like a cipher | (yet standing in rich place), i WT 1.02. 7
and will continue | the standing of his body. 1.02.431
here standing | to prate and talk for life and 3.02. 40
poor trespasses, | more monstrous standing by; 3.02.190
the spirits, | standing like stone with thee. 5.03. 42
standing on slippers, which his nimble haste JN 4.02.197
there be gallows standing in england when thou 1H4 1.02. 59 P
sheath, you bowcase, you vile standing tuck — 2.04.247 P
that his mountain sire, on mountain standing, H5 2.04. 57
though standing naked on a mountain top, | where 2H6 3.02.336
'tis but surmis'd whiles thou art standing by, 3.02.347
for standing by when richard stabb'd her son. R3 3.03. 17
you know the cause, sir, of my standing here. COR 2.03. 62
you into love, | standing your friendly lord. 2.03.190
like a great sea-mark, standing every flaw, 5.03. 74
how this grace | speaks his own standing! TIM 1.01. 31
talk not of standing. JC 3.01. 89
things standing thus unknown, shall i leave HAM 5.02.345
drinks the green mantle of the standing pool; LR 3.04.133 P
we | have us'd to conquer standing on the earth, ANT 3.07. 65
cupids | of silver, each on one foot standing, CYM 2.04. 90
and am right glad he is not standing here | to 5.05.296
our lodgings, standing bleak upon the sea, PER 3.02. 14
eye | of the fair breeder that is standing by." VEN 282
not suppress'd, for standing by her side, | his LUC 425

STANDING-BED 1 FR 0.0001 REL FR 0 V 1 P
his castle, his standing-bed and truckle-bed; WIV 4.05. 7 P

STANDING-BOWL 1 FR 0.0001 REL FR 1 V 0 P
say we drink this standing-bowl of wine to him. PER 2.03. 65

/STANDS 2 FR 0.0002 REL FR 1 V 1 P
thus /stands the case: 3H6 4.05. 4
/look /where /he /stands /and /glares! LR 3.06. 23 P

STANDS 166 FR 0.0187 REL FR 137 V 29 P
why then, how stands the matter with them? TGV 2.05. 20 P
when it stands well with him, it stands well 2.05. 22 P
stands well with him, it stands well with her. 2.05. 23 P
it stands under thee indeed. 2.05. 31 P
(which, unrevers'd, stands in effectual force) 3.01.225
here she stands: 5.04.129
and stands so firmly on his wive's frailty, yet WIV 2.01.233 P
thus stands it with me: MM 1.02.145
and thy head stands so tickle on thy shoulders 1.02.172 P
stands at a guard with envy; 1.03. 51
to fine the faults whose fine stands in record, 2.02. 40
yet, as the matter now stands, he will avoid 3.01.196 P
richer than innocency, stands for the facing. 3.02. 9 P
first, his integrity | stands without blemish; 5.01.108
that stands on tricks when i am undispos'd: ERR 1.02. 80
in what part of her body stands ireland? 3.02.116 P
consider how it stands upon my credit. 4.01. 68
degree | stands in attainder of eternal shame. LLL 1.01.157
i am the king, for so stands the comparison; 4.01. 79 P
for it stands too right. 5.02.565
cross'd, | it stands as an edict in destiny. MND 1.01.151
the fold stands empty in the drowned field, 2.01. 96
but since he stands obdurate, | and that no MV 4.01. 8
never to part with it, and here he stands. 5.01.171
down, and that which here stands up | is but a AYL 1.02.250
gallops withal, and who he stands still withal. 3.02.311 P
where in the purlieus of this forest stands | a 4.03. 76
i hope this reason stands for my excuse. SHR in.2. 124
it stands so that i may hardly tarry so long. in.2. 125 P
thus it stands: 1.01.179
signior hortensio, thus it stands with me: 1.02. 53
when he stands where i am and sees you there. 3.02. 40 P
and here she stands, touch her whoever dare, 3.02.233
then here's a man stands that has brought his AWW 2.01. 63
of my dear father's gift stands chief in power, 2.01.112
yet stands off | in differences so mighty. 2.03.120
best set thy lower part where thy nose stands. 2.03.252 P
or, the church stands by thy tabor, if thy tabor TN 3.01. 9 P
so stands this squire | offic'd with me. WT 1.02.171
(for, as the case now stands, it is a curse | he 2.03. 88
my life stands in the level of your dreams, 3.02. 81
which stands by like a weather-bitten conduit of 5.02. 55 P
as now it coldly stands), when first i woo'd her 5.03. 36
of him it holds, stands young plantagenet, | son JN 2.01.238
and he that stands upon a slipp'ry place | makes 3.04.137
and derby | stands here for god, his sovereign, R2 1.03.105
wherein the king stands generally condemn'd. 2.02.132
there stands the castle, by yon tuft of trees, 2.03. 53
fortune comes to years, | stands for my bounty. 2.03. 67
on what condition stands it and wherein? 2.03.107
it stands your grace upon to do him right. 2.03.138
bullingbrook — for yon methinks he stands — 3.03. 91
that stands upon your royal grandsire's bones, 3.03.106
sir john stands to his word, the devil shall 1H4 1.02.117 P
sirrah jack, thy horse stands behind the hedge; 2.02. 70 P
the land is burning, percy stands on high, | and 3.03.203
what, stands thou idle here? 5.03. 40
his back, and the whole frame stands upon pins. 2H4 3.02.144 P
so the question stands. 4.01. 53
now, cousin, wherefore stands our army still? 4.02. 98
though the truth of it stands off as gross | as H5 2.02.103
that stands upon the rolling restless stone — 3.06. 29

there stands your friend for the devil; 3.07.118 P
what is this castle call'd that stands hard by? 4.07. 88
for one fair french maid that stands in my way. 5.02.318 P
or whose will stands but mine? 1H6 1.03. 11
think at the north gate, for there stands lords. 1.04. 66
and stands upon the honor of his birth, | if he 2.04. 28
the burning torch in yonder turret stands. 3.02. 30
stands with the snares of war to tangle thee. 4.02. 22
the help of one stands me in little stead. 4.06. 31
stands on a tickle point now they are gone. 2H6 1.01.216
and shakes his head, and trembling stands aloof, 1.01.227
well, so it stands; 1.02.104
and, for my wife, i know not how it stands. 2.01.188
whose beam stands sure, whose rightful cause 2.01.201
look, look, it stands upright, | like lime–twigs 3.03. 15
thus stands my state, 'twixt cade and york 4.09. 31
it shall ne'er be said, while england stands, 4.10. 42
whoever got thee, there thy mother stands, | for 3H6 2.02.133
beseeching thee (if with thy will it stands) 2.03. 38
and rear it in the place your father's stands. 2.06. 86
like one that stands upon a promontory | and 3.02.135
yet here prince edward stands, king henry's son. 3.03. 73
if warwick knew in what estate he stands, | 'tis 4.03. 18
your horse stands ready at the park–corner. 4.05. 19
brave followers, yonder stands the thorny wood, 5.04. 67
see where his grace stands, 'tween two clergymen R3 3.07. 95
for it stands me much upon | to stop all hopes 4.02. 58
or else my kingdom stands on brittle glass. 4.02. 61
stands in the gap and trade of moe preferments, H8 5.01. 36
know | there's none stands under more calumnious 5.01.112
you not | how your state stands i' th' world, 5.01.127
then thus for you, my lord, it stands agreed, 5.02.122
he stands there like a mortar–piece to blow us. 5.03. 45 P
say he is a very man per se and stands alone. TRO 1.02. 15 P
troy in our weakness stands, not in her strength 1.03.137
achilles stands i' th' entrance of his tent. 3.03. 38
i wonder now how yonder city stands | when we 4.05.211
and stands colossus–wise, waving his beam, 5.05. 9
neither foolish in our stands | nor cowardly in COR 1.06. 2
but to come by him where he stands, by ones, by 2.03. 42 P
and manhood is call'd foolery when it stands 3.01.245
since that to both | it stands in like request? 3.02. 51
here stands my other son, a banish'd man, | and TIT 3.01. 99
lo by thy side where rape and murder stands; 5.02. 45
here stands the spring whom you have stain'd 5.02.170
how stands your dispositions to be married? ROM 1.03. 65
and here stands all your state: 3.03.166
day | stands tiptoe on the misty mountain tops. 3.05. 10
then, since the case so stands as now it doth, 3.05.216
and the high east | stands, as the capitol, JC 2.01.111
my credit now stands on such slippery ground 3.01.191
king | stands not within the prospect of belief, MAC 1.03. 74
but why | stands macbeth thus amazedly? 4.01.126
throne | by his own interdiction stands accus'd, 4.03.107
stands scotland where it did? 4.03.164
behold where stands | th' usurper's cursed head: 5.09. 20
upon whose influence neptune's empire stands HAM 1.01.119
nor stands it safe with us | to let his madness 3.03. 1
and how his audit stands who knows save heaven? 3.03. 82
here stands the man; 5.01. 16 P
sir, there she stands: LR 1.01.197
when it is mingled with regards that stands 1.01.239
tell why one's nose stands i' th' middle on 's 1.05. 19 P
my time | than stands on any shoulder that i see 2.02. 94
nature in you stands on the very verge | of his 2.04.147
being the worst | stands in some rank of praise. 2.04.258
stands still in esperance, lives not in fear. 4.01. 4
our preparation stands | in expectation of them. 4.04. 22
the main descry | stands on the hourly thought. 4.06.214
for my state | stands on me to defend, not to 5.01. 69
the cyprus wars | (which even now stands in act) OTH 1.01.151
for that it stands not in such warlike brace, 1.03. 24
who stands so eminent in the degree of this 2.01.236 P
and the condition of this country stands, i 2.03.301 P
and life, stands up | for the main soldier; ANT 1.02.190
to his love, which stands | an honorable trial. 1.03. 74
stands he, or sits he? 1.05. 19
it only stands | our lives upon to use our 2.01. 50
that stands upon the swell at the full of tide, 3.02. 49
whom in constancy you think stands so safe. CYM 1.04.126 P
thy mistress how | the case stands with her; 1.05. 67
of your isle, which stands | as neptune's park, 3.01. 18
yet the traitor | stands in worse case of woe. 3.04. 87
why stands he so perplex'd? 5.05.108
before thee stands this fair hesperides, | with PER 1.01. 27
here stands a lord, and there a lady weeping; 1.04. 47
when peers thus knit, a kingdom ever stands. 2.04. 58
and tyrus stands | in a litigious peace. 3.03. 2
this borrowed passion stands for true old woe; 4.04. 24
my temple stands in ephesus, hie thee thither, 5.01.240
it, | and, by mine honor, once again it stands, TNK 3.06.289
he that stands | in the /first place with arcite 4.02. 75
his nose stands high, a character of honor; 4.02.110
state | stands many a father with his child. 5.04. 3
legs, on his hind hoofs | /... on end he stands, 5.04. 77
stands on his hinder–legs with list'ning ear, VEN 698
for know, my heart stands armed in mine ear, 779
thus stands she in a trembling ecstasy, | till, 895
through the length of times he stands disgraced; LUC 718
as the poor frighted deer that stands at gaze, 1149
herds stands weeping, flocks all sleeping, PP 17.27
and nothing stands but for his scythe to mow: SON 60.12
hours, | but all alone stands hugely politic, 124.11
when most impeach'd stands least in thy control. 125.14
STAND'ST 15 FR 0.0017 REL FR 12 V 3 P
that stand'st between her father's ground and MND 5.01.175
in which predicament i say thou stand'st; MV 4.01.357
fair sun which shows me where thou stand'st, | i R2 4.01. 35
what, stand'st thou still, and hear'st such a 1H4 2.04. 80 P
though thou stand'st more sure than i could do, 2H4 4.05.202
by his treason, stand'st not thou attainted, 1H6 2.04. 92
lo, there thou stand'st, a breathing valiant man 4.02. 31
stand'st thou aloof upon comparison? 5.04.150
stand'st out? COR 1.01.241
sword | and, when it bows, stand'st up. 1.04. 54
with him if thou stand'st not i' th' state of 5.02. 64 P
but wherefore stand'st thou with thy weapon TIT 3.01. 48
no, thou stand'st single, th' art not on him yet TIM 2.02. 56 P
not to consider in what case thou stand'st ANT 3.13. 54
pisanio, thou that stand'st so for posthumus! CYM 3.05. 56
STAND–UNDER 1 FR 0.0001 REL FR 0 V 1 P
why, stand–under and under–stand is all one. TGV 2.05. 32 P
/STANIEL 1 FR 0.0001 REL FR 0 V 1 P
and with what wing the /staniel checks at it! TN 2.05.113 P
STANLEY 23 FR 0.0026 REL FR 23 V 0 P
with sir john stanley, in the isle of man. 2H6 2.03. 13
and sir john stanley is appointed now | to take 2.04. 77
stanley, i prithee go, and take me hence, | i 2.04. 91
come, stanley, shall we go? 2.04.104
now, my lord hastings and sir william stanley, 3H6 4.05. 1
stanley, i will requite thy forwardness. 4.05. 23
what think'st thou then of stanley? will not he? R3 3.01.167
one from the lord stanley. 3.02. 3
cannot my lord stanley sleep these tedious 3.02. 6
stanley did dream the boar did /rase our helms, 3.04. 82
how now, lord stanley, what's the news? 4.02. 46
stanley, he is your wive's son: 4.02. 87
stanley, look to your wife. 4.02. 92
my mind is chang'd. stanley, what news with you? 4.04.456
but leave behind | your son, george stanley. 4.04.495
my son george stanley is frank'd up in hold; 4.05. 3
sir gilbert talbot, sir william stanley, 4.05. 13
and here receive we from our father stanley 5.02. 5
where is lord stanley quarter'd, do you know? 5.03. 34
call up lord stanley, bid him bring his power. 5.03.290
what says lord stanley? 5.03.342
after the battle let george stanley die. 5.03.346
but tell me, is young george stanley living? 5.05. 9
STANLEY'S 1 FR 0.0001 REL FR 1 V 0 P
a pursuivant–at–arms | to stanley's regiment, R3 5.03. 60
STANZE 1 FR 0.0001 REL FR 1 V 0 P
let me hear a staff, a stanze, a verse; LLL 4.02.104
STANZO 1 FR 0.0001 REL FR 0 V 1 P
come, more, another stanzo. AYL 2.05. 18 P
STANZOS 1 FR 0.0001 REL FR 0 V 1 P
call you 'em stanzos? AYL 2.05. 19 P
STAPLE 1 FR 0.0001 REL FR 0 V 1 P
verbosity finer than the staple of his argument. LLL 5.01. 17 P
/STAPLES 1 FR 0.0001 REL FR 1 V 0 P
/with /massy /staples | /and /corresponsive /and TRO pr 17
STAR 50 FR 0.0056 REL FR 39 V 11 P
doth depend upon | a most auspicious star, whose TMP 1.02.182
at first i did adore a twinkling star, | but now TGV 2.06. 9
i will make a star chamber matter of it. WIV 1.01. 2 P
by welkin and her star! 1.03. 92
look, th' unfolding star calls up the shepherd. MM 4.02.203 P
near her, she would infect to the north star. ADO 2.01.250 P
but then there was a star danc'd, and under that 2.01.335 P
turk, there's no more sailing by the star. 3.04. 58 P
lights, | that give a name to every fixed star, LLL 1.01. 89
she (an attending star) scarce seen a light. 4.03.227
it shall be moon, or star, or what i list, | or SHR 4.05. 7
that i should love a bright particular star AWW 1.01. 86
parolles, you were born under a charitable star. 1.01.191 P
but /or every blazing star or at an earthquake, 1.03. 87 P
under the influence of the most receiv'd star, 2.01. 55 P
leg, it was form'd under the star of a galliard. TN 1.03.133 P
nine changes of the wat'ry star hath been | the WT 1.02. 1
happy star reign now! 1.02.363
over | by each particular star in heaven and 1.02.425
i see thy glory like a shooting star | fall to R2 2.04. 19
small most greatly lived | this star of england. H5 ep 6
a far more glorious star thy soul will make 1H6 1.01. 55
bright star of venus, fall'n down on the earth, 1.02.144
what low'ring star now envies thy estate, | that 2H6 3.01.206
cause | to wail the dimming of our shining star; R3 2.02.102
mercury from jove, | or like a star disorb'd? TRO 2.02. 46
lords, was't not a happy star | led us to rome, TIT 4.02. 32
but i am constant as the northern star, | of JC 3.01. 60
when yond same star that's westward from the HAM 1.01. 36
and the moist star | upon whose influence 1.01.118
being nature's livery, or fortune's star, | his 1.04. 32
"lord hamlet is a prince out of thy star; 2.02.141
that, as the star moves not but in his sphere, 4.07. 15
skill shall, like a star i' th' darkest night, 5.02.256
his goatish disposition on the charge of a star! LR 1.02.128 P
i am, had the maidenl'est star in the firmament 1.02.132 P
the star is fall'n. ANT 4.14.106
o eastern star! 5.02.308
our jovial star reign'd at his birth, and in CYM 5.04.105
had | upon his neck a mole, a sanguine star, 5.05.364
heavens make a star of him! PER 5.03. 79
to thee no star be dark! TNK 1.04. 1
that fortunate bright star, the fair emilia, 3.06.146
i' th' night, and you | the only star to shine. 5.03. 20
look how a bright star shooteth from the sky, VEN 815
from whom each lamp and shining star doth borrow 861
no comfortable star did lend his light, | no LUC 164
till whatsoever star that guides my moving SON 26. 9
it is the star to every wand'ring bark, | whose 116. 7
nor that full star that ushers in the even 132. 7
STAR–BLASTING 1 FR 0.0001 REL FR 0 V 1 P
bless thee from whirlwinds, star–blasting, and LR 3.04. 59 P
STAR–CROSS'D 1 FR 0.0001 REL FR 1 V 0 P
a pair of star–cross'd lovers take their life; ROM pr 6
STAR'D 3 FR 0.0003 REL FR 3 V 0 P
star'd each on other, and look'd deadly pale; R3 3.07. 26
was, | you star'd upon me with ungentle looks. JC 2.01.242
they star'd and were distracted; MAC 2.03.104
STARE 11 FR 0.0012 REL FR 10 V 1 P
sir, why stand you | in this strange stare? TMP 3.03. 95
i will stare him out of his wits; WIV 2.02.279 P
look not big, nor stamp, nor stare, nor fret, SHR 3.02.228
that makes him gasp, and stare, and catch the 2H6 3.02.371
why are you breathless, and why stare you so? JC 1.03. 2
men, wives, and children stare, cry out, and run 3.01. 97
that mak'st my blood cold, and my hair to stare? 4.03.280
when i do stare, see how the subject quakes. LR 4.06.108
nay, /an' you stare, we shall hear more anon. OTH 5.01.107
nay, stare not, masters, it is true indeed. 5.02.188
is in thy mind | that makes thee stare thus? CYM 3.04. 5
STARES 4 FR 0.0004 REL FR 4 V 0 P
cousin, that he stares and looks | so wildly? R2 5.03. 24
shall i be frighted when a madman stares? JC 4.03. 40
sometime he scuds far off, and there he stares, VEN 301
saw, | amazedly in her sad face he stares: LUC 1591
STAR–GAZERS 1 FR 0.0001 REL FR 1 V 0 P
that the star–gazers, having writ on death, VEN 509
STARING 7 FR 0.0008 REL FR 6 V 1 P
be /foul, | then nightly sings the staring owl, LLL 5.02.917
the bowl, | then nightly sings the staring owl, 5.02.926
they seem'd almost, with staring on one another, WT 5.02. 12 P
that ever wall–ey'd wrath or staring rage JN 4.03. 49
staring full ghastly, like a strangled man; 2H6 3.02.170
the staring ruffian shall it keep in quiet, VEN 1149
staring on priam's wounds with her old eyes, LUC 1448
STARINGS 1 FR 0.0001 REL FR 0 V 1 P
and to drinkings and swearings and starings, WIV 5.05.160 P
STARK 10 FR 0.0011 REL FR 8 V 2 P
not cuckold–mad — | but sure he is stark mad: ERR 2.01. 59
i think you are all mated, or stark mad. 5.01.282
that wench is stark mad or wonderful froward. SHR 1.01. 69
of the fives, stark spoil'd with the staggers, 3.02. 54 P
therefore on, or strip your sword stark naked; TN 3.04.251 P
done, | and then run mad indeed — stark mad! WT 3.02.183
many a nobleman lies stark and stiff | under the 1H4 5.03. 41
shall, stiff and stark and cold, appear like ROM 4.01.103
stark, as you see; CYM 4.02.209
and stood stark naked on the brook's green brim. PP 6.10
STARKLY 1 FR 0.0001 REL FR 1 V 0 P
when it lies starkly in the traveller's bones. MM 4.02. 67
STARK–NAK'D 1 FR 0.0001 REL FR 1 V 0 P
rather on nilus' mud | lay me stark–nak'd, and ANT 5.02. 59
STARLIGHT 3 FR 0.0003 REL FR 2 V 1 P
till candles, and starlight, and moonshine be WIV 5.05.102
by fountain clear, or spangled starlight sheen, MND 2.01. 29
she will find him by starlight. 5.01.314 P
STAR–LIKE 2 FR 0.0002 REL FR 2 V 0 P
shall star–like rise as great in fame as she was H8 5.04. 46
you, | whose star–like nobleness gave life and TIM 5.01. 63
STARLING 1 FR 0.0001 REL FR 1 V 0 P
i'll have a starling shall be taught to speak 1H4 1.03.224
STARR'D 1 FR 0.0001 REL FR 1 V 0 P
my third comfort | (starr'd most unluckily) is WT 3.02. 99
STARRY 1 FR 0.0001 REL FR 1 V 0 P
the starry welkin cover thou anon | with MND 3.02.356
/STARS 2 FR 0.0002 REL FR 2 V 0 P
/it /is /the /stars, | /the /stars /above /us, LR 4.03. 32
/the /stars /above /us, /govern /our /conditions 4.03. 33
STARS 82 FR 0.0092 REL FR 71 V 11 P
but truer stars did govern proteus' birth: TGV 2.07. 74
wilt thou reach stars, because they shine on 3.01.156
to ridiculous smiling — o, pardon me, my stars! LLL 3.01. 78 P
bright moon, and these thy stars, to shine 5.02.205
thus pour the stars down plagues for perjury. 5.02.394
and certain stars shot madly from their spheres, MND 2.01.153
thou coward, art thou bragging to the stars, 3.02.407
what stars do spangle heaven with such beauty, SHR 4.05. 31
happier the man whom favorable stars | allots 4.05. 40
whose baser stars do shut us up in wishes, AWW 1.01.183
be sanctified | by th' luckiest stars in heaven, 1.03.246
wherein toward me my homely stars have fail'd 2.05. 75
my stars shine darkly over me. TN 2.01. 3 P
in my stars i am above thee, but be not afraid 2.05.144 P
i thank my stars, i am happy. 2.05.170 P
jove and my stars be prais'd! 2.05.172 P
you would seek t' unsphere the stars with oaths, WT 1.02. 48
stars, stars, | and all eyes else dead coals! 5.01. 67
stars, stars, | and all eyes else dead coals! 5.01. 67
the stars, i see, will kiss the valleys first; 5.01.206
bidding me depend | upon thy stars, thy fortune, JN 3.01.126
now, you stars that move in your right spheres, 5.07. 74
and meteors fright the fixed stars of heaven, R2 2.04. 9
shall i so much dishonor my fair stars | on 4.01. 21
take purses go by the moon and the seven stars, 1H4 1.02. 14 P
two stars keep not their motion in one sphere, 5.04. 65
we have seen the seven stars. 2H4 2.04.187 P
tent to–night, are those stars or suns upon it? H5 3.07. 70 P
stars, my lord. 3.07. 71 P
and with them scourge the bad revolting stars 1H6 1.01. 4
but o malignant and ill–boding stars! 4.05. 6
may not be punish'd with my thwarting stars, 3H6 4.06. 22
for few men rightly temper with the stars; 4.06. 29
me, | the right and fortune of his happy stars, R3 3.07.172
lo at their birth good stars were opposite. 4.04.216
their coronets say so. these are stars indeed. H8 4.01. 54
as many farewells as be stars in heaven, | with TRO 4.04. 44
pibbles on the hungry beach | fillop the stars; COR 5.03. 59
earth–treading stars that make dark heaven light ROM 1.02. 25
some consequence yet hanging in the stars 1.04.107
two of the fairest stars in all the heaven, 2.02. 15
brightness of her cheek would shame those stars, 2.02. 19
die, | take him and cut him out in little stars, 3.02. 22
then i /defy you, stars! 5.01. 24
and shake the yoke of inauspicious stars | from 5.03.111
the fault, dear brutus, is not in our stars, JC 1.02.140
i cannot by the progress of the stars | give 2.01. 2
but signs of nobleness, like stars, shall shine MAC 1.04. 41
stars, hide your fires, | let not light see my 1.04. 50
as stars with trains of fire and dews of blood, HAM 1.01.117
make thy two eyes, like stars, start from their 1.05. 17
"doubt thou the stars are fire, | doubt that the 2.02.116
the wand'ring stars and makes them stand | like 5.01.256
the moon, and stars, as if we were villains on LR 1.02.121 P
reason why the seven stars are no moe than seven 1.05. 35 P
that their great stars | thron'd and set high? 3.01. 22
let me not name it to you, you chaste stars, OTH 5.02. 2
let all the number of the stars give light | to ANT 3.02. 65
moon and stars! 3.13. 95
when my good stars, that were my former guides, 3.13.145
mine his thoughts did kindle — that our stars, 5.01. 46
that knew the stars as i his characters; CYM 3.02. 28
they are worthy | to inlay heaven with stars. 5.05.352
that without covering, save yon field of stars, PER 1.01. 37
until our stars that frown lend us a smile. 1.04.108
yet cease your ire, you angry stars of heaven! 2.01. 1
had princes sit like stars about his throne, 2.03. 39
but her better stars | brought her to meteline, 5.03. 9
i am very cold, and all the stars are out too, TNK 3.04. 1
the little stars and all, that look like aglets. 3.04. 2
"i will be true, my stars, my fate," etc. 4.03. 57
our stars must glister with new fire, or be 5.01. 69
like stars asham'd of day, themselves withdrew. VEN 1032
where mortal stars as bright as heaven's LUC 13

but little stars may hide them when they list. 1008
and little stars shot from their fixed places, 1525
and the dove, | co–supremes and stars of love, PHT 51
not from the stars do i my judgment pluck, | and SON 14. 1
and, constant stars, in them i read such art 14.10
whereon the stars in secret influence comment; 15. 4
let those who are in favor with their stars | of 25. 1
when sparkling stars twire not, thou /gild'st 28.12
/START 1 FR 0.0001 REL FR 0 V 1 P
frame, and /start not so wildly from my affair. HAM 3.02.309 P
START 34 FR 0.0038 REL FR 31 V 3 P
but if he start, | it is the flesh of a WIV 5.05. 86
you have the start of me, i am dejected. 5.05.161 P
how if your husband start some other where? ERR 2.01. 30
blushing apparitions | to start into her face, a ADO 4.01.160
use your legs, take the start, run away." MV 2.02. 6 P
what's in "mother," | that you start at it? AWW 1.03.142
that the first face of neither on the start 3.02. 50
seven of my people, with an obedient start, make TN 2.05. 58 P
start not; WT 5.03.104
do but start | an echo with the clamor of thy JN 5.02.167
stirs | to rouse a lion than to start a hare! 1H4 1.03.198
you start away, | and lend no ear unto my 1.03.216
and start so often when thou sit'st alone? 2.03. 43
base inclination, and the start of spleen, | to 3.02.125
in the slips, | /straining upon the start. H5 3.01. 32
suddenly made him from my side to start | into 1H6 4.07. 12
and when i start, the envious people laugh, 2H6 2.04. 35
should make a start o'er seas and vanquish you? 4.08. 43
side, | tremble and start at wagging of a straw; R3 3.05. 7
should | so get the start of the majestic world JC 1.02.130
"brutus" will start a spirit as soon as "caesar. 1.02.147
good sir, why do you start, and seem to fear MAC 1.03. 51
start, eyes! 4.01.116
blame | his pester'd senses to recoil and start, 5.02. 23
slaughterous thoughts, | cannot once start me. 5.05. 15
two eyes, like stars, start from their spheres, HAM 1.05. 17
life in excrements, | start up and stand an end. 3.04.122
now fear i this will give it start again, 4.07.193
/bravery dost thou come | to start my quiet. OTH 1.01.101
unto a muss, kings would start forth | and cry, ANT 3.13. 91
then start amongst 'em | and, as an east wind, TNK 2.02. 12
thou hast the start now; 2.03. 8
'fore yourself | by some small start of time. 5.03. 38
"with this i did begin to start and cry, | and LUC 1639
/STARTED 2 FR 0.0002 REL FR 2 V 0 P
/it //rouge–mount, /at /which /name /i /started, R3 4.02.105
/then /away /she /started | /to /deal /with LR 4.03. 31
STARTED 3 FR 0.0003 REL FR 3 V 0 P
he started one poor heart of mine, in thee. TN 4.01. 59
and started when he look'd upon the tower, | as R3 3.04. 85
and then it started like a guilty thing | upon a HAM 1.01.148
STARTETH 1 FR 0.0001 REL FR 1 V 0 P
said, from her betumbled couch she starteth, LUC 1037
/STARTING 1 FR 0.0001 REL FR 1 V 0 P
/starting /thence /away | /to /what /may /be TRO pr 28
STARTING 4 FR 0.0004 REL FR 3 V 1 P
and starting so | he seem'd in running to devour 2H4 1.01. 46
with starting courage, | give with thy trumpet a TRO 4.05. 2
you mar all with this starting. MAC 5.01. 45 P
after this strange starting from your orbs, CYM 5.05.371
STARTING–HOLE 1 FR 0.0001 REL FR 0 V 1 P
what starting–hole? 1H4 2.04.263 P
STARTINGLY 1 FR 0.0001 REL FR 1 V 0 P
why do you speak so startingly and rash? OTH 3.04. 79
STARTLE 3 FR 0.0003 REL FR 3 V 0 P
patience herself would startle at this letter, AYL 4.03. 13
i'll startle you | worse than the sacring bell, H8 3.02.294
thou little know'st how thou dost startle me PER 5.01.146
STARTLES 3 FR 0.0003 REL FR 3 V 0 P
about, | startles and frights consideration, JN 4.02. 25
startles mine eyes, and makes me more amaz'd 5.02. 51
what fear is this which startles in your ears? ROM 5.03.194
STARTS 16 FR 0.0018 REL FR 15 V 1 P
you boggle shrewdly, every feather starts you. AWW 5.03.232
for she did speak in starts distractedly. TN 2.02. 21
mangling by starts the full course of their H5 ep 4
why starts thou? 2H6 4.01. 32
he bites his lip, and starts, | stops on a H8 3.02.113
speak a word | but it straight starts you. TRO 5.02.101
chance | that starts i' th' way before thee. COR 4.01. 37
drums in his ear, at which he starts and wakes, ROM 1.04. 86
and now falls on her bed, and then starts up, 3.03.100
o, these flaws and starts | (imposters to true MAC 3.04. 62
such unconstant starts are we like to have from LR 1.01.300 P
and by starts | his fretted fortunes give him ANT 4.12. 7
anon he starts at stirring of a feather; VEN 302
whereat she starts like one that spies an adder 878
auspicious to the hour, | even there he starts; LUC 348
by this starts collatine as from a dream, | and 1772
START–UP 1 FR 0.0001 REL FR 0 V 1 P
that young start–up hath all the glory of my ADO 1.03. 66 P
STARV'D 12 FR 0.0013 REL FR 9 V 3 P
the air hath starv'd the roses in her cheeks, TGV 4.04.154
are wolvish, bloody, starv'd, and ravenous. MV 4.01.138
am starv'd for meat, giddy for lack of sleep, SHR 4.03. 9
the turkeys in my pannier are quite starv'd. 1H4 2.01. 27 P
this same starv'd justice hath done nothing but 2H4 3.02.304 P
ay, come, you starv'd bloodhound. 5.04. 27 P
have stay'd in france, and starv'd in france, 2H6 1.01.135
it is too starv'd a subject for my sword. TRO 1.01. 93
for beauty starv'd with her severity | cuts ROM 1.01.219
we'll see 'em starv'd first. LR 5.03. 25
they are now starv'd for want of exercise; PER 1.04. 38
give them life whom hunger starv'd half dead. 1.04. 96
STARVE 17 FR 0.0019 REL FR 13 V 4 P
whilst i at home starve for a merry look: ERR 2.01. 88
when she did starve the general world beside LLL 2.01. 11
we must starve our sight | from lovers' food MND 1.01.222
with too much as they that starve with nothing. MV 1.02. 6 P
no, on the barren mountains let him starve; 1H4 1.03. 89
that wish'd him on the barren mountains starve. 1.03.159
i'll starve ere i'll rob a foot further. 2.02. 21 P
your grace may starve, perhaps, before that time 1H6 3.02. 48
ready to starve, and dare not touch his own. 2H6 1.01.229
he had better starve | than but once think his H8 5.02.167
never go home, here starve we out the night — TRO 5.10. 2
better it is to die, better to starve, | than COR 2.03.113
upon myself, | and so shall starve with feeding. 4.02. 51
be not, hang, beg, starve, die in the streets, ROM 3.05.192
aches contract and starve your supple joints! TIM 1.01.248
lest the bargain should catch cold and starve. CYM 1.04.167 P
nay then thou wilt starve sure; PER 2.01. 68 P
STARVED 5 FR 0.0005 REL FR 5 V 0 P
you drop manna in the way | of starved people. MV 5.01.295
do but behold yond poor and starved band, | and H5 4.02. 16
i fear me you but warm the starved snake, | who, 2H6 3.01.343
as frozen water to a starved snake. TIT 3.01.251
sight, | and by and by clean starved for a look; SON 75.10
STARVE–LACKEY 1 FR 0.0001 REL FR 0 V 1 P
and master starve–lackey the rapier and dagger MM 4.03. 14 P
STARVELING 5 FR 0.0005 REL FR 0 V 5 P
robin starveling, the tailor. MND 1.02. 58 P
robin starveling, you must play thisby's mother. 1.02. 60 P
starveling! 4.01.203 P
with me, and thou knowest he is no starveling. 1H4 2.01. 69 P
'sblood, you starveling, you /eel–skin, you 2.04.244 P
STARVES 1 FR 0.0001 REL FR 1 V 0 P
who starves the ears she feeds, and makes them PER 5.01.112
STARVETH 1 FR 0.0001 REL FR 1 V 0 P
need and oppression starveth in thy eyes, ROM 5.01. 70
STARVING 1 FR 0.0001 REL FR 1 V 0 P
starving for a time | of pell–mell havoc and 1H4 5.01. 81
/STATE 10 FR 0.0011 REL FR 8 V 2 P
and pluck commiseration of /his /state | from MV 4.01. 30
/the /resignation /of /thy /state /and /crown R2 4.01.179
/you /may /my /glories /and /my /state /depose, 4.01.192
/mine /own /tongue /deny /my /sacred /state, 4.01.209
/against /the /state /and /profit /of /this 4.01.225
/proud /majesty /a /subject, /state /a /peasant. 4.01.252
/that /lov'd /him, /as /the /state /stood /then, 2H4 4.01.113
/of /ancient /amities, /divisions /in /state, LR 1.02.146 P
/plumed /helm /thy /state /begins /to /threat, 4.02. 57
/something /he /left /imperfect /in /the /state, 4.03. 3 P
STATE 305 FR 0.0344 REL FR 280 V 25 P
and to him put | the manage of my state, as at TMP 1.02. 70
and to my state grew stranger, being transported 1.02. 76
set all hearts i' th' state | to what tune 1.02. 84
other two be brain'd like us, the state totters. 3.02. 6 P
highest queen of state, | great juno, comes, i 4.01.101
plead a new state in thy unrivall'd merit, | to TGV 5.04.144
and that, my state being gall'd with my expense, WIV 3.04. 5
in state as wholesome as in state 'tis fit, 5.05. 59
in state as wholesome as in state 'tis fit, 5.05. 59
love, the heavens themselves do guide the state; 5.05.232
acquaint her with the danger of my state; MM 1.02.179
by those that know the very nerves of state, 1.04. 53
the state, whereon i studied, | is like a good 2.04. 7
my vouch against you, and my place i' th' state, 2.04.156
trick of him to steal from the state, and usurp 3.02. 93 P
my business in this state | made me a looker–on 5.01.316
slander to th' state! | away with him to prison. 5.01.322
that's not my fault, he's master of my state. ERR 2.01. 95
whose weakness, married to thy /stronger state, 2.02.175
and to thy state of darkness hie thee straight: 4.04. 56
as a measure, full of state and ancientry; ADO 2.01. 77 P
so politic a state of evil that they will not 5.02. 63 P
conjoin'd | in the state of honorable marriage, 5.04. 30
a gait, a state, a brow, a breast, a waist, | a LLL 4.03.183
flat treason 'gainst the kingly state of youth. 4.03.289
so pair–taunt–like would i o'ersway his state 5.02. 67
trim gallants, full of courtship and of state. 5.02.363
keep some state in thy exit, and vanish. 5.02.594 P
the summer still doth tend upon my state; MND 3.01.155
when i told you | my state was nothing, i should MV 3.02.259
and doth impeach the freedom of the state, | if 3.02.278
will much impeach the justice of the state, 3.03. 29
soul, | from out the state of hellish cruelty! 3.04. 21
by the same example | will rush into the state. 4.01.222
venice, confiscate | unto the state of venice. 4.01.312
half | comes to the privy coffer of the state, 4.01.354
and yet, thy wealth being forfeit to the state, 4.01.365
the other half comes to the general state, 4.01.371
ay, for the state, not for antonio. 4.01.373
king be by, and then his state | empties itself, 5.01. 95
something that hath a reference to my state: AYL 1.03.127
thou art in a parlous state, shepherd. 3.02. 44 P
that were my state far worser than it is, | i SHR 1.02. 91
love | made me exchange my state with tranio, 5.01.125
disclose | the state of your affection, for your AWW 1.03.190
to her whose state is such that cannot choose 1.03.214
with any branch or image of thy state; 2.01.198
his valor, and my state that way is dangerous, 2.05. 11 P
lord, | the reasons of our state i cannot yield, 3.01. 10
above my fortunes, yet my state is well: TN 1.05.278
"above my fortunes, yet my state is well: 1.05.290
my state is desperate for my master's love; 2.02. 37
that cons state without book and utters it by 2.03.149 P
months married to her, sitting in my state — 2.05. 45 P
and then to have the humor of state; 2.05. 52 P
let thy tongue tang arguments of state; 2.05.151 P
let thy tongue /tang with arguments of state; 3.04. 70 P
in the streets, desperate of shame and state, 5.01. 64
briers and made | more homely than thy state. WT 4.04.426
beseech you | of your own state take care. 4.04.448
you pity not the state, nor the remembrance | of 5.01. 25
outfaced infant state, and done a rape | upon JN 2.01. 97
to me and to the state of my great grief | let 3.01. 70
with any long'd–for change or better state. 4.02. 8
my nobles leave me, and my state is braved, 4.02.243
the unowed interest of proud swelling state. 4.03.147
to any sovereign state throughout the world. 5.02. 82
put on | the lineal state and glory of the land! 5.07.102
or complot any ill | 'gainst us, our state, our R2 1.03.190
thy state of law is bond–slave to the law, | and 2.01.114
thy joys, friends, fortune, and thy state, | for 3.02. 72
bows | of double–fatal yew against thy state; 3.02.117
scoffing his state and grinning at his pomp, 3.02.163
the sky | the state and inclination of the day; 3.02.195
they will talk of state, for every one doth so 3.04. 27
poor queen, so that thy state might be no worse, 3.04.102
soul, | to think our former state a happy dream, 5.01. 18
now, | whose state and honor i for aye allow. 5.02. 40
but for the concord of my state and time | had 5.05. 47
first, to thy sacred state wish i all happiness. 5.06. 6
this chair shall be my state, this dagger my 1H4 2.04.378 P
thy state is taken for a join'd–stool, thy 2.04.380 P
ne'er seen but wond'red at, and so my state, 3.02. 57
soon kindled and soon burnt, carded his state, 3.02. 62
he hath more worthy interest to the state | than 3.02. 98
hand, | as ever off'red foul play in a state. 3.02.169
thou knowest in the state of innocency adam fell 3.03.165 P
i would the state of time had first been whole 4.01. 25
and in the neck of that, task'd the whole state; 4.03. 92
that you did nothing purpose 'gainst the state, 5.01. 43
but these mine eyes saw him in bloody state, 2H4 1.01.107
the great, | under the canopies of costly state, 3.01. 13
but that necessity so bow'd the state | that i 3.01. 73
down, royal state! 4.05.120
might make them look | too near unto my state. 4.05.212
speak in your state | what i have done that 5.02. 99
where it shall mingle with the state of floods, 5.02.132
that the great body of our state may go | in 5.02.136
accite | (as i before rememb'red) all our state, 5.02.142
divide | the state of man in divers functions, H5 1.02.184
but tell the dolphin i will keep my state, | be 1.02.273
with what great state he heard their embassy, 2.04. 32
whose state so many had the managing, | that ep 11
more blessed hap did ne'er befall our state. 1H6 1.06. 10
yes, when his holy state is touch'd so near. 3.01. 58
state holy or unhallow'd, what of that? 3.01. 59
pretend | malicious practices against his state. 4.01. 7
brave peers of england, pillars of the state, 2H6 1.01. 75
the state of normandy | stands on a tickle point 1.01.215
asleep, | to pry into the secrets of the state, 1.01.250
that were a state fit for his holiness. 1.03. 64
have practic'd dangerously against your state, 2.01.167
man, | there to be us'd according to your state. 2.04. 95
according to that state you shall be us'd. 2.04. 99
false allegations to o'erthrow his state? 3.01.181
that dread king that took our state upon him, 3.02.154
mischance unto my state by suffolk's means. 3.02.284
thus stands my state, 'twixt cade and york 4.09. 31
sufficeth that i have maintains my state | and 4.10. 22
king, | seditious to his grace and to the state. 5.01. 37
sturdy rebel sits, | even in the chair of state. 3H6 1.01. 51
and over the chair of state, where now he sits, 1.01.168
deadly, | i should lament thy miserable state. 1.04. 85
and had he match'd according to his state, | he 2.02.152
by my state i swear to thee | i speak no more 3.02. 93
it ill befits thy state | and birth that thou 3.03. 2
bona, | and replant henry in his former state. 3.03.198
majesty | to raise my state to title of a queen, 4.01. 68
though fortune's malice overthrow my state, | my 4.03. 46
seat, | and turn'd my captive state to liberty, 4.06. 3
my waned state for henry's regal crown. 4.07. 4
is prisoner to the foe, his state usurp'd, | his 5.04. 77
thy honor, state, and seat is due to me. R3 1.03.111
so stood the state when henry the sixt | was 2.03. 16
stood the state so? 2.03. 18
news, what news, in this our tott'ring state? 3.02. 37
think you, but that i know our state secure, | i 3.02. 81
death, | and i in better state than e'er i was. 3.02.104
your state of fortune, and your due of birth, 3.07.120
i am unfit for state and majesty. 3.07.205
tell me, what state, what dignity, what honor, 4.04.247
urge the necessity and state of times, | and be 4.04.416
sad, high, and working, full of state and woe: H8 pr 3
the state takes notice of the private difference 1.01.101
a single part in aught | pertains to th' state; 1.02. 42
to pepin or clotharius, they keep state so. 1.03. 10
that trick of state | was a deep envious one. 2.01. 44
my state now will but mock me. 2.01.101
be to the prejudice of her present state, | or 2.04.155
bearing a state of mighty moment in't | and 2.04.214
to wear our mortal state to come with her, 2.04.229
morning | papers of state he sent me to peruse, 3.02.121
part of business which | i bear i' th' state; 3.02.146
i not made you | the prime man of the state? 3.02.162
sacred person and | the profit of the state. 3.02.174
good, the state | of our despis'd nobility, our 3.02.290
this is the state of man: 3.02.352
in a rich chair of state, opposing freely | the 4.01. 67
and with the same full state pac'd back again 4.01. 93
an old man, broken with the storms of state, 4.02. 21
you not | how your state stands i' th' world, 5.01.127
who holds his state at door 'mongst pursuivants, 5.02. 24
with a general taint | of the whole state; 5.02. 64
for kindling such a combustion in the state. 5.03. 49 P
factious feasts, rails on our state of war, TRO 1.03.191
did move your greatness and this noble state 2.03.109
general | to call together all his state of war. 2.03.260
you are in the state of grace? 3.01. 15 P
the providence that's in a watchful state 3.03.196
durst never meddle) in the soul of state, 3.03.202
by priam and the general state of troy. 4.02. 67
hail, all the state of greece! 4.05. 65
the general state, i fear, | can scarce entreat 4.05.264
staves as lift them | against the roman state, COR 1.01. 69
and you slander | the helms o' th' state, who 1.01. 77
what ever have been thought /on in this state 1.02. 4
the state hath another, his wife another, and, i 2.01.108 P
power, | but was a petty servant to the state, 2.03.178
a place of potency and sway o' th' state, | if 2.03.182
disobedience, fed | the ruin of the state. 3.01.118
even when the navel of the state was touch'd, 3.01.123
that love the fundamental part of state | more 3.01.151
and bereaves the state | of that integrity which 3.01.158
time craves it as physic | for the whole state, 3.02. 34
from the volscian state to find you out there. 4.03. 11 P
our state thinks not so; 4.03. 16 P
is, and feasts the nobles of the state | at his 4.04. 9
and shows good husbandry for the volscian state, 4.07. 22
it was a bare petition of a state | to one whom 5.01. 20
i am an officer of state, and come | to speak 5.02. 3
if thou stand'st not i' th' state of hanging, or 5.02. 65 P
suits, | nor from the state nor private friends, 5.03. 18
and state of bodies would bewray what life | we 5.03. 95
he sits in his state, as a thing made for 5.04. 22 P
you lords and heads a' th' state, perfidiously 5.06. 90
to him that, for your honor and your state, TIT 1.01.259
and in this state she gallops night by night ROM 1.04. 70
more honorable state, more courtship lives | in 3.03. 34
and here stands all your state: 3.03.166

to move the heavens to smile upon my state, 4.03. 4
as are behoofeful for our state to–morrow. 4.03. 8
that state of fortune fall into my keeping, TIM 1.01.150
healths will make thee and thy state look ill, 1.02. 57 P
his promises fly so beyond his state | that what 1.02.197
hold, no reason | can sound his state in safety. 2.01. 13
had you not fully laid my state before me, 2.02.125
to have his pomp, and all what state compounds, 4.02. 35
best state, contentless, | hath a distracted and 4.03.245
th' eternal devil to keep his state in rome | as JC 1.02.160
of fear and warning | unto some monstrous state. 1.03. 71
and the state of a man, | like to a little 2.01. 67
thorough the hazards of this untrod state | with 3.01.136
to young octavius of the state of things. 3.01.296
by his plight, of the revolt | the newest state. MAC 1.02. 3
shakes so my single state of man that function 1.03.140
and our duties | are to your throne and state, 1.04. 25
when therewithal we shall have cause of state 3.01. 33
our hostess keeps her state, but in best time 3.04. 5
though in your state of honor i am perfect. 4.02. 66
snow, and the poor state | esteem him as a lamb, 4.03. 53
this bodes some strange eruption to our state. HAM 1.01. 69
other, | as it doth well appear unto our state, 1.01.101
in the most high and palmy state of rome, | a 1.01.113
th' imperial jointress to this warlike state, 1.02. 9
our state to be disjoint and out of frame, 1.02. 20
the safety and health of this whole state, | and 1.03. 21
something is rotten in the state of denmark. 1.04. 90
thereon, | let me be no assistant for a state, 2.02.166
'gainst fortune's state would treason have 2.02.511
him on to some confession | of his true state. 3.01. 10
th' expectation and rose of the fair state, 3.01.152
so far from cheer and from /your former state, 3.02.164
o wretched state! 3.03. 67
thy state is the more gracious, for 'tis a vice 5.02. 84 P
interest of territory, cares of state), | which LR 1.01. 50
reserve thy state, | and in thy best 1.01.149
shall find time | from this enormous state — 2.02.169
death on my state! 2.04.112
by some discretion that discerns your state 2.04.149
and speculations | intelligent of our state. 3.01. 25
with others whom the rigor of our state | forc'd 5.01. 22
for my state | stands on me to defend, not to 5.01. 68
rule in this realm, and the gor'd state sustain. 5.03.321
let loose on me the justice of the state | for OTH 1.01.139
for i do know the state | (how ever this may 1.01.147
side, | upon some present business of the state, 1.02. 90
himself, | or any of my brothers of the state, 1.02. 96
so was i bid report here to the state | by 1.03. 15
your special mandate for the state affairs 1.03. 72
please it your grace, on to the state affairs. 1.03.190
beseech you proceed to th' affairs of state. 1.03.220
most humbly therefore bending to your state, | i 1.03.235
something sure of state, | either from venice, 3.04.140
pray heaven it be state matters, as you think, 3.04.155
the business of the state does him offense, 4.02.166
of your fault be known | to the venetian state. 5.02.337
i have done the state some service, and they 5.02.339
turk | beat a venetian and traduc'd the state, 5.02.354
and to the state | this heavy act with heavy 5.02.370
and the time's state | made friends of them, ANT 1.02. 91
the business she hath broached in the state 1.02.171
as have not thrived | upon the present state, 1.03. 52
and speaks as loud | as his own state and ours, 1.04. 30
it hath been taught us from the primal state 1.04. 41
yet if you there | did practice on my state, 2.02. 39
in state of health thou say'st, and thou say'st 2.05. 56
quake in the present winter's state, and wish CYM 2.04. 5
which attends | in place of greater state. 3.03. 78
fitting my bounty and thy state, i'll give it; 5.05. 98
amazement shall drive courage from the state, PER 1.02. 26
from the dejected state wherein he is, | he 2.02. 46
cause, | and not to be a rebel to her state; 2.05. 62
shrouded in cloth of state, balm'd and 3.02. 65
though wayward fortune did malign my state, | my 5.01. 89
who, hearing of your melancholy state, | did 5.01.220
the intelligence of state came in the instant TNK 1.02.106
since in our terrene state petitions are not 1.03. 14
nor in a state of life; 1.04. 25
freed of this plight, and in their morning state 1.04. 34
o state of nature, fail together in me, | since 3.02. 31
on't to give half my state that both she and i 4.03. 67 P
i' th' self–same state | stands many a father 5.04. 2
could not have brought you to the state of men. STM II.C 67
gay skins with thought of their sharp state, III 18
unlock'd the treasure of his happy state; LUC 16
his honor, his affairs, his friends, his state, 45
that thou shalt see thy state, and pity mine." 644
let thy thoughts, low vassals to thy state" — 666
for greatest scandal waits on greatest state. 1006
nor laugh with his companions at thy state, 1066
began to clothe his wit in state and pride, 1809
and wear their brave state out of memory: SON 15. 8
eyes, | i all alone beweep my outcast state, 29. 2
haply i think on thee, and then my state | (like 29.10
that then i scorn to change my state with kings. 29.14
when i have seen such interchange of state, | or 64. 9
of state, | or state itself confounded to decay, 64.10
i see a better state to me belongs | than that 92. 7
thou wouldst use the strength of all thy state! 96.12
and brought to medicine a healthful state 118.11
if my dear love were but the child of state, 124. 1
they would change their state | and situation 128. 9
o, but with mine compare thou thine own state, 142. 3
but when she saw my woeful state, | straight in 145. 4
with others thou shouldst not abhor my state: 150.12
STATELIER 1 FR 0.0001 REL FR 1 V 0 P
a statelier pyramis to her i'll rear | than 1H6 1.06. 21
STATELY 11 FR 0.0012 REL FR 9 V 2 P
with slow but stately pace kept on his course, R2 5.02. 10
victory | we with our stately presence glorify, 1H6 1.01. 21
shall lay your stately and air–braving towers, 4.02. 13
here's a silly stately style indeed! 4.07. 72
that we spend the time | with stately triumphs, 3H6 5.07. 43
that like the stately /phoebe 'mongst her nymphs TIT 1.01.316
our empress' shame, and stately rome's disgrace! 4.02. 60
solemn march | goes slow and stately by them. HAM 1.02.202
and when from a stately cedar shall be lopp'd CYM 5.04.140 P
and when from a stately cedar shall be lopp'd 5.05.438 P
"to fill with worm–holes stately monuments, | to LUC 946
STATE'S 4 FR 0.0004 REL FR 4 V 0 P
thou must be hang'd at the state's charge. MV 4.01.367
the king's will or the state's allowance, | a H8 3.02.322
rather our state's defective for requital | than COR 2.02. 50
of whom, even to the state's best health, i have TIM 2.02.197
/STATES 1 FR 0.0001 REL FR 1 V 0 P
in /states unborn and accents yet unknown! JC 3.01.113
STATES 13 FR 0.0014 REL FR 13 V 0 P
our states are forfeit, seek not to undo us. LLL 5.02.425
according to the measure of their states. AYL 5.04.175
how like you this wild counsel, mighty states? JN 2.01.395
to set the exact wealth of all our states | all 1H4 4.01. 46
comets, importing change of times and states, 1H6 1.01. 2
for know, my lords, the states of christendom, 5.04. 96
jocund, and suppos'd their states were sure, R3 3.02. 84
the unity and married calm of states | quite TRO 1.03.100
and mighty states characterless are grated | to 3.02.188
of this sphere | to propagate their states. TIM 1.01. 67
forgetting thy great deeds when neighbor states, 4.03. 95
kings, queens, and states, | maids, matrons, nay CYM 3.04. 37
shaker of o'er–rank states, thou grand decider TNK 5.01. 63
STATESMAN 2 FR 0.0002 REL FR 1 V 1 P
appear to the envious a scholar, a statesman, MM 3.02.146 P
my parasite, my soldier, statesman, all. WT 1.02.168
STATESMEN 1 FR 0.0001 REL FR 1 V 0 P
bond–slaves and pagans shall our statesmen be. OTH 1.02. 99
STATE–STATUES 1 FR 0.0001 REL FR 1 V 0 P
here where we sit, or sit | state–statues only. H8 1.02. 88
STATILIUS 1 FR 0.0001 REL FR 1 V 0 P
statilius show'd the torchlight, but, my lord, JC 5.05. 2
STATION 7 FR 0.0008 REL FR 6 V 1 P
throngs, and puff | to win a vulgar station; COR 2.01.215
you, poor gentleman, take up some other station; 4.05. 30 P
now, if you have a station in the file, | not i' MAC 3.01.101
in the unshrinking station where he fought, 5.09. 8
and they in france of the best rank and station HAM 1.03. 73
a station like the herald mercury | new lighted 3.04. 58
her motion and her station are as one; ANT 3.03. 19
STATIST 1 FR 0.0001 REL FR 1 V 0 P
i do believe | (statist though i am none, nor CYM 2.04. 16
STATISTS 1 FR 0.0001 REL FR 1 V 0 P
i once did hold it, as our statists do, | a HAM 5.02. 33
STATUE 19 FR 0.0021 REL FR 17 V 2 P
my substance should be statue in thy stead. TGV 4.04.201
the princess hearing of her mother's statue, WT 5.02. 95 P
but we came | to see the statue of our queen. 5.03. 10
came to look upon, | the statue of her mother. 5.03. 14
the statue is but newly fix'd; 5.03. 47
i'll make the statue move indeed, descend, | and 5.03. 88
we'll set thy statue in some holy place, | and 1H6 3.03. 14
erect his statue and worship it, | and make my 2H6 3.02. 80
the primitive statue and oblique memorial of TRO 5.01. 54 P
as to jove's statue, and the commons made | a COR 2.01.266
for i will /raise her statue in pure gold, ROM 5.03.299
set this up with wax | upon old brutus' statue. JC 1.03.146
she dreamt to–night she saw my statue, | which, 2.02. 76
your statue spouting blood in many pipes, | in 2.02. 85
give him a statue with his ancestors. 3.02. 50
even at the base of pompey's statue | (which all 3.02.188
rather than a life, | a statue, than a breather. ANT 3.03. 21
does, | build his statue to make him glorious. PER 2.ch. 14
and dead, | statue contenting but the eye alone, VEN 213
/STATUES 1 FR 0.0001 REL FR 0 V 1 P
with any man that knows the /statues, he may ADO 3.03. 79 P
STATUES 4 FR 0.0004 REL FR 4 V 0 P
but, like dumb statues or breathing stones, R3 3.07. 25
cold statues of the youth, and, in a word, TRO 5.10. 20
tells him of trophies, statues, tombs, and VEN 1013
when wasteful war shall statues overturn, | and SON 55. 5
STATURE 6 FR 0.0006 REL FR 3 V 3 P
about my stature; TGV 4.04.158
if he be of any reasonable stature, he may creep WIV 3.03.130 P
what stature is she of? AYL 3.02.268 P
i for the limb, the thews, the stature, bulk, 2H4 3.02.259 P
that unmatch'd form and stature of blown youth HAM 3.01.159
her stature to an inch, as wand–like straight, PER 5.01.109
STATURES 1 FR 0.0001 REL FR 1 V 0 P
she hath made compare | between our statures: MND 3.02.291
STATUTE 4 FR 0.0004 REL FR 4 V 0 P
and follows close the rigor of the statute, | to MM 1.04. 67
his life | according to the statute of the town, ERR 1.02. 6
ere humane statute purg'd the gentle weal; MAC 3.04. 75
the statute of thy beauty thou wilt take, | thou SON 134. 9
STATUTE–CAPS 1 FR 0.0001 REL FR 1 V 0 P
well, better wits have worn plain statute–caps. LLL 5.02.281
/STATUTES 1 FR 0.0001 REL FR 1 V 0 P
/my /acts, /decrees, /and /statutes /i /deny; R2 4.01.213
STATUTES 9 FR 0.0010 REL FR 6 V 3 P
we have strict statutes and most biting laws MM 1.03. 19
that the strong statutes | stand like the 5.01.320
seal'd his rigorous statutes with their bloods, ERR 1.01. 9
against the laws and statutes of this town, 5.01.126
and to keep those statutes | that are recorded LLL 1.01. 17
then we are like to have biting statutes, unless 2H6 4.07. 17 P
his statutes cancell'd, and his treasure spent; 3H6 5.04. 79
more piercing statutes daily to chain up and COR 1.01. 84 P
time a great buyer of land, with his statutes, HAM 5.01.104 P
STAUNCH 2 FR 0.0002 REL FR 2 V 0 P
let my tears staunch the earth's dry appetite, TIT 3.01. 14
hoop should hold us staunch from edge to edge ANT 2.02.115
STAVE'S *(also staff)*
STAVE'S 1 FR 0.0001 REL FR 0 V 1 P
belzebub at the stave's end as well as a man in TN 5.01.285 P
/STAVES 1 FR 0.0001 REL FR 1 V 0 P
/their /armed /staves /in /charge, /their 2H4 4.01.118
STAVES 6 FR 0.0006 REL FR 4 V 2 P
such bearded hermits' staves as master shallow. 2H4 5.01. 64 P
look that my staves be sound, and not too heavy. R3 5.03. 65
amaze the welkin with your broken staves! 5.03.341
fetch me a dozen crab–tree staves, and strong H8 5.03. 8 P
at the heaven with your staves as lift them COR 1.01. 68
whose arms | are hir'd to bear their staves; MAC 5.07. 18
/STAY* 3 FR 0.0003 REL FR 3 V 0 P
/the /crown, /yet /still /with /me /they /stay. R2 4.01.199
/but /my /deeds /shall /stay /thy /fury /soon. 2H6 4.01.113
/thou /must /not /stay /behind. LR 3.06.101
STAY* 445 FR 0.0503 REL FR 380 V 65 P
to a bootless inquisition, | concluding, "stay: TMP 1.02. 36
no more of stay: TGV 1.03. 75
that tide will stay me longer than i should. 2.02. 15
if you think so, then stay at home and go not. 2.07. 62
stay with me a while; 3.01. 58
here if thou stay, thou canst not see thy love; 3.01.246
come, coz, come, coz, we stay for you. WIV 1.01.206 P
we stay for you. 1.01.301 P
he will not stay long. 1.04. 38 P
you bear witness that me have stay six or seven, 2.03. 36 P
jarteer — have i not stay for him to kill him? 3.01. 92 P
he sent me word to stay within. 3.05. 58 P
come, we stay too long. 4.01. 85 P
i'll be so bold as stay, sir, till she come down 4.05. 12 P
procure the vicar | to stay for me at church, 4.06. 49
but stay, i smell a man of middle–earth. 5.05. 80
stay a little while. MM 2.02. 26
stay a while, | and you shall be conducted. 2.03. 17
my stay must be stolen out of other affairs; 3.01.157 P
first, that your stay with him may not be long; 3.01.246 P
and that i have possess'd him my most stay | can 4.01. 43
there he must stay until the officer | arise to 4.02. 90
at flavio's house, | and tell him where i stay. 4.05. 7
stay, sir, stay a while. 5.01.349 P
stay, sir, stay a while. 5.01.349 P
and stay there, dromio, till i come to thee. ERR 1.02. 10
the chain unfinish'd made me stay thus long. 3.02.168
i'll to the mart and there for dromio stay: 3.02.184
they stay for nought at all | but for their 4.01. 91
faith, stay here this night, they will surely do 4.04.151 P
i could find in my heart to stay here still, and 4.04.155 P
i will not stay to–night for all the town: 4.04.157
i, sir, am dromio, pray let me stay. 5.01.337
stay, stand apart, i know not which is which. 5.01.365
i tell him we shall stay here at the least a ADO 1.01.149 P
i do but stay till your marriage be consummate, 3.02. 1 P
meet the prince in the night, you may stay him. 3.03. 76 P
man that knows the /statues, he may stay him; 3.03. 79 P
it is an offense to stay a man against his will. 3.03. 82 P
they stay for you to give your daughter to her 3.05. 54 P
o, stay but till then! 5.02. 45 P
and stay here in your court for three years' LLL 1.01. 52
no, my good lord, i have sworn to stay with you; 1.01.111
for you'll prove perjur'd if you make me stay. 2.01.113
i cannot stay thanksgiving. 2.01.193
o, stay, slave; 3.01.151 P
stay not thy compliment; 4.02.142 P
by whom shall i send this? — company? stay. 4.03. 75
aside the true folk, and let the traitors stay. 4.03.209
so shall we stay, mocking intended game, | and 5.02.155
nay, why dost thou stay? 5.02.626
madam, not so, i do beseech you stay. 5.02.728
there stay until the twelve celestial signs 5.02.797
i'll stay with patience, but the time is long. 5.02.835
to a morn of may), | there will i stay for thee. MND 1.01.168
how long within this wood intend you stay? 2.01.138
we shall chide downright, if i longer stay. 2.01.145
i will not stay thy questions. 2.01.235
stay, though thou kill me, sweet demetrius. 2.02. 84
stay, on thy peril; i alone will go. 2.02. 87
stay thou but here a while, | and by and by i 3.01. 86
pay, | if for his tender here i make some stay. 3.02. 87
why should he stay, whom love doth press to go? 3.02.184
stay, gentle helena; 3.02.245
you, i, | nor longer stay in your curst company. 3.02.341
courtesy, in all reason, we must stay the time. 5.01.255 P
but stay! 5.01.276
make no stay; 5.01.421
i should stay with the jew my master, who, god MV 2.02. 23 P
to offer to counsel me to stay with the jew. 2.02. 30 P
our masquing mates by this time for us stay. 2.06. 59
nine a' clock — our friends all stay for you. 2.06. 63
but stay the very riping of the time; 2.08. 40
it out in length, | to stay you from election. 3.02. 24
again, | no bed shall e'er be guilty of my stay, 3.02.326
i stay here on my bond. 4.01.242
i'll stay no longer question. 4.01.346
whether till the next night she had rather stay, 5.01.302
her exile, or have died to stay behind her. AYL 1.01.110 P
withal, that either you might stay him from his 1.01.133 P
you must if you stay here, for here is the place 1.02.144 P
let us now stay and see it. 1.02.148 P
i did not then entreat to have her stay, | it 1.03. 69
let me stay the growth of his beard, if thou 3.02.210 P
stay, jaques, stay. 5.04.194
stay, jaques, stay. 5.04.194
have | i'll stay to know at your abandon'd cave. 5.04.196
do you intend to stay with me to–night? SHR in.1. 81
and how my men will stay themselves from in.1. 134
but stay a while, what company is this? 1.01. 46
katherina, you may stay, | for i have more to 1.01.100
as though she bid me stay by her a week; 2.01.178
faith, mistress, then i have no cause to stay. 3.01. 86
i stay too long from her. 3.02.110
you would entreat me rather go than stay. 3.02.192
let us entreat you stay till after dinner. 3.02.198
are you content to stay? 3.02.201
i am content you shall entreat me stay, | but 3.02.202
but yet not stay, entreat me how you can. 3.02.203
now, if you love me, stay. 3.02.204
father, be quiet, he shall stay my leisure. 3.02.217
so shall you stay | till you have done your 4.02.110
and she to him, to stay him not too long, | i am 4.04. 30
stay, officer, he shall not go to prison. 5.01. 95 P
now pray thee, love, stay. 5.01.148
i'll stay at home | and pray god's blessing into AWW 1.03.253
o my sweet lord, that you will stay behind us! 2.01. 24
i shall stay here the forehorse to a smock, 2.01. 30
stay the king. 2.01. 49 P
i pray you stay not, but in haste to horse. 2.05. 87
shall i stay here to do't? 3.02.124
i thank you, and will stay upon your leisure. 3.05. 45
had, and here we'll stay | to see our widower's 5.03. 69
stay, royal sir. 5.03.295
i'll stay a month longer. TN 1.03.112 P
will you stay no longer? 2.01. 1 P
o, stay and hear, your true–love's coming, 2.03. 40

stay! 3.01.137
no, faith, i'll not stay a jot longer. 3.02. 1 P
i could not stay behind you. 3.03. 4
stay you by this gentleman till my return. 3.04.257 P
whither, my lord? cesario, husband, stay. 5.01.143
stay your thanks a while, | and pay them when WT 1.02. 9
no longer stay. 1.02. 16
my stay, | to you a charge and trouble. 1.02. 25
you had drawn oaths from him not to stay. 1.02. 29
but let him swear so, and he shall not stay, 1.02. 36
you'll stay? 1.02. 44
he'll stay, my lord. 1.02. 87
my last good deed was to entreat his stay; 1.02. 97
camillo, this great sir will yet stay longer. 1.02.212
he would not stay at your petitions, made | his 1.02.215
how came't, camillo, | that he did stay? 1.02.220
to be hang'd, | that wilt not stay her tongue. 2.03.110
must either stay to execute them thyself, or 4.02. 15 P
they cherish it to make it stay there; 4.03. 93 P
why, they stay at door, sir. 4.04.342 P
if they can but stay you | where you'll be loath 4.04.571
stay for an answer to your embassy, | lest JN 2.01. 44
vouchsafe awhile to stay, | and i shall show you 2.01.416
here's a stay | that shakes the rotten carcass 2.01.455
your grace shall stay behind | so strongly 3.03. 1
makes nice of no vild hold to stay him up. 3.04.138
stay yet, lord salisbury, i'll go with thee, 4.02. 96
as good to die and go, as die and stay. 4.03. 8
my heart hath one poor string to stay it by, 5.07. 55
what surety of the world, what hope, what stay, 5.07. 68
i do but stay behind | to do the office for thee 5.07. 70
as much good stay with thee as go with me! R2 1.02. 57
and stay | for nothing but his majesty's 1.03. 5
stay, the king hath thrown his warder down. 1.03.118
had i thy youth and cause, i would not stay. 1.03.305
be merry, for our time of stay is short. 2.01.223
but that they stay | the first departing of the 2.01.289
so, | stay, and be secret, and myself will go. 2.01.298
stay yet another day, thou trusty welshman. 2.04. 5
we will not stay. 2.04. 7
but stay, here come the gardeners. 3.04. 24
stay thy revengeful hand, thou hast no cause to 5.03. 42
fellow, give place, here is no longer stay. 5.05. 95
stay, and pause a while. 1H4 1.03.129
not, to it again, | we will stay your leisure. 1.03.258
anon, sir. pray stay a little, my lord. 2.04. 57 P
he is, sir john. i fear we shall stay too long. 4.02. 77 P
for god's sake, cousin, stay till all come in. 4.03. 29
stay and breathe a while. 5.04. 47
who then persuaded you to stay at home? 2H4 2.03. 15
a dozen captains stay at door for you. 2.04.372
own part, have a desire to stay with my friends, 3.02.225 P
mouldy, stay at home till you are past service; 3.02.250 P
where is he that will not stay so long | till 4.05. 80
i stay too long by thee, i weary thee. 4.05. 93
stay but a little, for my cloud of dignity | is 4.05. 98
doth the man of war stay all night, sir? 5.01. 29 P
it follows then the cat must stay at home, | yet H5 1.02.174
read | in your own losses, if he stay in france. 2.04.139
pray thee, corporal, stay. 3.02. 3 P
prince dolphin, you shall stay with us in roan. 3.05. 64
day, my /friends, and all things stay for me. 4.01.309
why do you stay so long, my lords of france? 4.02. 38
said their prayers, and they stay for death. 4.02. 56
i stay but for my /guidon; 4.02. 60
i must stay with the lackeys with the luggage of 4.04. 74 P
invites the king of england's stay at home; 5.pr. 37
go with the princes, or stay here with us? 5.02. 91
stay, stay thy hands! 1H6 1.02.104
stay, stay thy hands! 1.02.104
now beat them hence, why do you let them stay? 1.03. 54
now do thou watch, for i can stay no longer. 1.04. 18
our english troops retire, i cannot stay them; 1.05. 2
stay, my lord talbot, for my lady craves | to 2.03. 29
stay, lords and gentlemen, and pluck no more, 2.04. 39
are these feet, whose strengthless stay is numb 2.05. 13
stay, stay, i say! 3.01.103
stay, stay, i say! 3.01.103
stay, let thy humble handmaid speak to thee. 3.03. 42
if we both stay, we both are sure to die. 4.05. 20
then let me stay, and, father, do you fly. 4.05. 21
there is no hope that ever i will stay, | if the 4.05. 30
stay, go, do what you will, the like do i; 4.05. 50
by me they nothing gain and if i stay, | 'tis 4.06. 36
all these, and more, we hazard by thy stay; 4.06. 40
stay, my lord legate, you shall first receive 5.01. 51
o, stay! 5.03. 60
but, suffolk, stay, | thou mayest not wander in 5.03.187
if i longer stay, | we shall begin our ancient 2H6 1.01.143
stay, humphrey duke of gloucester! 2.03. 22
my stay, my guide, and lanthorn to my feet; 2.03. 25
witness my tears, i cannot stay to speak. 2.04. 86
stay, salisbury, | with the rude multitude till 3.02.134
thou that judgest all things, stay my thoughts, 3.02.136
o, let me stay, befall what may befall! 3.02.402
stay, whitmore, for thy prisoner is a prince, 4.01. 44
but stay, i'll read it over once again. 4.04. 14
and therefore in this city will i stay | and 4.04. 47
for a thousand years, i could stay no longer. 4.10. 6 P
can we outrun the heavens? good margaret, stay. 5.02. 73
stay by me, my lords, | and, soldiers, stay and 3H6 1.01. 31
and, soldiers, stay and lodge by me this night. 1.01. 32
arm'd as we are, let's stay within this house. 1.01. 38
i cannot stay to hear these articles. 1.01.180
be patient, gentle queen, and i will stay. 1.01.214
stay, gentle margaret, and hear me speak. 1.01.257
gentle son edward, thou wilt stay /with me? 1.01.259
but stay, what news? 1.02. 48
edward and richard, you shall stay with me, | my 1.02. 54
here must i stay, and here my life must end. 1.04. 26
nay, stay, let's hear the orisons he makes. 1.04.110
now thou art gone we have no staff, no stay. 2.01. 69
if warwick bid him stay. 2.01.188
stay we no longer, dreaming of renown, | but 2.01.199
why, that's my fortune too, therefore i'll stay. 2.02. 76
no, nor your manhood that durst make you stay. 2.02.108
stay, edward. 2.02.175
no, wrangling woman, we'll no longer stay, 2.02.176
and give them leave to fly that will not stay; 2.03. 50
o that my death would stay these ruthful deeds! 2.05. 95
nay, stay not to expostulate, make speed, | or 2.05.135
not that i fear to stay, but love to go 2.05.138
i'll stay above the hill, so both may shoot. 3.01. 5
here comes a man, let's stay till he be past. 3.01. 12
but stay thee, 'tis the fruits of love i mean. 3.02. 58
the more we stay, the stronger grows our foe. 3.03. 40
the more i stay, the more i'll succor thee. 3.03. 41
why stay we now? 3.03.251
how could he stay till warwick made return? 4.01. 5
i | stay not for the love of edward, but the 4.01.126
stay, or thou diest! 4.03. 27
but wherefore stay we? 'tis no time to talk. 4.05. 24
nay, stay, sir john, a while, and we'll debate 4.07. 51
stay, you that bear the corse, and set it down. R3 1.02. 33
stay, dog, for thou shalt hear me. 1.03.215
falling | strook me (that thought to stay him) 1.04. 19
nay, i prithee stay a little. 1.04.117 P
for this will out, and then i must not stay. 1.04.283
what stay had i but edward? and he's gone. 2.02. 74
what stay had we but clarence? and he's gone. 2.02. 75
for god sake let not us two stay at home; 2.02.147
toward /ludlow then, for we'll not stay behind. 2.02.154
stay, i will go with you. 2.04. 67
i do, my lord, but long i cannot stay there. 3.02.119
nay, like enough, for i stay dinner there. 3.02.121
prince, | to stay him from the fall of vanity; 3.07. 97
stay, yet look back with me unto the tower. 4.01. 97
o thou well skill'd in curses, stay awhile, 4.04.116
stay, madam, i must talk a word with you. 4.04.199
and /you, sir walter herbert — stay with me. 5.03. 28
stay, my lord, | and let your reason with your H8 1.01.129
stay there, sir, | and see the noble ruin'd man 2.01. 53
holiness | to stay the judgment o' th' divorce; 3.02. 33
stay! 3.02.232
stay, good my lords, | i have a little yet to 5.02.132
for all shall stay; 5.04. 75
nay, you must stay the cooling too, or ye may TRO 1.01. 26 P
she's a fool to stay behind her father, let her 1.01. 81 P
fall greeks, fail fame, honor or go or stay, 5.01. 43
i prithee stay. 5.02. 42
i pray you stay. 5.02. 43
nay, stay; 5.02. 52
stay a little while. 5.02. 54
why stay we then? 5.02.115
now if thou lose thy stay, | thou on him leaning 5.03. 60
stay yet. 5.10. 23
why stay we prating here? COR 1.01. 47 P
with t' other, | ere stay behind this business. 1.01.243
when blows have made me stay, i fled from words. 2.02. 72
we are not to stay all together, but to come by 2.03. 41 P
we stay here for the people. 2.03.150
mutiny were better put in hazard | than stay, 2.03.257
stay, hold, peace! 3.01.187
you shall stay too. 4.02. 15
nay, but thou shalt stay too. 4.02. 23
why stay we to be baited | with one that wants 4.02. 43
he could not stay to pick them in a pile | of 5.01. 25
stay! whence are you? 5.02. 1
throats are sentenc'd, and stay upon execution. 5.04. 8 P
stay, roman brethren! TIT 1.01.104
stay, madam, here is more belongs to her: 2.03.122
come, lucius, come, stay not to talk with them. 2.03.306
noble tribunes, stay! 3.01. 1
stay, father, for that noble hand of thine, 3.01.162
now stay your strife, what shall be is 3.01.192
thou art an exile, and thou must not stay. 3.01.284
stay, murtherous villains, will you kill your 4.02. 88
so that perforce you must needs stay a time. 4.03. 42
nay, nay, let rape and murder stay with me, | or 5.02.134
some stay to see him fast'ned in the earth. 5.03.183
i would thou wert so happy by thy stay | to hear ROM 1.01.158
she will not stay the siege of loving terms, 1.01.212
my house and welcome on their pleasure stay. 1.02. 37
stay, fellow, i can read. 1.02. 63 P
stay but a little, i will come again. 2.02.138
and i'll still stay, to have thee still forget, 2.02.174
and stay, good nurse — behind the abbey wall 2.04.187
peter, stay at the gate. 2.05. 20 P
can you not stay a while? 2.05. 29
say either, and i'll stay the circumstance. 2.05. 36
you shall not stay alone | till holy church 2.06. 36
why dost thou stay? 3.01.136
stay a while! 3.03. 75
but look thou stay not till the watch be set, 3.03.148
i must be gone and live, or stay and die. 3.05. 11
therefore stay yet, thou need'st not to be gone. 3.05. 16
i have more care to stay than will to go. 3.05. 23
stay, tybalt, stay! 4.03. 57
stay, tybalt, stay! 4.03. 57
here, tarry for the mourners, and stay dinner. 4.05.146 P
stay not, be gone; 5.03. 66
for fear of that, i still will stay with thee, 5.03.106
death | if i did stay to look on his intents. 5.03.134
stay then, i'll go alone. 5.03.135
stay not to question, for the watch is coming. 5.03.158
come go, good juliet, i dare no longer stay. 5.03.159
a great suspicion. stay the friar too. 5.03.187
i be gentle, stay thou for thy good morrow — TIM 1.01.179
let me stay at thine apperil, timon. 1.02. 33
stay, stay, here comes the fool with apemantus, 2.02. 46 P
stay, stay, here comes the fool with apemantus, 2.02. 46 P
if timon stay at home. 2.02. 91 P
women are more valiant | that stay at home, if 3.05. 48
our dinner will not recompense this long stay; 3.06. 33 P
stay, i will lend thee money, borrow none. 3.06.101
let's make no stay. 3.06.118 P
nay, stay thou out for earnest. 4.03. 48
o, let me stay, | and comfort you, my master. 4.03.533
if thou hat'st curses, | stay not; 4.03.535
stay not, all's in vain. 5.01.184
thy fill, but pass and stay not here thy gait." 5.04. 73
by this they stay for me | in pompey's porch; JC 1.03.125
if he should stay at home to-day for fear. 2.02. 43
well, | and, for thy humor, i will stay at home. 2.02. 56
hath begg'd that i will stay at home to-day. 2.02. 82
stay not to answer me, but get thee gone. 2.04. 2
why dost thou stay? 2.04. 3
yet stay awhile, | thou shalt not back till i 3.01.290
that will hear me speak, let 'em stay here; 3.02. 5
and, for my sake, stay here with antony. 3.02. 56
stay ho, and let us hear mark antony. 3.02. 62
will you stay awhile? 3.02.149
stay, countrymen. 3.02.206
let's stay and hear the will. 3.02.239
nothing but death shall stay me. 4.03.128
to stay the providence of some high powers 5.01.106
i prithee, strato, stay thou by thy lord. 5.05. 44
stay, you imperfect speakers, tell me more: MAC 1.03. 70
worthy macbeth, we stay upon your leisure. 1.03.148
now go to the door, and stay there till we call. 3.01. 72
i am so much a fool, should i stay longer, | it 4.02. 28
a crew of wretched souls | that stay his cure. 4.03.142
stay! speak, speak, i charge thee speak! HAM 1.01. 51
stay, illusion! 1.01.127
stay, and speak! 1.01.139
i pray thee stay with us, go not to wittenberg. 1.02.119
i stay too long — but here my father comes. 1.03. 52
good madam, stay awhile. 2.02.115
ay, my lord, they stay upon your patience. 3.02.107 P
'a will stay till you come. 4.03. 39 P
who shall stay you? 4.05.137
but stay, what noise? 4.07.162
no, not to stay the grinding of the axe, | my 5.02. 24
stay, give me drink. 5.02.282
let me not stay a jot for dinner, go get it LR 1.04. 8 P
follow me not, | stay here. 2.04. 60
but i will tarry, the fool will stay, | and let 2.04. 82
i can be patient, i can stay with regan, | i and 2.04.230
my lord, entreat him by no means to stay. 2.04.299
our troops set forth to-morrow, stay with us; 4.05. 16
stay till i have read the letter. 5.01. 47
stay yet, hear reason. 5.03. 82
cordelia, cordelia, stay a little. 5.03.272
to be producted (as, if i stay, i shall) OTH 1.01.146
determine, | either for her stay or going; 1.03.276
bade her wrong stay, and her displeasure fly; 2.01.153
why, stay, and hear me speak. 3.03. 31
nay, stay. thou shouldst be honest. 3.03.381
i will not stay to offend you. 4.01.247
stay you, good gentlemen. 5.01.105
you must not stay here longer, your dismission ANT 1.01. 26
therefore, o antony, stay not by his side. 2.03. 19
speak not against it, | i will not stay behind. 3.07. 19
i must stay his time. 3.13.155
married to your good service, stay till death. 4.02. 31
adjoining to the city | shall stay with us — 4.10. 6
stay for me! 4.14. 50
what should i stay — 5.02.313
nay, stay a little: CYM 1.01.109
stay, come not in. 3.06. 39
ere you depart, and thanks to stay and eat it. 3.06. 67
brother, stay here. | are we not brothers? 4.02. 2
i'll stay | till hasty polydore return, and 4.02.164
stay, sir king. 5.05.301
and stay your coming to present themselves. PER 2.02. 3
but stay, the knights are coming, we will 2.02. 58
we do our longing stay | to hear the rest untold 5.03. 83
if | you stay to see of us such spinsters, we TNK 1.03. 23
thou shalt stay and see | her bright eyes break 2.03. 8
stay, i'll tell you | after a draught or two 3.03. 18
stay, and edify. 3.05. 95
ladies, sit down, we'll stay it. 3.05. 99
and furnish'd with your old strength, i'll stay, 3.06. 37
stay a little; 3.06. 85
why her eyes command me | stay here to love her; 3.06.170
i cannot stay — | their fame has fir'd me so — 4.02.152
i will stay here, | it is enough my hearing 5.03. 6
pray yet stay a while, | and let me look upon ye ep 3
'tis in vain, i see, to stay ye; ep 9
each shadow makes him stop, each murmur stay, VEN 706
some twin'd about her thigh to make her stay. 873
they basely fly, and dare not stay the field. 894
the wind wars with his torch to make him stay, LUC 311
all these poor forbiddings could not stay him, 323
who with a ling'ring stay his course doth let, 328
so o'er this sleeping soul doth tarquin stay, 423
the stain upon his silver down will stay. 1012
that she her plaints a little while doth stay, 1364
then the conceit of this inconstant stay | sets SON 15. 9
through heavy sleep on sightless eyes doth stay! 43.12
from limits far remote, where thou dost stay. 44. 4
that to my use it might unused stay | from hands 48. 3
but like a sad slave stay and think of nought 57.11
being your vassal bound to stay your leisure. 58. 4
which for memorial still with thee shall stay. 74. 4
and life no longer than thy love will stay, 92. 3
in pursuit of the thing she would have stay; 143. 4
counsel may stop a while what will not stay; LC 159

/STAY'D 1 FR 0.0001 REL FR 1 V 0 P
/when /there /was /nothing /could /have /stay'd 2H4 4.01.121

STAY'D 40 FR 0.0045 REL FR 35 V 5 P
sir proteus, you are stay'd for. TGV 2.02. 19
he hath stay'd for a better man than thee. 3.01.376 P
for thou hast stay'd so long that going will 3.01.378 P
sixteen months, and longer might have stay'd, 4.01. 21
you have stay'd me in a happy hour, i was about ADO 4.01.283 P
here they stay'd an hour, | and talk'd apace; LLL 5.02.368
i would have stay'd till i had made you merry, MV 1.01. 60
and we are stay'd for at bassanio's feast. 2.06. 48
ay, celia, we stay'd her for your sake, | else AYL 1.03. 67
your ships are stay'd at venice, and the duke, SHR 4.02. 83
eye | hath stay'd upon some favor that it loves. TN 2.04. 24
besides, i have stay'd | to tire your royalty. WT 1.02. 14
whose leisure i have stay'd, have given him time JN 2.01. 58
but stay'd and made the western welkin blush, 5.05. 2
my lord of salisbury, we have stay'd ten days, R2 2.04. 1
retrait is made and execution stay'd. 2H4 4.03. 72
he came not through the chamber where we stay'd. 4.05. 56
she should have stay'd in france, and starv'd in 2H6 1.01.135
pardon, my liege, that i have stay'd so long. 3.01. 94
and, being protector, stay'd the soldiers' pay, 3.01.105
he never would have stay'd in france so long. 3.01.295
i have stay'd for thee, | god knows, in torment R3 4.04.163
ague | stay'd me a prisoner in my chamber when H8 1.01. 5

and he had stay'd by him, i would not have been COR 2.01.130 P
away, for thou hast stay'd us here too long. TIT 2.03.181
i could have stay'd here all the night | to hear ROM 3.03.159
so that my speed to mantua there was stay'd. 5.02. 12
am i not stay'd for, cinna? JC 1.03.136
am i not stay'd for? tell me. 1.03.139
would they had stay'd! MAC 1.03. 82
very like, /very /like. stay'd it long? HAM 1.02.236
shoulder of your sail, | and you are stay'd for. 1.03. 57
long stay'd he so. 2.01. 88
you stay'd well by't in egypt. ANT 2.02.176 P
i died whilst in the womb he stay'd | attending CYM 5.04. 37
good helicane, that stay'd at home, | not to eat PER 2.ch. 17
where she stay'd, | and fell, scarce to be got TNK 4.01.101
an oven that is stopp'd, or river stay'd, VEN 331
when tarquin did, but he was stay'd by thee. LUC 917
(and there she stay'd | till after a deep groan) 1275

STAYED 2 FR 0.0002 REL FR 2 V 0 P
of door, | and stayed the odds by adding four. LLL 3.01. 92
john, | was stayed by accident, and yesternight ROM 5.03.251

STAYEST 1 FR 0.0001 REL FR 1 V 0 P
stayest thou to vex me here? TGV 4.04. 61

STAYING 11 FR 0.0012 REL FR 10 V 1 P
besides, thy staying will abridge thy life. TGV 3.01.247
no longer staying but to give the mother MM 1.04. 86
who, but for staying on our controversy, | had ERR 5.01. 20
out of door, | staying the odds by adding four. LLL 3.01. 98
to devour the way, | staying no longer question. 2H4 1.01. 48
by staying there so long till all were lost. 2H6 3.01.299
sword make way for me, for here is no staying. 4.08. 60 P
there is staying | a gentleman, sent from the H8 4.02.105
upon the stygian banks | staying for waftage. TRO 3.02. 10
heads, | staying for thine to keep him company. ROM 3.01.128
when you sued staying, | then was the time for ANT 1.03. 33

STAYS* 43 FR 0.0048 REL FR 39 V 4 P
madam, | dinner is ready, and your father stays. TGV 1.02.128
my father stays my coming; 2.02. 13
that stays to bear my letters to my friends, 3.01. 53
that thy master stays for thee at the north–gate 3.01.373 P
that stays upon me, whose persuasion is | i come MM 4.01. 46
my mistress and her sister stays for you. ERR 1.02. 76
my master stays in the street. 3.01. 36
for he is bound to sea, and stays but for it. 4.01. 33
both wind and tide stays for this gentleman, 4.01. 46
that stays but till her owner comes aboard, 4.01. 86
sheep, | what ship of epidamium stays for me? 4.01. 94
my coach, which stays for us | at the park–gate; MV 3.04. 82
here stays without | a messenger with letters 4.01.107
more properly, stays me here at home unkept; AYL 1.01. 8 P
along by him | and never stays to greet him. 2.01. 54
who stays it still withal? 3.02.330 P
whatever fortune stays him from his word. SHR 3.02. 23
the tailor stays thy leisure, | to deck thy body 4.03. 59
most understand | bohemia stays here longer. WT 1.02.230
stays here longer. 1.02.230
stays in his course and plays the alchymist, JN 3.01. 78
stays but the summons of the appellant's trumpet R2 1.03. 4
and only stays but to behold the face | of that 1H4 1.03.275
please your grace, here my commission stays; 2H6 2.04. 76
what stays had i but they? and they are gone. R3 2.02. 76
my barge stays; H8 1.03. 63
sir, /he stays for you to conduct him thither. TRO 3.02. 3 P
with venomous wights she stays | as tediously as 4.02. 12
in love whereof, half hector stays at home; 4.05. 84
ajax, your guard, stays to conduct you home. 5.02.184
we follow thee. juliet, the county stays. ROM 1.03.104
being tasted, stays all senses with the heart. 2.03. 26
there stays a husband to make you a wife. 2.05. 69
calphurnia here, my wife, stays me at home: JC 2.02. 75
see, | sits in a foggy cloud, and stays for me. MAC 3.05. 35
my mother stays, | this physic but prolongs thy HAM 3.03. 95
the messengers of venice stays the meat. OTH 4.02.170
he stays upon your will. ANT 1.02.115
will, and tell her | her palamon stays for her; TNK 5.02. 26
come, your love palamon stays for you, child, 5.02. 41
she stays, exclaiming on the direful night, | he LUC 741
hie thee, | for methinks thou stays too long. PP 12.12
flesh stays no farther reason, | but, rising at SON 151. 8

STAY'ST 1 FR 0.0001 REL FR 1 V 0 P
why stay'st thou here, and go'st not to the duke R3 4.04.446

STEAD 31 FR 0.0035 REL FR 26 V 5 P
so it stead you, i will write | (please you TGV 2.01.113
my substance should be statue in thy stead. 4.04.201
can you so stead me | as bring me to the sight MM 1.04. 17
this wrong'd maid to stead up your appointment, 3.01.250 P
may you stead me? MV 1.03. 7 P
to fill up your grace's request in my stead. 4.01.161 P
thou shalt be master, tranio, in my stead; SHR 1.01.202
that you are the man | must stead us all, and me 1.02.264
to reave her | of what should stead her most? AWW 5.03. 87
bought | thy likeness, for in stead of thee, 1H4 5.03. 8
using the names of men in stead of men, | like 2H4 1.03. 57
drink'st thou oft, in stead of homage sweet, H5 4.01.250
in stead of gold, we'll offer up our arms, 1H6 1.01. 46
wounds will i lend the french in stead of eyes, 1.01. 87
in stead whereof sharp stakes pluck'd out of 1.01.117
renounce your soil, give sheep in lions' stead: 1.05. 29
the help of one stands me in little stead. 4.06. 31
had been the regent there in stead of me, | he 2H6 3.01.294
with these borne before us, in stead of maces, 4.07.135 P
urge it no more, lest that, in stead of words, 3H6 1.01. 98
in stead whereof let this supply the room: 2.06. 54
in stead of mounting barbed steeds | to fright R3 1.01. 10
five have i slain to–day in stead of him. 5.04. 12
but, saying thus, in stead of oil and balm, TRO 1.01. 61
were you in my stead, would you have heard | a COR 5.03.192
but, in their stead, | curses, not loud but deep MAC 5.03. 26
i could never better stead thee than now. OTH 1.03.339 P
and sail and high expense | can stead the quest. PER 3.ch. 21
the sooner her vile thoughts to stead, 4.ch. 41
what woman i may stead that is distress'd | does TNK 1.01. 36
in stead of love's coy touch, shall rudely tear LUC 669

STEADED 1 FR 0.0001 REL FR 1 V 0 P
necessaries, | which since have steaded much; TMP 1.02.165

STEADFAST 1 FR 0.0001 REL FR 1 V 0 P
her, with a steadfast eye | receives the scroll LUC 1339

STEADFAST–GAZING 1 FR 0.0001 REL FR 1 V 0 P
oppose thy steadfast–gazing eyes to mine, | see 2H6 4.10. 45

STEADFASTLY 1 FR 0.0001 REL FR 1 V 0 P
upon his hurt she looks so steadfastly, | that VEN 1063

STEADIER 1 FR 0.0001 REL FR 0 V 1 P
see if his head will stand steadier on a pole, 2H6 4.07. 95 P

STEADS 4 FR 0.0004 REL FR 4 V 0 P
it nothing steads us | to chide him from our AWW 3.07. 41
for lo | my intercession likewise steads my foe. ROM 2.03. 54
from the bench, | and minister in their steads! TIM 4.01. 6
and in their steads do ravens, crows, and kites JC 5.01. 84

STEAL 87 FR 0.0098 REL FR 64 V 23 P
we steal by line and level, and't like your TMP 4.01.239 P
"steal by line and level" is an excellent pass 4.01.243 P
should from her vesture chance to steal a kiss, TGV 2.04.160
this night intends to steal away your daughter; 3.01. 11
banished | for practicing to steal away a lady, 4.01. 46
the good humor is to steal at a minute's rest. WIV 1.03. 27 P
"steal!" 1.03. 29 P
time | shall master slender steal my nan away, 4.04. 74
"thou shalt not steal"? MM 1.02. 10 P
they put forth to steal. 1.02. 14 P
have authority | when judges steal themselves. 2.02.176
trick of him to steal from the state, and usurp 3.02. 92 P
us, | and bid her steal into the pleached bower, ADO 3.01. 7
what he is and steal out of your company. 3.03. 59 P
steal forth thy father's house to–morrow night; MND 1.01.164
through athens gates have we devis'd to steal. 1.01.213
the honey–bags steal from the humble–bees, | and 3.01.168
eye, | steal me a while from mine own company. 3.02.436
and thrift is blessing, if men steal it not. MV 1.03. 90
except to steal your thoughts, my gentle queen. 2.01. 12
methinks it should have power to steal both his 3.02.125
night | did jessica steal from the wealthy jew, 5.01. 15
what if we assay'd to steal | the clownish fool AYL 1.03.129
myself | did steal behind him as he lay along 2.01. 30
'twere good methinks to steal our marriage, SHR 3.02.140
long, | but on us both did haggish age steal on, AWW 1.02. 29
thy mind stand to't, boy, steal away bravely. 2.01. 29
by heaven, i'll steal away. 2.01. 33
most fain would steal | what law does vouch mine 2.05. 81
for with the dark, poor thief, i'll steal away. 3.02.129
it is that he will steal himself into a man's 3.06. 91 P
he will steal, sir, an egg out of a cloister. 4.03.250 P
here's nobody will steal that from thee. WT 4.04.631 P
'tis strange | he thus should steal upon us. 5.01.115
unless he do profane, steal, or usurp. R2 3.03. 81
the moon, under whose countenance we steal. 1H4 1.02. 29 P
i'll steal to glendower and lord mortimer, 1.03.295
we steal as in a castle, cock–sure; 2.01. 86 P
from whom you now must steal and take no leave, 3.01. 92
where shall i find one that can steal well? 3.03.188 P
me, i am as vigilant as a cat to steal cream. 4.02. 59 P
i think, to steal cream indeed, for thy theft 4.02. 60 P
shall we steal upon them, ned, at supper? 2H4 2.02.158 P
ears | to steal his sweet and honeyed sentences; H5 1.01. 50
they will steal any thing, and call it purchase. 3.02. 42 P
be, if he durst steal any thing adventurously. 4.04. 73 P
to england will i steal, and there i'll steal; 5.01. 87
to england will i steal, and there i'll steal; 5.01. 87
the fox barks not when he would steal the lamb. 2H6 3.01. 55
who cannot steal a shape that means deceit? 3.01. 79
i'll steal away. 3H6 1.01.212
stand you thus close to steal the bishop's deer? 4.05. 17
but, whiles he thought to steal the single ten, 5.01. 43
a man cannot steal, but it accuseth him; R3 1.04.135 P
that deceit should steal such gentle shape, 2.02. 27
the silent hours steal on, | and flaky darkness 5.03. 85
to steal from spiritual leisure a brief span H8 3.02.140
and easy it is | of a cut loaf to steal a shive, TIT 2.01. 87
and she steal love's sweet bait from fearful ROM 2.pr. 8
and steal immortal blessing from her lips, | who 3.03. 37
steal but a beggar's dog | and give it timon, TIM 2.01. 5
bound servants, steal; 4.01. 10
nothing can you steal | but thieves do lose it. 4.03.447
steal less for this i give you, | and gold 4.03.448
and will he steal out of his wholesome bed | to JC 2.01.264
i come not, friends, to steal away your hearts. 3.02.216
if 'a steal aught the whilst this play is HAM 3.02. 88
in their mouths to steal away their brains! OTH 2.03.291 P
it, | that he would steal away so guilty–like, 3.03. 39
hath a hundred times | woo'd me to steal it; 3.03.293
that which so often you did bid me steal. 3.03.309
no slander, they steal hearts. ANT 2.06.101 P
they induc'd to steal it? CYM 2.04.125
but first of all, | how we may steal from hence; 3.02. 62
which did steal | the eyes of young and old. PER 4.01. 40
may rather seem to steal in than be permitted. TNK 4.03. 75 P
steal thine own freedom, and complain on theft. VEN 160
lest she should steal a kiss and die forsworn. 726
mean | to stifle beauty and to steal his breath? 934
"such devils steal effects from lightless hell, LUC 1555
yet doth it steal sweet hours from love's SON 36. 8
although thou steal thee all my poverty; 40.10
and steal dead seeing of his living hue? 67. 6
the filching age will steal his treasure; 75. 6
but do thy worst to steal thyself away, | for 92. 1
whence didst thou steal thy sweet that smells, 99. 2
steal from his figure, and no pace perceiv'd, 104.10

STEALER 2 FR 0.0002 REL FR 1 V 1 P
the transgression is in the stealer. ADO 2.01.226 P
up | their deer to th' stand o' th' stealer; CYM 2.03. 70

STEALERS 1 FR 0.0001 REL FR 0 V 1 P
and do still, by these pickers and stealers. HAM 3.02.336 P

STEALETH 1 FR 0.0001 REL FR 1 V 0 P
this thought through the dark night he stealeth, LUC 729

/STEALING 1 FR 0.0001 REL FR 0 V 1 P
/mahu, /of /stealing; LR 4.01. 61 P

STEALING 18 FR 0.0020 REL FR 13 V 5 P
that time comes stealing on by night and day? ERR 4.02. 60
stealing her soul with many vows of faith, | and MV 5.01. 19
a bank of violets, | stealing and giving odor. TN 1.01. 7
wronging the ancientry, stealing, fighting — WT 3.03. 62 P
stealing away from his father with his clog at 4.04.678 P
be guilty of the stealing that sweet breath JN 4.03.136
or rather, of stealing a cade of herrings. 2H6 4.02. 33 P
being burnt i' th' hand for stealing of sheep. 4.02. 63 P
which, mellow'd by the stealing hours of time, R3 3.07.168
come hither for stealing out of a french hose. MAC 2.03. 13 P
"but age with his stealing steps | hath clawed HAM 5.01. 71
myself, and let me die, | stealing so poorly. CYM 4.02. 16
more it shap'd | unto my end of stealing them. 5.05.347
view | how she came stealing to the wayward boy! VEN 344
should by his stealing in disturb the feast?" 450
for stealing moulds from heaven that were divine 730
stealing unseen to west with this disgrace: SON 33. 8
stealing away the treasure of his spring; 63. 8

STEALS 14 FR 0.0015 REL FR 12 V 2 P
and as the morning steals upon the night, TMP 5.01. 65
me to her trencher and steals her capon's leg. TGV 4.04. 9 P
the hour steals on, i pray you, sir, dispatch. ERR 4.01. 52
nest, shows it his companion, and he steals it. ADO 2.01.224 P
that steals the color from bassanio's cheek — MV 3.02.244
foot of time | steals ere we can effect them. AWW 5.03. 42
bed, | away from light steals home my heavy son, ROM 1.01.137
warrant in that theft | which steals itself, MAC 2.03.146
look how it steals away! HAM 3.04.134
the robb'd that smiles steals something from the OTH 1.03.208
who steals my purse steals trash; 3.03.157
who steals my purse steals trash; 3.03.157
away he steals with open list'ning ear, | full LUC 283
which steals men's eyes and women's souls SON 20. 8

STEAL'T 1 FR 0.0001 REL FR 1 V 0 P
to such a trifle), | he begg'd of me to steal't. OTH 5.02.229

STEALTH 10 FR 0.0011 REL FR 9 V 1 P
the stealth of our most mutual entertainment MM 1.02.154
or if you like elsewhere, do it by stealth, ERR 3.02. 7
i told him of your stealth unto this wood. MND 3.02.310
my lord, fair helen told me of their stealth, 4.01.160
with an invisible and subtle stealth | to creep TN 1.05.297
or, if he do, it needs must be by stealth. ROM 3.05.215
and now ingratitude makes it worse than stealth. TIM 3.04. 27
who, in the lusty stealth of nature, take | more LR 1.02. 11
hog in sloth, fox in stealth, wolf in greediness 3.04. 93 P
thou by thy dial's shady stealth mayst know SON 77. 7

STEALTHY 1 FR 0.0001 REL FR 1 V 0 P
howl's his watch, thus with his stealthy pace, MAC 2.01. 54

STEAM 1 FR 0.0001 REL FR 1 V 0 P
she feedeth on the steam as on a prey, | and VEN 63

STEED 22 FR 0.0024 REL FR 22 V 0 P
bound and high curvet | of mars's fiery steed. AWW 2.03.283
mounted upon a hot and fiery steed, | which his R2 5.02. 8
speak terms of manage to thy bounding steed, 1H4 2.03. 49
steed threatens steed, in high and boastful H5 4.pr. 10
steed threatens steed, in high and boastful 4.pr. 10
the deadly–handed clifford slew my steed; 2H6 5.02. 9
as hot as perseus, spur thy phrygian steed, TRO 4.05.186
present the fair steed to my lady cressid. 5.05. 2
our steed the leg, the tongue our trumpeter, COR 1.01.117
here is the steed, we the caparison. 1.09. 12
my noble steed, known to the camp, i give him, 1.09. 61
i mean to stride your steed, and at all times 1.09. 71
dismounted from your snow–white goodly steed, TIT 2.03. 76
farewell the neighing steed and the shrill trump OTH 3.03.351
and soberly did mount an arm–gaunt steed, | who ANT 1.05. 48
brave a knight as e'er | did spur a noble steed. TNK 5.03.116
mounted upon a steed that emily | did first 5.04. 49
"vouchsafe, thou wonder, to alight thy steed, VEN 13
the steed is stalled up, and even now | to tie 39
the strong–neck'd steed, being tied unto a tree, 263
life | in limning out a well–proportioned steed, 290
or he his manage by th' well–doing steed. LC 112

STEED'S 1 FR 0.0001 REL FR 1 V 0 P
bare–headed, lower than his proud steed's neck, R2 5.02. 19

STEEDS 13 FR 0.0014 REL FR 13 V 0 P
i shall think or phoebus' steeds are founder'd TMP 4.01. 30
battle heard | loud 'larums, neighing steeds, SHR 1.02.206
his barbed steeds to stables, and his heart | to R2 3.03.117
hark how our steeds for present service neigh! H5 4.02. 8
and /their wounded steeds | fret fetlock deep in 4.07. 78
and once again bestride our foaming steeds, 3H6 2.01.183
so, underneath the belly of their steeds, | that 2.03. 20
that phaeton should check thy fiery steeds, 2.06. 12
brought from thence the thracian fatal steeds, 4.02. 21
in stead of mounting barbed steeds | to fright R3 1.01. 10
gallop apace, you fiery–footed steeds, | towards ROM 3.02. 1
his steeds to water at those springs | on CYM 2.03. 22
two such steeds might well | be by a pair of TNK 3.01. 20

/STEEL 1 FR 0.0001 REL FR 1 V 0 P
/fire /sparkling /through /sights /of /steel, 2H4 4.01.119

STEEL 73 FR 0.0082 REL FR 66 V 7 P
whom i with this obedient steel, three inches of TMP 2.01.283
no token but stones, for she's as hard as steel. TGV 1.01.141 P
golden touch could soften steel and stones, 3.02. 78
of troy become, | and by my side wear steel? WIV 1.03. 76
with wit or steel? 1.03. 93
not been made of faith, and my heart of steel, ERR 3.02.145
/one whose hard heart is button'd up with steel; 4.02. 34
draw not iron, for my heart | is true as steel. MND 2.01.197
poison with thee, or in bastinado, or in steel; AYL 5.01. 55 P
more sharp than filed steel, did spur me forth, TN 3.03. 5
pins and poking–sticks of steel; WT 4.04.226
for it with stamped coin, not stabbing steel, 4.04.725 P
now doth death line his dead chaps with steel, JN 2.01.352
and with thy blessings steel my lance's point, R2 1.03. 74
to lift shrewd steel against our golden crown, 3.02. 59
your fearful land | with hard bright steel, and 3.02.111
hard bright steel, and hearts harder than steel. 3.02.111
and never brandish more revengeful steel | over 4.01. 50
to crush our old limbs in ungentle steel. 1H4 5.01. 13
a scaly gauntlet now with joints of steel | must 2H4 1.01.146
then join you with them, like a rib of steel, 2.03. 54
them great meals of beef and iron and steel, H5 3.07.150 P
o god of battles, steel my soldiers' hearts, 4.01.289
that they suppos'd i could rend bars of steel, 1H6 1.04. 51
lean famine, quartering steel, and climbing fire 4.02. 11
turn on the bloody hounds with heads of steel, 4.02. 51
now, york, or never, steel thy fearful thoughts, 2H6 3.01.331
and he but naked, though lock'd up in steel, 3.02.234
steel, if thou turn the edge, or cut not out the 4.10. 56 P
the hope thereof makes clifford mourn in steel. 3H6 1.01. 58
shall we go throw away our coats of steel, | and 2.01.160
then, clifford, were thy heart as hard as steel, 2.01.201
steel thy melting heart | to hold thine own and 2.02. 41
and bloody steel grasp'd in their ireful hands, 2.05.132
that must round my brow | were red–hot steel, to R3 4.01. 60
and, as the long divorce of steel falls on me, H8 2.01. 76
enough, patroclus, | or give me ribs of steel! TRO 1.03.177

part | to steel a strong opinion to themselves? 1.03.353
shall more obey than to the edge of steel | or 3.01.152
as true as steel, as plantage to the moon, | as 3.02.177
or, like a gate of steel | fronting the sun, 3.03.121
but this thy countenance, still lock'd in steel, 4.05.195
when steel grows soft as the parasite's silk, COR 1.09. 45
trail your steel pikes. 5.06.150
and with a gad of steel will write these words, TIT 4.01.103
but metal, marcus, steel to the very back, | yet 4.03. 48
my heart is not compact of flint nor steel, 5.03. 88
sheathing the steel in my advent'rous body. 5.03.112
profaners of this neighbor-stained steel — ROM 1.01. 82
'warrant thee, my man's as true as steel. 2.04.198
and in my temper soft'ned valor's steel! 3.01.115
with piercing steel at bold mercutio's breast, 3.01.159
and to steel with valor | the melting spirits of JC 2.01.121
and as he pluck'd his cursed steel away, | mark 3.02.177
for piercing steel, and darts envenomed, | shall 5.03. 76
disdaining fortune, with his brandish'd steel, MAC 1.02. 17
nor steel, nor poison, | malice domestic, 3.02. 24
grapple them unto thy soul with hoops of steel, HAM 1.03. 63
again in complete steel | revisits thus the 1.04. 52
knees, and heart, with strings of steel, | be 3.03. 70
hath made the flinty and steel /couch of war OTH 1.03.230
i'll leave thee | now like a man of steel. ANT 4.04. 33
it is a throughfare for steel, if it be not hurt CYM 1.02. 10 P
his steel was in debt, it went o' th' backside 1.02. 12 P
by your furtherance i am cloth'd in steel, | and PER 2.01.154
strong-temper'd steel his stronger strength VEN 111
"art thou obdurate, flinty, hard as steel? 199
o, give it me, lest thy hard heart do steel it, 375
and grave, like water that doth eat in steel, LUC 755
to spoil antiquities of hammer'd steel, | and 951
nor gates of steel so strong, but time decays? SON 65. 8
unless my nerves were brass or hammered steel. 120. 4
prison my heart in thy steel bosom's ward, | but 133. 9
STEEL'D 5 FR 0.0005 REL FR 5 V 0 P
strong purpose, steel'd | the hearts of men, R2 5.02. 34
with lies well steel'd with weighty arguments, R3 1.01.148
you have steel'd 'em with your beauty. TNK 4.02.149
and being steel'd, soft sighs can never grave it VEN 376
that my steel'd sense or changes right or wrong. SON 112. 8
STEELED 4 FR 0.0004 REL FR 4 V 0 P
when | the steeled jailer is the friend of men. MM 4.02. 87
for from his metal was his party steeled, 2H4 1.01.116
so service shall with steeled sinews toil, | and H5 2.02. 36
give me my steeled coat, i'll fight for france. 1H6 1.01. 85
STEELY 2 FR 0.0002 REL FR 2 V 0 P
that they take place when virtue's steely bones AWW 1.01.103
broach'd with the steely point of clifford's 3H6 2.03. 16
STEEP* 11 FR 0.0012 REL FR 10 V 1 P
days will quickly steep themselves in night; MND 1.01. 7
here | come from the farthest steep of india? 2.01. 69
let fancy still my sense in lethe steep; TN 4.01. 62
i'll steep this letter in sack and make him eat 2H4 2.02.135 P
down, | and steep my senses in forgetfulness? 3.01. 8
to climb steep hills | requires slow pace at H8 1.01.131
let them pronounce the steep tarpeian death, COR 3.03. 88
show me the steep and thorny way to heaven, HAM 1.03. 48
horrible steep. | hark, do you hear the sea? LR 4.06. 3
do not steep thy heart | in such relenting dew LUC 1828
and his love-kindling fire did quickly steep SON 153. 3
STEEP'D 10 FR 0.0011 REL FR 10 V 0 P
there may be in the cup | a spider steep'd, and WT 2.01. 40
enemies | have steep'd their galls in honey, and H5 2.02. 30
steep'd in the faultless blood of pretty rutland R3 1.03.177
did to thy father, steep'd in rutland's blood — 4.04.275
and steep'd in blood? ROM 5.03.145
steep'd in the colors of their trade, their MAC 2.03.115
who this had seen, with tongue in venom steep'd, HAM 2.02.510
head, | steep'd me in poverty to the very lips, OTH 4.02. 50
that the conquering wine hath steep'd our sense ANT 2.07.107
deserve, | and yet are steep'd in favors; CYM 5.04.131
STEEP-DOWN 1 FR 0.0001 REL FR 1 V 0 P
wash me in steep-down gulfs of liquid fire! OTH 5.02.280
STEEPED 1 FR 0.0001 REL FR 1 V 0 P
cheeks | a napkin steeped in the harmless blood 3H6 2.01. 62
STEEPLE 3 FR 0.0003 REL FR 1 V 2 P
on a man's face, or a weathercock on a steeple! TGV 2.01.136
the whole parish, church, steeple, bells, and PER 2.01. 34 P
never have left till he cast bells, steeple, 2.01. 42 P
STEEPLES 2 FR 0.0002 REL FR 2 V 0 P
topples down | steeples and moss-grown towers. 1H4 3.01. 32
spout | till you have drench'd our steeples, LR 3.02. 3
STEEPS 1 FR 0.0001 REL FR 1 V 0 P
for he that steeps his safety in true blood JN 3.04.147
STEEP-UP 3 FR 0.0003 REL FR 3 V 0 P
hard | against the steep-up rising of the hill? LLL 4.01. 2
her stand she takes upon a steep-up hill. PP 9. 5
and having climb'd the steep-up heavenly hill, SON 7. 5
STEEPY 2 FR 0.0002 REL FR 2 V 0 P
bowing his head against the steepy mount | to TIM 1.01. 75
morn | hath travell'd on to age's steepy night, SON 63. 5
STEER* 4 FR 0.0004 REL FR 4 V 0 P
and yet the steer, the heckfer, and the calf WT 1.02.124
and you yourself shall steer the happy helm. 2H6 1.03.100
my conscience, i did steer | toward this remedy, H8 2.04.201
a rarer spirit never | did steer humanity; ANT 5.01. 32
STEERAGE 2 FR 0.0002 REL FR 2 V 0 P
but he that hath the steerage of my course ROM 1.04.112
so with his steerage shall your thoughts /grow PER 4.04. 19
STEER'D 1 FR 0.0001 REL FR 1 V 0 P
brings in some boats that are not steer'd. CYM 4.03. 46
STEERING 1 FR 0.0001 REL FR 1 V 0 P
steering with due course toward the isle of OTH 1.03. 34
STEERS* 2 FR 0.0002 REL FR 2 V 0 P
like youthful steers unyok'd, they take their 2H4 4.02.103
at the helm | a seeming mermaid steers; ANT 2.02.209
/STELL'D 1 FR 0.0001 REL FR 1 V 0 P
eye hath play'd the painter and hath /stell'd SON 24. 1
STELL'D 1 FR 0.0001 REL FR 1 V 0 P
to find a face where all distress is stell'd. LUC 1444
STELLED 1 FR 0.0001 REL FR 1 V 0 P
have buoy'd up | and quench'd the stelled fires; LR 3.07. 61
/STEM* 1 FR 0.0001 REL FR 1 V 0 P
industry they skip | from /stem to stern. PER 4.01. 63
STEM* 5 FR 0.0005 REL FR 5 V 0 P
two lovely berries moulded on one stem; MND 3.02.211
this is a stem | of that victorious stock; H5 2.04. 62
now declare, sweet stem from york's great stock, 1H6 2.05. 41
gust, | command an argosy to stem the waves. 3H6 2.06. 36
sail, so men obey'd | and fell below his stem. COR 2.02.107
STEMMING 1 FR 0.0001 REL FR 1 V 0 P
and stemming it with hearts of controversy; JC 1.02.109
STENCH 4 FR 0.0004 REL FR 4 V 0 P
thou odoriferous stench! JN 3.04. 26
so bees with smoke and doves with noisome stench 1H6 1.05. 23
pit, burning, scalding, | stench, consumption. LR 4.06.129
the winds | with stench of our slain lords. TNK 1.01. 47
STEP 31 FR 0.0035 REL FR 28 V 3 P
shall step by step attend | you and your ways, TMP 3.03. 78
shall step by step attend | you and your ways, 3.03. 78
stream, | and make a pastime of each weary step, TGV 2.07. 35
till the last step have brought me to my love, 2.07. 36
step into th' chamber, sir john. WIV 4.02. 11 P
now step i forth to whip hypocrisy. LLL 4.03.149
who after me hath many a weary step | limp'd in AYL 2.07.130
deadly divorce step between me and you! AWW 5.03.318
as your feet hits the ground they step on. TN 3.04.278 P
of such affections, | step forth mine advocate. WT 5.01.221
that none so small advantage shall step forth JN 3.04.151
wherein we step after a stranger, march | upon 5.02. 27
let's step into the shadow of these trees. R2 3.04. 25
twice for one step i'll groan, the way being 5.01. 91
step aside, and i'll show thee a /president. 1H4 2.04. 33 P
my judgment is we should not step too far 2H4 1.03. 20
they are as children but one step below, | even R3 4.04.301
the general's disdain'd | by him one step below, TRO 1.03.130
so every step, | exampled by the first pace that 1.03.131
my lord, to step out of these dreary dumps, TIT 1.01.391
so please you step aside, | i'll know his ROM 1.01.156
that is a step | on which i must fall down, or MAC 1.04. 48
what judgment | would step from this to this? HAM 3.04. 71
o, step between her and her fighting soul. 3.04.113
no unchaste action, or dishonored step, | that LR 1.01.228
one step i have advanc'd thee, if thou dost | as 5.03. 28
which, as a grise or step, may help these lovers OTH 1.03.200
sir, step you forth; CYM 5.05.130
each errant step beside is torment. TNK 3.02. 34
i'll no step further. 5.03. 1
should step as 'twere up to my country's head STM III 7
STEP-DAME 4 FR 0.0004 REL FR 4 V 0 P
like to a step-dame, or a dowager, | long MND 1.01. 5
pard to the hind, or step-dame to her son, | yea TRO 3.02.194
a father cruel, and a step-dame false, | a CYM 1.06. 1
betwixt a father by thy step-dame govern'd, | a 2.01. 58
/STEPHANO 1 FR 0.0001 REL FR 1 V 0 P
my friend /stephano, signify, i pray you, MV 5.01. 51
STEPHANO 16 FR 0.0018 REL FR 2 V 14 P
be said so again while stephano breathes at' TMP 2.02. 62 P
stephano! 2.02. 96 P
stephano! 2.02.100 P
if thou beest stephano, touch me, and speak to 2.02.100 P
but art thou not drown'd, stephano? 2.02.109 P
and art thou living, stephano? 2.02.112 P
o stephano, two neapolitans scap'd! 2.02.112 P
o stephano, hast any more of this? 2.02.133 P
wilt come? i'll follow stephano. 3.02.152 P
o king stephano! 4.01.222 P
o worthy stephano! 4.01.223 P
o king stephano! 4.01.226 P
is not this stephano, my drunken butler? 5.01.277
why, how now, stephano? 5.01.285 P
o, touch me not, i am not stephano, but a cramp. 5.01.286 P
stephano is my name, and i bring word | my MV 5.01. 28
STEPHEN *(also steven)*
STEPHEN 4 FR 0.0004 REL FR 4 V 0 P
as stephen sly, and old john naps of greece, SHR in.2. 93
and force perforce | keep stephen langton, JN 3.01.143
sir stephen scroop, besides a clergyman | of R2 3.03. 28
"king stephen was and-a worthy peer, | his OTH 2.03. 89
STEPMOTHERS 1 FR 0.0001 REL FR 1 V 0 P
after the slander of most stepmothers, CYM 1.01. 71
STEPP'D 7 FR 0.0008 REL FR 7 V 0 P
petruchio, since we are stepp'd thus far in, | i SHR 1.02. 83
the prince of wales stepp'd forth before the 1H4 5.02. 45
he stepp'd before me happily | for my example. H8 4.02. 10
by whose death he's stepp'd | into a great TIM 2.02.223
who in hot blood | hath stepp'd into the law, 3.05. 12
i am in blood | stepp'd in so far that, should i MAC 3.04.136
naked breast | stepp'd before targes of proof, CYM 5.05. 5
STEPPING 1 FR 0.0001 REL FR 1 V 0 P
not stepping o'er the bounds of modesty. ROM 4.02. 27
STEPS 28 FR 0.0031 REL FR 27 V 1 P
to measure kingdoms with his feeble steps; TGV 2.07. 10
dining-chamber but he steps me to her trencher 4.04. 8 P
tell her, we measure them by weary steps. LLL 5.02.194
how many weary steps | of many weary miles you 5.02.195
and turn two mincing steps | into a manly stride MV 3.04. 67
doth watch bianca's steps so narrowly, | 'twere SHR 3.02.139
my lord, | and leave you to your graver steps. WT 1.02.173
attend | the steps of wrong, should move you to JN 4.02. 57
we will untread the steps of damned flight, 5.04. 52
the sullen passage of thy weary steps | esteem R2 1.03.265
and thy steps no more | than a delightful 1.03.290
which with usurping steps do trample thee. 3.02. 17
measure our confines with such peaceful steps? 3.02.125
steps me a little higher than his vow | made to 1H4 4.03. 75
and threefold vengeance tend upon your steps! 2H6 3.02.304
soul | leads discontented steps in foreign soil, R3 4.04.312
in that file | where others tell steps with me. H8 1.02. 43
gone slightly o'er low steps and now are mounted 2.04.112
we'll consecrate the steps that ajax makes TRO 2.03.183
saucy controller of my private steps! TIT 2.03. 60
hear not my steps, which /way /they walk, for MAC 2.01. 57
"but age with his stealing steps | hath clawed HAM 5.01. 71
and decay, | have follow'd your sad steps — LR 5.03.290
steps in to cassio and entreats his pause; OTH 2.03.229
whose rudeness | answer'd my steps too loud. CYM 4.02.215
whose /delightful steps | shall make the gazer PER 2.01.158
sometime he trots, as if he told the steps, VEN 277
who sees the lurking serpent steps aside; LUC 362
STERILE 5 FR 0.0005 REL FR 2 V 3 P
and thy sea-marge, sterile and rocky-hard, TMP 4.01. 69
he hath, like lean, sterile, and bare land, 2H4 4.03.119 P
holy chase, | shake off their sterile curse. JC 1.02. 9
the earth, seems to me a sterile promontory; HAM 2.02.299 P
many, either to have it sterile with idleness or OTH 1.03.324 P
STERILITY 1 FR 0.0001 REL FR 1 V 0 P
into her womb convey sterility, | dry up in her LR 1.04.278
/STERLING 1 FR 0.0001 REL FR 1 V 0 P
/if /my /word /be /sterling /yet /in /england, R2 4.01.264
STERLING 2 FR 0.0002 REL FR 1 V 1 P
the one you may do with sterling money, and the 2H4 2.01.120 P
tenders for true pay, | which are not sterling. HAM 1.03.107
STERN* 34 FR 0.0038 REL FR 34 V 0 P
he, like you, | would not have been so stern. MM 2.02. 66
through the heart with your stern cruelty. MND 3.02. 59
i on the countenance | of stern command'ment. AYL 2.07.109
i guess | by the stern brow and waspish action 4.03. 9
for you are cold and stern, | and now you should AWW 4.02. 8
he hath a stern look, but a gentle heart. JN 4.01. 87
hand | of stern injustice and confused wrong. 5.02. 23
teaching stern murder how to butcher thee. R2 1.02. 32
is thought with child by the stern tyrant war, 2H4 in 14
to swearing and stern looks, defus'd attire, H5 5.02. 61
and sit at chiefest stern of public weal. 1H6 1.01.177
question her proudly, let thy looks be stern. 1.02. 62
why look you still so stern and tragical? 3.01.125
rough deeds of rage and stern impatience; 4.07. 8
shore, | or turn our stern upon a dreadful rock? 2H6 3.02. 91
mother took into her blameful bed | some stern, 3.02.213
suffolk's imperial tongue is stern and rough, 4.01.121
stern falconbridge commands the narrow seas, 3H6 1.01.239
thou stern, obdurate, flinty, rough, remorseless 1.04.142
is by the stern lord clifford done to death. 2.01.103
our stern alarums chang'd to merry meetings, R3 1.01. 7
that i, forsooth, am stern, and love them not? 1.03. 44
murther, stern murther, in the direst degree; 5.03.197
i have seen thee stern, and thou hast oft beheld COR 4.01. 24
what stern ungentle hands | hath lopp'd and TIT 2.04. 16
more stern and bloody than the centaurs' feast. 5.02.203
piteous action you convert | my stern effects, HAM 3.04.129
attend you here the door of our stern daughter? CYM 2.03. 37
industry they skip | from /stem to stern. PER 4.01. 63
stern, and yet noble, | which shows him hardy, TNK 4.02. 79
now, | even by the stern and direful god of war, VEN 98
and there we will unfold | to creatures stern, LUC 1147
men can cover crimes with bold stern looks, 1252
how many lambs might the stern wolf betray, | if SON 96. 9
STERNAGE 1 FR 0.0001 REL FR 1 V 0 P
grapple your minds to sternage of this navy, H5 3.pr. 18
STERNER 2 FR 0.0002 REL FR 2 V 0 P
will you sterner be | than he that dies and AYL 3.05. 6
ambition should be made of sterner stuff: JC 3.02. 92
STERNEST 1 FR 0.0001 REL FR 1 V 0 P
i would o'erstare the sternest eyes that look, MV 2.01. 27
STERNNESS 2 FR 0.0002 REL FR 2 V 0 P
flaunts, behold | the sternness of his presence? WT 4.04. 24
that equally canst poise sternness with pity, TNK 1.01. 86
STERN'ST 1 FR 0.0001 REL FR 1 V 0 P
bellman, | which gives the stern'st good-night. MAC 2.02. 4
STETERAT 3 FR 0.0003 REL FR 1 V 2 P
hic steterat priami regia celsa senis." SHR 3.01. 29
disguis'd thus to get your love, "hic steterat," 3.01. 34 P
i trust you not, "hic steterat priami," take 3.01. 43 P
STEVEN *(also stephen)*
STEVEN 1 FR 0.0001 REL FR 0 V 1 P
god and saint steven give you god-den. TIT 4.04. 42 P
STEW 2 FR 0.0002 REL FR 2 V 0 P
boil and bubble, | till it o'errun the stew; MM 5.01.319
in his court to mart | as in a romish stew, and CYM 1.06.152
STEWARD 22 FR 0.0024 REL FR 16 V 6 P
not call'd up her steward malvolio and bid him TN 2.03. 73 P
art any more than a steward? 2.03.114 P
if not, let me see thee a steward still, the 2.05.156 P
here comes the lady paulina's steward, he can WT 5.02. 26 P
his captain, steward, deputy, elect, | anointed, R2 4.01.126
be what thou wilt, i am fortune's steward — get 2H4 5.03.131 P
not as protector, steward, substitute, | or R3 3.07.133
is the first, and claims | to be high steward; H8 4.01. 18
'tis the same: high steward. 4.01. 41
plutus, the god of gold, | is but his steward. TIM 1.01.277
go to my steward. 2.02. 18
your steward puts me off, my lord, | and i am 2.02. 31
is not that his steward muffled so? 3.04. 41
i'll have it so. my steward! 3.04.108
hear you, master steward, where's our master? 4.02. 1
whilst i have gold, i'll be his steward still. 4.02. 50
nev'r did poor steward wear a truer grief | for 4.03.480
lasts | to entertain me as your steward still. 4.03.489
had i a steward | so true, so just, and now so 4.03.490
no more, i pray — and he's a steward. 4.03.498
said he gave unto | his steward a mighty sum. 5.01. 8
it is the false steward, that stole his master's HAM 4.05.173 P
STEWARD'S 1 FR 0.0001 REL FR 1 V 0 P
the lord steward's daughter — | do you remember TNK 3.03. 29
STEWARDS 1 FR 0.0001 REL FR 1 V 0 P
others but stewards of their excellence. SON 94. 8
STEWARDSHIP 2 FR 0.0002 REL FR 2 V 0 P
hath broken his staff, resign'd his stewardship, R2 2.02. 59
that hath dismiss'd us from our stewardship, 3.03. 78
STEW'D 9 FR 0.0010 REL FR 3 V 6 P
(three veneys for a dish of stew'd prunes) and, WIV 1.01.285 P
(when i was more than half stew'd in grease, 3.05.119 P
your honors' reverence) for stew'd pruins. MM 2.01. 90 P
no more faith in thee than in a stew'd prune, 1H4 3.03.112 P
he lives upon mouldy stew'd pruins and dried 2H4 2.04.146 P
sodden business! there's a stew'd phrase indeed! TRO 3.01. 41 P
stew'd in corruption, honeying and making love HAM 3.04. 93
stew'd in his haste, half breathless, /panting LR 2.04. 31
shalt be whipt with wire, and stew'd in brine, ANT 2.05. 65
STEWS 2 FR 0.0002 REL FR 1 V 1 P
his answer was, he would unto the stews, | and R2 5.03. 16
and i could get me but a wife in the stews, i 2H4 1.02. 54 P
STICK* 30 FR 0.0034 REL FR 21 V 9 P
for i can here disarm thee with this stick, TMP 1.02.473
on whose nature | nurture can never stick; 4.01.189
ground be overcharg'd, you were best stick her. TGV 1.01.102 P
unless you have a codpiece to stick pins on. 2.07. 56
only to stick it in their children's sight | for MM 1.03. 25
nay, friar, i am a kind of bur, i shall stick. 4.03.179 P

and stick musk–roses in thy sleek smooth head, MND 4.01. 3
that in mine ear i durst not stick a rose | lest JN 1.01.142
and yet he will not stick to say his face is a 2H4 1.02. 22 P
the knave will stick by thee, i can assure thee 5.03. 66 P
and i'll stick by him, sir. 5.03. 68 P
'a saw a flea stick upon bardolph's nose, and 'a H5 2.03. 40 P
thou this favor for me and stick it in thy cap. 4.07.154 P
that he that breaks a stick of gloucester's 2H6 1.02. 33
thy leg a stick compared with this truncheon; 4.10. 49
from our laws, | and stick them in our will. H8 1.02. 94
they will not stick to say you envied him, | and 2.02.126
tell you, they'll stick where they are thrown. TRO 3.02.112 P
let them say, to stick the heart of falsehood, 3.02.195
and stick i' th' wars | like a great sea–mark, COR 5.03. 73
and stick your rosemary | on this fair corse, ROM 4.05. 79
our fears in banquo | stick deep, and in his MAC 3.01. 49
of reverent priam, seem'd i' th' air to stick. HAM 2.02.479
will nothing stick our person to arraign | in 4.05. 93
i' th' darkest night, | stick fiery off indeed. 5.02.257
she knapp'd 'em o' th' coxcombs with a stick, LR 2.04.124 P
that he might stick | the small'st opinion on my OTH 4.02.108
you, leave me, | stick to your journal course: CYM 4.02. 10
humors that | stick misbecomingly on others, on TNK 5.03. 54
she will not stick to round me on th' ear, | to PP 18.51

STICKEST 1 FR 0.0001 REL FR 1 V 0 P
love, wherein thou stickest | up to the ears. ROM 1.04. 42

STICKING 4 FR 0.0004 REL FR 4 V 0 P
faithful loves, | sticking together in calamity. JN 3.04. 67
on the sheets his hair, you see, is sticking, 2H6 3.02.174
but screw your courage to the sticking place, MAC 1.07. 60
his secret murthers sticking on his hands; 5.02. 17

STICKLER–LIKE 1 FR 0.0001 REL FR 1 V 0 P
and, stickler–like, the armies separates. TRO 5.08. 18

STICKS* 13 FR 0.0014 REL FR 12 V 1 P
i'll bear him no more sticks, but follow thee, TMP 2.02.163
and so deep sticks it in my penitent heart MM 5.01.475
and envious disposition | sticks me at heart. AYL 1.02.242
this drum sticks sorely in your disposition. AWW 3.06. 44 P
opinion that so sticks on martius shall | of his COR 1.01.271
when every feather sticks in his own wing, TIM 2.01. 30
this avarice | sticks deeper, grows with more MAC 4.03. 85
which now, the fruit unripe, sticks on the tree, HAM 3.02.190
hates the slime | that sticks on filthy deeds. OTH 5.02.149
his speech sticks in my heart. ANT 1.05. 41
on, where she sticks | the queen of flowers. TNK 5.01. 44
mellow plum doth fall, the green sticks fast, VEN 527
lucretia's glove, wherein her needle sticks. LUC 317

STICK'ST 2 FR 0.0002 REL FR 1 V 1 P
thou stick'st a dagger in me. MV 3.01.110 P
'gainst thyself thou stick'st not to conspire, SON 10. 6

STIFF 12 FR 0.0013 REL FR 12 V 0 P
for with long travel i am stiff and weary. ERR 1.02. 15
in stiff unwieldy arms against thy crown; R2 3.02.115
many a nobleman lies stark and stiff | under the 1H4 5.03. 41
eye, | and passeth by with stiff unbowed knee, 2H6 3.01. 16
as the shrouds make at sea in a stiff tempest, H8 4.01. 72
but make you ready your stiff bats and clubs, COR 1.01.161
what, art thou stiff? 1.01.241
shall, stiff and stark and cold, appear like ROM 4.01.103
her blood is settled, and her joints are stiff; 4.05. 26
how stiff is my vild sense | that i stand up, LR 4.06.279
labienus | (this is stiff news) hath with his ANT 1.02.100
well corresponding | with your stiff age; CYM 3.03. 32

//STIFF–BORNE 1 FR 0.0001 REL FR 1 V 0 P
/could /restrain | /the //stiff–borne /action. 2H4 1.01.177

STIFFEN 1 FR 0.0001 REL FR 1 V 0 P
stiffen the sinews, /conjure up the blood, H5 3.01. 7

/STIFFLY 1 FR 0.0001 REL FR 1 V 0 P
grow not instant old, | but bear me /stiffly up. HAM 1.05. 95

STIFLE 4 FR 0.0004 REL FR 4 V 0 P
that you shall stifle in your own report, | and MM 2.04.158
the ocean, | enough to stifle such a villain up. JN 4.03.133
stifle the villain whose unstanched thirst 3H6 2.06. 83
mean | to stifle beauty and to steal his breath? VEN 934

STIFLED 3 FR 0.0003 REL FR 3 V 0 P
for i am stifled with this smell of sin. JN 4.03.113
i am stifled | with the mere rankness of their H8 4.01. 58
shall i not then be stifled in the vault, | to ROM 4.03. 33

STIGMATIC 2 FR 0.0002 REL FR 2 V 0 P
foul stigmatic, that's more than thou canst tell 2H6 5.01.215
nor dam, | but like a foul misshapen stigmatic, 3H6 2.02.136

STIGMATICAL 1 FR 0.0001 REL FR 1 V 0 P
unkind, | stigmatical in making, worse in mind. ERR 4.02. 22

STILE 2 FR 0.0002 REL FR 0 V 2 P
from frogmore, over the stile, this way. WIV 3.01. 33 P
both stile and gate, horse–way and foot–path. LR 4.01. 56 P

STILE–A 1 FR 0.0001 REL FR 1 V 0 P
foot–path way, | and merrily hent the stile–a; WT 4.03.124

/STILL 8 FR 0.0009 REL FR 8 V 0 P
/i /am, /but /still /my /griefs /are /mine. R2 4.01.191
/still /am /i /king /of /those. 4.01.193
/the /crown, /yet /still /with /me /they /stay. 4.01.199
/not /strike /it /thus /to /make /it /still. TIT 3.02. 14
/lest /we /remember /still /that /we /have /none 3.02. 30
/and /by /still /practice /learn /to /know /thy 3.02. 45
/that /still /would /manage /those /authorities LR 1.03. 17
/a /moral /fool, /sits /still /and /cries, 4.02. 58

STILL 622 FR 0.0703 REL FR 545 V 77 P
sit still, and hear the last of our sea–sorrow: TMP 1.02.170
for still 'tis beating in my mind, your reason 1.02.176
so you may continue, and laugh at nothing still. 2.01.179 P
and increasing, | hourly joys be still upon you! 4.01.108
or two i'll walk | to still my beating mind. 4.01.163
thy shape invisible retain thou still. 4.01.185
good my lord, give me thy favor still. 4.01.204
let grief and sorrow still embrace his heart 5.01.214
but since thou lov'st, love still, and thrive TGV 1.01. 9
this proves me still a sheep. 1.01. 82 P
keep tune there still, so you will sing it out. 1.02. 86
well — you'll still be too forward. 2.01. 11 P
since i saw her, and still i see her beautiful. 2.01. 67 P
sure, i think she holds them prisoners still. 2.04. 92
for love is still most precious in itself, | and 2.06. 24
well, your old vice still: 3.01.284 P
the more it grows, and fawneth on her still. 4.02. 15
heaven and fortune still rewards with plagues. 4.03. 31
did not i bid thee still mark me and do as i do? 4.04. 36 P
a slave, that still an end turns me to shame! 4.04. 62
o, 'tis the curse in love, and still approv'd, 5.04. 43
and youthful still, in your doublet and hose, WIV 3.01. 46 P
yet seek my father's love, still seek it, sir. 3.04. 19
you wrong me, sir, thus still to haunt my house. 3.04. 69
still swine eats all the draff. 4.02.107
afflicted, we two will still be the ministers. 4.02.218 P
doth all the winter–time, at still midnight, 4.04. 30
and, as you trip, still pinch him to your time. 5.05. 92
i'll be your tapster still. MM 1.02.108 P
yet still 'tis just. 1.02.123
pardon is still the nurse of second woe. 2.01.284
whose very comfort | is still a dying horror! 2.03. 42
to shun, | and yet run'st toward him still. 3.01. 13
what thou hast not, still thou striv'st to get, 3.01. 22
this rank offense, | so to offend him still. 3.01.100
still thus, and thus; still worse! 3.02. 53 P
still thus, and thus; still worse! 3.02. 53 P
procures she still? 3.02. 55 P
does bridget paint still, pompey? ha? 3.02. 79 P
admonition, and still forfeit in the same kind! 3.02.193 P
his friends still wrought reprieves for him; 4.02.135 P
you make my bonds still greater. 5.01. 8
habit, i am still | attorney'd at your service. 5.01.384
haste still pays haste, and leisure answers 5.01.410
doth quit like, and measure still for measure. 5.01.411
wise | as you, lord angelo, have still appear'd, 5.01.471
because their business still lies out a' door. ERR 2.01. 11
yet the gold bides still | that others touch and 2.01.110
o, soft, sir, hold you still; 3.02. 69
i cannot, nor i will not, hold me still, | my 4.02. 17
wilt thou still talk? 4.04. 44 P
i could find in my heart to stay here still, and 4.04.155 P
still did i tell him it was vild and bad. 5.01. 67
i see we still did meet each other's man, | and 5.01.387
i wonder that you will still be talking, signior ADO 1.01.116 P
god keep your ladyship still in that mind! 1.01.133 P
how still the evening is, | as hush'd on purpose 2.03. 38
it is the witness still of excellency | to put a 2.03. 46
you must call to the nurse and bid her still it. 3.03. 66 P
still and contemplative in living art. LLL 1.01. 14
he weeds the corn and still lets grow the 1.01. 96
still me? 1.01.254 P
for still her cheeks possess the same | which 1.02.105
rust, rapier, be still, drum, for your manager 1.02.181 P
whose will still wills | it should none spare 2.01. 50
by the heart's still rhetoric disclosed with 2.01.229
were still at odds, being but three. 3.01. 85
were still at odds, being but three. 3.01. 90
were still at odds, being but three. 3.01. 96
still a–repairing, ever out of frame, | and 3.01.191
but being watch'd that it may still go right! 3.01.193
you still wrangle with her, boyet, and she 4.01.117
my tears for glasses, and still make me weep. 4.03. 38
can you still dream and pore and thereon look? 4.03.294
still climbing trees in the hesperides? 4.03.338
they sparkle still the right promethean fire; 4.03.348
look what you do, you do it still i' th' dark. 5.02. 24
great reason: for past care is still past cure. 5.02. 28
that we may do it still without accompt. 5.02.200
yet still she is the moon, and i the man. 5.02.215
let's mock them still, as well known as 5.02.301
visit the speechless sick and still converse 5.02.851
i frown upon him; yet he loves me still. MND 1.01.194
(a time that lovers' flights doth still conceal) 1.01.212
yet hermia still loves you; 2.02.110
the summer still doth tend upon my state; 3.01.155
still thou mistak'st, | or else commit'st thy 3.02.345
he goes before me and still dares me on. 3.02.413
and, like limander, am i trusty still. 5.01.196
i should be still | plucking the grass to know MV 1.01. 17
it, | and if it stand, as you yourself still do, 1.01.136
still have i borne it with a patient shrug, 1.03.109
still more fool i shall appear | by the time i 2.09. 73
the world is still deceiv'd with ornament. 3.02. 74
still gazing in a doubt | whether those peals of 3.02.144
thee honest–true, | so let me find thee still. 3.04. 47
than to live still and write mine epitaph. 4.01.118
it is still her use | to let the wretched man 4.01.268
a daniel, still say i, a second daniel! 4.01.340
still quiring to the young–ey'd cherubins; 5.01. 62
my father, so thou hadst been still with me, i AYL 1.02. 11 P
but i did find him still mine enemy. 1.02.226
we still have slept together, | rose at an 1.03. 73
swans, | still we went coupled and inseparable. 1.03. 76
that is the way to make her scorn you still. 2.04. 22
why, we are still handling our ewes, and their 3.02. 53 P
gallops withal, and who he stands still withal. 3.02.311 P
who stays it still withal? 3.02.330 P
in the which women still give the lie to their 3.02.390 P
as firmly as yourself were still in place, | yea SHR 1.02.156
that she shall still be curst in company. 2.01.305
i should be arguing still upon that doubt. 3.01. 55
and with the clamor keep her still awake. 4.01.207
do, or think to do, | you are still crossing it. 4.03.193
besides, old gremio is heark'ning still, | and 4.04. 53
he was skillful enough to have liv'd still, if AWW 1.01. 30 P
sieve | i still pour in the waters of my love 1.03.203
waters of my love | and lack not to lose still. 1.03.204
i, | thy resolv'd patient, on thee still rely. 2.01.204
them on, and to keep them on, have them still. 2.04. 18 P
treasons, we still see them reveal themselves, 4.03. 22 P
a pox on him, he's a cat still. 4.03.275 P
still the fine's the crown; 4.04. 35
serve him still. 4.05. 46 P
what's to come is still unsure. TN 2.03. 49
let still the woman take | an elder than herself 2.04. 29
for still we prove | much in our vows, but 2.04.117
let me see thee a steward still, the fellow of 2.05.156 P
therefore in my presence still smile, dear my 2.05.177 P
"if not, let me see thee a servant still." 3.04. 55 P
still you keep o' th' windy side of the law; 3.04.164 P
and he went | still in this fashion, color, 3.04.382
let fancy still my sense in lethe steep; 4.01. 62
if it be thus to dream, still let me sleep! 4.01. 63
remain thou still in darkness. 4.02. 57 P
still so cruel? 5.01.110
still so constant, lord. 5.01.111
live you the marble–breasted tyrant still. 5.01.124
with toss–pots still had drunken heads, | for 5.01.403
still virginalling | upon his palm? WT 1.02.125
hold, | when you cast out, it still came home. 1.02.214
me, and thy places shall | still neighbor mine. 1.02.449
and speak to me as if | i were a baby still. 2.01. 6
mountain, and still winter | in storm perpetual, 3.02.212
both breed thee, pretty, | and still rest thine. 3.03. 49
and to be so still requires nothing but secrecy. 3.03.125 P
what you do | still betters what is done. 4.04.136
move still, still so, | and own no other 4.04.142
move still, still so, | and own no other 4.04.142
why, be so still; 4.04.631 P
and so still think of | the wrong i did myself; 5.01. 8
still, 'tis strange | he thus should steal upon 5.01.114
like an old tale still, which will have matter 5.02. 61 P
them not and think me still no gentleman born. 5.02.131 P
mock'd as ever | still sleep mock'd death. 5.03. 20
still methinks | there is an air comes from her. 5.03. 77
then, all stand still; 5.03. 95
or no, | that still i lay upon my mother's head, JN 1.01. 76
near or far off, well won is still well shot, 1.01.174
still secure | and confident from foreign 2.01. 27
that she is bound in honor still to do | what 2.01.522
do | what you in wisdom still vouchsafe to say. 2.01.523
that broker that still breaks the pate of faith, 2.01.568
or, if it must stand still, let wives with child 3.01. 89
still and anon cheer'd up the heavy time, 4.01. 47
many a poor man's son would have lien still, 4.01. 50
though to no use but still to look on you! 4.01.102
doth he still rage? 5.07. 11
as it on earth hath been thy servant still. 5.07. 73
each day still better other's happiness | until R2 1.01. 22
whose manners still our tardy, apish nation 2.01. 22
conceit is still deriv'd | from some forefather 2.02. 34
it shall be still thy true love's recompense. 2.03. 49
must fall, for heaven still guards the right. 3.02. 62
as thus to drop them still upon one place, 3.03.166
beasts, | i had been still a happy king of men. 5.01. 36
and thus still doing, thus he pass'd along. 5.02. 21
his face still combating with tears and smiles, 5.02. 32
our knees still kneel till to the ground they 5.03.106
is pointing still, in cleansing them from tears. 5.05. 54
it in snuff — and still he smil'd and talk'd: 1H4 1.03. 41
give it him | to keep his anger still in motion. 1.03.226
before the game is afoot thou still let'st slip. 1.03.278
what, stand'st thou still, and hear'st such a 2.04. 80 P
a plague of all cowards, i say still. 2.04.134 P
a plague of all cowards, still say i. 2.04.156 P
and roar'd for mercy, and still run and roar'd, 2.04.260 P
lie still, ye thief, and hear the lady sing in 3.01.233 P
then be still. 3.01.239 P
the crown, | had still kept loyal to possession, 3.02. 43
thou seest i am pacified still. 3.03.173 P
sweet beef, i must still be good angel to thee. 3.03.177 P
and god defend but still i should stand so, | so 4.03. 38
he will suspect us still, and find a time | to 5.02. 6
the better cherish'd, still the nearer death. 5.02. 15
by still dispraising praise valued with you, 5.02. 59
point, | still ending at the arrival of an hour. 5.02. 84
still unfold | the acts commenced on this ball 2H4 in 4
he may keep it still at a face royal, for a 1.02. 24 P
you'll be a fool still. 2.01.157 P
he is at oxford still, is he not? 3.02. 11 P
now, cousin, wherefore stands our army still? 4.02. 98
colevile shall be still your name, a traitor 4.03. 7 P
so shall you be still colevile of the dale. 4.03. 8 P
/write her fair words still in foulest terms? 4.04.104
lest rest and lying still might make them look 4.05.211
therefore still bear the balance and the sword, 5.02.103
the air, a charter'd libertine, is still, | and H5 1.01. 48
who hath been still a giddy neighbor to us; 1.02.145
and leave your england as dead midnight, still, 3.pr. 19
still be kind, | and eche out our performance 3.pr. 34
so god sa' me, 'tis shame to stand still, it is 3.02.111 P
doing is activity, and he will still be doing. 3.07. 99 P
he will keep that good name still. 3.07.102 P
solemn priests | sing still for richard's soul. 4.01.302
foul with chaw'd–grass, still and motionless; 4.02. 50
arms are set, like clocks, still to strike on; 1H6 1.02. 42
one that still motions war and never peace, 1.03. 63
sleeping or waking, must i still prevail, | or 2.01. 56
with his name the mothers still their babes? 2.03. 17
and keep me on the side where still i am. 2.04. 54
ah, thou shalt find us ready for thee still; 2.04.104
in your behalf still will i wear the same. 2.04.130
why look you still so stern and tragical? 3.01.125
lord, in heart desiring still | you may behold 4.01. 76
so let us still continue peace, and love. 4.01.161
under him, | and still enjoy thy regal dignity. 5.04.132
hang up your ensigns, let your drums be still, 5.04.174
and we will keep it still. 2H6 1.01.106
still revelling like lords till all be gone; 1.01.224
then, york, be still awhile, till time do serve. 1.01.248
and wilt thou still be hammering treachery, | to 1.02. 47
shall king henry be a pupil still | under the 1.03. 46
but still remember what the lord hath done. 2.01. 84
the king will labor still to save his life, 3.01.239
sweet somerset, be still. 3.01.304
madam, be still — with reverence may i say — 3.02.207
still lamenting and mourning for suffolk's death 4.04. 22
continue still in this so good a mind, | and 4.09. 17
and still proclaimeth, as he comes along, | his 4.09. 28
war hath given thee peace, for thou art still. 5.02. 29
heart, be wrathful still: 5.02. 70
but still, where danger was, still there i met 5.03. 11
still, where danger was, still there i met him, 5.03. 11
therefore be still. 3H6 2.02.122
hadst thou been meek, our title still had slept, 2.02.160
i'll never pause again, never stand still, 2.03. 30
what e'er it be, be thou still like thyself, 3.03. 15
mind | still ride in triumph over all mischance. 3.03. 18
reason may suffice, | that henry liveth still; 3.03. 72
and still is friend to him and margaret. 3.03.144
warwick, although my head still wear the crown, 4.06. 23
your grace hath still been fam'd for virtuous, 4.06. 26
and thou shalt still remain the duke of york. 5.01. 28
'tis even so, yet you are warwick still. 5.01. 47
yet lives our pilot still. 5.04. 6

that you might still have worn the petticoat, 5.05. 23
clarence still breathes, edward still lives and R3 1.01.161
still breathes, edward still lives and reigns; 1.01.161
and still, as you are weary of this weight, 1.02. 31
a murth'rous villain, and so still thou art. 1.03.133
the worm of conscience still begnaw thy soul! 1.03.221
and in that shame still live my sorrow's rage! 1.03.277
but still the envious flood | stopp'd in my soul 1.04. 37
o, they did urge it still unto the king! 2.01.138
before the days of change, still is it so. 2.03. 41
my lord of york will still be cross in talk. 3.01.126
because they have been still my adversaries; 3.02. 52
play the maid's part, still answer nay, and take 3.07. 51
but with his timorous dreams was still awak'd. 4.01. 84
still live they, and for ever let them last! 4.02. 7
that edward still should live true noble prince! 4.02. 16
is in the field, and still his power increaseth. 4.03. 48
that my woe–wearied tongue is still and mute. 4.04. 18
but that still use of grief makes wild grief 4.04.230
harp on it still shall i till heart–strings 4.04.365
sleeping and waking, o, defend me still! 5.03.117
the play may pass, if they be still and willing, H8 pr 11
him in eye | still him in praise, and being 1.01. 31
still exaction! 1.02. 52
if we shall stand still, | in fear our motion 1.02. 85
his accusations | he pleaded still not guilty, 2.01. 13
kept him a foreign man still, which so griev'd 2.02.128
still growing in a majesty and pomp, the which 2.03. 7
zeal and obedience he still bore your grace, 3.01. 63
all my full affections | still met the king? 3.01.130
object, he should still | dwell in his musings, 3.02.132
"ego et rex meus" | was still inscrib'd; 3.02.315
dignities, | a still and quiet conscience. 3.02.380
still in thy right hand carry gentle peace | to 3.02.445
where eagerly his sickness | pursu'd him still, 4.02. 25
so excellent in art, and still so rising, | that 4.02. 62
patience, be near me still, and set me lower; 4.02. 76
to th' broom–staff to me, i defied 'em still, 5.03. 55 P
they grow still too; 5.03. 68
royal infant — heaven still move about her! 5.04. 17
the good, | shall still be doubled on her. 5.04. 28
holy and heavenly thoughts still counsel her. 5.04. 29
still have i tarried. TRO 1.01. 22
yet god achilles still cries, "excellent! 1.03.169
the still and mental parts, | that do contrive 1.03.200
yet go we under our opinion still | that we have 1.03.382
you have the honey still, but these the gall; 2.02.144
to you | in resolution to keep helen still, 2.02.191
love, nothing but love, still love, still more! 3.01.115
love, nothing but love, still love, still more! 3.01.115
that it wounds, | but tickles still the sore. 3.01.120
so dying love lives still. 3.01.124
what, blushing still? 3.02.100 P
whom troy hath still denied, but this antenor, 3.03. 22
and still it might, and yet it may again, | if 3.03.185
i might have still held off, | and then you 4.02. 17
there lurks a still and dumb–discoursive devil 4.04. 90
your quondam wife swears still by venus' glove. 4.05.179
but this thy countenance, still lock'd in steel, 4.05.195
but still sweet love is food for fortune's tooth 4.05.293
lechery, still wars and lechery, nothing else 5.02.194 P
hold you still, i say; 5.03. 25
my love with words and errors still she feeds, 5.03.111
i'll haunt thee like a wicked conscience still, 5.10. 28
still cupboarding the viand, never bearing COR 1.01.100
people in what hatred | he still hath held them; 2.01.246
i do owe them still | my life and services. 2.02.133
if he should still malignantly remain | fast foe 2.03.183
say you ne'er had done't | (harp on that still) 2.03.252
of sight, yet will i still | be thus to them. 3.02. 5
in congregations, to yawn, be still, and wonder, 3.02. 11
have the power still | to banish your defenders, 3.03.127
still your own foes) deliver you as most 3.03.131
well | my hazards still have been your solace, 4.01. 28
you shall | hear from me still, and never of me 4.01. 52
whose meal and exercise | are still together, 4.04. 15
it, and rome | sits safe and still without him. 4.06. 37
do they still fly to th' roman? 4.07. 1
leave unburnt | and still to nose th' offense. 5.01. 28
for a noble man | still to remember wrongs? 5.03.155
but still subsisting | under your great command. 5.06. 72
in summer's drought i'll drop upon thee still, TIT 3.01. 19
now is a time to storm, why art thou still? 3.01.263
she's with the lion deeply still in league, 4.01. 98
and by her presence still renew his sorrows. 5.03. 42
alas that love, whose view is muffled still, ROM 1.01.171
she hath sworn that she will still live chaste? 1.01.217
i shall forget, to have thee still stand there, 2.02.172
and i'll still stay, to have thee still forget, 2.02.174
and i'll still stay, to have thee still forget, 2.02.174
two such opposed kings encamp them still | in 2.03. 27
still blush, as thinking their own kisses sin; 3.03. 39
but much of grief shows still some want of wit. 3.05. 73
what, still in tears? 3.05.129
for still thy eyes, which i may call the sea, 3.05.132
still my care hath been | to have her match'd; 3.05.177
not, | for he hath still been tried a holy man. 4.03. 29
for fear of that, i still will stay with thee, 5.03.106
we still have known thee for a holy man. 5.03.270
that time serves still. TIM 1.01.258
the most accursed thou, that still omit'st it. 1.01.259
still in motion | of raging waste? 2.01. 3
but rather one that smiles and still invites 2.01. 11
this is the old man still. 3.06. 61 P
but reserve still to give, lest your deities be 3.06. 72 P
we are fellows still, | serving alike in sorrow. 4.02. 18
for bounty, that makes gods, do still mar men. 4.02. 41
whilst i have gold, i'll be his steward still. 4.02. 50
be a whore still. 4.03. 84
i'll trust to your conditions, be whores still. 4.03.140
whore still, | paint till a horse may mire upon 4.03.147
the one is filling still, never complete; 4.03.244
and still thou liv'dst but as a breakfast to the 4.03.333 P
and, as my lord, | still serve him with my life. 4.03.471
lasts | to entertain me as your steward still. 4.03.489
suspect still comes where an estate is least. 4.03.514
at all times alike | men are not still the same; 5.01.122
go, live still; 5.01.188

him no further, thus you still shall find him. 5.01.213
bid every noise be still; peace yet again! JC 1.02. 14
and still as he refus'd it, the rabblement 1.02.244 P
fly not, stand still; 3.01. 83
and my misgiving still | falls shrewdly to the 3.01.145
doing himself offense, whilst we, lying still, 4.03.201
he thinks he still is at his instrument. 4.03.292
old cassius still! 5.01. 63
since the affairs of men rests still incertain, 5.01. 95
caesar, now be still, | i kill'd not thee with 5.05. 50
is our trouble, | which still we thank as love. MAC 1.06. 12
highness' pleasure, | still to return your own. 1.06. 28
in these cases | we still have judgment here, 1.07. 8
it, but still keep | my bosom franchis'd and 2.01. 27
i have thee not, and yet i see thee still. 2.01. 35
i see thee still; 2.01. 45
still it cried, "sleep no more!" 2.02. 38
'gainst nature still! 2.04. 27
(which still hath been both grave and prosperous 3.01. 21
thou marvel'st at my words, but hold thee still: 3.02. 54
pray you sit still. 3.04.107
angels are bright still, though the brightest 4.03. 22
brows of grace, | yet grace must still look so. 4.03. 24
here's the smell of the blood still. 5.01. 50 P
all annoyance, | and still keep eyes upon her. 5.01. 77
the confident tyrant | keeps still in dunsinane, 5.04. 9
outward walls, | the cry is still, "they come!" 5.05. 2
wife and children's ghosts will haunt me still. 5.07. 16
and let the angel whom thou still hast serv'd 5.08. 14
as harbingers preceding still the fates | and HAM 1.01.122
how is it that the clouds still hang on you? 1.02. 66
is death of fathers, and who still hath cried, 1.02.104
let it be tenable in your silence still, | and 1.02.247
till then sit still, my soul. 1.02.256
it waves me still. — | go on, i'll follow thee. 1.04. 78
still am i call'd. 1.04. 84
and still your fingers on your lips, i pray. 1.05.187
thou still hast been the father of good news. 2.02. 42
still harping on my daughter. 2.02.187 P
still on my daughter. 2.02.409 P
a silence in the heavens, the rack stand still, 2.02.484
whereon his brains still beating puts him thus 3.01.174
run | that our devices still are overthrown, 3.02.212
still better, and worse. 3.02.251 P
and do still, by these pickers and stealers. 3.02.336 P
since i am still possess'd | of those effects 3.03. 53
this counsellor | is now most still, most secret 3.04.214
it, | and nothing is at a like goodness still, 4.07.116
as peace should still her wheaten garland wear 5.02. 41
and let me still remain | the true blank of LR 1.01.158
and the remainders that shall still depend, | to 1.04.250
let me still take away the harms i fear, | not 1.04.329
the harms i fear, | not fear still to be taken. 1.04.330
infirmity doth still neglect all office 2.04.106
still through the hawthorn blows the cold wind: 3.04. 98 P
i will keep still with my philosopher. 3.04.176
his word was still, 'fie, foh, and fum, | i 3.04.183
contemn'd, | than still contemn'd and flatter'd. 4.01. 2
stands still in esperance, lives not in fear. 4.01. 4
heavens, deal so still! 4.01. 66
stand still. 4.06. 11
madam, sleeps still. 4.07. 13
still, still, far wide! 4.07. 49
still, still, far wide! 4.07. 49
other sorrows, | and it is still itself. OTH 1.03. 58
of spirit so still and quiet that her motion 1.03. 95
still question'd me the story of my life | from 1.03.129
but still the house affairs would draw her 1.03.147
i find it still, when i have /list to sleep. 2.01.104
to love him still for prating — let not thy 2.01.224 P
/'zounds, i bleed still, | i am hurt to th' 2.03.164
to follow still the changes of the moon | with 3.03.178
peace, and be still! 5.02. 46
still as the grave. 5.02. 94
property | which still should go with antony. ANT 1.01. 59
forth weeds | when our quick winds lie still, 1.02.110
they are so still, | or thou, the greatest 1.03. 37
still he mends. 1.03. 82
his cocks do win the battle still of mine, 2.03. 37
gods confound thee, dost thou hold there still? 2.05. 92
is of a holy, cold, and still conversation. 2.06.123 P
sweet octavia, | you shall hear from me still; 3.02. 60
and i see still | a diminution in our captain's 3.13.196
thee, would have still | followed thy heels. 4.05. 5
your emperor | continues still a jove. 4.06. 28
but being charg'd, we will be still by land, 4.11. 1
with her modest eyes | and still conclusion, 4.15. 28
how calm and gentle i proceeded still | in all 5.01. 75
still be't yours, | bestow it at your pleasure, 5.02.181
dost thou lie still? 5.02.296
our courtiers' | still seem as does the king's. CYM 1.01. 3
loss, so in our trifles | i still win of you. 1.01.121
no, but he fled forward still, toward your face. 1.02. 15 P
glove or hat or handkerchief | still waving, as 1.03. 12
which i will be ever to pay and yet pay still. 1.04. 37 P
she holds her virtue still, and i my mind. 1.04. 64 P
weeps she still, say'st thou? 1.05. 46
on, but think | thou hast thy mistress still; 1.05. 69
fast to your affection, | still close as sure. 1.06.139
if not, | let her lie still and dream. 2.03. 65
still i swear i love you. 2.03. 90
if you swear still, your recompense is still 2.03. 92
your recompense is still | that i regard it not. 2.03. 92
they are not constant, but are changing still: 2.05. 30
thou need'st | but keep that count'nance still. 3.04. 14
i am sick still, heart–sick. 4.02. 37
yet still it's strange | what cloten's being 4.02.181
good faith, | i tremble still with fear; 4.02.303
the dream's here still; 4.02.306
the heavens still must work. 4.03. 41
but to be still hot summer's tanlings and | the 4.04. 29
still going? 5.03. 64
'tis still a dream, or else such stuff as madmen 5.04.145
new matter still. 5.05.243
her, still pretending | the satisfaction of her 5.05.250
who hath upon him still that natural stamp. 5.05.366
made a law, | to keep her still and men in awe, PER 1.ch. 36
glass of light, i lov'd you, and could still, 1.01. 76

is still at tharsus, where each man | thinks all 2.ch. 11
o, still | thy deaf'ning, dreadful thunders, 3.01. 4
with us at sea it hath been still observ'd, and 3.01. 52 P
but even | your purse, still open, hath built 3.02. 47
which the people's prayers still fall upon you, 3.03. 19
mute, | that still records with moan; 4.ch. 27
still | this philoten contends in skill | with 4.ch. 29
deep, | untied i still my virgin knot will keep. 4.02.147
demanded that, | she would sit still and weep. 5.01.189
still confirmation! 5.03. 54
yet still is modesty, and still retains | more TNK pr 7
and still retains | more of the maid to sight pr 7
thus dost thou still make good | the tongue o' 1.01.226
but dead–cold winter must inhabit here still. 2.02. 45
i would hear you still. 2.02.111
first sees the enemy, shall i stand still, | and 2.02.194
that still blossom | as her bright eyes shine on 2.02.233
still as she tasted, should be doubled on her, 2.02.240
laid upon ye, | and do you still cry, "where?" 3.05. 7
but still before that flew | the lightning of 3.06. 84
a still temper, | no stirring in him, no 4.02. 28
stout–hearted, still, | but, when he stirs, a 4.02.130
and still among intermingle your petition of 4.03. 88 P
apprehension | which still is farther off it, go 5.01. 37
doctor, | methinks you are i' th' wrong still. 5.02. 27
from her, | but still preserve her in this way. 5.02.106
still "palamon!" 5.03. 71
upon my right side still i wore thy picture, 5.03. 73
"palamon" still? 5.03. 90
to live still, | have their good wishes; 5.04. 5
are sorry, still | are children in some kind. 5.04.133
have among yourselves, | command still audience. STM II.C 47
are incident, by his name | can still the rout? II.C 116
still she entreats, and prettily entreats, | for VEN 73
still is he sullen, still he low'rs and frets, 75
still is he sullen, still he low'rs and frets, 75
in that thy likeness still is left alive." 174
her eyes wooed still, his eyes disdain'd the 358
yet would my love to thee be still as much, 442
will never rise, so he will kiss her still. 480
and as they last, their verdour still endure, 507
what bargains may i make, still to be sealing? 512
she sinketh down, still hanging by his neck, 593
whose tushes never sheath'd he whetteth still, 617
"o, let him keep his loathsome cabin still! 637
ear, | to hearken if his foes pursue him still. 699
her heavy anthem still concludes in woe, | and 839
woe, | and still the choir of echoes answer so. 840
sorrow that friendly sighs sought still to dry; 964
which knows no pity, but is still severe; 1000
who bids them still consort with ugly night, 1041
whose downward eye still looketh for a grave, 1106
thy hasty spring still blasts and ne'er grows LUC 49
yet their ambition makes them still to fight, 68
that cloy'd with much, he pineth still for more. 98
pure thoughts are dead and still, | while lust 167
true valor still a true respect should have; 201
guilt being great, the fear doth still exceed; 229
urging the worser sense for vantage still; 249
they fright him, yet he still pursues his fear. 308
in his clear bed might have reposed still! 382
swell in their pride, the onset still expecting. 432
but she with vehement prayers urgeth still 475
but happy monarchs still are fear'd for love; 611
conceit | can comprehend in still imagination! 702
which in her prescience she controlled still, 727
and therefore would they still in darkness be, 752
and bids her eyes hereafter still be blind; 758
keep still possession of thy gloomy place, 803
"the nurse, to still her child, will tell my 813
and therefore still in night would cloist'red be 1085
like an unpractic'd swimmer plunging still, 1098
for burthen–wise i'll hum on tarquin still, 1133
extremity still urgeth such extremes. 1337
an humble gait, calm looks, eyes wailing still, 1508
and still on him she gaz'd, and gazing still, 1531
and still on him she gaz'd, and gazing still, 1531
so should my shame still rest upon record, | and 1643
but still pure | doth in her poison'd closet yet 1658
some of her blood still pure and red remain'd, 1742
and blood untainted still doth red abide, 1749
that like two spirits do suggest me still: PP 2. 2
touches so soft still conquer chastity. 4. 8
my love, the loss whereof still fearing! 7.10
crave, | for why i craved nothing of thee still. 10.10
think women still to strive with men, | to sin 18.43
their show, their substance still lives sweet. SON 5.14
age, | yet mortal looks adore his beauty still, 7. 7
the world will be thy widow and still weep, 9. 5
but his place, for still the world enjoys it, 9.10
that beauty still may live in thine or thee. 10.14
to give away yourself keeps yourself still, 16.13
which in my bosom's shop is hanging still, 24. 7
how far i toil, still farther off from thee. 28. 8
though thou repent, yet i have still the loss: 34.10
for still temptation follows where thou art. 41. 4
love, | thyself away are present still with me, 47.10
and i am still with them, and they with thee; 47.12
your praise shall still find room, | even in the 55.10
and they shall live, and he in them still green. 63.14
in black ink my love may still shine bright. 65.14
which for memorial still with thee shall stay. 74. 4
why write i still all one, ever the same, | and 76. 5
you, | and you and love are still my argument; 76.10
old, | so is my love still telling what is told. 76.14
you still shall live (such virtue hath my pen) 81.13
my tongue–tied muse in manners holds her still, 85. 1
still cry "amen" | to every hymn that able 85. 6
so love's face | may still seem love to me, 93. 3
yet seem'd it winter still, and, you away, | as 98.13
your eye i ey'd, | such seems your beauty still. 104. 3
your sweet hue, which methinks still doth stand, 104.11
be | to one, of one, still such, and ever so. 105. 4
kind, | still constant in a wondrous excellence, 105. 6
they had not still enough your worth to sing: 106.12
give full growth to that which still doth grow. 115.14
fears, | still losing when i saw myself to win? 119. 4
true | that better is by evil still made better, 119.10

thou goest onwards, still will pluck thee back, 126. 6
she may detain, but not still keep, her treasure 126.10
mine | thou wilt restore to be my comfort still: 134. 4
more than enough am i that vex thee still, | to 135. 3
the sea, all water, yet receives rain still, 135. 9
make but my name thy love, and love that still, 136.13
if thou turn back and my loud crying still. 143.14
which like two spirits do suggest me still: 144. 2
longing still | for that which longer nurseth 147. 1
love | a dateless lively heat, still to endure, 153. 6
some in her threaden fillet still did bide, LC 33
for his advantage still did wake and sleep. 123

STILL–BORN 1 FR 0.0001 REL FR 1 V 0 P
should be still–born, and that we now possess'd 2H4 1.03. 64

STILL–BREEDING 1 FR 0.0001 REL FR 1 V 0 P
beget | a generation of still–breeding thoughts; R2 5.05. 8

STILL–CLOSING 1 FR 0.0001 REL FR 1 V 0 P
stabs | kill the still–closing waters, as TMP 3.03. 64

STILL'D 2 FR 0.0002 REL FR 2 V 0 P
hath often still'd my brawling discontent. MM 4.01. 9
like the froward infant still'd with dandling, VEN 562

STILL–DISCORDANT 1 FR 0.0001 REL FR 1 V 0 P
the still–discordant wav'ring multitude, | can 2H4 in 19

STILLER 1 FR 0.0001 REL FR 1 V 0 P
for this from stiller seats we came, | our CYM 5.04. 69

STILLEST 1 FR 0.0001 REL FR 1 V 0 P
and in the calmest and most stillest night, 2H4 3.01. 28

STILL–GAZING 1 FR 0.0001 REL FR 1 V 0 P
in silent wonder of still–gazing eyes. LUC 84

STILLITORY 1 FR 0.0001 REL FR 1 V 0 P
for from the stillitory of thy face excelling VEN 443

STILL–LASTING 1 FR 0.0001 REL FR 1 V 0 P
which she shall purchase with still–lasting war. R3 4.04.344

STILLNESS 6 FR 0.0006 REL FR 5 V 1 P
pond, | and do a willful stillness entertain, MV 1.01. 90
soft stillness and the night | become the 5.01. 56
a man | as modest stillness and humility; H5 3.01. 4
but only in patient stillness while his rider 3.07. 23 P
the gravity and stillness of your youth | the OTH 2.03.191
with the number, | command them to a stillness. STM II.C 52

STILL–PEERING 1 FR 0.0001 REL FR 1 V 0 P
move the still–peering air | that sings with AWW 3.02.110

STILL–PINING 1 FR 0.0001 REL FR 1 V 0 P
but like still–pining tantalus he sits, | and LUC 858

STILL–SLAUGHTERED
1 FR 0.0001 REL FR 1 V 0 P
his naked armor of still–slaughtered lust, | and LUC 188

STILL–SOLICITING 1 FR 0.0001 REL FR 1 V 0 P
a still–soliciting eye, and such a tongue | that LR 1.01.231

STILL–STAND 1 FR 0.0001 REL FR 1 V 0 P
that makes a still–stand, running neither way. 2H4 2.03. 64

STILL–VEX'D 1 FR 0.0001 REL FR 1 V 0 P
to fetch dew | from the still–vex'd bermoothes, TMP 1.02.229

STILL–WAKING 1 FR 0.0001 REL FR 1 V 0 P
still–waking sleep, that is not what it is! ROM 1.01.181

STILLY 1 FR 0.0001 REL FR 1 V 0 P
night, | the hum of either army stilly sounds, H5 4.pr. 5

/STING 1 FR 0.0001 REL FR 1 V 0 P
/these /things /sting | /his /mind /so LR 4.03. 45

STING 29 FR 0.0032 REL FR 29 V 0 P
wouldst thou have a serpent sting thee twice? MV 4.01. 69
as sensual as the brutish sting itself, | and AYL 2.07. 66
thy sting is not so sharp | as friend rememb'red 2.07.188
if i be waspish, best beware my sting. SHR 2.01.210
who knows not where a wasp does wear his sting? 2.01.213
whose sting is sharper than the sword's, and WT 2.03. 87
in my heart–blood warm'd, that sting my heart! R2 3.02.131
a serpent that will sting thee to the heart. 5.03. 58
doth sting a child | that for the beauty thinks 2H6 3.01.229
in your breasts, will sting your hearts. 3.01.344
their touch affrights me as a serpent's sting. 3.02. 47
and care not who they sting in his revenge. 3.02.127
with whose envenomed and fatal sting, | your 3.02.267
who scapes the lurking serpent's mortal sting? 3H6 2.02. 15
for though they cannot greatly sting to hurt, 2.06. 94
his nose | will make this sting the sooner. H8 3.02. 56
till he hath lost his honey and his sting; TRO 5.10. 42
let not this wasp outlive, us both to sting. TIT 2.03.132
and then i grant we put a sting in him | that at JC 2.01. 16
and very wisely threat before you sting. 5.01. 38
of dog, | adder's fork and blind–worm's sting, MAC 4.01. 16
the serpent that did sting thy father's life HAM 1.05. 39
in her bosom lodge | to prick and sting her. 1.05. 88
serpents have | edge, sting, or operation. ANT 4.15. 26
disdainfully did sting | his high–pitch'd LUC 40
thing, | lies at the mercy of his mortal sting. 364
i think the honey guarded with a sting: 493
kill'd too soon by death's sharp sting! PP 10. 4
in thee hath neither sting, knot, nor confine, LC 265

STINGING 3 FR 0.0003 REL FR 3 V 0 P
each pinch more stinging | than bees that made TMP 1.02.329
yield stinging nettles to mine enemies; R2 3.02. 18
like stinging bees in hottest summer's day, TIT 5.01. 14

STINGLESS 1 FR 0.0001 REL FR 1 V 0 P
not stingless too? JC 5.01. 35

STINGS 11 FR 0.0012 REL FR 8 V 3 P
kill the bees that yield it with your stings! TGV 1.02.104
the wanton stings and motions of the sense; MM 1.04. 59
ah, what sharp stings are in her mildest words! AWW 3.04. 18
there is something in't that stings his nature; 4.03. 4 P
have but their stings and teeth newly ta'en out; 2H4 4.05.205
others, like soldiers, armed in their stings, H5 1.02.193
their softest touch as smart as lizards' stings! 2H6 3.02.325
some say the bee stings, but i say, 'tis the 4.02. 82 P
as venom toads, or lizards' dreadful stings. 3H6 2.02.138
to cool our raging motions, our carnal stings, OTH 1.03.331 P
than lead itself, stings more than nettles. TNK 5.01. 97

STINK 5 FR 0.0005 REL FR 1 V 4 P
indeed, it does stink in some sort, sir; MM 3.02. 28 P
sir, if your metaphor stink, i will stop my nose AWW 5.02. 12 P
they would but stink, and putrefy the air. 1H6 4.07. 90
the lady brach may stand by th' fire and stink. LR 1.04.113 P
as it were to stink afore the face of the gods. PER 4.06.136 P

STINKING 11 FR 0.0012 REL FR 6 V 5 P
sky, it seems, would pour down stinking pitch, TMP 1.02. 3
with stinking clothes that fretted in their own WIV 3.05.113 P
may buy land now as cheap as stinking mack'rel. 1H4 2.04.360 P
stinking and fly–blown lies here at our feet. 1H6 4.07. 76
john, it will be stinking law, for his breath 2H6 4.07. 11 P
to th' people, beg their stinking breaths. COR 2.01.236
cast | your stinking greasy caps in hooting at 4.06.131
such a deal of stinking breath because caesar JC 1.02.246 P
among twenty but can smell him that's stinking. LR 2.04. 71 P
smoky light | that's fed with stinking tallow: CYM 1.06.110
and let the stinking elder, grief, untwine | his 4.02. 59

STINKINGLY 1 FR 0.0001 REL FR 1 V 0 P
thy living is a life, | so stinkingly depending? MM 3.02. 27

STINKS 1 FR 0.0001 REL FR 0 V 1 P
for his breath stinks with eating toasted cheese 2H6 4.07. 12 P

STINT 5 FR 0.0005 REL FR 5 V 0 P
we must not stint | our necessary actions in the H8 1.02. 76
wings | he can at pleasure stint their melody; TIT 4.04. 86
and stint thou too, i pray thee, nurse, say i. ROM 1.03. 58
make war breed peace, make peace stint war, make
TIM 5.04. 83
she does, and swears she'll never stint, | make PER 4.04. 42

STINTED 2 FR 0.0002 REL FR 2 V 0 P
and, pretty fool, it stinted and said, "ay." ROM 1.03. 48
it stinted and said, "ay." 1.03. 57

STINTS 1 FR 0.0001 REL FR 1 V 0 P
half stints their strife before their strokes TRO 4.05. 93

STIR 87 FR 0.0098 REL FR 72 V 15 P
what hallowing and what stir is this to–day? TGV 5.04. 13
it had been anne page, would i might never stir! WIV 5.05.187 P
vigor, art and nature, | once stir my temper; MM 2.02.184
but stir not you till you have well determin'd 5.01.258
for i will not let him stir | till i have us'd ERR 5.01.102
i will determine this before i stir. 5.01.167
peace, stir not. ADO 3.03. 96 P
stir them /on, stir them on! LLL 5.02.689 P
stir them /on, stir them on! 5.02.689 P
stir up the athenian youth to merriments, MND 1.01. 12
but i will not stir from this place, do what 3.01.121 P
then stir demetrius up with bitter wrong; 3.02.361
i pray you, let none of your people stir me; 4.01. 38 P
now will i stir this gamester. AYL 1.01.164 P
shall we pass along | and never stir assailants. 1.03.114
watch, | when that the sleeping man should stir; 4.03.116
nay, then 'tis time to stir him from his trance. SHR 1.01.177
worthiness would stir it up where it wanted AWW 1.01. 9 P
and by all means stir on the youth to an answer. TN 3.02. 58 P
they are heavier | than all thy woes can stir; WT 3.02.209
that he would not stir his pettitoes till he had 4.04.607 P
the wrongs i have done thee stir | afresh within 5.01.148
proceed; | no foot shall stir. 5.03. 98
stir; 5.03.101
would i might never stir from off this place, JN 1.01.145
who dares not stir by day must walk by night, 1.01.172
and stir them up against a mightier task. 2.01. 55
i'll stir them to it. 2.01.415
i will not stir, nor winch, nor speak a word, 4.01. 80
if thou but frown on me, or stir thy foot, | or 4.03. 96
to stir against the butchers of his life! R2 1.02. 3
and what stir | keeps good old york there with 2.03. 51
temperate, | unapt to stir at these indignities, 1H4 1.03. 2
i fear my brother mortimer doth stir | about his 2.03. 81
seen, i could not stir | but like a comet i was 3.02. 46
good cousin, be advis'd, stir not to–night. 4.03. 5
all hell shall stir for this. H5 5.01. 68
and if i did but stir out of my bed, | ready 1H6 1.04. 55
what stir is this? 1.04. 98
no, stir not for your lives, let her pass by. 2H6 2.04. 18
nor stir at nothing, till the axe of death 2.04. 49
i will stir up in england some black storm 3.01.349
dares stir a wing if warwick shake his bells. 3H6 1.01. 47
as shall revenge his death before i stir. 1.01.100
shalt stir up in suffolk, norfolk, and in kent, 4.08. 12
(as i will meet thee, if thou stir abroad), | to 5.01. 96
that stir the king against the duke my brother. R3 1.03.330
stir with the lark to–morrow, gentle norfolk. 5.03. 56
i know 'twill stir him strongly; H8 3.02.218
some little memory of me will stir him | (i know 3.02.417
we may as well push against powle's as stir 'em. 5.03. 16
if renown made it not stir, was pleas'd to let COR 1.03. 12 P
too much of that | for which the people stir. 3.01. 53
to stir a mutiny in the mildest thoughts, | and TIT 4.01. 85
to move is to stir, and to be valiant is to ROM 1.01. 9 P
thou shalt not stir one foot to seek a foe. 1.01. 80
tush, i will stir about, | and all things shall 4.02. 39
come, stir, stir, stir! 4.04. 3
come, stir, stir, stir! 4.04. 3
come, stir, stir, stir! 4.04. 3
you do yourselves but wrong to stir me up, | let TIM 3.04. 53
there is no stir or walking in the streets; JC 1.03.127
do, | stir up their servants to an act of rage, 2.01.176
you shall not stir out of your house to–day. 2.02. 9
they would not have you to stir forth to–day. 2.02. 38
if i were dispos'd to stir | your hearts and 3.02.121
let me not stir you up | to such a sudden flood 3.02.210
nor the power of speech | to stir men's blood; 3.02.223
stir not until the signal. 5.01. 26
why, chance may crown me | without my stir. MAC 1.03.144
would at a dismal treatise rouse and stir | as 5.05. 12
and then they say no spirit dare stir abroad, HAM 1.01.161
on lethe wharf, | wouldst thou not stir in this. 1.05. 34
fit, | behind the arras hearing something stir, 4.01. 9
great | is not to stir without great argument, 4.04. 54
this case, should stir me most | to my revenge, 5.02.245
if you do stir abroad, go arm'd. LR 1.02.170 P
/'zounds, if i stir, | or do but lift this arm, OTH 2.03.207
if she will stir hither, i shall seem to notify 3.01. 28 P
but pray you stir no embers up. ANT 2.02. 13
i could not stir him. CYM 4.02. 38
din | express impatience, lest you stir up mine. 5.04.112
gentlemen, | why do you stir so early? PER 3.02. 12
comfort you, men must feed you, men stir you up. 4.02. 92 P
that, after holy tie and first night's stir, TNK pr 6
what recketh he his rider's angry stir, | his VEN 283
"show me the strumpet that began this stir, LUC 1471

STIRR'D 14 FR 0.0015 REL FR 14 V 0 P
i am sorry, sir, i have thus far stirr'd you; WT 5.03. 74
stirr'd up by god, thus boldly for his king. R2 4.01.133
and with your best endeavor have stirr'd up | my 2H6 3.01.163
thought of them would have stirr'd up remorse, 3H6 5.05. 64
stirr'd up by dorset, buckingham, and morton, R3 4.04.467
he was stirr'd | with such an agony he sweat H8 2.01. 32
this business, never desir'd | it to be stirr'd; 2.04.165
my mind is troubled, like a fountain stirr'd, TRO 3.03.308
like to a bubbling fountain stirr'd with wind, TIT 2.04. 23
what, brutus, are you stirr'd so early too? JC 2.02.110
all things else | you mainly were stirr'd up. HAM 4.07. 9
but stirr'd by cleopatra. ANT 1.01. 43
the senate hath stirr'd up the confiners | and CYM 4.02.337
muse | stirr'd by a painted beauty to his verse, SON 21. 2

STIRRER 1 FR 0.0001 REL FR 0 V 1 P
an early stirrer, by the rood! 2H4 3.02. 2 P

STIRRERS 1 FR 0.0001 REL FR 1 V 0 P
for our bad neighbor makes us early stirrers, H5 4.01. 6

STIRRETH 1 FR 0.0001 REL FR 1 V 0 P
he heareth not, he stirreth not, he moveth not, ROM 2.01. 15

STIRRING 23 FR 0.0026 REL FR 15 V 8 P
in | now in the stirring passage of the day, | a ERR 3.01. 99
you, | of such a merry, nimble, stirring spirit, LLL 5.02. 16
approve | this flower's force in stirring love. MND 2.02. 69
nor no ill luck stirring but what lights a' my MV 3.01. 95 P
an /ate, stirring him to blood and strife; JN 2.01. 63
be stirring as the time, be fire with fire, 5.01. 48
two arrant cowards, there's no equity stirring. 1H4 2.02.100 P
for bearing arms, for stirring up my subjects, 3H6 5.05. 15
good morrow, catesby, you are early stirring. R3 3.02. 36
e'en so; hector was stirring early. TRO 1.02. 51 P
i will keep where there is wit stirring, and 2.01.119 P
a stirring dwarf we do allowance give | before a 2.03.137
why then we shall have a stirring world again. COR 4.05.218 P
now, these hot days, is the mad blood stirring. ROM 3.01. 4
is thy master stirring? MAC 2.03. 42 P
is the king stirring, worthy thane? 2.03. 45
not a mouse stirring. HAM 1.01. 10
that attends the /general's /wife be stirring, OTH 3.01. 25 P
she is stirring, sir. 3.01. 28 P
that our stirring | can from the lap of egypt's ANT 2.01. 36
no stirring in him, no alacrity, | of all this TNK 4.02. 29
anon he starts at stirring of a feather; VEN 302
myself was stirring ere the break of day, | and LUC 1280

STIRRUP 4 FR 0.0004 REL FR 4 V 0 P
door | to hold my stirrup nor to take my horse? SHR 4.01.121
thou not kiss'd thy hand and held my stirrup? 2H6 4.01. 53
who bow'd but in my stirrup, bend like his COR 3.02.119
make sacred even his stirrup, and through him TIM 1.01. 82

STIRRUPS 1 FR 0.0001 REL FR 0 V 1 P
an old mothy saddle and stirrups of no kindred; SHR 3.02. 49 P

STIRS 19 FR 0.0021 REL FR 18 V 1 P
what wisdom stirs amongst you? WT 2.01. 21
you perceive she stirs. 5.03.103
that supernal judge that stirs good thoughts JN 2.01.112
the blood more stirs | to rouse a lion than to 1H4 1.03.197
there lies a downy feather which stirs not. 2H4 4.05. 32
a man that more detests, more stirs against, H8 5.02. 74
sooner catch the eye | /than what stirs not. TRO 3.03.184
the lady stirs. ROM 5.03.147
who stirs? LR 1.01.126
if it be you that stirs these daughters' hearts 2.04.274
this feather stirs, she lives! 5.03.266
he that stirs next to carve for his own rage OTH 2.03.173
look, he stirs. 4.01. 55
i think she stirs again. 5.02. 95
what you shall know mean time | of stirs abroad, ANT 1.04. 82
as the fits and stirs of 's mind | could best CYM 1.03. 12
as my giving out her beauty stirs up the lewdly PER 4.02.143 P
still, | but, when he stirs, a tiger. TNK 4.02.131
and careless lust stirs up a desperate courage, VEN 556

STIR'ST 2 FR 0.0002 REL FR 1 V 1 P
look how thou stir'st now! PER 2.01. 16 P
how thou stir'st, thou block! 3.02. 90

STITCHERY 1 FR 0.0001 REL FR 0 V 1 P
come, lay aside your stitchery, i must have you COR 1.03. 69 P

STITCHES 1 FR 0.0001 REL FR 0 V 1 P
and will laugh yourselves into stitches, follow TN 3.02. 69 P

/STITHIED 1 FR 0.0001 REL FR 1 V 0 P
but, by the forge that /stithied mars his helm, TRO 4.05.255

STITHY 1 FR 0.0001 REL FR 1 V 0 P
imaginations are as foul | as vulcan's stithy. HAM 3.02. 84

STOCCADOES 1 FR 0.0001 REL FR 0 V 1 P
your passes, stoccadoes, and i know not what. WIV 2.01.226 P

STOCCATO 1 FR 0.0001 REL FR 1 V 0 P
alla stoccato carries it away. ROM 3.01. 74

STOCK* 26 FR 0.0029 REL FR 18 V 8 P
what need a man care for a stock with a wench, TGV 3.01.309 P
with a wench, when she can knit him a stock? 3.01.310 P
to see thee pass thy puncto, thy stock, thy WIV 2.03. 26 P
would any of the stock of barrabas | had been MV 4.01.296
with a linen stock on one leg and a kersey SHR 3.02. 66 P
does indifferent well in a /dun–color'd stock. TN 1.03.135 P
we marry | a gentler scion to the wildest stock, WT 4.04. 93
of the true line and stock of charles the great, H5 1.02. 71
this is a stem | of that victorious stock; 2.04. 63
our scions, put in wild and savage stock, 3.05. 7
now declare, sweet stem from york's great stock, 1H6 2.05. 41
and in thy sons, fair slips of such a stock. 2H6 2.02. 58
and noble stock | was graft with crab–tree slip, 3.02.213
house, | to the corruption of a blemish'd stock; R3 3.07.122
/her royal stock graft with ignoble plants, 3.07.127
though from an humble stock, undoubtedly | was H8 4.02. 49
but for the stock, sir thomas, | i wish it 5.01. 22
long continued, and what stock he springs of — COR 2.03.237
not, | nor her, nor thee, nor any of thy stock. TIT 1.01.300
now, by the stock and honor of my kin, | to ROM 1.05. 58
so /inoculate our old stock but we shall relish HAM 3.01.117 P
queen, and you | recoil from your great stock. CYM 1.06.128
be jointed to the old stock, and freshly grow; 5.04.142 P
be jointed to the old stock, and freshly grow; 5.05.440 P
assur'd | came of a gentle kind and noble stock, PER 5.01. 68
he shall not boast who did thy stock pollute LUC 1063

STOCK'D 1 FR 0.0001 REL FR 1 V 0 P
who stock'd my servant? LR 2.04.188

STOCK–FISH 2 FR 0.0002 REL FR 0 V 2 P
out o' doors, and make a stock–fish of thee. TMP 3.02. 70 P
tongue, you bull's pizzle, you stock–fish! 1H4 2.04.245 P

STOCKFISH 1 FR 0.0001 REL FR 0 V 1 P
same day did i fight with one samson stockfish, 2H4 3.02. 32 P

STOCK–FISHES 1 FR 0.0001 REL FR 0 V 1 P
that he was begot between two stock–fishes. MM 3.02.109 P

STOCKING 1 FR 0.0001 REL FR 1 V 0 P
person of my master, | stocking his messenger. LR 2.02.132

STOCKINGS 13 FR 0.0014 REL FR 2 V 11 P
smocks, socks, foul stockings, greasy napkins, WIV 3.05. 90 P
than backs, no more stockings than legs, nor no SHR in.2. 9 P
in their new fustian, /their white stockings, 4.01. 48 P
remember who commended thy yellow stockings, and
TN 2.05.153 P
she did commend my yellow stockings of late, she 2.05.166 P
stout, in yellow stockings, and cross–garter'd, 2.05.171 P
he will come to her in yellow stockings, and 2.05.199 P
he's in yellow stockings. 3.02. 73 P
"remember who commended thy yellow stockings" — 3.04. 48 P
thy yellow stockings? 3.04. 49 P
to put on yellow stockings and to frown | upon 5.01.338
note how many pair of silk stockings thou hast, 2H4 2.02. 15 P
faith they have in tennis and tall stockings, H8 1.03. 30
STOCKINS 1 FR 0.0001 REL FR 1 V 0 P
no hat upon his head, his stockins fouled, HAM 2.01. 76
STOCKISH 1 FR 0.0001 REL FR 1 V 0 P
since nought so stockish, hard, and full of rage MV 5.01. 81
/STOCK–PUNISH'D 1 FR 0.0001 REL FR 0 V 1 P
to tithing, and /stock–punish'd and imprison'd; LR 3.04.135 P
STOCKS 21 FR 0.0023 REL FR 11 V 10 P
i have sat in the stocks for puddings he hath TGV 4.04. 30 P
the knave constable had set me i' th' stocks, i' WIV 4.05.120 P
had set me i' th' stocks, i' th' common stocks, 4.05.120 P
all that, and a pair of stocks in the town? ERR 3.01. 60
a pair of stocks, you rogue! SHR in.1. 2 P
let's be no stoics nor no stocks, i pray, | or 1.01. 31
him forth, h'as sat i' th' stocks all night, AWW 4.03.101 P
the stocks carry him. 4.03.106 P
instant disaster of his setting i' th' stocks; 4.03.111 P
sir, in a dungeon, i' th' stocks, or any where, 4.03.244 P
i well may give, | and in the stocks avouch it. WT 4.03. 22
like seely beggars | who, sitting in the stocks, R2 5.05. 26
here he lets me prate | like one i' th' stocks. COR 5.03.160
fetch forth the stocks! LR 2.02.125
call not your stocks for me, i serve the king, 2.02.128
fetch forth the stocks! 2.02.133
come, bring away the stocks! 2.02.139
hadst been set i' th' stocks for that question, 2.04. 64 P
not i' th' stocks, fool. 2.04. 87 P
who put my man i' th' stocks? 2.04.182
how came my man i' th' stocks? 2.04.198
STOICS 1 FR 0.0001 REL FR 1 V 0 P
let's be no stoics nor no stocks, i pray, | or SHR 1.01. 31
/STOKESLY 1 FR 0.0001 REL FR 1 V 0 P
/stokesly and gardiner, the one of winchester, H8 4.01.101
STOLE* 25 FR 0.0028 REL FR 19 V 6 P
or stole it, rather. TMP 5.01.300
jest how my father stole two geese out of a pen, WIV 3.04. 40 P
'twas the boy that stole your meat, and you'll ADO 2.01.199 P
warily | i stole into a neighbor thicket by, LLL 5.02. 94
the gentleman | that lately stole his daughter. MV 4.01.385
he stole from france, | as 'tis reported, for AWW 3.05. 52
he stole from florence, taking no leave, and i 5.03.143 P
and then i stole all courtesy from heaven, | and 1H4 3.02. 50
bardolph stole a lute–case, bore it twelve H5 3.02. 42 P
and in callice they stole a fire–shovel. 3.02. 45 P
north, | he slily stole away and left his men; 3H6 1.01. 3
with sleight and manhood stole to rhesus' tents 4.02. 20
of me, | and stole into the covert of the wood. ROM 1.01.125
y' have ungently, brutus, | stole from my bed; JC 2.01.238
and stole thence | the life o' th' building! MAC 2.03. 68
upon my secure hour thy uncle stole, | with HAM 1.05. 61
that from a shelf the precious diadem stole, 3.04.100
false steward, that stole his master's daughter. 4.05.173 P
at three and two years old, i stole these babes, CYM 3.03.101
stole these children | upon my banishment; 5.05.341
'tis the duke's, | and, to say true, i stole it. TNK 3.06. 55
but stole his blood and seem'd with him to bleed VEN 1056
now stole upon the time the dead of night, LUC 162
and he stole that word | from thy behavior; SON 79. 9
there my white stole of chastity i daff'd, LC 297
STOLEN 4 FR 0.0004 REL FR 3 V 1 P
my stay must be stolen out of other affairs; MM 3.01.158 P
hath | a lovely boy stolen from an indian king; MND 2.01. 22
when thou hast stolen away from fairy land, 2.01. 65
would he have stolen away | from sleeping hermia 3.02. 51
STOLEST 1 FR 0.0001 REL FR 0 V 1 P
thou stolest a cup of sack eighteen years ago, 1H4 2.04.314 P
STOL'N 62 FR 0.0070 REL FR 50 V 12 P
and should she thus be stol'n away from you, TGV 3.01. 15
sat in the stocks for puddings he hath stol'n, 4.04. 31 P
the other squirrel was stol'n from me by the 4.04. 55 P
to pardon him that hath from nature stol'n | a MM 2.04. 43
thou hast stol'n both mine office and my name: ERR 3.01. 44
who, as i take it, have stol'n his bird's nest. ADO 2.01.230 P
only, have a care that your bills be not stol'n. 3.03. 42 P
john is this morning secretly stol'n away. 4.02. 61 P
in my cousin's hand, stol'n from her pocket, 5.04. 89
great feast of languages, and stol'n the scraps. LLL 5.01. 37 P
and stol'n the impression of her fantasy | with MND 1.01. 32
thou toldst me they were stol'n unto this wood; 2.01.191
by night | and stol'n my love's heart from him? 3.02.284
they would have stol'n away, they would, 4.01.156
god's my life, stol'n hence, and left me asleep! 4.01.204 P
of double ducats, stol'n from me by my daughter! MV 2.08. 19
and precious stones, | stol'n by my daughter! 2.08. 21
has my fellow tranio stol'n your clothes? SHR 1.01.223 P
or you stol'n his? 1.01.224 P
scorn'd a fair color, or express'd it stol'n, AWW 5.03. 50
she has liv'd, | or how stol'n from the dead. WT 5.03.115
worcester is stol'n away to–night. 1H4 2.04.358 P
the truth, stol'n from my host at saint albons, 4.02. 46 P
he was some hilding fellow that had stol'n | the 2H4 1.01. 57
thou hast stol'n that which after some few hours 4.05.101
for he hath stol'n a pax, and hanged must 'a be H5 3.06. 40
to nurse, | was by a beggar–woman stol'n away, 2H6 4.02.143
from scotland am i stol'n, even of pure love, 3H6 3.01. 13
and ne'er have stol'n the breech from lancaster. 5.05. 24
with odd old ends stol'n forth of holy writ, R3 1.03.336
cardinal campeius | is stol'n away to rome, hath H8 3.02. 57
that we have stol'n what we do fear to keep! TRO 2.02. 93
but thieves unworthy of a thing so stol'n, 2.02. 94
with that robbery, thy stol'n name | coriolanus, COR 5.06. 88
and, on my life, hath stol'n him home to bed. ROM 2.01. 4
and their stol'n marriage–day | was tybalt's 5.03.233
that feeds and breeds by a composture stol'n TIM 4.03.441
for you have stol'n their buzzing, antony, | and JC 5.01. 37
are stol'n away and fled, which puts upon them MAC 2.04. 26
and when i have stol'n upon these son–in–laws, LR 4.06.186
she is abus'd, stol'n from me, and corrupted OTH 1.03. 60
hast stol'n it from her? 3.03.310
what sense had i in her stol'n hours of lust? 3.03.338
he that is robb'd, not wanting what is stol'n, 3.03.342
why have you stol'n upon us thus? ANT 3.06. 42
equal theirs | till they had stol'n our jewel. 4.15. 78
from their nursery | were stol'n, and to this CYM 1.01. 60
your ring may be stol'n too: 1.04. 90 P
being corrupted, | hath stol'n it from her? 2.04.117
for this was stol'n. 2.04.120
i have stol'n nought, nor would not, though i 3.06. 48
you shall not now be stol'n, you have locks upon 5.04. 1
who, by belarius stol'n, | for many years 5.05.455
had mine ear | stol'n some new air, or at TNK 1.03. 75
he restor'd her | as your stol'n jewel, and 5.04.119
poor helpless help, the treasure stol'n away, LUC 1056
with gold, but stol'n from forth thy gate. 1068
hath dear religious love stol'n from mine eye SON 31. 6
and even thence thou wilt be stol'n, i fear, 48.13
and buds of marjerom had stol'n thy hair; 99. 7
a third, nor red nor white, had stol'n of both, 99.10
but sweet or color it had stol'n from thee. 99.15
STOL'ST 1 FR 0.0001 REL FR 1 V 0 P
and stol'st away the ladies' hearts of france, 2H6 1.03. 52
STOMACH 46 FR 0.0052 REL FR 33 V 13 P
which rais'd in me | an undergoing stomach, to TMP 1.02.157
mine ears against | the stomach of my sense. 2.01.108
not turn me about, my stomach is not constant. 2.02.114 P
that you might kill your stomach on your meat, TGV 1.02. 68
you come not home, because you have no stomach:
ERR 1.02. 49
you have no stomach, having broke your fast: 1.02. 50
trencherman, he hath an excellent stomach. ADO 1.01. 52 P
eat when i have stomach, and wait for no man's 1.03. 15 P
despite of his quick wit and his queasy stomach, 2.01.383 P
you have no stomach, signior, fare you well. 2.03.256 P
when i do it i shall do it on a full stomach. LLL 1.02.149 P
the deepest loathing to the stomach brings, | or MND 2.02.138
nay, let me praise you while i have a stomach. MV 3.05. 87
plenty in it, it goes much against my stomach. AYL 3.02. 21 P
to them as you find your stomach serves you: SHR 1.01. 38
but if you have a stomach, to't a' god's name; 1.02.194
come, kate, sit down, i know you have a stomach. 4.01.158
and so dies with feeding his own stomach. AWW 1.01.143 P
as an old man loves money, with no stomach. 3.02. 16 P
why, if you have a stomach, to't, monsieur: 3.06. 64 P
and when my knightly stomach is suffic'd, | why JN 1.01.191
what is't that takes from thee | thy stomach, 1H4 2.03. 41
gan vail his stomach and did grace the shame 2H4 1.01.129
she either gives a stomach and no food — | such 4.04.105
or else a feast | and takes away the stomach — 4.04.107
we'll not offend one stomach with our play. H5 2.pr. 40
their villainy goes against my weak stomach, and 3.02. 53 P
that he which hath no stomach to this fight, 4.03. 35
amiss to cool a man's stomach this hot weather. 2H6 4.10. 9 P
all goodness | is poison to thy stomach. H8 3.02.283
he was a man | of an unbounded stomach, ever 4.02. 34
call some knight to arms | that hath a stomach, TRO 2.01.125
they think my little stomach to the war | and 3.03.220
day enough of hector, | if you have stomach. 4.05.264
where my stomach finds meat, or, rather, where i TIM 4.03.294 P
which gives men stomach to disgest his words JC 1.02.301
to some enterprise | that hath a stomach in't, HAM 1.01.100
i should answer | from a full–flowing stomach. LR 5.03. 74
my great revenge | had stomach for them all. OTH 5.02. 75
and make the wars alike against my stomach, ANT 2.02. 50
all, or, if you must believe, | stomach not all. 3.04. 12
ay, or a stomach. CYM 5.04. 2
if the sea's stomach be o'ercharg'd with gold, PER 3.02. 54
and it pierces and sharpens the stomach. 4.01. 28
a cuff, my stomach | not reconcil'd by reason. TNK 3.01.104
i am glad | you have so good a stomach. 3.03. 21
STOMACHERS 2 FR 0.0002 REL FR 2 V 0 P
golden quoifs and stomachers | for my lads to WT 4.04.224
you shall no more | be stomachers to my heart. CYM 3.04. 84
STOMACHING 1 FR 0.0001 REL FR 1 V 0 P
'tis not a time | for private stomaching. ANT 2.02. 9
STOMACH–QUALM'D 1 FR 0.0001 REL FR 1 V 0 P
or stomach–qualm'd at land, a dram of this CYM 3.04.190
STOMACHS 15 FR 0.0017 REL FR 13 V 2 P
for we have stomachs. TMP 3.03. 41
your stomachs are too young, | and abstinence LLL 4.03.290
that is done, sir, they have all stomachs! MV 3.05. 48 P
my banket is to close our stomachs up | after SHR 5.02. 9
then vail your stomachs, for it is no boot, 5.02.176
they have only stomachs to eat and none to fight H5 3.07.154 P
god, these nobles should such stomachs bear! 1H6 1.03. 90
for soldiers' stomachs always serve them well. 2.03. 80
how will their grudging stomachs be provok'd 4.01.141
the winds grow high, so do your stomachs, lords. 2H6 2.01. 53
to ease their stomachs with their bitter tongues TIT 3.01.233
'twill fill your stomachs, please you eat of it. 5.03. 29
if not, when you have stomachs. JC 5.01. 66
they are all but stomachs, and we all but food; OTH 3.04.104
our stomachs | will make what's homely savory; CYM 3.06. 32
STON'D 2 FR 0.0002 REL FR 0 V 2 P
some say he shall be ston'd; WT 4.04.778 P
remember "ston'd," and "flay'd alive." 4.04.804 P
STONE 62 FR 0.0070 REL FR 46 V 16 P
he is a stone, a very pibble stone, and has no TGV 2.03. 10 P
he is a stone, a very pibble stone, and has no 2.03. 10 P
he shall not have a stone to throw at his dog. WIV 1.04.112 P
a stone. 4.01. 32 P
and what is "a stone," william? 4.01. 33 P
that his appetite | is more to bread than stone: MM 1.03. 53
and this stone doth show | that i am that same MND 5.01.161
to church | and see the holy edifice of stone, MV 1.01. 30
i was in love i broke my sword upon a stone, and AYL 2.04. 47 P
because she brought stone jugs and no seal'd SHR in.2. 88
that's able to breathe life into a stone, AWW 2.01. 73
fool that has no more brain than a stone. TN 1.05. 85 P
i have said too much unto a heart of stone, 3.04.201
nor brass nor stone nor parchment bears not one, WT 1.02.360
is rotten | as ever oak or stone was sound. 2.03. 91
not a counterfeit stone, not a ribbon, glass, 4.04.597 P
chide me, dear stone, that i may say indeed 5.03. 24
does not the stone rebuke me | for being more 5.03. 37
stone rebuke me | for being more stone than it? 5.03. 38
the spirits, | standing like stone with thee. 5.03. 42
thus have wrought you (for the stone is mine), 5.03. 58
be stone no more; 5.03. 99
this precious stone set in the silver sea, R2 2.01. 46
lies | within the limits of yon lime and stone, 3.03. 26
and this worm–eaten /hold of ragged stone, 2H4 in 35
felt them, and they were as cold as any stone; H5 2.03. 24 P
and up'ard, and all was as cold as any stone. 2.03. 26 P
that stands upon the rolling restless stone — 3.06. 29
is fixed upon a spherical stone, which rolls, 3.06. 36 P
and here, sitting upon london stone, i charge 2H6 4.06. 2 P
at this sight | my heart is turn'd to stone; 5.02. 50
a base foul stone, made precious by the foil R3 5.03.250
we first put this dangerous stone a–rolling, H8 5.02.139
the fall of every phrygian stone will cost | a TRO 4.05.223
there is a word will priam turn to stone, | make 5.10. 18
that hunger broke stone walls, that dogs must COR 1.01.206
by, | and you recount your sorrows to a stone. TIT 3.01. 29
a stone is soft as wax, tribunes more hard than 3.01. 45
a stone is silent, and offendeth not, | and 3.01. 46
a bump as big as a young cock'rel's stone — | a ROM 1.03. 53
i am sorry i shall lose a stone by thee. TIM 4.03.370
that under cold stone | days and nights has MAC 4.01. 6
a grass–green turf, | at his heels a stone." HAM 4.05. 32
work like the spring that turneth wood to stone, 4.07. 20
if that her breath will mist or stain the stone, LR 5.03.263
no, my heart is turn'd to stone; OTH 4.01.183 P
o perjur'd woman, thou dost stone my heart, 5.02. 63
go to then — your considerate stone. ANT 2.02.110 P
source, and the first stone | drop in my neck; 3.13.160
i prais'd her as i rated her: so do i my stone. CYM 1.04. 77 P
sparkles this stone as it was wont, or is't not 2.04. 40
it to some pity, | though it were made of stone. TNK 1.01.129
and beef at four nobles a stone, list to me. STM II.C 3 P
more than flint, for stone at rain relenteth. VEN 200
liveless picture, cold and senseless stone, 211
that from the cold stone sparks of fire do fly, LUC 177
o, if no harder than a stone thou art, | melt at 593
stone him with hard'ned hearts, harder than 978
bright in these contents | than unswept stone, SON 55. 4
since brass, nor stone, nor earth, nor boundless 65. 1
who, moving others, are themselves as stone, 94. 3
each several stone, | with wit well blazon'd, LC 216
STONE–BOW 1 FR 0.0001 REL FR 0 V 1 P
o, for a stone–bow, to hit him in the eye! TN 2.05. 46 P
STONE–CUTTER 1 FR 0.0001 REL FR 0 V 1 P
a stone–cutter or a painter could not have made LR 2.02. 58 P
STONE–HARD 1 FR 0.0001 REL FR 1 V 0 P
till it was whetted on thy stone–hard heart | to R3 4.04.228
STONE'S 2 FR 0.0002 REL FR 2 V 0 P
the stone's too hard to come by. CYM 2.04. 46
that did amplify | each stone's dear nature, LC 210
/STONES 1 FR 0.0001 REL FR 1 V 0 P
/king /richard, /scrap'd /from /pomfret /stones; 2H4 1.01.205
STONES 63 FR 0.0071 REL FR 57 V 6 P
give her no token but stones, for she's as hard TGV 1.01.140 P
i throw thy name against the bruising stones, 1.02.108
he makes sweet music with th' enamell'd stones, 2.07. 28
golden touch could soften steel and stones, 3.02. 78
by gar, i will cut all his two stones; WIV 1.04.112 P
cracking the stones of the foresaid pruins — MM 2.01.107 P
or stones, whose rate are either rich or poor 2.02.150
curs'd be thy stones for thus deceiving me! MND 5.01.181
my cherry lips have often kiss'd thy stones, 5.01.190
thy stones with lime and hair knit /up /in /thee 5.01.191
and jewels, two stones, two rich and precious MV 2.08. 20
two stones, two rich and precious stones, 2.08. 20
she hath the stones upon her, and the ducats." 2.08. 22
crying, his stones, his daughter, and his ducats 2.08. 24
did feign that orpheus drew trees, stones, and 5.01. 80
sermons in stones, and good in every thing. AYL 2.01. 17
and but for our approach those sleeping stones, JN 2.01.216
o me, my uncle's spirit is in these stones. 4.03. 9
walls, | unpeopled offices, untrodden stones? R2 1.02. 69
and these stones | prove armed soldiers, ere her 3.02. 24
i'll make him a philosopher's two stones to me. 2H4 3.02.330 P
away, as swift as stones | enforced from the old H5 4.07. 61
with my nails digg'd stones out of the ground 1H6 1.04. 45
have fill'd their pockets full of pebble stones; 3.01. 80
nay, if we be forbidden stones, we'll fall to it 3.01. 89 P
not deck'd with diamonds and indian stones, 3H6 3.01. 63
who gave his blood to lime the stones together, 5.01. 84
or shall we beat the stones about thine ears? 5.01.108
inestimable stones, unvalued jewels, | all R3 1.04. 27
but, like dumb statues or breathing stones, 3.07. 25
i am not made of stones, | but penetrable to 3.07.224
pity, you ancient stones, those tender babes 4.01. 98
so foolish sorrows bids your stones farewell. 4.01.103
when water–drops have worn the stones of troy, TRO 3.02.186
thy knee bussing the stones (for in such COR 3.02. 75
that thy wives with spits and boys with stones 4.04. 5
therefore i tell my sorrows to the stones, | who TIT 3.01. 37
is soft as wax, tribunes more hard than stones; 3.01. 45
and on the ragged stones beat forth our souls, 5.03.133
plants, herbs, stones, and their true qualities; ROM 2.03. 16
strew — | o woe, thy canopy is dust and stones! 5.03. 13
with two stones moe than 's artificial one. TIM 2.02.111 P
one day he gives us diamonds, next day stones. 3.06.120
you blocks, you stones, you worse than senseless JC 1.01. 35
you are not wood, you are not stones, but men; 3.02.142
move | the stones of rome to rise and mutiny. 3.02.230
fear | the very stones prate of my whereabout, MAC 2.01. 58
stones have been known to move and trees to 3.04.122
form and cause conjoin'd, preaching to stones, HAM 3.04.126
harder than the stones whereof 'tis rais'd, LR 3.02. 64
rings, | their precious stones new lost; 5.03.191
o, /you are men of stones! 5.03.258
tears fell from her, and soft'ned the stones, OTH 4.03. 46
are there no stones in heaven | but what serves 5.02.234
the fiery orbs above and the twinn'd stones CYM 1.06. 35
spit, and throw stones, cast mire upon me, set 5.05.222
the gods throw stones of sulphur on me, if 5.05.240
that dwells in vegetives, in metals, stones; PER 3.02. 36
horse is arcite | trotting the stones of athens, TNK 5.04. 55
for stones dissolv'd to water do convert. LUC 592

and waste huge stones with little water–drops. 959
him with hard'ned hearts, harder than stones, 978
like stones of worth they thinly placed are, SON 52. 7
STONE–STILL 2 FR 0.0002 REL FR 2 V 0 P
i will not struggle, i will stand stone–still. JN 4.01. 76
stone–still, astonish'd with this deadly deed, LUC 1730
STONISH *(also astonish, etc.)*
STONISH 1 FR 0.0001 REL FR 0 V 1 P
o wonderful son, that can so stonish a mother! HAM 3.02.328 P
STONISH'D 1 FR 0.0001 REL FR 1 V 0 P
or stonish'd as night–wand'rers often are, VEN 825
STONY 8 FR 0.0009 REL FR 8 V 0 P
thou art come to answer | a stony adversary, an MV 4.01. 4
whom thou hast whetted on thy stony heart | to 2H4 4.05.107
and while 'tis mine, | it shall be stony. 2H6 5.02. 51
i, | even like a stony image, cold and numb. TIT 3.01.258
walls, | for stony limits cannot hold love out, ROM 2.02. 67
stains | the stony entrance of this sepulchre? 5.03.141
nor stony tower, nor walls of beaten brass, JC 1.03. 93
and break'st | the stony girths of cities: TNK 5.01. 56
STONY–HEARTED 1 FR 0.0001 REL FR 0 V 1 P
me, and the stony–hearted villains know it well 1H4 2.02. 26 P
STONY–STRATFORD 1 FR 0.0001 REL FR 1 V 0 P
night, i /hear, they lay at stony–stratford, R3 2.04. 1
/STOOD 1 FR 0.0001 REL FR 1 V 0 P
/that /lov'd /him, /as /the /state /stood /then, 2H4 4.01.113
STOOD 109 FR 0.0123 REL FR 95 V 14 P
whiles we stood here securing your repose, TMP 2.01.310
such men | whose heads stood in their breasts? 3.03. 47
love, and thou | hast strangely stood the test. 4.01. 7
i have stood on the pillory for geese he hath TGV 4.04. 32 P
what dangerous action, stood it next to death, 5.04. 41
which at that very distant time stood, as it MM 2.01. 92 P
i have stood by, my lord, and i have heard 5.01.138
but i guess, it stood in her chin, by the salt ERR 3.02.127 P
where stood belgia, the netherlands? 3.02.138 P
you have of late stood out against your brother, ADO 1.03. 21 P
upon me that i stood like a man at a mark, with 2.01.246 P
or else it stood upon the choice of friends — MND 1.01.139
stood now within the pretty flouriets' eyes 4.01. 55
then stood as fair | as any comer i have look'd MV 2.01. 20
that have stood by and seen our wishes prosper, 3.02.187
your fortune stood upon the caskets there, | and 3.02.201
a night | stood dido with a willow in her hand 5.01. 10
stood on th' extremest verge of the swift brook, AYL 2.01. 42
verse, and therefore stood lamely in the verse. 3.02.170 P
but see, while idly i stood looking on, | i SHR 1.01.150
way, | and there i stood amazed for a while, 2.01.155
with that she sighed as she stood, | with that AWW 1.03. 74
she stood, | with that she sighed as she stood, 1.03. 75
if her fortunes ever stood | necessitied to help 5.03. 84
noble she was, and thought | i stood engag'd; 5.03. 96
only myself stood out, | for which, if i be TN 3.03. 35
'twixt heaven and earth | might thus have stood, WT 5.01.133
o, thus she stood, | even with such life of 5.03. 34
in, | that so stood out against the holy church, JN 5.02. 71
and thus long have we stood | to watch the R2 3.03. 72
that beads of sweat have stood upon thy brow, 1H4 2.03. 58
attended him on bridges, stood in lanes, | laid 4.03. 70
hill | stood smiling to behold his lion's whelp H5 1.02.109
who disgrac'd, what terms the enemy stood on; 3.06. 74 P
when articles too nicely urg'd be stood on. 5.02. 94
so the maid that stood in the way for my wish 5.02.327 P
all the whole army stood agaz'd on him. 1H6 1.01.126
that basely fled when noble talbot stood. 4.05. 17
but when my angry guardant stood alone, 4.07. 9
as he stood by, whilest i, his forlorn duchess, 2H6 2.04. 45
back, | i stood upon the hatches in the storm; 3.02.103
how in our voiding lobby hast thou stood | and 4.01. 61
and stood against them, as the hope of troy 3H6 2.01. 51
you should not blemish it, if i stood by: R3 1.02.128
so stood the state when henry the sixt | was 2.03. 16
stood the state so? 2.03. 18
every man that stood | show'd like a mine. H8 1.01. 21
i stood i' th' level | of a full–charg'd 1.02. 2
who ever yet | have stood to charity, and 2.04. 86
methought | i stood not in the smile of heaven, 2.04.188
i weigh'd the danger which my realms stood in 2.04.198
my lord, we have | stood here observing him. 3.02.112
service that | hath thus stood for his country; COR 2.02. 41
he never stood | to ease his breast with panting 2.02.121
for once we stood up about the corn, he himself 2.03. 15 P
you have stood your limitation, and the tribunes 2.03.138
did claim no less | than what he stood for, so 2.03.187
when one but of my ordinance stood up | to speak 3.02. 12
we stood to't in good time. is this menenius? 4.06. 10
were inshell'd when martius stood for rome, 4.06. 45
and | your franchises, whereon you stood, 4.06. 86
you that stood so much | upon the voice of 4.06. 96
this monument five hundreth years hath stood, TIT 1.01.350
this minion stood upon her chastity, | upon her 2.03.124
then fresh tears | stood on her cheeks, as doth 3.01.112
three or four wenches, where i stood, cried, JC 1.02.272 P
caesar, i never stood on ceremonies, | yet now 2.02. 13
of caesar might | have stood against the world; 3.02.119
doubtful it stood, | as two spent swimmers that MAC 1.02. 7
whiles i stood rapt in the wonder of it, came 1.05. 6 P
i stood and heard them; 2.02. 21
why, it stood by her. 5.01. 22 P
all /those his lands | which he stood seiz'd of, HAM 1.01. 89
the graves stood /tenantless and the sheeted 1.01.115
as a painted tyrant, pyrrhus stood | /and, like 2.02.480
upon that head | where late the diadem stood, 2.02.507
that your grace hath screen'd and stood between 3.04. 3
stood challenger on mount of all the age | for 4.07. 28
him, | but yet, alas, stood i within his grace, LR 1.01.273
here stood he in the dark, his sharp sword out, 2.01. 38
seeing how loathly opposite i stood | to his 2.01. 49
as i stood here below, methought his eyes | were 4.06. 69
should have stood that night | against my fire, 4.07. 36
where each second | stood heir to th' first. OTH 1.01. 38
though our proper son | stood in your action. 1.03. 70
and stood within the blank of his displeasure 3.04.128
on each side her | stood pretty dimpled boys, ANT 2.02.202
if this division chance, ne'er stood between, 3.04. 13
whilst he stood up and spoke, | he was my master 5.01. 7
charmian liv'd but now, she stood and spake. 5.02.341
tremblingly she stood, | and on the sudden 5.02.343
child, and stood between | her and her fortunes. PER 4.03. 31
who stood equivalent with mighty kings, | but 5.01. 91
methought stood staggering whether he should TNK 4.01. 10
and i at this present stood unfeignedly on the 4.03. 68 P
things that ever stood in such a question. STM II.C 21
"how like a jade he stood, tied to the tree, VEN 391
with this she falleth in the place she stood, 1121
which in round drops upon their whiteness stood. 1170
that had narcissus seen her as she stood, LUC 265
that for achilles' image stood his spear, 1424
a head | stood for the whole to be imagined. 1428
stood many troyan mothers, sharing joy | to see 1431
both stood like old acquaintance in a trance, 1595
deed, | stood collatine and all his lordly crew, 1731
vastly stood | bare and unpeopled in this 1740
and stood stark naked on the brook's green brim. PP 6.10
he spying her, bounc'd in, whereas he stood; 6.13
and nice affections wavering stood in doubt | if LC 97
STOOL 11 FR 0.0012 REL FR 5 V 6 P
o, a stool and a cushion for the sexton. ADO 4.02. 2 P
sometime for three–foot stool mistaketh me; MND 2.01. 52
to comb your noddle with a three–legg'd stool, SHR 1.01. 64
now fetch me a stool hither by and by. 2H6 2.01.138 P
whipping, leap me over this stool and run away. 2.01.140 P
whip him till he leap over that same stool. 2.01.146 P
thou stool for a witch! TRO 2.01. 42 P
each man to his stool, with that spur as he TIM 3.06. 65 P
when all's done, | you look but on a stool. MAC 3.04. 67
merit thou wilt hear me, | rise from thy stool. ANT 2.07. 56
when on my three–foot stool i sit and tell | the CYM 3.03. 89
STOOLBALL 1 FR 0.0001 REL FR 1 V 0 P
why, play at stoolball: TNK 5.02. 74
STOOLS 1 FR 0.0001 REL FR 1 V 0 P
on their crowns, | and push us from our stools. MAC 3.04. 81
/STOOP 1 FR 0.0001 REL FR 1 V 0 P
/stoop, boys, this gate | instructs you how t' CYM 3.03. 2
STOOP 33 FR 0.0037 REL FR 30 V 3 P
why didst thou stoop then? TGV 1.02. 70
the jewel that we find, we stoop and take't, MM 2.01. 24
before his sister should her body stoop | to 2.04.182
stoop, i say, | her shoulder is with child. LLL 4.03. 87
and till she stoop, she must not be full–gorg'd, SHR 4.01.191
for grief is proud and makes his owner stoop. JN 3.01. 69
stoop low within those bounds we have o'erlook'd 5.04. 55
as to take up mine honor's pawn, then stoop. R2 1.01. 74
and make you stoop | unto the sovereign mercy of 2.03.156
stoop with oppression of their prodigal weight; 3.04. 31
cured, | stoop tamely to the foot of majesty. 2H4 4.02. 42
and i will stoop and humble my intents | to your 5.02.120
yet, when they stoop, they stoop with the like H5 4.01.107 P
when they stoop, they stoop with the like wing. 4.01.107 P
a straight back will stoop, a black beard will 5.02.160 P
compassion on the king commands me stoop, | or i
1H6 3.01.119
stoop then and set your knee against my foot, 3.01.168
i'll either make thee stoop and bend thy knee, 5.01. 61
wilt thou not stoop? 5.04. 26
now will ye stoop? 2H6 4.01.119
stoop to the block than these knees bow to any 4.01.125
than you should stoop unto a frenchman's mercy. 4.08. 48
who made the dolphin and the french to stoop, 3H6 1.01.108
and tam'd the king and made the dolphin stoop; 2.02.151
nor i, but stoop with patience to my fortune. 5.05. 6
before he should thus stoop to th' /herd, but COR 3.02. 32
and at thy mercy shall they stoop and kneel, TIT 5.02.118
stoop, romans, stoop, | and let us bathe our JC 3.01.105
stoop, romans, stoop, | and let us bathe our 3.01.105
stoop then, and wash. 3.01.111
as befits mine honor | to stoop in such a case. ANT 2.02. 98
mountain pine | and make him stoop to th' vale. CYM 4.02.176
and stoop to honor, not to foul desire. LUC 574
/STOOP'D 1 FR 0.0001 REL FR 1 V 0 P
chickens, the way which they /stoop'd eagles; CYM 5.03. 42
STOOP'D 5 FR 0.0005 REL FR 5 V 0 P
the very block | where claudio stoop'd to death, MM 5.01.415
book, | and as he stoop'd again to take it up, SHR 3.02.162
me, | have stoop'd my neck under your injuries, R2 3.01. 19
stoop'd his anointed head as low as death. 2H4 in 32
the holy eagle | stoop'd, as to foot us. CYM 5.04.116
STOOPING 6 FR 0.0006 REL FR 5 V 1 P
to most ignoble stooping. TMP 1.02.116
basis bowed, | as stooping to relieve him. 2.01.122
if it be worth stooping for, there it lies in TN 2.02. 15 P
land, | my stooping duty tenderly shall show. R2 3.03. 48
consul, which he lost | by lack of stooping — COR 5.06. 28
our tragedy, | here stooping to your clemency, HAM 3.02.150
STOOPS 5 FR 0.0005 REL FR 5 V 0 P
a golden mind stoops not to shows of dross. MV 2.07. 20
and virtue stoops and trembles at her frown; TIT 2.01. 11
with flaming top | stoops to his base, and with HAM 2.02.476
the grass stoops not, she treads on it so light, VEN 1028
the cedar stoops not to the base shrub's foot, LUC 664
/STOP 2 FR 0.0002 REL FR 2 V 0 P
/th' /obstructions /which /begin /to /stop 2H4 4.01. 65
/stop /her /there! LR 3.06. 54
STOP 105 FR 0.0118 REL FR 85 V 20 P
there, sir, stop. TMP 5.01.198
thy service — why dost thou stop my mouth? TGV 2.03. 45 P
stop there; 3.01.355 P
let me stop this way first. WIV 3.03.164 P
and so stop the air | by which he should revive; MM 2.04. 25
stop in your wind, sir; ERR 1.02. 53
i'll stop mine ears against the mermaid's song. 3.02.164
if you cannot, stop his mouth with a kiss, and ADO 2.01.310 P
peace, i will stop your mouth. 5.04. 98 P
proceeded well, to stop all good proceeding! LLL 1.01. 95
he knows not the stop. MND 5.01.120 P
but stop my house's ears, i mean my casements; MV 2.05. 34
is no bar | to stop the foreign spirits, but 2.07. 46
come, the full stop. 3.01. 15 P
to stop his wounds, lest he do bleed to death. 4.01.258
stop that, 'twill fly with the smoke out at the AYL 4.01.163 P
and if you cannot, best you stop your ears. SHR 4.03. 76
to stop up the displeasure he hath conceiv'd AWW 4.05. 75 P
nay, you need not to stop your nose, sir; 5.02. 10 P
if your metaphor stink, i will stop my nose, or 5.02. 12 P
spiritual counsel had, | shall stop or spur me. WT 2.01.187
her so | that we shall stop her exclamation. JN 2.01.558
john, to stop arthur's title in the whole, 2.01.562
not a calve's–skin stop that mouth of thine? 3.01.299
and stop this gap of breath with fulsome dust, 3.04. 32
yea, without stop, didst let thy heart consent, 4.02.239
to stop their marches 'fore we are inflam'd. 5.01. 7
even so must i run on, and even so stop. 5.07. 67
age, | but stop no wrinkle in his pilgrimage; R2 1.03.230
one kiss shall stop our mouths, and dumbly part; 5.01. 95
at that sad stop, my lord, | where rude 5.02. 4
for tears do stop the flood–gates of her eyes. 1H4 2.04.394
and stop all sight–holes, every loop from whence 4.01. 71
survey of all the world, | must have a stop. 5.04. 83
for which of you will stop | the vent of hearing 2H4 in 1
and of so easy and so plain a stop | that the in 17
deeds, | but in the end, to stop my ear indeed, 1.01. 79
in my mouth as offer to stop it with security. 1.02. 42 P
sir, do you mean to stop any of william's wages, 5.01. 23 P
turn head, and stop pursuit; H5 2.04. 69
who in proud heart | doth stop my cornets, were 1H6 4.03. 25
means | to stop effusion of our christian blood, 5.01. 9
send succors, lords, and stop the rage betime, 2H6 3.01.285
a breach that craves a quick expedient stop! 3.01.288
to have thee with thy lips to stop my mouth; 3.02.396
now death shall stop his dismal threat'ning 3H6 2.06. 58
and stop the rising of blood–sucking sighs, 4.04. 22
this fiend | to stop devoted charitable deeds? R3 1.02. 35
a word, | and then again begin, and stop again, 3.05. 3
to stop all hopes whose growth may damage me. 4.02. 59
to the lord mayor straight | to stop the rumor, H8 2.01.152
but stop their mouths with stubborn bits and 5.02. 58
as will stop the eye of helen's needle, for whom TRO 2.01. 80 P
stop my mouth. 3.02.133
to stop his ears against admonishment? 5.03. 2
oppos'd to hinder me, should stop my way, | /but 5.03. 57
stop, | or all will fall in broil. COR 3.01. 32
and stop those maims | of shame seen through thy 4.05. 86
army we can make, | might stop our countryman. 5.01. 38
nay then i'll stop your mouth. TIT 2.03.185
sirs, stop his mouth, and let him speak no more. 5.01.151
and stop their mouths if they begin to cry. 5.02.161
stop close their mouths, let them not speak a 5.02.164
sirs, stop their mouths, let them not speak to 5.02.167
therefore thy kinsmen are no stop to me. ROM 2.02. 69
stop there, stop there. 2.04. 94 P
stop there, stop there. 2.04. 94 P
thou desirest me to stop in my tale against the 2.04. 95 P
marriage, | to stop the inundation of her tears, 4.01. 12
stop thy unhallowed toil, vile montague! 5.03. 54
no care, no stop, so senseless of expense, TIM 2.02. 1
and what remains will hardly stop the mouth | of 2.02.147
that whoso please | to stop affliction, let him 5.01.210
to wind, to stop, to run directly on, | his JC 4.01. 32
upon this blasted heath you stop our way | with MAC 1.03. 77
stop up th' access and passage to remorse, 1.05. 44
stop it, marcellus. HAM 1.01.139
finger | to sound what stop she please. 3.02. 71
was converted might they not stop a beer–barrel? 5.01.212 P
clay, | might stop a hole to keep the wind away. 5.01.214
stop, stop! LR 2.01. 36
stop, stop! 2.01. 36
let's teach ourselves that honorable stop, | not OTH 2.03. 2
as hydra, such an answer would stop them all. 2.03.305 P
more impediments | than twenty times your stop. 5.02.264
against the blown rose may they stop their nose ANT 3.13. 39
teeth, | and send to darkness all that stop me. 3.13.181
discover to me | what both you spur and stop. CYM 1.06. 99
then began | a stop i' th' chaser; 5.03. 40
see clear | to stop the air would hurt them. PER 1.01.100
he'll stop the course by which it might be known 1.02. 23
how i might stop this tempest ere it came, | and 1.02. 98
what do you stop your ears? 4.02. 80 P
o, stop there a little! 5.01.160
stop no more holes but what you should. TNK 3.05. 83
stop, | as thou art just, thy noble ear against 3.06.173
keep, | to stop the loud pursuers in their yell, VEN 688
each shadow makes him stop, each murmur stay, 706
or as those bars which stop the hourly dial, LUC 327
or stop the headlong fury of his speed. 501
revenge on him that made me stop my breath. 1180
the tomb, | of his self–love, to stop posterity? SON 3. 8
injurious distance should not stop my way, | for 44. 2
what bounds, what course, what stop he makes!' LC 109
counsel may stop a while what will not stay; 159
STOPE *(also stoup)*
STOPE 2 FR 0.0002 REL FR 0 V 2 P
a stope of wine, maria! TN 2.03.120 P
lieutenant, i have a stope of wine, and here OTH 2.03. 30 P
STOPP'D 30 FR 0.0034 REL FR 28 V 2 P
i am, but stopp'd | and left me to a bootless TMP 1.02. 34
thou know'st, being stopp'd, impatiently doth TGV 2.07. 26
my ears are stopp'd and cannot hear good news, 3.01.206
and then, to be stopp'd in, like a strong WIV 3.05.112 P
when the suspicious head of theft is stopp'd. LLL 4.03.333
my liege, her ear | is stopp'd with dust: JN 4.02.120
no, it is stopp'd with other flattering sounds, R2 2.01. 17
that stopp'd by me to breathe his bloodied horse 2H4 1.01. 38
those waters from me which i would have stopp'd,
H5 4.06. 29
in our fortunes made | may readily be stopp'd. 2H6 5.02. 83
hath stopp'd the passage where thy words should 3H6 1.03. 22
i have not stopp'd mine ears to their demands, 4.08. 39
still the envious flood | stopp'd in my soul, R3 1.04. 38
the devil" — there the villain stopp'd; 4.03. 16
now civil wounds are stopp'd, peace lives again; 5.05. 40
not before the king, which stopp'd our mouths, H8 2.02. 8 P
he stopp'd the fliers, | and by his rare example COR 2.02.103
stopp'd your ears against | the general suit of 5.03. 5
sorrow concealed, like an oven stopp'd, | doth TIT 2.04. 36
grief of my son's exile hath stopp'd her breath. ROM 5.03.211
the fountain of your blood | is stopp'd, the MAC 2.03. 99
is stopp'd, the very source of it is stopp'd. 2.03. 99
well knows, | will not be rubb'd nor stopp'd. LR 2.02.154
no — his mouth is stopp'd; OTH 5.02. 71
breath, indeed, these hands have newly stopp'd. 5.02.202
/deafen'd parts, | which now are midway stopp'd. PER 5.01. 48
an oven that is stopp'd, or river stay'd, VEN 331
who like sluices stopp'd | the crystal tide that 956
her voice is stopp'd, her joints forget to bow, 1061

who, being stopp'd, the bounding banks o'erflows LUC 1119
STOPPED 1 FR 0.0001 REL FR 1 V 0 P
sense | to critic and to flatterer stopped are. SON 112.11
STOPPING 3 FR 0.0003 REL FR 2 V 1 P
stopping the career | of laughter with a sigh (a WT 1.02.286
stopping my greedy ear with their bold deeds, 2H4 1.01. 78
alexander, till 'a find it stopping a bunghole? HAM 5.01.204 P
/STOPPLE 1 FR 0.0001 REL FR 1 V 0 P
dame, | or with this paper shall i /stopple it. LR 5.03.156
STOPS 22 FR 0.0024 REL FR 18 V 4 P
into a lute-string and now govern'd by stops. ADO 3.02. 60 P
these be the stops that hinder study quite, LLL 1.01. 70
on the proudest he | that stops my way in padua. SHR 3.02.235
bohemia stops his ears, and threatens them WT 5.01.201
that follows our places stops the mouth of all H5 5.02.272 P
vexation almost stops my breath, | that sund'red 1H6 4.03. 41
why stops my lord? shall i not hear my task? 3H6 3.02. 52
mine eyes with tears | and stops my tongue, 3.03. 14
now stops thy spring, my sea shall suck them dry 4.08. 55
with me untir'd, | and stops he now for breath? R3 4.02. 45
stops on a sudden, looks upon the ground, | then H8 3.02.114
springs out into fast gait, then stops again, 3.02.116
look you, these are the stops. HAM 3.02.360 P
you would seem to know my stops, you would pluck 3.02.365 P
enough of this content, | it stops me here; OTH 2.01.197
therefore these stops of thine fright me the 3.03.120
heaven stops the nose at it, and the moon winks; 4.02. 77
and gins to chide, but soon she stops his lips, VEN 46
my restless discord loves no stops nor rests; LUC 1124
blow | the grief away that stops his answer so; 1664
task hath not said, | the protestation stops. 1700
and stops /her pipe in growth of riper days: SON 102. 8
/STOR'D 1 FR 0.0001 REL FR 1 V 0 P
here, with a cup that's /stor'd unto the brim — PER 2.03. 50
STOR'D 7 FR 0.0008 REL FR 6 V 1 P
i did not think the king so stor'd with friends. JN 5.04. 1
whereof they say | the city is well stor'd. COR 1.01.190
he's poor in no one fault, but stor'd with all. 2.01. 18 P
all the stor'd vengeances of heaven fall | on LR 2.04.162
were not this glorious casket stor'd with ill. PER 1.01. 77
their tables were stor'd full, to glad the sight 1.04. 28
are stor'd with corn to make your needy bread, 1.04. 95
/STORE 1 FR 0.0001 REL FR 1 V 0 P
/what /store /her /heart /is /made /an. LR 3.06. 54
STORE 43 FR 0.0048 REL FR 38 V 5 P
too small a pasture for such store of muttons. TGV 1.01. 99 P
for wenches, that thou call'st for such store, ERR 3.01. 34
is of that nature that to your huge store | wise LLL 5.02.377
i am debating of my present store, | and, by the MV 1.03. 53
and i have better news in store for you | than 5.01.274
which i did store to be my foster-nurse | when AYL 2.03. 40
and have prepar'd great store of wedding cheer, SHR 3.02.186
he bade me store up, as a triple eye, | safer AWW 2.01.108
and aid me with that store of power you have 5.01. 20
and your store | i think is not for idle markets TN 3.03. 45
and say, what store of parting tears were shed? R2 1.04. 5
no, ye fat chuffs, i would your store were here! 1H4 2.02. 89 P
drinking good and good store of fertile sherris, 2H4 4.03.121 P
many a pound of mine own proper store, | because 2H6 3.01.115
me, | nor store of treasons to augment my guilt. 3.01.169
may be possessed with some store of crowns, 3H6 2.05. 57
their aspects with store of childish drops: R3 1.02.154
if heaven have any grievous plague in store 1.03.216
we shall have | great store of room, no doubt, H8 5.03. 73
whereof we have ta'en good and good store — of COR 1.09. 32
how many sons hast thou of mine in store, | that TIT 1.01. 94
that, when she dies, with beauty dies her store. ROM 1.01.216
love, and you, among the store | one more, most 1.02. 22
i have an hour's talk in store for you; JC 2.02.121
for that | i do appoint him store of provender. 4.01. 30
th' vantage as would store the world they play'd OTH 4.03. 85 P
we have store to do't, | and they have earn'd ANT 4.01. 15
i do nothing doubt you have store of thieves; CYM 1.04. 97 P
withhold the vengeance that they had in store, PER 2.04. 4
to him, | store never hurts good governors. TNK 1.03. 6
but poorly rich, so wanteth in his store, | that LUC 97
pure chastity is rifled of her store, | and lust 692
fair sun that breeds the fat earth's store, | by 1837
but if store of crowns be scant, | no man will PP 20.35
let those whom nature hath not made for store, SON 11. 9
if from thyself to store thou wouldst convert; 14.12
sit, | i make my love ingrafted to this store: 37. 8
increasing store with loss, and loss with store; 64. 8
increasing store with loss, and loss with store; 64. 8
new, | and him as for a map doth nature store, 68.13
in whose confine immured is the store | which 84. 3
still, | and in abundance addeth to his store, 135.10
and let that pine to aggravate thy store; 146.10
STORE-HOUSE 3 FR 0.0003 REL FR 3 V 0 P
because i am the store-house and the shop | of COR 1.01.133
give forth | the corn a' th' store-house gratis, 3.01.114
the sacred store-house of his predecessors | and MAC 2.04. 34
STORE-HOUSES 1 FR 0.0001 REL FR 0 V 1 P
and their store-houses cramm'd with grain; COR 1.01. 81 P
STORE'S 1 FR 0.0001 REL FR 1 V 0 P
though in thy store's account i one must be, SON 136.10
STORES 1 FR 0.0001 REL FR 1 V 0 P
o, him she stores, to show what wealth she had SON 67.13
/STORIES 1 FR 0.0001 REL FR 1 V 0 P
/sad /stories /chanced /in /the /times /of /old. TIT 3.02. 83
STORIES 8 FR 0.0009 REL FR 7 V 1 P
to tell sad stories of my own mishaps. ERR 1.01.120
love's stories written in love's richest book. MND 2.02.122
and tell sad stories of the death of kings: R2 3.02.156
breeds no bate with telling of discreet stories; 2H4 2.04.250 P
their copious stories, oftentimes begun, | end VEN 845
tombs, and stories | his victories, his triumphs 1013
he stories to her ears her husband's fame, | won LUC 106
she told him stories to delight his /ear; PP 4. 5
/STORM 1 FR 0.0001 REL FR 1 V 0 P
/what, /i' /th' /storm? LR 4.03. 28
STORM 53 FR 0.0060 REL FR 47 V 6 P
you do assist the storm. TMP 1.01. 14 P
and another storm brewing, i hear it sing i' th' 2.02. 19 P
alas, the storm is come again! 2.02. 37 P
here shroud till the dregs of the storm be past. 2.02. 41 P
is the storm overblown? 2.02.110 P
moon-calf's gaberdine for fear of the storm. 2.02.112 P
so full of frost, of storm, and cloudiness? ADO 5.04. 42
why, look you how you storm! MV 1.03.137
began to scold and raise up such a storm | that SHR 1.01.172
carousing to his mates | after a storm, quaff'd 3.02.172
and still winter | in storm perpetual, could not WT 3.02.213
the storm begins. 3.03. 49
so foul a sky clears not without a storm, | pour JN 4.02.108
my tongue shall hush again this storm of war, 5.01. 20
and with a great heart heave away this storm. 5.02. 55
sing, | yet seek no shelter to avoid the storm; R2 2.01.264
i will stir up in england some black storm 2H6 3.01.349
back, | i stood upon the hatches in the storm; 3.02.103
i am resolv'd to bear a greater storm | than any 5.01.198
that keeps his leaves in spite of any storm, 5.01.206
renowned queen, with patience calm the storm, 3H6 3.03. 38
ay, now begins a second storm to rise, | for 3.03. 47
to help king edward in his time of storm, | as 4.07. 43
up, | for every cloud engenders not a storm. 5.03. 13
see | the water swell before a boist'rous storm. R3 2.03. 44
after the hideous storm that follow'd, was | a H8 1.01. 90
hollo, what storm is this? TIT 2.01. 25
when with a happy storm they were surpris'd, 2.03. 23
one hour's storm will drown the fragrant meads, 2.04. 54
now is a time to storm, why art thou still? 3.01.263
why, how now, kinsman, wherefore storm you so? ROM 1.05. 60
what storm is this that blows so contrary? 3.02. 64
for every storm that blows — i to bear this, TIM 4.03.266
the storm is up, and all is on the hazard. JC 5.01. 68
but, as we often see, against some storm, | a HAM 2.02.483
begins to rain, | and leave thee in the storm. LR 2.04. 81
let us withdraw, 'twill be a storm. 2.04.287
come out o' th' storm. 2.04.309
fie on this storm! 3.01. 49
think'st 'tis much that this contentious storm 3.04. 6
that bide the pelting of this pitiless storm, 3.04. 29
the sea, with such a storm as his bare head | in 3.07. 59
i' th' last night's storm i such a fellow saw, 4.01. 32
my downright violence and storm of fortunes OTH 1.03.249
by the /discandying of this pelleted storm, ANT 3.13.165
to daff't for our repose, shall hear a storm. 4.04. 13
a storm or robbery (call it what you will) CYM 3.03. 62
and what ensues in this fell storm | shall for PER 3.ch. 53
/thou storm, venomously | wilt thou spet all 3.01. 7
patience, good sir, do not assist the storm. 3.01. 19
died, | this world to me is a lasting storm, 4.01. 19
i could prevent this storm, and shun thy wrack! LUC 966
him, was he such a storm | as oft 'twixt may and LC 101
STORM-BEATEN 1 FR 0.0001 REL FR 1 V 0 P
to dry the rain on my storm-beaten face, | for SON 34. 6
STORMED 1 FR 0.0001 REL FR 1 V 0 P
to be so baited, scorn'd, and stormed at. R3 1.03.108
STORMING 1 FR 0.0001 REL FR 1 V 0 P
storming her world with sorrow's wind and rain. LC 7
STORMS 18 FR 0.0020 REL FR 16 V 2 P
such as sea-faring men provide for storms; ERR 1.01. 80
i will move storms; MND 1.02. 27 P
to watch the night in storms, the day in cold, SHR 5.02.150
show'rs last long, but sudden storms are short; R2 2.01. 35
witnessing storms to come, woe, and unrest. 2.04. 22
'gainst foreign storms than any home-bred 3H6 4.01. 38
brittany, | till storms be past of civil enmity. 4.06. 98
untimely storms makes men expect a dearth. R3 2.03. 35
they swell and grow, as terrible as storms. H8 3.01.164
an old man, broken with the storms of state, 4.02. 21
and valor's worth divide | in storms of fortune; TRO 1.03. 47
here grow no damned drugs, here are no storms, TIT 1.01.154
the ocean swells not so as aaron storms. 4.02.139
with frost, or grass beat down with storms. 4.04. 71
shipwracking storms and direful thunders /break, MAC 1.02. 26
they are greater storms and tempests than ANT 1.02.149 P
into so bright a day such black-fac'd storms, LUC 1518
foretell new storms to those already spent; 1589
STORMY 7 FR 0.0008 REL FR 7 V 0 P
like an unseasonable stormy day, | which makes R2 3.02.106
if you give o'er | to stormy passion, must 2H4 1.01.165
and suffolk's cloudy brow his stormy hate; 2H6 3.01.155
't 'as been a turbulent and stormy night. PER 3.02. 4
but like a stormy day, now wind, now rain, VEN 965
no cloudy show of stormy blust'ring weather LUC 115
against the stormy gusts of winter's day | and SON 13.11
STORY 78 FR 0.0088 REL FR 68 V 10 P
without the which this story | were most TMP 1.02.137
the strangeness of your story put | heaviness in 1.02.306
that shall be by and by. i remember the story. 3.02.147 P
(and if this be at all) a most strange story. 5.01.117
make it | go quick away — the story of my life, 5.01.305
i long | to hear the story of your life, which 5.01.313
that's on some shallow story of deep love, | how TGV 1.01. 21
that's a deep story of a deeper love, | for he 1.01. 23
to hear | the story of your loves discovered; 5.04.171
painted about with the story of the prodigal, WIV 4.05. 8 P
sir, make me not your story. MM 1.04. 30
the hand, | who hath a story ready for your ear. 4.01. 55
but here must end the story of my life, | and ERR 1.01.137
why, here begins his morning story right: 5.01.357
that thou began'st to twist so fine a story? ADO 1.01.311
deny | the story that is printed in her blood? 4.01.122
the story shall be chang'd: MND 2.01.230
for pyramus and thisby (says the story) did talk 3.01. 64 P
but all the story of the night told over, | and 5.01. 23
to tell this story, that you might excuse | his AYL 4.03.153
by her own letters, which makes her story true, AWW 4.03. 56 P
the story then goes false, you threw it him 5.03.229
let us from point to point this story know, | to 5.03.325
when weeping made you break the story off, | of R2 5.02. 2
it appears so by the story. 1H4 3.03.169 P
slight drollery, or the story of the prodigal, 2H4 2.01.144 P
our humble author will continue the story, with ep 28 P
this story shall the good man teach his son; H5 4.03. 56
vouchsafe to those that have not read the story, 5.pr. 1
our bending author hath pursu'd the story, | in ep 2
and if thou tell'st the heavy story right, 3H6 1.04.160
some dreadful story hanging on thy tongue? 2.01. 44
told the sad story of my father's death, | and R3 1.02.160
as index to the story we late talk'd of, | to 2.02.149
like /two children in their deaths' sad story. 4.03. 8
the very persons of our noble story | as they H8 pr 26
thought's compass, that former fabulous story, 1.01. 36
there was a lady once ('tis an old story) | that 2.03. 90
i fear, the story of his anger. 3.02.209
ear | the story of that baleful burning night, TIT 5.03. 83
many a story hath he told to thee, | and bid 5.03.164
that in gold clasps locks in the golden story; ROM 1.03. 92
for never was a story of more woe | than this of 5.03.309
well, honor is the subject of my story: JC 1.02. 92
become | a woman's story at a winter's fire, MAC 3.04. 64
thy story quickly. 5.05. 29
ears, | that are so fortified against our story, HAM 1.01. 32
his name's gonzago, the story is extant, and 3.02.262 P
draw thy breath in pain | to tell my story. 5.02.349
still question'd me the story of my life | from OTH 1.03.129
my story being done, | she gave me for my pains 1.03.158
i should but teach him how to tell my story, 1.03.165
iago /beckons me; now he begins the story. 4.01.131 P
conquer, | and earns a place i' th' story. ANT 3.13. 46
and their story is | no less in pity than his 5.02.361
rather than story him in his own hearing. CYM 1.04. 33 P
and the contents o' th' story. 2.02. 27
the story | proud cleopatra, when she met her 2.04. 69
o boys, this story | the world may read in me: 3.03. 55
have done, his spirits fly out | into my story; 3.03. 91
we'll mannerly demand thee of thy story, | so 3.06. 91
let me end the story: | i slew him there. 5.05.286
and it is said | for certain in our story, she PER 4.ch. 19
gaps to teach you, | the stages of our story. 4.04. 9
chances | into an honest house, our story says. 5.ch. 2
tell thy story; 5.01.134
i'll hear you more, to th' bottom of your story, 5.01.164
chaucer (of all admir'd) the story gives; TNK pr 13
nature now | shall make and act the story, the 5.03. 14
he, | "leave me, and then the story aptly ends; VEN 716
my brow, | the story of sweet chastity's decay, LUC 808
nurse, to still her child, will tell my story, 813
whose enchanting story | the credulous old priam 1521
tell | that you are you, so dignifies his story. SON 84. 8
upon thy part i can set down a story | of faults 88. 6
that tongue that tells the story of thy days 95. 5
in hue, | could make me any summer's story tell, 98. 7
a plaintful story from a sist'ring vale, | my LC 2
STOUP *(also stope)*
STOUP 1 FR 0.0001 REL FR 0 V 1 P
a stoup of wine! TN 2.03. 14 P
STOUPS 1 FR 0.0001 REL FR 1 V 0 P
set me the stoups of wine upon that table. HAM 5.02.267
STOUT 20 FR 0.0022 REL FR 19 V 1 P
and rifted jove's stout oak | with his own bolt; TMP 5.01. 45
i will be strange, stout, in yellow stockings, TN 2.05.170 P
my towns | with dreadful pomp of stout invasion! JN 4.02.173
dead | bears not alive so stout a gentleman. 1H4 5.04. 93
betwixt the stout lord talbot and the french. 1H6 1.01.106
i read | that stout pendragon in his litter sick 3.02. 95
'tis said the stout parisians do revolt, | and 5.02. 2
as stout and proud as he were lord of all, 2H6 1.01.187
of gallowglasses and stout kerns | is marching 4.09. 26
that as ulysses and stout diomede | with sleight 3H6 4.02. 19
a wise stout captain, and soon persuaded! 4.07. 30
how now, my hardy, stout, resolved mates, | are R3 1.03.339
for after the stout earl northumberland H8 4.02. 12
which often thus correcting thy stout heart, COR 3.02. 78
from tybalt hit the life | of stout mercutio, ROM 3.01.169
could draw to part them, was stout tybalt slain; 3.01.173
pluck stout men's pillows from below their heads TIM 4.03. 33
he finds thee in the stout norweyan ranks, MAC 1.03. 95
by his seeming | should be a stout man, by his TNK 4.02. 77
days, | when rocks impregnable are not so stout, SON 65. 7
STOUTER 1 FR 0.0001 REL FR 1 V 0 P
said | a stouter champion never handled sword. 1H6 3.04. 19
STOUT-HEARTED 2 FR 0.0002 REL FR 2 V 0 P
o love, | what a stout-hearted child thou art! TNK 2.06. 9
stout-hearted, still, | but, when he stirs, a 4.02.130
STOUTLY 4 FR 0.0004 REL FR 4 V 0 P
thou that so stoutly hath resisted me, | give me 3H6 2.05. 79
his bark is stoutly timber'd, and his pilot | of OTH 2.01. 48
talking of it, | and she speaks for you stoutly. 3.01. 44
not, faint heart, but stoutly say, 'so be it'* LUC 1209
STOUTNESS 2 FR 0.0002 REL FR 2 V 0 P
thy pride than fear | thy dangerous stoutness; COR 3.02.127
his stoutness | when he did stand for consul, 5.06. 26
STOVER 1 FR 0.0001 REL FR 1 V 0 P
and flat meads thatch'd with stover, them to TMP 4.01. 63
STOW 1 FR 0.0001 REL FR 1 V 0 P
clap her aboard to-morrow night and stow her, TNK 2.03. 32
STOWAGE 1 FR 0.0001 REL FR 1 V 0 P
being strange, | to have them in safe stowage. CYM 1.06.192
STOW'D 2 FR 0.0002 REL FR 1 V 1 P
safely stow'd. HAM 4.02. 1 P
foul thief, where hast thou stow'd my daughter? OTH 1.02. 62
STOWED 1 FR 0.0001 REL FR 1 V 0 P
the mariners all under hatches stowed, | who, TMP 1.02.230
STOWS 1 FR 0.0001 REL FR 1 V 0 P
and in her vaulty prison stows the day. LUC 119
STRACHY 1 FR 0.0001 REL FR 0 V 1 P
the lady of the strachy married the yeoman of TN 2.05. 40 P
STRAGGLERS 1 FR 0.0001 REL FR 1 V 0 P
let's whip these stragglers o'er the seas again; R3 5.03.327
STRAGGLING 2 FR 0.0002 REL FR 2 V 0 P
likewise enrich'd poor straggling soldiers with TIM 5.01. 6
like straggling slaves for pillage fighting, LUC 428
/STRAIGHT 3 FR 0.0003 REL FR 3 V 0 P
/let /it /command /a /mirror /hither /straight, R2 4.01.265
/let /us /make /ready /straight. TRO 4.04.144
/be /done, /i /will /arraign /them /straight. LR 3.06. 20
STRAIGHT 164 FR 0.0185 REL FR 143 V 21 P
i will answer it straight: WIV 1.01.115 P
we'll come dress you straight. 4.02. 83 P
go up, i'll bring linen for him straight. 4.02.101 P
go, send to falstaff straight. 4.04. 75
where a priest attends, | straight marry her. 4.06. 32
he can command, lets it straight feel the spur; MM 1.02.162
i will about it straight; 1.04. 85
he will come straight. 2.02. 1
and floating straight, obedient to the stream, ERR 1.01. 86
if any ship put out, then straight away. 3.02.185

to adriana, villain, hie thee straight: 4.01.102
go, dromio, there's the money, bear it straight, 4.02. 63
and to thy state of darkness hie thee straight: 4.04. 56
straight after did i meet him with a chain. 4.04.140
my servant straight was mute. LLL 5.02.277
lo, he is tilting straight! 5.02.483
i will be with thee straight. MND 3.02.403
which straight she gave me, and her fairy sent 4.01. 60
and not bethink me straight of dangerous rocks, MV 1.01. 31
a throstle sing, he falls straight a–cap'ring. 1.02. 61 P
and i will go and purse the ducats straight, 1.03.174
ay, marry, i'll be gone about it straight. 2.04. 24
with some moe ducats, and be with you straight. 2.06. 50
quick, i pray thee, draw the curtain straight; 2.09. 1
straight shall our nuptial rites be solemniz'd; 2.09. 6
i'll bring you to him straight. AYL 2.01. 69
i'll write it straight; 3.05.136
and if he chance to speak, be ready straight, SHR in.1. 52
we will fetch thee straight | adonis painted by in.2. 49
like the hazel–twig | is straight and slender, 2.01.254
i'll be with you straight. 4.01.167
i am for thee straight. 4.03.151 P
go call my men, and let us straight to him, 4.03.184
home, | and bid bianca make her ready straight; 4.04. 63
away, i say, and bring them hither straight. 5.02.105
i'll send her straight away. AWW 2.03.295
seem to know, is to know straight our purpose: 4.01. 19 P
i have wit enough to lie straight in my bed. TN 2.03.136 P
this will i tell my lady straight; 4.01. 30 P
deserves high speech) and straight | the shrug, WT 2.01. 70
he straight declin'd, droop'd, took it deeply, 2.03. 14
take it up straight. 2.03.135
/philip, determine what we shall do straight. JN 2.01.149
the king by me requests your presence straight. 4.03. 22
to my litter straight, | weakness possesseth me, 5.03. 16
straight let us seek, or straight we shall be 5.07. 79
let us seek, or straight we shall be sought; 5.07. 79
go, bushy, to the earl of wiltshire straight, R2 2.01.215
i will for refuge straight to bristow castle: 2.02.135
destruction straight shall dog them at the heels 5.03.139
by bullingbrook, | and straight am nothing. 5.05. 38
that we at our own charge shall ransom straight 1H4 1.03. 79
i will after straight | and tell him so, for i 1.03.126
deliver them up without their ransom straight, 1.03.260
well, i will back him straight. 2.03. 71
you are straight enough in the shoulders, you 2.04.148 P
of land, | and then he runs straight and even. 3.01.113
from hence, | and straight they shall be here. 3.01.225
i'll to clifton straight. 5.04. 46
supp'd is too hot, they'll come in straight. 2H4 2.04. 14 P
from him, give him air, he'll straight be well. 4.04.116
i'll be with you straight. 5.03. 44 P
will be thought we keep a bawdy–house straight. H5 2.01. 35 P
of god, | putting it straight in expedition. 2.02.191
straight to horse! 4.02. 15
your thoughts, straight back again to france. 5.pr. 45
good leg will fall, a straight back will stoop, 5.02.159 P
gather strength and march unto him straight. 1H6 4.01. 73
come go, i will dispatch the horsemen straight; 4.04. 40
you judge it straight a thing impossible | to 5.04. 47
sirrah, go fetch the beadle hither straight. 2H6 2.01.137
go call our uncle to our presence straight. 3.02. 15
unless lord suffolk straight be done to death, 3.02.244
and so will i, and write home for it straight. 4.01. 24
and issue forth and bid them battle straight. 3H6 1.02. 70
myself in person will straight follow you. 4.01.133
will thither straight, for willingness rids way, 5.03. 21
away with oxford to hames castle straight; 5.05. 2
i like you, lads, about your business straight. R3 1.03.353
you straight are on your knees for pardon, 2.01.125
send straight for him, | let him be crown'd, in 2.02. 97
who they shall be that straight shall post to 2.02.142
for by his face straight shall you know his 3.04. 53
i'll signify so much unto him straight. 3.07. 70
come, madam, you must straight to westminster, 4.01. 31
whom i will marry straight to clarence' daughter 4.02. 54
i will dispatch it straight. 4.02. 82
bid him levy straight | the greatest strength 4.04.449
he sent command to the lord mayor straight | to H8 2.01.151
straight | springs out into fast gait, then 3.02.115
go we to him straight. TRO 1.03.388
here i' th' orchard, i'll bring her straight. 3.02. 17 P
she's making her ready, she'll come straight. 3.02. 30 P
come, thou shalt bear a letter to him straight. 3.03.305
speak a word | but it straight starts you. 5.02.101
then straight his doubled spirit | requick'ned COR 2.02.116
that i'll straight do; 2.03.147
them now, | and straight disclaim their tongues? 3.01. 35
put him to choler straight, he hath been us'd 3.03. 25
speed thee straight | and make my misery serve 4.05. 87
away with him, and make a fire straight, | and TIT 1.01.127
body hearing it | should straight fall mad, or 2.03.104
but straight they told me they would bind me 2.03.106
straight will i bring you to the loathsome pit 2.03.193
ye draw home enough, and 'tis there straight. 4.03. 3
i beseech you follow straight. ROM 1.03.103 P
knees, that dream on cur'sies straight; 1.04. 72
lawyers' fingers, who straight dream on fees; 1.04. 73
o'er ladies' lips, who straight on kisses dream, 1.04. 74
by her fine foot, straight leg, and quivering 2.01. 19
they'll be in scarlet straight at any news. 2.05. 71
the county will be here with music straight, 4.04. 22
i'll be with thee straight. 5.01. 33
of twenty men, it would dispatch you straight. 5.01. 79
iron crow, and bring it straight | unto my cell. 5.02. 21
it him, it foals me straight | and able horses. TIM 2.01. 9
and thither will i straight to visit him; JC 3.02.265
we must straight make head; 4.01. 42
a hasty spark, | and straight is cold again. 4.03.113
is so much that thou wilt kill me straight: 5.04. 13
i'll call upon you straight; MAC 3.01.139
did he not straight | in pious rage the two 3.06. 11
we'll have a speech straight. HAM 2.02.431 P
'a will come straight. 3.04. 1
i'll be with you straight — go a little before. 4.04. 31
thee she is, therefore make her grave straight. 5.01. 4 P
i'll write straight to my sister | to hold my LR 1.03. 25
summon'd up their meiny, straight took horse, 2.04. 35

i'll tell you straight. 5.03.280
i'll see that straight. 5.03.288
straight satisfy yourself. OTH 1.01.137
we must straight employ you | against the 1.03. 48
my desdemona, i'll come to thee straight. 3.03. 87
a little while, | he will recover straight. 4.01. 57
stand behind this /bulk, straight will he come. 5.01. 1
to heaven and grace, | solicit for it straight. 5.02. 28
myself will straight aboard, and to the state 5.02.370
sister's view, | whither straight i'll lead you. ANT 2.02.168
bring thee word | straight how 'tis like to go. 4.12. 3
lawful counsel, and straight away for britain, CYM 1.04.165 P
crook'd noses, but to owe such straight arms, 3.01. 37 P
goodly gifts | and snatch them straight away? PER 3.01. 24
yield 'er, for she must overboard straight. 3.01. 53 P
to thy grave, but straight | must cast thee, 3.01. 59
wrench it open straight. 3.02. 53
her stature to an inch, as wand–like straight, 5.01.109
with thy twinkling eyes look right and straight TNK 3.05.117
the straight young boughs that blush with 3.06.243
she saw me, and straight sought the flood. 4.01. 95
i'll away straight. 5.02.101
breaketh his rein, and to her straight goes he. VEN 264
short ears, straight legs and passing strong, 297
and straight, in pity of his tender years, 1091
with the sceptre straight be strooken down? LUC 217
and as one shifts, another straight ensues: 1104
wit sets down is blotted straight with will; 1299
i'll murther straight, and then i'll slaughter 1634
i send them back again and straight grow sad. SON 45.14
speak of my lameness, and i straight will halt, 89. 3
and straight redeem | in gentle numbers time so 100. 5
i may be straight though they themselves be 121.11
enjoy'd no sooner but despised straight, | past 129. 5
bear thine eyes straight, though thy proud heart 140.14
state, | straight in her heart did mercy come, 145. 5

STRAIGHTEST 1 FR 0.0001 REL FR 1 V 0 P
amongst a grove the very straightest plant, 1H4 1.01. 82

STRAIGHT–PIGHT 1 FR 0.0001 REL FR 1 V 0 P
the shrine of venus or straight–pight minerva, CYM 5.05.164

STRAIGHTWAY 8 FR 0.0009 REL FR 8 V 0 P
straightway, at liberty; TMP 5.01.235
titania wak'd, and straightway lov'd an ass. MND 3.02. 34
wilt thou at ninny's tomb meet me straightway? 5.01.202
and straightway give thy soul to him thou 1H6 1.05. 7
is straightway /calm'd and boarded with a pirate 2H6 4.09. 33
we, like friends, will straightway go together. JC 2.02.127
to the sea–side straightway; ANT 3.11. 20
or else | thou art straightway with the fiends. CYM 3.05. 83

STRAIN* 31 FR 0.0035 REL FR 27 V 4 P
i hear | the strain of strutting chanticleer: TMP 1.02.386
unless he know some strain in me that i know not WIV 2.01. 87 P
all of the same strain were in the same distress 3.03.186 P
he is of a noble strain, of approv'd valor, and ADO 2.01.379 P
to strange sores strangely they strain the cure. 4.01.252
and let it answer every strain for strain, | as 5.01. 12
and let it answer every strain for strain, | as 5.01. 12
that strain again, it had a dying fall; TN 1.01. 4
and strain their cheeks to idle merriment — | a JN 3.03. 46
you strain too far. 1H4 4.01. 75
or swell my thoughts to any strain of pride, 2H4 4.05.170
and he is bred out of that bloody strain | that H5 2.04. 51
publication, make no strain | but that achilles, TRO 1.03.326
that so degenerate a strain as this | should 2.02.154
i do not strain at the position — | it is 3.03.112
such a case as mine a man may strain courtesy. ROM 2.04. 50 P
to build his fortune i will strain a little, TIM 1.01.143
the strain of man's bred out | into baboon and 1.01.250
praise his most vicious strain, | and call it 4.03.213
and strain what other means is left unto us | in 5.01.227
and touch thy instrument a strain or two? JC 4.03.257
o, if thou wert the noblest of thy strain, 5.01. 59
sir, you have show'd to–day your valiant strain, LR 5.03. 40
i am to pray you not to strain my speech | to OTH 3.03.218
note if your lady strain his entertainment 3.03.250
of common passage, but | a strain of rareness; CYM 3.04. 92
o noble strain! 4.02. 24
shame | to think of what a noble strain you are, PER 4.03. 24
they all strain court'sy who shall cope him VEN 888
so i at each sad strain will strain a tear, LUC 1131
so i at each sad strain will strain a tear, 1131

/STRAIN'D 1 FR 0.0001 REL FR 1 V 0 P
/troth, | /strain'd /purely /from /all /hollow TRO 4.05.169

STRAIN'D 6 FR 0.0006 REL FR 6 V 0 P
the quality of mercy is not strain'd, | it MV 4.01.184
so uncurrent i | have strain'd t' appear thus; WT 3.02. 50
i love thee in so strain'd a purity | that the TRO 4.04. 24
aught so good but, strain'd from that fair use, ROM 2.03. 19
and with strain'd pride | to come betwixt our LR 1.01.169
fool, | away with this strain'd mirth! TNK 3.03. 43

STRAINED 2 FR 0.0002 REL FR 2 V 0 P
this strained passion doth you wrong, my lord. 2H4 1.01.161
what strained touches rhetoric can lend, | thou, SON 82.10

/STRAINING 1 FR 0.0001 REL FR 1 V 0 P
in the slips, | /straining upon the start. H5 3.01. 32

STRAINING 3 FR 0.0003 REL FR 3 V 0 P
more straining on for plucking back, not WT 4.04.465
breast i'll burst with straining of my courage, 1H6 1.05. 10
straining harsh discords and unpleasing sharps. ROM 3.05. 28

STRAINS* 8 FR 0.0009 REL FR 7 V 1 P
as love is full of unbefitting strains, | all LLL 5.02.760
an instrument, and play false strains upon thee? AYL 4.03. 68 P
and more and richer, when he strains that lady. H8 4.01. 46
do not these high strains | of divination in our TRO 2.02.113
thou hast affected the /fine strains of honor, COR 5.03.149
it strains me past the compass of my wits. ROM 4.01. 47
strains his young nerves, and puts himself in CYM 3.03. 94
and other strains of woe, which now seem woe, SON 90.13

STRAIT 11 FR 0.0012 REL FR 10 V 1 P
(whom i believe to be most strait in virtue) MM 2.01. 9
and you are so strait | and so ingrateful, you JN 5.07. 42
some certain edicts and some strait decrees 1H4 4.03. 79
french hose off, and in your strait strossers. H5 3.07. 54 P
yet, notwithstanding such a strait edict, | were 2H6 3.02.258
way, | for honor travels in a strait so narrow, TRO 3.03.154
his means most short, his creditors most strait. TIM 1.01. 96
seen, all flying | through a strait lane; CYM 5.03. 7
that the strait pass was damm'd | with dead men 5.03. 11
is not this piece too strait? TNK 3.06. 86
back to the strait that forc'd him on so fast LUC 1670

STRAITED 1 FR 0.0001 REL FR 1 V 0 P
love or bounty, you were straited | for a reply, WT 4.04.354

STRAITER 1 FR 0.0001 REL FR 1 V 0 P
proceed no straiter 'gainst our uncle gloucester 2H6 3.02. 20

STRAITLY 1 FR 0.0001 REL FR 1 V 0 P
his majesty hath straitly given in charge | that R3 1.01. 85

STRAITNESS 1 FR 0.0001 REL FR 0 V 1 P
life answer the straitness of his proceeding, it MM 3.02.255 P

STRAITS 1 FR 0.0001 REL FR 0 V 1 P
i know into what straits of fortune she is AYL 5.02. 64 P

STRAND *(see strond, etc.)*

/STRANGE 2 FR 0.0002 REL FR 1 V 1 P
of my sudden /and /more /strange return. HAM 4.07. 47 P
i can call but now) i have heard /strange /news. LR 2.01. 87

STRANGE 262 FR 0.0296 REL FR 209 V 53 P
by accident most strange, bountiful fortune TMP 1.02.178
a sea–change | into something rich and strange. 1.02.402
what strange fish | hath made his meal on thee? 2.01.113
what a strange drowsiness possesses them! 2.01.199
this is a strange repose, to be asleep | with 2.01.213
i heard a humming | (and that a strange one too) 2.01.318
a strange fish! 2.02. 27 P
any strange beast there makes a man. 2.02. 31 P
misery acquaints a man with strange bedfellows; 2.02. 40 P
and observation strange, my meaner ministers 3.03. 87
sir, why stand you | in this strange stare? 3.03. 95
this is strange. 4.01.143
our skins with pinches, | make us strange stuff. 4.01.234
(and if this be at all) a most strange story. 5.01.117
they strengthen | from strange to stranger. 5.01.228
with strange and several noises | of roaring, 5.01.232
this is as strange a maze as e'er men trod, 5.01.242
this is a strange thing as e'er i look'd on. 5.01.290
she makes it strange, but she would be best TGV 1.02. 99
i'll tell you strange things of this knave ford, WIV 5.01. 27 P
strange things in hand, master /brook! 5.01. 29 P
this is strange. who hath got the right anne? 5.05.211 P
for thy complexion shifts to strange effects, MM 3.01. 24
sir, a strange picklock, which we have sent to 3.02. 17 P
doubt not, and the signet is not strange to you. 4.02.193 P
very day receives letters of strange tenor — 4.02.200 P
i should not think it strange, for 'tis a physic 4.06. 7
and she will speak most bitterly and strange. 5.01. 36
most strange! 5.01. 37
that angelo's forsworn, is it not strange? 5.01. 38
that angelo's a murtherer, is't not strange? 5.01. 39
a virgin–violator, | is it not strange? 5.01. 42
and strange? 5.01. 42
nay, it is ten times strange. 5.01. 42
than this is all as true as it is strange; 5.01. 44
he is sick, my lord, | of a strange fever. 5.01.152
this is a strange abuse. let's see thy face. 5.01.205
and, which was strange, the one so like the ERR 1.01. 51
ay, ay, antipholus, look strange and frown, 2.02.110
thyself i call it, being strange to me, | that, 2.02.121
as strange unto your town as to your talk, | who 2.02.149
to know the reason of this strange restraint. 3.01. 97
why, this is strange. 5.01.281
why look you strange on me? you know me well. 5.01.296
have written strange defeatures in my face: 5.01.300
i can tell you strange news that you yet dreamt ADO 1.02. 4 P
banquet, just so many strange dishes. 2.03. 21 P
to put a strange face on his own perfection. 2.03. 47
is it not strange that sheep's guts should hale 2.03. 59 P
be a fancy that he hath to strange disguises — 3.02. 32 P
there is some strange misprision in the princes. 4.01.185
but not for that dream i on this strange course, 4.01.212
for to strange sores strangely they strain the 4.01.252
the world so well as you — is not that strange? 4.01.268 P
as strange as the thing i know not. 4.01.269 P
and some such strange bull leapt your father's 5.04. 49
berowne, one of the strange queen's lords. LLL 4.02.130 P
we will with some strange pastime solace them, 4.03.374
without opinion, and strange without heresy. 5.01. 6 P
this begging is not strange. 5.02.210
o strange! MND 3.01.104 P
'tis strange, my theseus, that these lovers 5.01. 1
more strange than true. 5.01. 2
but, howsoever, strange and admirable. 5.01. 27
that is hot ice and wondrous strange snow. 5.01. 59
nature hath fram'd strange fellows in her time: MV 1.01. 51
you grow exceeding strange. 1.01. 67
so strange, outrageous, and so variable | as the 2.08. 13
thou'lt show thy mercy and remorse more strange 4.01. 20
strange | than is thy strange apparent cruelty; 4.01. 21
of a strange nature is the suit you follow, 4.01.177
you shall not know by what strange accident | i 5.01.278
we that are true lovers run into strange capers; AYL 2.04. 55 P
a voyage, he hath strange places cramm'd | with 2.07. 40
full of strange oaths, and bearded like the pard 2.07.150
all, | that ends this strange eventful history, 2.07.164
look you lisp and wear strange suits; 4.01. 34 P
in me what strange effect | would they work in 4.03. 52
if you please, that i can do strange things. 5.02. 59 P
here comes a pair of very strange beasts, which 5.04. 37 P
make conclusion | of these most strange events. 5.04.127
it would seem strange unto him when he wak'd. SHR in.1. 43
house, | as beaten hence by your strange lunacy. in.2. 29
signior baptista, will you be so strange? 1.01. 85
such a life, with such a wife, were strange! 1.02.193
that with your strange encounter much amaz'd me, 4.05. 54
impossible be strange attempts to those | that AWW 1.01.224
nay, 'tis strange, 'tis very strange, that is 2.03. 28 P
'tis strange, 'tis very strange, that is the 2.03. 28 P
strange is it that our bloods, | of color, 2.03.118
is not this a strange fellow, my lord, that so 3.06. 86 P
but o, strange men, | that can such sweet use 4.04. 21
why do you look so strange upon your wife? 5.03.168
i will be strange, stout, in yellow stockings, TN 2.05.170 P
he's coming, madam, but in very strange manner. 3.04. 8 P
this is as uncivil as strange. 3.04.253 P
but in conclusion put strange speech upon me. 5.01. 67
you throw a strange regard upon me, and by that 5.01.212
this is strange; WT 1.02.364
as by strange fortune | it came to us, i do in 2.03.179
for maids, so without bawdry, which is strange; 4.04.194 P

must to the king, and show our strange sights. 4.04.819 P
'tis strange | he thus should steal upon us. 5.01.114
a strange beginning: "borrowed majesty"! JN 1.01. 5
'tis strange to think how much king john hath 3.04.121
strong reasons makes strange actions. 3.04.182
wounds | with many legions of strange fantasies, 5.07. 18
'tis strange that death should sing. 5.07. 20
is a strange brooch in this all–hating world. R2 5.05. 66
and in thy face strange motions have appear'd, 1H4 2.03. 60
oftentimes breaks forth | in strange eruptions; 3.01. 27
and profited | in strange concealments, valiant 3.01.165
i see a strange confession in thine eye. 2H4 1.01. 94
is it not strange that desire should so many 2.04.260 P
studies his companions | like a strange tongue, 4.04. 69
'tis so strange, | that, though the truth of it H5 2.02.102
lord strange of blackmere, lord verdon of alton, 1H6 4.07. 65
devise strange deaths for small offenses done? 2H6 3.01. 59
you did devise | strange tortures for offenders, 3.01.122
'tis wondrous strange, the like yet never heard 3H6 2.01. 33
you'ld think it strange if i should marry her. 3.02.111
should juggle | men into such strange mysteries? H8 1.03. 2
'tis strange. 2.03. 36
this is strange to me. 2.03. 88
a strange tongue makes my cause more strange, 3.01. 45
a strange tongue makes my cause more strange, 3.01. 45
some strange commotion | is in his brain; 3.02.112
in most strange postures | we have seen him set 3.02.118
or have we some strange indian with the great 5.03. 34 P
in this | are dogg'd with two strange followers. TRO 1.03.364
and yet he loves himself. is't not strange? 2.03.161 P
or strange, or self–affected! 2.03.239
like to a strange soul upon the stygian banks 3.02. 9
am become | as new into the world, strange, 3.03. 12
a strange fellow here | writes me that man, how 3.03. 95
this is not strange, ulysses. 3.03.102
this is not strange at all. 3.03.111
doth conduce a fight | of this strange nature, 5.02.148
and a petition granted them — a strange one, COR 1.01.210
this is strange. 1.01.221
this is strange now. 2.01. 21 P
you are a pair of strange ones. 2.01. 79 P
there hath been in rome strange insurrections; 4.03. 13 P
supper, tell you most strange things from rome, 4.03. 41 P
a strange one as ever i look'd on. 4.05. 20 P
tell my master what a strange guest he has here. 4.05. 35 P
here's a strange alteration! 4.05.148 P
why makes thou it so strange? TIT 2.01. 81
thus, in this strange and sad habiliment, | i 5.02. 1
to ruminate strange plots of dire revenge; 5.02. 6
of some strange nature, letting it there stand ROM 2.01. 25
than those that have /more coying to be strange. 2.02.101
i should have been more strange, i must confess, 2.02.102
be thus afflicted with these strange flies, 2.04. 32 P
till strange love grow bold, | think true love 3.02. 15
strange dream, that gives a dead man leave to 5.01. 7
what strange, | which manifold record not TIM 1.01. 4
what a strange case was that! 3.02. 17 P
i'll show you how t' observe a strange event. 3.04. 17
mark how strange it shows, | timon in this 3.04. 21
strange, unusual blood, | when man's worst sin 4.02. 38
but in thy fortunes am unlearn'd and strange. 4.03. 57
strange times, that weep with laughing, not with 4.03.486
you bear too stubborn and too strange a hand JC 1.02. 35
to see the strange impatience of the heavens; 1.03. 61
and fearful, as these strange eruptions are. 1.03. 78
two or three of us have seen strange sights. 1.03.138
it seems to me most strange that men should fear 2.02. 35
that, methinks, is strange. 4.03.184
for certain she is dead, and by strange manner. 4.03.189
he look | that seems to speak things strange. MAC 1.02. 47
from whence | you owe this strange intelligence, 1.03. 76
thyself didst make | strange images of death. 1.03. 97
but 'tis strange; 1.03.122
like our strange garments, cleave not to their 1.03.145
as a book, where men | may read strange matters. 1.05. 63
strange screams of death, | and prophesying, 2.03. 56
i have seen | hours dreadful and things strange; 2.04. 3
horses (a thing most strange and certain), 2.04. 14
filling their hearers | with strange invention. 3.01. 32
this is more strange | than such a murther is. 3.04. 81
i have a strange infirmity, which is nothing 3.04. 85
you make me strange | even to the disposition 3.04.111
strange things i have in head, that will to hand 3.04.138
my strange and self–abuse | is the initiate fear 3.04.141
with this strange virtue, | he hath a heavenly 4.03.156
'tis strange. HAM 1.01. 64
this bodes some strange eruption to our state. 1.01. 69
'tis very strange. 1.02.220
but this most foul, strange, and unnatural. 1.05. 28
o day and night, but this is wondrous strange! 1.05.164
how strange or odd some'er i bear myself — | as 1.05.170
it is not very strange, for my uncle is king of 2.02.363 P
aye, nor 'tis not strange | that even our loves 3.02.200
this is most strange, | that she, whom even but LR 1.01.213
'tis strange that from their cold'st neglect 1.01.254
'tis strange. 1.02.117 P
o strange and fast'ned villain! 2.01. 77
thou art a strange fellow. a tailor make a man? 2.02. 56 P
'tis strange that they should so depart from 2.04. 1
the art of our necessities is strange | and can 3.02. 70
there is strange things toward, edmund, pray you 3.03. 19 P
but that thy strange mutations make us hate thee 4.01. 11
she gave strange eliads and most speaking looks 4.05. 25
she swore, in faith 'twas strange, 'twas passing OTH 1.03.160
in faith 'twas strange, 'twas passing strange; 1.03.160
from him that fled some strange indignity 2.03.245
o strange! 2.03.307 P
and certainly in strange unquietness. 3.04.133
that's strange. 4.02. 11
'tis a strange truth. 5.02.189
it is reported thou didst eat strange flesh, ANT 1.04. 67
for he hath laid strange courtesies and great 2.02.154
a strange invisible perfume hits the sense | of 2.02.212
y' have strange serpents there? 2.07. 24 P
'tis a strange serpent. 2.07. 48 P
there's strange news come, sir. 3.05. 2 P
is it not strange, canidius, | that from 3.07. 20
impossible | strange that his power should be. 3.07. 57
heard you of nothing strange about the streets? 4.03. 3
ay, is't not strange? 4.03. 19
content. 'tis strange. 4.03. 22
all strange and terrible events are welcome, 4.15. 3
and strange it is | that nature must compel us 5.01. 28
wants stuff | to vie strange forms with fancy; 5.02. 98
howsoe'er 'tis strange, | or that the negligence CYM 1.01. 65
but you know strange fowl light upon neighboring 1.04. 89 P
doth think she has | strange ling'ring poisons. 1.05. 34
he's strange and peevish. 1.06. 54
such an end thou seek'st — as base as strange. 1.06.144
and i am something curious, being strange, | to 1.06.191
he's a strange fellow himself, and knows it not. 2.01. 35 P
what a strange infection | is fall'n into thy 3.02. 3
yet still it's strange | what cloten's being 4.02.181
'tis strange. 4.03. 37
this was strange chance. 5.03. 51
'tis strange he hides him in fresh cups, soft 5.03. 71
but failing of her end by his strange absence, 5.05. 57
after this strange starting from your orbs, 5.05.371
'twas very strange. PER 2.04. 13
tyre, | fame answering the most strange inquire, 3.ch. 22
'tis most strange | nature should be so 3.02. 24
most strange. 3.02. 64
is not this strange? 3.02.106
what strange ruins, | since first we went to TNK 1.02. 13
have heard | strange howls this livelong night; 3.02. 12
these are strange conjurings. 3.06.201
these are strange questions. 4.01. 35
this is strange. 4.01.134
his head, | seem'd with strange art to hang. 5.04. 79
'tis strange if none be here — and, if he will ep 7
they bring in strange roots, which is merely to STM II.C 8 P
o strange excuse! VEN 791
o hard–believing love, how strange it seems! 985
th' impression of strange kinds | is form'd in LUC 1242
that millions of strange shadows on you tend? SON 53. 2
to new–found methods and to compounds strange? 76. 4
i will acquaintance strangle and look strange, 89. 8
writ in moods and frowns and wrinkles strange; 93. 8
to me are nothing novel, nothing strange; 123. 3
against strange maladies a sovereign cure. 153. 8
applied to cautels, all strange forms receives, LC 303

STRANGE–ACHIEVED 1 FR 0.0001 REL FR 1 V 0 P
the cank'red heaps of strange–achieved gold; 2H4 4.05. 71

STRANGE–DISPOSED 1 FR 0.0001 REL FR 1 V 0 P
indeed, it is a strange–disposed time; JC 1.03. 33

STRANGELY 28 FR 0.0031 REL FR 24 V 4 P
they vanish'd strangely. TMP 3.03. 40
love, and thou | hast strangely stood the test. 4.01. 7
of milan, who most strangely | upon this shore 5.01.160
your life, which must | take the ear strangely. 5.01.314
the duke is very strangely gone from hence; MM 1.04. 50
this unwonted putting–on, methinks strangely, 4.02.117 P
o mischief strangely thwarting! ADO 3.02.132 P
to strange sores strangely they strain the cure. 4.01.252
that thou commend it strangely to some place WT 2.03.182
land, | i find the people strangely fantasied, JN 4.02.144
were strangely clamorous to the frighted fields. 1H4 3.01. 39
you all look strangely on me, and you most. 2H4 5.02. 63
gone by him, or at least | strangely neglected? H8 3.02. 11
most strangely. 3.02. 29
all were woven | so strangely in one piece. 4.01. 81
the times and titles now are alter'd strangely 4.02.112
you are strangely troublesome. 5.02.129
please it our general pass strangely by him, TRO 3.03. 39
they pass by strangely. 3.03. 71
only i say | things have been strangely borne. MAC 3.06. 3
very strangely, they say. HAM 5.01.157 P
how strangely? 5.01.158 P
it is a day turn'd strangely. CYM 5.02. 17
of her it was | that we meet here so strangely; 5.05.272
to an honor'd triumph strangely furnished. PER 2.02. 53
so strangely, so unlike a noble kinsman, | to TNK 2.02.190
that time when thou shalt strangely pass, | and SON 49. 5
i have look'd on truth | askaunce and strangely: 110. 6

STRANGELY–VISITED 1 FR 0.0001 REL FR 1 V 0 P
but strangely–visited people, | all swoll'n and MAC 4.03.150

STRANGENESS 12 FR 0.0013 REL FR 11 V 1 P
the strangeness of your story put | heaviness in TMP 1.02.306
beating on | the strangeness of this business. 5.01.247
at his dishonor | than at the strangeness of it. MM 5.01.381
now ungird thy strangeness and tell me what i TN 4.01. 15 P
the strangeness of his alter'd countenance? 2H6 3.01. 5
here tend the savage strangeness he puts on, TRO 2.03.126
to use between your strangeness and his pride, 3.03. 45
put on | a form of strangeness as we pass along. 3.03. 51
this is above all strangeness. LR 4.06. 66
he shall in strangeness stand no farther off OTH 3.03. 12
she puts on outward strangeness, seems unkind: VEN 310
measure my strangeness with my unripe years; 524

/STRANGER 1 FR 0.0001 REL FR 1 V 0 P
to seek new friends and /stranger /companies. MND 1.01.219

STRANGER 50 FR 0.0056 REL FR 41 V 9 P
and to my state grew stranger, being transported TMP 1.02. 76
they strengthen | from strange to stranger. 5.01.228
but count the world a stranger for thy sake. TGV 5.04. 70
good signior, take the stranger to my house, ERR 4.01. 36
then swore he that he was a stranger here. 4.02. 9
a letter to a sequent of the stranger queen's, LLL 4.02.139 P
a stranger pyramus than e'er played here. MND 3.01. 88
and foot me as you spurn a stranger cur | over MV 1.03.118
nerissa, cheer yond stranger, bid her welcome. 3.02.237
at heart, | he sent me hither, stranger as i am, AYL 4.03.152
gentle sir, methinks you walk like a stranger. SHR 2.01. 86 P
own, | that, being a stranger in this city here, 2.01. 89
for her, they touch'd not any stranger sense. AWW 1.03.110 P
let him approach | a stranger, no offender; 5.03. 26
but three days, and already you are no stranger. TN 1.04. 4 P
which to a stranger, | unguided and unfriended, 3.03. 9
and the love of soul | to stranger blood, to JN 5.01. 11
wherein we step after a stranger, march | upon 5.02. 27
but tread the stranger paths of banishment. R2 1.03.143
o, had't been a stranger, not my child, | to 1.03.239
lord, | i am a stranger here in gloucestershire. 2.03. 3
the first that there did greet my stranger soul R3 1.04. 48
alas, poor lady! | she's a stranger now again. H8 2.03. 17
for | i am a most poor woman, and a stranger, 2.04. 15
and to be | acquainted with this stranger. 5.01.168
may | a stranger to those most imperial looks TRO 1.03.224
my child is yet a stranger in the world, | she ROM 1.02. 8
and therefore as a stranger give it welcome. HAM 1.05.165
and as a stranger to my heart and me | hold thee LR 1.01.115
in an extravagant and wheeling stranger | of OTH 1.01.136
and mak'st his ear | a stranger to thy thoughts. 3.03.144
of your knowing to a stranger of his quality. CYM 1.04. 30 P
signior, i thank him, makes no stranger of me: 1.04.101 P
none a stranger there | so merry and so gamesome 1.06. 59
it fit | a saucy stranger in his court to mart 1.06.151
did you hear of a stranger that's come to court 2.01. 32 P
a stranger, and i not know on't? 2.01. 34 P
who told you of this stranger? 2.01. 40 P
and by a stranger? 2.04.126
he seems to be a stranger; PER 2.02. 42
he well may be a stranger, for he comes | to an 2.02. 52
not me | unto a stranger knight to be so bold. 2.03. 67
tells me here, she'll wed the stranger knight, 2.05. 16
lord, | a stranger and distressed gentleman, 2.05. 46
your love and your affections | upon a stranger? 2.05. 78
where i am but a stranger. 5.01.114
that lends embracements unto every stranger. VEN 790
but she, that never cop'd with stranger eyes, LUC 99
when shall he think to find a stranger just 159
in the interest of thy bed | a stranger came, 1620

STRANGER'D 1 FR 0.0001 REL FR 1 V 0 P
with our curse, and stranger'd with our oath, LR 1.01.204

STRANGERS' 2 FR 0.0002 REL FR 2 V 0 P
grace must needs deserve all strangers' loves, H8 2.02.101
this is the strangers' case | and this your STM II.C 139

STRANGERS 26 FR 0.0029 REL FR 18 V 8 P
we being strangers here, how dar'st thou trust ERR 1.02. 60
what would these strangers? LLL 5.02.175
since you are strangers and come here by chance, 5.02.218
the four strangers seek for you, madam, to take MV 1.02.123 P
for the commodity that strangers have | with us 3.03. 27
i do desire we may be better strangers. AYL 3.02.258 P
thus strangers may be hal'd and abus'd. SHR 5.01.108 P
strangers and foes do sunder, and not kiss. AWW 2.05. 86
us some band of strangers i' th' adversary's 4.01. 14 P
to make us strangers to his looks of love. 1H4 1.03.290
strangers in court do take her for the queen. 2H6 1.03. 79
a noble troop of strangers, | for so they seem. H8 1.04. 53
not a happy star | led us to rome, strangers, TIT 4.02. 33
come let's away, the strangers all are gone. ROM 1.05.144
for no less, though we are but strangers to him. TIM 3.02. 4 P
laid upon myself, | for strangers to my nature. MAC 4.03.125
remove | the means that makes us strangers! 4.03.163
and strangers ne'er beheld but wond'red at; PER 1.04. 25
jump | as they are, here were to be strangers, TNK 1.02. 41
shall travel, ever strangers | to one another. 3.06.255
will come to that pass if strangers be suffer'd. STM II.C 4 P
but we will show no mercy upon the strangers. II.C 20 P
the removing of the strangers, which cannot II.C 70 P
imagine that you see the wretched strangers, II.C 74
you'll put down strangers, | kill them, cut II.C 119
to england, | why, you must needs be strangers; II.C 130

STRANGEST 5 FR 0.0005 REL FR 4 V 1 P
am a fellow o' th' strangest mind i' th' world; TN 1.03.113 P
here is the strangest controversy | come from JN 1.01. 44
this is the strangest tale that ever i heard. 1H4 5.04.154
this is the strangest fellow, brother john. 5.04.155
i'll show your grace the strangest sight — H8 5.02. 20

STRANGLE 7 FR 0.0008 REL FR 6 V 1 P
thus did he strangle serpents in his manus. LLL 5.02.591
fear | that makes thee strangle thy propriety. TN 5.01.147
strangle such thoughts as these with any thing WT 4.04. 47
from her womb | will serve to strangle thee; JN 4.03.129
mists | of vapors that did seem to strangle him. 1H4 1.02.203
strangle her in her bed, even the bed she hath OTH 4.01.207 P
i will acquaintance strangle and look strange, SON 89. 8

STRANGLED 5 FR 0.0005 REL FR 4 V 1 P
i shall as soon be strangled with a halter as 1H4 2.04.498 P
and you three shall be strangled on the gallows. 2H6 2.03. 8
staring full ghastly, like a strangled man; 3.02.170
he has strangled | his language in his tears. H8 5.01.156
and there die strangled ere my romeo comes? ROM 4.03. 35

STRANGLER 1 FR 0.0001 REL FR 0 V 1 P
will be the very strangler of their amity. ANT 2.06.122 P

STRANGLES 2 FR 0.0002 REL FR 2 V 0 P
strangles our dear vows | even in the birth of TRO 4.04. 37
and yet dark night strangles the travelling lamp MAC 2.04. 7

STRANGLING 2 FR 0.0002 REL FR 1 V 1 P
his enter and exit shall be strangling a snake; LLL 5.01.135 P
thee, | by strangling thee in her accursed womb, R3 4.04.138

STRAPPADO 1 FR 0.0001 REL FR 0 V 1 P
'zounds, and i were at the strappado, or all the 1H4 2.04.237 P

STRAPS 1 FR 0.0001 REL FR 0 V 1 P
let them hang themselves in their own straps. TN 1.03. 13 P

STRATAGEM 10 FR 0.0011 REL FR 6 V 4 P
he says he has a stratagem for't. AWW 3.06. 35 P
think your mystery in stratagem can bring this 3.06. 65 P
of my beard, and to say it was in stratagem. 4.01. 50 P
now | should be the father of some stratagem. 2H4 1.01. 8
be old utis, it will be an excellent stratagem. 2.04. 20 P
when, without stratagem, | but in plain shock H5 4.08.108
saint denis bless this happy stratagem! 1H6 3.02. 18
'tis policy and stratagem must do | that you TIT 2.01.104
know that this gold must coin a stratagem, 2.03. 5
it were a delicate stratagem, to shoe | a troop LR 4.06.184

STRATAGEMS 5 FR 0.0005 REL FR 5 V 0 P
is fit for treasons, stratagems, and spoils; MV 5.01. 85
for thee | to tutor thee in stratagems of war, 1H6 4.05. 2
what stratagems? 3H6 2.05. 89
offices | at any time to grace my stratagems. R3 3.05. 11
that heaven should practice stratagems | upon so ROM 3.05.209

STRATO 7 FR 0.0008 REL FR 7 V 0 P
strato, thou hast been all this while asleep; JC 5.05. 32
farewell to thee too, strato. 5.05. 33
i prithee, strato, stay thou by thy lord. 5.05. 44
wilt thou, strato? 5.05. 48
farewell, good strato. 5.05. 50
my master's man. strato, where is thy master? 5.05. 53
how died my master, strato? 5.05. 64

STRAW 20 FR 0.0022 REL FR 16 V 4 P

the strongest oaths are straw | to th' fire i' TMP 4.01. 52
i hear his straw rustle. MM 4.03. 36 P
they know his conditions and lay him in straw. AWW 4.03.258 P
no life | (i prize it not a straw), but for mine WT 3.02.110
to speak | shall blow each dust, each straw, JN 3.04.128
me your doublet and stuff me out with straw. 2H4 5.05. 82 P
a wisp of straw were worth a thousand crowns 3H6 2.02.144
side, | tremble and start at wagging of a straw; R3 3.05. 7
thrash the corn, then after burn the straw. TIT 2.03.123
will not debate the question of this straw. HAM 4.04. 26
but greatly to find quarrel in a straw | when 4.04. 55
where is this straw, my fellow? LR 3.02. 69
art thou that dost grumble there i' th' straw? 3.04. 45 P
arm it in rags, a pigmy's straw does pierce it. 4.06.167
and rogues forlorn | in short and musty straw? 4.07. 39
for me, i force not argument a straw, | since LUC 1021
she burnt with love, as straw with fire flameth, PP 7.13
burnt out love, as soon as straw out-burneth; 7.14
a belt of straw and ivy buds, | with coral 19.13
upon her head a platted hive of straw, | which LC 8

STRAWBERRIES 3 FR 0.0003 REL FR 3 V 0 P
i saw good strawberries in your garden there. R3 3.04. 32
i have sent for these strawberries. 3.04. 47
spotted with strawberries in your wive's hand? OTH 3.03.435

STRAWBERRY 1 FR 0.0001 REL FR 1 V 0 P
the strawberry grows underneath the nettle, H5 1.01. 60

STRAW-COLOR 1 FR 0.0001 REL FR 0 V 1 P
discharge it in either your straw-color beard, MND 1.02. 93 P

STRAWS 5 FR 0.0005 REL FR 5 V 0 P
when shepherds pipe on oaten straws | and merry LLL 5.02.903
but now i see our lances are but straws, | our SHR 5.02.173
for oaths are straws, men's faiths are H5 2.03. 51
make a mighty fire | begin it with weak straws. JC 1.03.108
spurns enviously at straws, speaks things in HAM 4.05. 6

STRAWY 1 FR 0.0001 REL FR 1 V 0 P
and there the strawy greeks, ripe for his edge, TRO 5.05. 24

STRAY 12 FR 0.0013 REL FR 11 V 1 P
he is drown'd | whom thus we stray to find, and TMP 3.03. 9
indeed a sheep doth very often stray, | and if TGV 1.01. 74
of day, | through this house each fairy stray. MND 5.01.402
she doth stray about | by holy crosses, where MV 5.01. 30
farewell, my liege, now no way can i stray; R2 1.03.206
strike up our drums, pursue the scatt'red stray; 2H4 4.02.120
but taken and impounded as a stray | the king of H5 1.02.160
lord of the soil come to seize me for a stray, 2H6 4.10. 25 P
i would not from your love make such a stray LR 1.01.209
torch is out, | lie down and stray no farther. ANT 4.14. 47
and if jove stray, who dares say jove doth ill? PER 1.01.104
stray lower, where the pleasant fountains lie. VEN 234

STRAY'D 3 FR 0.0003 REL FR 3 V 0 P
eye | stray'd his affection in unlawful love — ERR 5.01. 51
what if i stray'd no farther, but chose here? MV 2.07. 35
from our troops i stray'd | to gaze upon a TIT 5.01. 20

STRAYING 6 FR 0.0006 REL FR 6 V 0 P
full of straying shapes, of habits, and of forms LLL 5.02.763
seeking a way, and straying from the way, | not 3H6 3.02.176
win straying souls with modesty again, | cast H8 5.02. 99
o, thus i found her straying in the park, TIT 3.01. 88
this world's a city full of straying streets, TNK 1.05. 15
and chide thy beauty and thy straying youth, SON 41.10

STRAYS 3 FR 0.0003 REL FR 3 V 0 P
his fellows, | and strays about to find 'em. TMP 1.02.418
and so by many winding nooks he strays | with TGV 2.07. 31
binds the wretch and beats it when it strays, 2H6 3.01.211

STREAK 1 FR 0.0001 REL FR 1 V 0 P
and with the juice of this i'll streak her eyes, MND 2.01.257

STREAK'D 2 FR 0.0002 REL FR 2 V 0 P
all the eanlings which were streak'd and pied MV 1.03. 79
are our carnations and streak'd gillyvors, WT 4.04. 82

STREAKS 3 FR 0.0003 REL FR 3 V 0 P
the eastern clouds with streaks of light, | and ROM 2.03. 2
what envious streaks | do lace the severing 3.05. 7
the west yet glimmers with some streaks of day; MAC 3.03. 5

/STREAM 1 FR 0.0001 REL FR 1 V 0 P
/which /way /the /stream /of /time /doth /run, 2H4 4.01. 70

STREAM 35 FR 0.0039 REL FR 32 V 3 P
i'll be as patient as a gentle stream, | and TGV 2.07. 34
the very stream of his life, and the business he MM 3.02.142 P
and floating straight, obedient to the stream, ERR 1.01. 86
cut with her golden oars the silver stream, ADO 3.01. 27
would scatter all her spices on the stream, MV 1.01. 33
proper, my eye shall be the stream | and wat'ry 3.02. 46
first, for his weeping into the needless stream: AYL 2.01. 46
to forswear the full stream of the world and to 3.02.420 P
the rank of osiers by the murmuring stream 4.03. 79
love, that god most high, | do my sighs stream. AWW 2.03. 76
nobility in his proper stream o'erflows himself. 4.03. 25 P
how runs the stream? TN 4.01. 60
from whence this stream through muddy passages R2 5.03. 62
brow, | like bubbles in a late-disturbed stream, 1H4 2.03. 59
which swims against your stream of quality. 2H4 5.02. 34
of a rude stream that must for ever hide me. H8 3.02.364
the rich stream | of lords and ladies, having 4.01. 62
none, | but carries on the stream of his dispose TRO 2.03.164
will be there before the stream o' th' people; COR 2.03.261
till i find the stream | to cool this heat, a TIT 2.01.133
would through the airy region stream so bright ROM 2.02. 21
that 'gainst the stream of virtue they may TIM 4.01. 27
or offend the stream | of regular justice in 5.04. 60
till the lowest stream | do kiss the most JC 1.01. 59
weeping as fast as they stream forth thy blood, 3.01.201
shows his hoary leaves in the glassy stream, HAM 4.07.167
my boat sails freely, both with wind and stream. OTH 2.03. 63
body, | like to a vagabond flag upon the stream, ANT 1.04. 45
i have sent cloten's clotpole down the stream CYM 4.02.184
like wrinkled pebbles in a /glassy stream, | you TNK 1.01.112
and to follow | the common stream, 'twould bring 1.02. 10
any nymph, | that makes the stream seem flowers! 3.01. 9
and all in vain you strive against the stream, VEN 772
and then in key-cold lucrece' bleeding stream LUC 1774
o, how the channel to the stream gave grace! LC 285

STREAM'D 1 FR 0.0001 REL FR 1 V 0 P
her tear-distained eye | blue circles stream'd, LUC 1587

STREAMER 1 FR 0.0001 REL FR 1 V 0 P
that to thy laud | i may advance my streamer, TNK 5.01. 59

STREAMERS 1 FR 0.0001 REL FR 1 V 0 P
with silken streamers the young phoebus /fanning H5 3.pr. 6

STREAMING 1 FR 0.0001 REL FR 1 V 0 P
streaming the ensign of the christian cross R2 4.01. 94

STREAMS 13 FR 0.0014 REL FR 13 V 0 P
turns into yellow gold his salt green streams. MND 3.02.393
two such shores to two such streams made one, JN 2.01.443
out his innocent soul through streams of blood, R2 1.01.103
as many fresh streams meet in one salt sea; H5 1.02.209
grieve thee more than streams of foreign gore. 1H6 3.03. 55
as plays the sun upon the glassy streams, 5.03. 62
and make poor england weep in streams of blood! R3 5.05. 37
lave our honors in these flattering streams, MAC 3.02. 33
poison, or fire, or suffocating streams, | i'll OTH 3.03.389
the fresh streams ran by her, and murmur'd her 4.03. 44
the petty streams that pay a daily debt | to LUC 649
shall gush pure streams to purge my impure tale. 1078
gilding pale streams with heavenly alcumy; SON 33. 4

STREET 24 FR 0.0027 REL FR 15 V 9 P
hard by, at street end; he will be here anon. WIV 4.02. 39 P
should exhibit their petitions in the street? MM 4.04. 10 P
my master stays in the street. ERR 3.01. 36
tell her i am arrested in the street, | and that 4.01.106
desp'rately he hurried through the street — 5.01.140
in the street i met him, | and in his company 5.01.225
the street should see as she walk'd overhead. LLL 4.03.277
nor thrust your head into the public street | to MV 2.05. 32
what, in the midst of the street? SHR 5.01.144
he met the duke in the street, sir, of whom he AWW 4.03. 76 P
rated me the other day in the street about you, 1H4 1.02. 84 P
and yet he talk'd wisely, and in the street too. 1.02. 87 P
dinner to the lubber's head in lumbert street, 2H4 2.01. 29 P
the feats he hath done about turnbull street, 3.02.306 P
our windows are broke down in every street, 1H6 3.01. 84
up fish street! 2H6 4.08. 1 P
with a man for coughing in the street, because ROM 3.01. 25 P
o, the people in the street cry "romeo," | some 5.03.191
here the street is narrow; JC 2.04. 33
what, urge you your petitions in the street? 3.01. 11
cassius, go you into the other street, | and 3.02. 3
hop forty paces through the public street; ANT 2.02.229
upon me, set | the dogs o' th' street to bay me; CYM 5.05.223
or to go tiptoe | before the street be foul? TNK 1.02. 58

STREETS 55 FR 0.0062 REL FR 50 V 5 P
seeing her go thorough the streets, to know, sir WIV 4.05. 31 P
when in the streets he meets such golden gifts. ERR 3.02.183
you shall also make no noise in the streets; ADO 3.03. 35 P
o, if the streets were paved with thine eyes, LLL 4.03.274
as the dog jew did utter in the streets. MV 2.08. 14
are not the streets as free | for me as for you? SHR 1.02.231
i do not without danger walk these streets. TN 3.03. 25
here in the streets, desperate of shame and 5.01. 64
with me | from forth the streets of pomfret, JN 4.02.148
old men and beldames in the streets | do 4.02.185
they found him dead and cast into the streets, 5.01. 39
my heart when i beheld | in london streets, that R2 5.05. 77
for wisdom cries out in the streets, and no man 1H4 1.02. 89 P
grew a companion to the common streets, 3.02. 68
and feast and banquet in the open streets, | to 1H6 1.06. 13
uneath may she endure the flinty streets, | to 2H6 2.04. 8
thou didst ride in triumph through the streets. 2.04. 14
will we ride through the streets, and at every 4.07.136 P
broil | i see them lording it in london streets, 4.08. 45
shows of peace, | and not our streets with war! COR 3.03. 37
behold | dissentious numbers pest'ring streets, 4.06. 7
than when these fellows ran about the streets, 4.06. 28
be led | with manacles through our streets, or 5.03.115
but must my sons be slaughtered in the streets TIT 1.01.112
i will not re-salute the streets of rome, | or 1.01.326
kneel in the streets and beg for grace in vain. 1.01.455
sweet scrolls to fly about the streets of rome! 4.04. 16
look round about the wicked streets of rome, 5.02. 98
have thrice disturb'd the quiet of our streets, ROM 1.01. 91
if ever you disturb our streets again | your 1.01. 96
hath | forbid this bandying in verona streets. 3.01. 89
be not, hang, beg, starve, die in the streets, 3.05.192
why dost thou lead these men about the streets? JC 1.01. 28
to see great pompey pass the streets of rome; 1.01. 42
and drive away the vulgar from the streets; 1.01. 70
men, all in fire, walk up and down the streets. 1.03. 25
for my part, i have walk'd about the streets, 1.03. 46
there is no stir or walking in the streets; 1.03.127
my ancestors did from the streets of rome | the 2.01. 53
a lioness hath whelped in the streets, | and 2.02. 17
ghosts did shriek and squeal about the streets. 2.02. 24
run hence, proclaim, cry it about the streets. 3.01. 79
led in triumph | thorough the streets of rome? 5.01.109
did squeak and gibber in the roman streets. HAM 1.01.116
bak'd and impasted with the parching streets, 2.02.459
his delight, | proclaim him in the streets; OTH 1.01. 69
/faith, i must, she'll rail in the streets else. 4.01.163 P
we'll wander through the streets and note | the ANT 1.01. 53
to reel the streets at noon, and stand the 1.04. 20
heard you of nothing strange about the streets? 4.03. 3
should have shook lions into civil streets, 5.01. 16
for riches strew'd herself even in her streets; PER 1.04. 23
tyre, | and seen the desolation of your streets; 1.04. 89
this world's a city full of straying streets, TNK 1.05. 15
strong arms from forth her fair streets chased. LUC 1834

/STRENGTH 1 FR 0.0001 REL FR 1 V 0 P
/preserve /just /so /much /strength /in /us TIT 3.02. 2

STRENGTH 135 FR 0.0152 REL FR 124 V 11 P
and what strength i have's mine own, | which is TMP ep 2
or as one nail by strength drives out another, TGV 2.04.193
lists of all advice | my strength can give you. MM 1.01. 7
but of what strength and nature | i am not yet 1.01. 79
o, it is excellent | to have a giant's strength; 2.02.108
makes me with thy strength to communicate: ERR 2.02.176
me, | even in the strength and height of injury: 5.01.200
both strength of limb, and policy of mind, ADO 4.01.198
so tempted, and he had an excellent strength; LLL 1.02.174 P
have no more strength than her weak /prays. MND 3.02.250
you would abate the strength of your displeasure MV 5.01.198
do, to try with him the strength of my youth. AYL 1.02.172 P
have seen cruel proof of this man's strength. 1.02.175 P
the little strength that i have, i would it were 1.02.194 P
our strength as weak, our weakness past compare, SHR 5.02.174
it is | a charge too heavy for my strength, but AWW 3.03. 4
of him, of what strength they are afoot." 4.03.159 P
your opposite hath in him what youth, strength, TN 3.04.232 P
open air, before | i have got strength of limit. WT 3.02.106
they can behold | bright phoebus in his strength 4.04.124
and ampler strength indeed | than most have of 4.04.403
your strong hand shall help to give him strength JN 2.01. 33
strength match'd with strength, and power 2.01.330
strength match'd with strength, and power 2.01.330
upon thy stars, thy fortune, and thy strength, 3.01.126
with all religious strength of sacred vows. 3.01.229
that knit your sinews to the strength of mine. 5.02. 63
that hand which had the strength, even at your 5.02.137
if guilty dread have left thee so much strength R2 1.01. 73
to fear the foe, since fear oppresseth strength, 3.02.180
gives in your weakness strength unto your foe, 3.02.181
not with such strength denied | as is delivered 1H4 1.03. 25
and then i shall have no strength to repent. 3.03. 7 P
a rib of steel, | to make strength stronger; 2H4 2.03. 55
which to his former strength may be restored 3.01. 42
only, we want a little personal strength; 4.04. 8
and put the world's whole strength | into one 4.05. 44
that strength of speech is utterly denied me. 4.05.217
praised be god, and not our strength, for it! H5 4.07. 87
and for the other i have no strength in measure, 5.02.135 P
measure, yet a reasonable measure in strength. 5.02.136 P
all france with their chief assembled strength 1H6 1.01.139
where is my strength, my valor, and my force? 1.05. 1
o'ertake me if thou canst, i scorn thy strength. 1.05. 15
are his substance, sinews, arms, and strength, 2.03. 63
what is the trust or strength of foolish man? 3.02.112
cities, and seven walled towns of strength, 3.04. 7
then gather strength and march unto him straight 4.01. 73
thou princely leader of our english strength, 4.03. 17
having vow'd | to try his strength, forsaketh 5.05. 32
why, then from ireland come i with my strength, 2H6 3.01.380
tugg'd for life, and was by strength subdu'd. 3.02.173
shall fight with all the strength thou hast, 4.10. 50
and spend her strength with overmatching waves. 3H6 1.04. 21
robb'd my strong-knit sinews of their strength, 2.03. 4
no way to fly, nor strength to hold out flight. 2.06. 24
wrong, | inferreth arguments of mighty strength, 3.01. 49
unless my hand and strength could equal them. 3.02.145
or than for strength and safety of our country. 3.03.211
my blood, my want of strength, my sick heart 5.02. 8
our strength will be augmented | in every county 5.03. 22
and give more strength to that which hath too 5.04. 9
by the heavens' assistance and your strength, 5.04. 68
than buckingham and his rash-levied strength. R3 4.03. 50
the greatest strength and power that he can make 4.04.450
besides, the king's name is a tower of strength, 5.03. 12
are strong, and skillful to their strength, TRO 1.01. 7
strength should be lord of imbecility, | and the 1.03.114
in our weakness stands, not in her strength. 1.03.137
disguise the holy strength of their command, 2.03.127
a proof of strength she could not publish more, 5.02.113
i will wish her speedy strength, and visit her COR 1.03. 78 P
so | i' th' right and strength a' th' commons," 3.03. 14
and they | stand in their ancient strength. 4.02. 7
as ever in ambitious strength i did | contend 4.05.112
know'st | thy country's strength and weakness — 4.05.140
desperation | is all the policy, strength, and 4.06.127
does reason our petition with more strength 5.03.176
that you withdraw you, and abate your strength, TIT 1.01. 43
and led my country's strength successfully, 1.01.194
this for me, struck home to show my strength. 2.03.117
or, wanting strength to do thee so much good, 2.03.238
i have no strength to pluck thee to the brink. 2.03.241
nor i no strength to climb without thy help. 2.03.242
your consent gives strength to make /it fly. ROM 1.03. 99
women may fall, when there's no strength in men. 2.03. 80
thou hast the strength of will to /slay thyself, 4.01. 72
love give me strength! 4.01.125
and strength shall help afford. 4.01.125
and if you had the strength | of twenty men, it 5.01. 78
can be retentive to the strength of spirit; JC 1.03. 95
our arms in strength of malice, and our hearts 3.01.174
you do unbend your noble strength, to think | so MAC 2.02. 42
sprites | as by the strength of their illusion 3.05. 28
our castle's strength | will laugh a siege to 5.05. 2
with all the strength and armor of the mind | to HAM 3.03. 12
and will, and strength, and means | to do't. 4.04. 45
own purpose, | how in my strength you please. LR 2.01.112
moreover, to descry | the strength o' th' enemy. 4.05. 14
thy friendly hand | put strength enough to't. 4.06.231
is the guess of their true strength and forces, 5.01. 52
maugre thy strength, place, youth, and eminence, 5.03.132
the hated, grown to strength, | are newly grown ANT 1.03. 48
are in the field, a mighty strength they carry. 2.01. 17
what is his strength by land? 2.02.161
that which is the strength of their amity shall 2.06.128 P
i'll wrastle with you in my strength of love. 3.02. 62
very force entangles | itself with strength. 4.14. 49
our strength is all gone into heaviness, | that 4.15. 33
whose strength | i will confirm with oath, which CYM 2.04. 63
that possible strength might meet, would seek us 4.02.160
gods, put the strength o' th' leonati in me! 5.01. 31
renew thy strength; 5.05.150
thee i lay, whose wisdom's strength can bear it. PER 1.02.119
have scarce strength left to give them burial. 1.04. 49
ever he had on thee, who ow'st his strength, TNK 1.01. 88
in will | /o'er-wrastling strength in reason. 1.04. 45
you talk of feeding me to breed me strength; 3.01.119
could have restor'd | my lost strength to me, i 3.06. 6
yet | and furnish'd with your old strength, i'll 3.06. 37
by your own eyes, by strength, | in which you 3.06.205
fair and knightly strength to touch the pillar, 3.06.295
and shap'd just to that strength of nature STM III 4
and govern'd him in strength, though not in lust VEN 42
steel his stronger strength obeyed, | yet was he 111
who should say, "lo thus my strength is tried; 280
leaden slumber with live's strength doth fight, LUC 124
no object but her passion's strength renews; 1103
then little strength rings out the doleful knell 1495
what though she strive to try her strength, PP 18.31
and in mine own love's strength seem to decay, SON 23. 7
to leave poor me thou hast the strength of laws, 49.13
and strength by limping sway disabled, | and art 66. 8

thou wouldst use the strength of all thy state! 96.12
there is such strength and warrantise of skill 150. 7
STRENGTHEN 9 FR 0.0010 REL FR 9 V 0 P
they strengthen | from stranger to stranger. TMP 5.01.227
but now in arms you strengthen it with yours. JN 3.01.103
with pow'rful policy strengthen themselves, 3H6 1.02. 58
to strengthen and support king edward's place. 3.01. 52
and, to strengthen | that holy duty, out of dear H8 5.02.153
my faction if thou strengthen with thy friends, TIT 1.01.214
fearing to strengthen that impatience | which JC 2.01.248
strengthen your patience in our last night's HAM 5.01.294
way thou goest, | and the gods strengthen thee! PER 4.06.107
STRENGTHEN'D 1 FR 0.0001 REL FR 0 V 1 P
and kinreds are mightily strengthen'd. 2H4 2.02. 27 P
STRENGTHENS 1 FR 0.0001 REL FR 1 V 0 P
upon a sun | that strengthens what it looks on. TNK 3.01.121
STRENGTHLESS 4 FR 0.0004 REL FR 4 V 0 P
like strengthless hinges, buckle under life, 2H4 1.01.141
are these feet, whose strengthless stay is numb 1H6 2.05. 13
two strengthless doves will draw me through the VEN 153
heavy eye, knit brow, and strengthless pace, LUC 709
STRENGTH'NED 4 FR 0.0004 REL FR 4 V 0 P
strength'ned with what apology you think | may AWW 2.04. 50
strength'ned by interchangement of your rings, TN 5.01.159
alliance | would more have strength'ned this our 3H6 4.01. 37
my love is strength'ned, though more weak in SON 102. 1
STRENGTH'NING 1 FR 0.0001 REL FR 1 V 0 P
impairing henry, strength'ning misproud york. 3H6 2.06. 7
STRENGTH'S 1 FR 0.0001 REL FR 1 V 0 P
whose strength's abundance weakens his own heart SON 23. 4
STRENGTHS 7 FR 0.0008 REL FR 7 V 0 P
swords are now too massy for your strengths, TMP 3.03. 67
that done, dissever your united strengths, | and JN 2.01.388
he should draw his several strengths together, 2H4 1.03. 76
will, according to your strengths and qualities, 5.05. 69
rights fouler, strengths by strengths do fail. COR 4.07. 55
rights fouler, strengths by strengths do fail. 4.07. 55
conferring them on younger strengths, while we LR 1.01. 40
STRETCH 19 FR 0.0021 REL FR 17 V 2 P
dare no more stretch this finger of mine than he MM 5.01.314
their discharge did stretch his leathern coat AYL 2.01. 37
the gift doth stretch itself as 'tis receiv'd, AWW 2.01. 4
so far as my coin would stretch, and where it 1H4 1.02. 55 P
at, how shall we stretch our eye | when capital H5 2.02. 55
now set the teeth and stretch the nostril wide, 3.01. 15
receive | if you might please to stretch it. H8 2.03. 33
come, stretch thy chest, and let thy eyes spout TRO 4.05. 10
for requital | than we to stretch it out. COR 2.02. 51
that the precipitation might down stretch 3.02. 4
i stretch it out for that word "broad," which, ROM 2.04. 85 P
may well stretch so far | as to annoy us all; JC 2.01.159
will the line stretch out to th' crack of doom? MAC 4.01.117
observants | that stretch their duties nicely. LR 2.02.104
would stretch thy spirits up into the air. 4.02. 23
of this tough world | stretch him out longer. 5.03.316
there's not a minute of our lives should stretch ANT 1.01. 46
which swell'd so much that it did almost stretch CYM 3.01. 49
when you shall stretch yourself, and say but, TNK 3.01. 87
STRETCH'D 13 FR 0.0014 REL FR 11 V 2 P
ox hath therefore stretch'd his yoke in vain, MND 2.01. 93
extremely stretch'd and conn'd with cruel pain, 5.01. 80
there lay he, stretch'd along, like a wounded AYL 3.02.240 P
had it stretch'd so far, would have made nature AWW 1.01. 19 P
his nostrils stretch'd with struggling; 2H6 3.02.171
which stretch'd unto their servants, daughters, R3 3.05. 82
with the "knife," | he stretch'd him, and, with H8 1.02.204
'twixt his stretch'd footing and the scaffolage, TRO 1.03.156
and thus far having stretch'd it (here be with COR 3.02. 74
which my sinews shall be stretch'd upon him — 5.06. 44
have i in conquest stretch'd mine arm so far, JC 2.02. 66
our best friends made, our means stretch'd, 4.01. 44
your kindness | we have stretch'd thus far, let PER 5.01. 55
STRETCH'D–OUT 1 FR 0.0001 REL FR 1 V 0 P
thou most reverend for /thy stretch'd–out life, TRO 1.03. 61
STRETCHED 1 FR 0.0001 REL FR 1 V 0 P
rage, | and stretched metre of an antique song: SON 17.12
STRETCHES 3 FR 0.0003 REL FR 2 V 1 P
stretches itself beyond the hour of death. 2H4 4.04. 57
and it stretches | beyond you to your friends. H8 1.02.141
that stretches from an inch narrow to an ell ROM 2.04. 83 P
STRETCHING 2 FR 0.0002 REL FR 2 V 0 P
that the stretching of a span | buckles in his AYL 3.02.131
cribs, | upon uneasy pallets stretching thee, 2H4 3.01. 10
STRETCH–MOUTH'D 1 FR 0.0001 REL FR 0 V 1 P
and where some stretch–mouth'd rascal would, as WT 4.04.196 P

STREW *(also strow, etc.)*
STREW 13 FR 0.0014 REL FR 13 V 0 P
strew good luck, ouphes, on every sacred room, WIV 5.05. 57
my sweet friend, | to strew him o'er and o'er! WT 4.04.129
for it shall strew the footsteps of my rising. JN 1.01.216
that strew the green lap of the new–come spring? R2 5.02. 47
strew me over | with maiden flowers, that all H8 4.02.168
strew flowers before them! COR 5.05. 3
flower, with flowers thy bridal bed i strew — ROM 5.03. 12
nightly shall be to strew thy grave and weep. 5.03. 17
and strew this hungry churchyard with thy limbs. 5.03. 36
he came with flowers to strew his lady's grave, 5.03.281
and do you now strew flowers in his way, | that JC 1.01. 50
for she may strew | dangerous conjectures in HAM 4.05. 14
these herblets shall, which we upon you strew. CYM 4.02.287
/STREW'D 1 FR 0.0001 REL FR 1 V 0 P
/and /what's /to /come /is /strew'd /with /husks TRO 4.05.166
STREW'D 9 FR 0.0010 REL FR 8 V 1 P
for so i have strew'd it in the common ear, MM 1.03. 15
the house trimm'd, rushes strew'd, cobwebs swept SHR 4.01. 46 P
want, and whose delay, is strew'd with sweets, AWW 2.04. 44
out, | and strew'd repentant ashes on his head. JN 4.01.110
sweet maid, | and not have strew'd thy grave. HAM 5.01.246
smooth success | be strew'd before your feet! ANT 1.03.101
though i had found | gold strew'd i' th' floor. CYM 3.06. 49
wood–leaves and weeds i ha' strew'd his grave, 4.02.390
for riches strew'd herself even in her streets; PER 1.04. 23
STREWING 1 FR 0.0001 REL FR 1 V 0 P
fair love, strewing her way with flowers. LLL 4.03.377
STREWINGS 2 FR 0.0002 REL FR 1 V 1 P
o' th' night | are strewings fitt'st for graves. CYM 4.02.285
these strewings are for their chamber. TNK 2.01. 21 P
STREWMENTS 1 FR 0.0001 REL FR 1 V 0 P
her maiden strewments, and the bringing home HAM 5.01.233
STREW'ST 1 FR 0.0001 REL FR 1 V 0 P
why strew'st thou sugar on that bottled spider R3 1.03.241
STRICKEN *(also strook, strooken, struck, strucken)*
STRICKEN 1 FR 0.0001 REL FR 1 V 0 P
the clock hath stricken three. JC 2.01.192
STRICT 21 FR 0.0023 REL FR 21 V 0 P
that she make friends | to the strict deputy; MM 1.02.181
we have strict statutes and most biting laws 1.03. 19
but rather wishing a more strict restraint 1.04. 4
but there are other strict observances: LLL 1.01. 36
o me, with what strict patience have i sat, | to 4.03.163
this strict court of venice | must needs give MV 4.01.204
say | i was too strict to make mine own away; R2 1.03.244
some fathers feed upon | is my strict fast — i 2.01. 80
and i will call him to so strict account | that 1H4 3.02.149
side | must keep aloof from strict arbitrement, 4.01. 70
is all your strict preciseness come to this? 1H6 5.04. 67
shall be with such strict and severe covenants 5.04.114
you undergo too strict a paradox, | striving to TIM 3.05. 24
for law is strict, and war is nothing more. 3.05. 84
why this same strict and most observant watch HAM 1.01. 71
is strict in his arrest — o, i could tell you 5.02.337
though by the tenor of /our strict edict, | your PER 1.01.111
with this strict charge, even as he left his 2.01.125
that the strict fates had pleas'd you had 3.03. 8
she wildly breaketh from their strict embrace, VEN 874
keep the obsequy so strict. PHT 12
STRICTER 1 FR 0.0001 REL FR 1 V 0 P
take | no stricter render of me than my all. CYM 5.04. 17
STRICTEST 1 FR 0.0001 REL FR 1 V 0 P
and to the strictest decrees i'll write my name. LLL 1.01.117
STRICTLY 2 FR 0.0002 REL FR 2 V 0 P
the king hath strictly charg'd the contrary. R3 4.01. 17
she hath so strictly tied | her to her chamber, PER 2.05. 8
STRICTURE 1 FR 0.0001 REL FR 1 V 0 P
(a man of stricture and firm abstinence) | my MM 1.03. 12
STRIDE 6 FR 0.0006 REL FR 5 V 1 P
turn two mincing steps | into a manly stride; MV 3.04. 68
every tedious stride i make | will but remember R2 1.03.268
that every stride he makes upon my land | is 3.03. 92
and down like a peacock — a stride and a stand; TRO 3.03.252 P
i mean to stride your steed, and at all times COR 1.09. 71
or a debtor that not dares | to stride a limit. CYM 3.03. 35
/STRIDES 1 FR 0.0001 REL FR 1 V 0 P
with tarquin's ravishing /strides, towards his MAC 2.01. 55
STRIDES 2 FR 0.0002 REL FR 2 V 0 P
on the moment | follow his strides, his lobbies TIM 1.01. 80
slaves, | the strides /they victors made: CYM 5.03. 43
STRIDING 1 FR 0.0001 REL FR 1 V 0 P
striding the blast, or heaven's cherubin, hors'd MAC 1.07. 22
STRIFE 43 FR 0.0048 REL FR 43 V 0 P
the sweet breath of flattery conquers strife. ERR 3.02. 28
if i should as lion come in strife | into this MND 5.01.225
if thou keep promise, i shall end this strife, MV 2.03. 20
you, gentlemen, i will compound this strife. SHR 2.01.341
and to cut off all strife, here sit we down: 3.01. 21
wars is no strife | to the dark house and the AWW 2.03.291
with strife to please you, day exceeding day. ep 4
yet a barful strife! TN 1.04. 41
an /ate, stirring him to blood and strife; JN 2.01. 63
as thou liv'st in peace, die free from strife, R2 5.06. 27
nought rests for me in this tumultuous strife 1H6 1.03. 70
pray, uncle gloucester, mitigate this strife. 3.01. 88
confounded be your strife, | and perish ye, with 4.01.123
let me be umpeer in this doubtful strife. 4.01.151
but dies, betray'd to fortune by your strife. 4.04. 39
that such immanity and bloody strife | should 5.01. 13
hell, | an age of discord and continual strife? 5.05. 63
i pray, my lords, let me compound this strife. 2H6 2.01. 56
why, how now, sons and brother, at a strife? 3H6 1.02. 4
half stints their strife before their strokes TRO 4.05. 93
now stay your strife, what shall be is TIT 3.01.192
with their death bury their parents' strife. ROM pr 8
some twenty of them fought in this black strife, 3.01.178
artificial strife | lives in these touches, TIM 1.01. 37
either there is a civil strife in heaven, | or JC 1.03. 11
domestic fury and fierce civil strife | shall 3.01.263
both here and hence pursue me lasting strife, HAM 3.02.222
that future strife | may be prevented now. LR 1.01. 44
who were the opposites of this day's strife; 5.03. 42
to have their balmy slumbers wak'd with strife. OTH 2.03.258
that tell this fellow | be nothing of our strife; ANT 2.02. 80
hard, and harsher | than strife or war could be. TNK 1.02. 26
i'll choose, | and end their strife. 4.02. 3
nature that made thee with herself at strife, VEN 11
his art with nature's workmanship at strife, 291
a mischief worse than civil home–bred strife, 764
and in this aim there is such thwarting strife LUC 143
wife, | as in revenge or quittal of such strife; 236
as if between them twain there were no strife, 405
this forced league doth force a further strife, 689
red blood reek'd, to show the painter's strife, 1377
then son and father weep with equal strife | who 1791
and for the peace of you i hold such strife | as SON 75. 3
STRIFES 3 FR 0.0003 REL FR 2 V 1 P
one that, above all other strifes, contended MM 3.02.232 P
i would to god all strifes were well compounded. R3 2.01. 75
wilt thou sort an hour great strifes to end? LUC 899
/STRIKE 5 FR 0.0005 REL FR 5 V 0 P
/well, /let /it /strike. R3 4.02.112
/why /let /it /strike? 4.02.113
will /strike amazement to their drowsy spirits. TRO 2.02.210
/thou /canst /not /strike /it /thus /to /make TIT 3.02. 14
/what /dost /thou /strike /at, /marcus, /with 3.02. 52
STRIKE 161 FR 0.0182 REL FR 135 V 26 P
vent thy groans | as fast as mill–wheels strike. TMP 1.02.281
who mak'st a show but dar'st not strike, thy 1.02.471
the watch of his wit, by and by it will strike. 2.01. 13 P
can nothing speak? master, shall i strike? TGV 3.01.199 P
who wouldst thou strike? 3.01.200 P
why, sir, i'll strike nothing. i pray you — 3.01.203 P
gentlemen, let him /not strike the old woman. WIV 4.02.181 P
you have ta'en a special stand to strike at me, 5.05.235 P
'twould be my tyranny to strike and gall them MM 1.03. 36
who may, in th' ambush of my name, strike home, 1.03. 41
and strike you home without a messenger. ERR 1.02. 67
now you strike like the blind man. ADO 2.01.198 P
rearward of reproaches, | strike at thy life. 4.01.127
strike up, pipers. 5.04.128 P
that his own hand may strike his honor down LLL 1.01. 20
spurn me, strike me, | neglect me, lose me; MND 2.01.205
should i hurt her, strike her, kill her dead? 3.02.269
let her not strike me. 3.02.303
chid me hence and threat'ned me | to strike me, 3.02.313
and strike more dead | than common sleep of all 4.01. 81
i swear i'll cuff you, if you strike again. SHR 2.01.220
if you strike me, you are no gentleman, | and if 2.01.222
italian fields | where noble fellows strike. AWW 2.03.291
i know my lady will strike him. TN 3.02. 82 P
that will strike | where 'tis predominant; WT 1.02.201
to | a savor that may strike the dullest nostril 1.02.421
heavens themselves | do strike at my injustice. 3.02.147
come on. strike up. 4.04.161
come, strike up. 4.04.165
strike! 5.03. 98
strike all that look upon with marvel. 5.03.100
when i strike my foot | upon the bosom of the JN 4.01. 2
spleen to do me shame, | i'll strike thee dead. 4.03. 98
strike up the drums, and let the tongue of war 5.02.164
strike up our drums, to find this danger out. 5.02.179
and yet we strike not, but securely perish. R2 2.01.266
and they shall strike | your children yet unborn 3.03. 87
strike him, aumerle. 5.02. 85
clamorous groans, which strike upon my heart, 5.05. 56
hold in, such as will strike sooner than speak, 1H4 2.01. 77 P
now cannot i strike him, if i should be hang'd. 2.02. 73 P
strike! 2.02. 83 P
strike up our drums, pursue the scatt'red stray; 2H4 4.02.120
that must strike sail to spirits of vile sort! 5.02. 18
shall strike his father's crown into the hazard. H5 1.02.263
yea, strike the dolphin blind to look on us. 1.02.280
god's arm strike with us! 4.03. 5
wear if alive, i will strike it out soundly. 4.07.130 P
if that the soldier strike him, as i judge | by 4.07.176
i promis'd to strike him, if he did. 4.08. 30 P
'twas i indeed thou promisedst to strike, | and 4.08. 41
arms are set, like clocks, still to strike on; 1H6 1.02. 42
for none would strike a stroke in his revenge. 1.05. 35
should strike such terror to his enemies. 2.03. 24
strike those that hurt, and hurt not those that 3.03. 53
she shall not strike dame eleanor unreveng'd. 2H6 1.03.147
on our longboat's side | strike off his head. 4.01. 69
i say, and strike off his head presently, and 4.07.109 P
sir james cromer, and strike off his head, and 4.07.111 P
then strike up drums. 3H6 2.01.204
yet know thou, since we have begun to strike, 2.02.167
or strike, ungentle death! 2.03. 6
must strike her sail and learn a while to serve 3.03. 5
drummer, strike up, and let us march away. 4.07. 50
strike now, or else the iron cools. 5.01. 49
than bear so low a sail to strike to thee. 5.01. 52
strike up the drum, cry "courage!" 5.03. 24
or, by saint paul, i'll strike thee to my foot, R3 1.02. 41
heav'n with lightning strike the murth'rer dead; 1.02. 64
would they were basilisks, to strike thee dead! 1.02.150
strike! 1.04.159 P
strike alarum, drums! 4.04.149
strike, i say! 4.04.151
strike up the drum. 4.04.180
in trust) of him | things to strike honor sad. H8 1.02.126
and the rude son should strike his father dead; TRO 1.03.115
that do contrive how many hands shall strike 1.03.201
thou canst strike, canst thou? 2.01. 19 P
thou shouldst strike him. 2.01. 37 P
shall quite strike off all service i have done, 3.03. 29
strike not a stroke, but keep yourselves in 5.07. 3
strike, fellows, strike, this is the man i seek. 5.08. 10
strike, fellows, strike, this is the man i seek. 5.08. 10
strike a free march. 5.10. 30
strike at the heaven with your staves as lift COR 1.01. 68
shalt see me once more strike at tullus' face. 1.01.240
'tis sworn between us we shall ever strike 1.02. 35
the red pestilence strike all trades in rome, 4.01. 13
strike the proud cedars 'gainst the fiery sun, 5.03. 60
and my pretext to strike at him admits | a good 5.06. 19
and strike her home by force, if not by words; TIT 2.01.118
there speak, and strike, brave boys, and take 2.01.129
if i do wake, some planet strike me down, | that 2.04. 14
i strike quickly, being mov'd. ROM 1.01. 6 P
but thou art not quickly mov'd to strike. 1.01. 7 P
strike! 1.01. 73
strike, drum. 1.04.114
kin, | to strike him dead i hold it not a sin. 1.05. 59
spleen and fury, | that i may strike at athens. TIM 3.05.113
strike me the counterfeit matron, | it is her 4.03.113
hollow bones of man, strike their sharp shins, 4.03.152
strike up the drum towards athens! 4.03.169
we but offend him. strike! 4.03.175
let our drums strike. 5.04. 85
speak, strike, redress!" JC 2.01. 47
"speak, strike, redress!" 2.01. 55
am i entreated | to speak and strike? 2.01. 56
strike as thou didst at caesar; 4.03.105
my drink is ready, | she strike upon the bell. MAC 2.01. 32
who did strike out the light? 3.03. 19
new sorrows | strike heaven on the face, that it 4.03. 6
i cannot strike at wretched kerns, whose arms 5.07. 17
we have met with foes | that strike beside us. 5.07. 29
shall i strike it with my partisan? HAM 1.01.140
nights are wholesome, then no planets strike, 1.01.162
did my father strike my gentleman for chiding of LR 1.03. 1
you strike my people, | and your disorder'd 1.04.255
strike, you slave! 2.02. 41 P
strike! 2.02. 42 P
the king his master very late | to strike at me, 2.02.117
strike in their numb'd and mortified arms | pins 2.03. 15
strike her young bones, | you taking airs, with 2.04.163
strike flat the thick rotundity o' th' world! 3.02. 7
with this ungracious paper strike the sight | of 4.06.276
let the drum strike, and prove my title thine. 5.03. 81
he'll strike, and quickly too. 5.03.286
strike on the tinder, ho! OTH 1.01.140

in choler, and happily may strike at you — 2.01.273 P
as men in rage strike those that wish them best, 2.03.243
time, | strike off this score of absence. 3.04.179
i strike it, and it hurts my hand. 4.01.183 P
what? strike his wife? 4.01.272
or say they strike us, | or scant our former 4.03. 90
i have a mind to strike thee ere thou speak'st; ANT 2.05. 42
these hands do lack nobility that they strike 2.05. 82
strike the vessels ho! 2.07. 97
strike not by land, keep whole, provoke not 3.08. 3
i'll strike, and cry, "take all!" 4.02. 8
that heaven and earth may strike their sounds 4.08. 38
before i strike this bloody stroke, farewell. 4.14. 91
farewell, great chief. shall i strike now? 4.14. 93
let him that loves me strike me dead. 4.14.108
events as these | strike those that make them; 5.02.361
your cause doth strike my heart | with pity that CYM 1.06.118
if thou fear to strike and to make me certain it 3.04. 30 P
do his bidding, strike. 3.04. 71
the gods do mean to strike me | to death with 5.05.234
prince, pardon me, or strike me, if you please, PER 1.02. 46
the axe myself, | do but you strike the blow. 1.02. 59
the sinful father | seem'd not to strike, but 1.02. 78
o helicanus, strike me, honored sir, | give me a 5.01.190
there to strike | the inhospitable cleon, but i 5.01.252
yet in the field to strike a battle for her; TNK 2.02.252
ira, nec ignis" — | strike up, and lead her in. 3.05. 89
i'll warrant thee, i'll strike home. 3.06. 68
and twenty strike of oats, but he'll ne'er have 5.02. 65
seeing his beauty, thou shouldst strike at it: VEN 938
and not death's ebon dart to strike him dead. 948
strike the wise dumb, and teach the fool to 1146
his bow | to strike a poor unseasonable doe. LUC 581
and stall'd the deer that thou shouldst strike, PP 18. 2

STRIKERS 1 FR 0.0001 REL FR 0 V 1 P
no long–staff sixpenny strikers, none of these 1H4 2.01. 74 P

STRIKES 22 FR 0.0024 REL FR 19 V 3 P
this parting strikes poor lovers dumb. TGV 2.02. 20
calumny | the whitest virtue strikes. MM 3.02.187
ere i left him, and now the clock strikes one. ERR 4.02. 54
or not laugh'd at, strikes him into melancholy, ADO 2.01.148 P
with her, boyet, and she strikes at the brow. LLL 4.01.117
it strikes a man more dead than a great AYL 3.03. 14 P
strikes some scores away | from the great compt; AWW 5.03. 56
a puny subject strikes | at thy great glory. R2 3.02. 86
he that strikes the first stroke, i'll run him H5 2.01. 64 P
strikes his breast hard, and anon he casts | his H8 3.02.117
pyrrhus at priam drives, in rage strikes wide, HAM 2.02.472
he dies that strikes again. LR 2.02. 49
heavenly, | it strikes where it doth love. OTH 5.02. 22
for pompey's name strikes more | than could his ANT 1.04. 54
he that strikes | the venison first shall be the CYM 3.03. 74
strikes life into my speech and shows much more 3.03. 97
it strikes me, past | the hope of comfort. 4.03. 8
of wiving, | fairness which strikes the eye — 5.05.168
wrings her nose, he strikes her on the cheeks, VEN 475
being mov'd, he strikes, what e'er is in his way 623
and whom he strikes his crooked tushes slay. 624
strikes each in each by mutual ordering; SON 8.10

STRIKEST 2 FR 0.0002 REL FR 0 V 2 P
think i have no sense, thou strikest me thus? TRO 2.01. 23 P
incursions, thou strikest as slow as another. 2.01. 30 P

STRIKING 8 FR 0.0009 REL FR 7 V 1 P
shame to him whose cruel striking | kills for MM 3.02.267
the prince for striking him about bardolph. 2H4 1.02. 56 P
as he is striking, holds his infant up | and 4.01.210
his sword did ne'er leave striking in the field. 1H6 1.04. 81
he finds him | striking too short at greeks. HAM 2.02.469
that striking in our country's cause | fell CYM 5.04. 71
dead at first, what needs a second striking? VEN 250
anon his beating heart, alarum striking, | gives LUC 433

STRIK'ST 2 FR 0.0002 REL FR 2 V 0 P
but thou strik'st me | sorely, to say i did. WT 5.01. 17
thou strik'st not me, 'tis caesar thou defeat'st ANT 4.14. 68

STRING 6 FR 0.0006 REL FR 6 V 0 P
my heart hath one poor string to stay it by, JN 5.07. 55
to check time broke in a disordered string; R2 5.05. 46
harp not on that string, madam, that is past. R3 4.04.364
'twere something that would fret the string, H8 3.02.105
take but degree away, untune that string, | and TRO 1.03.109
mark how one string, sweet husband to another, SON 8. 9

STRINGHALT *(see springhalt)*

STRINGLESS 1 FR 0.0001 REL FR 1 V 0 P
his tongue is now a stringless instrument, R2 2.01.149

/STRINGS 1 FR 0.0001 REL FR 1 V 0 P
/grew /puissant /and /the /strings /of /life LR 5.03.217

STRINGS 11 FR 0.0012 REL FR 9 V 2 P
no, girl, i'll knit it up in silken strings, TGV 2.07. 45
how, out of tune on the strings? 4.02. 60 P
to draw with idle spiders' strings | most MM 3.02.275
apparel together, good strings to your beards, MND 4.02. 36 P
when such strings jar, what hope of harmony? 2H6 2.01. 55
and make the silken strings delight to kiss them TIT 2.04. 46
the strings, my lord, are false. JC 4.03.291
knees, and heart, with strings of steel, | be HAM 3.03. 70
had my purse | as if the strings were thine, OTH 1.01. 3
my heart was to thy rudder tied by th' strings, ANT 3.11. 57
you are a fair viol, and your sense the strings; PER 1.01. 81

STRIP 6 FR 0.0006 REL FR 4 V 2 P
and strip myself to death, as to a bed | that, MM 2.04.102
therefore on, or strip your sword stark naked; TN 3.04.251 P
given to the church, | would they strip from us; H5 1.01. 11
then will he strip his sleeve and show his scars 4.03. 47
strip thy own back, | thou hotly lusts to use LR 4.06.161
if such tricks as these strip you out of your OTH 2.01.171 P

STRIPES 4 FR 0.0004 REL FR 3 V 1 P
slave, | whom stripes may move, not kindness! TMP 1.02.345
offend me more than the stripes i have receiv'd, WT 4.03. 57 P
who wears my stripes impress'd upon him, that COR 5.06.107
hence with thy stripes, be gone! ANT 3.13.152

STRIPLING 2 FR 0.0002 REL FR 2 V 0 P
a proper stripling, and an amorous! SHR 1.02.143
a bachelor, and a handsome stripling too: R3 1.03.100

STRIPLINGS 1 FR 0.0001 REL FR 1 V 0 P
he, with two striplings (lads more like to run CYM 5.03. 19

/STRIPP'D 1 FR 0.0001 REL FR 1 V 0 P
/that /stripp'd /her /from /his /benediction, LR 4.03. 43

STRIPP'D 3 FR 0.0003 REL FR 2 V 1 P
there stripp'd himself, and here upon his arm AYL 4.03.146
or to drown my clothes, and say i was stripp'd. AWW 4.01. 53 P
she stripp'd it from her arm. CYM 2.04.101

STRIPPING 1 FR 0.0001 REL FR 1 V 0 P
how, in stripping it, | you more invest it! TMP 2.01.225

STRIV'D 1 FR 0.0001 REL FR 1 V 0 P
the city striv'd | god neptune's annual feast to PER 5.ch. 16

STRIVE 42 FR 0.0047 REL FR 42 V 0 P
good things will strive to dwell with't. TMP 1.02.460
i shall discharge | what i must strive to do. 3.01. 23
i were well awake, | i'ld strive to tell you. 5.01.230
when they strive to be | lords o'er their lords? LLL 4.01. 37
but if thou strive, poor soul, what art thou 4.01. 92
strive mightily, but eat and drink as friends. SHR 1.02.277
to strive for that which resteth in my choice. 3.01. 17
daughter and mother | so strive upon your pulse. AWW 1.03.169
i know i love in vain, strive against hope; 1.03.201
i cannot love her, nor will strive to do't. 2.03.145
thyself, if thou shouldst strive to choose. 2.03.146
we'll strive to bear it for your worthy sake 3.03. 5
i prithee do not strive against my vows. 4.02. 14
and we'll strive to please you every day. TN 5.01.408
your discontenting father strive to qualify, WT 4.04.532
when workmen strive to do better than well, JN 4.02. 28
not yourself, nor strive not with your breath, R2 2.01. 3
strive to speak big, and clap their female 3.02.114
that i may strive to kill it with a groan. 5.01.100
and often did i strive | to yield the ghost; R3 1.04. 36
i'll strive with troubled thoughts to take a nap 5.03.104
bid him strive | to the love o' th' commonalty; H8 1.02.169
princes, that strive by factions and by friends TIT 1.01. 18
sirs, strive no more: 3.01.177
here shall miss, our toil shall strive to mend. ROM pr 14
'gainst the stream of virtue they may strive, TIM 4.01. 27
run, | and i will strive with things impossible, JC 2.01.325
and milk of burgundy | strive to be interess'd, LR 1.01. 85
nay, /an' you strive — OTH 5.02. 81
that it did strive | in workmanship and value, CYM 2.04. 73
strive, man, and speak. 5.05.152
for though he strive | to killen bad, keep good PER 2.ch. 19
the hardy youths strive for the games of honor, TNK 2.02. 10
outstripping crows that strive to overfly them. VEN 324
and all in vain you strive against the stream, 772
nor sun nor wind will ever strive to kiss you: 1082
they both would strive who first should dry his 1092
enmity, | yet strive i to embrace mine infamy." LUC 504
what though she strive to try her strength, PP 18.31
think women still to strive with men, | to sin 18.43
world, and i must strive | to know my shames and SON 112. 5
since my appeal says i did strive to prove | the 117.13

STRIVED 1 FR 0.0001 REL FR 1 V 0 P
within whose face beauty and virtue strived LUC 52

/STRIVES 1 FR 0.0001 REL FR 1 V 0 P
/strives /in /his /little /world /of /man /to LR 3.01. 10

STRIVES 9 FR 0.0010 REL FR 8 V 1 P
where zeal strives to content, and the contents LLL 5.02.517
'tis often seen | adoption strives with nature, AWW 1.03.145
strives bullingbrook to be as great as we? R2 3.02. 97
ay, ay, so strives the woodcock with the gin. 3H6 1.04. 61
how fairly this lord strives to appear foul! TIM 3.03. 31 P
and by how much she strives to do him good, OTH 2.03.358
/whose every passion fully strives | to make ANT 1.01. 50
but, wretched as he is, he strives in vain, LUC 1665
thing we have not, mast'ring what not strives, LC 240

STRIVING 10 FR 0.0011 REL FR 10 V 0 P
her womb, which, for enlargement striving, 1H4 3.01. 30
advance our half–fac'd sun, striving to shine, 2H6 4.01. 98
face, | the fatal colors of our striving houses; 3H6 2.05. 98
the man you are, | with striving less to be so. COR 3.02. 20
striving to make an ugly deed look fair. TIM 3.05. 25
striving to better, oft we mar what's well. LR 1.04.346
this hurt you see, striving to apprehend him. 2.01.108
at least to frustrate striving, and to follow TNK 1.02. 9
as striving who should best become her grief; VEN 968
were it not sinful then, striving to mend, | to SON 103. 9

STRIV'ST 1 FR 0.0001 REL FR 1 V 0 P
what thou hast not, still thou striv'st to get, MM 3.01. 22

/STROKE* 3 FR 0.0003 REL FR 3 V 0 P
/upon /the /stroke /of /ten. R3 4.02.112
/that /like /a /jack /thou /keep'st /the /stroke 4.02.114
/in /the /most /terrible /and /nimble /stroke LR 4.07. 33

STROKE* 40 FR 0.0045 REL FR 37 V 3 P
himself with his good arms in lusty stroke | to TMP 2.01.120
one stroke | shall free thee from the tribute 2.01.292
even with the stroke and line of his great MM 4.02. 80
if such a one will smile and stroke his beard, ADO 5.01. 15
stroke your chins, and swear by your beards that AYL 1.02. 71 P
with bloodless stroke my heart doth gore; TN 2.05.106
win you this city without stroke or wound, JN 2.01.418
the wildest savagery, the vildest stroke, | that 4.03. 48
more welcome is the stroke of death to me | than R2 3.01. 31
faith, you may stroke him as gently as a puppy 2H4 2.04. 98 P
he that strikes the first stroke, i'll run him H5 2.01. 64 P
cowardly fled, not having struck one stroke. 1H6 1.01.134
for none would strike a stroke in his revenge. 1.05. 35
before we met, or that a stroke was given, 4.01. 22
free from oppression or the stroke of war, | my 5.03.155
thee, | i lay it naked to the deadly stroke, R3 1.02.177
upon the stroke of four. 3.02. 5
upon the stroke of four. 5.03.235
at one stroke has taken | for ever from the H8 2.01.117
that when the greatest stroke of fortune falls 2.02. 35
now play me nestor, hem, and stroke thy beard, TRO 1.03.165
strike not a stroke, but keep yourselves in 5.07. 3
wherein i had no stroke of mischief in it? TIT 5.01.110
and smilest upon the stroke that murders me. ROM 3.03. 23
fevers heap | on athens, ripe for stroke! TIM 4.01. 23
nor all deserve | the common stroke of war. 5.04. 22
if thou beest slain and with no stroke of mine, MAC 5.07. 15
but not without that harmful stroke which since LR 4.02. 77
when i did speak of some distressful stroke OTH 1.03.157
i knew | that stroke would prove the worst! 4.01.274
which to the tune of flutes kept stroke, and ANT 2.02.195
before i strike this bloody stroke, farewell. 4.14. 91
by some mortal stroke | she do defeat us; 5.01. 64
the stroke of death is as a lover's pinch, 5.02.295
th' great, | thou art past the tyrant's stroke; CYM 4.02.265
ere the stroke | of yet this scarce–cold battle, 5.05.468
what will | the fall o' th' stroke do damage? TNK 1.02.113
each stroke laments | the place whereon it falls 5.03. 4
now doth she stroke his cheek, now doth he frown VEN 45
the destinies will curse thee for this stroke: 945

/STROKES* 1 FR 0.0001 REL FR 1 V 0 P
so tender of rebukes that words are /strokes, CYM 3.05. 40

STROKES* 22 FR 0.0024 REL FR 22 V 0 P
wounds th' unsisting postern with these strokes. MM 4.02. 89
as you love strokes, so jest with me again. ERR 2.02. 8
that hath enrag'd him on to offer strokes, | as 2H4 4.01.209
and many strokes, though with a little axe, 3H6 2.01. 54
for strokes receiv'd and many blows repaid 2.03. 3
of bloody strokes and mortal–staring war. R3 5.03. 90
stints their strife before their strokes begin. TRO 4.05. 93
she strokes his cheek! 5.02. 51
not fierce and terrible | only in strokes, but, COR 1.04. 58
opposing laws with strokes, and here defying 3.03. 79
as now at last | given hostile strokes, and that 3.03. 97
women | 'tis fond to wail inevitable strokes, 4.01. 26
their fears of hostile strokes, their aches, TIM 5.01.199
good words are better than bad strokes, octavius JC 5.01. 29
in your bad strokes, brutus, you give good words 5.01. 30
so they | doubly redoubled strokes upon the foe. MAC 1.02. 38
but certain issue strokes must arbitrate, 5.04. 20
virtue itself scapes not calumnious strokes. HAM 1.03. 38
heav'ns' plagues | have humbled to all strokes. LR 4.01. 65
to follow faster, | as amorous of their strokes. ANT 2.02.197
and give me | sufficing strokes for death. 4.14.117
words are /strokes, | and strokes death to her. CYM 3.05. 41

STROK'ST 1 FR 0.0001 REL FR 1 V 0 P
thou strok'st me and made much of me, wouldst TMP 1.02.333

STROND 5 FR 0.0005 REL FR 4 V 1 P
which makes her seat of belmont colchis' strond, MV 1.01.171
when with his knees he kiss'd the cretan strond. SHR 1.01.170
so looks the strond whereon the imperious flood 2H4 1.01. 62
which were the hope o' th' strond, where she was H8 5.03. 53 P
and from the strond of dardan, where they fought LUC 1436

STRONDS 1 FR 0.0001 REL FR 1 V 0 P
broils | to be commenc'd in stronds afar remote. 1H4 1.01. 4

/STRONG 4 FR 0.0004 REL FR 4 V 0 P
/and /cracking /the /strong /warrant /of /an R2 4.01.235
/marshal /and /the /archbishop /are /strong. 2H4 2.03. 42
/within /whose /strong /immures | /the /ravish'd TRO pr 8
/with /his /strong /arms | /he /fastened /on /my LR 5.03.212

STRONG 206 FR 0.0232 REL FR 183 V 23 P
to thy strong bidding, task | ariel, and all his TMP 1.02.192
thee, and | my strong imagination sees a crown 2.01.208
(whose inward pinches therefore are most strong) 5.01. 77
and one so strong | that could control the moon, 5.01.269
to be stopp'd in, like a strong distillation, WIV 3.05.112 P
(even strong against that match | and firm for 4.06. 27
and in my heart the strong and swelling evil MM 2.04. 6
what king so strong | can tie the gall up in the 3.02.187
that the strong statutes | stand like the 5.01.320
if by strong hand you offer to break in | now in ERR 3.01. 98
more company! the fiend is strong within him. 4.04.107
anon, i wot not by what strong escape, | he 5.01.148
force | and strong encounter of my amorous tale; ADO 1.01.325
fetter strong madness in a silken thread, 5.01. 25
folly in fools bears not so strong a note | as LLL 5.02. 75
of strong prevailment in unhardened youth. MND 1.01. 35
thus weak, lost with their fears thus strong, 3.02. 27
such tricks hath strong imagination, | that, if 5.01. 18
the spirit of my father grows strong in me, and AYL 1.01. 70 P
to catch the strong fellow by the leg. 1.02.211 P
should fall into so strong a liking with old sir 1.03. 28 P
and wherefore are you gentle, strong, and 2.03. 6
though i look old, yet i am strong and lusty; 2.03. 47
let gentleness my strong enforcement be, | in 2.07.118
after some small space, being strong at heart, 4.03.151
where love's strong passion is impress'd in AWW 1.03.133
my reasons are most strong, and you shall know 4.02. 59
of him, how many horse the duke is strong." 4.03.130 P
mood, and smell somewhat strong of her strong 5.02. 5 P
smell somewhat strong of her strong displeasure. 5.02. 5 P
oil and fire, too strong for reason's force, 5.03. 7
to a strong mast that liv'd upon the sea; TN 1.02. 14
the back–trick simply as strong as any man in 1.03.124 P
ay, 'tis strong; 1.03.134 P
can bide the beating of so strong a passion | as 2.04. 94
to him, lad, some two thousand strong, or so. 3.02. 55 P
or any taint of vice whose strong corruption 3.04.356
to tell he longs to see his son were strong; WT 1.02. 34
that the verity of it is in strong suspicion. 5.02. 29 P
our strong possession and our right for us. JN 1.01. 39
your strong possession much more than your right 1.01. 40
till your strong hand shall help to give him 2.01. 33
his forces strong, his soldiers confident. 2.01. 61
thoughts | in any /breast of strong authority, 2.01.113
thou ever strong upon the stronger side! 3.01.117
so newly join'd in love, so strong in both, 3.01.240
before the curing of a strong disease, | even in 3.04.112
and pick strong matter of revolt and wrath | out 3.04.167
strong reasons makes strange actions. 3.04.182
have possess'd you with, and think them strong; 4.02. 41
and more, more strong than lesser is my fear, 4.02. 42
we cannot hold mortality's strong hand. 4.02. 82
strong as a tower in hope, i cry amen. R2 1.03.102
grows strong and great in substance and in power 3.02. 35
of faith, | to tie thee to my strong correction. 4.01. 77
that had not god, for some strong purpose, 5.02. 34
o heinous, strong, and bold conspiracy! 5.03. 59
not pardon twain, | but makes one pardon strong. 5.03.135
to bear our fortunes in our own strong arms, 1H4 1.03.298
the earl of westmerland, seven thousand strong, 4.01. 88
speedily, | with strong and mighty preparation. 4.01. 93
and when he was not six and twenty strong, 4.03. 56
and 'tis but wisdom to make strong against him. 4.04. 39
account | nothing so strong and fortunate as i. 5.01. 38
i think we are so /a body strong enough, | even 2H4 1.03. 66
and northumberland | are fifty thousand strong. 3.01. 96
fellow, young, strong, and of good friends. 3.02.103 P
our armor all as strong, our cause the best; 4.01.154
though it do work as strong | as aconitum or 4.04. 47
think we king harry strong; H5 2.04. 48
pains, and strong endeavors | to bring your most 5.02. 25

strong fixed is the house of lancaster, | and 1H6 2.05.102
i was six thousand strong | and that the french 4.01. 20
and strong enough to issue out and fight. 4.02. 20
the bastard to destroy, | came in strong rescue. 4.06. 26
and hell too strong for me to buckle with: 5.03. 28
bring the strong poison that i bought of him. 2H6 3.03. 18
that lays strong siege unto this wretch's soul, 3.03. 22
more | than bargulus the strong illyrian pirate. 4.01.108
henry hath money, you are strong and manly; 4.08. 51
or is he but retir'd to make him strong? 4.09. 9
till henry be more weak and i more strong. 5.01. 31
but i have reasons strong and forcible. 3H6 1.02. 3
and were i strong, i would not shun their fury. 1.04. 24
thou shalt know this strong right hand of mine 2.01.152
their power, i think, is thirty thousand strong. 2.01.177
the queen is valued thirty thousand strong, 5.03. 14
her faction will be full as strong as ours. 5.03. 17
to the rebels, and their power grows strong. R3 4.04.505
devis'd at first to keep the strong in awe: 5.03.310
our strong arms be our conscience, swords our 5.03.311
and make my vouch as strong | as shore of rock. H8 1.01.157
'twill require | a strong faith to conceal it. 2.01.145
teaching | and the strong course of my authority 5.02. 70
me a dozen crab–tree staves, and strong ones; 5.03. 8 P
the greeks are strong, and skillful to their TRO 1.01. 7
strong as the axle–tree | on which heaven rides, 1.03. 66
good arms, strong joints, true swords, and, 1.03.238
part | to steel a strong opinion to themselves? 1.03.353
but it was a strong composure a fool could 2.03. 99 P
no, noble ajax, you are as strong, as valiant, 2.03.148 P
of this my privacy | i have strong reasons. 3.03.191
but the strong base and building of my love | is 4.02.103
and violenteth in a sense as strong | as that 4.04. 4
my heart, | an esperance so obstinately strong, 5.02.121
strong as pluto's gates: 5.02.153
strong as heaven itself: 5.02.155
it is the purpose that makes strong the vow, 5.03. 23
let grow thy sinews till their knots be strong, 5.03. 33
they say poor suitors have strong breaths; COR 1.01. 60 P
they shall know we have strong arms too. 1.01. 61 P
of more strong link asunder than can ever 1.01. 71
conjectural marriages, making parties strong, 1.01.194
sir, 'tis fit | you make strong party, or defend 3.02. 94
as i hear, more strong | than are upon you yet. 3.02.140
make them be strong, and ready for this hint 3.03. 23
hath yok'd a nation strong, train'd up in arms. TIT 1.01. 30
why should you fear? is not your city strong? 4.04. 78
and see the ambush of our friends be strong, | i 5.03. 9
a reason mighty, strong, and effectual, | a 5.03. 43
and, in strong proof of chastity well arm'd, ROM 1.01.210
but i'll amerce you with so strong a fine | that 3.01.190
be strong and prosperous | in this resolve. 4.01.122
thou't go, strong thief, | when gouty keepers of TIM 4.03. 46
into strong shudders and to heavenly agues | th' 4.03.138
be strong in whore, allure him, burn him up, 4.03.142
when crouching marrow in the bearer strong 5.04. 9
therein, ye gods, you make the weak most strong; JC 1.03. 91
nor airless dungeon, nor strong links of iron, 1.03. 94
i think he will stand very strong with us. 2.01.142
i have made strong proof of my constancy, 2.01.299
o constancy, be strong upon my side, | set a 2.04. 6
your voice shall be as strong as any man's | in 3.01.177
ingratitude, more strong than traitors' arms, 3.02.185
for i am arm'd so strong in honesty | that they 4.03. 67
mark antony | have made themselves so strong — 4.03.154
you know that i held epicurus strong, | and his 5.01. 76
and his subject, | strong both against the deed; MAC 1.07. 14
i think, being too strong for him, though he 2.03. 39 P
nor our strong sorrow | upon the foot of motion. 2.03.124
things bad begun make strong themselves by ill. 3.02. 55
precious motives, those strong knots of love, 4.03. 27
of us, by strong hand | and terms compulsatory, HAM 1.01.102
my stronger guilt defeats my strong intent, 3.03. 40
yet must not we put the strong law on him. 4.03. 3
much unsinow'd, | but yet to me th' are strong. 4.07. 11
with how manifold and strong a bond | the child LR 2.01. 47
and the strong lance of justice hurtless breaks; 4.06.166
being strong on both sides, are equivocal. OTH 1.03.217
moor | at least into a jealousy so strong | that 2.01.301
with any strong or vehement importunity; 3.03.251
are to the jealious confirmations strong | as 3.03.323
if imputation and strong circumstances | which 3.03.406
cannot remove nor choke the strong conception 5.02. 55
these strong egyptian fetters i must break, | or ANT 1.02.116
the strong necessity of time commands | our 1.03. 42
pompey is strong at sea, | and it appears he is 1.04. 36
there's a strong fellow, menas. 2.07. 88
/bear as loud | as his strong sides can volley. 2.07.112
strong enobarb | is weaker than the wine, and 2.07.122
o'er your content these strong necessities, 3.06. 83
women are not | in their best fortunes strong, 3.12. 30
another antony | in her strong toil of grace. 5.02.348
this is not strong enough to be believ'd | of CYM 2.04.131
but from proof as strong as my grief and as 3.04. 24 P
i am weak with toil, yet strong in appetite. 3.06. 37
no less young, more strong, not beneath him in 4.01. 10 P
still observ'd, and we are strong in /custom; PER 3.01. 52 P
such strong renown as time shall never — 3.02. 48
we have, a strong wind will blow it to pieces, 4.02. 19 P
the gods will be strong with us for giving o'er. 4.02. 35 P
that with thy arm, as strong | as it is white, TNK 1.01. 79
more buckled with strong judgment, and their 1.03. 57
strong enough to laugh at misery | and bear the 2.02. 2
she takes strong note of me, | hath made me near 3.01. 17
i pray you | take comfort and be strong. 3.01.100
stand long, | and thy dogs be swift and strong! 3.05.155
whose twelve strong labors crown his memory, 3.06.176
his shoulders broad and strong, | arm'd long and 4.02. 84
are as a man would wish 'em, strong and clean. 4.02.114
his arms are brawny, | lin'd with strong sinews; 4.02.127
how insolence and strong hand should prevail, STM II.C 81
short ears, straight legs and passing strong, VEN 297
loseth his pride, and never waxeth strong. 420
and with his strong course opens them again. 960
my will is strong, past reason's weak removing: LUC 243
high winds, strong pirates, shelves and sands, 335
in me, | from me by strong assault it is bereft: 835
their father was too weak, and they too strong, 865
assail'd by night with circumstances strong | of 1262
"mine enemy was strong, my poor self weak | (and 1646
(and far the weaker with so strong a fear), | my 1647
by our strong arms from forth her fair streets 1834
"had women been so strong as men, | in faith, PP 18.35
resembling strong youth in his middle age, | yet SON 7. 6
to him that bears the strong offense's /cross. 34.12
be where you list, your charter is so strong, 58. 9
nor gates of steel so strong, but time decays? 65. 8
or what strong hand can hold his swift foot back 65.11
perceiv'st, which makes thy love more strong, 73.13
potions of eisel 'gainst my strong infection, 111.10
divert strong minds to th' course of alt'ring 115. 8
grows fairer than at first, more strong, far 119.12
all replication prompt and reason strong, | for LC 122
i strong o'er them, and you o'er me being strong 257
strong o'er them, and you o'er me being strong, 257

STRONG–BARR'D 1 FR 0.0001 REL FR 1 V 0 P
our former scruple in our strong–barr'd gates, JN 2.01.370

STRONG–BAS'D 1 FR 0.0001 REL FR 1 V 0 P
the strong–bas'd promontory | have i made shake, TMP 5.01. 46

STRONG–BESIEGED 1 FR 0.0001 REL FR 1 V 0 P
and from the walls of strong–besieged troy, LUC 1429

STRONG–BONDED 1 FR 0.0001 REL FR 1 V 0 P
and credent soul to that strong–bonded oath LC 279

/STRONGER 1 FR 0.0001 REL FR 1 V 0 P
whose weakness, married to thy /stronger state, ERR 2.02.175

STRONGER 40 FR 0.0045 REL FR 31 V 9 P
the ship were no stronger than a nutshell and as TMP 1.01. 47 P
(since i suppose we are made to be no stronger MM 2.04.132
not on a band but on a stronger thing: ERR 4.02. 50
i thy spirits were stronger than thy shames, ADO 4.01.125
that is stronger made | which was before barr'd 4.01.150
of /a lover is no stronger than the word of a AYL 3.04. 31 P
and nature, stronger than his just occasion, 4.03.129
the stronger part of it by her own letters, AWW 4.03. 55 P
in breaking 'em he is stronger than hercules. 4.03.253 P
ne'er been higher rear'd | with stronger blood, WT 1.02. 73
easier for advice, | or stronger for your need. 4.04.506
thou ever strong upon the stronger side! JN 3.01.117
be stronger with thee than the name of wife? 3.01.314
a rib of steel, | to make strength stronger; 2H4 2.03. 55
limb united, | grow stronger for the breaking. 4.01.221
what stronger breastplate than a heart untainted 2H6 3.02.232
the more we stay, the stronger grows our foe. 3H6 3.03. 40
when we grow stronger, then we'll make our claim 4.07. 59
more stronger to direct you than yourself, | if H8 1.01.147
say, | are you not stronger than you were? 2.03.100
so i grow stronger, you more honor gain. 5.02.215
with surety stronger than achilles' arm, | 'fore TRO 1.03.220
mine ears against your suits are stronger than COR 5.02. 88
and am not | of stronger earth than others. 5.03. 29
think you i am no stronger than my sex, | being JC 2.01.296
my stronger guilt defeats my strong intent, HAM 3.03. 40
is he that builds stronger than either the mason 5.01. 41 P
the gallows is built stronger than the church; 5.01. 48 P
who builds stronger than a mason, a shipwright, 5.01. 50 P
love shall grow stronger than it was before. OTH 2.03.325 P
heart, once be stronger than thy continent, ANT 4.14. 40
sure mine nails | are stronger than mine eyes. 5.02.224
a voucher, | stronger than ever law could make; CYM 2.02. 40
our kingdom is stronger than it was at that time 3.01. 35 P
and in time | may make some stronger head, the 4.02.139
that /blast gives heat and stronger glowing; PER 1.02. 41
steel his stronger strength obeyed, | yet was he VEN 111
rotten death make conquest of the stronger, LUC 1767
doth nightly make grief's length seem stronger. SON 28.14
whose action is no stronger than a flower? 65. 4

STRONGEST 9 FR 0.0010 REL FR 9 V 0 P
the strongest oaths are straw | to th' fire i' TMP 4.01. 52
i swear to thee, by cupid's strongest bow, | by MND 1.01.169
of repair and health, | the fit is strongest; JN 3.04.114
the strongest nerves and small inferior veins COR 1.01.138
conceit in weakest bodies strongest works, HAM 3.04.114
our lives upon to use our strongest hands. ANT 2.01. 51
whose death indeed the strongest in our censure, PER 2.04. 34
the strongest body shall it make most weak, VEN 1145
the strongest castle, tower, and town, | the PP 18.17

STRONG–FRAM'D 1 FR 0.0001 REL FR 0 V 1 P
i am strong–fram'd, he cannot prevail with me. R3 1.04.150 P

STRONG–HEARTED 1 FR 0.0001 REL FR 1 V 0 P
you valiant and strong–hearted enemies, | you TNK 5.01. 8

STRONG–JOINTED 1 FR 0.0001 REL FR 0 V 1 P
strong–jointed sampson! LLL 1.02. 73 P

STRONG–KNIT 2 FR 0.0002 REL FR 2 V 0 P
and large proportion of his strong–knit limbs. 1H6 2.03. 21
have robb'd my strong–knit sinews of their 3H6 2.03. 4

/STRONGLY 2 FR 0.0002 REL FR 2 V 0 P
/of /this | (/though /strongly /apprehended) 2H4 1.01.176
suspects, yet /strongly loves! OTH 3.03.170

STRONGLY 29 FR 0.0032 REL FR 25 V 4 P
in some passion | that works him strongly. TMP 4.01.144
your charm so strongly works 'em | that if you 5.01. 17
now are too too strongly embattled against me. WIV 2.02.250 P
i am affianc'd this man's wife as strongly | as MM 5.01.227
our late edict shall strongly stand in force: LLL 1.01. 11
which each to other hath so strongly sworn. 1.01.307
which appears most strongly | in bearing thus MV 3.04. 3
if it smell so strongly as thou speak'st of. AWW 5.02. 7 P
which was so strongly urg'd past my defense. JN 1.01.258
grace shall stay behind | so strongly guarded. 3.03. 2
who strongly hath set footing in this land: R2 2.02. 48
we all have strongly sworn to give him aid; 2.03.150
so strongly that they dare not meet each other; 1H4 2.02.106
and, princes, look you strongly arm to meet him. H5 2.04. 49
and fortify it strongly 'gainst the french. 3.03. 53
deliver'd strongly through my fixed teeth, 2H6 3.02.313
all these accus'd him strongly, which he fain H8 2.01. 24
i know 'twill stir him strongly; 3.02.218
'tis strongly wadg'd up in a blockhead; COR 2.03. 28 P
to satisfy my remembrance the more strongly. MAC 5.01. 34 P
great dunsinane he strongly fortifies. 5.02. 12
and she for him pleads strongly to the moor, OTH 2.03.355
more urgent touches, | do strongly speak to us; ANT 1.02.181
as strongly as the conscience does within, | to CYM 2.02. 36
but must be look'd to speedily and strongly. 3.05. 27
like meeting of two tides, fly strongly from us, TNK 3.06. 30
what did he note but strongly he desired? LUC 415
thy merit hath my duty strongly knit, | to thee SON 26. 2
you are so strongly in my purpose bred | that 112.13

STRONG–NECK'D 1 FR 0.0001 REL FR 1 V 0 P
the strong–neck'd steed, being tied unto a tree, VEN 263

STRONG–RIBB'D 1 FR 0.0001 REL FR 1 V 0 P
the strong–ribb'd bark through liquid mountains TRO 1.03. 40

STRONG'ST 2 FR 0.0002 REL FR 2 V 0 P
the strong'st suggestion | our worser genius can TMP 4.01. 26
that know the strong'st and surest way to get. R2 3.03.201

STRONG–TEMPER'D 1 FR 0.0001 REL FR 1 V 0 P
strong–temper'd steel his stronger strength VEN 111

STRONG–WING'D 1 FR 0.0001 REL FR 1 V 0 P
the strong–wing'd mercury should fetch thee up, ANT 4.15. 35

STROOK *(also stricken, strooken, struck, strucken)*

STROOK 55 FR 0.0062 REL FR 46 V 9 P
it strook mine ear most terribly. TMP 2.01.313
with their high wrongs i am strook to th' quick, 5.01. 25
it hath strook ten a' clock. WIV 5.02. 10 P
the windsor bell hath strook twelve; 5.05. 1 P
nay, he strook so plainly, i could too well feel ERR 2.01. 52 P
well strook! 3.01. 56
and with that word she strook me on the head, SHR 2.01.153
myself am strook in years, i must confess, | and 2.01.360
though i strook him first, yet it's no matter TN 4.01. 35 P
who strook this heat up after i was gone? 1H4 1.03.139
death hath not strook so fat a deer to–day, 5.04.107
and bending forward strook his armed heels 2H4 1.01. 44
your majesty, | how cold it strook my heart! 4.05.151
and strook me in my very seat of judgment; 5.02. 80
thou wert better thou hadst strook thy mother, 5.04. 10 P
has strook the glove which your majesty is take H5 4.08. 26 P
and his noble queen | well strook in years, fair R3 1.01. 92
and in falling | strook me (that thought to stay 1.04. 19
have strook more terror to the soul of richard 5.03.217
it hath strook. H8 5.01. 1
he chid andromache and strook his armorer, | and TRO 1.02. 6
cop'd hector in the battle and strook him down, 1.02. 34 P
of this cormorant war — | shall be strook off." 2.02. 7
whiles we have strook, | by interims and COR 1.06. 4
when most strook home, being gentle wounded, 4.01. 8
to banish him that strook more blows for rome 4.02. 19
shall have the drum strook up this afternoon. 4.05.215 P
even thou hast strook upon my crest, | and with TIT 1.01.364
what, hast not thou full often strook a doe, 2.01. 93
but new strook nine. ROM 1.01.161
the clock strook nine when i did send the nurse; 2.05. 1
fire i' th' flint | shows not till it be strook; TIM 1.01. 23
why i, that did love caesar when i strook him, JC 3.01.182
like a cur, behind | strook caesar on the neck. 5.01. 44
sinful macduff, | they were all strook for thee! MAC 4.03.225
'tis now strook twelf. HAM 1.01. 7
no, it is strook. 1.04. 4
of the scene | been strook so to the soul, that 2.02.591
your behavior hath strook her into amazement and 3.02.326 P
of the axe, | my head should be strook off. 5.02. 25
princes at a shot | so bloodily hast strook? 5.02.367
look'd black upon me, strook me with her tongue, LR 2.04.160
on the sudden | a roman thought hath strook him. ANT 1.02. 83
now, darting parthia, art thou strook, and now 3.01. 1
while i strook | the lean and wrinkled cassius, 3.11. 36
therein false strook, can take no greater wound, CYM 3.04.114
vessel of the world | strook the main–top! 4.02.320
the noble imogen to repent, and strook | me, 5.01. 10
tools to do't — strook down | some mortally, 5.03. 9
hear him groan, | nor feel him where he strook. 5.03. 70
unhappy was the clock | that strook the hour! 5.05.154
he should have strook, not spoke; PER 4.02. 65
he is a good one | as ever strook at head. TNK 5.03.109
which strook her sad, and then it faster rock'd, LUC 262
this said, he strook his hand upon his breast, 1842

STROOKEN *(also stricken, strook, struck, strucken)*

STROOKEN 6 FR 0.0006 REL FR 5 V 1 P
bows not his vassal head and, strooken blind, LLL 4.03.220
had thought to have strooken him with a cudgel, COR 4.05.150 P
he that is strooken blind cannot forget | the ROM 1.01.232
how like a deer, strooken by many princes, JC 3.01.209
why, let the strooken deer go weep, | the hart HAM 3.02.271
with the sceptre straight be strooken down? LUC 217

STROSSERS 1 FR 0.0001 REL FR 0 V 1 P
french hose off, and in your strait strossers. H5 3.07. 54 P

/STROVE 1 FR 0.0001 REL FR 1 V 0 P
/patience /and /sorrow /strove | /who /should LR 4.03. 16

STROVE 3 FR 0.0003 REL FR 3 V 0 P
who ever strove | to show her merit, that did AWW 1.01.226
of your friends | have i not strove to love, H8 2.04. 30
were there aught in me which strove to show TNK 5.01. 20

STROW *(also strew, etc.)*

STROW 1 FR 0.0001 REL FR 1 V 0 P
of her weed | to strow thy green with flowers. PER 4.01. 14

STROW'D 1 FR 0.0001 REL FR 1 V 0 P
whereon thou tread'st the presence strow'd, R2 1.03.289

STROWN 1 FR 0.0001 REL FR 1 V 0 P
sweet, | on my black coffin let there be strown. TN 2.04. 60

'STROY'D *(also destroy'd)*

'STROY'D 1 FR 0.0001 REL FR 1 V 0 P
what i have left behind | 'stroy'd in dishonor. ANT 3.11. 54

STRUCK *(also stricken, strook, strooken, strucken)*

/STRUCK 1 FR 0.0001 REL FR 1 V 0 P
/hath /sorrow /struck | /so /many /blows /upon R2 4.01.277

STRUCK 27 FR 0.0030 REL FR 25 V 2 P
of thousands that had struck anointed kings WT 1.02.358
deep shame had struck me dumb, made me break off JN 4.02.235
caliver worse than a struck fowl or a hurt wild 1H4 4.02. 19 P
shame | when cressy battle fatally was struck, H5 2.04. 54
cowardly fled, not having struck one stroke. 1H6 1.01.134
one of thy eyes and thy cheek's side struck off! 1.04. 75
whilst any trump did sound, or drum struck up, 1.04. 80
from the dolphin's crest thy sword struck fire, 4.06. 10
some sudden qualm hath struck me at the heart, 2H6 1.01. 54
then is sin struck down like an ox, and 4.02. 26 P
oft have i struck | those that i never saw, and 4.07. 81
those that i never saw, and struck them dead. 4.07. 82
gently down, as if they struck their friends. 3H6 2.01.132

that princely novice, was struck dead by thee? R3 1.04.222
when the alarum were struck than idly sit | to COR 2.02. 76
self he met, | and struck him on his knee. 2.02. 95
off, | and with a sudden reinforcement struck 2.02.113
my rage is gone, | and i am struck with sorrow. 5.06.147
this for me, struck home to show my strength. TIT 2.03.117
this dear sight | struck pale and bloodless, and 3.01.257
have struck but thus much show of fire from JC 1.02.177
that struck the foremost man of all this world 4.03. 22
but wail his fall | who i myself struck down. MAC 3.01.122
our rages, | struck with our well–steel'd darts. TNK 2.02. 51
struck dead at first, what needs a second VEN 250
his meaning struck her ere his words begun. 462
above a mortal pitch, that struck me dead? SON 86. 6

STRUCKEN *(also stricken, strook, strooken, struck)*

STRUCKEN 3 FR 0.0003 REL FR 2 V 1 P
the clock hath strucken twelve upon the bell: ERR 1.02. 45
caesar, 'tis strucken eight. JC 2.02.114
i'll not be strucken, my lord. LR 1.04. 85 P

STRUCK'ST 1 FR 0.0001 REL FR 0 V 1 P
tut, when struck'st thou one blow in the field? 2H6 4.07. 79 P

STRUGGLE 3 FR 0.0003 REL FR 3 V 0 P
i will not struggle, i will stand stone–still. JN 4.01. 76
so doth the cony struggle in the net. 3H6 1.04. 62
nay, do not struggle, for thou shalt not rise. VEN 710

STRUGGLES 1 FR 0.0001 REL FR 1 V 0 P
and when from thence he struggles to be gone, VEN 227

STRUGGLING 3 FR 0.0003 REL FR 3 V 0 P
his nostrils stretch'd with struggling; 2H6 3.02.171
o limed soul, that, struggling to be free, | art HAM 3.03. 68
struggling for passage, earth's foundation VEN 1047

/STRUMPET 1 FR 0.0001 REL FR 1 V 0 P
/impudent /strumpet! OTH 4.02. 81

STRUMPET 25 FR 0.0028 REL FR 23 V 2 P
never could the strumpet, | with all her double MM 2.02.182
o most unhappy strumpet! ERR 4.04.124
bay, | hugg'd and embraced by the strumpet wind! MV 2.06. 16
lean, rent, and beggar'd by the strumpet wind! 2.06. 19
great king, i am no strumpet, by my life; AWW 5.03.292
myself on every post | proclaim'd a strumpet; WT 3.02.102
that strumpet fortune, that usurping john! JN 3.01. 61
but i will chastise this high–minded strumpet. 1H6 1.05. 12
strumpet, thy words condemn thy brat and thee. 5.04. 84
consorted with that harlot, strumpet shore, R3 3.04. 71
thou protector of this damned strumpet, 3.04. 74
and bid that strumpet, your unhallowed dam, TIT 5.02.190
o, most true, she is a strumpet. HAM 2.02.236 P
out, out, thou strumpet fortune! 2.02.493
are not you a strumpet? OTH 4.02. 82
foul unlawful touch | be not to be a strumpet, i 4.02. 85
strumpet, i come. 5.01. 34
o notable strumpet! 5.01. 78
o, fie upon thee, strumpet! 5.01.121
i am no strumpet, but of life as honest | as you 5.01.122
out, strumpet! weep'st thou for him to my face? 5.02. 77
down, strumpet! 5.02. 79
pisanio, hath play'd the strumpet in my bed; CYM 3.04. 22 P
i have heard i am a strumpet, and mine ear, 3.04.113
"show me the strumpet that began this stir, LUC 1471

STRUMPETED 2 FR 0.0002 REL FR 2 V 0 P
thy flesh, | being strumpeted by thy contagion. ERR 2.02.144
and maiden virtue rudely strumpeted, | and right SON 66. 6

STRUMPET'S 3 FR 0.0003 REL FR 3 V 0 P
a strumpet's boldness, a divulged shame, AWW 2.01.171
(as 'tis the strumpet's plague | to beguile many OTH 4.01. 96
the world transform'd | into a strumpet's fool. ANT 1.01. 13

STRUMPETS 1 FR 0.0001 REL FR 1 V 0 P
saucy lictors | will catch at us like strumpets, ANT 5.02.215

STRUNG 2 FR 0.0002 REL FR 2 V 0 P
for orpheus' lute was strung with poets' sinews, TGV 3.02. 77
as bright apollo's lute, strung with his hair. LLL 4.03.340

STRUT 4 FR 0.0004 REL FR 3 V 1 P
up his head, as it were, and strut in his gait? WIV 1.04. 30 P
to strut before a wanton ambling nymph; R3 1.01. 17
laugh at 's while we strut | to our confusion. ANT 3.13.114
fires bright, | and britains strut with courage. CYM 3.01. 33

STRUTS 1 FR 0.0001 REL FR 1 V 0 P
that struts and frets his hour upon the stage, MAC 5.05. 25

STRUTTED 1 FR 0.0001 REL FR 0 V 1 P
man, have so strutted and bellow'd that i have HAM 3.02. 32 P

STRUTTING 2 FR 0.0002 REL FR 2 V 0 P
i hear | the strain of strutting chanticleer: TMP 1.02.386
and, like a strutting player, whose conceit TRO 1.03.153

STUBBLE 1 FR 0.0001 REL FR 1 V 0 P
will be his fire | to kindle their dry stubble; COR 2.01.258

STUBBLE–LAND 1 FR 0.0001 REL FR 1 V 0 P
show'd like a stubble–land at harvest–home. 1H4 1.03. 35

STUBBORN 25 FR 0.0028 REL FR 21 V 4 P
proud, disobedient, stubborn, lacking duty, TGV 3.01. 69
thou art said to have a stubborn soul | that MM 5.01.480
i fear these stubborn lines lack power to move. LLL 4.03. 53
(which is due to me) | to stubborn harshness. MND 1.01. 38
from stubborn turks, and tartars never train'd MV 4.01. 32
his wealth and ease | a stubborn will to please, AYL 2.05. 53
on purpose, that i may appear stubborn to him; TN 3.04. 67 P
upon some stubborn and uncourteous parts | we 5.01.361
and though authority be a stubborn bear, yet he WT 4.04.802 P
up, | upon your stubborn usage of the pope; JN 5.01. 18
as is the sepulchre in stubborn jewry | of the R2 2.01. 55
therefore was i created with a stubborn outside, H5 5.02.227 P
in ireland have i seen this stubborn cade 2H6 3.01.360
loyalty, | free from a stubborn opposite intent, 3.02.251
stubborn to justice, apt to accuse it, and H8 2.04.122
but to stubborn spirits | they swell and grow, 3.01.163
for your stubborn answer | about the giving–back 3.02.346
their mouths with stubborn bits and spur 'em 5.02. 58
his stubborn buckles, | with /these your white TRO 3.01.150
do not give advantage | to stubborn critics, apt 5.02.131
you bear too stubborn and too strange a hand JC 1.02. 35
bow, stubborn knees, and heart, with strings of HAM 3.03. 70
you stubborn ancient knave, you reverent LR 2.02.126
fortunes with this more stubborn and boist'rous OTH 1.03.228 P
all–fear'd gods, bow down your stubborn bodies. TNK 5.01. 13

STUBBORN–CHASTE 1 FR 0.0001 REL FR 1 V 0 P
as she is stubborn–chaste against all suit. TRO 1.01. 97

STUBBORNEST 1 FR 0.0001 REL FR 0 V 1 P
it is the stubbornest young fellow of france, AYL 1.01.142 P

STUBBORN–HARD 1 FR 0.0001 REL FR 1 V 0 P
are you more stubborn–hard than hammer'd iron? JN 4.01. 67

STUBBORNLY 1 FR 0.0001 REL FR 1 V 0 P
when stubbornly he did repugn the truth | about 1H6 4.01. 94

STUBBORNNESS 3 FR 0.0003 REL FR 3 V 0 P
that can translate the stubbornness of fortune AYL 2.01. 19
is a course | of impious stubbornness, 'tis HAM 1.02. 94
that even his stubbornness, his checks, his OTH 4.03. 20

STUCK* 23 FR 0.0026 REL FR 17 V 6 P
millions of false eyes | are stuck upon thee. MM 4.01. 60
with two pitch–balls stuck in her face for eyes; LLL 3.01.197
stuck with cloves. 5.02.648 P
he stuck them up before the fulsome ewes, | who MV 1.03. 86
a thing stuck on with oaths upon your finger, 5.01.168
at first | i stuck my choice upon her, ere my AWW 5.03. 45
my shroud of white, stuck all with yew, | o, TN 2.04. 55
and he gives me the stuck in with such a mortal 3.04.275 P
to me that all their other senses stuck in ears. WT 4.04.609 P
there stuck no plume in any english crest | that JN 2.01.317
all our lives shall be stuck full of eyes, | for 1H4 5.02. 8
it stuck upon him as the sun | in the grey vault 2H4 2.03. 18
he himself stuck not to call us the many–headed COR 2.03. 16 P
who, stuck and spangled /with /your flatteries, TIM 3.06. 91
that numberless upon me stuck as leaves | do on 4.03.263
of blessing, and "amen" | stuck in my throat. MAC 2.02. 30
if he by chance escape your venom'd stuck, | our HAM 4.07.161
the heav'ns, and therein stuck | a sun and moon, ANT 5.02. 79
constantly thou hast stuck to the bare fortune CYM 3.05.118 P
about her stuck | thousand fresh water–flowers TNK 4.01. 84
oak, | and in it stuck the favor of his lady. 4.02.138
her, stuck in as sweet flowers as the season is 4.03. 82 P
that maidens' eyes stuck over all his face. LC 81

STUDDED 2 FR 0.0002 REL FR 2 V 0 P
their harness studded all with gold and pearl. SHR in.2. 42
the studded bridle on a ragged bough | nimbly VEN 37

STUDENT 2 FR 0.0002 REL FR 1 V 1 P
negligent student! learn her by heart. LLL 3.01. 35 P
i prithee do not mock me, fellow student, | i HAM 1.02.177

STUDENTS 1 FR 0.0001 REL FR 1 V 0 P
another of these students at that time | was LLL 2.01. 64

STUDIED 17 FR 0.0019 REL FR 11 V 6 P
he hath studied her /well, and translated her WIV 1.03. 49 P
the state, whereon i studied, | is like a good MM 2.04. 7
i have studied eight or nine wise words to speak ADO 3.02. 71 P
now here is three studied ere ye'll thrice wink; LLL 1.02. 51 P
like one well studied in a sad ostent | to MV 2.02.196
from whence you have studied your questions. AYL 3.02.274 P
terms, | as had she studied to misuse me so. SHR 2.01.159
i can say little more than i have studied, and TN 1.05.178 P
what studied torments, tyrant, hast for me? WT 3.02.175
not be so loosely studied as to remember so weak 2H4 2.02. 8 P
studied so long, sat in the council–house 2H6 1.01. 90
more than could | my studied purposes requite, H8 3.02.168
as one that had been studied in his death, | to MAC 1.04. 9
for 'tis a studied, not a present thought, | by ANT 2.02.137
and am well studied for a liberal thanks, 2.06. 47
'tis known, i ever | have studied physic; PER 3.02. 32
o, 'twas a studied punishment, a death | beyond TNK 2.03. 4

STUDIENT 2 FR 0.0002 REL FR 0 V 2 P
the dice, and a good studient from his book, and WIV 3.01. 38 P
nor lean enough to be thought a good studient; TN 4.02. 8 P

STUDIES 13 FR 0.0014 REL FR 13 V 0 P
being transported | and rapt in secret studies. TMP 1.02. 77
made me neglect my studies, lose my time, | war TGV 1.01. 67
for interim to our studies shall relate, | in LLL 1.01.171
studies my lady? 5.02.837
of many desperate studies by his uncle, | whom AYL 5.04. 32
a course of learning and ingenious studies. SHR 1.01. 9
of man | after his studies or his usual pain? 3.01. 12
myself and them | bend their best studies — JN 4.02. 51
who studies day and night | to answer all the 1H4 1.03.184
all studies here i solemnly defy, | save how to 1.03.228
the prince but studies his companions | like a 2H4 4.04. 68
all your studies | make me a curse like this! H8 3.01.123
to use our utmost studies in your service. 3.01.174

STUDIOUS 2 FR 0.0002 REL FR 2 V 0 P
some to the studious universities. TGV 1.03. 10
but yet be wary in thy studious care. 1H6 2.05. 97

STUDIOUSLY 1 FR 0.0001 REL FR 1 V 0 P
with written pamphlets studiously devis'd? 1H6 3.01. 2

STUDS 2 FR 0.0002 REL FR 1 V 1 P
letters for her name fairly set down in studs, SHR 3.02. 62 P
ivy buds, | with coral clasps and amber studs: PP 19.14

STUDY 63 FR 0.0071 REL FR 50 V 13 P
those being all my study, | the government i TMP 1.02. 74
you make me study of that. 2.01. 83 P
my father | is hard at study; 3.01. 20
and study help for that which thou lament'st. TGV 3.01.244
do you study them both, master parson? WIV 3.01. 45 P
with profits of the mind — study and fast. MM 1.04. 61
no, and he were, i would burn my study. ADO 1.01. 80 P
sweetly creep | into his study of imagination, 4.01.225
that is, to live and study here three years. LLL 1.01. 35
not to see ladies, study, fast, not sleep. 1.01. 48
i only swore to study with your grace, | and 1.01. 51
what is the end of study, let me know. 1.01. 55
com' on then, i will swear to study so, | to 1.01. 59
as thus — to study where i well may dine, 1.01. 61
or study where to meet some mistress fine, 1.01. 63
study to break it and not break my troth. 1.01. 66
study knows that which yet it doth not know. 1.01. 68
these be the stops that hinder study quite, 1.01. 70
study me how to please the eye indeed | by 1.01. 80
study is like the heaven's glorious sun, | that 1.01. 84
so you, to study now it is too late, | climb 1.01.108
so study evermore is overshot: 1.01.142
while it doth study to have what it would, | it 1.01.143
and so to study three years is but short. 1.01.180
i have promised to study three years with the 1.02. 35 P
why, sir, is this such a piece of study? 1.02. 50 P
"three," and study three years in two words, the 1.02. 53 P
till painful study shall outwear three years, 2.01. 23
study his bias leaves, and makes his book thine 4.02.109
to fast, to study, and to see no woman — | flat 4.03.288
and where that you have vow'd to study, lords, 4.03.292
eyes, | and study too, the causer of your vow. 4.03.307
o, we have made a vow to study, lords, | and in 4.03.315
if it be, give it me, for i am slow of study. MND 1.02. 67 P
the one sleeps easily because he cannot study, AYL 3.02.321 P
my love deny, | and then i'll study how to die." 4.03. 63
it is my study | to seem despiteful and ungentle 5.02. 79
and therefore, tranio, for the time i study, SHR 1.01. 17
in brief, sir, study what you most affect. 1.01. 40
where did you study all this goodly speech? 2.01.262
alas, i took great pains to study it, and 'tis TN 1.05.194 P
to be more thankful to thee shall be my study, WT 4.02. 19 P
it hath it original from much grief, from study, 2H4 1.02.115 P
you would say it hath been all in all his study; H5 1.01. 42
and never noted in him any study, | any 1.01. 57
unless my study and my books be false, | the 1H6 2.04. 56
or who should study to prefer a peace, | if holy 3.01.110
and fitter is my study and my books | than 5.01. 22
his study is his tilt–yard, and his loves | are 2H6 1.03. 59
nor how to study for the people's welfare, | nor 3H6 4.03. 39
of tailors | to study fashions to adorn my body: R3 1.02.257
and with no little study, that my teaching | and H8 5.02. 69
knock at his study, where they say he keeps | to TIT 5.02. 5
fly away, | and all my study be to no effect? 5.02. 12
run to my study. ROM 3.03. 76
get me a taper in my study, lucius. JC 2.01. 7
for need, study a speech of some dozen lines, or HAM 2.02.541 P
sir, i shall study deserving. LR 1.01. 31 P
let your study | be to content your lord, who 1.01.276
what is your study? 3.04.158
and bids thee study on what fair demands | thou ANT 5.02. 10
the body of our sport, of no small study, | i TNK 3.05.121
study his bias leaves, and makes his book thine PP 5. 5

STUDYING 3 FR 0.0003 REL FR 2 V 1 P
that hath been long studying at rheims, as SHR 2.01. 80 P
i have been studying how i may compare | this R2 5.05. 1
night by night, in studying good for england. 2H6 3.01.111

STUDY'S 3 FR 0.0003 REL FR 3 V 0 P
ay, that is study's godlike recompense. LLL 1.01. 58
if study's gain be thus, and this be so, | study 1.01. 67
have found the ground of study's excellence 4.03.296

STUFF 52 FR 0.0058 REL FR 39 V 13 P
what stuff is this? TMP 2.01.254
we are such stuff | as dreams are made on; 4.01.156
our skins with pinches, | make us strange stuff. 4.01.234
o heavens, what stuff is here? MM 3.02. 4 P
to the centaur, fetch our stuff from thence; ERR 4.04.149
therefore away, to get our stuff aboard. 4.04.158
master, shall i fetch your stuff from shipboard? 5.01.409
dromio, what stuff of mine hast thou embark'd? 5.01.410
heart | of prouder stuff than that of beatrice. ADO 3.01. 50
i never knew man hold vile stuff so dear. LLL 4.03.272
this is the silliest stuff that ever i heard. MND 5.01.210 P
what stuff 'tis made of, whereof it is born, | i MV 1.01. 4
no, my good lord, it is more pleasing stuff. SHR in.2. 139
what, household stuff? in.2. 140 P
my household stuff, my field, my barn, | my 3.02.231
what masquing stuff is here? 4.03. 87
i gave him no order, i gave him the stuff. 4.03.118
to the garden for parsley to stuff a rabbit, and 4.04.101 P
youth's a stuff will not endure." TN 2.03. 52
do not seek to stuff | my head with more ill JN 4.02.133
with a foul traitor's name stuff i thy throat, R2 1.01. 44
go, i will stuff your purses full of crowns; 1H4 1.02.131 P
and such a deal of skimble–skamble stuff | as 3.01.152
merchant's venture of burdeaux stuff in him, you 2H4 2.04. 64 P
here's goodly stuff toward! 2.04.200 P
what stuff wilt have a kirtle of? 2.04.274 P
me your doublet and stuff me out with straw. 5.05. 82 P
there's in him stuff that puts him to these ends H8 1.01. 58
you are full of heavenly stuff, and bear the 3.02.137
at this fusty stuff | the large achilles, on his TRO 1.03.161
as stuff for these two to make paradoxes. 1.03.184
a grave as to stuff a botcher's cushion, or to COR 2.01. 88 P
who in spite put stuff | to some she–beggar and TIM 4.03.272
thy verse swells with stuff so fine and smooth 5.01. 84
ambition should be made of sterner stuff: JC 3.02. 92
o proper stuff! MAC 3.04. 59
cleanse the stuff'd bosom of that perilous stuff 5.03. 44
my lord, there was no such stuff in my thoughts. HAM 2.02.311 P
so i shall, | if it be made of penetrable stuff, 3.04. 36
that we are made of stuff so flat and dull 4.07. 31
king, it will stuff his suspicion more fully. LR 3.05. 21 P
yet do i hold it very stuff o' th' conscience OTH 1.02. 2
nature wants stuff | to vie strange forms with ANT 5.02. 97
think | so fair an outward and such stuff within CYM 1.01. 23
such boil'd stuff | as well might poison poison. 1.06.125
like his ancestry, | moulded the stuff so fair, 5.04. 49
or else such stuff as madmen | tongue and brain 5.04.145
did compound for her | a certain stuff, which, 5.05.255
the stuff we have, a strong wind will blow it to PER 4.02. 18 P
the circuit of my breast any gross stuff | to TNK 3.01. 46
what stuff she utters! 5.02. 68
stuff up his lust, as minutes fill up hours; LUC 297

STUFF'D 19 FR 0.0021 REL FR 12 V 7 P
i know they are stuff'd with protestations, TGV 4.04.129
to a man, stuff'd with all honorable virtues. ADO 1.01. 56 P
is so indeed, he is no less than a stuff'd man. 1.01. 58 P
of his cheek hath already stuff'd tennis–balls. 3.02. 47 P
i am stuff'd, cousin, i cannot smell. 3.04. 64 P
a maid, and stuff'd! 3.04. 65 P
in ivory coffers i have stuff'd my crowns; SHR 2.01.350
dion, whom you know | of stuff'd sufficiency. WT 2.01.185
my arms such eel–skins stuff'd, my face so thin JN 1.01.141
bombard of sack, that stuff'd cloak–bag of guts, 1H4 2.04.451 P
have not seen a hulk better stuff'd in the hold. 2H4 2.04. 65 P
but when we have stuff'd | these pipes and these COR 5.01. 53
stuff'd, as they say, with honorable parts, ROM 3.05.181
an alligator stuff'd, and other skins | of 5.01. 43
cleanse the stuff'd bosom of that perilous stuff MAC 5.03. 44
horribly stuff'd with epithites of war, | /and, OTH 1.01. 14
/hath stuff'd the hollow vessels with their PER 1.04. 67
are like the troyan horse was stuff'd within 1.04. 93
till either gorge be stuff'd, or prey be gone; VEN 58

STUFFING 2 FR 0.0002 REL FR 1 V 1 P
but for the stuffing — well, we are all mortal. ADO 1.01. 59 P
stuffing the ears of men with false reports. 2H4 in 8

STUFF'S 1 FR 0.0001 REL FR 0 V 1 P
what stuff's here? poor soul! TNK 4.03. 17 P

STUFFS 3 FR 0.0003 REL FR 3 V 0 P
rich garments, linens, stuffs, and necessaries, TMP 1.02.164

stuffs out his vacant garments with his form; JN 3.04. 97
rich stuffs, and ornaments of household, which H8 3.02.126
STUMBLE 9 FR 0.0010 REL FR 9 V 0 P
ay, madam, so you stumble not unheedfully. TGV 1.02. 3
did stumble with haste in his eyesight to be; LLL 2.01.239
it grows dark, he may stumble. 5.02.630
rein i let her run, | but she'll not stumble. WT 2.03. 52
would he not stumble? R2 5.05. 87
my tongue should stumble in mine earnest words, 2H6 3.02.316
for many men that stumble at the threshold | are 3H6 4.07. 11
times to–day my foot–cloth horse did stumble, R3 3.04. 84
wisely and slow, they stumble that run fast. ROM 2.03. 94
STUMBLED 4 FR 0.0004 REL FR 3 V 1 P
how he beat me because her horse stumbled, how SHR 4.01. 77 P
methought that gloucester stumbled, and in R3 1.04. 18
to–night | have my old feet stumbled at graves! ROM 5.03.122
i stumbled when i saw. LR 4.01. 19
STUMBLEST 1 FR 0.0001 REL FR 1 V 0 P
in night | so stumblest on my counsel? ROM 2.02. 53
STUMBLING 5 FR 0.0005 REL FR 3 V 2 P
being restrain'd to keep him from stumbling, SHR 3.02. 58 P
the stumbling night did part our weary pow'rs? JN 5.05. 18
in his flight, | stumbling in fear, was took. 2H4 1.01.131
than blind reason stumbling without fear. TRO 3.02. 72 P
revolts from true birth, stumbling on abuse. ROM 2.03. 20
STUMBLING–BLOCKS 1 FR 0.0001 REL FR 1 V 0 P
i would remove these tedious stumbling–blocks, 2H6 1.02. 64
STUMP 2 FR 0.0002 REL FR 2 V 0 P
my lord, | nor shall not while i have a stump. H8 1.03. 49
witness this wretched stump, witness these TIT 5.02. 22
/STUMPS 1 FR 0.0001 REL FR 1 V 0 P
/not /sigh, /nor /hold /thy /stumps /to /heaven, TIT 3.02. 42
STUMPS 2 FR 0.0002 REL FR 2 V 0 P
and if thy stumps will let thee play the scribe. TIT 2.04. 4
whiles that lavinia 'tween her stumps doth hold 5.02.182
STUNG 5 FR 0.0005 REL FR 4 V 1 P
than thine, thou serpent, never adder stung. MND 3.02. 73
nettled and stung with pismires, when i hear 1H4 1.03.240
i am stung like a tench. 2.01. 15 P
a serpent stung me, so the whole ear of denmark HAM 1.05. 36
of the other, as the stung | are of the adder. LR 5.01. 56
STUNK 1 FR 0.0001 REL FR 1 V 0 P
for they so stunk, | that all those eyes ador'd PER 2.04. 10
STUPEFIED 1 FR 0.0001 REL FR 1 V 0 P
you — or stupefied | or seeming so in skill — WT 2.01.165
STUPEFY 1 FR 0.0001 REL FR 1 V 0 P
has | will stupefy and dull the sense awhile, CYM 1.05. 37
STUPID 1 FR 0.0001 REL FR 1 V 0 P
is he not stupid | with age and alt'ring rheums? WT 4.04.398
STUPRUM 1 FR 0.0001 REL FR 1 V 0 P
"stuprum — chiron — demetrius." TIT 4.01. 78
STURDY 2 FR 0.0002 REL FR 2 V 0 P
my lords, look where the sturdy rebel sits, 3H6 1.01. 50
forceless flowers like sturdy trees support me; VEN 152
STY 5 FR 0.0005 REL FR 5 V 0 P
and here you sty me | in this hard rock, whiles TMP 1.02.342
that in the sty of the most deadly boar | my son R3 4.05. 2
honeying and making love | over the nasty sty! HAM 3.04. 94
which in thy absence is | no better than a sty? ANT 4.15. 62
ungentle fortune | have plac'd me in this sty, PER 4.06. 97
STYGIA 1 FR 0.0001 REL FR 1 V 0 P
calm these fits, | per stygia, per manes vehor. TIT 2.01.135
STYGIAN 1 FR 0.0001 REL FR 1 V 0 P
like to a strange soul upon the stygian banks TRO 3.02. 9
STYL'D 3 FR 0.0003 REL FR 3 V 0 P
to be styl'd | the under–hangman of his kingdom, CYM 2.03.129
in that honor | first nature styl'd it in — TNK 1.01. 83
and by thee | be styl'd the lord o' th' day. 5.01. 60
STYLE 19 FR 0.0021 REL FR 14 V 5 P
i can construe the action of her familiar style, WIV 1.03. 47 P
ford's a knave, and i will aggravate his style; 2.02.284 P
however they have writ the style of gods, | and ADO 5.01. 37
in so high a style, margaret, that no man living 5.02. 6 P
be it as the style shall give us cause to climb LLL 1.01.199 P
i am much deceived but i remember the style. 4.01. 96
of fortune | into so quiet and so sweet a style. AYL 2.01. 20
why, 'tis a boisterous and a cruel style, | a 4.03. 31
and a cruel style, | a style for challengers. 4.03. 32
count's master is of another style. AWW 2.03.195 P
means his grace, that he hath chang'd his style? 1H6 4.01. 50
here's a silly stately style indeed! 4.07. 72
hath, | writes not so tedious a style as this. 4.07. 74
whose large style | agrees not with the leanness 2H6 1.01.111
am i a queen in title and in style, | and must 1.03. 48
plain and not honest is too harsh a style. R3 4.04.360
theirs for their style i'll read, his for his SON 32.14
in others' works thou dost but mend the style, 78.11
his wit, | making his style admired every where. 84.12
STYX 2 FR 0.0002 REL FR 2 V 0 P
fly not, for shouldst thou take the river styx, TRO 5.04. 19
yet, | to hover on the dreadful shore of styx? TIT 1.01. 88
SUB 1 FR 0.0001 REL FR 0 V 1 P
gelida quando /pecus /omne sub umbra ruminat — LLL 4.02. 94 P
SUB–CONTRACTED 1 FR 0.0001 REL FR 1 V 0 P
'tis she is sub–contracted to this lord, | and i LR 5.03. 86
SUBDU'D 19 FR 0.0021 REL FR 18 V 1 P
nor this man's threats | to whom i am subdu'd, TMP 1.02.490
their cheer is the greater that i am subdu'd. ADO 1.03. 72 P
with her modern grace, | subdu'd me to her rate. AWW 5.03.217
charles the great, having subdu'd the saxons, H5 1.02. 46
and charles the great | subdu'd the saxons, and 1.02. 62
my heart and hands thou hast at once subdu'd. 1H6 1.02.109
tugg'd for life, and was by strength subdu'd. 2H6 3.02.173
by many hands your father was subdu'd, | but 3H6 2.01. 56
and being once subdu'd in armed tail, | sweet TRO 5.10. 43
nothing could have subdu'd nature | to such a LR 3.04. 70
my heart's subdu'd | even to the very quality of OTH 1.03.250
of one whose subdu'd eyes, | albeit unused to 5.02.348
caesar, thou hast subdu'd | his judgment too. ANT 3.13. 36
neck, his face subdu'd | to penetrative shame, 4.14. 74
of nature's, have subdu'd me | in my profession? CYM 5.02. 5
do, being sensually subdu'd | we lose our human TNK 1.01.232
for the subdu'd, | give them our present justice 5.03.131
and almost thence my nature is subdu'd | to what SON 111. 6
of pensiv'd and subdu'd desires the tender, LC 219
SUBDUE 11 FR 0.0012 REL FR 10 V 1 P
he doth with holy abstinence subdue | that in MM 4.02. 81
be called boy, but his glory is to subdue men. LLL 1.02.180 P
i think affliction may subdue the cheek, | but WT 4.04.576
which did subdue the greatest part of spain; 3H6 3.03. 82
him, if he do resist | subdue him at his peril. OTH 1.02. 81
subdue and poison this young maid's affections? 1.03.112
th' inclining desdemona to subdue | in any 2.03.340
and subdue my father | entirely to her love; 3.04. 59
the heaviest club, | subdue my worthiest self. ANT 4.12. 47
asprays do the fish, | subdue before they touch. TNK 1.01.139
her eye | upon the moment did her force subdue, LC 248
SUBDUED 1 FR 0.0001 REL FR 1 V 0 P
for then both parties nobly are subdued, | and 2H4 4.02. 90
SUBDUEMENTS 1 FR 0.0001 REL FR 1 V 0 P
despising many forfeits and subduements, | when TRO 4.05.187
SUBDUES 5 FR 0.0005 REL FR 5 V 0 P
but this virtuous maid | subdues me quite. MM 2.02.185
we may afford | to any lady that subdues a lord. LLL 4.01. 40
to make him worthy whose offense subdues him, COR 1.01.175
subdues and properties to his love and tendance TIM 1.01. 57
a touch more rare | subdues all pangs, all fears CYM 1.01.136
SUBDUING 2 FR 0.0002 REL FR 2 V 0 P
at once subduing | thy force and thy affection; TNK 1.01. 84
"so on the tip of his subduing tongue | all kind LC 120
/SUBJECT 4 FR 0.0004 REL FR 3 V 1 P
/proud /majesty /a /subject, /state /a /peasant. R2 4.01.252
/being /now /a /subject, | /i /have /a /king 4.01.307
/the /dry /suppeago /on /the /subject, /and /war TRO 2.03. 75 P
/for /he /himself /is /subject /to /his /birth: HAM 1.03. 18
SUBJECT 101 FR 0.0114 REL FR 82 V 19 P
subject his coronet to his crown, and bend | the TMP 1.02.114
be subject | to no sight but thine and mine, 1.02.301
swear upon that bottle to be thy true subject, 2.02.125 P
i'll swear myself thy subject. 2.02.152
the poor monster's my subject, and he shall not 3.02. 37 P
as i told thee before, i am subject to a tyrant, 3.02. 42
teach me, thy tempted subject, to excuse it! TGV 2.06. 8
of my beauty, and am i now a subject for them? WIV 2.01. 3 P
of that — that am as subject to heat as butter; 3.05.115 P
so | the general subject to a well–wish'd king MM 2.04. 27
greater file of the subject held the duke to be 3.02.136 P
and let the subject see, to make them know 5.01. 14
his subject am i not, | nor here provincial. 5.01.315
which of these sorrows is he subject to? ERR 5.01. 54
alone, it was the subject of my theme; 5.01. 65
i pray you choose another subject. ADO 5.01.137 P
i will have that subject newly writ o'er, that i LLL 1.02.115 P
the same weapons, subject to the same diseases, MV 3.01. 61 P
i am th' unhappy subject of these quarrels. 5.01.238
i rather will subject me to the malice | of a AYL 2.03. 36
such duty as the subject owes the prince, | even SHR 5.02.155
indeed, physics the subject, makes old hearts WT 1.01. 39 P
you'll leave yourself | hardly one subject. 2.03.112
to the faith and allegiance of a true subject, 3.02. 19 P
polixenes blameless, camillo a true subject, 3.02.133 P
your faithful subject i, a gentleman, | born in JN 1.01. 50
but we will make it subject to this boy. 2.01. 43
fears, | a widow, husbandless, subject to fears, 3.01. 14
o, let me have no subject enemies | when adverse 4.02.171
malice, | or worthily, as a good subject should, R2 1.01. 10
he is our subject, mowbray; 1.01.122
i am a subject, | and i challenge law. 2.03.133
a puny subject strikes | at thy great glory. 3.02. 86
i would my skill were subject to thy curse. 3.04.103
what subject can give sentence on his king? 4.01.121
and who sits here that is not richard's subject? 4.01.122
be judg'd by subject and inferior breath, | and 4.01.128
i speak to subjects, and a subject speaks, 4.01.132
cost | a naked subject to the weeping clouds 2H4 1.03. 61
very hardly, upon such a subject. 2.02. 44 P
the part of a careful friend and a true subject, 2.04.322 P
how subject we old men are to this vice of lying 3.02.303 P
and a famous true subject took him. 4.03. 64 P
most subject is the fattest soil to weeds, | and 4.04. 54
unto whose grace our passion is as subject | as H5 1.02.242
think, a subject | that sits in heart–grief and 2.02. 26
never did faithful subject more rejoice | at the 2.02.161
'tis a subject for a sovereign to reason on, and 3.07. 35 P
subject to the breath | of every fool whose 4.01.234
to be shame's scorn and subject of mischance! 1H6 4.06. 49
style, | and must be made a subject to a duke? 2H6 1.03. 49
having neither subject, wealth, nor diadem. 4.01. 82
was never subject long'd to be a king | as i do 4.09. 5
a king | as i do long and wish to be a subject. 4.09. 6
or why thou, being a subject as i am, | against 5.01. 19
i am too mean a subject for thy wrath, | be thou 3H6 1.03. 19
that's soon perform'd, because i am a subject. 3.02. 54
i am a subject fit to jest withal, | but far 3.02. 91
of storm, | as every loyal subject ought to do. 4.07. 44
and henry is my king, warwick his subject. 5.01. 38
speak like a subject, proud ambitious york! 5.05. 17
to–day shalt thou behold a subject die | for R3 3.03. 3
and prov'd the subject of mine own soul's curse, 4.01. 80
james tyrrel, and your most obedient subject. 4.02. 67
say i, her sovereign, am her subject low. 4.04.355
but she, your subject, loathes such sovereignty. 4.04.356
the subject will deserve it. H8 pr 7
most like a careful subject, have collected 1.02.130
his master would be serv'd before a subject, if 2.02. 8 P
yea, subject to your countenance — glad, or 2.04. 26
desperate to be honest), | and live a subject? 3.01. 87
that it outspeaks | possession of a subject. 3.02.128
a loyal and obedient subject is | therein 3.02.180
if a prince | may be beholding to a subject, i 5.02.191
it, | that am a poor and humble subject to you? 5.02.200
it is too starv'd a subject for my sword. TRO 1.01. 93
whose height commands as subject all the vale, 1.02. 3
or death unfam'd, | where helen is the subject. 2.02.160
stratagems | upon so soft a subject as myself! ROM 3.05.210
must be thy subject, who in spite put stuff | to TIM 4.03.272
thou be, that were not subject to a beast? 4.03.344 P
well, honor is the subject of my story: JC 1.02. 92
first, as i am his kinsman and his subject, MAC 1.07. 13
and near approaches | the subject of our watch. 3.03. 8
so nightly toils the subject of the land, | and HAM 1.01. 72
proportions are all made | out of his subject; 1.02. 33
be'st as poor for a subject as he's for a king, LR 1.04. 21 P
when i do stare, see how the subject quakes. 4.06.108
i hold you but a subject of this war, | not as a 5.03. 60
that your royalty | holds idleness your subject, ANT 1.03. 92
notes | of what commands i should be subject to, CYM 1.01.172
great king, a subject who | was call'd belarius. 5.05.316
how from the /finny subject of the sea | these PER 2.01. 48
making it subject to the tyranny | of mad VEN 737
whereat each tributary subject quakes, | as when 1045
sire, | subject and servile to all discontents, 1161
how can my muse want subject to invent | while SON 38. 1
words which writers use | of their fair subject, 82. 4
that to his subject lends not some small glory, 84. 6
mend, | to mar the subject that before was well? 103.10
as subject to time's love, or to time's hate, 124. 3
SUBJECTED 2 FR 0.0002 REL FR 2 V 0 P
dispose, | subjected tribute to commanding love, JN 1.01.264
subjected thus, | how can you say to me i am a R2 3.02.176
SUBJECTION 7 FR 0.0008 REL FR 5 V 2 P
whom i am now in ward, evermore in subjection. AWW 1.01. 5 P
services | and true subjection everlastingly. JN 5.07.105
were against all proportion of subjection. H5 4.01.146 P
perform | all parts of his subjection loyally. CYM 4.03. 19
i'll bring you in subjection. PER 2.05. 75
and by their mortal fault brought in subjection LUC 724
proud of subjection, noble by the sway, | what LC 108
SUBJECT'S 6 FR 0.0006 REL FR 4 V 2 P
speech, | in the devotion of a subject's love, R2 1.01. 31
every subject's duty is the king's, but every H5 4.01.176 P
the king's, but every subject's soul is his own. 4.01.177 P
the subject's grief | comes through commissions, H8 1.02. 56
thou show'dst a subject's shine, i a true PER 1.02.124
force the king | to be his subject's vassal, and TNK 5.01. 84
SUBJECTS' 6 FR 0.0006 REL FR 6 V 0 P
his, | and he our subjects' next degree in hope. R2 1.04. 36
where subjects' feet | may hourly trample on 3.03.156
to kings that fear their subjects' treachery? 3H6 2.05. 45
was ever king so griev'd for subjects' woe? 2.05.111
the care i had and have of subjects' good | on PER 1.02.118
where subjects' eyes do learn, do read, do look. LUC 616
/SUBJECTS 1 FR 0.0001 REL FR 1 V 0 P
/my /flatterers | /were /then /but /subjects; R2 4.01.307
SUBJECTS 60 FR 0.0067 REL FR 50 V 10 P
for i am all the subjects that you have, | which TMP 1.02.341
no marrying 'mong his subjects? 2.01.166 P
i few attendants, | and subjects none abroad. 5.01.167
think, i think and pray | to several subjects. MM 2.04. 2
thoughts are no subjects, | intents but merely 5.01.453
are their males' subjects and at their controls: ERR 2.01. 19
is bidden, he is none of the prince's subjects. ADO 3.03. 32 P
to meddle with none but the prince's subjects. 3.03. 34 P
varying in subjects as the eye doth roll | to LLL 5.02.764
even as the flourish when true subjects bow | to MV 3.02. 49
you men of angiers, and my loving subjects — JN 2.01.203
you loving men of angiers, arthur's subjects, 2.01.204
in brief, we are the king of england's subjects: 2.01.267
us, our state, our subjects, or our land. R2 1.03.190
revolt our subjects? 3.02.100
my subjects for a pair of carved saints, | and 3.03.152
i speak to subjects, and a subject speaks, 4.01.132
to bullingbrook are we sworn subjects now, 5.02. 39
and drive all thy subjects afore thee like a 1H4 2.04.137 P
doth not the king lack subjects? 2H4 1.02. 74 P
we are time's subjects, and time bids be gone. 1.03.110
how many thousand of my poorest subjects | are 3.01. 4
the subjects of his substitute, my father, | and 4.02. 28
had nobles richer and more loyal subjects, H5 1.02.127
his subjects to oppression and contempt, | and 2.02.172
as we his subjects have in wonder found, 2.04.135
losses we have borne, the subjects we have lost, 3.06.127 P
enough, if we know we are the king's subjects. 4.01.131 P
as can be desir'd in the hearts of his subjects. 4.07.161 P
amongst his subjects and his loyal friends, | as 1H6 3.01.181
of foot, | and, like true subjects, sons of your 4.01.166
yours, | and do him homage as obedient subjects, 4.02. 7
to save your subjects from such massacre | and 5.04.160
good, | the nevils are thy subjects to command. 2H6 2.02. 8
and we his subjects, sworn in all allegiance, 3H6 3.01. 70
and you were sworn true subjects unto me; 3.01. 78
for we were subjects but while you were king. 3.01. 81
we are true subjects to the king, king edward. 3.01. 94
subjects may challenge nothing of their 4.06. 6
his realm a slaughter–house, his subjects slain, 5.04. 78
for bearing arms, for stirring up my subjects, 5.05. 15
if not, that i am queen, you bow like subjects, R3 1.03.160
teach me to be your queen, and you my subjects: 1.03.251
live each of you the subjects to his hate, | and 1.03.301
or like obedient subjects follow him | to his 2.02. 45
that your subjects | are in great grievance: H8 1.02. 19
we must not rend our subjects from our laws, 1.02. 93
are subjects all | to envious and calumniating TRO 3.03.173
encounter such ridiculous subjects as you are. COR 2.01. 85 P
rebellious subjects, enemies to peace, ROM 1.01. 81
our subjects, sir, | will not endure his yoke; CYM 3.05. 4
publish we this peace | to all our subjects. 5.05.479
graces her subjects, and her thoughts the king PER 1.01. 13
and subjects punish'd that ne'er thought offense 1.02. 28
are arms to princes and bring joys to subjects. 1.02. 74
he gains from his subjects the name of good by 2.01.105 P
go search like nobles, like noble subjects, 2.04. 50
says, her subjects with foul insurrection | have LUC 722
to subjects worse have given admiring praise. SON 59.14
dark'ning thy pow'r to lend base subjects light? 100. 4
SUBMERG'D 1 FR 0.0001 REL FR 1 V 0 P
so half my egypt were submerg'd and made | a ANT 2.05. 94
/SUBMISSION 1 FR 0.0001 REL FR 1 V 0 P
/while /to /tutor /me | /to /this /submission. R2 4.01.167
SUBMISSION 10 FR 0.0011 REL FR 10 V 0 P
be not as extreme in submission as in offense; WIV 4.04. 11
to whom with all submission, on my knee, | i do JN 5.07.103
irregular, | find pardon on my true submission. 1H4 3.02. 28
thanks, | and in submission will attend on her. 1H6 2.02. 52
submission, dolphin? 4.07. 54
that all the court admir'd him for submission; 2H6 3.01. 12
york, i commend this kind submission; 5.01. 54
in all submission and humility | york doth 5.01. 58
fled | that in submission will return to us, R3 5.05. 17
o calm, dishonorable, vile submission! ROM 3.01. 73
SUBMISSIVE 4 FR 0.0004 REL FR 4 V 0 P
submissive fall his princely feet before, | and LLL 4.01. 90

and with a low submissive reverence | say, "what SHR in.1. 53
and with submissive loyalty of heart | ascribes 1H6 3.04. 10
on what submissive message art thou sent? 4.07. 53
SUBMIT 13 FR 0.0014 REL FR 12 V 1 P
when we should submit ourselves to an unknown AWW 2.03. 5 P
for i submit | my fancy to your eyes. 2.03.167
submit thee, boy. JN 2.01.159
his head, | unless he do submit himself to rome. 3.01.194
must he submit? R2 3.03.143
and do submit me to your highness' mercy. H5 2.02. 77
he shall submit, or i will never yield. 1H6 3.01.118
now winchester will not submit, i trow, | or be 5.01. 56
swear | to pay him tribute and submit thyself, 5.04.130
if you submit you to the people's voices, COR 3.03. 44
although the victor, we submit to caesar, | and CYM 5.05.460
reign, | we thus submit unto — our sovereign. PER 2.04. 39
submit you to these noble gentlemen, | entreat STM II.C 144
SUBMITS 1 FR 0.0001 REL FR 1 V 0 P
submits her to thy might, and of thee craves ANT 3.12. 17
SUBMITTING 1 FR 0.0001 REL FR 1 V 0 P
submitting me unto the perilous night; JC 1.03. 47
SUBORN 1 FR 0.0001 REL FR 1 V 0 P
who i did suborn | to do this piece of /ruthless R3 4.03. 4
SUBORNATION 4 FR 0.0004 REL FR 4 V 0 P
the detested blot | of murtherous subornation — 1H4 1.03.163
the duchess by his subornation, | upon my life, 2H6 3.01. 45
foul subornation is predominant, | and equity 3.01.145
of theft, | guilty of perjury and subornation, LUC 919
SUBORN'D 7 FR 0.0008 REL FR 7 V 0 P
or else thou art suborn'd against his honor | in MM 5.01.106
is't not enough thou hast suborn'd these women 5.01.306
thou hast suborn'd the goldsmith to arrest me. ERR 4.04. 82
what peer hath been suborn'd to grate on you? 2H4 4.01. 90
you have suborn'd this man | of purpose to 1H6 5.04. 21
but now i find i had suborn'd the witness, | and OTH 3.04.153
hence, thou suborn'd informer! SON 125.13
SUBORNED 2 FR 0.0002 REL FR 2 V 0 P
as if she had suborned some to swear | false 2H6 3.01.180
they were suborned. MAC 2.04. 24
/SUBSCRIB'D 1 FR 0.0001 REL FR 1 V 0 P
/subscrib'd it, gave't th' impression, plac'd it HAM 5.02. 52
SUBSCRIB'D 3 FR 0.0003 REL FR 2 V 1 P
reading the challenge, subscrib'd for cupid, and ADO 1.01. 41 P
but when i had subscrib'd | to mine own fortune, AWW 5.03. 96
subscrib'd by th' consuls and patricians, COR 5.06. 81
SUBSCRIBE 16 FR 0.0018 REL FR 12 V 4 P
unrivall'd merit, | to which i thus subscribe: TGV 5.04.145
way to save his life | (as i subscribe not that, MM 2.04. 89
hear from him, or i will subscribe him a coward. ADO 5.02. 58 P
oaths are pass'd, and now subscribe your names, LLL 1.01. 19
subscribe to your deep oaths, and keep it too. 1.01. 23
sir, to your pleasure humbly i subscribe; SHR 1.01. 81
of thy soldiership will subscribe for thee. AWW 3.06. 83 P
i will subscribe for thee, thou art both knave 4.05. 32 P
they shall subscribe them for large sums of gold R2 1.04. 50
if i have fewest, i subscribe in silence. 1H6 2.04. 44
i will subscribe, and say i wrong'd the duke. 2H6 3.01. 38
will you subscribe his thought, and say he is? TRO 2.03.147 P
done, | and we will all subscribe to thy advice: TIT 4.02.130
all cruels else subscribe; LR 3.07. 65
write to him | (i will subscribe) gentle adieus ANT 4.05. 14
or my hand subscribe | to any syllable that made PER 2.05. 69
SUBSCRIBED 1 FR 0.0001 REL FR 1 V 0 P
only he hath not yet subscribed this: H5 5.02.335
SUBSCRIBES 2 FR 0.0002 REL FR 2 V 0 P
for hector in his blaze of wrath subscribes | to TRO 4.05.105
my love looks fresh, and death to me subscribes, SON 107.10
SUBSCRIPTION 1 FR 0.0001 REL FR 1 V 0 P
you owe me no subscription. LR 3.02. 18
SUBSEQUENT 1 FR 0.0001 REL FR 1 V 0 P
small pricks | to their subsequent volumes) TRO 1.03.344
SUBSIDIES 1 FR 0.0001 REL FR 1 V 0 P
nor much oppress'd them with great subsidies, 3H6 4.08. 45
SUBSIDY 1 FR 0.0001 REL FR 0 V 1 P
and one shilling to the pound, the last subsidy. 2H6 4.07. 23 P
SUBSIST 1 FR 0.0001 REL FR 1 V 0 P
and heart | have faculty by nature to subsist, SON 122. 6
SUBSISTING 1 FR 0.0001 REL FR 1 V 0 P
but still subsisting | under your great command. COR 5.06. 72
/SUBSTANCE 2 FR 0.0002 REL FR 1 V 1 P
/there /lies /the /substance; R2 4.01.299
/for /the /very /substance /of /the /ambitious HAM 2.02.258 P
SUBSTANCE 40 FR 0.0045 REL FR 36 V 4 P
you take the sum and substance that i have. TGV 4.01. 15
for since the substance of your perfect self 4.02.123
if 'twere a substance, you would sure deceive it 4.02.126
my substance should be statue in thy stead. 4.04.201
i ken the wight; he is of substance good. WIV 1.03. 37 P
like a shadow flies when substance love pursues, 2.02.207
in his fortunes with the finger of my substance. 3.02. 75 P
thy substance, valued at the highest rate, ERR 1.01. 23
far | the substance of my praise doth wrong this MV 3.02.127
this shadow | doth limp behind the substance. 3.02.129
as makes it light or heavy in the substance | or 4.01.328
each substance of a grief hath twenty shadows, R2 2.02. 14
strong and great in substance and in power. 3.02. 35
all of one nature, of one substance bred, | did 1H4 1.01. 11
he hath put all my substance into that fat belly 2H4 2.01. 75 P
so indeed, but much of the father's substance! 3.02.131 P
their cold intent, tenure, and substance thus: 4.01. 9
i in chief address | the substance of my speech. 4.01. 32
but now the substance shall endure the like, 1H6 2.03. 38
then have i substance too. 2.03. 49
you are deceiv'd, my substance is not here; 2.03. 51
these are his substance, sinews, arms, and 2.03. 63
coronet, | and yet, in substance and authority, 5.04.135
that are the substance | of that great shadow i 2H6 1.01. 13
than can the substance of ten thousand soldiers R3 5.03.218
from each | the sixt part of his substance, to H8 1.02. 58
then, that you have sent innumerable substance 3.02.326
true, the purpose is perspicuous as substance, TRO 1.03.324
dear father, soul and substance of us all — TIT 1.01.374
which is as thin of substance as the air, | and ROM 1.04. 99
brags of his substance, not of ornament; 2.06. 31
despised substance of divinest show! 3.02. 77
doth all the noble substance of a doubt | to his HAM 1.04. 37
if aught within that little seeming substance, LR 1.01.198
hast heavy substance, bleed'st not, speak'st, 4.06. 52

man | is but a substance that must yield to you; PER 2.01. 3
their show, their substance still lives sweet. SON 5.14
that this shadow doth such substance give, 37.10
if the dull substance of my flesh were thought, 44. 1
what is your substance, whereof are you made, 53. 1
/SUBSTANCES 1 FR 0.0001 REL FR 1 V 0 P
/takes /false /shadows /for /true /substances. TIT 3.02. 80
SUBSTANCES 1 FR 0.0001 REL FR 1 V 0 P
wherever in your sightless substances | you wait MAC 1.05. 49
SUBSTANTIAL 4 FR 0.0004 REL FR 3 V 1 P
strings | most ponderous and substantial things! MM 3.02.276
but your reason was not substantial, why there ERR 2.02.104 P
acquitted by a true substantial form | and 2H4 4.01.171
dream, | too flattering–sweet to be substantial. ROM 2.02.141
SUBSTITUTE 11 FR 0.0012 REL FR 9 V 2 P
how will you do to content this substitute, and MM 3.01.188 P
wretched woman here | against our substitute! 5.01.133
woman | most wrongfully accus'd your substitute, 5.01.140
a substitute shines brightly as a king | until a MV 5.01. 94
god's is the quarrel, for god's substitute, R2 1.02. 37
the subjects of his substitute, my father, | and 2H4 4.02. 28
this devil here shall be my substitute; 2H6 3.01.371
not as protector, steward, substitute, | or R3 3.07.133
and afterward by substitute betroth'd | to bona, 3.07.181
we have there a substitute of most allow'd OTH 1.03.223 P
tyre, | i left behind an ancient substitute. PER 5.03. 51
SUBSTITUTED 2 FR 0.0002 REL FR 2 V 0 P
but who is substituted against the french, | i 2H4 1.03. 84
heir, | and substituted in the place of mine, TIT 4.02.159
SUBSTITUTES 4 FR 0.0004 REL FR 3 V 1 P
to him, and to his substitutes. MM 4.02.184 P
our substitutes at home shall have blank R2 1.04. 48
our substitutes in absence well invested, | and 2H4 4.04. 6
that are substitutes | under the lordly monarch 1H6 5.03. 5
SUBSTITUTION 1 FR 0.0001 REL FR 1 V 0 P
he was indeed the duke, out o' th' substitution, TMP 1.02.103
SUBSTRACTORS 1 FR 0.0001 REL FR 0 V 1 P
scoundrels and substractors that say so of him. TN 1.03. 34 P
SUBTILE 16 FR 0.0018 REL FR 16 V 0 P
thou subtile, perjur'd, false, disloyal man, TGV 4.02. 95
subtile as sphinx, as sweet and musical | as LLL 4.03.339
she is too subtile for thee, and her smoothness, AYL 1.03. 77
wherein you range under this subtile king! 1H4 1.03.169
a subtile knave, but yet it shall not serve. 2H6 2.01.102
was not incensed by his subtile mother | to R3 3.01.152
that the subtile traitor | this day had plotted, 3.05. 37
(for he is equal rav'nous | as he is subtile, H8 1.01.160
fine, | too subtile, potent, tun'd too sharp in TRO 3.02. 24
nor play at subtile games — fair virtues all, 4.04. 87
how comes it that the subtile queen of goths TIT 1.01.392
what subtile hole is this, | whose mouth is 2.03.198
when subtile greeks surpris'd king priam's troy. 5.03. 84
this is a subtile whore, | a closet lock and key OTH 4.02. 21
"for even as subtile sinon here is painted, | so LUC 1541
talk, | lest she some subtile practice smell — PP 18. 9
SUBTILE–WITTED 1 FR 0.0001 REL FR 1 V 0 P
or shall we think the subtile–witted french 1H6 1.01. 25
SUBTILLY 2 FR 0.0002 REL FR 2 V 0 P
that play'st so subtilly with a king's repose. H5 4.01.258
subtilly hath minist'red to have me dead, | lest ROM 4.03. 25
SUBTILTIES 1 FR 0.0001 REL FR 1 V 0 P
unlearned in the world's false subtilties. SON 138. 4
SUBTILTY 2 FR 0.0002 REL FR 2 V 0 P
'tis the king's subtilty to have my life. PER 2.05. 44
hare, | or at the fox which lives by subtilty, VEN 675
SUBTLE 21 FR 0.0023 REL FR 17 V 4 P
it must needs be of subtle, tender, and delicate TMP 2.01. 42 P
ay, and a subtle, as he most learnedly deliver'd 2.01. 45 P
am i subtle? WIV 3.01.101 P
with an invisible and subtle stealth | to creep TN 1.05.297
a subtle traitor needs no sophister. 2H6 5.01.191
for warwick is a subtle orator, | and lewis a 3H6 3.01. 33
edward be as true and just | as i am subtle, R3 1.01. 37
thy age confirm'd, proud, subtle, sly, and 4.04.172
admits no orifex for a point as subtle | as TRO 5.02.151
bolder, though not so subtle. COR 1.10. 17
like to a bowl upon a subtle ground, | i have 5.02. 20
go, suck the subtle blood o' th' grape, | till TIM 4.03.429
is not thy kindness subtle, covetous, | if not a 4.03.508
and let our hearts, as subtle masters do, | stir JC 2.01.175
distinguishes the swift, the slow, the subtle, MAC 3.01. 95
none, why, none — a slipper and subtle knave, a OTH 2.01.242 P
subtle as the fox for prey, | like warlike as CYM 3.03. 40
nor read the subtle shining secrecies | writ in LUC 101
swift subtle post, carrier of grisly care, 926
to mock the subtle in themselves beguil'd, | to 957
"in him a plenitude of subtle matter, | applied LC 302
SUBTLER 1 FR 0.0001 REL FR 1 V 0 P
never fortune | did play a subtler game. TNK 5.04.113
SUBTLETIES 1 FR 0.0001 REL FR 1 V 0 P
you do yet taste | some subtleties o' th' isle, TMP 5.01.124
SUBTLETY 1 FR 0.0001 REL FR 1 V 0 P
be it by gins, by snares, by subtlety, 2H6 3.01.262
SUBTLY 1 FR 0.0001 REL FR 1 V 0 P
subtly taints | even then when they sit idly in TRO 3.03.232
SUBURBS 8 FR 0.0009 REL FR 5 V 3 P
all houses in the suburbs of vienna must be MM 1.02. 95 P
houses of resort in the suburbs be pull'd down? 1.02.102 P
was (as they say) pluck'd down in the suburbs; 2.01. 65 P
in the south suburbs at the elephant | is best TN 3.03. 39
and how the english have the suburbs won. 1H6 1.04. 2
the english, in the suburbs close intrench'd, 1.04. 9
these | your faithful friends o' th' suburbs? H8 5.03. 72
dwell i but in the suburbs | of your good JC 2.01.285
SUBVERSION 1 FR 0.0001 REL FR 1 V 0 P
do seek subversion of thy harmless life? 2H6 3.01.208
SUBVERTS 1 FR 0.0001 REL FR 1 V 0 P
razeth your cities, and subverts your towns, 1H6 2.03. 65
/SUCCEDANT 1 FR 0.0001 REL FR 1 V 0 P
"in terram salicam mulieres ne /succedant," H5 1.02. 38
SUCCEED 16 FR 0.0018 REL FR 15 V 1 P
but only he, | owe and succeed thy weakness. MM 2.04.123
bertram, and succeed thy father | in manners, as AWW 1.01. 61
"no woman shall succeed in salique land"; H5 1.02. 39
of france and england, did this king succeed; ep 10
of the elder son | succeed before the younger, i 2H6 2.02. 52
but that the next heir should succeed and reign. 3H6 1.01.146
if you be king, why should not i succeed? 1.01.227

who should succeed the father but the son? 2.02. 94
living with her, | and all that shall succeed. H8 5.04. 23
whom worthily you would have now succeed, | and TIT 1.01. 40
ways than ever, | by him that shall succeed. MAC 4.03. 49
the effects he writes of succeed unhappily, /as LR 1.02.143 P
fortunes of the moor, | for they succeed on you. OTH 5.02.367
bethought what was past, what might succeed. PER 1.02. 83
an heir | that may succeed as his inheritor; 1.04. 64
the curse of heaven and men succeed their evils! 1.04.104
SUCCEEDED 1 FR 0.0001 REL FR 1 V 0 P
that downward hath succeeded in his house | from AWW 3.07. 23
SUCCEEDERS 2 FR 0.0002 REL FR 2 V 0 P
woes, | aery succeeders of /intestate joys, R3 4.04.128
the true succeeders of each royal house, | by 5.05. 30
SUCCEEDING 10 FR 0.0011 REL FR 9 V 1 P
not to be understood without bloody succeeding. AWW 2.03.191 P
to god, my king, and my succeeding issue, R2 1.03. 20
the fift | (succeeding his father bullingbrook) 1H6 2.05. 83
which, since, succeeding ages have re–edified. R3 3.01. 71
henry the seventh succeeding, truly pitying | my H8 2.01.112
an unlineal hand, | no son of mine succeeding. MAC 3.01. 63
to the succeeding royalty he leaves | the 4.03.155
succeeding from so fair a tree | as your fair PER 1.01.114
and sung by children in succeeding times. LUC 525
allow | for beauty's pattern to succeeding men. SON 19.12
SUCCEEDS 3 FR 0.0003 REL FR 3 V 0 P
court, | not amurath an amurath succeeds, | but 2H4 5.02. 48
and after summer evermore succeeds | barren 2H6 2.04. 2
comfort like to this | succeeds in unknown fate. OTH 2.01.193
SUCCESS 54 FR 0.0061 REL FR 47 V 7 P
and on a love–book pray for my success? TGV 1.01. 19
from thee by letters | of thy success in love, 1.01. 58
i'll send him certain word of my success. MM 1.04. 89
so, and doubt not but success | will fashion the ADO 4.01.234
i know he will be glad of our success; MV 3.02.240
your honor | but give me leave to try success, AWW 1.03.247
lordship sees the bottom of /his success in't, 3.06. 36 P
well, we cannot greatly condemn our success. 3.06. 55 P
i know not what the success will be, my lord, 3.06. 80 P
length a–piece, by an abstract of success. 4.03. 86 P
in whose success we are gentle — i beseech you, WT 1.02.394
to signify | not only my success in libya, sir, 5.01.166
and so success of mischief shall be born, | and 2H4 4.02. 47
not wish | success and conquest to attend on us. H5 2.02. 24
her aid she promis'd, and assur'd success; 1H6 1.02. 82
how shall i honor thee for this success? 1.06. 5
created, for his rare success in arms, | great 4.07. 62
success unto our valiant general, | and 5.02. 8
why should i not now have the like success? 3H6 1.02. 75
or whether 'twas report of her success, | or 2.01.125
hear | that things ill got had ever bad success? 2.02. 46
the queen hath best success when you are absent. 2.02. 74
weak, | as may appear by edward's good success, 3.03.146
enemies | and promise them success and victory. R3 4.04.194
and dangerous success of bloody wars, | as i 4.04.237
sleep, | dream of success and happy victory! 5.03.165
success or loss, what is or is not, serves | as TRO 1.03.183
pois'd | in this vild action, for the success, 1.03.340
nor fear of bad success in a bad cause, | can 2.02.117
if i might in entreaties find success — | as 4.05.149
tickled with good success, disdains the shadow COR 1.01.260
us, we will write | to rome of our success. 1.09. 75
i shall ere long have knowledge | of my success. 5.01. 62
and bring me their opinions of success. JC 2.02. 6
mistrust of my success hath done this deed. 5.03. 65
mistrust of good success hath done this deed. 5.03. 66
receiv'd, macbeth, | the news of thy success; MAC 1.03. 90
ill, | why hath it given me earnest of success, 1.03.132
"they met me in the day of success; 1.05. 2 P
and catch | with his surcease, success; 1.07. 4
not sure, though hoping, of this good success, LR 5.03.195
my speech should fall into such vild success OTH 3.03.222
and smooth success | be strew'd before your feet ANT 1.03.100
sir, good success! 2.04. 9
this is old, what is the success? 3.05. 6 P
would i might never | o'ertake pursu'd success, 5.02.103
whom | he serv'd with glory and admir'd success: CYM 1.01. 32
my divination) | success to th' roman host. 4.02.352
you and pray the gods | for success and return; TNK 1.01.209
of whose success i dare not | make any timorous 1.03. 2
and hasten the success, which doubt not will 4.03.100 P
i should | choose one, and pray for his success, 5.01.153
he look'd all grace and success, and he is 5.03. 69
and wordless so greets heaven for his success. LUC 112
SUCCESSANTLY 1 FR 0.0001 REL FR 1 V 0 P
then go successantly, and plead to him. TIT 4.04.113
SUCCESSES 3 FR 0.0003 REL FR 3 V 0 P
gods | lead their successes as we wish our own, COR 1.06. 7
and last general | in our well–found successes, 2.02. 44
tyrant, whose successes | makes heaven unfear'd, TNK 1.02. 63
SUCCESSFUL 6 FR 0.0006 REL FR 6 V 0 P
and perhaps with more successful words | than SHR 1.02.157
th' journey | prove as successful to the queen WT 3.01. 12
if god doth give successful end | to this debate 2H4 4.04. 1
which promiseth | successful fortune, steel thy 3H6 2.02. 41
successful in the battles that he fights, | with TIT 1.01. 66
and welcome, nephews, from successful wars, 1.01.172
SUCCESSFULLY 3 FR 0.0003 REL FR 2 V 1 P
yet he looks successfully. AYL 1.02.153 P
reign, | and 'tis my hope to end successfully. SHR 4.01.189
and led my country's strength successfully, TIT 1.01.194
/SUCCESSION 1 FR 0.0001 REL FR 0 V 1 P
/them /exclaim /against /their /own /succession? HAM 2.02.351 P
SUCCESSION 16 FR 0.0018 REL FR 13 V 3 P
contract, succession, | bourn, bound of land, TMP 2.01.152
for slander lives upon succession, | for ever ERR 3.01.105
cannot for all that dissuade succession, but AWW 3.05. 23 P
and a perpetual succession for it perpetually. 4.03.280 P
thou shalt), we'll bar thee from succession, WT 4.04.429
from my succession wipe me, father, i | am heir 4.04.480
a king | but by fair sequence and succession? R2 2.01.199
the state | than thou the shadow of succession. 1H4 3.02. 99
touching king henry's oath and your succession. 3H6 2.01.119
he swore consent to your succession, | his oath 2.01.172
what else? and that succession be determined. 4.06. 56
off | to the succession of new days this month. TIM 2.02. 20

the king himself for your succession in denmark? HAM 3.02.342 P
him | and his succession granted rome a tribute, CYM 3.01. 8
thinking to bar thee of succession, as | thou 3.03.102
proving his beauty by succession thine! SON 2.12
SUCCESSIVE 5 FR 0.0005 REL FR 5 V 0 P
born, | are now to have no successive degrees, MM 2.02. 98
as next the king he was successive heir, | and 2H6 3.01. 49
plead my successive title with your swords. TIT 1.01. 4
richer than that which four successive kings HAM 5.02.273
but now is black beauty's successive heir, | and SON 127. 3
SUCCESSIVELY 3 FR 0.0003 REL FR 3 V 0 P
so thou the garland wear'st successively. 2H4 4.05.201
or else reported | successively from age to age, R3 3.01. 73
but as successively, from blood to blood, | your 3.07.135
SUCCESSOR 1 FR 0.0001 REL FR 1 V 0 P
so his successor | was like to be the best. WT 5.01. 48
SUCCESSORS 2 FR 0.0002 REL FR 1 V 1 P
all his successors (gone before him) hath done't WIV 1.01. 14 P
whose grace | chalks successors their way, nor H8 1.01. 60
SUCCOR 14 FR 0.0015 REL FR 13 V 1 P
travel much oppressed, | and faints for succor. AYL 2.04. 75
sir nicholas gawsey hath for succor sent, | and 1H4 5.04. 45
be not dismay'd, for succor is at hand: 1H6 1.02. 50
o, send some succor to the distress'd lord! 4.03. 30
come, margaret, god, our hope, will succor us. 2H6 4.04. 55
the more i stay, the more i'll succor thee. 3H6 3.03. 41
'tis not his new–made bride shall succor him, 3.03.207
to keep them back that come to succor you. 4.07. 56
flying for succor to his servant banister, H8 2.01.109
far from his succor, from the king, from all 3.02.261
far some forty truncheoners draw to her succor, 5.03. 52 P
lucius, | and will revolt from me to succor him. TIT 4.04. 80
dead, | my heart can lend no succor to my head. PER 1.01.169
yet not for me, shine sun to succor flowers! PP 14.28
SUCCORS 4 FR 0.0004 REL FR 4 V 0 P
the proffered means of succors and redress. R2 3.02. 32
the dolphin, whom of succors we entreated, H5 3.03. 45
the levied succors that should lend him aid, 1H6 4.04. 23
send succors, lords, and stop the rage betime, 2H6 3.01.285
/SUCH 9 FR 0.0010 REL FR 7 V 2 P
call'd jove's tree, when it drops /such fruit. AYL 3.02.237 P
/how /able /such /a /work /to /undergo, | /to 2H4 1.03. 54
meet for rebellion /and /such /acts /as /yours. 4.02.117
/such /violent /hands /upon /her /tender /life. TIT 3.02. 22
/no /such /matter. HAM 2.02.267 P
to be made | /for /such /a /guest /is /meet." 5.01.121
/is /such /as /basest /and /contemned'st LR 2.02.143
/could /not /beget | /such /different /issues. 4.03. 35
/a /period | /to /such /as /love /not /sorrow, 5.03.206
SUCH 1522 FR 0.1720 REL FR 1218 V 304 P
i have with such provision in mine art | so TMP 1.02. 28
made such a sinner of his memory | to credit his 1.02.101
his art is of such pow'r, | it would control my 1.02.372
it eats and sleeps and hath such senses | as we 1.02.413
and hath such senses | as we have — such. 1.02.414
there's nothing ill can dwell in such a temple. 1.02.458
i will resist such entertainment till | mine 1.02.466
think'st there is no more such shapes as he, 1.02.479
space enough | have i in such a prison. 1.02.494
grac'd before with such a paragon to their queen 2.01. 75 P
i would with such perfection govern, sir, | t' 2.01.168
who are of such sensible and nimble lungs that 2.01.173 P
and says such baseness | had never like executor 3.01. 12
back, | than you should such dishonor undergo, 3.01. 27
that a monster should be such a natural! 3.02. 33 P
use such vigilance | as when they are fresh. 3.03. 16
if i should say i saw such /islanders | (for, 3.03. 29
i cannot too much muse | such shapes, such 3.03. 37
too much muse | such shapes, such gesture, and 3.03. 37
shapes, such gesture, and such sound expressing 3.03. 37
or that there were such men | whose heads stood 3.03. 46
with such love as 'tis now, the murkiest den, 4.01. 25
and i must use you | in such another trick. 4.01. 37
we are such stuff | as dreams are made on; 4.01.156
what do you mean | to dote thus on such luggage? 4.01.231
o brave new world | that has such people in't! 5.01.184
i have been in such a pickle since i saw you 5.01.282 P
i'll waste | with such discourse as, i not doubt 5.01.304
such another proof will make me cry "baa." TGV 1.01. 93 P
too small a pasture for such store of muttons. 1.01. 99 P
receiving them from such a worthless post. 1.01.153
as little by such toys as may be possible: 1.02. 79
o hateful hands, to tear such loving words! 1.02.102
to feed on such sweet honey | and kill the bees 1.02.103
the honor and regard of such a father. 2.04. 60
to see such lovers, thurio, as yourself: 2.04. 97
to have a look of such a worthy mistress. 2.04.108
nor to his service no such joy on earth: 2.04.139
and i as rich in having such a jewel | as twenty 2.04.169
thou shalt never get such a secret from me but 2.05. 39 P
of such divine perfection, as sir proteus. 2.07. 13
fit me with such weeds | as may beseem some 2.07. 42
beseeming such a wife as your fair daughter. 3.01. 66
advise me where i may have such a ladder. 3.01.122
by seven a' clock i'll get you such a ladder. 3.01.126
i'll get me one of such another length. 3.01.133
the grace that with such grace hath blest them, 3.01.146
feeling line | that may discover such integrity: 3.02. 76
will well become such sweet–complaining 3.02. 85
i was, and held me glad of such a doom. 4.01. 32
such as the fury of ungovern'd youth | thrust 4.01. 43
and i for such like petty crimes as these. 4.01. 50
and a man of such perfection | as we do in our 4.01. 55
no, we detest such vile base practices. 4.01. 71
the heaven such grace did lend her, | that she 4.02. 42
didst thou ever see me do such a trick? 4.04. 39 P
thanks is good enough for such a present. 4.04. 49 P
partly that i have need of such a youth | that 4.04. 64
how many women would do such a message? 4.04. 90
if i had such a tire, this face of mine | were 4.04.185
his love, | i'll get me such a color'd periwig. 4.04.191
such pearls as put out ladies' eyes, | for i had 5.02. 13
that such an ass should owe them. 5.02. 28
faith or love, | for such is a friend now! 5.04. 63
have took upon me | such an immodest raiment — 5.04.106
'twere pity two such friends should be long foes 5.04.118
to make such means for her as thou hast done, 5.04.137
done, | and leave her on such slight conditions. 5.04.138
o'er my exteriors with such a greedy intention, WIV 1.03. 66 P
good faith, it is such another nan; 1.04.150 P
trifling respect, i could come to such honor! 2.01. 45 P
and gave such orderly and well–behav'd reproof 2.01. 58 P
i never heard such a drawling, affecting rogue. 2.01.141 P
i will not believe such a cataian, though the 2.01.144 P
have brought her into such a canaries as 'tis 2.02. 60 P
could never have brought her to such a canary. 2.02. 63 P
in silk and gold, and in such alligant terms, 2.02. 68 P
terms, and in such wine and sugar of the best, 2.02. 68 P
but i defy all angels (in any such sort, as they 2.02. 73 P
such /brooks are welcome to me, that o'erflows 2.02.150 P
are welcome to me, that o'erflows such liquor. 2.02.151 P
know how easy it is to be such an offender. 2.02.189 P
have you importun'd her to such a purpose? 2.02.212 P
the devil himself hath not such a name. 2.02.300 P
there is such a league between my goodman and he 3.02. 25 P
let the court of france show me such another. 3.03. 54 P
believe me, there's no such thing in me. 3.03. 67 P
husband, to give him such cause of suspicion! 3.03.100 P
it be not so, that you have such a man here; 3.03.113 P
windsor at his heels, to search for such a one. 3.03.115 P
i am not such a sickly creature, i give heaven 3.04. 59 P
daughter | in such a righteous fashion as i do, 3.04. 79
through fire and water for such a kind heart. 3.04.103 P
well, /and i be serv'd such another trick, i'll 3.05. 6 P
you do ill to teach the child such words. 4.01. 65 P
an abstract for the remembrance of such places, 4.02. 62 P
by th' figure, and such daub'ry as this is, 4.02.177 P
you have heard of such a spirit, and well you 4.04. 35
her | of such contents as you will wonder at; 4.06. 13
against such lewdsters and their lechery | those 5.03. 21
worth | to undergo such ample grace and honor, MM 1.01. 23
near to the speech we had to such a purpose. 1.02. 78 P
and speechless dialect, | such as move men; 1.02.184
his offense | for i have had such faults; 2.01. 28
threepence — your honors have seen such dishes; 2.01. 93 P
that such a one and such a one were past cure of 2.01.110 P
that such a one and such a one were past cure of 2.01.110 P
faith, sir, few of any wit in such matters. 2.01.268 P
plays such fantastic tricks before high heaven 2.02.121
confess | a natural guiltiness such as is his, 2.02.139
'tis | such sense that my sense breeds with it. 2.02.142
with such gifts that heaven shall share with you 2.02.147
more fit to do another such offense | than die 2.03. 14
give up your body to such sweet uncleanness | as 2.04. 54
finding yourself desir'd of such a person, 2.04. 91
yet hath he in him such a mind of honor | that, 2.04.179
her body stoop | to such abhorr'd pollution. 2.04.183
none, but such remedy as, to save a head, | to 3.01. 61
in such a one as, you consenting to't, | would 3.01. 70
for such a warped slip of wilderness | ne'er 3.01.141
maw or clothe a back | from such a filthy vice; 3.02. 23
though music oft hath such a charm | to make bad 4.01. 14
no such example have we. 4.02. 97
purchas'd by such sin | for which the pardoner 4.02.108
for i would commune with you of such things 4.03.104
did you such a thing? 4.03.171 P
give notice to such men of sort and suit as are 4.04. 17 P
a dishonor'd life | with ransom of such shame. 4.04. 32
where you may have such vantage on the duke, 4.06. 11
and we hear | such goodness of your justice, 5.01. 6
of sense, | such a dependancy of thing on thing, 5.01. 62
that with such vehemency he should pursue 5.01.109
with such a time | when i'll depose i had him in 5.01.197
such a fellow is not to be talk'd withal. 5.01.344 P
i am sorry that such sorrow i procure, | and so 5.01.474
woman was delivered | of such a burthen male, ERR 1.01. 55
my wife, not meanly proud of two such boys, 1.01. 58
such as sea–faring men provide for storms; 1.01. 80
that in such haste i sent to seek his master? 2.01. 2
unfeeling fools can with such wrongs dispense: 2.01.103
what answer, sir? when spake i such a word? 2.02. 13
why is time such a niggard of hair, being, as it 2.02. 77 P
for wenches, that thou call'st for such store, 3.01. 34
he gains by death that hath such means to die: 3.02. 51
sir, such claim as you would lay to your horse, 3.02. 85 P
such a one as a man may not speak of without he 3.02. 90 P
possess'd with such a gentle sovereign grace, 3.02.160
of such enchanting presence and discourse, 3.02.161
when in the streets he meets such golden gifts. 3.02.183
who would be jealous then of such a one? 4.02. 23
methinks they are such a gentle nation that, but 4.04.153 P
but had he such a chain of thee, or no? 5.01.257
with me — | after so long grief, such nativity! 5.01.407
there was none such in the army of any sort. ADO 1.01. 33 P
die while she hath such meet food to feed it as 1.01.121 P
it worse, and 'twere such a face as yours were. 1.01.137 P
can the world buy such a jewel? 1.01.181 P
without spectacles, and i see no such matter. 1.01.190 P
and in such great letters as they write "here is 1.01.265 P
matter enough in me for such an embassage, and 1.01.280 P
such a man would win any woman in the world, if 2.01. 15 P
jest upon jest with such impossible conveyance 2.01.245 P
will but minister such assistance as i shall 2.01.369 P
to a contaminated stale, such a one as hero. 2.02. 25 P
there shall appear such seeming truth of hero's 2.02. 48 P
after he hath laugh'd at such shallow follies in 2.03. 10 P
by falling in love — and such a man is claudio. 2.03. 12 P
of me, he shall never make me such a fool. 2.03. 26 P
cannot sure hide himself in such reverence. 2.03.120 P
opinion of another's dotage, and no such matter; 2.03.217 P
sure, sure, such carping is not commendable. 3.01. 71
o, do not do your cousin such a wrong. 3.01. 87
no glory lives behind the back of such. 3.01.110
appear when there is no need of such vanity. 3.03. 22 P
and, for such kind of men, the less you meddle 3.03. 52 P
lady, i am not such a fool to think what i list, 3.04. 82 P
yet benedick was such another, and now is he 3.04. 87 P
nor fortune made such havoc of my means, | nor 4.01.195
but they shall find, awak'd in such a kind, 4.01.197
is there any way to show such friendship? 4.01.263 P
a very even way, but no such friend. 4.01.264 P
defend but god should go before such villains! 4.02. 20 P
but such a one whose wrongs do suit with mine. 5.01. 7
as thus for thus, and such a grief for such, 5.01. 13
as thus for thus, and such a grief for such, 5.01. 13
if such a one will smile and stroke his beard, 5.01. 15
but there is no such man, for, brother, men 5.01. 20
if it should give your age such cause of fear. 5.01. 56
ape, but then is an ape a doctor to such a man. 5.01.202 P
matter, | that you have such a february face, 5.04. 41
and some such strange bull leapt your father's 5.04. 49
'tis no such matter. then you do not love me? 5.04. 82
he shall endure such public shame as the rest of LLL 1.01.130 P
such is the simplicity of man to hearken after 1.01.217 P
why, sir, is this such a piece of study? 1.02. 50 P
thoughts, master, are mask'd under such colors. 1.02. 93 P
was very guilty of such a ballet some three ages 1.02.111 P
such short–liv'd wits do wither as they grow. 2.01. 54
delivers in such apt and gracious words | that 2.01. 73
with such bedecking ornaments of praise? 2.01. 79
long of you that spur me with such questions. 2.01.118
for such a sum from special officers | of 2.01.161
mean time receive such welcome at my hand | as 2.01.168
his face's own margent did cote such amazes 2.01.246
and such barren plants are set before us, that 4.02. 28
heaven's praise with such an earthly tongue." 4.02.118
as his your case is such; 4.03.129
faith infringed, which such zeal did swear? 4.03.144
a wife of such wood were felicity. 4.03.245
her feet were much too dainty for such tread! 4.03.275
world | teaches such beauty as a woman's eye? 4.03.309
out | such fiery numbers as the prompting eyes 4.03.319
such as the shortness of the time can shape, 4.03.375
i abhor such fanatical phantasimes, such 5.01. 17 P
such insociable and point–devise companions, 5.01. 18 P
companions, such rackers of ortography, as to 5.01. 19 P
sweet self are good at such eruptions and sudden 5.01.114 P
of such a merry, nimble, stirring spirit, | she 5.02. 16
the blood of youth burns not with such excess 5.02. 73
with such a zealous laughter, so profound, 5.02.116
there's no such sport as sport by sport 5.02.153
blessed are clouds, to do as such clouds do! 5.02.204
we can afford no more at such a price. 5.02.223
have not the grace to grace it with such show. 5.02.320
troth, | i never swore this lady such an oath. 5.02.451
whole world again | cannot pick out five such, 5.02.545
if for my love (as there is no such cause) | you 5.02.792
in such a presence here to plead my thoughts; MND 1.01. 61
their blood | to undergo such maiden pilgrimage; 1.01. 75
your frowns would teach my smiles such skill! 1.01.195
o that my prayers could such affection move! 1.01.197
a bill of properties, such as our play wants. 1.02.105 P
uttering such dulcet and harmonious breath 2.01.151
the wildest hath not such a heart as you. 2.01.229
such separation as may well be said | becomes a 2.02. 58
you do) | in such disdainful manner me to woo. 2.02.130
we will have such a prologue, and it shall be 3.01. 23 P
i am no such thing; 3.01. 43 P
you would not make me such an argument. 3.02.242
and i am such a tender ass, if my hair do but 4.01. 25 P
flower | hath such force and blessed power. 4.01. 74
music, ho, music, such as charmeth sleep! 4.01. 83
never did i hear | such gallant chiding; 4.01.115
so musical a discord, such sweet thunder. 4.01.118
lovers and madmen have such seething brains, 5.01. 4
such shaping fantasies, that apprehend | more 5.01. 5
such tricks hath strong imagination, | that, if 5.01. 18
why, gentle sweet, you shall see no such thing. 5.01. 87
and such a wall, as i would have you think, 5.01.157
should not use a long one for such a pyramus. 5.01.317 P
prodigious, such as are | despised in nativity, 5.01.412
and such a want–wit sadness makes of me, | that MV 1.01. 6
believe me, sir, had i such venture forth, | the 1.01. 15
that such a thing bechanc'd would make me sad? 1.01. 38
and other of such vinegar aspect | that they'll 1.01. 54
moan to be abridg'd | from such a noble rate, 1.01.127
i have a mind presages me such thrift | that i 1.01.175
cold decree — such a hare is madness the youth, 1.02. 19 P
you spurn'd me such a day, another time | you 1.03.127
sport, | if you repay me not on such a day, | in 1.03.146
day, | in such a place, such sum or sums as are 1.03.147
such sum or sums as are | express'd in the 1.03.147
content, in faith, i'll seal to such a bond, 1.03.152
you shall not seal to such a bond for me, | i'll 1.03.154
to fates and destinies, and such odd sayings, 2.02. 62 P
sisters three, and such branches of learning, is 2.02. 63 P
and in such eyes as ours appear not faults, 2.02.183
and such fair ostents of love | as shall 2.08. 44
shadows kiss, | such have but a shadow's bliss. 2.09. 67
thou spend'st such high–day wit in praising him. 2.09. 98
yourself, | hate counsels not in such a quality. 3.02. 6
such it is | as are those dulcet sounds in break 3.02. 50
which /make such wanton gambols with the wind 3.02. 93
sweet a bar | should sunder such sweet friends. 3.02.120
lord bassanio, where i stand, | such as i am. 3.02.150
and there is such confusion in my powers, | as, 3.02.177
but in such a habit | that they shall think we 3.04. 60
life, | for, having such a blessing in his lady, 3.05. 75
even such a husband | hast thou of me as she is 3.05. 83
of force | must yield to such inevitable shame 4.01. 57
their palates | be season'd with such viands"? 4.01. 97
yet in such rule that the venetian law | cannot 4.01.178
penance | of such misery doth she cut me off. 4.01.272
in such a night as this, | when the sweet wind 5.01. 1
in such a night | troilus methinks mounted the 5.01. 3
in such a night | did thisby fearfully o'ertrip 5.01. 6
in such a night | stood dido with a willow in 5.01. 9
in such a night | medea gathered the enchanted 5.01. 12
in such a night | did jessica steal from the 5.01. 14
in such a night | did young lorenzo swear he 5.01. 17
in such a night | did pretty jessica (like a 5.01. 20
such harmony is in immortal souls, | but whilst 5.01. 63
let no such man be trusted. 5.01. 88
a day, | such as the day is when the sun is hid. 5.01.126
have i spent, that i should come to such penury? AYL 1.01. 39 P
a villain that says such a father begot villains 1.01. 58 P
therefore allow me such exercises as may become 1.01. 72 P
he would not have spoke such a word. 1.01. 84 P
or brook such disgrace well as he shall run into 1.01.134 P
wits too dull to reason of such goddesses, /and 1.02. 53 P
making such pitiful dole over them that all the 1.02.130 P
i can tell you, there is such odds in the man. 1.02.159 P
yet such is now the duke's condition | that he 1.02.264
is it possible, on such a sudden, you should 1.03. 27 P

the wretched animal heav'd forth such groans 2.01. 36
when such a one as she, such is her neighbor? 2.07. 78
when such a one as she, such is her neighbor? 2.07. 78
and let my officers of such a nature | make an 3.01. 16
such a one is a natural philosopher. 3.02. 32 P
nut hath sourest rind, | such a nut is rosalind. 3.02.110
though it be pity to see such a sight, it well 3.02.242 P
but you are no such man; 3.02.382 P
of fathers, when there is such a man as orlando? 3.04. 39 P
'tis such fools as you | that makes the world 3.05. 52
is my love, | and in such a poverty of grace, 3.05.100
and you serve me such another trick, never come 4.01. 40 P
which such as you are fain to be beholding to 4.01. 59 P
ay, and twenty such. 4.01.119 P
a man that had a wife with such a wit, he might 4.01.165 P
old justice that examines all such offenders, 4.01.200 P
could not drop forth such giant–rude invention, 4.03. 34
such ethiop words, blacker in their effect 4.03. 35
did you ever hear such railing? 4.03. 46 P
eyne | have power to raise such love in mine, 4.03. 51
wilt thou love such a woman? 4.03. 67 P
description — | such garments and such years. 4.03. 85
description — | such garments and such years. 4.03. 85
it but time lost to hear such a foolish song. 5.03. 40 P
the fool's bolt, sir, and such dulcet diseases. 5.04. 64 P
fleet, | i would esteem him worth a dozen such. SHR in.1. 27
such as he hath observ'd in noble ladies | unto in.1. 111
such duty to the drunkard let him do, | with in.1. 113
tears, | an onion will do well for such a shift, in.1. 126
shoes, or such shoes as my toes look through the in.2. 11 P
o, that a mighty man of such descent, | of such in.2. 14
of such possessions, and so high esteem, in.2. 15
am i a lord, and have i such a lady? in.2. 68
why, sir, you know no house nor no such maid, in.2. 91
maid, | nor no such men as you have reckon'd up, in.2. 92
and twenty more such names and men as these, in.2. 95
such friends as time in padua shall beget. 1.01. 45
from all such devils, good lord deliver us! 1.01. 66
or, signior gremio, you, know any such, | prefer 1.01. 96
that love should of a sudden take such hold? 1.01.147
her face, | such as the daughter of agenor had, 1.01.168
began to scold and raise up such a storm | that 1.01.172
such wind as scatters young men through the 1.02. 50
'twixt such friends as we | few words suffice; 1.02. 65
o sir, such a life, with such a wife, were 1.02.193
such a life, with such a wife, were strange! 1.02.193
and twangling jack, with twenty such vild terms, 2.01.158
no such jade as you, if me you mean. 2.01.201
too light for such a swain as you to catch, 2.01.204
well aim'd of such a young one. 2.01.235
for such an injury would vex a very saint, 3.02. 28
/old /news, and such news as you never heard of! 3.02. 30 P
this mad–brain'd bridegroom took him such a cuff 3.02.163
and kiss'd her lips with such a clamorous smack 3.02.178
such a mad marriage never was before. 3.02.182
than feed it with such overroasted flesh. 4.01.175
disguise | for such a one as leaves a gentleman 4.02. 19
a gentleman | and makes a god of such a cullion. 4.02. 20
bless you with such grace | as 'longeth to a 4.02. 44
the taming–school! what, is there such a place? 4.02. 55
time, | and gentlewomen wear such caps as these. 4.03. 70
with such austerity as 'longeth to a father. 4.04. 7
best | we be affied and such assurance ta'en 4.04. 49
such war of white and red within her cheeks! 4.05. 30
what stars do spangle heaven with such beauty, 4.05. 31
sigh, | till i be brought to such a silly pass! 5.02.124
such duty as the subject owes the prince, | even 5.02.155
even such a woman oweth to her husband; 5.02.156
than lack it where there is such abundance. AWW 1.01. 10 P
such a man | might be a copy to these younger 1.02. 45
ability enough to make such knaveries yours. 1.03. 12 P
i have other holy reasons, such as they are. 1.03. 32 P
such friends are thine enemies, knave. 1.03. 41 P
that had put such difference betwixt their two 1.03.112 P
such were our faults, or then we thought them 1.03.135
to her whose state is such that cannot choose 1.03.214
such as his reading | and manifest experience 1.03.222
on his grace's cure | by such a day an' hour. 1.03.249
devil lead the measure, such are to be follow'd. 2.01. 56 P
but such traitors | his majesty seldom fears. 2.01. 96
and such thanks i give | as one near death to 2.01.130
but such a one, thy vassal, whom i know | is 2.01.199
when you put off that with such contempt? 2.02. 6 P
and indeed such a fellow, to say precisely, were 2.02. 12 P
an answer of such fitness for all questions? 2.02. 28 P
in such a business, give me leave to use | the 2.03.107
prepar'd i was not | for such a business; 2.05. 62
but in such a 'then' i write a 'never.'" 3.02. 60 P
such is his noble purpose, and, believe't, | the 3.02. 70
that twenty such rude boys might tend upon | and 3.02. 82
the count rossillion. know you such a one? 3.05. 49
and brokes with all that can in such a suit 3.05. 71
such i will have, whom i am sure he knows not 3.06. 23 P
e'en such as you speak to me. 4.01. 13 P
and knowing i had no such purpose? 4.01. 36 P
dead, you should be such a one | as you are now; 4.02. 7
my mother did but duty, such, my lord, | as you 4.02. 12
i see that men make rope's in such a scarre 4.02. 38
mine honor's such a ring, | my chastity's the 4.02. 45
sir, with such volubility, that you would think 4.03.253 P
of your army and made such pestiferous reports 4.03.305 P
that can such sweet use make of what they hate, 4.04. 22
sallets ere we light on such another herb. 4.05. 14 P
by him that in such intelligence hath seldom 4.05. 82 P
such a ring as this, | the last that e'er i took 5.03. 78
my aid | for such disguise as haply shall become TN 1.02. 54
i am not such an ass but i can keep my hand dry. 1.03. 74 P
ladyship takes delight in such a barren rascal. 1.05. 83 P
look you, sir, such a one i was this present. 1.05.234 P
o, such love | could be but recompens'd, though 1.05.252
with such a suff'ring, such a deadly life, | in 1.05.265
with such a suff'ring, such a deadly life, | in 1.05.265
i could not with such estimable wonder overfar 2.01. 27 P
for such as we are made /of, such we be. 2.02. 32
for such as we are made /of, such we be. 2.02. 32
rather than forty shillings i had such a leg, 2.03. 20 P
for such as i am, all true lovers are, | unstaid 2.04. 17
i would have men of such constancy put to sea, 2.04. 75 P
no other dowry with her but such another jest. 2.05.184 P
thou hast put him in such a dream, that when the 2.05.193 P
no such matter, sir. 3.01. 5 P
can ever believe such impossible passages of 3.02. 72 P
you have not seen such a thing as 'tis. 3.02. 80 P
are shuffled off with such uncurrent pay; 3.03. 16
i did some service, of such note indeed, | that, 3.03. 27
th' offense is not of such a bloody nature, 3.03. 30
but such a headstrong potent fault it is | that 3.04.204
a very devil, i have not seen such a firago. 3.04.274 P
me the stuck in with such a mortal motion that 3.04.276 P
reliev'd him with such sanctity of love, | and 3.04.361
methinks his words do from such passion fly 3.04.373
even such and so | in favor was my brother, and 3.04.380
the first that ever dissembled in such a gown. 4.02. 6 P
affairs and their dispatch | with such a smooth, 4.03. 19
with which such scathful grapple did he make 5.01. 56
father — | such a sebastian was my brother too; 5.01.233
why you have given me such clear lights of favor 5.01.336
and in such forms which here were presuppos'd 5.01.350
"madam, why laugh you at such a barren rascal? 5.01.375 P
we cannot with such magnificence — in so rare WT 1.01. 12 P
rooted betwixt them then such an affection, 1.01. 23 P
behind | but such a day to–morrow as to–day, 1.02. 64
are such allow'd infirmities that honesty | is 1.02.263
the king hath on him such a countenance | as he 1.02.368
give rest to th' minds of others — such as he, 2.01.191
here's such ado to make no stain a stain | as 2.02. 17
'tis such as you, | that creep like shadows by 2.03. 33
such as you | nourish the cause of his awaking. 2.03. 35
your evils, | than such as most seem yours. 2.03. 57
with such a kind of love as might become | a 3.02. 64
with a love even such, | so and no other, as 3.02. 65
if such thing be, thy mother | appear'd to me 3.03. 17
i have seen two such sights, by sea and by land! 3.03. 83 P
and give my scene such growing | as you had 4.01. 16
sir, of such a man, who hath a daughter of most 4.02. 41 P
can be thought to begin from such a cottage. 4.02. 43 P
strangle such thoughts as these with any thing 4.04. 47
with such delicate burthens of dildos and 4.04.194 P
know | she prizes not such trifles as these are. 4.04.357
should hold some counsel | in such a business. 4.04.410
point you where you shall have such receiving 4.04.526
house these seven years | be born another such. 4.04.579
there lies such secrets in this farthel and box, 4.04.756 P
no more such wives, therefore no wife. 5.01. 56
had she such power, | she had just cause. 5.01. 60
as was your former, but she shall be such | as, 5.01. 79
now have look'd on, | such goodly things as you? 5.01.178
with thought of such affections, | step forth 5.01.220
she was more worth such gazes | than what you 5.01.226
such a deal of wonder is broken out within this 5.02. 23 P
you see, there is such unity in the proofs. 5.02. 32 P
so and in such manner that it seem'd sorrow wept 5.02. 44 P
with countenance of such distraction that they 5.02. 47 P
i never heard of such another encounter, which 5.02. 56 P
of kings and princes, for by such was it acted. 5.02. 80 P
even with such life of majesty (warm life, | as 5.03. 35
him, | and if my legs were two such riding–rods, JN 1.01.140
my arms such eel–skins stuff'd, my face so thin 1.01.141
but who comes in such haste in riding–robes? 1.01.217
swords | in such a just and charitable war. 2.01. 36
such as she is, in beauty, virtue, birth, | is 2.01.432
man, | left to be finished by such as she, | and 2.01.438
o, two such silver currents when they join | do 2.01.441
and two such shores to two such streams made one 2.01.443
two such shores to two such streams made one, 2.01.443
two such controlling bounds shall you be, kings, 2.01.444
should be | in such a love so vile a lout as he. 2.01.509
make such unconstant children of ourselves, | as 3.01.243
when such profound respects do pull you on. 3.01.318
so hot a speed with such advice dispos'd, | such 3.04. 11
such temperate order in so fierce a cause, 3.04. 12
there was not such a gracious creature born. 3.04. 81
had you such a loss as i, | i could give better 3.04. 99
my head | when there is such disorder in my wit. 3.04.102
i am best pleas'd to be from such a deed. 4.01. 85
why do you bend such solemn brows on me? 4.02. 90
never such a pow'r | for any foreign preparation 4.02.110
that such an army could be drawn in france, 4.02.118
without this object, | form such another? 4.03. 45
eyes, | for villainy is not without such rheum, 4.03.108
the ocean, | enough to stifle such a villain up. 4.03.133
i am not glad that such a sore of time | should 5.02. 12
but such is the infection of the time, | that, 5.02. 20
but this effusion of such manly drops, | this 5.02. 49
but i, | and such as to my claim are liable, 5.02.101
too precious to be spent | with such a brabbler. 5.02.162
after such bloody toil, we bid good night, | and 5.05. 6
and brings from him such offers of our peace 5.07. 84
yet can i not of such tame patience boast | as R2 1.01. 52
such neighbor nearness to our sacred blood 1.01.119
o, god defend my soul from such deep sin! 1.01.187
shall wound my honor with such feeble wrong, 1.01.191
except the marshal and such officers | appointed 1.03. 44
such is the breath of kings. 1.03.215
to counterfeit oppression of such grief | that 1.04. 14
this land of such dear souls, this dear dear 2.01. 57
god, 'tis shame such wrongs are borne | in him, 2.01.238
why i should welcome such a guest as grief, 2.02. 7
such as it is, being tender, raw, and young, 2.03. 42
were i but now lord of such hot youth | as when 2.03. 99
measure our confines with such peaceful steps? 3.02.125
when such a sacred king should hide his head! 3.03. 9
such crimson tempest should bedrench | the fresh 3.03. 46
breast, | to answer twenty thousand such as you. 4.01. 59
wedding it, there is such length in grief. 5.01. 94
which with such gentle sorrow he shook off, 5.02. 31
even such, they say, as stand in narrow lanes 5.03. 8
back | of such as have before endur'd the like. 5.05. 30
upon whose dead corpse' there was such misuse, 1H4 1.01. 43
misuse, | such beastly shameless transformation, 1.01. 44
alone, i will lay him down such reasons for this 1.02.150 P
not with such strength denied | as is delivered 1.03. 25
harry percy then had said | to such a person, 1.03. 72
said | to such a person, and in such a place, 1.03. 72
at such a time, with all the rest retold, | may 1.03. 73
color her working with such deadly wounds, | nor 1.03.109
or you shall hear in such a kind from me | as 1.03.121
cousin" — | o, the devil take such cozeners! 1.03.255
and great oney'rs, such as can hold in, such as 2.01. 77 P
hold in, such as will strike sooner than speak, 2.01. 77 P
for moving such a dish of skim–milk with so 2.03. 33 P
such as we see when men restrain their breath 2.03. 61
a weasel hath not such a deal of spleen | as you 2.03. 78
stand'st thou still, and hear'st such a calling? 2.04. 80 P
a plague upon such backing! 2.04.151 P
pick thee out three such enemies again as that 2.04.367 P
it shall not wind with such a deep indent, | to 3.01.103
and such a deal of skimble–skamble stuff | as 3.01.152
shame, | in such a parley should i answer thee. 3.01.201
making such difference 'twixt wake and sleep 3.01.216
and givest such sarcenet surety for thy oaths 3.01.251
and such protest of pepper–gingerbread, | to 3.01.255
else, | could such inordinate and low desires, 3.02. 12
such poor, such bare, such lewd, such mean 3.02. 13
such poor, such bare, such lewd, such mean 3.02. 13
poor, such bare, such lewd, such mean attempts, 3.02. 13
poor, such bare, such lewd, such mean attempts, 3.02. 13
such barren pleasures, rude society, | as thou 3.02. 14
yet such extenuation let me beg | as, in reproof 3.02. 22
and dress'd myself in such humility | that i did 3.02. 51
a feast, | and wan by rareness such solemnity. 3.02. 59
seen, but with such eyes | as, sick and blunted 3.02. 76
gaze, | such as is bent on sunlike majesty, 3.02. 79
slept in his face and rend'red such aspect | as 3.02. 82
such attribution should the douglas have | as 4.01. 3
leisure to be sick | in such a justling time? 4.01. 18
and think how such an apprehension | may turn 4.01. 66
there is not such a word | spoke of in scotland 4.01. 84
and vaulted with such ease into his seat | as if 4.01.107
such as had been ask'd twice on the banes, such 4.02. 16 P
on the banes, such a commodity of warm slaves, 4.02. 17 P
such as fear the report of a caliver worse than 4.02. 18 P
i press'd me none but such toasts–and–butter, 4.02. 20 P
sores, and such as indeed were never soldiers, 4.02. 27 P
and such have i, to fill up the rooms of them as 4.02. 32 P
no eye hath seen such scarecrows. 4.02. 38 P
i did never see such pitiful rascals. 4.02. 64 P
being men of such great leading as you are, 4.03. 17
the breast of civil peace | such bold hostility, 4.03. 44
that you and i should meet upon such terms | as 5.01. 10
and such a flood of greatness fell on you, 5.01. 48
whereby we stand opposed by such means | as you 5.01. 67
want | such water–colors to impaint his cause, 5.01. 80
and chid his truant youth with such a grace | as 5.02. 62
never shall | a second time do such a courtesy. 5.02.100
gregory never did such deeds in arms as i have 5.03. 45 P
i like not such grinning honor as sir walter 5.03. 59 P
the prince of wales from such a field as this, 5.04. 12
i did not think thee lord of such a spirit. 5.04. 18
i did look for | of such an ungrown warrior. 5.04. 23
have taught us how to cherish such high deeds 5.05. 30
sway, | meeting the check of such another day, 5.05. 42
by the stern tyrant war, | and no such matter? 2H4 in 15
o, such a day! 1.01. 20
by travers | give then such instances of loss? 1.01. 56
even such a man, so faint, so spiritless, | so 1.01. 70
and make thee rich for doing me such wrong. 1.01. 90
lend to this weight such lightness with their 1.01.122
knew that we ventured on such dangerous seas 1.01.181
there is no honesty in such dealing, unless a 2.01. 36 P
be no more so familiarity with such poor people, 2.01.100 P
of words that come with such more than impudent 2.01.112 P
very hardly, upon such a subject. 2.02. 44 P
and keeping such vile company as thou art hath 2.02. 49 P
is't such a matter to get a pottle–pot's 2.02. 78 P
even such kin as the parish heckfers are to the 2.02.157 P
empty vessel bear such a huge full hogshead? 2.04. 62 P
a' my word, captain, there's none such here. 2.04.176 P
i cannot endure such a fustian rascal. 2.04.189 P
and such other gambol faculties 'a has, that 2.04.250 P
for the prince himself is such another, the 2.04.253 P
(though then, god knows, i had no such intent, 3.01. 72
such things become the hatch and brood of time, 3.01. 86
you had not four such swingebucklers in all the 3.02. 21 P
and i will take such order that thy friends 3.02.185 P
i shall ne'er see such a fellow. 3.02.286 P
with such powers | as might hold sortance with 4.01. 10
of the speech of peace that bears such grace, 4.01. 48
there is no need of any such redress, | or if 4.01. 95
peace | upon such large terms and so absolute 4.01.184
but our valuation shall be such | that every 4.01.187
weary | of dainty and such picking grievances, 4.01.196
he set abroach | in shadow of such greatness? 4.02. 15
and no food — | such are the poor, in health; 4.04.106
and takes away the stomach — such are the rich, 4.04.107
with such a deep demeanor in great sorrow | that 4.05. 84
make four dozen of such bearded hermits' staves 5.01. 63 P
having such a son | that would deliver up his 5.02.110
and let us choose such limbs of noble counsel 5.02.135
i have long dreamt of such a kind of man, | so 5.05. 49
which was never seen in such an assembly. ep 25 P
never was such a sudden scholar made; H5 1.01. 32
in a flood | with such a heady currance, 1.01. 34
for never two such kingdoms did contend 1.02. 24
that makes such waste in brief mortality. 1.02. 28
will raise your highness such a mighty sum | as 1.02.133
if we, with thrice such powers left at home, 1.02.217
him he hath made a match with such a wrangler 1.02.264
breed, by his sufferance, more of such a kind. 2.02. 46
such and so finely bolted didst thou seem. 2.02.137
to trouble himself with any such thoughts yet. 2.03. 22 P
for indeed three such antics do not amount to a 3.02. 31 P
decoct their cold blood to such valiant heat? 3.05. 20
and such fellows are perfit in the great 3.06. 69 P
services were done — at such and such a sconce, 3.06. 72 P
services were done — at such and such a sconce, 3.06. 72 P
at such and such a sconce, at such a breach, at 3.06. 72 P
a sconce, at such a breach, at such a convoy; 3.06. 73 P
you must learn to know such slanders of the age, 3.06. 80 P
we would have all such offenders so cut off; 3.06.107 P
though france himself and such another neighbor 3.06.157
or any such proverb so little kin to the purpose 3.07. 68 P
they could never wear such heavy head–pieces. 3.07.138 P
day and cry all, "we died at such a place" — 4.01.138 P

lost wherein such preparation was gain'd;		4.01.181 P
and, but for ceremony, such a wretch, | winding		4.01.278
to purge this field of such a hilding foe;		4.02. 29
to demonstrate the life of such a battle, | in		4.02. 54
such outward things dwell not in my desires.		4.03. 27
if thou encounter any such, apprehend him, and		4.07.158 P
and of such as have, | i humbly pray them to		5.pr. 2
the venom of such looks we fairly hope | have		5.02. 18
rusts | that should deracinate such savagery;		5.02. 47
terms, | such as will enter at a lady's ear,		5.02.100
thou wouldst find me such a plain king that thou		5.02.124 P
if thou would have such a one, take me!		5.02.165 P
endeavor for your french part of such a boy;		5.02.214 P
so be there 'twixt your kingdoms such a spousal,		5.02.362
whilst such a worthy leader, wanting aid, | unto	1H6	1.01.143
since they, so few, watch such a multitude.		1.01.161
suppose | they had such courage and audacity?		1.02. 36
god, these nobles should such stomachs bear!		1.03. 90
should strike such terror to his enemies.		2.03. 24
here, | it is of such a spacious lofty pitch,		2.03. 55
no, prelate, such is thy audacious wickedness,		3.01. 14
and know the office that belongs to such.		3.01. 55
that two such noble peers as ye should jar!		3.01. 70
and ere that we will suffer such a prince, | so		3.01. 97
fast | before he'll buy again at such a rate.		3.02. 43
whither away, sir john falstaff, in such haste?		3.02.104
grief | that such a valiant company are fled.		3.02.125
thou knowest the law of arms is such | that		3.04. 38
esteem none friends but such as are his friends,		4.01. 5
and none your foes but such as shall pretend		4.01. 6
or whether that such cowards ought to wear		4.01. 28
such as were grown to credit by the wars;		4.01. 36
of such as your oppression feeds upon,		4.01. 58
there should be found such false dissembling		4.01. 63
a cause | such factious emulations shall arise!		4.01.113
feeds in the bosom of such great commanders,		4.03. 48
my age was never tainted with such shame.		4.05. 46
and shall my youth be guilty of such blame?		4.05. 47
on that advantage, bought with such a shame,		4.06. 44
he speaks with such a proud commanding spirit.		4.07. 88
unnatural | that such immanity and bloody strife		5.01. 13
beauty's princely majesty is such, | 'confounds		5.03. 70
worth | to be the princely bride of such a lord,		5.03.152
such commendations as becomes a maid, | a virgin		5.03.177
presume | to send such peevish tokens to a king.		5.03.186
peace, | it shall be with such strict and severe		5.04.114
to save your subjects from such massacre | and		5.04.160
and of such great authority in france | as his		5.05. 41
i feel such sharp dissension in my breast,		5.05. 84
such fierce alarums both of hope and fear, | as		5.05. 85
such as my wit affords | and overjoy of heart	2H6	1.01. 30
such is the fullness of my heart's content.		1.01. 35
this peroration with such circumstance?		1.01.105
that shall make answer to such questions | as by		1.02. 80
and plac'd a choir of such enticing birds | that		1.03. 89
i never said nor thought any such matter.		1.03.188 P
good uncle, hide such malice;		2.01. 25
with such holiness can you do it?		2.01. 26
when such strings jar, what hope of harmony?		2.01. 55
such as my heart doth tremble to unfold:		2.01.162
honor and virtue, and convers'd with such | as,		2.01.191
and in thy sons, fair slips of such a stock.		2.02. 58
such as by god's book are adjudg'd to death.		2.03. 4
yet so he rul'd, and such a prince he was, | as		2.04. 44
heir, | and such high vaunts of his nobility,		3.01. 50
and well such losers may have leave to speak.		3.01.185
hide not thy poison with such sug'red words.		3.02. 45
yet, notwithstanding such a strait edict, | were		3.02.258
from such fell serpents as false suffolk is;		3.02.266
could send such message to their sovereign.		3.02.272
enough to purchase such another island, | so		3.03. 3
fight | be counterpois'd with such a petty sum!		4.01. 22
must not be shed by such a jaded groom.		4.01. 52
should die | by such a lowly vassal as thyself.		4.01.111
far be it we should honor such as these | with		4.01.123
spare none but such as go in clouted shoon,		4.02.185
they are thrifty honest men, and such | as would		4.02.186
why com'st thou in such haste?		4.04. 26
such aid as i can spare you shall command, | but		4.05. 6
sweep the court clean of such filth as thou art.		4.07. 32 P
and such abominable words as no christian ear		4.07. 39 P
court | and may enjoy such quiet walks as these?		4.10. 17
that living wrought me such exceeding trouble.		5.01. 70
may iden live to merit such a bounty, | and		5.01. 81
and such a piece of service will you do, | if		5.01.155
thou dispense with heaven for such an oath?		5.01.181
being opposites of such repairing nature.		5.03. 22
all, | and more such days as these to us befall!		5.03. 33
such hope have all the line of john of gaunt!	3H6	1.01. 19
patience is for poltroons, such as he.		1.01. 62
such a messenger | as shall revenge his death		1.01. 99
who can be patient in such extremes?		1.01.215
and giv'n unto the house of york such head | as		1.01.233
such safety finds | the trembling lamb environed		1.01.241
why com'st thou in such post?		1.02. 48
and not with such a cruel threat'ning look.		1.03. 17
such pity as my rapier's point affords.		1.03. 37
ay, to such mercy as his ruthless arm | with		1.04. 31
and in thy need such comfort come to thee | as		1.04.165
for all the rest is held at such a rate | as		2.02. 51
promise them such rewards | as victors wear at		2.03. 52
o heavy times, begetting such events!		2.05. 63
because he would avoid such bitter taunts		2.06. 66
no, never such an oath, nor will not now.		3.01. 73
gust, | such is the lightness of you common men.		3.01. 89
no, by my troth, i did not mean such love.		3.02. 64
o monstrous fault, to harbor such a thought!		3.02.164
to o'erbear such | as are of better person than		3.02.166
from such a cause as fills mine eyes with tears		3.03. 13
such it seems | as may beseem a monarch like		3.03.121
mine such as fill my heart with unhop'd joys.		3.03.172
be appeas'd | by such invention as i can devise?		4.01. 35
yet, to have join'd with france in such alliance		4.01. 36
but such as i (without your special pardon)		4.01. 87
ay, such a pleasure as incaged birds | conceive,		4.06. 12
if any such be here — as god forbid!		5.04. 48
and he that will not fight for such a hope | go		5.04. 55
not like the fruit of such a goodly tree.		5.06. 52
may such purple tears be alway shed | from those		5.06. 64
for i will buzz abroad such prophecies | that		5.06. 86
such as befits the pleasure of the court?		5.07. 44
by such despair i should accuse myself.	R3	1.02. 85
teach not thy lip such scorn;		1.02.171
made | for kissing, lady, not for such contempt.		1.02.172
no other harm but loss of such a lord.		1.03. 7
the loss of such a lord includes all harms.		1.03. 8
that fill his ears with such dissentious rumors.		1.03. 46
i would not spend another such a night | though		1.04. 5
had you such leisure in the time of death | to		1.04. 34
such hideous cries that with the very noise | i,		1.04. 60
hell, | such terrible impression made my dream.		1.04. 63
when thou hast broke it in such dear degree?		1.04.210
if two such murtherers as yourselves came to you		1.04.259
that deceit should steal such gentle shape,		2.02. 27
such news, my lord, as grieves me to report.		2.04. 39
keep you from them, and from such false friends!		3.01. 15
when that he bids good morrow with such spirit.		3.04. 50
when such ill dealing must be seen in thought.		3.06. 14
such troops of citizens to come to him, | his		3.07. 85
my lord, there needs no such apology.		3.07.104
rough cradle for such little pretty ones!		4.01.100
repays he my deep service | with such contempt?		4.02.120
wilt thou, o god, fly from such gentle lambs,		4.04. 22
when didst thou sleep when such a deed was done?		4.04. 24
and i, in such a desp'rate bay of death, | like		4.04.233
having bought love with such a bloody spoil.		4.04.290
therefore accept such kindness as i can.		4.04.310
but she, your subject, loathes such sovereignty.		4.04.356
such proclamation hath been made, my lord.		4.04.517
such noble scenes as draw the eye to flow, | we	H8	pr 4
such as give | their money out of hope they may		pr 7
to rank our chosen truth with such a show | as		pr 18
ones could have weigh'd | such a compounded one?		1.01. 12
that promises no element | in such a business.		1.01. 49
that such a keech can with his very bulk | take		1.01. 55
for the most part such | to whom as great a		1.01. 76
yea, such which breaks | the sides of loyalty,		1.02. 27
his training such | that he may furnish and		1.02.112
i remember | of such a time, being my sworn		1.02.191
should juggle | men into such strange mysteries?		1.03. 2
their clothes are after such a pagan cut to't,		1.03. 14
let me have such a bowl may hold my thanks,		1.04. 39
pledge it, madam, | for 'tis to such a thing —		1.04. 48
such a one, they all confess, | there is indeed,		1.04. 82
stirr'd | with such an agony he sweat extremely,		2.01. 33
and fit it with such furniture as suits | the		2.01. 99
heaven keep me from such counsel!		2.02. 37
they have sent me such a man i would have wish'd		2.02.100
for such receipt of learning is black–friars;		2.02.138
and heav'nly blessings | follow such creatures.		2.03. 58
but with thanks to god for such | a royal lady,		2.04.153
the region of my breast, which forc'd such way,		2.04.185
in sweet music is such art, | killing care and		3.01. 12
i am not such a truant since my coming, | as not		3.01. 43
suddenly an answer | in such a point of weight,		3.01. 71
wit, | and to such men of gravity and learning,		3.01. 73
looking | either for such men or such business.		3.01. 76
looking | either for such men or such business.		3.01. 76
woe upon ye | and all such false professors!		3.01.115
we are to cure such sorrows, not to sow 'em.		3.01.158
you, ever casts | such doubts, as false coin,		3.01.171
wit | to make a seemly answer to such persons.		3.01.178
i should be glad to hear such news as this		3.02. 24
which | i find at such proud rate, that it		3.02.127
that seal | you ask with such a violence, the		3.02.246
that therefore such a writ be sued against you,		3.02.341
such a noise arose | as the shrouds make at sea		4.01. 71
such joy | i never saw before.		4.01. 75
peace, and all such emblems | laid nobly on her;		4.01. 89
but such an honest chronicler as griffith.		4.02. 72
madam, such good dreams | possess your fancy.		4.02. 93
you cannot with such freedom purge yourself		5.01.102
such things have been done.		5.01.133
an ordinary groom is for such payment.		5.01.172
in daily thanks, that gave us such a prince,		5.02.150
but know i come not | to hear such flattery now,		5.02.159
monarch now alive may glory | in such an honor;		5.02.199
for kindling such a combustion in the state.		5.03. 49 P
loose shot, deliver'd such a show'r of pibbles,		5.03. 56 P
that mould up such a mighty piece as this is,		5.04. 26
of good women, | for such a one we show'd 'em.		ep 11
troy, | that find such cruel battle here within?	TRO	1.01. 3
but there was such laughing!		1.02.142 P
but there was such laughing!		1.02.165 P
i had rather be such a man as troilus than		1.02.245 P
you are such a woman, a man knows not at what		1.02.258 P
you are such another!		1.02.271 P
which were such | as agamemnon and the hand of		1.03. 62
in brass, and such again | as venerable nestor,		1.03. 64
such to–be–pitied and o'er–wrested seeming | he		1.03.157
and bears his head | in such a rein, in full as		1.03.189
if none of them have soul in such a kind, | we		1.03.285
now heavens forfend such scarcity of /youth!		1.03.302
and in such indexes (although small pricks | to		1.03.343
stomach, and such a one that dare | maintain —		2.01.125
act | such and no other than event doth form it,		2.02.120
such things as might offend the weakest spleen		2.02.128
the pleasures such a beauty brings with it,		2.02.147
thersites is a fool to serve such a fool, and		2.03. 64 P
here is such patchery, such juggling, and such		2.03. 71 P
here is such patchery, such juggling, and such		2.03. 71 P
such patchery, such juggling, and such knavery!		2.03. 72 P
worth | holds in his blood such swoll'n and hot		2.03.173
save such as doth revolve | and ruminate himself		2.03.187
nay, i care not for such words, no, no.		3.01. 75 P
no such matter, you are wide.		3.01. 88 P
even such a passion doth embrace my bosom:		3.02. 35
are there such?		3.02. 90 P
such are not we.		3.02. 90 P
troilus shall be such to cressid as what envy		3.02. 96 P
and weight | of such a winnowed purity in love!		3.02.167
since i have taken such pain to bring you		3.02.200 P
is such a wrest in their affairs | that their		3.03. 23
question me | why such unplausive eyes are bent,		3.03. 43
some thing not worth in me such rich beholding		3.03. 91
a tick in a sheep than such a valiant ignorance.		3.03.312 P
no man alive can love in such a sort | the thing		4.01. 24
with such a hell of pain and world of charge;		4.01. 58
with such a costly loss of wealth and friends.		4.01. 61
i shall have such a life!		4.02. 22
you are deceived, i think of no such thing.		4.02. 39
no more my grief, in such a precious loss.		4.04. 10
for we may live to have need of such a verse.		4.04. 22 P
as to one | that would be rid of such an enemy.		4.05.164
gods, proud man, | to answer such a question.		4.05.248
to such as boasting show their scars | a mock is		4.05.290
tetter, take and take again such preposterous		5.01. 23 P
poor world is pest'red with such water–flies,		5.01. 33 P
eyes too, and such an ache in my bones that,		5.03.105 P
with such a careless force and forceless care		5.05. 40
senators for that | they are not such as you.	COR	1.01.114
and feebling such as stand not in their liking		1.01.195
such a nature, | tickled with good success,		1.01.259
how honor would become such a person, that it		1.03. 10 P
h'as such a confirm'd countenance.		1.03. 59 P
if any such be here | (as it were sin to doubt)		1.06. 67
thank the gods | our rome hath such a soldier."		1.09. 9
meeting two such wealsmen as you are (i cannot		2.01. 54 P
they shall encounter such ridiculous subjects as		2.01. 85 P
dear, | such eyes the widows in corioles wear,		2.01.178
such a poother | as if that whatsoever god who		2.01.218
his ascent is not by such easy degrees as those		2.02. 25 P
i cannot bring | my tongue to such a pace.		2.03. 51
of such childish friendliness | to yield your		2.03.175
suffer't, and live with such as cannot rule,		3.01. 40
you are like to do such business.		3.01. 48
and such a one as he, who puts his "shall,"		3.01.105
but with such words that are but roted in | your		3.02. 55
(for in such business | action is eloquence, and		3.02. 75
you have put me now to such a part which never		3.02.105
and when such time they have begun to cry, | let		3.03. 19
to suffer lawful censure for such faults | as		3.03. 46
such as become a soldier | rather than envy you.		3.03. 56
this | so criminal, and in such capital kind,		3.03. 81
head, that he gives entrance to such companions?		4.05. 12 P
people | deserve such pity of him as the wolf		4.06.110
rome, such as was never | s' incapable of help.		4.06.119
intercession of such a decay'd dotant as you		5.02. 44 P
to flame in, with such weak breath as this?		5.02. 46 P
for such things as you, i can scarce think		5.02.103 P
not with such friends | that thought them sure		5.03. 7
i'll never | be such a gosling to obey instinct,		5.03. 35
which thou shalt thereby reap is such a name		5.03.143
in such a case the gods will not be good unto us		5.04. 31 P
of tribunes, such as you, | a sea and land full.		5.04. 54
ye draw, | and maintain such a quarrel openly?	TIT	2.01. 47
that for her love such quarrels may be broach'd,		2.01. 67
ye, and are you such fools | to square for this?		2.01. 99
and after conflict such as was suppos'd | the		2.03. 21
would make such fearful and confused cries, | as		2.03.102
terms | that ever ear did hear to such effect,		2.03.111
in pleasing smiles such murderous tyranny.		2.03.267
for such a sight will blind a father's eye.		2.04. 53
that blabb'd them with such pleasing eloquence,		3.01. 83
such with'red herbs as these | are meet for		3.01.177
ay, such a place there is where we did hunt | (o		4.01. 55
we had a thousand roman dames | at such a bay,		4.02. 42
gave aries such a knock | that down fell both		4.03. 72
of egall justice, us'd in such contempt?		4.04. 4
'cause they take vengeance of such kind of men.		5.02. 63
could not all hell afford you such a devil?		5.02. 86
it were convenient you had such a devil.		5.02. 90
oft have you heard me wish for such an hour,		5.02.159
why, such is love's transgression.	ROM	1.01.185
such as i love, and you, among the store | one		1.02. 22
such comfort as do lusty young men feel | when		1.02. 26
even such delight | among fresh fennel buds		1.02. 28
religion of mine eye | maintains such falsehood,		1.02. 89
i'll go along no such sight to be shown, | but		1.02.100
lady, such a man | as all the world — why, he's		1.03. 75
verona's summer hath not such a flower.		1.03. 77
the date is out of such prolixity:		1.04. 3
in a fair lady's ear, | such as would please;		1.05. 24
it fits when such a villain is a guest.		1.05. 75
to breathe such vows as lovers use to swear,		2.pr. 10
sea, | i should adventure for such merchandise.		2.02. 84
parting is such sweet sorrow, | that i shall say		2.02.184
two such opposed kings encamp them still | in		2.03. 27
the pox of such antic, lisping, affecting		2.04. 28 P
and in such a case as mine a man may strain		2.04. 50 P
such a case as yours constrains a man to bow in		2.04. 52 P
were lustier than he is, and twenty such jacks;		2.04.152 P
here's such a coil! come, what says romeo?		2.05. 65
but my true love is grown to such excess | i		2.06. 33
am i like such a fellow?		3.01. 10 P
nay, and there were two such, we should have		3.01. 15 P
what eye but such an eye would spy out such a		3.01. 21 P
but such an eye would spy out such a quarrel?		3.01. 21 P
the appertaining rage | to such a greeting.		3.01. 64
such a waggoner | as phaeton would whip you to		3.02. 2
i am not i, if there be such an ay;		3.02. 48
fiend | in mortal paradise of such sweet flesh?		3.02. 82
was ever book containing such vile matter | so		3.02. 83
deceit should dwell | in such a gorgeous palace!		3.02. 85
blister'd be thy tongue | for such a wish!		3.02. 91
is my dear son with such sour company!		3.03. 7
take heed, take heed, for such die miserable.		3.03.145
yet let me weep for such a feeling loss.		3.05. 74
shall give him such an unaccustom'd dram | that		3.05. 90
find thou the means, and i'll find such a man.		3.05.103
and joy comes well in such a needy time.		3.05.105
closet | to help me sort such needful ornaments		4.02. 34
madam, we have cull'd such necessaries | as are		4.03. 7
but i will watch you from such watching now.		4.04. 12
and doth it give me such a sight as this?		4.05. 42
and breath'd such life with kisses in my lips		5.01. 8
such soon–speeding gear | as will disperse		5.01. 60
such mortal drugs i have, but mantua's law | is		5.01. 66
there shall no figure at such rate be set | as		5.03.301
figures are | even such as they give out.	TIM	1.01.160
i could wish my best friend at such a feast.		1.02. 79 P
to feed | than such that do e'en enemies exceed.		1.02.204
on water to scald such chickens as you are.		2.02. 69 P
has friendship such a faint and milky heart,		3.01. 54

i to disfurnish myself against such a good time, 3.02. 45 P
i cannot pleasure such an honorable gentleman. 3.02. 56 P
i'd such a courage to do him good. 3.03. 24
of such a nature is his politic love. 3.03. 33 P
such may rail against great buildings. 3.04. 64 P
and with such sober and unnoted passion | he did 3.05. 21
your words have took such pains as if they 3.05. 26
if there be | such valor in the bearing, what 3.05. 46
base | to sue and be denied such common grace. 3.05. 94
leaves winter, such summer birds are men. 3.06. 32 P
such a house broke? 4.02. 5
affords | to such as may the passive drugs of it 4.03.254
i know none such, my lord. 5.01. 99
of none but such as you, and you of timon. 5.01.135
even such heaps and sums of love and wealth | as 5.01.152
till now myself and such | as slept within the 5.04. 5
nor are they such | that these great tow'rs, 5.04. 24
that you have no such mirrors as will turn JC 1.02. 56
live to be | in awe of such a thing as i myself. 1.02. 96
amaze me | a man of such a feeble temper should 1.02.129
both meet to hear and answer such high things. 1.02.170
looks with such ferret and such fiery eyes | as 1.02.186
looks with such ferret and such fiery eyes | as 1.02.186
sleek–headed men and such as sleep a–nights. 1.02.193
such men are dangerous. 1.02.195
and smiles in such a sort | as if he mock'd 1.02.205
such men as he be never at heart's ease | whiles 1.02.208
and utter'd such a deal of stinking breath 1.02.246 P
send | such dreadful heralds to astonish us. 1.03. 56
casca, and to such a man | that is no fleering 1.03.116
such instigations have been often dropp'd 2.01. 49
and such suffering souls | that welcome wrongs; 2.01.130
bad causes swear | such creatures as men doubt; 2.01.132
such an exploit have i in hand, ligarius, | had 2.01.318
to think that caesar bears such rebel blood 3.01. 40
my credit now stands on such slippery ground 3.01.191
and you, | than i will wrong such honorable men. 3.02.127
stir you up | to such a sudden flood of mutiny. 3.02.211
when comes such another? 3.02.252
my noble master will appear | such as he is, 4.02. 12
enough, | but not with such familiar instances, 4.02. 16
nor with such free and friendly conference, | as 4.02. 17
you wrong'd yourself to write in such a case. 4.03. 6
in such a time as this it is not meet | that 4.03. 7
be a dog, and bay the moon, | than such a roman. 4.03. 28
to lock such rascal counters from his friends, 4.03. 80
a friendly eye could never see such faults. 4.03. 90
love, and be friends, as two such men should be, 4.03.131
on such a full sea are we now afloat, | and we 4.03.222
never come such division 'tween our souls! 4.03.235
a peevish schoolboy, worthless of such honor, 5.01. 61
are yet two romans living such as these? 5.03. 98
rather have | such men my friends than enemies. 5.04. 29
shall i do such a deed? 5.05. 8
you stop our way | with such prophetic greeting? MAC 1.03. 78
were such things here as we do speak about? 1.03. 83
from this time | such i account thy love. 1.07. 39
going, | and such an instrument i was to use. 2.01. 43
there's no such thing: 2.01. 47
that such a hideous trumpet calls to parley 2.03. 82
and in such bloody distance, | that every minute 3.01.115
shame itself, | why do you make such faces? 3.04. 66
this is more strange | than such a murther is. 3.04. 82
can such things be, | and overcome us like a 3.04.109
when now i think you can behold such sights, 3.04.113
shall raise such artificial sprites | as by the 3.05. 27
of the most pious edward with such grace | that 3.06. 27
where such as thou mayst find him. 4.02. 82
better macbeth | than such an one to reign. 4.03. 66
in my most ill–compos'd affection such | a 4.03. 77
if such a one be fit to govern, speak. 4.03.101
such welcome and unwelcome things at once | 'tis 4.03.138
such sanctity hath heaven given his hand, | they 4.03.144
i cannot but remember such things were, | that 4.03.222
i would not have such a heart in my bosom for 5.01. 55 P
there would have been a time for such a word. 5.05. 18
such a one | am i to fear, or none. 5.07. 3
that ever scotland | in such an honor nam'd. 5.09. 30
such was the very armor he had on | when he the HAM 1.01. 60
and /why such daily /cast of brazen cannon, 1.01. 73
why such impress of shipwrights, whose sore task 1.01. 75
post | with such dexterity to incestious sheets! 1.02.157
girl, | unsifted in such perilous circumstance. 1.03.102
thou com'st in such a questionable shape | that 1.04. 43
effect | holds such an enmity with blood of man 1.05. 65
such as it is, and for my own poor part, | i 1.05.131
that you, at such times seeing me, never shall, 1.05.173
or such ambiguous giving out, to note | that you 1.05.178
but, sir, such wanton, wild, and usual slips 2.01. 22
or then, or then, with such or such, and, as you 2.01. 55
or then, or then, with such or such, and, as you 2.01. 55
"i saw him enter such a house of sale," 2.01. 58
he falls to such perusal of my face | as 'a 2.01. 87
your visitation shall receive such thanks | as 2.02. 25
on such regards of safety and allowance | as 2.02. 79
hath there been such a time — i would fain know 2.02.153
at such a time i'll loose my daughter to him. 2.02.162
my lord, there was no such stuff in my thoughts. 2.02.311 P
those you were wont to take such delight in, the 2.02.327 P
whose judgments in such matters cried in the top 2.02.438 P
as he is very potent with such spirits, | abuses 2.02.602
that show of such an exercise may color | your 3.01. 44
i could accuse me of such things that it were 3.01.122 P
what should such fellows as i do crawling 3.01.127 P
i would have such a fellow whipt for o'erdoing 3.02. 13 P
such love must needs be treason in my breast. 3.02.178
but, sir, such answer as i can make, you shall 3.02.322 P
and do such /bitter /business /as /the day 3.02.391
such an act | that blurs the grace and blush of 3.04. 40
o, such a deed | as from the body of contraction 3.04. 45
of choice, | to serve in such a difference. 3.04. 76
and there i see such black and /grained spots 3.04. 90
from a bat, a gib, | such dear concernings hide? 3.04.191
but such officers do the king best service in 4.02. 16 P
sure he that made us with such large discourse, 4.04. 36
witness this army of such mass and charge | led 4.04. 47
there's such divinity doth hedge a king | that 4.05.124
or is it some abuse, and no such thing? 4.07. 50
did not together pluck such envy from him | as 4.07. 74
and to such wondrous doing brought his horse, 4.07. 86
and gave you such a masterly report | for art 4.07. 96
into the land, | as if i had never been such." 5.01. 74
clay for to be made | for such a guest is meet." 5.01. 97
and with such maimed rites? 5.01.219
to sing a requiem and such rest to her | as to 5.01.237
what is he whose grief | bears such an emphasis, 5.01.255
with, ho, such bugs and goblins in my life, 5.02. 22
and with such coz'nage — is't not perfect 5.02. 67
and his infusion of such dearth and rareness as, 5.02.117 P
foolery, but it is such a kind of /gain–giving, 5.02.215 P
such a sight as this | becomes the field, but 5.02.401
sir, | election makes not up in such conditions. LR 1.01.206
i would not from your love make such a stray 1.01.209
her offense | must be of such unnatural degree 1.01.219
and such a tongue | that i am glad i have not, 1.01.231
for we | have no such daughter, nor shall ever 1.01.263
such unconstant starts are we like to have from 1.01.300 P
carry authority with such disposition as he 1.01.304 P
of nothing hath not such need to hide itself. 1.02. 34 P
he cannot be such a monster — 1.02. 94 P
sung, | that such a king should play bo–peep, 1.04.177
depend, | to be such men as may besort your age, 1.04.251
when one has caught her, | and such a daughter, 1.04.318
and thereto add such reasons of your own | as 1.04.338
well inform'd of them, and with such cautions, 2.01.102
natures of such deep trust we shall much need; 2.01.115
that such a slave as this should wear a sword, 2.02. 72
such smiling rogues as these, | like rats, oft 2.02. 73
hold more antipathy | than i and such a knave. 2.02. 88
and put upon him such a deal of man | that 2.02.120
to do upon respect such violent outrage. 2.04. 24
'tis on such ground and to such wholesome end 2.04.144
'tis on such ground and to such wholesome end 2.04.144
reservation to be followed | with such a number. 2.04.253
i will have such revenges on you both | that all 2.04.279
all the world shall — i will do such things — 2.04.280
that love night | love not such nights as these. 3.02. 43
such sheets of fire, such bursts of horrid 3.02. 46
sheets of fire, such bursts of horrid thunder, 3.02. 46
such groans of roaring wind and rain, i never 3.02. 47
in such a night | to shut me out? 3.04. 17
in such a night as this? 3.04. 19
defend you | from seasons such as these? 3.04. 32
to such a lowness but his unkind daughters. 3.04. 71
unaccommodated man is no more but such a poor, 3.04.107 P
but mice and rats, and such small deer, | have 3.04.138
so white, and such a traitor? 3.07. 37
the sea, with such a storm as his bare head | in 3.07. 59
the winged vengeance overtake such children. 3.07. 66
i' th' last night's storm i such a fellow saw, 4.01. 32
upon such sacrifices, my cordelia, | the gods 5.03. 20
and such addition as your honors | have more 5.03.302
if ever i did dream of such a matter, | abhor me OTH 1.01. 5
whip me such honest knaves. 1.01. 49
some soul, | and such a one do i profess myself. 1.01. 55
joy, | yet throw such /changes of vexation on't, 1.01. 72
with such loud reason to the cyprus wars 1.01.150
you not read, roderigo, | of some such thing? 1.01.174
and spoke such scurvy and provoking terms 1.02. 7
to the sooty bosom | of such a thing as thou — 1.02. 71
for if such actions may have passage free, 1.02. 98
for that it stands not in such warlike brace, 1.03. 24
(for such proceeding i am charg'd withal) | i 1.03. 93
and such fair question | as soul to soul 1.03.113
was my hint to speak — such was my process — 1.03.142
wish'd | that heaven had made her such a man. 1.03.163
with such accommodation and besort | as levels 1.03.238
and such things else of quality and respect | as 1.03.282
if i would time expend with such /a snipe | but 1.03.385
she was a wight (if ever such /wight were) — 2.01.158
if such tricks as these strip you out of your 2.01.171 P
if after every tempest come such calms, | may 2.01.185
should hazard such a place as his own second 2.03.139
at all, unless you repute yourself such a loser. 2.03.271 P
as hydra, such an answer would stop them all. 2.03.305 P
we have none such, sir. 3.01. 18 P
or feed upon such nice and waterish diet, | or 3.03. 15
for such things in a false disloyal knave | are 3.03.121
soul | to such exsufflicate and /blown surmises, 3.03.182
she that so young could give out such a seeming 3.03.209
my speech should fall into such vild success 3.03.222
foh, one may smell in such, a will most rank, 3.03.232
love no friend, sith love breeds such offense. 3.03.380
i gave her such a one; 'twas my first gift. 3.03.436
but such a handkerchief | (i am sure it was your 3.03.437
mind, and made of no such baseness | as jealious 3.04. 27
he was born | drew all such humors from him. 3.04. 31
to lose't or give't away were such perdition 3.04. 67
if my offense be of such mortal kind | that nor 3.04.115
and in such cases | men's natures wrangle with 3.04.143
nor of them look for such observancy | as fits 3.04.149
or heard him say — as knaves be such abroad, 4.01. 25
not invest herself in such shadowing passion 4.01. 40 P
grief | (a passion most /unsuiting such a man), 4.01. 77
'tis such another fitchew! 4.01.146 P
thrown such despite and heavy terms upon her, 4.02.116
such as she said my lord did say i was. 4.02.119
could not have laid such terms upon his callet. 4.02.121
i do not know; i am sure i am none such. 4.02.123
fie, there is no such man; it is impossible. 4.02.134
if any such there be, heaven pardon him! 4.02.135
o /heaven, that such companions thou'dst unfold, 4.02.141
some such squire he was | that turn'd your wit 4.02.145
i will show you such a necessity in his death 4.02.240 P
do abuse their husbands | in such gross kind? 4.03. 63
there be some such, no question. 4.03. 63
wouldst thou do such a deed for all the world? 4.03. 64
wouldst thou do such a deed for all the world? 4.03. 68
i would not do such a thing for a joint–ring, 4.03. 72 P
if i would do such a wrong | for the whole world 4.03. 78
i do not think there is any such woman. 4.03. 83
/god me such uses send, | not to pick bad from 4.03.104
that hast such noble sense of thy friend's wrong 5.01. 32
but with such general warranty of heaven | as i 5.02. 60
if heaven would make me such another world | of 5.02.144
thou'rt not such a villain. 5.02.174
(more than indeed belong'd to such a trifle), 5.02.228
what should such a fool | do with so good a wife 5.02.233
when such a mutual pair | and such a twain can ANT 1.01. 37
such a mutual pair | and such a twain can do't, 1.01. 38
with such full license as both truth and malice 1.02.108
the man from sicyon — is there such an one? 1.02.114
act upon her, she hath such a celerity in dying. 1.02.144 P
to such whose places under us require, | our 1.02.195
into the hearts of such as have not thrived 1.03. 51
labor | to bear such idleness so near the heart 1.03. 94
but to confound such time | that drums him from 1.04. 28
be chok'd with such another emphasis! 1.05. 68
have donn'd his helm | for such a petty war. 2.01. 34
i would you had her spirit in such another; 2.02. 62
you may pace easy, but not such a wife. 2.02. 64
would we had all such wives, that the men might 2.02. 65 P
as befits mine honor | to stoop in such a case. 2.02. 98
so tart a favor | to trumpet such good tidings! 2.05. 39
i made no such report. 2.05. 57
prove such a wife | as my thoughts make thee, 3.02. 25
by him, | this creature's no such thing. 3.03. 41
his power went out in such distractions as 3.07. 76
i never saw an action of such shame; 3.10. 21
such as i am, i come from antony. 3.12. 7
have nick'd his captainship, at such a point, 3.13. 8
of mankind, had | destroyed in such a shape. 4.08. 26
eros, now thy captain is | even such a body. 4.14. 13
i have liv'd in such dishonor that the gods 4.14. 56
by such poor passion as the maid that milks 4.15. 74
when such a spacious mirror's set before him, 5.01. 34
have shown to thee such a declining day, | or 5.01. 38
do not yourself such wrong, who are in this 5.02. 40
o, such another sleep, that i might see | but 5.02. 77
sleep, that i might see | but such another man! 5.02. 78
think you there was or might be such a man | as 5.02. 93
but if there be, nor ever were one such, | it's 5.02. 96
things of such dignity | as we greet modern 5.02.166
such as th' aspic leaves | upon the caves of 5.02.352
and therefore banish'd) is a creature such | as, CYM 1.01. 19
think | so fair an outward and such stuff within 1.01. 23
of issue, took such sorrow | that he quit being, 1.01. 37
to air yourself, | such parting were too petty. 1.01.111
him at certain hours | such thoughts and such; 1.03. 28
him at certain hours | such thoughts and such; 1.03. 28
and by such two that would by all likelihood 1.04. 50 P
come off and leave her in such honor as you have 1.04.152 P
doctor, | thou ask'st me such a question. 1.05. 11
of these thy compounds on such creatures as | we 1.05. 19
her malice with | a drug of such damn'd nature. 1.05. 36
of thy preferment, such | as thou'lt desire; 1.05. 71
'twixt two such shes would chatter this way, and 1.06. 40
sluttery, to such neat excellence oppos'd, 1.06. 44
hell should at one time | encounter such revolt. 1.06.112
such boil'd stuff | as well might poison poison. 1.06.125
(as i have such a heart that both mine ears 1.06.130
not | for such an end thou seek'st — as base as 1.06.144
such a holy witch | that he enchants societies 1.06.166
was there ever man had such luck? 2.01. 1 P
that such a crafty devil as is his mother 2.01. 52
such and such pictures; 2.02. 25
such and such pictures; 2.02. 25
such | th' adornment of her bed; 2.02. 25
the arras, figures, | why, such and such; 2.02. 27
the arras, figures, | why, such and such; 2.02. 27
hairs above thee, | were they all made such men. 2.03.136
to their approvers they are people such | that 2.04. 25
a second night of such sweet shortness which 2.04. 44
be many caesars, | ere such another julius. 3.01. 12
and, as i said, there is no moe such caesars. 3.01. 36 P
crook'd noses, but to owe such straight arms, 3.01. 37 P
such assaults | as would take in some virtue. 3.02. 8
was made so happy as | t' inherit such a haven. 3.02. 61
a goodly day not to keep house with such | whose 3.03. 1
such gain the cap of him that makes him fine, 3.03. 25
o, for such means, | though peril to my modesty, 3.04.151
you can borrow | from youth of such a season) 3.04.172
such, i mean, | where they should be reliev'd. 3.06. 7
such a foe, good heavens! 3.06. 27
and such a welcome as i'ld give to him | (after 3.06. 72
to him | (after long absence), such is yours. 3.06. 73
was that it was for not being such a smile; 4.02. 53
i have heard of such. 4.02. 72
it may be heard at court that such as we | cave 4.02.137
color | i'ld let a parish of such clotens blood, 4.02.168
alas, | there is no more such masters. 4.02.371
never | find such another master. 4.02.374
it said a century of prayers | (such as i can) 4.02.392
a doubt | in such a time nothing becoming you, 4.04. 15
and the disorder's such | as war were hoodwink'd 5.02. 15
the country base than to commit such slaughter, 5.03. 20
or else such stuff as madmen | tongue and brain 5.04.145
or a speaking such | as sense cannot untie. 5.04.147
going, but such as wink and will not use them. 5.04.186 P
never saw | such noble fury in so poor a thing; 5.05. 8
such precious deeds in one that promis'd nought 5.05. 9
she bore in hand to love | with such integrity, 5.05. 44
gentle princes | (for such and so they are) 5.05.337
bloody hands were wash'd) with such a peace. 5.05.485
will, | to compass such a /boundless happiness! PER 1.01. 24
this mercy shows we'll joy in such a son; 1.01.118
antiochus doth sin | in such a loathed manner; 1.01.147
if there be such a dart in princes' frowns, 1.02. 53
such griefs as you yourself do lay upon yourself 1.02. 66
o my distressed lord, even such our griefs are; 1.04. 7
makes such unquiet, that the ship | should house 2.ch. 31
such whales have i heard on a' th' land, who 2.01. 32 P
i would have kept such a jangling of the bells, 2.01. 41 P
with such a graceful courtesy delivered? 2.02. 41
fed | with such delightful pleasing harmony. 2.05. 28
who thought of such a thing?" 3.ch. 38
grisled north | disgorges such a tempest forth, 3.ch. 48
here is a thing too young for such a place, 3.01. 15
but such a night as this | till now i ne'er 3.02. 5
such strong renown as time shall never — 3.02. 48
such a maidenhead were no cheap thing, if men 4.02. 60 P
such a piece of slaughter | the sun and moon 4.03. 2
to such proceeding | who ever but his 4.03. 25
nor never shall do in such a place as this, she 4.05. 2 P

did you ever dream of such a thing? 4.05. 5 P
know this house to be a place of such resort, 4.06. 79 P
thy food is such | as hath been belch'd on by 4.06.168
she's such a one that, were i well assur'd 5.01. 67
thy sacred physic shall receive such pay | as 5.01. 74
and such a one | my daughter might have been. 5.01.107
some such thing | i said, and said no more but 5.01.132
and give you gold for such provision | as our 5.01.257
give me, | for such kindness must relieve me: 5.02. 4
the king my father gave you such a ring. 5.03. 39
fan | from me the witless chaff of such a writer TNK pr 19
which gives me such lamenting | as wakes my 1.01. 57
you, at such a season | as now it is with me, i 1.01. 60
key — like such a woman | as any of us three; 1.01. 94
indeed — | such heart–pierc'd demonstration! 1.01.124
and the number | to carry such a business, forth 1.01.162
as much sorry | i should be such a suitor; 1.01.188
some say, | groan under such a mast'ry. 1.01.231
i do bleed | when such i meet, and wish great 1.02. 21
where e'er i find them, but such most | that, 1.02. 32
and | such things to be, mere monsters. 1.02. 42
not scissor'd just | to such a favorite's glass? 1.02. 55
if | you stay to see of us such spinsters, we 1.03. 23
she would long | till she had such another, and 1.03. 69
the very lees of such (millions of rates) 1.04. 29
that with such a constant nobility enforce a 2.01. 33 P
canst not thou work such flowers in silk, wench? 2.02.127
of such a virtuous greatness that this lady, 2.02.257
thou bring'st such pelting scurvy news 2.02.266
such a vengeance | that, were i old and wicked, 2.03. 5
not far, sir. | are there such games to–day? 2.03. 64
and such as you never saw. 2.03. 65
to such a well–found wonder as thy worth, | for 2.05. 27
he made such scruples of the wrong he did | to 2.06. 25
get many more such prisoners and such daughters, 2.06. 38
get many more such prisoners and such daughters, 2.06. 38
to drop on such a mistress, expectation | most 3.01. 14
two such steeds might well | be by a pair of 3.01. 20
give me language such | as thou hast show'd me 3.01. 44
i have seen you move in such a place, which well 3.01. 63
despisings of our persons, and such poutings, 3.06. 33
but, loving such a lady, | and justifying my 3.06. 41
i never saw such valor. 3.06. 74
more | come near thee with such friendship. 3.06.103
for none but such dare die in these just trials. 3.06.105
do such a justice thou thyself wilt envy. 3.06.155
if such vows | stand for express will, all the 3.06.228
their knees | begg'd with such handsome pity, 4.01. 9
city made | with such a cry and swiftness that, 4.01. 98
two such young handsome men | shall never fall 4.02. 3
just such another wanton ganymede | set /jove 4.02. 15
and fights | of gods and such men near 'em. 4.02. 25
fear he cannot, | he shows no such soft temper. 4.02.103
promises | in such a body yet i never look'd on. 4.02.119
but such a manly color | next to an aborn; 4.02.124
they have i' th' tother place, such burning, 4.03. 32 P
as one would think, for such a trifle. 4.03. 46 P
sing to her such green songs of love as she says 4.03. 81 P
such a one i am, | and vow that lover never yet 5.01.124
o, what pity | enough for such a chance! 5.03. 60
better never born | than minister to such harm! 5.03. 66
that four such eyes should be so fix'd on one 5.03.145
sure shall please the gods | sooner than such, 5.04. 12
but such a vessel 'tis that floats but for | the 5.04. 83
i am not bold, | we have no such cause. ep 12
things that ever stood in such a question. STM II.C 21
had there such fellows liv'd when you were babes II.C 63
to find a nation of such barbarous temper | that II.C 131
god, | that i from such an humble bench of birth III 6
being wasted in such time–beguiling sport." VEN 24
so they were dew'd with such distilling showers. 66
then be my deer, since i am such a park, | no 239
fee, | he held such petty bondage in disdain, 394
were never four such lamps together mix'd, | had 489
and such disdain | that they have murd'red this 501
is twenty hundred kisses such a trouble?" 522
such nectar from his lips she had not suck'd. 572
beauty hath nought to do with such foul fiends. 638
drink tears, that thou provok'st such weeping? 949
was i | to be of such a weak and silly mind, 1016
when he was by, the birds such pleasure took, 1101
reck'ning his fortune at such high proud rate LUC 19
but king nor peer to such a peerless dame. 21
writ in the glassy margents of such books. 102
and such griefs sustain | that they prove 139
and in this aim there is such thwarting strife 143
such hazard now must doting tarquin make, 155
wife, | as in revenge or quittal of such strife; 236
who fears sinking where such treasure lies?" 280
but she, sound sleeping, fearing no such thing, 363
his hand, as proud of such a dignity, | smoking 437
such shadows are the weak brain's forgeries, 460
(rude ram, to batter such an ivory wall!), 464
with such black payment as thou hast pretended; 576
if in thy hope thou dar'st do such outrage, 605
must he in thee read lectures of such shame? 618
alas, how many bear such shameful blows, | which 832
evil, | when virtue is profan'd in such a devil! 847
being so bad, such numbers seek for thee? 896
such wretched hands such wretched blood should 999
such wretched hands such wretched blood should 999
for who so base would such an office have | as 1000
such danger to resistance did belong | that 1265
extremity still urgeth such extremes. 1337
such harmless creatures have a true respect | to 1347
such sweet observance in this work was had, 1385
fight, | making such sober action with his hand, 1403
and in their rage such signs of rage they bear, 1419
and to their hope they such odd action yield, 1433
into so bright a day such black–fac'd storms, 1518
blot with hell–born sin such saint–like forms. 1519
such signs of truth in his plain face she spied, 1532
she would have said, "can lurk in such a look"; 1535
but such a face should bear a wicked mind. 1540
"such devils steal effects from lightless hell, 1555
these contraries such unity do hold | only to 1558
such passion her assails | that patience is 1562
side, | seeing such emulation in their woe, 1808
such childish humor from weak minds proceeds; 1825
heart | in such relenting dew of lamentations, 1829
such looks as none could look but beauty's queen PP 4. 4
heaven's praise with such an earthly tongue. 5.14
spenser to me, whose deep conceit is such | as, 8. 7
that on himself such murd'rous shame commits. SON 9.14
in them i read such art | as truth and beauty 14.10
such heavenly touches ne'er touch'd earthly 17. 8
whilst i, whom fortune of such triumph bars, 25. 3
thy sweet love rememb'red such wealth brings, 29.13
why didst thou promise such a beauteous day, 34. 1
for no man well of such a salve can speak | that 34. 7
such civil war is in my love and hate, | that i 35.12
but do not so, i love thee in such sort, | as 36.13
that this shadow doth such substance give, 37.10
hang on such thorns, and play as wantonly, 54. 7
no shape so true, no truth of such account, 62. 6
for such a time do i now fortify | against 63. 9
when i have seen such interchange of state, | or 64. 9
in me thou seest the twilight of such day | as 73. 5
in me thou seest the glowing of such fire | that 73. 9
and for the peace of you i hold such strife | as 75. 3
and found such fair assistance in my verse | as 78. 2
you still shall live (such virtue hath my pen) 81.13
and such a counterpart shall fame his wit, 84.11
in sleep a king, but waking no such matter. 87.14
such is my love, to thee i so belong, | that for 88.13
but do not so, i love thee in such sort, | as 96.13
that, having such a scope to show her pride, 103. 2
your eye i ey'd, | such seems your beauty still. 104. 3
be | to one, of one, still such, and ever so. 105. 4
even such a beauty as you master now. 106. 8
such cherubins as your sweet self resemble, 114. 6
and they mourners seem | at such who, not born 127.11
white, | but no such roses see i in her cheeks, 130. 6
there is such strength and warrantise of skill 150. 7
him, was he such a storm | as oft 'twixt may and LC 101
make | what i should do again for such a sake. 322

SUCH–A–ONE 1 FR 0.0001 REL FR 0 V 1 P
this might be my lord such–a–one, that prais'd HAM 5.01. 84 P

SUCH–A–ONE'S 1 FR 0.0001 REL FR 0 V 1 P
that prais'd my lord such–a–one's horse, when 'a HAM 5.01. 85 P

SUCH–LIKE 9 FR 0.0010 REL FR 7 V 2 P
and even with such–like valor men hang and drown TMP 3.03. 59
and many such–like liberties of sin: ERR 1.02.102
and such–like toys as these | hath mov'd his R3 1.01. 60
liberality, and such–like, the spice and salt TRO 1.02.254 P
plate, jewels, and such–like trifles — nothing TIM 3.02. 22 P
and many such–like /as's of great charge, | that HAM 5.02. 43
they think delight | in such–like circumstance, VEN 844
in such–like circumstance, with such–like sport: 844
and with such–like flattering, | "pity but he PP 20.39

SUCK 24 FR 0.0027 REL FR 22 V 2 P
where the bee sucks, there suck i, | in a TMP 5.01. 88
they'll suck our breath, or pinch us black and ERR 2.02.192
i can suck melancholy out of a song, as a weasel AYL 2.05. 13 P
pride is to see my ewes graze and my lambs suck. 3.02. 77 P
to suck the sweets of sweet philosophy. SHR 1.01. 28
why then i suck my teeth, and catechize | my JN 1.01.192
but let thy spiders, that suck up thy venom, R2 3.02. 14
the noisome weeds which without profit suck 3.04. 38
to suck, to suck, the very blood to suck! H5 2.03. 56
to suck, to suck, the very blood to suck! 2.03. 56
to suck, to suck, the very blood to suck! 2.03. 56
and your fair show shall suck away their souls, 4.02. 17
as i suck blood, i will some mercy show. 4.04. 64
their mothers' moist'ned eyes babes shall suck, 1H6 1.01. 49
drones suck not eagles' blood, but rob beehives. 2H6 4.01.109
stops thy spring, my sea shall suck them dry, 3H6 4.08. 55
more spungy to suck in the sense of fear, | more TRO 2.02. 12
him that gat thee, she that gave thee suck; 2.03.241
and feed on curds and whey, and suck the goat, TIT 4.02.178
go, suck the subtle blood o' th' grape, | till TIM 4.03.429
to walk unbraced and suck up the humors | of the JC 2.01.262
signifies that from you great rome shall suck 2.02. 87
i have given suck, and know | how tender 'tis to MAC 1.07. 54
boats, | but suck them up to th' topmast. CYM 3.01. 22

SUCK'D 12 FR 0.0013 REL FR 11 V 1 P
trunk, | and suck'd my verdure out on't. TMP 1.02. 87
have suck'd up from the sea | contagious fogs; MND 2.01. 89
there, | food to the suck'd and hungry lioness? AYL 4.03.126
that was a man | when hector's grandsire suck'd. TRO 1.03.292
would say thou hadst suck'd wisdom from thy teat ROM 1.03. 68
death, that hath suck'd the honey of thy breath, 5.03. 92
that suck'd the honey of his /music vows, | now HAM 3.01.156
/comply, sir, with his dug before 'a suck'd it. 5.02.188 P
the blood of mine that's sib to him be suck'd TNK 1.02. 72
such nectar from his lips she had not suck'd. VEN 572
there lives a son that suck'd an earthly mother, 863
and suck'd the honey which thy chaste bee kept. LUC 840

SUCK'DST 1 FR 0.0001 REL FR 1 V 0 P
mother gave thee, when thou suck'dst her breast, 1H6 5.04. 28

SUCKING 6 FR 0.0006 REL FR 5 V 1 P
i will roar you as gently as any sucking dove; MND 1.02. 82 P
pluck the young sucking cubs from the she–bear, MV 2.01. 29
as fierce | as waters to the sucking of a gulf. H5 2.04. 10
fift | was in the mouth of every sucking babe, 1H6 3.01.196
as is the sucking lamb or harmless dove. 2H6 3.01. 71
kind | we sucking on her natural bosom find: ROM 2.03. 12

SUCKLE 2 FR 0.0002 REL FR 2 V 0 P
when she did suckle hector, look'd not lovelier COR 1.03. 41
to suckle fools and chronicle small beer. OTH 2.01.160

SUCKS 5 FR 0.0005 REL FR 4 V 1 P
all the infections that the sun sucks up | from TMP 2.02. 1
where the bee sucks, there suck i, | in a 5.01. 88
out of a song, as a weasel sucks eggs. AYL 2.05. 13 P
comes sneaking, and so sucks her princely eggs, H5 1.02.171
at my breast, | that sucks the nurse asleep? ANT 5.02.310

SUCK'ST 2 FR 0.0002 REL FR 2 V 0 P
valiantness was mine, thou suck'st it from me; COR 3.02.129
the milk thou suck'st from her did turn to TIT 2.03.144

SUDDEN 81 FR 0.0091 REL FR 72 V 9 P
then let us both be sudden. TMP 2.01.306
and, notwithstanding all her sudden quips, | the TGV 4.02. 12
upon a sudden, | as falstaff, she, and i are WIV 4.04. 52
of my mind, the sudden surprise of my powers, 5.05.123 P
o, that's sudden! MM 2.02. 83
but lest my liking might too sudden seem, | i ADO 1.01.314
but pardon me, i am too sudden bold; LLL 2.01.107
such eruptions and sudden breaking out of mirth, 5.01.114 P
the sudden hand of death close up mine eye! 5.02.815
is it possible, on such a sudden, you should AYL 1.03. 27 P
jealous in honor, sudden, and quick in quarrel, 2.07.151
the small acquaintance, my sudden wooing, nor 5.02. 6 P
my sudden wooing, nor /her sudden consenting; 5.02. 7 P
never any thing so sudden but the fight of two 5.02. 30 P
that love should of a sudden take such hold? SHR 1.01.147
whose sudden sight hath thrall'd my wounded eye. 1.01.220
so out of circumstance and sudden, tells us WT 5.01. 90
therefore i will be sudden, and dispatch. JN 4.01. 27
the better arm you to the sudden time | than if 5.06. 26
show'rs last long, but sudden storms are short; R2 2.01. 35
woman, do not so, | to make my end too sudden. 5.01. 17
their breath | on some great sudden hest. 1H4 2.03. 62
season, | for i am on the sudden something ill. 2H4 4.02. 80
coz, since sudden sorrow | serves to say thus, 4.02. 83
and as sudden | as flaws congealed in the spring 4.04. 34
never was such a sudden scholar made; H5 1.01. 32
word, | some sudden mischief may arise of it; 4.07.178
none durst come near for fear of sudden death. 1H6 1.04. 48
this sudden mischief never could have fall'n. 2.01. 59
rous'd on the sudden from their drowsy beds, 2.02. 23
as i with sudden and extemporal speech | purpose 3.01. 6
one sudden foil shall never breed distrust. 3.03. 11
thee how thou shalt escape | by sudden flight. 4.05. 11
somewhat too sudden, sirs, the warning is, | but 5.02. 14
will excuse | this sudden execution of my will. 5.05. 99
some sudden qualm hath struck me at the heart, 2H6 1.01. 54
and comment then upon his sudden death. 3.02.133
madam, what makes you in this sudden change? 3H6 4.04. 1
he's sudden, if a thing comes in his head. 5.05. 86
but, sirs, be sudden in the execution, | withal R3 1.03.345
this sudden stab of rancor i misdoubt; 3.02. 87
to–morrow, in my judgment, is too sudden, | for 3.04. 43
is that by sudden floods and fall of waters 4.04.510
of this peace, aboded | the sudden breach on't. H8 1.01. 94
stops on a sudden, looks upon the ground, | then 3.02.114
what sudden anger's this? 3.02.204
that's somewhat sudden; 3.02.394
how much her grace is alter'd on the sudden? 4.02. 96
which reformation must be sudden too, | my noble 5.02. 55
you were ever good at sudden commendations, 5.02.157
is like that mirth fate turns to sudden sadness. TRO 1.01. 40
who upon the sudden | clapp'd to their gates. COR 1.04. 50
on the sudden, | i warrant him consul. 2.01.221
off, | and with a sudden reinforcement struck 2.02.113
enemy, and revoke | your sudden approbation. 2.03.251
if thou be pleas'd with this my sudden choice, TIT 1.01.318
of goths | is of a sudden thus advanc'd in rome? 1.01.393
it is too rash, too unadvis'd, too sudden, | too ROM 2.02.118
where on a sudden one hath wounded me | that's 2.03. 50
o, let us hence, i stand on sudden haste. 2.03. 93
no sudden mean of death, though ne'er so mean, 3.03. 45
hath sorted out a sudden day of joy, | that thou 3.05.109
without a sudden calm, will overset | thy 3.05.136
hands full all, | in this so sudden business. 4.03. 12
casca, be sudden, for we fear prevention. JC 3.01. 19
stir you up | to such a sudden flood of mutiny. 3.02.211
and sudden push gives them the overthrow. 5.02. 5
sudden, malicious, smacking of every sin | that MAC 4.03. 59
and with a sudden vigor it doth /posset | and HAM 1.05. 68
even, | this sudden sending him away must seem 4.03. 8
the occasion of my sudden /and /more /strange 4.07. 47 P
beg | your sudden coming o'er to play with you. 4.07.105
he should those bearers put to sudden death, 5.02. 46
breeches, "then they for sudden joy did weep, LR 1.04.175
sir, he's rash and very sudden in choler, and OTH 2.01.272 P
and comforts of sudden respect and acquaintance, 4.02.189 P
but on the sudden | a roman thought hath strook ANT 1.02. 82
if in mirth, report | that i am sudden sick. 1.03. 5
she stood, | and on the sudden dropp'd. 5.02.344
quoth she, whereat a sudden pale, | like lawn VEN 589
are on the sudden wasted, thaw'd, and done, | as 749

/SUDDENLY 2 FR 0.0002 REL FR 0 V 2 P
him, /and /suddenly /contrive /the /means /of HAM 2.02.212 P
/king /of /france /is /so /suddenly /gone /back, LR 4.03. 1 P

SUDDENLY 51 FR 0.0057 REL FR 43 V 8 P
muse not that i thus suddenly proceed; TGV 1.03. 64
in the brew–house, and when i suddenly call you, WIV 3.03. 11 P
mistress ford desires you to come suddenly. 4.01. 6 P
and upon the grief of this suddenly died. ADO 4.02. 63 P
my coming, | and suddenly resolve me in my suit. LLL 2.01.110
madam, i will, if suddenly i may. 2.01.111
yet do not suddenly, for it may grieve him. MV 2.08. 34
argosies | are richly come to harbor suddenly. 5.01.277
'gainst the lady | will suddenly break forth. AYL 1.02.283
do this suddenly; 2.02. 19
be, | and buy it with your gold right suddenly. 2.04.100
but suddenly, | seeing orlando, it unlink'd 4.03.110
was ever match clapp'd up so suddenly? SHR 2.01.325
of florentines, will suddenly surprise him; AWW 3.06. 22 P
foretells | the great apollo suddenly will have WT 2.03.200
villain, | whose bowels suddenly burst out. JN 5.06. 30
suddenly taken, and hath sent post–haste | to R2 1.04. 55
when time is ripe, which will be suddenly, 1H4 1.03.294
i'll repent, and that suddenly, while i am in 3.03. 5 P
spirt up so suddenly into the clouds | and H5 3.05. 8
them, we will suddenly | pass our accept and 5.02. 81
chance is this that suddenly hath cross'd us? 1H6 1.04. 72
my charge, | do it without invention, suddenly, 3.01. 5
her words, | or nature makes me suddenly relent. 3.03. 59
heart | suddenly made him from my side to start 4.07. 12
and may ye both be suddenly surpris'd | by 5.03. 40
had not your man put up the fowl so suddenly, 2H6 2.01. 44
but suddenly | to nominate them all, it is 2.01.127
and that's not suddenly to be perform'd, | but 2.02. 67
for suddenly a grievous sickness took him, 3.02.370
speak suddenly, my lords, are we all friends? 3H6 4.02. 4
dead, | and i would have it suddenly perform'd. R3 4.02. 19
speak suddenly, be brief. 4.02. 20
to have him suddenly convey'd from hence. 4.04. 76
can make, | and meet me suddenly at salisbury. 4.04.451
but how to make ye suddenly an answer | in such H8 3.01. 70
he fell sick suddenly and grew so ill | he could 4.02. 15

still, when suddenly a file of boys behind 'em, 5.03. 55 P
i'll lay ye all | by th' heels, and suddenly; 5.03. 79
and suddenly, where injury of chance | puts back TRO 4.04. 33
and i myself | am like a prophet suddenly enrapt 5.03. 65
should straight fall mad, or else die suddenly. TIT 2.03.104
suddenly | i heard a child cry underneath a wall 5.01. 23
surpris'd him suddenly, and brought him hither 5.01. 38
at supper | you suddenly arose and walk'd about, JC 2.01.239
by the noise i made, | full suddenly he fled. LR 2.01. 56
it came in too suddenly, let it die as it was CYM 1.04.121 P
suddenly, woman. PER 3.01. 69
come, let's have her aboard suddenly. 4.01. 95 P
be suddenly revenged on my foe, | thine, mine, LUC 1683
good, | a shining gloss that vadeth suddenly, PP 13. 2
SU'D–FOR 1 FR 0.0001 REL FR 1 V 0 P
ask but mock, bestow | your su'd–for tongues? COR 2.03.208
SUE 28 FR 0.0031 REL FR 23 V 5 P
good sir john, i sue for yours — not to charge WIV 2.02.164 P
and let him learn to know, when maidens sue, MM 1.04. 80
blushes | that banish what they sue for. 2.04.163
to sue to live, i find i seek to die, | and, 3.01. 42
love with life that i will sue to be rid of it. 3.01.172 P
my soul should sue as advocate for thee: ERR 1.01.145
i love, i sue, i seek a wife — | a woman, that LLL 3.01.189
i will love, write, sigh, pray, sue, groan: 3.01.204
that you stand forfeit, being those that sue? 5.02.427
we were not born to sue, but to command, | which R2 1.01.196
by his attorneys–general to sue | his livery, 2.01.203
i am denied to sue my livery here, | and yet my 2.03.129
i do not sue to stand; 5.03.129
to sue his livery and beg his peace, | with 1H4 4.03. 62
they humbly sue unto your excellence | to have a 1H6 5.01. 4
grace, | begin your suits anew, and sue to him. 2H6 1.03. 39
what love, think'st thou, i sue so much to get? 3H6 3.02. 61
nor will i sue, although the king have mercies H8 2.01. 70
knew | love got so sweet as when desire did sue. TRO 1.02.291
base | to sue and be denied such common grace. TIM 3.05. 94
i must love you, and sue to know you better. LR 1.01. 30 P
sue to him again, and he's yours. OTH 2.03.275 P
i will rather sue to be despis'd than to deceive 2.03.277 P
or sue to you to do a peculiar profit | to your 3.03. 79
to their throne, decays | the thing we sue for. ANT 2.01. 5
if she perform, | she shall not sue unheard. 3.12. 24
i sue for exil'd majesty's repeal, | let him LUC 640
use, | and sue a friend came debtor for my sake, SON 134.11
SUED 6 FR 0.0006 REL FR 6 V 0 P
i never sued to friend nor enemy; R3 1.02.167
who sued to me for him? 2.01.107
for one being sued to, one that humbly sues; 4.04.100
that therefore such a writ be sued against you, H8 3.02.341
sons, | to whom i sued for my dear son's life; TIT 1.01.453
when you sued staying, | then was the time for ANT 1.03. 33
SUERLY *(also surely)*
SUERLY 1 FR 0.0001 REL FR 0 V 1 P
as valorously as i may, that sall i suerly do, H5 3.02.117 P
SUES 5 FR 0.0005 REL FR 5 V 0 P
my master sues to her; TGV 2.01.137
my proud heart sues, and prompts my tongue to R3 1.02.170
who sues, and kneels, and says, "god save the 4.04. 94
for one being sued to, one that humbly sues; 4.04.100
and to thee sues | to let him breathe between ANT 3.12. 13
SUETH 1 FR 0.0001 REL FR 1 V 0 P
'tis the french dolphin sueth to thee thus. 1H6 1.02.112
/SUFFER 2 FR 0.0002 REL FR 2 V 0 P
/our /arms /may /do, /what /wrongs /we /suffer, 2H4 4.01. 68
/my /good /brother /suffer /you /to /do /it? LR 4.02. 44
SUFFER 86 FR 0.0097 REL FR 66 V 20 P
i have suffered | with those that i saw suffer. TMP 1.02. 6
but doth suffer a sea–change | into something 1.02.401
this wooden slavery than to suffer | the 3.01. 62
my subject, and he shall not suffer indignity. 3.02. 37 P
would suffer him to spend his youth at home, TGV 1.03. 5
i do as truly suffer | as e'er i did commit. 5.04. 76
'tis my fault, master page. i suffer for it. WIV 3.03.218 P
you suffer for a pad conscience. 3.03.219 P
to this supposed, or else to let him suffer — MM 2.04. 97
so it doth appear | by the wrongs i suffer, and ERR 3.01. 16
wilt thou suffer them | to make a rescue? 4.04.110
us, | and will not suffer us to fetch him out, 5.01.157
it were pity but they should suffer salvation, ADO 3.03. 3 P
make those that do offend you suffer too. 5.01. 40
my good parts did you first suffer love for me? 5.02. 65 P
suffer love! 5.02. 66 P
i do suffer love indeed, for i love thee against 5.02. 66 P
i suffer for the truth, sir; LLL 1.01.311 P
and you must suffer him to take no delight nor 1.02.128 P
why will you suffer her to flout me thus? MND 3.02.327
and am arm'd | to suffer, with a quietness of MV 4.01. 12
what, will you not suffer me? SHR 2.01. 31
that would suffer her poor knight surpris'd AWW 1.03.115 P
rather than suffer question for your residence. 2.05. 38 P
under my poor instructions yet must suffer 4.04. 27
i am yours | upon your will to suffer. 4.04. 30
both suffer under this complaint we bring, | and 5.03.163
that suffer surfeit, cloyment, and revolt, | but TN 2.04. 99
violence, in the which three great ones suffer, WT 2.01.128
and settled project | may suffer alteration. 4.04.525
not he alone shall suffer what wit can make 4.04.772 P
to be honest, i see fortune would not suffer me: 4.04.832 P
go we, as well as haste will suffer us, | to JN 2.01.559
long | shall tender duty make me suffer wrong? R2 2.01.164
we see the very wrack that we must suffer, | and 2.01.267
detraction will not suffer it. 1H4 5.01.139 P
and suffer the condition of these times | to lay 2H4 4.01. 99
heavens, can you suffer hell so to prevail? 1H6 1.05. 9
and ere that we will suffer such a prince, | so 3.01. 97
and suffer you to breathe in fruitful peace, 5.04.127
either to suffer shipwrack, or arrive | where i 5.05. 8
suffer them now, and they'll o'ergrow the garden 2H6 3.01. 32
what, shall we suffer this? 3H6 1.01. 59
o god that seest it, do not suffer it! R3 1.03.270
patience, | i may not suffer you to visit them, 4.01. 16
or else you suffer | too hard an exclamation. H8 1.02. 51
as not thus to suffer | a man of his place, and 5.02. 29
if we suffer, | out of our easiness and childish 5.02. 59
the king will suffer but the little finger | of 5.02.141
you'll ne'er be good, | nor suffer others. TRO 4.02. 30
suffer us to famish, and their store–houses COR 1.01. 80 P
were to us all that do't and suffer it | a brand 3.01.301
to suffer lawful censure for such faults | as 3.03. 46
though they themselves did suffer by't, behold 4.06. 6
size that verity | would without lapsing suffer. 5.02. 19
and suffer not dishonor to approach | the TIT 1.01. 13
suffer thy brother marcus to inter | his noble 1.01.375
that will not suffer you to square yourselves, 2.01.124
stand by too and suffer every knave to use me at ROM 2.04.155 P
he's truly valiant that can wisely suffer | the TIM 3.05. 31
that suffer in exposure, let us meet | and MAC 2.03.127
of things disjoint, both the worlds suffer, 3.02. 16
more suffer, and more sundry ways than ever, 4.03. 48
whether 'tis nobler in the mind to suffer | the HAM 3.01. 56
then, or else shall 'a suffer not thinking on, 3.02.134 P
why does he suffer this mad knave now to knock 5.01.101 P
commands the mind | to suffer with the body. LR 2.04.109
my duty cannot suffer | t' obey in all your 3.04.148
part of his grief with me | to suffer with him. OTH 3.03. 54
thou hast no weapon, and perforce must suffer. 5.02.256
if they suffer our departure, death's the word. ANT 1.02.134 P
with patience more | than savages could suffer. 1.04. 61
only, | lest my remembrance suffer ill report; 2.02.156
quality after them, | to suffer all alike. 3.13. 34
he would not suffer me | to bring him to the CYM 1.01.170
may, without contradiction, suffer the report. 1.04. 55 P
why did you suffer jachimo, | slight thing of 5.04. 63
a roman with a roman's heart can suffer. 5.05. 81
see how belief may suffer by foul show! PER 4.04. 23
he will not suffer us to burn their bones, | to TNK 1.01. 43
bodies, let 'em suffer | the gall of hazard, so 2.02. 65
griefs, angers, fears, my friend shall suffer? 2.02.188
hast felt what sorrow was, | dream how i suffer! 2.02.277
that they will suffer these abominations LUC 1832
o, let me suffer (being at your beck) | th' SON 58. 5
why dost thou pine within and suffer dearth, 146. 3
/SUFFERANCE 1 FR 0.0001 REL FR 1 V 0 P
/the /mind /much /sufferance /doth /o'erskip, LR 3.06.106
SUFFERANCE 22 FR 0.0024 REL FR 16 V 6 P
lord, your sorrow hath eaten up my sufferance. WIV 4.02. 2 P
his death draw out | to ling'ring sufferance. MM 2.04.167
in corporal sufferance finds a pang as great 3.01. 79
a present remedy, at least a patient sufferance. ADO 1.03. 9 P
and made a push at chance and sufferance. 5.01. 38
jew, what should his sufferance be by christian MV 3.01. 70 P
court | are of consent and sufferance in this. AYL 2.02. 3
well, of sufferance comes ease. 2H4 5.04. 25 P
lest example | breed, by his sufferance, more of H5 2.02. 46
which /i in sufferance heartily will rejoice, 2.02.159
see his weakness, and admire our sufferance. 3.06.125 P
as thou shalt reign but by their sufferance. 3H6 1.01.234
'tis a sufferance panging | as soul and body's H8 2.03. 15
our sufferance is a gain to them. COR 1.01. 22 P
in authority, | against all noble sufferance. 3.01. 24
thy nature did commence in sufferance, time TIM 4.03.268
arms, and breath'd | our sufferance vainly. 5.04. 8
our yoke and sufferance show us womanish. JC 1.03. 84
the sufferance of our souls, the time's abuse — 2.01.115
hath seen a grievous wrack and sufferance | on OTH 2.01. 23
us, for | we have been too slight in sufferance. CYM 3.05. 35
and patience, tame to sufferance, bide each SON 58. 7
SUFFERANCES 1 FR 0.0001 REL FR 1 V 0 P
the seeming sufferances that you had borne, 1H4 5.01. 51
SUFFER'D 27 FR 0.0030 REL FR 14 V 13 P
that hath lately suffer'd by a thunderbolt. TMP 2.02. 36 P
sure as i live, he had suffer'd for't. TGV 4.04. 16 P
he hath kill'd, otherwise he had suffer'd for't. 4.04. 33 P
what i have suffer'd to bring this woman to evil WIV 3.05. 96 P
i suffer'd the pangs of three several deaths: 3.05.107 P
that for my sake you have suffer'd all this. 3.05.124 P
i have suffer'd more for their sakes — more 4.05.108 P
and have not they suffer'd? 4.05.110 P
over and above that you have suffer'd, i think 5.05.168 P
one day's error | have suffer'd wrong, go keep ERR 5.01.399
him, | and suffer'd him to go displeas'd away — MV 5.01.213
why have you suffer'd me to be imprison'd, TN 5.01.341
i do believe | hermione hath suffer'd death, and WT 3.03. 42
what your highness suffer'd under that shape, i H5 4.08. 53 P
lest, being suffer'd in that harmful slumber, 2H6 3.02.262
who, being suffer'd, with the bear's fell paw 5.01.153
which, being suffer'd, rivers cannot quench. 3H6 4.08. 8
out of the pain you suffer'd, gave no ear to't. H8 4.02. 8
and suffer'd me by th' voice of slaves to be COR 4.05. 77
offenses enforc'd, for which he suffer'd death. JC 3.02. 40 P
not as it hath power, but as it is suffer'd. LR 1.02. 51 P
distressful stroke | that my youth suffer'd. OTH 1.03.158
was your fellow too, | and suffer'd my command. ANT 4.02. 23
that i suffer'd | was all the harm i did. CYM 5.05.335
and suffer'd | your knees to wrong themselves. TNK 1.01. 55
will come to that pass if strangers be suffer'd. STM II.C 4 P
else, suffer'd, it will set the heart on fire: VEN 388
SUFFERED 7 FR 0.0008 REL FR 7 V 0 P
i have suffered | with those that i saw suffer. TMP 1.02. 5
he that hath suffered this disordered spring R2 3.04. 48
the one part suffered, the other will i do. COR 2.03.124
sir, your jewel | hath suffered under praise. TIM 1.01.165
companion maid | be suffered to come near him. PER 5.01. 78
art a man, and i | have suffered like a girl. 5.01.137
to weigh how once i suffered in your crime. SON 120. 8
SUFFERING 11 FR 0.0012 REL FR 9 V 2 P
now, | for suffering so the causes of our wrack. R2 2.01.269
for suffering flesh to be eaten in thy house, 2H4 2.04.344 P
your suffering in this dearth, you may as well COR 1.01. 67
long in spectatorship and crueller in suffering; 5.02. 66 P
than the judge, | if wisdom be in suffering. TIM 3.05. 51
and such suffering souls | that welcome wrongs; JC 2.01.130
may soon return to this our suffering country MAC 3.06. 48
eye discerning | thine honor from thy suffering, LR 4.02. 53
he so undertaking, | or they so suffering. CYM 4.02.143
which may her suffering ecstasy assuage, | 'tis LC 69
have of my suffering youth some feeling pity 178
/SUFFERS 2 FR 0.0002 REL FR 2 V 0 P
/who /alone /suffers, /suffers /most /i' /th' LR 3.06.104
/alone /suffers, /suffers /most /i' /th' /mind, 3.06.104
SUFFERS 10 FR 0.0011 REL FR 8 V 2 P
gives this sentence, | and he, that suffers. MM 2.02.107
that suffers under probation: TN 2.05.130 P
and never suffers matter of the world | enter TRO 2.03.186
the eagle suffers little birds to sing, | and is TIT 4.04. 83
suffers then | the nature of an insurrection. JC 2.01. 68
of his love or no | that thus he suffers for. HAM 3.01. 36
as one in suff'ring all that suffers nothing, 3.02. 66
sir, his defenement suffers no perdition in you, 5.02.112 P
worth | the shame which here it suffers. LR 2.04. 45
it suffers not in smiling pomp, nor falls SON 124. 6
SUFFER'ST 2 FR 0.0002 REL FR 2 V 0 P
that suffer'st more | of mortal griefs than do H5 4.01.241
why suffer'st thou thy sons, unburied yet, | to TIT 1.01. 87
SUFFER'T 1 FR 0.0001 REL FR 1 V 0 P
suffer't, and live with such as cannot rule, COR 3.01. 40
SUFFIC'D 4 FR 0.0004 REL FR 4 V 0 P
till he be first suffic'd, | oppress'd with two AYL 2.07.131
and when my knightly stomach is suffic'd, | why JN 1.01.191
true sorrow then is feelingly suffic'd | when LUC 1112
give, | that i in thy abundance am suffic'd, SON 37.11
SUFFICE 18 FR 0.0020 REL FR 13 V 5 P
let it suffice thee, mistress page — at the WIV 2.01. 10 P
if the love of a soldier can suffice — that i 2.01. 11 P
it shall suffice me; LLL 2.01.166
be the mark, to know thee shall suffice; 4.02.111
if that will not suffice, | i will be bound to MV 4.01.210
if this will not suffice, it must appear | that 4.01.213
let it suffice thee that i trust thee not. AYL 1.03. 55
'twixt such friends as we | few words suffice; SHR 1.02. 66
return again and suffice ourselves with the AWW 3.05. 10 P
let that suffice. WT 1.02.235
let that suffice, most forcible feeble. 2H4 3.02.167 P
it shall suffice, sir. 3.02.169 P
to prove him tyrant this reason may suffice, 3H6 3.03. 71
let that suffice you. OTH 3.04.131
let it suffice the greatness of your powers | to PER 2.01. 8
and have no more of life than may suffice | to 2.01. 74
let it then suffice | to drown /one woe, one LUC 1679
be the mark, to know thee shall suffice: PP 5. 7
SUFFICES 1 FR 0.0001 REL FR 0 V 1 P
demand of the prover, it suffices me thou art. TRO 2.03. 67 P
SUFFICETH 7 FR 0.0008 REL FR 7 V 0 P
sufficeth my reasons are both good and weighty. SHR 1.01.248
hear — | sufficeth i am come to keep my word, 3.02.106
sufficeth that i have maintains my state | and 2H6 4.10. 22
sufficeth not that we are brought to rome | to TIT 1.01.109
but it sufficeth | that brutus leads me on. JC 2.01.333
but it sufficeth that the day will end, | and 5.01.124
sufficeth | a roman with a roman's heart can CYM 5.05. 80
SUFFICIENCY 4 FR 0.0004 REL FR 3 V 1 P
to your sufficiency as your worth is able, | and MM 1.01. 8
but no man's virtue nor sufficiency | to be so ADO 5.01. 29
dion, whom you know | of stuff'd sufficiency. WT 2.01.185
there a substitute of most allow'd sufficiency, OTH 1.03.224 P
SUFFICIENT 19 FR 0.0021 REL FR 11 V 8 P
sorrow | be a sufficient ransom for offense, | i TGV 5.04. 75
not men in your ward sufficient to serve it? MM 2.01.267 P
or seven, the most sufficient of your parish. 2.01.273 P
to have you understand me that he is sufficient. MV 1.03. 17 P
the man is notwithstanding sufficient. 1.03. 26 P
him, | and pass my daughter a sufficient dower, SHR 4.04. 45
clerk, and some sufficient honest witnesses. 4.04. 94 P
provided me here half a dozen sufficient men? 2H4 3.02. 93 P
shall be a wall sufficient to defend | our H5 1.02.141
the concavities of it is not sufficient. 3.02. 60 P
your roof were not sufficient to contain't. 1H6 2.03. 56
dame | (had i sufficient skill to utter them) 5.05. 13
for your expenses and sufficient charge, | among 5.05. 92
and thine | were not revenge sufficient for me; 3H6 1.03. 26
were a sufficient briber for his life. TIM 3.05. 61
you'll never meet a more sufficient man. OTH 3.04. 91
our full senate | call all in all sufficient? 4.01.265
if i bring you no sufficient testimony that i CYM 1.04.149 P
and am sufficient | to tell the world 'tis but a TNK 2.02.102
SUFFICIENTLY 3 FR 0.0003 REL FR 2 V 1 P
which none without thee can sufficiently manage, WT 4.02. 15 P
endur'd, | but we will be reveng'd sufficiently. 1H6 1.04. 58
does speak sufficiently he's gone to travel. PER 1.03. 13
SUFFICING 1 FR 0.0001 REL FR 1 V 0 P
and give me | sufficing strokes for death. ANT 4.14.117
SUFFICIT 1 FR 0.0001 REL FR 0 V 1 P
satis quid sufficit. LLL 5.01. 1 P
SUFFIGANCE 1 FR 0.0001 REL FR 0 V 1 P
it shall be suffigance. ADO 3.05. 52 P
SUFFOCATE 3 FR 0.0003 REL FR 3 V 0 P
free, | and let not hemp his windpipe suffocate. H5 3.06. 43
for suffolk's duke, may he be suffocate, | that 2H6 1.01.124
this chaos, when degree is suffocate, | follows TRO 1.03.125
SUFFOCATING 1 FR 0.0001 REL FR 1 V 0 P
poison, or fire, or suffocating streams, | i'll OTH 3.03.389
SUFFOCATION 1 FR 0.0001 REL FR 0 V 1 P
it was a miracle to scape suffocation. WIV 3.05.117 P
SUFFOLK 72 FR 0.0081 REL FR 69 V 3 P
wounds) | the noble earl of suffolk also lies. H5 4.06. 10
suffolk first died, and york, all haggled over, 4.06. 11
he cries aloud, "tarry, my cousin suffolk! 4.06. 15
edward the duke of york, the earl of suffolk, 4.08.103
an earl i am, and suffolk am i call'd. 1H6 5.03. 53
say, earl of suffolk — if thy name be so — 5.03. 72
suffolk, what remedy? 5.03.132
speaks suffolk as he thinks? 5.03.141
margaret knows | that suffolk doth not flatter, 5.03.142
prayers | shall suffolk ever have of margaret. 5.03.174
but, suffolk, stay, | thou mayest not wander in 5.03.187
my noble lord of suffolk, or for that | my 5.05. 80
thus suffolk hath prevail'd, and thus he goes, 5.05.103
suffolk, arise. 2H6 1.01. 17
and william de la pole, marquess of suffolk, 1.01. 45 P
we here create thee the first duke of suffolk, 1.01. 64
suffolk, the new–made duke that rules the roast, 1.01.109
that suffolk should demand a whole fifteenth 1.01.133
and all together, with the duke of suffolk, 1.01.168
delay, | i'll to the duke of suffolk presently. 1.01.171
the pride of suffolk and the cardinal, | with 1.01.201
suffolk concluded on the articles, | the peers 1.01.217
and william de la pole, first duke of suffolk. 1.02. 30
and from the great and new–made duke of suffolk; 1.02. 95
yet am i suffolk and the cardinal's broker. 1.02.101
this is the duke of suffolk and not my lord 1.03. 9 P
"against the duke of suffolk, for enclosing the 1.03. 21 P
suffolk, let them go. 1.03. 40

SUFFOLK
my lord of suffolk, say, is this the guise, | is 1.03. 42
till suffolk gave two dukedoms for his daughter. 1.03. 87
i'll tell thee, suffolk, why i am unmeet: 1.03.165
what mean'st thou, suffolk? 1.03.180
/me what /fate /awaits the duke of suffolk?" 1.04. 32
"tell me what fate awaits the duke of suffolk?" 1.04. 64
why, suffolk, england knows thine insolence. 2.01. 31
for suffolk, he that can do all in all | with 2.04. 51
my lord of suffolk, buckingham, and york, 3.01. 39
well, suffolk, thou shalt not see me blush | nor 3.01. 98
my lord cardinal, and you, my lord of suffolk, 3.01.246
thrice-noble suffolk, 'tis resolutely spoke. 3.01.266
but i would have him dead, my lord of suffolk, 3.01.273
lord suffolk, you and i must talk of that event. 3.01.326
my lord of suffolk, within fourteen days | at 3.01.327
run to my lord of suffolk; 3.02. 1
what's the matter, suffolk? 3.02. 28
what, doth my lord of suffolk comfort me? 3.02. 39
why do you rate my lord of suffolk thus? 3.02. 56
by suffolk and the cardinal beauford's means. 3.02.124
are you the butcher, suffolk? 3.02.195
dares not warwick, if false suffolk dare him? 3.02.203
though suffolk dare him twenty thousand times. 3.02.206
unless lord suffolk straight be done to death, 3.02.244
from such fell serpents as false suffolk is; 3.02.266
o henry, let me plead for gentle suffolk! 3.02.289
ungentle queen, to call him gentle suffolk! 3.02.290
and let thy suffolk take his heavy leave. 3.02.306
enough, sweet suffolk, thou torment'st thyself, 3.02.329
thus is poor suffolk ten times banished, | once 3.02.357
enough, | so suffolk had thy heavenly company: 3.02.361
why only, suffolk, mourn i not for thee, | and 3.02.383
to france, sweet suffolk! 3.02.405
the duke of suffolk, william de la pole. 4.01. 45
the duke of suffolk muffled up in rags? 4.01. 46
come, suffolk, i must waft thee to thy death. 4.01.116
and suffolk dies by pirates. 4.01.138
ah, were the duke of suffolk now alive, | these 4.04. 41
my hope is gone, now suffolk is deceas'd. 4.04. 56
power | of essex, norfolk, suffolk, nor of kent, 3H6 1.01.156
shalt stir up in suffolk, norfolk, and in kent, 4.08. 12
the duke of suffolk is the first, and claims H8 4.01. 17
that should be | the duke of suffolk. 4.01. 41
left him at primero | with the duke of suffolk. 5.01. 8
SUFFOLK'S 10 FR 0.0011 REL FR 10 V 0 P
so did he turn and over suffolk's neck | he H5 4.06. 24
go, and be free again, as suffolk's friend. 1H6 5.03. 59
for suffolk's duke, may he be suffocate, | that 2H6 1.01.124
wink at the duke of suffolk's insolence, | at 2.02. 70
and suffolk's cloudy brow his stormy hate; 3.01.155
how often have i tempted suffolk's tongue | (the 3.02.114
mischance unto my state by suffolk's means. 3.02.284
omitting suffolk's exile, my soul's treasure? 3.02.382
suffolk's imperial tongue is stern and rough, 4.01.121
lamenting and mourning for suffolk's death? 4.04. 22
SUFFRAGE 1 FR 0.0001 REL FR 1 V 0 P
for my wounds' sake to give their suffrage. COR 2.02.138
SUFFRAGES 3 FR 0.0003 REL FR 3 V 0 P
here, | i ask your voices and your suffrages: TIT 1.01.218
what time i threw the people's suffrages | on 4.03. 19
forbear your suffrages. PER 2.04. 41
SUFF'RANCE 4 FR 0.0004 REL FR 3 V 1 P
for suff'rance is the badge of all our tribe. MV 1.03.110
and that her suff'rance made | almost each pang H8 5.01. 68
doth lesser blench at suff'rance than i do. TRO 1.01. 28
your last service was suff'rance, 'twas not 2.01. 95 P
SUFF'RED 6 FR 0.0006 REL FR 4 V 2 P
with a charm join'd to their suff'red labor, | i TMP 1.02.231
to make that worse, suff'red his kinsman march 1H4 4.03. 93
so did your son, | he was so suff'red; 2H4 2.03. 57
as for her greeks and troyans suff'red death. TRO 4.01. 75
truly in my youth i suff'red much extremity for HAM 2.02.190 P
in peace what already i have foolishly suff'red. OTH 4.02.180 P
SUFF'RERS 1 FR 0.0001 REL FR 0 V 1 P
nay, most likely, for they are noble suff'rers. TNK 2.01. 32 P
SUFF'RING 6 FR 0.0006 REL FR 6 V 0 P
with such a suff'ring, such a deadly life, | in TN 1.05.265
in suff'ring thus thy brother to be slaught'red, R2 1.02. 30
poison'd | with only suff'ring stain by him; COR 1.10. 18
as one in suff'ring all that suffers nothing, HAM 3.02. 66
suff'ring my friend for my sake to approve her. SON 42. 8
and sweetens, in the suff'ring pangs it bears, LC 272
SUGAR 15 FR 0.0017 REL FR 6 V 9 P
and in such wine and sugar of the best, and the WIV 2.02. 69 P
honey, and milk, and sugar: there is three. LLL 5.02.231
are sever'd lips, | parted with sugar breath; MV 3.02.119
to beauty is to have honey a sauce to sugar. AYL 3.03. 31 P
three pound of sugar, five pound of currants, WT 4.03. 38 P
and yet your fair discourse hath been as sugar, R2 2.03. 6
what says sir john sack and sugar? 1H4 1.02.114 P
i give thee this pennyworth of sugar, clapp'd 2.04. 23 P
my puny drawer to what end he gave me the sugar, 2.04. 31 P
for the sugar thou gavest me, 'twas a pennyworth 2.04. 58 P
if sack and sugar be a fault, god help the 2.04.470 P
more eloquence in a sugar touch of them than in H5 5.02.276 P
why strew'st thou sugar on that bottled spider R3 1.03.241
and pious action we do sugar o'er | the devil HAM 3.01. 47
these sentences, to sugar or to gall, | being OTH 1.03.216
SUGAR-CANDY 1 FR 0.0001 REL FR 0 V 1 P
one poor pennyworth of sugar-candy to make thee 1H4 3.03.160 P
SUGARSOP 1 FR 0.0001 REL FR 0 V 1 P
philip, walter, sugarsop, and the rest; SHR 4.01. 90 P
SUGGEST 8 FR 0.0009 REL FR 7 V 1 P
thee not this to suggest thee from thy master AWW 4.05. 45 P
death, | suggest his soon-believing adversaries, R2 1.01.101
and other devils that suggest by treasons | do H5 2.02.114
suggest but truth to my divining thoughts, 3H6 4.06. 69
we must suggest the people in what hatred | he COR 2.01.245
they do suggest at first with heavenly shows, OTH 2.03.352
that like two spirits do suggest me still, PP 2. 2
which like two spirits do suggest me still: SON 144. 2
SUGGESTED 6 FR 0.0006 REL FR 5 V 1 P
knowing that tender youth is soon suggested, | i TGV 3.01. 34
look into these faults, | suggested us to make. LLL 5.02.770
hath suggested thee | to make a second fall of R2 3.04. 75
say, suggested | at some time when his soaring COR 2.01.253
with tokens, as if they suggested for him. TNK 4.03. 92 P
suggested this proud issue of a king; LUC 37
SUGGESTETH 1 FR 0.0001 REL FR 1 V 0 P
gives false alarms, suggesteth mutiny, | and in VEN 651
SUGGESTION 10 FR 0.0011 REL FR 10 V 0 P
they'll take suggestion as a cat laps milk; TMP 2.01.288
the strong'st suggestion | our worser genius can 4.01. 26
say is kill'd to-night | on your suggestion. JN 4.02.166
and these | herein misled by your suggestion. 1H4 4.03. 51
mingled with venom of suggestion | (as, force 2H4 4.04. 45
by the suggestion of the queen's allies; R3 3.02.101
one that by suggestion | tied all the kingdom. H8 4.02. 35
why do i yield to that suggestion | whose horrid MAC 1.03.134
i'ld turn it all | to thy suggestion, plot, and LR 2.01. 73
by their suggestion gives a deadly groan. VEN 1044
SUGGESTIONS 3 FR 0.0003 REL FR 2 V 1 P
suggestions are to other as to me; LLL 1.01.158
he is in those suggestions for the young earl. AWW 3.05. 17 P
parts | against these giddy loose suggestions; JN 3.01.292
SUGGESTS 2 FR 0.0002 REL FR 1 V 1 P
spirit, what devil suggests this imagination? WIV 3.03.215 P
suggests the king our master | to this last H8 1.01.164
SUG'RED 5 FR 0.0005 REL FR 5 V 0 P
by fair persuasions, mix'd with sug'red words, 1H6 3.03. 18
hide not thy poison with such sug'red words. 2H6 3.02. 45
your grace attended to their sug'red words, R3 3.01. 13
but followed | the sug'red game before thee. TIM 4.03.259
thy sug'red tongue to bitter wormwood taste; LUC 893
SUING 2 FR 0.0002 REL FR 1 V 1 P
th' other curses a suing fellow and her TNK 4.03. 56 P
her eyes petitioners to his eyes suing, | his VEN 356
SUIS 3 FR 0.0003 REL FR 0 V 3 P
je pense que je suis le bon ecolier; H5 3.04. 13 P
je suis le gentilhomme de bonne maison; 4.04. 41 P
que dit-il? que je suis semblable a les anges? 5.02.111 P
/SUIT 4 FR 0.0004 REL FR 4 V 0 P
/you, /lords, /to /grant /the /commons' /suit? R2 4.01.154
/and /might /by /no /suit /gain /our /audience. 2H4 4.01. 76
to cease thy /suit, and leave me to my grief. ROM 2.02.152
when you come ashore, | i have another /suit. PER 5.01.261
SUIT 144 FR 0.0162 REL FR 113 V 31 P
to me inveterate, hearkens my brother's suit, TMP 1.02.122
hearken once again to the suit i made to thee? 3.02. 39 P
that i despise thee for thy wrongful suit, | and TGV 4.02.102
i hope my master's suit will be but cold, 4.04.181
sir proteus, what says silvia to my suit? 5.02. 1
shall i not lose my suit? WIV 1.04.143 P
give him a show of comfort in his suit, and lead 2.01. 95 P
hast thou no suit against my knight, my 2.01.212 P
if opportunity and humblest suit | cannot attain 3.04. 20
my suit then is desperate; 3.05.124 P
well; what's your suit? MM 2.02. 28
you granting of my suit, | if that be sin, i'll 2.04. 70
at the suit of master three-pile the mercer, for 4.03. 9 P
to such men of sort and suit as are to meet him. 4.04. 17 P
well, officer, arrest him at my suit. ERR 4.01. 69
i do arrest you, sir: you hear the suit. 4.01. 79
with words that in an honest suit might move. 4.02. 14
what, is he arrested? tell me at whose suit. 4.02. 43
i know not at whose suit he is arrested well; 4.02. 44
but /'a's in a suit of buff which 'rested him, 4.02. 45
say now, whose suit is he arrested at? 4.04.131
the first suit is hot and hasty, like a scotch ADO 2.01. 75 P
no means, she mocks all her wooers out of suit. 2.01.350 P
since many a wooer doth commence his suit | to 2.03. 50
surely suit ill spent and labor ill bestow'd. 3.02. 99 P
but such a one whose wrongs do suit with mine. 5.01. 7
my coming, | and suddenly resolve me in my suit. LLL 2.01.110
grace, | despite of suit, to see a lady's face. 5.02.129
berowne did swear himself out of all suit. 5.02.275
thanks | for my great suit so easily obtain'd. 5.02.739
the holy suit which fain it would convince, 5.02.746
what humble suit attends thy answer there. 5.02.839
and to trouble you with no more suit, unless you MV 1.02.103 P
moneys is your suit. 1.03.119
bestow upon your worship, and my suit is — 2.02.136 P
very brief, the suit is impertinent to myself, 2.02.137 P
i know thee well, thou hast obtain'd thy suit. 2.02.144
i have suit to you. 2.02.177
rather to put on | your boldest suit of mirth, 2.02.202
with, | what page's suit she hath in readiness. 2.04. 32
fare you well, your suit is cold." 2.07. 73
that i follow thus | a losing suit against him. 4.01. 62
of a strange nature is the suit you follow, 4.01.177
we will make it our suit to the duke that the AYL 1.02.181 P
that i did suit me all points like a man? 1.03.116
it is my only suit — | provided that you weed 2.07. 44
what, of my suit? 4.01. 86 P
out of your apparel, and yet out of your suit. 4.01. 88 P
some one be ready with a costly suit, | and ask SHR in.1. 59
him not | by any token of presumptuous suit, AWW 1.03.198
2.03. 76
3.05. 71
and brokes with all that can in such a suit 5.03.160
my suit, as i do understand, you know, | and ep 2
all is well ended, if this suit be won, | that
because she will admit no kind of suit, | no, TN 1.02. 45
if it be a suit from the count, i am sick, or 1.05.108 P
but, would you undertake another suit, | i had 3.01.108
i arrest thee at the suit of count orsino. 3.04.326 P
if spirits can assume both form and suit, | you 5.01.235
action | is now in durance, at malvolio's suit, 5.01.276
whereof the least | is not this suit of mine, WT 1.02.402
by long and vehement suit i was seduc'd | to JN 1.01.254
let it be our suit | that you have bid us ask 4.02. 62
the suit which you demand is gone and dead. 4.02. 84
pardon is all the suit i have in hand. R2 5.03.130
i arrest you at the suit of mistress quickly. 2H4 2.01. 45 P
of eastcheap, and he is arrested at my suit. 2.01. 71 P
if i had a suit to master shallow, i would humor 5.01. 71 P
cut and a horrid suit of the camp will do among H5 3.06. 77 P
description cannot suit itself in words | to 4.02. 53
i wear out my suit. 5.02.129 P
you may not, my lord, despise her gentle suit. 1H6 2.02. 47
pay recompense, if you will grant my suit. 5.03. 19
how canst thou tell she will deny thy suit, 5.03. 75
what answer makes your grace unto my suit? 5.03.150
should honor such as these | with humble suit. 2H6 4.01.124
i have a suit unto your lordship. 4.07. 3 P
her suit is now to repossess those lands, 3H6 3.02. 4
your highness shall do well to grant her suit; 3.02. 8
before the king will grant her humble suit. 3.02. 13
widow, we will consider of your suit, | and come 3.02. 16
accords not with the sadness of my suit. 3.02. 77
then no, my lord. my suit is at an end. 3.02. 81
her suit is granted for her husband's lands. 3.02.117
device | by this alliance to make void my suit. 3.03.142
and i no friends to back my suit /at /all | but R3 1.02.235
be not you spoke with but by mighty suit; 3.07. 46
if to reprove you for this suit of yours, | so 3.07.148
o, make them joyful, grant their lawful suit! 3.07.203
yet know, whe'er you accept our suit or no, 3.07.214
call him again, sweet prince, accept their suit. 3.07.221
may it please you to resolve me in my suit. 4.02.117
whereby his suit was granted | ere it was ask'd H8 1.01.186
half your suit | never name to us; 1.02. 10
salisbury, | made suit to come in 's presence; 1.02.197
too early and too late | for any suit of pounds; 2.03. 85
i have a suit which you must not deny me: 5.02.195
as she is stubborn-chaste against all suit. TRO 1.01. 97
carry it but by the suit of the gentry to him COR 2.01.238
humble weed, | how in his suit he scorn'd you; 2.03.222
your ears against | the general suit of rome; 5.03. 6
no, our suit | is that you reconcile them: 5.03.135
tribunes, i thank you, and this suit i make, TIT 1.01.223
and at my suit, sweet, pardon what is past. 1.01.431
then at my suit look graciously on him; 1.01.439
but now, my lord, what say you to my suit? ROM 1.02. 6
and then dreams he of smelling out a suit; 1.04. 78
that with your other noble parts you'll suit TIM 2.02. 23
thou hast some suit to caesar, hast thou not? JC 2.04. 27
brutus hath a suit | that caesar will not grant. 2.04. 42
(at your best leisure) this his humble suit. 3.01. 5
for mine's a suit | that touches caesar nearer. 3.01. 6
go | and presently prefer his suit to caesar. 3.01. 28
you told us of some suit, what is't, laertes? HAM 1.02. 43
suit the action to the word, the word to the 3.02. 17 P
wear black, for i'll have a suit of sables. 3.02.130 P
life i have spar'd at suit of his grey beard — LR 2.02. 63 P
in personal suit to make me his lieutenant, OTH 1.01. 9
desdemona to subdue | in any honest suit; 2.03.341
my suit to her | is that she will to virtuous 3.01. 34
every thing he does | with cassio's suit. 3.03. 26
when i have a suit | wherein i mean to touch 3.03. 80
this is a trick to put me from my suit. 3.04. 87
madam, my former suit. 3.04.110
i'll move your suit | and seek to effect it to 3.04.166
who having, by their own importunate suit, | or 4.01. 26
now, if this suit lay in bianca's /pow'r, | how 4.01.107
i will give over my suit and repent my unlawful 4.02.198 P
the same suit he wore when he took leave of my CYM 3.05.125 P
service thou dost me, fetch that suit hither. 3.05.127 P
with that suit upon my back will i ravish her; 3.05.137 P
of these italian weeds and suit myself | as does 5.01. 23
whose kinsmen have made suit | that their good 5.05. 71
in suit the place of 's bed and win this ring 5.05.185
more proclaiming | our suit shall be neglected. TNK 1.01.175
fit for my modest suit and your free granting. 3.06.235
or what great danger dwells upon my suit? VEN 206
the client breaks, as desperate in his suit. 336
and thy children's sake, | tender my suit; LUC 534
and bring him where his suit may be obtained? 898
assured trust, | and in thy suit be humble true; PP 18.20
grace, | and suit thy pity like in every part. SON 132.12
too early i attended | a youthful suit — it was LC 79
which late her noble suit in court did shun, 234
SUITABLE 1 FR 0.0001 REL FR 0 V 1 P
them, you gods, make suitable for destruction. TIM 3.06. 82 P
/SUITED 1 FR 0.0001 REL FR 1 V 0 P
/but /suited | /in /like /conditions /as /our TRO pr 24
SUITED 7 FR 0.0008 REL FR 4 V 3 P
by my troth, there's one meaning well suited. ADO 5.01.225 P
how oddly he is suited! MV 1.02. 74 P
o dear discretion, how his words are suited! 3.05. 65
wears her cap out of fashion, richly suited, but AWW 1.01.157 P
so went he suited to his watery tomb. TN 5.01.234
be better suited, | these weeds are memories of LR 4.07. 6
her eyes so suited, and they mourners seem | at SON 127.10
SUITING 1 FR 0.0001 REL FR 1 V 0 P
an' his whole function suiting | with forms to HAM 2.02.556
SUITOR 22 FR 0.0024 REL FR 19 V 3 P
and she hath taught her suitor, | he being her TGV 2.01.137
i am a woeful suitor to your honor, | please but MM 2.02. 27
she hath been a suitor to me for her brother, 5.01. 34
have been troubled with a pernicious suitor. ADO 1.01.129 P
that i drave my suitor from his mad humor of AYL 3.02.418 P
are you a suitor to the maid you talk of, yea or SHR 1.02.228
and since you do profess to be a suitor, | you 1.02.270
do make myself a suitor to your daughter, | unto 2.01. 90
i am your neighbor, and was suitor first. 2.01.334
now, in age, | is she become the suitor? WT 5.03.109
duty rememb'red, i will not be your suitor. 2H4 2.01.126 P
(and not provok'd by any suitor else), | aiming, R3 1.03. 64
nay, we must longer kneel; i am a suitor. H8 1.02. 9
i am an humble suitor to your virtues; TIM 3.05. 7
along, | and as a suitor will i give him this. JC 2.03. 12
suitor that i may | produce his body to the 3.01.227
and needs no other suitor but his likings | /to OTH 3.01. 48
i have been talking with a suitor here, | a man 3.03. 42
a foolish suitor to a wedded lady | that hath CYM 1.06. 2
as much sorry | i should be such a suitor; TNK 1.01.188
i am a suitor | that to your sword you will 3.01.114
and like a bold-fac'd suitor gins to woo him. VEN 6
SUITORS 18 FR 0.0020 REL FR 16 V 2 P
like humble/-visag'd suitors, his high will. LLL 2.01. 34
blow in from every coast | renowned suitors, and MV 1.01.169
of these princely suitors that are already come? 1.02. 34 P
because she will not be annoy'd with suitors. SHR 1.01.184
more, | suitors to her and rivals in my love; 1.02.122
is, | she may more suitors have, and me for one. 1.02.241
her father keeps from all access of suitors, 1.02.259
of all thy suitors here i charge /thee tell 2.01. 8
seek these suitors. AWW 5.03.151
no humble suitors press to speak for right, | no 3H6 3.01. 19
they say poor suitors have strong breaths; COR 1.01. 60 P
this lady, and myself, | are suitors to you. 5.03. 78
dismiss your followers, and, as suitors should, TIT 1.01. 44
what caesar doth, what suitors press to him. JC 2.04. 15

of senators, of praetors, common suitors, | will 2.04. 35
no heretics burn'd, but wenches' suitors; LR 3.02. 84
see suitors following, and not look behind: OTH 2.01.157
whiles we are suitors to their throne, decays ANT 2.01. 4
SUIT'S 1 FR 0.0001 REL FR 1 V 0 P
your suit's unprofitable; MM 5.01.455
SUITS 32 FR 0.0036 REL FR 22 V 10 P
being once perfected how to grant suits, | how TMP 1.02. 79
for some four suits of peach–color'd satin, MM 4.03. 10 P
on decay'd men and gives them suits of durance; ERR 4.03. 27 P
one out of suits with fortune, | that could give AYL 1.02.246
more suits you to conceive than i to speak of. 1.02.267
but therein suits | his folly to the mettle of 2.07. 81
look you lisp and wear strange suits; 4.01. 34 P
and see him dress'd in all suits like a lady; SHR in.1. 106
i will believe thou hast a mind that suits TN 1.02. 50
and suits well for a servant with my fortunes. 3.04. 6
be in man besides the king to effect your suits, WT 4.04.798 P
for obtaining of suits? 1H4 1.02. 71 P
yea, for obtaining of suits, whereof the hangman 1.02. 72 P
sure i have paid, two rogues in buckrom suits. 2.04.193 P
ay, four, in buckrom suits. 2.04.205 P
suits not in native colors with the truth; H5 1.02. 17
shall we go send them dinners and fresh suits, 4.02. 57
your several suits | have been consider'd and 1H6 5.01. 34
grace, | begin your suits anew, and sue to him. 2H6 1.03. 39
nor posted off their suits with slow delays; 3H6 4.08. 40
and in no worldly suits would he be mov'd, | to R3 3.07. 63
and fit it with such furniture as suits | the H8 2.01. 99
mine ears against your suits are stronger than COR 5.02. 88
fresh embassies and suits, | nor from the state 5.03. 17
horror from the time, | which now suits with it. MAC 2.01. 60
mother, | nor customary suits of solemn black, HAM 1.02. 78
these but the trappings and the suits of woe. 1.02. 86
show, | but mere /implorators of unholy suits, 1.03.129
who hath /had three suits to his back, six LR 3.04.136 P
amongst you as suits with gentlemen of your CYM 1.04. 29 P
and /make me put into contempt the suits | of 3.04. 89
they prevail'd, had their suits fairly granted: TNK 4.01. 27
SUIVEZ–VOUS 1 FR 0.0001 REL FR 0 V 1 P
suivez–vous le grand capitaine. H5 4.04. 66 P
SULLEN 19 FR 0.0021 REL FR 19 V 0 P
no, trust me, she is peevish, sullen, froward, TGV 3.01. 68
i love to cope him in these sullen fits, | for AYL 2.01. 67
'twas told me you were rough and coy and sullen, SHR 2.01.243
and when she is froward, peevish, sullen, sour, 5.02.157
wrath, | and sullen presage of your own decay. JN 1.01. 28
shorten my days thou canst with sullen sorrow, R2 1.03.227
the sullen passage of thy weary steps | esteem 1.03.265
lament, | and put on sullen black incontinent. 5.06. 48
and like bright metal on a sullen ground, | my 1H4 1.02.212
his tongue | sounds ever after as a sullen bell, 2H4 1.01.102
why are thine eyes fix'd to the sullen earth, 2H6 1.02. 5
old sullen playfellow | for tender princes — R3 4.01.101
array, | but, like a mishaved and sullen wench, ROM 3.03.143
our solemn hymns to sullen dirges change; 4.05. 88
now, apemantus (if thou wert not sullen), | i TIM 1.02.236
i am sick and sullen. ANT 1.03. 13
still is he sullen, still he low'rs and frets, VEN 75
at break of day arising | from sullen earth) SON 29.12
than you shall hear the surly sullen bell | give 71. 2
SULLENS 1 FR 0.0001 REL FR 1 V 0 P
and let them die that age and sullens have, R2 2.01.139
SULLIED *(also sallied, etc.)*
SULLIED 2 FR 0.0002 REL FR 2 V 0 P
hath sullied all his gloss of former honor | by 1H6 4.04. 6
to change your day of youth to sullied night, SON 15.12
SULLY 4 FR 0.0004 REL FR 2 V 2 P
that may not sully the chariness of our honesty. WIV 2.01. 99 P
sully | the purity and whiteness of my sheets WT 1.02.326
francis, your white canvas doublet will sully. 1H4 2.04. 75 P
before we further | sully our gloss of youth: TNK 1.02. 5
SULPH'ROUS 2 FR 0.0002 REL FR 2 V 0 P
when i to sulph'rous and tormenting flames HAM 1.05. 3
you sulph'rous and thought–executing fires, LR 3.02. 4
SULPHUR 5 FR 0.0005 REL FR 5 V 0 P
and yet to /charge thy sulphur with a bolt COR 5.03.152
upon the blood | burn like the mines of sulphur. OTH 3.03.329
roast me in sulphur! 5.02.279
the gods throw stones of sulphur on me, if CYM 5.05.240
or what fierce sulphur else, to this end made, TNK 5.04. 64
SULPHUROUS 5 FR 0.0005 REL FR 5 V 0 P
of sulphurous roaring the most mighty neptune TMP 1.02.204
thou rather with thy sharp and sulphurous bolt MM 2.02.115
there is the sulphurous pit, burning, scalding, LR 4.06.128
his celestial breath | was sulphurous to smell; CYM 5.04.115
gently quench | thy nimble, sulphurous flashes! PER 3.01. 6
SULTAN 1 FR 0.0001 REL FR 1 V 0 P
that won three fields of sultan solyman, | i MV 2.01. 26
/SULTRY 1 FR 0.0001 REL FR 0 V 1 P
yet methinks it is very /sultry and hot /for my HAM 5.02. 98 P
SULTRY 1 FR 0.0001 REL FR 0 V 1 P
my lord, it is very sultry — as 'twere — i HAM 5.02.100 P
/SUM 1 FR 0.0001 REL FR 1 V 0 P
/i /will /retort /the /sum /in /equipage. WIV 2.02. 1
SUM 58 FR 0.0065 REL FR 53 V 5 P
you take the sum and substance that i have. TGV 4.01. 15
beg thou, or borrow, to make up the sum, | and ERR 1.01.153
you know since pentecost the sum is due, | and 4.01. 1
even just the sum that i do owe to you | is 4.01. 7
wife | disburse the sum on the receipt thereof. 4.01. 38
either consent to pay this sum for me | or i 4.01. 72
i know the man; what is the sum he owes? 4.04.133
if any friend will pay the sum for him, | he 5.01.131
my life, | and pay the sum that may deliver me. 5.01.285
that is the sum of all: ADO 1.01.146 P
how much the gross sum of deuce–ace amounts to. LLL 1.02. 46 P
being but the one half of an entire sum 2.01.130
receiv'd that sum, yet there remains unpaid | a 2.01.133
for such a sum from special officers | of 2.01.161
i money nor commodity | to raise a present sum; MV 1.01.179
three thousand ducats — 'tis a good round sum. 1.03.103
such sum or sums as are | express'd in the 1.03.147
love | had been the very sum of my confession. 3.02. 36
but the full sum of me | is sum of something; 3.02.157
but the full sum of me | is sum of something; 3.02.158
than twenty times the value of the sum | that he 3.02.287
what sum owes he the jew? 3.02.297
it for him in the court, | yea, twice the sum. 4.01.210
giving thy sum of more | to that which had too AYL 2.01. 48
of a span | buckles in his sum of age; 3.02.132
king john, this is the very sum of all: JN 2.01.151
the sum of all | is that the king hath won, and 2H4 1.01.131
for what sum? 2.01. 72 P
what is the gross sum that i owe thee? 2.01. 84 P
to give a greater sum | than ever at one time H5 1.01. 79
will raise your highness such a mighty sum | as 1.02.133
the sum is paid, the traitors are agreed, | the 2.pr. 33
the sum of all our answer is but this: 3.06.163
master's command transporting a sum of money, be 4.01.152 P
receive | the sum of money which i promised 1H6 5.01. 52
fight | be counterpois'd with such a petty sum! 2H6 4.01. 22
the sum of all i can i have disclos'd. R3 2.04. 46
produce the grand sum of his sins, the articles H8 3.02.293
whose grossness little characters sum up; TRO 1.03.325
will you with compters sum | the past–proportion 2.02. 28
o, were the sum of these that i should pay TIT 5.03.158
excess | i cannot sum up sum of half my wealth. ROM 2.06. 34
excess | i cannot sum up sum of half my wealth. 2.06. 34
he owes nine thousand, besides my former sum, TIM 2.01. 2
i'd rather than the worth of thrice the sum 3.03. 22
and it should seem by th' sum | your master's 3.04. 30
said he gave unto | his steward a mighty sum. 5.01. 8
your sum of parts | did not together pluck such HAM 4.07. 73
all their quantity of love | make up my sum. 5.01.271
grates me, the sum. ANT 1.01. 18
should | parcel the sum of my disgraces by 5.02.163
overbuys me | almost the sum he pays. CYM 1.01.147
the sum of this, | brought hither to pentapolis, PER 3.ch. 33
has given a sum of money to her marriage, | a TNK 4.01. 23
"this fair child of mine | shall sum my count, SON 2.11
why dost thou use | so great a sum of sums, yet 4. 8
when as thy love hath cast his utmost sum, 49. 3
to leave for nothing all thy sum of good; 109.12
SUMLESS 1 FR 0.0001 REL FR 1 V 0 P
sea | with sunken wrack and sumless treasuries. H5 1.02.165
SUMMA 1 FR 0.0001 REL FR 1 V 0 P
dii faciant laudis summa sit ista tuae! 3H6 1.03. 48
/SUMMARY 1 FR 0.0001 REL FR 1 V 0 P
/and /have /the /summary /of /all /our /griefs 2H4 4.01. 73
SUMMARY 1 FR 0.0001 REL FR 1 V 0 P
the continent and summary of my fortune. MV 3.02.130
/SUMM'D 1 FR 0.0001 REL FR 1 V 0 P
/and /summ'd /the /accompt /of /chance /before 2H4 1.01.167
/SUMMER 1 FR 0.0001 REL FR 1 V 0 P
/common /people /swarm /like /summer /flies, 3H6 2.06. 8
SUMMER 62 FR 0.0070 REL FR 54 V 8 P
the bat's back i do fly | after summer merrily. TMP 5.01. 92
heed, ere summer comes or cuckoo–birds do sing. WIV 2.01.123
men was ever so, | since summer first was leavy. ADO 2.03. 73
why should proud summer boast | before the birds LLL 1.01.102
blow like sweet roses in this summer air. 5.02.293
these summer flies | have blown me full of 5.02.408
daws, | and maidens bleach their summer smocks, 5.02.906
an odorous chaplet of sweet summer buds | is, as MND 2.01.110
the spring, the summer, | the childing autumn, 2.01.111
the summer still doth tend upon my state; 3.01.155
sweet, | to show how costly summer was at hand, MV 2.09. 94
warm'd and cool'd by the same winter and summer, 3.01. 63 P
is like the mending of highways | in summer, 5.01.264
but with the word the time will bring on summer, AWW 4.04. 31
and for turning away, let summer bear it out. TN 1.05. 20 P
i think, this coming summer, the king of sicilia WT 1.01. 5 P
are summer songs for me and my aunts, | while we 4.03. 11
these are flow'rs | of middle summer, and i 4.04.107
there is so hot a summer in my bosom | that all JN 5.07. 30
is hack'd down, and his summer leaves all faded, R2 1.02. 20
our sighs and they shall lodge the summer corn, 3.03.162
farewell, all–hallown summer! 1H4 1.02.159 P
talk to me | in any summer house in christendom. 3.01.162
shadow will serve for summer, prick him, for we 2H4 3.02.133 P
o westmerland, thou art a summer bird, | which 4.04. 91
grew like the summer grass, fastest by night, H5 1.01. 65
moral ties me over to time and a hot summer; 5.02.313 P
expect saint martin's summer, halcyons' days, 1H6 1.02.131
and after summer evermore succeeds | barren 2H6 2.04. 2
and that thy summer bred us no increase, | we 3H6 2.02.164
they never then had sprung like summer flies; 2.06. 17
made glorious summer by this son of york; R3 1.01. 2
/which in their summer beauty kiss'd each other. 4.03. 13
that spoil'd your summer fields and fruitful 5.02. 8
to those men that sought him, sweet as summer. H8 4.02. 54
show not their mealy wings but to the summer, TRO 3.03. 79
than boys pursuing summer butterflies, | or COR 4.06. 94
the trees, though summer, yet forlorn and lean, TIT 2.03. 94
this goodly summer with your winter mix'd. 5.02.171
verona's summer hath not such a flower. ROM 1.03. 77
gossamers | that idles in the wanton summer air, 2.06. 19
swallow follows not summer more willing than we TIM 3.06. 29 P
leaves winter, such summer birds are men. 3.06. 32 P
this guest of summer, | the temple–haunting MAC 1.06. 3
o, ay, as summer flies are in the shambles, OTH 4.02. 66
if't be summer news, | smile to't before; CYM 3.04. 12
flowers | whilst summer lasts and i live here, 4.02.219
as a fair day in summer; wondrous fair. PER 2.05. 36
upon thy grave | while summer days doth last. 4.01. 17
summer shall come, and with her all delights, TNK 2.02. 44
lust's winter comes ere summer half be done; VEN 802
bee, | have no perfection of my summer left, LUC 837
youth like summer morn, age like winter weather, PP 12. 3
youth like summer brave, age like winter bare. 12. 4
for never–resting time leads summer on | to SON 5. 5
in thee thy summer ere thou be distill'd: 6. 2
but thy eternal summer shall not fade, | nor 18. 9
and true, | making no summer of another's green, 68.11
the summer's flow'r is to the summer sweet, 94. 9
for summer and his pleasures wait on thee, | and 97.11
not that the summer is less pleasant now | than 102. 9
ere you were born was beauty's summer dead. 104.14
SUMMER'D 1 FR 0.0001 REL FR 0 V 1 P
for maids, well summer'd and warm kept, are like H5 5.02.308 P
SUMMER'S 32 FR 0.0036 REL FR 29 V 3 P
a proper man as one shall see in a summer's day; MND 1.02. 87 P
and never, since the middle summer's spring, 2.01. 82
not yet on summer's death, nor on the birth | of WT 4.04. 80
snow | by thinking on fantastic summer's heat? R2 1.03.299
and lay the summer's dust with show'rs of blood 3.03. 43
sung by a fair queen in a summer's bow'r, | with 1H4 3.01.207
so that, as clear as is the summer's sun, | king H5 1.02. 86
make boot upon the summer's velvet buds, | which 1.02.194
the pridge as you shall see in a summer's day. 3.06. 64 P
look you, as you shall desire in a summer's day. 4.08. 22 P
in winter's cold and summer's parching heat, 2H6 1.01. 81
like to the summer's corn by tempest lodged. 3.02.176
went all afoot in summer's scalding heat, | that 3H6 5.07. 18
in summer's drought i'll drop upon thee still, TIT 3.01. 19
like stinging bees in hottest summer's day, 5.01. 14
this bud of love, by summer's ripening breath, ROM 2.02.121
'twas on a summer's evening, in his tent, | that JC 3.02.172
be, | and overcome us like a summer's cloud, MAC 3.04.110
but to be still hot summer's tanlings and | the CYM 4.04. 29
a summer's day will seem an hour but short, VEN 23
never did passenger in summer's heat | more 91
then were not summer's distillation left | a SON 5. 9
and summer's green all girded up in sheaves 12. 7
shall i compare thee to a summer's day? 18. 1
and summer's lease hath all too short a date; 18. 4
when summer's breath their masked buds discloses 54. 8
makes summer's welcome thrice more wish'd, more 56.14
o, how shall summer's honey breath hold out 65. 5
the summer's flow'r is to the summer sweet, 94. 9
and yet this time remov'd was summer's time, 97. 5
in hue, | could make me any summer's story tell, 98. 7
lays, | as philomel in summer's front doth sing, 102. 7
SUMMERS' 1 FR 0.0001 REL FR 1 V 0 P
from the forests shook three summers' pride, SON 104. 4
/SUMMERS 1 FR 0.0001 REL FR 1 V 0 P
palates who, not yet /two /summers younger, PER 1.04. 39
SUMMERS 6 FR 0.0006 REL FR 6 V 0 P
five summers have i spent in farthest greece, ERR 1.01.132
winters cannot blow away, | so many summers dry. WT 5.03. 51
till twice five summers have enrich'd our fields R2 1.03.141
short summers lightly have a forward spring. R3 3.01. 94
bladders, | this many summers in a sea of glory, H8 3.02.360
let two more summers wither in their pride, ROM 1.02. 10
SUMMER–SEEMING 1 FR 0.0001 REL FR 1 V 0 P
more pernicious root | than summer–seeming lust; MAC 4.03. 86
SUMMER–SWELLING 1 FR 0.0001 REL FR 1 V 0 P
disdain to root the summer–swelling flow'r | and TGV 2.04.162
SUMMIT 3 FR 0.0003 REL FR 3 V 0 P
or to the dreadful summit of the cliff | that HAM 1.04. 70
fix'd on the summit of the highest mount, | to 3.03. 18
from the dread summit of this chalky bourn. LR 4.06. 57
SUMMON 14 FR 0.0015 REL FR 14 V 0 P
now, madam, summon up your dearest spirits; LLL 2.01. 1
bridegroom's ear, | and summon him to marriage. MV 3.02. 53
summon a session, that we may arraign | our most WT 2.03.202
some trumpet summon hither to the walls | these JN 2.01.198
what lusty trumpet thus doth summon us? 5.02.117
summon a parley, we will talk with him. 1H6 3.03. 35
trumpeter, | summon their general unto the wall. 4.02. 2
i summon your grace to his majesty's parliament, 2H6 2.04. 70
my liege, i'll knock once more to summon them. 3H6 4.07. 16
and summon him to–morrow to the tower | to sit R3 3.01.172
summon the town. COR 1.04. 7
hark how these instruments summon to supper! OTH 4.02.169
light | do summon us to part and bid good night. VEN 534
i summon up remembrance of things past, | i sigh SON 30. 2
SUMMON'D 3 FR 0.0003 REL FR 3 V 0 P
why hath thy queen | summon'd me hither, to this TMP 4.01. 83
the people do admit you and are summon'd | to COR 2.03.143
those contents | they summon'd up their meiny, LR 2.04. 35
SUMMONERS 1 FR 0.0001 REL FR 1 V 0 P
and cry | these dreadful summoners grace. LR 3.02. 59
SUMMONS 9 FR 0.0010 REL FR 9 V 0 P
and on this green land | answer your summons; TMP 4.01.131
stays but the summons of the appellant's trumpet R2 1.03. 4
got your leave | to make this present summons. H8 2.04.220
a heavy summons lies like lead upon me, | and MAC 2.01. 6
knell, | that summons thee to heaven or to hell. 2.01. 64
ere to black hecat's summons | the shard–borne 3.02. 41
like a guilty thing | upon a fearful summons. HAM 1.01.149
and why you answer | this present summons? LR 5.03.121
what is the reason of this terrible summons? OTH 1.01. 82
SUMPTER 1 FR 0.0001 REL FR 1 V 0 P
persuade me rather to be slave and sumpter | to LR 2.04.216
SUMPTUOUS 4 FR 0.0004 REL FR 4 V 0 P
seldom but sumptuous, show'd like a feast, | and 1H4 3.02. 58
in marriage, with a large and sumptuous dowry. 1H6 5.01. 20
thy sumptuous buildings and thy wive's attire 2H6 1.03.130
is my apparel sumptuous to behold? 4.07.100
SUMPTUOUSLY 1 FR 0.0001 REL FR 1 V 0 P
stood, | which i have sumptuously re–edified. TIT 1.01.351
SUMS 17 FR 0.0019 REL FR 15 V 2 P
than stamps in gold, or sums in sealed bags; WIV 3.04. 16
such sum or sums as are | express'd in the MV 1.03.147
in padua | of greater sums than i have promised. SHR 3.02.135
with well–weighing sums of gold to corrupt him AWW 4.03.179 P
the sums i have collected shall express. JN 4.02.142
shall subscribe them for large sums of gold, R2 1.04. 50
large sums of gold and dowries with their wives, 2H6 1.01.129
levy great sums of money through the realm | for 3.01. 61
i doubt whether their legs be worth the sums TIM 1.02.232
why then preferr'd you not your sums and bills 3.04. 49
cut my heart in sums. 3.04. 92
even such heaps and sums of love and wealth | as 5.01.152
i did send to you | for certain sums of gold, JC 4.03. 70
have mingled sums | to buy a present for the CYM 1.06.186
it sums up thousands in a trice. 5.04.167 P
why dost thou use | so great a sum of sums, yet SON 4. 8
comes | their distract parcels in combined sums. LC 231
/SUN 5 FR 0.0005 REL FR 5 V 0 P
in thy treacherous ear | from /sun to /sun. R2 4.01. 55
in thy treacherous ear | from /sun to /sun. 4.01. 55
/standing /before /the /sun /of /bullingbrook, 4.01.261

/was /this /the /face | /that, /like /the /sun, 4.01.284
to the air | or dedicate his beauty to the /sun. ROM 1.01.153

SUN 254 FR 0.0287 REL FR 232 V 22 P

can have no note, unless the sun were post — TMP 2.01.248
all the infections that the sun sucks up | from 2.02. 1
the sun will set before i shall discharge | what 3.01. 22
i have bedimm'd | the noontide sun, call'd forth 5.01. 42
which now shows all the beauty of the sun, | and TGV 1.03. 86
star, | but now i worship a celestial sun. 2.06. 10
the sun begins to gild the western sky, | and 5.01. 1
then did the sun on dunghill shine. WIV 1.03. 63 P
i rather will suspect the sun with /cold | than 4.04. 7
have i laid my brain in the sun and dried it, 5.05.135 P
it is i | that, lying by the violet in the sun, MM 2.02.165
ere twice the sun hath made his journal greeting 4.03. 88
my woes end likewise with the evening sun. ERR 1.01. 27
at length the sun, gazing upon the earth, 1.01. 88
town, | dies ere the weary sun set in the west. 1.02. 7
when the sun shines, let foolish gnats make 2.02. 30
for gazing on your beams, fair sun, being by. 3.02. 56
bower, | where honeysuckles, ripened by the sun, ADO 3.01. 8
forbid the sun to enter, like favorites | made 3.01. 9
study is like the heaven's glorious sun, | that LLL 1.01. 84
"so sweet a kiss the golden sun gives not | to 4.03. 25
then thou, fair sun, which on my earth dost 4.03. 67
ay, as some days, but then no sun must shine. 4.03. 89
o, 'tis the sun that maketh all things shine! 4.03.242
in conflict that you get the sun of them. 4.03.366
the sun was not so true unto the day | as he to MND 3.02. 50
hecat's team | from the presence of the sun, 5.01.385
the shadowed livery of the burnish'd sun, | to MV 2.01. 2
a day, | such as the day is when the sun is hid. 5.01.126
if you would walk in absence of the sun. 5.01.128
ambition shun, | and loves to live i' th' sun, AYL 2.05. 39
who laid him down and bask'd him in the sun, 2.07. 15
a great cause of the night is lack of the sun; 3.02. 28 P
or, if not so, until the sun be set. SHR in.2. 120
and as the sun breaks through the darkest clouds 4.03.173
why so: this gallant will command the sun. 4.03.196
the moon! the sun — it is not moonlight now. 4.05. 3
i know it is the sun that shines so bright. 4.05. 5
and be it moon, or sun, or what you please; 4.05. 13
nay then you lie; it is the blessed sun. 4.05. 17
then, god be blest, it /is the blessed sun, 4.05. 18
but sun it is not, when you say it is not; 4.05. 19
that have been so bedazzled with the sun, | that 4.05. 46
error, i adore | the sun, that looks upon his AWW 1.03.206
ere twice the horses of the sun shall bring 2.01.161
the spinsters and the knitters in the sun, | and TN 2.04. 44
has been yonder i' the sun practicing behavior 2.05. 17 P
does walk about the orb like the sun, it shines 3.01. 39 P
this is the air, that is the glorious sun, 4.03. 1
were as twinn'd lambs that did frisk i' th' sun, WT 1.02. 67
of pruins, and as many of raisins o' th' sun. 4.03. 49 P
that goes to bed wi' th' sun | and with him 4.04.105
the self–same sun that shines upon his court 4.04.444
may | be thereat gleaned, for all the sun sees, 4.04.489
the sun looking with a southward eye upon him, 4.04.789 P
i think, | that e'er the sun shone bright on. 5.01. 95
that yon green boy shall have no sun to ripe JN 2.01.472
becomes a sun and makes your son a shadow. 2.01.500
to solemnize this day the glorious sun | stays 3.01. 77
the sun is in the heaven, and the proud day, 3.03. 34
crest | of the old, feeble, and day–wearied sun, 5.04. 35
the sun of heaven, methought, was loath to set, 5.05. 1
that sun that warms you here shall shine on me, R2 1.03.145
the setting sun, and music at the close, | as 2.01. 12
thy sun sets weeping in the lowly west, 2.04. 21
as doth the blushing discontented sun | from out 3.03. 63
by that fair sun which shows me where thou 4.01. 35
and the blessed sun himself a fair hot wench in 1H4 1.02. 9 P
idleness, | yet herein will i imitate the sun, 1.02.197
shall the blessed sun of heaven prove a micher 2.04.407 P
of may, | and gorgeous as the sun at midsummer; 4.01.102
worse than the sun in march, | this praise doth 4.01.111
how bloodily the sun begins to peer | above yon 5.01. 1
it stuck upon him as the sun | in the grey vault 2H4 2.03. 18
so that, as clear as is the summer's sun, | king H5 1.02. 86
up in the air, crown'd with the golden sun, 2.04. 58
on whom, as in despite, the sun looks pale, 3.05. 17
a largess universal, like the sun, | his liberal 4.pr. 43
go about to turn the sun to ice with fanning in 4.01.200 P
the sun doth gild our armor, up, my lords! 4.02. 1
the sun is high, and we outwear the day. 4.02. 63
for there the sun shall greet them, | and draw 4.03.100
kate, is the sun and the moon, or rather the sun 5.02.162 P
the moon, or rather the sun and not the moon; 5.02.163 P
than midday sun fierce bent against their faces. 1H6 1.01. 14
the sun with one eye vieweth all the world. 1.04. 84
as plays the sun upon the glassy streams, 5.03. 62
may never glorious sun reflex his beams | upon 5.04. 87
or count them happy that enjoys the sun? 2H6 2.04. 39
these dread curses, like the sun 'gainst glass, 3.02.330
hopeful colors | advance our half–fac'd sun, 4.01. 98
and takes her farewell of the glorious sun! 3H6 2.01. 22
three glorious suns, each one a perfect sun, 2.01. 26
now are they but one lamp, one light, one sun. 2.01. 31
show thy descent by gazing 'gainst the sun; 2.01. 92
this world frowns, and edward's sun is clouded. 2.03. 7
and whither fly the gnats but to the sun? 2.06. 9
leaves and fruit maintain'd with beauty's sun, 3.03.126
and when the morning sun shall raise his car 4.07. 80
the sun shines hot, and, if we use delay, | cold 4.08. 60
have been as piercing as the midday sun | to 5.02. 17
that will encounter with our glorious sun, | ere 5.03. 5
the sun that sear'd the wings of my sweet boy, 5.06. 23
unless to see my shadow in the sun | and descant R3 1.01. 26
as all the world is cheered by the sun, | so i 1.02.129
shine out, fair sun, till i have bought a glass, 1.02.262
and dallies with the wind and scorns the sun. 1.03.264
and turns the sun to shade — alas, alas! 1.03.265
when the sun sets, who doth not look for night? 2.03. 34
the weary sun hath made a golden set, | and by 5.03. 19
who saw the sun to–day? 5.03.277
the sun will not be seen to–day, | the sky doth 5.03.282
bulk | take up the rays o' th' beneficial sun, H8 1.01. 56
cloud puts on | by dark'ning my clear sun. 1.01.226
after | so many courses of the sun enthroned, 2.03. 6
as sun and showers | there had made a lasting 3.01. 7
no sun shall ever usher forth mine honors, | or 3.02.410
that sun, i pray, may never set! 3.02.415
cast thousand beams upon me, like the sun? 4.02. 89
where ever the bright sun of heaven shall shine, 5.04. 50
i have (as when the sun doth light a–scorn) TRO 1.01. 37
before the sun rose he was harness'd light, 1.02. 8
and it were better parch in afric sun | than in 1.03.369
that hector, by the /fift hour of the sun, 2.01.122
as sun to day, as turtle to her mate, | as iron 3.02.178
or, like a gate of steel | fronting the sun, 3.03.122
even then when they sit idly in the sun. 3.03.233
glory, | a thousand complete courses of the sun! 4.01. 28
the sun borrows of the moon when diomed keeps 5.01. 93 P
call, | constring'd in mass by the almighty sun, 5.02.173
look, hector, how the sun begins to set, | how 5.08. 5
even with the vail and dark'ning of the sun, 5.08. 7
of fire upon the ice, | or hailstone in the sun. COR 1.01.174
i had rather have one scratch my head i' th' sun 2.02. 75
strike the proud cedars 'gainst the fiery sun, 5.03. 60
as certain as i know the sun is fire. 5.04. 45
and the shouting romans, | make the sun dance. 5.04. 51
as when the golden sun salutes the morn, | and, TIT 2.01. 5
the /snake lies rolled in the cheerful sun, 2.03. 13
here never shines the sun, here nothing breeds, 2.03. 96
and stain the sun with fog, as sometime clouds 3.01.212
is the sun dimm'd, that gnats do fly in it? 4.04. 82
what boots it thee to call thyself a sun? 5.03. 18
an hour before the worshipp'd sun | peer'd forth ROM 1.01.118
but all so soon as the all–cheering sun | should 1.01.134
the all–seeing sun | ne'er saw her match since 1.02. 92
sitting in the sun under the dove–house wall. 1.03. 27
it is the east, and juliet is the sun. 2.02. 3
arise, fair sun, and kill the envious moon, 2.02. 4
now, ere the sun advance his burning eye, | the 2.03. 5
the sun not yet thy sighs from heaven clears, 2.03. 73
now is the sun upon the highmost hill | of this 2.05. 9
thy dog that hath lain asleep in the sun. 3.01. 26 P
night, | and pay no worship to the garish sun. 3.02. 25
it is some meteor that the sun /exhal'd | to be 3.05. 13
when the sun sets, the earth doth drizzle dew, 3.05.126
the sun, for sorrow, will not show his head. 5.03.306
men shut their doors against a setting sun. TIM 1.02.145
o blessed breeding sun, draw from the earth 4.03. 1
and her pale fire she snatches from the sun; 4.03.438
thou sun that comforts, burn! 5.01.131
sun, hide thy beams, timon hath done his reign. 5.01.223
here, as i point my sword, the sun arises, JC 2.01.106
o setting sun, | as in thy red rays thou dost 5.03. 60
the sun of rome is set. 5.03. 63
that will be ere the set of sun. MAC 1.01. 5
as whence the sun gins his reflection 1.02. 25
o, never | shall sun that morrow see! 1.05. 61
i gin to be a–weary of the sun, | and wish th' 5.05. 48
fire and dews of blood, | disasters in the sun; HAM 1.01.118
not so, my lord, i am too much in the sun. 1.02. 67
stars are fire, | doubt that the sun doth move, 2.02.117
for if the sun breed maggots in a dead dog, 2.02.181 P
let her not walk i' th' sun. 2.02.184 P
so many journeys may the sun and moon | make us 3.02.161
the sun no sooner shall the mountains touch, 4.01. 29
"'so would i 'a' done, by yonder sun, | and thou 4.05. 65
for, by the sacred radiance of the sun, | the LR 1.01.109
late eclipses in the sun and moon portend no 1.02.103 P
we make guilty of our disasters the sun, the 1.02.121 P
heaven's benediction com'st | to the warm sun! 2.02.162
you fen–suck'd fogs, drawn by the pow'rful sun, 2.04.167
though other things grow fair against the sun, OTH 2.03.376
i think the sun where he was born | drew all 3.04. 30
world | the sun to course two hundred compasses, 3.04. 71
should be now a huge eclipse | of sun and moon, 5.02.100
now of your mud by the operation of your sun. ANT 2.07. 27 P
before the sun shall see 's, we'll spill the 4.08. 3
o sun, thy uprise shall i see no more, | fortune 4.12. 18
o sun, | burn the great sphere thou mov'st in! 4.15. 9
and therein stuck | a sun and moon, which kept 5.02. 80
there could behold the sun with as firm eyes as CYM 1.04. 12 P
to hide me from the radiant sun, and solace | i' 1.06. 86
if caesar can hide the sun from us with a 3.01. 43 P
one score 'twixt sun and sun, | madam, 's enough 3.02. 68
one score 'twixt sun and sun, | madam, 's enough 3.02. 68
turbands on without | good morrow to the sun. 3.03. 7
hath britain all the sun that shines? 3.04.136
fear no more the heat o' th' sun, | nor the 4.02.258
by this sun that shines, | i'll thither. 4.04. 34
i am asham'd | to look upon the holy sun, to 4.04. 41
and in the beams o' th' sun | so vanish'd; 5.05.472
shield | is a black ethiope reaching at the sun; PER 2.02. 20
throne, | and he the sun for them to reverence; 2.03. 40
in our shadow, to scatter his crowns in the sun. 4.02.112 P
slaughter | the sun and moon ne'er look'd upon! 4.03. 3
showing the sun his teeth, grinning at the moon, TNK 1.01.100
lords | lie blist'ring 'fore the visitating sun, 1.01.146
and exclaim'd against | the horses of the sun, 1.02. 87
and paints the sun | with her chaste blushes! 2.02.139
the sun grows high, let's walk in. 2.02.148
mark how his virtue, like a hidden sun, | breaks 2.05. 23
to–morrow, by the sun, to do observance | to 2.05. 50
you are going now to look upon a sun | that 3.01.120
the sun has seen my folly. 3.04. 3
for, ere the sun set, both shall sleep for ever. 3.06.184
even as the sun with purple–color'd face | had VEN 1
the sun doth burn my face, i must remove." 186
shall cool the heat of this descending sun: 190
"the sun that shines from heaven shines but warm 193
warm, | and lo i lie between that sun and thee; 194
done, | between this heavenly and earthly sun. 198
like the fair sun, when in his fresh array | he 483
and as the bright sun glorifies the sky, | so is 485
to shame the sun by day and her by night. 732
as mountain snow melts with the midday sun. 750
rain, | but lust's effect is tempest after sun; 800
silver breast | the sun ariseth in his majesty, 856
nor sun nor wind will ever strive to kiss you: 1082
the sun doth scorn you and the wind doth hiss 1084
sun and sharp air | lurk'd like two thieves, to 1085
on, | under whose brim the gaudy sun would peep; 1088
dew | against the golden splendor of the sun! LUC 25
look as the fair and fiery–pointed sun, 372
or if thou wilt permit the sun to climb | his 775
as winter meads when sun doth melt their snow. 1218
but as the earth doth weep, the sun being set, 1226
by heaven's fair sun that breeds the fat earth's 1837
then thou, fair sun, that on this earth doth PP 3.10
scarce had the sun dried up the dewy morn, | and 6. 1
the sun look'd on the world with glorious eye, 6.11
yet not for me, shine sun to succor flowers! 14.28
couplement of proud compare | with sun and moon, SON 21. 6
breast, wherethrough the sun | delights to peep, 24.11
even so my sun one early morn did shine | with 33. 9
the world may stain when heaven's sun staineth. 33.14
clouds and eclipses stain both moon and sun, 35. 3
and scarcely greet me with that sun, thine eye, 49. 6
even of five hundreth courses of the sun, | show 59. 6
for as the sun is daily new and old, | so is my 76.13
my mistress' eyes are nothing like the sun; 130. 1
and truly not the morning sun of heaven | better 132. 5
the sun itself sees not till heaven clears. 148.12
which fortified her visage from the sun, LC 9

SUN–BEAMED 2 FR 0.0002 REL FR 2 V 0 P

"once to behold with your sun–beamed eyes, | — LLL 5.02.169
eyes, | — with your sun–beamed eyes" — 5.02.170

SUNBEAMS 1 FR 0.0001 REL FR 1 V 0 P

there vanish'd in the sunbeams, which portends CYM 4.02.350

SUN–BRIGHT 1 FR 0.0001 REL FR 1 V 0 P

myself | to be regarded in her sun–bright eye. TGV 3.01. 88

SUNBURN'D 1 FR 0.0001 REL FR 1 V 0 P

you sunburn'd sicklemen, of august weary, | come TMP 4.01.134

SUNBURNING 1 FR 0.0001 REL FR 0 V 1 P

whose face is not worth sunburning, that never H5 5.02.147 P

SUNBURNT 2 FR 0.0002 REL FR 1 V 1 P

every one to the world but i, and i am sunburnt. ADO 2.01.319 P
the grecian dames are sunburnt, and not worth TRO 1.03.282

SUNDAY 8 FR 0.0009 REL FR 7 V 1 P

together | that upon sunday is the wedding–day. SHR 2.01.298
i'll see thee hang'd on sunday first. 2.01.299
i will to venice, sunday comes apace. 2.01.322
and kiss me, kate, we will be married a' sunday. 2.01.324
on sunday next you know | my daughter katherine 2.01.393
now on the sunday following shall bianca | be 2.01.395
be as fair a' friday as helen is on sunday. TRO 1.01. 76 P
task | does not divide the sunday from the week, HAM 1.01. 76

SUNDAY–CITIZENS 1 FR 0.0001 REL FR 1 V 0 P

to velvet–guards and sunday–citizens. 1H4 3.01.256

SUNDAYS 2 FR 0.0002 REL FR 0 V 2 P

wear the print of it, and sigh away sundays. ADO 1.01.202 P
we may call it herb of grace a' sundays. HAM 4.05.183 P

SUNDER 9 FR 0.0010 REL FR 9 V 0 P

till, gnawing with my teeth my bonds in sunder, ERR 5.01.250
that vile wall, which did these lovers sunder; MND 5.01.132
sweet a bar | should sunder such sweet friends. MV 3.02.120
strangers and foes do sunder, and not kiss. AWW 2.05. 86
even as a splitted bark, so sunder we; 2H6 3.02.411
to sunder them that yoke so well together. 3H6 4.01. 23
no space of earth shall sunder our two hates. TRO 5.10. 27
in twain | to sunder his that was thine enemy? ROM 5.03.100
who, therefore angry, seems to part in sunder, LUC 388

SUNDERS 1 FR 0.0001 REL FR 1 V 0 P

and chides the sea that sunders him from thence, 3H6 3.02.138

SUND'RED 4 FR 0.0004 REL FR 4 V 0 P

shall we be sund'red? AYL 1.03. 98
that sund'red friends greet in the hour of death 1H6 4.03. 42
which so long sund'red friends should dwell upon R3 5.03.100
ev'n very here | i sund'red you. TNK 5.04.100

SUNDRY 6 FR 0.0006 REL FR 5 V 1 P

and indeed the sundry contemplation of my AYL 4.01. 17 P
the common eye | for sundry weighty reasons. MAC 3.01.125
more suffer, and more sundry ways than ever, 4.03. 48
and sundry blessings hang about his throne 4.03.158
extremity, that sharpens sundry wits, | makes me TNK 1.01.118
the sundry dangers of his will's obtaining; LUC 128

SUN–EXPELLING 1 FR 0.0001 REL FR 1 V 0 P

and threw her sun–expelling mask away, | the air TGV 4.04.153

SUNG 27 FR 0.0030 REL FR 22 V 5 P

thou hast by moonlight at her window sung | with MND 1.01. 30
to be sung | by an athenian eunuch to the harp." 5.01. 44
very pleasant thing indeed and sung lamentably. WT 4.04.190 P
and sung this ballad against the hard hearts of 4.04.277 P
to whom he sung, in rude harsh–sounding rhymes, JN 4.02.150
even now he sung. 5.07. 12
made on you all and sung to filthy tunes, let a 1H4 2.02. 45 P
sung by a fair queen in a summer's bow'r, | with 3.01.207
and sung those tunes to the overscutch'd 2H4 3.02.316 P
let there be sung non nobis and te deum, | the H5 4.08.123
that nothing sung but death to us and ours. 3H6 2.06. 57
and chatt'ring pies in dismal discords sung; 5.06. 48
music of the kingdom, | together sung te deum. H8 4.01. 92
where like a sweet melodious bird it sung TIT 3.01. 85
sung thee asleep, his loving breast thy pillow; 5.03.163
sudden joy did weep, | and i for sorrow sung, LR 1.04.176
to sing a song that old was sung, | from ashes PER 1.ch. 1
it hath been sung at festivals, | on ember–eves 1.ch. 5
or when to th' lute | she sung, and made the 4.ch. 26
i might well perceive | 'twas one that sung, and TNK 4.01. 58
me down | and list'ned to the words she sung, 4.01. 63
she sung much, but no sense; 4.01. 66
then she sung | nothing but "willow, willow, 4.01. 79
and then she wept, and sung again, and sigh'd, 4.01. 92
of love as she says palamon hath sung in prison. 4.03. 82 P
and sung by children in succeeding times. LUC 525
a thorn, | and there sung the dolefull'st ditty, PP 20.11

SUNK 4 FR 0.0004 REL FR 4 V 0 P

have sunk the sea within the earth or ere | it TMP 1.02. 11
are cast away, and sunk on goodwin sands. JN 5.05. 13
her bawdy veins, | a grecian's life hath sunk; TRO 4.01. 71
and see the brave day sunk in hideous night; SON 12. 2

SUNKEN 2 FR 0.0002 REL FR 1 V 1 P

a blue eye and sunken, which you have not; AYL 3.02.374 P
sea | with sunken wrack and sumless treasuries. H5 1.02.165

SUNLIKE 1 FR 0.0001 REL FR 1 V 0 P

gaze, | such as is bent on sunlike majesty, 1H4 3.02. 79

SUNNY 3 FR 0.0003 REL FR 3 V 0 P

fair | a sunny look of his would soon repair. ERR 2.01. 99
sweet moon, i thank thee for thy sunny beams; MND 5.01.272

and her sunny locks | hang on her temples like a MV 1.01.169
SUN–RISE 1 FR 0.0001 REL FR 1 V 0 P
be up at heaven and enter there | ere sun–rise, MM 2.02.153
SUNRISING 1 FR 0.0001 REL FR 1 V 0 P
bid him bring his power | before sunrising, lest R3 5.03. 61
SUN'S 10 FR 0.0011 REL FR 9 V 1 P
the sun's o'ercast with blood; JN 3.01.326
that melted at the sweet tale of the sun's? 1H4 2.04.122 P
and to sun's parching heat display'd my cheeks, 1H6 1.02. 77
lords, cold snow melts with the sun's hot beams: 2H6 3.01.223
like to the glorious sun's transparent beams, 3.01.353
that gives sweet tidings of the sun's uprise? TIT 3.01.159
ten times faster glides than the sun's beams, ROM 2.05. 5
that a prodigal course | is like the sun's, but TIM 3.04. 13
the sun's a thief, and with his great attraction 4.03.436
spread | but as the marigold at the sun's eye, SON 25. 6
SUNS 12 FR 0.0013 REL FR 11 V 1 P
tent to–night, are those stars or suns upon it? H5 3.07. 70 P
dazzle mine eyes, or do i see three suns? 3H6 2.01. 25
three glorious suns, each one a perfect sun, 2.01. 26
i bear | upon my target three fair shining suns. 2.01. 40
in my chamber when | those suns of glory, those H8 1.01. 6
when these suns | (for so they phrase 'em) by 1.01. 33
what, hath the firmament moe suns than one? TIT 5.03. 17
there were no suns to borrow of. TIM 4.03. 70
were all thy letters suns, i could not see. LR 4.06.140
why her two suns were cloud–eclipsed so, | nor LUC 1224
of those fair suns set in her mistress' sky, 1230
suns of the world may stain when heaven's sun SON 33.14
SUNSET 4 FR 0.0004 REL FR 4 V 0 P
but, ere sunset, | set armed discord 'twixt JN 3.01.110
but ere sunset i'll make thee curse the deed. 3H6 2.02.116
but for the sunset of my brother's son | it ROM 3.05.127
such day | as after sunset fadeth in the west, SON 73. 6
/SUNSHINE 2 FR 0.0002 REL FR 2 V 0 P
/send /him /many /years /of /sunshine /days! R2 4.01.221
/have /seen | /sunshine /and /rain /at /once; LR 4.03. 18
SUNSHINE 7 FR 0.0008 REL FR 7 V 0 P
vouchsafe to show the sunshine of your face, LLL 5.02.201
for thou mayst see a sunshine and a hail | in me AWW 5.03. 33
heart | and ripens in the sunshine of his favor, 2H4 4.02. 12
ne'er may he live to see a sunshine day | that 3H6 2.01.187
even then that sunshine brew'd a show'r for him, 2.02.156
but when we saw our sunshine made thy spring, 2.02.163
"love comforteth like sunshine after rain, | but VEN 799
SUP* 21 FR 0.0023 REL FR 11 V 10 P
now can i break my fast, dine, sup, and sleep, TGV 2.04.141
i am fain to dine and sup with water and bran; MM 4.03.153 P
man's blood in his belly than will sup a flea. LLL 5.02.692 P
old master the jew to sup to–night with my new MV 2.04. 18 P
but sup them well, and look unto them all, SHR in.1. 28
are they gone, and there they intend to sup. WT 5.02.103 P
me to–morrow night in eastcheap, there i'll sup. 1H4 1.02.193 P
will you sup with me, master gower? 2H4 2.01.188 P
sup any women with him? 2.02.151 P
and warwick | to sup with me to–morrow night. 2H6 1.04. 80
for you shall sup with jesu christ to–night. 5.01.214
if not in heaven, you'll surely sup in hell. 5.01.216
come, let us sup betimes, that afterwards | we R3 3.01.199
i will not sup to–night. 5.03. 48
you'll sup with me? COR 4.02. 49
i sup upon myself, | and so shall starve with 4.02. 50
will you sup with me to–night, casca? JC 1.02.288 P
go get thee in, and fetch me a sup of liquor. HAM 5.01. 60 P
will you sup there? OTH 4.01.164 P
i do entreat that we may sup together. 4.01.262
to camp this host, we all would sup together, ANT 4.08. 33
SUPER–DAINTY 1 FR 0.0001 REL FR 1 V 0 P
kate of kate–hall, my super–dainty kate, | for SHR 2.01.188
SUPERFICIAL 2 FR 0.0002 REL FR 1 V 1 P
a very superficial, ignorant, unweighing fellow. MM 3.02.139 P
this superficial tale | is but a preface of her 1H6 5.05. 10
SUPERFICIALLY 2 FR 0.0002 REL FR 1 V 1 P
now in hand | have gloz'd, but superficially, TRO 2.02.165
faith, sir, superficially. 3.01. 10 P
SUPERFLUITY 4 FR 0.0004 REL FR 1 V 3 P
superfluity comes sooner by white hairs, but MV 1.02. 8 P
as, one for superfluity, and another for use! 2H4 2.02. 17 P
would yield us but the superfluity while it were COR 1.01. 17 P
shall ha' means to vent | our musty superfluity. 1.01.226
SUPERFLUOUS 17 FR 0.0019 REL FR 14 V 3 P
i have no superfluous leisure; MM 3.01.157 P
that superfluous case | that hid the worse and LLL 5.02.387
see | cold wisdom waiting on superfluous folly. AWW 1.01.105
with this abundance of superfluous breath? JN 2.01.148
your highness pleas'd) | was once superfluous. 4.02. 4
superfluous branches | we lop away, that bearing R2 3.04. 63
shouldst be so superfluous to demand the time of 1H4 1.02. 11 P
it were superfluous, for /'s apparel is built 2H4 3.02.143 P
and dout them with superfluous courage, ha! H5 4.02. 11
that our superfluous lackeys and our peasants, 4.02. 26
a peace, and purchas'd | at a superfluous rate! H8 1.01. 99
in many places | gives me superfluous death. HAM 4.05. 96
beggars | are in the poorest thing superfluous. LR 2.04.265
let the superfluous and lust–dieted man, | that 4.01. 67
which had superfluous kings for messengers | not ANT 3.12. 5
with their superfluous riots, hear these tears! PER 1.04. 54
to say you're welcome were superfluous. 2.03. 2
SUPERFLUOUSLY 1 FR 0.0001 REL FR 0 V 1 P
for you bear a many superfluously, and 'twere H5 3.07. 74 P
SUPERFLUX 1 FR 0.0001 REL FR 1 V 0 P
that thou mayst shake the superflux to them, LR 3.04. 35
SUPERIOR 1 FR 0.0001 REL FR 1 V 0 P
the first pace that is sick | of his superior, TRO 1.03.133
SUPERIORS 1 FR 0.0001 REL FR 1 V 0 P
that golden hap which their superiors want. LUC 42
SUPERNAL 1 FR 0.0001 REL FR 1 V 0 P
from that supernal judge that stirs good JN 2.01.112
SUPERNATURAL 2 FR 0.0002 REL FR 1 V 1 P
and familiar things supernatural and causeless. AWW 2.03. 3 P
this supernatural soliciting | cannot be ill; MAC 1.03.130
SUPERPRAISE 1 FR 0.0001 REL FR 1 V 0 P
to vow, and swear, and superpraise my parts, MND 3.02.153
SUPERSCRIPT 1 FR 0.0001 REL FR 0 V 1 P
i will overglance the superscript: LLL 4.02.131 P
SUPERSCRIPTION 2 FR 0.0002 REL FR 1 V 1 P
or doth this churlish superscription | pretend 1H6 4.01. 53
read me the superscription of these letters, i TIM 2.02. 78 P
SUPERSERVICEABLE 1 FR 0.0001 REL FR 0 V 1 P
glass–gazing, superserviceable, finical rogue; LR 2.02. 18 P
SUPERSTITION 3 FR 0.0003 REL FR 3 V 0 P
and do not say 'tis superstition, that | i kneel WT 5.03. 43
that's your superstition. PER 3.01. 50
which superstition | here finds allowance — on TNK 5.04. 53
SUPERSTITIOUS 4 FR 0.0004 REL FR 4 V 0 P
you know | the superstitious idle–headed eld WIV 4.04. 36
been, out of fondness, superstitious to him? H8 3.01.131
superstitious girl | makes all these bodements. TRO 5.03. 79
for he is superstitious grown of late, | quite JC 2.01.195
SUPERSTITIOUSLY 2 FR 0.0002 REL FR 2 V 0 P
toys, | yet for this once, yea, superstitiously, WT 3.03. 40
y' are like one that superstitiously | do swear PER 4.03. 49
SUPER–SUBTLE 1 FR 0.0001 REL FR 0 V 1 P
barbarian and /a super–subtle venetian be not OTH 1.03.356 P
SUPERVISE 2 FR 0.0002 REL FR 1 V 1 P
let me supervise the /canzonet. LLL 4.02.120 P
that, on the supervise, no leisure bated, | no, HAM 5.02. 23
/SUPERVISOR 1 FR 0.0001 REL FR 1 V 0 P
would you, the /supervisor, grossly gape on? OTH 3.03.395
SUPP'D 7 FR 0.0008 REL FR 6 V 1 P
the room where they supp'd is too hot, they'll 2H4 2.04. 13 P
he has almost supp'd. MAC 1.07. 29
i have supp'd full with horrors; 5.05. 13
go know of cassio where he supp'd to–night. OTH 5.01.117
he supp'd at my house, but i therefore shake not 5.01.119
when we have supp'd, | we'll mannerly demand CYM 3.06. 90
fare well i could not, for i supp'd with sorrow. PP 14. 6
SUPPEAGO *(also sapego)*
/SUPPEAGO 1 FR 0.0001 REL FR 0 V 1 P
/now, /the /dry /suppeago /on /the /subject, TRO 2.03. 74 P
SUPPER 51 FR 0.0057 REL FR 21 V 30 P
she that you gaze on so as she sits at supper? TGV 2.01. 43 P
we'll wait upon your grace till after supper, 3.02. 95
and tell him i will not fail him at supper, for ADO 1.01.277 P
i came yonder from a great supper. 1.03. 42 P
let us to the great supper, their cheer is the 1.03. 71 P
was not count john here at supper? 2.01. 1 P
for the fool will eat no supper that night. 2.01.150 P
down to that nourishment which is called supper: LLL 1.01.238 P
let it be so hasted that supper be ready at the MV 2.02.115 P
soon at supper shalt thou see | lorenzo, who is 2.03. 5
i am bid forth to supper, jessica. 2.05. 11
is supper ready, the house trimm'd, rushes SHR 4.01. 45 P
go, rascals, go, and fetch my supper in. 4.01.139
daughter is to be brought by you to the supper. 4.04. 86 P
po, | it draws toward supper in conclusion so. JN 1.01.204
come home with me to supper, i'll lay | a plot R2 4.01.333
and unbuttoning thee after supper, and sleeping 1H4 1.02. 3 P
i have bespoke supper to–morrow night in 1.02.130 P
fat rogue will tell us when we meet at supper, 1.02.188 P
it to one of his company last night at supper, a 2.01. 57 P
item, anchoves and sack after supper ... 2s.6d.. 2.04.538 P
i hope you'll come to supper. 2H4 2.01.159 P
will you have doll tearsheet meet you at supper? 2.01.164 P
shall we steal upon them, ned, at supper? 2.02.158 P
like a man made after supper of a cheese–paring. 3.02.309 P
the mass, i have drunk too much sack at supper. 5.03. 14 P
our simple supper ended, give me leave | in this 2H6 2.02. 2
i guess, | to make a bloody supper in the tower. 3H6 5.05. 85
grandam, one night as we did sit at supper, | my R3 2.04. 10
and supper too, although thou know'st it not. 3.02.122
this night he makes a supper, and a great one, H8 1.03. 52
that if the king call for him at supper, you TRO 3.01. 77 P
i shall, between this and supper, tell you most COR 4.03. 40 P
whither? to supper? ROM 1.02. 73 P
the guests are come, supper serv'd up, you 1.03.100 P
supper is done, and we shall come too late. 1.04.105
she will indite him to some supper. 2.04.129 P
and come again to supper to him of purpose to TIM 3.01. 25 P
and yesternight at supper | you suddenly arose JC 2.01.238
to–night we hold a solemn supper, sir, | and MAC 3.01. 14
will fill up the time | 'twixt this and supper. 3.01. 25
at supper. HAM 4.03. 17 P
at supper? where? 4.03. 18 P
we'll go to supper i' th' morning. LR 3.06. 84 P
(being full of supper and distemp'ring draughts) OTH 1.01. 99
shall't be to–night at supper? 3.03. 57
/an' you'll come to supper to–night, you may; 4.01.159 P
hark how these instruments summon to supper! 4.02.169
antony sent to her, | invited her to supper. ANT 2.02.220
let's to supper, come, | and drown consideration 4.02. 44
for after supper long he questioned | with LUC 122
SUPPERS 1 FR 0.0001 REL FR 0 V 1 P
dinners and suppers and sleeping–hours excepted. AYL 3.02. 97 P
SUPPER–TIME 10 FR 0.0011 REL FR 9 V 1 P
for yet ere supper–time must i perform | much TMP 3.01. 95
and soon at supper–time i'll visit you, | and ERR 3.02.174
rest, | but we will visit you at supper–time. MV 2.02.206
nay, we will slink away in supper–time, 2.04. 1
and 'twill be supper–time ere you come there. SHR 4.03.190
cost me /a hundred crowns since supper–time. 5.02.128
now it is supper–time in orleance: 1H6 1.04. 59
it's supper–time, my lord, | it's /nine a' clock R3 5.03. 47
we will keep ourself | till supper–time alone; MAC 3.01. 43
it is now high supper–time, and the night grows OTH 4.02.242 P
SUPPING 1 FR 0.0001 REL FR 1 V 0 P
what tell'st thou me of supping? ERR 4.03. 65
SUPPLANT 6 FR 0.0006 REL FR 5 V 1 P
you did supplant your brother prospero. TMP 2.01.271
this hand, i will supplant some of your teeth. 3.02. 49 P
three | from milan did supplant good prospero, 3.03. 70
we must supplant those rough rug–headed kerns, R2 2.01.156
which fear, if better reasons can supplant, | i 2H6 3.01. 37
part, | and so supplant you for ingratitude, TIT 1.01.447
SUPPLE 6 FR 0.0006 REL FR 4 V 2 P
well, | and had the tribute of his supple knee, R2 1.04. 33
i will knead him, i'll make him supple. TRO 2.03.221 P
for supple knees | feed arrogance and are the 3.03. 48
having been supple and courteous to the people, COR 2.02. 26 P
each part, depriv'd of supple government, ROM 4.01.102
aches contract and starve your supple joints! TIM 1.01.248
SUPPLER 2 FR 0.0002 REL FR 2 V 0 P
i do beseech you | (that are of suppler joints) TMP 3.03.107
we have suppler souls | than in our priest–like COR 5.01. 55
SUPPLIANCE 1 FR 0.0001 REL FR 1 V 0 P
the perfume and suppliance of a minute — | no HAM 1.03. 9
SUPPLIANT 5 FR 0.0005 REL FR 5 V 0 P
him so, | when she for thy repeal was suppliant, TGV 3.01.236
fair grace and speech | of the poor suppliant, AWW 5.03.134
what shrill/–voic'd suppliant makes this eager R2 5.03. 75
heard you not what an humble suppliant | lord R3 1.01. 74
for /then hast made it like an humble suppliant. TIT 4.03.117
SUPPLIANT'S 1 FR 0.0001 REL FR 1 V 0 P
wilt thou be the humble suppliant's friend, LUC 897
SUPPLIANTS' 1 FR 0.0001 REL FR 1 V 0 P
and be more costly than | your suppliants' war! TNK 1.01.133
SUPPLIANTS 1 FR 0.0001 REL FR 1 V 0 P
scandall'd the suppliants for the people, call'd COR 3.01. 44
SUPPLICANT 1 FR 0.0001 REL FR 1 V 0 P
and supplicant their sighs to you extend | to LC 276
SUPPLICATION 4 FR 0.0004 REL FR 1 V 3 P
makes your grace to the rebels' supplication? 2H6 4.04. 8 P
to a molehill should | in supplication nod; COR 5.03. 31
can you with a grace deliver up a supplication? TIT 4.03.107 P
then here is a supplication for you; 4.03.109 P
SUPPLICATIONS 2 FR 0.0002 REL FR 0 V 2 P
we may deliver our supplications in the quill. 2H6 1.03. 3 P
are your supplications to his lordship? 1.03. 14 P
SUPPLIE 2 FR 0.0002 REL FR 0 V 2 P
o, je vous supplie, pour l'amour de dieu, me H5 4.04. 40 P
excusez–moi, je vous supplie, mon tres puissant 5.02.256 P
SUPPLIED 9 FR 0.0010 REL FR 8 V 1 P
which may be better supplied when i have made it AYL 1.02.192 P
these sovereign thrones, are all supplied, and TN 1.01. 37
which by thy younger brother is supplied, | and 1H4 3.02. 33
a hundred almshouses right well supplied; H5 1.01. 17
how well supplied with noble counsellors, | how 2.04. 33
chairs of justice | supplied with worthy men! COR 3.03. 35
isles | of kerns and /gallowglasses is supplied, MAC 1.02. 13
that, i being absent and my place supplied, | my OTH 3.03. 17
convinced or supplied them, cannot choose | but 4.01. 28
SUPPLIES 4 FR 0.0004 REL FR 4 V 0 P
and our supplies live largely in the hope | of 2H4 1.03. 12
down, | we have supplies to second our attempt; 4.02. 45
with furbish'd arms and new supplies of men, MAC 1.02. 32
'tis their fresh supplies. CYM 5.02. 16
SUPPLIEST 1 FR 0.0001 REL FR 0 V 1 P
all conveniency than suppliest me with the least OTH 4.02.177 P
SUPPLY 29 FR 0.0032 REL FR 23 V 6 P
soul | elected him our absence to supply, | lent MM 1.01. 18
therefore i prithee | supply me with the habit, 1.03. 46
and did supply thee at thy garden–house | in her 5.01.212
yet, to supply the ripe wants of my friend, MV 1.03. 63
supply your present wants, and take no doit | of 1.03.140
wants | for to supply the places at the table, SHR 3.02.247
you shall supply the bridegroom's place, | and 3.02.249
for the great supply, | that was expected by the JN 5.03. 9
and your supply, which you have wish'd so long, 5.05. 12
gold, | and send them after to supply our wants, R2 1.04. 51
why say you so? looks he not for supply? 1H4 4.03. 3
hope, | eating the air, and promise of supply, 2H4 1.03. 28
for the which supply, | admit me chorus to this H5 pr 31
the earl of salisbury craveth supply, | and 1H6 1.01.159
that thus delays my promised supply | of 4.03. 10
in stead whereof let this supply the room: 3H6 2.06. 54
and prince shall follow with a fresh supply. 3.03.237
shadow | to henry's body, and supply his place; 4.06. 50
to me in words, | but find supply immediate. TIM 2.01. 27
found time to use 'em toward a supply of money. 2.02.192 P
behalf, i come to entreat your honor to supply; 3.01. 18 P
your lordship to supply his instant use with so 3.02. 35 P
nor has he with him to | supply his life, or 4.02. 47
if he care not for't, he will supply us easily; 4.03.404 P
a while | for the supply and profit of our hope, HAM 2.02. 24
deliver me, and supply the place for your labor. LR 4.06.268 P
supply it with one gender of herbs or distract OTH 1.03.323 P
your coast, with a supply | of roman gentlemen, CYM 4.03. 25
crowns be scant, | no man will supply thy want. PP 20.36
SUPPLYANT 1 FR 0.0001 REL FR 1 V 0 P
of, whereunto your levy | must be supplyant. CYM 3.07. 14
SUPPLYING 1 FR 0.0001 REL FR 1 V 0 P
land, supplying every stage | with an augmented ANT 3.06. 54
SUPPLYMENT 1 FR 0.0001 REL FR 1 V 0 P
i will never fail | beginning nor supplyment. CYM 3.04.179
SUPPLY'T 1 FR 0.0001 REL FR 1 V 0 P
be in their dear rites, we would supply't. TNK 1.04. 9
SUPPORT 13 FR 0.0014 REL FR 12 V 1 P
support him by the arm. AYL 2.07.199
who, weak with age, cannot support myself. R2 2.02. 83
takes on the point of honor to support | so 5.03. 11
is numb | (unable to support this lump of clay), 1H6 2.05. 14
to strengthen and support king edward's place. 3H6 3.01. 52
title | a thousand pound a year, annual support, H8 2.03. 64
make edicts for usury, to support usurers; COR 1.01. 82 P
help the feeble up, | but to support him after. TIM 1.01.108
and in the most exact regard support | the LR 1.04.265
/durst thou support a publish'd traitor? 4.06.232
(alack, too weak the conflict to support!) 5.03.198
and i a heavy interim shall support | by his OTH 1.03.258
forceless flowers like sturdy trees support me; VEN 152
SUPPORTABLE 1 FR 0.0001 REL FR 1 V 0 P
and, supportable | to make the dear loss, have i TMP 5.01.145
SUPPORTANCE 2 FR 0.0002 REL FR 1 V 1 P
therefore draw, for the supportance of his vow. TN 3.04.300 P
give some supportance to the bending twigs. R2 3.04. 32
SUPPORTED 1 FR 0.0001 REL FR 1 V 0 P
supported his estate, nay, timon's money | has TIM 3.02. 69
SUPPORTER 2 FR 0.0002 REL FR 1 V 1 P
sheriff's post, and be the supporter to a bench, TN 1.05.148 P
that no supporter but the huge firm earth | can JN 3.01. 72
SUPPORTERS 1 FR 0.0001 REL FR 1 V 0 P
and good supporters are you. MM 5.01. 18
SUPPORTING 1 FR 0.0001 REL FR 1 V 0 P
of all this world | but for supporting robbers, JC 4.03. 23
SUPPOSAL 1 FR 0.0001 REL FR 1 V 0 P
holding a weak supposal of our worth, | or HAM 1.02. 18
/SUPPOS'D 1 FR 0.0001 REL FR 1 V 0 P
/suppos'd /sincere /and /holy /in /his /thoughts 2H4 1.01.202
SUPPOS'D 19 FR 0.0021 REL FR 17 V 2 P
i'll be suppos'd upon a book, his face is the MM 2.01.155 P
some fear, | how easy is a bush suppos'd a bear! MND 5.01. 22
i see no reason but suppos'd lucentio | must get SHR 2.01.407

must get a father, call'd — suppos'd vincentio; 2.01.408
which vainly i suppos'd the holy land. 2H4 4.05.238
idly suppos'd the founder of this law, | who H5 1.02. 59
that they suppos'd i could rend bars of steel, 1H6 1.04. 51
broils, | than yet can be imagin'd or suppos'd. 4.01.186
john cade, so term'd of our suppos'd father — 2H6 4.02. 31 P
jocund, and suppos'd their states were sure, R3 3.02. 84
it is suppos'd | he that meets hector issues TRO 1.03.346
and after conflict such as was suppos'd | the TIT 2.03. 21
i knew them all though they suppos'd me mad, 5.02.142
i aim'd so near when i suppos'd you lov'd. ROM 1.01.205
but to his foe suppos'd he must complain, | and 2.pr. 7
we tender our loves to him in this suppos'd TIM 5.01. 12
let my unsounded self, suppos'd a fool, | now LUC 1819
suppos'd as forfeit to a confin'd doom. SON 107. 4
sweetly suppos'd them mistress of his heart. LC 142

SUPPOSE 33 FR 0.0037 REL FR 32 V 1 P
young ferdinand, whom they suppose is drown'd, TMP 3.03. 92
and so suppose am i; TGV 4.02.113
(since i suppose we are made to be no stronger MM 2.04.132
and do suppose | what hath been cannot be. AWW 1.01.225
that he shall suppose no other but that he is 3.06. 25 P
yet i suppose him virtuous, know him noble, | of TN 1.05.258
as i suppose, to robert faulconbridge, | a JN 1.01. 52
i did suppose it should be on constraint, | but, 5.01. 28
brain | (which some suppose the soul's frail 5.07. 3
or suppose | devouring pestilence hangs in our R2 1.03.283
suppose the singing birds musicians, | the grass 1.03.288
mind, | if you suppose as fearing you it shook. 1H4 3.01. 22
is he so hasty that he doth suppose | my sleep 2H4 4.05. 60
suppose within the girdle of these walls | are H5 pr 19
suppose that you have seen | the well-appointed 3.pr. 3
suppose th' embassador from the french comes 3.pr. 28
who would e'er suppose | they had such courage 1H6 1.02. 35
if he suppose that i have pleaded truth, | from 2.04. 29
would you not suppose | your bondage happy, to 5.03.110
suppose, my lords, he did it unconstrain'd, 3H6 1.01.143
suppose this arm is for the duke of york, | and 2.04. 2
suppose they take offense without a cause; 4.01. 14
suppose that i am now my father's mouth: 5.05. 18
my lord, as you suppose | you should enjoy, were R3 1.03.150
as little joy you may suppose in me | that i 1.03.152
that we come short of our suppose so far | that TRO 1.03. 11
lose not so noble a friend on vain suppose, TIT 1.01.440
bid him suppose some good necessity | touches TIM 2.02.227
in a secure couch, | and to suppose her chaste! OTH 4.01. 72
and on this coast | suppose him now at anchor. PER 5.ch. 16
that you aptly will suppose | what pageantry, 5.02. 5
suppose thou dost defend me | from what is past: LUC 1684
where you may be, or your affairs suppose, | but SON 57.10

SUPPOSED 17 FR 0.0019 REL FR 16 V 1 P
let the supposed fairies pinch him sound, | and WIV 4.04. 62
the treasures of your body | to this supposed, MM 2.04. 97
and that supposed by the common rout | against ERR 3.01.101
gambols with the wind | upon supposed fairness, MV 3.02. 94
helen, | if you should tender your supposed aid, AWW 1.03.236
you must know | i am supposed dead. 4.04. 11
and to bloodshed, | wounding supposed peace. 2H4 4.05.195
and tell false edward, thy supposed king, | that 3H6 3.03.223
"go tell false edward, the supposed king, | that 4.01. 93
of these supposed crimes, to give me leave | by R3 1.02. 76
grief | it is supposed the fair creature died, ROM 5.03. 51
upon edmund, supposed earl of gloucester, that LR 5.03.112 P
that thaisa am i, supposed dead | and drown'd. PER 5.03. 35
death be adjunct, there's no death supposed. LUC 133
that dazzleth them, or else some shame supposed, 377
the sight which makes supposed terror true. 455
hearts, | which i by lacking have supposed dead, SON 31. 2

SUPPOSES 3 FR 0.0003 REL FR 2 V 1 P
and he supposes me travell'd to poland — | for MM 1.03. 14
while counterfeit supposes blear'd thine eyne. SHR 5.01.117
to morgan, whom he supposes to be a friar, from AWW 4.03.109 P

SUPPOSEST 1 FR 0.0001 REL FR 1 V 0 P
which thou supposest i have done to thee. R3 4.04.253

SUPPOSING 5 FR 0.0005 REL FR 5 V 0 P
supposing that they saw the king's ship wrack'd, TMP 1.02.236
supposing it a thing impossible, | for those SHR 1.02.123
he talks on now, | supposing that i lack'd it. ANT 2.02. 86
in your supposing once more put your sight: PER 5.ch. 21
so shall i live, supposing thou art true, | like SON 93. 1

SUPPOSITION 6 FR 0.0006 REL FR 4 V 2 P
and in that glorious supposition think | he ERR 3.02. 50
the supposition of the lady's death | will ADO 4.01.238
yet his means are in supposition: MV 1.03. 17 P
well, and to beguile the supposition of that AWW 4.03.300 P
supposition all our lives shall be stuck full of 1H4 5.02. 8
/one supposition, which if you will mark | you STM II.C 91

SUPPRESS 5 FR 0.0005 REL FR 5 V 0 P
to crown himself king and suppress the prince. 1H6 1.03. 68
well didst thou, richard, to suppress thy voice; 4.01.182
in what we can to bridle and suppress | the 2H6 1.01.200
to suppress | his further gait herein, in that HAM 1.02. 30
he sent out to suppress | his nephew's levies, 2.02. 61

SUPPRESS'D 5 FR 0.0005 REL FR 5 V 0 P
by your own counsel is suppress'd and kill'd. H5 2.02. 80
in whom the title rested, were suppress'd. 1H6 2.05. 92
till warwick or himself be quite suppress'd. 3H6 4.03. 6
slak'd, not suppress'd, for standing by her side LUC 425
on both sides thus is simple truth suppress'd. SON 138. 8

SUPPRESSETH 1 FR 0.0001 REL FR 1 V 0 P
heav'ns are just, and time suppresseth wrongs. 3H6 3.03. 77

SUPREMACY 5 FR 0.0005 REL FR 5 V 0 P
life, | an aweful rule, and right supremacy; SHR 5.02.109
or seek for rule, supremacy, and sway, | when 5.02.163
head, | so under him that great supremacy, JN 3.01.156
my spirit | /thy full supremacy thou knew'st, ANT 3.11. 59
did vail their crowns to his supremacy; PER 2.03. 42

SUPREME 9 FR 0.0010 REL FR 9 V 0 P
but as we, under /god, are supreme head, | so JN 3.01.155
fie, lords, that you, being supreme magistrates, 1H6 1.03. 57
lest he that is the supreme king of kings R3 2.01. 13
your fault that you resign | the supreme seat, 3.07.118
neither supreme, how soon confusion | may enter COR 3.01.110
with the consent of supreme jove, inform | thy 5.03. 71
my supreme crown of grief, and those repeated CYM 1.06. 4
kings, | imperious supreme of all mortal things. VEN 996
sick | the life of purity, the supreme fair, LUC 780

SUPS 5 FR 0.0005 REL FR 1 V 4 P
where sups he? 2H4 2.02.146 P
what exploit's in hand? where sups he to-night? TRO 3.01. 81 P
you must not know where he sups. 3.01. 86 P
sups the fair rosaline whom thou so loves, ROM 1.02. 83
he sups to-night with a harlotry, and thither OTH 4.02.233 P

SUR 2 FR 0.0002 REL FR 0 V 2 P
sur mes genoux /je vous donne mille H5 4.04. 54 P
je quand sur le possession de france, et quand 5.02.181 P

SUR-ADDITION 1 FR 0.0001 REL FR 1 V 0 P
so gain'd the sur-addition leonatus; CYM 1.01. 33

SURANCE *(also assurance)*

SURANCE 1 FR 0.0001 REL FR 1 V 0 P
now give some surance that thou art revenge — TIT 5.02. 46

SURCEASE 4 FR 0.0004 REL FR 4 V 0 P
do't, | lest i surcease to honor mine own truth, COR 3.02.121
shall keep his native progress, but surcease; ROM 4.01. 97
and catch | with his surcease, success; MAC 1.07. 4
if they surcease to be that should survive. LUC 1766

/SURE 4 FR 0.0004 REL FR 3 V 1 P
/model, | /consent /upon /a /sure /foundation, 2H4 1.03. 52
thou /sure and firm-set earth, | hear not my MAC 2.01. 56
/but /sure /the /bravery /of /his /grief /did HAM 5.02. 79
/nor /is /not, /sure. LR 1.02. 95 P

SURE 315 FR 0.0356 REL FR 229 V 86 P
for this, be sure, to-night thou shalt have TMP 1.02.325
and sure it waits upon | some god o' th' island. 1.02.389
most sure, the goddess | on whom these airs 1.02.422
sure it was the roar | of a whole herd of lions. 2.01.315
for he is sure i' th' island. 2.01.325
nay sure, i think she holds them prisoners still TGV 2.04. 92
and sure the match | were rich and honorable; 3.01. 63
for i am sure she is not buried. 4.02.107
'twere a substance, you would sure deceive it, 4.02.126
sure as i live, he had suffer'd for't. 4.04. 15 P
if we recover that, we are sure enough. 5.01. 12
she, | but, being mask'd, he was not sure of it; 5.02. 40
and less than this, i am sure you cannot give. 5.04. 25
as sure as his guts are made of puddings. WIV 2.01. 31 P
writ with blank space for different names (sure, 2.01. 76 P
for sure, unless he know some strain in me that 2.01. 87 P
i'll be sure to keep him above deck. 2.01. 90 P
my means, meed, i am sure, i have receiv'd none, 2.02.203 P
be sure of that — two other husbands. 3.02. 16 P
sure they sleep, he hath no use of them. 3.02. 31 P
sure he is by this — or will be presently. 4.01. 3 P
there are fairer things than poulcats sure. 4.01. 29 P
but are you sure of your husband now? 4.02. 6 P
in my house i am sure he is. 4.02.148 P
spirit of wantonness is sure scar'd out of him. 4.02.209 P
sure he'll come. 4.04. 77
sure, one of you does not serve heaven well, 4.05.125 P
are now so sure that nothing can dissolve us. 5.05.224
art thou sure of this? MM 1.02. 71 P
i am too sure of it; 1.02. 72 P
precise villains they are, that i am sure of, 2.01. 54 P
sure it is no sin, | or of the deadly seven it 3.01.109
are not mad | have sure more lack of reason. 5.01. 68
sure, luciana, it is two a' clock. ERR 2.01. 3
why, mistress, sure my master is horn-mad. 2.01. 57
not cuckold-mad — | but sure he is stark mad: 2.01. 59
sure ones then. 2.02. 93 P
nay, not sure, in a thing falsing. 2.02. 94 P
until i know this sure uncertainty, | i'll 2.02.185
sure these are but imaginary wiles, | and 4.03. 10
anon i'm sure the duke himself in person | comes 5.01.119
and sure (unless you send some present help) 5.01.176
as sure, my liege, as i do see your grace. 5.01.280
i am sure you both of you remember me. 5.01.292
i am sure thou dost! 5.01.304
sir, but i am sure i do not — and whatsoever a 5.01.305 P
you are both sure, and will assist me? ADO 1.03. 69 P
i am sure you know him well enough. 2.01.133 P
i am sure he is in the fleet; 2.01.142 P
sure my brother is amorous on hero and hath 2.01.155 P
no, sure, my lord, my mother cried, but then 2.01.334 P
knavery cannot sure hide himself in such 2.03.119 P
but are you sure | that benedick loves beatrice 3.01. 36
sure i think so, | and therefore certainly it 3.01. 56
sure, sure, such carping is not commendable. 3.01. 71
sure, sure, such carping is not commendable. 3.01. 71
yea, as sure as i have a thought or a soul. 4.01.330 P
come, cousin, i am sure you love the gentleman. 5.04. 84
then i am sure you know how much the gross sum LLL 1.02. 45 P
god of rhyme, for i am sure i shall turn sonnet. 1.02.184 P
o, nothing so sure, and thereby all forsworn. 4.03.279
dumaine is mine, as sure as bark on tree. 5.02.285
when i am sure you hate me with your hearts. MND 3.02.154
are you sure | that we are awake? 4.01.192
his discretion, i am sure, cannot carry his 5.01.235 P
when, i am very sure, | if they should speak, MV 1.01. 97
i am sure you are not launcelot, my boy. 2.02. 81 P
and i am sure margery your wife is my mother. 2.02. 89 P
i am sure he had more hair of his tail than i 2.02. 97 P
and in their ship i am sure lorenzo is not. 2.08. 3
why, i am sure, if he forfeit, thou wilt not 3.01. 51 P
for i am sure you can wish none from me; 3.02.191
i am sure the duke | will never grant this 3.03. 24
know him i shall, i am well sure of it. 5.01.229
and yet i am sure you are not satisfied | of 5.01.296
yonder sure they are coming. AYL 1.02.147 P
as sure i think did never man love so — | how 2.04. 29
cat will after kind, | so be sure will rosalind. 3.02.104
cage of rushes i am sure you /are not prisoner. 3.02.371 P
'tis pretty, sure, and very probable, | that 3.05. 11
nor i am sure there is no force in eyes | that 3.05. 26
but sure he's proud — and yet his pride becomes 3.05.114
sure it is hers. 4.03. 30
there is sure another flood toward, and these 5.04. 35 P
you and you are sure together, | as the winter 5.04.135
and i am sure, as many as have good beards, or ep 21 P
but sure that part | was aptly fitted and SHR in.1. 86
i would i were as sure of a good dinner. 1.02.217
this is a gift very grateful, i am sure of it. 2.01. 76 P
i will be sure my katherine shall be fine. 2.01.317
mistrust it not, for sure aeacides | was ajax, 3.01. 52
i am sure, sweet kate, this kindness merits 4.03. 41
but lend and give where she is sure to lose; AWW 1.03.215
be gone to-morrow, and be sure of this, | what i 1.03.255
but know i think, and think i know most sure, 2.01.157
uncertain life, and sure death. 2.03. 18 P
sure they are bastards to the english, the 2.03. 94 P
i am sure thy father drunk wine — but if thou 2.03. 99 P
will this capriccio hold in thee, art sure? 2.03.293
but i am sure the younger of our nature, | that 3.01. 17
whom i am sure he knows not from the enemy. 3.06. 23 P
but sure he is the prince of the world; 4.05. 49 P
i am sure i saw her wear it. 5.03. 91
i am sure care's an enemy to life. TN 1.03. 2 P
sure, my noble lord, | if she be so abandon'd to 1.04. 18
and i, that am sure i lack thee, may pass for a 1.05. 34 P
sure you have some hideous matter to deliver, 1.05.206 P
she loves me sure, the cunning of her passion 2.02. 22
he is sure possess'd, madam. 3.04. 9 P
he come, for sure the man is tainted in 's wits. 3.04. 13 P
you mistake, sir, i am sure; 3.04.226 P
tell him you are sure | all in bohemia's well; WT 1.02. 30
but i am sure 'tis safer to | avoid what's grown 1.02.432
so sure as this beard's grey — what will you 2.03.162
sure some scape. 3.03. 71 P
sure this robe of mine | does change my 4.04.134
a-life, for then we are sure they are true. 4.04.261 P
sure the gods do this year connive at us, and we 4.04.676 P
sure | when i shall see this gentleman, thy 5.01.120
for i am sure my heart wept blood. 5.02. 89 P
there is no sure foundation set on blood; JN 4.02.104
and be sure | i count myself in nothing else so R2 2.03. 45
but be sure | i will from henceforth rather be 1H4 1.03. 4
two i am sure i have paid, two rogues in buckrom 2.04.192 P
these promises are fair, the parties sure, | and 3.01. 1
"as god shall mend me," and "as sure as day"; 3.01.250 P
so should i be sure to be heart-burnt. 3.03. 50 P
i am sure they never learn'd that of me. 4.02. 71 P
i have paid percy, i have made him sure. 5.03. 47 P
but mine i am sure thou art, whoe'er thou be, 5.04. 37
therefore i'll make him sure, yea, and i'll 5.04.125 P
i am sure he is, to the hearing of any thing 2H4 1.02. 68 P
good master fang, hold him sure. 2.01. 25 P
he sure means brevity in breath, short-winded. 2.02.124 P
certain, 'tis certain, very sure, very sure. 3.02. 36 P
certain, 'tis certain, very sure, very sure. 3.02. 36 P
lead him hence, and see you guard him sure. 4.03. 75
though thou stand'st more sure than i could do, 4.05.202
face | of seeming sorrow, it is sure your own. 5.02. 29
sure we thank you. H5 1.02. 8
nay sure, he's not in hell; 2.03. 9 P
for i am sure, when he shall see our army, 3.05. 58
so should he be sure to be ransom'd, and a many 4.01.122 P
which i am sure will hang upon my tongue like a 5.02.179 P
gloucester, we'll meet to thy cost, be sure: 1H6 1.03. 82
if not of hell, the heavens sure favor him. 2.01. 47
'tis sure they found some place | but weakly 2.01. 73
am sure i scar'd the dolphin and his trull, 2.02. 28
i, as sure as english henry lives | and as his 3.02. 80
as sure as in this late-betrayed town | great 3.02. 82
so sure i swear to get the town, or die. 3.02. 84
if we both stay, we both are sure to die. 4.05. 20
he talks at randon; sure the man is mad. 5.03. 85
i'll be the first, sure. 2H6 1.03. 7 P
whose beam stands sure, whose rightful cause 2.01.201
death | hang over thee, as sure it shortly will; 2.04. 50
sirs, take away the duke, and guard him sure. 3.01.188
so the poor chicken should be sure of death. 3.01.251
for sure, my thoughts do hourly prophesy 3.02.283
the king hath sent him sure; 5.01. 13
then am i sure of victory. 3H6 4.01.147
fly, | if warwick take us we are sure to die. 4.04. 35
nay, be thou sure, i'll well requite thy 4.06. 10
ere ye come there, be sure to hear some news. 5.05. 48
a persecutor i am sure thou art. 5.06. 31
jocund, and suppos'd their states were sure, R3 3.02. 84
but sure i fear we shall not win him to it. 3.07. 80
for i am sure the emperor | paid ere he promis'd H8 1.01.185
to't, | that sure th' have worn out christendom. 1.03. 15
going, | for sure there's no converting of 'em. 1.03. 43
sure he does not, | he never was so womanish. 2.01. 37
loves and counsels, | be sure you be not loose; 2.01.127
how sad he looks! sure he is much afflicted. 2.02. 62
sure in that | i deem you an ill husband, and am 3.02.141
a sure and safe one, though thy master miss'd it 3.02.438
i am sure have shown at full their royal minds 4.01. 8
and sure those men are happy that shall have 'em 4.02.147
sure you know me? 5.02. 4
i'm sure | thou hast a cruel nature and a bloody 5.02.163
to the world than malice, | i'm sure, in me. 5.02.188
say as i say, for i am sure he is not hector. TRO 1.02. 67 P
nay, i am sure she does. 1.02.110 P
but i am sure none, unless the fiddler apollo 3.03.303 P
she was not, sure. 5.02.126
most sure she was. 5.02.126
my dreams will sure prove ominous to the day. 5.03. 6
and linger not our sure destructions on! 5.10. 9
a sure destruction. COR 2.01.243
if it were at liberty, 'twould sure southward. 2.03. 29 P
why, so he did, i am sure. 2.03.165
physic | that's sure of death without it — at 3.01.155
he shall, sure on't. 3.01.271
i understand thee well, and be thou sure, | when 4.07. 17
but sure if you | would be your country's 5.01. 35
such friends | that thought them sure of you. 5.03. 8
and sure as death i swore | i would not part a TIT 1.01.487
i warrant you, madam, we will make that sure. 2.03.133
farewell, my sons, see that you make her sure. 2.03.187
but sure some tereus hath deflow'red thee, | and 2.04. 26
'tis sure enough, and you knew how, | but if you 4.01. 95
sweet blowse, you are a beauteous blossom sure. 4.02. 72
mother, | as sure a card as ever won the set; 5.01.100
and whilst i at a banket hold him sure, | i'll 5.02. 76
and now i find it, therefore bind them sure, 5.02.160
is he sure bound? 5.02.165
because i would be sure to have all well, | to 5.03. 31
torments him so, that he will sure run mad. ROM 2.04. 5
sure wit! 2.04. 61 P
wild goose in one of thy wits than, i am sure, i 2.04. 73 P
so will ye, i am sure, that you love me. 4.01. 26
for i am sure you have your hands full all, | in 4.03. 11

be employ'd | now to guard sure their master. TIM 3.03. 39
certain as your waiting, | 'twere sure enough. 3.04. 48
'tis so, be sure of it. 3.06. 55 P
(for i must ever doubt, though ne'er so sure), 4.03.507
heard that i have gold, | i am sure you have. 5.01. 77
dead, sure, and this his grave. 5.03. 5
mean by that, but i am sure caesar fell down. JC 1.02.258 P
and after this let caesar seat him sure, | for 1.02.321
ere day | we will awake him and be sure of him. 1.03.164
and i am sure | it did not lie there when i went 2.01. 37
but if these | (as i am sure they do) bear fire 2.01.120
sure the boy heard me. 2.04. 42
ambitious, | and sure he is an honorable man. 3.02. 99
for i have seen more years, i'm sure, than ye. 4.03.132
i was sure your lordship did not give it me. 4.03.254
nay, i am sure it is, volumnius. 5.05. 21
i wish your horses swift and sure of foot; MAC 3.01. 37
but yet i'll make assurance double sure, | and 4.01. 83
great tyranny, lay thou thy basis sure, | for 4.03. 32
spoke what she should not, i am sure of that; 5.01. 48 P
at least i am sure it may be so in denmark. HAM 1.05.109
and sure i am two men there is not living | to 2.02. 20
hunts not the trail of policy so sure | as it 2.02. 47
but i thank you, and sure, dear friends, my 2.02.273 P
sense sure you have, | else could you not have 3.04. 71
have motion, but sure that sense | is apoplex'd, 3.04. 72
sure he that made us with such large discourse, 4.04. 36
though nothing sure, yet much unhappily. 4.05. 13
i am sure you make a wanton of me. 5.02.299
since i am sure my love's | more ponderous than LR 1.01. 77
sure i shall never marry like my sisters, | /to 1.01.103
sure her offense | must be of such unnatural 1.01.218
who i am sure is kind and comfortable. 1.04.306
such a daughter, | should sure to the slaughter, 1.04.319
i am sure on't, not a word. 2.01. 27
does not love her husband, | i am sure of that; 4.05. 24
most sure and vulgar; 4.06.210
not sure, though hoping, of this good success, 5.03.195
for, sir, | it is as sure as you are roderigo, OTH 1.01. 56
but thou must needs be sure | my spirits and my 1.01.102
and your noble self | i am sure is sent for. 1.02. 93
thou art sure of me — go make money. 1.03.364 P
but all will sure be well. 3.01. 42
no, sure, i cannot think it, | that he would 3.03. 38
for sure he fills it up with great ability — 3.03.247
villain, be sure thou prove my love a whore; 3.03.359
be sure of it. 3.03.360
a handkerchief | (i am sure it was your wive's) 3.03.438
sure, there's some wonder in this handkerchief; 3.04.101
something sure of state, | either from venice, 3.04.140
ply desdemona well, and you are sure on't. 4.01.106
are you sure of that? 4.01.226
i do not know; i am sure i am none such. 4.02.123
no — yes, sure — /o /heaven, roderigo! 5.01. 90
if she come in, she'll sure speak to my wife. 5.02. 96
the woman falls; sure he hath kill'd his wife. 5.02.236
with him at any game, | thou art sure to lose; ANT 2.03. 27
of thee, | that art not what th' art sure of. 2.05.103
if he do, sure he cannot weep't back again. 2.06.106 P
the token'd pestilence, | where death is sure. 3.10. 10
to be sure of that, | i will ask antony. 3.13. 62
for i am sure, | though you can guess what 3.13.120
for i am sure mine nails | are stronger than 5.02.223
o, sir, you are too sure an augurer; 5.02.334
ill often hurts more | than to be sure they do; CYM 1.06. 96
fast to your affection, | still close as sure. 1.06.139
i would i were so sure | to win the king as i am 2.04. 1
i am sure | she would not lose it. 2.04.123
none in the world. you did mistake him sure. 4.02.102
so well master'd, but be sure | no less belov'd. 4.02.383
than be cur'd | by th' sure physician, death, 5.04. 7
yourself that which i am sure you do not know, 5.04.181 P
i am sure hanging's the way of winking. 5.04.190 P
he, i am sure | he would have spoke to us. 5.05.125
this is sure fidele. 5.05.260
so sure as you your father's. 5.05.332
my pistol's length, | i'll make him sure enough; PER 1.01.167
if i do it not, i am sure to be hang'd at home. 1.03. 2 P
nay then thou wilt starve sure; 2.01. 68 P
we'll sure provide. 2.01.162 P
sure he's a gallant gentleman. 2.03. 32
sure all effectless; 5.01. 53
seems to dote, | how sure you are my daughter. 5.01.226
for i am sure | it has a noble breeder and a TNK pr 9
i am sure i shall not. 1.03. 85
but sure, my sister, | if i were ripe for your 1.03. 90
a thousand differing ways to one sure end. 1.05. 14
here, | i am sure, a more content, and all those 2.02.100
sure there cannot. 2.02.113
i could lie down, i am sure. 2.02.151
and then i am sure she would love me. 2.02.243
i am sure | to have my wife as jealous as a 2.03. 29
your father | sure is a happy sire then. 2.05. 9
he's well got sure. 2.05. 24
sure he cannot | be so unmanly as to leave me 2.06. 18
sure, of another | you would not hear me doubted 3.01. 60
and be sure | you tumble with audacity and 3.05. 35
yours, | of more authority, i am sure more love, 3.06.231
burst of clamor | is sure th' end o' th' combat. 5.03. 78
that sure shall please the gods | sooner than 5.04. 11
sure these things | not physick'd by respect STM III 12
from hands of falsehood, in sure wards of trust! SON 48. 4
sure i am the wits of former days | to subjects 59.13
and to be sure that is not false i swear, | a 131. 9
/SURECARD 1 FR 0.0001 REL FR 0 V 1 P
master /surecard, as i think? 2H4 3.02. 86 P
SURELY *(also suerly)*
SURELY 42 FR 0.0047 REL FR 27 V 15 P
i do, and surely | it is a sleepy language, and TMP 2.01.210
surely i think you have charms, la; WIV 2.02.103 P
act | freshly on me — 'tis surely for a name. MM 1.02.171
you do him wrong, surely. 3.02.129 P
sir, by your good favor — for surely, sir, a 4.02. 32 P
might, | but surely, master, not a rag of money. ERR 4.04. 86
here this night, they will surely do us no harm. 4.04.151 P
hero thinks surely she will die, for she says ADO 2.03.173 P
surely suit ill spent and labor ill bestow'd. 3.02. 99 P
surely i do believe your fair cousin is wrong'd. 4.01.259 P
surely a princely testimony, a goodly count, 4.01.315 P
count, count comfect, a sweet gallant surely! 4.01.317 P
i do live, | and surely as i live, i am a maid. 5.04. 64
he surely affected her for her wit. LLL 1.02. 88 P
none are so surely caught, when they are catch'd 5.02. 69
gone, | that youth is surely in their company. AYL 2.02. 16
a good matter, surely; SHR 1.01.251 P
for me, that i may surely keep mine oath, | i 4.02. 36
in gait and countenance surely like a father. 4.02. 65
ay, surely, mere the truth, i know his lady. AWW 3.05. 55
he pays you as surely as your feet hits the TN 3.04.277 P
for by this knot thou shalt so surely tie | thy JN 2.01.470
as surely as i live, my lord. R2 4.01.102
good phrases are surely, and ever were, very 2H4 3.02. 70 P
surely, by all the glory you have won, | and if 1H6 4.06. 50
his skin is surely lent him, | for he's inclin'd 2H6 3.01. 77
as surely as my soul intends to live | with that 3.02.153
if not in heaven, you'll surely sup in hell. 5.01.216
and wheresoe'er he is, he's surely dead. 3H6 2.06. 41
surely, sir, | there's in him stuff that puts H8 1.01. 57
yes, surely. 2.02.123
man, full surely | his greatness is a–ripening, 3.02.356
the devil was amongst 'em, i think, surely. 5.03. 59 P
for in this rapture i shall surely speak | the TRO 3.02.130
was above mine, | else surely his had equall'd. TIM 3.04. 32
surely, this man | was born of woman. 4.03.493
you do surely bar the door upon your own liberty HAM 3.02.338 P
that you shall surely find him, | lead to the OTH 1.01.157
yet surely cassio, i believe, receiv'd | from 2.03.244
i have surely seen him; CYM 5.05. 92
will you surely? TNK 5.02. 85
surely the gods | would have him die a bachelor, 5.03.116
SURER 3 FR 0.0003 REL FR 3 V 0 P
to effect | and surer bind this knot of amity, 1H6 5.01. 16
you are no surer, no, | than is the coal of fire COR 1.01.172
nay, he is your brother by the surer side, TIT 4.02.126
SUREST 2 FR 0.0002 REL FR 2 V 0 P
that know the strong'st and surest way to get. R2 3.03.201
disclos'd, | and open perils surest answered. JC 4.01. 47
/SURETIES 1 FR 0.0001 REL FR 1 V 0 P
/procure /your /sureties /for /your /days /of R2 4.01.159
/SURETY 3 FR 0.0003 REL FR 3 V 0 P
/with /a /double /surety /binds /his /followers. 2H4 1.01.191
the wound of peace is /surety, | /surety secure, TRO 2.02. 14
/surety secure, but modest doubt is call'd | the 2.02. 15
SURETY 18 FR 0.0020 REL FR 17 V 1 P
sir, have pity, | i'll be his surety. TMP 1.02.476
in surety of the which | one part of aquitaine LLL 2.01.134
frenchman became his surety and seal'd under for MV 1.02. 82 P
then you shall be his surety. 5.01.254
in the christian world | shall be my surety; AWW 4.04. 3
she call'd the saints to surety | that she would 5.03.108
the ring is sent for, | and he shall surety me. 5.03.297
and mak'st an oath the surety for thy truth JN 3.01.282
what surety of the world, what hope, what stay, 5.07. 68
and givest such sarcenet surety for thy oaths 1H4 3.01.251
impawn'd | some surety for a safe return again, 4.03.109
and all the peers', for surety of our leagues. H5 5.02.372
shall be the surety for their traitor father. 2H6 5.01.116
those | that for my surety will refuse the boys! 5.01.121
with surety stronger than achilles' arm, | 'fore TRO 1.03.220
give me some token for the surety of it. 5.02. 60
we'll surety him. COR 3.01.177
in that kind, | will do as if for surety. OTH 1.03.390
SURETY–LIKE 1 FR 0.0001 REL FR 1 V 0 P
he learn'd but surety–like to write for me SON 134. 7
SURFEIT 19 FR 0.0021 REL FR 16 V 3 P
and now excess of it will make me surfeit. TGV 3.01.222
as surfeit is the father of much fast, | so MM 1.02.126
for as a surfeit of the sweetest things | the MND 2.02.137
deceive, | so thou, my surfeit and my heresy, 2.02.141
are as sick that surfeit with too much as they MV 1.02. 6 P
make it less, | for fear i surfeit. 3.02.114
that surfeit on their ease, will day by day AWW 3.01. 18
that suffer surfeit, cloyment, and revolt, | but TN 2.04. 99
now comes the sick hour that his surfeit made, R2 2.02. 84
though not by war, by surfeit die your king, R3 1.03.196
than one voluptuously surfeit out of action. COR 1.03. 25 P
to, | and this the banket she shall surfeit on, TIT 5.02.193
morning taste | to cure thy o'ernight's surfeit? TIM 4.03.227
cure their surfeit | that craves a present TNK 1.01.190
that intemp'rate surfeit of her eye hath 4.03. 70 P
whereon they surfeit, yet complain on drouth: VEN 544
do surfeit by the eye and pine the maw; 602
the profit of excess | is but to surfeit, and LUC 139
thus do i pine and surfeit day by day, | or SON 75.13
/SURFEITED 1 FR 0.0001 REL FR 1 V 0 P
/their //over–greedy /love /hath /surfeited. 2H4 1.03. 88
SURFEITED 3 FR 0.0003 REL FR 3 V 0 P
they surfeited with honey and began | to loathe 1H4 3.02. 71
and the surfeited grooms | do mock their charge MAC 2.02. 5
therefore my hopes (not surfeited to death) OTH 2.01. 50
SURFEITER 1 FR 0.0001 REL FR 1 V 0 P
this amorous surfeiter would have donn'd his ANT 2.01. 33
/SURFEITING 1 FR 0.0001 REL FR 1 V 0 P
/and /with /our /surfeiting /and /wanton /hours 2H4 4.01. 55
SURFEITING 3 FR 0.0003 REL FR 3 V 0 P
his purpose surfeiting, he sends a warrant | for MM 5.01.102
that, surfeiting, | the appetite may sicken, and TN 1.01. 2
surfeiting in joys of love | with his new bride 2H6 1.01.251
SURFEITS 8 FR 0.0009 REL FR 6 V 2 P
by, | as one that surfeits thinking on a want. 2H6 3.02.348
what authority surfeits /on would relieve us. COR 1.01. 16 P
full | of the wars' surfeits to go rove with one 4.01. 46
often the surfeits of our own behavior — we LR 1.02.119 P
full surfeits and the dryness of his bones ANT 1.04. 27
no surfeits seek us; TNK 2.02. 86
surfeits, impostumes, grief, and damn'd despair VEN 743
love surfeits not, lust like a glutton dies; 803
SURFEIT–SWELL'D 1 FR 0.0001 REL FR 1 V 0 P
so surfeit–swell'd, so old, and so profane; 2H4 5.05. 50
SURFEIT–TAKING 1 FR 0.0001 REL FR 1 V 0 P
so surfeit–taking tarquin fares this night: LUC 698
SURGE 10 FR 0.0011 REL FR 9 V 1 P
breasted | the surge most swoll'n that met him. TMP 2.01.118
glowing–hot, in that surge, like a horse–shoe; WIV 3.05.121 P
brains | in cradle of the rude imperious surge, 2H4 3.01. 20
the furrowed sea, | breasting the lofty surge. H5 3.pr. 13
expecting ever when some envious surge | will in TIT 3.01. 96
whose liquid surge resolves | the moon into salt TIM 4.03.439
froth | the turbulent surge shall cover; 5.01.218
the murmuring surge, | that on th' unnumb'red LR 4.06. 20
the wind–shak'd surge, with high and monstrous OTH 2.01. 13
floats but for | the surge that next approaches. TNK 5.04. 84
SURGEON 12 FR 0.0013 REL FR 6 V 6 P
with the help of a surgeon he might yet recover, MND 5.01.310 P
have by some surgeon, shylock, on your charge, MV 4.01.257
for the love of god, a surgeon! TN 5.01.172 P
sot, didst see dick surgeon, sot? 5.01.197 P
some swearing, some crying for a surgeon, some H5 4.01.139 P
bleed, | opinion shall be surgeon to my hurt, 1H6 2.04. 53
go, villain, fetch a surgeon. ROM 3.01. 94
withal i am indeed, sir, a surgeon to old shoes; JC 1.01. 23 P
for your hurts, | myself will be your surgeon. OTH 2.03.254
o, help ho! light! a surgeon! 5.01. 30
from hence, | i'll fetch the general's surgeon. 5.01.100
that a man may deal withal and defy the surgeon? PER 4.06. 26 P
SURGEON'S 2 FR 0.0002 REL FR 1 V 1 P
content, i'll to the surgeon's. 1H6 3.01.146
the surgeon's box, or the patient's wound. TRO 5.01. 11 P
SURGEONS 3 FR 0.0003 REL FR 3 V 0 P
go get him surgeons. MAC 1.02. 44
let me have surgeons, | i am cut to th' brains. LR 4.06.192
all our surgeons | convent in their behoof, our TNK 1.04. 30
SURGERE 1 FR 0.0001 REL FR 0 V 1 P
is to be up betimes, and "deliculo surgere," TN 2.03. 3 P
SURGERY 5 FR 0.0005 REL FR 1 V 4 P
often tarr'd over with the surgery of our sheep; AYL 3.02. 63 P
honor hath no skill in surgery then? 1H4 5.01.133 P
his pike bent bravely, and to surgery bravely; 2H4 2.04. 51 P
the mere despair of surgery, he cures, | hanging MAC 4.03.152
ay, past all surgery. OTH 2.03.260 P
SURGES 5 FR 0.0005 REL FR 5 V 0 P
i saw him beat the surges under him, | and ride TMP 2.01.115
whom the blind waves and surges have devour'd. TN 5.01.229
on the dying deck, | hearing the surges threat; TIM 4.02. 21
like egg–shells mov'd upon their surges, crack'd CYM 3.01. 28
the god of this great vast, rebuke these surges, PER 3.01. 1
SURLY 11 FR 0.0012 REL FR 9 V 2 P
'tis like you'll prove a jolly surly groom, SHR 3.02.213
be opposite with a kinsman, surly with servants; TN 2.05.150 P
opposite with a kinsman, surly with servants; 3.04. 69 P
or if that surly spirit, melancholy, | had bak'd JN 3.03. 42
the sad–ey'd justice, with his surly hum, H5 1.02.202
still | under the surly gloucester's governance? 2H6 1.03. 47
see how the surly warwick mans the wall! 3H6 5.01. 17
ay, or surly borne — TRO 2.03.238
or else it would have gall'd his surly nature, COR 2.03.195
a lion, | who glaz'd upon me, and went surly by, JC 1.03. 21
than you shall hear the surly sullen bell | give SON 71. 2
SURMIS'D 1 FR 0.0001 REL FR 1 V 0 P
'tis but surmis'd whiles thou art standing by, 2H6 3.02.347
/SURMISE 1 FR 0.0001 REL FR 1 V 0 P
/and /surmise | /of /aids /incertain /should 2H4 1.03. 23
SURMISE 7 FR 0.0008 REL FR 7 V 0 P
by false intelligence or wrong surmise | hold me R3 2.01. 55
the thing whereat it trembles by surmise. TIT 2.03.219
of man that function | is smother'd in surmise, MAC 1.03.141
now gather, and surmise. HAM 2.02.108
owe | enchanted tarquin answers with surmise, LUC 83
brought | by deep surmise of others' detriment, 1579
down, | and on just proof surmise accumulate; SON 117.10
SURMISED 1 FR 0.0001 REL FR 1 V 0 P
of the thought | that gave't surmised shape. TRO 1.03. 17
SURMISES 4 FR 0.0004 REL FR 3 V 1 P
if i shall be condemn'd | upon surmises (all WT 3.02.112
rumor is a pipe | blown by surmises, jealousies, 2H4 in 16
soul | to such exsufflicate and /blown surmises, OTH 3.03.182
i speak not out of weak surmises, but from proof CYM 3.04. 23 P
SURMOUNT 2 FR 0.0002 REL FR 2 V 0 P
bethink thee on her virtues that surmount, 1H6 5.03.191
define, | as i all other in all worths surmount. SON 62. 8
SURMOUNTED 1 FR 0.0001 REL FR 1 V 0 P
"this hector far surmounted hannibal. LLL 5.02.670
SURMOUNTS 1 FR 0.0001 REL FR 1 V 0 P
and far surmounts our labor to attain it. R2 2.03. 64
/SURNAM'D 1 FR 0.0001 REL FR 1 V 0 P
/and /censorinus /that /was /so /surnam'd, | and COR 2.03.243
SURNAM'D 2 FR 0.0002 REL FR 2 V 0 P
"i pompey am, pompey surnam'd the big" — LLL 5.02.550
"pompey surnam'd the great, | that oft in field 5.02.552
SURNAME 3 FR 0.0003 REL FR 3 V 0 P
thereto witness may | my surname, coriolanus. COR 4.05. 68
country are requited | but with that surname — 4.05. 71
to his surname coriolanus 'longs more pride 5.03.170
SURNAMED 1 FR 0.0001 REL FR 1 V 0 P
surnamed pius | for many good and great deserts TIT 1.01. 23
SURPASS 1 FR 0.0001 REL FR 1 V 0 P
look when a painter would surpass the life | in VEN 289
SURPASSETH 1 FR 0.0001 REL FR 1 V 0 P
but she as far surpasseth sycorax | as great'st TMP 3.02.102
SURPASSING 1 FR 0.0001 REL FR 1 V 0 P
the temple much surpassing | the common praise WT 3.01. 2
SURPLICE 2 FR 0.0002 REL FR 1 V 1 P
it will wear the surplice of humility over the AWW 1.03. 94 P
let the priest in surplice white, | that PHT 13
SURPLUS 2 FR 0.0002 REL FR 1 V 1 P
it is a surplus of your grace, which never | my WT 5.03. 7
he hath faults (with surplus) to tire in COR 1.01. 45 P
SURPRIS'D 20 FR 0.0022 REL FR 19 V 1 P
they i cannot be, | who are surpris'd /withal; TMP 3.01. 93
armed in arguments — you'll be surpris'd. LLL 5.02. 84
maid, | and how she was beguiled and surpris'd, SHR in.2. 55
her poor knight surpris'd without rescue in the AWW 1.03.115 P
kin to jove's thunder, so surpris'd my sense, WT 3.01. 10
which he in this adventure hath surpris'd | to 1H4 1.01. 93
we had not been thus shamefully surpris'd. 1H6 2.01. 65
were there surpris'd and taken prisoners. 4.01. 26
and may ye both be suddenly surpris'd | by 5.03. 40
hath slain their governors, surpris'd our forts, 2H6 4.01. 89
why, buckingham, is the traitor cade surpris'd? 4.09. 8
his guard | or by his foe surpris'd at unawares; 3H6 4.04. 9
lavinia is surpris'd! TIT 1.01.284
surpris'd? by whom? 1.01.285

when with a happy storm they were surpris'd, 2.03. 23
lavinia, wert thou thus surpris'd, sweet girl? 4.01. 51
surpris'd him suddenly, and brought him hither 5.01. 38
when subtile greeks surpris'd king priam's troy. 5.03. 84
your castle is surpris'd; MAC 4.03.204
you see how easily she may be surpris'd. ANT 5.02. 35
SURPRISE 12 FR 0.0013 REL FR 9 V 3 P
of my mind, the sudden surprise of my powers, WIV 5.05.123 P
of florentines, will suddenly surprise him; AWW 3.06. 23 P
surprise her with discourse of my dear faith; TN 1.04. 25
them lay their heads together to surprise me. 2H6 4.08. 59 P
we may surprise and take him at our pleasure? 3H6 4.02. 17
him, | for i intend but only to surprise him. 4.02. 25
surprise me to the very brink of tears. TIM 5.01.156
the castle of macduff i will surprise, | seize MAC 4.01.150
pure surprise and fear | made me to quit the PER 3.02. 17
through which it enters to surprise her heart, VEN 890
this mutiny each part doth so surprise | that 1049
now serves the season that they may surprise LUC 166
SURPRISED 1 FR 0.0001 REL FR 1 V 0 P
i am surprised with an uncouth fear, | a TIT 2.03.211
SUR–REIN'D 1 FR 0.0001 REL FR 1 V 0 P
water, | a drench for sur–rein'd jades, their H5 3.05. 19
/SURRENDER 1 FR 0.0001 REL FR 1 V 0 P
/that /in /common /view | /he /may /surrender; R2 4.01.156
SURRENDER 4 FR 0.0004 REL FR 3 V 1 P
about surrender up of aquitaine | to her LLL 1.01.137
with my love and duty | i would surrender it. H8 1.04. 81
message | importing the surrender of those lands HAM 1.02. 23
this last surrender of his will but offend us. LR 1.01.305 P
SURREY 16 FR 0.0018 REL FR 12 V 4 P
surrey, thou liest. R2 4.01. 65
or live, | i dare meet surrey in a wilderness, 4.01. 74
go call the earls of surrey and of warwick; 2H4 3.01. 1
my lord of surrey, why look you so sad? R3 5.03. 2
saddle white surrey for the field to–morrow. 5.03. 64
thomas the earl of surrey and himself, | much 5.03. 69
he said the truth, and what said surrey then? 5.03.273
john duke of norfolk, thomas earl of surrey, 5.03.296
earl surrey was sent thither, and in haste too, H8 2.01. 43
within these forty hours surrey durst better 3.02.253
dare mate a sounder man than surrey can be, 3.02.274
and that the earl of surrey, with the rod. 4.01. 39
we'll hear the earl of surrey. STM II.C 31 P
we'll not hear my lord of surrey, no, no, no, no II.C 38 P
surrey, surrey! II.C 48 P
surrey, surrey! II.C 48 P
/SURVEY 2 FR 0.0002 REL FR 2 V 0 P
/we /first /survey /the /plot, /then /draw /the 2H4 1.03. 42
/should /we /survey | /the /plot /of /situation 1.03. 50
SURVEY 12 FR 0.0013 REL FR 11 V 1 P
i will survey th' inscriptions back again. MV 2.07. 14
queen of night, survey | with thy chaste eye, AYL 3.02. 2
wife | whose beauty did astonish the survey | of AWW 5.03. 16
and time, that takes survey of all the world, 1H4 5.04. 82
i am come to survey the tower this day; 1H6 1.03. 1
ta'en, | and to survey the bodies of the dead. 4.07. 57
and to survey his dead and earthy image, | what 2H6 3.02.147
let us survey the vantage of the ground. R3 5.03. 15
make but an interior survey of your good selves! COR 2.01. 40 P
too, | upon a just survey take titus' part, TIT 1.01.446
the which he will not ev'ry hour survey, | for SON 52. 3
rise, resty muse, my love's sweet face survey, 100. 9
SURVEYED 1 FR 0.0001 REL FR 1 V 0 P
verge | that ever was surveyed by english eye, R2 1.01. 94
SURVEYEST 1 FR 0.0001 REL FR 0 V 1 P
thou viewest, beholdest, surveyest, or seest. LLL 1.01.244 P
SURVEYING 1 FR 0.0001 REL FR 1 V 0 P
but the norweyan lord, surveying vantage, | with MAC 1.02. 31
SURVEYOR 5 FR 0.0005 REL FR 5 V 0 P
then, | to make the fox surveyor of the fold? 2H6 3.01.253
the duke of buckingham's surveyor? H8 1.01.115
my surveyor is false; 1.01.222
you were the duke's surveyor, and lost your 1.02.172
at which appear'd against him his surveyor, 2.01. 19
/SURVEYORS 1 FR 0.0001 REL FR 1 V 0 P
/question /surveyors, /know /our /own /estate, 2H4 1.03. 53
SURVEYS 1 FR 0.0001 REL FR 1 V 0 P
surveys | the singing masons building roofs of H5 1.02.197
SURVIVE 12 FR 0.0013 REL FR 12 V 0 P
of | her widowhood, be it that she survive me, SHR 2.01.124
and with his spirits sadly i survive, | to mock 2H4 5.02.125
tears, | if talbot but survive thy treachery. 1H6 3.02. 37
these that survive let rome reward with love; TIT 1.01. 82
rest, and we survive | to tremble under titus' 1.01.133
you that survive, and you that sleep in fame! 1.01.173
because the girl should not survive her shame, 5.03. 41
and so in spite of death thou dost survive, | in VEN 173
"yea, though i die, the scandal will survive, LUC 204
if they surcease to be that should survive. 1766
if thou survive my well–contented day, | when SON 32. 1
or you survive when i in earth am rotten, | from 81. 2
SURVIVES 2 FR 0.0002 REL FR 2 V 0 P
yet valentine thy friend | survives, to whom, TGV 4.02.109
i give him you, the noblest that survives, | the TIT 1.01.102
SURVIVING 2 FR 0.0002 REL FR 2 V 0 P
sage, | this dying virtue, this surviving shame, LUC 223
"so thy surviving husband shall remain | the 519
SURVIVOR 2 FR 0.0002 REL FR 2 V 0 P
fall of either | makes the survivor heir of all. COR 5.06. 18
and the survivor bound | in filial obligation HAM 1.02. 90
SUSAN 3 FR 0.0003 REL FR 2 V 1 P
susan and she — god rest all christian souls! ROM 1.03. 18
well, susan is with god, | she was too good for 1.03. 19
let the porter let in susan grindstone and nell. 1.05. 9 P
SUSPECT 42 FR 0.0047 REL FR 35 V 7 P
if i suspect without cause, why then make sport WIV 3.03.149 P
i suspect without cause, mistress, do i? 4.02.132 P
do, /and if you suspect me in any dishonesty. 4.02.134 P
i rather will suspect the sun with /cold | than 4.04. 7
and draw within the compass of suspect | th' ERR 3.01. 87
if you meet a thief, you may suspect him, by ADO 3.03. 50 P
dost thou not suspect my place? 4.02. 74 P
dost thou not suspect my years? 4.02. 75 P
whose own hard dealings teaches them suspect MV 1.03.161
all colors | no yellow in't, lest she suspect, WT 2.03.107
i do suspect thee very grievously. JN 4.03.134
thou dost suspect | that i have been disloyal to R2 5.02.104
he will suspect us still, and find a time | to 1H4 5.02. 6
if they were known, as the suspect is great, 2H6 1.03.136
for thousands more, that yet suspect no peril, 3.01.152
if my suspect be false, forgive me, god, | for 3.02.139
then you belike suspect these noblemen | as 3.02.186
axe, | but will suspect 'twas he that made the 3.02.190
vow, | that i may never have you in suspect. 3H6 4.01.142
for did i but suspect a fearful man, | he should 5.04. 44
thy friends suspect for traitors while thou R3 1.03.222
should | suspect me that i mean no good to him. 3.07. 89
i do suspect i have done some offense | that 3.07.111
if you suspect my husbandry or falsehood, | call TIM 2.02.155
thou wert the fox, the lion would suspect thee, 4.03.330 P
in whose breast | doubt and suspect, alas, are 4.03.512
suspect still comes where an estate is least. 4.03.514
for that i do suspect the lusty moor | hath OTH 2.01.295
nor ever heard — nor ever did suspect. 4.02. 2
if happily you my father do suspect | an 4.02. 44
and made you to suspect me with the moor. 4.02.147
may you suspect | who they should be that have 5.01. 78
i do suspect this trash | to be a party in this 5.01. 85
you did suspect | she had dispos'd with caesar, ANT 4.14.122
i do suspect you, madam, | but you shall do no CYM 1.05. 31
honor /him, | if he suspect i may dishonor him; PER 1.02. 21
is alive, | her rash suspect she doth extenuate, VEN 1010
"it shall suspect where is no cause of fear, 1153
fiend, | suspect i may (yet not directly tell): PP 2.10
the ornament of beauty is suspect, | a crow that SON 70. 3
if some suspect of ill mask'd not thy show, 70.13
that my angel be turn'd fiend | suspect i may, 144.10
SUSPECTED 8 FR 0.0009 REL FR 7 V 1 P
thy tongue, | that truth should be suspected. AWW 1.03.181
yet who would have suspected an ambush where i 4.03.302 P
makes sound opinion sick, and truth suspected, JN 4.02. 26
yet most suspected, as the time and place | doth ROM 5.03.224
person and a smooth dispose | to be suspected — OTH 1.03.398
give cause | to be suspected of more tenderness CYM 1.01. 94
i be suspected of | your carriage from the court 3.04.186
i half suspected | what you told me. TNK 4.01. 47
SUSPECTETH 1 FR 0.0001 REL FR 1 V 0 P
devil, | little suspecteth the false worshipper: LUC 86
SUSPECTING 1 FR 0.0001 REL FR 1 V 0 P
suspecting that we both were in a house | where ROM 5.02. 9
SUSPECTS 5 FR 0.0005 REL FR 5 V 0 P
falsely to draw me in these vile suspects. R3 1.03. 88
he liv'd from all attainder of suspects. 3.05. 32
my heart suspects more than mine eye can see. TIT 2.03.213
so far from doing harms | that he suspects none; LR 1.02.181
suspects, yet /strongly loves! OTH 3.03.170
SUSPEND 2 FR 0.0002 REL FR 1 V 1 P
it shall please you to suspend your indignation LR 1.02. 80 P
suspend thy purpose, if thou didst intend | to 1.04.276
SUSPENSE 1 FR 0.0001 REL FR 1 V 0 P
that you will clear yourself from all suspense. 2H6 3.01.140
/SUSPICION 1 FR 0.0001 REL FR 1 V 0 P
/so /we /shall /proceed | /without /suspicion. R2 4.01.157
SUSPICION 32 FR 0.0036 REL FR 22 V 10 P
husband, to give him such cause of suspicion! WIV 3.03.101 P
what cause of suspicion? 3.03.102 P
what cause of suspicion? 3.03.103 P
hath some special suspicion of falstaff's being 3.03.188 P
to make another experiment of his suspicion. 4.02. 36 P
one man but he will wear his cap with suspicion? ADO 1.01.198 P
and (out of all suspicion) she is virtuous. 2.03.160 P
theme, but nothing | of his ill–ta'en suspicion! WT 1.02.460
me | to have her honor true than your suspicion, 2.01.160
i have too much believ'd mine own suspicion. 3.02.151
that the verity of it is in strong suspicion. 5.02. 29 P
put between your holy looks | my ill suspicion. 5.03.149
see what a ready tongue suspicion hath! 2H4 1.01. 84
man and best indued | with some suspicion. H5 2.02.140
french, | because in york this breeds suspicion; 2H6 1.03.206
pray god he may acquit him of suspicion! 3.02. 25
suspicion always haunts the guilty mind; 3H6 5.06. 11
thus have we swept suspicion from our seat, 5.07. 13
did, | and yet go current from suspicion! R3 2.01. 95
intending deep suspicion, ghastly looks | are at 3.05. 8
so deep suspicion, where all faith was meant. H8 3.01. 53
vainglory) | never yet branded with suspicion? 3.01.128
to answer their suspicion with their lives. TIT 2.03.298
a great suspicion. stay the friar too. ROM 5.03.187
bring forth the parties of suspicion. 5.03.222
which puts upon them | suspicion of the deed. MAC 2.04. 27
king, it will stuff his suspicion more fully. LR 3.05. 21 P
true, | but i, for mere suspicion in that kind, OTH 1.03.389
issues nor to larger reach | than to suspicion. 3.03.220
and your suspicion is not without wit and 4.02.211 P
last, | and bid suspicion double–lock the door, VEN 448
from that suspicion which the world might bear LUC 1321
SUSPICIONS 1 FR 0.0001 REL FR 1 V 0 P
the changes of the moon | with fresh suspicions? OTH 3.03.179
SUSPICIOUS 5 FR 0.0005 REL FR 5 V 0 P
when the suspicious head of theft is stopp'd. LLL 4.03.333
that any one should therefore be suspicious | i 1H6 4.01.153
even so suspicious is this tragedy. 2H6 3.02.194
i spy a black, suspicious, threat'ning cloud, 3H6 5.03. 4
tongue makes my cause more strange, suspicious; H8 3.01. 45
SUSPIRATION 1 FR 0.0001 REL FR 1 V 0 P
black, | nor windy suspiration of forc'd breath, HAM 1.02. 79
SUSPIRE 2 FR 0.0002 REL FR 2 V 0 P
child, | to him that did but yesterday suspire, JN 3.04. 80
did he suspire, that light and weightless down 2H4 4.05. 33
SUSTAIN 16 FR 0.0018 REL FR 13 V 3 P
do take the prop | that doth sustain my house; MV 4.01.376
which should sustain the bound and high curvet AWW 2.03.282
good beauties, let me sustain no scorn; TN 1.05.175 P
like to the old vice, | your need to sustain; 4.02.125
to do them good i would sustain some harm. 3H6 3.02. 39
but that you shall sustain moe new disgraces H8 3.02. 5
that nature's fragile vessel doth sustain | in TIM 5.01.201
then weigh what loss your honor may sustain | if HAM 1.03. 29
if she sustain him and his hundred knights, LR 1.04.332
of him, entreat for him, or any way sustain him. 3.03. 6 P
rule in this realm, and the gor'd state sustain. 5.03.321
a better never did itself sustain | upon a OTH 5.02.260
long, the sides of nature | will not sustain it. ANT 1.03. 17
well then, sustain me. o! 3.11. 45
and i doubt not you sustain what y' are worthy CYM 1.04.115 P
and such griefs sustain | that they prove LUC 139
SUSTAIN'D 2 FR 0.0002 REL FR 2 V 0 P
prick'd on by public wrongs sustain'd in france, 1H6 3.02. 78
of an hundred knights | by you to be sustain'd, LR 1.01.134
SUSTAINING 4 FR 0.0004 REL FR 4 V 0 P
on their sustaining garments not a blemish, TMP 1.02.218
idle weeds that grow | in our sustaining corn. LR 4.04. 6
if thou dost weep for grief of my sustaining, LUC 1272
time seems long in sorrow's sharp sustaining; 1573
SUSTENANCE 1 FR 0.0001 REL FR 1 V 0 P
nor taken sustenance | but to prorogue his grief PER 5.01. 25
SUST'NANCE 1 FR 0.0001 REL FR 1 V 0 P
let him receive no sust'nance; TIT 5.03. 6
SUTLER 1 FR 0.0001 REL FR 1 V 0 P
for i shall sutler be | unto the camp, and H5 2.01.111
SUTTON 1 FR 0.0001 REL FR 0 V 1 P
we'll to sutton co'fil' to–night. 1H4 4.02. 3 P
SUUM* 2 FR 0.0002 REL FR 1 V 1 P
suum /cuique is our roman justice: TIT 1.01.280
says suum, mun, nonny. LR 3.04. 99 P
SWABBER 2 FR 0.0002 REL FR 1 V 1 P
"the master, the swabber, the boatswain, and i, TMP 2.02. 46
no, good swabber, i am to hull here a little TN 1.05.203 P
SWADDLING–CLOUTS *(also swathing, swathling)*
SWADDLING–CLOUTS 1 FR 0.0001 REL FR 0 V 1 P
there is not yet out of his swaddling–clouts. HAM 2.02.383 P
SWAG–BELLIED 1 FR 0.0001 REL FR 0 V 1 P
your german, and your swag–bellied hollander — OTH 2.03. 78 P
/SWAGGER 1 FR 0.0001 REL FR 0 V 1 P
and your ancient /swagger, /'a comes not in my 2H4 2.04. 84 P
SWAGGER 5 FR 0.0005 REL FR 0 V 5 P
if he swagger, let him not come here. 2H4 2.04. 73 P
he'll not swagger with a barbary hen, if her 2.04. 99 P
i am the worse when one says swagger. 2.04.105 P
will 'a swagger himself out on 's own eyes? TRO 5.02.136 P
swagger? OTH 2.03.280 P
SWAGGER'D *(also zwagger'd)*
SWAGGER'D 1 FR 0.0001 REL FR 0 V 1 P
a rascal that swagger'd with me last night; H5 4.07.126 P
SWAGGERER 1 FR 0.0001 REL FR 1 V 0 P
at this letter, | and play the swaggerer: AYL 4.03. 14
SWAGGERERS 3 FR 0.0003 REL FR 0 V 3 P
i'll no swaggerers, i am in good name and fame 2H4 2.04. 75 P
shut the door, there comes no swaggerers here; 2.04. 76 P
there comes no swaggerers here. 2.04. 81 P
SWAGGERING 6 FR 0.0006 REL FR 1 V 5 P
with a swaggering accent sharply twang'd off, TN 3.04.180 P
by swaggering could i never thrive, | for the 5.01.399
hang him, swaggering rascal! 2H4 2.04. 71 P
not liv'd all this while to have swaggering now. 2.04. 78 P
receive," says he, "no swaggering companions." 2.04. 94 P
but i do not love swaggering, by my troth. 2.04.104 P
SWAGG'RER 1 FR 0.0001 REL FR 0 V 1 P
he's no swagg'rer, hostess, a tame cheater, i' 2H4 2.04. 97 P
SWAGG'RERS 2 FR 0.0002 REL FR 0 V 2 P
no, i'll no swagg'rers. 2H4 2.04. 96 P
i cannot abide swagg'rers. 2.04.109 P
SWAGG'RING 2 FR 0.0002 REL FR 2 V 0 P
what hempen home–spuns have we swagg'ring here, MND 3.01. 77
wassail, and the swagg'ring up–spring reels; HAM 1.04. 9
SWAIN 23 FR 0.0026 REL FR 17 V 6 P
thou gentle nymph, cherish thy forlorn swain. TGV 5.04. 12
costard the swain and he shall be our sport, LLL 1.01.179
there did i see that low–spirited swain, that 1.01.247 P
which i apprehended with the aforesaid swain, i 1.01.274 P
key, give enlargement to the swain, bring him 3.01. 5 P
fetch hither the swain, he must carry me a 3.01. 49 P
i shoot thee at the swain. 3.01. 65
by my soul, a swain, a most simple clown! 4.01.140
this swain, because of his great limb or joint, 5.01.127 P
the swain, pompey the great; 5.02.534 P
from off the head of this athenian swain, | that MND 4.01. 65
that young swain that you saw here but erewhile, AYL 2.04. 89
too light for such a swain as you to catch, SHR 2.01.204
you peasant swain! 4.01.129
god, | golden apollo, a poor humble swain, | as WT 4.04. 30
what fair swain is this | which dances with your 4.04.166
how prettily th' young swain seems to wash | the 4.04.366
soft, swain, awhile, beseech you. 4.04.391
like a hedge–born swain | that doth presume to 1H6 4.01. 43
not me begotten of a shepherd swain, | but 5.04. 37
obscure and lousy swain, king henry's blood, 2H6 4.01. 50
speak, captain, shall i stab the forlorn swain? 4.01. 65
life | to be no better than a homely swain, | to 3H6 2.05. 22
SWAIN'S 1 FR 0.0001 REL FR 1 V 0 P
you have obscur'd | with a swain's wearing, and WT 4.04. 9
SWAINS 4 FR 0.0004 REL FR 4 V 0 P
what is she, | that all our swains commend her? TGV 4.02. 40
true swains in love shall in the world to come TRO 3.02.173
onward to troy with the blunt swains he goes, LUC 1504
all our pleasure known to us poor swains, | all PP 17.29
SWALLOW* 17 FR 0.0019 REL FR 14 V 3 P
that come before the swallow dares, and take WT 4.04.119
now swallow down that lie. R2 1.01.132
do you think me a swallow, an arrow, or a bullet 2H4 4.03. 32 P
ostridge, and swallow my sword like a great pin, 2H6 4.10. 29 P
may that ground gape, and swallow me alive, 3H6 1.01.161
whose envious gulf did swallow up his life. 5.06. 25
as thou dost swallow up this good king's blood, R3 1.02. 66
surge | will in his brinish bowels swallow him. TIT 3.01. 97
now to the goths, as swift as swallow flies, 4.02.172
like to the earth swallow her own increase. 5.02.191
the swallow follows not summer more willing than TIM 3.06. 29 P
let prisons swallow 'em, | debts wither 'em to 4.03.530
waves | confound and swallow navigation up; MAC 4.01. 54
a capable and wide revenge | swallow them up. OTH 3.03.460
none here, nor the seas | swallow their youth. TNK 2.02. 88
open'd their mouths to swallow venus' liking. VEN 248
which seem'd to swallow up his sound advice, LUC 1409
SWALLOW'D 16 FR 0.0018 REL FR 7 V 9 P
it should the good ship so have swallow'd and TMP 1.02. 12
as cold as if i had swallow'd snowballs for WIV 3.05. 23 P
swallow'd his vows whole, pretending in her MM 3.01.226 P
/as if you swallow'd love with singing love, LLL 3.01. 15 P

thou art easier swallow'd than a flap–dragon. 5.01. 41 P
and anon swallow'd with yest and froth, as WT 3.03. 93 P
capital crimes, chew'd, swallow'd, and digested, H5 2.02. 56
and half our sailors swallow'd in the flood? 3H6 5.04. 5
troy, | and blind oblivion swallow'd cities up, TRO 3.02.187
i think they have swallow'd one another. 5.04. 34 P
and, her attendants absent, swallow'd fire. JC 4.03.156
of his jaw, first mouth'd, to be last swallow'd. HAM 4.02. 19 P
if they had swallow'd poison, 'twould appear ANT 5.02.345
by the queen's dram she swallow'd. CYM 5.05.381
gaping till they swallow'd the whole parish, PER 2.01. 33 P
because he should have swallow'd me too, and 2.01. 39 P
SWALLOWED 7 FR 0.0008 REL FR 7 V 0 P
that, being daily swallowed by men's eyes, 1H4 3.02. 70
that shall be swallowed in this controversy. H5 2.04.109
th' interview | that swallowed so much treasure, H8 1.01.166
earth hath swallowed all my hopes but she; ROM 1.02. 14
being proud, swallowed some part a' th' earth. PER 4.04. 39
than they whose whole is swallowed in confusion. LUC 1159
past reason hated as a swallowed bait | on SON 129. 7
SWALLOWING 8 FR 0.0009 REL FR 8 V 0 P
with open mouth swallowing a tailor's news, JN 4.02.195
come near your sight | for fear of swallowing; 1H4 5.01. 64
for swallowing the treasure of the realm. 2H6 4.01. 74
and almost should'red in the swallowing gulf R3 3.07.128
i may be pluck'd into the swallowing womb | of TIT 2.03.239
i pray his absence | proceed by swallowing that; CYM 3.05. 58
"what is thy body but a swallowing grave, VEN 757
a swallowing gulf that even in plenty wanteth. LUC 557
SWALLOW'S 1 FR 0.0001 REL FR 1 V 0 P
hope is swift and flies with swallow's wings, R3 5.02. 23
SWALLOWS* 4 FR 0.0004 REL FR 3 V 1 P
way, and runs like swallows o'er the plain. TIT 2.02. 24
swallows the old rat and the ditch–dog; LR 3.04.132 P
that it engluts and swallows other sorrows, OTH 1.03. 57
swallows have built | in cleopatra's sails their ANT 4.12. 3
SWAM *(also swom)*
SWAM 2 FR 0.0002 REL FR 0 V 2 P
i swam, ere i could recover the shore, five and TMP 3.02. 13 P
i will scarce think you have swam in a gundello. AYL 4.01. 38 P
SWAN 9 FR 0.0010 REL FR 8 V 1 P
were also, jupiter, a swan for the love of leda. WIV 5.05. 6 P
i am the /cygnet to this pale faint swan | who JN 5.07. 21
so doth the swan her downy cygnets save, 1H6 5.03. 56
as i have seen a swan | with bootless labor swim 3H6 1.04. 19
and i will make thee think thy swan a crow. ROM 1.02. 87
i will play the swan, | and die in music. OTH 5.02.247
but if the like the snow–white swan desire, LUC 1011
and now this pale swan in her wat'ry nest 1611
music can, | be the death–divining swan, | lest PHT 15
SWAN–LIKE 1 FR 0.0001 REL FR 1 V 0 P
then, if he lose, he makes a swan–like end, MV 3.02. 44
SWAN'S 3 FR 0.0003 REL FR 3 V 0 P
can never turn the swan's black legs to white, TIT 4.02.102
inform her tongue — the swan's down feather, ANT 3.02. 48
in a great pool a swan's nest. CYM 3.04.139
SWANS 1 FR 0.0001 REL FR 1 V 0 P
and wheresoe'er we went, like juno's swans, AYL 1.03. 75
SWARE *(also swore)*
SWARE 2 FR 0.0002 REL FR 1 V 1 P
whistle, and sware they were his fancies or his 2H4 3.02.318 P
lord junius brutus sware for lucrece' rape, TIT 4.01. 91
/SWARM 1 FR 0.0001 REL FR 1 V 0 P
/the /common /people /swarm /like /summer /flies 3H6 2.06. 8
SWARM 4 FR 0.0004 REL FR 4 V 0 P
and from this swarm of fair advantages | you 1H4 5.01. 55
who in unnecessary action swarm | about our H5 4.02. 27
the common people by numbers swarm to us. 3H6 4.02. 2
villainies of nature | do swarm upon him) from MAC 1.02. 12
SWARMING 2 FR 0.0002 REL FR 2 V 0 P
wholesome herbs | swarming with caterpillars? R2 3.04. 47
with the plebeians swarming at their heels, | go H5 5.pr. 27
/SWART 1 FR 0.0001 REL FR 1 V 0 P
your /swart cimmerian | doth make your honor of TIT 2.03. 72
SWART 3 FR 0.0003 REL FR 2 V 1 P
swart, like my shoe, but her face nothing like ERR 3.02.102 P
lame, foolish, crooked, swart, prodigious, JN 3.01. 46
and, whereas i was black and swart before, 1H6 1.02. 84
SWART–COMPLEXION'D 1 FR 0.0001 REL FR 1 V 0 P
so flatter i the swart–complexion'd night, SON 28.11
SWARTH 1 FR 0.0001 REL FR 1 V 0 P
he's swarth and meagre, of an eye as heavy | as TNK 4.02. 27
SWARTHS *(also swath*)*
SWARTHS 1 FR 0.0001 REL FR 0 V 1 P
without book and utters it by great swarths; TN 2.03.150 P
SWARTHY 1 FR 0.0001 REL FR 1 V 0 P
her fair) | shows julia but a swarthy ethiope. TGV 2.06. 26
SWASHERS 1 FR 0.0001 REL FR 0 V 1 P
as i am, i have observ'd these three swashers. H5 3.02. 29 P
SWASHING *(also washing*)*
SWASHING 1 FR 0.0001 REL FR 1 V 0 P
we'll have a swashing and a martial outside, AYL 1.03.120
SWATH* *(also swarths)*
SWATH* 2 FR 0.0002 REL FR 2 V 0 P
fall down before him like a mower's swath. TRO 5.05. 25
thou like us from our first swath proceeded TIM 4.03.252
SWATHING *(also swaddling–clouts, swathling)*
SWATHING 1 FR 0.0001 REL FR 1 V 0 P
i' th' swathing clothes the other, from their CYM 1.01. 59
SWATHLING 1 FR 0.0001 REL FR 1 V 0 P
hath this hotspur, mars in swathling clothes, 1H4 3.02.112
/SWAY 1 FR 0.0001 REL FR 1 V 0 P
/pride /of /kingly /sway /from /out /my /heart; R2 4.01.206
SWAY 36 FR 0.0040 REL FR 35 V 1 P
confederates | (so dry he was for sway) wi' th' TMP 1.02.112
and to behold his sway, | i will, as 'twere a MM 1.03. 43
but, were you wedded, you would bear some sway. ERR 2.01. 28
and let my counsel sway you in this case. ADO 4.01.201
art | you sway the motion of demetrius' heart. MND 1.01.193
but mercy is above this sceptred sway, | it is MV 4.01.193
thy huntress' name that my full life doth sway. AYL 3.02. 4
peace, | or seek for rule, supremacy, and sway, SHR 5.02.163
m.o.a.i. doth sway my life." TN 2.05.107
"m.o.a.i. doth sway my life." 2.05.110 P
sway | in this uncivil and unjust extent 4.01. 52
so, | she could not sway her house, command her 4.03. 17
this sway of motion, this commodity, | makes it JN 2.01.578
to gripe the general sway into your hand, 1H4 5.01. 57
rebellion in this land shall lose his sway, 5.05. 41
let us sway on and face them in the field. 2H4 4.01. 24
it is because no one should sway but he, | no 1H6 3.01. 37
a gentler heart did never sway in court; 3.02.135
for though usurpers sway the rule a while, | yet 3H6 3.03. 76
no, warwick, thou art worthy of the sway, | to 4.06. 32
the which, most mighty for thy place and sway, TRO 1.03. 60
bear the great sway of his affairs with reason, 2.02. 35
in my way | than sway with them in theirs. COR 2.01.204
a place of potency and sway o' th' state, | if 2.03.182
that she do give her sorrow so much sway; ROM 4.01. 10
when all the sway of earth | shakes like a thing JC 1.03. 3
come | give solely sovereign sway and masterdom. MAC 1.05. 70
the mind i sway by, and the heart i bear, 5.03. 9
the sway, revenue, execution of the rest, LR 1.01.137
old men, if your sweet sway | allow obedience, 2.04.190
and proceed | i' th' sway of your own will. 4.07. 19
in our loves, | and sway our great designs! ANT 2.02.148
you gods that made me man, and sway in love, PER 1.01. 19
and strength by limping sway disabled, | and art SON 66. 8
might | with insufficiency my heart to sway, 150. 2
proud of subjection, noble by the sway, | what LC 108
/SWAY'D 1 FR 0.0001 REL FR 0 V 1 P
bots, /sway'd in the back and shoulder–shotten, SHR 3.02. 55 P
SWAY'D 7 FR 0.0008 REL FR 7 V 0 P
the will of man is by his reason sway'd; MND 2.02.115
but sway'd and fashion'd by the hand of heaven. MV 1.03. 93
and god forgive them that so much have sway'd 1H4 3.02.130
henry, hadst thou sway'd as kings should do, 3H6 2.06. 14
minds sway'd by eyes are full of turpitude. TRO 5.02.112
i have not known when his affections sway'd JC 2.01. 20
but was indeed | sway'd from the point, by 3.01.219
SWAYING 1 FR 0.0001 REL FR 1 V 0 P
or rather swaying more upon our part | than H5 1.01. 73
SWAYS 8 FR 0.0009 REL FR 6 V 2 P
sways it to the mood | of what it likes or MV 4.01. 51
so sways she level in her husband's heart. TN 2.04. 31
which sways usurpingly these several titles, JN 1.01. 13
that sways the earth this climate overlooks, 2.01.344
now sways it this way, like a mighty sea 3H6 2.05. 5
now sways it that way, like the self–same sea 2.05. 7
but a mad lord, and nought but humors sways him. TIM 3.06.112 P
in the oppression of aged tyranny, who sways, LR 1.02. 50 P
SWAY'ST 1 FR 0.0001 REL FR 1 V 0 P
with thy sweet fingers when thou gently sway'st SON 128. 3
/SWEAR 2 FR 0.0002 REL FR 2 V 0 P
and /swear i got them in the gallia wars. H5 5.01. 89
/o, /do /not /swear, /my /lord /of /buckingham. R3 3.07.220
SWEAR 263 FR 0.0297 REL FR 198 V 65 P
though every drop of water swear against it, TMP 1.01. 59
swear by this bottle how thou cam'st hither — i 2.02.120 P
i'll swear upon that bottle to be thy true 2.02.125 P
here; swear then how thou escap'dst. 2.02.127 P
come, swear to that; 2.02.142 P
swear. 2.02.143 P
i'll swear myself thy subject. 2.02.152
come on then; down, and swear. 2.02.153 P
whether this be, | or be not, i'll not swear. 5.01.123
love bade me swear, and love bids me forswear. TGV 2.06. 6
for me (by this pale queen of night i swear), 4.02.100
think not i flatter, for i swear i do not — 4.03. 12
and yet he would not swear; WIV 2.01. 58 P
this would make mercy swear and play the tyrant. MM 3.02.194 P
i swear i will not die to–day for any man's 4.03. 59 P
though they would swear down each particular 5.01.243
(as i have heard him swear there's one 5.01.510
there did this perjur'd goldsmith swear me down ERR 5.01.227
dog bark at a crow than a man swear he loves me. ADO 1.01.132 P
i dare swear he is no hypocrite, but prays from 1.01.151 P
if you swear, my lord, you shall not be forsworn 1.01.153 P
i heard him swear his affection. 2.01.168 P
yet he woos, | yet will he swear he loves. 2.03. 52
she would swear the gentleman should be her 3.01. 62
would you not swear, | all you that see her, 4.01. 38
do not swear and eat it. 4.01.275 P
i will swear by it that you love me, and i will 4.01.276 P
before this friar, and swear to marry her. 5.04. 57
are much deceiv'd, for they did swear you did. 5.04. 79
com' on then, i will swear to study so, | to LLL 1.01. 59
swear me to this, and i will ne'er say no. 1.01. 69
we will read it, i swear. 4.01. 58
and how most sweetly 'a will swear! 4.01.146
make me forsworn, how shall i swear to love? 4.02.105
thou for whom jove would swear | juno but an 4.03.115
faith infringed, which such zeal did swear? 4.03.144
that i may swear beauty doth beauty lack, | if 4.03.247
consider what you first did swear unto: 4.03.287
berowne did swear himself out of all suit. 5.02.275
not so, my lord, it is not so, i swear; 5.02.359
yet swear not, lest ye be forsworn again. 5.02.832
i swear to thee, by cupid's strongest bow, | by MND 1.01.169
and swear | a merrier hour was never wasted 2.01. 56
move me | on the first view to say, to swear, i 3.01.141
to vow, and swear, and superpraise my parts, 3.02.153
i swear by that which i will lose for thee, | to 3.02.252
but as yet, i swear, | i cannot truly say how i 4.01.147
though nestor swear the jest be laughable. MV 1.01. 56
come into the court and swear that i have a poor 1.02. 71 P
i swear | the best–regarded virgins of our clime 2.01. 9
or swear before you choose, if you choose wrong 2.01. 40
table, which doth offer to swear upon a book, i 2.02.159 P
talk with respect, and swear but now and then, 2.02.191
by jacob's staff i swear | i have no mind of 2.05. 36
albeit i'll swear that i do know your tongue. 2.06. 27
to these injunctions every one doth swear | that 2.09. 17
to venice that swear he cannot choose but break. 3.01.114 P
when i was with him i have heard him swear | to 3.02.284
that men shall swear i have discontinued school 3.04. 75
by my soul i swear | there is no power in the 4.01.240
which i did make him swear to keep for ever. 4.02. 14
did young lorenzo swear he lov'd her well, 5.01. 18
by yonder moon i swear you do me wrong; 5.01.142
and made him swear | never to part with it, and 5.01.170
off, | and swear i lost the ring defending it. 5.01.178
and that which you did swear to keep for me, | i 5.01.225
hearing of these many friends | i swear to thee, 5.01.242
swear by your double self, | and there's an oath 5.01.245
and by my soul i swear | i never more will break 5.01.247
here, lord bassanio, swear to keep this ring. 5.01.256
and swear by your beards that i am a knave. AYL 1.02. 72 P
but if you swear by that that is not, you are 1.02. 76 P
i swear to thee, youth, by the white hand of 3.02.394 P
and what they swear in poetry may be said as 3.03. 21 P
but why did he swear he would come this morning, 3.04. 18 P
you have heard him swear downright he was. 3.04. 29 P
country copulatives, to swear and to forswear, 5.04. 56 P
her legs that one shall swear she bleeds, | and SHR in.2. 58
here i swear | i'll plead for you myself, but 2.01. 14
i swear i'll cuff you, if you strike again. 2.01.220
you that durst swear that your mistress bianca 4.02. 12
i dare swear this is the right vincentio. 5.01. 99 P
swear, if thou dar'st. 5.01.101 P
nay, i dare not swear it. 5.01.102 P
i will tell truth, by grace itself i swear. AWW 1.03.220
an idle lord, i swear. 2.05. 49 P
and then to return and swear the lies he forges. 4.01. 23 P
i would swear i recover'd it. 4.01. 62 P
what is not holy, that we swear not by, | but 4.02. 23
if i should swear by jove's great attributes | i 4.02. 25
to swear by him whom i protest to love | that i 4.02. 28
that you fly them as you swear them lordship, 5.03.156
he knows i am no maid, and he'll swear to't; 5.03.290
i'll swear i am a maid, and he knows not. 5.03.291
(by the very fangs of malice i swear) i am not TN 1.05.184 P
we men may say more, swear more, but indeed 2.04.116
by innocence i swear, and by my youth, | i have 3.01.157
him, draw, and, as thou draw'st, swear horrible; 3.04.178 P
and whom, by heaven i swear, i tender dearly, 5.01.126
o, do not swear! 5.01.170
and all those sayings will i over swear, | and 5.01.269
but let him swear so, and he shall not stay, WT 1.02. 36
swear his thought over | by each particular star 1.02.424
swear by this sword | thou wilt perform my 2.03.168
i swear to do this — though a present death 2.03.184
you here shall swear upon this sword of justice, 3.02.124
all this we swear. 3.02.130
i'll swear for 'em. 4.04.155
will you swear | never to marry but by my free 5.01. 69
that which you hear you'll swear you see, there 5.02. 31 P
i will swear to the prince thou art as honest a 5.02.156 P
you may say it, but not swear it. 5.02.158 P
not swear it, now i am a gentleman? 5.02.159 P
let boors and franklins say it, i'll swear it. 5.02.160 P
a true gentleman may swear it in the behalf of 5.02.163 P
and i'll swear to the prince thou art a tall 5.02.163 P
but i'll swear it, and i would thou wouldst be a 5.02.167 P
and by this hand i swear, | that sways the earth JN 2.01.343
gone to swear a peace? 3.01. 1
to brag and stamp and swear | upon my party! 3.01.122
the truth thou art unsure | to swear, swears 3.01.284
else what a mockery should it be to swear! 3.01.285
but thou dost swear only to be forsworn, | and 3.01.286
and most forsworn, to keep what thou dost swear; 3.01.287
albeit we swear | a voluntary zeal and an 5.02. 9
and by that sword i swear | which gently laid my R2 1.01. 78
to swear him in the justice of his cause. 1.03. 10
swear by the duty that y' owe to god | (our part 1.03.180
i swear. 1.03.191
they shall not live within this world, i swear, 5.03.142
i will swear | i love thee infinitely. 1H4 2.03.101
and said he would swear truth out of england but 2.04.306 P
garments with it and swear it was the blood of 2.04.311 P
heart, you swear like a comfit–maker's wife: 3.01.247 P
swear me, kate, like a lady as thou art, | a 3.01.253
way given to virtue, i would swear by thy face; 3.03. 34 P
and when he heard him swear and vow to god | he 4.03. 60
us, | and you did swear that oath at doncaster, 5.01. 42
make him sure, yea, and i'll swear i kill'd him. 5.04.125 P
thou didst swear to me upon a parcel–gilt goblet 2H4 2.01. 86 P
of windsor, thou didst swear to me then, as i 2.01. 91 P
and swear here, by the honor of my blood, | my 4.02. 55
have you a ruffin that will swear, drink, dance, 4.05.124
and i dare swear you borrow not that face | of 5.02. 28
now by /gadslugs i swear i scorn the term; H5 2.01. 30
let us swear | that you are worth your breeding, 3.01. 27
by my hand i swear, and my father's soul, the 3.02. 90 P
swear by her foot, that she may tread out the 3.07. 95 P
they shall have none, i swear, but these my 4.03.123
horribly revenge — i eat and eat — i swear — 5.01. 48 P
there is not enough leek to swear by. 5.01. 50 P
by which honor i dare not swear thou lovest me, 5.02.222 P
then shall i swear to kate, and you to me, | and 5.02.373
so sure i swear to get the town, or die. 1H6 3.02. 84
you fled for vantage, every one will swear; 4.05. 28
upon condition thou wilt swear | to pay him 5.04.129
then swear allegiance to his majesty, | as thou 5.04.169
all, | swear like a ruffian, and demean himself 2H6 1.01.188
as if she had suborned some to swear | false 3.01.180
and therefore by his majesty i swear, | whose 3.02.285
but when i swear, it is irrevocable. 3.02.294
and they jointly swear | to spoil the city and 4.04. 52
it is great sin to swear unto a sin, | but 5.01.182
mock thee, clifford, swear as thou wast wont. 3H6 2.06. 76
but did you never swear and break an oath? 3.01. 72
ah, simple men, you know not what you swear! 3.01. 83
by my state i swear to thee | i speak no more 3.02. 93
myself have often heard him say, and swear, 3.03.123
didst thou not hear me swear i would not do it? 5.05. 74
a man cannot swear, but it checks him; R3 1.04.136 P
dissemble not your hatred, swear your love. 2.01. 8
so thrive i, as i truly swear the like! 2.01. 11
so prosper i, as i swear perfect love! 2.01. 16
and so swear i. 2.01. 28
now by saint paul i swear | i will not dine 3.04. 76
i swear — 4.04.368
if something thou wouldst swear to be believ'd, 4.04.372
swear then by something that thou hast not 4.04.373
what canst thou swear by now? 4.04.387
swear not by time to come, for that thou hast 4.04.395

you would swear directly | their very noses had H8 1.03. 8
i swear, 'tis better to be lowly born, | and 2.03. 19
i swear again, i would not be a queen | for all 2.03. 45
knaves as corrupt | to swear against you? 5.01.133
i swear he is true–hearted, and a soul | none 5.01.154
i swear to you, i think helen loves him better TRO 1.02.107 P
swear the oaths now to her that you have sworn 3.02. 41 P
they say all lovers swear more performance than 3.02. 84 P
by venus' hand i swear, | no man alive can love 4.01. 23
what did you swear you would bestow on me? 5.02. 25
i did swear patience. 5.02. 84
be gone, i say, the gods have heard me swear. 5.03. 15
i'll swear 'tis a very pretty boy. COR 1.03. 57 P
i heard him swear, | were he to stand for consul 2.01.231
and here i swear by all the roman gods, | sith TIT 1.01.322
and here in sight of heaven to rome i swear, 1.01.329
and swear unto my soul to right your wrongs. 3.01.278
and swear with me, as with the woeful fere | and 4.01. 89
unless thou swear to me my child shall live. 5.01. 68
swear that he shall, and then i will begin. 5.01. 70
who should i swear by? 5.01. 71
even by my god i swear to thee i will. 5.01. 86
that makes dainty, | she i'll swear hath corns. ROM 1.05. 20
to breathe such vows as lovers use to swear, 2.pr. 10
o, swear not by the moon, th' inconstant moon, 2.02.109
what shall i swear by? 2.02.112
do not swear at all; 2.02.112
or, if thou wilt, swear by thy gracious self, 2.02.113
well, do not swear. 2.02.116
and when i do, i swear | it shall be romeo, whom 3.05.121
swear against objects, | put armor on thine ears TIM 4.03.123
although i know you'll swear, terribly swear 4.03.137
terribly swear | into strong shudders and to 4.03.137
and let us swear our resolution. JC 2.01.113
swear priests and cowards, and men cautelous, 2.01.129
unto bad causes swear | such creatures as men 2.01.131
that could swear in both the scales against MAC 2.03. 9 P
and must they all be hang'd that swear and lie? 4.02. 51 P
swear. HAM 1.05.149
fellow in the cellarage, | consent to swear. 1.05.152
of this that you have seen, | swear by my sword. 1.05.154
swear. 1.05.155
swear by my sword, | never to speak of this that 1.05.159
swear by his sword. 1.05.161
that you know aught of me — this do swear, | so 1.05.179
swear. 1.05.181
madam, i swear i use no art at all. 2.02. 96
were good, my lord, i durst swear it were his; LR 1.02. 64 P
by jupiter, i swear no. 2.04. 21
by juno, i swear ay. 2.04. 22
keep thy word's justice, swear not, commit not 3.04. 81 P
i will not swear these are my hands. 4.07. 54
swear? OTH 2.03.280 P
i swear 'tis better to be much abus'd | than but 3.03.336
unproper beds | which they dare swear peculiar; 4.01. 69
in venice, | though i should swear i saw't. 4.01.243
come swear it, damn thyself, | lest, being like 4.02. 35
swear thou art honest. 4.02. 38
or i could make him swear | the shes of italy CYM 1.03. 28
and would undergo what's spoken, i swear. 1.04.141 P
when a gentleman is dispos'd to swear, it is not 2.01. 10 P
still i swear i love you. 2.03. 90
if you swear still, your recompense is still 2.03. 92
if you will swear you have not done't, you lie, 2.04.144
might break out and swear | he'ld fetch us in; 4.02.140
think me speaking, though i swear to silence; PER 1.02. 19
i'll swear she's dead, | and thrown into the sea 4.01. 98
do swear to th' gods that winter kills the flies 4.03. 50
swear 'em never more | to make me their TNK 3.06.252
swear nature's death for framing thee so fair. VEN 744
that one would swear he saw them quake and LUC 1393
another, smother'd, seems to pelt and swear, 1418
and swear i found you where you did fulfill 1635
his scarlet lust came evidence to swear | that 1650
make me forsworn, how shall i swear to love? PP 5. 1
thou for whom jove would swear | juno but an 16.15
so bold, | although i swear it to myself alone. SON 131. 8
and to be sure that is not false i swear, | a 131. 9
then will i swear beauty herself is black, | and 132.13
swear to thy blind soul that i was thy will, 136. 2
and swear that brightness doth not grace the day 150. 4
or made them swear against the thing they see; 152.12
eye, | to swear against the truth so foul a lie! 152.14

SWEARER 1 FR 0.0001 REL FR 0 V 1 P
i do believe the swearer. what with me? WIV 2.02. 39 P

SWEARERS 3 FR 0.0003 REL FR 0 V 3 P
then the liars and swearers are fools; MAC 4.02. 56 P
there are liars and swearers enow to beat the 4.02. 57 P
our cavalleria, and make our swearers priests. PER 4.06. 12 P

SWEAREST 1 FR 0.0001 REL FR 0 V 1 P
swearest thou, ungracious boy? 1H4 2.04.445 P

SWEARING 25 FR 0.0028 REL FR 17 V 8 P
i am damn'd in hell for swearing to gentlemen my WIV 2.02. 10 P
for my love some other way than swearing by it. ADO 4.01.327 P
and swearing till my very /roof was dry | with MV 3.02.204
we shall have old swearing | that they did give 4.02. 15
no more was this knight, swearing by his honor, AYL 1.02. 77 P
our life, swearing that we | are mere usurpers, 2.01. 60
lunatic, | a madcap ruffian and a swearing jack, SHR 2.01.288
nay, let me alone for swearing. TN 3.04.183 P
swearing allegiance and the love of soul | to JN 5.01. 10
got with swearing "lay by," and spent with 1H4 1.02. 36 P
"we died at such a place" — some swearing, some H5 4.01.138 P
to swearing and stern looks, defus'd attire, 5.02. 61
swearing that you withhold his levied host, 1H6 4.04. 31
swearing both | they prosper best of all when i 3H6 2.05. 17
the policy of those crafty swearing rascals, TRO 5.04. 10 P
and hale him up and down, all swearing, if | the COR 5.04. 37
ay, or drinking, fencing, swearing, quarrelling, HAM 2.01. 25
(though you in swearing shake the throned gods), ANT 1.03. 28
vows, | which break themselves in swearing! 1.03. 31
jack–an–apes must take me up for swearing, as if CYM 2.01. 4 P
no swearing: 2.04.143
swearing i slew him, seeing thee embrace him. LUC 518
swearing, unless i took all patiently, | i 1641
each kiss her oaths of true love swearing! PP 7. 8

thou art twice forsworn, to me love swearing; SON 152. 2

SWEARINGS 2 FR 0.0002 REL FR 1 V 1 P
and to drinkings and swearings and starings, WIV 5.05.160 P
and all those swearings keep as true in soul TN 5.01.270

SWEARS 31 FR 0.0035 REL FR 20 V 11 P
swears he will shoot no more, but play with TMP 4.01.100
for he swears he'll turn me away. WIV 3.03. 32 P
of none but him, and swears he was carried out, 4.02. 31 P
he swears she's a witch, forbade her my house, 4.02. 86 P
no, and swears she never will. ADO 2.03.125 P
hercules that only tells a lie, and swears it. 4.01.322 P
and in that kind swears you do more usurp | than AYL 2.01. 27
speaks brave words, swears brave oaths, and 3.04. 41 P
he hath been a courtier, he swears. 5.04. 42 P
to her, and rails, and swears, and rates, that SHR 4.01.184
"when he swears oaths, bid him drop gold, and AWW 4.03.223
yond young fellow swears he will speak with you. TN 1.05.139 P
he thinks, nay, with all confidence he swears, WT 1.02.414
to swear, swears only not to be forsworn, | else JN 3.01.284
and by the honorable tomb he swears | that R2 3.03.105
this swears he, as he is /a /prince, /is just, 3.03.119
so much that he swears thou art to marry his 2H4 2.02.128 P
join'd–stools, and swears with a good grace, and 2.04.248 P
that hath authority over him that swears. 3H6 1.02. 24
your quondam wife swears still by venus' glove. TRO 4.05.179
and keeps the oath which by that god he swears, TIT 5.01. 80
being thus frighted, swears a prayer or two, ROM 1.04. 87
why, one that swears and lies. MAC 4.02. 47 P
hark you, he swears; CYM 2.04.122
by jupiter he swears. 2.04.122
he swears | never to wash his face, nor cut his PER 4.04. 27
she does, and swears she'll never stint, | make 4.04. 42
and by her fair immortal hand she swears | from VEN 80
and therefore lucrece swears he did her wrong, LUC 1462
when my love swears that she is made of truth, PP 1. 1
when my love swears that she is made of truth, SON 138. 1

SWEAR'ST 6 FR 0.0006 REL FR 5 V 1 P
that swear'st grace o'erboard, not an oath on TMP 5.01.219
for thou swear'st to me thou art honest. AYL 3.03. 25 P
by what thou swear'st against the thing thou JN 3.01.281
thou swear'st against the thing thou swear'st, 3.01.281
yet, if thou swear'st, | thou mayest prove false ROM 2.02. 91
apollo, king, | thou swear'st thy gods in vain. LR 1.01.161

SWEAR'T 3 FR 0.0003 REL FR 2 V 1 P
i have heard her swear't. TN 1.03.111 P
i'll swear't. WT 3.02.203
nay, but swear't. HAM 1.05.145

/SWEAT 2 FR 0.0002 REL FR 2 V 0 P
/sweat now, make haste! ERR 4.02. 29
/at /this /time | /we /sweat /and /bleed: LR 5.03. 55

SWEAT 41 FR 0.0046 REL FR 32 V 9 P
should produce | without sweat or endeavor: TMP 2.01.161
what with the war, what with the sweat, what MM 1.02. 83 P
with targe and shield did make my foe to sweat, LLL 5.02.553
the ploughman lost his sweat, and the green corn MND 2.01. 94
for, wooing here until i sweat again, | and MV 3.02.203
why sweat they under burthens? 4.01. 95
when service sweat for duty, not for meed! AYL 2.03. 58
where none will sweat but for promotion, | and 2.03. 60
why, do not your courtier's hands sweat? 3.02. 55 P
of a mutton as wholesome as the sweat of a man? 3.02. 57 P
rage like an angry boar chafed with sweat? SHR 1.02.202
sake | with burden of our armor here we sweat. JN 2.01. 92
sweat in this business and maintain this war? 5.02.102
that beads of sweat have stood upon thy brow, 1H4 2.03. 58
me, and i mean not to sweat extraordinarily. 2H4 1.02.210 P
or shall i sweat for you? 4.03. 12 P
if i do sweat, they are the drops of thy lovers, 4.03. 12 P
falstaff shall die of a sweat, unless already 'a ep 30 P
sweat drops of gallant youth in our rich fields! H5 3.05. 25
drops bloody sweat from his war–wearied limbs, 1H6 4.04. 18
if you do sweat to put a tyrant down, | you R3 5.03.255
and follow'd with the general throng and sweat H8 pr 28
did almost sweat to bear | the pride upon them, 1.01. 24
stirr'd | with such an agony he sweat extremely, 2.01. 33
till then i'll sweat and seek about for eases, TRO 5.10. 55
our thoughts, | which makes me sweat with wrath. COR 1.04. 27
done, and sav'd | your husband so much sweat. 4.01. 19
thing to make | mine eyes to sweat compassion. 5.03.196
a chilling sweat o'erruns my trembling joints, TIT 2.03.212
i have sweat to see his honor. TIM 3.02. 26 P
gold, | to groan and sweat under the business, JC 4.01. 22
if arguing make us sweat, | the proof of it will 5.01. 48
napkins enow about you, here you'll sweat for't. MAC 2.03. 6 P
bear, | to grunt and sweat under a weary life, HAM 3.01. 76
to live | in the rank sweat of an enseamed bed, 3.04. 92
the buffet | with knaves that smells of sweat: ANT 1.04. 21
the sweat of industry would dry and die, | but CYM 3.06. 31
must recompense itself | with its own sweat; TNK 1.01.154
by this the love–sick queen began to sweat, VEN 175
with pearly sweat resembling dew of night. LUC 396
see the laboring pioner | begrim'd with sweat, 1381

SWEATEN 1 FR 0.0001 REL FR 1 V 0 P
grease that's sweaten | from the murderer's MAC 4.01. 65

SWEATING 10 FR 0.0011 REL FR 8 V 2 P
here's mistress page at the door, sweating, and WIV 3.03. 86 P
bare–headed, sweating, knocking at the taverns, 2H4 2.04.359
travel, and sweating with desire to see him, 5.05. 24 P
and in good time, here comes the sweating lord. R3 3.01. 24
for here's a young and sweating devil here OTH 3.04. 42
'tis sweating labor | to bear such idleness so ANT 1.03. 93
such most | that, sweating in an honorable toil, TNK 1.02. 33
with this she seizeth on his sweating palm, VEN 25
since sweating lust on earth usurp'd his name, 794
he faintly flies, sweating with guilty fear; LUC 740

SWEATS 5 FR 0.0005 REL FR 3 V 2 P
she sweats, a man may go over shoes in the grime ERR 3.02.103 P
falstaff sweats to death, | and lards the lean 1H4 2.02.108
sweats in the eye of phoebus, and all night H5 4.01.273
he sweats not to overthrow your almain; OTH 2.03. 83 P
princely blood flows in his cheek, he sweats, CYM 3.03. 93

SWEAT'ST 1 FR 0.0001 REL FR 0 V 1 P
alas, poor ape, how thou sweat'st! 2H4 2.04.217 P

SWEATY 2 FR 0.0002 REL FR 1 V 1 P
hands, and threw up their sweaty night–caps, and JC 1.02.246 P
that this sweaty haste | doth make the night HAM 1.01. 77

SWEEP 13 FR 0.0014 REL FR 12 V 1 P
sever themselves and madly sweep the sky, | so, MND 3.02. 23
with ears that sweep away the morning dew; 4.01.121
before, | to sweep the dust behind the door. 5.01.390
"sweep on, you fat and greasy citizens, | 'tis AYL 2.01. 55
and like a peacock sweep along his tail; 1H6 3.03. 6
that kiss'd the queen shall sweep the ground, 2H6 4.01. 75
am the besom that must sweep the court clean of 4.07. 31 P
unless we sweep 'em from the door with cannons H8 5.03. 13
what a sweep of vanity comes this way! TIM 1.02.132
with barefac'd power sweep him from my sight, MAC 3.01.118
the thoughts of love, | may sweep to my revenge. HAM 1.05. 31
they bear the mandate — they must sweep my way, 3.04.204
some friends that will | sweep your way for you. ANT 3.11. 17

SWEEPS 3 FR 0.0003 REL FR 3 V 0 P
that sweeps through our land | with pennons H5 3.05. 48
she sweeps it through the court with troops of 2H6 1.03. 77
and lo, where george of clarence sweeps along, 3H6 5.01. 76

SWEEPSTAKE *(see swoopstake)*

/SWEET 3 FR 0.0003 REL FR 3 V 0 P
emptying our bosoms of their counsel /sweet, MND 1.01.216
/had /my /sweet /harry /had /but /half /their 2H4 2.03. 43
/the /sweet /and /bitter /fool | /will LR 1.04.144

SWEET 873 FR 0.0986 REL FR 696 V 177 P
and, sweet sprites, /the /burthen /bear. TMP 1.02.380
their fury and my passion | with its sweet air; 1.02.394
'twas a sweet marriage, and we prosper well in 2.01. 73 P
my sweet mistress | weeps when she sees me work, 3.01. 11
but these sweet thoughts do even refresh my 3.01. 14
sounds, and sweet airs, that give delight and 3.02.136
marvellous sweet music! 3.03. 19
no sweet aspersion shall the heavens let fall 4.01. 18
sweet now, silence! 4.01.124
sweet lord, you play me false. 5.01.172
days | to the sweet glances of thy honor'd love, TGV 1.01. 4
sweet valentine, adieu! 1.01. 11
sweet proteus, no; 1.01. 56
to feed on such sweet honey | and kill the bees 1.02.103
to the sweet julia" — that i'll tear away — 1.02.122
hear sweet discourse, converse with noblemen, 1.03. 31
sweet love, sweet lines, sweet life! 1.03. 45
sweet love, sweet lines, sweet life! 1.03. 45
sweet love, sweet lines, sweet life! 1.03. 45
sweet ornament that decks a thing divine — | ah 2.01. 4
yourself, sweet lady, for you gave the fire. 2.04. 37 P
omitting the sweet benefit of time | to clothe 2.04. 65
sweet lady, entertain him | to be my 2.04.104
not so, sweet lady, but too mean a servant | to 2.04.107
sweet lady, entertain him for your servant. 2.04.110
sweet, except not any, | except thou wilt except 2.04.154
forswear not thyself, sweet youth, for i am not 2.05. 3 P
he makes sweet music with th' enamell'd stones, 2.07. 28
you, a sweet virtue in a maid with clean hands. 3.01.278 P
"item, she hath a sweet mouth." 3.01.327 P
lady's chamber–window | with some sweet consort; 3.02. 83
therefore, sweet proteus, my direction–giver, 3.02. 89
i grant, sweet love, that i did love a lady; 4.02.105
sweet lady, let me rake it from the earth. 4.02.115
i give thee this | for thy sweet mistress' sake, 4.04.177
dispatch, sweet gentlemen, and follow me. 5.02. 48
nay, conceive me, conceive me, sweet coz; WIV 1.01.242 P
how now, sweet frank, why art thou melancholy? 2.01.150 P
the sweet woman leads an ill life with him. 2.02. 89 P
ah, sweet anne page! 3.01. 40 P
o sweet anne page! 3.01. 70 P
o sweet anne page! 3.01.114 P
o sweet sir john! 3.03. 47 P
therefore no more turn me to him, sweet nan. 3.04. 2
once to–night | give my sweet nan this ring. 3.04.100
he's a–birding, sweet sir john. 4.02. 8 P
how now, sweet heart! 4.02. 12 P
go, go, sweet sir john. 4.02. 80 P
nay, good, sweet husband! 4.02.180 P
must my sweet nan present the fairy queen; 4.06. 20
mistress page is come with me, sweet heart. 5.05. 23 P
give up your body to such sweet uncleanness | as MM 2.04. 54
sweet sister, let me live. 3.01.132
for 'tis a physic | that's bitter to sweet end. 4.06. 8
sweet isabel, take my part! 5.01.430
sweet isabel, do yet but kneel by me. 5.01.437
some other mistress hath thy sweet aspects: ERR 2.02.111
look sweet, speak fair, become disloyalty; 3.02. 11
when the sweet breath of flattery conquers 3.02. 28
sweet mistress — what your name is else, i know 3.02. 29
o, train me not, sweet mermaid, with thy note, 3.02. 45
as good to wink, sweet love, as look on night. 3.02. 58
my food, my fortune, and my sweet hope's aim, 3.02. 63
call thyself sister, sweet, for i am thee: 3.02. 66
sweet recreation barr'd, what doth ensue | but 5.01. 78
sweet prince, sweet prince, against that woman there! 5.01.197
"o sweet benedick! ADO 2.03.148 P
she's an excellent sweet lady, and (out of all 2.03.159 P
of the false sweet bait that we lay for it. 3.01. 33
as much as to say, the sweet youth's in love. 3.02. 52 P
good morrow, sweet hero. 3.04. 40 P
sweet prince, you learn me noble thankfulness. 4.01. 30
sweet prince, why speak not you? 4.01. 63
if this sweet lady lie not guiltless here 4.01.169
what offense, sweet beatrice? 4.01.282 P
tarry, sweet beatrice. 4.01.292 P
sweet hero, she is wrong'd, she is sland'red, 4.01.312 P
count, count comfect, a sweet gallant surely! 4.01.317 P
you have kill'd a sweet lady, and her death 5.01.148 P
have among you kill'd a sweet and innocent lady. 5.01.191 P
sweet prince, let me go no farther to mine 5.01.230 P
sweet hero, now thy image doth appear | in the 5.01.251
pray thee, sweet mistress margaret, deserve well 5.02. 1 P
sweet beatrice, wouldst thou come when i call'd 5.02. 42 P
sweet, let me see your face. 5.04. 55
sweet lord, and why? LLL 1.01.126
or, for thy more sweet understanding, a woman. 1.01.264 P
of punishment, by thy sweet grace's officer, 1.01.267 P
and shall, at the least of thy sweet notice, 1.01.275 P
most sweet hercules! 1.02. 67 P
and, sweet my child, let them be men of good 1.02. 68 P
sweet invocation of a child, most pretty and 1.02. 97 P
so sweet and voluble is his discourse. 2.01. 76
sweet health and fair desires consort your grace 2.01.177
she is a most sweet lady. 2.01.207

no sheep, sweet lamb, unless we feed on your 2.01.220
sweet air! 3.01. 4 P
sweet smoke of rhetoric! 3.01. 63
by thy favor, sweet welkin, i must sigh in thy 3.01. 67
by my sweet soul, i mean setting thee at liberty 3.01.123 P
my sweet ounce of man's flesh, my incony jew! 3.01.135
gardon, o sweet gardon! 3.01.170 P
most sweet gardon! 3.01.171 P
here, sweet, put up this — 'twill be thine 4.01.107
o' my troth, most sweet jests, most incony 4.01.142
not to anger bent, is music and sweet fire. 4.02.116
trip and go, my sweet, deliver this paper into 4.02.141 P
sweet clown, sweeter fool, sweetest lady! 4.03. 16 P
proceed, sweet cupid, thou hast thump'd him with 4.03. 22 P
"so sweet a kiss the golden sun gives not | to 4.03. 25
sweet leaves, shade folly. 4.03. 42
in love, i hope — sweet fellowship in shame. 4.03. 47
o sweet maria, empress of my love, | these 4.03. 54
sweet misprision! 4.03. 96
youth unmeet, | youth so apt to pluck a sweet. 4.03.112
sweet lords, sweet lovers, o, let us embrace! 4.03.210
sweet lords, sweet lovers, o, let us embrace! 4.03.210
and ethiops of their sweet complexion crack. 4.03.264
as sweet and musical | as bright apollo's lute, 4.03.339
salt /wave of the mediterraneum, a sweet touch, 5.01. 59 P
at your sweet pleasure, for the mountain. 5.01. 85 P
sir, it is the king's most sweet pleasure and 5.01. 87 P
the word is well cull'd, chose, sweet, and apt, 5.01. 93 P
but, sweet heart, let that pass. 5.01.105 P
is — but, sweet heart, i do implore secrety — 5.01.109 P
would have me present the princess (sweet chuck) 5.01.111 P
the curate and your sweet self are good at such 5.01.114 P
sweet hearts, we shall be rich ere we depart, 5.02. 1
take thou this, my sweet, and give me thine, 5.02.132
curtsy, sweet hearts — and so the measure ends. 5.02.221
white–handed mistress, one sweet word with thee. 5.02.230
seventh sweet, adieu. 5.02.234
let it not be sweet. 5.02.236
they are, with your sweet breaths puff'd out. 5.02.267
blow like sweet roses in this summer air. 5.02.293
dismask'd, their damask sweet commixture shown, 5.02.296
the ladies call him sweet; 5.02.329
a blister on his sweet tongue, with my heart, 5.02.335
all hail, sweet madam, and fair time of day! 5.02.339
gentle sweet, | your wits makes wise things 5.02.373
teach us, sweet madam, for our rude 5.02.431
expense of thy royal sweet breath as will utter 5.02.523 P
that is all one, my fair, sweet, honey monarch, 5.02.527 P
before the legs of this sweet lass of france." 5.02.555
and so adieu, sweet jude! 5.02.626
sweet lord longaville, rein thy tongue. 5.02.656 P
the sweet war–man is dead and rotten, sweet 5.02.660 P
sweet war–man is dead and rotten, sweet chucks, 5.02.661 P
sweet royalty, bestow on me the sense of hearing 5.02.663 P
i do adore thy sweet grace's slipper. 5.02.667 P
sweet bloods, i both may and will. 5.02.708 P
ay, sweet my lord, and so i take my leave. 5.02.872
sweet majesty, vouchsafe me — 5.02.879 P
hold the plough for her sweet love three year. 5.02.884 P
relent, sweet hermia, and, lysander, yield | thy MND 1.01. 91
and she, sweet lady, dotes, | devoutly dotes, 1.01.108
and your tongue's sweet air | more tuneable than 1.01.183
tongue should catch your tongue's sweet melody. 1.01.189
farewell, sweet playfellow, pray thou for us; 1.01.220
she never had so sweet a changeling. 2.01. 23
those, that hobgoblin call you, and sweet puck, 2.01. 40
an odorous chaplet of sweet summer buds | is, as 2.01.110
with sweet musk–roses and with eglantine; 2.01.252
a sweet athenian lady is in love | with a 2.01.260
with melody | sing in our sweet lullaby, | lulla 2.02. 14
o, take the sense, sweet, of my innocence! 2.02. 45
and good night, sweet friend. 2.02. 60
thy love ne'er alter till thy sweet life end! 2.02. 61
stay, though thou kill me, sweet demetrius. 2.02. 84
and run through fire i will for thy sweet sake. 2.02.103
can, | deserve a sweet look from demetrius' eye, 2.02.127
"thisby, the flowers of odious savors sweet" — 3.01. 82
"odors savors sweet; 3.01. 84
fear, | and left sweet pyramus translated there; 3.02. 32
wink each at other, hold the sweet jest up; 3.02.239
sweet, do not scorn her so. 3.02.247
what change is this, | sweet love? 3.02.263
what, wilt thou hear some music, my sweet love? 4.01. 27
or say, sweet love, what thou desirest to eat. 4.01. 30
good hay, sweet hay, hath no fellow. 4.01. 33 P
so doth the woodbine the sweet honeysuckle 4.01. 42
seest thou this sweet sight? 4.01. 46
seeking sweet favors for this hateful fool, | i 4.01. 49
now, my titania, wake you, my sweet queen. 4.01. 75
so musical a discord, such sweet thunder. 4.01.118
and he is a very paramour for a sweet voice. 4.02. 12 P
o sweet bully bottom! 4.02. 19 P
let us hear, sweet bottom. 4.02. 33 P
nor garlic, for we are to utter sweet breath; 4.02. 43 P
but to hear them say, it is a sweet comedy. 4.02. 44 P
why, gentle sweet, you shall see no such thing. 5.01. 87
trust me, sweet, | out of this silence yet i 5.01. 99
anon comes pyramus, sweet youth and tall, | and 5.01.144
and thou, o wall, o sweet, o lovely wall, | that 5.01.174
thou wall, o wall, o sweet and lovely wall, 5.01.176
sweet moon, i thank thee for thy sunny beams; 5.01.272
hath spied him already with those sweet eyes. 5.01.321 P
a tomb | must cover thy sweet eyes. 5.01.329
sweet friends, to bed. 5.01.368
bless, | through this palace, with sweet peace, 5.01.418
you would be, sweet madam, if your miseries were MV 1.02. 3 P
most beautiful pagan, most sweet jew! 2.03. 11 P
sweet friends, your patience for my long abode; 2.06. 21
so are you, sweet, | even in the lovely garnish 2.06. 44
sweet, adieu. 2.09. 77
a day in april never came so sweet, | to show 2.09. 93
so sweet a bar | should sunder such sweet 3.02.119
sweet a bar | should sunder such sweet friends. 3.02.120
friends and countrymen, | sweet portia, welcome. 3.02.224
o sweet portia, | here are a few of the 3.02.250
"sweet bassanio, my ships have all miscarried, 3.02.315 P
and now, good sweet, say thy opinion, | how dost 3.05. 71
when the sweet wind did gently kiss the trees 5.01. 2
sweet soul, let's in, and there expect their 5.01. 49
how sweet the moonlight sleeps upon this bank! 5.01. 54
the night | become the touches of sweet harmony. 5.01. 57
i am never merry when i hear sweet music. 5.01. 69
to a modest gaze, | by the sweet power of music; 5.01. 79
nor is not moved with concord of sweet sounds, 5.01. 84
sweet portia, | if you did know to whom i gave 5.01.192
what should i say, sweet lady? 5.01.215
sweet doctor, you shall be my bedfellow — 5.01.284
sweet lady, you have given me life and living, 5.01.286
sweet masters, be patient, for your father's AYL 1.01. 63 P
i pray thee, rosalind, sweet my coz, be merry. 1.02. 1 P
therefore, my sweet rose, my dear rose, be merry 1.02. 23 P
shall we part, sweet girl? 1.03. 98
hath not old custom made this life more sweet 2.01. 2
sweet are the uses of adversity, | which, like 2.01. 12
of fortune | into so quiet and so sweet a style. 2.01. 20
o my sweet master! 2.03. 3
his merry note | unto the sweet bird's throat, 2.05. 4
sweet, say on. 3.02.250 P
come, sweet audrey, | we must be married, or we 3.03. 96
not — o sweet oliver, | o brave oliver, | leave 3.03. 99
sweet phebe, do not scorn me, do not, phebe; 3.05. 1
sweet youth, i pray you chide a year together, 3.05. 64
sweet phebe — 3.05. 83
sweet phebe, pity me. 3.05. 84
ay, sweet rosalind. 4.01.187 P
chewing the food of sweet and bitter fancy, | lo 4.03.101
why, how now, ganymed, sweet ganymed? 4.03.157
a ding, ding, | sweet lovers love the spring. 5.03. 21
beards, or good faces, or sweet breaths, will, ep 22 P
wrapp'd in sweet clothes, rings put upon his SHR in.1. 38
and burn sweet wood to make the lodging sweet. in.1. 49
and burn sweet wood to make the lodging sweet. in.1. 49
i smell sweet savors, and i feel soft things. in.2. 71
to suck the sweets of sweet philosophy. 1.01. 28
for the love i bear my sweet bianca, if i can by 1.01.110 P
sweet bianca! 1.01.139 P
o yes, i saw sweet beauty in her face, | such as 1.01.167
sacred and sweet was all i saw in her. 1.01.176
and tell me now, sweet friend, what happy gale 1.02. 48
in speech, yet sweet as spring–time flowers. 2.01.246
marry, so i mean, sweet katherine, in thy bed; 2.01.267
farewell, sweet masters both, i must be gone. 3.01. 85
hope, | and marry sweet bianca with consent. 3.02.137
give away myself | to this most patient, sweet, 3.02.195
fear not, sweet wench, they shall not touch thee 3.02.238
shall sweet bianca practice how to bride it? 3.02.251
nay, good sweet kate, be merry. 4.01.143
will you give thanks, sweet kate, or else shall 4.01.159
while you, sweet dear, prove mistress of my 4.02. 10
i am sure, sweet kate, this kindness merits 4.03. 41
tell me, sweet kate, and tell me truly too, 4.05. 28
sweet kate, embrace her for her beauty's sake. 4.05. 34
budding virgin, fair, and fresh, and sweet, 4.05. 37
pardon, sweet father. 5.01.112
lives my sweet son? 5.01.112
then pardon him, sweet father, for my sake. 5.01.130
come, my sweet kate: 5.01.149
to be short, what not, that's sweet and happy. 5.02.110
of every line and trick of his sweet favor. AWW 1.01. 96
his faith, his sweet disaster; 1.01.173
o my sweet lord, that you will stay behind us! 2.01. 24
sweet monsieur parolles! 2.01. 39 P
sweet practicer, thy physic i will try, | that 2.01.185
what's the matter, sweet heart? 2.03.268 P
what, what, sweet heart? 2.03.271 P
your mother was | when your sweet self was got. 4.02. 10
i love thee | by love's own sweet constraint, 4.02. 16
shaking off so good a wife and so sweet a lady. 4.03. 7 P
they cannot be too sweet for the king's tartness 4.03. 82 P
that can such sweet use make of what they hate, 4.04. 22
as well as thorns, | and be as sweet as sharp. 4.04. 33
sir, she was the sweet marjorom of the sallet, 4.05. 16 P
be this sweet helen's knell, and now forget her. 5.03. 67
helen, that's dead, | was a sweet creature; 5.03. 78
in a sweet verbal brief, it did concern | your 5.03.137
the bitter past, more welcome is the sweet. 5.03.334
it came o'er my ear like the sweet sound | that TN 1.01. 5
'tis not so sweet now as it was before. 1.01. 8
her sweet perfections with one self king! 1.01. 38
away before me to sweet beds of flow'rs, 1.01. 39
sweet sir andrew! 1.03. 46 P
some mollification for your giant, sweet lady. 1.05.204 P
most sweet lady — 1.05.221 P
nature's own sweet and cunning hand laid on. 1.05.240
i had such a leg, and so sweet a breath to sing, 2.03. 21 P
plenty, | then come kiss me, sweet and twenty; 2.03. 51
very sweet and contagious, i' faith. 2.03. 55 P
sweet sir toby, be patient for to–night. 2.03.131 P
love, | in the sweet pangs of it remember me; 2.04. 16
not a flower, not a flower sweet, | on my black 2.04. 59
in my presence still smile, dear my sweet, i 2.05.177 P
sweet lady, ho, ho. 3.04. 17 P
i think we do know the sweet roman hand. 3.04. 28 P
to bed? ay, sweet heart, and i'll come to thee. 3.04. 30 P
pardon me, sweet one, even for the vows | we 5.01.214
mean time, sweet sister, | we will not part from 5.01.384
sweet villain! WT 1.02.136
why, my sweet lord? 2.01. 4
the climate's delicate, the air most sweet, 3.01. 1
why, then comes in the sweet o' the year, | for 4.03. 3
with hey, the sweet birds, o, how they sing! 4.03. 6
a footman, sweet sir, a footman. 4.03. 65 P
no, good sweet sir; 4.03. 79 P
sweet sir, much better than i was: 4.03.111 P
no, good–fac'd sir, no, sweet sir. 4.03.115 P
prosper you, sweet sir! 4.03.118 P
you see, sweet maid, we marry | a gentler scion 4.04. 92
to make you garlands of, and my sweet friend, 4.04.128
when you speak, sweet, | i'ld have you do it 4.04.136
was crow, | gloves as sweet as damask roses, 4.04.220
me a tawdry–lace and a pair of sweet gloves. 4.04.250 P
bed of majesty again | with a sweet fellow to't? 5.01. 34
o sweet paulina, | make me to think so twenty 5.03. 70
for this affliction has a taste as sweet | as 5.03. 76
sir," says question, "i, sweet sir, at yours"; JN 1.01.199
but from the inward motion to deliver | sweet, 1.01.213
the inward motion to deliver | sweet, sweet, 1.01.213
sweet, sweet, sweet poison for the age's tooth, 1.01.213
nothing but a calve's–skin, most sweet lout. 3.01.220
shame hath spoil'd the sweet word's taste, 3.04.110
the foul corruption of a sweet child's death. 4.02. 81
soul, | kneeling before this ruin of sweet life, 4.03. 65
my date of life out for his sweet live's loss. 4.03.106
be guilty of the stealing that sweet breath 4.03.136
to seek sweet safety out | in vaults and prisons 5.02.142
o my sweet sir, news fitting to the night, 5.06. 19
and happily may your sweet self put on | the 5.07.101
the daintiest last, to make the end most sweet: R2 1.03. 68
draws the sweet infant breath of gentle sleep; 1.03.133
things sweet to taste prove in digestion sour. 1.03.236
england's ground, farewell, sweet soil, adieu; 1.03.306
save bidding farewell to so sweet a guest | as 2.02. 8
to so sweet a guest | as my sweet richard. 2.02. 9
so your sweet majesty, | looking awry upon your 2.02. 20
making the hard way sweet and delectable. 2.03. 7
sweet love, i see, changing his property, 3.02.135
forth | of that sweet way i was in to despair! 3.02.205
sweet peace conduct his sweet soul to the bosom 4.01.103
sweet peace conduct his sweet soul to the bosom 4.01.103
i am sworn brother, sweet, | to grim necessity, 5.01. 20
pomp | she came adorned hither like sweet may, 5.01. 79
sweet york, sweet husband, be not of that mind, 5.02.107
sweet york, sweet husband, be not of that mind, 5.02.107
sweet york, be patient. hear me, gentle liege. 5.03. 91
the word is short, but not so short as sweet, 5.03.117
how sour sweet music is | when time is broke, 5.05. 42
who is sweet fortune's minion and her pride, 1H4 1.01. 83
and i prithee, sweet wag, when thou art a king, 1.02. 16 P
marry then, sweet wag, when thou art king, let 1.02. 23 P
not my hostess of the tavern a most sweet wench? 1.02. 40 P
not a buff jerkin a most sweet robe of durance? 1.02. 42 P
but i prithee, sweet wag, shall there be gallows 1.02. 59 P
comparative, rascalliest, sweet young prince. 1.02. 80 P
good morrow, sweet hal. 1.02.112 P
now, my good sweet honey lord, ride with us 1.02.160 P
to see him shine so brisk and smell so sweet, 1.03. 54
to put down richard, that sweet lovely rose, 1.03.175
tell me, sweet lord, what is't that takes from 2.03. 40
but, sweet ned — to sweeten which name of ned, 2.04. 21 P
"o my sweet harry," says she, "how many hast 2.04.105 P
that melted at the sweet tale of the sun's? 2.04.121 P
how now, my sweet creature of bumbast, how long 2.04.326 P
weep not, sweet queen, for trickling tears are 2.04.391
banish poins, but for sweet jack falstaff, kind 2.04.475 P
makes welsh as sweet as ditties highly penn'd, 3.01.206
o, my sweet beef, i must still be good angel to 3.03.177 P
should, | where now remains a sweet reversion, 4.01. 53
day, | england did never owe so sweet a hope, 5.02. 67
and i will take it as a sweet disgrace | and 2H4 1.01. 89
sweet earl, divorce not wisdom from your honor, 1.01.162
yea, i thank your pretty sweet wit for it. 1.02.206 P
alas, sweet wife, my honor is at pawn, | and, 2.03. 7
i' faith, sweet heart, methinks now you are in 2.04. 22 P
good captain pistol, not here, sweet captain. 2.04.138 P
me some sack, and, sweet heart, lie thou there. 2.04.183
sweet knight, i kiss thy neaf. 2.04.186 P
ah, you sweet little rogue, you! 2.04.216 P
now, the lord bless that sweet face of thine! 2.04.293 P
well, sweet jack, have a care of thyself. 2.04.380 P
sweet prince, speak low, | the king your father 4.05. 16
yet not so sound, and half so deeply sweet, | as 4.05. 26
sweet princes, what i did, i did in honor, | led 5.02. 35
sweet sir, sit, i'll be with you anon, most 5.03. 26 P
sit, i'll be with you anon, most sweet sir, sit. 5.03. 27 P
be merry, now comes in the sweet a' th' night. 5.03. 51 P
sweet knight, thou art now one of the greatest 5.03. 87 P
o sweet pistol! 5.03.132 P
god save thee, my sweet boy! 5.05. 43
ears | to steal his sweet and honeyed sentences; H5 1.01. 50
sweet men, come to him. 2.01.120 P
under the sweet shade of your government. 2.02. 28
use lenity, sweet chuck! 3.02. 25
with cheerful semblance and sweet majesty; 4.pr. 40
drink'st thou oft, in stead of homage sweet, 4.01.250
may make a peaceful and a sweet retire | from 4.03. 86
tarry, sweet soul, for mine, then fly abreast, 4.06. 17
the pretty and sweet manner of it forc'd | those 4.06. 28
christian–like accord | in their sweet bosoms, 5.02.354
with sweet enlargement doth dismiss me hence. 1H6 2.05. 30
now declare, sweet stem from york's great stock, 2.05. 41
sweet king! 3.01.131
for, sweet prince, | and if your grace mark 3.01.151
employ thee then, sweet virgin, for our good. 3.03. 16
forgive me, country, and sweet countrymen, | and 3.03. 81
and this is mine, sweet henry, favor him. 4.01. 81
i dare presume, sweet prince, he thought no harm 4.01.179
thy life to me is sweet. 4.06. 55
sweet madam, give me hearing in a cause. 5.03.106
thanks, reignier, happy for so sweet a child, 5.03.148
farewell, sweet madam! 5.03.175
joan, sweet daughter joan, i'll die with thee! 5.04. 6
with whose sweet smell the air shall be perfum'd 2H6 1.01.255
o nell, sweet nell, if thou dost love thy lord, 1.02. 17
it | with sweet rehearsal of my morning's dream. 1.02. 24
but list to me, my humphrey, my sweet duke: 1.02. 35
sweet aunt, be quiet, 'twas against her will. 1.03.143
sweet york, begin; 2.02. 7
sweet nell, ill can thy noble mind abrook | the 2.04. 10
sweet somerset, be still. 3.01.304
enough, sweet suffolk, thou torment'st thyself, 3.02.329
thy body, | and then it liv'd in sweet elysium. 3.02.399
to france, sweet suffolk! 3.02.405
and bandetto slave | murder'd sweet tully; 4.01.136
sweet is the country, because full of riches, 4.07. 62
assist me then, sweet warwick, and i will, | for 3H6 1.01. 28
sweet father, do so, set it on your head. 1.01.115
pardon me, margaret, pardon me, sweet son, | the 1.01.228
think | how sweet a thing it is to wear a crown, 1.02. 29
sweet clifford, hear me speak before i die: 1.03. 18
sweet clifford, pity me! 1.03. 36
these tears are my sweet rutland's obsequies, 1.04.147
cloth thou dipp'dst in blood of my sweet boy, 1.04.157
in the harmless blood | of sweet young rutland, 2.01. 63

sweet duke of york, our prop to lean upon, | now 2.01. 68
ope | and give sweet passage to my sinful soul! 2.03. 41
away, away! once more, sweet lords, farewell. 2.03. 48
how sweet! 2.05. 41
my heart, sweet boy, shall be thy sepulchre, 2.05.115
nay, take me with thee, good sweet exeter; 2.05.137
even as thou wilt, sweet warwick, let it be; 2.06. 99
sweet widow, by my state i swear to thee | i 3.02. 93
and witch sweet ladies with my words and looks. 3.02.150
but welcome, sweet clarence, my daughter shall 4.02. 12
sweet oxford, and my loving montague, | and all 4.08. 30
farewell, sweet lords, let's meet at coventry. 4.08. 32
if thou be there, sweet brother, take my hand, 5.02. 34
sweet rest his soul! 5.02. 48
thanks, gentle somerset, sweet oxford, thanks. 5.04. 58
world, | to meet with joy in sweet jerusalem. 5.05. 8
o ned, sweet ned, speak to thy mother, boy! 5.05. 51
how sweet a plant have you untimely cropp'd! 5.05. 62
deathsmen, you have rid this sweet young prince! 5.05. 67
sweet clarence, do thou do it. 5.05. 73
and i, the hapless male to one sweet bird, 5.06. 15
the sun that sear'd the wings of my sweet boy, 5.06. 23
i seal upon the lips of this sweet babe. 5.07. 29
sweet saint, for charity, be not so curst. R3 1.02. 49
so i might live one hour in your sweet bosom. 1.02.124
never came poison from so sweet a place. 1.02.146
thine eyes, sweet lady, have infected mine. 1.02.149
tongue could never learn sweet smoothing word; 1.02.168
cropp'd the golden prime of this sweet prince 1.02.247
because sweet flow'rs are slow and weeds make 2.04. 15
welcome, sweet prince, to london, to your 3.01. 1
sweet prince, the untainted virtue of your years 3.01. 7
thence, | so sweet is zealous contemplation. 3.07. 94
call him again, sweet prince, accept their suit. 3.07.221
foes to my rest and my sweet sleep's disturbers, 4.02. 73
thou sing'st sweet music. 4.02. 78
the most replenished sweet work of nature | that 4.03. 18
when holy harry died, and my sweet son. 4.04. 25
my damned son that thy two sweet sons smother'd. 4.04.134
the purple sap from her sweet brother's body, 4.04.277
with the sweet silent hours of marriage joys; 4.04.330
but how long fairly shall her sweet life last? 4.04.352
sweet blunt, make some good means to speak with 5.03. 40
and ample interchange of sweet discourse | which 5.03. 99
life, | they are a sweet society of fair ones. H8 1.04. 14
sweet ladies, will it please you sit? 1.04. 19
by your leave, sweet ladies. 1.04. 25
sweet heart, | i were unmannerly to take you out 1.04. 94
sweet partner, | i must not yet forsake you. 1.04.103
me, | make of your prayers one sweet sacrifice, 2.01. 77
an able man to leave | so sweet a bedfellow? 2.02.142
bitter than | 'tis sweet at first t' acquire — 2.03. 9
(if thy rare qualities, sweet gentleness, | thy 2.04.138
in sweet music is such art, | killing care and 3.01. 12
that sweet aspect of princes, and their ruin, 3.02.369
to those men that sought him, sweet as summer. 4.02. 54
and, sweet lady, does | deserve our better 5.01. 25
sweet pandarus — TRO 1.01. 86
good niece, do, sweet niece cressida. 1.02.179 P
knew | love got so sweet as when desire did sue. 1.02.291
like one besotted on your sweet delights. 2.02.143
the heavens, lord, thou art of sweet composure. 2.03.240
you speak your fair pleasure, sweet queen. 3.01. 48 P
well, sweet queen, you are pleasant with me. 3.01. 62 P
go to, sweet queen, go to — commends himself 3.01. 66 P
sweet queen, sweet queen, that's a sweet queen 3.01. 70 P
sweet queen, sweet queen, that's a sweet queen 3.01. 70 P
sweet queen, that's a sweet queen — i' faith — 3.01. 70 P
and to make a sweet lady sad is a sour offense. 3.01. 72 P
what says my sweet queen, my very very sweet 3.01. 79 P
says my sweet queen, my very very sweet queen? 3.01. 80 P
what says my sweet queen? 3.01. 84 P
now, sweet queen. 3.01. 95 P
in love with a thing you have, sweet queen. 3.01. 98 P
by my troth, sweet /lord, thou hast a fine 3.01.107 P
sweet lord, who's a–field to–day? 3.01.133 P
farewell, sweet queen. 3.01.145 P
i will, sweet queen. 3.01.147 P
sweet helen, i must woo you | to help unarm our 3.01.149
sweet, above thought i love /thee! 3.01.159
th' imaginary relish is so sweet | that it 3.02. 19
build there, carpenter, the air is sweet. 3.02. 51 P
dreg espies my sweet lady in the fountain of our 3.02. 66 P
sweet, bid me hold my tongue, | for in this 3.02.129
and shall, albeit sweet music issues thence. 3.02.134
your leave, sweet cressid! 3.02.140
sweet, rouse yourself, and the weak wanton cupid 3.03.222
go call thersites hither, sweet patroclus. 3.03.234
then, sweet my lord, i'll call mine uncle down, 4.02. 2
tell me, sweet uncle, what's the matter? 4.02. 81 P
no soul so near me | as the sweet troilus. 4.02. 99
here, here, here he comes. /ah, sweet ducks! 4.04. 11 P
most dearly welcome to the greeks, sweet lady. 4.05. 18
may i, sweet lady, beg a kiss of you? 4.05. 47
shall i, sweet lord, be bound to you so much, 4.05.284
but still sweet love is food for fortune's tooth 4.05.293
my sweet patroclus, i am thwarted quite | from 5.01. 37
good night, sweet lord menelaus. 5.01. 74
sweet draught! 5.01. 75 P
"sweet," quoth 'a! 5.01. 75 P
sweet sink, sweet sewer. 5.01. 75 P
sweet sink, sweet sewer. 5.01. 76 P
sweet sir, you honor me. 5.01. 86
now, my sweet guardian! hark, a word with you. 5.02. 7
sweet honey greek, tempt me no more to folly. 5.02. 18
bid me do any thing but that, sweet greek. 5.02. 27
notes of sally, for the heavens, sweet brother. 5.03. 14
unarm, sweet hector. 5.03. 25
sweet honey and sweet notes together fail. 5.10. 44
sweet honey and sweet notes together fail. 5.10. 44
sweet madam. COR 1.03. 49 P
come, good sweet lady. 1.03.107 P
and live you yet? o my sweet lady, pardon. 2.01.180
most sweet voices! 2.03.112
voices, thank you, | your most sweet voices. 2.03.172
them not lick | the sweet which is their poison. 3.01.157
i prithee now, sweet son, as thou hast said | my 3.02.107
come, my sweet wife, my dearest mother, and | my 4.01. 48
a kiss | long as my exile, sweet as my revenge! 5.03. 45
of my joys, | sweet cell of virtue and nobility, TIT 1.01. 93
sweet mercy is nobility's true badge. 1.01.119
thanks, sweet lavinia. 1.01.273
there lie thy bones, sweet mutius, with thy 1.01.387
and at my suit, sweet, pardon what is past. 1.01.431
come, come, sweet emperor — come, andronicus — 1.01.456
nay, nay, sweet emperor, we must all be friends. 1.01.479
sweet heart, look back. 1.01.481
and so repose, sweet gold, for their unrest, 2.03. 8
under their sweet shade, aaron, let us sit, 2.03. 16
hounds and horns and sweet melodious birds | be 2.03. 27
ah, my sweet moor, sweeter to me than life! 2.03. 51
sweet lords, entreat her hear me but a word. 2.03.138
so should i rob my sweet sons of their fee. 2.03.179
sweet huntsman — bassianus 'tis we mean — | do 2.03.269
go home, call for sweet water, wash thy hands. 2.04. 6
those sweet ornaments | whose circling shadows 2.04. 18
harmony | which that sweet tongue hath made, 2.04. 49
my sons' sweet blood will make it shame and 3.01. 15
where like a sweet melodious bird it sung 3.01. 85
melodious bird it sung | sweet varied notes, 3.01. 86
sweet father, cease your tears, for at your 3.01.136
that gives sweet tidings of the sun's uprise? 3.01.159
sweet father, if i shall be thought thy son, 3.01.179
bear thou my hand, sweet wench, between thy 3.01.282
alas, sweet aunt, i know not what you mean. 4.01. 4
read to thee | sweet poetry and tully's orator. 4.01. 14
but pardon me, sweet aunt, | and, madam, if my 4.01. 26
lavinia, wert thou thus surpris'd, sweet girl? 4.01. 51
give signs, sweet girl, for here are none but 4.01. 61
sit down, sweet niece; 4.01. 65
and kneel, sweet boy, the roman hector's hope, 4.01. 88
sweet blowse, you are a beauteous blossom sure. 4.02. 72
sweet scrolls to fly about the streets of rome! 4.04. 16
the old andronicus | with words more sweet, and 4.04. 90
and now, sweet emperor, be blithe again, | and 4.04.111
not die | so sweet a death as hanging presently. 5.01.146
o sweet revenge, now do i come to thee, | and, 5.02. 67
i know thou dost, and, sweet revenge, farewell. 5.02.148
both her sweet hands, her tongue, and that more 5.02.175
o now, sweet boy, give them their latest kiss! 5.03.169
ere he can spread his sweet leaves to the air ROM 1.01.152
a choking gall, and a preserving sweet. 1.01.194
now seeming sweet, convert to bitt'rest gall. 1.05. 92
and she steal love's sweet bait from fearful 2.pr. 8
temp'ring extremities with extreme sweet. 2.pr. 14
a rose | by any other word would smell as sweet; 2.02. 44
look thou but sweet, | and i am proof against 2.02. 72
sweet, good night! 2.02.120
as sweet repose and rest | come to thy heart as 2.02.123
sweet montague, be true. 2.02.137
sweet, so would i, | yet i should kill thee with 2.02.182
parting is such sweet sorrow, | that i shall say 2.02.184
would i were sleep and peace, so sweet to rest! 2.02.187
what early tongue so sweet saluteth me? 2.03. 32
is it not then well serv'd in to a sweet goose? 2.04. 81 P
my words would bandy her to my sweet love, | and 2.05. 14
now, good sweet nurse — o lord, why lookest 2.05. 21
good, thou shamest the music of sweet news | by 2.05. 23
sweet, sweet, sweet nurse, tell me, what says my 2.05. 54
sweet, sweet, sweet nurse, tell me, what says my 2.05. 54
sweet, sweet, sweet nurse, tell me, what says my 2.05. 54
o sweet juliet, | thy beauty hath made me 3.01.113
fiend | in mortal paradise of such sweet flesh? 3.02. 82
adversity's sweet milk, philosophy, | to comfort 3.03. 55
do so, and bid my sweet prepare to chide. 3.03.162
some say the lark makes sweet division; 3.05. 29
for sweet discourses in our times to come. 3.05. 53
o sweet my mother, cast me not away! 3.05.198
to live an unstain'd wife to my sweet love. 4.01. 88
sweet heart! 4.05. 3
marry, sir, because silver hath a sweet sound. 4.05.131 P
ah me, how sweet is love itself possess'd, 5.01. 10
sweet flower, with flowers thy bridal bed i 5.03. 12
which with sweet water nightly i will dew, | or, 5.03. 14
be small love amongest these sweet knaves, | and TIM 1.01.249
would most resemble sweet instruments hung up in 1.02. 98 P
pardon him, sweet timandra, for his wits | are 4.03. 89
the sweet degrees that this brief world affords 4.03.253
o thou sweet king–killer, and dear divorce 4.03.381
that which melteth fools — i mean sweet words, JC 3.01. 42
good friends, sweet friends, let me not stir you 3.02.210
show you sweet caesar's wounds, poor, poor, dumb 3.02.225
sweet remembrancer! MAC 3.04. 36
sweet bodements! 4.01. 96
pour the sweet milk of concord into hell, 4.03. 98
and with some sweet oblivious antidote | cleanse 5.03. 43
'tis sweet and commendable in your nature, HAM 1.02. 87
forward, not permanent, sweet, not lasting, 1.03. 8
it an honest method, as wholesome as sweet, and 2.02.444 P
sweet gertrude, leave us two, | for we have 3.01. 28
words of so sweet breath compos'd | as made 3.01. 97
o, help him, you sweet heavens! 3.01.133 P
like sweet bells jangled, out of time and harsh; 3.01.158
here, sweet lord, at your service. 3.02. 53
sweet, leave me here a while, | my spirits grow 3.02.225
is there not rain enough in the sweet heavens 3.03. 45
and sweet religion makes | a rhapsody of words. 3.04. 47
no more, sweet hamlet! 3.04. 96
o, 'tis most sweet | when in one line two crafts 3.04.209
alas, sweet lady, what imports this song? 4.05. 27
"larded all with sweet flowers, | which bewept 4.05. 38
sweet ladies, good night, good night. 4.05. 72 P
dear maid, kind sister, sweet ophelia! 4.05.159
end — "for bonny sweet robin is all my joy." 4.05.187
love, did love, | methought it was very sweet, 5.01. 62
which could say, "good morrow, sweet lord! 5.01. 83 P
how dost thou, sweet lord?" 5.01. 83 P
sweets to the sweet, farewell! 5.01.243
thy bride–bed to have deck'd, sweet maid, | and 5.01.245
sweet lord, if your lordship were at leisure, i 5.02. 89 P
good night, sweet prince, | and flights of 5.02.359
my boy, between a bitter fool and a sweet one? LR 1.04.138 P
o, let me not be mad, not mad, sweet heaven! 1.05. 46
old men, if your sweet sway | allow obedience, 2.04.190
spouse, set not thy sweet heart on proud array. 3.04. 82 P
and broke them in the sweet face of heaven: 3.04. 89 P
farewell, sweet lord, and sister. 3.07. 21
bless thy sweet eyes, they bleed. 4.01. 54
sweet marjorum. 4.06. 93 P
now, sweet lord, | you know the goodness i 5.01. 6
amen to that, sweet powers! OTH 2.01.195
o my sweet, | i prattle out of fashion, and i 2.01.205
o sweet england! 2.03. 88 P
not now, sweet desdemon, some other time. 3.03. 55
the sooner, sweet, for you. 3.03. 56
shall ever medicine thee to that sweet sleep 3.03.332
pioners and all, had tasted her sweet body, | so 3.03.346
in sleep i heard him say, "sweet desdemona, 3.03.419
cry, "o sweet creature!" 3.03.422
indeed, sweet love, i was coming to your house. 3.04.171
sweet bianca, | take me this work out. 3.04.179
how now, my sweet bianca? how now? how now? 4.01.156 P
a sweet woman! 4.01.179 P
why, sweet othello? 4.01.239
who art so lovely fair and smell'st so sweet 4.02. 68
he that is yours, sweet lady. 4.02.101
and have their palates both for sweet and sour, 4.03. 95
o my dear cassio, my sweet cassio! 5.01. 76
so sweet was ne'er so fatal. 5.02. 20
sweet soul, take heed, | take heed of perjury, 5.02. 50
out of tune, | and sweet revenge grows harsh. 5.02.116
sweet desdemona, o sweet mistress, speak! 5.02.121
sweet desdemona, o sweet mistress, speak! 5.02.121
lord alexas, sweet alexas, most any thing alexas ANT 1.02. 1 P
him marry a woman that cannot go, sweet isis, i 1.02. 64 P
most sweet queen — 1.03. 31
no, sweet octavia, | you shall hear from me 3.02. 59
you have heard on't, sweet? 3.07. 23
one word, sweet queen: 4.15. 45
let me report to him | your sweet dependancy, 5.02. 26
as sweet as balm, as soft as air, as gentle — 5.02.311
sweet sovereign, | leave us to ourselves, and CYM 1.01.154
quite unpeople her | of liegers for her sweet; 1.05. 80
i dedicate myself to your sweet pleasure, | more 1.06.136
after, a wonderful sweet air, with admirable 2.03. 18 P
with every thing that pretty is, my lady sweet, 2.03. 25
good morrow, fairest: sister, your sweet hand. 2.03. 86
a second night of such sweet shortness which 2.04. 44
a pudency so rosy the sweet view on't | might 2.05. 11
the dish, | poor tributary rivers as sweet fish. 4.02. 36
below the violet, | not wagging his sweet head; 4.02.173
him in fresh cups, soft beds, | sweet words; 5.03. 72
cast | from her his dearest one, | sweet imogen? 5.04. 62
ascension is | more sweet than our blest fields. 5.04.117
not more resembles that sweet rosy lad | who 5.05.121
therefore to make his entrance more sweet, PER 2.03. 64
to you | for your sweet music this last night. 2.05. 26
o your sweet queen! 3.03. 7
i'll leave you, my sweet lady, for a while. 4.01. 47
my thanks, sweet madam. 4.01. 49
she questionless with her sweet harmony, | and 5.01. 45
to his bones sweet sleep! TNK pr 29
yet most quaint, | and sweet thyme true; 1.01. 6
all dear nature's children sweet, | lie 'fore 1.01. 13
sweet, keep it as my token. 1.01.217
presently gives it so sweet a rebuke that i 2.01. 43 P
the sweet embraces of a loving wife, | loaden 2.02. 30
and, sweet companions, let's rehearse by any 2.03. 56
sweet, you must be ready — | and you, emilia — 2.05. 48
sweet palamon — 3.01. 92
but if it did, yours is too tart, sweet cousin. 3.03. 26
all hail, sweet ladies! 3.05.100
take twenty, domine. — how does my sweet heart? 3.05.148
i'll give you cause, sweet cousin. 3.06. 69
you love most — wars, and this sweet lady — 3.06.203
or the sweet compassion | of those two ladies; 4.01. 11
"o fair, o sweet," etc. 4.01.114
good heaven, | what a sweet face has arcite! 4.02. 7
ask me now, sweet sister — | i may go look! 4.02. 51
the same, my lord. | are they not sweet ones? 4.02.121
her, stuck in as sweet flowers as the season is 4.03. 83 P
for palamon can sing, and palamon is sweet, and 4.03. 87 P
o, then, most soft sweet goddess, | give me the 5.01.126
sweet, solitary, white as chaste, and pure | as 5.01.139
'tis a sweet one, | and will perfume me finely 5.02. 88
yes, sweet heart, | and i am glad my cousin 5.02. 90
come, sweet, we'll go to dinner, | and then 5.02.107
i will not, sweet. 5.02.112
ear | that are most /dearly sweet and bitter. 5.04. 47
"the field's chief flower, sweet above compare, VEN 8
and one sweet kiss shall pay this comptless debt 84
is love so light, sweet boy, and may it be 155
sweet bottom grass and high delightful plain, 236
for one sweet look thy help i would assure thee, 371
welcomes the warm approach of sweet desire; 386
ears' deep sweet music, and heart's deep sore 432
lips, sweet seals in my soft lips imprinted, 511
her arms do lend his neck a sweet embrace; 539
the heavenly moisture, that sweet coral mouth, 542
"sweet boy," she says, "this night i'll waste in 583
been gone," quoth she, "sweet boy, ere this, 613
nor thy soft hands, sweet lips, and crystal eyne 633
with this he breaketh from the sweet embrace 811
in the sweet channel of her bosom dropp'd; 958
no," quoth she, "sweet death, i did but jest, 997
the flowers are sweet, their colors fresh and 1079
but true sweet beauty liv'd and died with him. 1080
find sweet beginning, but unsavory end; 1138
sweet issue of a more sweet–smelling sire — 1178
wherein i will not kiss my sweet love's flow'r." 1188
for one sweet grape who will the vine destroy? LUC 215
whereat she smiled with so sweet a cheer | that 264
covers the shame that follows sweet delight." 357
to make the breach and enter this sweet city. 469
knighthood, gentry, and sweet friendship's oath, 569
entombs her outcry in her lips' sweet fold. 679
my brow, | the story of sweet chastity's decay, 808
the adder hisses where the sweet birds sing, 871
make her moans mad with their sweet melody, 1108
conclusion | who, having two sweet babes, when 1161
such sweet observance in this work was had, 1385
and drop sweet balm in priam's painted wound, 1466
sweet love, what spite hath thy fair color spent 1600
in thy sweet semblance my old age new born, 1759

then live, sweet lucrece, live again and see 1770
sweet cytherea, sitting by a brook | with young PP 4. 1
not to anger bent, is music and sweet fire. 5.12
if music and sweet poetry agree, | as they must 8. 1
thou lov'st to hear the sweet melodious sound 8. 9
"did i see a fair sweet youth | here in these 9. 9
sweet rose, fair flower, untimely pluck'd, soon 10. 1
o, sweet shepherd, hie thee, | for methinks thou 12.11
youth unmeet, | youth, so apt to pluck a sweet. 16.14
clear wells spring not, sweet birds sing not, 17.25
farewell, sweet /lass, thy like ne'er was | for 17.33
thy like ne'er was | for a sweet content, the 17.34
thyself thy foe, to thy sweet self too cruel. SON 1. 8
thou of thyself thy sweet self dost deceive, 4.10
their show, their substance still lives sweet. 5.14
make sweet some vial; 6. 3
mark how one string, sweet husband to another, 8. 9
and your sweet semblance to some other give. 13. 4
when your sweet issue your sweet form should 13. 8
your sweet issue your sweet form should bear. 13. 8
and you must live drawn by your own sweet skill. 16.14
and make the earth devour her own sweet brood; 19. 2
to show me worthy of /thy sweet respect: 26.12
for thy sweet love rememb'red such wealth brings 29.13
when to the sessions of sweet silent thought | i 30. 1
to that sweet thief which sourly robs from me. 35.14
yet doth it steal sweet hours from love's 36. 8
into my verse | thine own sweet argument, too 38. 3
were it not thy sour leisure gave sweet leave 39.10
sweet flattery! 42.14
can bring him to his sweet up-locked treasure, 52. 2
by that sweet ornament which truth doth give! 54. 2
for that sweet odor which doth in it live. 54. 4
sweet roses do not so, | of their sweet deaths 54.11
of their sweet deaths are sweetest odors made: 54.12
sweet love, renew thy force, be it not said 56. 1
never cut from memory | my sweet love's beauty, 63.12
that i in your sweet thoughts would be forgot, 71. 7
/ruin'd choirs, where late the sweet birds sang. 73. 4
o, know, sweet love, i always write of you, 76. 9
and arts with thy sweet graces graced be; 78.12
i grant, sweet love, thy lovely argument 79. 5
thy sweet beloved name no more shall dwell, 89.10
that in thy face sweet love should ever dwell; 93.10
grow, | if thy sweet virtue answer not thy show! 93.14
the summer's flow'r is to the summer sweet, 94. 9
how sweet and lovely dost thou make the shame 95. 1
nor the sweet smell | of different flowers in 98. 5
they were but sweet, but figures of delight, 98.11
sweet thief, whence didst thou steal thy sweet 99. 2
whence didst thou steal thy sweet that smells, 99. 2
but sweet or color it had stol'n from thee. 99.15
rise, resty muse, my love's sweet face survey, 100. 9
so your sweet hue, which methinks still doth 104.11
then, in the blazon of sweet beauty's best, | of 106. 5
nothing, sweet boy, but yet, like prayers divine 108. 5
the most sweet favor or deformed'st creature, 113.10
such cherubins as your sweet self resemble, 114. 6
for compound sweet forgoing simple savor, 125. 7
thy lovers withering as thy sweet self grow'st; 126. 4
sweet beauty hath no name, no holy bow'r, | but 127. 7
with thy sweet fingers when thou gently sway'st 128. 3
still, | to thy sweet will making addition thus. 135. 4
thus far for love my love-suit, sweet, fulfill. 136. 4
that nothing me, a something, sweet, to thee. 136.12
come, | chiding that tongue that, ever sweet, 145. 6
lest guilty of my faults thy sweet self prove: 151. 4
what's sweet to do, to do will aptly find: LC 88
when winds breathe sweet, unruly though they be. 103
"'but, o my sweet, what labor is't to leave 239
lending soft audience to my sweet design, | and 278

SWEET-COMPLAINING 1 FR 0.0001 REL FR 1 V 0 P
well become such sweet-complaining grievance. TGV 3.02. 85

SWEETEN 8 FR 0.0009 REL FR 6 V 2 P
there's not a grain of it the face to sweeten WT 2.01.156
sweet ned — to sweeten which name of ned, i 1H4 2.04. 22 P
sweeten the bitter mock you sent his majesty, H5 2.04.122
nor heel the high lavolt, nor sweeten talk, TRO 4.04. 86
then sweeten with thy breath | this neighbor air ROM 2.06. 26
of arabia will not sweeten this little hand. MAC 5.01. 51 P
good apothecary, | sweeten my imagination. LR 4.06.131
live here, fidele, | i'll sweeten thy sad grave. CYM 4.02.220

SWEETENS 1 FR 0.0001 REL FR 1 V 0 P
and sweetens, in the suff'ring pangs it bears, LC 272

SWEETER 19 FR 0.0021 REL FR 17 V 2 P
enemy, | aiming at silvia as a sweeter friend. TGV 2.06. 30
death or life | shall thereby be the sweeter. MM 3.01. 6
sweet clown, sweeter fool, sweetest lady! LLL 4.03. 17 P
methinks it sounds much sweeter than by day. MV 5.01.100
softer and sweeter than the lustful bed | on SHR in.2. 38
for she is sweeter than perfume itself | to whom 1.02.152
as hazel-nuts, and sweeter than the kernels. 2.01.255
but sweeter than the lids of juno's eyes | or WT 4.04.121
gives not the hawthorn bush a sweeter shade | to 3H6 2.05. 42
a sweeter and a lovelier gentleman, | fram'd in R3 1.02.242
that thy babes were sweeter than they were, 4.04.120
ah, my sweet moor, sweeter to me than life! TIT 2.03. 51
that last is true — the sweeter rest was mine. ROM 2.03. 43
to make society | the sweeter welcome, we will MAC 3.01. 42
o, the world hath not a sweeter creature! OTH 4.01.184 P
sweeter to you | that have a sharper known; CYM 3.03. 30
sweeter | than her gold buttons on the boughs, TNK 3.01. 5
like the great-ey'd juno's, but far sweeter, 4.02. 20
knight he spoke of, | but of a face far sweeter; 4.02. 95

SWEETEST 27 FR 0.0030 REL FR 23 V 4 P
as in the sweetest bud | the eating canker TGV 1.01. 42
in mine eye she is the sweetest lady that ever i ADO 1.01.187 P
sweet clown, sweeter fool, sweetest lady! LLL 4.03. 17 P
for as a surfeit of the sweetest things | the MND 2.02.137
with sweetest touches pierce your mistress' ear, MV 5.01. 67
sweetest nut hath sourest rind, | such a nut is AYL 3.02.109
he that sweetest rose will find, | must find 3.02.111
as the last taste of sweets, is sweetest last, R2 2.01. 13
now comes in the sweetest morsel of the night, 2H4 2.04.367 P
and lull'd with sound of sweetest melody? 3.01. 14
their sweetest shade a grove of cypress trees! 2H6 3.02.323
the sweetest sleep and fairest-boding dreams R3 5.03.227
thou hast the sweetest face i ever look'd on. H8 4.01. 43
sir, my mistress is the sweetest lady — lord, ROM 2.04.199 P
the sweetest honey | is loathsome in his own 2.06. 11
upon the sweetest flower of all the field. 4.05. 29
for thou hast kill'd the sweetest innocent OTH 5.02.199
you the sourest points with sweetest terms, ANT 2.02. 24
and, sweetest, fairest, | as i my poor self did CYM 1.01.118
o sweetest, fairest lily! 4.02.201
who though they feed | on sweetest flowers, yet PER 1.01.133
"the fairest, sweetest, and best lies here, 4.04. 34
and loathsome canker lives in sweetest bud. SON 35. 4
of their sweet deaths are sweetest odors made: 54.12
a crow that flies in heaven's sweetest air. 70. 4
for canker vice the sweetest buds doth love, 70. 7
for sweetest things turn sourest by their deeds; 94.13

SWEET-FAC'D 2 FR 0.0002 REL FR 1 V 1 P
i see by you i am a sweet-fac'd youth. ERR 5.01.419
for pyramus is a sweet-fac'd man; MND 1.02. 86 P

SWEETHEART 2 FR 0.0002 REL FR 1 V 1 P
wherefore, sweetheart? what's your metaphor? TN 1.03. 71 P
trey, blanch, and sweetheart, see, they bark at LR 3.06. 63

SWEETHEART'S 1 FR 0.0001 REL FR 1 V 0 P
take your sweetheart's hat | and pluck it o'er WT 4.04.650

SWEETING 5 FR 0.0005 REL FR 4 V 1 P
how fares my kate? what, sweeting, all amort? SHR 4.03. 36
trip no further, pretty sweeting; TN 2.03. 42
ay, marry, sweeting, if we could do that, 1H6 3.03. 21
thy wit is a very bitter sweeting, it is a most ROM 2.04. 79 P
all's well /now, sweeting; OTH 2.03.252

SWEETLY 35 FR 0.0039 REL FR 31 V 4 P
the air breathes upon us here most sweetly. TMP 2.01. 47 P
smelling so sweetly, all musk, and so rushling, WIV 2.02. 66 P
lips away, | that so sweetly were forsworn, MM 4.01. 2
how sweetly you do minister to love, | that know ADO 1.01.312
so you walk softly, and look sweetly, and say 2.01. 88 P
th' idea of her life shall sweetly creep | into 4.01.224
when tongues speak sweetly, then they name her LLL 3.01.166
and how most sweetly 'a will swear! 4.01.146
holofernes, the epithites are sweetly varied, 4.02. 9 P
the crow doth sing as sweetly as the lark | when MV 5.01.102
since my conversion | so sweetly tastes, being AYL 4.03.137
plain | she sings as sweetly as a nightingale; SHR 2.01.171
but riddle-like lives sweetly where she dies! AWW 1.03.217
speak sweetly, man, although thy looks be sour. R2 3.02.193
that erst brought sweetly forth | the freckled H5 5.02. 48
words sweetly plac'd and /modestly directed. 1H6 5.03.179
shade, | all which secure and sweetly he enjoys, 3H6 2.05. 50
whence that tender spray did sweetly spring, | i 2.06. 50
sweetly in force unto her fair live's end. R3 4.04.351
and sweetly | in all the rest show'd a most H8 2.01. 35
o trespass sweetly urg'd! ROM 1.05.109
show'r of your gifts, | and sweetly felt it. TIM 5.01. 71
to sound more sweetly in great caesar's ear JC 3.01. 50
the air | nimbly and sweetly recommends itself MAC 1.06. 2
it smells most sweetly in my sense. PER 3.02. 60
before the ladies see us, and do sweetly, | and TNK 2.03. 57
and sweetly, by a figure, trace and turn, boys. 3.05. 21
and sweetly we will do it, master gerrold. 3.05. 22
bodies, | and carry it sweetly and deliverly, 3.05. 29
th' one sweetly flatters, th' other feareth harm LUC 172
light, | and canopied in darkness sweetly lay, 398
yet at my parting sweetly did she smile, | in PP 14. 7
they do but sweetly chide thee, who confounds SON 8. 7
which time and thoughts so sweetly dost deceive, 39.12
sweetly suppos'd them mistress of his heart. LC 142

SWEETMEATS 2 FR 0.0002 REL FR 2 V 0 P
nosegays, sweetmeats — messengers | of strong MND 1.01. 34
their breath with sweetmeats tainted are. ROM 1.04. 76

SWEET'NED 1 FR 0.0001 REL FR 1 V 0 P
but theirs is sweet'ned with the hope to have R2 2.03. 13

SWEETNESS 13 FR 0.0014 REL FR 13 V 0 P
their saucy sweetness that do coin heaven's MM 2.04. 45
and began | to loathe the taste of sweetness, 1H4 3.02. 72
jealousy infected | the sweetness of affiance! H5 2.02.127
tun'd too sharp in sweetness | for the capacity TRO 3.02. 24
follow'd me so near (o, our lives' sweetness! LR 5.03.185
mortality, | and drown me with their sweetness. PER 5.01.194
her twinning cherries shall their sweetness fall TNK 1.01.178
feed | upon the sweetness of a noble beauty, 2.03. 11
of what a fiery sparkle and quick sweetness, 4.02. 13
that, having two fair gauds of equal sweetness, 4.02. 53
and having felt the sweetness of the spoil, VEN 553
looks should nothing thence but sweetness tell. SON 93.12
so, being full of your ne'er-cloying sweetness, 118. 5

/SWEETS 1 FR 0.0001 REL FR 1 V 0 P
from every flower | /the /virtuous /sweets, 2H4 4.05. 75

SWEETS 17 FR 0.0019 REL FR 17 V 0 P
there's half a dozen sweets. LLL 5.02.234
to suck the sweets of sweet philosophy. SHR 1.01. 28
want, and whose delay, is strew'd with sweets, AWW 2.04. 44
as the last taste of sweets, is sweetest last, R2 2.01. 13
nor with thy sweets comfort his ravenous sense, 3.02. 13
my /unblown flow'rs, new-appearing sweets! R3 4.04. 10
sweets to the sweet, farewell! HAM 5.01.243
melt their sweets | on blossoming caesar; ANT 4.12. 22
with sweets that shall the truest sight beguile; VEN 1144
the sweets we wish for turn to loathed sours LUC 867
sweets with sweets war not, joy delights in joy. SON 8. 2
sweets with sweets war not, joy delights in joy. 8. 2
since sweets and beauties do themselves forsake, 12.11
to the wide world and all her fading sweets: 19. 7
o, in what sweets dost thou thy sins enclose! 95. 4
and sweets grown common lose their dear delight. 102.12
to be forbod the sweets that seems so good | for LC 164

SWEET-SAVOR'D 1 FR 0.0001 REL FR 1 V 0 P
that never meat sweet-savor'd in thy taste, ERR 2.02.117

SWEET-SEASON'D 1 FR 0.0001 REL FR 1 V 0 P
or as sweet-season'd showers are to the ground; SON 75. 2

SWEET-SMELLING 1 FR 0.0001 REL FR 1 V 0 P
sweet issue of a more sweet-smelling sire — VEN 1178

SWEET'ST 4 FR 0.0004 REL FR 4 V 0 P
the sweet'st, dear'st creature's dead, and WT 3.02.201
destroy'd the sweet'st companion that e'er man 5.01. 11
two of the sweet'st companions in the world. CYM 5.05.349
but slave to slavery my sweet'st friend must be? SON 133. 4

SWEET-SUGGESTING 1 FR 0.0001 REL FR 1 V 0 P
o sweet-suggesting love, if thou hast sinn'd, TGV 2.06. 7

SWELL 21 FR 0.0023 REL FR 20 V 1 P
their understanding | begins to swell, and the TMP 5.01. 80
do but behold the tears that swell in me, | and LLL 4.03. 35
was wont to swell like round and orient pearls, MND 4.01. 54
where great additions swell 's, and virtue none, AWW 2.03.127
for 'tis polixenes | has made thee swell thus. WT 2.01. 62
or swell my thoughts to any strain of pride, 2H4 4.05.170
and swell so much the higher by their ebb. 3H6 4.08. 56
see | the water swell before a boist'rous storm. R3 2.03. 44
but to stubborn spirits | they swell and grow, H8 3.01.164
i took the blow — unless it swell past hiding, TRO 1.02.269 P
and, not to swell our spirit, | he shall be TIM 3.05.101
and i have seen | th' ambitious ocean swell, and JC 1.03. 7
why now blow wind, swell billow, and swim bark! 5.01. 67
or swell the curled waters 'bove the main, LR 3.01. 6
and swell his sail with thine own pow'rful OTH 2.01. 78
swell, bosom, with thy fraught, | for 'tis of 3.03.449
swell with the touches of those flower-soft ANT 2.02.210
that stands upon the swell at the full of tide, 3.02. 49
then but beginning | to swell about the blossom) TNK 1.03. 68
to the shoulder-piece | gently they swell, like 4.02.128
swell in their pride, the onset still expecting. LUC 432

SWELL'D 5 FR 0.0005 REL FR 4 V 1 P
should i have been when i had been swell'd! WIV 3.05. 17 P
as with the tide swell'd up unto his height, 2H4 2.03. 63
and cydnus swell'd above the banks, or for | the CYM 2.04. 71
which swell'd so much that it did almost stretch 3.01. 49
for beauty that made barren the swell'd boast 5.05.162

SWELLETH 1 FR 0.0001 REL FR 1 V 0 P
burneth more hotly, swelleth with more rage; VEN 332

SWELLING 25 FR 0.0028 REL FR 24 V 1 P
and in my heart the strong and swelling evil MM 2.04. 6
by something showing a more swelling port | than MV 1.01.124
is as rough | as are the swelling adriatic seas, SHR 1.02. 74
did never float upon the swelling tide | to do JN 2.01. 74
the unowed interest of proud swelling state. 4.03.147
the swelling difference of your settled hate. R2 1.01.201
thou pourest down from these swelling heavens 1H4 3.01.199
and monarchs to behold the swelling scene! H5 pr 4
why, here he comes, swelling like a turkey-cock. 5.01. 14 P
from envious malice of thy swelling heart. 1H6 3.01. 26
my mildness hath allay'd their swelling griefs, 3H6 4.08. 42
between these swelling wrong-incensed peers. R3 2.01. 52
/flowing and swelling o'er with arts and TRO 4.04. 78
ten thousand swelling toads, as many urchins, TIT 2.03.101
the venomous malice of my swelling heart! 5.03. 13
as happy prologues to the swelling act | of the MAC 1.03.128
noble swelling spirits | that hold their honors OTH 2.03. 55
poison, 'twould appear | by external swelling; ANT 5.02.346
hallowed clouds commend their swelling incense TNK 5.01. 4
and swelling passion doth provoke a pause. VEN 218
like a milch doe, whose swelling dugs do ache, 875
swelling on either side to want his bliss; LUC 389
within your hollow swelling feathered breasts, 1122
even so the maid with swelling drops gan wet 1228
the battle sought | with swelling ridges, and 1439

SWELLINGS 1 FR 0.0001 REL FR 0 V 1 P
no matter for his swellings nor his turkey-cocks H5 5.01. 16 P

/SWELLS 1 FR 0.0001 REL FR 1 V 0 P
/that /swells /with /silence /in /the /tortur'd R2 4.01.298

SWELLS 9 FR 0.0010 REL FR 8 V 1 P
for the water swells a man; WIV 3.05. 16 P
so high above his limits swells the rage | of R2 3.02.109
here lurks no treason, here no envy swells, TIT 1.01.153
the ocean swells not so as aaron storms. 4.02.139
thy verse swells with stuff so fine and smooth TIM 5.01. 84
comfort seem'd to come | discomfort swells. MAC 1.02. 28
o, how this mother swells up toward my heart! LR 2.04. 56
the higher nilus swells, | the more it promises; ANT 2.07. 20
turns not, but swells the higher by this let. LUC 646

SWELL'ST 1 FR 0.0001 REL FR 1 V 0 P
swell'st thou, proud heart? R2 3.03.140

SWELT'RED 1 FR 0.0001 REL FR 1 V 0 P
has thirty-one | swelt'red venom sleeping got, MAC 4.01. 8

SWENO 1 FR 0.0001 REL FR 1 V 0 P
that now | sweno, the norways' king, craves MAC 1.02. 59

SWEPT 2 FR 0.0002 REL FR 1 V 1 P
rushes strew'd, cobwebs swept, the servingmen in SHR 4.01. 47 P
thus have we swept suspicion from our seat, 3H6 5.07. 13

SWERVE 4 FR 0.0004 REL FR 3 V 1 P
that you swerve not from the smallest article of MM 4.02.103 P
i the fairest youth | that ever made eye swerve, WT 4.04.374
if i be false, or swerve a hair from truth, TRO 3.02.184
but, alas, i swerve. CYM 5.04.129

SWERVING 3 FR 0.0003 REL FR 3 V 0 P
constant in spirit, not swerving with the blood, H5 2.02.133
offended reputation, | a most unnoble swerving. ANT 3.11. 50
and so my patent back again is swerving. SON 87. 8

SWIFT 74 FR 0.0083 REL FR 70 V 4 P
but this swift business | i must uneasy make, TMP 1.02.451
and perfected by the swift course of time. TGV 1.03. 23
love, lend me wings to make my purpose swift, 2.06. 42
heaven, | intends you for his swift ambassador, MM 3.01. 57
make a swift return, | for i would commune with 4.03.103
maid, | it was the swift celerity of his death, 5.01.394
having so swift and excellent a wit | as she is ADO 3.01. 89
as swift as lead, sir. LLL 3.01. 57 P
you are too swift, sir, to say so. 3.01. 61
courses as swift as thought in every power, 4.03.327
swift as a shadow, short as any dream, | brief MND 1.01.144
for night's swift dragons cut the clouds full 3.02.379
my eyes, my lord, can look as swift as yours: MV 3.02.197
stood on th' extremest verge of the swift brook, AYL 2.01. 42
and why not the swift foot of time? 3.02.306 P
by my faith, he is very swift and sententious. 5.04. 62 P
thy greyhounds are as swift | as breathed stags; SHR in.2. 47
a good swift simile, but something currish. 5.02. 54
wishing clocks more swift? WT 1.02.289
good mind of camillo tardied | my swift command, 3.02.163
it not a crime | to me, or my swift passage, 4.01. 5
forewearied in this action of swift speed, JN 2.01.233
be swift like lightning in the execution, | and R2 1.03. 79
with all swift speed you must away to france. 5.01. 54
upon agreement, of swift severn's flood, | who 1H4 1.03.103
whose swift wrath beat down | the never-daunted 2H4 1.01.109
you, prince dolphin, with all swift dispatch, H5 2.04. 6
thus with imagin'd wing our swift scene flies 3.pr. 1
and teach lavoltas high and swift corantos, 3.05. 33
away, as swift as stones | enforced from the old 4.07. 61

so swift a pace hath thought that even now | you 5.pr. 15
another would fly swift, but wanteth wings; 1H6 1.01. 75
take all the swift advantage of the hours. R3 4.01. 48
true hope is swift and flies with swallow's 5.02. 23
in all swift haste. TRO 1.01.116
but his evasion, wing'd thus swift with scorn, 2.03.114
light boats sail swift, though greater hulks 2.03.266
and give me swift transportance to these fields 3.02. 11
that mouldeth goblins swift as frenzy's thoughts 5.10. 29
good uncle marcus, see how swift she comes. TIT 4.01. 3
now to the goths, as swift as swallow flies, 4.02.172
jet, | to hale thy vengeful waggon swift away, 5.02. 51
she would be as swift in motion as a ball; ROM 2.05. 13
too swift arrives as tardy as too slow. 2.06. 15
thou art swift | to enter in the thoughts of 5.01. 35
it requires swift foot. TIM 5.01.228
beauteous and swift, the minions of their race, MAC 2.04. 15
i wish your horses swift and sure of foot; 3.01. 37
the valued file | distinguishes the swift, the 3.01. 95
that a swift blessing | may soon return to this 3.06. 47
i, with wings as swift | as meditation or the HAM 1.05. 29
that swift as quicksilver it courses through 1.05. 66
our posts shall be swift and intelligent betwixt LR 3.07. 11 P
he, swift of foot, | outran my purpose; OTH 2.03.232
to furnish me with some swift means of death 3.03.478
reapers, people | ingross'd by swift impress. ANT 3.07. 36
if swift thought break it not, a swifter mean 4.06. 34
slow his soul sail'd on, | how swift his ship. CYM 1.03. 14
swift, swift, you dragons of the night, that 2.02. 48
swift, swift, you dragons of the night, that 2.02. 48
make swift the pangs | of my queen's travails! PER 3.01. 13
stand long, | and thy dogs be swift and strong! TNK 3.05.155
he finds 'em, | he's swift to hale 'em his. 4.02.134
by whose swift aid | their mistress mounted VEN 1190
with swift intent he goes | to quench the coal LUC 46
swift subtle post, carrier of grisly care, 926
and how swift and short | his time of folly and 991
whose swift obedience to her mistress hies; 1215
with swift pursuit to venge this wrong of mine, 1691
these present–absent with swift motion slide. SON 45. 4
by those swift messengers return'd from thee, 45.10
find, | when swift extremity can seem but slow? 51. 6
what strong hand can hold his swift foot back? 65.11
sets down her babe and makes all swift dispatch 143. 3

SWIFTER 14 FR 0.0015 REL FR 13 V 1 P
arrows, bullets, wind, thought, swifter things. LLL 5.02.261
every where, | swifter than the moon's sphere; MND 2.01. 7
about the wood go swifter than the wind, | and 3.02. 94
go, | swifter than arrow from the tartar's bow. 3.02.101
compass soon, | swifter than the wand'ring moon. 4.01. 98
the swifter speed the better. WT 4.04.669
with swifter spleen than powder can enforce, JN 2.01.448
that arrows fled not swifter toward their aim 2H4 1.01.123
come off and on swifter than he that gibbets on 3.02.263 P
that doth renew swifter than blood decays! TRO 3.02.163
it was which caus'd | our swifter composition. COR 3.01. 3
and, swifter than his tongue, | his /agile arm ROM 3.01.165
not, a swifter mean | shall outstrike thought, ANT 4.06. 34
run | swifter than wind upon a field of corn, TNK 2.03. 77

SWIFTEST 6 FR 0.0006 REL FR 6 V 0 P
my territories | longer than swiftest expedition TGV 3.01.164
ay, madam, with the swiftest wing of speed. AWW 3.02. 73
therefore, dear boy, mount on my swiftest horse, 1H6 4.05. 9
that swiftest wing of recompense is slow | to MAC 1.04. 17
the swiftest harts have posted you by land, CYM 2.04. 27
and had let go by | the swiftest hours, observed LC 60

SWIFT–FOOTED 1 FR 0.0001 REL FR 1 V 0 P
and do what e'er thou wilt, swift–footed time, SON 19. 6

SWIFTLY 8 FR 0.0009 REL FR 6 V 2 P
are of suppler joints) follow them swiftly, TMP 3.03.107
your praise is come too swiftly home before you. AYL 2.03. 9
softly and swiftly, sir, for the priest is ready SHR 5.01. 1 P
which must be ev'n as swiftly followed as | i WT 1.02.409
how swiftly will this feeble the woman's tailor 2H4 3.02.268 P
when arm in arm they both came swiftly running, 1H6 2.02. 29
tidings, as swiftly as the posts could run, 3H6 2.01.109
jealous of catching, swiftly doth forsake him, VEN 321

SWIFTNESS 5 FR 0.0005 REL FR 4 V 1 P
even with the swiftness of putting on. TN 2.05.172 P
that may with reasonable swiftness add | more H5 1.02.306
by violent swiftness that which we run at, | and H8 1.01.142
it shall find | the harm of unscann'd swiftness, COR 3.01.311
city made | with such a cry and swiftness that, TNK 4.01. 98

SWIFT–WINGED 2 FR 0.0002 REL FR 2 V 0 P
swift–winged with desire to get a grave, | as 1H6 2.05. 15
that our swift–winged souls may catch the king's R3 2.02. 44

SWILL'D 1 FR 0.0001 REL FR 1 V 0 P
swill'd with the wild and wasteful ocean. H5 3.01. 14

SWILLS 1 FR 0.0001 REL FR 1 V 0 P
swills your warm blood like wash and makes his R3 5.02. 9

SWIM 15 FR 0.0017 REL FR 12 V 3 P
to swim, to dive into the fire, to ride | on the TMP 1.02.191
i can swim like a duck, i'll be sworn. 2.02.128 P
though thou canst swim like a duck, thou art 2.02.131 P
again | ere the leviathan can swim a league. MND 2.01.174
if he fall in, good night, or sink or swim. 1H4 1.03.194
with bootless labor swim against the tide, | and 3H6 1.04. 20
say you can swim, alas, 'tis but a while; 5.04. 29
like little wanton boys that swim on bladders, H8 3.02.359
thou take the river styx, | i would swim after. TRO 5.04. 20
this angry flood, | and swim to yonder point?" JC 1.02.104
why now blow wind, swell billow, and swim bark! 5.01. 67
be contented, 'tis a naughty night to swim in. LR 3.04.111 P
and almost breathless swim | in this deep water. TNK pr 24
for not to swim | i' th' aid o' th' current were 1.02. 7
swim with your bodies, | and carry it sweetly 3.05. 28

SWIMMER 2 FR 0.0002 REL FR 1 V 1 P
but in loving, leander the good swimmer, troilus ADO 5.02. 31 P
like an unpractic'd swimmer plunging still, LUC 1098

SWIMMERS 1 FR 0.0001 REL FR 1 V 0 P
as two spent swimmers that do cling together MAC 1.02. 8

SWIMMING 2 FR 0.0002 REL FR 1 V 1 P
which she with pretty and with swimming gait MND 2.01.130
poor tom, that eats the swimming frog, the toad, LR 3.04.129 P

SWIMS 3 FR 0.0003 REL FR 3 V 0 P
he's undrown'd, | as he that sleeps here swims. TMP 2.01.238
which swims against your stream of quality. 2H4 5.02. 34
upon your favors swims with fins of lead, | and COR 1.01.180

SWINE 12 FR 0.0013 REL FR 11 V 1 P
still swine eats all the draff. WIV 4.02.107
enough for a flint, pearl enough for a swine: LLL 4.02. 89 P
o monstrous beast, how like a swine he lies! SHR in.1. 34
to hug with swine, to seek sweet safety out | in JN 5.02.142
this foul swine | is now even in the centry of R3 5.02. 10
in a baser temple | than where swine feed! TIM 5.01. 49
killing swine. MAC 1.03. 2
to hovel thee with swine and rogues forlorn | in LR 4.07. 38
whilst the angry swine | flies like a parthian TNK 2.02. 49
that i lay fatting like a swine, to fight, | and 3.06. 12
with javeling's point a churlish swine to gore, VEN 616
the loving swine | sheath'd unaware the tusk in 1115

SWINE–DRUNK 1 FR 0.0001 REL FR 0 V 1 P
is his best virtue, for he will be swine–drunk, AWW 4.03.255 P

SWINE–HERDS 1 FR 0.0001 REL FR 0 V 1 P
three neat–herds, three swine–herds, that have WT 4.04.325 P

SWINE–KEEPING 1 FR 0.0001 REL FR 0 V 1 P
prodigals lately come from swine–keeping, from 1H4 4.02. 35 P

SWING'D 8 FR 0.0009 REL FR 2 V 6 P
i thank you, you swing'd me for my love, which TGV 2.01. 82 P
now will he be swing'd for reading my letter — 3.01.382 P
been i' th' church, i would have swing'd him, or WIV 5.05.185 P
have swing'd him, or he should have swing'd me. 5.05.186 P
in your retirement, i had swing'd him soundly. MM 5.01.130
saint george, that swing'd the dragon, and e'er JN 2.01.288
i will have you as soundly swing'd for this — 2H4 5.04. 19 P
famish'd correctioner, if you be not swing'd, 5.04. 21 P

SWINGE 2 FR 0.0002 REL FR 2 V 0 P
swinge me them soundly forth unto their husbands SHR 5.02.104
for the great swinge and rudeness of his poise, TRO 1.03.207

SWINGEBUCKLERS 1 FR 0.0001 REL FR 0 V 1 P
not four such swingebucklers in all the inns a' 2H4 3.02. 22 P

SWINISH 2 FR 0.0002 REL FR 2 V 0 P
when in swinish sleep | their drenched natures MAC 1.07. 67
and with swinish phrase | soil our addition, and HAM 1.04. 19

SWINSTEAD 2 FR 0.0002 REL FR 2 V 0 P
tell him toward swinstead, to the abbey there. JN 5.03. 8
set on toward swinstead. 5.03. 16

SWISSERS 1 FR 0.0001 REL FR 1 V 0 P
where is my swissers? HAM 4.05. 98

SWITCHES *(also swits)*

SWITCHES 1 FR 0.0001 REL FR 0 V 1 P
these are but switches to 'em. H8 5.03. 9 P

SWITHOLD 1 FR 0.0001 REL FR 1 V 0 P
"swithold footed thrice the 'old, | he met the LR 3.04.120

SWITS *(also switches)*

SWITS 2 FR 0.0002 REL FR 0 V 2 P
swits and spurs, swits and spurs, or i'll cry a ROM 2.04. 69 P
swits and spurs, swits and spurs, or i'll cry a 2.04. 69 P

SWITZERS *(see swissers)*

SWOLL'N 7 FR 0.0008 REL FR 6 V 1 P
breasted | the surge most swoll'n that met him. TMP 2.01.118
of beastliness, that swoll'n parcel of dropsies, 1H4 2.04.450 P
the big year, swoll'n with some other grief, 2H4 in 13
in his blood such swoll'n and hot discourse TRO 2.03.173
all swoll'n and ulcerous, pitiful to the eye, MAC 4.03.151
him, if he i' th' blood–siz'd field lay swoll'n, TNK 1.01. 99
all swoll'n with chafing, down adonis sits, VEN 325

SWOM *(also swam)*

SWOM 2 FR 0.0002 REL FR 1 V 1 P
swom ashore, man, like a duck. TMP 2.02.128 P
love, | and yet you never swom the hellespont. TGV 1.01. 26

SWOON *(also sound*, etc., swoonds, swoun, swound, etc.)*

SWOON 3 FR 0.0003 REL FR 3 V 0 P
i swoon almost with fear. MND 2.02.154
many will swoon when they do look on blood. AYL 4.03.158
or else i swoon with this dead–killing news! R3 4.01. 35

SWOONDS 1 FR 0.0001 REL FR 1 V 0 P
swoonds rather, for so bad a prayer as his | was ANT 4.09. 26

SWOOP 1 FR 0.0001 REL FR 1 V 0 P
chickens, and their dam, | at one fell swoop? MAC 4.03.219

SWOOPSTAKE 1 FR 0.0001 REL FR 1 V 0 P
is't writ in your revenge | that, swoopstake, HAM 4.05.143

/SWORD 2 FR 0.0002 REL FR 2 V 0 P
/that /by /indictment /and /by /dint /of /sword 2H4 4.01.126
/arms, /arms, /sword, /fire! LR 3.06. 55

SWORD 346 FR 0.0391 REL FR 295 V 51 P
put thy sword up, traitor, | who mak'st a show TMP 1.02.470
sword, pike, knife, gun, or need of any engine, 2.01.162
draw thy sword. 2.01.292
if i were young again, the sword should end it. WIV 1.01. 41 P
it is petter that friends is the sword, and end 1.01. 42 P
day with playing at sword and dagger with a 1.01.283 P
but i have a sword, and it shall bite upon my 2.01.131 P
with my long sword i would have made you four 2.01.228 P
mine oyster, | which i with sword will open. 2.02. 4
be old and of the peace, if i see a sword out, 2.03. 45 P
the sword and the word? 3.01. 44 P
not the king's crown, nor the deputed sword, MM 2.02. 60
he who the sword of heaven will bear | should be 3.02.261
some get within him, take his sword away: ERR 5.01. 34
mart, | and thereupon i drew my sword on you; 5.01.263
nor ever didst thou draw thy sword on me; 5.01.267
by my sword, beatrice, thou lovest me. ADO 4.01.274 P
nay, never lay thy hand upon thy sword, | i fear 5.01. 54
in faith, my hand meant nothing to my sword. 5.01. 57
if drawing my sword against the humor of LLL 1.02. 59 P
dumaine was at my service, and his sword: 5.02.276
there's an eye | wounds like a leaden sword. 5.02.481
i'll slash, i'll do it by the sword. 5.02.695 P
hippolyta, i woo'd thee with my sword, | and won MND 1.01. 16
word | is that vile name to perish on my sword! 2.02.107
pyramus must draw a sword to kill himself; 3.01. 11 P
he is defil'd | that draws a sword on thee. 3.02.411
out, sword, and wound | the pap of pyramus; 5.01.296
come, trusty sword, | come, blade, my breast 5.01.343
or with a base and boist'rous sword enforce | a AYL 2.03. 32
i was in love i broke my sword upon a stone, and 2.04. 47 P
in the which hope i blush, and hide my sword. 2.07.119
his brother here, and put him to the sword; 5.04.158
an old rusty sword ta'en out of the town armory, SHR 3.02. 46 P
up, and no sword worn | but one to dance with! AWW 2.01. 32
my sword and yours are kin. 2.01. 40 P
it was this very sword entrench'd it. 2.01. 44 P
whilst i can shake my sword or hear the drum. 2.05. 91
to tell him that his sword can never win | the 3.02. 93
the turn, or the breaking of my spanish sword. 4.01. 47 P
trust a man again for keeping his sword clean, 4.03.145 P
rust, sword! 4.03.337
would thou mightst never draw sword again. TN 1.03. 62 P
i would i might never draw sword again. 1.03. 64 P
therefore on, or strip your sword stark naked; 3.04.251 P
put up your sword. 3.04.312
pray, sir, put your sword up, if you please. 3.04.321 P
do, cuff him soundly, but never draw thy sword. 3.04.393 P
if thou dar'st tempt me further, draw thy sword. 4.01. 42
you drew your sword upon me without cause, | but 5.01.188
swear by this sword | thou wilt perform my WT 2.03.168
you here shall swear upon this sword of justice, 3.02.124
desiring thee to lay aside the sword | which JN 1.01. 12
your sword is bright, sir, put it up again. 4.03. 79
put up thy sword betime, | or i'll so maul you 4.03. 98
tongue speaks, my right drawn sword may prove. R2 1.01. 46
and by that sword i swear | which gently laid my 1.01. 78
civil wounds plough'd up with neighbors' sword; 1.03.128
lay on our royal sword your banish'd hands; 1.03.179
base | to stain the temper of my knightly sword. 4.01. 29
that lie shall lie so heavy on my sword, | that 4.01. 66
breathless and faint, leaning upon my sword, 1H4 1.03. 32
and through, my sword hack'd like a hand–saw — 2.04.168 P
art thou to hack thy sword as thou hast done, 2.04.261 P
in earnest, how came falstaff's sword so hack'd? 2.04.304 P
thou hadst fire and sword on thy side, and yet 2.04.317 P
and here draw i | a sword, whose temper i intend 5.02. 93
thee, king harry, | this sword hath ended him. 5.03. 9
now, by my sword, i will kill all his coats; 5.03. 26
lend me thy sword. 5.03. 40
i prithee lend me thy sword. 5.03. 43
i prithee lend me thy sword. 5.03. 49 P
if percy be alive, thou gets not my sword, but 5.03. 51 P
wound my thoughts worse than thy sword my flesh. 5.04. 80
bravely hast thou flesh'd | thy maiden sword. 5.04.131
i would make him eat a piece of my sword. 5.04.153 P
fell | under the wrath of noble hotspur's sword, 2H4 in 30
whose well–laboring sword | had three times 1.01.127
give me my sword and cloak. 2.04.366
the word with my sword to be a soldier–like word 3.02. 75 P
turning the word to sword and life to death. 4.02. 10
there is not now a rebel's sword unsheath'd, 4.04. 86
to trip the course of law and blunt the sword 5.02. 87
therefore still bear the balance and the sword, 5.02.103
th' unstained sword that you have us'd to bear, 5.02.114
should famine, sword, and fire | crouch for H5 pr 7
how you awake our sleeping sword of war — | we 1.02. 22
with /blood and sword and fire, to win your 1.02.131
and hides a sword, from hilts unto the point, 2.pr. 9
it will endure cold as another man's sword will; 2.01. 10 P
nym, show thy valor, and put up your sword. 2.01. 44 P
by this sword, he that makes the first thrust, 2.01. 99 P
by this sword, i will. 2.01.100 P
sword is an oath, and oaths must have their 2.01.101
and sword and shield, | in bloody field, | doth 3.02. 9
he hath a killing tongue and a quiet sword; 3.02. 34 P
the sword, the mace, the crown imperial, | the 4.01.261
or mangled shalt thou be by this my sword. 4.04. 39
his bruised helmet and his bended sword | before 5.pr. 18
bringing rebellion broached on his sword, | how 5.pr. 32
his bleeding sword 'twixt england and fair 5.02.355
fortune made his sword; ep 6
his brandish'd sword did blind men with his 1H6 1.01. 10
enacted wonders with his sword and lance: 1.01.122
here is my keen–edg'd sword, | deck'd with /five 1.02. 98
and fightest with the sword of deborah. 1.02.105
not to wear, handle, or use any sword, weapon, 1.03. 78 P
his sword did ne'er leave striking in the field. 1.04. 81
the cry of talbot serves me for a sword, | for i 2.01. 79
i girt thee with the valiant sword of york: 3.01.170
o, turn the edged sword another way, | strike 3.03. 52
lets fall his sword before your highness' feet, 3.04. 9
said | a stouter champion never handled sword. 3.04. 19
law of arms is such | that whoso draws a sword, 3.04. 39
and left us to the rage of france his sword. 4.06. 3
till with thy warlike sword, despite of fate, 4.06. 8
from the dolphin's crest thy sword struck fire, 4.06. 10
the sword of orleance hath not made me smart; 4.06. 42
knee, | his bloody sword he brandish'd over me, 4.07. 6
did flesh his puny sword in frenchmen's blood! 4.07. 36
duke of suffolk, | and girt thee with the sword. 2H6 1.01. 65
my sword should shed hot blood, mine eyes no 1.01.118
against this proud protector with my sword! 2.01. 36
come with thy two–hand sword. 2.01. 45
and that my sword be stain'd | with heart–blood 2.02. 65
are up | and put the englishmen unto the sword. 3.01.284
but here's a vengeful sword, rusted with ease, 3.02.198
but with our sword we wip'd away the blot; 4.01. 40
broke be my sword, my arms torn and defac'd, 4.01. 42
come and get thee a sword, though made of a lath 4.02. 1 P
i fear neither sword nor fire. 4.02. 59 P
he need not fear the sword, for his coat is of 4.02. 60 P
we will have the mayor's sword borne before us. 4.03. 14 P
many simple souls | should perish by the sword! 4.04. 11
hath my sword therefore broke through london 4.08. 23 P
my sword make way for me, for here is no staying 4.08. 59 P
fie on myself, that have a sword, and yet am 4.10. 2 P
ostridge, and swallow my sword like a great pin, 4.10. 29 P
let this my sword report what speech forbears. 4.10. 54
sword, i will hallow thee for this thy deed, 4.10. 67
and as i thrust thy body in with my sword, | so 4.10. 78
words, | except a sword or sceptre balance it. 5.01. 9
so let it help me now against thy sword, | as i 5.02. 24
sword, hold thy temper; 5.02. 70
now, by my sword, well hast thou fought to–day; 5.03. 15
ay, with my sword. 3H6 1.02. 53
kill me with thy sword | and not with such a 1.03. 16
unsheathe your sword, and dub him presently. 2.02. 59
draw thy sword in right. 2.02. 62
unsheathe your sword, good father; 2.02. 80
then, executioner, unsheathe thy sword. 2.02.123
thou shalt be the third, /and this sword hold. 5.01. 75
here sheathe thy sword, i'll pardon thee my 5.05. 70
see how my sword weeps for the poor king's death 5.06. 63
black–fac'd clifford shook his sword at him; R3 1.02.158
lo here i lend thee this sharp–pointed sword, 1.02.174
take up the sword again, or take up me. 1.02.183

well, well, put up your sword. 1.02.196
him on the costard with the hilts of thy sword, 1.04.155 P
a greater gift? o, that's the sword to it. 3.01.116
is the sword unsway'd? 4.04.469
think on me, | and fall thy edgeless sword. 5.03.135
think on me, | and fall thy edgeless sword. 5.03.163
if you do free your children from the sword, 5.03.261
and i know his sword | hath a sharp edge; H8 1.01.109
feel | my sword i' th' life–blood of thee else. 3.02.277
it is too starv'd a subject for my sword. TRO 1.01. 93
look you how his sword is bloodied, and his helm 1.02.232 P
the great hector's sword had lack'd a master, 1.03. 76
since the first sword was drawn about this 2.02. 18
you know a sword employ'd is perilous, | and 2.02. 40
when helenus beholds | a grecian and his sword, 2.02. 43
without a heart to dare, or sword to draw, 2.02.157
if to my sword his fate be not the glory, | a 4.01. 27
if e'er thou stand at mercy of my sword, | name 4.04.114
wherein my sword had not impressure made | /of 4.05.131
aunt, should by my mortal sword | be drained! 4.05.134
thou hast hung /thy advanced sword i' th' air, 4.05.188
by vulcan's skill, | my sword should bite it. 5.02.171
in his descent than shall my prompted sword 5.02.175
even in the fan and wind of your fair sword, 5.03. 41
nor you, my brother, with your true sword drawn, 5.03. 56
rest, sword, thou hast thy fill of blood and 5.08. 4
my half–supp'd sword, that frankly would have 5.08. 19
lay aside their ruth | and let me use my sword, COR 1.01.198
when it spit forth blood | at grecian sword, 1.03. 43
who sensibly outdares his senseless sword | and, 1.04. 53
make you a sword of me? 1.06. 76
heart consent to take | a bribe to pay my sword. 1.09. 38
true sword to sword, i'll potch at him some way, 1.10. 15
true sword to sword, i'll potch at him some way, 1.10. 15
his sword, death's stamp, | where it did mark, 2.02.107
how often he had met you, sword to sword; 3.01. 13
how often he had met you, sword to sword; 3.01. 13
down with that sword! 3.01.225
bred i' th' wars | since 'a could draw a sword, 3.01.319
tribe before him, | his good sword in his hand. 4.02. 25
here i cleep | the anvil of my sword, and do 4.05.110
and does achieve as soon | as draw his sword; 4.07. 24
with what he would say, let him feel your sword, 5.06. 55
or more, his tribe, | to use my lawful sword! 5.06.129
from where he circumscribed with his sword, TIT 1.01. 68
goths have given me leave to sheathe my sword. 1.01. 85
emperor, do i consecrate | my sword, my chariot, 1.01.249
and with my sword i'll keep this door safe. 1.01.288
to him that flourish'd for her with his sword. 1.01.310
and that my sword upon thee shall approve, | and 2.01. 35
give me a sword, i'll chop off my hands too, 3.01. 72
give it me, my sword shall soon dispatch it. 4.02. 86
sooner this sword shall plough thy bowels up. 4.02. 87
put up thy sword, | or manage it to part these ROM 1.01. 68
what noise is this? give me my long sword ho! 1.01. 75
a crutch, a crutch! why call you for a sword? 1.01. 76
my sword, i say! 1.01. 77
the fiery tybalt, with his sword prepar'd, 1.01.109
of a tavern, claps me his sword upon the table, 3.01. 6 P
will you pluck your sword out of his pilcher by 3.01. 80 P
what heart, head, sword, force, means, but is TIM 2.02.167
hath in her more destruction than thy sword, 4.03. 63
but for thy sword and fortune, trod upon them — 4.03. 96
let not thy sword skip one. 4.03.111
virgin's cheek | make soft thy trenchant sword; 4.03.116
and shakes his threat'ning sword | against the 5.01.166
with thy smile | than hew to't with thy sword. 5.04. 46
city, | and i will use the olive with my sword: 5.04. 82
besides — i ha' not since put up my sword — JC 1.03. 19
here, as i point my sword, the sun arises, 2.01.106
look, | i draw a sword against conspirators; 5.01. 51
when think you that the sword goes up again? 5.01. 52
have added slaughter to the sword of traitors. 5.01. 55
i was not born to die on brutus' sword. 5.01. 58
now be a freeman, and with this good sword, 5.03. 41
is cover'd, as 'tis now, | guide thou the sword. 5.03. 45
even with the sword that kill'd thee. 5.03. 46
come, cassius' sword, and find titinius' heart. 5.03. 90
hold then my sword, and turn away thy face, 5.05. 47
i held the sword, and he did run on it. 5.05. 65
hold, take my sword. MAC 2.01. 4
give me my sword. 2.01. 9
and dare me to the desert with thy sword; 3.04.103
fife, give to th' edge o' th' sword | his wife, 4.01.151
let us rather | hold fast the mortal sword, and 4.03. 3
or wear it on my sword, yet my poor country 4.03. 46
and it hath been | the sword of our slain kings. 4.03. 87
be this the whetstone of your sword, let grief 4.03.228
with my sword | i'll prove the lie thou speak'st 5.07. 10
or else my sword with an unbattered edge | i 5.07. 19
the roman fool, and die | on mine own sword? 5.08. 2
my voice is in my sword, thou bloodier villain 5.08. 7
with thy keen sword impress as make me bleed. 5.08. 10
upon my sword. HAM 1.05.147
indeed, upon my sword, indeed. 1.05.148
of this that you have seen, | swear by my sword. 1.05.154
and lay your hands again upon my sword. 1.05.158
swear by my sword, | never to speak of this that 1.05.159
swear by his sword. 1.05.161
his antique sword, | rebellious to his arm, lies 2.02.469
but with the whiff and wind of his fell sword 2.02.473
for lo his sword, | which was declining on the 2.02.477
with less remorse than pyrrhus' bleeding sword 2.02.491
in mincing with his sword her /husband's limbs, 2.02.514
soldier's, scholar's, eye, tongue, sword, | th' 3.01.151
up, sword, and know thou a more horrid hent: 3.03. 88
looks raw and red | after the danish sword, and 4.03. 61
no trophy, sword, nor hatchment o'er his bones, 4.05.215
you may choose | a sword unbated, and in a /pass 4.07.138
and, for /that purpose, i'll anoint my sword. 4.07.140
in cunning i must draw my sword upon you. LR 2.01. 29
here stood he in the dark, his sharp sword out, 2.01. 38
with his prepared sword he charges home | my 2.01. 51
that such a slave as this should wear a sword, 2.02. 72
give me thy sword. a peasant stand up thus? 3.07. 80
act, bending his sword | to his great master, 4.02. 74
the sword is out | that must destroy thee. 4.06.229
to be tender–minded | does not become a sword. 5.03. 32
draw thy sword, | that, if my speech offend a 5.03.126
say thou "no," | this sword, this arm, and my 5.03.140
this sword of mine shall give them instant way 5.03.150
take my sword. 5.03.251
and cassio following him with determin'd sword OTH 2.03.227
what was he that you follow'd with your sword? 2.03.285 P
forth my sword; 5.01. 10
almost persuade | justice to break her sword! 5.02. 17
i care not for thy sword, i'll make thee known, 5.02.165
fie, | your sword upon a woman? 5.02.224
but every puny whipster gets my sword. 5.02.244
it was a sword of spain, the ice–brook's temper 5.02.253
that, with this little arm and this good sword, 5.02.262
wrench his sword from him. 5.02.288
now, by /my sword — ANT 1.03. 82
upon your sword | sit laurel victory, and smooth 1.03. 99
i did not think to draw my sword 'gainst pompey, 2.02.153
she made great caesar lay his sword to bed; 2.02.227
on him, whilst | i wore his sword philippan. 2.05. 23
know | if 'twill tie up thy discontented sword, 2.06. 6
yet with parthian blood thy sword is warm, | the 3.01. 6
that | without the which a soldier and his sword 3.01. 28
do you misdoubt | this sword, and these my 3.07. 63
at philippi kept | his sword e'en like a dancer, 3.11. 36
and that | my sword, made weak by my affection, 3.11. 67
and answer me declin'd, sword against sword, 3.13. 27
and answer me declin'd, sword against sword, 3.13. 27
i and my sword will earn our chronicle. 3.13.175
/on reason, | it eats the sword it fights with. 3.13.199
she has robb'd me of my sword. 4.14. 23
i, that with my sword | quarter'd the world, and 4.14. 57
draw that thy honest sword, which thou hast worn 4.14. 79
my sword is drawn. 4.14. 88
this sword but shown to caesar, with this 4.14.112
draw thy sword, and give me | sufficing strokes 4.14.116
this is his sword, | i robb'd his wound of it; 5.01. 24
chastity, you shall answer me with your sword. CYM 1.04.163 P
pure honor gains or loses | your sword or mine, 2.04. 60
to master caesar's sword, | made lud's–town with 3.01. 31
whose use the sword of caesar | hath too much 3.01. 55
what shall i need to draw my sword, the paper 3.04. 32
whose edge is sharper than the sword, whose 3.04. 34
look | i draw the sword myself, take it, and hit 3.04. 67
best draw my sword; 3.06. 25
and if mine enemy | but fear the sword like me, 3.06. 26
out, sword, and to a sore purpose! 4.01. 22 P
with his own sword, | which he did wave against 4.02.149
have threaten'd | our prisoners with the sword. 5.05. 78
came to me | with his sword drawn, foam'd at the 5.05.276
me, | this sword shall prove he's honor's enemy. PER 2.05. 64
draw thy fear'd sword | that does good turns to TNK 1.01. 48
under the shadow of his sword may cool us; 1.01. 92
good light, | had i a sword, i would kill thee. 2.02.265
off me and this hand | but owner of a sword! 3.01. 33
had i a sword, | and these house–clogs away — 3.01. 42
to clear his own way with the mind and sword 3.01. 56
y'ave seen me use my sword | against th' advice 3.01. 59
quit me of these cold gyves, give me a sword, 3.01. 72
a good sword in thy hand, and do but say | that 3.01. 75
shall be at your choice | both sword and armor. 3.01. 89
that to your sword you will bequeath this plea, 3.01.115
a sword and armor. 3.03. 50
and that sword he refuses, | if it but hold, i 3.06. 14
i would have nothing hurt thee but my sword, | a 3.06. 87
take my sword, i hold it better. 3.06. 89
my sword | is in my hand, and, if thou kill'st 3.06. 96
and on his thigh a sword | hung by a curious 4.02. 85
his throne and sword, but given him his own name STM II.C 103
draw not thy sword to guard iniquity, | for it LUC 626
and then against my heart he set his sword, 1640
nor mars his sword nor war's quick fire shall SON 55. 7

SWORD–AND–BUCKLER 1 FR 0.0001 REL FR 1 V 0 P
and that same sword–and–buckler prince of wales, 1H4 1.03.230

SWORDER 2 FR 0.0002 REL FR 2 V 0 P
a roman sworder and bandetto slave | murder'd 2H6 4.01.135
and be stag'd to th' show | against a sworder! ANT 3.13. 31

SWORD–HILTS 1 FR 0.0001 REL FR 1 V 0 P
i prithee | hold thou my sword–hilts, whilest i JC 5.05. 28

SWORDMEN 1 FR 0.0001 REL FR 0 V 1 P
fellows, and like to prove most sinewy swordmen. AWW 2.01. 60 P

SWORD'S 4 FR 0.0004 REL FR 4 V 0 P
whose sting is sharper than the sword's, and WT 2.03. 87
by heaven, i think my sword's as sharp as yours. JN 4.03. 82
within my sword's length set him; MAC 4.03.234
i may not wish | more than my sword's edge on't. TNK 3.01. 96

/SWORDS 1 FR 0.0001 REL FR 1 V 0 P
/no /less /working /than /are /swords /and /bows TRO 1.03.355

SWORDS 69 FR 0.0078 REL FR 58 V 11 P
of whom your swords are temper'd, may as well TMP 3.03. 62
your swords are now too massy for your strengths 3.03. 67
come, lay their swords to pawn. WIV 3.01.110 P
and come with naked swords: ERR 4.04.145
i see these witches are afraid of swords. 4.04.147
each one with ireful passion, with drawn swords, 5.01.151
give us the swords, we have bucklers of our own. ADO 5.02. 18 P
seem to say we will do no harm with our swords, MND 3.01. 18 P
and so we measur'd swords and parted. AYL 5.04. 87 P
peace of heaven is theirs that lift their swords JN 2.01. 35
lest unadvis'd you stain your swords with blood. 2.01. 45
with unhack'd swords, and helmets all unbruis'd, 2.01.254
the swords of soldiers are his teeth, his fangs, 2.01.353
there shall your swords and lances arbitrate R2 1.01.200
lend friends, and friends their helpful swords. 3.03.132
or to the place of diff'rence call the swords 2H4 4.01.179
and draw no swords but what are sanctified. 4.04. 4
we bear our civil swords and native fire | as 5.05.106
him whose wrongs gives edge unto the swords H5 1.02. 27
and sheath'd their swords for lack of argument. 3.01. 21
of honor edged | more sharper than your swords, 3.05. 39
if it come to the arbitrement of swords, can try 4.01.160 P
whose dreadful swords were never drawn in vain, 2H6 4.01. 92
go to ward, | they'll pawn their swords /for my 5.01.113
were by the swords of common soldiers slain. 3H6 1.01. 9
if not, our swords shall plead it in the field. 1.01.103
thus doth he force the swords of wicked men | to R3 5.01. 23
your standards, draw your willing swords. 5.03.264
strong arms be our conscience, swords our law! 5.03.311
be those with swords? TRO 1.02.209 P
swords! 1.02.210 P
good arms, strong joints, true swords, and, 1.03.238
not bear it so, 'a should eat swords first. 2.03.217 P
the venom'd vengeance ride upon our swords, 5.03. 47
had rather see the swords and hear a drum than COR 1.03. 55 P
that we with smoking swords may march from hence 1.04. 11
great charms | misguide thy opposers' swords! 1.05. 22
filling the air with swords advanc'd and darts, 1.06. 61
since | he lurch'd all swords of the garland. 2.02.101
all the swords | in italy, and her confederate 5.03.207
masters all, be quiet, | put up your swords. 5.06.134
plead my successive title with your swords. TIT 1.01. 4
and with our swords, upon a pile of wood, 1.01.128
that in your country's service drew your swords, 1.01.175
patricians, draw your swords, and sheathe them 1.01.204
put up your swords, you know not what you do. ROM 1.01. 65
in thine eye | than twenty of their swords! 2.02. 72
what mean these masterless and gory swords | to 5.03.142
up to the elbows, and besmear our swords; JC 3.01.107
of half that worth as those your swords, made 3.01.155
to you our swords have leaden points, mark 3.01.173
abroad, and turns our swords | in our own proper 5.03. 95
but swords i smile at, weapons laugh to scorn, MAC 5.07. 12
six barb'ry horses against six french swords, HAM 5.02.161 P
keep up your bright swords, for the dew will OTH 1.02. 59
swords out, and tilting one at other's /breast, 2.03.183
for that i heard the clink and fall of swords, 2.03.234
our italy | shines o'er with civil swords; ANT 1.03. 45
entertained cause enough | to draw their swords; 2.01. 47
true reports | that drew their swords with you. 2.02. 48
o' th' time | died with their swords in hand; CYM 1.01. 36
to be put to the arbiterment of swords, and by 1.04. 50 P
my body's mark'd | with roman swords, and my 3.03. 57
our good swords now | (better the red–ey'd god TNK 2.02. 20
and grasp | our good swords in our hands, i 2.02.209
with him bring | two swords and two good armors. 3.06. 3
honor | in public question with their swords. 3.06.222
may fairly carry | our swords and cause along; 3.06.260
it seem'd they would debate with angry swords. LUC 1421

SWORE *(also sware)*

SWORE 56 FR 0.0063 REL FR 39 V 17 P
call'd me dromio, swore i was assur'd to her, ERR 3.02.141 P
then swore he that he was a stranger here. 4.02. 9
and true he swore, though yet forsworn he were. 4.02. 10
i too, and he swore he would marry her to–night. ADO 2.01.169 P
swore he would meet her as he was appointed next 3.03.160 P
he swore he would never marry, and yet now in 3.04. 88 P
"for he swore a thing to me on monday night, 5.01.167 P
they swore you did. 5.04. 76
they swore that you were almost sick for me. 5.04. 80
they swore that you were well–nigh dead for me. 5.04. 81
i only swore to study with your grace, | and LLL 1.01. 51
you swore to that, berowne, and to the rest. 1.01. 53
by yea and nay, sir, then i swore in jest. 1.01. 54
and swore | a better speech was never spoke 5.02.109
he swore that he did hold me dear | as precious 5.02.444
troth, | i never swore this lady such an oath. 5.02.451
i had no judgment when to her i swore. MND 3.02.134
same | to whom you swore a secret pilgrimage, MV 1.01.120
and swore he would pay him again when he was 1.02. 81 P
you swore to me, when i did give /it you, | that 5.01.152
that swore by his honor they were good pancakes, AYL 1.02. 63 P
and swore by his honor the mustard was naught. 1.02. 64 P
and they shook hands and swore brothers. 5.04.102 P
by gogs–wouns," quoth he, and swore so loud, SHR 3.02.160
he stamp'd and swore | as if the vicar meant to 3.02.167
how he swore, how she pray'd that never pray'd 4.01. 79 P
my leave, | in resolution as i swore before. 4.02. 43
though i swore i leapt from the window of the AWW 4.01. 55 P
even on that altar where we swore to you | dear JN 5.04. 19
lucifer cuckold and swore the devil his true 1H4 2.04.337 P
swore little, dic'd not above seven times — a 3.03. 15 P
swore him assistance, and perform'd it too. 4.03. 65
you swore to us, | and you did swear that oath 5.01. 41
to this we swore our aid. 5.01. 46
i can see my glove in his cap, which he swore, H5 4.07.129 P
he swore consent to your succession, | his oath 3H6 2.01.172
and swore with sobs | that he would labor my R3 1.04.245
helen herself swore th' other day that troilus, TRO 1.02. 93 P
that swore to ride before him to the field. 4.04.142
and sure as death i swore | i would not part a TIT 1.01.487
with their fear, who swore they saw | men, all JC 1.03. 24
and then i swore thee, saving of thy life, 5.03. 38
of their nation | he swore had neither motion, HAM 4.07.101
swore as many oaths as i spake words, and broke LR 3.04. 88 P
she swore, in faith 'twas strange, 'twas passing OTH 1.03.160
swore to cymbeline | i was confederate with the CYM 3.03. 67
and swore | with his own single hand he'd take 4.02.120
to lose, | but that he swore to take, our lives? 4.02.125
his sword drawn, foam'd at the mouth, and swore, 5.05.276
the truest princess | that ever swore her faith. 5.05.417
at it, and swore he would see her to–morrow. PER 4.02.108 P
his /nemean hide, | and swore his sinews thaw'd. TNK 1.01. 69
she swore by wine and bread she would not break. 3.05. 47
in which you swore i went beyond all women, 3.06.206
i | believ'd it was his, for she swore it was, 5.01.117
he doth again repeat, and that they swore. LUC 1848

SWORN 139 FR 0.0157 REL FR 98 V 41 P
i can swim like a duck, i'll be sworn. TMP 2.02.129 P
come to me, | and i'll be sworn 'tis true. 3.03. 26
nay, i'll be sworn, i have sat in the stocks for TGV 4.04. 30 P
fenton, i'll be sworn on a book she loves you. WIV 1.04.145 P
that i would have sworn his disposition would 2.01. 60 P
i'll be sworn, | as my mother was, the first 2.02. 37
i am sworn of the peace. 2.03. 53 P
ay, i'll be sworn. 3.03. 29 P
may in the sworn twelve have a thief or two MM 2.01. 20
were you sworn to the duke, or to the deputy? 4.02.182 P
i will be sworn these ears of mine | heard you ERR 5.01.260
he hath every month a new sworn brother. ADO 1.01. 72 P
trust myself, though i had sworn the contrary, 1.01.196 P
to be true, though, i'll be sworn, if he be so, 2.01.297 P
i will not be sworn but love may transform me to 2.03. 23 P

i would have sworn it had, my lord, especially 2.03.116 P
and i'll be sworn upon't that he loves her, 5.04. 85
have sworn for three years' term to live with me LLL 1.01. 16
if you are arm'd to do, as sworn to do, 1.01. 22
so much, dear liege, i have already sworn, 1.01. 34
or, having sworn too hard–a–keeping oath, 1.01. 65
no, my good lord, i have sworn to stay with you; 1.01.111
yet, confident, i'll keep what i have sworn, 1.01.114
which each to other hath so strongly sworn. 1.01.307
hear me, dear lady: i have sworn an oath. 2.01. 97
i hear your grace hath sworn out house–keeping: 2.01.104
my hand is sworn | ne'er to pluck thee from thy 4.03.109
or keeping what is sworn, you will prove fools. 4.03.353
the king is my love sworn. 5.02.282
since when, i'll be sworn, he wore none but a 5.02.713 P
i'll be sworn, if thou be launcelot, thou art MV 2.02. 91 P
i have sworn an oath that i will have my bond. 3.03. 5
and by our holy sabaoth have i sworn | to have 4.01. 36
i dare be sworn for him he would not leave it, 5.01.172
that my nerissa shall be sworn on is, | whether 5.01.301
he had sworn it away before ever he saw those AYL 1.02. 79 P
although before the solemn priest i have sworn, AWW 2.03.269
bedded her, and sworn to make the 'not' eternal. 3.02. 21 P
and what to your sworn counsel i have spoken 3.07. 9
how have i sworn! 4.02. 20
he had sworn to marry me | when his wife's dead; 4.02. 71
sir toby will be sworn that i am no fox, but he TN 1.05. 79 P
i'll be sworn thou art; 1.05.291
as thou usest him, and thy sworn enemy, andrew 3.04.169 P
and, having sworn truth, ever will be true. 4.03. 33
now my sworn friend and then mine enemy; WT 1.02.167
own mouth — thereon | his execution sworn. 1.02.446
and i'll be sworn you would believe my saying, 2.01. 63
i dare be sworn. 2.02. 27
i should blush | to see you so attir'd — sworn, 4.04. 13
nuptial, which | we two have sworn shall come. 4.04. 51
thou hast sworn my love to be. 4.04.306
thou hast sworn it more to me: 4.04.307
and trust, his sworn brother, a very simple 4.04.596 P
been sworn my soldier, bidding me depend | upon JN 3.01.125
unswear faith sworn, and on the marriage–bed 3.01.245
since thou swor'st is sworn against thyself, 3.01.268
for that which thou hast sworn to do amiss | is 3.01.270
kept, | but thou hast sworn against religion, 3.01.280
i have sworn to do it; 4.01. 58
yet am i sworn, and i did purpose, boy, | with 4.01.123
thus hath he sworn, | and i with him, and many 5.04. 16
disgrace | neglected my sworn duty in that case. R2 1.01.134
the noble duke hath sworn his coming is | but 2.03.148
we all have strongly sworn to give him aid; 2.03.150
which i have sworn to weed and pluck away. 2.03.167
comprising all that may be sworn or said, | his 3.03.111
i am sworn brother, sweet, | to grim necessity, 5.01. 20
to bullingbrook are we sworn subjects now, 5.02. 39
i am sworn brother to a leash of drawers, and 1H4 2.04. 6 P
i'll be sworn upon all the books in england, i 2.04. 49 P
and i'll be sworn i have power to shame him 3.01. 60
no, i'll be sworn, i make as good use of it as 3.03. 29 P
a hair, and i'll be sworn my pocket was pick'd. 3.03. 60 P
no, i'll be sworn, unless you call three fingers 4.02. 73 P
troth | sworn to us in your younger enterprise. 5.01. 71
whom i have weekly sworn to marry since i 2H4 1.02.241 P
a' gaunt as if he had been sworn brother to him, 3.02.321 P
and i'll be sworn 'a ne'er saw him but once in 3.02.321 P
and we'll be all three sworn brothers to france. H5 2.01. 12 P
and sworn unto the practices of france | to kill 2.02. 90
to us | than cambridge is, hath likewise sworn. 2.02. 93
as two yoke–devils sworn to either's purpose, 2.02.106
nym and bardolph are sworn brothers in filching, 3.02. 44 P
i have sworn to take him a box a' th' ear; 4.07.127 P
remember, lords, your oaths to henry sworn: 1H6 1.01.162
a dreadful oath, sworn with a solemn tongue! 2H6 3.02.158
lord say, jack cade hath sworn to have thy head. 4.04. 19
against thy oath and true allegiance sworn, 5.01. 20
hast thou not sworn allegiance unto me? 5.01.179
and we his subjects, sworn in all allegiance, 3H6 3.01. 70
and you were sworn true subjects unto me; 3.01. 78
but i return his sworn and mortal foe. 3.03.257
whom thou wast sworn to cherish and defend. R3 1.04.208
thou art sworn as deeply to effect what we 3.01.158
seal | he solemnly had sworn that what he spoke H8 1.02.165
of such a time, being my sworn servant, | the 1.02.191
i'll be sworn 'tis true; TRO 1.02.173 P
corse, i'll be sworn and sworn upon't she never 2.03. 32 P
corse, i'll be sworn and sworn upon't she never 2.03. 32 P
the oaths now to her that you have sworn to me. 3.02. 42 P
it's more than i know, i'll be sworn. 4.02. 52 P
no, i'll be sworn. 4.05. 45
gaging me to keep | an oath that i have sworn. 5.01. 42
you have sworn patience. 5.02. 62
'tis sworn between us we shall ever strike COR 1.02. 35
i'll be sworn they are true. 2.01.143 P
will, sir, flatter my sworn brother, the people, 2.03. 96 P
what may be sworn by, both divine and human, 3.01.141
friends now fast sworn, | whose double bosoms 4.04. 12
so did i, i'll be sworn. 4.05.160 P
our general has sworn you out of reprieve and 5.02. 49 P
i dare be sworn you were; 5.03.194
then she hath sworn that she will still live ROM 1.01.217
or, if thou wilt not, be but sworn my love, 2.02. 35
thy dear love sworn but hollow perjury, 3.03.128
once, i am sworn not to give regard to you. TIM 1.02.245 P
he's a sworn rioter; 3.05. 67
out, had i so sworn as you | have done to this. MAC 1.07. 58
we have sworn, my lord, already. HAM 1.05.147
'tis deeply sworn. 3.02.225
nothing. i have sworn, i am firm. LR 1.01.245
commit not with man's sworn spouse, set not thy 3.04. 82 P
to both these sisters have i sworn my love; 5.01. 55
i dare be sworn i think that he is honest. OTH 3.03.125
thou art sworn, eros, | that when the exigent ANT 4.14. 62
madam, as thereto sworn by your command | (which 5.02.198
her attendants are | all sworn and honorable. CYM 2.04.125
i'll be sworn. 2.04.143
thy oath remember, thou hast sworn to do't. PER 4.01. 1
ear, and i am sworn | to do my work with haste. 4.01. 69
i am sworn, | and will dispatch. 4.01. 90
i have sworn. TNK 3.06.157
when they had sworn to this advised doom, | they LUC 1849
my hand hath sworn | ne'er to pluck thee from PP 16.11
for i have sworn thee fair, and thought thee SON 147.13
for i have sworn deep oaths of thy deep kindness 152. 9
for i have sworn thee fair; 152.13
that's to ye sworn to none was ever said, | for LC 180

SWORN'T 1 FR 0.0001 REL FR 1 V 0 P
i have sworn't. HAM 1.05.112

SWOR'ST 3 FR 0.0003 REL FR 3 V 0 P
which once thou swor'st was worth the looking on MM 5.01.208
what since thou swor'st is sworn against thyself JN 3.01.268
swor'st thou not then | to do this when i bade ANT 4.14. 81

SWOUN *(also sound*, etc., swoon, swoonds, swound, etc.)*

SWOUN 1 FR 0.0001 REL FR 1 V 0 P
doth she swoun? 3H6 5.05. 45

SWOUND 7 FR 0.0008 REL FR 5 V 2 P
now counterfeit to swound; AYL 3.05. 17
i am no woman, i'll not swound at it. JN 5.06. 22
unto the lodging where i first did swound? 2H4 4.05.233
and swound for what's to come upon thee. COR 5.02. 67 P
what cause do you think i have to swound? 5.02.101 P
i swound to see thee. TIM 4.03.368
but soft, i pray you; what, did caesar swound? JC 1.02.251

SWOUNDED 2 FR 0.0002 REL FR 0 V 2 P
some swounded, all sorrow'd. WT 5.02. 91 P
chok'd caesar, for he swounded, and fell down at JC 1.02.248 P

'SWOUNDS *(also 'zounds)*

'SWOUNDS 2 FR 0.0002 REL FR 2 V 0 P
hah, 'swounds, i should take it; HAM 2.02.576
'swounds, show me what thou't do. 5.01.274

SWOUNDS 1 FR 0.0001 REL FR 1 V 0 P
play the foolish throngs with one that swounds, MM 2.04. 24

SWUM *(see swam, swom)*

SWUNG 1 FR 0.0001 REL FR 1 V 0 P
he swung about his head and cut the winds, | who ROM 1.01.111

SYCAMORE 3 FR 0.0003 REL FR 3 V 0 P
under the cool shade of a sycamore | i thought LLL 5.02. 89
underneath the grove of sycamore | that westward ROM 1.01.121
"the poor soul sat /sighing by a sycamore tree, OTH 4.03. 40

SYCORAX 7 FR 0.0008 REL FR 7 V 0 P
hast thou forgot | the foul witch sycorax, who TMP 1.02.258
this damn'd witch sycorax, | for mischiefs 1.02.263
damn'd, which sycorax | could not again undo. 1.02.290
this island's mine by sycorax my mother, | which 1.02.331
all the charms | of sycorax, toads, beetles, 1.02.340
saw a woman | but only sycorax my dam and she; 3.02.101
but she as far surpasseth sycorax | as great'st 3.02.102

SYLLA 1 FR 0.0001 REL FR 1 V 0 P
thou grown great | and, like ambitious sylla, 2H6 4.01. 84

SYLLABLE 12 FR 0.0013 REL FR 10 V 2 P
to th' syllable. TMP 1.02.501
find | by every syllable a faithful verity. MM 4.03.126
even to the utmost syllable of your worthiness. AWW 3.06. 71 P
no, not a syllable: H8 1.01.195
and who dare speak | one syllable against him? 5.01. 39
my soul | of every syllable that here was spoke. TRO 5.02.117
and yell'd out | like syllable of dolor. MAC 4.03. 8
to day, | to the last syllable of recorded time; 5.05. 21
thou deni'st the least syllable of thy addition. LR 2.02. 24 P
each syllable that breath made up between them. OTH 4.02. 5
to any syllable that made love to you. PER 2.05. 70
i will believe you by the syllable | of what you 5.01.167

SYLLABLES 2 FR 0.0002 REL FR 1 V 1 P
compound with the major part of your syllables; COR 2.01. 59 P
though but bastards and syllables | of no 3.02. 56

SYLLOGISM 1 FR 0.0001 REL FR 0 V 1 P
if that this simple syllogism will serve, so; TN 1.05. 50 P

SYMBOLS 1 FR 0.0001 REL FR 1 V 0 P
all seals and symbols of redeemed sin, | his OTH 2.03.344

SYMPATHIZ'D 3 FR 0.0003 REL FR 2 V 1 P
a message well sympathiz'd — a horse to be LLL 3.01. 51 P
when with like semblance it is sympathiz'd. LUC 1113
wert truly sympathiz'd | in true plain words by SON 82.11

SYMPATHIZE 5 FR 0.0005 REL FR 4 V 1 P
the senseless brands will sympathize | the heavy R2 5.01. 46
then with the losers let it sympathize, | for 1H4 5.01. 7
and the men do sympathize with the mastiffs in H5 3.07.147 P
as rous'd with rage, with rage doth sympathize, TRO 1.03. 52
we sympathize. 4.01. 26

SYMPATHIZED 1 FR 0.0001 REL FR 1 V 0 P
place | that by this sympathized one day's error ERR 5.01.398

SYMPATHY 12 FR 0.0013 REL FR 8 V 4 P
go to then, there's sympathy. WIV 2.01. 7 P
then there's more sympathy. 2.01. 8 P
would you desire better sympathy? 2.01. 10 P
or, if there were a sympathy in choice, | war, MND 1.01.141
if that thy valure stand on sympathy, | there is R2 4.01. 33
soul, | if sympathy of love unite our thoughts. 2H6 1.01. 23
o, what a sympathy of woe is this, | as far from TIT 3.01.148
o woeful sympathy! ROM 3.03. 85
loveliness in favor, sympathy in years, manners, OTH 2.01.229 P
like it, which | i'll keep, if but for sympathy. CYM 5.04.150
this solemn sympathy poor venus noteth, | over VEN 1057
enforc'd by sympathy | of those fair suns set in LUC 1229

SYNAGOGUE 2 FR 0.0002 REL FR 0 V 2 P
go, tubal, and meet me at our synagogue; MV 3.01.129 P
go, good tubal, at our synagogue, tubal. 3.01.130 P

SYNOD 6 FR 0.0006 REL FR 5 V 1 P
of many parts | by heavenly synod was devis'd, AYL 3.02.150
gods sit in hourly synod about thy particular COR 5.02. 69 P
gods, | in general synod take away her power! HAM 2.02.494
and goddesses, | all the whole synod of them! ANT 3.10. 5
will cry | to th' shining synod of the rest CYM 5.04. 89
able to lock jove from a synod, shall | by TNK 1.01.176

SYNODS 1 FR 0.0001 REL FR 1 V 0 P
and us, | it hath in solemn synods been decreed, ERR 1.01. 13

SYRACUSA 5 FR 0.0005 REL FR 5 V 0 P
merchant of syracusa, plead no more. ERR 1.01. 3
in syracusa was i born, and wed | unto a woman, 1.01. 36
but seven years since, in syracusa, boy, | thou 5.01.321
i ne'er saw syracusa in my life. 5.01.326
during which time he ne'er saw syracusa: 5.01.329

SYRACUSE 1 FR 0.0001 REL FR 1 V 0 P
no, sir, not i, i came from syracuse. ERR 5.01.364

SYRACUSIAN 7 FR 0.0008 REL FR 7 V 0 P
be seen | at any syracusian marts and fairs; ERR 1.01. 17
if any syracusian born | come to the bay of 1.01. 18
well, syracusian; 1.01. 28
this very day a syracusian merchant | is 1.02. 3
to see a reverent syracusian merchant, | who put 5.01.124
speak freely, syracusian, what thou wilt. 5.01.286
i tell thee, syracusian, twenty years | have i 5.01.327

SYRACUSIANS 1 FR 0.0001 REL FR 1 V 0 P
both by the syracusians and ourselves, | to ERR 1.01. 14

SYRIA 6 FR 0.0006 REL FR 6 V 0 P
shook, from syria | to lydia and to ionia, ANT 1.02.102
one of my place in syria, his lieutenant, | for 3.01. 18
of egypt, made her | of lower syria, cyprus, 3.06. 10
to ptolomy he assign'd | syria, cilicia, and 3.06. 16
caesar through syria | intends his journey, and 5.02.200
his chiefest seat, | the fairest in all syria — PER 1.ch. 19

SYRUPS 2 FR 0.0002 REL FR 2 V 0 P
with wholesome syrups, drugs, and holy prayers, ERR 5.01.104
nor all the drowsy syrups of the world | shall OTH 3.03.331

'T *(also it and contractions with 't)*

'T 10 FR 0.0011 REL FR 9 V 1 P
can 't no other, | but, i your daughter, he must AWW 1.03.165
't may — i grant. WT 1.02.114
't has done, upon the premises, but justice; H8 2.01. 63
't 'as been prov'd. TIM 1.02. 49 P
't 'as been done; 1.02.144
is't true? can 't be? 2.02.203
't 'as been a turbulent and stormy night. PER 3.02. 4
't 'ad been a kindness | becoming well thy /fact 4.03. 11
't may be she joy'd to jest at my exile, | 't PP 14. 9
't may be again, to make me wander thither: 14.10

T'* *(also the, to, too)*

/T'* 6 FR 0.0006 REL FR 3 V 3 P
an ass, if he go about /t' expound this dream. MND 4.01.207 P
within /t' /one year it will make itself two, AWW 1.01.147 P
thy cheeks | confess it, /t' /one to th' other, 1.03.177
with any safety this sport /t' the upshot. TN 4.02. 71 P
/t' /undeck /the /pompous /body /of /a /king; R2 4.01.250
by circumstance /t' /accuse thy cursed self. R3 1.02. 80

T'* 82 FR 0.0092 REL FR 78 V 4 P
how to deny them, who t' advance, and who | to TMP 1.02. 80
govern, sir, | t' excel the golden age. 2.01.169
forgo the purpose | that you resolv'd t' effect. 3.03. 13
to learn his wit t' exchange the bad for better. TGV 2.06. 13
would seem in me t' affect speech and discourse, MM 1.01. 4
a golden mesh t' entrap the hearts of men MV 3.02.122
t' achieve that maid | whose sudden sight hath SHR 1.01.219
not i, | it is too hard a knot for me t' untie! TN 2.02. 41
madam, i am most apt t' embrace your offer. 5.01.320
though you would seek t' unsphere the stars with WT 1.02. 48
please you t' accept it — that the queen is 2.01.131
so uncurrent i | have strain'd t' appear thus; 3.02. 50
t' one is my sovereign, whom both my oath | and R2 2.02.112
t' other again | is my kinsman, whom the king 2.02.113
master tisick, the debuty, t' other day, and, as 2H4 2.04. 85 P
t' envelop and contain celestial spirits. H5 1.01. 31
we must not only arm t' invade the french, | but 1.02.136
she vaunted 'mongst her minions t' other day, 2H6 1.03. 84
whiles i live, t' account this world but hell, 3H6 3.02.169
t' avoid the censures of the carping world. R3 3.05. 68
th' king) t' appoint | who should attend on him? H8 1.01. 74
from | the king t' attach lord montacute, and 1.01.217
bitter than | 'tis sweet at first t' acquire — 2.03. 9
i shall not fail t' approve the fair conceit 2.03. 74
woman, much too weak | t' oppose your cunning. 2.04.107
is my duty | t' attend your highness' pleasure. 5.01. 91
t' invite the troyan lords after the combat | to TRO 3.03.236
a' th' t' other side, the policy of those crafty 5.04. 9 P
soft, here comes sleeve and t' other. 5.04. 18 P
lean upon one crutch, and fight with t' other, COR 1.01.242
evident as a chair | t' extol what it hath done. 4.07. 53
desire not | t' allay my rages and revenges with 5.03. 85
and | intends t' appear before the people, 5.06. 7
t' appease their groaning shadows that are gone. TIT 1.01.126
by day and night t' attend him carefully, | and 4.03. 28
my back a' t' other side — ah, my back, my back ROM 2.05. 50
i'll show you how t' observe a strange event. TIM 3.04. 17
which the gods grant thee t' attain to! 4.03.328 P
t' accept my grief, and whilst this poor wealth 4.03.488
t' hold what distance | his wisdom can provide. MAC 3.06. 44
poor, innocent lamb | t' appease an angry god. 4.03. 17
had made his course t' illume that part of HAM 1.01. 37
do, t' express his love and friending to you, 1.05.185
/dev'l hath power | t' assume a pleasing shape, 2.02.600
t' have seen what i have seen, see what i see! 3.01.161
should patch a wall t' expel the /winter's flaw! 5.01.216
mountain you have made | t' o'ertop old pelion, 5.01.253
you | t' avert your liking a more worthier way LR 1.01.211
nature is asham'd | almost t' acknowledge hers. 1.01.213
not been born than not t' have pleas'd me better 1.01.234
a–twain | which are t' intrinse t' unloose; 2.02. 75
a–twain | which are t' intrinse t' unloose; 2.02. 75
t' obey in all your daughters' hard commands. 3.04.149
to go, my lord, | his wits begin t' unsettle. 3.04.162
t' appear | where you shall hold your session. 5.03. 53
t' assume a semblance | that very dogs disdain'd 5.03.188
i had thought t' have yerk'd him here under the OTH 1.02. 5
would ever have, t' incur a general mock, | run 1.02. 69
charter in your voice | t' assist my simpleness. 1.03.246
not almost a fault | t' incur a private check. 3.03. 67
i would do much | t' atone them, for the love i 4.01.233
roderigo meant t' have sent this damned villain; 5.02.316
birthday, | i had thought t' have held it poor; ANT 3.13.185
yet t' imagine | an antony were nature's piece 5.02. 98
t' encounter me with orisons, for then | i am in CYM 1.03. 32
t' entreat your grace but in a small request, 1.06.181
t' enjoy thy banish'd lord and this great land! 2.01. 65
would testify, t' enrich mine inventory. 2.02. 30
have need | t' employ you towards this roman. 2.03. 63
as far, t' enjoy | a second night of such sweet 2.04. 43
was made so happy as | t' inherit such a haven. 3.02. 61
gate | instructs you how t' adore the heavens, 3.03. 3
and but disguise | that which, t' appear itself, 3.04.145
death, who is the key | t' unbar these locks. 5.04. 8
men | be like a beacon fir'd t' amaze your eyes. PER 1.04. 87
the mutiny he there hastes t' oppress, | says to 3.ch. 29
t' instruct me 'gainst a capital grief indeed — TNK 1.01.123
next, vouchsafe t' afford | (if ever, love, thy LUC 1305

in love, t' anticipate | the ills that were not, SON 118. 9
and age in love loves not t' have years told. 138.12
my spirits t' attend this double voice accorded, LC 3
believ'd her eyes when they t' assail begun, 262
T 1 FR 0.0001 REL FR 1 V 0 P
i had a wound here that was like a t, | but now ANT 4.07. 7
TA *(also th'*, thou)*
TA 1 FR 0.0001 REL FR 0 V 1 P
thou wo't, wo't ta? 2H4 2.01. 58 P
TABER *(also taper)*
TABER 1 FR 0.0001 REL FR 0 V 1 P
also, to burn the knight with my taber. WIV 4.04. 69 P
TABLE 41 FR 0.0046 REL FR 23 V 18 P
who art the table wherein all my thoughts | are TGV 2.07. 3
gentleman-like dogs, under the duke's table. 4.04. 18 P
the dinner is on the table. WIV 1.01.261 P
commandements, but scrap'd one out of the table. MM 1.02. 9 P
a table full of welcome makes scarce one dainty ERR 3.01. 23
please you to gratify the table with a grace, i LLL 4.02.155 P
if any man in italy have a fairer table, which MV 2.02.158 P
go to thy fellows, bid them cover the table, 3.05. 59 P
for the table, sir, it shall be serv'd in; 3.05. 61 P
sit down and feed, and welcome to our table. AYL 2.07.105
in his waning age | set foot under thy table. SHR 2.01.402
wants | for to supply the places at the table, 3.02.247
in our heart's table — heart too capable | of AWW 1.01. 95
at upper end o' th' table, now i' th' middle; WT 4.04. 59
his son a guest | that best becomes the table. 4.04.396
drawn in the flattering table of her eye. JN 2.01.503
drawn in the flattering table of her eye! 2.01.504
chamber, at the round table by a sea-coal fire, 2H4 2.01. 88 P
and wait upon him at his table as drawers. 2.02.172 P
i here divorce myself | both from thy table, 3H6 1.01.248
kings | hath in the table of his law commanded R3 1.04.196
you may worst | of all this table say so. H8 5.02.114
at priam's royal table do i sit, | and when fair TRO 1.01. 29
not serv'd thyself in to my table so many meals? 2.03. 42 P
giber for the table than a necessary bencher in COR 2.01. 82 P
set at upper end o' th' table; 4.05.193 P
by the entreaty and grant of the whole table. 4.05.200 P
their talk at table, and their thanks at end; 4.07. 4
claps me his sword upon the table, and says, ROM 3.01. 7 P
go, | let him have a table by himself, | for he TIM 1.02. 30
taste, touch, all, pleas'd from thy table rise; 1.02.126
so much left to furnish out | a moderate table. 3.04.115
if there sit twelve women at the table, let a 3.06. 78 P
anon we'll drink a measure | the table round. MAC 3.04. 12
i drink to th' general joy o' th' whole table, 3.04. 88
from the table of my memory | i'll wipe away all HAM 1.05. 98
two dishes, but to one table — that's the end. 4.03. 24 P
god be at your table! 4.05. 44 P
that were wont to set the table on a roar? 5.01.191 P
set me the stoups of wine upon that table. 5.02.267
thy beauty's form in table of my heart; SON 24. 2
TABLE-BOOK 2 FR 0.0002 REL FR 1 V 1 P
pomander, brooch, table-book, ballad, knife, WT 4.04.598 P
think, | if i had play'd the desk or table-book, HAM 2.02.136
TABLED 1 FR 0.0001 REL FR 0 V 1 P
of his endowments had been tabled by his side, CYM 1.04. 6 P
TABLE'S 1 FR 0.0001 REL FR 1 V 0 P
the table's full. MAC 3.04. 45
TABLES 12 FR 0.0013 REL FR 11 V 1 P
that, when he plays at tables, chides the dice LLL 5.02.326
be not lisping to his /master's old tables, his 2H4 2.04.266 P
and therefore will he wipe his tables clean 4.01.199
and wide unclasp the tables of their thoughts TRO 4.05. 60
more light, you knaves, and turn the tables up; ROM 1.05. 27
we may again | give to our tables meat, sleep to MAC 3.06. 34
did coldly furnish forth the marriage tables. HAM 1.02.181
my tables — meet it is i set it down | that one 1.05.107
in prison, yet | you clasp young cupid's tables. CYM 3.02. 39
their tables were stor'd full, to glad the sight PER 1.04. 28
thy gift, thy tables, are within my brain | full SON 122. 1
to trust those tables that receive thee more: 122.12
TABLE-SPORT 1 FR 0.0001 REL FR 0 V 1 P
let me for ever be your table-sport. WIV 4.02.162 P
TABLET 1 FR 0.0001 REL FR 1 V 0 P
this tablet lay upon his breast, wherein | our CYM 5.04.109
TABLE-TALK 1 FR 0.0001 REL FR 1 V 0 P
no, pray thee, let it serve for table-talk; MV 3.05. 88
TABOR 8 FR 0.0009 REL FR 3 V 5 P
then i beat my tabor, | at which, like unback'd TMP 4.01.175
now had he rather hear the tabor and the pipe; ADO 2.03. 14 P
or i will play | on the tabor to the worthies, LLL 5.01.154
dost thou live by thy tabor? TN 3.01. 2 P
or, the church stands by thy tabor, if thy tabor 3.01. 10 P
by thy tabor, if thy tabor stand by the church. 3.01. 10 P
would never dance again after a tabor and pipe; WT 4.04.182 P
the shepherd knows not thunder from a tabor COR 1.06. 25
TABORER 2 FR 0.0002 REL FR 1 V 1 P
i would i could see this taborer; TMP 3.02.151 P
draw up the company. where's the taborer? TNK 3.05. 23
TABORINES 1 FR 0.0001 REL FR 1 V 0 P
ear, | make mingle with our rattling taborines, ANT 4.08. 37
/TABORINS 1 FR 0.0001 REL FR 1 V 0 P
/beat /loud /the /taborins, let the trumpets TRO 4.05.275
TABORS 1 FR 0.0001 REL FR 1 V 0 P
tabors and cymbals, and the shouting romans, COR 5.04. 50
TACITURNITY 1 FR 0.0001 REL FR 1 V 0 P
pandar | have not more gift in taciturnity. TRO 4.02. 73
TACK 3 FR 0.0003 REL FR 3 V 0 P
and we shall tack about | and something do to TNK pr 26
up with a course or two, and tack about, boys! 3.04. 10
tack about! 4.01.152
TACK'D 1 FR 0.0001 REL FR 0 V 1 P
shirt is two napkins tack'd together and thrown 1H4 4.02. 43 P
TACKLE 5 FR 0.0005 REL FR 5 V 0 P
nor tackle, sail, nor mast, the very rats TMP 1.02.147
the tackle of my heart is crack'd and burn'd, JN 5.07. 52
upon the hempen tackle ship-boys climbing; H5 3.pr. 8
the silken tackle | swell with the touches of ANT 2.02.209
see the sports, then every man to 's tackle! TNK 2.03. 55
TACKLED 1 FR 0.0001 REL FR 1 V 0 P
and bring thee cords made like a tackled stair, ROM 2.04.189
TACKLE'S 1 FR 0.0001 REL FR 1 V 0 P
though thy tackle's torn, | thou show'st a noble COR 4.05. 61
TACKLES 1 FR 0.0001 REL FR 1 V 0 P
our slaught'red friends the tackles; 3H6 5.04. 15
TACKLING 2 FR 0.0002 REL FR 2 V 0 P
like a poor bark of sails and tackling reft, R3 4.04.234
for the tackling | let me alone. TNK 4.01.145
TACKLINGS 1 FR 0.0001 REL FR 1 V 0 P
the friends of france our shrouds and tacklings? 3H6 5.04. 18
TADDLE *(also tittle-tattling)*
TADDLE 1 FR 0.0001 REL FR 0 V 1 P
there is no tiddle taddle nor pibble babble in H5 4.01. 70 P
TADPOLE *(also todpole)*
TADPOLE 1 FR 0.0001 REL FR 1 V 0 P
i'll broach the tadpole on my rapier's point. TIT 4.02. 85
TA'EN *(also taken)*
TA'EN 97 FR 0.0109 REL FR 84 V 13 P
but valentine, if he be ta'en, must die. TGV 3.01.234
was eve's legacy, and cannot be ta'en from her. 3.01.339 P
i'll have my brains ta'en out and butter'd, and WIV 3.05. 7 P
though you have ta'en a special stand to strike 5.05.234 P
i have ta'en a due and wary note upon't. MM 4.01. 37
might in the times to come have ta'en revenge, 4.04. 30
i thought to have ta'en you at the porpentine; ERR 3.02.167
and i was ta'en for him, and he for me, | and 5.01.388
and he hath ta'en you newly into his grace, ADO 1.03. 22 P
he hath ta'en th' infection. hold it up. 2.03.121 P
ha' ta'en a couple of as arrant knaves as any in 3.05. 31 P
my lord, your brother john is ta'en in flight, 5.04.125
the prince of arragon hath ta'en his oath, | and MV 2.09. 2
your grace hath ta'en great pains to qualify 4.01. 7
leave thee till he hath ta'en thy life by some AYL 1.01.152 P
hath ta'en displeasure 'gainst his gentle niece, 1.02.278
that from the hunter's aim had ta'en a hurt, 2.01. 34
of bare distress hath ta'en from me the show 2.07. 95
he hath ta'en his bow and arrows and is gone 4.03. 4 P
and how was that ta'en up? 5.04. 48 P
no profit grows where is no pleasure ta'en. SHR 1.01. 39
therefore this order hath baptista ta'en, | that 1.02.126
well ta'en, and like a buzzard. 2.01.206
an old rusty sword ta'en out of the town armory, 3.02. 46 P
nay, i have ta'en you napping, gentle love, 4.02. 46
we be affied and such assurance ta'en | as shall 4.04. 49
that, were i ta'en here, it would scarce be TN 3.03. 28
that i, dear brother, be now ta'en for you! 3.04.376
my money and apparel ta'en from me, and these WT 4.03. 62 P
is assailed in our tent, | and ta'en, i fear. JN 3.02. 7
arthur ta'en prisoner? 3.04. 7
by some damn'd hand was robb'd and ta'en away. 5.01. 41
and, madam, there is order ta'en for you, | with R2 5.01. 53
a dozen of them here have ta'en the sacrament, 5.02. 97
but whether they be ta'en or slain we hear not. 5.06. 4
if i be ta'en, i'll peach for this. 1H4 2.02. 44 P
four of us here have ta'en a thousand pound this 2.04.159 P
right | according to our threefold order ta'en? 3.01. 70
discomfited great douglas, ta'en him once, 3.02.114
on, | and, his corruption being ta'en from us, 5.02. 22
that noble worcester | so soon ta'en prisoner, 2H4 1.01.126
you have ta'en up, | under the counterfeited 4.02. 26
the prince hath ta'en it hence. 4.05. 59
have but their stings and teeth newly ta'en out; 4.05.205
ten thousand french have ta'en the sacrament 1H6 4.02. 28
too late comes rescue, he is ta'en or slain; 4.04. 42
i come to know what prisoners thou hast ta'en, 4.07. 56
miracle, | thou art allotted to be ta'en by me; 5.03. 55
if you be ta'en, we then should see the bottom 2H6 5.02. 78
had he been ta'en, we should have heard the news 3H6 2.01. 4
be not ta'en tardy by unwise delay. R3 4.01. 51
that you have ta'en a tardy sluggard here. 5.03.225
us, | and then, as we have ta'en the sacrament, 5.05. 18
to see you ta'en from liberty, to look on | the H8 1.01.205
and high note's | ta'en of your many virtues, 2.03. 60
is stol'n away to rome, hath ta'en no leave, 3.02. 57
fellow, and hath ta'en much pain | in the king's 3.02. 72
i should have ta'en some pains to bring together 5.01.119
patroclus ta'en or slain, and palamedes | sore TRO 5.05. 13
ajax hath ta'en aeneas! 5.06. 22
i'll be ta'en too, | or bring him off. 5.06. 24
whereof we have ta'en good and good store — of COR 1.09. 32
we render you the tenth, to be ta'en forth, 1.09. 34
the town is ta'en! 1.10. 1
you should have ta'en th' advantage of his 2.03.198
they have ta'en note of us; keep on your way. 4.02. 10
because the law hath ta'en revenge on them. TIT 3.01.117
let me be ta'en, let me be put to death, | i am ROM 3.05. 17
that hath ta'en her hence to make me wail, 4.05. 31
he's ta'en. JC 5.03. 32
to see my best friend ta'en before my face! 5.03. 35
room ho! tell antony, brutus is ta'en. 5.04. 16
brutus is ta'en, brutus is ta'en, my lord! 5.04. 18
brutus is ta'en, brutus is ta'en, my lord! 5.04. 18
he is or ta'en or slain. 5.05. 3
that you have ta'en these tenders for true pay, HAM 1.03.106
and rewards | hast ta'en with equal thanks; 3.02. 68
if hamlet from himself be ta'en away, | and when 5.02.234
o, i have ta'en | too little care of this! LR 3.04. 32
king lear hath lost, he and his daughter ta'en. 5.02. 6
that i have ta'en away this old man's daughter, OTH 1.03. 78
hath ta'en your part — to have so much to do 3.03. 73
i'll have the work ta'en out, | and give't iago. 3.03.296
honest iago hath ta'en order for't. 5.02. 72
force him think i have pick'd the lock and ta'en CYM 2.02. 41
to be unbent when thou hast ta'en thy stand, 3.04.108
my throat, i have ta'en | his head from him. 4.02.150
hast done, | home art gone, and ta'en thy wages. 4.02.261
you | should have ta'en vengeance on my faults, 5.01. 8
prevented it, she had | ta'en off by poison. 5.05. 47
thou do demand a prisoner, | the noblest ta'en. 5.05.100
quite crack'd, | i having ta'en the forfeit. 5.05.208
which, being ta'en, would cease | the present 5.05.255
have you ta'en of it? 5.05.258
till now grown up | had been ta'en from you, and STM II.C 66
had ta'en his last leave of the weeping morn, VEN 2
know | her honor is ta'en prisoner by the foe, LUC 1608
TAFFATA 4 FR 0.0004 REL FR 2 V 2 P
beauties no richer than rich taffata. LLL 5.02.159
taffata phrases, silken terms precise, 5.02.406
tailor make thy doublet of changeable taffata, TN 2.04. 74 P
a fair hot wench in flame-color'd taffata; 1H4 1.02. 10 P
TAFFETY 1 FR 0.0001 REL FR 0 V 1 P
as your french crown for your taffety punk, as AWW 2.02. 22 P
TAG 1 FR 0.0001 REL FR 1 V 0 P
will you hence | before the tag return, whose COR 3.01.247
TAG-RAG 1 FR 0.0001 REL FR 0 V 1 P
if the tag-rag people did not clap him and hiss JC 1.02.258 P
TAH 2 FR 0.0002 REL FR 0 V 2 P
"rah, tah, tah," would 'a say, "bounce," would 2H4 3.02.284 P
"rah, tah, tah," would 'a say, "bounce," would 3.02.284 P
TAIL 26 FR 0.0029 REL FR 18 V 8 P
monster indeed if they were set in his tail. TMP 3.02. 11 P
in thy tail! TGV 2.03. 49 P
if he shake his tail and say nothing, it will. 2.05. 36 P
chin than dobbin my fill-horse has on his tail. MV 2.02. 95 P
seem then that dobbin's tail grows backward. 2.02. 96 P
had more hair of his tail than i have of my face 2.02. 97 P
in his tail. SHR 2.01.214
what, with my tongue in your tail? 2.01.218
and like a peacock sweep along his tail; 1H6 3.03. 6
hath clapp'd his tail between his legs and cried 2H6 5.01.154
come, tie his body to my horse's tail, | along TRO 5.08. 21
he's dead, and at the murtherer's horse's tail, 5.10. 4
and being once subdu'd in armed tail, | sweet 5.10. 43
and sometime comes she with a tithe-pig's tail ROM 1.04. 79
thither sail, | and, like a rat without a tail, MAC 1.03. 9
with my mother under the dragon's tail, and my LR 1.02.129 P
to change the cod's head for the salmon's tail; OTH 2.01.155
o, thereby hangs a tail. 3.01. 8 P
if we do fear this body hath a tail | more CYM 4.02.144
carry your tail without offense | or scandal to TNK 3.05. 34
unless by th' tail | and with thy teeth thou 3.05. 49
the bavian, with long tail and eke long tool, 3.05.132
and, for a jig, come cut and long tail to him! 5.02. 49
thin mane, thick tail, broad buttock, tender VEN 298
through his mane and tail the high wind sings, 305
he vails his tail that, like a falling plume, 314
TAILOR 35 FR 0.0039 REL FR 14 V 21 P
yet a tailor might scratch her where e'er she TMP 2.02. 53
of thine shall be a tailor to thee and shall WIV 3.03. 34 P
even now a tailor call'd me in his shop, | and ERR 4.03. 7
robin starveling, the tailor. MND 1.02. 58 P
and "tailor" cries, and falls into a cough; 2.01. 54
knew the tailor that made the wings she flew MV 3.01. 27 P
the tailor stays thy leisure, | to deck thy body SHR 4.03. 59
come, tailor, let us see these ornaments; 4.03. 61
come, tailor, let us see't. 4.03. 86
what a' devil's name, tailor, call'st thou this? 4.03. 92
hortensio, say thou wilt see the tailor paid. 4.03.164
tailor, i'll pay thee for thy gown to-morrow, 4.03.166
pray you, sir, who's his tailor? AWW 2.05. 16 P
he, sir, 's a good workman, a very good tailor. 2.05. 19 P
and the tailor make thy doublet of changeable TN 2.04. 74 P
'tis the next way to turn tailor, or be 1H4 3.01.259 P
a woman's tailor, sir. 2H4 3.02.150 P
may, but if he had been a man's tailor, he'd 'a' 3.02.152 P
well said, good woman's tailor! 3.02.158 P
prick the woman's tailor. 3.02.161 P
i would thou wert a man's tailor, that thou 3.02.164 P
will this feeble the woman's tailor run off! 3.02.268 P
with his yard and the tailor with his last, the ROM 1.02. 40 P
not fall out with a tailor for wearing his new 3.01. 27 P
faith, here's an english tailor come hither for MAC 2.03. 13 P
come in, tailor, here you may roast your goose. 2.03. 14 P
a tailor made thee. LR 2.02. 55 P
thou art a strange fellow. a tailor make a man? 2.02. 56 P
a tailor, sir. 2.02. 58 P
too dear, | with that he call'd the tailor lown; OTH 2.03. 92
who was made by him that made the tailor, not be CYM 4.01. 4 P
no, nor thy tailor, rascal, | who is thy 4.02. 81
thou precious varlet, | my tailor made them not. 4.02. 84
bond to follow him | follows his tailor, haply TNK 1.02. 51
are not you a tailor? 4.01.108
TAILOR'S 2 FR 0.0002 REL FR 1 V 1 P
with open mouth swallowing a tailor's news, JN 4.02.195
you tailor's yard, you sheath, you bowcase, you 1H4 2.04.246 P
TAILORS' 1 FR 0.0001 REL FR 1 V 0 P
when nobles are their tailors' tutors; LR 3.02. 83
TAILORS 6 FR 0.0006 REL FR 3 V 3 P
i have undone three tailors, i have had four AYL 5.04. 46 P
and entertain a score or two of tailors | to R3 1.02.256
fill the court with quarrels, talk, and tailors. H8 1.03. 20
is nothing but to rust iron, increase tailors, COR 4.05.220 P
him, it shows to man the tailors of the earth; ANT 1.02.163 P
than some, whose tailors are as dear as yours, CYM 2.03. 79
TAILS 3 FR 0.0003 REL FR 3 V 0 P
is goads, thorns, nettles, tails of wasps), WT 1.02.329
tickle't out | of the jades' tails to-morrow. TNK 2.03. 29
clapping their proud tails to the ground below, VEN 923
TAINT 16 FR 0.0018 REL FR 15 V 1 P
wise /men, folly-fall'n, quite taint their wit. TN 3.01. 68
him now, lest the device take air and taint. 3.04.132 P
or any taint of vice whose strong corruption 3.04.356
come | taint the condition of this present hour, 5.01.357
never yet taint with love, i send the king. 1H6 5.03.183
to taint that honor every good tongue blesses, H8 3.01. 55
and odious, | i will not taint my mouth with, 3.02.332
with a general taint | of the whole state; 5.02. 63
main opinion crush | in taint of our best man. TRO 1.03.373
remove to dunsinane | i cannot taint with fear. MAC 5.03. 3
taint not thy mind, nor let thy soul contrive HAM 1.05. 85
your fore-vouch'd affection | fall into taint; LR 1.01.221
that my disports corrupt and taint my business, OTH 1.03.271
may defeat my life, | but never taint my love. 4.02.161
to taint his nobler heart and brain | with CYM 5.04. 65
not taint mine eye | with dread sights it may TNK 5.03. 9
TAINTED 19 FR 0.0021 REL FR 15 V 4 P
corrupt, corrupt, and tainted in desire! WIV 5.05. 90
whether thou art tainted or free. MM 1.02. 43 P
madness, pray heaven his wisdom be not tainted! 4.04. 5 P
a fair presence, though your heart be tainted; ERR 3.02. 13
may season give | to her foul tainted flesh! ADO 4.01.143
in law, what plea so tainted and corrupt | but, MV 3.02. 75
i am a tainted wether of the flock, | meetest 4.01.114
a very tainted fellow, and full of wickedness. AWW 3.02. 87
he come, for sure the man is tainted in 's wits. TN 3.04. 13 P
my age was never tainted with such shame. 1H6 4.05. 46
corrupt and tainted with a thousand vices, 5.04. 45
and nero will be tainted with remorse | to hear 3H6 3.01. 40

as a man sorely tainted, to his answer, | he H8 4.02. 14
their breath with sweetmeats tainted are. ROM 1.04. 76
if thy faith be not tainted with the breach of CYM 3.04. 26 P
a settled valor | (not tainted with extremes) TNK 4.02.101
for by our ears our hearts oft tainted be; LUC 38
which by him tainted shall for him be spent, 1182
which seems to weep upon the tainted place, 1746

TAINTING 3 FR 0.0003 REL FR 1 V 2 P
above | punish my life for tainting of my love! TN 5.01.138
speaking too loud, or tainting his discipline, OTH 2.01.268 P
a dram, you cannot preserve it from tainting. CYM 1.04.136 P

TAINTS 5 FR 0.0005 REL FR 5 V 0 P
subtly taints | even then when they sit idly in TRO 3.03.232
which out of daily fortune ever taints | the COR 4.07. 38
the taints and blames i laid upon myself, | for MAC 4.03.124
that they may seem the taints of liberty, | the HAM 2.01. 32
his taints and honors | wag'd equal with him. ANT 5.01. 30

TAINTURE 1 FR 0.0001 REL FR 1 V 0 P
gloucester, see here the tainture of thy nest, 2H6 2.01.184

/TAKE 10 FR 0.0011 REL FR 9 V 1 P
/that /king /again, | /and /take /thou /this!" 2H4 1.03.107
/i /take /not /on /me /here /as /a /physician, 4.01. 60
/to /take /is /not /to /give. R3 1.02.202
/sirs, /take /up /the /corse. 1.02.225
/come, /take /away. TIT 3.02. 81
/he /runs, | /and /bids /what /will /take /all. LR 3.01. 15
/robed /man /of /justice, /take /thy /place, 3.06. 36
/mouth, | /thy /sheep /shall /take /no /harm." 3.06. 44
/i /here /take /my /oath /before /this 3.06. 46 P
/to /take /the /safest /occasion /by /the /front OTH 3.01. 49

TAKE 1270 FR 0.1435 REL FR 975 V 295 P
take in the topsail. TMP 1.01. 6 P
let's take leave of him. 1.01. 64
thing she did | they would not take her life. 1.02.267
go take this shape | and hither come in't. 1.02.303
which any print of goodness wilt not take, 1.02.352
unto these yellow sands, | and then take hands: 1.02.376
good lord, how you take it! 2.01. 81 P
will guard your person while you take your rest, 2.01.197
they'll take suggestion as a cat laps milk; 2.01.288
open–ey'd conspiracy | his time doth take. 2.01.302
four legs, who hath got, as i take it, an ague. 2.02. 66 P
keep him tame, i will not take too much for him; 2.02. 76 P
and much less take | what i shall die to want. 3.01. 78
give him blows, | and take his bottle from him. 3.02. 65
take thou that. 3.02. 76 P
your monster, and the devil take your fingers! 3.02. 81 P
the next advantage | will we take throughly. 3.03. 14
worthily purchas'd, take my daughter. 4.01. 14
therefore take heed, | as hymen's lamps shall 4.01. 22
into lust, to take away | the edge of that day's 4.01. 28
if i should take a displeasure against you, look 4.01.202 P
nobler reason, 'gainst my fury | do i take part. 5.01. 27
the rest, and let no man take care for himself; 5.01.257 P
one) had plotted with them | to take my life. 5.01.274
take with you your companions. 5.01.293
ass | was i to take this drunkard for a god, 5.01.297
where you shall take your rest | for this one 5.01.302
your life, which must | take the ear strangely. 5.01.314
now let us take our leave. TGV 1.01. 56
to set it together, take it for your pains. 1.01.117 P
no, not so much as "take this for thy pains." 1.01.143 P
take the paper; 1.02. 46
to take a paper up that i let fall. 1.02. 71
if you respect them, best to take them up. 1.02.131
lest he should take exceptions to my love, | and 1.03. 81
and yet take this again — and yet i thank you 2.01.118
writ, | but (since unwillingly) take them again. 2.01.123
nay, take them. 2.01.124
why, if it please you, take it for your labor; 2.01.133
here, take you this. 2.02. 6
to take a note of what i stand in need of, | to 2.07. 84
i now am full resolv'd to take a wife | and turn 3.01. 76
wife | and turn her out to who will take her in: 3.01. 77
take no repulse, what ever she doth say; 3.01.100
you take the sum and substance that i have. 4.01. 15
tell us this: have you any thing to take to? 4.01. 40
i take your offer, and will live with you, 4.01. 68
sir proteus, as i take it. 4.02. 90
than he, to take a fault upon me that he did, i 4.04. 14 P
go presently, and take this ring with thee, 4.04. 71
come, shadow, come, and take this shadow up, 4.04.197
take but possession of her with a touch — | i 5.04.130
take thou thy silvia, for thou hast deserv'd her 5.04.147
take your vizaments in that. WIV 1.01. 39 P
then lucifer take all! 1.03. 76
here, take the humor–letter; 1.03. 77 P
take the honor. 2.01. 46 P
take heed, have open eye, for thieves do foot by 2.01.122
take heed, ere summer comes or cuckoo–birds do 2.01.123
she will, say what she will, take all, pay all, 2.02.118 P
help to bear it, sir john, take all, or half, 2.02.172 P
take your rapier, jack, i vill tell you how i 2.03. 13 P
villainy, take your rapier. 2.03. 16 P
well, i will take him, then torture my wife, 3.02. 40 P
if he take her, let him take her simply. 3.02. 76 P
if he take her, let him take her simply. 3.02. 76 P
staggering) take this basket on your shoulders. 3.03. 12 P
to take an ill advantage of his absence. 3.03.109 P
go take up these clothes here quickly. 3.03.146 P
take away these chalices. 3.05. 28 P
she does so take on with her men; 3.05. 39 P
i will now take the lecher; 3.05.144 P
sirs, take the basket again on your shoulders. 4.02.108 P
come, come, take it up. 4.02.111 P
will you take up your wive's clothes? 4.02.141 P
where we may take him, and disgrace him for it. 4.04. 15
the devil take one party and his dam the other! 4.05.106 P
time | to take her by the hand and bid her go, 4.06. 37
when you see your time, take her by the hand, 5.03. 2 P
come, will this wood take fire? 5.05. 88
i will never take you for my love again, but i 5.05.117 P
why? did you take her in /green? 5.05.208 P
take thy commission. MM 1.01. 47
therefore take your honors. 1.01. 52
i take my leave of you. 1.04. 90
i'll take my leave, | and leave you to the 2.01.135
if your worship will take order for the drabs 2.01.234 P
as it is an evil, | and take the shame with joy. 2.03. 36
wherein (let no man hear me) i take pride, 2.04. 10
as easy | falsely to take away a life true made 2.04. 47
to do't, | i'll take it as a peril to my soul, 2.04. 65
to take life | from thine own sister's shame? 3.01.138
take my defiance! 3.01.142
were it in death to take this poor maid from the 3.01.231 P
and, sir, we take him to be a thief too, sir, 3.02. 16 P
take him to prison, officer. 3.02. 31
if you take it not patiently, why, your mettle 3.02. 76 P
of a codpiece to take away the life of a man! 3.02.115 P
take, o, take those lips away, | that so sweetly 4.01. 1
take, o, take those lips away, | that so sweetly 4.01. 1
take then this your companion by the hand, | who 4.01. 54
she'll take the enterprise upon her, father, 4.01. 65
if you will take it on you to assist him, it 4.02. 10 P
for, as i take it, it is almost day. 4.02.105 P
pray you take note of it; 5.01. 80
the warrant's for yourself; take heed to't. 5.01. 83
take him hence; 5.01.311
go take her hence, and marry her instantly. 5.01.377
sweet isabel, take my part! 5.01.430
bed would break, | and take her hence in horror. 5.01.436
and pray thee take this mercy to provide | for 5.01.484
take him to prison, | and see our pleasure 5.01.520
jailer, take him to thy custody. ERR 1.01.155
many a man would take you at your word, | and go 1.02. 17
there, take you that, sir knave. 1.02. 92
nay, and you will not, sir, i'll take my heels. 1.02. 94
hold, take thou that, and that. 2.02. 23
and take unmingled thence that drop again, 2.02.127
as take from me thyself and not me too. 2.02.129
though my cates be mean, take them in good part; 3.01. 28
and as a /bed i'll take /them, and there lie, 3.02. 49
good signior, take the stranger to my house, 4.01. 36
and with you take the chain, and bid my wife 4.01. 37
some get within him, take his sword away: 5.01. 34
for god's sake take a house! 5.01. 36
and take perforce my husband from the abbess. 5.01.117
whilst to take order for the wrongs i went, 5.01.146
he cries for you, and vows, if he can take you, 5.01.182
there, take it, and much thanks for my good 5.01.393
vouchsafe to take the pains | to go with us into 5.01.394
what key shall a man take you to go in the song? ADO 1.01.186 P
and take her hearing prisoner with the force 1.01.324
he meant to take the present time by the top, 1.02. 14 P
impossible you should take true root but by the 1.03. 23 P
therefore i will even take sixpence in earnest 2.01. 40 P
who, as i take it, have stol'n his bird's nest. 2.01.230 P
count, take of me my daughter, and with her my 2.01.302 P
me to an oyster, but i'll take my oath on it, 2.03. 24 P
and i take him to be valiant. 2.03.188 P
those thanks than you take pains to thank me. 2.03.251 P
you take pleasure then in the message? 2.03.253 P
so much as you may take upon a knive's point and 2.03.254 P
"any pains that i take for you is as easy as 2.03.261 P
if i do not take pity of her, i am a villain; 2.03.262 P
nor take no shape nor project of affection, 3.01. 55
why then take no note of him, but let him go, 3.03. 28 P
peaceable way for you, if you do take a thief, 3.03. 58 P
take their examination yourself, and bring it me 3.05. 49 P
there, leonato, take her back again. 4.01. 31
take not away thy heavy hand, | death is the 4.01.115
bear her in hand until they come to take hands, 4.01.304 P
indeed | as i dare take a serpent by the tongue. 5.01. 90
expect your coming, | to–night i take my leave. 5.01.297
no, that you shall not till you take her hand, 5.04. 56
thee, but, by this light, i take thee for pity. 5.04. 93 P
thought of it, i would take desire prisoner, and LLL 1.02. 61 P
you must suffer him to take no delight nor no 1.02.128 P
take away this villain, shut him up. 1.02.153 P
it was well done of you to take him at his word. 2.01.217
go, tenderness of years, take this key, give 3.01. 4 P
doth the inconsiderate take salve for l'envoy, 3.01. 78 P
(good my glass), take this for telling true: 4.01. 18
hold, take thou this, my sweet, and give me 5.02.132
thine, | so shall berowne take me for rosaline. 5.02.133
take hands. 5.02.219
why take we hands then? 5.02.220
fair lord — | take that for your fair lady. 5.02.240
take all and wean it, it may prove an ox. 5.02.250
but that you take what doth to you belong, | it 5.02.381
but take it, sir, again. 5.02.453
we will take some care. 5.02.510
pick out five such, take each one in his vein. 5.02.545
take away the conqueror, take away alisander. 5.02.572 P
take away the conqueror, take away alisander. 5.02.572 P
master, let me take you a button–hole lower. 5.02.700 P
ay, sweet my lord, and so i take my leave. 5.02.872
i will kiss thy royal finger, and take leave. 5.02.882 P
take time to pause, and by the next new moon — MND 1.01. 83
take comfort; 1.01.202
flute, you must take thisby on you. 1.02. 44 P
take pains, be perfit; 1.02.108 P
take heed the queen come not within his sight; 2.01. 19
and ere i take this charm from off her sight 2.01.183
her sight | (as i can take it with another herb) 2.01.184
take thou some of it, and seek through this 2.01.259
thou dost wake, | do it for thy true–love take; 2.02. 28
o, take the sense, sweet, of my innocence! 2.02. 45
when i did him at this advantage take, | an 3.02. 16
to break loose — take on as you would follow, 3.02.258
she shall not, though you take her part. 3.02.322
speak not of helena, | take not her part. 3.02.333
to take from thence all error with his might, 3.02.368
known, | that every man should take his own, 3.02.459
take this transformed scalp | from off the head 4.01. 64
robin, take off this head. 4.01. 80
come, my queen, take hands with me, | and rock 4.01. 85
and take your places, ladies. 5.01. 84
our sport shall be to take what they mistake; 5.01. 90
i trust to take of truest thisby sight. 5.01.275
tongue, lose thy light, | moon, take thy flight, 5.01.305
consecrate, | every fairy take his gait, | and 5.01.416
i take it your own business calls on you, | and MV 1.01. 63
seek for you, madam, to take their leave; 1.02.124 P
i think i may take his bond. 1.03. 27 P
and what of him? did he take interest? 1.03. 75
no, not take interest, not, as you would say, 1.03. 76
for when did friendship take | a breed for 1.03.133
and take no doit | of usance for my moneys, and 1.03.140
if he will take it, so, if not, adieu; 1.03.169
you must take your chance, | and either not 2.01. 38
use your legs, take the start, run away." 2.02. 6 P
take heed, honest launcelot, take heed, honest 2.02. 7 P
honest launcelot, take heed, honest /gobbo," or, 2.02. 7 P
take leave of thy old master, and inquire | my 2.02.153
i'll take my leave of the jew in the twinkling. 2.02.167 P
pray thee take pain | to allay with some cold 2.02.185
hold here, take this. 2.04. 19
how i shall take her from her father's house, 2.04. 30
there, take it, prince, and if my form lie there 2.07. 61
too griev'd a heart | to take a tedious leave; 2.07. 77
take what wife you will to bed, | i will ever be 2.09. 70
if he forfeit, thou wilt not take his flesh. 3.01. 52 P
to discharge the jew, | he would not take it. 3.02.274
take this same letter, | and use thou all th' 3.04. 47
and here, i take it, is the doctor come. 4.01.168
you are welcome, take your place. 4.01.170
take thrice thy money, bid me tear the bond. 4.01.234
take then thy bond, take thou thy pound of flesh 4.01.308
then thy bond, take thou thy pound of flesh, 4.01.308
i take this offer then; 4.01.318
why doth the jew pause? take thy forfeiture. 4.01.335
nay, take my life and all, pardon not that: 4.01.374
you take my house when you do take the prop 4.01.375
you take my house when you do take the prop 4.01.375
you take my life | when you do take the means 4.01.376
when you do take the means whereby i live. 4.01.377
i wish you well, and so i take my leave. 4.01.420
take some remembrance of us, as a tribute, | not 4.01.422
and for your love i'll take this ring from you. 4.01.427
do not draw back your hand, i'll take no more, 4.01.428
give order to my servants that they take | no 5.01.119
since you do take it, love, so much at heart. 5.01.145
and neither man nor master would take aught 5.01.183
let not me take him then, | for if i do, i'll 5.01.236
gave me his countenance seems to take from me. AYL 1.01. 18 P
i would not take this hand from thy throat till 1.01. 60 P
have taught my love to take thy father for mine; 1.02. 12 P
all the beholders take his part with weeping. 1.02.131 P
you will take little delight in it, i can tell 1.02.158 P
o, they take the part of a better wrastler than 1.03. 22 P
and do not seek to take your change upon you, 1.03.102
take that, and he that doth the ravens feed, 2.03. 43
and bid him take that for coming a–night to jane 2.04. 48 P
and take upon command what help we have | that 2.07.125
i prithee take the cork out of thy mouth that i 3.02.202 P
nay, but the devil take mocking. 3.02.214 P
but take a taste of my finding him, and relish 3.02.233 P
which i take to be either a fool or a cipher. 3.02.290 P
and this way will i take upon me to wash your 3.02.422 P
i will not take her on gift of any man. 3.03. 68 P
cry the man mercy, love him, take his offer; 3.05. 61
so take her to thee, shepherd. 3.05. 63
lack of matter, you might take occasion to kiss. 4.01. 75 P
i take some joy to say you are, because i would 4.01. 89 P
then you must say, "i take thee, rosalind, for 4.01.135 P
i take thee, rosalind, for wife. 4.01.137 P
ask you for your commission, but i do take thee, 4.01.139 P
you shall never take her without her answer, 4.01.172 P
answer, unless you take her without her tongue. 4.01.173 P
take thou no scorn to wear the horn, | it was a 4.02. 13
will the faithful offer take | of me and all 4.03. 60
i pray you, will you take him by the arm? 4.03.162
take a good heart and counterfeit to be a man. 4.03.173 P
and therefore take the present time, | with a 5.03. 30
mine, sir, to take that that no man else will. 5.04. 59 P
when seven justices could not take up a quarrel, 5.04. 99 P
here's eight that must take hands | to join in 5.04.128
conduct, purposely to take | his brother here, 5.04.157
trust me, i take him for the better dog. SHR in.1. 25
then take him up, and manage well the jest. in.1. 45
take him up gently and to bed with him, | and in.1. 72
go, sirrah, take them to the buttery, | and give in.1. 102
and take a lodging fit to entertain | such 1.01. 44
i knew not what to take and what to leave? 1.01.104
light on them, would take her with all faults, 1.01.129 P
but i had as lief take her dowry with this 1.01.131 P
that love should of a sudden take such hold? 1.01.147
take my color'd hat and cloak. 1.01.207
for a while i take my leave | to see my friends 1.02. 1
take your paper too, | and let me have them very 1.02.150
take you the lute, and you the set of books. 2.01.106
take this of me, kate of my consolation — 2.01.190
o slow–wing'd turtle, shall a buzzard take thee? 2.01.207
and so i take my leave, and thank you both. 2.01.398
take you your instrument, play you the whiles, 3.01. 22
"hic steterat priami," take heed he hear us not, 3.01. 43 P
good master, take it not unkindly, pray, | that 3.01. 57
b mi, bianca, take him for thy lord, | c fa ut, 3.01. 75
book, | and as he stoop'd again to take it up, 3.02.162
"now take them up," quoth he, "if any list." 3.02.165
and therefore here i mean to take my leave. 3.02.188
that take it on you at the first so roundly. 3.02.214
place, | and let bianca take her sister's room. 3.02.250
the weather, a taller man than i will take cold. 4.01. 11 P
door | to hold my stirrup nor to take my horse? 4.01.121
take that, and mend the plucking /off the other. 4.01.148
there, take it to you, trenchers, cups, and all. 4.01.165
and here i take the like unfeigned oath, | never 4.02. 32
shall win my love, and so i take my leave, | in 4.02. 42
take /in your love, and then let me alone. 4.02. 71
look that you take upon you as you should; 4.02.109
here, take away this dish. 4.03. 44
take thou the bill, give me thy mete–yard, and 4.03.151 P
go take it up unto thy master's use. 4.03.157
take up my mistress' gown for thy master's use! 4.03.158 P
take up my mistress' gown to his master's use! 4.03.162
go take it hence, be gone, and say no more. 4.03.165
take no unkindness of his hasty words. 4.03.167
take you assurance of her, cum privilegio ad 4.04. 92 P
to th' church take the priest, clerk, and some 4.04. 94 P
knavery, to take upon you another man's name. 5.01. 36 P
take heed, signior baptista, lest you be 5.01. 98 P
that they take place when virtue's steely bones AWW 1.01.103

those girls of italy, take heed of them. 2.01. 19
after them, and take a more dilated farewell. 2.01. 57 P
too, or take off thine | by wond'ring how thou 2.01. 89
which great love grant, and so i take my leave. 2.03. 85
be not afraid that i your hand should take, 2.03. 89
i dare not say i take you, but i give | me and 2.03.102
then, young bertram, take her, she's thy wife. 2.03.105
here, take her hand, | proud scornful boy, 2.03.150
take her by the hand, | and tell her she is 2.03.173
i take her hand. 2.03.176
thou hast a son shall take this disgrace off me, 2.03.235 P
that you will take your instant leave a' th' 2.04. 48
when i should take possession of the bride, 2.05. 26
you | that presently you take your way for home, 2.05. 64
i take my young lord to be a very melancholy man 3.02. 3 P
and would you take the letter of her? 3.04. 1
well, diana, take heed of this french earl. 3.05. 11 P
we'll take your offer kindly. 3.05.101
take this purse of gold, | and let me buy your 3.07. 14
swear not by, | but take the high'st to witness. 4.02. 24
here, take my ring! 4.02. 51
i'll order take my mother shall not hear. 4.02. 55
that he might take a measure of his own 4.03. 33 P
do, i'll take the sacrament on't, how and which 4.03.136 P
to take heed of the allurement of one count 4.03.214 P
he swears oaths, bid him drop gold, and take it; 4.03.223
he ne'er pays after–debts, take it before, | and 4.03.226
you, and take your leave of all your friends. 4.03.311 P
which i take to be too little for pomp to enter. 4.05. 51 P
marry, as i take it, to rossillion, | whither i 5.01. 28
let's take the instant by the forward top; 5.03. 39
howe'er it pleases you to take it so, | the ring 5.03. 88
take him away. 5.03.120
take her away, i do not like her now, | to 5.03.281
take her away. 5.03.285
your gentle hands lend us, and take our hearts. ep 6
means my niece to take the death of her brother TN 1.03. 1 P
hope to see a huswife take thee between her legs 1.03.103 P
are they like to take dust, like mistress mall's 1.03.127 P
take the fool away. 1.05. 38 P
do you not hear, fellows? take away the lady. 1.05. 39 P
the lady bade take away the fool, therefore i 1.05. 52 P
the fool, therefore i say again, take her away. 1.05. 53 P
sir, i bade them take away you. 1.05. 54 P
take away the fool, gentlemen. 1.05. 71 P
i protest i take these wise men that crow so at 1.05. 88 P
is to take those things for bird–bolts that you 1.05. 92 P
and it would please you to take leave of her, 2.03.100 P
i do not, never trust me, take it how you will. 2.03.188 P
let still the woman take | an elder than herself 2.04. 29
no pains, sir, i take pleasure in singing, sir. 2.04. 68 P
and does not toby take you a blow o' the lips 2.05. 67 P
eleven places — my niece shall take note of it, 3.02. 36 P
him now, lest the device take air and taint. 3.04.131 P
give them way till he take leave, and presently 3.04.198 P
i have his horse to take up the quarrel. 3.04.292 P
have done offense, i take the fault on me; 3.04.313
take him away, he knows i know him well. 3.04.331
take and give back affairs and their dispatch 4.03. 18
sir, let your bounty take a nap, i will awake it 5.01. 48 P
take him aside. 5.01.100
fear not, cesario, take thy fortunes up, | be 5.01.148
farewell, and take her, but direct thy feet 5.01.168
when at bohemia | you take my lord, i'll give WT 1.02. 40
honest friend, | will you take eggs for money? 1.02.161
will take again your queen as yours at first, 1.02.336
please your highness | to take the urgent hour. 1.02.465
take the boy to you; 2.01. 1
to laughter, as i take it, | if the good truth 2.01.198
for present vengeance, | take it on her. 2.03. 23
unless he take the course that you have done — 2.03. 48
when she will take the rein i let her run, | but 2.03. 51
take up the bastard, | take't up, i say; 2.03. 76
once more, take her hence. 2.03.112
hast | a heart so tender o'er it, take it hence, 2.03.133
take it up straight. 2.03.135
go, take it to the fire, | for thou set'st on 2.03.141
take it up. 2.03.183
with camillo to take away the life of our 3.02. 16 P
though devis'd | and play'd to take spectators. 3.02. 37
take her hence; 3.02.149
take your patience to you, | and i'll say 3.02.231
i'll take it up for pity — yet i'll tarry till 3.03. 76 P
look thee here, take up, take up, boy; 3.03.116 P
look thee here, take up, take up, boy; 3.03.116 P
now take upon me, in the name of time, | to use 4.01. 3
or take away with thee the very services thou 4.02. 16 P
i will even take my leave of you, and pace 4.03.112 P
it is my father's will i should take on me | the 4.04. 71
and take | the winds of march with beauty; 4.04.119
come, take your flow'rs. 4.04.132
with mopsa, thou shouldst take no money of me, 4.04.232 P
your heart is full of something that does take 4.04.346
i take thy hand, this hand, | as soft as dove's 4.04.362
take hands, a bargain! 4.04.383
beseech you | of your own state take care. 4.04.448
you, | but as you shake off one to take another; 4.04.569
subdue the cheek, | but not take in the mind. 4.04.577
earnest, but i cannot with conscience take it. 4.04.646 P
take your sweetheart's hat | and pluck it o'er 4.04.650
it should take joy | to see her in your arms. 5.01. 80
it seem'd sorrow wept to take leave of them, for 5.02. 45 P
pow'r | to take off so much grief from you as he 5.03. 55
indeed, descend, | and take you by the hand; 5.03. 89
thou shouldst a husband take by my consent, | as 5.03.136
and take her by the hand, whose worth and 5.03.144
then take my king's defiance from my mouth, JN 1.01. 21
brother, take you my land, i'll take my chance. 1.01.151
brother, take you my land, i'll take my chance. 1.01.151
that will take pains to blow a horn before her? 1.01.219
o, take his mother's thanks, a widow's thanks, 2.01. 32
but, ass, i'll take that burthen from your back, 2.01.145
which heaven shall take in nature of a fee; 2.01.170
speed then to take advantage of the field. 2.01.297
makes it take head from all indifferency, | from 2.01.579
with my vex'd spirits i cannot take a truce, 3.01. 17
evils that take leave, | on their departure most 3.04.114
his words do take possession of my bosom. 4.01. 32
by slaves that take their humors for a warrant 4.02.209
heaven take my soul, and england keep my bones! 4.03. 10
how easy dost thou take all england up | from 4.03.142
take again | from this my hand, as holding of 5.01. 2
to cudgel you and make you take the hatch, | to 5.02.138
he means to recompense the pains you take | by 5.04. 15
how did he take it? who did taste to him? 5.06. 28
nor let my kingdom's rivers take their course 5.07. 38
peace | as we with honor and respect may take, 5.07. 85
much strength | as to take up mine honor's pawn, R2 1.01. 74
i take it up, and by that sword i swear | which 1.01. 78
take but my shame, | and i resign my gage. 1.01.175
one, | take honor from me, and my life is done. 1.01.183
i take my leave before i have begun, | for 1.02. 60
then let us take a ceremonious leave | and 1.03. 50
and craves to kiss your hand and take his leave. 1.03. 53
my loving lord, i take my leave of you; 1.03. 63
take from my mouth the wish of happy years. 1.03. 94
return again, and take an oath with thee. 1.03.178
my lord, no leave take i, for i will ride, | as 1.03.251
i have too few to take my leave of you, | when 1.03.255
take herford's rights away, and take from time 2.01.195
away, and take from time | his charters and his 2.01.195
hold, take my ring. 2.02. 92
you on | to take advantage of the absent time, 2.03. 79
my comfort is, that heaven will take our souls, 3.01. 33
take special care my greetings be delivered. 3.01. 39
take not, good cousin, further than you should, 3.03. 16
on yon proud man should take it off again | with 3.03.135
bagot, forbear, thou shalt not take it up. 4.01. 30
you shall not only take the sacrament | to bury 4.01.328
take the correction, mildly kiss the rod, | and 5.01. 32
take leave and part, for you must part forthwith 5.01. 70
thus give i mine, and thus take i thy heart. 5.01. 96
part | to take on me to keep and kill thy heart. 5.01. 98
the devil take henry of lancaster and thee! 5.05.102
take hence the rest, and give them burial here. 5.05.118
the guilt of conscience take thou for thy labor, 5.06. 41
and pride of their contention did take horse, 1H4 1.01. 60
for we that take purses go by the moon and the 1.02. 14 P
where shall we take a purse to–morrow, jack? 1.02. 98 P
cousin" — | o, the devil take such cozeners! 1.03.255
'tis dangerous to take a cold, to sleep, to 2.03. 8 P
they take it already upon their salvation, that 2.04. 9 P
son of england prove a thief and take purses? 2.04.410 P
i would your grace would take me with you. 2.04.460 P
from whom you now must steal and take no leave, 3.01. 92
here come our wives, and let us take our leave. 3.01.189
shall i not take mine ease in mine inn but i 3.03. 80 P
come let us take a muster speedily. 4.01.133
and if it do, take it for thy labor, and if it 4.02. 7 P
and if it make twenty, take them all, i'll 4.02. 8 P
i am content that he shall take the odds | of 5.01. 97
and, will they take the offer of our grace, 5.01.106
we offer fair, take it advisedly. 5.01.114
or take away the grief of a wound? 5.01.132 P
thou gets not my sword, but take my pistol, if 5.03. 51 P
adieu, and take thy praise with thee to heaven! 5.04. 99
i'll take it upon my death, i gave him this 5.04.150 P
and i will take it as a sweet disgrace | and 2H4 1.01. 89
men of all sorts take a pride to gird at me. 1.02. 6 P
he would not take his band and yours, he lik'd 1.02. 32 P
this apoplexy, as i take it, is a kind of 1.02.111 P
looks upon me will take me without weighing, and 1.02.166 P
by the lord, i take but two shirts out with me, 1.02.209 P
perforce a third | must take up us. 1.03. 73
alas the day, take heed of him! 2.01. 13 P
being you are to take soldiers up in counties as 2.01.187 P
or to take note how many pair of silk stockings 2.02. 14 P
"i will now take my leave of these six dry, 2.04. 7 P
on, therefore take heed what guests you receive. 2.04. 93 P
all to a merriment, if you take not the heat. 2.04.298 P
who take the ruffian /billows by the top, 3.01. 22
i will take your counsel, | and were these 3.01.106
and i will take such order that thy friends 3.02.185 P
mowbray, you overween to take it so; 4.01.147
then take, my lord of westmerland, this schedule 4.01.166
i take your princely word for these redresses. 4.02. 66
steers unyok'd, they take their courses | east, 4.02.103
i pray you take me up, and bear me hence | into 4.04.131
but wherefore did he take away the crown? 4.05. 88
god put /it in thy mind to take it hence, | that 4.05.178
carriage is caught, as men take diseases, one of 5.01. 76 P
therefore let men take heed of their company. 5.01. 77 P
from the court, i take it there's but two ways, 5.03.110 P
i would not take a /knighthood for my fortune. 5.03.126 P
let us take any man's horses, the laws of 5.03.136 P
take all his company along with him. 5.05. 92
take them away. 5.05. 95
therefore take heed how you impawn our person, H5 1.02. 21
we charge you, in the name of god, take heed; 1.02. 23
whereof take you one quarter into france, | and 1.02.215
their promises, | ere he take ship for france; 2.pr. 30
for i can take, and pistol's cock is up, | and 2.01. 52
take up the english short, and let them know 2.04. 72
and to take mercy | on the poor souls for whom 2.04.103
if i should take from another's pocket to put 3.02. 49 P
theise eyes of mine take themselves to slomber, 3.02.114 P
if you take the matter otherwise than is meant, 3.02.125 P
take pity of your town and of your people, 3.03. 28
and i will take up that with "give the devil his 3.07.116 P
if you would take the pains but to examine the 4.01. 68 P
by this hand i will take thee a box on the ear. 4.01.215 P
do it, though i take thee in the king's company. 4.01.219 P
take from them now | the sense of reck'ning, /if 4.01.290
i will the banner from a trumpet take, | and use 4.02. 61
take it, brave york. 4.03.132
fury shall abate, and i | the crowns will take. 4.04. 48
the devil take order now! 4.05. 22
was called philip of macedon, as i take it. 4.07. 21 P
mark you now, to take the tales out of my mouth, 4.07. 42 P
take a trumpet, herald, | ride thou unto the 4.07. 56
and not a man of them that we shall take | shall 4.07. 64
i have sworn to take him a box a' th' ear; 4.07.127 P
which your majesty is take out of the helmet of 4.08. 27 P
i beseech you take it for your own fault and not 4.08. 53 P
take it, god, | for it is none but thine! 4.08.111
or take that praise from god | which is his only 4.08.115
when you take occasions to see leeks hereafter, 5.01. 55 P
verily and in truth you shall take it, or i have 5.01. 61 P
i take thy groat in earnest of revenge. 5.01. 63
king, | and take with you free power to ratify, 5.02. 86
if thou canst love me for this, take me! 5.02.150 P
take a fellow of plain and uncoin'd constancy, 5.02.153 P
if thou would have such a one, take me! 5.02.165 P
and take me, take a soldier; 5.02.165 P
and take me, take a soldier; 5.02.166 P
take a soldier, take a king. 5.02.166 P
take a soldier, take a king. 5.02.166 P
to constantinople and take the turk by the beard 5.02.209 P
moi'ty, take the word of a king and a bachelor. 5.02.215 P
the looks of an empress, take me by the hand, 5.02.236 P
take her, fair son, and from her blood raise up 5.02.348
my lord of burgundy, we'll take your oath, | and 5.02.371
in your fair minds let this acceptance take. ep 14
/reignier, duke of anjou, doth take his part; 1H6 1.01. 94
ten thousand soldiers with me i will take, 1.01.155
i do remember it, and here take my leave, | to 1.01.165
father, i warrant you, take you no care, | i'll 1.04. 21
sirs, take your places and be vigilant. 2.01. 1
i'll be so bold to take what they have left. 2.01. 78
in that thou laidst a trap to take my life, | as 3.01. 22
if holy churchmen take delight in broils? 3.01.111
take heed, be wary how you place your words, 3.02. 3
and dare not take up arms like gentlemen. 3.02. 70
now will we take some order in the town, 3.02.126
we'll pull his plumes and take away his train, 3.03. 7
and the rest will take thee in their arms. 3.03. 77
and in our coronation take your place. 3.04. 27
hark ye; not so; in witness, take ye that. 3.04. 37
now, governor of paris, take your oath: 4.01. 3
much less to take occasion from their mouths 4.01.130
let me persuade you take a better course. 4.01.132
then god take mercy on brave talbot's soul, 4.03. 34
and take foul scorn to fawn on him by sending. 4.04. 35
then here i take my leave of thee, fair son, 4.05. 52
pause, and take thy breath; 4.06. 4
go take their bodies hence. 4.07. 91
then take my soul — my body, soul, and all, 5.03. 22
kneel down and take my blessing, good my girl. 5.04. 25
take her away, for she hath liv'd too long, | to 5.04. 34
and therefore take this compact of a truce, 5.04.163
take therefore shipping, post, my lord, to 5.05. 87
and therefore i will take the nevils' parts, 2H6 1.01.240
here, hume, take this reward. 1.02. 85
hume, if you take not heed, you shall go near 1.02.102
take this fellow in, and send for his master 1.03. 33 P
strangers in court do take her for the queen. 1.03. 79
by water shall he die, and take his end. 1.04. 33
stafford, take her to thee. 1.04. 52
"by water shall he die, and take his end." 1.04. 65
follow the knave, and take this drab away. 2.01.153
and here, tom, take all the money that i have. 2.03. 76 P
touching the duke of york, i will take my death, 2.03. 88 P
take away his weapon. 2.03. 95 P
go, take hence that traitor from our sight, 2.03.100
your grace, we'll take her from the sheriff. 2.04. 17
my nell, i take my leave. 2.04. 74
now | to take her with him to the isle of man. 2.04. 78
stanley, i prithee go, and take me hence, | i 2.04. 91
take heed, my lord, the welfare of us all 3.01. 80
sirs, take away the duke, and guard him sure. 3.01.188
ere you can take due orders for a priest. 3.01.274
nay, then a shame take all! 3.01.307
then, noble york, take thou this task in hand. 3.01.318
whiles i take order for mine own affairs. 3.01.320
i take it kindly. 3.01.346
lords, take your places; 3.02. 19
and let thy suffolk take his heavy leave. 3.02.306
embrace, and kiss, and take ten thousand leaves, 3.02.354
and take my heart with thee. 3.02.408
be not so rash, take ransom, let him live. 4.01. 28
would (but that they dare not) take our parts. 4.02.187
then linger not, my lord, away, take horse. 4.04. 54
take him away, and behead him. 4.07. 96 P
go, take him away, i say, and strike off his 4.07.109 P
go to cheapside and take up commodities upon our 4.07.127 P
with burthens, take your houses over your heads, 4.08. 29 P
take heed, lest by your heat you burn yourselves 5.01.160
i mean to take possession of my right. 3H6 1.01. 44
conditionally that here thou take an oath | to 1.01.196
this oath i willingly take and will perform. 1.01.201
and thus most humbly i do take my leave. 1.02. 61
o, let me pray before i take my death! 1.03. 35
it is war's prize to take all vantages, | and 1.04. 59
whilest we breathe, take time to do him dead. 1.04.108
there, take the crown, and, with the crown, my 1.04.164
hard–hearted clifford, take me from the world, 1.04.167
now, lords, take leave until we meet again, 2.03. 42
my flock, | so many hours must i take my rest, 2.05. 32
and i, that, haply, take them from him now, 2.05. 58
mother for a father's death | take on with me, 2.05.104
nay, take me with thee, good sweet exeter; 2.05.137
god forbid that, for he'll take vantages. 3.02. 25
till youth take leave and leave you to the 3.02. 35
but you will take exceptions to my boon. 3.02. 46
i take my leave with many thousand thanks. 3.02. 56
say that king edward take thee for his queen? 3.02. 89
issue of their bodies | to take their rooms, ere 3.02.132
could, | and, like a sinon, take another troy. 3.02.190
where i must take like seat unto my fortune, 3.03. 10
that they'll take no offense at our abuse. 4.01. 13
suppose they take offense without a cause; 4.01. 14
we may surprise and take him at our pleasure? 4.02. 17
come on, my masters, each man take his stand, 4.03. 1
vow | never to lie and take his natural rest 4.03. 5
fly, | if warwick take us we are sure to die. 4.04. 35
fair lords, take leave and stand not to reply. 4.08. 23
comfort, my lord! and so i take my leave. 4.08. 28
and take the great–grown traitor unawares. 4.08. 63
come, warwick, take the time, kneel down, kneel 5.01. 48
if thou be there, sweet brother, take my hand, 5.02. 34
and take his thanks that yet hath nothing else. 5.04. 59
for god's sake, take away this captive scold. 5.05. 29
nay, take away this scolding crook–back, rather. 5.05. 30
take that, the likeness of this railer here. 5.05. 38

sprawl'st thou? take that, to end thy agony. 5.05. 39
if heaven will take the present at our hands. R3 1.01.120
which done, god take king edward to his mercy, 1.01.151
take up the sword again, or take up me. 1.02.183
take up the sword again, or take up me. 1.02.183
to take her in her heart's extremest hate, 1.02.231
and take deep traitors for thy dearest friends! 1.03.223
o buckingham, take heed of yonder dog! 1.03.288
seize on him, furies, take him unto torment!" 1.04. 57
take the devil in thy mind, and believe him not; 1.04.147 P
take him on the costard with the hilts of thy 1.04.154 P
take heed; 1.04.199
take not the quarrel from his pow'rful arm; 1.04.217
take that! 1.04.269
take thou the fee and tell him what i say, | for 1.04.277
/hastings and rivers, take each other's hand, 2.01. 7
take heed you dally not before your king, | lest 2.01. 12
to take our brother clarence to your grace. 2.01. 77
i fear thy justice will take hold | on me and 2.01.132
that you take with unthankfulness his doing. 2.02. 90
if you will presently take horse with him, | and 3.02. 16
which i presume he'll take in gentle part. 3.04. 20
now will i go to take some privy order | to draw 3.05.106
the maid's part, still answer nay, and take it. 3.07. 51
take on his grace the sovereignty thereof, | but 3.07. 79
your gracious self to take on you the charge 3.07.131
take to your royal self | this proffer'd benefit 3.07.195
i do beseech you take it not amiss, | i cannot 3.07.206
grace, | and so most joyfully we take our leave. 3.07.245
and take thy office from thee on my peril. 4.01. 25
take all the swift advantage of the hours. 4.01. 48
i will take order for her keeping close. 4.02. 52
i humbly take my leave. 4.03. 35
therefore take with thee my most grievous curse, 4.04.188
if i did take the kingdom from your sons, | to 4.04.294
there, take thou that, till thou bring better 4.04.508
some one take order buckingham be brought | to 4.04.537
we must both give and take, my loving lord. 5.03. 6
strive with troubled thoughts to take a nap, 5.03.104
bulk | take up the rays o' th' beneficial sun, H8 1.01. 56
(and take it from a heart that wishes towards 1.01.103
(which, as i take it, is a kind of puppy | to 1.01.175
arise, and take place by us. 1.02. 10
repeat your will and take it. 1.02. 13
we should take root here where we sit, or sit 1.02. 87
why, we take | from every tree, lop, bark, and 1.02. 95
take good heed | you charge not in your spleen a 1.02.173
i say, take heed; 1.02.175
one would take it, | that never see 'em pace 1.03. 11
there, i take it, | they may, cum privilegio, 1.03. 33
you that side, i'll take the charge of this. 1.04. 20
thanks, and pray 'em take their pleasures. 1.04. 74
have your grace | find out, and he will take it. 1.04. 84
i were unmannerly to take you out | and not to 1.04. 95
'gainst me, that i cannot take peace with; 2.01. 85
put me off, | and take your good grace from me? 2.04. 22
take thy lute, wench, my soul grows sad with 3.01. 1
would leave your griefs, and take my counsel. 3.01. 92
take heed, for heaven's sake take heed, lest at 3.01.110
take heed, for heaven's sake take heed, lest at 3.01.110
for if | it did take place, "i do," quoth he, 3.02. 34
take notice, lords, he has a loyal breast, | for 3.02.200
yet i know | a way, if it take right, in spite 3.02.219
now, who'll take it? 3.02.250
there take an inventory of all i have, | to the 3.02.451
you come to take your stand here, and behold 4.01. 2
i take it, she that carries up the train | is 4.01. 51
and heartily entreats you take good comfort. 4.02.119
i'll take my leave. 5.01. 9
answer, you must take | your patience to you, 5.01.104
you take a precipit for no leap of danger, | and 5.01.139
it stands agreed, | i take it, by all voices: 5.02.123
i take my cause | out of the gripes of cruel men 5.02.134
respect him, | take him, and use him well; 5.02.189
do you take the court for parish garden? 5.03. 2 P
with this kiss take my blessing: 5.04. 10
some come to take their ease, | and sleep an act ep 2
let them take heed of troilus; TRO 1.02. 57 P
a daughter a goddess, he should take his choice. 1.02.237 P
take but degree away, untune that string, | and 1.03.109
he bade me take a trumpet, | and to this purpose 1.03.263
for, whosomever you take him to be, he is ajax. 2.01. 64 P
i take to–day a wife, and my election | is led 2.02. 61
if ye take not that little little less than 2.03. 12 P
for this time will i take my leave, my lord. 3.02.139
and you take leave till to–morrow morning — 3.02.141 P
take the instant way, | for honor travels in a 3.03.153
a valiant greek, aeneas, take his hand, 4.01. 8
a bugbear take him! 4.02. 33 P
the devil take antenor! 4.02. 75 P
lips blow to their deities, take thee from me. 4.04. 27
i'll take that winter from your lips, fair lady; 4.05. 24
both take and give. 4.05. 37
the kiss you take is better than you give; 4.05. 38
and i have seen thee pause and take thy breath, 4.05.192
tetter, take and take again such preposterous 5.01. 23 P
tetter, take and take again such preposterous 5.01. 23 P
any man may sing her, if he can take her cliff; 5.02. 10 P
he that takes that doth take my heart withal. 5.02. 82
but, now you have it, take it. 5.02. 90
a burning devil take them! 5.02.196 P
to take that course by your consent and voice, 5.03. 74
hector, i take my leave. 5.03. 89
fly not, for shouldst thou take the river styx, 5.04. 19
go, go, my servant, take thou troilus' horse, 5.05. 1
take heed, the quarrel's most ominous to us. 5.07. 20 P
the devil take thee, coward! 5.07. 23 P
is my day's work done, i'll take /good breath. 5.08. 3
take these rats thither | to gnaw their garners. COR 1.01.249
which was | to take in many towns ere (almost) 1.02. 24
take your commission, hie you to your bands, 1.02. 26
he that retires, i'll take him for a volsce, 1.04. 28
take | convenient numbers to make good the city, 1.05. 11
take your choice of those | that best can aid 1.06. 65
but cannot make my heart consent to take | a 1.09. 37
if you take it as a pleasure to you in being so. 2.01. 31 P
i will be bold to take my leave of you. 2.01. 96 P
take my cap, jupiter, and i thank thee. 2.01.105 P
and | take to you, as your predecessors have, 2.02.143
have chose a consul that will from them take 2.03.214
gap of both, and take | the one by th' other. 3.01.111
no, take more! 3.01.140
here's he that would take from you all your 3.01.181
myself | take up a brace o' th' best of them, 3.01.243
all | than to take in a town with gentle words, 3.02. 59
and schoolboys' tears take up | the glasses of 3.02.116
do not take | his rougher /accents for malicious 3.03. 54
that the very hour | you take it off again? 3.03. 61
that you have contriv'd to take | from rome all 3.03. 63
take good cominius | with thee a while. 4.01. 34
take my prayers with you. 4.02. 44
are in a ripe aptness to take all power from the 4.03. 23 P
you take my part from me, sir, i have the most 4.03. 50 P
broke their sleep | to take the one the other, 4.04. 20
you, poor gentleman, take up some other station; 4.05. 29 P
and take our friendly senators by th' hands, 4.05.132
revenges, take | th' one half of my commission, 4.05.137
but i take him to be the greater soldier. 4.05.167 P
take this along, i writ it for thy sake, | and 5.02. 90
take him up. 5.06.147
nor wish no less, and so i take my leave. TIT 1.01.402
too, | upon a just survey take titus' part, 1.01.446
take up this good old man, and cheer the heart 1.01.457
take this of me: 2.01.108
and strike, brave boys, and take your turns; 2.01.129
take it up, i pray thee, | and give the king 2.03. 46
'tis pity they should take him for a stag. 2.03. 71
andronicus himself did take it up. 2.03.294
come, brother, take a head, | and in this hand 3.01.279
come and take choice of all my library, | and so 4.01. 34
this done, see that you take no longer days, 4.02.165
sirs, take you to your tools. 4.03. 6
war | take wreak on rome for this ingratitude, 4.03. 34
to take up a matter of brawl betwixt my uncle 4.03. 93 P
go take him away and hang him presently. 4.04. 45
'cause they take vengeance of such kind of men. 5.02. 63
business, | and take my ministers along with me. 5.02.133
the empress' sons i take them, chiron, demetrius 5.02.154
good uncle, take you in this barbarous moor, 5.03. 4
you, therefore, draw nigh and take your places. 5.03. 24
o, take this warm kiss on thy pale cold lips, 5.03.153
do them that kindness, and take leave of them. 5.03.171
and, being dead, let birds on her take pity. 5.03.200
a pair of star–cross'd lovers take their life; ROM pr 6
i will take the wall of any man or maid of 1.01. 12 P
maidenheads, take it in what sense thou wilt. 1.01. 26 P
they must take it /in sense that feel it. 1.01. 27 P
let us take the law of our sides, let them begin 1.01. 38 P
as i pass by, and let them take it as they list. 1.01. 40 P
take thou some new infection to thy eye, | and 1.02. 49
and take our good meaning, for our judgment sits 1.04. 46
where's potpan, that he helps not to take away? 1.05. 2 P
be brisk a while, and the longer liver take all. 1.05. 15 P
therefore be patient, take no note of him; 1.05. 71
then move not while my prayer's effect i take. 1.05.106
which is no part of thee, | take all myself. 2.02. 49
i take thee at thy word. 2.02. 49
thou wilt say "ay," | and i will take thy word; 2.02. 91
speak any thing against me, i'll take him down, 2.04.150 P
which, as i take it, is a gentleman–like offer. 2.04.178 P
could you not take some occasion without giving? 3.01. 43 P
take the "villain" back again | that late thou 3.01.125
could not take truce with the unruly spleen | of 3.01.157
die, | take him and cut him out in little stars, 3.02. 22
take up those cords. 3.02.132
and death, not romeo, take my maidenhead! 3.02.137
and bid him come to take his last farewell. 3.02.143
take heed, take heed, for such die miserable. 3.03.145
take heed, take heed, for such die miserable. 3.03.145
and see how he will take it at your hands. 3.05.125
soft, take me with you, take me with you, wife. 3.05.141
soft, take me with you, take me with you, wife. 3.05.141
take thou this vial, being then in bed, | and 4.01. 93
hold, take these keys and fetch more spices, 4.04. 1
you take your pennyworths now; 4.05. 4
ay, let the county take you in your bed, | he'll 4.05. 10
then be not poor, but break it, and take this. 5.01. 74
hold, take this letter; 5.03. 23
but chiefly to take thence from her dead finger 5.03. 30
take thou that; 5.03. 41
arms, take your last embrace! 5.03.113
to help to take her from her borrowed grave, 5.03.248
came i to take her from her kindred's vault, 5.03.254
so thou apprehend'st it, take it for thy labor. TIM 1.01.209 P
i take no heed of thee; 1.02. 35 P
my lord, you take us even at the best. 1.02.152
you may take my word, my lord; 1.02.214
i take all and your several visitations | so 1.02.218
take the bonds along with you, | and have the 2.01. 34
no counsel, take no warning by my coming. 3.01. 26 P
must i take th' cure upon me? 3.03. 12
and take down th' int'rest into their glutt'nous 3.04. 52
we cannot take this for answer, sir. 3.04. 77
tear me, take me, and the gods fall upon you! 3.04. 99
take my deserts to his, and join 'em both; 3.05. 78
soft, take thy physic first — thou too — and 3.06.100
take thou that too, with multiplying bans! 4.01. 34
not | one friend to take his fortune by the arm, 4.02. 7
let each take some; 4.02. 27
i'll take the gold thou givest me, | not all thy 4.03.130
take the bridge quite away | of him that, his 4.03.158
get thee away, and take | thy beagles with thee. 4.03.174
first mend /my company, take away thyself. 4.03.283
take wealth and lives together, | do, /villains, 4.03.433
thou singly honest man, | here, take; 4.03.524
neither wish i | you take much pains to mend. 5.01. 89
you'll take it ill. 5.01. 90
thine and ours, to take | the captainship, thou 5.01.160
and take our goodly aged men by th' beards, 5.01.172
to stop affliction, let him take his haste, 5.01.210
the character i'll take with wax; 5.03. 6
nature loathes, take thou the destin'd tenth, 5.04. 33
it is not square to take | on those that are, 5.04. 36
good cinna, take this paper, | and look you lay JC 1.03.142
to himself — take thought and die for caesar; 2.01.187
take heed of cassius; 2.03. 1 P
and take good note | what caesar doth, what 2.04. 14
i go to take my stand, | to see him pass on to 2.04. 25
next, caius cassius, do i take your hand; 3.01.186
mark antony, here take you caesar's body. 3.01.244
how the people take | the cruel issue of these 3.01.293
he would not take the crown, | therefore 'tis 3.02.112
take up the body. 3.02.256
art afoot, | take thou what course thou wilt! 3.02.261
then take we down his load, and turn him off 4.01. 25
if that thou be'st a roman, take it forth. 4.03.103
and we must take the current when it serves, 4.03.223
thy instrument, | i'll take it from thee; 4.03.272
therefore our everlasting farewell take: 5.01.115
i slew the coward, and did take it from him. 5.03. 4
in parthia did i take thee prisoner, | and then 5.03. 37
here, take thou the hilts, | and when my face is 5.03. 43
run, | where never roman shall take note of him. 5.03. 50
but hold thee, take this garland on thy brow; 5.03. 85
enemy | shall ever take alive the noble brutus; 5.04. 22
octavius, then take him to follow thee, | that 5.05. 66
so humbly take my leave. MAC 1.04. 47
and take my milk for gall, you murth'ring 1.05. 48
hold, take my sword. 2.01. 4
take thee that too. 2.01. 5
and take the present horror from the time, 2.01. 59
but we'll take to–morrow. 3.01. 22
take any shape but that, and my firm nerves 3.04.101
double sure, | and take a bond of fate: 4.01. 84
proud, and take no care | who chafes, who frets, 4.01. 90
i take my leave of you; 4.02. 22
i take my leave at once. 4.02. 30
if you will take a homely man's advice, | be not 4.02. 68
fear not yet | to take upon you what is yours. 4.03. 70
heaven look on, | and would not take their part? 4.03.224
unlock her closet, take forth paper, fold it, 5.01. 6 P
take thy face hence. 5.03. 19
we | shall take upon 's what else remains to do, 5.06. 5
and will not let belief take hold of him HAM 1.01. 24
and this, i take it, | is the main motive of our 1.01.104
take thy fair hour, laertes, time be thine, 1.02. 62
we in our peevish opposition | take it to heart? 1.02.101
as of a father, for, let the world take note, 1.02.108
'a was a man, take him for all in all, | i shall 1.02.187
take each man's censure, but reserve thy 1.03. 69
most humbly do i take my leave, my lord. 1.03. 82
as it is a–making, | you must not take for fire. 1.03.120
shall in the general censure take corruption 1.04. 35
take you, as 'twere, some distant knowledge of 2.01. 13
rank | as may dishonor him, take heed of that, 2.01. 21
your bait of falsehood take this carp of truth, 2.01. 60
take this from this, if this be otherwise. 2.02.156
my lord, i will take my leave of you. 2.02.213 P
you cannot take from me any thing that i will 2.02.215 P
those you were wont to take such delight in, the 2.02.327 P
gods, | in general synod take away her power! 2.02.494
take them in. 2.02.533 P
hah, 'swounds, i should take it; 2.02.576
or to take arms against a sea of troubles, | and 3.01. 58
take these again, for to the noble mind | rich 3.01. 99
would cost you a groaning to take off mine edge. 3.02.249 P
i'll take the ghost's word for a thousand pound. 3.02.286 P
to take him in the purging of his soul, | when 3.03. 85
take thy fortune; 3.04. 32
tell us where 'tis, that we may take it thence, 4.02. 7
take you me for a spunge, my lord? 4.02. 14 P
the devil take thy soul! 5.01.259
i prithee take thy fingers from my throat. 5.01.260
i take him to be a soul of great article, and 5.02.116 P
against the which he has impawn'd, as i take it, 5.02.149 P
with laertes, or that you will take longer time. 5.02.199 P
come, hamlet, come, and take this hand from me. 5.02.225
here, hamlet, take my napkin, rub thy brows. 5.02.288
take up the bodies. 5.02.401
lord whose hand must take my plight shall carry LR 1.01.101
bear, | our potency made good, take thy reward. 1.01.172
the gods to their dear shelter take thee, maid, 1.01.182
with our oath, | take her, or leave her? 1.01.205
and here i take cordelia by the hand, | duchess 1.01.243
upon, | be it lawful i take up what's cast away. 1.01.253
take | more composition and fierce quality 1.02. 11
sirrah, you were best take my coxcomb. 1.04. 97 P
there, take my coxcomb. 1.04.101 P
take heed, sirrah — the whip. 1.04.110 P
by her, that else will take the thing she begs, 1.04.248
nuncle lear, tarry, take the fool with thee. 1.04.315 P
let me still take away the harms i fear, | not 1.04.329
take you some company, and away to horse. 1.04.336
my father hath set guard to take my brother, 2.01. 16
and take vanity the puppet's part against the 2.02. 36 P
the king must take it ill | that he, so slightly 2.02.145
take vantage, heavy eyes, not to behold | this 2.02.171
to take the basest and most poorest shape | that 2.03. 7
to take the indispos'd and sickly fit | for the 2.04.111
i pray you, sir, take patience. 2.04.138
send down, and take my part. 2.04.192
o regan, will you take her by the hand? 2.04.194
open this purse and take | what it contains. 3.01. 45
doth from my senses take all feeling else, 3.04. 13
take physic, pomp, | expose thyself to feel what 3.04. 33
take heed o' th' foul fiend. 3.04. 80 P
and let this tyrannous night take hold upon you, 3.04.151
good my lord, take his offer, go into th' house. 3.04.156
let him take the fellow. 3.04.177
take him you on. 3.04.178
is better than the open air, take it thankfully. 3.06. 1 P
my tears begin to take his part so much, | they 3.06. 60
good friend, i prithee take him in thy arms; 3.06. 88
take up thy master; 3.06. 92
take up, take up, | and follow me, that will to 3.06. 95
take up, take up, | and follow me, that will to 3.06. 95
we are bound to take upon your traitorous father 3.07. 8 P
nay then come on, and take the chance of anger. 3.07. 79
here, take this purse, thou whom the heav'ns' 4.01. 64
where was his son when they did take his eyes? 4.02. 88
he that helps him take all my outward worth. 4.04. 10
therefore i do advise you take this note: 4.05. 29
i would not take this from report; 4.06.141
take that of me, my friend, who have the power 4.06.169

if thou wilt weep my fortunes, take my eyes. 4.06.176
you ever–gentle gods, take my breath from me, 4.06.217
lest that th' infection of his fortune take 4.06.233
villain, take my purse: 4.06.246
you do me wrong to take me out o' th' grave: 4.07. 44
which of them shall i take? 5.01. 57
to take the widow | exasperates, makes mad her 5.01. 59
take the shadow of this tree | for your good 5.02. 1
some officers take them away. 5.03. 1
and take upon 's the mystery of things | as if 5.03. 16
take them away. 5.03. 19
take thou this note; 5.03. 27
take thou my soldiers, prisoners, patrimony; 5.03. 75
take my sword. 5.03.251
i take it much unkindly | that thou, iago, who OTH 1.01. 1
nor doth the general care | take hold on me; 1.03. 55
not only take away, but let your sentence | even 1.03.119
take up this mangled matter at the best; 1.03.173
whereof i take this that you call love to be a 1.03.331 P
down, | /then take thy auld cloak about thee." 2.03. 96
madam, i'll take my leave. 3.03. 30
to move you, | his present reconciliation take; 3.03. 47
would take no notice, nor build yourself a 3.03.150
my lord, i take my leave. 3.03.241
i once more take my leave. 3.03.257
take mine office. 3.03.375
take note, take note, o world, | to be direct 3.03.377
take note, take note, o world, | to be direct 3.03.377
and take heed on't, | make it a darling like 3.04. 65
sweet bianca, | take me this work out. 3.04.180
take it, and do't, and leave me for this time. 3.04.191
i was a fine fool to take it. 4.01.150 P
i must take out the work? 4.01.150 P
some minx's token, and i must take out the work? 4.01.153 P
you had it, i'll take out no work on't. 4.01.155 P
take me from this world with treachery and 4.02.215 P
and one), you may take him at your pleasure. 4.02.237 P
here, at thy hand; be bold, and take thy stand. 5.01. 7
this is othello's ancient, as i take it. 5.01. 51
sweet soul, take heed, | take heed of perjury, 5.02. 50
take heed of perjury, thou art on thy death–bed. 5.02. 51
take you this weapon | which i have /here 5.02.239
take but good note, and you shall see in him ANT 1.01. 11
take in that kingdom, and enfranchise that; 1.01. 23
their deities to take the wife of a man from him 1.02.162 P
i should take you | for idleness itself. 1.03. 92
i take no pleasure | in aught an eunuch has. 1.05. 9
i learn you take things ill which are not so — 2.02. 29
knot, take antony | octavia to his wife; 2.02.126
take no offense that i would not offend you; 2.05. 99
take your time. 2.06. 23
how you take | the offers we have sent you. 2.06. 30
you here a man prepar'd | to take this offer; 2.06. 41
no, antony, take the lot; 2.06. 62
here they might take two thieves kissing. 2.06. 96 P
i shall take it, sir; 2.06.134 P
they take the flow o' th' nile | by certain 2.07. 17
seeks, and will not take when once 'tis offer'd, 2.07. 83
come, let's all take hands, | till that the 2.07.106
all take hands. 2.07.108
take heed you fall not. 2.07.129
you take from me a great part of myself; 3.02. 24
thou must not take my former sharpness ill. 3.03. 35
take from his heart, take from his brain, from 3.07. 11
take from his heart, take from his brain, from 3.07. 11
cut the ionian sea, | and take in toryne? 3.07. 23
i have a ship | laden with gold, take that, 3.11. 5
take it. 3.11. 11
take the hint | which my despair proclaims: 3.11. 18
all–disgraced friend, | or take his life there. 3.12. 23
take hence this jack and whip him. 3.13. 93
take him hence. 3.13.101
to let a fellow that will take rewards | and say 3.13.123
i'll strike, and cry, "take all!" 4.02. 8
now the witch take me, if i meant it thus! 4.02. 37
you take me in too dolorous a sense, | for i 4.02. 39
and snatch 'em up, as we take hares, behind: 4.07. 13
let him take thee | and hoist thee up to the 4.12. 33
take me up. 4.14.138
good sirs, take heart, | we'll bury him; 4.15. 85
fashion, | and make death proud to take us. 4.15. 88
if thou please | to take me to thee, as i was to 5.01. 10
and take a queen | worth many babes and beggars! 5.02. 47
for the queen, | i'll take her to my guard. 5.02. 67
take to you no hard thoughts. 5.02.117
i'll take my leave. 5.02.133
take thou no care, it shall be heeded. 5.02.268
come then, and take the last warmth of my lips. 5.02.291
nay, i will take thee too: 5.02.312
take up her bed, | and bear her women from the 5.02.356
take it, heart, | but keep it till you woo CYM 1.01.112
i did not take my leave of him, but had | most 1.03. 25
for this time is ended, | take your own way. 1.05. 31
i humbly take my leave. 1.05. 45
but take it for thy labor. 1.05. 61
nay, i prithee take it, | it is an earnest of a 1.05. 64
boot, my son, | who shall take notice of thee. 1.05. 70
i have given him that | which, if he take, shall 1.05. 79
is warm'd by th' rest — and take it thankfully. 1.06. 28
take my pow'r i' th' court for yours. 1.06.179
may it please you | to take them in protection? 1.06.193
jack–an–apes must take me up for swearing, as if 2.01. 4 P
and this her son | cannot take two from twenty, 2.01. 55
take not away the taper, leave it burning; 2.02. 5
he cannot choose but take this service i have 2.03. 34 P
here, take this too, | it is a basilisk unto 2.04.106
and take your ring again, 'tis not yet won. 2.04.114
there, take thy hire, and all the fiends of hell 2.04.129
which then they had to take from 's, to resume 3.01. 15
such assaults | as would take in some virtue. 3.02. 9
wrath, should he take me in his dominion, could 3.02. 41 P
take notice that i am in cambria, at 3.02. 43 P
morgan call'd, | they take for natural father. 3.03.107
thy tongue | may take off some extremity, which 3.04. 17
let thine own hands take away her life. 3.04. 27 P
look | i draw the sword myself, take it, and hit 3.04. 67
therein false strook, can take no greater wound, 3.04.114
well, madam, we must take a short farewell, 3.04.185
if savage, | take or lend. 3.06. 24
with his own single hand he'ld take us in, 4.02.121
to lose, | but that he swore to take, our lives? 4.02.125
that by the top doth take the mountain pine 4.02.175
wilt take thy chance with me? 4.02.382
and give me leave, | i'll take the better care; 4.04. 45
if each of you should take this course, how many 5.01. 3
great the answer be | britains must take. 5.03. 80
take | no stricter render of me than my all. 5.04. 16
men, | who of their broken debtors take a third, 5.04. 19
for imogen's dear life take mine, and though 5.04. 22
though light, take pieces for the figure's sake; 5.04. 25
if you will take this audit, take this life, 5.04. 27
if you will take this audit, take this life, 5.04. 27
our son is good, | take off his miseries. 5.04. 86
be directed by some that take upon them to know, 5.04.180 P
or to take upon yourself that which i am sure 5.04.180 P
the offender, | and take him from our presence. 5.05.301
take him hence, | the whole world shall not save 5.05.320
take that life, beseech you, | which i so often 5.05.414
i have power | to take thy life from thee. PER 1.02. 57
or private treason | will take away your life. 1.02.105
i'll take thy word for faith, not ask thine oath 1.02.120
why, d' ye take it, and the gods give thee good 2.01.146 P
daughter, so you are — here take your place. 2.03. 18
he may my proffer take for an offense, | since 2.03. 68
since men take women's gifts for impudence. 2.03. 69
take i your wish, i leap into the seas, 2.04. 43
loath to bid farewell, we take our leaves. 2.05. 13
obedient to their dooms, | will take the crown. 3.ch. 33
take in your arms this piece | of your dead 3.01. 17
for the sake of it | be manly, and take comfort. 3.01. 22
your lady | take from my heart all thankfulness! 3.03. 4
so i take my leave. 3.03. 30
see again, | a vestal livery will i take me to, 3.04. 10
life | /seeks to take off by treason's knife, 4.ch. 14
leonine, take her by the arm, walk with her. 4.01. 29
wife, take her in, instruct her what she has to 4.02. 54 P
boult, take you the marks of her, the color of 4.02. 57 P
o, take her home, mistress, take her home. 4.02.123 P
o, take her home, mistress, take her home. 4.02.123 P
but for't, | making, to take our imagination, 4.04. 3
you must take some pains to work her to your 4.06. 63 P
we must take another course with you! 4.06.121 P
boult, take her away, use her at thy pleasure. 4.06.141 P
to take from you the jewel you hold so dear. 4.06.154 P
take me home again | and prostitute me to the 4.06.189
their ashes, nor to take th' offense | of mortal TNK 1.01. 44
take some note | that for our crowned heads we 1.01. 51
now 'twill take form, the heats are gone 1.01.152
now you may take him | drunk with his victory. 1.01.157
dowagers, take hands, | let us be widows to our 1.01.165
in't will | take hostage of thee for a hundred, 1.01.184
thing, nor be so hardy | ever to take a husband. 1.01.205
one salmon, you shall take a number of minnows. 2.01. 4 P
no hard oppressor | dare take this from us; 2.02. 85
but take heed to your kindness though! 2.02.125
honor, would be loath | to take example by her. 2.02.146
and take one with you? 2.02.151
madness if i hazard thee | and take thy life, i 2.02.203
blushing virgin, should take manhood to her, 2.02.258
devils take 'em | that are so envious to me! 2.02.262
and you shall see her | take a new lesson out, 2.03. 35
well, sir, | take your own time. come, boys. 2.03. 69
take your choice, and what | you want at any 2.05. 54
love of mine | will take more root within him. 2.06. 28
i pray you | take comfort and be strong. 3.01.100
come, take courage, | you shall not die thus 3.03. 5
a fire ill take her! does she flinch now? 3.05. 52
go take her, | and fluently persuade her to a 3.05. 86
take twenty, domine. — how does my sweet heart? 3.05.148
this i'll take. 3.06. 52
prithee take mine, good cousin. 3.06. 65
take my sword, i hold it better. 3.06. 89
he that faints now, shame take him! 3.06.121
then take my life, i'll woo thee to't. 3.06.156
i'll be cut a–pieces | before i take this oath. 3.06.257
else, never trifle, | but take our lives, duke. 3.06.261
will you, arcite, | take these conditions? 3.06.264
to me than begging | to take my life so basely. 3.06.267
you | content to take th' other to your husband? 3.06.274
and take heed, as you are gentlemen, this 3.06.303
you must ev'n take it patiently. 4.01.115
take heed: 4.03. 34 P
take upon you, young sir her friend, the name of 4.03. 75 P
i do take | thy signs auspiciously, and in thy 5.01. 66
take to thy grace | me thy vow'd soldier, who do 5.01. 94
let him | take off my wheaten garland, or else 5.01.160
well she knew | what hour my fit would take me. 5.02. 10
take her offer. 5.02.110
take emilia, | and with her all the world's joy. 5.04. 90
take her. 5.04. 95
the gods my justice | take from my hand, and 5.04.121
life | to take prerogative and tithe of knees STM III 9
till he take truce with her contending tears, VEN 82
his testy master goeth about to take him, | when 319
thee, | to take advantage on presented joy; 405
they that thrive well take counsel of their 640
lo in this hollow cradle take thy rest, | my 1185
the shame that from them no device can take, LUC 535
unwholesome weeds take root with precious 870
ground, | my resolution, husband, do thou take, 1200
"do not take away | my sorrow's interest, let no 1796
or he refus'd to take /her figured proffer, PP 4.10
and would not take her meaning nor her pleasure. 11.12
as take the pain but cannot pluck the pelf. 14.12
take counsel of some wiser head, | neither too 18. 5
me, | unless thou take that honor from thy name. SON 36.12
take all my comfort of thy worth and truth. 37. 4
take all my loves, my love, yea, take them all, 40. 1
take all my loves, my love, yea, take them all, 40. 1
that time will come and take my love away. 64.12
which by and by black night doth take away, 73. 7
brain, | to take a new acquaintance of thy mind. 77.12
from hence your memory death cannot take, 81. 3
alone, that thou mayst take | all this away, and 91.13
take heed, dear heart, of this large privilege, 95.13
and take thou my oblation, poor but free, 125.10
the statute of thy beauty thou wilt take, | thou 134. 9
yet what the best is take the worst to be. 137. 4
take all these similes to your own command, LC 227

TAKE–A 1 FR 0.0001 REL FR 0 V 1 P
come, take–a your rapier, and come after my heel WIV 1.04. 59 P

TAKEN *(also ta'en)*
TAKEN 96 FR 0.0108 REL FR 58 V 38 P
you have taken it wiselier than i meant you TMP 2.01. 21 P
humanely taken, all, all lost, quite lost; 4.01.190
now you have taken the pains to set it together, TGV 1.01.116 P
nay, i was taken up for laying them down; 1.02.132
twenty times, and have taken him by the chain; WIV 1.01.295 P
there will be pity taken on you. MM 1.02.109 P
and in our sight they three were taken up | by ERR 1.01.110
and i, | and the twin dromio, all were taken up; 5.01.351
commodity, being taken up of these men's bills. ADO 3.03.178 P
manner of it is, i was taken with the manner. LLL 1.01.202 P
the form, and taken following her into the park, 1.01.207 P
a year's imprisonment to be taken with a wench. 1.01.288 P
i was taken with none, sir, i was taken with a 1.01.289 P
taken with none, sir, i was taken with a damsel. 1.01.289 P
i was taken with a maid. 1.01.296 P
for true it is, i was taken with jaquenetta, and 1.01.312 P
i know, | to be o'erheard and taken napping so. 4.03.128
to be cut off and taken | in what part of your MV 1.03.150
a pound of man's flesh taken from a man | is not 1.03.165
forfeiture, | to be so taken at thy peril, jew. 4.01.344
for what he hath taken away from thy father AYL 1.02. 19 P
hellespont and being taken with the cramp was 4.01.104 P
his taken labors bid him me forgive; AWW 3.04. 12
it is reported that he has taken their great'st 3.05. 5 P
whatsome'er he is, | he's bravely taken here. 3.05. 52
sir, of whom he hath taken a solemn leave. 4.03. 77 P
his confession is taken, and it shall be read to 4.03.113 P
have suspected an ambush where i was taken? 4.03.302 P
well penn'd, i have taken great pains to con it. TN 1.05.174 P
me my pains, to have taken it away yourself. 2.02. 6 P
his very genius hath taken the infection of the 3.04.129 P
was this taken | by any understanding pate but WT 1.02.222
so, without | my present vengeance taken. 1.02.281
have taken | the shapes of beasts upon them. 4.04. 26
if you had not taken yourself with the manner. 4.04.728 P
eyes, | have taken treasure from her lips — 5.01. 54
passing these flats, are taken by the tide — JN 5.06. 40
suddenly taken, and hath sent post–haste | to R2 1.04. 55
was by the rude hands of that welshman taken, 1H4 1.01. 41
taken from us it is: 2.04.161 P
years ago, and wert taken with the manner, and 2.04.315 P
choler, my lord, if rightly taken. 2.04.324 P
no, if rightly taken, halter. 2.04.325 P
thy state is taken for a join'd–stool, thy 2.04.380 P
art hath in reason taken from me all ostentation 2H4 2.02. 50 P
valor, taken sir john colevile of the dale, a 4.03. 38 P
defended | but taken and impounded as a stray H5 1.02.160
your fathers taken by the silver beards, | and 3.03. 36
nothing taken but paid for; 3.06.110 P
what prisoners of good sort are taken, uncle? 4.08. 75
talbot is taken, whom we wont to fear; 1H6 1.02. 14
were there surpris'd and taken prisoners. 4.01. 26
for i think i have taken my last draught in this 2H6 2.03. 73 P
say he be taken, rack'd, and tortured, | i know 3.01.376
my gracious lord, henry your foe is taken, | and 3H6 3.02.118
ay, almost slain, for he is taken prisoner, 4.04. 7
load, | taken from paul's to be interred there; R3 1.02. 30
and your brother york | have taken sanctuary. 3.01. 28
my liege, the duke of buckingham is taken — 4.04.531
at one stroke has taken | for ever from the H8 2.01.117
out of pity taken | a load would sink a navy — 3.02.382
nor, i'll assure you, better taken, sir. 4.01. 12
if troy be not taken till these two undermine it TRO 2.03. 8 P
since i have taken such pain to bring you 3.02.200 P
and might well | be taken from the people. COR 2.02.146
he was not taken well, he had not din'd: 5.01. 50
the fresh taste be taken from that clearness, TIT 3.01.128
he says that he hath taken them down again, for 4.03. 82 P
prince will doom thee death | if thou art taken. ROM 3.01.135
romeo, arise, | thou wilt be taken. 3.03. 75
if i would not have taken him at a word, i would JC 1.02.267 P
but there's no heed to be taken of them; 1.02.274 P
the affairs of men | which, taken at the flood, 4.03.219
now i have taken heart thou vanishest. 4.03.287
weighing delight and dole, | taken to wife; HAM 1.02. 14
the harms i fear, | not fear still to be taken. LR 1.04.330
if he be taken, he shall never more | be fear'd 2.01.110
duke's to blame in this, 'twill be ill taken. 2.02.159
of being taken by the insolent foe | and sold to OTH 1.03.137
thou hast taken against me a most just exception 4.02.207 P
your power and your command is taken off, | and 5.02.331
peep forth, but 'tis as soon | taken as seen; ANT 1.04. 54
caesar has taken toryne. 3.07. 55
lord, pardon — i dare not, | lest i be taken. 4.15. 23
o cleopatra! thou art taken, queen. 5.02. 38
lucius is taken. CYM 5.03. 84
me, that we have taken | no care to your best PER 4.01. 37
i must have your maidenhead taken off, or the 4.06.127 P
nor taken sustenance | but to prorogue his grief 5.01. 25
my lord is taken | heart–deep with your distress TNK 1.01.104
had they been taken | when their last hurts were 1.04. 25
and like enough the duke hath taken notice 2.02.227
"his shackles will betray him, he'll be taken, 4.01. 70
worth's unknown, although his highth be taken. SON 116. 8
have no leisure taken | to weigh how once i 120. 7
me from myself thy cruel eye hath taken, | and 133. 5

TAKER 3 FR 0.0003 REL FR 2 V 1 P
pestilence, and the taker runs presently mad. ADO 1.01. 88 P
veins | that the life–weary taker may fall dead, ROM 5.01. 62
bait | on purpose laid to make the taker mad: SON 129. 8

/TAKES 1 FR 0.0001 REL FR 1 V 0 P
/him, | /he /takes /false /shadows /for /true TIT 3.02. 80

TAKES 100 FR 0.0113 REL FR 80 V 20 P
the sun, | and by and by a cloud takes all away. TGV 1.03. 87
to fast, like one that takes diet; 2.01. 24 P
my daughter takes his going grievously. 3.02. 14
say) one that takes upon him to be a dog indeed, 4.04. 12 P
and yet she takes exceptions at your person. 5.02. 3
he so takes on yonder with my husband; WIV 4.02. 22 P
there he blasts the tree, and takes the cattle, 4.04. 32

takes note of what is done, and like a prophet MM 2.02. 94
look when i serve him so, he takes it /ill. ERR 2.01. 12
that takes pity on decay'd men and gives them 4.03. 26 P
me, sorrow abides and happiness takes his leave. ADO 1.01.102 P
love takes the meaning in love's conference: MND 2.02. 46
night, that from the eye his function takes, 3.02.177
noble respect | takes it in might, not merit. 5.01. 92
it blesseth him that gives and him that takes. MV 4.01.187
but the same tradition takes not away my blood, AYL 1.01. 48 P
ay, for a turtle, as he takes a buzzard. SHR 2.01.208
of her sorrows takes all livelihood from her AWW 1.01. 51 P
hath in't a bond | whereof the world takes note. 1.03.189
lady, takes great exceptions to your ill hours. TN 1.03. 5 P
i marvel your ladyship takes delight in such a 1.05. 83 P
he takes on him to understand so much, and 1.05.140 P
come to me again | to tell me how he takes it. 1.05.282
ill of the devil, how he takes it at heart! 3.04.101 P
chafes, how it rages, how it takes up the shore! WT 3.03. 89 P
that takes away by any secret course | thy JN 3.01.178
the last leave of thee takes my weeping eye. R2 1.02. 74
takes on the point of honor to support | so 5.03. 11
each takes his fellow for an officer. 1H4 2.02.107
what is't that takes from thee | thy stomach, 2.03. 40
much | as on the other side it takes from you. 3.01.110
takes on him to reform | some certain edicts and 4.03. 78
and time, that takes survey of all the world, 5.04. 82
says he, that takes upon him not to conceive. 2H4 2.02.114 P
or else a feast | and takes away the stomach — 4.04.107
and takes him by the beard, kisses the gashes H5 4.06. 13
believe your majesty takes no scorn to wear the 4.07.102 P
she takes upon her bravely at first dash. 1H6 1.02. 71
belike your lordship takes us then for fools, 3.02. 62
and as the butcher takes away the calf | and 2H6 3.01.210
and takes her farewell of the glorious sun! 3H6 2.01. 22
whose soul is that which takes her heavy leave? 2.06. 42
and, weakling, warwick takes his gift again, 5.01. 37
the state takes notice of the private difference H8 1.01.101
and she takes upon her to spy a white hair on TRO 1.02.139 P
you of this man that takes me for the general? 3.03.262 P
of thee and me, and sighs, and takes my glove, 5.02. 79
he that takes that doth take my heart withal. 5.02. 82
there, and every where, he leaves and takes, 5.05. 26
state, whose course will on | the way it takes, COR 1.01. 70
fish, who takes it | by sovereignty of nature. 4.07. 34
takes from aufidius a great part of blame. 5.06.145
for now he firmly takes me for revenge, | and, TIT 5.02. 73
takes no accompt | how things go from him, nor TIM 2.02. 3
takes virtuous copies to be wicked; 3.03. 31 P
often | drowns him and takes his valor prisoner. 3.05. 68
insane root | that takes the reason prisoner? MAC 1.03. 85
the desire, but it takes away the performance. 2.03. 30 P
it sets him on, and it takes him off; 2.03. 33 P
bosoms, | whose execution takes your enemy off, 3.01.104
fortune nothing | takes from his high respect. 3.06. 29
no fairy takes, nor witch hath power to charm, HAM 1.01.163
the king doth wake to–night and takes his rouse, 1.04. 8
and indeed it takes | from our achievements, 1.04. 20
a hideous crash | takes prisoner pyrrhus' ear; 2.02.477
that patient merit of th' unworthy takes, | when 3.01. 73
takes off the rose | from the fair forehead of 3.04. 42
what cannot be preserv'd when fortune takes, OTH 1.03.206
he takes her by the palm; 2.01.167 P
i look on you | as one that takes his leave. ANT 4.02. 29
mardian, | and bring me how he takes my death. 4.13. 10
the king he takes the babe | to his protection, CYM 1.01. 40
he takes his part | to draw upon an exile. 1.01.165
takes prisoner the wild motion of mine eye, 1.06.103
guilt within my bosom | takes off my manhood. 5.02. 2
who takes offense | at that would make me glad? PER 2.05. 71
lychorida, her nurse, she takes, | and so to sea 3.ch. 43
that old time, as he passes by, takes with him. TNK 2.02.104
that way he takes | i purpose is my way too. 2.06. 17
she takes strong note of me, | hath made me near 3.01. 17
he does no wrongs, | nor takes none. 4.02.135
as apt as new–fall'n snow takes any dint. VEN 354
full gently now she takes him by the hand, | a 361
while she takes all she can, not all she listeth 564
my boding heart pants, beats, and takes no rest, 647
she takes him by the hand, and that is cold, 1124
which once corrupted takes the worser part; LUC 294
he takes it from the rushes where it lies, | and 318
him, | he takes for accidental things of trial; 326
having two sweet babes, when death takes one, 1161
weeps, the other takes in hand | no cause, but 1235
at last he takes her by the bloodless hand, 1597
her stand she takes upon a steep–up hill. PP 9. 5
none takes pity on thy pain. 20.20
breed, to brave him when he takes thee hence. SON 12.14
you, | as he takes from you, i ingraft you new. 15.14
as a decrepit father takes delight | to see his 37. 1
'that horse his mettle from his rider takes: LC 107
and controversy hence a question takes, 110
and he takes and leaves, | in either's aptness, 305

TAKEST 1 FR 0.0001 REL FR 1 V 0 P
think i am dead, and that even here thou takest, R2 5.01. 38

TAKE/'T 1 FR 0.0001 REL FR 1 V 0 P
and they will take/'t, so; LR 2.02.100

TAKE'T 14 FR 0.0015 REL FR 8 V 6 P
if thou beest a devil, take't as thou list. TMP 3.02.129 P
the jewel that we find, we stoop and take't, MM 2.01. 24
do, he'll smile, and take't for a great favor. TN 3.02. 83 P
give't or take't. 3.04.240 P
i'll take't upon me. WT 2.02. 30
take up the bastard, | take't up, i say; 2.03. 77
'twill not, sir thomas lovell, take't of me — H8 5.01. 30
there's laying on, take't off who will, as they TRO 1.02.207 P
take't, 'tis yours. what is't? COR 1.09. 81
for, take't of my soul, my lord leans wondrously TIM 3.04. 70 P
and let him take't at worst — for their knives 5.01.178
i take't, 'tis later, sir. MAC 2.01. 3
to take't again perforce! monster ingratitude! LR 1.05. 39 P
which as i take't we shall, for his best force ANT 4.11. 2

TAKETH 2 FR 0.0002 REL FR 1 V 1 P
and for i know she taketh most delight | in SHR 1.01. 92
into mauritania and taketh away with him the OTH 4.02.224 P

TAKING 33 FR 0.0037 REL FR 23 V 10 P
what a taking was he in when your husband ask'd WIV 3.03.180 P
you'll mar the light by taking it in snuff; LLL 5.02. 22
nor borrow | by taking nor by giving of excess, MV 1.03. 62
yet art thou good for nothing but taking up, and AWW 2.03.207 P
he stole from florence, taking no leave, and i 5.03.143 P
it be to report your lord's taking of this. TN 2.02. 11 P
sin, | for which the heavens, taking angry note, WT 5.01.173
but taking note of thy abhorr'd aspect, JN 4.02.224
for taking so the head, your whole head's length R2 3.03. 14
the manner of their taking may appear | at large 5.06. 9
a man is through with them in honest taking up, 2H4 1.02. 40 P
you out for taking their names upon you before 2.04.143 P
and then imagine me taking your part, | and in 5.02. 96
then, taking him from thence that is not there, R3 3.01. 53
who now are here, taking their leaves of me, COR 4.05.133
taking thy part, hath rush'd aside the law, ROM 3.03. 26
do now, | taking the measure of an unmade grave. 3.03. 70
the worst is filthy, and would not hold taking, TIM 1.02.154 P
pella | for taking bribes here of the sardians; JC 4.03. 3
for taking one's part that's out of favor. LR 1.04. 99 P
unusual vigilance | does not attend my taking. 2.03. 5
young bones, | you taking airs, with lameness! 2.04.164
thee from whirlwinds, star–blasting, and taking! 3.04. 60 P
in it a jewel | well worth a poor man's taking. 4.06. 29
be rid of him devise | his speedy taking off. 5.01. 65
oft | (when he hath mus'd of taking kingdoms in) ANT 3.13. 83
on me a cruelty, by taking | antony's course, 5.02.129
should we be taking leave | as long a term as CYM 1.01.106
flat, for taking a beggar without less quality. 1.04. 23 P
to try your taking of a false report, which hath 1.06.173
nation, | taking advantage of our misery, PER 1.04. 66
mind, | taking no notice that she is so nigh, VEN 341
but she in worser taking, | from sleep disturbed LUC 453

TAKING–OFF 1 FR 0.0001 REL FR 1 V 0 P
against | the deep damnation of his taking–off; MAC 1.07. 20

TAK'ST 12 FR 0.0013 REL FR 10 V 2 P
sycorax my mother, | which thou tak'st from me. TMP 1.02.332
he's a better woodman than thou tak'st him for. MM 4.03.162 P
thou tak'st | true delight | in the sight | of MND 3.02.454
if thou tak'st more | or less than a just pound, MV 4.01.326
rich stake drawn, | and tak'st it all for jest. WT 1.02.249
tak'st up the princess by that forced baseness 2.03. 79
call it a travel that thou tak'st for pleasure. R2 1.03.262
if thou tak'st leave, thou wert better be hang'd 2H4 1.02. 89 P
adieu, poor soul, that tak'st thy leave of it! R3 4.01. 90
but, whatsoe'er thou tak'st me for, i'm sure H8 5.02.163
thou tak'st up | thou know'st not what; CYM 1.05. 60
mak'st | with the breath thou giv'st and tak'st, PHT 19

TALBONITES 1 FR 0.0001 REL FR 1 V 0 P
but burning fatal to the talbonites! 1H6 3.02. 28

TALBOT 74 FR 0.0083 REL FR 74 V 0 P
warwick and talbot, salisbury and gloucester, H5 4.03. 54
betwixt the stout lord talbot and the french. 1H6 1.01.106
what? wherein talbot overcame, is't so? 1.01.107
wherein lord talbot was o'erthrown. 1.01.108
where valiant talbot above human thought 1.01.121
spying his undaunted spirit, | "a talbot! 1.01.128
a talbot!" 1.01.128
thrust talbot with a spear into the back, | whom 1.01.138
is talbot slain then? 1.01.141
talbot is taken, whom we wont to fear; 1.02. 14
talbot, my life, my joy, again return'd? 1.04. 23
speak unto talbot, nay, look up to him. 1.04. 89
talbot, farewell, thy hour is not yet come. 1.05. 13
ascend, brave talbot, we will follow thee. 2.01. 28
and here will talbot mount, or make his grave. 2.01. 34
i think this talbot be a fiend of hell. 2.01. 46
the cry of talbot serves me for a sword, | for i 2.01. 79
'tis thought, lord talbot, when the fight began, 2.02. 22
princely train | call ye the warlike talbot, for 2.02. 35
here is the talbot, who would speak with him? 2.02. 37
by message crav'd, so is lord talbot come. 2.03. 13
is this the talbot, so much fear'd abroad | that 2.03. 16
stay, my lord talbot, for my lady craves | to 2.03. 29
that talbot is but shadow of himself? 2.03. 62
victorious talbot, pardon my abuse. 2.03. 67
nor misconster | the mind of talbot, as you did 2.03. 74
tears, | if talbot but survive thy treachery. 3.02. 37
or else let talbot perish with this shame. 3.02. 57
if talbot do but thunder, rain will follow. 3.02. 59
for talbot means no goodness by his looks. 3.02. 72
lord talbot, do not so dishonor me: 3.02. 90
what? will you fly, and leave lord talbot? 3.02.107
warlike and martial talbot, burgundy | enshrines 3.02.118
what wills lord talbot pleaseth burgundy. 3.02.130
let frantic talbot triumph for a while, | and 3.03. 5
burgundy | to leave the talbot and to follow us. 3.03. 20
there goes the talbot, with his colors spread, 3.03. 31
when talbot hath set footing once in france 3.03. 64
so farewell, talbot, i'll no longer trust thee. 3.03. 84
is this the lord talbot, uncle gloucester, 3.04. 13
why then lord talbot there shall talk with him, 4.01. 68
english john talbot, captains, /calls you forth, 4.02. 3
upon no christian soul but english talbot. 4.02. 30
and saint george, talbot and england's right, 4.02. 55
burdeaux with his power | to fight with talbot. 4.03. 5
renowned talbot doth expect my aid, | and i am 4.03. 12
spur to the rescue of the noble talbot, | who 4.03. 19
else farewell talbot, france, and england's 4.03. 23
this seven years did not talbot see his son, 4.03. 37
what joy shall noble talbot have | to bid his 4.03. 39
this expedition was by york and talbot | too 4.04. 2
the over–daring talbot | hath sullied all his 4.04. 5
that, talbot dead, great york might bear the 4.04. 9
from bought and sold lord talbot, | who, ring'd 4.04. 13
about, | and talbot perisheth by your default. 4.04. 28
hath now entrapp'd the noble–minded talbot: 4.04. 37
and fly would talbot never, though he might. 4.04. 44
if he be dead, brave talbot, then adieu! 4.04. 45
o young john talbot, i did send for thee | to 4.05. 1
is my name talbot? 4.05. 12
that basely fled when noble talbot stood. 4.05. 17
the regent hath with talbot broke his word, 4.06. 2
where is john talbot? 4.06. 4
of mine | which thou didst force from talbot, my 4.06. 24
before young talbot from old talbot fly | the 4.06. 46
before young talbot from old talbot fly | the 4.06. 46
if son to talbot, die at talbot's foot. 4.06. 53
o, where's young talbot? 4.07. 2
"young talbot was not born | to be the pillage 4.07. 40
valiant lord talbot, earl of shrewsbury, 4.07. 61
lord talbot of goodrig and urchinfield, | lord 4.07. 64
is talbot slain, the frenchmen's only scourge, 4.07. 77
i trust the ghost of talbot is not there. 5.02. 16
sir gilbert talbot, sir william stanley, R3 4.05. 13

TALBOT'S 14 FR 0.0015 REL FR 14 V 0 P
belief, | i go to certify her talbot's here. 1H6 2.03. 32
to think that you have aught but talbot's shadow 2.03. 46
or else reproach be talbot's greatest fame! 3.02. 76
doth stop my cornets, were in talbot's place! 4.03. 25
then god take mercy on brave talbot's soul, 4.03. 34
that talbot's name might be in thee reviv'd, 4.05. 3
the world will say, he is not talbot's blood, 4.05. 16
have won, | and if i fly, i am not talbot's son. 4.06. 51
if son to talbot, die at talbot's foot. 4.06. 53
young talbot's valor makes me smile at thee. 4.07. 4
now my old arms are young john talbot's grave. 4.07. 32
how the young whelp of talbot's, raging wood, 4.07. 35
i think this upstart is old talbot's ghost, | he 4.07. 87
all will be ours, now bloody talbot's slain. 4.07. 96

TALBOTS 2 FR 0.0002 REL FR 2 V 0 P
all the talbots in the world, to save my life. 1H6 3.02.108
two talbots, winged through the lither sky, | in 4.07. 21

/TALE 4 FR 0.0004 REL FR 3 V 1 P
/to /bid /aeneas /tell /the /tale /twice /o'er TIT 3.02. 27
/my /aunt /merry /with /some /pleasing /tale. 3.02. 47
i chiefly lov'd, 'twas aeneas' /tale to dido, HAM 2.02.446 P
/the /most /piteous /tale /of /lear /and /him LR 5.03.215

TALE 111 FR 0.0125 REL FR 80 V 31 P
your tale, sir, would cure deafness. TMP 1.02.106
my tale provokes that question. 1.02.140
if you trouble him any more in 's tale, by this 3.02. 49 P
now forward with your tale. 3.02. 83 P
in thy tale. TGV 2.03. 48 P
that peradventures shall tell you another tale, WIV 1.01. 77 P
peace–a your tongue. — speak–a your tale. 1.04. 81 P
well, thereby hangs a tale. 1.04.149 P
there is an old tale goes, that herne the hunter 4.04. 28
age | this tale of herne the hunter for a truth. 4.04. 38
this gentleman told somewhat of my tale — MM 5.01. 84
thou hast, | rely upon it till my tale be heard, 5.01.365
rage, | is a mad tale he told to–day at dinner, ERR 4.03. 88
like the old tale, my lord: ADO 1.01.216 P
force | and strong encounter of my amorous tale; 1.01.325
indeed that tells a heavy tale for him. 3.02. 61 P
answer for that, and now forward with thy tale. 3.03.102 P
shifted out of thy tale into telling me of the 3.03.142 P
times good night — i tell this tale vildly, i 3.03.148 P
'fore god, they are both in a tale. 4.02. 31 P
even so: my tale is told. LLL 5.02.720
ever read, | could ever hear by tale or history, MND 1.01.133
the wisest aunt, telling the saddest tale, 2.01. 51
and, when the tale is told, bid her be judge MV 4.01.276
i could match this beginning with an old tale. AYL 1.02.120 P
and thereby hangs a tale." 2.07. 28
saving your tale, petruchio, i pray | let us SHR 2.01. 71
saddles into the dirt, and thereby hangs a tale. 4.01. 58 P
this 'tis to feel a tale, not to hear a tale. 4.01. 63 P
this 'tis to feel a tale, not to hear a tale. 4.01. 63 P
and therefore 'tis call'd a sensible tale; 4.01. 64 P
tell thou the tale. 4.01. 72 P
if he be credulous, and trust my tale, | i'll 4.02. 67
my widow says, thus she conceives her tale. 5.02. 24
pray you sit by us, | and tell 's a tale. WT 2.01. 23
of this present, as my tale | now seems to it. 4.01. 14
which is call'd true, is so like an old tale, 5.02. 28 P
like an old tale still, which will have matter 5.02. 61 P
you, should be hooted at | like an old tale; 5.03.117
your tale must be how he employ'd my mother. JN 1.01. 98
be well advis'd, tell o'er thy tale again. 3.01. 5
then speak again, not all thy former tale, | but 3.01. 25
but this one word, whether thy tale be true. 3.01. 26
tell him this tale, and from the mouth of 3.01.152
life is as tedious as a twice–told tale | vexing 3.04.108
done, | this act is as an ancient tale new told, 4.02. 18
cuts off his tale and talks of arthur's death. 4.02.202
face, | as bid me tell my tale in express words, 4.02.234
my death's sad tale may yet undeaf his ear. R2 2.01. 16
too well, too well thou tell'st a tale so ill. 3.02.121
my tongue hath but a heavier tale to say. 3.02.197
griefs, | tell thou the lamentable tale of me, 5.01. 44
key, | that no man enter till my tale be done. 5.03. 37
good uncle, tell your tale — i have done. 1H4 1.03.256
that his tale to me may be nothing but "anon." 2.04. 32 P
that melted at the sweet tale of the sun's? 2.04.122 P
mark now how a plain tale shall put you down. 2.04.255 P
i thank him that he cuts me from my tale, | for 5.02. 90
this is the strangest tale that ever i heard. 5.04.154
and death approach not ere my tale be done. 1H6 2.05. 62
this superficial tale | is but a preface of her 5.05. 10
i think i should have told your grace's tale. 2H6 3.01. 44
short tale to make, we at saint albons met, 3H6 2.01.120
then he was urg'd to tell my tale again: R3 3.07. 31
prepare her ears to hear a wooer's tale; 4.04.327
an honest tale speeds best being plainly told. 4.04.358
then plainly to her tell my loving tale. 4.04.359
when thou mayest tell thy tale the nearest way? 4.04.461
and every tongue brings in a several tale, | and 5.03.194
and every tale condemns me for a villain. 5.03.195
shall tell me another tale when th' other's come TRO 1.02. 85 P
to end a tale of length, | troy in our weakness 1.03.136
i shall tell you | a pretty tale. COR 1.01. 90
not think to fob off our disgrace with a tale. 1.01. 94 P
after your way his tale pronounc'd shall bury 5.06. 57
no sooner had they told this hellish tale, | but TIT 2.03.105
for that they will not intercept my tale. 3.01. 40
this is the tragic tale of philomel, | and 4.01. 47
sport, | she sounded almost at my pleasing tale, 5.01.119
rome's young captain, let him tell the tale, 5.03. 94
tell | a whispering tale in a fair lady's ear, ROM 1.05. 23
desirest me to stop in my tale against the hair. 2.04. 95 P
thou wouldst else have made thy tale large. 2.04. 97 P
for i was come to the whole depth of my tale, 2.04. 99 P
is longer than the tale thou dost excuse. 2.05. 34
of breath | is not so long as is a tedious tale. 5.03.230
as thick as tale | /came post with post, and MAC 1.03. 97
it is a tale | told by an idiot, full of sound 5.05. 26
i could a tale unfold whose lightest word HAM 1.05. 15

and he repell'd, a short tale to make, | fell 2.02.146
say on, he's for a jig or a tale of bawdry, or 2.02.500 P
ride, run, mar a curious tale in telling it, and LR 1.04. 33 P
list a brief tale, | and when 'tis told, o, that 5.03.182
i will a round unvarnish'd tale deliver | of my OTH 1.03. 90
i think this tale would win my daughter too. 1.03.171
whereby hangs a tale, sir? 3.01. 9 P
face, | for i will make him tell the tale anew: 4.01. 84
come, mistress, you must tell 's another tale. 5.01.125
who tells me true, though in his tale lie death, ANT 1.02. 98
thou wouldst have told this tale for virtue, not CYM 1.06.143
she hath been reading late | the tale of tereus; 2.02. 45
not standing here | to tell this tale of mine. 5.05.297
and thereby hangs a tale. TNK 3.03. 41
if the tale we have told | (for 'tis no other) ep 12
for to a pretty ear she tunes her tale. VEN 74
she trembles at his tale, | and on his neck her 591
cold, | she whispers in his ears a heavy tale, 1125
shall plead for me and tell my loving tale. LUC 480
gush pure streams to purge my impure tale." 1078
and when thou com'st thy tale to tell, | smooth PP 18. 7
and down i laid to list the sad–tun'd tale, LC 4

TALENT* *(also talons)*

TALENT* 4 FR 0.0004 REL FR 0 V 4 P
a rare talent! LLL 4.02. 62 P
if a talent be a claw, look how he claws him 4.02. 63 P
be a claw, look how he claws him with a talent. 4.02. 64 P
hal, i was not an eagle's talent in the waist, i 1H4 2.04.330 P

TALENTS* 18 FR 0.0020 REL FR 11 V 7 P
that are fools, let them use their talents. TN 1.05. 15 P
ay, my good lord, five talents is his debt, TIM 1.01. 95
three talents on the present; in future, all. 1.01.141
to your free heart, i do return those talents, 1.02. 6
let the request be fifty talents. 2.02.193 P
send o' th' instant | a thousand talents to me. 2.02.199
of friends, | i clear'd him with five talents. 2.02.226
to be rememb'red | with those five talents. 2.02.229
great and instant occasion to use fifty talents, 3.01. 19 P
the lord lucullus to borrow so many talents, nay 3.02. 12 P
ne'er have denied his occasion so many talents. 3.02. 24 P
to supply his instant use with so many talents. 3.02. 36 P
he cannot want fifty — five hundred talents. 3.02. 38
mine, fifty talents. 3.04. 93 P
in you, which i account his, beyond all talents. CYM 1.06. 80
face, | seize with thine eagle's talents. PER 4.03. 48
the beaks of ravens, talents of the kites, | and TNK 1.01. 41
"'and lo behold these talents of their hair, LC 204

TALE–PORTER 1 FR 0.0001 REL FR 0 V 1 P
midwive's name to't, one mistress tale–porter, WT 4.04.270 P

TALE'S 1 FR 0.0001 REL FR 1 V 0 P
a sad tale's best for winter. WT 2.01. 25

TALES 25 FR 0.0028 REL FR 20 V 5 P
at this time | i will tell no tales. TMP 5.01.129
my tales of love were wont to weary you; TGV 2.04.126
i can tell thee pretty tales of the duke. MM 4.03.166 P
my good wit out of the "hundred merry tales" — ADO 2.01.130 P
words | that aged ears play truant at his tales, LLL 2.01. 74
and both as light as tales. MND 3.02.133
he hears merry tales and smiles not. MV 1.02. 48 P
yours, if you talk of tales, and so farewell. SHR 2.01.217
occasion more mine eyes will tell tales of me. TN 2.01. 42 P
madam, we'll tell tales. R2 3.04. 10
good old folks and let them tell /thee tales 5.01. 41
and heard thee murmur tales of iron wars, 1H4 2.03. 48
me beg | as, in reproof of many tales devis'd, 3.02. 23
mark you now, to take the tales out of my mouth, H5 4.07. 43 P
in seeking tales and informations | against this H8 5.02.145
and bid thee bear his pretty tales in mind, TIT 5.03.165
nor tell tales of thee to high–judging jove. LR 2.04.228
and sing, and tell old tales, and laugh | at 5.03. 12
truths would be tales, | where now half tales be ANT 2.02.133
be tales, | where now half tales be truths. 2.02.134
you may then revolve what tales i have told you CYM 3.03. 14
here, | and by relating tales of others' griefs, PER 1.04. 2
remember, cousin, | else there be tales abroad. TNK 3.03. 38
sad tales doth tell | to pencill'd pensiveness LUC 1496
how many tales to please me hath she coined, PP 7. 9

/TALK 4 FR 0.0004 REL FR 4 V 0 P
/of /woe, /that /thus /dost /talk /in /signs! TIT 3.02. 12
/handle /not /the /theme, /to /talk /of /hands, 3.02. 29
/fie, /how /franticly /i /square /my /talk, 3.02. 31
/i /pray /talk /me /of /cassio. OTH 3.04. 92

TALK 208 FR 0.0235 REL FR 147 V 61 P
prithee no more; thou dost talk nothing to me. TMP 2.01.171
his fit now, and does not talk after the wisest. 2.02. 73 P
sit then and talk with her, she is thine own. 4.01. 32
what sad talk was that | wherewith my brother TGV 1.03. 1
"item, she doth talk in her sleep." 3.01.329 P
matter for that, so she sleep not in her talk. 3.01.331 P
doth this sir proteus that we talk on | often 4.02. 73
ill, when you talk of war. 5.02. 16
we had an hour's talk of that wart. WIV 1.04.151 P
we have an hour's talk with you. 2.01.167 P
break their talk, mistress quickly, my kinsman 3.04. 22 P
why, does he talk of him? 4.02. 30 P
master fenton, talk not to me, my mind is heavy; 4.06. 1 P
i talk not of your soul; MM 2.04. 57
i would the duke we talk of were return'd again. 3.02.173 P
if bawdy talk offend you, we'll have very little 4.03.178 P
as strange unto your town as to your talk, | who ERR 2.02.149
we talk with goblins, owls, and sprites; 2.02.190
wilt thou still talk? 4.04. 44 P
god help, poor souls, how idlely do they talk! 4.04.129
come, talk not of her; ADO 2.01.255 P
a week married, they would talk themselves mad. 2.01.354 P
because you talk of wooing, i will sing, | since 2.03. 49
now you talk of a sheet of paper, i remember a 2.03.134 P
and down, | our talk must only be of benedick. 3.01. 17
my talk to thee must be how benedick | is sick 3.01. 20
for the watch to babble and to talk, is most 3.03. 36 P
we will rather sleep than talk, we know what 3.03. 37 P
talk with a ruffian at her chamber–window, | who 4.01. 91
talk with a man out at a window! 4.01.309 P
also, the watch heard them talk of one deformed. 5.01.308 P
we'll talk with margaret, | how her acquaintance 5.01.331
if any man be seen to talk with a woman within LLL 1.01.129 P
mirth, | i never spent an hour's talk withal. 2.01. 68
we will talk no more of this matter. 3.01.118 P
come, you talk greasily, your lips grow foul. 4.01.137
i'll prove her fair, or talk till doomsday here. 4.03.270
with visages display'd, to talk and greet. 5.02.144
the story) did talk through the chink of a wall. MND 3.01. 64 P
for he doth nothing but talk of his horse, and MV 1.02. 41 P
sell with you, talk with you, walk with you, and 1.03. 35 P
talk you of young master launcelot? 2.02. 48 P
talk you of young master launcelot? 2.02. 50 P
what 'a will, we talk of young master launcelot. 2.02. 54 P
beseech you, talk you of young master launcelot. 2.02. 58 P
talk not of master launcelot, father, for the 2.02. 60 P
talk with respect, and swear but now and then, 2.02.191
not have my father | see me in talk with thee. 2.03. 9
prolixity or crossing the plain highway of talk, 3.01. 12 P
what talk you of the posy or the value? 5.01.151
out of service, let us talk in good earnest. AYL 1.03. 26 P
here, a young man and an old in solemn talk. 2.04. 21 P
never talk to me, i will weep. 3.04. 1 P
but what talk we of fathers, when there is such 3.04. 38 P
but since that thou canst talk of love so well, 3.05. 94
then god buy you, and you talk in blank verse. 4.01. 31 P
and practice rhetoric in your common talk, SHR 1.01. 35
sirrah, be gone, or talk not, i advise you. 1.02. 44
are you a suitor to the maid you talk of, yea or 1.02.228
talk not to me, i will go sit and weep, | till i 2.01. 35
they call me katherine that do talk of me. 2.01.184
yours, if you talk of tales, and so farewell. 2.01.217
nor hast thou pleasure to be cross in talk; 2.01.249
but what talk i of this? 4.01. 89 P
talk not, signior gremio; 5.01. 96 P
here is a wonder, if you talk of a wonder. 5.02.106
much repairs me | to talk of your good father. AWW 1.02. 31
get you gone, sir, i'll talk with you more anon. 1.03. 64 P
i long to talk with the young noble soldier. 4.05.103 P
i had talk of you last night; 5.02. 53 P
i heard my lady talk of it yesterday; TN 1.03. 15 P
to prate and talk for life and honor 'fore | who WT 3.02. 41
deserv'd | all tongues to talk their bitt'rest. 3.02.216
see a thing to talk on when thou art dead and 3.03. 81 P
my father and the gentlemen are in sad talk, and 4.04.310 P
but what talk we of these traitorly rascals, 4.04.791 P
told him i heard them talk of a farthel and i 5.02.116 P
if i talk to him, with his innocent prate | he JN 4.01. 25
and when they talk of him, they shake their 4.02.188
let's talk of graves, of worms, and epitaphs, R2 3.02.145
let's choose executors and talk of wills; 3.02.148
i see | i talk but idly, and you laugh at me. 3.03.171
they will talk of state, for every one doth so 3.04. 27
amongst much other talk, that very time, | i 4.01. 14
well | the very time aumerle and you did talk. 4.01. 61
and talk so like a waiting–gentlewoman | of guns 1H4 1.03. 55
i'll talk to you | when you are better temper'd 1.03.234
than feed on cates and have him talk to me | in 3.01.161
talk not of dying, i am out of fear | of death 4.01.135
never talk of it. 2H4 1.01. 54
i talk not of his majesty. 1.02.105 P
have labor'd so hard, you should talk so idlely! 2.02. 29 P
where i think they will talk of mad shallow yet. 3.02. 15 P
argument | is all too heavy to admit much talk. 5.02. 24
think, when we talk of horses, that you see them H5 pr 26
you must not dare, for shame, to talk of mercy, 2.02. 81
the trumpet call us to the breach, and we talk, 3.02.109 P
high constable, you talk of horse and armor? 3.07. 8 P
the maiden cities you talk of may wait on her; 5.02.326 P
in private will i talk with thee apart. 1H6 1.02. 69
my lord, methinks, is very long in talk. 1.02.118
must your bold verdict enter talk with lords?" 3.01. 63
talk like the vulgar sort of market men | that 3.02. 4
summon a parley, we will talk with him. 3.03. 35
why then lord talbot there shall talk with him, 4.01. 68
then talk no more of flight, it is no boot; 4.06. 52
lady, wherefore talk you so? 5.03.108
i come to talk of commonwealth affairs. 2H6 1.03.154
his highness' pleasure is to talk with him. 2.01. 71
lord suffolk, you and i must talk of that event. 3.01.326
hale him away, and let him talk no more. 4.01.131
thee that usually talk of a noun and a verb, and 4.07. 39 P
talk not of france, sith thou hast lost it all. 3H6 1.01.110
and men may talk of kings, and why not i? 3.01. 58
i will not hence, till with my talk and tears 3.03.158
my lords, forbear this talk; 4.01. 6
but wherefore stay we? 'tis no time to talk. 4.05. 24
what talk you of debating? 4.07. 53
let him see our commission, and talk no more. R3 1.04. 90 P
my lord of york will still be cross in talk. 3.01.126
be thou so too, and so break off the talk, | and 3.01.177
go on before, i'll talk with this good fellow. 3.02. 95
man | the men you talk of came into my mind. 3.02.117
stay, madam, i must talk a word with you. 4.04.199
that fill the court with quarrels, talk, and H8 1.03. 20
if i chance to talk a little wild, forgive me; 1.04. 26
then we shall have 'em | talk us to silence. 1.04. 45
i told your grace they would talk anon. 1.04. 49
let me have it; | i do not talk much. 2.01.146
how you do talk! 2.03. 44
i would somebody had heard her talk yesterday, TRO 1.01. 45 P
what do you talk of? 1.02. 44 P
nay, if we talk of reason, | /let's shut our 2.02. 46
to talk with him, and to behold his visage, 3.03.240
nor heel the high lavolt, nor sweeten talk, 4.04. 86
to our own selves bend we our needful talk. 4.04.139
be silent, /boy, i profit not by thy talk. 5.01. 15 P
because you talk of pride now — will you not be COR 2.01. 25 P
you talk of pride: 2.01. 38 P
what do ye talk? 3.01.315
i talk of you: 3.02. 13
i talk of that, that know it. 3.03. 84
come, what talk you | of martius? 4.06. 46
their talk at table, and their thanks at end; 4.07. 4
if you have heard your general talk of rome 5.02. 9
away, and talk not, trouble us no more. TIT 1.01.478
come, lucius, come, stay not to talk with them. 2.03.306
now talk at pleasure of your safety. 4.02.134
for i must talk of murthers, rapes, and 5.01. 63
titus, i am come to talk with thee. 5.02. 16
no, not a word, how can i grace my talk, 5.02. 17
thou didst know me, thou wouldst talk with me. 5.02. 20
and talk of them when he was dead and gone. 5.03.166
what, drawn and talk of peace? ROM 1.01. 70
give leave a while, | we must talk in secret. 1.03. 8
"marry" is the very theme | i came to talk of. 1.03. 64
true, i talk of dreams, | which are the children 1.04. 96
this wind you talk of blows us from ourselves: 1.04.104
that loves to hear himself talk, and will speak 2.04.148 P
we talk here in the public haunt of men. 3.01. 50
talk no more. 3.03. 60
let's talk, it is not day. 3.05. 25
talk not to me, for i'll not speak a word. 3.05.202
or am i mad, hearing him talk of juliet, | to 5.03. 80
go hence to have more talk of these sad things; 5.03.307
no talk of timon, nothing of him expect. TIM 5.02. 14
it will not let you eat, nor talk, nor sleep; JC 2.01.252
comfort your bed, | and talk to you sometimes? 2.01.285
i have an hour's talk in store for you; 2.02.121
talk not of standing. 3.01. 89
do not talk of him | but as a property. 4.01. 39
the deep of night is crept upon our talk, | and 4.03.226
ill spirit, i would hold more talk with thee. 4.03.288
stand fast, titinius; we must out and talk. 5.01. 22
country round, | hang those that talk of fear. MAC 5.03. 36
as to give words or talk with the lord hamlet. HAM 1.03.134
upon the talk of the pois'ning? 3.02.289 P
i will talk further with you. LR 3.01. 43
go you and maintain talk with the duke, that my 3.03. 15 P
first let me talk with this philosopher. 3.04.154
i'll talk a word with this same learned theban. 3.04.157
and hear poor rogues | talk of court news; 5.03. 14
and we'll talk with them too — | who loses and 5.03. 14
watch him tame, and talk him out of patience; OTH 3.03. 23
it evermore about her | to kiss and talk to. 3.03.296
do not talk to me, emilia; 4.02.102
come, come; you talk. 4.03. 25
talk you of killing? 5.02. 33
and we shall talk before we fight. ANT 2.06. 2
if idle talk will once be necessary, | i'll not 5.02. 50
never talk on't: | she hath been colted by him. CYM 2.04.132
we'll talk of that hereafter. 3.02. 66
talk thy tongue weary, speak. 3.04.112
princes, it is too late to talk of love, | and PER 2.03.112
you talk of pirithous' and theseus' love: TNK 1.03. 55
we will talk more of this when the solemnity is 2.01. 12 P
bequeath this plea, | and talk of it no more. 3.01.116
you talk of feeding me to breed me strength; 3.01.119
are faint — then i'll talk further with you. 3.03. 7
with us, | make talk for fools and cowards. 3.03. 12
we were not bred to talk, man. 3.06. 28
"what, canst thou talk?" VEN 427
mine ears, that to your wanton talk attended, 809
mingling my talk with tears, my grief with LUC 797
sometime 'tis mad and too much talk affords. 1106
have a true respect | to talk in deeds, while 1348
begins to talk, but through his lips do throng 1783
tell, | smooth not thy tongue with filed talk, PP 18. 8

/TALK'D 3 FR 0.0003 REL FR 3 V 0 P
/neck, | /have /talk'd /of /monmouth's /grave. 2H4 2.03. 45
to–day the lords you /talk'd of are beheaded. R3 3.02. 91
and therefore have i little /talk'd of love, ROM 4.01. 7

TALK'D 28 FR 0.0031 REL FR 20 V 8 P
i think there are, sir, i heard them talk'd of. WIV 1.01.288 P
spirit, | and to be talk'd with in sincerity, MM 1.04. 36
such a fellow is not to be talk'd withal. 5.01.344 P
what man was he talk'd with you yesternight ADO 4.01. 83
i talk'd with no man at that hour, my lord. 4.01. 86
here they stay'd an hour, | and talk'd apace; LLL 5.02.369
that talk'd of her, have talk'd amiss of her. SHR 2.01.291
that talk'd of her, have talk'd amiss of her. 2.01.291
and talk'd of sathan and of limbo and of furies AWW 5.03.260 P
know'st | he dies to me again when talk'd of. WT 5.01.120
i mark'd him not, and yet he talk'd very wisely, 1H4 1.02. 86 P
i regarded him not, and yet he talk'd wisely, 1.02. 87 P
it in snuff — and still he smil'd and talk'd: 1.03. 41
and thou hast talk'd | of sallies and retires, 2.03. 50
rheumatic, and talk'd | of the whore of babylon. H5 2.03. 38 P
as index to the story we late talk'd of, | to R3 2.02.149
my uncle rivers talk'd how i did grow | more 2.04. 11
makes fear'd and talk'd of more than seen — COR 4.01. 31
i'll have you talk'd with anon. 4.05. 17 P
i nurs'd her daughter that you talk'd withal; ROM 1.05.115
though they be not to be talk'd on, yet they are 2.05. 42 P
could they say, till now, that talk'd of rome, JC 1.02.154
good gentlemen, he hath much talk'd of you, HAM 2.02. 19
you have been talk'd of since your travel much, 4.07. 71
edmund and i have talk'd, | and more convenient LR 4.05. 30
dispatch we | the business we have talk'd of. ANT 2.02.166
then she talk'd of you, sir — | that you must TNK 4.01. 76
he did complain him, | and talk'd of virtue: LUC 846

TALKER 2 FR 0.0002 REL FR 2 V 0 P
fare you well! i'll grow a talker for this gear. MV 1.01.110
lord, have great care | i be not found a talker. H8 2.02. 78

TALKERS 1 FR 0.0001 REL FR 1 V 0 P
talkers are no good doers. R3 1.03.350

TALKEST 3 FR 0.0003 REL FR 0 V 3 P
talkest thou nothing but of ladies? TN 4.02. 26 P
thou talkest of an admirable conceited fellow. WT 4.04.202 P
what talkest thou to me of the hangman? 1H4 2.01. 66 P

TALKING 24 FR 0.0027 REL FR 10 V 14 P
he will be talking. TMP 2.01. 27 P
we were talking that our garments seem now as 2.01. 97 P
now lead the way without any more talking. 2.02.174 P
even for this time i spend in talking to thee. TGV 4.02.104
i wonder that you will still be talking, signior ADO 1.01.116 P
a good old man, sir, he will be talking; 3.05. 33 P
say you are, because i would be talking of her. AYL 4.01. 90 P
will weary you then no longer with idle talking. 5.02. 52 P
talking with the deceiving father of a deceitful SHR 4.04. 82 P
he finds that now scarce to be worth talking of; TN 3.04.299 P
and talking of the alps and apennines, | the JN 1.01.202
me from my tale, | for i profess not talking; 1H4 5.02. 91
/than now to see you here an iron man, talking, 2H4 4.02. 8
talking of hawking; 2H6 2.01. 49
what, talking with a priest, lord chamberlain? R3 3.02.113
hold my thanks, | and save me so much talking. H8 1.04. 40
else | this talking lord can lay upon my credit, 3.02.265
what were you talking of when i came? TRO 1.02. 47 P
that were we talking of, and of his anger. 1.02. 52 P

have you not done talking yet? 3.02.101 P
no more talking on't; COR 1.01. 12 P
the general and his wife are talking of it, OTH 3.01. 43
i have been talking with a suitor here, | a man 3.03. 42
i was the other day talking on the sea–bank with 4.01.133 P
TALKS 14 FR 0.0015 REL FR 9 V 5 P
is he, and talks of the basket too, howsoever he WIV 4.02. 91 P
love talks with better knowledge, and knowledge MM 3.02.150 P
who talks within there? ho, open the door! ERR 3.01. 38
'tis but a peevish boy — yet he talks well — AYL 3.05.110
talks as familiarly of roaring lions | as maids JN 2.01.459
he talks to me that never had a son. 3.04. 91
cuts off his tale and talks of arthur's death. 4.02.202
and talks as familiarly of john a' gaunt as if 2H4 3.02.320 P
who talks of my nation? H5 3.02.124 P
he talks at randon; sure the man is mad. 1H6 5.03. 85
he talks of wood; it is some carpenter. 5.03. 90
sometime he talks as if duke humphrey's ghost 2H6 3.02.373
a corslet with his eye, talks like a knell, and COR 5.04. 21 P
the honor is sacred which he talks on now, ANT 2.02. 85
TALK'ST 7 FR 0.0008 REL FR 4 V 3 P
to suggest thee from thy master thou talk'st of; AWW 4.05. 45 P
say, what art thou talk'st of kings and queens? 3H6 3.01. 55
ay, but thou talk'st as if thou wert a king. 3.01. 59
damned strumpet, | talk'st thou to me of "ifs"? R3 3.04. 75
thou talk'st of nothing. ROM 1.04. 96
without those means thou talk'st of, didst thou TIM 4.03.313 P
poor prattler, how thou talk'st! MAC 4.02. 64 P
TALL 38 FR 0.0043 REL FR 23 V 15 P
how tall was she? TGV 4.04.157
but he is as tall a man of his hands as any is WIV 1.04. 25 P
have made you four tall fellows skip like rats. 2.01.229 P
you were good soldiers and tall fellows; 2.02. 11 P
if tall, a lance ill–headed; ADO 3.01. 64
the cowslips tall her pensioners be, | in their MND 2.01. 10
and with her personage, her tall personage, 3.02.292
anon comes pyramus, sweet youth and tall, | and 5.01.144
the carcasses of many a tall ship lie buried, as MV 3.01. 6 P
because that i am more than common tall, | that AYL 1.03.115
he is not very tall — yet for his years he's 3.05.118
is not very tall — yet for his years he's tall; 3.05.118
th' art a tall fellow; SHR 4.04. 17
he's as tall a man as any's in illyria. TN 1.03. 20 P
i am not tall enough to become the function well 4.02. 6 P
the prince thou art a tall fellow of thy hands WT 5.02.164 P
i know thou art no tall fellow of thy hands and 5.02.165 P
thou wouldst be a tall fellow of thy hands. 5.02.167 P
ay, by any means prove a tall fellow. 5.02.170 P
venture to be drunk, not being a tall fellow, 5.02.172 P
by the duke of britain | with eight tall ships, R2 2.01.286
which many a good tall fellow had destroyed | so 1H4 1.03. 62
sir john falstaff, a tall gentleman, by heaven, 2H4 3.02. 61 P
master bardolph, and welcome, my tall fellow. 5.01. 58 P
for women are shrows, both short and tall; 5.03. 33
thy spirits are most tall. H5 2.01. 68
spoke like a tall man that respects thy R3 1.04.152 P
faith they have in tennis and tall stockings, H8 1.03. 30
a very tall man! ROM 2.04. 30 P
and yond tall anchoring bark, | diminish'd to LR 4.06. 18
that he may bless this bay with his tall ship, OTH 2.01. 79
bid you alexas | bring me word how tall she is. ANT 2.05.118
and carry back to sicily much tall youth | that 2.06. 7
is she as tall as me? 3.03. 11
of their ladies, | like tall ships under sail; TNK 2.02. 12
ones, | and humble with a ferula the tall ones, 3.05.112
palamon," | and "palamon was a tall young man." 4.01. 82
boat, | he of tall building and of goodly pride. SON 80.12
TALLER 2 FR 0.0002 REL FR 1 V 1 P
the liker you; few taller are so young. LLL 5.02.836
the weather, a taller man than i will take cold. SHR 4.01. 11 P
TALLEST 2 FR 0.0002 REL FR 1 V 1 P
the thickest and the tallest. LLL 4.01. 47 P
the thickest and the tallest! 4.01. 48
TALLIES 1 FR 0.0001 REL FR 1 V 0 P
nor need i tallies thy dear love to score; SON 122.10
TALLOW 5 FR 0.0005 REL FR 1 V 4 P
jove, or who can blame me to piss my tallow? WIV 5.05. 15 P
her rags and the tallow in them will burn a ERR 3.02. 98 P
call in ribs, call in tallow. 1H4 2.04.111 P
a wassail candle, my lord, all tallow; 2H4 1.02.158 P
smoky light | that's fed with stinking tallow: CYM 1.06.110
TALLOW–CATCH 1 FR 0.0001 REL FR 0 V 1 P
thou whoreson, obscene, greasy tallow–catch — 1H4 2.04.228 P
TALLOW–FACE 1 FR 0.0001 REL FR 1 V 0 P
you tallow–face! ROM 3.05.157
TALLY 1 FR 0.0001 REL FR 0 V 1 P
had no other books but the score and the tally, 2H6 4.07. 35 P
TALONS *(also talent*, etc.)*
TALONS 2 FR 0.0002 REL FR 2 V 0 P
where are his talons? 2H6 3.02.196
so doves do peck the falcon's piercing talons, 3H6 1.04. 41
TAM* *(also dam*)*
TAM* 3 FR 0.0003 REL FR 2 V 1 P
the tevil and his tam! WIV 1.01.149 P
dominator poli, | tam lentus audis scelera? TIT 4.01. 82
tam lentus vides? 4.01. 82
TAM'D 5 FR 0.0005 REL FR 4 V 1 P
for it hath tam'd my old master and my new SHR 4.01. 24 P
now go thy ways, thou hast tam'd a curst shrow. 5.02.188
a wonder, by your leave, she will be tam'd so. 5.02.189
and tam'd the king and made the dolphin stoop; 3H6 2.02.151
a wild bird being tam'd with too much handling, VEN 560
'TAME 1 FR 0.0001 REL FR 1 V 0 P
cat, | to 'tame and havoc more than she can eat. H5 1.02.173
/TAME 1 FR 0.0001 REL FR 1 V 0 P
/quickly /down /to /tame /these /vild /offenses, LR 4.02. 47
TAME 41 FR 0.0046 REL FR 30 V 11 P
if i can recover him, and keep him tame, and get TMP 2.02. 69 P
if i can recover him, and keep him tame, i will 2.02. 76 P
make tigers tame, and huge leviathans | forsake TGV 3.02. 79
to be what i would not shall not make me tame. WIV 3.05.150 P
you could not with more tame a tongue desire it; MM 2.02. 46
if justice cannot tame you, she shall ne'er ADO 5.01.206 P
you are a tame man, go! MND 3.02.259
(for i see love hath made thee a tame snake) and AYL 4.03. 70 P
for i am he am born to tame you, kate, | and SHR 2.01.276
'tis a world to see | how tame, when men and 2.01.312
he that knows better how to tame a shrew, | now 4.01.210
ay, and he'll tame her. 4.02. 53
to tame a shrew and charm her chattering tongue. 4.02. 58
i have kept of them tame, and know their natures AWW 2.05. 45 P
praise, and make 's | as fat as tame things. WT 1.02. 92
rage, | and make them tame to their obedience! JN 4.02.262
up, | and tame the savage spirit of wild war, 5.02. 74
yet can i not of such tame patience boast | as R2 1.01. 52
lions make leopards tame. 1.01.174
their courage with hard labor tame and dull, 1H4 4.03. 23
who, never so tame, so cherish'd and lock'd up, 5.02. 10
no swagg'rer, hostess, a tame cheater, i' faith, 2H4 2.04. 97 P
that still use of grief makes wild grief tame, R3 4.04.230
for those that tame wild horses | pace 'em not H8 5.02. 56
two curs shall tame each other; TRO 1.03.389
you must be watch'd ere you be made tame, must 3.02. 44 P
weep seas, live in fire, eat rocks, tame tigers; 3.02. 78 P
made tame and most familiar to my nature; 3.03. 10
his remedies are tame: COR 4.06. 2
be not too tame neither, but let your own HAM 3.02. 16 P
i am tame, sir. pronounce. 3.02.310 P
at your age | the heyday in the blood is tame, 3.04. 69
a most poor man, made tame to fortune's blows, LR 4.06.221
rest, | i'll watch him tame, and talk him out of OTH 3.03. 23
i'll tame you; PER 2.05. 75
he has a tongue will tame tempests, | and make TNK 2.03. 16
the tiger would be tame and gently hear him; VEN 1096
slaughter, | to tame the unicorn and lion wild, LUC 956
weak and cold, | youth is wild, and age is tame. PP 12. 8
and patience, tame to sufferance, bide each SON 58. 7
showing fair nature is both kind and tame; LC 311
TAMED 1 FR 0.0001 REL FR 1 V 0 P
up | the lees and dregs of a flat tamed piece; TRO 4.01. 63
TAMELY 3 FR 0.0003 REL FR 3 V 0 P
cured, | stoop tamely to the foot of majesty. 2H4 4.02. 42
if we live thus tamely, | to be thus jaded by a H8 3.02.279
father, fool me not so much | to bear it tamely; LR 2.04.276
/TAMENESS 1 FR 0.0001 REL FR 0 V 1 P
/that /trusts /in /the /tameness /of /a /wolf, LR 3.06. 18 P
TAMENESS 1 FR 0.0001 REL FR 0 V 1 P
madness i ever yet beheld seem'd but tameness, WIV 4.02. 27 P
TAMER 1 FR 0.0001 REL FR 1 V 0 P
tamer than sleep, fonder than ignorance, | less TRO 1.01. 10
TAMES 2 FR 0.0002 REL FR 1 V 1 P
but thou know'st winter tames man, woman, and SHR 4.01. 23 P
continuance tames the one, the other wild, LUC 1097
TAMING 1 FR 0.0001 REL FR 1 V 0 P
thee, | taming my wild heart to thy loving hand. ADO 3.01.112
TAMING–SCHOOL 2 FR 0.0002 REL FR 2 V 0 P
faith, he is gone unto the taming–school. SHR 4.02. 54
the taming–school! what, is there such a place? 4.02. 55
/TAMORA 1 FR 0.0001 REL FR 1 V 0 P
/for /thyself, /and /that's /for /tamora. TIT 3.02. 74
TAMORA 24 FR 0.0027 REL FR 24 V 0 P
thracian tyrant in his tent | may favor tamora, TIT 1.01.139
(when goths were goths and tamora was queen), 1.01.140
and therefore, lovely tamora, queen of goths, 1.01.315
behold, i choose thee, tamora, for my bride, 1.01.319
if ever tamora | were gracious in those princely 1.01.428
this day shall be a love–day, tamora. 1.01.491
now climbeth tamora olympus' top, | safe out of 2.01. 1
so tamora. 2.01. 9
hark, tamora, the empress of my soul, | which 2.03. 40
ay, come, semiramis, nay, barbarous tamora, 2.03.118
o tamora, thou bearest a woman's face — 2.03.136
o tamora, be call'd a gentle queen, | and with 2.03.168
here, tamora, though griev'd with killing grief. 2.03.260
o tamora, was ever heard the like? 2.03.276
tamora, was it you? 2.03.293
the lustful sons of tamora | performers of this 4.01. 79
for this care of tamora, | herself and hers are 4.02.170
become | high–witted tamora to gloze with all; 4.04. 35
if tamora entreat him, then he will, | for i can 4.04. 95
fields, | and be adveng'd on cursed tamora. 5.01. 16
well | for our proud empress, mighty tamora. 5.02. 26
know, thou sad man, i am not tamora; 5.02. 28
of this was tamora delivered, | the issue of an 5.03.120
as for that ravenous tiger tamora, | no funeral 5.03.195
TAMORA'S 1 FR 0.0001 REL FR 1 V 0 P
here, | and at my lovely tamora's entreats, | i TIT 1.01.483
TAMWORTH 1 FR 0.0001 REL FR 1 V 0 P
from tamworth thither is but one day's march. R3 5.02. 13
TAN 1 FR 0.0001 REL FR 1 V 0 P
tan sacred beauty, blunt the sharp'st intents, SON 115. 7
TANDEM 1 FR 0.0001 REL FR 1 V 0 P
quo usque tandem? here is a woman wanting. TNK 3.05. 38
/TANG* 1 FR 0.0001 REL FR 0 V 1 P
let thy tongue /tang with arguments of state; TN 3.04. 70 P
TANG* 2 FR 0.0002 REL FR 1 V 1 P
for she had a tongue with a tang, | would cry to TMP 2.02. 50
let thy tongue tang arguments of state; TN 2.05.150 P
TANGLE 4 FR 0.0004 REL FR 4 V 0 P
you must lay lime to tangle her desires | by TGV 3.02. 68
life, | i think she means to tangle my eyes too! AYL 3.05. 44
stands with the snares of war to tangle thee. 1H6 4.02. 22
fly thou how thou canst, they'll tangle thee. 2H6 2.04. 55
TANGLED 3 FR 0.0003 REL FR 2 V 1 P
his speech was like a tangled chain; MND 5.01.125 P
"perceive | my king is tangled in affection to H8 3.02. 35
look how a bird lies tangled in a net, | so VEN 67
TANK *(also dank*, thank)*
TANK 1 FR 0.0001 REL FR 0 V 1 P
me tank you for dat. WIV 2.03. 72 P
TANLINGS 1 FR 0.0001 REL FR 1 V 0 P
but to be still hot summer's tanlings and | the CYM 4.04. 29
TANN'D 2 FR 0.0002 REL FR 1 V 1 P
his hide is so tann'd with his trade that 'a HAM 5.01.170 P
beated and chopp'd with tann'd antiquity, | mine SON 62.10
TANNER 2 FR 0.0002 REL FR 0 V 2 P
there's best's son, the tanner of wingham — 2H6 4.02. 22 P
a tanner will last you nine year. HAM 5.01.168 P
TANNER'S 1 FR 0.0001 REL FR 1 V 0 P
him | and the tanner's daughter to let slip now; TNK 2.03. 44
TANQUAM 1 FR 0.0001 REL FR 0 V 1 P
novi /hominem tanquam te. LLL 5.01. 9 P
TANTA 1 FR 0.0001 REL FR 0 V 1 P
tanta est erga te mentis integritas, regina H8 3.01. 40 P
TANTAENE 1 FR 0.0001 REL FR 1 V 0 P
tantaene animis caelestibus irae? 2H6 2.01. 24
TANTALUS' 1 FR 0.0001 REL FR 1 V 0 P
her, | that worse than tantalus' is her annoy, VEN 599
TANTALUS 1 FR 0.0001 REL FR 1 V 0 P
but like still–pining tantalus he sits, | and LUC 858
TAP* 3 FR 0.0003 REL FR 0 V 3 P
he shall draw, he shall tap. WIV 1.03. 11 P
grace, my lord, tap for tap, and so part fair. 2H4 2.01.193 P
grace, my lord, tap for tap, and so part fair. 2.01.193 P
TAPE 2 FR 0.0002 REL FR 1 V 1 P
will you buy any tape, | or lace for your cape, WT 4.04.315
ballad, knife, tape, glove, shoe–tie, bracelet, 4.04.599 P
TAPER *(also taber)*
TAPER 9 FR 0.0010 REL FR 9 V 0 P
my inch of taper will be burnt and done, | and R2 1.03.223
hole, | which, like a taper in some monument, TIT 2.03.228
get me a taper in my study, lucius. JC 2.01. 7
the taper burneth in your closet, sir. 2.01. 35
now sit we close about this taper here, | and 4.03.164
how ill this taper burns! 4.03.275
give me a taper! OTH 1.01.141
take not away the taper, leave it burning; CYM 2.02. 5
the flame o' th' taper | bows toward her, and 2.02. 19
TAPER–LIGHT 2 FR 0.0002 REL FR 2 V 0 P
or with taper–light | to seek the beauteous eye JN 4.02. 14
i might | waste it for you like taper–light. PER 1.ch. 16
TAPERS 7 FR 0.0008 REL FR 7 V 0 P
with rounds of waxen tapers on their heads, WIV 4.04. 51
him sound, | and burn him with their tapers. 4.04. 63
tapers they are, with your sweet breaths puff'd LLL 5.02.267
day was done | and tapers burnt to bedward! COR 1.06. 32
and tapers burn so bright, and every thing | in TIT 1.01.324
now, by the burning tapers of the sky, | that 4.02. 89
get moe tapers; OTH 1.01.166
/TAPESTRIES 1 FR 0.0001 REL FR 0 V 1 P
bed–hangers and these fly–bitten /tapestries. 2H4 2.01.147 P
TAPESTRY 5 FR 0.0005 REL FR 3 V 2 P
desk | that's cover'd o'er with turkish tapestry ERR 4.01.104
hercules in the smirch'd worm–eaten tapestry, ADO 3.03.137 P
my hangings all of tyrian tapestry; SHR 2.01.349
my plate and the tapestry of my dining–chambers.
2H4 2.01.141 P
was hang'd | with tapestry of silk and silver; CYM 2.04. 69
TAP–HOUSE 1 FR 0.0001 REL FR 0 V 1 P
i never come into any room in a tap–house, but i MM 2.01.209 P
TAPP'D 1 FR 0.0001 REL FR 1 V 0 P
hast thou tapp'd out and drunkenly carous'd. R2 2.01.127
TAPSTER 14 FR 0.0015 REL FR 1 V 13 P
a tapster is a good trade. WIV 1.03. 16 P
a wither'd servingman a fresh tapster. 1.03. 18 P
i'll be your tapster still. MM 1.02.108 P
what's to do here, thomas tapster? 1.02.112 P
a tapster, sir; 2.01. 63 P
a tapster, a poor widow's tapster. 2.01.198 P
a tapster, a poor widow's tapster. 2.01.198 P
come you hither to me, master tapster. 2.01.213 P
what's your name, master tapster? 2.01.213 P
howsoever you color it in being a tapster, are 2.01.220 P
reck'ning, it fitteth the spirit of a tapster. LLL 1.02. 41 P
lover is no stronger than the word of a tapster; AYL 3.04. 31 P
pregnancy is made a tapster, and his quick wit 2H4 1.02.170 P
informs the tapster to inflame the reck'ning. TNK 3.05.130
TAPSTER'S 1 FR 0.0001 REL FR 0 V 1 P
indeed a tapster's arithmetic may soon bring his TRO 1.02.113 P
TAPSTERS 4 FR 0.0004 REL FR 2 V 2 P
i would not have you acquainted with tapsters; MM 2.01.205 P
sons to younger brothers, revolted tapsters, and 1H4 4.02. 29 P
thine ears (like tapsters that bade welcome) TIM 4.03.215
like shrill–tongu'd tapsters answering every VEN 849
TAR *(see tarre)*
TAR 3 FR 0.0003 REL FR 1 V 2 P
she lov'd not the savor of tar nor of pitch, TMP 2.02. 52
and would you have us kiss tar? AYL 3.02. 64 P
civet is of a baser birth than tar, the very 3.02. 68 P
TARDIED 1 FR 0.0001 REL FR 1 V 0 P
but that the good mind of camillo tardied | my WT 3.02.162
/TARDILY 1 FR 0.0001 REL FR 1 V 0 P
/those /that /could /speak /low /and /tardily 2H4 2.03. 26
TARDINESS 1 FR 0.0001 REL FR 1 V 0 P
a tardiness in nature | which often leaves the LR 1.01.235
TARDY 13 FR 0.0014 REL FR 11 V 2 P
say, is your tardy master now at hand? ERR 2.01. 44
nay, and you be so tardy, come no more in my AYL 4.01. 51 P
whose manners still our tardy, apish nation R2 2.01. 22
these tardy tricks of yours will, on my life, 2H4 4.03. 28
some tardy cripple bare the countermand, | that R3 2.01. 90
be not ta'en tardy by unwise delay. 4.01. 51
that you have ta'en a tardy sluggard here. 5.03.225
o my lord, y' are tardy; H8 1.04. 7
the prince must think me tardy and remiss, TRO 4.04.141
too swift arrives as tardy as too slow. ROM 2.06. 15
however he puts on this tardy form. JC 1.02.299
now this overdone, or come tardy off, though it HAM 3.02. 25 P
do you not come your tardy son to chide, | that, 3.04.106
TARDY–GAITED 1 FR 0.0001 REL FR 1 V 0 P
and chide the cripple tardy–gaited night, | who H5 4.pr. 20
TARENTUM 1 FR 0.0001 REL FR 1 V 0 P
that from tarentum and brundusium | he could so ANT 3.07. 21
TARGE 1 FR 0.0001 REL FR 1 V 0 P
oft in field with targe and shield did make my LLL 5.02.553
TARGES 2 FR 0.0002 REL FR 2 V 0 P
edges and bear back | our targes undinted. ANT 2.06. 39
naked breast | stepp'd before targes of proof, CYM 5.05. 5
TARGET 6 FR 0.0006 REL FR 4 V 2 P
but took all their seven points in my target, 1H4 2.04.202 P
i bear | upon my target three fair shining suns. 3H6 2.01. 40
once more to hew thy target from thy brawn, | or COR 4.05.120
knight shall use his foil and target, the lover HAM 2.02.321 P
and target. ANT 1.03. 82
worth, | for it was sometime target to a king; PER 2.01.137
TARGETS 3 FR 0.0003 REL FR 3 V 0 P
a noise of targets, or to see a fellow | in a H8 pr 15
bear our hack'd targets like the men that owe ANT 4.08. 31
sin, | ay, and the targets to put off the shame; PER 1.01.140
TARPEIAN 5 FR 0.0005 REL FR 5 V 0 P
bear him to th' rock tarpeian, and from thence COR 3.01.212
he shall be thrown down the tarpeian rock | with 3.01.265
heels, | or pile ten hills on the tarpeian rock, 3.02. 3
let them pronounce the steep tarpeian death, 3.03. 88

of precipitation | from off the rock tarpeian, 3.03.103
TARQUIN 31 FR 0.0035 REL FR 30 V 1 P
in the repulse of tarquin seven hurts i' th' COR 2.01.150 P
when tarquin made a head for rome, he fought 2.02. 88
beg at the gates, like tarquin and his queen. TIT 3.01.298
or slunk not saturnine, as tarquin erst, | that 4.01. 63
the tarquin drive when he was call'd a king. JC 2.01. 54
our tarquin thus | did softly press the rushes CYM 2.02. 12
lust–breathed tarquin leaves the roman host, LUC 3
which tarquin view'd in her fair face's field, 72
owe | enchanted tarquin answers with surmise, 83
for then is tarquin brought unto his bed, 120
as one of which doth tarquin lie revolving | the 127
such hazard now must doting tarquin make, 155
these worlds in tarquin new ambition bred, | who 411
so o'er this sleeping soul doth tarquin stay, 423
so surfeit–taking tarquin fares this night: 698
"were tarquin night, as he is but night's child, 785
line, | how tarquin wronged me, i collatine. 819
would else have come to me | when tarquin did, 917
with some mischance cross tarquin in his flight. 968
at time, at tarquin, and uncheerful night, | in 1024
of that true type hath tarquin rifled me. 1050
for burthen–wise i'll hum on tarquin still, 1133
my stained blood to tarquin i'll bequeath, 1181
how tarquin must be us'd, read it in me: 1195
and for my sake serve thou false tarquin so. 1197
till after a deep groan) "tarquin from hence?" 1276
of day, | and ere i rose was tarquin gone away. 1281
to me came tarquin armed to beguild | with 1544
so did i tarquin, so my troy did perish. 1547
look'd black, and that false tarquin stain'd. 1743
yet sometime "tarquin" was pronounced plain, 1786
TARQUIN'S 13 FR 0.0014 REL FR 13 V 0 P
tarquin's self he met, | and struck him on his COR 2.02. 94
with tarquin's ravishing /strides, towards his MAC 2.01. 55
for he the night before, in tarquin's tent, LUC 15
"in tarquin's likeness i did entertain thee; 596
and fright her crying babe with tarquin's name; 814
will couple my reproach to tarquin's shame; 816
face, | and tarquin's eye may read the mot afar, 830
i fear'd by tarquin's falchion to be slain, 1046
thought he blush'd, as knowing tarquin's lust, 1354
but tarquin's shape came in her mind the while, 1536
would break, | she throws forth tarquin's name: 1717
and so to publish tarquin's foul offense; 1852
consent | to tarquin's everlasting banishment. 1855
TARQUINS 1 FR 0.0001 REL FR 1 V 0 P
rome, | no, not th' expulsion of the tarquins. COR 5.04. 43
TARR'D 1 FR 0.0001 REL FR 0 V 1 P
and they are often tarr'd over with the surgery AYL 3.02. 62 P
/TARRE 2 FR 0.0002 REL FR 1 V 1 P
pride alone | must /tarre the mastiffs on, as TRO 1.03.390
/it /no /sin /to /tarre /them /to /controversy. HAM 2.02.353 P
TARRE 1 FR 0.0001 REL FR 1 V 0 P
snatch at his master that doth tarre him on. JN 4.01.116
TARRIANCE 2 FR 0.0002 REL FR 2 V 0 P
it presently, | i am impatient of my tarriance. TGV 2.07. 90
a longing tarriance for adonis made | under an PP 6. 4
TARRIED 4 FR 0.0004 REL FR 4 V 0 P
have i not tarried? TRO 1.01. 16
have i not tarried? 1.01. 19
still have i tarried. 1.01. 22
held off, | and then you would have tarried. 4.02. 18
TARRIES 2 FR 0.0002 REL FR 1 V 1 P
a bohemian–tartar tarries the coming down of thy WIV 4.05. 20 P
old nestor tarries; TRO 5.01. 80
TARRY 45 FR 0.0050 REL FR 22 V 23 P
you'll lose the tide, if you tarry any longer. TGV 2.03. 36 P
tarry i here, i but attend on death, | but, fly 3.01.186
by my trot, i tarry too long. WIV 1.04. 62 P
tarry you a little–a while. 1.04. 88 P
it is not good you tarry here. 1.04.111 P
nay, tarry, i ll go along with thee.JPfMM 4.03.165 P
by the sergeant to tarry for the hoy delay. ERR 4.03. 39 P
tarry, sweet beatrice. ADO 4.01.292 P
tarry, good beatrice. by this hand, i love thee. 4.01.324 P
tarry, rash wanton! am not i thy lord? MND 2.01. 63
it good, | and tarry for the comfort of the day. 2.02. 38
i pray you tarry, pause a day or two | before MV 3.02. 1
tarry a little, there is something else. 4.01.305
tarry, jew, | the law hath yet another hold on 4.01.346
thou know'st where i will tarry. 4.02. 18
i'll tarry no longer with you. AYL 3.02.291 P
it stands so that i may hardly tarry so long. SHR in.2. 125 P
i will therefore tarry in despite of the flesh in.2. 127 P
tarry, petruchio, i must go with thee, | for in 1.02.117
i chafe you if i tarry. let me go. 2.01.241
i cannot tarry. 4.04. 99 P
if you will tarry, holy pilgrim, | but till the AWW 3.05. 39
if you tarry longer, | i shall give worse TN 4.01. 19
up for pity — yet i'll tarry till my son come; WT 3.03. 77 P
if you will not, tarry at home and be hang'd. 1H4 1.02.132 P
ye, yedward, if i tarry at home and go not, i'll 1.02.134 P
well, come what will, i'll tarry at home. 1.02.145 P
go drink with you, but i cannot tarry dinner. 2H4 3.02.192 P
he cries aloud, "tarry, my cousin suffolk! H5 4.06. 15
tarry, sweet soul, for mine, then fly abreast, 4.06. 17
leave me, or tarry, edward will be king, | and 3H6 4.01. 65
better do so than tarry and be hang'd. 4.05. 26
i will not tarry; H8 2.04.132
a cake out of the wheat must tarry the grinding. TRO 1.01. 15 P
but you must tarry the bolting. 1.01. 17 P
but you must tarry the leavening. 1.01. 20 P
prithee tarry, | you men will never tarry. 4.02. 15
prithee tarry, | you men will never tarry. 4.02. 16
both /at /once, to those | that go or tarry. 5.01. 78
fair, | and tarry with him till i turn again. TIT 5.02.141
we'll in here, tarry for the mourners, and stay ROM 4.05.146 P
in ourselves | than tarry till they push us. JC 5.05. 25
will measure your lubber's length again, tarry; LR 1.04. 91 P
nuncle lear, tarry, take the fool with thee. 1.04.315 P
but i will tarry, the fool will stay, | and let 2.04. 82
TARRYING 4 FR 0.0004 REL FR 4 V 0 P
and thisby, tarrying in mulberry shade, | his MND 5.01.148
there is no tarrying here; TRO 2.03.258
fly, fly, my lord, there is no tarrying here. JC 5.05. 30
there is nor flying hence, nor tarrying here. MAC 5.05. 47
TARSUS *(see tharsus)*
TART 3 FR 0.0003 REL FR 3 V 0 P
another way, | the news is not so tart. LR 4.02. 87
so tart a favor | to trumpet such good tidings! ANT 2.05. 38
but if it did, yours is too tart, sweet cousin. TNK 3.03. 26
TARTAR* 4 FR 0.0004 REL FR 3 V 1 P
no, he's in tartar limbo, worse than hell: ERR 4.02. 32
out, tawny tartar, out! MND 3.02.263
to the gates of tartar, thou most excellent TN 2.05.205 P
world, | he might return to vasty tartar back, H5 2.02.123
TARTAR'S 4 FR 0.0004 REL FR 4 V 0 P
go, | swifter than arrow from the tartar's bow. MND 3.02.101
through flinty tartar's bosom would peep forth AWW 4.04. 7
scarf, | bearing a tartar's painted bow of lath, ROM 1.04. 5
eclipse, | nose of turk and tartar's lips, MAC 4.01. 29
TARTARS 1 FR 0.0001 REL FR 1 V 0 P
and tartars never train'd | to offices of tender MV 4.01. 32
TARTLY 1 FR 0.0001 REL FR 0 V 1 P
how tartly that gentleman looks! ADO 2.01. 3 P
TARTNESS 2 FR 0.0002 REL FR 0 V 2 P
cannot be too sweet for the king's tartness. AWW 4.03. 83 P
the tartness of his face sours ripe grapes. COR 5.04. 17 P
TASK 34 FR 0.0038 REL FR 33 V 1 P
to thy strong bidding, task | ariel, and all his TMP 1.02.192
this my mean task | would be as heavy to me as 3.01. 4
a heavier task could not have been impos'd ERR 1.01. 31
but had a rougher task in hand | than to drive ADO 1.01.299
but now to task the tasker: LLL 2.01. 20
and your task shall be, | with all the fierce 5.02.852
snores, | all with weary task foredone. MND 5.01.374
and stir them up against a mightier task. JN 2.01. 55
the task he undertakes | is numb'ring sands and R2 2.02.145
overblown, | an easy task it is to win our own. 3.02.191
i task the earth to the like, forsworn aumerle, 4.01. 52
nay, task me to my word, approve me, lord. 1H4 4.01. 9
some things of weight | that task our thoughts, H5 1.02. 6
therefore let every man now task his thought, 1.02.309
farewell, my masters, to my task will i. 1H6 1.01.152
i have perform'd my task, and was espous'd; 2H6 1.01. 9
then, noble york, take thou this task in hand. 3.01.318
but sound the trumpets, and about our task. 3H6 2.01.200
why stops my lord? shall i not hear my task? 3.02. 52
an easy task, 'tis but to love a king. 3.02. 53
come let me see what task i have to do. TIT 3.01.275
and day by day i'll do this heavy task, | so 5.02. 58
a while, | for nature puts me to a heavy task. 5.03.150
whose sore task | does not divide the sunday HAM 1.01. 75
and dare not task my weakness with any more. OTH 2.03. 42 P
unarm, eros, the long day's task is done, | and ANT 4.14. 35
rages, | thou thy worldly task hast done, | home CYM 4.02.260
received | the danger of the task you undertake. PER 1.01. 2
love's provocations, zeal, a mistress' task, TNK 1.04. 41
his day's hot task hath ended in the west; VEN 530
in that high task hath done her beauty wrong, LUC 80
"then be this all the task it hath to say: 1618
but she, that yet her sad task hath not said, 1699
lest the world should task you to recite | what SON 72. 1
TASK'D 3 FR 0.0003 REL FR 3 V 0 P
the gallants shall be task'd: LLL 5.02.126
and in the neck of that, task'd the whole state; 1H4 4.03. 92
like to a harvest–man /that's task'd to mow | or COR 1.03. 36
TASKER 1 FR 0.0001 REL FR 1 V 0 P
but now to task the tasker: LLL 2.01. 20
TASKING 2 FR 0.0002 REL FR 2 V 0 P
while other sports are tasking of their minds, WIV 4.06. 30
tell me, tell me, | how show'd his tasking? 1H4 5.02. 50
TASKS 3 FR 0.0003 REL FR 2 V 1 P
o, these are barren tasks, too hard to keep, LLL 1.01. 47
lie by an emperor's side and command him tasks. OTH 4.01.185 P
babes | do it with gentle means and easy tasks. 4.02.112
TASSEL *(see tossel)*
TASSEL–GENTLE *(also tercel)*
TASSEL–GENTLE 1 FR 0.0001 REL FR 1 V 0 P_
voice, | to lure this tassel–gentle back again! ROM 2.02.159
TASTE 95 FR 0.0107 REL FR 80 V 15 P
he shall taste of my bottle; TMP 2.02. 74 P
will't please you taste of what is here? 3.03. 42
you do yet taste | some subtleties o' th' isle, 5.01.123
that never meat sweet–savor'd in thy taste, ERR 2.02.117
which we /of taste and feeling are — for those LLL 4.02. 29
tongue proves dainty bacchus gross in taste. 4.03.336
nor hath love's mind of any judgment taste; MND 1.01.236
but, as in health, come to my natural taste, 4.01.174
man's hand is not able to taste, his tongue to 4.01.212 P
something grow to, he had a kind of taste — MV 2.02. 18 P
didst rob it of some taste of tediousness. 2.03. 3
teeth, sans eyes, sans taste, sans every thing. AYL 2.07.166
for a taste: 3.02.100 P
but take a taste of my finding him, and relish 3.02.233 P
please your honor taste of these conserves? SHR in.2. 3
malvolio, and taste with a distemper'd appetite. TN 1.05. 91 P
taste your legs, sir, put them to motion. 3.01. 78 P
what you mean by bidding me taste my legs. 3.01. 80 P
purposely on others, to taste their valor. 3.04.244 P
word deserves | to taste of thy most worst? WT 3.02.179
for this affliction has a taste as sweet | as 5.03. 76
can taste the free breath of a sacred king? JN 3.01.148
shame hath spoil'd the sweet word's taste, 3.04.110
never to taste the pleasures of the world, 4.03. 68
how did he take it? who did taste to him? 5.06. 28
things sweet to taste prove in digestion sour. R2 1.03.236
as the last taste of sweets, is sweetest last, 2.01. 13
as praises, of whose taste the wise are /fond, 2.01. 18
you, feel want, | taste grief, need friends: 3.02.176
they might have liv'd to bear and he to taste 3.04. 62
taste of it first, as thou art wont to do. 5.05. 99
is he good, but to taste sack and drink it? 1H4 2.04.455 P
done, | without the taste of danger and reproof. 3.01.173
and began | to loathe the taste of sweetness, 3.02. 72
come let me taste my horse, | who is to bear me 4.01.119
have of their puissance made a little taste. 2H4 2.03. 52
shall to the king taste of this action, | that, 4.01.190
look to taste the due | meet for rebellion /and 4.02.116
this bitter taste | yields his engrossments to 4.05. 78
him life | after the taste of much correction. H5 2.02. 51
the taste whereof god of his mercy give | you 2.02.179
them that we shall take | shall taste our mercy. 4.07. 65
taste of your wine and see what cates you have, 1H6 2.03. 79
do you like the taste? 3.02. 44
worse than gall, the daintiest that they taste! 2H6 3.02.322
let them not live to taste this land's increase R3 5.05. 38
for here the troyans taste our dear'st repute TRO 1.03.337
and i will give a taste thereof forthwith | to 1.03.387
be, | when that the wat'ry palates taste indeed 3.02. 21
i do beseech you, as in way of taste, | to give 3.03. 13
her, | not palating the taste of her dishonor, 4.01. 60
the grief is fine, full, perfect, that i taste, 4.04. 3
why, my negation hath no taste of madness. 5.02.127
the great'st taste | most palates theirs. COR 3.01.103
have we not had a taste of his obedience — 3.01.316
long | till the fresh taste be taken from that TIT 3.01.128
when it did taste the wormwood on the nipple ROM 1.03. 30
to season love, that of it doth not taste! 2.03. 72
and in the taste confounds the appetite. 2.06. 13
shall we in | and taste lord timon's bounty? TIM 1.01.274
timon, and to all | that of his bounties taste! 1.02.123
taste, touch, all, pleas'd from thy table rise; 1.02.126
with ice, caudle thy morning taste | to cure thy 4.03.226
the valiant never taste of death but once. JC 2.02. 33
friends, go in, and taste some wine with me, 2.02.126
and, in some taste, is lepidus but so: 4.01. 34
i have almost forgot the taste of fears. MAC 5.05. 9
come give us a taste of your quality, come, a HAM 2.02.431 P
this but as an essay or taste of my virtue. LR 1.02. 45 P
she will taste as like this as a crab does to a 1.05. 18 P
from rest, | and must needs taste his folly. 2.04.291
ere i taste bread, thou art in nothing less 5.03. 94
all friends shall taste | the wages of their 5.03.303
shall come into no true taste again but by the OTH 2.01.276 P
her humor, shall be assur'd | to taste of too. CYM 1.05. 82
pisanio, | i'll now taste of thy drug. 4.02. 38
joyful too, | for they shall taste our comfort. 5.05.403
to taste the fruit of yon celestial tree | (or PER 1.01. 21
must have inventions to delight the taste, 1.04. 40
cup | and her prosperities so largely taste, 1.04. 53
shall you, and taste gentlemen of all fashions. 4.02. 78 P
led you to this banket shall | taste to you all. TNK 5.04. 23
dainties to taste, fresh beauty for the use, VEN 164
"but o, what banquet wert thou to the taste, 445
fast, | or being early pluck'd is sour to taste. 528
whose precious taste her thirsty lips well knew, 543
add to his flow, but alter not his taste." LUC 651
his taste delicious, in digestion souring, 699
thy sug'red tongue to bitter wormwood taste; 893
not know | the stained taste of violated troth; 1059
by willful taste of what thyself refusest. SON 40. 8
and of this book this learning mayst thou taste. 77. 4
so /shall i taste | at first the very worst of 90.11
nor taste, nor smell, desire to be invited | to 141. 7
the one a palate hath that needs will taste, LC 167
TASTED 9 FR 0.0010 REL FR 8 V 1 P
yet never have you tasted our reward, | or been 1H6 3.04. 22
praise us as we are tasted, allow us as we prove TRO 3.02. 91 P
being tasted, stays all senses with the heart. ROM 2.03. 26
own part, | i never tasted timon in my life, TIM 3.02. 77
sir, | having often of your open bounty tasted, 5.01. 58
pioners and all, had tasted her sweet body, | so OTH 3.03.346
apparent | that you have tasted her in bed, my CYM 2.04. 57
still as she tasted, should be doubled on her, TNK 2.02.240
yet mayst thou well be tasted. VEN 128
TASTEFUL 1 FR 0.0001 REL FR 1 V 0 P
their sweetness fall | upon thy tasteful lips, TNK 1.01.179
TASTES 4 FR 0.0004 REL FR 4 V 0 P
since my conversion | so sweetly tastes, being AYL 4.03.137
i know not how it tastes, though it be dish'd WT 3.02. 72
how tastes it? H8 2.03. 89
how tastes your victuals? TNK 3.03. 24
TASTING 2 FR 0.0002 REL FR 2 V 0 P
which they themselves not feel, but tasting it, ADO 5.01. 22
thou art unpaid for, | by tasting of our wrath? CYM 5.05.308
TATTER'D *(also tatt'red, totter'd, etc.)*
TATTER'D 1 FR 0.0001 REL FR 1 V 0 P
thorough tatter'd clothes /small vices do appear LR 4.06.164
TATTLE 1 FR 0.0001 REL FR 1 V 0 P
then let the ladies tattle what they please. TIT 4.02.168
TATTLING 2 FR 0.0002 REL FR 0 V 2 P
pray you do so, she's a very tattling woman. WIV 3.03. 91 P
like my lady's eldest son, evermore tattling. ADO 2.01. 10 P
TATTLINGS 1 FR 0.0001 REL FR 0 V 1 P
peace your tattlings! what is "fair," william? WIV 4.01. 25 P
TATT'RED 1 FR 0.0001 REL FR 1 V 0 P
which late i noted | in tatt'red weeds, with ROM 5.01. 39
TAUGHT' 1 FR 0.0001 REL FR 1 V 0 P
who taught' this? WT 2.01. 11
TAUGHT 54 FR 0.0061 REL FR 41 V 13 P
taught thee each hour | one thing or other. TMP 1.02.354
you taught me language, and my profit on't | is, 1.02.363
troll the catch | you taught me but while–ere? 3.02.118
how angerly i taught my brow to frown, | when TGV 1.02. 62
and she hath taught her suitor, | he being her 2.01.137
herself hath taught her love himself to write 2.01.168
i have taught him, even as one would say 4.04. 5 P
rate, and that hath taught me to say this: WIV 2.02.206 P
one that hath taught me more wit than ever i 4.05. 60 P
love, and it hath taught me to rhyme and to be LLL 4.03. 12 P
you taught me first to beg, and now methinks MV 4.01.439
their feeding, they are taught their manage, and AYL 1.01. 12 P
nothing. i am not taught to make any thing. 1.01. 30 P
i could have taught my love to take thy father 1.02. 12 P
old religious uncle of mine taught me to speak, 3.02.344 P
he taught me how to know a man in love; 3.02.370 P
than hath been taught by any of my trade; SHR 3.01. 69
then hast thou taught hortensio to be untoward. 4.05. 79
i will show myself highly fed and lowly taught. AWW 2.02. 4 P
in yourself, sir, or were you taught to find me? 2.04. 34 P
taught him to face me out of his acquaintance, TN 5.01. 88
you taught me how to know the face of right, JN 5.02. 88
that taught me craft | to counterfeit oppression R2 1.04. 13
they whom youth and ease have taught to glose. 2.01. 10
i'll have a starling shall be taught to speak 1H4 1.03.224
have taught us how to cherish such high deeds 5.05. 30
what foolish master taught you these manners, 2H4 2.01.189 P
me not, he was a fool that taught me me. 2.01.192 P
cade, the duke of york hath taught you this. 2H6 4.02.154
hath that poor monarch taught thee to insult? 3H6 1.04.124

that taught his son the office of a fowl! 5.06. 19
you well serv'd, you would be taught your duty. R3 1.03.249
you are not to be taught | that you have many H8 2.04.158
of me more must be heard of, say i taught thee; 3.02.434
o, do not learn her wrath — she taught it thee; TIT 2.03.143
taught thee to make vast neptune weep for aye TIM 5.04. 78
he must be taught, and train'd, and bid go forth JC 4.01. 35
which, being taught, return | to plague th' MAC 1.07. 9
taught me to shift | into a madman's rags, t' LR 5.03.187
it hath been taught us from the primal state ANT 1.04. 41
your great knowing | should learn, being taught, CYM 2.03. 98
friends, | the boy hath taught us manly duties. 4.02.397
where i was taught | of your chaste daughter the 5.05.193
who hath taught | my frail mortality to know PER 1.01. 41
you had taught | how insolence and strong hand STM II.C 80
hath taught them scornful tricks, and such VEN 501
those eyes that taught all other eyes to see? 952
when craft hath taught her thus to say: PP 18.34
decay, | ruin hath taught me thus to ruminate, SON 64.11
eyes, that taught the dumb on high to sing, 78. 5
by spirits taught to write | above a mortal 86. 5
and that your love taught it this alcumy, | to 114. 4
gentle doom, | and taught it thus anew to greet: 145. 8
who taught thee how to make me love thee more, 150. 9
TAUGHT'ST 1 FR 0.0001 REL FR 1 V 0 P
me to curse him that thou taught'st this ill! LUC 996
TAUNT 7 FR 0.0008 REL FR 5 V 2 P
i liv'd to stand at the taunt of one that makes WIV 5.05.143 P
did not her kitchen maid rail, taunt, and scorn ERR 4.04. 74
taunt him with the license of ink. TN 3.02. 44 P
becomes it thee to taunt his valiant age, | and 1H6 3.02. 54
to taunt and scorn you thus opprobriously? R3 3.01.153
and taunt my faults | with such full license as ANT 1.02.107
the best of men, | to taunt at slackness. 3.07. 27
TAUNTED 1 FR 0.0001 REL FR 1 V 0 P
when i had at my pleasure taunted her, | and she MND 4.01. 57
TAUNTING 1 FR 0.0001 REL FR 1 V 0 P
i'll write to him a very taunting letter, | and AYL 3.05.134
/TAUNTINGLY 1 FR 0.0001 REL FR 1 V 0 P
it /tauntingly replied | to th' discontented COR 1.01.110
TAUNTS 7 FR 0.0008 REL FR 7 V 0 P
with scoffs and scorns and contumelious taunts. 1H6 1.04. 39
and after many scorns, many foul taunts, | they 3H6 2.01. 64
because he would avoid such bitter taunts 2.06. 66
of those gross taunts that oft i have endur'd. R3 1.03.105
uncle, | he prettily and aptly taunts himself: 3.01.134
nay, but his taunts. COR 1.01.255
and with taunts | did gibe my missive out of ANT 2.02. 73
TAURUS'* 2 FR 0.0002 REL FR 2 V 0 P
that pure congealed white, high taurus' snow, MND 3.02.141
see, thou hast shot off one of taurus' horns. TIT 4.03. 70
TAURUS 4 FR 0.0004 REL FR 2 V 2 P
were we not born under taurus? TN 1.03.138 P
taurus? that/'s sides and heart. 1.03.139 P
they say, one taurus. ANT 3.07. 78
taurus! 3.08. 1
/TAVERN 1 FR 0.0001 REL FR 0 V 1 P
/me /to /the /tavern /and /made /me /drunk, /and WIV 1.01.126 P
TAVERN 9 FR 0.0010 REL FR 3 V 6 P
not my hostess of the tavern a most sweet wench? 1H4 1.02. 40 P
pox have i to do with my hostess of the tavern? 1.02. 48 P
lie, ye rogue, 'tis going to the king's tavern. 2.02. 57 P
thee in the night betwixt tavern and tavern; 3.03. 44 P
thee in the night betwixt tavern and tavern; 3.03. 44 P
o, i could wish this tavern were my drum! 3.03.206
and i will see what physic the tavern affords. 1H6 3.01.147
when he enters the confines of a tavern, claps ROM 3.01. 6 P
makes it more like a tavern or a brothel | than LR 1.04.245
TAVERN–BILLS 1 FR 0.0001 REL FR 0 V 1 P
to no more payments, fear no more tavern–bills, CYM 5.04.159 P
TAVERN–RECKONINGS 1 FR 0.0001 REL FR 0 V 1 P
any thing in thy pocket but tavern–reckonings, 1H4 3.03.158 P
TAVERNS 3 FR 0.0003 REL FR 2 V 1 P
and given to fornications, and to taverns, and WIV 5.05.158 P
inquire at london, 'mongst the taverns there, R2 5.03. 5
bare–headed, sweating, knocking at the taverns, 2H4 2.04.359
TAVY'S *(also davy's)*
TAVY'S 1 FR 0.0001 REL FR 0 V 1 P
no scorn to wear the leek upon saint tavy's day. H5 4.07.103 P
TAWDRY–LACE 1 FR 0.0001 REL FR 0 V 1 P
you promis'd me a tawdry–lace and a pair of WT 4.04.250 P
TAWNY 7 FR 0.0008 REL FR 6 V 1 P
the ground indeed is tawny. TMP 2.01. 55 P
the worth of many a knight | from tawny spain, LLL 1.01.173
out, tawny tartar, out! MND 3.02.263
we shall your tawny ground with your red blood H5 3.06.161
privileged place — | blue coats to tawny coats! 1H6 1.03. 47
"peace, tawny slave, half me and half thy dame. TIT 5.01. 27
and devotion of their view | upon a tawny front; ANT 1.01. 6
TAWNY–COATS 1 FR 0.0001 REL FR 1 V 0 P
out, tawny–coats! 1H6 1.03. 56
TAWNY/–FINN'D 1 FR 0.0001 REL FR 1 V 0 P
far off, i will betray | tawny/–finn'd fishes; ANT 2.05. 12
/TAX 1 FR 0.0001 REL FR 1 V 0 P
fall, | shall /tax my fears of little vanity, AWW 5.03.122
TAX 10 FR 0.0011 REL FR 9 V 1 P
to appear most bright | when it doth tax itself; MM 2.04. 79
to th' duke himself, to tax him with injustice? 5.01.310
niece, you tax signior benedick too much, but ADO 1.01. 46 P
tax not so bad a voice | to slander music any 2.03. 44
pride | that can therein tax any private party? AYL 2.07. 71
tax of impudence, | a strumpet's boldness, a AWW 2.01.170
because i would not tax the needy commons, 2H6 3.01.116
they tax our policy, and call it cowardice, TRO 1.03.197
i'll warrant she'll tax him home, | and, as you HAM 3.03. 29
i tax not you, you elements, with unkindness; LR 3.02. 16
TAXATION 5 FR 0.0005 REL FR 3 V 2 P
you'll be whipt for taxation one of these days. AYL 1.02. 85 P
bring no overture of war, no taxation of homage; TN 1.05.209 P
taxation? H8 1.02. 37
and what taxation? 1.02. 38
it alike with us, | know you of this taxation? 1.02. 40
TAXATIONS 2 FR 0.0002 REL FR 2 V 0 P
his burthenous taxations notwithstanding, | but R2 2.01.260
for, upon these taxations, | the clothiers all, H8 1.02. 30

TAX'D 4 FR 0.0004 REL FR 3 V 1 P
as he hath generally tax'd their whole sex AYL 3.02.349 P
for silence, | but never tax'd for speech. AWW 1.01. 68
all the spots a' th' world tax'd and debosh'd, 5.03.206
makes us traduc'd and tax'd of other nations. HAM 1.04. 18
TAXES 1 FR 0.0001 REL FR 1 V 0 P
the commons hath he pill'd with grievous taxes, R2 2.01.246
TAXING 2 FR 0.0002 REL FR 2 V 0 P
why then my taxing like a wild goose flies, AYL 2.07. 86
both taxing me and gaging me to keep | an oath TRO 5.01. 41
/TE 1 FR 0.0001 REL FR 1 V 0 P
why, this is just | "aio /te, aeacida, romanos 2H6 1.04. 62
TE 8 FR 0.0009 REL FR 5 V 3 P
che non te /vede, che non te /prechia. LLL 4.02. 98
che non te /vede, che non te /prechia. 4.02. 98
novi /hominem tanquam te. 5.01. 9 P
but so, | "redime te captum quam queas minimo." SHR 1.01.162
je te prie, m'enseignez; H5 3.04. 4 P
let there be sung non nobis and te deum, | the 4.08.123
tanta est erga te mentis integritas, regina H8 3.01. 40 P
music of the kingdom, | together sung te deum. 4.01. 92
/TEACH 1 FR 0.0001 REL FR 1 V 0 P
/teach /her /not /thus /to /lay | /such /violent TIT 3.02. 21
TEACH 118 FR 0.0133 REL FR 93 V 25 P
and teach me how | to name the bigger light, and TMP 1.02.334
i'll teach you how to flow. 2.01.222
teach me, thy tempted subject, to excuse it! TGV 2.06. 8
would say precisely, "thus i would teach a dog." 4.04. 6 P
and i will teach a scurvy jack–a–nape priest to WIV 1.04.109 P
we'll teach him to know turtles from jays. 3.03. 42 P
you do ill to teach the child such words. 4.01. 65 P
i will teach the children their behaviors; 4.04. 67 P
i'll teach you how you shall arraign your MM 2.03. 21
teach her the way. 2.04. 19
teach sin the carriage of a holy saint; ERR 3.02. 14
teach me, dear creature, how to think and speak: 3.02. 33
and teach your ears to list me with more heed. 4.01.101
my love is thine to teach; ADO 1.01.291
teach it but how, | and thou shalt see how apt 1.01.291
i will but teach them to sing, and restore them 2.01.232 P
i will teach you how to humor your cousin, that 2.01.380 P
to teach a teacher ill beseemeth me. LLL 2.01.108
shall i teach you to know? 4.01.108
action and accent did they teach him there: 5.02. 99
teach us, sweet madam, for our rude 5.02.431
then let us teach our trial patience, | because MND 1.01.152
o, teach me how you look, and with what art 1.01.192
your frowns would teach my smiles such skill! 1.01.195
i can easier teach twenty what were good to be MV 1.02. 16 P
not learning more than the fond eye doth teach, 2.09. 27
the villainy you teach me, i will execute, and 3.01. 71 P
i could teach you | how to choose right, but 3.02. 10
doth teach me answers for deliverance! 3.02. 38
and that same prayer doth teach us all to render 4.01.201
you teach me how a beggar should be answer'd. 4.01.440
unless you could teach me to forget a banish'd AYL 1.02. 5 P
light on a fit man to teach her that wherein she SHR 1.01.111 P
and bow'd her hand to teach her fingering; 2.01.150
art, | to teach you gamouth in a briefer sort, 3.01. 67
for she seems a mistress | to most that teach. WT 4.04.583
at mine hostess' door, | teach us some fence! JN 2.01.290
o, if thou teach me to believe this sorrow, 3.01. 29
teach thou this sorrow how to make me die, | and 3.01. 30
humorous ladyship is by | to teach thee safety! 3.01.120
the spirit of the time shall teach me speed. 4.02.176
or teach thy hasty spleen to do me shame, | i'll 4.03. 97
teach thy necessity to reason thus: R2 1.03.277
and if i were thy nurse, thy tongue to teach, 5.03.113
say "pardon," king, let pity teach thee how. 5.03.116
dost thou teach pardon pardon to destroy? 5.03.120
why, i can teach you, cousin, to command | the 1H4 3.01. 55
and i can teach thee, coz, to shame the devil 3.01. 57
humane principle i would teach them should be, 2H4 4.03.123 P
creatures that by a rule in nature teach | the H5 1.02.188
as fear may teach us out of late examples | left 2.04. 12
of grosser blood, | and teach them how to war. 3.01. 25
and teach lavoltas high and swift corantos, 3.05. 33
see his greatness and to teach others how they 4.01.185 P
this story shall the good man teach his son; 4.03. 56
let a welsh correction teach you a good english 5.01. 78 P
will you vouchsafe to teach a soldier terms, 5.02. 99
my royal cousin, teach you our princess english? 5.02.282 P
my lord, teach your cousin to consent winking. 5.02.304 P
lord, if you will teach her to know my meaning; 5.02.307 P
and will not you maintain the thing you teach, 1H6 3.01.129
persuade | than i am able to instruct or teach; 4.01.159
ah, gloucester, teach me to forget myself! 2H6 2.04. 27
teach not thy lip such scorn; R3 1.02.171
but since you teach me how to flatter you, 1.02.223
teach me to be your queen, and you my subjects: 1.03.251
serve me well, and teach yourselves that duty! 1.03.252
and teach me how to curse mine enemies! 4.04.117
revolving this will teach thee how to curse. 4.04.123
want of wisdom, you, that best should teach us, H8 5.02. 48
therefore this maxim out of love i teach: TRO 1.02.292
soaring insolence | shall teach the people — COR 2.01.255
and by my body's action teach my mind | a most 3.02.122
when did the tiger's young ones teach the dam? TIT 2.03.142
o, let me teach thee! 2.03.158
no, boy, not so, i'll teach thee another course. 4.01.119
o, let me teach you how to knit again | this 5.03. 70
o, teach me how i should forget to think. ROM 1.01.226
farewell, thou canst not teach me to forget. 1.01.237
o, she doth teach the torches to burn bright! 1.05. 44
i'll teach them to prevent wild alcibiades' TIM 5.01.203
it is a creature that i teach to fight, | to JC 4.01. 31
herein i teach you | how you shall bid god 'ield MAC 1.06. 12
here, that we but teach | bloody instructions, 1.07. 8
we'll teach you to drink /deep ere you depart. HAM 1.02.175
marry, i will teach you: 1.03.105
that you must teach me. 2.02.283 P
and that, i hope, will teach you to imagine — 4.07. 35
i'll teach you differences. LR 1.04. 89 P
sirrah, i'll teach thee a speech. 1.04.115 P
no, lad, teach me. 1.04.139 P
a schoolmaster that can teach thy fool to lie — 1.04.179 P
knave, you reverent braggart, | we'll teach you. 2.02.127

to teach thee there's no laboring i' th' winter. 2.04. 68 P
i should but teach him how to tell my story, OTH 1.03.165
child, | for thy escape would teach me tyranny, 1.03.197
let's teach ourselves that honorable stop, | not 2.03. 2
a knave teach me my duty? 2.03.147 P
be as your fancies teach you; 3.03. 88
those that do teach young babes | do it with 4.02.111
teach me, | alcides, thou mine ancestor, thy ANT 4.12. 43
see if 'twill teach us to forget our own? PER 1.04. 3
your honor and your goodness teach me to't 3.03. 26
of me, who stand /i' /th' gaps to teach you, 4.04. 8
boast, | and will undertake all these to teach. 4.06.185
but can you teach all this you speak of? 4.06.188 P
and like young eagles teach 'em | boldly to gaze TNK 2.02. 34
i would quickly teach thee | what 'twere to 2.02.209
i were dumb, yet his proceedings teach thee. VEN 406
bleed, | and fear doth teach it divination: 670
the wise dumb, and teach the fool to speak. 1146
he learn'd to sin, and thou didst teach the way? LUC 630
teach me to curse him that thou taught'st this 996
"o, teach me how to make mine own excuse, | or 1653
on th' ear, | to teach my tongue to be so long. PP 18.52
doth teach that ease and that repose to say, SON 50. 3
i teach thee how | to make him seem long hence, 101.13
if i might teach thee wit, better it were, 140. 5
TEACHER 2 FR 0.0002 REL FR 1 V 1 P
to teach a teacher ill beseemeth me. LLL 2.01.108
way to turn tailor, or be redbreast teacher. 1H4 3.01.260 P
TEACHERS 2 FR 0.0002 REL FR 2 V 0 P
that he may furnish and instruct great teachers H8 1.02.113
thus may poor fools | believe false teachers. CYM 3.04. 85
TEACHES 8 FR 0.0009 REL FR 5 V 3 P
he teaches him to "hic" and to "hac," which WIV 4.01. 66 P
world | teaches such beauty as a woman's eye? LLL 4.03.309
yes, yes, he teaches boys the horn–book. 5.01. 46 P
whose own hard dealings teaches them suspect MV 1.03.161
nerissa teaches me what to believe — | i'll die 5.01.207
woes, | and teaches me to kill or hang myself. JN 3.04. 56
nature teaches beasts to know their friends. COR 2.01. 6 P
but what i am, want teaches me to think on: PER 2.01. 72
/TEACHEST 1 FR 0.0001 REL FR 1 V 0 P
/but /teachest /me /the /way | /how /to /lament R2 4.01.301
TEACHEST 4 FR 0.0004 REL FR 4 V 0 P
thou teachest me. OTH 5.01. 33
thou teachest like a fool: the way to lose him. ANT 1.03. 10
thou teachest me, o valiant eros, what | i 4.14. 96
and that thou teachest how to make one twain, SON 39.13
TEACHETH 3 FR 0.0003 REL FR 3 V 0 P
which teacheth thee that thou and i am one. AYL 1.03. 97
that teacheth tricks eleven and twenty long, SHR 4.02. 57
teacheth this prostrate and exterior bending. 2H4 4.05.148
TEACHING 15 FR 0.0017 REL FR 14 V 1 P
one of the twenty to follow mine own teaching. MV 1.02. 17 P
i thank thee, jew, for teaching me that word. 4.01.341
write, | teaching all that read to know | the AYL 3.02.138
and undertake the teaching of the maid: SHR 1.01.192
stand by and mark the manner of his teaching. 4.02. 5
and hope both teaching him the practice) | to a TN 1.02. 13
teaching stern murder how to butcher thee. R2 1.02. 32
this is his uncle's teaching; 1H4 1.01. 96
teaching his duteous land | audacious cruelty. 4.03. 44
spirit | of teaching and of learning instantly. 5.02. 64
whole realm by your teaching and your chaplains' H8 5.02. 51
that my teaching | and the strong course of my 5.02. 69
teaching the sheets a whiter hue than white, VEN 398
teaching decrepit age to tread the measures; 1148
teaching them thus to use it in the fight, LUC 62
TEAM 7 FR 0.0008 REL FR 5 V 2 P
but a team of horse shall not pluck that from me TGV 3.01.267 P
by the triple hecat's team | from the presence MND 5.01.384
my land spares my team and gives me leave to inn AWW 1.03. 44 P
the hour before the heavenly–harness'd team 1H4 3.01.218
drawn with a team of little atomi | over men's ROM 1.04. 57
either i am | the forehorse in the team, or i am TNK 1.02. 59
them, | wishing adonis had his team to guide, VEN 179
/TEAR* 2 FR 0.0002 REL FR 2 V 0 P
/are /apt /enough /to /dislocate /and /tear LR 4.02. 65
/now /and /then /an /ample /tear /trill'd /down 4.03. 12
TEAR* 85 FR 0.0096 REL FR 72 V 13 P
o hateful hands, to tear such loving words! TGV 1.02.102
to the sweet julia" — that i'll tear away — 1.02.122
did not this cruel–hearted cur shed one tear. 2.03. 10 P
now the dog all this while sheds not a tear, nor 2.03. 31 P
will break | as easily as i do tear his paper. 4.04.131
ah, do not tear away thyself from me; ERR 2.02.124
and tear the stain'd skin off my harlot brow, 2.02.136
but truth of her, | these hands shall tear her; ADO 4.01.191
thou shin'st in every tear that i do weep, | no LLL 4.03. 32
these numbers will i tear, and write in prose! 4.03. 55
how now, what is in you? why dost thou tear it? 4.03.196
play ercles rarely, or a part to tear a cat in, MND 1.02. 29 P
will you tear | impatient answers from my gentle 3.02.286
take thrice thy money, bid me tear the bond. MV 4.01.234
feast, | if ever from your eyelids wip'd a tear, AYL 2.07.116
dearly, | him will i tear out of that cruel eye, TN 5.01.127
on one another, to tear the cases of their eyes. WT 5.02. 12 P
this hair i tear is mine, | my name is constance JN 3.04. 45
my teeth shall tear | the slavish motive of R2 1.01.192
o, let no noble eye profane a tear | for me, if 1.03. 59
did grace our hollow parting with a tear. 1.04. 9
us, | except like curs to tear us all to pieces. 2.02.139
do me good, | and never borrow any tear of thee. 3.04. 23
here did she fall a tear, here in this place 3.04.104
may tear a passage thorough the flinty ribs | of 5.05. 20
or i will tear the reckoning from his heart. 1H4 3.02.152
thee what, corporal bardolph, i could tear her. 2H4 2.04.154 P
he hath a tear for pity, and a hand | open as 4.04. 31
the walls they'll tear down than forsake the 1H6 1.02. 40
or tear the lions out of england's coat; 1.05. 28
to tear the garter from thy craven's leg, 4.01. 15
and for thy sake have i shed many a tear. 5.04. 19
they will by violence tear him from your palace, 2H6 3.02.246
father, tear the crown from the usurper's head. 3H6 1.01.114
that not a tear can fall for rutland's death? 1.04. 88
i'll aid thee tear for tear, | and let our 2.05. 76
i'll aid thee tear for tear, | and let our 2.05. 76

ay, ay, for this i draw in many a tear, | and 4.04. 21
these eyes, which never shed remorseful tear — R3 1.02.155
time | my manly eyes did scorn an humble tear; 1.02.164
may (if they think it well) let fall a tear; H8 pr 6
i did not think to shed a tear | in all my 3.02.428
valiant, | but i am weaker than a woman's tear, TRO 1.01. 9
tear my bright hair and scratch my praised 4.02.107
how 'twas, he did so set his teeth and tear it. COR 1.03. 64 P
to tear with thunder the wide cheeks a' th' air, 5.03.151
their base throats tear | with giving him glory. 5.06. 52
tear him to pieces! 5.06.120 P
i wot, | thy napkin cannot drink a tear of mine, TIT 3.01.140
why, i have not another tear to shed. 3.01.266
stab them, or tear them on thy chariot–wheels, 5.02. 47
tear for tear, and loving kiss for kiss, | thy 5.03.156
tear for tear, and loving kiss for kiss, | thy 5.03.156
had i it written, i would tear the word. ROM 2.02. 57
else would i tear the cave where echo lies, 2.02.161
sit | of an old tear that is not wash'd off yet. 2.03. 76
thou speak, then mightst thou tear thy hair, 3.03. 68
by heaven, i will tear thee joint by joint, 5.03. 35
tear me, take me, and the gods fall upon you! TIM 3.04. 99
tear him to pieces, he's a conspirator. JC 3.03. 28 P
tear him for his bad verses, tear him for his 3.03. 30 P
tear him for his bad verses, tear him for his bad verses. 3.03. 30 P
tear him, tear him! 3.03. 35 P
tear him, tear him! 3.03. 35 P
hand | cancel and tear to pieces that great bond MAC 3.02. 49
in pious rage the two delinquents tear, | that 3.06. 12
periwig–pated fellow tear a passion to totters, HAM 3.02. 9 P
and in his grave rain'd many a tear" — | fare 4.05.167
woo't fight, woo't fast, woo't tear thyself? 5.01.275
is it not as this mouth should tear this hand LR 3.04. 15
i'll tear her all to pieces. OTH 3.03.431
fall not a tear, i say, one of them rates | all ANT 3.11. 69
o, that i had her here, to tear her limb–meal! CYM 2.04.147
sinon's weeping | did scandal many a holy tear, 3.04. 60
i see one eye of yours conceives a tear, | the TNK 5.03.137
of love's coy touch, shall rudely tear thee; LUC 669
desperate, with her nails her flesh doth tear; 739
"let him have time to tear his curled hair, 981
so i at each sad strain will strain a tear, 1131
many a dry drop seem'd a weeping tear, | shed 1375
that with my nails her beauty i may tear. 1472
for every tear he falls a troyan bleeds; 1551
how many a holy and obsequious tear | hath dear SON 31. 5
and often kiss'd, and often /gan to tear; LC 51
lies | in the small orb of one particular tear! 289

TEAR–DISTAINED 1 FR 0.0001 REL FR 1 V 0 P
and round about her tear–distained eye | blue LUC 1586

TEAR–FALLING 1 FR 0.0001 REL FR 1 V 0 P
tear–falling pity dwells not in this eye. R3 4.02. 65

TEARFUL 1 FR 0.0001 REL FR 1 V 0 P
lad, | with tearful eyes add water to the sea, 3H6 5.04. 8

TEARING 6 FR 0.0006 REL FR 5 V 1 P
tearing the thracian singer in their rage." MND 5.01. 49
for tearing a poor whore's ruff in a bawdy–house 2H4 2.04.144 P
and the father tearing | his country's bowels COR 5.03.102
no tearing, lady, i perceive you know it. LR 5.03.158
then in the midst a tearing groan did break ANT 4.14. 31
tearing of papers, breaking rings a–twain, LC 6

TEARS' 1 FR 0.0001 REL FR 1 V 0 P
/loneliness, and find | your salt tears' head. AWW 1.03.172

/TEARS* 10 FR 0.0011 REL FR 10 V 0 P
/bucket /down /and /full /of /tears /am /i, R2 4.01.188
/with /mine /own /tears /i /wash /away /my /balm 4.01.207
/mine /eyes /are /full /of /tears, /i /cannot 4.01.244
/that /all /the /tears /that /thy /poor /eyes TIT 3.02. 18
/the /lamenting /fool /in //sea–salt /tears. 3.02. 20
/she /drinks /no /other /drink /but /tears, 3.02. 37
/tender /sapling, /thou /art /made /of /tears, 3.02. 50
/and /tears /will /quickly /melt /thy /life 3.02. 51
might change or cease, /tears /his /white /hair, LR 3.01. 7
/her /smiles /and /tears | /were /like /a 4.03. 18

TEARS* 317 FR 0.0358 REL FR 290 V 27 P
his tears runs down his beard like winter's TMP 5.01. 16
the tide is now — nay, not thy tide of tears, TGV 2.02. 14
but see how i lay the dust with my tears. 2.03. 32 P
were dry, i am able to fill it with my tears; 2.03. 52 P
with nightly tears, and daily heart–sore sighs, 2.04.132
a thousand oaths, an ocean of his tears, | and 2.07. 69
his tears pure messengers sent from his heart, 2.07. 77
a sea of melting pearl, which some call tears; 3.01.226
nor silver–shedding tears | could penetrate her 3.01.232
altar of her beauty | you sacrifice your tears, 3.02. 73
be dry, and with your tears | moist it again, 3.02. 74
which i so lively acted with my tears | that my 4.04.169
left her in her tears, and dried not one of them MM 3.01.225 P
and he, a marble to her tears, is wash'd with 3.01.229 P
to drown me in thy /sister's flood of tears. ERR 3.02. 46
and never rise until my tears and prayers | have 5.01.115
did he break out into tears? ADO 1.01. 24 P
sobs, beats her heart, tears her hair, prays, 2.03.147 P
of her foulness, | wash'd it with tears? 4.01.154
your overkindness doth wring tears from me. 5.01.293
doth thy face through tears of mine give light. LLL 4.03. 31
do but behold the tears that swell in me, | and 4.03. 35
then thou /wilt keep | my tears for glasses, and 4.03. 38
in your tears | there is no certain princess 4.03.153
to check their folly, passion's solemn tears. 5.02.118
raining the tears of lamentation | for the 5.02.809
wishes and tears, poor fancy's followers. MND 1.01.155
that will ask some tears in the true performing 1.02. 25 P
not with salt tears; 2.02. 92
scorn and derision never come in tears. 3.02.123
to conjure tears up in a poor maid's eyes | with 3.02.158
like tears that did their own disgrace bewail. 4.01. 56
but more merry tears | the passion of loud 5.01. 69
come, tears, confound, | out, sword, and wound 5.01.295
tears exhibit my tongue. MV 2.03. 10 P
and even there, his eye being big with tears, 2.08. 46
a' my breathing, no tears but a' my shedding. 3.01. 96 P
i assure thee (and almost with tears i speak it) AYL 1.01.153 P
i should have given him tears unto entreaties, 1.02.238
and the big round tears | cours'd one another 2.01. 38
of the swift brook, | augmenting it with tears. 2.01. 43
giving her them again, said with weeping tears, 2.04. 53 P
inconstant, full of tears, full of smiles; 3.02.412 P
to consider that tears do not become a man. 3.04. 3 P
tears our recountments had most kindly bath'd, 4.03.140
it is to be all made of sighs and tears, | and 5.02. 84
bid him shed tears, as being overjoyed | to see SHR in.1. 120
gift | to rain a shower of commanded tears, | an in.1. 125
so workmanly the blood and tears are drawn. in.2. 60
and till the tears that she hath shed for thee in.2. 64
your commendations, madam, get from her tears. AWW 1.01. 47 P
and these great tears grace his remembrance more 1.01. 80
grief would have tears, and sorrow bids me speak 3.04. 42
some other times we drown our gain in tears! 4.03. 68 P
with adorations, fertile tears, | with groans TN 1.05.255
more | will i my master's tears to you deplore. 3.01.162
i should my tears let fall upon your cheek, 5.01.240
here which burns | worse than tears drown. WT 2.01.112
prison, then abound in tears | as i come out; 2.01.120
and tears shed there | shall be my recreation. 3.02.239
him, whose daughter | his tears proclaim'd his, 5.01.160
leave of them, for their joy waded in tears. 5.02. 46 P
i would fain say, bleed tears; 5.02. 89 P
first gentleman–like tears that ever we shed. 5.02.145 P
much work for tears in many an english mother, JN 2.01.303
out at mine eyes in tender womanish tears. 4.01. 36
near these eyes, would drink my tears, | and 4.01. 62
rage | presented to the tears of soft remorse. 4.03. 50
my heart hath melted at a lady's tears, | being 5.02. 47
o that there were some virtue in my tears, 5.07. 44
and knows not how to do it but with tears. 5.07.109
and say, what store of parting tears were shed? R2 1.04. 5
for sorrow's eyes, glazed with blinding tears, 2.02. 16
with tears drawn from her eyes by your foul 3.01. 15
plays fondly with her tears and smiles in 3.02. 9
as if the world were all dissolv'd to tears, 3.02.108
at meeting tears the cloudy cheeks of heaven. 3.03. 57
we'll make foul weather with despised tears; 3.03.161
and make some pretty match with shedding tears? 3.03.165
tears show their love, but want their remedies. 3.03.203
your hearts of sorrow, and your eyes of tears. 4.01.332
and wash him fresh again with true–love tears. 5.01. 10
his face still combating with tears and smiles, 5.02. 32
his eyes do drop no tears, his prayers are in 5.03.101
is pointing still, in cleansing them from tears. 5.05. 54
so sighs, and tears, and groans | show minutes, 5.05. 57
not, sweet queen, for trickling tears are vain. 1H4 2.04.391
for tears do stop the flood–gates of her eyes. 2.04.394
i do not speak to thee in drink but in tears; 2.04.415 P
with tears of innocency and terms of zeal, | my 4.03. 63
when richard, with his eye brimful of tears, 2H4 3.01. 67
me | is tears and heavy sorrows of the blood, 4.05. 38
washing with kindly tears his gentle cheeks, 4.05. 83
let all the tears that should bedew my hearse 4.05.113
but for my tears, | the moist impediments unto 4.05.138
that shall convert those tears | by number into 5.02. 60
and on your head | turning the widows' tears, H5 2.04.106
and on it have bestowed more contrite tears, 4.01.296
how shall we then behold their natural tears? 4.02. 13
came into mine eyes | and gave me up to tears. 4.06. 32
our isle be made a nourish of salt tears, | and 1H6 1.01. 50
were our tears wanting to this funeral, | these 1.01. 82
behold | my sighs and tears, and will not once 3.01.108
thou shalt rue this treason with thy tears, | if 3.02. 36
return thee therefore with a flood of tears, 3.03. 56
sword should shed hot blood, mine eyes no tears. 2H6 1.01.118
mine eyes are full of tears, my heart of grief. 2.03. 17
to see my tears and hear my deep–fet groans. 2.04. 33
witness my tears, i cannot stay to speak. 2.04. 86
for i should melt at an offender's tears, | and 3.01.126
and gloucester's case | with sad unhelpful tears, 3.01.218
might liquid tears or heart–offending groans 3.02. 60
me drown'd on shore | with tears as salt as sea, 3.02. 96
to drain | upon his face an ocean of salt tears, 3.02.143
that i may dew it with my mournful tears; 3.02.340
and with the southern clouds contend in tears, 3.02.384
pray'rs and tears have mov'd me, gifts could 4.07. 68
tears virginal | shall be to me even as the dew 5.02. 52
these tears are my sweet rutland's obsequies, 3H6 1.04.147
so | that hardly can i check my eyes from tears. 1.04.151
see, ruthless queen, a hapless father's tears! 1.04.156
boy, | and i with tears do wash the blood away. 1.04.158
upon my soul, the hearers will shed tears; 1.04.161
yea, even my foes will shed fast–falling tears, 1.04.162
and that will quickly dry thy melting tears. 1.04.174
burns me up with flames that tears would quench. 2.01. 84
tears then for babes; 2.01. 86
ten days ago i drown'd these news in tears; 2.01.104
my tears shall wipe away these bloody marks; 2.05. 71
be blind with tears, and break o'ercharg'd with 2.05. 78
for slaughter of my son | shed seas of tears, 2.05.106
her tears will pierce into a marble heart; 3.01. 38
to hear and see her plaints, her brinish tears. 3.01. 41
and wet my cheeks with artificial tears, | and 3.02.184
from such a cause as fills mine eyes with tears 3.03. 13
i will not hence, till with my talk and tears 3.03.158
lest with my sighs or tears i blast or drown 4.04. 23
my mercy dried their water–flowing tears; 4.08. 43
thy tears would wash this cold congealed blood 5.02. 37
gentlemen, what i should say | my tears gainsay; 5.04. 74
may such purple tears be alway shed | from those 5.06. 64
eyes of thine from mine have drawn salt tears, R3 1.02.153
and wet his grave with my repentant tears) | i 1.02.215
with curses in her mouth, tears in her eyes, 1.02.232
drop millstones, when fools' eyes fall tears. 1.03.352
how can we aid you with our kindred tears? 2.02. 63
send forth plenteous tears to drown the world! 2.02. 70
me, threefold distress'd, | pour all your tears. 2.02. 87
the liquid drops of tears that you have shed 4.04.321
for i myself have many tears to wash | hereafter 4.04.389
i would these dewy tears were from the ground. 5.03.284
my drops of tears | i'll turn to sparks of fire. H8 2.04. 72
may have a tomb of orphants' tears wept on him! 3.02.399
continual meditations, tears, and sorrows, | he 4.02. 28
he has strangled | his language in his tears. 5.01.157
man, those joyful tears show thy true /heart. 5.02.208
i'll spring up in his tears an' 'twere a nettle TRO 1.02.175 P
vows, gifts, tears, and love's full sacrifice, 1.02.282
and i will fill them with prophetic tears. 2.02.102
practice your eyes with tears! 2.02.108
kiss, | distasted with the salt of broken tears. 4.04. 48
where are my tears? 4.04. 53 P
their eyes o'ergalled with recourse of tears, 5.03. 55
where senators shall mingle tears with smiles; COR 1.09. 3
carries noise, and behind him he leaves tears: 2.01.159 P
and schoolboys' tears take up | the glasses of 3.02.116
come leave your tears: 4.01. 1
thy tears are salter than a younger man's, | and 4.01. 22
but at his nurse's tears | he whin'd and roar'd 5.06. 96
name not the god, thou boy of tears! 5.06.100
to re–salute his country with his tears, | tears TIT 1.01. 75
tears of true joy for his return to rome. 1.01. 76
victorious titus, rue the tears i shed, | a 1.01.105
shed, | a mother's tears in passion for her son; 1.01.106
lo at this tomb my tributary tears | i render 1.01.159
with tears of joy | shed on this earth for thy 1.01.161
no man shed tears for noble mutius, | he lives 1.01.389
let it be your glory | to see her tears, but be 2.03.140
i pour'd forth tears in vain | to save your 2.03.163
i beg this boon, with tears not lightly shed, 2.03.289
will whole months of tears thy father's eyes? 2.04. 55
and for these bitter tears which now you see 3.01. 6
heart's deep languor, and my soul's sad tears: 3.01. 13
let my tears staunch the earth's dry appetite, 3.01. 14
in winter with warm tears i'll melt the snow, 3.01. 20
before) | my tears are now prevailing orators. 3.01. 26
they humbly at my feet | receive my tears, and 3.01. 42
thou hast no hands to wipe away thy tears, | nor 3.01.106
then fresh tears | stood on her cheeks, as doth 3.01.111
and made a brine–pit with our bitter tears? 3.01.129
sweet father, cease your tears, for at your 3.01.136
his napkin, with /his true tears all bewet, 3.01.146
if any power pities wretched tears, | to that i 3.01.208
then must my earth with her continual tears 3.01.228
and make them blind with tributary tears; 3.01.269
beheld his tears, and laugh'd so heartily | that 5.01.116
and bid the owners quench them with their tears. 5.01.134
kill'd her for whom my tears have made me blind. 5.03. 49
but floods of tears will drown my oratory, | and 5.03. 90
our father's tears despis'd, and basely cozen'd 5.03.101
who drown'd their enmity in my true tears, | and 5.03.107
near | to shed obsequious tears upon this trunk. 5.03.152
my tears will choke me if i ope my mouth. 5.03.175
with tears augmenting the fresh morning's dew, ROM 1.01.132
being vex'd, a sea nourish'd with loving tears. 1.01.192
such falsehood, then turn tears to /fires; 1.02. 89
nor tears nor prayers shall purchase out abuses; 3.01.193
back, foolish tears, back to your native spring, 3.02.102
wash they his wounds with tears? 3.02.130
on the ground, with his own tears made drunk. 3.03. 83
thy tears are womanish, thy wild acts /denote 3.03.110
wilt thou wash him from his grave with tears? 3.05. 70
what, still in tears? 3.05.129
may call the sea, | do ebb and flow with tears; 3.05.133
who, raging with thy tears, and they with them, 3.05.135
for venus smiles not in a house of tears. 4.01. 8
marriage, | to stop the inundation of her tears, 4.01. 12
poor soul, thy face is much abus'd with tears. 4.01. 29
the tears have got small victory by that, | for 4.01. 30
wrong'st it more than tears with that report. 4.01. 32
dry up your tears, and stick your rosemary | on 4.05. 79
yet nature's tears are reason's merriment. 4.05. 83
or, wanting that, with tears distill'd by moans. 5.03. 15
surge resolves | the moon into salt tears; TIM 4.03.440
surprise me to the very brink of tears. 5.01.156
banks, and weep your tears | into the channel, JC 1.01. 58
there is tears for his love; 3.02. 27 P
if you have tears, prepare to shed them now. 3.02.169
i owe moe tears | to this dead man than you 5.03.101
in every eye, | that tears shall drown the wind. MAC 1.07. 25
let's away, | our tears are not yet brew'd. 2.03.124
like niobe, all tears — why, she, /even /she — HAM 1.02.149
ere yet the salt of most unrighteous tears | had 1.02.154
not turn'd his color and has tears in 's eyes. 2.02.520 P
tears in his eyes, distraction in his aspect, 2.02.555
he would drown the stage with tears, | and 2.02.562
want true color — tears perchance for blood. 3.04.130
tears seven times salt | burn out the sense and 4.05.155
poor ophelia, | and therefore i forbid my tears. 4.07.186
with cadent tears fret channels in her cheeks, LR 1.04.285
that these hot tears, which break from me 1.04.298
my tears begin to take his part so much, | they 3.06. 60
virtues of the earth, | spring with my tears! 4.04. 17
my mourning and importun'd tears hath pitied. 4.04. 26
that mine own tears | do scald like molten lead. 4.07. 46
be your tears wet? 4.07. 70
and often did beguile her of her tears, | when i OTH 1.03.156
if that the earth could teem with woman's tears, 4.01.245
proceed you in your tears. 4.01.256
am i the motive of these tears, my lord? 4.02. 43
her salt tears fell from her, and soft'ned the 4.03. 46
i must weep, | but they are cruel tears. 5.02. 21
drops tears as fast as the arabian trees | their 5.02.350
call her winds and waters sighs and tears; ANT 1.02.148 P
and indeed the tears live in an onion that 1.02.169 P
to me, and say the tears | belong to egypt. 1.03. 77
'tis so, and the tears of it are wet. 2.07. 49 P
feats, whilst they with joyful tears | wash the 4.08. 9
with tears as sovereign as the blood of hearts, 5.01. 41
my tears that fall | prove holy water on thee! CYM 5.05.268
wanting breath to speak, help me with tears. PER 1.04. 19
with their superfluous riots, hear these tears! 1.04. 54
nor come we to add sorrow to your tears, | but 1.04. 90
o, no tears, | lychorida, no tears. 3.03. 38
o, no tears, | lychorida, no tears. 3.03. 39
shot through and biggest tears o'ershow'r'd, 4.04. 26
a tempest, which his mortal vessel tears, | and 4.04. 30
when we with tears parted pentapolis, | the king 5.03. 38
there, through my tears, | like wrinkled pebbles TNK 1.01.111
heavy cheers, | sacred vials fill'd with tears, 1.05. 5
and while i live, | this day i give to tears. 5.04. 98
wash your foul minds with tears, and those same STM II.C 108
she with her tears | doth quench the maiden VEN 49
till he take truce with her contending tears, 82
they burn too, i'll quench them with my tears. 192
with tears which chorus–like her eyes did rain. 360
dismiss your vows, your feigned tears, your 425
which through the crystal tears gave light, 491
"dost thou drink tears, that thou provok'st such 949

o, how her eyes and tears did lend and borrow! 961
her eye seen in the tears, tears in her eye, 962
her eye seen in the tears, tears in her eye, 962
sighs dry her cheeks, tears make them wet again. 966
whereat her tears began to turn their tide, 979
whose wonted lily white | with purple tears, 1054
my sighs are blown away, my salt tears gone, 1071
would strive who first should dry his tears. 1092
green–dropping sap, which she compares to tears. 1176
nor children's tears nor mothers' groans LUC 431
i know repentant tears ensue the deed, 502
tears harden lust, though marble /wear with 560
by her untimely tears, her husband's love, | by 570
be moved with my tears, my sighs, my groans. 588
art, | melt at my tears and be compassionate! 594
cooling his hot face in the chastest tears 682
her tears should drop on them perpetually. 686
mingling my talk with tears, my grief with 797
likes dumps when time is kept with tears. 1127
"on what occasion break | those tears from thee, 1271
if tears could help, mine own would do me good. 1274
sighs and groans and tears may grace the fashion 1319
and with my tears quench troy that burns so long 1468
to see those borrowed tears that sinon sheeds! 1549
priam's trust false sinon's tears doth flatter, 1560
she tears the senseless sinon with her nails, 1564
her eyes, though sod in tears, look'd red and 1592
of hard misfortune, carv'd /in /it with tears. 1713
to check the tears in collatinus' eyes. 1817
her oaths, her tears, and all were jestings. PP 7.12
complain, | scarce i could from tears refrain; 20.16
but those tears are pearl which thy love sheeds, SON 34.13
/nought by elements so slow | but heavy tears, 44.14
what potions have i drunk of siren tears 119. 1
that is so vex'd with watching and with tears? 148.10
cunning love, with tears thou keep'st me blind, 148.13
brine | that seasoned woe had pelleted in tears, LC 18
even there resolv'd my reason into tears, 296
TEARSHEET 7 FR 0.0008 REL FR 1 V 6 P
will you have doll tearsheet meet you at supper? 2H4 2.02.163 P
mistress quickly and mistress doll tearsheet. 2.02.153 P
this doll tearsheet should be some road. 2.02.166 P
mistress tearsheet would fain hear some music. 2.04. 11 P
mistress tearsheet! 2.04.385 P
bid mistress tearsheet come to my master. 2.04.387 P
doll tearsheet she by name, and her espouse. H5 2.01. 77
TEAR–STAIN'D 1 FR 0.0001 REL FR 1 V 0 P
my tear–stain'd eyes to see her miseries. 2H6 2.04. 16
TEAT 2 FR 0.0002 REL FR 2 V 0 P
even at thy teat thou hadst thy tyranny; TIT 2.03.145
say thou hadst suck'd wisdom from thy teat. ROM 1.03. 68
TECHY *(also tetchy)*
TECHY 1 FR 0.0001 REL FR 1 V 0 P
to see it techy and fall out wi' th' dug! ROM 1.03. 32
TEDER 1 FR 0.0001 REL FR 1 V 0 P
and with a larger teder may he walk | than may HAM 1.03.125
TEDIOSITY 1 FR 0.0001 REL FR 1 V 0 P
what tediosity and disensanity | is here among TNK 3.05. 2
TEDIOUS 49 FR 0.0055 REL FR 40 V 9 P
with twenty watchful, weary, tedious nights: TGV 1.01. 31
you are a tedious fool. MM 2.01.115 P
being often read, | grown /sere and tedious; 2.04. 9
neighbors, you are tedious. ADO 3.05. 18 P
mine own part, if i were as tedious as a king, i 3.05. 21 P
the tedious minutes i with her have spent. MND 2.02.112
o weary night, o long and tedious night, | abate 3.02.431
"a tedious brief scene of young pyramus | and 5.01. 56
tedious and brief? 5.01. 58
lord, it is too long, | which makes it tedious; 5.01. 64
his tedious measures with the unbated fire MV 2.06. 11
too griev'd a heart | to take a tedious leave; 2.07. 77
respect it is not in the court, it is tedious. AYL 3.02. 19 P
what tedious homily of love have you wearied 3.02.155 P
knowing no burthen of heavy tedious penury. 3.02.324 P
tedious it were to tell, and harsh to hear — SHR 3.02.105
that is the brief and the tedious of it, and AWW 2.03. 29 P
life is as tedious as a twice–told tale | vexing JN 3.04.108
every tedious stride i make | will but remember R2 1.03.268
within me grief hath kept a tedious fast; 2.01. 75
in winter's tedious nights sit by the fire 5.01. 40
next, | thinking his prattle to be tedious, 5.02. 26
to sport would be as tedious as to work; 1H4 1.02.205
son | can trace me in the tedious ways of art, 3.01. 47
o, he is as tedious | as a tired horse, a 3.01.157
ordained is to raise this tedious siege, | and 1H6 1.02. 53
hath, | writes not so tedious a style as this. 4.07. 74
i would remove these tedious stumbling–blocks, 2H6 1.02. 64
weaves tedious snares to trap mine enemies. 3.01.340
and, for the time shall not seem tedious, | i'll 3H6 3.01. 9
'tis better, sir, than to be tedious. R3 1.04. 89 P
our crosses on the way | have made it tedious, 3.01. 5
my lord stanley sleep these tedious nights? 3.02. 6
brief abstract and record of tedious days, 4.04. 28
and in a tedious sampler sew'd her mind; TIT 2.04. 39
so tedious is this day | as is the night before ROM 3.02. 28
of breath | is not so long as is a tedious tale. 5.03.230
away, thou tedious rogue! TIM 4.03.369
no more, | returning were as tedious as go o'er. MAC 3.04.137
these tedious old fools! HAM 2.02.219 P
i would beguile | the tedious day with sleep. 3.02.227
it were a tedious difficulty, i think, | to OTH 3.03.397
more tedious than the dial eightscore times? 3.04.175
i see a man's life is a tedious one, | i have CYM 3.06. 1
pray, but be not tedious, for | the gods are PER 4.01. 68
'twould be too tedious to repeat, | but the main 5.01. 28
her song was tedious and outwore the night, VEN 841
my woes are tedious, though my words are brief." LUC 1309
like dying coals burnt out in tedious nights. 1379
TEDIOUSLY 2 FR 0.0002 REL FR 2 V 0 P
and ugly witch doth limp | so tediously away. H5 4.pr. 22
wights she stays | as tediously as hell, but TRO 4.02. 13
TEDIOUSNESS 4 FR 0.0004 REL FR 3 V 1 P
all thy tediousness on me, ah? ADO 3.05. 23 P
didst rob it of some taste of tediousness. MV 2.03. 3
the tediousness and process of my travel. R2 2.03. 12
and tediousness the limbs and outward flourishes HAM 2.02. 91
TEEM 3 FR 0.0003 REL FR 3 V 0 P
teem with new monsters, whom thy upward face TIM 4.03.190
if she must teem, | create her child of spleen, LR 1.04.281
if that the earth could teem with woman's tears, OTH 4.01.245
TEEMING 6 FR 0.0006 REL FR 6 V 0 P
the bare fallow brings | to teeming foison, even MM 1.04. 43
this nurse, this teeming womb of royal kings, R2 2.01. 51
is not my teeming date drunk up with time? 5.02. 91
oft the teeming earth | is with a kind of colic 1H4 3.01. 27
breath blows down | the teeming ceres' foison, TNK 5.01. 53
the teeming autumn, big with rich increase, SON 97. 6
TEEMS 3 FR 0.0003 REL FR 3 V 0 P
idleness, and nothing teems | but hateful docks, H5 5.02. 51
and infinite breast | teems and feeds all; TIM 4.03.179
each minute teems a new one. MAC 4.03.176
TEEN 6 FR 0.0006 REL FR 6 V 0 P
to think o' th' teen that i have turn'd you to, TMP 1.02. 64
of sighs, of groans, of sorrow, and of teen! LLL 4.03.162
and each hour's joy wrack'd with a week of teen. R3 4.01. 96
and yet, to my teen be it spoken, i have but ROM 1.03. 13
my face is full of shame, my heart of teen, VEN 808
or my affection put to th' smallest teen, | or LC 192
/TEETH 2 FR 0.0002 REL FR 2 V 0 P
/get /some /little /knife /between /thy /teeth, TIT 3.02. 16
you show'd your /teeth like apes, and fawn'd JC 5.01. 41
TEETH 61 FR 0.0069 REL FR 47 V 14 P
this hand, i will supplant some of your teeth. TMP 3.02. 49 P
"item, she hath no teeth." TGV 3.01.340 P
well, the best is, she hath no teeth to bite. 3.01.344 P
in despite of the teeth of all rhyme and reason, WIV 5.05.125 P
must be lock'd within the teeth and the lips. MM 3.02.135 P
yea, dost thou jeer and flout me in the teeth? ERR 2.02. 22
till, gnawing with my teeth my bonds in sunder, 5.01.250
snapp'd off with two old men without teeth. ADO 5.01.116 P
to show his teeth as white as whale's bone; LLL 5.02.332
they'll not show their teeth in way of smile MV 1.01. 55
most true, i have lost my teeth in your service. AYL 1.01. 83 P
sans teeth, sans eyes, sans taste, sans every 2.07.166
my very lips might freeze to my teeth, my tongue SHR 4.01. 7 P
ask questions and sing, pick his teeth and sing. AWW 3.02. 8 P
i know by the picking on 's teeth. WT 4.04.753 P
why then i suck my teeth, and catechize | my JN 1.01.192
the swords of soldiers are his teeth, his fangs, 2.01.353
and to part by th' teeth | the unowed interest 4.03.146
my teeth shall tear | the slavish motive of R2 1.01.192
doubly portcullis'd with my teeth and lips, 1.03.167
and that would set my teeth nothing an edge, 1H4 3.01.131
thrown | a brave defiance in king henry's teeth, 5.02. 42
have but their stings and teeth newly ta'en out; 2H4 4.05.205
puff i' thy teeth, most recreant coward base! 5.03. 92
the "solus" in thy teeth, and in thy throat, H5 2.01. 48
now set the teeth and stretch the nostril wide, 3.01. 15
rather with their teeth | the walls they'll tear 1H6 1.02. 39
stones, we'll fall to it with our teeth. 3.01. 90 P
deliver'd strongly through my fixed teeth, 2H6 3.02.313
biting statutes, unless his teeth be pull'd out. 4.07. 17 P
for one to thrust his hand between his teeth, 3H6 1.04. 57
teeth hadst thou in thy head when thou wast born 5.06. 53
"o, jesus bless us, he is born with teeth!" 5.06. 75
that had his teeth before his eyes | to worry R3 4.04. 49
manner | daring th' event to th' teeth, are all H8 1.02. 36
how 'twas, he did so set his teeth and tear it. COR 1.03. 64 P
wash their faces, | and keep their teeth clean. 2.03. 61
their mouths, why rule you not their teeth? 3.01. 36
thy other hand | gnawing with thy teeth, and be TIT 3.01.261
thou my hand, sweet wench, between thy teeth. 3.01.282
i'll lay fourteen of my teeth — | and yet, to ROM 1.03. 12
cannot live | out of the teeth of emulation. JC 2.03. 14
and conn'd by rote, | to cast into my teeth. 4.03. 99
defiance, traitors, hurl we in your teeth. 5.01. 64
will venom breed, | no teeth for th' present. MAC 3.04. 30
even to the teeth and forehead of our faults, HAM 3.03. 63
that i /shall live and tell him to his teeth, 4.07. 56
chill pick your teeth, zir. LR 4.06.244 P
throw your vild guesses in the devil's teeth, OTH 3.04.184
by isis, i will give thee bloody teeth, | if ANT 1.05. 70
him, he not /took't, | or did it from his teeth. 3.04. 10
but now i'll set my teeth, | and send to 3.13.180
with thy sharp teeth this knot intrinsicate | of 5.02.304
so sharp are hunger's teeth, that man and wife PER 1.04. 45
showing the sun his teeth, grinning at the moon, TNK 1.01.100
by th' tail | and with thy teeth thou hold, will 3.05. 50
if you do, | your teeth will bleed extremely. 3.05. 81
the iron bit he crusheth 'tween his teeth, VEN 269
who did not whet his teeth at him again, | but 1113
but through his teeth, as if the name he tore. LUC 1787
pluck the keen teeth from the fierce tiger's SON 19. 3
TEIPSUM 1 FR 0.0001 REL FR 1 V 0 P
medice, teipsum — | protector, see to't well, 2H6 2.01. 51
TELAMON 1 FR 0.0001 REL FR 1 V 0 P
o, he's more mad | than telamon for his shield; ANT 4.13. 2
TELAMONIUS 1 FR 0.0001 REL FR 1 V 0 P
and now, like ajax telamonius, | on sheep or 2H6 5.01. 26
/TELL 8 FR 0.0009 REL FR 8 V 0 P
and how accompanied? /canst /thou /tell /that? 2H4 4.04. 52
"/tell /me what /fate /awaits the duke of 2H6 1.04. 32
/tell /him, /and /spare /not. R3 1.03.113
/tell /over /your /woes /again /by /viewing 4.04. 39
/to /tell /you, /fair /beholders, /that /our TRO pr 26
/to /bid /aeneas /tell /the /tale /twice /o'er TIT 3.02. 27
/tell /me /but /this: STM II.C 114
that every word doth almost /tell my name, SON 76. 7
TELL 1118 FR 0.1263 REL FR 760 V 358 P
tell your piteous heart | there's no harm done. TMP 1.02. 14
you have often | begun to tell me what i am, but 1.02. 34
of any thing the image, tell me, that | hath 1.02. 43
then tell me | if this might be a brother. 1.02.117
thou hast. where was she born? speak. tell me. 1.02.260
one. tell. 2.01. 15 P
then tell me, | who's the next heir of naples? 2.01.244
they'll tell the clock to any business that | we 2.01.289
this will shake your shaking, i can tell you, 2.02. 84 P
you cannot tell who's your friend. 2.02. 85 P
tell not me. 3.02. 1 P
wilt thou tell a monstrous lie, being but half a 3.02. 28 P
this will i tell my master. 3.02.115
tell me, heavenly bow, | if venus or her son, as 4.01. 86
at this time | i will tell no tales. 5.01.129
i were well awake, | i'ld strive to tell you. 5.01.230
tell me, panthino, what sad talk was that TGV 1.03. 1
then tell me, whither were i best to send him? 1.03. 24
go to, sir; tell me, do you know madam silvia? 2.01. 14 P
but tell me: dost thou know my lady silvia? 2.01. 42 P
now tell me: how do all from whence you came? 2.04.122
but tell me true, will't be a match? 2.05. 34 P
i tell thee, my master is become a hot lover. 2.05. 51 P
why, i tell thee, i care not, though he burn 2.05. 52 P
to lesson me and tell me some good mean | how 2.07. 5
that fits as well as "tell me, good my lord, 2.07. 50
but tell me, wench, how will the world repute me 2.07. 59
now tell me, proteus, what's your will with me? 3.01. 3
when would you use it? pray, sir, tell me that. 3.01.123
but what woman, i will not tell myself; 3.01.269 P
i will try thee. tell me this: who begot thee? 3.01.293 P
why then will i tell thee — that thy master 3.01.372 P
why didst not tell me sooner? 3.01.380 P
tell us this: have you any thing to take to? 4.01. 40
i tell you what launce, his man, told me: 4.02. 75 P
tell my lady | i claim the promise for her 4.04. 86
tell him from me, | one julia, that his changing 4.04.118
please you, i'll tell you as we pass along, 5.04.168
shall i tell you a lie? WIV 1.01. 68 P
that peradventures shall tell you another tale, 1.01. 77 P
where's simple, my man? can you tell, cousin? 1.01.134 P
my honest lads, i will tell you what i am about. 1.03. 38 P
tell master parson evans i will do what i can 1.04. 33 P
but notwithstanding (to tell you in your ear, i 1.04.102 P
i can tell you that by the way, i praise heaven 1.04.140 P
and i will tell your worship more of the wart 1.04.159 P
tell him, cavaleiro justice; 2.01.198 P
tell him, bully–rook. 2.01.198 P
hark, i will tell you what our sport shall be. 2.01.210 P
recourse to him and tell him my name is /brook 2.01.215 P
and let me tell you in your ear, she's as 2.02. 97 P
and one (i tell you) that will not miss you 2.02. 98 P
and she bade me tell your worship that her 2.02.100 P
but i pray thee tell me this: 2.02.108 P
i will tell you, sir, if you will give me the 2.02.176 P
i shall be with her (i may tell you) by her own 2.02.262 P
jack, i vill tell you how i vill kill him. 2.03. 13 P
i had as lief you would tell me of a mess of 3.01. 63 P
i cannot tell what the dickens his name is my 3.02. 19 P
my nursh–a quickly tell me so mush. 3.02. 65 P
me into everlasting liberty if i tell you of it; 3.03. 31 P
go tell thy master i am alone. 3.03. 36 P
nay, i must tell you, so you do; 3.03. 83 P
i come before to tell you. 3.03.115 P
i'll tell you my dream. 3.03.161 P
my uncle can tell you good jests of him. 3.04. 39 P
tell mistress anne the jest how my father stole 3.04. 39 P
they can tell you how things go better than i 3.04. 65 P
well, i will visit her, tell her so. 3.05. 49 P
i will tell her. 3.05. 52 P
shall we tell our husbands how we have serv'd 4.02.213 P
and till he tell the truth, | let the supposed 4.04. 61
he'll tell me all his purpose. 4.04. 77
i tell you for good will, look you. 4.05. 79 P
i cannot tell vat is dat; 4.05. 86 P
i tell you for good will; 4.05. 89 P
i will tell you — he beat me grievously, in the 5.01. 20 P
go along with me, i'll tell you all, master 5.01. 24 P
i'll tell you strange things of this knave ford, 5.01. 27 P
tell her master slender hath married her 5.05.173 P
when need you tell me that? 5.05.190 P
did not i tell you how you should know my 5.05.194 P
but rather tell me, | when i, that censure him, MM 2.01. 28
come, tell me true, it shall be the better for 2.01.221 P
is pretty orders beginning, i can tell you: 2.01.236 P
i'll tell him of you. 2.02. 2
did not i tell thee yea? 2.02. 8
i would tell what 'twere to be a judge, | and 2.02. 69
and you tell me that he shall die for't. 2.04.143
an outstretch'd throat i'll tell the world aloud 2.04.153
did i tell this, | who would believe me? 2.04.171
i'll tell him yet of angelo's request, | and fit 2.04.186
i know none. can you tell me of any? 3.02. 87 P
canst thou tell if claudio die to–morrow, or no? 3.02.169 P
that he hath forc'd me to tell him he is indeed 3.02.253 P
i pray you tell me, hath any body inquir'd for 4.01. 16 P
tell him he must awake, and that quickly too. 4.03. 30 P
i can tell thee pretty tales of the duke. 4.03.166 P
at flavio's house, | and tell him where i stay. 4.05. 7
is this the man | that you did tell us of? 5.01.325
to tell sad stories of my own mishaps. ERR 1.01.120
tell me this, i pray: 1.02. 53
tell me, and dally not, where is the money? 1.02. 59
and tell me how thou hast dispos'd thy charge. 1.02. 73
i pray you, master, tell me. 2.02. 21
shall i tell you why? 2.02. 42 P
own handwriting would tell you what i think. 3.01. 14
sir, i'll tell you when, and you'll tell me 3.01. 39
tell you when, and you'll tell me wherefore. 3.01. 39
he comes too late, | and so tell your master. 3.01. 50
can you tell? 3.01. 52
can you tell for whose sake? 3.01. 57
what i should think of this, i cannot tell: 3.02.179
give her this key, and tell her, in the desk 4.01.103
tell her i am arrested in the street, | and that 4.01.106
what, is he arrested? tell me at whose suit. 4.02. 43
suit of buff which 'rested him, that can i tell. 4.02. 45
tell me, was he arrested on a band? 4.02. 49
and tell his wife that, being lunatic, | he 4.03. 93
i tell you, 'twill sound harshly in her ears. 4.04. 7
still did i tell him it was vild and bad. 5.01. 67
mistress, upon my life, i tell you true; 5.01.180
but tell me yet, dost thou not know my voice? 5.01.301
err — | tell me thou art my son antipholus. 5.01.319
i tell thee, syracusian, twenty years | have i 5.01.327
if thou art she, tell me, where is that son 5.01.348
what then became of them i cannot tell; 5.01.355
than you must expect of me to tell you how. ADO 1.01. 17 P
i tell him we shall stay here at the least a 1.01.148 P
i pray thee tell me truly how thou lik'st her. 1.01.178 P
jack, to tell us cupid is a good hare–finder and 1.01.184 P
i would your grace would constrain me to tell. 1.01.207 P
him, and tell him i will not fail him at supper, 1.01.276 P
disguise, | and tell fair hero i am claudio, 1.01.322

i can tell you strange news that you yet dreamt 1.02. 4 P
go you and tell her of it. 1.02. 23 P
tell him there is measure in every thing, and so 2.01. 71 P
to tell you true, i counterfeit him. 2.01.116 P
will you not tell me who told you so? 2.01.125 P
nor will you not tell me who you are? 2.01.127 P
know the gentleman, i'll tell him what you say. 2.01.144 P
she cannot endure to hear tell of a husband. 2.01.347 P
go in with me, and i will tell you my drift. 2.01.387 P
spare not to tell him that he hath wrong'd his 2.02. 22 P
tell them that you know that hero loves me, 2.02. 34 P
i cannot tell; 2.03. 23 P
i cannot tell what to think of it but that she 2.03. 99 P
sit you — you heard my daughter tell you how. 2.03.111 P
i pray you tell benedick of it, and hear what 'a 2.03.170 P
we go seek benedick, and tell him of her love? 2.03.199 P
never tell him, my lord. 2.03.201 P
and tell her i and ursley | walk in the orchard, 3.01. 4
and did they bid you tell her of it, madam? 3.01. 39
but who dare tell her so? 3.01. 74
yet tell her of it, hear what she will say. 3.01. 81
i came hither to tell you, and, circumstances 3.02.102 P
times good night — i tell this tale vildly, i 3.03.148 P
vildly, i should first tell thee how the prince, 3.03.149 P
my soul doth tell me hero is belied, | and that 5.01. 42
i'll tell thee how beatrice prais'd thy wit the 5.01.159 P
but i must tell thee plainly, claudio undergoes 5.02. 56 P
and i pray thee now tell me, for which of my bad 5.02. 59 P
and now tell me, how doth your cousin? 5.02. 88 P
did i not tell you she was innocent? 5.04. 1
i'll tell you largely of fair hero's death. 5.04. 69
i'll tell thee what, prince: 5.04.100 P
this letter will tell you more. LLL 1.01.188 P
in two words, the dancing horse will tell you. 1.02. 54 P
tell me precisely of what complexion. 1.02. 81 P
i will tell thee wonders. 1.02.139 P
i am less proud to hear you tell my worth | than 2.01. 17
tell him, the daughter of the king of france, 2.01. 30
but tell me, how was there a costard broken in a 3.01.111 P
i will tell you sensibly. 3.01.113 P
can you tell me by your wit | what was a month 4.02. 34
sir, tell not me of the father, i do fear 4.02.149 P
thought can think, nor tongue of mortal tell." 4.03. 40
where lies thy grief, o, tell me, good dumaine? 4.03.169
this audience, and i shall tell you more. 4.03.206
for, sir, to tell you plain, | i'll find a 4.03.268
for i must tell thee it will please his grace 5.01.101 P
shall i tell you a thing? 5.01.145 P
the princess bids you tell | how many inches 5.02.192
tell her, we measure them by weary steps. 5.02.194
i will go tell him of fair hermia's flight; MND 1.01.246
tell you i do not /nor i cannot love you? 2.01.201
tell them that i pyramus am not pyramus, but 3.01. 20 P
another prologue must tell he is not a lion. 3.01. 34 P
and tell them plainly he is snug the joiner. 3.01. 45 P
o, once tell true; 3.02. 68
tell true, even for my sake! 3.02. 68
nor is he dead, for aught that i can tell. 3.02. 76
i pray thee, tell me then that he is well. 3.02. 77
did not you tell me i should know the man | by 3.02.348
in our flight | tell me how it came this night 4.01.100
i was — there is no man can tell what. 4.01.208 P
for if i tell you, i am /no true athenian. 4.02. 30 P
i will tell you every thing, right as it fell 4.02. 31 P
all that i will tell you is, that the duke hath 4.02. 34 P
i have to say is to tell you that the lanthorn 5.01.257 P
but tell not me; MV 1.01. 39
i tell thee what, antonio — | i love thee, and 1.01. 86
i'll tell thee more of this another time; 1.01.100
tell me now what lady is the same | to whom you 1.01.119
that you to-day promis'd to tell me of? 1.01.121
i cannot tell, i make it breed as fast. 1.03. 96
pray you tell me this: 1.03.162
i tell thee, lady, this aspect of mine | hath 2.01. 8
can you tell me whether one launcelot, that 2.02. 46 P
young gentleman, but i pray you tell me, is my 2.02. 71 P
well, old man, i will tell you news of your son. 2.02. 78 P
you may tell every finger i have with my ribs. 2.02.106 P
tell gentle jessica | i will not fail her; 2.04. 19
i must needs tell thee all. 2.04. 29
worship was wont to tell me i could do nothing 2.05. 8 P
tell me for more certainty, | albeit i'll swear 2.06. 26
you were best to tell antonio what you hear, 2.08. 33
tell me once more what title thou dost bear: 2.09. 35
but tell us, do you hear whether antonio have 3.01. 42 P
tell me where is fancy bred, | or in the heart 3.02. 63
i pray you tell me how my good friend doth. 3.02.233
jailer, look to him, tell not me of mercy. 3.03. 1
a fine bragging youth, and tell quaint lies, 3.04. 69
and twenty of these puny lies i'll tell, | that 3.04. 74
i'll tell thee all my whole device | when i am 3.04. 81
i'll tell my husband, launcelot, what you say. 3.05. 27 P
on what compulsion must i? tell me that. 4.01.183
wife, | tell her the process of antonio's end, 4.01.274
most thankfully, | and so i pray you tell him; 4.02. 10
tell him there's a post come from my master, 5.01. 46 P
can you tell if rosalind, the duke's daughter, AYL 1.01.105 P
i'll tell thee, charles, it is the stubbornest 1.01.141 P
yet tell us the manner of the wrastling. 1.02.112 P
i will tell you the beginning; 1.02.113 P
will take little delight in it, i can tell you, 1.02.159 P
in mine eye, i can tell who should down. 1.02.214 P
and pray you tell me this: 1.02.268
but i can tell you that of late this duke | hath 1.02.277
tell me whereon the /likelihood depends. 1.03. 57
go seek him, tell him i would speak with him. 2.07. 7
fie on thee! i can tell what thou wouldst do. 2.07. 62
of your fortune, | go to my cave and tell me. 2.07.197
most petitionary vehemence, tell me who it is. 3.02.190 P
i prithee tell me who is it quickly, and speak 3.02.197 P
i'll tell you who time ambles withal, who time 3.02.309 P
so love-shak'd, i pray you tell me your remedy. 3.02.368 P
and, i tell you, deserves as well a dark house 3.02.400 P
tell me where it is. 3.02.428 P
by the way you shall tell me where in the forest 3.02.431 P
good priest that can tell you what marriage is. 3.03. 85 P
for i must tell you friendly in your ear, | sell 3.05. 59
now tell me how long you would have her after 4.01.143 P
i'll tell thee, aliena, i cannot be out of the 4.01.215 P
i pray you tell it. 4.03. 97
i do not shame | to tell you what i was, since 4.03.136
to tell this story, that you might excuse | his 4.03.153
i pray you tell your brother how well i 4.03.167 P
did your brother tell you how i counterfeited to 5.02. 25 P
shepherd, tell this youth what 'tis to love. 5.02. 83
another tell him of his hounds and horse, | and SHR in.1. 61
for i tell you, sirs, | if you should smile, he in.1. 98
tell him from me, as he will win my love, | he in.1. 109
tell me thy mind, for i have pisa left | and am 1.01. 21
i cannot tell; 1.01.131 P
sir, tell me, is it possible | that love should 1.01.146
tell me thine first. 1.01.191
and tell me now, sweet friend, what happy gale 1.02. 48
tell me her father's name, and 'tis enough; 1.02. 94
i'll tell you what, sir, and she stand him but a 1.02.112 P
i'll tell you news indifferent good for either. 1.02.180
and do you tell me of a woman's tongue, | that 1.02.207
tell me, i beseech you, which is the readiest 1.02.219
of all thy suitors here i charge /thee tell 2.01. 8
gentlemen | to my daughters, and tell them both, 2.01.109
then tell me, if i get your daughter's love, 2.01.119
for i tell you, father, | i am as peremptory as 2.01.130
i did but tell her she mistook her frets, | and 2.01.149
why then i'll tell her plain | she sings as 2.01.170
i tell you 'tis incredible to believe | how much 2.01.306
and tell us what occasion of import | hath all 3.02.102
tedious it were to tell, and harsh to hear — 3.02.105
i'll tell you, sir lucentio: 3.02.158
good grumio, tell me, how goes the world? 4.01. 33 P
tell thou the tale. 4.01. 72 P
i tell thee, kate, 'twas burnt and dried away, 4.01.170
i tell you, sir, she bears me fair in hand. 4.02. 3
now tell me, i pray, | you that durst swear that 4.02. 11
i tell thee, litio, this is wonderful. 4.02. 15
first, tell me, have you ever been at pisa? 4.02. 93
i cannot tell, i fear 'tis choleric. 4.03. 22
my tongue will tell the anger of my heart, | or 4.03. 77
i tell thee, i, that thou hast marr'd her gown. 4.03.114
and, if you will, tell what hath happened: 4.04. 64
i cannot tell — /except they are busied about a 4.04. 91 P
tell me, sweet kate, and tell me truly too, 4.05. 28
tell me, sweet kate, and tell me truly too, 4.05. 28
i pray you tell signior lucentio that his father 5.01. 27 P
tell me, thou villain, where is my son lucentio? 5.01. 89 P
why, tell me, is not this my cambio? 5.01.122
i pray you tell me what you meant by that. 5.02. 27
i charge thee tell these headstrong women | what 5.02.130
tell me thy reason why thou wilt marry. AWW 1.03. 27 P
tell my gentlewoman i would speak with her — 1.03. 68 P
therefore tell me true, | but tell me then, 'tis 1.03.175
tell me true, | but tell me then, 'tis so; 1.03.176
work in me for thine avail, | to tell me truly. 1.03.185
wherefore? tell true. 1.03.219
i will tell truth, by grace itself i swear. 1.03.220
her by the hand, | and tell her she is thine; 2.03.174
i must tell thee, sirrah, i write man; 2.03.198 P
i would not tell you what i would, my lord. 2.05. 84
here they come will tell you more. 3.02. 43 P
to tell him that his sword can never win | the 3.02. 93
parted, tell me what a sprat you shall find him, 3.06.104 P
go tell the count rossillion, and my brother, 4.01. 89
then pray you tell me, | if i should swear by 4.02. 24
i will tell you a thing, but you shall let it 4.03. 10 P
to live this present hour, i will tell true. 4.03.161 P
be a-weary of thee, and i tell thee so before, 4.05. 57 P
and i was about to tell you, since i heard of 4.05. 69 P
tell me, sirrah — but tell me true, i charge 5.03.234
me, sirrah — but tell me true, i charge you, 5.03.234
i'll never tell you. 5.03.284
and tell them, there thy fixed foot shall grow TN 1.04. 17
nay, either tell me where thou hast been, or i 1.05. 1 P
i can tell thee where that saying was born, of 1.05. 9 P
tell him he shall not speak with me. 1.05.146 P
i pray you tell me if this be the lady of the 1.05.171 P
tell me your mind — i am a messenger. 1.05.205 P
come to me again | to tell me how he takes it. 1.05.282
tell him i'll none of it. 1.05.302
occasion more mine eyes will tell tales of me. 2.01. 42 P
my lady bade me tell you that, though she 2.03. 96 P
us, possess us, tell us something of him. 2.03.138 P
tell her, my love, more noble than the world, 2.04. 81
her, | tell her, i hold as giddily as fortune; 2.04. 84
you tell her so. 2.04. 92
by my troth, i'll tell thee, i am almost sick 3.01. 46 P
i prithee tell me what thou think'st of me. 3.01.138
tell me that. 3.02. 9 P
did not i tell you? 3.04. 92 P
thing would make me tell them how much i lack of 3.04.303 P
thy strangeness and tell me what i shall vent to 4.01. 16 P
this will i tell my lady straight; 4.01. 30 P
jolly robin, | tell me how thy lady does." 4.02. 73
i tell thee i am as well in my wits as any man 4.02.106 P
but tell me true, are you not mad indeed, or do 4.02.113 P
believe me, i am not, i tell thee true. 4.02.115 P
now my foes tell me plainly i am an ass; 5.01. 18 P
and tell me, in the modesty of honor, | why you 5.01.335
tell me why! 5.01.344
tell him you are sure | all in bohemia's well; WT 1.02. 30
to tell he longs to see his son were strong; 1.02. 34
i prithee tell me; 1.02. 91
sir, i will tell you, | since i am charg'd in 1.02.406
pray you sit by us, | and tell 's a tale. 2.01. 23
i will tell it softly, | yond crickets shall not 2.01. 30
tell her, emilia, | i'll use that tongue i have. 2.02. 49
tell me what blessings i have here alive, | that 3.02.107
awake), i tell you | 'tis rigor and not law. 3.02.113
i cannot tell, good sir, for which of his 4.03. 88 P
several tunes faster than you'll tell money; 4.04.184 P
'tis in request, i can tell you. 4.04.291 P
oath full well, | thou to me thy secrets tell. 4.04.301
and tell him plainly | the self-same sun that 4.04.443
what i do next shall be to tell the king | of 4.04.662
is no other way but to tell the king she's a 4.04.688 P
i will tell the king all, every word, yea, and 4.04.699 P
tell me (for you seem to be honest plain men) 4.04.793 P
and tell me for what dull part in't | you chose 5.01. 64
tell me, mine own, | where hast thou been 5.03.123
tell me, how if my brother, | who, as you say, JN 1.01.120
anon i'll tell thee more. 1.01.232
then tell us, shall your city call us lord, | in 2.01.263
tell me, who knows. 2.01.543
be well advis'd, tell o'er thy tale again. 3.01. 5
tell me, thou fellow, is not france forsworn? 3.01. 62
tell him this tale, and from the mouth of 3.01.152
so tell the pope, all reverence set apart | to 3.01.159
and tell me how you would bestow yourself. 3.01.225
i'll tell thee what, my friend, | he is a very 3.03. 60
face, | as bid me tell my tale in express words, 4.02.234
return, and tell him so. 4.03. 27
there, tell the king, he may inquire us out. 4.03.115
i'll tell thee what; 4.03.120
and come ye now to tell me john hath made | his 5.02. 91
how goes the day with us? o, tell me, hubert. 5.03. 1
tell him toward swinstead, to the abbey there. 5.03. 8
a monk, i tell you, a resolved villain, | whose 5.06. 29
i'll tell thee, hubert, half my power this night 5.06. 39
tell me, moreover, hast thou sounded him, | if R2 1.01. 8
what will ensue hereof, there's none can tell; 2.01.212
my lord, i had forgot to tell your lordship: 2.02. 93
my lords of england, let me tell you this: 2.03.140
tell her i send to her my kind commends; 3.01. 38
and all goes worse than i have power to tell. 3.02.120
and tell sad stories of the death of kings: 3.02.156
tell bullingbrook — for yon methinks he stands 3.03. 91
madam, we'll tell tales. 3.04. 10
good duke of york's | that tell black tidings. 3.04. 71
good old folks and let them tell /thee tales 5.01. 41
griefs, | tell thou the lamentable tale of me, 5.01. 44
my lord, you told me you would tell the rest, 5.02. 1
can no man tell me of my unthrifty son? 5.03. 1
tell us how near is danger | that we may arm us 5.03. 47
tell me, gentle friend, | how went he under him? 5.05. 81
old, | and bootless 'tis to tell you we will go; 1H4 1.01. 29
as well as waiting in the court, i can tell you. 1.02. 70 P
this same fat rogue will tell us when we meet at 1.02.187 P
i tell thee, | he durst as well have met the 1.03.115
i will after straight | and tell him so, for i 1.03.127
good uncle, tell your tale — i have done. 1.03.256
ay, when, canst tell? 2.01. 39 P
i heard him tell it to one of his company last 2.01. 56 P
sleep, to drink, but i tell you, my lord fool, 2.03. 9 P
let him tell the king: 2.03. 34 P
tell me, sweet lord, what is't that takes from 2.03. 40
and if thou wilt not tell me all things true. 2.03. 88
nay, tell me if you speak in jest or no. 2.03. 99
and tell me flatly i am no proud jack like 2.04. 11 P
i tell thee, ned, thou hast lost much honor that 2.04. 20 P
i tell thee what, hal, if i tell thee a lie, 2.04.193 P
hal, if i tell thee a lie, spit in my face, call 2.04.193 P
come, tell us your reason; 2.04.233 P
the world, i would not tell you on compulsion. 2.04.238 P
faith, tell me now in earnest, how came 2.04.303 P
but tell me, hal, art not thou horrible afeard? 2.04.365 P
and tell me now, thou naughty varlet, tell me, 2.04.431 P
thou naughty varlet, tell me, where hast thou 2.04.432 P
leave | to tell you once again that at my birth 3.01. 36
tell truth and shame the devil. 3.01. 58
while you live, tell truth and shame the devil! 3.01. 61
i tell you what: 3.01.153
shall i tell you, cousin? 3.01.167
tell her that she and my aunt percy | shall 3.01.194
tell me else, | could such inordinate and low 3.02. 11
that men would tell their children, "this is he" 3.02. 48
but wherefore do i tell these news to thee? 3.02.121
why, harry, do i tell thee of my foes, | which 3.02.122
day | be bold to tell you that i am your son, 3.02.134
i have heard the prince tell him, i know not how 3.03. 83 P
i prithee tell me, doth he keep his bed? 4.01. 21
the king, i can tell you, looks for us all, we 4.02. 56 P
but tell me, jack, whose fellows are these that 4.02. 61 P
tell your nephew | the prince of wales doth join 5.01. 85
so tell your cousin, and bring me word | what he 5.01.109
lord douglas, go you and tell him so. 5.02. 32
tell me, tell me, | how show'd his tasking? 5.02. 49
tell me, tell me, | how show'd his tasking? 5.02. 49
there did he pause, but let me tell the world, 5.02. 65
because some tell me that thou art a king. 5.03. 5
they tell thee true. 5.03. 6
why didst thou tell me that thou wert a king? 5.03. 24
shall find no boy's play here, i can tell you. 5.04. 76 P
did you not tell me this fat man was dead? 5.04.132
tell thou the earl | that the lord bardolph doth 2H4 1.01. 2
my lord, i'll tell you what: 1.01. 51
is apter than thy tongue to tell thy arrand. 1.01. 69
morton, | tell thou an earl his divination lies, 1.01. 88
boy, tell him i am deaf. 1.02. 66 P
the name of rebellion can tell how to make it. 1.02. 77 P
and give me leave to tell you you lie in your 1.02. 84 P
i give thee leave to tell me so? 1.02. 87 P
what tell you me of it? be it as it is. 1.02.114 P
i cannot tell. 1.02.168 P
tell me how many good young princes would do so, 2.02. 29 P
shall i tell thee one thing, poins? 2.02. 32 P
the push of your one thing that you will tell. 2.02. 38 P
i tell thee it is not meet that i should be sad, 2.02. 39 P
father is sick, albeit i could tell to thee — 2.02. 41 P
but i tell thee, my heart bleeds inwardly that 2.02. 47 P
tilly-fally, sir john, ne'er tell me; 2.04. 83 P
now 'a said so, i can tell whereupon. 2.04. 91 P
i tell thee what, corporal bardolph, i could 2.04.153 P
will you tell me, master shallow, how to choose 3.02.257 P
to tell you from his grace | that he will give 4.01.140
fall | as those that i am come to tell you of! 4.04. 96
heard he the good news yet? | tell it him. 4.05. 12
pretty little tiny kickshaws, tell william cook. 5.01. 28 P
dead, | and tell him who hath sent me after him. 5.02. 41
i'll tell thee what, thou damn'd tripe-visag'd 5.04. 8 P
i'll tell you what, you thin man in a censer, i 5.04. 18 P
my lord, i'll tell you, that self bill is urg'd H5 1.01. 1
uncurbed plainness | tell us the dolphin's mind. 1.02.245
tell him he hath made a match with such a 1.02.264
but tell the dolphin i will keep my state, | be 1.02.273
and tell the pleasant prince this mock of his 1.02.281
whose name | tell you the dolphin i am coming on 1.02.291

and tell the dolphin | his jest will savor but 1.02.294
i cannot tell — things must be as they may. 2.01. 20 P
must be conclusions — well, i cannot tell. 2.01. 25 P
and tell the legions, "i can never win | a soul 2.02.124
tell you the duke, it is not so good to come to 3.02. 57 P
you, i will be so bold as to tell you i know the 3.02.140 P
i tell you what, captain gower: 3.06. 82 P
a hole in his coat, i will tell him my mind. 3.06. 84 P
i can tell your majesty, the duke is a prave man 3.06. 96 P
tell him we could have rebuk'd him at harflew, 3.06.120 P
and tell him, for conclusion, he hath betray'd 3.06.134 P
back, | and tell thy king i do not seek him now, 3.06.140
who when they were in health, i tell thee, 3.06.148
go therefore tell thy master here i am; 3.06.153
yet, god before, tell him we will come on, 3.06.156
so tell your master. 3.06.166
i tell thee, constable, my mistress wears his 3.07. 60 P
tell him i'll knock his leek about his pate 4.01. 54
quarrels enow, if you could tell how to reckon. 4.01.223 P
tell the constable | we are but warriors for the 4.03.108
and my poor soldiers tell me, yet ere night, 4.03.116
shall yield them little, tell the constable. 4.03.125
tell him my fury shall abate, and i | the crowns 4.04. 47
i tell you, captain, if you look in the maps of 4.07. 23 P
i'll tell you there is good men porn at monmouth 4.07. 52 P
go and tell them so. 4.07. 65
i tell thee truly, herald, | i know not if the 4.07. 83
plood out of your pody, i can tell you that. 4.07.107 P
i can tell you it will serve you to mend your 4.08. 68 P
this note doth tell me of ten thousand french 4.08. 80
please your majesty, to tell how many is kill'd? 4.08.118 P
i will tell you asse my friend, captain gower: 5.01. 4 P
and then i will tell him a little piece of my 5.01. 13 P
pardonnez-moi, i cannot tell wat is "like me." 5.02.108 P
i cannot tell wat is dat. 5.02.177 P
i will tell thee in french, which i am sure will 5.02.178 P
i cannot tell. 5.02.195 P
can any of your neighbors tell, kate? 5.02.196 P
and therefore tell me, most fair katherine, will 5.02.233 P
mine ear withal, but i will tell thee aloud, 5.02.239 P
i cannot tell wat is /baiser en anglish. 5.02.262 P
the circumstance i'll tell you more at large. 1H6 1.01.109
and therefore tell her i return great thanks, 2.02. 51
i tell you, madam, were the whole frame here, 2.03. 54
but tell me, keeper, will my nephew come? 2.05. 17
o, tell me when my lips do touch his cheeks, 2.05. 39
and in that ease, i'll tell thee my disease. 2.05. 44
believe me, lords, my tender years can tell, 3.01. 71
we came but to tell you | that we are here. 3.02. 73
but tell me whom thou seek'st. 4.07. 59
how canst thou tell she will deny thy suit, 5.03. 75
first let me tell you whom you have condemn'd: 5.04. 36
any passion of inflaming /love, | i cannot tell; 5.05. 83
tell me, and i'll requite it | with sweet 2H6 1.02. 23
i tell thee, pole, when in the city tours | thou 1.03. 50
i'll tell thee, suffolk, why i am unmeet: 1.03.165
tell me, what are these? 1.03.180
the duchess, i tell you, expects performance of 1.04. 1 P
"tell me what fate awaits the duke of suffolk?" 1.04. 64
come to the king and tell him what miracle. 2.01. 60
good fellow, tell us here the circumstance, 2.01. 72
tell me, good fellow, cam'st thou here by chance 2.01. 85
tell me, sirrah, what's my name? 2.01.115
to tell my love unto his dumb deaf trunk, | and 3.02.144
go, salisbury, and tell them all from me, | i 3.02.279
and i am sent to tell his majesty | that even 3.02.377
go tell this heavy message to the king. 3.02.379
i tell thee, jack cade the clothier means to 4.02. 4 P
go to, sirrah, tell the king from me, that, for 4.02.156 P
i tell you that that lord say hath gelded the 4.02.164 P
tell me: 4.07. 97
be as free as heart can wish or tongue can tell. 4.07.125 P
tell him i'll send duke edmund to the tower; 4.09. 38
tell kent from me, she hath lost her best man, 4.10. 73 P
tell me, my friend, art thou the man that slew 5.01. 71
stigmatic, that's more than thou canst tell. 5.01.215
speak thou for me and tell them what i did. 3H6 1.01. 16
tell me, may not a king adopt an heir? 1.01.135
come, cousin, let us tell the queen these news. 1.01.182
norfolk, | and tell him privily of our intent. 1.02. 39
to tell thee whence thou cam'st, of whom deriv'd 1.04.119
i come to tell you things sith then befall'n. 2.01.106
foes | tell our devotion with revengeful arms? 2.01.164
clifford, tell me, didst thou never hear | that 2.02. 45
i'll tell thee what befell me on a day | in this 3.01. 10
and tell me then, have you not broke your oaths? 3.01. 79
how many children hast thou, widow? tell me. 3.02. 26
now tell me, madam, do you love your children? 3.02. 36
i'll tell you how these lands are to be got. 3.02. 42
to tell thee plain, i aim to lie with thee. 3.02. 69
to tell you plain, i had rather lie in prison. 3.02. 70
i can tell you both | her suit is granted for 3.02.116
be plain, queen margaret, and tell thy grief; 3.03. 19
to tell the passion of my sovereign's heart, 3.03. 62
you tell a pedigree | of threescore and two 3.03. 92
now, warwick, tell me, even upon thy conscience, 3.03.113
tell me for truth the measure of his love | unto 3.03.120
and as for clarence, as my letters tell me, 3.03.208
and tell false edward, thy supposed king, | that 3.03.223
tell him, in hope he'll prove a widower shortly, 3.03.227
tell him, my mourning weeds are laid aside, 3.03.229
tell him from me that he hath done me wrong, 3.03.231
now tell me, brother clarence, what think you 4.01. 1
i mind to tell him plainly what i think. 4.01. 8
tell me some reason why the lady grey | should 4.01. 25
tell me their words as near as thou canst guess 4.01. 90
"go tell false edward, the supposed king, | that 4.01. 93
"tell him, in hope he'll prove a widower shortly 4.01. 99
"tell him," quoth she, "my mourning weeds are 4.01.104
"tell him from me that he hath done me wrong, 4.01.110
tell me if you love warwick more than me? 4.01.137
and tell what answer | lewis and the lady bona 4.03. 55
and tell me who is victor, york or warwick? 5.02. 6
dick, i tell ye all | i am your better, traitors 5.05. 35
i'll tell you what, i think it is our way, | if R3 1.01. 78
i tell thee, fellow, | he that doth naught with 1.01. 98
o wonderful, when devils tell the /troth! 1.02. 73
if i thought that, i tell thee, homicide, 1.02.125

i cannot tell, the world is grown so bad | that 1.03. 69
and tell them 'tis the queen and her allies 1.03.329
tell them that god bids us do good for evil: 1.03.334
i pray you tell me. 1.04. 8
i am afraid, methinks, to hear you tell it. 1.04. 65
back to the duke of gloucester and tell him so. 1.04.116 P
you scarcely have the hearts to tell me so, 1.04.175
tell him, when that our princely father york 1.04.235
take thou the fee and tell him what i say, | for 1.04.277
good grandam, tell us, is our father dead? 2.02. 1
if 'twere not she, i cannot tell who told me. 2.04. 34
not | to tell us whether they will come or no! 3.01. 23
i'll tell you what, my cousin buckingham — 3.01. 89
encourage him, and tell him all our reasons; 3.01.175
tell him, catesby, | his ancient knot of 3.01.181
tell him his fears are shallow, without instance 3.02. 25
i'll go, my lord, and tell him what you say. 3.02. 34
i tell thee, man, 'tis better with me now | than 3.02. 98
but now i tell thee (keep it to thyself) | this 3.02.102
sir richard ratcliffe, let me tell thee this: 3.03. 2
tell me what they deserve | that do conspire my 3.04. 59
that by great preservation | we live to tell it, 3.05. 37
tell them how edward put to death a citizen 3.05. 76
tell them, when that my mother went with child 3.05. 86
then he was urg'd to tell my tale again: 3.07. 31
tell him, myself, the mayor and aldermen, | in 3.07. 66
and so once more return and tell his grace. 3.07. 91
i cannot tell if to depart in silence, | or 3.07.141
when thou shalt tell the process of their death. 4.03. 32
tell me, thou villain-slave, where are my 4.04.144
tell me, what state, what dignity, what honor, 4.04.247
tell her thou mad'st away her uncle clarence, 4.04.281
tell her the king, that may command, entreats. 4.04.345
then plainly to her tell my loving tale. 4.04.359
mighty liege, tell me your highness' pleasure, 4.04.447
when thou mayest tell thy tale the nearest way? 4.04.461
then tell me, what makes he upon the seas? 4.04.473
the news i have to tell your majesty | is that 4.04.509
sir christopher, tell richmond this from me: 4.05. 1
but tell me, where is princely richmond now? 4.05. 9
tell me, how fares our loving mother? 5.03. 82
tell the clock there. 5.03.276
but tell me, is young george stanley living? 5.05. 9
i cannot tell | what heaven hath given him — H8 1.01. 66
in that file | where others tell steps with me. 1.02. 43
the king nor 's heirs | (tell you the duke) 1.02.169
thus they pray'd | to tell your grace, that, 1.04. 66
pray tell 'em thus much from me: 1.04. 77
are a churchman, or, i'll tell you, cardinal, 1.04. 88
i'll tell you in a little. 2.01. 11
pray tell him | you met him half in heaven. 2.01. 87
longer than i have time to tell his years; 2.01. 91
i must tell you, | you tender more your person's 2.04.115
ye tell me what ye wish for both — my ruin. 3.01. 98
i pray you tell me, | if what i now pronounce 3.02.162
i should tell you | you have as little honesty 3.02.270
that i can tell you too. 4.01. 24
as i walk thither, | i'll tell ye more. 4.01.117
didst thou not tell me, griffith, as thou ledst 4.02. 5
prithee, good griffith, tell me how he died. 4.02. 9
tell him, in death i blest him, | for so i will. 4.02.163
and, let me tell you, it will ne'er be well — 5.01. 29
day, | sir (i may tell it you), i think i have 5.01. 42
i have news to tell you. 5.01. 94
i was about to tell thee — when my heart, | as TRO 1.01. 34
o pandarus, i tell thee, pandarus — | when i do 1.01. 48
when i do tell thee there my hopes lie drown'd, 1.01. 49
i tell thee i am mad | in cressid's love; 1.01. 51
and so i'll tell her the next time i see her. 1.01. 82 P
tell me, apollo, for thy daphne's love, | what 1.01. 98
lay about him to-day, i can tell them that, and 1.02. 56 P
i can tell them that too. 1.02. 58 P
you shall tell me another tale when th' other's 1.02. 84 P
i'll tell you them all by their names as they 1.02.182 P
he's one of the flowers of troy, i can tell you. 1.02.187 P
he has a shrowd wit, i can tell you, and he's 1.02.191 P
good boy, tell him i come. 1.02.275 P
tell him of nestor, one that was a man | when 1.03.291
tell him from me | i'll hide my silver beard in 1.03.295
/will tell him that my lady | was fairer than 1.03.298
at thy heel, and tell what thou art by inches, 2.01. 48 P
in his head, /i'll tell you what i say of him. 2.01. 74 P
because your speech hath none that tell him so? 2.02. 36
then tell me, patroclus, what's achilles? 2.03. 44 P
then tell me, i pray thee, what's thersites? 2.03. 46 P
then tell me, patroclus, what art thou? 2.03. 48 P
thou must tell that knowest. 2.03. 50 P
o, tell, tell. 2.03. 51 P
o, tell, tell. 2.03. 51 P
go and tell him | we come to speak with him, and 2.03.121
go tell him this, and add, | that if he overhold 2.03.132
tell him so. 2.03.138
they are burs, i can tell you, they'll stick 3.02.111 P
tell him i humbly desire the valiant ajax to 3.03.273 P
and tell me, noble diomed — faith, tell me true 4.01. 52
tell me, noble diomed — faith, tell me true, 4.01. 52
did not i tell you? 4.02. 34
tell me, sweet uncle, what's the matter? 4.02. 81 P
troilus, | tell you the lady what she is to do, 4.03. 4
why tell you me of moderation? 4.04. 2
but i can tell that in each grace of these 4.04. 89
i tell thee, lord of greece, | she is as far 4.04.123
i'll tell thee, diomed, | this brave shall oft 4.04.136
the worthiest of them tell me name by name; 4.05.160
tell me, you heavens, in which part of his body 4.05.242
i tell thee, yea. 4.05.251
wert thou an oracle to tell me so, | i'd not 4.05.252
my lord ulysses, tell me, i beseech you, | in 4.05.277
but gentle tell me, of what honor was | this 4.05.287
i'll tell you what — 5.02. 21
fo, fo, come, tell a pin. you are forsworn. 5.02. 22
come, tell me whose it was. 5.02. 88
and by herself, i will not tell you whose. 5.02. 92
but if i tell how these two did //co-act, 5.02.118
enrapt | to tell thee that this day is ominous: 5.03. 66
deeds worth praise, and tell you them at night. 5.03. 93
were curs'd, i cannot tell what to think on't. 5.03.106 P
tell her i have chastis'd the amorous troyan, 5.05. 4

you understand me not that tell me so. 5.10. 11
who shall tell priam so, or hecuba? 5.10. 15
i tell you, friends, most charitable care | have COR 1.01. 65
i shall tell you | a pretty tale. 1.01. 89
sir, i shall tell you. 1.01.107
i will tell you; 1.01.124
i tell thee, daughter, i sprang not more in joy 1.03. 15 P
tell valeria | we are fit to bid her welcome. 1.03. 43
and i'll tell you excellent news of your husband 1.03. 89 P
will the time serve to tell? 1.06. 46
if i should tell thee o'er this thy day's work, 1.09. 1
tell me one thing that i shall ask you. 2.01. 13 P
they lie deadly that tell you have good faces. 2.01. 61 P
if he show us his wounds and tell us his deeds, 2.03. 6 P
so, if he tell us his noble deeds, we must also 2.03. 8 P
we must also tell him our noble acceptance of 2.03. 8 P
we do, sir, tell us what hath brought you to't. 2.03. 63 P
and tell those friends | they have chose a 2.03.213
tell me of corn! 3.01. 61
and tell me | in peace what each of them by th' 3.02. 43
tell these sad women | 'tis fond to wail 4.01. 25
i'll tell thee what — yet go! 4.02. 22
this lies glowing, i can tell you, and is almost 4.03. 25 P
supper, tell you most strange things from rome, 4.03. 40 P
prithee tell my master what a strange guest he 4.05. 34 P
why, thou mars, i tell thee, | we have a power 4.05.118
face, methought — i cannot tell how to term it. 4.05.156 P
look you, one cannot tell how to say that. 4.05.169 P
o slaves, i can tell you news — news, you 4.05.172 P
tell not me! | i know this cannot be. 4.06. 56
i tell you, he does sit in gold, his eye | red 5.01. 63
i tell thee, fellow, | thy general is my lover. 5.02. 13
has he din'd, canst thou tell? 5.02. 34 P
tell me not | wherein i seem unnatural; 5.03. 83
this boy, that cannot tell what he would have, 5.03.174
go tell the lords a' th' city i am here. 5.06. 1
sir, i cannot tell, | we must proceed as we do 5.06. 14
but tell the traitor, in the highest degree | he 5.06. 84
proud and ambitious tribune, canst thou tell? TIT 1.01.202
tell me, andronicus, doth this motion please 1.01.243
(whether by device or no, the heavens can tell). 1.01.395
i tell you, lords, you do but plot your deaths 2.01. 78
more | that womanhood denies my tongue to tell. 2.03.174
o, tell me who it is, for ne'er till now | was i 2.03.220
so now go tell, and if thy tongue can speak, 2.04. 1
therefore i tell my sorrows to the stones, | who 3.01. 37
nor tongue to tell me who hath mart'red thee. 3.01.107
tell him it was a hand that warded him | from 3.01.194
o, tell me, did you see aaron the moor? 4.02. 52
i tell you, younglings, not enceladus, | with 4.02. 93
tell the empress from me, i am of age | to keep 4.02.104
go to the empress, tell her this i said. 4.02.145
and tell them both the circumstance of all, 4.02.156
tell him it is for justice and for aid, | and 4.03. 15
tell me, can you deliver an oration to the 4.03. 98 P
knock at my door, and tell me what he says. 4.03.119
tell on thy mind, i say thy child shall live. 5.01. 69
tell him revenge is come to join with him, | and 5.02. 7
and in their ears tell them my dreadful name, 5.02. 39
tell him the emperor and the empress too | feast 5.02.127
whiles i go tell my lord the emperor | how i 5.02.138
tell us, old man, how shall we be employ'd? 5.02.149
what, was she ravish'd? tell who did the deed. 5.03. 53
tell us what sinon hath bewitch'd our ears, | or 5.03. 85
rome's young captain, let him tell the tale, 5.03. 94
yet tell me not, for i have heard it all: ROM 1.01.174
tell me in sadness, who is that you love? 1.01.199
what, shall i groan and tell thee? 1.01.200
groan? why, no; | but sadly tell me, who? 1.01.201
vow | do i live dead that live to tell it now. 1.01.224
now i'll tell you without asking. 1.02. 78 P
faith, i can tell her age unto an hour. 1.03. 11
tell me, daughter juliet, | how stands your 1.03. 64
that i have worn a visor and could tell | a 1.05. 22
will you tell me that? 1.05. 39
i tell you, he that can lay hold of her | shall 1.05.116
a name | i know not how to tell thee who i am. 2.02. 54
how camest thou hither, tell me, and wherefore? 2.02. 62
his help to crave, and my dear hap to tell. 2.02.189
i'll tell thee ere thou ask it me again. 2.03. 48
i'll tell thee as we pass, but this i pray, 2.03. 63
'tis no less, i tell ye, for the bawdy hand of 2.04.112 P
can any of you tell me where i may find the 2.04.118 P
i can tell you, but young romeo will be older 2.04.120 P
but first let me tell ye, if ye should lead her 2.04.165 P
heart, and, i' faith, i will tell her as much. 2.04.173 P
what wilt thou tell her, nurse? 2.04.175 P
i will tell her, sir, that you do protest, which 2.04.177 P
her sometimes and tell her that paris is the 2.04.204 P
though news be sad, yet tell them merrily; 2.05. 22
sweet, sweet nurse, tell me, what says my love? 2.05. 54
o holy friar, o tell me, holy friar, | where's 3.03. 81
o, tell me, friar, tell me, | in what vile part 3.03.105
o, tell me, friar, tell me, | in what vile part 3.03.105
tell me, that i may sack | the hateful mansion. 3.03.107
my lord, i'll tell my lady you will come. 3.03.161
a' thursday let it be — a' thursday, tell her, 3.04. 20
but now i'll tell thee joyful tidings, girl. 3.05.104
i pray you tell my lord and father, madam, | i 3.05.120
here comes your father, tell him so yourself; 3.05.124
i tell thee what: 3.05.161
go in, and tell my lady i am gone, | having 3.05.231
tell me not, friar, that thou hearest of this, 4.01. 50
unless thou tell me how i may prevent it. 4.01. 51
give me, give me! o, tell not me of fear! 4.01.121
send for the county, go tell him of this. 4.02. 23
vault, | and presently took post to tell it you. 5.01. 21
tell me, good my friend, | what torch is yond, 5.03.124
go tell the prince, run to the capulets, | raise 5.03.177
else i should tell him well (i' faith, i should) TIM 1.02.161
i'll tell you true, i'll call to you. 1.02.217
hand, thus — but tell him | my uses cry to me; 2.01. 19
you tell me true. 2.02.154
but i can tell you one thing, my lord, and which 3.02. 4 P
i tell you, denied, my lord. 3.02. 16 P
and tell him this from me, i count it one of my 3.02. 55 P
i need not tell him that, he knows you are too 3.04. 39 P
tell out my blood. 3.04. 94

i'll tell you more anon. 3.06. 59 P
if thou wilt, | tell them there i have gold; 4.03.289
but tell me true | (for i must ever doubt, 4.03.506
tell him of an intent | that's coming toward him 5.01. 20
then let him know, and tell him timon speaks it, 5.01.175
i cannot choose but tell him that i care not, 5.01.177
and tell them that, to ease them of their griefs 5.01.198
tell my friends, | tell athens, in the sequence 5.01.207
tell athens, in the sequence of degree, | from 5.01.208
tell me, good brutus, can you see your face? JC 1.02. 51
i cannot tell what you and other men | think of 1.02. 93
tell you | what hath proceeded worthy note 1.02.180
casca will tell us what the matter is. 1.02.189
i rather tell thee what is to be fear'd | than 1.02.211
and tell me truly what thou think'st of him. 1.02.214
tell us what hath chanc'd to–day | that caesar 1.02.217
tell us the manner of it, gentle casca. 1.02.234
can as well be hang'd as tell the manner of it: 1.02.235 P
nay, and i tell you that, i'll ne'er look you i' 1.02.281 P
i could tell you more news too. 1.02.284 P
am i not stay'd for? tell me. 1.03.139
but when i tell him he hates flatterers | he 2.01.207
within the bond of marriage, tell me, brutus, 2.01.280
tell me your counsels, i will not disclose 'em. 2.01.298
here's decius brutus, he shall tell them so. 2.02. 57
and tell them that i will not come to–day. 2.02. 62
tell them so, decius. 2.02. 64
to be afeard to tell greybeards the truth? 2.02. 67
decius, go tell them caesar will not come. 2.02. 68
lest i be laugh'd at when i tell them so. 2.02. 70
love | to your proceeding bids me tell you this; 2.02.103
ere i can tell thee what thou shouldst do there. 2.04. 5
so tell them, publius. 3.01. 91
tell him, so please him come unto this place, 3.01.140
back with speed, and tell him what hath chanc'd. 3.01.287
hie hence, and tell him so. 3.01.290
i have o'ershot myself to tell you of it. 3.02.150
i tell you that which you yourselves do know, 3.02.224
i must tell you then: 3.02.237
let me tell you, cassius, you yourself | are 4.03. 9
now as you are a roman tell me true. 4.03.187
then like a roman bear the truth i tell: 4.03.188
to tell thee thou shalt see me at philippi. 4.03.283
and tell me what thou not'st about the field. 5.03. 22
room ho! tell antony, brutus is ta'en. 5.04. 16
i'll tell /the news. 5.04. 17
or memorize another golgotha, | i cannot tell — MAC 1.02. 41
stay, you imperfect speakers, tell me more: 1.03. 70
the instruments of darkness tell us truths, 1.03.124
sir, can you tell | where he bestows himself? 3.06. 23
tell me, thou unknown power — 4.01. 69
that i may tell pale–hearted fear it lies, | and 4.01. 85
tell me, if your art | can tell so much, shall 4.01.101
if your art | can tell so much, shall banquo's 4.01.102
i tell you yet again, banquo's buried; 5.01. 63 P
angel whom thou still hast serv'd | tell thee, 5.08. 15
good now, sit down, and tell me, he that knows, HAM 1.01. 70
but the great cannon to the clouds shall tell, 1.02.126
one with moderate haste might tell a hundreth. 1.02.237
and that in way of caution — i must tell you, 1.03. 95
ignorance, but tell | why thy canoniz'd bones, 1.04. 46
forbid | to tell the secrets of my prison–house, 1.05. 14
good my lord, tell it. 1.05.119
my lord, come from the grave | to tell us this. 1.05.126
it is an honest ghost, that let me tell you. 1.05.138
as i perceiv'd it (i must tell you that) 2.02.133
i will tell you why, so shall my anticipation 2.02.293 P
which, i tell you, must show fairly outwards, 2.02.373 P
prophesy, he comes to tell me of the players, 2.02.386 P
my lord, i have news to tell you. 2.02.389 P
my lord, i have news to tell you. 2.02.390 P
you need not tell us what lord hamlet said, | we 3.01.179
players cannot keep /counsel, they'll tell all. 3.02.142 P
will 'a tell us what this show meant? 3.02.143 P
show, he'll not shame to tell you what it means. 3.02.145 P
ere you go to bed, | and tell you what i know. 3.03. 35
tell him his pranks have been too broad to bear 3.04. 2
tell us where 'tis, that we may take it thence, 4.02. 7
my lord, you must tell us where the body is, and 4.02. 25 P
tell him that by his license fortinbras | craves 4.04. 2
tell me, laertes, | why thou art thus incens'd. 4.05.126
for england, of them i have much to tell thee. 4.06. 29 P
but tell me | why you /proceeded not against 4.07. 5
that i /shall live and tell him to his teeth, 4.07. 56
i tell thee she is, therefore make her grave 5.01. 3 P
ay, tell me that, and unyoke. 5.01. 52 P
marry, now i can tell. 5.01. 53 P
mass, i cannot tell. 5.01. 55 P
and will not tell him of his action of battery? 5.01.102 P
cannot you tell that? 5.01.146 P
every fool can tell that. 5.01.146 P
now get you to my lady's /chamber, and tell her, 5.01.193 P
prithee, horatio, tell me one thing. 5.01.195 P
i tell thee, churlish priest, | a minist'ring 5.01.240
very sultry — as 'twere — i cannot tell how. 5.02.101 P
strict in his arrest — o, i could tell you — 5.02.337
draw thy breath in pain | to tell my story. 5.02.349
so tell him, with th' occurrents, more and less, 5.02.357
to tell him his commandment is fulfill'd, | that 5.02.370
tell me, my daughters | (since now we will LR 1.01. 48
from my throat, | i'll tell thee thou dost evil. 1.01.166
pow'r that made me, | i tell you all her wealth. 1.01.208
go you and tell my daughter i would speak with 1.04. 76 P
prithee tell him, so much the rent of his land 1.04.134 P
who is it that can tell me who i am? 1.04.230
i'll tell thee. 1.04.296
how far your eyes may pierce i cannot tell: 1.04.345
like an apple, yet i can tell what i can tell. 1.05. 16 P
like an apple, yet i can tell what i can tell. 1.05. 16 P
what canst tell, boy? 1.05. 17 P
thou canst tell why one's nose stands i' th' 1.05. 19 P
canst tell how an oyster makes his shell? 1.05. 25 P
but i can tell why a snail has a house. 1.05. 27 P
prithee, if thou lov'st me, tell me. 2.02. 6 P
for thy daughters as thou canst tell in a year. 2.04. 55 P
tell the hot duke that — | no, but not yet, may 2.04.104
go tell the duke, and 's wife, i'ld speak with 2.04.116
nor tell tales of thee to high–judging jove. 2.04.228
and she will tell you who that fellow is | that 3.01. 48
when usurers tell their gold i' th' field, | and 3.02. 91
thou sayest the king grows mad, i'll tell thee, 3.04.165
true to tell thee, | the grief hath craz'd my 3.04.169
tell me whether a madman be a gentleman or a 3.06. 9 P
friend, | tell me what more thou know'st. 4.02. 97
that of thy death and business i can tell. 4.06.278
tell me but truly, but then speak the truth, 5.01. 8
and sing, and tell old tales, and laugh | at 5.03. 12
i'll tell you straight. 5.03.280
he's a good fellow, i can tell you that; 5.03.285
/tush, never tell me! OTH 1.01. 1
that comes to tell you your daughter and the 1.01.115 P
my manners tell me | we have your wrong rebuke. 1.01.129
to th' very moment that he bade me tell it; 1.03.133
i should but teach him how to tell my story, 1.03.165
what tidings can you tell /me of my lord? 2.01. 88
first, i must tell thee this: 2.01.218 P
place again, he shall tell me i am a drunkard! 2.03.303 P
/i'll tell you what you shall do. 2.03.314 P
tell her there's one cassio entreats her a 3.01. 25 P
tell me, othello. 3.03. 68
tell me but this, | have you not sometimes seen 3.03.433
to tell you where he lodges, is to tell you 3.04. 8 P
you where he lodges, is to tell you where i lie. 3.04. 8 P
tell him i have mov'd my lord on his behalf, and 3.04. 18 P
face, | for i will make him tell the tale anew: 4.01. 84
now he importunes him | to tell it o'er. 4.01.114
i cannot tell. 4.02.111
i tell you 'tis not very well. 4.02.196 P
dost thou in conscience think — tell me, emilia 4.03. 61
come, mistress, you must tell 's another tale. 5.01.125
and tell my lord and lady what hath happ'd. 5.01.127
but did you ever tell him she was false? 5.02.178
if it be love indeed, tell me how much. ANT 1.01. 14
nay, come, tell iras hers. 1.02. 43 P
prithee tell her but a worky–day fortune. 1.02. 54 P
which seem'd to tell them his remembrance lay 1.05. 57
i will tell you. 2.02.190 P
but let ill tidings tell | themselves when they 2.05. 87
be pleas'd to tell us | (for this is from the 2.06. 29
tell me of that? 2.07. 53
i'll tell you in your ear. 3.02. 46
the neighs of horse to tell of her approach, 3.06. 45
tell him he wears the rose | of youth upon him; 3.13. 20
tell him, i am prompt | to lay my crown at 's 3.13. 75
tell him, from his all–obeying breath i hear 3.13. 77
back to caesar, | tell him thy entertainment. 3.13.140
and what is done, tell him he has | hipparchus, 3.13.148
mock not, enobarbus, | i tell you true. 4.06. 25
tell them your feats, whilst they with joyful 4.08. 9
auguries | say they know not, they cannot tell, 4.12. 5
mardian, go tell him i have slain myself; 4.13. 7
to tell them that this world did equal theirs 4.15. 77
tell him he mocks | the pauses that he makes. 5.01. 2
but i will tell you at some meeter season. 5.01. 49
antony | did tell me of you, bade me trust you, 5.02. 13
his beggar, you must tell him | that majesty, to 5.02. 16
pray you tell him | i am his fortune's vassal, 5.02. 28
i cannot tell. 5.02. 72
you laugh when boys or women tell their dreams; 5.02. 74
i am loath to tell you what i would you knew. 5.02.107
love makes religion to obey), | i tell you this: 5.02.200
but pray you tell me, | is she sole child to th' CYM 1.01. 55
ere i could tell him | how i would think on him 1.03. 26
i'll tell thee on the instant thou art then | as 1.05. 50
tell thy mistress how | the case stands with her 1.05. 66
i hope it be not gone to tell my lord | that i 2.03.147
read, and tell me | how far 'tis thither. 3.02. 49
th' way | tell me how wales was made so happy as 3.02. 60
when on my three–foot stool i sit and tell | the 3.03. 89
his service, tell him | wherein you're happy — 3.04.173
no wonder, | when rich ones scarce tell true. 3.06. 12
i cannot tell; 4.02.103
and tell the fishes he's the queen's son, cloten 4.02.153
a leg of rome shall not return to tell | what 5.03. 92
end, i think you'll never return to tell one. 5.04.184 P
i tell thee, fellow, there are none want eyes to 5.04.185 P
i'll tell you, sir, in private, if you please 5.05.115
not standing here | to tell this tale of mine. 5.05.297
all syria — | i tell you what mine authors say. PER 1.ch. 20
tell thee, with speechless tongues and semblance 1.01. 36
but i must tell you, now my thoughts revolt, 1.01. 78
braid yourself too near for me to tell it. 1.01. 93
heaven, to tell the earth is throng'd | by man's 1.01.101
nor tell the world antiochus doth sin | in such 1.01.146
go tell their general we attend him here, | to 1.04. 79
sea | these fishers tell the infirmities of men, 2.01. 49
why, i'll tell you. 2.01. 99 P
and i'll tell you, he hath a fair daughter, and 2.01.108 P
and furthermore tell him, we desire to know of 2.03. 73
to the pothecary, | and tell me how it works. 3.02. 10
and i prithee tell me, how dost thou find the 4.02. 96 P
prithee tell me one thing first. 4.06.156 P
if i should tell my history, it would seem 5.01.118
tell thy story; 5.01.134
most wise in general, tell me, if thou canst, 5.01.183
she never would tell | her parentage; 5.01.187
tell me but that, | for truth can never be 5.01.200
but tell me now | my drown'd queen's name, as in 5.01.204
she shall tell thee all; 5.01.216
tell helicanus, my marina, tell him | o'er, 5.01.224
my marina, tell him | o'er, point by point, for 5.01.224
awake, and tell thy dream. 5.01.249
eftsoons i'll tell thee why. 5.01.255
tell him, if he i' th' blood–siz'd field lay TNK 1.01. 99
tell us | when we know all ourselves, and let us 1.02.114
or tell of babes broach'd on the lance, or women 1.03. 20
i can tell you they are princes. 2.01. 20 P
to tell the world 'tis but a gaudy shadow | that 2.02.103
i cannot tell what you have done; 2.02.156
dirge, | and tell to memory my death was noble, 2.06. 16
tell me, o lady fortune | (next after emily my 3.01. 15
i'll tell you | after a draught or two more. 3.03. 18
he would tell me | news from all parts o' th' 3.04. 12
and she fail me once — you can tell, arcas, 3.05. 46
i can tell your fortune. 3.05. 78
tell ten — i have pos'd him. 3.05. 79
pray thee tell me, cousin, | where got'st thou 3.06. 53
that i may tell my soul he shall not have her. 3.06.179
i'll tell you quickly. 4.01. 52
them with her | and hither came to tell you. 4.01.103
but she shall never have him, tell her so, | for 4.01.122
faith, i'll tell you; 4.03. 30 P
will, and tell her | her palamon stays for her; 5.02. 25
i prithee run | and tell me how it goes. 5.03. 71
thing | i shall be glad of, prithee tell her so. 5.04. 30
the calkins | did rather tell than trample; 5.04. 56
i'll tell you: STM II.C 80
this' a sound fellow i tell you, let's mark him. II.C 89 P
tell me, love's master, shall we meet to–morrow? VEN 585
"more i could tell, but more i dare not say, 805
lies, | do tell her she is dreadfully beset, LUC 444
shall plead for me and tell my loving tale. 480
nurse, to still her child, will tell my story, 813
"but tell me, girl, when went" (and there she 1275
when more is felt than one hath power to tell. 1288
sad tales doth tell | to pencill'd pensiveness 1496
and tell thy grief, that we may give redress. 1603
to tell them all with one poor tired tongue. 1617
fiend, | suspect i may (yet not directly tell): PP 2.10
and when thou com'st thy tale to tell, | smooth 18. 7
look in thy glass and tell the face thou viewest SON 3. 1
but not to tell of good or evil luck, | of 14. 3
nor can i fortune to brief minutes tell, 14. 5
i tell the day, to please him, thou art bright, 28. 9
and heavily from woe to woe tell o'er | the sad 30.10
of you, if he can tell | that you are you, so 84. 7
wrong, | and haply of our old acquaintance tell. 89.12
looks should nothing thence but sweetness tell. 93.12
in hue, | could make me any summer's story tell, 98. 7
than of your graces and your gifts to tell; 103.12
tell me thou lov'st elsewhere, but in my sight, 139. 5
though not to love, yet, love, to tell me so, 140. 6
fiend | suspect i may, yet not directly tell, 144.10
my soul doth tell my body that he may | triumph 151. 7
hour, | let it not tell your judgment i am old, LC 73
"'how mighty then you are, o, hear me tell! 253

TELL–A 2 FR 0.0002 REL FR 0 V 2 P
do not you tell–a me dat i shall have anne page WIV 1.04.116 P
but it is tell–a me dat you make grand 4.05. 86 P

TELLER 1 FR 0.0001 REL FR 1 V 0 P
the nature of bad news infects the teller. ANT 1.02. 95

TELLEST 1 FR 0.0001 REL FR 0 V 1 P
what tellest thou me of black and blue? WIV 4.05.114 P

TELLING 27 FR 0.0030 REL FR 16 V 11 P
one | who having into truth, by telling of it, TMP 1.02.100
prove as hard to you in telling your mind. TGV 1.01.139 P
i telling you then (if you be rememb'red) that MM 2.01.109 P
out of thy tale into telling me of the fashion? ADO 3.03.142 P
say it is so, he is, in telling true — but so. LLL 1.01.225 P
(good my glass), take this for telling true: 4.01. 18
the wisest aunt, telling the saddest tale, MND 2.01. 51
telling the bushes that thou look'st for wars, 3.02.408
we will have no telling. SHR 5.02.132
telling them i know my place as i would they TN 2.05. 53 P
gard'ner, for telling me these news of woe, R2 3.04.100
and telling me the sovereignest thing on earth 1H4 1.03. 57
coz, to shame the devil | by telling truth: 3.01. 58
with telling me of the moldwarp and the ant, 3.01.147
telling us she had a good dish of prawns, 2H4 2.01. 96 P
breeds no bate with telling of discreet stories; 2.04.250 P
with eleanor, for telling but her dream? 2H6 1.02. 52
threat you me with telling of the king? R3 1.03.112
last longer telling than thy kindness' date. 4.04.255
i can watch you for telling how i took the blow TRO 1.02.268 P
i am one that, telling true under him, must say COR 5.02. 32 P
mar a curious tale in telling it, and deliver a LR 1.04. 33 P
but for bragging and telling her fantastical OTH 2.01.223 P
though i lose | the praise of it by telling, you ANT 2.06. 43
give | is telling you that i am poor of thanks, CYM 2.03. 89
your breath cool yourself, telling your haste. PER 1.01.159
old, | so is my love still telling what is told. SON 76.14

/TELLS 1 FR 0.0001 REL FR 1 V 0 P
/tells /them /he /doth /bestride /a /bleeding 2H4 1.01.207

TELLS 50 FR 0.0056 REL FR 37 V 13 P
and tells you currish thanks is good enough for TGV 4.04. 49 P
and tells me 'tis a thing impossible | i should WIV 3.04. 9
may be he tells you true. 3.04. 11
tells me there is three cozen–germans that has 4.05. 76 P
besides, he tells me that, if peradventure | he MM 4.06. 5
but she tells to your highness simple truth! ERR 5.01.211
my cousin tells him in his ear that he is in her ADO 2.01.315 P
my daughter tells us all. 2.03.133 P
indeed that tells a heavy tale for him. 3.02. 61 P
as valiant as hercules that only tells a lie, 4.01.322 P
there's something tells me (but it is not love) MV 3.02. 4
he tells me flatly there's no mercy for me in 3.05. 32 P
you, sir, he tells you flatly what his mind is. SHR 1.02. 77 P
he tells her something | that makes her blood WT 4.04.159
he's simple, and tells much. 4.04.345
sudden, tells us | 'tis not a visitation fram'd, 5.01. 90
gracing the scroll that tells of this war's loss JN 2.01.348
he tells us arthur is deceas'd to–night. 4.02. 85
sir, the sound that tells what hour it is | are R2 5.05. 55
the rest the paper tells. 2H4 2.01.135
there is a thing within my bosom tells me | that 4.01.181
back, | tells harry that the king doth offer him H5 3.pr. 29
a saving faith within me tells me thou shalt, i 5.02.204 P
my conscience tells me you are innocent. 2H6 3.01.141
my conscience tells me he is lawful king. 3H6 1.01.150
whiles warwick tells his title, smooths the 3.01. 48
was wont to hold me but while one tells twenty. R3 1.04.119 P
he tells you rightly. H8 3.01. 97
troyan, he is awake, | he tells thee so himself. TRO 1.03.256
the augurer tells me we shall have news to–night COR 2.01. 1 P
accursed be that tongue that tells me so, | for MAC 5.08. 17
he tells me, my dear gertrude, he hath found HAM 2.02. 54
and tells me nero is an angler in the lake of LR 3.06. 6 P
what damned minutes tells he o'er | who dotes, OTH 3.03.169
now he tells how she pluck'd him to my chamber. 4.01.141 P
who tells me true, though in his tale lie death, ANT 1.02. 98
than she which by her death our caesar tells, 4.14. 61
for her physician tells me | she hath pursu'd 5.02.354
who tells us life's but breath, to trust it PER 1.01. 46
which tells /me in that glory once he was; 2.03. 38

she tells me here, she'll wed the stranger 2.05. 16
hear nothing but the clock that tells our woes; TNK 2.02. 42
king of pigmies, | for he tells fortunes rarely. 3.04. 16
him i do not love that tells close offices | the 5.01.122
he tells her, no, to-morrow he intends | to hunt VEN 587
she tells them 'tis a causeless fantasy | and 897
tells him of trophies, statues, tombs, and 1013
marking what he tells | with trembling fear, as LUC 510
when i do count the clock that tells the time, SON 12. 1
that tongue that tells the story of thy days 95. 5
TELL'ST 11 FR 0.0012 REL FR 11 V 0 P
what tell'st thou me of supping? ERR 4.03. 65
thou tell'st me there is murder in mine eye: AYL 3.05. 10
unless thou tell'st me where thou hadst this AWW 5.03.283
too well, too well thou tell'st a tale so ill. R2 3.02.121
yet tell'st thou not how thou wert entertain'd. 1H6 1.04. 38
and if thou tell'st the heavy story right, 3H6 1.04.160
this thou tell'st me, | as true thou tell'st me, TRO 1.01. 59
as true thou tell'st me, when i say i love her, 1.01. 60
what tell'st thou me of robbing? OTH 1.01.105
thou tell'st the world | it is not worth ANT 5.02.297
done is more | unlike than this thou tell'st. CYM 5.05.354
TELL-TALE 5 FR 0.0005 REL FR 4 V 1 P
i warrant you, no tell-tale nor no breed-bate. WIV 1.04. 12 P
clean | and keep no tell-tale to his memory 2H4 4.01.200
let not the heavens hear these tell-tale women R3 4.04.150
to such a man | that is no fleering tell-tale. JC 1.03.117
"make me not object to the tell-tale day, | the LUC 806
TELL-TALES 2 FR 0.0002 REL FR 2 V 0 P
shall these papers lie like tell-tales here? TGV 1.02.130
we are no tell-tales, madam, fear you not. MV 5.01.123
TELLUS' 1 FR 0.0001 REL FR 1 V 0 P
neptune's salt wash and tellus' orbed ground, HAM 3.02.156
TELLUS 4 FR 0.0004 REL FR 2 V 2 P
hic est /sigeia tellus; SHR 3.01. 28
son unto vincentio of pisa, "/sigeia tellus," 3.01. 33 P
i know you not, "hic est /sigeia tellus," i 3.01. 43 P
i will rob tellus of her weed | to strow thy PER 4.01. 13
TEMPER 38 FR 0.0043 REL FR 32 V 6 P
where you may temper her by your persuasion | to TGV 3.02. 64
vigor, art and nature, | once stir my temper; MM 2.02.184
the poison of that lies in you to temper. ADO 2.02. 21 P
but a hot temper leaps o'er a cold decree — MV 1.02. 19 P
my lord, | you know /your father's temper. WT 4.04.467
a noble temper dost thou show in this, | and JN 5.02. 40
base | to stain the temper of my knightly sword. R2 4.01. 29
he holds your temper in a high respect, | and 1H4 3.01.168
whose temper i intend to stain | with the best 5.02. 93
what man of good temper would endure this 2H4 2.01. 81 P
his temper therefore must be well observ'd. 4.04. 36
o that the living harry had the temper | of he, 5.02. 15
if thou canst love a fellow of this temper, kate H5 5.02.146 P
two blades, which bears the better temper, 1H6 2.04. 13
and temper clay with blood of englishmen. 2H6 3.01.311
sword, hold thy temper; 5.02. 70
for few men rightly temper with the stars; 3H6 4.06. 29
hearts of most hard temper | melt and lament for H8 2.03. 11
i know you have a gentle, noble temper, | a soul 3.01.165
you keep a constant temper. COR 5.02. 94
and temper him with all the art i have, | to TIT 4.04.109
small, | and with this hateful liquor temper it, 5.02.199
and in my temper soft'ned valor's steel! ROM 3.01.115
but a man | to bear a poison, i would temper it, 3.05. 97
his comfortable temper has forsook him, he's TIM 3.04. 71 P
a man of such a feeble temper should | so get JC 1.02.129
and our hearts | of brothers' temper, do receive 3.01.175
and, to that dauntless temper of his mind, | he MAC 3.01. 51
the waters that you loose, | to temper clay. LR 1.04.304
keep me in temper, i would not be mad! 1.05. 47
was a sword of spain, the ice-brook's temper — OTH 5.02.253
the buckles on his breast, reneges all temper, ANT 1.01. 8
patient after the noble temper of your lordship. CYM 2.03. 5 P
oft importun'd me | to temper poisons for her, 5.05.250
their valiant temper | men lose when they TNK 3.01. 66
a still temper, | no stirring in him, no 4.02. 28
fear he cannot, | he shows no such soft temper. 4.02.103
to find a nation of such barbarous temper | that STM II.C 131
TEMPERALITY 1 FR 0.0001 REL FR 0 V 1 P
now you are in an excellent good temperality. 2H4 2.04. 23 P
TEMPERANCE 9 FR 0.0010 REL FR 5 V 4 P
be of subtle, tender, and delicate temperance. TMP 2.01. 43 P
"temperance" was a delicate wench. 2.01. 44 P
a gentleman of all temperance. MM 3.02.237 P
he cannot | be rein'd again to temperance; COR 3.03. 28
acquire and beget a temperance that may give it HAM 3.02. 7 P
do awake him, | i doubt /not of his temperance. LR 4.07. 23
though you can guess what temperance should be, ANT 3.13.121
o, temperance, lady! 5.02. 48
thou blowest the fire when temperance is thaw'd, LUC 884
TEMPERATE 8 FR 0.0009 REL FR 7 V 1 P
come, temperate nymphs, and help to celebrate TMP 4.01.132
she is not hot, but temperate as the morn; SHR 2.01.294
peace, lady, pause, or be more temperate. JN 2.01.195
such temperate order in so fierce a cause, 3.04. 12
my blood hath been too cold and temperate, 1H4 1.03. 1
whiles yet the cool and temperate wind of grace H5 3.03. 30
there was a more temperate fire under the pot of TRO 1.02.146 P
thou art more lovely and more temperate: SON 18. 2
TEMPERATELY 2 FR 0.0002 REL FR 2 V 0 P
nay, temperately; your promise. COR 3.03. 67
my pulse, as yours, doth temperately keep time, HAM 3.04.140
TEMPER'D 9 FR 0.0010 REL FR 8 V 1 P
of whom your swords are temper'd, may as well TMP 3.03. 62
blood | and lack of temper'd judgment afterward. MM 5.01.473
were so righteously temper'd as mine is to thee. AYL 1.02. 14 P
to you | when you are better temper'd to attend. 1H4 1.03.235
but he that temper'd thee, bade thee stand up, H5 2.02.118
as green as ajax', and your brain so temper'd, TRO 2.03.254
when was my lord so much ungently temper'd | to 5.03. 1
i thought thy disposition better temper'd. ROM 3.03.115
served, | it is a poison temper'd by himself. HAM 5.02.328
/TEMPERS 1 FR 0.0001 REL FR 1 V 0 P
'tis she | that /tempers him to this extremity. R3 1.01. 65
TEMPERS 1 FR 0.0001 REL FR 1 V 0 P
in whom the tempers and the minds of all TRO 1.03. 57
TEMPEST 48 FR 0.0054 REL FR 44 V 4 P
perform'd to point the tempest that i bade thee? TMP 1.02.194
i did say so, | when first i rais'd the tempest. 5.01. 6
in this last tempest. 5.01.153
what tempest, i trow, threw this whale (with so WIV 2.01. 64 P
let there come a tempest of provocation, i will 5.05. 21 P
well | beteem them from the tempest of my eyes. MND 1.01.131
so, by a roaring tempest on the flood, | a whole JN 3.04. 1
cloak and center can | hold out this tempest. 4.03.156
it was my breath that blew this tempest up, 5.01. 17
this show'r, blown up by tempest of the soul, 5.02. 50
this low'ring tempest of your home-bred hate, R2 1.03.187
but, lords, we hear this fearful tempest sing, 2.01.263
such crimson tempest should bedrench | the fresh 3.03. 46
foretells a tempest and a blust'ring day. 1H4 5.01. 6
temper would endure this tempest of exclamation? 2H4 2.01. 81 P
when tempest of commotion, like the south 2.04.363
therefore in fierce tempest is he coming, | in H5 2.04. 99
and this fell tempest shall not cease to rage 2H6 3.01.351
when from thy shore the tempest beat us back, 3.02.102
like to the summer's corn by tempest lodged. 3.02.176
like to a ship that, having scap'd a tempest, 4.09. 32
to keep thee from the tempest of the field. 5.01.197
blown with the windy tempest of my heart | upon 3H6 2.05. 86
bowl'd, and hideous tempest shook down trees; 5.06. 46
o, then began the tempest to my soul! R3 1.04. 44
the britain navy is dispers'd by tempest. 4.04.521
that this tempest, | dashing the garment of this H8 1.01. 92
as the shrouds make at sea in a stiff tempest, 4.01. 72
but, in the wind and tempest of her frown, TRO 1.03. 26
heart | that dies in tempest of thy angry frown. TIT 1.01.458
to calm this tempest whirling in the court; 4.02.160
now, | did i go through a tempest dropping fire. JC 1.03. 10
gently, for in the very torrent, tempest, and, HAM 3.02. 6 P
friendship will it lend you 'gainst the tempest. LR 3.02. 62
/this tempest in my mind | doth from my senses 3.04. 12
this tempest will not give me leave to ponder 3.04. 24
the desperate tempest hath so bang'd the turks, OTH 2.01. 21
were parted | with foul and violent tempest. 2.01. 34
if after every tempest come such calms, | may 2.01.185
how i might stop this tempest ere it came, | and PER 1.02. 98
grisled north | disgorges such a tempest forth, 3.ch. 48
maid, | born in a tempest when my mother died, 4.01. 18
he bears | a tempest, which his mortal vessel 4.04. 30
did you not name a tempest, | a birth, and death 5.03. 33
to shelter thee from tempest and from rain: VEN 238
wrack to the seaman, tempest to the field, 454
rain, | but lust's effect is tempest after sun; 800
this windy tempest, till it blow up rain, | held LUC 1788
TEMPESTS 6 FR 0.0006 REL FR 5 V 1 P
tempests are kind and salt waves fresh in love. TN 3.04.384
i have seen tempests when the scolding winds JC 1.03. 5
tempests themselves, high seas, and howling OTH 2.01. 68
greater storms and tempests than almanacs can ANT 1.02.149 P
he has a tongue will tame tempests, | and make TNK 2.03. 16
that looks on tempests and is never shaken; SON 116. 6
TEMPEST-TOSS'D 1 FR 0.0001 REL FR 1 V 0 P
be lost, | yet it shall be tempest-toss'd. MAC 1.03. 25
TEMPEST-TOSSED 1 FR 0.0001 REL FR 1 V 0 P
calm, will overset | thy tempest-tossed body. ROM 3.05.137
TEMPESTUOUS 2 FR 0.0002 REL FR 2 V 0 P
heart, | and like as rigor of tempestuous gusts 1H6 5.05. 5
scatter'd by winds and high tempestuous gusts, TIT 5.03. 69
TEMPLE* 35 FR 0.0039 REL FR 32 V 3 P
there's nothing ill can dwell in such a temple. TMP 1.02.458
as he was appointed next morning at the temple, ADO 3.03.161 P
ay, in the temple, in the town, the field, | you MND 2.01.238
for in the temple, by and by, with us | these 4.01.180
and he did bid us follow to the temple. 4.01.197
the duke is coming from the temple, and there is 4.02. 15 P
first, forward to the temple; MV 2.01. 44
for here we have no temple but the wood, no AYL 3.03. 50 P
in post | to sacred delphos, to apollo's temple, WT 2.01.183
the temple much surpassing | the common praise 3.01. 2
meet me to-morrow in the temple hall | at two 1H4 3.03.199
within their chiefest temple i'll erect | a tomb 1H6 2.02. 12
within the temple hall we were too loud, | the 2.04. 3
grown to this faction in the temple garden, 2.04.125
we sent unto the temple, unto his chamber, | and 2.05. 19
ground, | then lays his finger on his temple; H8 3.02.115
from purest snow | and hangs on dian's temple — COR 5.03. 67
you deserve | to have a temple built you. 5.03.207
that he is worshipp'd in a baser temple | than TIM 5.01. 48
hath broke ope | the lord's anointed temple, and MAC 2.03. 68
in thews and /bulk, but, as this temple waxes, HAM 1.03. 12
keep unshak'd | that temple, thy fair mind, that CYM 2.01. 64
it would fly | from so divine a temple to commix 4.02. 55
his birth, and in | our temple was he married. 5.04.106
the temple | of virtue was she; 5.05.220
and smoke the temple with our sacrifices. 5.05.398
and in the temple of great jupiter | our peace 5.05.482
ye speak, | diana's temple is not distant far, PER 3.04. 13
my temple stands in ephesus, hie thee thither, 5.01.240
at ephesus the temple see, | our king and all 5.02. 17
her, and plac'd her | here in diana's temple. 5.03. 25
how she came plac'd here in the temple; 5.03. 67
forward to th' temple! TNK 1.01.130
besides, his soul's fair temple is defaced, | to LUC 719
her sacred temple spotted, spoil'd, corrupted, 1172
TEMPLE-HAUNTING 1 FR 0.0001 REL FR 1 V 0 P
the temple-haunting /marlet does approve, | by MAC 1.06. 4
TEMPLES* 15 FR 0.0017 REL FR 15 V 0 P
the solemn temples, the great globe itself, TMP 4.01.153
for she his hairy temples then had rounded MND 4.01. 51
hang on her temples like a golden fleece, MV 1.01.170
when living blood doth in these temples beat, JN 2.01.108
that rounds the mortal temples of a king | keeps R2 3.02.161
adorn his temples with a coronet, | and yet, in 1H6 5.04.134
glory, | and rob his temples of the diadem, 3H6 1.04.104
had grac'd the tender temples of my child, | and R3 4.04.383
from the dead temples of this bloody wretch 5.05. 5
/throng our large temples with the shows of COR 3.03. 36
your temples burned in their cement, and | your 4.06. 85
thy temples should be planted presently | with TIT 2.03. 62
rub him about the temples. OTH 4.01. 52
and deck the temples of those gods that hate us; TNK 2.02. 23
let the temples | burn bright with sacred fires, 5.01. 2
TEMPORAL 7 FR 0.0008 REL FR 7 V 0 P
of temporal royalties | he thinks me now TMP 1.02.110
whose minds are dedicate | to nothing temporal. MM 2.02.155
his sceptre shows the force of temporal power, MV 4.01.190
for all the temporal lands, which men devout H5 1.01. 9
is this an hour for temporal affairs? H8 2.02. 72
though't be temporal, | yet, if that quarrel, 2.03. 13
so children temporal fathers do appease; CYM 5.04. 12
TEMPORARY 1 FR 0.0001 REL FR 1 V 0 P
and holy, | not scurvy, nor a temporary meddler, MM 5.01.145
TEMPORIZ'D 1 FR 0.0001 REL FR 1 V 0 P
been much better, if | he could have temporiz'd. COR 4.06. 17
TEMPORIZE 3 FR 0.0003 REL FR 2 V 1 P
well, you will temporize with the hours. ADO 1.01.274 P
and will not temporize with my entreaties. JN 5.02.125
if i could temporize with my affections, | or TRO 4.04. 6
TEMPORIZER 1 FR 0.0001 REL FR 1 V 0 P
or else a hovering temporizer, that | canst with WT 1.02.302
TEMP'RANCE 2 FR 0.0002 REL FR 2 V 0 P
ask god for temp'rance, that's th' appliance H8 1.01.124
as justice, verity, temp'rance, stableness, MAC 4.03. 92
TEMP'RATE 1 FR 0.0001 REL FR 1 V 0 P
who can be wise, amaz'd, temp'rate, and furious, MAC 2.03.108
TEMP'RATELY 2 FR 0.0002 REL FR 2 V 0 P
he cannot temp'rately transport his honors COR 2.01.224
and temp'rately proceed to what you would | thus 3.01.218
TEMP'RED 1 FR 0.0001 REL FR 1 V 0 P
until his ink were temp'red with love's sighs: LLL 4.03.344
TEMP'RING 3 FR 0.0003 REL FR 2 V 1 P
i have him already temp'ring between my finger 2H4 4.03.130 P
temp'ring extremities with extreme sweet. ROM 2.pr. 14
what wax so frozen but dissolves with temp'ring, VEN 565
TEMPS 1 FR 0.0001 REL FR 0 V 1 P
par la grace de dieu, et en peu de temps. H5 3.04. 41 P
TEMPT 31 FR 0.0035 REL FR 31 V 0 P
nor doth she tempt; MM 2.02.164
ah, luciana, did he tempt thee so? ERR 4.02. 1
with what persuasion did he tempt thy love? 4.02. 13
sathan, avoid! i charge thee tempt me not. 4.03. 48
devils soonest tempt, resembling spirits of LLL 4.03.253
tempt not too much the hatred of my spirit, MND 2.01.211
do not tempt my misery, | lest that it make me TN 3.04.349
if thou dar'st tempt me further, draw thy sword. 4.01. 42
but durst not tempt a minister of honor, | lest WT 2.02. 48
you tempt him overmuch. 5.01. 73
nor tempt the danger of my true defense, | lest JN 4.03. 84
and tempt us not to bear above our power! 5.06. 38
you tempt the fury of my three attendants, 1H6 4.02. 10
gold | will tempt unto a close exploit of death? R3 4.02. 35
and will, no doubt, tempt him to any thing. 4.02. 39
ay, if the devil tempt you to do good. 4.04.419
when we will tempt the frailty of our powers, TRO 4.04. 96
sweet honey greek, tempt me no more to folly. 5.02. 18
and tempt not yet the brushes of the war. 5.03. 34
good gentle youth, tempt not a desp'rate man. ROM 5.03. 59
but wherefore did you so much tempt the heavens? JC 1.03. 53
and tempt the rheumy and unpurged air | to add 2.01.266
tempt me no farther. 4.03. 36
what? durst not tempt him? 4.03. 62
what if it tempt you toward the flood, my lord, HAM 1.04. 69
let the bloat king tempt you again to bed, 3.04.182
follow him at foot, tempt him with speed aboard. 4.03. 54
let not my worser spirit tempt me again | to die LR 4.06.218
their virtue tempts, and they tempt heaven. OTH 4.01. 8
tempt him not so too far; ANT 1.03. 11
and now, to tempt, all liberty /procur'd. LC 252
TEMPTATION 5 FR 0.0005 REL FR 4 V 1 P
for i am that way going to temptation, | where MM 2.02.158
is that temptation that doth goad us on | to sin 2.02.181
devil be within, and that temptation without, i MV 1.02. 97 P
for still temptation follows where thou art. SON 41. 4
stone, | unmoved, cold, and to temptation slow, 94. 4
TEMPTATIONS 1 FR 0.0001 REL FR 1 V 0 P
temptations have since then been born to 's: WT 1.02. 77
TEMPTED 15 FR 0.0017 REL FR 14 V 1 P
teach me, thy tempted subject, to excuse it! TGV 2.06. 8
'tis one thing to be tempted, escalus, | another MM 2.01. 17
the tempter, or the tempted, who sins most, ha? 2.02.163
i never tempted her with word too large, | but, ADO 4.01. 52
yet was sampson so tempted, and he had an LLL 1.02.173 P
had he been adam, he had tempted eve. 5.02.322
might so have tempted him as you have done, 1H4 3.01.172
how often have i tempted suffolk's tongue | (the 2H6 3.02.114
mine ear hath tempted judgment to desire. 3H6 3.03.133
who from my cabin tempted me to walk | upon the R3 1.04. 12
shall i be tempted of the devil thus? 4.04.418
that tempts most cunningly, but be not tempted. TRO 4.04. 91
shall i be tempted to infringe my vow | in the COR 5.03. 20
peace, peace, you durst not so have tempted him. JC 4.03. 59
not to be tempted would she be enur'd, | and now LC 251
TEMPTER 2 FR 0.0002 REL FR 2 V 0 P
the tempter, or the tempted, who sins most, ha? MM 2.02.163
that th' unexperient gave the tempter place, LC 318
TEMPTERS 2 FR 0.0002 REL FR 2 V 0 P
women are shrewd tempters with their tongues. 1H6 1.02.123
from fairies and the tempters of the night CYM 2.02. 9
TEMPTETH 2 FR 0.0002 REL FR 2 V 0 P
evil | tempteth my better angel from my side; PP 2. 6
evil | tempteth my better angel from my /side, SON 144. 6
TEMPTING 6 FR 0.0006 REL FR 6 V 0 P
thy lips, those kissing cherries, tempting grow! MND 3.02.140
then with kind embracements, tempting kisses, SHR in.1. 118
too venturous | in tempting of your patience; H8 1.02. 55
"the tender spring upon thy tempting lip | shows VEN 127
yet from mine ear the tempting tune is blown; 778
hers, by thy beauty tempting her to thee, SON 41.13
TEMPTINGS 1 FR 0.0001 REL FR 1 V 0 P
thebes and the temptings in't before we further TNK 1.02. 4
TEMPTS 6 FR 0.0006 REL FR 4 V 2 P
the fiend is at mine elbow and tempts me, saying MV 2.02. 3 P
the devil tempts thee here | in likeness of a JN 3.01.208
devil | that tempts most cunningly, but be not TRO 4.04. 91
a whore fight for a whore, he tempts judgment. 5.07. 22 P
the devil their virtue tempts, and they tempt OTH 4.01. 8
unto a greater uproar tempts his veins. LUC 427
/TEN 2 FR 0.0002 REL FR 2 V 0 P
/roof | /did /keep /ten /thousand /men? R2 4.01.283

/upon /the /stroke /of /ten. R3 4.02.112
TEN 159 FR 0.0179 REL FR 113 V 46 P
mightst lie drowning | the washing of ten tides! TMP 1.01. 58
she that dwells | ten leagues beyond man's life; 2.01.247
they will lay out ten to see a dead indian. 2.02. 33 P
ten times more gentle than her father's crabbed; 3.01. 8
if there be ten, shrink not, but down with 'em. TGV 4.01. 2
own, who is a dog as big as ten of yours, and 4.04. 58 P
i sit at ten pounds a week. WIV 1.03. 8 P
absence from his house between ten and eleven. 2.02. 84 P
ten and eleven? 2.02. 85 P
ten and eleven. 2.02. 92 P
say i shall be with her between ten and eleven; 2.02.264 P
do so. between nine and ten, say'st thou? 3.05. 53 P
it hath strook ten a' clock. 5.02. 10 P
that went to sea with the ten commandements, but MM 1.02. 8 P
that offend that way but for ten year together, 2.01.239 P
if this law hold in vienna ten year, i'll rent 2.01.241 P
proclaim an enshield beauty ten times louder 2.04. 80
nay, call us ten times frail, | for we are soft 2.04.128
nay, it is ten times strange. 5.01. 42
nay, it is ten times true, for truth is truth 5.01. 45
you, though it cost me ten nights' watchings. ADO 2.01.372 P
he would have walk'd ten mile afoot to see a 2.03. 16 P
and now will he lie ten nights awake carving the 2.03. 17 P
we have ten proofs to one that blood hath the 2.03.164 P
and excellent fashion, yours is worth ten on't. 3.04. 23 P
a play there is, my lord, some ten words long, MND 5.01. 61
but by ten words, my lord, it is too long, 5.01. 63
o, ten times faster venus' pigeons fly | to seal MV 2.06. 5
being ten times undervalued to tried gold? 2.07. 53
times more fair, ten thousand times more rich, 3.02.154
and i be pleas'd to give ten thousand ducats 4.01. 45
i will be bound to pay it ten times o'er, | on 4.01.211
i been judge, thou shouldst have had ten more, 4.01.399
within these ten days if that thou beest found AYL 1.03. 43
eye, | says very wisely, "it is ten a' clock. 2.07. 22
i love her ten times more than e'er i did. SHR 2.01.161
yet i have fac'd it with a card of ten. 2.01.405
'tis ten to one it maim'd you /two outright. 5.02. 62
by being once lost, may be ten times found; AWW 1.01.131 P
if one be good, | there's yet one good in ten." 1.03. 79
what, one good in ten? 1.03. 80 P
one good woman in ten, madam, which is a 1.03. 82 P
one in ten, quoth 'a? 1.03. 85 P
as fit as ten groats is for the hand of an 2.02. 21 P
ten a' clock: 4.01. 24 P
ten thousand years together, naked, fasting, WT 3.02.211
were no age between ten and three–and–twenty, or 3.03. 59 P
even to that drop ten thousand wiry /friends JN 3.04. 64
to train ten thousand english to their side, 3.04.175
to men in joy, but grief makes one hour ten. R2 1.03.261
my lord of salisbury, we have stay'd ten days, 2.04. 1
ten thousand bloody crowns of mothers' sons 3.03. 96
the cheapest of us is ten groats too dear. 5.05. 68
ten thousand bold scots, two and twenty knights, 1H4 1.01. 68
if thou darest not stand for ten shillings. 1.02.141 P
is threescore and ten miles afoot with me, and 2.02. 25 P
some eight or ten. 2.02. 64 P
ten times more dishonorable ragged than an old 4.02. 30 P
wherein the fortune of ten thousand men | must 4.04. 9
that if we wrought out life 'twas ten to one, 2H4 1.01.182
let it be ten pound, if thou canst. 2.01.147 P
and ten times better than the nine worthies. 2.04.220 P
'tis not ten years gone | since richard and 3.01. 57
a score of good ewes may be worth ten pounds. 3.02. 51 P
and here's four harry ten shillings in french 3.02.221 P
not to come near our person by ten mile. 5.05. 65
by ten | we shall have each a hundred englishmen H5 3.07.156
but one ten thousand of those men in england 4.03. 17
bardolph and nym had ten times more valor than 4.04. 70 P
this note doth tell me of ten thousand french 4.08. 80
so that, in these ten thousand they have lost, 4.08. 87
ten thousand soldiers with me i will take, 1H6 1.01.155
one to ten! 1.02. 34
that now our loss might be ten times so much? 2.01. 53
and that the french were almost ten to one, 4.01. 21
ten thousand french have ta'en the sacrament 4.02. 28
ten to one | we shall not find like opportunity. 5.04.157
i could set my ten commandements in your face. 2H6 1.03.142
by these ten bones, my lords, he did speak them 1.03.190 P
and, ten to one, old joan had not gone out. 2.01. 4
ten, my lord. 2.04. 5
ten is the hour that was appointed me | to watch 2.04. 6
shall blow ten thousand souls to heaven or hell; 3.01.350
quitting thee thereby of ten thousand shames, 3.02.218
embrace, and kiss, and take ten thousand leaves, 3.02.354
thus is poor suffolk ten times banished, | once 3.02.357
the three–hoop'd pot shall have ten hoops, and i 4.02. 67 P
well, he shall be beheaded for it ten times. 4.07. 24 P
better ten thousand base–born cades miscarry 4.08. 47
let ten thousand devils come against me, and 4.10. 61 P
me, and give me but the ten meals i have lost, 4.10. 62 P
france | when as the enemy hath been ten to one; 3H6 1.02. 74
and ten to one is no impeach of valor. 1.04. 60
o, ten times more, than tigers of hyrcania. 1.04.155
ten days ago i drown'd these news in tears; 2.01.104
these words will cost ten thousand lives this 2.02.177
mine ten times so much. 2.05.112
i and ten thousand in this luckless realm | had 2.06. 18
that would be ten days' wonder at the least. 3.02.113
but, whiles he thought to steal the single ten, 5.01. 43
and ten to one you'll meet him in the tower. 5.01. 46
now welcome more, and ten times more belov'd, 5.01.103
and some ten voices cried, "god save king R3 3.07. 36
of ten times double gain of happiness. 4.04.324
my heart is ten times lighter than my looks. 5.03. 3
than can the substance of ten thousand soldiers 5.03.218
ten times more ugly | than ever they were fair. H8 1.02.117
o' my conscience, | wish him ten fadom deep. 2.01. 51
'tis ten to one this play can never please | all ep 1
to us | (had it our name) the value of one ten, TRO 2.02. 23
lend me ten thousand eyes, | and i will fill 2.02.101
'a would have ten shares. 2.03.220 P
vowing more than the perfection of ten, and 3.02. 87 P
cracking ten thousand curbs | of more strong COR 1.01. 70
heels, | or pile ten hills on the tarpeian rock, 3.02. 3
this morning for ten thousand of your throats 5.04. 56
ten years are spent since first he undertook TIT 1.01. 31
ten thousand swelling toads, as many urchins, 2.03.101
but that i cannot do ten thousand more. 5.01.144
ten thousand worse than ever yet i did | would i 5.03.187
which ten times faster glides than the sun's ROM 2.05. 5
"banished," | hath slain ten thousand tybalts. 3.02.114
inch | ten thousand dollars to our general use. MAC 1.02. 62
threescore and ten i can remember well, | within 2.04. 1
with ten thousand warlike men | already at a 4.03.134
lent us good siward, and ten thousand men; 4.03.190
there is ten thousand — 5.03. 13
is to be one man pick'd out of ten thousand. HAM 2.02.179 P
we shall obey, were she ten times our mother. 3.02.333 P
to whose /huge spokes ten thousand lesser things 3.03. 19
woe | fall ten times /treble on that cursed head 5.01.247
ten? LR 2.04.261
ten masts at each make not the altitude | which 4.06. 53
nine or ten times | i had thought t' have yerk'd OTH 1.02. 4
'tis not yet ten o' th' clock. 2.03. 13 P
ten thousand harms, more than the ills i know, ANT 1.02.129
being barber'd ten times o'er, goes to the feast 2.02.224
when you have well deserv'd ten times as much 2.06. 77
for in every ten that they make, the devils mar 5.02.277 P
i will lay you ten /thousand ducats to your ring CYM 1.04.127 P
your mistress, my ten thousand ducats are yours, 1.04.150 P
above ten thousand meaner moveables | would 2.02. 29
ten chas'd by one | are now each one the 5.03. 48
i lov'd my lips the better ten days after. TNK 2.04. 26
or two, or three, or ten. 3.03. 36
tell ten — i have pos'd him. 3.05. 79
your cousin | has ten times more offended, for i 3.06.181
and at ten years old | they must be all gelt for 4.01.132
ten kisses short as one, one long as twenty: VEN 22
what is ten hundred touches unto thee? 519
could rule them both without ten women's wit." 1008
he ten times pines that pines beholding food, LUC 1115
thee, | or ten times happier be it ten for one; SON 6. 8
thee, | or ten times happier be it ten for one; 6. 8
ten times thyself were happier than thou art, 6. 9
art, | if ten of thine ten times refigur'd thee, 6.10
art, | if ten of thine ten times refigur'd thee, 6.10
this wish i have, then ten times happy me! 37.14
ten times more in worth | than those old nine 38. 9
TENABLE 1 FR 0.0001 REL FR 1 V 0 P
let it be tenable in your silence still, | and HAM 1.02.247
TENANT 2 FR 0.0002 REL FR 2 V 0 P
i have been your tenant, and your father's LR 4.01. 13
have been your tenant, and your father's tenant, 4.01. 13
TENANTIUS' 1 FR 0.0001 REL FR 1 V 0 P
our fealty and tenantius' right | with honor to CYM 5.04. 73
TENANTIUS 1 FR 0.0001 REL FR 1 V 0 P
but had his titles by tenantius, whom | he CYM 1.01. 31
/TENANTLESS 1 FR 0.0001 REL FR 1 V 0 P
the graves stood /tenantless and the sheeted HAM 1.01.115
TENANTLESS 1 FR 0.0001 REL FR 1 V 0 P
leave not the mansion so long tenantless, | lest TGV 5.04. 8
TENANTS 6 FR 0.0006 REL FR 5 V 1 P
you may have drawn together | your tenants, 1H4 3.01. 89
where be thy tenants and thy followers? R3 4.04.480
your office | on the complaint o' th' tenants. H8 1.02.173
for that outlives a thousand tenants. HAM 5.01. 44 P
make weak–made women tenants to their shame. LUC 1260
a quest of thoughts, all tenants to the heart, SON 46.10
TENCH 2 FR 0.0002 REL FR 0 V 2 P
i am stung like a tench. 1H4 2.01. 15 P
like a tench? 2.01. 16 P
TEND* *(also attend, etc.)*
/TEND* 2 FR 0.0002 REL FR 2 V 0 P
/they /tend /the /crown, /yet /still /with /me R2 4.01.199
/let /us /address /to /tend /on /hector's /heels TRO 4.04.146
TEND* 24 FR 0.0027 REL FR 22 V 2 P
tend to th' master's whistle. TMP 1.01. 6 P
when i am drowsy, and tend on no man's business; ADO 1.03. 16 P
the summer still doth tend upon my state; MND 3.01.155
that twenty such rude boys might tend upon | and AWW 3.02. 82
who didst thou leave to tend his majesty? JN 5.06. 32
while they do tend the profit of the land. 2H6 1.01.204
and threefold vengeance tend upon your steps! 3.02.304
so many hours must i tend my flock, | so many 3H6 2.05. 31
go thou to richard, and good angels tend thee! R3 4.01. 92
here tend the savage strangeness he puts on, TRO 2.03.126
ajax commands the guard to tend on you. 5.01. 72
if it were so that our request did tend | to COR 5.03.132
you spirits | that tend on mortal thoughts, MAC 1.05. 41
the time invests you, go, your servants tend. HAM 1.03. 83
his affections do not that way tend, | nor what 3.01.162
and hitherto doth love on fortune tend, | for 3.02.206
th' associates tend, and every thing is bent 4.03. 45
twice so many | have a command to tend you? LR 2.04.263
tend me to–night; ANT 4.02. 24
tend me to–night two hours, i ask no more, | and 4.02. 32
that millions of strange shadows on you tend? SON 53. 2
what should i do but tend | upon the hours and 57. 1
for to no other pass my verses tend | than of 103.11
hard, | whereto his invis'd properties did tend; LC 212
TENDANCE 4 FR 0.0004 REL FR 4 V 0 P
my brethren mortal, | must give my tendance to. H8 3.02.149
subdues and properties to his love and tendance TIM 1.01. 57
his strides, his lobbies fill with tendance, 1.01. 80
by watching, weeping, tendance, kissing, to CYM 5.05. 53
TENDED 5 FR 0.0005 REL FR 5 V 0 P
not | four, or five, women once that tended me? TMP 1.02. 47
from whence thou cam'st, how tended on, but rest AWW 2.01.207
three months this youth hath tended upon me, TN 5.01. 99
riotous knights | that tended upon my father? LR 2.01. 95
so many mermaids, tended her i' th' eyes, | and ANT 2.02.207
/TENDER* 3 FR 0.0003 REL FR 3 V 0 P
/such /violent /hands /upon /her /tender /life. TIT 3.02. 22
/alas, /the /tender /boy, /in /passion /mov'd, 3.02. 48
/peace, /tender /sapling, /thou /art /made /of 3.02. 50
TENDER* 151 FR 0.0170 REL FR 132 V 19 P
it must needs be of subtle, tender, and delicate TMP 2.01. 42 P
your content | tender your own good fortune? 2.01.270
who once again | i tender to thy hand. 4.01. 5
them, your affections | would become tender. 5.01. 19
were't not affection chains thy tender days | to TGV 1.01. 3
even so by love the young and tender wit | is 1.01. 47
knowing that tender youth is soon suggested, | i 3.01. 34
i thank you, madam, that you tender her. 4.04.140
whose life's as tender to me as my soul! 5.04. 37
there is, as 'twere, a tender, a kind of tender, WIV 1.01.208 P
a tender, a kind of tender, made afar off by sir 1.01.208 P
had he twenty heads to tender down | on twenty MM 2.04.180
for thou dost fear the soft and tender fork | of 3.01. 16
but that her tender shame | will not proclaim 4.04. 23
some tender money to me, some invite me; ERR 4.03. 4
him, | he shall not die, so much we tender him. 5.01.132
wisdom and blood combating in so tender a body, ADO 2.03.164 P
if she should make tender of her love, 'tis very 2.03.179 P
part sadness and melancholy, my tender juvenal? LLL 1.02. 8 P
why tender juvenal? why tender juvenal? 1.02. 12 P
why tender juvenal? why tender juvenal? 1.02. 12 P
i spoke it tender juvenal as a congruent 1.02. 13 P
to thy young days, which we may nominate tender. 1.02. 15 P
may | make tender of to thy true worthiness. 2.01.170
than are the tender horns of cockled snails. 4.03.335
pay, | if for his tender here i make some stay. MND 3.02. 87
and tender me (forsooth) affection, | but by 3.02.230
and i am such a tender ass, if my hair do but 4.01. 25 P
be amiss, | when simpleness and duty tender it. 5.01. 83
never train'd | to offices of tender courtesy. MV 4.01. 33
yes, here i tender it for him in the court, 4.01.209
your brother is but young and tender, and for AYL 1.01.129 P
i do, which i tender dearly, though i say i am a 5.02. 70 P
i charge thee, tender well my hounds | (brach SHR in.1. 16
you | you have show'd a tender fatherly regard, 2.01.286
helen, | if you should tender your supposed aid, AWW 1.03.236
i come to tender it, and my appliance, | with 2.01.113
those tender limbs of thine to the event | of 3.02.104
a suit | corrupt the tender honor of a maid. 3.05. 72
but the many will be too chill and tender, and 4.05. 53 P
five removes come short | to tender it herself. 5.03.132
and whom, by heaven i swear, i tender dearly, TN 5.01.126
so far beneath your soft and tender breeding, 5.01.323
(which never tender lady hath borne greater) WT 2.02. 22
you, that are thus so tender o'er his follies, 2.03.128
that hast | a heart so tender o'er it, take it 2.03.133
(thoughts high for one so tender) cleft the 3.02.196
as cruel for thee | as thou art tender to't. 4.04.441
is aboard, tender your persons to his presence, 4.04.796 P
for she was as tender | as infancy and grace. 5.03. 26
out at mine eyes in tender womanish tears. JN 4.01. 36
should move you to mew up | your tender kinsman, 4.02. 58
and the like tender of our love we make, | to 5.07.106
long | shall tender duty make me suffer wrong? R2 2.01.164
and prick my tender patience to those thoughts 2.01.207
my gracious lord, i tender you my service, 2.03. 41
such as it is, being tender, raw, and young, 2.03. 42
and show'd thou mak'st some tender of my life 1H4 5.04. 49
sir john, thy tender lambkin now is king; 2H4 5.03.116
care | and tender preservation of our person, H5 2.02. 59
but we our kingdom's safety must so tender, 2..02.175
lo, whilest i waited on my tender lambs, | and 1H6 1.02. 76
believe me, lords, my tender years can tell, 3.01. 71
my tender years, and let us not forgo | that for 4.01.149
peace, | and lay them gently on thy tender side. 5.03. 49
hath been | a virgin from her tender infancy, 5.04. 50
for that | my tender youth was never yet attaint 5.05. 81
the ruthless flint doth cut my tender feet, 2H6 2.04. 34
i tender so the safety of my liege. 3.01.277
me, | i thank them for their tender loving care; 3.02.280
eyes, | yet, in protection of their tender ones, 3H6 2.02. 28
as thou didst kill our tender brother rutland, 2.02.115
from whence that tender spray did sweetly spring 2.06. 50
that | of whom you seem to have so tender care? 4.06. 66
to me | as well i tender you and all of yours! R3 2.04. 72
the tender prince | would fain have come with me 3.01. 28
the tender love i bear your grace, my lord, 3.04. 63
pure heart's love, to greet the tender prince. 4.01. 4
those tender babes | whom envy hath immur'd 4.01. 98
old sullen playfellow | for tender princes — 4.01.102
ah, my tender babes! 4.04. 9
whose hand soever lanch'd their tender hearts, 4.04.225
put in her tender heart th' aspiring flame | of 4.04.328
can make seem pleasing to her tender years? 4.04.342
had grac'd the tender temples of my child, | and 4.04.383
which now, two tender bedfellows for dust, | thy 4.04.385
i tender not thy beauteous princely daughter! 4.04.405
lest, being seen, thy brother, tender george, 5.03. 95
to your highness' hand | i tender my commission; H8 2.02.103
o, 'tis a tender place, and i must leave her. 2.02.143
what kind of my obedience i should tender. 2.03. 66
you tender more your person's honor than | your 2.04.116
he puts forth | the tender leaves of hopes, 3.02.353
blaze of wrath subscribes | to tender objects, TRO 4.05.106
my country's good with a respect more tender, COR 3.03.112
too great oppression for a tender thing. ROM 1.04. 24
is love a tender thing? 1.04. 25
to smooth that rough touch with a tender kiss. 1.05. 96
with tender juliet /match'd is now not fair. 2.pr. 4
which name i tender | as dearly as mine own — 3.01. 71
i will make a desperate tender | of my child's 3.04. 12
a whining mammet, in her fortune's tender, | to 3.05.184
tender down | their services to lord timon. TIM 1.01. 54
whom fortune's tender arm | with favor never 4.03.250
we tender our loves to him in this suppos'd 5.01. 12
how tender 'tis to love the babe that milks me; MAC 1.07. 55
night, | scarf up the tender eye of pitiful day, 3.02. 47
tender yourself more dearly, | or (not to crack HAM 1.03.107
/wringing it thus) you'll tender me a fool. 1.03.109
which we do tender, as we dearly grieve | for 4.03. 41
charge | led by a delicate and tender prince, 4.04. 48
highness offer'd, | nor will you tender less. LR 1.01.195
which, in the tender of a wholesome weal, 1.04.211
whether a maid so tender, fair, and happy, | so OTH 1.02. 66
let me my service tender on your lips. CYM 1.06.140
is material | to th' tender of our present. 1.06.208
to do those duties which | you tender to her; 2.03. 51
so tender of rebukes that words are /strokes, 3.05. 40
and true preferment shall tender itself to thee. 3.05.154 P
then why should we be tender | to let an 4.02.126
find, and be embrac'd by a piece of tender air; 5.04.140 P

so tender over his occasions, true, | so feat, 5.05. 87
find, and be embrac'd by a piece of tender air; 5.05.437 P
the piece of tender air, thy virtuous daughter, 5.05.446
were clipt about | with this most tender air. 5.05.452
villainy | so well as soft and tender flattery. PER 4.04. 45
mercy, all our best | their best skill tender! TNK 1.04. 47
when that shall be seen, i tender my consent. 2.01. 14 P
and before the gods | tender their holy prayers. 5.01. 2
then from this gather | how i should tender you. 5.01. 25
and, to piece her portion, | tender her this. 5.04. 32
rein, | under her other was the tender boy, VEN 32
"the tender spring upon thy tempting lip | shows 127
mane, thick tail, broad buttock, tender hide; 298
her other tender hand his fair cheek feels: 352
this canker that eats up love's tender spring, 656
as caterpillars do the tender leaves. 798
or as the snail, whose tender horns being hit, 1033
and straight, in pity of his tender years, 1091
and thy children's sake, | tender my suit; LUC 534
unapt for tender smell, or speedy flight, | make 695
"unruly blasts wait on the tender spring, 869
the tender nibbler would not touch the bait, PP 4.11
his tender heir might bear his memory: SON 1. 4
and, tender chorl, mak'st waste in niggarding: 1.12
as tender nurse her babe from faring ill. 22.12
are gone | in tender embassy of love to thee, 45. 6
did exceed | the barren tender of a poet's debt; 83. 4
leap | to kiss the tender inward of thy hand, 128. 6
nor tender feeling to base touches prone, | nor 141. 6
of pensiv'd and subdu'd desires the tender, LC 219

TENDER–BODIED 1 FR 0.0001 REL FR 0 V 1 P
yet he was but tender–bodied and the only son of COR 1.03. 6 P

TENDER'D 3 FR 0.0003 REL FR 3 V 0 P
at her father's churlish feet she tender'd, TGV 3.01.227
have breath'd out | that e'er devotion tender'd! TN 5.01.115
nor to us hath tender'd | the duty of the day. CYM 3.05. 31

TENDER–DYING 1 FR 0.0001 REL FR 1 V 0 P
when death doth close his tender–dying eyes, 1H6 3.03. 48

TENDER–FEELING 1 FR 0.0001 REL FR 1 V 0 P
to tread them with her tender–feeling feet. 2H6 2.04. 9

TENDER–HEARTED 1 FR 0.0001 REL FR 1 V 0 P
aumerle, thou weep'st, my tender–hearted cousin! R2 3.03.160

TENDER–HEFTED 1 FR 0.0001 REL FR 1 V 0 P
thy tender–hefted nature shall not give | thee LR 2.04.171

/TENDERLY 1 FR 0.0001 REL FR 0 V 1 P
/that /so /tenderly /and /entirely /loves /him. LR 1.02. 96 P

TENDERLY 6 FR 0.0006 REL FR 4 V 2 P
you that have been so tenderly officious | with WT 2.03.159
beseech you tenderly apply to her | some 3.02.152
o good sir, tenderly, o! 4.03. 70 P
land, | my stooping duty tenderly shall show. R2 3.03. 48
and will as tenderly be led by th' nose | as OTH 1.03.401
mean time, look tenderly to the two prisoners. TNK 2.01. 19 P

TENDER–MINDED 1 FR 0.0001 REL FR 1 V 0 P
to be tender–minded | does not become a sword. LR 5.03. 31

TENDERNESS 13 FR 0.0014 REL FR 10 V 3 P
a resolution fetch | from flow'ry tenderness? MM 3.01. 82
go, tenderness of years, take this key, give LLL 3.01. 4 P
the tenderness of her nature became as a prey to AWW 4.03. 51 P
its tenderness! WT 1.02.152
do, | make blind itself with foolish tenderness. 1H4 3.02. 91
for doing these fair rites of tenderness. 5.04. 98
love, and filial tenderness | shall, o dear 2H4 4.05. 39
as well we know your tenderness of heart | and R3 3.07.210
melted with tenderness and /kind compassion, 4.03. 7
my conscience first receiv'd a tenderness, H8 2.04.171
not of a woman's tenderness to be, | requires COR 5.03.129
her delicate tenderness will find itself abus'd, OTH 2.01.232 P
to be suspected of more tenderness | than doth CYM 1.01. 94

TENDERS 4 FR 0.0004 REL FR 4 V 0 P
kiss, | thy brother marcus tenders on thy lips. TIT 5.03.157
of late made many tenders | of his affection to HAM 1.03. 99
do you believe his tenders, as you call them? 1.03.103
that you have ta'en these tenders for true pay, 1.03.106

TENDER–SMELLING 1 FR 0.0001 REL FR 1 V 0 P
"no" in /this, most tender–smelling knight. LLL 5.02.566

TENDER'ST 1 FR 0.0001 REL FR 1 V 0 P
why tender'st thou that paper to me with | a CYM 3.04. 11

TENDER'T 1 FR 0.0001 REL FR 1 V 0 P
ransom for offense, | i tender't here: TGV 5.04. 76

TENDING* 6 FR 0.0006 REL FR 5 V 1 P
thoughts tending to ambition, they do plot R2 5.05. 18
thoughts tending to content flatter themselves 5.05. 23
all tending to the good of their adversaries. COR 4.03. 41 P
all tending to the great opinion | that rome JC 1.02.318
grace his speech | tending to caesar's glories, 3.02. 58
give him tending, | he brings great news. MAC 1.05. 37

TEND'RED 2 FR 0.0002 REL FR 2 V 0 P
"adieu," | the honey fee of parting tend'red is: VEN 538
tend'red | the humble salve which wounded bosoms SON 120.11

TEND'RER 1 FR 0.0001 REL FR 1 V 0 P
his tend'rer cheek receives her soft hand's VEN 353

TEND'RING* 5 FR 0.0005 REL FR 5 V 0 P
tend'ring their own worth from where they were LLL 2.01.244
tend'ring the precious safety of my prince, R2 1.01. 32
alone, | tend'ring my ruin and assail'd of none, 1H6 4.07. 10
tend'ring my person's safety, hath appointed R3 1.01. 44
tend'ring our sister's honor and our own. TIT 1.01.476

TENDS* 8 FR 0.0009 REL FR 8 V 0 P
lysander, whereto tends all this? MND 3.02.256
and being not done, where doing tends to ill, JN 3.01.272
tends that thou wouldst speak to the duke of R2 2.01.232
tends to god's glory and my country's weal. 1H6 5.01. 27
his daughter speak, commands, tends service. LR 2.04.102
whereto we see in all things nature tends — OTH 3.03.231
save when command to your dismission tends, CYM 2.03. 52
there's no motion | that tends to vice in man, 2.05. 21

/TENEDOS 1 FR 0.0001 REL FR 1 V 0 P
/to /tenedos /they /come, | /and /the TRO pr 11

TENEMENT 1 FR 0.0001 REL FR 1 V 0 P
it — | like to a tenement or pelting farm. R2 2.01. 60

TENEMENTS 1 FR 0.0001 REL FR 1 V 0 P
to forfeit all your goods, lands, tenements, H8 3.02.342

/TENFOLD 1 FR 0.0001 REL FR 1 V 0 P
/and /cannot /passionate /our /tenfold /grief TIT 3.02. 6

TENFOLD 1 FR 0.0001 REL FR 1 V 0 P
comfort, and tenfold | for thy good valor. ANT 4.07. 15

TENNER *(also tenor, tenure, etc.)*

TENNER 1 FR 0.0001 REL FR 1 V 0 P
to speak, before thy noble grace, this tenner; TNK 3.05.123

TENNIS 3 FR 0.0003 REL FR 3 V 0 P
faith they have in tennis and tall stockings, H8 1.03. 30
in 's rouse, | there falling out at tennis"; HAM 2.01. 57
i think he might be brought to play at tennis. TNK 5.02. 56

TENNIS–BALLS 2 FR 0.0002 REL FR 1 V 1 P
of his cheek hath already stuff'd tennis–balls. ADO 3.02. 47 P
tennis–balls, my liege. H5 1.02.258

TENNIS–COURT 1 FR 0.0001 REL FR 1 V 0 P
in that vast tennis–court, hath made the ball PER 2.01. 60

TENNIS–COURT–KEEPER 1 FR 0.0001 REL FR 0 V 1 P
but that the tennis–court–keeper knows better 2H4 2.02. 18 P

TENOR *(also tenner, tenure, etc.)*

TENOR 11 FR 0.0012 REL FR 9 V 2 P
very day receives letters of strange tenor — MM 4.02.200 P
apollo said, | is't not the tenor of his oracle, WT 5.01. 38
my good lord, | i guess their tenor. 1H4 4.04. 7
misuse the tenor of thy kinsman's trust? 5.05. 5
discharge a horrible oath, whose tenor | was, H8 1.02.206
owl go learn me the tenor of the proclamation, TRO 2.01. 90 P
this is the tenor of the emperor's writ: CYM 3.07. 1
though by the tenor of /our strict edict, | your PER 1.01.111
are letters brought, the tenor these: 3.ch. 24
who is a servant for | the tenor of /thy speech; TNK 1.01. 90
are you, that, 'gainst the tenor of my laws, 3.06.133

TENS 1 FR 0.0001 REL FR 1 V 0 P
thou shalt have more | than two tens to a score. LR 1.04.127

/TENT* 1 FR 0.0001 REL FR 1 V 0 P
/shall /attend /you /presently /at /your /tent. LR 5.01. 33

TENT* 79 FR 0.0089 REL FR 70 V 9 P
i shall beat you to your tent, and prove a MM 2.01.248 P
should be presented at our tent to us. LLL 5.02.307
gone to her tent. 5.02.311
a file with the duke's other letters in my tent. AWW 4.03.205 P
is sad and passionate at your highness' tent. JN 2.01.544
my mother is assailed in our tent, | and ta'en, 3.02. 6
my lord of westmerland, lead him to his tent. 1H4 5.04. 8
come, my lord, i'll lead you to your tent. 5.04. 9
at my tent | the douglas is; 5.05. 22
the armor that i saw in your tent to–night, are H5 3.07. 70 P
walking from watch to watch, from tent to tent, 4.pr. 30
walking from watch to watch, from tent to tent, 4.pr. 30
knight, | collect them all together at my tent. 4.01.287
carried away all that was in the king's tent; 4.07. 8 P
pray thee go seek him, and bring him to my tent. 4.07.168 P
convey me salisbury into his tent, | and then 1H6 1.04.110
herald, conduct me to the dolphin's tent, | to 4.07. 51
we twain will go into his highness' tent. 2H6 5.01. 55
that with the king here resteth in his tent? 3H6 4.03. 10
wherefore else guard we his royal tent | but to 4.03. 21
this is his tent, and see where stand his guard. 4.03. 23
here pitch our tent, even here in bosworth field R3 5.03. 1
up with my tent! 5.03. 7
up with the tent! 5.03. 14
give me some ink and paper in my tent; 5.03. 23
morning | desire the earl to see me in my tent. 5.03. 32
in to my tent, the dew is raw and cold. 5.03. 46
and all my armor laid into my tent? 5.03. 51
about the mid of night come to my tent | and 5.03. 77
of all that i had murther'd | came to my tent, 5.03.205
came to my tent and cried on victory. 5.03.231
this found i on my tent this morning. 5.03.303
and in his tent | lies mocking our designs. TRO 1.03.145
keeps his tent like him, | makes factious feasts 1.03.190
what would you 'fore our tent? 1.03.215
is this great agamemnon's tent, i pray you? 1.03.216
so shall each lord of greece, from tent to tent. 1.03.307
so shall each lord of greece, from tent to tent. 1.03.307
the tent that searches | to th' bottom of the 2.02. 16
within his tent, but ill dispos'd, my lord. 2.03. 77
we saw him at the opening of his tent, | he is 2.03. 84
dear lord, go you and greet him in his tent. 2.03.179
achilles stands i' th' entrance of his tent. 3.03. 38
alive | and case thy reputation in thy tent, 3.03.187
valorous hector to come unarm'd to my tent, and 3.03.275 P
desires you to invite hector to his tent — 3.03.285 P
next | to feast with me and see me at my tent. 4.05.229
first, all you peers of greece, go to my tent; 4.05.271
at menelaus' tent, most princely troilus. 4.05.279
so much, | after we part from agamemnon's tent, 4.05.285
who keeps the tent now? 5.01. 10 P
come, come, thersites, help to trim my tent; 5.01. 45
follow his torch, he goes to calchas' tent. 5.01. 85
come, come, enter my tent. 5.01. 87
troyan drab, and uses the traitor calchas' tent. 5.01. 97 P
be sent | to pray achilles see us at our tent. 5.09. 8
ingratitude, | and tent themselves with death. COR 1.09. 31
so, to our tent; 1.09. 73
go we to our tent. 1.09. 92
'tis a sore upon us | you cannot tent yourself. 3.01.235
the smiles of knaves | tent in my cheeks, and 3.02.116
you that banish'd him | a mile before his tent, 5.01. 5
upon the thracian tyrant in his tent | may favor TIT 1.01.138
'twas on a summer's evening, in his tent, | that JC 3.02.172
then in my tent, cassius, enlarge your griefs, 4.02. 46
no man | come to our tent till we have done our 4.02. 51
here in the tent. 4.03.240
i'll have them sleep on cushions in my tent. 4.03.243
i pray you, sirs, lie in my tent and sleep; 4.03.246
and bring us word unto octavius' tent | how 5.04. 31
within my tent his bones to–night shall lie, 5.05. 78
observe his looks, | i'll tent him to the quick. HAM 2.02.597
she is not well, convey her to my tent. LR 5.03.106
and at thy tent is now | unloading of his mules. ANT 4.06. 22
go with me to my tent, where you shall see | how 5.01. 73
no greater wound, | nor tent to bottom that. CYM 3.04.115
our hearts | are in his army, in his tent. TNK 1.03. 17
making my arms his field, his tent my bed. VEN 108
for he the night before, in tarquin's tent, LUC 15

TENTED 1 FR 0.0001 REL FR 1 V 0 P
us'd | their dearest action in the tented field; OTH 1.03. 85

TENTH 10 FR 0.0011 REL FR 9 V 1 P
the tenth of mankind | would hang themselves. WT 1.02.199
also, king lewis the tenth, | who was sole heir H5 1.02. 77
the tenth of august last this dreadful lord, 1H6 1.01.110
charge, | among the people gather up a tenth. 5.05. 93
and discharging less than the tenth part of one. TRO 3.02. 87 P
we render you the tenth, to be ta'en forth, COR 1.09. 34
nature loathes, take thou the destin'd tenth, TIM 5.04. 33
if, on the tenth day following, | thy banish'd LR 1.01.176
a sixt, a tenth, letting them thrive again | on CYM 5.04. 20
be thou the tenth muse, ten times more in worth SON 38. 9

TENTHS 1 FR 0.0001 REL FR 1 V 0 P
if we have lost so many tenths of ours, | to TRO 2.02. 21

TEN–TIMES–BARR'D–UP 1 FR 0.0001 REL FR 1 V 0 P
a jewel in a ten–times–barr'd–up chest | is a R2 1.01.180

TENT–ROYAL 1 FR 0.0001 REL FR 1 V 0 P
bring home | to the tent–royal of their emperor; H5 1.02.196

TENTS 20 FR 0.0022 REL FR 17 V 3 P
some entertainment for them in their tents. LLL 4.03.370
whip to our tents, as roes /run o'er land. 5.02.309
and sigh'd his soul toward the grecian tents, MV 5.01. 5
costly apparel, tents, and canopies, | fine SHR 2.01.352
adversaries, when we bring him to our own tents. AWW 3.06. 27 P
of sallies and retires, of trenches, tents, | of 1H4 2.03. 51
lie within fifteen hundred paces of your tents. H5 3.07.126 P
and from the tents | the armorers, accomplishing 4.pr. 11
with sleight and manhood stole to rhesus' tents 3H6 4.02. 20
under our tents i'll play the ease–dropper, | to R3 5.03.221
and look how many grecian tents do stand TRO 1.03. 79
thy brass voice through all these lazy tents, 1.03.257
midway between your tents and walls of troy, 1.03.278
clatpoles ere i come any more to your tents. 2.01.118 P
will with a trumpet 'twixt our tents and troy 2.01.123
desire | my famous cousin to our grecian tents. 4.05.151
and, worthy warrior, welcome to our tents. 4.05.200
you /vile abominable tents, | thus proudly 5.10. 23
mark antony is in your tents, my lord; JC 5.03. 10
are those my tents where i perceive the fire? 5.03. 13

TENURE *(also tenner, tenor)*

TENURE 10 FR 0.0011 REL FR 10 V 0 P
the tenure of them doth but signify | my health TGV 3.01. 56
seal doth warrant | the tenure of my book; ADO 4.01.167
when it is paid according to the tenure. MV 4.01.235
was writing of it, | it bears an angry tenure. AYL 4.03. 11
their cold intent, tenure, and substance thus: 2H4 4.01. 9
lord, | to see perform'd the tenure of my word. 5.05. 71
myself have letters of the self–same tenure. JC 4.03.171
their tenure good, i trust. CYM 2.04. 36
here folds she up the tenure of her woe, | her LUC 1310
in me, | the scope and tenure of thy jealousy? SON 61. 8

TENURES* 2 FR 0.0002 REL FR 1 V 1 P
whose tenures and particular effects | you have H5 5.02. 72
his cases, his tenures, and his tricks? HAM 5.01.100 P

TERCEL *(also tassel–gentle)*

TERCEL 1 FR 0.0001 REL FR 0 V 1 P
out ere i part you — the falcon as the tercel, TRO 3.02. 52 P

TEREU 2 FR 0.0002 REL FR 2 V 0 P
now would she cry, | "tereu, tereu," by and by; PP 20.14
now would she cry, | "tereu, tereu," by and by; 20.14

TEREUS' 1 FR 0.0001 REL FR 1 V 0 P
and treats of tereus' treason and his rape — TIT 4.01. 48

TEREUS 4 FR 0.0004 REL FR 4 V 0 P
but sure some tereus hath deflow'red thee, | and TIT 2.04. 26
a craftier tereus, cousin, hast thou met, | and 2.04. 41
she hath been reading late | the tale of tereus; CYM 2.02. 45
while thou on tereus descants better skill. LUC 1134

TERM 27 FR 0.0030 REL FR 19 V 8 P
margaret hero, hear margaret term me claudio; ADO 2.02. 44 P
sworn for three years' term to live with me, LLL 1.01. 16
as, not to see a woman in that term, | which i 1.01. 37
with a woman within the term of three years, he 1.01.130 P
you shall this twelvemonth term from day to day 5.02.850
which, to term in gross, | is an unlesson'd girl MV 3.02.158
for they sleep between term and term, and then AYL 3.02.332 P
for they sleep between term and term, and then 3.02.332 P
habits | (methinks i so should term them) and WT 3.01. 5
spoke of in scotland as this term of fear. 1H4 4.01. 85
now by /gadslugs i swear i scorn the term; H5 2.01. 30
but what's that pucelle whom they term so pure? 1H6 2.01. 20
till term of eighteen months | be full expir'd. 2H6 1.01. 67
i would not, as they term it, praise her, but i TRO 1.01. 44 P
face, methought — i cannot tell how to term it. COR 4.05.156 P
sir) show themselves (as we term it) his friends 4.05.208 P
and expire the term | of a despised life clos'd ROM 1.04.109
bear thee can afford | no better term than this: 3.01. 61
in filial obligation for some term | to do HAM 1.02. 91
doom'd for a certain term to walk the night, 1.05. 10
whether i in any just term am affin'd | to love OTH 1.01. 39
leave | as long a term as yet we have to live, CYM 1.01.107
the holding or loss of that you term her frail. 1.04. 96 P
mollis aer, and mollis aer | we term it mulier; 5.05.448
(which nev'r heard scurril term, into whose port TNK 5.01.147
and that which we profanely term our fortunes STM III 2
away, | for term of life thou art assured mine, SON 92. 2

TERMAGANT 2 FR 0.0002 REL FR 0 V 2 P
or that hot termagant scot had paid me scot and 1H4 5.04.114 P
such a fellow whipt for o'erdoing termagant, it HAM 3.02. 13 P

TERM'D 6 FR 0.0006 REL FR 5 V 1 P
but chiefly | him that you term'd, sir, "the TMP 5.01. 15
not now | worthily term'd them merciless to us! ERR 1.01. 99
is beauford term'd a kite? 2H6 3.02.196
john cade, so term'd of our suppos'd father — 4.02. 31 P
is term'd the civill'st place of all this isle: 4.07. 61
and your true rights be term'd a poet's rage, SON 17.11

TERMED 1 FR 0.0001 REL FR 1 V 0 P
which by the sign thereof was termed so. R3 3.05. 79

TERMINATIONS 1 FR 0.0001 REL FR 0 V 1 P
her breath were as terrible as her terminations, ADO 2.01.249 P

TERMLESS 1 FR 0.0001 REL FR 1 V 0 P
like unshorn velvet on that termless skin, LC 94

TERMS 81 FR 0.0091 REL FR 64 V 17 P
i can do to keep the terms of my honor precise. WIV 2.02. 22 P
and in such alligant terms, and in such wine and 2.02. 68 P
stand under the adoption of abominable terms, 2.02.295 P
terms! 2.02.296 P
and the terms | for common justice, y' are as MM 1.01. 10
that is, were i under the terms of death, | th' 2.04.100
planet, nor i cannot woo in festival terms. ADO 5.02. 41 P
at tables, chides the dice | in honorable terms; LLL 5.02.327
taffata phrases, silken terms precise, 5.02.406

her, | and she in mild terms begg'd my patience, MND 4.01. 58
i like not fair terms and a villain's mind. MV 1.03.179
in terms of choice i am not soly led | by nice 2.01. 13
as you would say in plain terms, gone to heaven. 2.02. 65 P
to have defended it | with any terms of zeal, 5.01.205
sun, | and rail'd on lady fortune in good terms, AYL 2.07. 16
in good set terms, and yet a motley fool. 2.07. 17
and twangling jack, with twenty such vild terms, SHR 2.01.158
all this chat aside, | thus in plain terms: 2.01.269
name of justice, | without all terms of pity. AWW 2.03.166
more than light airs and recollected terms | of TN 2.04. 5
i call thee by the most modest terms, for i am 4.02. 32 P
whom thou, in terms so bloody and so dear, 5.01. 71
these terms of treason doubled down his throat. R2 1.01. 57
on equal terms to give /him chastisement? 4.01. 22
with many holiday and lady terms | he questioned 1H4 1.03. 46
speak terms of manage to thy bounding steed, 2.03. 49
with tears of innocency and terms of zeal, | my 4.03. 63
that you and i should meet upon such terms | as 5.01. 10
i'll gild it with the happiest terms i have. 5.04.158
pardon, and terms of love to all of you? 5.05. 3
peace | upon such large terms and so absolute 2H4 4.01.184
so, like gross terms, | the prince will in the 4.04. 73
/write her fair words still in foulest terms? 4.04.104
out of six fashions, which is four terms, or two 5.01. 80 P
you with my rapier, as i may, in fair terms. H5 2.01. 57 P
i would prick your guts a little in good terms, 2.01. 58 P
cut thy throat one time or other in fair terms, 2.01. 70 P
who disgrac'd, what terms the enemy stood on; 3.06. 74 P
and thou hast given me most bitter terms. 4.08. 42
will you vouchsafe to teach a soldier terms, 5.02. 99
we have consented to all terms of reason. 5.02.329 P
thou hast astonish'd me with thy high terms. 1H6 1.02. 93
among which terms he us'd his lavish tongue 2.05. 47
with other vile and ignominious terms: 4.01. 97
the bolder to salute my king | with ruder terms, 2H6 1.01. 30
i would invent as bitter searching terms, | as 3.02.311
the duke of somerset, whom he terms a traitor. 4.09. 30
in any case, be not too rough in terms, | for he 4.09. 44
but thou wilt brave me with these saucy terms? 4.10. 36
flint, | i am so angry at these abject terms; 5.01. 25
hath made her break out into terms of rage! 3H6 1.01.265
becomes it thee to be thus bold in terms 2.02. 85
his master's child, as worshipfully he terms it, R3 3.04. 39
like a chime a–mending, with terms /unsquar'd, TRO 1.03.159
her possession up | on terms of base compulsion! 2.02.153
should enlarge itself | to wrathful terms. 5.02. 38
and all the bitterest terms | that ever ear did TIT 2.03.110
she will not stay the siege of loving terms, ROM 1.01.212
in terms of friendship with thine enemies. JC 3.01.203
bloodier villain | than terms can give thee out! MAC 5.08. 8
by strong hand | and terms compulsatory, those HAM 1.01.103
i would not, in plain terms, from this time 1.03.132
the terms of our estate may not endure | hazard 3.03. 5
lost, | a sister driven into desp'rate terms, 4.07. 26
but in my terms of honor | i stand aloof, and 5.02.246
parted you in good terms? LR 1.02.156 P
that indiscretion finds | and dotage terms so. 2.04.197
and spoke such scurvy and provoking terms OTH 1.02. 7
and in terms like bride and groom | devesting 2.03.180
thrown such despite and heavy terms upon her, 4.02.116
could not have laid such terms upon his callet. 4.02.121
you the sourest points with sweetest terms, ANT 2.02. 24
he could not | but pay me terms of honor, cold 3.04. 7
if you seek us afterwards in other terms, you CYM 3.01. 79 P
the sore terms we stand upon with the gods will PER 4.02. 34 P
pleas'd | to show in generous terms your griefs, TNK 3.01. 54
defy me in these fair terms, and you show | more 3.06. 25
present stood unfeignedly on the same terms. 4.03. 69 P
may any terms acquit me from this chance? LUC 1706
buy terms divine in selling hours of dross; SON 146.11
"and long upon these terms i held my city, LC 176

TERRA 2 FR 0.0002 REL FR 1 V 1 P
anon falleth like a crab on the face of terra, LLL 4.02. 7 P
nothing but this; 'tis "bona terra, mala gens." 2H6 4.07. 56

TERRAM 1 FR 0.0001 REL FR 1 V 0 P
"in terram salicam mulieres ne /succedant," H5 1.02. 38

TERRAS 1 FR 0.0001 REL FR 1 V 0 P
terras astraea reliquit; TIT 4.03. 4

TERRE 1 FR 0.0001 REL FR 1 V 0 P
via! les eaux et terre. H5 4.02. 4

TERRENE 2 FR 0.0002 REL FR 2 V 0 P
alack, our terrene moon | is now eclips'd, and ANT 3.13.153
since in our terrene state petitions are not TNK 1.03. 14

/TERRESTRIAL 1 FR 0.0001 REL FR 0 V 1 P
/give /me /thy /hand, /terrestrial; WIV 3.01.106 P

TERRESTRIAL 1 FR 0.0001 REL FR 1 V 0 P
but when from under this terrestrial ball | he R2 3.02. 41

/TERRIBLE 1 FR 0.0001 REL FR 1 V 0 P
/in /the /most /terrible /and /nimble /stroke LR 4.07. 33

TERRIBLE 27 FR 0.0030 REL FR 21 V 6 P
for mischiefs manifold and sorceries terrible TMP 1.02.264
her breath were as terrible as her terminations, ADO 2.01.248 P
example, that so terrible shows in the wrack of AWW 3.05. 22 P
upon him, speak what terrible language you will. 4.01. 3 P
for it comes to pass oft that a terrible oath, TN 3.04.179 P
terrible hell | make war upon their spotted R2 3.02.133
my name were not so terrible to the enemy as it 2H4 1.02.218 P
withal | how terrible in constant resolution, H5 2.04. 35
then lend the eye a terrible aspect; 3.01. 9
of death, | a terrible and unavoided danger; 1H6 4.05. 8
where death's approach is seen so terrible! 2H6 3.03. 6
hell, | such terrible impression made my dream. R3 1.04. 63
they swell and grow, as terrible as storms. H8 3.01.164
wish, not fierce and terrible | only in strokes, COR 1.04. 57
and lascivious town | our terrible approach. TIM 5.04. 2
hand, | most bloody, fiery, and most terrible. JC 1.03.130
in one day, | and i the elder and more terrible; 2.02. 47
norway himself, with terrible numbers, MAC 1.02. 51
up | each corporal agent to this terrible feat. 1.07. 80
death, | and prophesying, with accents terrible, 2.03. 57
in the affliction of these terrible dreams 3.02. 18
have been perform'd | too terrible for the ear. 3.04. 77
needed then that terrible dispatch of it into LR 1.02. 32 P
what is the reason of this terrible summons? OTH 1.01. 82
all strange and terrible events are welcome, ANT 4.15. 3
on our terrible seas, | like egg–shells mov'd CYM 3.01. 27
a terrible child–bed hast thou had, my dear, PER 3.01. 56

TERRIBLY 3 FR 0.0003 REL FR 2 V 1 P
it strook mine ear most terribly. TMP 2.01.313
and you should do it too terribly, you would MND 1.02. 74 P
terribly swear | into strong shudders and to TIM 4.03.137

TERRITORIES 11 FR 0.0012 REL FR 11 V 0 P
but if thou linger in my territories | longer TGV 3.01.163
claim | to this fair island and the territories, JN 1.01. 10
arms, | from out the circle of his territories. 5.02.136
therefore we banish you our territories. R2 1.03.139
welcome, brave earl, into our territories! 1H6 5.03.146
with more than half the gallian territories, 5.04.139
that all your interest in those territories | is 2H6 3.01. 84
death, | or banished fair england's territories, 3.02.245
me, | who am prepar'd against your territories, COR 4.05.134
powers | are ent'red in the roman territories, 4.06. 40
rages | upon our territories, and have already 4.06. 77

TERRITORY 2 FR 0.0002 REL FR 2 V 0 P
no more | to seek a living in our territory. AYL 3.01. 8
interest of territory, cares of state), | which LR 1.01. 50

TERROR 35 FR 0.0039 REL FR 34 V 1 P
lent him our terror, dress'd him with our love, MM 1.01. 19
stick it in their children's sight | for terror, 1.03. 26
make it | their perch and not their terror. 2.01. 4
now, to our perjury to add more terror, | we are LLL 5.02.470
ignorant, will breed no terror in the youth; TN 3.04.189 P
try all, both joy and terror | of good and bad, WT 4.01. 1
night, | thou hate and terror to prosperity, JN 3.04. 28
meet | with no less terror than the elements R2 3.03. 55
that would divorce this terror from my heart" — 5.04. 9
is | that doth with awe and terror kneel to it! 2H4 4.05.176
here, said they, is the terror of the french, 1H6 1.04. 42
and what a terror he had been to france. 2.02. 17
should strike such terror to his enemies. 2.03. 24
our nation's terror and their bloody scourge! 4.02. 16
your kingdom's terror and black nemesis? 4.07. 78
days — | so full of dismal terror was the time. R3 1.04. 7
as if thou were distraught and mad with terror? 3.05. 4
and die in terror of thy guiltiness! 5.03.170
have strook more terror to the soul of richard 5.03.217
'tis his aspect of terror. H8 5.01. 88
peace, plenty, love, truth, terror, | that were 5.04. 47
made the coward | turn terror into sport; COR 2.02.105
that with his sons, a terror to our foes, | hath TIT 1.01. 29
whose name was once our terror, now our comfort, 5.01. 10
for exile hath more terror in his look, | much ROM 3.03. 13
together with the terror of the place — | as in 4.03. 38
the unaccustom'd terror of this night, | and the JC 2.01.199
there is no terror, cassius, in your threats; 4.03. 66
it is the cowish terror of his spirit | that LR 4.02. 12
in him, he brings not | a jot of terror to us. TNK 1.02. 95
which with cold terror doth men's minds confound VEN 1048
but coward–like with trembling terror die. LUC 231
what terror 'tis! 453
the sight which makes supposed terror true. 455
mood, | effects of terror and dear modesty, LC 202

TERRORS 6 FR 0.0006 REL FR 3 V 3 P
there should be terrors in him that he should WIV 4.04. 22 P
hence is it that we make trifles of terrors, AWW 2.03. 4 P
beating and hanging are terrors to me. WT 4.03. 29 P
all the foul terrors in dark–seated hell — 2H6 3.02.328
but they shall be | the terrors of the earth! LR 2.04.282
he had not apprehension | of roaring terrors; CYM 4.02.111

TERTIAN 1 FR 0.0001 REL FR 0 V 1 P
he is so shak'd of a burning quotidian tertian, H5 2.01.119 P

TERTIO 1 FR 0.0001 REL FR 0 V 1 P
primo, secundo, tertio, is a good play, and the TN 5.01. 36 P

TEST 4 FR 0.0004 REL FR 4 V 0 P
love, and thou | hast strangely stood the test. TMP 4.01. 7
let there be some more test made of my mettle MM 1.01. 48
bring me to the test, | and /i the matter will HAM 3.04.142
without more wider and more /overt test | than OTH 1.03.107

TESTAMENT 12 FR 0.0013 REL FR 9 V 3 P
poor allottery my father left me by testament, AYL 1.01. 74 P
he, "thou mak'st a testament | as worldlings do, 2.01. 47
conferr'd by testament to th' sequent issue, AWW 5.03.197
to open | the purple testament of bleeding war; R2 3.03. 94
devout | by testament have given to the church, H5 1.01. 10
he seal'd | a testament of noble–ending love. 4.06. 27
help salisbury to make his testament. 1H6 1.05. 17
performance is a kind of will or testament TIM 5.01. 28
let but the commons hear this testament — JC 3.02.130
the will! the testament! 3.02.154 P
have hearken'd to their father's testament. PER 4.02. 99 P
be spent, | and as his due writ in my testament. LUC 1183

TESTED 1 FR 0.0001 REL FR 1 V 0 P
not with fond sicles of the tested gold, | or MM 2.02.149

TESTER *(also testril)*

TESTER 2 FR 0.0002 REL FR 1 V 1 P
tester i'll have in pouch when thou shalt lack, WIV 1.03. 87
hold, there's a tester for thee. 2H4 3.02.277 P

/TESTERN'D 1 FR 0.0001 REL FR 0 V 1 P
bounty, i thank you, you have /testern'd me; TGV 1.01.145 P

TESTIFY 7 FR 0.0008 REL FR 4 V 3 P
to testify your bounty, i thank you, you have TGV 1.01.144 P
why, here is the note of the fashion to testify. SHR 4.03.130 P
yet, can testify | she was the first fruit of my 1H6 5.04. 12
the bricks are alive at this day to testify it; 2H6 4.02.149 P
no warmth, no /breath shall testify thou livest; ROM 4.01. 98
ten thousand meaner moveables | would testify, CYM 2.02. 30
wight did die, | as yon grim looks do testify. PER 1.ch. 40

TESTIMONIED 1 FR 0.0001 REL FR 0 V 1 P
let him be but testimonied in his own MM 3.02.144 P

TESTIMONIES 2 FR 0.0002 REL FR 1 V 1 P
were testimonies against his worth and credit MM 5.01.244
the testimonies whereof lies bleeding in me. CYM 3.04. 22 P

TESTIMONY 13 FR 0.0014 REL FR 6 V 7 P
and from this testimony of your own sex | (since MM 2.04.131
for testimony whereof, one in the prison, | that 5.01.465
surely a princely testimony, a goodly count, ADO 4.01.316 P
and done in the testimony of a good conscience. LLL 4.02. 2 P
there is too great testimony in your complexion AYL 4.03.170 P
and by other warranted testimony. AWW 2.05. 5 P
seal'd in my function, by my testimony; TN 5.01.161
me word 'tis done | (and by good testimony) or WT 2.03.137
and | the testimony on my part no other | but 3.02. 24
your majesty is pear me testimony and witness, H5 4.08. 35 P
face | for testimony of her foul proceedings. TIT 5.03. 8
derive from him better testimony of his intent, LR 1.02. 81 P
you no sufficient testimony that i have enjoy'd CYM 1.04.149 P

TESTINESS 1 FR 0.0001 REL FR 0 V 1 P
having power of his testiness, shall turn all CYM 4.01. 21 P

TESTRIL *(also tester)*

TESTRIL 1 FR 0.0001 REL FR 0 V 1 P
there's a testril of me too. TN 2.03. 33 P

TESTY 9 FR 0.0010 REL FR 8 V 1 P
that, like a testy babe, will scratch the nurse TGV 1.02. 58
and lead these testy rivals so astray | as one MND 3.02.358
and finds the testy gentleman so hot | that he R3 3.04. 37
proud, violent, testy magistrates (alias fools) COR 2.01. 44 P
i stand and crouch | under your testy humor? JC 4.03. 46
ras'd, and testy wrath | could never be her mild PER 1.01. 17
his testy master goeth about to take him, | when VEN 319
true grief is fond and testy as a child, | who LUC 1094
as testy sick men, when their deaths be near, SON 140. 7

TETCHY *(also techy)*

TETCHY 2 FR 0.0002 REL FR 2 V 0 P
to me, | tetchy and wayward was thy infancy; R3 4.04.169
pandar, | and he's as tetchy to be woo'd to woo, TRO 1.01. 96

TETHER *(see teder)*

TETTER 3 FR 0.0003 REL FR 2 V 1 P
and the rivell'd fee–simple of the tetter, take TRO 5.01. 23 P
measles | which we disdain should tetter us, yet COR 3.01. 79
mine, | and a most instant tetter bark'd about, HAM 1.05. 71

TEVIL *(also devil, dev'l)*

TEVIL 1 FR 0.0001 REL FR 0 V 1 P
the tevil and his tam! WIV 1.01.149 P

TEWKSBURY 7 FR 0.0008 REL FR 6 V 1 P
his wit's as thick as tewksbury mustard, there's 2H4 2.04.241 P
that they do hold their course toward tewksbury. 3H6 5.03. 19
since, | stabb'd in my angry mood at tewksbury? R3 1.02.241
tower, | and edward, my poor son, at tewksbury. 1.03.119
that stabb'd me in the field by tewksbury: 1.04. 56
who told me, in the field at tewksbury, | when 2.01.112
stab'st me in my prime of youth | at tewksbury. 5.03.120

/TEXT 1 FR 0.0001 REL FR 1 V 0 P
/no /more, /the /text /is /foolish. LR 4.02. 37

TEXT 12 FR 0.0013 REL FR 6 V 6 P
yea, and text underneath, "here dwells benedick ADO 5.01.183 P
for society, saith the text, is the happiness of LLL 4.02.162 P
and certes the text most infallibly concludes it 4.02.163 P
fair as a text b in a copy–book. 5.02. 42
will bless it, and approve it with a text, MV 3.02. 79
now, sir, what is your text? TN 1.05.220 P
where lies your text? 1.05.223 P
you are now out of your text; 1.05.232 P
your exposition on the holy text | than now to 2H4 4.02. 7
that's a certain text. ROM 4.01. 21
pardon old gower — this long's the text. PER 2.ch. 40
say, | the text is old, the orator too green, VEN 806

TH'* *(also the, they, thou, thy)*

/TH'* 27 FR 0.0030 REL FR 21 V 6 P
armado /a' /th' /one side — o, a most dainty LLL 4.01.144
/son /and /heir /to /th' /earl /of /arundel, R2 2.01.280
/you /cast /th' /event /of /war, /my /noble 2H4 1.01.166
/early /spring | /we /see /th' /appearing /buds, 1.03. 39
/after /th' /admired /heels /of /bullingbrook, 1.03.105
/and /purge /th' /obstructions /which /begin /to 4.01. 65
/from /th' /athenian /bay | /put /forth /toward TRO pr 6
or my heart will be blown up by /th' /root. 4.04. 54 P
that /for /th' poorest piece | will bear the COR 3.03. 32
martius should be join'd /wi' /th' volscians — 4.06. 89
that /th' runaway's eyes may wink, and romeo ROM 3.02. 6
and borrowing dulleth /th' edge of husbandry. HAM 1.03. 77
a thing a little soil'd /wi' /th' working, 2.01. 40
/dungeons, /denmark /being /one /o' /th' /worst. 2.02.246 P
/shall /we /to /th' /court? 2.02.265 P
/whose /lungs /are /tickle /a' /th' /sere, and 2.02.324 P
and let me speak to /th' yet unknowing world 5.02.379
as he's for a king, /th' art poor enough. LR 1.04. 22 P
/you /are /o' /th' /commission, | /sit /you /too 3.06. 38
/alone /suffers, /suffers /most /i' /th' /mind, 3.06.104
/what, /i' /th' /storm? 4.03. 28
/i' /th' /night? 4.03. 28
/the /poor /distressed /lear's /i' /th' /town, 4.03. 38
thou hast, | they'll grind /th' /one the other. ANT 3.05. 15
and with /th' /ostent of war will look so huge, PER 1.02. 25
of me, who stand /i' /th' gaps to teach you, 4.04. 8
/th' other, "this fire!" TNK 4.03. 53 P

TH'* 1397 FR 0.1579 REL FR 1133 V 264 P
speak to th' mariners. TMP 1.01. 3 P
tend to th' master's whistle. 1.01. 6 P
let's all sink wi' th' king. 1.01. 63
that the sea, mounting to th' welkin's cheek, 1.02. 4
to think o' th' teen that i have turn'd you to, 1.02. 64
set all hearts i' th' state | to what tune 1.02. 84
he was indeed the duke, out o' th' substitution, 1.02.103
and executing th' outward face of royalty | with 1.02.104
wi' th' king of naples | to give him annual 1.02.112
mark his condition, and th' event, then tell me 1.02.117
which was, that he, in lieu o' th' premises, 1.02.123
one midnight | fated to th' purpose, did antonio 1.02.129
gates of milan, and, i' th' dead of darkness, 1.02.130
the ministers for th' purpose hurried thence 1.02.131
us, | to cry to th' sea, that roar'd to us; 1.02.149
to sigh | to th' winds, whose pity, sighing back 1.02.150
the precursors | o' th' dreadful thunder–claps, 1.02.202
hast dispos'd, | and all the rest o' th' fleet. 1.02.226
and for the rest o' th' fleet | (which i 1.02.232
what is the time o' th' day? 1.02.239
to do me business in the veins o' th' earth 1.02.255
with child, | and here was left by th' sailors. 1.02.270
go make thyself like a nymph o' th' sea; 1.02.301
and show'd thee all the qualities o' th' isle, 1.02.337
you do keep from me | the rest o' th' island. 1.02.344
i' th' air, or th' earth? 1.02.388
i' th' air, or th' earth? 1.02.388
and sure it waits upon | some god o' th' island. 1.02.390
wench, | to th' most of men this is a caliban, 1.02.481
all corners else o' th' earth | let liberty make 1.02.492
to th' syllable. 1.02.501
that's offer'd, | comes to th' entertainer — 2.01. 17
his good arms in lusty stroke | to th' shore, 2.01.121
at | which end o' th' beam should bow. 2.01.132
so is the dear'st o' th' loss. 2.01.136
i' th' commonwealth i would, by contraries, 2.01.148

it is the quality o' th' climate. 2.01.200
th' occasion speaks thee, and | my strong 2.01.207
the man i' th' moon's too slow — till new–born 2.01.249
for he is sure i' th' island. 2.01.325
me with urchin–shows, pitch me i' th' mire, 2.02. 5
storm brewing, i hear it sing i' th' wind. 2.02. 20 P
my cellar is in a rock by th' sea–side, where my 2.02.135 P
out o' th' moon, i do assure thee. 2.02.138 P
i was the man i' th' moon, when time was. 2.02.139 P
the man i' th' moon? 2.02.146 P
i'll show thee every fertile inch o' th' island; 2.02.148
th' harmony of their tongues hath into bondage 3.01. 41
i, | beyond all limit of what else i' th' world, 3.01. 72
if th' other two be brain'd like us, the state 3.02. 6 P
a custom with him | i' th' afternoon to sleep. 3.02. 88
with weariness | to th' dulling of my spirits. 3.03. 6
i' th' name of something holy, sir, why stand 3.03. 94
therefore my son i' th' ooze is bedded; 3.03.100
oaths are straw | to th' fire i' th' blood. 4.01. 53
oaths are straw | to th' fire i' th' blood. 4.01. 53
thou thyself dost air — the queen o' th' sky, 4.01. 70
i' th' filthy–mantled pool beyond your cell, 4.01.182
there dancing up to th' chins, that the foul 4.01.183
thou here, | this is the mouth o' th' cell. 4.01.216
with their high wrongs i am strook to th' quick, 5.01. 25
th' affliction of my mind amends, with which | i 5.01.115
you do yet taste | some subtleties o' th' isle, 5.01.124
he makes sweet music with th' enamell'd stones, TGV 2.07. 28
by penitence th' eternal's wrath's appeas'd: 5.04. 81
makes him run through all th' sins: 5.04.112
i bruis'd my shin th' other day with playing at WIV 1.01.283 P
be there bears i' th' town? 1.01.287 P
plod away i' th' hoof! 1.03. 82
though the priest o' th' town commended him for 2.01.145 P
good mine host o' th' garter, a word with you. 2.01.203 P
alas, i had rather be set quick i' th' earth, 3.04. 86
a blind bitch's puppies, fifteen i' th' litter; 3.05. 11 P
step into th' chamber, sir john. 4.02. 11 P
no, i'll come no more i' th' basket. 4.02. 49 P
by spells, by th' figure, and such daub'ry as 4.02.177 P
nay, by th' mass, that he did not; 4.02.202 P
the knave constable had set me i' th' stocks, i' 4.05.119 P
had set me i' th' stocks, i' th' common stocks, 4.05.120 P
we'll couch i' th' castle–ditch till we see the 5.02. 1 P
stag, and the fattest, i think, i' th' forest. 5.05. 13 P
th' expressure that it bears, green let it be, 5.05. 67
if it had not been i' th' church, i would have 5.05.185 P
th' offense is holy that she hath committed, 5.05.225
that to th' observer doth thy history | fully MM 1.01. 28
to th' hopeful execution do i leave you | of 1.01. 59
fellow, why dost thou show me thus to th' world? 1.02.116
hung by th' wall | so long that nineteen zodiacs 1.02.167
who may, in th' ambush of my name, strike home, 1.03. 41
could have attain'd th' effect of your own 2.01. 13
if he took you a box o' th' ear, you might have 2.01.180 P
if the first that did th' edict infringe | had 2.02. 92
thou'rt i' th' right, girl, more o' that. 2.02.129
in itself, | that skins the vice o' th' top. 2.02.136
th' impression of keen whips i'ld wear as rubies 2.04.101
my unsoil'd name, th' austereness of my life, 2.04.155
my vouch against you, and my place i' th' state, 2.04.156
hooking both right and wrong to th' appetite, 2.04.176
for all th' accommodations that thou bear'st 3.01. 14
and deliberate word | nips youth i' th' head, 3.01. 90
that thus can make him bite the law by th' nose, 3.01.108
is't not drown'd i' th' last rain? 3.02. 49 P
and advis'd him for th' entertainment of death. 3.02.213 P
what news abroad i' th' world? 3.02.221 P
so disguise shall by th' disguised | pay with 3.02.280
none but only a repair i' th' dark, | and that i 4.01. 42
th' one has my pity; 4.02. 61
that wounds th' unsisting postern with these 4.02. 89
for the fault's love is th' offender friended. 4.02.113
who is to be executed in th' afternoon? 4.02.129 P
look, th' unfolding star calls up the shepherd. 4.02.203 P
you let it be proclaim'd betimes i' th' morn. 4.04. 16 P
for truth is truth | to th' end of reck'ning. 5.01. 46
she speaks this in th' infirmity of sense. 5.01. 47
him in mine arms | with all th' effect of love. 5.01.199
then to glance from him | to th' duke himself, 5.01.310
to th' rack with him! 5.01.311
slander to th' state! | away with him to prison. 5.01.322
for claudio's, | th' offense pardons itself. 5.01.534
hath homely age th' alluring beauty took | from ERR 2.01. 89
of suspect | th' unviolated honor of your wife. 3.01. 88
to a curtal dog, and made me turn i' th' wheel. 3.02.146
by th' way we met | my wife, her sister, and a 5.01.235
a mountain of affection th' one with th' other. ADO 2.01.367 P
a mountain of affection th' one with th' other. 2.01.367 P
he hath ta'en th' infection. hold it up. 2.03.121 P
th' idea of her life shall sweetly creep | into 4.01.224
th' endeavor of this present breath may buy LLL 1.01. 5
or vainly comes th' admired princess hither. 1.01.140
th' anointed sovereign of sighs and groans, 3.01.182
th' allusion holds in the exchange. 4.02. 41 P
i say, th' allusion holds in the exchange. 4.02. 44 P
we are much out a' th' way. 4.03. 74
look what you do, you do it still i' th' dark. 5.02. 24
o that i knew he were but in by th' week! 5.02. 61
do not you know my lady's foot by th' squier, 5.02.474
maintained by the owl, th' other by the cuckoo. 5.02.892 P
marking th' embarked traders on the flood; MND 2.01.127
her brother's noontide with th' antipodes. 3.02. 55
myself the man i' th' moon do seem to be. 5.01.245
how is it else the man i' th' moon? 5.01.248 P
the lanthorn is the moon, i the man i' th' moon, 5.01.258 P
you, | and you embrace th' occasion to depart. MV 1.01. 64
monday last at six a' clock i' th' morning, 2.05. 25 P
on ash we'nsday was four year in th' afternoon. 2.05. 27 P
i will survey th' inscriptions back again. 2.07. 14
which pries not to th' interior, but, like the 2.09. 28
before | to signify th' approaching of his lord, 2.09. 88
which makes me fear th' enjoying of my love; 3.02. 29
come forth to view | the issue of th' exploit. 3.02. 60
and use thou all th' endeavor of a man | in 3.04. 48
and others, when the bagpipe sings i' th' nose, 4.01. 49
i am th' unhappy subject of these quarrels. 5.01.238
stood on th' extremest verge of the swift brook, AYL 2.01. 42
compliment is like th' encounter of two dog–apes 2.05. 26 P
ambition shun, | and loves to live i' th' sun, 2.05. 39
i met a fool i' th' forest, | a motley fool. 2.07. 12
cleanse the foul body of th' infected world, 2.07. 60
and all th' embossed sores and headed evils, 2.07. 67
it will be the earliest fruit i' th' country; 3.02.119 P
whose heart th' accustom'd sight of death makes 3.05. 4
him that cupid hath clapp'd him o' th' shoulder, 4.01. 48 P
we are for you, sit i' th' middle. 5.03. 10 P
measure heap'd in joy, to th' measures fall. 5.04.179
and once again a pot o' th' smallest ale. SHR in.2. 75
but th' art too much my friend, | and i'll not 1.02. 63
gabr'el's pumps were all unpink'd i' th' heel; 4.01.133
error i' th' bill, sir, error i' th' bill! 4.03.145 P
error i' th' bill, sir, error i' th' bill! 4.03.145 P
you are i' th' right, sir, 'tis for my mistress. 4.03.156 P
th' art a tall fellow; 4.04. 17
to th' church take the priest, clerk, and some 4.04. 93 P
th' ambition in my love thus plagues itself: AWW 1.01. 90
steely bones | looks bleak i' th' cold wind. 1.01.104
the florentines and senoys are by th' ears, 1.02. 1
jowl horns together like any deer i' th' herd. 1.03. 55 P
in ten, madam, which is a purifying a' th' song. 1.03. 83 P
thy cheeks | confess it, /t' /one to th' other, 1.03.177
be sanctified | by th' luckiest stars in heaven, 1.03.246
and of his old experience th' only darling, | he 2.01.107
whipt, or i would send them to th' turk, to make 2.03. 88 P
the place is dignified by th' doer's deed. 2.03.126
thou hast to pull at a smack a' th' contrary. 2.03.225 P
to th' wars! 2.03.275
what th' import is, | i know not yet. 2.03.276
to th' wars, my boy, to th' wars! 2.03.278
to th' wars, my boy, to th' wars! 2.03.278
that dwell in't jades, | therefore to th' war! 2.03.285
she's very well, and wants nothing i' th' world; 2.04. 4 P
away, th' art a knave. 2.04. 28 P
sir, "before a knave th' art a knave," that's 2.04. 30 P
a knave," that's "before me th' art a knave." 2.04. 30 P
you will take your instant leave a' th' king, 2.04. 48
to–morrow to th' field. 3.01. 23
and our isbels a' th' country are nothing like 3.02. 13 P
like your old ling and your isbels a' th' court. 3.02. 14 P
worthy sake | to th' extreme edge of hazard. 3.03. 6
perchance he's hurt i' th' battle. 3.05. 87 P
i know th' art valiant, and to the possibility 3.06. 82 P
by this same coxcomb that we have i' th' wind, 3.06.114
good captain, let me be th' interpreter. 4.01. 7 P
us some band of strangers i' th' adversary's 4.01. 15 P
which were the greatest obloquy i' th' world 4.02. 44
which were the greatest obloquy i' th' world 4.02. 48
him forth, h'as sat i' th' stocks all night, 4.03.101 P
instant disaster of his setting i' th' stocks; 4.03.110 P
whether one captain dumaine be i' th' camp, a 4.03.176 P
me this other day to turn him out a' th' band. 4.03.200 P
sir, in a dungeon, i' th' stocks, or any where, 4.03.244 P
of it, and cut th' entail from all remainders, 4.03.279 P
e'en a crow a' th' same nest; 4.03.286 P
natural rebellion, done i' th' blade of youth, 5.03. 6
we do bury | th' incensing relics of it. 5.03. 25
th' inaudible and noiseless foot of time 5.03. 41
all that | he gave it to a commoner a' th' camp, 5.03.194
conferr'd by testament to th' sequent issue, 5.03.197
with all the spots a' th' world tax'd and 5.03.206
and boarded her i' th' wanton way of youth. 5.03.211
come, come, to th' purpose. 5.03.241 P
what's that to th' purpose? TN 1.03. 21 P
he plays o' th' viol–de–gamboys, and speaks 1.03. 25 P
his brains turn o' th' toe like a parish–top. 1.03. 42 P
sir, i have not you by th' hand. 1.03. 66 P
i pray you bring your hand to th' butt'ry–bar, 1.03. 70 P
she'll none o' th' count. 1.03.109 P
i am a fellow o' th' strangest mind i' th' world 1.03.113 P
am a fellow o' th' strangest mind i' th' world; 1.03.113 P
th' art a scholar; 2.03. 13 P
anne, and ginger shall be hot i' th' mouth too. 2.03.118 P
th' art i' th' right. 2.03.119 P
th' art i' th' right. 2.03.119 P
if thou hast her not i' th' end, call me cut. 2.03.187 P
but let concealment, like a worm i' th' bud, 2.04.111
and baited it with all th' unmuzzled thoughts 3.01.119
i saw't i' th' orchard. 3.02. 7 P
of a flea, i'll eat the rest of th' anatomy. 3.02. 62 P
like a pedant that keeps a school i' th' church. 3.02. 76 P
th' offense is not of such a bloody nature, 3.03. 30
to th' elephant. 3.03. 48
carry his water to th' wise woman. 3.04.102 P
still you keep o' th' windy side of the law; 3.04.164 P
thou shalt hold th' opinion of pythagoras ere i 4.02. 58 P
like to th' egyptian thief at point of death, 5.01.118
h'as hurt me, and there's th' end on't. 5.01.197 P
his eyes were set at eight i' th' morning. 5.01.199 P
one day shall crown th' alliance on't, so please 5.01.318
no tongue that moves, none, none i' th' world, WT 1.02. 20
i love thee not a jar o' th' clock behind | what 1.02. 43
was not my lord | the verier wag o' th' two? 1.02. 66
were as twinn'd lambs that did frisk i' th' sun, 1.02. 67
i' th' sun, | and bleat the one at th' other. 1.02. 68
th' offenses we have made you do we'll answer, 1.02. 83
but to th' goal: 1.02. 96
but once before i spoke to th' purpose? 1.02.100
i have spoke to th' purpose twice: 1.02.106
th' other for some while a friend. 1.02.108
to sigh, as 'twere | the mort o' th' deer — o, 1.02.118
you would seek us, | we are yours i' th' garden. 1.02.178
while i speak this) holds his wife by th' arm, 1.02.193
th' entreaties of your mistress? 1.02.234
give scandal to the blood o' th' prince my son 1.02.330
what is the news i' th' court? 1.02.367
wafting his eyes to th' contrary and falling | a 1.02.372
at several posterns | clear them o' th' city. 1.02.439
present | th' abhorr'd ingredient to his eye, 2.01. 43
my saying, | howe'er you lean to th' nayward. 2.01. 64
spotless | i' th' eyes of heaven and to you — i 2.01.132
all other circumstances | made up to th' deed), 2.01.179
the oracle | give rest to th' minds of others — 2.01.191
credulity will not | come up to th' truth. 2.01.193
and honor from th' access of gentle visitors. 2.02. 10
these dangerous, unsafe lunes i' th' king, 2.02. 28
undertake to be | her advocate to th' loud'st. 2.02. 37
how he may soften at the sight o' th' child: 2.02. 38
cause were not in being — part o' th' cause, 2.03. 3
might we lay th' old proverb to your charge, 2.03. 97
from those you sent to th' oracle are come | an 2.03.194
are both landed, | hasting to th' court. 2.03.197
solemn, and unearthly | it was i' th' off'ring! 3.01. 8
and the ear–deaf'ning voice o' th' oracle, | kin 3.01. 9
if th' event o' th' journey | prove as 3.01. 11
if th' event o' th' journey | prove as 3.01. 11
great apollo | turn all to th' best! 3.01. 15
hurried | here to this place, i' th' open air, 3.02.105
there is no truth at all i' th' oracle. 3.02.140
made fault | i' th' boldness of your speech. 3.02.218
he is touch'd | to th' noble heart. 3.02.222
best haste, and go not | too far i' th' land; 3.03. 11
am glad at heart | to be so rid o' th' business. 3.03. 15
the spirits o' th' dead | may walk again. 3.03. 16
of him what he is, fetch me to th' sight of him. 3.03.134 P
and you shall help to put him i' th' ground. 3.03.137 P
i do | to th' freshest things now reigning, and 4.01. 13
th' effects of his fond jealousies so grieving 4.01. 18
i mentioned a son o' th' king's, which florizel 4.01. 22
which follows after, | is th' argument of time. 4.01. 29
of pruins, and as many of raisins o' th' sun. 4.03. 49 P
i' th' name of me — 4.03. 51 P
the gracious mark o' th' land, you have obscur'd 4.04. 8
(as it must be) by th' pow'r of the king. 4.04. 37
i prithee darken not | the mirth o' th' feast. 4.04. 42
at upper end o' th' table, now i' th' middle; 4.04. 59
at upper end o' th' table, now i' th' middle; 4.04. 59
that which you are, mistress o' th' feast. 4.04. 68
should take on me | the hostess–ship o' th' day. 4.04. 72
the fairest flow'rs o' th' season | are our 4.04. 81
that goes to bed wi' th' sun | and with him 4.04.105
i had some flow'rs o' th' spring that might 4.04.113
i wish you | a wave o' th' sea, that you might 4.04.141
hath ribbons of all the colors i' th' rainbow; 4.04.204 P
handle, though they come to him by th' gross; 4.04.206 P
or thou goest to th' grange, or mill. 4.04.303
but they themselves are o' th' mind (if it be 4.04.329 P
but jumps twelve foot and a half by th' squier. 4.04.339 P
bolted | by th' northern blasts twice o'er. 4.04.365
how prettily th' young swain seems to wash | the 4.04.366
by th' pattern of mine own thoughts i cut out 4.04.382
that must be | i' th' virtue of your daughter. 4.04.387
nature crush the sides o' th' earth together, 4.04.478
i' th' love | that i have borne your father? 4.04.516
but as th' unthought–on accident is guilty | to 4.04.538
forgiveness, | as 'twere i' th' father's person; 4.04.550
th' one | he chides to hell and bids the other 4.04.552
her breeding as | she is i' th' rear 'our birth. 4.04.581
thus we set on, camillo, to th' sea–side. 4.04.668
also, to smell out work for th' other senses. 4.04.673 P
to th' palace, and it like your worship. 4.04.716 P
what's i' th' farthel? 4.04.754 P
this hour, if i may come to th' speech of him. 4.04.758 P
great alexander | left his to th' worthiest; 5.01. 48
welcome hither, | as is the spring to th' earth. 5.01.152
too | expos'd this paragon to th' fearful usage 5.01.153
pains, much less | th' adventure of her person? 5.01.156
could not say if th' importance were joy or 5.02. 18 P
th' advantage of his absence took the king, JN 1.01.102
brother by th' mother's side, give me your hand; 1.01.163
for thou wast got i' th' way of honesty. 1.01.181
and all th' unsettled humors of the land, | rash 2.01. 66
against th' /invulnerable clouds of heaven, 2.01.252
without th' assistance of a mortal hand. 3.01.158
holding th' eternal spirit, against her will, 3.04. 18
doth make the fault the worse by th' excuse: 4.02. 31
request | th' enfranchisement of arthur, whose 4.02. 52
and find th' inheritance of this poor child, 4.02. 97
th' uncleanly savors of a slaughter–house, | for 4.03.112
and to part by th' teeth | the unowed interest 4.03.146
had three times slain th' appearance of the king 2H4 1.01.128
to frown upon th' enrag'd northumberland! 1.01.152
you may thank th' unquiet time for your quiet 1.02.150 P
but answer in th' effect of your reputation, and 2.01.130 P
by this hand, to th' infernal deep, with erebus 2.04.157 P
are you not hurt i' th' groin? 2.04.210 P
you have hurt him, sir, i' th' shoulder. 2.04.214 P
what says th' almanac to that? 2.04.264 P
till thy return — well, hearken a' th' end. 2.04.280 P
no abuse, ned, i' th' world, honest ned, none. 2.04.318 P
for th' other, i owe her money, and whether she 2.04.339 P
look to th' door there, francis. 2.04.352 P
would have clapp'd i' th' clout at twelve score, 3.02. 46 P
for th' other, sir john, let me see: 3.02.120 P
peter bullcalf o' th' green! 3.02.172 P
by the mass, i could anger her to th' heart. 3.02.204 P
well said, th' art a good fellow. 3.02.239 P
well said, i' faith, wart, th' art a good scab. 3.02.276 P
to us th' /imagin'd voice of god himself, | the 4.02. 19
th' unguided days | and rotten times that you 4.04. 59
th' incessant care and labor of his mind | hath 4.04.118
and never live to show th' incredulous world 4.05.153
a friend i' th' court is better than a penny in 5.01. 31 P
of woncote against clement perkes a' th' hill. 5.01. 39 P
led by th' impartial conduct of my soul; 5.02. 36
send to prison | th' immediate heir of england! 5.02. 71
in me, | and, in th' administration of his law, 5.02. 75
th' unstained sword that you have us'd to bear, 5.02.114
be merry, now comes in the sweet a' th' night. 5.03. 51 P
come, | i'll pledge you a mile to th' bottom." 5.03. 54
their proud hoofs i' th' receiving earth; H5 pr 27
turning th' accomplishment of many years | into pr 30
which in th' eleventh year of the last king's 1.01. 2
king beside, | a thousand pounds by th' year. 1.01. 19
came | and whipt th' offending adam out of him, 1.01. 29
than cherishing th' exhibiters against us; 1.01. 74
what was th' impediment that broke this off? 1.01. 90
shall we call in th' ambassador, my liege? 1.02. 3
convey'd himself as th' heir to th' lady lingare 1.02. 74
himself as th' heir to th' lady lingare, 1.02. 74
hath shook and trembled at th' ill neighborhood. 1.02.154
th' advised head defends itself at home; 1.02.179
on, and we'll digest | th' abuse of distance; 2.pr. 32
twelve and one, ev'n at the turning o' th' tide; 2.03. 13 P

borne with th' invisible and creeping wind, 3.pr. 11
a city on th' inconstant billows dancing; 3.pr. 15
suppose th' embassador from the french comes 3.pr. 28
for look you, th' athversary — you may discuss 3.02. 60 P
expedition and knowledge in th' aunchiant wars, 3.02. 78 P
upon th' enraged soldiers in their spoil, | as 3.03. 25
th' athversary was have possession of the pridge 3.06. 93 P
the perdition of th' athversary hath been very 3.06. 98 P
for th' effusion of our blood, the muster of his 3.06.130 P
/if th' opposed numbers | pluck their hearts 4.01.291
valor than this roaring devil i' th' old play, 4.04. 71 P
i have sworn to take him a box a' th' ear; 4.07.128 P
favor | may haply purchase him a box a' th' ear. 4.07.173
and little loss, | on one part and on th' other? 4.08.111
i humbly pray them to admit th' excuse | of time 5.pr. 3
like to the senators of th' antique rome, | with 5.pr. 26
news have i that my doll is dead i' th' spittle 5.01. 81
whose want gives growth to th' imperfections 5.02. 69
i can, | to view th' artillery and munition, 1H6 1.01.168
or else was wrangling somerset in th' error? 2.04. 6
or make my will th' advantage of my good. 2.05.129
writ to your grace from th' duke of burgundy. 4.01. 12
yet call th' embassadors, and as you please, 5.01. 24
from being regent | i' th' parts of france, till 2H6 1.01. 67
more like a soldier than a man o' th' church, 1.01.186
but, as i think, it was by th' cardinal), | and 1.02. 27
th' uncivil kerns of ireland are in arms, | and 3.01.310
it is not worth th' enjoying. 3.01.334
being burnt i' th' hand for stealing of sheep. 4.02. 63 P
others to th' inns of court; 4.07. 2 P
give him a box o' th' ear, and that will make 4.07. 86 P
see, buckingham, somerset comes with th' queen. 5.01. 83
by th' mass, so did we all. 5.03. 16
is this th' alliance that he seeks with france? 3H6 3.03.177
did i let pass th' abuse done to my niece? 3.03.188
edward's fruit, true heir to th' english crown. 4.04. 24
th' untimely fall of virtuous lancaster. R3 1.02. 4
i dare adventure to be sent to th' tow'r. 1.03.115
which may make you and him to rue at th' other. 3.02. 14
this princely presence | to doom th' offenders, 3.04. 65
th' unsatiate greediness of his desire, | and 3.07. 7
th' earldom of /herford, and the moveables, 4.02. 90
th' adulterate hastings, rivers, vaughan, grey, 4.04. 69
th' advancement of your children, gentle lady. 4.04.242
put in her tender heart th' aspiring flame | of 4.04.328
th' imperial metal, circling now thy head, | had 4.04.382
and th' ensuing night | made it a fool and H8 1.01. 27
bulk | take up the rays o' th' beneficial sun, 1.01. 56
call'd upon | for high feats done to th' crown, 1.01. 61
(without the privity o' th' king) t' appoint 1.01. 74
is it therefore | th' ambassador is silenc'd? 1.01. 97
that's th' appliance only | which your disease 1.01.124
he's gone to th' king; 1.01.128
to th' king i'll say't, and make my vouch as 1.01.157
th' interview | that swallowed so much treasure, 1.01.165
and like a glass | did break i' th' wrenching. 1.01.167
cardinal | the articles o' th' combination drew 1.01.169
to as much end | as give a crutch to th' dead. 1.01.172
is a kind of puppy | to th' old dam, treason), 1.01.176
his highness' pleasure | you shall to th' tower. 1.01.207
the king | is pleas'd you shall to th' tower, 1.01.213
these are the limbs o' th' plot. 1.01.220
a monk o' th' chartreux. 1.01.221
i stood i' th' level | of a full-charg'd 1.02. 2
manner | daring th' event to th' teeth, are all 1.02. 36
manner | daring th' event to th' teeth, are all 1.02. 36
a single part in aught | pertains to th' state; 1.02. 42
they are | most pestilent to th' hearing, and, 1.02. 49
bear 'em, | the back is sacrifice to th' load. 1.02. 50
every tree, lop, bark, and part o' th' timber; 1.02. 96
bid him strive | to the love o' th' commonalty; 1.02.170
your office | on the complaint o' th' tenants. 1.02.173
by th' devil's illusions | the monk might be 1.02.178
father meant to act upon | th' usurper richard, 1.02.196
by day and night, | he's traitor to th' height. 1.02.214
is but merely | a fit or two o' th' face — but 1.03. 7
to't, | that sure th' have worn out christendom. 1.03. 15
th' have left their barge and landed, | and 1.04. 54
is the banket ready | i' th' privy chamber? 1.04. 99
when he was brought again to th' bar, to hear 2.01. 31
to th' water side i must conduct your grace; 2.01. 95
th' are breath i not believe in. 2.02. 53
deliver this with modesty to th' queen. 2.02.136
there 'long'd | no more to th' crown but that. 2.03. 49
read, | and on all sides th' authority allow'd; 2.04. 4
if not, i' th' name of god, | your pleasure be 2.04. 56
yea, the elect o' th' land, who are assembled 2.04. 60
and display'd th' effects | of disposition 2.04. 86
that man i' th' world who shall report he has 2.04.135
then mark th' inducement. 2.04.170
speeches utter'd | by th' bishop of bayonne, 2.04.173
i' th' progress of this business, | ere a 2.04.176
of life to't than | the grave does to th' dead; 2.04.192
(well worthy the best heir o' th' world) should 2.04.196
for no dislike i' th' world against the person 2.04.224
creature | that's paragon'd o' th' world. 2.04.231
if you cannot | bar his access to th' king, 3.02. 17
and came to th' eye o' th' king, wherein was 3.02. 31
and came to th' eye o' th' king, wherein was 3.02. 31
holiness | to stay the judgment o' th' divorce; 3.02. 33
has left the cause o' th' king unhandled, and 3.02. 58
look'd he | o' th' inside of the paper? 3.02. 78
cause, that she should lie i' th' bosom of | our 3.02.100
and what expense by th' hour | seems to flow 3.02.108
how, i' th' name of thrift, | does he rake this 3.02.109
part of business which | i bear i' th' state; 3.02.146
to th' good of your most sacred person and | the 3.02.173
of it, as i' th' contrary | the foulness is the 3.02.182
'tis th' accompt | of all that world of wealth i 3.02.210
"to th' pope"? 3.02.220
feel | my sword i' th' life-blood of thee else. 3.02.277
packets | you writ to th' pope against the king. 3.02.287
fall into th' compass of a praemunire — | that 3.02.340
among the crowd i' th' abbey, where a finger 4.01. 57
a man in much esteem with th' king, and truly 4.01.109
king has made him master | o' th' jewel house, 4.01.111
which | is to th' court, and there ye shall be 4.01.115
my legs like loaden branches bow to th' earth, 4.02. 2

i' th' presence | he would say untruths, and be 4.02. 37
speak of two | the most remark'd i' th' kingdom. 5.01. 33
is made master | o' th' rolls, and the king's 5.01. 35
th' archbishop | is the king's hand and tongue, 5.01. 37
incens'd the lords o' th' council that he is 5.01. 43
pray'rs remember | th' estate of my poor queen. 5.01. 74
you not | how your state stands i' th' world, 5.01.127
justice and the truth o' th' question carries 5.01.130
carries | the due o' th' verdict with it. 5.01.131
vehemency | th' occasion shall instruct you. 5.01.149
you be convey'd to th' tower a prisoner; 5.02.124
way of mercy | but i must needs to th' tower, my 5.02.128
let some o' th' guard be ready there. 5.02.130
receive him, | and see him safe i' th' tower. 5.02.132
good master porter, i belong to th' larder. 5.03. 4 P
belong to th' gallows, and be hang'd, ye rogue! 5.03. 6 P
should you do, but knock 'em down by th' dozens? 5.03. 33 P
which were the hope o' th' strond, where she was 5.03. 53 P
at length they came to th' broom-staff to me, i 5.03. 54 P
these | your faithful friends o' th' suburbs? 5.03. 72
i'll lay ye all | by th' heels, and suddenly; 5.03. 79
th' are come already from the christening. 5.03. 83
you i' th' chamblet, get up o' th' rail, | i'll 5.03. 89
you i' th' chamblet, get up o' th' rail, | i'll 5.03. 89
unspotted lily shall she pass | to th' ground, 5.04. 62
i'll meddle nor make no more i' th' matter. TRO 1.01. 83 P
so do all men, unless th' are drunk, sick, or 1.02. 17 P
th' other's not come to't. 1.02. 84 P
tell me another tale when th' other's come to't. 1.02. 85 P
helen herself swore th' other day that troilus, 1.02. 93 P
she came to him th' other day into the compass'd 1.02.110 P
idle head, you would eat chickens i' th' shell. 1.02.134 P
he's one o' th' soundest judgments in troy, 1.02.192 P
besides th' applause and approbation | the which 1.03. 59
th' unworthiest shows as fairly in the mask. 1.03. 84
tent that searches | to th' bottom of the worst. 2.02. 17
without some image of th' affected merit. 2.02. 60
untent his person and share th' air with us? 2.03.168
walk here i' th' orchard, i'll bring her 3.02. 16 P
th' imaginary relish is so sweet | that it 3.02. 19
you draw backward, we'll put you i' th' fills. 3.02. 46 P
as the tercel, for all the ducks i' th' river. 3.02. 53 P
but she'll bereave you a' th' deeds too, if she 3.02. 56 P
as iron to adamant, as earth to th' centre, 3.02.179
when th' have said as false | as air, as water, 3.02.191
th' advantage of the time prompts me aloud | to 3.03. 2
achilles stands i' th' entrance of his tent. 3.03. 38
till he behold them formed in th' applause 3.03.119
formed in th' applause | where th' are extended; 3.03.120
apprehended here immediately | th' unknown ajax. 3.03.125
slightly shakes his parting guest by th' hand, 3.03.166
finds bottom in th' uncomprehensive depth, 3.03.198
for if hector break not his neck i' th' combat, 3.03.259 P
would he were knock'd i' th' head! 4.02. 34
you fillip me a' th' head. 4.05. 45
mock not /that /i affect th' untraded /oath, 4.05.178
thou hast hung /thy advanced sword i' th' air, 4.05.188
sciaticas, lime-kills i' th' palm, incurable 5.01. 22 P
that doth invert th' attest of eyes and ears, 5.02.122
youth, | i am to-day i' th' vein of chivalry. 5.03. 32
for th' love of all the gods, | let's leave the 5.03. 44
th' effect doth operate another way. 5.03.109
a' th' t' other side, the policy of those crafty 5.04. 9 P
the other side a' th' city is risen; COR 1.01. 47 P
to th' capitol! 1.01. 48 P
our business is not unknown to th' senate; 1.01. 57 P
and you slander | the helms o' th' state, who 1.01. 77
a gulf it did remain | i' th' midst a' th' body, 1.01. 99
a gulf it did remain | i' th' midst a' th' body, 1.01. 99
where th' other instruments | did see and hear, 1.01.101
replied | to th' discontented members, the 1.01.111
be restrain'd, | who is the sink a' th' body — 1.01.122
the court, the heart, to th' seat o' th' brain, 1.01.136
the court, the heart, to th' seat o' th' brain, 1.01.136
rightly | touching the weal a' th' common, you 1.01.151
for that, being one o' th' lowest, basest, 1.01.157
they'll sit by th' fire, and presume to know 1.01.191
presume to know | what's done i' th' capitol; 1.01.192
they would hang them on the horns a' th' moon, 1.01.213
were half to half the world by th' ears, and he 1.01.233
your company to th' capitol, where i know | our 1.01.244
though he perform | to th' utmost of a man, and 1.01.268
you'll find | th' have not prepar'd for us. 1.02. 30
no better than picture-like to hang by th' wall, 1.03. 11 P
see him pluck aufidius down by th' hair; 1.03. 30
to th' pot, i warrant him. 1.04. 47
call thither all the officers a' th' town, 1.05. 27
him, or pitying, threat'ning th' other; 1.06. 36
are you lords a' th' field? 1.06. 47
their bands i' th' vaward are the /antiates, 1.06. 53
by th' blood we have shed together, by th' vows 1.06. 57
by th' vows | we have made to endure friends, 1.06. 57
our guider, come, to th' roman camp conduct us. 1.07. 7
revenge | wrench up thy power to th' highest. 1.08. 11
shall attend and shrug, | i' th' end admire; 1.09. 5
trumpets shall | i' th' field prove flatterers, 1.09. 43
let him be made an overture for th' wars! 1.09. 46
with all th' applause and clamor of the host, 1.09. 64
bear | th' addition nobly ever! 1.09. 66
good addition | to th' fairness of my power. 1.09. 73
a treaty find | i' th' part that is at mercy? 1.10. 7
by th' elements, | if e'er again i meet him 1.10. 10
go you to th' city, | learn how 'tis held, and 1.10. 27
the city, i mean of us a' th' right-hand file? 2.01. 22 P
i' th' shoulder and i' th' left arm. 2.01.147 P
i' th' shoulder and i' th' left arm. 2.01.147 P
the repulse of tarquin seven hurts i' th' body. 2.01.150 P
one i' th' neck, and two i' th' thigh — there's 2.01.151 P
one i' th' neck, and two i' th' thigh — there's 2.01.151 P
their nicely gawded cheeks to th' wanton spoil 2.01.217
never would he | appear i' th' market-place, nor 2.01.233
his wounds | to th' people, beg their stinking 2.01.236
and carry with us ears and eyes for th' time, 2.01.269
masters a' th' people, | we do request your 2.02. 51
i had rather have one scratch my head i' th' sun 2.02. 75
and i' th' consul's view | slew three opposers. 2.02. 93
he prov'd best man i' th' field, and for his 2.02. 97
alone he ent'red | the mortal gate of th' city, 2.02.111

show them th' unaching scars which i should hide 2.02.148
of our proceedings here on th' market-place; 2.02.159
be at once to all the points a' th' compass. 2.03. 24 P
and ran | from th' noise of our own drums." 2.03. 54
well then, i pray, your price a' th' consulship? 2.03. 73 P
remains | that, in th' official marks invested, 2.03.140
myself again, | repair to th' senate-house. 2.03.148
that you bear | i' th' body of the weal; 2.03.181
a place of potency and sway o' th' state, | if 2.03.182
malignantly remain | fast foe to th' plebeii, 2.03.184
you should have ta'en th' advantage of his 2.03.198
you | th' apprehension of his present portance, 2.03.224
springs of — | the noble house o' th' martians; 2.03.238
have drawn your number, | repair to th' capitol. 2.03.254
to th' capitol, come. 2.03.260
will be there before the stream o' th' people; 2.03.261
the people, | the tongues o' th' common mouth. 3.01. 22
give way, he shall to th' market-place. 3.01. 31
laid falsely | i' th' plain way of his merit. 3.01. 61
you speak a' th' people | as if you were a god, 3.01. 80
being but | the horn and noise o' th' monster's, 3.01. 95
gap of both, and take | the one by th' other. 3.01.112
well, on to th' market-place. 3.01.112
give forth | the corn a' th' store-house gratis, 3.01.114
being press'd to th' war, | even when the navel 3.01.122
being i' th' war, | their mutinies and revolts, 3.01.125
th' accusation | which they have often made 3.01.127
in time | break ope the locks a' th' senate, and 3.01.138
it would, | for th' ill which doth control't. 3.01.161
their obedience fails | to th' greater bench. 3.01.166
be meet, | and throw their power i' th' dust. 3.01.170
innovator, | a foe to th' public weal. 3.01.175
you, tribunes | to th' people! 3.01.190
upon the part o' th' people, in whose power | we 3.01.209
bear him to th' rock tarpeian, and from thence 3.01.212
though calved i' th' porch o' th' capitol! 3.01.239
though calved i' th' porch o' th' capitol! 3.01.239
myself | take up a brace o' th' best of them, 3.01.243
and suffer it | a brand to th' end a' th' world. 3.01.302
and suffer it | a brand to th' end a' th' world. 3.01.302
he has been bred i' th' wars | since 'a could 3.01.318
before he should thus stoop to th' /herd, but 3.02. 32
the violent fit a' th' time craves it as physic 3.02. 33
return to th' tribunes. 3.02. 36
friends, | i' th' war do grow together; 3.02. 43
in peace what each of them by th' other lose 3.02. 44
now it lies you on to speak | to th' people; 3.02. 53
nor by th' matter which your heart prompts you, 3.02. 54
and the eyes of th' ignorant | more learned than 3.02. 76
i have been i' th' market-place; 3.02. 93
to th' market-place! 3.02.104
which never | i shall discharge to th' life. 3.02.106
tongue can do | i' th' way of flattery further. 3.02.137
that we have procur'd | set down by th' pole? 3.03. 10
so | i' th' right and strength a' th' commons," 3.03. 14
so | i' th' right and strength a' th' commons," 3.03. 14
and power i' th' truth a' th' cause. 3.03. 18
and power i' th' truth a' th' cause. 3.03. 18
piece | will bear the knave by th' volume. 3.03. 33
th' honor'd gods | keep rome in safety, and the 3.03. 33
which show | like graves i' th' holy churchyard. 3.03. 51
the fires i' th' lowest hell fold in the people! 3.03. 68
to th' rock, to th' rock with him! 3.03. 75
to th' rock, to th' rock with him! 3.03. 75
capital kind, | deserves th' extremest death. 3.03. 82
doth distribute it — in the name a' th' people, 3.03. 99
i' th' people's name, | i say it shall be so. 3.03.104
breath i hate | as reek a' th' rotten fens, 3.03.121
chance | that starts i' th' way before thee. 4.01. 37
doth ever cool | i' th' absence of the needer. 4.01. 44
the hoarded plague a' th' gods | requite your 4.02. 11
billeted, already in th' entertainment, and to 4.03. 44 P
now th' art troublesome. 4.05. 16 P
i cannot get him out o' th' house. 4.05. 21 P
i' th' city of kites and crows. 4.05. 42 P
i' th' city of kites and crows? 4.05. 43 P
and suffer'd me by th' voice of slaves to be 4.05. 77
of all the men i' th' world | i would have 4.05. 81
and that to prove more fortunes | th' art tir'd, 4.05. 94
and take our friendly senators by th' hands, 4.05.132
take | th' one half of my commission, and set 4.05.138
he is simply the rarest man i' th' world. 4.05.161 P
set at upper end o' th' table; 4.05.192 P
turns up the white o' th' eye to his discourse. 4.05.196 P
our general is cut i' th' middle, and but one 4.05.197 P
and sowl the porter of rome gates by th' ears. 4.05.201 P
caius martius was | a worthy officer i' th' war, 4.06. 30
clusters, | who did hoot him out o' th' city. 4.06.123
i ever said we were i' th' wrong when we 4.06.154 P
do they still fly to th' roman? 4.07. 1
and is no less apparent | to th' vulgar eye, 4.07. 21
not moving | from th' casque to th' cushion, but 4.07. 43
not moving | from th' casque to th' cushion, but 4.07. 43
lie in th' interpretation of the time, | and 4.07. 50
till he had forg'd himself a name a' th' fire 5.01. 14
leave unburnt | and still to nose th' offense. 5.01. 28
if thou stand'st not i' th' state of hanging, or 5.02. 64 P
i neither care for th' world nor your general; 5.02.102 P
you must report to th' volscian lords, how 5.03. 3
sink, my knee, i' th' earth; 5.03. 50
which by th' interpretation of full time | may 5.03. 69
and stick i' th' wars | like a great sea-mark, 5.03. 73
his name remains | to th' ensuing age abhorr'd." 5.03.148
to tear with thunder the wide cheeks a' th' air, 5.03.151
here he lets me prate | like one i' th' stocks. 5.03.160
see you yond coign a' th' capitol, yond 5.04. 1 P
rome, | no, not th' expulsion of the tarquins. 5.04. 43
tide, | as the recomforted through th' gates. 5.04. 48
go tell the lords a' th' city i am here. 5.06. 1
bid them repair to th' market-place, where i, 5.06. 3
to the antiates | than shame to th' romans; 5.06. 80
subscrib'd by th' consuls and patricians, 5.06. 81
together with the seal a' th' senate, what | we 5.06. 82
you lords and heads a' th' state, perfidiously 5.06. 90
silk, never admitting | counsel a' th' war; 5.06. 96
and his fame folds in | this orb o' th' earth. 5.06.125
help, three a' th' chiefest soldiers; 5.06.148
th' effects of sorrow for his valiant sons, TIT 4.04. 30

sent from th' infernal kingdom | to ease the 5.02. 30
nor bide th' encounter of assailing eyes, | nor ROM 1.01.213
to see it techy and fall out wi' th' dug! 1.03. 32
nay, by th' rood, | she could have run and 1.03. 36
you kiss by th' book. 1.05.110
o, swear not by the moon, th' inconstant moon, 2.02.109
th' exchange of thy love's faithful vow for mine 2.02.127
i know them both; th' other's a jeweller. TIM 1.01. 8
the fire i' th' flint | shows not till it be 1.01. 22
to th' dumbness of the gesture | one might 1.01. 33
the base o' th' mount | is rank'd with all 1.01. 64
the maid is fair, a' th' youngest for a bride, 1.01.123
right, if doing nothing be death by th' law. 1.01.194 P
to be flatter'd is worthy o' th' flatterer. 1.01.227 P
i will fly, like a dog, the heels a' th' ass. 1.01.272 P
fie, th' art a churl. 1.02. 26
th' art an athenian, therefore welcome. 1.02. 35 P
honest water, which ne'er left man i' th' mire. 1.02. 59
thou stand'st single, th' art not on him yet. 2.02. 56 P
yea, 'gainst th' authority of manners, pray'd 2.02.138
call me before th' exactest auditors, | and set 2.02.156
bid 'em send o' th' instant | a thousand talents 2.02.198
must i take th' cure upon me? 3.03. 12
may prove an argument of laughter | to th' rest, 3.03. 21
and it should seem by th' sum | your master's 3.04. 30
and take down th' int'rest into their glutt'nous 3.04. 52
will fare so harshly o' th' trumpet's sound; 3.06. 34 P
he gave me a jewel th' other day, and now he has 3.06.112 P
to general filths | convert o' th' instant, 4.01. 7
master's bed, | thy mistress is o' th' brothel! 4.01. 13
sow all th' athenian bosoms, and their crop | be 4.01. 29
th' unkindest beast more kinder than mankind. 4.01. 36
th' athenians both within and out that wall! 4.01. 38
knit and break religions, bless th' accurs'd, 4.03. 35
embalms and spices | to th' april day again. 4.03. 42
th' art quick, | but yet i'll bury thee; 4.03. 45
is this th' athenian minion, whom the world 4.03. 81
agues | th' immortal gods that hear you. 4.03.139
with all th' abhorred births below crisp heaven 4.03.183
so i shall mend mine own, by th' lack of thine. 4.03.284
and th' hadst hated meddlers sooner, thou 4.03.309 P
i'll say th' hast gold; 4.03.393
go, suck the subtle blood o' th' grape, | till 4.03.429
then, if thou /grant'st th' art a man, i have 4.03.474
promising is the very air o' th' time; 5.01. 22
th' art indeed the best, | thou counterfeit'st 5.01. 81
it is our part and promise to th' athenians | to 5.01.120
th' athenians, | by two of their most reverend 5.01.128
be as a cantherizing to the root o' th' tongue, 5.01.133
drive back | of alcibiades th' approaches wild, 5.01.164
and take our goodly aged men by th' beards, 5.01.172
there's not a whittle in th' unruly camp | but i 5.01.180
his fellowship i' th' cause against your city, 5.02. 12
approach the fold and cull th' infected forth, 5.04. 43
dead, | entomb'd upon the very hem o' th' sea, 5.04. 66
set honor in one eye and death i' th' other, JC 1.02. 86
th' eternal devil to keep his state in rome | as 1.02.160
you that, i'll ne'er look you i' th' face again. 1.02.282 P
and i have seen | th' ambitious ocean swell, and 1.03. 7
th' abuse of greatness is when it disjoins 2.01. 18
nor th' insuppressive mettle of our spirits, 2.01.134
till he unseam'd him from the nave to th' chops, MAC 1.02. 22
husband's to aleppo gone, master o' th' tiger; 1.03. 7
th' art kind. 1.03. 12
quarters that they know | i' th' shipman's card. 1.03. 17
that look not like th' inhabitants o' th' earth, 1.03. 41
that look not like th' inhabitants o' th' earth, 1.03. 41
i' th' name of truth, | are ye fantastical, or 1.03. 52
to th' self–same tune and words. who's here? 1.03. 88
in viewing o'er the rest o' th' self–same day, 1.03. 94
it is too full o' th' milk of human kindness 1.05. 17
stop up th' access and passage to remorse, 1.05. 44
nor keep peace between | th' effect and /it! 1.05. 47
look like th' innocent flower, | but be the 1.05. 65
if th' assassination | could trammel up the 1.07. 2
being taught, return | to plague th' inventor. 1.07. 10
commends th' ingredience of our poison'd chalice 1.07. 11
itself, | and falls on th' other — how now? 1.07. 28
"i would," | like the poor cat i' th' adage? 1.07. 45
you and i perform upon | th' unguarded duncan? 1.07. 70
eyes are made the fools o' th' other senses, 2.01. 44
th' attempt, and not the deed, | confounds us. 2.02. 10
hark! who lies i' th' second chamber? 2.02. 17
who's there, i' th' name of belzebub? 2.03. 4 P
that hang'd himself on th' expectation of plenty 2.03. 5 P
who's there, in th' other devil's name? 2.03. 7 P
go the primrose way to th' everlasting bonfire. 2.03. 19 P
and, as they say, | lamentings heard i' th' air; 2.03. 56
events | new hatch'd to th' woeful time. 2.03. 59
and stole thence | the life o' th' building! 2.03. 69
th' expedition of my violent love | outrun the 2.03.110
readiness, | and meet i' th' hall together. 2.03.134
by th' clock 'tis day, | and yet dark night 2.04. 6
to th' amazement of mine eyes | that look'd 2.04. 19
the list, | and champion me to th' utterance! 3.01. 71
not i' th' worst rank of manhood, say't, | and i 3.01.102
acquaint you with the perfect spy o' th' time, 3.01.129
and the crow | makes wing to th' rooky wood; 3.02. 51
note of expectation | already are i' th' court. 3.03. 11
from hence to th' palace gate | make it their 3.03. 13
here i'll sit i' th' midst. 3.04. 10
thou art the best o' th' cut–throats, | yet he's 3.04. 16
will venom breed, | no teeth for th' present. 3.04. 30
blood hath been shed ere now, i' th' olden time, 3.04. 74
i drink to th' general joy o' th' whole table, 3.04. 88
i drink to th' general joy o' th' whole table, 3.04. 88
the arm'd rhinoceros, or th' hyrcan tiger, 3.04.100
at the pit of acheron | meet me i' th' morning; 3.05. 16
i am for th' air; 3.05. 20
got, | boil thou first i' th' charmed pot. 4.01. 9
shark, | root of hemlock digg'd i' th' dark, 4.01. 25
chawdron, | for th' ingredience of our cau'dron. 4.01. 34
pains, | and every one shall share i' th' gains. 4.01. 40
if th' hadst rather hear it from our mouths, 4.01. 62
will the line stretch out to th' crack of doom? 4.01.117
fife, give to th' edge o' th' sword | his wife, 4.01.151
fife, give to th' edge o' th' sword | his wife, 4.01.151
and best knows | the fits o' th' season. 4.02. 17
th' untimely emptying of the happy throne, | and 4.03. 68
begin | to doubt th' equivocation of the fiend 5.05. 42
and wish th' estate o' th' world were now undone 5.05. 49
and wish th' estate o' th' world were now undone 5.05. 49
and live to be the show and gaze o' th' time! 5.08. 24
behold where stands | th' usurper's cursed head: 5.09. 21
th' extravagant and erring spirit hies | to his HAM 1.01.154
th' imperial jointress to this warlike state, 1.02. 9
bear't that th' opposed may beware of thee. 1.03. 67
said, old mole, canst work i' th' earth so fast? 1.05.162
i saw him yesterday, or th' other day, | or then 2.01. 54
with what, i' th' name of god? 2.01. 73
it, | sith nor th' exterior nor the inward man 2.02. 6
him | so much from th' understanding of himself, 2.02. 9
th' embassadors from norway, my good lord, | are 2.02. 40
give first admittance to th' embassadors; 2.02. 51
to give th' assay of arms against your majesty. 2.02. 71
let her not walk i' th' sun. 2.02.184 P
any thing, but to th' purpose. 2.02.278 P
then, th' appurtenance of welcome is fashion and 2.02.371 P
am i not i' th' right, old jephthah? 2.02.410 P
"the rugged pyrrhus, like th' hyrcanian beast — 2.02.450
when he lay couched in th' ominous horse, | hath 2.02.454
of his fell sword | th' unnerved father falls. 2.02.474
of reverent priam, seem'd i' th' air to stick. 2.02.479
gives me the lie i' th' throat | as deep as to 2.02.574
if't be th' affliction of his love or no | that 3.01. 35
th' oppressor's wrong, the proud man's contumely 3.01. 70
that patient merit of th' unworthy takes, | when 3.01. 73
th' expectation and rose of the fair state, 3.01.152
th' observ'd of all observers, quite, quite down 3.01.154
neither having th' accent of christians nor the 3.02. 31 P
my lord, you play'd once i' th' university, you 3.02. 99 P
i was kill'd i' th' capitol; 3.02.103 P
jest, poison in jest — no offense i' th' world. 3.02.235 P
'a poisons him i' th' garden for his estate. 3.02.261 P
by th' mass and 'tis, like a camel indeed. 3.02.378 P
may one be pardon'd and retain th' offense? 3.03. 56
or in th' incestious pleasure of his bed, | at 3.03. 90
by | th' important acting of your dread command? 3.04.108
and with th' incorporal air do hold discourse? 3.04.118
and, as the sleeping soldiers in th' alarm, 3.04.120
'tis so, th' offender's scourge is weigh'd, 4.03. 6
not there, seek him i' th' other place yourself. 4.03. 34 P
th' associates tend, and every thing is bent 4.03. 45
seal'd and done | that else leans on th' affair. 4.03. 57
this is th' imposthume of much wealth and peace, 4.04. 27
of thinking too precisely on th' event — | a 4.04. 41
says she hears | there's tricks i' th' world, 4.05. 5
to think they would lay him i' th' cold ground. 4.05. 70 P
and where th' offense is, let the great axe fall 4.05.219
it came from th' embassador that was bound for 4.06. 10 P
much unsinow'd, | but yet to me th' are strong. 4.07. 11
but to the quick of th' ulcer: 4.07.123
to cut his throat i' th' church. 4.07.126
and must th' inheritor himself have no more, ha? 5.01.112 P
of /all the days i' th' year, i came to't that 5.01.143 P
how long will a man lie i' th' earth ere he rot? 5.01.163 P
now hath lien you i' th' earth three and twenty 5.01.173 P
alexander look'd a' this fashion i' th' earth? 5.01.198 P
lay her i' th' earth, | and from her fair and 5.01.238
wilt thou know | th' effect of what i wrote? 5.02. 37
folded the writ up in the form of th' other, 5.02. 51
/subscrib'd it, gave't th' impression, plac'd it 5.02. 52
popp'd in between th' election and my hopes, 5.02. 65
would dozy th' arithmetic of memory, and yet but 5.02.114 P
skill shall, like a star i' th' darkest night, 5.02.256
your grace has laid the odds a' th' weaker side. 5.02.261
as th' art a man, | give me the cup. 5.02.342
to th' embassadors of england gives | this 5.02.351
but i do prophesy th' election lights | on 5.02.355
so tell him, with th' occurrents, more and less, 5.02.357
had it th' ability of life to thank you. 5.02.373
mistook | fall'n on th' inventors' heads: 5.02.385
the name, and all th' addition to a king; LR 1.01.136
that stands | aloof from th' entire point. 1.01.240
we must do something, and i' th' heat. 1.01.308 P
bed, | go to th' creating a whole tribe of fops, 1.02. 14
is to the bastard edmund | as to th' legitimate. 1.02. 18
edmund the base | shall /top th' legitimate. 1.02. 21
the lady brach may stand by th' fire and stink. 1.04.112 P
i have cut the egg i' th' middle and eat up the 1.04.158 P
clovest thy /crown i' th' middle and gav'st away 1.04.160 P
o' both sides, and left nothing i' th' middle. 1.04.188 P
you are too much of late i' th' frown. 1.04.190 P
is much o' th' savor | of other your new pranks. 1.04.237
th' untented woundings of a father's curse 1.04.300
when i have show'd th' unfitness — how now, 1.04.333
well, well, th' event. 1.04.348
why one's nose stands i' th' middle on 's face? 1.05. 19 P
he's coming hither, now i' th' night, i' th' 2.01. 24
coming hither, now i' th' night, i' th' haste, 2.01. 24
a bond | the child was bound to th' father; 2.01. 48
in the quarrel's right, rous'd to th' encounter, 2.01. 54
comes too short | which can pursue th' offender. 2.01. 89
to have th' expense and waste of his revenues. 2.01.100
i' th' mire. 2.02. 5 P
i'll make a sop o' th' moonshine of you, you 2.02. 32 P
though they had been but two years o' th' trade. 2.02. 60 P
under th' allowance of your great aspect, 2.02.106
what was th' offense you gave him? 2.02.114
tied by the heads, dogs and bears by th' neck, 2.04. 8 P
and bears by th' neck, monkeys by th' loins, and 2.04. 9 P
neck, monkeys by th' loins, and men by th' legs. 2.04. 9 P
arrant whore, | ne'er turns the key to th' poor. 2.04. 53
and thou hadst been set i' th' stocks for that 2.04. 64 P
to teach thee there's no laboring i' th' winter. 2.04. 68 P
not i' th' stocks, fool. 2.04. 87 P
to the eels when she put 'em i' th' paste alive; 2.04.123 P
she knapp'd 'em o' th' coxcombs with a stick, 2.04.124 P
thy half o' th' kingdom hast thou not forgot, 2.04.180
good sir, to th' purpose. 2.04.181
who put my man i' th' stocks? 2.04.182
why not by th' hand, sir? 2.04.195
how came my man i' th' stocks? 2.04.198
choose | to wage against the enmity o' th' air, 2.04.209
come out o' th' storm. 2.04.309
strike flat the thick rotundity o' th' world! 3.02. 7
cannot carry | th' affliction nor the fear. 3.02. 49
when usurers tell their gold i' th' field, | and 3.02. 91
sea, | thou'dst meet the bear i' th' mouth. 3.04. 11
art thou that dost grumble there i' th' straw? 3.04. 44 P
take heed o' th' foul fiend. 3.04. 80 P
good my lord, take his offer, go into th' house. 3.04.156
in, fellow, there, into th' hovel; 3.04.174
we'll go to supper i' th' morning. 3.06. 84 P
i am tied to th' stake, and i must stand the 3.07. 54
one side will mock another; th' other too. 3.07. 71
i' th' last night's storm i such a fellow saw, 4.01. 32
as flies to wanton boys are we to th' gods, 4.01. 36
hence a mile or twain | i' th' way toward dover, 4.01. 43
moreover, to descry | the strength o' th' enemy. 4.05. 14
when shall i come to th' top of that same hill? 4.06. 1
that on th' unnumb'red idle pebble chafes, 4.06. 21
are now within a foot | of th' extreme verge. 4.06. 26
upon the crown o' th' cliff, what thing was that 4.06. 67
i' th' clout, i' th' clout — hewgh! 4.06. 91 P
i' th' clout, i' th' clout — hewgh! 4.06. 92 P
who have the power | to seal th' accuser's lips. 4.06.170
let me have surgeons, | i am cut to th' brains. 4.06.193
lest that th' infection of his fortune take 4.06.233
nay, come not near th' old man; 4.06.240 P
th' untun'd and jarring senses, o, wind up | of 4.07. 15
and proceed | i' th' sway of your own will. 4.07. 19
you do me wrong to take me out o' th' grave: 4.07. 44
with th' ancient of war on our proceeding. 5.01. 32
we two alone will sing like birds i' th' cage; 5.03. 9
of great ones, | that ebb and flow by th' moon. 5.03. 19
about it, and write happy when th' hast done. 5.03. 35
why he appears | upon this call o' th' trumpet. 5.03.119
and from th' extremest upward of thy head | to 5.03.137
by th' law of war thou wast not bound to answer 5.03.153
if more, the more th' hast wrong'd me. 5.03.169
th' hast spoken right, 'tis true. 5.03.174
(be brief in it) to th' castle, for my writ | is 5.03.246
mine eyes are not o' th' best; 5.03.280
but he, sir, had th' election; OTH 1.01. 27
where each second | stood heir to th' first. 1.01. 38
at this odd–even and dull watch o' th' night, 1.01.123
yet do i hold it very stuff o' th' conscience 1.02. 2
consider | th' importancy of cyprus to the turk, 1.03. 20
but altogether lacks th' abilities | that rhodes 1.03. 25
to th' very moment that he bade me tell it; 1.03.133
of hair–breadth scapes i' th' imminent deadly 1.03.136
beseech you proceed to th' affairs of state. 1.03.220
th' affair cries haste, | and speed must answer 1.03.276
at nine i' th' morning here we'll meet again. 1.03.279
where shall we meet i' th' morning? 1.03.373 P
and will as tenderly be led by th' nose | as 1.03.401
and quench the guards of th' ever–fixed pole; 2.01. 15
even till we make the main and th' aerial blue 2.01. 39
on the brow o' th' sea | stand ranks of people, 2.01. 53
and in th' essential vesture of creation | does 2.01. 64
paradoxes to make fools laugh i' th' alehouse. 2.01.139 P
and main exercise, th' incorporate conclusion. 2.01.262 P
'tis not yet ten o' th' clock. 2.03. 14 P
to th' platform, masters, come, let's set the 2.03.120
a just equinox, | the one as long as th' other. 2.03.125
i bleed still, | i am hurt to th' death. 2.03.165
most easy | th' inclining desdemona to subdue 2.03.340
in naples, that they speak i' th' nose thus? 3.01. 4 P
and, to th' advantage, i, being here, took't up. 3.03.312
the spirit–stirring drum, th' ear–piercing fife, 3.03.352
th' immortal jove's dread clamors counterfeit, 3.03.356
speak, is't out o' th' way? 3.04. 80
may be th' letter mov'd him; 4.01.235
nor send you out o' th' way? 4.02. 7
the world | even from the east to th' west! 4.02.144
get you to bed on th' instant, i will be 4.03. 7 P
i might do't as well i' th' dark. 4.03. 67
why, the wrong is but a wrong i' th' world; 4.03. 80 P
and as many to th' vantage as would store the 4.03. 84 P
kill men i' th' dark? 5.01. 63
o, bear him /out o' th' air. 5.01.104
and that th' affrighted globe | did yawn at 5.02.100
he lies to th' heart. 5.02.156
i took by th' throat the circumcised dog, | and 5.02.355
the soothsayer that you prais'd so to th' queen? ANT 1.02. 3 P
going on, | the sides o' th' world may danger. 1.02.192
are, or cease, | as you shall give th' advice. 1.03. 68
there | a man who is th' /abstract of all faults 1.04. 9
time we twain | did show ourselves i' th' field, 1.04. 74
like to the time o' th' year between the 1.05. 51
auguring hope | says it will come to th' full. 2.01. 11
terms, | nor curstness grow to th' matter. 2.02. 25
offended, and with you | chiefly i' th' world; 2.02. 33
the third o' th' world is yours, which with a 2.02. 63
and did want | of what i was i' th' morning; 2.02. 77
us staunch from edge to edge | a' th' world, i 2.02.116
so many mermaids, tended her i' th' eyes, | and 2.02.207
and antony | enthron'd i' th' market–place, did 2.02.215
whistling to th' air, which, but for vacancy, 2.02.216
that to come | shall all be done by th' rule. 2.03. 7
for my peace, | i' th' east my pleasure lies. 2.03. 41
give me mine angle, we'll to th' river; 2.05. 10
th' art an honest man. 2.05. 47
for the best turn i' th' bed. 2.05. 59
of thee, | that art not what th' art sure of. 2.05.103
to scourge th' ingratitude that despiteful rome 2.06. 22
the beds i' th' east are soft, and thanks to you 2.06. 50
the least wind i' th' world will blow them down. 2.07. 2 P
them to his entreaty, and himself to th' drink. 2.07. 8 P
they take the flow o' th' nile | by certain 2.07. 17
o' th' nile | by certain scales i' th' pyramid; 2.07. 18
by th' height, the lowness, or the mean, if 2.07. 19
i think th' art mad. the matter? 2.07. 56
be a child o' th' time. 2.07.100
which he achiev'd by th' minute, lost his favor. 3.01. 20
who does i' th' wars more than his captain can 3.01. 21
of parthia | we have jaded out o' th' field. 3.01. 34
i' th' market–place, on a tribunal silver'd, 3.06. 3
i' th' common show–place, where they exercise. 3.06. 12
she | in th' abiliments of the goddess isis 3.06. 17
we had not rated him | his part o' th' isle. 3.06. 26
the trees by th' way | should have borne men, 3.06. 46
are levying | the kings o' th' earth for war. 3.06. 68

only th' adulterous antony, most large | in his 3.06. 93
a charge we bear i' th' war, | and, as the 3.07. 16
from th' head of /actium | beat th' approaching 3.07. 51
head of /actium | beat th' approaching caesar. 3.07. 52
let th' egyptians | and the phoenicians go 3.07. 63
by hercules, i think i am i' th' right. 3.07. 67
set we our squadrons on yond side o' th' hill, 3.09. 1
th' antoniad, the egyptian admiral, | with all 3.10. 2
i' th' midst o' th' fight, | when vantage like a 3.10. 11
i' th' midst o' th' fight, | when vantage like a 3.10. 11
my heart was to thy rudder tied by th' strings, 3.11. 57
with half the bulk o' th' world play'd as i 3.11. 64
a child as soon | as i' th' command of caesar. 3.13. 25
unstate his happiness and be stag'd to th' show 3.13. 30
conquer, | and earns a place i' th' story. 3.13. 46
and shot their fires | into th' abysm of hell. 3.13.147
music i' th' air. 4.03. 13
o thou day o' th' world, | chain mine arm'd neck 4.08. 13
hour, | we must return to th' court of guard. 4.09. 2
shall embattle | by th' second hour i' th' morn. 4.09. 4
shall embattle | by th' second hour i' th' morn. 4.09. 4
let us bear him | to th' court of guard; 4.09. 31
i would they'ld fight i' th' fire or i' th' air; 4.10. 3
i would they'ld fight i' th' fire or i' th' air; 4.10. 3
'tis well th' art gone, | if it be well to live; 4.12. 39
let me lodge lichas on the horns o' th' moon, 4.12. 45
to th' monument! 4.13. 3
to th' monument! 4.13. 6
to th' monument! 4.13. 10
see behind me | th' inevitable prosecution of 4.14. 65
look out o' th' other side your monument, | his 4.15. 8
darkling stand | the varying shore o' th' world! 4.15. 11
not th' imperious show | of the full-fortun'd 4.15. 23
i liv'd, the greatest prince o' th' world, | the 4.15. 54
the crown o' th' earth doth melt. 4.15. 63
may frame herself | to th' way she's forc'd to. 5.01. 56
and would gladly | look him i' th' face. 5.02. 32
my master's bounty by | th' undoing of yourself. 5.02. 44
course, and lighted | the little o, th' earth. 5.02. 81
sole sir o' th' world, | i cannot project mine 5.02.120
of my spirits | through th' ashes of my chance. 5.02.174
acknowledg'd, | put we i' th' roll of conquest. 5.02.181
boy my greatness | i' th' posture of a whore. 5.02.221
truly, she makes a very good report o' th' worm; 5.02.255 P
yes, forsooth; i wish you joy o' th' worm. 5.02.279 P
such as th' aspic leaves | upon the caves of 5.02.352
who in the wars o' th' time | died with their CYM 1.01. 35
to th' more mature | a glass that feated them, 1.01. 48
you tell me, | is she sole child to th' king? 1.01. 56
i' th' swathing clothes the other, from their 1.01. 59
so soon as i can win th' offended king, | i will 1.01. 75
was in debt, it went o' th' backside the town. 1.02. 13 P
would thou grew'st unto the shores o' th' haven, 1.03. 1
and my neighbor's on th' approbation of what i 1.04.124 P
your ill opinion and th' assault you have made 1.04.162 P
she is alone th' arabian bird, and i | have lost 1.06. 17
middle of my heart | is warm'd by th' rest — 1.06. 28
it cannot be i' th' eye: 1.06. 39
nor i' th' judgment: 1.06. 41
nor i' th' appetite: 1.06. 43
sun, and solace | i' th' dungeon by a snuff! 1.06. 87
the feeler's soul | to th' oath of loyalty; 1.06.102
take my pow'r i' th' court for yours. 1.06.179
is material | to th' tender of our present. 1.06.208
i am not vex'd more at any thing in th' earth; 2.01. 17 P
and if thou canst awake by four o' th' clock, 2.02. 6
the flame o' th' taper | bows toward her, and 2.02. 19
to see th' enclosed lights, now canopied | under 2.02. 21
such | th' adornment of her bed; 2.02. 26
and the contents o' th' story. 2.02. 27
does within, | to th' madding of her lord. 2.02. 37
the crimson drops | i' th' bottom of a cowslip. 2.02. 39
to th' trunk again, and shut the spring of it. 2.02. 47
you are most bound to th' king, | who lets go by 2.03. 44
up | their deer to th' stand o' th' stealer; 2.03. 70
up | their deer to th' stand o' th' stealer; 2.03. 70
do here pronounce | by th' very truth of it, i 2.03.108
with scraps o' th' court, it is no contract, 2.03.115
enlargement by | the consequence o' th' crown, 2.03.121
i leave /you, sir, | to th' worst of discontent. 2.03.155
he'll grant the tribute, send th' arrearages, 2.04. 13
the roof o' th' chamber | with golden cherubins 2.04. 87
i will go there and do't, i' th' court, before 2.04.148
boats, | but suck them up to th' topmast. 3.01. 22
it did almost stretch | the sides o' th' world, 3.01. 50
to th' smothering of the sense), how far it is 3.02. 58
and by th' way | tell me how wales was made so 3.02. 59
than the sands | that run i' th' clock's behalf. 3.02. 73
we house i' th' rock, yet use thee not so hardly 3.03. 8
have never wing'd from view o' th' nest, nor 3.03. 28
the art o' th' court, | as hard to leave as keep 3.03. 46
the toil o' th' war, | a pain that only seems to 3.03. 49
i' th' name of fame and honor which dies i' th' 3.03. 51
name of fame and honor which dies i' th' search, 3.03. 51
but up to th' mountains! 3.03. 73
venison first shall be the lord o' th' feast, 3.03. 75
boys know little they are sons to th' king, 3.03. 80
up thus meanly | i' th' cave /wherein /they bow, 3.03. 83
breaks that sigh | from th' inward of thee? 3.04. 6
and, for i am richer than to hang by th' walls, 3.04. 52
ta'en thy stand, | th' elected deer before thee? 3.04.109
if you'll back to th' court — 3.04.130
i' th' world's volume | our britain seems as of 3.04.137
th' ambassador, | lucius the roman, comes to 3.04.141
that will be given to th' loud of noise we make. 3.05. 44
my dear lord, | thou art one o' th' false ones. 3.06. 15
there is cold meat i' th' cave, we'll browse on 3.06. 38
though i had found | gold strew'd i' th' floor. 3.06. 49
the night to th' owl and morn to th' lark less 3.06. 93
to th' owl and morn to th' lark less welcome. 3.06. 93
i am near to th' place where they should meet, 4.01. 1 P
'tis the ninth hour o' th' morn. 4.02. 30
th' imperious seas breeds monsters; 4.02. 35
to th' field, to th' field! 4.02. 42
to th' field, to th' field! 4.02. 42
know him, 'tis | cloten, the son o' th' queen. 4.02. 65
thou shalt know | i am son to th' queen. 4.02. 93
mountain pine | and make him stoop to th' vale. 4.02.176
o' th' floor; 4.02.212
to th' grave! 4.02.233
got the mannish crack, sing him to th' ground, 4.02.236
nay, cadwal, we must lay his head to th' east, 4.02.255
fear no more the heat o' th' sun, | nor the 4.02.258
fear no more the frown o' th' great, | thou art 4.02.264
nor th' all-dreaded thunder-stone. 4.02.271
herbs that have on them cold dew o' th' night 4.02.284
have i not found it | murd'rous to th' senses? 4.02.328
with the next benefit o' th' wind. 4.02.342
my divination) | success to th' roman host. 4.02.352
even to the note o' th' king, or i'll fall in 4.03. 44
pray, sir, to th' army. 4.04. 31
i am brought hither | among th' italian gentry, 5.01. 18
gods, put the strength o' th' leonati in me! 5.01. 31
to shame the guise o' th' world, i will begin 5.01. 32
we have th' advantage of the ground, | the lane 5.02. 11
grin like lions | upon the pikes o' th' hunters. 5.03. 39
then began | a stop i' th' chaser; 5.03. 40
in hard voyages, became | the life o' th' need. 5.03. 45
their friends | o'erborne i' th' former wave. 5.03. 48
resist are grown | the mortal bugs o' th' field. 5.03. 51
to be i' th' field, and ask "what news?" 5.03. 65
than we | that draw his knives i' th' war. 5.03. 73
great the slaughter is | here made by th' roman; 5.03. 79
silly habit, | that gave th' affront with them. 5.03. 87
bring him to th' king. 5.03. 94
am i better | than one that's sick o' th' gout, 5.04. 5
than be cur'd | by th' sure physician, death, 5.04. 7
that he deserv'd the praise o' th' world, | as 5.04. 50
the geck and scorn | o' th' other's villainy? 5.04. 68
will cry | to th' shining synod of the rest 5.04. 89
arise my knights o' th' battle. 5.05. 20
like romans, | and not o' th' court of britain. 5.05. 25
work | her son into th' adoption of the crown; 5.05. 56
nay, nay, to th' purpose. 5.05.178
that all th' abhorred things o' th' earth amend 5.05.216
that all th' abhorred things o' th' earth amend 5.05.216
upon me, set | the dogs o' th' street to bay me; 5.05.223
wrought by th' hand | of his queen mother, which 5.05.361
and in the beams o' th' sun | so vanish'd; 5.05.472
th' imperial caesar, should again unite | his 5.05.474
yon celestial tree | (or die in th' adventure), PER 1.01. 22
come away, or i'll fetch th' with a wanton. 2.01. 17 P
such whales have i heard on a' th' land, who 2.01. 33 P
come, queen a' th' feast — | for, daughter, so 2.03. 17
to th' court of king simonides | are letters 3.ch. 23
th' unfriendly elements | forgot thee utterly, 3.01. 57
bring your grace e'en to the edge a' th' shore, 3.03. 35
which makes /her both th' /heart and place | of 4.ch. 10
or when to th' lute | she sung, and made the 4.ch. 25
to equal any single crown a' th' earth | i' th' 4.03. 8
crown a' th' earth | i' th' justice of compare! 4.03. 9
do swear to th' gods that winter kills the flies 4.03. 50
being proud, swallowed some part a' th' earth. 4.04. 39
the meanest bird | that flies i' th' purer air! 4.06.102
i'll hear you more, to th' bottom of your story, 5.01.164
rise, th' art my child. 5.01.213
shall raze you out o' th' book of trespasses TNK 1.01. 33
their ashes, nor to take th' offense | of mortal 1.01. 44
sword | that does good turns to th' world; 1.01. 49
him, if he i' th' blood-siz'd field lay swoll'n, 1.01. 99
he that will all the treasure know o' th' earth 1.01.114
forward to th' temple! 1.01.130
leave not out a jot | o' th' sacred ceremony. 1.01.131
that your fame | knolls in the ear o' th' world. 1.01.134
none fit for th' dead! 1.01.141
and that work presents itself to th' doing: 1.01.151
think, | did i not by th' abstaining of my joy, 1.01.189
thou still make good | the tongue o' th' world. 1.01.227
i' th' aid o' th' current were almost to sink, 1.02. 8
i' th' aid o' th' current were almost to sink, 1.02. 8
and bare weeds | the gain o' th' martialist, who 1.02. 16
your pity, | but th' unconsider'd soldier? 1.02. 31
or i am none | that draw i' th' sequent trace. 1.02. 60
which rips my bosom | almost to th' heart's — 1.02. 62
what will | the fall o' th' stroke do damage? 1.02.113
let th' event, | that never-erring arbitrator, 1.02.113
and power | i' th' least of these was dreadful, 1.03. 39
made too proud the bed, took leave o' th' moon 1.03. 52
the one of th' other may be said to water 1.03. 58
th' impartial gods, who from the mounted heavens 1.04. 4
by th' helm of mars, i saw them in the war, 1.04. 17
i' th' mean time, look tenderly to the two 2.01. 19 P
martyr'd as 'twere i' th' deliverance, will 2.01. 41 P
lord arcite, you must presently to th' duke; 2.02.221
boys in athens | blow wind i' th' breech on 's, 2.03. 47
this must be done i' th' woods. 2.03. 50
he's excellent i' th' woods, | bring him to th' 2.03. 53
bring him to th' plains, his learning makes no 2.03. 54
this fellow has a vengeance trick o' th' hip. 2.03. 70
the athenians pay it | to th' heart of ceremony. 3.01. 4
th' enamell'd knacks o' th' mead or garden! 3.01. 7
th' enamell'd knacks o' th' mead or garden! 3.01. 7
thou, o jewel | o' th' wood, o' th' world, hast 3.01. 10
thou, o jewel | o' th' wood, o' th' world, hast 3.01. 10
me use my sword | against th' advice of fear. 3.01. 60
should break out, though i' th' sanctuary. 3.01. 62
and | perfumes to kill the smell o' th' prison; 3.01. 86
night, | and darkness lord o' th' world! 3.02. 4
play o' th' virginals? 3.03. 34
tell me | news from all parts o' th' world. 3.04. 13
where's the rest o' th' music? 3.05. 31
we may go whistle; all the fat's i' th' fire. 3.05. 39
unless by th' tail | and with thy teeth thou 3.05. 49
now to be frampal, now to piss o' th' nettle! 3.05. 57
comes i' th' nick, as mad as a march hare. 3.05. 73
let him play | qui passa o' th' bells and bones. 3.05. 86
those are o' th' least; 3.06. 64
or i will make th' advantage of this hour | mine 3.06.123
my knees shall grow to th' ground but i'll get 3.06.192
better they fall by th' law than one another. 3.06.225
you | content to take th' other to your husband? 3.06.274
is gone to th' wood to gather mulberries. 4.01. 68
set it to th' north. 4.01.143
and now direct your course to th' wood, where 4.01.144
'tis a sore life they have i' th' tother place, 4.03. 32 P
up to the nav'l, and in ice up to th' heart, and 4.03. 43 P
th' heart, and there th' offending part burns, 4.03. 44 P
th' other curses a suing fellow and her 4.03. 55 P
i would destroy th' offender, coz, i would, 5.01. 23
and i' th' self-same place | to seat something i 5.01. 27
expels the seeds of fear and th' apprehension 5.01. 36
and by thee | be styl'd the lord o' th' day. 5.01. 60
and cur'st the world | o' th' plurisy of people! 5.01. 66
mars's drum | and turn th' alarm to whispers; 5.01. 81
first, by your leave, | i' th' way of honesty. 5.02. 20
doctor, | methinks you are i' th' wrong still. 5.02. 27
and casts himself th' accounts | of all his hay 5.02. 58
yours to command i' th' way of honesty. 5.02. 71
how far is't now to th' end o' th' world, my 5.02. 72
how far is't now to th' end o' th' world, my 5.02. 72
and that would be a blot i' th' business. 5.02. 81
are they i' th' field? 5.02.100
this trial is as 'twere i' th' night, and you 5.03. 19
burst of clamor | is sure th' end o' th' combat. 5.03. 78
burst of clamor | is sure th' end o' th' combat. 5.03. 78
arcite's body | within an inch o' th' pyramid, 5.03. 80
anon | th' assistants made a brave redemption, 5.03. 82
set both thine ears to th' business. 5.03. 92
his race | should show i' th' world too godlike. 5.03.118
each part of him to th' all i have spoke, your 5.03.121
two emulous philomels beat the ear o' th' night 5.03.124
that hath outliv'd | the love o' th' people, yea 5.04. 2
i' th' self-same state | stands many a father 5.04. 2
dancing as 'twere to th' music | his own hoofs 5.04. 59
kinsman hath confess'd the right o' th' lady 5.04.116
you would have us upon th' hip, would you? STM II.C 18 P
ay, by th' mass, will we, more. II.C 58 P
th' art a good house-keeper and i thank thy good II.C 58 P
luggage | plodding to th' ports and coasts for II.C 76
sin | which oft th' apostle did forewarn us of, II.C 94
king, | as he is clement if th' offender mourn, II.C 123
so indeed, | that tremble at th' imagination? VEN 668
whereat th' impartial gazer late did wonder, 748
th' one sweetly flatters, th' other feareth harm LUC 172
one sweetly flatters, th' other feareth harm, 172
having solicited th' eternal power | that his 345
in his dim mist th' aspiring mountains hiding, 548
have time to wail th' abusing of his time. 994
th' impression of strange kinds | is form'd in 1242
th' adulterate death of lucrece and her groom. 1645
she will not stick to round me on th' ear, | to PP 18.51
thee, | which used lives th' executor to be. SON 4.14
stars twire not, thou /gild'st th' even: 28.12
and moan th' expense of many a vanish'd sight; 30. 8
th' offender's sorrow lends but weak relief | to 34.11
or at your hand th' account of hours to crave, 58. 3
beck) | th' imprison'd absence of your liberty, 58. 6
your love and pity doth th' impression fill 112. 1
divert strong minds to th' course of alt'ring 115. 8
whereto th' inviting time our fashion calls; 124. 8
th' expense of spirit in a waste of shame | is 129. 1
better becomes the grey cheeks of th' east, 132. 6
ill, | th' uncertain sickly appetite to please. 147. 4
their poor balls are tied | to th' orbed earth; LC 25
or he his manage by th' well-doing steed. 112
like fools that in th' imagination set | the 136
or my affection put to th' smallest teen, | or 192
with th' annexions of fair gems enrich'd, | and 208
that th' unexperient gave the tempter place, 318

THAISA 10 FR 0.0011 REL FR 10 V 0 P

note it not you, thaisa? PER 2.03. 57
than | to say my mother's name was thaisa? 5.01.210
thaisa was my mother, who did end | the minute i 5.01.211
did wed | at pentapolis the fair thaisa. 5.03. 4
look, thaisa is | recovered. 5.03. 27
the voice of dead thaisa! 5.03. 34
that thaisa am i, supposed dead | and drown'd. 5.03. 35
flesh of thy flesh, thaisa, | thy burden at the 5.03. 46
embrace him, dear thaisa, this is he. 5.03. 55
thaisa, | this prince, the fair-betrothed of 5.03. 70

THALIARD 6 FR 0.0006 REL FR 6 V 0 P

thaliard — you are of our chamber, thaliard, PER 1.01.151
thaliard — you are of our chamber, thaliard, 1.01.151
faithfulness | we will advance you, thaliard. 1.01.154
thaliard, adieu! 1.01.168
lord thaliard from antiochus is welcome. 1.03. 30
how thaliard came full bent with sin | and hid 2.ch. 23

THAMES 7 FR 0.0008 REL FR 0 V 7 P

it in the muddy ditch close by the thames side. WIV 3.03. 16 P
and to be thrown in the thames? 3.05. 6 P
let me pour in some sack to the thames water; 3.05. 22 P
dish) to be thrown into the thames, and cool'd, 3.05.120 P
as i have been into thames, ere i will leave her 3.05.127 P
he could wish himself in thames up to the neck; H5 4.01.115 P
throw them into thames! 2H6 4.08. 3 P

/THAN 15 FR 0.0017 REL FR 14 V 1 P

/i /am /greater /than /a /king; R2 4.01.305
/likely /to /fall /in /than /to /get /o'er; 2H4 1.01.171
/more /than /that /being /which /was /like /to 1.01.179
/and /nice | /with /others /than /with /him! 2.03. 41
/our /griefs /heavier /than /our /offenses. 4.01. 69
/grac'd /and /did, /more /than /the /king — 4.01.137
text | /than now to see you here an iron man, 4.02. 8
/divide /thy /lips, /than /we /are /confident, TRO 1.03. 72
/no /less /working /than /are /swords /and /bows 1.03.355
sooner catch the eye | /than what stirs not. 3.03.184
a speedier course /than ling'ring languishment TIT 2.01.110
/than /will /preserve /just /so /much /strength 3.02. 2
/quality /no /longer /than /they /can /sing? HAM 2.02.347 P
/man's /life's /no /more /than /to /say "/one." 5.02. 74
/rather /lose /the /battle /than /that /sister LR 5.01. 18

THAN 2006 FR 0.2267 REL FR 1521 V 485 P

none that i more love than myself. TMP 1.01. 20 P
they are louder than the weather, or our office. 1.01. 36 P
we are less afraid to be drown'd than thou art. 1.01. 44 P
the ship were no stronger than a nutshell and as 1.01. 47 P
i am, nor that i am more better | than prospero, 1.02. 20
and rather like a dream than an assurance | that 1.02. 45
thee more profit | than other princess' can, 1.02.173
not a blemish, | but fresher than before; 1.02.219
pinch more stinging | than bees that made 'em. 1.02.330
rock, | who hadst deserv'd more than a prison. 1.02.362
better nature, sir, | than he appears by speech. 1.02.498
you have spoken truer than you purpos'd. 2.01. 20 P

have taken it wiselier than i meant you should. 2.01. 21 P
being rather new dy'd than stain'd with salt 2.01. 64 P
his word is more than the miraculous harp. 2.01. 87 P
making | than we bring men to comfort them. 2.01.135
i am more serious than my custom; 2.01.219
why, they were no worse | than now they are. 2.01.262
garments sit upon me, | much feater than before. 2.01.273
no better than the earth he lies upon, | if he 2.01.281
ten times more gentle than her father's crabbed; 3.01. 8
back, | than you should such dishonor undergo, 3.01. 27
have i seen | more that i may call men than you, 3.01. 51
more endure | this wooden slavery than to suffer 3.01. 62
than of | our human generation you shall find 3.03. 32
of you there present | are worse than devils. 3.03. 36
(worse than any death | can be at once) shall 3.03. 77
i'll seek him deeper than e'er plummet sounded, 3.03.101
bring a corollary, | rather than want a spirit. 4.01. 58
done little better than play'd the jack with us. 4.01.197 P
that's more to me than my wetting; 4.01.211 P
make them | than pard or cat o' mountain. 4.01.261
as they, be kindlier mov'd than thou art? 5.01. 24
rarer action is | in virtue than in vengeance. 5.01. 28
and deeper than did ever plummet sound | i'll 5.01. 56
much weaker | than you may call to comfort you; 5.01.147
and there is in this business more than nature 5.01.243
than (living dully sluggardiz'd at home) | wear TGV 1.01. 7
love, | for he was more than over shoes in love. 1.01. 24
less than a pound shall serve me for carrying 1.01.105 P
to plead for love deserves more fee than hate. 1.02. 48
that tide will stay me longer than i should. 2.02. 15
truth hath better deeds than words to grace it. 2.02. 18
stone, and has no more pity in him than a dog. 2.03. 11 P
to feed on your blood than live in your air. 2.04. 28 P
than how? 2.05. 44 P
i to myself am dearer than a friend, | for love 2.06. 23
youth | of greater time than i shall show to be. 2.07. 48
than, by concealing it, heap on your head | a 3.01. 19
more than quick words do move a woman's mind. 3.01. 91
and think my patience, more than thy desert, 3.01.159
thank me for this more than for all the favors 3.01.161
my territories | longer than swiftest expedition 3.01.164
and why not death, rather than living torment? 3.01.170
she hath more qualities than a water–spaniel, 3.01.272 P
only carry, therefore is she better than a jade. 3.01.277 P
"item, she hath more hair than wit, and more 3.01.353 P
more hair than wit, and more faults than hairs, 3.01.354 P
faults than hairs, and more wealth than faults." 3.01.354 P
"item, she hath more hair than wit" — 3.01.358 P
more hair than wit? 3.01.359 P
salt, and therefore it is more than the salt; 3.01.361 P
hair that covers the wit is more than the wit, 3.01.362 P
"and more faults than hairs" — 3.01.364 P
"and more wealth than faults." 3.01.367 P
he hath stay'd for a better man than thee. 3.01.376 P
longer than i prove loyal to your grace | let me 3.02. 20
are you sadder than you were before? 4.02. 54 P
if i had not had more wit than he, to take a 4.04. 14 P
would better fit his chamber than this shadow. 4.04.120
she hath been fairer, madam, than she is: 4.04.149
o, sir, i find her milder than she was, | and 5.02. 2
eyes, | for i had rather wink than look on them. 5.02. 14
eglamour | than for the love of reckless silvia. 5.02. 52
love | than hate of eglamour that goes with her. 5.02. 54
more to cross that love | than hate for silvia, 5.02. 56
a thousand more mischances than this one | have 5.03. 3
i better brook than flourishing peopled towns: 5.04. 3
a smaller boon than this i cannot beg, | and 5.04. 24
and less than this, i am sure you cannot give. 5.04. 25
rather than have false proteus rescue me. 5.04. 35
thou'dst two, | and that's far worse than none: 5.04. 51
better have none | than plural faith, which is 5.04. 52
to change their shapes than men their minds. 5.04.109
than men their minds? 5.04.110
i warrant you, my lord — more grace than boy. 5.04.166
i had rather than forty shillings i had my book WIV 1.01.198 P
i will do a greater thing than that, upon your 1.01.240 P
i'll rather be unmannerly than troublesome. 1.01.312 P
in windsor knows more of anne's mind than i do, 1.04.129 P
than i do, nor can do more than i do with her, i 1.04.129 P
keep place together than the hundred psalms to 2.01. 62 P
and what he gets more of her than sharp words, 2.01.183 P
i had rather hear them scold than fight. 2.01.232 P
in windsor leads a better life than she does: 2.02.117 P
i'll make more of thy old body than i have done. 2.02.139 P
in better plight for a lender than you are; 2.02.166 P
my ambling gelding, than my wife with herself. 2.02.305 P
three hours too soon than a minute too late. 2.02.312 P
go before you like a man than follow him like a 3.02. 6 P
i shall be rather prais'd for this than mock'd; 3.02. 47 P
with her for more money than i'll speak of. 3.02. 56 P
i had rather than a thousand pound he were out 3.03.123 P
heaven make you better than your thoughts! 3.03.204 P
found thee of more value | than stamps in gold, 3.04. 16
can tell you how things go better than i can. 3.04. 66 P
(when i was more than half stew'd in grease, 3.05.118 P
there are fairer things than poulcats sure. 4.01. 28 P
he is a better scholar than i thought he was. 4.01. 80 P
better shame than murther. 4.02. 45 P
any extremity rather than a mischief. 4.02. 74 P
the sun with /cold | than thee with wantonness. 4.04. 8
there is no better way than that they spoke of. 4.04. 16
taught me more wit than ever i learn'd before in 4.05. 60 P
more than the villainous inconstancy of man's 4.05.108 P
a hundred pound in gold more than your loss. 4.06. 5
better a little chiding than a great deal of 5.03. 10 P
more fertile–fresh than all the field to see; 5.05. 68
yokes | become the forest better than the town? 5.05.108
more grave and wrinkled than the aims and ends MM 1.03. 5
none better knows than you | how i have ever 1.03. 7
time the rod | /becomes more mock'd than fear'd; 1.03. 27
would have seem'd | than in lord angelo. 1.03. 34
that his appetite | is more to bread than stone: 1.03. 53
cut a little, | than fall, and bruise to death. 2.01. 6
a thief or two | guiltier than him they try. 2.01. 21
is a more respected person than any of us all. 2.01.166 P
hath she had any more than one husband? 2.01.201 P
heaven | with less respect than we do minister 2.02. 86
and gnarled oak | than the soft myrtle; 2.02.117

more betray our sense | than woman's lightness? 2.02.169
i would do more than that, if more were needful. 2.03. 9
to do another such offense | than die for this. 2.03. 15
then was your sin of heavier kind than his. 2.03. 28
better please me | than to demand what 'tis. 2.04. 33
this, | i had rather give my body than my soul. 2.04. 56
sins | stand more for number than for accompt. 2.04. 58
beauty ten times louder | than beauty could, 2.04. 81
than that a sister, by redeeming him, | should 2.04.107
of your brother | a merriment than a vice. 2.04.116
no stronger | than faults may shake our frames), 2.04.133
in't, | which seems a little fouler than it is, 2.04.146
more than our brother is our chastity. 2.04.185
winters more respect | than a perpetual honor. 3.01. 76
or to be worse than worst | of those that 3.01.125
die by the law than my son should be unlawfully 3.01.190 P
signify that craft, being richer than innocency, 3.02. 9 P
than merry at any thing which profess'd to make 3.02.235 P
others paying | than by self–offenses weighing. 3.02.266
is a more penitent trade than your bawd — he 4.02. 50 P
more depends on it than we must yet deliver. 4.02.125 P
greater forfeit to the law than angelo who hath 4.02.158 P
upon this, more than thanks and good fortune, by 4.02.178 P
attempt you, i will go further than i meant, to 4.02.191 P
he's a better woodman than thou tak'st him for. 4.03.162 P
sir, your company is fairer than honest. 4.03.175 P
than this is all as true as it is strange; 5.01. 44
there is another comfort than this world, | that 5.01. 49
charges she moe than me? 5.01.200
not better than he, by her own report. 5.01.273 P
dare no more stretch this finger of mine than he 5.01.314
this may prove worse than hanging. 5.01.360 P
lord, | i should be guiltier than my guiltiness, 5.01.367
at his dishonor | than at the strangeness of it. 5.01.381
of my hidden pow'r | than let him so be lost. 5.01.393
fearing death, | than that which lives to fear. 5.01.398
that i crave death more willingly than mercy: 5.01.476
that apprehends no further than this world, 5.01.481
impos'd | than i to speak my griefs unspeakable: ERR 1.01. 32
reserve them till a merrier hour than this: 1.02. 69
why should their liberty than ours be more? 2.01. 10
of more pre–eminence than fish and fowls, | are 2.01. 23
unkindness blunts it more than marble hard. 2.01. 93
but there's many a man hath more hair than wit. 2.02. 83 P
am better than thy dear self's better part. 2.02.123
grace you show not | than our earth's wonder, 3.02. 32
than our earth's wonder, more than earth divine. 3.02. 32
she'll burn a week longer than the whole world. 3.02.100 P
longer from head to foot than from hip to hip: 3.02.113 P
more | than i stand debted to this gentleman. 4.01. 31
ah, but i think him better than i say, | and yet 4.02. 25
no, he's in tartar limbo, worse than hell: 4.02. 32
and owes more than he's worth to season. 4.02. 58
more exploits with his mace than a morris–pike. 4.03. 28 P
poisons more deadly than a mad dog's tooth. 5.01. 70
bett'red expectation than you must expect of me ADO 1.01. 16 P
are no faces truer than those that are so wash'd 1.01. 27 P
is it to weep at joy than to joy at weeping! 1.01. 28 P
is so indeed, he is no less than a stuff'd man. 1.01. 58 P
he is sooner caught than the pestilence, and the 1.01. 87 P
my dog bark at a crow than a man swear he loves 1.01.132 P
of my tongue is better than a beast of yours. 1.01.139 P
can afford her, that were she other than she is, 1.01.174 P
more blood with love than i will get again with 1.01.251 P
hand | than to drive liking to the name of love. 1.01.300
need the bridge much broader than the flood? 1.01.316
be a canker in a hedge than a rose in his grace, 1.03. 28 P
be disdain'd of all than to fashion a carriage 1.03. 29 P
too curst is more than curst. 2.01. 21 P
he that hath a beard is more than a youth, and 2.01. 36 P
and he that hath no beard is less than a man; 2.01. 37 P
and he that is more than a youth is not for me, 2.01. 38 P
is not for me, and he that is less than a man, i 2.01. 39 P
god make men of some other mettle than earth. 2.01. 60 P
jester, that i was duller than a great thaw, 2.01.244 P
rather than hold three words' conference with 2.01.270 P
bear no less likelihood than to see me at her 2.02. 42 P
a voice | to slander music any more than once. 2.03. 45
her, rather than she will bate one breath of her 2.03.176 P
that she will rather die than give any sign of 2.03.227 P
for those thanks than you take pains to thank me 2.03.251 P
for those thanks than you took pains to thank 2.03.260 P
to praise him more than ever man did merit. 3.01. 19
heart | of prouder stuff than that of beatrice. 3.01. 50
it were a better death than die with mocks, 3.01. 79
and i | believe it better than reportingly. 3.01.116
indeed he looks younger than he did, by the loss 3.02. 48 P
we will rather sleep than talk, we know what 3.03. 37 P
the fashion wears out more apparel than the man. 3.03.140 P
that is an old man and no honester than i. 3.05. 15 P
and 'twere a thousand pound more than 'tis, for 3.05. 25 P
are more intemperate in your blood | than venus, 4.01. 60
i thy spirits were stronger than thy shames, 4.01.125
than that which maiden modesty doth warrant, 4.01.179
of his soul, | than when she liv'd indeed. 4.01.230
shape | than i can lay it down in likelihood. 4.01.236
be friends with me than fight with mine enemy. 4.01.298 P
for my love some other way than swearing by it. 4.01.326 P
that you are little better than false knaves, 4.02. 21 P
and this is more, masters, than you can deny. 4.02. 60 P
my griefs cry louder than advertisement. 5.01. 32
seal with my death than repeat over to my shame. 5.01.241 P
no longer in monument than the bell rings and 5.02. 79 P
's | than this for whom we rend'red up this woe. 5.03. 33
why, no, no more than reason. 5.04. 74
troth, no, no more than reason. 5.04. 77
staff more reverent than one tipp'd with horn. 5.04.123 P
than those that walk and wot not what they are. LLL 1.01. 91
than wish a snow in may's new–fangled shows; 1.01.106
than for that angel knowledge you can say, | yet 1.01.113
it doth amount to one more than two. 1.02. 47 P
and yet a better love than my master. 1.02.121 P
i am more bound to you than your fellows, for 1.02.151 P
the plea of no less weight | than aquitaine, a 2.01. 8
worth | than you much willing to be counted wise 2.01. 18
court, | than seek a dispensation for his oath, 2.01. 87
lent, | than aquitaine, so gelded as it is. 2.01.148
why, it is a fairer name than french crown! 3.01.141 P

better than remuneration, aleven–pence–farthing 3.01.170 P
the boy, | than whom no mortal so magnificent! 3.01.178
fair payment for foul words is more than due. 4.01. 19
that more for praise than purpose meant to kill. 4.01. 29
more fairer than fair, beautiful than beauteous, 4.01. 62 P
more fairer than fair, beautiful than beauteous, 4.01. 63 P
than beauteous, truer than truth itself, have 4.01. 63 P
those parts that do fructify in us more than he. 4.02. 29
o, 'tis more than need. 4.03.285
than are the tender horns of cockled snails. 4.03.335
of his verbosity finer than the staple of his 5.01. 17 P
thou art easier swallow'd than a flap–dragon. 5.01. 42 P
beauties no richer than rich taffata. 5.02.159
cutting a smaller hair than may be seen; 5.02.258
their conceits have wings | fleeter than arrows, 5.02.261
that more than all the world i did respect her. 5.02.437
to have one show worse than the king's and his 5.02.513
greater than great, great, great, great pompey! 5.02.685 P
man's blood in his belly than will sup a flea. 5.02.692 P
but more devout than this /in our respects 5.02.782
our letters, madam, show'd much more than jest. 5.02.785
if this, or more than this, i would deny, | to 5.02.813
than that which withering on the virgin thorn MND 1.01. 77
my love is more than his; 1.01.100
and (which is more than all these boasts can be) 1.01.103
broke | (in number more than ever women spoke), 1.01.176
air | more tuneable than lark to shepherd's ear 1.01.184
every where, | swifter than the moon's sphere; 2.01. 7
with me) | than to be used as you use your dog? 2.01.210
prove | more fond on her than she upon her love; 2.01.266
if so, my eyes are oft'ner wash'd than hers. 2.02. 93
a more fearful wild–fowl than your lion living; 3.01. 32 P
a stranger pyramus than e'er played here. 3.01. 88
this falls out better than i could devise. 3.02. 35
for with doubler tongue | than thine, thou 3.02. 73
about the wood go swifter than the wind, | and 3.02. 94
go, | swifter than arrow from the tartar's bow. 3.02.101
than all yon fiery oes and eyes of light. 3.02.188
this you should pity rather than despise. 3.02.235
thou canst compel no more than she entreat. 3.02.249
have no more strength than her weak /prays. 3.02.250
i say i love thee more than he can do. 3.02.254
can you do me greater harm than hate? 3.02.271
because she is something lower than myself, 3.02.304
your hands than mine are quicker for a fray; 3.02.342
the villain is much lighter–heel'd than i; 3.02.415
than common sleep of all these /five the sense. 4.01. 82
compass soon, | swifter than the wand'ring moon. 4.01. 98
more strange than true. 5.01. 2
more than cool reason ever comprehends. 5.01. 6
one sees more devils than vast hell can hold; 5.01. 9
together, | more witnesseth than fancy's images, 5.01. 25
more than to us | wait in your royal walks, your 5.01. 30
no worse of them than they of themselves, they 5.01.215 P
less than an ace, man; 5.01.308 P
vailing her high top lower than her ribs | to MV 1.01. 28
than my heart cool with mortifying groans. 1.01. 82
of nothing, more than any man in all venice. 1.01.115 P
than my faint means would grant continuance. 1.01.125
than if you had made waste of all i have. 1.01.157
and she is fair and, fairer than that word, | of 1.01.162
than to be one of the twenty to follow mine own 1.02. 16 P
a bone in his mouth than to either of these. 1.02. 52 P
he hath a horse better than the neapolitan's, a 1.02. 58 P
bad habit of frowning than the count palentine; 1.02. 59 P
he is a little worse than a man, and when he is 1.02. 88 P
he is worst, he is little better than a beast. 1.02. 89 P
by some other sort than your father's imposition 1.02.104 P
i had rather he should shrive me than wive me. 1.02.131 P
father, who, being more than sand–blind, high 2.02. 36 P
more hair on thy chin than dobbin my fill–horse 2.02. 95 P
had more hair of his tail than i have of my face 2.02. 97 P
him a livery | more guarded than his fellows'; 2.02.155
and whiter than the paper it writ on | is the 2.04. 13
and he sleeps by day | more than the wild–cat. 2.05. 48
made, than they are wont | to keep obliged faith 2.06. 6
are, | are with more spirit chased than enjoy'd. 2.06. 13
desire no more delight | than to be under sail, 2.06. 68
but more than these, in love i do deserve. 2.07. 34
so rich a gem | was set in worse than gold. 2.07. 55
not learning more than the fond eye doth teach, 2.09. 27
did i deserve no more than a fool's head? 2.09. 59
thy flesh and hers than between jet and ivory, 3.01. 40 P
between your bloods than there is between red 3.01. 41 P
than young alcides, when he did redeem | the 3.02. 55
i view the fight than thou that mak'st the fray. 3.02. 62
rather threaten'st than dost promise aught, 3.02.105
thy paleness moves me more than eloquence, | and 3.02.106
hearts of men | faster than gnats in cobwebs. 3.02.123
happier than this, | she is not bred so dull but 3.02.161
no more pertains to me, my lord, than you; 3.02.200
have told you | that i was worse than nothing; 3.02.260
flesh | than twenty times the value of the sum 3.02.287
appears | than any that draws breath in italy. 3.02.296
work | than customary bounty can enforce you. 3.04. 9
to the commonwealth than you can the getting up 3.05. 38 P
much that the moor should be more than reason; 3.05. 41 P
but if she be less than an honest woman, she is 3.05. 41 P
woman, she is indeed more than i took her for. 3.05. 42 P
strange | than is thy strange apparent cruelty; 4.01. 21
have | a weight of carrion flesh than to receive 4.01. 41
more than a lodg'd hate and a certain loathing 4.01. 60
seek to soften that — than which what's harder? 4.01. 79
than to live still and write mine epitaph. 4.01.118
the throned monarch better than his crown. 4.01.189
how much more elder art thou than thy looks! 4.01.251
shows herself more kind | than is her custom. 4.01.268
had been her husband rather than a christian! 4.01.297
thou shalt have justice more than thou desir'st. 4.01.316
if thou tak'st more | or less than a just pound, 4.01.327
there's more depends on this than on the value. 4.01.434
methinks it sounds much sweeter than by day. 5.01.100
be thought | no better a musician than the wren. 5.01.106
no more than i am well acquitted of. 5.01.138
it must appear in other ways than words, 5.01.140
no higher than thyself, the judge's clerk, | a 5.01.163
and bid him keep it better than the other. 5.01.255
better news in store for you | than you expect. 5.01.275

ay, better than him i am before knows me. AYL 1.01. 43 P
no further offend you than becomes me for my 1.01. 79 P
less belov'd of her uncle than his own daughter, 1.01.111 P
(yet i know not why) hates nothing more than he. 1.01.166 P
i show more mirth than i am mistress of, and 1.02. 3 P
than with safety of a pure blush thou mayst in 1.02. 28 P
well, and overthrown | more than your enemies. 1.02.255
more suits you to conceive than i to speak of. 1.02.267
are dearer than the natural bond of sisters. 1.02.276
hereafter, in a better world than this, | i 1.02.284
take the part of a better wrastler than myself! 1.03. 23 P
charge thee be not thou more griev'd than i am. 1.03. 92
beauty provoketh thieves sooner than gold. 1.03.110
because that i am more than common tall, | that 1.03.115
i'll have no worse a name than jove's own page, 1.03.124
life more sweet | than that of painted pomp? 2.01. 3
more free from peril than the envious court? 2.01. 4
than doth your brother that hath banish'd you. 2.01. 28
cannot recompense me better | than to die well, 2.03. 76
part, i had rather bear with you than bear you. 2.04. 12 P
thou speak'st wiser than thou art ware of. 2.04. 57 P
and wish, for her sake more than for mine own, 2.04. 76
more at your request than to please myself. 2.05. 23 P
thy conceit is nearer death than thy powers. 2.06. 8 P
more than your force move us to gentleness. 2.07.103
presents more woeful pageants than the scene 2.07.138
civet is of a baser birth than tar, the very 3.02. 68 P
had in them more feet than the verses would bear 3.02.165 P
to these particulars is more than to answer in a 3.02.228 P
is something finer than you could purchase in so 3.02.341 P
yourself, than seeming the lover of any other. 3.02.383 P
she is apter to do than to confess she does. 3.02.389 P
worse than jove in a thatch'd house! 3.03. 11 P
a man more dead than a great reckoning in a 3.03. 15 P
a wall'd town is more worthier than a village, 3.03. 59 P
man more honorable than the bare brow of a 3.03. 61 P
and by how much defense is better than no skill, 3.03. 62 P
by so much is a horn more precious than to want. 3.03. 63 P
better to be married of him than of another, for 3.03. 91 P
something browner than judas's. 3.04. 8 P
lover is no stronger than the word of a tapster; 3.04. 31 P
than he that dies and lives by bloody drops? 3.05. 7
you | than without candle may go dark to bed — 3.05. 39
i see no more in you than in the ordinary | of 3.05. 42
times a properer man | than she a woman. 3.05. 52
than any of her lineaments can show her. 3.05. 56
i had rather hear you chide than this man woo. 3.05. 65
me, | for i am falser than vows made in wine. 3.05. 73
than thine own gladness that thou art employ'd. 3.05. 98
and faster than his tongue | did make offense, 3.05.116
more lusty red | than that mix'd in his cheek; 3.05.122
have more cause to hate him than to love him, 3.05.128
i am so; i do love it better than laughing. 4.01. 4 P
to every modern censure worse than drunkards. 4.01. 7 P
fool to make me merry than experience to make me 4.01. 28 P
better jointure, i think, than you make a woman. 4.01. 56 P
he hath a rosalind of a better leer than you. 4.01. 67 P
or i should think my honesty ranker than my wit. 4.01. 84 P
more jealous of thee than a barbary cock–pigeon 4.01.150 P
hen, more clamorous than a parrot against rain, 4.01.151 P
against rain, more new–fangled than an ape, more 4.01.152 P
an ape, more giddy in my desires than a monkey. 4.01.153 P
with no less religion than if thou wert indeed 4.01.197 P
in their effect | than in their countenance. 4.03. 36
the woman low, | and browner than her brother." 4.03. 88
but kindness, nobler ever than revenge, | and 4.03.128
and nature, stronger than his just occasion, 4.03.129
ay, and greater wonders than that. 5.02. 28 P
for a greater esteem than may in some little 5.02. 56 P
i durst go no further than the lie 5.04. 85 P
i am for other than for dancing measures. 5.04.193
is no more unhandsome than to see the lord the ep 2 P
he is no less than what we say he is. SHR in.1. 71
no better than a poor and loathsome beggar. in.1. 123
for i have no more doublets than backs, no more in.2. 9 P
than backs, no more stockings than legs, nor no in.2. 10 P
than legs, nor no more shoes than feet — nay, in.2. 10 P
nay, sometime more feet than shoes, or such in.2. 11 P
softer and sweeter than the lustful bed | on in.2. 38
ay, fleeter than the roe. in.2. 48
beautiful | than any woman in this waning age. in.2. 63
to seek their fortunes farther than at home, 1.02. 51
that were my state far worser than it is, | i 1.02. 91
have no more eyes to see withal than a cat. 1.02.115 P
for she is sweeter than perfume itself | to whom 1.02.152
perhaps with more successful words | than you — 1.02.158
and were his daughter fairer than she is, | she 1.02.240
and let it be more than alcides' twelve. 1.02.256
face | which i could fancy more than any other. 2.01. 12
have been more kindly beholding to you than any, 2.01. 78 P
which i have bettered rather than decreas'd. 2.01.118
i love her ten times more than e'er i did. 2.01.161
as hazel–nuts, and sweeter than the kernels. 2.01.255
that love bianca more | than words can witness, 2.01.336
father hath no less | than three great argosies, 2.01.378
and she can have no more than all i have; 2.01.382
than hath been taught by any of my trade; 3.01. 69
a penny, | a horse and a man | is more than one, 3.02. 85
in padua | of greater sums than i have promised. 3.02.135
curster than she? why, 'tis impossible. 3.02.154
you would entreat me rather go than stay. 3.02.192
the weather, a taller man than i will take cold. 4.01. 11 P
by this reck'ning he is more shrew than she. 4.01. 85 P
than feed it with such overroasted flesh. 4.01.175
alas, sir, it is worse for me than so! 4.02. 88
that which spites me more than all these wants, 4.03. 11
and rather than it shall, i will be free, | even 4.03. 79
sir, the conceit is deeper than you think for: 4.03.161
what, is the jay more precious than the lark, 4.03.175
or is the adder better than the eel, | because 4.03.177
and if you please to like | no worse than i, 4.04. 33
and therefore, if you say no more than this, 4.04. 43
better once than never, for never too late. 5.01.150
it wanted rather than lack it where there is AWW 1.01. 10 P
thought you affect a sorrow than to have — 1.01. 53 P
able for thine enemy | rather in power than use, 1.01. 66
remembrance more | than those i shed for him. 1.01. 81
your pie and your porridge than in your cheek; 1.01.159 P
frank nature, rather curious than in haste, 1.02. 20
lies richer in your thoughts than on his tomb. 1.02. 49
thy marriage, sooner than thy wickedness. 1.03. 38 P
there is more owing her than is paid, and more 1.03.104 P
and more shall be paid her than she'll demand. 1.03.105 P
late more near her than i think she wish'd me. 1.03.106 P
i care no more for than i do for heaven, | so i 1.03.164
inclusive were | more than they were in note. 1.03.227
something in't | more than my father's skill, 1.03.243
amaz'd me more | than i dare blame my weakness. 2.01. 85
eye, | safer than mine own two, more dear. 2.01.109
use to be made than alone the recov'ry of the 2.03. 36 P
my mouth no more were broken than these boys', 2.03. 60
be in this choice than throw ames–ace for my 2.03. 78 P
our acts we them derive | than our foregoers. 2.03.137
no more pity of his age than i would have of — 2.03.240 P
honorable personages than the commission of your 2.03.261 P
rather than suffer question for your residence. 2.05. 38 P
spoken better of you than you have or will to 2.05. 47 P
and rather muse than ask why i entreat you, 2.05. 65
for my respects are better than they seem, | and 2.05. 66
greater than shows itself at the first view | to 2.05. 68
none better than to let him fetch off his drum, 3.06. 19 P
no more than a fish loves water. 3.06. 85 P
to do, and dares better be damn'd than to do't? 3.06. 89 P
they shall be no more than needful there, if 4.03. 80 P
there, if they were more than they can commend. 4.03. 81 P
in breaking 'em he is stronger than hercules. 4.03.253 P
advanc'd by the king than by that red–tail'd 4.05. 6 P
his fisnomy is more hotter in france than there. 4.05. 40 P
night, and with more haste | than is his use. 5.01. 24
you beg more than "word" then. 5.02. 40 P
and deeper than oblivion we do bury | th' 5.03. 24
which better than the first, o dear heaven, 5.03. 71
mystery more science | than i have in this ring. 5.03.104
win me to believe, | more than to see this ring. 5.03.120
than for to think that i would sink it here. 5.03.181
prove your honor | than in my thought it lies. 5.03.184
faith, i know more than i'll speak. 5.03.256 P
as i said, but more than that, he lov'd her, for 5.03.259 P
i'll confine myself no finer than i am. TN 1.03. 10 P
i have no more wit than a christian or an 1.03. 84 P
bounds, | rather than make unprofited return. 1.04. 22
youth | than in a nuntio's of more grave aspect. 1.04. 28
"better a witty fool than a foolish wit." 1.05. 36 P
fool that has no more brain than a stone. 1.05. 85 P
kind of fools no better than the fools' zanies. 1.05. 89 P
i can say little more than i have studied, and 1.05.178 P
rather to wonder at you than to hear you. 1.05.198 P
i had rather than forty shillings i had such a 2.03. 20 P
art any more than a steward? 2.03.114 P
my lady's favor at any thing more than contempt, 2.03.122 P
more than light airs and recollected terms | of 2.04. 5
still the woman take | an elder than herself, so 2.04. 30
sooner lost and worn, | than women's are. 2.04. 35
then let thy love be younger than thyself, | or 2.04. 36
tell her, my love, more noble than the world, 2.04. 81
more, but indeed | our shows are more than will; 2.04.117
a more exalted respect than any one else that 2.05. 27 P
at your heels than fortunes before you. 2.05.137 P
than i understand what you mean by bidding me 3.01. 79 P
they were blanks, rather than fill'd with me! 3.01.104
to solicit that | than music from the spheres. 3.01.110
better | to fall before the lion than the wolf! 3.01.129
would it be better, madam, than i am? 3.01.143
more soon | than love that would seem hid: 3.01.148
count's servingman than ever she bestow'd upon 3.02. 6 P
commendation with woman than report of valor. 3.02. 38 P
his face into more lines than is in the new map, 3.02. 79 P
more sharp than filed steel, did spur me forth, 3.03. 5
is bought more oft than begg'd or borrow'd. 3.04. 3
no worse man than sir toby to look to me! 3.04. 65 P
lady would not lose him for more than i'll say. 3.04.105 P
more approbation than ever proof itself would 3.04.181 P
had rather go with sir priest than sir knight. 3.04.271 P
than you have heard him brag to you he will. 3.04.317
i cannot do for you | than what befalls myself. 3.04.337
i hate ingratitude more in a man | than lying, 3.04.355
paltry boy, and more a coward than a hare. 3.04.386 P
thou art more puzzled than the egyptians in 4.02. 43 P
i am no more mad than you are; 4.02. 48 P
if you be no better in your wits than a fool. 4.02. 90 P
advantage thee more than ever the bearing of 4.02.111 P
after him i love | more than i love these eyes, 5.01.135
more than i love these eyes, more than my life, 5.01.135
more, by all mores, than e'er i shall love wife. 5.01.136
i had rather than forty pound i were at home. 5.01.177 P
would have tickled you othergates than he did. 5.01.194 P
is not more twin | than these two creatures. 5.01.224
may rather pluck on laughter than revenge, | if 5.01.366
tougher, brother, | than you can put us to't. WT 1.02. 16
for me less easy to commit | than you to punish. 1.02. 59
will draw in | more than the common blocks. 1.02.225
eye–glass | is thicker than a cuckold's horn), 1.02.269
spoke what did become you less | than this; 1.02.283
our gentry than our parents' noble names, | in 1.02.393
worse than the great'st infection | that e'er 1.02.423
avoid what's grown than question how 'tis born. 1.02.433
than one condemn'd by the king's own mouth — 1.02.445
which often hath no less prevail'd than so | on 2.01. 54
here which burns | worse than tears drown. 2.01.112
than when i feel and see her no farther trust 2.01.136
and i had rather glib myself than they | should 2.01.149
i had rather you did lack than i, my lord, 2.01.158
me | to have her honor true than your suspicion, 2.01.160
satisfied and need no more | than what i know, 2.01.190
passion more, alas, | than the queen's life? 2.03. 29
innocent soul, | more free than he is jealous. 2.03. 30
your evils, | than such as most seem yours. 2.03. 57
and no less honest | than you are mad; 2.03. 72
whose sting is sharper than the sword's, and 2.03. 87
accusation | than your own weak–hing'd fancy) 2.03.119
better burn it now | than curse it then. 2.03.157
in more than this deed does require! 2.03.190
which is more | than history can pattern, though 3.02. 36
what they did | than to perform it first. 3.02. 57
more than mistress of | which comes to me in 3.02. 59
the gods themselves | (wotting no more than i) 3.02. 76
which to deny concerns more than avails; 3.02. 86
is indeed | more criminal in thee than it), so 3.02. 89
easiest passage | look for no less than death. 3.02. 91
himself commended, | no richer than his honor. 3.02.170
they are heavier | than all thy woes can stir; 3.02.209
receive much better | than to be pitied of thee. 3.02.234
fear the wolf will sooner find than the master. 3.03. 67 P
warmer that got this than the poor thing is here 3.03. 75 P
both roaring louder than the sea or weather. 3.03.101 P
not to have had thee than thus to want thee. 4.02. 13 P
than they are in losing them when they have 4.02. 27 P
to his princely exercises than formerly he hath 4.02. 33 P
of her is extended more than can be thought to 4.02. 43 P
rags to lay on thee, rather than have these off. 4.03. 55 P
of them offend me more than the stripes i have 4.03. 57 P
sweet sir, much better than i was: 4.03.111 P
honor, nor my lusts | burn hotter than my faith. 4.04. 35
no more than were i painted i would wish | this 4.04.101
but sweeter than the lids of juno's eyes | or 4.04.121
but smacks of something greater than herself, 4.04.158
several tunes faster than you'll tell money; 4.04.184 P
points more than all the lawyers in bohemia can 4.04.205 P
that have more in them than you'ld think, sister 4.04.216 P
he hath promis'd you more than that, or there be 4.04.237 P
it, and witnesses more than my pack will hold. 4.04.284 P
and he, and more | than he, and men — the earth 4.04.371
force and knowledge | more than was ever man's, 4.04.375
i shall have more than you can dream of yet, 4.04.388
strength indeed | than most have of his age. 4.04.404
briers and made | more homely than thy state. 4.04.426
no, not our kin, | farre than deucalion off. 4.04.431
that i may call thee something more than man 4.04.535
the other grow | faster than thought or time. 4.04.554
promising | than a wild dedication of yourselves 4.04.566
paid down | more penitence than done trespass. 5.01. 4
holy | than to rejoice the former queen is well? 5.01. 30
what holier than, for royalty's repair, | for 5.01. 31
your writing now | is colder than that theme, 5.01.100
that she is a woman | more worth than any man; 5.01.111
(he bade me say so) more than all the sceptres, 5.01.146
since you ow'd no more to time | than i do now. 5.01.220
worth such gazes | than what you look on now. 5.01.227
stone rebuke me | for being more stone than it? 5.03. 38
strong possession much more than your right, JN 1.01. 40
sir, | than was his will to get me, as i think. 1.01.133
france, for france, for it is more than need. 1.01.179
a foot of honor better than i was, | but many a 1.01.182
than now the english bottoms have waft o'er 2.01. 73
father geffrey | than thou and john in manners, 2.01.127
than e'er the coward hand of france can win. 2.01.158
to you | than the constraint of hospitable zeal 2.01.244
in this hot trial more than we of france, 2.01.342
a greater pow'r than we denies all this, | and 2.01.368
where should he find it fairer than in blanch? 2.01.427
where should he find it purer than in blanch? 2.01.429
whose veins bound richer blood than lady blanch? 2.01.431
this union shall do more than battery can | to 2.01.446
with swifter spleen than powder can enforce, 2.01.448
his | but buffets better than a fist of france. 2.01.465
all i see in you is worthy love, | than this: 2.01.518
no longer than we well could wash our hands | to 3.01.234
than keep in peace that hand which thou dost 3.01.261
than arm thy constant and thy nobler parts 3.01.291
be stronger with thee than the name of wife? 3.01.314
no more than he that threats. to arms let's hie! 3.01.347
as i, | i could give better comfort than you do. 3.04.100
matter breeds for you | than i have nam'd! 3.04.171
i warrant i love you more than you do me. 4.01. 31
are you more stubborn–hard than hammer'd iron? 4.01. 67
when workmen strive to do better than well, 4.02. 28
than did the fault before it was so patch'd. 4.02. 34
and more, more strong than lesser is my fear, 4.02. 42
we do no further ask | than whereupon our weal, 4.02. 65
frowns | more upon humor than advis'd respect. 4.02.214
mind | than to be butcher of an innocent child. 4.02.259
presented thee more hideous than thou art. 4.02.266
is much more general than these lines import. 4.03. 17
thou art more deep damn'd than prince lucifer. 4.03.122
than had i seen the vaulty top of heaven 5.02. 52
nor met with fortune other than at feasts, 5.02. 58
peace, | and be no further harmful than in show. 5.02. 77
whom he hath us'd rather for sport than need) 5.02.175
time | than if you had at leisure known of this. 5.06. 27
he is more patient | than when you left him; 5.07. 12
doth more solicit me than your exclaims | to R2 1.02. 2
more than my dancing soul doth celebrate | this 1.03. 91
me no more | than an unstringed viol or a harp, 1.03.162
no more | than a delightful measure or a dance, 1.03.291
doth never rankle more | than when he bites, but 1.03.303
than they whom youth and ease have taught to 2.01. 10
are men's ends mark'd than their lives before. 2.01. 11
writ in remembrance more than things long past. 2.01. 14
thy death–bed is no lesser than thy land, 2.01. 95
whose compass is no bigger than thy head, | and 2.01.101
the waste is no whit lesser than thy land. 2.01.103
is it not more than shame to shame it so? 2.01.112
than was that young and princely gentleman. 2.01.175
more hath he spent in peace than they in wars. 2.01.255
more than with parting from my lord the king. 2.02. 13
find shapes of grief, more than himself, to wail 2.02. 22
more than your lord's departure weep not — more 2.02. 25
joy is little less in joy | than hope enjoyed. 2.03. 16
less value is my company | than your good words. 2.03. 20
and much more, much more than twice all this, 3.01. 28
of death to me | than bullingbrook to england. 3.01. 32
off, my gracious lord, | than this weak arm. 3.02. 65
than can my care–tun'd tongue deliver him! 3.02. 92
hard bright steel, and hearts harder than steel. 3.02.111
and all goes worse than i have power to tell. 3.02.120
three judases, each one thrice worse than judas! 3.02.132
mistake not, uncle, further than you should. 3.03. 15
take not, good cousin, further than you should, 3.03. 16
meet | with no less terror than the elements 3.03. 55
further scope | than for his lineal royalties, 3.03.113
great | as is my grief, or lesser than my name! 3.03.137
love | than my unpleased eye see your courtesy. 3.03.193
thou, thou little better thing than earth, 3.04. 78
so, | i speak no more than every one doth know. 3.04. 91

crowns | than bullingbrook's return to england, 4.01. 17
not be many hours of age | more than it is, ere 5.01. 58
better far off than, near, be ne'er the near. 5.01. 88
bare-headed, lower than his proud steed's neck, 5.02. 19
it is no more | than my poor life must answer. 5.02. 83
more than thou hast, and with it joy thy life. 5.06. 26
to be done | than out of anger can be uttered. 1H4 1.01.107
truly, little better than one of the wicked. 1.02. 94 P
third, if he fight longer than he sees reason, 1.02.185 P
by how much better than my word i am, | by so 1.02.210
than that which hath no foil to set it off. 1.02.215
mighty and to be fear'd, than my condition, 1.03. 6
stirs | to rouse a lion than to start a hare! 1.03.198
than i by letters shall direct your course. 1.03.293
could be better bit than i have been since the 2.01. 17 P
picking of purses than giving direction doth 2.01. 51 P
such as will strike sooner than speak, and speak 2.01. 77 P
sooner than speak, and speak sooner than drink, 2.01. 78 P
sooner than drink, and drink sooner than pray; 2.01. 79 P
to the night than to fern-seed for your walking 2.01. 89 P
no more valor in that poins than in a wild duck. 2.02.101 P
his own barn better than he loves our house. 2.03. 5 P
yet no farther wise | than harry percy's wife; 2.03.108
english in his life than "eight shillings and 2.04. 25 P
fellow should have fewer words than a parrot, 2.04. 99 P
yet a coward is worse than a cup of sack with 2.04.126 P
if they speak more or less than truth, they are 2.04.171 P
to say i know more harm in him than in myself, 2.04.466 P
than in myself, were to say more than i know. 2.04.467 P
than one of these same metre ballet-mongers. 3.01.128
a railing wife, | worse than a smoky house. 3.01.159
than feed on cates and have him talk to me | in 3.01.161
as if thou never walk'st further than finsbury. 3.01.252
little | more than a little is by much too much. 3.02. 73
the state | than thou the shadow of succession. 3.02. 99
and, being no more in debt to years than thou, 3.02.103
no more faith in thee than in a stew'd prune, 3.03.112 P
nor no more truth in thee than in a drawn fox, 3.03.113 P
thou seest i have more flesh than another man, 3.03.167 P
in my heart's love hath no man than yourself. 4.01. 8
his health was never better worth than now. 4.01. 27
present want | seems more than we shall find it. 4.01. 45
than if the earl were here, for men must think, 4.01. 79
worse than the sun in march, | this praise doth 4.01.111
of a caliver worse than a struck fowl or a hurt 4.02. 19 P
in their bellies no bigger than pins' heads, and 4.02. 22 P
dishonorable ragged than an old feaz'd ancient: 4.02. 31 P
sir john, 'tis more than time that i were there, 4.02. 54 P
steps me a little higher than his vow | made to 4.03. 75
nor claim no further than your new-fall'n right, 5.01. 44
making you ever better than his praise | by 5.02. 58
better consider what you have to do | than i, 5.02. 77
i need no more weight than mine own bowels. 5.03. 35 P
with lustier maintenance than i did look for 5.04. 22
than those proud titles thou hast won of me. 5.04. 79
wound my thoughts worse than thy sword my flesh. 5.04. 80
brings other news | than they have learnt of me. 2H4 in 39
smooth comforts false, worse than true wrongs. in 40
more than he haply may retail from me. 1.01. 32
is apter than thy tongue to tell thy arrand. 1.01. 69
toward their aim | than did our soldiers, aiming 1.01.124
'tis more than time, and, my most noble lord, 1.01.187
it, he might have moe diseases than he knew for. 1.02. 5 P
to laughter more than i invent or is invented on 1.02. 9 P
service for any other reason than to set me off, 1.02. 13 P
to be worn in my cap than to wait at my heels. 1.02. 15 P
in the palm of my hand than he shall get one /of 1.02. 21 P
procure him better assurance than bardolph. 1.02. 32 P
it is worse shame to beg than to be on the worst 1.02. 76 P
were it worse than the name of rebellion can 1.02. 77 P
if you say i am any other than an honest man. 1.02. 85 P
eaten to death with a rust than to be scour'd to 1.02.219 P
age and covetousness than 'a can part young 1.02.229 P
much smaller than the smallest of his thoughts, 1.03. 30
it is more than for some, my lord, it is for all 2.01. 73 P
come with such more than impudent sauciness from 2.01.112 P
the tennis-court-keeper knows better than i, for 2.02. 19 P
among wits of no higher breeding than thine. 2.02. 36 P
the world keeps the road-way better than thine: 2.02. 59 P
when you were more /endear'd to it than now, 2.03. 11
better than i was. hem! 2.04. 30 P
to me — 'twas no longer ago than wed'sday last, 2.04. 86 P
i'll drink no more than will do me good, for no 2.04.119 P
and ten times better than the nine worthies. 2.04.221 P
no more conceit in him than is in a mallet. 2.04.242 P
i love thee better than i love e'er a scurvy 2.04.272 P
a better than thou: 2.04.287 P
than in the perfum'd chambers of the great, 3.01. 12
is better /accommodated than with a wife. 3.02. 67 P
me, there are other men fitter to go out than i. 3.02.115 P
here is two more call'd than your number, you 3.02.188 P
off and on swifter than he that gibbets on the 3.02.263 P
duer paid to the hearer than the turk's tribute. 3.02.307 P
our battle is more full of names than yours, 4.01.152
it was more of his courtesy than your deserving. 4.03. 43 P
you should have won them dearer than you have. 4.03. 67
shall better speak of you than you deserve. 4.03. 85
had the wit, 'twere better than your dukedom. 4.03. 86 P
place in his affection | than all thy brothers. 4.04. 23
it more | than as your honor and as your renown, 4.05.145
though thou stand'st more sure than i could do, 4.05.202
be, | which i with more than with a common pain 4.05.223
i' th' court is better than a penny in purse. 5.01. 31 P
no worse than they are backbitten, sir, for they 5.01. 34 P
upon me | than i have drawn it in my fantasy. 5.02. 13
than a joint burden laid upon us all. 5.02. 55
gape | for thee thrice wider than for other men. 5.05. 54
than cherishing th' exhibiters against us; H5 1.01. 74
sum | than ever at one time the clergy yet | did 1.01. 80
a net | than amply to imbar their crooked titles 1.02. 94
she hath been then more fear'd than harm'd, my 1.02.155
cat, | to 'tame and havoc more than she can eat. 1.02.173
when thousands weep more than did laugh at it. 1.02.296
better fear'd and lov'd | than is your majesty. 2.02. 26
sooner than quittance of desert and merit, 2.02. 34
less for bounty bound to us | than cambridge is, 2.02. 93
and i repent my fault more than my death, 2.02.152
than i do at this hour joy o'er myself, 2.02.163
and more than carefully it us concerns | to 2.04. 2
no, with no more than if we heard that england 2.04. 24
to weigh | the enemy more mighty than he seems, 2.04. 44
of no less celerity | than that of thought. 3.pr. 3
of the roman disciplines, than is a puppy-dog. 3.02. 73 P
if you take the matter otherwise than is meant, 3.02.126 P
of honor edged | more sharper than your swords, 3.05. 39
advantage is a better soldier than rashness. 3.06.120 P
i have | almost no better than so many french; 3.06.147
hoof is more musical than the pipe of hermes. 3.07. 17 P
told that by one that knows him better than you. 3.07.105 P
were better than a churlish turf of france. 4.01. 15
then you are a better than the king. 4.01. 43 P
his affections are higher mounted than ours, yet 4.01.106 P
that's more than we know. 4.01.129 P
ay, or more than we should seek after; 4.01.130 P
of their damnation than he was before guilty of 4.01.175 P
more | of mortal griefs than do thy worshippers? 4.01.242
happy, being fear'd, | than they in fearing. 4.01.249
than from it issued forced drops of blood. 4.01.297
which likes me better than to wish us one. 4.03. 77
ten times more valor than this roaring devil i' 4.04. 70 P
whilst /by /a slave, no gentler than my dog, 4.05. 15
his eyes are humbler than they us'd to be. 4.07. 67
you peradventure than is in your knowledge to 4.08. 4 P
know to be no petter than a fellow, look you now 5.01. 7 P
you urge me farther than to say "do you in faith 5.02.128 P
a sugar touch of them than in the tongues of the 5.02.277 P
harry of england than a general petition of 5.02.279 P
his arms spread wider than a dragon's wings; 1H6 1.01. 11
than midday sun fierce bent against their faces. 1.01. 14
awe, | more than god or religious churchmen may. 1.01. 40
soul will make | than julius caesar or bright — 1.01. 56
more than three hours the fight continued, 1.01.120
walls they'll tear down than forsake the siege. 1.02. 40
he may mean more than we poor men do know: 1.02.122
we do no otherwise than we are will'd. 1.03. 10
this cardinal's more haughty than the devil. 1.03. 85
rather than i would be so pill'd esteem'd: 1.04. 33
i'll rear | than rhodope's /of memphis ever was. 1.06. 22
than the rich-jewell'd coffer of darius, 1.06. 25
more venturous or desperate than this. 2.01. 45
no, truly, 'tis more than manners will; 2.02. 54
i find thou art no less than fame hath bruited, 2.03. 68
and more than may be gathered by thy shape. 2.03. 69
the law, | good faith, i am no wiser than a daw. 2.04. 18
and that i'll prove on better men than somerset, 2.04. 98
was nothing less than bloody tyranny. 2.05.100
will see his burial better than his life. 2.05.121
more than well beseems | a man of thy profession 3.01. 19
who preferreth peace | more than i do, except i 3.01. 34
grieve thee more than streams of foreign gore. 3.03. 55
and after meet you, sooner than you would. 3.04. 45
i more incline to somerset than york: 4.01.154
persuade | than i am able to instruct or teach; 4.01.159
broils, | than yet can be imagin'd or suppos'd. 4.01.186
two mightier troops than that the dolphin led, 4.03. 7
rather than life preserv'd with infamy. 4.05. 33
ay, rather than i'll shame my mother's womb. 4.05. 35
than can yourself yourself in twain divide. 4.05. 49
books | than wanton dalliance with a paramour. 5.01. 23
more vile | than is a slave in base servility; 5.03.113
with more than half the gallian territories, 5.04.139
i'll rather keep | that which i have than, 5.04.145
why, what, i pray, is margaret more than that? 5.05. 36
her father is no better than an earl, | although 5.05. 37
where reignier sooner will receive than give. 5.05. 47
worth | than to be dealt in by attorneyship. 5.05. 56
spirit | (more than in women commonly is seen) 5.05. 71
love, | but prosper better than the troyan did. 5.05.106
no kinder sign of love | than this kind kiss. 2H6 1.01. 19
than all the princes in the land beside. 1.01.176
more like a soldier than a man o' th' church, 1.01.186
but can do more in england than the king. 1.03. 71
all | cannot do more in england than the nevils: 1.03. 73
more like an empress than duke humphrey's wife. 1.03. 78
was better worth than all my father's lands, 1.03. 86
sandy plains | than where castles mounted stand. 1.04. 37
plains | than where castles mounted stand." 1.04. 69
that mounts no higher than a bird can soar. 2.01. 14
no more than well becomes | so good a quarrel 2.01. 27
but you have done more miracles than i: 2.01.159
what plain proceedings is more plain than this? 2.02. 53
than when thou wert protector to thy king. 2.03. 27
or more afraid to fight, than is the appellant, 2.03. 57
sheriff, farewell, and better than i fare, 2.04.100
what's more dangerous than this fond affiance! 3.01. 74
unless thou wert more loyal than thou art. 3.01. 96
i say no more than truth, so help me god! 3.01.120
far truer spoke than meant. 3.01.183
for what's more miserable than discontent? 3.01.201
believe me, lords, were none more wise than i — 3.01.231
more than mistrust, that shows him worthy death. 3.01.242
betimes | than bring a burthen of dishonor home 3.01.298
might happily have prov'd far worse than his. 3.01.306
what, worse than nought? 3.01.307
faster than spring-time show'rs comes thought on 3.01.337
my brain, more busy than the laboring spider, 3.01.339
than from true evidence of good esteem | he be 3.02. 21
be woe for me, more wretched than he is. 3.02. 73
because thy flinty heart, more hard than they, 3.02. 99
his eyeballs further out than when he lived, 3.02.169
stronger breastplate than a heart untainted! 3.02.232
gall, worse than gall, the daintiest that they 3.02.322
loather a hundred times to part than die. 3.02.355
from thee to die were torture more than death. 3.02.401
more | than bargulus the strong illyrian pirate. 4.01.108
stoop to the block than these knees bow to any 4.01.125
pole | than stand uncover'd to the vulgar groom. 4.01.128
more can i bear than you dare execute. 4.01.130
no better sign of a brave mind than a hard hand. 4.02. 20 P
and more than that, he can speak french, and 4.02.166 P
rather than bloody war shall cut them short, 4.04. 12
for any that calls me other than lord mortimer. 4.06. 6 P
when honester men than thou go in their hose and 4.07. 50 P
than you should stoop unto a frenchman's mercy. 4.08. 48
and could command no more content than i? 4.09. 2
i am far better born than is the king; 5.01. 28
storm | than any thou canst conjure up to-day; 5.01.199
stigmatic, that's more than thou canst tell. 5.01.215
than drops of blood were in my father's veins. 3H6 1.01. 97
my title's good, and better far than his. 1.01.130
rather than have made that savage duke thine 1.01.224
of france, but worse than wolves of france, 1.04.111
tongue more poisons than the adder's tooth! 1.04.112
o, ten times more, than tigers of hyrcania. 1.04.155
it, | you love the breeder better than the male. 2.01. 42
words would add more anguish than the wounds. 2.01. 99
or more than common fear of clifford's rigor, 2.01.126
keep | than in possession any jot of pleasure. 2.02. 53
your legs did better service than your hands. 2.02.104
helen of greece was fairer far than thou, 2.02.146
life | to be no better than a homely swain, | to 2.05. 22
sheep | than doth a rich embroider'd canopy | to 2.05. 44
grief more than common grief! 2.05. 94
here sits a king more woeful than you are. 2.05.124
more than my body's parting with my soul. 2.06. 4
more than i seem, and less than i was born to; 3.01. 56
more than i seem, and less than i was born to; 3.01. 56
'tis better said than done, my gracious lord. 3.02. 90
i speak no more than what my soul intends, | and 3.02. 94
and that is more than i will yield unto. 3.02. 96
no more than when my daughters call thee mother. 3.02.101
that's a day longer than a wonder lasts. 3.02.114
than to accomplish twenty golden crowns! 3.02.152
such | as are of better person than myself, 3.02.167
i'll drown more sailors than the mermaid shall, 3.02.186
i'll slay more gazers than the basilisk, | i'll 3.02.187
nestor, | deceive more slily than ulysses could, 3.02.189
and thou no more art prince than she is queen. 3.03. 80
and more than so, my father, | even in the 3.03.103
and better 'twere you troubled him than france. 3.03.155
for matching more for wanton lust than honor, 3.03.210
or than for strength and safety of our country. 3.03.211
foreign storms than any home-bred marriage. 4.01. 38
'tis better using france than trusting france. 4.01. 42
and meaner than myself have had like fortune. 4.01. 71
against your majesty | than all the rest, 4.01.109
tell me if you love warwick more than me? 4.01.137
i rather wish you foes than hollow friends. 4.01.139
i like it better than a dangerous honor. 4.03. 17
better do so than tarry and be hang'd. 4.05. 26
now then it is more than needful | forthwith 4.06. 53
he | must help you more than you are hurt by me. 4.06. 76
then why should they love edward more than me? 4.08. 47
than bear so low a sail to strike to thee. 5.01. 52
more than the nature of a brother's love! 5.01. 79
than jephthah when he sacrific'd his daughter. 5.01. 91
than if thou never hadst deserv'd our hate. 5.01.104
the brothers | more than with ruthless waves, 5.04. 36
what's worse than murtherer, that i may name it? 5.05. 58
point | than can my ears that tragic history. 5.06. 28
thy mother felt more than a mother's pain, | and 5.06. 49
and yet brought forth less than a mother's hope, 5.06. 50
touches me deeper than you can imagine. R3 1.01.112
the death of thee | than i can wish to wolves — 1.02. 19
him | than i am made by my young lord and thee! 1.02. 28
advance thy halberd higher than my breast, | or, 1.02. 40
fairer than tongue can name thee, let me have 1.02. 81
fouler than heart can think thee, thou canst 1.02. 83
for he was fitter for that place than earth. 1.02.108
he lives, that loves thee better than he could. 1.02.141
'tis more than you deserve; 1.02.222
(whom god preserve better than you would wish!) 1.03. 59
she may do more, sir, than denying that: 1.03. 93
maid | than a great queen with this condition, 1.03.107
ay, and much better blood than his or thine. 1.03.125
than death can yield me here by my abode. 1.03.168
'tis better, sir, than to be tedious. 1.04. 89 P
life | than edward will for tidings of my death. 1.04.231
more than the infant that is born to-night. 2.01. 72
deserve not worse than wretched clarence did, 2.01. 94
it so, | 'tis more than we deserve or i expect. 2.03. 37
talk'd how i did grow | more than my brother. 2.04. 12
to touch his growth nearer than he touch'd mine. 2.04. 25
distinguish of a man | than of his outward show, 3.01. 10
then he is more beholding to you than i. 3.01.107
a greater gift than that i'll give my cousin. 3.01.115
than some that have accus'd them wear their hats 3.02. 93
than when thou met'st me last where now we meet. 3.02. 99
death, | and i in better state than e'er i was. 3.02.104
he knows no more of mine than i of yours, | or i 3.04. 11
yours, | or i of his, my lord, than you of mine. 3.04. 12
than my lord hastings no man might be bolder, 3.04. 29
can lesser hide his love or hate than he, | for 3.04. 52
which we more hunt for than the grace of god! 3.04. 97
no less importing than our general good, | are 3.07. 68
than in my greatness covet to be hid | and in 3.07.163
no farther than the tower, and, as i guess, 4.01. 8
than thou hast made me by my dear lord's death!" 4.01. 76
no more than with my soul i mourn for yours. 4.01. 88
than buckingham and his rash-levied strength. 4.03. 50
that thy babes were sweeter than they were, 4.04.120
were, | and he that slew them fouler than he is. 4.04.121
than all the complete armor that thou wear'st! 4.04.190
than ever you /or yours by me were harm'd! 4.04.239
last longer telling than thy kindness' date. 4.04.255
in love | than is the doting title of a mother; 4.04.300
my heart is ten times lighter than my looks. 5.03. 3
is my beaver easier than it was? 5.03. 50
than can the substance of ten thousand soldiers 5.03.218
more than i have said, loving countrymen, | the 5.03.237
had rather have us win than him they follow: 5.03.244
why, what is that to me | more than to richmond? 5.03.286
what shall i say more than i have inferr'd? 5.03.314
the king enacts more wonders than a man, 5.04. 2
more stronger to direct you than yourself, | if H8 1.01.147
you know no more than others? 1.02. 44
me, | i have no further gone in this than by | a 1.02. 69
but benefit no further | than vainly longing. 1.02. 81
ten times more ugly | than ever they were fair. 1.02.118
abusing better men than they can be | out of a 1.03. 28
would show a worse sin than ill doctrine. 1.03. 60
his person | more worthy this place than myself, 1.04. 79
have mercies | more than i dare make faults. 2.01. 71
longer than i have time to tell his years; 2.01. 91

yet i am richer than my base accusers, | that 2.01.104
me | a little happier than my wretched father. 2.01.120
ensuing evil, if it fall, | greater than this. 2.01.142
for it grows again | fresher than e'er it was, 2.01.155
to leave a thousandfold more bitter than | 'tis 2.03. 8
than to be perk'd up in a glist'ring grief | and 2.03. 21
in your way | for more than blushing comes to. 2.03. 42
no less flowing | than marchioness of pembroke; 2.03. 63
more than my all is nothing: 2.03. 67
nor my wishes | more worth than empty vanities; 2.03. 69
honor's train | is longer than his foreskirt. 2.03. 98
say, | are you not stronger than you were? 2.03.100
you tender more your person's honor than | your 2.04.116
do no more offices of life to't than | the grave 2.04.191
for him, | there's more in't than fair visage. 3.02. 88
show'r'd on me daily have been more than could 3.02.167
more | on you than any, so your hand and heart, 3.02.186
be more | to me, your friend, than any. 3.02.190
good i ever labor'd | more than mine own; 3.02.192
till i find more than will or words to do it 3.02.236
better | have burnt that tongue than said so. 3.02.254
dare mate a sounder man than surrey can be, 3.02.274
i'll startle you | worse than the sacring bell, 3.02.295
i had rather want those than my head. 3.02.309
more pangs and fears than wars or women have; 3.02.370
far | than my weak–hearted enemies dare offer. 3.02.390
corruption wins not more than honesty. 3.02.444
honors to his age | than man could give him, he 4.02. 68
in them a wilder nature than the business | that 5.01. 15
to your ear | much weightier than this work. 5.01. 18
under more calumnious tongues | than i myself, 5.01.113
i mean in perjur'd witness, than your master, 5.01.136
they shall no more prevail than we give way to. 5.01.143
place, | defacers of a public peace than i do. 5.02. 76
more than, i fear, you are provided for. 5.02. 92
lord, | become a churchman better than ambition; 5.02. 98
than but once think his place becomes thee not. 5.02.168
ye, i see, | more out of malice than integrity, 5.02.180
and fair purgation to the world than malice, 5.02.187
and fair virtue | than this pure soul shall be. 5.04. 25
TRO valiant, | but i am weaker than a woman's tear, 1.01. 9
tamer than sleep, fonder than ignorance, | less 1.01. 10
tear, | tamer than sleep, fonder than ignorance, 1.01. 10
less valiant than the virgin in the night, | and 1.01. 11
doth lesser blench at suff'rance than i do. 1.01. 28
yesternight fairer than ever i saw her look, or 1.01. 32 P
hair were not somewhat darker than helen's — 1.01. 41 P
i speak no more than truth. 1.01. 64 P
no, hector is not a better man than troilus. 1.02. 79 P
him above, his complexion is higher than his. 1.02.102 P
you, i think helen loves him better than paris. 1.02.108 P
becomes him better than any man in all phrygia. 1.02.122 P
esteems her no more than i esteem an addle egg. 1.02.131 P
and his helm more hack'd than hector's, and how 1.02.233 P
be such a man as troilus than agamemnon and all 1.02.245 P
the greeks achilles, a better man than troilus. 1.02.248 P
than in the glass of pandar's praise may be; 1.02.285
men prize the thing ungain'd more than it is. 1.02.289
annoyance by the breeze | than by the tiger; 1.03. 49
should lift their bosoms higher than the shores, 1.03.112
with surety stronger than achilles' arm, | 'fore 1.03.220
that holds his honor higher than his ease, | and 1.03.266
/seeks his praise more than he fears his peril, 1.03.267
that loves his mistress more than in confession 1.03.269
and her worth | in other arms than hers — to 1.03.272
truer, | than ever greek did couple in his arms, 1.03.276
him that my lady | was fairer than his grandam, 1.03.299
than in the pride and salt scorn of his eyes, 1.03.370
his crest that prouder than blue iris bends. 1.03.379
oration without book than thou learn /a prayer 2.01. 18 P
hast no more brain than i have in mine elbows, 2.01. 43 P
bobb'd his brain more than he has beat my bones. 2.01. 70 P
though no man lesser fears the greeks than i 2.02. 8
than hector is. 2.02. 14
to make the service greater than the god, | and 2.02. 57
which you priz'd | richer than sea and land? 2.02. 92
act | such and no other than event doth form it, 2.02.120
i am no more touch'd than all priam's sons; 2.02.126
blood | than to make up a free determination 2.02.170
have ears more deaf than adders to the voice 2.02.172
in all humanity | than wife is to the husband? 2.02.176
than the performance of our heaving spleens, | i 2.02.196
little little less than little wit from them 2.03. 13 P
fraction is more our wish than their faction. 2.03. 99 P
if any thing more than your sport and pleasure 2.03.108
greater | than in the note of judgment; 2.03.125
and worthier than himself | here tend the savage 2.03.125
what is he more than another? 2.03.142 P
no more than what he thinks he is. 2.03.143 P
think he thinks himself a better man than i am? 2.03.145 P
of that we hold an idol more than he? 2.03.189
shall more obey than to the edge of steel | or 3.01.152
you shall do more | than all the island kings — 3.01.154
gives us more palm in beauty than we have, | yea 3.01.157
my heart beats thicker than a feverous pulse, 3.02. 36
more dregs than water, if my /fears have eyes. 3.02. 67 P
finds safer footing than blind reason stumbling 3.02. 72 P
imposition enough than for us to undergo any 3.02. 80 P
swear more performance than they are able, and 3.02. 85 P
vowing more than the perfection of ten, and 3.02. 86 P
and discharging less than the tenth part of one. 3.02. 87 P
truth can speak truest not truer than troilus. 3.02. 98 P
perchance, my lord, i show more craft than love, 3.02.153
that doth renew swifter than blood decays! 3.02.163
and simpler than the infancy of truth. 3.02.170
shall shake him more | than if not look'd on. 3.03. 54
though less than yours in /past, must o'ertop 3.03.164
a little gilt, | more laud than gilt o'erdusted. 3.03.179
than breath or pen can give expressure to. 3.03.204
much | to throw down hector than polyxena. 3.03.208
is not more loath'd than an effeminate man | in 3.03.218
rather be a tick in a sheep than such a valiant 3.03.312 P
borne to greece | than cressid borne from troy. 4.01. 48
with wings more momentary–swift than thought. 4.02. 14
it's more than i know, i'll be sworn. 4.02. 51 P
more bright in zeal than the devotion which 4.04. 26
the kiss you take is better than you give; 4.05. 38
action | is more vindicative than jealous love. 4.05.107

but there's more in me than thou understand'st. 4.05.240
him when he leers than i will a serpent when he 5.01. 90 P
rather leave to see hector than not to dog him. 5.01. 95 P
'twas one's that lov'd me better than you will. 5.02. 89
divides more wider than the sky and earth, | and 5.02.149
in his descent than shall my prompted sword 5.02.175
do more for an almond than he for a commodious 5.02.194 P
abhorr'd | than spotted livers in the sacrifice. 5.03. 18
holds honor far more precious–dear than life. 5.03. 28
in you, | which better fits a lion than a man. 5.03. 38
is the cur ajax prouder than the cur achilles, 5.04. 14 P
are all resolv'd rather to die than to famish? COR 1.01. 4 P
of more strong link asunder than can ever 1.01. 71
no, | than is the coal of fire upon the ice, 1.01.173
better be held nor more attain'd than by | a 1.01.265
more than his singularity, he goes | upon this 1.01.278
(who is of more worse hated than of you), | and 1.02. 13
wherein he won honor than in the embracements of 1.03. 4 P
that it was no better than picture–like to hang 1.03. 11 P
he was a man–child than now in first seeing he 1.03. 16 P
alike, and none less dear than thine and my good 1.03. 23 P
for their country than one voluptuously surfeit 1.03. 25 P
it more becomes a man | than gilt his trophy. 1.03. 40
than hector's forehead when it spit forth blood 1.03. 42
and hear a drum than look upon his schoolmaster. 1.03. 56 P
no, nor a man that fears you less than he, 1.04. 14
you less than he, | that's lesser than a little. 1.04. 15
our walls | rather than they shall pound us up; 1.04. 17
and fight | with hearts more proof than shields. 1.04. 25
that you may be abhorr'd | farther than seen, 1.04. 33
drop is rather physical | than dangerous to me. 1.05. 19
friend no less | than those she placeth highest! 1.05. 24
more than i know the sound of martius' tongue 1.06. 26
they did budge | from rascals worse than they. 1.06. 45
fear | /lesser his person than an ill report; 1.06. 70
and that his country's dearer than himself; 1.06. 72
i do hate thee | worse than a promise–breaker. 1.08. 2
a serpent i abhor | more than thy fame and envy. 1.08. 4
'twere a concealment | worse than a theft, no 1.09. 22
worse than a theft, no less than a traducement, 1.09. 22
more cruel to your good report than grateful 1.09. 54
buttock of the night than with the forehead of 2.01. 52 P
giber for the table than a necessary bencher in 2.01. 82 P
of no better report than a horse–drench. 2.01.118 P
in my way | than sway with them in theirs. 2.01.204
than carry it but by the suit of the gentry to 2.01.238
than have him hold that purpose and to put it 2.01.240
for the world | than camels in their war, who 2.01.251
with greater devotion than they can render it 2.02. 19 P
for requital | than we to stretch it out. 2.02. 51
a kinder value of the people than | he hath 2.02. 59
more pertinent | than the rebuke you give it. 2.02. 64
to heal again | than hear say how i got them. 2.02. 70
when the alarum were struck than idly sit | to 2.02. 76
for honor | than /one /on /'s ears to hear it? 2.02. 81
he covets less | than misery itself would give, 2.02.127
choice is rather to have my hat than my heart, i 2.03. 99 P
than crave the hire which first we do deserve. 2.03.114
rather than fool it so, | let the high office 2.03.121
did claim no less | than what he stood for, so 2.03.187
make them of no more voice | than dogs, that are 2.03.216
more after our commandment than as guided | by 2.03.230
what you rather must do | than what you should, 2.03.233
mutiny were better put in hazard | than stay, 2.03.257
a graver bench | than ever frown'd in greece. 3.01.107
my reasons, | more worthier than their voices. 3.01.120
you that will be less fearful than discreet; 3.01.150
of state | more than you doubt the change on't; 3.01.152
trial | than the severity of the public power, 3.01.268
to no further harm | than so much loss of time. 3.01.283
(which, i dare vouch, is more than that he hath, 3.01.298
all | than to take in a town with gentle words, 3.02. 59
than spend a fawn upon 'em | for the inheritance 3.02. 67
of th' ignorant | more learned than the ears), 3.02. 77
in a fiery gulf | than flatter him in a bower. 3.02. 92
it is my more dishonor | than thou of them. 3.02.125
thy mother rather feel thy pride than fear | thy 3.02.126
as i hear, more strong | than are upon you yet. 3.02.141
shall i be charg'd no further than this present? 3.03. 42
such as become a soldier | rather than envy you. 3.03. 57
more holy and profound, than mine own life, | my 3.03.113
thy tears are salter than a younger man's, | and 4.01. 22
makes fear'd and talk'd of more than seen — 4.01. 31
more than a wild exposture to each chance | that 4.01. 36
after it is done | than when it was a–doing. 4.02. 5
blows for rome | than thou hast spoken words? 4.02. 20
moe noble blows than ever thou wise words, | and 4.02. 21
'tis an honester service than to meddle with thy 4.05. 47 P
i'd not believe them more | than thee, all–noble 4.05.106
heart | than when i first my wedded mistress saw 4.05.117
and more a friend than e'er an enemy; 4.05.146
there was more in him than i could think. 4.05.158 P
but a greater soldier than he, you wot one. 4.05.162 P
more bastard children than war's a destroyer of 4.05.225 P
than see | our tradesmen singing in their shops, 4.06. 7
than when these fellows ran about the streets, 4.06. 28
can | no more atone than violent'st contrariety. 4.06. 73
a thing | made by some other deity than nature, 4.06. 91
than boys pursuing summer butterflies, | or 4.06. 94
than i thought he would | when first i did 4.07. 9
not to be other than one thing, not moving 4.07. 42
more than the instant army we can make, | might 5.01. 37
suppler souls | than in our priest–like fasts: 5.01. 56
love thee no worse than thy old father menenius 5.02. 70 P
shall poison rather | than pity note how much. 5.02. 87
mine ears against your suits are stronger than 5.02. 88
and am not | of stronger earth than others. 5.03. 29
more impression show | than that of common sons. 5.03. 52
whilst with no softer cushion than the flint | i 5.03. 53
how more unfortunate than all living women | are 5.03. 97
grace to both parts | than seek the end of one, 5.03.122
march to assault thy country than to tread 5.03.123
will move him more | than can our reasons. 5.03.158
'longs more pride | than pity to our prayers. 5.03.171
with more strength | than thou hast to deny't. 5.03.177
shall bear | a better witness back than words, 5.03.204
he has wings, he's more than a creeping thing. 5.04. 14 P
his mother now than an eight–year–old horse. 5.04. 17 P

is no more mercy in him than there is milk in a 5.04. 28 P
that we look'd | for no less spoil than glory — 5.06. 43
my country's love | than when i parted hence, 5.06. 72
doth more than counterpoise a full third part 5.06. 77
to the antiates | than shame to th' romans; 5.06. 80
than his that shakes for age and feebleness. TIT 1.01.188
rather than rob me of the people's hearts! 1.01.207
can make you greater than the queen of goths. 1.01.269
my lord, you are unjust, and more than so, | in 1.01.292
renowmed titus, more than half my soul — 1.01.373
eyes | than is prometheus tied to caucasus. 2.01. 17
world, | i love lavinia more than all the world. 2.01. 72
glideth by the mill | than wots the miller of, 2.01. 86
better than he have worn vulcan's badge. 2.01. 89
lucrece was not more chaste | than this lavinia, 2.01.109
never hopes more heaven than rests in thee, 2.03. 41
ah, my sweet moor, sweeter to me than life! 2.03. 51
o, keep me from their worse than killing lust, 2.03.175
my heart suspects more than mine eye can see. 2.03.213
by my soul, were there worse end than death, 2.03.302
that could have better sew'd than philomel. 2.04. 43
than youthful april shall with all his show'rs. 3.01. 18
in some sort they are better than the tribunes, 3.01. 39
is soft as wax, tribunes more hard than stones; 3.01. 45
hath hurt me more than had he kill'd me dead: 3.01. 92
spurn | is dear lavinia, dearer than my soul. 3.01.102
my youth can better spare my blood than you, 3.01.165
more than remembrance of my father's death. 3.01.240
these miseries are more than may be borne. 3.01.243
he loves his pledges dearer than his life. 3.01.291
read to her sons than she hath read to thee 4.01. 13
i think she means that there were more than one 4.01. 38
than foemen's marks upon his batt'red shield, 4.01.127
led us to rome, strangers, and more than so, 4.02. 33
coal–black is better than another hue, | in that 4.02. 99
wrung with wrongs more than our backs can bear. 4.03. 49
plight | than prosecute the meanest or the best 4.04. 33
than baits to fish, or honey–stalks to sheep, 4.04. 91
and that more dear | than hands or tongue, her 5.02.176
for worse than philomel you us'd my daughter, 5.02.194
and worse than progne i will be reveng'd. 5.02.195
more stern and bloody than the centaurs' feast. 5.02.203
what, hath the firmament moe suns than one? 5.03. 17
and have a thousand times more cause than he 5.03. 51
or more than any living man could bear. 5.03.127
ten thousand worse than ever yet i did | would i 5.03.187
younger than she are happy mothers made. ROM 1.02. 12
not mad, but bound more than a madman is; 1.02. 54
one fairer than my love! 1.02. 92
younger than you, | here in verona, ladies of 1.03. 69
than your consent gives strength to make /it fly 1.03. 99
comes | in shape no bigger than an agot–stone 1.04. 55
and more inconstant than the wind, who woos 1.04.100
that thou, her maid, art far more fair than she. 2.02. 6
in thine eye | than twenty of their swords! 2.02. 72
than death prorogued, wanting of thy love. 2.02. 78
than those that have /more coying to be strange. 2.02.101
and make her airy tongue more hoarse than /mine, 2.02.162
and yet no farther than a wanton's bird, | that 2.02.177
more than prince of cats. 2.04. 19 P
more of the wild goose in one of thy wits than, 2.04. 73 P
is not this better now than groaning for love? 2.04. 88 P
you have found him than he was when you sought 2.04.121 P
more in a minute than he will stand to in a 2.04.148 P
take him down, and 'a were lustier than he is, 2.04.151 P
ten times faster glides than the sun's beams, 2.05. 5
is longer than the tale thou dost excuse. 2.05. 34
though his face be better than any man's, yet 2.05. 40 P
conceit, more rich in matter than in words, 2.06. 30
more or a hair less in his beard than thou hast. 3.01. 18 P
bear thee can afford | no better term than this: 3.01. 61
but love thee better than thou canst devise, 3.01. 69
and, swifter than his tongue, | his /agile arm 3.01.165
whiter than new snow upon a raven's back. 3.02. 19
than the death/–darting eye of cockatrice. 3.02. 47
some word there was, worser than tybalt's death, 3.02.108
what less than dooms–day is the prince's doom? 3.03. 9
more terror in his look, | much more than death. 3.03. 14
courtship lives | in carrion flies than romeo; 3.03. 35
joy | than thou went'st forth in lamentation. 3.03.154
i have more care to stay than will to go. 3.05. 23
whom you know i hate, | rather than paris. 3.05.123
being spoke behind your back, than to your face. 4.01. 28
thou wrong'st it more than tears with that 4.01. 32
if, rather than to marry county paris, | thou 4.01. 71
o, bid me leap, rather than marry paris, | from 4.01. 77
than these poor compounds that thou mayest not 5.01. 82
far | than empty tigers or the roaring sea. 5.03. 39
can vengeance be pursued further than death? 5.03. 55
by heaven, i love thee better than myself, | for 5.03. 64
than with that hand that cut thy youth in twain 5.03. 99
a greater power than we can contradict | hath 5.03.153
of more woe | than this of juliet and her romeo. 5.03.310
lives in these touches, livelier than life. TIM 1.01. 38
few things loves better | than to abhor himself; 1.01. 60
some better than his value — on the moment 1.01. 79
blows of fortune's | more pregnantly than words. 1.01. 92
more rais'd | than one which holds a trencher. 1.01.120
are ye to my fortunes | than my fortunes to me. 1.02. 20
a breakfast of enemies than a dinner of friends. 1.02. 77 P
more of you to myself than you can with modesty 1.02. 93 P
can we call our own than the riches of our 1.02.103 P
to feed | than such that do e'en enemies exceed. 1.02.204
with more than common thanks i will receive it. 1.02.208
my horse and buy twenty moe | better than he, 2.01. 8
with two stones moe than 's artificial one. 2.02.111 P
milky heart, | it turns in less than two nights? 3.01. 55
i'd rather than the worth of thrice the sum 3.03. 22
timon in this should pay more than he owes; 3.04. 22
and now ingratitude makes it worse than stealth. 3.04. 27
who can speak broader than he that has no house 3.04. 63 P
and the ass more captain than the lion, the 3.05. 49
fellow | loaden with irons wiser than the judge, 3.05. 50
i'm worse than mad. 3.05.105
not summer more willing than we your lordship. 3.06. 30 P
meat be belov'd more than the man that gives it. 3.06. 76 P
rather than render back, out with your knives, 4.01. 9
th' unkindest beast more kinder than mankind. 4.01. 36

and more than that i know thee | i not desire to 4.03. 58
hath in her more destruction than thy sword, 4.03. 63
i love thee better now than e'er i did. 4.03.233
wretched being, | worse than the worst, content. 4.03.247
at duty, more than i could frame employment; 4.03.262
i had rather be a beggar's dog than apemantus. 4.03.356 P
are poison, and he slays | moe than you rob. 4.03.433
what vilder thing upon the earth than friends, 4.03.463
those that would mischief me than those that do! 4.03.468
for his undone lord than mine eyes for you. 4.03.481
methinks thou art more honest now than wise; 4.03.502
in a baser temple | than where swine feed! 5.01. 49
than their offense can weigh down by the dram; 5.01.151
with thy smile | than hew to't with thy sword. 5.04. 46
you stones, you worse than senseless things! JC 1.01. 35
i hear a tongue shriller than all the music 1.02. 16
than that poor brutus, with himself at war, 1.02. 46
love | the name of honor more than i fear death. 1.02. 89
why should that name be sounded more than yours? 1.02.143
but it was fam'd with more than with one man? 1.02.153
villager | than to repute himself a son of rome 1.02.173
whiles they behold a greater than themselves, 1.02.209
thee what is to be fear'd | than what i fear; 1.02.212
put it by thrice, every time gentler than other; 1.02.230 P
a man no mightier than thyself, or me, | in 1.03. 76
his affections sway'd | more than his reason. 2.01. 21
what other bond | than secret romans, that have 2.01.125
other oath | than honesty to honesty engag'd 2.01.127
for he can do no more than caesar's arm | when 2.01.182
think you i am no stronger than my sex, | being 2.01.296
well | that caesar is more dangerous than he. 2.02. 45
is there no voice more worthy than my own, | to 3.01. 49
basis /lies along | no worthier than the dust! 3.01.116
shall it not grieve thee dearer than thy death, 3.01.196
it would become me better than to close | in 3.01.202
it shall advantage more than do us wrong. 3.01.242
brutus' love to caesar was no less than his. 3.02. 19 P
and die all slaves, than that caesar were dead, 3.02. 23 P
no more to caesar than you shall do to brutus. 3.02. 37 P
there's not a nobler man in rome than antony. 3.02.116
and you, | than i will wrong such honorable men. 3.02.127
ingratitude, more strong than traitors' arms, 3.02.185
octavius, i have seen more days than you, | and 4.01. 18
be a dog, and bay the moon, | than such a roman. 4.03. 28
abler than yourself | to make conditions. 4.03. 31
and drop my blood for drachmaes than to wring 4.03. 73
but brutus makes mine greater than they are. 4.03. 87
a heart | dearer than pluto's mine, richer than 4.03.102
dearer than pluto's mine, richer than gold: 4.03.102
him better | than ever thou lovedst cassius. 4.03.107
for i have seen more years, i'm sure, than ye. 4.03.132
good words are better than bad strokes, octavius 5.01. 29
to this dead man than you shall see me pay. 5.03.102
rather have | such men my friends than enemies. 5.04. 29
in ourselves | than tarry till they push us. 5.05. 25
losing day | more than octavius and mark antony 5.05. 37
lesser than macbeth, and greater. MAC 1.03. 65
prospect of belief, | no more than to be cawdor. 1.03. 75
fears | are less than horrible imaginings: 1.03.138
more is thy due than more than all can pay. 1.04. 21
more is thy due than more than all can pay. 1.04. 21
they have more in them than mortal knowledge. 1.05. 3 P
dost fear to do | than wishest should be undone. 1.05. 25
scarcely more | than would make up his message. 1.05. 37
greater than both, by the all-hail hereafter! 1.05. 55
and, to be more than what you were, you would 1.07. 50
is't known who did this more than bloody deed? 2.04. 22
lest our old robes sit easier than our new! 2.04. 38
rather than so, come fate into the list, | and 3.01. 70
no less material to me | than is his father's, 3.01.136
than by destruction dwell in doubtful joy. 3.02. 7
than on the torture of the mind to lie | in 3.02. 21
'tis better thee without than he within. 3.04. 14
for unkindness | than pity for mischance. 3.04. 42
this is more strange | than such a murther is. 3.04. 82
here's another, | more potent than the first. 4.01. 76
shall have more vices than it had before, | more 4.03. 47
more suffer, and more sundry ways than ever, 4.03. 48
better macbeth | than such an one to reign. 4.03. 66
more pernicious root | than summer-seeming lust; 4.03. 86
thee, | oft'ner upon her knees than on her feet, 4.03.110
and delight | no less in truth than life. 4.03.130
more needs she the divine than the physician. 5.01. 74
thyself a hotter name | than any is in hell. 5.07. 7
bloodier villain | than terms can give thee out! 5.08. 8
is not this something more than fantasy? HAM 1.01. 54
more than the scope | of these delated articles 1.02. 37
than is the throne of denmark to thy father. 1.02. 49
a little more than kin, and less than kind. 1.02. 65
a little more than kin, and less than kind. 1.02. 65
than that which dearest father bears his son 1.02.111
but no more like my father | than i to hercules. 1.02.153
a countenance more | in sorrow than in anger. 1.02.232
than the main voice of denmark goes withal. 1.03. 28
giving more light than heat, extinct in both 1.03.118
at a higher rate | than a command to parle. 1.03.123
teder may he walk | than may be given you. 1.03.126
more honor'd in the breach than the observance. 1.04. 16
and duller shouldst thou be than the fat weed 1.05. 32
than are dreamt of in your philosophy. 1.05.167
than your particular demands will touch it. 2.01. 12
more grief to hide, than hate to utter love. 2.01.116
more than his father's death, that thus hath put 2.02. 8
pleasures more into command | than to entreaty. 2.02. 29
there is something in this more than natural, if 2.02.367 P
more appear like entertainment than yours. 2.02.375 P
is nearer to heaven than when i saw you last, by 2.02.426 P
sweet, and by very much more handsome than fine. 2.02.445 P
with less remorse than pyrrhus' bleeding sword 2.02.491
have a bad epitaph than their ill report while 2.02.526 P
i'll have grounds | more relative than this — 2.02.604
it | than is my deed to my most painted word. 3.01. 52
have, | than fly to others that we know not of? 3.01. 81
my lord, have better commerce than with honesty? 3.01.109 P
what it is to a bawd than the force of honesty 3.01.112 P
offenses at my beck than i have thoughts to put 3.01.125 P
clowns speak no more than is set down for them, 3.02. 39 P
think i am easier to be play'd on than a pipe? 3.02.370 P
'tis meet that some more audience than a mother, 3.03. 31
were thicker than itself with brother's blood, 3.03. 44
with more impiteous haste | than young laertes, 4.05.102
this nothing's more than matter. 4.05.174
than settled age his sables and his weeds, 4.07. 80
indeed your father's son | more than in words? 4.07.126
hang themselves, more than their even-christen. 5.01. 28 P
he that builds stronger than either the mason, 5.01. 41 P
the gallows is built stronger than the church; 5.01. 48 P
who builds stronger than a mason, a shipwright, 5.01. 50 P
/too, than the length and breadth of a pair of 5.01.109 P
why he more than another? 5.01.169 P
i lay | worse than the mutines in the /bilboes. 5.02. 6
richer than that which four successive kings 5.02.273
i am more an antique roman than a dane. 5.02.341
more affected the duke of albany than cornwall. LR 1.01. 2 P
by order of law, some year elder than this, who 1.01. 20 P
i love you more than /words can wield the matter 1.01. 55
dearer than eyesight, space, and liberty, 1.01. 56
no less than life, with grace, health, beauty, 1.01. 58
sure my love's | more ponderous than my tongue. 1.01. 78
and pleasure, | than that conferr'd on goneril. 1.01. 82
draw | a third more opulent than your sisters'? 1.01. 86
i crave no more than hath your highness offer'd, 1.01.194
way | than on a wretch whom nature is asham'd 1.01.212
hadst not been born than not t' have pleas'd me 1.01.234
more composition and fierce quality | than doth, 1.02. 13
worse than brutish! 1.02. 77 P
any further delay than this very evening. 1.02. 93 P
i do profess to be no less than i seem, to serve 1.04. 13 P
own jealous curiosity than as a very pretense 1.04. 70 P
have more than thou showest, | speak less than 1.04.118
thou showest, | speak less than thou knowest, 1.04.119
than thou knowest, | lend less than thou owest, 1.04.120
than thou owest, | ride more than thou goest, 1.04.121
than thou goest, | learn more than thou trowest, 1.04.122
thou trowest, | set less than thou throwest; 1.04.123
thou shalt have more | than two tens to a score. 1.04.127
i had rather be any kind o' thing than a fool, 1.04.186 P
i am better than thou art now, i am a fool, thou 1.04.193 P
a tavern or a brothel | than a grac'd palace. 1.04.246
show'st thee in a child | than the sea-monster. 1.04.261
feel | how sharper than a serpent's tooth it is 1.04.288
sir, more knave than fool, after your master. 1.04.314
safer than trust too far. 1.04.328
of wisdom | than prais'd for harmful mildness. 1.04.344
any thing you know than comes from her demand 1.05. 3 P
stars are no moe than seven is a pretty reason. 1.05. 35 P
seen drunkards | do more than this in sport. 2.01. 35
hold more antipathy | than i and such a knave. 2.02. 88
my time | than stands on any shoulder that i see 2.02. 94
ends | than twenty silly-ducking observants 2.02.103
'tis worse than murther | to do upon respect 2.04. 23
having more man than wit about me, drew. 2.04. 42
value her desert | than she to scant her duty. 2.04.140
discerns your state | better than you yourself. 2.04.150
allow not nature more than nature needs, | man's 2.04.266
that i am much more | than my out-wall, open 3.01. 45
few words, but, to effect, more than all yet: 3.01. 52
a dry house is better than this rain-water out 3.02. 11 P
i am a man | more sinn'd against than sinning. 3.02. 60
(more harder than the stones whereof 'tis rais'd 3.02. 64
when priests are more in word than matter; 3.02. 81
between the dukes, and a worse matter than that. 3.03. 9 P
no less than all. 3.03. 24
wert better in a grave than to answer with thy 3.04.101 P
is man no more than this? 3.04.103 P
here is better than the open air, take it 3.06. 1 P
i never done you | than now to bid you hold. 3.07. 75
contemn'd, | than still contemn'd and flatter'd. 4.01. 2
i am worse than e'er i was. 4.01. 26
is he for my hand | than for your lady's. 4.05. 32
in better phrase and matter than thou didst. 4.06. 8
methinks he seems no bigger than his head. 4.06. 16
was kinder to his father than my daughters | got 4.06.115
exalt himself, | more than in your addition. 5.03. 68
nothing less | than i have here proclaim'd thee. 5.03. 95
thou worse than any name, read thine own evil. 5.03.157
i am no less in blood than thou art, edmund; 5.03.168
would hourly die | rather than die at once!), 5.03.187
as your honors | have more than merited. 5.03.303
of a battle knows | more than a spinster — OTH 1.01. 24
command with years | than with your weapons. 1.02. 61
that, as it more concerns the turk than rhodes, 1.03. 22
more than pertains to feats of broils and battle 1.03. 87
than these thin habits and poor likelihoods | of 1.03.108
weapons rather use | than their bare hands. 1.03.175
i had rather to adopt a child than get it. 1.03.191
your son-in-law is far more fair than black. 1.03.290
i could never better stead thee than now. 1.03.339 P
do it a more delicate way than drowning. 1.03.354 P
in compassing thy joy than to be drown'd and go 1.03.360 P
him more in the soldier than in the scholar. 2.01.166 P
in their natures more than is native to them), 2.01.216 P
further conscionable than in putting on the mere 2.01.239 P
this is a more exquisite song than the other. 2.03. 98 P
thou dost deliver more or less than truth, 2.03.219
than it should do offense to michael cassio; 2.03.222
there is more sense in that than in reputation. 2.03.268 P
a punishment more in policy than in malice, even 2.03.274 P
sue to be despis'd than to deceive so good a 2.03.277 P
goodness not to do more than she is requested. 2.03.322 P
love shall grow stronger than it was before. 2.03.325 P
no farther off | than in a politic distance. 3.03. 13
shall rather die | than give thy cause away. 3.03. 28
issues nor to larger reach | than to suspicion. 3.03.220
sees and knows more, much more, than he unfolds. 3.03.243
dungeon | than keep a corner in the thing i love 3.03.272
prerogativ'd are they less than the base; 3.03.274
to be much abus'd | than but to know't a little. 3.03.337
been born a dog | than answer my wak'd wrath! 3.03.363
canst thou to damnation add | greater than that. 3.03.373
eyes do see them bolster | more than their own. 3.03.400
and more i will | than for myself i dare. 3.04.131
more tedious than the dial eightscore times? 3.04.175
you well assur'd, | no more than he'll unswear. 4.01. 31
me all conveniency than suppliest me with the 4.02.177 P
build on thee a better opinion than ever before. 4.02.206 P
i have greater reason to believe now than ever 4.02.213 P
how goes it now? he looks gentler than he did. 4.03. 11
but that my coat is better than thou know'st. 5.01. 25
nor scar that whiter skin of hers than snow, 5.02. 4
she comes more nearer earth than she was wont, 5.02.110
more worthy heaven | than thou wast worthy her. 5.02.161
than what he found himself was apt and true. 5.02.177
(more than indeed belong'd to such a trifle), 5.02.228
more impediments | than twenty times your stop. 5.02.264
threw a pearl away | richer than all his tribe; 5.02.348
more fell than anguish, hunger, or the sea! 5.02.362
you shall be yet far fairer than you are. ANT 1.02. 17
you shall be more beloving than beloved. 1.02. 23
o, excellent, i love long life better than figs. 1.02. 32 P
former fortune | than that which is to approach. 1.02. 34
am i not an inch of fortune better than she? 1.02. 58 P
you were but an inch of fortune better than i, 1.02. 60 P
ten thousand harms, more than the ills i know, 1.02.129
storms and tempests than almanacs can report. 1.02.149 P
higher than both in blood and life, stands up 1.02.190
is not more manlike | than cleopatra; 1.04. 6
nor the queen of ptolomy | more womanly than he; 1.04. 7
hereditary, | rather than purchas'd; 1.04. 14
what he cannot change, | than what he chooses. 1.04. 15
name strikes more | than could his war resisted. 1.04. 55
with patience more | than savages could suffer. 1.04. 61
no more than my residing here at rome | might be 2.02. 37
no worse a husband than the best of men; 2.02.128
caesar and he are greater friends than ever. 2.05. 48
that they strike | a meaner than myself, since i 2.05. 83
i cannot hate thee worser than i do, | if thou 2.05. 90
that call'd me timelier than my purpose hither; 2.06. 51
made more in the marriage than the love of the 2.06.119 P
all, four days, | than drink so much in one. 2.07.103
strong enobarb | is weaker than the wine, and 2.07.123
than by our deed | acquire too high a fame when 3.01. 14
ever won | more in their officer than person. 3.01. 17
who does i' th' wars more than his captain can 3.01. 21
choice of loss | than gain which darkens him. 3.01. 24
she shows a body rather than a life, | a statue, 3.03. 20
rather than a life, | a statue, than a breather. 3.03. 21
i were not yours | than /yours so branchless. 3.04. 24
is never more admir'd | than by the negligent. 3.07. 25
'twas a shame no less | than was his loss, to 3.13. 11
case thou stand'st | further than he is /caesar. 3.13. 55
a lion's whelp | than with an old one dying. 3.13. 95
expect victorious life | than death and honor. 4.02. 44
queen's a squire | more tight at this than thou; 4.04. 15
o antony, | nobler than my revolt is infamous, 4.09. 19
o, he's more mad | than telamon for his shield; 4.13. 2
not more in parting | than greatness going off. 4.13. 6
heart, once be stronger than thy continent, 4.14. 40
than she which by her death our caesar tells, 4.14. 61
thrice-nobler than myself! 4.14. 95
which in thy absence is | no better than a sty? 4.15. 62
keep decorum, must | no less beg than a kingdom. 5.02. 18
these thoughts of horror further than you shall 5.02. 63
know | we will extenuate rather than enforce. 5.02.125
i had rather seel my lips than to my peril 5.02.146
of no more trust | than love that's hir'd! 5.02.155
sure mine nails | are stronger than mine eyes. 5.02.224
i heard of one of them no longer than yesterday, 5.02.251 P
story is | no less in pity than his glory which 5.02.362
no more obey the heavens than our courtiers' CYM 1.01. 2
crush him together rather than unfold | his 1.01. 26
of more tenderness | than doth become a man. 1.01. 95
be a pinch in death | more sharp than this is. 1.01.131
but that my master rather play'd than fought 1.01.162
senseless linen, happier therein than i! 1.03. 7
he was less furnish'd than now he is with that 1.04. 9 P
be weigh'd rather by her value than his own, 1.04. 15 P
have been often bound for no less than my life. 1.04. 27 P
rather than story him in his own hearing. 1.04. 33 P
with what i heard than in my every action to be 1.04. 45 P
and less attemptable than any the rarest of our 1.04. 61 P
more than the world enjoys. 1.04. 79 P
against your confidence than her reputation; 1.04.111 P
with no more advantage than the opportunity of a 1.04.129 P
more than the locking up the spirits a time, 1.05. 41
ill often hurts more | than to be sure they do; 1.06. 96
more noble than that runagate to your bed, | and 1.06.137
sets him off, | more than a mortal seeming. 1.06.171
wooer | more hateful than the foul expulsion is 2.01. 60
than that horrid act | of the divorce he'ld make 2.01. 61
fresh lily, | and whiter than the sheets! 2.02. 16
a voucher, | stronger than ever law could make; 2.02. 40
that's more | than some, whose tailors are as 2.03. 79
i had rather | you felt than make't my boast. 2.03.111
in meaner parties | (yet who than he more mean?) 2.03.117
he never can meet more mischance than come | to 2.03.132
in my respect than all the hairs above thee, 2.03.135
in our not-fearing britain than have tidings 2.04. 19
are men more order'd than when julius caesar 2.04. 21
they are made | than they are to their virtues, 2.04.112
sign about her, | more evident than this; 2.04.120
no whit less | than in his feats deserving it), 3.01. 7
kingdom is stronger than it was at that time; 3.01. 35 P
that hath moe kings his servants than | thyself 3.01. 63
more goddess-like than wife-like, such assaults 3.02. 8
where horses have been nimbler than the sands 3.02. 72
no costlier than would fit | a franklin's 3.02. 76
in a safer hold | than is the full-wing'd eagle. 3.03. 21
life | is nobler than attending for a check; 3.03. 22
richer than doing nothing for a /bable; 3.03. 23
prouder than rustling in unpaid-for silk: 3.03. 24
more pious debts to heaven than in all | the 3.03. 72
whose edge is sharper than the sword, whose 3.04. 34
and, for i am richer than to hang by th' walls, 3.04. 52
ourself | to show less sovereignty than they, 3.05. 6
like | a thing more made of malice than of duty, 3.05. 33
all courtly parts more exquisite | than lady, 3.05. 72
in more respect than my noble and natural person 3.05.135 P
in fullness | is sorer than to lie for need; 3.06. 13
and falsehood | is worse in kings than beggars. 3.06. 14
behold divineness | no elder than a boy! 3.06. 44
that had a court no bigger than this cave, 3.06. 82
more slavish did i ne'er than answering | a 4.02. 73
body hath a tail | more perilous than the head. 4.02.145

time into a crutch, | than have seen this. 4.02.201
are worse | than priests and fanes that lie. 4.02.242
was he | that (otherwise than noble nature did) 4.02.364
thou mov'st no less with thy complaining than 4.02.375
not sooner | than thine own worth prefer thee. 4.02.386
and rather father thee than master thee. 4.02.395
can affront no less | than what you hear of. 4.03. 30
than be so, | better to cease to be. 4.04. 30
must murther wives much better than themselves 5.01. 4
men know | more valor in me than my habits show. 5.01. 30
work | more plentiful than tools to do't — 5.03. 9
the country base than to commit such slaughter, 5.03. 20
fairer | than those for preservation cas'd, or 5.03. 22
at the things you hear | than to work any. 5.03. 55
or hath moe ministers than we | that draw his 5.03. 72
am i better | than one that's sick o' th' gout, 5.04. 5
groan so in perpetuity than be cur'd | by th' 5.04. 6
art fetter'd | more than my shanks and wrists. 5.04. 9
i repent, | i cannot do it better than in gyves, 5.04. 14
than in gyves, | desir'd more than constrain'd. 5.04. 15
take | no stricter render of me than my all. 5.04. 17
i know you are more clement than vild men, | who 5.04. 18
ascension is | more sweet than our blest fields. 5.04.117
world, a garment | nobler than that it covers! 5.04.135
i am merrier to die than thou art to live. 5.04.171 P
thou shalt be then freer than a jailer; 5.04.196 P
who worse than a physician | would this report 5.05. 27
no more kin to me | than i to your highness; 5.05.113
while nature will | than die ere i hear more. 5.05.152
her honor confident | than i did truly find her, 5.05.188
o' th' earth amend | by being worse than they. 5.05.217
that caus'd a lesser villain than myself, | a 5.05.219
leonatus, and | be villainy less than 'twas! 5.05.225
this man is better than the man he slew, | as 5.05.302
more of thee merited than a band of clotens 5.05.304
done is more | unlike than this thou tell'st. 5.05.354
he's more secure to keep it shut than shown; PER 1.01. 95
blush not in actions blacker than the night 1.01.135
please, | i cannot be much lower than my knees. 1.02. 47
decrease not, but grow faster than the years; 1.02. 85
day serves not light more faithful than i'll be. 1.02.110
more with begging than we can do with working. 2.01. 64 P
and have no more of life than may suffice | to 2.01. 74
i would wish no better office than to be beadle. 2.01. 93 P
he had need mean better than his outward show 2.02. 48
practic'd more the whipstock than the lance. 2.02. 51
were more than you expect, or more than's fit, 2.03. 5
'tis more by fortune, lady, than my merit. 2.03. 12
h'as done no more than other knights have done, 2.03. 34
thy loss is more than can thy portage quit 3.01. 35
endowments greater | than nobleness and riches. 3.02. 28
than to be thirsty after tottering honor, | or 3.02. 40
not be more dear to my respect | than yours, my 3.03. 34
and yourself, | with more than foreign heart. 4.01. 33
three, and they can do no more than they can do; 4.02. 7 P
much less in blood than virtue, yet a princess 4.03. 7
i had rather than twice the worth of her she had 4.06. 1 P
no less than it gives a good report to a number 4.06. 40 P
diseases have been sold dearer than physic — 4.06. 98
she were a thornier piece of ground than she is, 4.06.145 P
any of these ways are yet better than this; 4.06.177
brought forth, and am | no other than i appear. 5.01.105
is it no more to be your daughter than | to say 5.01.209
no mortal officer | more like a god than you. 5.03. 63
more of the maid to sight than husband's pains. TNK pr 8
my fam'd works makes lighter | than robin hood!" pr 21
not juno's mantle fairer than your tresses, 1.01. 63
our kinsman | (then weaker than your eyes) laid 1.01. 67
more power on him | than ever he had on thee, 1.01. 88
than a dove's motion when the head's pluck'd off 1.01. 98
will long last and be more costly than | your 1.01.132
is more | than others' labored meditance; 1.01.136
your premeditating | more than their actions; 1.01.137
whereto i am going, | greater than any /war. 1.01.172
me | than all the actions that i have foregone 1.01.173
and | thou shalt remember nothing more than what 1.01.185
dear palamon, dearer in love than blood, | and 1.02. 1
hard, and harsher | than strife or war could be. 1.02. 26
and maid may be | more than in sex /dividual. 1.03. 82
thyself) | than i will trust a sickly appetite, 1.03. 89
assurance | that we, more than his pirithous, 1.03. 95
rather than a gap | should be in their dear 1.04. 8
our richest balms, | rather than niggard, waste; 1.04. 32
concern us | much more than thebes is worth. 1.04. 33
rather than have 'em | freed of this plight, and 1.04. 33
rather have 'em | prisoners to us than death. 1.04. 37
our dole more deadly looks than dying; 1.05. 3
out to be better lin'd than it can appear to me 2.01. 5 P
sir, i demand no more than your own offer, and i 2.01. 10 P
of their captivity than i of ruling athens. 2.01. 38 P
of any two that lov'd | better than we do, 2.02.113
thou art baser in it than a cutpurse. 2.02.211
run | swifter than wind upon a field of corn, 2.03. 77
and somewhat better than your rank i'll use you. 2.05. 43
higher than all the rest, spreads like a plane 2.06. 5
better have endur'd cold iron than done it. 2.06. 10
fresher than may, sweeter | than her gold 3.01. 5
sweeter | than her gold buttons on the boughs, 3.01. 6
i may not wish | more than my sword's edge on't. 3.01. 96
and you show | more than a mistress to me; 3.06. 26
shall threaten me | i fear less than my fortune. 3.06.125
o heaven, | what more than man is this! 3.06.157
for i gave him | more mercy than you found, sir, 3.06.182
sir, your offenses | being no more than his. 3.06.183
lives, invent a way | safer than banishment. 3.06.218
better they fall by th' law than one another. 3.06.225
'tis worse to me than begging | to take my life 3.06.266
distemper'd | /far worse than now she shows. 4.01.120
far sweeter, | smoother than pelops' shoulder! 4.02. 21
braver spirits | than these they have brought 4.02. 74
his complexion | nearer a brown than black; 4.02. 79
he's somewhat bigger than the knight he spoke of 4.02. 94
at some time of the moon than at other some, is 4.03. 2 P
and penn'd by no worse man than giraldo, 4.03. 12 P
may rather seem to steal in than be permitted. 4.03. 75 P
your ire is more than mortal; 5.01. 14
phoebus thou | add'st flames, hotter than his; 5.01. 91
yet is heavier | than lead itself, stings more 5.01. 97
than lead itself, stings more than nettles. 5.01. 97
that lover never yet made sigh | truer than i. 5.01.126
allow'st no more blood than will make a blush, 5.01.141
see a wren hawk at a fly | than this decision. 5.03. 3
falls, and sounds more like | a bell than blade. 5.03. 6
better never born | than minister to such harm! 5.03. 66
could | no more be hid in him than fire in flax, 5.03. 98
than humble banks can go to law with waters 5.03. 99
a life more worthy from him than all women, | i 5.03.143
sure shall please the gods | sooner than such, 5.04. 12
to me deserving | than i can quite or speak of. 5.04. 35
the calkins | did rather tell than trample; 5.04. 56
which he frets at rather | than any jot obeys; 5.04. 71
that arcite's legs, being higher than his head, 5.04. 78
more in our country than they do in their own. STM II.C 6 P
forgiven | is safer wars than ever you can make, II.C 112
"thrice fairer than myself," thus she began, VEN 7
stain to all nymphs, more lovely than a man, 9
more white and red than doves or roses are: 10
more thirst for drink than she for this good 92
nay, more than flint, for stone at rain 200
teaching the sheets a whiter hue than white, 398
her, | that worse than tantalus' is her annoy, 599
are better proof than thy spear's point can 626
"and more than so, presenteth to mine eye | the 661
a mischief worse than civil home-bred strife, 764
and every tongue more moving than your own, 776
her more than haste is mated with delays, | like 909
him go, | rather than triumph in so false a foe. LUC 77
more than his eyes were open'd to the light. 105
paying more slavish tribute than they owe. 299
with more than admiration he admired | her azure 418
worse than a slavish wipe or birth-hour's blot; 537
o, if no harder than a stone thou art, | melt at 593
but she hath lost a dearer thing than life, 687
and lust, the thief, far poorer than before. 693
o, deeper sin than bottomless conceit | can 701
him with hard'ned hearts, harder than stones, 978
wilder to him than tigers in their wildness. 980
than they whose whole is swallowed in confusion. 1159
ill, | no more than wax shall be accounted evil, 1245
for more it is than i can well express, | and 1286
when more is felt than one hath power to tell. 1288
see sad sights moves more than hear them told, 1324
sounds make lesser noise than shallow fords, 1329
"at ardea to my lord with more than haste." 1332
speed more than speed but dull and slow she 1336
upon the galled shore, and than | retire again, 1440
in me moe woes than words are now depending, 1615
but more than "he" her poor tongue could not 1718
brighter than glass, and yet as glass is, PP 7. 3
softer than wax, and yet as iron rusty: 7. 4
paler for sorrow than her milk-white dove, | for 9. 3
silly queen, with more than love's good will, 9. 7
she showed hers, he saw more wounds than one, 9.13
and yet thou lefts me more than i did crave, 10. 9
inconstancy | more in women than in men remain. 17.12
ten times thyself were happier than thou art, SON 6. 9
shall hate be fairer lodg'd than gentle love? 10.10
no longer yours than you yourself here live: 13. 2
with means more blessed than my barren rhyme? 16. 4
much liker than your painted counterfeit: 16. 8
scorn'd, like old men of less truth than tongue, 17.10
an eye more bright than theirs, less false in 20. 5
how can i then be elder than thou art? 22. 8
more than that tongue that more hath more 23.12
a dearer birth than this his love had brought 32.11
excusing /thy sins more than /thy sins are; 35. 8
than those old nine which rhymers invocate, 38.10
what hast thou then more than thou hadst before? 40. 2
to bear love's wrong than hate's known injury. 40.12
for thou /not farther than my thoughts canst 47.11
more sharp to me than spurring to his side, 50.12
bright in these contents | than unswept stone, 55. 4
said | thy edge should blunter be than appetite, 56. 2
whose action is no stronger than a flower? 65. 4
by seeing farther than the eye hath shown. 69. 8
dead | than you shall hear the surly sullen bell 71. 2
lie, | to do more for me than mine own desert, 72. 6
i | than niggard truth would willingly impart: 72. 8
than both your poets can in praise devise. 83.14
which can say more | than this rich praise, that 84. 2
thy love is /better than high birth to me, 91. 9
richer than wealth, prouder than garments' cost, 91.10
richer than wealth, prouder than garments' cost, 91.10
cost, | of more delight than hawks or horses be; 91.11
and life no longer than thy love will stay, 92. 3
than that which on thy humor doth depend. 92. 8
lilies that fester smell far worse than weeds. 94.14
give my love fame faster than time wastes life, 100.13
than when her mournful hymns did hush the night, 102.10
than when it hath my added praise beside. 103. 4
than of your graces and your gifts to tell; 103.12
and more, much more than in my verse can sit, 103.13
than public means which public manners breeds. 111. 4
grows fairer than at first, more strong, far 119.12
and gain by ills thrice more than i have spent. 119.14
'tis better to be vile than vile esteemed, 121. 1
than think that we before have heard them told. 123. 8
which proves more short than waste or ruining? 125. 4
making dead wood more blest than living lips: 128.12
coral is far more red than her lips' red; 130. 2
than in the breath that from my mistress reeks. 130. 8
more than enough am i that vex thee still, | to 135. 3
is more than my o'erpress'd defense can bide? 139. 8
than the true gouty landlord which doth owe them LC 140

THANE 25 FR 0.0028 REL FR 23 V 2 P
the worthy thane of rosse. MAC 1.02. 45
whence cam'st thou, worthy thane? 1.02. 48
the thane of cawdor, began a dismal conflict, 1.02. 53
no more that thane of cawdor shall deceive | our 1.02. 63
hail, macbeth, hail to thee, thane of glamis! 1.03. 48
hail, macbeth, hail to thee, thane of cawdor! 1.03. 49
by sinel's death i know i am thane of glamis, 1.03. 71
the thane of cawdor lives | a prosperous 1.03. 72
and thane of cawdor too; went it not so? 1.03. 87
he bade me, from him, call thee thane of cawdor; 1.03.105
in which addition, hail, most worthy thane, 1.03.106
the thane of cawdor lives; 1.03.108
who was the thane lives yet, | but under heavy 1.03.109
glamis, and thane of cawdor! 1.03.116
when those that gave the thane of cawdor to me 1.03.119
unto the crown, | besides the thane of cawdor. 1.03.122
i am thane of cawdor. 1.03.133
the king, who all-hail'd me 'thane of cawdor, 1.05. 7 P
our thane is coming. 1.05. 34
your face, my thane, is as a book, where men 1.05. 62
where's the thane of cawdor? 1.06. 20
why, worthy thane, | you do unbend your noble 2.02. 41
is the king stirring, worthy thane? 2.03. 45
beware macduff, | beware the thane of fife. 4.01. 72
the thane of fife had a wife; 5.01. 42 P

THANES 5 FR 0.0005 REL FR 5 V 0 P
sons, kinsmen, thanes, | and you whose places MAC 1.04. 35
then fly, false thanes, | and mingle with the 5.03. 7
doctor, the thanes fly from me. 5.03. 49
fight, | the noble thanes do bravely in the war, 5.07. 26
my thanes and kinsmen, | henceforth be earls, 5.09. 28

THANK *(also dank*, tank)*

/THANK 2 FR 0.0002 REL FR 2 V 0 P
/and /i /thank /thee, /king, | /for /thy /great R2 4.01.299
/shall /find | /some /that /will /thank /you, LR 3.01. 37

THANK 306 FR 0.0346 REL FR 209 V 97 P
heavens thank you for't! TMP 1.02.175
i thank thee, master. 1.02.293
sir, you may thank yourself for this great loss, 2.01.124
thank you. wondrous heavy. 2.01.198
i thank my noble lord. 3.02. 38 P
come with a thought. i thank thee. ariel! come. 4.01.164
i thank thee for that jest; 4.01.241 P
to testify your bounty, i thank you, you have TGV 1.01.144 P
i thank you, you swing'd me for my love, which 2.01. 82 P
i thank you, gentle servant — 'tis very clerkly 2.01.108
yet take this again — and yet i thank you — 2.01.118
'tis indeed, madam, we thank the giver. 2.04. 35 P
proteus, i thank thee for thine honest care, 3.01. 22
thank me for this more than for all the favors 3.01.161
i thank you for your own. 4.02. 24
i thank you for your music, gentlemen. 4.02. 86
i thank you, madam, that you tender her. 4.04.140
and she shall thank you for't, if e'er you know 4.04.179
i thank your grace; 5.04.148
i thank you for my venison, master shallow. WIV 1.01. 79 P
and i thank you always with my heart, la! 1.01. 84 P
sir, i thank you. 1.01. 86 P
sir, i thank you; by yea and no, i do. 1.01. 87 P
no, i thank you, forsooth, heartily; 1.01.267 P
i am not a-hungry, i thank you, forsooth. 1.01.270 P
i thank you as much as though i did. 1.01.279 P
i had rather walk here, i thank you. 1.01.282 P
i'll eat nothing, i thank you, sir. 1.01.302 P
i thank thee for that humor. 1.03. 64 P
can do more than i do with her, i thank heaven. 1.04.130 P
good body, i thank thee. 2.02.142 P
marry, i thank you for it; 3.04. 52 P
i thank you for that good comfort. 3.04. 52 P
i ne'er made my will yet, i thank heaven. 3.04. 58 P
i thank thee; 3.04. 99
i thank your worship. 4.05. 55 P
i thank you. fare you well. MM 1.01. 75
i thank you, good friend lucio. 1.02.192
i humbly thank you. 1.04. 87
ay, sir; whom i thank heaven is an honest woman. 2.01. 72 P
marry, i thank your good worship for it. 2.01.182 P
marry, i thank your worship for it. 2.01.189 P
i thank your worship. 2.01.208 P
thank you, good pompey; 2.01.244 P
i thank your worship for your good counsel; 2.01.252 P
i humbly thank you. 2.01.279 P
i humbly thank you. 3.01. 41
most holy sir, i thank you. 3.01. 47
i thank you for this comfort. 3.01.268 P
i thank thee, varrius, thou hast made good haste 4.05. 11
i thank him, i bare home upon my shoulders: ERR 2.01. 73
well, sir, i thank you. 2.02. 49 P
thank me, sir, for what? 2.02. 50 P
i will discharge my bond, and thank you too. 4.01. 13
but he, i thank him, gnaw'd in two my cords: 5.01.290
i thank god and my cold blood, i am of your ADO 1.01.130 P
i thank you. 1.01.157 P
i am not of many words, but i thank you. 1.01.158 P
that a woman conceiv'd me, i thank her; 1.01.238 P
yea, my lord, i thank it — poor fool, it keeps 2.01.314 P
fair beatrice, i thank you for your pains. 2.03.249 P
those thanks than you take pains to thank me. 2.03.251 P
those thanks than you took pains to thank me" — 2.03.260 P
together, and thank god you are rid of a knave. 3.03. 30 P
i thank god i am as honest as any man living 3.05. 13 P
i' faith, i thank him, he hath bid me to a 5.01.154 P
my lord, for your many courtesies i thank you. 5.01.189 P
i thank you, princes, for my daughter's death; 5.01.268
i thank thee for thy care and honest pains. 5.01.314
thee of thy prisoner, and i thank thee. 5.01.320 P
i thank god i have as little patience as another LLL 1.02.164 P
i thank your worship, god be wi' you! 3.01.150 P
i thank my beauty, i am fair that shoot, | and 4.01. 11
and thank you too; 4.02.161 P
nay, i have verses too, i thank berowne; 5.02. 34
and lord berowne (i thank him) is my dear. 5.02.457
i thank you, gracious lords, | for all your fair 5.02.729
o, shall i say, i thank you, gentle wife? 5.02.826
mine ear, i thank it, brought me to thy sound. MND 3.02.182
sweet moon, i thank thee for thy sunny beams; 5.01.272
i thank thee, moon, for shining now so bright; 5.01.273
i thank my fortune for it, | my ventures are not MV 1.01. 41
even for that i thank you; 2.01. 22
i thank god, i thank god. 3.01.102 P
i thank god, i thank god. 3.01.102 P
i thank thee, good tubal, good news, good news! 3.01.106 P
i thank your lordship, you have got me one. 3.02.196
i thank your honor. 3.02.226
i thank you for your wish, and am well pleas'd 3.04. 43
i thank thee, jew, for teaching me that word. 4.01.341
i thank you, madam. 5.01.133
charles, i thank thee for thy love to me, which AYL 1.01.137 P

let us go thank him, and encourage him. 1.02.240
can i not say, i thank you? 1.02.249
i thank you, sir; 1.02.268
i thank it. 2.05. 12 P
well then, if ever i thank any man, i'll thank 2.05. 25 P
then, if ever i thank any man, i'll thank you; 2.05. 26 P
i thank ye, and be blest for your good comfort! 2.07.135
i thank you most for him. 2.07.169
i scarce can speak to thank you for myself. 2.07.170
i thank you for your company, but, good faith, i 3.02.253 P
fashion sake, i thank you too for your society. 3.02.256 P
against it, and i thank god i am not a woman, to 3.02.348 P
not a slut, though i thank the gods i am foul. 3.03. 38 P
and thank heaven, fasting, for a good man's love 3.05. 58
ay, sir, i thank god. 5.01. 24 P
"thank god" — a good answer. art rich? 5.01. 25 P
we thank your honor. SHR in.1. 80
i thank thee, thou shalt not lose by it. in.2. 99
thou'dst thank me but a little for my counsel; 1.02. 61
and so i take my leave, and thank you both. 2.01.398
and friends, i thank you for your pains. 3.02.184
i thank you all | that have beheld me give away 3.02.193
i thank you, sir. 4.03. 47
i thank you, sir. 4.04. 48
i thank my good father, i am able to maintain it 5.01. 76 P
i thank thee for that gird, good tranio. 5.02. 58
thank your majesty. AWW 1.02. 76
bosom, and i thank you for your honest care. 1.03.126 P
we thank you, maiden, | but may not be so 2.01.114
we understand it, and thank heaven for you. 2.03. 65
i thank you, and will stay upon your leisure. 3.05. 45
i humbly thank you. 3.05. 96
for which live long to thank both heaven and me! 4.02. 67
i humbly thank you, sir. 4.03.156 P
a bold charter, but i thank my god it holds yet. 4.05. 93 P
but rather make you thank your pains for it. 5.01. 33
so, i thank thee; 5.03.322 P
i thank thee. lead me on. TN 1.02. 64
i thank you. here comes the count. 1.04. 9 P
i thank you for your pains. 1.05.283
i thank my stars, i am happy. 2.05.170 P
jove, i thank thee. 2.05.178 P
with one "we thank you" many thousands moe WT 1.02. 8
with all my heart i thank thee for my father! JN 1.01.270
o heaven! i thank you, hubert. 4.01.131
we thank you both, yet one but flatters us, | as R2 1.01. 25
i thank my liege that in regard of me | he 1.03.216
i thank thee, gentle percy, and be sure | i 2.03. 45
"i thank you, countrymen." 5.02. 20
we thank thee, gentle percy, for thy pains, 5.06. 11
exton, i thank thee not, for thou hast wrought 5.06. 34
what thing? why, a thing to thank god on. 1H4 3.03.117 P
i am no thing to thank god on, i would thou 3.03.118 P
i can but thank you. 4.01. 13
i thank him that he cuts me from my tale, | for 5.02. 90
and even in thy behalf i'll thank myself | for 5.04. 97
i thank your grace for this high courtesy, 5.05. 32
you may thank th' unquiet time for your quiet 2H4 1.02.150 P
yea, i thank your pretty sweet wit for it. 1.02.206 P
i must wait upon my good lord here, i thank you, 2.01.184 P
fare you well, gentlemen both, i thank you. 3.02.290 P
thyself away gratis, and i thank thee for thee. 4.03. 70 P
i thank thee with my heart, kind master bardolph 5.01. 57 P
by god's liggens, i thank thee. 5.03. 65 P
sure we thank you. H5 1.02. 8
his present and your pains we thank you for. 1.02.260
i thank you. god be with you! 4.01. 61 P
some of you, thank love for my blindness, who 5.02.316 P
we thank you all. 2H6 1.01. 38
we thank you all for this great favor done | in 1.01. 71
i humbly thank your royal majesty. 1.03.211
clear as day, i thank god and saint albon. 2.01.105 P
we thank you, lords. 2.02. 64
i thank you all. 2.03. 72 P
fellow, thank god, and the good wine in thy 2.03. 95 P
i thank thee, /meg, these words content me much. 3.02. 26
me, | i thank them for their tender loving care; 3.02.280
i thank you, good people — there shall be no 4.02. 72 P
sir, i thank god, i have been so well brought up 4.02.105 P
soldiers, i thank you all; 5.01. 45
i thank thee, clifford. 5.01.125
i thank you, richard. 5.03. 16
yes, i agree, and thank you for your motion. 3H6 3.03.244
and chiefly therefore i thank god and thee. 4.06. 17
let him thank me that holp to send him thither; R3 1.02.107
i thank my god for my humility. 2.01. 73
i thank you, good my lord, and thank you all. 3.01. 19
i thank you, good my lord, and thank you all. 3.01. 19
i thank you, gentle uncle. 3.01.102
i would, that i might thank you as you call me. 3.01.123
i thank your honor. 3.02.107
i thank thee, good sir john, with all my heart. 3.02.109
i thank his grace, i know he loves me well; 3.04. 14
how do i thank thee that this carnal cur | preys 4.04. 56
ay, i thank god, my father, and yourself. 4.04.156
and from my heart's love i do thank thee for it. 4.04.261
i thank your grace: H8 1.01. 2
thank your majesty. 1.02. 13
by my faith, | and thank your lordship. 1.04. 25
and thank the holy conclave for their loves; 2.02. 99
here are some will thank you, | if you speak 3.01. 46
my lords, i thank you both for your good wills, 3.01. 68
i thank my memory, i yet remember | some of 3.02.303
shall know it, and, no doubt, shall thank you. 3.02.348
king has cur'd me, | i humbly thank his grace; 3.02.381
i thank you, sir; 4.01. 20
i thank you, honest lord. 4.02.160
i humbly thank your highness, | and am right 5.01.108
ah, my good lord of winchester — i thank you, 5.02. 93
thank you, good lord archbishop. 5.04. 8
i thank ye heartily; 5.04. 13
i thank ye all. 5.04. 69
must all see the queen, and she must thank ye, 5.04. 73
thank the heavens, lord, thou art of sweet TRO 2.03.240
i thank you for that; 3.02.104 P
i thank thee, hector. 4.05.138
i thank thee, most imperious agamemnon. 4.05.172
i thank your ladyship; well, good madam. COR 1.03. 54 P
"we thank the gods | our rome hath such a 1.09. 8
i thank you, general; 1.09. 36
howbeit, i thank you. 1.09. 70
take my cap, jupiter, and i thank thee. 2.01.106 P
o, he is wounded, i thank the gods for't. 2.01.121 P
whom | we met here both to thank and to remember 2.02. 47
here was "i thank you for your voices, thank you 2.03.171
was "i thank you for your voices, thank you, 2.03.171
thank you, sir, farewell. 4.04. 11
i thank you all and here dismiss you all, | and TIT 1.01. 57
tribunes, i thank you, and this suit i make, 1.01.223
i thank your majesty, and her, my lord. 1.01.460
i humbly thank him, and i thank you all. 5.01. 18
i humbly thank him, and i thank you all. 5.01. 18
why then i thank you all. ROM 1.05.123
i thank you, honest gentlemen, good night. 1.05.124
romeo shall thank thee, daughter, for us both. 2.06. 22
"proud," and "i thank you," and "i thank you not 3.05.150
and "i thank you," and "i thank you not," | and 3.05.150
thank me no thankings, nor proud me no prouds, 3.05.152
humbly i thank your lordship. TIM 1.01.149
i thank you, you shall hear from me anon. 1.01.153
i am to thank you for't. 1.02.151
i thank you, sir. 3.01. 3 P
how shall i thank him, think'st thou? 3.02. 32 P
i thank them, and would send them back the 5.01.137
i thank you for your pains and courtesy. JC 2.02.115
now, brutus, thank yourself; 5.01. 45
i thank thee, brutus, | that thou hast prov'd 5.05. 58
i thank you, gentlemen. MAC 1.03.129
is our trouble, | which still we thank as love. 1.06. 12
for your pains, | and thank us for your trouble. 1.06. 14
i thank you, doctor. 4.03.145
time, we thank you for your well–took labor. HAM 2.02. 83
i am /even poor in thanks — but i thank you, 2.02.273 P
i humbly thank you, well, /well, /well. 3.01. 91
i humbly thank you, sir. 4.04. 29
of it, and so i thank you for your good counsel. 4.05. 71 P
i thank you, keep the door. 4.05.116
i humbly thank you, sir. 5.02. 82
i thank your lordship, it is very hot. 5.02. 94 P
had it th' ability of life to thank you. 5.02.373
i thank thee, fellow. LR 1.04. 87 P
my friendly knave, i thank thee, there's earnest 1.04. 93 P
for him i thank your grace. 2.01.117
to thank thee for the love thou show'dst the 4.02. 95
i thank you, sir, that's all. 4.06.214
i thank you, sir. 4.06.216
thank you, sir. 5.03.310
humbly i thank your grace. OTH 1.03. 70
i thank you, valiant cassio. 2.01. 87
make the moor thank me, love me, and reward me, 2.01.308
i humbly thank you for't. 3.01. 39
i thank you. 3.03. 10
i thank you for this profit, and from hence 3.03.379
i humbly thank your ladyship. 3.04.168
i thank you. how does lieutenant cassio? 4.01.222
madam, good night; i humbly thank your ladyship. 4.03. 3
thank you. ANT 2.02. 28
i must thank him only, | lest my remembrance 2.02.155
humbly, sir, i thank you. 2.02.244
a halter'd neck which does the hangman thank 3.13.130
i thank you all, | for doughty–handed are you, 4.08. 4
i thank you, sir. 5.02.105
i humbly thank your highness. CYM 1.01.175
this worthy signior, i thank him, makes no 1.04.101 P
i thank you for your pains: 1.06.203
sir (i thank her), that. 2.04.100
thus defied, | i thank thee for myself. 3.01. 68
amen! i thank thee. 3.04.193
then, and thank | the man that gave them thee. 4.02. 84
i thank you. 4.02.292
i thank you. 4.03. 32
ne'er thank thy master. 5.05. 96
i humbly thank your highness. 5.05.100
antiochus, i thank thee, who hath taught | my PER 1.01. 41
i thank thee for't, and heaven forbid | that 1.02. 61
i thank you, sir. 2.01. 84
i thank thee for't. 2.01.133
we thank your grace. 2.03. 52
i thank him. 2.03. 76
i thank both him and you, and pledge him freely. 2.03. 78
i thank thee. mariner, say, what coast is this? 3.01. 72
knees, thank the holy gods as loud | as thunder 5.01.198
how possibly preserved, and who to thank 5.03. 57
you have made me | (i thank you, cousin arcite) TNK 2.02. 96
'tis a benefit, | a mercy i must thank 'em for; 2.03. 2
schoolmaster, i thank you. 3.05.151
i thank thee, arcite, | thou art yet a fair foe; 3.06. 7
that my embraces | might thank ye, not my blows. 3.06. 23
thank you, arcite. 3.06. 65
i thank ye. 3.06. 90
thank ye, doctor. 5.02. 23
i thank him for his gentle patience, | he's a 5.02. 43
house–keeper and i thank thy good worship for my STM II.C 59 P
then thank him not for that which he doth say, SON 79.13

THANK'D 10 FR 0.0011 REL FR 6 V 4 P
their blades, which, god be thank'd, hurt not. ADO 5.01.188 P
honest exceeding poor man and, god be thank'd, MV 2.02. 53 P
and you shall find yourself to be well thank'd, AWW 5.01. 36
i, is the doer of this, and he is to be thank'd. TN 3.04. 83 P
but, heav'n be thank'd, it is but voluntary. JN 5.01. 29
well, god be thank'd for these rebels, they 1H4 3.03.190 P
but, god be thank'd, there is no need of me, R3 3.07.165
go not you hence | till i have thank'd you. TIM 1.01.245
she thank'd me, | and bade me, if i had a friend OTH 1.03.163
and yet he has not thank'd me | for what i have TNK 2.06. 21

THANKED 2 FR 0.0002 REL FR 2 V 0 P
now lord be thanked for my good amends! SHR in.2. 97
but god be thanked for prevention, | which /i in H5 2.02.158

THANKFUL 22 FR 0.0024 REL FR 14 V 8 P
i will be thankful | to any happy messenger from TGV 2.04. 52
speaks like a most thankful and reverent youth, ADO 5.01.315 P
are set before us, that we thankful should be — LLL 4.02. 28
/in whom it is acute, and i am thankful for it. 4.02. 71 P
god will send more, if the man will be thankful. AYL 3.02.210 P
she's apt to learn and thankful for good turns. SHR 2.01.165
generally thankful. AWW 2.03. 38 P
yet am i thankful. 4.03.330
for the which | i shall continue thankful. 5.01. 17
it is jove's doing, and jove make me thankful! TN 3.04. 75 P
i will live to be thankful to thee for't. 4.02. 82 P
to be more thankful to thee shall be my study, WT 4.02. 18 P
i am thankful to you, and i'll go along | by H8 1.01.150
your presence, | and ye shall find me thankful. 5.04. 72
encount'ring, | may give you thankful sacrifice. COR 1.06. 9
i will most thankful be, and thanks to men | of TIT 1.01.215
not proud you have, but thankful that you have. ROM 3.05.146
but thankful even for hate that is meant love. 3.05.148
why, sir, give the gods a thankful sacrifice. ANT 1.02.161 P
so soon | is by your fancies' thankful doom. PER 5.02. 20
the gods requite you all, and make her thankful! TNK 5.04. 36
let us be thankful | for that which is, and with 5.04.134

THANKFULLY 8 FR 0.0009 REL FR 6 V 2 P
and thankfully rest debtor for the first. MV 1.01.152
his ring i do accept most thankfully, | and so i 4.02. 9
most thankfully, my lord. TIM 1.02.157
most thankfully, my lord. 5.01. 91
is better than the open air, take it thankfully. LR 3.06. 2 P
is warm'd by th' rest — and take it thankfully. CYM 1.06. 28
towards him might | be us'd more thankfully. 1.06. 79
will do graciously, i will thankfully receive. PER 4.06. 60 P

THANKFULNESS 6 FR 0.0006 REL FR 5 V 1 P
sweet prince, you learn me noble thankfulness. ADO 4.01. 30
we therefore have great cause of thankfulness, H5 2.02. 32
lend me a heart replete with thankfulness! 2H6 1.01. 20
next, | accept my thankfulness. COR 5.04. 59
sprinkle our society with thankfulness. TIM 3.06. 71 P
your lady | take from my heart all thankfulness! PER 3.03. 4

THANKING 1 FR 0.0001 REL FR 1 V 0 P
the charge and thanking | shall be for me, and, AWW 3.05. 98

THANKINGS 3 FR 0.0003 REL FR 3 V 0 P
many and hearty thankings to you both. MM 5.01. 4
thank me no thankings, nor proud me no prouds, ROM 3.05.152
place, and grac'd | the thankings of a king. CYM 5.05.407

THANKLESS 3 FR 0.0003 REL FR 3 V 0 P
shed for my thankless country are requited | but COR 4.05. 70
whose thankless natures (o abhorred spirits!) TIM 5.01. 60
tooth it is | to have a thankless child! LR 1.04.289

THANK'S 1 FR 0.0001 REL FR 1 V 0 P
evermore thank's the exchequer of the poor, R2 2.03. 65

/THANKS 1 FR 0.0001 REL FR 1 V 0 P
/thanks, noble clarence, worthy brother, thanks. 3H6 5.07. 30

THANKS 179 FR 0.0202 REL FR 154 V 25 P
you cannot, give thanks you have liv'd so long, TMP 1.01. 24 P
tells you currish thanks is good enough for such TGV 4.04. 49 P
she thanks you. 4.04.138
for the which she thanks you a thousand times — WIV 2.02. 82 P
the glory of a creditor, | both thanks and use. MM 1.01. 40
he should receive his punishment in thanks: 1.04. 28
thanks, dear isabel. 3.01.105
upon this, more than thanks and good fortune, by 4.02.178 P
cannot but yield you forth to public thanks, 5.01. 7
thanks, good friend escalus, for thy much 5.01.528
thanks, provost, for thy care and secrecy, | we 5.01.530
some other give me thanks for kindnesses; ERR 4.03. 5
take it, and much thanks for my good cheer. 5.01.393
me up, i likewise give her most humble thanks; ADO 1.01.240 P
more pains for those thanks than you take pains 2.03.250 P
more pains for those thanks than you took pains 2.03.259 P
pains that i take for you is as easy as thanks." 2.03.262 P
why, give god thanks, and make no boast of it, 3.03. 19 P
thanks to you all, and leave us. 5.03. 28
if your ladyship would say, "thanks, pompey," i LLL 5.02.556
great thanks, great pompey. 5.02.557 P
coming too short of thanks | for my great suit 5.02.738
thanks, good egeus. what's the news with thee? MND 1.01. 21
and for this intelligence | if i have thanks, it 1.01.249
the kinder we, to give them thanks for nothing. 5.01. 89
thanks, courteous wall; 5.01.178
thanks, i' faith, for silence is only MV 1.01.111
your wife would give you little thanks for that 4.01.288
and when a man thanks me heartily, methinks i AYL 2.05. 27 P
a penny and he renders me the beggarly thanks. 2.05. 29 P
as many matters as he, but i give heaven thanks, 2.05. 36 P
a thousand thanks, signior gremio. SHR 2.01. 84 P
if she do bid me pack, i'll give her thanks, 2.01.177
will you give thanks, sweet kate, or else shall 4.01.159
sure, sweet kate, this kindness merits thanks. 4.03. 41
the poorest service is repaid with thanks, | and 4.03. 45
must think, which never | returns us thanks. AWW 1.01.186
my thanks and duty are your majesty's. 1.02. 23
and such thanks i give | as one near death to 2.01.130
proffers not took reap thanks for their reward. 2.01.147
thanks, sir; all the rest is mute. 2.03. 77
but thanks be given, she's very well, and wants 2.04. 3 P
but i con him no thanks for't, in the nature he 4.03.152 P
nothing, but let him have thanks. 4.03.171 P
bosom would peep forth | and answer thanks. 4.04. 8
i can no other answer make but thanks, | and TN 3.03. 14
answer make but thanks, | and thanks, and ever. 3.03. 15
would be fill'd up, my brother, with our thanks, WT 1.02. 4
stay your thanks a while, | and pay them when 1.02. 9
fees | when you depart, and save your thanks. 1.02. 54
for this | i'll blush you thanks. 4.04.584
now he thanks the old shepherd, which stands by 5.02. 54 P
i give heaven thanks i was not like to thee! JN 1.01. 83
o, take his mother's thanks, a widow's thanks, 2.01. 32
o, take his mother's thanks, a widow's thanks, 2.01. 32
i have a kind soul that would give thanks, | and 5.07.108
with "thanks, my countrymen, my loving friends," R2 1.04. 34
all my treasury | is yet but unfelt thanks, 2.03. 61
thanks, gentle uncle. 3.01. 42
thanks, noble peer! 5.05. 67
and thy father is to give me thanks for it. 2H4 2.04.323 P
i shall deliver so. thanks to your highness. H5 3.06.167
you, upon his knees, a thousand thanks, and he 4.04. 60 P
thanks, good my /countryman. 4.07.110
and therefore tell her i return great thanks, 1H6 2.02. 51
thanks, /gentlemen. 2.04.131
thanks, gentle duke. 3.02.121
or been reguerdon'd with so much as thanks, 3.04. 23
thanks, reignier, happy for so sweet a child, 5.03.148
reignier of france, i give thee kingly thanks, 5.03.163

thanks, uncle winchester, | gloucester, york, 2H6 1.01. 68
to entertain my vows of thanks and praise! 4.09. 14
and so, with thanks and pardon to you all, | i 4.09. 20
thanks, gentle norfolk. 3H6 1.01. 31
i take my leave with many thousand thanks. 3.02. 56
my love till death, my humble thanks, my prayers 3.02. 62
let me give humble thanks for all at once. 3.03.221
thanks, good montgomery; 4.07. 45
thanks, brave montgomery, and thanks unto you 4.07. 77
brave montgomery, and thanks unto you all. 4.07. 77
thanks, gentle somerset, sweet oxford, thanks. 5.04. 58
thanks, gentle somerset, sweet oxford, thanks. 5.04. 58
and take his thanks that yet hath nothing else. 5.04. 59
discharge the common sort | with pay and thanks, 5.05. 88
/thanks, noble clarence, worthy brother, thanks. 5.07. 30
to give them thanks | that were the cause of my R3 1.01.127
"thanks, gentle citizens and friends," quoth i, 3.07. 38
your love deserves my thanks, but my desert 3.07.154
kind sister, thanks, we'll enter all together. 4.01. 11
heart of it, | thanks you for this great care. H8 1.02. 2
and give thanks | to you that chok'd it. 1.02. 3
let me have such a bowl may hold my thanks, 1.04. 39
for which i pay 'em | a thousand thanks, and 1.04. 74
thanks, my good lord chamberlain. 2.02. 61
vouchsafe to speak my thanks and my obedience, 2.03. 71
but with thanks to god for such | a royal lady, 2.04.153
i | can nothing render but allegiant thanks, 3.02.176
who return'd her thanks | in the great'st 5.01. 64
much are we bound to heaven | in daily thanks, 5.02.150
and between, but small thanks for my labor. TRO 1.01. 72 P
oft have you (often have you thanks therefore) 3.03. 20
and he replies, "thanks, agamemnon." 3.03.261 P
please you, save the thanks this prince expects. 4.04.117
by mars his gauntlet, thanks! 4.05.177
thanks and good night to the greeks' general. 5.01. 73
accept distracted thanks. 5.02.189
thanks. COR 1.01.164
a certain number | (though thanks to all) must i 1.06. 81
their talk at table, and their thanks at end; 4.07. 4
good will | must have that thanks from rome, 5.01. 46
we have all | great cause to give great thanks. 5.04. 60
thanks, gentle tribune, noble brother marcus. TIT 1.01.171
and thanks to men | of noble minds is honorable 1.01.215
i give thee thanks in part of thy deserts, | and 1.01.236
thanks, noble titus, father of my life! 1.01.253
thanks, sweet lavinia. 1.01.273
thanks, gentle romans, may i govern so, | to 5.03.147
as much to him, else is his thanks too much. ROM 2.06. 23
sir, but she will none, she /gives you thanks. 3.05.139
doth she not give us thanks? 3.05.142
doubled with thanks and service, from whose help TIM 1.02. 7
feasts are too proud to give thanks to the gods. 1.02. 61
with more than common thanks i will receive it. 1.02.208
the gods require our thanks. 3.06. 69 P
o, a root, dear thanks! 4.03.192
yet thanks i must you con | that you are thieves 4.03.425
the captainship, thou shalt be met with thanks, 5.01.161
to give thee from our royal master thanks, MAC 1.03.101
thanks for your pains. 1.03.117
that the proportion both of thanks and payment 1.04. 19
thanks, sir; the like to you! 2.01. 30
thanks to your majesty. 3.04. 2
they encounter thee with their hearts' thanks. 3.04. 9
thanks for that: 3.04. 27
e'er thou art, for thy good caution, thanks; 4.01. 73
so thanks to all at once and to each one, | whom 5.09. 40
for this relief much thanks. HAM 1.01. 8
for all, our thanks. 1.02. 16
your visitation shall receive such thanks | as 2.02. 25
thanks, rosencrantz and gentle guildenstern. 2.02. 33
thanks, guildenstern and gentle rosencrantz. 2.02. 34
beggar that i am, i am /even poor in thanks — 2.02.272 P
friends, my thanks are too dear a halfpenny. 2.02.273 P
and rewards | hast ta'en with equal thanks; 3.02. 68
thanks, dear my lord. 3.03. 35
where should we have our thanks? 5.02.372
he which finds him shall deserve our thanks, LR 2.01. 61
hearty thanks; 4.06.224
thanks you, the valiant of /this warlike isle, OTH 2.01. 43
not with vain thanks, but with acceptance 3.03.470
and am well studied for a liberal thanks, ANT 2.06. 47
beds i' th' east are soft, and thanks to you, 2.06. 50
thanks to my lord. 3.04. 28
commend thy acts, | make her thanks bless thee. 4.08. 13
now, good friends, | and have my thanks for all. 4.14.140
mine own as i | will kneel to him with thanks. 5.02. 21
farewell, and thanks! 5.02.207
thanks, good sir, | you're kindly welcome. CYM 1.06. 13
thanks, fairest lady. 1.06. 31
thanks, madam, well. 1.06. 52
my humble thanks. 1.06.180
the thanks i give | is telling you that i am 2.03. 88
give | is telling you that i am poor of thanks, 2.03. 89
thanks, royal sir. 3.05. 1
ere you depart, and thanks to stay and eat it. 3.06. 67
thanks, sir. 3.06. 94
displace our heads where (thanks, /ye gods!) 4.02.122
thanks, jupiter! 5.04.119
thanks, fortune, yet, that, after all /thy PER 2.01.121
he thanks your grace; 2.03. 86
thanks, gentlemen, to all, all have done well; 2.03.107
madam, my thanks and prayers. 3.03. 34
my recompense is thanks, that's all, | yet my 3.04. 17
my thanks, sweet madam. 4.01. 49
thanks, sir. TNK 1.03. 11
thanks, theseus. 2.05. 32
game, i give thee thanks | for this fair token, 5.01.132
to the gods | our thanks that you are living. 5.04.101
give thyself the thanks if aught in me | worthy SON 38. 5
THANKSGIVING 2 FR 0.0002 REL FR 1 V 1 P
that, in the thanksgiving before meat, do relish MM 1.02. 15 P
i cannot stay thanksgiving. LLL 2.01.193
THAN'S 1 FR 0.0001 REL FR 1 V 0 P
were more than you expect, or more than's fit, PER 2.03. 5
THARSUS 16 FR 0.0018 REL FR 15 V 1 P
thee then, and to tharsus | intend my travel, PER 1.02.115
this tharsus, o'er which i have the government, 1.04. 21
the misery of tharsus may be theirs. 1.04. 55
is still at tharsus, where each man | thinks all 2.ch. 11
and that in tharsus was not best | longer for 2.ch. 25
we are near tharsus. 3.01. 73 P
o, make for tharsus! 3.01. 77
our fast–growing scene must find | at tharsus, 4.ch. 7
the petty wrens of tharsus will fly hence | and 4.03. 22
winds have brought | this king to tharsus — 4.04. 18
leaves tharsus and again embarks. 4.04. 27
the king my father did in tharsus leave me, 5.01.170
thou that wast born at sea, buried at tharsus, 5.01.196
she is not dead at tharsus, as she should have 5.01.215
my purpose was for tharsus, there to strike 5.01.252
she at tharsus | was nurs'd with cleon, who at 5.03. 7
THAS 3 FR 0.0003 REL FR 0 V 3 P
hold, wart, traverse! thas, thas, thas. 2H4 3.02.272 P
hold, wart, traverse! thas, thas, thas. 3.02.272 P
hold, wart, traverse! thas, thas, thas. 3.02.272 P
/THASOS 1 FR 0.0001 REL FR 1 V 0 P
come therefore, and to /thasos send his body; JC 5.03.104
THAT *(also dat)*
/THAT 113 FR 0.0127 REL FR 99 V 14 P
THAT 11725 FR 1.3253 REL FR 9413 V 2312 P
THATCH 2 FR 0.0002 REL FR 2 V 0 P
like roping icicles | upon our houses' thatch, H5 3.05. 24
and thatch your poor thin roofs | with burthens TIM 4.03.145
THATCH'D 3 FR 0.0003 REL FR 1 V 2 P
and flat meads thatch'd with stover, them to TMP 4.01. 63
why then your visor should be thatch'd. ADO 2.01. 98 P
worse than jove in a thatch'd house! AYL 3.03. 11 P
/THAT'S 5 FR 0.0005 REL FR 5 V 0 P
/all /my /sins /are /writ, /and /that's /myself. R2 4.01.275
/paris /sleeps — /and /that's /the /quarrel. TRO pr 10
/but /that's /no /welcome. 4.05.165
like to a harvest–man /that's task'd to mow | or COR 1.03. 36
/for /thyself, /and /that's /for /tamora. TIT 3.02. 74
THAT/'S 4 FR 0.0004 REL FR 1 V 3 P
yet behind, that/'s meet you all should know. MM 5.01.539
taurus? that/'s sides and heart. TN 1.03.139 P
should be "by this fire, that/'s god's angel." 1H4 3.03. 35 P
well, then that/'s the humor of't. H5 2.01.116 P
THAT'S 436 FR 0.0492 REL FR 284 V 152 P
why, that's my spirit! TMP 1.02.215
that's my noble master! 1.02.299
stain'd | with grief (that's beauty's canker), 1.02.416
when every grief is entertain'd that's offer'd, 2.01. 16
he were that which now he's like — that's dead, 2.01.282
there was a noise, | that's verily. 2.01.321
that's a brave god, and bears celestial liquor. 2.02.117
that's most certain. 3.02. 56 P
when that's gone, | he shall drink nought but 3.02. 65
that's not the tune. 3.02.124
as diminish | one dowle that's in my plume. 3.03. 65
but remember | (for that's my business to you) 3.03. 69
that's more to me than my wetting; 4.01.211 P
why, that's my dainty ariel! 5.01. 95
our remembrances with | a heaviness that's gone. 5.01.200
that's on some shallow story of deep love, | how TGV 1.01. 21
that's a deep story of a deeper love, | for he 1.01. 23
nod–ay — why, that's "noddy." 1.01.112 P
fire that's closest kept burns most of all. 1.02. 30
nay, that's certain; 2.01. 36 P
that's because the one is painted, and the other 2.01. 56 P
that's the letter i writ to her friend. 2.01.160 P
why, he that's tied here, crab, my dog. 2.03. 40 P
yet hath sir proteus (for that's his name) 2.04. 67
and that's the reason i love him so little. 2.04.206
that thou art banish'd — o, that's the news! 3.01.219
but that's all one, if he be but one knave. 3.01.265 P
that's as much as to say, "can she so?" 3.01.307 P
that's as much as to say "bastard virtues," that 3.01.318 P
she cannot, for that's writ down she is slow of; 3.01.349 P
that's monstrous. o, that that were out! 3.01.365 P
that's not so, sir; we are your enemies. 4.01. 8
that's her chamber. 4.04. 86
and that's her cause of sorrow. 4.04.147
we'll follow him that's fled — | the thicket is 5.03. 10
thou'dst two, | and that's far worse than none: 5.04. 51
common friend, that's without faith or love, 5.04. 62
that's my humor. WIV 1.01.132 P
that's meat and drink to me, now. 1.01.294 P
anne's mind — that's neither here nor there. 1.04.106 P
'od's heartlings, that's a pretty jest indeed! 3.04. 57 P
that's my master, master doctor. 3.04. 85 P
and that's a good root. 4.01. 54 P
that's good too; 5.02. 8 P
lest the oil that's in me should set hell on 5.05. 35 P
marry, sir, that's claudio, signior claudio. MM 1.02. 64 P
and that's my pith | of business 'twixt you and 1.04. 70
for that's the utmost of his pilgrimage. 2.01. 36
o, that's sudden! 2.02. 83
that's well said. 2.02.109
it doth know | that's like my brother's fault. 2.02.138
and that's not good. 2.04. 75
he is a motion generative, that's infallible. 3.02.112 P
not consent to die this day, that's certain. 4.03. 56 P
for 'tis a physic | that's bitter to sweet end. 4.06. 8
that's i, and't like your grace. 5.01. 74
that's he indeed. 5.01. 77
that's somewhat madly spoken. 5.01. 89
compact with her that's gone, think'st thou thy 5.01.242
worth and credit | that's seal'd in approbation? 5.01.245
that's the way; for women are light at midnight. 5.01.279 P
that's not my fault, he's master of my state. ERR 2.01. 95
more common, for that's nothing but words. 3.01. 25
have at you with another, that's — when? 3.01. 52
that's my sister. 3.02. 60
that's a fault that water will mend. 3.02.105 P
quarters, that's an ell and three quarters, will 3.02.110 P
ay, that's my name. 3.02.165
desk | that's cover'd o'er with turkish tapestry 4.01.104
"god damn me," that's as much to say, "god make 4.03. 54 P
that's a question; how shall we try it? 5.01.422
why, that's spoken like an honest drovier; ADO 2.01.194 P
rich she shall be, that's certain; 2.03. 30 P
not a note of mine that's worth the noting. 2.03. 55
that's her torment. 2.03.125 P
nay, that's impossible, she may wear her heart 2.03.203 P
that's the scene that i would see, which will be 2.03.217 P
pains to thank me" — that's as much as to say, 2.03.260 P
that's as much as to say, the sweet youth's in 3.02. 52 P
nay, that's certain, we have the exhibition to 4.02. 5 P
yea, marry, that's the eftest way; 4.02. 36 P
but that's no matter, let him kill one first. 5.01. 81
almost the copy of my child that's dead, | and 5.01.289
and that's great marvel, loving a light wench. LLL 1.02.123 P
that's hereby. 1.02.136 P
reputes me a cannon, and the bullet, that's he; 3.01. 64
hath sold him a bargain, a goose, that's flat. 3.01.101
a fat l'envoy — ay, that's a fat goose. 3.01.104
o, that's the latin word for three farthings: 3.01.137 P
cain's birth, that's not five weeks old as yet? 4.02. 35
you weigh me not? o, that's you care not for me. 5.02. 27
why, that's the way to choke a gibing spirit, 5.02.858
that's too long for a play. 5.02.878
that's all one; MND 1.02. 49 P
ay, that's a colt indeed, for he doth nothing MV 1.02. 40 P
that's a month before | this bond expires, i do 1.03.157
why, that's the lady. 2.07. 31
why, that's the lady, all the world desires her. 2.07. 38
stamp'd in gold, but that's insculp'd upon; 2.07. 57
that's certain. 3.01. 26 P
that's certain, if the devil may be her judge. 3.01. 32 P
nay, that's true, that's very true. 3.01.125 P
nay, that's true, that's very true. 3.01.125 P
ripe, and that's the right virtue of the medlar. AYL 3.02.120 P
that's no matter; 3.02.167 P
o, that's a brave man! 3.04. 40 P
but that's all one; 3.05.133
has a huswive's hand — but that's no matter. 4.03. 27
that's your device. SHR 1.01.193
why, that's nothing; 1.02.111 P
morrow, kate — for that's your name, i hear. 2.01.182
that's but a cavil; he is old, i young. 2.01.390
and that's a wonder. 2.01.409
why, that's all one. 3.02. 81 P
now, by my mother's son, and that's myself, | it 4.05. 6
that's my office. 5.02. 36
to be short, what not, that's sweet and happy. 5.02.110
that's for advantage. AWW 1.01.201 P
that's able to breathe life into a stone, 2.01. 73
marry, that's a bountiful answer that fits all 2.02. 15 P
that's it i would have said, the very same. 2.03. 25 P
the devil it is that's thy master. 2.03.249 P
a young man married is a man that's marr'd; 2.03.298
a knave," that's "before me th' art a knave." 2.04. 30 P
that's the loss of men, though it be the getting 3.02. 41 P
that's all the fault. 3.06.112
well, that's set down. 4.03.147 P
well, that's set down. 4.03.155 P
well, that's set down. 4.03.174 P
my lord that's gone made himself much sport out 4.05. 64 P
offense, | crying, "that's good that's gone." 5.03. 60
offense, | crying, "that's good that's gone." 5.03. 60
and ev'ry hair that's on't, helen, that's dead, 5.03. 77
and ev'ry hair that's on't, helen, that's dead, 5.03. 77
one that's dead is quick — | and now behold the 5.03.303
any thing that's mended is but patch'd; TN 1.05. 47 P
that's as much to say as i wear not motley in my 1.05. 56 P
for that's it that always makes a good voyage of 2.04. 77 P
ay, that's the theme, | to her in haste. 2.04.122
that's me, i warrant you. 2.05. 79 P
nay, that's certain. 3.01. 14 P
that's a degree to love. 3.01.123
for meddle you must, that's certain, or forswear 3.04.252 P
that's all one. 5.01.196 P
one sir topas, sir, but that's all one. 5.01.373 P
but that's all one, our play is done, | and 5.01.407
sir, that's to–morrow. WT 1.02. 10
why, that's my bawcock. 1.02.121
why, that's some comfort. | what? camillo there? 1.02.208
not you seen, camillo | (but that's past doubt; 1.02.268
then the world and all that's in't is nothing, 1.02.293
nay, that's a mock. 2.01. 14
that's enough. 2.03. 30
i, nor any | but one that's here — and that's 2.03. 84
any | but one that's here — and that's himself; 2.03. 84
that's true enough, | though 'tis a saying, sir, 3.02. 57
but that's not to the point. 3.03. 89 P
that's a good deed. 3.03.133 P
that's likewise part of my intelligence; 4.02. 45 P
dates, none — that's out of my note; 4.03. 46 P
that's the rogue that put me into this apparel. 4.03.103 P
tooth, or the fann'd snow that's bolted | by th' 4.04.364
o, that's the case of the shepherd's son. 4.04.816 P
is none worthy, | respecting her that's gone. 5.01. 35
there | my mate, that's never to be found again, 5.03.134
i am not worth this coil that's made for me. JN 2.01.165
that's the curse of rome. 3.01.207
that's as york thrives to beat back bullingbrook R2 2.02.144
why, that's well said. 1H4 1.02.144 P
that's flat. 1.03.218
that's even as fair as — at hand, quoth the 2.01. 49 P
undertake is dangerous" — why, that's certain. 2.03. 7 P
nay, that's past praying for, i have pepper'd 2.04.191 P
and that's the dearest grace it renders you — 3.01.180
thou mine, | and that's a feeling disputation, 3.01.203
that's the worst tidings that i hear of /yet. 4.01.127
march through coventry with them, that's flat. 4.02. 39 P
but that's all one, they'll find linen enough on 4.02. 47 P
no, that's certain, i am not a double man; 5.04.138 P
and as the thing that's heavy in itself | upon 2H4 1.01.119
that's to make him eat twenty of his words. 2.02.137 P
and that's a marvellous searching wine, and it 2.04. 27 P
why, that's well said; 2.04. 31 P
that's fifty–five year ago. 3.02.210 P
man cannot make him laugh, but that's no marvel, 4.03. 89 P
"a cup of wine that's brisk and fine, | and 5.03. 46
live so long as i may, that's the certain of it; H5 2.01. 14 P
terms, as i may, and that's the humor of it. 2.01. 59 P
that now i will have: that's the humor of it. 2.01. 97 P
bad humors on the knight, that's the even of it. 2.01.122 P
that's mercy, but too much security. 2.02. 44
that's all the riches i got in his service. 2.03. 44 P
and that's but unwholesome food, they say. 2.03. 57 P
a! that's a foul fault. 3.02.136 P

say, that's a valiant flea that dare eat his 3.07.145 P
that's more than we know. 4.01.129 P
that's a perilous shot out of an elder–gun, that 4.01.197 P
that's a lie in thy throat. 4.08. 16 P
nay, that's right; 5.01. 1 P
must die, | for that's the end of human misery. 1H6 3.02.137
tush, that's a wooden thing! 5.03. 89
a married man! that's most intolerable. 5.04. 79
for that's the golden mark i seek to hit. 2H6 1.01.243
that's some wrong indeed. 1.03. 19 P
why, that's well said. what color is my gown of? 2.01.109
and that's not suddenly to be perform'd, | but 2.02. 67
that's bad enough, for i am but reproach; 2.04. 96
why, that's well said. 3.02. 8
that's false. 4.02.140
alexander iden, that's my name, | a poor esquire 5.01. 74
stigmatic, that's more than thou canst tell. 5.01.215
true, clifford, that's richard duke of york. 3H6 1.01. 83
why, that's my fortune too, therefore i'll stay. 2.02. 76
tut, that's a foolish observation. 2.06.108
why, so i am — in mind, and that's enough. 3.01. 60
that's soon perform'd, because i am a subject. 3.02. 54
that's a day longer than a wonder lasts. 3.02.114
ay, that's the first thing that we have to do, 4.03. 62
that's not my fear, my meed hath got me fame: 4.08. 38
or else you famish — that's a threefold death. 5.04. 32
it were lost sorrow to wail one that's lost. R3 2.02. 11
woe to that land that's govern'd by a child! 2.03. 11
a greater gift? o, that's the sword to it. 3.01.116
that's th' appliance only | which your disease H8 1.01.124
that's clapp'd upon the court gate. 1.03. 18
that's christian care enough. 2.02.130
that's to say, | i meant to rectify my 2.04.203
creature | that's paragon'd o' th' world. 2.04.231
that's somewhat sudden; 3.02.394
that's news indeed. 3.02.402
must no more call it york–place, that's past; 4.01. 95
you are a sectary, | that's the plain truth. 5.02.106
by all that's holy, he had better starve | than 5.02.167
abus'd extremely, and to cry, "that's witty!" ep 6
that's true, make no question of that. TRO 1.02.160 P
that's aeneas; 1.02.186 P
that's antenor. 1.02.190 P
that's hector, that, that, look you, that; 1.02.199 P
that's helenus. 1.02.219 P
that's helenus. 1.02.220 P
that's helenus. 1.02.221 P
that's deiphobus. 1.02.227 P
and that's one of the chiefest of them too. 1.02.266 P
that's done, as near as the extremest ends | of 1.03.167
that's their /fame in peace. 1.03.236
that's to't indeed, sir. 3.01. 20 P
sweet queen, that's a sweet queen — i' faith — 3.01. 70 P
the providence that's in a watchful state 3.03.196
his horse, for that's the more capable creature. 3.03.306 P
that's my mind too. good morrow, lord aeneas. 4.01. 7
but that's no argument for kissing now, | for 4.05. 27
you less than he, | that's lesser than a little. COR 1.04. 15
done | as you have done — that's what i can; 1.09. 16
as you have been — that's for my country: 1.09. 17
chests in corioles, and the gold that's in them. 2.01.132 P
and that's as easy | as to set dogs on sheep — 2.01.256
that's a brave fellow; 2.02. 5 P
that's off, that's off; 2.02. 60
that's off, that's off; 2.02. 60
that's thousand to one good one — when you now 2.02. 79
but that's no matter, the greater part carries 2.03. 37 P
physic | that's sure of death without it — at 3.01.155
what has he done to rome that's worthy death? 3.01.296
to go rove with one | that's yet unbruis'd. 4.01. 47
that's worthily | as any ear can hear. 4.01. 53
yet his nature | in that's no changeling, and i 4.07. 11
back, that's the utmost of your having, back! 5.02. 57 P
that's curdied by the frost from purest snow 5.03. 66
that's my brave boy! 5.03. 76
for love of her that's gone, | perhaps, she TIT 4.01. 43
ay, that's my boy! 4.01.110
that you are both decipher'd, that's the news, 4.02. 8
"ad jovem," that's for you; 4.03. 54
"ad martem," that's for myself; 4.03. 55
and when thou find'st a man that's like thyself, 5.02. 99
nay, that's not so. ROM 1.04. 44
the earth that's nature's mother is her tomb; 2.03. 9
that's my good son, but where hast thou been 2.03. 47
one hath wounded me | that's by me wounded; 2.03. 51
that's as much as to say, such a case as yours 2.04. 52 P
ah, mocker, that's the /dog's name. 2.04.209 P
perchance she cannot meet him — that's not so. 2.05. 3
that's a certain text. 4.01. 21
ay, that's well known; TIM 1.01. 3
nay, that's most fix'd. 1.01. 9
that's a deed thou't die for. 1.01.193 P
that's a lascivious apprehension. 1.01.208 P
that's not feign'd, he is so. 1.01.224 P
who lives that's not depraved or depraves? 1.02.140
and he that's once denied will hardly speed. 3.02. 62
what, he's poor, and that's revenge enough. 3.04. 63 P
under that's above me. 4.03.292
him of an intent | that's coming toward him. 5.01. 21
that's well spoke. 5.01.193
that's all i seek, | and am, moreover, suitor JC 3.01.226
nay, that's certain: 3.02. 69
that's as much as to say, they are fools that 3.03. 17 P
that's not an office for a friend, my lord. 5.05. 29
he that's coming | must be provided for; MAC 1.05. 66
this murtherous shaft that's shot | hath not yet 2.03.141
unnatural, | even like the deed that's done. 2.04. 11
the worm that's fled | hath nature that in time 3.04. 28
grease that's sweaten | from the murderer's 4.01. 65
for the whole space that's in the tyrant's grasp 4.03. 36
no mind that's honest | but in it shares some 4.03.197
no man that's born of woman | shall e'er have 5.03. 6
brandish'd by man that's of a woman born. 5.07. 13
when yond same star that's westward from the HAM 1.01. 36
in the same figure, like the king that's dead. 1.01. 41
open to incontinency — | that's not my meaning. 2.01. 31
beautified ophelia" — that's an ill phrase, a 2.02.111 P
that's very true, my lord. 2.02.180 P
indeed that's out of the air. 2.02.208 P
that's good, "/mobled /queen" /is /good. 2.02.504 P
that's villainous, and shows a most pitiful 3.02. 43 P
that's a fair thought to lie between maids' legs 3.02.118 P
that's wormwood! 3.02.181 P
you see yonder cloud that's almost in shape of a 3.02.376 P
for who, that's but a queen, fair, sober, wise, 3.04.189
two dishes, but to one table — that's the end. 4.03. 24 P
that drop of blood that's calm proclaims me 4.05.118
there's rosemary, that's for remembrance; 4.05.175 P
and there is pansies, that's for thoughts. 4.05.176 P
that's two of his weapons — but well. 5.02.146 P
that's the french bet against the danish. 5.02.162 P
that's most certain, and with you; LR 1.01.286 P
that's my fear. 1.02.166 P
for taking one's part that's out of favor. 1.04. 99 P
that's a sheal'd peascod. 1.04.200 P
she that's a maid now, and laughs at my 1.05. 51
that's something yet: 2.03. 21
among twenty but can smell him that's stinking. 2.04. 71 P
or rather a disease that's in my flesh, | which 2.04.222
and a codpiece — that's a wise man and a fool. 3.02. 40 P
part in my heart | that's sorry yet for thee. 3.02. 73
which came from one that's of a neutral heart, 3.07. 48
i thank you, sir, that's all. 4.06.214
and that's true too. 5.02. 11
that's as we list to grace him. 5.03. 61
that's but a trifle here. 5.03.296
as well to see the vessel that's come in | as to OTH 2.01. 37
hast thou for her that's foul and foolish? 2.01.140 P
by me that's said or done amiss this night, 2.03.201
ay, that's the way; 2.03.387
something that's brief; 3.01. 2
o, that's an honest fellow. 3.03. 5
but in a man that's just | they're close 3.03.122
into the vale of years (yet that's not much), 3.03.266
/faith, that's with watching, 'twill away again. 3.03.285
that's a fault. 3.04. 55
her honor is an essence that's not seen; 4.01. 16
that's not so good now. 4.01. 23
/'zounds, that's fulsome! 4.01. 36 P
think every bearded fellow that's but yok'd 4.01. 66
that's not amiss, | but yet keep time in all. 4.01. 91
nay, that's not your way. 4.01.186 P
nay, that's certain. 4.01.195 P
that's fouler. 4.01.203 P
that's strange. 4.02. 11
his scorn i approve" — | nay, that's not next. 4.03. 53 P
that's one of them. 5.01. 61
o, that's well said: 5.01. 98
one more, and that's the last. 5.02. 19
that's he that was othello; here i am. 5.02.284
but that's a fable. 5.02.286
sir, you and i must part, but that's not it; ANT 1.03. 87
his wife that's dead did trespasses to caesar; 2.01. 40
that's our offer. 2.06. 39
that's the next to do. 2.06. 59
that's twice. 2.07. 62
that's not so good. he cannot like her long. 3.03. 14
let him appear that's come from antony. 3.12. 1
that's my brave lord! 3.13.176
sometime we see a cloud that's dragonish, | a 4.14. 2
and impatience does | become a dog that's mad. 4.15. 80
of no more trust | than love that's hir'd! 5.02.155
nay, that's certain. 5.02.222
why, that's the way | to fool their preparation, 5.02.224
most miserable | is the /desire that's glorious. CYM 1.06. 7
smoky light | that's fed with stinking tallow: 1.06.110
did you hear of a stranger that's come to court 2.01. 32 P
why should i write this down, that's riveted, 2.02. 43
late, for that's the reason i was up so early. 2.03. 33 P
but that's no fault of his. 2.03. 57
that's more | than some, whose tailors are as 2.03. 78
damn'd paper, | black as the ink that's on thee! 3.02. 20
that's false to 's bed? 3.04. 44
if any thing that's civil, speak; 3.06. 23
that's all i reak. 4.02.154
not lack | the flower that's like thy face, pale 4.02.221
that's love, | to have them fall no more: 5.01. 12
am i better | than one that's sick o' th' gout, 5.04. 5
that's not my desire. 5.04. 21
any thing | that's due to all the villains past, 5.05.212
life, | for that's an article within our law, PER 1.01. 88
that's the least fear; 1.04. 71
is an armed knight that's conquered by a lady; 2.02. 26
a burning torch that's turned upside down; 2.02. 32
holding out gold that's by the touchstone tried; 2.02. 37
a withered branch, that's only green at top; 2.02. 43
here, with a cup that's /stor'd unto the brim — 2.03. 50
that's as much as you would be denied | of your 2.03.105
love, | and that's the mark i know you level at. 2.03.113
that's your superstition. 3.01. 50
my recompense is thanks, that's all, | yet my 3.04. 17
the blood of mine that's sib to him be suck'd TNK 1.02. 72
the maid flavina) | love any that's call'd man. 1.03. 85
that's arcite looks out. 2.01. 48 P
no, sir, no, that's palamon. 2.01. 49 P
that's a good wench! 2.02.124
that's as we bargain, madam. 2.02.152
that's nothing. 2.02.160
my masters, i'll be there, that's certain. 2.03. 24
but that's all one, i'll go through, let her 2.03. 31
thing, | i care for nothing, and that's palamon. 3.02. 6
that's no matter, | we'll argue that hereafter. 3.03. 4
anger, | as you love any thing that's honorable. 3.06. 27
that's well said. 3.06. 49
that's mine then. | i'll arm you first. 3.06. 52
methinks, of him that's first with palamon. 4.02. 90
o, he that's freckle–fac'd? 4.02.120
that's all one, if ye make a noise. 5.02. 16
that's but a niceness. 5.02. 20
but that's all one, 'tis nothing to our purpose. 5.02. 32
that's fine indeed. 5.02. 50
alas, that's nothing. 5.02. 57
that's a fine maid! 5.02. 70
that's all one, i will have you. 5.02. 85
before god, that's as true as the gospel. STM II.C 88 P
the colt that's back'd and burthen'd being young VEN 419
as the fleet–foot roe that's tir'd with chasing, 561
but gold that's put to use more gold begets." 768
face remains alive that's worth the viewing? 1076
bud, | a brittle glass that's broken presently: PP 13. 4
that's for thyself to breed another thee, | or SON 6. 7
that's to ye sworn to none was ever said, | for LC 180

THAW 6 FR 0.0006 REL FR 3 V 3 P
a man of continual dissolution and thaw. WIV 3.05.116 P
that i was duller than a great thaw, huddling ADO 2.01.244 P
belly, ere i should come by a fire to thaw me. SHR 4.01. 9 P
whose blush doth thaw the consecrated snow TIM 4.03.385
melt, | thaw, and resolve itself into a dew! HAM 1.02.130
do not you feel it thaw you? TNK 3.03. 18

THAW'D 5 FR 0.0005 REL FR 5 V 0 P
that i did love, for now my love is thaw'd, TGV 2.04.200
that will be thaw'd from the true quality | with JC 3.01. 41
his /nemean hide, | and swore his sinews thaw'd. TNK 1.01. 69
are on the sudden wasted, thaw'd, and done, | as VEN 749
thou blowest the fire when temperance is thaw'd, LUC 884

THAWING 1 FR 0.0001 REL FR 1 V 0 P
thawing cold fear, that mean and gentle all H5 4.pr. 45

THAWS 1 FR 0.0001 REL FR 1 V 0 P
where phoebus' fire scarce thaws the icicles, MV 2.01. 5

THE *(also d'*, de*, t'*, th'*)*

/THE 278 FR 0.0314 REL FR 223 V 55 P

THE 27457 FR 3.1037 REL FR 20835 V 6622 P

THEATRE 6 FR 0.0006 REL FR 4 V 2 P
this wide and universal theatre | presents more AYL 2.07.137
securely on their battlements | as in a theatre, JN 2.01.375
as in a theatre the eyes of men, | after a R2 5.02. 23
as they use to do the players in the theatre, i JC 1.02.261 P
that done, repair to pompey's theatre. 1.03.152
allowance, o'erweigh a whole theatre of others. HAM 3.02. 28 P

THEBAN 2 FR 0.0002 REL FR 2 V 0 P
i'll talk a word with this same learned theban. LR 3.04.157
to our theban hounds, | that shook the aged TNK 2.02. 46

THEBES 14 FR 0.0015 REL FR 14 V 0 P
when i from thebes came last a conqueror. MND 5.01. 51
and pecks of crows in the foul fields of thebes. TNK 1.01. 42
thebes and the temptings in't before we further 1.02. 4
to school, may we perceive | walking in thebes! 1.02. 15
the soldier in | the cranks and turns of thebes? 1.02. 28
this is virtue | of no respect in thebes. 1.02. 36
i spake of thebes, | how dangerous, if we will 1.02. 36
to him, and pronounces | ruin to thebes; 1.02. 92
our services stand now for thebes, not creon. 1.02. 99
some of thebes have told 's | they are sisters' 1.04. 15
concern us | much more than thebes is worth. 1.04. 33
o cousin arcite, | where is thebes now? 2.02. 7
he shall see thebes again and call to arms | the 2.02.248
me thou deem'st at thebes, | and therein 3.01. 26

/THEE 39 FR 0.0044 REL FR 36 V 3 P

THEE 3384 FR 0.3825 REL FR 2690 V 694 P

THEE'T 1 FR 0.0001 REL FR 1 V 0 P
villainy, | in thee't had been good service. ANT 2.07. 75

THEFT 17 FR 0.0019 REL FR 16 V 1 P
if /'a be in debt and theft, and a sergeant in ERR 4.02. 61
when the suspicious head of theft is stopp'd. LLL 4.03.333
there's honor in the theft. AWW 2.01. 34
for thy theft hath already made thee butter. 1H4 4.02. 60 P
keeps | and useth it to patronage his theft. 1H6 3.01. 48
o theft most base, | that we have stol'n what we TRO 2.02. 92
'twere a concealment | worse than a theft, no COR 1.09. 22
for there is boundless theft | in limited TIM 4.03.427
in their rough power | has uncheck'd theft. 4.03.444
there's warrant in that theft | which steals MAC 2.03.145
and scape /detecting, i will pay the theft. HAM 3.02. 89
of life, when life itself | yields to the theft. LR 4.06. 44
euriphile | (whom for the theft i wedded), stole CYM 5.05.341
steal thine own freedom, and complain on theft. VEN 160
but robb'd and ransack'd by injurious theft. LUC 838
"guilty thou art of murther and of theft, 918
but, for his theft, in pride of all his growth SON 99.12

/THEFTS 1 FR 0.0001 REL FR 1 V 0 P
/we /would /give /much /to /use /violent /thefts TRO 5.03. 21

THEFTS 1 FR 0.0001 REL FR 0 V 1 P
his thefts were too open; WIV 1.03. 25 P

/THEIR 41 FR 0.0046 REL FR 35 V 6 P
in their new fustian, /their white stockings, SHR 4.01. 48 P
/the /action /of /their /bodies /from /their 2H4 1.01.195
/action /of /their /bodies /from /their /souls, 1.01.195
/that /their /weapons /only | /seem'd /on /our 1.01.197
/but, /for /their /spirits /and /souls, | /this 1.01.198
/commonwealth /is /sick /of /their /own /choice, 1.03. 87
/their //over–greedy /love /hath /surfeited. 1.03. 88
/would /turn /their /own /perfection /to /abuse 2.03. 27
/sweet /harry /had /but /half /their /numbers, 2.03. 43
/construe /the /times /to /their /necessities, 4.01.102
/mounted /and /both /roused /in /their /seats, 4.01.116
/their /neighing /coursers /daring /of /the 4.01.117
/their /armed /staves /in /charge, /their 4.01.118
/staves /in /charge, /their /beavers /down, 4.01.118
/their /eyes /of /fire /sparkling /through 4.01.119
/he /down /himself /and /all /their /lives 4.01.125
/and /all /their /prayers /and /love | /were 4.01.135
and /their wounded steeds | fret fetlock deep in H5 4.07. 78
/orgillous, /their /high /blood /chaf'd, | /have TRO pr 2
/to /the /port /of /athens /sent /their /ships pr 3
/that /wore | /their /crownets /regal, /from pr 6
/and /their /vow /is /made | /to /ransack /troy, pr 7
/there /disgorge | /their /warlike /fraughtage. pr 13
/greeks /do /pitch | /their /brave /pavilions. pr 15
ere /your grandsires had nails /on /their /toes, 2.01.105 P
/their /loving /well /compos'd /with /gift /of 4.04. 77
/as /begging /hermits /in /their /holy /prayers. TIT 3.02. 41
/their /endeavor /keeps /in /the /wonted /pace; HAM 2.02.338 P
/most /like, /if /their /means /are /no /better) 2.02.349 P
/their /writers /do /them /wrong, /to /make 2.02.350 P
/them /exclaim /against /their /own /succession? 2.02.351 P
and unwholesome in /their thoughts and whispers 4.05. 82
/with /eyeless /rage | /catch /in /their /fury, LR 3.01. 9
//belly–pinched /wolf | /keep /their /fur /dry, 3.01. 14
/at /point | /to /show /their /open /banner. 3.01. 34
/i'll /see /their /trial /first, /bring /in 3.06. 35
/trial /first, /bring /in /their /evidence. 3.06. 35
/the /heavens /do /not /their /visible /spirits 4.02. 46
/ere /they /have /done /their /mischief, 4.02. 55
/by /those /that /feel /their /sharpness. 5.03. 57

they give /their greeting to the citadel. OTH 2.01. 94
THEIR 2274 FR 0.2570 REL FR 1986 V 288 P
with colors fairer painted their foul ends. TMP 1.02.143
on their sustaining garments not a blemish, 1.02.218
with a charm join'd to their suff'red labor, | i 1.02.231
allaying both their fury and my passion | with 1.02.393
thy nerves are in their infancy again | and have 1.02.485
hold notwithstanding their freshness and glosses 2.01. 63 P
before with such a paragon to their queen. 2.01. 76 P
surges under him, | and ride upon their backs. 2.01.116
the bottom run | by their own fear or sloth. 2.01.228
mine eyes open'd, | i saw their weapons drawn. 2.01.320
way, and mount | their pricks at my footfall; 2.02. 12
and their labor | delight in them /sets off; 3.01. 1
th' harmony of their tongues hath into bondage 3.01. 41
their manners are more gentle, kind, than of 3.03. 32
since | they have left their viands behind; 3.03. 41
such men | whose heads stood in their breasts? 3.03. 47
valor men hang and drown | their proper selves. 3.03. 60
ministers | their several kinds have done. 3.03. 88
are all knit up | in their distractions. 3.03. 90
at a time, | i'll fight their legions o'er. 3.03.103
their great guilt | (like poison given to work a 3.03.104
may prosperous be, | and honor'd in their issue. 4.01.105
art | i have from their confines call'd to enact 4.01.121
the minute of their plot | is almost come. 4.01.141
smote the air | for breathing in their faces; 4.01.173
beat the ground | for kissing of their feet; 4.01.174
yet always bending | towards their project. 4.01.175
like unback'd colts, they prick'd their ears, 4.01.176
advanc'd their eyelids, lifted up their noses 4.01.177
lifted up their noses | as they smelt music. 4.01.177
so i charm'd their ears | that calf–like they my 4.01.178
and thorns, | which ent'red their frail shins. 4.01.181
that the foul lake | o'erstunk their feet. 4.01.184
charge my goblins that they grind their joints 4.01.258
shorten up their sinews | with aged cramps, and 4.01.259
a feeling | of their afflictions, and shall not 5.01. 22
one of their kind, that relish all as sharply 5.01. 23
though with their high wrongs i am strook to th' 5.01. 25
my charms i'll break, their senses i'll restore, 5.01. 31
at my command | have wak'd their sleepers, op'd, 5.01. 49
to work mine end upon their senses that | this 5.01. 53
so their rising senses | begin to chase the 5.01. 66
fumes that mantle | their clearer reason. 5.01. 68
their understanding | begins to swell, and the 5.01. 79
so much admire | that they devour their reason, 5.01.155
scarce think | their eyes do offices of truth, 5.01.156
of truth, their words | are natural breath; 5.01.156
please you repeat their names, i'll show my mind TGV 1.02. 7
they do not love that do not show their love. 1.02. 31
o, they love least that let men know their love. 1.02. 32
put forth their sons to seek preferment out: 1.03. 7
some to the wars, to try their fortune there; 1.03. 8
and to commend their service to his will. 1.03. 42
to seal our happiness with their consents! 1.03. 49
for it appears by their bare liveries that they 2.04. 45 P
as twenty seas, if all their sand were pearl, 2.04.170
if i lose them, thus find i by their loss — 2.06. 21
of their disguising and pretended flight, | who, 2.06. 37
dumb jewels often in their silent kind | more 3.01. 90
flatter and praise, commend, extol their graces; 3.01.102
o, could their master come and go as lightly, 3.01.142
while i, their king, that thither them importune 3.01.145
they should harbor where their lord should be." 3.01.149
that indeed know not their fathers, and 3.01.319 P
to their instruments | tune a deploring dump — 3.02. 83
hours, | unless it be to come before their time, 5.01. 5
time, | so much they spur their expedition. 5.01. 6
are my mates, that make their wills their law, 5.04. 14
are my mates, that make their wills their law, 5.04. 14
women to change their shapes than men their 5.04.109
to change their shapes than men their minds. 5.04.109
than men their minds? 5.04.110
and let them be recall'd from their exile; 5.04.155
dispose of them as thou know'st their deserts. 5.04.159
may give the dozen white luces in their coat. WIV 1.01. 16 P
host hath had the measuring of their weapons, 2.01.207 P
and lords, and gentlemen, with their coaches; 2.02. 64 P
what they think in their hearts they may effect, 2.02.307 P
they will break their hearts but they will 2.02.308 P
let them keep their limbs whole and hack our 3.01. 77 P
come, lay their swords to pawn. 3.01.110 P
break their talk, mistress quickly, my kinsman 3.04. 22 P
they mistook their erection. 3.05. 40 P
were call'd forth by their mistress to carry me 3.05. 98 P
they took me on their shoulders; 3.05.100 P
met the jealous knave their master in the door, 3.05.101 P
once or twice what they had in their basket. 3.05.102 P
clothes that fretted in their own grease. 3.05.114 P
him and the rest of their company from their 4.02. 34 P
and the rest of their company from their sport, 4.02. 35 P
always use to discharge their birding–pieces. 4.02. 58 P
if they can find in their hearts the poor 4.02.217 P
and three or four more of their growth, we'll 4.04. 49
with rounds of waxen tapers on their heads, 4.04. 51
on their heads, | and rattles in their hands. 4.04. 52
upon their sight, | we two in great amazedness 4.04. 55
in their so sacred paths he dares to tread | in 4.04. 60
him sound, | and burn him with their tapers. 4.04. 63
i will teach the children their behaviors; 4.04. 67 P
would whip me with their fine wits till i were 4.05. 99 P
i have suffer'd more for their sakes — more 4.05.108 P
while other sports are tasking of their minds, 4.06. 30
against such lewdsters and their lechery | those 5.03. 21
no man their works must eye. 5.05. 48
but those as sleep and think not on their sins, 5.05. 53
fairies use flow'rs for their charactery. 5.05. 73
but do not like to stage me to their eyes; MM 1.01. 68
well | their loud applause and aves vehement; 1.01. 70
captain and all the rest from their functions; 1.02. 13 P
like rats that ravin down their proper bane, | a 1.02.129
only to stick it in their children's sight | for 1.03. 25
when evil deeds have their permissive pass, 1.03. 38
as school–maids change their names | by vain 1.04. 47
all their petitions are as freely theirs | as 1.04. 82
make it | their perch and not their terror. 2.01. 4
make it | their perch and not their terror. 2.01. 4
do nothing but use their abuses in common houses 2.01. 42 P
thieves for their robbery have authority | when 2.02.175
to make me know | the nature of their crimes, 2.03. 7
to a well–wish'd king | quit their own part, and 2.04. 28
where their untaught love | must needs appear 2.04. 29
their saucy sweetness that do coin heaven's 2.04. 45
men their creation mar | in profiting by them. 2.04.127
bidding the law make curtsy to their will, 2.04.175
from their abominable and beastly touches | i 3.02. 24
make thee the father of their idle dream | and 4.01. 63
idle dream | and rack thee in their fancies. 4.01. 64
at the gates, | there to give up their pow'r. 4.03.132
they should exhibit their petitions in the 4.04. 10 P
who, wanting guilders to redeem their lives, ERR 1.01. 8
seal'd his rigorous statutes with their bloods, 1.01. 9
those, for their parents were exceeding poor, 1.01. 56
and, knowing whom it was their hap to save, 1.01.113
healthful welcome to their shipwrack'd guests, 1.01.114
and would have reft the fishers of their prey, 1.01.115
had not their /bark been very slow of sail; 1.01.116
therefore homeward did they bend their course. 1.01.117
time is their master, and when they see time, 2.01. 8
why should their liberty than ours be more? 2.01. 10
because their business still lies out a' door. 2.01. 11
are their males' subjects and at their controls: 2.01. 19
are their males' subjects and at their controls: 2.01. 19
are masters to their females, and their lords: 2.01. 24
are masters to their females, and their lords: 2.01. 24
then let your will attend on their accords. 2.01. 25
do their gay vestments his affections bait? 2.01. 94
declining their rich aspect to the hot breath of 3.02.135 P
stay for nought at all | but for their owner, 4.01. 92
for servants must their masters' minds fulfill. 4.01.113
me | as if i were their well–acquainted friend, 4.03. 2
i know it by their pale and deadly looks. 4.04. 93
who give their eyes the liberty of gazing? 5.01. 53
to the citizens | by rushing in their houses, 5.01.143
both, | and you the calendars of their nativity, 5.01.405
will you walk in to see their gossiping? 5.01.420
as being a profess'd tyrant to their sex? ADO 1.01.169 P
war–thoughts | have left their places vacant, in 1.01.302
vacant, in their rooms | come thronging soft and 1.01.302
their cheer is the greater that i am subdu'd. 1.03. 71 P
all hearts in love use their own tongues. 2.01.177
if their singing answer your saying, by my faith 2.01.234 P
i will presently go learn their day of marriage. 2.02. 56 P
it seems her affections have their full bent. 2.03.223 P
are they that hear their detractions and can put 2.03.229 P
that advance their pride | against that power 3.01. 10
have by this play'd their parts with beatrice, 3.02. 77 P
well, give them their charge, neighbor dogberry. 3.03. 7 P
i, but god send every one their heart's desire! 3.04. 60 P
take their examination yourself, and bring it me 3.05. 49 P
and you shall recount their particular duties 4.01. 2 P
honor, | and if their wisdoms be misled in this, 4.01.187
call forth the watch that are their accusers. 4.02. 35 P
i will go before and show him their examination. 4.02. 65 P
their counsel turns to passion, which before 5.01. 23
how they might hurt their enemies — if they 5.01. 98
so, though very many have been beside their wit. 5.01.128 P
you break jests as braggards do their blades, 5.01.187 P
hearken after their offense, my lord. 5.01.212 P
thirdly, i ask thee what's their offense; 5.01.221 P
and, to conclude, what you lay to their charge. 5.01.223 P
let fame, that all hunt after in their lives, LLL 1.01. 1
i can but say their protestation over: 1.01. 33
have no more profit of their shining nights 1.01. 90
wrong | have chose as umpeer of their mutiny. 1.01.169
for prisoners to be too silent in their words, 1.02.164 P
all his behaviors did make their retire | to the 2.01.234
all senses to that sense did make their repair, 2.01.240
tend'ring their own worth from where they were 2.01.244
when they strive to be | lords o'er their lords? 4.01. 38
for their sons are well tutor'd by you, and 4.02. 74 P
and their daughters profit very greatly under 4.02. 75 P
mehercle, if their sons be /ingenious, they 4.02. 78 P
if their daughters be capable, i will put it to 4.02. 79 P
away, the gentles are at their game, and we will 4.02.166 P
when their fresh rays have smote | the night of 4.03. 27
and ethiops of their sweet complexion crack. 4.03.264
for fear their colors should be wash'd away. 4.03.267
scarce show a harvest of their heavy toil; 4.03.323
above their functions and their offices. 4.03.329
above their functions and their offices. 4.03.329
some entertainment for them in their tents. 4.03.370
are they | that charge their breath against us? 5.02. 88
their herald is a pretty knavish page, | that 5.02. 97
making the bold wag by their praises bolder. 5.02.108
to check their folly, passion's solemn tears. 5.02.118
their purpose is to parley, to court, and dance, 5.02.122
their several counsels they unbosom shall | to 5.02.141
nor to their penn'd speech render we no grace, 5.02.147
of the fairest dames | that ever turn'd their — 5.02.161
their "eyes," villain, their "eyes." 5.02.162 P
their "eyes," villain, their "eyes." 5.02.162 P
"that /ever turn'd their eyes to mortal views! 5.02.163
know their minds, boyet. 5.02.175
that some plain man recount their purposes. 5.02.177
so sensible | seemeth their conference, their 5.02.260
their conceits have wings | fleeter than arrows, 5.02.260
or ever but in vizards show their faces? 5.02.271
they will again be here | in their own shapes; 5.02.288
fair ladies mask'd are roses in their bud; 5.02.295
dismask'd, their damask sweet commixture shown, 5.02.296
do, | if they return in their own shapes to woo? 5.02.299
their shallow shows and prologue vildly penn'd, 5.02.305
and their rough carriage so ridiculous, | should 5.02.306
they are infected, in their hearts it lies; 5.02.420
their form confounded makes most form in mirth, 5.02.519
great things laboring perish in their birth. 5.02.520
these four worthies in their first show thrive, 5.02.538
a–coming will speak their mind in some other 5.02.585 P
therefore met your loves | in their own fashion, 5.02.784
with the clamors of their own dear groans, 5.02.864
daws, | and maidens bleach their summer smocks, 5.02.906
thrice blessed they that master so their blood MND 1.01. 74
emptying our bosoms of their counsel /sweet, 1.01.216
if i do it, let the audience look to their eyes. 1.02. 26 P
you should fright the ladies out of their wits, 1.02. 80 P
be, | in their gold coats spots you see: 2.01. 11
favors, | in those freckles live their savors. 2.01. 13
that all their elves for fear | creep into 2.01. 30
mislead night–wanderers, laughing at their harm? 2.01. 39
you do their work, and they shall have good luck 2.01. 41
then the whole quire hold their hips and loff, 2.01. 55
and waxen in their mirth, and neeze, and swear 2.01. 56
you come | to give their bed joy and prosperity. 2.01. 73
that they have overborne their continents. 2.01. 92
the human mortals want their winter here; 2.01.101
angry winter, change | their wonted liveries; 2.01.113
by their increase, now knows not which is which. 2.01.114
we are their parents and original. 2.01.117
and certain stars shot madly from their spheres, 2.01.153
and i will overhear their conference. 2.01.187
some war with rere–mice for their leathren wings 2.02. 4
things growing are not ripe until their season, 2.02.117
i see their knavery. 3.01.120 P
and for night–tapers crop their waxen thighs 3.01.169
sort, | who pyramus presented, in their sport, 3.02. 14
their sense thus weak, lost with their fears 3.02. 27
thus weak, lost with their fears thus strong, 3.02. 27
for briers and thorns at their apparel snatch; 3.02. 29
shall we their fond pageant see? 3.02.114
so born, | in their nativity all truth appears. 3.02.125
sort, | as this their jangling i esteem a sport. 3.02.353
till o'er their brows death–counterfeiting sleep 3.02.364
burial, | already to their wormy beds are gone. 3.02.384
for fear lest day should look their shames upon, 3.02.385
like tears that did their own disgrace bewail. 4.01. 56
and their heads are hung | with ears that sweep 4.01.120
i wonder of their being here together. 4.01.131
go, bid the huntsmen wake them with their horns. 4.01.138
my lord, fair helen told me of their stealth, 4.01.160
of this their purpose hither to this wood, | and 4.01.161
and all their minds transfigur'd so together, 5.01. 24
tearing the thracian singer in their rage." 5.01. 49
which never labor'd in their minds till now; 5.01. 73
and now have toiled their unbreathed memories 5.01. 74
unless you can find sport in their intents, 5.01. 79
throttle their practic'd accent in their fears, 5.01. 97
throttle their practic'd accent in their fears, 5.01. 97
and, by their show, | you shall know all, that 5.01.116
you, the wall is down that parted their fathers. 5.01.352 P
nature's hand | shall not in their issue stand; 5.01.410
in nativity, | shall upon their children be. 5.01.414
as they fly by them with their woven wings. MV 1.01. 14
some that will evermore peep through their eyes, 1.01. 52
that they'll not show their teeth in way of 1.01. 55
hearing them, would call their brothers fools. 1.01. 99
virtuous, and holy men at their death have good 1.02. 28 P
have acquainted me with their determinations, 1.02.101 P
which is indeed to return to their home, and to 1.02.102 P
seek for you, madam, to take their leave; 1.02.124 P
and in their ship i am sure lorenzo is not. 2.08. 3
they have the wisdom by their wit to lose. 2.09. 81
puts bars between the owners and their rights! 3.02. 19
sand, wear yet upon their chins | the beards of 3.02. 84
sings i' th' nose, | cannot contain their urine: 4.01. 50
to wag their high tops and to make no noise 4.01. 76
let their beds | be made as soft as yours, and 4.01. 95
and let their palates | be season'd with such 4.01. 96
that 'scuse serves many men to save their gifts, 4.01.444
soul, let's in, and there expect their coming. 5.01. 49
which is the hot condition of their blood, | if 5.01. 74
sound, | or any air of music touch their ears, 5.01. 76
their savage eyes turn'd to a modest gaze, | by 5.01. 78
are | to their right praise and true perfection! 5.01.108
a messenger before, | to signify their coming. 5.01.118
besides that they are fair with their feeding, AYL 1.01. 12 P
their feeding, they are taught their manage, and 1.01. 13 P
being ever from their cradles bred together, 1.01.108 P
he will put on us, as pigeons feed their young. 1.02. 94 P
with bills on their necks, "be it known unto all 1.02.123 P
lie, the poor old man, their father, making such 1.02.130 P
if their purgation did consist in words, | they 1.03. 53
have | that do outface it with their semblances. 1.03.122
should in their own confines with forked heads 2.01. 24
forked heads | have their round haunches gor'd. 2.01. 25
that their discharge did stretch his leathern 2.01. 37
in their assign'd and native dwelling–place. 2.01. 63
found the bed untreasur'd of their mistress. 2.02. 7
gone, | that youth is surely in their company. 2.02. 16
of men | their graces serve them but as enemies? 2.03. 11
and having that do choke their service up | even 2.03. 61
at seventeen years many their fortunes seek, 2.03. 73
nay, i care not for their names, they owe me 2.05. 21 P
they have their exits and their entrances, | and 2.07.141
they have their exits and their entrances, | and 2.07.141
and in their barks my thoughts i'll character, 3.02. 6
our ewes, and their fells you know are greasy. 3.02. 54 P
trees with writing love–songs in their barks. 3.02.260 P
he hath generally tax'd their whole sex withal. 3.02.350 P
plants with carving "rosalind" on their barks; 3.02.361 P
women still give the lie to their consciences. 3.02.391 P
say | i'll prove a busy actor in their play. 3.04. 59
who shut their coward gates on atomies, | should 3.05. 13
words, blacker in their effect | than in their 4.03. 35
in their effect | than in their countenance. 4.03. 36
and all their lands restor'd to /them again 5.04.164
according to the measure of their states. 5.04.175
observ'd in noble ladies | unto their lords, by SHR in.1. 112
their harness studded all with gold and pearl. in.2. 42
their love is not so great, hortensio, but we 1.01.106 P
to seek their fortunes farther than at home, 1.02. 51
how the young folks lay their heads together! 1.02.139 P
if you accept them, then their worth is great. 2.01.101
and tell them both, | these are their tutors. 2.01.110
they do consume the thing that feeds their fury. 2.01.133
fathers commonly | do get their children; 2.01.410
swept, the servingmen in their new fustian, 4.01. 47 P
out of their saddles into the dirt, and thereby 4.01. 57 P
let their heads be slickly comb'd, their blue 4.01. 90 P
be slickly comb'd, their blue coats brush'd, and 4.01. 91 P
and their garters of an indifferent knit; 4.01. 92 P
let them curtsy with their left legs and not 4.01. 93 P
master's horse–tail till they kiss their hands. 4.01. 94 P

kindness in women, not their beauteous looks, 4.02. 41
or both dissemble deeply their affections; 4.04. 42
me them soundly forth unto their husbands. 5.02.104
add | unto their losses twenty thousand crowns, 5.02.113
what duty they do owe their lords and husbands. 5.02.131
AWW in her they are the better for their simpleness; 1.01. 44 P
to those | that weigh their pains in sense, and 1.01.225
till their own scorn return to them unnoted 1.02. 34
ere they can hide their levity in honor. 1.02. 35
and bow'd his eminent top to their low ranks, 1.02. 43
his humility, | in their poor praise he humbled. 1.02. 45
judgments are | mere fathers of their garments; 1.02. 62
constancies | expire before their fashions." 1.02. 63
and sickness | debate it at their leisure. 1.02. 75
howsome'er their hearts are sever'd in religion, 1.03. 53 P
sever'd in religion, their heads are both one: 1.03. 53 P
put such difference betwixt their two estates; 1.03.112 P
behaviors | that in their kind they speak it. 1.03.179
embowell'd of their doctrine, have left off 1.03.241
proffers not took reap thanks for their reward. 2.01.147
bring | their fiery torcher his diurnal ring, 2.01.162
have kept of them tame, and know their natures. 2.05. 46 P
that surfeit on their ease, will day by day 3.01. 18
that he has taken their great'st commander, and 3.05. 5 P
you may know by their trumpets. 3.05. 9 P
their promises, enticements, oaths, tokens, and 3.05. 18 P
camp i'll show, | their force, their purposes; 4.01. 85
camp i'll show, | their force, their purposes; 4.01. 85
till they attain to their abhorr'd ends; 4.03. 23 P
dare not shake the snow from off their cassocks, 4.03.168 P
which are their own right by the law of nature. 4.05. 61 P
not knowing them until we know their grave. 5.03. 62
destroy our friends and after weep their dust; 5.03. 64
at that time that i knew of their going to bed, 5.03.263 P
TN let them hang themselves in their own straps. 1.03. 13 P
that are fools, let them use their talents. 1.05. 15 P
in women's waxen hearts to set their forms! 2.02. 30
free maids that weave their thread with bones, 2.04. 45
that their business might be every thing and 2.04. 76 P
be every thing and their intent every where, for 2.04. 77 P
alas, their love may be call'd appetite, | no 2.04. 97
thy fates open their hands, let thy blood and 2.05.147 P
he must observe their mood on whom he jests, 3.01. 62
wise /men, folly–fall'n, quite taint their wit. 3.01. 68
purposely on others, to taste their valor. 3.04.244 P
more puzzled than the egyptians in their fog. 4.02. 44 P
take and give back affairs and their dispatch 4.03. 18
foolish boldness brought thee to their mercies 5.01. 70
'gainst knaves and thieves men shut their gate, 5.01.395
WT they were train'd together in their childhoods; 1.01. 22 P
since their more mature dignities and royal 1.01. 25 P
necessities made separation of their society, 1.01. 26 P
separation of their society, their encounters 1.01. 26 P
the heavens continue their loves! 1.01. 32 P
was born desire yet their life to see him a man. 1.01. 40 P
gates open'd, | as mine, against their will. 1.02.198
eyes | to see alike mine honor as their profits 1.02.310
their profits | (their own particular thrifts), 1.02.311
star in heaven and | by all their influences, 1.02.426
never | saw i men scour so on their way. 2.01. 35
i ey'd them | even to their ships. 2.01. 36
ay, and privy | to this their late escape. 2.01. 95
added to their familiarity | (which was as gross 2.01.175
make their pastime at my sorrow: 2.03. 24
casting their savageness aside, have done | like 2.03.188
sir, their speed | hath been beyond accompt. 2.03.197
counsel and aid them, for their better safety, 3.02. 20 P
deserv'd | all tongues to talk their bitt'rest. 3.02.216
them shall | the causes of their death appear 3.02.237
their sacred wills be done! 3.03. 7
no less unhappy, their issue not being gracious, 4.02. 27 P
them when they have approv'd their virtues. 4.02. 28 P
themselves | (humbling their deities to love) 4.04. 26
their transformations | were never for a piece 4.04. 31
there is an art which in their piedness shares 4.04. 87
stomachers | for my lads to give their dears; 4.04.225
will they wear their plackets where they should 4.04.243 P
plackets where they should bear their faces? 4.04.243 P
one three of them, by their own report, sir, 4.04.337 P
to her service, | or to their own perdition. 4.04.378
who | do their best office, if they can but stay 4.04.571
herd to me that all their other senses stuck in 4.04.608 P
i pick'd and cut most of their festival purses; 4.04.614 P
be smil'd at, their offenses being so capital? 4.04.792 P
will have fulfill'd their secret purposes; 5.01. 36
be contrary, | oppose against their wills. 5.01. 46
was not full a month | between their births. 5.01.118
having both their country quitted | with this 5.01.192
on one another, to tear the cases of their eyes. 5.02. 12 P
there was speech in their dumbness, language in 5.02. 13 P
their dumbness, language in their very gesture; 5.02. 14 P
leave of them, for their joy waded in tears. 5.02. 46 P
the same instant of their master's death and in 5.02. 69 P
appearing in the blossoms of their fortune. 5.02.125 P
JN some sins do bear their privilege on earth, 1.01.261
he that perforce robs lions of their hearts 1.01.268
shadowing their right under your wings of war. 2.01. 14
peace of heaven is theirs that lift their swords 2.01. 35
have sold their fortunes at their native homes, 2.01. 69
have sold their fortunes at their native homes, 2.01. 69
bearing their birthrights proudly on their backs 2.01. 70
their birthrights proudly on their backs, | to 2.01. 70
the interruption of their churlish drums | cuts 2.01. 76
their proud contempt that beats his peace to 2.01. 88
the cannons have their bowels full of wrath, 2.01.210
their iron indignation 'gainst your walls; 2.01.212
by the compulsion of their ordinance | by this 2.01.218
by this time from their fixed beds of lime | had 2.01.219
though all these english and their discipline 2.01.261
were harbor'd in their rude circumference. 2.01.262
to verify our title with their lives. 2.01.277
souls | that to their everlasting residence, 2.01.284
their armors, that march'd hence so 2.01.315
dy'd in the dying slaughter of their foes. 2.01.323
and stand securely on their battlements | as in 2.01.374
their battering cannon charged to the mouths, 2.01.382
till their soul–fearing clamors have brawl'd 2.01.383
shall rain their drift of bullets on this town. 2.01.412
urge them while their souls | are capable of 2.01.475
pray that their burthens may not fall this day, 3.01. 90
lest that their hopes prodigiously be cross'd; 3.01. 91
but in despair die under their black weight. 3.01.297
and in their rage, i having hold of both, | they 3.01.329
and strain their cheeks to idle merriment — | a 3.03. 46
i tore them from their bonds, and cried aloud, 3.04. 70
as they have given these hairs their liberty!" 3.04. 72
but now i envy at their liberty, | and will 3.04. 73
and will again commit them to their bonds, 3.04. 74
on their departure most of all show evil. 3.04.115
of all his people, and freeze up their zeal, 3.04.150
to train ten thousand english to their side, 3.04.175
what may be wrought out of their discontent, 3.04.179
now that their souls are topful of offense. 3.04.180
should use to do me wrong | deny their office; 4.01.118
they do confound their skill in covetousness, 4.02. 29
to sound the purposes of all their hearts, 4.02. 48
myself and them | bend their best studies — 4.02. 51
go | and thrust thyself into their companies; 4.02.167
i have a way to win their loves again. 4.02.168
young arthur's death is common in their mouths, 4.02.187
when they talk of him, they shake their heads, 4.02.188
by slaves that take their humors for a warrant 4.02.209
throw this report on their incensed rage, | and 4.02.261
rage, | and make them tame to their obedience! 4.02.262
to stop their marches 'fore we are inflam'd. 5.01. 7
go i to make the french lay down their arms. 5.01. 24
that borrow their behaviors from the great, 5.01. 51
as i have bank'd their towns? 5.02.104
their thimbles into armed gauntlets change, 5.02.156
their needl's to lances, and their gentle hearts 5.02.157
and their gentle hearts | to fierce and bloody 5.02.157
when english measure backward their own ground 5.05. 3
and brought prince henry in their company, | at 5.06. 34
in their continuance will not feel themselves. 5.07. 14
in their throng and press to that last hold, 5.07. 19
sings | his soul and body to their lasting rest. 5.07. 24
nor let my kingdom's rivers take their course 5.07. 38
R2 from false mowbray their first head and spring. 1.01. 97
let them lay by their helmets and their spears, 1.03.119
let them lay by their helmets and their spears, 1.03.119
and both return back to their chairs again. 1.03.120
can change their moons and bring their times 1.03.220
change their moons and bring their times about, 1.03.220
how he did seem to dive into their hearts | with 1.04. 25
as 'twere to banish their affects with him. 1.04. 30
for their advantage and your highness' loss. 1.04. 41
breathe truth that breathe their words in pain. 2.01. 8
are men's ends mark'd than their lives before. 2.01. 11
fear'd by their breed, and famous by their birth 2.01. 52
by their breed, and famous by their birth, 2.01. 52
renowned for their deeds as far from home, | for 2.01. 53
can sick men play so nicely with their names? 2.01. 84
that their events can never fall out good. 2.01.214
grievous taxes, | and quite lost their hearts; 2.01.247
ancient quarrels, and quite lost their hearts. 2.01.248
with all their powerful friends, are fled to him 2.02. 55
commons, for their love | lies in their purses, 2.02.129
for their love | lies in their purses, and whoso 2.02.130
by so much fills their hearts with deadly hate. 2.02.131
weary lords | shall make their way seem short, 2.03. 17
is held | by bushy, bagot, and their complices, 2.03.165
as well assured richard their king is dead. 2.04. 17
rebels wound thee with their horses' hoofs. 3.02. 7
and heavy–gaited toads lie in their way, | doing 3.02. 15
of night being pluck'd from off their backs, 3.02. 45
they break their faith to god as well as us. 3.02.101
which makes the silver rivers drown their shores 3.02.107
have arm'd their thin and hairless scalps 3.02.112
and clap their female joints | in stiff unwieldy 3.02.114
thy very beadsmen learn to bend their bows | of 3.02.116
if we prevail, their heads shall pay for it. 3.02.126
make war upon their spotted souls for this! 3.02.134
again uncurse their souls, their peace is made 3.02.137
their souls, their peace is made | with heads, 3.02.137
ay, all of them at bristow lost their heads. 3.02.142
some poisoned by their wives, some sleeping 3.02.159
my lord, wise men ne'er sit and wail their woes, 3.02.178
and oppose not myself | against their will. 3.03. 19
when their thund'ring shock | at meeting tears 3.03. 56
to pay their aweful duty to our presence? 3.03. 76
have torn their souls by turning them from us, 3.03. 83
lend friends, and friends their helpful swords. 3.03.132
may hourly trample on their sovereign's head; 3.03.157
two kinsmen digg'd their graves with weeping 3.03.169
tears show their love, but want their remedies. 3.03.203
tears show their love, but want their remedies. 3.03.203
which like unruly children make their sire 3.04. 30
stoop with oppression of their prodigal weight; 3.04. 31
to bear and he to taste | their fruits of duty. 3.04. 63
their fortunes both are weigh'd. 3.04. 84
ere thou bid good night, to quite their griefs, 5.01. 43
and send the hearers weeping to their beds. 5.01. 45
through casements darted their desiring eyes 5.02. 14
and interchangeably set down their hands, | to 5.02. 98
as thriftless sons their scraping fathers' gold. 5.03. 69
and, for they cannot, die in their own pride. 5.05. 22
who, sitting in the stocks, refuge their shame, 5.05. 26
bearing their own misfortunes on the back | of 5.05. 29
they jar | their watches on unto mine eyes, the 5.05. 52
for though it have holp mad men to their wits, 5.05. 62
the manner of their taking may appear | at large 5.06. 9
1H4 whose arms were moulded in their mother's womb, 1.01. 23
as by discharge of their artillery | and shape 1.01. 57
and pride of their contention did take horse, 1.01. 60
balk'd in their own blood, did sir walter see 1.01. 69
who then, affrighted with their bloody looks, 1.03.104
deliver them up without their ransom straight, 1.03.260
into) for their own credit sake make all whole. 2.01. 72 P
for they pray continually to their saint, the 2.01. 80 P
up and down on her, and make her their boots. 2.01. 82 P
what, the commonwealth their boots? 2.01. 83 P
have i not all their letters to meet me in arms 2.03. 27 P
such as we see when men restrain their breath 2.03. 61
and can call them all by their christen names, 2.04. 8 P
they take it already upon their salvation, that 2.04. 9 P
more ado but took all their seven points in my 2.04.201 P
their points being broken — 2.04.214 P
down fell their hose. 2.04.215 P
these lies are like their father that begets 2.04.225 P
bound them, and were masters of their wealth. 2.04.254 P
both which i have had, but their date is out, 2.04.503 P
and hold their level with thy princely heart? 3.02. 17
that men would tell their children, "this is he" 3.02. 48
loud shouts and salutations from their mouths, 3.02. 53
had his great name profaned with their scorns, 3.02. 64
but rather drows'd and hung their eyelids down, 3.02. 81
aspect | as cloudy men use to their adversaries, 3.02. 83
receive | money and order for their furniture. 3.03.202
they come like sacrifices in their trim, | and 4.01.113
with hearts in their bellies no bigger than 4.02. 21 P
heads, and they have bought out their services; 4.02. 22 P
rooms of them as have bought out their services, 4.02. 33 P
faith, for their poverty, i know not where they 4.02. 70 P
not where they had that, and for their bareness, 4.02. 71 P
and now their pride and mettle is asleep, 4.03. 22
their courage with hard labor tame and dull, 4.03. 23
gifts before him, proffer'd him their oaths, 4.03. 71
gave him their heirs as pages, followed him 4.03. 72
my good lord, | i guess their tenor. 4.04. 7
wait on us, | and they shall do their office. 5.01.112
for, on their answer, will we set on them, | and 5.01.119
two stars keep not their motion in one sphere, 5.04. 65
reward valor bear the sin upon their own heads. 5.04.150 P
2H4 stopping my greedy ear with their bold deeds, 1.01. 78
to this weight such lightness with their fear 1.01.122
that arrows fled not swifter toward their aim 1.01.123
than did our soldiers, aiming at their safety, 1.01.124
the shame | of those that turn'd their backs, 1.01.130
and bunches of keys at their girdles, and if a 1.02. 39 P
so, their fathers being so sick as yours at this 2.02. 30 P
for they never prick their finger but they say, 2.02.112 P
have of their puissance made a little taste. 2.03. 52
you out for taking their names upon you before 2.04.143 P
because their legs are both of a bigness, and 'a 2.04.244 P
hair will turn scales between their haberdepois. 2.04.254 P
curling their monstrous heads and hanging them 3.01. 23
who in their seeds | and weak beginning lie 3.01. 84
their cold intent, tenure, and substance thus: 4.01. 9
hazard | and fearful meeting of their opposite. 4.01. 16
i judge their number | upon or near the rate of 4.01. 21
how far forth you do like their articles. 4.02. 53
your powers unto their several counties, | as we 4.02. 61
that all their eyes may bear those tokens home 4.02. 64
they know their duties. 4.02.101
steers unyok'd, they take their courses | east, 4.02.103
for thin drink doth so over–cool their blood, 4.03. 91 P
petty spirits muster me all to their captain, 4.03.111 P
in, | that the united vessel of their blood, 4.04. 44
and their memory | shall as a pattern or a 4.04. 75
the seasons change their manners, as the year 4.04.123
fathers | have broke their sleep with thoughts, 4.05. 68
sleep with thoughts, their brains with care, 4.05. 68
brains with care, | their bones with industry; 4.05. 69
their sons with arts and martial exercises; 4.05. 73
to upbraid | my gain of it by their assistances, 4.05.193
have but their stings and teeth newly ta'en out; 4.05.205
their spirits are so married in conjunction with 5.01. 68 P
with the imputation of being near their master; 5.01. 73 P
therefore let men take heed of their company. 5.01. 77 P
how many nobles then should hold their places, 5.02. 17
but all are banish'd till their conversations 5.05.100
H5 printing their proud hoofs i' th' receiving pr 27
health | shall drop their blood in approbation 1.02. 19
yet their own authors faithfully affirm | that 1.02. 43
for some dishonest manners of their life, 1.02. 49
besides, their writers say, | king pepin, which 1.02. 64
a net | than amply to imbar their crooked titles 1.02. 94
with half their forces the full pride of france, 1.02.112
and with your puissant arm renew their feats. 1.02.116
you are their heir, you sit upon their throne; 1.02.117
you are their heir, you sit upon their throne; 1.02.117
hearts have left their bodies here in england, 1.02.128
o, let their bodies follow, my dear liege, 1.02.130
others, like soldiers, armed in their stings, 1.02.193
bring home | to the tent–royal of their emperor; 1.02.196
in | their heavy burthens at his narrow gate, 1.02.201
this his mock mock out of their dear husbands; 1.02.285
mock mothers from their sons, mock castles down; 1.02.286
shake in their fear, and with pale policy | seek 2.pr. 14
and by their hands this grace of kings must die, 2.pr. 28
die, | if hell and treason hold their promises, 2.pr. 29
and they may have their throats about them at 2.01. 21 P
by the prick of their needles but it will be 2.01. 34 P
is an oath, and oaths must have their course. 2.01.101
as if allegiance in their bosoms sate | crowned 2.02. 4
us | will cut their passage through the force of 2.02. 16
enemies | have steep'd their galls in honey, and 2.02. 30
in their dear care | and tender preservation of 2.02. 58
their cheeks are paper. 2.02. 74
as dogs upon their masters, worrying you. 2.02. 83
their faults are open, | arrest them to the 2.02.142
law, | and god acquit them of their practices! 2.02.144
with what great state he heard their embassy, 2.04. 32
most spend their mouths when what they seem to 2.04. 70
behold the ordinance on their carriages, | with 3.pr. 26
and sheath'd their swords for lack of argument. 3.01. 21
with men's pockets as their gloves or their 3.02. 48 P
pockets as their gloves or their handkerchers; 3.02. 48 P
their villainy goes against my weak stomach, and 3.02. 52 P
upon th' enraged soldiers in their spoil, | as 3.03. 25
and their most reverend heads dash'd to the 3.03. 37
whiles the mad mothers with their howls confus'd 3.03. 39
into the clouds | and overlook their grafters? 3.05. 9
is not their climate foggy, raw, and dull, | on 3.05. 16
looks pale, | killing their fruit with frowns? 3.05. 18
drench for sur–rein'd jades, their barley–broth, 3.05. 19
decoct their cold blood to such valiant heat? 3.05. 20
poor we call them in their native lords! 3.05. 26
give | their bodies to the lust of english youth 3.05. 30
his soldiers sick and famish'd in their march; 3.05. 57
to lay apart their particular functions and 3.07. 38 P
for if their heads had any intellectual armor, 3.07.137 P
their mastiffs are of unmatchable courage. 3.07.141 P

a russian bear and have their heads crush'd like 3.07.144 P
coming on, leaving their wits with their wives; 3.07.149 P
coming on, leaving their wits with their wives; 3.07.149 P
and through their paly flames | each battle sees 4.pr. 8
proud of their numbers and secure in soul, | the 4.pr. 17
by their watchful fires | sit patiently and inly 4.pr. 23
and their gesture sad, | investing lank–lean 4.pr. 25
minding true things by what their mock'ries be. 4.pr. 53
'tis good for men to love their present pains 4.01. 18
break up their drowsy grave, and newly move 4.01. 22
some upon their wives left poor behind them, 4.01.139 P
they owe, some upon their children rawly left. 4.01.141 P
of any thing, when blood is their argument? 4.01.143 P
for they purpose not their death when they 4.01.158 P
their death when they purpose their services. 4.01.158 P
some, making the wars their bulwark, that have 4.01.164 P
is the king guilty of their damnation than he 4.01.174 P
beat us, for they bear them on their shoulders; 4.01.227 P
opposed numbers | pluck their hearts from them. 4.01.292
who twice a day their wither'd hands hold up 4.01.299
mount them, and make incision in their hides, 4.02. 9
that their hot blood may spin in english eyes, 4.02. 10
how shall we then behold their natural tears? 4.02. 13
and your fair show shall suck away their souls, 4.02. 17
scarce blood enough in all their sickly veins 4.02. 20
yond island carrions, desperate of their bones, 4.02. 39
their ragged curtains poorly are let loose, 4.02. 41
big mars seems bankrout in their beggar'd host, 4.02. 43
candlesticks, | with torch–staves in their hand; 4.02. 46
and their poor jades | lob down their heads, 4.02. 46
and their poor jades | lob down their heads, 4.02. 47
the gum down–roping from their pale–dead eyes, 4.02. 48
and in their pale dull mouths the /gimmal'd bit 4.02. 49
and their executors, the knavish crows, | fly 4.02. 51
fly o'er them all, impatient for their hour. 4.02. 52
they have said their prayers, and they stay for 4.02. 56
and give their fasting horses provender, | and 4.02. 58
the king himself is rode to view their battle. 4.03. 2
be in their flowing cups freshly rememb'red. 4.03. 55
and hold their manhoods cheap whiles any speaks 4.03. 66
the french are bravely in their battles set, 4.03. 69
that their souls | may make a peaceful and a 4.03. 85
their poor bodies | must lie and fester. 4.03. 87
and those that leave their valiant bones in 4.03. 98
and draw their honors reeking up to heaven, 4.03.101
leaving their earthly parts to choke your clime, 4.03.102
the french have reinforc'd their scatter'd men. 4.06. 36
so do our vulgar drench their peasant limbs | in 4.07. 77
yerk out their armed heels at their dead masters 4.07. 80
out their armed heels at their dead masters, 4.07. 80
in safety, and dispose | of their dead bodies! 4.07. 83
did grow, wearing leeks in their monmouth caps, 4.07.100 P
the names of those their nobles that lie dead: 4.08. 91
which cannot in their huge and proper life | be 5.pr. 5
with the plebeians swarming at their heels, | go 5.pr. 27
go forth and fetch their conqu'ring caesar in; 5.pr. 28
against the french that met them in their bent 5.02. 16
looks we fairly hope | have lost their quality, 5.02. 19
defective in their natures, grow to wildness. 5.02. 55
blind, though they have their eyes, and then 5.02.309 P
all, | according to their firm proposed natures. 5.02.334
other's happiness, | may cease their hatred; 5.02.352
christian–like accord | in their sweet bosoms, 5.02.354
to make divorce of their incorporate league; 5.02.366
by starts the full course of their glory. ep 4
and, for their sake, | in your fair minds let ep 13
than midday sun fierce bent against their faces. 1H6 1.01. 14
when at their mothers' moist'ned eyes babes 1.01. 49
of eyes, | to weep their intermissive miseries. 1.01. 88
enclosed were they with their enemies. 1.01.136
whom all france with their chief assembled 1.01.139
four of their lords i'll change for one of ours. 1.01.151
they want their porridge and their fat 1.02. 9
want their porridge and their fat bull–beeves: 1.02. 9
and have their provender tied to their mouths, 1.02. 11
and have their provender tied to their mouths, 1.02. 11
food, | do rush upon us as their hungry prey. 1.02. 28
rather with their teeth | the walls they'll tear 1.02. 39
some odd gimmors or device | their arms are set, 1.02. 42
women are shrewd tempters with their tongues. 1.02.123
are from their hives and houses driven away. 1.05. 24
when others sleep upon their quiet beds, 2.01. 6
as fitting best to quittance their deceit 2.01. 14
let us resolve to scale their flinty bulwarks. 2.01. 27
the other yet may rise against their force. 2.01. 32
within their chiefest temple i'll erect | a tomb 2.02. 12
rous'd on the sudden from their drowsy beds, 2.02. 23
men | could not prevail with all their oratory, 2.02. 49
to give their censure of these rare reports. 2.03. 10
with his name the mothers still their babes? 2.03. 17
spent, | wax dim, as drawing to their exigent; 2.05. 9
heir, | i lost my liberty, and they their lives. 2.05. 81
as princes do their courts, when they are cloy'd 2.05.105
have fill'd their pockets full of pebble stones; 3.01. 80
that many have their giddy brains knock'd out; 3.01. 83
men | that come to gather money for their corn. 3.02. 5
poor market folks that come to sell their corn. 3.02. 15
they that of late were daring with their scoffs 3.02.113
their powers are marching unto paris–ward. 3.03. 30
and the rest will take thee in their arms. 3.03. 77
well | to bear with their perverse objections; 4.01.129
much less to take occasion from their mouths 4.01.130
how will their grudging stomachs be provok'd 4.01.141
this factious bandying of their favorites, | but 4.01.190
trumpeter, | summon their general unto the wall. 4.02. 2
if you forsake the offer of their love. 4.02. 14
our nation's terror and their bloody scourge! 4.02. 16
sacrament | to rive their dangerous artillery 4.02. 29
some light horsemen, and peruse their wings. 4.02. 43
with him and made their march for burdeaux. 4.03. 8
now they meet where both their lives are done. 4.03. 38
hew them to pieces, hack their bones asunder, 4.07. 47
give me their bodies, that i may bear them hence 4.07. 85
and give them burial as beseems their worth. 4.07. 86
go take their bodies hence. 4.07. 91
but from their ashes shall be rear'd | a phoenix 4.07. 92
i have, my lord, and their intent is this: 5.01. 3
how doth your grace affect their motion? 5.01. 7

so let them have their answers every one. 5.01. 25
to us, | else ruin combat with their palaces! 5.02. 7
repeat their semblance often on the seas, | that 5.03.193
and sold their bodies for their country's 5.04.106
sold their bodies for their country's benefit, 5.04.106
and therein reverenc'd for their lawful king. 5.04.140
so worthless peasants bargain for their wives, 5.05. 53
large sums of gold and dowries with their wives, 2H6 1.01.129
clapping their hands, and crying with loud voice 1.01.160
while these do labor for their own preferment, 1.01.181
'tis thine they give away, and not their own. 1.01.221
may make cheap pennyworths of their pillage 1.01.222
and smooth my way upon their headless necks; 1.02. 65
patience, good lady, wizards know their times. 1.04. 15
spirits walk, and ghosts break up their graves, 1.04. 19
lay hands upon these traitors and their trash. 1.04. 41
they know their master loves to be aloft, | and 2.01. 11
heaping confusion on their own heads thereby! 2.01.183
and call these foul offenders to their answers, 2.01.199
they in seeking that | shall find their deaths, 2.02. 76
giddy multitude do point | and nod their heads, 2.04. 22
nod their heads, and throw their eyes on thee! 2.04. 22
gloucester, hide thee from their hateful looks, 2.04. 23
and each of them had twenty times their power, 2.04. 61
i never robb'd the soldiers of their pay, | nor 3.01.108
and lowly words were ransom for their fault. 3.01.127
i know their complot is to have my life; 3.01.147
happy, | and prove the period of their tyranny, 3.01.149
but mine is made the prologue to their play; 3.01.151
will not conclude their plotted tragedy. 3.01.153
and given me notice of their villainies. 3.01.370
their touch affrights me as a serpent's sting. 3.02. 47
he that loos'd them forth their brazen caves, 3.02. 89
and would not dash me with their ragged sides, 3.02. 98
an angry hive of bees | that want their leader, 3.02.126
myself have calm'd their spleenful mutiny, 3.02.128
could send such message to their sovereign. 3.02.272
me, | i thank them for their tender loving care; 3.02.280
poison be their drink! 3.02.321
their sweetest shade a grove of cypress trees! 3.02.323
their chiefest prospect murd'ring basilisks! 3.02.324
their softest touch as smart as lizards' stings! 3.02.325
their music frightful as the serpent's hiss, 3.02.326
who with their drowsy, slow, and flagging wings 4.01. 5
graves, and from their misty jaws | breathe foul 4.01. 6
here shall they make their ransom on the sand, 4.01. 10
or with their blood stain this discolored shore. 4.01. 11
lord, and picardy | hath slain their governors, 4.01. 89
argo, their thread of life is spun. 4.02. 29 P
agree like brothers, and worship me their lord. 4.02. 75 P
may, even in their wives' and children's sight, 4.02.179
be hang'd up for example at their doors. 4.02.180
will parley with jack cade their general. 4.04. 13
call false caterpillars, and intend their death. 4.04. 37
the sight of me is odious in their eyes; 4.04. 46
the citizens fly and forsake their houses; 4.04. 50
men than thou go in their hose and doublets. 4.07. 50 P
and work in their shirt too, as myself, for 4.07. 52 P
and command that their wives be as free as heart 4.07.124 P
i see them lay their heads together to surprise 4.08. 58 P
and humbly thus, with halters on their necks, 4.09. 11
go to ward, | they'll pawn their swords /for my 5.01.113
shall be the surety for their traitor father. 5.01.116
the sons of york, thy betters in their birth, 5.01.119
shall be their father's bail, and bane to those 5.01.120
and here comes clifford to deny their bail. 5.01.123
sons, he says, shall give their words for him. 5.01.137
that with the very shaking of their chains 5.01.145
and manacle the bearard in their chains, | if 5.01.149
to quell the rebels and their complices. 5.01.212
whom angry heavens do make their minister, 5.02. 34
no more will i their babes. 5.02. 52
and we will live | to see their day, and them 5.02. 89
and they have troops of soldiers at their beck? 3H6 1.01. 68
and seiz'd upon their towns and provinces. 1.01.109
ay, and their colors, often borne in france, 1.01.127
as thou shalt reign but by their sufferance. 1.01.234
soldiers should have toss'd me on their pikes, 1.01.244
i hear their drums. 1.02. 69
ah, whither shall i fly to scape their hands? 1.03. 1
here, their lives and thine | were not revenge 1.03. 25
and hung their rotten coffins up in chains, | it 1.03. 28
and till i root out their accursed line, | and 1.03. 32
and i am faint, and cannot fly their fury; 1.04. 23
and were i strong, i would not shun their fury. 1.04. 24
desperate thieves, all hopeless of their lives, 1.04. 42
so triumph thieves upon their conquer'd booty, 1.04. 63
trull | upon their woes whom fortune captivates! 1.04.115
that beggars mounted run their horse to death. 1.04.127
that robb'd my soldiers of their heated spleen; 2.01.124
their weapons like to lightning came and went; 2.01.129
gently down, as if they struck their friends. 2.01.132
and of their feather many moe proud birds, 2.01.170
their power, i think, is thirty thousand strong. 2.01.177
as the rocks cheer them that fear their wrack: 2.02. 5
to whom do lions cast their gentle looks? 2.02. 11
not to the beast that would usurp their den. 2.02. 12
and doves will peck in safeguard of their brood. 2.02. 18
unreasonable creatures feed their young, | and 2.02. 26
and though man's face be fearful to their eyes, 2.02. 27
eyes, | yet, in protection of their tender ones, 2.02. 28
make war with him that climb'd unto their nest, 2.02. 31
offering their own lives in their young's 2.02. 32
their own lives in their young's defense? 2.02. 32
a thousand men have broke their fasts to–day 2.02.127
if thou deny, their blood upon thy head, | for 2.02.129
robb'd my strong–knit sinews of their strength, 2.03. 4
so, underneath the belly of their steeds, | that 2.03. 20
that stain'd their fetlocks in his smoking blood 2.03. 21
may plant courage in their quailing breasts, 2.03. 54
here's the heart that triumphs in their death, 2.04. 8
to shepherds looking on their silly sheep | than 2.05. 43
to kings that fear their subjects' treachery? 2.05. 45
no more words till they have flow'd their fill. 2.05. 72
whiles lions war and battle for their dens, 2.05. 74
dens, | poor harmless lambs abide their enmity. 2.05. 75
and bloody steel grasp'd in their ireful hands, 2.05.132
for at their hands i have deserv'd no pity. 2.06. 26

pity they should lose their father's lands. 3.02. 31
and all the unlook'd–for issue of their bodies 3.02.131
issue of their bodies | to take their rooms, ere 3.02.132
and with their helps only defend ourselves: 4.01. 45
my love, forbear to fawn upon their frowns. 4.01. 75
and their true sovereign whom they must obey? 4.01. 78
tell me their words as near as thou canst guess 4.01. 90
shall have wars, and pay for their presumption. 4.01.114
may challenge nothing of their sov'reigns, | but 4.06. 6
they quite forget their loss of liberty. 4.06. 15
i have not stopp'd mine ears to their demands, 4.08. 39
nor posted off their suits with slow delays; 4.08. 40
my pity hath been balm to heal their wounds, 4.08. 41
my mildness hath allay'd their swelling griefs, 4.08. 42
my mercy dried their water–flowing tears; 4.08. 43
i have not been desirous of their wealth, | nor 4.08. 44
and swell so much the higher by their ebb. 4.08. 56
have sold their lives unto the house of york, 5.01. 74
that they do hold their course toward tewksbury. 5.03. 19
lords, wise men ne'er sit and wail their loss, 5.04. 1
but cheerly seek how to redress their harms. 5.04. 2
and men ne'er spend their fury on a child. 5.05. 57
men for their sons, wives for their husbands, 5.06. 41
men for their sons, wives for their husbands, 5.06. 41
orphans for their parents' timeless death — 5.06. 42
and seek their ruin that usurp'd our right? 5.06. 73
have we mow'd down in tops of all their pride! 5.07. 4
ne'er spurr'd their coursers at the trumpet's 5.07. 9
that in their chains fetter'd the kingly lion, 5.07. 11
open their congeal'd mouths and bleed afresh! R3 1.02. 56
that laid their guilt upon my guiltless 1.02. 98
sham'd their aspects with store of childish 1.02.154
that all the standers–by had wet their cheeks 1.02.162
to both their deaths shalt thou be accessary. 1.02.191
their kingdom's loss, my woeful banishment, 1.03.192
and then hurl down their indignation | on thee, 1.03.219
death, and hell have set their marks on him, 1.03.292
on him, | and all their ministers attend on him. 1.03.293
princes have but their titles for their glories, 1.04. 78
princes have but their titles for their glories, 1.04. 78
so that between their titles and low name 1.04. 82
what lawful quest have given their verdict up 1.04.184
to hurl upon their heads that break his law. 1.04.200
why wither not the leaves that want their sap? 2.02. 42
all springs reduce their currents to mine eyes, 2.02. 68
their woes are parcell'd, mine is general. 2.02. 81
clouds are seen, wise men put on their cloaks; 2.03. 32
for me to joy and weep their gain and loss; 2.04. 59
your grace attended to their sug'red words, 3.01. 13
but look'd not on the poison of their hearts. 3.01. 14
hate, | i live to look upon their tragedy. 3.02. 59
jocund, and suppos'd their states were sure, 3.02. 84
they, for their truth, might better wear their 3.02. 92
might better wear their heads | than some that 3.02. 92
some that have accus'd them wear their hats. 3.02. 93
upon my body with their hellish charms? 3.04. 62
then be your eyes the witness of their evil. 3.04. 67
that by their witchcraft thus have marked me. 3.04. 72
and both are ready in their offices | at any 3.05. 10
which stretch'd unto their servants, daughters, 3.05. 82
i bid them that did love their country's good 3.07. 21
at lower end of the hall, hurl'd up their caps, 3.07. 35
and devout religious men | are at their beads, 3.07. 93
friends, | and by their vehement instigation, 3.07.139
o, make them joyful, grant their lawful suit! 3.07.203
call him again, sweet prince, accept their suit. 3.07.221
hath he set bounds between their love and me? 4.01. 20
i am their mother, who shall bar me from them? 4.01. 21
i am their father's mother, i will see them. 4.01. 22
their aunt i am in law, in love their mother; 4.01. 23
their aunt i am in law, in love their mother; 4.01. 23
then bring me to their sights. 4.01. 24
like /two children in their deaths' sad story. 4.03. 8
another | within their alablaster innocent arms. 4.03. 11
their lips were four red roses on a stalk, 4.03. 12
/which in their summer beauty kiss'd each other. 4.03. 13
a book of prayers on their pillow lay, | which 4.03. 14
when thou shalt tell the process of their death. 4.03. 32
to worry lambs and lap their gentle blood, 4.04. 50
untimely smoth'red in their dusky graves. 4.04. 70
only reserv'd their factor to buy souls | and 4.04. 72
windy attorneys to their client's woes, | aery 4.04.127
and therefore level not to hit their lives. 4.04.203
lo at their birth good stars were opposite. 4.04.216
no, to their lives ill friends were contrary. 4.04.217
indeed, and by their uncle cozen'd | of comfort, 4.04.223
whose hand soever lanch'd their tender hearts, 4.04.225
up to some scaffold, there to lose their heads. 4.04.243
advantaging their love with interest | of ten 4.04.323
deep and dead, poor infants, in their graves. 4.04.363
ungovern'd youth, to wail it /in their age; 4.04.392
old barren plants, to wail it with their age. 4.04.394
'tis thought that richmond is their admiral; 4.04.437
safe–conducting the rebels from their ships? 4.04.482
they should serve their sovereign in the west? 4.04.485
to the rebels, and their power grows strong. 4.04.505
and towards london do they bend their power, 4.05. 17
men | to turn their own points in their masters' 5.01. 24
turn their own points in their masters' bosoms; 5.01. 24
six or seven thousand is their utmost power. 5.03. 10
put in their hands thy bruising irons of wrath, 5.03.110
your friends are up and buckle on their armor. 5.03.211
methought their souls whose bodies richard 5.03.230
whom their o'ercloyed country vomits forth | to 5.03.318
these famish'd beggars weary of their lives, 5.03.329
our fathers | have in their own land beaten, 5.03.334
hark, i hear their drum. 5.03.337
inter their bodies as become their births. 5.05. 15
inter their bodies as become their births. 5.05. 15
that long have frown'd upon their enmity! 5.05. 21
and lancaster, | divided in their dire division, 5.05. 28
and let their heirs (god, if thy will be so) 5.05. 32
give | their money out of hope they may believe, H8 pr 8
i'll undertake may see away their shilling pr 12
how they clung | in their embracement, as they 1.01. 10
their dwarfish pages were | as cherubins, all 1.01. 22
them, that their very labor | was to them as a 1.01. 25
by their heralds challeng'd | the noble spirits 1.01. 34

whose grace | chalks successors their way, nor 1.01. 60
that have | by this so sicken'd their estates, 1.01. 82
have broke their backs with laying manors on 'em 1.01. 84
england and france might through their amity 1.01.181
hath flaw'd the heart | of all their loyalties; 1.02. 22
and yet must | perforce be their acquaintance. 1.02. 47
tongues spit their duties out, and cold hearts 1.02. 61
their curses now | live where their prayers did; 1.02. 62
their curses now | live where their prayers did; 1.02. 63
example, in their issue | are to be fear'd. 1.02. 90
directly | their very noses had been councillors 1.03. 9
their clothes are after such a pagan cut to't, 1.03. 14
with all their honorable points of ignorance 1.03. 26
honest men, | or pack to their old playfellows. 1.03. 33
the lag end of their lewdness and be laugh'd at. 1.03. 35
physic, their diseases | are grown so catching. 1.03. 36
red wine first must rise | in their fair cheeks, 1.04. 44
th' have left their barge and landed, | and 1.04. 54
what are their pleasures? 1.04. 64
but leave their flocks, and under your fair 1.04. 70
thanks, and pray 'em take their pleasures. 1.04. 74
nor build their evils on the graves of great men 2.01. 67
too many curses on their heads | that were the 2.01.138
in christian kingdoms) | have their free voices. 2.02. 93
and thank the holy conclave for their loves; 2.02. 99
york, are join'd with me their servant | in the 2.02.105
their arguments | be now produc'd and heard. 2.04. 67
as't please | yourself pronounce their office. 2.04.115
my appearance make | in any of their courts. 2.04.134
to village curs, | bark when their fellows do: 2.04.161
of the sea, | hung their heads, and then lay by. 3.01. 11
pray their graces | to come near. 3.01. 18
what can be their business | with me, a poor 3.01. 19
i do not like their coming. 3.01. 21
should be good men, their affairs as righteous. 3.01. 22
you speak truth, for their poor mistress' sake; 3.01. 47
all the world should crack their duty to you 3.02.193
duty to you | and throw it from their soul, 3.02.194
no doubt | in time will find their fit rewards. 3.02.245
that sweet aspect of princes, and their ruin, 3.02.369
am sure have shown at full their royal minds — 4.01. 8
as, let 'em have their rights, they are ever 4.01. 9
of those that claim their offices this day | by 4.01. 15
their coronets say so. these are stars indeed. 4.01. 54
stifled | with the mere rankness of their joy. 4.01. 59
flew up, and had their faces | been loose, this 4.01. 74
to th' earth, | willing to leave their burthen. 4.02. 3
in brass, their virtues | we write in water. 4.02. 45
that they may have their wages duly paid 'em, 4.02.150
her two hands, and she | sleep in their graves. 5.01. 32
their practices | must bear the same proportion, 5.01.128
shade thy person | under their blessed wings! 5.01.161
by some that hate me | (god turn their hearts! 5.02. 15
i never sought their malice) | to quench mine 5.02. 15
but their pleasures | must be fulfill'd, and i 5.02. 18
dance attendance on their lordships' pleasures, 5.02. 31
pace 'em not in their hands to make 'em gentle, 5.02. 57
but stop their mouths with stubborn bits and 5.02. 58
prayers then would seek you, not their fears. 5.02.118
or the limbs of limehouse, their dear brothers, 5.03. 63 P
beaten corn, | and hang their heads with sorrow. 5.04. 32
and by those claim their greatness, not by blood 5.04. 38
some come to take their ease, | and sleep an act ep 2
if they hold when their ladies bid 'em clap. ep 14
TRO are strong, and skillful to their strength, 1.01. 7
fierce to their skill, and to their fierceness 1.01. 8
to their skill, and to their fierceness valiant, 1.01. 8
all whites are ink | writing their own reproach, 1.01. 57
robb'd many beasts of their particular additions 1.02. 20 P
tell you them all by their names as they pass by 1.02.182 P
making their way | with those of nobler bulk! 1.03. 36
calm of states | quite from their fixure! 1.03.101
should lift their bosoms higher than the shores, 1.03.112
should lose their names, and so should justice 1.03.118
of their observant toil the enemies' weight — 1.03.203
or those that with the fineness of their souls 1.03.209
that's their /fame in peace. 1.03.236
our dear'st repute | with their fin'st palate; 1.03.338
small pricks | to their subsequent volumes) 1.03.344
would they but fat their thoughts | with this 2.02. 48
that in their country did them that disgrace 2.02. 95
craves | all dues be rend'red to their owners: 2.02.174
of partial indulgence | to their benumbed wills, 2.02.179
will /strike amazement to their drowsy spirits. 2.02.210
i was advertis'd their great general slept, 2.02.211
without drawing their massy irons and cutting 2.03. 16 P
their fraction is more our wish than their 2.03. 98 P
fraction is more our wish than their faction. 2.03. 99 P
do in our eyes begin to lose their gloss, | yea, 2.03.119
disguise the holy strength of their command, 2.03.127
and /cull their flower, ajax shall cope the best 2.03.264
and all my powers do their bestowing lose, 3.02. 37
grown | too headstrong for their mother. 3.02.123
world to come | approve their truth by troilus. 3.02.174
when their rhymes, | full of protest, of oath 3.02.174
is such a wrest in their affairs | that their 3.03. 23
that their negotiations all must slack, 3.03. 24
to send their smiles before them to achilles, 3.03. 72
show not their mealy wings but to the summer, 3.03. 79
do thoughts unveil in their dumb cradles. 3.03.200
which | cold lips blow to their deities, take 4.04. 27
powers, | presuming on their changeful potency. 4.04. 97
some with cunning gild their copper crowns, 4.04.105
and wide unclasp the tables of their thoughts 4.05. 60
aeneas | consent upon the order of their fight, 4.05. 90
half stints their strife before their strokes 4.05. 93
stints their strife before their strokes begin. 4.05. 93
do buss the clouds, | must kiss their own feet. 4.05.221
to such as boasting show their scars | a mock is 4.05.290
let grow thy sinews till their knots be strong, 5.03. 33
their eyes o'ergalled with recourse of tears, 5.03. 55
that gods and men | address their dangers in. 5.10. 14
COR an inventory to particularize their abundance; 1.01. 21 P
and their store–houses cramm'd with grain; 1.01. 80 P
for examine | their counsels and their cares; 1.01.150
for examine | their counsels and their cares; 1.01.150
what's their seeking? 1.01.188
for corn at their own rates, whereof they say 1.01.189
and feebling such as stand not in their liking 1.01.195
not in their liking | below their cobbled shoes. 1.01.196
would the nobility lay aside their ruth | and 1.01.197
these shreds | they vented their complainings, 1.01.209
they threw their caps | as they would hang them 1.01.212
horns a' th' moon, | /shouting their emulation. 1.01.214
five tribunes to defend their vulgar wisdoms, 1.01.215
their vulgar wisdoms, | of their own choice. 1.01.216
take these rats thither | to gnaw their garners. 1.01.250
some parcels of their power are forth already, 1.02. 32
had eleven die nobly for their country than one 1.03. 24 P
lartius are set down before their city corioles; 1.03. 99 P
then shall we hear their 'larum, and they ours. 1.04. 9
their noise be our instruction. ladders ho! 1.04. 22
they fear us not, but issue forth their city. 1.04. 23
stand fast, we'll beat them to their wives, | as 1.04. 41
who upon the sudden | clapp'd to their gates. 1.04. 51
see here these movers that do prize their hours 1.05. 4
gods | lead their successes as we wish our own, 1.06. 7
i saw our party to their trenches driven, | and 1.06. 12
briefly we heard their drums. 1.06. 16
how lies their battle? 1.06. 51
side | they have plac'd their men of trust? 1.06. 52
their bands i' th' vaward are the /antiates, 1.06. 53
vaward are the /antiates, | of their best trust; 1.06. 54
o'er them aufidius, | their very heart of hope. 1.06. 55
shall say against their hearts, "we thank the 1.09. 8
we may articulate | for their own good and ours. 1.09. 78
up | their rotten privilege and custom 'gainst 1.10. 23
nature teaches beasts to know their friends. 2.01. 6 P
all the peace you make in their cause is calling 2.01. 78 P
i had rather be their servant in my way | than 2.01.203
their nicely gawded cheeks to th' wanton spoil 2.01.217
but they | upon their ancient malice will forget 2.01.228
to th' people, beg their stinking breaths. 2.01.236
have made them mules, silenc'd their pleaders, 2.01.247
and | dispropertied their freedoms, holding them 2.01.248
for the world | than camels in their war, who 2.01.251
war, who have their provand | only for bearing 2.01.251
will be his fire | to kindle their dry stubble; 2.01.258
and their blaze | shall darken him for ever. 2.01.258
ladies and maids their scarfs and handkerchers, 2.01.264
a shower and thunder with their caps and shouts. 2.01.267
the true knowledge he has in their disposition, 2.02. 13 P
he did not care whether he had their love or no, 2.02. 16 P
but he seeks their hate with greater devotion 2.02. 18 P
that may fully discover him their opposite. 2.02. 20 P
he dislikes, to flatter them for their love. 2.02. 23 P
to have them at all into their estimation and 2.02. 28 P
planted his honors in their eyes and his actions 2.02. 29 P
and his actions in their hearts that for their 2.02. 29 P
their hearts that for their tongues to be silent 2.02. 30 P
people, | but tie him not to be their bedfellow. 2.02. 65
for my wounds' sake to give their suffrage. 2.02.138
sir, the people | must have their voices; 2.02.140
them for the hire | of their breath only! 2.02.150
and their consent of one direct way should be at 2.03. 23 P
bid them wash their faces, | and keep their 2.03. 60
wash their faces, | and keep their teeth clean. 2.03. 61
since the wisdom of their choice is rather to 2.03. 98 P
that does appear, | their needless vouches? 2.03.117
five hundred, and their friends to piece 'em. 2.03.212
that will from them take | their liberties, make 2.03.215
almost all | repent in their election. 2.03.255
is, he fall in rage | with their refusal, both 2.03.259
and this shall seem, as partly 'tis, their own, 2.03.262
in our ages see | their banners wave again. 3.01. 8
them now, | and straight disclaim their tongues? 3.01. 35
you being their mouths, why rule you not their 3.01. 36
their mouths, why rule you not their teeth? 3.01. 36
my nobler friends, | i crave their pardons. 3.01. 65
coin words till their decay against those 3.01. 78
not | a man of their infirmity. 3.01. 82
they choose their magistrate, | and such a one 3.01.104
people give | one that speaks thus their voice? 3.01.119
my reasons, | more worthier than their voices. 3.01.120
their mutinies and revolts, wherein they show'd 3.01.126
deeds express | what's like to be their words: 3.01.133
them not lick | the sweet which is their poison. 3.01.157
their obedience fails | to th' greater bench. 3.01.165
be meet, | and throw their power i' th' dust. 3.01.170
are the people's mouths, | and we their hands. 3.01.271
for the inheritance of their loves and safeguard 3.02. 68
thou art their soldier, and, being bred in 3.02. 81
in asking their good loves, but thou wilt frame 3.02. 84
as she speaks, why, their hearts were yours; 3.02. 87
i'll mountebank their loves, | cog their hearts 3.02.132
cog their hearts from them, and come home 3.02.133
allow their officers, and are content | to 3.03. 45
call me their traitor, thou injurious tribune! 3.03. 69
buy | their mercy at the price of one fair word, 3.03. 91
seeking means | to pluck away their power, as 3.03. 96
your enemies, with nodding of their plumes, 3.03.126
say their great enemy is gone, and they | stand 4.02. 6
and they | stand in their ancient strength. 4.02. 7
to come upon them in the heat of their division. 4.03. 18 P
and to pluck from them their tribunes for ever. 4.03. 24 P
all tending to the good of their adversaries. 4.03. 42 P
the centurions and their charges, distinctly 4.03. 43 P
i am joyful to hear of their readiness, and am 4.03. 46 P
passions and whose plots have broke their sleep 4.04. 19
grow dear friends | and interjoin their issues. 4.04. 22
who now are here, taking their leaves of me, 4.05.133
man in blood, they will out of their burrows, 4.05.211 P
as it were, a parcel of their feast, and to be 4.05.216 P
and to be executed ere they wipe their lips. 4.05.217 P
than see | our tradesmen singing in their shops, 4.06. 8
and going | about their functions friendly. 4.06. 9
news is coming | that turns their countenances. 4.06. 60
and have already | o'erborne their way, consum'd 4.06. 78
your temples burned in their cement, and | your 4.06. 85
he is their god; 4.06. 90
their talk at table, and their thanks at end; 4.07. 4
their talk at table, and their thanks at end; 4.07. 4
and their people | will be as rash in the repeal 4.07. 31
only their ends | you have respected; 5.03. 4
their latest refuge | was to send him; 5.03. 11
their base throats tear | with giving him glory. 5.06. 52
TIT these that i bring unto their latest home, 1.01. 83
home, | with burial amongst their ancestors. 1.01. 84
make way to lay them by their bretheren. 1.01. 89
before this earthy prison of their bones, | that 1.01. 99
for valiant doings in their country's cause? 1.01.113
these are their brethren, whom your goths beheld 1.01.122
and for their brethren slain | religiously they 1.01.123
t' appease their groaning shadows that are gone. 1.01.126
make this his latest farewell to their souls. 1.01.149
send thee by me, their tribune and their trust, 1.01.181
send thee by me, their tribune and their trust, 1.01.181
in right and service of their noble country. 1.01.197
all, | and rase their faction and their family, 1.01.451
all, | and rase their faction and their family, 1.01.451
and so repose, sweet gold, for their unrest, 2.03. 8
that have their alms out of the empress' chest. 2.03. 9
under their sweet shade, aaron, let us sit, 2.03. 16
let us sit down and mark their yellowing noise; 2.03. 20
and wash their hands in bassianus' blood. 2.03. 45
which dreads not yet their lives' destruction. 2.03. 50
the whilst their own birds famish in their nests 2.03.154
whilst their own birds famish in their nests; 2.03.154
o, keep me from their worse than killing lust, 2.03.175
so should i rob my sweet sons of their fee. 2.03.179
no, let them satisfice their lust on thee. 2.03.180
i did, my lord, yet let me be their bail, | for 2.03.295
to answer their suspicion with their lives. 2.03.298
to answer their suspicion with their lives. 2.03.298
and tribunes with their tongues doom men to 3.01. 47
to rescue my two brothers from their death, 3.01. 49
witness the sorrow that their sister makes. 3.01.119
and that shall be the ransom for their fault. 3.01.156
to ransom my two nephews from their death; 3.01.172
for fear they die before their pardon come. 3.01.175
their heads, i mean. 3.01.202
when they do hug him in their melting bosoms. 3.01.213
to ease their stomachs with their bitter tongues 3.01.233
ease their stomachs with their bitter tongues. 3.01.233
to thee sent back — | thy grief their sports! 3.01.238
even in their throats that hath committed them. 3.01.274
and see their blood or die with this reproach. 4.01. 94
their mother's bedchamber should not be safe 4.01.108
ay, with my dagger in their bosoms, grandsire. 4.01.118
the old man hath found their guilt, | and sends 4.02. 26
that wound beyond their feeling to the quick. 4.02. 28
and how by this their child shall be advanc'd, 4.02.157
they have wish'd that lucius were their emperor. 4.04. 77
wings | he can at pleasure stint their melody; 4.04. 86
signifies what hate they bear their emperor, 5.01. 3
led by their master to the flow'red fields, 5.01. 15
indeed i was their tutor to instruct them. 5.01. 98
that codding spirit had they from their mother, 5.01. 99
make poor men's cattle break their necks, | set 5.01.132
and bid the owners quench them with their tears. 5.01.134
oft have i digg'd up dead men from their graves, 5.01.135
set them upright at their dear friends' door, 5.01.136
even when their sorrows almost was forgot, | and 5.01.137
and on their skins, as on the bark of trees, 5.01.138
and in their ears tell them my dreadful name, 5.02. 39
and find out /murderers in their guilty /caves; 5.02. 52
and when thy car is loaden with their heads, | i 5.02. 53
and will o'erreach them in their own devices, 5.02.143
a pair of cursed hell–hounds and their dame. 5.02.144
and stop their mouths if they begin to cry. 5.02.161
stop close their mouths, let them not speak a 5.02.164
sirs, stop their mouths, let them not speak to 5.02.167
let me go grind their bones to powder small, 5.02.198
and in that paste let their vile heads be bak'd. 5.02.200
and see them ready against their mother comes. 5.02.205
whereof their mother daintily hath fed, | eating 5.03. 61
for their fell faults our brothers were beheaded 5.03.100
who drown'd their enmity in my true tears, | and 5.03.107
and op'd their arms to embrace me as a friend. 5.03.108
o now, sweet boy, give them their latest kiss! 5.03.169
ROM a pair of star–cross'd lovers take their life; pr 6
doth with their death bury their parents' strife pr 8
with their death bury their parents' strife. pr 8
the fearful passage of their death–mark'd love, pr 9
and the continuance of their parents' rage, pr 10
which, but their children's end, nought could pr 11
quarrel is between our masters and us their men. 1.01. 20 P
i will cut off their heads. 1.01. 23 P
the heads of the maids, or their maidenheads, 1.01. 25 P
cast by their grave beseeming ornaments | to 1.01. 93
let two more summers wither in their pride, 1.02. 10
my house and welcome on their pleasure stay. 1.02. 37
tickle the senseless rushes with their heels. 1.04. 36
because their breath with sweetmeats tainted are 1.04. 76
this is the hag, when maids lie on their backs, 1.04. 92
ladies that have their toes | unplagu'd with 1.05. 16
my flesh tremble in their different greeting. 1.05. 90
to twinkle in their spheres till they return. 2.02. 17
in thine eye | than twenty of their swords! 2.02. 72
sweet, | and i am proof against their enmity. 2.02. 73
i have night's cloak to hide me from their eyes, 2.02. 75
my life were better ended by their hate, | than 2.02. 77
goes toward love as schoolboys from their books, 2.02.156
plants, herbs, stones, and their true qualities; 2.03. 16
love then lies | not truly in their hearts, but 2.03. 68
not truly in their hearts, but in their eyes. 2.03. 68
o, their bones, their bones! 2.04. 35 P
o, their bones, their bones! 2.04. 35 P
and in their triumph die, like fire and powder, 2.06. 10
they are but beggars that can count their worth, 2.06. 32
draw, benvolio, beat down their weapons. 3.01. 86
his /agile arm beats down their fatal points, 3.01.166
lovers can see to do their amorous rites | by 3.02. 8
do their amorous rites | by their own beauties, 3.02. 9
still blush, as thinking their own kisses sin; 3.03. 39
for it was bad enough before their spite. 4.01. 31
for i'll try if they can lick their fingers. 4.02. 4 P
turn from their office to black funeral: 4.05. 85
move them no more by crossing their high will. 4.05. 95
which their keepers call | a lightning before 5.03. 89
and know their spring, their head, their true 5.03.218
and know their spring, their head, their true 5.03.218
their spring, their head, their true descent, 5.03.218
and their stol'n marriage–day | was tybalt's 5.03.233

their course of love, the tidings of her death; 5.03.287
tender down | their services to lord timon. TIM 1.01. 55
of this sphere | to propagate their states. 1.01. 67
mountain's top | even on their knees and /hands, 1.01. 87
in the owners | are prized by their masters. 1.01.171
me to see so many dip their meat in one man's 1.02. 41 P
good for their meat, and safer for their lives. 1.02. 45
good for their meat, and safer for their lives. 1.02. 45
men should drink with harness on their throats. 1.02. 52
in cases that keeps their sounds to themselves. 1.02. 99 P
to forget their faults, i drink to you. 1.02.107 P
ladies? what are their wills? 1.02.118 P
bears that office to signify their pleasures. 1.02.120 P
best senses | acknowledge thee their patron, and 1.02.124
music, make their welcome! 1.02.129
dies that bears not one spurn to their graves 1.02.141
spurn to their graves | of their friends' gift? 1.02.142
men shut their doors against a setting sun. 1.02.145
his land's put to their books. 1.02.200
i doubt whether their legs be worth the sums 1.02.232
honest fools lay out their wealth on curtsies. 1.02.235
commend me to their loves; 2.02.190 P
but they do shake their heads, and i am here 2.02.202
have their ingratitude in them hereditary: 2.02.215
their blood is cak'd, 'tis cold, it seldom flows 2.02.216
timon's money | has paid his men their wages. 3.02. 70
all these | owes their estates unto him. 3.03. 5
and with their faint reply this answer join: 3.03. 25
that were ne'er acquainted with their wards 3.03. 37
be employ'd | now to guard sure their master. 3.03. 39
down th' int'rest into their glutt'nous maws. 3.04. 52
many do keep their chambers are not sick; 3.04. 73
our masters may throw their caps at their money. 3.04.101 P
our masters may throw their caps at their money. 3.04.101 P
and let the foes quietly cut their throats 3.05. 44
i have kept back their foes, | while they have 3.05.105
while they have told their money, and let out 3.05.106
and let out | their coin upon large interest — 3.05.107
from the bench, | and minister in their steads! 4.01. 6
that their limbs may halt | as lamely as their 4.01. 24
limbs may halt | as lamely as their manners! 4.01. 25
bosoms, and their crop | be general leprosy! 4.01. 29
that their society (as their friendship) may 4.01. 31
that their society (as their friendship) may 4.01. 31
slink all away, leave their false vows with him, 4.02. 11
stout men's pillows from below their heads. 4.03. 33
them diseases, leaving with thee their lust. 4.03. 85
dimpled smiles from fools exhaust their mercy; 4.03.120
hollow bones of man, strike their sharp shins, 4.03.152
hug their diseas'd perfumes, and have forgot 4.03.207
one winter's brush | fell from their boughs, and 4.03.265
in their rough power | has uncheck'd theft. 4.03.443
second masters, | upon their first lord's neck. 4.03.506
and may diseases lick up their false bloods! 4.03.532
gave life and influence | to their whole being! 5.01. 64
by two of their most reverend senate, greet thee 5.01.129
and send forth us to make their sorrowed render, 5.01.149
than their offense can weigh down by the dram; 5.01.151
and write in thee the figures of their love, 5.01.154
take't at worst — for their knives care not, 5.01.178
great triumphers | in their applauding gates. 5.01.197
tell them that, to ease them of their griefs, 5.01.198
their fears of hostile strokes, their aches, 5.01.199
their fears of hostile strokes, their aches, 5.01.199
their pangs of love, with other incident throes 5.01.200
only be men's works, and death their gain! 5.01.222
ingratitude with loves | above their quantity. 5.04. 18
ours | were not erected by their hands from whom 5.04. 23
cunning in excess, | hath broke their hearts. 5.04. 29
shall make their harbor in our town till we 5.04. 53
sir, to wear out their shoes, to get myself into JC 1.01. 29 P
see whe'er their basest metal be not mov'd; 1.01. 61
they vanish tongue–tied in their guiltiness. 1.01. 62
holy chase, | shake off their sterile curse. 1.02. 9
fear the people | choose caesar for their king. 1.02. 80
his coward lips did from their color fly, | and 1.02.122
mark him, and write his speeches in their books, 1.02.126
men at some time are masters of their fates; 1.02.139
howted, and clapp'd their chopp'd hands, and 1.02.245 P
hands, and threw up their sweaty night–caps, and 1.02.245 P
he desir'd their worships to think it was his 1.02.270 P
and forgave him with all their hearts. 1.02.273 P
if caesar had stabb'd their mothers, they would 1.02.274 P
smil'd at one another, and shook their heads; 1.02.283 P
that noble minds keep ever with their likes; 1.02.311
transformed with their fear, who swore they saw 1.03. 24
"these are their reasons, they are natural"; 1.03. 30
but men may construe things after their fashion, 1.03. 34
all these things change from their ordinance, 1.03. 66
their natures, and preformed faculties, | to 1.03. 67
have thews and limbs like to their ancestors; 1.03. 81
sir, their hats are pluck'd about their ears, 2.01. 73
sir, their hats are pluck'd about their ears, 2.01. 73
and half their faces buried in their cloaks, 2.01. 74
and half their faces buried in their cloaks, 2.01. 74
do, | stir up their servants to an act of rage, 2.01.176
who did hide their faces | even from darkness. 2.01.277
and bring me their opinions of success. 2.02. 6
graves have yawn'd and yielded up their dead; 2.02. 18
cowards die many times before their deaths, 2.02. 32
came smiling and did bathe their hands in it. 2.02. 79
you will not come, | their minds may change. 2.02. 96
the men that gave their country liberty. 3.01.118
(which like dumb mouths do ope their ruby lips 3.01.260
their infants quartered with the hands of war; 3.01.268
i will hear cassius, and compare their reasons, 3.02. 9
the good is oft interred with their bones; 3.02. 76
beasts, | and men have lost their reason. 3.02.105
and dip their napkins in his sacred blood; 3.02.133
and, dying, mention it within their wills, 3.02.135
it as a rich legacy | unto their issue. 3.02.137
many then shall die, their names are prick'd. 4.01. 1
and some that smile have in their hearts, i fear 4.01. 50
make gallant show and promise of their mettle; 4.02. 24
they fall their crests, and like deceitful jades 4.02. 26
bid our commanders lead their charges off | a 4.02. 48
from the hard hands of peasants their vile trash 4.03. 74
prepare to lodge their companies to–night. 4.03.140
bending their expedition toward philippi. 4.03.170
senators that died | by their proscriptions, 4.03.178
all the voyage of their life | is bound in 4.03.220
their battles are at hand; 5.01. 4
tut, i am in their bosoms, and i know 5.01. 7
their bloody sign of battle is hung out, | and 5.01. 14
no, caesar, we will answer on their charge. 5.01. 24
for you have stol'n their buzzing, antony, | and 5.01. 37
and in their steads do ravens, crows, and kites 5.01. 84
their shadows seem | a canopy most fatal, under 5.01. 86
didst thou not hear their shouts? 5.03. 83
that do cling together | and choke their art. MAC 1.02. 9
these skipping kerns to trust their heels, | but 1.02. 30
these | so wither'd and so wild in their attire, 1.03. 40
cleave not to their mould | but with the aid of 1.03.145
to make their audit at your highness' pleasure, 1.06. 27
which would be worn now in their newest gloss, 1.07. 34
and that their fitness now | does unmake you. 1.07. 53
their drenched natures lies as in a death, 1.07. 68
of his own chamber, and us'd their very daggers, 1.07. 76
in heaven, | their candles are all out. 2.01. 5
grooms | do mock their charge with snores. 2.02. 6
i have drugg'd their possets, | that death and 2.02. 6
i laid their daggers ready, | he could not miss 2.02. 11
but they did say their prayers, and address'd 2.02. 22
list'ning their fear, i could not say "amen," 2.02. 26
grooms withal, | for it must seem their guilt. 2.02. 54
their hands and faces were all badg'd with blood 2.03.102
so were their daggers, which unwip'd we found 2.03.103
which unwip'd we found | upon their pillows. 2.03.104
steep'd in the colors of their trade, their 2.03.115
their daggers | unmannerly breech'd with gore. 2.03.115
beauteous and swift, the minions of their race, 2.04. 15
turn'd wild in nature, broke their stalls, flung 2.04. 16
his predecessors | and guardian of their bones. 2.04. 35
as upon thee, macbeth, their speeches shine — 3.01. 7
not confessing | their cruel parricide, filling 3.01. 31
filling their hearers | with strange invention. 3.01. 31
and so i do commend you to their backs. 3.01. 38
night's black agents to their preys do rouse. 3.02. 53
hence to th' palace gate | make it their walk. 3.03. 14
they encounter thee with their hearts' thanks. 3.04. 9
with twenty mortal murthers on their crowns, 3.04. 80
as by the strength of their illusion | shall 3.05. 28
for donalbain | to kill their gracious father? 3.06. 10
though castles topple on their warders' heads; 4.01. 56
do slope | their heads to their foundations; 4.01. 58
do slope | their heads to their foundations; 4.01. 58
i should cut off the nobles for their lands, 4.03. 79
their malady convinces | the great assay of art; 4.03.142
hanging a golden stamp about their necks, | put 4.03.153
lives | expire before the flowers in their caps, 4.03.172
the tyrant has not batter'd at their peace? 4.03.178
women fight, | to doff their dire distresses. 4.03.188
be't their comfort | we are coming thither. 4.03.188
what, all my pretty chickens, and their dam, 4.03.218
heaven look on, | and would not take their part? 4.03.224
not for their own demerits, but for mine, | fell 4.03.226
but for mine, | fell slaughter on their souls. 4.03.227
and the pow'rs above | put on their instruments. 4.03.239
ay, but their sense are shut. 5.01. 25 P
which have walk'd in their sleep who have died 5.01. 60 P
their sleep who have died holily in their beds. 5.01. 61 P
to their deaf pillows will discharge their 5.01. 73
their deaf pillows will discharge their secrets. 5.01. 73
for their dear causes | would to the bleeding 5.02. 3
that even now | protest their first of manhood. 5.02. 11
but, in their stead, | curses, not loud but deep 5.03. 26
thoughts speculative their unsure hopes relate, 5.04. 19
whose arms | are hir'd to bear their staves; 5.07. 18
that speak my salutation in their minds; 5.09. 23
marcellus and barnardo, on their watch, | in the HAM 1.02.197
by their oppress'd and fear–surprised eyes, 1.02.203
too oft before their buttons be disclos'd, | and 1.03. 40
friends thou hast, and their adoption tried, 1.03. 62
extinct in both | even in their promise, as it 1.03.119
not of that dye which their investments show, 1.03.128
as in their birth, wherein they are not guilty 1.04. 25
by their o'ergrowth of some complexion | oft 1.04. 27
hearsed in death, | have burst their cerements; 1.04. 48
two eyes, like stars, start from their spheres, 1.05. 17
for out a' doors he went without their helps, 2.01. 96
and to the last bended their light on me. 2.01. 97
have grey beards, that their faces are wrinkled, 2.02.197 P
their eyes purging thick amber and plum–tree gum 2.02.198 P
their residence, both in reputation and profit, 2.02.329 P
i think their inhibition comes by the means of 2.02.332 P
and a damned light | to their lord's murther. 2.02.461
a bad epitaph than their ill report while you 2.02.526 P
lord, i will use them according to their desert. 2.02.527 P
they have proclaim'd their malefactions: 2.02.592
we may of their encounter frankly judge, | and 3.01. 33
with this regard their currents turn awry, | and 3.01. 86
their perfume lost, | take these again, for to 3.01. 98
you) in the ear | of all their conference. 3.01.185
my operant powers their functions leave to do, 3.02.174
their own enactures with themselves destroy. 3.02.197
thoughts are ours, their ends none of our own: 3.02.213
/grained spots | as will /not leave their tinct. 3.04. 91
me, | that i must be their scourge and minister. 3.04.175
but i will delve one yard below their mines, 3.04.208
who like not in their judgment, but their eyes, 4.03. 5
who like not in their judgment, but their eyes, 4.03. 5
trick of fame | go to their graves like beds, 4.04. 62
botch the words up fit to their own thoughts, 4.05. 10
of our ship, so i alone became their prisoner. 4.06. 20 P
and guildenstern hold their course for england, 4.06. 28 P
who, dipping all his faults in their affection, 4.07. 19
the scrimers of their nation | he swore had 4.07.100
till that her garments, heavy with their drink, 4.07.181
hang themselves, more than their even–christen. 5.01. 28 P
could not with all their quantity of love | make 5.01.270
finger'd their packet, and in fine withdrew | to 5.02. 15
manners, to /unseal | their grand commission; 5.02. 18
wear | and stand a comma 'tween their amities, 5.02. 42
their defeat | does by their own insinuation 5.02. 58
defeat | does by their own insinuation grow. 5.02. 59
french rapiers and poniards, with their assigns, 5.02.149 P
horses against six french swords, their assigns, 5.02.161 P
and do but blow them to their trial, the bubbles 5.02.193 P
i will forestall their repair hither, and say 5.02.218 P
let all the battlements their ord'nance fire. 5.02.270
he never gave commandement for their death. 5.02.374
in our court have made their amorous sojourn, LR 1.01. 47
the gods to their dear shelter take thee, maid, 1.01.182
'tis strange that from their cold'st neglect 1.01.254
foppish, | and know not how their wits to wear, 1.04.168
wits to wear, | their manners are so apish." 1.04.169
might in their working do you that offense, 1.04.212
this our court, infected with their manners, 1.04.243
rabble make servants of their betters. 1.04.256
regard support | the worships of their name. 1.04.266
he may enguard his dotage with their pow'rs, 1.04.326
that in the natures of their lords rebel, 2.02. 76
and turn their halcyon beaks | with every gale 2.02. 78
with every gale and vary of their masters, 2.02. 79
observants | that stretch their duties nicely. 2.02.104
rogues and cowards | but ajax is their fool. 2.02.125
seeking to give | losses their remedies." 2.02.170
strike in their numb'd and mortified arms | pins 2.03. 15
sometime with prayers, | enforce their charity. 2.03. 20
my lord, when at their home | i did commend your 2.04. 27
those contents | they summon'd up their meiny, 2.04. 35
and attend | the leisure of their answer, gave 2.04. 37
that wear rags | do make their children blind, 2.04. 49
that bear bags | shall see their children kind. 2.04. 51
all that follow their noses are led by their 2.04. 69 P
their noses are led by their eyes but blind men, 2.04. 69 P
or at their chamber–door i'll beat the drum 2.04.118
these daughters' hearts | against their father, 2.04.275
procure | must be their schoolmasters. 2.04.304
that their great stars | thron'd and set high? 3.01. 22
of the dark, | and make them keep their caves. 3.02. 45
o'er our heads, | find out their enemies now. 3.02. 51
in) return, and force | their scanted courtesy. 3.02. 67
when brewers mar their malt with water; 3.02. 82
when nobles are their tailors' tutors; 3.02. 83
when usurers tell their gold i' th' field, | and 3.02. 91
when i desir'd their leave that i might pity him 3.03. 2 P
should have thus little mercy on their flesh? 3.04. 73
though their injunction be to bar my doors, 3.04.150
we to th' gods, | they kill us for their sport. 4.01. 37
quit the house on purpose that their punishment 4.02. 93
go to, they are not men o' their words: 4.06.104 P
to know our enemies' minds, we rip their hearts, 4.06.260
rip their hearts, | their papers is more lawful. 4.06.261
had you not been their father, these white 4.07. 29
here is the guess of their true strength and 5.01. 52
their going hence even as their coming hither, 5.02. 10
their going hence even as their coming hither, 5.02. 10
until their greater pleasures first be known 5.03. 2
as we shall find their merits and our safety 5.03. 44
my name, have in my name | took their discharge. 5.03.105
rings, | their precious stones new lost; 5.03.191
even so. cover their faces. 5.03.243
friends shall taste | the wages of their virtue, 5.03.304
and all foes | the cup of their deservings. 5.03.305
keep yet their hearts attending on themselves, OTH 1.01. 51
throwing but shows of service on their lords, 1.01. 52
and when they have lin'd their coats, | do 1.01. 53
my spirits and my place have in their power | to 1.01.103
even now stands in act) that, for their souls, 1.01.151
fadom they have none | to lead their business; 1.01.153
cannot but feel this wrong as 'twere their own; 1.02. 97
and now they do restem | their backward course, 1.03. 38
frank appearance | their purposes toward cyprus. 1.03. 39
us'd | their dearest action in the tented field; 1.03. 85
whose heads | /do /grow beneath their shoulders. 1.03.145
men do their broken weapons rather use | than 1.03.174
weapons rather use | than their bare hands. 1.03.175
these moors are changeable in their wills — 1.03.347 P
bang'd the turks, | that their designment halts. 2.01. 22
and sufferance | on most part of their fleet. 2.01. 24
they do discharge their shot of courtesy; 2.01. 56
do omit | their mortal natures, letting go 2.01. 72
then a nobility in their natures more than is 2.01.216 P
they met so near with their lips that their 2.01.259 P
near with their lips that their breaths embrac'd 2.01.259 P
well — happiness to their sheets! 2.03. 29 P
that hold their honors in a wary distance, | the 2.03. 56
to have their balmy slumbers wak'd with strife. 2.03.258
put an enemy in their mouths to steal away their 2.03.290 P
in their mouths to steal away their brains! 2.03.291 P
lord, | is the immediate jewel of their souls. 3.03.156
the pranks | they dare not show their husbands; 3.03.203
their best conscience | is not to leave't undone 3.03.203
creatures ours, | and not their appetites! 3.03.270
dangerous conceits are in their natures poisons, 3.03.326
eyes do see them bolster | more than their own. 3.03.400
that in their sleeps will mutter their affairs; 3.03.417
that in their sleeps will mutter their affairs; 3.03.417
things, | though great ones are their object. 3.04.145
the devil their virtue tempts, and they tempt 4.01. 8
who having, by their own importunate suit, | or 4.01. 26
i kiss the instrument of their pleasures. 4.01.218
the purest of their wives | is foul as slander. 4.02. 18
that there be women do abuse their husbands | in 4.03. 62
but i do think it is their husbands' faults | if 4.03. 86
say that they slack their duties, | and pour our 4.03. 87
know | their wives have sense like them; 4.03. 94
and have their palates both for sweet and sour, 4.03. 95
the ills we do, their ills instruct us so. 4.03.103
that men must lay their murthers on your neck. 5.02.170
as the arabian trees | their medicinable gum. 5.02.351
the office and devotion of their view | upon a ANT 1.01. 5
if it lay in their hands to make me a cuckold, 1.02. 76 P
of them, jointing their force 'gainst caesar, 1.02. 92
when it pleaseth their deities to take the wife 1.02.162 P
pawn their experience to their present pleasure, 1.04. 32
pawn their experience to their present pleasure, 1.04. 32
shine on those | that make their looks by his; 1.05. 56
whiles we are suitors to their throne, decays 2.01. 4
entertained cause enough | to draw their swords; 2.01. 47
how the fear of us | may cement their divisions, 2.01. 48
and their contestation | was theme for you — 2.02. 43
true reports | that drew their swords with you. 2.02. 48

our conditions | so diff'ring in their acts. 2.02.114
all great fears, which now import their dangers, 2.02.132
to follow faster, | as amorous of their strokes. 2.02.197
i' th' eyes, | and made their bends adornings. 2.02.208
my bended hook shall pierce | their slimy jaws; 2.05. 13
faces are true, whatsome'er their hands are. 2.06. 97 P
that seems to tie their friendship together will 2.06.121 P
will be the very strangler of their amity. 2.06.122 P
is the strength of their amity shall prove the 2.06.128 P
prove the immediate author of their variance. 2.06.129 P
some o' their plants are ill rooted already, the 2.07. 1 P
and, when we are put off, fall to their throats: 2.07. 72
ever won | more in their officer than person. 3.01. 17
they are his shards, and he their beetle, so. 3.02. 20
and all the unlawful issue that their lust 3.06. 7
already, will their good thoughts call from him. 3.06. 21
things to destiny | hold unbewail'd their way. 3.06. 85
and their tongues rot | that speak against us! 3.07. 15
their ships are yare, yours heavy. 3.07. 38
with all their sixty, fly and turn the rudder. 3.10. 3
cowards | to run and show their shoulders. 3.11. 8
women are not | in their best fortunes strong, 3.12. 30
judgments are | a parcel of their fortunes, and 3.13. 32
against the blown rose may they stop their nose 3.13. 39
have empty left their orbs, and shot their fires 3.13.146
and shot their fires | into th' abysm of hell. 3.13.146
i'll force | the wine peep through their scars. 3.13.190
early though't be, have on their riveted trim, 4.04. 22
them home | with clouts about their heads. 4.07. 6
let us score their backs, | and snatch 'em up, 4.07. 12
nightingale, | we have beat them to their beds. 4.08. 19
and earth may strike their sounds together, 4.08. 38
their preparation is to–day by sea, | we please 4.10. 1
where their appointment we may best discover, 4.10. 8
may best discover, | and look on their endeavor. 4.10. 9
have built | in cleopatra's sails their nests. 4.12. 4
grimly, | and dare not speak their knowledge. 4.12. 6
they cast their caps up and carouse together 4.12. 12
to whom i gave | their wishes, do discandy, melt 4.12. 22
melt their sweets | on blossoming caesar; 4.12. 22
have by their brave instruction got upon me | a 4.14. 98
civil streets, | and citizens to their dens. 5.01. 17
you laugh when boys or women tell their dreams; 5.02. 74
stuck | a sun and moon, which kept their course, 5.02. 80
to induce | their mediation, must i be unfolded 5.02.170
in their thick breaths, | rank of gross diet, 5.02.211
be enclouded, | and forc'd to drink their vapor. 5.02.213
that's the way | to fool their preparation, and 5.02.225
and to conquer | their most absurd intents. 5.02.226
devils do the gods great harm in their women; 5.02.276 P
the gods give men | to excuse their after wrath. 5.02.287
thy thoughts | touch their effects in this: 5.02.330
the manner of their deaths? 5.02.337
and their story is | no less in pity than his 5.02.361
although they wear their faces to the bent | of CYM 1.01. 13
o' th' time | died with their swords in hand; 1.01. 36
for which their father, | then old and fond of 1.01. 36
the other, from their nursery | were stol'n, and 1.01. 59
which, by their graces, i will keep. 1.04. 87 P
and apply | allayments to their act, and by them 1.05. 22
them gather | their several virtues and effects. 1.05. 23
how mean soe'er, that have their honest wills, 1.06. 8
of rich and exquisite form, their values great, 1.06.190
and pawn mine honor for their safety. 1.06.194
mary–buds begin to ope their golden eyes; 2.03. 24
what | if i do line one of their hands? 2.03. 67
up | their deer to th' stand o' th' stealer; 2.03. 70
to knit their souls | (on whom there is no more 2.03.117
whose remembrance | is yet fresh in their grief. 2.04. 15
julius caesar | smil'd at their lack of skill, 2.04. 22
but found their courage | worthy his frowning at 2.04. 22
their discipline | (now wing–led with their 2.04. 23
discipline | (now wing–led with their courages) 2.04. 24
known | to their approvers they are people such 2.04. 25
their tenure good, i trust. 2.04. 36
standing, nicely | depending on their brands. 2.04. 91
they are made | than they are to their virtues, 2.04.112
in a true hate, to pray they have their will: 2.05. 34
like egg–shells mov'd upon their surges, crack'd 3.01. 28
for | their liberties are now in arms, a 3.01. 74
and keep their impious turbands on without 3.03. 6
their thoughts do hit | the roofs of palaces, 3.03. 83
euriphile, | thou wast their nurse; 3.03.104
they took thee for their mother, | and every day 3.03.104
would you in their serving | (and with what 3.04.170
your valiant britains have their wishes in it. 3.05. 20
virtue | which their own conscience seal'd them, 3.06. 84
to the numbers and the time | of their dispatch. 3.07. 16
is the very description of their meeting–place, 4.01. 24 P
i'm not their father, yet who this should be 4.02. 28
in them both, | mingle their spurs together. 4.02. 58
their royal blood enchaf'd, as the rud'st wind 4.02.174
those rich–left heirs that let their fathers lie 4.02.226
upon their faces. 4.02.285
their pleasures here are past, so /is their pain 4.02.290
pleasures here are past, so /is their pain. 4.02.290
(i fast and pray'd for their intelligence) thus: 4.02.347
and unnatural revolts | during their use, and 4.04. 7
that when they hear their roman horses neigh, 4.04. 17
behold their quarter'd fires, have both their 4.04. 18
fires, have both their eyes | and ears so cloy'd 4.04. 18
that they will waste their time upon our note, 4.04. 20
their blood thinks scorn | till it fly out and 4.04. 53
'tis their fresh supplies. 5.02. 16
more charming | with their own nobleness, which 5.03. 33
some their friends | o'erborne i' th' former 5.03. 47
to–day how many would have given their honors 5.03. 66
their honors | to have sav'd their carcasses! 5.03. 67
men, | who of their broken debtors take a third, 5.04. 19
letting them thrive again | on their abatement. 5.04. 21
some of them too that die against their wills. 5.04.202 P
that their good souls may be appeas'd with 5.05. 72
appeas'd with slaughter | of you their captives, 5.05. 73
briefly die their joys | that place them on the 5.05.106
of nature should again | do their due functions. 5.05.258
their nurse, euriphile | (whom for the theft i 5.05.340
their dear loss, | the more of you 'twas felt, 5.05.345
covering heavens | fall on their heads like dew! 5.05.351
let our crooked smokes climb to their nostrils 5.05.477
and lords and ladies in their lives | have read PER 1.ch. 7
sit, | to knit in her their best perfections. 1.01. 11
why cloud they not their sights perpetually, 1.01. 74
in vice their law's their will; 1.01.103
in vice their law's their will; 1.01.103
all love the womb that their first being bred, 1.01.107
that have their first conception by misdread, 1.02. 12
from whence | they have their nourishment? 1.02. 56
that kings should let their ears hear their 1.02. 62
should let their ears hear their faults hid! 1.02. 62
if heaven slumber while their creatures want, 1.04. 16
they may awake their helpers to comfort them. 1.04. 17
their tables were stor'd full, to glad the sight 1.04. 28
although they gave their creatures in abundance, 1.04. 36
those mothers who, to nousle up their babes, 1.04. 42
with their superfluous riots, hear these tears! 1.04. 54
stuff'd the hollow vessels with their power | to 1.04. 67
the semblance | of their white flags display'd, 1.04. 72
go tell their general we attend him here, | to 1.04. 79
but to relieve them of their heavy load; 1.04. 91
the curse of heaven and men succeed their evils! 1.04.104
and from their wat'ry empire recollect | all 2.01. 50
how well this honest mirth becomes their labor! 2.01. 95
as jewels lose their glory if neglected, | so 2.02. 12
so princes their renowns if not respected. 2.02. 13
marshal, the rest, as they deserve their grace. 2.03. 19
did vail their crowns to his supremacy; 2.03. 42
he's both their parent, and he is their grave, 2.03. 46
he's both their parent, and he is their grave, 2.03. 46
and that their measures are as excellent. 2.03.103
these knights unto their several lodgings! 2.03.109
to–morrow all for speeding do their best. 2.03.115
that all those eyes ador'd them ere their fall 2.04. 11
scorn now their hand should give them burial. 2.04. 12
and now at length they overflow their banks. 2.04. 24
mouth, | are the blither for their drouth. 3.ch. 8
twice six moons, | he, obedient to their dooms, 3.ch. 32
omit we all their dole and woe. 3.ch. 42
their vessel shakes | on neptune's billow; 3.ch. 44
half the flood | hath their keel cut. 3.ch. 46
the good gods | throw their best eyes upon't! 3.01. 37
begin to part | their fringes of bright gold. 3.02.100
the master calls, and trebles their confusion. 4.01. 64
come, the gods have done their part in you. 4.02. 70 P
have hearken'd to their father's testament. 4.02. 99 P
on her, | but cast their gazes on marina's face; 4.03. 33
since they do better thee in their command. 4.06.162
you, there's no going but by their consent. 4.06.197 P
of noble race, | who pour their bounty on her; 5.ch. 10
mortality, | and drown me with their sweetness. 5.01.194
through whom the gods have shown their power; 5.03. 60
we'll celebrate their nuptials, and ourselves 5.03. 80
roses, their sharp spines being gone, | not TNK 1.01. 1
being gone, | not royal in their smells alone, 1.01. 2
royal in their smells alone, | but in their hue; 1.01. 3
oxlips in their cradles growing, | marigolds on 1.01. 10
and bridegroom's feet, | blessing their sense! 1.01. 15
he will not suffer us to burn their bones, | to 1.01. 43
to urn their ashes, nor to take th' offense | of 1.01. 44
your premeditating | more than their actions; 1.01.137
her twinning cherries shall their sweetness fall 1.01.178
cure their surfeit | that craves a present 1.01.190
force, | or sentencing for aye their vigor dumb, 1.01.195
descend again into their throats and have not 1.02. 82
yet they | must yield their tribute there. 1.03. 8
heavens infuse | in their best–temper'd pieces, 1.03. 10
cannot weep | when our friends don their helms, 1.03. 19
or women | that have sod their infants in (and 1.03. 21
their knot of love | tied, weav'd, entangled, 1.03. 41
and their needs | the one of th' other may be 1.03. 57
to water | their intertangled roots of love, but 1.03. 59
yet do effect | rare issues by their operance, 1.03. 63
the mounted heavens | view us their mortal herd, 1.04. 5
behold who err, | and in their time chastise. 1.04. 6
than a gap | should be in their dear rites, we 1.04. 9
as may be judg'd | by their appointment. 1.04. 15
/prisoner told me | when i inquired their names? 1.04. 22
been taken | when their last hurts were given, 1.04. 26
all our surgeons | convent in their behoof, our 1.04. 31
their lives concern us | much more than thebes 1.04. 32
freed of this plight, and in their morning state 1.04. 34
mercy, all our best | their best skill tender! 1.04. 47
these strewings are for their chamber. 2.01. 21 P
and they have all the world in their chamber. 2.01. 25 P
out of bondage, making misery their mirth, and 2.01. 34 P
have no more sense of their captivity than i of 2.01. 38 P
but nothing of their own restraint and disasters 2.01. 40 P
they would not make us their object. 2.01. 52 P
out of their sight! 2.01. 52 P
hung with the painted favors of their ladies, 2.02. 11
and in their songs curse ever–blinded fortune 2.02. 38
that shook the aged forest with their echoes, 2.02. 47
none here, nor the seas | swallow their youth. 2.02. 88
and had their epitaphs, the people's curses. 2.02.110
see how near art can come near their colors. 2.02.149
in a field | that their crowns' titles tried. 3.01. 22
their valiant temper | men lose when they 3.01. 66
save when my lids scour'd off their /brine. 3.02. 28
but i say, where's their women? 3.05. 25
spouse, that welcomes to their cost | the galled 3.05.128
the misadventure of their own eyes kill 'em; 3.06.190
upon their lives; but with their banishments. 3.06.214
upon their lives; but with their banishments. 3.06.214
if you desire their lives, invent a way | safer 3.06.217
honor | in public question with their swords. 3.06.222
how their lives | might breed the ruin of my 3.06.239
and in their funeral songs for these two cousins 3.06.248
for heaven's sake save their lives, and banish 3.06.251
'em never more | to make me their contention, or 3.06.253
a great likelihood | of both their pardons; 4.01. 7
upon their knees | begg'd with such handsome 4.01. 8
they prevail'd, had their suits fairly granted: 4.01. 27
the prisoners have their lives. 4.01. 28
with chaplets on their heads of daffadillies, 4.01. 73
i'll choose, | and end their strife. 4.02. 3
their weeping mothers, | following the dead–cold 4.02. 4
following the dead–cold ashes of their sons, 4.02. 5
should clap their wings and sing | to all the 4.02. 23
return'd, | and with them their fair knights. 4.02. 67
their fame has fir'd me so — till they appear. 4.02.153
again to execute their preordain'd faculties, 4.03. 72 P
her with palamon in their mouths and appear with 4.03. 92 P
out of square in her into their former law and 4.03. 96 P
and before the gods | tender their holy prayers. 5.01. 2
hallowed clouds commend their swelling incense 5.01. 4
his globy eyes | had almost drawn their spheres, 5.01.114
make a blush, | which is their order's robe: 5.01.142
she shall see deeds of honor in their kind 5.03. 12
knights must kindle | their valor at your eye. 5.03. 30
that remain with you could wish their office 5.03. 35
wish their office | to any of their enemies. 5.03. 36
spirit do incite | the princes to their proof! 5.03. 57
for they would glance their eyes | toward my 5.03. 61
their single share, | their nobleness peculiar 5.03. 86
their nobleness peculiar to them, gives | the 5.03. 87
the gods by their divine arbitrement | have 5.03.107
o' th' night | with their contentious throats, 5.03.125
since i know | their lives but pinch 'em. 5.03.133
to live still, | have their good wishes; 5.04. 6
the gods will show their glory in a life | that 5.04. 43
more in our country than they do in their own. STM II.C 6 P
they are o'er the bank of their obedience, II.C 39
plague on them, they will not hold their peace. II.C 53 P
their babies at their backs, with their poor II.C 75
their babies at their backs, with their poor II.C 75
with their poor luggage | plodding to th' ports II.C 75
for other ruffians, as their fancies wrought, II.C 84
kill them, cut their throats, possess their II.C 120
them, cut their throats, possess their houses, II.C 120
whet their detested knives against your throats, II.C 134
entreat their mediation to the king, | give up II.C 145
fear their gay skins with thought of their sharp III 18
gay skins with thought of their sharp state, III 18
but rather famish them amid their plenty, VEN 20
each leaning on their elbows and their hips. 44
each leaning on their elbows and their hips. 44
flowers that are not gath'red in their prime 131
herbs for their smell, and sappy plants to bear: 165
for men will kiss even by their own direction." 216
open'd their mouths to swallow venus' liking. 248
they wither in their prime, prove nothing worth: 418
as if from thence they borrowed all their shine. 488
these mine eyes, true leaders to their queen, 503
o, never let their crimson liveries wear! 506
and as they last, their verdour still endure, 507
the sheep are gone to fold, birds to their nest, 532
their lips together glued, fall to the earth. 546
that thrive well take counsel of their friends. 640
to make the cunning hounds mistake their smell, 686
keep, | to stop the loud pursuers in their yell, 688
ceasing their clamorous cry till they have 693
then do they spend their mouths: 695
anon their loud alarums he doth hear, | and now 700
their light blown out in some mistrustful wood, 826
their copious stories, oftentimes begun, | end 845
she wildly breaketh from their strict embrace, 874
finding their enemy to be so curst, | they all 887
like soldiers when their captain once doth yield 893
clapping their proud tails to the ground below, 923
shaking their scratch'd ears, bleeding as they 924
whereat her tears began to turn their tide, 979
where they resign their office and their light 1039
where they resign their office and their light 1039
by their suggestion gives a deadly groan. 1044
that from their dark beds once more leap her 1050
flowers are sweet, their colors fresh and trim, 1079
the fishes spread on it their golden gills; 1100
some other in their bills | would bring him 1102
their virtue lost, wherein they late excell'd, 1131
they that love best their loves shall not enjoy. 1164
which in round drops upon their whiteness stood. 1170
their mistress mounted through the empty skies, 1191
holding their course to paphos, where their 1193
where their queen | means to immure herself, and 1193
that golden hap which their superiors want. LUC 42
the golden age to gild | their silver cheeks, 61
silver cheeks, and call'd it then their shield, 61
proving from world's minority their right: 67
yet their ambition makes them still to fight, 68
in their pure ranks his traitor eye encloses, 73
could pick no meaning from their parling looks, 100
they scatter and unloose it from their bond, 136
sin | to wish that i their father had not been. 210
mine eyes forgo their light, my false heart 228
so cross him with their opposite persuasion, 286
who, flatt'red by their leader's jocund show, 296
and as their captain, so their pride doth grow, 298
and as their captain, so their pride doth grow, 298
he in the worst sense consters their denial: 324
are but dreams till their effects be tried, 353
by their high treason is his heart misled, 369
then had they seen the period of their ill! 380
and holy–thoughted lucrece to their sight | must 384
eyes like marigolds had sheath'd their light, 397
save of their lord no bearing yoke they knew, 409
swell in their pride, the onset still expecting. 432
the hot charge, and bids them do their liking. 434
left their round turrets destitute and pale. 441
where their dear governess and lady lies, | do 443
and fright her with confusion of their cries. 445
who, angry that the eyes fly from their lights, 461
thy kinsmen hang their heads at this disdain, 521
and thou, the author of their obloquy, | shalt 523
bequeath not to their lot | the shame that from 534
are nature's faults, not their own infamy." 539
blow these pitchy vapors from their biding, 550
hind'ring their present fall by this dividing; 551
to soften it with their continual motion; 591
their own transgressions partially they smother: 634
that from their own misdeeds askaunce their eyes 637
from their own misdeeds askaunce their eyes! 637
that pay a daily debt | to their salt sovereign, 650
with their fresh falls' haste | add to his flow, 650
these slaves be king, and thou their slave; 659
thou their fair life, and they thy fouler grave; 661

thou loathed in their shame, they in thy pride. 662
and by their mortal fault brought in subjection 724
her foresight could not forestall their will. 728
be, | to have their unseen sin remain untold; 753
for they their guilt with weeping will unfold, 754
let their exhal'd unwholesome breaths make sick 779
that in their smoky ranks his smoth'red light 783
as palmers' chat makes short their pilgrimage. 791
to cross their arms and hang their heads with 793
cross their arms and hang their heads with mine, 793
to mask their brows and hide their infamy, | but 794
to mask their brows and hide their infamy, | but 794
or kings be breakers of their own behests? 852
who in their pride do presently abuse it; 864
their father was too weak, and they too strong, 865
to hold their cursed–blessed fortune long. 866
thy heinous hours wait on them as their pages. 910
and smear with dust their glitt'ring golden 945
to blot old books and alter their contents, | to 948
and let mild women to him lose their mildness, 979
wilder to him than tigers in their wildness. 980
the little birds that tune their morning's joy 1107
make her moans mad with their sweet melody, 1108
stern, sad tunes to change their kinds; 1147
as winter meads when sun doth melt their snow. 1218
who in a salt–wav'd ocean quench their light, 1231
their gentle sex to weep are often willing, 1237
and then they drown their eyes or break their 1239
they drown their eyes or break their hearts. 1239
then call them not the authors of their ill, 1244
their smoothness, like a goodly champaign plain, 1247
poor women's faces are their own faults' books. 1253
make weak–made women tenants to their shame. 1260
but they whose guilt within their bosoms lie 1342
lie | imagine every eye beholds their blame, 1343
that two red fires in both their faces blazed; 1353
and dying eyes gleam'd forth their ashy lights, 1378
you might behold triumphing in their faces; 1388
their face their manners most expressly told: 1397
their face their manners most expressly told: 1397
as if some mermaid did their ears entice, | some 1411
and in their rage such signs of rage they bear, 1419
when their brave hope, bold hector, march'd to 1430
to see their youthful sons bright weapons wield, 1432
and to their hope they such odd action yield, 1433
that through their light joy seemed to appear 1434
and their ranks began | to break upon the galled 1439
join, and shoot their foam at simois' banks. 1442
them words, and she their looks doth borrow. 1498
and little stars shot from their fixed places, 1525
when their glass fell wherein they view'd their 1526
glass fell wherein they view'd their faces. 1526
to think their dolor others have endured. 1582
and so did kill | the lechers in their deed. 1637
knights, by their oaths, should right poor 1694
we are their offspring, and they none of ours. 1757
the old bees die, the young possess their hive: 1769
life, | answer'd their cries, "my daughter!" 1806
side, | seeing such emulation in their woe, 1808
then jointly to the ground their knees they bow, 1846
hath his hope, and eyes their wished sight: PP 14.22
not, | green plants bring not forth their dye; 17.26
and see the shepherds feed their flocks, | by 19. 6
of love, | as chorus to their tragic scene. PHT 52
no posterity, | 'twas not their infirmity, | it 60
leese but their show, their substance still SON 5.14
their show, their substance still lives sweet. 5.14
vaunt in their youthful sap, at height decrease, 15. 7
and wear their brave state out of memory: 15. 8
so should my papers (yellowed with their age) 17. 9
be thy love, and thy love's use their treasure. 20.14
yet eyes this cunning want to grace their art, 24.13
let those who are in favor with their stars | of 25. 1
princes' favorites their fair leaves spread 25. 5
and in themselves their pride lies buried, | for 25. 7
for at a frown they in their glory die. 25. 8
who all their parts of me to thee did give: 31.11
their images i lov'd i view in thee, | and thou 31.13
reserve them for my love, not for their rhyme, 32. 7
theirs for their style i'll read, his for his 32.14
way, | hiding thy brav'ry in their rotten smoke? 34. 4
who lead thee in their riot even there | where 41.11
and by their verdict is determined | the clear 46.11
when summer's breath their masked buds discloses 54. 8
but, for their virtue only is their show, | they 54. 9
but, for their virtue only is their show, | they 54. 9
of their sweet deaths are sweetest odors made: 54.12
shore, | so do our minutes hasten to their end, 60. 2
sea, | but sad mortality o'ersways their power, 65. 2
churls, their thoughts (although their eyes were 69.11
their thoughts (although their eyes were kind) 69.11
showing their birth and where they did proceed? 76. 8
my use, | and under thee their poesy disperse. 78. 4
words which writers use | of their fair subject, 82. 4
and their gross painting might be better us'd 82.13
reserve their character with golden quill | and 85. 3
making their tomb the womb wherein they grew? 86. 4
when other petty griefs have done their spite, 90.10
some glory in their birth, some in their skill, 91. 1
some glory in their birth, some in their skill, 91. 1
some in their wealth, some in their body's force 91. 2
in their wealth, some in their body's force, 91. 2
some in their garments, though new–fangled ill, 91. 3
some in their hawks and hounds, some in their 91. 4
in their hawks and hounds, some in their horse; 91. 4
they are the lords and owners of their faces, 94. 7
others but stewards of their excellence. 94. 8
for sweetest things turn sourest by their deeds; 94.13
got | which for their habitation chose out thee, 95.10
like widowed wombs after their lords' decease: 97. 8
or from their proud lap pluck them where they 98. 8
and sweets grown common lose their dear delight. 102.12
i see their antique pen would have express'd 106. 7
so all their praises are but prophecies | of 106. 9
and the sad augurs mock their own presage, 107. 6
have mine eyes out of their spheres been fitted 119. 7
which in their wills count bad what i think good 121. 8
that level | at my abuses reckon up their own; 121.10
by their rank thoughts my deeds must not be 121.12
all men are bad and in their badness reign. 121.14
pitiful thrivers, in their gazing spent? 125. 8
yet so they mourn, becoming of their woe, | that 127.13
they would change their state | and situation 128. 9
that they elsewhere might dart their injuries: 139.12
as testy sick men, when their deaths be near, 140. 7
no news but health from their physicians know; 140. 8
that have profan'd their scarlet ornaments, 142. 6
robb'd others' beds' revenues of their rents. 142. 8
sometimes her levell'd eyes their carriage ride, LC 22
sometime diverted their poor balls are tied | to 24
sometimes they do extend | their view right on; 26
anon their gazes lend | to every place at once, 26
bidding them find their sepulchres in mud, 46
big discontent so breaking their contents. 56
wind | upon his lips their silken parcels hurls. 87
all aids, themselves made fairer by their place, 117
yet their purpos'd trim | piec'd not his grace, 118
ask'd their own wills, and made their wills obey 133
their own wills, and made their wills obey. 133
that did his picture get | to serve their eyes, 135
to serve their eyes, and in it put their mind, 135
they sought their shame that so their shame did 187
sought their shame that so their shame did find, 187
by how much of me their reproach contains. 189
figuring that they their passions likewise lent 199
"'and lo behold these talents of their hair, 204
their kind acceptance weepingly beseech'd, 207
weak sights their sickly radiance do amend; 214
be, | since i their altar, you enpatron me. 224
comes | their distract parcels in combined sums. 231
have emptied all their fountains in my well, 255
and supplicant their sighs to you extend | to 276
flame through water which their hue encloses. 287

THEIRS 34 FR 0.0038 REL FR 31 V 3 P

let's assist them, | for our case is as theirs. TMP 1.01. 55
this love of theirs myself have often seen, TGV 3.01. 24
all their petitions are as freely theirs | as MM 1.04. 82
the effect of my intent is to cross theirs: LLL 5.02.138
to make theirs ours and ours none but our own; 5.02.154
must be your imagination then, and not theirs. MND 5.01.214 P
my place as i would they should do theirs — to TN 2.05. 54 P
eyes | blind with the pin and web but theirs, WT 1.02.291
with the pin and web but theirs, theirs only, 1.02.291
peace of heaven is theirs that lift their swords JN 2.01. 35
and made his majesty the bawd to theirs. 3.01. 59
his, | as theirs, so mine, and all be as it is. R2 2.01.146
but theirs is sweet'ned with the hope to have 2.03. 13
if they miscarry, theirs shall second them, 2H4 4.02. 46
we are in god's hand, brother, not in theirs. H5 3.06.169
theirs for the earth's increase, mine for my 2H6 3.02.385
at mine, sir, and theirs that love music. TRO 3.01. 24 P
in my way | than sway with them in theirs. COR 2.01.204
the great'st taste | most palates theirs. 3.01.104
in whose power | we were elected theirs, martius 3.01.210
forsooth, hereafter theirs, so far | as thou 3.02. 85
i, | even in theirs and in the commons' ears, 5.06. 4
when theirs are dry, for romeo's banishment. ROM 3.02.131
so is theirs and ours. TIM 3.04. 6
shall to thee blot out what wrongs were theirs, 5.01.153
your servants ever | have theirs, themselves, MAC 1.06. 26
themselves, and what is theirs, in compt, | to 1.06. 26
to tell them that this world did equal theirs ANT 4.15. 77
the misery of tharsus may be theirs. PER 1.04. 55
theirs has more ground, is more maturely TNK 1.03. 56
or theirs whose desperate hands themselves do VEN 765
an eye more bright than theirs, less false in SON 20. 5
theirs for their style i'll read, his for his 32.14
lands and mansions, theirs in thought assign'd, LC 138

THEISE *(also 's*, these, th's)*

THEISE 1 FR 0.0001 REL FR 0 V 1 P

mess, ere theise eyes of mine take themselves to H5 3.02.114 P

THEM *(also 'em, 'um)*

/THEM 29 FR 0.0032 REL FR 21 V 8 P

come, hang /them /on this line. TMP 4.01.193
ay, sir; i'll call /them to you. WIV 4.03. 7 P
bring /me to hear /them speak, where i may be MM 3.01. 52 P
and as a /bed i'll take /them, and there lie, ERR 3.02. 49
and all their lands restor'd to /them again AYL 5.04.164
/that, /by /confessing /them, /the /souls /of R2 4.01.226
/a /troop | /to /read /a /lecture /of /them? 4.01.232
/yet /salt /water /blinds /them /not /so /much 4.01.245
/word, /rebellion, /it /had /froze /them /up, 2H4 1.01.199
/tells /them /he /doth /bestride /a /bleeding 1.01.207
as the malice of /this age shapes /them, /are 1.02.173 P
/as /despair | /that /frosts /will /bite /them. 1.03. 41
/let /them /alone. 2.03. 41
/the /loud /trumpet /blowing /them /together; 4.01.120
/it /is /further /agreed /between /them, that 2H6 1.01. 50 P
eat, timon, and abhor /them. TIM 4.03.397
/the /common /stages — /so /they /call /them — HAM 2.02.343 P
/their /writers /do /them /wrong, /to /make 2.02.350 P
/to /make /them /exclaim /against /their /own 2.02.350 P
/it /no /sin /to /tarre /them /to /controversy. 2.02.353 P
/be /done, /i /will /arraign /them /straight. LR 3.06. 20
/ay, /sir, /she /took /them, /read /them /in /my 4.03. 11
/she /took /them, /read /them /in /my /presence, 4.03. 11
biting falchion | i would have made /them skip. 5.03.278
unpin me — have grace and favor /in /them. OTH 4.03. 21
cold and sickly | he vented /them, most narrow ANT 3.04. 8
shuns not to break one will crack /them both; PER 1.02.121
how lost thou /them? 5.01.140
yes, for /them | that have wild consciences. TNK 3.03. 23

THEM 2046 FR 0.2312 REL FR 1552 V 494 P

let's assist them, | for our case is as theirs. TMP 1.01. 54
put the wild waters in this roar, allay them. 1.02. 2
how to deny them, who t' advance, and who | to 1.02. 80
in troops i have dispers'd them 'bout the isle. 1.02.220
thy purposes | with words that made them known. 1.02.358
hark now i hear them — ding–dong bell. 1.02.405
i am the best of them that speak this speech, 1.02.430
their infancy again | and have no vigor in them. 1.02.486
as fresh as when we put them on first in afric, 2.01. 70 P
moe widows in them of this business' making 2.01.134
making | than we bring men to comfort them. 2.01.135
what a strange drowsiness possesses them! 2.01.199
say this were death | that now hath seiz'd them, 2.01.261
(for else his project dies) to keep them living. 2.01.299
and their labor | delight in them /sets off; 3.01. 2
some thousands of these logs, and pile them up, 3.01. 10
we are three of them; 3.02. 6 P
for without them | he's but a sot, as i am; 3.02. 92
he has brave utensils (for so he calls them) 3.02. 96
and in these fits i leave them, while i visit 3.03. 91
all three of them are desperate: 3.03.104
are of suppler joints) follow them swiftly, 3.03.107
and hinder them from what this ecstasy | may now 3.03.108
what this ecstasy | may now provoke them to. 3.03.109
incite them to quick motion, for i must | bestow 4.01. 39
flat meads thatch'd with stover, them to keep; 4.01. 63
at last i left them | i' th' filthy–mantled pool 4.01.181
i will plague them all, | even to roaring. 4.01.192
and more pinch–spotted make them | than pard or 4.01.260
let them be hunted soundly. 4.01.262
as you gave in charge, | just as you left them; 5.01. 9
and the remainder mourning over them, | brimful 5.01. 13
works 'em | that if you now beheld them, your 5.01. 18
go, release them, ariel. 5.01. 30
i'll fetch them, sir. 5.01. 32
not one of them | that yet looks on me, or would 5.01. 82
being awake, enforce them to this place; 5.01.100
i do forgive | thy rankest fault — all of them; 5.01.132
merciful, | i have curs'd them without cause. 5.01.179
even in a dream, were we divided from them, 5.01.239
one of them | is a plain fish, and no doubt 5.01.265
one) had plotted with them | to take my life. 5.01.273
he leaves his friends to dignify them more; TGV 1.01. 64
receiving them from such a worthless post. 1.01.153
you would be fing'ring them, to anger me. 1.02. 98
thus will i fold them one upon another; 1.02.125
if you respect them, best to take them up. 1.02.131
if you respect them, best to take them up. 1.02.131
nay, i was taken up for laying them down; 1.02.132
i see you have a month's mind to them. 1.02.134
with them shall proteus go — | and in good time 1.03. 43
no, boy, but as well as i can do them. 2.01. 92 P
writ, | but (since unwillingly) take them again. 2.01.123
nay, take them. 2.01.124
you writ them, sir, at my request, | but i will 2.01.126
sir, at my request, | but i will none of them; 2.01.127
i would have had them writ more movingly. 2.01.128
belike that now she hath enfranchis'd them 2.04. 90
sure, i think she holds them prisoners still. 2.04. 92
friends are well and have them much commended. 2.04.123
i left them all in health. 2.04.124
and made them watchers of mine own heart's 2.04.135
why then, how stands the matter with them? 2.05. 21 P
if i keep them, i needs must lose myself; 2.06. 20
if i lose them, thus find i by their loss — 2.06. 21
you must needs have them with a codpiece, madam. 2.07. 53
base men, that use them to so base effect! 2.07. 73
to my friends, | and i am going to deliver them. 3.01. 54
the tenure of them doth but signify | my health 3.01. 56
and slaves they are to me that send them flying: 3.01.141
my herald thoughts in thy pure bosom rest them, 3.01.144
i, their king, that thither them importune, | do 3.01.145
the grace that with such grace hath blest them, 3.01.146
so much of bad already hath possess'd them. 3.01.207
with them, upon her knees, her humble self, 3.01.228
whose whiteness so became them | as if but now 3.01.229
let me read them. 3.01.289 P
master, be one of them; 4.01. 38
you would have them always play but one thing? 4.02. 70 P
eyes, | for i had rather wink than look on them. 5.02. 14
o, ay; and pities them. 5.02. 26
that such an ass should owe them. 5.02. 28
for friar laurence met them both, | as he in 5.02. 37
much to do | to keep them from uncivil outrages. 5.04. 17
forgive them what they have committed here | and 5.04.154
and let them be recall'd from their exile; 5.04.155
thou hast prevail'd, i pardon them and thee; 5.04.158
dispose of them as thou know'st their deserts. 5.04.159
we three to hear it and end it between them. WIV 1.01.143 P
i think there are, sir, i heard them talk'd of. 1.01.288 P
let them wag; 1.03. 6 P
i will be cheaters to them both, and they shall 1.03. 70 P
and west indies, and i will trade to them both. 1.03. 72 P
of my beauty, and am i now a subject for them? 2.01. 3 P
he will print them, out of doubt; 2.01. 77 P
do you think there is truth in them? 2.01.172 P
but i would be loath to turn them together. 2.01.186 P
i think, hath appointed them contrary places; 2.01.208 P
i had rather hear them scold than fight. 2.01.231 P
/god bless them and make them his servants! 2.02. 52 P
/god bless them and make them his servants! 2.02. 53 P
the best courtier of them all (when the court 2.02. 61 P
as sip on a cup with the proudest of them all, 2.02. 76 P
fare thee well, commend me to them both. 2.02.131 P
she is my prize, or ocean whelm them all! 2.02.137
let them say 'tis grossly done, so it be fairly 2.02.142 P
eye upon my follies, as you hear them unfolded, 2.02.186 P
do you study them both, master parson? 3.01. 45 P
keep them asunder; 3.01. 71 P
disarm them, and let them question. 3.01. 76 P
disarm them, and let them question. 3.01. 76 P
let them keep their limbs whole and hack our 3.01. 77 P
sure they sleep, he hath no use of them. 3.02. 32 P
i ha' told them over and over, they lack no 3.03. 18 P
carry them to the laundress in datchet–mead; 3.03.147 P
i will do what i can for them all three, for so 3.04.107 P
and give them to a dog for a new–year's gift. 3.05. 8 P
who ask'd them once or twice what they had in 3.05.102 P
of such places, and goes to them by his note. 4.02. 63 P
let them say of me, "as jealous as ford, that 4.02.163 P
shall have my horses, but i'll make them pay; 4.03. 9 P
i'll sauce them. 4.03. 9 P
i'll sauce them, come. 4.03. 11 P
let them from forth a sawpit rush at once | with 4.04. 54
then let them all encircle him about, | and, 4.04. 57
i'll go buy them vizards. 4.04. 70
i may not conceal them, sir. 4.05. 44 P
conceal them, or thou diest. 4.05. 45 P
speak well of them, varletto. 4.05. 64 P
they threw me off from behind one of them, in a 4.05. 68 P
speciously one of them. 4.05.111 P

those that betray them do no treachery. 5.03. 22
are fairies, he that speaks to them shall die. 5.05. 47
pinch them, arms, legs, backs, shoulders, sides, 5.05. 54
as thoughts do blow them, higher and higher. 5.05. 98
as your worth is able, | and let them work. MM 1.01. 9
torches do, | not light them for themselves; 1.01. 33
of us, 'twere all alike | as if we had them not. 1.01. 35
too, but that a wise burgher put in for them. 1.02.100 P
hide our love | till time had made them for us. 1.02.153
have gone round | and none of them been worn; 1.02.169
'twould be my tyranny to strike and gall them 1.03. 36
strike and gall them | for what i bid them do; 1.03. 37
theirs | as they themselves would owe them. 1.04. 83
come, bring them away. 2.01. 41 P
bring them away. 2.01. 43 P
and (as i say) paying for them very honestly; 2.01.102 P
hoping you'll find good cause to whip them all. 2.01.137
draw you, master froth, and you will hang them. 2.01.206 P
are chosen, they are glad to choose me for them. 2.01.270 P
become them with one half so good a grace | as 2.02. 62
'tis wit in them, | but in the less foul 2.02.127
are either rich or poor | as fancy values them; 2.02.151
do me the common right | to let me see them, and 2.03. 6
that i may minister | to them accordingly. 2.03. 8
men their creation mar | in profiting by them. 2.04.128
that bear in them one and the self–same tongue, 2.04.173
on twenty bloody blocks, he'ld yield them up, 2.04.181
and dried not one of them with his comfort; 3.01.226 P
a marble to her tears, is wash'd with them, but 3.01.230 P
answer'd, he would never bring them to light. 3.02.178 P
angelo hath seen them both, and will discover 4.02.172 P
i know them both. 4.02.195 P
put them in secret holds, both barnardine and 4.03. 87
to angelo | (the provost, he shall bear them), 4.03. 94
reports, but the best is, he lives not in them. 4.03.160 P
and bid them bring the trumpets to the gate. 4.05. 9
see, to make them know | that outward courtesies 5.01. 14
she and that friar, | i saw them at the prison. 5.01.135
for many of them are neither maid, widow, nor 5.01.180 P
some more mightier member | that sets them on. 5.01.238
and punish them to your height of pleasure. 5.01.240
there is another friar that set them on, | let 5.01.248
here till he come and enforce them against him. 5.01.266 P
but, for those earthly faults, i quit them all, 5.01.483
forc'd me to seek delays for them and me. ERR 1.01. 74
not now | worthily term'd them merciless to us! 1.01. 99
and, for the sake of them thou sorrowest for, 1.01.121
what have befall'n of them and /thee till now. 1.01.123
in quest of them (unhappy), ah, lose myself. 1.02. 40
reserve them till a merrier hour than this: 1.02. 69
perchance you will not bear them patiently. 1.02. 86
doubtfully, that i could scarce understand them. 2.01. 54 P
scanted /men in hair he hath given them in wit. 2.02. 81 P
name them. 2.02. 96 P
if we obey them not, this will ensue: 2.02.191
though my cates be mean, take them in good part; 3.01. 28
go bid them let us in. 3.01. 30
at the door, master, bid them welcome hither. 3.01. 68
and the tallow in them will burn a poland winter 3.02. 98 P
cliffs, but i could find no whiteness in them. 3.02.127 P
are tir'd, gives them a sob and 'rests them; 4.03. 25 P
are tir'd, gives them a sob and 'rests them; 4.03. 26 P
on decay'd men and gives them suits of durance; 4.03. 27 P
here's that, i warrant you, will pay them all. 4.04. 10
wilt thou suffer them | to make a rescue? 4.04.110
let's call more help | to have them bound again. 4.04.146
bind dromio too, and bear them to my house. 5.01. 35
of more aid, | we came again to bind them. 5.01.154
fled | into this abbey, whither we pursu'd them, 5.01.155
between them they will kill the conjurer. 5.01.177
in this the madman justly chargeth them. 5.01.213
along with them | they brought one pinch, a 5.01.237
who deciphers them? 5.01.335
by force took dromio and my son from them, | and 5.01.353
what then became of them i cannot tell; 5.01.355
from you, | and dromio my man did bring them me. 5.01.386
meet but there's a skirmish of wit between them. ADO 1.01. 64 P
because i will not do them the wrong to mistrust 1.01.243 P
the bull's horns and set them in my forehead, 1.01.264 P
horse to hire," let them signify under my sign, 1.01.266 P
as the /event stamps them, but they have a good 1.02. 7 P
for he both pleases men and angers them, and 2.01.141 P
any ill, i will leave them at the next turning. 2.01.154 P
i will but teach them to sing, and restore them 2.01.232 P
them to sing, and restore them to the owner. 2.01.233 P
husbands, if a maid could come by them. 2.01.325 P
only to despite them, i will endeavor any thing. 2.02. 31 P
tell them that you know that hero loves me, 2.02. 34 P
offer them instances, which shall bear no less 2.02. 41 P
and bring them to see this the very night before 2.02. 45 P
then sigh not so, but let them go, | and be you 2.03. 66
for either he avoids them with great discretion, 2.03.191 P
or undertakes them with a most christian–like 2.03.192 P
their detractions and can put them to mending. 2.03.230 P
'tis a truth, i can bear them witness; 2.03.231 P
but i persuaded them, if they lov'd benedick, 3.01. 41
that were a punishment too good for them, if 3.03. 5 P
if they should have any allegiance in them, 3.03. 5 P
well, give them their charge, neighbor dogberry. 3.03. 7 P
and bid those that are drunk get them to bed. 3.03. 43 P
why then let them alone till they are sober. 3.03. 45 P
may say they are not the men you took them for. 3.03. 48 P
men, the less you meddle or make with them, why, 3.03. 53 P
sometimes fashioning them like pharaoh's 3.03.133 P
two of them did, the prince and claudio, but the 3.03.154 P
which first possess'd them, partly by the dark 3.03.156 P
by the dark night, which did deceive them, but 3.03.157 P
and one deformed is one of them; 3.03.169 P
for the letter that begins them all, h. 3.04. 56 P
and we would have them this morning examin'd 3.05. 47 P
i'll wait upon them, i am ready. 3.05. 56 P
that shall drive some of them to a non–come; 3.05. 62 P
in language | without offense to utter them. 4.01. 98
two of them have the very bent of honor, | and 4.01.186
the proudest of them shall well hear of it. 4.01.192
of friends, | to quit me of them throughly. 4.01.200
let them come before master constable. 4.02. 8 P
yea, marry, let them come before me. 4.02. 9 P
come let them be opinion'd. 4.02. 67 P
let them be in the hands — 4.02. 68 P
come, bind them. 4.02. 72 P
and all of them that thus dishonor her. 5.01. 44
i know them, yea, | and what they weigh, even to 5.01. 92
i doubt we should have been too young for them. 5.01.119 P
also, the watch heard them talk of one deformed. 5.01.308 P
if you use them, margaret, you must put in the 5.02. 20 P
for them all together, which maintain'd so 5.02. 62 P
admit any good part to intermingle with them. 5.02. 64 P
to bind me, or undo me — one of them. 5.04. 20
to fright them hence with that dread penalty. LLL 1.01.127
and he that breaks them in the least degree 1.01.156
let them be men of good repute and carriage. 1.02. 68 P
as i have read, sir, and the best of them too. 1.02. 84 P
beside | and prodigally gave them all to you. 2.01. 12
to–morrow you shall have a sight of them. 2.01.165
did point you to buy them, along as you pass'd; 2.01.245
and make them men of note — do you note? 3.01. 24 P
do the wise think them other? 3.01. 80
daughters be capable, i will put it to them: 4.02. 80 P
advance your standards, and upon them, lords; 4.03.364
pell–mell, down with them! 4.03.365
in conflict that you get the sun of them. 4.03.366
and win them too; 4.03.369
some entertainment for them in their tents. 4.03.370
from the park let us conduct them thither; 4.03.371
we will with some strange pastime solace them, 4.03.374
last of the five vowels, if "you" repeat them; 5.01. 54 P
i will repeat them — a,e,i — 5.01. 55 P
will you find men worthy enough to present them? 5.01.125 P
to the worthies, and let them dance the hay. 5.01.154
and not a man of them shall have the grace, 5.02.128
why, that they have, and bid them so be gone. 5.02.182
ask them how many inches | is in one mile: 5.02.188
tell her, we measure them by weary steps. 5.02.194
let's mock them still, as well known as 5.02.301
let us complain to them what fools were here, 5.02.302
the stairs, as he treads on them, kiss his feet. 5.02.330
i dare not call them fools; 5.02.371
i do forswear them, and i here protest, | by 5.02.410
it pleas'd them to think me worthy of pompey the 5.02.505 P
go bid them prepare. 5.02.509 P
let them not approach. 5.02.511
but you have out–fac'd them all. 5.02.623 P
stir them /on, stir them on! 5.02.689 P
stir them /on, stir them on! 5.02.689 P
and in our maiden council rated them | at 5.02.779
we did not cote them so. 5.02.786
call them forth quickly, we will do so. 5.02.889 P
well | beteem them from the tempest of my eyes. MND 1.01.131
you were best to call them generally, man by man 1.02. 2 P
and desire you, to con them by to–morrow night; 1.02.100 P
creep into acorn–cups and hide them there. 2.01. 31
tell them that i pyramus am not pyramus, but 3.01. 20 P
this will put them out of fear. 3.01. 22 P
and tell them plainly he is snug the joiner. 3.01. 45 P
this is a knavery of them to make me afeard. 3.01.113 P
honest neighbors will not make them friends. 3.01.146 P
and light them at the fiery glow–worm's eyes, 3.01.170
made senseless things begin to do them wrong, 3.02. 28
i led them on in this distracted fear, | and 3.02. 31
bearing the badge of faith to prove them true? 3.02.127
and from each other look thou lead them thus, 3.02.363
up and down, | i will lead them up and down; 3.02.397
goblin, lead them up and down. 3.02.399
uncouple in the western valley, let them go. 4.01.107
go, bid the huntsmen wake them with their horns. 4.01.138
this wood, | and i in fury hither followed them, 4.01.162
and i do not doubt but to hear them say, it is a 4.02. 44 P
turns them to shapes and gives to aery nothing 5.01. 16
go bring them in; 5.01. 84
the kinder we, to give them thanks for nothing. 5.01. 89
where i have seen them shiver and look pale, 5.01. 95
worst are no worse, if imagination amend them. 5.01.212 P
imagine no worse of them than they of themselves 5.01.215 P
lay them in gore, | since you have shore | with 5.01.339
the petty traffickers | that cur'sy to them, do MV 1.01. 13
that cur'sy to them, do them reverence, | as 1.01. 13
as they fly by them with their woven wings. 1.01. 14
almost damn those ears | which, hearing them, 1.01. 99
you shall seek all day ere you find them, and 1.01.117 P
day ere you find them, and when you have them, 1.01.118 P
means | to hold a rival place with one of them, 1.01.174
i pray thee over–name them, and as thou namest 1.02. 36 P
thee over–name them, and as thou namest them, i 1.02. 37 P
and as thou namest them, i will describe them; 1.02. 37 P
is not one among them but i dote on his very 1.02.109 P
and i pray god grant them a fair departure. 1.02.111 P
he stuck them up before the fulsome ewes, | who 1.03. 86
whose own hard dealings teaches them suspect 1.03.161
the unbated fire | that he did pace them first? 2.06. 12
the one of them contains my picture, prince: 2.07. 11
is the complexion of them all to leave the dam. 3.01. 29 P
no news of them? 3.01. 91 P
one of them show'd me a ring that he had of your 3.01.118 P
i am lock'd in one of them; 3.02. 40
valor's excrement | to render them redoubted! 3.02. 88
making them lightest that wear most of it. 3.02. 91
the skull that bred them in the sepulchre. 3.02. 96
but her eyes — | how could he see to do them? 3.02.124
i give them with this ring, | which when you 3.02.171
we'll play with them the first boy for a 3.02.213 P
bring them i pray thee with imagin'd speed 3.04. 52
wish, for all that, that i had not kill'd them; 3.04. 73
go in, sirrah, bid them prepare for dinner. 3.05. 46 P
then bid them prepare dinner! 3.05. 50 P
go to thy fellows, bid them cover the table, 3.05. 58 P
i would not draw them, i would have my bond. 4.01. 87
and in slavish parts, | because you bought them. 4.01. 93
shall i say to you, | "let them be free! 4.01. 94
marry them to your heirs! 4.01. 94
i have them ready. 4.01.256
ay, sacrifice them all | here to this devil, to 4.01.286
me your gloves, i'll wear them for your sake, 4.01.426
but we'll outface them, and outswear them too. 4.02. 17
but we'll outface them, and outswear them too. 4.02. 17
you shall perceive them make a mutual stand, 5.01. 77
ay, and i'll give them him without a fee. 5.01.290
shall i keep your hogs and eat husks with them? AYL 1.01. 38 P
therefore he gives them good leave to wander. 1.01.103 P
by our beards (if we had them) thou art. 1.02. 74 P
pitiful dole over them that all the beholders 1.02.131 P
i attend them with all respect and duty. 1.02.167 P
cast away upon curs, throw some of them at me. 1.03. 5 P
paths, our very petticoats will catch them. 1.03. 15 P
i could shake them off my coat; 1.03. 16 P
hem them away. 1.03. 18 P
to fright the animals and to kill them up | in 2.01. 62
can it be possible that no man saw them? 2.02. 1
of men | their graces serve them but as enemies? 2.03. 11
whom i took two cods and, giving her them again, 2.04. 53 P
i give heaven thanks, and make no boast of them. 2.05. 37 P
of all opinion that grows rank in them | that i 2.07. 46
your lips will feel them the sooner. 3.02. 60 P
why do you infect yourself with them? 3.02.114 P
peace, you dull fool, i found them on a tree. 3.02.115 P
o yes, i heard them all, and more, too, for some 3.02.164 P
for some of them had in them more feet than the 3.02.165 P
for some of them had in them more feet than the 3.02.165 P
of my verses with reading them ill–favoredly. 3.02.262 P
goldsmiths' wives, and conn'd them out of rings? 3.02.272 P
i prithee recount some of them. 3.02.357 P
a man has good horns, and knows no end of them. 3.03. 54 P
the noblest deer hath them as huge as the rascal 3.03. 57 P
fantastical knave of them all shall flout me out 3.03.107 P
the very ice of chastity is in them. 3.04. 17 P
swears brave oaths, and breaks them bravely, 3.04. 42 P
if mine eyes can wound, now let them kill thee. 3.05. 16
when he that speaks them pleases those that hear 3.05.112
from time to time and worms have eaten them, but 4.01.107 P
clubs cannot part them. 5.02. 41 P
themselves, one of them thought but of an if, as 5.04.100 P
by your simp'ring, none of you hates them), that ep 16 P
but sup them well, and look unto them all, SHR in.1. 28
but sup them well, and look unto them all, in.1. 28
bid them come near. in.1. 79
go, sirrah, take them to the buttery, | and give in.1. 102
and give them friendly welcome every one. in.1. 103
let them want nothing that my house affords. in.1. 104
ladies | unto their lords, by them accomplished; in.1. 112
i'll in to counsel them; in.1. 136
thy hounds shall make the welkin answer them in.2. 45
marry, i will, let them play it. in.2. 137 P
fall to them as you find your stomach serves you 1.01. 38
on them to look and practice by myself. 1.01. 83
you, know any such, | prefer them hither; 1.01. 97
and a man could light on them, would take her 1.01.129 P
visit his countrymen, and banquet them? 1.01.197
you, sir, i'll have them very fairly bound — 1.02.145
too, | and let me have them very well perfum'd; 1.02.151
unbind my hands, i'll pull them off myself, 2.01. 4
if you accept them, then their worth is great. 2.01.101
gentlemen | to my daughters, and tell them both, 2.01.109
bid them use them well. 2.01.110
bid them use them well. 2.01.110
quoth she, "i'll fume with them." 2.01.152
conster them. 3.01. 30
"now take them up," quoth he, "if any list." 3.02.165
nay, let them go, a couple of quiet ones. 3.02.240
a fire, and they are coming after to warm them. 4.01. 5 P
let them curtsy with their left legs and not 4.01. 92 P
call them forth. 4.01. 97 P
i call them forth to credit her. 4.01.104 P
why, she comes to borrow nothing of them. 4.01.105 P
from florence, and must here deliver them. 4.02. 90
among them know you one vincentio? 4.02. 96
i pray thee moralize them. 4.04. 81 P
i have seen them in the church together, god 5.01. 41 P
go fetch them hither. 5.02.103
swinge me them soundly forth unto their husbands 5.02.104
away, i say, and bring them hither straight. 5.02.105
might with effects of them follow our friends, AWW 1.01.184
till their own scorn return to them unnoted 1.02. 34
his equal had awak'd them, and his honor, 1.02. 38
low ranks, | making them proud of his humility, 1.02. 44
would demonstrate them now | but goers backward. 1.02. 47
he scatter'd not in ears, but grafted them, | to 1.02. 54
deservings, when of ourselves we publish them. 1.03. 7 P
for i know you lack not folly to commit them, 1.03. 11 P
may the world know them? 1.03. 34 P
were our faults, or then we thought them none. 1.03.135
me | in heedfull'st reservation to bestow them, 1.03.225
those girls of italy, take heed of them. 2.01. 19
be more expressive to them, for they wear 2.01. 52 P
after them, and take a more dilated farewell. 2.01. 57 P
grapes, and if my royal fox | could reach them. 2.01. 72
oft does them by the weakest minister: 2.01.137
more, more, a hundred of them. 2.02. 42 P
not much commendation to them. 2.02. 67 P
peruse them well. 2.03. 61
and they were sons of mine, i'd have them whipt, 2.03. 87 P
them whipt, or i would send them to th' turk, to 2.03. 87 P
when rather from our acts we them derive | than 2.03.136
you had my prayers to lead them on, and to keep 2.04. 17 P
my prayers to lead them on, and to keep them on, 2.04. 18 P
them on, and to keep them on, have them still. 2.04. 18 P
i have kept of them tame, and know their natures 2.05. 45 P
seem, | and my appointments have in them a need 2.05. 67
at the first view | to you that know them not. 2.05. 69
that can fly from us | shall on them settle. 3.01. 21
which of them both | is dearest to me, i have no 3.04. 38
beware of them, diana; 3.05. 18 P
many a maid hath been seduc'd by them, and the 3.05. 21 P
are lim'd with the twigs that threatens them. 3.05. 24 P
some hurts, and say i got them in exploit. 4.01. 37 P
keep him muffled | till we do hear from them. 4.01. 91
and you shall know them | when back again this 4.02. 59
treasons, we still see them reveal themselves, 4.03. 22 P
would be proud, if our faults whipt them not, 4.03. 73 P
demand them singly. 4.03.183 P
i'll after them. 4.03.340
which, in the minority of them both, his majesty 4.05. 72 P
foot of time | steals ere we can effect them. 5.03. 42
not knowing them until we know their grave. 5.03. 62
and that you fly them as you swear them lordship 5.03.156

that you fly them as you swear them lordship, 5.03.156
can nor will deny | but that i know them. 5.03.167
you have them ill to friend | till your deeds 5.03.182
them ill to friend | till your deeds gain them; 5.03.183
i did go between them, as i said, but more than 5.03.259 P
was in that credit with them at that time that i 5.03.262 P
let them hang themselves in their own straps. TN 1.03. 12 P
are you full of them? 1.03. 77 P
ay, sir, i have them at my fingers' ends. 1.03. 78 P
and tell them, there thy fixed foot shall grow 1.04. 17
well, god give them wisdom that have it; 1.05. 14 P
that are fools, let them use their talents. 1.05. 15 P
sir, i bade them take away you. 1.05. 54 P
item, two grey eyes, with lids to them; 1.05.248 P
and sing them loud even in the dead of night; 1.05.271
for your love, to lay any of them on you. 2.01. 7 P
telling them i know my place as i would they 2.05. 53 P
let thy blood and spirit embrace them, and, to 2.05.147 P
nicely with words may quickly make them wanton. 3.01. 15 P
are very rascals since bonds disgrac'd them. 3.01. 21 P
so false, i am loath to prove reason with them. 3.01. 25 P
i will conster to them whence you come; 3.01. 56 P
taste your legs, sir, put them to motion. 3.01. 78 P
oxen and wain–ropes cannot hale them together. 3.02. 60 P
answer'd in repaying | what we took from them, 3.03. 34
"and some have greatness thrust upon them." 3.04. 45 P
this will so fright them both that they will 3.04.195 P
give them way till he take leave, and presently 3.04.197 P
would make me tell them how much i lack of a man 3.04.303 P
who hath made this havoc with them? 5.01.203 P
and some have greatness thrown upon them." 5.01.372 P
there rooted betwixt them then such an affection WT 1.01. 23 P
thanks a while, | and pay them when you part. 1.02. 10
your dread "verily," | one of them you shall be. 1.02. 56
see good and evil, | inclining to them both. 1.02.304
at several posterns | clear them o' th' city. 1.02.439
behind the tuft of pines i met them; 2.01. 34
i ey'd them | even to their ships. 2.01. 35
yea, a very trick | for them to play at will. 2.01. 52
any of them? 2.02. 12
unsafe lunes i' th' king, beshrew them! 2.02. 28
they should not laugh if i could reach them, nor 2.03. 25
together with the dam | commit them to the fire! 2.03. 96
(methinks i so should term them) and the 3.01. 5
didst counsel and aid them, for their better 3.02. 20 P
faults i make, when i shall come to know them, 3.02.219
upon them shall | the causes of their death 3.02.236
if any where i have them, 'tis by the sea–side, 3.03. 67 P
the poor souls roar'd, and the sea mock'd them; 3.03.100 P
i witness to | the times that brought them in; 4.01. 12
must either stay to execute them thyself, or 4.02. 16 P
they are in losing them when they have approv'd 4.02. 28 P
but they are most of them means and bases; 4.03. 43 P
but one puritan amongst them, and he sings 4.03. 44 P
the loathsomeness of them offend me more than 4.03. 56 P
o, pardon, that i name them! 4.04. 7
have taken | the shapes of beasts upon them. 4.04. 27
address yourself to entertain them sprightly, 4.04. 53
barren, and i care not | to get slips of them. 4.04. 85
wherefore, gentle maiden, | do you neglect them? 4.04. 86
in gillyvors, | and do not call them bastards. 4.04. 99
the dibble in earth to set one slip of them; 4.04.100
methinks i play as i have seen them do | in 4.04.133
the ord'ring your affairs, | to sing them too. 4.04.140
he utters them as he had eaten ballads and all 4.04.185 P
that have more in them than you'ld think, sister 4.04.216 P
i was promis'd them against the feast, but they 4.04.235 P
are in sad talk, and we'll not trouble them. 4.04.311 P
one three of them, by their own report, sir, 4.04.337 P
these good men are pleas'd, let them come in; 4.04.341 P
'tis time to part them. 4.04.344
i would not prize them | without her love; 4.04.375
for her, employ them all, | commend them and 4.04.376
commend them and condemn them to her service, 4.04.377
commend them and condemn them to her service, 4.04.377
care | to have them recompens'd as thought on. 4.04.520
lie, but we pay them for it with stamped coin, 4.04.724 P
are rich, but he wears them not handsomely. 4.04.749 P
if he think it fit to shore them again, and that 4.04.837 P
to him will i present them, there may be matter 4.04.841 P
forget your evil, | with them, forgive yourself. 5.01. 6
i cannot forget | my blemishes in them, and so 5.01. 8
and left them | more rich for what they yielded. 5.01. 54
friends, | bring them to our embracement. 5.01.114
sceptres, | and those that bear them, living. 5.01.147
and threatens them | with divers deaths in death 5.01.201
by your desires, | i am friend to them and you. 5.01.231
a notable passion of wonder appear'd in them; 5.02. 16 P
it seem'd sorrow wept to take leave of them, for 5.02. 45 P
told him i heard them talk of a farthel and i 5.02.116 P
say you see them not and think me still no 5.02.130 P
unlawful business | i am about, let them depart. 5.03. 97
let them approach. JN 1.01. 47
his parts, | and finds them perfect richard. 1.01. 90
and stir them up against a mightier task. 2.01. 55
with them a bastard of the king's deceas'd, 2.01. 65
let them be welcome then, we are prepar'd. 2.01. 83
wilt thou resign them and lay down thy arms? 2.01.154
let us hear them speak | whose title they admit, 2.01.199
that did display them when we first march'd 2.01.320
leave them as naked as the vulgar air. 2.01.387
and when that we have dash'd them to the ground, 2.01.405
i'll stir them to it. 2.01.415
join | do glorify the banks that bound them in; 2.01.442
to these two princes, if you marry them. 2.01.445
urge them while their souls | are capable of 2.01.475
as true as i believe you think them false | that 3.01. 27
your breeches best may carry them. 3.01.201
our pray'rs come in, | if thou vouchsafe them. 3.01.294
so heavy as thou shalt not shake them off, | but 3.01.296
i tore them from their bonds, and cried aloud, 3.04. 70
and will again commit them to their bonds, 3.04. 74
she looks upon them with a threat'ning eye. 3.04.120
away his natural cause | and call them meteors, 3.04.157
and with hot irons must i burn them out. 4.01. 59
with this same very iron to burn them out. 4.01.124
have possess'd you with, and think them strong; 4.02. 41
both for myself and them — but, chief of all, 4.02. 49
for the which myself and them | bend their best 4.02. 50
the copy of your speed is learn'd by them; 4.02.113
bring them before me. 4.02.169
i will seek them out. 4.02.169
and fly, like thought, from them to me again. 4.02.175
rage, | and make them tame to their obedience! 4.02.262
at whose request the king hath pardon'd them, 5.06. 35
these lincoln washes have devoured them; 5.06. 41
leaves them invisible, and his siege is now 5.07. 16
the salt in them is hot. 5.07. 45
of the world in arms, | and we shall shock them. 5.07.117
then call them to our presence; R2 1.01. 15
let them lay by their helmets and their spears, 1.03.119
ere further leisure yield them further means 1.04. 40
they shall subscribe them for large sums of gold 1.04. 50
gold, | and send them after to supply our wants, 1.04. 51
and let them die that age and sullens have, 2.01.139
urge doubts to them that fear. 2.01.299
and whoso empties them | by so much fills their 2.02.130
if judgment lie in them, then so do we, 2.02.133
draws out our miles and makes them wearisome, 2.03. 5
to rouse his wrongs and chase them to the bay. 2.03.128
see them delivered over | to execution and the 3.01. 29
my lord northumberland, see them dispatch'd. 3.01. 35
ay, all of them at bristow lost their heads. 3.02.142
and let them go | to ear the land that hath some 3.02.211
discharge my followers, let them hence away, 3.02.217
have torn their souls by turning them from us, 3.03. 83
as thus to drop them still upon one place, 3.03.166
to come at traitors' calls and do them grace. 3.03.181
hear, | although apparent guilt be seen in them, 4.01.124
shall feel this day as sharp to them as thorn. 4.01.323
good old folks and let them tell /thee tales 5.01. 41
his proud steed's neck, | bespake them thus: 5.02. 20
a dozen of them here have ta'en the sacrament, 5.02. 97
against them both my true joints bended be. 5.03. 98
his, then let them have | that mercy which true 5.03.109
straight shall dog them at the heels. 5.03.139
but i will have them if i once know where. 5.03.143
is pointing still, in cleansing them from tears. 5.05. 54
take hence the rest, and give them burial here. 5.05.118
for he that brought them, in the very heat | and 1H4 1.01. 59
if you and i do not rob them, cut this head off 1.02.165 P
how shall we part with them in setting forth? 1.02.167 P
forth before or after them and appoint them a 1.02.169 P
after them and appoint them a place of meeting, 1.02.170 P
have no sooner achiev'd but we'll set upon them. 1.02.173 P
they shall not see — i'll tie them in the wood; 1.02.178 P
our vizards we will change after we leave them; 1.02.179 P
well, for two of them, i know them to be as 1.02.183 P
i know them to be as true–bred cowards as ever 1.02.183 P
he call'd them untaught knaves, unmannerly, | to 1.03. 43
and if the devil come and roar for them, | i 1.03.125
come and roar for them, | i will not send them. 1.03.126
power | did gage them both in an unjust behalf 1.03.173
from the north to south, | and let them grapple. 1.03.197
i'll keep them all! 1.03.213
by god, he shall not have a scot of them, | no, 1.03.214
i'll keep them, by this hand. 1.03.216
deliver them up without their ransom straight, 1.03.260
you four shall front them in the narrow lane; 2.02. 60 P
how many be there of them? 2.02. 63 P
down with them! 2.02. 83 P
down with them! 2.02. 85 P
fleece them! 2.02. 85 P
stand close, i hear them coming. 2.02. 97 P
are they not some of them set forward already? 2.03. 28 P
and crack'd crowns, | and pass them current too. 2.03. 94
and can call them all by their christen names, 2.04. 7 P
away, you rogue, dost thou not hear them call? 2.04. 78 P
dozen more are at the door, shall i let them in? 2.04. 83 P
let them alone awhile, and then open the door. 2.04. 84 P
nether–stocks, and mend them and foot them too. 2.04.117 P
nether–stocks, and mend them and foot them too. 2.04.117 P
england, and one of them is fat and grows old, 2.04.131 P
give me them that will face me. 2.04.151 P
with a dozen of them two hours together. 2.04.165 P
let them speak; 2.04.170 P
and bound them. 2.04.176 P
they were bound, every man of them, or i am a 2.04.179 P
what, fought you with them all? 2.04.184 P
but if i fought not with fifty of them, i am a 2.04.186 P
pray god you have not murd'red some of them. 2.04.190 P
past praying for, i have pepper'd two of them. 2.04.192 P
lies are like their father that begets them, 2.04.226 P
we two saw you four set on four and bound them, 2.04.254 P
our noses with speargrass to make them bleed, 2.04.310 P
shall i let them in? 2.04.490 P
one of them is well known, my gracious lord, | a 2.04.510
let's see what they be. read them. 2.04.534 P
but will they come when you do call for them? 3.01. 54
parts besides, | beguiling them of commendation. 3.01.187
and god forgive them that so much have sway'd 3.02.130
i have given them away to bakers' wives, they 3.03. 69 P
bakers' wives, they have made bolters of them. 3.03. 70 P
let them coin his nose, let them coin his cheeks 3.03. 78 P
them coin his nose, let them coin his cheeks. 3.03. 78 P
i laud them, i praise them. 3.03.191 P
i laud them, i praise them. 3.03.192 P
let them come! 4.01.112
war | all hot and bleeding will we offer them. 4.01.115
and if it make twenty, take them all, i'll 4.02. 8 P
to fill up the rooms of them as have bought out 4.02. 32 P
i'll not march through coventry with them, 4.02. 39 P
for indeed i had the most of them out of prison. 4.02. 41 P
thence, | who with them was a rated sinew too, 4.04. 17
for, on their answer, will we set on them, | and 5.01.119
i cannot read them now. 5.02. 80
fair | when the intent of bearing them is just. 5.02. 88
to all those | that wear those colors on them. 5.04. 27
let them that should reward valor bear the sin 5.04.149 P
and not a man of them brings other news | than 2H4 in 38
a man is through with them in honest taking up, 1.02. 40 P
keep them off, bardolph. 2.01. 54 P
i beseech you i may have redress against them. 2.01.108 P
me not, he was a fool that taught them me. 2.01.192 P
shall we steal upon them, ned, at supper? 2.02.158 P
times, | and be like them to percy troublesome. 2.03. 4
then join you with them, like a rib of steel, 2.03. 54
all our loves, | first let them try themselves. 2.03. 56
why then cover and set them down, and see if 2.04. 10 P
i make them? 2.04. 42 P
gluttony and diseases make, i make them not. 2.04. 43 P
names upon you before you have earn'd them. 2.04.144 P
nay, rather damn them with | king cerberus, and 2.04.167
let them play. 2.04.227 P
than i love e'er a scurvy young boy of them all. 2.04.273 P
for one of them, she's in hell already, and 2.04.338 P
bid them o'er–read these letters | and well 3.01. 2
these letters | and well consider of them. 3.01. 3
curling their monstrous heads and hanging them 3.01. 23
then let us meet them like necessities; 3.01. 93
and had the best of them all at commandement. 3.02. 24 P
let me see them, i beseech you. 3.02. 95 P
let them appear as i call; 3.02. 99 P
let them do so, let them do so. 3.02. 99 P
let them do so, let them do so. 3.02. 99 P
the just proportion that we gave them out. 4.01. 23
let us sway on and face them in the field. 4.01. 24
you shall enjoy them, every thing set off | that 4.01.143
of heaven and him | have here upswarm'd them. 4.02. 30
if they miscarry, theirs shall second them, 4.02. 46
pleaseth your grace to answer them directly 4.02. 52
i like them all, and do allow them well, | and 4.02. 54
i like them all, and do allow them well, | and 4.02. 54
let them have pay, and part. 4.02. 70
i know it will well please them. 4.02. 71
and, ere they be dismiss'd, let them march by. 4.02. 96
and not a tongue of them all speaks any other 4.03. 19 P
you should have won them dearer than you have. 4.03. 67
humane principle i would teach them should be, 4.03.123 P
let them go. 4.03.128 P
image of my youth, | is overspread with them; 4.04. 56
found some months asleep and leapt them over. 4.04.124
i cut them off, and had a purpose now | to lead 4.05.209
lest rest and lying still might make them look 4.05.211
he, by conversing with them, is turn'd into a 5.01. 67 P
i pray thee now deliver them like a man of this 5.03. 97 P
if there's but two ways, either to utter them, 5.03.111 P
two ways, either to utter them, or conceal them. 5.03.111 P
take them away. 5.05. 95
that you see them | printing their proud hoofs H5 pr 26
carry them here and there, jumping o'er times, pr 29
and rather choose to hide them in a net | than 1.02. 93
the blood and courage that renowned them | runs 1.02.118
urn, | tombless, with no remembrance over them. 1.02.229
days, | not measuring what use we made of them. 1.02.268
wasteful vengeance | that shall fly with them; 1.02.284
convey them with safe conduct. 1.02.297
may have their throats about them at that time, 2.01. 22 P
act | for which we have in head assembled them? 2.02. 18
read them, and know i know your worthiness. 2.02. 69
cause | that admiration did not hoop at them; 2.02.108
open, | arrest them to the answer of the law, 2.02.143
law, | and god acquit them of their practices! 2.02.144
bear them hence. 2.02.181
i put my hand into the bed and felt them, and 2.03. 23 P
we'll give them present audience. 2.04. 67
go, and bring them. 2.04. 67
they seem to threaten | runs far before them. 2.04. 71
and let them know | of what a monarchy you are 2.04. 72
and in them behold | upon the hempen tackle 3.pr. 7
cannon touches, | and down goes all before them. 3.pr. 34
of grosser blood, | and teach them how to war. 3.01. 25
i am boy to them all three, but all they three, 3.02. 29 P
i must leave them, and seek some better service. 3.02. 51 P
use mercy to them all for us, dear uncle. 3.03. 54
poor we call them in their native lords! 3.05. 26
and on to–morrow bid them march away. 3.06.172
tongues, and my horse is argument for them all. 3.07. 35 P
some of them will fall to–morrow, i hope. 3.07. 72 P
first go yourself to hazard, ere you have them. 3.07. 88 P
give them great meals of beef and iron and steel 3.07.149 P
presented them unto the gazing moon | so many 4.pr. 27
bids them good morrow with a modest smile, | and 4.pr. 33
and calls them brothers, friends, and countrymen 4.pr. 34
do my good morrow to them, and anon | desire 4.01. 26
them, and anon | desire them all to my pavilion. 4.01. 27
some upon their wives left poor behind them, 4.01.140 P
a black matter for the king that led them to it; 4.01.145 P
have on them the guilt of premeditated and 4.01.162 P
beat us, for they bear them on their shoulders; 4.01.227 P
knight, | collect them all together at my tent. 4.01.287
soldiers' hearts, | possess them not with fear! 4.01.290
take from them now | the sense of reck'ning, /if 4.01.290
opposed numbers | pluck their hearts from them. 4.01.292
mount them, and make incision in their hides, 4.02. 9
and dout them with superfluous courage, ha! 4.02. 11
what, will you have them weep our horses' blood? 4.02. 12
leaving them but the shales and husks of men. 4.02. 18
let us but blow on them, | the vapor of our 4.02. 23
the vapor of our valor will o'erturn them. 4.02. 24
and our air shakes them passing scornfully. 4.02. 42
fly o'er them all, impatient for their hour. 4.02. 52
shall we go send them dinners and fresh suits, 4.02. 57
horses provender, | and after fight with them? 4.02. 59
bid them achieve me, and then sell my bones. 4.03. 91
for there the sun shall greet them, | and draw 4.03.100
soldiers' heads | and turn them out of service. 4.03.119
which if they have as i will leave 'um them, 4.03.124
shall yield them little, tell the constable. 4.03.125
if they will fight with us, bid them come down, 4.07. 58
if they'll do neither, we will come to them, 4.07. 60
and make them skirr away, as swift as stones 4.07. 61
and not a man of them that we shall take | shall 4.07. 64
go and tell them so. 4.07. 65
field | to book our dead, and then to bury them; 4.07. 73
at their dead masters, | killing them twice. 4.07. 81
follow, and see there be no harm between them. 4.07.182
not read the story, | that i may prompt them; 5.pr. 2
i humbly pray them to admit th' excuse | of time 5.pr. 3
to order peace between them — and omit | all 5.pr. 39
and /swear i got them in the gallia wars. 5.01. 89
which hitherto have borne in them | against the 5.02. 15
against the french that met them in their bent 5.02. 16
the king hath heard them; 5.02. 74

with better heed | to re–survey them, we will 5.02. 81
our gracious brother, i will go with them. 5.02. 92
i'll ask them. 5.02.197 P
that, when i come to woo ladies, i fright them. 5.02.228 P
in a sugar touch of them than in the tongues of 5.02.277 P
yes, my lord, you see them perspectively: 5.02.320 P
and with them scourge the bad revolting stars 1H6 1.01. 4
with purpose to relieve and follow them, 1.01.133
we will rush on them. 1.02. 18
and hunger will enforce them to be more eager. 1.02. 38
of old i know them; 1.02. 39
by my consent, we'll even let them alone. 1.02. 44
drive them from orleance and be immortaliz'd. 1.02.148
or we'll burst them open, if that you come not 1.03. 28
now beat them hence, why do you let them stay? 1.03. 54
now beat them hence, why do you let them stay? 1.03. 54
father, i know, and oft have shot at them, 1.04. 3
three days have i watch'd | if i could see them. 1.04. 17
i'll never trouble you, if i may spy them. 1.04. 22
great fear of my name 'mongst them were spread 1.04. 50
our english troops retire, i cannot stay them; 1.05. 2
a woman clad in armor chaseth them. 1.05. 3
let them practice and converse with spirits. 2.01. 25
and lay new platforms to endamage them. 2.01. 77
we'll follow them with all the power we have. 2.02. 33
towns, | and in a moment makes them desolate. 2.03. 66
for soldiers' stomachs always serve them well. 2.03. 80
that charles the dolphin may encounter them. 3.02. 9
hearts, | because i ever found them as myself. 3.02. 98
and join'st with them will be thy slaughter–men. 3.03. 75
be patient, lords, and give them leave to speak. 4.01. 82
both are my kinsmen, and i love them both. 4.01.155
it is too late, i cannot send them now. 4.04. 1
hew them to pieces, hack their bones asunder, 4.07. 47
that i in rage might shoot them at your faces! 4.07. 80
that i may bear them hence | and give them 4.07. 85
and give them burial as beseems their worth. 4.07. 86
to keep them here, | they would but stink, and 4.07. 89
i'll bear them hence; 4.07. 92
so we be rid of them, do with /'em what thou 4.07. 94
so let them have their answers every one. 5.01. 25
see them guarded | and safely brought to dover, 5.01. 48
commit them to the fortune of the sea. 5.01. 50
peace be amongst them if they turn to us, | else 5.02. 6
is, | but we will presently provide for them. 5.02. 15
peace, | and lay them gently on thy tender side. 5.03. 49
keeping them prisoner underneath /her wings. 5.03. 57
dame | (had i sufficient skill to utter them) 5.05. 13
it is further agreed between them, that the 2H6 1.01. 58 P
for, were there hope to conquer them again, | my 1.01.117
myself did win them both. 1.01.119
ireland, | in bringing them to civil discipline, 1.01.195
i cannot blame them all, what is't to them? 1.01.220
i cannot blame them all, what is't to them? 1.01.220
the silly owner of the goods | weeps over them, 1.01.226
to call them both a pair of crafty knaves. 1.02.103
let me see them. 1.03. 14 P
suffolk, let them go. 1.03. 40
so one by one we'll weed them all at last, | and 1.03. 99
prove them, and i lie open to the law; 1.03.156
he did speak them to me in the garret one night, 1.03.191 P
and let these have a day appointed them | for 1.03.207
away with them to prison; 1.03.218 P
away with them, let them be clapp'd up close, 1.04. 50
away with them, let them be clapp'd up close, 1.04. 50
these news, as fast as horse can carry them — 1.04. 74
now open them. 2.01.103
but suddenly | to nominate them all, it is 2.01.128
let them be whipt through every market town, 2.01.155
at buckingham, and all the crew of them, | till 2.02. 72
here let them end it, and god defend the right! 2.03. 55
to tread them with her tender–feeling feet. 2.04. 9
or count them happy that enjoys the sun? 2.04. 39
and each of them had twenty times their power, 2.04. 61
suffer them now, and they'll o'ergrow the garden 3.01. 32
i never gave them condign punishment. 3.01.130
'twill make them cool in zeal unto your grace. 3.01.177
thou never didst them wrong, nor no man wrong; 3.01.209
for there i'll ship them all for ireland. 3.01.329
'twas men i lack'd, and you will give them me; 3.01.345
and he that loos'd them forth their brazen caves 3.02. 89
and bid them blow towards england's blessed 3.02. 90
and call'd them blind and dusky spectacles, 3.02.112
makes them thus forward in his banishment. 3.02.253
go, salisbury, and tell them all from me, | i 3.02.279
me, | i thank them for their tender loving care; 3.02.280
and had i not been cited so by them, | yet did i 3.02.281
a plague upon them! 3.02.309
wherefore should i curse them? 3.02.309
heart would break, | should i not curse them. 3.02.321
and turns the force of them upon thyself. 3.02.332
he hath no eyes, the dust hath blinded them. 3.03. 14
set, | it is our pleasure one of them depart; 4.01.140
i see them, i see them! 4.02. 21 P
i see them, i see them! 4.02. 21 P
come, come, let's fall in with them. 4.02. 30 P
and i will apparel them all in one livery, that 4.02. 74 P
the elder of them, being put to nurse, | was by 4.02.142
assail them with the army of the king. 4.02.175
proclaim them traitors that are up with cade, 4.02.177
rather than bloody war shall cut them short, 4.04. 12
me, | and could it not enforce them to relent, 4.04. 17
hath given them heart and courage to proceed. 4.04. 35
until a power be rais'd to put them down. 4.04. 40
bridge, killing all those that withstand them. 4.05. 4 P
but i am troubled here with them myself; 4.05. 7
come, then, let's go fight with them. 4.06. 13 P
down with them all. 4.07. 2 P
to call poor men before them about matters they 4.07. 42 P
moreover, thou hast put them in prison, and 4.07. 43 P
they could not read, thou hast hang'd them, when 4.07. 44 P
yet to recover them would lose my life. 4.07. 66
those that i never saw, and struck them dead. 4.07. 82
head, and bring them both upon two poles hither. 4.07.112 P
let them kiss one another, for they lov'd well 4.07.130 P
now part them again, lest they consult about the 4.07.132 P
the streets, and at every corner have them kiss. 4.07.136 P
throw them into thames! 4.08. 2 P
retreat or parley when i command them kill? 4.08. 5 P
and here pronounce free pardon to them all 4.08. 9
let them break your backs with burthens, take 4.08. 28 P
broil | i see them lording it in london streets, 4.08. 45
name of henry the fift hales them to an hundred 4.08. 57 P
mischiefs, and makes them leave me desolate. 4.08. 58 P
i see them lay their heads together to surprise 4.08. 58 P
ten meals i have lost, and i'd defy them all. 4.10. 62 P
let them obey that knows not how to rule; 5.01. 6
i'll send them all as willing as i live. 5.01. 51
if thou dar'st bring them to the baiting–place. 5.01.150
to see their day, and them our fortune give. 5.02. 89
i know our safety is to follow them, | for, as i 5.03. 23
shall we after them? 5.03. 27
after them! 5.03. 28
nay, before them, if we can. 5.03. 28
speak thou for me and tell them what i did. 3H6 1.01. 16
ah, know you not the city favors them, | and 1.01. 67
turn this way, henry, and regard them not. 1.01.189
accurs'd be he that seeks to make them foes! 1.01.205
will follow mine, if once they see them spread; 1.01.252
come, we'll after them. 1.01.256
i'll write unto them and entreat them fair; 1.01.271
i'll write unto them and entreat them fair; 1.01.271
and i, i hope, shall reconcile them all. 1.01.273
in them i trust, for they are soldiers, | witty, 1.02. 42
think'st thou that we fear them? 1.02. 53
i'll win them, fear it not. 1.02. 60
and issue forth and bid them battle straight. 1.02. 70
i'll open them. 1.03. 11
my sons, god knows what hath bechanced them; 1.04. 6
'tis virtue that doth make them most admir'd, 1.04.130
'tis government that makes them seem divine, 1.04.132
who having pinch'd a few and made them cry, 2.01. 16
and stood against them, as the hope of troy 2.01. 51
i cheer'd them up with justice of our cause, 2.01.133
and we, in them, no hope to win the day, | so 2.01.136
as the rocks cheer them that fear their wrack: 2.02. 5
who hath not seen them, even with those wings 2.02. 29
for shame, my liege, make them your president! 2.02. 33
defy them then, or else hold close thy lips. 2.02.118
and give them leave to fly that will not stay; 2.03. 50
and call them pillars that will stand to us; 2.03. 51
promise them such rewards | as victors wear at 2.03. 52
and i, that, haply, take them from him now, 2.05. 58
yield both my life and them | to some man else, 2.05. 59
bear thee hence, and let them fight that will, 2.05.121
for vengeance comes along with them. 2.05.134
think you, lords, that clifford fled with them? 2.06. 37
yet look to have them buzz to offend thine ears. 2.06. 95
for how can i help them and not myself? 3.01. 21
and would you not do much to do them good? 3.02. 38
to do them good i would sustain some harm. 3.02. 39
then get your husband's lands, to do them good. 3.02. 40
what service wilt thou do me if i give them? 3.02. 44
for by that loss i will not purchase them. 3.02. 73
herein your highness wrongs both them and me. 3.02. 75
unless my hand and strength could equal them. 3.02.145
i'll undertake to land them on our coast, | and 3.03.205
shall waft them over with our royal fleet. 3.03.253
god forbid that i should wish them sever'd 4.01. 21
to sunder them that yoke so well together. 4.01. 23
in them, and in ourselves, our safety lies. 4.01. 46
me their words as near as thou canst guess them. 4.01. 90
let them go, here is | the duke. 4.03. 29
for, till i see them here, by doubtful fear | my 4.06. 62
my liege, i'll knock once more to summon them. 4.07. 16
to keep them back that come to succor you. 4.07. 56
nor much oppress'd them with great subsidies, 4.08. 45
stops thy spring, my sea shall suck them dry, 4.08. 55
as good to chide the waves as speak them fair. 5.04. 24
for well i wot ye blaze to burn them out. 5.04. 71
go bear them hence, i will not hear them speak. 5.05. 4
go bear them hence, i will not hear them speak. 5.05. 4
had, | the thought of them would have stirr'd up 5.05. 64
with them, the two brave bears, warwick and 5.07. 10
that dogs bark at me as i halt by them — | why, R3 1.01. 23
since that our brother dubb'd them gentlewomen, 1.01. 82
to give them thanks | that were the cause of my 1.01.127
say that i slew them not? 1.02. 89
beauty hath, and made them blind with weeping. 1.02.166
wear both of them, for both of them are thine. 1.02.205
wear both of them, for both of them are thine. 1.02.205
and between them and my lord chamberlain, | and 1.03. 38
and sent to warn them to his royal presence. 1.03. 39
that i, forsooth, am stern, and love them not? 1.03. 44
i do remember them too well: 1.03.117
and then, to dry them, gav'st the duke a clout 1.03.176
o, let them keep it till thy sins be ripe, | and 1.03.218
that stand high have many blasts to shake them, 1.03.258
the lips of those that breathe them in the air. 1.03.285
god pardon them that are the cause thereof! 1.03.314
to pray for them that have done scath to us. 1.03.316
and tell them 'tis the queen and her allies 1.03.329
tell them that god bids us do good for evil: 1.03.334
but none can help our harms by wailing them. 2.02.103
and with them sir thomas vaughan, prisoners. 2.04. 43
who hath committed them? 2.04. 44
god keep you from them, and from such false 3.01. 15
heart, | thinking on them, go i unto the tower. 3.01.150
well, let them rest. 3.01.157
some that have accus'd them wear their hats. 3.02. 93
to hear her prayer for them, as now for us! 3.03. 20
i do beseech you send for some of them. 3.04. 33
tell them how edward put to death a citizen 3.05. 76
tell them, when that my mother went with child 3.05. 86
you thrive well, bring them to baynard's castle, 3.05. 98
bid them both | meet me within this hour at 3.05.104
i bid them that did love their country's good 3.07. 21
which when i saw, i reprehended them, | and 3.07. 27
and if you plead as well for them | as i can say 3.07. 52
at their beads, 'tis much to draw them thence, 3.07. 93
o, make them joyful, grant their lawful suit! 3.07.203
if you deny them, all the land will rue it. 3.07.222
call them again. 3.07.224
patience, | i may not suffer you to visit them, 4.01. 16
i am their mother, who shall bar me from them? 4.01. 21
i am their father's mother, i will see them. 4.01. 22
or shall they last, and we rejoice in them? 4.02. 6
still live they, and for ever let them last! 4.02. 7
let me have open means to come to them, | and 4.02. 76
and soon i'll rid you from the fear of them. 4.02. 77
and so i left them both, | to bear this tidings 4.03. 21
but didst thou see them dead? 4.03. 27
the chaplain of the tower hath buried them, 4.03. 29
and throw them in the entrails of the wolf? 4.04. 23
then would i hide my bones, not rest them here. 4.04. 33
factor to buy souls | and send them thither; 4.04. 73
were, | and he that slew them fouler than he is. 4.04.121
my words are dull, o, quicken them with thine! 4.04.124
thy woes will make them sharp and pierce like 4.04.125
orators of miseries, | let them have scope! 4.04.130
enemies | and promise them success and victory. 4.04.194
but in your daughter's womb i bury them; 4.04.423
unarm'd, and unresolv'd to beat them back. 4.04.436
the aid | of buckingham to welcome them ashore. 4.04.439
he, mistrusting them, | hois'd sail, and made 4.04.526
and who doth lead them but a paltry fellow, 5.03.323
and in record left them the heirs of shame. 5.03.335
upon them! 5.03.351
let them not live to taste this land's increase 5.05. 38
think you see them great, | and follow'd with H8 pr 27
was then present, saw them salute on horseback, 1.01. 8
beheld them when they lighted, how they clung 1.01. 9
did almost sweat to bear | the pride upon them, 1.01. 25
their very labor | was to them as a painting. 1.01. 26
best, now worst, | as presence did present them: 1.01. 30
able to maintain | the many to them 'longing, 1.02. 32
all in uproar, | and danger serves among them. 1.02. 37
wholesome | to those which would not know them, 1.02. 46
and cold hearts freeze | allegiance in them; 1.02. 62
from our laws, | and stick them in our will. 1.02. 94
of beauty | shall shine at full upon them. 1.04. 60
well, let him have them: 2.02. 10
that they had gather'd a wise council to them 2.04. 51
or shortly after | this world had air'd them. 2.04.194
and force them with a constancy, the cardinal 3.02. 2
the cardinal | cannot stand under them. 3.02. 3
presently | he did unseal them, and the first he 3.02. 79
his faults lie open to the laws, let them, | not 3.02.334
to which | she was often cited by them, but 4.01. 29
lofty and sour to them that lov'd him not, | but 4.02. 53
have | in them a wilder nature than the business 5.01. 15
this morning see | you do appear before them. 5.01.145
this ring | deliver them, and your appeal to us 5.01.151
and your appeal to us | there make before them. 5.01.152
lay about him to–day, i can tell them that, and TRO 1.02. 56 P
let them take heed of troilus; 1.02. 57 P
i can tell them that too. 1.02. 58 P
'tis just to each of them; he is himself. 1.02. 71 P
hairs on your chin — and one of them is white." 1.02.158 P
stand up here and see them as they pass toward 1.02.178 P
i'll tell you them all by their names as they 1.02.182 P
and that's one of the chiefest of them too. 1.02.267 P
and call them shames which are indeed nought 1.03. 19
hands shall strike | when fitness calls them on, 1.03.202
looks | know them from eyes of other mortals? 1.03.225
if none of them have soul in such a kind, | we 1.03.285
soul in such a kind, | we left them all at home. 1.03.286
i see them not with my old eyes, what are they? 1.03.365
sharp /at reasons, | you are so empty of them. 2.02. 34
when we have soil'd them, nor the remainder 2.02. 70
that in their country did them that disgrace 2.02. 95
and i will fill them with prophetic tears. 2.02.102
less than little wit from them that they have, 2.03. 13 P
desires, in all fair measure, fairly guide them! 3.01. 45 P
in, after falling out, may make them three. 3.01.103 P
son, | yea, let them say, to stick the heart of 3.02.195
call them all pandars. 3.02.202 P
to send their smiles before them to achilles, 3.03. 72
the love that lean'd on them as slippery too, 3.03. 85
heat them, and they retort that heat again | to 3.03.101
nor doth he of himself know them for aught, 3.03.118
till he behold them formed in th' applause 3.03.119
i will go meet them; 4.02. 70
distinct breath and consign'd kisses to them, 4.04. 45
bid them have patience, she shall come anon. 4.04. 52
set them down | for sluttish spoils of 4.05. 61
hector would have them fall upon him thus. 4.05.137
desire them home. 4.05.157
the worthiest of them tell me name by name; 4.05.160
a burning devil take them! 5.02.196 P
your fair sword, | you bid them rise and live. 5.03. 42
spur them to ruthful work, rein them from ruth. 5.03. 48
spur them to ruthful work, rein them from ruth. 5.03. 48
of valor, to appear | this morning to them. 5.03. 70
deeds worth praise, and tell you them at night. 5.03. 93
i would fain see them meet, that that same young 5.04. 5 P
i'll seek them. 5.04. 35 P
our sufferance is a gain to them. COR 1.01. 22 P
at the heaven with your staves as lift them 1.01. 68
make it, and | your knees to them (not arms) 1.01. 74
like fathers, | when you curse them as enemies. 1.01. 78
but it proceeds or comes from them to you, | and 1.01.153
and a petition granted them — a strange one, 1.01.210
as they would hang them on the horns a' th' moon 1.01.213
what is granted them? 1.01.214
nay, let them follow. 1.01.248
to martius, | though martius earn'd them not; 1.01.274
stand fast, we'll beat them to their wives, | as 1.04. 41
'tis for the followers fortune widens them, 1.04. 44
fliers at the very heels, | with them he enters; 1.04. 50
hangmen would | bury with those that wore them, 1.05. 7
down with them! 1.05. 8
tribunes for them!), 1.06. 43
o'er them aufidius, | their very heart of hope. 1.06. 54
keep your duties, | as i have set them down. 1.07. 2
chests in corioles, and the gold that's in them. 2.01.132 P
the gods grant them true! 2.01.141 P
greetings, | but with them change of honors. 2.01.198
in my way | than sway with them in theirs. 2.01.204
that he will give them make i as little question 2.01.230
people in what hatred | he still hath held them; 2.01.246
to 's power he would | have made them mules, 2.01.247
dispropertied their freedoms, holding them, | in 2.01.248
and sore blows | for sinking under them. 2.01.253

have flatter'd the people, who ne'er lov'd them; 2.02. 8 P
his noble carelessness lets them plainly see't. 2.02. 14 P
'twixt doing them neither good nor harm; 2.02. 17 P
he dislikes, to flatter them for their love. 2.02. 23 P
any further deed to have them at all into their 2.02. 27 P
the people than | he hath hereto priz'd them at. 2.02. 60
to heal again | than hear say how i got them. 2.02. 70
but your people, | i love them as they weigh — 2.02. 74
rewards | his deeds with doing them, and is 2.02.128
i do owe them still | my life and services. 2.02.133
and entreat them | for my wounds' sake to give 2.02.137
put them not to't. 2.02.141
to brag unto them, "thus i did, and thus!" 2.02.147
show them th' unaching scars which i should hide 2.02.148
as if i had receiv'd them for the hire | of 2.02.149
our purpose to them, and to our noble consul 2.02.152
he will require them | as if he did contemn what 2.02.156
what he requested | should be in them to give. 2.02.158
we'll inform them | of our proceedings here on 2.02.158
tongues into those wounds and speak for them; 2.03. 7 P
must also tell him our noble acceptance of them. 2.03. 9 P
i got them in my country's service, when | some 2.03. 52
you must desire them | to think upon you. 2.03. 55
bid them wash their faces, | and keep their 2.03. 60
the people, to earn a dearer estimation of them; 2.03. 97 P
nod and be off to them most counterfeitly; 2.03.100 P
will not seal your knowledge with showing them. 2.03.109 P
have chose a consul that will from them take 2.03.214
make them of no more voice | than dogs, that are 2.03.215
let them assemble; 2.03.217
let them go on; 2.03.255
when time shall prompt them, to make road | upon 3.01. 5
i do despise them! 3.01. 22
for they do prank them in authority, | against 3.01. 23
must these have voices, that can yield them now, 3.01. 34
have you not set them on? 3.01. 37
the people cry you mock'd them; 3.01. 42
when corn was given them gratis, you repin'd, 3.01. 43
for the people, call'd them | time–pleasers, 3.01. 44
not to them all. 3.01. 46
have you inform'd them sithence? 3.01. 47
how? i inform them? 3.01. 47
meiny, let them | regard me as i do not flatter, 3.01. 66
in soothing them we nourish 'gainst our senate 3.01. 69
by mingling them with us, the honor'd number, 3.01. 72
us, yet sought | the very way to catch them. 3.01. 80
if you are not, | let them have cushions by you. 3.01.101
they show'd | most valor, spoke not for them. 3.01.127
let them not lick | the sweet which is their 3.01.156
on fair ground | i could beat forty of them. 3.01.242
myself | take up a brace o' th' best of them, 3.01.243
let them pull all about mine ears, present me 3.02. 1
of sight, yet will i still | be thus to them. 3.02. 6
who was wont | to call them woollen vassals, 3.02. 9
you had not show'd them how ye were dispos'd 3.02. 22
let them hang! 3.02. 23
for them? 3.02. 38
do it to the gods, | must i then do't to them? 3.02. 39
in peace what each of them by th' other lose 3.02. 44
go to them, with this bonnet in thy hand, | and 3.02. 73
thus far having stretch'd it (here be with them) 3.02. 74
or say to them, | thou art their soldier, and, 3.02. 80
must i go show them my unbarb'd sconce? 3.02. 99
it is my more dishonor | than thou of them. 3.02.125
cog their hearts from them, and come home 3.02.133
let them accuse me by invention; 3.02.143
have you collected them by tribes? 3.03. 11
death, for fine, or banishment, then let them, 3.03. 15
i shall inform them. 3.03. 18
let them not cease, but with a din confus'd 3.03. 20
make them be strong, and ready for this hint 3.03. 23
this hint | when we shall hap to give't them. 3.03. 24
let them pronounce the steep tarpeian death, 3.03. 88
make invincible | the heart that conn'd them. 4.01. 11
bid them all home, he's gone; 4.02. 1
bid them home. 4.02. 5
dismiss them home. | here comes his mother. 4.02. 7
you have told them home, | and, by my troth, you 4.02. 48
and hope to come upon them in the heat of their 4.03. 18 P
and to pluck from them their tribunes for ever. 4.03. 24 P
the day serves well for them now. 4.03. 31 P
i think, that shall set them in present action. 4.03. 47 P
true," i'd not believe them more | than thee, 4.05.105
of rome, | or rudely visit them in parts remote, 4.05.142
in parts remote, | to fright them, ere destroy. 4.05.143
with fire, and took | what lay before them. 4.06. 79
he leads them like a thing | made by some other 4.06. 90
and defense | that rome can make against them. 4.06.128
first he was | a noble servant to them, but he 4.07. 36
as he hath spices of them all — not all, | for 4.07. 46
he could not stay to pick them in a pile | of 5.01. 25
and with our fair entreaties haste them on. 5.01. 74
push'd out your gates the very defender of them, 5.02. 40 P
such friends | that thought them sure of you. 5.03. 8
constrains them weep and shake with fear and 5.03.100
no, our suit | is that you reconcile them: 5.03.136
when we banish'd him, we respected not them; 5.04. 33 P
we'll meet them, | and help the joy. 5.04. 61
strew flowers before them! 5.05. 3
deliver them this paper. 5.06. 2
bid them repair to th' market–place, where i, 5.06. 3
make way to lay them by their bretheren. TIT 1.01. 89
draw near them then in being merciful: 1.01.118
and with loud 'larums welcome them to rome. 1.01.147
and sheathe them not | till saturninus be rome's 1.01.204
people's hearts, and wean them from themselves. 1.01.211
will ye bestow them friendly on andronicus? 1.01.219
receive them then, the tribute that i owe, 1.01.251
alone, | i'll find a day to massacre them all, 1.01.450
and make them know what 'tis to let a queen 1.01.454
the cause were known to them it most concerns, 2.01. 50
but be your heart to them | as unrelenting flint 2.03.140
no, let them satisfice their lust on thee. 2.03.180
now will i fetch the king to find them here, 2.03.206
'tis not an hour since i left them there. 2.03.256
we know not where you left them all alive, | but 2.03.257
sirs, drag them from the pit unto the prison, 2.03.283
there let them bide until we have devis'd | some 2.03.284
some never–heard–of tortering pain for them. 2.03.285
accursed, if the /fault be prov'd in them — 2.03.291
thou shalt not bail them, see thou follow me. 2.03.299
let them not speak a word, the guilt is plain, 2.03.301
death, | that end upon them should be executed. 2.03.303
come, lucius, come, stay not to talk with them. 2.03.306
make the silken strings delight to kiss them, 2.04. 46
would not then have touch'd them for his life! 2.04. 47
yet plead i must, | and bootless unto them. 3.01. 36
now all the service i require of them | is that 3.01. 77
that blabb'd them with such pleasing eloquence, 3.01. 83
perchance because she knows them innocent. 3.01.115
because the law hath ta'en revenge on them. 3.01.117
dry, | with miry slime left on them by a flood? 3.01.126
i'll deceive them both; 3.01.186
say i account of them | as jewels purchas'd at 3.01.197
then be my passions bottomless with them! 3.01.217
woes, | but like a drunkard must i vomit them. 3.01.231
to weep with them that weep doth ease some deal, 3.01.244
and make them blind with tributary tears; 3.01.269
even in their throats that hath committed them. 3.01.274
open them, boy. 4.01. 32
or else to heaven she heaves them for revenge. 4.01. 40
sons | presents that i intend to send them both. 4.01.116
and sends them weapons wrapp'd about with lines 4.02. 27
although she lave them hourly in the flood. 4.02.103
and tell them both the circumstance of all, 4.02.156
and who should find them but the empress' 4.03. 74
but give them to his master for a present. 4.03. 76
he says that he hath taken them down again, for 4.03. 82 P
myself hath often heard them say, | when i have 4.04. 74
trim sport for them which had the doing of it. 5.01. 96
indeed i was their tutor to instruct them. 5.01. 98
and bid the owners quench them with their tears. 5.01.134
and set them upright at their dear friends' door 5.01.136
can couch for fear, but i will find them out, 5.02. 38
and in their ears tell them my dreadful name, 5.02. 39
stab them, or tear them on thy chariot–wheels, 5.02. 47
stab them, or tear them on thy chariot–wheels, 5.02. 47
goths, | or at the least make them his enemies. 5.02. 79
wrong, | and i will be revenged on them all. 5.02. 97
go thou with them, and in the emperor's court 5.02.104
i pray thee do on them some violent death, 5.02.108
and on them shalt thou ease thy angry heart. 5.02.119
feast at my house, and he shall feast with them. 5.02.128
i knew them all though they suppos'd me mad, 5.02.142
and will o'erreach them in their own devices, 5.02.143
the empress' sons i take them, chiron, demetrius 5.02.154
name, | and therefore bind them, gentle publius. 5.02.157
caius and valentine, lay hands on them. 5.02.158
and now i find it, therefore bind them sure, 5.02.160
close their mouths, let them not speak a word. 5.02.164
look that you bind them fast. 5.02.165
stop their mouths, let them not speak to me, 5.02.167
but let them hear what fearful words i utter. 5.02.168
so, now bring them in, for i'll play the cook, 5.02.204
and see them ready against their mother comes. 5.02.205
go fetch them hither to us presently. 5.03. 59
countless and infinite, yet would i pay them! 5.03.159
and talk of them when he was dead and gone. 5.03.166
o now, sweet boy, give them their latest kiss! 5.03.169
do them that kindness, and take leave of them. 5.03.171
do them that kindness, and take leave of them. 5.03.171
us take the law of our sides, let them begin. ROM 1.01. 38 P
as i pass by, and let them take it as they list. 1.01. 40 P
i will bite my thumb at them, which is disgrace 1.01. 43 P
them, which is disgrace to them if they bear it. 1.01. 43 P
beat them down! 1.01. 73
i drew to part them. 1.01.108
not having that which, having, makes them short. 1.01.164
whose names are written there, and to them say, 1.02. 36
find them out whose names are written here! 1.02. 38 P
but let them measure us by what they will, 1.04. 9
we'll measure them a measure and be gone. 1.04. 10
and soar with them above a common bound. 1.04. 18
that presses them and learns them first to bear, 1.04. 93
that presses them and learns them first to bear, 1.04. 93
to bear, | making them women of good carriage. 1.04. 94
but passion lends them power, time means, to 2.pr. 13
and but thou love me, let them find me here; 2.02. 76
two such opposed kings encamp them still | in 2.03. 27
though news be sad, yet tell them merrily; 2.05. 22
follow me close, for i will speak to them. 3.01. 37
men's eyes were made to look, and let them gaze; 3.01. 54
their fatal points, | and 'twixt them rushes; 3.01.167
for, ere i | could draw to part them, was stout 3.01.173
some twenty of them fought in this black strife, 3.01.178
that hath new robes | and may not wear them. 3.02. 31
will you go to them? 3.02.129
love, | misshapen in the conduct of them both, 3.03.131
bed, | which heavy sorrow makes them apt unto. 3.03.157
who, raging with thy tears, and they with them, 3.05.135
and from my soul too, else beshrew them both. 3.05.227
turn to another, this shall slay them both. 4.01. 59
things that, to hear them told, have made me 4.01. 86
how canst thou try them so? 4.02. 5
i'll call them back again to comfort me. 4.03. 17
that living mortals, hearing them, run mad — 4.03. 48
and all things change them to the contrary. 4.05. 90
move them no more by crossing their high will. 4.05. 95
law | is death to any he that utters them. 5.01. 67
think upon these gone, | let them affright thee. 5.03. 61
lips, | haply some poison yet doth hang on them, 5.03.165
with instruments upon them, fit to open | these 5.03.200
i married them, and their stol'n marriage–day 5.03.233
i know them both; th' other's a jeweller. TIM 1.01. 8
i saw them speak together. 1.01. 62
amongst them all, | whose eyes are on this 1.01. 67
why dost thou call them knaves? 1.01.181
thou know'st them not. 1.01.181
pray entertain them, give them guide to us. 1.01.243
pray entertain them, give them guide to us. 1.01.243
that game, we must not dare | to imitate them; 1.02. 13
and all the madness is, he cheers them up too. 1.02. 42 P
methinks they should invite them without knives: 1.02. 44
thou weep'st to make them drink, timon. 1.02.109 P
there comes with them a forerunner, my lord, 1.02.119 P
i pray let them be admitted. 1.02.121 P
let's be provided to show them entertainment. 1.02.179
i shall accept them fairly; 1.02.184
i'll hunt with him, and let them be receiv'd, 1.02.190
do so, my friends. see them well entertain'd. 2.02. 44
brought in my accompts, | laid them before you; 2.02.134
you would throw them off, | and say you /found 2.02.134
off, | and say you /found them in mine honesty. 2.02.135
are crown'd, | that i account them blessings; 2.02.182
way) | to them to use your signet and your name, 2.02.201
you gods, reward them! 2.02.213
have their ingratitude in them hereditary: 2.02.215
i charge thee, invite them all, let in the tide 3.04.116
his outsides, to wear them like his raiment, 3.05. 33
but he hath conjur'd me beyond them, and i must 3.06. 12 P
women at the table, let a dozen of them be — as 3.06. 79 P
common /lag of people — what is amiss in them, 3.06. 81 P
are to me nothing, so in nothing bless them, and 3.06. 83 P
is divídant, touch them with several fortunes, 4.03. 5
and give them title, knee, and approbation 4.03. 37
thou saw'st them, when i had prosperity. 4.03. 78
i see them now, then was a blessed time. 4.03. 79
give them diseases, leaving with thee their lust 4.03. 85
but for thy sword and fortune, trod upon them — 4.03. 96
the gods confound them all in thy conquest, 4.03.104
writ, | but set them down horrible traitors. 4.03.119
wear them, betray with them. 4.03.147
wear them, betray with them. 4.03.147
thou dost affect my manners, and dost use them. 4.03.199
bid them flatter thee. 4.03.231
if thou wilt, | tell them there i have gold; 4.03.289
i would my tongue could rot them off! 4.03.365
close impossibilities, | and mak'st them kiss! 4.03.388
by thy virtue | set them into confounding odds, 4.03.391
fit i meet them. 5.01. 54
what you are | make them best seen and known. 5.01. 69
hang them, or stab them, drown them in a draught 5.01.102
hang them, or stab them, drown them in a draught 5.01.102
them, or stab them, drown them in a draught, 5.01.102
confound them by some course, and come to me, 5.01.103
name them, my lord, let's know them. 5.01.105
name them, my lord, let's know them. 5.01.105
speak to them, noble timon. 5.01.130
i thank them, and would send them back the 5.01.137
thank them, and would send them back the plague, 5.01.137
the plague, | could i but catch it for them. 5.01.138
of their love, | ever to read them thine. 5.01.155
become your lips as they pass thorough them. 5.01.195
commend me to them, | and tell them that, to 5.01.197
and tell them that, to ease them of their griefs 5.01.198
tell them that, to ease them of their griefs, 5.01.198
uncertain voyage, i will some kindness do them: 5.01.202
i'll teach them to prevent wild alcibiades' 5.01.203
should fall | for private faults in them. 5.04. 26
when they are in great danger, i recover them. JC 1.01. 24 P
draw them to tiber banks, and weep your tears 1.01. 58
if you do find them deck'd with ceremonies. 1.01. 65
so do you too, where you perceive them thick. 1.01. 71
know | that i do fawn on men and hug them hard, 1.02. 75
men and hug them hard, | and after scandal them; 1.02. 76
write them together, yours is as fair a name; 1.02.144
sound them, it doth become the mouth as well; 1.02.145
weigh them, it is as heavy; 1.02.146
according as he pleas'd and displeas'd them, as 1.02.260 P
his doublet, and offer'd them his throat to cut. 1.02.265 P
but there's no heed to be taken of them; 1.02.274 P
the gods, | incenses them to send destruction. 1.03. 13
heaven hath infus'd them with these spirits, 1.03. 69
to make them instruments of fear and warning 1.03. 70
give so much light that i may read by them. 2.01. 45
been often dropp'd | where i have took them up. 2.01. 50
do you know them? 2.01. 72
that by no means i may discover them | by any 2.01. 75
yes, every man of them; 2.01. 90
if he improve them, may well stretch so far | as 2.01.159
impossible, | yea, get the better of them. 2.01.326
things are beyond all use, | and i do fear them. 2.02. 26
here's decius brutus, he shall tell them so. 2.02. 57
and tell them that i will not come to–day. 2.02. 62
tell them so, decius. 2.02. 64
decius, go tell them caesar will not come. 2.02. 68
lest i be laugh'd at when i tell them so. 2.02. 70
if you shall send them word you will not come, 2.02. 95
i am ashamed i did yield to them. 2.02.106
bid them prepare within; 2.02.118
so tell them, publius. 3.01. 91
reasons, | when severally we hear them rendered. 3.02. 10
the evil that men do lives after them, | the 3.02. 75
i will not do them wrong; 3.02.125
if you have tears, prepare to shed them now. 3.02.169
have, alas, i know not, | that made them do it. 3.02.214
poor, dumb mouths, | and bid them speak for me. 3.02.226
he hath left them you, | and to your heirs for 3.02.249
notice of the people, | how i had mov'd them. 3.02.271
he shall but bear them as the ass bears gold, 4.01. 21
of yours hides wrongs, | and when you do them — 4.02. 41
bid them move away; 4.02. 45
i do not, till you practice them on me. 4.03. 88
you shall not come to them. 4.03.127
the enemy, marching along by them, | by them 4.03.207
them, | by them shall make a fuller number up, 4.03.208
along ourselves, and meet them at philippi. 4.03.225
i'll have them sleep on cushions in my tent. 4.03.243
here, | answering before we do demand of them. 5.01. 6
rob the hybla bees, | and leave them honeyless. 5.01. 35
hands, | unless thou bring'st them with thee. 5.01. 57
let them set on at once; 5.02. 3
and sudden push gives them the overthrow. 5.02. 5
ride, ride, messala, let them all come down. 5.02. 6
all that serv'd brutus, i will entertain them. 5.05. 60
this was the noblest roman of them all: 5.05. 68
and common good to all, made one of them. 5.05. 72
as the water has, | and these are of them. MAC 1.03. 80
defense, | and pour'd them down before him. 1.03.100
of cawdor to me | promis'd no less to them? 1.03.120
where every day i turn | the leaf to read them. 1.03.152
they have more in them than mortal knowledge. 1.05. 3 P
when i burnt in desire to question them further, 1.05. 4 P
old, | and the late dignities heap'd up to them, 1.06. 19

i think not of them; 2.01. 21
that which hath made them drunk hath made me 2.02. 1
what hath quench'd them hath given me fire. 2.02. 2
that death and nature do contend about them, 2.02. 7
i stood and heard them; 2.02. 21
prayers, and address'd them | again to sleep. 2.02. 22
go carry them, and smear | the sleepy grooms 2.02. 46
no man's life was to be trusted with them. 2.03.105
do repent me of my fury, | that i did kill them. 2.03.107
let's not consort with them; 2.03.135
which puts upon them | suspicion of the deed. 2.04. 26
if there come truth from them — | as upon thee, 3.01. 6
bring them before us. 3.01. 47
of king upon me, | and bade them speak to him; 3.01. 58
for them the gracious duncan have i murther'd, 3.01. 65
in the vessel of my peace | only for them, and 3.01. 67
to make them kings — the seeds of banquo kings! 3.01. 69
who wrought with them, and all things else that 3.01. 81
from the bill | that writes them all alike: 3.01.100
indeed have died | with them they think on? 3.02. 11
but in them nature's copy's not eterne. 3.02. 38
there's not a one of them but in his house | i 3.04.130
and let them fight | against the churches; 4.01. 52
smiles upon me, | and points at them for his. 4.01.124
ride, | and damn'd all those that trust them! 4.01.139
who must hang them? 4.02. 54 P
enow to beat the honest men and hang up them. 4.02. 58 P
good and loyal, | destroying them for wealth. 4.03. 84
i have no relish of them, but abound | in the 4.03. 95
air, | where hearing should not latch them. 4.03.195
which shall possess them with the heaviest sound 4.03.202
heaven rest them now! 4.03.227
revenges burn in them; 5.02. 3
near birnan wood | shall we well meet them; 5.02. 6
bring me no more reports, let them fly all. 5.03. 1
hear'st thou of them? 5.03. 56
here let them lie | till famine and the ague eat 5.05. 3
them lie | till famine and the ague eat them up. 5.05. 4
we might have met them dareful, beard to beard, 5.05. 6
beard to beard, | and beat them backward home. 5.05. 7
all our trumpets speak, give them all breath, 5.06. 9
i see lives, the gashes | do better upon them. 5.08. 3
i would not wish them to a fairer death. 5.09. 15
the rivals of my watch, bid them make haste. HAM 1.01. 13
i think i hear them. stand ho! who is there? 1.01. 14
and bow them to your gracious leave and pardon. 1.02. 56
appears before them, and with solemn march 1.02.201
solemn march | goes slow and stately by them. 1.02.202
and i with them the third night kept the watch, 1.02.208
though all the earth o'erwhelm them, to men's 1.02.257
grapple them unto thy soul with hoops of steel, 1.03. 63
do you believe his tenders, as you call them? 1.03.103
that for some vicious mole of nature in them, 1.04. 24
thyself do grace to them, and bring them in. 2.02. 53
thyself do grace to them, and bring them in. 2.02. 53
we coted them on the way, and hither are they 2.02.317 P
happily he is the second time come to them, for 2.02.384 P
unless things mortal move them not at all, 2.02.516
do you hear, let them be well us'd, for they are 2.02.523 P
lord, i will use them according to their desert. 2.02.527 P
use them after your own honor and dignity — the 2.02.531 P
take them in. 2.02.533 P
a sea of troubles, | and by opposing, end them. 3.01. 59
i pray you now receive them. 3.01. 94
did, | and, with them, words of so sweet breath 3.01. 97
at my beck than i have thoughts to put them in, 3.01.125 P
to put them in, imagination to give them shape, 3.01.126 P
to give them shape, or time to act them in. 3.01.126 P
know well enough what monsters you make of them. 3.01.139 P
journeymen had made men, and not made them well, 3.02. 34 P
clowns speak no more than is set down for them, 3.02. 40 P
for there be of them that will themselves laugh 3.02. 40 P
will you two help to hasten them? 3.02. 50 P
to give them seals never my soul consent! 3.02.399
since nature makes them partial, should o'erhear 3.03. 32
preaching to stones, | would make them capable. 3.04.127
the compost on the weeds | to make them ranker. 3.04.152
below their mines, | and blow them at the moon. 3.04.209
you must translate, 'tis fit we understand them. 4.01. 2
and let them know both what we mean to do | and 4.01. 39
he keeps them, like /an /ape an apple, in the 4.02. 17 P
i see a cherub that sees them. 4.03. 48 P
who commands them, sir? 4.04. 13
as her winks and nods and gestures yield them, 4.05. 11
let them guard the door. 4.05. 98
and for my means, i'll husband them so well, 4.05.139
will you know them then? 4.05.145
pelican, | repast them with my blood. 4.05.148
let them come in. 4.06. 4 P
valor, and in the grapple i boarded them. 4.06. 19 P
i am to do a /good turn for them. 4.06. 22 P
for england, of them i have much to tell thee. 4.06. 29 P
direct me | to him from whom you brought them. 4.06. 34
my bow again, | but not where i have aim'd them. 4.07. 24
from hamlet? who brought them? 4.07. 38
sailors, my lord, they say, i saw them not. 4.07. 39
he receiv'd them | of him that brought them. 4.07. 40
he receiv'd them | of him that brought them. 4.07. 41
laertes, you shall hear them. 4.07. 41
motion, guard, nor eye, | if you oppos'd them. 4.07.102
cull-cold maids do dead men's fingers call them. 4.07.171
the breeding, but to play at loggats with them? 5.01. 92 P
the wand'ring stars and makes them stand | like 5.01.256
pluck them asunder. 5.01.264
let them throw | millions of acres on us, till 5.01.280
shapes our ends, | rough-hew them how we will — 5.02. 11
in the dark | grop'd i to find out them, had my 5.02. 14
as love between them like the palm might 5.02. 40
but in the imputation laid on him by them, in 5.02.142 P
which carries them through and through the most 5.02.191 P
opinions, and do but blow them to their trial, 5.02.193 P
give them the foils, young osric. 5.02.259
part them, they are incens'd. 5.02.302
she sounds to see them bleed. 5.02.308
conferring them on younger strengths, while we LR 1.01. 40
bid them farewell, cordelia, though unkind, 1.01.260
that infirm and choleric years bring with them. 1.01.299 P
as in part i understand them, are to blame. 1.02. 42 P
from us till our oldness cannot relish them. 1.02. 48 P
if i gave them all my living, i'ld keep my 1.04.107 P
for when thou gav'st them the rod, and put'st 1.04.173 P
from me perforce, | should make thee worth them. 1.04.299
from my sister | been well inform'd of them, and 2.01.102
the night before there was no purpose in them 2.04. 3
i did commend your highness' letters to them, 2.04. 28
well, my good lord, i have inform'd them so. 2.04. 98
"inform'd" them? dost thou understand me, man? 2.04. 99
the duke, and 's wife, i'ld speak with them — 2.04.116
bid them come forth and hear me, | or at their 2.04.117
chanc'd to slack ye, | we could control them. 2.04.246
or the hard rein which both of them hath borne 3.01. 27
of the dark, | and make them keep their caves. 3.02. 45
that thou mayst shake the superflux to them, 3.04. 35
and broke them in the sweet face of heaven: 3.04. 89 P
tom will throw his head at them. 3.06. 64 P
then let them anatomize regan; 3.06. 76 P
say they are persian, but let them be chang'd. 3.06. 81 P
flew on him, and amongst them fell'd him dead, 4.02. 76
our preparation stands | in expectation of them. 4.04. 23
who make them honors | of men's impossibilities, 4.06. 73
i prithee put them off. 4.07. 8
these white flakes | did challenge pity of them. 4.07. 30
which of them shall i take? 5.01. 57
some officers take them away. 5.03. 1
first be known | that are to censure them. 5.03. 3
and we'll talk with them too — | who loses and 5.03. 14
take them away. 5.03. 19
the good-years shall devour them, flesh and fell 5.03. 24
go follow them to prison. 5.03. 27
i do require them of you, so to use them | as we 5.03. 43
so to use them | as we shall find their merits 5.03. 43
lances in our eyes | which do command them. 5.03. 51
dispose of them, of me; 5.03. 76
this sword of mine shall give them instant way 5.03.150
by nursing them, my lord. 5.03.182
i was contracted to them both; 5.03.229
i'ld use them so | that heaven's vault should 5.03.259
she lov'd and hated, | one of them we behold. 5.03.282
bear them from hence. 5.03.319
evades them with a bumbast circumstance OTH 1.01. 13
on their lords, | do well thrive by them; 1.01. 53
daughters' minds | by what you see them act. 1.01.171
your bright swords, for the dew will rust them. 1.02. 59
in /these news | that gives them credit. 1.03. 2
have there injointed them with an after fleet. 1.03. 35
ancient, conduct them; 1.03.121
and i lov'd her that she did pity them. 1.03.168
would teach me tyranny, | to hang clogs on them. 1.03.198
and bring them after in the best advantage. 1.03.297
what ribs of oak, when mountains melt on them, 2.01. 8
cyprus, | i have found great love amongst them. 2.01.205
in their natures more than is native to them), 2.01.217 P
by the means i shall then have to prefer them; 2.01.278 P
here, at the door; i pray you call them in. 2.03. 46 P
he held them sixpence all too dear, | with that 2.03. 91
like bride and groom | devesting them for bed; 2.03.181
i found them close together | at blow and thrust 2.03.237
they were | when you yourself did part them. 2.03.239
as men in rage strike those that wish them best, 2.03.243
as hydra, such an answer would stop them all. 2.03.305 P
make the net | that shall enmesh them all. 2.03.362
thy words before thou giv'st them breath, 3.03.119
and fear your looks, | she lov'd them most. 3.03.208
i think, | to bring them to that prospect; 3.03.398
damn them then, | if ever mortal eyes do see 3.03.398
if ever mortal eyes do see them bolster | more 3.03.399
a capable and wide revenge | swallow them up. 3.03.460
that is, make questions, and by them answer. 3.04. 17 P
nor of them look for such observancy | as fits 3.04.149
the devil's teeth, | from whence you have them. 3.04.185
convinced or supplied them, cannot choose | but 4.01. 28
i would do much | t' atone them, for the love i 4.01.233
each syllable that breath made up between them. 4.02. 5
o fie upon them! 4.02.145
any sense | delighted them /in any other form; 4.02.155
told me she hath receiv'd them and return'd me 4.02.188 P
know | their wives have sense like them; 4.03. 94
then let them use us well; 4.03.102
else let them know, | the ills we do, their ills 4.03.102
i think that one of them is hereabout, | and 5.01. 57
that's one of them. 5.01. 61
my great revenge | had stomach for them all. 5.02. 75
let heaven and men and devils, let them all, 5.02.221
the one of them imports | the death of cassio to 5.02.310
nay, hear them, antony. ANT 1.01. 19
three kings in a forenoon, and widow them all. 1.02. 27 P
and the time's state | made friends of them, 1.02. 92
italy, | upon the first encounter, drave them. 1.02. 94
we see how mortal an unkindness is to them; 1.02.134 P
it were pity to cast them away for nothing, 1.02.138 P
though, between them and a great cause, they 1.02.139 P
makes the sea serve them, which they ear and 1.04. 49
which seem'd to tell them his remembrance lay 1.05. 57
were't not that we stand up against them all, 2.01. 44
to lend me arms and aid when i requir'd them, 2.02. 88
to forget them quite | were to remember that the 2.02.100
that | the winds were love-sick with them; 2.02.194
my knee shall bow my prayers | to them for you. 2.03. 4
and, as i draw them up, | i'll think them every 2.05. 13
them up, | i'll think them every one an antony, 2.05. 14
and fair words to them. 2.06. 66
the least wind i' th' world will blow them down. 2.07. 3 P
reconciles them to his entreaty, and himself to 2.07. 7 P
lepidus, | keep off them, for you sink. 2.07. 60
indeed he plied them both with excellent praises 3.02. 14
that your love | can equally move with them. 3.04. 36
and throw between them all the food thou hast, 3.05. 14
their lust | since then hath made between them. 3.06. 8
and goddesses, | all the whole synod of them! 3.10. 5
rashness, and they them | for fear and doting. 3.11. 14
one of them rates | all that is won and lost. 3.11. 69
so to them both. 3.12. 24
outward | do draw the inward quality after them, 3.13. 33
should i find them | so saucy with the hand of 3.13. 97
and gnats of nile | have buried them for prey! 3.13.167
do so, we'll speak to them, and to-night i'll 3.13.189
mean you, sir, | to give them this discomfort? 4.02. 34
we had droven them home | with clouts about 4.07. 5
tell them your feats, whilst they with joyful 4.08. 9
nightingale, | we have beat them to their beds. 4.08. 19
our hack'd targets like the men that owe them. 4.08. 31
is to-day by sea, | we please them not by land. 4.10. 2
bid them all fly; 4.12. 15
bid them all fly, be gone. 4.12. 17
this pine is bark'd, | that overtopp'd them all. 4.12. 24
eye beck'd forth my wars and call'd them home, 4.12. 26
lips that power, | thus would i wear them out. 4.15. 40
in feeding them with those my former fortunes 4.15. 53
to tell them that this world did equal theirs 4.15. 77
to that destruction which i'll guard them from 5.02.132
i heard of one of them no longer than yesterday, 5.02.251 P
i do not see them bleed. 5.02.338
who was last with them? 5.02.338
and these fig leaves | have slime upon them, 5.02.352
events as these | strike those that make them; 5.02.361
his glory which | brought them to be lamented. 5.02.363
to th' more mature | a glass that feated them, CYM 1.01. 49
mark it), the eldest of them at three years old, 1.01. 58
the search so slow, | that could not trace them! 1.01. 65
would have broke mine eye-strings, crack'd them, 1.03. 17
those things i bid you do, get them dispatch'd, 1.03. 39
who has the note of them? 1.05. 2
to try the vigor of them, and apply | allayments 1.05. 21
and by them gather | their several virtues and 1.05. 22
hath nature given them eyes | to see this 1.06. 32
being strange, | to have them in safe stowage. 1.06.192
may it please you | to take them in protection? 1.06.193
since | my lord hath interest in them, i will 1.06.195
in them, i will keep them | in my bedchamber. 1.06.195
i will make bold | to send them to you, only for 1.06.198
of him and might not spend them at my pleasure. 2.01. 5 P
no, my lord; nor crop the ears of them. 2.01. 13 P
am poor of thanks, | and scarce can spare them. 2.03. 90
allure false hearts, | and be false with them. 2.04. 35
masterless leave both | to who shall find them. 2.04. 61
being so near the truth as i will make them, 2.04. 62
her andirons | (i had forgot them) were two 2.04. 89
married | to that your diamond, i'll keep them. 2.04. 98
i'll write against them, | detest them, curse 2.05. 32
write against them, | detest them, curse them; 2.05. 33
write against them, | detest them, curse them; 2.05. 33
the very devils cannot plague them better. 2.05. 35
boats, | but suck them up to th' topmast. 3.01. 22
other of them may have crook'd noses, but to owe 3.01. 36 P
so caesar shall not find them. 3.01. 76
griefs are med'cinable, that is one of them, 3.02. 33
but have a fog in them | that i cannot look 3.02. 79
the city's usuries, | and felt them knowingly; 3.03. 46
and nature prompts them | in simple and low 3.03. 84
doublet, hat, hose, all | that answer to them. 3.04.170
and she, of all compounded, | outsells them all. 3.05. 74
that have afflictions on them, knowing 'tis | a 3.06. 10
virtue | which their own conscience seal'd them, 3.06. 84
i'ld change my sex to be companion with them, 3.06. 87
fortune put them into my hand! 4.01. 23 P
that grief and patience, rooted in them both, 4.02. 57
thou precious varlet, | my tailor made them not. 4.02. 84
then, and thank | the man that gave them thee. 4.02. 85
at fools i laugh, not fear them. 4.02. 96
in this place we left them. 4.02.107
they grow, | and set them on lud's-town. 4.02.123
that an invisible instinct should frame them 4.02.177
that wildly grows in them but yields a crop | as 4.02.180
herbs that have on them cold dew o' th' night 4.02.284
the ground that gave them first has them again: 4.02.289
the ground that gave them first has them again: 4.02.289
malice and lucre in them | have laid this woe 4.02.324
to them the legions garrison'd in gallia, 4.02.333
when expect you them? 4.02.341
to the note o' th' king, or i'll fall in them. 4.03. 44
all other doubts, by time let them be clear'd, 4.03. 45
till it fly out and show them princes born. 4.04. 54
that's love, | to have them fall no more: 5.01. 13
and make them dread it, to the doers' thrift. 5.01. 15
silly habit, | that gave th' affront with them. 5.03. 87
to tell | what crows have peck'd them here. 5.03. 93
letting them thrive again | on their abatement. 5.04. 20
be directed by some that take upon them to know, 5.04.180 P
want eyes to direct them the way i am going, but 5.04.186 P
going, but such as wink and will not use them. 5.04.187 P
and there be some of them too that die against 5.04.202 P
that place them on the truth of girls and boys. 5.05.107
those arts they have as i | could put into them. 5.05.339
more it shap'd | unto my end of stealing them. 5.05.347
from your orbs, | you may reign in them now! 5.05.372
how first met them? 5.05.386
let them be joyful too, | for they shall taste 5.05.402
objects to prepare | this body, like to them, to PER 1.01. 44
see clear | to stop the air would hurt them. 1.01.100
/'schew no course to keep them from the light. 1.01.136
court mine eyes, and mine eyes shun them, | and 1.02. 6
which care of them, not pity of myself — | who 1.02. 29
fence the roots they grow by and defend them — 1.02. 31
and finding little comfort to relieve them, | i 1.02. 99
thought it princely charity to grieve for them. 1.02.100
fetch breath that may proclaim them louder, that 1.04. 15
they may awake their helpers to comfort them. 1.04. 17
like one another's glass to trim them by; 1.04. 27
yet those which see them fall | have scarce 1.04. 48
have scarce strength left to give them burial. 1.04. 49
but to relieve them of their heavy load; 1.04. 91
and give them life whom hunger starv'd half dead 1.04. 96
what pitiful cries they made to us to help them, 2.01. 21 P
a plague on them, they ne'er come but i look to 2.01. 25 P
him, and at last devour them all at a mouthful. 2.01. 32 P
hath made the ball | for them to play upon, 2.01. 61
here's them in our country of greece gets more 2.01. 63 P
you'll remember from whence you had them. 2.01.152 P
return them, we are ready; 2.02. 4
throne, | and he the sun for them to reverence; 2.03. 40
and gives them what he will, not what they crave 2.03. 47
give to every one that come | to honor them; 2.03. 61
in those that practice them they are, my lord. 2.03.104
that all those eyes ador'd them ere their fall 2.04. 11

scorn now their hand should give them burial. 2.04. 12
upon the winds command, bind them in brass, 3.01. 3
in brass, | having call'd them from the deep! 3.01. 4
goodly gifts | and snatch them straight away? 3.01. 24
have fresh ones, what e'er we pay for them. 4.02. 11 P
ay, to eleven, and brought them down again. 4.02. 16 P
i accuse them not. 4.02. 71
traveller, we should lodge them with this sign. 4.02.114 P
like motes and shadows see them move a while, 4.04. 21
faith, my acquaintance lies little amongst them. 4.06.196 P
therefore i will make them acquainted with your 4.06.198 P
not but i shall find them tractable enough. 4.06.199 P
the ears she feeds, and makes them hungry, | the 5.01.112
them hungry, | the more she gives them speech. 5.01.113
call | and give them repetition to the /life. 5.01.246
may we see them? 5.03. 25
perch or sing, | or with them any discord bring, TNK 1.01. 23
of our dead kings, that we may chapel them; 1.01. 50
unto the helmeted bellona use them | and pray 1.01. 75
humane grace | affords them dust and shadow. 1.01.145
either presuming them to have some force, | or 1.01.194
i pity | decays where e'er i find them, but such 1.02. 32
let them break and fall | off me with that 1.02. 73
have sod their infants in (and after eat them) 1.03. 21
yet fate hath brought them off. 1.03. 41
lords, and honor them | with treble ceremony — 1.04. 7
by th' helm of mars, i saw them in the war, 1.04. 17
i fix'd my note | constantly on them; 1.04. 20
speedily | from our kind air, to them unkind, 1.04. 38
i heard them reported in the battle to be the 2.01. 29 P
i' th' deliverance, will break from one of them; 2.01. 42 P
it is a holiday to look on them. 2.01. 53 P
howsoev'r | you skip them in me, and with them, 3.01. 52
howsoev'r | you skip them in me, and with them, 3.01. 52
who have in them | a sense to know a man unarm'd 3.02. 15
if one of them were dead, as one must, are you 3.06.273
and to second them, | that truly noble prince 4.01. 12
i left them with her | and hither came to tell 4.01.102
return'd, | and with them their fair knights. 4.02. 67
my fair sister, | you must love one of them. 4.02. 68
speak, | you that have seen them, what they are. 4.02. 72
and let them repair to her with palamon in their 4.03. 91 P
and have hotly ask'd them | if they had mothers; 5.01.105
a man | of eighty winters — this i told them — 5.01.108
know best, i pray them he | be made your lot. 5.03. 39
their nobleness peculiar to them, gives | the 5.03. 87
give them our present justice, since i know 5.03.132
what you will have them, but not men of wisdom. STM II.C 37
with the number, | command them to a stillness. II.C 52
a plague on them, they will not hold their peace II.C 53 P
the dev'l cannot rule them. II.C 54 P
grant them removed and grant that this your II.C 72
your unreverent knees, | make them your feet: II.C 111
kill them, cut their throats, possess their II.C 120
to your comforts, | but charter'd unto them? II.C 138
which might accite thee to embrace and hug them, III 16
more do thou in serpents' natures think them, III 17
but rather famish them amid their plenty, VEN 20
making them red and pale with fresh variety — 21
to fan and blow them dry again she seeks. 52
for where they lay the shadow had forsook them, 176
with burning eye did hotly overlook them, 178
they burn too, i'll quench them with my tears. 192
as they were mad, unto the wood they hie them, 323
outstripping crows that strive to overfly them. 324
o, what a war of looks was then between them! 355
his eyes saw her eyes as they had not seen them, 357
hath taught them scornful tricks, and such 501
me, | and pay them at thy leisure, one by one. 518
love breaks through, and picks them all at last. 576
doth make them droop with grief and hang the 666
if thou destroy them not in dark obscurity? 760
she, marking them, begins a wailing note, | and 835
anon she hears them chaunt it lustily, | and all 869
she tells them 'tis a causeless fantasy | and 897
bids them leave quaking, bids them fear no more 899
them leave quaking, bids them fear no more — 899
gazed, | infusing them with dreadful prophecies: 928
and with his strong course opens them again. 960
sighs dry her cheeks, tears make them wet again. 966
thy weal and woe are both of them extremes; 987
could rule them both without ten women's wit." 1008
who bids them still consort with ugly night, 1041
he fed them with his sight, they him with 1104
which of them both should underprop her fame. LUC 53
teaching them thus to use it in the fight, 62
yet their ambition makes them still to fight, 68
lest between them both it should be kill'd, 74
she reflects so bright | that dazzleth them, or 377
as if between them twain there were no strife, 405
the hot charge, and bids them do their liking. 434
in darkness daunts them with more dreadful 462
the shame that from them no device can take, 535
her tears should drop on them perpetually. 686
not themselves but he that gives them knows! 833
even in the moment that we call them ours. 868
thy heinous hours wait on them as their pages. 910
a thousand crosses keep them from thy aid: 912
but little stars may hide them when they list. 1008
old woes, not infant sorrows, bear them mild; 1096
of strange kinds | is form'd in them by force, 1243
then call them not the authors of their ill, 1244
yet save that labor, for i have them here. 1290
words, till action might become them better. 1323
see sad sights moves more than hear them told, 1324
one would swear he saw them quake and tremble. 1393
she lends them words, and she their looks doth 1498
hold | only to flatter fools and make them bold: 1559
she modestly prepares to let them know | her 1607
to tell them all with one poor tired tongue. 1617
rome herself in them doth stand disgraced) | by 1833
nothing could be used to turn them both to gain, PP 15.10
show, | the tricks and toys that in them lurk, 18.39
the cock that treads them shall not know. 18.40
then, | when time with age shall them attaint. 18.46
but in them it were a wonder. PHT 32
so between them love did shine, | that the 33
in them i read such art | as truth and beauty SON 14.10
let them say more that like of hearsay well, | i 21.13
compare them with the bett'ring of the time, 32. 5
reserve them for my love, not for their rhyme, 32. 7
take all my loves, my love, yea, take them all, 40. 1
i send them back again and straight grow sad. 45.14
and i am still with them, and they with thee; 47.12
and they shall live, and he in them still green. 63.14
when in the least of them my life hath end; 92. 6
from their proud lap pluck them where they grew; 98. 8
crow or dove, it shapes them to your feature. 113.12
therefore to give them from me was i bold, | to 122.11
and rather make them born to our desire | than 123. 7
than think that we before have heard them told. 123. 8
give them /thy fingers, me thy lips to kiss. 128.14
as those whose beauties proudly make them cruel; 131. 2
or made them swear against the thing they see; 152.12
bidding them find their sepulchres in mud, LC 46
and laboring in moe pleasures to bestow them 139
the true gouty landlord which doth owe them. 140
sweetly suppos'd them mistress of his heart. 142
love made them not, with acture they may be, 185
harm have i done to them, but ne'er was harmed, 194
nature hath charg'd me that i hoard them not, 220
but yield them up where i myself must render: 221
i strong o'er them, and you o'er me being strong 257
and, veil'd in them, did win whom he would maim. 312
which like a cherubin above them hover'd. 319

/THEME 2 FR 0.0002 REL FR 2 V 0 P
/in /a /theme /so //bloody–fac'd /as /this, 2H4 1.03. 22
/o, /handle /not /the /theme, /to /talk /of TIT 3.02. 29

THEME 30 FR 0.0034 REL FR 28 V 2 P
and the merchant | have just our theme of woe; TMP 2.01. 6
well, i am your theme. WIV 5.05.161 P
to me she speaks, she moves me for her theme: ERR 2.02.181
alone, it was the subject of my theme; 5.01. 65
and this weak and idle theme, | no more yielding MND 5.01.427
ay, that's the theme, | to her in haste. TN 2.04.122
comfort | the gracious queen, part of his theme, WT 1.02.459
your writing now | is colder than that theme, 5.01.100
a son who is the theme of honor's tongue, 1H4 1.01. 81
it is a theme as fluent as the sea; H5 3.07. 33 P
with your theme, i could | o'ermount the lark. H8 2.03. 93
hector, | she is a theme of honor and renown, TRO 2.02.199
o deadly gall, and theme of all our scorns, 4.05. 30
name her not now, sir, she's a deadly theme. 4.05.181
apt, without a theme | for depravation, to 5.02.131
honor and advance | the theme of our assembly. COR 2.02. 57
see here he comes, and i must ply my theme. TIT 5.02. 80
that "marry" is the very theme | i came to talk ROM 1.03. 63
to the swelling act | of the imperial theme. MAC 1.03.129
whose common theme | is death of fathers, and HAM 1.02.103
i will fight with him upon this theme | until my 5.01.266
o my son, what theme? 5.01.268
and their contestation | was theme for you — ANT 2.02. 44
big of this gentleman, our theme, deceas'd | as CYM 1.01. 39
to ears and tongues | be theme and hearing ever) 3.01. 4
and when a soldier was the theme, my name | was 3.03. 59
since that our theme is haste, | i stamp this TNK 1.01.215
and leave this idle theme, this bootless chat; VEN 422
fall again | into your idle over–handled theme. 770
if that he made a theme for disputation, | the LUC 822

THEMES 2 FR 0.0002 REL FR 2 V 0 P
upon power, and throw forth greater themes | for COR 1.01.220
three themes in one, which wondrous scope SON 105.12

/THEMSELVES 2 FR 0.0002 REL FR 1 V 1 P
/should /grow /themselves /to /common /players HAM 2.02.348 P
/seem /vild, | /filths /savor /but /themselves. LR 4.02. 39

THEMSELVES 173 FR 0.0195 REL FR 136 V 37 P
i wish mine eyes | would, with themselves, shut TMP 2.01.192
i'll restore, | and they shall be themselves. 5.01. 32
had instance and argument to commend themselves. WIV 2.02.247 P
which they'll do fast enough of themselves, and 4.01. 67 P
love, the heavens themselves do guide the state; 5.05.232
torches do, | not light them for themselves; MM 1.01. 33
dead to infliction, to themselves are dead, 1.03. 28
theirs | as they themselves would owe them. 1.04. 83
spleens, | would all themselves laugh mortal. 2.02.123
have authority | when judges steal themselves. 2.02.176
ay, as the glasses where they view themselves, 2.04.125
a week married, they would talk themselves mad. ADO 2.01.354 P
to that grief | which they themselves not feel, 5.01. 22
they not, think you, hang themselves to–night? LLL 5.02.270
o lord, sir, the parties themselves, the actors, 5.02.499 P
days will quickly steep themselves in night; MND 1.01. 7
as waggish boys in game themselves forswear, 1.01.240
sever themselves and madly sweep the sky, | so, 3.02. 23
they willfully themselves exile from light, 3.02.386
no worse of them than they of themselves, they 5.01.216 P
see | the pretty follies that themselves commit, MV 2.06. 37
they in themselves, good sooth, are too too 2.06. 42
so may the outward shows be least themselves — 3.02. 73
that souls of animals infuse themselves | into 4.01.132
lords have put themselves into voluntary exile AYL 1.01.101 P
and could not bear themselves without the verse, 3.02.170 P
and betray themselves to every modern censure 4.01. 6 P
but when the parties were met themselves, one of 5.04.100 P
how my men will stay themselves from laughter SHR in.1. 134
for they wear themselves in the cap of the time; AWW 2.01. 53 P
created for men to breathe themselves upon thee. 2.03.256 P
we still see them reveal themselves, till they 4.03. 23 P
cassocks, lest they shake themselves to pieces. 4.03.169 P
some that humble themselves may, but the many 4.05. 52 P
let them hang themselves in their own straps. TN 1.03. 13 P
o heavens themselves! 3.04.357
give fools money get themselves a good report — 4.01. 22 P
crabbed months had sour'd themselves to death, WT 1.02.102
the tenth of mankind | would hang themselves. 1.02.200
and why he left your court, the gods themselves 3.02. 75
and the heavens themselves | do strike at my 3.02.146
the gods themselves | (humbling their deities to 4.04. 25
that have made themselves all men of hair. 4.04.326 P
they call themselves saltiers, and they have a 4.04.326 P
but they themselves are o' th' mind (if it be 4.04.329 P
forswear themselves as often as they speak. 5.01.200
churlish thoughts themselves should be your JN 2.01.519
/friends | do glue themselves in sociable grief, 3.04. 65
the french fight coldly, and retire themselves. 5.03. 13
in their continuance will not feel themselves. 5.07. 14
press to that last hold, | confound themselves. 5.07. 20
for violent fires soon burn out themselves; R2 2.01. 34
stand bare and naked, trembling at themselves? 3.02. 46
thoughts tending to content flatter themselves 5.05. 23
will they adventure upon the exploit themselves, 1H4 1.02.172 P
when they have lost and forfeited themselves? 1.03. 88
that have show'd themselves humors since the old 2.04. 93 P
all the rest | turn'd on themselves, like dull 2H4 1.01.118
now enrag'd with grief, | are thrice themselves. 1.01.145
wherein the noble youth did dress themselves: 2.03. 22
all our loves, | first let them try themselves. 2.03. 56
touch ground | and dash themselves to pieces. 4.01. 18
i know not how they sold themselves, but thou, 4.03. 68 P
thin potations and to addict themselves to sack. 4.03.125 P
on ground, | confound themselves with working. 4.04. 41
him, do bear themselves like foolish justices; 5.01. 66 P
how smooth and even they do bear themselves! H5 2.02. 3
theise eyes of mine take themselves to slomber, 3.02.115 P
shall think themselves accurs'd they were not 4.03. 65
that can rhyme themselves into ladies' favors, 5.02.156 P
they do always reason themselves out again. 5.02.157 P
and, banding themselves in contrary parts, | do 1H6 3.01. 81
are glad and fain by flight to save themselves. 3.02.114
peers and chief nobility | destroy'd themselves, 4.01.147
with pow'rful policy strengthen themselves, 3H6 1.02. 58
they have demean'd themselves | like men born to 1.04. 7
tyrants themselves wept when it was reported. R3 1.03.184
if they fall, they dash themselves to pieces. 1.03.259
domestic broils | clean overblown, themselves, 2.04. 61
make war upon themselves, brother to brother, 2.04. 62
that think themselves as safe | as thou and i, 3.02. 66
spicery they will breed | selves of themselves, 4.04.425
want of means, poor rats, had hang'd themselves. 5.03.331
and with a care exempt themselves from fear; H8 1.02. 89
that freeze, | bow themselves when he did sing. 3.01. 5
the heavens themselves, the planets, and this TRO 1.03. 85
part | to steel a strong opinion to themselves? 1.03.353
walls will stand till they fall of themselves. 2.03. 9 P
emulous missions 'mongst the gods themselves, 3.03.189
wounds heal ill that men do give themselves. 3.03.229
valor and pride excel themselves in hector, 4.05. 79
till when | they needs must show themselves, COR 1.02. 21
with rushes, | they'll open of themselves. 1.04. 19
and they smart | to hear themselves rememb'red. 1.09. 29
ingratitude, | and tent themselves with death. 1.09. 31
do not flatter, and | therein behold themselves. 3.01. 68
(look you, sir) show themselves (as we term it) 4.05.207 P
though they themselves did suffer by't, behold 4.06. 6
people's hearts, and wean them from themselves. TIT 1.01.211
when no friends are by, men praise themselves. 5.03.118
they were living, warm'd themselves on thine! 5.03.168
i wonder men dare trust themselves with men. TIM 1.02. 43
but the gods themselves have provided that i 1.02. 89 P
in cases that keeps their sounds to themselves. 1.02.100 P
why do fond men expose themselves to battle, 3.05. 42
they may strive, | and drown themselves in riot! 4.01. 28
but men — men are the things themselves. 4.03.321 P
nor on the beasts themselves, the birds and 4.03.424
whiles they behold a greater than themselves, JC 1.02.209
clean from the purpose of the things themselves. 1.03. 35
what watchful cares do interpose themselves 2.01. 98
the heavens themselves blaze forth the death of 2.02. 31
the multitude, beside themselves with fear, 3.01.180
mark antony | have made themselves so strong — 4.03.154
seek to hide themselves | in drops of sorrow. MAC 1.04. 34
question them further, they made themselves air, 1.05. 5 P
your servants ever | have theirs, themselves, 1.06. 26
they have made themselves, and that their 1.07. 53
things bad begun make strong themselves by ill. 3.02. 55
many | as will to greatness dedicate themselves, 4.03. 75
but if the gods themselves did see her then, HAM 2.02.512
be of them that will themselves laugh to set on 3.02. 40 P
their own enactures with themselves destroy. 3.02.197
in this world to drown or hang themselves, more 5.01. 28 P
your age, | which know themselves and you. LR 1.04.252
the injuries that they themselves procure | must 2.04.303
imaginations lose | the knowledge of themselves. 4.06.284
cordelia, | the gods themselves throw incense. 5.03. 21
your eldest daughters have foredone themselves, 5.03.292
keep yet their hearts attending on themselves, OTH 1.01. 51
have lin'd their coats, | do themselves homage. 1.01. 54
tempests themselves, high seas, and howling 2.01. 68
the devils themselves | should fear to seize 4.02. 36
they would make themselves whores but they'ld ANT 1.02. 77 P
vows, | which break themselves in swearing! 1.03. 31
pregnant they should square between themselves, 2.01. 45
for vildest things | become themselves in her, 2.02.238
ill tidings tell | themselves when they be felt. 2.05. 88
that i may say | the gods themselves do weep! 5.02.300
and makes | diana's rangers false themselves, CYM 2.03. 69
saw i figures | so likely to report themselves. 2.04. 83
fiends of hell | divide themselves between you! 2.04.130
that did attend themselves and had the virtue 3.06. 83
must murther wives much better than themselves 5.01. 4
and stay your coming to present themselves. PER 2.02. 3
and hundreds call themselves | your creatures, 3.02. 44
they will but please themselves upon her, | not 4.01.100
and suffer'd | your knees to wrong themselves. TNK 1.01. 56
have to themselves | been death's most horrid 1.01.143
they themselves, some say, | groan under such a 1.01.230
if one be mad, or hang or drown themselves, 4.03. 35 P
and they themselves become | the executioners. 5.04.121
rot, and consume themselves in little time. VEN 132
things growing to themselves are growth's abuse. 166
theirs whose desperate hands themselves do slay, 765
do burn themselves for having so offended." 810
if pleas'd themselves, others they think delight 843
like stars asham'd of day, themselves withdrew. 1032
blind they are, and keep themselves enclosed. LUC 378
each in her sleep themselves so beautify, | as 404
men's faults do seldom to themselves appear, 633
the same disgrace which they themselves behold; 751
which not themselves but he that gives them 833
to mock the subtle in themselves beguil'd, | to 957
grieving themselves to guess at others' smarts, 1238
together, | to themselves yet either neither, PHT 43
since sweets and beauties do themselves forsake, SON 12.11

and in themselves their pride lies buried, | for 25. 7
and unrespected fade, | die to themselves. 54.11
who, moving others, are themselves as stone, 94. 3
incertainties now crown themselves assur'd, 107. 7
may be straight though they themselves be bevel; 121.11
all aids, themselves made fairer by their place, LC 117

THEN *(also den*)*

/THEN 39 FR 0.0044 REL FR 35 V 4 P

/then heigh–ho, the holly! AYL 2.07.182
what is thy sentence /then but speechless death, R2 1.03.172
/well /then, /amen. 4.01.173
/the /commons /will /not /then /be /satisfied. 4.01.272
/and /then /be /gone /and /trouble /you /no 4.01.303
/my /flatterers | /were /then /but /subjects; 4.01.307
/then /give /me /leave /to /go. 4.01.313
/what /hath /then /befall'n? 2H4 1.01.177
/survey /the /plot, /then /draw /the /model, 1.03. 42
/then /must /we /rate /the /cost /of /the 1.03. 44
/what /do /we /then /but /draw /anew /the /model 1.03. 46
give /then repose | to the wet //sea–boy in an 3.01. 26
/that /lov'd /him, /as /the /state /stood /then, 4.01.113
/and /then /that /henry /bullingbrook /and /he, 4.01.115
/then, /then, /when /there /was /nothing /could 4.01.121
/then, /then, /when /there /was /nothing /could 4.01.121
/then /threw /he /down /himself /and /all /their 4.01.125
/the /earl /of /herford /was /reputed /then 4.01.129
/on /whom /fortune /would /then /have /smil'd? 4.01.131
/my /flesh, | /then /thus /i /thump /it /down. TIT 3.02. 11
/then /pardon /me /for /reprehending /thee, 3.02. 69
for /then hast made it like an humble suppliant. 4.03.117
/then /is /the /world /one. HAM 2.02.244 P
/why /then /'tis /none /to /you; 2.02.249 P
/why /then /your /ambition /makes /it /one. 2.02.252 P
/then /are /our /beggars /bodies, /and /our 2.02.263 P
/then /senseless /ilium, | seeming to feel this 2.02.474
/but /then /the /mind /much /sufferance /doth LR 3.06.106
/then, /prithee, get thee away. 4.01. 41
/and /now /and /then /an /ample /tear /trill'd 4.03. 12
/o, /then /it /mov'd /her. 4.03. 15
/then /away /she /started | /to /deal /with 4.03. 31
/shunn'd /my /abhorr'd /society, /but /then, 5.03.211
/twice /then /the /trumpets /sounded, | /and 5.03.218
down, | /then take thy auld cloak about thee." OTH 2.03. 96
faults that are not), that your wisdom /then, 3.03.148
if she be false, /o, /then heaven /mocks itself! 3.03.278
/then laid his leg | /over my thigh, and /sigh'd 3.03.424
/then /lord have mercy on me! 5.02. 57

THEN 2341 FR 0.2646 REL FR 1871 V 470 P

work you then. TMP 1.01. 42 P
for then thou wast not | out three years old. 1.02. 40
then tell me | if this might be a brother. 1.02.117
i, not rememb'ring how i cried out then, | will 1.02.133
and then i'll bring thee to the present business 1.02.136
alack, what trouble | was i then to you! 1.02.152
who being then appointed | master of this design 1.02.162
would i flame distinctly, | then meet and join. 1.02.201
then all afire with me, the king's son, 1.02.212
with hair up–staring (then like reeds, not hair) 1.02.213
as thou report'st thyself, was then her servant, 1.02.271
then was this island | (save for the son that 1.02.281
and then i lov'd thee | and show'd thee all the 1.02.336
unto these yellow sands, | and then take hands: 1.02.376
my affections | are then most humble; 1.02.483
but then exactly do | all points of my command. 1.02.500
then wisely, good sir, weigh | our sorrow with 2.01. 8
we would so, and then go a–batfowling. 2.01.185 P
why | doth it not then our eyelids sink? 2.01.201
then tell me, | who's the next heir of naples? 2.01.244
my brother's servants | were then my fellows, 2.01.274
then let us both be sudden. 2.01.306
then like hedgehogs which | lie tumbling in my 2.02. 10
then to sea, boys, and let her go hang!" 2.02. 54
here; swear then how thou escap'dst. 2.02.127 P
come on then; down, and swear. 2.02.153 P
my husband then? 3.01. 87
mum then, and no more. — proceed. 3.02. 51 P
wilt thou destroy him then? 3.02.114
that, if i then had wak'd after long sleep, 3.02.139
and then, in dreaming, | the clouds methought 3.02.140
then, as my /gift, and thine own acquisition 4.01. 13
sit then and talk with her, she is thine own. 4.01. 32
then i beat my tabor, | at which, like unback'd 4.01.175
these men, my lords, | then say if they be true. 5.01.268
i should have been a sore one then. 5.01.289 P
then to the elements | be free, and fare thou 5.01.318
if lost, why then a grievous labor won; TGV 1.01. 33
twenty to one then he is shipp'd already, | and 1.01. 72
you conclude that my master is a shepherd then, 1.01. 77 P
why then my horns are his horns, whether i wake 1.01. 79 P
wouldst thou then counsel me to fall in love? 1.02. 2
then thus: of many good i think him best. 1.02. 21
why didst thou stoop then? 1.02. 70
then let it lie for those that it concerns. 1.02. 73
heavy? belike it hath some burden then? 1.02. 82
then tell me, whither were i best to send him? 1.03. 24
why then this may be yours — for this is but 2.01. 2
what should i see then? 2.01. 74 P
boy, then you are in love — for last morning 2.01. 79 P
if it please me, madam, what then? 2.01.132
why then we'll make exchange: 2.02. 6
of my mistress then. 2.04. 6 P
well then i'll double your folly. 2.04. 21 P
welcome him then according to his worth — 2.04. 83
nay then he should be blind, and, being blind, 2.04. 93
then speak the truth by her; 2.04.151
then let her alone. 2.04.167
must use, | and then i'll presently attend you. 2.04.189
how then? shall he marry her? 2.05. 16 P
why then, how stands the matter with them? 2.05. 20 P
the conclusion is then, that it will. 2.05. 38 P
then let me go, and hinder not my course: 2.07. 33
why then your ladyship must cut your hair. 2.07. 44
if you think so, then stay at home and go not. 2.07. 62
then never dream on infamy, but go. 2.07. 64
nay then no matter; 3.01. 58
then let her beauty be her wedding–dow'r, | for 3.01. 78
why then i would resort to her by night. 3.01.110
why then a ladder, quaintly made of cords, | to 3.01.117
then let me see thy cloak — | i'll get me one 3.01.132
who then? his spirit? 3.01.195 P
what then? 3.01.197 P
then in dumb silence will i bury mine, | for 3.01.208
what news then in your paper? 3.01.285 P
for then she need not be wash'd and scour'd. 3.01.312 P
then may i set the world on wheels, when she can 3.01.315 P
what then? 3.01.371 P
why then will i tell thee — that thy master 3.01.372 P
then you must undertake to slander him. 3.02. 38
then know that i have little wealth to lose. 4.01. 11
know, then, that some of us are gentlemen, 4.01. 42
then to silvia let us sing, | that silvia is 4.02. 49
and then i offer'd her mine own, who is a dog as 4.04. 57 P
nay then the wanton lies; my face is black. 5.02. 10
why then | she's fled unto that peasant 5.02. 34
whose dear sake thou didst then rend thy faith 5.04. 47
then i am paid; 5.04. 77
know then, i here forget all former griefs, 5.04.142
by these gloves, then 'twas he. WIV 1.01.165 P
by this hat, then he in the red face had it; 1.01.170 P
ay, you spake in latin then too: 1.01.180 P
why then let kibes ensue. 1.03. 32 P
then did the sun on dunghill shine. 1.03. 63 P
then lucifer take all! 1.03. 76
go to then, there's sympathy. 2.01. 7 P
then there's more sympathy. 2.01. 8 P
i was then frugal of my mirth. 2.01. 27 P
well — i do then; 2.01. 40 P
why then the world's mine oyster, | which i with 2.02. 3
good maid then. 2.02. 36 P
and then you may come and see the picture, she 2.02. 86 P
nay, but do so then, and, look you, he may come 2.02.124 P
of what quality was your love then? 2.02.214 P
i could drive her then from the ward of her 2.02.248 P
then she plots, then she ruminates, then she 2.02.305 P
then she plots, then she ruminates, then she 2.02.306 P
she plots, then she ruminates, then she devises; 2.02.306 P
then i have as much mock–vater as de englishman. 2.03. 62 P
let us wag then. 2.03. 97 P
i will take him, then torture my wife, pluck the 3.02. 40 P
go to then. 3.03. 40 P
without cause, why then make sport at me, then 3.03.150 P
then make sport at me, then let me be your jest, 3.03.150 P
alas, how then? 3.04. 3
cannot attain it, why then hark you hither! 3.04. 21
till then farewell, sir; 3.04. 92
his frailty, and then judge of my merit. 3.05. 51 P
and then, to be stopp'd in, like a strong 3.05.112 P
my suit then is desperate; 3.05.124 P
i will then address me to my appointment. 3.05.133 P
why then you are utterly sham'd, and he's but a 4.02. 42 P
i'll go out then. 4.02. 65 P
page, have you any way then to unfool me again? 4.02.115 P
come, to the forge with it, then shape it. 4.02.223 P
then let them all encircle him about, | and, 4.04. 57
and then another fault in the semblance of a 5.05. 9 P
upon my life then, you took the wrong. 5.05.189 P
then no more remains | but that: MM 1.01. 7
why then all the dukes fall upon the king. 1.02. 2 P
then, if you speak, you must not show your face, 1.04. 12
you being then (if you be rememb'red) cracking 2.01.106 P
i telling you then (if you be rememb'red) that 2.01.109 P
why, very well then — 2.01.114 P
why, very well then; i hope here be truths. 2.01.133 P
good then; 2.01.156 P
sir, in my poor opinion, they will to't then. 2.01.234 P
i had a brother then. 2.02. 42
should it then be thus? 2.02. 68
and mercy then will breathe within your lips, 2.02. 78
for then i pity those i do not know, | which a 2.02.101
so then it seems your most offenseful act | was 2.03. 26
then was your sin of heavier kind than his. 2.03. 28
then i shall pose you quickly. 2.04. 51
then must your brother die. 2.04.104
were not you then as cruel as the sentence 2.04.109
then, isabel, live chaste, and, brother, die; 2.04.184
so then you hope of pardon from lord angelo? 3.01. 1
well, then imprison him. 3.02. 66 P
you will not bail me then, sir? 3.02. 81 P
then, pompey, nor now. 3.02. 82 P
how should he be made then? 3.02.107 P
take then this your companion by the hand, | who 4.01. 54
they will then ere't be long. 4.02. 76
which he corrects, then were he tyrannous, | but 4.02. 84
marry, then ginger was not much in request, for 4.03. 7 P
then is there here one master caper, at the suit 4.03. 9 P
then have we here young dizzy, and young master 4.03. 12 P
this letter then to friar peter give; 4.03.137
which shall then have no power to stand against 4.04. 13 P
one lucio | as then the messenger — 5.01. 74
i wish you now then. 5.01. 79
for yourself, pray heaven you then | be perfect. 5.01. 81
then, o you blessed ministers above, | keep me 5.01.115
a widow then? 5.01.175 P
why, you are nothing then: 5.01.177 P
he was drunk then, my lord, it can be no better. 5.01.188 P
then is your cause gone too. 5.01.300
and then to glance from him | to th' duke 5.01.309
and a coward, as you then reported him to be? 5.01.334 P
then, good prince, | no longer session hold upon 5.01.370
immediate sentence then, and sequent death, | is 5.01.373
as i was then | advertising and holy to your 5.01.382
then, angelo, thy fault's thus manifested; 5.01.412
and left the ship, then sinking–ripe, to us. ERR 1.01. 77
if no, then thou art doom'd to die. 1.01.154
and then return and sleep within mine inn, | for 1.02. 14
town, | and then go to my inn and dine with me? 1.02. 23
farewell till then. 1.02. 30
then let your will attend on their accords. 2.01. 25
then he hath wasted it. 2.01. 90
then is he the ground | of my defeatures. 2.01. 97
first — for flouting me, and then wherefore — 2.02. 45
well, sir, then 'twill be dry. 2.02. 59 P
sure ones then. 2.02. 93 P
certain ones then. 2.02. 95 P
it, | that thou art then estranged from thyself? 2.02.120
keep then fair league and truce with thy true 2.02.145
how can she thus then call us by our names, 2.02.166
then for her wealth's sake use her with more 3.02. 6
then, gentle brother, get you in again; 3.02. 25
transform me then, and to your pow'r i'll yield. 3.02. 40
i, then well i know | your weeping sister is no 3.02. 41
then she bears some breadth? 3.02.112 P
you, | and then receive my money for the chain. 3.02.175
if any ship put out, then straight away. 3.02.185
then you will bring the chain to her yourself? 4.01. 40
comes aboard, | and then, sir, she bears away. 4.01. 87
then swore he that he was a stranger here. 4.02. 9
then pleaded i for you. 4.02. 11
first he did praise my beauty, then my speech. 4.02. 15
who would be jealous then of such a one? 4.02. 23
and then were you hind'red by the sergeant to 4.03. 39 P
avoid then, fiend! 4.03. 65
the consequence is then, thy jealous fits | hath 5.01. 85
then let your servants bring my husband forth. 5.01. 93
then they fled | into this abbey, whither we 5.01.154
even for the blood | that then i lost for thee, 5.01.194
could witness it, for he was with me then, | who 5.01.220
then fairly i bespoke the officer | to go in 5.01.233
then all together | they fell upon me, bound me, 5.01.246
and then you fled into this abbey here, | from 5.01.264
what then became of them i cannot tell; 5.01.355
what i told you then | i hope i shall have 5.01.375
we'll draw cuts for the senior, till then, lead 5.01.423
nay then thus: 5.01.424
signior benedick, no, for then were you a child. ADO 1.01.107 P
then is courtesy a turncoat. 1.01.124 P
i look for an earthquake too then. 1.01.273 P
then after to her father will i break, | and the 1.01.326
then half signior benedick's tongue in count 2.01. 11 P
well then, go you into hell. 2.01. 42 P
and then comes repentance, and with his bad legs 2.01. 77 P
why then your visor should be thatch'd. 2.01. 98 P
them, and then they laugh at him and beat him. 2.01.141 P
and then there's a partridge wing sav'd, for the 2.01.148 P
how then? sick? 2.01.291 P
mother cried, but then there was a star danc'd, 2.01.335 P
sad but when she sleeps, and not ever sad then; 2.01.344 P
go then, find me a meet hour to draw don pedro 2.02. 33 P
then sigh not so, but let them go, | and be you 2.03. 66
then sigh not so, etc. 2.03. 74
then down upon her knees she falls, weeps, sobs, 2.03.146 P
you take pleasure then in the message? 2.03.253 P
then go we near her, that her ear lose nothing 3.01. 32
if it prove so, then loving goes by haps: 3.01.105
be consummate, and then go i toward arragon. 3.02. 2 P
and then the two bears will not bite one another 3.02. 77 P
if you love her then, to–morrow wed her; 3.02.114 P
why then take no note of him, but let him go, 3.03. 28 P
why then let them alone till they are sober. 3.03. 45 P
if they make you not then the better answer, you 3.03. 46 P
why then depart in peace, and let the child wake 3.03. 69 P
the church–bench till two, and then all to bed. 3.03. 90 P
stand thee close then under this penthouse, for 3.03.103 P
then, if your husband have stables enough, 3.04. 47 P
why then, some be of laughing, as, ah, ha, he! 4.01. 21 P
why then you are no maiden. 4.01. 87
why seek'st thou then to cover with excuse 4.01.174
lack'd and lost, | why then we rack the value; 4.01.220
then we find | the virtue that possession would 4.01.220
then shall he mourn, | if ever love had interest 4.01.230
why then god forgive me! 4.01.281 P
in hand until they come to take hands, and then, 4.01.304 P
nay then give him another staff, this last was 5.01.138 P
i shall meet, and till then peace be with him. 5.01.193 P
he is then a giant to an ape, but then is an ape 5.01.201 P
ape, but then is an ape a doctor to such a man. 5.01.201 P
to–morrow then i will expect your coming, 5.01.296
will you then write me a sonnet in praise of my 5.02. 4 P
o, stay but till then! 5.02. 45 P
"then" is spoken; 5.02. 46 P
other weeds, | and then to leonato's we will go. 5.03. 31
why then she's mine. 5.04. 55
why then your uncle and the prince and claudio 5.04. 75
why then my cousin, margaret, and ursula | are 5.04. 78
'tis no such matter. then you do not love me? 5.04. 82
and then grace us in the disgrace of death; LLL 1.01. 3
and then, to sleep but three hours in the night, 1.01. 42
by yea and nay, sir, then i swore in jest. 1.01. 54
com' on then, i will swear to study so, | to 1.01. 59
something then in rhyme. 1.01. 99
then for the place where? 1.01.240 P
may one day smile again, and till then, sit thee 1.01.314 P
then i am sure you know how much the gross sum 1.02. 45 P
then if she fear, or be to blame, | by this you 1.02.103
i will be welcome then — conduct me thither. 2.01. 96
how needless was it then | to ask the question? 2.01.116
nay then will i be gone. 2.01.127
if then the king your father will restore | but 2.01.137
then was venus like her mother, for her father 2.01.256
what then, do you see? 2.01.257
thump then, and i flee. 3.01. 65
then call'd you for the l'envoy. 3.01.107 P
then the boy's fat l'envoy, the goose that you 3.01.109
o, why then three–farthing worth of silk. 3.01.149 P
tongues speak sweetly, then they name her name, 3.01.166
then, forester, my friend, where is the bush 4.01. 7
kill, | and shooting well is then accounted ill. 4.01. 25
if wounding, then it was to show my skill, 4.01. 28
if thou strive, poor soul, what art thou then? 4.01. 92
well then i am the shooter. 4.01.114
if my hand be out, then belike your hand is in. 4.01.135
then will she get the upshoot by cleaving the 4.01.136
put l to sore, then sorel jumps from thicket, 4.02. 58
sore, then l to sore makes fifty sores o' sorel: 4.02. 60
then thou /wilt keep | my tears for glasses, and 4.03. 37
then thou, fair sun, which on my earth dost 4.03. 67
if broken then, it is no fault of mine: 4.03. 69
ay, as some days, but then no sun must shine. 4.03. 89
why then incision | would let her out in saucers 4.03. 95
my eyes are then no eyes, nor i berowne. 4.03.228
passes praise, then praise too short doth blot. 4.03.237
no devil will fright thee then so much as she. 4.03.271
then, as she goes, what upward lies | the street 4.03.276
then leave this chat, and, good berowne, now 4.03.280

have at you then, affection's men–at–arms. 4.03.286
then when ourselves we see in ladies' eyes, 4.03.312
o, then his lines would ravish savage ears | and 4.03.345
then fools you were these women to forswear, 4.03.352
saint cupid, then! and, soldiers, to the field! 4.03.363
then homeward every man attach the hand | of his 4.03.372
and then the king will court thee for his dear. 5.02.131
come on then, wear the favors most in sight. 5.02.136
many, | the measure then of one is eas'ly told. 5.02.190
then in our measure do but vouchsafe one change. 5.02.209
play, music, then! 5.02.211
why take we hands then? 5.02.220
then cannot we be bought; 5.02.226
in private then. 5.02.229
nay then two treys, and if you grow so nice, 5.02.232
then die a calf, before your horns do grow. 5.02.253
bleat softly then, the butcher hears you cry. 5.02.255
then wish me better, i will give you leave. 5.02.342
vouchsafe it then. 5.02.344
there, then, that vizard, that superfluous case 5.02.387
when you then were here, | what did you whisper 5.02.435
and then we, | following the signs, woo'd but 5.02.468
then shall hector be whipt for jaquenetta that 5.02.680 P
then, at the expiration of the year, | come 5.02.804
hence /hermit then — my heart is in thy breast. 5.02.816
then, if i have much love, i'll give you some. 5.02.830
i'll serve thee true and faithfully till then. 5.02.831
then, if sickly ears, | deaf'd with the clamors 5.02.863
will hear your idle scorns, continue then, | and 5.02.865
a twelvemonth an' a day, | and then 'twill end. 5.02.878
the cuckoo then on every tree | mocks married 5.02.898
the cuckoo then on every tree | mocks married 5.02.907
be /foul, | then nightly sings the staring owl, 5.02.917
the bowl, | then nightly sings the staring owl, 5.02.926
and then the moon, like to a silver bow | /new MND 1.01. 9
why should not i then prosecute my right? 1.01.105
if then true lovers have been ever cross'd, | it 1.01.150
then let us teach our trial patience, | because 1.01.152
then | steal forth thy father's house to–morrow 1.01.163
o then, what graces in my love do dwell, | that 1.01.206
then to the wood will he to–morrow night 1.01.247
then read the names of the actors; 1.02. 9 P
and then you will play barefac'd. 1.02. 98 P
then slip i from her bum, down topples she, 2.01. 53
and then the whole quire hold their hips and 2.01. 55
then i must be thy lady; 2.01. 64
do you amend it then; 2.01.118
(her womb then rich with my young squire) 2.01.131
the next thing then she waking looks upon | (be 2.01.179
then how can it be said i am alone, | when all 2.01.225
then, for the third part of a minute, hence, 2.02. 2
then to your offices, and let me rest. 2.02. 8
oath, | so then two bosoms and a single troth. 2.02. 50
then by your side no bed–room me deny; 2.02. 51
say i — | and then end life when i end loyalty! 2.02. 63
then be content. 2.02.110
then i well perceive you are not nigh: 2.02.155
why, then may you leave a casement of the great 3.01. 56 P
then, there is another thing: 3.01. 61 P
if that may be, then all is well. 3.01. 72 P
then, what it was that next came in her eye, 3.02. 2
hast thou slain him then? 3.02. 66
i pray thee, tell me then that he is well. 3.02. 77
then fate o'errules, that, one man holding troth 3.02. 92
then will two at once woo one; 3.02.118
why then you left me (o, the gods forbid!) 3.02.276
then stir demetrius up with bitter wrong; 3.02.361
then crush this herb into lysander's eye; 3.02.366
and then i will her charmed eye release | from 3.02.376
follow me then | to plainer ground. 3.02.403
when i come where he calls, then he is gone. 3.02.414
nay then thou mock'st me. 3.02.426
for she his hairy temples then had rounded 4.01. 51
i then did ask of her her changeling child; 4.01. 59
then, my queen, in silence sad | trip we after 4.01. 95
why then, we are awake. 4.01.198
if he come not, then the play is marr'd. 4.02. 5 P
consider then, we come but in despite. 5.01.112
it must be your imagination then, and not theirs 5.01.213 P
then know that i as snug the joiner am | a lion 5.01.223
and then came pyramus. 5.01.270 P
why then you are in love. MV 1.01. 46
then let us say you are sad | because you are 1.01. 47
well, we will leave you then till dinner–time. 1.01.105
then do but say to me what i should do | that in 1.01.158
then is there the county palentine. 1.02. 45 P
what say you then to falconbridge, the young 1.02. 66 P
pirates, and then there is the peril of waters, 1.03. 24 P
well then, your bond; 1.03. 68
who then conceiving did in eaning time | fall 1.03. 87
then, let me see, the rate — 1.03.104
well then, it now appears you need my help. 1.03.114
go to then, you come to me, and you say, 1.03.115
then meet me forthwith at the notary's; 1.03.172
then stood as fair | as any comer i have look'd 2.01. 20
good fortune then! 2.01. 45
it should seem then that dobbin's tail grows 2.02. 96 P
and then to scape drowning thrice, and to be in 2.02.163 P
why then you must. 2.02.180
talk with respect, and swear but now and then, 2.02.191
then it was not for nothing that my nose fell 2.05. 23 P
clamber not you up to the casements then, | nor 2.05. 31
for wives, | i'll watch as long for you then. 2.06. 24
if you choose that, then i am yours withal. 2.07. 12
i'll then nor give nor hazard aught for lead. 2.07. 21
and if my form lie there, | then i am yours. 2.07. 62
then farewell heat, and welcome frost! 2.07. 75
why then to thee, thou silver treasure house! 2.09. 34
how many then should cover that stand bare? 2.09. 44
how much low peasantry would then be gleaned 2.09. 46
and then it is the complexion of them all to 3.01. 29 P
how to choose right, but then i am forsworn. 3.02. 11
but if mine, then yours, | and so all yours. 3.02. 17
then confess | what treason there is mingled 3.02. 26
well then, confess and live. 3.02. 35
away then! 3.02. 40
then, if he lose, he makes a swan–like end, 3.02. 44
he may win, | and what is music then? 3.02. 48
then music is | even as the flourish when true 3.02. 48
therefore then, thou gaudy gold, | hard food for 3.02.101
from this finger, then parts life from hence; 3.02.184
o, then be bold to say bassanio's dead! 3.02.185
and then i told you true. 3.02.256
i should then have told you | that i was worse 3.02.259
double six thousand, and then treble that, 3.02.300
wife, | and then away to venice to your friend; 3.02.304
to see me pay his debt, and then i care not! 3.03. 36
then i'll repent, | and wish, for all that, that 3.04. 72
truly then i fear you are damn'd both by father 3.05. 15 P
then bid them prepare dinner! 3.05. 50 P
will you cover then, sir? 3.05. 53 P
then, howsome'er thou speak'st, 'mong other 3.05. 89
and then 'tis thought | thou'lt show thy mercy 4.01. 19
then must the jew be merciful. 4.01.182
and earthly power doth then show likest god's 4.01.196
why then thus it is: 4.01.244
take then thy bond, take thou thy pound of flesh 4.01.308
i take this offer then; 4.01.318
why then the devil give him good of it! 4.01.345
king be by, and then his state | empties itself, 5.01. 95
and then the boy, his clerk, | that took some 5.01.181
you would not then have parted with the ring. 5.01.202
let not me take him then, | for if i do, i'll 5.01.236
then you shall be his surety. 5.01.254
when i am absent, then lie with my wife. 5.01.285
what mar you then, sir? AYL 1.01. 31 P
what shall be our sport then? 1.02. 30 P
by my knavery (if i had it) then i were. 1.02. 75 P
then shall we be news–cramm'd. 1.02. 95 P
then there were two cousins laid up, when the 1.03. 7 P
(as i do trust i am not), then, dear uncle, 1.03. 50
then, good my liege, mistake me not so much | to 1.03. 64
i did not then entreat to have her stay, | it 1.03. 69
then open not thy lips: 1.03. 82
pronounce that sentence then on me, my liege, 1.03. 85
rosalind lacks then the love | which teacheth 1.03. 96
then, being there alone, | left and abandoned of 2.01. 49
sullen fits, | for then he's full of matter. 2.01. 68
o, thou didst then never love so heartily! 2.04. 33
well then, if ever i thank any man, i'll thank 2.05. 25 P
and then he drew a dial from his poke, | and, 2.07. 20
and then, from hour to hour, we rot and rot; 2.07. 27
there then! 2.07. 83
how then? 2.07. 83
what then? 2.07. 83
it do him right, | then he hath wrong'd himself. 2.07. 85
why then my taxing like a wild goose flies, 2.07. 86
then forbear your food a little while, | whiles, 2.07.127
then the whining schoolboy, with his satchel 2.07.145
and then the lover, | sighing like furnace, with 2.07.147
then a soldier, | full of strange oaths, and 2.07.149
and then the justice, | in fair round belly with 2.07.153
then thou art damn'd. 3.02. 35 P
good manners, then thy manners must be wicked, 3.02. 42 P
sheaf and bind, | then to cart with rosalind. 3.02.108
you, and then i shall graff it with a medlar. 3.02.117 P
then it will be the earliest fruit i' th' 3.02.118 P
then there is no true lover in the forest, else 3.02.302 P
term, and then they perceive not how time moves. 3.02.332 P
revenue — then your hose should be ungarter'd, 3.02.378 P
then entertain him, then forswear him; 3.02.416 P
then entertain him, then forswear him; 3.02.416 P
now weep for him, then spit at him; 3.02.417 P
do you wish then that the gods had made me 3.03. 23 P
then one of you will prove a shrunk panel, and 3.03. 87 P
then shall you know the wounds invisible | that 3.05. 30
loose now and then | a scatt'red smile, and that 3.05.103
why then 'tis good to be a post. 4.01. 9 P
then, to have seen much, and to have nothing, is 4.01. 23 P
nay then god buy you, and you talk in blank 4.01. 31 P
then she puts you to entreaty, and there begins 4.01. 79 P
then, in mine own person, i die. 4.01. 93 P
then love me, rosalind. 4.01.115 P
why then, can one desire too much of a good 4.01.123 P
then you must say, "i take thee, rosalind, for 4.01.135 P
then sing him home. 4.02. 12
how then might your prayers move? 4.03. 55
my love deny, | and then i'll study how to die." 4.03. 63
then should i know you by description — | such 4.03. 84
well then, take a good heart and counterfeit to 4.03.173 P
then learn this of me: 5.01. 40 P
why then to–morrow i cannot serve your turn for 5.02. 48 P
i will weary you then no longer with idle 5.02. 51 P
know of me then (for now i speak to some purpose 5.02. 52 P
believe then, if you please, that i can do 5.02. 58 P
of an if, as, "if you said so, then i said so"; 5.04.101 P
then is there mirth in heaven, | when earthly 5.04.108
and shape be true, | why then my love adieu! 5.04.121
every town, | high wedlock then be honored. 5.04.144
what a case am i in then, that am neither a good ep 7 P
would not the beggar then forget himself? SHR in.1. 41
then take him up, and manage well the jest. in.1. 45
and then with kind embracements, tempting kisses in.1. 118
free for a husband, and then have to't afresh. 1.01.139 P
nay, then 'tis time to stir him from his trance. 1.01.177
then it follows thus: 1.01.201
when i am alone, why then i am tranio; 1.01.243
and then i know after who comes by the worst. 1.02. 14
first, | then had not grumio come by the worst. 1.02. 35
petruchio, shall i then come roundly to thee, 1.02. 59
if wealthily, then happily in padua. 1.02. 76
then well one more may fair bianca have; 1.02.243
the younger then is free, and not before. 1.02.262
o then belike you fancy riches more: 2.01. 16
nay then you jest, and now i well perceive | you 2.01. 19
if that be jest, then all the rest was so. 2.01. 22
if you accept them, then their worth is great. 2.01.101
a little in the orchard, | and then to dinner. 2.01.112
then tell me, if i get your daughter's love, 2.01.119
why then thou canst not break her to the lute? 2.01.147
why then i'll tell her plain | she sings as 2.01.170
a word, | then i'll commend her volubility, 2.01.175
my remedy is then to pluck it out. 2.01.211
and if no gentleman, why then no arms. 2.01.223
then show it me. 2.01.232
and then let kate be chaste and dian sportful! 2.01.261
nay then good night our part! 2.01.301
then at my farm | i have a hundred milch–kine to 2.01.356
why then the maid is mine from all the world, 2.01.384
then give me leave to have prerogative, | and 3.01. 6
then give me leave to read philosophy, | and 3.01. 13
faith, mistress, then i have no cause to stay. 3.01. 86
what then? 3.02. 37 P
nay then, | do what thou canst, i will not go 3.02.207
for then she never looks upon her lure. 4.01.192
then we are rid of litio. 4.02. 49
take /in your love, and then let me alone. 4.02. 71
but then up farther, and as far as rome, | and 4.02. 75
then go with me to make the matter good. 4.02.115
why then the beef, and let the mustard rest. 4.03. 26
nay then i will not, you shall have the mustard, 4.03. 27
then both or one, or any thing thou wilt. 4.03. 29
why then the mustard without the beef. 4.03. 30
nay then, thou lov'st it not; 4.03. 42
you shall have one too, | and not till then. 4.03. 72
god–a–mercy, grumio, then he shall have no odds. 4.03.153 P
where then do you know best | we be affied and 4.04. 48
then at my lodging, and it like you. 4.04. 55
then thus: 4.04. 82 P
and then? 4.04. 87 P
will be pleas'd, then wherefore should i doubt? 4.04.106
nay then you lie; it is the blessed sun. 4.05. 17
then, god be blest, it /is the blessed sun, 4.05. 18
then hast thou taught hortensio to be untoward. 4.05. 79
and then come back to my /master's as soon as i 5.01. 5 P
then thou wert best say that i am not lucentio. 5.01.103 P
then pardon him, sweet father, for my sake. 5.01.130
why then let's home again. 5.01.147
then never trust me if i be afeard. 5.02. 17
bush, | and then pursue me as you draw your bow. 5.02. 47
a hundred then. 5.02. 74
nay then she must needs come. 5.02. 88
then vail your stomachs, for it is no boot, 5.02.176
for then we wound our modesty and make foul the
AWW 1.03. 5 P
as she stood, | and gave this sentence then: 1.03. 76
were our faults, or then we thought them none. 1.03.135
tell me true, | but tell me then, 'tis so; 1.03.176
then i confess | here on my knee, before high 1.03.191
then give pity | to her whose state is such that 1.03.213
of my thoughts | happily been absent then. 1.03.235
then here's a man stands that has brought his 2.01. 63
my duty then shall pay me for my pains. 2.01.125
then shalt thou give me with thy kingly hand 2.01.193
why then, young bertram, take her, she's thy 2.03.105
good, very good, it is so then. 2.03.265 P
then my dial goes not true. 2.05. 6 P
i have then sinn'd against his experience and 2.05. 10 P
body that i am father to, then call me husband; 3.02. 59 P
but in such a 'then' i write a 'never.'" 3.02. 60 P
then hast thou all again. 3.02.102
then go thou forth, | and fortune play upon thy 3.03. 6
and then you cannot, | by the good aid that i of 3.07. 10
you see it lawful then. 3.07. 30
why then to–night | let us assay our plot, which 3.07. 43
and then to return and swear the lies he forges. 4.01. 23 P
till then i'll keep him dark and safely lock'd. 4.01. 94
she then was honest. 4.02. 11
then pray you tell me, | if i should swear by 4.02. 24
unto my sick desires, | who then recovers. 4.02. 36
adieu till then, then fail not. 4.02. 64
adieu till then, then fail not. 4.02. 64
we shall not then have his company to–night? 4.03. 27 P
what will count rossillion do then? 4.03. 41 P
you beg more than "word" then. 5.02. 40 P
then shall we have a match. 5.03. 30
then if you know | that you are well acquainted 5.03.105
the story then goes false, you threw it him 5.03.229
where did you find it then? 5.03.274
ours be your patience then, and yours our parts; ep 5
he was a bachelor then. TN 1.02. 29
and then 'twas fresh in murmur (as, you know, 1.02. 32
then leaving her | in the protection of his son, 1.02. 37
my tongue blabs, then let mine eyes not see. 1.02. 63
then hadst thou had an excellent head of hair. 1.03. 95 P
say i do speak with her, my lord, what then? 1.04. 23
o, then unfold the passion of my love, 1.04. 24
you are resolute then? 1.05. 21 P
the dry fool drink, then is the fool not dry; 1.05. 44 P
and then show you the heart of my message. 1.05.190 P
you must know of me then, antonio, my name is 2.01. 16 P
to be up after midnight and to go to bed then, 2.03. 8 P
plenty, | then come kiss me, sweet and twenty; 2.03. 51
and then to break promise with him and make a 2.03.127 P
she is not worth thee then. 2.04. 27
then let thy love be younger than thyself, | or 2.04. 36
i'll pay thy pleasure then. 2.04. 69
must she not then be answer'd? 2.04. 92
and then to have the humor of state; 2.05. 52 P
does not toby take you a blow o' the lips then? 2.05. 68 P
but then there is no consonancy in the sequel; 2.05.129 P
and then i comes behind. 2.05.135 P
if you will then see the fruits of the sport, 2.05.197 P
why then methinks 'tis time to smile again. 3.01.126
then westward–ho! 3.01.134
then think you right: i am not what i am. 3.01.141
you should then have accosted her, and with some 3.02. 21 P
why then build me thy fortunes upon the basis of 3.02. 33 P
never trust me then; 3.02. 58 P
do not then walk too open. 3.03. 37
nay then i must have an ounce or two of this 4.01. 43 P
then you are mad indeed, if you be no better in 4.02. 89 P
where's antonio then? 4.03. 4
then lead the way, good father, and heavens so 4.03. 34
why then the worse for my friends and the better 5.01. 22 P
art, and then thou art | as great as that thou 5.01.149
then he's a rogue, and a passy–measures /pavin. 5.01.200 P
look then to be well edified when the fool 5.01.290 P
well, grant it then, | and tell me, in the 5.01.334
then cam'st in smiling, | and in such forms 5.01.349
rooted betwixt them then such an affection, WT 1.01. 23 P
we'll part the time between 's then; 1.02. 18
but let him say so then, and let him go; 1.02. 35
your guest then, madam. 1.02. 56

not your jailer then, | but your kind hostess. 1.02. 59
you were pretty lordings then? 1.02. 62
temptations have since then been born to 's: 1.02. 77
your precious self had then not cross'd the eyes 1.02. 79
then didst thou utter, | "i am yours for ever." 1.02.104
and then to sigh, as 'twere | the mort o' th' 1.02.117
then 'tis very credent | thou mayst co–join with 1.02.142
how like, methought, i then was to this kernel, 1.02.159
now my sworn friend and then mine enemy; 1.02.167
if i then deny it, | 'tis none of mine. 1.02.266
thought, then say | my wife's a /hobby–horse, 1.02.275
why then the world and all that's in't is 1.02.293
my lord, | go then; 1.02.343
o then, my best blood turn | to an infected 1.02.417
turn then my freshest reputation to | a savor 1.02.420
of these days, and then you'ld wanton with us, 2.01. 18
nay, come sit down; then on. 2.01. 29
come on then, | and give't me in mine ear. 2.01. 31
you scarce can right me throughly, then, to say 2.01. 99
prison, then abound in tears | as i come out; 2.01.120
good for thee, | what dost thou then in prison? 2.02. 4
pray you then, | conduct me to the queen. 2.02. 6
then 'twere past all doubt | you'ld call your 2.03. 81
better burn it now | than curse it then. 2.03.157
rare | even then will rush to knowledge. 3.01. 21
do), | i doubt not then but innocence shall make 3.02. 30
and that since then | you have not dar'd to 3.02.128
done, | and then run mad indeed — stark mad! 3.02.183
thou art perfect then, our ship hath touch'd 3.03. 1
and then for the land–service, to see how the 3.03. 94 P
why, then comes in the sweet o' the year, | for 4.03. 3
here and there, | i then do most go right. 4.03. 18
bouget, | then my account i well may give, | and 4.03. 21
and then, death, death! 4.03. 53 P
been since an ape–bearer, then a process–server, 4.03. 95 P
then he compass'd a motion of the prodigal son, 4.03. 96 P
then fare thee well, i must go buy spices for 4.03.116 P
which then will speak, that you must change this 4.04. 39
then make /your garden rich in gillyvors, | and 4.04. 98
a–life, for then we are sure they are true. 4.04.261 P
then whither goest? 4.04.308
can dream of yet, | enough then for your wonder. 4.04.389
then, till the fury of his highness settle, 4.04.471
and then | let nature crush the sides o' th' 4.04.477
then list to me. 4.04.541
go to then. 4.04.692 P
and then your blood had been the dearer by i 4.04.704 P
then 'nointed over with honey, set on the head 4.04.783 P
then stand till he be three quarters and a dram 4.04.785 P
then recover'd again with aqua–vitae or some 4.04.786 P
then, raw as he is (and in the hottest day 4.04.787 P
then, even now, | i might have look'd upon my 5.01. 52
then i'ld shriek, that even your ears | should 5.01. 65
then, good my lords, bear witness to his oath. 5.01. 72
never till then. 5.01. 84
and then i lost | (all mine own folly) the 5.01.134
then have you lost a sight which was to be seen, 5.02. 42 P
then asks bohemia forgiveness; 5.02. 52 P
then embraces his son–in–law; 5.02. 52 P
then again worries he his daughter with clipping 5.02. 53 P
the child were even then lost when it was found. 5.02. 72 P
shepherd's daughter (so he then took her to be), 5.02.118 P
and then the two kings call'd my father brother; 5.02.141 P
and then the prince, my brother, and the 5.02.142 P
that | i kneel and then implore her blessing. 5.03. 44
but then you'll think | (which i protest against 5.03. 89
then, all stand still; 5.03. 95
her die again, for then | you kill her double. 5.03.106
then take my king's defiance from my mouth, JN 1.01. 21
you came not of one mother then, it seems. 1.01. 58
then, good my liege, let me have what is mine, 1.01.114
then, if he were my brother's, | my brother 1.01.125
shall then my father's will be of no force | to 1.01.130
why then i suck my teeth, and catechize | my 1.01.192
and then comes answer like an absey book: 1.01.196
then, good my mother, let me know my father; 1.01.249
till then, fair boy, | will i not think of home, 2.01. 30
well, then to work! 2.01. 37
and then we shall repent each drop of blood 2.01. 48
then turn your forces from this paltry siege, 2.01. 54
let them be welcome then, we are prepar'd. 2.01. 83
how comes it then that thou art call'd a king, 2.01.107
be pleased then | to pay that duty which you 2.01.246
and then our arms, like to a muzzled bear, 2.01.249
then tell us, shall your city call us lord, | in 2.01.263
acknowledge then the king, and let me in. 2.01.269
then god forgive the sin of all those souls 2.01.283
speed then to take advantage of the field. 2.01.297
then let confusion of one part confirm | the 2.01.359
till then, blows, blood, and death! 2.01.360
then, in a moment, fortune shall cull forth 2.01.391
then after fight who shall be king of it? 2.01.400
why then defy each other, and pell–mell | make 2.01.406
speak then, prince dolphin, can you love this 2.01.524
then do i give volquessen, touraine, maine, 2.01.527
my virtue then shall be | to say there is no 2.01.595
then speak again, not all thy former tale, | but 3.01. 25
o boy, then where art thou? 3.01. 34
i would not care, i then would be content, | for 3.01. 48
be content, | for then i should not love thee; 3.01. 49
then, by the lawful power that i have, | thou 3.01.172
o then tread down my need, and faith mounts up; 3.01.215
and then we shall be blest | to do your pleasure 3.01.251
ill, | the truth is then most done not doing it. 3.01.273
then know | the peril of our curses light on 3.01.294
well then, france shall rue. 3.01.325
then, in despite of brooded watchful day, | i 3.03. 52
then with a passion would i shake the world, 3.04. 39
for then 'tis like i should forget myself. 3.04. 49
then, have i reason to be fond of grief? 3.04. 98
john may stand, then arthur needs must fall: 3.04.139
may then make all the claim that arthur did. 3.04.143
and then the hearts | of all his people shall 3.04.164
that you must use me ill, | why then you must. 4.01. 56
alas, i then have chid away my friend! 4.01. 86
then feeling what small things are boisterous 4.01. 94
then i, as one that am the tongue of these | to 4.02. 47
why then your fears, which (as they say) attend 4.02. 56
how wildly then walks my estate in france! 4.02.128
then let the worst unheard fall on your head. 4.02.136
then shall this hand and seal | witness against 4.02.217
to–morrow morning let us meet him then. 4.03. 18
or rather then set forward, for 'twill be | two 4.03. 19
then pause not; 5.01. 14
away then with good courage! 5.01. 78
why should i then be false, since it is true 5.04. 28
brief then; and what's the news? 5.06. 18
and then all this thou seest is but a clod | and 5.07. 57
and then my soul shall wait on thee to heaven, 5.07. 72
it seems you know not then so much as we. 5.07. 81
thither shall it then; 5.07.100
which then our leisure would not let us hear, R2 1.01. 5
then call them to our presence; 1.01. 15
as to take up mine honor's pawn, then stoop. 1.01. 74
then, bullingbrook, as low as to thy heart 1.01.124
then, dear my liege, mine honor let me try; 1.01.184
where then, alas, may i complain myself? 1.02. 42
why then i will. 1.02. 44
why then the champions are prepar'd, and stay 1.03. 5
then let us take a ceremonious leave | and 1.03. 50
then thus i turn me from my country's light, 1.03.176
why at our justice seem'st thou then to low'r? 1.03.235
then england's ground, farewell, sweet soil, 1.03.306
which then blew bitterly against our faces, 1.04. 7
then all too late comes counsel to be heard, 2.01. 27
my life, | how happy then were my ensuing death! 2.01. 68
convey me to my bed, then to my grave; 2.01.137
let not to–morrow then ensue to–day; 2.01.197
then thus: 2.01.277
if then we shall shake off our slavish yoke, 2.01.291
then, thrice–gracious queen, | more than your 2.02. 24
then wherefore dost thou hope he is not shipp'd? 2.02. 45
if judgment lie in them, then so do we, 2.02.133
then with directions to repair to ravenspurgh. 2.03. 35
then learn to know him now, this is the duke. 2.03. 40
but then more "why?" 2.03. 92
o, then how quickly should this arm of mine, 2.03.103
o then my father, | will you permit that i shall 2.03.118
then thieves and robbers range abroad unseen 3.02. 39
then murthers, treasons, and detested sins, 3.02. 44
then if angels fight, | weak men must fall, for 3.02. 61
then i must not say no. 3.03.209
then set before my face the lord aumerle. 4.01. 6
'tis very true, you were in presence then, | and 4.01. 62
then true noblesse would | learn him forbearance 4.01.119
me, | and then betwixt me and my married wife. 5.01. 73
then whither he goes, thither let me go. 5.01. 85
then, as i said, the duke, great bullingbrook, 5.02. 7
no matter then who see it. 5.02. 58
we'll keep him here, then what is that to him? 5.02.100
then give me leave that /i may turn the key, 5.03. 36
his, then let them have | that mercy which true 5.03.109
"come, little ones," and then again, | "it is as 5.05. 15
then treasons make me wish myself a beggar, 5.05. 33
then crushing penury | persuades me i was better 5.05. 34
then am i king'd again, and by and by | think 5.05. 36
then let me hear | of you, my gentle cousin 1H4 1.01. 30
it seems then that the tidings of this broil 1.01. 47
then would i have his harry and he mine. 1.01. 90
well, how then? come, roundly, roundly. 1.02. 22 P
marry then, sweet wag, when thou art king, let 1.02. 23 P
then art thou damn'd for keeping thy word with 1.02.120 P
well then, once in my days i'll be a madcap. 1.02.142 P
by the lord, i'll be a traitor then, when thou 1.02.146 P
and then will they adventure upon the exploit 1.02.171 P
i then, all smarting with my wounds being cold, 1.03. 49
what e'er lord harry percy then had said | to 1.03. 71
wrong or any way impeach | what then he said, so 1.03. 76
shall our coffers then | be emptied to redeem a 1.03. 85
who then, affrighted with their bloody looks, 1.03.104
then let not him be slandered with revolt. 1.03.112
my wive's brother, then his cheek look'd pale, 1.03.142
and then it was when the unhappy king | (whose 1.03.148
you, did king richard then | proclaim my brother 1.03.155
nay, then i cannot blame his cousin king, | that 1.03.158
this fawning greyhound then did proffer me! 1.03.252
then once more to your scottish prisoners: 1.03.259
and then the power of scotland, and of york, 1.03.280
a jordan, and then we leak in your chimney, and 2.01. 20 P
from your encounter, then they light on us. 2.02. 62 P
let us share, and then to horse before day. 2.02. 98 P
why is he not then? 2.03. 4 P
well, do not then, for since you love me not, 2.03. 97
why then your brown bastard is your only drink! 2.04. 73 P
let them alone awhile, and then open the door. 2.04. 84 P
if thou didst, then behold that compound. 2.04.122 P
face of the earth, then am i a shotten herring. 2.04.129 P
unbound the rest, and then come in the other. 2.04.182 P
poor old jack, then am i no two–legg'd creature. 2.04.188 P
breathe a while, and then to it again, and when 2.04.249 P
then did we two set on you four, and, with a 2.04.255 P
as thou hast done, and then say it was in fight! 2.04.262 P
and then to beslubber our garments with it and 2.04.310 P
what a rascal art thou then, to praise him so 2.04.351 P
why then, it is like, if there come a hot june 2.04.361 P
if then thou be son to me, here lies the point: 2.04.405 P
if then the tree may be known by the fruit, as 2.04.428 P
as the fruit by the tree, then, peremptorily i 2.04.429 P
then many an old host that i know is damn'd. 2.04.471 P
then pharaoh's /lean kine are to be lov'd. 2.04.473 P
then the earth shook to see the heavens on fire, 3.01. 24
of land, | and then he runs straight and even. 3.01.113
let me understand you then, | speak it in welsh. 3.01.117
nay, if you melt, then will she run mad. 3.01.209
then should you be nothing but musical, for you 3.01.232 P
then be still. 3.01.239 P
we'll but seal, | and then to horse immediately. 3.01.266
and then i stole all courtesy from heaven, | and 3.02. 50
as thou art to this hour was richard then | when 3.02. 94
and even as i was then is percy now. 3.02. 96
and then i shall have no strength to repent. 3.03. 6 P
you confess then you pick'd my pocket? 3.03.168 P
you give him then advantage. 4.03. 2
then to the point. 4.03. 89
then with the losers let it sympathize, | for 5.01. 7
you have not sought it, how comes it then? 5.01. 27
how then? 5.01.131 P
honor hath no skill in surgery then? 5.01.133 P
'tis insensible then? 5.01.138 P
then are we all /undone; 5.02. 3
know then, my name is douglas, | and i do haunt 5.03. 3
why then i see | a very valiant rebel of the 5.04. 61
and by, | till then in blood by noble percy lie. 5.04.110
but if i be not jack falstaff, then am i a jack. 5.04.139 P
then, brother john of lancaster, to you | this 5.05. 25
then this remains, that we divide our power. 5.05. 34
by travers | give then such instances of loss? 2H4 1.01. 56
then was that noble worcester | so soon ta'en 1.01.125
than to set me off, why then i have no judgment. 1.02. 14 P
gentleman in hand, and then stand upon security! 1.02. 37 P
taking up, then they must stand upon security. 1.02. 40 P
then set your knighthood and your soldiership 1.02. 83 P
as i was then advis'd by my learned counsel in 1.02.134 P
the question then, lord hastings, standeth thus: 1.03. 15
thou didst swear to me then, as i was washing 2.01. 91 P
wife, come in then and call me gossip quickly? 2.01. 94 P
belike then my appetite was not princely got, 2.02. 9 P
who then persuaded you to stay at home? 2.03. 15
then join you with them, like a rib of steel, 2.03. 54
why then cover and set them down, and see if 2.04. 10 P
our minister, was by then — "neighbor quickly," 2.04. 88 P
then to you, mistress dorothy, i will charge you 2.04.121 P
then feed and be fat, my fair calipolis. 2.04.179
then death rock me asleep, abridge my doleful 2.04.197
why then let grievous, ghastly, gaping wounds 2.04.198
why does the prince love him so then? 2.04.243 P
i shall drive you then to confess the willful 2.04.311 P
abuse, and then i know how to handle you. 2.04.312 P
then (happy) low, lie down! 3.01. 30
why then good morrow to you all, my lords. 3.01. 35
then you perceive the body of our kingdom | how 3.01. 38
then check'd and rated by northumberland, | did 3.01. 68
bullingbrook ascends my throne" | (though then, 3.01. 72
that great northumberland, then false to him, 3.01. 89
are these things then necessities? 3.01. 92
then let us meet them like necessities; 3.01. 93
'a must then to the inns a' court shortly. 3.02. 13 P
you were call'd lusty shallow then, cousin. 3.02. 16 P
then was jack falstaff, now sir john, a boy, and 3.02. 24 P
she was then a bona roba. 3.02.205 P
marry, then, mouldy, bullcalf, feeble, and 3.02.248 P
i was then sir dagonet in arthur's show — there 3.02.280 P
and then he burst his head for crowding among 3.02.322 P
then, my lord, | unto your grace do i in chief 4.01. 30
then reason will our hearts should be as good. 4.01.155
say you not then our offer is compell'd. 4.01.156
then take, my lord of westmerland, this schedule 4.01.166
grace of york, in god's name then set forward. 4.01.225
for then both parties nobly are subdued, | and 4.02. 90
well then, colevile is your name, a knight is 4.03. 5 P
when every thing is ended, then you come. 4.03. 27
let it shine, then. 4.03. 57 P
into a kind of male green–sickness, and then, 4.03. 93 P
and then the vital commoners and inland petty 4.03.109 P
then get thee gone, and dig my grave thyself, 4.05.110
then plain and right must my possession be, 4.05.222
how many nobles then should hold their places, 5.02. 17
why then be sad, | but entertain no more of it, 5.02. 53
i then did use the person of your father, | the 5.02. 73
father, | the image of his power lay then in me, 5.02. 74
and then imagine me taking your part, | and in 5.02. 96
come, cousin silence — and then to bed. 5.03. 4 P
why then say an old man can do somewhat. 5.03. 78 P
then, pistol, lay thy head in furies' lap. 5.03.106
why then lament therefore. 5.03.108
till then i banish thee, on pain of death, | as 5.05. 63
first my fear, then my cur'sy, last my speech. ep 1 P
not, then the gentlemen do not agree with the ep 23 P
then should the warlike harry, like himself, H5 pr 5
then go we in, to know his embassy; 1.01. 95
then hear me, gracious sovereign, and you peers, 1.02. 33
of their life, | establish'd then this law: 1.02. 50
then doth it well appear the salique law | was 1.02. 54
she hath been then more fear'd than harm'd, my 1.02.155
france win, | then with scotland first begin." 1.02.168
it follows then the cat must stay at home, | yet 1.02.174
thus then in few: 1.02.245
but till the king come forth, and not till then, 2.pr. 41
thou wilt not, why then be enemies with me too. 2.01.103 P
well, then that/'s the humor of't. 2.01.116 P
then, richard earl of cambridge, there is yours; 2.02. 66
then forth, dear countrymen! 2.02.189
then i felt to his knees, and so up'ard and 2.03. 24 P
but then he was rheumatic, and talk'd of the 2.03. 38 P
it fits us then to be as provident | as fear may 2.04. 11
he bids you then resign | your crown and kingdom 2.04. 93
ears, | then imitate the action of the tiger; 3.01. 6
then lend the eye a terrible aspect; 3.01. 9
what is it then to me, if impious war, | arrayed 3.03. 15
why then rejoice therefore. 3.06. 52
a rogue, that now and then goes to the wars, to 3.06. 68 P
well then, i know thee. 3.06.115
then did they imitate that which i compos'd to 3.07. 43 P
o then belike she was old and gentle, and you 3.07. 52 P
be warn'd by me then: 3.07. 56 P
and then, give them great meals of beef and iron 3.07.149 P
then shall we find to–morrow they have only 3.07.153 P
a while, | and then i would no other company. 4.01. 32
then you are a better than the king. 4.01. 43 P
the figo for thee then! 4.01. 60
then i would he were here alone; 4.01.121 P
then if they die unprovided, no more is the king 4.01.173 P
you pay him then. 4.01.197 P
then, if ever thou dar'st acknowledge it, i will 4.01.209 P
how shall we then behold their natural tears? 4.02. 13
then let the trumpets sound | the tucket sonance 4.02. 34
then, joyfully, my noble lord of bedford, | my 4.03. 8
then will he strip his sleeve and show his scars 4.03. 47
then shall our names, | familiar in his mouth as 4.03. 51
bid them achieve me, and then sell my bones. 4.03. 91
mark then abounding valor in our english: 4.03.104
shall — my ransom then | will soon be levied. 4.03.120
tarry, sweet soul, for mine, then fly abreast, 4.06. 17
then every soldier kill his prisoners, | give 4.06. 37

field | to book our dead, and then to bury them; 4.07. 73
then call we this the field of agincourt, 4.07. 90
then keep thy vow, sirrah, when thou meet'st the 4.07.144 P
and then to callice, and to england then, 4.08.125
and then to callice, and to england then, 4.08.125
then brook abridgment, and your eyes advance 5.pr. 44
and then i will tell him a little piece of my 5.01. 13 P
since then my office hath so far prevail'd, 5.02. 29
well then: 5.02. 75
then if you urge me farther than to say "do you 5.02.127 P
and what say'st thou then to my love? 5.02.167 P
am yours, then yours is france and you are mine. 5.02.176 P
le possession de moi — let me see, what then? 5.02.183 P
then i will kiss your lips, kate. 5.02.257 P
can you blame her then, being a maid yet ros'd 5.02.295 P
they are then excus'd, my lord, when they see 5.02.302 P
then, good my lord, teach your cousin to consent 5.02.304 P
their eyes, and then they will endure handling, 5.02.309 P
i pray you then, in love and dear alliance, 5.02.345
then shall i swear to kate, and you to me, | and 5.02.373
is talbot slain then? 1H6 1.01.141
and then i will proclaim young henry king. 1.01.169
then come a' god's name, i fear no woman. 1.02.102
hence, | then will i think upon a recompense. 1.02.116
thou with an eagle art inspired then. 1.02.141
see the coast clear'd, and then we will depart. 1.03. 89
then broke i from the officers that led me, 1.04. 44
and then we'll try what these dastard frenchmen 1.04.111
embrace we then this opportunity | as fitting 2.01. 13
then how, or which way, should they first break 2.01. 71
then i see our wars | will turn unto a peaceful 2.02. 44
ne'er trust me then; 2.02. 48
well then, alone (since there's no remedy) | i 2.02. 57
if thou be he, then art thou prisoner. 2.03. 33
then have i substance too. 2.03. 49
then say at once if i maintain'd the truth; 2.04. 5
judge you, my lord of warwick, then between us. 2.04. 10
then for the truth and plainness of the case, 2.04. 46
and if thou be not then created york, | i will 2.04.119
my soul shall then be satisfied. 2.05. 21
and even since then hath richard been obscur'd, 2.05. 26
thy father, earl of cambridge then, deriv'd 2.05. 84
thou dost then wrong me, as that slaughterer 2.05.109
roam thither then. 3.01. 51
then be at peace, except ye thirst for blood. 3.01.117
stoop then and set your knee against my foot, 3.01.168
presently, | and then do execution on the watch. 3.02. 35
belike your lordship takes us then for fools, 3.02. 62
then be it so. 3.02.100
and then depart to paris to the king, | for 3.02.128
employ thee then, sweet virgin, for our good. 3.03. 16
then thus it must be, this doth joan devise: 3.03. 17
ill, | who then but english henry will be lord, 3.03. 66
see then, thou fight'st against thy countrymen 3.03. 74
then judge, great lords, if i have done amiss; 4.01. 27
he then, that is not furnish'd in this sort, 4.01. 39
why then lord talbot there shall talk with him, 4.01. 68
then gather strength and march unto him straight 4.01. 73
first let me know, and then i'll answer you. 4.01. 88
and then your highness shall command a peace. 4.01.117
betwixt ourselves let us decide it then. 4.01.119
if we be english deer, be then in blood, | not 4.02. 48
then god take mercy on brave talbot's soul, 4.03. 34
if he be dead, brave talbot, then adieu! 4.04. 45
then let me stay, and, father, do you fly. 4.05. 21
if death be so apparent, then both fly. 4.05. 44
then here i take my leave of thee, fair son, 4.05. 52
then leaden age, | quicken'd with youthful 4.06. 12
then talk no more of flight, it is no boot; 4.06. 52
then follow thou thy desp'rate sire of crete, 4.06. 54
death been french, then death had died to-day. 4.07. 28
then i perceive that will be verified | henry 5.01. 30
then march to paris, royal charles of france, 5.02. 4
then on, my lords, and france be fortunate! 5.02. 21
then take my soul — my body, soul, and all, 5.03. 22
a wife, | then how can margaret be thy paramour? 5.03. 82
and then i need not crave his courtesy. 5.03.105
then call our captains and our colors forth, 5.03.128
i'll over then to england with this news, | and 5.03.167
then, joan, discover thine infirmity, | that 5.04. 60
murther not then the fruit within my womb, 5.04. 63
then lead me hence; 5.04. 86
must he be then as shadow of himself? 5.04.133
then swear allegiance to his majesty, | as thou 5.04.169
how shall we then dispense with that contract, 5.05. 28
then yield, my lords, and here conclude with me 5.05. 77
why should he then protect our sovereign, | he 2H6 1.01.165
then let's make haste away, and look unto the 1.01.208
then, york, be still awhile, till time do serve. 1.01.248
then will i raise aloft the milk-white rose, 1.01.254
nay, eleanor, then must i chide outright. 1.02. 41
and then we may deliver our supplications in the 1.03. 2 P
then let him be denay'd the regentship. 1.03.104
resign it then and leave thine insolence. 1.03.122
why then, thou know'st what color jet is of? 2.01.111
then, saunder, sit there, the lying'st knave 2.01.123
then send for one presently. 2.01.136
then thus: 2.02. 9
then, father salisbury, kneel we together, | and 2.02. 59
thump? then see thou thump thy master well. 2.03. 84 P
and shall i then be us'd reproachfully? 2.04. 97
me seemeth then it is no policy, | respecting 3.01. 23
and were't not madness then, | to make the fox 3.01.252
nay then, this spark will prove a raging fire, 3.01.302
nay, then a shame take all! 3.01.307
then, noble york, take thou this task in hand. 3.01.318
why, then from ireland come i with my strength, 3.01.380
why then dame /margaret was ne'er thy joy. 3.02. 79
what did i then, but curs'd the gentle gusts, 3.02. 88
and comment then upon his sudden death. 3.02.133
then you belike suspect these noblemen | as 3.02.186
thy body, | and then it liv'd in sweet elysium. 3.02.399
then show me where he is, | i'll give a thousand 3.03. 12
they have the more need to sleep now then. 4.02. 3 P
then is sin struck down like an ox, and 4.02. 26 P
be brave then, for your captain is brave, and 4.02. 64 P
nay, then he is a conjurer. 4.02. 92 P
go to then, i ask but this: 4.02.170 P
but then are we in order when we are most out of 4.02.189 P
then linger not, my lord, away, take horse. 4.04. 54
come, then, let's go fight with them. 4.06. 13 P
mass, 'twill be sore law then, for he was thrust 4.07. 8 P
then we are like to have biting statutes, unless 4.07. 16 P
ye shall have a hempen /caudle then, and the 4.07. 90 P
and then break into his son-in-law's house, sir 4.07.110 P
then, heaven, set ope thy everlasting gates | to 4.09. 13
i know thee not, why then should i betray thee? 4.10. 32
then, buckingham, i do dismiss my pow'rs. 5.01. 44
then what intends these forces thou dost bring? 5.01. 60
then, york, unloose thy long-imprisoned thoughts 5.01. 88
and if words will not, then our weapons shall. 5.01.140
then nobly, york, 'tis for a crown thou fight'st 5.02. 16
but then aeneas bare a living load — | nothing 5.02. 64
we then should see the bottom | of all our 5.02. 78
assist me then, sweet warwick, and i will, | for 3H6 1.01. 28
then leave me not, my lords, be resolute, | i 1.01. 43
what then? 1.01.136
and if he may, then am i lawful king; 1.01.137
till then, i'll follow her. 1.01.262
then, seeing 'twas he that made you to depose, 1.02. 26
then let my father's blood open it again, | he 1.03. 23
then let me die, for now thou hast no cause. 1.03. 45
tears then for babes; 2.01. 86
i come to tell you things sith then befall'n. 2.01.106
i, then in london, keeper of the king, 2.01.111
then, clifford, were thy heart as hard as steel, 2.01.201
then strike up drums. 2.01.204
why then it sorts, brave warriors. let's away. 2.01.209
be it with resolution then to fight. 2.02. 77
then 'twas my turn to fly, and now 'tis thine. 2.02.105
defy them then, or else hold close thy lips. 2.02.118
then, executioner, unsheathe thy sword. 2.02.123
even then that sunshine brew'd a show'r for him, 2.02.156
then let the earth be drunken with our blood! 2.03. 23
sometime the flood prevails, and then the wind; 2.05. 9
now one the better, then another best; 2.05. 10
when this is known, then to divide the times: 2.05. 30
they never then had sprung like summer flies; 2.06. 17
then the world goes hard | when clifford cannot 2.06. 77
and then to brittany i'll cross the sea | to 2.06. 97
by this account then, margaret may win him, 3.01. 35
art then forsaken, as thou went'st forlorn! 3.01. 54
and tell me then, have you not broke your oaths? 3.01. 79
his land then seiz'd on by the conqueror. 3.02. 3
then i'll warrant you all your lands, | and if 3.02. 21
nay then whip me; he'll rather give her two. 3.02. 28
be pitiful, dread lord, and grant it then. 3.02. 32
then get your husband's lands, to do them good. 3.02. 40
why then i will do what your grace commands. 3.02. 49
as red as fire? nay then, her wax must melt. 3.02. 51
why then, thy husband's lands i freely give thee 3.02. 55
why then you mean not as i thought you did. 3.02. 65
why then thou shalt not have thy husband's lands 3.02. 71
why then mine honesty shall be my dower, | for 3.02. 72
then no, my lord. my suit is at an end. 3.02. 81
why then i do but dream on sovereignty, | like 3.02.134
well, say there is no kingdom then for richard; 3.02.146
and am i then a man to be belov'd? 3.02.163
then, since this earth affords no joy to me 3.02.165
person, | and then to crave a league of amity, 3.03. 53
then warwick disannuls great john of gaunt, 3.03. 81
then further: 3.03.119
then, warwick, thus: 3.03.134
then 'tis but reason that i be releas'd | from 3.03.147
then, england's messenger, return in post, | and 3.03.222
and then none but i shall turn his jest to sorrow. 3.03.261
then this is mine opinion: 4.01. 29
if it be so, then both depart to him; 4.01.138
then am i sure of victory. 4.01.147
then, gentle clarence, welcome unto warwick, 4.02. 6
why then, let's on our way in silent sort. 4.02. 28
to-morrow then belike shall be the day, | if 4.03. 7
embassade | then i degraded you from being king, 4.03. 33
nay, then i see that edward needs must down. 4.03. 42
then, for his mind, be edward england's king, 4.03. 48
then is my sovereign slain? 4.04. 6
till then fair hope must hinder live's decay; 4.04. 16
but, madam, where is warwick then become? 4.04. 25
but whither shall we then? 4.05. 20
come then, away, let's ha' no more ado. 4.05. 27
prevail, | i then crave pardon of your majesty. 4.06. 8
why then, though loath, yet must i be content. 4.06. 48
now then it is more than needful | forthwith 4.06. 53
what then remains, we being thus arriv'd | from 4.07. 7
ay, say you so? the gates shall then be opened. 4.07. 29
then fare you well, for i will hence again, | i 4.07. 48
we grow stronger, then we'll make our claim; 4.07. 59
till then, 'tis wisdom to conceal our meaning. 4.07. 60
then be it as you will; 4.07. 65
then why should they love edward more than me? 4.08. 47
then clarence is at hand, i hear his drum. 5.01. 11
why then 'tis mine, if but by warwick's gift. 5.01. 35
why then i would not fly. 5.02. 33
why, courage then! 5.04. 37
then in god's name, lords, | be valiant, and 5.04. 81
then, clarence, do it thou. 5.05. 71
executing, | why then thou art an executioner. 5.06. 33
then, since the heavens have shap'd my body so, 5.06. 78
and then, to purge his fear, i'll be thy death. 5.06. 88
clarence, thy turn is next, and then the rest, 5.06. 90
for then i'll marry warwick's youngest daughter. R3 1.01.153
when they are gone, then must i count my gains. 1.01.162
then say they were not slain. 1.02. 89
why then he is alive. 1.02. 91
then god grant me too | thou mayst be damned for 1.02.102
then bid me kill myself, and i will do it. 1.02.186
then never /was /man true. 1.02.195
say then my peace is made. 1.02.197
grave, | and then return lamenting to my love. 1.02.261
and then deny her aiding hand therein | and lay 1.03. 95
we follow'd then our lord, our sovereign king. 1.03.146
and then, to dry them, gav'st the duke a clout 1.03.176
his curses then, from bitterness of soul 1.03.178
northumberland, then present, wept to see it. 1.03.186
why then give way, dull clouds, to my quick 1.03.195
and then hurl down their indignation | on thee, 1.03.219
i cry thee mercy then; 1.03.234
but then i sigh, and, with a piece of scripture, 1.03.333
o, then began the tempest to my soul! 1.04. 44
then came wand'ring by | a shadow like an angel, 1.04. 52
why, then he'll say we stabb'd him sleeping. 1.04.105 P
and then throw him into the malmsey-butt in the 1.04.155 P
will you then | spurn at his edict, and fulfill 1.04.197
who made thee then a bloody minister, | when 1.04.220
for this will out, and then i must not stay. 1.04.283
then say at once what is it thou requests. 2.01. 99
then you conclude, my grandam, he is dead. 2.02. 12
then be it so, and go we to determine | who they 2.02.141
toward /ludlow then, for we'll not stay behind. 2.02.154
then, masters, look to see a troublous world. 2.03. 9
no doubt shall then, and till then, govern well. 2.03. 15
no doubt shall then, and till then, govern well. 2.03. 15
for then this land was famously enrich'd | with 2.03. 19
then the king | had virtuous uncles to protect 2.03. 20
when great leaves fall, then winter is at hand; 2.03. 33
then, taking him from thence that is not there, 3.01. 53
then where you please, and shall be thought most 3.01. 66
then he is more beholding to you than i. 3.01.107
then i see you will part but with light gifts! 3.01.118
what think'st thou then of stanley? will not he? 3.01.167
well then, no more but this: 3.01.169
what then? 3.02. 9
then certifies your lordship that this night 3.02. 10
then was i going prisoner to the tower, | by the 3.02.100
then curs'd she richard, then curs'd she 3.03. 18
curs'd she richard, then curs'd she buckingham, 3.03. 18
she buckingham, | then curs'd she hastings. 3.03. 19
to-morrow then i judge a happy day. 3.04. 6
then be your eyes the witness of their evil. 3.04. 67
and then again begin, and stop again, | as if 3.05. 3
my princely father, then had wars in france, 3.05. 88
as being got, your father then in france, | and 3.07. 10
then he was urg'd to tell my tale again: 3.07. 31
will not the mayor then and his brethren come? 3.07. 44
know then, it is your fault that you resign 3.07.117
then, on the other side, i check'd my friends. 3.07.150
and then, in speaking, not to incur the last — 3.07.152
then, good my lord, take to your royal self 3.07.195
then i salute you with this royal title — 3.07.239
to-morrow then we will attend your grace, | and 3.07.244
then bring me to their sights. 4.01. 24
that dear saint which then i weeping follow'd — 4.01. 69
murther her brothers and then marry her — 4.02. 62
in charge | beget your happiness, be happy then, 4.03. 26
farewell till then. 4.03. 35
then fiery expedition be my wing, | jove's 4.03. 54
then would i hide my bones, not rest them here. 4.04. 33
i call'd thee then vain flourish of my fortune; 4.04. 82
i call'd thee then poor shadow, painted queen, 4.04. 83
if so then, be not tongue-tied; 4.04.132
then patiently hear my impatience. 4.04.157
do then, but i'll not hear. 4.04.160
then know that from my soul i love thy daughter. 4.04.256
well then, who dost thou mean shall be her king? 4.04.265
then haply will she weep. 4.04.273
nay then indeed she cannot choose but hate thee, 4.04.289
go then, my mother, to thy daughter go, | make 4.04.325
then plainly to her tell my loving tale. 4.04.359
swear then by something that thou hast not 4.04.373
then by myself — 4.04.374
why then, by /god — 4.04.377
then tell me, what makes he upon the seas? 4.04.473
where is thy power then, to beat him back? 4.04.479
go then, and muster men; 4.04.494
why then all-souls' day is my body's doomsday. 5.01. 12
then in god's name march! 5.02. 22
then fly. 5.03.185
why, then 'tis time to arm and give direction. 5.03.236
then if you fight against god's enemy, | god 5.03.253
then, in the name of god and all these rights, 5.03.263
he said the truth, and what said surrey then? 5.03.273
then he disdains to shine, for by the book | he 5.03.278
if not to heaven, then hand in hand to hell. 5.03.313
and then, as we have ta'en the sacrament, | we 5.05. 18
then, in a moment, see | how soon this H8 pr 29
and, if you can be merry then, i'll say | a man pr 31
i was then present, saw them salute on horseback 1.01. 8
then you lost | the view of earthly glory. 1.01. 13
well, we shall then know more, and buckingham 1.01.118
then we shall have 'em | talk us to silence. 1.04. 44
let me see then, | by all your good leaves, 1.04. 84
and then let's dream | who's best in favor. 1.04.107
then deputy of ireland, who remov'd, | earl 2.01. 42
hear what i say, and then go home and lose me. 2.01. 57
for then my guiltless blood must cry against 'em 2.01. 68
then give my charge up to sir nicholas vaux, 2.01. 96
believe me, there's an ill opinion spread then, 2.02.124
then you are weakly made; 2.03. 40
you may then spare that time. 2.04. 5
then mark th' inducement. 2.04.170
th' bishop of bayonne, then french embassador, 2.04.173
then follows, that | i weigh'd the danger which 2.04.197
which | i then did feel full sick, and yet not 2.04.205
i then mov'd you, | my lord of canterbury, and 2.04.218
of the sea, | hung their heads, and then lay by. 3.01. 11
clear, 'tis i must snuff it, | then out it goes. 3.02. 97
ground, | then lays his finger on his temple; 3.02.115
springs out into fast gait, then stops again, 3.02.116
and then to breakfast with | what appetite you 3.02.202
then makes him nothing. 3.02.208
nay then, farewell! 3.02.222
it must be himself then. 3.02.251
then, that in all you writ to rome, or else | to 3.02.313
then, that, without the knowledge | either of 3.02.316
then, that you have sent innumerable substance 3.02.326
nips his root, | and then he falls as i do. 3.02.358
o my lord, | must i then leave you? 3.02.422
how can man then | (the image of his maker) hope 3.02.441
then if thou fall'st, o cromwell, | thou fall'st 3.02.448
then rose again and bow'd her to the people; 4.01. 85
his promises were, as he then was, mighty; 4.02. 41
for then, and not till then, he felt himself, 4.02. 65
for then, and not till then, he felt himself, 4.02. 65
embalm me, | then lay me forth. 4.02.171

toward the king first, then his laws, in filling 5.02. 50
and what follows then? 5.02. 62
men's prayers then would seek you, not their 5.02.118
then thus for you, my lord, it stands agreed, 5.02.122
shall then be his, and like a vine grow to him. 5.04. 49
TRO so, traitor, then she comes when she is thence. 1.01. 31
come go we then together. 1.01.116
then you say as i say, for i am sure he is not 1.02. 67 P
then troilus should have too much: 1.02.101 P
then she's a merry greek indeed. 1.02.109 P
why, go to then. 1.02.127 P
and then to be bak'd with no date in the pie, 1.02.256 P
date in the pie, for then the man's date is out. 1.02.257 P
swell past hiding, and then it's past watching. 1.02.269 P
then though my heart's content firm love doth 1.02.294
why then, you princes, | do you with cheeks 1.03. 17
for then the bold and coward, | the wise and 1.03. 23
where's then the saucy boat | whose weak 1.03. 42
fled under shade, why then the thing of courage, 1.03. 51
then every thing include itself in power, 1.03.119
and then, forsooth, the faint defects of age 1.03.172
on /the attentive bent, | and then to speak. 1.03.253
if then one is, or hath, /or means to be, | that 1.03.289
why then we do our main opinion crush | in taint 1.03.372
run — say so — did not the general run then? 2.01. 6 P
then would come some matter from him; 2.01. 8 P
feel then. 2.01. 11 P
speak then, thou /whinid'st leaven, speak; 2.01. 14 P
who marvels then, when helenus beholds | a 2.02. 42
then i say, | well may we fight for her whom, we 2.02.160
if helen then be wife to sparta's king, | as it 2.02.183
then there's achilles, a rare enginer! 2.03. 7 P
then if she that lays thee out says thou art a 2.03. 31 P
then tell me, patroclus, what's achilles? 2.03. 44 P
then tell me, i pray thee, what's thersites? 2.03. 46 P
then tell me, patroclus, what art thou? 2.03. 48 P
then will ajax lack matter, if he have lost his 2.03. 94 P
why was my cressid then so hard to win? 3.02.116
how were i then uplifted! 3.02.168
keep then the path, | for emulation hath a 3.03.155
then what they do in present, | though less than 3.03.163
then marvel not, thou great and complete man, 3.03.181
o, then beware! 3.03.228
even then when they sit idly in the sun. 3.03.233
then, sweet my lord, i'll call mine uncle down, 4.02. 2
good morrow then. 4.02. 6
held off, | and then you would have tarried. 4.02. 18
you bring me to do — and then you flout me too. 4.02. 26
nay then. 4.02. 54 P
i must then to the grecians? 4.04. 55
die i a villain then! 4.04. 83
why, beg then. 4.05. 48
why then, for venus' sake, give me a kiss | when 4.05. 49
never's my day, and then a kiss of you. 4.05. 52
a maiden battle then? o, i perceive you. 4.05. 87
why then will i no more. 4.05.119
sir, i foretold you then what would ensue. 4.05.217
why art thou then exasperate, thou idle 5.01. 30 P
nay, but do then, | and let your mind be coupled 5.02. 14
nay then — 5.02. 20
/but will you then? 5.02. 58
why then farewell, | thou never shalt mock 5.02. 98
farewell till then. 5.02.106
then conclude | minds sway'd by eyes are full of 5.02.111
why stay we then? 5.02.115
hector, then 'tis wars. 5.03. 49
then is he yonder, | and there the strawy greeks 5.05. 23
why then fly on, i'll hunt thee for thy hide. 5.06. 31
till then i'll sweat and seek about for eases, 5.10. 55
COR what then? 1.01.119
what then? 1.01.120
what then? 1.01.120
well, what then? 1.01.122
then we shall ha' means to vent | our musty 1.01.225
then, worthy martius, | attend upon cominius to 1.01.236
giddy censure | will then cry out of martius, "o 1.01.269
had he died in the business, madam, how then? 1.03. 19 P
then his good report should have been my son; 1.03. 20 P
bloody brow | with his mail'd hand then wiping, 1.03. 35
fare you well then. 1.03.107 P
well, then farewell. 1.03.111 P
then shall we hear their 'larum, and they ours. 1.04. 9
then, valiant titus, take | convenient numbers 1.05. 11
their trenches driven, | and then i came away. 1.06. 13
in manacles, | then reason safely with you. 1.09. 58
but then aufidius was within my view, | and 1.09. 85
what then, sir? 2.01. 42 P
why then you should discover a brace of 2.01. 43 P
and then rejourn the controversy of threepence 2.01. 71 P
being advanc'd, declines, and then men die. 2.01.161
then our office may, | during his power, go 2.01.222
it shall be to him then as our good wills: 2.01.242
our then dictator, | whom with all praise i 2.02. 89
then straight his doubled spirit | requick'ned 2.02.116
it then remains | that you do speak to the 2.02.134
well then, i pray, your price a' th' consulship? 2.03. 73 P
tullus aufidius then had made new head? 3.01. 1
so then the volsces stand but as at first, 3.01. 4
why then should i be consul? 3.01. 50
if he have power, | then vail your ignorance; 3.01. 98
well, what then? 3.01.130
what must be, was law, | then were they chosen; 3.01.168
speak briefly then, | for we are peremptory to 3.01.283
is not then respected | for what before it was. 3.01.305
menenius, | be you then as the people's officer. 3.01.328
well, what then? what then? 3.02. 36
well, what then? what then? 3.02. 36
do it to the gods, | must i then do't to them? 3.02. 39
at thy choice then. 3.02.123
well, mildly be it then. mildly! 3.02.145
death, for fine, or banishment, then let them, 3.03. 15
then he speaks | what's in his heart, and that 3.03. 28
say then; 'tis true, i ought so. 3.03. 62
then if i would | speak that — 3.03.115
what then? 4.02. 25
what then? | he'ld make an end of thy posterity. 4.02. 25
is it ended then? 4.03. 16 P
then know me not, | lest that thy wives with 4.04. 4
then thou dwell'st with daws too? 4.05. 44 P
then if thou hast | a heart of wreak in thee, 4.05. 84
to prove more fortunes | th' art tir'd, then, in 4.05. 94
why then we shall have a stirring world again. 4.05.218 P
because they then less need one another. 4.05.231 P
then shortly art thou mine. 4.07. 57
as cominius is return'd, | unheard — what then? 5.01. 43
is cold, and then | we pout upon the morning, 5.01. 51
to my request, | and then i'll set upon him. 5.01. 58
then you should hate rome, as he does. 5.02. 38 P
then the honor'd mould | wherein this trunk was 5.03. 22
then let the pibbles on the hungry beach 5.03. 58
then let the mutinous winds | strike the proud 5.03. 59
run away till i am bigger, but then i'll fight. 5.03.128
city be afire, | and then i'll speak a little. 5.03.182
TIT rome, | then let my father's honors live in me, 1.01. 7
rome, | keep then this passage to the capitol, 1.01. 12
draw near them then in being merciful: 1.01.118
then, madam, stand resolv'd, but hope withal 1.01.135
be candidatus then and put it on, | and help to 1.01.185
then, if you will elect by my advice, | crown 1.01.228
receive them then, the tribute that i owe, 1.01.251
how, sir? are you in earnest then, my lord? 1.01.277
let not young mutius then, that was thy joy, 1.01.382
is she not then beholding to the man | that 1.01.396
receive him then to favor, saturnine, | that 1.01.421
then hear me speak indifferently for all; 1.01.430
then at my suit look graciously on him; 1.01.439
lest then the people, and patricians too, | upon 1.01.445
and then let me alone, | i'll find a day to 1.01.449
then, aaron, arm thy heart, and fit thy thoughts 2.01. 12
what, is lavinia then become so loose, | or 2.01. 65
then why should he despair that knows to court 2.01. 91
why then it seems some certain snatch or so 2.01. 95
then should not we be tir'd with this ado. 2.01. 98
would it offend you then | that both should 2.01.100
single you thither then this dainty doe, | and 2.01.117
come on then, horse and chariots let us have, 2.02. 18
and then they call'd me foul adulteress, 2.03.109
thrash the corn, then after burn the straw. 2.03.123
what beg'st thou then? fond woman, let me go. 2.03.172
nay then i'll stop your mouth. 2.03.185
then all too late i bring this fatal writ, | the 2.03.264
he would not then have touch'd them for his life 2.04. 47
how happy art thou then, | from these devourers 3.01. 56
will it consume me? let me see it then. 3.01. 62
then fresh tears | stood on her cheeks, as doth 3.01.111
if they did kill thy husband, then be joyful, 3.01.116
then have i kept it to a worthy end. 3.01.173
then i'll go fetch an axe. 3.01.184
do then, dear heart, for heaven shall hear our 3.01.210
then be my passions bottomless with them! 3.01.217
then into limits could i bind my woes: 3.01.220
then must my sea be moved with her sighs; 3.01.227
then must my earth with her continual tears 3.01.228
then give me leave, for losers will have leave 3.01.232
then which way shall i find revenge's cave? 3.01.270
but if you hunt these bear-whelps, then beware, 4.01. 96
leaves abroad, | and where's our lesson then? 4.01.106
why, then she is the devil's dam: 4.02. 65
then let no man but i | do execution on my flesh 4.02. 83
then sit we down and let us all consult. 4.02.132
then let the ladies tattle what they please. 4.02.168
then, when you come to pluto's region, | i pray 4.03. 13
and, kinsmen, then we may go pipe for justice. 4.03. 24
then here is a supplication for you; 4.03.109 P
approach you must kneel, then kiss his foot, 4.03.111 P
kiss his foot, then deliver up your pigeons, and 4.03.111 P
up your pigeons, and then look for your reward. 4.03.112 P
then is all safe, the anchor in the port. 4.04. 38
then i have brought up a neck to a fair end. 4.04. 48 P
then cheer thy spirit, for know thou, emperor, 4.04. 88
if tamora entreat him, then he will, | for i can 4.04. 95
then go successantly, and plead to him. 4.04.113
swear that he shall, and then i will begin. 5.01. 70
and then i'll come and be thy waggoner, | and 5.02. 48
then, gracious auditory, be it known to you 5.03. 96
ROM no, for then we should be colliers. 1.01. 2 P
which then most sought where most might not be 1.01.127
why then, o brawling love! 1.01.176
then she hath sworn that she will still live 1.01.217
such falsehood, then turn tears to /fires; 1.02. 89
for i had then laid wormwood to my dug, 1.03. 26
my lord and you were then at mantua — | nay, i 1.03. 28
years, | for then she could stand high-lone; 1.03. 36
and then my husband — god be with his soul! 1.03. 39
thus then in brief: 1.03. 73
o then i see queen mab hath been with you. 1.04. 53
lovers' brains, and then they dream of love; 1.04. 71
and then dreams he of smelling out a suit; 1.04. 78
asleep, | then he dreams of another benefice. 1.04. 81
and then dreams he of cutting foreign throats, 1.04. 83
and then anon | drums in his ear, at which he 1.04. 85
some five and twenty years, and then we mask'd. 1.05. 37
o then, dear saint, let lips do what hands do, 1.05.103
then move not while my prayer's effect i take. 1.05.106
then have my lips the sin that they have took. 1.05.108
why then i thank you all. 1.05.123
come on, then let's to bed. 1.05.125
go then, for 'tis in vain | to seek him here 2.01. 41
i will not fail, 'tis twenty year till then. 2.02.169
or if not so, then here i hit it right — | our 2.03. 41
my good son, but where hast thou been then? 2.03. 47
then plainly know my heart's dear love is set 2.03. 57
young men's love then lies | not truly in their 2.03. 67
pronounce this sentence then: 2.03. 79
why then is my pump well flower'd. 2.04. 60 P
and is it not then well serv'd in to a sweet 2.04. 81 P
then hie you hence to friar lawrence' cell, 2.05. 68
then love-devouring death do what he dare, | it 2.06. 7
then sweeten with thy breath | this neighbor air 2.06. 26
life | of stout mercutio, and then tybalt fled; 3.01.169
then, dreadful trumpet, sound the general doom, 3.02. 67
all this is comfort, wherefore weep i then? 3.02.107
then "banished" | is death misterm'd. 3.03. 20
o, then i see that /madmen have no ears. 3.03. 61
then mightst thou speak, then mightst thou tear 3.03. 68
thou speak, then mightst thou tear thy hair, 3.03. 68
welcome then. 3.03. 80
and now falls on her bed, and then starts up, 3.03.100
up, | and tybalt calls, and then on romeo cries, 3.03.101
on romeo cries, | and then down falls again. 3.03.102
set, | for then thou canst not pass to mantua, 3.03.149
well, get you gone, a' thursday be it then. 3.04. 30
then, window, let day in, and let life out. 3.05. 41
for then i hope thou wilt not keep him long, 3.05. 63
then weep no more. 3.05. 88
and then i hope thou wilt be satisfied. 3.05. 92
man, | and then to have a wretched puling fool, 3.05.183
then, since the case so stands as now it doth, 3.05.216
till then adieu, and keep this holy kiss. 4.01. 43
then is it likely thou wilt undertake | a thing 4.01. 73
hold then. 4.01. 89
take thou this vial, being then in bed, | and 4.01. 93
and then awake as from a pleasant sleep. 4.01.106
then, as the manner of our country is, | /in thy 4.01.109
shall i be married then to-morrow morning? 4.03. 22
shall i not then be stifled in the vault, | to 4.03. 33
you will not then? 4.05.110 P
i will then give it you soundly. 4.05.112 P
then will i give you the serving-creature. 4.05.116 P
then will i lay the serving-creature's dagger on 4.05.117 P
then have at you with my wit! 4.05.123 P
/oppress, | then music with her silver sound" — 4.05.128
"then music with her silver sound | with speedy 4.05.142
then she is well and nothing can be ill: 5.01. 17
then i /defy you, stars! 5.01. 24
then be not poor, but break it, and take this. 5.01. 74
who bare my letter then to romeo? 5.02. 13
whistle then to me | as signal that thou hearest 5.03. 7
wilt thou provoke me? then have at thee, boy! 5.03. 70
stay then, i'll go alone. 5.03.135
then i'll be brief. 5.03.169
and then will i be general of your woes, | and 5.03.219
then say at once what thou dost know in this. 5.03.228
then comes she to me, | and with wild looks bid 5.03.239
then gave i her (so tutor'd by my art) | a 5.03.243
then all alone, | at the prefixed hour of her 5.03.252
but then a noise did scare me from the tomb, 5.03.262
and then in post he came from mantua | to this 5.03.273
on him, | and then i ran away to call the watch. 5.03.285
TIM then i repent not. 1.01.184 P
then i lie not. 1.01.219 P
then thou liest: 1.01.222 P
what wouldst do then, apemantus? 1.01.228 P
then, as in grateful virtue i am bound | to your 1.02. 5
all those flatterers were thine enemies then, 1.02. 82 P
enemies then, that then thou mightst kill 'em — 1.02. 82 P
when all's spent, he'ld be cross'd then, and he 1.02.162
why then another time i'll hear thee. 1.02.178
upon thee, and then thou wouldst sin the faster. 1.02.240 P
thou wilt not hear me now, thou shalt not then. 1.02.248 P
nor then silenc'd when | "commend me to your 2.01. 17
will little learning die then that day thou art 2.02. 82 P
do it then, that we may account thee a 2.02.104 P
why then preferr'd you not your sums and bills 3.04. 49
then they could smile, and fawn upon his debts, 3.04. 51
my lords, then, under favor, pardon me | if i 3.05. 40
why then, women are more valiant | that stay at 3.05. 47
who then dares to be half so kind again? 4.02. 40
then what should war be? 4.03. 62
then the rot returns | to thine own lips again. 4.03. 65
but then renew i could not, like the moon; 4.03. 69
i see them now, then was a blessed time. 4.03. 79
well, more gold — what then? 4.03.149
'tis, then, because thou dost not keep a dog, 4.03.200
then, timon, presently prepare thy grave; 4.03.377
then, if thou /grant'st th' art a man, i have 4.03.474
then i know thee not. 4.03.476
then i love thee, | because thou art a woman, 4.03.482
then this breaking of his | has been but a try 5.01. 8
then do we sin against our own estate, | when we 5.01. 41
but where one villain is, then him abandon. 5.01.111
then let him know, and tell him timon speaks it, 5.01.175
then, dear countryman, | bring in thy ranks, but 5.04. 38
then there's my glove; 5.04. 54
JC then, brutus, i have much mistook your passion, 1.02. 48
to all the rout, then hold me dangerous. 1.02. 78
then must i think you would not have it so. 1.02. 81
till then, my noble friend, chew upon this: 1.02.171
i should not then ask casca what had chanc'd. 1.02.220
hand thus, and then the people fell a-shouting. 1.02.223 P
then he offer'd it to him again; 1.02.240 P
then he put it by again; 1.02.241 P
and then he offer'd it the third time; 1.02.242 P
till then, think of the world. 1.02.307
good night then, casca; 1.03. 39
i know where i will wear this dagger then; 1.03. 89
and why should caesar be a tyrant then? 1.03.103
then i know | my answer must be made. 1.03.113
and then i grant we put a sting in him | that at 2.01. 16
round, | he then unto the ladder turns his back, 2.01. 25
then lest he may, prevent. 2.01. 28
the mortal instruments | are then in council; 2.01. 67
suffers then | the nature of an insurrection. 2.01. 68
o then, by day | where wilt thou find a cavern 2.01. 79
with valor | the melting spirits of women, then, 2.01.122
then leave him out. 2.01.152
to cut the head off and then hack the limbs — 2.01.163
o, that we then could come by caesar's spirit, 2.01.169
he says he does, being then most flattered. 2.01.208
be that the uttermost, and fail not then. 2.01.214
then you scratch'd your head, | and too 2.01.243
this were true, then should i know this secret. 2.01.291
follow me then. 2.01.334
et tu, brute? — then fall, caesar! 3.01. 77
grant that, and then is death a benefit; 3.01.103
then walk we forth, even to the market-place, 3.01.108
stoop then, and wash. 3.01.111
and then we will deliver you the cause | why i, 3.01.181
if then thy spirit look upon us now, | shall it 3.01.195
then, in a friend, it is cold modesty. 3.01.213
prepare the body then, and follow us. 3.01.253
then follow me, and give me audience, friends. 3.02. 2
if then that friend demand why brutus rose 3.02. 20 P
then none have i offended. 3.02. 36 P

what cause withholds you then to mourn for him? 3.02.103
you will compel me then to read the will? 3.02.157
then make a ring about the corpse of caesar, 3.02.158
then burst his mighty heart, | and, in his 3.02.186
then i, and you, and all of us fell down, 3.02.191
away then, come, seek the conspirators. 3.02.232
i must tell you then: 3.02.237
then to answer every man directly and briefly, 3.03. 15 P
these many then shall die, their names are 4.01. 1
then take we down his load, and turn him off 4.01. 25
then in my tent, cassius, enlarge your griefs, 4.02. 46
then like a roman bear the truth i tell: 4.03.188
then, with your will, go on; 4.03.224
well; then i shall see thee again? 4.03.284
why, i will see thee at philippi then. 4.03.286
then is this | the very last time we shall speak 5.01. 97
what are you then determined to do? 5.01. 99
then, if we lose this battle, | you are 5.01.107
if not, why then this parting was well made. 5.01.118
why then lead on. 5.01.122
the day will end, | and then the end is known. 5.01.125
and then i swore thee, saving of thy life, 5.03. 38
peace then, no words. 5.05. 7
hold then my sword, and turn away thy face, 5.05. 47
octavius, then take him to follow thee, | that 5.05. 66
speak then to me, who neither beg nor fear MAC 1.03. 60
till then, enough. come, friends. 1.03.156
in every point twice done, and then done double, 1.06. 15
done, then 'twere well | it were done quickly. 1.07. 1
then, as his host, | who should against his 1.07. 14
what beast was't then | that made you break this 1.07. 47
when you durst do it, then you were a man; 1.07. 49
did then adhere, and yet you would make both: 1.07. 52
how easy is it then! 2.02. 65
see, and then speak yourselves. 2.03. 73
then 'tis most like | the sovereignty will fall 2.04. 29
while then, god be with you! 3.01. 43
then prophet–like | they hail'd him father to a 3.01. 58
well then, now | have you consider'd of my 3.01. 74
then be thou jocund; 3.02. 40
then stand with us. 3.03. 4
then 'tis he; 3.03. 9
'tis banquo's then. 3.04. 13
then comes my fit again. 3.04. 20
love and health to all, | then i'll sit down. 3.04. 87
if trembling i inhabit then, protest me | the 3.04.104
blood, | then the charm is firm and good. 4.01. 38
then live, macduff; 4.01. 82
then you'll buy 'em to sell again. 4.02. 41
then the liars and swearers are fools; 4.02. 56 P
why then, alas, | do i put up that womanly 4.02. 77
one — two — why then 'tis time to do't. 5.01. 36 P
who then shall blame | his pester'd senses to 5.02. 22
then fly, false thanes, | and mingle with the 5.03. 7
upon the stage, | and then is heard no more. 5.05. 26
then yield thee, coward, | and live to be the 5.08. 23
then he is dead? 5.09. 9
by his worth, for then | it hath no end. 5.09. 11
why then, god's soldier be he! 5.09. 13
and myself, | the bell then beating one — HAM 1.01. 39
and then it started like a guilty thing | upon a 1.01.148
and then they say no spirit dare stir abroad, 1.01.161
nights are wholesome, then no planets strike, 1.01.162
but even then the morning cock crew loud, | and 1.02.218
then saw you not his face? 1.02.229
till then sit still, my soul. 1.02.256
then, if he says he loves you, | it fits your 1.03. 24
then weigh what loss your honor may sustain | if 1.03. 29
be wary then, best safety lies in fear: 1.03. 43
day, | thou canst not then be false to any man. 1.03. 80
it then draws near the season | wherein the 1.04. 5
it will not speak, then i will follow it. 1.04. 63
how say you then, would heart of man once think 1.05.121
then we'll shift our ground. 1.05.156
and then, sir, does 'a this — 'a does — what 2.01. 49
or then, or then, with such or such, and, as you 2.01. 55
or then, or then, with such or such, and, as you 2.01. 55
then goes he to the length of all his arm, | and 2.01. 85
mad let us grant him then, and now remains 2.02.100
and then i prescripts gave her, | that she 2.02.142
make, | fell into a sadness, then into a fast, 2.02.147
be you and i behind an arras then, | mark the 2.02.163
then i would you were so honest a man. 2.02.176 P
then you live about her waist, or in the middle 2.02.232 P
then is doomsday near. 2.02.238 P
nay then i have an eye of you! 2.02.290 P
why did ye laugh then, when i said, "man 2.02.313 P
come then, th' appurtenance of welcome is 2.02.371 P
sir, a' monday morning, 'twas then indeed. 2.02.388 P
"then came each actor on his ass" — 2.02.395
what follows then, my lord? 2.02.414 P
god wot," | and then, you know, "it came to pass 2.02.417 P
but if the gods themselves did see her then, 2.02.512
question of the play be then to be consider'd. 3.02. 43 P
nay then let the dev'l wear black, for i'll have 3.02.129 P
then there's hope a great man's memory may 3.02.131 P
'a must build churches then, or else shall 'a 3.02.133 P
why then belike he likes it not, perdy. 3.02.294
then thus she says: 3.02.326 P
then i will come to my mother by and by. 3.02.383 P
then i'll look up. 3.03. 50
what then? 3.03. 64
and am i then revenged, | to take him in the 3.03. 84
then trip him, that his heels may kick at heaven 3.03. 93
nay, then i'll set those to you that can speak. 3.04. 17
then what i have to do | will want true color — 3.04.129
why then the polack never will defend it. 4.04. 23
how stand i then, | that have a father kill'd, a 4.04. 56
"then up he rose and donn'd his clo'es, | and 4.05. 52
will you know them then? 4.05.145
and then this "should" is like a spendthrift's 4.07.122
alas, then she is drown'd? 4.07.183
what woman then? 5.01.132 P
see, | till then in patience our proceeding be. 5.01.299
i would it /might /be hangers till then. 5.02.160 P
then hamlet does it not, hamlet denies it. 5.02.236
who does it then? 5.02.237
then, venom, to thy work. 5.02.322
then poor cordelia! LR 1.01. 76
thy truth then be thy dow'r! 1.01.108
then leave her, sir, for, by the pow'r that made 1.01.207
i am sorry then you have so lost a father | that 1.01.246
then must we look from his age to receive not 1.01.296 P
well then, | legitimate edgar, i must have your 1.02. 15
what needed then that terrible dispatch of it 1.02. 32 P
then 'tis like the breath of an unfee'd lawyer, 1.04.129 P
breeches, "then they for sudden joy did weep, 1.04.175
shame, that then necessity | will call discreet 1.04.213
be then desir'd | by her, that else will take 1.04.247
nay then — 1.04.347
then i prithee be merry, thy wit shall not go 1.05. 11 P
you may do then in time. fare you well, sir. 2.01. 13 P
no marvel then, though he were ill affected: 2.01. 98
why then i care not for thee. 2.02. 8 P
at legs, then he wears wooden nether–stocks. 2.04. 10 P
dismissing half your train, come then to me. 2.04.204
if then they chanc'd to slack ye, | we could 2.04.245
then let fall | your horrible pleasure. 3.02. 18
then shall the realm of albion | come to great 3.02. 85
then comes the time, who lives to see't, | that 3.02. 93
i'll pray, and then i'll sleep. 3.04. 27
then let them anatomize regan; 3.06. 76 P
nay then come on, and take the chance of anger. 3.07. 79
then edgar was abus'd. 3.07. 91
welcome then, | thou unsubstantial air that i 4.01. 6
my son | came then into my mind, and yet my mind 4.01. 34
yet my mind | was then scarce friends with him. 4.01. 35
when i inform'd him, then he call'd me sot, 4.02. 8
then shall you go no further. 4.02. 11
why then your other senses grow imperfect | by 4.06. 5
then kill, kill, kill, kill, kill, kill! 4.06.187
then there's life in't. 4.06.202 P
then am i the prisoner, and his bed my jail; 4.06.266 P
then be't so, my good lord. how does the king? 4.07. 12
tell me but truly, but then speak the truth, 5.01. 8
let's then determine | with th' ancient of war 5.01. 31
now then, we'll use | his countenance for the 5.01. 62
mist or stain the stone, | why then she lives. 5.03.264
i would not follow him then. OTH 1.01. 40
we then have done you bold and saucy wrongs; 1.01.128
'tis certain then for cyprus. 1.03. 43
and then have we a prescription to die, when 1.03.309 P
men being in love have then a nobility in their 2.01.216 P
by the means i shall then have to prefer them; 2.01.278 P
why then let a soldier drink." 2.03. 73
why, very well then; 2.03.118 P
you must not think then that i am drunk. 2.03.118 P
and then, but now | (as if some planet had 2.03.181
and what's he then that says i play the villain? 2.03.336
and then for her | to win the moor, were/'t to 2.03.342
how am i then a villain, | to counsel cassio to 2.03.348
then put up your pipes in your bag, for i'll 3.01. 19 P
you have not been a–bed then? 3.01. 31
to–morrow dinner then? 3.03. 58
why then to–morrow night, /or tuesday morn; 3.03. 60
as if thou then hadst shut up in thy brain 3.03.114
why then i think cassio's an honest man. 3.03.129
why, go to then. 3.03.208
even then this forked plague is fated to us 3.03.276
damn them then, | if ever mortal eyes do see 3.03.398
what then? 3.03.400
how then? 3.03.400
and then, sir, would he gripe and wring my hand; 3.03.421
then kiss me hard, | as if he pluck'd up kisses 3.03.422
and /kiss'd, and then | /cried, "cursed fate 3.03.425
then would to /god that i had never seen't! 3.04. 77
something of moment then. 3.04.138
what then? 4.01. 11
why then 'tis hers, my lord, and, being hers, 4.01. 12
first to be hang'd, and then to confess. 4.01. 39 P
there's many a beast then in a populous city, 4.01. 63
and then, of so gentle a condition! 4.01.192 P
you have seen nothing then? 4.02. 1
but then i saw no harm, and then i heard | each 4.02. 4
and then i heard | each syllable that breath 4.02. 4
i cry you mercy then. 4.02. 88
why, then othello and desdemona return again to 4.02.222 P
but what said he then? 4.03. 55
then let them use us well; 4.03.102
nobody come? then shall i bleed to death. 5.01. 45
put out the light, and then put out the light: 5.02. 7
then heaven | have mercy on me! 5.02. 33
for you're fatal then | when your eyes roll so. 5.02. 37
he found it then; 5.02. 66
then murther's out of tune, | and sweet revenge 5.02.115
i thought so then — i'll kill myself for grief 5.02.192
look in upon me then and speak with me, | or, 5.02.257
then must you speak | of one that lov'd not 5.02.343
then must thou needs find out new heaven, new ANT 1.01. 17
pray then, foresee me one. 1.02. 16 P
then belike my children shall have no names. 1.02. 35 P
then we bring forth weeds | when our quick winds 1.02.109
why then we kill all our women. 1.02.133 P
you had then left unseen a wonderful piece of 1.02.153 P
women but fulvia, then had you indeed a cut, and 1.02.166 P
you sued staying, | then was the time for words; 1.03. 34
no going then; 1.03. 34
then bid adieu to me, and say the tears | belong 1.03. 77
thy palate then did deign | the roughest berry 1.04. 63
cold in blood, | to say as i said then! 1.05. 75
serves for the matter that is then born in't. 2.02. 10
then, noble partners, | the rather for i 2.02. 22
nay then. 2.02. 28
sir, | he fell upon me, ere admitted, then; 2.02. 75
and then when poisoned hours had bound me up 2.02. 90
go to then — your considerate stone. 2.02.110 P
import their dangers, | would then be nothing. 2.02.133
then put my tires and mantles on him, whilst | i 2.05. 22
nay then i'll run. 2.05. 73
then, to send | measures of wheat to rome. 2.06. 36
know then | i came before you here a man 2.06. 39
then so much have i heard; 2.06. 67
then is caesar and he for ever knit together. 2.06.115 P
then shall the sighs of octavia blow the fire up 2.06.126 P
i fear me you'll be in till then. 2.07. 33 P
the third part then is drunk. 2.07. 92
while i'll place you, then the boy shall sing. 2.07.110
then, /world, thou /hast a pair of chaps — no 3.05. 13
their lust | since then hath made between them. 3.06. 8
then does he say he lent me | some shipping 3.06. 26
but then, in his armenia | and other of his 3.06. 35
nor must not then be yielded to in this. 3.06. 38
from 's time, | what should not then be spar'd. 3.07. 12
but if we fail, | we then can do't at land. 3.07. 53
why then good night indeed. 3.10. 29
well then, sustain me. o! 3.11. 45
the itch of his affection should not then | have 3.13. 7
the queen shall then have courtesy, so she 3.13. 15
thus then, thou most renown'd: 3.13. 53
then, antony — but now — well, on. 4.04. 38
come on then, he may recover yet. 4.09. 33
then in the midst a tearing groan did break 4.14. 31
dead then? 4.14. 34
seal then, and all is done. 4.14. 49
on my command, | thou then wouldst kill me. 4.14. 67
come then; 4.14. 78
swor'st thou not then | to do this when i bade 4.14. 81
turn from me then that noble countenance, 4.14. 85
then let it do at once | the thing why thou hast 4.14. 88
why, there then. 4.14. 94
come then; 4.14.101
then is it sin | to rush into the secret house 4.15. 80
and then, what's brave, what's noble, | let's 4.15. 86
he'll lead me then in triumph? 5.02.109
come then, and take the last warmth of my lips. 5.02.291
crown's /awry, | i'll mend it, and then play — 5.02.319
poison'd then. 5.02.340
show attend this funeral, | and then to rome. 5.02.365
then old and fond of issue, took such sorrow CYM 1.01. 37
if my shirt were bloody, then to shift it. 1.02. 5 P
then wav'd his handkerchief? 1.03. 6
air, and then | have turn'd mine eye and wept. 1.03. 21
with orisons, for then | i am in heaven for him; 1.03. 32
he was then of a crescent note, expected to 1.04. 2 P
but i could then have look'd on him without the 1.04. 4 P
and then his banishment. 1.04. 18 P
with so mortal a purpose as then each bore, upon 1.04. 41 P
sir, i was then a young traveller, rather 1.04. 43 P
on cats and dogs, | then afterward up higher; 1.05. 39
i'll tell thee on the instant thou art then | as 1.05. 50
and then myself, i chiefly, | that set thee on 1.05. 72
the remedy then born — discover to me | what 1.06. 98
should i (damn'd then) | slaver with lips as 1.06.104
then by–peeping in an eye | base and illustrious 1.06.108
and then a whoreson jack–an–apes must take me up 2.01. 3 P
i have read three hours then. 2.02. 3
rich words to it — and then let her consider. 2.03. 18 P
of his remembrance on't, | and then she's yours. 2.03. 44
he was expected then, | but not approach'd. 2.04. 38
then, if you can | be pale, i beg but leave to 2.04. 95
which then they had to take from 's, to resume 3.01. 15
we do say then to caesar, | our ancestor was 3.01. 53
receive it from me then: 3.01. 65
then, true pisanio, | who long'st like me to see 3.02. 52
and you may then revolve what tales i have told 3.03. 14
then was i as a tree | whose boughs did bend 3.03. 60
even then | the princely blood flows in his 3.03. 92
then thou look'dst like a villain; 3.04. 48
on, how thy memory | will then be pang'd by me. 3.04. 95
do't, and to bed then. 3.04.100
wherefore then | didst undertake it? 3.04.101
then, madam, | i thought you would not back 3.04.115
as honest, then | my purpose would prove well. 3.04.118
at court, | then not in britain must you bide. 3.04.135
where then? 3.04.135
well then, here's the point: 3.04.153
then, sir: 3.05. 98
which will then be a torment to her contempt. 3.05.139 P
then i'll enter. 3.06. 24
my father's sons, then had my prize | been less, 3.06. 76
hence then, and thank | the man that gave them 4.02. 84
those lines of favor | which then he wore. 4.02.105
then why should we be tender | to let an 4.02.126
then on good ground we fear, | if we do fear 4.02.143
we'll speak it then. 4.02.242
come on then, and remove him. 4.02.257
he'll then instruct us of this body. 4.02.360
though cloten then but young, you see, not wore 4.04. 23
then began | a stop i' th' chaser; 5.03. 39
to pick that bolt, | then free for ever! 5.04. 11
whose father then (as men report | thou orphans' 5.04. 39
then, jupiter, thou king of gods, | why hast 5.04. 77
then shall posthumus end his miseries, britain 5.04.143 P
your death has eyes in 's head then; 5.04.178 P
i'll be hang'd then. 5.04.195 P
thou shalt be then freer than a jailer; 5.04.196 P
and then a mind put in't, either our brags 5.05.176
pieces of gold 'gainst this which then he wore 5.05.183
letter of my master's | then in my pocket, which 5.05.280
have at it then, by leave. 5.05.315
then spare not the old father. 5.05.327
punishment before | for that which i did then. 5.05.344
a fitment for | the purpose i then follow'd. 5.05.410
sinks my knee, | as then your force did. 5.05.414
then shall posthumus end his miseries, britain 5.05.440 P
this' antioch, then; PER 1.ch. 17
i'll make my will then, and, as sick men do 1.01. 47
scorning advice, read the conclusion then; 1.01. 56
then give my tongue like leave to love my head. 1.01.108
and until then your entertain shall be | as doth 1.01.119
then were it certain you were not so bad | as 1.01.125
then, lest my life be cropp'd to keep you clear, 1.01.141
then it is thus: 1.02. 11
lading's in our haven, | and then return to us. 1.02. 50
attend me then: 1.02. 70
tyre, i now look from thee then, and to tharsus 1.02.115
i'll then discourse our woes, felt several years 1.04. 18
be quiet then, as men should be, | till he hath 2.ch. 5
canst thou catch any fishes then? 2.01. 66 P
nay then thou wilt starve sure; 2.01. 68 P
then i'll turn craver too, and so i shall scape 2.01. 88 P
why, are /your beggars whipt then? 2.01. 90
till then, rest your debtor. 2.01.143
then honor be but a goal to my will, | this day 2.01.165

follow me then. lord helicane, a word. 2.04. 21
wrong not yourself then, noble helicane; 2.04. 26
then you love us, we you, and we'll clasp hands: 2.04. 57
then, as you are as virtuous as fair, | resolve 2.05. 67
and then with what haste you can, get you to bed 2.05. 93
then give you up to the mask'd neptune and | the 3.03. 36
the fitter then the gods should have her. 4.01. 10
to defend you by men, then men must comfort you, 4.02. 91 P
be it so then, | yet none does know but you how 4.03. 28
patience then, | and think you now are all in 4.04. 50
are almost run, | more a little, and then dumb. 5.02. 2
'twas helicanus then. 5.03. 53
wreath | was then nor thresh'd nor blasted; TNK 1.01. 65
our kinsman | (then weaker than your eyes) laid 1.01. 67
then, bootless toil must recompense itself 1.01.153
who then shall offer | to mars's so scorn'd 1.02. 19
then, if | you stay to see of us such spinsters, 1.03. 22
which shall be then | beyond further requiring. 1.03. 25
th' moon | (which then look'd pale at parting) 1.03. 53
what she lik'd | was then of me approv'd, what 1.03. 65
then but beginning | to swell about the blossom) 1.03. 67
then like men use 'em. 1.04. 28
then start amongst 'em | and, as an east wind, 2.02. 12
rude and impatient, then, like chastity, | she 2.02.141
well, agree then. 2.02.152
you love her then? 2.02.158
why then would you deal so cunningly, | so 2.02.189
and then i am sure she would love me. 2.02.243
and if he lose her then, he's a cold coward. 2.02.253
then i am resolv'd, i will not go. 2.02.269
i must | constrain you then; 2.02.270
why then have with ye, boys! 2.03. 27
see the sports, then every man to 's tackle! 2.03. 55
then, i lov'd him, | extremely lov'd him, 2.04. 14
he bows his noble body, then salutes me thus: 2.04. 23
what says the law then? 2.04. 31
your father | sure is a happy sire then. 2.05. 9
prince, i shall not then | freeze in my saddle. 2.05. 47
if the law | find me, and then condemn me for't, 2.06. 14
i am then | kissing the man they look for. 2.06. 36
and then they fight like compell'd bears, would 3.01. 68
of one meal lend me — come before me then, | a 3.01. 74
done me, yea, my life, | if then thou carry't; 3.01. 78
nay then — 3.01.118
if i whoop'd, what then? 3.02. 9
many together, | and then they /fed on him. 3.02. 19
how stand i then? 3.02. 20
are faint — then i'll talk further with you. 3.03. 7
pray sit down then, and let me entreat you | by 3.03. 13
then i'll leave you; | you are a beast now. 3.03. 46
then would i make | a carreck of a cockleshell, 3.04. 13
and "then let be," and no man understand me? 3.05. 10
and nods, and hums, | and then cries, "rare!" 3.05. 16
then do you, | as once did meleager and the boar 3.05. 17
and now and then a favor and a frisk. 3.05. 30
couple then, | and see what's wanting. 3.05. 32
then mine host | and his fat spouse, that 3.05.127
then the beast–eating clown, and next the fool, 3.05.131
then i shall quit you. 3.06. 24
and both upon our guards, then let our fury, 3.06. 29
and then to whom the birthright of this beauty 3.06. 31
then as i am an honest man, and love | with all 3.06. 50
that's mine then. | i'll arm you first. 3.06. 52
stand off then. 3.06. 89
then all the world will scorn us, | and say we 3.06.115
then come what can come, | thou shalt know, 3.06.127
then take my life, i'll woo thee to't. 3.06.156
nay then i'll in too. 3.06.201
be wise then | and here forget 'em; 3.06.222
o all ye gods, despise me then. 3.06.258
he's a villain then. 3.06.264
he that she refuses | must die then. 3.06.281
make choice then. 3.06.285
come shake hands again then, | and take heed, as 3.06.302
i then left my angle | to his own skill, came 4.01. 59
and list'ned to the words she sung, for then, 4.01. 63
him, he'll be taken, | and what shall i do then? 4.01. 71
then she talk'd of you, sir — | that you must 4.01. 76
then she sung | nothing but "willow, willow, 4.01. 79
and then she wept, and sung again, and sigh'd, 4.01. 92
she is then distemper'd | /far worse than now 4.01.119
and when he's angry, then a settled valor | (not 4.02.100
and then will she be out of love with aeneas. 4.03. 15 P
then, if it be your chance to come where the 4.03. 21 P
then will i make palamon a nosegay, then let him 4.03. 26 P
make palamon a nosegay, then let him mark me — 4.03. 26 P
a nosegay, then let him mark me — then — 4.03. 27 P
and then howls; 4.03. 55 P
alas, what then? 4.03. 61 P
then from this gather | how i should tender you. 5.01. 24
our intercession then | must be to him that 5.01. 45
then blend your spirits with mine, | you whose 5.01. 72
o, then, most soft sweet goddess, | give me the 5.01.126
then she told me | she would watch with me 5.02. 8
'twas very ill done then. 5.02. 13
then if she will be honest, | she has the path 5.02. 22
we'll to bed then. 5.02. 86
go to dinner, | and then we'll play at cards. 5.02.108
and then we'll sleep together? 5.02.110
well, well then, at your pleasure. 5.03. 34
then he has won. 5.03. 68
higher, | anon the other, then again the first, 5.03.126
list then: 5.04. 48
victor's wreath | even then fell off his head; 5.04. 80
saw her, and | even then proclaim'd your fancy. 5.04.118
then it goes hard, i see. ep 5
he that has | lov'd a young handsome wench then, ep 6
have at the worst can come, then! ep 10
then what a rough and riotous charge have you STM II.C 55
what do you then, | rising 'gainst him that god II.C 104
then with her windy sighs and golden hairs | to VEN 51
then why not lips on lips, since eyes in eyes? 120
then wink again, | and i will wink, so shall the 121
then mightst thou pause, for then i were not for 137
thou pause, for then i were not for thee, | but 137
then woo thyself, be of thyself rejected; 159
sometime she shakes her head, and then his hand, 223
then be my deer, since i am such a park, | no 239
then, like a melancholy malcontent, | he vails 313
o, what a war of looks was then between them! 355
then love's deep groans i never shall regard, 377
it, | unless it be a boar, and then i chase it; 410
incorporate then they seem, face grows to face. 540
but then woos best when most his choice is 570
when he did frown, o, had she then gave over, 571
then do they spend their mouths: 695
"then shalt thou see the dew–bedabbled wretch 703
he, | "leave me, and then the story aptly ends; 716
"but if thou fall, o, then imagine this, | the 721
"nay then," quoth adon, "you will fall again 769
and then my little heart were quite undone, | in 783
"hadst thou but bid beware, then he had spoke, 943
then join they all together, | like many clouds 971
then, gentle shadow (truth i must confess), | i 1001
and then she reprehends her mangling eye, | that 1065
then would adonis weep; 1090
face, why then i know | he thought to kiss him, 1109
what needeth then apology be made | to set forth LUC 31
then virtue claims from beauty beauty's red, 59
silver cheeks, and call'd it then their shield, 61
for then is tarquin brought unto his bed, 120
so then we do neglect | the thing we have, and 152
then where is truth, if there be no self–trust? 158
then looking scornfully, he doth despise | his 187
then my digression is so vile, so base, | that 202
lay, | then white as lawn, the roses took away. 259
which strook her sad, and then it faster rock'd, 262
"why hunt i then for color or excuses? 267
"then childish fear, avaunt, debating, die! 274
then who fears sinking where such treasure lies? 280
fact, | how can they then assist me in the act? 350
"then love and fortune be my gods, my guide! 351
then had they seen the period of their ill! 380
then collatine again by lucrece' side | in his 381
if thou deny, then force must work my way, | for 513
"then for thy husband and thy children's sake, 533
myself a weakling, do not then ensnare me; 584
then kings' misdeeds cannot be hid in clay. 609
when most unseen, then most doth tyrannize. 676
and then with lank and lean discolor'd cheek, 708
"so then he hath it when he cannot use it, | and 862
how comes it then, vile opportunity, | being so 895
o, hear me then, injurious, shifting time! 930
true sorrow then is feelingly suffic'd | when 1112
then let it not be call'd impiety, | if in this 1174
and then they drown their eyes or break their 1239
then call them not the authors of their ill, 1244
for then the eye interprets to the ear | the 1325
then little strength rings out the doleful knell 1495
looks for night, and then she longs for morrow, 1571
"then be this all the task it hath to say: 1618
murther straight, and then i'll slaughter thee, 1634
and then against my heart he set his sword, 1640
let it then suffice | to drown /one woe, one 1679
then live, sweet lucrece, live again and see 1770
and then in key–cold lucrece' bleeding stream 1774
then son and father weep with equal strife | who 1791
then jointly to the ground their knees they bow, 1846
then thou, fair sun, that on this earth doth PP 3.10
if broken, then it is no fault of mine. 3.12
then fell she on her back, fair queen, and 4.13
then must the love be great 'twixt thee and me, 8. 3
me," | and then she clipt adonis in her arms; 11. 6
then lullaby, the learned man hath got the lady 15.15
and then too late she will repent | that thus 18.27
as men, | in faith, you had not had it then." 18.36
there is no heaven, /be holy then, | when time 18.45
thee move, | then live with me, and be my love. 19.16
once do frown, | then farewell his great renown; 20.46
then being ask'd where all thy beauty lies, SON 2. 5
then, beauteous niggard, why dost thou abuse 4. 5
then how when nature calls thee to be gone, 4.11
then were not summer's distillation left | a 5. 9
then let not winter's ragged hand deface | in 6. 1
then what could death do if thou shouldst depart 6.11
then of thy beauty do i question make | that 12. 9
then you were | /yourself again after yourself's 13. 6
then the conceit of this inconstant stay | sets 15. 9
and then believe me, my love is as fair | as any 21.10
then look i death my days should expiate. 22. 4
how can i then be elder than thou art? 22. 8
o, let my books be then the eloquence | and dumb 23. 9
then happy i, that love and am beloved | where i 25.13
then may i dare to boast how i do love thee, 26.13
till then, not show my head where thou mayst 26.14
but then begins a journey in my head | to work 27. 3
for then my thoughts (from far where i abide) 27. 5
how can i then return in happy plight | that am 28. 1
haply i think on thee, and then my state | (like 29.10
that then i scorn to change my state with kings. 29.14
then can i drown an eye (unus'd to flow) | for 30. 5
then can i grieve at grievances foregone, | and 30. 9
o, then voutsafe me but this loving thought: 32. 9
so then i am not lame, poor, nor despis'd, 37. 9
this wish i have, then ten times happy me! 37.14
what hast thou then more than thou hadst before? 40. 2
then if for my love thou my love receivest, | i 40. 5
then she loves but me alone. 42.14
when most i wink, then do mine eyes best see, 43. 1
then thou, whose shadow shadows doth make bright 43. 5
for then, despite of space, i would be brought, 44. 3
no matter then although my foot did stand | upon 44. 5
this told, i joy, but then no longer glad, | i 45.13
with my love's picture then my eye doth feast, 47. 5
o, what excuse will my poor beast then find, 51. 5
then should i spur though mounted on the wind, 51. 7
then can no horse with my desire keep pace; 51. 9
then, churls, their thoughts (although their 69.11
then thou alone kingdoms of hearts shouldst owe. 70.14
if thinking on me then should make you woe. 71. 8
so then thou hast but lost the dregs of life, 74. 9
then better'd that the world may see my pleasure 75. 8
then thank him not for that which he doth say, 79.13
then if he thrive and i be cast away, | the 80.13
then others for the breath of words respect, 85.13
then lack'd i matter, that enfeebled mine. 86.14
thou gav'st, thy own worth then not knowing, 87. 9
then hate me when thou wilt, if ever, now, | now 90. 1
then need i not to fear the worst of wrongs, 92. 5
then do thy office, muse; 101.13
our love was new, and then but in the spring, 102. 5
were it not sinful then, striving to mend, | to 103. 9
then, in the blazon of sweet beauty's best, | of 106. 5
then give me welcome, next my heaven the best, 110.13
pity me then, and wish i were renew'd, | whilst 111. 8
pity me then, dear friend, and i assure ye 111.13
yet then my judgment knew no reason why | my 115. 3
might i not then say, "now i love you best," 115.10
love is a babe, then might i not say so, | to 115.13
now, | and for that sorrow which i then did feel 120. 2
and soon to you, as you to me then, tend'red 120.11
if snow be white, why then her breasts are dun; 130. 3
let it then as well beseem thy heart | to mourn 132.10
then will i swear beauty herself is black, | and 132.13
but then my friend's heart let my poor heart 133.10
thou canst not then use rigor in my jail: 133.12
then in the number let me pass untold, | though 136. 9
and then thou lovest me, for my name is will. 136.14
then, soul, live thou upon thy servant's loss, 146. 9
and death once dead, there's no more dying then. 146.14
then love doth well denote | love's eye is not 148. 7
no marvel then though i mistake my view, | the 148.11
then, gentle cheater, urge not my amiss, | lest 151. 3
"'o, then advance of yours that phraseless hand, LC 225
"'how mighty then you are, o, hear me tell! 253
whose sights till then were levell'd on my face, 282

/THENCE 4 FR 0.0004 REL FR 4 V 0 P

/thence we look'd toward england, | and cited up R3 1.04. 13
/starting /thence /away | /to /what /may /be TRO pr 28
/were /in /her /eyes, /which, /parted /thence, LR 4.03. 21
still the house affairs would draw her /thence, OTH 1.03.147

THENCE 97 FR 0.0109 REL FR 92 V 5 P

what foul play had we, that we came from thence? TMP 1.02. 60
play (as thou say'st) were we heav'd thence, 1.02. 62
the ministers for th' purpose hurried thence 1.02.131
thence i have follow'd it, | or it hath drawn me 1.02.394
for, coming thence, | my son is lost and (in my 2.01.109
and thence retire me to my milan, where | every 5.01.311
rock, | and throw it thence into the raging sea. TGV 1.02.119
thankful | to any happy messenger from thence. 2.04. 53
and thence she cannot be convey'd away. 3.01. 37
what, were you banish'd thence? 4.01. 23
go to thy lady's grave and call hers thence, 4.02.116
for thence will not i to–day. MM 4.03. 63 P
and from thence, | by cold gradation and 4.03. 99
and take unmingled thence that drop again, ERR 2.02.127
and did not i in rage depart from thence? 4.04. 76
to the centaur, fetch our stuff from thence; 4.04.149
rushing in their houses, bearing thence | rings, 5.01.143
they fell upon me, bound me, bore me thence, 5.01.247
and thence from athens turn away our eyes, | to MND 1.01.218
to take from thence all error with his might, 3.02.368
and i, seeing this, came thence for very shame, SHR 3.02.180
we met him thitherward, for thence we came; AWW 3.02. 53
thence it came | that she whom all men prais'd 5.03. 52
is | by law and process of great nature thence WT 2.02. 58
and from thence have brought | this seal'd–up 3.02.126
most royal sir, from thence; 5.01.159
thence | (a prosperous south–wind friendly) we 5.01.160
who would be thence that has the benefit of 5.02.109 P
i fear will issue thence | the foul corruption JN 4.02. 80
so he that doth redeem her thence might wear 1H4 1.03.206
and at the time of my departure thence | he was 4.01. 23
and what with owen glendower's absence thence, 4.04. 16
spake with one, my lord, that came from thence, 2H4 1.01. 25
and thence to france shall we convey you safe, H5 2.pr. 37
and thence discover how with most advantage 1H6 1.04. 12
from thence to england, where i hope ere long 4.01.171
from thence, unto the place of execution. 2H6 2.03. 6
'tis not the land i care for, wert thou thence; 3.02.359
'twas not your valor, clifford, drove me thence. 3H6 2.02.107
they prosper best of all when i am thence. 2.05. 18
and chides the sea that sunders him from thence, 3.02.138
and brought from thence the thracian fatal 4.02. 21
lord — | and shipp'd from thence to flanders? 4.05. 21
and what these sorrows could not thence exhale, R3 1.02.165
then, taking him from thence that is not there, 3.01. 53
i shall return before your lordship thence. 3.02.120
at their beads, 'tis much to draw them thence, 3.07. 93
gave notice | he was from thence discharg'd? H8 2.04. 34
so, traitor, then she comes when she is thence. TRO 1.01. 31
sorts, | for womanish it is to be from thence. 1.01.107
and shall, albeit sweet music issues thence. 3.02.134
'tis not four days gone | since i heard thence; COR 1.02. 7
and from thence | into destruction cast him. 3.01.212
pursue him to his house and pluck him thence, 3.01.307
to rome but that | thou art thence banish'd, we 4.05.128
in the repeal, as hasty | to expel him thence. 4.07. 33
our general | will no more hear from thence. 5.02. 6
and, being anger'd, puffs away from thence, ROM 1.04.102
but chiefly to take thence from her dead finger 5.03. 30
and stole thence | the life o' th' building! MAC 2.03. 68
and thence | against the undivulg'd pretense i 2.03.130
thence to be wrench'd with an unlineal hand, 3.01. 62
and thence it is | that i to your assistance do 3.01.122
from thence, the sauce to meat is ceremony, 3.04. 35
and i must be from thence! | my wife kill'd too? 4.03.212
thence to a watch, thence into a weakness, HAM 2.02.148
thence to a watch, thence into a weakness, 2.02.148
thence to /a lightness, and, by this declension, 2.02.149
tell us where 'tis, that we may take it thence, 4.02. 7
of my redemption thence | and portance in my OTH 1.03.138
but the free comfort which from thence he hears; 1.03.213
to be discarded thence! 4.02. 60
if you will watch his going thence (which i will 4.02.235 P
mine ear must pluck it thence. ANT 1.05. 42
would i had never come from thence, nor you 2.03. 11 P
and i will bring from thence that honor of hers CYM 1.04.130 P
as from thence | sorrow were ever ras'd, and PER 1.01. 16
the heat i have from thence doth little harm, VEN 195
and when from thence he struggles to be gone, 227
as if from thence they borrowed all their shine. 488
he carries thence incaged in his breast. 582

he like a thievish dog creeps sadly thence, LUC 736
he thence departs a heavy convertite, | she 743
and bids it leap from thence, where it may find 760
his eye drops fire, no water thence proceeds; 1552
harmful knife, that thence her soul unsheathed; 1724
they did conclude to bear dead lucrece thence, 1850
and even thence thou wilt be stol'n, i fear, SON 48.13
where thou art, why should i haste me thence? 51. 3
i was not sick of any fear from thence: 86.12
looks should nothing thence but sweetness tell. 93.12
thence comes it that my name receives a brand, 111. 5
and almost thence my nature is subdu'd | to what 111. 6
but thence i learn, and find the lesson true, 118.13
and thence this slander, as i think, proceeds. 131.14
true to bondage, would not break from thence, LC 34
and did thence remove | to spend her living in 237

THEORIC 3 FR 0.0003 REL FR 2 V 1 P
that had the whole theoric of war in the knot of AWW 4.03.142 P
of life | must be the mistress to this theoric; H5 1.01. 52
than a spinster — unless the bookish theoric, OTH 1.01. 24

THERE *(also dere)*

/THERE 27 FR 0.0030 REL FR 21 V 6 P
/there /shouldst /thou /find /one /heinous R2 4.01.233
/for /there /it /is, /crack'd /in /an /hundred 4.01.289
/there /lies /the /substance; 4.01.299
/are /enforc'd /from /our /most /quiet /there 2H4 4.01. 71
/when /there /was /nothing /could /have /stay'd 4.01.121
/if /your /father /had /been /victor /there, 4.01.132
why, /there thou hast it; R3 4.02. 72
/in /troy, /there /lies /the /scene. TRO pr 1
/the //deep–drawing /barks /do /there /disgorge pr 12
/lie /there /for /pavement /to /the /abject 3.03.162
aye be call'd | go in to troy and say /there, 5.10. 17
/there! TIM 1.01.247
/one, /in /which /there /are /many /confines, HAM 2.02.245 P
/for /there /is /nothing /either /good /or /bad, 2.02.249 P
/but /there /is, /sir, /an /aery /of /children, 2.02.339 P
/there /has /been /much /to /do /on /both /sides 2.02.352 P
/there /was /for /a /while /no /money /bid /for 2.02.354 P
/o, /there /has /been /much /throwing /about /of 2.02.358 P
/what /is /the /issue /of /the /business /there. 5.02. 72
/motley /here, | /the /other /found /out /there. LR 1.04.147
/from /france /there /comes /a /power | /into 3.01. 30
/stop /her /there! 3.06. 54
/there /she /shook | /the /holy /water /from 4.03. 29
/louder /the /music /there! 4.07. 24
/was /big /in /clamor, /came /there /in /a /man, 5.03.209
/sounded, | /and /there /i /left /him /tranc'd. 5.03.219
his sons /he /there proclaim'd the /kings of ANT 3.06. 13

THERE 1932 FR 0.2184 REL FR 1324 V 608 P
so, | lie there, my art. TMP 1.02. 25
art | so safely ordered that there is no soul — 1.02. 29
there they hoist us, | to cry to th' sea, that 1.02.148
the still–vex'd bermoothes, there she's hid; 1.02.229
is there more toil? 1.02.242
and left thee there, where thou didst vent thy 1.02.280
foot it featly here and there, | and, sweet 1.02.379
thou think'st there is no more such shapes as he 1.02.479
and the rarest that e'er came there. 2.01.100 P
would i had never | married my daughter there! 2.01.109
what a blow was there given! 2.01.180 P
a wink beyond, | but doubt discovery there. 2.01.243
'twixt which regions | there is some space. 2.01.257
there be that can rule naples | as well as he 2.01.262
there was a noise, | that's verily. 2.01.320
not a holiday fool there but would give a piece 2.02. 29 P
there would this monster make a man; 2.02. 30 P
any strange beast there makes a man. 2.02. 31 P
there is no other shelter hereabout. 2.02. 38 P
there be some sports are painful, and their 3.01. 1
my heart fly to your service, there resides, 3.01. 65
was there ever man a coward that hath drunk so 3.02. 27 P
there thou mayst brain him, | having first 3.02. 88
now i will believe | that there are unicorns; 3.03. 22
that in arabia | there is one tree, the phoenix' 3.03. 23
one phoenix | at this hour reigning there. 3.03. 24
for some of you there present | are worse than 3.03. 35
who would believe that there were mountaineers, 3.03. 44
or that there were such men | whose heads stood 3.03. 46
sounded, | and with him there lie mudded. 3.03.102
retire into my cell, | and there repose. 4.01.162
there dancing up to th' chins, that the foul 4.01.183
there is not only disgrace and dishonor in that, 4.01.209 P
silver! there it goes, silver! 4.01.256
there, tyrant, there! 4.01.257
there, tyrant, there! 4.01.257
there stand, | for you are spell–stopp'd. 5.01. 60
where the bee sucks, there suck i, | in a 5.01. 88
there i couch when owls do cry. 5.01. 90
there shalt thou find the mariners asleep 5.01. 98
both in naples, | the king and queen there! 5.01.150
how many goodly creatures are there here! 5.01.182
there, sir, stop. 5.01.198
and there is in this business more than nature 5.01.243
there are yet missing of your company | some few 5.01.254
expects my coming, there to see me shipp'd. TGV 1.01. 54
there! 1.02. 46
keep tune there still, so you will sing it out. 1.02. 86
there wanteth but a mean to fill your song. 1.02. 92
some to the wars, to try their fortune there; 1.03. 8
there shall he practice tilts and tournaments, 1.03. 30
how now? what letter are you reading there? 1.03. 51
there is no news, my lord, but that he writes 1.03. 56
for what i will, i will, and there an end. 1.03. 65
excellent device, was there ever heard a better, 2.01.139
letter hath she deliver'd, and there an end. 2.01.161 P
there 'tis. 2.03. 19 P
why, there 'tis; 2.03. 28 P
i confess | there is no woe to his correction, 2.04.138
there is no reason but i shall be blind. 2.04.212
but there i leave to love where i should love. 2.06. 18
and there i'll rest, as after much turmoil | a 2.07. 37
there is a messenger | that stays to bear my 3.01. 52
there is a lady in /milano here | whom i affect; 3.01. 81
night, | there is no music in the nightingale; 3.01.179
the day, | there is no day for me to look upon. 3.01.181
there is a proclamation that you are vanish'd. 3.01.217 P
her, | with many bitter threats of biding there. 3.01.238

there — and saint nicholas be thy speed! 3.01.300 P
stop there; 3.01.355 P
if there be ten, shrink not, but down with 'em. 4.01. 2
have you long sojourn'd there? 4.01. 20
and, being help'd, inhabits there. 4.02. 48
he had not been there (bless the mark!) 4.04. 18 P
ursula, bring my picture there. 4.04.117
there, hold! 4.04.127
here, youth, there is my purse; 4.04.176
and, were there sense in his idolatry, | my 4.04.200
patrick's cell this even, and there she was not. 5.02. 42
there is our captain. 5.03. 10
and full as much (for more there cannot be) | i 5.04. 38
coat, there is but three skirts for yourself, in WIV 1.01. 29 P
there is no fear of got in a riot. 1.01. 37 P
and there is also another device in my prain, 1.01. 43 P
there is anne page, which is daughter to master 1.01. 45 P
is falstaff there? 1.01. 67 P
the knight sir john is there, and i beseech you 1.01. 70 P
who's there? 1.01. 74 P
dog, and a fair dog — can there be more said? 1.01. 97 P
there is three umpires in this matter, as i 1.01.137 P
page (fidelicet master page) and there is myself 1.01.139 P
there is, as 'twere, a tender, a kind of tender, 1.01.207 P
but if there be no great love in the beginning, 1.01.246 P
be there bears i' th' town? 1.01.287 P
i think there are, sir, i heard them talk'd of. 1.01.288 P
and there dwells one mistress quickly, which is 1.02. 2 P
there is no remedy; 1.03. 33 P
me, he'll find the young man there, and be mad! 1.04. 65 P
anne's mind — that's neither here nor there. 1.04.106 P
who's within there, ho? 1.04.131 P
who's there, i trow? 1.04.132 P
do you think there is truth in them? 2.01.172 P
there is either liquor in his pate, or money in 2.01.190 P
there is a fray to be fought between sir hugh 2.01.200 P
and what they made there, i know not. 2.01.236 P
there is one mistress ford, sir — i pray come a 2.02. 44 P
yet there has been knights, and lords, and 2.02. 63 P
of them all, and yet there has been earls, nay 2.02. 76 P
from home, but she hopes there will come a time. 2.02.102 P
it, for if there be a kind woman in windsor, she 2.02.120 P
there is a gentlewoman in this town, her 2.02.191 P
enlargeth her mirth so far that there is shrewd 2.02.223 P
there is money, spend it, spend it; 2.02.231 P
to see thee here, to see thee there, to see thee 2.03. 25 P
sir hugh is there, is he? 2.03. 76 P
he is there. 2.03. 77 P
there will we make our peds of roses, | and a 3.01. 19
there comes my master, master shallow, and 3.01. 31 P
there is reasons and causes for it. 3.01. 48 P
there is such a league between my goodman and he 3.02. 25 P
bids me search — there i shall find falstaff. 3.02. 46 P
as the earth is firm that falstaff is there. 3.02. 49 P
and there empty it in the muddy ditch close by 3.03. 15 P
there is a gentleman, my dear friend; 3.03.121 P
he's too big to go in there. what shall i do? 3.03.134 P
is there not a double excellency in this? 3.03.176 P
if there be any pody in the house, and in the 3.03.210 P
be–gar nor i too; there is no–bodies. 3.03.213 P
if there is one, i shall make two in the company 3.03.234 P
if there be one or two, i shall make–a the turd. 3.03.236 P
what? while you were there? 3.05. 79 P
while i was there. 3.05. 80 P
there was the rankest compound of villainous 3.05. 91 P
and how long lay you there? 3.05. 94 P
truly, i thought there had been one number more, 4.01. 23 P
there are fairer things than poulcats sure. 4.01. 28 P
there they always use to discharge their 4.02. 57 P
he will seek there, on my word. 4.02. 60 P
there is no hiding you in the house. 4.02. 63 P
there is no woman's gown big enough for him; 4.02. 69 P
there was one convey'd out of my house yesterday 4.02.145 P
why may not he be there again? 4.02.147 P
if you find a man there, he shall die a flea's 4.02.150 P
and methinks there would be no period to the 4.02.221 P
there is no better way than that they spoke of. 4.04. 16
methinks there should be terrors in him that he 4.04. 22 P
there is an old tale goes, that herne the hunter 4.04. 28
and there he blasts the tree, and takes the 4.04. 32
why yet there want not many that do fear | in 4.04. 39
art thou there? 4.05. 17 P
there was, mine host, an old fat woman even now 4.05. 24 P
was there a wise woman with thee? 4.05. 58 P
ay, that there was, mine host, one that hath 4.05. 59 P
there is a friend of mine come to town, tells me 4.05. 76 P
tells me there is three cozen–germans that has 4.05. 77 P
they say there is divinity in odd numbers, 5.01. 3 P
sir john? art thou there, my deer? my male deer? 5.05. 16 P
let there come a tempest of provocation, i will 5.05. 20 P
there pinch the maids as blue as bilberry; 5.05. 45
the doctor at the dean'ry, and there married. 5.05.203 P
where there was no proportion held in love. 5.05.222
there is our commission, | from which we would MM 1.01. 13
there is a kind of character in thy life, | that 1.01. 27
let there be some more test made of my mettle 1.01. 48
there went but a pair of shears between us. 1.02. 27 P
as there may between the lists and the velvet. 1.02. 29 P
what? is there a maid with child by him? 1.02. 91 P
there will be pity taken on you. 1.02.109 P
enter, | and there receive her approbation. 1.02.178
youth | there is a prone and speechless dialect, 1.02.183
adultery, and all uncleanliness there. 2.01. 81 P
night in russia | when nights are longest there. 2.01.135
once, sir? there was nothing done to her once. 2.01.141 P
there is pretty orders beginning, i can tell you 2.01.236 P
are there not men in your ward sufficient to 2.01.266 P
there is no remedy. 2.01.285
there shall be order for't. 2.02. 25
there is a vice that most i do abhor, | and most 2.02. 29
knock there, and ask your heart what it doth 2.02.137
that shall be up at heaven and enter there | ere 2.02.152
raze the sanctuary | and pitch our evils there? 2.02.171
there rest. 2.03. 36
who's there? 2.04. 17
might there not be a charity in sin | to save 2.04. 63
and that there were | no earthly mean to save 2.04. 94
who's there? 3.01. 45

is there no remedy? 3.01. 60
but is there any? 3.01. 62
there is a devilish mercy in the judge, | if 3.01. 64
there spake my brother; 3.01. 85
there my father's grave | did utter forth a 3.01. 85
hold you there! 3.01.173 P
there she lost a noble and renown'd brother, in 3.01.219 P
there, at the moated grange, resides this 3.01.264 P
if there be no remedy for it but that you will 3.02. 1 P
is there none of pygmalion's images newly made 3.02. 45 P
but that there is so great a fever on goodness, 3.02.222 P
there is scarce truth enough alive to make 3.02.226 P
there have i made my promise upon the heavy 4.01. 34
are there no other tokens | between you 'greed 4.01. 40
what ho, abhorson! where's abhorson, there? 4.02. 20 P
but what mystery there should be in hanging, if 4.02. 39 P
there he must stay until the officer | arise to 4.02. 90
yet i believe there comes | no countermand; 4.02. 96
there is written in your brow, provost, honesty 4.02.153 P
then is there here one master caper, at the suit 4.03. 9 P
who makes that noise there? 4.03. 25 P
there died this morning of a cruel fever | one 4.03. 70
at the gates, | there to give up their pow'r. 4.03.132
the gates, and /redeliver our authorities there? 4.04. 6 P
there is another comfort than this world, | that 5.01. 49
being come to knowledge that there was complaint 5.01.153
and five years since there was some speech of 5.01.217
as there comes light from heaven, and words from 5.01.225
as there is sense in truth, and truth in virtue, 5.01.226
there is another friar that set them on, | let 5.01.248
there was a friar told me of this man. 5.01.479
there had she not been long but she became | a ERR 1.01. 49
there is your money that i had to keep. 1.02. 8
and stay there, dromio, till i come to thee. 1.02. 10
who, falling there to find his fellow forth 1.02. 37
there, take you that, sir knave. 1.02. 92
for, in conclusion, he did beat me there. 2.01. 74
was there ever any man thus beaten out of season 2.02. 47
this time have prov'd there is no time for all 2.02.100 P
substantial, why there is no time to recover. 2.02.105 P
who talks within there? ho, open the door! 3.01. 38
what a coil is there, dromio? 3.01. 48
there was blow for blow. 3.01. 56
are you there, wife? you might have come before. 3.01. 63
there is something in the wind, that we cannot 3.01. 69
there will we dine. 3.01.111
but to spite my wife) | upon mine hostess there. 3.01.119
and as a /bed i'll take /them, and there lie, 3.02. 49
i'll to the mart and there for dromio stay: 3.02.184
perchance i will be there as soon as you. 4.01. 39
turkish tapestry | there is a purse of ducats; 4.01.105
well, sir, there rest in your foolery. 4.03. 34 P
is there any ships puts forth to–night? 4.03. 35 P
there is my hand, and let it feel your ear. 4.04. 53
and did not she herself revile me there? 4.04. 72
sans fable, she herself revil'd you there. 4.04. 73
that here and there his fury had committed. 5.01.147
and now he's there, past thought of human reason 5.01.189
justice, sweet prince, against that woman there! 5.01.197
that goldsmith there, were he not pack'd with 5.01.219
there did this perjur'd goldsmith swear me down 5.01.227
vault at home | there left me and my man, both 5.01.249
sir, he din'd with her there, at the porpentine. 5.01.276
there, take it, and much thanks for my good 5.01.393
embrace thy brother there, rejoice with him. 5.01.414
there is a fat friend at your master's house, 5.01.415
him letters, and there appears much joy in him, ADO 1.01. 21 P
there are no faces truer than those that are so 1.01. 26 P
there was none such in the army of any sort. 1.01. 32 P
there is a kind of merry war betwixt signior 1.01. 61 P
is there no young squarer now that will make a 1.01. 81 P
there is no measure in the occasion that breeds, 1.03. 3 P
and there heard it agreed upon that the prince 1.03. 61 P
and there will the devil meet me like an old 2.01. 43 P
and there live we as merry as the day is long. 2.01. 49 P
tell him there is measure in every thing, and so 2.01. 71 P
her terminations, there were no living near her, 2.01.249 P
mother cried, but then there was a star danc'd, 2.01.335 P
and there shall appear such seeming truth of 2.02. 47 P
i have known when there was no music with him 2.03. 13 P
there was never counterfeit of passion came so 2.03.104 P
and there will she sit in her smock till she 2.03.132 P
let there be the same net spread for her, and 2.03.213 P
there shalt thou find my cousin beatrice 3.01. 2
there will she hide her, | to listen our propose 3.01. 11
there is no appearance of fancy in him, unless 3.02. 31 P
some woman, there is no believing old signs. 3.02. 41 P
if there be any impediment, i pray you discover 3.02. 93 P
where i should wed, there will i shame her. 3.02.125 P
let that appear when there is no need of such 3.03. 21 P
and there be any matter of weight chances, call 3.03. 85 P
for the wedding being there to–morrow, there is 3.03. 93 P
there to–morrow, there is a great coil to–night. 3.03. 93 P
i thought there would a scab follow. 3.03. 99 P
appointed next morning at the temple, and there, 3.03.161 P
is there any harm in "the heavier for a husband" 3.04. 34 P
there thou prick'st her with a thistle. 3.04. 76 P
there, leonato, take her back again. 4.01. 31
there is not chastity enough in language 4.01. 97
and in her eye there hath appear'd a fire | to 4.01.162
there is some strange misprision in the princes. 4.01.185
is there any way to show such friendship? 4.01.263 P
there is no love in you. 4.01.293 P
but there is no such man, for, brother, men 5.01. 20
for there was never yet philosopher | that could 5.01. 35
there thou speak'st reason; 5.01. 41
in a false quarrel there is no true valor. 5.01.120 P
for my lord lack–beard there, he and i shall 5.01.192 P
there will i leave you too, for here comes one 5.02. 93 P
hang thou there upon the tomb, | praising her 5.03. 9
there is no staff more reverent than one tipp'd 5.04.123 P
but there are other strict observances: LLL 1.01. 36
term, | which i hope well is not enrolled there; 1.01. 38
the which i hope is not enrolled there; 1.01. 41
which i hope well is not enrolled there. 1.01. 46
but is there no quick recreation granted? 1.01.161
ay, that there is. 1.01.162
there did i see that low–spirited swain, that 1.01.247 P

is there not a ballet, boy, of the king and the		1.02.109 P
there is no evil angel but love.		1.02.172 P
students at that time | was there with him, if i		2.01. 65
yet there remains unpaid | a hundred thousand		2.01.133
me, how was there a costard broken in a shin?		3.01.111 P
till there be more matter in the shin.		3.01.119 P
there is remuneration, for the best ward of mine		3.01.131 P
park, | and in her train there is a gentle lady:		3.01.165
so were there a patch set on learning, to see		4.02. 31
by earth, she is not, corporal, there you lie.		4.03. 84
there is no certain princess that appears;		4.03.154
what present hast thou there?		4.03.187
ay marry, there — some flattery for this evil.		4.03.282
do we not likewise see our learning there?		4.03.314
there is the very remuneration i had of thy		5.01. 72 P
action and accent did they teach him there:		5.02. 99
honey, and milk, and sugar: there is three.		5.02.231
there, then, that vizard, that superfluous case		5.02.387
what, are there but three?		5.02.487
there is five in the first show.		5.02.540
there, an't shall please you, a foolish mild man		5.02.580 P
but there are worthies a–coming will speak their		5.02.584 P
if for my love (as there is no such cause) | you		5.02.792
there stay until the twelve celestial signs		5.02.797
what humble suit attends thy answer there.		5.02.839
how chance the roses there do fade so fast?	MND	1.01.129
or, if there were a sympathy in choice, | war,		1.01.141
there, gentle hermia, may i marry thee;		1.01.161
to a morn of may), | there will i stay for thee.		1.01.168
there my lysander and myself shall meet;		1.01.217
there will we rehearse;		1.02.102 P
and there we may rehearse most obscenely and		1.02.107 P
creep into acorn–cups and hide them there.		2.01. 31
swear | a merrier hour was never wasted there.		2.01. 57
hast thou the flower there?		2.01.247
ay, there it is.		2.01.248
there sleeps titania sometime of the night,		2.01.253
and there the snake throws her enamell'd skin,		2.01.255
hermia, sleep thou there, | and never mayst thou		2.02.135
there are things in this comedy of pyramus and		3.01. 9 P
for there is not a more fearful wild–fowl than		3.01. 31 P
and there indeed let him name his name, and tell		3.01. 44 P
but there is two hard things:		3.01. 47 P
then, there is another thing:		3.01. 62 P
fear, | and left sweet pyramus translated there;		3.02. 32
there is no following her in this fierce vein.		3.02. 82
to helen is it home return'd, | there to remain.		3.02.173
approach, ghosts, wand'ring here and there,		3.02.381
yea, art thou there?		3.02.411
there lies your love.		4.01. 78
there shall the pairs of faithful lovers be		4.01. 91
i was — there is no man can tell what.		4.01.208 P
and there is two or three lords and ladies more		4.02. 16 P
is there no play | to ease the anguish of a		5.01. 36
there is a brief how many sports are ripe.		5.01. 42
a play there is, my lord, some ten words long,		5.01. 61
for in all the play | there is not one word apt,		5.01. 65
think no scorn | to meet at ninus' tomb, there,		5.01.138
to meet at ninus' tomb, there, there to woo.		5.01.138
he dares not come there for the candle;		5.01.249 P
are all dead, there need none to be blam'd.		5.01.357 P
and the issue, there create, | ever shall be		5.01.405
there where your argosies with portly sail	MV	1.01. 9
there are a sort of men whose visages | do cream		1.01. 88
but what warmth is there in your affection		1.02. 33 P
first, there is the neapolitan prince.		1.02. 39 P
then is there the county palentine.		1.02. 45 P
for there is not one among them but i dote on		1.02.109 P
and there is a forerunner come from a fift, the		1.02.124 P
there be land–rats and water–rats, water–thieves		1.03. 22 P
pirates, and then there is the peril of waters,		1.03. 24 P
even there where merchants most do congregate,		1.03. 49
to a notary, seal me there | your single bond;		1.03.144
and say there is much kindness in the jew.		1.03.153
come on, in this there can be no dismay, | my		1.03.180
why, there they show | something too liberal.		2.02.184
but fare thee well, there is a ducat for thee,		2.03. 4
there are my keys.		2.05. 12
there is some ill a–brewing towards my rest,		2.05. 17
what, are there masques?		2.05. 28
for all this — there will come a christian by,		2.05. 42
who's there?		2.06. 60
pause there, morocco, | and weigh thy value with		2.07. 24
there, take it, prince, and if my form lie there		2.07. 61
take it, prince, and if my form lie there,		2.07. 61
whose empty eye | there is a written scroll!		2.07. 64
but there the duke was given to understand		2.08. 7
there miscarried | a vessel of our country		2.08. 29
love | as shall conveniently become you there."		2.08. 45
and even there, his eye being big with tears,		2.08. 46
behold, there stand the caskets, noble prince.		2.09. 4
too long a pause for that which you find there.		2.09. 53
some there be that shadows kiss, | such have but		2.09. 66
there be fools alive, iwis, | silver'd o'er, and		2.09. 68
madam, there is alighted at your gate | a young		2.09. 86
yet it lives there uncheck'd that antonio hath a		3.01. 2 P
there is more difference between thy flesh and		3.01. 39 P
your bloods than there is between red wine and		3.01. 41 P
there i have another bad match.		3.01. 44 P
why, there, there, there, there!		3.01. 83 P
why, there, there, there, there!		3.01. 83 P
why, there, there, there, there!		3.01. 83 P
why, there, there, there, there!		3.01. 83 P
there came divers of antonio's creditors in my		3.01.113 P
what treason there is mingled with your love.		3.02. 27
there may as well be amity and life | 'tween		3.02. 30
there is no /vice so simple but assumes | some		3.02. 81
and there is such confusion in my powers, | as,		3.02.177
there doth appear | among the buzzing pleased		3.02.179
your fortune stood upon the caskets there, | and		3.02.201
his letter there | will show you his estate.		3.02.235
there are some shrowd contents in yond same		3.02.243
there must be needs a like proportion | of		3.04. 14
there is a monast'ry two miles off, | and there		3.04. 31
two miles off, | and there we will abide.		3.04. 32
i shall be there before thee.		3.04. 55
there is but one hope in it that can do you any		3.05. 6 P
there must be something else | pawn'd with the		3.05. 81
some men there are love not a gaping pig;		4.01. 47
as there is no firm reason to be rend'red | why		4.01. 53
there is no force in the decrees of venice.		4.01.102
to cut the forfeiture from that bankrout there.		4.01.122
needs give sentence 'gainst the merchant there.		4.01.205
there is no power in venice | can alter a decree		4.01.218
i swear | there is no power in the tongue of man		4.01.241
are there balance here to weigh | the flesh?		4.01.255
tarry a little, there is something else.		4.01.305
soul, let's in, and there expect their coming.		5.01. 49
but there is come a messenger before, | to		5.01.117
what man is there so much unreasonable, | if you		5.01.203
had you been there, i think you would have		5.01.221
there you shall find that portia was the doctor,		5.01.269
was the doctor, | nerissa there her clerk.		5.01.270
there you shall find three of your argosies		5.01.276
there do i give to you and jessica, | from the		5.01.291
in, | and charge us there upon inter'gatories,		5.01.298
and there begins my sadness.	AYL	1.01. 4 P
my blood, were there twenty brothers betwixt us.		1.01. 48 P
and there they live like the old robin hood of		1.01.115 P
there is not one so young and so villainous this		1.01.154 P
indeed there is fortune too hard for nature,		1.02. 48 P
there comes an old man and his three sons —		1.02.118 P
ribs, that there is little hope of life in him.		1.02.128 P
but is there any else longs to see this broken		1.02.141 P
is there yet another dotes upon rib–breaking?		1.02.142 P
i can tell you, there is such odds in the man.		1.02.159 P
there is but one sham'd that was never gracious;		1.02.187 P
then there were two cousins laid up, when the		1.03. 7 P
lie there what hidden woman's fear there will —		1.03.119
lie there what hidden woman's fear there will —		1.03.119
then, being there alone, | left and abandoned of		2.01. 49
upon that poor and broken bankrupt there?"		2.01. 57
who's there?		2.03. 1
there is nothing | that you will feed on;		2.04. 85
lack of a dinner if there live any thing in this		2.06. 17 P
there then!		2.07. 83
there is an old poor man, | who after me hath		2.07.129
hang there, my verse, in witness of my love,		3.02. 1
but as there is no more plenty in it, it goes		3.02. 20 P
there lay he, stretch'd along, like a wounded		3.02.240 P
there was no thought of pleasing you when she		3.02.266 P
there i shall see mine own figure.		3.02.289 P
then there is no true lover in the forest, else		3.02.302 P
foot can fall, he thinks himself too soon there.		3.02.329 P
courtship too well, for there he fell in love.		3.02.346 P
there were none principal, they were all like		3.02.353 P
there is a man haunts the forest, that abuses		3.02.359 P
there is none of my uncle's marks upon you.		3.02.369 P
that there shall not be one spot of love in't.		3.02.423 P
is there none here to give the woman?		3.03. 67 P
nay certainly there is no truth in him.		3.04. 20 P
of fathers, when there is such a man as orlando?		3.04. 39 P
thou tell'st me there is murder in mine eye:		3.05. 10
with a pin, and there remains | some scar of it;		3.05. 21
nor i am sure there is no force in eyes | that		3.05. 26
there was a pretty redness in his lip, | a		3.05.120
there be some women, silvius, had they mark'd		3.05.124
you to entreaty, and there begins new matter.		4.01. 79 P
and in all this time there was not any man died		4.01. 96 P
marry, to say she came to seek you there.		4.01.171 P
did he leave him there, | food to the suck'd and		4.03.125
there stripp'd himself, and here upon his arm		4.03.146
there is more in it. cousin ganymed!		4.03.159
there is too great testimony in your complexion		4.03.169 P
there is a youth here in the forest lays claim		5.01. 6 P
there was never any thing so sudden but the		5.02. 30 P
you are there followed by a faithful shepherd —		5.02. 81
though there was no great matter in the ditty,		5.03. 34 P
there is sure another flood toward, and these		5.04. 35 P
then is there mirth in heaven, | when earthly		5.04.108
if there be truth in sight, you are my daughter.		5.04.118
if there be truth in sight, you are my rosalind.		5.04.119
there is much matter to be heard and learn'd.		5.04.185
there is a lord will hear you play to–night;	SHR	in.1. 93
there, there, hortensio, will you any wife?		1.01. 56
there, there, hortensio, will you any wife?		1.01. 56
man, there be good fellows in the world, and a		1.01.128 P
comes there any more of it?		1.01.251 P
is there any man has rebus'd your worship?		1.02. 6 P
who goes there?		1.02.140 P
way, | and there i stood amazed for a while,		2.01.155
there is, there is.		2.01.231
there is, there is.		2.01.231
and there it is in writing, fairly drawn.		3.01. 70
and say, "lo, there is mad petruchio's wife,		3.02. 19
when he stands where i am and sees you there.		3.02. 41 P
and here and there piec'd with packthread.		3.02. 62 P
the door is open, sir, there lies your way;		3.02.210
you know there wants no junkets at the feast.		3.02.248
there.		4.01. 62 P
there was no link to color peter's hat, | and		4.01.134
there were none fine but adam, rafe, and gregory		4.01.136
there, take it to you, trenchers, cups, and all.		4.01.165
here i'll fling the pillow, there the bolster,		4.01.201
the taming–school! what, is there such a place?		4.02. 55
there will we mount, and thither walk on foot.		4.03.186
and well we may come there by dinner–time.		4.03.188
and 'twill be supper–time ere you come there.		4.03.190
there doth my father lie;		4.04. 56
and there this night | we'll pass the business		4.04. 56
i am to padua, there to visit | a son of mine,		4.05. 56
the fouler fortune mine, and there an end.		5.02. 98
than lack it where there is such abundance.	AWW	1.01. 10 P
what hope is there of his majesty's amendment?		1.01. 11 P
qualities, there commendations go with pity:		1.01. 42 P
there is no living, none, | if bertram be away.		1.01. 84
there is none.		1.01.118 P
is there no military policy how virgins might		1.01.121 P
and there was never virgin /got till virginity		1.01.128 P
there shall your master have a thousand loves,		1.01.166
to grow there and to bear — "let me not live"		1.02. 55
what they are, there were no fear in marriage,		1.03. 51 P
there is more owing her than is paid, and more		1.03.103 P
there is a remedy, approv'd, set down, | to cure		1.03.228
there do muster true gait, eat, speak, and move		2.01. 53 P
and most oft there | where most it promises;		2.01.142
most fruitfully, i am there before my legs.		2.02. 70 P
why, there 'tis, so say i too.		2.03. 15 P
you shall read it in what–do–ye–call there.		2.03. 22 P
cheek for ever, | we'll ne'er come there again."		2.03. 72
be patient, there is no fettering of authority.		2.03.237 P
is there any unkindness between my lord and you,		2.05. 32 P
there can be no kernel in this light nut;		2.05. 43 P
/e'en that you have there.		3.02. 18 P
if there be breadth enough in the world, i will		3.02. 23 P
nay, there is some comfort in the news, some		3.02. 36 P
find you that there?		3.02. 76
whoever shoots at him, i set him there;		3.02.112
though there were no further danger known but		3.05. 26 P
there is a gentleman that serves the count		3.05. 56
there was excellent command — to charge in with		3.06. 48 P
have prevented, if he had been there to command.		3.06. 54 P
if there be here german, or dane, low dutch,		4.01. 71
remain there but an hour, nor speak to me.		4.02. 58
a wife of me, though there my hope be done.		4.02. 65
there is something in't that stings his nature;		4.03. 3 P
i hear there is an overture of peace.		4.03. 39 P
and, there residing, the tenderness of her		4.03. 50 P
they shall be no more than needful there, if		4.03. 81 P
either it is there, or it is upon a file with		4.03.204 P
be the officer at a place there call'd mile–end,		4.03.269 P
there is no remedy, sir, but you must die.		4.03.303 P
we shall speak of you there.		4.03.329 P
was misled with a snipt–taffata fellow there,		4.05. 2 P
his fisnomy is more hotter in france than there.		4.05. 40 P
against your son, there is no fitter matter.		4.05. 76 P
whether there be a scar under't or no, the		4.05. 95 P
i have been sometimes there.		5.01. 11
is there no exorcist | beguiles the truer office		5.03.304
there is your ring, | and, look you, here's your		5.03.310
receiveth as the sea, nought enters there, | of	TN	1.01. 11
there is a fair behavior in thee, captain, | and		1.02. 47
drink to her as long as there is a passage in my		1.03. 39 P
there thy fixed foot shall grow | till thou have		1.04. 17
as there is no true cuckold but calamity, so		1.05. 51 P
there is no slander in an allow'd fool, though		1.05. 94 P
there is at the gate a young gentleman much		1.05. 99 P
else would i very shortly see thee there.		2.01. 46
worth stooping for, there it lies in your eye;		2.02. 15 P
come on, there is sixpence for you.		2.03. 31 P
in delay there lies no plenty, | then come kiss		2.03. 50
"there dwelt a man in babylon, lady, lady!"		2.03. 78 P
is there no respect of place, persons, nor time		2.03. 91 P
sir toby, there you lie.		2.03.107
virtuous, there shall be no more cakes and ale?		2.03.115 P
sweet, | on my black coffin let there be strown.		2.04. 60
true lover never find my grave, | to weep there!		2.04. 66
say that some lady, as perhaps there is, | hath		2.04. 89
there is no woman's sides | can bide the beating		2.04. 93
lie thou there;		2.05. 21 P
there is example for't:		2.05. 39 P
curtsies there to me —		2.05. 61 P
capacity, there is no obstruction in this.		2.05.117 P
but then there is no consonancy in the sequel;		2.05.129 P
i think i saw your wisdom there.		3.01. 41 P
there lies your way, due west.		3.01.134
there is no love–broker in the world can more		3.02. 36 P
there is no way but this, sir andrew.		3.02. 39 P
let there be gall enough in thy ink, though thou		3.02. 49 P
for there is no christian that means to be sav'd		3.02. 70 P
there shall you have me.		3.03. 42
why, there's for thee, and there, and there.		4.01. 26
why, there's for thee, and there, and there.		4.01. 26
against him, if there be any law in illyria.		4.01. 35 P
and hear thou there how many fruitless pranks		4.01. 55
who calls there?		4.02. 20 P
i say there is no darkness but ignorance, in		4.02. 42 P
and i say there was never man thus abus'd.		4.02. 46 P
fool, there was never man so notoriously abus'd;		4.02. 87 P
yet there he was, and there i found this credit,		4.03. 6
yet there he was, and there i found this credit,		4.03. 6
there, before him, | and underneath that		4.03. 24
that most ingrateful boy there by your side		5.01. 77
do i stand there?		5.01.226
nor can there be that deity in my nature | of		5.01.227
and there rooted betwixt them then such an	WT	1.01. 23 P
i think there is not in the world either malice		1.01. 33 P
if there were no other excuse why they should		1.01. 43 P
there is no tongue that moves, none, none i' th'		1.02. 20
were there necessity in your request, although		1.02. 22
to let him there a month behind the gest		1.02. 41
two lads that thought there was no more behind		1.02. 63
shall 's attend you there?		1.02.178
there have been | (or i am much deceiv'd)		1.02.190
and many a man there is (even at this present,		1.02.192
why, that's some comfort. | what? camillo there?		1.02.209
there is a sickness | which puts some of us in		1.02.384
so that there be not | too much hair there, but		2.01. 9
so that there be not | too much hair there, but		2.01. 10
there was a man —		2.01. 29
was he met there? his train? camillo with him?		2.01. 33
there may be in the cup | a spider steep'd, and		2.01. 39
there is a plot against my life, my crown;		2.01. 47
do not weep, good fools, | there is no cause.		2.01.119
there is no lady living | so meet for this great		2.02. 43
who's there?		2.03. 9
/what noise there, ho?		2.03. 39
with lady margery, your midwife there, | to save		2.03.160
of our dominions, and that there thou leave it		2.03.177
there is no truth at all i' th' oracle.		3.02.140
how now there?		3.02.147
and tears shed there | shall be my recreation.		3.02.239
in bohemia, | there weep and leave it crying;		3.03. 32
there lie, and there thy character;		3.03. 47
there lie, and there thy character;		3.03. 47
there these, | which may, if fortune please,		3.03. 47
i would there were no age between ten and		3.03. 59 P
for there is nothing in the between but getting		3.03. 61 P
there your charity would have lack'd footing.		3.03.110 P
if there be any of him left, i'll bury it.		3.03.131 P
air'd abroad, i desire to lay my bones there.		4.02. 6 P
and when i wander here and there, | i then do		4.03. 17
i shall there have money, or any thing i want.		4.03. 81 P
they cherish it to make it stay there;		4.03. 93 P

give me those flow'rs there, dorcas. 4.04. 73
there is an art which in their piedness shares 4.04. 87
say there be; 4.04. 88
i think there is not half a kiss to choose | who 4.04.175
promis'd you more than that, or there be liars. 4.04.238 P
there is no manners left among maids? 4.04.242 P
is there not milking–time? 4.04.244 P
sir, there are cozeners abroad, therefore it 4.04.253 P
master, there is three carters, three shepherds, 4.04.324 P
and there present yourself and your fair 4.04.544
asks thee there, son, forgiveness, | as 'twere 4.04.549
but that you have your father's bosom there, 4.04.563
i am bound to you. | there is some sap in this. 4.04.565
there shall not at your father's house these 4.04.578
i think you know my fortunes | do all lie there. 4.04.591
by this means being there | so soon as you 4.04.619
no remedy. | have you done there? 4.04.657
there is no other way but to tell the king she's 4.04.687 P
there is that in this farthel will make him 4.04.707 P
your affairs there? 4.04.717 P
either push on or pluck back thy business there; 4.04.738 P
the farthel there? 4.04.754 P
there lies such secrets in this farthel and box, 4.04.756 P
will i present them, there may be matter in it. 4.04.841 P
there is none worthy, | respecting her that's 5.01. 34
there was not full a month | between their 5.01.117
there was speech in their dumbness, language in 5.02. 13 P
you see, there is such unity in the proofs. 5.02. 32 P
there might you have beheld one joy crown 5.02. 43 P
there was casting up of eyes, holding up of 5.02. 46 P
who was most marble there chang'd color; 5.02. 90 P
are they gone, and there they intend to sup. 5.02.103 P
thought she had some great matter there in hand, 5.02.104 P
and there was the first gentleman–like tears 5.02.144 P
still methinks | there is an air comes from her. 5.03. 78
will wing me to some wither'd bough and there 5.03.133
for ere thou canst report, i will be there; JN 1.01. 25
there with the emperor | to treat of high 1.01.100
from france to england, there to live in peace. 2.01. 90
there stuck no plume in any english crest | that 2.01.317
that daughter there of spain, the lady blanch, 2.01.423
if that the dolphin there, thy princely son, 2.01.484
there should be | in such a love so vile a lout 2.01.508
rail, | and say there is no sin but to be rich; 2.01.594
shall be | to say there is no vice but beggary. 2.01.596
there is no tongue hath power to curse him right 3.01.183
there where my fortune lives, there my life dies 3.01.338
where my fortune lives, there my life dies. 3.01.338
austria's head lie there, | while philip 3.02. 3
there is a soul counts thee her creditor, | and 3.03. 21
there was not such a gracious creature born. 3.04. 81
my head | when there is such disorder in my wit. 3.04.102
if but a dozen french | were there in arms, they 3.04.174
is there no remedy? 4.01. 90
that there were but a mote in yours, | a grain, 4.01. 91
feeling what small things are boisterous there, 4.01. 94
there is no malice in this burning coal; 4.01.108
there is no sure foundation set on blood; 4.02.104
but there is little reason in your grief; 4.03. 30
away toward bury, to the dolphin there! 4.03.114
there, tell the king, he may inquire us out. 4.03.115
there is not yet so ugly a fiend of hell | as 4.03.123
nothing there holds out | but dover castle. 5.01. 30
the lion in his den, | and fright him there? 5.01. 58
and make him tremble there? 5.01. 58
and there | where honorable rescue and defense 5.02. 17
and even there, methinks an angel spake. 5.02. 64
there end thy brave, and turn thy face in peace; 5.02.159
tell him toward swinstead, to the abbey there. 5.03. 8
who's there? 5.06. 1
there is so hot a summer in my bosom | that all 5.07. 30
o that there were some virtue in my tears, 5.07. 44
and there the poison | is as a fiend confin'd to 5.07. 46
pale trembling coward, there i throw my gage, R2 1.01. 69
norfolk, throw down, we bid, there is no boot. 1.01.164
there shall your swords and lances arbitrate 1.01.200
there to behold | our cousin herford and fell 1.02. 45
and what shall good old york there see | but 1.02. 67
and what hear there for welcome but my groans? 1.02. 70
let him not come there | to seek out sorrow that 1.02. 71
there lives or dies, true to king richard's 1.03. 86
there is no virtue like necessity. 1.03.278
but to the next high way, and there i left him. 1.04. 4
hold out my horse, and i will first be there. 2.01.300
to–day, as i came by, i called there — | but i 2.02. 94
what, are there no posts dispatch'd for ireland? 2.02.103
carts, | and bring away the armor that is there. 2.02.107
the earl of wiltshire is already there. 2.02.136
what power the duke of york had levied there, 2.03. 34
keeps good old york there with his men of war? 2.03. 52
there stands the castle, by yon tuft of trees, 2.03. 53
castle, | and there repose you for this night. 2.03.161
keeps death his court, and there the antic sits, 3.02.162
go to flint castle, there i'll pine away — | a 3.02.209
there lies | two kinsmen digg'd their graves 3.03.168
there is my gage, the manual seal of death, 4.01. 25
there is my gage, aumerle, in gage to thine. 4.01. 34
and that thou art so, there i throw my gage, 4.01. 46
there is my honor's pawn, | engage it to the 4.01. 55
in proof whereof, there is my honor's pawn, 4.01. 70
there is /my bond of faith, | to tie thee to my 4.01. 76
and there at venice gave | his body to that 4.01. 97
is there no plot | to rid the realm of this 4.01.324
and, madam, there is order ta'en for you, | with 5.01. 53
my guilt be on my head, and there an end. 5.01. 69
wedding it, there is such length in grief. 5.01. 94
you will be there, i know. 5.02. 54
who is within there? 5.02. 74
inquire at london, 'mongst the taverns there, 5.03. 5
for there, they say, he daily doth frequent, 5.03. 6
thou hast a traitor in thy presence there. 5.03. 40
i do repent me, read not my name there, | my 5.03. 52
thine eye begins to speak, set thy tongue there; 5.03.125
that many have and others must /sit there; 5.05. 27
when all athwart there came | a post from wales 1H4 1.01. 36
upon whose dead corpse' there was such misuse, 1.01. 43
on holy–rood day, the gallant hotspur there, 1.01. 52
yea, there thou mak'st me sad, and mak'st me sin 1.01. 78
give thee thy due, thou hast paid all there. 1.02. 53 P
shall there be gallows standing in england when 1.02. 59 P
there are pilgrims going to canterbury with rich 1.02.125 P
yourself and i will not be there; 1.02.164 P
me to–morrow night in eastcheap, there i'll sup. 1.02.193 P
came there a certain lord, neat, and trimly 1.03. 33
who therewith angry, when it next came there, 1.03. 40
there is ne'er a king christen could be better 2.01. 16 P
there are other troyans that thou dream'st not 2.01. 69 P
how many be there of them? 2.02. 63 P
thou need'st him, there thou shalt find him. 2.02. 71 P
lord, i could be well contented to be there, in 2.03. 2 P
is there not my father, my uncle, and myself? 2.03. 23 P
is there not besides the douglas? 2.03. 26 P
is there no virtue extant? 2.04.118 P
there is nothing but roguery to be found in 2.04.124 P
there lives not three good men unhang'd in 2.04.130 P
and poins there? 2.04.143 P
there be four of us here have ta'en a thousand 2.04.158 P
if there were not two or three and fifty upon 2.04.187 P
seven? why, there were but four even now. 2.04.203 P
there is a nobleman of the court at door would 2.04.287 P
well, he is there too, and one mordake, and a 2.04.356 P
is like, if there come a hot june and this civil 2.04.361 P
there is a thing, harry, which thou hast often 2.04.410 P
and yet there is a virtuous man whom i have 2.04.417 P
i speak it, there is virtue in that falstaff; 2.04.430 P
there is a devil haunts thee in the likeness of 2.04.447 P
there are two gentlemen | have in this robbery 2.04.519
what there is else, keep close, we'll read it at 2.04.542 P
there let him sleep till day. 2.04.543 P
for there will be a world of water shed | upon 3.01. 93
why, there is it. 3.03. 13 P
for there he is in his robes, burning, burning. 3.03. 32 P
if there were any thing in thy pocket but 3.03.157 P
there shalt thou know thy charge, and there 3.03.201
and there receive | money and order for their 3.03.201
what letters hast thou there? 4.01. 13
for, as he writes, there is no quailing now, 4.01. 39
there is not such a word | spoke of in scotland 4.01. 84
there is more news: 4.01.124
'tis more than time that i were there, and you 4.02. 55 P
and you too, but my powers are there already. 4.02. 55 P
wales, | there without ransom to lie forfeited; 4.03. 96
and let there be impawn'd | some surety for a 4.03.108
not fear, | there is douglas and lord mortimer. 4.04. 22
no, mortimer is not there. 4.04. 23
but there is mordake, vernon, lord harry percy, 4.04. 24
and there is my lord of worcester, and a head 4.04. 25
and so there is; 4.04. 27
in both your armies there is many a soul | shall 5.01. 83
there is no seeming mercy in the king. 5.02. 34
grace | as if he mast'red there a double spirit 5.02. 63
there did he pause, but let me tell the world, 5.02. 65
there is percy. 5.04.139 P
in poison there is physic, and these news, 2H4 1.01.137
what's he that goes there? 1.02. 58 P
is there not wars? 1.02. 72 P
is there not employment? 1.02. 73 P
when there were matters against you for your 1.02.132 P
there is not a white hair in your face but 1.02.160 P
there is not a dangerous action can peep out his 1.02.212 P
there is no honesty in such dealing, unless a 2.01. 36 P
with thee when thou keepest not racket there; 2.02. 20 P
there 'tis, boy. 2.02. 93 P
well, there is sixpence to preserve thee. 2.02. 95 P
there were two honors lost, yours and your son's 2.03. 16
but i must go and meet with danger there, | or 2.03. 48
there am i, | till time and vantage crave my 2.03. 67
what the devil hast thou brought there? 2.04. 1 P
and told him there were five more sir johns, and 2.04. 6 P
see thee again or no, there is nobody cares. 2.04. 67 P
shut the door, there comes no swaggerers here; 2.04. 76 P
there comes no swaggerers here. 2.04. 80 P
there comes none here. 2.04. 94 P
me some sack, and, sweet heart, lie thou there. 2.04.183
for the boy, there is a good angel about him, 2.04.335 P
marry, there is another indictment upon thee, 2.04.343 P
look to th' door there, francis. 2.04.353 P
and there are twenty weak and wearied posts 2.04.356
there is a history in all men's lives, 3.01. 80
there was i, and little john doit of 3.02. 19 P
by my troth, i was not there. 3.02. 39 P
me, there are other men fitter to go out than i. 3.02.114 P
show — there was a little quiver fellow, and 'a 3.02.281 P
let time shape, and there an end. 3.02.332 P
there is no need of any such redress, | or if 4.01. 95
or if there were, it not belongs to you. 4.01. 96
there is a thing within my bosom tells me | that 4.01.181
say, with the hook–nos'd fellow of rome, "there, 4.03. 41 P
dries me there all the foolish and dull and 4.03. 98 P
and there will i visit master robert shallow, 4.03.129 P
he is not there to–day, he dines in london. 4.04. 51
there is not now a rebel's sword unsheath'd, 4.04. 86
let there be no noise made, my gentle friends, 4.05. 1
why doth the crown lie there upon his pillow, 4.05. 21
there lies a downy feather which stirs not. 4.05. 32
there is your crown; 4.05.142
even there my life must end. 4.05.235
but bear me to that chamber, there i'll lie, 4.05.239
not be admitted, there is no excuse shall serve, 5.01. 5 P
for william cook — are there no young pigeons? 5.01. 17 P
there is many complaints, davy, against that 5.01. 40 P
there is my hand. 5.02.117
and lusty lads roam here and there | so merrily, 5.03. 20
and, my little soldier there, be merry. 5.03. 31 P
and i might see you there, davy! 5.03. 61 P
why, there spoke a king. 5.03. 69 P
look who's at door there ho! 5.03. 71 P
there hath been a man or two kill'd about her. 5.04. 6 P
as if there were nothing else to be done but to 5.05. 26 P
there roar'd the sea, and trumpet–clangor sounds 5.05. 40
carry them here and there, jumping o'er times, H5 pr 29
save that there were not time enough to hear, 1.01. 84
there is no bar | to make against your highness' 1.02. 35
there left behind and settled certain french; 1.02. 47
or there we'll sit, | ruling in large and ample 1.02.225
you cannot revel into dukedoms there. 1.02.253
but i will rise there with so full a glory 1.02.278
there is the playhouse now, there must you sit, 2.pr. 36
there is the playhouse now, there must you sit, 2.pr. 36
when time shall serve, there shall be smiles — 2.01. 6 P
she will plod — there must be conclusions — 2.01. 24 P
then, richard earl of cambridge, there is yours; 2.02. 66
there yours, lord scroop of masham; 2.02. 67
what read you there | that have so cowarded and 2.02. 74
his finger's end, i knew there was but one way; 2.03. 15 P
i hop'd there was no need to trouble himself 2.03. 21 P
even in your hearts, there will he rake for it. 2.04. 98
for there is none of you so mean and base | that 3.01. 29
plow up all, if there is not better directions. 3.02. 63 P
and there is throats to be cut, and works to be 3.02.111 P
works to be done, and there ish nothing done, so 3.02.112 P
correction, there is not many of your nation — 3.02.121 P
when there is more better opportunity to be 3.02.138 P
and there is an end. 3.02.140 P
there remain, | and fortify it strongly 'gainst 3.03. 52
there is very excellent services committed at 3.06. 3 P
there is an aunchient lieutenant there at the 3.06. 12 P
is an aunchient lieutenant there at the pridge, 3.06. 12 P
and there is gallant and most prave passages. 3.06. 92 P
there be nothing compell'd from the villages; 3.06.109 P
will cap that proverb with "there is flattery in 3.07.114 P
there stands your friend for the devil; 3.07.118 P
upon his royal face there is no note | how dread 4.pr. 35
there is some soul of goodness in things evil, 4.01. 4
that there is no tiddle taddle nor pibble babble 4.01. 70 P
there is much care and valor in this welshman. 4.01. 84
who goes there? 4.01. 91 P
i am afeard there are few die well that die in a 4.01.141 P
besides, there is no king, be his cause never so 4.01.159 P
there. 4.01.212 P
there is not work enough for all our hands, 4.02. 19
for there the sun shall greet them, | and draw 4.03.100
of it, for there is none to guard it but boys. 4.04. 76 P
there is a river in macedon, and there is also 4.07. 26 P
and there is also moreover a river at monmouth. 4.07. 27 P
is to my fingers, and there is salmons in both. 4.07. 31 P
well, for there is figures in all things. 4.07. 33 P
i'll tell you there is good men porn at monmouth 4.07. 52 P
follow, and see there be no harm between them. 4.07.182
there is more good toward you peradventure than 4.08. 3 P
it, if there is any martial law in the world. 4.08. 44 P
hold, there is twelvepence for you, and i pray 4.08. 63 P
there lie dead | one hundred twenty–six; 4.08. 82
there are but sixteen hundred mercenaries; 4.08. 88
let there be sung non nobis and te deum, | the 4.08.123
grant him there; 5.pr. 7
there seen, | heave him away upon your winged 5.pr. 7
there must we bring him; 5.pr. 42
there is occasions and causes why and wherefore 5.01. 3 P
there is one goat for you. 5.01. 29 P
come, there is sauce for it. 5.01. 34 P
there is not enough leek to swear by. 5.01. 50 P
hold you, there is a groat to heal your pate. 5.01. 58 P
and there my rendezvous is quite cut off. 5.01. 83
to england will i steal, and there i'll steal; 5.01. 87
view, | what rub or what impediment there is, 5.02. 33
to the which, as yet, | there is no answer made. 5.02. 75
his glass for love of any thing he sees there, 5.02.148 P
there is more eloquence in a sugar touch of them 5.02.276 P
so be there 'twixt your kingdoms such a spousal, 5.02.362
here, there, and every where, enrag'd he slew. 1H6 1.01.124
his ransom there is none but i shall pay: 1.01.148
and for his safety there i'll best devise. 1.01.172
henry's death, i fear, there is conveyance. 1.03. 2
who's there, that knocks so imperiously? 1.03. 5
think at the north gate, for there stands lords. 1.04. 66
and now there rests no other shift but this, 2.01. 75
there hath at least five frenchmen died to–night 2.02. 9
some words there grew 'twixt somerset and me; 2.05. 46
within a loathsome dungeon, there to pine, | was 2.05. 57
now she is there, how will she specify | here is 3.02. 21
and there will we be too, ere it be long, | or 3.02. 75
and there erects | thy noble deeds as valor's 3.02.119
for there young henry with his nobles lie. 3.02.129
there goes the talbot, with his colors spread, 3.03. 31
well, miscreant, i'll be there as soon as you, 3.04. 44
were there surpris'd and taken prisoners. 4.01. 26
there should be found such false dissembling 4.01. 63
why then lord talbot there shall talk with him, 4.01. 68
there is my pledge, accept it, somerset. 4.01.120
beside, what infamy will there arise, | when 4.01.143
i fear we should have seen decipher'd there 4.01.184
there comes the ruin, there begins confusion. 4.01.194
there comes the ruin, there begins confusion. 4.01.194
on either hand thee there are squadrons pitch'd, 4.02. 23
lo, there thou stand'st, a breathing valiant man 4.02. 31
and whiles the honorable captain there | drops 4.04. 17
there is no hope that ever i will stay, | if the 4.05. 30
and there died | my icarus, my blossom, in his 4.07. 15
i trust the ghost of talbot is not there. 5.02. 16
there all is marr'd; there lies a cooling card. 5.03. 84
there all is marr'd; there lies a cooling card. 5.03. 84
but there remains a scruple in that too; 5.03. 93
yes, there is remedy enough, my lord. 5.03.135
there minotaurs and ugly treasons lurk. 5.03.189
maid, | spare for no faggots, let there be enow. 5.04. 56
think she knows not well | (there were so many) 5.04. 81
for, were there hope to conquer them again, | my 2H6 1.01.117
so, there goes our protector in a rage. 1.01.147
what seest thou there? 1.02. 7
where are you there? 1.02. 68
who is there? 1.03. 33 P
what, madam, are you there? 1.04. 43
who's within there, ho? 1.04. 78
saunder, sit there, the lying'st knave | in 2.01.123
this staff of honor raught, there let it stand, 2.03. 43
well, i will be there. 2.04. 73
man, | there to be us'd according to your state. 2.04. 95
to signify that rebels there are up | and put 3.01.283
for, being green, there is great hope of help. 3.01.287
had been the regent there in stead of me, | he 3.01.294
by staying there so long till all were lost. 3.01.299
thy fortune, york, hadst thou been regent there, 3.01.305
for there i'll ship them all for ireland. 3.01.329

which with the heart there cools and ne'er 3.02.166
were there a serpent seen, with forked tongue, 3.02.259
for where thou art, there is the world itself, 3.02.362
there let his head and liveless body lie, 4.01.142
the field is honorable, and there was he born, 4.02. 51 P
there shall be in england seven halfpenny loaves 4.02. 65 P
you, good people — there shall be no money; 4.02. 72 P
who's there? 4.02. 84 P
knock him down there. 4.06. 8 P
there shall not a maid be married, but she shall 4.07.121 P
and there cut off thy most ungracious head, 4.10. 82
so lie thou there; 5.02. 66
still, where danger was, still there i met him, 5.03. 11
3H6 he durst not sit there, had your father liv'd. 1.01. 63
wouldst have left thy dearest heart–blood there 1.01.223
had i been there, which am a silly woman, | the 1.01.243
there, take the crown, and, with the crown, my 1.04.164
they set the same, and there it doth remain, 2.01. 66
are you there, butcher? o, i cannot speak! 2.02. 95
there is no wrong, but every thing is right. 2.02.132
whoever got thee, there thy mother stands, | for 2.02.133
to whom god will, there be the victory! 2.05. 15
your father's head, which clifford placed there; 2.06. 53
there to be crowned england's royal king; 2.06. 88
well, say there is no kingdom then for richard; 3.02.146
for i have heard that she was there in place. 4.01.103
who goes there? 4.03. 26
what are they that fly there? 4.03. 28
there shall i rest secure from force and fraud. 4.04. 33
so, lie thou there. 5.02. 1
if thou be there, sweet brother, take my hand, 5.02. 34
tread on the sand, why, there you quickly sink; 5.04. 30
ere ye come there, be sure to hear some news. 5.05. 48
R3 worship, | anthony woodvile, her brother there, 1.01. 67
i think there is no man /is secure | but the 1.01. 71
load, | taken from paul's to be interred there; 1.02. 30
to white–friars, there attend my coming. 1.02.226
world, | thou cacodemon, there thy kingdom is. 1.03.143
and there awake god's gentle–sleeping peace. 1.03.287
where eyes did once inhabit, there were crept 1.04. 30
the first that there did greet my stranger soul 1.04. 48
there lies the duke asleep, and there the keys. 1.04. 95
there lies the duke asleep, and there the keys. 1.04. 95
there, hastings, i will never more remember 2.01. 23
there wanteth now our brother gloucester here 2.01. 43
in him there is a hope of government, | which, 2.03. 12
or by his father there were none at all; 2.03. 24
then, taking him from thence that is not there, 3.01. 53
you break no privilege nor charter there. 3.01. 54
my grandam told me he was murd'red there. 3.01.145
at crosby house, there shall you find us both. 3.01.190
besides, he says there are two councils kept; 3.02. 12
gramercy, fellow. there, drink that for me. 3.02.106
i do, my lord, but long i cannot stay there. 3.02.119
nay, like enough, for i stay dinner there. 3.02.121
i saw good strawberries in your garden there. 3.04. 32
look to the drawbridge there! 3.05. 15
there, at your meet'st /advantage of the time, 3.05. 74
my lord, there needs no such apology. 3.07.104
but, god be thank'd, there is no need of me, 3.07.165
and much i need to help you, were there need: 3.07.166
to gratulate the gentle princes there. 4.01. 10
there to be crowned richard's royal queen. 4.01. 32
there is no more but so; 4.02. 80
the devil" — there the villain stopp'd; 4.03. 16
and there the little souls of edward's children 4.04.192
up to some scaffold, there to lose their heads. 4.04.243
there is no other way, | unless thou couldst put 4.04.285
and there they hull, expecting but the aid | of 4.04.438
why, what wouldst thou do there before i go? 4.04.454
there let him sink, and be the seas on him! 4.04.463
white–liver'd runagate, what doth he there? 4.04.464
what heir of york is there alive but we? 4.04.471
there, take thou that, till thou bring better 4.04.508
there is my purse to cure that blow of thine. 4.04.514
is there a murtherer here? 5.03.184
there is no creature loves me, | and if i die no 5.03.200
'zounds, who is there? 5.03.208
tell the clock there. 5.03.276
i think there be six richmonds in the field; 5.04. 11
H8 since a fresh admirer | of what i saw there. 1.01. 4
there is no english soul | more stronger to 1.01.146
there have been commissions | sent down among 1.02. 20
for | there is no primer baseness. 1.02. 67
let there be letters writ to every shire, | of 1.02.103
i'm glad 'tis there. 1.03. 21
there, i take it, | they may, cum privilegio, 1.03. 33
ay, marry, | there will be woe indeed, lords; 1.03. 39
there will be | the beauty of this kingdom, i'll 1.03. 53
look out there, some of ye. 1.04. 50
there should be one amongst 'em, by his person 1.04. 78
there is indeed, which they would have your 1.04. 83
were you there? 2.01. 5
stay there, sir, | and see the noble ruin'd man 2.01. 53
there cannot be those numberless offenses 2.01. 84
prepare there, | the duke is coming. 2.01. 97
the king's soul, and there scatters | dangers, 2.02. 26
who's there? ha? 2.02. 63
who's there, i say? 2.02. 64
who's there? 2.02. 73
there ye shall meet about this weighty business. 2.02.139
although there 'long'd | no more to th' crown 2.03. 48
there is hope | all will be well. 2.03. 55
there was a lady once ('tis an old story) | that 2.03. 90
the wisest prince that there had reign'd by many 2.04. 49
there must i be unloos'd, although not there 2.04.148
although not there | at once and fully satisfied 2.04.148
and showers | there had made a lasting spring. 3.01. 8
there sits a judge | that no king can corrupt. 3.01.100
there be moe wasps that buzz about his nose 3.02. 55
again, there is sprung up | an heretic, an 3.02.101
it may well be, | there is a mutiny in 's mind. 3.02.120
and wot you what i found | there (on my 3.02.123
is there no way to cure this? 3.02.216
many more there are, | which, since they are of 3.02.330
there is, betwixt that smile we would aspire to, 3.02.368
there was the weight that pull'd me down. 3.02.407
there take an inventory of all i have, | to the 3.02.451
man living | could say, "this is my wife" there, 4.01. 80
however, yet there is no great breach; 4.01.106
to th' court, and there ye shall be my guests; 4.01.115
there is staying | a gentleman, sent from the 4.02.105
of which there is not one, i dare avow | (and 4.02.142
and if there be | no great offense belongs to't, 5.01. 11
there are that dare, and i myself have ventur'd 5.01. 40
and your appeal to us | there make before them. 5.01.152
who waits there? 5.02. 4
there, my lord: 5.02. 22
who waits there? 5.02. 39
nor is there living | (i speak it with a single 5.02. 72
there to remain till the king's further pleasure 5.02.125
is there no other way of mercy | but i must 5.02.127
let some o' th' guard be ready there. 5.02.130
look there, my lords; 5.02.133
was rather | (if there be faith in men) meant 5.02.186
there is a fellow somewhat near the door, he 5.03. 39 P
he stands there like a mortar–piece to blow us. 5.03. 46 P
there was a haberdasher's wife of small wit near 5.03. 46 P
and there they are like to dance these three 5.03. 64 P
make way there for the princess. 5.03. 87
there were no more comparison between the women!
TRO 1.01. 42 P
when i do tell thee there my hopes lie drown'd, 1.01. 49
will leave all as i found it, and there an end. 1.01. 88 P
her bed is india, there she lies, a pearl; 1.01.100
because not there. 1.01.106
and, like as there were husbandry in war, 1.02. 7
there is among the greeks | a lord of troyan 1.02. 12
there is no man hath a virtue that he hath not a 1.02. 24 P
but there was such laughing! 1.02.142 P
but there was a more temperate fire under the 1.02.146 P
but there was such laughing! 1.02.165 P
look you there, there's no jesting; 1.02.206 P
there be hacks! 1.02.207 P
there is amongst the greeks achilles, a better 1.02.247 P
at your own house, there he unarms him. 1.02.274 P
if there be one among the fair'st of greece 1.03.265
but if there be not in our grecian /mould | a 1.03.293
there is seen | the baby figure of the giant 1.03.344
you see him there? do you? 2.01. 57 P
but the fool will not — he there, that he! 2.01. 84 P
look you there. 2.01. 84 P
lies in your sinews, or else there be liars. 2.01. 99 P
i will keep where there is wit stirring, and 2.01.118 P
priam, | there is no lady of more softer bowels, 2.02. 11
there can be no evasion | to blench from this 2.02. 67
and jove forbid there should be done amongst us 2.02.127
there is a law in each well–order'd nation | to 2.02.180
why, there you touch'd the life of our design: 2.02.194
who's there? 2.03. 23 P
who's there? 2.03. 38 P
there is no tarrying here; 2.03.258
of paris my lord, who is there in person; 3.01. 31 P
build there, carpenter, the air is sweet. 3.02. 51 P
in all cupid's pageant there is presented no 3.02. 75 P
are there such? 3.02. 90 P
till it hath travell'd and is /mirror'd there 3.03.110
though in and of him there be much consisting, 3.03.116
heavens, what a man is there! 3.03.126
what things there are | most /abject in regard, 3.03.127
there is a mystery (with whom relation | durst 3.03.201
as who should say there were wit in this head, 3.03.255 P
this head, and 'twould out — and so there is; 3.03.256 P
see, ho! who is that there? 4.01. 1
is the prince there in person? 4.01. 3
to calchas' house, and there to render him, 4.01. 38
or, if you please, | haste there before us. 4.01. 41
my brother troilus lodges there to–night. 4.01. 43
there is no help. 4.01. 48
who's there? 4.02. 42 P
who's there? 4.02. 45
there is at hand | paris your brother, and 4.02. 60
a priest there off'ring to it his own heart. 4.03. 9
there was never a truer rhyme. 4.04. 21 P
that there is no maculation in thy heart; 4.04. 64
there lurks a still and dumb–discoursive devil 4.04. 90
his blows are well dispos'd. there, ajax! 4.05.116
there is expectance here from both the sides, 4.05.146
there they stand yet, and modestly i think | the 4.05.222
his body | shall i destroy him — whether there, 4.05.243
him — whether there, or there, or there? 4.05.243
him — whether there, or there, or there? 4.05.243
for i'll not kill thee there, nor there, nor 4.05.254
for i'll not kill thee there, nor there, nor 4.05.254
i'll not kill thee there, nor there, nor there, 4.05.254
there in the full convive we. 4.05.272
there diomed doth feast with him to–night, | who 4.05.280
had she no lover there | that wails her absence? 4.05.288
and the goodly transformation of jupiter there, 5.01. 54 P
yonder 'tis, | there where we see the lights. 5.01. 68
it is prodigious, there will come some change; 5.01. 93 P
there is between my will and all offenses | a 5.02. 53
sith yet there is a credence in my heart, | an 5.02.120
delight, | if there be rule in unity itself, 5.02.141
within my soul there doth conduce a fight | of 5.02.147
what says she there? 5.03.107 P
wind, to wind, there turn and change together. 5.03.110
/young knave's sleeve of troy there in his helm. 5.04. 4 P
ass, that loves the whore there, might send that 5.04. 6 P
there is a thousand hectors in the field: 5.05. 19
on galathe his horse | and there lacks work; 5.05. 21
anon he's there afoot, | and there they fly or 5.05. 21
and there they fly or die, like scaling sculls 5.05. 22
and there the strawy greeks, ripe for his edge, 5.05. 24
here, there, and every where, he leaves and 5.05. 26
ay, there, there. 5.05. 43
ay, there, there. 5.05. 43
ha, art thou there? 5.06. 8
there is a word will priam turn to stone, | make 5.10. 18
there is no more to say. 5.10. 22
COR there was a time when all the body's members 1.01. 96
o, good madam, there can be none yet. 1.03. 91 P
there came news from him last night. 1.03. 92 P
there is aufidius. 1.04. 20
there is the man of my soul's hate, aufidius, 1.05. 10
at home, upon my brother's guard, even there, 1.10. 25
there will be large cicatrices to show the 2.01.147 P
give way there, and go on! 2.01.193
faith, there hath been many great men that have 2.02. 7 P
and there be many that they have lov'd, they 2.02. 9 P
to the people, there was never a worthier man. 2.03. 38 P
there, coriolanus. 2.03.145
we will be there before the stream o' th' people 2.03.261
i wish i had a cause to seek him there, | to 3.01. 19
though there the people had more absolute pow'r, 3.01.116
we'll attend you there; 3.01.330
by th' other lose | that they combine not there. 3.02. 45
yet, were there but this single plot to lose, 3.02.102
if he evade us there, | enforce him with his 3.03. 2
and that is there which looks | with us to break 3.03. 29
there is a world elsewhere. 3.03.135
from the volscian state to find you out there. 4.03. 11 P
there hath been in rome strange insurrections; 4.03. 13 P
knew by his face that there was something in him 4.05.154 P
hang'd but i thought there was more in him than 4.05.158 P
there is a slave, whom we have put in prison, 4.06. 38
general talk of rome | and of his friends there, 5.02. 10
finger, there is some hope the ladies of rome, 5.04. 5 P
but i say there is no hope in't; 5.04. 7 P
there is differency between a grub and a 5.04. 11 P
there is no more mercy in him than there is milk 5.04. 27 P
mercy in him than there is milk in a male tiger, 5.04. 28 P
there was it — | for which my sinews shall be 5.06. 43
but there to end | where he was to begin, and 5.06. 64
making a treaty where | there was a yielding — 5.06. 68
have writ your annals true, 'tis there | that, 5.06.113
TIT there greet in silence, as the dead are wont, 1.01. 90
there shall we consummate our spousal rites. 1.01.337
there lie thy bones, sweet mutius, with thy 1.01.387
there will the lovely roman ladies troop; 2.01.113
and many unfrequented plots there are, | fitted 2.01.115
there speak, and strike, brave boys, and take 2.01.129
there serve your lust, shadowed from heaven's 2.01.130
'tis not an hour since i left them there. 2.03.256
there let them bide until we have devis'd | some 2.03.284
by my soul, were there worse end than death, 2.03.302
if there were reason for these miseries, | then 3.01.219
hie to the goths and raise an army there, | and 3.01.285
some book there is that she desires to see. 4.01. 31
i think she means that there were more than one 4.01. 38
ay, more there was; 4.01. 39
ay, such a place there is where we did hunt | (c 4.01. 55
hunt | (o, had we never, never hunted there!), 4.01. 56
i know | there is enough written upon this earth 4.01. 84
keep there. 4.02.134
there to dispose this treasure in mine arms, 4.02.173
ye draw home enough, and 'tis there straight. 4.03. 3
why, there it goes, god give his lordship joy! 4.03. 77
alas, sir, i never came there. 4.03. 90 P
in the people's ears, there nought hath pass'd, 4.04. 7
if there be devils, would i were a devil, | to 5.01.147
there is a messenger from rome | desires to be 5.01.152
task, | so thou destroy rapine and murder there. 5.02. 59
never wags | but in her company there is a moor; 5.02. 88
and in the emperor's court | there is a queen, 5.02.105
why, there they are, both baked in this pie; 5.03. 60
there let him stand and rave and cry for food. 5.03.180
ROM many a morning hath he there been seen, | with 1.01.131
persons out | whose names are written there, and 1.02. 36
but in that crystal scales let there be weigh'd 1.02. 96
and find delight writ there with beauty's pen; 1.03. 82
we cannot be here and there too. 1.05. 14 P
and the demesnes that there adjacent lie, | that 2.01. 20
letting it there stand | till she had laid it 2.01. 25
what if her eyes were there, they in her head? 2.02. 18
there lies more peril in thine eye | than twenty 2.02. 71
i shall forget, to have thee still stand there, 2.02.172
couch his limbs, there golden sleep doth reign. 2.03. 38
was i with you there for the goose? 2.04. 74 P
thing when thou wast not there for the goose. 2.04. 76 P
stop there, stop there. 2.04. 94 P
stop there, stop there. 2.04. 94 P
and there she shall at friar lawrence' cell | be 2.04.181
this afternoon, sir? well, she shall be there. 2.04.186 P
o, there is a nobleman in town, one paris, that 2.04.201 P
there stays a husband to make you a wife. 2.05. 69
him on the drawer, when indeed there is no need. 3.01. 9 P
nay, and there were two such, we should have 3.01. 15 P
there lies that tybalt. 3.01.139
there lies the man, slain by young romeo, | that 3.01.144
what hast thou there? 3.02. 34
i am not i, if there be such an ay; 3.02. 48
some word there was, worser than tybalt's death, 3.02.108
death | was woe enough if it had ended there; 3.02.115
there is no end, no limit, measure, bound, | in 3.02.125
there is no world without verona walls, | but 3.03. 17
who's there? 3.03. 74
there on the ground, with his own tears made 3.03. 83
there art thou happy. 3.03.137
there art thou happy. 3.03.138
there art thou happy. 3.03.140
some half a dozen friends, | and there an end. 3.04. 28
the hour, | for in a minute there are many days. 3.05. 45
shall happily make thee there a joyful bride. 3.05.115
he shall not make me there a joyful bride. 3.05.117
is there no pity sitting in the clouds, | that 3.05.196
to rouse thee from thy bed, there art thou dead. 4.01.108
no, not till thursday, there is time enough. 4.02. 36
lie thou there. 4.03. 23
and there die strangled ere my romeo comes? 4.03. 35
now, fellow, what is there? 4.04. 14
there she lies, | flower as she was, deflowered 4.05. 36
hold, there is forty ducats; 5.01. 59
there is thy gold, worse poison to men's souls, 5.01. 80
to juliet's grave, for there must i use thee. 5.01. 86
so that my speed to mantua there was stay'd. 5.02. 12
death, lie thou there, by a dead man interr'd. 5.03. 87
and death's pale flag is not advanced there. 5.03. 96
tybalt, liest thou there in thy bloody sheet? 5.03. 97
who's there? 5.03.122
how long hath he been there? 5.03.130
well where i should be, | and there i am. 5.03.150
thy husband in thy bosom there lies dead; 5.03.155
there rust, and let me die. 5.03.170

is the place, there where the torch doth burn. 5.03.171
romeo, there dead, was husband to that juliet, 5.03.231
and she, there dead, /that romeo's faithful wife 5.03.232
or in my cell there would she kill herself. 5.03.242
vault, | if i departed not and left him there. 5.03.277
there shall no figure at such rate be set | as 5.03.301
what have you there? TIM 1.01. 25
what have you there, my friend? 1.01.154
that there should be small love amongst these 1.01.249
but where there is true friendship, there needs 1.02. 18
there is true friendship, there needs none. 1.02. 18
ye have got a humor there | does not become a 1.02. 26
lord, there are certain ladies most desirous of 1.02.116 P
there comes with them a forerunner, my lord, 1.02.119 P
there, | taste, touch, all, pleas'd from thy 1.02.125
ladies, there is an idle banquet attends you, 1.02.155
there is no crossing him in 's humor, | else i 1.02.160
there are certain nobles of the senate | newly 1.02.174
too, there would be none left to rail upon thee, 1.02.239 P
there will little learning die then that day 2.02. 82 P
will you leave me there? 2.02. 90 P
within there! 2.02.185
and what hast thou there under thy cloak, pretty 3.01. 14 P
there was very little honor show'd in't. 3.02. 19 P
if there be | such valor in the bearing, what 3.05. 45
if there were no foes, that were enough | to 3.05. 69
if there sit twelve women at the table, let a 3.06. 78 P
what art thou there? speak. 4.03. 49
there were no suns to borrow of. 4.03. 70
if thou wilt, | tell them there i have gold; 4.03.289
when there is nothing living but thee, thou 4.03.355 P
there is no leprosy but what thou speak'st. 4.03.362
for there is boundless theft | in limited 4.03.427
there is no time so miserable but a man may be 4.03.456 P
there does not live a man." 5.03. 4
arms, and there have sate | the livelong day, JC 1.01. 40
when went there by an age since the great flood 1.02.152
enough, | when there is in it but one only man. 1.02.157
there was a brutus once that would have brook'd 1.02.159
why, there was a crown offer'd him; 1.02.221 P
there was more foolery yet, if i could remember 1.02.287 P
either there is a civil strife in heaven, | or 1.03. 11
and there were drawn | upon a heap a hundred 1.03. 22
send word to you he would be there to-morrow. 1.03. 38
who's there? 1.03. 41
there is no stir or walking in the streets; 1.03.127
is decius brutus and trebonius there? 1.03.148
sure | it did not lie there when i went to bed. 2.01. 38
no, sir, there are moe with him. 2.01. 72
and in the spirit of men there is no blood; 2.01.168
there is no fear in him; 2.01.190
nay, we will all of us be there to fetch him. 2.01.212
there is one within, | besides the things that 2.02. 14
when beggars die there are no comets seen; 2.02. 30
there is but one mind in all these men, and it 2.03. 5 P
i would have had thee there and here again | ere 2.04. 4
ere i can tell thee what thou shouldst do there. 2.04. 5
and there | speak to great caesar as he comes 2.04. 37
is there no voice more worthy than my own, | to 3.01. 49
quality | there is no fellow in the firmament. 3.01. 62
there is no harm intended to your person, | nor 3.01. 90
there is no hour so fit | as caesar's death's 3.01.153
there shall i try, | in my oration, how the 3.01.292
if there be any in this assembly, any dear 3.02. 17 P
there is tears for his love; 3.02. 27 P
my heart is in the coffin there with caesar, 3.02.106
methinks there is much reason in his sayings. 3.02.108
i fear there will a worse come in his place. 3.02.111
now lies he there, | and none so poor to do him 3.02.119
o, what a fall was there, my countrymen! 3.02.190
peace there, hear the noble antony. 3.02.207 P
there were an antony | would ruffle up your 3.02.227
there are no tricks in plain and simple faith; 4.02. 22
there is no terror, cassius, in your threats; 4.03. 66
there is my dagger, | and here my naked breast; 4.03.100
there is some grudge between 'em; 4.03.125
him off | if at philippi we do face him there, 4.03.211
there is a tide in the affairs of men | which, 4.03.218
there is no more to say? 4.03.229
two mighty eagles fell, and there they perch'd, 5.01. 80
and where i did begin, there shall i end; 5.03. 24
there is so much that thou wilt kill me straight 5.04. 13
fly, fly, my lord, there is no tarrying here. 5.05. 30
there to meet with macbeth. MAC 1.01. 7
there if i grow, | the harvest is your own. 1.04. 32
who's there? 2.01. 10
who's there? what ho! 2.02. 8
there are two lodg'd together. 2.02. 23
they must lie there. 2.02. 46
who's there, i' th' name of belzebub? 2.03. 3 P
who's there, in th' other devil's name? 2.03. 7 P
who's there? 2.03. 12 P
there, the murtherers, | steep'd in the colors 2.03.114
well, may you see things well done there: 2.04. 37
if there come truth from them — | as upon thee, 3.01. 6
there is none but he | whose being i do fear; 3.01. 53
who's there? 3.01. 71
now go to the door, and stay there till we call. 3.01. 72
there shall be done | a deed of dreadful note. 3.02. 43
give us a light there, ho! 3.03. 9
there the grown serpent lies; 3.04. 28
prithee see there! 3.04. 67
were out, the man would die, | and there an end; 3.04. 79
the moon | there hangs a vap'rous drop profound, 3.05. 24
come in, without there! 4.01.135
for there are liars and swearers enow to beat 4.02. 57 P
shade, and there | weep our sad bosoms empty. 4.03. 1
perchance even there where i did find my doubts. 4.03. 25
there would be hands uplifted in my right; 4.03. 42
there cannot be | that vulture in you to devour 4.03. 73
there grows | in my most ill-compos'd affection 4.03. 76
there are a crew of wretched souls | that stay 4.03.141
man's knell | is there scarce ask'd for who, and 4.03.171
there ran a rumor | of many worthy fellows that 4.03.182
what a sigh is there! 5.01. 53 P
there is siward's son, | and many unrough youths 5.02. 9
him does condemn | itself for being there? 5.02. 25
there is ten thousand — 5.03. 13
for where there is advantage to be given, | both 5.04. 11
there would have been a time for such a word. 5.05. 18
there is nor flying hence, nor tarrying here. 5.05. 47
there thou shouldst be; 5.07. 20
who's there? HAM 1.01. 1
i think i hear them. stand ho! who is there? 1.01. 14
say — | what, is horatio there? 1.01. 19
hath in the skirts of norway here and there 1.01. 97
if there be any good thing to be done | that may 1.01.130
i would i had been there. 1.02.234
there — my blessing with thee! 1.03. 57
and there assume some other horrible form, 1.04. 72
hamlet, what /a falling-off was there | from me, 1.05. 47
past | that youth and observation copied there, 1.05.101
so, uncle, there you are. 1.05.110
there needs no ghost, my lord, come from the 1.05.125
yes, by saint patrick, but there is, horatio, 1.05.136
art thou there, truepenny? 1.05.150
there are more things in heaven and earth, 1.05.166
or "if we list to speak," or "there be, and if 1.05.177
and there put on him | what forgeries you please 2.01. 19
there was 'a gaming, there o'ertook in 's rouse, 2.01. 56
there was 'a gaming, there o'ertook in 's rouse, 2.01. 56
in 's rouse, | there falling out at tennis"; 2.01. 57
and sure i am two men there is not living | to 2.02. 20
hath there been such a time — i would fain know 2.02.153
this be madness, yet there is method in't. 2.02.205 P
you go to seek the lord hamlet, there he is. 2.02.220 P
and there is a kind of confession in your looks, 2.02.279 P
my lord, there was no such stuff in my thoughts. 2.02.311 P
there is something in this more than natural, if 2.02.367 P
there are the players. 2.02.369 P
great baby you see there is not yet out of his 2.02.383 P
i remember one said there were no sallets in the 2.02.441 P
and there did seem in him a kind of joy | to 3.01. 18
there, my lord. 3.01.101
o, there be players that i have seen play — and 3.02. 28 P
for there be of them that will themselves laugh 3.02. 40 P
there is a play to-night before the king, | one 3.02. 75
part of him to kill so capital a calf there. 3.02.106 P
little fears grow great, great love grows there. 3.02.172
is there no offense in't? 3.02.232 P
but is there no sequel at the heels of this 3.02.329 P
and there is much music, excellent voice, in 3.02.367 P
is there not rain enough in the sweet heavens 3.03. 45
there is no shuffling, there the action lies 3.03. 61
there the action lies | in his true nature, and 3.03. 61
of an innocent love | and sets a blister there, 3.04. 44
and there i see such black and /grained spots 3.04. 90
do you see nothing there? 3.04.131
why, look you there! 3.04.134
it had been so with us had we been there. 4.01. 13
if your messenger find him not there, seek him 4.03. 34 P
go seek him there. 4.03. 38 P
would make one think there might be thought, 4.05. 12
and there is pansies, that's for thoughts. 4.05.176 P
there lives within the very flame of love | a 4.07.114
and delays as many | as there are tongues, are 4.07.121
venom'd stuck, | our purpose may hold there. 4.07.162
there is a willow grows askaunt the brook, 4.07.166
there, on the pendant boughs her crownet weeds 4.07.172
why, there thou say'st, and the more pity that 5.01. 26 P
there is no ancient gentlemen but gard'ners, 5.01. 29 P
o, methought there — a — was nothing — a — 5.01. 64
'a shall recover his wits there, or, if 'a do 5.01.151 P
or, if 'a do not, 'tis no great matter there. 5.01.152 P
'twill not be seen in him there, there the men 5.01.154 P
in him there, there the men are as mad as he. 5.01.154 P
must there no more be done? 5.01.235
in my heart there was a kind of fighting | that 5.02. 4
himself, there are no tongues else for 's turn. 5.02.184 P
there is special providence in the fall of a 5.02.219 P
look to the queen there ho! 5.02.303
in thee there is not half an hour's life. 5.02.315
mother fair, there was good sport at his making, LR 1.01. 23 P
give me the map there. 1.01. 37
sir, there she stands: 1.01.197
your grace, | she's there, and she is yours. 1.01.201
there is further compliment of leave-taking 1.01.302 P
i am no honest man if there be any good meaning 1.02.173 P
what says the fellow there? 1.04. 46 P
there, take my coxcomb. 1.04.101 P
be not speedy, i shall be there afore you. 1.05. 4 P
to sojourn at my house, | i'll not be there. 2.01.104
life and honor, | there shall he sit till noon. 2.02.134
the night before there was no purpose in them 2.04. 3
my duty kneeling, came there a reeking post, 2.04. 30
i set him there, sir; 2.04.199
who's there, besides foul weather? 3.01. 1
there is division | (although as yet the face of 3.01. 19
for there was never yet fair woman but she made 3.02. 35 P
who's there? 3.02. 39
repose you there, while i to this hard house 3.02. 63
there is division between the dukes, and a worse 3.03. 8 P
there is part of a power already footed: 3.03. 13 P
there is strange things toward, edmund, pray you 3.03. 19 P
save what beats there — filial ingratitude! 3.04. 14
give me thy hand. who's there? 3.04. 41 P
art thou that dost grumble there i' th' straw? 3.04. 44 P
there could i have him now — and there — and 3.04. 61 P
there could i have him now — and there — and 3.04. 62 P
and there — and there again — and there. 3.04. 62 P
and there — and there again — and there. 3.04. 62 P
who's there? what is't you seek? 3.04.127
what are you there? your names? 3.04.128
in, fellow, there, into th' hovel; 3.04.174
is there any cause in nature that make these 3.06. 77 P
there is a litter ready, lay him in't, | and 3.06. 90
who's there? 3.07. 27
how now? who's there? 4.01. 24
there is a cliff, whose high and bending head 4.01. 73
there is means, madam. 4.04. 11
himself in person there? 4.05. 2
hairs in my beard ere the black ones were there. 4.06. 98 P
not peace at my bidding, there i found 'em, 4.06.103 P
there i found 'em, there i smelt 'em out. 4.06.103 P
there is the sulphurous pit, burning, scalding, 4.06.128
o ho, are you there with me? 4.06.145 P
there thou mightst behold the great image of 4.06.157 P
there is nothing done, if he return the 4.06.265 P
that will prove | what is avouched there. 5.01. 44
and many treasons, | there is my pledge. 5.03. 93
if there be more, more woeful, hold it in, | for 5.03.203
look there, look there! 5.03.312
look there, look there! 5.03.312
others there are | who, trimm'd in forms and OTH 1.01. 49
what is the matter there? 1.01. 83
and there will i be with him. 1.01.159
is there not charms | by which the property of 1.01.171
holla, stand there! 1.02. 56
have there injointed them with an after fleet. 1.03. 35
and though we have there a substitute of most 1.03.223 P
/i /would /not there reside, | to put my father 1.03.241
there are many events in the womb of time which 1.03.369 P
dull with the act of sport, there should be, 2.01.227 P
without the which there were no expectation of 2.01.280 P
and there is full liberty of feasting from this 2.02. 9 P
and there be souls must be sav'd, and there be 2.03.103 P
be sav'd, and there be souls must not be sav'd. 2.03.103 P
there comes a fellow crying out for help, | and 2.03.226
there is more sense in that than in reputation. 2.03.267 P
there are more ways to recover the general again 2.03.272 P
repair there to me. 3.02. 4
as if there were some monster in thy thought 3.03.107
and on the proof, there is no more but this — 3.03.191
if there be cords, or knives, | poison, or fire, 3.03.388
there are a kind of men, so loose of soul, 3.03.416
lodging and say he lies here, or he lies there, 3.04. 12 P
there is no other way: 3.04.107
in your chamber, and know not who left it there! 4.01.153 P
there, give it your hobby-horse. 4.01.154 P
will you sup there? 4.01.164 P
is there division 'twixt my lord and cassio? 4.01.231
but there, where i have garner'd up my heart, 4.02. 57
turn thy complexion there, | patience, thou 4.02. 62
fie, there is no such man; it is impossible. 4.02.134
if any such there be, heaven pardon him! 4.02.135
there is especial commission come from venice to 4.02.220 P
dismiss your attendant there. 4.03. 8 P
'tis neither here nor there. 4.03. 59
that there be women do abuse their husbands | in 4.03. 62
there be some such, no question. 4.03. 63
i do not think there is any such woman. 4.03. 83
there stand i in much peril. 5.01. 21
who's there? 5.01. 48
what are you there? 5.01. 59
o, help me there! 5.01. 60
who's there? othello? 5.02. 23
being done, there is no pause. 5.02. 82
who's there? 5.02. 89
there lies your niece, | whose breath, indeed, 5.02.201
are there no stones in heaven | but what serves 5.02.234
that there he dropp'd it for a special purpose 5.02.322
there is besides, in roderigo's letter, | how he 5.02.324
if there be any cunning cruelty | that can 5.02.333
from sicyon how the news? speak there! ANT 1.02.113
the man from sicyon — is there such an one? 1.02.114
i do think there is mettle in death, which 1.02.143 P
if there were no more women but fulvia, then had 1.02.165 P
worn out, there are members to make new. 1.02.164 P
o, never was there queen | so mightily betrayed! 1.03. 24
shouldst know | there were a heart in egypt. 1.03. 41
you shall find there | a man who is th' 1.04. 8
i must not think there are | evils enow to 1.04. 10
there would he anchor his aspect, and die | with 1.05. 33
yet if you there | did practice on my state, 2.02. 38
at a breakfast, and but twelve persons there; 2.02.180 P
there she appear'd indeed; 2.02.188 P
there, | my music playing far off, i will betray 2.05. 10
if thou so yield him, there is gold, and here 2.05. 28
gods confound thee, dost thou hold there still? 2.05. 92
ghosted, | there saw you laboring for him. 2.06. 14
julius caesar | grew fat with feasting there. 2.06. 65
there i deny my land service. 2.06. 94 P
but there is never a fair woman has a true face. 2.06. 99 P
y' have strange serpents there? 2.07. 24 P
all there is thine. 2.07. 73
on, there, pass along! 3.01. 37
us, why should not we | be there in person? 3.07. 6
of my kingdom, will | appear there for a man. 3.07. 18
can he be there in person? 3.07. 56
and there i will attend | what further comes. 3.10. 31
some wine, within there, and our viands! 3.11. 73
all-disgraced friend, | or take his life there. 3.12. 23
to lay my crown at 's feet, and there to kneel. 3.13. 76
approach there! 3.13. 89
within our files there are, | of those that 4.01. 12
there did dissuade | great herod to incline 4.06. 12
heart, and there | ride on the pants triumphing! 4.08. 15
we'ld fight there too. 4.10. 4
there lock yourself, and send him word you are 4.13. 4
there is left us | ourselves to end ourselves. 4.14. 21
why, there then. 4.14. 94
there, diomed, there. 4.14.114
there, diomed, there. 4.14.114
art thou there, diomed? 4.14.116
and there is nothing left remarkable | beneath 4.15. 67
i dreamt there was an emperor antony. 5.02. 76
for his bounty, | there was no winter in't; 5.02. 87
think you there was or might be such a man | as 5.02. 93
but if there be, nor ever were one such, | it's 5.02. 96
make way there! caesar! 5.02.111
hast thou the pretty worm of nilus there, | that 5.02.243
for indeed, there is no goodness in the worm. 5.02.266 P
a way there, a way for caesar! 5.02.333
there is a vent of blood, and something blown; 5.02.349
there would be something failing | in him that CYM 1.01. 21
but that there is this jewel in the world | that 1.01. 91
there cannot be a pinch in death | more sharp 1.01.130
there might have been, | but that my master 1.01.161
would there had been some hurt done! 1.02. 34 P
we had very many there could behold the sun with 1.04. 12 P
or if there were wealth enough for the /purchase 1.04. 83 P
let there be covenants drawn between 's. 1.04.143 P
but there is | no danger in what show of death 1.05. 39
none a stranger there | so merry and so gamesome 1.06. 59

there is a frenchman his companion, one | an 1.06. 64
was there ever man had such luck? 2.01. 1 P
is there no derogation in't? 2.01. 42 P
who's there? my woman? helen? 2.02. 1
there the window; 2.02. 25
who's there that knocks? 2.03. 77
there is gold for you, | sell me your good 2.03. 82
(on whom there is no more dependancy | but brats 2.03.118
in the britain court | when you were there? 2.04. 38
let there be no honor | where there is beauty; 2.04.108
let there be no honor | where there is beauty; 2.04.109
there, take thy hire, and all the fiends of hell 2.04.129
as hell can hold, | were there no more but it. 2.04.141
i will go there and do't, i' th' court, before 2.04.148
is there no way for men to be, but women | must 2.05. 1
there be many caesars, | ere such another julius 3.01. 11
and, as i said, there is no moe such caesars. 3.01. 36 P
to lie in watch there and to think on him? 3.04. 41
thy master is not there, who was indeed | the 3.04. 70
there is a prohibition so divine | that cravens 3.04. 77
even there, thou villain posthumus, will i kill 3.05.131 P
there shall she see my valor, which will then be 3.05.138 P
she can scarce be there yet. 3.05.150 P
there is cold meat i' th' cave, we'll browse on 3.06. 38
it is great morning. come away! — who's there? 4.02. 61
fool, an empty purse, | there was no money in't. 4.02.114
but if there be | yet left in heaven as small a 4.02.303
there vanish'd in the sunbeams, which portends 4.02.350
alas, | there is no more such masters. 4.02.371
there wants no diligence in seeking him, | and 4.03. 20
we'll higher to the mountains, there secure us. 4.04. 8
that is my bed too, lads, and there i'll lie. 4.04. 52
there was a fourth man, in a silly habit, | that 5.03. 86
who's there? 5.03. 88
there are none want eyes to direct them the way 5.04.185 P
there are verier knaves desire to live, for all 5.04.200 P
and there be some of them too that die against 5.04.201 P
there were desolation of jailers and gallowses! 5.04.204 P
is there more? 5.05. 48
your daughter's chastity — there it begins. 5.05.179
thou scornful page, | there lie thy part. 5.05.229
my boys, | there was our error. 5.05.260
hang there like fruit, my soul, | till the tree 5.05.263
let me end the story: | i slew him there. 5.05.287
set on there! 5.05.484
who attends us there? PER 1.01.150
if there be such a dart in princes' frowns, 1.02. 53
here stands a lord, and there a lady weeping; 1.04. 47
ground's the lowest, and we are half way there. 1.04. 78
and there are princes and knights come from all 2.01.109 P
to my desires, i could wish to make one there. 2.01.112 P
there are certain condolements, certain vails. 2.01.150 P
if in his grave he rest, we'll find him there; 2.04. 30
the mutiny he there hastes t' oppress, | says to 3.ch. 29
slack the bolins there! 3.01. 43 P
there will i visit cleon, for the babe | cannot 3.01. 78
there i'll leave it | at careful nursing. 3.01. 79
so, lift there. 3.02. 49
the music there! 3.02. 91
my /eaning time, but whether there | delivered, 3.04. 6
a niece of mine | shall there attend you. 3.04. 16
at ephesus, | unto diana there 's a votaress. 4.ch. 4
walk with leonine, the air is quick there, | and 4.01. 27
if there be not a conscience to be us'd in every 4.02. 11 P
there was a spaniard's mouth wat'red, and he 4.02. 99 P
but to have divinity preach'd there! 4.05. 4 P
but there never came her like in meteline. 4.06. 28 P
we there him /lost, | where, driven before the 5.ch. 13
sir, there is a barge put off from meteline, 5.01. 3
there is some of worth would come aboard; 5.01. 9
but there is something glows upon my cheek, 5.01. 95
o, stop there a little! 5.01.160
there, when my maiden priests are met together 5.01.242
there to strike | the inhospitable cleon, but i 5.01.252
found there rich jewels, recovered her, and 5.03. 24
and call'd marina | for she was yielded there. 5.03. 48
yet there, my queen, | we'll celebrate their 5.03. 79
in reverend cerimon there well appears | the 5.03. 93
there constant to eternity it lives. TNK pr 14
book of trespasses | all you are set down there. 1.01. 34
you cannot read it there. 1.01.111
there, through my tears, | like wrinkled pebbles 1.01.111
which is not catching | where there is faith? 1.02. 46
what canon is there | that does command my 1.02. 55
yet they | must yield their tribute there. 1.03. 8
doubtless | there is a best, and reason has no 1.03. 48
is there record of any two that lov'd | better 2.02.112
sure there cannot. 2.02.113
were there not maids enough? 2.02.121
there is no remedy. 2.02.274
is but a heap of ruins, | and no redress there. 2.03. 20
my masters, i'll be there, that's certain. 2.03. 24
and i'll be there. 2.03. 25
arcas will be there. 2.03. 37
and there i'll be, for our town, and here again, 2.03. 48
for our town, and here again, | and there again. 2.03. 49
not far, sir. | are there such games to–day? 2.03. 64
yes, marry, are there; 2.03. 64
the duke himself | will be in person there. 2.03. 66
venture, | and in some poor disguise be there. 2.03. 79
but in my heart was palamon, and there, | lord, 2.04. 17
and there he shall keep close | till i provide 2.06. 6
and where there is a path of ground i'll venture 2.06. 33
there shall be at your choice | both sword and 3.01. 88
you must guess | i have an office there. 3.01.110
there you have | a vantage o'er me, but enjoy't 3.01.121
what did she there, coz? 3.03. 34
remember, cousin, | else there be tales abroad. 3.03. 38
there was a time | when young men went a–hunting 3.03. 39
"thus let be," and "there let be," | and "then 3.05. 9
there are you, | close in the thicket. 3.05. 12
mark there! 3.05. 17
and there he met with brave gallants of war, 3.05. 61
"there was three fools fell out about an howlet: 3.05. 67
and me my love! is there aught else to say? 3.06. 93
if there be | a place prepar'd for those that 3.06. 98
(if there be a right in seeing | and first 3.06.147
but there be new conditions, which you'll hear 4.01. 29
there is at least two hundred now with child by 4.01.129
now with child by him — | there must be four. 4.01.130
lie there, arcite! 4.02. 43
there shall want no bravery. 4.02.154
to pieces with love, we shall come there, and do 4.03. 24 P
and there shall we be put in a cauldron of lead 4.03. 36 P
and there boil like a gammon of bacon that will 4.03. 38 P
th' heart, and there th' offending part burns, 4.03. 43 P
to hear there a proud lady and a proud city–wife 4.03. 51 P
were there aught in me which strove to show 5.01. 20
there | require of him the hearts of lions and 5.01. 38
far better, | for there the cure lies mainly. 5.02. 8
ho there, doctor! 5.02. 18
what shall we do there, wench? 5.02. 74
what is there else to do? 5.02. 75
content, | if we shall keep our wedding there. 5.02. 76
for there, i will assure you, we shall find 5.02. 77
they are. | you bear a charge there too. 5.02.101
'gainst the which there is | no deafing — but 5.03. 8
pardon me, | if i were there, i'ld wink. 5.03. 18
you must be there; 5.03. 18
there is but envy in that light which shows 5.03. 21
it is much better | i am not there. 5.03. 65
there were no woman | worth so compos'd a man! 5.03. 85
had there such fellows liv'd when you were babes STM II.C 63
sound | when there is no addition but a rebel II.C 118
my country's head | and give the law out there. III 8
look in mine eyeballs, there thy beauty lies; VEN 119
love keeps his revels where there are but twain; 123
foreknowing well, if there he came to lie, | why 245
why, there love liv'd, and there he could not 246
there love liv'd, and there he could not die. 246
sometime he scuds far off, and there he stares, 301
with her the horse, and left adonis there. 322
"for there his smell with others being mingled, 691
and will not let a false sound enter there, 780
there lives a son that suck'd an earthly mother, 863
and there another licking of his wound, 915
and there, all smoth'red up, in shade doth sit, 1035
but by a kiss thought to persuade him there; 1114
there shall not be one minute in an hour 1187
thither, | he makes excuses for his being there. LUC 114
and in this aim there is such thwarting strife 143
then where is truth, if there be no self–trust? 158
there is no hate in loving; 240
night–wand'ring weasels shriek to see him there; 307
auspicious to the hour, | even there he starts; 348
as if between them twain there were no strife, 405
winking, there appears | quick–shifting antics, 458
and lo there falls into thy boundless flood 653
for there it revels, and when that decays, | the 713
she like a wearied lamb lies panting there; 737
she there remains a hopeless castaway; 744
let there bechance him pitiful mischances | to 976
and there we will unfold | to creatures stern, 1146
(and there she stay'd | till after a deep groan) 1275
a thousand lamentable objects there, | in scorn 1373
there might you see the laboring pioner 1380
and from the tow'rs of troy there would appear 1382
and here and there the painter interlaces | pale 1390
there pleading might you see grave nestor stand, 1401
for much imaginary work was there, | conceit 1422
no rightful plea might plead for justice there. 1649
win his heart she touch'd him here and there — PP 4. 7
for his approach that often there had been. 6. 8
in love, | there a nay is plac'd without remove. 17. 8
other help for him i see that there is none. 17.36
and chiefly there | where thy desert may merit 18.14
there is no heaven, /be holy then, | when time 18.45
there will we sit upon the rocks, | and see the 19. 5
there will i make thee a bed of roses, | with a 19. 9
a thorn, | and there sung the dolefull'st ditty, 20.11
number there in love was slain. PHT 28
on | to hideous winter and confounds him there, SON 5. 6
nor draw no lines there with thine antique pen; 19.10
and there reigns love and all love's loving 31. 3
in our two loves there is but one respect, 36. 5
who lead thee in their riot even there | where 41.11
if there be nothing new, but that which is 59. 1
and for this sin there is no remedy, | it is so 62. 3
there lives more life in one of your fair eyes 83.13
for there can live no hatred in thine eye, 93. 5
survey, | if time have any wrinkle graven there; 100.10
and there appears a face | that overgoes my 103. 6
finding the first conceit of love there bred, 108.13
alas, 'tis true i have gone here and there, 110. 1
to be diseas'd ere that there was true needing. 118. 8
and in some perfumes is there more delight 130. 7
and will, thy soul knows, is admitted there; 136. 3
there is such strength and warrantise of skill 150. 7
came there for cure, and this by that i prove: 154.13
if that from him there may be aught applied LC 68
"many there were that did his picture get | to 134
even there resolv'd my reason into tears, 296
there my white stole of chastity i daff'd, 297

THEREABOUT 1 FR 0.0001 REL FR 0 V 1 P
and thereabout of it especially when he speaks HAM 2.02.447 P

THEREABOUTS 3 FR 0.0003 REL FR 2 V 1 P
i will say true — "or thereabouts," set down, AWW 4.03.149 P
be intelligent to me, 'tis thereabouts: WT 1.02.378
ay, are you thereabouts? ANT 3.10. 28

THEREAFTER 1 FR 0.0001 REL FR 0 V 1 P
thereafter as they be, a score of good ewes may 2H4 3.02. 50 P

/THEREAT 1 FR 0.0001 REL FR 1 V 0 P
to his great master, who, /thereat enraged, LR 4.02. 75

THEREAT 2 FR 0.0002 REL FR 2 V 0 P
nor the pomp that may | be thereat gleaned, for WT 4.04.489
and yet detested life not shrink thereat! TIT 3.01.247

THEREBY 27 FR 0.0030 REL FR 21 V 6 P
thereby to find | that which thyself hast now TGV 3.01. 31
well, thereby hangs a tale. WIV 1.04.149 P
death or life | shall thereby be the sweeter. MM 3.01. 6
o, nothing so sure, and thereby all forsworn. LLL 4.03.279
thereby to have defeated you and me: MND 4.01.157
and thereby hangs a tale." AYL 2.07. 28
meaning thereby that grapes were made to eat and 5.01. 35 P
saddles into the dirt, and thereby hangs a tale. SHR 4.01. 58 P
up, that thou thereby | mayst smile at this. TN 4.01. 56
and thereby for sealing | the injury of tongues WT 1.02.337
yet indirection thereby grows direct, | and JN 3.01.276
but little vantage shall i reap thereby; R2 1.03.218
to counterfeit dying, when a man thereby liveth, 1H4 5.04.118 P
as little shall the frenchmen gain thereby. 1H6 5.04.115
heaping confusion on their own heads thereby! 2H6 2.01.183
quitting thee thereby of ten thousand shames, 3.02.218
for thereby is england main'd, and fain to go 4.02.162 P
thereby to see the minutes how they run: 3H6 2.05. 25
thereby to destroy | the volsces whom you serve, COR 5.03.133
which thou shalt thereby reap is such a name 5.03.143
here, | that he thereby may have a likely guess, TIT 2.03.207
and is not careful what they mean thereby, 4.04. 84
thereby shall we shadow | the numbers of our MAC 5.04. 5
o, thereby hangs a tail. OTH 3.01. 8 P
and thereby hangs a tale. TNK 3.03. 41
that thereby beauty's rose might never die, SON 1. 2
and meant thereby | thou shouldst print more, 11.13

/THEREFORE 2 FR 0.0002 REL FR 2 V 0 P
/therefore /no /no, /for /i /resign /to /thee. R2 4.01.202
/empress' /moor, /therefore /i /kill'd /him. TIT 3.02. 67

THEREFORE 654 FR 0.0739 REL FR 497 V 157 P
therefore wast thou | deservedly confin'd into TMP 1.02.360
therefore, my lord — 2.01. 23
therefore bear up and board 'em. 3.02. 2 P
therefore my son i' th' ooze is bedded; 3.03.100
therefore take heed, | as hymen's lamps shall 4.01. 22
therefore speak softly, | all's hush'd as 4.01.206
(whose inward pinches therefore are most strong) 5.01. 77
therefore i am no sheep. TGV 1.01. 88 P
therefore thou art a sheep. 1.01. 92 P
therefore i pray you go. 1.03. 89
now therefore would i have thee to my tutor 3.01. 84
only carry, therefore is she better than a jade. 3.01.277 P
not their fathers, and therefore have no names. 3.01.319 P
salt, and therefore it is more than the salt; 3.01.360 P
therefore it must with circumstance be spoken 3.02. 36
therefore the office is indifferent, | being 3.02. 44
therefore, as you unwind her love from him, 3.02. 51
therefore, sweet proteus, my direction–giver, 3.02. 89
therefore, above the rest, we parley to you: 4.01. 58
of yours, and therefore the gift the greater. 4.04. 58 P
therefore know /thou, for this i entertain thee. 4.04. 70
therefore i know she is about my height. 4.04.164
therefore i pray you stand not to discourse, 5.02. 44
therefore be gone, solicit me no more. 5.04. 40
i claim her not, and therefore she is thine. 5.04.135
therefore precisely, can you carry your good WIV 1.01.230 P
therefore no more turn me to him, sweet nan. 3.04. 2
hold therefore, angelo: MM 1.01. 42
therefore take your honors. 1.01. 52
therefore indeed, my father, | i have on angelo 1.03. 39
therefore i prithee | supply me with the habit, 1.03. 45
dost thou detest her therefore? 2.01. 74 P
therefore your best appointment make with speed, 3.01. 59
therefore prepare yourself to death. 3.01.167 P
therefore fasten your ear on my advisings: 3.01.197 P
therefore you speak unskillfully; 3.02.146 P
and therefore i beseech you | look forward on 4.03. 57
forbear it therefore, give your cause to heaven. 4.03.124
therefore hence away! 4.06. 15
therefore by law thou art condemn'd to die. ERR 1.01. 25
and therefore homeward did they bend their 1.01.117
therefore, merchant, i'll limit thee this day 1.01.150
therefore give out you are of epidamium, | lest 1.02. 1
time himself is bald, and therefore, to the 2.02.107 P
i know thou canst, and therefore see thou do it. 2.02.139
and therefore 'tis high time that i were hence. 3.02.157
therefore make present satisfaction, | or i'll 4.01. 5
were chain'd together, and therefore came not. 4.01. 26
therefore away, to get our stuff aboard. 4.04.158
and therefore let me have him home with me. 5.01.101
therefore depart, and leave him here with me. 5.01.108
therefore, most gracious duke, with thy command 5.01.159
breeds, therefore the sadness is without limit. ADO 1.03. 4 P
therefore i have decreed not to sing in my cage. 1.03. 33 P
therefore i will even take sixpence in earnest 2.01. 39 P
therefore all hearts in love use their own 2.01.177
farewell therefore hero! 2.01.182
therefore your grace may well say i have lost it 2.01.281 P
and therefore certainly it were not good | she 3.01. 57
therefore let benedick, like cover'd fire, 3.01. 77
therefore bear you the lanthorn. 3.03. 24 P
therefore know i have earn'd of don john a 3.03.108 P
therefore i will die a woman with grieving. 4.01.323 P
therefore give me no counsel, | my griefs cry 5.01. 31
and therefore will come. 5.02. 25 P
therefore i will depart unkiss'd. 5.02. 53 P
therefore is it most expedient for the wise, if 5.02. 83 P
and therefore never flout at me for what i have 5.04.107 P
therefore play, music. 5.04.121 P
therefore, brave conquerors — for so you are, LLL 1.01. 8
therefore this article is made in vain, | or 1.01.139
and therefore welcome the sour cup of prosperity 1.01.313 P
and therefore apt, because quick. 1.02. 23 P
their words, and therefore i will say nothing. 1.02.164 P
as another man, and therefore i can be quiet. 1.02.166 P
and therefore too much odds for a spaniard's 1.02.176 P
therefore to 's seemeth it a needful course, 2.01. 25
him to passion, and therefore let's hear it. 4.03.198
therefore of all hands must we be forsworn. 4.03.215
and therefore is she born to make black fair. 4.03.257
and therefore red, that would avoid dispraise, 4.03.260
and therefore, finding barren practicers, 4.03.322
therefore let us devise | some entertainment for 4.03.369
therefore i'll darkly end the argument. 5.02. 23
indeed i weigh not you, and therefore light. 5.02. 26
therefore i do it, and i make no doubt | the 5.02.151
therefore meet. 5.02.237
therefore change favors, and, when they repair, 5.02.292
i will, and therefore keep it. 5.02.442
therefore as he is, an ass, let him go. 5.02.625
form'd by the eye and therefore, like the eye, 5.02.762
therefore, ladies, | our love being yours, the 5.02.770
and therefore met your loves | in their own 5.02.783
full of dear guiltiness, and therefore this: 5.02.791
therefore if you my favor mean to get, | a 5.02.820
therefore, fair hermia, question your desires, MND 1.01. 67

therefore hear me, hermia: 1.01.156
and therefore is wing'd cupid painted blind. 1.01.235
and therefore is love said to be a child, 1.01.238
therefore you must needs play pyramus. 1.02. 88 P
therefore the winds, piping to us in vain, | as 2.01. 88
the ox hath therefore stretch'd his yoke in vain 2.01. 93
therefore the moon, the governess of floods, 2.01.103
therefore pursue me not. 2.01.188
face, | therefore i think i am not in the night, 2.01.222
therefore no marvel though demetrius | do, as a 2.02. 96
should of another therefore be abus'd! 2.02.134
therefore another prologue must tell he is not a 3.01. 34 P
therefore go with me. 3.01.156
and if i could, what should i get therefore? 3.02. 78
here therefore for a while i will remain. 3.02. 83
therefore be out of hope, of question, of doubt; 3.02.279
hie therefore, robin, overcast the night; 3.02.355
love, therefore, and tongue–tied simplicity | in 5.01.104
therefore my merchandise makes me not sad. MV 1.01. 45
of these | that therefore only are reputed wise 1.01. 96
therefore speak. 1.01.160
therefore go forth, | try what my credit can in 1.01.179
it is no mean happiness, therefore, to be seated 1.02. 7 P
therefore the lott'ry that he hath devis'd in 1.02. 28 P
made him, and therefore let him pass for a man. 1.02. 56 P
therefore for fear of the worst, i pray thee set 1.02. 95 P
therefore i pray you lead me to the caskets | to 2.01. 23
therefore be advis'd. 2.01. 42
therefore i part with him, and part with him 2.05. 49
and therefore, like herself, wise, fair, and 2.06. 56
therefore forbear a while. 3.02. 3
therefore then, thou gaudy gold, | hard food for 3.02.101
i'll have my bond, and therefore speak no more. 3.03. 13
therefore he hates me. 3.03. 24
therefore go. 3.03. 31
praising of myself, | therefore no more of it. 3.04. 23
and therefore haste away, | for we must measure 3.04. 83
therefore, i promise you, i fear you. 3.05. 2 P
therefore be a' good cheer, for truly i think 3.05. 5 P
therefore i do beseech you | make no moe offers, 4.01. 80
therefore, jew, | though justice be thy plea, 4.01.197
therefore lay bare your bosom. 4.01.252
therefore prepare thee to cut off the flesh. 4.01.324
down therefore, and beg mercy of the duke. 4.01.363
therefore thou must be hang'd at the state's 4.01.367
you press me far, and therefore i will yield. 4.01.425
therefore the poet | did feign that orpheus drew 5.01. 79
therefore i scant this breathing courtesy. 5.01.141
therefore be well advis'd | how you do leave me 5.01.234
therefore allow me such exercises as may become AYL 1.01. 71 P
therefore he gives them good leave to wander. 1.01.103 P
therefore, out of my love to you, i came hither 1.01.131 P
therefore use thy discretion — i had as lief 1.01.145 P
therefore, my sweet rose, my dear rose, be merry 1.02. 22 P
reputation shall not therefore be mispris'd. 1.02.181 P
doth it therefore ensue that you should love his 1.03. 31 P
therefore devise with me how we may fly, 1.03.100
page, | and therefore look you call me ganymed. 1.03.125
therefore my age is as a lusty winter, | frosty, 2.03. 52
therefore courage, good aliena. 2.04. 7 P
and therefore put i on the countenance | of 2.07.108
and therefore sit you down in gentleness | and 2.07.124
therefore heaven nature charg'd | that one body 3.02.141
verse, and therefore stood lamely in the verse. 3.02.170 P
and therefore i pray the gods make me honest. 3.03. 33 P
is the single man therefore bless'd? 3.03. 58 P
good cause as one would desire, therefore weep. 3.04. 5 P
must you be therefore proud and pitiless? 3.05. 40
therefore beware my censure, and keep your 4.01.195 P
therefore, you clown, abandon — which is in the 5.01. 47 P
therefore tremble and depart. 5.01. 57 P
therefore put you in your best array, bid your 5.02. 71 P
and therefore take the present time, | with a 5.03. 30
a beggar, therefore to beg will not become me. ep 10 P
therefore paucas pallabris, let the world slide. SHR in.1. 5 P
i will therefore tarry in despite of the flesh in.2. 127 P
therefore they thought it good you hear a play, in.2. 134
and therefore, tranio, for the time i study, 1.01. 17
and therefore has he closely mew'd her up, 1.01.183
and therefore frame your manners to the time. 1.01.227
and therefore, if thou know | one rich enough to 1.02. 66
and therefore let me be thus bold with you | to 1.02.104
therefore this order hath baptista ta'en, | that 1.02.126
let specialties be therefore drawn between us, 2.01.126
for dainties are all kates, and therefore, kate, 2.01.189
here's no crab, and therefore look not sour. 2.01.230
and therefore, setting all this chat aside, 2.01.268
therefore ha' done with words; 3.02.116
and therefore here i mean to take my leave. 3.02.188
o, ay, curtis, ay, and therefore fire, fire; 4.01. 19 P
in every office but thine, and therefore fire. 4.01. 36 P
there's fire ready, and therefore, good grumio, 4.01. 39 P
why, therefore fire, for i have caught extreme 4.01. 44 P
all ready; and therefore, i pray thee, news. 4.01. 52 P
and therefore 'tis call'd a sensible tale; 4.01. 64 P
and therefore be not — cock's passion, silence! 4.01.117 P
and therefore frolic, we will hence forthwith, 4.03.182
and therefore, if you say no more than this, 4.04. 43
chance to need thee at home, therefore leave us. 5.01. 3 P
but not frighted me, therefore i'll sleep again. 5.02. 43
therefore a health to all that shot and miss'd. 5.02. 51
and therefore /for assurance | let's each one 5.02. 65
for't a little, though therefore i die a virgin. AWW 1.01.133 P
therefore tell me true, | but tell me then, 'tis 1.03.175
that dwell in't jades, | therefore to th' war! 2.03.285
therefore away, and leave her bravely; 2.03.299
therefore am i found | so much unsettled. 2.05. 62
therefore we marvel much our cousin france 3.01. 7
therefore dare not | say what i think of it, 3.01. 13
therefore we must every one be a man of his own 4.01. 16 P
therefore your oaths | are words and poor 4.02. 29
therefore i'll lie with him | when i am buried. 4.02. 72
therefore once more to this captain dumaine. 4.03.247 P
therefore you must die. 4.03.307 P
and therefore, goaded with most sharp occasions, 5.01. 14
and therefore know how far i may be pitied. 5.03.161
therefore i will not speak what i know. 5.03.265 P
too fine in thy evidence, therefore stand aside. 5.03.269 P
therefore, good youth, address thy gait unto her TN 1.04. 15
bade take away the fool, therefore i say again, 1.05. 53 P
so much, and therefore comes to speak with you. 1.05.141 P
that too, and therefore comes to speak with you. 1.05.144 P
therefore i shall crave of you your leave, that 2.01. 5 P
therefore it charges me in manners the rather to 2.01. 14 P
let us therefore eat and drink. 2.03. 13 P
therefore in my presence still smile, dear my 2.05.176 P
i would therefore my sister had had no name, sir 3.01. 16 P
for that i woo, thou therefore hast no cause; 3.01.154
therefore this letter, being so excellently 3.04.188 P
therefore, if you hold your life at any price, 3.04.230 P
therefore get you on, and give him his desire. 3.04.247 P
therefore on, or strip your sword stark naked; 3.04.250 P
therefore draw, for the supportance of his vow. 3.04.299 P
therefore perpend, my princess, and give ear. 5.01.299 P
and therefore, like a cipher | (yet standing in WT 1.02. 6
therefore mark my counsel, | which must be ev'n 1.02.408
if therefore you dare trust my honesty, | that 1.02.434
therefore proceed. 3.02.108
therefore bring forth, | and in apollo's name, 3.02.117
therefore betake thee | to nothing but despair. 3.02.209
and only therefore | desire to breed by me. 4.04.102
abroad, therefore it behooves men to be wary. 4.04.254 P
therefore, i pray you, | as you have ever been 4.04.492
therefore discase thee instantly (thou must 4.04.633 P
steel, therefore they do not give us the lie. 4.04.725 P
thee thy business, i am therefore no courtier? 4.04.736 P
me as these are, | therefore i will not disdain. 4.04.747
no more such wives, therefore no wife. 5.01. 56
therefore follow me | and mark what way i make. 5.01.232
therefore i keep it | /lonely, apart. 5.03. 17
therefore, good mother, | to whom am i beholding JN 1.01.238
to parley or to fight, therefore prepare. 2.01. 78
for our advantage — therefore hear us first: 2.01.206
with wrongs, and therefore full of fears, | a 3.01. 13
therefore, since law itself is perfect wrong, 3.01.189
therefore to arms! 3.01.255
therefore thy later vows, against thy first, 3.01.288
therefore never, never | must i behold my pretty 3.04. 88
and therefore mark: 3.04.130
therefore i will be sudden, and dispatch. 4.01. 27
therefore, to be possess'd with double pomp, 4.02. 9
therefore 'twere reason you had manners now. 4.03. 31
therefore thy threat'ning colors now wind up, 5.02. 73
therefore commend me; R2 1.02. 71
therefore we banish you our territories. 1.03.139
words are but as thoughts, therefore be bold. 2.01.276
and therefore personally i lay my claim | to my 2.03.135
king, | therefore we will disperse ourselves. 2.04. 4
therefore no dancing, girl, some other sport. 3.04. 9
therefore, friends, | as far as to the sepulchre 1H4 1.01. 18
therefore we meet not now. 1.01. 30
and therefore lost that title of respect | which 1.03. 8
either envy, therefore, or misprision | is 1.03. 27
therefore i say — 1.03.187
jack falstaff, and therefore more valiant, being 2.04.477 P
their date is out, and therefore i'll hide me. 2.04.504 P
than another man, and therefore more frailty. 3.03.167 P
therefore make haste. 4.04. 40
hence therefore, every leader to his charge, 5.01.118
therefore i'll none of it, honor is a mere 5.01.140 P
therefore, good cousin, let not harry know, | in 5.02. 24
therefore i'll make him sure, yea, and i'll 5.04.124 P
therefore, sirrah, with a new wound in your 5.04.127 P
hence therefore, thou nice crutch! 2H4 1.01.145
fire–brand, and therefore i call him her dream. 2.02. 90 P
on, therefore take heed what guests you receive. 2.04. 93 P
therefore captains had need look to't. 2.04.150 P
and therefore will he wipe his tables clean 4.01.199
and therefore be assur'd, my good lord marshal, 4.01.218
therefore be merry, coz, since sudden sorrow 4.02. 83
therefore rouse up fear and trembling, and do 4.03. 14 P
therefore let me have right, and let desert 4.03. 54 P
therefore omit him not, blunt not his love, 4.04. 27
his temper therefore must be well observ'd. 4.04. 36
therefore my grief | stretches itself beyond the 4.04. 56
therefore thou best of gold art /worst /of gold. 4.05.160
therefore, my harry, | be it thy course to busy 4.05.212
therefore i beseech you let him be countenanc'd. 5.01. 51 P
therefore let men take heed of their company. 5.01. 77 P
therefore still bear the balance and the sword, 5.02.103
why then lament therefore. 5.03.108
and therefore we must needs admit the means H5 1.01. 68
therefore take heed how you impawn our person, 1.02. 21
therefore doth heaven divide | the state of man 1.02.183
therefore to france, my liege! 1.02.213
therefore with frank and with uncurbed plainness 1.02.244
he therefore sends you, meeter for your spirit, 1.02.254
and therefore, living hence, did give ourself 1.02.270
therefore, my lords, omit no happy hour | that 1.02.300
therefore let our proportions for these wars 1.02.304
therefore let every man now task his thought, 1.02.309
and doting death is near, | therefore exhale. 2.01. 62
we therefore have great cause of thankfulness, 2.02. 32
get you therefore hence, | poor miserable 2.02.177
he is dead, | and we must ern therefore. 2.03. 6
therefore caveto be thy counsellor. 2.03. 53
therefore the dukes of berri and of britain, 2.04. 4
therefore, i say, 'tis meet we all go forth | to 2.04. 21
therefore in fierce tempest is he coming, | in 2.04. 99
men, and therefore he scorns to say his prayers, 3.02. 37 P
weak stomach, and therefore i must cast it up. 3.02. 53 P
therefore to our best mercy give yourselves, 3.03. 3
therefore, you men of harflew, | take pity of 3.03. 27
therefore, great king, | we yield our town and 3.03. 47
therefore, lord constable, haste on montjoy, 3.05. 61
therefore go speak, the duke will hear thy voice 3.06. 46
why then rejoice therefore. 3.06. 52
bid him therefore consider of his ransom, which 3.06.125 P
go therefore tell thy master here i am; 3.06.153
the greater therefore should our courage be. 4.01. 2
therefore, when he sees reason of fears, as we 4.01.108 P
therefore should every soldier in the wars do as 4.01.178 P
therefore i beseech your highness pardon me. 4.08. 55 P
he could not therefore handle an english cudgel. 5.01. 76 P
and thou must therefore needs prove a good 5.02.205 P
therefore was i created with a stubborn outside, 5.02.226 P
and therefore tell me, most fair katherine, will 5.02.233 P
therefore, queen of all, katherine, break thy 5.02.244 P
therefore patiently and yielding. 5.02.274 P
and therefore tell her i return great thanks, 1H6 2.02. 51
it, | and therefore frame the law unto my will. 2.04. 9
therefore, good uncle, for my father's sake, 2.05. 51
and therefore haste i to the parliament, 2.05.127
that therefore i have forg'd, or am not able 3.01. 12
therefore, my loving lords, our pleasure is 3.01.157
and rulers over roan, | therefore we'll knock. 3.02. 12
return thee therefore with a flood of tears, 3.03. 56
therefore stand up, and for these good deserts 3.04. 25
be packing therefore, thou that wast a knight; 4.01. 46
that any one should therefore be suspicious | i 4.01.153
and therefore, as we hither came in peace, | so 4.01.160
therefore, dear boy, mount on my swiftest horse, 4.05. 9
and therefore are we certainly resolv'd | to 5.01. 37
and therefore to be wooed: 5.03. 78
therefore to be won. 5.03. 79
and therefore take this compact of a truce, 5.04.163
therefore, my lord protector, give consent 5.05. 23
and therefore may be broke without offense. 5.05. 35
and therefore, lords, since he affects her most, 5.05. 59
take therefore shipping, post, my lord, to 5.05. 87
and therefore i will take the nevils' parts, 2H6 1.01.240
therefore i beseech your majesty, do not cast 1.03.201 P
master hume, we are therefore provided. 1.04. 3 P
for purposely therefore | left i the court, to 2.03. 52
and therefore, peter, have at thee with a 2.03. 89 P
and therefore do they cry, though you forbid, 3.02.264
and therefore by his majesty i swear, | whose 3.02.285
therefore bring forth the soldiers of our prize, 4.01. 8
i'll give it, sir, and therefore spare my life. 4.01. 23
and therefore to revenge it shalt thou die, 4.01. 26
therefore, when merchant–like i sell revenge, 4.01. 41
and therefore shall it charm thy riotous tongue. 4.01. 64
therefore come you with us and let him go. 4.01.141
and therefore should we be magistrates. 4.02. 18 P
therefore am i of an honorable house. 4.02. 49 P
therefore yield, or die. 4.02.127
nay, 'tis too true; therefore he shall be king. 4.02.147
therefore deny it not. 4.02.149 P
ay, marry, will we; therefore get ye gone. 4.02.153
can speak french, and therefore he is a traitor. 4.02.167 P
no, no, and therefore we'll have his head. 4.02.173 P
therefore thus will i reward thee: 4.03. 5 P
think therefore on revenge and cease to weep. 4.04. 3
thee, | therefore away with us to killingworth. 4.04. 44
and therefore in this city will i stay | and 4.04. 47
and therefore am i bold and resolute. 4.04. 60
and therefore yet relent, and save my life. 4.07.117
hath my sword therefore broke through london 4.08. 23 P
his is the right, and therefore pardon me. 3H6 1.01.148
they seek revenge, and therefore will not yield. 1.01.190
now you are heir, therefore enjoy it now. 1.02. 12
therefore to arms! 1.02. 28
and therefore fortify your hold, my lord. 1.02. 52
therefore — 1.03. 34
therefore die. 1.03. 47
why, therefore warwick came to seek you out, 2.01.166
out, | and therefore comes my brother montague. 2.01.167
why, that's my fortune too, therefore i'll stay. 2.02. 76
therefore be still. 2.02.122
are at our backs, and therefore hence amain. 2.05.133
therefore i came unto your majesty. 3.02. 41
now therefore be it known to noble lewis, | that 3.03. 23
look therefore, lewis, that by this league and 3.03. 74
therefore, at last, i firmly am resolv'd | you 3.03.219
and therefore i'll uncrown him ere't be long. 3.03.232
therefore delay not, give thy hand to warwick, 3.03.246
therefore, in brief, | tell me their words as 4.01. 89
and therefore i'll uncrown him ere't be long." 4.01.111
now therefore let us hence, and lose no hour, 4.01.148
come therefore let us fly while we may fly, | if 4.04. 34
and chiefly therefore i thank god and thee. 4.06. 17
therefore, that i may conquer fortune's spite 4.06. 19
and therefore i yield thee my free consent. 4.06. 36
therefore, lord oxford, to prevent the worst, 4.06. 96
come therefore, let's about it speedily. 4.06.102
therefore be resolute. 5.04. 61
therefore no more but this: 5.04. 76
therefore, not "good lord." 5.06. 5
and therefore, since i cannot prove a lover | to R3 1.01. 28
therefore be gone. 1.02. 48
but i know none, and therefore am no beast. 1.02. 72
therefore for god's sake entertain good comfort, 1.03. 4
and therefore cannot have the hearts to do it. 1.04.176
never, my lord, therefore prepare to die. 1.04.180
therefore i say with noble buckingham, | that it 2.02.138
and therefore, in mine opinion, cannot have it. 3.01. 52
and therefore is he idle? 3.01.105
therefore he sends to know your lordship's 3.02. 15
therefore — to speak, and to avoid the first, 3.07.151
i am bound by oath, and therefore pardon me. 4.01. 27
therefore take with thee my most grievous curse, 4.04.188
and therefore level not to hit their lives. 4.04.203
therefore present to her — as sometimes 4.04.274
therefore accept such kindness as i can. 4.04.310
therefore, dear mother — i must call you so — 4.04.412
no, my good lord, therefore mistrust me not. 4.04.478
no, my good lord, therefore be patient. 5.01. 2
despair therefore and die! 5.03.120
therefore, for goodness sake, and as you are H8 pr 23
is it therefore | th' ambassador is silenc'd? 1.01. 96
therefore best | not wake him in his slumber. 1.01.121
it shall be therefore bootless | that longer you 2.04. 61
therefore, madam, | it's fit this royal session 2.04. 65
therefore i say again, | i utterly abhor, yea, 2.04. 80
therefore in him | it lies to cure me, and the 2.04.100
therefore go on, | for no dislike i' th' world 2.04.223
that therefore such a writ be sued against you, 3.02.341
kin to me, therefore she's not so fair as helen. TRO 1.01. 74 P
therefore this maxim out of love i teach: 1.02.292
and therefore is the glorious planet sol | in 1.03. 89
therefore 'tis meet achilles meet not hector. 1.03.357
therefore i beat thee. 2.01. 67 P
oft have you (often have you thanks therefore) 3.03. 20

therefore no kiss. 4.05. 39
therefore achilles, but what e'er, know this: 4.05. 77
therefore come back. 5.03. 67
you know me dutiful, therefore, dear sir, | let 5.03. 72
therefore i beseech you, | in sign of what you COR 1.09. 25
therefore be it known, | as to us, to all the 1.09. 58
therefore, for coriolanus neither to care 2.02. 11 P
therefore please you, | most reverend and grave 2.02. 41
you sooth'd not, therefore hurt not; 2.02. 73
therefore follow me, and i'll direct you how you 2.03. 45 P
therefore, beseech you, i may be consul. 2.03.102 P
and therefore give you our voices heartily. 2.03.105 P
therefore let him be consul. 2.03.134 P
your voices therefore." 2.03.170
beat for barking | as therefore kept to do so. 2.03.217
therefore beseech you — | you that will be less 3.01.149
therefore lay hold of him; 3.01.211
and therefore law shall scorn him further trial 3.01.267
therefore it is decreed | he dies to-night. 3.01.287
therefore, most absolute sir, if thou wilt have 4.05.136
therefore i'll watch him | till he be dieted to 5.01. 56
therefore let's hence, | and with our fair 5.01. 73
therefore, fellow, | i must have leave to pass. 5.02. 22
therefore go back. 5.02. 27 P
therefore go back. 5.02. 33 P
therefore back to rome, and prepare for your 5.02. 47 P
therefore be gone. 5.02. 87
may hang upon your hardness, therefore hear us. 5.03. 91
therefore shall he die, | and i'll renew me in 5.06. 47
therefore at your vantage, | ere he express 5.06. 53
and therefore, lovely tamora, queen of goths, TIT 1.01.315
she is a woman, therefore may be woo'd, | she is 2.01. 82
woo'd, | she is a woman, therefore may be won, 2.01. 83
won, | she is lavinia, therefore must be lov'd. 2.01. 84
therefore away with her, and use her as you will 2.03.166
therefore i tell my sorrows to the stones, | who 3.01. 37
and therefore mine shall save my brothers' lives 3.01.166
are meet for plucking up, and therefore mine. 3.01.178
therefore, my lords, it highly us concerns | by 4.03. 27
therefore, great lords, be as your titles 5.01. 5
careful to observe, | therefore i urge thy oath; 5.01. 78
therefore thou shalt vow | by that same god, 5.01. 81
thou hast the odds of me, therefore no more. 5.02. 19
i am, therefore come down and welcome me. 5.02. 43
therefore called so | 'cause they take vengeance 5.02. 62
name, | and therefore bind them, gentle publius. 5.02.157
and now i find it, therefore bind them sure, 5.02.160
and therefore do we what we are commanded. 5.02.163
please you, therefore, draw nigh and take your 5.03. 24
therefore, if thou art mov'd, thou run'st away. ROM 1.01. 10 P
'tis true, and therefore women, being the weaker 1.01. 15 P
therefore i will push montague's men from the 1.01. 16 P
therefore be patient, take no note of him; 1.05. 71
therefore thy kinsmen are no stop to me. 2.02. 69
and therefore thou mayest think my behavior 2.02. 99
therefore pardon me, | and not impute this 2.02.104
therefore thy earliness doth me assure | thou 2.03. 39
and therefore, if you should deal double with 2.04.168 P
therefore do nimble-pinion'd doves draw love, 2.05. 7
and therefore hath the wind-swift cupid wings. 2.05. 8
therefore love moderately: 2.06. 14
therefore farewell, i see thou knowest me not. 3.01. 65
that thou hast done me, therefore turn and draw. 3.01. 67
therefore use none. 3.01.194
therefore we'll have some half a dozen friends, 3.04. 27
therefore stay yet, thou need'st not to be gone. 3.05. 16
therefore have done. 3.05. 72
and therefore have i little /talk'd of love, 4.01. 7
therefore, out of thy long-experienc'd time, 4.01. 60
therefore he that cannot lick his fingers goes 4.02. 7 P
in dear employment — therefore hence be gone. 5.03. 32
i must indeed, and therefore came i hither. 5.03. 58
therefore he will be, timon. TIM 1.01.129
th' art an athenian, therefore welcome. 1.02. 36 P
thou art a soldier, therefore seldom rich, | it 1.02.222
therefore be abhorr'd | all feasts, societies, 4.03. 20
therefore, 'tis not amiss | we tender our loves 5.01. 11
lord, but therefore | came not my friend nor i. 5.01. 78
therefore so please thee to return with us, 5.01.159
therefore, timon — 5.01.167
therefore i will, sir, thus: 5.01.168
but let not therefore my good friends be griev'd JC 1.02. 43
therefore, good brutus, be prepar'd to hear; 1.02. 66
and therefore are they very dangerous. 1.02.210
therefore it is meet | that noble minds keep 1.02.310
and therefore think him as a serpent's egg, 2.01. 32
therefore thou sleep'st so sound. 2.01.233
therefore i took your hands, but was indeed 3.01.218
therefore 'tis certain he was not ambitious. 3.02.113
therefore let our alliance be combin'd, | our 4.01. 43
and chastisement doth therefore hide his head. 4.03. 16
therefore our everlasting farewell take: 5.01.115
fly therefore, noble cassius, fly far off. 5.03. 11
come therefore, and to /thasos send his body; 5.03.104
and therefore cawdor | shall sleep no more — MAC 2.02. 39
therefore much drink may be said to be an 2.03. 30 P
therefore to horse, | and let us not be dainty 2.03.143
therefore i have entreated him along | with us HAM 1.01. 26
therefore our sometime sister, now our queen, 1.02. 8
and therefore must his choice be circumscrib'd 1.03. 22
and therefore as a stranger give it welcome. 1.05.165
therefore, /since brevity is the soul of wit, 2.02. 90
therefore no more, but to the matter: 3.02.324 P
therefore prepare you. 3.03. 2
therefore prepare thyself, | the bark is ready, 4.03. 43
therefore this project | should have a back or 4.07.152
poor ophelia, | and therefore i forbid my tears. 4.07.186
give it start again, | therefore let's follow. 4.07.194
thee she is, therefore make her grave straight. 5.01. 3 P
lie out on't, sir, and therefore 'tis not yours; 5.01.123 P
dead, not for the quick, therefore thou liest. 5.01.126 P
since he is /better'd, we have therefore odds. 5.02.263
therefore beseech you | t' avert your liking a LR 1.01.210
therefore be gone, | without our grace, our love 1.01.264
therefore i pray you | that to our sister you do 2.04.150
i have no way, and therefore want no eyes; 4.01. 18
therefore great france | my mourning and 4.04. 25
therefore i do advise you take this note: 4.05. 29
therefore, thou happy father, | think that the 4.06. 72
i therefore apprehend and do attach thee | for OTH 1.02. 77
and therefore little shall i grace my cause | in 1.03. 88
i therefore vouch again | that with some 1.03.103
you must therefore be content to slubber the 1.03.226 P
most humbly therefore bending to your state, | i 1.03.235
i therefore beg it not | to please the palate of 1.03.261
therefore put money in thy purse. 1.03.352 P
therefore make money. 1.03.358 P
therefore my hopes (not surfeited to death) 2.01. 50
who let us not therefore blame. 2.03. 15 P
therefore be merry, cassio, | for thy solicitor 3.03. 26
therefore these stops of thine fright me the 3.03.120
therefore, as i am bound, | receive it from me. 3.03.195
wit, and therefore i will attempt the doing it. 3.04. 22 P
most veritable, therefore look to't well. 3.04. 76
therefore be double damn'd: 4.02. 37
therefore, good emilia, | give me my nightly 4.03. 15
supp'd at my house, but i therefore shake not. 5.01.119
therefore confess thee freely of thy sin; 5.02. 53
is come from caesar, therefore hear it, antony. ANT 1.01. 27
therefore, dear isis, keep decorum, and fortune 1.02. 73 P
hence, | therefore be deaf to my unpitied folly, 1.03. 98
wrong this presence, therefore speak no more. 2.02.109
therefore, o antony, stay not by his side. 2.03. 19
therefore | make space enough between you. 2.03. 23
and therefore have we | our written purposes 2.06. 3
i have lost command, | therefore i pray you. 3.11. 24
i dare him therefore | to lay his gay 3.13. 25
the scars upon your honor, therefore, he | does 3.13. 58
in our name, | are therefore to be pitied. 5.02.179
therefore be cheer'd, | make not your thoughts 5.02.184
and therefore banish'd) is a creature such | as, CYM 1.01. 19
therefore i shall beseech you, if you please 1.06.205
you are a fool granted, therefore your issues, 2.01. 46 P
our good deed, | though rome be therefore angry. 3.01. 58
it fits us therefore ripely | our chariots and 3.05. 22
i love her therefore, but | disdaining me and 3.05. 74
the hazard therefore due fall on me by | the 4.04. 46
therefore, good heavens, | hear patiently my 5.01. 21
and therefore instantly this prince must die, PER 1.01.148
therefore, my lord, go travel for a while, 1.02.106
therefore to make his entrance more sweet, 2.03. 64
therefore each one betake him to his rest; 2.03.114
therefore look to it. 2.05. 39
therefore hear you, mistress, either frame 2.05. 81
therefore briefly yield 'er, for she must 3.01. 52 P
therefore let's have fresh ones, what e'er we 4.02. 10 P
therefore, if in our youths we could pick up 4.02. 32 P
therefore say what a paragon she is, and thou 4.02.140 P
therefore the earth, fearing to be o'erflowed, 4.04. 40
therefore i will make them acquainted with your 4.06.197 P
therefore, sir, | as i shall here make trial of TNK 1.01.192
therefore we must | with him stand to the mercy 1.02.101
therefore none but arcite | in this kind is so 3.01. 91
therefore this blest morning | shall be the last 3.06. 13
therefore, most modest queen, | he of the two 5.01.157
therefore no marvel though thy horse be gone. VEN 390
"and therefore hath she brib'd the destinies 733
"therefore, despite of fruitless chastity, 751
green, | therefore, in sadness, now i will away; 807
"and therefore would he put his bonnet on, 1087
therefore that praise which collatine doth owe LUC 82
who, therefore angry, seems to part in sunder, 388
and therefore would they still in darkness be, 752
and therefore now i need not fear to die. 1052
and therefore still in night would cloist'red be 1085
and therefore are they form'd as marble will; 1241
and therefore lucrece swears he did her wrong, 1462
therefore i'll lie with love, and love with me, PP 1.13
o, therefore, love, be of thyself so wary | as i SON 22. 9
gentle thou art, and therefore to be won, 41. 5
beauteous thou art, therefore to be assailed; 41. 6
therefore desire (of /perfect'st love being made 51.10
therefore are feasts so solemn and so rare, 52. 5
and therefore mayest without attaint o'erlook 82. 2
and therefore art enforc'd to seek anew | some 82. 7
and therefore to your fair no painting set; 83. 2
and therefore have i slept in your report, 83. 5
therefore in that i cannot know thy change. 93. 6
therefore, like her, i sometime hold my tongue, 102.13
therefore my verse, to constancy confin'd, | one 105. 7
therefore to give them from me was i bold, | to 122.11
and therefore we admire | what thou dost foist 123. 5
therefore my mistress' eyes are raven black, 127. 9
therefore i lie with her, and she with me, | and 138.13
and therefore from my face she turns my foes, 139.11
/THEREIN 1 FR 0.0001 REL FR 1 V 0 P
/me /that /glass, /and /therein /will /i /read. R2 4.01.276
THEREIN 62 FR 0.0070 REL FR 53 V 9 P
and my father's precepts | i therein do forget. TMP 3.01. 59
thou lov'st, love still, and thrive therein, TGV 1.01. 9
my youthful travel therein made me happy, | or 4.01. 34
since therein she doth evitate and shun | a WIV 5.05.228
you are therein in the right. MM 2.01. 96 P
therein do men from children nothing differ. ADO 5.01. 33
for pyramus therein doth kill himself. MND 5.01. 67
which therein works a miracle in nature, MV 3.02. 90
and therein do account myself well paid. 4.01.417
pride | that can therein tax any private party? AYL 2.07. 71
but therein suits | his folly to the mettle of 2.07. 81
and therein wealthiest | that i protest i simply AWW 2.03. 66
nor are you therein, by my life, deceiv'd, | you TN 5.01.262
in my serious trust | and therein negligent; WT 1.02.247
and my profit therein the heaping friendships. 4.02. 19 P
that makes himself (but for our honor therein) 4.04.436
and therein am i constant to my profession. 4.04.682 P
(our part therein we banish with yourselves) R2 1.03.181
and therein fasting, hast thou made me gaunt. 2.01. 81
and, therein laid — there lies | two kinsmen 3.03.168
for therein should we read | the very bottom and 1H4 4.01. 49
work your thoughts, and therein see a siege; H5 3.pr. 25
town, | placing therein some expert officers, 1H6 3.02.127
and therein reverenc'd for their lawful king. 5.04.140
therein thou wrong'st thy children mightily. 3H6 3.02. 74
ay, therein clarence shall not want his part. 4.06. 57
and then deny her aiding hand therein | and lay R3 1.03. 95
he is my son — ay, and therein my shame, | yet 2.02. 29
his gracious pleasure any way therein. 3.04. 17
and am /glad | to have you therein my companion. H8 3.02.143
and obedient subject is | therein illustrated; 3.02.181
soon bring his particulars therein to a total. TRO 1.02.114 P
i therein would have found issue. COR 1.03. 21 P
do not flatter, and | therein behold themselves. 3.01. 68
though therein you can never be too noble, | but 3.02. 40
his hate, | and therein show'd like enemies. 4.06.114
and therein, hellish dog, thou hast undone her. TIT 4.02. 77
doubting your present assistance therein. TIM 3.01. 20 P
therein, ye gods, you make the weak most strong; JC 1.03. 91
therein, ye gods, you tyrants do defeat; 1.03. 92
therein our letters do not well agree; 4.03.176
therein the patient | must minister to himself. MAC 5.03. 45
safety and allowance | as therein are set down. HAM 2.02. 80
comforting therein, that when old robes are worn ANT 1.02.164 P
though you be therein curious, the least cause 3.02. 35
sir, you therein throw away | the absolute 3.07. 41
the heav'ns, and therein stuck | a sun and moon, 5.02. 79
senseless linen, happier therein than i! CYM 1.03. 7
you are a friend, and therein the wiser. 1.04.134 P
tends, | and therein you are senseless. 2.03. 53
therein false strook, can take no greater wound, 3.04.114
therein i must play the workman. 4.01. 6 P
therein | he was as calm as virtue) he began 5.05.173
we give, and therein may | use honor with you. PER 3.01. 25
if neglection | should therein make me vile, the 3.03. 21
thebes, | and therein wretched, although free. TNK 3.01. 27
being therein train'd | and of kind manage; 5.04. 68
and therein heartens up his servile powers, LUC 295
and therein so ensconc'd his secret evil, | that 1515
sun | delights to peep, to gaze therein on thee. SON 24.12
so dost thou too, and therein dignified. 101. 4
and therein show'st | thy lovers withering as 126. 3
THEREOF 40 FR 0.0045 REL FR 36 V 4 P
only, in lieu thereof, dispatch me hence. TGV 2.07. 88
and thereof comes the proverb: 3.01.304 P
wife | disburse the sum on the receipt thereof. ERR 4.01. 38
and thereof comes that the wenches say, "god 4.03. 53 P
and thereof came it that the man was mad. 5.01. 68
and thereof comes it that his head is light. 5.01. 72
thereof the raging fire of fever bred, | and 5.01. 75
sir, the contempts thereof are as touching me. LLL 1.01.190 P
and, in lieu thereof, impose on thee nothing but 3.01.129 P
since all the power thereof it doth apply | to 5.02. 77
with demetrius thought to have spoke thereof; MND 1.01.112
behove my knowledge | thereof to be inform'd, WT 1.02.396
thereof most worthy, were i the fairest youth 4.04.373
let king cophetua know the truth thereof. 2H4 5.03.102
i'll turn my part thereof into thy throat. 1H6 2.04. 79
even to affright thee with the view thereof. 2H6 5.01.207
the hope thereof makes clifford mourn in steel. 3H6 1.01. 58
lest in revenge thereof, sith god is just, | he 1.03. 41
but god he knows thy share thereof is small. 1.04.129
the want thereof makes thee abominable. 1.04.133
the bruit thereof will bring you many friends. 4.07. 64
far be it from my heart, the thought thereof! R3 1.03.149
in me | that i enjoy, being the queen thereof. 1.03.153
a little joy enjoys the queen thereof, | for i 1.03.154
my part thereof that i have done to her. 1.03.307
god pardon them that are the cause thereof! 1.03.314
the benefit thereof is always granted | to those 3.01. 48
forward | upon his party for the gain thereof; 3.02. 47
which by the sign thereof was termed so. 3.05. 79
take on his grace the sovereignty thereof, | but 3.07. 79
his grace not being warn'd thereof before: 3.07. 86
but the respects thereof are nice and trivial, 3.07.175
from all the impure blots and stains thereof; 3.07.234
the least of you shall share his part thereof. 5.03.268
and i will give a taste thereof forthwith | to TRO 1.03.387
it, | that romeo should, upon receipt thereof, ROM 3.05. 98
as my great power thereof may give thee sense, HAM 4.03. 59
she dares not thereof make discovery, | lest he LUC 1314
and in the praise thereof spends all his might, SON 80. 3
for maiden-tongu'd he was, and thereof free; LC 100
THEREON 8 FR 0.0009 REL FR 8 V 0 P
thereon dependant, for your brother's life — MM 5.01.406
can you still dream and pore and thereon look? LLL 4.03.294
own mouth — thereon | his execution sworn. WT 1.02.445
thereon i pawn my credit and mine honor. 3H6 3.03.116
thereon engrave | "edward" and "york"; R3 4.04.272
and be not from his reason fall'n thereon, | let HAM 2.02.165
i'll guard them from | if thereon you rely. ANT 5.02.133
who, if it wink, shall thereon fall and die. LUC 1139
/THERE'S 2 FR 0.0002 REL FR 1 V 1 P
and cheese /and /there's /the /humor /of /it. WIV 2.01.136 P
/there's /for /thyself, /and /that's /for TIT 3.02. 74
THERE'S 413 FR 0.0466 REL FR 245 V 168 P
tell your piteous heart | there's no harm done. TMP 1.02. 15
but there's more work. 1.02.238
there's wood enough within. 1.02.314
forth, i say, there's other business for thee. 1.02.315
there's nothing ill can dwell in such a temple. 1.02.458
of that there's none, or little. 2.01. 52 P
distinctly, | there's meaning in thy snores. 2.01.218
they say there's but five upon this isle: 3.02. 5 P
there's something else to do. 4.01.126
there's another garment for't. 4.01.244 P
there's not a hair on 's head but 'tis a TGV 3.01.191 P
there's some great matter she'ld employ me in. 4.03. 3
ay, there's the point, sir. WIV 1.01.222 P
there's pippins and cheese to come. 1.02. 12 P
hold, there's money for thee. 1.04.155 P
go to then, there's sympathy. 2.01. 7 P
then there's more sympathy. 2.01. 8 P
there's the short and the long. 2.01.132 P
there's my purse, i am yet thy debtor. 2.02.132 P
there's one master /brook below would fain speak 2.02.144 P
rogue's coffer, and there's my harvest-home. 2.02.275 P
believe me, there's no such thing in me. 3.03. 67 P
let that persuade thee there's something 3.03. 69 P
there's for thy pains. 3.04.100
there's a hole made in your best coat, master 3.05.141 P
and there's her thrumm'd hat and her muffler too 4.02. 78 P
o you panderly rascals, there's a knot, a /ging, 4.02.117 P
there's his chamber, his house, his castle, his 4.05. 6 P

there's an old woman, a fat woman, gone up into 4.05. 11 P
there's not a soldier of us all, that, in the MM 1.02. 14 P
there's one yonder arrested and carried to 1.02. 60 P
but there's a woman with maid by him. 1.02. 92 P
and there's madam juliet. 1.02.115 P
the death of claudio — | but there's no remedy. 2.01.281
ay, touch him; there's the vein. 2.02. 70
there's many have committed it. 2.02. 89
there's some in hope. 4.02. 78
there's other of our friends | will greet us 4.05. 12
(as i have heard him swear himself there's one 5.01.510
there's more behind that is more gratulate. 5.01.529
there's none but asses will be bridled so. ERR 2.01. 14
there's nothing situate under heaven's eye | but 2.01. 16
in good time — there's a time for all things. 2.02. 65 P
there's no time for a man to recover his hair 2.02. 72 P
but there's many a man hath more hair than wit. 2.02. 82 P
without a fin, there's a fowl without a feather: 3.01. 82
you, to the porpentine, | for there's the house. 3.01.117
there's none but witches do inhabit here, | and 3.02.156
there's no man is so vain | that would refuse so 3.02.180
there's a bark of epidamium | that stays but 4.01. 85
go, dromio, there's the money, bear it straight, 4.02. 63
there's not a man i meet but doth salute me | as 4.03. 1
they never meet but there's a skirmish of wit ADO 1.01. 63 P
there's her cousin, and she were not possess'd 1.01.190 P
graces will appear, and there's an end. 2.01.124 P
and then there's a partridge wing sav'd, for the 2.01.149 P
there's little of the melancholy element in her, 2.01.342 P
there's not a note of mine that's worth the 2.03. 55
to dinner" — there's a double meaning in that. 2.03.258 P
there's no true drop of blood in him to be truly 3.02. 18 P
turk, there's no more sailing by the star. 3.04. 57 P
there's goodly catching of cold. 3.04. 65 P
there's a double tongue, there's two tongues." 5.01.169 P
there's a double tongue, there's two tongues." 5.01.169 P
by my troth, there's one meaning well suited. 5.01.225 P
there's for thy pains. 5.01.317 P
there's not one wise man among twenty that will 5.02. 73 P
there's villainy abroad; LLL 1.01.188 P
there's the moral. 3.01. 86 P
there's thy guerdon; 3.01.169
there's no such sport as sport by sport 5.02.153
there's half a dozen sweets. 5.02.234
there's an eye | wounds like a leaden sword. 5.02.480
there's something tells me (but it is not love) MV 3.02. 4
he tells me flatly there's no mercy for me in 3.05. 32 P
shylock, there's thrice thy money off'red thee. 4.01.227
there's more depends on this than on the value. 4.01.434
tell him there's a post come from my master, 5.01. 46 P
there's not the smallest orb which thou 5.01. 60
double self, | and there's an oath of credit. 5.01.246
there's no news at the court, sir, but the old AYL 1.01. 98 P
thou art thy father's daughter, there's enough. 1.03. 58
there's no clock in the forest. 3.02.300 P
there's a girl goes before the priest, and 4.01.139 P
house doth keep itself, | there's none within. 4.03. 82
you say, there's small choice in rotten apples. SHR 1.01.134 P
there's fire ready, and therefore, good grumio, 4.01. 39 P
ay, there's the villainy. 4.03.144 P
why, there's a wench! 5.02.180
there's little can be said in't, 'tis against AWW 1.01.135 P
if one be good, | there's yet one good in ten." 1.03. 79
there's something in't | more than my father's 1.03.242
there's honor in the theft. 2.01. 34
my lord, there's one arriv'd, | if you will see 2.01. 79
there's a simple putting off. 2.02. 41 P
there's one grape yet; 2.03. 99 P
lord and master's married, there's news for you. 2.03.243 P
there's letters from my mother; 2.03.276
why, these balls bound, there's noise in it. 2.03.297
there's nothing here that is too good for him 3.02. 80
of enjoin'd penitents | there's four or five, to 3.05. 95
there's place and means for every man alive. 4.03.339
hold thee, there's my purse. 4.05. 44 P
faith, there's a dozen of 'em, with delicate 4.05.104 P
there's a cardecue for you. 5.02. 32 P
so there's my riddle: 5.03.303
for saying so, there's gold. TN 1.02. 18
tut, there's life in't, man. 1.03.111 P
there's one at the gate. 1.05.125 P
there's a testril of me too. 2.03. 33 P
there's for thy pains. 2.04. 67
hold, there's expenses for thee. 3.01. 43 P
i warrant there's vinegar and pepper in't. 3.04.144 P
there's something in me that reproves my fault; 3.04.203
there's no remedy, sir, he will fight with you 3.04.296 P
sir andrew, there's no remedy, the gentleman 3.04.305 P
but there's no remedy, i shall answer it. 3.04.333
hold, there's half my coffer. 3.04.347
in nature there's no blemish but the mind; 3.04.367
there's money for thee. 4.01. 19
now, sir, have i met you again? there's for you. 4.01. 24 P
why, there's for thee, and there, and there. 4.01. 26
there's something in't | that is deceivable. 4.03. 20
shalt not be the worse for me, there's gold. 5.01. 27 P
there's another. 5.01. 35 P
h'as hurt me, and there's th' end on't. 5.01.196 P
nay, there's comfort in't, | whiles other men WT 1.02.196
physic for't there's none. 1.02.200
there's some ill planet reigns; 2.01.105
there's not a grain of it the face to sweeten 2.01.156
there's no virtue whipt out of the court. 4.03. 91 P
sirs, | for you there's rosemary and rue; 4.04. 74
there's scarce a maid westward but she sings it. 4.04.289 P
there's no disjunction to be made, but by | (as 4.04.529
(thou must think there's a necessity in't) and 4.04.634 P
be the worst, yet hold thee, there's some boot. 4.04.636 P
there's magic in thy majesty, which has | my 5.03. 39
there's time enough for that; 5.03.128
james, | there's toys abroad; JN 1.01.232
there's a good mother, boy, that blots thy 2.01.132
there's a good grandame, boy, that would blot 2.01.133
there's a good grandame. 2.01.163
there's law and warrant, lady, for my curse. 3.01.184
there's nothing in this world can make me joy: 3.04.107
there's few or none do know me; 4.03. 3
so it be new, there's no respect how vile — R2 2.01. 25
what will ensue hereof, there's none can tell; 2.01.212
there's neither honesty, manhood, nor good 1H4 1.02.139 P
there's a franklin in the wild of kent hath 2.01. 54 P
there's money of the king's coming down the hill 2.02. 54 P
there's enough to make us all. 2.02. 58 P
two arrant cowards, there's no equity stirring. 2.02.100 P
there's no more valor in that poins than in a 2.02.101 P
there's villainous news abroad. 2.04.333 P
i think there's no man speaks better welsh. 3.01. 49
ball of wildfire, there's no purchase in money. 3.03. 40 P
there's neither faith, truth, nor womanhood in 3.03.110 P
there's no more faith in thee than in a stew'd 3.03.112 P
but, sirrah, there's no room for faith, truth, 3.03.153 P
there's not a shirt and a half in all my company 4.02. 42 P
there's honor for you! 5.03. 32 P
there's not three of my hundred and fifty left 5.03. 36 P
there's that will sack a city. 5.03. 53 P
honor comes unlook'd for, and there's an end. 5.03. 61 P
yea, marry, there's the point! 2H4 1.03. 18
humors, there's not a better wench in england. 2.01.148 P
there's a letter for you. 2.02.100 P
say, "there's some of the king's blood spilt." 2.02.113 P
there's for your silence. 2.02.161 P
there's a whole merchant's venture of burdeaux 2.04. 63 P
a' my word, captain, there's none such here. 2.04.176 P
there's no more conceit in him than is in a 2.04.241 P
hold, there's a tester for thee. 3.02.276 P
there's never none of these demure boys come to 4.03. 90 P
there's a merry heart! 5.03. 23 P
there's a dish of leather–coats for you. 5.03. 41 P
there's one pistol come from the court with news 5.03. 80 P
from the court, i take it there's but two ways, 5.03.110 P
but there's a saying very old and true, | "if H5 1.02.166
there's nought in france | that can be with a 1.02.251
and there's an end. 2.01. 10 P
and — pauca, there's enough too! 2.01. 79
there's not, i think, a subject | that sits in 2.02. 26
in peace there's nothing so becomes a man | as 3.01. 3
there's for thy labor, montjoy. 3.06.158
there's five to one; 4.03. 4
there's not a piece of feather in our host — 4.03.112
'tis certain there's not a boy left alive, and 4.07. 5 P
be not amaz'd, there's nothing hid from me; 1H6 1.02. 68
there's none protector of the realm but i. 1.03. 12
well then, alone (since there's no remedy) | i 2.02. 57
there's reason he should be displeas'd at it. 2H6 1.01.155
there's two of you, the devil make a third, 3.02.303
for there's no better sign of a brave mind than 4.02. 19 P
there's best's son, the tanner of wingham — 4.02. 21 P
ay, there's the question; 4.02.141
there's an army gather'd together in smithfield. 4.06. 11 P
there's thy reward, be gone. 3H6 3.03.233
us, | that there's no hop'd–for mercy with the 5.04. 35
and there's for twitting me with perjury. 5.05. 40
there's no doubt his majesty | will soon recover R3 1.03. 1
there's many a gentle person made a jack. 1.03. 72
there's nothing differs but the outward fame. 1.04. 83
there's few or none will entertain it. 1.04.131 P
there's some conceit or other likes him well, 3.04. 49
i think there's never a man in christendom | can 3.04. 51
there's none else by. 5.03.182
there's in him stuff that puts him to these ends H8 1.01. 58
or proclaim | there's difference in no persons. 1.01.139
ah ha, | there's mischief in this man. 1.02.187
there's something more would out of thee; 1.02.202
there's his period, | to sheathe his knife in us 1.02.209
going, | for sure there's no converting of 'em. 1.03. 43
there's fresher air, my lord, | in the next 1.04.101
there's my creed. 2.02. 50
believe me, there's an ill opinion spread then, 2.02.124
for living murmurers | there's places of rebuke. 2.02.131
there's nothing i have done yet, o' my 3.01. 30
there's order given for her coronation. 3.02. 46
for him, | there's more in't than fair visage. 3.02. 88
know | there's none stands under more calumnious 5.01.112
'tis well there's one above 'em yet. 5.02. 27
by holy mary, butts, there's knavery. 5.02. 33
there's some of ye, i see, | more out of malice 5.02.179
there's a trim rabble let in. 5.03. 71
and there's troilus will not come far behind him TRO 1.02. 56 P
o jupiter, there's no comparison. 1.02. 62 P
there's a fellow! 1.02.200 P
there's a brave man, niece. 1.02.200 P
there's a countenance! 1.02.202 P
look you there, there's no jesting; 1.02.206 P
there's laying on, take't off who will, as they 1.02.206 P
there's a man, niece! 1.02.228 P
there's ulysses and old nestor, whose wit was 2.01.104 P
there's for you, patroclus. 2.01.116 P
there's not the meanest spirit on our party 2.02.156
then there's achilles, a rare enginer! 2.03. 7 P
sodden business! there's a stew'd phrase indeed! 3.01. 41 P
hark, there's one up. 4.02. 18
there's all the reach of it. 4.04.108
thou, trumpet, there's my purse. 4.05. 6
there's language in her eye, her cheek, her lip, 4.05. 55
there's many a greek and troyan dead | since 4.05.214
but there's more in me than thou understand'st. 4.05.240
and there's all the love they bear us. COR 1.01. 85 P
they say there's grain enough? 1.01.196
and, i think, there's one at home for you. 2.01.109 P
yes certain, there's a letter for you, i saw't. 2.01.113 P
in troth, there's wondrous things spoke of him. 2.01.137 P
two i' th' thigh — there's nine that i know. 2.01.151 P
only | there's one thing wanting, which i doubt 2.01.201
in that there's comfort. 2.01.226
there's in all two worthy voices begg'd. 2.03. 80 P
there's some among you have beheld me fighting; 3.01.223
there's no remedy, | unless, by not so doing, 3.02. 26
there's no more to be said, but he is banish'd 3.03.117
things as you, i can scarce think there's any, 5.02.103 P
there's no man in the world | more bound to 's 5.03.158
whilst | 'twixt you there's difference; 5.06. 17
why, there's the privilege your beauty bears. TIT 4.02.116
yet there's as little justice as at land. 4.03. 9
and, sith there's no justice in earth nor hell, 4.03. 50
to effect, | there's not a god left unsolicited. 4.03. 61
there's not a hollow cave or lurking–place, | no 5.02. 35
there's meed for meed, death for a deadly deed! 5.03. 66
women may fall, when there's no strength in men. ROM 2.03. 80
there's a french salutation to your french slop. 2.04. 44 P
there's no trust, | no faith, no honesty in men, 3.02. 85
there's a fearful point! 4.03. 32
it doth so, holy sir, and there's my master, 5.03.128
and there's none | can truly say he gives if he TIM 1.02. 10
there's much example for't: 1.02. 46 P
this and my food are equals, there's no odds; 1.02. 60
bleeding new, my lord, there's no meat like 'em; 1.02. 78 P
there's the fool hangs on your back already. 2.02. 54 P
there's not so much left to furnish out | a 3.04.114
there's nothing level in our cursed natures 4.03. 19
there's gold to pay thy soldiers, | make large 4.03.127
there's more gold. 4.03.164
there's a medlar for thee, eat it. 4.03.304 P
there's more gold. 4.03.445
there's never a one of you but trusts a knave 5.01. 93
there's gold; 5.01.112
there's payment, hence! 5.01.113
there's not a whittle in th' unruly camp | but i 5.01.180
then there's my glove; 5.04. 54
but there's no heed to be taken of them; JC 1.02.273 P
there's a bargain made. 1.03.120
there's two or three of us have seen strange 1.03.138
might change his nature, there's the question. 2.01. 13
but there's but one in all doth hold his place. 3.01. 65
there's not a nobler man in rome than antony. 3.02.116
there's no art | to find the mind's construction MAC 1.04. 11
there's husbandry in heaven, | their candles are 2.01. 4
there's no such thing: 2.01. 47
there's one did laugh in 's sleep, and one cried 2.02. 20
instant, | there's nothing serious in mortality: 2.03. 93
where we are, | there's daggers in men's smiles; 2.03.140
there's warrant in that theft | which steals 2.03.145
which steals itself, when there's no mercy left. 2.03.146
there's comfort yet, they are assailable. 3.02. 39
there's but one down; the son is fled. 3.03. 20
there's blood upon thy face. 3.04. 13
there's not a one of them but in his house | i 3.04.130
but there's no bottom, none, | in my 4.03. 60
there's knocking at the gate. 5.01. 66 P
there's never a villain dwelling in all denmark HAM 1.05.123
there's no offense, my lord. 1.05.135
ay, there's the rub, | for in that sleep of 3.01. 64
there's the respect | that makes calamity of so 3.01. 67
there's something in his soul | o'er which his 3.01.164
then there's hope a great man's memory may 3.02.131 P
there's letters seal'd, and my two schoolfellows 3.04.202
there's matter in these sighs, these profound 4.01. 1
says she hears | there's tricks i' th' world, 4.05. 5
there's such divinity doth hedge a king | that 4.05.124
there's rosemary, that's for remembrance; 4.05.175 P
there's fennel for you, and columbines. 4.05.180 P
there's rue for you, and here's some for me; 4.05.181 P
there's a daisy. 4.05.184 P
there's a letter for you, sir — it came from 4.06. 9 P
there's another. 5.01. 98 P
us | there's a divinity that shapes our ends, 5.02. 10
there's the cunning of it. LR 1.02. 59 P
there's son against father: 1.02.110 P
there's father against child. 1.02.111 P
pray ye go, there's my key. 1.02.170 P
there's a great abatement of kindness appears as 1.04. 60 P
i thank thee, there's earnest of thy service. 1.04. 94 P
there's mine, beg another of thy daughters. 1.04.108 P
to teach thee there's no laboring i' th' winter. 2.04. 68 P
men, and there's not a nose among twenty but can 2.04. 70 P
for many miles about | there's scarce a bush. 2.04.302
there's your press–money. 4.06. 86 P
there's my gauntlet, i'll prove it on a giant. 4.06. 90 P
there's hell, there's darkness, | there is the 4.06.127
there's hell, there's darkness, | there is the 4.06.127
there's money for thee. 4.06.131
then there's life in't. 4.06.202 P
there's my exchange. 5.03. 97
why, there's no remedy. OTH 1.01. 35
there's no composition in /these news | that 1.03. 1
there's one gone to the harbor? 2.01.120
there's none so foul and foolish thereunto, 2.01.141
there's a poor piece of gold for thee. 3.01. 23 P
tell her there's one cassio entreats her a 3.01. 25 P
nay, yet there's more in this. 3.03.130
ay, there's the point; 3.03.228
there's magic in the web of it. 3.04. 69
sure, there's some wonder in this handkerchief; 3.04.101
there's matter in't indeed, if he be angry. 3.04.139
there's many a beast then in a populous city, 4.01. 63
there's millions now alive | that nightly lie in 4.01. 67
there's fall'n between him and my lord | an 4.01.224
chaste, and true, | there's no man happy; 4.02. 18
there's money for your pains. 4.02. 93
why, now i see there's mettle in thee, and even 4.02.204 P
there's beggary in the love that can be reckon'd ANT 1.01. 15
there's not a minute of our lives should stretch 1.01. 46
there's a palm presages chastity, if nothing 1.02. 47 P
there's a great spirit gone! 1.02.122
i know by that same eye there's some good news. 1.03. 19
sir, you and i have lov'd, but there's not it; 1.03. 88
there's my hand. 2.02.148
why, there's more gold. 2.05. 31
but there's no goodness in thy face, if antony 2.05. 37
there's the point. 2.06. 31
i saw you last, | there's a change upon you. 2.06. 53
there's a strong fellow, menas. 2.07. 88
hoo, says 'a. there's my cap. 2.07.134
there's nothing in her yet. 3.03. 24
there's gold for thee, | thou must not take my 3.03. 34
there's strange news come, sir. 3.05. 2 P
there's hope in't yet. 3.13.176
come on, my queen, | there's sap in't yet. 3.13.191
there's dolabella sent from caesar; call him. 5.02.324
there's none abroad so wholesome as that you CYM 1.02. 3 P
there's all i'll do for you. 1.05. 87
there's an italian come, and, 'tis thought, one 2.01. 37 P
love, | where there's another man. 2.04.110
for there's no motion | that tends to vice in 2.05. 20

come, there's no more tribute to be paid. 3.01. 34 P
and there's an end. 3.01. 82 P
there's no more to say: 3.02. 81
prithee think | there's livers out of britain. 3.04.140
prithee away, | there's more to be consider'd; 3.04.181
and there's no answer | that will be given to 3.05. 43
nor seek for danger | where there's no profit. 4.02.163
to the king's party there's no going. 4.04. 9
there's business in these faces. 5.05. 23
no, no, alack, | there's other work in hand. 5.05.103
where when men been, there's seldom ease, | for PER 2.ch. 28
there's nothing can be minist'red to nature 3.02. 8
there's no hope she will return. 4.01. 98
thou sayest true, there's two unwholesome, a' 4.02. 21 P
there's no farther necessity of qualities can 4.02. 48 P
there's no way to be rid on't but by the way to 4.06. 15 P
well, there's for you, leave us. 4.06. 45 P
you, there's no going but by their consent. 4.06.197 P
assured | beyond its power there's nothing; TNK 1.02. 65
and earth, | there's nothing in thee honest. 3.03. 46
there's all things needful — files and shirts 3.03. 48
yonder's the sea, and there's a ship. 3.04. 5
and there's a rock lies watching under water; 3.04. 6
there's a leak sprung, a sound one. 3.04. 8
there's a dainty mad woman, master, | comes i' 3.05. 72
there's another, | a little man, but of a tough 4.02.116
the blessed spirits — as there's a sight now! 4.03. 22 P
there's a curtsy! 5.02. 70
there's many a man alive that hath outliv'd 5.04. 1
and there's no doubt, but mercy may be found if STM II.C 147
death be adjunct, there's no death supposed. LUC 133
and death once dead, there's no more dying then. SON 146.14

THERE'T 1 FR 0.0001 REL FR 0 V 1 P
o lord, sir! — why, there't serves well again. AWW 2.02. 62 P

THERETO 19 FR 0.0021 REL FR 18 V 1 P
my heart accords thereto, | and yet a thousand TGV 1.03. 90
adding thereto, moreover, | that he would wed me LLL 5.02.446
vanquish'd thereto by the fair grace and speech AWW 5.03.133
life i gave him, and did thereto add | my love, TN 5.01. 80
a gentleman, thereto | clerk–like experienc'd, WT 1.02.391
the justice of your hearts will thereto add 2.01. 67
if my reason | will thereto be obedient, i have 4.04.483
out of our demands, | and we'll consign thereto. H5 5.02. 90
whom i with pain have wooed and won thereto; 1H6 5.03.138
serve, if he | can thereto frame his spirit. COR 3.02. 97
thereto witness may | my surname, coriolanus. 4.05. 67
add thereto a tiger's chawdron, | for th' MAC 4.01. 33
thereto prick'd on by a most emulate pride, HAM 1.01. 83
and thereto add such reasons of your own | as LR 1.04.338
if she be black, and thereto have a wit, OTH 2.01.132
madam, as thereto sworn by your command | (which ANT 5.02.198
so out of thought, and thereto so o'ergrown, CYM 4.04. 33
with pain, | being thereto not compelled. PER 3.02. 26
of, and thereto make an addition of some other TNK 4.03. 84 P

THEREUNTO 3 FR 0.0003 REL FR 2 V 1 P
points of ignorance | pertaining thereunto, as H8 1.03. 27
first asking you pardon thereunto, recount the HAM 4.07. 46 P
there's none so foul and foolish thereunto, OTH 2.01.141

THEREUPON 8 FR 0.0009 REL FR 6 V 2 P
mart, | and thereupon i drew my sword on you; ERR 5.01.263
for me, | and thereupon these errors are arose. 5.01.389
foul words — and thereupon i will kiss thee. ADO 5.02. 50 P
and thereupon thou speak'st the fairest shoot. LLL 4.01. 12
word, | and thereupon i drink unto your grace. 2H4 4.02. 68
the rest, | and thereupon give me your daughter. H5 5.02.347
and thereupon he sends you this good news, R3 3.02. 48
i dare thereupon pawn the moi'ty of my estate to CYM 1.04.108 P

THEREWITH 3 FR 0.0003 REL FR 3 V 0 P
who therewith angry, when it next came there, 1H4 1.03. 40
therewith fantastic garlands did she make | of HAM 4.07.168
how may the duke be therewith satisfied, | whose OTH 1.02. 88

THEREWITHAL 9 FR 0.0010 REL FR 8 V 1 P
give her that ring and therewithal | this letter TGV 4.04. 85
that my poor mistress, moved therewithal, | wept 4.04.170
and therewithal | remit thy other forfeits. MM 5.01.519
me, | and therewithal took measure of my body. ERR 4.03. 9
and therewithal to win me, if you please, LLL 5.02.848
and therewithal | came to this vault to die, and ROM 5.03.289
when therewithal we shall have cause of state MAC 3.01. 33
but therewithal the unruly waywardness that LR 1.01.298 P
and therewithal the best, or let her beauty CYM 2.04. 33

THERSITES' 1 FR 0.0001 REL FR 1 V 0 P
thersites' body, is as good as ajax', | when CYM 4.02.252

/THERSITES 3 FR 0.0003 REL FR 1 V 2 P
/when /rank /thersites /opes /his /mastic /jaws, TRO 1.03. 73
/proceed, /thersites. 2.03. 57 P
/achilles /is /a /fool, /thersites /is /a /fool, 2.03. 59 P

THERSITES 22 FR 0.0024 REL FR 5 V 17 P
of war, | bold as an oracle, and sets thersites, TRO 1.03.192
thersites! 2.01. 1 P
thersites! 2.01. 4 P
mistress thersites! 2.01. 36 P
how now, thersites, what's the matter, man? 2.01. 56
good words, thersites. 2.01. 88 P
what, with me too, thersites? 2.01.103 P
no more words, thersites, peace! 2.01.113 P
how now, thersites? 2.03. 1 P
thersites? 2.03. 23 P
good thersites, come in and rail. 2.03. 23 P
thersites, my lord. 2.03. 39 P
thy lord, thersites. 2.03. 46 P
then tell me, i pray thee, what's thersites? 2.03. 47 P
thersites is a fool to serve such a fool, and 2.03. 64 P
come in with me, thersites. 2.03. 70 P
who, thersites? 2.03. 92 P
go call thersites hither, sweet patroclus. 3.03.234
thou must be my ambassador /to /him, thersites. 3.03.267 P
here comes thersites. 5.01. 4
come, come, thersites, help to trim my tent; 5.01. 45
me /not what i would be if i were not thersites, 5.01. 65 P

THESE *(also 's*, theise, th's)*

/THESE 20 FR 0.0022 REL FR 17 V 3 P
/well /remember | /the /favors /of /these /men. R2 4.01.168
/but /that /you /read | /these /accusations, 4.01.223
/and /these /grievous /crimes | /committed /by 4.01.223
/lord, /dispatch, /read /o'er /these /articles. 4.01.243
/and /these /external /manners /of /laments 4.01.296
/what /trust /is /in /these /times? 2H4 1.03.100
some guard /these /traitors to the block of 4.02.122
"/these /wounds /i /had /on /crispin's /day." H5 4.03. 48
first let me ask of /these | if they can brook i 2H6 5.01.109
with /these your white enchanting fingers TRO 3.01.151
and what needs /these tricks? 5.01. 12 P
rump and potato finger, tickles /these together! 5.02. 56 P
/as /will /revenge /these /bitter /woes /of TIT 3.02. 3
/but /i, /of /these, /will /wrest /an /alphabet, 3.02. 44
/leave /these /bitter /deep /laments, | /make 3.02. 46
/these /are /now /the /fashion, /and /so HAM 2.02.341 P
/quickly /down /to /tame /these /vild /offenses, LR 4.02. 47
/to /let /these /hands /obey /my /blood, | /they 4.02. 64
/these /things /sting | /his /mind /so 4.03. 45
there's no composition in /these news | that OTH 1.03. 1

THESE 1399 FR 0.1581 REL FR 1168 V 231 P
what cares these roarers for the name of king? TMP 1.01. 16 P
if you can command these elements to silence, 1.01. 21 P
come unto these yellow sands, | and then take 1.02.375
sure, the goddess | on whom these airs attend! 1.02.423
you cram these words into mine ears against 2.01.107
did it to minister occasion to these gentlemen, 2.01.173 P
heavens keep him from these beasts! 2.01.324
and these are devils. 2.02. 88 P
if any be trinculo's legs, these are they. 2.02.104 P
these be fine things, and if they be not sprites 2.02.116
i must remove | some thousands of these logs, 3.01. 10
but these sweet thoughts do even refresh my 3.01. 14
yourself, | he's safe for these three hours. 3.01. 21
give us kind keepers, heavens! what were these? 3.03. 20
(for, certes, these are people of the island), 3.03. 30
and these, mine enemies, are all knit up | in 3.03. 89
and in these fits i leave them, while i visit 3.03. 91
bids thee leave these, and with her sovereign 4.01. 72
may i be bold | to think these spirits? 4.01.120
and these fresh nymphs encounter every one | in 4.01.137
these our actors | (as i foretold you) were all 4.01.148
say again, where didst thou leave these varlots? 4.01.170
it hither, | for stale to catch these thieves. 4.01.187
i perceive these lords | at this encounter do so 5.01.153
these are not natural events, they strengthen 5.01.227
probable) of every | these happen'd accidents; 5.01.250
if these be true spies which i wear in my head, 5.01.259 P
o setebos, these be brave spirits indeed! 5.01.261
what things are these, my lord antonio? 5.01.264
mark but the badges of these men, my lords, 5.01.267
these three have robb'd me, and this demi–devil 5.01.272
two of these fellows you | must know and own, 5.01.274
nuptial | of these our dear–belov'd solemnized, 5.01.310
shall these papers lie like tell–tales here? TGV 1.02.130
for any or for all these exercises | he said 1.03. 11
marry, by these special marks: 2.01. 18 P
are all these things perceiv'd in me? 2.01. 33 P
but you are so without these follies, that these 2.01. 38 P
follies, that these follies are within you, and 2.01. 38 P
in these affairs to aid me with thy counsel. 2.04.185
all these are servants to deceitful men. 2.07. 72
these are the villains | that all the travellers 4.01. 5
my riches are these poor habiliments, | of which 4.01. 13
and i for such like petty crimes as these. 4.01. 50
is he among these? 4.02. 37 P
where have you been these two days loitering? 4.04. 44
these likelihoods confirm her flight from hence: 5.02. 43
these are my mates, that make their wills their 5.04. 14
nor of heaven nor earth, for these are pleas'd; 5.04. 80
these banish'd men, that i have kept withal, 5.04.152
have done any time these three hundred years. WIV 1.01. 13 P
ay, by these gloves, did he, or i would i might 1.01.153 P
pence a–piece of yead miller — by these gloves. 1.01.157 P
by these gloves, then 'twas he. 1.01.165 P
you hear all these matters denied, gentlemen; 1.01.186 P
wife, bid these gentlemen welcome. 1.01.194 P
hold, sirrah, bear you these letters tightly; 1.03. 79
sail like my pinnace to these golden shores. 1.03. 80
these knights will hack, and so thou shouldst 2.01. 52 P
i warrant he hath a thousand of these letters, 2.01. 75 P
and these are of the second edition. 2.01. 76 P
but these that accuse him in his intent towards 2.01.174 P
in these times you stand on distance: 2.01.225 P
and to these violent proceedings all my 3.02. 43 P
like a many of these lisping hawthorn buds, that 3.03. 71 P
are these your letters, knight? 3.03.140 P
go take up these clothes here quickly. 3.03.146 P
besides these, other bars he lays before me, 3.04. 7
take away these chalices. 3.05. 28 P
did he send you both these letters at an instant 4.04. 3 P
i shall make my master glad with these tidings. 4.05. 56 P
see you these, husband? 5.05.107
do not these fair yokes | become the forest 5.05.107
and these are not fairies? 5.05.121 P
within these three days his head to be chopp'd MM 1.02. 69 P
are not these large enough? 1.04. 2
if these be good people in a commonweal that do 2.01. 41 P
prove it before these varlets here, thou 2.01. 86 P
why do you put these sayings upon me? 2.02.133
fie, these filthy vices! 2.04. 42
as these black masks | proclaim an enshield 2.04. 79
death we fear | that makes these odds all even. 3.01. 41
run with these false and most contrarious 4.01. 61
wounds th' unsisting postern with these strokes. 4.02. 89
find, within these two days he will be here. 4.02.198 P
into amazement how these things should be; 4.02.204 P
command these fretting waters from your eyes 4.03.146
these letters at fit time deliver me. 4.05. 1
perceive | these poor informal women are no more 5.01.236
have well determin'd | upon these slanderers. 5.01.259
sir, did you set these women on to slander lord 5.01.288 P
is't not enough thou hast suborn'd these women 5.01.306
first, provost, let me bail these gentle three. 5.01.357
dromio, come, these jests are out of season, ERR 1.02. 68
man, more divine, the master of all these, 2.01. 20
and you use these blows long, i must get a 2.02. 37 P
known unto these, and to myself disguis'd? 2.02.214
sure these are but imaginary wiles, | and 4.03. 10
you minion, you, are these your customers? 4.04. 60
free from these slanders and this open shame! 4.04. 67
is't good to soothe him in these contraries? 4.04. 79
but with these nails i'll pluck out these false 4.04.104
with these nails i'll pluck out these false eyes 4.04.104
i see these witches are afraid of swords. 4.04.147
these ears of mine thou know'st did hear thee; 5.01. 26
which of these sorrows is he subject to? 5.01. 54
to none of these, except it be the last, 5.01. 55
why bear you these rebukes, and answer not? 5.01. 89
for these deep shames and great indignities. 5.01.254
these people saw the chain about his neck. 5.01.259
i will be sworn these ears of mine | heard you 5.01.260
i never came within these abbey walls, | nor 5.01.266
all these old witnesses — i cannot err — 5.01.318
one of these men is genius to the other: 5.01.333
and so of these, which is the natural man, | and 5.01.334
these two antipholus', these two so like, | and 5.01.358
these two antipholus', these two so like, | and 5.01.358
and these two dromios, one in semblance — 5.01.359
these are the parents to these children, | which 5.01.361
these are the parents to these children, | which 5.01.361
for me, | and thereupon these errors are arose. 5.01.389
these ducats pawn i for my father here. 5.01.390
how many hath he kill'd and eaten in these wars? ADO 1.01. 43 P
he hath done good service, lady, in these wars. 1.01. 48 P
but hear these ill news with the ears of claudio 2.01.173
may i be so converted and see with these eyes? 2.03. 22 P
why, these are very crotchets that he speaks — 2.03. 56
and sentences and these paper bullets of the 2.03.240 P
to you, which these hobby–horses must not hear. 3.02. 73 P
commodity, being taken up of these men's bills. 3.03.178 P
these gloves the count sent me — they are an 3.04. 62 P
we are now to examination these men. 3.05. 59 P
that she were a maid, | by these exterior shows? 4.01. 40
are these things spoken, or do i but dream? 4.01. 66
sir, they are spoken, and these things are true. 4.01. 67
these things, come thus to light, | smother her 4.01.111
to burn the errors that these princes hold 4.01.163
but truth of her, | these hands shall tear her; 4.01.191
you in the prince's name accuse these men. 4.02. 38 P
master constable, let these men be bound, and 4.02. 64 P
officers, what offense have these men done? 5.01.213 P
these shallow fools have brought to light, who 5.01.233 P
which of these is he? 5.01.261
bring you these fellows on. 5.01.331
a whole bookful of these quondam carpet–mongers, 5.02. 32 P
the grosser manner of these world's delights LLL 1.01. 29
and die, | with all these living in philosophy. 1.01. 32
o, these are barren tasks, too hard to keep, 1.01. 47
your oath is pass'd to pass away from these. 1.01. 49
these be the stops that hinder study quite, 1.01. 70
these earthly godfathers of heaven's lights, 1.01. 88
these oaths and laws will prove an idle scorn. 1.01.309
another of these students at that time | was 2.01. 64
these are complements, these are humors, these 3.01. 22 P
these are complements, these are humors, these 3.01. 22 P
these betray nice wenches that would be betray'd 3.01. 23 P
wenches that would be betray'd without these; 3.01. 24 P
men that most are affected to these. 3.01. 25 P
i am all these three. 3.01. 46 P
o heresy in fair, fit for these days! 4.01. 22
one a' these maids' girdles for your waist 4.01. 50
these are begot in the ventricle of memory, 4.02. 68 P
i fear these stubborn lines lack power to move. 4.03. 53
these numbers will i tear, and write in prose! 4.03. 55
thou thus to reprove | these worms for loving, 4.03.152
will these turtles be gone? 4.03.208
did these rent lines show some love of thine? 4.03.216
then fools you were these women to forswear, 4.03.352
or for men's sake, the /authors of these women, 4.03.356
now to plain–dealing, lay these glozes by: 4.03.367
shall we resolve to woo these girls of france? 4.03.368
this, and these /pearls, to me sent longaville. 5.02. 53
ay, or i would these hands might never part. 5.02. 57
loves | woo contrary, deceiv'd by these removes. 5.02.135
what would these strangers? 5.02.175
bright moon, and these thy stars, to shine 5.02.205
look how you butt yourself in these sharp mocks! 5.02.251
are these the breed of wits so wondered at? 5.02.266
these summer flies | have blown me full of 5.02.408
these lords are visited; 5.02.422
no, they are free that gave these tokens to us. 5.02.424
and if these four worthies in their first show 5.02.538
these four will change habits, and present the 5.02.539
and by these badges understand the king. 5.02.754
heavenly eyes, that look into these faults, 5.02.769
challenge me, challenge me by these deserts, 5.02.805
to flatter up these powers of mine with rest, 5.02.814
with threefold love i wish you all these three. 5.02.825
these ladies' courtesy | might well have made 5.02.875
and (which is more than all these boasts can be) MND 1.01.103
these are the forgeries of jealousy; 2.01. 81
lull'd in these flowers with dances and delight; 2.01.254
lord, what fools these mortals be! 3.02.115
how can these things in me seem scorn to you, 3.02.126
these vows are hermia's. 3.02.130
have you with these contriv'd | to bait me with 3.02.196
thou seest these lovers seek a place to fight; 3.02.354
and lead these testy rivals so astray | as one 3.02.358
from these that my poor company detest. 3.02.434
how came these things to pass? 4.01. 78
than common sleep of all these /five the sense. 4.01. 82
and rock the ground whereon these sleepers be. 4.01. 86
was found | with these mortals on the ground. 4.01.102
what nymphs are these? 4.01.127
begin these wood–birds but to couple now? 4.01.140
with us | these couples shall eternally be knit. 4.01.181
these things seem small and undistinguishable, 4.01.187
methinks i see these things with parted eye, 4.01.189
where are these lads? where are these hearts? 4.02. 25 P
where are these lads? where are these hearts? 4.02. 25 P
strange, my theseus, that these lovers speak of. 5.01. 1
i never may believe | these antic fables, nor 5.01. 3
these antic fables, nor these fairy toys. 5.01. 3
that vile wall, which did these lovers sunder; 5.01.132
by moonshine did these lovers think no scorn 5.01.137
why, all these should be in the lanthorn; 5.01.260 P
for all these are in the moon. 5.01.261 P
these lily lips, | this cherry nose, | these 5.01.330
this cherry nose, | these yellow cowslip cheeks, 5.01.332

slumb'red here | while these visions did appear. 5.01.426
i do know of these | that therefore only are MV 1.01. 95
i must be one of these same dumb wise men, | for 1.01.106
he hath devis'd in these three chests of gold, 1.02. 29 P
towards any of these princely suitors that are 1.02. 34 P
a bone in his mouth than to either of these. 1.02. 52 P
god defend me from these two! 1.02. 53 P
not fear, lady, the having any of these lords. 1.02.101 P
was | between these woolly breeders in the act, 1.03. 83
and for these courtesies | i'll lend you thus 1.03.128
within these two months, that's a month before 1.03.157
o father abram, what these christians are, 1.03.160
see these letters deliver'd, put the liveries to 2.02.116 P
these things being bought and orderly bestowed, 2.02.170
these foolish drops do something drown my manly 2.03. 13 P
but more than these, in love i do deserve. 2.07. 34
one of these three contains her heavenly picture 2.07. 48
to these injunctions every one doth swear | that 2.09. 17
o, these deliberate fools! 2.09. 80
rebels it at these years? 3.01. 35 P
o, these naughty times | puts bars between the 3.02. 18
and these assume but valor's excrement | to 3.02. 87
move these eyes? 3.02.116
this house, these servants, and this same myself 3.02.170
these griefs and losses have so bated me | that 3.03. 32
and twenty of these puny lies i'll tell, | that 3.04. 74
a thousand raw tricks of these bragging jacks, 3.04. 77
these be the christian husbands. 4.01.295
for, by these blessed candles of the night, 5.01.220
i am th' unhappy subject of these quarrels. 5.01.238
and in the hearing of these many friends | i 5.01.241
you are not satisfied | of these events at full. 5.01.297
you'll be whipt for taxation one of these days. AYL 1.02. 85 P
"be it known unto all men by these presents." 1.02.124 P
what passion hangs these weights upon my tongue? 1.02.257
these burs are in my heart. 1.03. 16 P
but, turning these jests out of service, let us 1.03. 25 P
within these ten days if that thou beest found 1.03. 43
are not these woods | more free from peril than 2.01. 3
these are counsellors | that feelingly persuade 2.01. 10
i love to cope him in these sullen fits, | for 2.01. 67
quail | to bring again these foolish runaways. 2.02. 21
o unhappy youth, | come not within these doors! 2.03. 17
thou art not for the fashion of these times, 2.03. 59
with weeping tears, "wear these for my sake." 2.04. 53 P
o rosalind, these trees shall be my books, | and 3.02. 5
heaven would that she these gifts should have, 3.02.153
didst thou hear these verses? 3.02.163 P
should be hang'd and carv'd upon these trees? 3.02.173 P
to say ay and no to these particulars is more 3.02.227 P
these time ambles withal. 3.02.324 P
nor the lover's, which is all these: 4.01. 15 P
but these are all lies: 4.01.106 P
for these two hours, rosalind, i will leave thee 4.01.177 P
and in these degrees have they made a pair of 5.02. 37 P
nonino, | these pretty country folks would lie, 5.03. 24
from hence i go | to make these doubts all even. 5.04. 25
toward, and these couples are coming to the ark. 5.04. 36 P
all these you may avoid but the lie direct; 5.04. 97 P
make conclusion | of these most strange events. 5.04.127
how thus we met, and these things finish. 5.04.140
that bring these tidings to this fair assembly. 5.04.153
out of these convertites | there is much matter 5.04.184
we'll begin these rites, | as we do trust 5.04.197
please your honor taste of these conserves? SHR in.2. 3
and banish hence these abject lowly dreams. in.2. 32
these fifteen years you have been in a dream, in.2. 79
these fifteen years! in.2. 81
and twenty more such names and men as these, in.2. 95
to make a stale of me amongst these mates? 1.01. 58
execute — | to make one among these wooers. 1.01.247
spake you not these words plain, "sirrah, knock 1.02. 40 P
hortensio, to what end are all these words? 1.02.248
but for these other /gawds, | unbind my hands, 2.01. 3
sirrah, lead these gentlemen | to my daughters, 2.01.108
and tell them both, | these are their tutors. 2.01.110
devilish spirit, | "frets, call you these?" 2.01.152
these i will assure her, | and twice as much, 2.01.379
sirrah, i will not bear these braves of thine. 3.01. 15
come, where be these gallants? who's at home? 3.02. 87
see not your bride in these unreverent robes, 3.02.112
me, | as i can change these poor accoutrements, 3.02.119
where be these knaves? 4.01.120
and bring along these rascal knaves with thee? 4.01.131
what dogs are these? 4.01.162
as we watch these kites | that bate and beat and 4.01.195
in all these circumstances i'll instruct you; 4.02.120
that which spites me more than all these wants, 4.03. 11
come, tailor, let us see these ornaments; 4.03. 61
time, | and gentlewomen wear such caps as these. 4.03. 70
even in these honest mean habiliments; 4.03.170
love wrought these miracles. 5.01.124
how likes gremio these quick–witted folks? 5.02. 38
i charge thee tell these headstrong women | what 5.02.130
and these great tears grace his remembrance more AWW 1.01. 80
yet these fix'd evils sit so fit in him, | that 1.01.102
a man | might be a copy to these younger times; 1.02. 46
if ever we are nature's, these are ours. 1.03.129
these warlike principles | do not throw from you 2.01. 1
my mouth no more were broken than these boys', 2.03. 60
these boys are boys of ice, they'll none have 2.03. 93 P
fair, | in these to nature she's immediate heir; 2.03.132
and these breed honor. 2.03.133
why, these balls bound, there's noise in it. 2.03.297
these things shall be done, sir. 2.05. 15 P
tokens, and all these engines of lust, are not 3.05. 19 P
same knave | that leads him to these places. 3.05. 83
nothing acquainted with these businesses, | and 3.07. 5
within these three hours 'twill be time enough 4.01. 24 P
mule, if you prattle me into these perils. 4.01. 43 P
in the mean time, what hear you of these wars? 4.03. 38 P
and between these main parcels of dispatch 4.03. 90 P
seek these suitors. 5.03.151
come hither, count, do you know these women? 5.03.165
if it were yours by none of all these ways, 5.03.275
these sovereign thrones, are all supplied, and TN 1.01. 37
these clothes are good enough to drink in, and 1.03. 11 P
enough to drink in, and so be these boots too; 1.03. 12 P
but he'll have but a year in all these ducats. 1.03. 23 P
art thou good at these kickshawses, knight? 1.03.115 P
wherefore are these things hid? 1.03.125 P
wherefore have these gifts a curtain before 'em? 1.03.126 P
if the duke continue these favors towards you, 1.04. 1 P
i protest i take these wise men that crow so at 1.05. 88 P
men that crow so at these set kind of fools no 1.05. 89 P
here — a plague o' these pickle–herring! 1.05.120 P
if you will lead these graces to the grave | and 1.05.242
of these most brisk and giddy–paced times. 2.04. 6
these be her very c's, her u's, and her t's, and 2.05. 86 P
for every one of these letters are in my name. 2.05.141 P
drives me to these habits of her liking. 2.05.169 P
would not a pair of these have bred, sir? 3.01. 49 P
your travel, | being skilless in these parts; 3.03. 9
love, | the rather by these arguments of fear, 3.03. 12
i do not without danger walk these streets. 3.03. 25
these wise men that give fools money get 4.01. 21 P
that i shake off these names you give me. 5.01. 73
after him i love | more than i love these eyes, 5.01.135
is not more twin | than these two creatures. 5.01.224
so please you, these things further thought on, 5.01.316
in every one of these no man is free | but that WT 1.02.251
these, my lord, | are such allow'd infirmities 1.02.262
is nothing, nor nothing have these nothings, 1.02.295
to a fine new prince | one of these days, and 2.01. 18
(and these petty brands | that calumny doth use — o 2.01. 71
itself), these shrugs, these hums and ha's, 2.01. 74
itself), these shrugs, these hums and ha's, 2.01. 74
to put apart these your attendants, i | shall 2.02. 13
these dangerous, unsafe lunes i' th' king, 2.02. 28
what needs these hands? 2.03.127
the bastard brains with these my proper hands 2.03.140
these lords, my noble fellows, if they please, 2.03.143
these proclamations, | so forcing faults upon 3.01. 15
yet | that any of these bolder vices wanted 3.02. 55
do not repent these things, for they are heavier 3.02.208
come, and lead me | to these sorrows. 3.02.243
there these, | which may, if fortune please, 3.03. 47
would any but these boil'd–brains of nineteen 3.03. 64 P
i have not wink'd since i saw these sights. 3.03.105 P
pluck but off these rags; 4.03. 52 P
rags to lay on thee, rather than have these off. 4.03. 55 P
me, and these detestable things put upon me. 4.03. 62 P
these your unusual weeds to each part of you 4.04. 1
or how | should i, in these my borrowed flaunts, 4.04. 23
one of these two must be necessities, | which 4.04. 38
with these forc'd thoughts, i prithee darken not 4.04. 41
strangle such thoughts as these with any thing 4.04. 47
you bid | these unknown friends to 's welcome, 4.04. 65
these keep | seeming and savor all the winter 4.04. 74
these are flow'rs | of middle summer, and i 4.04.106
o, these i lack, | to make you garlands of, and 4.04.127
you have of these pedlars, that have more in 4.04.215 P
to whistle /off these secrets, but you must be 4.04.245 P
pray let's see these four threes of herdsmen. 4.04.336 P
since these good men are pleas'd, let them come 4.04.340 P
know | she prizes not such trifles as these are. 4.04.357
come on, | contract us 'fore these witnesses. 4.04.390
thou | these rural latches to his entrance open, 4.04.438
one of these is true: 4.04.575
not at your father's house these seven years 4.04.578
not the air of the court in these enfoldings? 4.04.731 P
yet nature might have made me as these are, 4.04.746
but what talk we of these traitorly rascals, 4.04.791 P
i will bring these two moles, these blind ones, 4.04.836 P
i will bring these two moles, these blind ones, 4.04.836 P
stir | afresh within me, and these thy offices, 5.01.149
who now | has these poor men in question. 5.01.198
i thought of her, | even in these looks i made. 5.01.228
see you these clothes? 5.02.130 P
you were best say these robes are not gentlemen 5.02.132 P
ay, and have been so any time these four hours. 5.02.136 P
your crown'd brother and these your contracted 5.03. 5
no! not these twenty years. 5.03. 84
which sways usurpingly these several titles, JN 1.01. 13
to enforce these rights so forcibly withheld. 1.01. 18
to whom am i beholding for these limbs? 1.01.239
these eyes, these brows, were moulded out of his 2.01.100
these eyes, these brows, were moulded out of his 2.01.100
when living blood doth in these temples beat, 2.01.108
with these crystal beads heaven shall be brib'd 2.01.171
to cry aim | to these ill–tuned repetitions. 2.01.197
hither to the walls | these men of angiers; 2.01.199
these flags of france, that are advanced here 2.01.207
siege | and merciless proceeding by these french 2.01.214
in warlike march these greens before your town, 2.01.242
though all these english and their discipline 2.01.261
put thee down, 'gainst whom these arms we bear, 2.01.346
why stand these royal fronts amazed thus? 2.01.356
by heaven, these scroyles of angiers flout you, 2.01.373
i'd play incessantly upon these jades, | even 2.01.385
as we will ours, against these saucy walls, 2.01.404
to these two princes, if you marry them. 2.01.445
what say these young ones? 2.01.521
poictiers, and anjou, these five provinces, 2.01.528
be these sad signs confirmers of thy words? 3.01. 24
arm, you heavens, against these perjur'd kings! 3.01.107
set armed discord 'twixt these perjur'd kings! 3.01.111
well, ruffian, i must pocket up these wrongs, 3.01.200
and shall these hands, so lately purg'd of blood 3.01.239
parts | against these giddy loose suggestions; 3.01.292
and ring these fingers with thy household worms, 3.04. 31
reason | how i may be deliver'd of these woes, 3.04. 55
"o that these hands could so redeem my son | as 3.04. 71
as they have given these hairs their liberty!" 3.04. 72
heat me these irons hot, and look thou stand 4.01. 1
these eyes that never did nor never shall | so 4.01. 57
approaching near these eyes, would drink my 4.01. 62
even with the fierce looks of these bloody men. 4.01. 73
nay, hear me, hubert, drive these men away, 4.01. 78
thrust but these men away, and i'll forgive you, 4.01. 82
i'll fill these dogged spies with false reports; 4.01.128
i, as one that am the tongue of these | to sound 4.02. 47
hast made me giddy | with these ill tidings. 4.02.132
why seek'st thou to possess me with these fears? 4.02.203
o me, my uncle's spirit is in these stones. 4.03. 9
is much more general than these lines import. 4.03. 17
return the president to these lords again, 5.02. 3
both they and we, perusing o'er these notes, 5.02. 5
where these two christian armies might combine 5.02. 37
commend these waters to those baby eyes | that 5.02. 56
have i not heard these islanders shout out 5.02.103
and cull'd these fiery spirits from the world, 5.02.114
passing these flats, are taken by the tide — 5.06. 40
these lincoln washes have devoured them; 5.06. 41
you breathe these dead news in as dead an ear. 5.07. 65
now these her princes are come home again, 5.07.115
these terms of treason doubled down his throat. R2 1.01. 57
that all the treasons for these eighteen years, 1.01. 95
be ready to direct these home alarms. 1.01.205
appointed to direct these fair designs. 1.03. 45
while we return these dukes what we decree. 1.03.122
the language i have learnt these forty years, 1.03.159
he is gone, and with him go these thoughts. 1.04. 37
to deck our soldiers for these irish wars. 1.04. 62
these words hereafter thy tormentors be! 2.01.136
and, for these great affairs do ask some charge, 2.01.159
he hath not money for these irish wars, | his 2.01.259
all these, well furnished by the duke of britain 2.01.285
how shall we do for money for these wars? 2.02.104
i | know how or which way to order these affairs 2.02.109
these high wild hills and rough uneven ways 2.03. 4
and these, and all, are all amiss employed. 2.03.132
well, well, i see the issue of these arms. 2.03.152
these signs forerun the death or fall of kings. 2.04. 15
bring forth these men. 3.01. 1
and these stones | prove armed soldiers, ere her 3.02. 24
let's step into the shadow of these trees. 3.04. 25
gard'ner, for telling me these news of woe, 3.04.100
these differences shall all rest under gage 4.01. 86
but heaven hath a hand in these events, | to 5.02. 37
do these justs and triumphs hold? 5.02. 52
to oxford, or where e'er these traitors are. 5.03.141
these were his very words. 5.04. 3
father, and these two beget | a generation of 5.05. 7
and these same thoughts people this little world 5.05. 9
how these vain weak nails | may tear a passage 5.05. 19
to chase these pagans in those holy fields, 1H4 1.01. 24
temperate, | unapt to stir at these indignities, 1.03. 2
and but for these vile guns | he would himself 1.03. 63
blood–stained with these valiant combatants. 1.03.107
yea, on his part i'll empty all these veins, 1.03.133
shall it for shame be spoken in these days, | or 1.03.170
off | by him for whom these shames ye underwent? 1.03.179
none of these mad mustachio purple–hu'd 2.01. 74 P
to turn true man and to leave these rogues, i am 2.02. 23 P
i must leave you within these two hours. 2.03. 36
o, what portents are these? 2.03. 62
these four came all afront, and mainly thrust at 2.04.200 P
seven, by these hilts, or i am a villain else. 2.04.206 P
these nine in buckrom that i told thee of — 2.04.211 P
these lies are like their father that begets 2.04.225 P
how couldst thou know these men in kendal green 2.04.231 P
my lord, do you see these meteors? 2.04.319 P
do you behold these exhalations? 2.04.320 P
it as like one of these harlotry players as ever 2.04.395 P
if he have robb'd these men, | he shall be 2.04.521
these promises are fair, the parties sure, | and 3.01. 1
of many men | i do not bear these crossings. 3.01. 35
these signs have mark'd me extraordinary, | and 3.01. 40
nor shall we need his help these fourteen days. 3.01. 87
than one of these same metre ballet–mongers. 3.01.128
thou pourest down from these swelling heavens 3.01.199
be drawn, i'll away within these two hours, and 3.01.261 P
but wherefore do i tell these news to thee? 3.02.121
were enrich'd with any other injuries but these, 3.03.161 P
well, god be thank'd for these rebels, they 3.03.190 P
these letters come from your father. 4.01. 14
jack, whose fellows are these that come after? 4.02. 62 P
and pardon absolute for yourself and these 4.03. 50
these things indeed you have articulate, 5.01. 72
for doing these fair rites of tenderness. 5.04. 98
that freely rend'red me these news for true. 2H4 1.01. 27
but these mine eyes saw him in bloody state, 1.01.107
in poison there is physic, and these news, 1.01.137
so little regard in these costermongers' times 1.02.168 P
but for these foolish officers, i beseech you i 2.01.107 P
i do desire deliverance from these officers, 2.01.127 P
worth a thousand of these bed–hangers and these 2.01.146 P
of these bed–hangers and these fly–bitten 2.01.146 P
what foolish master taught you these manners, 2.01.189 P
but indeed these humble considerations make me 2.02. 11 P
these, and those that were thy peach–color'd 2.02. 16 P
o yet, for god's sake, go not to these wars! 2.03. 9
"i will now take my leave of these six dry, 2.04. 7 P
these villains will make the word as odious as 2.04.147 P
these be good humors indeed! 2.04.163
my troth, captain, these are very bitter words. 2.04.170 P
afore i'll be in these tirrits and frights. 2.04.205 P
i have known thee these twenty–nine years, come 2.04.382 P
bid them o'er–read these letters | and well 3.01. 2
did speak these words, now prov'd a prophecy? 3.01. 69
are these things then necessities? 3.01. 92
and these unseasoned hours perforce must add 3.01.105
and were these inward wars once out of hand, 3.01.107
these fellows woll do well, master shallow. 3.02.287 P
as i return, i will fetch off these justices. 3.02.302 P
my friends and brethren in these great affairs, 4.01. 6
and these noble lords | had not been here to 4.01. 38
now) | hath put us in these ill–beseeming arms, 4.01. 84
and suffer the condition of these times | to lay 4.01. 99
these griefs shall be with speed redress'd, 4.02. 59
i take your princely word for these redresses. 4.02. 66
i promis'd you redress of these same grievances 4.02.113
most shallowly did you these arms commence, 4.02.118
these tardy tricks of yours will, on my life, 4.03. 28
there's never none of these demure boys come to 4.03. 90 P
and pause us, till these rebels, now afoot, 4.04. 9
and wherefore should these good news make me 4.04.102
you do know these fits | are with his highness 4.04.114
no, no, he cannot long hold out these pangs. 4.04.117
all these bold fears | thou seest with peril i 4.05.195
of he, the worst of these three gentlemen! 5.02. 16
why, here it is, welcome these pleasant days! 5.03.141

suppose within the girdle of these walls | are H5 pr 19
awake remembrance of these valiant dead, | and 1.02.115
or lay these bones in an unworthy urn, 1.02.228
when we have match'd our rackets to these balls, 1.02.261
therefore let our proportions for these wars 1.02.304
yield the crow a pudding one of these days. 2.01. 88 P
god, his grace is bold to trust these traitors. 2.02. 1
and my noble peers, | these english monsters! 2.02. 85
of his greener days | and these he masters now. 2.04.137
these cull'd and choice–drawn cavaliers to 3.pr. 24
have in these parts from morn till even fought, 3.01. 20
these be good humors! 3.02. 26 P
as i am, i have observ'd these three swashers. 3.02. 28 P
ay, but these english are shrowdly out of beef. 3.07.152 P
now, if these men do not die well, it will be a 4.01.144 P
if these men have defeated the law and outrun 4.01.166 P
no, not all these, thrice–gorgeous ceremony, 4.01.266
not all these, laid in bed majestical, | can 4.01.267
and a sweet retire | from off these fields, 4.03. 87
shall have none, i swear, but these my joints; 4.03.123
be these the wretches that we play'd at dice for 4.05. 8
upon these words i came and cheer'd him up. 4.06. 20
that i have fin'd these bones of mine for ransom 4.07. 69
added to these, | of knights, esquires, and 4.08. 83
so that, in these ten thousand they have lost, 4.08. 87
patches will i get unto these cudgell'd scars, 5.01. 88
peace | should not expel these inconveniences, 5.02. 66
for these fellows of infinite tongue, that can 5.02.155 P
in between the /paction of these kingdoms, | to 5.02.365
cease these jars and rest your minds in peace. 1H6 1.01. 44
these news would cause him once more yield the 1.01. 67
these tidings would call forth her flowing tides 1.01. 83
away with these disgraceful wailing robes! 1.01. 86
lords, view these letters full of bad mischance. 1.01. 89
maid, is't thou wilt do these wondrous feats? 1.02. 64
these women are shrewd tempters with their 1.02.123
days, | since i have entered into these wars. 1.02.132
where be these warders, that they wait not here? 1.03. 3
god, these nobles should such stomachs bear! 1.03. 90
and even these three days have i watch'd | if i 1.04. 16
then we'll try what these dastard frenchmen dare 1.04.111
to give their censure of these rare reports. 2.03. 10
and i will chain these legs and arms of thine, 2.03. 39
that hast by tyranny these many years | wasted 2.03. 40
how can these contrarieties agree? 2.03. 59
these are his substance, sinews, arms, and 2.03. 63
but in these nice sharp quillets of the law, 2.04. 17
and know us by these colors for thy foes, | for 2.04.105
for these my friends in spite of thee shall wear 2.04.106
and these grey locks, the pursuivants of death, 2.05. 5
these eyes, like lamps whose wasting oil is 2.05. 8
yet are these feet, whose strengthless stay is 2.05. 13
the reason mov'd these warlike lords to this 2.05. 70
and makes him roar these accusations forth. 3.01. 40
these are the city–gates, the gates of roan, 3.02. 1
these haughty words of hers | have batt'red me 3.03. 78
and for these good deserts | we here create you 3.04. 25
disgracing of these colors that i wear | in 3.04. 29
to be our regent in these parts of france; 4.01.163
these eyes, that see thee now well colored, 4.02. 37
all these, and more, we hazard by thy stay; 4.06. 40
all these are sav'd if thou wilt fly away. 4.06. 41
these words of yours draw life–blood from my 4.06. 43
my spirit can no longer bear these harms. 4.07. 30
him that thou magnifi'st with all these titles 4.07. 75
o, that i could but call these dead to life, 4.07. 81
for clothing me in these grave ornaments. 5.01. 54
these news, my lords, may cheer our drooping 5.02. 1
i kiss these fingers for eternal peace, | and 5.03. 48
and peace established between these realms. 5.03. 92
mov'd with remorse of these outrageous broils, 5.04. 97
voice, | by sight of these our baleful enemies. 5.04.122
most of all these reasons bindeth us | in our 5.05. 60
and shall these labors and these honors die? 2H6 1.01. 95
and shall these labors and these honors die? 1.01. 95
all, | these counties were the keys of normandy. 1.01.114
those provinces these arms of mine did conquer, 1.01.120
while these do labor for their own preferment, 1.01.181
i would remove these tedious stumbling–blocks, 1.02. 64
we'll see these things effected to the full. 1.02. 84
and buzz these conjurations in her brain. 1.02. 99
and not the least of these | but can do more in 1.03. 70
and he of these that can do most of all | cannot 1.03. 72
not all these lords do vex me half so much | as 1.03. 75
these are no women's matters. 1.03.117
tell me, what are these? 1.03.180
his words were these: 1.03.183
say, man, were these thy words? 1.03.186
by these ten bones, my lords, he did speak them 1.03.190 P
and let these have a day appointed them | for 1.03.207
lay hands upon these traitors and their trash. 1.04. 41
see you well guerdon'd for these good deserts. 1.04. 46
my lords, these oracles | are hardly attain'd, 1.04. 70
thither goes these news, as fast as horse can 1.04. 74
i saw not better sport these seven years' day; 2.01. 2
good queen, and whet not on these furious peers, 2.01. 33
and call these foul offenders to their answers, 2.01.199
do you as i do in these dangerous days: 2.02. 69
all these could not procure me any scathe | so 2.04. 62
these few days' wonder will be quickly worn. 2.04. 69
made me collect these dangers in the duke. 3.01. 35
tut, these are petty faults to faults unknown, 3.01. 64
my lord, these faults are easy, quickly answer'd 3.01.133
ah, gracious lord, these days are dangerous: 3.01.142
that these great lords, and margaret our queen, 3.01.207
i thank thee, /meg, these words content me much. 3.02. 26
but all in vain are these mean obsequies, | and 3.02.146
the least of all these signs were probable. 3.02.178
then you belike suspect these noblemen | as 3.02.186
cease, gentle queen, these execrations, | and 3.02.305
and these dread curses, like the sun 'gainst 3.02.330
that thou mightst think upon these by the seal, 3.02.344
what news are these! 3.02.380
and so should these, if i might have my will. 4.01. 27
ay, but these rags are no part of the duke; 4.01. 47
god, to shoot forth thunder | upon these paltry, 4.01.105
far be it we should honor such as these | with 4.01.123
stoop to the block than these knees bow to any 4.01.125
and as for these whose ransom we have set, | it 4.01.139
they have been up these two days. 4.02. 2 P
as for these silken–coated slaves, i pass not, 4.02.128
these kentish rebels would be soon appeas'd! 4.04. 42
be it known unto thee by these presence, even 4.07. 29 P
these cheeks are pale for watching for your good 4.07. 85
these hands are free from guiltless 4.07.102
for with these borne before us, in stead of 4.07.134 P
never have given out these arms till you had 4.08. 26 P
and ask him what's the reason of these arms. 4.09. 37
these five days have i hid me in these woods and 4.10. 2 P
days have i hid me in these woods and durst not 4.10. 3 P
court | and may enjoy such quiet walks as these? 4.10. 17
but thou wilt brave me with these saucy terms? 4.10. 36
i have eat no meat these five days, yet, come 4.10. 39 P
to know the reason of these arms in peace; 5.01. 18
flint, | i am so angry at these abject terms; 5.01. 25
then what intends these forces thou dost bring? 5.01. 60
that gold must round engirt these brows of mine, 5.01. 99
they may astonish these fell–lurking curs. 5.01.146
are these thy bears? 5.01.148
nothing so heavy as these woes of mine. 5.02. 65
all, | and more such days as these to us befall! 5.03. 33
i vow by heaven these eyes shall never close. 3H6 1.01. 24
plantagenet, of thee and these thy sons, | thy 1.01. 95
i cannot stay to hear these articles. 1.01.180
come, cousin, let us tell the queen these news. 1.01.182
and long live thou, and these thy forward sons! 1.01.203
these tears are my sweet rutland's obsequies, 1.04.147
my soul flies through these wounds to seek out 1.04.178
ten days ago i drown'd these news in tears; 2.01.104
my royal father, cheer these noble lords, | and 2.02. 78
these words will cost ten thousand lives this 2.02.177
till either death hath clos'd these eyes of mine 2.03. 31
and cheers these hands that slew thy sire and 2.04. 9
my tears shall wipe away these bloody marks; 2.05. 71
o that my death would stay these ruthful deeds! 2.05. 95
how will the country for these woeful chances 2.05.107
these arms of mine shall be thy winding–sheet; 2.05.114
so shalt thou sinow both these lands together, 2.06. 91
to london | to see these honors in possession. 2.06.110
i'll tell you how these lands are to be got. 3.02. 42
from these our henry lineally descends. 3.03. 87
methinks these peers of france should smile at 3.03. 91
my lord ambassador, these letters are for you, 3.03.163
these from our king unto your majesty. 3.03.165
and, madam, these for you; 3.03.166
these words have turn'd my hate to love, | and i 3.03.199
these soldiers shall be levied, | and thou, lord 3.03.251
at my depart, these were his very words: 4.01. 92
these were her words, utt'red with mild disdain: 4.01. 98
but what said warwick to these injuries? 4.01.107
all the rest, discharg'd me with these words: 4.01.109
these news i must confess are full of grief, 4.04. 13
me, in these conflicts | what may befall him, to 4.06. 94
these gates must not be shut | but in the night 4.07. 35
no, exeter, these graces challenge grace; 4.08. 48
hark, hark, my lord, what shouts are these? 4.08. 51
and he shall pardon thee these outrages. 5.01. 24
these eyes, that now are dimm'd with death's 5.02. 16
what of these? 5.04. 15
all these the enemies to our poor bark. 5.04. 28
should, if a coward heard her speak these words, 5.04. 40
to entertain these fair well–spoken days, | i am R3 1.01. 29
and hate the idle pleasures of these days. 1.01. 31
these (as i learn) and such–like toys as these 1.01. 60
and such–like toys as these | hath mov'd his 1.01. 60
by the self–same hand that made these wounds! 1.02. 11
lo, in these windows that let forth thy life | i 1.02. 12
o, cursed be the hand that made these holes! 1.02. 14
of these supposed crimes, to give me leave | by 1.02. 76
of these known evils, but to give me leave | by 1.02. 79
of the timeless deaths | of these plantagenets, 1.02.118
these nails should rent that beauty from my 1.02.126
these eyes could not endure that beauty's wrack; 1.02.127
these eyes, which never shed remorseful tear — 1.02.155
and what these sorrows could not thence exhale, 1.02.165
that it may please you leave these sad designs 1.02.210
god, her conscience, and these bars against me, 1.02.234
falsely to draw me in these vile suspects. 1.03. 88
thou hadst call'd me all these bitter names. 1.03.235
death | to gaze upon these secrets of the deep? 1.04. 35
keeper, i have done these things | (that now 1.04. 66
between these swelling wrong–incensed peers. 2.01. 52
i am the mother of these griefs: 2.02. 80
these babes for clarence weep, /and /so /do /i; 2.02. 84
my lord stanley sleep these tedious nights? 3.02. 6
rood, | i do not like these several councils, i. 3.02. 76
i have sent for these strawberries. 3.04. 47
which now the loving haste of these our friends, 3.05. 54
and yet within these five hours hastings liv'd, 3.06. 8
these both put off, a poor petitioner, | a 3.07.183
but shall we wear these glories for a day? 4.02. 5
here in these confines slily have i lurk'd, | to 4.04. 3
these english woes shall make me smile in france 4.04.115
let not the heavens hear these tell–tale women 4.04.150
yet to beat down these rebels here at home. 4.04.530
god give us leisure for these rites of love! 5.03.101
then, in the name of god and all these rights, 5.03.263
i would these dewy tears were from the ground. 5.03.284
let's whip these stragglers o'er the seas again; 5.03.327
lash hence these overweening rags of france, 5.03.328
these famish'd beggars weary of their lives, 5.03.329
and not these bastard britains, whom our fathers 5.03.333
shall these enjoy our lands? 5.03.336
that would reduce these bloody days again, | and 5.05. 36
when these suns | (for so they phrase 'em) by H8 1.01. 33
what had he | to do in these fierce vanities? 1.01. 54
in him stuff that puts him to these ends; 1.01. 58
these are the limbs o' th' plot. 1.01.220
on you as putter–on | of these exactions, yet 1.02. 25
for, upon these taxations, | the clothiers all, 1.02. 30
these exactions | (whereof my sovereign would 1.02. 47
when these so noble benefits shall prove | not 1.02.115
these very words | i've heard him utter to his 1.02.135
our ladies | will have of these trim vanities! 1.03. 38
some of these | should find a running banket, 1.04. 11
were but now confessor | to one or two of these! 1.04. 16
pray sit between these ladies. 1.04. 24
you, if these fair ladies | pass away frowning. 1.04. 32
fair conduct | crave leave to view these ladies, 1.04. 71
a dozen healths | to drink to these fair ladies, 1.04.106
all these accus'd him strongly, which he fain 2.01. 24
and despairs, and all these for his marriage. 2.02. 28
and out of all these to restore the king, | he 2.02. 29
'tis most true | these news are every where; 2.02. 38
look into these affairs see this main end, | the 2.02. 40
from these sad thoughts that work too much upon 2.02. 57
these reverend fathers, men | of singular 2.04. 58
the cure is to | remove these thoughts from you; 2.04.102
to declare, in hearing | of all these ears (for, 2.04.147
by some of these | the queen is put in anger. 2.04.161
i may perceive | these cardinals trifle with me; 2.04.237
you wrong the king's love with these fears, 3.01. 81
your virtues | with these weak women's fears. 3.01.169
moe new disgraces | with these you bear already. 3.02. 6
within these forty hours surrey durst better 3.02.253
i yet remember | some of these articles, and out 3.02.304
and from these shoulders, | these ruin'd pillars 3.02.381
these ruin'd pillars, out of pity taken | a load 3.02.382
of all these learned men she was divorc'd, | and 4.01. 32
these i know. 4.01. 37
their coronets say so. these are stars indeed. 4.01. 54
to whom he gave these words: 4.02. 20
these are the whole contents, and, good my lord, 4.02.154
stand these poor people's friend, and urge the 4.02.157
these should be hours for necessities, | not for 5.01. 2
repose, and not for us | to waste these times. 5.01. 5
will these please you? 5.02.203
these are but switches to 'em. 5.03. 8 P
these are the youths that thunder at a playhouse 5.03. 60 P
there they are like to dance these three days; 5.03. 65 P
where are these porters? 5.03. 69
these lazy knaves? 5.03. 70
are all these | your faithful friends o' th' 5.03. 71
marshalsea shall hold ye play these two months. 5.03. 86
she, "which of these hairs is paris my husband?" TRO 1.02.163 P
defend my beauty, and you, to defend all these; 1.02.263 P
and at all these wards i lie, at a thousand 1.02.263 P
what grief hath set these jaundies o'er your 1.03. 2
had lack'd a master, | but for these instances: 1.03. 77
as stuff for these two to make paradoxes. 1.03.184
and in the imitation of these twain — | who, as 1.03.185
thy brass voice through all these lazy tents, 1.03.257
do not these high strains | of divination in our 2.02.113
for what, alas, can these my single arms? 2.02.135
you have the honey still, but these the gall; 2.02.144
is, these moral laws | of nature and of nations 2.02.184
troy be not taken till these two undermine it, 2.03. 8 P
we are too well acquainted with these answers, 2.03.113
at whose request do these men play? 3.01. 29 P
these lovers cry, o ho, they die! 3.01.121
and give me swift transportance to these fields 3.02. 11
what mean these fellows? know they not achilles? 3.03. 70
save these men's looks, who do methinks find out 3.03. 90
to see these grecian lords! 3.03.138
glorious deeds, but in these fields of late, 3.03.188
but i can tell that in each grace of these 4.04. 89
o, these encounterers, so glib of tongue, | that 4.05. 58
but i'll endeavor deeds to match these words, 4.05.259
let these threats alone | till accident or 4.05.261
and too little brain, these two may run mad, but 5.01. 49 P
but if i tell how these two did //co–act, 5.02.118
superstitious girl | makes all these bodements. 5.03. 80
what sounds are these? COR 1.01. 46 P
that in these several places of the city | you 1.01.185
with thousands of these quarter'd slaves, as 1.01.199
nay, these are almost thoroughly persuaded; 1.01.201
with these shreds | they vented their 1.01.208
martius, | attend upon cominius to these wars. 1.01.237
take these rats thither | to gnaw their garners. 1.01.249
these are the words — i think | i have the 1.02. 7
these three lead on this preparation | whither 1.02. 15
how far off lie these armies? 1.04. 8
see here these movers that do prize their hours 1.05. 4
with those that wore them, these base slaves, 1.05. 7
if these shows be not outward, which of you 1.06. 77
within these three hours, tullus, | alone i 1.08. 7
may these same instruments, which you profane, 1.09. 41
these are the ushers of martius: 2.01.158 P
these | in honor follows coriolanus. 2.01.164
with the least cause these his new honors, which 2.01.229
may i change these garments? 2.03.146
behold, these are the tribunes of the people, 3.01. 21
are these your herd? 3.01. 33
must these have voices, that can yield them now, 3.01. 34
should the people do with these bald tribunes? 3.01.164
your wife, your son, these senators, the nobles; 3.02. 65
tell these sad women | 'tis fond to wail 4.01. 25
one seven years | from these old arms and legs, 4.01. 56
tullus aufidius /will appear well in these wars, 4.03. 34 P
an heir | of these fair edifices 'fore my wars 4.04. 3
than when these fellows ran about the streets, 4.06. 28
these are a side that would be glad to have 4.06.150
but one of these — | as he hath spices of them 4.07. 45
these pipes and these conveyances of our blood 5.01. 54
these pipes and these conveyances of our blood 5.01. 54
these eyes are not the same i wore in rome. 5.03. 38
to wait on fortune till | these wars determine. 5.03.120
these that survive let rome reward with love; TIT 1.01. 82
these that i bring unto their latest home, 1.01. 83
were piety in thine, it is in these. 1.01.115
these are their brethren, whom your goths beheld 1.01.122
with these our late–deceased emperor's sons. 1.01.184
forget | the least of these unspeakable deserts, 1.01.256
warrants these words in princely courtesy. 1.01.272
agree these deeds with that proud brag of thine, 1.01.306
o monstrous! what reproachful words are these? 1.01.308
these words are razors to my wounded heart. 1.01.314
nor thou, nor these, confederates in the deed 1.01.344
and with these boys mine honor thou hast wounded 1.01.365
my lord, to step out of these dreary dumps, 1.01.391
these words, these looks, infuse new life in me. 1.01.461
these words, these looks, infuse new life in me. 1.01.461
i do remit these young men's heinous faults. 1.01.484
these lovers will not keep the peace. 2.01. 37

to cool this heat, a charm to calm these fits, 2.01.134
no, madam, these are no venereal signs. 2.03. 37
ay, for these slips have made him noted long, 2.03. 86
these two have 'ticed me hither to this place: 2.03. 92
how these were they that made away his brother. 2.03.208
and for these bitter tears which now you see 3.01. 6
for these, tribunes, in the dust i write | my 3.01. 12
that shall distill from these two ancient /urns, 3.01. 17
rome could afford no tribunes like to these. 3.01. 44
then, | from these devourers to be banished! 3.01. 57
such with'red herbs as these | are meet for 3.01.177
and do not break into these deep extremes. 3.01.215
if there were reason for these miseries, | then 3.01.219
these miseries are more than may be borne. 3.01.243
for these two heads do seem to speak to me, 3.01.271
till all these mischiefs be return'd again, 3.01.273
what means my niece lavinia by these signs? 4.01. 8
which is it, girl, of these? 4.01. 32
mortal revenge upon these traitorous goths, 4.01. 93
but if you hunt these bear–whelps, then beware, 4.01. 96
and with a gad of steel will write these words, 4.01.103
will blow these sands like sibyl's leaves abroad 4.01.105
for these base bondmen to the yoke of rome. 4.01.109
why, lords, what wrongs are these! 4.04. 1
however these disturbers of our peace | buzz in 4.04. 6
shall be no shelter to these outrages, | but he 4.04. 22
the meanest or the best | for these contempts. 4.04. 34
these tidings nip me, and i hang the head | as 4.04. 70
art thou not sorry for these heinous deeds? 5.01.123
wretched stump, witness these crimson lines, 5.02. 22
witness these trenches made by grief and care, 5.02. 23
these are my ministers, and come with me. 5.02. 60
know you these two? 5.02.153
parle, | these quarrels must be quietly debated. 5.03. 20
sheaf, | these broken limbs again into one body. 5.03. 72
chief architect and plotter of these woes. 5.03.122
had titus to revenge | these wrongs unspeakable, 5.03.126
these sorrowful drops upon thy blood/–stain'd 5.03.154
o, were the sum of these that i should pay 5.03.158
how many thousand times hath these poor lips, 5.03.167
that hath been breeder of these dire events. 5.03.178
from forth the fatal loins of these two foes | a ROM pr 5
art thou drawn among these heartless hinds? 1.01. 66
sword, | or manage it to part these men with me. 1.01. 69
these happy masks that kiss fair ladies' brows, 1.01.230
and these, who, often drown'd, could never die, 1.02. 90
i was your mother much upon these years | that 1.03. 72
show a fair presence and put off these frowns, 1.05. 73
he hath hid himself among these trees | to be 2.01. 30
love's light wings did i o'erperch these walls, 2.02. 66
tips with silver all these fruit–tree tops — 2.02.108
if e'er thou wast thyself and these woes thine, 2.03. 77
thou and these woes were all for rosaline. 2.03. 78
/phantasimes, these new tuners of accent! 2.04. 29 P
be thus afflicted with these strange flies, 2.04. 32 P
with these strange flies, these fashion–mongers, 2.04. 33 P
these fashion–mongers, these /pardon–me's, who 2.04. 33 P
these violent delights have violent ends, | and 2.06. 9
for now, these hot days, is the mad blood 3.01. 4
thou art like one of these fellows that, when he 3.01. 5 P
leap to these arms untalk'd of and unseen! 3.02. 7
these griefs, these woes, these sorrows make me 3.02. 89
these griefs, these woes, these sorrows make me 3.02. 89
griefs, these woes, these sorrows make me old. 3.02. 89
these times of woe afford no times to woo. 3.04. 8
not, and all these woes shall serve | for sweet 3.05. 52
ay, madam, from the reach of these my hands. 3.05. 85
these are news indeed! 3.05.123
environed with all these hideous fears, | and 4.03. 50
hold, take these keys and fetch more spices, 4.04. 1
life and these lips have long been separated. 4.05. 27
/cure lives not | in these confusions. 4.05. 66
o, pardon me for bringing these ill news, 5.01. 22
than these poor compounds that thou mayest not 5.01. 82
romeo | hath had no notice of these accidents; 5.02. 27
fly hence and leave me, think upon these gone, 5.03. 60
what mean these masterless and gory swords | to 5.03.142
we see the ground whereon these woes do lie, 5.03.179
but the true ground of all these piteous woes 5.03.180
upon them, fit to open | these dead men's tombs. 5.03.201
a while, | till we can clear these ambiguities, 5.03.217
where be these enemies? 5.03.291
go hence to have more talk of these sad things; 5.03.307
all these spirits thy power | hath conjur'd to TIM 1.01. 6
artificial strife | lives in these touches, 1.01. 38
ay, marry, what of these? 1.01. 83
shall demonstrate these quick blows of fortune's 1.01. 91
these pencill'd figures are | even such as they 1.01.159
thou art timon's dog, and these knaves honest. 1.01.180
be small love amongest these sweet knaves, | and 1.01.249
what needs these feasts, pomps, and vainglories? 1.02.242 P
read me the superscription of these letters, i 2.02. 79 P
of winter show'rs, | these flies are couch'd. 2.02.172
and in some sort these wants of mine are crown'd 2.02.181
or by these | shall i try friends. 2.02.182
distasteful looks, and these hard fractions, 2.02.211
these old fellows | have their ingratitude in 2.02.214
give't these fellows | to whom 'tis instant due. 2.02.229
may these add to the number that may scald thee! 3.01. 51
lord timon myself, these gentlemen can witness; 3.02. 50 P
all these | owes their estates unto him. 3.03. 4
these debts may well be call'd desperate ones, 3.04.101 P
for these my present friends, as they are to me 3.06. 82 P
and these looks of care? 4.03.205
shame not these woods | by putting on the 4.03.208
will these moist trees, | that have outliv'd the 4.03.223
rid me these villains from your companies; 5.01.101
and i'll beweep these comforts, worthy senators. 5.01.158
these words become your lips as they pass 5.01.195
these walls of ours | were not erected by their 5.04. 22
nor are they such | that these great tow'rs, 5.04. 25
these well express in thee thy latter spirits: 5.04. 74
why dost thou lead these men about the streets? JC 1.01. 28
these growing feathers pluck'd from caesar's 1.01. 72
i do believe that these applauses are | for some 1.02.133
how i have thought of this, and of these times, 1.02.164
rome | under these hard conditions as this time 1.02.174
a crown neither, 'twas one of these coronets — 1.02.238 P
when these prodigies | do so conjointly meet, 1.03. 28
"these are their reasons, they are natural"; 1.03. 30
consider the true cause | why all these fires, 1.03. 63
all these fires, why all these gliding ghosts, 1.03. 63
why all these things change from their ordinance 1.03. 66
heaven hath infus'd them with these spirits, 1.03. 69
and fearful, as these strange eruptions are. 1.03. 78
but life, being weary of these worldly bars, 1.03. 96
be factious for redress of all these griefs, 1.03.118
and so bestow these papers as you bade me. 1.03.151
would run to these and these extremities; 2.01. 31
would run to these and these extremities; 2.01. 31
know i these men that come along with you? 2.01. 89
if these be motives weak, break off betimes, 2.01.116
but if these | (as i am sure they do) bear fire 2.01.119
it may be these apparent prodigies, | the 2.01.198
o caesar, these things are beyond all use, | and 2.02. 25
for these predictions | are to the world in 2.02. 28
and these does she apply for warnings and 2.02. 80
there is but one mind in all these men, and it 2.03. 5 P
these couchings and these lowly courtesies 3.01. 36
these couchings and these lowly courtesies 3.01. 36
that i am meek and gentle with these butchers! 3.01.255
shall in these confines with a monarch's voice 3.01.272
take | the cruel issue of these bloody men, 3.01.294
these are gracious drops. 3.02.194
these many then shall die, their names are 4.01. 1
and though we lay these honors on this man | to 4.01. 19
should the wars do with these jigging fools? 4.03.137
do face him there, | these people at our back. 4.03.212
and give these bills | unto the legions on the 5.02. 1
these tidings will well comfort cassius. 5.03. 54
are yet two romans living such as these? 5.03. 98
compell'd these skipping kerns to trust their MAC 1.02. 30
what are these | so wither'd and so wild in 1.03. 39
as the water has, | and these are of them. 1.03. 80
before, these weird sisters saluted me, and 1.05. 8 P
but in these cases | we still have judgment here 1.07. 7
as they had seen me with these hangman's hands. 2.02. 25
these deeds must not be thought | after these 2.02. 30
deeds must not be thought | after these ways; 2.02. 31
why did you bring these daggers from the place? 2.02. 45
in the affliction of these terrible dreams 3.02. 18
lave our honors in these flattering streams, 3.02. 33
o, these flaws and starts | (impostors to true 3.04. 62
that by the help of these (with him above | to 3.06. 32
where are these gentlemen? 4.01.155
what are these faces? 4.02. 79
all these are portable, | with other graces 4.03. 89
these evils thou repeat'st upon thyself | hath 4.03.112
by many of these trains hath sought to win me 4.03.118
were on the quarry of these murther'd deer | to 4.03.206
what, will these hands ne'er be clean? 5.01. 43 P
drug, | would scour these english hence? 5.03. 56
and be these juggling fiends no more believ'd, 5.08. 19
and yet, by these i see, | so great a day as 5.09. 2
that was and is the question of these wars. HAM 1.01.111
the scope | of these delated articles allow. 1.02. 38
these indeed seem, | for they are actions that a 1.02. 83
these but the trappings and the suits of woe. 1.02. 86
to give these mourning duties to your father. 1.02. 88
deliver, | upon the witness of these gentlemen, 1.02.194
two nights together had these gentlemen, 1.02.196
your father, | these hands are not more like. 1.02.212
and these few precepts in thy memory | look thou 1.03. 58
that you have ta'en these tenders for true pay, 1.03.106
these blazes, daughter, | giving more light than 1.03.117
the form of plausive manners — that these men, 1.04. 30
these are but wild and whirling words, my lord. 1.05.133
give him this money and these notes, reynaldo. 2.01. 1
you laying these slight sallies on my son, | as 2.01. 39
and bring these gentlemen where hamlet is. 2.02. 37
"in her excellent white bosom, these, etc." 2.02.113 P
o dear ophelia, i am ill at these numbers. 2.02.120 P
these tedious old fools! 2.02.219 P
these are the only men. 2.02.401 P
i'll have these players | play something like 2.02.594
of these we told him, | and there did seem in 3.01. 17
and drive his purpose into these delights. 3.01. 27
compos'd | as made these things more rich. 3.01. 98
take these again, for to the noble mind | rich 3.01. 99
this answer, hamlet, these words are not mine. 3.02. 97 P
and do still, by these pickers and stealers. 3.02.336 P
govern these ventages with your fingers and 3.02.357 P
look you, these are the stops. 3.02.360 P
but these cannot i command to any utt'rance of 3.02.361 P
these words like daggers enter in my ears. 3.04. 95
for in the fatness of these pursy times | virtue 3.04.153
there's matter in these sighs, these profound 4.01. 1
matter in these sighs, these profound heaves — 4.01. 1
good sir, whose powers are these? 4.04. 9
last, and as much containing as all these, | her 4.05. 87
this, give these fellows some means to the king, 4.06. 14 P
these good fellows will bring thee where i am. 4.06. 26 P
i will /give you way for these your letters, 4.06. 32
me | why you /proceeded not against these feats, 4.07. 6
these to your majesty, this to the queen. 4.07. 37
when these are gone, | the woman will be out. 4.07.188
did these bones cost no more the breeding, but 5.01. 91 P
that, on the view and knowing of these contents, 5.02. 44
these foils have all a length? 5.02.265
give order that these bodies | high on a stage 5.02.377
unknowing world | how these things came about. 5.02.380
of all these bounds, even from this line to this LR 1.01. 63
these late eclipses in the sun and moon portend 1.02.103 P
o, these eclipses do portend these divisions! 1.02.136 P
o, these eclipses do portend these divisions! 1.02.136 P
other day, what should follow these eclipses. 1.02.141 P
i am none of these, my lord, i beseech your 1.04. 82 P
these dispositions which of late transport you 1.04.221
that these hot tears, which break from me 1.04.298
go you before to gloucester with these letters. 1.05. 1 P
such smiling rogues as these, | like rats, oft 2.02. 73
these kind of knaves i know, which in this 2.02.101
none of these rogues and cowards | but ajax is 2.02.124
these are unsightly tricks. 2.04.157
if it be you that stirs these daughters' hearts 2.04.274
whereof, perchance, these are but furnishings — 3.01. 29
that love night | love not such nights as these. 3.02. 43
and cry | these dreadful summoners grace. 3.02. 59
these injuries the king now bears will be 3.03. 11 P
defend you | from seasons such as these? 3.04. 32
any cause in nature that make these hard hearts? 3.06. 78 P
these hairs which thou dost ravish from my chin 3.07. 38
upon these eyes of thine i'll set my foot. 3.07. 68
your father's tenant, | these fourscore years. 4.01. 14
that these our nether crimes | so speedily can 4.02. 79
and when i have stol'n upon these son–in–laws, 4.06.186
let's see these pockets; 4.06.256
these weeds are memories of those worser hours; 4.07. 7
these white flakes | did challenge pity of them. 4.07. 29
i will not swear these are my hands. 4.07. 54
the skill i have | remembers not these garments; 4.07. 66
for these domestic and particular broils | are 5.01. 30
to both these sisters have i sworn my love; 5.01. 55
shall we not see these daughters and these 5.03. 7
we not see these daughters and these sisters? 5.03. 7
back do i toss these treasons to thy head, 5.03.147
i am old now, | and these same crosses spoil me. 5.03.279
these fellows have some soul, | and such a one OTH 1.01. 54
(as in these cases where the aim reports, | 'tis 1.03. 6
for since these arms of mine had seven years' 1.03. 83
than these thin habits and poor likelihoods | of 1.03.108
these things to hear | would desdemona seriously 1.03.145
may help these lovers | /into /your /favor. 1.03.200
these sentences, to sugar or to gall, | being 1.03.216
these moors are changeable in their wills — 1.03.346 P
these are old fond paradoxes to make fools laugh 2.01.138 P
if such tricks as these strip you out of your 2.01.171 P
now for want of these requir'd conveniences, her 2.01.231 P
when these /mutualities so marshal the way, hard 2.01.261 P
of that will i cause these of cyprus to mutiny, 2.01.274 P
for, besides these beneficial news, it is the 2.02. 6 P
are these, i pray you, wind instruments? 3.01. 6 P
these letters give, iago, to the pilot, | and by 3.02. 1
therefore these stops of thine fright me the 3.03.120
where virtue is, these are more virtuous. 3.03.186
that we can call these delicate creatures ours, 3.03.269
within these three days let me hear thee say 3.03.472
am i the motive of these tears, my lord? 4.02. 43
hark how these instruments summon to supper! 4.02.169
prithee shroud me | in one of these same sheets. 4.03. 25
lay by these — "— willow, willow" — | prithee 4.03. 48 P
o, these men, these men! 4.03. 60
o, these men, these men! 4.03. 60
these may be counterfeits; 5.01. 43
where be these bloody thieves? 5.01. 63
these bloody accidents must excuse my manners 5.01. 94
these are portents; 5.02. 45
breath, indeed, these hands have newly stopp'd. 5.02.202
when you shall these unlucky deeds relate, 5.02.341
these strong egyptian fetters i must break, | or ANT 1.02.116
rare indeed | whom these things cannot blemish), 1.04. 23
these hands do lack nobility that they strike 2.05. 82
these quicksands, lepidus, | keep off them, for 2.07. 59
these three world–sharers, these competitors, 2.07. 70
these three world–sharers, these competitors, 2.07. 70
these drums, these trumpets, flutes! 2.07.131
these drums, these trumpets, flutes! 2.07.131
we bid a loud farewell | to these great fellows. 2.07.133
spring, | and these the showers to bring it on. 3.02. 44
no midway | 'twixt these extremes at all. 3.04. 20
o'er your content these strong necessities, 3.06. 83
thou hast forespoke my being in these wars, 3.07. 3
but these offers, | which serve not for his 3.07. 32
you misdoubt | this sword, and these my wounds? 3.07. 63
i shall return once more | to kiss these lips, i 3.13.174
thou hast seen these signs, | they are black 4.14. 7
i made these wars for egypt, and the queen, 4.14. 15
these thoughts of horror further than you shall 5.02. 63
these same whoreson devils do the gods great 5.02.275 P
and these fig leaves | have slime upon them, 5.02.351
high events as these | strike those that make 5.02.360
left these notes | of what commands i should be CYM 1.01.171
i embrace these conditions, let us have articles 1.04.156 P
we will have these things set down by lawful 1.04.164 P
commanded of me these most poisonous compounds, 1.05. 8
of these thy compounds on such creatures as | we 1.05. 19
the seeing these effects will be | both noisome 1.05. 25
now canopied | under these windows, white and 2.02. 22
in these fear'd /hopes | i barely gratify your 2.04. 6
be | you bees that make these locks of counsel! 3.02. 36
i'll tread these flats. 3.03. 11
this rock and these demesnes have been my world, 3.03. 70
these boys know little they are sons to th' king 3.03. 80
at three and two years old, i stole these babes, 3.03.101
old servant, | i have not seen these two days. 3.05. 55
i would these garments were come. 3.05.132 P
multitudes, | could not outpeer these twain. 3.06. 86
these are kind creatures. 4.02. 32
i saw him not these many years, and yet | i know 4.02. 66
thou blazon'st | in these two princely boys! 4.02.171
even so | these herblets shall, which we upon 4.02.287
these flow'rs are like the pleasures of the 4.02.296
flies, as deep | as these poor pickaxes can dig; 4.02.389
these present wars shall find i love my country, 4.03. 43
me | of these italian weeds and suit myself | as 5.01. 23
these three, | three thousand confident, in act 5.03. 28
death, who is the key | t' unbar these locks. 5.04. 8
take this life, | and cancel these cold bonds. 5.04. 28
there's business in these faces. 5.05. 23
these her women | can trip me, if i err, who 5.05. 34
how comes these staggers on me? 5.05.233
these two young gentlemen, that call me father 5.05.328
these gentle princes | (for such and so they are 5.05.336
are) these twenty years | have i train'd up; 5.05.337
stole these children | upon my banishment; 5.05.341
the benediction of these covering heavens | fall 5.05.350
if these be they, i know not how to wish | a 5.05.355
these, | and your three motives to the battle, 5.05.387
all o'erjoy'd, | save these in bonds. 5.05.402
the soldier that did company these three | in 5.05.408
as these before thee, thou thyself shalt bleed. PER 1.01. 58
these mouths who, but of late, earth, sea, and 1.04. 34
with their superfluous riots, hear these tears! 1.04. 54
and these our ships, you happily may think | are 1.04. 92

we would purge the land of these drones, that 2.01. 46 P
sea | these fishers tell the infirmities of men, 2.01. 49
in honor of whose birth these triumphs are, 2.02. 5
these cates resist me, he not thought upon. 2.03. 29
these knights unto their several lodgings! 2.03.109
are letters brought, the tenor these: 3.ch. 24
the god of this great vast, rebuke these surges, 3.01. 1
get fire and meat for these poor men. 3.02. 3
you, should at these early hours | shake off the 3.02. 22
these roguing thieves serve the great pirate 4.01. 96
or that these pirates, | not enough barbarous, 4.02. 65
these blushes of hers must be quench'd with some 4.02.124 P
neither of these are so bad as thou art, | since 4.06.161
any of these ways are yet better than this; 4.06.177
boast, | and will undertake all these to teach. 4.06.185
here of these /shores? 5.01.103
and how achiev'd you these endowments which 5.01.116
how came you in these parts? 5.01.169
i threw her overboard with these very arms. 5.03. 19
be buried | a second time within these arms. 5.03. 44
i freely lend | to do these poor queens service. TNK 1.01.199
these poor slight sores | need not a plantin; 1.02. 60
mind nurse equal | to these so diff'ring twins. 1.03. 33
and power | i' th' least of these was dreadful, 1.03. 39
these strewings are for their chamber. 2.01. 21 P
these hands shall never draw 'em out like 2.02. 24
even from the bottom of these miseries, | from 2.02. 56
i'll have a gown full of 'em — and of these: 2.02.128
keep these flowers, | we'll see how near art can 2.02.148
it so) as ever | these eyes yet look'd on. 2.04. 11
best, and wrastle, | that these times can allow. 2.05. 4
if these signs | of prisonment were off me and 3.01. 31
with these hands | void of appointment, that 3.01. 39
had i a sword, | and these house–clogs away — 3.01. 43
quit me of these cold gyves, give me a sword, 3.01. 72
these impediments | will i file off; 3.01. 84
food took i none these two days — | sipp'd some 3.02. 26
and, good now, | no more of these vain parleys; 3.03. 10
defy me in these fair terms, and you show | more 3.06. 25
for none but such dare die in these just trials. 3.06.105
else of after–ages | for these lost cousins. 3.06.188
these are strange conjurings. 3.06.201
mercy on these princes. 3.06.211
can these two live, | and have the agony of love 3.06.218
the goodly mothers that have groan'd for these, 3.06.245
and in their funeral songs for these two cousins 3.06.248
will you, arcite, | take these conditions? 3.06.264
these are men! 3.06.265
for me, a hair shall never fall of these men. 3.06.287
these are strange questions. 4.01. 35
and all these must be boys, | he has the trick 4.01.131
yet these that we count errors may become him: 4.02. 31
alone | and only beautiful, and these the eyes, 4.02. 38
these the bright lamps of beauty, that command 4.02. 39
braver spirits | than these they have brought 4.02. 74
must these men die too? 4.02.112
we | the sails that must these vessels port even 5.01. 29
shall confound | both these brave knights, and i 5.01.167
having these virtues, | i think he might be 5.02. 55
i'll warrant you within these three or four days 5.02.104
so it far'd | good space between these kinsmen; 5.03.129
it with the palsy, for these bastards of dung — STM II.C 12 P
submit you to these noble gentlemen, | entreat II.C 144
sure these things | not physick'd by respect III 12
these blue–vein'd violets whereon we lean VEN 125
lie, | these forceless flowers like sturdy trees 152
these lovely caves, these round enchanting pits, 247
these lovely caves, these round enchanting pits, 247
and these mine eyes, true leaders to their queen 503
would root these beauties as he roots the mead. 636
pursue these fearful creatures o'er the downs, 677
"and not the least of all these maladies | but 745
so she at these sad signs draws up her breath, 929
part is youth, and beats these from the stage. LUC 278
but all these poor forbiddings could not stay 323
"so, so," quoth he, "these lets attend the time, 330
these worlds in tarquin new ambition bred, | who 411
which blow these pitchy vapors from their biding 550
if all these petty ills shall change thy good, 656
"so shall these slaves be king, and thou their 659
these means, as frets upon an instrument, 1140
a pretty while these pretty creatures stand, 1233
and one man's lust these many lives confounds. 1489
these contraries such unity do hold | only to 1558
these water–galls in her dim element | foretell 1588
that they will suffer these abominations 1832
here in these brakes deep–wounded with a boar, PP 9.10
and if these pleasures may thee move, | then 19.15
these pretty pleasures might me move | to live 19.19
these are certain signs to know | faithful 20.55
for these dead birds sigh a prayer. PHT 67
yet in these thoughts myself almost despising, SON 29. 9
these poor rude lines of thy deceased lover, 32. 4
or any of these all, or all, or more, | entitled 37. 6
if my slight muse do please these curious days, 38.13
these present–absent with swift motion slide. 45. 4
for when these quicker elements are gone | in 45. 5
you shall shine more bright in these contents 55. 3
his beauty shall in these black lines be seen, 63.13
tir'd with all these, for restful death i cry: 66. 1
tir'd with all these, from these would i be gone 66.13
with all these, from these would i be gone, 66.13
in days long since, before these last so bad. 67.14
before these bastard signs of fair were born, 68. 3
cannot contain | commit to these waste /blanks, 77.10
these offices, so oft as thou wilt look, | shall 77.13
but these particulars are not my measure, | all 91. 7
all these i better in one general best. 91. 8
as with your shadow i with these did play. 98.14
for we, which now behold these present days, 106.13
these blenches gave my heart another youth, 110. 7
/... these rebel pow'rs that thee array, | why 146. 2
these often bath'd she in her fluxive eyes, LC 50
"and long upon these terms i held my city, 176
"'and lo behold these talents of their hair, 204
"'lo all these trophies of affections hot, | of 218
for these, of force, must your oblations be, 223
take all these similes to your own command, 227

"'now all these hearts that do on mine depend, 274
THESEUS' 5 FR 0.0005 REL FR 5 V 0 P
for theseus' perjury and unjust flight; TGV 4.04.168
perchance till after theseus' wedding–day. MND 2.01.139
play | intended for great theseus' nuptial day. 3.02. 12
dance in duke theseus' house triumphantly, | and 4.01. 89
you talk of pirithous' and theseus' love: TNK 1.03. 55
THESEUS 20 FR 0.0022 REL FR 20 V 0 P
happy be theseus, our renowned duke! MND 1.01. 20
to theseus must be wedded, and you come | to 2.01. 72
hippolyta, | knowing i know thy love to theseus? 2.01. 76
of faithful lovers be | wedded, with theseus, 4.01. 92
'tis strange, my theseus, that these lovers 5.01. 1
here, mighty theseus. 5.01. 38
theseus (who where he threats appalls) hath sent TNK 1.02. 90
i think | theseus cannot be umpire to himself, 1.03. 45
me from the arm | of the all–noble theseus, for 1.03. 93
noble theseus, | to purchase name, and do my 2.05. 25
thanks, theseus. 2.05. 32
come forth and fear not, here's no theseus. 3.03. 3
hold thy word, theseus. 3.06.136
and thou shalt see me, theseus, | do such a 3.06.154
we seek not | thy breath of mercy, theseus. 3.06.158
thou shalt have pity of us both, o theseus, | if 3.06.172
almost all men, and yet i yielded, theseus — 3.06.207
o duke theseus, | the goodly mothers that have 3.06.244
we dare not fail thee, theseus. 3.06.305
for musicians, | and sing the wars of theseus. 4.01.134
THESSALIAN 1 FR 0.0001 REL FR 1 V 0 P
and dewlapp'd like thessalian bulls; MND 4.01.122
THESSALY 2 FR 0.0002 REL FR 2 V 0 P
horn, | in crete, in sparta, nor in thessaly. MND 4.01.126
the boar of thessaly | was never so emboss'd. ANT 4.13. 2
THETIS' 3 FR 0.0003 REL FR 3 V 0 P
and achilles' horse | makes many thetis' sons. TRO 1.03.212
now, great thetis' son! 3.03. 94
hath thetis' birth–child on the heavens bestowed PER 4.04. 41
THETIS 3 FR 0.0003 REL FR 3 V 0 P
ruffian boreas once enrage | the gentle thetis, TRO 1.03. 39
we'll to our ship, | away, my thetis! ANT 3.07. 60
thetis, being proud, swallowed some part a' th' PER 4.04. 39
THEWS 3 FR 0.0003 REL FR 2 V 1 P
care i for the limb, the thews, the stature, 2H4 3.02.258 P
have thews and limbs like to their ancestors; JC 1.03. 81
does not grow alone | in thews and /bulk, but, HAM 1.03. 12
THEY *(also th'*)*
/THEY 41 FR 0.0046 REL FR 26 V 15 P
/they /carried /me /to /the /tavern /and /made WIV 1.01.125 P
that by and by disguis'd /they will be here. LLL 5.02. 96
i am, as /they say, but to parfect one man in 5.02.501 P
i am like you, /they say. WT 1.02.208
/were /they /not /mine? R2 4.01.168
/did /they /not /sometimes /cry "/all /hail!" 4.01.169
/they /tend /the /crown, /yet /still /with /me 4.01.199
/the /crown, /yet /still /with /me /they /stay. 4.01.199
/but /they /can /see /a /sort /of /traitors 4.01.246
/they /shall /be /satisfied. 4.01.273
/and /they /did /fight /with /queasiness, 2H4 1.01.196
/they /that, /when /richard /liv'd, /would /have 1.03.101
/whom /they /doted /on | /and /bless'd /and 4.01.136
/to /tenedos /they /come, | /and /the TRO pr 11
/they /are /oppos'd /already. 4.05. 94
/as /they /contend /with /thee /in /courtesy. 4.05.206
are /they thy ministers? what are they call'd? TIT 5.02. 61
hear not my steps, which /way /they walk, for MAC 2.01. 57
/how /comes /it? /do /they /grow /rusty? HAM 2.02.337 P
/the /common /stages — /so /they /call /them — 2.02.342 P
/what, /are /they /children? 2.02.345 P
/how /are /they /escoted? 2.02.346 P
/will /they /pursue /the /quality /no /longer 2.02.346 P
/quality /no /longer /than /they /can /sing? 2.02.347 P
/will /they /not /say /afterwards, /if /they 2.02.347 P
/if /they /should /grow /themselves /to /common 2.02.348 P
/ay, /that /they /do, /my /lord — /hercules 2.02.361 P
/they cry, "choose we, laertes shall be king!" 4.05.107
/they /did /make /love /to /this /employment, 5.02. 57
/as /flatteries, /when /they /are /seen /abus'd. LR 1.03. 20
/monopoly /out, /they /would /have /part /an't. 1.04.153 P
/they /will /not /let /me /have /all /the /fool 1.04.154 P
/which /they /will /make /an /obedient /father. 1.04.235 P
/no, /no, /they /would /not. 2.04. 19
/yes, /they /have. 2.04. 20
/ere /they /have /done /their /mischief, 4.02. 55
/they /are /apt /enough /to /dislocate /and 4.02. 65
/'tis /so, /they /are /afoot. 4.03. 49
/they /say /edgar, /his /banish'd /son, /is 4.07. 89 P
up thus meanly | i' th' cave /wherein /they bow, CYM 3.03. 83
slaves, | the strides /they victors made: 5.03. 43
THEY 2577 FR 0.2913 REL FR 1850 V 727 P
they are louder than the weather, or our office. TMP 1.01. 36 P
poor souls, they perish'd. 1.02. 9
wherefore did they not | that hour destroy us? 1.02.138
dear, they durst not, | so dear the love my 1.02.140
in few, they hurried us aboard a bark, | bore us 1.02.144
where they prepared | a rotten carcass of a butt 1.02.145
there they hoist us, | to cry to th' sea, that 1.02.148
but are they, ariel, safe? 1.02.217
they all have met again | and are upon the 1.02.233
supposing that they saw the king's ship wrack'd, 1.02.236
thing she did | they would not take her life. 1.02.267
for that vast of night that they may work, | all 1.02.327
at the first sight | they have chang'd eyes. 1.02.442
they are both in either's pow'rs; 1.02.451
this is a caliban, | and they to him are angels. 1.02.482
so they are. 1.02.486
being, as they were, drench'd in the sea, hold 2.01. 62 P
and nimble lungs that they always use to laugh 2.01.174 P
i find | they are inclin'd to do so. 2.01.193
they fell together all, as by consent; 2.01.203
they dropp'd, as by a thunder–stroke. 2.01.204
why, they were no worse | than now they are. 2.01.261
why, they were no worse | than now they are. 2.01.262
were then my fellows, now they are my men. 2.01.274
that stand 'twixt me and milan, candied be they, 2.01.279
candied be they, | and melt ere they molest! 2.01.280
but | for every trifle are they set upon me, 2.02. 8
when they will not give a doit to relieve a lame 2.02. 31 P
they will lay out ten to see a dead indian. 2.02. 32 P

if any be trinculo's legs, these are they. 2.02.105 P
be fine things, and if they be not sprites. 2.02.116
so glad of this as they i cannot be, | who are 3.01. 92
they say there's but five upon this isle: 3.02. 5 P
where should they be set else? 3.02. 10 P
monster indeed if they were set in his tail. 3.02. 11 P
they all do hate him | as rootedly as i. 3.02. 94
for, now they are oppress'd with travail, they 3.03. 15
are oppress'd with travail, they | will not, nor 3.03. 15
use such vigilance | as when they are fresh. 3.03. 17
i should report this now, would they believe me? 3.03. 28
who, though they are of monstrous shape, yet, 3.03. 31
(although they want the use of tongue) a kind 3.03. 38
they vanish'd strangely. 3.03. 40
since | they have left their viands behind; 3.03. 41
thee of thy son, alonso, | they have bereft; 3.03. 76
they now are in my pow'r; 3.03. 90
young ferdinand, whom they suppose is drown'd, 3.03. 92
it is my promise, | and they expect it from me. 4.01. 42
since they did plot | the means that dusky dis 4.01. 88
here thought they to have done | some wanton 4.01. 94
bless this twain, that they may prosperous be, 4.01.104
told you, sir, they were red–hot with drinking, 4.01.171
so full of valor that they smote the air | for 4.01.172
like unback'd colts, they prick'd their ears, 4.01.176
lifted up their noses | as they smelt music. 4.01.178
that calf–like they my lowing follow'd through 4.01.179
charge my goblins that they grind their joints 4.01.258
hark, they roar! 4.01.261
they cannot boudge till your release. 5.01. 11
that relish all as sharply | passion as they, be 5.01. 24
they being penitent, | the sole drift of my 5.01. 28
i'll restore, | and they shall be themselves. 5.01. 32
o heavens, that they were living both in naples, 5.01.149
that they were, i wish | myself were mudded in 5.01.150
so much admire | that they devour their reason, 5.01.155
though the seas threaten, they are merciful, | i 5.01.178
they strengthen | from strange to stranger. 5.01.227
these men, my lords, | then say if they be true. 5.01.268
where should they | find this grand liquor that 5.01.279
they do not love that do not show their love. TGV 1.02. 31
o, they love least that let men know their love. 1.02. 32
which they would have the profferer construe "ay 1.02. 56
yet here they shall not lie, for catching cold. 1.02.133
they are all perceiv'd without ye. 2.01. 34 P
without me? they cannot. 2.01. 35 P
eyes had the lights they were wont to have when 2.01. 71 P
are they not lamely writ? 2.01. 91 P
madam, they are for you. 2.01.125
they are for you. 2.01.127
bare liveries that they live by your bare words. 2.04. 46 P
they say that love hath not an eye at all. 2.04. 96
marry, after they clos'd in earnest, they parted 2.05. 12 P
in earnest, they parted very fairly in jest. 2.05. 12 P
what, are they broken? 2.05. 18 P
no, they are both as whole as a fish. 2.05. 19 P
haply when they have judg'd me fast asleep, 3.01. 25
lord, they have devis'd a mean | how he her 3.01. 38
be they of much import? 3.01. 55
ne'er so black, say they have angels' faces. 3.01.103
and slaves they are to me that send them flying: 3.01.141
would lodge where, senseless, they are lying! 3.01.143
i curse myself, for they are sent by me, | that 3.01.148
that they should harbor where their lord should 3.01.149
thou reach stars, because they shine on thee? 3.01.156
mine, | for they are harsh, untuneable, and bad. 3.01.209
them | as if but now they waxed pale for woe: 3.01.230
that they may hold excus'd our lawless lives; 4.01. 52
which since i know they virtuously are plac'd, 4.03. 38
i know they are stuff'd with protestations, 4.04.129
time, | so much they spur their expedition. 5.01. 6
that they are out by lease. 5.02. 29
that leads toward mantua, whither they are fled. 5.02. 47
they love me well; 5.04. 16
forgive them what they have committed here | and 5.04.154
they are reformed, civil, full of good, | and 5.04.156
they may give the dozen white luces in their WIV 1.01. 16 P
and being fap, sir, was, as they say, cashier'd; 1.01.178 P
they will not sit till you come. 1.01.278 P
'em, they are very ill–favor'd rough things. 1.01.298 P
them both, and they shall be exchequers to me. 1.03. 70 P
they shall be my east and west indies, and i 1.03. 71 P
but they do no more adhere and keep place 2.01. 61 P
men — very rogues, now they be out of service. 2.01.176 P
were they his men? 2.01.177 P
marry, were they. 2.01.178 P
and what they made there, i know not. 2.01.236 P
are they so? 2.02. 52 P
you, they could never get an eye–wink of her. 2.02. 71 P
(in any such sort, as they say) but in the way 2.02. 73 P
they could never get her so much as sip on a cup 2.02. 74 P
wife acquainted each other how they love me? 2.02.110 P
they have not so little grace, i hope. 2.02.111 P
have discretion, as they say, and know the world 2.02.130 P
will they yet look after thee? 2.02.140 P
for they say, if money go before, all ways do 2.02.168 P
they say the jealous wittolly knave hath masses 2.02.271 P
yet they are devils' additions, the names of 2.02.298 P
and what they think in their hearts they may 2.02.307 P
what they think in their hearts they may effect, 2.02.307 P
they will break their hearts but they will 2.02.308 P
will break their hearts but they will effect. 2.02.308 P
sure they sleep, he hath no use of them. 3.02. 31 P
good plots, they are laid, and our revolted 3.02. 39 P
told them over and over, they lack no direction. 3.03. 18 P
why, what have you to do whither they bear it? 3.03.155 P
they can tell you how things go better than i 3.04. 65 P
as little remorse as they would have drown'd a 3.05. 10 P
they mistook their erection. 3.05. 39 P
they convey'd me into a buck–basket. 3.05. 86 P
they took me on their shoulders; 3.05.100 P
once or twice what they had in their basket. 3.05.102 P
had been one number more, because they say, 4.01. 24 P
there they always use to discharge their 4.02. 57 P
him at the door with it, as they did last time. 4.02. 96 P
direct my men what they shall do with the basket 4.02. 99 P
if they can find in their hearts the poor 4.02.217 P
at court, and they are going to meet him. 4.03. 3 P

they speak english? 4.03. 6 P
they shall have my horses, but i'll make them 4.03. 8 P
they have had my /house a week at command. 4.03. 9 P
they must come off. 4.03. 11 P
there is no better way than that they spoke of. 4.04. 16
what are they? let us know. 4.05. 42 P
they were nothing but about mistress anne page, 4.05. 46 P
eton, they threw me off from behind one of them, 4.05. 67 P
they are gone but to meet the duke, villain, do 4.05. 71 P
meet the duke, villain, do not say they be fled. 4.05. 72 P
they would melt me out of my fat drop by drop, 4.05. 97 P
i warrant they would whip me with their fine 4.05. 99 P
and so they shall be both bestow'd. 4.05.107 P
and have not they suffer'd? 4.05.110 P
for they must all be mask'd and vizarded) | that 4.06. 40
they say there is divinity in odd numbers, 5.01. 3 P
they are all couch'd in a pit hard by herne's 5.03. 13 P
meeting, they will at once display to the night. 5.03. 15 P
they are fairies, he that speaks to them shall 5.05. 47
four times in the thought they were not fairies, 5.05.122 P
of all rhyme and reason, that they were fairies. 5.05.126 P
waste | thyself upon thy virtues, they on thee. MM 1.01. 31
they put forth to steal. 1.02. 13 P
they shall stand for seed. 1.02. 99 P
they had gone down too, but that a wise burgher 1.02. 99 P
but when they weep and kneel, | all their 1.04. 81
theirs | as they themselves would owe them. 1.04. 83
a thief or two | guiltier than him they try. 2.01. 21
what benefactors are they? 2.01. 52 P
are they not malefactors? 2.01. 52 P
your honor, i know not well what they are; 2.01. 54 P
but precise villains they are, that i am sure of 2.01. 54 P
what quality are they of? 2.01. 58 P
was (as they say) pluck'd down in the suburbs; 2.01. 64 P
they are not china dishes, but very good dishes. 2.01. 94 P
you wot of, unless they kept very good diet, as 2.01.111 P
in his courses till thou know'st what they are. 2.01.188 P
they will draw you, master froth, and you will 2.01.205 P
sir, in my poor opinion, they will to't then. 2.01.233 P
they do you wrong to put you so oft upon't. 2.01.265 P
as they are chosen, they are glad to choose me 2.01.269 P
are chosen, they are glad to choose me for them. 2.01.269 P
degrees, | but here they live, to end. 2.02. 99
ay, as the glasses where they view themselves, 2.04.125
which are as easy broke as they make forms. 2.04.126
blushes | that banish what they sue for. 2.04.163
they say this angelo was not made by man and 3.02.104 P
in his house–eaves, because they are lecherous. 3.02.176 P
events, with a prayer they may prove prosperous, 3.02.238 P
they will then ere't be long. 4.02. 76
now are they come. 4.02. 85
difficulties are but easy when they are known. 4.02.205 P
or they shall beat out my brains with billets. 4.03. 55 P
but they say the duke will be here to–morrow. 4.03.155 P
too many of him already, sir, if they be true; 4.03.168 P
they would else have married me to the rotten 4.03.173 P
they should exhibit their petitions in the 4.04. 10 P
though they would swear down each particular 5.01.243
they have confess'd you did. 5.01.289 P
although by /confiscation they are ours, | we do 5.01.423
they say best men are moulded out of faults, 5.01.439
but ere they came — o, let me say no more! ERR 1.01. 94
and in our sight they three were taken up | by 1.01.110
therefore homeward did they bend their course. 1.01.117
could all my travels warrant me they live. 1.01.139
which princes, would they, may not disannul, 1.01.144
they say this town is full of cozenage: 1.02. 97
time is their master, and when they see time, 2.01. 8
they can be meek that have no other cause: 2.01. 33
for they say, every why hath a wherefore. 2.02. 43 P
that at dinner they should not drop in his 2.02. 98 P
i'll say as they say, and persever so, | and in 2.02.215
they stand at the door, master, bid them welcome 3.01. 68
they stay for nought at all | but for their 4.01. 91
they appear to men like angels of light, light 4.03. 55 P
they must be bound and laid in some dark room. 4.04. 94
god help, poor souls, how idlely do they talk! 4.04.129
god, for thy mercy! they are loose again. 4.04.144
here this night, they will surely do us no harm. 4.04.151 P
you saw they speak us fair, give us gold: 4.04.152 P
methinks they are such a gentle nation that, but 4.04.153 P
see where they come, we will behold his death. 5.01.128
then they fled | into this abbey, whither we 5.01.154
whose beard they have sing'd off with brands of 5.01.171
they threw on him | great pails of puddled mire 5.01.172
between them they will kill the conjurer. 5.01.177
they are both forsworn: 5.01.212
along with them | they brought one pinch, a 5.01.238
then all together | they fell upon me, bound me, 5.01.247
and me they left with those of epidamium. 5.01.354
they never meet but there's a skirmish of wit ADO 1.01. 63 P
women, they would else have been troubled with a 1.01.128 P
such great letters as they write "here is good 1.01.265 P
are they good? 1.02. 6 P
/event stamps them, but they have a good cover; 1.02. 7 P
they show well outward. 1.02. 8 P
them, and then they laugh at him and beat him. 2.01.142 P
nay, if they lead to any ill, i will leave them 2.01.153 P
so they sell bullocks. 2.01.195 P
sin upon purpose, because they would go thither; 2.01.259 P
my lord, if they were but a week married, they 2.01.353 P
a week married, they would talk themselves mad. 2.01.354 P
they will scarcely believe this without trial. 2.02. 40 P
have howl'd thus, they would have hang'd him, 2.03. 80 P
be, when they hold one an opinion of another's 2.03.216 P
they have the truth of this from hero; 2.03.221 P
they seem to pity the lady. 2.03.222 P
they say i will bear myself proudly, if i 2.03.225 P
they say too that she will rather die than give 2.03.226 P
happy are they that hear their detractions and 2.03.229 P
they say the lady is fair; 2.03.230 P
and did they bid you tell her of it, madam? 3.01. 39
they did entreat me to acquaint her of it, | but 3.01. 40
but i persuaded them, if they lov'd benedick, 3.01. 41
misprising what they look on, and her wit 3.01. 52
for the which i hear what they say of him. 3.02. 58 P
bears will not bite one another when they meet. 3.02. 78 P
yea, or else it were pity but they should suffer 3.03. 2 P
if they should have any allegiance in them, 3.03. 5 P
or george seacole, for they can write and read. 3.03. 12 P
true, and they are to meddle with none but the 3.03. 33 P
how if they will not? 3.03. 44 P
why then let them alone till they are sober. 3.03. 45 P
if they make you not then the better answer, you 3.03. 46 P
you may say they are not the men you took them 3.03. 47 P
may, but i think they that touch pitch will be 3.03. 57 P
ones, poor ones may make what price they will. 3.03.115 P
and thought they margaret was hero? 3.03.153 P
the duchess of milan's gown that they praise so. 3.04. 16 P
o, that exceeds, they say. 3.04. 17 P
count sent me — they are an excellent perfume. 3.04. 62 P
as, god help, i would desire they were, but, in 3.05. 11 P
as they say, "when the age is in, the wit is out 3.05. 34 P
they stay for you to give your daughter to her 3.05. 54 P
what men daily do, not knowing what they do! 4.01. 20 P
sir, they are spoken, and these things are true. 4.01. 67
confess'd the vile encounters they have had | a 4.01. 93
fie, fie, they are not to be named, my lord, 4.01. 95
they know that do accuse me, i know none. 4.01.177
if they speak but truth of her, | these hands 4.01.190
if they wrong her honor, | the proudest of them 4.01.191
but they shall find, awak'd in such a kind, 4.01.197
to strange sores strangely they strain the cure. 4.01.252
bear her in hand until they come to take hands, 4.01.304 P
write down, that they hope they serve god; 4.02. 18 P
write down, that they hope they serve god; 4.02. 18 P
'fore god, they are both in a tale. 4.02. 30 P
have you writ down, that they are none? 4.02. 31 P
to that grief | which they themselves not feel, 5.01. 22
however they have writ the style of gods, | and 5.01. 37
and what they weigh, even to the utmost scruple 5.01. 93
how they might hurt their enemies — if they 5.01. 98
might hurt their enemies — if they durst — 5.01. 98
marry, sir, they have committed false report; 5.01.215 P
moreover, they have spoken untruths; 5.01.216 P
secondarily, they are slanders; 5.01.217 P
sixt and lastly, they have belied a lady; 5.01.217 P
thirdly, they have verified unjust things; 5.01.218 P
and, to conclude, they are lying knaves. 5.01.219 P
first, i ask thee what they have done; 5.01.220 P
sixt and lastly, why they are committed; 5.01.222 P
my villainy they have upon record, which i had 5.01.240 P
they say he wears a key in his ear and a lock 5.01.308 P
vice, and they are dangerous weapons for maids. 5.02. 21 P
they were never so truly turn'd over and over as 5.02. 34 P
a state of evil that they will not admit any 5.02. 63 P
songs of woe, | round about her tomb they go. 5.03. 15
they swore you did. 5.04. 76
are much deceiv'd, for they did swear you did. 5.04. 79
they swore that you were almost sick for me. 5.04. 80
they swore that you were well–nigh dead for me. 5.04. 81
than those that walk and wot not what they are. LLL 1.01. 91
they are both the varnish of a complete man. 1.02. 43 P
your fellows, for they are but lightly rewarded. 1.02.152 P
nothing, master moth, but what they look upon. 1.02.162 P
they say so most that most his humors know. 2.01. 53
such short–liv'd wits do wither as they grow. 2.01. 54
berowne they call him, but a merrier man, 2.01. 66
are they all in love, | that every one her own 2.01. 77
my lips are no common, though several they be. 2.01.223
their own worth from where they were glass'd, 2.01.244
tongues speak sweetly, then they name her name, 3.01.166
name her name, | and rosaline they call her. 3.01.167
when they strive to be | lords o'er their lords? 4.01. 37
marvellous well shot, for they both did hit /it. 4.01.130
be /ingenious, they shall want no instruction; 4.02. 78 P
did they please you, sir nathaniel? 4.02.150 P
they have pitch'd a toil: 4.03. 2 P
for so they say the fool said, and so say i, and 4.03. 4 P
and they thy glory through my grief will show. 4.03. 36
did they, quoth you? 4.03.217
they are the ground, the books, the academes, 4.03.299
they sparkle still the right promethean fire; 4.03.348
they are the books, the arts, the academes, 4.03.349
they have been at a great feast of languages, 5.01. 36 P
they have liv'd long on the alms–basket of words 5.01. 38 P
ad dunghill, at the fingers' ends, as they say. 5.01. 78 P
they are worse fools to purchase mocking so. 5.02. 59
are so surely caught, when they are catch'd, 5.02. 69
what are they | that charge their breath against 5.02. 87
action and accent did they teach him there: 5.02. 99
and ever and anon they made a doubt | presence 5.02.101
with that they all did tumble on the ground, 5.02.115
but what, but what, come they to visit us? 5.02.119
they do, they do; 5.02.120
they do, they do; 5.02.120
know | by favors several which they did bestow. 5.02.125
and will they so? 5.02.126
they do it but in mockery merriment, | and mock 5.02.139
their several counsels they unbosom shall | to 5.02.141
but shall we dance, if they desire us to't? 5.02.145
and they, well mock'd, depart away with shame. 5.02.156
they will not answer to that epithet; 5.02.171
they do not mark me, and that brings me out. 5.02.173
if they do speak our language, 'tis our will 5.02.176
know what they would. 5.02.178
what would they, say they? 5.02.180
what would they, say they? 5.02.180
why, that they have, and bid them so be gone. 5.02.182
they say that they have measur'd many a mile 5.02.186
they say that they have measur'd many a mile 5.02.186
if they have measured many, | the measure then 5.02.189
tapers they are, with your sweet breaths puff'd 5.02.267
well–liking wits they have — gross gross, fat 5.02.268
will they not, think you, hang themselves 5.02.270
they were all in lamentable cases! 5.02.273
immediately they will again be here | in their 5.02.287
be | they will digest this harsh indignity. 5.02.289
will they return? 5.02.290
they will, they will, god knows, | and leap for 5.02.290
they will, they will, god knows, | and leap for 5.02.290
leap for joy, though they are lame with blows: 5.02.291
therefore change favors, and, when they repair, 5.02.292
do, | if they return in their own shapes to woo? 5.02.299
and wonder what they were, and to what end 5.02.304
here they stay'd an hour, | and talk'd apace; 5.02.368
they did not bless us with one happy word. 5.02.370
when they are thirsty, fools would fain have 5.02.372
they are infected, in their hearts it lies; 5.02.420
they have the plague, and caught it of your eyes 5.02.421
no, they are free that gave these tokens to us. 5.02.424
they would know | whether the three worthies 5.02.485
berowne, they will shame us; 5.02.511
i say they shall not come. 5.02.514
but we will put it, as they say, to fortuna de 5.02.530 P
but if they will not, throw away that spirit, 5.02.867
thrice blessed they that master so their blood MND 1.01. 74
duchess and the ladies, that they would shrike; 1.02. 76 P
they would have no more discretion but to hang 1.02. 80 P
and now they never meet in grove or green, | by 2.01. 28
but they do square, that all their elves for 2.01. 30
do their work, and they shall have good luck. 2.01. 41
that they have overborne their continents. 2.01. 92
thou toldst me they were stol'n unto this wood; 2.01.191
are hated most of those they did deceive, | so 2.02.140
why do they run away? 3.01.112 P
make an ass of me, to fright me, if they could; 3.01.121 P
will not stir from this place, do what they can. 3.01.122 P
will sing, that they shall hear i am not afraid. 3.01.123 P
and they shall fetch thee jewels from the deep, 3.01.158
when they him spy, | as wild geese that the 3.02. 19
the noise they make | will cause demetrius to 3.02.116
now i perceive they have conjoin'd all three 3.02.193
when they next wake, all this derision | shall 3.02.370
they willfully themselves exile from light, 3.02.386
heavens shield lysander, if they mean a fray! 3.02.447
when in a wood of crete they bay'd the bear 4.01.113
no doubt they rose up early to observe | the 4.01.132
they would have stol'n away, they would, 4.01.156
they would have stol'n away, they would, 4.01.156
for they shall hang out for the lion's claws. 4.02. 41 P
what are they that do play it? 5.01. 71
he says they can do nothing in this kind. 5.01. 88
our sport shall be to take what they mistake; 5.01. 90
poor souls, they are content | to whisper. 5.01.133
at large discourse, while here they do remain. 5.01.151
no worse of them than they of themselves, they 5.01.215 P
of themselves, they may pass for excellent men. 5.01.216 P
as they fly by them with their woven wings. MV 1.01. 14
they lose it that do buy it with much care. 1.01. 75
if they should speak, would almost damn those 1.01. 98
you have them, they are not worth the search. 1.01.118 P
they are as sick that surfeit with too much as 1.02. 5 P
with too much as they that starve with nothing. 1.02. 6 P
they would be better if well follow'd. 1.02. 11 P
they have acquainted me with their 1.02.101 P
why, there they show | something too liberal. 2.02.184
i am not bid for love, they flatter me, | but 2.05. 13
and they have conspir'd together. 2.05. 22 P
made, than they are wont | to keep obliged faith 2.06. 6
for if they could, cupid himself would blush 2.06. 38
they in themselves, good sooth, are too too 2.06. 42
from the four corners of the earth they come 2.07. 39
but they come | as o'er a brook to see fair 2.07. 46
they have in england | a coin that bears the 2.07. 55
duke | they were not with bassanio in his ship. 2.08. 11
he wrung bassanio's hand, and so they parted. 2.08. 49
when they do choose, | they have the wisdom by 2.09. 80
they have the wisdom by their wit to lose. 2.09. 81
the goodwins, i think they call the place, a 3.01. 4 P
of many a tall ship lie buried, as they say, if 3.01. 6 P
eyes, | they have o'erlook'd me and divided me: 3.02. 15
on the balls of mine, | seem they in motion? 3.02.118
so do i, my lord, | they are entirely welcome. 3.02.225
of the state, | if they deny him justice. 3.02.279
see our husbands | before they think of us. 3.04. 59
shall they see us? 3.04. 59
they shall, nerissa; 3.04. 60
that they shall think we are accomplished | with 3.04. 61
which i denying, they fell sick and died. 3.04. 71
that is done, sir, they have all stomachs! 3.05. 48 P
some that are mad if they behold a cat; 4.01. 48
do all men kill the things they do not love? 4.01. 66
when they are fretten with the gusts of heaven; 4.01. 77
why sweat they under burthens? 4.01. 95
that they did give the rings away to men; 4.02. 16
kiss the trees | and they did make no noise, in 5.01. 3
if they but hear perchance a trumpet sound, | or 5.01. 75
are they return'd? 5.01.116
madam, they are not yet; 5.01.116
give order to my servants that they take | no 5.01.119
besides that they are fair with their feeding, AYL 1.01. 12 P
their feeding, they are taught their manage, and 1.01. 12 P
daughter, and never two ladies lov'd as they do. 1.01.112 P
they say he is already in the forest of arden, 1.01.114 P
and there they live like the old robin hood of 1.01.116 P
they say many young gentlemen flock to him every 1.01.116 P
carelessly, as they did in the golden world. 1.01.118 P
that swore by his honor they were good pancakes, 1.02. 64 P
where you are, they are coming to perform it. 1.02.115 P
yonder they lie, the poor old man, their father, 1.02.129 P
the wrastling, and they are ready to perform it. 1.02.145 P
yonder sure they are coming. 1.02.147 P
they are but burs, cousin, thrown upon thee in 1.03. 13 P
o, they take the part of a better wrastler than 1.03. 22 P
words, | they are as innocent as grace itself. 1.03. 54
speak to the people, and they pity her. 1.03. 79
they found the bed untreasur'd of their mistress 2.02. 7
and she believes, where ever they are gone, 2.02. 15
else are they very wretched. 2.04. 68
i care not for their names, they owe me nothing. 2.05. 21 P
but that they call compliment is like th' 2.05. 26 P
young and fair, | they have the gift to know it; 2.07. 38
and they that are most galled with my folly, 2.07. 50
galled with my folly, | they most must laugh. 2.07. 51
and why, sir, must they so? 2.07. 51
if they will patiently receive my medicine. 2.07. 61
they have their exits and their entrances, | and 2.07.141
and they are often tarr'd over with the surgery 3.02. 62 P
they that reap must sheaf and bind, | then to 3.02.107
for they sleep between term and term, and then 3.02.331 P
term, and then they perceive not how time moves. 3.02.332 P
they were all like one another as halfpence are, 3.02.353 P
and the reason why they are not so punish'd and 3.02.402 P

and what they swear in poetry may be said as		3.03. 21 P
in poetry may be said as lovers they do feign.		3.03. 22 P
as horns are odious, they are necessary.		3.03. 52 P
but join you together as they join wainscot;		3.03. 87 P
they are both the confirmer of false reckonings.		3.04. 32 P
had they mark'd him | in parcels as i did, would		3.05.124
they say you are a melancholy fellow.		4.01. 3 P
very good orators, when they are out, they will		4.01. 76 P
when they are out, they will spit, and for		4.01. 76 P
so do all thoughts, they are wing'd.		4.01.142 P
orlando, men are april when they woo, december		4.01.147 P
are april when they woo, december when they wed;		4.01.148 P
maids are may when they are maids, but the sky		4.01.148 P
maids, but the sky changes when they are wives.		4.01.149 P
strange effect | would they work in mild aspect?		4.03. 53
many will swoon when they do look on blood.		4.03.158
and my sister no sooner met but they look'd;		5.02. 33 P
no sooner look'd but they lov'd;		5.02. 34 P
no sooner lov'd but they sigh'd;		5.02. 34 P
no sooner sigh'd but they ask'd one another the		5.02. 35 P
knew the reason but they sought the remedy:		5.02. 36 P
in these degrees have they made a pair of stairs		5.02. 37 P
to marriage, which they will climb incontinent,		5.02. 38 P
they are in the very wrath of love, and they		5.02. 39 P
the very wrath of love, and they will together.		5.02. 40 P
they shall be married to–morrow;		5.02. 42 P
this carol they began that hour, | with a hey,		5.03. 26
as those that fear they hope, and know they fear		5.04. 4
those that fear they hope, and know they fear.		5.04. 4
and they shook hands and swore brothers.		5.04.101 P
yet to good wine they do use good bushes;		ep 5 P
when they do homage to this simple peasant.	SHR	in.1. 135
they say that i have dream'd | and slept above		in.2. 112
therefore they thought it good you hear a play,		in.2. 134
than perfume itself | to whom they go to.		1.02.153
they do consume the thing that feeds their fury.		2.01.133
that /shake not, though they blow perpetually.		2.01.141
they call me katherine that do talk of me.		2.01.184
as if they saw some wondrous monument, | some		3.02. 95
ay, sir, they be ready;		3.02.205 P
they shall go forward, kate, at thy command.		3.02.222
sweet wench, they shall not touch thee, kate!		3.02.238
went they not quickly, i should die with		3.02.241
a fire, and they are coming after to warm them.		4.01. 4 P
master's horse–tail till they kiss their hands.		4.01. 94 P
are they all ready?		4.01. 95 P
they are.		4.01. 96 P
yet, as they are, here are they come to meet you		4.01.138
as they are, here are they come to meet you.		4.01.138
see how they kiss and court!		4.02. 27
if not, elsewhere they meet with charity;		4.03. 6
/except they are busied about a counterfeit		4.04. 91 P
but they may chance to need thee at home,		5.01. 2 P
believe me, sir, they butt together well.		5.02. 39
they sit conferring by the parlor fire.		5.02.102
if they deny to come, | swinge me them soundly		5.02.103
what duty they do owe their lords and husbands.		5.02.131
to offer war where they should kneel for peace,		5.02.162
when they are bound to serve, love, and obey.		5.02.164
they are virtues and traitors too.	AWW	1.01. 43 P
in her they are the better for their simpleness;		1.01. 44 P
that they take place when virtue's steely bones		1.01.103
freely have they leave | to stand on either part		1.02. 14
but they may jest | till their own scorn return		1.02. 33
ere they can hide their levity in honor.		1.02. 35
if they were, | his equal had awak'd them, and		1.02. 37
they that least lend it you shall lack you first		1.02. 68
for they say barnes are blessings.		1.03. 25 P
i have other holy reasons, such as they are.		1.03. 33 P
if men could be contented to be what they are,		1.03. 51 P
they may jowl horns together like any deer i'		1.03. 54 P
for her, they touch'd not any stranger sense.		1.03.109 P
behaviors | that in their kind they speak it.		1.03.179
inclusive were | more than they were in note.		1.03.227
he, that they cannot help him, | they, that they		1.03.238
cannot help him, | they, that they cannot help.		1.03.239
cannot help him, | they, that they cannot help.		1.03.239
how shall they credit | a poor unlearned virgin,		1.03.239
they say our french lack language to deny | if		2.01. 20
french lack language to deny | if they demand.		2.01. 21
for they wear themselves in the cap of the time;		2.01. 53 P
hath told the thievish minutes how they pass,		2.01.166
they say miracles are past, and we have our		2.03. 1 P
hast power to choose, and they none to forsake.		2.03. 56
do all they deny her?		2.03. 86 P
and they were sons of mine, i'd have them whipt,		2.03. 86 P
sure they are bastards to the english, the		2.03. 94 P
o my parolles, they have married me!		2.03.272
which they distill now in the curbed time, | to		2.04. 45
for my respects are better than they seem, | and		2.05. 66
welcome shall they be;		3.01. 19
when better fall, for your avails they fell.		3.01. 22
here they come will tell you more;		3.02. 42 P
come, for if they do approach the city, we shall		3.05. 1 P
they say the french count has done most		3.05. 3 P
lost our labor, they are gone a contrary way.		3.05. 8 P
of lust, are not the things they go under.		3.05. 20 P
but that they are lim'd with the twigs that		3.05. 23 P
thither they send one another.		3.05. 31 P
hark you, they come this way.		3.05. 38
so, now they come.		3.05. 75
they begin to smoke me, and disgraces have of		4.01. 27 P
they will say, "came you off with so little?"		4.01. 38 P
they told me that your name was fontibell.		4.02. 1
till they attain to their abhorr'd ends;		4.03. 23 P
if they were not cherish'd by our virtues.		4.03. 74 P
they shall be no more than needful there, if		4.03. 80 P
there, if they were more than they can commend.		4.03. 81 P
there, if they were more than they can commend.		4.03. 81 P
they cannot be too sweet for the king's tartness		4.03. 82 P
of him, of what strength they are afoot."		4.03.159 P
cassocks, lest they shake themselves to pieces.		4.03.169 P
but they know his conditions and lay him in		4.03.257 P
that can such sweet use make of what they hate,		4.04. 22
they are not herbs, you knave, they are		4.05. 18 P
are not herbs, you knave, they are nose–herbs.		4.05. 18 P
'em, sir, they shall be jades' tricks, which are		4.05. 60 P
to remain with me till they meet together.		4.05. 87 P
or, ere they meet, in me, o nature, cesse!		5.03. 72
do they charge me further?		5.03.167
already, unless thou canst say they are married.		5.03.268 P
let thy curtsies alone, they are scurvy ones.		5.03.323 P
they say, she hath abjur'd the /company | and	TN	1.02. 40
and they be not, let them hang themselves in		1.03. 12 P
they are scoundrels and substractors that say so		1.03. 34 P
who are they?		1.03. 35 P
they that add, moreov'r, he's drunk nightly in		1.03. 36 P
are they like to take dust, like mistress mall's		1.03.126 P
for they shall yet belie thy happy years, | that		1.04. 30
those wits that think they have thee do very oft		1.05. 33 P
faith, so they say, but i think it rather		2.03. 11 P
thou wilt drop, that they come from my niece,		2.03.165 P
and so they are;		2.04. 40
alas, that they are so!		2.04. 40
to die, even when they to perfection grow!		2.04. 41
they lack retention.		2.04. 96
in faith, they are as true of heart as we.		2.04.106
my place as i would they should do theirs — to		2.05. 54 P
they that dally nicely with words may quickly		3.01. 14 P
would they were blanks, rather than fill'd with		3.01.104
and they have been grand–jurymen since before		3.02. 16 P
fright them both that they will kill one another		3.04.195 P
as your feet hits the ground they step on.		3.04.278 P
they say he has been fencer to the sophy.		3.04.278 P
they have laid me here in hideous darkness.		4.02. 29 P
they have here propertied me, keep me in		4.02. 91 P
and do all they can to face me out of my wits.		4.02. 92 P
that they may fairly note this act of mine!		4.03. 35
sir, they praise me and make an ass of me.		5.01. 17 P
they say, poor gentleman, he's much distract.		5.01.280
so it skills not much when they are deliver'd.		5.01.288 P
alas, poor fool, how have they baffled thee!		5.01.369
may, though they cannot praise us, as little	WT	1.01. 15 P
they were train'd together in their childhoods;		1.01. 22 P
embassies, that they have seem'd to be together,		1.01. 29 P
they that went on crutches ere he was born		1.01. 39 P
would they else be content to die?		1.01. 42 P
no other excuse why they should desire to live.		1.01. 43 P
they would desire to live on crutches till he		1.01. 45 P
as now they are, and making practic'd smiles,		1.02.116
they say it is a copy out of mine.		1.02.122
yet they say we are | almost as like as eggs;		1.02.129
but were they false | as o'er–dy'd blacks, as		1.02.131
they would do that | which should undo more		1.02.311
yet black brows, they say, | become some women		2.01. 8
fourteen they shall not see | to bring false		2.01.147
they are co–heirs, | and i had rather glib		2.01.148
and i had rather glib myself than they | should		2.01.149
from the oracle | they will bring all, whose		2.01.186
they should not laugh if i could reach them, nor		2.03. 25
these lords, my noble fellows, if they please,		2.03.143
wolves and bears, they say, | casting their		2.03.187
twenty–three days | they have been absent.		2.03.199
divine | behold our human actions (as they do),		3.02. 29
less impudence to gainsay what they did | than		3.02. 56
girls of nine), o, think what they have done,		3.02.182
for they are heavier | than all thy woes can		3.02.208
a day i'll visit | the chapel where they lie,		3.02.239
they have scar'd away two of my best sheep,		3.03. 65 P
they were warmer that got this than the poor		3.03. 75 P
they are never curst but when they are hungry.		3.03.130 P
they are never curst but when they are hungry.		3.03.131 P
than they are in losing them when they have		4.02. 27 P
are in losing them when they have approv'd their		4.02. 28 P
a man, they say, that from very nothing, and		4.02. 38 P
with hey, the sweet birds, o, how they sing!		4.03. 6
but they are most of them means and bases;		4.03. 43 P
they cherish it to make it stay there;		4.03. 92 P
and i think they are given | to men of middle		4.04.107
ere they can behold | bright phoebus in his		4.04.123
they call him doricles, and boasts himself | to		4.04.168
handle, though they come to him by th' gross;		4.04.206 P
he sings 'em over as they were gods or goddesses		4.04.208 P
the feast, but they come not too late now.		4.04.236 P
will they wear their plackets where they should		4.04.243 P
wear their plackets where they should bear their		4.04.243 P
'tis well they are whisp'ring.		4.04.247 P
a–life, for then we are sure they are true.		4.04.261 P
they call themselves saltiers, and they have a		4.04.326 P
and they have a dance which the wenches say is a		4.04.327 P
of gambols, because they are not in't;		4.04.328 P
but they themselves are o' th' mind (if it be		4.04.329 P
why, they stay at door, sir.		4.04.342 P
if they can but stay you | where you'll be loath		4.04.571
they throng who should buy first, as if my		4.04.600 P
if they have overheard me now — why, hanging.		4.04.626 P
of this escape and whither they are bound;		4.04.663
and they often give us soldiers the lie, but we		4.04.723 P
steel, therefore they do not give us the lie.		4.04.725 P
and that the complaint they have to the king		4.04.838 P
and left them | more rich for what they yielded.		5.01. 55
they are come.		5.01.123
they kneel, they kiss the earth;		5.01.199
they kneel, they kiss the earth;		5.01.199
forswear themselves as often as they speak.		5.01.200
they seem'd almost, with staring on one another,		5.02. 11 P
they look'd as they had heard of a world		5.02. 14 P
they look'd as they had heard of a world		5.02. 14 P
with it, which they know to be his character;		5.02. 34 P
such distraction that they were to be known by		5.02. 48 P
are they return'd to the court?		5.02. 93 P
done hermione that they say one would speak to		5.02.101 P
with all greediness of affection are they gone,		5.02.103 P
are they gone, and there they intend to sup.		5.02.103 P
least they desire (upon this push) to trouble		5.03.129
and they shall say, when richard me begot, | if	JN	1.01.274
they are at hand, | to parley or to fight,		2.01. 77
let us hear them speak | whose title they admit,		2.01.200
and ready mounted are they to spit forth | their		2.01.211
they shoot but calm words folded up in smoke,		2.01.229
while they weigh so even, | we hold our town for		2.01.332
whence they gape and point | at your industrious		2.01.375
o, two such silver currents when they join | do		2.01.441
mark how they whisper.		2.01.475
but they will quake and tremble all this day.		3.01. 18
of peace, | heaven knows they were besmear'd and		3.01.236
of both, | they whirl asunder and dismember me.		3.01.330
as they have given these hairs their liberty!"		3.04. 72
to check his reign, but they will cherish it;		3.04.152
but they will pluck away his natural cause | and		3.04.156
they would be as a call | to train ten thousand		3.04.174
they do confound their skill in covetousness,		4.02. 29
which (as they say) attend | the steps of wrong,		4.02. 56
they burn in indignation.		4.02.103
for when you should be told they do prepare,		4.02.114
the tidings comes that they are all arriv'd.		4.02.115
not knowing what they fear, but full of fear.		4.02.146
whom they say is kill'd to–night | on your		4.02.165
my lord, they say five moons were seen to–night;		4.02.182
and when they talk of him, they shake their		4.02.188
when they talk of him, they shake their heads,		4.02.188
if they did, | this ship–boy's semblance hath		4.03. 3
again | after they heard young arthur was alive?		5.01. 38
they found him dead and cast into the streets,		5.01. 39
what, shall they seek the lion in his den, | and		5.01. 57
be said, | they saw we had a purpose of defense.		5.01. 76
both they and we, perusing o'er these notes,		5.02. 5
if they miscarry, we miscarry too.		5.04. 3
they say king john, sore sick, hath left the		5.04. 6
them, | and they are all about his majesty.		5.06. 36
high–stomach'd are they both and full of ire,	R2	1.01. 18
who, when they see the hour's ripe on earth,		1.02. 7
that they may break his foaming courser's back,		1.02. 51
what is six winters? they are quickly gone.		1.03.260
whereto, when they shall know what men are rich,		1.04. 49
they shall subscribe them for large sums of gold		1.04. 50
but they say the tongues of dying men | enforce		2.01. 5
words are scarce, they are seldom spent in vain,		2.01. 7
for they breathe truth that breathe their words		2.01. 8
than they whom youth and ease have taught to		2.01. 10
love they to live that love and honor have.		2.01.138
else | but only they have privilege to live.		2.01.158
led | by flatterers, and what they will inform,		2.01.242
more hath he spent in peace than they in wars.		2.01.255
perhaps they had ere this, but that they stay		2.01.289
but that they stay | the first departing of the		2.01.289
the nobles they are fled, the commons they are		2.02. 88
nobles they are fled, the commons they are cold,		2.02. 88
why have they dar'd to march | so many miles		2.03. 92
castle, which they say is held | by bushy, bagot		2.03.164
leap, | the one in fear to lose what they enjoy,		2.04. 13
barkloughly castle call they this at hand?		3.02. 1
and when they from thy bosom pluck a flower,		3.02. 19
men | did triumph in my face, and they are fled;		3.02. 77
they break their faith to god as well as us.		3.02.101
that they have let the dangerous enemy | measure		3.02.124
i warrant they have made peace with bullingbrook		3.02.127
peace have they made with him indeed, my lord.		3.02.128
would they make peace?		3.02.133
some haunted by the ghosts they have deposed,		3.02.158
and they shall strike | your children yet unborn		3.03. 87
for on my heart they tread now whilst i live,		3.03.158
our sighs and they shall lodge the summer corn,		3.03.162
till they have fretted us a pair of graves		3.03.167
they well deserve to have | that know the		3.03.200
they will talk of state, for every one doth so		3.04. 27
what, are they dead?		3.04. 54
they are;		3.04. 54
they might have liv'd to bear and he to taste		3.04. 62
thieves are not judg'd but they are by to hear,		4.01.123
hearts of men, they must perforce have melted,		5.02. 35
for aught i know, my lord, they do.		5.02. 53
for there, they say, he daily doth frequent,		5.03. 6
even such, they say, as stand in narrow lanes		5.03. 8
knees still kneel till to the ground they grow;		5.03.106
they shall not live within this world, i swear,		5.03.142
to ambition, they do plot | unlikely wonders:		5.05. 18
and, for they cannot, die in their own pride.		5.05. 22
that they are not the first of fortune's slaves,		5.05. 24
and in this thought they find a kind of ease,		5.05. 28
and with sighs they jar | their watches on unto		5.05. 51
but whether they be ta'en or slain we hear not.		5.06. 4
they love not poison that do poison need, | nor		5.06. 38
where they did spend a sad and bloody hour, | as	1H4	1.01. 56
in cradle–clothes our children where they lay,		1.01. 88
and when they have the booty, if you and i do		1.02.164 P
and then will they adventure upon the exploit		1.02.171 P
which they shall have no sooner achiev'd but		1.02.172 P
yea, but 'tis like that they will know us by our		1.02.174 P
tut, our horses they shall not see — i'll tie		1.02.177 P
yea, but i doubt they will be too hard for us.		1.02.181 P
but when they seldom come, they wish'd for come,		1.02.206
but when they seldom come, they wish'd for come,		1.02.206
when they have lost and forfeited themselves?		1.03. 88
three times they breath'd and three times did		1.03.102
they breath'd and three times did they drink,		1.03.102
and so they shall.		1.03.281
why, they will allow us ne'er a jordan, and then		2.01. 19 P
they will along with company, for they have		2.01. 45 P
along with company, for they have great charge.		2.01. 46 P
they are up already, and call for eggs and		2.01. 59 P
they will away presently.		2.01. 60 P
if they meet not with saint nicholas' clerks,		2.01. 61 P
i lie, for they pray continually to their saint,		2.01. 79 P
prey on her, for they ride up and down on her,		2.01. 81 P
if they scape from your encounter, then they		2.02. 61 P
from your encounter, then they light on us.		2.02. 62 P
'zounds, will they not rob us?		2.02. 65 P
they hate us youth.		2.02. 85 P
so strongly that they dare not meet each other;		2.02.106
and are they not some of them set forward		2.03. 28 P
they take it already upon their salvation, that		2.04. 9 P
a good boy (by the lord, so they call me!),		2.04. 13 P
they call drinking deep, dyeing scarlet, and		2.04. 15 P
you breathe in your watering, they cry "hem!"		2.04. 16 P
if they speak more or less than truth, they are		2.04.171 P
they are villains and the sons of darkness.		2.04.171 P
no, no, they were not bound.		2.04.177 P
you rogue, they were bound, every man of them,		2.04.178 P
what think you they portend?		2.04.322 P
we shall buy maidenheads as they buy hobnails,		2.04.363 P
'sblood, my lord, they are false.		2.04.443 P
at the door, they are come to search the house.		2.04.490 P
let's see what they be. read them.		2.04.534 P

but will they come when you do call for them? 3.01. 54
from hence, | and straight they shall be here. 3.01.225
they surfeited with honey and began | to loathe 3.02. 71
on his helm | would they were multitudes, and on 3.02.143
a mighty and a fearful head they are, | if 3.02.167
bakers' wives, they have made bolters of them. 3.03. 70 P
house is turn'd bawdy–house, they pick pockets. 3.03. 99 P
these rebels, they offend none but the virtuous. 3.03.191 P
on high, | and either we or they must lower lie. 3.03.204
under whose government come they along? 4.01. 19
they come like sacrifices in their trim, | and 4.01.113
heads, and they have bought out their services; 4.02. 22 P
wide betwixt the legs, as if they had gyves on, 4.02. 40 P
john, methinks they are exceeding poor and bare, 4.02. 68 P
their poverty, i know not where they had that, 4.02. 71 P
i am sure they never learn'd that of me. 4.02. 71 P
and all the rest | to whom they are directed. 4.04. 4
if you knew | how much they do import, you would 4.04. 5
doubt not, my lord, they shall be well oppos'd. 4.04. 33
this encounter, | if once they join in trial. 5.01. 85
and, will they take the offer of our grace, 5.01.106
both he and they and you, yea, every man | shall 5.01.107
wait on us, | and they shall do their office. 5.01.112
they tell thee true. 5.03. 6
have led my ragamuffins where they are pepper'd; 5.03. 36 P
left alive, and they are for the town's end, to 5.03. 37 P
they grow like hydra's heads. 5.04. 25
they did me too much injury | that ever said i 5.04. 51
they wound my thoughts worse than thy sword my 5.04. 80
i'll follow, as they say, for reward. 5.04.162 P
brings other news | than they have learnt of me. 2H4 in 39
tongues | they bring smooth comforts false, in 40
taking up, then they must stand upon security. 1.02. 40 P
i had as live they would put ratsbane in my 1.02. 41 P
our english nation, if they have a good thing, 1.02.215 P
back unarm'd, | they baying him at the heels. 1.03. 80
whereby i told thee they were ill for a green 2.01. 97 P
saying that ere long they should call me madam? 2.01.101 P
master gower, if they become me not, he was a 2.01.191 P
the worst that they can say of me is that i am a 2.02. 66 P
for they never prick their finger but they say, 2.02.112 P
for they never prick their finger but they say, 2.02.112 P
nay, they will be kin to us, or they will fetch 2.02.117 P
be kin to us, or they will fetch it from japhet. 2.02.117 P
if they get ground and vantage of the king, 2.03. 53
the room where they supp'd is too hot, they'll 2.04. 13 P
and they will put on two of our jerkins and 2.04. 16 P
and they be once in a calm, they are sick. 2.04. 37 P
and they be once in a calm, they are sick. 2.04. 38 P
you, you are the weaker vessel, as they say, the 2.04. 60 P
they would truncheon you out for taking their 2.04.142 P
they say poins has a good wit. 2.04.239 P
but, ere they come, bid them o'er–read these 3.01. 2
and in two year after | were they at wars. 3.01. 60
they say the bishop and northumberland | are 3.01. 95
where i think they will talk of mad shallow yet. 3.02. 14 P
thereafter as they be, a score of good ewes may 3.02. 50 P
is, when a man is, as they say, accommodated, or 3.02. 78 P
they are your likeliest men, and i would have 3.02.255 P
whistle, and sware they were his fancies or his 3.02.318 P
and, by the ground they hide, i judge their 4.01. 21
if they miscarry, theirs shall second them, 4.02. 46
with speed redress'd, | upon my soul they shall. 4.02. 60
hark how they shout! 4.02. 87
and, ere they be dismiss'd, let them march by. 4.02. 96
will not go off until they hear you speak. 4.02.100
they know their duties. 4.02.101
steers unyok'd, they take their courses | east, 4.02.103
if i do sweat, they are the drops of thy lovers, 4.03. 13 P
of thy lovers, and they weep for thy death; 4.03. 13 P
had they been rul'd by me, | you should have won 4.03. 66
i know not how they sold themselves, but thou, 4.03. 68 P
fish–meals, that they fall into a kind of male 4.03. 92 P
and then, when they marry, they get wenches. 4.03. 93 P
and then, when they marry, they get wenches. 4.03. 94 P
they are generally fools and cowards, which some 4.03. 94 P
and, when they stand against you, may they fall 4.04. 95
may they fall | as those that i am come to tell 4.04. 95
me, for they do observe | unfather'd heirs and 4.04.121
for this they have engrossed and pil'd up | the 4.05. 70
for this they have been thoughtful to invest 4.05. 72
well, davy, for they are arrant knaves, and will 5.01. 32 P
no worse than they are backbitten, sir, for they 5.01. 34 P
sir, for they have marvail's foul linen. 5.01. 35 P
they, by observing him, do bear themselves like 5.01. 66 P
of society that they flock together in consent, 5.01. 70 P
blessed are they that have been my friends, and 5.03.137 P
say they. 5.03.140
'twill be two a' clock ere they come from the 5.05. 3 P
and so they are. 5.05.102
given to the church, | would they strip from us; H5 1.01. 11
why the law salique, that they have in france, 1.02. 11
but this, which they produce from pharamond: 1.02. 37
they would hold up this salique law | to bar 1.02. 91
they know your grace hath cause, and means, and 1.02.125
they of those marches, gracious sovereign, 1.02.140
they have a king, and officers of sorts, | where 1.02.190
which pillage they with merry march bring home 1.02.195
that men are merriest when they are from home. 1.02.272
they sell the pasture now to buy the horse, 2.pr. 5
i cannot tell — things must be as they may. 2.01. 20 P
and they may have their throats about them at 2.01. 21 P
they shall be apprehended by and by. 2.02. 2
how smooth and even they do bear themselves! 2.02. 3
the king hath note of all that they intend, | by 2.02. 6
by interception which they dream not of. 2.02. 7
look ye how they change! 2.02. 73
seem they grave and learned? 2.02.128
come they of noble family? 2.02.129
seem they religious? 2.02.130
or are they spare in diet, | free from gross 2.02.131
felt them, and they were as cold as any stone; 2.03. 24 P
they say he cried out of sack. 2.03. 27 P
'a did, and said they were dev'ls incarnate. 2.03. 31 P
and that's but unwholesome food, they say. 2.03. 57 P
their mouths when what they seem to threaten 2.04. 70
i am boy to them all three, but all they three, 3.02. 29 P
but all they three, though they would serve me, 3.02. 30 P
they will steal any thing, and call it purchase. 3.02. 41 P
and in callice they stole a fire–shovel. 3.02. 45 P
they would have me as familiar with men's 3.02. 47 P
if they march along | unfought withal, but i 3.05. 11
where have they this mettle? 3.05. 15
and they will give | their bodies to the lust of 3.05. 29
they bid us to the english dancing–schools, 3.05. 32
and they will learn you by rote where services 3.06. 71 P
and this they con perfitly in the phrase of war, 3.06. 75 P
war, which they trick up with new–tun'd oaths; 3.06. 76 P
who when they were in health, i tell thee, 3.06.148
i hope they will not come upon us now. 3.06.168
then did they imitate that which i compos'd to 3.07. 43 P
they that ride so, and ride not warily, fall 3.07. 56 P
had any apprehension, they would run away. 3.07.135 P
that they lack; 3.07.137 P
they could never wear such heavy head–pieces. 3.07.138 P
they will eat like wolves and fight like devils. 3.07.150 P
we find to–morrow they have only stomachs to eat 3.07.153 P
they are our outward consciences | and preachers 4.01. 8
yet, when they stoop, they stoop with the like 4.01.107 P
when they stoop, they stoop with the like wing. 4.01.107 P
poor behind them, some upon the debts they owe, 4.01.140 P
for how can they charitably dispose of any thing 4.01.142 P
for they purpose not their death when they 4.01.157 P
not their death when they purpose their services 4.01.158 P
native punishment, though they can outstrip men, 4.01.168 P
men, they have no wings to fly from god. 4.01.168 P
where they fear'd the death, they have borne 4.01.171 P
fear'd the death, they have borne life away; 4.01.172 P
and where they would be safe, they perish. 4.01.173 P
and where they would be safe, they perish. 4.01.173 P
then if they die unprovided, no more is the king 4.01.173 P
impieties for the which they are now visited. 4.01.176 P
and to teach others how they should prepare. 4.01.185 P
twenty french crowns to one they will beat us, 4.01.226 P
beat us, for they bear them on their shoulders; 4.01.226 P
happy, being fear'd, | than they in fearing. 4.01.249
they have said their prayers, and they stay for 4.02. 56
said their prayers, and they stay for death. 4.02. 56
of fighting men they have full threescore 4.03. 3
besides, they all are fresh. 4.03. 4
think themselves accurs'd they were not here; 4.03. 65
god, why should they mock poor fellows thus? 4.03. 92
buried in your dunghills, | they shall be fam'd; 4.03.100
or they will pluck | the gay new coats o'er the 4.03.117
if they do this — | as, if god please, they 4.03.119
as, if god please, they shall — my ransom then 4.03.120
they shall have none, i swear, but these my 4.03.123
which if they have as i will leave 'um them, 4.03.124
with a wooden dagger, and they are both hang'd, 4.04. 72 P
with /mistful eyes, or they will issue too. 4.06. 34
they have burn'd and carried away all that was 4.07. 7 P
if they will fight with us, bid them come down, 4.07. 58
they do offend our sight. 4.07. 59
his eyes are humbler than they us'd to be. 4.07. 67
they call it agincourt. 4.07. 89
they did, fluellen. 4.07. 96
so that, in these ten thousand they have lost, 4.08. 87
and much more cause, | did they this harry. 5.pr. 35
they do always reason themselves out again. 5.02.157 P
maids in france to kiss before they are married, 5.02.266 P
and they should sooner persuade harry of england 5.02.278 P
yet they do wink and yield, as love is blind and 5.02.300 P
they are then excus'd, my lord, when they see 5.02.302 P
my lord, when they see not what they do. 5.02.302 P
blind, though they have their eyes, and then 5.02.303 P
their eyes, and then they will endure handling, 5.02.309 P
for they are all girdled with maiden walls that 5.02.310 P
that they lost france, and made his england 5.02.321 P
how were they lost? what treachery was us'd? ep 12
me they concern, regent i am of france. 1H6 1.01. 68
hedges | they pitched in the ground confusedly, 1.01. 84
enclosed were they with their enemies. 1.01.118
since they, so few, watch such a multitude. 1.01.136
they want their porridge and their fat 1.01.161
either they must be dieted like mules | and have 1.02. 9
or piteous they will look, like drowned mice. 1.02. 10
fled, | but that they left me midst my enemies. 1.02. 12
suppose | they had such courage and audacity? 1.02. 24
this town, for they are hare–brain'd slaves, 1.02. 36
else ne'er could they hold out so as they do. 1.02. 37
else ne'er could they hold out so as they do. 1.02. 43
my words, | for they are certain and unfallible. 1.02. 43
where be these warders, that they wait not here? 1.02. 59
they may vex us with shot or with assault. 1.03. 3
once in contempt they would have barter'd me; 1.04. 13
in open market–place produc'd they me | to be a 1.04. 31
here, said they, is the terror of the french, 1.04. 40
in iron walls they deem'd me not secure; 1.04. 42
that they suppos'd i could rend bars of steel, 1.04. 49
bed, | ready they were to shoot me to the heart. 1.04. 51
one, | and view the frenchmen how they fortify. 1.04. 56
they call'd us for our fierceness english dogs, 1.04. 61
when they shall hear how we have play'd the men. 1.05. 25
but what's that pucelle whom they term so pure? 1.06. 16
a maid, they say. 2.01. 20
how, or which way, should they first break in? 2.01. 21
'tis sure they found some place | but weakly 2.01. 71
i'll be so bold to take what they have left. 2.01. 73
they did amongst the troops of armed men | leap 2.01. 78
when arm in arm they both came swiftly running, 2.02. 24
guests | are often welcomest when they are gone. 2.02. 29
for pale they look with fear, as witnessing 2.02. 56
this blot that they object against your house 2.04. 63
they labored to plant the rightful heir, | i 2.04.116
heir, | i lost my liberty, and they their lives. 2.05. 80
when they are cloy'd | with long continuance in 2.05. 81
so perish they | that grudge one thought against 2.05.105
like peasant footboys do they keep the walls, 3.01.174
they that of late were daring with their scoffs 3.02. 69
for ever should they be expuls'd from france, 3.02.113
but when they heard he was thine enemy, | they 3.03. 25
they set him free without his ransom paid, | in 3.03. 71
if they perceive dissension in our looks, | and 3.03. 72
as well they may upbraid me with my crown, 4.01.139
and they shall find dear deer of us, my friends. 4.01.156
they are return'd, my lord, and give it out 4.02. 54
we lose, they daily get; 4.03. 3
and now they meet where both their lives are 4.03. 32
whiles they each other cross, | lives, honors, 4.03. 38
within six hours they will be at his aid. 4.03. 52
in yours they will, in you all hopes are lost. 4.04. 41
by me they nothing gain and if i stay, | 'tis 4.05. 25
they would but stink, and putrefy the air. 4.06. 36
they humbly sue unto your excellence | to have a 4.07. 90
peace be amongst them if they turn to us, | else 5.01. 4
see, they forsake me! 5.02. 6
charms, | and try if they can gain your liberty. 5.03. 24
it shall be so, disdain they ne'er so much. 5.03. 32
they please us well. 5.03. 98
for grief that they are past recovery; 2H6 1.01. 63
while they do tend the profit of the land. 1.01.116
stands on a tickle point now they are gone. 1.01.204
'tis thine they give away, and not their own. 1.01.216
and will they undertake to do me good? 1.01.221
this they have promised, to show your highness 1.02. 77
they, knowing dame eleanor's aspiring humor, 1.02. 78
they say, "a crafty knave does need no broker," 1.02. 97
if they were known, as the suspect is great, 1.02.100
they know their master loves to be aloft, | and 1.03.136
till they come to berwick, from whence they came 2.01. 11
they come to berwick, from whence they came. 2.01.156
which now they hold by force and not by right; 2.01.156
till they have snar'd the shepherd of the flock, 2.02. 30
'tis that they seek; 2.02. 73
and they in seeking that | shall find their 2.02. 75
look how they gaze! 2.02. 75
small curs are not regarded when they grin, 2.04. 20
'tis to be fear'd they all will follow him. 3.01. 18
what are they that think it? 3.01. 30
beshrew the winners, for they play'd me false! 3.01.107
even so remorseless have they borne him hence; 3.01.184
how they affect the house and claim of york. 3.01.213
i know no pain they can inflict upon him | will 3.01.375
because thy flinty heart, more hard than they, 3.01.377
and care not who they sting in his revenge. 3.02. 99
until they hear the order of his death. 3.02.127
they will by violence tear him from your palace, 3.02.129
they say, by him the good duke humphrey died; 3.02.246
they say, in him they fear your highness' death; 3.02.248
they say, in him they fear your highness' death; 3.02.249
they say, in care of your most royal person, 3.02.249
and therefore do they cry, though you forbid, 3.02.254
that they will guard you, whe'er you will or no, 3.02.264
worth, | they say is shamefully bereft of life. 3.02.265
by them, | yet did i purpose as they do entreat; 3.02.269
worse than gall, the daintiest that they taste! 3.02.282
can i make men live, whe'er they will or no? 3.02.322
here shall they make their ransom on the sand, 3.03. 10
they have been up these two days. 4.01. 10
they have the more need to sleep now then. 4.02. 2 P
one livery, that they may agree like brothers, 4.02. 3 P
they use to write it on the top of letters; 4.02. 74 P
for they are thrifty honest men, and such | as 4.02.100 P
and such | as would (but that they dare not) 4.02.186
they are all in order, and march toward us. 4.02.187
they fell before thee like sheep and oxen, and 4.02.188 P
they call false caterpillars, and intend their 4.03. 3 P
o graceless men! they know not what they do. 4.04. 37
o graceless men! they know not what they do. 4.04. 38
and they jointly swear | to spoil the city and 4.04. 38
for they have won the bridge, killing all those 4.04. 52
them about matters they were not able to answer. 4.05. 2 P
them in prison, and because they could not read, 4.07. 42 P
only for that cause they have been most worthy 4.07. 44 P
shall pay to me her maidenhead ere they have it. 4.07. 45 P
for they lov'd well when they were alive. 4.07.123 P
for they lov'd well when they were alive. 4.07.131 P
lest they consult about the giving up of some 4.07.131 P
here they be that dare and will disturb thee. 4.07.132 P
unto all they meet. 4.08. 6
/these | if they can brook i bow a knee to man. 4.08. 46
i know, ere they will have me go to ward, 5.01.110
see where they come, i'll warrant they'll make 5.01.112
they may astonish these fell–lurking curs. 5.01.122
and they have troops of soldiers at their beck? 5.01.146
they seek revenge, and therefore will not yield. 3H6 1.01. 68
will follow mine, if once they see them spread; 1.01.190
and spread they shall be, to thy foul disgrace, 1.01.252
in them i trust, for they are soldiers, | witty, 1.01.253
they have demean'd themselves | like men born to 1.02. 42
so cowards fight when they can fly no further, 1.04. 7
see, see, they join, embrace, and seem to kiss, 1.04. 40
kiss, | as if they vow'd some league inviolable. 2.01. 29
now are they but one lamp, one light, one sun. 2.01. 30
they took his head, and on the gates of york 2.01. 31
and on the gates of york | they set the same, 2.01. 65
gently down, as if they struck their friends. 2.01. 66
but all in vain, they had no heart to fight, 2.01.132
which sometime they have us'd with fearful 2.01.135
and in the towns, as they do march along, 2.02. 30
darraign your battle, for they are at hand. 2.02. 70
bootless is flight, they follow us with wings, 2.02. 72
they prosper best of all when i am thence. 2.03. 12
thereby to see the minutes how they run: 2.05. 18
pass'd over to the end they were created, 2.05. 25
no more words till they have flow'd their fill. 2.05. 39
they never then had sprung like summer flies; 2.05. 72
they mock thee, clifford, swear as thou wast 2.06. 17
for though they cannot greatly sting to hurt, 2.06. 76
'twere pity they should lose their father's 2.06. 94
unless abroad they purchase great alliance? 3.02. 31
suppose they take offense without a cause; 3.03. 70
they are but lewis and warwick, i am edward, 4.01. 14
and their true sovereign whom they must obey? 4.01. 15
nay, whom they shall obey, and love thee too, 4.01. 78
too, | unless they seek for hatred at my hands; 4.01. 79
which if they do, yet will i keep thee safe, 4.01. 80
and they shall feel the vengeance of my wrath. 4.01. 81
they shall have wars, and pay for their 4.01. 82
they are so link'd in friendship | that young 4.01.114
they are already or quickly will be landed. 4.01.116
what are they that fly there? 4.01.132
they quite forget their loss of liberty. 4.03. 28
4.06. 15

nor forward of revenge, though they much err'd. 4.08. 46
then why should they love edward more than me? 4.08. 47
they are at hand, and you shall quickly know. 5.01. 15
where slept our scouts, or how are they seduc'd, 5.01. 19
for they no doubt | will issue out again and bid 5.01. 62
that they do hold their course toward tewksbury. 5.03. 19
they that stabb'd caesar shed no blood at all, 5.05. 53
and made the forest tremble when they roar'd. 5.07. 12
and hither have they sent it for her ransom. 5.07. 40
too, | for they that were your enemies are his, R3 1.01.130
when they are gone, then must i count my gains. 1.01.162
then say they were not slain. 1.02. 89
but dead they are, and, devilish slave, by thee. 1.02. 90
would they were basilisks, to strike thee dead! 1.02.150
i would they were, that i might die at once; 1.02.151
for now they kill me with a living death. 1.02.152
they do me wrong, and i will not endure it! 1.03. 42
they love his grace but lightly | that fill his 1.03. 45
they that stand high have many blasts to shake 1.03.258
and if they fall, they dash themselves to pieces 1.03.259
if they fall, they dash themselves to pieces. 1.03.259
i will not think but they ascend the sky, | and 1.03.286
now they believe it, and withal whet me | to be 1.03.331
they often feel a world of restless cares; 1.04. 81
they that set you on | to do this deed will hate 1.04.254
look'd pale when they did hear of clarence' 2.01.137
o, they did urge it still unto the king! 2.01.138
what stays had i but they? and they are gone. 2.02. 76
what stays had i but they? and they are gone. 2.02. 76
/i /for /an /edward /weep, so do not they. 2.02. 85
who they shall be that straight shall post to 2.02.142
better it were they all came by his father, | or 2.03. 23
and were they to be rul'd, and not to rule, 2.03. 29
night, i /hear, they lay at stony–stratford, 2.04. 1
and at northampton they do rest to–night. 2.04. 2
to–morrow, or next day, they will be here. 2.04. 3
they say my son of york | has almost overta'en 2.04. 6
marry (they say) my uncle grew so fast | that he 2.04. 27
but they were none. 3.01. 16
not | to tell us whether they will come or no! 3.01. 23
so wise so young, they say do never live long. 3.01. 79
and if they live, i hope i need not fear. 3.01.148
because they have been still my adversaries; 3.02. 52
that they which brought me in my master's hate, 3.02. 58
for they account his head upon the bridge. 3.02. 70
i know they do, and i have well deserv'd it. 3.02. 71
lords at pomfret, when they rode from london, 3.02. 83
and they indeed had no cause to mistrust; 3.02. 85
they, for their truth, might better wear their 3.02. 92
friends at pomfret, they do need the priest, 3.02.114
tell me what they deserve | that do conspire my 3.04. 59
to doom th' offenders, whosoe'er they be: 3.04. 65
i say, my lord, they have deserved death. 3.04. 66
if they have done this deed, my noble lord — 3.04. 73
they smile at me who shortly shall be dead. 3.04.107
be patient, they are friends — ratcliffe and 3.05. 21
and did they so? 3.07. 23
no, so god help me, they spake not a word, | but 3.07. 24
what tongueless blocks were they! 3.07. 42
would they not speak? 3.07. 42
or shall they last, and we rejoice in them? 4.02. 6
still live they, and for ever let them last! 4.02. 7
say, have i thy consent that they shall die? 4.02. 23
are they that i would have thee deal upon: 4.02. 74
albeit they were flesh'd villains, bloody dogs, 4.03. 6
conscience and remorse | they could not speak; 4.03. 21
boot, because both they | match'd not the high 4.04. 65
that thy babes were sweeter than they were, 4.04.120
though what they will impart | help nothing else 4.04.130
help nothing else, yet do they ease the heart. 4.04.131
they shall be praying nuns, not weeping queens; 4.04.202
they are as children but one step below, | even 4.04.301
where in that nest of spicery they will breed 4.04.424
and there they hull, expecting but the aid | of 4.04.438
are they not now upon the western shore, 4.04.481
what do they in the north, | when they should 4.04.484
when they should serve their sovereign in the 4.04.485
they have not been commanded, mighty king. 4.04.486
on the banks | if they were his assistants, yea 4.04.524
him, they came from buckingham | upon his party. 4.04.525
is colder /tidings, yet they must be told. 4.04.534
and towards london do they bend their power, 4.05. 17
if by the way they be not fought withal. 4.05. 18
which they upon the adverse faction want. 5.03. 13
that they may crush down with a heavy fall | the 5.03.111
and wherefore should they, since that i myself 5.03.202
had rather have us win than him they follow: 5.03.244
for what is he they follow? 5.03.245
they thus directed, we will follow | in the main 5.03.298
you sleeping safe, they bring to you unrest; 5.03.320
they would restrain the one, distain the other. 5.03.322
here | may (if they think it well) let fall a H8 pr 6
give | their money out of hope they may believe, pr 8
the play may pass, if they be still and willing, pr 11
only they | that come to hear a merry, bawdy pr 13
of our noble story | as they were living. pr 27
beheld them when they lighted, how they clung 1.01. 9
lighted, how they clung | in their embracement, 1.01. 9
in their embracement, as they grew together, 1.01. 10
which had they, what four thron'd ones could 1.01. 11
and, to–morrow, they | made britain india: 1.01. 20
'twas said they saw but one, and no discerner 1.01. 32
when these suns | (for so they phrase 'em) by 1.01. 34
they did perform | beyond thought's compass, 1.01. 35
that never | they shall abound as formerly. 1.01. 83
and they were ratified | as he cried, "thus let 1.01.170
they vent reproaches | most bitterly on you as 1.02. 23
they are | most pestilent to th' hearing, and, 1.02. 48
they say | they are devis'd by you, or else you 1.02. 50
they say | they are devis'd by you, or else you 1.02. 51
they turn to vicious forms, ten times more ugly 1.02.117
ten times more ugly | than ever they were fair. 1.02.118
though they be never so ridiculous | (nay, let 1.03. 3
or two o' th' face — but they are shrewd ones, 1.03. 7
for when they hold 'em, you would swear directly 1.03. 8
to pepin or clotharius, they keep state so. 1.03. 10
they have all new legs, and lame ones. 1.03. 11
they must either | (for so run the conditions) 1.03. 23
of fool and feather that they got in france, 1.03. 25
abusing better men than they can be | out of a 1.03. 28
the faith they have in tennis and tall stockings 1.03. 30
they may, cum privilegio, "/oui" away | the lag 1.03. 34
i am glad they are going, | for sure there's no 1.03. 42
most liberal, | they are set here for examples. 1.03. 62
true, they are so; 1.03. 62
should find a running banket, ere they rested, 1.04. 12
life, | they are a sweet society of fair ones. 1.04. 14
i would i were, | they should find easy penance. 1.04. 17
i told your grace they would talk anon. 1.04. 49
a noble troop of strangers, | for so they seem. 1.04. 54
because they speak no english, thus they pray'd 1.04. 65
english, thus they pray'd | to tell your grace, 1.04. 65
this night to meet here, they could do no less 1.04. 68
(out of the great respect they bear to beauty) 1.04. 69
they have done my poor house grace; 1.04. 73
what say they? 1.04. 82
such a one, they all confess, | there is indeed, 1.04. 82
which they would have your grace | find out, and 1.04. 83
this duke as much | they love and dote on; 2.01. 52
be what they will, i heartily forgive 'em; 2.01. 65
yet let 'em look they glory not in mischief, 2.01. 66
when they once perceive | the least rub in your 2.01.128
found again | but where they mean to sink ye. 2.01.131
they were young and handsome, and of the best 2.02. 3 P
when they were ready to set out for london, a 2.02. 4 P
must now confess, if they have any goodness, 2.02. 90
they have sent me such a man i would have wish'd 2.02.100
they will not stick to say you envied him, | and 2.02.126
are so mingled | that they have caught the king; 2.03. 77
that they had gather'd a wise council to them 2.04. 51
the lord help, | they vex me past my patience. 2.04.131
enemies, that know not | why they are so, but, 2.04.160
her male issue | or died where they were made, 2.04.193
would they speak with me? 3.01. 17
they will'd me say so, madam. 3.01. 18
they should be good men, their affairs as 3.01. 22
they that must weigh out my afflictions, | they 3.01. 88
they that my trust must grow to, live not here. 3.01. 89
they are (as all my other comforts) far hence 3.01. 90
princes kiss obedience, | so much they love it; 3.01.163
but to stubborn spirits | they swell and grow, 3.01.164
that evermore they pointed | to th' good of your 3.02.172
but, thus much, they are foul ones. 3.02.300
some of these articles, and out they shall. 3.02.304
which, since they are of you, and odious, | i 3.02.331
they are ever forward | in celebration of this 4.01. 9
they that bear | the cloth of honor over her, 4.01. 47
faces | been loose, this day they had been lost. 4.01. 75
they promis'd me eternal happiness, | and 4.02. 90
music leave, | they are harsh and heavy to me. 4.02. 95
the last is for my men (they are the poorest, 4.02.148
that they may have their wages duly paid 'em, 4.02.150
affairs that walk | (as they say spirits do) at 5.01. 14
they say in great extremity, and fear'd | she'll 5.01. 19
he is | (for so i know he is, they know he is) 5.01. 44
with which they moved | have broken with the 5.01. 46
if they shall fail, i, with mine enemies, | will 5.01.123
they shall no more prevail than we give way to. 5.01.143
if they shall chance, | in charging you with 5.01.145
they would shame to make me | wait else at door, 5.02. 16
is this the honor they do one another? 5.02. 26
they had parted so much honesty among 'em — 5.02. 28
bits and spur 'em | till they obey the manage. 5.02. 59
be what they will, may stand forth face to face, 5.02. 82
should find respect | for what they have been. 5.02.111
they are too thin and base to hide offenses. 5.02.160
how got they in, and be hang'd? 5.03. 17 P
are under the line, they need no other penance: 5.03. 43 P
they fell on, i made good my place; 5.03. 53 P
at length they came to th' broom–staff to me, i 5.03. 54 P
and there they are like to dance these three 5.03. 64 P
they grow still too; 5.03. 68
from all parts they are coming, | as if we kept 5.03. 68
when they pass back from the christening. 5.03. 74
if they smile, | and say 'twill do, i know ep 11
if they hold when their ladies bid 'em clap. ep 14
i would not, as they term it, praise her, but i TRO 1.01. 44 P
in how many fadoms deep | they lie indrench'd. 1.01. 51
and whither go they? 1.02. 2
blood, nephew to hector, | they call him ajax. 1.02. 14
they say he is a very man per se and stands 1.02. 15 P
they say he yesterday cop'd hector in the battle 1.02. 33 P
they laugh'd not so much at the hair as at his 1.02.154 P
hark, they are coming from the field. 1.02.177 P
up here and see them as they pass toward ilion? 1.02.178 P
you them all by their names as they pass by, but 1.02.183 P
laying on, take't off who will, as they say. 1.02.207 P
they tax our policy, and call it cowardice, 1.03.197
they call this bed–work, mapp'ry, closet–war, 1.03.205
they place before his hand that made the engine, 1.03.208
but when they would seem soldiers, they have 1.03.237
when they would seem soldiers, they have galls, 1.03.237
i see them not with my old eyes, what are they? 1.03.365
would they but fat their thoughts | with this 2.02. 48
walls will stand till they fall of themselves. 2.03. 9 P
less than little wit from them that they have, 2.03. 13 P
that ajax makes | when they go from achilles. 2.03.184
who play they to? 3.01. 21 P
he? no! she'll none of him. they two are twain. 3.01.101 P
these lovers cry, o ho, they die! 3.01.121
why, they are vipers. 3.01.132 P
i long to hear how they sped to–day. 3.01.142 P
when they charge on heaps | the enemy flying. 3.02. 28
what should they grant? 3.02. 64 P
make devils of cherubins, they never see truly. 3.02. 69 P
they say all lovers swear more performance than 3.02. 84 P
swear more performance than they are able, and 3.02. 85 P
yet reserve an ability that they never perform; 3.02. 86 P
they that have the voice of lions and the act of 3.02. 88 P
and the act of hares, are they not monsters? 3.02. 89 P
kindred, though they be long ere they be woo'd, 3.02.110 P
though they be long ere they be woo'd, they are 3.02.110 P
ere they be woo'd, they are constant being won. 3.02.111 P
they are burs, i can tell you, they'll stick 3.02.111 P
tell you, they'll stick where they are thrown. 3.02.112 P
well know they what they speak that speak so 3.02.152
well know they what they speak that speak so 3.02.152
and they will almost | give us a prince of blood 3.03. 25
what mean these fellows? know they not achilles? 3.03. 70
they pass by strangely. 3.03. 71
they were us'd to bend, | to send their smiles 3.03. 71
to come as humbly as they us'd to creep | to 3.03. 73
which when they fall, as being slippery standers 3.03. 84
such rich beholding | as they have often given. 3.03. 92
and they retort that heat again | to the first 3.03.101
they clap the lubber ajax on the shoulder, | as 3.03.139
for they pass'd by me | as misers do by beggars, 3.03.142
which are devour'd | as fast as they are made, 3.03.149
they all rush by | and leave you /hindmost; 3.03.159
then what they do in present, | though less than 3.03.163
though they are made and moulded of things past, 3.03.177
they think my little stomach to the war | and 3.03.220
even then when they sit idly in the sun. 3.03.233
dispraise the thing that they desire to buy, 4.01. 77
how earnestly they knock! 4.02. 40
they are at hand and ready to effect it. 4.02. 68
i would they had broke 's neck! 4.02. 76 P
or shall they be divided | by any voice or order 4.05. 69
they call him troilus, and on him erect | a 4.05.108
they are in action. 4.05.113
i would they could. 4.05.207
there they stand yet, and modestly i think | the 4.05.222
too much brain and too little blood they do, 5.01. 50 P
they say he keeps a troyan drab, and uses the 5.01. 96 P
they are polluted off'rings, more abhorr'd 5.03. 17
they are at it, hark! 5.03. 95
now they are clapper–clawing one another; 5.04. 1 P
they set me up, in policy, that mongril cur, 5.04. 12 P
i think they have swallow'd one another. 5.04. 33 P
and there they fly or die, like scaling sculls 5.05. 22
if they would yield us but the superfluity while COR 1.01. 17 P
we might guess they reliev'd us humanely; 1.01. 18 P
but they think we are too dear. 1.01. 19 P
they have had inkling this fortnight what we 1.01. 58 P
they say poor suitors have strong breaths; 1.01. 59 P
they shall know we have strong arms too. 1.01. 60 P
they ne'er car'd for us yet. 1.01. 79 P
if the wars eat us not up, they will; 1.01. 85 P
and there's all the love they bear us. 1.01. 86 P
senators for that | they are not such as you. 1.01.114
helps | in this our fabric, if that they — 1.01.119
the former agents, if they did complain, | what 1.01.123
that natural competency | whereby they live. 1.01.140
whereof they say | the city is well stor'd. 1.01.189
they say? 1.01.190
they say there's grain enough? 1.01.196
for though abundantly they lack discretion, 1.01.202
discretion, | yet are they passing cowardly. 1.01.203
they are dissolv'd. 1.01.204
they said they were an–hungry; 1.01.205
they said they were an–hungry; 1.01.205
these shreds | they vented their complainings, 1.01.209
they threw their caps | as they would hang them 1.01.212
as they would hang them on the horns a' th' moon 1.01.213
they have a leader, | tullus aufidius, that will 1.01.228
that they of rome are ent'red in our counsels, 1.02. 2
"they have press'd a power, but it is not known 1.02. 9
till when | they needs must show themselves, 1.02. 21
if they set down before 's, for the remove 1.02. 28
yet, they say, all the yarn she spun in ulysses' 1.03. 82 P
they nothing doubt prevailing, and to make it 1.03. 99 P
yonder comes news: a wager they have met. 1.04. 1
they lie in view, but have not spoke as yet. 1.04. 4
then shall we hear their 'larum, and they ours. 1.04. 9
our walls | rather than they shall pound us up; 1.04. 17
o, they are at it! 1.04. 21
they fear us not, but issue forth their city. 1.04. 23
they do disdain us much beyond our thoughts, 1.04. 26
to their wives, | as they us to our trenches. 1.04. 42
see, they have shut him in. 1.04. 47
a' th' town, | where they shall know our mind. 1.05. 28
which told me they had beat you to your trenches 1.06. 40
mouse ne'er shunn'd the cat as they did budge 1.06. 44
they did budge | from rascals worse than they. 1.06. 45
side | they have plac'd their men of trust? 1.06. 52
those are they | that most are willing. 1.06. 66
and they smart | to hear themselves rememb'red. 1.09. 28
should they not, | well might they fester 1.09. 29
well might they fester 'gainst ingratitude, 1.09. 30
and what they are that must | be hostages for 1.10. 28
prayer of the people, for they love not martius. 2.01. 5 P
men, yet they lie deadly that tell you have good 2.01. 61 P
must become mockers if they shall encounter such 2.01. 85 P
titus lartius writes they fought together, but 2.01.127 P
i'll be sworn they are true. 2.01.143 P
but they | upon their ancient malice will forget 2.01.227
come, come, they are almost here. 2.02. 1 P
three, they say; 2.02. 3 P
and there be many that they have lov'd, they 2.02. 9 P
that they have lov'd, they know not wherefore; 2.02. 9 P
so that, if they love they know not why, they 2.02. 10 P
so that, if they love they know not why, they 2.02. 10 P
know not why, they hate upon no better a ground. 2.02. 11 P
to care whether they love or hate him manifests 2.02. 12 P
greater devotion than they can render it him, 2.02. 19 P
make way, they are coming. 2.02. 36 P
but your people, | i love them as they weigh — 2.02. 74
and look'd upon things precious as they were 2.02.125
neither will they bate | one jot of ceremony. 2.02.140
may they perceive 's intent! 2.02.156
i know they do attend us. 2.02.160
to issue out of one skull, they would fly east, 2.03. 22 P
i would they would forget me, like the virtues 2.03. 57
'tis a condition they account gentle. 2.03. 97 P
they have chose a consul that will from them 2.03.214
they are worn, lord consul, so | that we shall 3.01. 6
against the volsces for they had so vildly 3.01. 10
for they do prank them in authority, | against 3.01. 23
but that | which they have given to beggars. 3.01. 74
you are plebeians, | if they be senators; 3.01.102
and they are no less, | when, both your voices 3.01.102
they choose their magistrate, | and such a one 3.01.104
i say they nourish'd disobedience, fed | the 3.01.117
they know the corn | was not our recompense, 3.01.120

well assur'd | they ne'er did service for't; 3.01.122
was touch'd, | they would not thread the gates. 3.01.124
and revolts, wherein they show'd | most valor, 3.01.126
which they have often made against the senate, 3.01.128
and in true fear | they gave us our demands." 3.01.135
what must be, was law, | then were they chosen; 3.01.168
i would they were barbarians, as they are, 3.01.237
i would they were barbarians, as they are, 3.01.237
not romans, as they are not, | though calved i' 3.01.238
and o'erbear | what they are us'd to bear? 3.01.249
i would they were a–bed! 3.01.260
i would they were in tiber! 3.01.261
dispos'd | ere they lack'd power to cross you. 3.02. 23
by th' other lose | that they combine not there. 3.02. 45
were fit for thee to use as they to claim, | in 3.02. 83
for they have pardons, being ask'd, as free | as 3.02. 88
they to dust should grind it | and throw't 3.02.103
for they are prepar'd | with accusations, as i 3.02.139
and when they hear me say, "it shall be so | i' 3.03. 13
and when such time they have begun to cry, | let 3.03. 19
nor check my courage for what they can give, 3.03. 92
and they | stand in their ancient strength. 4.02. 6
they say she's mad. 4.02. 9
they have ta'en note of us; keep on your way. 4.02. 10
they are in a most warlike preparation, and hope 4.03. 17 P
that they are in a ripe aptness to take all 4.03. 23 P
of the senators but they stand bald before him. 4.05.194 P
but when they shall see, sir, his crest up again 4.05.210 P
man in blood, they will out of their burrows, 4.05.211 P
and to be executed ere they wipe their lips. 4.05.217 P
because they then less need one another. 4.05.231 P
they are rising, they are rising. 4.05.233 P
they are rising, they are rising. 4.05.233 P
though they themselves did suffer by't, behold 4.06. 6
and they follow him | against us brats with no 4.06. 92
for his best friends, if they | should say, "be 4.06.111
they charg'd him even | as those should do that 4.06.112
you are they | that made the air unwholesome, 4.06.129
to have | this true which they so seem to fear. 4.06.151
do they still fly to th' roman? 4.07. 1
of a state | to one whom they had punish'd. 5.01. 21
which they did refuse | and cannot now accept, 5.03. 14
down, and this unnatural scene | they laugh at. 5.03.185
to break our necks, they respect not us. 5.04. 33 P
hark, how they joy! 5.04. 57
they are near the city? 5.04. 60
slain | religiously they ask a sacrifice: TIT 1.01.124
let's hew his limbs till they be clean consum'd. 1.01.129
in rome | how furious and impatient they be, 2.01. 76
when with a happy storm they were surpris'd, 2.03. 23
sons | to back thy quarrels, whatsoe'er they be. 2.03. 54
'tis pity they should take him for a stag. 2.03. 71
and when they show'd me this abhorred pit, 2.03. 98
they told me, here, at dead time of the night, 2.03. 99
no sooner had they told this hellish tale, | but 2.03.105
but straight they told me they would bind me 2.03.106
straight they told me they would bind me here 2.03.106
and then they call'd me foul adulteress, 2.03.109
come, | this vengeance on me had they executed: 2.03.113
how these were they that made away his brother. 2.03.208
what, are they in this pit? 2.03.286
they shall be ready at your highness' will, | to 2.03.297
fear not thy sons, they shall do well enough. 2.03.305
wept, | because they died in honor's lofty bed. 3.01. 11
if they did hear, | they would not mark me; 3.01. 33
if they did hear, | they would not mark me; 3.01. 34
if they did mark, | they would not pity me; 3.01. 34
if they did mark, | they would not pity me; 3.01. 35
who, though they cannot answer my distress, 3.01. 38
yet in some sort they are better than the 3.01. 39
for that they will not intercept my tale. 3.01. 40
weep, they humbly at my feet | receive my tears, 3.01. 41
me, | and, were they but attired in grave weeds, 3.01. 43
o happy man, they have befriended thee! 3.01. 52
for they have fought for rome, and all in vain; 3.01. 73
and they have nurs'd this woe, in feeding life; 3.01. 74
in bootless prayer have they been held up, | and 3.01. 75
up, | and they have serv'd me to effectless use. 3.01. 76
she weeps because they kill'd her husband, 3.01.114
if they did kill thy husband, then be joyful, 3.01.116
no, no, they would not do so foul a deed; 3.01.118
how they are stain'd like meadows yet not dry, 3.01.125
for fear they die before their pardon come. 3.01.175
when they do hug him in their melting bosoms. 3.01.213
then let the ladies tattle what they please. 4.02.168
they hither march amain, under conduct | of 4.04. 65
and they have wish'd that lucius were their 4.04. 77
and is not careful what they mean thereby, 4.04. 84
signifies what hate they bear their emperor, 5.01. 3
and how desirous of our sight they are. 5.01. 4
they never do beget a coal–black calf. 5.01. 32
they cut thy sister's tongue, and ravish'd her, 5.01. 92
that codding spirit had they from their mother, 5.01. 99
that bloody mind i think they learn'd of me, 5.01.101
and they shall be immediately delivered. 5.01.161
where they say he keeps | to ruminate strange 5.02. 5
are /they thy ministers? what are they call'd? 5.02. 61
'cause they take vengeance of such kind of men. 5.02. 63
good lord, how like the empress' sons they are! 5.02. 64
death, | they have been violent to me and mine. 5.02.109
and at thy mercy shall they stoop and kneel, 5.02.118
bid him encamp his soldiers where they are. 5.02.126
i knew them all though they suppos'd me mad, 5.02.142
and stop their mouths if they begin to cry. 5.02.161
receive the blood, and when that they are dead, 5.02.197
they ravish'd her, and cut away her tongue, 5.03. 57
and they, 'twas they, that did her all this 5.03. 58
and they, 'twas they, that did her all this 5.03. 58
why, there they are, both baked in this pie; 5.03. 60
were they that murd'red our emperor's brother, 5.03. 98
and they it were that ravished our sister. 5.03. 99
my scars can witness, dumb although they are, 5.03.114
when they were living, warm'd themselves on 5.03.168
they must take it /in sense that feel it. ROM 1.01. 27 P
me they shall feel while i am able to stand, and 1.01. 28 P
as i pass by, and let them take it as they list. 1.01. 41 P
nay, as they dare. 1.01. 42 P
them, which is disgrace to them if they bear it. 1.01. 43 P
neighbor–stained steel — | will they not hear? 1.01. 83
being black, puts us in mind they hide the fair. 1.01.231
whither should they come? 1.02. 71
but let them measure us by what they will, 1.04. 9
in bed asleep, while they do dream things true. 1.04. 52
atomi | over men's noses as they lie asleep. 1.04. 58
lovers' brains, and then they dream of love; 1.04. 71
one or two men's hands, and they unwash'd too, 1.05. 4 P
ay, pilgrim, lips that they must use in pray'r. 1.05.102
they pray — grant thou, lest faith turn to 1.05.104
then have my lips the sin that they have took. 1.05.108
as maids call medlars, when they laugh alone. 2.01. 36
to twinkle in their spheres till they return. 2.02. 17
what if her eyes were there, they in her head? 2.02. 18
if they do see thee, they will murther thee. 2.02. 70
if they do see thee, they will murther thee. 2.02. 70
i would not for the world they saw thee here. 2.02. 74
at lovers' perjuries, | they say, jove laughs. 2.02. 93
wisely and slow, they stumble that run fast. 2.03. 94
that they cannot sit at ease on the old bench? 2.04. 34 P
lead her in a fool's paradise, as they say, it 2.04.166 P
were a very gross kind of behavior, as they say; 2.04.167 P
but old folks — many feign as they were dead, 2.05. 16
and a body, though they be not to be talk'd on, 2.05. 42 P
not to be talk'd on, yet they are past compare. 2.05. 42 P
fire and powder, | which as they kiss consume. 2.06. 11
they are but beggars that can count their worth, 2.06. 32
they have made worms' meat of me. 3.01.107
and to't they go like lightning, for, ere i 3.01.172
wash they his wounds with tears? 3.02.130
they may seize | on the white wonder of dear 3.03. 35
they are free men, but i am banished: 3.03. 42
how should they when that wise men have no eyes? 3.03. 62
hark how they knock! 3.03. 74
o, now i would they had chang'd voices too, 3.05. 32
what are they, beseech your ladyship? 3.05.106
who, raging with thy tears, and they with them, 3.05.135
stuff'd, as they say, with honorable parts, 3.05.181
for i'll try if they can lick their fingers. 4.02. 4 P
they are all forth. 4.02. 44
fest'ring in his shroud, where, as they say, 4.03. 43
they call for dates and quinces in the pastry. 4.04. 2
call peter, he will show thee where they are. 4.04. 17
it thee, | so fearful were they of infection. 5.02. 16
o lord, they fight! i will go call the watch. 5.03. 71
at the point of death | have they been merry, 5.03. 89
figures are | even such as they give out. TIM 1.01.160
are they not athenians? 1.01.182 P
o, they eat lords; 1.01.206 P
so they come by great bellies. 1.01.206 P
they say, my lords, "ira furor brevis est," 1.02. 28
methinks they should invite them without knives: 1.02. 44
lest they should spy my windpipe's dangerous 1.02. 51
so they were bleeding new, my lord, there's no 1.02. 78 P
they were the most needless creatures living, 1.02. 96 P
they only now come but to feast thine eyes. 1.02.127
they dance? 1.02.133
they are madwomen. 1.02.133
they are fairly welcome. 1.02.176
ay, would they serv'd us! 2.02. 93 P
to borrow of your masters, they approach sadly, 2.02.100 P
but they enter my master's house merrily, and go 2.02.101 P
but they do shake their heads, and i am here 2.02.202
they answer, in a joint and corporate voice, 2.02.204
that now they are at fall, want treasure, cannot 2.02.205
cannot | do what they would, are sorry; 2.02.206
but yet they could have wish'd — they know not 2.02.207
yet they could have wish'd — they know not — 2.02.207
cold–moving nods, | they froze me into silence. 2.02.213
'tis lack of kindly warmth they are not kind; 2.02.217
they have all been touch'd and found base metal, 3.03. 6
base metal, | for they have all denied him. 3.03. 7
have they denied him? 3.03. 7
then they could smile, and fawn upon his debts, 3.04. 51
they have e'en put my breath from me, the slaves 3.04.103
words have took such pains as if they labor'd 3.05. 26
while they have told their money, and let out 3.05.106
if they will fare so harshly o' th' trumpet's 3.06. 34 P
table, let a dozen of them be — as they are. 3.06. 79 P
my present friends, as they are to me nothing, 3.06. 83 P
bless them, and to nothing are they welcome. 3.06. 84 P
'gainst the stream of virtue they may strive, 4.01. 27
if one be, | so are they all; 4.03. 16
they love thee not that use thee; 4.03. 84
they never flatter'd thee. 4.03.270
they mock'd thee for too much curiosity; 4.03.302 P
load our purposes | with what they travail for, 5.01. 15
they confess | toward thee forgetfulness too 5.01.143
become your lips as they pass thorough them. 5.01.195
we stand much hazard if they bring not timon. 5.02. 5
nor are they such | that these great tow'rs, 5.04. 24
nor are they living | who were the motives that 5.04. 26
shame, that they wanted cunning in excess, 5.04. 28
against our rampir'd gates and they shall ope, 5.04. 47
when they are in great danger, i recover them. JC 1.01. 24 P
they vanish tongue–tied in their guiltiness. 1.01. 62
when could they say, till now, that talk'd of 1.02.154
as they pass by, pluck casca by the sleeve, 1.02.179
whiles they behold a greater than themselves, 1.02.209
and therefore are they very dangerous. 1.02.210
they shouted thrice; what was the last cry for? 1.02.226
as they use to do the players in the theatre, i 1.02.260 P
their mothers, they would have done no less. 1.02.275 P
throw, | as if they came from several citizens, 1.02.317
with their fear, who swore they saw | men, all 1.03. 24
"these are their reasons, they are natural": 1.03. 30
they are portentous things | unto the climate 1.03. 31
things | unto the climate that they point upon. 1.03. 32
indeed, they say, the senators to–morrow | mean 1.03. 85
by this they stay for me | in pompey's porch; 1.03.125
they are the faction. 2.01. 77
they are all welcome. 2.01. 97
but if these | (as i am sure they do) bear fire 2.01.120
they murther caesar!" 2.02. 3
when they shall see | the face of caesar, they 2.02. 11
see | the face of caesar, they are vanished. 2.02. 12
stood on ceremonies, | yet now they fright me. 2.02. 14
they would not have you to stir forth to–day. 2.02. 38
they could not find a heart within the beast. 2.02. 40
if caesar hide himself, shall they not whisper, 2.02.100
they are all fire, and every one doth shine; 3.01. 64
and this the bleeding business they have done. 3.01.168
our hearts you see not, they are pitiful; 3.01.169
weeping as fast as they stream forth thy blood, 3.01.201
that mothers shall but smile when they behold 3.01.267
so are they all, all honorable men), | come i to 3.02. 83
and they would go and kiss dead caesar's wounds, 3.02.132
they were traitors; honorable men! 3.02.153
they were villains, murderers. 3.02.155 P
they that have done this deed are honorable. 3.02.212
what private griefs they have, alas, i know not, 3.02.213
they are wise and honorable, | and will no doubt 3.02.214
and that they know full well | that gave me 3.02.219
belike they had some notice of the people, | how 3.02.270
as much as to say, they are fools that marry. 3.03. 17 P
but when they should endure the bloody spur, 4.02. 25
they fall their crests, and like deceitful jades 4.02. 26
they mean this night in sardis to be quarter'd. 4.02. 28
honesty | that they pass by me as the idle wind, 4.03. 68
but brutus makes mine greater than they are. 4.03. 87
though they do appear | as huge as high olympus. 4.03. 91
'tis not meet | they be alone. 4.03.126
for they have grudg'd us contribution. 4.03.206
they mean to warn us at philippi here, 5.01. 5
their bosoms, and i know | wherefore they do it. 5.01. 8
they could be content | to visit other places, 5.01. 8
fasten in our thoughts that they have courage; 5.01. 11
they stand, and would have parley. 5.01. 21
but for your words, they rob the hybla bees, 5.01. 34
two mighty eagles fell, and there they perch'd, 5.01. 80
this morning are they fled away and gone, | and 5.01. 83
they are, my lord. 5.03. 14
now they are almost on him. 5.03. 30
and hark, they shout for joy. 5.03. 32
and did not they | put on my brows this wreath 5.03. 81
in ourselves | than tarry till they push us. 5.05. 25
he, | did that they did in envy of great caesar; 5.05. 70
i must report they were | as cannons overcharg'd MAC 1.02. 36
so they | doubly redoubled strokes upon the foe. 1.02. 37
except they meant to bathe in reeking wounds, 1.02. 39
thee as thy wounds, | they smack of honor both. 1.02. 44
all the other, | and the very ports they blow, 1.03. 15
blow, | all the quarters that they know | i' th' 1.03. 16
whither are they vanish'd? 1.03. 80
would they had stay'd! 1.03. 82
my liege, | they are not yet come back. 1.04. 3
which do but what they should, by doing every 1.04. 26
"they met me in the day of success; 1.05. 1 P
they have more in them than mortal knowledge. 1.05. 3 P
question them further, they made themselves air, 1.05. 4 P
made themselves air, into which they vanish'd. 1.05. 5 P
where they /most breed and haunt, i have 1.06. 9
they have made themselves, and that their 1.07. 53
their very daggers, | that they have done't? 1.07. 77
to you they have show'd some truth. 2.01. 21
contend about them, | whether they live or die. 2.02. 8
alack, i am afraid they have awak'd, | and 'tis 2.02. 9
that they did wake each other. 2.02. 21
but they did say their prayers, and address'd 2.02. 22
as they had seen me with these hangman's hands. 2.02. 25
say "amen," | when they did say "god bless us!" 2.02. 27
they must lie there. 2.02. 46
they pluck out mine eyes. 2.02. 56
our chimneys were blown down, and, as they say, 2.03. 55
they star'd and were distracted; 2.03.104
as they would make | war with mankind. 2.04. 17
'tis said, they eat each other. 2.04. 18
they did so — to th' amazement of mine eyes 2.04. 19
alas the day, | what good could they pretend? 2.04. 24
they were suborned. 2.04. 24
made good, | may they not be my oracles as well, 3.01. 9
they are, my lord, without the palace gate. 3.01. 46
when first they put the name of king upon me, 3.01. 57
they hail'd him father to a line of kings. 3.01. 59
upon my head they plac'd a fruitless crown, 3.01. 60
indeed have died | with them they think on? 3.02. 11
to our hearts, | disguising what they are. 3.02. 35
there's comfort yet, they are assailable. 3.02. 39
friends, | for my heart speaks they are welcome. 3.04. 8
they encounter thee with their hearts' thanks. 3.04. 9
but now they rise again | with twenty mortal 3.04. 79
it will have blood, they say; 3.04.121
more shall they speak; 3.04.133
which must be acted ere they may be scann'd. 3.04.139
they should find | what 'twere to kill a father; 3.06. 19
where are they? 4.01.133
came they not by you? 4.01.137
infected be the air whereon they ride, | and 4.01.138
come bring me where they are. 4.01.156
or else climb upward | to what they were before. 4.02. 25
with what i get, i mean, and so do they. 4.02. 33
poor birds they are not set for. 4.02. 36
and must they all be hang'd that swear and lie? 4.02. 51 P
so grafted | that, when they shall be open'd, 4.03. 52
heaven given his hand, | they presently amend. 4.03.145
in their caps, | dying or e'er they sicken. 4.03.173
they were well at peace when i did leave 'em. 4.03.179
what concern they? 4.03.195
the heaviest sound | that ever yet they heard. 4.03.203
sinful macduff, | they were all strook for thee! 4.03.225
that way are they coming. 5.02. 6
outward walls, | the cry is still, "they come!" 5.05. 2
were they not forc'd with those that should be 5.05. 5
they have tied me to a stake; 5.07. 1
they say he parted well, and paid his score, 5.09. 18
for which, they say, your spirits oft walk in HAM 1.01.138
and then they say no spirit dare stir abroad, 1.01.161
for they are actions that a man might play, 1.02. 84
within his truncheon's length, whilst they, 1.02.204
to me | in dreadful secrecy impart they did, 1.02.207
where, as they had delivered, both in time, 1.02.209
and they in france of the best rank and station 1.03. 73
do not believe his vows, for they are brokers, 1.03.127
they clip us drunkards, and with swinish phrase 1.04. 19
as in their birth, wherein they are not guilty 1.04. 25
his virtues else, be they as pure as grace, | as 1.04. 33

i am sorry they offend you, heartily, | yes, 1.05.134
or "there be, and if they might," | or such 1.05.177
how, and who, what means, and where they keep, 2.01. 8
drift of question | that they do know my son, 2.01. 11
that they may seem the taints of liberty, | the 2.01. 32
as they fell out by time, by means, and place, 2.02.127
gum, and that they have a plentiful lack of wit, 2.02.199 P
and hither are they coming to offer you service. 2.02.318 P
what players are they? 2.02.326 P
how chances it they travel? 2.02.329 P
do they hold the same estimation they did when i 2.02.334 P
the same estimation they did when i was in the 2.02.334 P
are they so follow'd? 2.02.335 P
no indeed are they not. 2.02.336 P
them, for they say an old man is twice a child. 2.02.385 P
for they are the abstract and brief chronicles 2.02.524 P
own honor and dignity — the less they deserve, 2.02.532 P
they have proclaim'd their malefactions: 2.02.592
they are here about the court, | and, as i think 3.01. 19
they have already order | this night to play 3.01. 20
shall live, the rest shall keep as they are. 3.01.149 P
them well, they imitated humanity so abominably. 3.02. 34 P
that they are not a pipe for fortune's finger 3.02. 70
they are coming to the play. 3.02. 90
ay, my lord, they stay upon your patience. 3.02.107 P
tree, | but fall unshaken when they mellow be. 3.02.191
no, no, they do but jest, poison in jest — no 3.02.234 P
they fool me to the top of my bent. 3.02.384 P
they bear the mandate — they must sweep my way, 3.04.204
they bear the mandate — they must sweep my way, 3.04.204
o, here they come. 4.02. 4 P
they are of norway, sir. 4.04. 10
they yawn at it | and botch the words up fit to 4.05. 9
they say the owl was a baker's daughter. 4.05. 42 P
of this, but when they ask you what it means, 4.05. 47 P
young men will do't, if they come to't, | by 4.05. 60
if they come to't, | by cock, they are to blame. 4.05. 61
but weep to think they would lay him i' th' cold 4.05. 69 P
when sorrows come, they come not single spies, 4.05. 78
how cheerfully on the false trail they cry! 4.05.110
them so well, | they shall go far with little. 4.05.140
"they bore him barefac'd on the bier, | /hey 4.05.165
but they wither'd all when my father died. 4.05.185 P
they say 'a made a good end — "for bonny sweet 4.05.185 P
and they shall hear and judge 'twixt you and me. 4.05.206
or by collateral hand | they find us touch'd, we 4.05.208
what are they that would speak with me? 4.06. 1 P
they say they have letters for you. 4.06. 2 P
they say they have letters for you. 4.06. 2 P
means to the king, they have letters for him. 4.06. 15 P
on the instant they got clear of our ship, so i 4.06. 19 P
they have dealt with me like thieves of mercy, 4.06. 20 P
thieves of mercy, but they knew what they did: 4.06. 21 P
thieves of mercy, but they knew what they did: 4.06. 21 P
yet are they much too light for the /bore of the 4.06. 26 P
sailors, my lord, they say, i saw them not. 4.07. 39
they were given me by claudio. 4.07. 40
for a quality | wherein, they say, you shine. 4.07. 73
and they can well on horseback, but this gallant 4.07. 84
upon another's heel, | so fast they follow. 4.07.164
and, mermaid–like, awhile they bore her up, 4.07.176
they hold up adam's profession. 5.01. 31 P
they are sheep and calves which seek out 5.01.116 P
very strangely, they say. 5.01.157 P
was converted might they not stop a beer–barrel? 5.01.212 P
who is this they follow? 5.01.218
the corse they follow did with desp'rate hand 5.01.220
to my brains, | they had begun the play. 5.02. 31
/employment, | they are not near my conscience. 5.02. 58
to my purposes, they follow the king's pleasure. 5.02.200 P
part them, they are incens'd. 5.02.302
they bleed on both sides. how is it, my lord? 5.02.304
husbands, if they say | they love you all? LR 1.01. 99
husbands, if they say | they love you all? 1.01.100
loath to call | your faults as they are named. 1.01.271
why brand they us | with base? 1.02. 9
what two crowns shall they be? 1.04.157 P
breeches, "then they for sudden joy did weep, 1.04.175
because they are not eight. 1.05. 37 P
for they are yet but ear–/bussing arguments? 2.01. 7 P
not i. pray you, what are they? 2.01. 9 P
if they not thought the profits of my death 2.01. 75
'tis they have put him on the old man's death, 2.01. 99
that if they come to sojourn at my house, | i'll 2.01.103
though they had been but two years o' th' trade. 2.02. 59 P
and they will take/'t, so; 2.02.100
'tis strange that they should so depart from 2.04. 1
they durst not do't; 2.04. 22
they could not, would not do't. 2.04. 23
way | thou mightst deserve, or they impose, this 2.04. 26
of intermission, | which presently they read; 2.04. 34
those contents | they summon'd up their meiny, 2.04. 35
they are sick? 2.04. 88
they are weary? 2.04. 88
they have travell'd all the night? 2.04. 89
are they "inform'd" of this? 2.04.103
if then they chanc'd to slack ye, | we could 2.04.245
what they are yet, i know not, but they shall be 2.04.281
but they shall be | the terrors of the earth! 2.04.281
the injuries that they themselves procure | must 2.04.303
and what they may incense him to, being apt | to 2.04.306
they took from me the use of mine own house, 3.03. 3 P
his part so much, | they mar my counterfeiting. 3.06. 61
blanch, and sweetheart, see, they bark at me. 3.06. 63
you will say they are persian, but let them be 3.06. 80 P
where they boast | to have well–armed friends. 3.07. 19
thee they may hurt. 4.01. 17
we to th' gods, | they kill us for their sport. 4.01. 37
bless thy sweet eyes, they bleed. 4.01. 54
where was his son when they did take his eyes? 4.02. 88
no, they cannot touch me for /coining; 4.06. 83 P
they flatter'd me like a dog, and told me i had 4.06. 96 P
go to, they are not men o' their words: 4.06.104 P
they told me i was every thing. 4.06.104 P
down from the waist they are centaurs, | though 4.06.124
you have some cause, they have not. 4.07. 74
the battle done, and they within our power, 5.01. 67
flesh and fell, | ere they shall make us weep! 5.03. 25
all the same, and they are ready | to–morrow, or 5.03. 52
for they yet glance by and scarcely bruise, 5.03.149
instant way | where they shall rest for ever. 5.03.151
produce the bodies, be they alive or dead. 5.03.231
and when they have lin'd their coats, | do OTH 1.01. 53
another of his fadom they have none | to lead 1.01.152
are they married, think you? 1.01.167
truly, i think they are. 1.01.168
is it they? 1.02. 32
indeed, they are disproportioned; 1.03. 2
but though they jump not on a just accompt | (as 1.03. 5
yet do they all confirm | a turkish fleet, and 1.03. 7
and now they do restem | their backward course, 1.03. 37
they have us'd | their dearest action in the 1.03. 84
not enshelter'd and embay'd, they are drown'd; 2.01. 18
for they were parted | with foul and violent 2.01. 33
th' sea | stand ranks of people, and they cry, 2.01. 54
they do discharge their shot of courtesy; 2.01. 56
they give /their greeting to the citadel. 2.01. 94
would they were clyster–pipes for your sake! 2.01.177 P
may the winds blow till they have waken'd death! 2.01.186
(as they say base men being in love have then a 2.01.215 P
they met so near with their lips that their 2.01.259 P
o, they are our friends — but one cup, i'll 2.03. 37 P
where are they? 2.03. 45 P
with flowing cups, | and they watch too. 2.03. 59
but here they come. 2.03. 61
'fore /god, they have given me a rouse already. 2.03. 64 P
where indeed they are most potent in potting; 2.03. 76 P
even as again they were | when you yourself did 2.03.238
desperate of my fortunes if they check me /here. 2.03.331 P
they do suggest at first with heavenly shows, 2.03.352
how poor are they that have not patience! 2.03.370
in naples, that they speak i' th' nose thus? 3.01. 4 P
ay, marry, are they, sir. 3.01. 7 P
but (as they say) to hear music the general does 3.01. 16 P
(save that they say the wars must make example 3.03. 65
men should be what they seem, | or those that be 3.03.126
those that be not, would they might seem none! 3.03.127
certain, men should be what they seem. 3.03.128
why, say they are vild and false, | as where's 3.03.136
in venice they do let /god see the pranks | they 3.03.202
the pranks | they dare not show their husbands; 3.03.203
prerogativ'd are they less than the base; 3.03.274
were they as prime as goats, as hot as monkeys, 3.03.403
they are all but stomachs, and we all but food; 3.04.104
they eat us hungerly, and when they are full 3.04.105
and when they are full | they belch us. 3.04.105
and when they are full | they belch us. 3.04.106
they are not ever jealious for the cause, | but 3.04.160
they that mean virtuously, and yet do so, | the 4.01. 7
their virtue tempts, and they tempt heaven. 4.01. 8
if they do nothing, 'tis a venial slip; 4.01. 9
they have it very oft that have it not. 4.01. 17
them, cannot choose | but they must blab — 4.01. 29
we say lie on her, when they belie her. 4.01. 36 P
unproper beds | which they dare swear peculiar; 4.01. 69
so, so, so, so; they laugh that wins. 4.01.122 P
for, as i think, they do command him home, 4.01.236
what? did they never whisper? 4.02. 6
had they rain'd | all kind of sores and shames 4.02. 48
as would store the world they play'd for. 4.03. 85 P
say that they slack their duties, | and pour our 4.03. 87
or say they strike us, | or scant our former 4.03. 90
they see, and smell, | and have their palates 4.03. 94
what is it that they do | when they change us 4.03. 96
that they do | when they change us for others? 4.03. 97
who they should be that have thus mangled you? 5.01. 79
i must weep, | but they are cruel tears. 5.02. 21
they are loves i bear to you. 5.02. 40
yet i hope, i hope, | they do not point on me. 5.02. 46
done the state some service, and they know't — 5.02.339
fortunes of the moor, | for they succeed on you. 5.02.367
look where they come! ANT 1.01. 10
they would make themselves whores but they'ld 1.02. 77 P
if they suffer our departure, death's the word. 1.02.134 P
a great cause, they should be esteem'd nothing. 1.02.139 P
they are greater storms and tempests than 1.02.148 P
they are so still, | or thou, the greatest 1.03. 37
since my becomings kill me when they do not 1.03. 96
which they ear and wound | with keels of every 1.04. 49
many hot inroads | they make in italy; 1.04. 51
they shall assist | the deeds of justest men. 2.01. 1
that what they do delay, they not deny. 2.01. 3
that what they do delay, they not deny. 2.01. 3
are in the field, a mighty strength they carry. 2.01. 17
i know they are in rome together, | looking for 2.01. 19
'twere pregnant they should square between 2.01. 45
for they have entertained cause enough | to draw 2.01. 46
the water which they beat to follow faster, | as 2.02.196
/glow the delicate cheeks which they did cool, 2.02.204
which they did cool, | and what they undid did. 2.02.205
other women cloy | the appetites they feed, but 2.02.236
these hands do lack nobility that they strike 2.05. 82
ill tidings tell | themselves when they be felt. 2.05. 88
lie they upon thy hand, | and be undone by 'em! 2.05.105
but that they would | have one man but a man? 2.06. 18
here they might take two thieves kissing. 2.06. 95 P
no slander, they steal hearts. 2.06.101 P
they have made him drink alms–drink. 2.07. 5 P
as they pinch one another by the disposition, he 2.07. 6 P
thus do they, sir: 2.07. 17
they take the flow o' th' nile | by certain 2.07. 17
they know, | by th' height, the lowness, or the 2.07. 18
they are so. 2.07. 28 P
they have dispatch'd with pompey, he is gone; 3.02. 2
they are his shards, and he their beetle, so. 3.02. 20
most part, too, they are foolish that are so. 3.03. 31
sat | caesarion, whom they call my father's son, 3.06. 6
i' th' common show–place, where they exercise. 3.06. 12
they say, one taurus. 3.07. 78
toward peloponnesus are they fled. 3.10. 30
rashness, and they them | for fear and doting. 3.11. 14
against the blown rose may they stop their nose 3.13. 39
so haply are they friends to antony. 3.13. 48
store to do't, | and they have earn'd the waste. 4.01. 16
look, they weep, | and i, an ass, am onion–ey'd. 4.02. 34
they do retire. 4.07. 8
they are beaten, sir, and our advantage serves 4.07. 11
feats, whilst they with joyful tears | wash the 4.08. 9
and they say we shall embattle | by th' second 4.09. 3
sea is given, | they have put forth the haven — 4.10. 7
yet they are not join'd. 4.12. 1
the auguries | say they know not, they cannot 4.12. 5
auguries | say they know not, they cannot tell, 4.12. 5
they cast their caps up and carouse together 4.12. 12
these signs, | they are black vesper's pageants. 4.14. 8
they do not go together. 4.15. 47
equal theirs | till they had stol'n our jewel. 4.15. 78
shall they hoist me up, | and show me to the 5.02. 55
they show'd his back above | the element they 5.02. 89
his back above | the element they liv'd in. 5.02. 90
i'll catch thine eyes | though they had wings. 5.02.157
but he that will believe all that they say, 5.02.256 P
say, shall never be sav'd by half that they do. 5.02.257 P
for in every ten that they make, the devils mar 5.02.277 P
if they had swallow'd poison, 'twould appear 5.02.345
although they wear their faces to the bent | of CYM 1.01. 13
that is not | glad at the thing they scowl at. 1.01. 15
no guess in knowledge | which way they went. 1.01. 61
they were again together; 1.01.151
they were parted | by gentlemen at hand. 1.01.163
i would they were in afric both together, 1.01.167
i would they had not come between us. 1.02. 22 P
here they are, madam. 1.05. 5
ill often hurts more | than to be sure they do; 1.06. 96
they are in a trunk, | attended by my men. 1.06.196
they dare not fight with me because of the queen 2.01. 18 P
rubies unparagon'd, | how dearly they do't! 2.02. 18
they say it will penetrate. 2.03. 12 P
hairs above thee, | were they all made such men. 2.03.136
they failing, | i must die much your debtor. 2.04. 7
known | to their approvers they are people such 2.04. 25
so they must, | or do your honor injury. 2.04. 79
of no more bondage be to where they are made 2.04.111
they are made | than they are to their virtues, 2.04.112
they induc'd to steal it? 2.04.125
for even to vice | they are not constant, but 2.05. 30
in a true hate, to pray they have their will: 2.05. 34
which then they had to take from 's, to resume 3.01. 15
boys know little they are sons to th' king, 3.03. 80
nor cymbeline dreams that they are alive. 3.03. 81
they think they are mine, and, though train'd up 3.03. 82
they think they are mine, and, though train'd up 3.03. 82
they took thee for their mother, | and every day 3.03.104
morgan call'd, | they take for natural father. 3.03.107
are they not but in britain? 3.04.137
ourself | to show less sovereignty than they, 3.05. 6
such, i mean, | where they should be reliev'd. 3.06. 8
been so, that they | had been my father's sons, 3.06. 75
i am near to th' place where they should meet, 4.01. 1 P
they grow, | and set them on lud's–town. 4.02.122
he so undertaking, | or they so suffering. 4.02.143
they are as gentle | as zephyrs blowing below 4.02.171
they are here in readiness. 4.02.336
and they come | under the conduct of bold 4.02.339
for it seems | they crave to be demanded. 4.02.362
that when they hear their roman horses neigh, 4.04. 17
that they will waste their time upon our note, 4.04. 20
cam'st thou from where they made the stand? 5.03. 1
gan to look | the way that they did, and to grin 5.03. 38
forthwith they fly | chickens, the way which 5.03. 41
chickens, the way which they /stoop'd eagles; 5.03. 42
heavens, how they wound | some slain before, 5.03. 46
'tween man and man they weigh not every stamp; 5.04. 24
they went hence so soon as they were born. 5.04.126
they went hence so soon as they were born. 5.04.126
o' th' earth amend | by being worse than they. 5.05.217
arms alone, | they were not born for bondage. 5.05.306
call me father | and think they are my sons, are 5.05.329
they are the issue of your loins, my liege, 5.05.330
gentle princes | (for such and so they are) 5.05.337
those arts they have as i | could put into them. 5.05.338
for they are worthy | to inlay heaven with stars 5.05.351
if these be they, i know not how to wish | a 5.05.355
joyful too, | for they shall taste our comfort. 5.05.403
but custom what they did begin | was with long PER 1.ch. 29
here they stand martyrs, slain in cupid's wars; 1.01. 38
gripe not at earthly joys as erst they did; 1.01. 49
my riches to the earth from whence they came; 1.01. 52
how they may be, and yet in two, | as you will 1.01. 70
why cloud they not their sights perpetually, 1.01. 74
few love to hear the sins they love to act; 1.01. 92
are, who though they feed | on sweetest flowers, 1.01.132
on sweetest flowers, yet they poison breed. 1.01.133
our men be vanquish'd ere they do resist, | and 1.02. 27
which fence the roots they grow by and defend 1.02. 31
they do abuse the king that flatter him, | for 1.02. 38
fits kings as they are men, for they may err. 1.02. 43
fits kings as they are men, for they may err. 1.02. 43
from whence | they have their nourishment? 1.02. 56
it, | for who digs hills because they do aspire 1.04. 5
here they are but felt, and seen with mischief's 1.04. 8
like to groves, being topp'd, they higher rise. 1.04. 9
they may awake their helpers to comfort them. 1.04. 17
bore heads so high they kiss'd the clouds, | and 1.04. 24
although they gave their creatures in abundance, 1.04. 36
they are now starv'd for want of exercise; 1.04. 38
to eat those little darlings whom they lov'd. 1.04. 44
white flags display'd, they bring us peace, 1.04. 72
but bring they what they will and what they can, 1.04. 76
but bring they what they will and what they can, 1.04. 76
but bring they what they will and what they can, 1.04. 76
what pitiful cries they made to us to help them, 2.01. 21 P
they say they're half fish, half flesh. 2.01. 24 P
them, they ne'er come but i look to be wash'd. 2.01. 25 P
never leave gaping till they swallow'd the whole 2.01. 33 P
o, sir, things must be as they may; 2.01.113 P
they are, my liege, | and stay your coming to 2.02. 2
marshal, the rest, as they deserve their grace. 2.03. 19
gives them what he will, not what they crave. 2.03. 47
since they love men in arms as well as beds. 2.03. 98
in those that practice them they are, my lord. 2.03.104
withhold the vengeance that they had in store, 2.04. 4
for they so stunk, | that all those eyes ador'd 2.04. 10
and now at length they overflow their banks. 2.04. 24

so, | they are well dispatch'd; 2.05. 15
they were too rough | that threw her in the sea. 3.02. 79
of fortune, though they haunt you mortally, 3.03. 6
be't when they weav'd the sleided silk | with 4.ch. 21
and with a dropping industry they skip | from 4.01. 62
pirate valdes, | and they have seiz'd marina. 4.01. 97
perhaps they will but please themselves upon her 4.01.100
whom they have ravish'd must by me be slain. 4.01.102
three, and they can do no more than they can do; 4.02. 7 P
three, and they can do no more than they can do; 4.02. 8 P
and they with continual action are even as good 4.02. 8 P
blow it to pieces, they are so pitifully sodden. 4.02. 19 P
no cheap thing, if men were as they have been. 4.02. 61 P
they listen'd to me as they would have hearken'd 4.02. 98 P
listen'd to me as they would have hearken'd to 4.02. 98 P
thou sayest true, i' faith, so they must: 4.02.126 P
ay, by my faith, they shall not be chang'd yet. 4.02.135 P
though they did change me to the meanest bird 4.06.101
since they do better thee in their command. 4.06.162
sir, they shall be brought you to my house, 5.03. 26
that him and his they in his palace burn; 5.03. 98
much money gi'n, | if they stand sound and well; TNK pr 3
soon as they /move, as asprays do the fish, 1.01.138
asprays do the fish, | subdue before they touch. 1.01.139
they themselves, some say, | groan under such a 1.01.230
where not to be ev'n jump | as they are, here 1.02. 41
and what they win in't, boot and glory; 1.02. 70
yet they | must yield their tribute there. 1.03. 7
eat them) | the brine they wept at killing 'em. 1.03. 22
they two have cabin'd | in many as dangerous as 1.03. 35
they have skiff'd | torrents whose roaring 1.03. 37
and they have | fought out together where 1.03. 39
where, phoenix–like, | they died in perfume. 1.03. 71
have told 's | they are sisters' children, 1.04. 16
for they were a mark | worth a god's view. 1.04. 20
'tis right — those, those. | they are not dead? 1.04. 24
had they been taken | when their last hurts were 1.04. 25
'twas possible | they might have been recovered. 1.04. 27
yet they breathe | and have the name of men. 1.04. 27
it be for great ones, yet they seldom come: 2.01. 3 P
i can tell you they are princes. 2.01. 20 P
'tis pity they are in prison, and 'twere pity 2.01. 22 P
in prison, and 'twere pity they should be out. 2.01. 22 P
i do think they have patience to make any 2.01. 23 P
and they have all the world in their chamber. 2.01. 25 P
they are fam'd to be a pair of absolute men. 2.01. 26 P
they stand a grise above the reach of report. 2.01. 28 P
nay, most likely, for they are noble suff'rers. 2.01. 31 P
i marvel how they would have look'd had they 2.01. 32 P
they would have look'd had they been victors, 2.01. 33 P
do they so? 2.01. 36 P
it seems to me they have no more sense of their 2.01. 37 P
they eat well, look merrily, discourse of many 2.01. 38 P
came privately in the night, and so did they. 2.01. 47 P
look yonder they are! 2.01. 48 P
they would not make us their object. 2.01. 51 P
garlands, | ere they have time to wish 'em ours. 2.02. 17
the gall of hazard, so they grow together, 2.02. 66
they must not, say they could; 2.02. 67
they must not, say they could; 2.02. 67
we had died as they do, ill old men, unwept, 2.02.109
or were they all hard–hearted? 2.02.122
they could not be to one so fair. 2.02.123
near the gods in nature, they should fear her; 2.02.242
what pastimes are they? 2.03. 66
yet they that knew me | would say it was my best 2.05. 13
i am then | kissing the man they look for. 2.06. 37
this is a solemn rite | they owe bloom'd may, 3.01. 3
men lose when they incline to treachery, | and 3.01. 67
and then they fight like compell'd bears, would 3.01. 68
compell'd bears, would fly | were they not tied. 3.01. 69
news from earth, they shall get none but this — 3.01. 80
sir, they call | the scatter'd to the banket. 3.01.108
why may't not be | they have made prey of him? 3.02. 13
they howl'd many together, | and then they /fed 3.02. 18
many together, | and then they /fed on him. 3.02. 19
how they cry! 3.04. 8
may they kill him without lets, | and the ladies 3.05.156
i have said they die; 3.06.224
better they fall by th' law than one another. 3.06.225
thousand blossoms, | because they may be rotten? 3.06.244
where ever they shall travel, ever strangers 3.06.255
they cannot both enjoy you. 3.06.275
they are princes | as goodly as your own eyes, 3.06.275
i cannot, sir, they are both too excellent: 3.06.286
they are welcome. 4.01. 18
they that nev'r begg'd | but they prevail'd, had 4.01. 26
they that nev'r begg'd | but they prevail'd, had 4.01. 27
i hope they are good. 4.01. 30
they are honorable, | how good they'll prove, i 4.01. 30
here they are. 4.01.103
years old | they must be all gelt for musicians, 4.01.133
they come from all parts of the dukedom to him. 4.01.136
speak, | you that have seen them, what they are. 4.02. 72
braver spirits | than these they have brought 4.02. 74
the same, my lord. | are they not sweet ones? 4.02.121
yes, they are well. 4.02.121
they show | great and fine art in nature. 4.02.122
to the shoulder–piece | gently they swell, like 4.02.128
are they all thus? 4.02.141
they are all the sons of honor. 4.02.141
they would show | bravely about the titles of 4.02.144
weep not, till they weep blood. 4.02.148
their fame has fir'd me so — till they appear. 4.02.153
'tis a sore life they have i' th' tother place, 4.03. 32 P
o, they have shrowd measure! 4.03. 33 P
or hang or drown themselves, thither they go — 4.03. 35 P
got maids with child, they are in this place. 4.03. 42 P
they shall stand in fire up to the nav'l, and in 4.03. 42 P
they may return and settle again to execute 4.03. 71 P
but they are now in a most extravagant vagary. 4.03. 73 P
with tokens, as if they suggested for him. 4.03. 92 P
they have a noble work in hand will honor | the 5.01. 6
sir, they enter. 5.01. 7
and have hotly ask'd them | if they had mothers; 5.01.106
one, a woman, | and women 'twere they wrong'd. 5.01.107
were i to lose one — they are equal precious — 5.01.155
to marry us, for here they are nice and foolish. 5.02. 79
are they i' th' field? 5.02.100
they are. | you bear a charge there too. 5.02.100
for they would glance their eyes | toward my 5.03. 61
they said that palamon had arcite's body 5.03. 79
were they metamorphis'd | both into one — o, 5.03. 84
they are coming off. 5.03.103
a grain of honor | they not o'erweigh us. 5.04. 19
made (for, as they say, from iron | came music's 5.04. 60
and they themselves become | the executioners. 5.04.121
argo they eat more in our country than they do STM II.C 5 P
more in our country than they do in their own. II.C 6 P
they bring in strange roots, which is merely to II.C 8 P
they breed sore eyes and 'tis enough to infect II.C 10 P
of dung — as you know they grow in dung — have II.C 13 P
whiles they are o'er the bank of their obedience II.C 39
thus will they bear down all things. II.C 40
plague on them, they will not hold their peace. II.C 53 P
so they were dew'd with such distilling showers. VEN 66
though mine be not so fair, yet are they red — 116
for where they lay the shadow had forsook them, 176
like misty vapors when they blot the sky, 184
if they burn too, i'll quench them with my tears 192
and whe'er he run or fly they know not whether; 304
as they were mad, unto the wood they hie them, 323
as they were mad, unto the wood they hie them, 323
his eyes saw her eyes as they had not seen them, 357
they wither in their prime, prove nothing worth: 418
for where a heart is hard they make no batt'ry." 426
would they not wish the feast might ever last, 447
as if from thence they borrowed all their shine. 488
that they have murd'red this poor heart of mine, 502
"long may they kiss each other for this cure! 505
and as they last, their verdour still endure, 507
are they not quickly told, and quickly gone? 520
incorporate then they seem, face grows to face. 540
whereon they surfeit, yet complain on drouth: 544
they that thrive well take counsel of their 640
their clamorous cry till they have singled 693
then do they spend their mouths: 695
others they think delight | in such–like 843
she says, "'tis so," they answer all, "'tis so," 851
they all strain court'sy who shall cope him 888
they basely fly, and dare not stay the field. 894
and childish error that they are afraid; 898
their scratch'd ears, bleeding as they go. 924
whereon with fearful eyes they long have gazed, 927
they bid thee crop a weed, thou pluck'st a 946
crystals, where they view'd each other's sorrow, 963
then join they all together, | like many clouds 972
where they resign their office and their light 1039
her eyes are mad that they have wept till now. 1062
they both would strive who first should dry his 1092
fed them with his sight, they him with berries. 1104
she looks upon his lips, and they are pale, 1123
as if they heard the woeful words she told; 1126
their virtue lost, wherein they late excell'd, 1131
they that love best their loves shall not enjoy. 1164
that oft they interchange each other's seat. LUC 70
that what they have not, that which they possess 135
what they have not, that which they possess, 135
they scatter and unloose it from their bond, 136
and so by hoping more they have but less, | or, 137
that they prove bankrout in this poor rich gain. 140
now serves the season that they may surprise 166
paying more slavish tribute than they owe. 299
but as they open, they all rate his ill, | which 304
but as they open, they all rate his ill, | which 304
they fright him, yet he still pursues his fear. 308
and they would stand auspicious to the hour, 347
fact, | how can they then assist me in the act? 350
but blind they are, and keep themselves enclosed 378
o, had they in that darksome prison died, | then 379
then had they seen the period of their ill! 380
but they must ope, this blessed league to kill, 383
lay, | till they might open to adorn the day. 399
save of their lord no bearing yoke they knew, 409
they knew, | and him by oath they truly honored: 410
and they, like straggling slaves for pillage 428
they, must'ring to the quiet cabinet | where 442
when they in thee the like offenses prove. 613
their own transgressions partially they smother: 634
o, how are they wrapp'd in with infamies | that 636
thou nobly base, they basely dignified; 660
thou their fair life, and they thy fouler grave; 661
thou loathed in their shame, they in thy pride. 662
balk | the prey wherein by nature they delight, 697
"they think not but that every eye can see | the 750
the same disgrace which they themselves behold; 751
and therefore would they still in darkness be, 752
for they their guilt with weeping will unfold, 754
their father was too weak, and they too strong, 865
thee, | but they ne'er meet with opportunity. 903
they buy thy help, but sin ne'er gives a fee, 913
but little stars may hide them when they list. 1008
gnats are unnoted wheresoe'er they fly, | but 1014
they that lose half with greater patience bear 1158
than they whose whole is swallowed in confusion. 1159
and then they drown their eyes or break their 1239
and therefore are they form'd as marble will; 1241
poor women's faults that they are so fulfill'd 1258
but they whose guilt within their bosoms lie 1342
and in their rage such signs of rage they bear, 1419
it seem'd they would debate with angry swords. 1421
and to their hope they such odd action yield, 1433
from the strond of dardan, where they fought, 1436
they join, and shoot their foam at simois' banks 1442
glass fell wherein they view'd their faces. 1526
and they that watch see time how slow it creeps. 1575
with this they all at once began to say, | her 1709
we are their offspring, and they none of ours. 1757
if they surcease to be that should survive. 1766
yet neither may possess the claim they lay. 1794
that they will suffer these abominations 1832
then jointly to the ground their knees they bow, 1846
he doth again repeat, and that they swore. 1848
when they had sworn to this advised doom, | they 1849
they did conclude to bear dead lucrece thence, 1850
as they must needs (the sister and the brother), PP 8. 2
senseless trees they cannot hear thee, 20.21
thee, | ruthless bears they will not cheer thee. 20.22
one be prodigal, | bountiful they will him call; 20.38
addict to vice, | quickly him they will entice; 20.42
women he be bent, | they have at commandement. 20.44
they that fawn'd on him before | use his company 20.47
so they loved as love in twain | had the essence PHT 25
flowers distill'd, though they with winter meet, SON 5.13
they do but sweetly chide thee, who confounds 8. 7
and die as fast as they see others grow, | and 12.12
they draw but what they see, know not the heart. 24.14
they draw but what they see, know not the heart. 24.14
for at a frown they in their glory die. 25. 8
and thou (all they) hast all the all of me. 31.14
and though they be outstripp'd by every pen, 32. 6
and they are rich, and ransom all ill deeds. 34.14
for all the day they view things unrespected, 43. 2
but when i sleep, in dreams they look on thee, 43. 3
and i am still with them, and they with thee; 47.12
or, if they sleep, thy picture in my sight 47.13
like stones of worth they thinly placed are, 52. 7
they live unwoo'd, and unrespected fade, | die 54.10
hungry eyes even till they wink with fullness, 56. 6
that, when they see | return of love, more blest 56.11
whether we are mended, or whe'er better they, 59.11
and they shall live, and he in them still green. 63.14
they look into the beauty of thy mind, | and 69. 9
and that, in guess, they measure by thy deeds, 69.10
showing their birth and where they did proceed? 76. 8
yet when they have devis'd | what strained 82. 9
making their tomb the womb wherein they grew? 86. 4
they that have pow'r to hurt and will do none, 94. 1
that do not do the thing they most do show, 94. 2
slow, | they rightly do inherit heaven's graces, 94. 5
they are the lords and owners of their faces, 94. 7
or, if they sing, 'tis with so dull a cheer 97.13
from their proud lap pluck them where they grew; 98. 8
they were but sweet, but figures of delight, 98.11
and, for they look'd but with divining eyes, 106.11
they had not still enough your worth to sing: 106.12
am, and they that level | at my abuses reckon up 121. 9
may be straight though they themselves be bevel; 121.11
shown, | unless this general evil they maintain: 121.13
they are but dressings of a former sight. 123. 4
so suited, and they mourners seem | at such who, 127.10
yet so they mourn, becoming of their woe, | that 127.13
they would change their state | and situation 128. 9
to say they err i dare not be so bold, 131. 7
thine eyes i love, and they, as pitying me, 132. 1
and all they foul that thy complexion lack. 132.14
that they behold and see not what they see? 137. 2
that they behold and see not what they see? 137. 2
they know what beauty is, see where it lies, 137. 3
to this false plague are they now transferred. 137.14
that they elsewhere might dart their injuries: 139.12
eyes, | for they in thee a thousand errors note, 141. 2
but 'tis my heart that loves what they despise, 141. 3
or if they have, where is my judgment fled, 148. 3
that censures falsely what they see aright? 148. 4
or made them swear against the thing they see; 152.12
as they did batt'ry to the spheres intend; LC 23
sometimes they do extend | their view right on; 25
by | the swiftest hours, observed as they flew, 60
when winds breathe sweet, unruly though they be. 103
the goodly objects which abroad they find | of 137
love made them not, with acture they may be, 185
they sought their shame that so their shame did 187
figuring that they their passions likewise lent 199
believ'd her eyes when they t' assail begun, 262
it break, with bleeding groans they pine, | and 275

THEY'LD 3 FR 0.0003 REL FR 2 V 1 P
would make themselves whores but they'ld do't! ANT 1.02. 78 P
i would they'ld fight i' th' fire or i' th' air; 4.10. 3
every day | they'ld fight about you; TNK 3.06.221

/THEY'LL 1 FR 0.0001 REL FR 0 V 1 P
/the /fool /to /myself, /they'll /be /snatching. LR 1.04.155 P

THEY'LL 48 FR 0.0054 REL FR 36 V 12 P
they'll take suggestion as a cat laps milk; TMP 2.01.288
they'll tell the clock to any business that | we 2.01.289
but they'll nor pinch, | fright me with 2.02. 4
which they'll do fast enough of themselves, and WIV 4.01. 66 P
i'll warrant they'll have him publicly sham'd, 4.02.220 P
to send him word they'll meet him in the park at 4.04. 17 P
practic'd well to this, or they'll nev'r do't. 4.04. 66
if they'll do you any good. MM 1.02.143
and when they see time, | they'll go or come; ERR 2.01. 9
they'll suck our breath, or pinch us black and 2.02.192
knock elsewhere, to see if they'll disdain me. 3.01.121
away, they'll kill us. 4.04.146
which they'll know | by favors several which LLL 5.02.124
we were descried, they'll mock us now downright. 5.02.389
that they'll not show their teeth in way of MV 1.01. 55
as we do trust they'll end, in true delights. AYL 5.04.198
boys are boys of ice, they'll none have /her. AWW 2.03. 93 P
and they'll be for the flow'ry way that leads to 4.05. 53 P
if this prove true, they'll pay for't. WT 2.01.146
one, they'll find linen enough on every hedge. 1H4 4.02. 47 P
they'll fill a pit as well as better. 4.02. 66 P
supp'd is too hot, they'll come in straight. 2H4 2.04. 14 P
they'll be in fresher robes, or they will pluck H5 4.03.117
if they'll do neither, we will come to them, 4.07. 60
the walls they'll tear down than forsake the 1H6 1.02. 40
but, if i bow, they'll say it was for fear. 4.05. 29
fly thou how thou canst, they'll tangle thee. 2H6 2.04. 55
them now, and they'll o'ergrow the garden, | and 3.01. 32
go to ward, | they'll pawn their swords /for my 5.01.113
they come, i'll warrant they'll make it good. 5.01.122
but when the duke is slain, they'll quickly fly. 3H6 1.01. 69
that they'll take no offense at our abuse. 4.01. 13
none think flattery, for they'll find 'em truth. H8 5.04. 16
so, 'tis clear, | they'll say 'tis naught; ep 5
foul wares, | and think perchance they'll sell; TRO 1.03.359
tell you, they'll stick where they are thrown. 3.02.112 P
thy stained name, | and they'll seem glorious. 5.02.180
they'll sit by th' fire, and presume to know COR 1.01.191
with rushes, | they'll open of themselves. 1.04. 19
but i fear | they'll roar him in again. 4.06.124
home, | they'll give him death by inches. 5.04. 39

they'll be in scarlet straight at any news. ROM 2.05. 71
players cannot keep /counsel, they'll tell all. HAM 3.02.142 P
they'll have me whipt for speaking true; LR 1.04.183 P
here they'll be, man. ANT 2.07. 1 P
thou hast, | they'll grind /th' /one the other. 3.05. 15
the gods hear, i hope | they'll pardon it. CYM 4.02.379
honorable, | how good they'll prove, i know not. TNK 4.01. 31
THEY'RE 10 FR 0.0011 REL FR 8 V 2 P
when women cannot love where they're belov'd! TGV 5.04. 44
they're busy within, you were best knock louder. SHR 5.01. 14 P
they're here with me already, whisp'ring, WT 1.02.217
they're come from the field. TRO 3.01.148
they're welcome all, let 'em have kind TIM 1.02.128
in a man that's just | they're close dilations, OTH 3.03.123
the cause, | but jealious for they're jealious. 3.04.161
they say they're half fish, half flesh. PER 2.01. 25 P
fill'd, | and wishes fall out as they're will'd. 5.02. 16
/wi' leave, they're called | arcite and palamon. TNK 1.04. 22
/THICK 1 FR 0.0001 REL FR 1 V 0 P
/and /speaking /thick (/which /nature /made /his 2H4 2.03. 24
THICK 39 FR 0.0044 REL FR 31 V 8 P
thou shalt be pinch'd | as thick as honeycomb, TMP 1.02.329
is thick inlaid with patens of bright gold. MV 5.01. 59
muddy, ill-seeming, thick, bereft of beauty, SHR 5.02.143
o lord, sir! — thick, thick, spare not me. AWW 2.02. 45 P
o lord, sir! — thick, thick, spare not me. 2.02. 45 P
in me | thoughts that would thick my blood. WT 1.02.171
had bak'd thy blood and made it heavy, thick, JN 3.03. 43
his wit's as thick as tewksbury mustard, there's 2H4 2.04.241 P
that his dimensions to any thick sight were 3.02.313 P
thine's too thick to shine. 4.03. 58 P
this shoulder was ordain'd so thick to heave, 3H6 5.07. 23
abound, as thick as thought could make 'em, and H8 3.02.195
and bears his blushing honors thick upon him; 3.02.354
dews of heaven fall thick in blessings on her! 4.02.133
so do you too, where you perceive them thick. JC 1.01. 71
my sight was ever thick; 5.03. 21
as thick as tale | /came post with post, and MAC 1.03. 97
make thick my blood, | stop up th' access and 1.05. 43
come, thick night, | and pall thee in the 1.05. 50
by a drab, | make the gruel thick and slab. 4.01. 32
their eyes purging thick amber and plum–tree gum HAM 2.02.198 P
thick and unwholesome in /their thoughts and 4.05. 82
let her paint an inch thick, to this favor she 5.01.194 P
strike flat the thick rotundity o' th' world! LR 3.02. 7
why do you send so thick? ANT 1.05. 63
in their thick breaths, | rank of gross diet, 5.02.211
dissolve, thick cloud, and rain, that i may say 5.02.299
he furnaces | the thick sighs from him, whiles CYM 1.06. 67
say, and speak thick | (love's counsellor should 3.02. 56
anon | a rout, confusion thick. 5.03. 41
and thick slumber | hangs upon mine eyes. PER 5.01.234
our losses fall so thick we must needs leave. TNK pr 32
the far shore, thick set with reeds and sedges, 4.01. 54
and curl'd, thick twin'd like ivy/–tods, | not 4.02.104
but a most thick and profound melancholy. 4.03. 49 P
thin mane, thick tail, broad buttock, tender VEN 298
his short thick neck cannot be easily harmed; 627
and let thy musty vapors march so thick | that LUC 782
words, so thick come in his poor heart's aid, 1784
THICK–COMING 1 FR 0.0001 REL FR 1 V 0 P
as she is troubled with thick–coming fancies, MAC 5.03. 38
THICKEN 1 FR 0.0001 REL FR 1 V 0 P
and this may help to thicken other proofs | that OTH 3.03.430
THICKENS 2 FR 0.0002 REL FR 2 V 0 P
light thickens, and the crow | makes wing to th' MAC 3.02. 50
thy lustre thickens | when he shines by. ANT 2.03. 28
THICKER 3 FR 0.0003 REL FR 3 V 0 P
eye–glass | is thicker than a cuckold's horn), WT 1.02.269
my heart beats thicker than a feverous pulse, TRO 3.02. 36
were thicker than itself with brother's blood, HAM 3.03. 44
THICKEST 4 FR 0.0004 REL FR 3 V 1 P
the thickest and the tallest. LLL 4.01. 47 P
the thickest and the tallest! 4.01. 48
you are the thickest here. 4.01. 51
methought he bore him in the thickest troop | as 3H6 2.01. 13
THICKET 6 FR 0.0006 REL FR 6 V 0 P
fled — | the thicket is beset, he cannot scape. TGV 5.03. 11
put l to sore, then sorel jumps from thicket, LLL 4.02. 58
warily | i stole into a neighbor thicket by, 5.02. 94
hither | into this chiefest thicket of the park. 3H6 4.05. 3
the hart achilles | keeps thicket. TRO 2.03.259
there are you, | close in the thicket. TNK 3.05. 13
THICK–EY'D 1 FR 0.0001 REL FR 1 V 0 P
to thick–ey'd musing and curst melancholy? 1H4 2.03. 46
THICK–GROWN 1 FR 0.0001 REL FR 1 V 0 P
under this thick–grown brake we'll shroud 3H6 3.01. 1
THICK–LIPP'D 1 FR 0.0001 REL FR 1 V 0 P
come on, you thick–lipp'd slave, i'll bear you TIT 4.02.175
THICK–LIPS 1 FR 0.0001 REL FR 1 V 0 P
what a /full fortune does the thick–lips owe OTH 1.01. 66
THICK–PLEACH'D 1 FR 0.0001 REL FR 0 V 1 P
walking in a thick–pleach'd alley in mine ADO 1.02. 9 P
THICK–RIBBED 1 FR 0.0001 REL FR 1 V 0 P
in thrilling region of thick–ribbed ice; MM 3.01.122
THICK–SIGHTED 1 FR 0.0001 REL FR 1 V 0 P
thick–sighted, barren, lean, and lacking juice, VEN 136
THICK–SKIN 2 FR 0.0002 REL FR 1 V 1 P
what, thick–skin? WIV 4.05. 2 P
the shallowest thick–skin of that barren sort, MND 3.02. 13
THIDIAS 2 FR 0.0002 REL FR 2 V 0 P
try thy cunning, thidias, | make thine own edict ANT 3.12. 31
my name is thidias. 3.13. 73
THIEF 72 FR 0.0081 REL FR 42 V 30 P
bottle, or a thief to walk my ambling gelding, WIV 2.02.304 P
may in the sworn twelve have a thief or two MM 2.01. 20
and, sir, we take him to be a thief too, sir, 3.02. 16 P
every true man's apparel fits your thief. 4.02. 43 P
if it be too little for your thief, your true 4.02. 44 P
if it be too big for your thief, your thief 4.02. 45 P
your thief, your thief thinks it little enough; 4.02. 46 P
so every true man's apparel fits your thief. 4.02. 47 P
that angelo is an adulterous thief, | an 5.01. 40
what simple thief brags of his own /attaint? ERR 3.02. 16
nay, he's a thief too: 4.02. 59
if you meet a thief, you may suspect him, by ADO 3.03. 50 P
if we know him to be a thief, shall we not lay 3.03. 54 P
peaceable way for you, if you do take a thief, 3.03. 58 P
thou not what a deformed thief this fashion is? 3.03.124 P
'a has been a vile thief this seven year; 3.03.126 P
i say, what a deformed thief this fashion is, 3.03.131 P
a true man, or a thief, that gallops so? LLL 4.03.185
you thief of love! MND 3.02.283
the thief gone with so much, and so much to find MV 3.01. 92 P
so much, and so much to find the thief, and no 3.01. 93 P
with a thief to the gallows; AYL 3.02.327 P
but, like a timorous thief, most fain would AWW 2.05. 81
for with the dark, poor thief, i'll steal away. 3.02.129
notable pirate, thou salt–water thief! TN 5.01. 69
antonio never yet was thief or pirate, | though 5.01. 74
like to th' egyptian thief at point of death, 5.01.118
so when this thief, this traitor bullingbrook, R2 3.02. 47
do not thou, when thou art king, hang a thief. 1H4 1.02. 62 P
who, i rob? i a thief? not i, by my faith. 1.02.138 P
(for recreation sake) prove a false thief, for 1.02.156 P
rather let me have it as you are a false thief. 2.01. 94 P
son of england prove a thief and take purses? 2.04.410 P
lie still, ye thief, and hear the lady sing in 3.01.234 P
o for a fine thief, of the age of two and twenty 3.03.188 P
welcome, my little tiny thief, and welcome 2H4 5.03. 57 P
or foul felonious thief that fleec'd poor 2H6 3.01.129
and like a thief to come to rob my grounds, 4.10. 34
the thief doth fear each bush an officer. 3H6 5.06. 12
for a very little thief of occasion will rob you COR 2.01. 29 P
as good a trick as ever hangman serv'd thief. TIM 2.02. 95 P
thou't go, strong thief, | when gouty keepers of 4.03. 46
the sun's a thief, and with his great attraction 4.03.436
the moon's an arrant thief, | and her pale fire 4.03.437
the sea's a thief, whose liquid surge resolves 4.03.439
the earth's a thief, | that feeds and breeds by 4.03.440
each thing's a thief. 4.03.442
like a giant's robe | upon a dwarfish thief. MAC 5.02. 22
pinion him like a thief, bring him before us. LR 3.07. 23
how yond justice rails upon yond simple thief. 4.06.152 P
which is the justice, which is the thief? 4.06.154 P
down with him, thief! OTH 1.02. 57
o thou foul thief, where hast thou stow'd my 1.02. 62
that smiles steals something from the thief; 1.03.208
you have been a great thief by sea. ANT 2.06. 92 P
a cunning thief, or a (that way) accomplish'd CYM 1.04. 92 P
makes the true man kill'd and saves the thief; 2.03. 71
nay, sometime hangs both thief and true man. 2.03. 72
yield thee, thief. 4.02. 75
thou injurious thief, | hear but my name, and 4.02. 86
egregious murtherer, thief, any thing | that's 5.05.211
than myself, | a sacrilegious thief, to do't. 5.05.220
a curse upon him, die he like a thief, | that PER 4.06.114
and art | a very thief in love, a chaffy lord, TNK 3.01. 41
which drives the creeping thief to some regard; LUC 305
and lust, the thief, far poorer than before. 693
thou ravisher, thou traitor, thou false thief, 888
at his own shadow let the thief run mad, 997
to that sweet thief which sourly robs from me. SON 35.14
i do forgive thy robb'ry, gentle thief, 40. 9
care, | art left the prey of every vulgar thief. 48. 8
sweet thief, whence didst thou steal thy sweet 99. 2
THIEF–STOL'N 1 FR 0.0001 REL FR 1 V 0 P
had i been thief–stol'n, | as my two brothers, CYM 1.06. 5
THIEVERY 2 FR 0.0002 REL FR 2 V 0 P
it's an honorable kind of thievery. TGV 4.01. 39
like workmen, i'll example you with thievery: TIM 4.03.435
THIEVE'S 1 FR 0.0001 REL FR 0 V 1 P
i am accurs'd to rob in that thieve's company. 1H4 2.02. 10 P
THIEVES 46 FR 0.0052 REL FR 33 V 13 P
it hither, | for stale to catch these thieves. TMP 4.01.187
have open eye, for thieves do foot by night. WIV 2.01.122
the laws | that thieves do pass on thieves? MM 2.01. 23
the laws | that thieves do pass on thieves? 2.01. 23
thieves for their robbery have authority | when 2.02.175
you shall please to play the thieves for wives, MV 2.06. 23
beauty provoketh thieves sooner than gold. AYL 1.03.110
forth thy weapon, we are beset with thieves; SHR 3.02.236
'gainst knaves and thieves men shut their gate, TN 5.01.395
then thieves and robbers range abroad unseen R2 3.02. 39
thieves are not judg'd but they are by to hear, 4.01.123
body be call'd thieves of the day's beauty. 1H4 1.02. 25 P
mean thou shalt have the hanging of the thieves, 1.02. 67 P
a plague upon it when thieves cannot be true one 2.02. 27 P
the thieves have bound the true men. 2.02. 93 P
thou and i rob the thieves and go merrily to 2.02. 94 P
the thieves are all scattered and possess'd with 2.02.105
and the rest of the thieves are at the door; 2.04. 87 P
do you think i keep thieves in my house? 3.03. 55 P
and pretty traps to catch the petty thieves. H5 1.02.177
so desperate thieves, all hopeless of their 3H6 1.04. 42
so triumph thieves upon their conquer'd booty, 1.04. 63
but thieves unworthy of a thing so stol'n, TRO 2.02. 94
make the hoar leprosy ador'd, place thieves, TIM 4.03. 36
now, thieves? 4.03.412 P
soldiers, not thieves. 4.03.413 P
we are not thieves, but men that much do want. 4.03.415
i must you con | that you are thieves profess'd, 4.03.426
rascal thieves, | here's gold. 4.03.428
cut throats, | all that you meet are thieves. 4.03.446
nothing can you steal | but thieves do lose it. 4.03.448
of the prosperous gods, | as thieves to keepers. 5.01.184
they have dealt with me like thieves of mercy, HAM 4.06. 21 P
knaves, thieves, and treachers by spherical LR 1.02.123 P
thieves, thieves! OTH 1.01. 79
thieves, thieves! 1.01. 79
thieves, thieves! 1.01. 81
thieves, thieves! 1.01. 81
where be these bloody thieves? 5.01. 63
here they might take two thieves kissing. ANT 2.06. 96 P
i do nothing doubt you have store of thieves; CYM 1.04. 97 P
these roguing thieves serve the great pirate PER 4.01. 96
rich preys make true men thieves; VEN 724
as one with treasure laden, hemm'd with thieves; 1022
sun and sharp air | lurk'd like two thieves, to 1086
save thieves, and cares, and troubled minds that LUC 126
THIEVISH 7 FR 0.0008 REL FR 7 V 0 P
enforce | a thievish living on the common road? AYL 2.03. 33
hath told the thievish minutes how they pass, AWW 2.01.166
or walk in thievish ways, or bid me lurk | where ROM 4.01. 79
he should keep unknown | from thievish ears, LUC 35
he like a thievish dog creeps sadly thence, 736
for truth proves thievish for a prize so dear. SON 48.14
know | time's thievish progress to eternity. 77. 8
THIEV'RY 1 FR 0.0001 REL FR 1 V 0 P
a robber's haste | crams his rich thiev'ry up, TRO 4.04. 43
THIGH 13 FR 0.0014 REL FR 10 V 3 P
a gallant curtle–axe upon my thigh, | a AYL 1.03.117
with a new wound in your thigh, come you along 1H4 5.04.128 P
my death, i gave him this wound in the thigh. 5.04.151 P
one i' th' neck, and two i' th' thigh — there's COR 2.01.151 P
fine foot, straight leg, and quivering thigh, ROM 2.01. 19
myself a voluntary wound | here, in the thigh; JC 2.01.301
/then laid his leg | /over my thigh, and /sigh'd OTH 3.03.425
did itself sustain | upon a soldier's thigh. 5.02.261
hand, | his foot mercurial, his martial thigh, CYM 4.02.310
and on his thigh a sword | hung by a curious TNK 4.02. 85
some twin'd about her thigh to make her stay. VEN 873
boar, | deep in the thigh, a spectacle of ruth! PP 9.11
see, in my thigh," quoth she, "here was the sore 9.12
/THIGHS 1 FR 0.0001 REL FR 1 V 0 P
our /thighs pack'd with wax, our mouths with 2H4 4.05. 76
THIGHS 4 FR 0.0004 REL FR 3 V 1 P
and for night–tapers crop their waxen thighs MND 3.01.169
no, sir, it is legs and thighs. TN 1.03.140 P
on, | his cushes on his thighs, gallantly arm'd, 1H4 4.01.105
till that his thighs with darts | were almost 2H6 3.01.362
THILL–HORSE *(see fill–horse)*
THILLS *(see fills*)*
THIMBLE 2 FR 0.0002 REL FR 1 V 1 P
thou liest, thou thread, thou thimble, | thou SHR 4.03.107
though thy little finger be arm'd in a thimble. 4.03.148 P
THIMBLES 1 FR 0.0001 REL FR 1 V 0 P
their thimbles into armed gauntlets change, JN 5.02.156
/THIN 2 FR 0.0002 REL FR 2 V 0 P
and on old hiems' /thin and icy crown | an MND 2.01.109
/with /this /thin /helm? LR 4.07. 35
THIN 22 FR 0.0024 REL FR 18 V 4 P
and | are melted into air, into thin air, | and, TMP 4.01.150
say so, master, if your garments were thin. ERR 3.01. 70
hard lodging and thin weeds | nip not the gaudy LLL 5.02.801
but that his beard grew thin and hungerly, | and SHR 3.02.175
are like to have a thin and slender pittance. 4.04. 61
my face so thin | that in mine ear i durst not JN 1.01.141
we will not line his thin bestained cloak | with 4.03. 24
have arm'd their thin and hairless scalps R2 3.02.112
for thin drink doth so over–cool their blood, 2H4 4.03. 91 P
be, to forswear thin potations and to addict 4.03.124 P
in | so thin that life looks through /and /will 4.04.120
i'll tell you what, you thin man in a censer, i 5.04. 18 P
come, you thin thing, come, you rascal. 5.04. 30 P
his cold thin drink out of his leather bottle, 3H6 2.05. 48
and did give himself | (all thin and naked) to R3 2.01.118
they are too thin and base to hide offenses. H8 5.02.160
which is as thin of substance as the air, | and ROM 1.04. 99
and thatch your poor thin roofs | with burthens TIM 4.03.145
into milk, | the thin and wholesome blood. HAM 1.05. 70
than these thin habits and poor likelihoods | of OTH 1.03.108
thin mane, thick tail, broad buttock, tender VEN 298
and from his lips did fly | thin winding breath, LUC 1407
THIN/–BELLIED 1 FR 0.0001 REL FR 0 V 1 P
cross'd on your thin/–bellied doublet like a LLL 3.01. 19 P
/THINE 4 FR 0.0004 REL FR 4 V 0 P
/do /that /office /of /thine /own /good /will R2 4.01.177
/side /my /hand, /and /on /that /side /thine. 4.01.183
/no /lord /of /thine, /thou /haught /insulting 4.01.254
/being /now /trimm'd /in /thine /own /desires, 2H4 1.03. 94
THINE 494 FR 0.0558 REL FR 429 V 65 P
wipe thou thine eyes, have comfort. TMP 1.02. 25
come, | the very minute bids thee ope thine ear. 1.02. 37
be subject | to no sight but thine and mine, 1.02.302
my quaint ariel, | hark in thine ear. 1.02.318
know thine own meaning, but wouldst gabble like 1.02.356
the fringed curtains of thine eye advance | and 1.02.409
the setting of thine eye and cheek proclaim | a 2.01.229
how does thine ague? 2.02.136 P
and thine own acquisition | worthily purchas'd, 4.01. 13
sit then and talk with her, she is thine own. 4.01. 32
which may make this island | thine own for ever, 4.01.218
mine eyes, ev'n sociable to the show of thine, 5.01. 63
let me embrace thine age, whose honor cannot 5.01.121
proteus, i thank thee for thine honest care, TGV 3.01. 22
a cloak as long as thine will serve the turn? 3.01.131
or, at the least, in hers sepulchre thine. 4.02.117
do not name silvia thine; 5.04.128
i claim her not, and therefore she is thine. 5.04.135
i grant it, for thine own, what e'er it be. 5.04.151
by me, thine own true knight, | by day or night, WIV 2.01. 14
but let thine inherit first, for i protest mine 2.01. 73 P
this secrecy of thine shall be a tailor to thee 3.03. 34 P
i see how thine eye would emulate the diamond. 3.03. 55 P
it is thine host, thine ephesian, calls. 4.05. 17 P
it is thine host, thine ephesian, calls. 4.05. 18 P
are not thine own so proper as to waste MM 1.01. 30
i will, out of thine own confession, learn to 1.02. 37 P
for thine own bowels, which do call thee /sire, 3.01. 29
to take life | from thine own sister's shame? 3.01.139
am pale at mine heart to see thine eyes so red; 4.03.152 P
a vow'd contract, | was fast belock'd in thine; 5.01.210
so great a charge from thine own custody? ERR 1.02. 61
vow | that never words were music to thine ear, 2.02.114
ear, | that never object pleasing in thine eye, 2.02.115
come, i will fasten on this sleeve of thine: 2.02.173
thou hast thine own form. 2.02.198
my love is thine to teach; ADO 1.01.291
and the conclusion is, she shall be thine. 1.01.327
do not live, hero, do not ope thine eyes; 4.01.123
is claudio thine enemy? 4.01.300 P
thine, claudio, thine, i say. 5.01. 72
thine, claudio, thine, i say. 5.01. 72
thine, in all complements of devoted and LLL 1.01.276 P
thine, in the dearest design of industry, don 4.01. 86 P
put up this — 'twill be thine another day. 4.01.107
his bias leaves, and makes his book thine eyes, 4.02.109
"did not the heavenly rhetoric of thine eye, 4.03. 58
did these rent lines show some love of thine? 4.03.216
o, if the streets were paved with thine eyes, 4.03.274
take thou this, my sweet, and give me thine, 5.02.132
and, by this virgin palm now kissing thine, | i 5.02.806

palm now kissing thine, | i will be thine; 5.02.807
"if i were fair, thisby, i were only thine." MND 3.01.103
for with doubler tongue | than thine, thou 3.02. 73
to what, my love, shall i compare thine eyne? 3.02.138
but that my nails can reach unto thine eyes. 3.02.298
right, | of thine or mine, is most in helena. 3.02.337
thou wak'st, with thine own fool's eyes peep. 4.01. 84
shalt not know the sound of thine own tongue. MV 1.01.109
but lend it rather to thine enemy, | who, if he 1.03.135
a pound of that same merchant's flesh is thine, 4.01.299
i swear to thee, even by thine own fair eyes, 5.01.242
lands and all things that thou dost call thine AYL 3.01. 9
than thine own gladness that thou art employ'd. 3.05. 98
death, how foul and loathsome is thine image! SHR in.1. 35
tell me thine first. 1.01.191
but thine doth fry. 2.01.338
sirrah, i will not bear these braves of thine. 3.01. 15
but say, what to thine old news? 3.02. 42 P
curtis, in every office but thine, and therefore 4.01. 36 P
lend thine ear. 4.01. 60 P
while counterfeit supposes blear'd thine eyne. 5.01.117
while i with self-same kindness welcome thine. 5.02. 5
be able for thine enemy | rather in power than AWW 1.01. 65
thee, else thou diest in thine unthankfulness, 1.01.211 P
and thine ignorance makes thee away. 1.01.211 P
such friends are thine enemies, knave. 1.03. 41 P
wet, | the many-color'd iris, rounds thine eye? 1.03.152
and thine eyes | see it so grossly shown in thy 1.03.177
as heaven shall work in me for thine avail, | to 1.03.184
too, or take off thine | by wond'ring how thou 2.01. 89
try, | that ministers thine own death if i die. 2.01.186
fair maid, send forth thine eye. 2.03. 52
it is in us to plant thine honor where | we 2.03.156
do thine own fortunes that obedient right 2.03.160
speak, thine answer. 2.03.166
her by the hand, | and tell her she is thine; 2.03.174
if thou engrossest all the griefs are thine, 3.02. 65
those tender limbs of thine to the event | of 3.02.104
may report my flight | to consolate thine ear. 3.02.128
the first truth that e'er thine own tongue was 4.01. 33 P
my house, mine honor, yea, my life, be thine, 4.02. 52
thine, as he vow'd to thee in thine ear, 4.03.231 P
as he vow'd to thee in thine ear, parolles." 4.03.231 P
for this description of thine honesty? 4.03.263 P
as thy lord, | to call his fortunes thine. TN 1.04. 40
thine eye | hath stay'd upon some favor that it 2.04. 23
to him in thine own voice, and bring me word how 4.02. 66 P
bloody and so dear, | hast made thine enemies? 5.01. 72
that thine own trip shall be thine overthrow? 5.01.167
that thine own trip shall be thine overthrow? 5.01.167
plaintiff and the judge | of thine own cause. 5.01.355
taken | by any understanding pate but thine? WT 1.02.223
canst with thine eyes at once see good and evil, 1.02.303
do't not, thou split'st thine own. 1.02.349
thy life, | with what thou else call'st thine. 2.03.138
my great profaneness 'gainst thine oracle! 3.02.154
of my poor babe, according to thine oath, 3.03. 30
both breed thee, pretty, | and still rest thine. 3.03. 49
i have of thee, thine own goodness hath made. 4.02. 12 P
or i'll be thine, my fair, | or not my father's; 4.04. 42
own, nor any thing to any, if | i be not thine. 4.04. 45
take by my consent, | as i by thine a wife: 5.03.137
born, | doth he lay claim to thine inheritance? JN 1.01. 72
that for thine own gain shouldst defend mine 1.01.242
this toil of ours should be a work of thine; 2.01. 93
thy son as true | as thine was to thy husband, 2.01.125
thou and thine usurp | the dominations, 2.01.175
what means that hand upon that breast of thine? 3.01. 21
why holds thine eye that lamentable rheum, 3.01. 22
sh' adulterates hourly with thine uncle john, 3.01. 56
not a calve's-skin stop that mouth of thine? 3.01.299
o, thine honor, lewis, thine honor! 3.01.316
o, thine honor, lewis, thine honor! 3.01.316
father, i may not wish the fortune thine; 3.01.333
hear me without thine ears, and make reply 3.03. 49
hubert, throw thine eye | on yon young boy. 3.03. 59
i will not touch thine eye | for all the 4.01.121
for all the treasure that thine uncle owes. 4.01.122
go, bear him in thine arms. 4.03.139
that shall reverberate all as loud as thine. 5.02.170
and another shall | (as loud as thine) rattle 5.02.172
the cruel pangs of death | right in thine eye. 5.04. 60
why may not i demand | of thine affairs, as well 5.06. 5
withhold thine indignation, mighty heaven, | and 5.06. 37
ah, gaunt, his blood was thine! R2 1.02. 22
to safeguard thine own life | the best way is to 1.02. 35
i espy | virtue with valor couched in thine eye. 1.03. 98
even in the glasses of thine eyes | i see thy 1.03.208
there is my gage, aumerle, in gage to thine. 4.01. 34
hath bullingbrook depos'd | thine intellect? 5.01. 28
wilt thou not hide the trespass of thine own? 5.02. 89
is he not thine own? 5.02. 94
thine eye begins to speak, set thy tongue there; 5.03.125
or in thy piteous heart plant thou thine ear, 5.03.126
i do see | danger and disobedience in thine eye. 1H4 1.03. 16
tying thine ear to no tongue but thine own! 1.03.238
tying thine ear to no tongue but thine own! 1.03.238
i pray thee lend me thine. 2.01. 38 P
lay thine ear close to the ground, and list if 2.02. 32 P
hang thyself in thine own heir-apparent garters! 2.02. 43 P
why dost thou bend thine eyes upon the earth, 2.03. 42
ago, jack, since thou sawest thine own knee? 2.04.328 P
but chiefly a villainous trick of thine eye, and 2.04.404 P
truth, nor honesty in this bosom of thine; 3.03.154 P
i see a strange confession in thine eye. 2H4 1.01. 94
among wits of no higher breeding than thine. 2.02. 36 P
the world keeps the road-way better than thine: 2.02. 59 P
thine, by yea and no, which is as much as to say 2.02.131 P
and begin to patch up thine old body for heaven? 2.04.233 P
now, the lord bless that sweet face of thine! 2.04.293 P
is thine hostess here of the wicked? 2.04.328 P
some few hours | were thine without offense, and 4.05.102
and bid the merry bells ring to thine ear | that 4.05.111
a foutre for thine office! 5.03.115
what office thou wilt in the land, 'tis thine. 5.03.124 P
for this revolt of thine, methinks, is like H5 2.02.141
give me any gage of thine, and i will wear it in 4.01.208 P
here's my glove; give me another of thine. 4.01.211 P
my soul shall thine keep company to heaven; 4.06. 16
take it, god, | for it is none but thine! 4.08.112
thing he sees there, let thine eye be thy cook. 5.02.149 P
but thy speaking of my tongue, and i thine, most 5.02.191 P
hand, and say, "harry of england, i am thine"; 5.02.237 P
but i will tell thee aloud, "england is thine, 5.02.239 P
"england is thine, ireland is thine, france is 5.02.239 P
ireland is thine, france is thine, and henry 5.02.240 P
is thine, and henry plantagenet is thine"; 5.02.240 P
that thou nor none of thine shall be let in. 1H6 1.03. 21
and i will chain these legs and arms of thine, 2.03. 39
first, lean thine aged back against mine arm, 2.05. 43
i trust ere long to choke thee with thine own, 3.02. 46
but when they heard he was thine enemy, | they 3.03. 71
base, | and misbegotten blood i spill of thine, 4.06. 22
the conquest, charles, it shall be thine, | let 5.02. 19
then, joan, discover thine infirmity, | that 5.04. 60
'tis thine they give away, and not their own. 2H6 1.01.221
why are thine eyes fix'd to the sullen earth, 1.02. 5
what is thine? 1.03. 15 P
resign it then and leave thine insolence. 1.03.122
not half so bad as thine to england's king, 1.04. 47
thine eyes and thoughts | beat on a crown, the 2.01. 19
why, suffolk, england knows thine insolence. 2.01. 31
matter, | in thine own person answer thy abuse. 2.01. 40
let me see thine eyes. 2.01.103
what's thine own name? 2.01.121
this dishonor in thine age | will bring thy head 2.03. 18
and ban thine enemies, both mine and thine! 2.04. 25
and ban thine enemies, both mine and thine! 2.04. 25
run, go, help, help! o henry, ope thine eyes! 3.02. 35
look not upon me, for thine eyes are wounding. 3.02. 51
hast thou not spirit to curse thine enemy? 3.02.308
if thou hadst been in thine own slaughter-house; 4.03. 5 P
upon thine honor, is he prisoner? 5.01. 42
that head of thine doth not become a crown: 5.01. 96
war, | and shame thine honorable age with blood? 5.01.170
for this is thine and not king henry's heirs'. 3H6 1.01. 27
and thine, lord clifford, and you both have 1.01. 55
i am thine. 1.01. 76
the crown to thee and to thine heirs for ever, 1.01.195
than have made that savage duke thine heir, 1.01.224
thine heir, | and disinherited thine only son. 1.01.225
but thou prefer'st thy life before thine honor; 1.01.246
here, their lives and thine | were not revenge 1.03. 25
and if thine eyes can water for his death, | i 1.04. 82
hath thy fiery heart so parch'd thine entrails 1.04. 87
either that is thine, or else thou wert not his. 2.01. 94
to hold thine own and leave thine own with him. 2.02. 42
to hold thine own and leave thine own with him. 2.02. 42
then 'twas my turn to fly, and now 'tis thine. 2.02.105
o warwick, i do bend my knee with thine, | and 2.03. 33
and in this vow do chain my soul to thine! 2.03. 34
any life be left in thee, | throw up thine eye! 2.05. 85
for from my heart thine image ne'er shall go; 2.05.116
yet look to have them buzz to offend thine ears. 2.06. 95
no, harry, harry, 'tis no land of thine; 3.01. 15
and mine with hers, and thine, and margaret's. 3.03.218
that only warwick's daughter shall be thine. 3.03.248
sweet clarence, my daughter shall be thine. 4.02. 12
or shall we beat the stones about thine ears? 5.01.108
that warwick's bones may keep thine company. 5.02. 4
thine uncles and myself | have in our armors 5.07. 16
thine eyes, sweet lady, have infected mine. R3 1.02.149
those eyes of thine from mine have drawn salt 1.02.153
wear both of them, for both of them are thine. 1.02.205
ay, and much better blood than his or thine. 1.03.125
no sleep close up that deadly eye of thine, 1.03.224
o, if thine eye be not a flatterer, | come thou 1.04.264
have i | (thine being but a moi'ty of my moan) 2.02. 60
rise, and lend thine ear. 4.02. 79
god witness with me, i have wept for thine. 4.04. 60
my words are dull, o, quicken them with thine! 4.04.124
whisper the spirits of thine enemies | and 4.04.193
till that my nails were anchor'd in thine eyes; 4.04.232
all — | will i withal endow a child of thine; 4.04.250
in her consists my happiness and thine; 4.04.406
there is my purse to cure that blow of thine. 4.04.514
now, and provide | for thine own future safety. H8 3.02.421
folly and ignorance, be thine in great revenue! TRO 2.03. 29 P
but he that disciplin'd thine arms to fight, 2.03.244
now, ajax, hold thine own! 4.05.114
why dost thou so oppress me with thine eye? 4.05.241
none less dear than thine and my good martius, i COR 1.03. 23 P
thou mad'st thine enemies shake, as if the world 1.04. 60
that with the fusty plebeians hate thine honors, 1.09. 7
i charge thee, | and follow to thine answer. 3.01.176
rather | follow thine enemy in a fiery gulf 3.02. 91
within thine eyes sate twenty thousand deaths, 3.03. 70
a younger man's, | and venomous to thine eyes. 4.01. 23
volscians' ears, | and harsh in sound to thine. 4.05. 59
that wilt revenge | thine own particular wrongs, 4.05. 86
wilt have | the leading of thine own revenges, 4.05.137
strength and weakness — thine own ways: 4.05.140
when, caius, rome is thine, | thou art poor'st 4.07. 56
and to poor we | thine enmity's most capital; 5.03.104
and so i love and honor thee and thine, | thy TIT 1.01. 49
titus, unkind and careless of thine own, | why 1.01. 86
for king and commonweal | were piety in thine, 1.01.115
agree these deeds with that proud brag of thine, 1.01.306
were gracious in those princely eyes of thine, 1.01.429
choice, | lavinia is thine elder brother's hope. 2.01. 74
and with thine own hands kill me in this place! 2.03.169
i bring consuming sorrow to thine age. 3.01. 61
or shall we cut away our hands like thine? 3.01.130
good titus, dry thine eyes. 3.01.138
thou, poor man, hast drown'd it with thine own. 3.01.141
stay, father, for that noble hand of thine, 3.01.162
stand by me, lucius, do not fear thine aunt. 4.01. 5
as who should say, "old lad, i am thine own." 4.02.121
shalt thou know her by thine own proportion, 5.02.106
and ours with thine, befall what fortune will. 5.03. 3
why hast thou slain thine only daughter thus? 5.03. 55
they were living, warm'd themselves on thine! 5.03.168
to have it press'd | with more of thine. ROM 1.01.188
by giving liberty unto thine eyes: 1.01.227
were not i thine only nurse, | i would say thou 1.03. 67
thus from my lips, by thine, my sin is purg'd. 1.05.107
there lies more peril in thine eye | than twenty 2.02. 71
sleep dwell upon thine eyes, peace in thy breast 2.02.186
if e'er thou wast thyself and these woes thine, 2.03. 77
heads, | staying for thine to keep him company. 3.01.128
flask, | is set afire by thine own ignorance, 3.03.133
and thou dismemb'red with thine own defense. 3.03.134
that pierc'd the fearful hollow of thine ear; 3.05. 3
in twain | to sunder his that was thine enemy? 5.03.100
this man of thine | attempts her love. TIM 1.01.125
let me stay at thine apperil, timon. 1.02. 33
all those flatterers were thine enemies then, 1.02. 81 P
they only now come but to feast thine eyes. 1.02.127
this fell whore of thine | hath in her more 4.03. 62
then the rot returns | to thine own lips again. 4.03. 66
as thine is now, held with a brace of harlots. 4.03. 80
put armor on thine ears and on thine eyes, 4.03.124
put armor on thine ears and on thine eyes, 4.03.124
thou gav'st thine ears (like tapsters that bade 4.03.215
so i shall mend mine own, by th' lack of thine. 4.03.284
thee and make thine own self the conquest of thy 4.03.337 P
make thine epitaph, | that death in me at 4.03.379
needs | stand for a villain in thine own work? 5.01. 38
wilt thou whip thine own faults in other men? 5.01. 39
that thou art even natural in thine art. 5.01. 85
of their love, | ever to read them thine. 5.01.155
and of our athens, thine and ours, to take | the 5.01.160
thy glove, | or any token of thine honor else, 5.04. 50
the heavens speed thee in thine enterprise! JC 2.04. 41
in terms of friendship with thine enemies. 3.01.203
seeing those beads of sorrow stand in thine, 3.01.284
come now, keep thine oath; 5.03. 40
thrice to thine, and thrice to mine, | and MAC 1.03. 35
do contend | which should be thine or his. 1.03. 93
hail, most worthy thane, | for it is thine. 1.03.107
that i may pour my spirits in thine ear, | and 1.05. 26
to be the same in thine own act and valor | as 1.07. 40
life, | and live a coward in thine own esteem, 1.07. 43
that will ravin up | thine own live's means! 2.04. 29
is thine and my poor country's to command: 4.03.132
those linen cheeks of thine | are counsellors to 5.03. 16
too much charg'd | with blood of thine already. 5.08. 6
take thy fair hour, laertes, time be thine, HAM 1.02. 62
and let thine eye look like a friend on denmark. 1.02. 69
to thine own self be true, | and it must follow, 1.03. 78
thine evermore, most dear lady, whilst this 2.02.123 P
hamlet, this deed, for thine especial safety — 4.03. 40
words to speak in thine ear will make thee dumb, 4.06. 25 P
/he that thou knowest thine, hamlet." 4.06. 30 P
to thine own peace. 4.07. 61
i think it be thine indeed, for thou liest in't. 5.01.122 P
dost lie in't, to be in't and say it is thine. 5.01.126 P
hamlet, this pearl is thine, | here's to thy 5.02.282
death come not upon thee, | nor thine on me! 5.02.331
what feast is toward in thine eternal cell, 5.02.365
to thine and albany's /issue | be this perpetual LR 1.01. 66
to thee and thine hereditary ever | remain this 1.01. 79
but as /a pawn | to wage against thine enemies, 1.01.156
me still remain | the true blank of thine eye. 1.01.159
me, recreant, | on thine allegiance, hear me! 1.01.167
france, let her be thine, for we | have no such 1.01.262
thou bor'st thine ass on thy back o'er the dirt. 1.04.161 P
the rod, and put'st down thine own breeches, 1.04.174 P
her eyes are fierce, but thine | do comfort, and 2.04.172
prithee go in thyself, seek thine own ease. 3.04. 23
with thine and all that offer to defend him, 3.06. 94
upon these eyes of thine i'll set my foot. 3.07. 68
eye discerning | thine honor from thy suffering, 4.02. 53
show'dst the king, | and to revenge thine eyes. 4.02. 96
i remember thine eyes well enough. 4.06.136 P
look with thine ears; 4.06.151 P
hark in thine ear: 4.06.153 P
that eyeless head of thine was first fram'd 4.06.227
wipe thine eyes; 5.03. 23
the walls is thine. 5.03. 76
nor in thine, lord. 5.03. 80
let the drum strike, and prove my title thine. 5.03. 81
thou worse than any name, read thine own evil. 5.03.157
say if i do, the laws are mine, not thine; 5.03.159
had my purse | as if the strings were thine, OTH 1.01. 3
thine hath no less reason. 1.03.366 P
swell his sail with thine own pow'rful breath, 2.01. 78
i will gyve thee in thine own courtship. 2.01.170 P
these stops of thine fright me the more; 3.03.120
that lov'st to make thine honesty a vice! 3.03.376
i will make proof of thine. 5.01. 26
/forth of my heart those charms, thine eyes, are 5.01. 35
this deed of thine is no more worthy heaven 5.02.160
this look of thine will hurl my soul from heaven 5.02.274
and that blood of thine | is caesar's homager; ANT 1.01. 30
no messenger but thine, and all alone, 1.01. 52
(it wounds thine honor that i speak it now) 1.04. 69
or i'll spurn thine eyes | like balls before me; 2.05. 63
or sky inclips, | is thine, if thou wilt ha't. 2.07. 69
all there is thine. 2.07. 73
e'er thy tongue | hath so betray'd thine act. 2.07. 78
how i convey my shame out of thine eyes | by 3.11. 52
be't so, declare thine office. 3.12. 10
add more, | from thine invention, offers. 3.12. 29
make thine own edict for thy pains, which we 3.12. 32
come, good fellow, put thine iron on. 4.04. 3
from caesar's camp | say "i am none of thine." 4.05. 9
infamous, | forgive me in thine own particular, 4.09. 20
and her fortunes mingled | with thine entirely. 4.14. 25
thee such a declining day, | or look on thine; 5.01. 39
but i'll catch thine eyes | though they had 5.02.156
cassibelan, thine uncle | (famous in caesar's CYM 3.01. 5
than | thyself domestic officers) thine enemy. 3.01. 64
let thine own hands take away her life. 3.04. 27 P
and thine own? 3.04.104
have not i | an arm as big as thine? 4.02. 77
not sooner | than thine own worth prefer thee. 4.02.386
wipe thine eyes: 4.02.402
by thine own tongue thou art condemn'd, and must 5.05.298
desert, because thine eye | presumes to reach, PER 1.01. 32
the rest (hark in thine ear) as black as incest, 1.02. 76
take thy word for faith, not ask thine oath: 1.02.120
thou hast the harvest out of thine own report. 4.02.141 P
which, to betray, dost, with thine angel's face, 4.03. 47

face, | seize with thine eagle's talents. 4.03. 48
what canst thou wish thine enemy to be? 4.06.158
if thine, considered, prove the thousand part 5.01.135
call'st thou her thine? TNK 3.01. 38
and do but say | that emily is thine, i will 3.01. 76
is mutual — | in me, thine, and in thee, mine. 3.06. 96
look to thine own well, arcite. 3.06.131
fires | did scorch his mortal son, thine him. 5.01. 92
thy priest, | am humbled 'fore thine altar. 5.01.143
sacred silver mistress, lend thine ear | (which 5.01.146
i think so, but i know not thine own will: 5.01.171
set both thine ears to th' business. 5.03. 92
i'll close thine eyes, prince; 5.04. 96
but my lips with those fair lips of thine — VEN 115
the kiss shall be thine own as well as mine. 117
"bid me discourse, i will enchant thine ear, 145
"is thine own heart to thine own face affected? 157
"is thine own heart to thine own face affected? 157
steal thine own freedom, and complain on theft. 160
that thine may live, when thou thyself art dead; 172
thine eye darts forth the fire that burneth me, 196
poor queen of love, in thine own law forlorn, 251
my heart all whole as thine, thy heart my wound! 370
eyes' shrowd tutor, that hard heart of thine, 500
"alas, he nought esteems that face of thine, 631
and so 'tis thine, but know, it is as good | to 1181
not | to darken her whose light excelleth thine; LUC 191
the fault is thine, | for those thine eyes 482
for those thine eyes betray thee unto mine. 483
done, some worthless slave of thine i'll slay, 515
to kill thine honor with thy live's decay; 516
thyself art mighty, for thine own sake leave me; 583
"how will thy shame be seeded in thine age, 603
"if, collatine, thine honor lay in me, | from me 834
an accessary by thine inclination | to all sins 922
eyes | of all the greeks that are thine enemies. 1470
and here in troy, for trespass of thine eye, 1476
on thee and thine this night i will inflict, 1630
"'for some hard–favor'd groom of thine,' quoth 1632
revenged on my foe, | thine, mine, his own. 1684
did not the heavenly rhetoric of thine eye, PP 3. 1
his bias leaves, and makes his book thine eyes, 5. 5
thine eye jove's lightning seems, thy voice his 5.11
when as thine eye hath chose the dame, | and 18. 1
but thou, contracted to thine own bright eyes, SON 1. 5
within thine own bud buriest thy content, | and, 1.11
to say within thine own deep–sunken eyes | were 2. 7
proving his beauty by succession thine! 2.12
so thou through windows of thine age shalt see, 3.11
die single, and thine image dies with thee. 3.14
art, | if ten of thine ten times refigur'd thee, 6.10
be death's conquest and make worms thine heir. 6.14
or else receiv'st with pleasure thine annoy? 8. 4
by unions married, do offend thine ear, | they 8. 6
that beauty still may live in thine or thee. 10.14
in one of thine, from that which thou departest, 11. 2
youngly thou bestow'st | thou mayst call thine, 11. 4
but from thine eyes my knowledge i derive, | and 14. 9
nor draw no lines there with thine antique pen; 19.10
which in thy breast doth live, as thine in me: 22. 7
thou gav'st me thine not to give back again. 22.14
that hath his windows glazed with thine eyes. 24. 8
and thine for me | are windows to my breast, 24.10
but that i hope some good conceit of thine | in 26. 7
that due of many, now is thine alone. 31.12
into my verse | thine own sweet argument, too 38. 3
the pain be mine, but thine shall be the praise. 38.14
all mine was thine, before thou hadst this more. 40. 4
thee, | thine, by thy beauty being false to me. 41.14
and scarcely greet me with that sun, thine eye, 49. 6
those same tongues that give thee so thine own, 69. 6
my spirit is thine, the better part of me. 74. 8
thine eyes, that taught the dumb on high to sing 78. 5
whose influence is thine, and born of thee: 78.10
stay, | for it depends upon that love of thine. 92. 4
for there can live no hatred in thine eye, 93. 5
counting no old thing old, thou mine, i thine, 108. 7
thine eyes i love, and they, as pitying me, 132. 1
perforce am thine, and all that is in me. 133.14
so now i have confess'd that he is thine, | and 134. 1
not once vouchsafe to hide my will in thine? 135. 6
wound me not with thine eye but with thy tongue, 139. 3
dear heart, forbear to glance thine eye aside; 139. 6
bear thine eyes straight, though thy proud heart 140.14
o, but with mine compare thou thine own state, 142. 3
or, if it do, not from those lips of thine, 142. 5
whom thine eyes woo as mine importune thee. 142.10
defect, | commanded by the motion of thine eyes? 149.12
for thou art all, and all things else are thine. LC 266

THINE'S 2 FR 0.0002 REL FR 0 V 2 P
thine's too heavy to mount. 2H4 4.03. 56 P
thine's too thick to shine. 4.03. 58 P

THIN–FAC'D 1 FR 0.0001 REL FR 0 V 1 P
and a coxcomb and a knave, a thin–fac'd knave, a TN 5.01.207 P

/THING 4 FR 0.0004 REL FR 4 V 0 P
/what /thing, /in /honor, /had /my /father /lost 2H4 4.01.111
/of /itself | /after /the /thing /it /loves. HAM 4.05.164
/madness | /allows /itself /to /any /thing. LR 3.07.105
/thou /changed /and //self–cover'd /thing, /for 4.02. 62

THING 545 FR 0.0616 REL FR 362 V 183 P
ground, long heath, brown /furze, any thing. TMP 1.01. 67 P
of any thing the image, tell me, that | hath 1.02. 43
thou liest, malignant thing! 1.02.257
for one thing she did | they would not take her 1.02.266
dull thing, i say so; 1.02.285
taught thee each hour | one thing or other. 1.02.355
but wouldst gabble like | a thing most brutish, 1.02.357
i might call him | a thing divine, for nothing 1.02.419
a single thing, as i am now, that wonders | to 1.02.433
here is every thing advantageous to life. 2.01. 50 P
i know thou dar'st, | but this thing dare not — 3.02. 55
i will requite you with as good a thing, | at 5.01.169
be cheerful | and think of each thing well. 5.01.251
this thing of darkness i | acknowledge mine. 5.01.275
this is a strange thing as e'er i look'd on. 5.01.290
sweet ornament that decks a thing divine — | ah TGV 2.01. 4
should i have wish'd a thing, it had been he. 2.04. 82
fire, | bears no impression of the thing it was. 2.04.202
that longs for every thing that he can come by. 3.01.125
now, of another thing she may, and that cannot i 3.01.351 P
tell us this: have you any thing to take to? 4.01. 40
she excels each mortal thing | upon the dull 4.02. 51
you would have them always play but one thing? 4.02. 71 P
i would always have one play but one thing. 4.02. 72
'tis a foul thing when a cur cannot keep himself 4.04. 10 P
quoth i, "'twas i did the thing you wot of." 4.04. 27 P
i will do a greater thing than that, upon your WIV 1.01.240 P
and the boy never need to understand any thing; 2.02.128 P
i shall discover a thing to you, wherein i must 2.02.184 P
believe me, there's no such thing in me. 3.03. 67 P
any thing. 3.03.233 P
and tells me 'tis a thing impossible | i should 3.04. 9
and what a thing should i have been when i had 3.05. 16 P
i hold you as a thing enskied, and sainted, | by MM 1.04. 34
'tis one thing to be tempted, escalus, | another 2.01. 17
to be tempted, escalus, | another thing to fall. 2.01. 18
a one were past cure of the thing you wot of, 2.01.111 P
a book, his face is the worst thing about him. 2.01.156 P
if his face be the worst thing about him, how 2.01.157 P
and your bum is the greatest thing about you, so 2.01.217 P
is like a good thing, being often read, | grown 2.04. 8
for i can speak | against the thing i say. 2.04. 60
i something do excuse the thing i hate, | for 2.04.119
i do lose a thing | that none but fools would 3.01. 7
death is a fearful thing. 3.01.115
i have spirit to do any thing that appears not 3.01.206 P
why, what a ruthless thing is this in him, for 3.02.114 P
than merry at any thing which profess'd to make 3.02.236 P
if any thing fall to you upon this, more than 4.02.178 P
this is a thing that angelo knows not, for he 4.02.199 P
if you have any thing to say to me, come to my 4.03. 62 P
did you such a thing? 4.03.171 P
of sense, | such a dependancy of thing on thing, 5.01. 62
of sense, | such a dependancy of thing on thing, 5.01. 62
in that he did the thing for which he died; 5.01.449
commends me to the thing i cannot get: ERR 1.02. 34
nay, not sure, in a thing falsing. 2.02. 94 P
not on a band but on a stronger thing: 4.02. 50
rings, jewels, any thing his rage did like. 5.01.144
tell him there is measure in every thing, and so ADO 2.01. 72 P
in every good thing. 2.01.152 P
only to despite them, i will endeavor any thing. 2.02. 32 P
and one on shore, | to one thing constant never. 2.03. 65
in every thing but in loving benedick. 2.03.162 P
if i see any thing to–night why i should not 3.02.123 P
it is the only thing for a qualm. 3.04. 75 P
doth not every earthly thing | cry shame upon 4.01.120
as strange as the thing i know not. 4.01.269 P
come, bid me do any thing for thee. 4.01.288 P
two gowns, and every thing handsome about him. 4.02. 85 P
"for he swore a thing to me on monday night, 5.01.167 P
what a pretty thing man is when he goes in his 5.01.199 P
virtuous | in any thing that i do know by her. 5.01.303
for man is a giddy thing, and this is my 5.04.108 P
so, | to know the thing i am forbid to know: LLL 1.01. 60
but like of each thing that in season grows. 1.01.107
it doth forget to do the thing it should; 1.01.144
and when it hath the thing it hunteth most, 1.01.145
sadness is one and the self–same thing, dear imp 1.02. 5 P
do one thing for me that i shall entreat. 3.01.153
you'll not be perjur'd, 'tis a hateful thing; 4.03.155
when shall you see me write a thing in rhyme, 4.03.179
shall i tell you a thing? 5.01.145 P
any thing like? 5.02. 39
the next thing then she waking looks upon | (be MND 2.01.179
but do it when the next thing he espies | may be 2.01.262
wake when some vile thing is near. 2.02. 34
a lion among ladies, is a most dreadful thing; 3.01. 31 P
i am no such thing; 3.01. 43 P
then, there is another thing: 3.01. 62 P
vile thing, let loose; 3.02.260
parted eye, | when every thing seems double. 4.01.190
a paramour is, god bless us, a thing of naught. 4.02. 14 P
i will tell you every thing, right as it fell 4.02. 31 P
for never any thing can be amiss, | when 5.01. 82
why, gentle sweet, you shall see no such thing. 5.01. 87
that such a thing bechanc'd would make me sad? MV 1.01. 38
it is that — any thing now! 1.01.113
i will do any thing, nerissa, ere i will be 1.02. 99 P
a thing not in his power to bring to pass, | but 1.03. 92
rack, | where men enforced do speak any thing. 3.02. 33
and i must freely have the half of any thing 3.02.249
hates any man the thing he would not kill? 4.01. 67
you may as well do any thing most hard, | as 4.01. 78
you, merchant, have you any thing to say? 4.01.263
a thing stuck on with oaths upon your finger, 5.01.168
modesty | to urge the thing held as a ceremony? 5.01.206
as you, | i'll not deny him any thing i have, 5.01.227
while i live i'll fear no other thing | so sore, 5.01.306
nothing. i am not taught to make any thing. AYL 1.01. 30 P
into, in that it is a thing of his own search, 1.01.135 P
to deny so fair and excellent ladies any thing. 1.02.185 P
sermons in stones, and good in every thing. 2.01. 17
that little cares for buying any thing. 2.04. 90
assuredly the thing is to be sold. 2.04. 96
if this uncouth forest yield any thing savage, i 2.06. 6 P
a dinner if there live any thing in this desert. 2.06. 17 P
teeth, sans eyes, sans taste, sans every thing. 2.07.166
and every thing about you demonstrating a 3.02.380 P
something and for no passion truly any thing, as 3.02.414 P
is it a true thing? 3.03. 18 P
the best thing in him | is his complexion; 3.05.115
then, can one desire too much of a good thing? 4.01.124 P
lusty horn | is not a thing to laugh to scorn. 4.02. 18
so sweetly tastes, being the thing i am. 4.03.137
there was never any thing so sudden but the 5.02. 30 P
how bitter a thing it is to look into happiness 5.02. 44 P
to have her and death were both one thing. 5.04. 17
a poor virgin, sir, an ill–favor'd thing, sir, 5.04. 58 P
he's as good at any thing, and yet a fool. 5.04.105 P
love, to labor and effect one thing specially. SHR 1.01.118 P
one thing more rests, that thyself execute — 1.01.246
supposing it a thing impossible, | for those 1.02.123
o this learning, what a thing it is! 1.02.159
ay, when the special thing is well obtain'd, 2.01.128
they do consume the thing that feeds their fury. 2.01.133
barn, | my horse, my ox, my ass, my any thing; 3.02.232
the carpets laid, and every thing in order? 4.01. 50 P
then both or one, or any thing thou wilt. 4.03. 29
sun, | that every thing i look on seemeth green; 4.05. 47
will you any thing with it? AWW 1.01.164 P
in every thing i wait upon his will. 2.04. 54
upon oath, never trust my judgment in any thing. 3.06. 33 P
i will tell you a thing, but you shall let it 4.03. 10 P
he can have every thing in him by wearing his 4.03.146 P
i could endure any thing before but a cat, and 4.03.237 P
he has every thing that an honest man should not 4.03.259 P
simply the thing i am | shall make me live. 4.03.333
what he'll utter, | that will speak any thing? 5.03.209
of a wife you see, | the name and not the thing. 5.03.308
any thing that's mended is but patch'd; TN 1.05. 47 P
and — one thing more — that you be never so 2.02. 9 P
my lady's favor at any thing more than contempt, 2.03.122 P
is, or any thing constantly but a time–pleaser, 2.03.147 P
might be every thing and their intent every 2.04. 77 P
i will do every thing that thou wilt have me. 2.05.179 P
by maidhood, honor, truth, and every thing, | i 3.01.150
you have not seen such a thing as 'tis. 3.02. 81 P
why, every thing adheres together, that no dram 3.04. 78 P
a little thing would make me tell them how much 3.04.302 P
any thing. 5.01. 4 P
and grew a twenty years removed thing | while 5.01. 89
and the rain, | a foolish thing was but a toy, 5.01.391
women say so — | that will say any thing. WT 1.02.131
if ever fearful | to do a thing, where i the 1.02.259
my design, and i | remain a pinch'd thing; 2.01. 51
o thou thing! 2.01. 82
any thing, my lord, | that my ability may 2.03.163
to save the innocent — any thing possible. 2.03.167
on thy side, | poor thing, condemn'd to loss! 2.03.192
if such thing be, thy mother | appear'd to me 3.03. 17
that got this than the poor thing is here. 3.03. 76 P
if thou'lt see a thing to talk on when thou art 3.03. 80 P
'tis a sickness denying thee any thing; 4.02. 2 P
i shall there have money, or any thing i want. 4.03. 82 P
i cannot be | mine own, nor any thing to any, if 4.04. 44
strangle such thoughts as these with any thing 4.04. 47
and the thing she took to quench it | she would 4.04. 61
so she does any thing, though i report it | that 4.04.177
down, or a very pleasant thing indeed and sung 4.04.189 P
at us, and we may do any thing extempore. 4.04.677 P
and any thing that is fitting to be known — 4.04.720 P
that any thing he sees, which moves his liking, JN 2.01.512
having no external thing to lose | but the word 2.01.571
thou swear'st against the thing thou swear'st, 3.01.281
i had a thing to say, | but i will fit it with 3.03. 25
i had a thing to say, but let it go. 3.03. 33
at some thing it grieves, | more than with R2 2.02. 12
divides one thing entire to many objects, | like 2.02. 17
and every thing is left at six and seven. 2.02.122
thou, thou little better thing than earth, 3.04. 78
our scene is alt'red from a serious thing, | and 5.03. 79
and telling me the sovereignest thing on earth 1H4 1.03. 57
a weaver, i could sing psalms, or any thing. 2.04.134 P
there is a thing, harry, which thou hast often 2.04.411 P
man, | for any thing he shall be charg'd withal, 2.04.517
go, you thing, go. 3.03.115 P
say, what thing? what thing? 3.03.116 P
say, what thing? what thing? 3.03.116 P
what thing? why, a thing to thank god on. 3.03.117 P
what thing? why, a thing to thank god on. 3.03.117 P
i am no thing to thank god on, i would thou 3.03.118 P
if there were any thing in thy pocket but 3.03.157 P
friends with my father and may do any thing. 3.03.182 P
rob me the exchequer the first thing thou doest, 3.03.183 P
he that but fears the thing he would not know 2H4 1.01. 85
and as the thing that's heavy in itself | upon 1.01.119
is not able to invent any thing that intends to 1.02. 8 P
am sure he is, to the hearing of any thing good. 1.02. 68 P
hot day, and i brandish any thing but a bottle, 1.02.211 P
our english nation, if they have a good thing, 1.02.215 P
a good wit will make use of any thing. 1.02.248 P
you, he's an infinitive thing upon my score. 2.01. 24 P
shall i tell thee one thing, poins? 2.02. 32 P
faith, and let it be an excellent good thing. 2.02. 34 P
the push of your one thing that you will tell. 2.02. 37 P
for in every thing the purpose must weigh with 2.02.175 P
by the mass, i was call'd any thing, and i would 3.02. 17 P
and i would have done any thing indeed too, and 3.02. 18 P
be accommodated — which is an excellent thing. 3.02. 80 P
has nobody to do any thing about her when i am 3.02.231 P
every thing set off | that might so much as 4.01.143
there is a thing within my bosom tells me | that 4.01.181
to say thus, some good thing comes to–morrow. 4.02. 84
when every thing is ended, then you come. 4.03. 27
and every thing lies level to our wish. 4.04. 7
it is a wonderful thing to see the semblable 5.01. 64 P
if thou want'st any thing, and wilt not call, 5.03. 56 P
come, you thin thing, come, you rascal. 5.04. 30 P
jest, | presume not that i am the thing i was, 5.05. 56
where (for any thing i know) falstaff shall die ep 30 P
and any thing that may not misbecome | the H5 2.04.118
they will steal any thing, and call it purchase. 3.02. 42 P
aunchient, it is not a thing to rejoice at; 3.06. 53 P
thou mak'st use of any thing. 3.07. 66 P
how can they charitably dispose of any thing, 4.01.143 P
be, if he durst steal any thing adventurously. 4.04. 73 P
if i owe you any thing, i will pay you in 5.01. 64 P
attire, | and every thing that seems unnatural. 5.02. 62
dignity, | any thing in or out of our demands, 5.02. 89
his glass for love of any thing he sees there, 5.02.148 P
and will not you maintain the thing you teach, 1H6 3.01.129
that for a toy, a thing of no regard, | king 4.01.145
tush, that's a wooden thing! 5.03. 89
you judge it straight a thing impossible | to 5.04. 47
how now, fellow? wouldst any thing with me? 2H6 1.03. 10 P
now, sirs, have you dispatch'd this thing? 3.02. 6
cask | that ever did contain a thing of worth. 3.02.410
the first thing we do, let's kill all the 4.02. 76 P
is not this a lamentable thing, that of the skin 4.02. 79 P
for i did but seal once to a thing, and i was 4.02. 83 P
you shall have pay and every thing you wish. 5.01. 47
armor, any thing i have | is his to use, so 5.01. 52

think | how sweet a thing it is to wear a crown, 3H6 1.02. 29
there is no wrong, but every thing is right. 2.02.132
and never will i undertake the thing | wherein 2.06.101
i see the lady hath a thing to grant, | before 3.02. 12
'tis a happy thing | to be the father unto many 3.02.104
ay, that's the first thing that we have to do, 4.03. 62
yet in this one thing let me blame your grace, 4.06. 30
he's sudden, if a thing comes in his head. 5.05. 86
you may partake of any thing we say: R3 1.01. 89
or any creeping venom'd thing that lives! 1.02. 20
are you now going to dispatch this thing? 1.03.340
out of towns and cities for a dangerous thing, 1.04.142 P
he was the wretched'st thing when he was young, 2.04. 18
'tis a vile thing to die, my gracious lord, 3.02. 62
and will, no doubt, tempt him to any thing. 4.02. 39
if to have done the thing you gave in charge 4.03. 25
yet one thing more, good captain, do for me — 5.03. 33
a thing devised by the enemy. 5.03.306
the tract of ev'ry thing | would by a good H8 1.01. 40
nought rebell'd, | order gave each thing view; 1.01. 44
that follow'd, was | a thing inspir'd, and, not 1.01. 91
pledge it, madam, | for 'tis to such a thing — 1.04. 48
every thing that heard him play, | even the 3.01. 9
if ye be any thing but churchmen's habits) | put 3.01.117
to th' king, never attempt | any thing on him; 3.02. 18
ye appear in every thing may bring my ruin! 3.02.242
before | this happy child, did i get any thing. 5.04. 65
he hath the joints of every thing, but every TRO 1.02. 28 P
but every thing so out of joint that he is a 1.02. 28 P
cousin, i told you a thing yesterday, think on't 1.02.170 P
any thing, he cares not; 1.02.210 P
men prize the thing ungain'd more than it is. 1.02.289
fled under shade, why then the thing of courage, 1.03. 51
each thing /meets | in mere oppugnancy: 1.03.110
then every thing include itself in power, 1.03.119
thou art by inches, thou thing of no bowels, 2.01. 49 P
to guard a thing not ours nor worth to us | (had 2.02. 22
but thieves unworthy of a thing so stol'n, 2.02. 94
if any thing more than your sport and pleasure 2.03.108
niece is horribly in love with a thing you have, 3.01. 97 P
i shall surely speak | the thing i shall repent. 3.02.131
some thing not worth in me such rich beholding 3.03. 91
proves | that no man is the lord of any thing, 3.03.115
virtue seek | remuneration for the thing it was; 3.03.170
in such a sort | the thing he means to kill, 4.01. 25
dispraise the thing that they desire to buy, 4.01. 77
you are deceived, i think of no such thing. 4.02. 39
bid me do any thing but that, sweet greek. 5.02. 27
that a thing inseparate | divides more wider 5.02.148
will give me any thing for the intelligence of 5.02.192 P
fortune of this girl, and what one thing, what 5.03.103 P
bastard in valor, in every thing illegitimate. 5.07. 18 P
and were i any thing but what i am, | i would COR 1.01.231
madam, i will obey you in every thing hereafter. 1.03.103 P
tell me one thing that i shall ask you. 2.01. 13 P
you know neither me, yourselves, nor any thing. 2.01. 68 P
only | there's one thing wanting, which i doubt 2.01.201
from face to foot | he was a thing of blood, 2.02.109
you must think, if we give you any thing, we 2.03. 71 P
it is a purpos'd thing, and grows by plot, | to 3.01. 38
hence, rotten thing! 3.01.178
but a small thing would make it flame again; 4.03. 20 P
thou noble thing, more dances my rapt heart 4.05.116
as between | the young'st and oldest thing. 4.06. 69
he leads them like a thing | made by some other 4.06. 90
not to be other than one thing, not moving 4.07. 42
the thing i have forsworn to grant may never 5.03. 80
you have said you will not grant us any thing; 5.03. 87
it is no little thing to make | mine eyes to 5.03.195
he has wings, he's more than a creeping thing. 5.04. 14 P
in his state, as a thing made for alexander. 5.04. 22 P
and every thing | in readiness for hymenaeus TIT 1.01.324
when every thing doth make a gleeful boast? 2.03. 11
and one thing more | that womanhood denies my 2.03.173
the thing whereat it trembles by surmise. 2.03.219
o wondrous thing! 2.03.286
now, what a thing it is to be an ass! 4.02. 25
and hast a thing within thee called conscience, 5.01. 75
o any thing, of nothing first /create! ROM 1.01.177
but, i pray, can you read any thing you see? 1.02. 60 P
in the pantry, and every thing in extremity. 1.03.102 P
too great oppression for a tender thing. 1.04. 24
is love a tender thing? 1.04. 25
hands, and they unwash'd too, 'tis a foul thing. 1.05. 5 P
and yet i wish but for the thing i have. 2.02.132
why, is not this a lamentable thing, grandsire, 2.04. 31 P
never with me for any thing when thou wast not 2.04. 75 P
and 'a speak any thing against me, i'll take him 2.04.150 P
truly it were an ill thing to be off'red to any 2.04.169 P
when 'twas a little prating thing — o, there is 2.04.201 P
dog | and little mouse, every unworthy thing, 3.03. 31
a thing like death to chide away this shame, 4.01. 74
child, | but one thing to rejoice and solace in, 4.05. 47
leave me, and do the thing i bid thee do. 5.01. 30
put this in any liquid thing you will | and 5.01. 77
o, much i fear some ill unthrifty thing. 5.03.136
a thing slipp'd idlely from me. TIM 1.01. 20
but i can tell you one thing, my lord, and which 3.02. 4 P
believe't that we'll do any thing for gold. 4.03.150
what vilder thing upon the earth than friends, 4.03.463
live to be | in awe of such a thing as i myself. JC 1.02. 96
that could be mov'd to smile at any thing. 1.02.207
said, if he had done or said any thing amiss, he 1.02.270 P
did cicero say any thing? 1.02.278
the sway of earth | shakes like a thing unfirm? 1.03. 4
why, saw you any thing more wonderful? 1.03. 14
to illuminate | so vile a thing as caesar! 1.03.111
will bear no color for the thing he is, 2.01. 29
between the acting of a dreadful thing | and the 2.01. 63
for he will never follow any thing | that other 2.01.151
how weak a thing | the heart of woman is! 2.04. 39
pluck down forms, windows, any thing. 3.02.259 P
and in this mood will give us any thing. 3.02.267
every thing is well. 4.03.236
art thou any thing? 4.03.278
yes, that thou didst. didst thou see any thing? 4.03.297
ay. saw you any thing? 4.03.304
alas, thou hast misconstrued every thing! 5.03. 84
octavius' tent | how every thing is chanc'd. 5.04. 32
to throw away the dearest thing he ow'd, | as MAC 1.04. 10
by doing every thing | safe toward your love and 1.04. 26
there's no such thing: 2.01. 47
horses (a thing most strange and certain), 2.04. 14
of this, good peers, | but as a thing of custom. 3.04. 96
provide, | your charms and every thing beside. 3.05. 19
yet my heart | throbs to know one thing: 4.01.101
what, has this thing appear'd again to–night? HAM 1.01. 21
if there be any good thing to be done | that may 1.01.130
and then it started like a guilty thing | upon a 1.01.148
common | as any the most vulgar thing to sense, 1.02. 99
form of the thing, each word made true and good, 1.02.210
do to that, | being a thing immortal as itself? 1.04. 67
as 'twere a thing a little soil'd /wi' /th' 2.01. 40
take from me any thing that i will not more 2.02.215 P
any thing, but to th' purpose. 2.02.278 P
/french falc'ners — fly at any thing we see; 2.02.430 P
the play's the thing | wherein i'll catch the 2.02.604
is not more ugly to the thing that helps it 3.01. 51
for any thing so o'erdone is from the purpose of 3.02. 20 P
you now, how unworthy a thing you make of me! 3.02.363 P
the king is a thing — 4.02. 28 P
a thing, my lord? 4.02. 29 P
tend, and every thing is bent | for england. 4.03. 45
for every thing is seal'd and done | that else 4.03. 56
or is it some abuse, and no such thing? 4.07. 50
can save the thing from death | that is but 4.07.145
prithee, horatio, tell me one thing. 5.01.195 P
i should impart a thing to you from his majesty. 5.02. 90 P
if your mind dislike any thing, obey it. 5.02.217 P
trice of time | commit a thing so monstrous, to LR 1.01.217
nor so old to dote on her for any thing. 1.04. 38 P
i had rather be any kind o' thing than a fool, 1.04.186 P
by her, that else will take the thing she begs, 1.04.248
no further with any thing you know than comes 1.05. 3 P
and i have one thing, of a queasy question, 2.01. 17
beggars | are in the poorest thing superfluous. 2.04.265
of my note | commend a dear thing to you. 3.01. 19
who gives any thing to poor tom? 3.04. 51 P
thou art the thing itself: 3.04.106 P
the lowest and most dejected thing of fortune, 4.01. 3
what thing was that | which parted from you? 4.06. 67
that thing you speak of, | i took it for a man; 4.06. 77
to say "ay" and "no" to every thing that i said! 4.06. 99 P
they told me i was every thing. 4.06.105 P
you shall have any thing. 4.06.193
great thing of us forgot! 5.03.237
gentle, and low, an excellent thing in woman. 5.03.274
sir, i will answer any thing. OTH 1.01.120
you not read, roderigo, | of some such thing? 1.01.174
to the sooty bosom | of such a thing as thou — 1.02. 71
of years, of country, credit, every thing, | to 1.03. 97
beguile | the thing i am by seeming otherwise. 2.01.123
which thing to do, | if this poor trash of 2.01.302
he's never any thing but your true servant. 3.03. 9
i'll intermingle every thing he does | with 3.03. 25
your honor | to scan this thing no farther; 3.03.245
than keep a corner in the thing i love | for 3.03.272
do not you chide; i have a thing for you. 3.03.301
you have a thing for me? it is a common thing — 3.03.302
you have a thing for me? it is a common thing — 3.03.302
can any thing be made of this? 3.04. 10 P
hath he said any thing? 4.01. 29
an old thing 'twas, but it express'd her fortune 4.03. 29
the world's a huge thing; 4.03. 69
i would not do such a thing for a joint–ring, 4.03. 73 P
why, any thing: 5.02.293
whom every thing becomes — to chide, to laugh, ANT 1.01. 49
sweet alexas, most any thing alexas, almost most 1.02. 1 P
in each thing give him way, cross him in nothing 1.03. 9
last thing he did, dear queen, | he kiss'd — 1.05. 39
to their throne, decays | the thing we sue for. 2.01. 5
what manner o' thing is your crocodile? 2.07. 41 P
by him, | this creature's no such thing. 3.03. 41
i have one thing more to ask him yet, good 3.03. 45
do at once | the thing why thou hast drawn it. 4.14. 89
the breaking of so great a thing should make | a 5.01. 14
to do that thing that ends all other deeds, 5.02. 5
that is not | glad at the thing they scowl at. CYM 1.01. 15
he that hath miss'd the princess is a thing 1.01. 16
thou basest thing, avoid hence, from my sight! 1.01.125
o disloyal thing, | that shouldst repair my 1.01.131
thou foolish thing! 1.01.150
the other is not a thing for sale, and only the 1.04. 84 P
expect | to be depender on a thing that leans? 1.05. 58
it is a thing i made, which hath the king | five 1.05. 62
i am not vex'd more at any thing in th' earth; 2.01. 17 P
first, a very excellent good conceited thing; 2.03. 17 P
with every thing that pretty is, my lady sweet, 2.03. 25
this is a thing | which you might from relation 2.04. 85
would be interpreted a thing perplex'd | beyond 3.04. 7
man, a thing | the most disdain'd of fortune. 3.04. 19
like | a thing more made of malice than of duty, 3.05. 33
for he believes | it is a thing most precious. 3.05. 59
(i forgot to ask him one thing, i'll remember't 3.05.131 P
that is the second thing that i have commanded 3.05.152 P
if any thing that's civil, speak; 3.06. 23
yet this imperceiverant thing loves him in my 4.01. 14 P
a thing | more slavish did i ne'er than 4.02. 72
ay, and that | from one bad thing to worse, not 4.02.134
thou blessed thing, | jove knows what man thou 4.02.206
what thing is't that i never | did see man die, 4.04. 35
came crying 'mongst his foes, | a thing of pity! 5.04. 47
did you suffer jachimo, | slight thing of italy, 5.04. 64
never saw | such noble fury in so poor a thing; 5.05. 8
this one thing only | i will entreat: 5.05. 83
i see a thing | bitter to me as death; 5.05.103
the same dead thing alive. 5.05.123
any thing | that's due to all the villains past, 5.05.211
you was not thought by me | a precious thing. 5.05.242
i left out one thing which the queen confess'd, 5.05.244
the thing the which is flattered, but a spark PER 1.02. 40
let me ask you one thing: 2.05. 32
who thought of such a thing?" 3.ch. 38
here is a thing too young for such a place, 3.01. 15
thou canst not do a thing in the world so soon 4.01. 3
such a maidenhead were no cheap thing, if men 4.02. 61 P
did you ever dream of such a thing? 4.05. 5 P
i'll do any thing now that is virtuous, but i am 4.05. 8 P
prithee tell me one thing first. 4.06.156 P
come now, your one thing. 4.06.157 P
do any thing but this thou doest. 4.06.174
some such thing | i said, and said no more but 5.01.132
no needful thing omitted. 5.03. 68
for, to say truth, it were an endless thing, TNK pr 22
and the bear's, | and vault to every thing! 1.01. 54
henceforth i'll not dare | to ask you any thing, 1.01.204
omit not any thing | in the pretended 1.01.209
and even each thing | our haste does leave 1.04. 11
our thing of learning /says so — | where he 2.03. 51
thou think'st thyself the happier thing to be 3.01. 25
i'll bring you every needful thing. 3.01. 99
hath grief slain fear, and, but for one thing, 3.02. 5
anger, | as you love any thing that's honorable. 3.06. 27
me | a thing as soon to die as thee to say it, 3.06.159
that you would nev'r deny me any thing | fit for 3.06.234
shall any thing that loves me perish for me? 3.06.241
and palamon is sweet, and ev'ry good thing. 4.03. 87 P
which never yet | beheld thing maculate — look 5.01.145
if she entreat again, do any thing, | lie with 5.02. 17
'tis the latest thing | i shall be glad of, 5.04. 29
although we grant you get the thing you seek? STM II.C 69
alone, | thing like a man, but of no woman bred! VEN 214
of things long since, or any thing ensuing? 1078
perchance that envy of so rich a thing, LUC 39
so then we do neglect | the thing we have, and 153
"what win i if i gain the thing i seek? 211
pain pays the income of each precious thing: 334
barr'd him from the blessed thing he sought. 340
but she, sound sleeping, fearing no such thing, 363
mar not the thing that cannot be amended. 578
for kings like gods should govern every thing. 602
no outrageous thing | from vassal actors can be 607
the lesser thing should not the greater hide: 663
but she hath lost a dearer thing than life, 687
man, the mightier is the thing | that makes him 1004
thus cavils she with every thing she sees: 1093
holds disputation with each thing she views, 1101
every thing did banish moan, | save the PP 20. 7
when i consider every thing that grows | holds SON 15. 1
by adding one thing to my purpose nothing. 20.12
or some fierce thing replete with too much rage, 23. 3
i sigh the lack of many a thing i sought, | and 30. 3
eye, | when love converted from the thing it was 49. 7
that in your will | (though you do any thing) he 57.14
that do not do the thing they most do show, 94. 2
hath put a spirit of youth in every thing, 98. 3
one thing expressing, leaves out difference. 105. 8
counting no old thing old, thou mine, i thine, 108. 7
in pursuit of the thing she would have stay; 143. 4
or made them swear against the thing they see; 152.12
labor is't to leave | the thing we have not, LC 240
against the thing he sought he would exclaim: 313

THING'S 2 FR 0.0002 REL FR 2 V 0 P

each thing's a thief. TIM 4.03.442
why yet i live to say, "this thing's to do," HAM 4.04. 44

/THINGS 3 FR 0.0003 REL FR 3 V 0 P

/things /present /worst. 2H4 1.03.108
/leaving /free /things /and /happy /shows LR 3.06.105
/these /things /sting | /his /mind /so 4.03. 45

THINGS 366 FR 0.0413 REL FR 297 V 69 P

good things will strive to dwell with't. TMP 1.02.460
i would, by contraries, | execute all things; 2.01.149
all things in common nature should produce 2.01.160
these be fine things, and if they be not sprites 2.02.116
that will /not let you | believe things certain. 5.01.125
what things are these, my lord antonio? 5.01.264
i see things too, although you judge i wink. TGV 1.02.136
are all these things perceiv'd in me? 2.01. 33 P
for good things should be prais'd. 3.01.347 P
three things that women highly hold in hate. 3.02. 33
indeed, to be, as it were, a dog at all things. 4.04. 13 P
'em, they are very ill–favor'd rough things. WIV 1.01.299 P
can tell you how things go better than i can. 3.04. 65 P
there are fairer things than poulcats sure. 4.01. 28 P
i would not have things cool. 4.02.224 P
i had other things to have spoken with her too 4.05. 40 P
you shall hear how things go, and, i warrant, to 4.05.122 P
i'll tell you strange things of this knave ford, 5.01. 27 P
strange things in hand, master /brook! 5.01. 29 P
but so sound as things that are hollow. MM 1.02. 56 P
dost thou desire her foully for those things 2.02.173
strings | most ponderous and substantial things! 3.02.276
into amazement how these things should be; 4.02.204 P
for i would commune with you of such things 4.03.104
in good time — there's a time for all things. ERR 2.02. 65 P
have prov'd there is no time for all things. 2.02.101 P
friendship is constant in all other things ADO 2.01.175
will you look to those things i told you of? 2.01.337 P
brief, too, to have all things answer my mind. 2.01.361 P
are these things spoken, or do i but dream? 4.01. 66
sir, they are spoken, and these things are true. 4.01. 67
these things, come thus to light, | smother her 4.01.111
thirdly, they have verified unjust things; 5.01.219 P
well, i am glad that all things sorts so well. 5.04. 7
things hid and barr'd, you mean, from common LLL 1.01. 57
to things of sale a seller's praise belongs: 4.03.236
o, 'tis the sun that maketh all things shine! 4.03.242
arrows, bullets, wind, thought, swifter things. 5.02.261
sweet, | your wits makes wise things foolish. 5.02.374
wise things seem foolish and rich things but 5.02.378
things seem foolish and rich things but poor. 5.02.378
when great things laboring perish in their birth 5.02.520
so quick bright things come to confusion. MND 1.01.149
things base and vile, holding no quantity, 1.01.232
things growing are not ripe until their season, 2.02.117
for as a surfeit of the sweetest things | the 2.02.137
there are things in this comedy of pyramus and 3.01. 9 P
but there is two hard things: 3.01. 48 P
made senseless things begin to do them wrong, 3.02. 28
some hats, from yielders all things catch. 3.02. 30
and those things do best please me | that befall 3.02.120
how can these things in me seem scorn to you, 3.02.126
monster's view, and all things shall be peace. 3.02.377
how came these things to pass? 4.01. 78

these things seem small and undistinguishable, 4.01.187
methinks i see these things with parted eye, 4.01.189
bodies forth | the forms of things unknown, the 5.01. 15
but wonder on till truth make all things plain. 5.01.128
these things being bought and orderly bestowed, MV 2.02.170
all things that are, | are with more spirit 2.06. 12
i am enjoin'd by oath to observe three things: 2.09. 9
/hear other things: 3.04. 23
'mong other things | i shall disgest it. 3.05. 89
do all men kill the things they do not love? 4.01. 66
two things provided more, that for this favor 4.01.386
grant me two things, i pray you, | not to deny 4.01.423
how many things by season season'd are | to 5.01.107
and we will answer all things faithfully. 5.01.299
i thought that all things had been savage here, AYL 2.07.107
thy lands and all things that thou dost call 3.01. 9
eyes, that are the frail'st and softest things, 3.05. 12
if you please, that i can do strange things. 5.02. 59 P
when earthly things made even | atone together. 5.04.109
how thus we met, and these things finish. 5.04.140
i smell sweet savors, and i feel soft things. SHR in.2. 71
we will have rings and things, and fine array; 2.01.323
brass, and all things that belongs | to house or 2.01.355
and all things answerable to this portion. 2.01.359
my crupper, with many things of worthy memory, 4.01. 82 P
companions, is all ready, and all things neat? 4.01.114 P
all things is ready. how near is our master? 4.01.115 P
ruffs and cuffs, and fardingales, and things, 4.03. 56
thou hast fac'd many things. 4.03.122 P
to join like likes, and kiss like native things. AWW 1.01.223
senses | all but new things disdain; 1.02. 61
it is not so with him that all things knows | as 2.01.149
i see things may serve long, but not serve ever. 2.02. 58 P
make modern and familiar things supernatural and 2.03. 3 P
from lowest place /when virtuous things proceed, 2.03.125
she's very well indeed, but for two things. 2.04. 9 P
what two things? 2.04. 10 P
these things shall be done, sir. 2.05. 15 P
of lust, are not the things they go under. 3.05. 20 P
as we are ourselves, what things are we! 4.03. 20 P
make trivial price of serious things we have, 5.03. 61
and things which would derive me ill will to 5.03.264 P
wherefore are these things hid? TN 1.03.125 P
is to take those things for bird–bolts that you 1.05. 92 P
i can hardly forbear hurling things at him. 3.02. 81 P
with the memorials and the things of fame | that 3.03. 23
you are idle shallow things, i am not of your 3.04.124 P
so please you, these things further thought on, 5.01.316
praise, and make 's | as fat as tame things. WT 1.02. 92
thou dost make possible things not so held, 1.02.139
with all the nearest things to my heart, as well 1.02.236
do not repent these things, for they are heavier 3.02.208
thou met'st with things dying, i with things 3.03.114 P
with things dying, i with things new–born. 3.03.114 P
i do | to th' freshest things now reigning, and 4.01. 13
me, and these detestable things put upon me. 4.03. 62 P
we'll buy the other things anon. 4.04.274 P
things known betwixt us three, i'll write you 4.04.560
show those things you found about her, those 4.04.696 P
things you found about her, those secret things, 4.04.697 P
if thou be'st capable of things serious, thou 4.04.764 P
might have spoken a thousand things that would 5.01. 21
now have look'd on, | such goodly things as you? 5.01.178
my father will grant precious things as trifles. 5.01.222
this day all things begun come to ill end, | yea JN 3.01. 94
feeling what small things are boisterous there, 4.01. 94
all things that you should use to do me wrong 4.01.117
things sweet to taste prove in digestion sour. R2 1.03.236
writ in remembrance more than things long past. 2.01. 14
which for things true weeps things imaginary. 2.02. 27
which for things true weeps things imaginary. 2.02. 27
things past redress are now with me past care. 2.03.171
as thoughts of things divine, are intermix'd 5.05. 12
provide us all things necessary, and meet me 1H4 1.02.192 P
and if thou wilt not tell me all things true. 2.03. 88
wherein villainous, but in all things? 2.04.458 P
i may for some things true, wherein my youth 3.02. 26
these things indeed you have articulate, 5.01. 72
and those two things i confess i cannot help. 2H4 2.02. 68 P
and are etceteras no things? 2.04.184
of the main chance of things | as yet not come 3.01. 83
such things become the hatch and brood of time, 3.01. 86
are these things then necessities? 3.01. 92
things that are mouldy lack use. 3.02.107 P
see, sons, what things you are! 4.05. 64
be | as things acquainted and familiar to us, 5.02.139
as nail in door. the things i speak are just. 5.03.121
admit the means | how things are perfected. H5 1.01. 69
him, of some things of weight | that task our 1.02. 5
that many things, having full reference | to one 1.02.205
and all things thought upon | that may with 1.02.305
i cannot tell — things must be as they may. 2.01. 20 P
minding true things by what their mock'ries be. 4.pr. 53
there is some soul of goodness in things evil, 4.01. 4
day, my /friends, and all things stay for me. 4.01.309
such outward things dwell not in my desires. 4.03. 27
all things are ready, if our minds be so. 4.03. 71
well, for there is figures in all things. 4.07. 33 P
of time, of numbers, and due course of things, 5.pr. 4
and causes why and wherefore in all things. 5.01. 4 P
after that things are set in order here, | we'll 1H6 2.02. 32
if all things fall out right, | i shall as 2.03. 4
for things that are not to be remedied. 3.03. 4
we'll see these things effected to the full. 2H6 1.02. 84
beadles in your town, and things call'd whips? 2.01.134
a' god's name see the lists and all things fit; 2.03. 54
for things are often spoke and seldom meant; 3.01.268
is all things well, | according as i gave 3.02. 11
o thou that judgest all things, stay my thoughts 3.02.136
small things make base men proud. 4.01.106
and henceforward all things shall be in common. 4.07. 18 P
as all things shall redound unto your good. 4.09. 47
i come to tell you things sith then befall'n. 3H6 2.01.106
hear | that things ill got had ever bad success? 2.02. 46
keeper, i have done these things | (that now R3 1.04. 66
in common worldly things 'tis call'd ungrateful 2.02. 91
in weightier things you'll say a beggar nay. 3.01.119
is all things ready for the royal time? 3.04. 4
is, my liege, and all things are in readiness. 5.03. 52
things now | that bear a weighty and a serious H8 pr 1
will of heav'n | be done in this and all things! 1.01.210
but you frame | things that are known alike, 1.02. 45
things done well | and with a care exempt 1.02. 88
things done without example, in their issue 1.02. 90
in trust) of him | things to strike honor sad. 1.02.126
because all those things you have done of late 3.02.338
such things have been done. 5.01.133
things won are done, joy's soul lies in the TRO 1.02.287
of the giant mass | of things to come at large. 1.03.346
such things as might offend the weakest spleen 2.02.128
things small as nothing, for request's sake only 2.03.169
through the sight i bear in things to /come, | i 3.03. 4
what things there are | most /abject in regard, 3.03.127
what things again most dear in the esteem, | and 3.03.129
though they are made and moulded of things past, 3.03.177
since things in motion sooner catch the eye 3.03.183
centre of the earth, | drawing all things to it. 4.02.105
digest things rightly | touching the weal a' COR 1.01.150
besides, if things go well, | opinion that so 1.01.270
in troth, there's wondrous things spoke of him. 2.01.137 P
and look'd upon things precious as they were 2.02.125
what custom wills, in all things should we do't, 2.03.118
for your voices have | done many things, some 2.03.130
that of all things upon the earth he hated 3.01. 14
things created | to buy and sell with groats, to 3.02. 9
tell you most strange things from rome, all 4.03. 41 P
should from yond cloud speak divine things, 4.05.104
y' are goodly things, you voices! 4.06.146
th' vulgar eye, that he bears all things fairly, 4.07. 21
for such things as you, i can scarce think 5.02.103 P
if thou do this, i'll show thee wondrous things, TIT 5.01. 55
but i have done a thousand dreadful things | as 5.01.141
in bed asleep, while they do dream things true. ROM 1.04. 52
things have fall'n out, sir, so unluckily | that 3.04. 1
things that, to hear them told, have made me 4.01. 86
and all things shall be well, i warrant thee, 4.02. 40
things for the cook, sir, but i know not what. 4.04. 15
all things that we ordained festival, | turn 4.05. 84
and all things change them to the contrary. 4.05. 90
go hence to have more talk of these sad things; 5.03.307
that few things loves better | than to abhor TIM 1.01. 59
things of like value differing in the owners 1.01.170
takes no accompt | how things go from him, nor 2.02. 4
grief too, as i understand how all things go. 3.06. 18 P
what things in the world canst thou nearest 4.03.318 P
but men — men are the things themselves. 4.03.321 P
moe things like men! 4.03.397
to mend, | and nothing brings me all things. 5.01.188
you stones, you worse than senseless things! JC 1.01. 35
but by reflection, by some other things. 1.02. 53
both meet to hear and answer such high things. 1.02.170
they are portentous things | unto the climate 1.03. 31
but men may construe things after their fashion, 1.03. 34
clean from the purpose of the things themselves. 1.03. 35
why all these things change from their ordinance 1.03. 66
run, | and i will strive with things impossible, 2.01.325
the things that threaten'd me | ne'er look'd but 2.02. 10
besides the things that we have heard and seen, 2.02. 15
o caesar, these things are beyond all use, | and 2.02. 25
to young octavius of the state of things. 3.01.296
and things unluckily charge my fantasy. 3.03. 2
and now, octavius, | listen great things. 4.01. 41
some worthy cause to wish | things done undone; 4.02. 9
and partly credit things that do presage. 5.01. 78
apt thoughts of men | the things that are not? 5.03. 69
he look | that seems to speak things strange. MAC 1.02. 47
and seem to fear | things that do sound so fair? 1.03. 52
were such things here as we do speak about? 1.03. 83
dull brain was wrought | with things forgotten. 1.03.150
strength, to think | so brain–sickly of things. 2.02. 43
drink, sir, is a great provoker of three things. 2.03. 25 P
what three things does drink especially provoke? 2.03. 26 P
i have seen | hours dreadful and things strange; 2.04. 3
well, may you see things well done there: 2.04. 37
and all things else that might | to half a soul 3.01. 81
things without all remedy | should be without 3.02. 11
but let the frame of things disjoint, both the 3.02. 16
good things of day begin to droop and drowse, 3.02. 52
things bad begun make strong themselves by ill. 3.02. 55
can such things be, | and overcome us like a 3.04.109
strange things i have in head, that will to hand 3.04.138
only i say | things have been strangely borne. 3.06. 3
he has borne all things well, and i do think 3.06. 17
things at the worst will cease, or else climb 4.02. 24
though all things foul would wear the brows of 4.03. 23
such welcome and unwelcome things at once | 'tis 4.03.138
i cannot but remember such things were, | that 4.03.222
and none serve with him but constrained things, 5.04. 13
in that, and all things, will we show our duty. HAM 1.02. 40
things rank and gross in nature | possess it 1.02.136
there are more things in heaven and earth, 1.05.166
unless things mortal move them not at all, 2.02.516
compos'd | as made these things more rich. 3.01. 98
accuse me of such things that it were better my 3.01.122 P
to whose /huge spokes ten thousand lesser things 3.03. 19
speaks things in doubt | that carry but half 4.05. 6
all things else | you mainly were stirr'd up. 4.07. 8
things standing thus unknown, shall i leave 5.02.345
unknowing world | how these things came about. 5.02.380
be a maid long, unless things be cut shorter. LR 1.05. 52
all the world shall — i will do such things — 2.04.280
that things might change or cease, /tears /his 3.01. 7
things that love night | love not such nights as 3.02. 42
is strange | and can make vild things precious. 3.02. 71
there is strange things toward, edmund, pray you 3.03. 19 P
leave to ponder | on things would hurt me more. 3.04. 25
belike | some things — i know not what. 4.05. 21
seem | to see the things thou dost not. 4.06.172
and take upon 's the mystery of things | as if 5.03. 16
her, | for i'll refer me to all things of sense, OTH 1.02. 64
these things to hear | would desdemona seriously 1.03.145
and such things else of quality and respect | as 1.03.282
be unworthy of his place that does those things. 2.03.102 P
i remember a mass of things, but nothing 2.03.288 P
though other things grow fair against the sun, 2.03.376
two things are to be done: 2.03.382
for such things in a false disloyal knave | are 3.03.121
as where's that palace whereinto foul things 3.03.137
whereto we see in all things nature tends — 3.03.231
men's natures wrangle with inferior things, 3.04.144
all things shall be well. 4.02.171
is't you, sir, that know things? ANT 1.02. 9 P
things that are past are done with me. 1.02. 97
rare indeed | whom these things cannot blemish), 1.04. 23
i learn you take things ill which are not so — 2.02. 29
for vildest things | become themselves in her, 2.02.237
the ptolomies' pyramises are very goodly things; 2.07. 35 P
but let determin'd things to destiny | hold 3.06. 84
and things outward | do draw the inward quality 3.13. 32
for the things he speaks | may concern caesar. 4.09. 24
shall remember | as things but done by chance. 5.02.120
exactly valued, | not petty things admitted. 5.02.140
things of such dignity | as we greet modern 5.02.166
are misthought | for things that others do; 5.02.177
prize with you | of things that merchants sold. 5.02.184
of him, but had | most pretty things to say. CYM 1.03. 26
those things i bid you do, get them dispatch'd, 1.03. 39
we will have these things set down by lawful 1.04.165 P
since doubting things go ill often hurts more 1.06. 95
thus | draws us a profit from all things we see; 3.03. 18
in simple and low things to prince it much 3.03. 85
fear not, 'tis empty of all things but grief. 3.04. 69
father cowards and base things sire base: 4.02. 26
all solemn things | should answer solemn 4.02.191
rather to wonder at the things you hear | than 5.03. 54
that all th' abhorred things o' th' earth amend 5.05.216
o, sir, things must be as they may; PER 2.01.113 P
and | such things to be, mere monsters. TNK 1.02. 42
she (i sigh and spoke of) were things innocent, 1.03. 60
where, having bound things scatter'd, we will 1.04. 48
look merrily, discourse of many things, but 2.01. 39 P
men are mad things. 2.02.126
i would do things | of such a virtuous greatness 2.02.256
of his gyves | might call fell things to listen, 3.02. 15
there's all things needful — files and shirts 3.03. 48
and unto him i utter learned things | and many 3.05. 14
his body, | and guides his arm to brave things. 4.02.102
how do things fare? 5.04. 45
that we should things desire which do cost us 5.04.110
heavenly charmers, | what things you make of us! 5.04.132
you are the simplest things that ever stood in STM II.C 21
thus will they bear down all things. II.C 40
alas, poor things, what is it you have got, II.C 68
sure these things | not physick'd by respect III 12
things growing to themselves are growth's abuse. VEN 166
if springing things be any jot diminish'd, 417
things out of hope are compass'd oft with 567
in hand with all things, nought at all effecting 912
kings, | imperious supreme of all mortal things. 996
what canst thou boast | of things long since, or 1078
ill we leave to be | the things we are, for that LUC 149
him, | he takes for accidental things of trial; 326
to stamp the seal of time in aged things, | to 941
to feed oblivion with decay of things, | to blot 947
seemed to appear | (like bright things stain'd) 1435
for sportive words and utt'ring foolish things. 1813
strike, | let reason rule things worthy blame, PP 18. 3
and all things rare | that heaven's air in this SON 21. 7
i summon up remembrance of things past, | i sigh 30. 2
but things remov'd that hidden in /thee lie! 31. 8
for all the day they view things unrespected, 43. 2
and so should you, to love things nothing worth. 72.14
for sweetest things turn sourest by their deeds; 94.13
and all things turns to fair that eyes can see! 95.12
truths translated, and for true things deem'd. 96. 8
of the wide world, dreaming on things to come, 107. 2
to make of monsters and things indigest | such 114. 5
strong minds to th' course of alt'ring things: 115. 8
in things of great receipt with ease we prove 136. 7
in things right true my heart and eyes have 137.13
whence hast thou this becoming of things ill, 150. 5
for thou art all, and all things else are thine. LC 266

/THINK 5 FR 0.0005 REL FR 4 V 1 P

/yet /amen, /if /heaven /do /think /him /me. R2 4.01.175
but i /think your grace, | out of the pain you H8 4.02. 7
/yet /i /think /we /are /not /brought /so /low, TIT 3.02. 76
/we /think /not /so, /my /lord. HAM 2.02.248 P
/we /scarcely /think /our /miseries /our /foes. LR 3.06.103

THINK 1102 FR 0.1245 REL FR 760 V 342 P

i do not think thou canst, for then thou wast TMP 1.02. 40
to think o' th' teen that i have turn'd you to, 1.02. 64
sin | to think but nobly of my grandmother. 1.02.119
i think he will carry this island home in his 2.01. 91 P
i do think, a king | (i would, not so!), 3.01. 60
when i shall think or phoebus' steeds are 4.01. 30
may i be bold | to think these spirits? 4.01.120
dost thou think so, spirit? 5.01. 19
i rather think | you have not sought her help, 5.01.141
and scarce think | their eyes do offices of 5.01.155
if i did think, sir, i were well awake, | i'ld 5.01.229
be cheerful | and think of each thing well. 5.01.251
think on thy proteus, when thou, happ'ly, seest TGV 1.01. 12
truly, sir, i think you'll hardly win her. 1.01.133 P
then thus: of many good i think him best. 1.02. 21
i think him so, because i think him so. 1.02. 24
i think him so, because i think him so. 1.02. 24
yet he, of all the rest, i think best loves ye. 1.02. 28
and sent, i think, from proteus. 1.02. 38
i think your lordship is not ignorant | how his 1.03. 25
'twere good, i think, your lordship sent him 1.03. 29
i look on you, i can hardly think you my master. 2.01. 32 P
perchance you think too much of so much pains? 2.01.112
i think crab my dog be the sourest–natur'd dog 2.03. 5 P
you have an exchequer of words and, i think, no 2.04. 44 P
i think 'tis no unwelcome news to you. 2.04. 81
sure, i think she holds them prisoners still. 2.04. 92
if you think so, then stay at home and go not. 2.07. 62
and think my patience, more than thy desert, 3.01.159
unless it be to think that she is by, | and feed 3.01.176
yet i have the wit to think my master is a kind 3.01.264 P
and also, i think, thou art not ignorant | how 3.02. 25
ay, but she'll think that it is spoke in hate. 3.02. 34
she bids me think how i have been forsworn | in 4.02. 10
trust me, i think 'tis almost day. 4.02.137 P

think not i flatter, for i swear i do not — 4.03. 12
but think upon my grief, a lady's grief, | and 4.03. 28
he did, i think verily he had been hang'd for't; 4.04. 14 P
not so; i think she lives. 4.04. 75
to think upon her woes i do protest | that i 4.04.144
i think she doth; 4.04.147
when she did think my master lov'd her well, 4.04.150
i weep myself to think upon thy words. 4.04.175
i think, | if i had such a tire, this face of 4.04.184
and think thee worthy of an empress' love. 5.04.141
what think you of this page, my lord? 5.04.164
i think the boy hath grace in him; he blushes. 5.04.165
ay — i think my cousin meant well. WIV 1.01.257 P
i think there are, sir, i heard them talk'd of. 1.01.288 P
i shall think the worse of fat men, as long as i 2.01. 55 P
i think the best way were to entertain him with 2.01. 66 P
what doth he think of us? 2.01. 83 P
do you think there is truth in them? 2.01.172 P
i do not think the knight would offer it; 2.01.173 P
and, i think, hath appointed them contrary 2.01.208 P
surely i think you have charms, la; 2.02.103 P
must let you understand i think myself in better 2.02.165 P
and what they think in their hearts they may 2.02.307 P
i think you know him: 3.01. 60 P
i think, if your husbands were dead, you two 3.02. 14 P
i think i shall drink in pipe–wine first with 3.02. 89 P
i think my husband hath some special suspicion 3.03.187 P
and bid her think what a man is: 3.05. 50 P
think of that — a man of my kidney. 3.05.114 P
think of that — that am as subject to heat as 3.05.115 P
think of that — hissing–hot — think of that, 3.05.121 P
hissing–hot — think of that, master /brook. 3.05.122 P
i think you have kill'd the poor woman. 4.02.187 P
yea and no, i think the oman is a witch indeed. 4.02.192 P
what think you? 4.02.206 P
he will never, i think, in the way of waste, 4.02.212 P
so think i too. 4.04. 25 P
fault in the semblance of a fowl — think on't, 5.05. 10 P
stag, and the fattest, i think, i' th' forest. 5.05. 13 P
i think the devil will not have me damn'd, lest 5.05. 34 P
but those as sleep and think not on their sins, 5.05. 53
do not fly, i think we have watch'd you now. 5.05.103
sir john, do you think, though we would have 5.05.146 P
i think to repay that money will be a biting 5.05.168 P
if i did not think it had been anne page, would 5.05.186 P
i think so, when i took a boy for a girl. 5.05.190 P
what figure of us think you he will bear? MM 1.01. 16
what think you of it? 1.01. 21
nor do i think the man of safe discretion | that 1.01. 71
for i think thou never wast where grace was said 1.02. 18 P
i think, or in any religion. 1.02. 23 P
i think thou dost; 1.02. 36 P
i think i have done myself wrong, have i not? 1.02. 40 P
not see | we tread upon, and never think of it. 2.01. 26
which, i think, is a very ill house too. 2.01. 66 P
i think no less. 2.01.138
let not your worship think me the poor duke's 2.01.177 P
what do you think of the trade, pompey? 2.01.225 P
what's a' clock, think you? 2.01.276 P
i do think that you might pardon him, | and 2.02. 49
o, think on that, | and mercy then will breathe 2.02. 77
hail to you, provost! so i think you are. 2.03. 1
as i do think, to–morrow. 2.03. 16
when i would pray and think, i think and pray 2.04. 1
think, i think and pray | to several subjects. 2.04. 1
i think it well; 2.04.130
think you i can a resolution fetch | from 3.01. 81
dost thou think, claudio, | if i would yield him 3.01. 96
what should i think? 3.01.139
if you think well to carry this as you may, the 3.01.256 P
what think you of it? 3.01.258 P
do thou but think | what 'tis to cram a maw or 3.02. 21
but where is he, think you? 3.02. 89 P
is it true, think you? 3.02.106 P
if you think it meet, compound with him by the 4.02. 23 P
you will think you have made no offense, if the 4.02.185 P
one would think it were mistress overdone's own 4.03. 2 P
that stabb'd pots, and i think forty more — all 4.03. 18 P
do we jest now, think you? 4.03. 49 P
i should not think it strange, for 'tis a physic 4.06. 7
sir, i think, if you handled her privately, she 5.01.275 P
guiltiness, | to think i can be undiscernible, 5.01.368
which i did think with slower foot came on, 5.01.395
i partly think | a due sincerity governed his 5.01.445
no, sir, i think the meat wants that i have. ERR 2.02. 55 P
or sleep i now and think i hear all this? 2.02.183
i think thou art in mind, and so am i. 2.02.196
own handwriting would tell you what i think. 3.01. 14
i think thou art an ass. 3.01. 15
teach me, dear creature, how to think and speak: 3.02. 33
and in that glorious supposition think | he 3.02. 50
and i think, if my breast had not been made of 3.02.145
'tis time, i think, to trudge, pack, and be gone 3.02.153
what i should think of this, i cannot tell: 3.02.179
but this i think, there's no man is so vain 3.02.180
ah, but i think him better than i say, | and yet 4.02. 25
i think he brings the money. 4.04. 8
and, i think, when he hath lam'd me, i shall beg 4.04. 38 P
speak softly, yonder, as i think, he walks. 5.01. 9
i think i had, i never did deny it. 5.01. 23
by this i think the dial points at five. 5.01.118
from whence, i think, you are come by miracle. 5.01.265
i think you all have drunk of circe's cup. 5.01.271
i think you are all mated, or stark mad. 5.01.282
i think it be, sir, i deny it not. 5.01.379
i think i did, sir, i deny it not. 5.01.381
by dromio, but i think he brought it not. 5.01.383
i think this is your daughter. ADO 1.01.104 P
i would have you think so; 1.01.210 P
do you think i do not know you by your excellent 2.01.121 P
but did you think the prince would have serv'd 2.01.195 P
i told him, and i think i told him true, that 2.01.215 P
lady, i think your blazon to be true, though, 2.01.296 P
i think i told your lordship a year since, how 2.02. 12 P
i think not. 2.03. 23 P
i did never think that lady would have lov'd any 2.03. 93 P
i cannot tell what to think of it but that she 2.03.100 P
i should think this a gull, but that the 2.03.118 P
were it good, think you? 2.03.172 P
i did never think to marry. 2.03.228 P
i did not think i should live till i were 2.03.243 P
sure i think so, | and therefore certainly it 3.01. 56
you may think i love you not; 3.02. 95 P
for my brother, i think he holds you well, and 3.02. 97 P
think you of a worse title, and i will fit her 3.02.110 P
i will not think it. 3.02.118 P
who think you the most desartless man to be 3.03. 9 P
may, but i think they that touch pitch will be 3.03. 56 P
nay, by'r lady, that i think 'a cannot. 3.03. 77 P
by'r lady, i think it be so. 3.03. 83 P
troth, i think your other rebato were better. 3.04. 6 P
i think you would have me say, "saving your 3.04. 31 P
none, i think, and it be the right husband and 3.04. 35 P
you may think perchance that i think you are in 3.04. 81 P
think perchance that i think you are in love. 3.04. 81 P
i am not such a fool to think what i list, nor i 3.04. 82 P
what i list, nor i list not to think what i can, 3.04. 83 P
to think what i can, nor indeed i cannot think, 3.04. 84 P
if i would think my heart out of thinking, that 3.04. 84 P
dead, i think. 4.01.113
for, did i think thou wouldst not quickly die, 4.01.124
think you in your soul the count claudio hath 4.01.328 P
as you hear of me, so think of me. 4.01.334 P
i think he be angry indeed. 5.01.141 P
call beatrice to you, who i think hath legs. 5.02. 24 P
in spite of your heart, i think. 5.02. 68 P
and how long is that, think you? 5.02. 81 P
friar, i must entreat your pains, i think. 5.04. 18
the sight whereof i think you had from me, 5.04. 25
i think he thinks upon the savage bull. 5.04. 43
dost thou think i care for a satire or an 5.04.102 P
i will think nothing to any purpose that the 5.04.105 P
claudio, i did think to have beaten thee, but in 5.04.109 P
think not on him till to–morrow. 5.04.127 P
when i was wont to think no harm all night, LLL 1.01. 44
i think scorn to sigh; 1.02. 63 P
since, but i think now 'tis not to be found; 1.02.112 P
do the wise think them other? 3.01. 80
i know not, but i think it was not he. 4.01. 3
how far dost thou excel | no thought can think, 4.03. 40
i think no less. 5.02. 55
will they not, think you, hang themselves 5.02.270
but this i think, | when they are thirsty, fools 5.02.371
sea–sick, i think, coming from muscovy. 5.02.393
it pleas'd them to think me worthy of pompey the 5.02.505 P
i think hector was not so clean–timber'd. 5.02.638 P
face, | therefore i think i am not in the night, MND 2.01.222
we'll rest us, hermia, if you think it good, 2.02. 37
if you think i come hither as a lion, it were 3.01. 42 P
why should you think that i should woo in scorn? 3.02.122
you speak not as you think. it cannot be. 3.02.191
you perhaps may think, | because she is 3.02.303
and think no more of this night's accidents 4.01. 68
but, as i think — for truly would i speak, 4.01.149
do not you think | the duke was here, and bid us 4.01.194
that you should think, we come not to offend, 5.01.109
by moonshine did these lovers think no scorn 5.01.137
and such a wall, as i would have you think, 5.01.157
my love thou art, my love i think. 5.01.194
think what thou wilt, i am thy lover's grace; 5.01.195
think but this, and all is mended, | that you 5.01.424
but i should think of shallows and of flats, MV 1.01. 26
shall i have the thought | to think on this, and 1.01. 37
antonio | is sad to think upon his merchandise. 1.01. 40
i think he bought his doublet in italy, his 1.02. 74 P
what think you of the scottish lord, his 1.02. 77 P
i think the frenchman became his surety and 1.02. 82 P
it was bassanio — as i think, so was he call'd. 1.02.115 P
i think i may take his bond. 1.03. 26 P
i cannot think you are my son. 2.02. 87 P
i know not what i shall think of that; 2.02. 88 P
i pray thee, good leonardo, think on this: 2.02.169
'twere damnation | to think so base a thought; 2.07. 50
or shall i think in silver she's immur'd, 2.07. 52
i think he only loves the world for him. 2.08. 50
the goodwins, i think they call the place, a 3.01. 4 P
which makes me think that this antonio, | being 3.04. 16
see our husbands | before they think of us. 3.04. 59
that they shall think we are accomplished | with 3.04. 61
a' good cheer, for truly i think you are damn'd. 3.05. 5 P
i think the best grace of wit will shortly turn 3.05. 44 P
shylock, the world thinks, and i think so too, 4.01. 17
i pray you think you question with the jew: 4.01. 70
and i think | the nightingale, if she should 5.01.103
i think you would have begg'd | the ring of me 5.01.221
spirit of my father, which i think is within me, AYL 1.01. 23 P
let me see — what think you of falling in love? 1.02. 25 P
so much | to think my poverty is treacherous. 1.03. 65
for i think you have no money in your purse. 2.04. 13 P
as sure i think did never man love so — | how 2.04. 29
i think of as many matters as he, but i give 2.05. 35 P
i think he be transform'd into a beast, | for i 2.07. 1
brother's mouth | of what we think against thee. 3.01. 12
dost thou think, though i am caparison'd like a 3.02.194 P
when i think, i must speak. 3.02.250 P
i think 'twas made of atalanta's heels. 3.02.276 P
do you think so? 3.04. 21 P
yes, i think he is not a pick–purse nor a 3.04. 22 P
i do think him as concave as a cover'd goblet or 3.04. 23 P
yes, when he is in — but i think he is not in. 3.04. 27 P
life, | i think she means to tangle my eyes too! 3.05. 44
that i shall think it a most plenteous crop | to 3.05.101
think not i love him, though i ask for him; 3.05.109
or i will scarce think you have swam in a 4.01. 37 P
a better jointure, i think, than you make a 4.01. 56 P
or i should think my honesty ranker than my wit. 4.01. 84 P
your hour, i will think you the most pathetical 4.01.191 P
i verily did think | that her old gloves were on 4.03. 25
a body would think this was well counterfeited! 4.03.166 P
a saying, "the fool doth think he is wise, but 5.01. 31 P
by how much i shall think my brother happy in 5.02. 47 P
what think you, if he were convey'd to bed, SHR in.1. 37
believe me, lord, i think he cannot choose. in.1. 42
part | as he shall think by our true diligence in.1. 70
i think 'twas soto that your honor means. in.1. 88
he, | although i think 'twas in another sense — 1.01.215
she would think scolding would do little good 1.02.109 P
think you a little din can daunt mine ears? 1.02.199
and so i pray you all to think yourselves. 2.01.113
i think she'll sooner prove a soldier, | iron 2.01.145
i know you think to dine with me to–day, | and 3.02.185
and think it not the worst of all your fortunes 4.02.105
as thou shalt think on prating whilst thou 4.03.113
sir, the conceit is deeper than you think for: 4.03.161
let's see, i think 'tis now some seven a' clock, 4.03.187
look what i speak, or do, or think to do, | you 4.03.192
i think i shall command your welcome here; 5.01. 12
pray what do you think is his name? 5.01. 80 P
i think thou hast the veriest shrew of all. 5.02. 64
i think it would be the death of the king's AWW 1.01. 22 P
i think not on my father, | and these great 1.01. 79
a bright particular star | and think to wed it, 1.01. 87
think him a great way fool, soly a coward; 1.01.101
and show what we alone must think, which never 1.01.185
remember thee, i will think of thee at court. 1.01.189 P
i especially think, under mars. 1.01.193 P
when he was retrograde, i think rather. 1.01.198 P
why think you so? 1.01.199 P
and i think i shall never have the blessing of 1.03. 24 P
late more near her than i think she wish'd me. 1.03.107 P
my lord your son made me to think of this; 1.03.232
but think you, helen, | if you should tender 1.03.235
but know i think, and think i know most sure, 2.01.157
but know i think, and think i know most sure, 2.01.157
i think, sir, you can eat none of this homely 2.02. 46 P
you were lately whipt, sir, as i think. 2.02. 50 P
'fore god, i think so. 2.03. 45 P
fair one, i think not so. 2.03. 98
i did think thee, for two ordinaries, to be a 2.03.201 P
i think thou wast created for men to breathe 2.03.255 P
strength'ned with what apology you think | may 2.04. 50
i think so. 2.05. 50 P
therefore dare not | say what i think of it, 3.01. 14
think upon patience. 3.02. 48
the rather for i think i know your hostess | as 3.05. 42
you came, i think, from france? 3.05. 46
think you it is so? 3.05. 54
do you think i am so far deceiv'd in him? 3.06. 6 P
if you think your mystery in stratagem can bring 3.06. 65 P
do you think he will make no deed at all of this 3.06. 94 P
he must think us some band of strangers i' th' 4.01. 14 P
and what think you he hath confess'd? 4.03.111 P
i think i have his letter in my pocket. 4.03.200 P
that you would think truth were a fool. 4.03.254 P
than for to think that i would sink it here. 5.03.181
if he does think | he had not my virginity. 5.03.185
i think she has. 5.03.210
i think thee now some common customer. 5.03.286
perchance he is not drown'd — what think you, TN 1.02. 5
fair lady, do you think you have fools in hand? 1.03. 65 P
why, i think so. 1.03. 74 P
never in your life, i think, unless you see 1.03. 82 P
and i think i have the back–trick simply as 1.03.123 P
i did think, by the excellent constitution of 1.03.132 P
i think not so, my lord. 1.04. 29
those wits that think they have thee do very oft 1.05. 33 P
i think his soul is in hell, madonna. 1.05. 68 P
what think you of this fool, malvolio? 1.05. 73 P
one would think his mother's milk were scarce 1.05.161 P
but i think it rather consists of eating and 2.03. 11 P
dost thou think, because thou art virtuous, 2.03.115 P
do not think i have wit enough to lie straight 2.03.136 P
he shall think, by the letters that thou wilt 2.03.164 P
i think it well, my lord. 2.04. 35
what should i think on't? 2.05. 28 P
i think i saw your wisdom there. 3.01. 41 P
for him, i think not on him. 3.01.103
what might you think? 3.01.117
thoughts | that tyrannous heart can think? 3.01.120
that you do think you are not what you are. 3.01.139
if i think so, i think the same of you. 3.01.140
if i think so, i think the same of you. 3.01.140
then think you right: i am not what i am. 3.01.141
i think oxen and wain–ropes cannot hale them 3.02. 59 P
your store | i think is not for idle markets, 3.03. 46
i think we do know the sweet roman hand. 3.04. 28 P
good sir topas, do not think i am mad; 4.02. 29 P
i think nobly of the soul, and no way approve 4.02. 55 P
i would not have you to think that my desire of 5.01. 46 P
i think you set nothing by a bloody coxcomb. 5.01.191 P
think of me as you please. 5.01.309 P
on, | to think me as well a sister as a wife, 5.01.317
i think, this coming summer, the king of sicilia WT 1.01. 5 P
i think there is not in the world either malice 1.01. 33 P
and 'tis pow'rful — think it — | from east, 1.02.202
i think most understand | bohemia stays here 1.02.229
resides not in that man that does not think) 1.02.272
dost think i am so muddy, so unsettled, | to 1.02.325
son | (who i do think is mine and love as mine), 1.02.331
in honor and by him | that i think honorable. 1.02.408
leave me, | and think upon my bidding. 2.03.207
which not to have done i think had been in me 3.02. 67
girls of nine), o, think what they have done, 3.02.182
might be some allay (or i o'erween to think so), 4.02. 8 P
whose simplicity i think it not uneasy to get 4.02. 49 P
blush | to see you so attir'd — sworn, i think, 4.04. 13
even now i tremble | to think your father, by 4.04. 19
and i think they are given | to men of middle 4.04.107
i think you have | as little skill to fear as i 4.04.151
i think so too; 4.04.172
i think there is not half a kiss to choose | who 4.04.175
you would think a smock were a she–angel, he so 4.04.209 P
that have more in them than you'ld think, sister 4.04.216 P
ay, good brother, or go about to think. 4.04.217 P
is it true, think you? 4.04.266 P
is it true too, think you? 4.04.282 P
i cannot speak, nor think, | nor dare to know 4.04.451
i not purpose it. | i think, camillo? 4.04.473
i needs must think it honesty. 4.04.487
i think | you have heard of my poor services, i' 4.04.515
if you may please to think i love the king | and 4.04.521
i think affliction may subdue the cheek, | but 4.04.576
i think you know my fortunes | do all lie there. 4.04.590
(thou must think there's a necessity in't) and 4.04.634 P

think you so, sir? 4.04.771 P
if he think it fit to shore them again, and that 4.04.837 P
and so still think of | the wrong i did myself; 5.01. 8
i think so. 5.01. 16
the most peerless piece of earth, i think, 5.01. 94
you see them not and think me still no gentleman 5.02.131 P
on't, lest your fancy | may think anon it moves. 5.03. 61
transported that | he'll think anon it lives. 5.03. 70
make me to think so twenty years together! 5.03. 71
but then you'll think | (which i protest against 5.03. 89
those that think it is unlawful business | i am 5.03. 96
is well known — and, as i think, one father; JN 1.01. 60
sir, | than was his will to get me, as i think. 1.01.133
will i not think of home, but follow arms. 2.01. 31
i think | his father never was so true begot — 2.01.129
as true as i believe you think them false | that 3.01. 27
and, by my troth, i think thou lov'st me well. 3.03. 55
come, grin on me, and i will think thou smil'st, 3.04. 34
son, | or madly think a babe of clouts were he. 3.04. 58
'tis strange to think how much king john hath 3.04.121
nay, you may think my love was crafty love, 4.01. 53
have possess'd you with, and think them strong; 4.02. 41
think you i bear the shears of destiny? 4.02. 91
what e'er you think, good words, i think, were 4.03. 28
e'er you think, good words, i think, were best. 4.03. 28
sir richard, what think you? 4.03. 41
or have you read, or heard, or could you think? 4.03. 42
or do you almost think, although you see, | that 4.03. 43
by heaven, i think my sword's as sharp as yours. 4.03. 82
that you shall think the devil is come from hell 4.03.100
i did not think the king so stor'd with friends. 5.04. 1
where i may think the remnant of my thoughts 5.04. 46
i did not think to be so sad to-night | as this 5.05. 15
hubert, i think. 5.06. 6
thou mayst befriend me so much as to think | i 5.06. 10
if you think meet, this afternoon will post | to 5.07. 94
and for we think the eagle-winged pride | of R2 1.03.129
think not the king did banish thee, | but thou 1.03.279
which honor and allegiance cannot think. 2.01.208
think what you will, we seize into our hands 2.01.209
as, /though on thinking on no thought i think, 2.02. 31
and though you think that all, as you have done, 3.03. 82
'twill make me think the world is full of rubs, 3.04. 4
what, think you the king shall be deposed? 3.04. 67
soul, | to think our former state a happy dream, 5.01. 18
think i am dead, and that even here thou takest, 5.01. 38
thou shalt think, | though he divide the realm 5.01. 59
he shall think that thou, which knowest the way 5.01. 62
by | think that i am unking'd by bullingbrook, 5.05. 37
what think you, coz, | of this young percy'i 1H4 1.01. 91
redeeming time when men think least i will. 1.02.217
but that i think his father loves him not | and 1.03.231
as what i think might be, but what i know | is 1.03.273
the king will always think him in our debt, 1.03.286
and think we think ourselves unsatisfied, | till 1.03.287
and think we think ourselves unsatisfied, | till 1.03.287
i think this be the most villainous house in all 2.01. 14 P
i think it be two a' clock. 2.01. 33 P
i think you are more beholding to the night than 2.01. 88 P
i shall think the better of myself, and thee, 2.04.273 P
what think you they portend? 2.04.322 P
carriage, and, as i think, his age some fifty, 2.04.424 P
i think it is good morrow, is it not? 2.04.524
indeed, my lord, i think it be two a' clock. 2.04.525
i think there's no man speaks better welsh. 3.01. 49
by that time will our book, i think, be drawn. 3.01.221
do not think so, you shall not find it so, | and 3.02.129
see thy face but i think upon hell-fire and 3.03. 31 P
if i did not think thou hadst been an ignis 3.03. 39 P
why, sir john, what do you think, sir john? 3.03. 54 P
do you think i keep thieves in my house? 3.03. 55 P
dost thou think i'll fear thee as i fear thy 3.03.150 P
nor did he think it meet | to lay so dangerous 4.01. 33
and think how such an apprehension | may turn 4.01. 66
than if the earl were here, for men must think, 4.01. 79
as heart can think. 4.01. 84
that you would think that i had a hundred and 4.02. 33 P
i think, to steal cream indeed, for thy theft 4.02. 60 P
his head, | i do not think a braver gentleman, 5.01. 89
i think thou art enamored | on his follies. 5.02. 69
i did not think thee lord of such a spirit. 5.04. 18
i am the prince of wales, and think not, percy, 5.04. 63
i cannot think, my lord, your son is dead. 2H4 1.01.104
i think you are fall'n into the disease, for you 1.02.118 P
i think we are so /a body strong enough, | even 1.03. 66
i think i am as like to ride the mare, if i have 2.01. 78 P
what wouldst thou think of me if i should weep? 2.02. 52 P
i would think thee a most princely hypocrite. 2.02. 54 P
a blessed fellow to think as every man thinks. 2.02. 57 P
every man would think me an hypocrite indeed. 2.02. 59 P
your most worshipful thought to think so? 2.02. 61 P
the good-year, do you think i would deny her? 2.04.177 P
so, i did not think thou wast within hearing. 2.04.309 P
no, i think thou art not, i think thou art quit 2.04.342 P
thou art not, i think thou art quit for that. 2.04.342 P
the law, for the which i think thou wilt howl. 2.04.345 P
where i think they will talk of mad shallow yet. 3.02. 14 P
come two of sir john falstaff's men, as i think. 3.02. 54 P
master /surecard, as i think? 3.02. 86 P
what think you, sir john? 3.02.102 P
i think it is my lord of westmerland. 4.01. 26
off | that might so much as think you enemies. 4.01.144
i think you are sir john falstaff, and in that 4.03. 16 P
do you think me a swallow, an arrow, or a bullet 4.03. 32 P
i think he's gone to hunt, my lord, at windsor. 4.04. 14
and dead almost, my liege, to think you were, 4.05.156
and hear (i think) the very latest counsel 4.05.182
indeed i think the young king loves you not. 5.02. 9
majesty, | sits not so easy on me as you think. 5.02. 45
you are, i think, assur'd i love you not. 5.02. 64
i did not think master silence had been a man of 5.03. 37 P
by'r lady, i think 'a be, but goodman puff of 5.03. 89 P
think, when we talk of horses, that you see them H5 pr 26
and the hour, i think, is come | to give him 1.01. 92
think you not that the pow'rs we bear with us 2.02. 15
there's not, i think, a subject | that sits in 2.02. 26
comfort him, bid him 'a should not think of god; 2.03. 20 P
but though we think it so, it is no matter. 2.04. 42
think we king harry strong; 2.04. 48
o, do but think | you stand upon the rivage and 3.pr. 13
by cheshu, i think 'a will plow up all, if there 3.02. 63 P
i think it be. 3.02. 69 P
captain macmorris, i think, look you, under your 3.02.120 P
peradventure i shall think you do not use me 3.02.127 P
i think in my very conscience he is as valiant a 3.06. 13 P
my part, i think the duke hath lost never a man, 3.06. 99 P
i think he will eat all he kills. 3.07. 92 P
is it meet, think you, that we should also, look 4.01. 78 P
i think it be; 4.01. 87 P
but i think we shall never see the end of it. 4.01. 90 P
speak it to you, i think the king is but a man, 4.01.101 P
i think he would not wish himself any where but 4.01.119 P
him that escapes, it were not sin to think that, 4.01.183 P
think not upon the fault | my father made in 4.01.293
shall think themselves accurs'd they were not 4.03. 65
i think alexander the great was born in macedon. 4.07. 19 P
i think it is in macedon where alexander is porn 4.07. 22 P
what think you, captain fluellen? 4.07.131 P
do you think i'll be forsworn? 4.08. 12 P
that thou wouldst think i had sold my farm to 5.02.125 P
or shall we think the subtile-witted french 1H6 1.01. 25
i think by some odd gimmors or device | their 1.02. 41
hence, | then will i think upon a recompense. 1.02.116
i think at the north gate, for there stands 1.04. 66
i think this talbot be a fiend of hell. 2.01. 46
to think that you have aught but talbot's shadow 2.03. 46
and think me honored | to feast so great a 2.03. 81
and say withal, i think he held the right. 2.04. 38
think not, although in writing i preferr'd | the 3.01. 10
i think the duke of burgundy will fast | before 3.02. 42
i think her old familiar is asleep. 3.02.122
o, think upon the conquest of my father, | my 4.01.148
i think this upstart is old talbot's ghost, | he 4.07. 87
damsel of france, i think i have you fast: 5.03. 30
i think she knows not well | (there were so many 5.04. 80
but, as i think, it was by th' cardinal), | and 2H6 1.02. 27
it is enough, i'll think upon the questions. 1.02. 82
beldam, i think we watch'd you at an inch. 1.04. 42
ay, my lord cardinal, how think you by that? 2.01. 16
and yet, i think, jet did he never see. 2.01.112
and would ye not think /his cunning to be great, 2.01.130
this news, i think, hath turn'd your weapon's 2.01.176
for i think i have taken my last draught in this 2.03. 73 P
but soft, i think she comes, and i'll prepare 2.04. 15
for whilest i think i am thy married wife | and 2.04. 28
to think upon my pomp shall be my hell. 2.04. 41
i think i should have told your grace's tale. 3.01. 44
what are they that think it? 3.01.107
say as you think, and speak it from your souls: 3.01.247
and think it but a minute spent in sport. 3.02.338
that thou mightst think upon these by the seal, 3.02.344
what, think you much to pay two thousand crowns, 4.01. 18
the nobility think scorn to go in leather aprons 4.02. 12 P
think therefore on revenge and cease to weep. 4.04. 3
i think he hath a very fair warning. 4.06. 10 P
and i think this word "sallet" was born to do me 4.10. 10 P
but thou mistakes me much to think i do. 5.01.130
think you 'twere prejudicial to his crown? 3H6 1.01.144
think not that henry shall be so depos'd. 1.01.153
do but think | how sweet a thing it is to wear a 1.02. 28
think but upon the wrong he did us all, | and 1.04.173
i think it cites us, brother, to the field, 2.01. 34
their power, i think, is thirty thousand strong. 2.01.177
but think you, lords, that clifford fled with 2.06. 37
i think /his understanding is bereft. 2.06. 60
for, as we think, | you are the king king edward 3.01. 68
i think he means to beg a child of her. 3.02. 27
you'ld think it strange if i should marry her. 3.02.111
what think you | of this new marriage with the 4.01. 1
i mind to tell him plainly what i think. 4.01. 8
and montague, | speak freely what you think. 4.01. 28
i hear, yet say not much, but think the more. 4.01. 83
else might i think that clarence, edward's 4.02. 10
had i not reason, think ye, to make haste, | and 5.06. 72
i think there is no man /is secure | but the R3 1.01. 71
i'll tell you what, i think it is our way, | if 1.01. 78
fouler than heart can think thee, thou canst 1.02. 83
which i think proceeds | from wayward sickness 1.03. 28
cannot a plain man live and think no harm, | but 1.03. 51
for i did think | that thou hadst call'd me all 1.03.234
i will not think but they ascend the sky, | and 1.03.286
bid gloucester think /of this, and he will weep. 1.04.239
think you my uncle did dissemble, grandam? 2.02. 31
i cannot think it. hark, what noise is this? 2.02. 33
and so in me, and so (i think) in all. 2.02.134
think you, my lord, this little prating york 3.01.151
i'll send some packing that yet think not on't. 3.02. 61
that think themselves as safe | as thou and i, 3.02. 66
think you, but that i know our state secure, | i 3.02. 81
your grace, we think, should soonest know his 3.04. 9
i think there's never a man in christendom | can 3.04. 51
think you we are turks or infidels? 3.05. 41
i think the duke will not be spoke withal. 3.07. 57
you might haply think | tongue-tied ambition, 3.07.144
think now what i would speak. 4.02. 10
o, let me think on hastings, and be gone | to 4.02.121
mean time, but think how i may do thee good, 4.03. 33
think that thy babes were sweeter than they were 4.04.120
what do you think? 4.04.258
even so. how think you of it? 4.04.267
think how thou stab'st me in my prime of youth 5.03.119
think on the tower and me. 5.03.126
to-morrow in the battle think on me, | and fall 5.03.134
think upon grey, and let thy soul despair! 5.03.141
think upon vaughan, and with guilty fear | let 5.03.142
awake and think our wrongs in richard's bosom 5.03.144
think on lord hastings. 5.03.156
to-morrow in the battle think on me, | and fall 5.03.162
o, in the battle think on buckingham, | and die 5.03.169
i think there be six richmonds in the field; 5.04. 11
here | may (if they think it well) let fall a H8 pr 6
think ye see | the very persons of our noble pr 25
think you see them great, | and follow'd with pr 27
grievingly i think | the peace between the 1.01. 87
to think an english courtier may be wise | and 1.03. 22
they rested, | i think would better please 'em. 1.04. 13
i do not think he fears death. 2.01. 37
and lately, | as all think, for this business. 2.01.161
i think you have hit the mark; 2.01.165
let's think in private more. 2.01.169
he will have all, i think. 2.02. 11
the most convenient place that i can think of 2.02.137
but i pray you, | what think you of a duchess? 2.03. 38
it faints me | to think what follows. 2.03.104
what do you think me? 2.03.107
foe, and think not | at all a friend to truth. 2.04. 83
now i think on't, | they should be good men, 3.01. 21
can you think, lords, | that any englishman dare 3.01. 83
pray think us | those we profess, peacemakers, 3.01.166
i think by this he is. 3.02. 83
if we did think | his contemplation were above 3.02.130
time | to think upon the part of business which 3.02.145
i did not think to shed a tear | in all my 3.02.428
cloaks | (doublets, i think) flew up, and had 4.01. 74
you), i think i have | incens'd the lords o' th' 5.01. 42
for i must think of that which company | would 5.01. 75
i think your highness saw this many a day. 5.02. 21
do you think, my lords, | the king will suffer 5.02.140
and think with wagging of your tongue to win me; 5.02.162
than but once think his place becomes thee not. 5.02.168
the devil was amongst 'em, i think, surely. 5.03. 59 P
and the words i utter | let none think flattery, 5.04. 16
day, no man think | h'as business at his house; 5.04. 74
you, i think helen loves him better than paris. TRO 1.02.107 P
i think his smiling becomes him better than any 1.02.121 P
choose but laugh to think how she tickled his 1.02.135 P
i told you a thing yesterday, think on't. 1.02.171 P
i think he went not forth to-day. 1.02.220 P
and doth think it rich | to hear the wooden 1.03.154
and wake him to the answer, think you? 1.03.332
foul wares, | and think perchance they'll sell; 1.03.359
but i think thy horse will sooner con an oration 2.01. 17 P
dost thou think i have no sense, thou strikest 2.01. 22 P
thou art proclaim'd fool, i think. 2.01. 25 P
we may not think the justness of each act | such 2.02.119
lest perchance he think | we dare not move the 2.03. 81
not sin | if you do say we think him over-proud 2.03.123
do you not think he thinks himself a better man 2.03.144 P
they think my little stomach to the war | and 3.03.220
what think you of this man that takes me for the 3.03.262 P
as heart can think or courage execute. 4.01. 14
you are deceived, i think of no such thing. 4.02. 39
think it an altar, and thy brother troilus | a 4.03. 8
do you think i will? 4.04. 92
the prince must think me tardy and remiss, 4.04.141
yet, and modestly i think | the fall of every 4.05.222
diomed. calchas, i think. where's your daughter? 5.02. 3
think we had mothers, do not give advantage | to 5.02.130
rather think this not cressid. 5.02.133
were curs'd, i cannot tell what to think on't. 5.03.106 P
i think they have swallow'd one another. 5.04. 33 P
but they think we are too dear. COR 1.01. 19 P
yet you must not think to fob off our disgrace 1.01. 94 P
what do you think, | you, the great toe of this 1.01.154
the words — i think | i have the letter here; 1.02. 7
nor did you think it folly | to keep your great 1.02. 19
but, i think, you'll find | th' have not 1.02. 29
in troth, i think she would. 1.03.106 P
i do not think. 1.06. 46
if any think brave death outweighs bad life, 1.06. 71
and wouldst do so, i think, should we encounter 1.10. 9
what i think, i utter, and spend my malice in my 2.01. 53 P
and, i think, there's one at home for you. 2.01.109 P
and make us think | rather our state's defective 2.02. 49
and truly i think if all our wits were to issue 2.03. 21 P
think you so? 2.03. 25 P
you must desire them | to think upon you. 2.03. 56
think upon me? 2.03. 56
you must think, if we give you any thing, we 2.03. 71 P
nature | would think upon you for your voices, 2.03.188
and do you think | that his contempt shall not 2.03.201
i think 'twill serve, if he | can thereto frame 3.02. 96
think | upon the wounds his body bears, which 3.03. 49
your name, i think, is adrian. 4.03. 2 P
and am the man, i think, that shall set them in 4.03. 47 P
i think our fellows are asleep. 4.05. 2 P
dost not | think me for the man i am, necessity 4.05. 56
there was more in him than i could think. 4.05.159 P
i think he is; 4.05.162 P
i think not so. 4.06. 33
sir, i beseech you, think you he'll carry rome? 4.07. 27
i think he'll be to rome | as is the aspray to 4.07. 33
i think he'll hear me. 5.01. 48
think to front his revenges with the easy groans 5.02. 41 P
can you think to blow out the intended fire your 5.02. 45 P
what cause do you think i have to swound? 5.02.100 P
things as you, i can scarce think there's any, 5.02.103 P
delivers us thus chang'd | makes you think so. 5.03. 40
think with thyself | how more unfortunate than 5.03. 96
the last, i think | might have found easy fines; 5.06. 63
dost thou think | i'll grace thee with that 5.06. 87
to thee, | o, think my son to be as dear to me! TIT 1.01.108
and think you not how dangerous | it is to jet 2.01. 63
he that had wit would think that i had none, 2.03. 1
have i not reason, think you, to look pale? 2.03. 91
that woe is me to think upon thy woes, | more 3.01.239
there, | and if ye love me, as i think you do, 3.01.286
i think she means that there were more than one 4.01. 38
i blush to think upon this ignomy. 4.02.115
hither | to use as you think needful of the man. 5.01. 39
that bloody mind i think they learn'd of me, 5.01.101
and yet i think | few come within the compass of 5.01.125
be rul'd by me, forget to think of her. ROM 1.01.225
o, teach me how i should forget to think. 1.01.226
in penalty alike, and 'tis not hard, i think, 1.02. 2
ere we may think her ripe to be a bride. 1.02. 11
and i will make thee think thy swan a crow. 1.02. 87
laugh | to think it should leave crying and say, 1.03. 51
well, think of marriage now; 1.03. 69
marry, that, i think, be young petruchio. 1.05.131
birds would sing and think it were not night. 2.02. 22
therefore thou mayest think my behavior light, 2.02. 99
bold, | think true love acted simple modesty. 3.02. 16
doth not she think me an old murtherer, | now i 3.03. 94

i think she will /be rul'd | in all respects by 3.04. 13
look to't, think on't, i do not use to jest. 3.05.189
i think it best you married with the county. 3.05.217
i think you are happy in this second match, 3.05.222
as you think fit to furnish me to–morrow? 4.02. 35
dream, that gives a dead man leave to think! 5.01. 7
fly hence and leave me, think upon these gone, 5.03. 60
i think | he told me paris should have married 5.03. 77
him talk of juliet, | to think it was so? 5.03. 81
what dost thou think 'tis worth? TIM 1.01.213 P
we should think ourselves for ever perfect. 1.02. 87 P
o you gods, think i, what need we have any 1.02. 95 P
ho, ho! i laugh to think that babe a bastard. 1.02.112 P
i think no usurer but has a fool to his servant; 2.02. 98 P
conscience lack | to think i shall lack friends? 2.02.176
nev'r speak or think | that timon's fortunes 2.02.230
i would i could not think it! 2.02.232
and does he think so backwardly of me now, 3.03. 18
and i cannot think but, in the end, the 3.03. 29 P
and i think | one business does command us all; 3.04. 3
what do you think the hour? 3.04. 8
i cannot think but your age has forgot me, | it 3.05. 92
i think this honorable lord did but try us this 3.06. 2 P
i should think so. 3.06. 9 P
think not on't, sir. 3.06. 44 P
think it a bastard, whom the oracle | hath 4.03.121
think thy slave man rebels, and by thy virtue 4.03.390
then must i think you would not have it so. JC 1.02. 81
what you and other men | think of this life; 1.02. 94
their worships to think it was his infirmity. 1.02.271 P
till then, think of the world. 1.02.307
and therefore think him as a serpent's egg, 2.01. 32
i think we are too bold upon your rest. 2.01. 86
to think that or our cause or our performance 2.01.135
i think he will stand very strong with us. 2.01.142
i think it is not meet, | mark antony, so well 2.01.155
and for mark antony, think not of him; 2.01.181
alas, good cassius, do not think of him. 2.01.185
think you i am no stronger than my sex, | being 2.01.296
think you to walk forth? 2.02. 8
the heart of brutus earns to think upon! 2.02.129
to think that caesar bears such rebel blood 3.01. 40
he'll think your mother chides, and leave you so 4.03.123
i did not think you could have been so angry. 4.03.143
what do you think | of marching to philippi 4.03.196
i do not think it good. 4.03.198
here it is, i think. 4.03.274
i think it is the weakness of mine eyes | that 4.03.276
when think you that the sword goes up again? 5.01. 52
think not, thou noble roman, | that ever brutus 5.01.110
think upon what hath chanc'd; MAC 1.03.153
i think not of them; 2.01. 21
strength, to think | so brain–sickly of things. 2.02. 42
i am afraid to think what i have done; 2.02. 48
his lie, and, i think, being too strong for him, 2.03. 39 P
indeed have died | with them they think on? 3.02. 11
think of this, good peers, | but as a thing of 3.04. 95
when now i think you can behold such sights, 3.04.113
borne all things well, and i do think | that, 3.06. 17
may be rightly just, | what ever i shall think. 4.03. 31
i think our country sinks beneath the yoke: 4.03. 39
i think withal | there would be hands uplifted 4.03. 41
i think, but dare not speak. 5.01. 79
i think i hear them. stand ho! who is there? HAM 1.01. 14
what think you on't? 1.01. 55
i think it be no other but e'en so. 1.01.108
nature | that we with wisest sorrow think on him 1.02. 6
woe, and think of us | as of a father, for, let 1.02.107
yet, within a month — | let me not think on't! 1.02.146
i think it was to /see my mother's wedding. 1.02.178
my lord, i think i saw him yesternight. 1.02.189
and we did think it writ down in our duty | to 1.02.222
think it no more: 1.03. 10
i do not know, my lord, what i should think. 1.03.104
think yourself a baby | that you have ta'en 1.03.105
i think it lacks of twelf. 1.04. 3
think of it. 1.04. 74
say you then, would heart of man once think it? 1.05.121
as i perchance hereafter shall think meet | to 1.05.171
and i do think, or else this brain of mine 2.02. 46
read, | answer, and think upon this business. 2.02. 82
what do you think of me? 2.02.129
but what might you think, | when i had seen this 2.02.131
or my dear majesty your queen here, think, | if 2.02.135
love with idle sight, | what might you think? 2.02.139
do you think /'tis this? 2.02.151
to think, my lord, if you delight not in man, 2.02.315 P
i think their inhibition comes by the means of 2.02.332 P
and, as i think, they have already order | this 3.01. 20
what think you on't? 3.01.175
him where | your wisdom best shall think. 3.01.187
nay, do not think i flatter, | for what 3.02. 56
do you think i meant country matters? 3.02.116 P
i think nothing, my lord. 3.02.117 P
i do believe you think what now you speak, | but 3.02.186
so think thou wilt no second husband wed, | but 3.02.214
do you think i am easier to be play'd on than a 3.02.369 P
indeed would make one think there might be 4.05. 12
choose but weep to think they would lay him i' 4.05. 69 P
you must not think | that we are made of stuff 4.07. 30
be shook with danger | and think it pastime. 4.07. 33
not that i think you did not love your father, 4.07.110
let's further think of this, | weigh what 4.07.148
mine ache to think on't. 5.01. 93 P
i think it be thine indeed, for thou liest in't. 5.01.122 P
whose do you think it was? 5.01.177 P
dost thou think alexander look'd a' this fashion 5.01.197 P
does it not, think thee, stand me now upon — 5.02. 63
i do not think so; 5.02.210 P
thou wouldst not think how ill all's here about 5.02.212 P
i think our father will hence to–night. LR 1.01.284 P
we shall further think of it. 1.01.307 P
respect of that, i would fain think it were not. 1.02. 65 P
think you so? 1.02. 89 P
i think the world's asleep. 1.04. 48 P
be silent when i think your highness wrong'd. 1.04. 65 P
that i'll resume the shape which thou dost think 1.04.309
"thou unpossessing bastard, dost thou think, 2.01. 67

regan, i think /you are; 2.04.129
i know what reason | i have to think so. 2.04.130
i cannot think my sister in the least | would 2.04.141
your passion | must be content to think you old, 2.04.235
you think i'll weep: 2.04.282
way to loyalty, something fears me to think of. 3.05. 3 P
he that will think to live till he be old, 3.07. 69
fellow saw, | which made me think a man a worm. 4.01. 33
edmund, i think, is gone, | in pity of his 4.05. 11
think that the clearest gods, who make them 4.06. 73
you know me not | till time and i think meet. 4.07. 11
i think this lady | to be my child cordelia. 4.07. 68
ay, so i think. 5.03.293
to do you service and you think we are ruffians, OTH 1.01.110 P
are they married, think you? 1.01.167
truly, i think they are. 1.01.168
i think i can discover him, if you please | to 1.01.178
by janus, i think no. 1.02. 33
what is the matter, think you? 1.02. 38
we must not think the turk is so unskillful | to 1.03. 27
i think this tale would win my daughter too. 1.03.171
that you think | i will your serious and great 1.03.266
what else needful your good grace shall think 1.03.286
she that could think, and nev'r disclose her 2.01.156
prating — let not thy discreet heart think it. 2.01.225 P
and i dare think he'll prove to desdemona | a 2.01.290
do not think, gentlemen, i am drunk: 2.03.113 P
you must not think then that i am drunk. 2.03.118 P
good lieutenant, i think you think i love you. 2.03.311 P
good lieutenant, i think you think i love you. 2.03.311 P
i think it freely; 2.03.329 P
and i think the issue will be, i shall have so 2.03.366 P
if you think fit, or that it may be done, | give 3.01. 51
no, sure, i cannot think it, | that he would 3.03. 38
i did not think he had been acquainted with her. 3.03. 99
what dost thou think? 3.03.105
think, my lord? 3.03.105
think, my lord? 3.03.106
i think thou dost; 3.03.117
i dare be sworn i think that he is honest. 3.03.125
i think so too. 3.03.126
why then i think cassio's an honest man. 3.03.129
i do not think but desdemona's honest. 3.03.225
long live she so! and long live you to think so! 3.03.226
i think my wife be honest, and think she is not; 3.03.384
i think my wife be honest, and think she is not; 3.03.384
i think that thou art just, and think thou art 3.03.385
that thou art just, and think thou art not. 3.03.385
it were a tedious difficulty, i think, | to 3.03.397
i think the sun where he was born | drew all 3.04. 30
nay, we must think men are not gods, | nor of 3.04.148
pray heaven it be state matters, as you think, 3.04.155
and think it no addition, nor my wish, | to have 3.04.194
will you think so? 4.01. 1
think so, iago? 4.01. 1
hers, | she may, i think, bestow't on any man. 4.01. 13
think every bearded fellow that's but yok'd 4.01. 66
alas, poor rogue, i think, /i' /faith, she loves 4.01.111
to my wit, do not think it so unwholesome. 4.01.120 P
for, as i think, they do command him home, 4.01.236
if you think other, | remove your thought; 4.02. 13
/by /this /hand, i think it is scurvy, and begin 4.02.193 P
death that you shall think yourself bound to put 4.02.241 P
dost thou in conscience think — tell me, emilia 4.03. 61
/good troth, i think thou wouldst not. 4.03. 70
/by /my troth, i think i should, and undo't when 4.03. 71 P
i do not think there is any such woman. 4.03. 83
but i do think it is their husbands' faults | if 4.03. 86
i think it is. 4.03. 98
i think it doth. 4.03. 99
it makes us, or it mars us, think on that, | and 5.01. 4
i think that one of them is hereabout, | and 5.01. 57
think on thy sins. 5.02. 40
i think she stirs again. 5.02. 95
i think upon't, i think — i smell't — o 5.02.191
i think upon't, i think — i smell't — o 5.02.191
so speaking as i think, alas, i die. 5.02.251
befall'n, | which, as i think, you know not. 5.02.308
you think none but your sheets are privy to your ANT 1.02. 41 P
i do think there is mettle in death, which 1.02.142 P
why should i think you can be mine, and true 1.03. 27
or | /vouchsaf'd to think he had partners. 1.04. 8
i must not think there are | evils enow to 1.04. 10
the borders maritime | lack blood to think on't, 1.04. 52
you think of him too much. 1.05. 6
and think | what venus did with mars. 1.05. 17
think on me, | that am with phoebus' amorous 1.05. 27
i did not think | this amorous surfeiter would 2.01. 32
him, although i think | not mov'd by antony. 2.01. 41
i did not think to draw my sword 'gainst pompey, 2.02.153
them up, | i'll think them every one an antony, 2.05. 14
i did not think, sir, to have met you here. 2.06. 49
at sea, i think. 2.06. 84 P
i think the policy of that purpose made more in 2.06.118 P
i think so too. 2.06.120 P
i think th' art mad. the matter? 2.07. 56
and, though thou think me poor, i am the man 2.07. 64
bards, poets, cannot | think, speak, cast, write 3.02. 17
i think so, charmian: 3.03. 16
and i do think she's thirty. 3.03. 28
by hercules, i think i am i' th' right. 3.07. 67
think, and die. 3.13. 1
caesar must think, | when one so great begins to 4.01. 6
think you there was or might be such a man | as 5.02. 93
you must think this, look you, that the worm 5.02.262 P
you must not think i am so simple but i know the 5.02.272 P
though i think the king | be touch'd at very CYM 1.01. 9
i do not think | so fair an outward and such 1.01. 22
him | how i would think on him at certain hours 1.03. 27
safely, i think; 1.04. 54 P
whom in constancy you think stands so safe. 1.04.126 P
will this hold, think you? 1.04.170 P
she doth think she has | strange ling'ring 1.05. 33
dost thou think in time | she will not quench, 1.05. 46
think what a chance thou changest on, but think 1.05. 68
on, but think | thou hast thy mistress still; 1.05. 68
think on my words. 1.05. 75
think on my words. 1.05. 85

can my sides hold, to think that man, who knows 1.06. 69
if he shall think it fit | a saucy stranger in 1.06.150
not easily, i think. 2.01. 45 P
will force him think i have pick'd the lock and 2.02. 41
to report of you | what i shall think is good? 2.03. 85
i do think | i saw't this morning; 2.03.144
and i think | he'll grant the tribute, send th' 2.04. 12
they think they are mine, and, though train'd up 3.03. 82
to lie in watch there and to think on him? 3.04. 41
and i grieve myself | to think, when thou shalt 3.04. 93
prithee think | there's livers out of britain. 3.04.139
i am most glad | you think of other place. 3.04.141
sir, as i think. 3.05.107 P
and truly, i would think thee an honest man. 3.05.113 P
o jove, i think | foundations fly the wretched: 3.06. 6
now i think on thee, | my hunger's gone; 3.06. 15
victuals, i should think | here were a fairy. 3.06. 40
prithee, fair youth, | think us no churls; 3.06. 64
for thou art a way, | i think, to liberty; 5.04. 4
i think he would change places with his officer; 5.04.174 P
end, i think you'll never return to tell one. 5.04.183 P
so think of your estate. 5.05. 74
augustus lives to think on't; 5.05. 82
think more and more | what's best to ask. 5.05.109
what think you? 5.05.122
but think her bond of chastity quite crack'd, 5.05.207
think that you are upon a rock, and now | throw 5.05.262
call me father | and think they are my sons, are 5.05.329
think death no hazard in this enterprise. PER 1.01. 5
act, | will think me speaking, though i swear to 1.02. 19
and justly too, i think, you fear the tyrant, 1.02.103
you happily may think | are like the troyan 1.04. 92
breath | nothing to think on but ensuing death. 2.01. 7
but what i am, want teaches me to think on: 2.01. 72
what do you think of my daughter, sir? 2.05. 33
i know, | may be (nor can i think the contrary) 2.05. 79
as you think meet. most wretched queen! 3.01. 54
my lord, but think | your grace, that fed my 3.03. 17
our bringing up of poor bastards — as i think, 4.02. 14 P
i think i shall have something to do with you. 4.02. 86 P
i think you'll turn a child again. 4.03. 4
shame | to think of what a noble strain you are, 4.03. 24
king to tharsus — think /his pilot thought, 4.04. 18
then, | and think you now are all in metelin. 4.04. 51
i did not think | thou couldst have spoke so 4.06.102
of heavy pericles think this his bark; 5.ch. 22
no better choice, and think me rarely to wed. 5.01. 69
i do think so. 5.01.101
i think thou saidst | thou hadst been toss'd 5.01.129
it may be | you think me an imposture. 5.01.177
think, dear duke, think | what beds our slain TNK 1.01.139
duke, think | what beds our slain kings have! 1.01.139
lips, what wilt thou think | of rotten kings or 1.01.179
yet i think, | did i not by th' abstaining of my 1.01.188
i think the echoes of his shames have deaf'd 1.02. 80
i think | theseus cannot be umpire to himself, 1.03. 44
i do think they have patience to make any 2.01. 23 P
by my troth, i think fame but stammers 'em, they 2.01. 27 P
me, let me perish | if i think this our prison! 2.02. 62
let's think this prison holy sanctuary | to keep 2.02. 71
i do not think it possible our friendship 2.02.114
i think i should not, madam. 2.02.124
what think you of this beauty? 2.02.153
us, i disclaim | if thou once think upon her! 2.02.174
do you think me | unworthy of her sight? 2.02.191
the schoolmaster, | keep touch, do you think? 2.03. 41
i did not think a week could have restor'd | my 3.06. 5
to delay it longer | would make the world think, 3.06. 11
i shall think either, | well done, a noble 3.06. 23
if you think so, cousin, | you are deceived, for 3.06. 47
thy prison — | think well what that deserves; 3.06.140
i am, and, which is more, dares think her his. 3.06.149
think how you maim your honor | (for now i am 3.06.237
though i think | i never shall enjoy her, yet 3.06.267
nor think he dies with interest in this lady. 3.06.298
i do not think she was very well, for, now | you 4.01. 36
i think you can. 4.01.106
i will, sir, | and truly what i think. 4.02. 73
o my soft–hearted sister, what think you? 4.02.147
a very grievous punishment, as one would think, 4.03. 46 P
what think you of her, sir? 4.03. 58 P
i think she has a perturb'd mind, which i cannot 4.03. 59 P
i did think so too, and would account i had a 4.03. 66 P
think you but thus, | that, were there aught in 5.01. 19
i think so, but i know not thine own will: 5.01.171
why, do you think she is not honest, sir? 5.02. 30
what think you of this horse? 5.02. 55
i think he might be brought to play at tennis. 5.02. 56
do you think he'll have me? 5.02. 92
do you think so too? 5.02. 93
i did think | good palamon would miscarry, yet i 5.03.100
miscarry, yet i knew not | why i did think so. 5.03.102
verily i think so, | a right good creature, more 5.04. 33
what would you think | to be thus us'd? STM II.C 138
more do thou in serpents' natures think them, III 17
be | that thou should think it heavy unto thee? VEN 156
for sharply he did think to reprehend her, 470
others they think delight | in such–like 843
when shall he think to find a stranger just LUC 159
i think the honey guarded with a sting: 493
"think but how vile a spectacle it were | to 631
"they think not but that every eye can see | the 750
to those that live and think no shame of me. 1204
to think their dolor others have endured. 1582
that she might think me some untutor'd youth, PP 1. 3
think women still to strive with men, | to sin 18.43
so lively shown, | made me think upon mine own. 20.18
haply i think on thee, and then my state | (like SON 29.10
but if the while i think on thee, dear friend, 30.13
as soon as think the place where he would be. 44. 8
you, | nor think the bitterness of absence sour, 57. 7
but like a sad slave stay and think of nought 57.11
i think good thoughts whilst other write good 85. 5
no bitterness that i will bitter think, | nor 111.11
in their wills count bad what i think good? 121. 8
than think that we before have heard them told. 123. 8
i think my love as rare | as any she belied with 130.13
and thence this slander, as i think, proceeds. 131.14

think all but one, and me in that one will. 135.14
why should my heart think that a several plot, 137. 9
that she might think me some untutor'd youth, 138. 3
do i not think on thee when i forgot | am of 149. 3
whereon the thought might think sometime it saw LC 10

THINKEST 5 FR 0.0005 REL FR 3 V 2 P
thou thinkest i am in sport. ADO 1.01.177 P
o, thou thinkest | to serve me last that i may R2 3.04. 94
thou thinkest me as far in the devil's book as 2H4 2.02. 45 P
reignier, is't thou that thinkest to beguile me? 1H6 1.02. 65
or if thou thinkest i am too quickly won, | i'll ROM 2.02. 95

/THINKING 1 FR 0.0001 REL FR 0 V 1 P
/good /or /bad, /but /thinking /makes /it /so. HAM 2.02.250 P

THINKING 48 FR 0.0054 REL FR 31 V 17 P
and thinking on it makes me cry "alas!" TGV 4.04. 84
hath he any thinking? WIV 3.02. 31 P
belike, thinking me remiss in mine office, MM 4.02.115 P
she told me, not thinking i had been myself, ADO 2.01.242 P
and bad thinking do not wrest true speaking, 3.04. 33 P
if i would think my heart out of thinking, that 3.04. 85 P
thinking that i mean him, but therein suits AYL 2.07. 81
i can live no longer by thinking. 5.02. 50 P
i was thinking with what manners i might safely AWW 4.05. 88 P
crow, | thinking this voice an armed englishman; JN 5.02.145
his hand | by thinking on the frosty caucasus? R2 1.03.295
snow | by thinking on fantastic summer's heat? 1.03.299
as, /though on thinking on no thought i think, 2.02. 31
next, | thinking his prattle to be tedious, 5.02. 26
coming to look on you, thinking you dead, | and 2H4 4.05.155
desire to see him, thinking of nothing else, 5.05. 25 P
whose music, to my thinking, pleas'd the king. 5.05.108
he was thinking of civil wars when he got me; H5 5.02.225 P
by, | as one that surfeits thinking on a want. 2H6 3.02.348
good | that is too cold in thinking of it now. R3 1.03.311
heart, | thinking on them, go i unto the tower. 3.01.150
but, thinking that | we are a queen (or long H8 2.04. 70
thinking it harder for our mistress to devise TRO 3.02. 78 P
thy master now lies thinking on his bed | of 5.02. 78
thinking upon his services, took from you | th' COR 2.03.223
with pride, ambitious past all thinking, 4.06. 31
still blush, as thinking their own kisses sin; ROM 3.03. 39
not worth my thinking. how now, poet? TIM 1.01.214 P
i am thinking | what i shall say i have provided 5.01. 32
but for all that, to my thinking, he would fain JC 1.02.239 P
but, to my thinking, he was very loath to lay 1.02.241 P
thinking by this face | to fasten in our 5.01. 10
or thinking by our late dear brother's death HAM 1.02. 19
or else shall 'a suffer not thinking on, with 3.02.134 P
of thinking too precisely on th' event — | a 4.04. 41
i am thinking, brother, of a prediction i read LR 1.02.140 P
on, | 'tis probable, and palpable to thinking. OTH 1.02. 76
little in her heart, | and chides with thinking. 2.01.107
probal to thinking, and indeed the course | to 2.03.338
it were enough | to put him to ill thinking. 3.04. 29
the time shall not | outgo my thinking on you. ANT 3.02. 61
goodness the hugeness of your unworthy thinking. CYM 1.04.145 P
thinking to bar thee of succession, as | thou 3.03.102
i am thinking of the poor men that were cast PER 2.01. 18 P
thus vainly thinking that she thinks me young, PP 1. 5
if thinking on me then should make you woe. SON 71. 8
a thousand groans, but thinking on thy face, 131.10
thus vainly thinking that she thinks me young, 138. 5

THINKINGS 3 FR 0.0003 REL FR 3 V 0 P
i am wrapp'd in dismal thinkings. AWW 5.03.128
i am afraid | his thinkings are below the moon, H8 3.02.134
i prithee speak to me as to thy thinkings, | as OTH 3.03.131

THINKS 68 FR 0.0076 REL FR 51 V 17 P
temporal royalties | he thinks me now incapable; TMP 1.02.111
but thurio thinks not so. TGV 3.02. 16
belike she thinks that proteus hath forsook her? 4.04.146
your thief, your true man thinks it big enough; MM 4.02. 44 P
your thief, your true thief thinks it little enough; 4.02. 46 P
who thinks he knows that he ne'er knew my body, 5.01.203
but knows he thinks that he knows isabel's. 5.01.204
one that thinks a man always going to bed and ERR 4.03. 32 P
commence his suit | to her he thinks not worthy, ADO 2.03. 51
hero thinks surely she will die, for she says 2.03.173 P
is the clapper, for what his heart thinks, his 3.02. 13 P
i think he thinks upon the savage bull. 5.04. 43
demetrius thinks not so; MND 1.01.228
that thinks he hath done well in people's eyes, MV 3.02.142
shylock, the world thinks, and i think so too, 4.01. 17
foot can fall, he thinks himself too soon there. AYL 3.02.328 P
that thinks with oaths to face the matter out. SHR 2.01.289
he that is giddy thinks the world turns round. 5.02. 20
"he that is giddy thinks the world turns round": 5.02. 26
i hope your lordship thinks not him a soldier. AWW 2.05. 1 P
ring, and thinks himself made in the unchaste 4.03. 18 P
or whether he thinks it were not possible with 4.03.179 P
which he thinks is a patent for his sauciness, 4.05. 66 P
so cramm'd (as he thinks) with excellencies, TN 2.03.151 P
that little thinks she has been sluic'd in 's WT 1.02.194
he thinks, nay, with all confidence he swears, 1.02.414
a blessed fellow to think as every man thinks. 2H4 2.02. 57 P
i pray you, what thinks he of our estate? H5 4.01. 96 P
thinks thou the fiery fever will go out | with 4.01.253
hath fall'n into the hands of one (as he thinks) 4.04. 61 P
a third thinks, without expense at all, | by 1H6 1.01. 76
speaks suffolk as he thinks? 5.03.141
child | that for the beauty thinks it excellent. 2H6 3.01.230
and not a thought but thinks on dignity. 3.01.338
and thinks he that the chirping of a wren, | by 3.02. 42
but little thinks we shall be of her council. 3H6 1.01. 36
belike he thinks me henry. 4.01. 96
cousin of exeter, what thinks your lordship? 4.08. 34
ape, | he thinks that you should bear me on your R3 3.01.131
my daughter's mother thinks it with her soul. 4.04.257
and, when he thinks, good easy man, full surely H8 3.02.356
no more than what he thinks he is. TRO 2.03.143 P
do you not think he thinks himself a better man 2.03.144 P
for what he has he gives, what thinks he shows, 4.05.101
our state thinks not so; COR 4.03. 17 P
and so he thinks, and is no less apparent | to 4.07. 20
let him that thinks of me so abjectly | know TIT 2.03. 4
he thinks, with jove in heaven, or some where 4.03. 41
and calls herself revenge, and thinks me mad. 5.02.185
being free itself, it thinks all others so. TIM 2.02.233
a lean and hungry look, | he thinks too much; JC 1.02.195
he thinks he still is at his instrument. 4.03.292
that thinks men honest that but seem to be so, OTH 1.03.400
he thinks, being twenty times of better fortune, ANT 4.02. 3
their blood thinks scorn | till it fly out and CYM 4.04. 53
each man | thinks all is writ he /speken can; PER 2.ch. 12
sir, my daughter thinks very well of you, | ay, 2.05. 37
she thinks not so; peruse this writing else. 2.05. 41
be one of those that thinks | the petty wrens of 4.03. 21
she thinks he could not die, he is not dead; VEN 1060
now thinks he that her husband's shallow tongue LUC 78
that thinks she hath beheld some ghastly sprite, 451
but long she thinks till he return again, | and 1359
and both she thinks too long with her remaining. 1572
thus vainly thinking that she thinks me young, PP 1. 5
(though you do any thing) he thinks no ill. SON 57.14
thus vainly thinking that she thinks me young, 138. 5
what largeness thinks in paradise was sawn. LC 91

THINK'ST 47 FR 0.0053 REL FR 37 V 10 P
and think'st it much to tread the ooze | of the TMP 1.02.252
thou think'st there is no more such shapes as he 1.02.479
what think'st thou of the fair sir eglamour? TGV 1.02. 9
what think'st thou of the rich mercatio? 1.02. 12
what think'st thou of the gentle proteus? 1.02. 14
let me have | what thou think'st meet, and is 2.07. 58
think'st thou i am so shallow, so conceitless, 4.02. 96
thou think'st not of this now. 4.04. 34 P
shall i do any good, think'st thou? WIV 1.04.142 P
think'st thou i'll endanger my soul gratis? 2.02. 15 P
is he at master ford's already, think'st thou? 4.01. 2 P
with her that's gone, think'st thou thy oaths, MM 5.01.242
think'st thou i jest? ERR 2.02. 23
what think'st thou? ADO 5.01.117 P
think'st thou, hortensio, though her father be SHR 1.01.123 P
i prithee tell me what thou think'st of me. TN 3.01.138
what think'st thou of his opinion? 4.02. 54 P
think'st thou, for that i insinuate, /that toze WT 4.04.734 P
hound of crete, think'st thou my spouse to get? H5 2.01. 73
card'nal, if thou think'st on heaven's bliss, 2H6 3.03. 27
think'st thou that i will leave my kingly throne 3H6 1.01.124
think'st thou that we fear them? 1.02. 53
if so thou think'st, vex him with eager words. 2.06. 68
what love, think'st thou, i sue so much to get? 3.02. 61
think'st thou i am an executioner? 5.06. 30
what think'st thou? R3 3.01.161
what think'st thou then of stanley? will not he? 3.01.167
what think'st thou — will our friends prove all 5.03.213
what think'st thou, norfolk? 5.03.301
think'st thou to catch my life so pleasantly TRO 4.05.249
think'st thou it honorable for a noble man COR 5.03.154
o, think'st thou we shall ever meet again? ROM 3.05. 51
how shall i thank him, think'st thou? TIM 3.02. 33 P
what, think'st | that the bleak air, thy 4.03.221
and tell me truly what thou think'st of him. JC 1.02.214
i would not be the villain that thou think'st MAC 4.03. 35
think'st thou that duty shall have dread to LR 1.01.147
that justly think'st and hast most rightly said! 1.01.183
thou think'st 'tis much that this contentious 3.04. 6
what will i do, think'st thou? OTH 1.03.303 P
if thou but think'st him wrong'd, and mak'st his 3.03.143
think'st thou i'ld make a life of jealousy? 3.03.177
where think'st thou he is now? ANT 1.05. 19
and what thou think'st his very action speaks 3.12. 35
now, iras, what think'st thou? 5.02.207
proceeded | (unless thou think'st me devilish), CYM 1.05. 16
thou think'st thyself the happier thing to be TNK 3.01. 25

THINK'T 3 FR 0.0003 REL FR 3 V 0 P
only in this disguise i think't no sin | to AWW 4.02. 75
i do not think't. HAM 5.02.295
let's think't unsafe | to come in to the cry OTH 5.01. 43

THINLY 3 FR 0.0003 REL FR 3 V 0 P
and old cakes of roses | were thinly scattered, ROM 5.01. 48
other proofs | that do demonstrate thinly. OTH 3.03.431
like stones of worth they thinly placed are, SON 52. 7

THIRD *(also turd)*

THIRD 70 FR 0.0079 REL FR 47 V 23 P
this | is the third man that e'er i saw; TMP 1.02.446
have given you here a third of mine own life, 4.01. 3
where | every third thought shall be my grave. 5.01.312
"whip him out," says the third. TGV 4.04. 22 P
this is the third time; WIV 5.01. 2 P
men, | a third is fled, that had a hand in it. ADO 5.01.267
the third he caper'd, and cried, "all goes well. LLL 5.02.113
then, for the third part of a minute, hence, MND 2.02. 2
upon the rialto, he hath a third at mexico, a MV 1.03. 20 P
wrought in his behalf) | the third possessor; 1.03. 74
ay, he was the third — 1.03. 74
this third, dull lead, with warning all as blunt 2.07. 8
she wept for the death of a third husband. 3.01. 10 P
a third cannot be match'd, unless the devil 3.01. 77 P
so he serv'd the second, and so the third. AYL 1.02.129 P
the third, the reply churlish; 5.04. 93 P
third, or fourth, or fift borough, i'll answer SHR in.1. 13 P
another bear the ewer, the third a diaper, | and in.1. 57
the second mads him, and a third drowns him. TN 1.05.133 P
for he's in the third degree of drink, he's 1.05.135 P
and let the fool make a third, where he shall 2.03.174 P
and the old saying is, the third pays for all. 5.01. 37 P
the second and the third, nine, and some five; WT 2.01.145
my third comfort | (starr'd most unluckily) is 3.02. 98
and for the third, if he fight longer than he 1H4 1.02.185 P
perforce a third | must take up us. 2H4 1.03. 72
turnbull street, and every third word a lie, 3.02.307 P
your great predecessor, king edward the third. H5 1.02.248
henry lord scroop of masham, and the third, 2.pr. 24
edward the third, he bids you then resign | your 2.04. 93
and the third hour of drowsy morning /name. 4.pr. 16
a third thinks, without expense at all, | by 1H6 1.01. 76
during the time edward the third did reign. 1.02. 31
third son to the third edward, king of england. 2.04. 84
third son to the third edward, king of england. 2.04. 84
of edward king, the third of that descent; 2.05. 66
clarence, third son | to king edward the third; 2.05. 75
clarence, third son | to king edward the third; 2.05. 76
edward the third, my lords, had seven sons: 2H6 2.02. 10
and the third, | lionel duke of clarence; 2.02. 12
the third son, duke of clarence, from whose line 2.02. 34
the fourth son, york claims it from the third; 2.02. 55
there's two of you, the devil make a third, 3.02.303
and thou shalt be the third, /and this sword 3H6 5.01. 75
profan'd, dishonor'd, and the third usurp'd. R3 4.04.367
the third day comes a frost, a killing frost, H8 3.02.355
he comes the third time home with the oaken COR 2.01.124 P
doth more than counterpoise a full third part 5.06. 77
rests, one, two, and the third in your bosom: ROM 2.04. 23 P
and then he offer'd it the third time; JC 1.02.243 P
he put it the third time by; 1.02.243 P
a third is like the former. MAC 4.01.115
and i with them the third night kept the watch, HAM 1.02.208
hit, | or quit in answer of the third exchange, 5.02.269
come, for the third, laertes, you do but dally. 5.02.297
remain this ample third of our fair kingdom, LR 1.01. 80
draw | a third more opulent than your sisters'? 1.01. 86
with my two daughters' dow'rs digest the third; 1.01.128
and did the third a blessing against his will; 1.04.103 P
let him appear by the third sound of the trumpet 5.03.113 P
the third o' th' world is yours, which with a ANT 2.02. 63
'a bears the third part of the world, man; 2.07. 90 P
the third part then is drunk. 2.07. 92
so the poor third is up, till death enlarge his 3.05. 12 P
the third is, that thou wilt be a voluntary mute CYM 3.05.152 P
men, | who of their broken debtors take a third, 5.04. 19
and with the third? PER 2.02. 28
the third, of antioch; 2.02. 28
he said nay, | the third he said it was a hawk, TNK 3.05. 70
a third, nor red nor white, had stol'n of both, SON 99.10

/THIRDBOROUGH 1 FR 0.0001 REL FR 0 V 1 P
i must go fetch the /thirdborough. SHR in.1. 12 P

THIRDLY 2 FR 0.0002 REL FR 0 V 2 P
thirdly, they have verified unjust things; ADO 5.01.218 P
thirdly, i ask thee what's their offense; 5.01.221 P

THIRD'S 3 FR 0.0003 REL FR 3 V 0 P
who after edward the third's death reign'd as 2H6 2.02. 20
to edmund langley, edward the third's fift /son, 2.02. 46
two may keep counsel when the third's away. TIT 4.02.144

THIRDS 2 FR 0.0002 REL FR 1 V 1 P
but /one that lies three thirds and uses a known AWW 2.05. 29 P
yet what man | thirds his own worth (the case is TNK 1.02. 96

THIRST 8 FR 0.0009 REL FR 7 V 1 P
and with saciety seeks to quench his thirst. SHR 1.01. 24
king, my master, whom | i so much thirst to see. WT 4.04.513
dost thou thirst, base troyan, | to have me fold H5 5.01. 19
then be at peace, except ye thirst for blood. 1H6 3.01.117
stifle the villain whose unstanched thirst 3H6 2.06. 83
in hunger for bread, not in thirst for revenge. COR 1.01. 24 P
to all, and him, we thirst, | and all to all. MAC 3.04. 90
more thirst for drink than she for this good VEN 92

THIRSTING 1 FR 0.0001 REL FR 1 V 0 P
the rascal people, thirsting after prey, | join 2H6 4.04. 51

THIRSTS 1 FR 0.0001 REL FR 1 V 0 P
much blood let forth | and more thirsts after. AWW 3.01. 4

THIRSTY 8 FR 0.0009 REL FR 8 V 0 P
a thirsty evil, and when we drink we die. MM 1.02.130
when they are thirsty, fools would fain have LLL 5.02.372
none so dry or thirsty | will deign to sip or SHR 5.02.144
no more the thirsty entrance of this soil 1H4 1.01. 5
brother's blood the thirsty earth hath drunk, 3H6 2.03. 15
my heart is thirsty for that noble pledge. JC 4.03.160
than to be thirsty after tottering honor, | or PER 3.02. 40
whose precious taste her thirsty lips well knew, VEN 543

THIRTEEN 5 FR 0.0005 REL FR 4 V 1 P
from her birth | had numb'red thirteen years. TN 5.01.245
that day that made my sister thirteen years. 5.01.248
lions | as maids of thirteen do of puppy-dogs! JN 2.01.460
in thirteen battles salisbury o'ercame; 1H6 1.04. 78
goes up and down in from fourscore to thirteen, TIM 2.02.113 P

THIRTIES 1 FR 0.0001 REL FR 1 V 0 P
about the world have times twelve thirties been, HAM 3.02.158

THIRTIETH 1 FR 0.0001 REL FR 0 V 1 P
of england ere the thirtieth of may next ensuing 2H6 1.01. 49 P

THIRTY 27 FR 0.0030 REL FR 19 V 8 P
the shore, five and thirty leagues off and on. TMP 3.02. 14 P
ay, and the time seems thirty unto me, | being SHR in.2. 114
(for aught i see) two and thirty, a peep out? 1.02. 33 P
thirty fadom. AWW 4.01. 58 P
of as able body as when he number'd thirty. 4.05. 81 P
full thirty thousand marks of english coin. JN 2.01.530
at supper, how thirty at least he fought with, 1H4 1.02.188 P
with fire any time this two and thirty years, 3.03. 48 P
have thirty miles to ride yet ere dinner-time. 3.03.198
to thirty thousand. 4.01.130
kiss me, and bid me fetch thee thirty shillings? 2H4 2.01.102 P
asia, | which cannot go but thirty mile a day, 2.04.165
upon or near the rate of thirty thousand. 4.01. 22
their power, i think, is thirty thousand strong. 3H6 2.01.177
for with a band of thirty thousand men | comes 2.02. 68
whom thou obey'dst thirty and six years, | and 3.03. 96
the queen is valued thirty thousand strong, 5.03. 14
by'r lady, thirty years. ROM 1.05. 33
his son is thirty. 1.05. 39
till caesar's three and thirty wounds | be well JC 5.01. 53
full thirty times hath phoebus' cart gone round HAM 3.02.155
and thirty dozen moons with borrowed sheen 3.02.157
been sexton here, man and boy, thirty years. 5.01.162 P
some five or six and thirty of his knights, LR 3.07. 16
of thirty sail; OTH 1.03. 37
and i do think she's thirty. ANT 3.03. 28
his age some six and thirty. TNK 4.02.139

THIRTY-ONE 1 FR 0.0001 REL FR 1 V 0 P
days and nights has thirty-one | swelt'red venom MAC 4.01. 7

THIRTY-THREE 1 FR 0.0001 REL FR 1 V 0 P
thirty-three years have i but gone in travail ERR 5.01.401

THIS' 7 FR 0.0008 REL FR 5 V 2 P
this' a good friar, belike! MM 5.01.131
my lord, this' my daughter here asleep, | and MND 4.01.128
why, this' a heavy chance 'twixt him and you, SHR 1.02. 46
marry, this' /miching mallecho, it means HAM 3.02.137 P
this' a good block. LR 4.06.183
this' antioch, then; PER 1.ch. 17
nay, this' a sound fellow i tell you, let's mark STM II.C 89 P

THIS *(also thus, tis)*

/THIS 64 FR 0.0072 REL FR 57 V 7 P

THIS 7074 FR 0.7996 REL FR 5794 V 1280 P

THISBY 31 FR 0.0035 REL FR 14 V 17 P
and most cruel death of pyramus and thisby. MND 1.02. 12 P

flute, you must take thisby on you. 1.02. 44 P
what is thisby? a wand'ring knight? 1.02. 45 P
and i may hide my face, let me play thisby too. 1.02. 51 P
thy thisby dear, and lady dear!" 1.02. 53 P
and, flute, you thisby. 1.02. 56 P
of pyramus and thisby that will never please. 3.01. 10 P
you know, pyramus and thisby meet by moonlight. 3.01. 49 P
for pyramus and thisby (says the story) did talk 3.01. 63 P
that cranny shall pyramus and thisby whisper. 3.01. 71 P
speak, pyramus. thisby, stand forth. 3.01. 81 P
"thisby, the flowers of odious savors sweet" — 3.01. 82
so hath thy breath, my dearest thisby dear. 3.01. 85
"if i were fair, thisby, i were only thine." 3.01.103
anon his thisby must be answered, | and forth my 3.02. 18
in any case, let thisby have clean linen; 4.02. 39 P
scene of young pyramus | and his love thisby; 5.01. 57
this beauteous lady thisby is certain. 5.01.130
the trusty thisby, coming first by night, | did 5.01.140
and thisby, tarrying in mulberry shade, | his 5.01.148
through which the lovers, pyramus and thisby, 5.01.159
no thisby do i see. 5.01.179
thisby! 5.01.194
here comes thisby. 5.01.262 P
well run, thisby. 5.01.266 P
i trust to take of truest thisby sight. 5.01.275
is gone before thisby comes back and finds her 5.01.313 P
which pyramus, which thisby, is the better: 5.01.319 P
thus thisby ends; 5.01.346
a night | did thisby fearfully o'ertrip the dew, MV 5.01. 7
hildings and harlots, thisby a grey eye or so, ROM 2.04. 42 P
THISBY'S 7 FR 0.0008 REL FR 3 V 4 P
robin starveling, you must play thisby's mother. MND 1.02. 60 P
myself, thisby's father; 1.02. 63 P
and finds his trusty thisby's mantle slain; 5.01.145
alack, | i fear my thisby's promise is forgot! 5.01.173
"deceiving me" is thisby's cue. 5.01.185 P
chink, | to spy and i can hear my thisby's face. 5.01.193
pyramus and hang'd himself in thisby's garter, 5.01.359 P
THISNE 2 FR 0.0002 REL FR 0 V 2 P
i'll speak in a monstrous little voice, "thisne! MND 1.02. 52 P
thisne! 1.02. 53 P
THISTLE 2 FR 0.0002 REL FR 0 V 2 P
there thou prick'st her with a thistle. ADO 3.04. 76 P
a red-hipp'd humble-bee on the top of a thistle; MND 4.01. 12 P
THISTLES 1 FR 0.0001 REL FR 1 V 0 P
teems | but hateful docks, rough thistles, H5 5.02. 52
/THITHER 1 FR 0.0001 REL FR 0 V 2 P
/and /dare /scarce /come /thither. HAM 2.02.344 P
THITHER 97 FR 0.0109 REL FR 76 V 21 P
and thither will i bring thee, valentine. TGV 1.01. 55
good, i think, your lordship sent him thither: 1.03. 29
how shall i best convey the ladder thither? 3.01.128
i, their king, that thither them importune, | do 3.01.145
thither provok'd and instigated by his distemper WIV 3.05. 76 P
and let us two devise to bring him thither. 4.04. 27
in this shape when you have brought him thither, 4.04. 45
go say i sent thee thither. MM 3.02. 64 P
thither i must, although against my will, | for ERR 4.01.112
our dinner done, and he not coming thither, | i 5.01.224
come, let us thither, this may prove food to my ADO 1.03. 65 P
sin upon purpose, because they would go thither; 2.01.260 P
i'll bring you thither, my lord, if you'll 3.02. 3 P
i will be welcome then — conduct me thither. LLL 2.01. 96
from the park let us conduct them thither; 4.03.371
majesty | command me any service to her thither? 5.02.312
to have his sight thither and back again. MND 1.01.251
come, you and i will thither presently, | and in MV 4.01.455
remains but that i kindle the boy thither, which AYL 1.01.173 P
we'll lead you thither. 4.03.161
thither will i invite the duke and all 's 5.02. 14 P
unless you will accompany me thither. SHR 1.02.106
there will we mount, and thither walk on foot. 4.03.186
thither must i, and here i leave you, sir. 5.01. 10
in hand at court, | thither we bend again. AWW 3.02. 55
return you thither? 3.02. 72
"i am saint jaques' pilgrim, thither gone. 3.04. 4
thither they send one another. 3.05. 31 P
i fear, the angle that plucks our son thither. WT 4.02. 46 P
to get the cause of my son's resort thither. 4.02. 50 P
me too; let me go thither. 4.04.302
thither with all greediness of affection are 5.02.102 P
shall we thither, and with our company piece the 5.02.107 P
nay, i would have you go before me thither. JN 1.01.155
thither shall it then; 5.07.100
thither will i with you, for little office R2 2.02.137
and, till so much blood thither come again, 3.02. 78
then whither he goes, thither let me go. 5.01. 85
kate, | whither i go, thither shall you go too; 1H4 2.03.115
hal'd thither | by most mechanical and dirty 2H4 5.05. 35
not fail with me, | but thither would i hie." H5 3.02. 17
roam thither then. 1H6 3.01. 51
thither goes these news, as fast as horse can 2H6 1.04. 74
that somerset be sent as regent thither: 3.01.290
and thither i will send you matthew goffe. 4.05. 10
and, somerset, we will commit thee thither, 4.09. 39
/is thither gone to crave the french king's 3H6 3.01. 30
will thither straight, for willingness rids way, 5.03. 21
down to hell, and say i sent thee thither — | i 5.06. 67
let him thank me that holp to send him thither; R3 1.02.107
and thither bear your treasure and your goods. 2.04. 69
factor to buy souls | and send them thither; 4.04. 73
when thou com'st thither — dull unmindful 4.04.445
from tamworth thither is but one day's march. 5.02. 13
where 'twill not extend, | thither he darts it. H8 1.01.112
earl surrey was sent thither, and in haste too, 2.01. 43
as i walk thither, | i'll tell ye more. 4.01.116
for me? | must i go like a traitor thither? 5.02.131
to the sport abroad — are you bound thither? TRO 1.01.115
sir, /he stays for you to conduct him thither. 3.02. 4 P
from agamemnon's tent, | to bring me thither? 4.05.286
by calamity | thither where more attends you, COR 1.01. 76
take these rats thither | to gnaw their garners. 1.01.249
but i cannot go thither. 1.03. 79 P
call thither all the officers a' th' town, 1.05. 27
bring me word thither | how the world goes, that 1.10. 31
single you thither then this dainty doe, | and TIT 2.01.117
go thither, and with unattainted eye | compare ROM 1.02. 85
we'll to dinner thither. 2.04.141 P
i will bring you thither. 3.02.129
or i will drag thee on a hurdle thither. 3.05.155
thee thither in a whirlwind. TIM 4.03.288
thither come, | and let my grave-stone be your 5.01.218
and thither will i straight to visit him; JC 3.02.265
but in a sieve i'll thither sail, | and, like a MAC 1.03. 8
well, i will thither. 2.04. 36
thither he | will come to know his destiny. 3.05. 16
thither macduff | is gone to pray the holy king, 3.06. 29
be't their comfort | we are coming thither. 4.03.189
in heaven, send thither to see; HAM 4.03. 33 P
but to follow him thither with modesty enough 5.01.207 P
certain venetians, and thither comes the bauble, OTH 4.01.134 P
with a harlotry, and thither will i go to him — 4.02.233 P
i had never come from thence, nor you thither. ANT 2.03. 12 P
monument, | his guard have brought him thither. 4.15. 9
thither write, my queen, | and with mine eyes CYM 1.01. 99
read, and tell me | how far 'tis thither. 3.02. 50
a week, why may not i | glide thither in a day? 3.02. 52
pray how far thither? 4.02.292
by this sun that shines, | i'll thither. 4.04. 35
sinful dame | made many princes thither frame PER 1.ch. 32
thither, gentle mariner, | alter thy course for 3.01. 74
my temple stands in ephesus, hie thee thither, 5.01.240
or hang or drown themselves, thither they go — TNK 4.03. 35 P
far from the purpose of his coming thither, | he LUC 113
't may be again, to make me wander thither: PP 14.10
and thither hied, a sad distemper'd guest; SON 153.12
THITHERWARD 1 FR 0.0001 REL FR 1 V 0 P
we met him thitherward, for thence we came; AWW 3.02. 53
THOAS 1 FR 0.0001 REL FR 1 V 0 P
is slain, | amphimachus and thoas deadly hurt, TRO 5.05. 12
/THOMAS 2 FR 0.0002 REL FR 1 V 1 P
/thomas, /son /and /heir /to /th' /earl /of R2 2.01.280
under sir /thomas erpingham. H5 4.01. 94 P
THOMAS 51 FR 0.0057 REL FR 46 V 5 P
what's to do here, thomas tapster? MM 1.02.112 P
against the duke of norfolk, thomas mowbray? R2 1.01. 6
against the duke of norfolk, thomas mowbray? 1.01. 29
now, thomas mowbray, do i turn to thee, | and 1.01. 35
thomas of norfolk, what say'st thou to this? 1.01.110
but thomas, my dear lord, my life, my gloucester 1.02. 16
my name is thomas mowbray, duke of norfolk, 1.03. 16
in lists, on thomas mowbray, duke of norfolk, 1.03. 38
go bear this lance to thomas duke of norfolk. 1.03.103
to prove the duke of norfolk, thomas mowbray, 1.03.107
here standeth thomas mowbray, duke of norfolk, 1.03.110
sir thomas erpingham, sir john ramston, | sir 2.01.283
john, a boy, and page to thomas mowbray, duke of 2H4 3.02. 25 P
thomas wart! 3.02.136 P
is not his brother thomas of clarence with him? 4.04. 16
nothing but well to thee, thomas of clarence. 4.04. 19
loves thee, and thou dost neglect him, thomas. 4.04. 21
learn this, thomas, | and thou shalt prove a 4.04. 41
why art thou not at windsor with him, thomas? 4.04. 50
sir thomas grey, knight, of northumberland, H5 2.pr. 25
of high treason, by the name of thomas grey, 2.02.149 P
good morrow, old sir thomas erpingham. 4.01. 13
lend me thy cloak, sir thomas. 4.01. 24
sir thomas gargrave, and sir william glansdale, 1H6 1.04. 63
sir thomas gargrave, hast thou any life? 1.04. 88
against my master, thomas horner, for saying 2H6 1.03. 26 P
the sixt was thomas of woodstock, duke of 2.02. 16
and with them sir thomas vaughan, prisoners. R3 2.04. 43
sir thomas lovel and lord marquess dorset, 4.04.518
and rice ap thomas, with a valiant crew, | and 4.05. 15
thomas the earl of surrey and himself, | much 5.03. 69
john duke of norfolk, thomas earl of surrey, 5.03.296
the cardinal's and sir thomas lovell's heads H8 1.02.185
what news, sir thomas lovell? 1.03. 16
sir thomas, | whither were you a-going? 1.03. 49
come, good sir thomas, | we shall be late else, 1.03. 64
sir thomas lovell, had the cardinal | but half 1.04. 10
your grace, sir thomas bullen's daughter — 1.04. 92
sir thomas lovell, is the banket ready | i' th' 1.04. 98
sir thomas lovell, i as free forgive you | as i 2.01. 82
that sir thomas more is chosen | lord chancellor 3.02.393
thomas cromwell, | a man in much esteem with th' 4.01.108
good hour of night, sir thomas! 5.01. 5
i did, sir thomas, and left him at primero 5.01. 7
not yet, sir thomas lovell. 5.01. 10
but for the stock, sir thomas, | i wish it 5.01. 22
hear me, sir thomas, y' are a gentleman | of 5.01. 27
'twill not, sir thomas lovell, take't of me — 5.01. 30
yes, yes, sir thomas, | there are that dare, and 5.01. 39
he's a rank weed, sir thomas, | and we must root 5.01. 52
good night, sir thomas. 5.01. 54
THONG 1 FR 0.0001 REL FR 1 V 0 P
throwing the base thong from his bending crest, VEN 395
/THORN 2 FR 0.0002 REL FR 2 V 0 P
is sworn | ne'er to pluck thee from thy /thorn; LLL 4.03.110
sworn | ne'er to pluck thee from thy /thorn, PP 16.12
THORN 11 FR 0.0012 REL FR 11 V 0 P
than that which withering on the virgin thorn MND 1.01. 77
this man, with lantern, dog, and bush of thorn, 5.01.135
this thorn | doth to our rose of youth rightly AWW 1.03.129
shall feel this day as sharp to them as thorn. R2 4.01.323
and plant this thorn, this canker, bullingbrook? 1H4 1.03.176
pluck a red rose from off this thorn with me. 1H6 2.04. 33
hath not thy rose a thorn, plantagenet? 2.04. 69
can so young a thorn begin to prick? 3H6 5.05. 13
rude, too boist'rous, and it pricks like thorn. ROM 1.04. 26
"and whiles against a thorn thou bear'st thy LUC 1135
forlorn, | lean'd her breast up-till a thorn, PP 20.10
THORN-BUSH 2 FR 0.0002 REL FR 0 V 2 P
man i' th' moon, this thorn-bush my thorn-bush, MND 5.01.259 P
this thorn-bush my thorn-bush, and this dog my 5.01.259 P
THORNIER 1 FR 0.0001 REL FR 0 V 1 P
and if she were a thornier piece of ground than PER 4.06.144 P
THORNS 16 FR 0.0018 REL FR 15 V 1 P
briers, sharp furzes, pricking goss, and thorns, TMP 4.01.180
come in with a bush of thorns and a lantern, and MND 3.01. 60 P
for briers and thorns at their apparel snatch; 3.02. 29
you barely leave our thorns to prick ourselves, AWW 4.02. 19
when briers shall have leaves as well as thorns, 4.04. 32
which being spotted | is goads, thorns, nettles, WT 1.02.329
but o, the thorns we stand upon! 4.04.585
among the thorns and dangers of this world. JN 4.03.141
to mow down thorns that would annoy our foot 2H6 3.01. 67
that rents the thorns, and is rent with the 3H6 3.02.175
rents the thorns, and is rent with the thorns, 3.02.175
and to those thorns that in her bosom lodge | to HAM 1.05. 87
i know what thorns the growing rose defends, | i LUC 492
roses have thorns, and silver fountains mud, SON 35. 2
hang on such thorns, and play as wantonly, 54. 7
the roses fearfully on thorns did stand, | /one 99. 8
THORNY 8 FR 0.0009 REL FR 8 V 0 P
thorny hedgehogs, be not seen, | newts and MND 2.02. 10
the thorny point | of bare distress hath ta'en AYL 2.07. 94
or daphne roaming through a thorny wood, SHR in.2. 57
and i — like one lost in a thorny wood, | that 3H6 3.02.174
brave followers, yonder stands the thorny wood, 5.04. 67
but the sharp thorny points | of my alleged H8 2.04.225
show me the steep and thorny way to heaven, HAM 1.03. 48
the thorny brambles and embracing bushes, | as VEN 629
THOROUGH *(also through, etc.)*
THOROUGH 20 FR 0.0022 REL FR 19 V 1 P
sent to her, seeing her go thorough the streets, WIV 4.05. 31 P
the court of his eye, peeping thorough desire: LLL 2.01.235
thorough bush, thorough brier, | over park, over MND 2.01. 3
over dale, | thorough bush, thorough brier, 2.01. 3
thorough flood, thorough fire, | i do wander 2.01. 5
over pale, | thorough flood, thorough fire, | i 2.01. 5
and thorough this distemperature we see | the 2.01.106
a little pin | bores thorough his castle wall, R2 3.02.170
may tear a passage thorough the flinty ribs | of 5.05. 20
with cain go wander thorough shades of night, 5.06. 43
his power to build it, who, half thorough, 2H4 1.03. 59
the false revolting normans thorough thee 2H6 4.01. 87
do never give | but thorough lust and laughter. TIM 4.03.485
become your lips as they pass thorough them. 5.01.195
thorough the hazards of this untrod state | with JC 3.01.136
led in triumph | thorough the streets of rome? 5.01.109
thorough tatter'd clothes /small vices do appear LR 4.06.164
look thorough a casement to allure false hearts, CYM 2.04. 34
it pierc'd me thorough, | and though you call my PER 4.03. 35
to show her bleeding body thorough rome, | and LUC 1851
THOROUGHLY 4 FR 0.0004 REL FR 3 V 1 P
begin his wooing that would thoroughly woo her, SHR 1.01.144 P
again, | to look into this business thoroughly, 2H6 2.01.198
nay, we shall heat you thoroughly anon. 5.01.159
nay, these are almost thoroughly persuaded; COR 1.01.201
/THOSE 10 FR 0.0011 REL FR 9 V 1 P
/still /am /i /king /of /those. R2 4.01.193
/for /those /that /could /speak /low /and 2H4 2.03. 26
/even /by /those /men /that /most /have /done 4.01. 79
/the /vaunt /and /firstlings /of /those /broils, TRO pr 27
all /those his lands | which he stood seiz'd of, HAM 1.01. 88
/clown /shall /make /those /laugh /whose /lungs 2.02.323 P
/that /still /would /manage /those /authorities LR 1.03. 17
/fools /do /those /villains /pity /who /are 4.02. 54
/those /happy /smilets | /that /play'd /on /her 4.03. 19
/by /those /that /feel /their /sharpness. 5.03. 57
THOSE 604 FR 0.0682 REL FR 531 V 73 P
i have suffered | with those that i saw suffer. TMP 1.02. 6
those being all my study, | the government i 1.02. 74
those are pearls that were his eyes: 1.02.399
burnt up those logs that you are enjoin'd to 3.01. 17
then let it lie for those that it concerns. TGV 1.02. 73
those at her father's churlish feet she tender'd 3.01.227
and all those oaths | descended into perjury, to 5.04. 48
i'll be drunk with those that have the fear of WIV 1.01.183 P
those that betray them do no treachery. 5.03. 22
but those as sleep and think not on their sins, 5.05. 53
and what shall become of those in the city? MM 1.02. 97 P
as those cheek-roses | proclaim you are no less! 1.04. 16
as those that feed grow full, as blossoming time 1.04. 41
by those that know the very nerves of state, 1.04. 53
those many had not dar'd to do that evil | if 2.02. 91
for then i pity those i do not know, | which a 2.02.101
dost thou desire her foully for those things 2.02.173
of those that lawless and incertain thought 3.01.126
take, o, take those lips away, | that so sweetly 4.01. 1
and those eyes, the break of day, | lights that 4.01. 3
away with those giglets too, and with the other 5.01.347 P
but, for those earthly faults, i quit them all, 5.01.483
those, for their parents were exceeding poor, ERR 1.01. 56
dispers'd those vapors that offended us, | and 1.01. 89
if i should pay your worship those again, 1.02. 85
not a man of those but he hath the wit to lose 2.02. 84 P
who are those at the gate? 3.01. 48
he broke from those that had the guard of him, 5.01.149
and me they left with those of epidamium. 5.01.354
no faces truer than those that are so wash'd. ADO 1.01. 27 P
will you look to those things i told you of? 2.01.337 P
no more pains for those thanks than you take 2.03.250 P
no more pains for those thanks than you took 2.03.259 P
and bid those that are drunk get them to bed. 3.03. 43 P
or those pamp'red animals | that rage in savage 4.01. 60
in angel whiteness beat away those blushes, 4.01.161
to those that wring under the load of sorrow, 5.01. 28
make those that do offend you suffer too. 5.01. 40
the night, | those that slew thy virgin knight, 5.03. 13
and to keep those statutes | that are recorded LLL 1.01. 17
than those that walk and wot not what they are. 1.01. 91
manner and form following, sir, all those three: 1.01.205 P
all those three i will prove. 3.01. 37 P
for those parts that do fructify in us more than 4.02. 29
the gift is good in those /in whom it is acute, 4.02. 71 P
those thoughts to me were oaks, to thee like 4.02.108
where all those pleasures live that art would 4.02.110
where i will prove those verses to be very 4.02.158 P
to those fresh morning drops upon the rose, | as 4.03. 26
to shine | (those clouds removed) upon our 5.02.206
write "lord have mercy on us" on those three: 5.02.419
that you stand forfeit, being those that sue? 5.02.427
those heavenly eyes, that look into these faults 5.02.769
ever to be true | to those that make us both — 5.02.774
those be rubies, fairy favors, | in those MND 2.01. 12
favors, | in those freckles live their savors. 2.01. 13
those, that hobgoblin call you, and sweet puck, 2.01. 40
are hated most of those they did deceive, | so 2.02.140
and those things do best please me | that befall 3.02.120
ripe in show | thy lips, those kissing cherries, 3.02.140
hath spied him already with those sweet eyes. 5.01.321 P

speak, would almost damn those ears | which, MV 1.01. 98
parti–color'd lambs, and those were jacob's. 1.03. 88
is | as are those dulcet sounds in break of day 3.02. 51
so are those crisped snaky golden locks, | which 3.02. 92
whether those peals of praise be his or no, | so 3.02.145
"nearest his heart," those are the very words. 4.01.254
for those that she makes fair she scarce makes AYL 1.02. 37 P
and those that she makes honest she makes very 1.02. 38 P
away before ever he saw those pancakes or that 1.02. 79 P
those that are good manners at the court are as 3.02. 45 P
cast away my physic but on those that are sick. 3.02.359 P
the sight of lovers feedeth those in love. 3.04. 57
he that speaks them pleases those that hear. 3.05.112
those that are in extremity of either are 4.01. 5 P
as those that fear they hope, and know they fear 5.04. 4
in this forest let us do those ends | that here 5.04.170
for those defects i have before rehears'd, SHR 1.02.124
to instruct her fully in those sciences, 2.01. 57
where are those" — | sit down, kate, and 4.01.141
as those two eyes become that heavenly face? 4.05. 32
and dart not scornful glances from those eyes, 5.02.137
i have those hopes of her good that her AWW 1.01. 39 P
remembrance more | than those i shed for him. 1.01. 81
impossible be strange attempts to those | that 1.01.224
and put you in the catalogue of those | that 1.03.143
my loving greetings | to those of mine in court. 1.03.253
(those bated that inherit but the fall | of the 2.01. 13
those girls of italy, take heed of them. 2.01. 19
most admirable! i have seen those wars. 2.01. 26
as one near death to those that wish him live. 2.01.131
not one of those but had a noble father. 2.03. 62
gift | shall furnish me to those italian fields 2.03.290
those tender limbs of thine to the event | of 3.02.104
officer he is in those suggestions for the young 3.05. 17 P
you give away heaven's vows, and those are mine; 5.03.171
when you, and those poor number saved with you, TN 1.02. 10
and those that are fools, let them use their 1.05. 15 P
those wits that think they have thee do very oft 1.05. 33 P
is to take those things for bird–bolts that you 1.05. 92 P
as to upbraid you with those kindnesses | that i 3.04.351
for i am one of those gentle ones that will use 4.02. 32 P
and all those sayings will i over swear, | and 5.01.269
and all those swearings keep as true in soul 5.01.270
in those unfledg'd days was my wife a girl; WT 1.02. 78
other men have gates, and those gates open'd, 1.02.197
even as bad as those | that vulgars give bold'st 2.01. 93
in those foundations which i build upon, | the 2.01.101
from those you sent to th' oracle are come | an 2.03.194
past all shame | (those of your fact are so), so 3.02. 85
give me those flow'rs there, dorcas. 4.04. 73
you weary those that refresh us. 4.04.335 P
and those that you'll procure from king leontes? 4.04.621
show those things you found about her, those 4.04.696 P
things you found about her, those secret things, 4.04.696 P
but those that are germane to him (though 4.04.773 P
you are one of those | would have him wed again. 5.01. 23
but few, | and those but mean. 5.01. 93
sceptres, | and those that bear them, living. 5.01.147
here come those i have done good to against my 5.02.124 P
and that those veins | did verily bear blood? 5.03. 64
those that think it is unlawful business | i am 5.03. 96
draws those heaven–moving pearls from his poor JN 2.01.169
and but for our approach those sleeping stones, 2.01.216
as many and as well–born bloods as those — 2.01.278
then god forgive the sin of all those souls 2.01.283
our colors do return in those same hands | that 2.01.319
rescue those breathing lives to die in beds, 2.01.419
lewis have blanch, and blanch those provinces? 3.01. 3
and leave those woes alone which i alone | am 3.01. 64
and hang a calve's–skin on those recreant limbs. 3.01.129
o, that a man should speak those words to me! 3.01.130
and hang a calve's–skin on those recreant limbs. 3.01.131
and hang a calve's–skin on those recreant limbs. 3.01.133
i'll send those powers o'er to your majesty. 3.03. 70
bind up those tresses. 3.04. 61
note | in the fair multitude of those her hairs! 3.04. 62
that i have seen inhabit in those cheeks? 4.02.107
under whose conduct came those pow'rs of france 4.02.129
and those thy fears might have wrought fears in 4.02.236
trust not those cunning waters of his eyes, 4.03.107
commend these waters to those baby eyes | that 5.02. 56
he is forsworn if e'er those eyes of yours 5.04. 31
stoop low within those bounds we have o'erlook'd 5.04. 55
but since correction lieth in those hands R2 1.02. 4
some of those seven are dried by nature's course 1.02. 14
some of those branches by the destinies cut; 1.02. 15
and those his golden beams to you here lent 1.03.146
should dying men flatter with those that live? 2.01. 88
no, no, men living flatter those that die. 2.01. 89
of those physicians that first wounded thee. 2.01. 99
we must supplant those rough rug–headed kerns, 2.01.156
and prick my tender patience to those thoughts 2.01.207
is near the hate of those love not the king. 2.02.128
why have those banish'd and forbidden legs 2.03. 90
those whom you curse | have felt the worst of 3.02.138
and told him of those triumphs held at oxford. 5.03. 14
those opposed eyes, | which, like the meteors of 1H4 1.01. 9
to chase these pagans in those holy fields, 1.01. 24
over whose acres walk'd those blessed feet 1.01. 25
by those welshwomen done as may not be | without 1.01. 45
and gadshill shall rob those men that we have 1.02.163 P
those prisoners in your highness' name demanded, 1.03. 23
the lives of those that he did lead to fight 1.03. 82
no more but one tongue for all those wounds, 1.03. 96
those mouthed wounds, which valiantly he took, 1.03. 97
those same noble scots | that are your prisoners 1.03.212
those prisoners you shall keep. 1.03.218
hath butler brought those horses from the 2.03. 67
so, | and those musicians that shall play to you 3.01.223
and even those some | envy your great deservings 4.03. 34
for nothing can seem foul to those that win. 5.01. 8
even those we love | that are misled upon your 5.01.104
fatal to all those | that wear those colors on 5.04. 26
to all those | that wear those colors on them. 5.04. 27
than those proud titles thou hast won of me. 5.04. 79
the shame | of those that turn'd their backs, 2H4 1.01.130
and those that were thy peach–color'd once, or 2.02. 16 P
and god knows whether those that /bawl out the 2.02. 23 P
and those two things i confess i cannot help. 2.02. 68 P
even like those that are kin to the king, for 2.02.111 P
says he, "receive those that are civil, for," 2.04. 89 P
and sung those tunes to the overscutch'd 3.02.316 P
that all their eyes may bear those tokens home 4.02. 64
fall | as those that i am come to tell you of! 4.04. 96
those precepts cannot be serv'd; 5.01. 13 P
that shall convert those tears | by number into 5.02. 60
so will i those that kept me company. 5.05. 59
they of those marches, gracious sovereign, H5 1.02.140
save those to god, that run before our business. 1.02.303
those that were your father's enemies | have 2.02. 29
what see you in those papers that you lose | so 2.02. 72
as gardeners do with ordure hide those roots 2.04. 39
that those whom you call'd fathers did beget you 3.01. 23
and those few i have | almost no better than so 3.06.146
tent to–night, are those stars or suns upon it? 3.07. 70 P
a heavy reckoning to make, when all those legs, 4.01.136 P
he was before guilty of those impieties for the 4.01.175 P
but one ten thousand of those men in england 4.03. 17
and those that leave their valiant bones in 4.03. 98
those waters from me which i would have stopp'd, 4.06. 29
besides, we'll cut the throats of those we have, 4.07. 63
the names of those their nobles that lie dead: 4.08. 91
vouchsafe to those that have not read the story, 5.pr. 1
will to her dispraise those parts in me that you 5.02.200 P
or the loss of those great towns | will make him 1H6 1.01. 63
with those clear rays which she infus'd on me 1.02. 85
and for those wrongs, those bitter injuries, 2.05.124
and for those wrongs, those bitter injuries, 2.05.124
especially for those occasions | at eltam place 3.01.154
and those occasions, uncle, were of force: 3.01.156
strike those that hurt, and hurt not those that 3.03. 53
those that hurt, and hurt not those that help. 3.03. 53
and those two counties i will undertake | your 5.03.158
those provinces these arms of mine did conquer, 2H6 1.01.120
or, if he were not privy to those faults, | yet, 3.01. 47
that all your interest in those territories | is 3.01. 84
if those that care to keep your royal person 3.01.173
will make him say i mov'd him to those arms. 3.01.378
the lives of those which we have lost in fight 4.01. 21
that those which fly before the battle ends 4.02.178
bridge, killing all those that withstand them. 4.05. 3 P
oft have i struck | those that i never saw, and 4.07. 82
and bane to those | that for my surety will 5.01.120
that we are those which chas'd you from the 3H6 1.01. 90
the loss of those three lords torments my heart; 1.01.270
in blood of those that had encount'red him. 1.04. 13
even with those wings | which sometime they have 2.02. 29
and hearten those that fight in your defense. 2.02. 79
her suit is now to repossess those lands, 3.02. 4
those gracious words revive my drooping thoughts 3.03. 21
and all those friends that deign to follow me. 4.07. 39
those will i muster up; 4.08. 11
those powers that the queen | hath rais'd in 5.03. 7
thy very beams will dry those vapors up, | for 5.03. 12
from those that wish the downfall of our house! 5.06. 65
those eyes of thine from mine have drawn salt R3 1.02.153
are daily given to ennoble those | that scarce 1.03. 80
and lay those honors on your high desert. 1.03. 96
of those gross taunts that oft i have endur'd. 1.03.105
my lord of gloucester, in those busy days, 1.03.144
exceeding those that i can wish upon thee, | o, 1.03.217
the lips of those that breathe them in the air. 1.03.285
to cut off those that have offended him. 1.04.219
with hate in those where i expect most love! 2.01. 35
those uncles which you want were dangerous; 3.01. 12
to those whose dealings have deserv'd the place 3.01. 49
and those who have the wit to claim the place. 3.01. 50
this day those enemies are put to death, | and i 3.02.103
and thus i took the vantage of those few: 3.07. 37
those tender babes | whom envy hath immur'd 4.01. 98
tyrrel, i mean those bastards in the tower. 4.02. 75
thou drown the sad remembrance of those wrongs 4.04.252
to ask those on the banks | if they were his 4.04.523
those whom we fight against | had rather have us 5.03.243
and slaughtered those that were the means to 5.03.249
those that can pity, here | may (if they think H8 pr 5
those that come to see | only a show or two, and pr 9
in my chamber when | those suns of glory, those 1.01. 6
those suns of glory, those two lights of men, 1.01. 6
and those of true condition, that your subjects 1.02. 19
wholesome | to those which would not know them, 1.02. 46
leave those remnants | of fool and feather that 1.03. 24
blist'red breeches, and those types of travel, 1.03. 31
but those that sought it i could wish more 2.01. 64
there cannot be those numberless offenses 2.01. 84
by our servants, by those men we lov'd most; 2.01.122
for those you make friends | and give your 2.01.127
and allay those tongues | that durst disperse it 2.01.152
pray think us | those we profess, peacemakers, 3.01.167
those articles, my lord, are in the king's hand: 3.02.299
i had rather want those than my head. 3.02.309
because all those things you have done of late 3.02.338
last, cherish those hearts that hate thee; 3.02.443
of those that claim their offices this day | by 4.01. 15
had i not known those customs | i should have 4.01. 20
those men are happy, and so are all are near her 4.01. 50
were those that went on each side of the queen? 4.01.100
but to those men that sought him, sweet as 4.02. 54
those twins of learning that he rais'd in you, 4.02. 58
and sure those men are happy that shall have 'em 4.02.147
princely care foreseeing those fell mischiefs 5.01. 49
till further trial in those charges | which will 5.01.103
i weigh not, | being of those virtues vacant. 5.01.125
for those that tame wild horses | pace 'em not 5.02. 56
man, those joyful tears show thy true /heart. 5.02.208
and those about her | from her shall read the 5.04. 36
and by those claim their greatness, not by blood 5.04. 38
but those, we fear, | w' have frighted with our ep 3
who were those went by? TRO 1.02. 1
be those with swords? 1.02.209 P
making their way | with those of nobler bulk! 1.03. 37
or those that with the fineness of their souls 1.03.209
may | a stranger to those most imperial looks 1.03.224
that can from hector bring those honors off, 1.03.334
and those biles did run — say so — did not the 2.01. 5 P
thou art bought and sold among those of any wit, 2.01. 46 P
to stand the push and enmity of those | this 2.02.137
nation | to curb those raging appetites that are 2.02.181
curse depending on those that war for a placket. 2.03. 20 P
out of those many regist'red in promise, | which 3.03. 15
but honor for those honors | that are without 3.03. 81
those scraps are good deeds past, which are 3.03.148
those wounds heal ill that men do give 3.03.229
sleep kill those pretty eyes, | and give as soft 4.02. 4
both /at /once, to those | that go or tarry. 5.01. 77
as if those organs /had /deceptious functions, 5.02.123
the policy of those crafty swearing rascals, 5.04. 9 P
hangmen would | bury with those that wore them, COR 1.05. 7
whilst i, with those that have the spirit, will 1.05. 13
friend no less | than those she placeth highest! 1.05. 24
take your choice of those | that best can aid 1.06. 65
those are they | that most are willing. 1.06. 66
do send, dispatch | those centuries to our aid; 1.07. 3
and stand upon my common part with those | that 1.09. 39
be content to bear with those that say you are 2.01. 60 P
and end, but will | lose those he hath won. 2.01.226
ascent is not by such easy degrees as those who, 2.02. 25 P
put our tongues into those wounds and speak for 2.03. 7 P
and tell those friends | they have chose a 2.03.213
words till their decay against those measles 3.01. 78
sir, those cold ways, | that seem like prudent 3.01.219
be in request | with those that have but little. 3.01.251
with old menenius and those senators | that 3.03. 7
those whose great power must try him — even 3.03. 80
worth | as i can of those mysteries which heaven 4.02. 35
spite, | to be full quit of those my banishers, 4.05. 83
and stop those maims | of shame seen through thy 4.05. 86
let me commend thee first to those that shall 4.05.144
as those should do that had deserv'd his hate, 4.06.113
to fail in the disposing of those chances 4.07. 40
i am one of those; 5.01. 29
or those doves' eyes, | which can make gods 5.03. 27
every flaw, | and saving those that eye thee! 5.03. 75
'tis thou, and those, that have dishonored me. TIT 1.01.425
were gracious in those princely eyes of thine, 1.01.429
thrust those reproachful speeches down his 2.01. 55
those sweet ornaments | whose circling shadows 2.04. 18
and he hath cut those pretty fingers off | that 2.04. 42
had the monster seen those lily hands | tremble 2.04. 44
from those bloody hands | throw your mistempered ROM 1.01. 86
and too soon marr'd are those so early made. 1.02. 13
find those persons out | whose names are written 1.02. 35
but i am sent to find those persons whose names 1.02. 42 P
brightness of her cheek would shame those stars, 2.02. 19
than those that have /more coying to be strange. 2.02.101
and if i cannot, i'll find those that shall. 2.04.152 P
and all those twenty could but kill one life. 3.01.179
mercy but murders, pardoning those that kill. 3.01.197
or those eyes /shut, that makes thee answer ay, 3.02. 49
for who is living, if those two are gone? 3.02. 68
take up those cords. 3.02.132
ay, those attires are best, but, gentle nurse, 4.03. 1
matter, get thee gone, | and hire those horses; 5.01. 33
give me those flowers. 5.03. 9
all those which were his fellows but of late — TIM 1.01. 78
letter he desires | to those have shut him up, 1.01. 98
'tis rated | as those which sell would give; 1.01.169
to your free heart, i do return those talents, 1.02. 6
those healths will make thee and thy state look 1.02. 56 P
would all those flatterers were thine enemies 1.02. 81 P
and spend our flatteries to drink those men 1.02.137
i should fear those that dance before me now 1.02.143
to be rememb'red | with those five talents. 2.02.229
like those that under hot ardent zeal would set 3.03. 32 P
which is past depth | to those that, without 3.05. 13
all those, for this? 3.05.108
o thou wall | that girdles in those wolves, dive 4.01. 2
for those milk paps, | that through the 4.03.116
who, without those means thou talk'st of, didst 4.03.313 P
those that would mischief me than those that do! 4.03.468
those that would mischief me than those that do! 4.03.468
for those that were, it is not square to take 5.04. 36
it is not square to take | on those that are, 5.04. 37
spare thy athenian cradle and those kin | which 5.04. 40
wrath must fall | with those that have offended; 5.04. 42
those enemies of timon's and mine own | whom you 5.04. 56
and those our droplets which | from niggard 5.04. 76
but those that understood him smil'd at one JC 1.02.282 P
those that have known the earth so full of 1.03. 45
and those sparks of life | that should be in a 1.03. 57
those that with haste will make a mighty fire 1.03.107
of half that worth as those your swords, made 3.01.155
seeing those beads of sorrow stand in thine, 3.01.284
those that will hear me speak, let 'em stay here 3.02. 5
those that will follow cassius, go with him; 3.02. 6
are those my tents where i perceive the fire? 5.03. 13
whether he was combin'd | with those of norway, MAC 1.03.112
when those that gave the thane of cawdor to me 1.03.119
/are not | those in commission yet return'd? 1.04. 2
against those honors deep and broad wherewith 1.06. 17
for those of old, | and the late dignities 1.06. 18
when we have mark'd with blood those sleepy two 1.07. 75
those of his chamber, as it seem'd, had done't. 2.03.101
those that macbeth hath slain. 2.04. 23
and with those | that would make good of bad, 2.04. 40
attend those men | our pleasure? 3.01. 44
using those thoughts which should indeed have 3.02. 10
our graves must send | those that we bury back, 3.04. 71
which is nothing | to those that know me. 3.04. 86
thou hast no speculation in those eyes | which 3.04. 94
ride, | and damn'd all those that trust them! 4.01.139
those precious motives, those strong knots of 4.03. 27
precious motives, those strong knots of love, 4.03. 27
yet i have known those which have walk'd in 5.01. 60 P
those he commands move only in command, 5.02. 19
those linen cheeks of thine | are counsellors to 5.03. 16
country round, | hang those that talk of fear. 5.03. 36
they not forc'd with those that should be ours, 5.05. 5
throw down, | and show like those you are. 5.06. 2
those clamorous harbingers of blood and death. 5.06. 10
those foresaid lands | so by his father lost; HAM 1.01.103
importing the surrender of those lands | lost by 1.02. 23

or ere those shoes were old | with which she 1.02.147
those friends thou hast, and their adoption 1.03. 62
natural gifts were poor | to those of mine! 1.05. 52
and to those thorns that in her bosom lodge | to 1.05. 87
and his commission to employ those soldiers, 2.02. 74
even those you were wont to take such delight in 2.02.327 P
and those that would make mouths at him while my 2.02.364 P
and makes us rather bear those ills we have, 3.01. 80
those that are married already (all but one) 3.01.148 P
and let those that play your clowns speak no 3.02. 38 P
and blest are those | whose blood and judgment 3.02. 68
fear it is | to keep those many many bodies safe 3.03. 9
of those effects for which i did the murther: 3.03. 54
nay, then i'll set those to you that can speak. 3.04. 17
we'll put on those shall praise your excellence, 4.07.131
it does well to those that do ill. 5.01. 47 P
here hung those lips that i have kiss'd i know 5.01.188 P
he should those bearers put to sudden death, 5.02. 46
i | return those duties back as are right fit, LR 1.01. 97
nor are those empty–hearted whose low sounds 1.01.153
will you, with those infirmities she owes, 1.01.202
on those contents | they summon'd up their meiny 2.04. 34
for those that mingle reason with your passion 2.04.234
from those that she calls servants or from mine? 2.04.244
those wicked creatures yet do look well–favor'd 2.04.256
this flesh begot | those pelican daughters. 3.04. 75
these weeds are memories of those worser hours; 4.07. 7
repair those violent harms that my two sisters 4.07. 27
you are one of those that will not serve god, if OTH 1.01.108 P
those are the raised father and his friends. 1.02. 29
and hath all those requisites in him that folly 2.01.246 P
be unworthy of his place that does those things. 2.03.102 P
those legs that brought me to a part of it. 2.03.187
as men in rage strike those that wish them best, 2.03.243
town, | and silence those whom this vild brawl 2.03.256
or those that be not, would they might seem none 3.03.127
and have not those soft parts of conversation 3.03.264
alive | that nightly lie in those unproper beds 4.01. 68
those that do teach young babes | do it with 4.02.111
i have laid those sheets you bade me on the bed. 4.03. 22
/forth of my heart those charms, thine eyes, are 5.01. 35
those his goodly eyes, | that o'er the files and ANT 1.01. 2
to be entangled with those mouth–made vows, 1.03. 30
and it appears he is belov'd of those | that 1.04. 37
for he would shine on those | that make their 1.05. 55
could not with graceful eyes attend those wars 2.02. 60
with the touches of those flower–soft hands, 2.02.210
his ministers | of us and those that love you. 3.06. 89
are those that often have 'gainst pompey fought; 3.07. 37
of those that serv'd mark antony but late, 4.01. 13
'tis one of those odd tricks which sorrow shoots 4.02. 14
grace grow where those drops fall, my hearty 4.02. 38
would thou and those thy scars had once 4.05. 2
plant those that have revolted in the vant, 4.06. 8
and with those hands, that grasp'd the heaviest 4.12. 46
in feeding them with those my former fortunes 4.15. 53
those that do die of it do seldom or never 5.02.247 P
events as these | strike those that make them; 5.02.361
those things i bid you do, get them dispatch'd, CYM 1.03. 39
ay, and the approbation of those that weep this 1.04. 19 P
yet the dew's on ground, gather those flowers; 1.05. 1
master doctor, have you brought those drugs? 1.05. 4
those she has | will stupefy and dull the sense 1.05. 36
of grief, and those repeated | vexations of it! 1.06. 4
blessed be those, | how mean soe'er, that have 1.06. 7
his steeds to water at those springs | on 2.03. 22
you were inspir'd to do those duties which | you 2.03. 50
though those that are betray'd | do feel the 3.04. 85
undergo those employments wherein i should have 3.05.110 P
be those the garments? 3.05.146 P
reckon'd, but of those | who worship dirty gods. 3.06. 54
with those legions | which i have spoke of, 3.07. 12
i cannot find those runagates, that villain 4.02. 62
those runagates? 4.02. 63
he made those clothes, | which, as it seems, 4.02. 82
those that i reverence, those i fear — the wise 4.02. 95
those that i reverence, those i fear — the wise 4.02. 95
i'll follow those that even now fled hence, 4.02. 98
time hath nothing blurr'd those lines of favor 4.02.104
those rich–left heirs that let their fathers lie 4.02.226
that we the horrider may seem to those | which 4.02.331
the want is but to put those pow'rs in motion 4.03. 31
fairer | than those for preservation cas'd, or 5.03. 22
made good the passage, cried to those that fled, 5.03. 23
those that would die or e'er resist are grown 5.03. 50
or at least | those which i heav'd to head! 5.05.157
those arts they have as i | could put into them. 5.05.338
if you, born in those latter times, | when wit's PER 1.ch. 11
and by those fearful objects to prepare | this 1.01. 43
for wisdom sees those men | blush not in actions 1.01.134
those palates who, not yet /two /summers younger 1.04. 39
those mothers who, to nousle up their babes, 1.04. 42
to eat those little darlings whom they lov'd. 1.04. 44
yet those which see them fall | have scarce 1.04. 48
let those cities that of plenty's cup | and her 1.04. 52
i'll show you those in troubles reign, | losing 2.ch. 7
in those that practice them they are, my lord. 2.03.104
heaven came and shrivell'd up | those bodies, 2.04. 10
that all those eyes ador'd them ere their fall 2.04. 11
/midwife gentle | to those that cry by night, 3.01. 12
cases to those heavenly jewels | which pericles 3.02. 98
be one of those that thinks | the petty wrens of 4.03. 21
those that with cords, knives, drams, TNK 1.01.142
those best affections that the heavens infuse 1.03. 9
but those we will depute which shall invest 1.04. 10
what are those? 1.04. 13
'tis right — those, those. | they are not dead? 1.04. 23
'tis right — those, those. | they are not dead? 1.04. 23
never more | must we behold those comforts, 2.02. 9
and deck the temples of those gods that hate us; 2.02. 23
palamon, | those hopes are prisoners with us. 2.02. 26
and all those pleasures | that woo the wills of 2.02.100
shall be led | to those that love eternally. 2.02.117
first with mine eye of all those beauties in her 2.02.168
am not i liable to those affections, | those 2.02.187
those joys, griefs, angers, fears, my friend 2.02.188
and to those gentle uses gave me life. 2.05. 7
we are a few of those collected here | that 3.05.103
those are o' th' least; 3.06. 64
a place prepar'd for those that sleep in honor, 3.06. 99
or the sweet compassion | of those two ladies; 4.01. 12
yet i may bind those wounds up, that must open 4.02. 1
all those beauties | she sows into the births of 4.02. 8
their swelling incense | to those above us. 5.01. 5
i am | to those that prate and have done, no 5.01.119
to those that boast and have not, a defier; 5.01.120
to those that would and cannot, a rejoicer. 5.01.121
those that remain with you could wish their 5.03. 35
those darker humors that | stick misbecomingly 5.03. 53
you | to lead those that the dev'l cannot rule. STM II.C 56
and those same hands | that you like rebels lift II.C 108
but my lips with those fair lips of thine — VEN 115
graze on my lips, and if those hills be dry, 233
love made those hollows, if himself were slain, 243
as those poor birds that helpless berries saw. 604
of those fair arms which bound him to her breast 812
those eyes that taught all other eyes to see? 952
his all too timeless speed, if none of those. LUC 44
to those two armies that would let him go, 76
those that much covet are with gain so fond, 134
or as those bars which stop the hourly dial, 327
for those thine eyes betray thee unto mine. 483
to those that live and think no shame of me. 1204
of those fair suns set in her mistress' sky, 1230
those proud lords to blame | make weak–made 1259
"on what occasion break | those tears from thee, 1271
that one might see those far–off eyes look sad. 1386
the spring that those shrunk pipes had fed, 1455
the painter was no god to lend her those, | and 1461
to see those borrowed tears that sinon sheeds! 1549
those round clear pearls of his, that move thy 1553
foretell new storms to those already spent; 1589
(speaking to those that came with collatine), 1689
those thoughts to me like oaks, to thee like PP 5. 4
where all those pleasures live that art can 5. 6
the boy he should not pass those grounds. 9. 8
to this urn let those repair | that are either PHT 65
and being frank she lends to those are free: SON 4. 4
those hours that with gentle work did frame 5. 1
which happies those that pay the willing loan; 6. 6
let those whom nature hath not made for store, 11. 9
as those gold candles fix'd in heaven's air: 21.12
let those who are in favor with their stars | of 25. 1
and all those friends which i thought buried. 31. 4
but those tears are pearl which thy love sheeds, 34.13
so shall those blots that do with me remain, 36. 3
than those old nine which rhymers invocate, 38.10
those pretty wrongs that liberty commits | when 41. 1
by those swift messengers return'd from thee, 45.10
save where you are how happy you make those. 57.12
and all those beauties whereof now he's king 63. 6
in him those holy antique hours are seen, 68. 9
those parts of thee that the world's eye doth 69. 1
but those same tongues that give thee so thine 69. 6
upon those boughs which shake against the cold, 73. 3
and thou shalt find | those children nurs'd, 77.11
what a mansion have those vices got | which for 95. 9
so are those errors that in thee are seen | to 96. 7
drawn after you, you pattern of all those. 98.12
those lines that i before have writ do lie, 115. 1
even those that said i could not love you dearer 115. 2
to trust those tables that receive thee more: 122.12
do i envy those jacks that nimble leap | to kiss 128. 5
state | and situation with those dancing chips, 128.10
as those whose beauties proudly make them cruel; 131. 2
as those two /mourning eyes become thy face. 132. 9
or, if it do, not from those lips of thine, 142. 5
be it lawful i love thee as thou lov'st those 142. 9
those lips that love's own hand did make 145. 1
those that can see thou lov'st, and i am blind. 149.14
how coldly those impediments stand forth | of LC 269

THOU *(also ta, th'*)*

/THOU 55 FR 0.0062 REL FR 50 V 5 P

THOU 5800 FR 0.6556 REL FR 4550 V 1250 P

THOU'DST 11 FR 0.0012 REL FR 9 V 2 P

hast no faith left now, unless thou'dst two, TGV 5.04. 50
thou'dst thank me but a little for my counsel; SHR 1.02. 61
would thou'dst be rul'd by me! TN 4.01. 64
and thou shouldst, thou'dst anger ladies. TIM 1.01.205 P
thou'dst courtier be again, | wert thou not 4.03.241
poor bird, thou'dst never fear the net nor lime, MAC 4.02. 34
for that question, thou'dst well deserv'd it. LR 2.04. 65 P
thou'dst shun a bear, | but if /thy flight lay 3.04. 9
sea, | thou'dst meet the bear i' th' mouth. 3.04. 11
precipitating), | thou'dst shiver'd like an egg: 4.06. 51
o /heaven, that such companions thou'dst unfold, OTH 4.02.141

/THOUGH 5 FR 0.0005 REL FR 5 V 0 P

/though all the world's vastidity you had, | to MM 3.01. 68
as, /though on thinking on no thought i think, R2 2.02. 31
/cares /i /give /i /have, /though /given /away, 4.01.198
/though /some /of /you, /with /pilate, /wash 4.01.239
/of /this | (/though /strongly /apprehended) 2H4 1.01.176

THOUGH 687 FR 0.0776 REL FR 529 V 158 P

though the ship were no stronger than a nutshell TMP 1.01. 46 P
though every drop of water swear against it, 1.01. 59
but thy vild race | (though thou didst learn) 1.02.359
though this island seem to be desert — 2.01. 35 P
all were sea–swallow'd, though some cast again, 2.01.251
though thou canst swim like a duck, thou art 2.02.131 P
did lie, | though fools at home condemn 'em. 3.03. 27
who, though they are of monstrous shape, yet, 3.03. 31
my bottle, though i be o'er ears for my labor. 4.01.213 P
though with their high wrongs i am strook to th' 5.01. 25
by whose aid | (weak masters though ye be) i 5.01. 41
i do forgive thee, | unnatural though thou art. 5.01. 79
though the seas threaten, they are merciful, | i 5.01.178
though the chameleon love can feed on the air, i TGV 2.01.172 P
and though myself have been an idle truant, 2.04. 64
i care not, though he burn himself in love. 2.05. 52 P
though ne'er so black, say they have angels' 3.01.103
thy letters may be here, though thou art hence, 3.01.250
as thou lov'st silvia (though not for thyself) 3.01.257
though his false finger have profan'd the ring, 4.04.136
(though you respect not aught your servant doth) 5.04. 20
for though i cannot remember what i did when you WIV 1.01.171 P
in his country, simple though i stand here. 1.01.219 P
but what though? 1.01.275 P
i thank you as much as though i did. 1.01.280 P
for though love use reason for his precisian, he 2.01. 4 P
though the priest o' th' town commended him for 2.01.144 P
though page be a secure fool, and stands so 2.01.233 P
though i had never so good means as desire to 2.02.182 P
some say that, though she appear honest to me, 2.02.221 P
been a great fighter, though now a man of peace. 2.03. 43 P
page, though i now be old and of the peace, if i 2.03. 44 P
though we are justices and doctors and churchmen 2.03. 46 P
though what i am i cannot avoid, yet to be what 3.05.149 P
that slender, though well landed, is an idiot; 4.04. 86
though twenty thousand worthier come to crave 4.04. 90
though we would have thrust virtue out of our 5.05.146 P
though you have ta'en a special stand to strike 5.05.234 P
though first in question, is thy secondary. MM 1.01. 46
though it do well, i do not relish well | their 1.01. 69
though you change your place, you need not 1.02.107 P
though 'tis my familiar sin | with maids to seem 1.04. 31
their names | by vain though apt affection. 1.04. 48
law hath not been dead, though it hath slept. 2.02. 90
because authority, though it err like others, 2.02.134
though he hath fall'n by prompture of the blood, 2.04.178
beggar, though she smelt brown bread and garlic. 3.02.183 P
though my chance is now | to use it for my time. 3.02.217
him hide, | though angel on the outward side! 3.02.272
though music oft hath such a charm | to make bad 4.01. 14
being a murtherer, though he were my brother. 4.02. 62
though sometimes you do blench from this to that 4.05. 5
though they would swear down each particular 5.01.243
which, though thou wouldst deny, denies thee 5.01.413
which though myself would gladly have embrac'd, ERR 1.01. 69
so, | for we may pity, though not pardon thee. 1.01. 97
but, though thou art adjudged to the death, 1.01.146
no marvel though she pause — | they can be meek 2.01. 32
but though my cates be mean, take them in good 3.01. 28
a fair presence, though your heart be tainted; 3.02. 13
though others have the arm, show us the sleeve: 3.02. 23
and true he swore, though yet forsworn he were. 4.02. 10
my tongue, though not my heart, shall have his 4.02. 18
heart prays for him, though my tongue do curse. 4.02. 28
me, | though most dishonestly he doth deny it. 5.01. 3
though now this grained face of mine be hid | in 5.01.312
trust myself, though i had sworn the contrary, ADO 1.01.195 P
this (though i cannot be said to be a flattering 1.03. 30 P
it is the base (though bitter) disposition of 2.01.207 P
though she were endow'd with all that adam had 2.01.251 P
i think your blazon to be true, though, i'll be 2.01.297 P
you, though it cost me ten nights' watchings. 2.01.371 P
writ to me, yea, though i love him, i should." 2.03.144 P
man in the city, and though i be but a poor man, 3.05. 26 P
no, though he thought his accusation true. 4.01.233
and though you know my inwardness and love | is 4.01.245
i am gone, though i am here; 4.01.293 P
though it be not written down, yet forget not 4.02. 77 P
so, though very many have been beside their wit. 5.01.127 P
what though care kill'd a cat, thou hast mettle 5.01.132 P
the mind shall banquet, though the body pine; LLL 1.01. 25
and though i have for barbarism spoke more 1.01.112
good lord boyet, my beauty, though but mean, 2.01. 13
and shape to win grace though he had no wit. 2.01. 60
though so denied fair harbor in my house. 2.01.174
my lips are no common, though several they be. 2.01.223
though argus were her eunuch and her guard. 3.01.199
a giving hand, though foul, shall have fair 4.01. 23
though to myself forsworn, to thee i'll faithful 4.02.107
gracious, though few have the grace to do it. 5.01.140 P
leap for joy, though they are lame with blows: 5.02.291
a world of torments though i should endure, | i 5.02.353
though my mocks come home by me, i will now be 5.02.634 P
and though the mourning brow of progeny | forbid 5.02.744
stay, though thou kill me, sweet demetrius. MND 2.02. 84
therefore no marvel though demetrius | do, as a 2.02. 96
what though he love your hermia? 2.02.109
lord, what though? 2.02.109
a bird the lie, though he cry "cuckoo" never so? 3.01.135 P
you for it, | though i alone do feel the injury. 3.02.219
what though i be not so in grace as you, | so 3.02.232
i pray you, though you mock me, /gentlemen, 3.02.299
she shall not, though you take her part. 3.02.322
and though she be but little, she is fierce. 3.02.325
my legs are longer though, to run away. 3.02.343
though nestor swear the jest be laughable. MV 1.01. 56
his father, though i say't, is an honest 2.02. 52 P
old man, and, though i say it, though old man, 2.02.139 P
though i say it, though old man, yet poor man, 2.02.139 P
but though i am a daughter to his blood, | i am 2.03. 18
and so, though yours, not yours. 3.02. 20
though for myself alone | i would not be 3.02.150
though justice be thy plea, consider this, 4.01.198
though not for me, yet for your vehement oaths, 5.01.155
though yet i know no wise remedy how to avoid it AYL 1.01. 24 P
though nature hath given us wit to flout at 1.02. 45 P
though i look old, yet i am strong and lusty; 2.03. 47
though in thy youth thou wast as true a lover 2.04. 26
though thou the waters warp, | thy sting is not 2.07.187
retreat, though not with bag and baggage, yet 3.02.161 P
thou think, though i am caparison'd like a man, 3.02.195 P
though it be pity to see such a sight, it well 3.02.242 P
for though he go as softly as foot can fall, he 3.02.327 P
not a slut, though i thank the gods i am foul. 3.03. 38 P
but what though? 3.03. 51 P
what though you have no beauty — | as, by my 3.05. 37
though all the world could see, | none could be 3.05. 78
think not i love him, though i ask for him; 3.05.109
for though he comes slowly, he carries his house 4.01. 54 P
many a fair year though hero had turn'd nun, if 4.01.101 P
i tender dearly, though i say i am a magician. 5.02. 71 P
though there was no great matter in the ditty, 5.03. 34 P
though to have her and death were both one thing 5.04. 17
for though you lay here in this goodly chamber, SHR in.2. 84
shall i be appointed hours, as though, belike, 1.01.103
though the nature of our quarrel yet never 1.01.114 P
hortensio, though her father be very rich, any 1.01.124 P
though it pass your patience and mine to endure 1.01.126 P

though she have as many diseases as two and 1.02. 80 P
though she chide as loud | as thunder when the 1.02. 95
i know her father, though i know not her, | and 1.02.101
one, | though paris came in hope to speed alone. 1.02.245
though little fire grows great with little wind, 2.01.134
that /shake not, though they blow perpetually. 2.01.141
as though she bid me stay by her a week; 2.01.178
methinks he looks as though he were in love; 3.01. 88
though he be blunt, i know him passing wise; 3.02. 24
though he be merry, yet withal he's honest. 3.02. 25
would katherine had never seen him though! 3.02. 26
word, | though in some part enforced to digress, 3.02.107
though bride and bridegroom wants | for to 3.02.246
to marry with her though she would entreat. 4.02. 33
though thy little finger be arm'd in a thimble. 4.03.147 P
at last, though long, our jarring notes agree, 5.02. 1
this bird you aim'd at, though you hit her not; 5.02. 50
'twas i won the wager, though you hit the white, 5.02.186
'twas pretty, though a plague, | to see him AWW 1.01. 92
our virginity, though valiant in the defense, 1.01.115 P
for't a little, though therefore i die a virgin. 1.01.133 P
i am poor, though many of the rich are damn'd, 1.03. 17 P
though honesty be no puritan, yet it will do no 1.03. 93 P
star, and though the devil lead the measure, 2.01. 55 P
though more to know could not be more to trust 2.01.206
do so ever, though i took him at 's prayers. 2.05. 41 P
of men, though it be the getting of children. 3.02. 42 P
and, though i kill him not, i am the cause | his 3.02.115
though little he do feel it, set down sharply. 3.04. 33
though there were no further danger known but 3.05. 26 P
though my estate be fall'n, i was well born, 3.07. 4
though you understand it not yourselves, no 4.01. 3 P
though i swore i leapt from the window of the 4.01. 55 P
a wife of me, though there my hope be done. 4.02. 65
though i know his brains are forfeit to the next 4.03.190 P
though time seem so adverse and means unfit. 5.01. 26
though you are a fool and a knave, you shall eat 5.02. 53 P
though my revenges were high bent upon him | and 5.03. 10
though yet he never harm'd me, here i quit him. 5.03.299
dead though she be, she feels her young one kick 5.03.302
and though that nature with a beauteous wall TN 1.02. 48
an allow'd fool, though he do nothing but rail; 1.05. 94 P
discreet man, though he do nothing but reprove. 1.05. 96 P
though you were crown'd | the nonpareil of 1.05.253
sir, though it was said she much resembled me, 2.01. 25 P
though i could not with such estimable wonder 2.01. 27 P
though i seem to drown her remembrance again 2.01. 31 P
you that, though she harbors you as her kinsman, 2.03. 96 P
my life upon't, young though thou art, thine eye 2.04. 23
though our silence be drawn from us with cars, 2.05. 63 P
for all this, though it be as rank as a fox. 2.05.123 P
though i would not have it grow on my chin. 3.01. 47 P
in thy ink, though thou write with a goose–pen, 3.02. 49 P
(though so much | as might have drawn one to a 3.03. 6
not black in my mind, though yellow in my legs. 3.04. 26 P
though now you have no sea–cap on your head. 3.04.330
though i strook him first, yet it's no matter 4.01. 35 P
though ignorance were as dark as hell; 4.02. 46 P
and though 'tis wonder that enwraps me thus, 4.03. 3
for though my soul disputes well with my sense, 4.03. 9
though it please you to be one of my friends. 5.01. 25 P
though i confess, on base and ground enough, 5.01. 75
though lately we intended | to keep in darkness 5.01.152
little faith, though thou hast too much fear. 5.01.171
though you have put me into darkness, and given 5.01.303 P
though, i confess, much like the character; 5.01.346
may, though they cannot praise us, as little WT 1.01. 15 P
their encounters (though not personal) hath been 1.01. 27 P
they have seem'd to be together, though absent; 1.01. 29 P
though you would seek t' unsphere the stars with 1.02. 48
though you perceive me not how i give line. 1.02.181
were sin | as deep as that, though true. 1.02.284
though he does bear some signs of me, yet you 2.01. 57
though i am satisfied and need no more | than 2.01.189
though a present death | had been more merciful. 2.03.184
though devis'd | and play'd to take spectators. 3.02. 36
though 'tis a saying, sir, not due to me. 3.02. 58
tastes, though it be dish'd | for me to try how. 3.02. 72
though i with death and with | reward did 3.02.163
though a devil | would have shed water out of 3.02.192
though i am not bookish, yet i can read 3.03. 72 P
though i have for the most part been air'd 4.02. 5 P
i am most constant, | though destiny say no. 4.04. 46
though i report it | that should be silent. 4.04.177
handle, though they come to him by th' gross; 4.04.206 P
though full of our displeasure, yet we free thee 4.04.433
though the pennyworth on his side be the worst, 4.04.635 P
though i am not naturally honest, i am so 4.04.712 P
are germane to him (though remov'd fifty times) 4.04.774 P
which though it be great pity, yet it is 4.04.775 P
and though authority be a stubborn bear, yet he 4.04.801 P
but though my case be a pitiful one, i hope i 4.04.814 P
whom | (though bearing misery) i desire my life 5.01.137
though fortune, visible an enemy, | should chase 5.01.216
though credit be asleep and not an ear open: 5.02. 62 P
mine eyes (caught the water though not the fish) 5.02. 83 P
appears she lives, | though yet she speak not. 5.03.118
what though? JN 1.01.169
which, though i will not practice to deceive, 1.01.214
though all these english and their discipline 2.01.261
though churlish thoughts themselves should be 2.01.519
and though thou now confess thou didst but jest, 3.01. 16
though you and all the kings of christendom 3.01.162
though you, and all the rest so grossly led, 3.01.168
though indirect, | yet indirection thereby grows 3.01.275
though that my death were adjunct to my act, 3.03. 57
the iron of itself, though heat red–hot, 4.01. 61
though to no use but still to look on you! 4.01.102
this we prescribe, though no physician; R2 1.01.154
and though thou livest and breathest, | yet art 1.02. 24
though this be all, do not so quickly go; 1.02. 64
though banish'd, yet a true–born englishman. 1.03.309
though richard my live's counsel would not hear, 2.01. 15
o no, thou diest, though i the sicker be. 2.01. 91
though death be poor, it ends a mortal woe. 2.01.152
though rebels wound thee with their horses' 3.02. 7
and though you think that all, as you have done, 3.03. 82
though you are old enough to be my heir. 3.03.205
though being all too base | to stain the temper 4.01. 28
and, though mine enemy, restor'd again | to all 4.01. 88
though he divide the realm and give thee half, 5.01. 60
though i be old, | i doubt not but to ride as 5.02.114
for though it have holp mad men to their wits, 5.05. 62
for though mine enemy thou hast ever been, 5.06. 28
though i did wish him dead, | i hate the 5.06. 39
salvation, that though i be but prince of wales, 1H4 2.04. 9 P
for though the camomile, the more it is trodden 2.04.400 P
kitten'd, though yourself had never been born. 3.01. 19
though sometimes it show greatness, courage, 3.01.179
though i could scape shot–free at london, i fear 5.03. 30 P
though many dearer, in this bloody fray. 5.04.108
of this gunpowder percy though he be dead. 5.04.122 P
though he have his own lanthorn to light him. 2H4 1.02. 48 P
though it be a shame to be on any side but one, 1.02. 75 P
your lordship, though not clean past your youth, 1.02. 97 P
well, you shall have it, though i pawn my gown. 2.01.158 P
me, though it discolors the complexion of my 2.02. 4 P
though that be sick, it dies not. 2.02.105 P
bullingbrook ascends my throne" | (though then, 3.01. 72
and though we here fall down, | we have supplies 4.02. 44
though it do work as strong | as aconitum or 4.04. 47
though thou stand'st more sure than i could do, 4.05.202
though no man be assur'd what grace to find, 5.02. 30
though in pure truth it was corrupt and naught, H5 1.02. 73
for government, though high, and low, and lower, 1.02.180
it is a simple one, but what though? 2.01. 8 P
though patience be a tir'd /mare, yet she will 2.01. 23 P
though cambridge, scroop, and grey, in their 2.02. 58
though the truth of it stands off as gross | as 2.02.103
(though war nor no known quarrel were in 2.04. 17
but though we think it so, it is no matter. 2.04. 42
but all they three, though they would serve me, 3.02. 30 P
thou to harry of england, though we seem'd dead, 3.06.119 P
though 'tis no wisdom to confess so much | unto 3.06.143
though france himself and such another neighbor 3.06.157
the organs, though defunct and dead before, 4.01. 21
though it appear a little out of fashion, 4.01. 83
for, though i speak it to you, i think the king 4.01.101 P
and though his affections are higher mounted 4.01.106 P
native punishment, though they can outstrip men, 4.01.167 P
do it, though i take thee in the king's company. 4.01.219 P
though all that i can do is nothing worth, 4.01.303
though we upon this mountain's basis by | took 4.02. 30
dying like men, though buried in your dunghills, 4.03. 99
though he be as good a gentleman as the devil is 4.07.137 P
who, though i speak it before his face, if he be 5.02.241 P
blind, though they have their eyes, and then 5.02.309 P
i know thee well, though never seen before. 1H6 1.02. 67
though thy speech doth fail, | one eye thou hast 1.04. 82
for though he seem with forged quaint conceit 4.01.102
out, | though ne'er so cunningly you smother it. 4.01.110
and fly would talbot never, though he might. 4.04. 44
for though her father be the king of naples, 5.03. 94
what though i be enthrall'd, he seems a knight, 5.03.101
what though the common people favor him, 2H6 1.01.158
though humphrey's pride | and greatness of his 1.01.172
though in this place most master wear no 1.03.146
with ignominious words, though clerkly couch'd, 3.01.179
though suffolk dare him twenty thousand times. 3.02.206
unworthy though thou art, i'll cope with thee, 3.02.230
and he but naked, though lock'd up in steel, 3.02.234
and therefore do they cry, though you forbid, 3.02.264
though standing naked on a mountain top, | where 3.02.336
though parting be a fretful corrosive, | it is 3.02.403
and get thee a sword, though made of a lath; 4.02. 1 P
a mind, | and henry, though he be infortunate, 4.09. 18
brother, though i be youngest, give me leave. 3H6 1.02. 1
though the odds be great, | i doubt not, uncle, 1.02. 71
to prick thy finger, though to wound his heart. 1.04. 55
and many strokes, though with a little axe, 2.01. 54
and though man's face be fearful to their eyes, 2.02. 27
you that are king, though he do wear the crown, 2.02. 90
and though the edge hath something hit ourselves 2.02.166
that led calm henry, though he were a king, | as 2.06. 34
for (though before his face i speak the words) 2.06. 39
for though they cannot greatly sting to hurt, 2.06. 94
for though usurpers sway the rule a while, | yet 3.03. 76
that, though i want a kingdom, yet in marriage 4.01.121
though fortune's malice overthrow my state, | my 4.03. 46
why then, though loath, yet must i be content. 4.06. 48
nor forward of revenge, though they much err'd. 4.08. 46
what though the mast be now blown overboard, 5.04. 3
and, though unskillful, why not ned and i | for 5.04. 19
keep our course (though the rough wind say no) 5.04. 22
what though i kill'd her husband and her father? R3 1.01.154
though i wish thy death, | i will not be thy 1.02.184
though not by war, by surfeit die your king, 1.03.196
though 'twere to buy a world of happy days — 1.04. 6
no marvel, lord, though it affrighted you; 1.04. 64
though we have spent our harvest of this king, 2.02.115
for now he lives in fame though not in life. 3.01. 88
though what they will impart | help nothing else 4.04.130
though far more cause, yet much less spirit to 4.04.197
and, though we leave it with a root, thus hack'd H8 1.02. 97
though they be never so ridiculous | (nay, let 1.03. 3
i would not be so sick though for his place. 2.02. 82
(though he be grown so desperate to be honest), 3.01. 86
to him (though now the time | gives way to us) i 3.02. 15
what though i know her virtuous | and well 3.02. 97
(though all the world should crack their duty to 3.02.193
it from their soul, though perils did | abound, 3.02.194
sure and safe one, though thy master miss'd it. 3.02.438
though from an humble stock, undoubtedly | was 4.02. 49
and though he were unsatisfied in getting 4.02. 55
the other, though unfinish'd, yet so famous, 4.02. 61
though in her cradle, yet now promises | upon 5.04. 18
then though my heart's content firm love doth TRO 1.02.294
his brain as barren | as banks of libya (though, 1.03.328
though no man lesser fears the greeks than i 2.02. 8
no marvel though you bite so sharp /at reasons, 2.02. 33
sail swift, though greater hulks draw deep. 2.03.266
kindred, though they be long ere they be woo'd, 3.02.110 P
but, though i lov'd you well, i woo'd you not, 3.02.126
though in and of him there be much consisting, 3.03.116
though less than yours in /past, must o'ertop 3.03.164
though they are made and moulded of things past, 3.03.177
though the great bulk achilles be thy guard, 4.04.128
i reak not though i end my life to–day. 5.06. 26
though not for me, yet for /your aching bones. 5.10. 50
though soft–conscienc'd men can be content to COR 1.01. 37 P
and though that all at once" — | you, my good 1.01.140
"though all at once cannot | see what i do 1.01.142
for though abundantly they lack discretion, 1.01.202
though he perform | to th' utmost of a man, and 1.01.267
to martius, | though martius earn'd them not; 1.01.274
honors, though indeed | in aught he merit not. 1.01.275
got in fear, | though you were born in rome!" 1.03. 34
though thou speakest truth, | methinks thou 1.06. 13
though i could wish | you were conducted to a 1.06. 62
a certain number | (though thanks to all) must i 1.06. 81
bolder, though not so subtle. 1.10. 17
and though i must be content to bear with those 2.01. 59 P
though peradventure some of the best of 'em were 2.01. 92 P
though there the people had more absolute pow'r, 3.01.116
as they are, | though in rome litter'd; 3.01.238
though calved i' th' porch o' th' capitol! 3.01.239
though therein you can never be too noble, | but 3.02. 40
though but bastards and syllables | of no 3.02. 56
believe't not lightly — though i go alone, 4.01. 29
though thy tackle's torn, | thou show'st a noble 4.05. 61
your territories, | though not for rome itself. 4.05.135
though they themselves did suffer by't, behold 4.06. 6
best, and though we willingly consented to his 4.06.144 P
no, though it were as virtuous to lie as to live 5.02. 26 P
though i owe | my revenge properly, my remission 5.02. 83
love i have | (though i show'd sourly to him) 5.03. 13
an evident calamity, though we had | our wish, 5.03.112
aufidius, though i cannot make true wars, | i'll 5.03.190
though in this city he | hath widowed and 5.06.150
though /chance of war hath wrought this change TIT 1.01.264
lavinia, though you left me like a churl, | i 1.01.486
though bassianus be the emperor's brother, 2.01. 88
madam, though venus govern your desires, 2.03. 30
the trees, though summer, yet forlorn and lean, 2.03. 94
o, be to me, though thy hard heart say no, 2.03.155
here, tamora, though griev'd with killing grief. 2.03.260
who, though they cannot answer my distress, 3.01. 38
"let not your sorrow die, though i am dead." 5.01.140
i knew them all though they suppos'd me mad, 5.02.142
may stand in number, though in reck'ning none. ROM 1.02. 33
do not move, though grant for prayers' sake. 1.05.105
thou art thyself, though not a montague. 2.02. 39
though news be sad, yet tell them merrily; 2.05. 22
though his face be better than any man's, yet 2.05. 40 P
and a body, though they be not to be talk'd on, 2.05. 42 P
but not possess'd it, and, though i am sold, 3.02. 27
romeo can, | though heaven cannot. 3.02. 41
no sudden mean of death, though ne'er so mean, 3.03. 45
to comfort thee though thou art banished. 3.03. 56
for though /fond nature bids us all lament, 4.05. 82
though you hear now (too late), yet now's a time TIM 2.02.143
for no less, though we are but strangers to him. 3.02. 3 P
though his right arm might purchase his own time 3.05. 76
ay, though it look like thee. 4.03.308 P
(for i must ever doubt, though ne'er so sure), 4.03.507
whom, though in general part we were oppos'd, 5.02. 7
an ag'd interpreter, though young in days. 5.03. 8
though thou abhorr'dst in us our human griefs, 5.04. 75
though now we must appear bloody and cruel, | as JC 3.01.165
though last, not least in love, yours, good 3.01.189
who, though he had no hand in his death, shall 3.02. 42 P
and though we lay these honors on this man | to 4.01. 19
venom of your spleen | though it do split you; 4.03. 48
though they do appear | as huge as high olympus. 4.03. 91
though his bark cannot be lost, | yet it shall MAC 1.03. 24
thou shalt get kings, though thou be none. 1.03. 67
for him, though he took up my legs sometime, yet 2.03. 40 P
and though i could | with barefac'd power sweep 3.01.117
though our lives — 3.01.126
though you untie the winds, and let them fight 4.01. 52
though the yesty waves | confound and swallow 4.01. 53
though bladed corn be lodg'd, and trees blown 4.01. 55
though castles topple on their warders' heads; 4.01. 56
though palaces and pyramids do slope | their 4.01. 57
though the treasure | of nature's /germains 4.01. 58
though in your state of honor i am perfect. 4.02. 66
are bright still, though the brightest fell. 4.03. 22
though all things foul would wear the brows of 4.03. 23
though the main part | pertains to you alone. 4.03.198
though thou call'st thyself a hotter name | than 5.07. 6
though birnan wood be come to dunsinane, | and 5.08. 30
i'll cross it, though it blast me. HAM 1.01.127
though yet of hamlet our dear brother's death 1.02. 1
from whence though willingly i came to denmark 1.02. 52
though hell itself should gape | and bid me hold 1.02.244
though all the earth o'erwhelm them, to men's 1.02.257
youth to itself rebels, though none else near. 1.03. 44
though i am native here | and to the manner born 1.04. 14
our achievements, though perform'd at height, 1.04. 21
though lewdness court it in a shape of heaven, 1.05. 54
so /lust, though to a radiant angel link'd, 1.05. 55
though it were hid indeed | within the centre. 2.02.158
though i most powerfully and potently believe, 2.02.201 P
though this be madness, yet there is method in't 2.02.205 P
though by your smiling you seem to say so. 2.02.309 P
for murther, though it have no tongue, will 2.02.593
what he spake, though it lack'd form a little, 3.01.163
tardy off, though it makes the unskillful laugh, 3.02. 25 P
though in the mean time some necessary question 3.02. 42 P
yet, though i distrust, | discomfort you, my 3.02.165
me what instrument you will, though you fret me, 3.02.371 P
i not, | though inclination be as sharp as will. 3.03. 39
though nothing sure, yet much unhappily. 4.05. 13
for though i am not splenitive /and rash, | yet 5.01.261
definement suffers no perdition in you, though, 5.02.113 P
though this knave came something saucily to the LR 1.01. 21 P
though the fork invade | the region of my heart; 1.01.144
though not to have it | hath lost me in your 1.01.232
bid them farewell, cordelia, though unkind, 1.01.260
though the wisdom of nature can reason it thus 1.02.104 P
so your face bids me, though you say nothing. 1.04.196 P
and course of yours | though i condemn not, yet, 1.04.342
for though she's as like this as a crab's like 1.05. 15 P

though thou didst produce | my very character), 2.01. 71
no marvel then, though he were ill affected: 2.01. 98
you rogue, for though it be night, yet the moon 2.02. 31 P
though they had been but two years o' th' trade. 2.02. 59 P
though i should win your displeasure to entreat 2.02.112 P
fit, | though the rain it raineth every day." 3.02. 77
though their injunction be to bar my doors, 3.04.150
though the conflict be sore between that and my 3.05. 22 P
though well we may not pass upon his life 3.07. 24
they are centaurs, | though women all above; 4.06.125
though that the queen on special cause is here, 4.06.215
though he had bit me, should have stood that 4.07. 36
wretched though i seem, | i can produce a 5.01. 42
not sure, though hoping, of this good success, 5.03.195
and, though he in a fertile climate dwell, OTH 1.01. 70
though that his joy be joy, | yet throw such 1.01. 71
though i do hate him as i do hell–pains, | yet, 1.01.154
though in the trade of war i have slain men, 1.02. 1
but though they jump not on a just accompt | (as 1.03. 5
though our proper son | stood in your action. 1.03. 69
and though we have there a substitute of most 1.03.223 P
though he speak of comfort | touching the 2.01. 31
learn of him, emilia, though he be thy husband. 2.01.162 P
though true advantage never present itself; 2.01.244 P
(though peradventure | i stand accomptant for as 2.01.292
though he had twinn'd with me, both at a birth, 2.03.212
though cassio did some little wrong to him, | as 2.03.242
though other things grow fair against the sun, 2.03.376
though i am bound to every act of duty, | i am 3.03.134
though i perchance am vicious in my guess | (as 3.03.145
speak of her, though i may fear | her will, 3.03.235
haggard, | though that her jesses were my dear 3.03.261
'tis a shrewd doubt, though it be but a dream, 3.03.429
things, | though great ones are their object. 3.04.145
in venice, | though i should swear i saw't. 4.01.243
will (though he do shake me off | to beggarly 4.02.157
and though we have some grace, | yet have we 4.03. 92
will speak, | though tongues were out of use. 5.01.110
make thee known, | though i lost twenty lives. 5.02.166
be not afraid though you do see me weapon'd; 5.02.266
though thou deny me a matter of more weight; ANT 1.02. 68 P
who tells me true, though in his tale lie death, 1.02. 98
were pity to cast them away for nothing, though, 1.02.138 P
(though you in swearing shake the throned gods), 1.03. 28
though age from folly could not give me freedom, 1.03. 57
fought'st against | (though daintily brought up) 1.04. 60
and though i make this marriage for my peace, 2.03. 40
again, | though i am mad, i will not bite him. 2.05. 80
though it be honest, it is never good | to bring 2.05. 85
though he be painted one way like a gorgon, 2.05.116
though i lose | the praise of it by telling, you 2.06. 42
though it cannot be denied what i have done by 2.06. 89 P
and, though thou think me poor, i am the man 2.07. 64
though you be therein curious, the least cause 3.02. 35
though my reason | sits in the wind against me. 3.10. 35
what though you fled | from that great face of 3.13. 4
though you can guess what temperance should be, 3.13.121
girl, though grey | do something mingle with our 4.08. 19
darts, | though enemy, lost aim and could not? 4.14. 71
though he be honorable — 5.02.108
though written in our flesh, we shall remember 5.02.119
i'll catch thine eyes | though they had wings. 5.02.157
though i think the king | be touch'd at very CYM 1.01. 9
though the king | hath charg'd you should not 1.01. 82
words you send, | though ink be made of gall. 1.01.101
though the catalogue of his endowments had been 1.04. 5 P
her nothing, though i profess myself her adorer, 1.04. 68 P
a repulse, though your attempt (as you call it) 1.04.118 P
a languishing death, | but though slow, deadly. 1.05. 10
though this a heavenly angel, hell is here. 2.02. 50
and though it be allowed in meaner parties 2.03.116
i do believe | (statist though i am none, nor 2.04. 16
me present hunger | to feed again, though full. 2.04.138
our good deed, | though rome be therefore angry. 3.01. 58
though forfeiters you cast in prison, yet | you 3.02. 38
and, though train'd up thus meanly | i' th' cave 3.03. 82
though those that are betray'd | do feel the 3.04. 85
that though his actions were not visible, yet 3.04.149
though peril to my modesty, not death on't, | i 3.04.152
though i had found | gold strew'd i' th' floor. 3.06. 48
though his /humor | was nothing but mutation, ay 4.02.132
though valor | becomes thee well enough. 4.02.155
though now our voices | have got the mannish 4.02.235
and though he came our enemy, remember | he was 4.02.245
though mean and mighty, rotting | together, have 4.02.246
and though you took his life, as being our foe, 4.02.250
and do | no harm by it, though the gods hear, i 4.02.378
though cloten then but young, you see, not wore 4.04. 23
though you, it seems, come from the fliers? 5.03. 2
life take mine, and though | 'tis not so dear, 5.04. 22
though light, take pieces for the figure's sake; 5.04. 25
out, though with the loss | of many a bold one, 5.05. 70
britain harm, | though he have serv'd a roman. 5.05. 91
yea, though thou do demand a prisoner, | the 5.05. 99
though you did love this youth, i blame ye not, 5.05.267
a dangerous speech, | though haply well for you. 5.05.314
though by the tenor of /our strict edict, | your PER 1.01.111
are, who though they feed | on sweetest flowers, 1.01.132
think me speaking, though i swear to silence; 1.02. 19
for though he strive | to killen bad, keep good 2.ch. 19
and though it was mine own, part of my heritage, 2.01.123
it in rage, though calm'd have given't again. 2.01.132
for though | this king were great, his greatness 2.04. 13
of fortune, though they haunt you mortally, 3.03. 6
hair of mine remain, | though i show /ill in't. 3.03. 30
my good will is great, though the gift small. 3.04. 18
though not his /prime consent, he did not flow 4.03. 27
and though you call my course unnatural, | you 4.03. 36
though most ungentle fortune | have plac'd me in 4.06. 96
though they did change me to the meanest bird 4.06.101
though wayward fortune did malign my state, | my 5.01. 89
enough, | though doubts did ever sleep. 5.01.202
you shall hear | scenes, though below his art, TNK pr 28
it to some pity, | though it were made of stone. 1.01.129
though much unlike | you should be so 1.01.186
ingots, | which, though he won, he had not; 1.02. 18
though i know | his ocean needs not my poor 1.03. 6
though craving seriousness and skill, pass'd 1.03. 28
though happily her careless /wear) i followed 1.03. 73
(though in't i know thou dost believe thyself) 1.03. 88
the prison i keep, though it be for great ones, 2.01. 3 P
but take heed to your kindness though! 2.02.125
i'll be hang'd though, | if he dare venture. 2.03. 71
should break out, though i' th' sanctuary. 3.01. 62
though it be rusty, and the charity | of one 3.01. 73
i first appear, though rude, and raw, and muddy, 3.05.122
i had not said i lov'd her, | though i had died; 3.06. 41
but use your gauntlets though. 3.06. 64
though i think | i never shall enjoy her, yet 3.06.267
coz, i would, | though parcel of myself. 5.01. 24
part is play'd, and, though it were too short, 5.04.102
govern'd him in strength, though not in lust. VEN 42
though mine be not so fair, yet are they red — 116
though of a man's complexion, | for men will 215
dog shall rouse thee, though a thousand bark." 240
though nothing but my body's bane would cure 372
therefore no marvel though thy horse be gone. 390
though i were dumb, yet his proceedings teach 406
though neither eyes nor ears to hear nor see, 437
what though the rose have prickles, yet 'tis 574
lovers' hours are long, though seeming short. 842
though weak–built hopes persuade him to LUC 130
though death be adjunct, there's no death 133
"yea, though i die, the scandal will survive, 204
harden lust, though marble /wear with raining. 560
though men can cover crimes with bold stern 1252
my woes are tedious, though my words are brief." 1309
his face, though full of cares, yet show'd 1503
though woe be heavy, yet it seldom sleeps, | and 1574
it easeth some, though none it ever cured, | to 1581
her eyes, though sod in tears, look'd red and 1592
though my gross blood be stain'd with this abuse 1655
i do believe her (though i know she lies) | that PP 1. 2
though to myself forsworn, to thee i'll constant 5. 3
bad in the best, though excellent in neither. 7.18
slack | to proffer, though she put thee back. 18.24
what though her frowning brows be bent, | her 18.25
what though she strive to try her strength, 18.31
flowers distill'd, though they with winter meet, SON 5.13
though yet, heaven knows, it is but as a tomb 17. 3
though not so bright | as those gold candles 21.11
and each (though enemies to /either's reign) 28. 5
and though they be outstripp'd by every pen, 32. 6
though thou repent, yet i have still the loss: 34.10
though in our lives a separable spite, | which 36. 6
which though it alter not love's sole effect, 36. 7
save where thou art not, though i feel thou art, 48.10
then should i spur though mounted on the wind, 51. 7
that in your will | (though you do any thing) he 57.14
i am to wait, though waiting so be hell, | not 58.13
o no, thy love, though much, is not so great, 61. 9
my sweet love's beauty, though my lover's life: 63.12
though i (once gone) to all the world must die; 81. 6
whose love to you | (though words come hindmost) 85.12
prove thee virtuous, though thou art forsworn. 88. 4
some in their garments, though new–fangled ill, 91. 3
may still seem love to me, though alter'd new: 93. 3
sweet, | though to itself it only live and die, 94.10
is strength'ned, though more weak in seeming, 102. 1
i love not less, though less the show appear; 102. 2
though absence seem'd my flame to qualify! 109. 2
though in my nature reign'd | all frailties that 109. 9
though rosy lips and cheeks | within his bending 116. 9
i may be straight though they themselves be 121.11
her audit (though delay'd) answer'd must be, 126.11
though in thy store's account i one must be, 136.10
i do believe her, though i know she lies, | that 138. 2
though not to love, yet, love, to tell me so, 140. 6
eyes straight, though thy proud heart go wide. 140.14
no marvel then though i mistake my view, | the 148.11
o, though i love what others do abhor, | with 150.11
though slackly braided in loose negligence. LC 35
"though in me you behold | the injury of many a 71
when winds breathe sweet, unruly though they be. 103
though reason weep and cry, 'it is thy last.' 168
melting, though our drops this diff'rence bore: 300

THOUGH'T 4 FR 0.0004 REL FR 4 V 0 P

though't be temporal, | yet, if that quarrel, H8 2.03. 13
though't be a sportful combat, | yet in the TRO 1.03.335
good will is show'd, though't come too short, ANT 2.05. 8
early though't be, have on their riveted trim, 4.04. 22

/THOUGHT 6 FR 0.0006 REL FR 5 V 1 P

/i /thought /you /had /been /willing /to /resign R2 4.01.190
/and /very /well /appointed, /as /i /thought, 3H6 2.01.113
/complainant, /i /will /learn /thy /thought; TIT 3.02. 39
which i best /thought it fit | to answer from LR 2.01.123
/since /his /coming /forth /is /thought /of, 4.03. 4 P
/that /thought /abuses /you. 5.01. 11

THOUGHT 399 FR 0.0451 REL FR 322 V 77 P

thought is free." TMP 3.02.123
here thought they to have done | some wanton 4.01. 94
come with a thought. i thank thee. ariel! come. 4.01.164
i thought to have told thee of it, but i fear'd 4.01.168
father | for his advice, nor thought i had one. 5.01.191
where | every third thought shall be my grave. 5.01.312
wit with musing weak, heart sick with thought. TGV 1.01. 69
ay — if you thought your love not cast away. 1.02. 26
where i thought the remnant of mine age | should 3.01. 74
dead | if i in thought felt not her very sorrow. 4.04.172
trust me, i thought on her. she'll fit it. WIV 2.01.161 P
would any man have thought this? 2.02.291 P
truly, i thought there had been one number more, 4.01. 23 P
he is a better scholar than i thought he was. 4.01. 80 P
that likewise have we thought upon, and thus: 4.04. 47
three or four times in the thought they were not 5.05.122 P
from whom we thought it meet to hide our love MM 1.02.152
holy father, throw away that thought; 1.03. 1
i thought, by the readiness in the office, you 2.01.261 P
let it not sound a thought upon your tongue 2.02.140
of those that lawless and incertain thought 3.01.126
with a thought that more depends on it than we 4.02.124 P
of your honor, | i thought your marriage fit; 5.01.420
i thought it was a fault, but knew it not, | yet 5.01.463
was carried towards corinth, as we thought. ERR 1.01. 87
up | by fishermen of corinth, as we thought. 1.01.111
i thought to have ask'd you. 3.01. 55
i thought to have ta'en you at the porpentine; 3.02.167
belike you thought our love would last too long 4.01. 25
now he's there, past thought of human reason. 5.01.189
by my troth, i speak my thought. ADO 1.01.224 P
it is past the infinite of thought. 2.03.101 P
me, i would have thought her spirit had been 2.03.114 P
you are thought here to be the most senseless 3.03. 22 P
i thought there would a scab follow. 3.03. 99 P
and thought they margaret was hero? 3.03.153 P
excellently, if the hair were a thought browner; 3.04. 14 P
thought i thy spirits were stronger than thy 4.01.125
no, though he thought his accusation true. 4.01.233
yea, as sure as i have a thought or a soul. 4.01.330 P
and it will go near to be thought so shortly. 4.02. 22 P
say to you, it is thought you are false knaves. 4.02. 28 P
deliver me from the reprobate thought of it, i LLL 1.02. 61 P
thou enforcest laughter — thy silly thought, my 3.01. 76 P
how far dost thou excel | no thought can think, 4.03. 40
courses as swift as thought in every power, 4.03.327
i thought to close mine eyes some half an hour; 5.02. 90
arrows, bullets, wind, thought, swifter things. 5.02.261
and with demetrius thought to have spoke thereof MND 1.01.112
through athens i am thought as fair as she. 1.01.227
of every man's name, which is thought fit, 1.02. 5 P
i thought you lord of more true gentleness. 2.02.132
would blow me to an ague when i thought | what MV 1.01. 23
shall i have the thought | to think on this, and 1.01. 36
and shall i lack the thought | that such a thing 1.01. 37
'twere damnation | to think so base a thought; 2.07. 50
o sinful thought! 2.07. 54
i thought upon antonio when he told me, | and 2.08. 31
and yet a maiden hath no tongue but thought — 3.02. 8
and then 'tis thought | thou'lt show thy mercy 4.01. 19
would be thought | no better a musician than the 5.01.105
never so much as in a thought unborn | did i AYL 1.03. 51
i thought that all things had been savage here, 2.07.107
there was no thought of pleasing you when she 3.02.266 P
and certainly a woman's thought runs before her 4.01.141 P
friends told me as much, and i thought no less. 4.01.184 P
bastard of venus that was begot of thought, 4.01.212 P
i thought thy heart had been wounded with the 5.02. 22 P
themselves, one of them thought but of an if, as 5.04.100 P
therefore they thought it good you hear a play, SHR in.2. 134
true, | i never thought it possible or likely. 1.01.149
'tis thought your deer does hold you at a bay. 5.02. 56
lest it be rather thought you affect a sorrow AWW 1.01. 52 P
she thought, i dare vow for her, they touch'd 1.03.109 P
were our faults, or then we thought them none. 1.03.135
not be kill'd so soon as i thought he would. 3.02. 38 P
noble she was, and thought | i stood engag'd; 5.03. 95
the heavens have thought well on thee, lafew, 5.03.150
lay a more noble thought upon mine honor | than 5.03.180
prove your honor | than in my thought it lies. 5.03.184
'tis thought among the prudent he would quickly TN 1.03. 32 P
now, sir, thought is free. 1.03. 69 P
and i thought that, i'd forswear it. 1.03. 88 P
o, if i thought that, i'd beat him like a dog! 2.03.141 P
she pin'd in thought, | and with a green and 2.04.112
plague on't, and i thought he had been valiant, 3.04.283 P
nor lean enough to be thought a good studient; 4.02. 7 P
so please you, these things further thought on, 5.01.316
i had thought, sir, to have held my peace until WT 1.02. 28
two lads that thought there was no more behind 1.02. 63
or thought (for cogitation | resides not in that 1.02.271
to have nor eyes nor ears nor thought, then say 1.02.275
swear his thought over | by each particular star 1.02.424
so have we thought it good | from our free 2.01.193
fie, fie, no thought of him; 2.03. 18
the very thought of my revenges that way 2.03. 19
i did in time collect myself and thought | this 3.03. 38
more than can be thought to begin from such a 4.02. 43 P
the life to come, i sleep out the thought of it. 4.03. 30 P
it was thought she was a woman and was turn'd 4.04.278 P
that thought to fill his grave in quiet; 4.04.454
care | to have them recompens'd as thought on. 4.04.520
have you thought on | a place whereto you'll go? 4.04.536
the other grow | faster than thought or time. 4.04.554
if i thought it were a piece of honesty to 4.04.680 P
is as bitter | upon thy tongue as in my thought. 5.01. 19
with thought of such affections, | step forth 5.01.220
i thought of her, | even in these looks i made. 5.01.227
i thought she had some great matter there in 5.02.104 P
if i had thought the sight of my poor image 5.03. 57
for i saw her, | as i thought, dead; 5.03.140
and fly, like thought, from them to me again. JN 4.02.175
the dreadful motion of a murderous thought, 4.02.255
could thought, without this object, | form such 4.03. 44
or sin of thought | be guilty of the stealing 4.03.135
be great in act, as you have been in thought. 5.01. 45
thou hast a perfect thought. 5.06. 6
us | so much as of a thought of ill in him. R2 1.01. 86
as, /though on thinking on no thought i think, 2.02. 31
i had thought, my lord, to have learn'd his 2.03. 24
'tis thought the king is dead; 2.04. 7
because we thought ourself thy lawful king; 3.03. 74
to drive away the heavy thought of care? 3.04. 2
you would have thought the very windows spake, 5.02. 12
for no thought is contented. 5.05. 11
and in this thought they find a kind of ease, 5.05. 28
and with a thought seven of the eleven i paid. 1H4 2.04.217 P
look red, that it may be thought i have wept, 2.04.386 P
in this fine age were not thought flattery, 4.01. 2
it will be thought | by some that know not why 4.01. 62
i thought your honor had already been at 4.02. 52 P
is thought with child by the stern tyrant war, 2H4 in 14
but if without him we be thought too feeble, 1.03. 19
that day, that it is a shame to be thought on. 2.01. 36 P
i had thought weariness durst not have attach'd 2.02. 2 P
it would be every man's thought, and thou art a 2.02. 56 P
never a man's thought in the world keeps the 2.02. 58 P
your most worshipful thought to think so? 2.02. 61 P
"you are an honest woman, and well thought on, 2.04. 92 P
whereby 'a may be thought to be accommodated — 3.02. 79 P
to give admittance to a thought of fear. 4.01.151
sir john falstaff, and in that thought yield me. 4.03. 17 P
poor and old motion, the expedition of thought? 4.03. 34 P
i never thought to hear you speak again. 4.05. 91

thy wish was father, harry, to that thought: 4.05. 92
it must be thought on. H5 1.01. 7
for we have now no thought in us but france, 1.02.302
and all things thought upon | that may with 1.02.305
therefore let every man now task his thought, 1.02.309
and honor's thought | reigns solely in the 2.pr. 3
but it will be thought we keep a bawdy–house 2.01. 35 P
of no less celerity | than that of thought. 3.pr. 3
his prayers, lest 'a should be thought a coward; 3.02. 38 P
ale–wash'd wits, is wonderful to be thought on. 3.06. 79 P
but that we thought not good to bruise an injury 3.06.122 P
i thought upon one pair of english legs | did 3.06.149
he hath not told his thought to the king? 4.01. 99 P
throngs, | if any order might be thought upon. 4.05. 21
so swift a pace hath thought that even now | you 5.pr. 15
in the quick forge and working–house of thought, 5.pr. 23
you thought, because he could not speak english 5.01. 75 P
where valiant talbot above human thought 1H6 1.01.121
'tis thought, lord talbot, when the fight began, 2.02. 22
i thought i should have seen some hercules, | a 2.03. 19
that grudge one thought against your majesty! 3.01.175
dare presume, sweet prince, he thought no harm. 4.01.179
for i always thought | it was both impious and 5.01. 11
chaste, and immaculate in very thought, | whose 5.04. 51
and may that thought, when i imagine ill 2H6 1.02. 19
above the reach or compass of thy thought? 1.02. 46
i thought king henry had resembled thee | in 1.03. 53
i never said nor thought any such matter. 1.03.188 P
i thought as much, he would be above the clouds. 2.01. 15
fellow, | which he had thought to have murther'd 2.03.104
'tis thought, my lord, that you took bribes of 3.01.104
is it but thought so? 3.01.107
spring–time show'rs comes thought on thought, 3.01.337
spring–time show'rs comes thought on thought, 3.01.337
and not a thought but thinks on dignity. 3.01.338
as being thought to contradict your liking, 3.02.252
and thought thee happy when i shook my head? 4.01. 55
i have thought upon it, it shall be so. 4.07. 13 P
i thought ye would never have given out these 4.08. 25 P
far be the thought of this from henry's heart, 3H6 1.01. 70
and in thy thought o'errun my former time; 1.04. 45
why then you mean not as i thought you did. 3.02. 65
o miserable thought! 3.02.151
o monstrous fault, to harbor such a thought! 3.02.164
i thought, at least, he would have said the king 5.01. 29
but, whiles he thought to steal the single ten, 5.01. 43
i thought no less; 5.04. 62
had, | the thought of them would have stirr'd up 5.05. 64
i thought it would have mounted. 5.06. 62
g, | it follows in his thought that i am he. R3 1.01. 59
'tis very grievous to be thought upon. 1.01.141
if i thought that, i tell thee, homicide, 1.02.125
far be it from my heart, the thought thereof! 1.03.149
well thought upon, i have it here about me. 1.03.343
falling | strook me (that thought to stay him) 1.04. 19
i thought thou hadst been resolute. 1.04.113 P
he little thought of this divided friendship. 1.04.238
my brother kill'd no man, his fault was thought, 2.01.105
i thought my mother and my brother york | would 3.01. 20
and shall be thought most fit | for your best 3.01. 66
when such ill dealing must be seen in thought. 3.06. 14
having no more but thought of what thou wast 4.04.107
'tis thought that richmond is their admiral; 4.04.437
as to the tower, i thought — i would have H8 1.02.194
the very thought of this fair company | clapp'd 1.04. 8
hence i took a thought | this was a judgment on 2.04.194
holy men i thought ye, | upon my soul, two 3.01.102
she now begs | that little thought, when she set 3.01.183
abound, as thick as thought could make 'em, and 3.02.195
i had thought | they had parted so much honesty 5.02. 27
i had thought i had had men of some 5.02.170
ill thought on of her, and ill thought /on of TRO 1.01. 70 P
thought on of her, and ill thought /on of you; 1.01. 71 P
and that unbodied figure of the thought | that 1.03. 16
it was thought meet | paris should do some 2.02. 72
whom aristotle thought | unfit to hear moral 2.02.166
will you subscribe his thought, and say he is? 2.03.147 P
sweet, above thought i love /thee! 3.01.159
o that i thought it could be in a woman — | as, 3.02.158
keeps place with thought and almost, like the 3.03.199
(or rather call my thought a certain knowledge) 4.01. 42
to thy senses | as infants empty of all thought! 4.02. 6
with wings more momentary–swift than thought. 4.02. 14
nor dignifies an impare thought with breath; 4.05.103
a thought of added honor torn from hector. 4.05.145
what ever have been thought /on in this state COR 1.02. 4
i thought to crush him in an equal force, | true 1.10. 14
'tis thought | that martius shall be consul. 2.01.260
but 'tis thought of every one coriolanus will 2.02. 3 P
and to make us no better thought of, a little 2.03. 14 P
i had thought to have strooken him with a cudgel 4.05.149 P
i were hang'd but i thought there was more in 4.05.158 P
than i thought he would | when first i did 4.07. 9
such friends | that thought them sure of you. 5.03. 8
grace him only | that thought he could do more: 5.03. 16
'tis thought you have a goodly gift in horning, TIT 2.03. 67
whose souls is not corrupted as 'tis thought. 3.01. 9
sweet father, if i shall be thought thy son, 3.01.179
and, being credulous in this mad thought, | i'll 5.02. 74
i thought all for the best. ROM 3.01.104
who ever would have thought it? 3.02. 42
i thought thy disposition better temper'd. 3.03.115
it may be thought we held him carelessly, 3.04. 25
we scarce thought us blest | that god had lent 3.05.164
proportion'd as one's thought would wish a man, 3.05.182
have i thought /long to see this morning's face, 4.05. 41
o, this same thought did but forerun my need, 5.01. 53
that thought is bounty's foe; TIM 2.02.232
rest, and 'mongst lords /i be thought a fool. 3.03. 21
what's to be thought of him? 5.01. 2
athens, who have thought | on special dignities, 5.01.141
how i have thought of this, and of these times, JC 1.02.164
to himself — take thought and die for caesar; 2.01.187
i wonder none of you have thought of him. 2.01.217
and valiant roman, | i never thought him worse. 3.01.139
so you thought him, | and took his voice who 4.01. 15
i will be here again, even with a thought. 5.03. 19
only in a general honest thought | and common 5.05. 71
my thought, whose murther yet is but fantastical MAC 1.03.139
this have i thought good to deliver thee, my 1.05. 10 P
a foolish thought, to say a sorry sight. 2.02. 19
these deeds must not be thought | after these 2.02. 30
i had thought to have let in some of all 2.03. 18 P
which you thought had been | our innocent self? 3.01. 77
always thought | that i require a clearness: 3.01.131
upon a thought | he will again be well. 3.04. 54
who cannot want the thought, how monstrous | it 3.06. 8
he knows thy thought: 4.01. 69
my thoughts with acts, be it thought and done: 4.01.149
blisters our tongues, | was once thought honest; 4.03. 13
yet who would have thought the old man to have 5.01. 39 P
who (as 'tis thought) by self and violent hands 5.09. 36
in what particular thought to work i know not, HAM 1.01. 67
nor any unproportion'd thought his act. 1.03. 60
is sicklied o'er with the pale cast of thought, 3.01. 84
bellow'd that i have thought some of nature's 3.02. 33 P
that's a fair thought to lie between maids' legs 3.02.118 P
but in our circumstance and course of thought 3.03. 83
a thought which quarter'd hath but one part 4.04. 42
would make one think there might be thought, 4.05. 12
thought and afflictions, passion, hell itself, 4.05.188
so far he topp'd /my thought, | that i, in 4.07. 88
i thought thy bride–bed to have deck'd, sweet 5.01.245
i thought the king had more affected the duke of LR 1.01. 1 P
and thought to set my rest | on her kind nursery 1.01.123
as my great patron thought on in my prayers — 1.01.142
i had thought, by making this well known unto 1.04.205
if they not thought the profits of my death 2.01. 75
had he been where he thought, | by this had 4.06. 44
he thought, | by this had thought been past. 4.06. 45
the main descry | stands on the hourly thought. 4.06.214
i thought it fit | to send the old and miserable 5.03. 45
well thought on. 5.03.251
o, she deceives me | past thought! OTH 1.01.166
i had thought t' have yerk'd him here under the 1.02. 5
is dress'd in — if we make thought of this, 1.03. 26
ay, so i thought. how many, as you guess? 1.03. 36
and it is thought abroad that 'twixt my sheets 1.03.387
the thought whereof | doth, like a poisonous 2.01.296
i had thought you had receiv'd some bodily wound 2.03.266 P
but for a satisfaction of my thought, | no 3.03. 97
why of thy thought, iago? 3.03. 98
as if there were some monster in thy thought 3.03.107
if thou dost love me, | show me thy thought. 3.03.116
he thought 'twas witchcraft — but i am much to 3.03.211
let me be thought too busy in my fears | (as 3.03.253
i saw't not, thought it not; 3.03.339
if you think other, | remove your thought; 4.02. 14
either in discourse of thought or actual deed, 4.02.153
to do | a murther, which i thought a sacrifice. 5.02. 65
i told him what i thought, and told no more 5.02.176
i thought so then — i'll kill myself for grief 5.02.192
this did i fear, but thought he had no weapon; 5.02.360
on the sudden | a roman thought hath strook him. ANT 1.02. 83
she is cunning past man's thought. 1.02.145
very necessity of this thought, that i, | your 2.02. 58
for 'tis a studied, not a present thought, | by 2.02.137
you are abus'd | beyond the mark of thought; 3.06. 87
i little thought | you would have followed. 3.11. 55
birthday, | i had thought t' have held it poor; 3.13.185
if swift thought break it not, a swifter mean 4.06. 34
a swifter mean | shall outstrike thought, but 4.06. 35
shall outstrike thought, but thought will do't, 4.06. 35
horse, even with a thought | the rack dislimns, 4.14. 9
whose heart i thought i had, for she had mine — 4.14. 16
and, 'tis thought, one of leonatus' friends. CYM 2.01. 37 P
that i thought her | as chaste as unsunn'd snow. 2.05. 12
husband, shall be thought | put on for villainy; 3.04. 55
false aeneas, | were in his time thought false; 3.04. 59
madam, | i thought you would not back again. 3.04.116
and thought | to have begg'd or bought what i 3.06. 46
i thought he slept, and put | my clouted brogues 4.02.213
for so i thought i was a cave–keeper, | and cook 4.02.298
yourself | so out of thought, and thereto so 4.04. 33
'tis thought the old man and his sons were 5.03. 85
my heart, | that thought her like her seeming. 5.05. 65
that box i gave you was not thought by me | a 5.05.241
that headless man | i thought had been my lord. 5.05.300
lov'd, | continu'd so, until we thought he died. 5.05.380
for many years thought dead, are now reviv'd, 5.05.456
nor ask advice of any other thought | but PER 1.01. 62
subjects punish'd that ne'er thought offense: 1.02. 28
i thought it princely charity to grieve for them 1.02.100
thought nought too curious, are ready now | to 1.04. 43
i thought as much. 1.04. 62
or pay you with unthankfulness in thought, | be 1.04.102
these cates resist me, he not thought upon. 2.03. 29
never did thought of mine levy offense; 2.05. 52
who thought of such a thing?" 3.ch. 38
upon you, | must in your child be thought on. 3.03. 20
king to tharsus — think /his pilot thought, 4.04. 18
judgment good | that thought you worthy of it. 4.06. 94
your first thought is more | than others' TNK 1.01.135
i, seeing, thought he was a goodly man; 2.04. 8
and greatest, | i would be thought a soldier. 2.05. 15
come between, | and chop on some cold thought! 3.01. 13
fear their gay skins with thought of their sharp STM III 18
for all my mind, my thought, my busy care, | is VEN 383
whose vultur thought doth pitch the price so 551
the thought of it doth make my faint heart bleed 669
why then i know | he thought to kiss him, and 1110
but by a kiss thought to persuade him there; 1114
but some untimely thought did instigate | his LUC 43
within his thought her heavenly image sits, 288
that shuts him from the heaven of his thought, 338
the fault unknown is as a thought unacted. 527
ev'n in this thought through the dark night he 729
and the dire thought of his committed evil 972
"nor shall he smile at thee in secret thought, 1065
for lucrece thought he blush'd to see her shame, 1344
she thought he blush'd, as knowing tarquin's 1354
the more she thought he spied in her some 1358
which all this time hath overslipp'd her thought 1576
ah, thought i, thou mourn'st in vain! PP 20.19
o, change thy thought, that i may change my mind SON 10. 9
good conceit of thine | in thy soul's thought 26. 8
when to the sessions of sweet silent thought | i 30. 1
and all those friends which i thought buried. 31. 4
o, then voutsafe me but this loving thought: 32. 9
if the dull substance of my flesh were thought, 44. 1
for nimble thought can jump both sea and land 44. 7
but ah, thought kills me that i am not thought, 44. 9
but ah, thought kills me that i am not thought, 44. 9
the first my thought, the other my desire, 45. 3
nor dare i question with my jealious thought 57. 9
i should in thought control your times of 58. 2
this thought is as a death, which cannot choose 64.13
nothing that the thought of hearts can mend; 69. 2
i found (or thought i found) you did exceed 83. 3
but that is in my thought, whose love to you 85.11
whilst it hath thought itself so blessed never? 119. 6
i have sworn thee fair, and thought thee bright, 147.13
whereon the thought might think sometime it saw LC 10
lands and mansions, theirs in thought assign'd, 138
thought characters and words merely but art, 174

THOUGHTEN 1 FR 0.0001 REL FR 1 V 0 P
me, be you thoughten | that i came with no ill PER 4.06.108

THOUGHT–EXECUTING 1 FR 0.0001 REL FR 1 V 0 P
you sulph'rous and thought–executing fires, LR 3.02. 4

THOUGHTFUL 1 FR 0.0001 REL FR 1 V 0 P
for this they have been thoughtful to invest 2H4 4.05. 72

THOUGHT'S 2 FR 0.0002 REL FR 2 V 0 P
they did perform | beyond thought's compass, H8 1.01. 36
fleet–wing'd duty with thought's feathers flies. LUC 1216

THOUGHTS' 2 FR 0.0002 REL FR 2 V 0 P
welcome, dear cousin, my thoughts' sovereign, R3 3.01. 2
and that thou thoughts' thy griefs might equal PER 5.01.131

/THOUGHTS 4 FR 0.0004 REL FR 4 V 0 P
/i /have /shook /off /the /regal /thoughts R2 4.01.163
/sincere /and /holy /in /his /thoughts, | /he's 2H4 1.01.202
/o /thoughts /of /men /accurs'd! 1.03.107
/opinion, /whose /wrong /thoughts /defile /thee, LR 3.06.112

THOUGHTS 266 FR 0.0300 REL FR 246 V 20 P
to know | did never meddle with my thoughts. TMP 1.02. 22
would, with themselves, shut up my thoughts. 2.01.192
but these sweet thoughts do even refresh my 3.01. 14
thy thoughts i cleave to. what's thy pleasure? 4.01.165
i do begin to have bloody thoughts. 4.01.221 P
whose high imperious thoughts have punish'd me TGV 2.04.130
who art the table wherein all my thoughts | are 2.07. 3
his love sincere, his thoughts immaculate, | his 2.07. 76
"my thoughts do harbor with my silvia nightly, 3.01.140
my herald thoughts in thy pure bosom rest them, 3.01.144
and manage it against despairing thoughts. 3.01.249
a little time will melt her frozen thoughts, 3.02. 9
one julia, that his changing thoughts forget, 4.04.119
heaven make you better than your thoughts! WIV 3.03.205 P
as thoughts do blow them, higher and higher. 5.05. 98
thoughts are no subjects, | intents but merely MM 5.01.453
are no subjects, | intents but merely thoughts. 5.01.454
about thy thoughts and counsels of thy heart! ADO 4.01.102
to turn all beauty into thoughts of harm, | and 4.01.107
most maculate thoughts, master, are mask'd under LLL 1.02. 92 P
your own good thoughts excuse me, and farewell. 2.01.175
those thoughts to me were oaks, to thee like 4.02.108
in such a presence here to plead my thoughts; MND 1.01. 61
as due to love as thoughts and dreams and sighs, 1.01.154
teaches them suspect | the thoughts of others! MV 1.03.162
except to steal your thoughts, my gentle queen. 2.01. 12
heaven and thy thoughts are witness that thou 2.06. 32
and employ your chiefest thoughts | to courtship 2.08. 43
as doubtful thoughts, and rash–embrac'd despair, 3.02.109
fair thoughts and happy hours attend on you! 3.04. 41
punish me not with your hard thoughts, wherein i AYL 1.02.184 P
and in their barks my thoughts i'll character, 3.02. 6
so do all thoughts, they are wing'd. 4.01.142 P
call home thy ancient thoughts from banishment, SHR in.2. 31
maid, | bend thoughts and wits to achieve her. 1.01.179
words can witness, or your thoughts can guess. 2.01.336
yet if thy thoughts, bianca, be so humble | to 3.01. 89
be forg'd in your thoughts be servants to you! AWW 1.01. 75
lies richer in your thoughts than on his tomb. 1.02. 49
king, | had from the conversation of my thoughts 1.03.234
if seriously i may convey my thoughts | in this 2.01. 81
humbly entreating from your royal thoughts | a 2.01.127
late | was in my nobler thoughts most base, is 2.03.171
make me but like my thoughts, and i shall prove 3.03. 10
ever a friend whose thoughts more truly labor 4.04. 17
when saucy trusting of the cozen'd thoughts 4.04. 23
sir, for my thoughts, you have them ill to 5.03.182
for his thoughts, | would they were blanks, TN 3.01.103
i come to whet your gentle thoughts | on his 3.01.105
and baited it with all th' unmuzzled thoughts 3.01.119
boy, with me, my thoughts are ripe in mischief. 5.01.129
in me | thoughts that would thick my blood. WT 1.02.171
with thoughts so qualified as your charities 2.01.113
jealousies | to bloody thoughts and to revenge, 3.02.159
of the young prince, whose honorable thoughts 3.02.195
thoughts | (thoughts high for one so tender) 3.02.196
business, and lay aside the thoughts of sicilia. 4.02. 52 P
with these forc'd thoughts, i prithee darken not 4.04. 41
strangle such thoughts as these with any thing 4.04. 47
by th' pattern of mine own thoughts i cut out 4.04.382
that supernal judge that stirs good thoughts JN 2.01.112
though churlish thoughts themselves should be 2.01.519
day, | i would into thy bosom pour my thoughts. 3.03. 53
it makes the course of thoughts to fetch about, 4.02. 24
where i may think the remnant of my thoughts 5.04. 46
pride | of sky–aspiring and ambitious thoughts, R2 1.03.130
he is gone, and with him go these thoughts. 1.04. 37
and prick my tender patience to those thoughts 2.01.207
nay, let us share thy thoughts, as thou dost 2.01.273
thy words are but as thoughts, therefore be bold 2.01.276
should i do so, i should belie my thoughts. 2.02. 77
high be our thoughts. 3.02. 89
beget | a generation of still–breeding thoughts; 5.05. 8
and these same thoughts people this little world 5.05. 9
as thoughts of things divine, are intermix'd 5.05. 12
thoughts tending to ambition, they do plot 5.05. 18
thoughts tending to content flatter themselves 5.05. 23

my thoughts are minutes, and with sighs they jar 5.05. 51
but let him from my thoughts. 1H4 1.01. 91
into the good thoughts of the world again; 1.03.182
your majesty's good thoughts away from me! 3.02.131
they wound my thoughts worse than thy sword my 5.04. 80
but thoughts, the slaves of life, and life, 5.04. 81
much smaller than the smallest of his thoughts, 2H4 1.03. 30
fathers | have broke their sleep with thoughts, 4.05. 68
thou hid'st a thousand daggers in thy thoughts, 4.05.106
or swell my thoughts to any strain of pride, 4.05.170
question your royal thoughts, make the case 5.02. 91
thy doll, and helen of thy noble thoughts, | is 5.05. 33
piece out our imperfections with your thoughts; H5 pr 23
for 'tis your thoughts that now must deck our pr 28
some things of weight | that task our thoughts, 1.02. 6
you, my gentle knight, give me your thoughts. 2.02. 14
to trouble himself with any such thoughts yet. 2.03. 22 P
work, work your thoughts, and therein see a 3.pr. 25
a name that in my thoughts becomes me best, | if 3.03. 6
seen, | heave him away upon your winged thoughts 5.pr. 8
and your eyes advance | after your thoughts, 5.pr. 45
avouch the thoughts of your heart with the looks 5.02.235 P
an army have i muster'd in my thoughts, 1H6 1.01.101
my thoughts are whirled like a potter's wheel, 1.05. 19
in dumb significants proclaim your thoughts: 2.04. 26
beside, i fear me, if thy thoughts were sifted, 3.01. 24
as i am sick with working of my thoughts. 5.05. 86
soul, | if sympathy of love unite our thoughts. 2H6 1.01. 23
lord, | banish the canker of ambitious thoughts! 1.02. 18
and bears his thoughts above his falcon's pitch. 2.01. 12
thine eyes and thoughts | beat on a crown, the 2.01. 19
now, york, or never, steel thy fearful thoughts, 3.01.331
thou that judgest all things, stay my thoughts, 3.02.136
my thoughts that labor to persuade my soul 3.02.137
my thoughts do hourly prophesy | mischance unto 3.02.283
breast from harboring foul deceitful thoughts. 4.07.103
more like a king, more kingly in my thoughts; 5.01. 29
york, unloose thy long-imprisoned thoughts, 5.01. 88
those gracious words revive my drooping thoughts 3H6 3.03. 21
my thoughts aim at a further matter: 4.01.125
conceive, when, after many moody thoughts, | at 4.06. 13
suggest but truth to my divining thoughts, 4.06. 69
dive, thoughts, down to my soul — here clarence R3 1.01. 41
nearer in bloody thoughts, /but not in blood, 2.01. 93
the history of all her secret thoughts. 3.05. 28
whiles, in the mildness of your sleepy thoughts, 3.07.123
to sanctuary, and good thoughts possess thee! 4.01. 93
love, | immaculate devotion, holy thoughts, | i 4.04.404
strive with troubled thoughts to take a nap, 5.03.104
private, | full of sad thoughts and troubles. H8 2.02. 15
from these sad thoughts that work too much upon 2.02. 57
the cure is to | remove these thoughts from you; 2.04.102
holy and heavenly thoughts still counsel her. 5.04. 29
and when fair cressid comes into my thoughts — TRO 1.01. 30
would they but fat their thoughts | with this 2.02. 48
matter of the world | enter his thoughts, save 2.03.187
fair queen, fair thoughts be your fair pillow! 3.01. 45 P
and hot blood begets hot thoughts, and hot 3.01.129 P
hot thoughts, and hot thoughts beget hot deeds, 3.01.130 P
love — hot blood, hot thoughts, and hot deeds? 3.01.132 P
my thoughts were like unbridled children grown 3.02.122
to angle for your thoughts, but you are wise, 3.02.155
do thoughts unveil in their dumb cradles. 3.03.200
who, in your thoughts, deserves fair helen best, 4.01. 54
and wide unclasp the tables of their thoughts 4.05. 60
mouldeth goblins swift as frenzy's thoughts. 5.10. 29
they do disdain us much beyond our thoughts, COR 1.04. 26
inform | thy thoughts with nobleness, that thou 5.03. 72
how fair the tribune speaks to calm my thoughts! TIT 1.01. 46
and her to whom my thoughts are humbled all, 1.01. 51
aaron, arm thy heart, and fit thy thoughts, | to 2.01. 12
away with slavish weeds and servile thoughts! 2.01. 18
o, that delightful engine of her thoughts, 3.01. 82
doth fat me with the very thoughts of it! 3.01.203
to stir a mutiny in the mildest thoughts, | and 4.01. 85
lord of my life, commander of my thoughts, 4.04. 28
king, be thy thoughts imperious, like thy name. 4.04. 81
love's heralds should be thoughts, | which ten ROM 2.05. 4
me above the ground with cheerful thoughts. 5.01. 5
to enter in the thoughts of desperate men! 5.01. 36
assurance bless your thoughts! TIM 2.02.180
upon that were my thoughts tiring when we 3.06. 4 P
of mine hath buried | thoughts of great value, JC 1.02. 50
you in | with all kind love, good thoughts, and 3.01.176
to fasten in our thoughts that they have courage 5.01. 11
why dost thou show to the apt thoughts of men 5.03. 68
you spirits | that tend on mortal thoughts, MAC 1.05. 41
restrain in me the cursed thoughts that nature 2.01. 8
be not lost | so poorly in your thoughts. 2.02. 69
using those thoughts which should indeed have 3.02. 10
my former speeches have but hit your thoughts, 3.06. 1
to crown my thoughts with acts, be it thought 4.01.149
which you are, my thoughts cannot transpose: 4.03. 21
reconcil'd my thoughts | to thy good truth and 4.03.116
thoughts speculative their unsure hopes relate, 5.04. 19
direness, familiar to my slaughterous thoughts, 5.05. 14
my thoughts and wishes bend again toward france, HAM 1.02. 55
give thy thoughts no tongue, | nor any 1.03. 59
with thoughts beyond the reaches of our souls? 1.04. 56
swift | as meditation or the thoughts of love, 1.05. 30
my lord, there was no such stuff in my thoughts. 2.02.312 P
at my beck than i have thoughts to put them in, 3.01.125 P
our thoughts are ours, their ends none of our 3.02.213
but die thy thoughts when thy first lord is dead 3.02.215
thoughts black, hands apt, drugs fit, and time 3.02.255
my words fly up, my thoughts remain below: 3.03. 97
words without thoughts never to heaven go. 3.03. 98
my thoughts be bloody, or be nothing worth! 4.04. 66
botch the words up fit to their own thoughts, 4.05. 10
and unwholesome in /their thoughts and whispers 4.05. 82
and there is pansies, that's for thoughts. 4.05.177 P
in madness, thoughts and remembrance fitted. 4.05.178 P
free me so far in your most generous thoughts, 5.02.242
bear free and patient thoughts. LR 4.06. 80
so should my thoughts be sever'd from my griefs, 4.06.282
what, in ill thoughts again? 5.02. 9
to put my father in impatient thoughts | by OTH 1.03.242
whose footing here anticipates our thoughts | a 2.01. 76
to the history of lust and foul thoughts. 2.01.258 P
villainous thoughts, roderigo! 2.01.260 P
and give thy worst of thoughts | the worst of 3.03.132
utter my thoughts? 3.03.136
and mak'st his ear | a stranger to thy thoughts. 3.03.144
and wisdom, | to let you know my thoughts. 3.03.154
/by /heaven, i'll know thy thoughts. 3.03.162
such vild success | which my thoughts aim'd not. 3.03.223
rank, | foul disproportions, thoughts unnatural. 3.03.233
even so my bloody thoughts, with violent pace, 3.03.457
and could almost read | the thoughts of people. 3.04. 58
this while with leaden thoughts been press'd, 3.04.177
our worser thoughts heavens mend! ANT 1.02. 62 P
thy freer thoughts | may not fly forth of egypt. 1.05. 11
prove such a wife | as my thoughts make thee, 3.02. 26
already, will their good thoughts call from him. 3.06. 21
break to powder, | and finish all foul thoughts. 4.09. 18
but please your thoughts | in feeding them with 4.15. 52
heart | where mine his thoughts did kindle — 5.01. 46
these thoughts of horror further than you shall 5.02. 63
take to you no hard thoughts. 5.02.117
cheer'd, | make not your thoughts your prisons; 5.02.185
thy thoughts | touch their effects in this: 5.02.329
him at certain hours | such thoughts and such; CYM 1.03. 28
lust and rank thoughts, hers, hers; 2.05. 24
their thoughts do hit | the roofs of palaces, 3.03. 83
and her thoughts the king | of every virtue PER 1.01. 13
but i must tell you, now my thoughts revolt, 1.01. 78
why should this change of thoughts, | the sad 1.02. 1
by jove, i wonder, that is king of thoughts, 2.03. 28
my actions are as noble as my thoughts, | that 2.05. 59
the sooner her vile thoughts to stead, 4.ch. 41
convey, | unless your thoughts went on my way. 4.ch. 50
his steerage shall your thoughts /grow /on — 4.04. 19
and to her father turn our thoughts again, 5.ch. 12
and said no more but what my thoughts | did 5.01.133
so, but alters to | the quality of his thoughts; TNK 5.03. 48
let me set up before your thoughts, good friends STM II.C 90
once more the engine of her thoughts began: VEN 367
the one doth flatter thee in thoughts unlikely, 989
in likely thoughts the other kills thee quickly. 990
did sting | his high-pitch'd thoughts, that LUC 41
for unstain'd thoughts do seldom dream on evil; 87
pure thoughts are dead and still, | while lust 167
and justly thus controls his thoughts unjust: 189
and die, unhallowed thoughts, before you blot 192
and with good thoughts makes dispensation, 248
that his foul thoughts might compass his fair 346
thoughts are but dreams till their effects be 353
let him return, and flatt'ring thoughts retire; 641
"so let thy thoughts, low vassals to thy state" 666
those thoughts to me like oaks, to thee like PP 5. 4
for then my thoughts (from far where i abide) SON 27. 5
yet in these thoughts myself almost despising, 29. 9
to entertain the time with thoughts of love, 39.11
which time and thoughts so sweetly dost deceive, 39.12
this title is impanelled | a quest of thoughts, 46.10
and in his thoughts of love doth share a part. 47. 8
thou /not farther than my thoughts canst move, 47.11
churls, their thoughts (although their eyes were 69.11
that i in your sweet thoughts would be forgot, 71. 7
so are you to my thoughts as food to life, | or 75. 1
i think good thoughts whilst other write good 85. 5
me for my dumb thoughts, speaking in effect. 85.14
that did my ripe thoughts in my brain inhearse, 86. 3
for, bending all my loving thoughts on thee, 88.10
what e'er thy thoughts or thy heart's workings 93.11
gor'd mine own thoughts, sold cheap what is most 110. 3
by their rank thoughts my deeds must not be 121.12
my thoughts and my discourse as madmen's are, 147.11
to dwell with him in thoughts, or to remain | in LC 129

THOUGHT-SICK 1 FR 0.0001 REL FR 1 V 0 P
is thought-sick at the act. HAM 3.04. 51

THOUGHT'ST 1 FR 0.0001 REL FR 1 V 0 P
thou thought'st to help me, and such thanks i AWW 2.01.130

THOU'LDST 1 FR 0.0001 REL FR 1 V 0 P
thou'ldst have, great glamis, | that which cries MAC 1.05. 22

THOU'LT 16 FR 0.0018 REL FR 11 V 5 P
tut, man, i mean thou'lt lose the flood, and, in TGV 2.03. 41 P
thou'lt show thy mercy and remorse more strange MV 4.01. 20
if thou'lt see a thing to talk on when thou art WT 3.03. 80 P
if thou'lt bear a part, thou shalt hear; 4.04.292 P
o, like a book of sport thou'lt read me o'er; TRO 4.05.239
come, thou'lt do my message, wilt thou not? TIT 4.01.117
and let his very breath whom thou'lt observe TIM 4.03.212
thou'lt be afraid to hear it. MAC 5.07. 5
nay, and thou'lt mouth, | i'll rant as well as HAM 5.01.283
as the wind sits, thou'lt catch cold shortly. LR 1.04.101 P
thou'lt have me whipt for lying; 1.04.183 P
thou'lt not believe | with how deprav'd a 2.04.136
either say thou'lt do't, | or thrive by other 5.03. 33
thou'lt come no more, | never, never, never, 5.03.308
of thy preferment, such | as thou'lt desire; CYM 1.05. 72
thou'lt torture me to leave unspoken that 5.05.139

THOU'RT 20 FR 0.0022 REL FR 15 V 5 P
fetch us in fuel, and be quick, thou'rt best, TMP 1.02.366
thou'rt an emperor — caesar, keiser, and WIV 1.03. 9 P
thou'rt a gentleman. 2.01.193 P
thou'rt a good boy. 3.03. 33 P
thou'rt a three-pil'd piece, i warrant thee. MM 1.02. 32 P
thou'rt i' th' right, girl, more o' that. 2.02.129
thou'rt by no means valiant, | for thou dost 3.01. 15
if thou art rich, thou'rt poor, | for, like an 3.01. 25
thou'rt condemn'd, | but, for those earthly 5.01.482
but taking up, and that thou'rt scarce worth. AWW 2.03.208 P
go play, mamillius, thou'rt an honest man. WT 1.02.211
thou'rt like to have | a lullaby too rough. 3.03. 54
thou'rt damn'd as black — nay, nothing is so JN 4.03.121
thou'rt mad to say it! MAC 1.05. 31
if thou'rt noble, | i do forgive thee. LR 5.03.166
for i know thou'rt full of love and honesty, OTH 3.03.118
thou'rt not such a villain. 5.02.174
thou'rt poison to my blood. CYM 1.01.128
thou'rt my good youth — my page; 5.05.118
thou'rt dead. 5.05.299

/THOUSAND 4 FR 0.0004 REL FR 3 V 1 P
he ask'd me for a /thousand marks in gold: ERR 2.01. 61
/i, /in /twelve /thousand, /none. R2 4.01.171
/roof | /did /keep /ten /thousand /men? 4.01.283
i will lay you ten /thousand ducats to your ring CYM 1.04.127 P

THOUSAND 346 FR 0.0391 REL FR 272 V 74 P
now would i give a thousand furlongs of sea for TMP 1.01. 65 P
a thousand, thousand! 3.01. 91
a thousand, thousand! 3.01. 91
sometimes a thousand twangling instruments 3.02.137
and yet a thousand times it answers "no." TGV 1.03. 91
madam and mistress, a thousand good morrows. 2.01. 96 P
sir valentine and servant! to you two thousand. 2.01.100 P
(please you command) a thousand times as much; 2.01.114
pence, thou shalt have five thousand welcomes. 2.05. 10 P
with twenty thousand soul-confirming oaths. 2.06. 16
a thousand oaths, an ocean of his tears, | and 2.07. 69
sir eglamour, a thousand times good morrow. 4.03. 6
for i have heard him say a thousand times | his 4.04.134
a thousand more mischances than this one | have 5.03. 3
then rend thy faith | into a thousand oaths; 5.04. 48
i warrant he hath a thousand of these letters, WIV 2.01. 74 P
two thousand, fair woman, and i'll vouchsafe 2.02. 42 P
for the which she thanks you a thousand times — 2.02. 82 P
marriage vow, and a thousand other her defenses, 2.02.249 P
peds of roses, | and a thousand fragrant posies. 3.01. 20
in pabylon — | and a thousand vagram posies. 3.01. 25
i had rather than a thousand pound he were out 3.03.123 P
a omans as i will desires among five thousand, 3.03.221 P
though twenty thousand worthier come to crave 4.04. 90
and shun | a thousand irreligious cursed hours 5.05.229
to three thousand dolors a year. MM 1.02. 50 P
to prison was worth five thousand of you all. 1.02. 61 P
for thou exists on many a thousand grains | that 3.01. 20
yet in this life | lie hid moe thousand deaths; 3.01. 40
i'll pray a thousand prayers for thy death, | no 3.01.145
he would have paid for the nursing a thousand. 3.02.119 P
thousand escapes of wit | make thee the father 4.01. 62
unless a thousand marks be levied | to quit the ERR 1.01. 21
where is the thousand marks thou hadst of me? 1.02. 81
but not a thousand marks between you both. 1.02. 84
"where is the thousand marks i gave thee, 2.01. 65
and shrive you of a thousand idle pranks. 2.02.208
and charg'd him with a thousand marks in gold, 3.01. 8
i buy a thousand pound a year! i buy a rope! 4.01. 21
it will cost him a thousand pound ere 'a be ADO 1.01. 90 P
working this, and thy fee is a thousand ducats. 2.02. 53 P
she tore the letter into a thousand halfpence; 2.03.140 P
i have earn'd of don john a thousand ducats. 3.03.109 P
bids me a thousand times good night — i tell 3.03.147 P
yea, and 'twere a thousand pound more than 'tis, 3.05. 24 P
they have had | a thousand times in secret. 4.01. 94
i have mark'd | a thousand blushing apparitions 4.01.159
a thousand innocent shames | in angel whiteness 4.01.160
he had receiv'd a thousand ducats of don john 4.02. 47 P
three thousand times within this three years' LLL 1.01.150
the payment of a hundred thousand crowns, 2.01.129
there remains unpaid | a hundred thousand more, 2.01.134
to have repaid | a hundred thousand crowns, and 2.01.143
/on payment of a hundred thousand crowns, | to 2.01.144
for he hath been five thousand year a boy. 5.02. 11
i am compar'd to twenty thousand fairs. 5.02. 37
some thousand verses of a faithful lover. 5.02. 50
as it should pierce a hundred thousand hearts; MND 2.01.160
three thousand ducats — well. MV 1.03. 1 P
three thousand ducats for three months, and 1.03. 9 P
three thousand ducats: 1.03. 26 P
up the gross | of full three thousand ducats. 1.03. 56
ay, ay, three thousand ducats. 1.03. 65
three thousand ducats — 'tis a good round sum. 1.03.103
a cur can lend three thousand ducats?" 1.03.122
gone, cost me two thousand ducats in frankford! 3.01. 84 P
two thousand ducats in that, and other precious, 3.01. 86 P
a thousand times more fair, ten thousand times 3.02.154
times more fair, ten thousand times more rich, 3.02.154
with them the first boy for a thousand ducats. 3.02.214 P
for me, three thousand ducats. 3.02.298
pay him six thousand, and deface the bond; 3.02.299
double six thousand, and then treble that, 3.02.300
a thousand raw tricks of these bragging jacks, 3.04. 77
flesh than to receive | three thousand ducats. 4.01. 42
and i be pleas'd to give ten thousand ducats 4.01. 45
for thy three thousand ducats here is six. 4.01. 84
if every ducat in six thousand ducats | were in 4.01. 85
in lieu whereof | three thousand ducats, due 4.01.411
which did refuse three thousand ducats of me, 5.01.211
me by will but poor a thousand crowns, and, as AYL 1.01. 2 P
and yet give no thousand crowns neither. 1.01. 86 P
o yes, into a thousand similes. 2.01. 45
into a thousand that i have forgotten. 2.04. 32
you are a thousand times a properer man | than 3.05. 51
that will divide a minute into a thousand parts, 4.01. 45 P
but a part of the thousand part of a minute in 4.01. 46 P
the poor world is almost six thousand years old, 4.01. 95 P
which bars a thousand harms and lengthens life. SHR in.2. 136
fair leda's daughter had a thousand wooers, 1.02.242
a thousand thanks, signior gremio. 2.01. 84 P
and in possession twenty thousand crowns. 2.01.122
besides two thousand ducats by the year | of 2.01.369
two thousand ducats by the year of land! 2.01.372
he'll woo a thousand, 'point the day of marriage 3.02. 15
add | unto their losses twenty thousand crowns, 5.02.113
there shall your master have a thousand loves, AWW 1.01.166
a known truth to pass a thousand nothings with, 2.05. 30 P
her, i'll add three thousand crowns | to what is 3.07. 35
five or six thousand, but very weak and 4.03.131 P
"five or six thousand horse," i said — i will 4.03.148 P
amounts not to fifteen thousand pole, half of 4.03.167 P
we may pick a thousand sallets ere we light on 4.05. 14 P
is his wife, | that ring's a thousand proofs. 5.03.199
why, he has three thousand ducats a year. TN 1.03. 22 P
a thousand thousand sighs to save, | lay me, o, 2.04. 63
a thousand thousand sighs to save, | lay me, o, 2.04. 63
to him, lad, some two thousand strong, or so. 3.02. 55 P
to do you rest, a thousand deaths would die. 5.01.133
thou hast said to me a thousand times | thou 5.01.267
slaughters a thousand waiting upon that. WT 1.02. 93
's | with one soft kiss a thousand furlongs ere 1.02. 95

many thousand on 's | have the disease, and 1.02.206
a thousand knees, | ten thousand years together, 3.02.210
ten thousand years together, naked, fasting, 3.02.211
of april, forty thousand fadom above water, and 4.04.277 P
might have spoken a thousand things that would 5.01. 21
twice fifteen thousand hearts of england's breed JN 2.01.275
full thirty thousand marks of english coin. 2.01.530
and thou possessed with a thousand wrongs; 3.03. 41
even to that drop ten thousand wiry /friends 3.04. 64
to train ten thousand english to their side, 3.04.175
told of a many thousand warlike french | that 4.02.199
i'll find a thousand shifts to get away. 4.03. 7
a thousand businesses are brief in hand, | and 4.03.158
that mowbray hath receiv'd eight thousand nobles R2 1.01. 88
a thousand flatterers sit within thy crown, 2.01.100
you pluck a thousand dangers on your head, | you 2.01.205
you lose a thousand well–disposed hearts, | and 2.01.206
eight tall ships, three thousand men of war, 2.01.286
bid her send me presently a thousand pound. 2.02. 91
from forth the ranks of many thousand french, 2.03.102
thou shalt have twelve thousand fighting men! 3.02. 70
but now the blood of twenty thousand men | did 3.02. 76
is not the king's name twenty thousand names? 3.02. 85
ten thousand bloody crowns of mothers' sons 3.03. 96
the offer of an hundred thousand crowns | than 4.01. 16
i have a thousand spirits in one breast, | to 4.01. 58
breast, | to answer twenty thousand such as you. 4.01. 59
taken, | a thousand of his people butchered, 1H4 1.01. 42
ten thousand bold scots, two and twenty knights, 1.01. 68
i will give thee for it a thousand pound. 2.04. 61 P
but i would give a thousand pound i could run as 2.04.147 P
of us here have ta'en a thousand pound this day 2.04.159 P
and one mordake, and a thousand blue–caps more. 2.04.357 P
hang in the air a thousand leagues from hence, 3.01.224
and i will die a hundred thousand deaths | ere 3.02.158
a hundred thousand rebels die in this. 3.02.160
thou hast sav'd me a thousand marks in links and 3.03. 42 P
this other day you ought him a thousand pound. 3.03.134 P
sirrah, do i owe you a thousand pound? 3.03.135 P
a thousand pound, hal? 3.03.136 P
the earl of westmerland, seven thousand strong, 4.01. 88
to thirty thousand. 4.01.130
wherein the fortune of ten thousand men | must 4.04. 9
he that will caper with me for a thousand marks, 2H4 1.02.193 P
lordship lend me a thousand pound to furnish me 1.02.223 P
to five and twenty thousand men of choice, | and 1.03. 11
whether our present five and twenty thousand 1.03. 16
what, is the king but five and twenty thousand? 1.03. 68
is worth a thousand of these bed–hangers and 2.01.146 P
but many thousand reasons hold me back. 2.03. 66
how many thousand of my poorest subjects | are 3.01. 4
and northumberland | are fifty thousand strong. 3.01. 96
upon or near the rate of thirty thousand. 4.01. 22
if i had a thousand sons, the first humane 4.03.122 P
thou hid'st a thousand daggers in thy thoughts, 4.05.106
have bestow'd the thousand pound i borrow'd of 5.05. 12 P
master shallow, i owe you a thousand pound. 5.05. 73 P
john, let me have five hundred of my thousand. 5.05. 84 P
into a thousand parts divide one man, | and make H5 pr 24
six thousand and two hundred good esquires; 1.01. 14
king beside, | a thousand pounds by th' year. 1.01. 19
so may a thousand actions, once afoot, | /end in 1.02.211
for many a thousand widows | shall this his mock 1.02.284
fighting men they have full threescore thousand. 4.03. 3
but one ten thousand of those men in england 4.03. 17
why, now thou hast unwish'd five thousand men; 4.03. 76
you, upon his knees, a thousand thanks, and he 4.04. 59 P
this note doth tell me of ten thousand french 4.08. 80
gentlemen, | eight thousand and four hundred; 4.08. 85
so that, in these ten thousand they have lost, 4.08. 87
having full scarce six thousand in his troop, 1H6 1.01.112
by three and twenty thousand of the french | was 1.01.113
ten thousand soldiers with me i will take, 1.01.155
a thousand souls to death and deadly night. 2.04.127
i was six thousand strong | and that the french 4.01. 20
ten thousand french have ta'en the sacrament 4.02. 28
corrupt and tainted with a thousand vices, 5.04. 45
it dies, and if it had a thousand lives. 5.04. 75
i rest perplexed with a thousand cares. 5.05. 95
shall blow ten thousand souls to heaven or hell; 2H6 3.01.350
his paly lips | with twenty thousand kisses, and 3.02.142
though suffolk dare him twenty thousand times. 3.02.206
quitting thee thereby of ten thousand shames, 3.02.218
through whom a thousand sighs are breath'd for 3.02.345
embrace, and kiss, and take ten thousand leaves, 3.02.354
i'll give a thousand pound to look upon him. 3.03. 13
a thousand crowns, or else lay down your head. 4.01. 16
what, think you much to pay two thousand crowns, 4.01. 18
better ten thousand base–born cades miscarry 4.08. 47
shall have a thousand crowns for his reward. 4.08. 67
have a lease of my life for a thousand years, i 4.10. 6 P
me, and get a thousand crowns of the king by 4.10. 27 P
let ten thousand devils come against me, and 4.10. 61 P
we give thee for reward a thousand marks, | and 5.01. 79
for thousand yorks he shall not hide his head, 5.01. 85
i would break a thousand oaths to reign one year 3H6 1.02. 17
she is hard by with twenty thousand men; 1.02. 51
what, with five thousand men? 1.02. 66
for a thousand causes | i would prolong a while 1.04. 51
their power, i think, is thirty thousand strong. 2.01.177
will but amount to five and twenty thousand, 2.01.181
for with a band of thirty thousand men | comes 2.02. 68
a thousand men have broke their fasts to–day 2.02.127
a wisp of straw were worth a thousand crowns 2.02.144
words will cost ten thousand lives this day. 2.02.177
if you contend, a thousand lives must wither. 2.05.102
i and ten thousand in this luckless realm | had 2.06. 18
i take my leave with many thousand thanks. 3.02. 56
thou and oxford, with five thousand men, | shall 3.03.234
the queen is valued thirty thousand strong, 5.03. 14
that many a thousand | which now mistrust no 5.06. 37
england, | and cited up a thousand heavy times, R3 1.04. 14
methoughts i saw a thousand fearful wracks; 1.04. 24
a thousand men that fishes gnaw'd upon; 1.04. 25
every man's conscience is a thousand men, | to 5.02. 17
six or seven thousand is their utmost power. 5.03. 10
my conscience hath a thousand several tongues, 5.03.193
than can the substance of ten thousand soldiers 5.03.218
a thousand hearts are great within my bosom. 5.03.347
general throng and sweat | of thousand friends; H8 pr 29
for which i pay 'em | a thousand thanks, and 1.04. 74
to which title | a thousand pound a year, annual 2.03. 64
a thousand pounds a year for pure respect? 2.03. 95
bright faces | cast thousand beams upon me, like 4.02. 89
this one christening will beget a thousand, here 5.03. 37 P
upon this land a thousand thousand blessings, 5.04. 19
upon this land a thousand thousand blessings, 5.04. 19
at all these wards i lie, at a thousand watches. TRO 1.02.264 P
every tithe soul, 'mongst many thousand dismes, 2.02. 19
price hath launch'd above a thousand ships, 2.02. 82
lend me ten thousand eyes, | and i will fill 2.02.101
for emulation hath a thousand sons | that one by 3.03.156
glory, | a thousand complete courses of the sun! 4.01. 28
that with so many thousand sighs | did buy each 4.04. 39
there is a thousand hectors in the field: 5.05. 19
cracking ten thousand curbs | of more strong COR 1.01. 70
a hundred thousand welcomes! 2.01.183
that's thousand to one good one — when you now 2.02. 79
within thine eyes sate twenty thousand deaths, 3.03. 70
a thousand welcomes! 4.05.145
this morning for ten thousand of your throats 5.04. 56
a thousand deaths | would i propose to achieve TIT 2.01. 79
a thousand fiends, a thousand hissing snakes, 2.03.100
a thousand fiends, a thousand hissing snakes, 2.03.100
ten thousand swelling toads, as many urchins, 2.03.101
a hand that warded him | from thousand dangers, 3.01.195
i would we had a thousand roman dames | at such 4.02. 41
and that would she for twenty thousand more. 4.02. 45
ay, that i had not done a thousand more. 5.01.124
but i have done a thousand dreadful things | as 5.01.141
but that i cannot do ten thousand more. 5.01.144
show me a thousand that hath done thee wrong, 5.02. 96
and have a thousand times more cause than he 5.03. 51
how many thousand times hath these poor lips, 5.03.167
ten thousand worse than ever yet i did | would i 5.03.187
i warrant, and i should live a thousand years, ROM 1.03. 46
a thousand times good night! 2.02.154
a thousand times the worse, to want thy light. 2.02.155
ay, a thousand times. peter! 2.04.214 P
"banished," | hath slain ten thousand tybalts. 3.02.114
with twenty hundred thousand times more joy 3.03.153
him with above compare | so many thousand times? 3.05.239
a thousand moral paintings i can show | that TIM 1.01. 90
and late, five thousand; 2.01. 1
to varro and to isidore | he owes nine thousand, 2.01. 2
send o' th' instant | a thousand talents to me. 2.02.199
yes, mine's three thousand crowns; what's yours? 3.04. 28
five thousand mine. 3.04. 29
five thousand crowns, my lord. 3.04. 95 P
five thousand drops pays that. 3.04. 96
a thousand pieces. 3.06. 21 P
a thousand pieces? 3.06. 22 P
live a thousand years, | i shall not find myself JC 3.01.159
inch | ten thousand dollars to our general use. MAC 1.02. 62
with ten thousand warlike men | already at a 4.03.134
lent us good siward, and ten thousand men; 4.03.190
there is ten thousand — 5.03. 13
him threescore thousand crowns in annual fee, HAM 2.02. 73
is to be one man pick'd out of ten thousand. 2.02.179 P
the heart–ache and the thousand natural shocks 3.01. 61
i'll take the ghost's word for a thousand pound. 3.02.287 P
to whose /huge spokes ten thousand lesser things 3.03. 19
two thousand souls and twenty thousand ducats 4.04. 25
two thousand souls and twenty thousand ducats 4.04. 25
see | the imminent death of twenty thousand men, 4.04. 60
for that outlives a thousand tenants. 5.01. 44 P
he hath bore me on his back a thousand times. 5.01.186 P
forty thousand brothers | could not with all 5.01.269
shall break into a hundred thousand flaws | or LR 2.04.285
to have a thousand with red burning spits | come 3.06. 15
he had a thousand noses, | horns welk'd and 4.06. 70
o, that the slave had forty thousand lives! OTH 3.03.442
o, a thousand, a thousand times. 4.01.192 P
o, a thousand, a thousand times. 4.01.192 P
the act of shame | a thousand times committed. 5.02.212
ten thousand harms, more than the ills i know, ANT 1.02.129
hold by land, | and our twelve thousand horse. 3.07. 59
a thousand, sir, | early though't be, have on 4.04. 21
until | of many thousand kisses the poor last 4.15. 20
your mistress, my ten thousand ducats are yours, CYM 1.04.150 P
above ten thousand meaner moveables | would 2.02. 29
yearly three thousand pounds, which, by thee, 3.01. 9
three thousand confident, in act as many — 5.03. 29
with thousand doubts | how i might stop this PER 1.02. 97
three or four thousand chequins were as pretty a 4.02. 26 P
i cannot be bated one doit of a thousand pieces. 4.02. 51 P
prove the thousand part | of my endurance, thou 5.01.135
but forty thousand fold we had rather have 'em TNK 1.04. 36
a thousand differing ways to one sure end. 1.05. 14
loaden with kisses, arm'd with thousand cupids, 2.02. 31
a thousand chances, | were we from hence, would 2.02. 94
her, | if he be noble arcite — thousand ways! 2.02.255
young boughs that blush with thousand blossoms, 3.06.243
thousand fresh water–flowers of several colors, 4.01. 85
meed | a thousand honey secrets shalt thou know. VEN 16
dog shall rouse thee, though a thousand bark." 240
a thousand ways he seeks | to mend the hurt that 477
"a thousand kisses buys my heart from me, | and 517
he cranks and crosses with a thousand doubles: 682
"if love have lent you twenty thousand tongues, 775
a thousand spleens bear her a thousand ways, 907
a thousand spleens bear her a thousand ways, 907
where herself herself beheld | a thousand times, 1130
wrapp'd and confounded in a thousand fears, LUC 456
a thousand crosses keep them from thy aid: 912
would purchase thee a thousand thousand friends, 963
would purchase thee a thousand thousand friends, 963
a thousand lamentable objects there, | in scorn 1373
like a thousand vanquish'd men in bloody fight! PP 17.24
bed of roses, | with a thousand fragrant posies, 19.10
after a thousand victories once foil'd, | is SON 25.10
a thousand groans, but thinking on thy face, 131.10
eyes, | for they in thee a thousand errors note, 141. 2
a thousand favors from a maund she drew, | of LC 36

THOUSANDFOLD 4 FR 0.0004 REL FR 4 V 0 P
as brings a thousandfold more care to keep 3H6 2.02. 52
a thousandfold it doth. 2.05. 46
which | to leave a thousandfold more bitter than H8 2.03. 8
but more in troilus thousandfold i see | than in TRO 1.02.284

THOUSANDS 17 FR 0.0019 REL FR 13 V 4 P
i must remove | some thousands of these logs, TMP 3.01. 10
for a pension of thousands to be paid from the TN 2.05.181 P
with one "we thank you" many thousands moe WT 1.02. 8
of thousands that had struck anointed kings 1.02.358
i have look'd on thousands, who have sped the 1.02.389
to feast upon whole thousands of the french. JN 5.02.178
one on his side fights, thousands will fly. R2 2.02.147
soldier that is the leader of so many thousands. 2H4 3.02.167 P
when thousands weep more than did laugh at it. H5 1.02.296
for thousands more, that yet suspect no peril, 2H6 3.01.152
by my life, | that promises moe thousands; H8 2.03. 97
with thousands of these quarter'd slaves, as COR 1.01.199
have you that charitable title from thousands, TIM 1.02. 91 P
england have i offer | of goodly thousands. MAC 4.03. 44
mine, 'tis his, and has been slave to thousands; OTH 3.03.158
and thousands more | of semblable import — but ANT 3.04. 2
it sums up thousands in a trice. CYM 5.04.167 P

THOUSANDTH *(see thousand)*

THOU'ST* 2 FR 0.0002 REL FR 1 V 1 P
if thou thou'st him some thrice, it shall not be TN 3.02. 45 P
if thou dost deny | thou'st made me cuckold. CYM 2.04.146

THOU'T 8 FR 0.0009 REL FR 4 V 4 P
thou't forget me when i am gone. 2H4 2.04.277 P
thou't set me a–weeping and thou say'st so. 2.04.278 P
thy day's work, | thou't not believe thy deeds: COR 1.09. 2
that's a deed thou't die for. TIM 1.01.193 P
thou wast born a bastard, and thou't die a bawd. 2.02. 84 P
thou't go, strong thief, | when gouty keepers of 4.03. 46
heart before, | to say thou't enter friendly. 5.04. 49
'swounds, show me what thou't do. HAM 5.01.274

THRACIAN 5 FR 0.0005 REL FR 5 V 0 P
tearing the thracian singer in their rage." MND 5.01. 49
brought from thence the thracian fatal steeds, 3H6 4.02. 21
revenge | upon the thracian tyrant in his tent TIT 1.01.138
as cerberus at the thracian poet's feet. 2.04. 51
the thracian king, adallas; ANT 3.06. 71

THRALL 7 FR 0.0008 REL FR 7 V 0 P
mean time look gracious on thy prostrate thrall. 1H6 1.02.117
long time thy shadow hath been thrall to me, 2.03. 36
and make me die the thrall of margaret's curse, R3 4.01. 45
love makes young men thrall and old men dote, VEN 837
and made her thrall | to living death and pain LUC 725
i, | love hath forlorn me, living in thrall; PP 17.14
for men diseas'd, but i, my mistress' thrall, SON 154.12

THRALL'D 2 FR 0.0002 REL FR 2 V 0 P
whose sudden sight hath thrall'd my wounded eye. SHR 1.01.220
nor sense to ecstasy was ne'er so thrall'd | but HAM 3.04. 74

THRALLDOM 1 FR 0.0001 REL FR 1 V 0 P
you | from this earth's thralldom to the joys of R3 1.04.248

THRALLED 1 FR 0.0001 REL FR 1 V 0 P
falls | under the blow of thralled discontent, SON 124. 7

THRALLS 1 FR 0.0001 REL FR 1 V 0 P
were the slaves of drink and thralls of sleep? MAC 3.06. 13

THRASH *(also thresh'd, etc.)*

THRASH 2 FR 0.0002 REL FR 1 V 1 P
thou art here but to thrash troyans, and thou TRO 2.01. 45 P
first thrash the corn, then after burn the straw TIT 2.03.123

THRASONICAL 2 FR 0.0002 REL FR 0 V 2 P
behavior vain, ridiculous, and thrasonical. LLL 5.01. 12 P
rams, and caesar's thrasonical brag of "i came, AYL 5.02. 31 P

THREAD 21 FR 0.0023 REL FR 18 V 3 P
fetter strong madness in a silken thread, ADO 5.01. 25
he draweth out the thread of his verbosity finer LLL 5.01. 16 P
o fates, come, come, | cut thread and thrum, MND 5.01.286
you have shore | with shears his thread of silk. 5.01.341
thou liest, thou thread, thou thimble, | thou SHR 4.03.107
brav'd in mine own house with a skein of thread? 4.03.110
marry, sir, with needle and thread. 4.03.120
beat me to death with a bottom of brown thread. 4.03.137 P
free maids that weave their thread with bones, TN 2.04. 45
any silk, any thread, | any toys for your head WT 4.04.318
the smallest thread | that ever spider twisted JN 4.03.127
my life should sail | are turned to one thread, 5.07. 54
to thread the postern of a small needle's eye." R2 5.05. 17
and let not bardolph's vital thread be cut H5 3.06. 47
his thread of life had not so soon decay'd. 1H6 1.01. 34
argo, their thread of life is spun. 2H6 4.02. 29 P
was touch'd, | they would not thread the gates. COR 3.01.124
and with a silken thread plucks it back again, ROM 2.02.180
and pure grief | shore his old thread in twain. OTH 5.02.206
or till the destinies do cut his thread of life. PER 1.02.108
is, when the thread of hazard is once spun, | a STM III 20

THREADBARE 2 FR 0.0002 REL FR 1 V 1 P
a threadbare juggler and a fortune–teller, | a ERR 5.01.240
so he had need, for 'tis threadbare. 2H6 4.02. 7 P

THREADEN 2 FR 0.0002 REL FR 2 V 0 P
behold the threaden sails, | borne with th' H5 3.pr. 10
some in her threaden fillet still did bide, LC 33

THREADING 1 FR 0.0001 REL FR 1 V 0 P
thus out of season, threading dark–ey'd night: LR 2.01.119

THREADS 1 FR 0.0001 REL FR 1 V 0 P
her hair like golden threads play'd with her LUC 400

/THREAT 1 FR 0.0001 REL FR 1 V 0 P
/plumed /helm /thy /state /begins /to /threat, LR 4.02. 57

THREAT 12 FR 0.0013 REL FR 12 V 0 P
and threat the glory of my precious crown. R2 3.03. 90
threat you me with telling of the king? R3 1.03.112
and every one did threat | to–morrow's vengeance 5.03.205
you so desperate grown to threat your friends? TIT 2.01. 40
and threat me i shall never come to bliss | till 3.01.272
on the dying deck, | hearing the surges threat; TIM 4.02. 21
and very wisely threat before you sting. JC 5.01. 38
whiles i threat, he lives: MAC 2.01. 60
to let an arrogant piece of flesh threat us, CYM 4.02.127
of bristly pikes that ever threat his foes, VEN 620
little frosts that sometime threat the spring, LUC 331
when a black–fac'd cloud the world doth threat, 547

THREATEN 11 FR 0.0012 REL FR 11 V 0 P
though the seas threaten, they are merciful, | i TMP 5.01.178
with | reward did threaten and encourage him, WT 3.02.164
look grimly | and threaten present blusters. 3.03. 4
threaten the threat'ner, and outface the brow JN 5.01. 49

their mouths when what they seem to threaten H5 2.04. 70
shelves and rocks that threaten us with wrack. 3H6 5.04. 23
to threaten me with death is most unlawful. R3 1.04.188
an eye like mars, to threaten and command, | a HAM 3.04. 57
upon the present state, whose numbers threaten, ANT 1.03. 52
and what to come shall threaten me | i fear less TNK 3.06.124
that command | and threaten love, and what young 4.02. 40

THREATEN'D 3 FR 0.0003 REL FR 3 V 0 P
the things that threaten'd me | ne'er look'd but JC 2.02. 10
curst speech | i threaten'd to discover him; LR 2.01. 66
have threaten'd | our prisoners with the sword. CYM 5.05. 77

THREATENS 9 FR 0.0010 REL FR 8 V 1 P
this casket threatens. MV 2.07. 18
are lim'd with the twigs that threatens them. AWW 3.05. 24 P
and threatens them | with divers deaths in death WT 5.01.201
it is the prince of wales that threatens thee, 1H4 5.04. 42
steed threatens steed, in high and boastful H5 4.pr. 10
threatens more | than bargulus the strong 2H6 4.01.107
with man's act, | threatens his bloody stage. MAC 2.04. 6
with whom each minute threatens life or death. PER 1.03. 24
the holy gods as loud | as thunder threatens us. 5.01.199

THREATEN'ST 1 FR 0.0001 REL FR 1 V 0 P
which rather threaten'st than dost promise aught MV 3.02.105

THREATEST 1 FR 0.0001 REL FR 1 V 0 P
injurious duke, that threatest where's no cause. 2H6 1.04. 48

THREAT'NED 8 FR 0.0009 REL FR 5 V 3 P
and has threat'ned to put me into everlasting WIV 3.03. 30 P
her my house, and hath threat'ned to beat her. 4.02. 87 P
but he hath chid me hence and threat'ned me | to MND 3.02.312
save unscratch'd your city's threat'ned cheeks, JN 2.01.225
this friendly treaty of our threat'ned town? 2.01.481
the law that threat'ned death becomes thy friend ROM 3.03.139
and threat'ned me with death, going in the vault 5.03.276
if i die for/'t (as no less is threat'ned me), LR 3.03. 18 P

THREAT'NER 1 FR 0.0001 REL FR 1 V 0 P
threaten the threat'ner, and outface the brow JN 5.01. 49

THREAT'NING 20 FR 0.0022 REL FR 20 V 0 P
having bound up the threat'ning twigs of birch, MM 1.03. 24
excludes all pity from our threat'ning looks: ERR 1.01. 10
fie, fie, unknit that threat'ning unkind brow, SHR 5.02.136
she looks upon them with a threat'ning eye. JN 3.04.120
therefore thy threat'ning colors now wind up, 5.02. 73
march without the noise of threat'ning drum, R2 3.03. 51
this is his claim, his threat'ning, and my H5 2.04.110
and not with such a cruel threat'ning look. 3H6 1.03. 17
death shall stop his dismal threat'ning sound, 2.06. 58
i spy a black, suspicious, threat'ning cloud, 5.03. 4
him, or pitying, threat'ning th' other; COR 1.06. 36
to tremble under titus' threat'ning look. TIT 1.01.134
advanc'd above pale envy's threat'ning reach. 2.01. 4
threat'ning the welkin with his big–swoll'n face 3.01.223
with all his threat'ning band of typhon's brood, 4.02. 94
and shakes his threat'ning sword | against the TIM 5.01.166
to be exalted with the threat'ning clouds; JC 1.03. 8
threat'ning the flames | with bisson rheum, a HAM 2.02.505
again, and fleet, threat'ning most sea–like. ANT 3.13.171
threat'ning cloud–kissing ilion with annoy, LUC 1370

THREAT'NINGLY 1 FR 0.0001 REL FR 1 V 0 P
before i speak, too threat'ningly replies. AWW 2.03. 81

THREATS 17 FR 0.0019 REL FR 17 V 0 P
nor this man's threats | to whom i am subdu'd, TMP 1.02.489
her, | with many bitter threats of biding there. TGV 3.01.238
thy threats have no more strength than her weak MND 3.02.250
who with her head nimble in threats approach'd AYL 4.03.109
sir, spare your threats. WT 3.02. 91
no more than he that threats. to arms let's hie! JN 3.01.347
and threats | shall be the war that henry means 3H6 1.01. 72
clifford, how i scorn his worthless threats! 1.01.101
let these threats alone | till accident or TRO 4.05.261
who threats, in course of this revenge, to do TIT 4.04. 67
to battle, | and not endure all threats? TIM 3.05. 43
there is no terror, cassius, in your threats; JC 4.03. 66
his liberty is full of threats to all, | to you HAM 4.01. 14
and threats the throat of that his officer ANT 3.05. 18
theseus (who where he threats appalls) hath sent TNK 1.02. 90
ev'ry blow that falls | threats a brave life, 5.03. 4
whose crooked beak threats, if he mount, he dies LUC 508

THREE *(also tree*)*

/THREE 2 FR 0.0002 REL FR 2 V 0 P
as from a conduit with /three issuing spouts, TIT 2.04. 30
from nine till twelve | is /three long hours, ROM 2.05. 11

THREE 354 FR 0.0400 REL FR 212 V 142 P
for then thou wast not | out three years old. TMP 1.02. 41
i with this obedient steel, three inches of it, 2.01.283
yourself, | he's safe for these three hours. 3.01. 21
we are three of them; 3.02. 5 P
you are three men of sin, whom destiny, | that 3.03. 53
that you three | from milan did supplant good 3.03. 69
all three of them are desperate: 3.03.104
brother, and yours, abide all three distracted, 5.01. 12
whom three hours since | were wrack'd upon this 5.01.136
your eld'st acquaintance cannot be three hours. 5.01.186
which, but three glasses since, we gave out 5.01.223
these three have robb'd me, and this demi–devil 5.01.272
three things that women highly hold in hate. TGV 3.02. 33
when three or four of his blind brothers and 4.04. 4 P
into the company of three or four gentleman–like 4.04. 17 P
the forest is not three leagues off; 5.01. 11
have done any time these three hundred years. WIV 1.01. 13 P
coat, there is but three skirts for yourself, in 1.01. 29 P
there is three umpires in this matter, as i 1.01.137 P
myself (fidelicet myself) and the three party is 1.01.140 P
we three to hear it and end it between them. 1.01.142 P
i keep but three men and a boy yet, till my 1.01.274 P
fence (three veneys for a dish of stew'd prunes) 1.01.284 P
my good friends for three reprieves for you and 2.02. 7 P
better three hours too soon than a minute too 2.02.312 P
looks handsome in three hundred pounds a year! 3.04. 33
i will do what i can for them all three, for so 3.04.107 P
i suffer'd the pangs of three several deaths: 3.05.108 P
three of master ford's brothers watch the door 4.02. 51 P
/germans /desire to have three of your horses. 4.03. 1 P
and three or four more of their growth, we'll 4.04. 49
set spurs and away, like three german devils, 4.05. 69 P
three german devils, three doctor faustuses. 4.05. 69 P
tells me there is three cozen–germans that has 4.05. 77 P
i was three or four times in the thought they 5.05.121 P
to three thousand dolors a year. MM 1.02. 50 P
within these three days his head to be chopp'd 1.02. 69 P
first, provost, let me bail these gentle three. 5.01.357
and in our sight they three were taken up | by ERR 1.01.110
but her name /and three quarters, that's an ell 3.02.109 P
quarters, that's an ell and three quarters, will 3.02.110 P
which doth amount to three odd ducats more 4.01. 30
he was not three leagues off when i left him. ADO 1.01. 3 P
rather than hold three words' conference with 2.01.270 P
if you three will but minister such assistance 2.01.369 P
you three, berowne, dumaine, and longaville, LLL 1.01. 15
have sworn for three years' term to live with me 1.01. 16
i am resolved, 'tis but a three years' fast: 1.01. 24
that is, to live and study here three years. 1.01. 35
and then, to sleep but three hours in the night, 1.01. 42
stay here in your court for three years' space. 1.01. 52
and bide the penance of each three years' day. 1.01.115
with a woman within the term of three years, he 1.01.130 P
three thousand times within this three years' 1.01.150
thousand times within this three years' space; 1.01.150
and so to study three years is but short. 1.01.180
manner and form following, sir, all those three: 1.01.206 P
promised to study three years with the duke. 1.02. 35 P
which the base vulgar do call three. 1.02. 48 P
now here is three studied ere ye'll thrice wink; 1.02. 51 P
easy it is to put "years" to the word "three," 1.02. 52 P
"three," and study three years in two words, the 1.02. 53 P
of all the four, or the three, or the two, or 1.02. 79 P
guilty of such a ballet some three ages since, 1.02.112 P
no penance, but 'a must fast three days a week. 1.02.129 P
till painful study shall outwear three years, 2.01. 23
all those three i will prove. 3.01. 37 P
i am all these three. 3.01. 46 P
and three times as much more — and yet nothing 3.01. 47 P
were still at odds, being but three. 3.01. 85
were still at odds, being but three. 3.01. 90
were still at odds, being but three. 3.01. 96
o, that's the latin word for three farthings: 3.01.137 P
three farthings — remuneration. 3.01.138 P
and, among three, to love the worst of all, | a 3.01.195
/overcame, three. 4.01. 71 P
not care a pin, if the other three were in. 4.03. 18 P
all three of you, to be thus much o'ershot? 4.03.158
but i a beam do find in each of three. 4.03.160
that you three fools lack'd me fool to make up 4.03.203
i will play three myself. 5.01.143 P
honey, and milk, and sugar: there is three. 5.02.231
write "lord have mercy on us" on those three: 5.02.419
whether the three worthies shall come in or no. 5.02.486
what, are there but three? 5.02.487
it is vara fine, | for every one pursents three. 5.02.488
and three times thrice is nine. 5.02.488
i hope, sir, three times thrice, sir — 5.02.491
by jove, i always took three threes for nine. 5.02.495 P
with threefold love i wish you all these three. 5.02.825
hold the plough for her sweet love three year. 5.02.884 P
now i perceive they have conjoin'd all three MND 3.02.193
yet but three? 3.02.437
three and three, | we'll hold a feast in great 4.01.184
three and three, | we'll hold a feast in great 4.01.184
and there is two or three lords and ladies more 4.02. 16 P
to wear away this long age of three hours 5.01. 33
"the thrice three muses mourning for the death 5.01. 52
o sisters three, | come, come to me, | with 5.01.336
so shall all the couples three | ever true in 5.01.407
he hath devis'd in these three chests of gold, MV 1.02. 29 P
three thousand ducats — well. 1.03. 1 P
ay, sir, for three months. 1.03. 2 P
for three months — well. 1.03. 3 P
three thousand ducats for three months, and 1.03. 9 P
three thousand ducats for three months, and 1.03. 9 P
three thousand ducats: 1.03. 26 P
up the gross | of full three thousand ducats. 1.03. 56
ay, ay, three thousand ducats. 1.03. 65
and for three months. 1.03. 66
i had forgot — three months — you told me so. 1.03. 67
three thousand ducats — 'tis a good round sum. 1.03.103
three months from twelve; 1.03.104
a cur can lend three thousand ducats?" 1.03.122
of thrice three times the value of this bond. 1.03.159
that won three fields of sultan solyman, | i 2.01. 26
and such odd sayings, the sisters three, and 2.02. 63 P
one of these three contains her heavenly picture 2.07. 48
i am enjoin'd by oath to observe three things: 2.09. 9
for me, three thousand ducats. 3.02.298
flesh than to receive | three thousand ducats. 4.01. 42
for thy three thousand ducats here is six. 4.01. 84
some three or four of you | go give him 4.01.147
in lieu whereof | three thousand ducats, due 4.01.411
which did refuse three thousand ducats of me, 5.01.211
there you shall find three of your argosies 5.01.276
duke, and three or four loving lords have put AYL 1.01.100 P
there comes an old man and his three sons — 1.02.118 P
three proper young men, of excellent growth and 1.02.121 P
the eldest of the three wrastled with charles, 1.02.125 P
a moment threw him, and broke three of his ribs, 1.02.127 P
and content is without three good friends; 3.02. 25 P
i have, since i was three year old, convers'd 5.02. 60 P
with mine enemy, i have undone three tailors, i 5.04. 46 P
i'll leave her houses three or four as good, SHR 2.01.366
father hath no less | than three great argosies, 2.01.378
my lessons make no music in three parts. 3.01. 60
am i but three inches? 4.01. 27 P
ere three days pass, which hath as long lov'd me 4.02. 38
him up ever since he was three years old, and 5.01. 82 P
we three are married, but you two are sped. 5.02.185
but /one that lies three thirds and uses a known AWW 2.05. 29 P
and clap upon you two or three probable lies. 3.06. 98 P
her, i'll add three thousand crowns | to what is 3.07. 35
within these three hours 'twill be time enough 4.01. 24 P
three great oaths would scarce make that be 4.01. 59 P
not three hours' travel from this very place. TN 1.02. 23
why, he has three thousand ducats a year. 1.03. 22 P
and speaks three or four languages word for word 1.03. 26 P
he hath known you but three days, and already 1.04. 3 P
did you never see the picture of "we three"? 2.03. 17 P
in a catch that will draw three souls out of one 2.03. 59 P
a peg–a–ramsey, and "three merry men be we." 2.03. 76 P
get ye all three into the box–tree; 2.05. 15 P
having been three months married to her, sitting 2.05. 44 P
i'll get 'em all three all ready. 3.01. 91 P
souls and bodies hath he divorc'd three, and his 3.04.237 P
sir, may put you in mind — one, two, three. 5.01. 40 P
and for three months before, | no int'rim, not a 5.01. 94
three months this youth hath tended upon me, 5.01. 99
three crabbed months had sour'd themselves to WT 1.02.102
violence, in the which three great ones suffer, 2.01.128
be she honor–flaw'd, | i have three daughters: 2.01.144
sir, it is three days since i saw the prince. 4.02. 29 P
three pound of sugar, five pound of currants, 4.03. 37 P
have a kinsman not past three quarters of a mile 4.03. 80 P
'tis in three parts. 4.04.293 P
master, there is three carters, three shepherds, 4.04.324 P
there is three carters, three shepherds, three 4.04.324 P
three shepherds, three neat–herds, three 4.04.325 P
three neat–herds, three swine–herds, that have 4.04.325 P
one three of them, by their own report, sir, 4.04.337 P
not the worst of the three but jumps twelve foot 4.04.339 P
sir, | you have undone a man of fourscore three, 4.04.453
things known betwixt us three, i'll write you 4.04.560
then stand till he be three quarters and a dram 4.04.785 P
of all this isle, | three foot of it doth hold; JN 4.02.100
constance in a frenzy died | three days before; 4.02.123
are wrack'd three nights ago on goodwin sands; 5.03. 11
come the three corners of the world in arms, 5.07.116
three parts of that receipt i had for callice R2 1.01.126
we three are but thyself, and, speaking so, 2.01.275
eight tall ships, three thousand men of war, 2.01.286
we three here part that ne'er shall meet again. 2.02.143
mann'd with three hundred men, as i have heard, 2.03. 54
three judases, each one thrice worse than judas! 3.02.132
'tis full three months since i did see him last. 5.03. 2
three times they breath'd and three times did 1H4 1.03.102
they breath'd and three times did they drink, 1.03.102
of kent hath brought three hundred marks with 2.01. 55 P
with three or four loggerheads amongst three or 2.04. 4 P
or four loggerheads amongst three or four score 2.04. 5 P
there lives not three good men unhang'd in 2.04.130 P
there were not two or three and fifty upon poor 2.04.187 P
three misbegotten knaves in kendal green came at 2.04.221 P
world pick thee out three such enemies again as 2.04.367 P
have in this robbery lost three hundred marks. 2.04.520
three times hath henry bullingbrook made head 3.01. 63
divided it | into three limits very equally: 3.01. 72
money that i borrow'd — three or four times, 3.03. 18 P
hal, three or four bonds of forty pound a–piece, 3.03.101 P
fifty soldiers, three hundred and odd pounds. 4.02. 14 P
unless you call three fingers in the ribs bare. 4.02. 73 P
there's not three of my hundred and fifty left 5.03. 37 P
three knights upon our party slain to–day, | a 5.05. 6
had three times slain th' appearance of the king 2H4 1.01.128
lord, i was born about three of the clock in the 1.02.187 P
as the times do brawl, | /are in three heads: 1.03. 71
so is the unfirm king | in three divided, and 1.03. 74
gaping wounds | untwind the sisters three! 2.04.199
i have three pound to free mouldy and bullcalf. 3.02.244 P
of he, the worst of these three gentlemen! 5.02. 16
and three corrupted men, | one, richard earl of H5 2.pr. 22
and we'll be all three sworn brothers to france. 2.01. 12 P
three or four times. 2.03. 19 P
as i am, i have observ'd these three swashers. 3.02. 28 P
i am boy to them all three, but all they three, 3.02. 29 P
i am boy to them all three, but all they three, 3.02. 29 P
for indeed three such antics do not amount to a 3.02. 31 P
twelve leagues, and sold it for three halfpence. 3.02. 43 P
of english legs | did march three frenchmen. 3.06.150
by three and twenty thousand of the french | was 1H6 1.01.113
more than three hours the fight continued, 1.01.120
and even these three days have i watch'd | if i 1.04. 16
you tempt the fury of my three attendants, 4.02. 10
and you three shall be strangled on the gallows. 2H6 2.03. 8
shall, after three days' open penance done, 2.03. 11
and now we three have spoke it, | it skills not 3.01.280
infection in this air | but three days longer, 3.02.288
if after three days' space thou here be'st found 3.02.295
by the king, and three times thrice by thee. 3.02.358
i have seen him whipt three market–days together 4.02. 58 P
three times to–day i holp him to his horse, 5.03. 8
him to his horse, | three times bestrid him; 5.03. 9
and it hath pleas'd him that three times to–day 5.03. 18
the loss of those three lords torments my heart; 3H6 1.01.270
three times did richard make a lane to me, | and 1.04. 9
dazzle mine eyes, or do i see three suns? 2.01. 25
three glorious suns, each one a perfect sun, 2.01. 26
i bear | upon my target three fair shining suns. 2.01. 40
nay, bear three daughters; 2.01. 41
three, my most gracious lord. 3.02. 29
three dukes of somerset, threefold /renown'd 5.07. 5
her lord, whom i, some three months since, R3 1.02.240
blest his three sons with his victorious arm, 1.04.236
you three on me, threefold distress'd, | pour 2.02. 86
three times to–day my foot–cloth horse did 3.04. 84
and towards three or four a' clock | look for 3.05.101
i do know | kinsmen of mine, three at the least, H8 1.01. 81
pursu'd him still, and three nights after this, 4.02. 25
fire–drake did i hit three times on the head, 5.03. 44 P
and three times was his nose discharg'd against 5.03. 44 P
there they are like to dance these three days; 5.03. 65 P
know he has not past three or four hairs on his TRO 1.02.112 P
and yet will he, within three pound, lift as 1.02.116 P
he never saw three and twenty. 1.02.235 P
prove this troth with my three drops of blood. 1.03.301
in, after falling out, may make them three. 3.01.104 P
i'll give you boot, i'll give you three for one. 4.05. 40
these three lead on this preparation | whither COR 1.02. 15
was forc'd to wheel | three or four miles about, 1.06. 20
within these three hours, tullus, | alone i 1.08. 7
/you are three | that rome should dote on; 2.01.186
three, they say; 2.02. 3 P
and i' th' consul's view | slew three opposers. 2.02. 94
where being three parts melted away with rotten 2.03. 31 P
can, | and three examples of the like hath been 4.06. 51
help, three a' th' chiefest soldiers; 5.06.148
three civil brawls, bred of an airy word, | by ROM 1.01. 89
three words, dear romeo, and good night indeed. 2.02.142
and earth, all three do meet | in thee at once, 3.03.120
the curfew–bell hath rung, 'tis three a' clock. 4.04. 4

within this three hours will fair juliet wake. 5.02. 25
three talents on the present; in future, all. TIM 1.01.141
you three serve three usurers? 2.02. 91 P
you three serve three usurers? 2.02. 92 P
are you three usurers' men? 2.02. 96 P
here's three solidares for thee; 3.01. 43 P
three? 3.03. 9
yes, mine's three thousand crowns; what's yours? 3.04. 28
three or four wenches, where i stood, cried, JC 1.02.271 P
there's two or three of us have seen strange 1.03.138
three parts of him | is ours already, and the 1.03.154
the clock hath stricken three. 2.01.192
he should stand | one of the three to share it? 4.01. 15
till caesar's three and thirty wounds | be well 5.01. 53
'tis three a' clock, and, romans, yet ere night 5.03.109
when shall we three meet again? MAC 1.01. 1
i dreamt last night of the three weird sisters: 2.01. 20
drink, sir, is a great provoker of three things. 2.03. 25 P
what three things does drink especially provoke? 2.03. 26 P
had i three ears, i'ld hear thee. 4.01. 78
'tis two or three, my lord, that bring you word 4.01.141
within this three mile may you see it coming; 5.05. 36
one part wisdom | and ever three parts coward — HAM 4.04. 43
argues an act, and an act hath three branches — 5.01. 11 P
this three years i have took note of it: 5.01.139 P
lien you i' th' earth three and twenty years. 5.01.173 P
three of the carriages, in faith, are very dear 5.02.150 P
assigns, and three liberal-conceited carriages; 5.02.162 P
and him, he shall not exceed you three hits. 5.02.167 P
that we have divided | in three our kingdom; LR 1.01. 38
here's three on 's are sophisticated. 3.04.105 P
who hath /had three suits to his back, six 3.04.135 P
all three | now marry in an instant. 5.03.229
three great ones of the city, | in personal suit OTH 1.01. 8
the senate hath sent about three several quests 1.02. 46
you had not kiss'd your three fingers so oft, 2.01.173 P
three else of cyprus, noble swelling spirits 2.03. 55
the time, but let it not | exceed three days. 3.03. 63
within these three days let me hear thee say 3.03.472
two or three groan. 5.01. 42
let me be married to three kings in a forenoon, ANT 1.02. 27 P
three kings i had newly feasted, and did want 2.02. 76
to you all three, | the senators alone of this 2.06. 8
these three world-sharers, these competitors, 2.07. 70
the other three are sealing. 3.02. 3
three in egypt | cannot make better note. 3.03. 22
and within three days | you with your children 5.02.201
mark it), the eldest of them at three years old, CYM 1.01. 58
i have read three hours then. 2.02. 3
one, two, three: 2.02. 51
yearly three thousand pounds, which, by thee, 3.01. 9
at three and two years old, i stole these babes, 3.03.101
these three, | three thousand confident, in act 5.03. 28
three thousand confident, in act as many — 5.03. 29
for three performers are the file when all | the 5.03. 30
we will die all three, | but i will prove that 5.05.310
the service that you three have done is more 5.05.353
o, what, am i | a mother to the birth of three? 5.05.369
and your three motives to the battle, with | i 5.05.388
the soldier that did company these three | in 5.05.408
we have but poor three, and they can do no more PER 4.02. 7 P
three or four thousand chequins were as pretty a 4.02. 26 P
a man who for this three months hath not spoken 5.01. 24
we are three queens, whose sovereigns fell TNK 1.01. 39
key — like such a woman | as any of us three; 1.01. 95
and three better lads nev'r danc'd | under green 2.03. 38
or two, or three, or ten. 3.03. 36
"there was three fools fell out about an howlet: 3.05. 67
thou wor'st that day the three kings fell, but 3.06. 71
accompanied | with three fair knights, appear 3.06.292
three or four | i saw from far off cross her — 4.01. 99
i'll warrant you within these three or four days 5.02.104
her sight dazzling makes the wound seem three, VEN 1064
three times with sighs she gives her sorrow fire LUC 1604
a lording's daughter, the fairest one of three, PP 15. 1
three winters cold | have from the forests shook SON 104. 3
from the forests shook three summers' pride, 104. 4
three beauteous springs to yellow autumn turn'd 104. 5
three april perfumes in three hot junes burn'd, 104. 7
three april perfumes in three hot junes burn'd, 104. 7
three themes in one, which wondrous scope 105.12
which three till now never kept seat in one. 105.14
THREE-A 1 FR 0.0001 REL FR 1 V 0 P
gallants of war, | by one, by two, by three-a. TNK 3.05. 62
THREE-AND-TWENTY
1 FR 0.0001 REL FR 0 V 1 P
were no age between ten and three-and-twenty, or WT 3.03. 60 P
THREE-FARTHING 1 FR 0.0001 REL FR 0 V 1 P
o, why then three-farthing worth of silk. LLL 3.01.149 P
THREE-FARTHINGS 1 FR 0.0001 REL FR 1 V 0 P
should say, "look where three-farthings goes!" JN 1.01.143
THREEFOLD 10 FR 0.0011 REL FR 10 V 0 P
'tis threefold too little for carrying a letter TGV 1.01.109
my oath | provokes me to this threefold perjury. 2.06. 5
with threefold love i wish you all these three. LLL 5.02.825
right | according to our threefold order ta'en? 1H4 3.01. 70
and threefold vengeance tend upon your steps! 2H6 3.02.304
or else you famish — that's a threefold death. 3H6 5.04. 32
threefold /renown'd | for hardy and undoubted 5.07. 5
you three on me, threefold distress'd, | pour R3 2.02. 86
the threefold world divided, he should stand JC 4.01. 14
a torment thrice threefold thus to be crossed. SON 133. 8
THREE-FOOT 2 FR 0.0002 REL FR 2 V 0 P
sometime for three-foot stool mistaketh me; MND 2.01. 52
when on my three-foot stool i sit and tell | the CYM 3.03. 89
THREE-HEADED 1 FR 0.0001 REL FR 1 V 0 P
club kill'd cerberus, that three-headed canus; LLL 5.02.589
THREE-HOOP'D 1 FR 0.0001 REL FR 0 V 1 P
the three-hoop'd pot shall have ten hoops, and i 2H6 4.02. 66 P
THREE-HOURS 1 FR 0.0001 REL FR 1 V 0 P
when i, thy three-hours wife, have mangled it? ROM 3.02. 99
THREE-INCH 1 FR 0.0001 REL FR 0 V 1 P
away, you three-inch fool! i am no beast. SHR 4.01. 26 P
THREE-LEGG'D 1 FR 0.0001 REL FR 1 V 0 P
to comb your noddle with a three-legg'd stool, SHR 1.01. 64
THREE-MAN 2 FR 0.0002 REL FR 0 V 2 P
for the shearers (three-man song-men all, and WT 4.03. 42 P
if i do, fillip me with a three-man beetle. 2H4 1.02.228 P
THREE-NOOK'D 1 FR 0.0001 REL FR 1 V 0 P
the three-nook'd world | shall bear the olive ANT 4.06. 5
THREEPENCE 5 FR 0.0005 REL FR 1 V 4 P
in a fruit-dish, a dish of some threepence — MM 2.01. 93 P
froth, i could not give you threepence again. 2.01.103 P
the fairest house in it after threepence a bay. 2.01.242 P
a threepence bow'd would hire me, | old as i am, H8 2.03. 36
the controversy of threepence to a second day of COR 2.01. 72 P
THREE-PIL'D 2 FR 0.0002 REL FR 1 V 1 P
thou'rt a three-pil'd piece, i warrant thee. MM 1.02. 32 P
three-pil'd hyperboles, spruce affection, LLL 5.02.407
THREE-PILE 2 FR 0.0002 REL FR 0 V 2 P
at the suit of master three-pile the mercer, for MM 4.03. 10 P
and in my time wore three-pile, but now i am out WT 4.03. 14 P
THREE-QUARTERS 1 FR 0.0001 REL FR 1 V 0 P
thou yard, three-quarters, half-yard, quarter, SHR 4.03.108
THREES 4 FR 0.0004 REL FR 1 V 3 P
by jove, i always took three threes for nine. LLL 5.02.495 P
and will by twos and threes at several posterns WT 1.02.438
pray let's see these four threes of herdsmen. 4.04.336 P
he stands, by ones, by twos, and by threes. COR 2.03. 43 P
THREESCORE 8 FR 0.0009 REL FR 5 V 3 P
i never see a bachelor of threescore again? ADO 1.01.199 P
uneven ground is threescore and ten miles afoot 1H4 2.02. 25 P
fifty, or, by'r lady, inclining to threescore; 2.04.425 P
fighting men they have full threescore thousand. H5 4.03. 3
tell a pedigree | of threescore and two years — 3H6 3.03. 93
threescore and ten i can remember well, | within MAC 2.04. 1
gives him threescore thousand crowns in annual HAM 2.02. 73
and threescore year would make the world away. SON 11. 8
THREE-SUITED 1 FR 0.0001 REL FR 0 V 1 P
shallow, beggarly, three-suited, hundred-pound, LR 2.02. 16 P
THRENE 1 FR 0.0001 REL FR 1 V 0 P
whereupon it made this threne | to the phoenix PHT 49
THREREABOUTS 1 FR 0.0001 REL FR 0 V 1 P
of the age of two and twenty or threreabouts! 1H4 3.03.189 P
THRESH'D *(also thrash)*
THRESH'D 1 FR 0.0001 REL FR 1 V 0 P
wreath | was then nor thresh'd nor blasted; TNK 1.01. 65
THRESHER 1 FR 0.0001 REL FR 1 V 0 P
or like /an /idle thresher with a flail, | fell 3H6 2.01.131
THRESHOLD 6 FR 0.0006 REL FR 5 V 1 P
fell over the threshold, and broke my shin. LLL 3.01.117
you spurn a stranger cur | over your threshold; MV 1.03.119
for many men that stumble at the threshold | are 3H6 4.07. 11
i'll not over the threshold till my lord return COR 1.03. 75 P
my wedded mistress saw | bestride my threshold. 4.05.118
the threshold grates the door to have him heard, LUC 306
/THREW 3 FR 0.0003 REL FR 3 V 0 P
/own /life /hung /upon /the /staff /he /threw), 2H4 4.01.124
/then /threw /he /down /himself /and /all /their 4.01.125
/burst /heaven, /threw /him /on /my /father, LR 5.03.214
THREW 28 FR 0.0031 REL FR 23 V 5 P
and threw her sun-expelling mask away, | the air TGV 4.04.153
i trow, threw this whale (with so many tuns of WIV 2.01. 64 P
eton, they threw me off from behind one of them, 4.05. 67 P
they threw on him | great pails of puddled mire ERR 5.01.172
which charles in a moment threw him, and broke AYL 1.02.127 P
he threw his eye aside, | and mark what object 4.03.102
and threw the sops all in the sexton's face, SHR 3.02.173
which contain'd the name | of her that threw it. AWW 5.03. 95
false, you threw it him | out of a casement. 5.03.229
come, sir, you peevishly threw it to her; TN 2.02. 13 P
threw off his spirit, his appetite, his sleep, WT 2.03. 16
threw dust and rubbish on king richard's head. R2 5.02. 6
threw many a northward look to see his father 2H4 2.03. 13
over suffolk's neck | he threw his wounded arm, H5 4.06. 25
with diamonds, | and threw it towards thy land. 2H6 3.02.108
they threw their caps | as they would hang them COR 1.01.212
as you threw caps up will he tumble down, | and 4.06.135
what time i threw the people's suffrages | on TIT 4.03. 19
hands, and threw up their sweaty night-caps, and JC 1.02.245 P
threw a pearl away | richer than all his tribe; OTH 5.02.347
doing bad, | threw him ashore, to give him glad. PER 2.ch. 38
they were too rough | that threw her in the sea. 3.02. 80
i threw her overboard with these very arms. 5.03. 19
threw unwilling light | upon the wide wound that VEN 1051
himself on her self-slaught'red body threw, LUC 1733
"i hate" from hate away she threw, | and sav'd SON 145.13
jet, | which one by one she in a river threw, LC 38
art, | threw my affections in his charmed power, 146
/THREW'ST 1 FR 0.0001 REL FR 1 V 0 P
/that /threw'st /dust /upon /his /goodly /head 2H4 1.03.103
THRICE 64 FR 0.0072 REL FR 51 V 13 P
but twice, or thrice, was "proteus" written down TGV 1.02.114
not mine twice or thrice in that last article. 3.01.356 P
why, he hath not been thrice in my company! WIV 2.01. 26 P
ere she sleep, has thrice her prayers said, 5.05. 50
he hath twice or thrice cut cupid's bow-string, ADO 3.02. 10 P
how many is one thrice told? LLL 1.02. 39 P
now here is three studied ere ye'll thrice wink; 1.02. 51 P
and three times thrice is nine. 5.02.488
i hope, sir, three times thrice, sir — 5.02.491
thrice blessed they that master so their blood MND 1.01. 74
"the thrice three muses mourning for the death 5.01. 52
of thrice three times the value of this bond. MV 1.03.159
and then to scape drowning thrice, and to be in 2.02.164 P
shylock, there's thrice thy money off'red thee. 4.01.227
take thrice thy money, bid me tear the bond. 4.01.234
pay the bond thrice | and let the christian go. 4.01.318
and he is thrice a villain that says such a AYL 1.01. 58 P
a pair of old breeches thrice turn'd; SHR 3.02. 44 P
with, should be once heard and thrice beaten. AWW 2.05. 31 P
if thou thou'st him some thrice, it shall not be TN 3.02. 45 P
and say, "thrice welcome, drowned viola!" 5.01.241
thrice bow'd before me, | and, gasping to begin WT 3.03. 24
for she hath privately twice or thrice a day, 5.02.105 P
three judases, each one thrice worse than judas! R2 3.02.132
thrice from the banks of wye | and 1H4 3.01. 64
i'll give thrice so much land | to any 3.01.135
thrice hath this hotspur, mars in swathling 3.02.112
now enrag'd with grief, | are thrice themselves. 2H4 1.01.145
the river hath thrice flowed, no ebb between, 4.04.125
gape | for thee thrice wider than for other men. 5.05. 54
if we, with thrice such powers left at home, H5 1.02.217
thrice within this hour | i saw him down; 4.06. 4
thrice up again, and fighting; 4.06. 5
and galling at this gentleman twice or thrice. 5.01. 75 P
bastard of orleance, thrice welcome to us. 1H6 1.02. 47
thrice is he arm'd that hath his quarrel just; 2H6 3.02.233
by the king, and three times thrice by thee. 3.02.358
thrice i led him off, | persuaded him from any 5.03. 9
to me, | and thrice cried, "courage, father! 3H6 1.04. 10
this thrice worthy and right valiant lord TRO 2.03.190
and thy parts of nature | thrice fam'd beyond, 2.03.243
battles thrice six | i have seen, and heard of; COR 2.03.128
have thrice disturb'd the quiet of our streets, ROM 1.01. 91
i'd rather than the worth of thrice the sum TIM 3.03. 22
they shouted thrice; what was the last cry for? JC 1.02.226
was the crown offer'd him thrice? 1.02.228
was't, and he put it by thrice, every time 1.02.229 P
thrice hath calphurnia in her sleep cried out, 2.02. 2
i thrice presented him a kingly crown, | which 3.02. 96
a kingly crown, | which he did thrice refuse. 3.02. 97
thrice to thine, and thrice to mine, | and MAC 1.03. 35
about, | thrice to thine, and thrice to mine, 1.03. 35
to mine, | and thrice again, to make up nine. 1.03. 36
thrice the brinded cat hath mew'd. 4.01. 1
thrice, and once the hedge-pig whin'd. 4.01. 2
thrice he walk'd | by their oppress'd and HAM 1.02.202
and thrice his head thus waving up and down, 2.01. 90
with hecat's ban thrice blasted, thrice 3.02.258
hecat's ban thrice blasted, thrice /infected, 3.02.258
"swithold footed thrice the 'old, | he met the LR 3.04.120
"thrice fairer than myself," thus she began, VEN 7
makes summer's welcome thrice more wish'd, more SON 56.14
and gain by ills thrice more than i have spent. 119.14
a torment thrice threefold thus to be crossed. 133. 8
THRICE-BLESSED 1 FR 0.0001 REL FR 1 V 0 P
thrice-blessed chance, | to drop on such a TNK 3.01. 13
THRICE-CROWNED 1 FR 0.0001 REL FR 1 V 0 P
and thou, thrice-crowned queen of night, survey AYL 3.02. 2
THRICE-DOUBLE 1 FR 0.0001 REL FR 1 V 0 P
what a thrice-double ass | was i to take this TMP 5.01.296
THRICE-DRIVEN 1 FR 0.0001 REL FR 1 V 0 P
/couch of war | my thrice-driven bed of down. OTH 1.03.231
THRICE-FAIR 1 FR 0.0001 REL FR 1 V 0 P
so, thrice-fair lady, stand i, even so, | as MV 3.02.146
THRICE-FAMED 1 FR 0.0001 REL FR 1 V 0 P
laid | upon the life of this thrice-famed duke. 2H6 3.02.157
THRICE-GENTLE 1 FR 0.0001 REL FR 1 V 0 P
alas, thrice-gentle cassio, | my advocation is OTH 3.04.122
THRICE-GORGEOUS 1 FR 0.0001 REL FR 1 V 0 P
no, not all these, thrice-gorgeous ceremony, H5 4.01.266
THRICE-GRACIOUS 2 FR 0.0002 REL FR 2 V 0 P
then, thrice-gracious queen, | more than your R2 2.02. 24
i shall hereafter, my thrice-gracious lord, | be 1H4 3.02. 92
THRICE-NOBLE 4 FR 0.0004 REL FR 4 V 0 P
thrice-noble lord, let me entreat of you | to SHR in.2. 118
thy thrice-noble cousin, | harry bullingbrook, R2 3.03.103
thrice-noble suffolk, 'tis resolutely spoke. 2H6 3.01.266
thrice-noble titus, spare my first-born son! TIT 1.01.120
THRICE-NOBLER 1 FR 0.0001 REL FR 1 V 0 P
thrice-nobler than myself! ANT 4.14. 95
THRICE-PUISSANT 1 FR 0.0001 REL FR 1 V 0 P
and my thrice-puissant liege | is in the very H5 1.02.119
THRICE-RENOWNED 1 FR 0.0001 REL FR 1 V 0 P
why, so you are, my thrice-renowned lord. R3 4.02. 13
THRICE-REPURED 1 FR 0.0001 REL FR 1 V 0 P
taste indeed | love's thrice-repured nectar? TRO 3.02. 22
THRICE-VALIANT 2 FR 0.0002 REL FR 2 V 0 P
well have we done, thrice-valiant countrymen, H5 4.06. 1
to send for lucius, thy thrice-valiant son, TIT 5.02.112
THRICE-VICTORIOUS
1 FR 0.0001 REL FR 1 V 0 P
the thrice-victorious lord of falconbridge, 1H6 4.07. 67
THRICE-WORTHY 2 FR 0.0002 REL FR 0 V 2 P
thrice-worthy gentleman! LLL 5.01.144 P
valorous, and thrice-worthy seigneur of england. H5 4.04. 62 P
THRIFT 12 FR 0.0013 REL FR 11 V 1 P
i am about thrift. WIV 1.03. 43 P
french thrift, you rogues — myself and skirted 1.03. 84
i have a mind presages me such thrift | that i MV 1.01.175
on me, my bargains, and my well-won thrift, 1.03. 50
and thrift is blessing, if men steal it not. 1.03. 90
how, i' th' name of thrift, | does he rake this H8 3.02.109
that from my first have been inclin'd to thrift, TIM 1.01.118
thrift, thrift, horatio! HAM 1.02.180
thrift, thrift, horatio! 1.02.180
of the knee | where thrift may follow fawning. 3.02. 62
marriage move | are base respects of thrift, but 3.02.183
and make them dread it, to the doers' thrift. CYM 5.01. 15
THRIFTLESS 4 FR 0.0004 REL FR 4 V 0 P
what thriftless sighs shall poor olivia breathe? TN 2.02. 39
as thriftless sons their scraping fathers' gold. R2 5.03. 69
thriftless ambition, that will ravin up | thine MAC 2.04. 28
were an all-eating shame, and thriftless praise. SON 2. 8
THRIFTS 1 FR 0.0001 REL FR 1 V 0 P
their profits | (their own particular thrifts), WT 1.02.311
THRIFTY 5 FR 0.0005 REL FR 4 V 1 P
but, like a thrifty goddess, she determines MM 1.01. 38
find — | a proverb never stale in thrifty mind. MV 2.05. 55
the thrifty hire i sav'd under your father, AYL 2.03. 39
for they are thrifty honest men, and such | as 2H6 4.02.186
of cuckolds, a thrifty shoeing-horn in a chain, TRO 5.01. 55 P
THRILL 2 FR 0.0002 REL FR 1 V 1 P
and to thrill and shake | even at the crying of JN 5.02.143
doth not thy blood thrill at it? 1H4 2.04.370 P
THRILL'D 1 FR 0.0001 REL FR 1 V 0 P
a servant that he bred, thrill'd with remorse, LR 4.02. 73
THRILLING 1 FR 0.0001 REL FR 1 V 0 P
in thrilling region of thick-ribbed ice; MM 3.01.122
THRILLS 1 FR 0.0001 REL FR 1 V 0 P
have a faint cold fear thrills through my veins, ROM 4.03. 15
THRIVE 62 FR 0.0070 REL FR 54 V 8 P
thou lov'st, love still, and thrive therein, TGV 1.01. 9
it is a life that i have desir'd. i will thrive. WIV 1.03. 19 P
we will thrive, lads, we will thrive. 1.03. 74 P
we will thrive, lads, we will thrive. 1.03. 74 P
these four worthies in their first show thrive, LLL 5.02.538
this was a way to thrive, and he was blest; MV 1.03. 89
here do i choose, and thrive i as i may! 2.07. 60
happily to wive and thrive as best i may. SHR 1.02. 56

honors thrive, | when rather from our acts we AWW 2.03.135
he cannot thrive, | unless her prayers, whom 3.04. 26
being fool'd, by fool'ry thrive! 4.03.338
would not have knaves thrive long under /her? 5.02. 32 P
by swaggering could i never thrive, | for the TN 5.01.399
is the time that the unjust man doth thrive. WT 4.04.674 P
grandam, i will not wish thy wishes thrive: JN 3.01.334
so thrive it in your game! 4.02. 95
mine innocence and saint george to thrive! R2 1.03. 84
as i intend to thrive in this new world, 4.01. 78
ill mayst thou thrive if thou grant any grace! 5.03. 99
good brother, we shall thrive, i trust. 1H4 1.03.300
for if lord percy thrive not, ere the king 4.04. 36
and wholesome berries thrive and ripen best H5 1.01. 61
now thrive the armorers, and honor's thought 2.pr. 3
and so thrive richard as thy foes may fall! 1H6 3.01.173
say that he thrive, as 'tis great like he will, 2H6 3.01.379
if we mean to thrive and do good, break open the 4.03. 15 P
as i intend, clifford, to thrive to–day, | it 5.02. 17
and, if we thrive, promise them such rewards 3H6 2.03. 52
so thrive i, as i truly swear the like! R3 2.01. 11
our former hatred, so thrive i and mine! 2.01. 24
if you thrive well, bring them to baynard's 3.05. 98
so thrive i in my enterprise | and dangerous 4.04.236
so thrive i in my dangerous affairs | of hostile 4.04.398
but if i thrive, the gain of my attempt | the 5.03.267
live, and thrive! COR 4.06. 23
so thrive my soul — ROM 2.02.153
why should it thrive and turn to nutriment TIM 3.01. 58
like physicians, | thrive, give him over; 3.03. 12
if i thrive well, i'll visit thee again. 4.03.170
and seek to thrive | by that which has undone 4.03.210
us, not to have us thrive in our mystery. 4.03.453 P
and so farewell and thrive. 4.03.533
i wish your enterprise to–day may thrive. JC 3.01. 13
he wish'd to–day our enterprise might thrive. 3.01. 16
if this letter speed | and my invention thrive, LR 1.02. 20
let copulation thrive; 4.06.114
if ever thou wilt thrive, bury my body, | and 4.06.247
pray that the right may thrive. 5.02. 2
say thou'lt do't, | or thrive by other means. 5.03. 34
on their lords, | do well thrive by them; OTH 1.01. 53
how i did thrive in this fair lady's love, | and 1.03.125
and if to–morrow | our navy thrive, i have an ANT 4.03. 10
well, well, | we shall thrive now. 4.04. 9
letting them thrive again | on their abatement. CYM 5.04. 20
his comforts thrive, his trials well are spent. 5.04.104
sir, if you thrive, you'll remember from whence PER 2.01.151 P
as you wish your womb may thrive with fair ones, TNK 1.01. 27
by cocklight, | 'twill never thrive else. 4.01.113
they that thrive well take counsel of their VEN 640
and that his beauty may the better thrive, 1011
as truth and beauty shall together thrive | if SON 14.11
then if he thrive and i be cast away, | the 80.13

THRIVED 2 FR 0.0002 REL FR 2 V 0 P
into the hearts of such as have not thrived ANT 1.03. 51
so he thrived | that he is promis'd to be wived PER 5.02. 9

THRIVERS 1 FR 0.0001 REL FR 1 V 0 P
pitiful thrivers, in their gazing spent? SON 125. 8

THRIVES 5 FR 0.0005 REL FR 5 V 0 P
how does your lady, and how thrives your love? TGV 2.04.125
that's as york thrives to beat back bullingbrook R2 2.02.144
like to rise, | who thrives, and who declines; COR 1.01.193
pompey | thrives in our idleness. ANT 1.04. 76
love thrives not in the heart that shadows LUC 270

THRIVETH 1 FR 0.0001 REL FR 1 V 0 P
but blessed bankrout that by love so thriveth! VEN 466

THRIVING 2 FR 0.0002 REL FR 2 V 0 P
free undertaking cannot miss | a thriving issue. WT 2.02. 43
crown, | to her go i, a jolly thriving wooer. R3 4.03. 43

THROAT *(also troat)*

THROAT 52 FR 0.0058 REL FR 36 V 16 P
a pox o' your throat, you bawling, blasphemous, TMP 1.01. 40 P
with an outstretch'd throat i'll tell the world MM 2.04.153
a note, sometime through the throat, /as if you LLL 3.01. 14 P
in the world but lie, and lie in my throat. 4.03. 12 P
to move wild laughter in the throat of death? 5.02.855
this hand from thy throat till this other had AYL 1.01. 60 P
his merry note | unto the sweet bird's throat, 2.05. 4
the note lies in 's throat if he say i said so. SHR 4.03.132 P
is a passage in my throat and drink in illyria. TN 1.03. 39 P
but thou liest in thy throat, that is not the 3.04.157 P
with a foul traitor's name stuff i thy throat, R2 1.01. 44
these terms of treason doubled down his throat. 1.01. 57
the false passage of thy throat thou liest. 1.01.125
aside, i had lied in my throat if i had said so. 2H4 1.02. 82 P
you you lie in your throat if you say i am any 1.02. 85 P
the "solus" in thy teeth, and in thy throat, H5 2.01. 48
i will cut thy throat one time or other in fair 2.01. 69 P
/or i will fetch thy rim out at thy throat | in 4.04. 14
bid him prepare, for i will cut his throat. 4.04. 32
every soldier to cut his prisoner's throat. 4.07. 10 P
that's a lie in thy throat. 4.08. 16 P
i'll turn my part thereof into thy throat. 1H6 2.04. 79
an ox, and iniquity's throat cut like a calf. 2H6 4.02. 27 P
and next his throat unto the butcher's knife. 3H6 5.06. 9
in thy foul throat thou li'st! R3 1.02. 93
came, | ready to catch each other by the throat, 1.03.188
seeking for richmond in the throat of death. 5.04. 5
achilles be thy guard, | i'll cut thy throat. TRO 4.04.129
my throat of war be turn'd, | which quier'd with COR 3.02.112
my throat to thee and to thy ancient malice; 4.05. 96
unbuckling helms, fisting each other's throat, 4.05.125
my hearth, | presented to my knife his throat. 5.06. 30
those reproachful speeches down his throat, TIT 2.01. 55
hath doubtfully pronounc'd the throat shall cut, TIM 4.03.122
love before | the /reverend'st throat in athens. 5.01.182
his doublet, and offer'd them his throat to cut. JC 1.02.266 P
of blessing, and "amen" | stuck in my throat. MAC 2.02. 30
that it did, sir, i' the very throat on me; 2.03. 38 P
my lord, his throat is cut; 3.04. 15
doth with his lofty and shrill–sounding throat HAM 1.01.151
gives me the lie i' th' throat | as deep as to 2.02.574
to cut his throat i' th' church. 4.07.126
i prithee take thy fingers from my throat. 5.01.260
or, whilst i can vent clamor from my throat, LR 1.01.165
he lies there, were to lie in mine own throat. OTH 3.04. 13 P
i took by th' throat the circumcised dog, | and 5.02.355
i melt and pour | down thy ill–uttering throat. ANT 2.05. 35
and threats the throat of that his officer 3.05. 18
sword, the paper | hath cut her throat already! CYM 3.04. 33
which he did wave against my throat, i have 4.02.150
even in his throat — unless it be the king — PER 2.05. 56
and make him, to the scorn of his hoarse throat, TNK 5.01. 88

THROATS 29 FR 0.0032 REL FR 21 V 8 P
whose throats had hanging at 'em | wallets of TMP 3.03. 45
a pox o' your throats! MM 4.03. 24 P
cut the villains' throats! 1H4 2.02. 84 P
they may have their throats about them at that H5 2.01. 21 P
we keep knives to cut one another's throats? 2.01. 92 P
and there is throats to be cut, and works to be 3.02.111 P
but when our throats are cut, he may be ransom'd 4.01.193 P
besides, we'll cut the throats of those we have, 4.07. 63
we will not fly but to our enemies' throats. 1H6 1.01. 98
cut both the villains' throats; 2H6 4.01. 20
our throats are sentenc'd, and stay upon COR 5.04. 7 P
this morning for ten thousand of your throats 5.04. 56
their base throats tear | with giving him glory. 5.06. 52
even in their throats that hath committed them. TIT 3.01.274
this one hand yet is left to cut your throats, 5.02.181
and now prepare your throats. 5.02.196
and then dreams he of cutting foreign throats, ROM 1.04. 83
men should drink with harness on their throats. TIM 1.02. 52
and let the foes quietly cut their throats 3.05. 44
your knives, | and cut your trusters' throats! 4.01. 10
cut throats, | all that you meet are thieves. 4.03.445
care not, | while you have throats to answer. 5.01.179
whose rude throats | th' immortal jove's dread OTH 3.03.355
we have us'd our throats in egypt. ANT 2.06.134 P
and, when we are put off, fall to their throats: 2.07. 72
descend again into their throats and have not TNK 1.02. 82
o' th' night | with their contentious throats, 5.03.125
kill them, cut their throats, possess their STM II.C 120
whet their detested knives against your throats, II.C 134

THROBBING 2 FR 0.0002 REL FR 2 V 0 P
here may his head lie on my throbbing breast; 2H6 4.04. 5
my throbbing heart shall rock thee day and night VEN 1186

THROBS 1 FR 0.0001 REL FR 1 V 0 P
yet my heart | throbs to know one thing: MAC 4.01.101

THROCA 1 FR 0.0001 REL FR 0 V 1 P
throca movousus, cargo, cargo, cargo. AWW 4.01. 65 P

THROE 1 FR 0.0001 REL FR 1 V 0 P
and that gave to me | many a groaning throe. H8 2.04.200

THROES 4 FR 0.0004 REL FR 4 V 0 P
indeed, | which throes thee much to yield. TMP 2.01.231
love, with other incident throes | that nature's TIM 5.01.200
with labor, and throes forth | each minute some. ANT 3.07. 80
lent not me her aid, | but took me in my throes, CYM 5.04. 44

THROMULDO 1 FR 0.0001 REL FR 0 V 1 P
boskos thromuldo boskos. AWW 4.01. 68 P

THRON'D *(also enthron'd, throne)*

THRON'D 4 FR 0.0004 REL FR 4 V 0 P
a very echo to the seat | where love is thron'd. TN 2.04. 22
what four thron'd ones could have weigh'd | such H8 1.01. 11
pleasant hill | feign'd fortune to be thron'd. TIM 1.01. 64
that their great stars | thron'd and set high? LR 3.01. 23

THRONE 68 FR 0.0076 REL FR 66 V 2 P
arabia | there is one tree, the phoenix' throne, TMP 3.03. 23
be sometime honor'd for his burning throne! MM 5.01.293
'fore whose throne 'tis needful, | ere i can AWW 4.04. 3
shepherd's note since we have left our throne WT 1.02. 2
bed, which owe | a moi'ty of the throne, a great 3.02. 39
draw our throne into a sheep–cote! 4.04.779 P
the lands and waters 'twixt your throne and his 5.01.144
here is my throne, bid kings come bow to it. JN 3.01. 74
directly lead | thy foot to england's throne. 3.04.130
lives or dies, true to king richard's throne, R2 1.03. 86
this royal throne of kings, this sceptred isle, 2.01. 40
shall see us rising in our throne, the east, 3.02. 50
ascend his throne, descending now from him, 4.01.111
in god's name i'll ascend the regal throne. 4.01.113
the mounting bullingbrook ascends my throne, 5.01. 56
to pluck him headlong from the usurped throne. 5.01. 65
that roan shall be my throne. 1H4 2.03. 70
and shake the peace and safety of our throne. 3.02.117
my cousin bullingbrook ascends my throne" 2H4 3.01. 71
god and his angels guard your sacred throne, H5 1.02. 7
lives, and services | to this imperial throne. 1.02. 35
you are their heir, you sit upon their throne; 1.02.117
when i do rouse me in my throne of france. 1.02.275
the throne he sits on, nor the tide of pomp 4.01.264
i'll hale the dolphin headlong from his throne, 1H6 1.01.149
endeavor'd my advancement to the throne. 2.05. 69
i pray, | but one imperious in another's throne? 3.01. 44
gone, | may honorable peace attend thy throne! 2H6 2.03. 38
was ever king that joy'd an earthly throne | and 4.09. 1
before i see thee seated in that throne | which 3H6 1.01. 22
thou factious duke of york, descend my throne, 1.01. 74
and shall i stand, and thou sit in my throne? 1.01. 84
thou that i will leave my kingly throne, 1.01.124
for chair and dukedom, throne and kingdom say, 2.01. 93
the next degree is england's royal throne; 2.01.193
and see him seated in the regal throne. 4.03. 64
likely in time to bless a regal throne. 4.06. 74
once more we sit in england's royal throne, 5.07. 1
and plant your joys in living edward's throne. R3 2.02.100
to jut | upon the innocent and aweless throne. 2.04. 52
shall lose the royalty of england's throne. 3.04. 40
the supreme seat, the throne majestical, | the 3.07.118
but we will plant some other in the throne, | to 3.07.216
and affecting one sole throne, | without COR 4.06. 32
of a god but eternity and a heaven to throne in. 5.04. 24 P
you are but newly planted in your throne; TIT 1.01.444
for 'tis a throne where honor may be crown'd ROM 3.02. 93
my bosom's lord sits lightly in his throne, 5.01. 3
this throne, this fortune, and this hill, TIM 1.01. 73
and our duties | are to your throne and state, MAC 1.04. 25
th' untimely emptying of the happy throne, | and 4.03. 68
since that the truest issue of thy throne | by 4.03.106
and sundry blessings hang about his throne 4.03.158
than is the throne of denmark to thy father. HAM 1.02. 49
you are the most immediate to our throne, | and 1.02.109
i could as well be brought | to knee his throne, LR 2.04.214
thy crown and hearted throne | to tyrannous hate OTH 3.03.448
i will piece | her opulent throne with kingdoms. ANT 1.05. 46
whiles we are suitors to their throne, decays 2.01. 4
the barge she sat in, like a burnish'd throne, 2.02.191
beggar, wouldst have made my throne | a seat for CYM 1.01.141
i will pursue her | even to augustus' throne. 3.05.101
the gods have made | preservers of my throne. 5.05. 2
had princes sit like stars about his throne, PER 2.03. 39
possess | the high throne in his heart. TNK 1.03. 96
his throne and sword, but given him his own name STM II.C 103
who, like a king perplexed in his throne, | by VEN 1043
from this fair throne to heave the owner out. LUC 413

THRONED 4 FR 0.0004 REL FR 4 V 0 P
he took | at a fair vestal throned by /the west, MND 2.01.158
the throned monarch better than his crown. MV 4.01.189
(though you in swearing shake the throned gods), ANT 1.03. 28
as on the finger of a throned queen | the basest SON 96. 5

THRONES 2 FR 0.0002 REL FR 2 V 0 P
these sovereign thrones, are all supplied, and TN 1.01. 37
sit, gods, upon your thrones, and smile at troy! TRO 5.10. 7

/THRONG 1 FR 0.0001 REL FR 1 V 0 P
/throng our large temples with the shows of COR 3.03. 36

THRONG 16 FR 0.0018 REL FR 13 V 3 P
go — a short knife and a throng! WIV 2.02. 18 P
be quiet, people. wherefore throng you hither? ERR 5.01. 38
they throng who should buy first, as if my WT 4.04.600 P
in their throng and press to that last hold, JN 5.07. 19
nor the throng of words that come with such more 2H4 2.01.111 P
i'll to the throng: H5 4.05. 22
throng many doubtful hollow–hearted friends, R3 4.04.435
throng to the bar, crying all, "guilty! 5.03.199
and follow'd with the general throng and sweat H8 pr 28
that many maz'd considerings did throng | and 2.04.186
i have seen the dumb men throng to see him, and COR 2.01.262
fellow, come from the throng, look upon caesar. JC 1.02. 21
the throng that follows caesar at the heels, 2.04. 34
variable passions throng her constant woe, | as VEN 967
throng her inventions, which shall go before. LUC 1302
but through his lips do throng | weak words, so 1783

THRONG'D 5 FR 0.0005 REL FR 5 V 0 P
thou wilt be throng'd to shortly. TIM 4.03.394
throng'd to? 4.03.394
heaven, to tell the earth is throng'd | by man's PER 1.01.101
a man throng'd up with cold, my veins are chill, 2.01. 73
here one being throng'd bears back, all boll'n LUC 1417

THRONGING 3 FR 0.0003 REL FR 3 V 0 P
come thronging soft and delicate desires, | all ADO 1.01.303
where be the thronging troops that followed thee R3 4.04. 96
which, thronging through her lips, so vanisheth LUC 1041

/THRONGS 1 FR 0.0001 REL FR 1 V 0 P
/troop /in /the /throngs /of /military /men; 2H4 4.01. 62

THRONGS 5 FR 0.0005 REL FR 5 V 0 P
so play the foolish throngs with one that MM 2.04. 24
to smother up the english in our throngs, | if H5 4.05. 20
flamens | do press among the popular throngs, COR 2.01.214
all feasts, societies, and throngs of men! TIM 4.03. 21
nor cutpurses come not to throngs; LR 3.02. 90

THROSTLE 2 FR 0.0002 REL FR 1 V 1 P
bill, | the throstle with his note so true, MND 3.01.127
if a throstle sing, he falls straight a–cap'ring MV 1.02. 60 P

THROTTLE 1 FR 0.0001 REL FR 1 V 0 P
throttle their practic'd accent in their fears, MND 5.01. 97

THROUGH *(also thorough, etc.)*

/THROUGH 2 FR 0.0002 REL FR 2 V 0 P
/when /through /proud /london /he /came /sighing 2H4 1.03.104
/fire /sparkling /through /sights /of /steel, 4.01.119

THROUGH 305 FR 0.0344 REL FR 254 V 51 P
through all the signories it was the first, TMP 1.02. 71
me, | might i but through my prison once a day 1.02.491
my master through his art foresees the danger 2.01.297
trod indeed | through forth–rights and meanders! 3.03. 3
that calf–like they my lowing follow'd through 4.01.179
you, and shine through you like the water in an TGV 2.01. 39 P
come, i'll convey thee through the city–gate; 3.01.254
as he in penance wander'd through the forest; 5.02. 38
makes him run through all th' sins: 5.04.112
or else you had look'd through the grate, like a WIV 2.02. 9 P
slender, go you through the town to frogmore. 2.03. 75 P
go about the fields with me through frogmore, i 2.03. 86 P
a woman would run through fire and water for 3.04.103 P
of lust and late–walking through the realm. 5.05.145 P
some piece of money, and go through with all. MM 2.01.271 P
roaming clean through the bounds of asia, | and, ERR 1.01.133
desp'rately he hurried through the street — 5.01.140
valor, | goes foremost in report through italy. ADO 3.01. 97
slander hath gone through and through her heart, 5.01. 68
slander hath gone through and through her heart, 5.01. 68
not this speech like iron through your blood? 5.01.245
and sing a note, sometime through the throat, LLL 3.01. 14 P
with singing love, sometime through /the nose, 3.01. 16 P
through the transparent bosom of the deep, | as 4.03. 30
as doth thy face through tears of mine give 4.03. 31
and they thy glory through my grief will show. 4.03. 36
through the velvet leaves the wind, | all unseen 4.03.103
thrust thy sharp wit quite through my ignorance, 5.02.398
seen the day of wrong through the little hole of 5.02.723 P
through athens gates have we devis'd to steal. MND 1.01.213
through athens i am thought as fair as she. 1.01.227
which is thought fit, through all athens, to 1.02. 5 P
not thou lead him through the glimmering night 2.01. 77
thou some of it, and seek through this grove: 2.01.259
through the forest have i gone, | but athenian 2.02. 66
and run through fire i will for thy sweet sake. 2.02.103
that through thy bosom makes me see thy heart. 2.02.105
his face must be seen through the lion's neck, 3.01. 37 P
and he himself must speak through, saying thus, 3.01. 38 P
the story) did talk through the chink of a wall. 3.01. 64 P
and through that cranny shall pyramus and thisby 3.01. 70 P
through bog, through bush, through brake, 3.01.107
through bog, through bush, through brake, 3.01.107
bog, through bush, through brake, through brier: 3.01.107
bog, through bush, through brake, through brier: 3.01.107
that the moon | may through the centre creep, 3.02. 54
i, | pierc'd through the heart with your stern 3.02. 59
and through wall's chink, poor souls, they are 5.01.133
through which the lovers, pyramus and thisby, 5.01.159
through which the fearful lovers are to whisper. 5.01.164
me thy chink, to blink through with mine eyne! 5.01.177

o wicked wall, through whom i see no bliss! 5.01.180
enter now, and i am to spy her through the wall. 5.01.186 P
o, kiss me through the hole of this vild wall! 5.01.200
through the house give glimmering light | by the 5.01.391
of day, | through this house each fairy stray. 5.01.402
through this palace, with sweet peace, | and the 5.01.418
some that will evermore peep through their eyes, MV 1.01. 52
spirit, lest through thy wild behavior | i be 2.02.187
shall lose a hair through bassanio's fault. 3.02.302
thus most invectively he pierceth through | the AYL 2.01. 58
and i will through and through | cleanse the 2.07. 59
and i will through and through | cleanse the 2.07. 59
wind, | through all the world bears rosalind. 3.02. 91
within an hour, and pacing through the forest, 4.03.100
look into happiness through another man's eyes! 5.02. 44 P
shoes as my toes look through the overleather. SHR in.2. 12 P
or daphne roaming through a thorny wood, in.2. 57
a merchant of great traffic through the world, 1.01. 12
wind as scatters young men through the world 1.02. 50
and through the instrument my pate made way, 2.01.154
as on a pillory, looking through the lute, 2.01.156
how she waded through the dirt to pluck him off 4.01. 78 P
as the sun breaks through the darkest clouds, 4.03.173
heaven hath through me restor'd the king to AWW 2.03. 64
i need not open, for i look through thee. 2.03.215 P
he shall be whipt through the army with this 4.03.233 P
through flinty tartar's bosom would peep forth 4.04. 7
how he glisters | through my rust! WT 3.02.171
of january | would blow you through and through. 4.04.112
of january | would blow you through and through. 4.04.112
king | and through him what's nearest to him, 4.04.522
your gallery | have we pass'd through, not 5.03. 11
but as i travell'd hither through the land, | i JN 4.02.143
take their course | through my burn'd bosom, nor 5.07. 39
out his innocent soul through streams of blood, R2 1.01.103
through the false passage of thy throat thou 1.01.125
dear for her reputation through the world, | is 2.01. 58
even through the hollow eyes of death | i spy 2.01.270
whilst bullingbrook, through our security, 3.02. 34
and darts his light through every guilty hole, 3.02. 43
through brazen trumpet send the breath of parley 3.03. 33
i am press'd to death through want of speaking! 3.04. 72
through casements darted their desiring eyes 5.02. 14
yet through both | i see some sparks of better 5.03. 20
from whence this stream through muddy passages 5.03. 62
at | by breaking through the foul and ugly mists 1H4 1.02.202
i am eight times thrust through the doublet, 2.04.166 P
through the doublet, four through the hose, my 2.04.167 P
the hose, my buckler cut through and through, my 2.04.167 P
my buckler cut through and through, my sword 2.04.168 P
through all the kingdoms that acknowledge christ 3.02.111
thou that art like enough, through vassal fear, 3.02.124
you shall march | through gloucestershire; 3.02.176
should go so general current through the world. 4.01. 5
our soldiers shall march through; 4.02. 2 P
i'll not march through coventry with them, 4.02. 39 P
this have i rumor'd through the peasant towns 2H4 in 33
and if a man is through with them in honest 1.02. 40 P
and the lightness of his wife shines through it; 1.02. 47 P
my lord, through a red lattice, and i could 2.02. 79 P
the ale-wive's petticoat and so peep'd through. 2.02. 83 P
happiest youth, viewing his progress through, 3.01. 54
you give me leave to go through gloucestershire, 4.03. 82 P
i'll through gloucestershire, and there will i 4.03.128 P
thin that life looks through /and /will /break 4.04.120
he came not through the chamber where we stay'd. 4.05. 56
cut their passage through the force of france, H5 2.02. 16
draw the huge bottoms through the furrowed sea, 3.pr. 12
let it pry through the portage of the head 3.01. 10
that sweeps through our land | with pennons 3.05. 48
charge that, in our marches through the country, 3.06.109 P
camp to camp, through the foul womb of night, 4.pr. 4
and through their paly flames | each battle sees 4.pr. 8
absence, | seek through your camp to find you. 4.01.286
and faintly through a rusty beaver peeps. 4.02. 44
proclaim it, westmerland, through my host, 4.03. 34
kill his prisoners, | give the word through. 4.06. 38
and be it death proclaimed through our host | to 4.08.114
his bended sword | before him through the city. 5.pr. 19
/wont through a secret grate of iron bars | in 1H6 1.04. 10
here, through this grate, i count each one, 1.04. 60
so much applauded through the realm of france? 2.02. 36
that it will glimmer through a blindman's eye. 2.04. 24
begun through malice of the bishop's men. 3.01. 75
too, | hath been enacted through your enmity. 3.01.116
through which our policy must make a breach. 3.02. 2
and we will make thee famous through the world. 3.03. 13
two talbots, winged through the lither sky, | in 4.07. 21
whether it be through force of your report, | my 5.05. 79
she sweeps it through the court with troops of 2H6 1.03. 77
let them be whipt through every market town, 2.01.155
thou didst ride in triumph through the streets. 2.04. 14
levy great sums of money through the realm | for 3.01. 61
tears as salt as sea, through thy unkindness. 3.02. 96
deliver'd strongly through my fixed teeth, 3.02.313
through whom a thousand sighs are breath'd for 3.02.345
and i proclaim'd a coward through the world! 4.01. 43
of maces, will we ride through the streets, and 4.07.135 P
my sword therefore broke through london gates, 4.08. 23 P
will he conduct you through the heart of france, 4.08. 36
and hell, have through the very middest of you! 4.08. 61 P
(as well we may, if not through your neglect), 5.02. 80
march'd through the city to the palace gates. 3H6 1.01. 92
my soul flies through these wounds to seek out 1.04.178
for through this laund anon the deer will come, 3.01. 2
hath pass'd in safety through the narrow seas, 4.08. 3
do through the clouds behold this present hour, R3 5.01. 8
from troop to troop | went through the army, 5.03. 71
see his pride | peep through each part of him. H8 1.01. 69
england and france might through their amity 1.01.181
the subject's grief | comes through commissions, 1.02. 57
the rough brake | that virtue must go through. 1.02. 76
that through our intercession this revokement 1.02.106
strong-ribb'd bark through liquid mountains cut, TRO 1.03. 40
send thy brass voice through all these lazy 1.03.257
this, sir, is proclaim'd through all our host: 2.01.121
law | of nature be corrupted through affection, 2.02.177
he's not yet through warm. 2.03.221 P

through the sight i bear in things to /come, | i 3.03. 4
cruel way | through ranks of greekish youth, and 4.05.185
sort, dragg'd through the shameful field. 5.10. 5
as he dare, | i'll through and through you! 5.10. 26
as he dare, | i'll through and through you! 5.10. 26
i send it through the rivers of your blood, COR 1.01.135
and, through the cranks and offices of man, 1.01.137
i am half through: 2.03.123
a beggar's tongue | make motion through my lips, 3.02.118
let a guard | attend us through the city. 3.03.141
those maims | of shame seen through thy country, 4.05. 87
be led | with manacles through our streets, or 5.03.115
ne'er through an arch so hurried the blown tide, 5.04. 47
tide, | as the recomforted through th' gates. 5.04. 48
i pried me through the crevice of a wall, | when TIT 5.01.114
trudge about | through fair verona, find those ROM 1.02. 35
gallops night by night | through lovers' brains, 1.04. 71
soft, what light through yonder window breaks? 2.02. 2
would through the airy region stream so bright 2.02. 21
black eye, run through the ear with a love-song, 2.04. 14 P
when presently through all thy veins shall run 4.01. 95
have a faint cold fear thrills through my veins, 4.03. 15
as will disperse itself through all the veins 5.01. 61
stirrup, and through him | drink the free air. TIM 1.01. 82
that through the window/-bars bore at men's eyes 4.03.117
and he looks | quite through the deeds of men. JC 1.02.203
now, | did i go through a tempest dropping fire. 1.03. 10
look, in this place ran cassius' dagger through; 3.02.174
through this the well-beloved brutus stabb'd, 3.02.176
are rid like madmen through the gates of rome. 3.02.269
that ran through caesar's bowels, search this 5.03. 42
is fair, | hover through the fog and filthy air. MAC 1.01. 12
what a haste looks through his eyes! 1.02. 46
time and the hour runs through the roughest day. 1.03.147
nor heaven peep through the blanket of the dark 1.05. 53
your spirits shine through you. 3.01.127
something | you may discern of him through me, 4.03. 15
figure | comes armed through our watch, so like HAM 1.01.110
must die, | passing through nature to eternity. 1.02. 73
that swift as quicksilver it courses through 1.05. 66
through your dominions for this enterprise, | on 2.02. 78
may go a progress through the guts of a beggar. 4.03. 31 P
that our drift look through our bad performance, 4.07.151
which carries them through and through the most 5.02.192 P
them through and through the most /profound and 5.02.192 P
may carry through itself to that full issue LR 1.04. 3
"through the sharp hawthorn blow the /cold winds 3.04. 46 P
the foul fiend hath led through fire and through 3.04. 52 P
fiend hath led through fire and through flame, 3.04. 52 P
and through flame, through /ford and whirlpool, 3.04. 53 P
still through the hawthorn blows the cold wind: 3.04. 98 P
i ran it through, even from my boyish days | to OTH 1.03.132
the bruis'd heart was pierced through the /ear. 1.03.219
to lash the rascals naked through the world 4.02.143
i have made my way through more impediments 5.02.263
we'll wander through the streets and note | the ANT 1.01. 53
hop forty paces through the public street; 2.02.229
spur through media, | mesopotamia, and the 3.01. 7
is gone, | through whom i might command it? 3.03. 6
bring him through the bands. 3.12. 25
i'll force | the wine peep through their scars. 3.13.190
through proof of harness to my heart, and there 4.08. 15
through alexandria make a jolly march, | bear 4.08. 30
and may, through all the world; 5.02.134
of my spirits | through th' ashes of my chance. 5.02.174
caesar through syria | intends his journey, and 5.02.200
to seek through the regions of the earth | for CYM 1.01. 20
have a fog in them | that i cannot look through. 3.02. 80
are arch'd so high that giants may jet through 3.03. 5
would seek us through | and put us to our answer 4.02.160
seen, all flying | through a strait lane; 5.03. 7
some falling | merely through fear, that the 5.03. 11
peep through thy marble mansion, help, | or we 5.04. 87
when shall i hear all through? 5.05.382
so through lud's-town march, | and in the temple 5.05.481
made up this garment through the rough seams of PER 2.01.149 P
through which secret art, | by turning o'er 3.02. 32
your honor has through ephesus pour'd forth 3.02. 43
through you, increase our wonder, and sets up 3.02. 96
i have gone through for this piece you see. 4.02. 43 P
sir, hast thou cried her through the market? 4.02. 93 P
with sighs shot through and biggest tears 4.04. 26
and make a batt'ry through his /deafen'd parts, 5.01. 47
through whom the gods have shown their power; 5.03. 60
there, through my tears, | like wrinkled pebbles TNK 1.01.111
if labor through, | our gain but life and 1.02. 11
and clamors through the wild air flying! 1.05. 6
the wills of men to vanity | i see through now, 2.02.102
but that's all one, i'll go through, let her 2.03. 31
hidden sun, | breaks through his baser garments. 2.05. 24
and i'll go seek him through the world that is 3.04. 23
cousin, thrust the buckle | through far enough. 3.06. 62
through a small glade cut by the fishermen, | i 4.01. 64
tainted with extremes) runs through his body, 4.02.101
whose youth, like wanton boys through bonfires, 5.01. 86
and costliness of spirit look'd through him, it 5.03. 97
shake, which partly comes through the eating of STM II.C 14 P
like a dive-dapper peering through a wave, | who VEN 86
strengthless doves will draw me through the sky, 153
for through his mane and tail the high wind 305
which through the crystal tears gave light, 491
yet love breaks through, and picks them all at 576
as fearful of him, part, through whom he rushes. 630
the many musits through the which he goes | are 683
and homeward through the dark laund runs apace, 813
through which it enters to surprise her heart, 890
a second fear through all her sinews spread, 903
but through the flood-gates breaks the silver 959
their mistress mounted through the empty skies, 1191
through little vents and crannies of the place LUC 310
that through the length of times he stands 718
ev'n in this thought through the dark night he 729
through night's black bosom should not peep 788
which, thronging through her lips, so vanisheth 1041
revealing day through every cranny spies, | and 1086
of eyes, | why pry'st thou through my window? 1089
through which i may convey this troubled soul. 1176

through crystal walls each little mote will peep 1251
that dying fear through all her body spread, 1266
the very eyes of men through loop-holes thrust, 1383
that through their light joy seemed to appear 1434
as through an arch the violent roaring tide 1667
and through her wounds doth fly | live's lasting 1728
but through his lips do throng | weak words, so 1783
but through his teeth, as if the name he tore. 1787
and falls, through wind, before the fall should PP 10. 6
through the velvet leaves the wind | all unseen 16. 5
how sighs resound through heartless ground, 17.23
so thou through windows of thine age shalt see, SON 3.11
for through the painter must you see his skill 24. 5
'tis not enough that through the cloud thou 34. 5
through heavy sleep on sightless eyes doth stay! 43.12
beggar'd of blood to blush through lively veins, 67.10
sake, | so him i lose through my unkind abuse. 134.12
some beauty peep'd through lettice of sear'd age LC 14
roses | that flame through water which their hue 287

THROUGHFARE 1 FR 0.0001 REL FR 0 V 1 P
it is a throughfare for steel, if it be not hurt CYM 1.02. 10 P

THROUGHFARES 1 FR 0.0001 REL FR 1 V 0 P
of wide arabia are as throughfares now | for MV 2.07. 42

/THROUGHLY 1 FR 0.0001 REL FR 1 V 0 P
/and /period /will /be /throughly /wrought, LR 4.07. 95

THROUGHLY 12 FR 0.0013 REL FR 11 V 1 P
the next advantage | will we take throughly. TMP 3.03. 14
lodge thee till thy wound be throughly heal'd; TGV 1.02.112
if he had been throughly mov'd, you should have WIV 1.04. 90 P
my lord, we'll do it throughly. MM 5.01.259
of friends, | to quit me of them throughly. ADO 4.01.200
i am informed throughly of the cause. MV 4.01.173
now do your duty throughly, i advise you. SHR 4.04. 11
you scarce can right me throughly, then, to say WT 2.01. 99
good occasion | most throughly to be winnowed, H8 5.01.110
i'll be reveng'd | most throughly for my father. HAM 4.05.137
caius lucius | will do 's commission throughly. CYM 2.04. 12
i am throughly weary. 3.06. 36

THROUGHOUT 7 FR 0.0008 REL FR 7 V 0 P
son, | a man well known throughout all italy. SHR 2.01. 69
to any sovereign state throughout the world. JN 5.02. 82
and ne'er throughout the year to church thou 1H6 1.01. 42
not out the bells aloud throughout the town? 1.06. 11
away, and throughout every town | proclaim them 2H6 4.02.176
and follow thee my lord throughout the world. ROM 2.02.148
from high to low throughout, that whoso please TIM 5.01.209

THROUGH'T 1 FR 0.0001 REL FR 1 V 0 P
and the true blood which peeps fairly through't, WT 4.04.148

/THROW 1 FR 0.0001 REL FR 1 V 0 P
/when /the /king /did /throw /his /warder /down 2H4 4.01.123

THROW 107 FR 0.0121 REL FR 88 V 19 P
i throw thy name against the bruising stones, TGV 1.02.108
rock, | and throw it thence into the raging sea. 1.02.119
stand, sir, and throw us that you have about ye. 4.01. 3
he shall not have a stone to throw at his dog. WIV 1.04.112 P
thy impatience, throw cold water on thy choler. 2.03. 85 P
creep in here, and throw foul linen upon him, as 3.03.130 P
holy father, throw away that thought; MM 1.03. 1
i'd throw it down for your deliverance | as 3.01.104
abate throw at novum, and the whole world again LLL 5.02.544
but if they will not, throw away that spirit, 5.02.867
upon thy eyes i throw | all the power this charm MND 2.02. 78
the greater throw | may turn by fortune from the MV 2.01. 33
not one to throw at a dog. AYL 1.03. 3 P
cast away upon curs, throw some of them at me. 1.03. 5 P
a little, he will throw a figure in her face, SHR 1.02.113 P
off with that bable, throw it under-foot. 5.02.122
warlike principles | do not throw from you; AWW 2.01. 2
in this choice than throw ames-ace for my life. 2.03. 78 P
or i will throw thee from my care for ever 2.03.162
come, throw it o'er my face. TN 1.05.165
sir, or i'll throw your dagger o'er the house. 4.01. 28 P
can fool no more money out of me at this throw. 5.01. 42 P
you throw a strange regard upon me, and by that 5.01.212
hubert, throw thine eye | on yon young boy. JN 3.03. 59
the lily, | to throw a perfume on the violet, 4.02. 12
throw this report on their incensed rage, | and 4.02.261
pale trembling coward, there i throw my gage, R2 1.01. 69
throw down, my son, the duke of norfolk's gage. 1.01.161
and, norfolk, throw down his. 1.01.162
norfolk, throw down, we bid, there is no boot. 1.01.164
myself i throw, dread sovereign, at thy foot, 1.01.165
cousin, throw up your gage, do you begin. 1.01.186
and throw the rider headlong in the lists, | a 1.02. 52
what reverence he did throw away on slaves, 1.04. 27
throw death upon thy sovereign's enemies. 3.02. 22
with solemn reverence, throw away respect, 3.02.172
and that thou art so, there i throw my gage, 4.01. 46
by heaven, i'll throw at all! 4.01. 57
that norfolk lies, here do i throw down this, 4.01. 84
when this loose behavior i throw off | and pay 1H4 1.02.208
villain's head, throw the quean in the channel. 2H4 2.01. 47 P
throw me in the channel? 2.01. 48 P
i'll throw thee in the channel. 2.01. 48 P
nay, pray you throw none away, the skin is good H5 5.01. 54 P
nod their heads, and throw their eyes on thee! 2H6 2.04. 22
madam, your penance done, throw off this sheet, 2.04.105
throw them into thames! 4.08. 2 P
throw in the frozen bosoms of our part | hot 5.02. 35
and in that hope i throw mine eyes to heaven, 3H6 1.04. 37
shall we go throw away our coats of steel, | and 2.01.160
i throw my hands, mine eyes, my heart to thee, 2.03. 36
any life be left in thee, | throw up thine eye! 2.05. 85
look here, i throw my infamy at thee. 5.01. 82
i'll throw thy body in another room, | and 5.06. 92
and then throw him into the malmsey-butt in the R3 1.04.155 P
and throw them in the entrails of the wolf? 4.04. 23
bed, | throw over her the veil of infamy. 4.04.209
duty to you | and throw it from their soul, H8 3.02.194
viands | we do not throw in unrespective sieve, TRO 2.02. 71
an act that very chance doth throw upon him — 3.03.131
much | to throw down hector than polyxena. 3.03.208
for i will throw my glove to death himself 4.04. 63
upon power, and throw forth greater themes | for COR 1.01.220
be meet, | and throw their power i' th' dust. 3.01.170
subtle ground, | i have tumbled past the throw; 5.02. 21

which made me down to throw my books, and fly — TIT 4.01. 25
but throw her forth to beasts and birds to prey: 5.03.198
throw your mistempered weapons to the ground, ROM 1.01. 87
you would throw them off, | and say you /found TIM 2.02.134
our masters may throw their caps at their money. 3.04.100 P
were i like thee, i'd throw away myself. 4.03.219
throw thy glove, | or any token of thine honor 5.04. 49
in several hands, in at his windows throw, | as JC 1.02.316
and throw this | in at his window; 1.03.144
to throw away the dearest thing he ow'd, | as MAC 1.04. 10
in the poison'd entrails throw; 4.01. 5
from the murderer's gibbet throw | into the 4.01. 66
from her bed, throw her night–gown upon her, 5.01. 5 P
throw physic to the dogs, i'll none of it. 5.03. 47
your leavy screens throw down, | and show like 5.06. 1
before my body | i throw my warlike shield. 5.08. 33
we pray you throw to earth | this unprevailing HAM 1.02.106
o, throw away the worser part of it, | and /live 3.04.157
and either /... the devil or throw him out, 3.04.169
let them throw | millions of acres on us, till 5.01.280
and in the cup an /union shall he throw, 5.02.272
tom will throw his head at them. LR 3.06. 64 P
throw this slave | upon the dunghill. 3.07. 96
cordelia, | the gods themselves throw incense. 5.03. 21
joy, | yet throw such /changes of vexation on't, OTH 1.01. 72
in | as to throw out our eyes for brave othello, 2.01. 38
throw your vild guesses in the devil's teeth, 3.04.184
of yours, but not that dog i shall throw it to. 4.01.143 P
begin to throw | pompey the great and all his ANT 1.02.187
and throw between them all the food thou hast, 3.05. 14
sir, you therein throw away | the absolute 3.07. 41
throw my heart | against the flint and hardness 4.09. 15
me | to throw my sceptre at the injurious gods, 4.15. 76
spit, and throw stones, cast mire upon me, set CYM 5.05.222
the gods throw stones of sulphur on me, if 5.05.240
why did you throw your wedded lady /from you? 5.05.261
you are upon a rock, and now | throw me again. 5.05.263
the good gods | throw their best eyes upon't! PER 3.01. 37
i'll throw my body out, | and leap the garden, TNK 2.02.215
some say, began to throw | her bow away, and 5.01. 93
lord, how mine eyes throw gazes to the east! PP 14.13
in so profound abysm i throw all care | of SON 112. 9
THROWER–OUT 1 FR 0.0001 REL FR 1 V 0 P
hath made thy person for the thrower–out | of my WT 3.03. 29
THROWEST 1 FR 0.0001 REL FR 1 V 0 P
thou trowest, | set less than thou throwest; LR 1.04.123
/THROWING 1 FR 0.0001 REL FR 0 V 1 P
/has /been /much /throwing /about /of /brains. HAM 2.02.358 P
THROWING 11 FR 0.0012 REL FR 8 V 3 P
so throwing him into the water will do him a WIV 3.03.183 P
to him, and excuse his throwing into the water, 3.03.194 P
mad about his throwing into the water. 4.01. 5 P
your eye | by throwing it on any other object, MM 5.01. 23
throwing it aside | and stemming it with hearts JC 1.02.108
and wail, | for, with throwing thus my head, LR 3.06. 72
throwing but shows of service on their lords, OTH 1.01. 52
jealousies, | throwing restraint upon us; 4.03. 90
but | disdaining me and throwing favors on | the CYM 3.05. 75
throwing the base thong from his bending crest, VEN 395
bed, | throwing his mantle rudely o'er his arm, LUC 170
THROWN 34 FR 0.0038 REL FR 24 V 10 P
and to be thrown in the thames? WIV 3.05. 6 P
i was thrown into the ford; 3.05. 36 P
like a dutch dish) to be thrown into the thames, 3.05.119 P
master /brook, i will be thrown into etna, as i 3.05.126 P
you say he has been thrown in the rivers, and 4.04. 20 P
that she this day hath shameless thrown on me. ERR 5.01.202
my better parts | are all thrown down, and that AYL 1.02.250
cousin, thrown upon thee in holiday foolery; 1.03. 13 P
lame, | and unregarded age in corners thrown. 2.03. 42
and thrown into neglect the pompous court? 5.04.182
in florence was it from a casement thrown me, AWW 5.03. 93
my poor corpse, where my bones shall be thrown. TN 2.04. 62
and some have greatness thrown upon them." 5.01.371 P
stay, the king hath thrown his warder down. R2 1.03.118
waste of idle hours hath quite thrown down. 3.04. 66
which our profane hours here have thrown down. 5.01. 25
but dust was thrown upon his sacred head, 5.02. 30
tack'd together and thrown over the shoulders 1H4 4.02. 44 P
for i have thrown | a brave defiance in king 5.02. 41
tell you, they'll stick where they are thrown. TRO 3.02.112 P
he shall be thrown down the tarpeian rock | with COR 3.01.265
thine, | that hath thrown down so many enemies, TIT 3.01.163
how much salt water thrown away in waste, | to ROM 2.03. 71
from our companion thrown into his grave, | so TIM 4.02. 9
flints, and pebbles should be thrown on her. HAM 5.01.231
thrown out his angle for my proper life, | and 5.02. 66
dow'rless daughter, king, thrown to my chance, LR 1.01.256
i found it thrown in at the casement of my 1.02. 60 P
thrown such despite and heavy terms upon her, OTH 4.02.116
to be exil'd, and thrown | from leonati seat, CYM 5.04. 59
and having thrown him from your wat'ry grave, PER 2.01. 10
swear she's dead, | and thrown into the sea. 4.01. 99
had not o'erboard thrown me | for to seek my 4.02. 66
morn this lady was | thrown upon this shore. 5.03. 23
THROWS 15 FR 0.0017 REL FR 14 V 1 P
he throws upon the gross world's baser slaves; LLL 1.01. 30
and there the snake throws her enamell'd skin, MND 2.01.255
how far that little candle throws his beams! MV 5.01. 90
thus king henry throws away his crutch | before 2H6 3.01.189
and he that throws not up his cap for joy 3H6 2.01.196
bran together | he throws without distinction. COR 3.01.321
metellus cimber throws before thy seat | an JC 3.01. 34
of effects, throws a more safer voice on you. OTH 1.03.225 P
harmless lightning) throws her eye | on him, her CYM 5.05.394
throws down one mountain to cast up a higher. PER 1.04. 6
and on his neck her yoking arms she throws. VEN 592
she throws her eyes about the painting round, LUC 1499
would break, | she throws forth tarquin's name: 1717
but now he throws that shallow habit by, 1814
anon he comes, and throws his mantle by, | and PP 6. 9
THROW'T 2 FR 0.0002 REL FR 2 V 0 P
should grind it | and throw't against the wind. COR 3.02.104
i'll throw't into the creek | behind our rock, CYM 4.02.151
THRUM 1 FR 0.0001 REL FR 1 V 0 P
o fates, come, come, | cut thread and thrum, MND 5.01.286
THRUMM'D 1 FR 0.0001 REL FR 0 V 1 P
and there's her thrumm'd hat and her muffler too WIV 4.02. 78 P
THRUSH 1 FR 0.0001 REL FR 1 V 0 P
heigh, /with /heigh, the thrush and the jay! WT 4.03. 10
THRUST 58 FR 0.0065 REL FR 36 V 22 P
very duke | which was thrust forth of milan, who TMP 5.01.160
was milan thrust from milan, that his issue 5.01.205
slave, that will thrust himself into secrets. TGV 3.01.383 P
youth | thrust from the company of aweful men. 4.01. 44
though we would have thrust virtue out of our WIV 5.05.147 P
and thou wilt needs thrust thy neck into a yoke, ADO 1.01.200 P
thrust thy sharp wit quite through my ignorance, LLL 5.02.398
nor thrust your head into the public street | to MV 2.05. 32
and i have thrust myself into this maze, SHR 1.02. 55
understand what advice shall thrust upon thee, AWW 1.01.210 P
and some have greatness thrust upon 'em. TN 2.05.146 P
"and some have greatness thrust upon them." 3.04. 45 P
and it you cannot thrust a bodkin's point. WT 3.03. 85 P
froth, as you'ld thrust a cork into a hogshead. 3.03. 93 P
thrust but these men away, and i'll forgive you, JN 4.01. 82
go | and thrust thyself into their companies; 4.02.167
haste | had falsely thrust upon contrary feet, 4.02.198
for thou shalt thrust thy hand as deep | into 5.02. 60
yea, thrust this enterprise into my heart, | and 5.02. 90
come | to thrust his icy fingers in my maw, 5.07. 37
where doth the world thrust forth a vanity — R2 2.01. 24
affairs | thus disorderly thrust into my hands, 2.02.110
i am eight times thrust through the doublet, 1H4 2.04.166 P
four came all afront, and mainly thrust at me. 2.04.200 P
can peep out his head but i am thrust upon it. 2H4 1.02.213 P
i can close with him, i care not for his thrust. 2.01. 19 P
you, can thrust me from a level consideration. 2.01.113 P
wine, i'll thrust my knife in your mouldy chaps, 2.04.129 P
for god's sake thrust him down stairs. 2.04.188 P
thrust him down stairs! 2.04.190 P
methought 'a made a shrewd thrust at your belly. 2.04.211 P
name, for you might have thrust him and all his 3.02.325 P
he that makes the first thrust, i'll kill him; H5 2.01. 99 P
thrust in between the /paction of these kingdoms 5.02.365
thrust talbot with a spear into the back, | whom 1H6 1.01.138
lord, | and thou be thrust out like a fugitive? 3.03. 67
thrust from the crown | by shameful murther of a 2H6 4.01. 94
for he was thrust in the mouth with a spear, and 4.07. 9 P
and as i thrust thy body in with my sword, | so 4.10. 78
so wish i, i might thrust thy soul to hell. 4.10. 79
unless he seek to thrust you out perforce. 3H6 1.01. 34
for one to thrust his hand between his teeth, 1.04. 57
how dare you thrust yourselves | into my private H8 2.02. 64
so if the time thrust forth | a cause for thy COR 4.01. 40
shall join | to thrust the lie unto him. 5.06.109
thrust those reproachful speeches down his TIT 2.01. 55
the weaker vessels, are ever thrust to the wall; ROM 1.01. 16 P
from the wall, and thrust his maids to the wall. 1.01. 17 P
arm | an envious thrust from tybalt hit the life 3.01.168
i come to have thee thrust me out of doors. TIM 1.02. 25
go thrust him out at gates, and let him smell LR 3.07. 93
found them close together | at blow and thrust, OTH 2.03.238
that thrust had been mine enemy indeed, | but 5.01. 24
cousin, thrust the buckle | through far enough. TNK 3.06. 61
backward she push'd him, as she would be thrust, VEN 41
the very eyes of men through loop–holes thrust, LUC 1383
false creeping craft and perjury should thrust 1517
way, | each trifle under truest bars to thrust, SON 48. 2
THRUSTETH 1 FR 0.0001 REL FR 1 V 0 P
the lion dying thrusteth forth his paw, | and R2 5.01. 29
THRUSTING 4 FR 0.0004 REL FR 3 V 1 P
by thrusting out a torch from yonder tower, 1H6 3.02. 23
brutus, thrusting this report | into his ears; JC 5.03. 74
i may say "thrusting" it; 5.03. 75
that we are evil in, by a divine thrusting on. LR 1.02.126 P
THRUSTS 5 FR 0.0005 REL FR 4 V 1 P
he thrusts me himself into the company of three TGV 4.04. 16 P
thrusts forth his horns again into the world, COR 4.06. 44
while we were interchanging thrusts and blows, ROM 1.01.113
that every minute of his being thrusts | against MAC 3.01.116
on | that sometimes anger thrusts into his hide, SON 50.10
TH'S *(also 's*, theise, these)*
TH'S 1 FR 0.0001 REL FR 0 V 1 P
that i shall leave you one a' th's days; TRO 5.03.104 P
THUMB 12 FR 0.0013 REL FR 3 V 9 P
is not quantity enough for that worthy's thumb, LLL 5.01.131 P
another, with his finger and his thumb, | cried, 5.02.111
and 'twixt his finger and his thumb he held | a 1H4 1.03. 37
temp'ring between my finger and my thumb, and 2H4 4.03.131 P
his finger and his thumb as one would set up a COR 4.05.153 P
i will bite my thumb at them, which is disgrace ROM 1.01. 42 P
do you bite your thumb at us, sir? 1.01. 44 P
i do bite my thumb, sir. 1.01. 45 P
do you bite your thumb at us, sir? 1.01. 46 P
no, sir, i do not bite my thumb at you, sir, but 1.01. 50 P
my thumb at you, sir, but i bite my thumb, sir. 1.01. 51 P
here i have a pilot's thumb, | wrack'd as MAC 1.03. 28
THUMB–RING 1 FR 0.0001 REL FR 0 V 1 P
could have crept into any alderman's thumb–ring. 1H4 2.04.331 P
/THUMBS 1 FR 0.0001 REL FR 0 V 1 P
these ventages with your fingers and /thumbs, HAM 3.02.358 P
THUMBS 1 FR 0.0001 REL FR 1 V 0 P
by the pricking of my thumbs, | something wicked MAC 4.01. 44
/THUMP 1 FR 0.0001 REL FR 1 V 0 P
/my /flesh, | /then /thus /i /thump /it /down. TIT 3.02. 11
THUMP 5 FR 0.0005 REL FR 1 V 4 P
thump then, and i flee. LLL 3.01. 65
of dildos and fadings, "jump her and thump her"; WT 4.04.195 P
thump. 2H6 2.03. 83 P
thump? then see thou thump thy master well. 2.03. 84 P
thump? then see thou thump thy master well. 2.03. 84 P
THUMP'D 2 FR 0.0002 REL FR 1 V 1 P
thou hast thump'd him with thy bird–bolt under LLL 4.03. 23 P
in their own land beaten, bobb'd, and thump'd, R3 5.03.334
/THUNDER 1 FR 0.0001 REL FR 1 V 0 P
/against /the /deep //dread–bolted /thunder? LR 4.07. 32
THUNDER 52 FR 0.0058 REL FR 47 V 5 P
if it should thunder as it did before, i know TMP 2.02. 22 P
the winds did sing it to me, and the thunder, 3.03. 97
to the dread rattling thunder | have i given 5.01. 44
let it thunder to the tune of "green–sleeves," WIV 5.05. 19 P
could great men thunder | as jove himself does, MM 2.02.110
officer | would use his heaven for thunder, 2.02.113
his heaven for thunder, | nothing but thunder! 2.02.114
lightning bears, thy voice his dreadful thunder, LLL 4.02.115
so musical a discord, such sweet thunder. MND 4.01.118
as thunder when the clouds in autumn crack. SHR 1.02. 96
and heaven's artillery thunder in the skies? 1.02.204
with groans that thunder love, with sighs of TN 1.05.256
kin to jove's thunder, so surpris'd my sense, WT 3.01. 10
the thunder of my cannon shall be heard. JN 1.01. 26
our thunder from the south | shall rain their 2.01.411
hast thou not spoke like thunder on my side? 3.01.124
ear, | and mock the deep–mouth'd thunder; 5.02.173
fall like amazing thunder on the casque | of thy R2 1.03. 81
in thunder and in earthquake, like a jove, H5 2.04.100
and that engenders thunder in his breast, | and 1H6 3.01. 39
if talbot do but thunder, rain will follow. 3.02. 59
god, to shoot forth thunder | upon these paltry, 2H6 4.01.104
thy voice is thunder, but thy looks are humble. R3 1.04.167
are the youths that thunder at a playhouse and H8 5.03. 60 P
and say in thunder, "achilles go to him." TRO 2.03.199
the shepherd knows not thunder from a tabor COR 1.06. 25
a shower and thunder with their caps and shouts. 2.01.267
his trident, | or jove for 's power to thunder. 3.01.256
to tear with thunder the wide cheeks a' th' air, 5.03.151
in thunder, lightning, or in rain? MAC 1.01. 2
fear it lies, | and sleep in spite of thunder. 4.01. 86
shall bruit again, | respeaking earthly thunder. HAM 1.02.128
anon the dreadful thunder | doth rend the region 2.02.486
'gainst parricides did all the thunder bend, LR 2.01. 46
and thou, all–shaking thunder, | strike flat the 3.02. 6
nor rain, wind, thunder, fire are my daughters. 3.02. 15
sheets of fire, such bursts of horrid thunder, 3.02. 46
what is the cause of thunder? 3.04.155
when the thunder would not peace at my bidding, 4.06.102 P
in heaven | but what serves for the thunder? OTH 5.02.235
and shake the orb, | he was as rattling thunder. ANT 5.02. 86
he came in thunder, his celestial breath | was CYM 5.04.114
thunder above, and deeps below, | makes such PER 2.ch. 30
rain, and thunder, remember earthly man | is but 2.01. 2
thunder shall not so awake the beds of eels as 4.02.142 P
the holy gods as loud | as thunder threatens us. 5.01.199
methought i heard a dreadful clap of thunder TNK 3.06. 83
like ivy/–tods, | not to undo with thunder. 4.02.105
hollow womb resounds like heaven's thunder; VEN 268
lightning seems, thy voice his dreadful thunder, PP 5.11
'pointing to each his thunder, rain, and wind, SON 14. 6
o, that forc'd thunder from his heart did fly, LC 325
THUNDER–BEARER 1 FR 0.0001 REL FR 1 V 0 P
i do not bid the thunder–bearer shoot, | nor LR 2.04.227
THUNDERBOLT 4 FR 0.0004 REL FR 2 V 2 P
that hath lately suffer'd by a thunderbolt. TMP 2.02. 36 P
if i had a thunderbolt in mine eye, i can tell AYL 1.02.214 P
who is to bear me like a thunderbolt | against 1H4 4.01.120
some innocents scape not the thunderbolt. ANT 2.05. 77
THUNDERBOLTS 2 FR 0.0002 REL FR 2 V 0 P
be ready, gods, with all your thunderbolts, JC 4.03. 81
vaunt–couriers of oak–cleaving thunderbolts, LR 3.02. 5
THUNDER–CLAPS 1 FR 0.0001 REL FR 1 V 0 P
the precursors | o' th' dreadful thunder–claps, TMP 1.02.202
THUNDER–DARTER 1 FR 0.0001 REL FR 0 V 1 P
o thou great thunder–darter of olympus, forget TRO 2.03. 10 P
THUNDERER 1 FR 0.0001 REL FR 1 V 0 P
how dare you ghosts | accuse the thunderer, CYM 5.04. 95
THUNDER–LIKE 1 FR 0.0001 REL FR 1 V 0 P
and | the thunder–like percussion of thy sounds, COR 1.04. 59
THUNDER–MASTER 1 FR 0.0001 REL FR 1 V 0 P
no more, thou thunder–master, show | thy spite CYM 5.04. 30
THUNDER'S 2 FR 0.0002 REL FR 2 V 0 P
o, that my tongue were in the thunder's mouth! JN 3.04. 38
secure of thunder's crack or lightning flash, TIT 2.01. 3
THUNDERS 7 FR 0.0008 REL FR 7 V 0 P
who thunders to his captives blood and death, 3H6 2.01.127
by him that thunders, thou hast lusty arms! TRO 4.05.136
that thunders, lightens, opens graves, and roars JC 1.03. 74
shipwracking storms and direful thunders /break, MAC 1.02. 26
that roars so loud and thunders in the index? HAM 3.04. 52
by jove that thunders! ANT 3.13. 85
still | thy deaf'ning, dreadful thunders, gently PER 3.01. 5
THUNDER–STONE 2 FR 0.0002 REL FR 2 V 0 P
see, | have bar'd my bosom to the thunder–stone; JC 1.03. 49
nor th' all–dreaded thunder–stone. CYM 4.02.271
THUNDER–STROKE 2 FR 0.0002 REL FR 1 V 1 P
they dropp'd, as by a thunder–stroke. TMP 2.01.204
i took him to be kill'd with a thunder–stroke. 2.02.108 P
THUND'REST 1 FR 0.0001 REL FR 1 V 0 P
coward, that thund'rest with thy tongue, | and TIT 2.01. 58
THUND'RING 1 FR 0.0001 REL FR 1 V 0 P
when their thund'ring shock | at meeting tears R2 3.03. 56
THURIO 23 FR 0.0026 REL FR 20 V 3 P
master, sir thurio frowns on you. TGV 2.04. 3 P
what, angry, sir thurio? do you change color? 2.04. 23 P
sir thurio borrows his wit from your ladyship's 2.04. 38 P
silvia, i speak to you, and you, sir thurio; 2.04. 84
to see such lovers, thurio, as yourself: 2.04. 97
come, sir thurio, | go with me. 2.04.117
for thurio, he intends, shall wed his daughter; 2.06. 39
sir thurio, give us leave, i pray, a while, | we 3.01. 1
you have determin'd to bestow her | on thurio, 3.01. 14
to match my friend sir thurio to my daughter. 3.01. 62
sir thurio, fear not but that she will love you 3.02. 1
but thurio thinks not so. 3.02. 16
the match between sir thurio and my daughter? 3.02. 23
the love of valentine, and love sir thurio? 3.02. 30
it follows not that she will love sir thurio. 3.02. 50
but you, sir thurio, are not sharp enough: 3.02. 67
and now i must be as unjust to thurio: 4.02. 2
but here comes thurio. 4.02. 16
ay, gentle thurio, for you know that love | will 4.02. 19
sir thurio, fear not you, i will so plead, 4.02. 82
my father would enforce me marry | vain thurio, 4.03. 17
how now, thurio? 5.02. 31
thurio, give back, or else embrace thy death; 5.04.126
THURIO'S 1 FR 0.0001 REL FR 1 V 0 P
some sly trick blunt thurio's dull proceeding. TGV 2.06. 41
THURSDAY 17 FR 0.0019 REL FR 15 V 2 P
or, francis, a' thursday; 1H4 2.04. 66 P
forward, | on thursday we ourselves will march. 3.02.174

THURSDAY

i shall receive money a' thursday, shalt have a 2H4 2.04.275 P
a' thursday let it be — a' thursday, tell her, ROM 3.04. 20
a' thursday let it be — a' thursday, tell her, 3.04. 20
but what say you to thursday? 3.04. 28
my lord, i would that thursday were to–morrow. 3.04. 29
well, get you gone, a' thursday be it then. 3.04. 30
marry, my child, early next thursday morn, | the 3.05.112
fettle your fine joints 'gainst thursday next, 3.05.153
get thee to church a' thursday, | or never after 3.05.161
thursday is near, lay hand on heart, advise. 3.05.190
on thursday, sir? the time is very short. 4.01. 1
that may be must be, love, on thursday next. 4.01. 20
juliet, on thursday early will i rouse ye; 4.01. 42
on thursday next be married to this county. 4.01. 49
no, not till thursday, there is time enough. 4.02. 36

THUS *(also this)*
/THUS 8 FR 0.0009 REL FR 8 V 0 P
/that /rise /thus /nimbly /by /a /true /king's R2 4.01.318
/i /am /thus /bold /to /put /your /grace /in R3 4.02.110
/my /flesh, | /then /thus /i /thump /it /down. TIT 3.02. 11
/of /woe, /that /thus /dost /talk /in /signs! 3.02. 12
/not /strike /it /thus /to /make /it /still. 3.02. 14
/teach /her /not /thus /to /lay | /such /violent 3.02. 21
and /thus a while the fit will work on him; HAM 5.01.285
/thus it is, general: OTH 2.03.224
THUS 841 FR 0.0950 REL FR 733 V 108 P
i, thus neglecting worldly ends, all dedicated TMP 1.02. 89
he being thus lorded, | not only with what my 1.02. 97
know thus far forth: 1.02.177
the purpose cherish | whiles thus you mock it! 2.01.225
thus, sir: 2.01.231
whiles you, doing thus, | to the perpetual wink 2.01.284
my mistress, dearest, | and i thus humble ever. 3.01. 87
he is drown'd | whom thus we stray to find, and 3.03. 9
what do you mean | to dote thus on such luggage? 4.01.231
hath sever'd us, | and brought us thus together? 5.01.188
i am) | should censure thus on lovely gentlemen. TGV 1.02. 19
then thus: of many good i think him best. 1.02. 21
and thus i search it with a sovereign kiss. 1.02.113
thus will i fold them one upon another; 1.02.125
muse not that i thus suddenly proceed; 1.03. 64
thus have i shunn'd the fire for fear of burning 1.03. 78
that makes me, reasonless, to reason thus? 2.04.198
that thus without advice begin to love her? 2.04.208
marry, thus: 2.05. 22 P
if i lose them, thus find i by their loss — 2.06. 21
and should she thus be stol'n away from you, 3.01. 15
thus, for my duty's sake, i rather chose | to 3.01. 17
i am thus early come to know what service | it 4.03. 9
would say precisely, "thus i would teach a dog." 4.04. 6 P
unrivall'd merit, | to which i thus subscribe: 5.04.145
i cannot be thus satisfied. WIV 2.01.188 P
you wrong me, sir, thus still to haunt my house. 3.04. 69
being thus cramm'd in the basket, a couple of 3.05. 97 P
been into thames, ere i will leave her thus. 3.05.128 P
borrow'd of the pronoun, and be thus declin'd, 4.01. 41 P
if i cry out thus upon no trail, never trust me 4.02.197 P
that likewise have we thought upon, and thus: 4.04. 47
now, thus it rests: 4.06. 34
he would never else cross me thus. 5.05. 36 P
thus, what with the war, what with the sweat, MM 1.02. 82 P
fellow, why dost thou show me thus to th' world? 1.02.116
thus can the demigod, authority, | make us pay 1.02.120
thus stands it with me: 1.02.145
be sorry should be thus foolishly lost at a game 1.02.190 P
fewness and truth, 'tis thus: 1.04. 39
should it then be thus? 2.02. 68
or my son, | it should be thus with him: 2.02. 82
why does my blood thus muster to my heart, 2.04. 20
thus wisdom wishes to appear most bright | when 2.04. 78
reason thus with life: 3.01. 6
that thus can make him bite the law by th' nose, 3.01.108
still thus, and thus; still worse! 3.02. 53 P
still thus, and thus; still worse! 3.02. 53 P
to bring you thus together 'tis no sin, | sith 4.01. 72
thus fail not to do your office, as you will 4.02.125 P
woe, | as i, thus wrong'd, hence unbelieved go! 5.01.119
shall we thus permit | a blasting and a 5.01.121
unjust | thus to retort your manifest appeal, 5.01.301
then, angelo, thy fault's thus manifested; 5.01.412
i so deserv'd of you, | that you extol me thus? 5.01.503
the children thus dispos'd, my wife and i, ERR 1.01. 83
thus have you heard me sever'd from my bliss, 1.01.118
what, wilt thou flout me thus unto my face, 1.02. 91
me, | that like a football you do spurn me thus? 2.01. 83
mad, | that thus so madly thou didst answer me? 2.02. 12
there ever any man thus beaten out of season, 2.02. 47
thus i mend it: 2.02.106 P
when were you wont to use my sister thus? 2.02.153
how can she thus then call us by our names, 2.02.166
to counterfeit thus grossly with your slave, 2.02.169
the chain unfinish'd made me stay thus long. 3.02.168
thou art a villain to impeach me thus: 5.01. 29
my lord, in truth, thus far i witness with him: 5.01.255
nay then thus: 5.01.424
were thus much overheard by a man of mine. ADO 1.02. 10 P
why are you thus out of measure sad? 1.03. 2 P
thus answer i in name of benedick, | but hear 2.01.172
you think the prince would have serv'd you thus? 2.01.196 P
thus goes every one to the world but i, and i am 2.01.318 P
thus far can i praise him: 2.01.378 P
who is thus like to be cozen'd with the 2.02. 38 P
of a maid — that you have discover'd thus. 2.02. 40 P
he had been a dog that should have howl'd thus, 2.03. 80 P
thus, pretty lady, | i am sorry for thy much 4.01. 98
these things, come thus to light, | smother her 4.01.111
who smirched thus and mir'd with infamy, | i 4.01.133
if you go on thus, you will kill yourself, | and 5.01. 1
and 'tis not wisdom thus to second grief 5.01. 2
as thus for thus, and such a grief for such, 5.01. 13
as thus for thus, and such a grief for such, 5.01. 13
and all of them that thus dishonor her. 5.01. 44
thus did she an hour together trans–shape thy 5.01.170 P
masters, that you are thus bound to your answer? 5.01.227 P
as thus — to study where i well may dine, LLL 1.01. 61
if study's gain be thus, and this be so, | study 1.01. 67
marry, thus much i have learnt: 2.01. 84
thus came your argument in; 3.01.108
thus will i save my credit in the shoot: 4.01. 26
thus expecting thy reply, i profane my lips on 4.01. 84 P
thus dost thou hear the nemean lion roar 4.01. 88
what grace hast thou thus to reprove | these 4.03.151
all three of you, to be thus much o'ershot? 4.03.158
are we betrayed thus to thy over–view? 4.03.173
it is religion to be thus forsworn: 4.03.360
and with his royal finger, thus, dally with my 5.01.103 P
depart, | if fairings come thus plentifully in. 5.02. 2
"thus must thou speak," and "thus thy body bear" 5.02.100
must thou speak," and "thus thy body bear"; 5.02.100
one rubb'd his elbow thus, and fleer'd, and 5.02.109
and are apparell'd thus, | like muscovites or 5.02.120
thus change i like the moon. 5.02.212
will you not dance? how come you thus estranged? 5.02.213
thus pour the stars down plagues for perjury. 5.02.394
forestall our sport, to make us thus untrue? 5.02.473
thus did he strangle serpents in his manus. 5.02.591
sin, | thus purifies itself and turns to grace. 5.02.776
for thus sings he, | "cuckoo; 5.02.899
for thus sings he, | "cuckoo; 5.02.908
how canst thou thus for shame, titania, | glance MND 2.01. 74
i charge thee hence, and do not haunt me thus. 2.02. 85
do, as a monster, fly my presence thus. 2.02. 97
and he himself must speak through, saying thus, 3.01. 38 P
or let him hold his fingers thus, and through 3.01. 70 P
their sense thus weak, lost with their fears 3.02. 27
thus weak, lost with their fears thus strong, 3.02. 27
you would not do me thus much injury. 3.02.148
why will you suffer her to flout me thus? 3.02.327
and from each other look thou lead them thus, 3.02.363
a knavish lad, | thus to make poor females mad. 3.02.441
thus hath he lost sixpence a day during his life 4.02. 19 P
curs'd be thy stones for thus deceiving me! 5.01.181
thus have i, wall, my part discharged so; 5.01.204
and, being done, thus wall away doth go. 5.01.205
thus die i, thus, thus, thus. 5.01.300
thus die i, thus, thus, thus. 5.01.300
thus die i, thus, thus, thus. 5.01.300
thus die i, thus, thus, thus. 5.01.300
and thus she means, videlicet — 5.01.323 P
thus thisby ends; 5.01.346
courtesies | i'll lend you thus much moneys"? MV 1.03.129
hood mine eyes | thus with my hat, and sigh and 2.02.194
blush | to see me thus transformed to a boy. 2.06. 39
thus losers part. 2.07. 77
thus hath the candle sing'd the moth. 2.09. 79
thus ornament is but the guiled shore | to a 3.02. 97
is it your dear friend that is thus in trouble? 3.02.291
in bearing thus the absence of your lord. 3.04. 4
thus when i shun scylla, your father, i fall 3.05. 16 P
launcelot, if you thus get my wife into corners! 3.05. 30 P
that i follow thus | a losing suit against him. 4.01. 61
i have spoke thus much | to mitigate the justice 4.01.202
why then thus it is: 4.01.244
thus men may grow wiser every day. AYL 1.02.137 P
entreaties, | ere he should thus have ventur'd. 1.02.239
thus must i from the smoke into the smother, 1.02.287
thus do all traitors! 1.03. 52
and thus the hairy fool, | much marked of the 2.01. 40
"thus misery doth part | the flux of company." 2.01. 51
thus most invectively he pierceth through | the 2.01. 58
thus it goes: 2.05. 49 P
thus we may see," quoth he, "how the world wags. 2.07. 23
hear | the motley fool thus moral on the time, 2.07. 29
art thou thus bolden'd, man, by thy distress? 2.07. 91
thus rosalind of many parts | by heavenly synod 3.02.149
and thus i cur'd him, and this way will i take 3.02.421 P
can a woman rail thus? 4.03. 42 P
your body more seeming, audrey), as thus, sir. 5.04. 69 P
reason wonder may diminish | how thus we met, 5.04.140
glad that you thus continue your resolve | to SHR 1.01. 27
thus it stands: 1.01.179
then it follows thus: 1.01.201
signior hortensio, thus it stands with me: 1.02. 53
petruchio, since we are stepp'd thus far in, | i 1.02. 83
and therefore let me be thus bold with you | to 1.02.104
was ever gentleman thus griev'd as i? 2.01. 37
all this chat aside, | thus in plain terms: 2.01.269
father, 'tis thus: 2.01.290
well, gentlemen, | i am thus resolv'd: 2.01.393
tellus," disguis'd thus to get your love, "hic 3.01. 33 P
that i have been thus pleasant with you both. 3.01. 58
were it better i should rush in thus: 3.02. 91
not i, believe me, thus i'll visit her. 3.02.114
but thus, i trust, you will not marry her. 3.02.115
good sooth, even thus; 3.02.116
fellow, you — and thus much for greeting. 4.01.112 P
and serve it thus to me that love it not? 4.01.164
thus have i politicly begun my reign, | and 'tis 4.01.188
and thus i'll curb her mad and headstrong humor. 4.01.209
pack of you | that triumph thus upon my misery! 4.03. 34
then thus: 4.04. 82 P
thus the bowl should run, | and not unluckily 4.05. 24
thus strangers may be hal'd and abus'd. 5.01.108 P
thus i conceive by him. 5.02. 22
my widow says, thus she conceives her tale. 5.02. 24
th' ambition in my love thus plagues itself: AWW 1.01. 90
thus, indian–like, | religious in mine error, i 1.03.204
but, my good lord, 'tis thus: 2.01. 68
thus he his special nothing ever prologues. 2.01. 92
the blushes in my cheeks thus whisper me, | "we 2.03. 69
her intents, | which thus she hath prevented. 3.04. 22
and let me buy your friendly help thus far, 3.07. 15
thus your own proper wisdom | brings in the 4.02. 49
my niece to take the death of her brother thus? TN 1.03. 2 P
that, yet thus far i will boldly publish her: 2.01. 28 P
and i have heard herself come thus near, that, 2.05. 25 P
i extend my hand to him thus, quenching my 2.05. 65 P
and her t's, and thus makes she her great p's. 2.05. 87 P
she thus advises thee that sighs for thee. 2.05.152 P
but rather reason thus with reason fetter: 3.01.155
we may carry it thus, for our pleasure and his 3.04.137 P
will it be ever thus? 4.01. 47
if it be thus to dream, still let me sleep! 4.01. 63
sir topas, never was man thus wrong'd. 4.02. 28 P
and i say there was never man thus abus'd. 4.02. 47 P
and though 'tis wonder that enwraps me thus, 4.03. 3
but to read his right wits is to read thus; 5.01.299 P
and thus the whirligig of time brings in his 5.01.376 P
is breeding | that changes thus his manners. WT 1.02.375
finding | myself thus alter'd with't. 1.02.384
for 'tis polixenes | has made thee swell thus. 2.01. 62
knowledge, that | you thus have publish'd me! 2.01. 98
as you feel doing thus — and see withal | the 2.01.153
it is but weakness | to bear the matter thus — 2.03. 2
you, that are thus so tender o'er his follies, 2.03.128
at least thus much: 2.03.165
(thus by apollo's great divine seal'd up) 3.01. 19
but thus, if pow'rs divine | behold our human 3.02. 28
so uncurrent i | have strain'd t' appear thus; 3.02. 50
that for thy mother's fault art thus expos'd 3.03. 50
not to have had thee than thus to want thee. 4.02. 13 P
heir, | that thus affects a sheep–hook! 4.04.420
how often have i told you 'twould be thus! 4.04.474
thus we set on, camillo, to th' sea–side. 4.04.668
thus your verse | flow'd with her beauty once. 5.01.101
'tis strange | he thus should steal upon us. 5.01.115
'twixt heaven and earth | might thus have stood, 5.01.133
o, thus she stood, | even with such life of 5.03. 34
of my poor image | would thus have wrought you 5.03. 58
i am sorry, sir, i have thus far stirr'd you; 5.03. 74
thus, after greeting, speaks the king of france JN 1.01. 2
"my dear sir," | thus, leaning on mine elbow, i 1.01.194
why stand these royal fronts amazed thus? 2.01.356
thou shalt be punish'd for thus frighting me, 3.01. 11
from the mouth of england | add thus much more, 3.01.153
this must not be thus borne. 4.02.101
i saw a smith stand with his hammer, thus, | the 4.02.193
thus have i yielded up into your hand | the 5.01. 1
what lusty trumpet thus doth summon us? 5.02.117
king, | for thus his royalty doth speak in me: 5.02.129
thus hath he sworn, | and i with him, and many 5.04. 16
but now a king, now thus. 5.07. 66
in suff'ring thus thy brother to be slaught'red, R2 1.02. 30
and why thou comest thus knightly clad in arms, 1.03. 12
hither | thus plated in habiliments of war, 1.03. 28
then thus i turn me from my country's light, 1.03.176
teach thy necessity to reason thus: 1.03.277
and thus expiring do foretell of him: 2.01. 32
then thus: 2.01.277
affairs | thus disorderly thrust into my hands, 2.02.110
this covenant makes, my hand thus seals it. 2.03. 50
had you first died, and he been thus trod down, 2.03.126
and humor'd thus, | comes at the last and with a 3.02.168
subjected thus, | how can you say to me i am a 3.02.176
parley | into his ruin'd ears, and thus deliver: 3.03. 34
and thus long have we stood | to watch the 3.03. 72
northumberland, say thus the king returns: 3.03.121
as thus to drop them still upon one place, 3.03.166
thus high at least, although your knee be low. 3.03.195
you thus employed, i will go root away | the 3.04. 37
stirr'd up by god, thus boldly for his king. 4.01.133
thus give i mine, and thus take i thy heart. 5.01. 96
thus give i mine, and thus take i thy heart. 5.01. 96
his proud steed's neck, | bespake them thus: 5.02. 20
and thus still doing, thus he pass'd along. 5.02. 21
and thus still doing, thus he pass'd along. 5.02. 21
the word itself | against the word, | as thus: 5.05. 15
thus play i in one person many people, | and 5.05. 31
fire | that staggers thus my person. 5.05.109
came from the north, and thus it did import: 1H4 1.01. 51
and resolution thus fubb'd as it is with the 1.02. 60 P
your son in scotland being thus employed, 1.03.265
what a plague mean ye to colt me thus? 2.02. 37 P
o my good lord, why are you thus alone? 2.03. 37
and thus hath so bestirr'd thee in thy sleep, 2.03. 57
here i lay, and thus i bore my point. 2.04.195 P
took all their seven points in my target, thus. 2.04.202 P
thus did i keep my person fresh and new, | my 3.02. 55
of his oath–breaking, which he mended thus, | by 5.02. 37
name, that in battle thus | thou crossest me? 5.03. 1
and i do haunt thee in the battle thus | because 5.03. 4
o douglas, hadst thou fought at holmedon thus, 5.03. 14
art, whoe'er thou be, | and thus i win thee. 5.04. 38
thus ever did rebellion find rebuke. 5.05. 1
but what need i thus | my well–known body to 2H4 in 20
thou wouldst say, "your son did thus and thus; 1.01. 76
thou wouldst say, "your son did thus and thus; 1.01. 76
your brother thus; 1.01. 77
thus have you heard our cause and known our 1.03. 1
the question then, lord hastings, standeth thus: 1.03. 15
but do you use me thus, ned? 2.02.138 P
well, thus we play the fools with the time, and 2.02.142 P
"the time shall come," thus did he follow it, 3.01. 75
court–gate, when 'a was a crack not thus high; 3.02. 31 P
and 'a would manage you his piece thus, and 'a 3.02.282 P
their cold intent, tenure, and substance thus: 4.01. 9
thus do the hopes we have in him touch ground 4.01. 17
since sudden sorrow | serves to say thus, some 4.02. 84
will you thus break your faith? 4.02.112
would be sorry, my lord, but it should be thus. 4.03. 31 P
crown as having sense, | and thus upbraided it: 4.05.158
thus, my most royal liege, | accusing it, i put 4.05.164
marry, sir, thus; 5.01. 13 P
o god, that right should thus overcome might! 5.04. 24 P
look you, he must seem thus to the world. 5.05. 78 P
being valu'd thus: H5 1.01. 11
thus runs the bill. 1.01. 19
thus then in few: 1.02.245
if that same demon that hath gull'd thee thus 2.02.121
and thus thy fall hath left a kind of blot | to 2.02.138
thus comes the english with full power upon us, 2.04. 1
from him, and thus he greets your majesty: 2.04. 76
thus says my king: 2.04.120
thus with imagin'd wing our swift scene flies 3.pr. 1
or, guilty in defense, be thus destroy'd? 3.03. 43
thus says my king: 3.06.118 P
yet, forgive me, god, | that i do brag thus! 3.06.151
once writ a sonnet in his praise and began thus: 3.07. 40 P
thus may we gather honey from the weed, | and 4.01. 11
god, why should they mock poor fellows thus? 4.03. 92
i know this, and thus i challenge it. 4.08. 8 P
to cry amen to that, thus we appear. 5.02. 21
kate, dost thou understand thus much english? 5.02.193 P
and thus in latin, praeclarissimus filius noster 5.02.340 P

thus far, with rough and all–unable pen, | our ep 1
that plotted thus our glory's overthrow? 1H6 1.01. 24
'tis the french dolphin sueth to thee thus. 1.02.112
shall i be flouted thus by dunghill grooms? 1.03. 14
thus contumeliously should break the peace! 1.03. 58
thus joan de pucelle hath perform'd her word. 1.06. 3
thus are poor servitors, | when others sleep 2.01. 5
we had not been thus shamefully surpris'd. 2.01. 65
or durst not for his craven heart say thus. 2.04. 87
ay, noble uncle, thus ignobly us'd, | your 2.05. 35
was, for that (young richard thus remov'd, 2.05. 71
thus the mortimers, | in whom the title rested, 2.05. 91
then thus it must be, this doth joan devise: 3.03. 17
say, gentlemen, what makes you thus exclaim? 4.01. 83
to harry king of england, | and thus he would: 4.02. 5
that thus delays my promised supply | of 4.03. 10
that thus we die, while remiss traitors sleep. 4.03. 29
thus, while the vulture of sedition | feeds in 4.03. 47
blood, and in disgrace | bespoke him thus: 4.06. 21
once i encount'red him, and thus i said: 4.07. 37
proud majestical high scorn | he answer'd thus: 4.07. 40
whose maiden blood, thus rigorously effus'd, 5.04. 52
it is thus agreed | that peaceful truce shall be 5.04.116
charles, and the rest, it is enacted thus: 5.04.123
thus suffolk hath prevail'd, and thus he goes, 5.05.103
thus suffolk hath prevail'd, and thus he goes, 5.05.103
and thus, i fear, at last | hume's knavery will 2H6 1.02.104
as thus | to name the several colors we do wear. 2.01.125
then thus: 2.02. 9
thus got the house of lancaster the crown. 2.02. 29
thus droops this lofty pine and hangs his sprays 2.03. 45
thus eleanor's pride dies in her youngest days. 2.03. 46
thus sometimes hath the brightest day a cloud, 2.04. 1
land, | methinks i should not thus be led along, 2.04. 30
thus are my blossoms blasted in the bud, | and 3.01. 89
knife and traitors' rage | be thus upbraided, 3.01.175
thus king henry throws away his crutch | before 3.01.189
thus is the shepherd beaten from thy side, | and 3.01.191
why do you rate my lord of suffolk thus? 3.02. 56
makes them thus forward in his banishment. 3.02.253
even thus two friends condemn'd | embrace, and 3.02.353
thus is poor suffolk ten times banished, | once 3.02.357
therefore thus will i reward thee: 4.03. 5 P
that thus you do exclaim you'll go with him? 4.08. 35
and humbly thus, with halters on their necks, 4.09. 11
thus stands my state, 'twixt cade and york 4.09. 31
from ireland thus comes york to claim his right, 5.01. 1
us | that thus he marcheth with thee arm in arm? 5.01. 57
thus war hath given thee peace, for thou art 5.02. 29
thy chair–days, thus | to die in ruffian battle? 5.02. 48
thus do i hope to shake king henry's head. 3H6 1.01. 20
fight it out, and not stand cavilling thus. 1.01.117
which makes thee thus presumptuous and proud, 1.01.157
hath he deserv'd to lose his birthright thus? 1.01.219
thus do i leave thee. 1.01.255
come, son, away, we may not linger thus. 1.01.263
why do we linger thus? 1.02. 32
while you are thus employ'd, what resteth more, 1.02. 44
and thus most humbly i do take my leave. 1.02. 61
and i, to make thee mad, do mock thee thus. 1.04. 90
becomes it thee to be thus bold in terms 2.02. 85
o margaret, thus 'twill be, and thou, poor soul, 3.01. 53
then, warwick, thus: 3.03.134
well, i will arm me, being thus forewarn'd. 4.01.113
thus /stands the case: 4.05. 4
stand you thus close to steal the bishop's deer? 4.05. 17
rest, | yet thus far fortune maketh us amends, 4.07. 2
we being thus arriv'd | from ravenspurgh haven 4.07. 7
and thus i seal my truth, and bid adieu. 4.08. 29
thus yields the cedar to the axe's edge, | whose 5.02. 11
thus far our fortune keeps an upward course, 5.03. 1
it is his policy | to haste thus fast, to find 5.04. 63
and thus i prophesy, that many a thousand 5.06. 37
thus have we swept suspicion from our seat, 5.07. 13
on me, that halts and am misshapen thus? R3 1.02.250
but thus his simple truth must be abus'd | with 1.03. 52
thus have you breath'd your curse against 1.03.239
and thus i clothe my naked villainy | with odd 1.03.335
that thus i have resign'd to you my charge. 1.04. 97
much more to be thus opposite with heaven, | for 2.02. 94
thus, like the formal vice, iniquity, | i 3.01. 82
to taunt and scorn you thus opprobriously? 3.01.153
that by their witchcraft thus have marked me. 3.04. 72
proceed thus rashly in the villain's death, 3.05. 43
nay, for a need, thus far come near my person: 3.05. 85
"thus saith the duke, thus hath the duke 3.07. 32
saith the duke, thus hath the duke inferr'd" — 3.07. 32
and thus i took the vantage of those few: 3.07. 37
the last — | definitively thus i answer you: 3.07.153
thus high, by thy advice | and thy assistance, 4.02. 3
and is it thus? 4.02.119
"o, thus," quoth dighton, "lay the gentle babes. 4.03. 9
"thus, thus," quoth forrest, "girdling one 4.03. 10
"thus, thus," quoth forrest, "girdling one 4.03. 10
when dighton thus told on, "we smothered | the 4.03. 17
thus hath the course of justice whirl'd about, 4.04.105
of war | thus will i drown your exclamations. 4.04.154
shall i be tempted of the devil thus? 4.04.418
thus doth he force the swords of wicked men | to 5.01. 23
thus margaret's curse falls heavy on my neck: 5.01. 25
thus far into the bowels of the land | have we 5.02. 3
plain, | and thus my battle shall be ordered: 5.03.292
they thus directed, we will follow | in the main 5.03.298
they were ratified | as he cried, "thus let be!" H8 1.01.171
and pav'd with gold, the emperor thus desir'd, 1.01.188
that thus the cardinal | does buy and sell his 1.01.191
though we leave it with a root, thus hack'd, 1.02. 97
english, thus they pray'd | to tell your grace, 1.04. 65
pray tell 'em thus much from me: 1.04. 77
you that thus far have come to pity me, | hear 2.01. 56
yet thus far we are one in fortunes: 2.01.121
that thus you should proceed to put me off, 2.04. 21
to this point, | and thus far clear him. 2.04.168
thus it came; 2.04.170
thus hulling in | the wild sea of my conscience, 2.04.200
have i liv'd thus long (let me speak myself, 3.01.125
and am i thus rewarded? 3.01.133
thus importing | the several parcels of his 3.02.124
if we live thus tamely, | to be thus jaded by a 3.02.279
to be thus jaded by a piece of scarlet, 3.02.280
but, thus much, they are foul ones. 3.02.300
and thus far hear me, cromwell, | and when i am 3.02.431
yet thus far, griffith, give me leave to speak 4.02. 32
life | and able means, we had not parted thus. 4.02.153
wherefore frowns he thus? 5.01. 87
it fits we thus proceed, or else no witness 5.01.107
as not thus to suffer | a man of his place, and 5.02. 29
then thus for you, my lord, it stands agreed, 5.02.122
thus far, | my most dread sovereign, may it like 5.02.182
i will say thus much for him, if a prince | may 5.02.190
is verified | of thee, which says thus, "do my 5.02.210
my noble partners and myself thus pray | all 5.04. 5
but, saying thus, in stead of oil and balm, TRO 1.01. 61
when with your blood you daily paint her thus. 1.01. 91
think i have no sense, thou strikest me thus? 2.01. 23 P
why, how now, ajax, wherefore do ye thus? 2.01. 55
his evasions have ears thus long. 2.01. 69 P
thus once again says nestor from the greeks: 2.02. 2
thus to persist | in doing wrong extenuates not 2.02.186
shall the elephant ajax carry it thus? 2.03. 3 P
what moves ajax thus to bay at him? 2.03. 90 P
but his evasion, wing'd thus swift with scorn, 2.03.114
a whoreson dog, that shall palter with us thus! 2.03.233
but, marry, thus, my lord: 3.01. 63 P
o cressid, how often have i wish'd me thus! 3.02. 61 P
me, | 'twas not my purpose thus to beg a kiss. 3.02.137
or that persuasion could but thus convince me 3.02.164
and your great love to me restrains you thus. 3.03.221
but /he's out of tune thus. 3.03.301 P
now, | for thus popp'd paris in his hardiment, 4.05. 28
and parted thus you and your argument. 4.05. 29
thus says aeneas, one that knows the youth 4.05.110
did in great ilion thus translate him to me. 4.05.112
hector would have them fall upon him thus. 4.05.137
of envy, thou, what means thou to curse thus? 5.01. 26 P
thy goodly armor thus hath cost thy life. 5.08. 2
pleas'd with this dainty bait, thus goes to bed. 5.08. 20
thus proudly /pight upon our phrygian plains, 5.10. 24
thus is the poor agent despis'd! 5.10. 36 P
thus accus'd it: COR 1.01. 97
ne'er came from the lungs, but even thus — 1.01.108
not rash like his accusers, and thus answered: 1.01.129
methinks i see him stamp thus, and call thus: 1.03. 32
methinks i see him stamp thus, and call thus: 1.03. 32
thus it is: 1.03. 96 P
to aufidius thus | i will appear, and fight. 1.05. 19
martius, and i have | before–time seen him thus. 1.06. 24
minded, | wave thus to express his disposition, 1.06. 74
service that | hath thus stood for his country; 2.02. 41
his pupil age | man–ent'red thus, he waxed like 2.02. 99
to brag unto them, "thus i did, and thus!" 2.02.147
to brag unto them, "thus i did, and thus!" 2.02.147
and the honor go | to one that would do thus. 2.03.123
and with his hat, thus waving it in scorn, | "i 2.03.167
thus to have said, | as you were fore–advis'd, 2.03.190
one thus descended, | that hath beside well in 2.03.245
have you thus | given hydra here to choose an 3.01. 92
people give | one that speaks thus their voice? 3.01.119
thus we debase | the nature of our seats and 3.01.135
to what you would | thus violently redress. 3.01.219
of sight, yet will i still | be thus to them. 3.02. 6
before he should thus stoop to th' /herd, but 3.02. 32
and thus far having stretch'd it (here be with 3.02. 74
which often thus correcting thy stout heart, 3.02. 78
for you, the city, thus i turn my back; 3.03.134
i am most fortunate thus accidentally to 4.03. 37 P
dismiss'd me | thus, with his speechless hand. 5.01. 67
the sorrow that delivers us thus chang'd | makes 5.03. 39
nay, go not from us thus. 5.03.131
whose chronicle thus writ: 5.03.145
you, you'll rejoice | that he is thus cut off. 5.06.138
that have been thus forward in my right, | i TIT 1.01. 56
that hast thus lovingly reserv'd | the cordial 1.01.165
sons, | confederates all thus to dishonor me. 1.01.303
dishonored thus and challenged of wrongs? 1.01.340
of goths | is of a sudden thus advanc'd in rome? 1.01.393
only thus much i give your grace to know: 1.01.413
o, thus i found her straying in the park, 3.01. 88
thou not guess wherefore she plies thee thus? 4.01. 15
why lifts she up her arms in sequence thus? 4.01. 37
lavinia, wert thou thus surpris'd, sweet girl? 4.01. 51
why do the emperor's trumpets flourish thus? 4.02. 49
wilt thou betray thy noble mistress thus? 4.02.106
on him that thus doth tyrannize o'er me. 4.03. 20
case, | to see thy noble uncle thus distract? 4.03. 26
ever seen | an emperor in rome thus overborne, 4.04. 2
troubled, confronted thus, and, for the extent 4.04. 3
shall we be thus afflicted in his wreaks, | his 4.04. 11
thus it shall become | high–witted tamora to 4.04. 34
even thus he rates the babe — | "for i must 5.01. 33
thus, in this strange and sad habiliment, | i 5.02. 1
why art thou thus attir'd, andronicus? 5.03. 30
why hast thou slain thine only daughter thus? 5.03. 55
thus then in brief: ROM 1.03. 73
and, being thus frighted, swears a prayer or two 1.04. 87
thus from my lips, by thine, my sin is purg'd. 1.05.107
what man art thou that thus bescreen'd in night 2.02. 52
that we should be thus afflicted with these 2.04. 32 P
what devil art thou that dost torment me thus? 3.02. 43
is it more sin to wish me thus forsworn, | or to 3.05.236
earth, | thus i enforce thy rotten jaws to open, 5.03. 47
thus with a kiss i die. 5.03.120
and thus far i confirm you. TIM 1.02. 94 P
thus honest fools lay out their wealth on 1.02.235
and the cap | plays in the right hand, thus — 2.01. 19
that i am thus encount'red | with clamorous 2.02. 36
made your minister | thus to excuse yourself. 2.02.132
thus part we rich in sorrow, parting poor. 4.02. 29
thus much of this will make | black white, foul 4.03. 28
thou wast told thus; 4.03.214
thus would i eat it. 4.03.282
the malice of mankind that he thus advises us, 4.03.452 P
go, live rich and happy, | but thus condition'd: 4.03.526
'twas time and griefs | that fram'd him thus. 5.01.123
therefore i will, sir, thus: 5.01.168
him no further, thus you still shall find him. 5.01.213
have struck but thus much show of fire from JC 1.02.177
he put it by with the back of his hand thus, and 1.02.223 P
and after that, he came thus sad away? 1.02.276
and, thus unbraced, casca, as you see, | have 1.03. 48
no color for the thing he is, | fashion it thus: 2.01. 30
i found | this paper, thus seal'd up, and i am 2.01. 37
thus must i piece it out: 2.01. 51
it is not for your health thus to commit | your 2.01.235
i am to blame to be thus waited for. 2.02.119
thus, brutus, did my master bid me kneel; 3.01.123
thus did mark antony bid me fall down; 3.01.124
and, being prostrate, thus he bade me say: 3.01.125
caesar when i strook him, | have thus proceeded. 3.01.183
wherein hath caesar thus deserv'd your loves? 3.02.236
for so much trash as may be grasped thus? 4.03. 26
caesar liv'd, he durst not thus have mov'd me. 4.03. 58
thus do go, about, about, | thrice to thine, and MAC 1.03. 34
that which cries, "thus thou must do," if thou 1.05. 23
business which informs | thus to mine eyes. 2.01. 49
howl's his watch, thus with his stealthy pace, 2.01. 54
who was it that thus cried? 2.02. 41
to be thus is nothing, | but to be safely thus. 3.01. 47
to be thus is nothing, | but to be safely thus. 3.01. 48
and to a notion craz'd | say, "thus did banquo." 3.01. 83
my lord is often thus, | and hath been from his 3.04. 52
but why | stands macbeth thus amazedly? 4.01.126
to fright you thus methinks i am too savage; 4.02. 70
action with her, to seem thus washing her hands. 5.01. 29 P
all mortal consequences have pronounc'd me thus: 5.03. 5
thus twice before, and jump at this dead hour, HAM 1.01. 65
time of meeting, | thus much the business is: 1.02. 27
middle of the night, | been thus encount'red. 1.02.199
/wringing it thus) you'll tender me a fool. 1.03.109
the kettle–drum and trumpet thus bray out | the 1.04. 11
steel | revisits thus the glimpses of the moon, 1.04. 53
let's follow. 'tis not fit thus to obey him. 1.04. 88
thus was i, sleeping, by a brother's hand | of 1.05. 74
with arms encumb'red thus, or this headshake, 1.05.174
as thus, "i know his father and his friends, 2.01. 14
he closes thus: 2.01. 53
truth, | and thus do we of wisdom and of reach, 2.01. 61
and, with his other hand thus o'er his brow, 2.01. 86
and thrice his head thus waving up and down, 2.01. 90
death, that thus hath put him | so much from th' 2.02. 8
whether aught, to us unknown, afflicts him thus, 2.02. 17
thus it remains, and the remainder thus. 2.02.104
thus it remains, and the remainder thus. 2.02.104
thus: 2.02.112 P
and my young mistress thus i did bespeak: 2.02.140
i hold it not honesty to have it thus set down, 2.02.202 P
fire, | and thus o'er–sized with coagulate gore, 2.02.462
of his love or no | that thus he suffers for. 3.01. 36
thus conscience does make cowards /of /us /all, 3.01. 82
and thus the native hue of resolution | is 3.01. 83
have in quick determination | thus set it down: 3.01.169
whereon his brains still beating puts him thus 3.01.174
not saw the air too much with your hand, thus, 3.02. 5 P
some must sleep, | thus runs the world away. 3.02.274
then thus she says: 3.02.326 P
that thus hath cozen'd you at hoodman–blind? 3.04. 77
how long hath she been thus? 4.05. 67
tell me, laertes, | why thou art thus incens'd. 4.05.127
to his good friends thus wide i'll ope my arms, 4.05.146
persuade revenge, | it could not move thus. 4.05.170
and tell him to his teeth, | "thus didst thou." 4.07. 57
sir, | what is the reason that you use me thus? 5.01.289
being thus benetted round with /villainies — 5.02. 29
thus has he, and many more of the same breed 5.02.188 P
things standing thus unknown, shall i leave 5.02.345
sith thus thou wilt appear, | freedom lives LR 1.01.180
thus kent, o princes, bids you all adieu, 1.01.186
kent banish'd thus? 1.02. 23
wisdom of nature can reason it thus and thus, 1.02.105 P
wisdom of nature can reason it thus and thus, 1.02.105 P
does lear walk thus? 1.04.227
speak thus? 1.04.227
that thou hast power to shake my manhood thus, 1.04.297
thus out of season, threading dark–ey'd night: 2.01.119
why dost thou use me thus? i know thee not. 2.02. 11 P
thus to rail on one that is neither known of 2.02. 25 P
messenger, | should have him thus restrained. 2.02.147
should have thus little mercy on their flesh? 3.04. 73
he said it would be thus, poor banish'd man. 3.04.164
censur'd, that nature thus gives way to loyalty, 3.05. 3 P
and wail, | for, with throwing thus my head, 3.06. 72
hospitable favors | you should not ruffle thus. 3.07. 41
give me thy sword. a peasant stand up thus? 3.07. 80
yet better thus, and known to be contemn'd, 4.01. 1
and when your mistress hears thus much from you, 4.05. 34
why i do trifle thus with his despair | is done 4.06. 33
thus might he pass indeed; 4.06. 47
sense will ne'er accommodate | his master thus. 4.06. 82
should ev'n die with pity | to see another thus. 4.07. 53
alack, why thus? 5.03.240
the thick–lips owe | if he can carry't thus! OTH 1.01. 67
i thus would play and trifle with your reverence 1.01.132
justice of the state | for thus deluding you. 1.01.140
with his free duty recommends you thus, | and 1.03. 41
hath thus beguil'd your daughter of herself, 1.03. 66
'tis in ourselves that we are thus or thus. 1.03.320 P
'tis in ourselves that we are thus or thus. 1.03.320 P
thus do i ever make my fool my purse; 1.03.383
but my muse labors, | and thus she is deliver'd: 2.01.128
lay thy finger thus; 2.01.221 P
our general cast us thus early for the love of 2.03. 14 P
but is he often thus? 2.03.128
how comes it, michael, you are thus forgot? 2.03.188
matter | that you unlace your reputation thus, 2.03.194
how came you thus recover'd? 2.03.295 P
in naples, that they speak i' th' nose thus? 3.01. 4 P
wear your eyes thus, not jealious nor secure. 3.03.198
all my fond love thus do i blow to heaven. 3.03.445
it is not words that shakes me thus. 4.01. 42 P
thus credulous fools are caught, | and many 4.01. 45
and many worthy and chaste dames even thus, 4.01. 46
/by /this /hand, falls me thus about my neck — 4.01.135 P
is't frailty that thus errs? 4.03. 99
who they should be that have thus mangled you? 5.01. 79

i am sorry to find you thus; 5.01. 81
of life as honest | as you that thus abuse me. 5.01.123
be thus when thou art dead, and i will kill thee 5.02. 18
why he hath thus ensnar'd my soul and body? 5.02.302
the circumcised dog, | and smote him — thus. 5.02.356
the nobleness of life | is to do thus — when ANT 1.01. 37
common liar, who | thus speaks of him at rome; 1.01. 61
'tis thus: 1.02. 97
thus did i desire it. 1.02.122
it cannot be thus long, the sides of nature 1.03. 16
our armies, and to fight, | i should do thus. 2.02. 27
thus we are agreed. 2.06. 57
and thus it may be. 2.06.132 P
thus do they, sir: 2.07. 17
look, here i have you, thus i let you go, | and 3.02. 63
he's walking in the garden — thus, and spurns 3.05. 16
let rome be thus | inform'd. 3.06. 19
why have you stol'n upon us thus? 3.06. 42
to come thus was i not constrain'd, but did it 3.06. 56
thus then, thou most renown'd: 3.13. 53
now the witch take me, if i meant it thus! 4.02. 37
sooth law, i'll help. thus it must be. 4.04. 8
and see | thy master thus with pleach'd arms, 4.14. 73
thus i do escape the sorrow | of antony's death. 4.14. 94
to do thus | i learnt of thee. 4.14.102
lips that power, | thus would i wear them out. 4.15. 40
what art thou that dar'st | appear thus to us? 5.01. 5
the gods | will have it thus, my master and my 5.02.116
if thus thou vanishest, thou tell'st the world 5.02.297
only, thus far you shall answer: CYM 1.04.157 P
having thus far proceeded | (unless thou 1.05. 15
what, dear sir, | thus raps you? are you well? 1.06. 51
the love i bear him | made me to fan you thus, 1.06.177
our tarquin thus | did softly press the rushes 2.02. 12
her breathing that | perfumes the chamber thus. 2.02. 19
but as a monument, | thus in a chapel lying! 2.02. 33
she hath bought the name of whore thus dearly. 2.04.128
thus defied, | i thank thee for myself. 3.01. 67
to apprehend thus | draws us a profit from all 3.03. 17
and, though train'd up thus meanly | i' th' cave 3.03. 82
say, "thus mine enemy fell, | and thus i set my 3.03. 91
and thus i set my foot on 's neck," even then 3.03. 92
is in thy mind | that makes thee stare thus? 3.04. 5
one but painted thus | would be interpreted a 3.04. 6
thus may poor fools | believe false teachers. 3.04. 84
thus far, and so farewell. 3.05. 1
our expectation that it would be thus | hath 3.05. 28
thus did he answer me; 4.02. 41
soft, what are you | that fly me thus? 4.02. 71
thus smiling, as some fly had tickled slumber, 4.02.210
his arms thus leagu'd. 4.02.213
(i fast and pray'd for their intelligence) thus: 4.02.347
for i wish'd | thou shouldst be color'd thus. 5.01. 2
and thus, unknown, | pitied nor hated, to the 5.01. 27
why hast thou thus adjourn'd | the graces for 5.04. 78
but since the gods | will have it thus, that 5.05. 79
being thus quench'd | of hope, not longing, mine 5.05.195
his belief in her renown | with tokens thus, and 5.05.203
in her renown | with tokens thus, and thus; 5.05.203
o my gentle brothers, | have we thus met? 5.05.375
thus ready for the way of life or death, | i PER 1.01. 54
and yet the end of all is bought thus dear, 1.01. 98
then it is thus: 1.02. 11
the motto thus, in spanish: 2.02. 27
the motto thus: 2.02. 38
in framing an artist, art hath thus decreed, 2.03. 15
reign, | we thus submit unto — our sovereign. 2.04. 39
when peers thus knit, a kingdom ever stands. 2.04. 58
and being join'd, i'll thus your hopes destroy, 2.05. 86
find | our paragon to all reports thus blasted, 4.01. 35
thus time we waste, and long leagues make short; 4.04. 1
marina thus the brothel scapes, and chances 5.ch. 1
your kindness | we have stretch'd thus far, let 5.01. 55
was it not thus? 5.01. 98
is like to be, | that thus hath made me weep. 5.01.185
thus dost thou still make good | the tongue o' TNK 1.01.226
as we are men | thus should we do, being 1.01.232
and here being thus together, | we are an 2.02. 78
why are you mov'd thus? 2.02.183
he bows his noble body, then salutes me thus: 2.04. 23
thus much for law or kindred! 2.04. 32
beauty, | thus let me seal my vow'd faith. 2.05. 39
'tis your passion | that thus mistakes, the 3.01. 49
take courage, | you shall not die thus beastly. 3.03. 6
have i said, "thus let be," and "there let be," 3.05. 9
are making battle, thus like knights appointed, 3.06.134
man calls me traitor, | let me say thus much: 3.06.161
thus i ordain it, | and, by mine honor, once 3.06.288
prettiest posies — "thus our true love's tied," 4.01. 90
are they all thus? 4.02.141
ev'n thus all day long. 4.03. 18 P
think you but thus, | that, were there aught in 5.01. 19
for he that was thus good | encount'red yet his 5.03.122
as he thus went counting | the flinty pavement, 5.04. 58
thus will they bear down all things. STM II.C 40
what would you think | to be thus us'd? II.C 139
it is in heaven that i am thus and thus, | and III 1
it is in heaven that i am thus and thus, | and III 1
"thrice fairer than myself," thus she began, VEN 7
"thus he that overrul'd i overswayed, | leading 109
who should say, "lo thus my strength is tried; 280
thus she replies: 385
thus stands she in a trembling ecstasy, | till, 895
divorce of love" — thus chides she death — 932
thus hoping that adonis is alive, | her rash 1009
"'tis true, 'tis true, thus was adonis slain: 1111
thus weary of the world, away she hies, | and 1189
teaching them thus to use it in the fight, LUC 62
and to the flame thus speaks advisedly: 180
and justly thus controls his thoughts unjust: 189
thus, graceless, holds he disputation | 'tween 246
by reprobate desire thus madly led, | the roman 300
thus treason works ere traitors be espied. 361
thus he replies: 477
"thus i forestall thee, if thou mean to chide, 484
when thus thy vices bud before thy spring? 604
frantic with grief thus breathes she forth her 762
thus cavils she with every thing she sees: 1093
yet with the fault i thus far can dispense: 1279
at last she thus begins: 1303
and turn'd it thus, "it cannot be, i find, | but 1539
thus ebbs and flows the current of her sorrow, 1569
her by the bloodless hand, | and thus begins: 1598
why art thou thus attir'd in discontent? 1601
and his untimely frenzy thus awaketh: 1675
thus vainly thinking that she thinks me young, PP 1. 5
since that our faults in love thus smother'd be. 1.14
"even thus," quoth she, "the warlike god 11. 5
"even thus," quoth she, "the warlike god unlac'd 11. 7
"even thus," quoth she, "he seized on my lips," 11. 9
thus art with arms contending was victor of the 15.13
will repent | that thus dissembled her delight; 18.28
when craft hath taught her thus to say: 18.34
thus of every grief in heart | he with thee doth 20.53
property was thus appalled, | that the self was PHT 37
lo thus by day my limbs, by night my mind, | for SON 27.13
loving offenders, thus i will excuse ye: 42. 5
moiety and the dear heart's part — | as thus: 46.13
"thus far the miles are measur'd from thy friend 50. 4
thus can my love excuse the slow offense | of my 51. 1
but love, for love, thus shall excuse my jade: 51.12
decay, | ruin hath taught me thus to ruminate, 64.11
thus is his cheek the map of days outworn, 68. 1
/thy outward thus with outward praise is crown'd 69. 5
thus do i pine and surfeit day by day, | or 75.13
thus have i had thee as a dream doth flatter: 87.13
the forward violet thus did i chide: 99. 1
my most true mind thus maketh mine untrue. 113.14
accuse me thus: 117. 1
thus policy in love, t' anticipate | the ills 118. 9
a torment thrice threefold thus to be crossed. 133. 8
still, | to thy sweet will making addition thus. 135. 4
thus far for love my love-suit, sweet, fulfill. 136. 4
thus vainly thinking that she thinks me young, 138. 5
on both sides thus is simple truth suppress'd. 138. 8
only my plague thus far i count my gain, | that 141.13
gentle doom, | and taught it thus anew to greet: 145. 8
i held my city, | till thus he gan besiege me: LC 177
"thus merely with the garment of a grace, | the 316

THWACK 4 FR 0.0004 REL FR 1 V 3 P
stay, | we'll thwack him hence with distaffs. WT 1.02. 37
here's he that was wont to thwack our general, COR 4.05.178 P
why do you say, "thwack our general"? 4.05.180 P
i do not say, "thwack our general," but he was 4.05.181 P

THWART 3 FR 0.0003 REL FR 3 V 0 P
slave, | abetting him to thwart me in my mood! ERR 2.02.170
trial did draw | bias and thwart, not answering TRO 1.03. 15
and be a thwart disnatur'd torment to her. LR 1.04.283

THWARTED 4 FR 0.0004 REL FR 3 V 1 P
if crooked fortune had not thwarted me. TGV 4.01. 22
scorn'd my nation, thwarted my bargains, cool'd MV 3.01. 57 P
i am thwarted quite | from my great purpose in TRO 5.01. 37
we can contradict | hath thwarted our intents. ROM 5.03.154

THWARTING 4 FR 0.0004 REL FR 3 V 1 P
o mischief strangely thwarting! ADO 3.02.132 P
may not be punish'd with my thwarting stars, 3H6 4.06. 22
is now against thwarting /the wayward seas, PER 4.04. 10
and in this aim there is such thwarting strife LUC 143

/THWARTINGS 1 FR 0.0001 REL FR 1 V 0 P
had been | the /thwartings of your dispositions, COR 3.02. 21

THY *(also th'*)*
/THY 69 FR 0.0078 REL FR 66 V 3 P
THY 4291 FR 0.4850 REL FR 3673 V 618 P

THYME *(also tine*)*
THYME 2 FR 0.0002 REL FR 2 V 0 P
i know a bank where the wild thyme blows, MND 2.01.249
yet most quaint, | and sweet thyme true; TNK 1.01. 6

THYREUS *(see thidias)*

/THYSELF 3 FR 0.0003 REL FR 3 V 0 P
/thou /provok'st /thyself /to /cast /him /up. 2H4 1.03. 96
/there's /for /thyself, /and /that's /for TIT 3.02. 74
/and /thyself /bewray | /when /false /opinion, LR 3.06.111

THYSELF 236 FR 0.0266 REL FR 191 V 45 P
he whom next thyself | of all the world i lov'd, TMP 1.02. 68
as thou report'st thyself, was then her servant, 1.02.271
go make thyself like a nymph o' th' sea; 1.02.301
and hast put thyself | upon this island as a spy 1.02.455
and trinculo and thyself shall be viceroys. 3.02.108 P
thou beest a man, show thyself in thy likeness. 3.02.128 P
where thou thyself dost air — the queen o' th' 4.01. 70
forswear not thyself, sweet youth, for i am not TGV 2.05. 3 P
that which thyself hast now disclos'd to me. 3.01. 32
the love | i ever bore my daughter, or thyself. 3.01.167
as thou lov'st silvia (though not for thyself) 3.01.257
friend | survives, to whom, thyself art witness, 4.02.109
/his grave | assure thyself my love is buried. 4.02.114
thyself hast lov'd, and i have heard thee say 4.03. 18
why, thou must be thyself. WIV 3.04. 3
and 'tis the very riches of thyself | that now i 3.04. 17
thyself and thy belongings | are not thine own MM 1.01. 29
proper as to waste | thyself upon thy virtues, 1.01. 31
for example, thou thyself art a wicked villain, 1.02. 25 P
thou art not thyself, | for thou exists on many 3.01. 19
say to thyself, | from their abominable and 3.02. 23
it, | that thou art then estranged from thyself? ERR 2.02.120
thyself i call it, being strange to me, | that, 2.02.121
ah, do not tear away thyself from me; 2.02.124
as take from me thyself and not me too. 2.02.129
why prat'st thou to thyself, and answer'st not? 2.02.193
sing, siren, for thyself, and i will dote; 3.02. 47
it is thyself, mine own self's better part: 3.02. 61
call thyself sister, sweet, for i am thee: 3.02. 66
art dromio, thou art my man, thou art thyself. 3.02. 76 P
what woman's man, and how besides thyself? 3.02. 80 P
but art not thou thyself giddy with the fashion ADO 3.03.141 P
no, not so, villain, thou beliest thyself. 5.01.265
for thyself? LLL 4.01. 83 P
but do not love thyself, then thou /wilt keep 4.03. 37
thyself shalt see the act; MV 4.01.314
beg that thou mayst have leave to hang thyself, 4.01.364
no higher than thyself, the judge's clerk, | a 5.01.163
thou hast rail'd on thyself. AYL 1.01. 62 P
comfort a little, cheer thyself a little. 2.06. 5 P
for thou thyself hast been a libertine, | as 2.07. 65
one thing more rests, that thyself execute — SHR 1.01.246
thy pains not us'd must by thyself be paid. AWW 2.01.146
thou wrong'st thyself, if thou shouldst strive 2.03.146
do not plunge thyself too far in anger, lest 2.03.211 P
off, | but give thyself unto my sick desires, 4.02. 35
whether dost thou profess thyself — a knave or 4.05. 22 P
thou kept'st a wife herself, thyself a maid. 5.03.330
then let thy love be younger than thyself, | or TN 2.04. 36
to inure thyself to what thou art like to be, 2.05.148 P
put thyself into the trick of singularity. 2.05.151 P
niece shall take note of it, and assure thyself, 3.02. 36 P
put thyself into the trick of singularity"; 3.04. 71 P
but my hope is better, and so look to thyself. 3.04.168 P
endeavor thyself to sleep, and leave thy vain 4.02. 96 P
hast thou forgot thyself? 5.01.141
open thy white hand | /and clap thyself my love; WT 1.02.104
next to thyself and my young rover, he's 1.02.176
death to thyself but to thy lewd-tongu'd wife, 2.03.172
now bless thyself: 3.03.113 P
must either stay to execute them thyself, or 4.02. 16 P
hast thou denied thyself a faulconbridge? JN 1.01.251
we like not this, thou dost forget thyself. 3.01.134
since thou swor'st is sworn against thyself, 3.01.268
thyself, | and may not be performed by thyself, 3.01.269
thy first, | is in thyself rebellion to thyself; 3.01.289
thy first, | is in thyself rebellion to thyself; 3.01.289
look to thyself, thou art in jeopardy. 3.01.346
dust, | and be a carrion monster like thyself. 3.04. 33
go | and thrust thyself into their companies; 4.02.167
or wouldst thou drown thyself, | put but a 4.03.130
would bear thee from the knowledge of thyself, 5.02. 35
edward's seven sons, whereof thyself art one, R2 1.02. 11
which art possess'd now to depose thyself. 2.01.108
be not thyself; 2.01.198
we three are but thyself, and, speaking so, 2.01.275
look to thyself, | thou hast a traitor in thy 5.03. 39
hang thyself in thine own heir-apparent garters! 1H4 2.02. 43 P
when thou hast tir'd thyself in base comparisons 2.04.250 P
harry, withdraw thyself, thou bleedest too much. 5.04. 2
boys | seek percy and thyself about the field, 5.04. 32
i will assay thee, and defend thyself. 5.04. 34
wert an honest man, thyself and the money too. 2H4 2.01. 85 P
well, sweet jack, have a care of thyself. 2.04.380 P
like a kind fellow, gavest thyself away gratis, 4.03. 69 P
then get thee gone, and dig my grave thyself, 4.05.110
and withal devise something to do thyself good. 5.03.134 P
which thou thyself hast given her woeful breast. 1H6 3.03. 51
fie, de la pole, disable not thyself. 5.03. 67
that for thyself; 5.03.185
swear | to pay him tribute and submit thyself, 5.04.130
to tumble down thy husband and thyself | from 2H6 1.02. 48
and look thyself be faultless, thou wert best. 2.01.185
that thou thyself wast born in bastardy; 3.02.223
enough, sweet suffolk, thou torment'st thyself, 3.02.329
and turns the force of them upon thyself. 3.02.332
should die | by such a lowly vassal as thyself. 4.01.111
or hast thou a mark to thyself, like a honest 4.02.103 P
and thou thyself a shearman, art thou not? 4.02.133
and thou behavedst thyself as if thou hadst been 4.03. 4 P
it must and shall be so. content thyself. 3H6 1.01. 85
how hast thou injur'd both thyself and us! 1.01.179
to seek to put me down and reign thyself. 1.01.200
thou hast undone thyself, thy son, and me, | and 1.01.232
ah, warwick, why hast thou withdrawn thyself? 2.03. 14
brother | to execute the like upon thyself — 2.04. 10
what e'er it be, be thou still like thyself, 3.03. 15
of thee thyself and all thy complices, | edward 4.03. 44
ay, but thou usest to forswear thyself. 5.05. 75
and thyself, the sea | whose envious gulf did 5.06. 24
make | no excuse current but to hang thyself. R3 1.02. 84
excused | for doing worthy vengeance on thyself, 1.02. 87
curse not thyself, fair creature — thou art 1.02.132
thyself a queen, for me that was a queen, 1.03.201
fool, thou whet'st a knife to kill thyself. 1.03.243
how dost thou feel thyself now? 1.04.120 P
wherein thyself shalt highly be employ'd. 3.01.180
but now i tell thee (keep it to thyself) | this 3.02.102
glory, | to feed my humor wish thyself no harm. 4.01. 64
thyself is self-misus'd. 4.04.374
ratcliffe, thyself — or catesby — where is he? 4.04.441
fool, of thyself speak well; 5.03.192
love thyself last, cherish those hearts that H8 3.02.443
but it is no matter, thyself upon thyself! TRO 2.03. 27 P
but it is no matter, thyself upon thyself! 2.03. 27 P
hast thou not serv'd thyself in to my table so 2.03. 42 P
if thou wouldst not entomb thyself alive | and 3.03.186
thou dost thyself and all our troy deceive. 5.03. 90
loves, but thou wilt frame | thyself, forsooth, COR 3.02. 85
but owe thy pride thyself. 3.02.130
dreamt of encounters 'twixt thyself and me; 4.05.123
think with thyself | how more unfortunate than 5.03. 96
let marcus, lucius, or thyself, old titus, | or TIT 3.01.152
in hope thyself should govern rome and me. 4.04. 60
o barbarous, beastly villains like thyself! 5.01. 97
and when thou find'st a man that's like thyself, 5.02. 99
what boots it thee to call thyself a sun? 5.03. 18
thou art thyself, though not a montague. ROM 2.02. 39
if e'er thou wast thyself and these woes thine, 2.03. 77
arise, one knocks. good romeo, hide thyself. 3.03. 71
wilt thou slay thyself, | and slay thy lady that 3.03.116
/lives, | by doing damned hate upon thyself? 3.03.118
thou hast the strength of will to /slay thyself, 4.01. 72
buy food, and get thyself in flesh. 5.01. 84
what, thyself? TIM 1.01.231 P
shouldst have kept one to thyself, for i mean to 1.01.265 P
hang thyself! 1.01.267 P
thou wilt give away thyself in paper shortly. 1.02.241 P
contain thyself, good friend. 2.02. 26
no, 'tis to thyself. come away. 2.02. 53 P
so hateful to thee, | that art thyself a man? 4.03. 53
and, thy fury spent, | confounded be thyself! 4.03.129
thou hast cast away thyself, being like thyself, 4.03.220
thou hast cast away thyself, being like thyself, 4.03.220
dost please thyself in't? 4.03.238
thou wouldst have plung'd thyself | in general 4.03.255
first mend /my company, take away thyself. 4.03.283
thou shouldst have lov'd thyself better now. 4.03.310 P
wouldst thou have thyself fall in the confusion 4.03.324 P
hated all mankind, | and thou redeem'st thyself. 4.03.500
canst not paint a man | so bad as is thyself. 5.01. 32

a man no mightier than thyself, or me, | in JC 1.03. 76
awake, and see thyself! 2.01. 46
nothing afeard of what thyself didst make MAC 1.03. 96
dear duff, i prithee contradict thyself, | and 2.03. 89
thyself and office deftly show! 4.01. 68
these evils thou repeat'st upon thyself | hath 4.03.112
though thou call'st thyself a hotter name | than 5.07. 6
as thou art to thyself. HAM 1.01. 59
thyself do grace to them, and bring them in. 2.02. 53
therefore prepare thyself, | the bark is ready, 4.03. 43
me not to the purpose, confess thyself — 5.01. 39 P
woo't fight, woo't fast, woo't tear thyself? 5.01.275
prithee go in thyself, seek thine own ease. LR 3.04. 23
expose thyself to feel what wretches feel, 3.04. 34
see thyself, devil! 4.02. 59
old unhappy traitor, | briefly thyself remember; 4.06.229
drown thyself? OTH 1.03.336 P
if thou wilt needs damn thyself, do it a more 1.03.353 P
a pox of drowning thyself, it is clean out of 1.03.358 P
canst cuckold him, thou dost thyself a pleasure, 1.03.369 P
content thyself a while. 2.03.378
come swear it, damn thyself, | lest, being like 4.02. 35
thyself art coming | to see perform'd the ANT 5.02.330
do't as from thyself. CYM 1.05. 67
his servants than | thyself domestic officers) 3.01. 64
put thyself | into a havior of less fear, ere 3.04. 8
be here, | poor house, that keep'st thyself! 3.06. 36
thou thyself thou blazon'st | in these two 4.02.170
one half so well | as when thou grew'st thyself. 4.02.203
thou dost approve thyself the very same; 4.02.380
away, boy, from the troops, and save thyself; 5.02. 14
boy, | thou hast look'd thyself into my grace, 5.05. 94
as well descended as thyself, and hath | more of 5.05.303
yon sometimes famous princes, like thyself, PER 1.01. 34
as these before thee, thou thyself shalt bleed. 1.01. 58
that thou wouldst tremble to receive thyself. 1.02. 69
which love to all, of which thyself art one, 1.02. 94
storm, venomously | wilt thou spet all thyself? 3.01. 8
blow, and split thyself. 3.01. 44 P
thou dost startle me | to call thyself marina. 5.01.147
(though in't i know thou dost believe thyself) TNK 1.03. 88
thou think'st thyself the happier thing to be 3.01. 25
put thyself | upon thy present guard — 3.06.121
do such a justice thou thyself wilt envy. 3.06.155
then woo thyself, be of thyself rejected; VEN 159
then woo thyself, be of thyself rejected; 159
that thine may live, when thou thyself art dead; 172
on his back doth lie | an image like thyself, 664
"so in thyself thyself art made away, | a 763
"so in thyself thyself art made away, | a 763
thyself art mighty, for thine own sake leave me; LUC 583
honor thyself to rid me of this shame, | for if 1031
kill both thyself and her for yielding so." 1036
is it revenge to give thyself a blow | for his 1823
night to–night, and length thyself to–morrow. PP 14.30
thyself thy foe, to thy sweet self too cruel. SON 1. 8
thou spend | upon thyself thy beauty's legacy? 4. 2
for having traffic with thyself alone, | thou of 4. 9
thou of thyself thy sweet self dost deceive, 4.10
that's for thyself to breed another thee, | or 6. 7
ten times thyself were happier than thou art, 6. 9
so thou, thyself outgoing in thy noon, 7.13
that thou consum'st thyself in single life? 9. 2
to any, | who for thyself art so unprovident. 10. 2
that 'gainst thyself thou stick'st not to 10. 6
or to thyself at least kind–hearted prove: 10.12
if from thyself to store thou wouldst convert; 14.12
love, be of thyself so wary | as i, not for 22. 9
give thyself the thanks if aught in me | worthy 38. 5
when thou thyself dost give invention light? 38. 8
by willful taste of what thyself refusest. 40. 8
love, | thyself away are present still with me, 47.10
since what he owes thee thou thyself dost pay. 79.14
thyself thou gav'st, thy own worth then not 87. 9
but do thy worst to steal thyself away, | for 92. 1

TIB 1 FR 0.0001 REL FR 1 V 0 P
custrel that comes inquiring for his tib. PER 4.06.166

TIBER 8 FR 0.0009 REL FR 7 V 1 P
hot wine with not a drop of allaying tiber in't; COR 2.01. 49 P
i would they were in tiber! 3.01.261
that tiber trembled underneath her banks | to JC 1.01. 45
draw them to tiber banks, and weep your tears 1.01. 58
the troubled tiber chafing with her shores, 1.02.101
so from the waves of tiber | did i the tired 1.02.114
and new–planted orchards, | on this side tiber; 3.02.249
let rome in tiber melt, and the wide arch | of ANT 1.01. 33

TIBERIO 1 FR 0.0001 REL FR 1 V 0 P
the son and heir of old tiberio. ROM 1.05.129

TIB'S 1 FR 0.0001 REL FR 0 V 1 P
punk, as tib's rush for tom's forefinger, as a AWW 2.02. 23 P

'TICED *(also entice, etc.)*

'TICED 1 FR 0.0001 REL FR 1 V 0 P
these two have 'ticed me hither to this place: TIT 2.03. 92

TICK 1 FR 0.0001 REL FR 0 V 1 P
i had rather be a tick in a sheep than such a TRO 3.03.312 P

/TICKLE 1 FR 0.0001 REL FR 0 V 1 P
/whose /lungs /are /tickle /a' /th' /sere, and HAM 2.02.324 P

TICKLE 10 FR 0.0011 REL FR 3 V 7 P
thy head stands so tickle on thy shoulders that MM 1.02.172 P
such a tender ass, if my hair do but tickle me, MND 4.01. 26 P
if you tickle us, do we not laugh? MV 3.01. 65 P
and to tickle our noses with speargrass to make 1H4 2.04.309 P
nay, i'll tickle ye for a young prince, i' faith 2.04.444 P
i'll tickle your catastrophe. 2H4 2.01. 60 P
stands on a tickle point now they are gone. 2H6 1.01.216
he'll tickle it for his concupy. TRO 5.02.177 P
tickle the senseless rushes with their heels. ROM 1.04. 36
fine this tyrant | can tickle where she wounds! CYM 1.01. 85

TICKLEBRAIN 1 FR 0.0001 REL FR 0 V 1 P
peace, good pint–pot, peace, good ticklebrain. 1H4 2.04.397 P

TICKLED 6 FR 0.0006 REL FR 4 V 2 P
he would have tickled you othergates than he did TN 5.01.193 P
she's tickled now; 2H6 1.03.150
but laugh to think how she tickled his chin. TRO 1.02.136 P
tickled with good success, disdains the shadow COR 1.01.260
thus smiling, as some fly had tickled slumber, CYM 4.02.210
to be so tickled, they would change their state SON 128. 9

TICKLES 2 FR 0.0002 REL FR 1 V 1 P
that it wounds, | but tickles still the sore. TRO 3.01.120
rump and potato finger, tickles /these together! 5.02. 56 P

TICKLE'T 2 FR 0.0002 REL FR 2 V 0 P
to–day, i'll tickle't out | of the jades' tails TNK 2.03. 28
he'll tickle't up | in two hours, if his hand be 4.01.138

/TICKLING 1 FR 0.0001 REL FR 1 V 0 P
/now /expectation, /tickling /skittish /spirits, TRO pr 20

TICKLING 6 FR 0.0006 REL FR 5 V 1 P
mocks, | which is as bad as die with tickling. ADO 3.01. 80
the trout that must be caught with tickling. TN 2.05. 22 P
that smooth–fac'd gentleman, tickling commodity, JN 2.01.573
which else runs tickling up and down the veins, 3.03. 44
tickling a parson's nose as 'a lies asleep, ROM 1.04. 80
mock with thy tickling beams eyes that are LUC 1090

TICKLISH 1 FR 0.0001 REL FR 1 V 0 P
of their thoughts | to every ticklish reader! TRO 4.05. 61

TICK–TACK 1 FR 0.0001 REL FR 0 V 1 P
be thus foolishly lost at a game of tick–tack. MM 1.02.190 P

TIDDLE *(also tittle–tattling)*

TIDDLE 1 FR 0.0001 REL FR 0 V 1 P
that there is no tiddle taddle nor pibble babble H5 4.01. 70 P

'TIDE *(also betide)*

'TIDE 2 FR 0.0002 REL FR 2 V 0 P
'tide life, 'tide death, i come without delay. MND 5.01.203
'tide life, 'tide death, i come without delay. 5.01.203

TIDE 42 FR 0.0047 REL FR 37 V 5 P
and the approaching tide | will shortly fill the TMP 5.01. 80
the tide is now — nay, not thy tide of tears, TGV 2.02. 14
the tide is now — nay, not thy tide of tears, 2.02. 14
that tide will stay me longer than i should. 2.02. 15
ass, you'll lose the tide, if you tarry any 2.03. 36 P
what's the unkindest tide? 2.03. 39 P
lose the tide, and the voyage, and the master, 2.03. 50 P
both wind and tide stays for this gentleman, ERR 4.01. 46
did never float upon the swelling tide | to do JN 2.01. 74
me, cousin, for i was amaz'd | under the tide; 4.02.138
passing these flats, are taken by the tide — 5.06. 40
what a tide of woes | comes rushing on this R2 2.02. 98
may turn the tide of fearful faction, | and 1H4 4.01. 67
as with the tide swell'd up unto his height, 2H4 2.03. 63
the tide of blood in me | hath proudly flow'd in 5.02.129
came pouring like the tide into a breach, | with H5 1.02.149
twelve and one, ev'n at the turning o' th' tide; 2.03. 13 P
sand, that look to be wash'd off the next tide. 4.01. 98 P
nor the tide of pomp | that beats upon the high 4.01.264
provokes the mightiest hulk against the tide, 1H6 5.05. 6
with bootless labor swim against the tide, | and 3H6 1.04. 20
forc'd by the tide to combat with the wind; 2.05. 6
for this is he that moves both wind and tide. 3.03. 48
it boots not to resist both wind and tide. 4.03. 59
how thou canst, have wind and tide thy friend, 5.01. 53
bestride the rock, the tide will wash you off, 5.04. 31
alas, i know not, how gets the tide in? H8 5.03. 18
/carriage /of /this /action | rode on his tide. TRO 2.03.132
like to an ent'red tide, they all rush by | and 3.03.159
important business, | the tide whereof is now. 5.01. 83
ne'er through an arch so hurried the blown tide, COR 5.04. 47
who marks the waxing tide grow wave by wave, TIT 3.01. 95
them all, let in the tide | of knaves once more; TIM 3.04.116
man | that ever lived in the tide of times. JC 3.01.257
there is a tide in the affairs of men | which, 4.03.218
goes to and back, /lackeying the varying tide, ANT 1.04. 46
that stands upon the swell at the full of tide, 3.02. 49
the crystal tide that from her two cheeks fair VEN 957
whereat her tears began to turn their tide, 979
quoth he, "my uncontrolled tide | turns not, but LUC 645
as through an arch the violent roaring tide 1667
held back his sorrow's tide, to make it more; 1789

TIDES 6 FR 0.0006 REL FR 5 V 1 P
mightst lie drowning | the washing of ten tides! TMP 1.01. 58
whose foot spurns back the ocean's roaring tides JN 2.01. 24
be set | among the high tides in the calendar? 3.01. 86
tidings would call forth her flowing tides. 1H6 1.01. 83
he keeps his tides well. TIM 1.02. 56 P
like meeting of two tides, fly strongly from us, TNK 3.06. 30

/TIDINGS 1 FR 0.0001 REL FR 1 V 0 P
power landed at milford | is colder /tidings, R3 4.04.534

TIDINGS 55 FR 0.0062 REL FR 52 V 3 P
i shall make my master glad with these tidings. WIV 4.05. 56 P
out of thy mouth that i may drink thy tidings. AYL 3.02.203 P
that bring these tidings to this fair assembly. 5.04.153
pardon, my lord, for me and for my tidings. AWW 2.01. 61
the tidings comes that they are all arriv'd. JN 4.02.115
hast made me giddy | with these ill tidings. 4.02.132
say | how near the tidings of our comfort is. R2 2.01.272
and yet we hear no tidings from the king, 2.04. 3
is so arm'd | to bear the tidings of calamity. 3.02.105
good duke of york's | that tell black tidings. 3.04. 71
and how, | /cam'st thou by this ill tidings? 3.04. 80
it seems then that the tidings of this broil 1H4 1.01. 47
that's the worst tidings that i hear of /yet. 4.01.127
now, travers, what good tidings comes with you? 2H4 1.01. 33
umfrevile turn'd me back | with joyful tidings, 1.01. 35
good tidings, my lord hastings! 4.02.106
and tidings do i bring, and lucky joys, | and 5.03. 95
sad tidings bring i to you out of france, | of 1H6 1.01. 58
these tidings would call forth her flowing tides 1.01. 83
what tidings send our scouts? i prithee speak. 5.02. 10
what tidings with our cousin buckingham? 2H6 2.01.161
health and glad tidings to your majesty! 4.09. 7
heard | the happy tidings of his good escape. 3H6 2.01. 7
tidings, as swiftly as the posts could run, 2.01.109
life | than edward will for tidings of my death. R3 1.04.231
despiteful tidings, o unpleasing news! 4.01. 36
both, | to bear this tidings to the bloody king. 4.03. 22
the tidings that i bring | will make my boldness H8 5.01.158
first, the gods bless you for your tidings; COR 5.04. 58
that gives sweet tidings of the sun's uprise? TIT 3.01.159
sirrah, what tidings? 4.03. 79
these tidings nip me, and i hang the head | as 4.04. 70
and for my tidings gave me twenty kisses. 5.01.120
i bring thee tidings of the prince's doom. ROM 3.03. 8
but now i'll tell thee joyful tidings, girl. 3.05.104
their course of love, the tidings of her death; 5.03.287
for with her death | that tidings came. JC 4.03.155
these tidings will well comfort cassius. 5.03. 54
the ears of brutus | as tidings of this sight. 5.03. 78
what is your tidings? MAC 1.05. 30
when i came hither to transport the tidings, 4.03.181
what tidings can you tell /me of my lord? OTH 2.01. 88
general, that upon certain tidings now arriv'd, 2.02. 2 P
ram thou thy fruitful tidings in mine ears, ANT 2.05. 24
so tart a favor | to trumpet such good tidings! 2.05. 39
but let ill tidings tell | themselves when they 2.05. 87
sword but shown to caesar, with this tidings, 4.14.112
but it is tidings | to wash the eyes of kings. 5.01. 27
in our not–fearing britain than have tidings CYM 2.04. 19
who did promise | to yield me often tidings. 4.03. 39
no tidings of him? 5.05. 10
but tidings to the contrary | are brought your PER 2.ch. 15
and give the tidings ear | that are most /dearly TNK 5.04. 46
and yet she hears no tidings of her love. VEN 867
hand, | and gaz'd for tidings in my eager eyes, LUC 254

TIDY 1 FR 0.0001 REL FR 0 V 1 P
thou whoreson little tidy bartholomew boar–pig, 2H4 2.04.231 P

TIE 25 FR 0.0028 REL FR 22 V 3 P
wrench awe from fools and tie the wiser souls MM 2.04. 14
can tie the gall up in the slanderous tongue? 3.02.188
shave the head, and tie the beard, and say it 4.02.175 P
tie up my lover's tongue, bring him silently. MND 3.01.201
only sin | and hellish obstinacy tie thy tongue, AWW 1.03.180
for by this knot thou shalt so surely tie | thy JN 2.01.470
of faith, | to tie thee to my strong correction. R2 4.01. 77
they shall not see — i'll tie them in the wood; 1H4 1.02.177 P
come, tie his body to my horse's tail, | along TRO 5.08. 21
people, | but tie him not to be their bedfellow. COR 2.02. 65
will (too late) | tie leaden pounds to 's heels. 3.01.312
are with a most indissoluble tie | for ever knit MAC 3.01. 17
not feel wrongs | which tie him to an answer. LR 4.02. 14
tie up the libertine in a field of feasts, ANT 2.01. 23
know | if 'twill tie up thy discontented sword, 2.06. 6
find the band that seems to tie their friendship 2.06.121 P
will tie you to the numbers and the time | of CYM 3.07. 15
honor, | or tie my pleasure up in silken bags, PER 3.02. 41
that, after holy tie and first night's stir, TNK pr 6
sir, by our tie of marriage — 3.06.195
i tie you to your word now; 3.06.236
even now | to tie the rider she begins to prove. VEN 40
will tie the hearers to attend each line, | how LUC 818
praise cannot be so thy praise | to tie up envy, SON 70.12
call, | whereto all bonds do tie me day by day; 117. 4

TIED 33 FR 0.0037 REL FR 24 V 9 P
it is no matter if the tied were lost; TGV 2.03. 37 P
it is the unkindest tied that ever any man tied. 2.03. 38 P
it is the unkindest tied that ever any man tied. 2.03. 38 P
why, he that's tied here, crab, my dog. 2.03. 40 P
and the master, and the service, and the tied! 2.03. 51 P
pleasure is, | and i am tied to be obedient — SHR 1.01.212
i'll not be tied to hours nor 'pointed times, 3.01. 19
from his liking, | where you were tied in duty; WT 5.01.213
were i tied to run afoot | even to the frozen R2 1.01. 63
remov'd my horse, and tied him i know not where. 1H4 2.02. 11 P
and have their provender tied to their mouths, 1H6 1.02. 11
king, | and not be tied unto his brother's will. 3H6 4.01. 66
the spaniard, tied by blood and favor to her, H8 2.02. 89
his goodness, | tied it by letters–patents. 3.02.250
one that by suggestion | tied all the kingdom. 4.02. 36
cressid is mine, tied with the bonds of heaven. TRO 5.02.154
eyes | than is prometheus tied to caucasus. TIT 2.01. 17
they have tied me to a stake; MAC 5.07. 1
horses are tied by the heads, dogs and bears by LR 2.04. 8 P
regan, she hath tied | sharp–tooth'd unkindness, 2.04.134
i am tied to th' stake, and i must stand the 3.07. 54
my heart was to thy rudder tied by th' strings, ANT 3.11. 57
to whose kindnesses i am most infinitely tied. CYM 1.06. 23 P
my horse is tied up safe; 4.01. 22 P
she hath so strictly tied | her to her chamber, PER 2.05. 8
their knot of love | tied, weav'd, entangled, TNK 1.03. 42
compell'd bears, would fly | were they not tied. 3.01. 69
"thus our true love's tied," | "this you may 4.01. 90
the strong–neck'd steed, being tied unto a tree, VEN 263
"how like a jade he stood, tied to the tree, 391
whereto the judgment of my heart is tied? SON 137. 8
sometime diverted their poor balls are tied | to LC 24
her hair, nor loose nor tied in formal plat, 29

TIED–UP 1 FR 0.0001 REL FR 1 V 0 P
to unloose this tied–up justice when you pleas'd MM 1.03. 32

TIES 4 FR 0.0004 REL FR 3 V 1 P
this moral ties me over to time and a hot summer H5 5.02.312 P
ties up my tongue and will not let me speak. ROM 4.05. 32
you mingle eyes | with one that ties his points? ANT 3.13.157
and all the ties between us, i disclaim | if TNK 2.02.173

TIGER 16 FR 0.0018 REL FR 15 V 1 P
and let us to the tiger all to dinner; ERR 3.01. 95
mild hind | makes speed to catch the tiger — MND 2.01.233
and this is he that did the tiger board, | when TN 5.01. 62
paw, | a fasting tiger safer by the tooth, JN 3.01.260
ears, | then imitate the action of the tiger; H5 3.01. 6
the tiger will be mild whiles she doth mourn; 3H6 3.01. 39
the tiger now hath seiz'd the gentle hind; R3 2.04. 50
annoyance by the breeze | than by the tiger; TRO 1.03. 49
mercy in him than there is milk in a male tiger, COR 5.04. 28 P
this ravenous tiger, this accursed devil; TIT 5.03. 5
as for that ravenous tiger tamora, | no funeral 5.03.195
husband's to aleppo gone, master o' th' tiger; MAC 1.03. 7
the arm'd rhinoceros, or th' hyrcan tiger, 3.04.100
still, | but, when he stirs, a tiger. TNK 4.02.131
the tiger would be tame and gently hear him; VEN 1096
to slay the tiger that doth live by slaughter, LUC 955

TIGER–FOOTED 1 FR 0.0001 REL FR 1 V 0 P
this tiger–footed rage, when it shall find | the COR 3.01.310

TIGER'S 4 FR 0.0004 REL FR 4 V 0 P
o tiger's heart wrapp'd in a woman's hide! 3H6 1.04.137
when did the tiger's young ones teach the dam? TIT 2.03.142
add thereto a tiger's chawdron, | for th' MAC 4.01. 33
the keen teeth from the fierce tiger's /jaws, SON 19. 3

/TIGERS 1 FR 0.0001 REL FR 1 V 0 P
/tigers, /not /daughters, /what /have /you LR 4.02. 40

TIGERS 9 FR 0.0010 REL FR 8 V 1 P
make tigers tame, and huge leviathans | forsake TGV 3.02. 79
o, ten times more, than tigers of hyrcania. 3H6 1.04.155
weep seas, live in fire, eat rocks, tame tigers; TRO 3.02. 78 P
that rome is but a wilderness of tigers? TIT 3.01. 54
tigers must prey, and rome affords no prey | but 3.01. 55

far | than empty tigers or the roaring sea. ROM 5.03. 39
go great with tigers, dragons, wolves, and bears TIM 4.03.189
the hearts of lions and | the breath of tigers, TNK 5.01. 40
wilder to him than tigers in their wildness. LUC 980

TIGHT 3 FR 0.0003 REL FR 3 V 0 P
is tight and yare, and bravely rigg'd as when TMP 5.01.224
two galliasses | and twelve tight galleys. SHR 2.01.379
queen's a squire | more tight at this than thou; ANT 4.04. 15

TIGHTLY 2 FR 0.0002 REL FR 1 V 1 P
hold, sirrah, bear you these letters tightly; WIV 1.03. 79
he will clapper–claw thee tightly, bully. 2.03. 65 P

/TIKE 1 FR 0.0001 REL FR 1 V 0 P
or /lym, | or bobtail /tike or trundle–tail, LR 3.06. 70

TIKE 1 FR 0.0001 REL FR 1 V 0 P
base tike, call'st thou me host? H5 2.01. 29

TILE 2 FR 0.0002 REL FR 1 V 1 P
brains are forfeit to the next tile that falls. AWW 4.03.190 P
have, as learned authors utter, wash'd a tile, TNK 3.05. 40

/TILL 6 FR 0.0006 REL FR 4 V 2 P
/till /we /had /his /assistance /by /the /hand. 2H4 1.03. 21
my good friends, i'll leave you /till night. HAM 2.02.547 P
with weight | /till our scale turn the beam. 4.05.158
but /till that time | i do receive your offer'd 5.02.250
at curfew, and walks /till /the first cock; LR 3.04.116 P
and, /till she come, as truly as to heaven | i OTH 1.03.122

TILL 687 FR 0.0776 REL FR 560 V 127 P
blow till thou burst thy wind, if room enough! TMP 1.01. 7 P
and peg thee in his knotty entrails till | thou 1.02.295
till thou didst seek to violate | the honor of 1.02.347
i will resist such entertainment till | mine 1.02.466
till new–born chins | be rough and razorable; 2.01.249
i will here shroud till the dregs of the storm 2.02. 40 P
and now farewell | till half an hour hence. 3.01. 91
do not approach | till thou dost hear me call. 4.01. 50
shall be paid | till hymen's torch be lighted; 4.01. 97
never till this day | saw i him touch'd with 4.01.144
they cannot boudge till your release. 5.01. 11
till when, be cheerful | and think of each thing 5.01.250
shall lodge thee till thy wound be throughly TGV 1.02.112
till i have found each letter in the letter, 1.02.116
that a man is never undone till he be hang'd, 2.05. 5 P
welcome to a place till some certain shot be 2.05. 6 P
better forbear till proteus make return. 2.07. 14
till the last step have brought me to my love, 2.07. 36
write till your ink be dry, and with your tears 3.02. 74
we'll wait upon your grace till after supper, 3.02. 95
three men and a boy yet, till my mother be dead. WIV 1.01.275 P
they will not sit till you come. 1.01.278 P
till the wicked fire of lust have melted him in 2.01. 67 P
till he hath pawn'd his horses to mine host of 2.01. 96 P
by your leave, sir. i am sick till i see her. 3.02. 28 P
never saw him so gross in his jealousy till now. 3.03.189 P
till then farewell, sir; 3.04. 92
and till he tell the truth, | let the supposed 4.04. 61
be so bold as stay, sir, till she come down. 4.05. 13 P
with their fine wits till i were as crestfall'n 4.05.100 P
i knew not what 'twas to be beaten till lately. 5.01. 26 P
i' th' castle–ditch till we see the light of our 5.02. 2 P
that it may stand till the perpetual doom | in 5.05. 58
but till 'tis one a' clock, | our dance of 5.05. 74
till candles, and starlight, and moonshine be 5.05.102
till thou art able to woo her in good english. 5.05.133 P
hide our love | till time had made them for us. MM 1.02.153
till custom make it | their perch and not their 2.01. 3
in his courses till thou know'st what they are. 2.01.187 P
ever till now, | when men were fond, i smil'd 2.02.185
free your life, | but fetter you till death. 3.01. 66
friar, till eating and drinking be put down. 3.02.103 P
fact, till now in the government of lord angelo, 4.02.136 P
master barnardine, awake till you are executed, 4.03. 32 P
this reprobate till he were well inclin'd, | and 4.03. 74
till you have heard me in my true complaint 5.01. 24
to her eyes, | till she herself confess it. 5.01.162
i did but smile till now. 5.01.233
but stir not you till you have well determin'd 5.01.258
you to abide here till he come and enforce them 5.01.265 P
speak not you to him till we call upon you. 5.01.285 P
boil and bubble, | till it o'errun the stew; 5.01.319
thou hast, | rely upon it till my tale be heard, 5.01.365
governed his deeds, | till he did look on me. 5.01.447
made | to epidamium, till my factor's death, ERR 1.01. 41
what have befall'n of them and /thee till now. 1.01.123
and stay there, dromio, till i come to thee. 1.02. 10
till that, i'll view the manners of the town, 1.02. 12
mart, | and afterward consort you till bed–time: 1.02. 28
farewell till then. 1.02. 30
reserve them till a merrier hour than this: 1.02. 69
she that doth fast till you come home to dinner; 1.02. 89
till he come home again, i would forbear. 2.01. 31
i, sir? i never saw her till this time. 2.02.162
let him knock till it ache. 3.01. 58
if she lives till doomsday, she'll burn a week 3.02. 99 P
where i will walk till thou return to me. 3.02.151
i owe you none, till i receive the chain. 4.01. 64
i do obey thee, till i give thee bail. 4.01. 80
that stays but till her owner comes aboard, 4.01. 86
on, officer, to prison till it come. 4.01.108
but till this afternoon his passion | ne'er 5.01. 47
till i have brought him to his wits again, | or 5.01. 96
till i have us'd the approved means i have, 5.01.103
till, raising of more aid, | we came again to 5.01.153
till, gnawing with my teeth my bonds in sunder, 5.01.250
i never saw you in my life till now. 5.01.297
and till this present hour | my heavy burthen 5.01.402
we'll draw cuts for the senior, till then, lead 5.01.423
no, not till a hot january. ADO 1.01. 94 P
will hold it as a dream till it appear itself; 1.02. 20 P
the full show of this till you may do it without 1.03. 20 P
not till god make men of some other mettle than 2.01. 59 P
faster and faster, till he sink into his grave. 2.01. 79 P
time goes on crutches till love have all his 2.01.358 P
not till monday, my dear son, which is hence a 2.01.359 P
oath on it, till he have made /an oyster of me, 2.03. 25 P
but till all graces be in one woman, one woman 2.03. 28 P
she sit in her smock till she have writ a sheet 2.03.132 P
did not think i should live till i were married. 2.03.244 P
i do but stay till your marriage be consummate, 3.02. 1 P
wonder not till further warrant. 3.02.112 P
her no farther till you are my witnesses. 3.02.128 P
bear it coldly but till midnight, and let the 3.02.129 P
why then let them alone till they are sober. 3.03. 45 P
us go sit here upon the church–bench till two, 3.03. 89 P
i shall meet, and till then peace be with him. 5.01.193 P
o, stay but till then! 5.02. 45 P
and yield your dead, | till death be uttered, 5.03. 20
no, that you shall not till you take her hand, 5.04. 56
think not on him till to–morrow. 5.04.127 P
may one day smile again, and till then, sit thee LLL 1.01.314 P
forbear till this company be past. 1.02.126 P
till painful study shall outwear three years, 2.01. 23
not till it leave the rider in the mire. 2.01.120
till there be more matter in the shin. 3.01.119 P
not a sore, till now made sore with shooting. 4.02. 57
i'll prove her fair, or talk till doomsday here. 4.03.270
what wert thou | till this madman show'd thee? 5.02.338
from morn till night, out of his pavilion. 5.02.654
and till that /instant shut | my woeful self up 5.02.807
i'll serve thee true and faithfully till then. 5.02.831
from lovers' food till morrow deep midnight. MND 1.01.223
perchance till after theseus' wedding–day. 2.01.139
grove | till i torment thee for this injury. 2.01.147
thy love ne'er alter till thy sweet life end! 2.02. 61
so i, being young, till now ripe not to reason; 2.02.118
whom i do love and will do till my death. 3.02.167
till o'er their brows death–counterfeiting sleep 3.02.364
league whose date till death shall never end. 3.02.373
groves may tread | even till the eastern gate, 3.02.391
here will i rest me till the break of day. 3.02.446
which never labor'd in their minds till now; 5.01. 73
but wonder on till truth make all things plain. 5.01.128
and i, like helen, till the fates me kill. 5.01.197
i would have stay'd till i had made you merry, MV 1.01. 60
well, we will leave you then till dinner–time. 1.01.105
so i will not rest till i have run some ground. 2.02.104 P
the curse never fell upon our nation till now, i 3.01. 85 P
our nation till now, i never felt it till now. 3.01. 86 P
and swearing till my very /roof was dry | with 3.02.204
but, till i come again, | no bed shall e'er be 3.02.325
so fare you well till we shall meet again. 3.04. 40
till thou canst rail the seal from off my bond, 4.01.139
that you would wear it till your hour of death, 5.01.153
nor i in yours | till i again see mine! 5.01.192
whether till the next night she had rather stay, 5.01.302
till i were couching with the doctor's clerk. 5.01.305
hand from thy throat till this other had pull'd AYL 1.01. 60 P
i will not till i please. 1.01. 66 P
and never leave thee till he hath ta'en thy life 1.01.151 P
upon my body | even till i shrink with cold, i 2.01. 9
from /seventeen years till now almost fourscore 2.03. 71
be ware of mine own wit till i break my shins 2.04. 59 P
he, | "call me not fool till heaven hath sent me 2.07. 19
sea, | till that the weary very means do ebb? 2.07. 73
nor shalt not, till necessity be serv'd. 2.07. 89
this fruit | till i and my affairs are answered. 2.07. 99
till he be first suffic'd, | oppress'd with two 2.07.131
and we will nothing waste till you return. 2.07.134
till thou canst quit thee by thy brother's mouth 3.01. 11
seeming monstrous till his fellow–fault came to 3.02.355 P
but till that time | come not thou near me; 3.05. 31
not, | as till that time i shall not pity thee. 3.05. 34
it, till you met your wive's wit going to your 4.01.167 P
i'll go find a shadow, and sigh till he come. 4.01.217 P
and till the tears that she hath shed for thee SHR in.2. 64
or have i dream'd till now? in.2. 69
friendly maintain'd till by helping baptista's 1.01.137 P
o tranio, till i found it to be true, | i never 1.01.148
that till the father rid his hands of her, 1.01.181
i will not sleep, hortensio, till i see her, 1.02.103
till katherine the curst have got a husband. 1.02.128
and weep, | till i can find occasion of revenge. 2.01. 36
let us entreat you stay till after dinner. 3.02.198
no, nor to–morrow — not till i please myself. 3.02.209
for me, i'll not be gone till i please myself. 3.02.212
master's horse–tail till they kiss their hands. 4.01. 94 P
and till she stoop, she must not be full–gorg'd, 4.01.191
till you have done your business in the city. 4.02.111
you shall have one too, | and not till then. 4.03. 72
sigh, | till i be brought to such a silly pass! 5.02.124
was never virgin /got till virginity was first AWW 1.01.128 P
till their own scorn return to them unnoted 1.02. 34
the blessing of god till i have issue a' my body 1.03. 25 P
nor would i have him till i do deserve him, 1.03.199
till honor be bought up, and no sword worn | but 2.01. 32
"till i have no wife, i have nothing in france." 3.02. 74 P
"till i have no wife, i have nothing in france." 3.02. 99 P
holy pilgrim, | but till the troops come by, | i 3.05. 40
keep him muffled | till we do hear from them. 4.01. 91
till then i'll keep him dark and safely lock'd. 4.01. 94
ay, so you serve us | till we serve you; 4.02. 18
adieu till then, then fail not. 4.02. 64
till they attain to their abhorr'd ends; 4.03. 23 P
not till after midnight; 4.03. 29 P
we will not meddle with him till he come; 4.03. 35 P
to remain with me till they meet together. 4.05. 87 P
them ill to friend | till your deeds gain them; 5.03.183
the element itself, till seven years' heat, TN 1.01. 25
world | till i had made mine own occasion mellow 1.02. 43
not drink to my niece till his brains turn o' 1.03. 41 P
fixed foot shall grow | till thou have audience. 1.04. 18
and shall do till the pangs of death shake him. 1.05. 75 P
sir, till she be married, and fools are as like 3.01. 33 P
pleasure and his penance, till our very pastime, 3.04.138 P
give them way till he take leave, and presently 3.04.198 P
stay you by this gentleman till my return. 3.04.258 P
ne'er believe a madman till i see his brains. 4.02.116 P
sir, lullaby to your bounty till i come again. 5.01. 45 P
do not embrace me till each circumstance | of 5.01.251
desire to live on crutches till he had one. WT 1.01. 46 P
i must be patient till the heavens look | with 2.01.106
up for pity — yet i'll tarry till my son come; 3.03. 77 P
then, till the fury of his highness settle, 4.04.471
my dignity would last | but till 'twere known! 4.04.476
not stir his pettitoes till he had both tune and 4.04.607 P
then stand till he be three quarters and a dram 4.04.785 P
this young man in pawn till i bring it you. 4.04.808 P
as he says, your pawn till it be brought you. 4.04.823 P
not have an heir | till his lost child be found? 5.01. 40
we shall not marry till thou bid'st us. 5.01. 82
never till then. 5.01. 84
whose honor and whose honesty till now | endur'd 5.01.194
how attentiveness wounded his daughter, till, 5.02. 87 P
to be found again, | lament till i am lost. 5.03.135
would not cease | till she had kindled france, JN 1.01. 33
to my home i will no more return | till angiers, 2.01. 22
even till that england, hedg'd in with the main, 2.01. 26
even till that utmost corner of the west 2.01. 29
till then, fair boy, | will i not think of home, 2.01. 30
till your strong hand shall help to give him 2.01. 33
till that time | have we ramm'd up our gates 2.01.271
till you compound whose right is worthiest, | we 2.01.281
till then, blows, blood, and death! 2.01.360
and till it be undoubted, we do lock | our 2.01.369
till their soul–fearing clamors have brawl'd 2.01.383
even till unfenced desolation | leave them as 2.01.386
lov'd myself | till now infixed i beheld myself 2.01.502
till this advantage, this vile–drawing bias, 2.01.577
name, | which till this time my tongue did ne'er 3.01.307
me, till i have pleas'd | my discontented peers! 4.02.126
till i have set a glory to this hand, | by 4.03. 71
not till i sheathe it in a murtherer's skin. 4.03. 80
return | till my attempt so much be glorified 5.02.111
by, | which holds but till thy news be uttered, 5.07. 56
till i have told this slander of his blood | how R2 1.01.113
till twice five summers have enrich'd our fields 1.03.141
which, till my infant fortune comes to years, 2.03. 66
in love | till you did make him misinterpret me, 3.01. 18
and, till so much blood thither come again, 3.02. 78
till time lend friends, and friends their 3.03.132
till they have fretted us a pair of graves 3.03.167
give richard leave to live till richard die? 3.03.174
till thou the lie–giver and that lie do lie | in 4.01. 68
all rest under gage | till norfolk be repeal'd. 4.01. 87
gage | till we assign you to your days of trial. 4.01.106
to keep him safely till his day of trial. 4.01.153
and he and i | will keep a league till death. 5.01. 22
ground | till bullingbrook have pardoned thee. 5.02.117
key, | that no man enter till my tale be done. 5.03. 37
till thou give joy, until thou bid me joy | by 5.03. 95
our knees still kneel till to the ground they 5.03.106
i never long'd to hear a word till now, | say 5.03.115
pleas'd, till he be eas'd | with being nothing. 5.05. 40
till he hath found a time to pay us home. 1H4 1.03.288
till fields, and blows, and groans applaud our 1.03.302
to drive away the time till falstaff come, i 2.04. 28 P
there let him sleep till day. 2.04.543 P
till i have learn'd thy language, for thy tongue 3.01.205
meet and ne'er part till one drop down a corse. 4.01.123
for god's sake, cousin, stay till all come in. 4.03. 29
and by, | till then in blood by noble percy lie. 5.04.110
let us not leave till all our own be won. 5.05. 44
won, | came not till now to dignify the times, 2H4 1.01. 22
i was never mann'd with an agot till now, but i 1.02. 17 P
till that the nobles and the armed commons 2.03. 51
am i, | till time and vantage crave my company. 2.03. 68
ever i dress myself handsome till thy return — 2.04.280 P
come prick bullcalf till he roar again. 3.02.176 P
mouldy, stay at home till you are past service; 3.02.251 P
your part, bullcalf, grow till you come unto it. 3.02.252 P
till sack commences it and sets it in act and 4.03.116 P
and pause us, till these rebels, now afoot, 4.04. 9
till that his passions, like a whale on ground, 4.04. 40
till his friend sickness /have determin'd me? 4.05. 81
shall see him laugh till his face be like a wet 5.01. 84 P
till you do live to see a son of mine | offend 5.02.105
in me | hath proudly flow'd in vanity till now; 5.02.130
till then i banish thee, on pain of death, | as 5.05. 63
but all are banish'd till their conversations 5.05.100
france, till satisfied | that fair queen isabel, H5 1.02. 80
but till the king come forth, and not till then, 2.pr. 41
but till the king come forth, and not till then, 2.pr. 41
have in these parts from morn till even fought, 3.01. 20
harflew | till in her ashes she lies buried. 3.03. 9
good to bruise an injury till it were full ripe. 3.06.122 P
if we no more meet till we meet in heaven, 4.03. 7
an honor in thy cap | till i do challenge it. 4.08. 60
till harry's back–return again to france. 5.pr. 41
to wear it in my cap till i see him once again, 5.01. 12 P
downright oaths, which i never use till urg'd, 5.02.145 P
recreants, | fight till the last gasp; 1H6 1.02.127
till by broad spreading it disperse to nought. 1.02.135
till you conclude that he upon whose side | the 2.04. 40
and, till thou be restor'd, thou art a yeoman. 2.04. 95
and humble service till the point of death. 3.01.167
till bones and flesh and sinews fall away, | so 3.01.192
because till now we never saw your face. 3.04. 24
till with thy warlike sword, despite of fate, 4.06. 8
till mischief and despair | drive you to break 5.04. 90
be gone, i say, for, till you do return, | i 5.05. 94
till term of eighteen months | be full expir'd. 2H6 1.01. 67
still revelling like lords till all be gone; 1.01.224
then, york, be still awhile, till time do serve. 1.01.248
till henry, surfeiting in joys of love | with 1.01.251
till suffolk gave two dukedoms for his daughter. 1.03. 87
till we have brought duke humphrey in disgrace. 1.03. 96
till france be won into the dolphin's hands. 1.03.170
on his will | till paris was besieg'd, famish'd, 1.03.172
for, till thou speak, thou shalt not pass from 1.04. 27
whip him till he leap over that same stool. 2.01.145 P
till they come to berwick, from whence they came 2.01.156
death reign'd as king | till henry bullingbrook, 2.02. 21
king, | who kept him in captivity till he died. 2.02. 42
till lionel's issue fails, his should not reign. 2.02. 56
but i am not your king | till i be crown'd, and 2.02. 65
till they have snar'd the shepherd of the flock, 2.02. 73
nothing, till the axe of death | hang over thee, 2.04. 49
by staying there so long till all were lost. 3.01.299
till that his thighs with darts | were almost 3.01.362
with the rude multitude till i return. 3.02.135
at my horse heels till i do come to london, 4.03. 13 P
given out these arms till you had recover'd your 4.08. 26 P
till henry be more weak and i more strong. 5.01. 31
till then, i'll follow her. 3H6 1.01.262
mine, boys? not till king henry be dead. 1.02. 10
and till i root out their accursed line, | and 1.03. 32

doubt, | till my bad angel fire my good one out. 144.14
the sun itself sees not till heaven clears. 148.12
i held my city, | till thus he gan besiege me: LC 177
till now did ne'er invite, nor never vise. 182
whose sights till then were levell'd on my face, 282
TILLAGE 1 FR 0.0001 REL FR 1 V 0 P
womb | disdains the tillage of thy husbandry? SON 3. 6
TILL'D 1 FR 0.0001 REL FR 0 V 1 P
and till'd with excellent endeavor of drinking 2H4 4.03.120 P
TILL'T 1 FR 0.0001 REL FR 1 V 0 P
the fire that mounts the liquor till't run o'er H8 1.01.144
TILLY–FALLY 1 FR 0.0001 REL FR 0 V 1 P
tilly–fally, sir john, ne'er tell me; 2H4 2.04. 83 P
TILLY–VALLY 1 FR 0.0001 REL FR 0 V 1 P
tilly–vally. TN 2.03. 78 P
TILT 1 FR 0.0001 REL FR 1 V 0 P
to play with mammets and to tilt with lips. 1H4 2.03. 92
TILTER 2 FR 0.0002 REL FR 0 V 2 P
and master forthlight the tilter, and brave MM 4.03. 16 P
the heart of his lover, as a puisne tilter, that AYL 3.04. 43 P
TILTH 2 FR 0.0002 REL FR 2 V 0 P
bourn, bound of land, tilth, vineyard, none; TMP 2.01.153
womb | expresseth his full tilth and husbandry. MM 1.04. 44
TILTING 3 FR 0.0003 REL FR 3 V 0 P
/of his heart's meteors tilting in his face? ERR 4.02. 6
lo, he is tilting straight! LLL 5.02.483
swords out, and tilting one at other's /breast, OTH 2.03.183
TILTS 2 FR 0.0002 REL FR 2 V 0 P
there shall he practice tilts and tournaments, TGV 1.03. 30
but that he tilts | with piercing steel at bold ROM 3.01.158
TILT–YARD 2 FR 0.0002 REL FR 1 V 1 P
'a ne'er saw him but once in the tilt–yard, and 2H4 3.02.322 P
his study is his tilt–yard, and his loves | are 2H6 1.03. 59
/TIMANDRA 1 FR 0.0001 REL FR 1 V 0 P
/phrynia and /timandra had gold of him. TIM 5.01. 5
TIMANDRA 2 FR 0.0002 REL FR 2 V 0 P
art thou timandra? TIM 4.03. 82
pardon him, sweet timandra, for his wits | are 4.03. 89
TIMBER 2 FR 0.0002 REL FR 1 V 1 P
a shrunk panel, and like green timber warp, warp AYL 3.03. 88 P
every tree, lop, bark, and part o' th' timber; H8 1.02. 96
TIMBER'D 2 FR 0.0002 REL FR 2 V 0 P
too slightly timber'd for so /loud /a /wind, HAM 4.07. 22
his bark is stoutly timber'd, and his pilot | of OTH 2.01. 48
/TIMBRIA 1 FR 0.0001 REL FR 1 V 0 P
/dardan /and /timbria, /helias, /chetas, /troien TRO pr 16
TIM'D 1 FR 0.0001 REL FR 1 V 0 P
whose every motion | was tim'd with dying cries. COR 2.02.110
/TIME 11 FR 0.0012 REL FR 10 V 1 P
say, | but i will fit it with some better /time. JN 3.03. 26
/which /way /the /stream /of /time /doth /run, 2H4 4.01. 70
/all /our /griefs | (/when /time /shall /serve) 4.01. 74
/you /shall /say, /indeed, /it /is /the /time, 4.01.103
/from /the /king /or /in /the /present /time, 4.01.106
/the /prophet /could /not /at /that /time R3 4.02.100
with which the /time will load him. H8 5.01. 37
the /time has been, | that when the brains were MAC 3.04. 77
/him /even /o'er /the /time /he /has /lost. LR 4.07. 79
/'tis /time /to /look /about, /the /powers /of 4.07. 91 P
/at /this /time | /we /sweat /and /bleed: 5.03. 54
TIME 1133 FR 0.1280 REL FR 922 V 211 P
'tis time | i should inform thee farther. TMP 1.02. 22
remember | a time before we came unto this cell? 1.02. 39
else | in the dark backward and abysm of time? 1.02. 50
as at that time | through all the signories it 1.02. 70
can, that have more time | for vainer hours, and 1.02.173
what is the time o' th' day? 1.02.239
the time 'twixt six and now | must by us both be 1.02.240
before the time be out? no more! 1.02.246
not since widow dido's time. 2.01. 77 P
why, in good time. 2.01. 96 P
lack some gentleness, | and time to speak it in. 2.01.139
open–ey'd conspiracy | his time doth take. 2.01.302
i was the man i' th' moon, when time was. 2.02.139 P
and many a time | th' harmony of their tongues 3.01. 40
as you like this, give me the lie another time. 3.02. 77 P
after a little time | i'll beat him too. 3.02. 85
but one fiend at a time, | i'll fight their 3.03.102
(like poison given to work a great time after) 3.03.105
we shall lose our time, | and all be turn'd to 4.01.247
and time | goes upright with his carriage. 5.01. 2
on the sixt hour, at which time, my lord, | you 5.01. 4
at this time | i will tell no tales. 5.01.128
but wherefore waste i time to counsel thee TGV 1.01. 51
me, | made me neglect my studies, lose my time, 1.01. 67
you | to let him spend his time no more at home, 1.03. 14
i have consider'd well his loss of time, | and 1.03. 19
and perfected by the swift course of time. 1.03. 23
them shall proteus go — | and in good time! 1.03. 44
i am resolv'd that thou shalt spend some time 1.03. 66
or else for want of idle time, could not again 2.01.166
ay, sir, and done too — for this time. 2.04. 30 P
omitting the sweet benefit of time | to clothe 2.04. 65
and here he means to spend his time a while. 2.04. 80
in, | by longing for that food so long a time. 2.07. 17
youth | of greater time than i shall show to be. 2.07. 48
besides, the fashion of the time is chang'd) 3.01. 86
will give thee time to leave our royal court, 3.01.165
time is the nurse and breeder of all good. 3.01.245
the time now serves not to expostulate: 3.01.253
a little time will melt her frozen thoughts, 3.02. 9
a little time, my lord, will kill that grief. 3.02. 15
even for this time i spend in talking to thee. 4.02.104
and at that time i made her weep agood, | for i 4.04.165
hours, | unless it be to come before their time, 5.01. 5
o time most accurst! 5.04. 71
and have done any time these three hundred years WIV 1.01. 12 P
was like an unskillful singer, he kept not time. 1.03. 26 P
of the wart the next time we have confidence, 1.04.159 P
i have seen the time, with my long sword i would 2.01.228 P
from home, but she hopes there will come a time. 2.02.102 P
give me so much of your time in exchange of it, 2.02.233 P
for at that time the jealous rascally knave her 2.02.265 P
pray you use your patience in good time. 3.01. 82 P
and smell like bucklersbury in simple time — i 3.03. 73 P
no, heaven so speed me in my time to come! 3.04. 12
carried out, the last time he search'd for him, 4.02. 32 P
him at the door with it, as they did last time. 4.02. 96 P
help to search my house this one time. 4.02.160 P
and in that time | shall master slender steal my 4.04. 73
from time to time i have acquainted you | with 4.06. 8
from time to time i have acquainted you | with 4.06. 8
when slender sees his time | to take her by the 4.06. 36
this is the third time; 5.01. 2 P
i say, time wears, hold up your head and mince. 5.01. 7 P
when you see your time, take her by the hand, 5.03. 2 P
and, as you trip, still pinch him to your time. 5.05. 92
'tis time i were chok'd with a piece of toasted 5.05.138 P
as time and our concernings shall importune, MM 1.01. 56
hide our love | till time had made them for us. 1.02.153
use, in time the rod | /becomes more mock'd than 1.03. 26
as blossoming time | that from the seedness the 1.04. 41
had time coher'd with place, or place with 2.01. 11
which at that very distant time stood, as it 2.01. 92 P
the time is yet to come that she was ever 2.01.168 P
so for this time, pompey, fare you well. 2.01.250 P
the office, you had continu'd in it some time. 2.01.262 P
at any time 'fore noon. 2.02.160
this night's the time | that i should do what i 3.01.100
in good time. 3.01.179 P
between which time of the contract and limit of 3.01.215 P
that the time may have all shadow and silence in 3.01.247 P
was with child by him in the duke's time; 3.02.200 P
though my chance is now | to use it for my time. 3.02.218
much upon this time have i promis'd here to meet 4.01. 17 P
the time is come even now. 4.01. 21 P
you shall have your full time of imprisonment, 4.02. 12 P
i have been an unlawful bawd time out of mind, 4.02. 15 P
the smallest article of it, neither in time, 4.02.104 P
and i will have more time to prepare me, or they 4.03. 54 P
these letters at fit time deliver me. 4.05. 1
a forted residence 'gainst the tooth of time 5.01. 12
now is your time. 5.01. 19
are i' the wrong | to speak before your time. 5.01. 87
and with ripened time | unfold the evil which is 5.01.116
he in time may come to clear himself; 5.01.150
with such a time | when i'll depose i had him in 5.01.197
since which time of five years | i never spake 5.01.222
in very good time. 5.01.285 P
but fitter time for that. 5.01.493
time is their master, and when they see time, ERR 2.01. 8
time is their master, and when they see time, 2.01. 8
for urging it the second time to me. 2.02. 46
in good time, sir: what's that? 2.02. 57 P
learn to jest in good time — there's a time for 2.02. 64 P
in good time — there's a time for all things. 2.02. 65 P
as the plain bald pate of father time himself. 2.02. 70 P
there's no time for a man to recover his hair 2.02. 72 P
why is time such a niggard of hair, being, as it 2.02. 77 P
you would all this time have prov'd there is no 2.02.100 P
have prov'd there is no time for all things. 2.02.101 P
/e'en no time to recover hair lost by nature. 2.02.102 P
substantial, why there is no time to recover. 2.02.105 P
time himself is bald, and therefore, to the 2.02.106 P
the time was once, when thou unurg'd wouldst vow 2.02.113
i, sir? i never saw her till this time. 2.02.162
the porter for this time, sir, and my name is 3.01. 43
why at this time the doors are made against you. 3.01. 93
'tis time, i think, to trudge, pack, and be gone 3.02.153
and therefore 'tis high time that i were hence. 3.02.157
bear it with you, lest i come not time enough. 4.01. 41
no, no, the bell, 'tis time that i were gone: 4.02. 53
as if time were in debt! 4.02. 57
time is a very bankrout and owes more than he's 4.02. 58
that time comes stealing on by night and day? 4.02. 60
where would you had remain'd until this time, 4.04. 66
his word might bear my wealth at any time. 5.01. 8
during which time he ne'er saw syracusa: 5.01.329
well, as time shall try: ADO 1.01.260 P
"in time the savage bull doth bear the yoke." 1.01.261
in the mean time, good signior benedick, repair 1.01.275 P
he meant to take the present time by the top, 1.02. 15 P
good cousin, have a care this busy time. 1.02. 27 P
in the mean time let me be that i am, and seek 1.03. 36 P
music, cousin, if you be not woo'd in good time. 2.01. 70 P
time goes on crutches till love have all his 2.01.357 P
hence a just sevennight, and a time too brief, 2.01.360 P
claudio, the time shall not go dully by us. 2.01.363 P
for in the mean time i will so fashion the 2.02. 46 P
five a' clock, cousin, 'tis time you were ready. 3.04. 52 P
pray you, for you see it is a busy time with me. 3.05. 5 P
time hath not yet so dried this blood of mine, 4.01.193
by this time our sexton hath reform'd signior 5.01.254 P
to specify, when time and place shall serve, 5.01.256 P
that liv'd in the time of good neighbors. 5.02. 77 P
mean time let wonder seem familiar, | and to the 5.04. 70
when, spite of cormorant devouring time, | th' LLL 1.01. 4
fit in his place and time. 1.01. 98
the time when? 1.01.235 P
so much for the time when. 1.01.238 P
as an appertinent title to your old time, which 1.02. 17 P
another of these students at that time | was 2.01. 64
what time a' day? 2.01.121
mean time receive such welcome at my hand | as 2.01.168
joan, or spend a minute's time | in pruning me? 4.03.180
and since her time are colliers counted bright. 4.03.263
such as the shortness of the time can shape, 4.03.375
no time shall be omitted | that will be time, 4.03.378
no time shall be omitted | that will be time, 4.03.379
as concerning some entertainment of time, some 5.01.119 P
all hail, sweet madam, and fair time of day! 5.02.339
the extreme parts of time extremely forms | all 5.02.740
for your fair sakes have we neglected time, 5.02.755
as bombast and as lining to the time; 5.02.781
a time methinks too short | to make a 5.02.788
i'll stay with patience, but the time is long. 5.02.835
four nights will quickly dream away the time; MND 1.01. 8
take time to pause, and by the next new moon — 1.01. 83
before the time i did lysander see, | seem'd 1.01.204
(a time that lovers' flights doth still conceal) 1.01.212
in the mean time i will draw a bill of 1.02.105 P
that very time i saw (but thou couldst not) 2.01.155
when we have chid the hasty–footed time | for 3.02.200
how shall we beguile | the lazy time, if not 5.01. 41
courtesy, in all reason, we must stay the time. 5.01.255 P
lovers, to bed, 'tis almost fairy time. 5.01.364
now it is the time of night | that the graves, 5.01.379
nature hath fram'd strange fellows in her time: MV 1.01. 51
i'll tell thee more of this another time; 1.01.100
debts | wherein my time something too prodigal 1.01.129
and herein spend but time | to wind about my 1.01.153
lady, in your father's time, a venetian, a 1.02.113 P
who then conceiving did in eaning time | fall 1.03. 87
many a time and oft | in the rialto you have 1.03.106
me such a day, another time | you call'd me dog; 1.03.127
our masquing mates by this time for us stay. 2.06. 59
but stay the very riping of the time; 2.08. 40
fool i shall appear | by the time i linger here. 2.09. 74
i speak too long, but 'tis to peize the time, 3.02. 22
my lord and lady, it is now our time, | that 3.02.186
you | even at that time i may be married too. 3.02.194
my maid nerissa and myself mean time | will live 3.02.309
that do converse and waste the time together, 3.04. 12
waste no time in words, | but get thee gone. 3.04. 54
mean time the court shall hear bellario's letter 4.01.149
we trifle time. 4.01.298
but music for the time doth change his nature. 5.01. 82
to him every day, and fleet the time carelessly, AYL 1.01.118 P
it is the first time that ever i heard breaking 1.02.138 P
you will try in time, in despite of a fall. 1.03. 25 P
i was too young that time to value her, | but 1.03. 71
if you outstay the time, upon mine honor, | and 1.03. 88
devise the fittest time and safest way | to hide 1.03.135
and willingly could waste my time in it. 2.04. 95
hear | the motley fool thus moral on the time, 2.07. 29
lose and neglect the creeping hours of time; 2.07.112
and one man in his time plays many parts, | his 2.07.142
i was never so berhym'd since pythagoras' time, 3.02.177 P
you should ask me what time o' day; 3.02.300 P
detect the lazy foot of time as well as a clock. 3.02.304 P
and why not the swift foot of time? 3.02.306 P
time travels in divers paces with divers persons 3.02.308 P
i'll tell you who time ambles withal, who time 3.02.309 P
who time ambles withal, who time trots withal, 3.02.310 P
who time trots withal, who time gallops withal, 3.02.310 P
who ambles time withal? 3.02.318 P
these time ambles withal. 3.02.325 P
term, and then they perceive not how time moves. 3.02.333 P
at which time would i, being but a moonish youth 3.02.409 P
but till that time | come not thou near me; 3.05. 31
and when that time comes, | afflict me with thy 3.05. 32
not, | as till that time i shall not pity thee. 3.05. 34
silvius, the time was that i hated thee; 3.05. 92
and in all this time there was not any man died 4.01. 96 P
men have died from time to time and worms have 4.01.107 P
died from time to time and worms have eaten them 4.01.107 P
time is the old justice that examines all such 4.01.199 P
examines all such offenders, and let time try. 4.01.200 P
we shall find a time, audrey, patience, gentle 5.01. 1 P
in spring time, the only pretty /ring time, 5.03. 19
in spring time, the only pretty /ring time, 5.03. 19
country folks would lie, | in spring time, etc. 5.03. 25
a life was but a flower, | in spring time, etc. 5.03. 29
and therefore take the present time, | with a 5.03. 30
crowned with the prime, | in spring time, etc. 5.03. 33
sir, we kept time, we lost not our time. 5.03. 37 P
sir, we kept time, we lost not our time. 5.03. 38 P
i count it but time lost to hear such a foolish 5.03. 39 P
the first time that i ever saw him | methought 5.04. 28
mean time, forget this new–fall'n dignity, | and 5.04.176
well, you are come to me in happy time, | the SHR in.1. 90
nap, | but did i never speak of all that time? in.2. 82
ay, and the time seems thirty unto me, | being in.2. 114
being all this time abandon'd from your bed. in.2. 115
and therefore, tranio, for the time i study, 1.01. 17
such friends as time in padua shall beget. 1.01. 45
master, it is no time to chide you now, 1.01.159
nay, then 'tis time to stir him from his trance. 1.01.177
sirrah, come hither, 'tis no time to jest, | and 1.01.226
and therefore frame your manners to the time. 1.01.227
gremio, 'tis now no time to vent our love; 1.02.178
have i not in my time heard lions roar? 1.02.200
in good time! 2.01.195
in time i may believe, yet i mistrust. 3.01. 51
the morning wears, 'tis time we were at church. 3.02.111
i'll have no bigger, this doth fit the time, 4.03. 69
well, | according to the fashion and the time. 4.03. 95
i did not bid you mar it to the time. 4.03. 97
and time it is, when raging war is /done, | to 5.02. 2
practices he hath persecuted time with hope, and AWW 1.01. 14 P
the process but only the losing of hope by time. 1.01. 16 P
answer the time of request. 1.01.155 P
he did look far | into the service of the time, 1.02. 27
and at this time | his tongue obey'd his hand. 1.02. 40
for they wear themselves in the cap of the time; 2.01. 53 P
if i break time, or flinch in property | of what 2.01.187
so make the choice of thy own time, for i, | thy 2.01.203
i play the noble huswife with the time, | to 2.02. 60
a second time receive | the confirmation of my 2.03. 49
as your due, time claims, he does acknowledge, 2.04. 42
which they distill now in the curbed time, | to 2.04. 45
which holds not color with the time, nor does 2.05. 59
in fine, delivers me to fill the time, | herself 3.07. 33
that time and place with this deceit so lawful 3.07. 38
three hours 'twill be time enough to go home. 4.01. 25 P
that what in time proceeds | may token to the 4.02. 62
in the mean time, what hear you of these wars? 4.03. 37 P
from the time of his remembrance to this very 4.03.109 P
time was, i did him a desired office, | dear 4.04. 5
but with the word the time will bring on summer, 4.04. 31
our waggon is prepar'd, and time revives us. 4.04. 34
in happy time! 5.01. 6
though time seem so adverse and means unfit. 5.01. 26
bent upon him | and watch'd the time to shoot. 5.03. 11
the time is fair again. 5.03. 36
whole, | not one word more of the consumed time. 5.03. 38
th' inaudible and noiseless foot of time 5.03. 41
with them at that time that i knew of their 5.03.262 P
and at that time he got his wife with child. 5.03.301
what else may hap, to time i will commit, | only TN 1.02. 60
i had bestow'd that time in the tongues that i 1.03. 92 P
'tis not that time of moon with me to make one 1.05.200 P
o time, thou must untangle this, not i, | it is 2.02. 40

'tis not the first time i have constrain'd one 2.03. 67 P
to gabble like tinkers at this time of night? 2.03. 88 P
no respect of place, persons, nor time in you? 2.03. 92 P
we did keep time, sir, in our catches. sneck up! 2.03. 93 P
and pleasure will be paid, one time or another. 2.04. 70 P
the treasure of your time with a foolish knight" 2.05. 78 P
jests, | the quality of persons, and the time; 3.01. 63
why then methinks 'tis time to smile again. 3.01.126
the clock upbraids me with the waste of time. 3.01.130
gilt of this opportunity you let time wash off, 3.02. 25 P
albeit the quality of the time and quarrel 3.03. 31
you beguile the time and feed your knowledge 3.03. 41
at which time we will bring the device to the 3.04.139 P
what's that to us? the time goes by; away! 3.04.364
note, | what time we will our celebration keep 4.03. 30
be | when time hath sow'd a grizzle on thy case? 5.01.165
me till each circumstance | of place, time, 5.01.252
you shall from this time be | your master's 5.01.325
and thus the whirligig of time brings in his 5.01.376 P
when that is known and golden time convents, | a 5.01.382
mean time, sweet sister, | we will not part from 5.01.384
time as long again | would be fill'd up, my WT 1.02. 3
we'll part the time between 's then; 1.02. 18
good time encounter her! 2.01. 20
she is, something before her time, deliver'd. 2.02. 23
let him be, | until a time may serve. 2.03. 22
wife, | whom for this time we pardon. 2.03.173
speedy, | the time is worth the use on't. 3.01. 14
my lord, and fear | we have landed in ill time: 3.03. 3
i did in time collect myself and thought | this 3.03. 38
error, | now take upon me, in the name of time, 4.01. 3
which follows after, | is th' argument of time. 4.01. 29
if ever you have spent time worse ere now; 4.01. 30
if never, yet that time himself doth say, | he 4.01. 31
prince florizel, and in my time wore three–pile, 4.03. 13 P
i bless the time | when my good falcon made her 4.04. 14
spring that might | become your time of day — 4.04.114
now in good time! 4.04.163
'tis time to part them. 4.04.344
thou, churl, for this time, | though full of our 4.04.432
at this time | he will allow no speech (which i 4.04.467
myself and fortune | tug for the time to come. 4.04.497
the other grow | faster than thought or time. 4.04.554
so that in this time of lethargy i pick'd and 4.04.614 P
i see this is the time that the unjust man doth 4.04.674 P
have done the time more benefit and grac'd 5.01. 22
as every present time doth boast itself | above 5.01. 96
remember since you ow'd no more to time | than i 5.01.219
but he at that time, overfond of the shepherd's 5.02.117 P
ay, and have been so any time these four hours. 5.02.136 P
'tis time; 5.03. 99
there's time enough for that; 5.03.128
perform'd in this wide gap of time since first 5.03.154
to treat of high affairs touching that time. JN 1.01.101
and in the mean time sojourn'd at my father's; 1.01.103
full fourteen weeks before the course of time. 1.01.113
for he is but a bastard to the time | that doth 1.01.207
have given him time | to land his legions all as 2.01. 58
and the hand of time | shall draw this brief 2.01.102
by this time from their fixed beds of lime | had 2.01.219
till that time | have we ramm'd up our gates 2.01.271
name, | which till this time my tongue did ne'er 3.01.307
old time the clock–setter, that bald sexton time 3.01.324
time the clock–setter, that bald sexton time! 3.01.324
and creep time ne'er so slow, | yet it shall 3.03. 31
still and anon cheer'd up the heavy time, 4.01. 47
being urged at a time unseasonable. 4.02. 20
mean time but ask | what you would have reform'd 4.02. 43
the spirit of the time shall teach me speed. 4.02.176
this gentle offer of the perilous time. 4.03. 13
be stirring as the time, be fire with fire, 5.01. 48
have thou the ordering of this present time. 5.01. 77
i am not glad that such a sore of time | should 5.02. 12
but such is the infection of the time, | that, 5.02. 20
we hold our time too precious to be spent | with 5.02.161
the better arm you to the sudden time | than if 5.06. 26
o, let us pay the time but needful woe, | since 5.07.110
mean time, let this defend my loyalty: R2 1.01. 67
by this time, had the king permitted us, | one 1.03.194
how long a time lies in one little word! 1.03.213
thou canst help time to furrow me with age, 1.03.229
thy grief is but thy absence for a time. 1.03.258
joy absent, grief is present for that time. 1.03.259
when time shall call him home from banishment, 1.04. 21
for sleeping england long time have i watch'd, 2.01. 77
his time is spent, our pilgrimage must be. 2.01.154
away, and take from time | his charters and his 2.01.195
next | we will for ireland, and 'tis time, i 2.01.218
be merry, for our time of stay is short. 2.01.223
to plashy too, | but time will not permit. 2.02.121
you on | to take advantage of the absent time, 2.03. 79
art come | before the expiration of thy time, 2.03.111
o, call back yesterday, bid time return, | and 3.02. 69
side, | for time hath set a blot upon my pride. 3.02. 81
the time hath been, | would you have been so 3.03. 11
till time lend friends, and friends their 3.03.132
/we at time of year | do wound the bark, the 3.04. 57
in that dead time when gloucester's death was 4.01. 10
amongst much other talk, that very time, | i 4.01. 14
well | the very time aumerle and you did talk. 4.01. 61
many a time hath banish'd norfolk fought | for 4.01. 92
the time shall not be many hours of age | more 5.01. 57
well, bear you well in this new spring of time, 5.02. 50
is not my teeming date drunk up with time? 5.02. 91
ha, ha, keep time! 5.05. 42
how sour sweet music is | when time is broke, 5.05. 43
to check time broke in a disordered string; 5.05. 46
but for the concord of my state and time | had 5.05. 47
had not an ear to hear my true time broke. 5.05. 48
i wasted time, and now doth time waste me; 5.05. 49
i wasted time, and now doth time waste me; 5.05. 49
for now hath time made me his numb'ring clock: 5.05. 50
but my time | runs posting on in bullingbrook's 5.05. 58
if thou love me, 'tis time thou wert away. 5.05. 96
find we a time for frighted peace to pant | and 1H4 1.01. 2
now, hal, what time of day is it, lad? 1.02. 1 P
devil hast thou to do with the time of the day? 1.02. 6 P
be so superfluous to demand the time of the day. 1.02. 11 P
call'd her to a reckoning many a time and oft. 1.02. 50 P
the poor abuses of the time want countenance. 1.02.156 P
redeeming time when men think least i will. 1.02.217
at such a time, with all the rest retold, | may 1.03. 73
days, | or fill up chronicles in time to come, 1.03.171
yet time serves wherein you may redeem | your 1.03.180
in richard's time — what do you call the place? 1.03.242
till he hath found a time to pay us home. 1.03.288
when time is ripe, which will be suddenly, 1.03.294
what time do you mean to come to london? 2.01. 41 P
time enough to go to bed with a candle, i 2.01. 43 P
his company hourly any time this two and twenty 2.02. 16 P
have nam'd uncertain, the time itself unsorted, 2.03. 12 P
ned, to drive away the time till falstaff come, 2.04. 28 P
do not only marvel where thou spendest thy time, 2.04.399 P
for i myself at this time have employ'd him. 2.04.513
a shorter time shall send me to you, lords, 3.01. 90
by that time will our book, i think, be drawn. 3.01.221
the hope and expectation of thy time | is ruin'd 3.02. 36
for the time will come | that i shall make this 3.02.144
yea, even the slightest worship of his time, 3.02.151
of yours with fire any time this two and thirty 3.03. 47 P
leisure to be sick | in such a justling time? 4.01. 18
and at the time of my departure thence | he was 4.01. 23
i would the state of time had first been whole 4.01. 25
sir john, 'tis more than time that i were there, 4.02. 54 P
know the king | knows at what time to promise, 4.03. 53
in short time after, he depos'd the king, | soon 4.03. 90
staff of office did i break | in richard's time, 5.01. 35
boldly did outdare | the dangers of the time. 5.01. 41
king, | what with the injuries of a wanton time, 5.01. 50
starving for a time | of pell–mell havoc and 5.01. 81
and find a time | to punish this offense in 5.02. 6
o gentlemen, the time of life is short! 5.02. 81
never shall | a second time do such a courtesy. 5.02.100
what, is it a time to jest and dally now? 5.03. 55 P
and time, that takes survey of all the world, 5.04. 82
'sblood, 'twas time to counterfeit, or that hot 5.04.113 P
for this i shall have time enough to mourn; 2H4 1.01.136
ragged'st hour that time and spite dare bring 1.01.151
'tis more than time, and, my most noble lord, 1.01.187
god give your lordship good time of day. 1.02. 94 P
some relish of the saltness of time in you, and 1.02. 98 P
you may thank th' unquiet time for your quiet 1.02.150 P
we are time's subjects, and time bids be gone. 1.03.110
doth this become your place, your time, and 2.01. 66
fathers being so sick as yours at this time is. 2.02. 31 P
thus we play the fools with the time, and the 2.02.142 P
the time was, father, that you broke your word 2.03. 10
am i, | till time and vantage crave my company. 2.03. 68
to blame | so idly to profane the precious time, 2.04.362
"the time shall come," thus did he follow it, 3.01. 75
"the time will come, that foul sin, gathering 3.01. 76
such things become the hatch and brood of time, 3.01. 86
'tis the more time thou wert us'd. 3.02.106 P
mouldy, it is time you were spent. 3.02.117 P
let time shape, and there an end. 3.02.332 P
the time misord'red doth, in common sense, 4.02. 33
one time or other break some gallows' back. 4.03. 29
but, being moody, give him time and scope, 4.04. 39
the prince will in the perfectness of time 4.04. 74
say it did so a little time before | that our 4.04.127
for now a time is come to mock at form. 4.05.118
myself | to welcome the condition of the time, 5.02. 11
o, if i had had time to have made new liveries, 5.05. 11 P
but that the scambling and unquiet time | did H5 1.01. 4
sum | than ever at one time the clergy yet | did 1.01. 80
save that there was not time enough to hear, 1.01. 84
as never did the clergy at one time | bring in 1.02.134
but when time shall serve, there shall be smiles 2.01. 6 P
may have their throats about them at that time, 2.01. 22 P
cut thy throat one time or other in fair terms, 2.01. 69 P
now he weighs time | even to the utmost grain; 2.04.137
it is no time to discourse, so chrish save me. 3.02.105 P
it is no time to discourse. 3.02.107 P
that is well, i warrant you, when time is serve. 3.06. 66 P
'tis not the first time you were overshot. 3.07.124 P
now is it time to arm. 3.07.154 P
now entertain conjecture of a time | when 4.pr. 1
dying, the time was blessedly lost wherein such 4.01.181 P
be angry with you, if the time were convenient. 4.01.204 P
fly — | and time hath worn us into slovenry. 4.03.114
humbly pray them to admit th' excuse | of time, 5.pr. 4
as in good time he may, from ireland coming, 5.pr. 31
i will desire you to live in the mean time, and 5.01. 33 P
to our sister, | health and fair time of day; 5.02. 3
have lost, or do not learn for want of time, 5.02. 57
moral ties me over to time and a hot summer; 5.02.312 P
small time, but in that small most greatly lived ep 5
england ne'er had a king until his time: 1H6 1.01. 8
during the time edward the third did reign. 1.02. 31
mean time look gracious on thy prostrate thrall. 1.02.117
'twas time, i trow, to wake and leave our beds, 2.01. 41
i'll sort some other time to visit you. 2.03. 27
long time thy shadow hath been thrall to me, 2.03. 36
mean time your cheeks do counterfeit our roses; 2.04. 62
were growing time once ripened to my will. 2.04. 99
mean time, in signal of my love to thee, 2.04.121
which in the time of henry nam'd the fift | was 3.01.195
his days may finish ere that hapless time. 3.01.200
defer no time, delays have dangerous ends, 3.02. 33
grace may starve, perhaps, before that time. 3.02. 48
to my determin'd time thou gav'st new date. 4.06. 9
now the time is come | that france must vail her 5.03. 24
now cursed be the time | of thy nativity! 5.04. 26
then, york, be still awhile, till time do serve. 2H6 1.01.248
next time i'll keep my dreams unto myself, | and 1.02. 53
look to't in time, | she'll hamper thee, and 1.03.144
last time, i danc'd attendance on his will 1.03.171
the time of night when troy was set on fire, 1.04. 17
the time when screech–owls cry and ban–dogs howl 1.04. 18
that time best fits the work we have in hand. 1.04. 20
and many time and oft | myself have heard a 2.01. 91
we know the time since he was mild and affable, 3.01. 9
when every one will give the time of day, | he 3.01. 14
which time will bring to light in smooth duke 3.01. 65
to keep, until your further time of trial. 3.01.138
over whom, in time to come, i hope to reign, 4.02.130
(in whose time boys went to span–counter for 4.02.157 P
for many a time, but for a sallet, my brain–pan 4.10. 11 P
and many a time, when i have been dry and 4.10. 12 P
of one or both of us the time is come. 5.02. 13
forgets | aged contusions and all brush of time, 5.03. 3
'tis not enough our foes are this time fled, 5.03. 21
and creep into it far before thy time? 3H6 1.01.237
and in thy thought o'errun my former time; 1.04. 45
whilest we breathe, take time to do him dead. 1.04.108
but in this troublous time what's to be done? 2.01.159
what time the shepherd, blowing of his nails, 2.05. 3
which in the time of death he gave our father. 2.06. 67
and, for the time shall not seem tedious, | i'll 3.01. 9
and come some other time to know our mind. 3.02. 17
to cross me from the golden time i look for! 3.02.127
heav'ns are just, and time suppresseth wrongs. 3.03. 77
a silly time | to make prescription for a 3.03. 93
brother, the time and case requireth haste, 4.05. 18
but wherefore stay we? 'tis no time to talk. 4.05. 24
likely in time to bless a regal throne. 4.06. 74
shut | but in the night or in the time of war. 4.07. 36
to help king edward in his time of storm, | as 4.07. 43
come, warwick, take the time, kneel down, kneel 5.01. 48
if she have time to breathe, be well assur'd 5.03. 16
the night–crow cried, aboding luckless time; 5.06. 45
and now what rests but that we spend the time 5.07. 42
sent before my time | into this breathing world, R3 1.01. 20
why, i, in this weak piping time of peace, 1.01. 24
peace, | have no delight to pass away the time, 1.01. 25
mean time, this deep disgrace in brotherhood 1.01.111
mean time, have patience. 1.01.116
good time of day unto my gracious lord! 1.01.122
in that sad time | my manly eyes did scorn an 1.02.163
good time of day unto your royal grace! 1.03. 18
mean time, god grants that i have need of you. 1.03. 76
'tis time to speak, my pains are quite forgot. 1.03.116
in all which time you and your husband grey 1.03.126
days — | so full of dismal terror was the time. 1.04. 7
had you such leisure in the time of death | to 1.04. 34
and in good time, | here comes sir richard 2.01. 45
and, princely peers, a happy time of day! 2.01. 48
and in good time, here comes the sweating lord. 3.01. 24
now in good time, here comes the duke of york. 3.01. 95
is all things ready for the royal time? 3.04. 4
but you, my honorable lords, may name the time, 3.04. 18
in happy time, here comes the duke himself. 3.04. 21
i prophesy the fearfull'st time to thee | that 3.04.104
offices | at any time to grace my stratagems. 3.05. 11
there, at your meet'st /advantage of the time, 3.05. 74
france, | and, by true computation of the time, 3.05. 89
have any time recourse unto the princes. 3.05.109
which, mellow'd by the stealing hours of time, 3.07.168
graces both | a happy and a joyful time of day! 4.01. 6
and in good time, here the lieutenant comes. 4.01. 12
within so small a time, my woman's heart 4.01. 78
mean time, but think how i may do thee good, 4.03. 33
thou didst prophesy the time would come | that i 4.04. 79
about, | and left thee but a very prey to time, 4.04.106
the time to come. 4.04.387
that thou hast wronged in the time o'erpast; 4.04.388
myself have many tears to wash | hereafter time, 4.04.390
hereafter time, for time past wrong'd by thee. 4.04.390
swear not by time to come, for that thou hast 4.04.395
where and what time your majesty shall please. 4.04.489
this is the day which, in king edward's time, 5.01. 13
much about cock–shut time, from troop to troop 5.03. 70
with best advantage will deceive the time, | and 5.03. 92
the leisure and the fearful time | cuts off the 5.03. 97
why, then 'tis time to arm and give direction. 5.03.236
the leisure and enforcement of the time 5.03.238
enrich the time to come with smooth–fac'd peace, 5.05. 33
all the whole time | i was my chamber's prisoner H8 1.01. 12
men might say | till this time pomp was single, 1.01. 15
hast thou heard him | at any time speak aught? 1.02.146
i remember | of such a time, being my sworn 1.02.191
'tis time to give 'em physic, their diseases 1.03. 36
beaten | a long time out of play, may bring his 1.03. 45
longer than i have time to tell his years; 2.01. 91
and when old time shall lead him to his end, 2.01. 93
you'll find a most unfit time to disturb him. 2.02. 60
by this time | i know your back will bear a 2.03. 98
you may then spare that time. 2.04. 5
in the course | and process of this time, you 2.04. 38
i will be bold with time and your attention: 2.04.169
let me have time and counsel for my cause. 3.01. 79
if you omit | the offer of this time, i cannot 3.02. 4
to him (though now the time | gives way to us) i 3.02. 15
you have scarce time | to steal from spiritual 3.02.139
sir, | for holy offices i have a time; 3.02.144
a time | to think upon the part of business 3.02.144
no doubt | in time will find their fit rewards. 3.02.245
but that time offer'd sorrow, | this, general 4.01. 6
like rams | in the old time of war, would shake 4.01. 78
that gentle physic given in time had cur'd me; 4.02.122
that it may find | good time, and live; 5.01. 22
come, lords, we trifle time away; 5.02.212
blessings, | which time shall bring to ripeness. 5.04. 20
are like to hear | for this play at this time, ep 9
and so i'll tell her the next time i see her. TRO 1.01. 82 P
the gods are above, time must friend or end. 1.02. 77 P
be you my time to bring it to some shape. 1.03.313
as honor, loss of time, travail, expense, 2.02. 4
foes, | and fame in time to come canonize us, 2.02.202
for this time will i take my leave, my lord. 3.02.139
when time is old /and hath forgot itself, | when 3.02.185
th' advantage of the time prompts me aloud | to 3.03. 2
fortunes, sequest'ring from me all | that time, 3.03. 9
time hath, my lord, a wallet at his back, 3.03.145
for time is like a fashionable host | that 3.03.165
subjects all | to envious and calumniating time. 3.03.174
than an effeminate man | in time of action. 3.03.219
the bitter disposition of the time | will have 4.01. 49
time, force, and death, | do to this body what 4.02.101
justles roughly by | all time of pause, rudely 4.04. 35
injurious time now with a robber's haste | crams 4.04. 42
appointment fresh and fair, | anticipating time. 4.05. 2
that hast so long walk'd hand in hand with time. 4.05.203
i have seen the time. 4.05.210

all, | and that old common arbitrator, time, 4.05.225
i will the second time, | as i would buy thee, 4.05.237
place is dangerous, | the time right deadly. 5.02. 39
and at that time bequeath you my diseases. 5.10. 56
there was a time when all the body's members COR 1.01. 96
it will in time | win upon power, and throw 1.01.219
will the time serve to tell? 1.06. 46
and from this time, | for what he did before 1.09. 62
dries, 'tis time | it should be look'd to. 1.09. 93
in which time i will make a lip at the physician 2.01.115 P
he comes the third time home with the oaken 2.01.125 P
and 'twas time for him too, i'll warrant him 2.01.129 P
at some time when his soaring insolence | shall 2.01.254
teach the people — which time shall not want, 2.01.255
and carry with us ears and eyes for th' time, 2.01.269
and is content | to spend the time to end it. 2.02.129
the dust on antique time would lie unswept, 2.03.119
ready, when time shall prompt them, to make road 3.01. 5
which will in time | break ope the locks a' th' 3.01.137
one time will owe another. 3.01.241
to no further harm | than so much loss of time. 3.01.283
the violent fit a' th' time craves it as physic 3.02. 33
and when such time they have begun to cry, | let 3.03. 19
from time to time | envied against the people, 3.03. 94
from time to time | envied against the people, 3.03. 94
so if the time thrust forth | a cause for thy 4.01. 40
the fittest time to corrupt a man's wife is when 4.03. 32 P
we stood to't in good time. is this menenius? 4.06. 10
this is a happier and more comely time | than 4.06. 27
lie in th' interpretation of the time, | and 4.07. 50
yet one time he did call me by my name. 5.01. 9
to infringe my vow | in the same time 'tis made? 5.03. 21
which by th' interpretation of full time | may 5.03. 69
this boy, to keep your name | living to time. 5.03.127
that so short a time can alter the condition of 5.04. 9 P
'tis the first time that ever | i was forc'd to 5.06.104
they told me, here, at dead time of the night, TIT 2.03. 99
to make us wonder'd at in time to come. 3.01.135
now is a time to storm, why art thou still? 3.01.263
what time i threw the people's suffrages | on 4.03. 19
we may, | till time beget some careful remedy. 4.03. 30
so that perforce you must needs stay a time. 4.03. 42
even in the time | when it should move ye to 5.03. 91
many a time he danc'd thee on his knee, | sung 5.03.162
for this time all the rest depart away. ROM 1.01. 98
in good time! 1.02. 44 P
and since that time it is aleven years, | for 1.03. 35
time out a' mind the fairies' coachmakers. 1.04. 61
marry, 'tis time. 1.05. 85
but passion lends them power, time means, to 2.pr. 13
where and what time thou wilt perform the rite, 2.02.146
he fights as you sing prick–song, keeps time, 2.04. 21 P
where thou shalt live till we can find a time 3.03.150
and he shall signify from time to time | every 3.03.170
and he shall signify from time to time | every 3.03.170
that we have had no time to move our daughter. 3.04. 2
and joy comes well in such a needy time. 3.05.105
madam, in happy time, what day is that? 3.05.111
on thursday, sir? the time is very short. 4.01. 1
my lord, we must entreat the time alone. 4.01. 40
therefore, out of thy long–experienc'd time, 4.01. 60
in the mean time, against thou shalt awake, 4.01.113
we shall be much unfurnish'd for this time. 4.02. 10
no, not till thursday, there is time enough. 4.02. 36
i wake before the time that romeo | come to 4.03. 31
ay, you have been a mouse–hunt in your time, 4.04. 11
o woeful time! 4.05. 30
most miserable hour that e'er time saw | in 4.05. 44
uncomfortable time, why cam'st thou now | to 4.05. 60
not a dump we, 'tis no time to play now. 4.05.109 P
the time and my intents are savage–wild, | more 5.03. 37
mean time forbear, | and let mischance be slave 5.03.220
as the time and place | doth make against me, of 5.03.224
mean time i writ to romeo, | that he should 5.03.246
being the time the potion's force should cease. 5.03.249
some minute ere the time | of her awakening, 5.03.257
life | be sacrific'd some hour before his time, 5.03.268
we'll share a bounteous time | in different TIM 1.01.254
what time a' day is't, apemantus? 1.01.256
time to be honest. 1.01.257
that time serves still. 1.01.258
why then another time i'll hear thee. 1.02.178
the time is unagreeable to this business. 2.02. 40
you make me marvel wherefore ere this time | had 2.02.124
you hear now (too late), yet now's a time: 2.02.143
my occasions have found time to use 'em toward a 2.02.192 P
many a time and often i ha' din'd with him, and 3.01. 23 P
and canst use the time well, if the time use 3.01. 36 P
use the time well, if the time use thee well. 3.01. 37 P
to me) that this is no time to lend money, 3.01. 42 P
but in the mean time he wants less, my lord. 3.02. 39
i to disfurnish myself against such a good time, 3.02. 45 P
it pleases time and fortune to lie heavy | upon 3.05. 10
though his right arm might purchase his own time 3.05. 76
the good time of day to you, sir. 3.06. 1 P
it does; but time will — and so — 3.06. 63 P
i see them now, then was a blessed time. 4.03. 79
in sufferance, time | hath made thee hard in't. 4.03.268
there is no time so miserable but a man may be 4.03.457 P
nothing at this time but my visitation; 5.01. 18
promising is the very air o' th' time; 5.01. 22
'twas time and griefs | that fram'd him thus. 5.01.122
time, with his fairer hand, | offering the 5.01.123
till now you have gone on and fill'd the time 5.04. 3
now the time is flush, | when crouching marrow 5.04. 8
many a time and oft | have you climb'd up to JC 1.01. 37
men at some time are masters of their fates; 1.02.139
and find a time | both meet to hear and answer 1.02.169
under these hard conditions as this time | is 1.02.174
put it by thrice, every time gentler than other; 1.02.230 P
and then he offer'd it the third time; 1.02.243 P
he put it the third time by; 1.02.243 P
for this time i will leave you; 1.02.303
indeed, it is a strange–disposed time; 1.03. 33
'tis time to part. 2.01.193
o, what a time have you chose out, brave caius, 2.01.314
and you are come in very happy time | to bear my 2.02. 60
say, | "break up the senate till another time, 2.02. 98
trebonius knows his time; 3.01. 25
that we shall die we know, 'tis but the time, 3.01. 99
that have abridg'd | his time of fearing death. 3.01.105
remember | the first time ever caesar put it on; 3.02.171
in such a time as this it is not meet | that 4.03. 7
i'll know his humor, when he knows his time. 4.03.136
i know young bloods look for a time of rest. 4.03.262
the very last time we shall speak together: 5.01. 98
fall, so to prevent | the time of life — arming 5.01.105
time is come round, | and where i did begin, 5.03. 23
i shall find time, cassius; 5.03.103
i shall find time. 5.03.103
fellow, wilt thou bestow thy time with me? 5.05. 61
if you can look into the seeds of time, | and MAC 1.03. 58
time and the hour runs through the roughest day. 1.03.147
and at more time, | the interim having weigh'd 1.03.153
referr'd me to the coming on of time with 'hail, 1.05. 9 P
to beguile the time, | look like the time; 1.05. 63
to beguile the time, | look like the time; 1.05. 64
but here, upon this bank and /shoal of time, 1.07. 6
from this time | such i account thy love. 1.07. 38
nor time, nor place, | did then adhere, and yet 1.07. 51
away, and mock the time with fairest show: 1.07. 81
that business, | if you would grant the time. 2.01. 24
and take the present horror from the time, 2.01. 59
come in time! 2.03. 5 P
events | new hatch'd to th' woeful time. 2.03. 59
this chance, | i had liv'd a blessed time; 2.03. 92
within the volume of which time i have seen 2.04. 2
lord, as will fill up the time | 'twixt this and 3.01. 24
ay, my good lord. our time does call upon 's. 3.01. 36
let every man be master of his time | till seven 3.01. 40
acquaint you with the perfect spy o' th' time, 3.01.129
but in best time | we will require her welcome. 3.04. 5
hath nature that in time will venom breed, | no 3.04. 29
blood hath been shed ere now, i' th' olden time, 3.04. 74
only it spoils the pleasure of the time. 3.04. 97
"you'll rue the time | that clogs me with this 3.06. 42
harpier cries, "'tis time, 'tis time." 4.01. 3
harpier cries, "'tis time, 'tis time." 4.01. 3
pay his breath | to time and mortal custom. 4.01.100
time, thou anticipat'st my dread exploits: 4.01.144
as i shall find the time to friend, i will. 4.03. 10
and yet seem cold, the time you may so hoodwink. 4.03. 72
at no time broke my faith, would not betray 4.03.128
now is the time of help; 4.03.186
what, at any time, have you heard her say? 5.01. 12 P
one — two — why then 'tis time to do't. 5.01. 36 P
the time approaches | that will with due 5.04. 16
the time has been, my senses would have cool'd 5.05. 10
there would have been a time for such a word. 5.05. 18
to day, | to the last syllable of recorded time; 5.05. 21
and live to be the show and gaze o' th' time! 5.08. 24
the time is free. 5.09. 21
we shall not spend a large expense of time 5.09. 26
which would be planted newly with the time, | as 5.09. 31
we will perform in measure, time, and place. 5.09. 39
what art thou that usurp'st this time of night, HAM 1.01. 46
so hallowed, and so gracious is that time. 1.01.164
now for ourself, and for this time of meeting, 1.02. 26
take thy fair hour, laertes, time be thine, 1.02. 62
where, as they had delivered, both in time, 1.02.209
the time invests you, go, your servants tend. 1.03. 83
very oft of late | given private time to you, 1.03. 92
from this time | be something scanter of your 1.03.120
would not, in plain terms, from this time forth, 1.03.132
the time is out of joint — o cursed spite, 1.05.188
your rest here in our court | some little time, 2.02. 14
will | as to expend your time with us a while 2.02. 23
and at our more considered time we'll read, 2.02. 81
mean time, we thank you for your well–took labor 2.02. 83
why day is day, night night, and time is time, 2.02. 88
why day is day, night night, and time is time, 2.02. 88
were nothing but to waste night, day, and time; 2.02. 89
as they fell out by time, by means, and place, 2.02.127
hath there been such a time — i would fain know 2.02.153
at such a time i'll loose my daughter to him. 2.02.162
happily he is the second time come to them, for 2.02.384 P
the abstract and brief chronicles of the time. 2.02.525 P
for who would bear the whips and scorns of time, 3.01. 69
a paradox, but now the time gives it proof. 3.01.114 P
to give them shape, or time to act them in. 3.01.126 P
like sweet bells jangled, out of time and harsh; 3.01.158
age and body of the time his form and pressure. 3.02. 24 P
though in the mean time some necessary question 3.02. 42 P
a second time i kill my husband dead, | when 3.02.184
black, hands apt, drugs fit, and time agreeing, 3.02.255
'tis now the very witching time of night, | when 3.02.388
that, laps'd in time and passion, lets go by 3.04.107
my pulse, as yours, doth temperately keep time, 3.04.140
if his chief good and market of his time | be 4.04. 34
o, from this time forth, | my thoughts be bloody 4.04. 65
father, | but that i know love is begun by time, 4.07.111
time qualifies the spark and fire of it. 4.07.113
weigh what convenience both of time and means 4.07.149
which time she chaunted snatches of old lauds, 4.07.177
to contract — o — the time for — a — my 5.01. 63
fellow might be in 's time a great buyer of land 5.01.104 P
to sudden death, | not shriving time allow'd. 5.02. 47
it is the breathing time of day with me. 5.02.174 P
on, only got the tune of the time and, out of an 5.02.190 P
with laertes, or that you will take longer time. 5.02.199 P
in happy time. 5.02.205 P
but /till that time | i do receive your offer'd 5.02.250
had i but time — as this fell sergeant, death, 5.02.336
mean time we shall express our darker purpose. LR 1.01. 36
should in this trice of time | commit a thing so 1.01.216
time shall unfold what plighted cunning hides, 1.01.280
and soundest of his time hath been but rash; 1.01.295 P
we have seen the best of our time. 1.02.112 P
until some little time hath qualified the heat 1.02.161 P
have thee beaten for being old before thy time. 1.05. 42 P
you may do then in time. fare you well, sir. 2.01. 13 P
i have seen better faces in my time | than 2.02. 93
some time i shall sleep out, the rest i'll 2.02.156
and shall find time | from this enormous state 2.02.168
some other time for that. 2.04.133
and in good time you gave it. 2.04.250
then comes the time, who lives to see't, | that 3.02. 93
merlin shall make, for i live before his time. 3.02. 96 P
wolves had at thy gate howl'd that /dearn time, 3.07. 63
the first time that we smell the air | we wawl 4.06.179
not, time and place will be fruitfully offer'd. 4.06.264 P
and in the mature time | with this ungracious 4.06.275
you know me not | till time and i think meet. 4.07. 11
when time shall serve, let but the herald cry, 5.01. 48
we will greet the time. 5.01. 54
know thou this, that men | are as the time is: 5.03. 31
and more, much more, the time will bring it out. 5.03.164
the time will not allow the compliment | which 5.03.234
nay, send in time. 5.03.248
the weight of this sad time we must obey, 5.03.324
he, in good time, must his lieutenant be, | and OTH 1.01. 32
wears out his time, much like his master's ass, 1.01. 47
and what's to come of my despised time | is 1.01.161
till fit time | of law and course of direct 1.02. 85
in this time of the night? 1.02. 94
we must obey the time. 1.03.300
many events in the womb of time which will be 1.03.370 P
if i would time expend with such /a snipe | but 1.03.385
after some time, to abuse othello's /ear | that 1.03.395
which the time shall more favorably minister. 2.01.269 P
him in, | on some odd time of his infirmity, 2.03.127
as the time, the place, and the condition of 2.03.300 P
or any man living, may be drunk at a time, man. 2.03.314 P
witchcraft, | and wit depends on dilatory time. 2.03.373
/do, /good /my /friend. in happy time, iago. 3.01. 30
i will bestow you where you shall have time | to 3.01. 54
not now, sweet desdemon, some other time. 3.03. 55
i prithee name the time, but let it not | exceed 3.03. 62
that came a–wooing with you, and so many a time, 3.03. 71
leave it to time. 3.03.245
in the mean time, | let me be thought too busy 3.03.252
a man that all his time | hath founded his good 3.04. 93
but i shall, in a more continuate time, | strike 3.04.178
take it, and do't, and leave me for this time. 3.04.191
that's not amiss, | but yet keep time in all. 4.01. 92
me | the fixed figure for the time of scorn | to 4.02. 54
what time? 4.02.138
from this time forth i never will speak word. 5.02.304
the time, the place, the torture, o, enforce it! 5.02.369
not confound the time with conference harsh; ANT 1.01. 45
in time we hate that which we often fear. 1.03. 12
you sued staying, | then was the time for words; 1.03. 34
the strong necessity of time commands | our 1.03. 42
but to confound such time | that drums him from 1.04. 28
'tis time we twain | did show ourselves i' th' 1.04. 73
land i can be able | to front this present time. 1.04. 79
what you shall know mean time | of stirs abroad, 1.04. 81
that i might sleep out this great gap of time 1.05. 5
pinches black, | and wrinkled deep in time? 1.05. 29
like to the time o' th' year between the 1.05. 51
'tis not a time | for private stomaching. 2.02. 8
every time | serves for the matter that is then 2.02. 9
you shall have time to wrangle in when you have 2.02.105 P
time calls upon 's. 2.02.157
all which time | before the gods my knee shall 2.03. 2
that time? 2.05. 18
in mine ears, | that long time have been barren. 2.05. 25
take your time. 2.06. 23
be a child o' th' time. 2.07.100
the time shall not | outgo my thinking on you. 3.02. 60
the mean time, lady, | i'll raise the 3.04. 25
be you not troubled with the time, which drives 3.06. 82
his heart, take from his brain, from 's time, 3.07. 11
to try thy eloquence, now 'tis time; 3.12. 26
and at this time most easy 'tis to do't: 3.13.144
i must stay his time. 3.13.155
the next time i do fight, | i'll make death love 3.13.191
mean time | laugh at his challenge. 4.01. 5
the time of universal peace is near. 4.06. 4
do't, the time is come. 4.14. 67
and time is at his period. 4.14.107
he shall in time be ready. 5.01. 72
who in the wars o' th' time | died with their CYM 1.01. 35
puts to him all the learnings that his time 1.01. 43
for this time leave me. 1.01.178
this gentleman at that time vouching (and upon 1.04. 58 P
doctor, your service for this time is ended, 1.05. 30
more than the locking up the spirits a time, 1.05. 41
dost thou think in time | she will not quench, 1.05. 46
that all the plagues of hell should at one time 1.06.111
i have outstood my time, which is material | to 1.06.207
time, time! 2.02. 51
time, time! 2.02. 51
some more time | must wear the print of his 2.03. 42
but abide the change of time, | quake in the 2.04. 4
yet my mother seem'd | the dian of that time. 2.05. 7
kingdom is stronger than it was at that time; 3.01. 35 P
and for the gap | that we shall make in time, 3.02. 63
to heaven than in all | the fore–end of my time. 3.03. 73
false aeneas, | were in his time thought false; 3.04. 59
the time inviting thee? 3.04.105
but to win time | to lose so bad employment, in 3.04.109
we'll even | all that good time will give us. 3.04.182
but from this time forth | i wear it as your 3.05. 13
the cure whereof, my lord, | 'tis time must do. 3.05. 38
she said upon a time (the bitterness of it i now 3.05.133 P
will tie you to the numbers and the time | of 3.07. 15
beyond him in the advantage of the time, above 4.01. 12 P
we'll leave you for this time, go in, and rest. 4.02. 43
but time hath nothing blurr'd those lines of 4.02.104
i wish my brother make good time with him, | you 4.02.108
and in time | may make some stronger head, the 4.02.138
to have turn'd my leaping time into a crutch, 4.02.200
and in a time | when fearful wars point at me; 4.03. 6
the time is troublesome. 4.03. 21
withdraw, | and meet the time as it seeks us. 4.03. 33
all other doubts, by time let them be clear'd, 4.03. 45
a doubt | in such a time nothing becoming you, 4.04. 15
that they will waste their time upon our note, 4.04. 20
the time seems long, their blood thinks scorn 4.04. 53
'tis now the time | to ask of whence you are. 5.05. 15
in which time she purpos'd, | by watching, 5.05. 52
and, in time | (when she had fitted you with her 5.05. 54
is living, let the time run on | to good or bad. 5.05.128

upon a time — unhappy was the clock | that 5.05.153
but in short time | all offices of nature should 5.05.256
but nor the time nor place | will serve our long 5.05.391
but being play'd upon before your time, | hell PER 1.01. 84
if by which time our secret be undone, | this 1.01.117
'tis time to fear when tyrants seems to kiss. 1.02. 79
safe, | that time of both this truth shall ne'er 1.02.123
and waste the time, which looks for other revels 2.03. 93
if in which time expir'd he not return, | i 2.04. 47
and time that is so briefly spent | with your 3.ch. 12
nor have i time | to give thee hallow'd to thy 3.01. 58
such strong renown as time shall never — 3.02. 48
even on my /eaning time, but whether there 3.04. 6
only i carried winged time | post /on the lame 4.ch. 47
and held a mawkin | not worth the time of day. 4.03. 35
thus time we waste, and long leagues make short; 4.04. 1
advanc'd in time to great and high estate. 4.04. 16
kings, | but time hath rooted out my parentage, 5.01. 92
be buried | a second time within these arms. 5.03. 44
play do not keep | a little dull time from us, TNK pr 31
you were that time fair; 1.01. 62
o grief and time, | fearful consumers, you will 1.01. 69
but touch the ground for us no longer time 1.01. 97
can, fitt'st time | for best solicitation? 1.01.169
once with a time when i enjoy'd a playfellow; 1.03. 50
behold who err, | and in their time chastise. 1.04. 6
i' th' mean time, look tenderly to the two 2.01. 19 P
garlands, | ere they have time to wish 'em ours. 2.02. 17
world 'tis but a gaudy shadow | that old time, 2.02.104
well, sir, | take your own time. come, boys. 2.03. 69
and what | you want at any time, let me but know 2.05. 55
'twill disturb us, | we shall have time enough. 3.03. 16
there was a time | when young men went a–hunting 3.03. 39
which you'll hear of | at better time. 4.01. 30
is more at some time of the moon than at other 4.03. 1 P
time comes on. 5.01.136
'fore yourself | by some small start of time. 5.03. 38
long time his eye | will dwell upon his object; 5.03. 48
an offense, | which crav'd that very time. 5.03. 64
let's go off, | and bear us like the time. 5.04.137
make use of time, let not advantage slip, VEN 129
rot, and consume themselves in little time. 132
the time is spent, her object will away, | and 255
by the rights of time thou needs must have, | if 759
"wonder of time," quoth she, "this is my spite, 1133
now stole upon the time the dead of night, LUC 162
"so, so," quoth he, "these lets attend the time, 330
make war against proportion'd course of time; 774
thou grant'st no time for charitable deeds: 908
"misshapen time, copesmate of ugly night, 925
o, hear me then, injurious, shifting time! 930
to stamp the seal of time in aged things, | to 941
"let him have time to tear his curled hair, 981
let him have time against himself to rave, | let 982
let him have time of time's help to despair, 983
let him have time to live a loathed slave, | let 984
let him have time a beggar's orts to crave, 985
and time to see one that by alms doth live 986
"let him have time to see his friends his foes, 988
let him have time to mark how slow time goes 990
let him have time to mark how slow time goes 990
to mark how slow time goes | in time of sorrow, 991
short | his time of folly and his time of sport; 992
short | his time of folly and his time of sport; 992
have time to wail th' abusing of his time. 994
have time to wail th' abusing of his time. 994
"o time, thou tutor both to good and bad, 995
at time, at tarquin, and uncheerful night, | in 1024
likes dumps when time is kept with tears. 1127
the weary time she cannot entertain, | for now 1361
and time doth weary time with her complaining; 1570
and time doth weary time with her complaining; 1570
short time seems long in sorrow's sharp 1573
and they that watch see time how slow it creeps. 1575
which all this time hath overslipp'd her thought 1576
shows me a bare–bon'd death by time outworn. 1761
"o time, cease thou thy course and last no 1765
when time shall serve, be thou not slack | to PP 18.23
then, | when time with age shall them attaint. 18.46
die, | but as the riper should by time decease, SON 1. 3
now is the time that face should form another, 3. 2
despite of wrinkles, this thy golden time. 3.12
for never–resting time leads summer on | to 5. 5
when i do count the clock that tells the time, 12. 1
that thou among the wastes of time must go, 12.10
where wasteful time debateth with decay | to 15.11
and all in war with time for love of you, | as 15.13
way | make war upon this bloody tyrant, time? 16. 2
who will believe my verse in time to come | if 17. 1
but were some child of yours alive that time, 17.13
when in eternal lines to time thou grow'st. 18.12
devouring time, blunt thou the lion's paws, 19. 1
and do what e'er thou wilt, swift–footed time, 19. 6
yet do thy worst, old time: 19.13
compare them with the bett'ring of the time, 32. 5
to entertain the time with thoughts of love, 39.11
which time and thoughts so sweetly dost deceive, 39.12
another time mine eye is my heart's guest, | and 47. 7
against that time (if ever that time come) 49. 1
against that time (if ever that time come) 49. 1
against that time when thou shalt strangely pass 49. 5
against that time do i insconce me here | within 49. 9
so is the time that keeps you as my chest, | or 52. 9
unswept stone, besmear'd with sluttish time. 55. 4
i have no precious time at all to spend, | nor 57. 3
that you yourself may privilege your time | to 58.10
and time that gave doth now his gift confound. 60. 8
time doth transfix the flourish set on youth, 60. 9
for such a time do i now fortify | against 63. 9
that time will come and take my love away. 64.12
nor gates of steel so strong, but time decays? 65. 8
/thy worth the greater, being woo'd of time, 70. 6
that time of year thou mayst in me behold | when 73. 1
why with the time do i not glance aside | to 76. 3
and yet this time remov'd was summer's time, 97. 5
and yet this time remov'd was summer's time, 97. 5
redeem | in gentle numbers time so idly spent; 100. 6
survey, | if time have any wrinkle graven there; 100.10
give my love fame faster than time wastes life, 100.13
when in the chronicle of wasted time | i see 106. 1
praises are but prophecies | of this our time, 106.10
now with the drops of this most balmy time | my 107. 9
where time and outward form would show it dead. 108.14
just to the time, not with the time exchang'd, 109. 7
just to the time, not with the time exchang'd, 109. 7
but reckoning time, whose million'd accidents 115. 5
and given to time your own dear–purchas'd right; 117. 6
as i by yours, y' have pass'd a hell of time, 120. 6
time, thou shalt not boast that i do change: 123. 1
whereto th' inviting time our fashion calls; 124. 8
to this i witness call the fools of time, 124.13
may time disgrace and wretched /minutes kill. 126. 8
time had not scythed all that youth begun, | nor LC 12

TIME–BEGUILING 1 FR 0.0001 REL FR 1 V 0 P
being wasted in such time–beguiling sport." VEN 24

TIME–BETTERING 1 FR 0.0001 REL FR 1 V 0 P
some fresher stamp of the time–bettering days. SON 82. 8

TIME–BEWASTED 1 FR 0.0001 REL FR 1 V 0 P
my oil–dried lamp and time–bewasted light R2 1.03.221

TIME–HONORED 1 FR 0.0001 REL FR 1 V 0 P
old john of gaunt, time–honored lancaster, R2 1.01. 1

TIMELESS 9 FR 0.0010 REL FR 9 V 0 P
being unprevented, to your timeless grave. TGV 3.01. 21
the bloody office of his timeless end. R2 4.01. 5
out, | must i behold thy timeless cruel death? 1H6 5.04. 5
as guilty of duke humphrey's timeless death. 2H6 3.02.187
orphans for their parents' timeless death — 3H6 5.06. 42
is not the causer of the timeless deaths | of R3 1.02.117
writ, | the complot of this timeless tragedy, TIT 2.03.265
poison, i see, hath been his timeless end. ROM 5.03.162
did instigate | his all too timeless speed, if LUC 44

TIMELIER 1 FR 0.0001 REL FR 1 V 0 P
that call'd me timelier than my purpose hither; ANT 2.06. 51

TIMELY 5 FR 0.0005 REL FR 5 V 0 P
my life, | and happy were i in my timely death, ERR 1.01.138
he did command me to call timely on him, | i MAC 2.03. 46
lated traveller apace | to gain the timely inn, 3.03. 7
either are past remedies, or, timely knowing, CYM 1.06. 97
bright orient pearl, alack, too timely shaded! PP 10. 3

TIMELY–PARTED 1 FR 0.0001 REL FR 1 V 0 P
oft have i seen a timely–parted ghost, | of ashy 2H6 3.02.161

TIME–PLEASER 1 FR 0.0001 REL FR 0 V 1 P
or any thing constantly but a time–pleaser, an TN 2.03.148 P

TIME–PLEASERS 1 FR 0.0001 REL FR 1 V 0 P
people, call'd them | time–pleasers, flatterers, COR 3.01. 45

TIME'S 38 FR 0.0043 REL FR 37 V 1 P
and careful hours with time's deformed hand ERR 5.01.299
o time's extremity, | hast thou so crack'd and 5.01.308
time's pace is so hard that it seems the length AYL 3.02.316 P
but let time's news | be known when 'tis brought WT 4.01. 26
that the time's enemies may not have this | to JN 4.02. 61
for the present time's so sick, | that present 5.01. 14
the slaves of life, and life, time's fool, | and 1H4 5.04. 81
we are time's subjects, and time bids be gone. 2H4 1.03.110
foretelling this same time's condition | and the 3.01. 78
and the old folk (time's doting chronicles) 4.04.126
of fortune, trencher–friends, time's flies, TIM 3.06. 96
how rarely does it meet with this time's guise, 4.03.465
the sufferance of our souls, the time's abuse — JC 2.01.115
'tis the time's plague, when madmen lead the LR 4.01. 46
and the time's state | made friends of them, ANT 1.02. 91
with news the time's with labor, and throes 3.07. 80
your time's expir'd, | either expound now, or PER 1.01. 89
whereby i see that time's the king of men, 2.03. 45
time's office is to fine the hate of foes, | to LUC 936
"time's glory is to calm contending kings, | to 939
let him have time of time's help to despair, 983
in her the painter had anatomiz'd | time's ruin, 1451
and nothing 'gainst time's scythe can make SON 12.13
that life repair | which this time's pencil, or 16.10
but when in thee time's furrows i behold, | then 22. 3
and with old woes new wail my dear time's waste; 30. 4
i must attend time's leisure with my moan, 44.12
with time's injurious hand crush'd and o'erworn, 63. 2
when i have seen by time's fell hand defaced 64. 1
shall time's best jewel from time's chest lie 65.10
time's best jewel from time's chest lie hid? 65.10
know | time's thievish progress to eternity. 77. 8
and make time's spoils despised every where. 100.12
alas, why, fearing of time's tyranny, | might i 115. 9
love's not time's fool, though rosy lips and 116. 9
as subject to time's love, or to time's hate, 124. 3
as subject to time's love, or to time's hate, 124. 3
in thy power | dost hold time's fickle glass, 126. 2

/TIMES 3 FR 0.0003 REL FR 3 V 0 P
/what /trust /is /in /these /times? 2H4 1.03.100
/construe /the /times /to /their /necessities, 4.01.102
/sad /stories /chanced /in /the /times /of /old. TIT 3.02. 83

TIMES 219 FR 0.0247 REL FR 181 V 38 P
ten times more gentle than her father's crabbed; TMP 3.01. 8
and yet a thousand times it answers "no." TGV 1.03. 91
(please you command) a thousand times as much; 2.01.114
sir eglamour, a thousand times good morrow. 4.03. 6
for i have heard him say a thousand times | his 4.04.134
that i have wept a hundred several times. 4.04.145
i have seen sackerson loose twenty times, and WIV 1.01.295 P
in these times you stand on distance: 2.01.225 P
for the which she thanks you a thousand times — 2.02. 82 P
i was three or four times in the thought they 5.05.122 P
no? a dozen times at least. MM 1.02. 20 P
proclaim an enshield beauty ten times louder 2.04. 80
nay, call us ten times frail, | for we are soft 2.04.128
made in crimes, | making practice on the times, 3.02.274
drunk many times a day, if not many days 4.02.149 P
might in the times to come have ta'en revenge, 4.04. 30
nay, it is ten times strange. 5.01. 42
nay, it is ten times true, for truth is truth 5.01. 45
mercy to provide | for better times to come. 5.01.485
not once, nor twice, but twenty times you have. ERR 3.02.172
her mother hath many times told me so. ADO 1.01.105 P
for she'll be up twenty times a night, and there 2.03.131 P
bids me a thousand times good night — i tell 3.03.148 P
they have had | a thousand times in secret. 4.01. 94
three thousand times within this three years' LLL 1.01.150
and three times as much more — and yet nothing 3.01. 47 P
and wait the season, and observe the times, 5.02. 63
and three times thrice is nine. 5.02.488
i hope, sir, three times thrice, sir — 5.02.491
of thrice three times the value of this bond. MV 1.03.159
o, ten times faster venus' pigeons fly | to seal 2.06. 5
being ten times undervalued to tried gold? 2.07. 53
pick'd from the chaff and ruin of the times | to 2.09. 48
"the fire seven times tried this: 2.09. 63
seven times tried that judgment is, | that did 2.09. 64
o, these naughty times | puts bars between the 3.02. 18
the seeming truth which cunning times put on 3.02.100
you | i would be trebled twenty times myself, 3.02.153
a thousand times more fair, ten thousand times 3.02.154
times more fair, ten thousand times more rich, 3.02.154
flesh | than twenty times the value of the sum 3.02.287
gold | to pay the petty debt twenty times over. 3.02.307
many that have at times made moan to me; 3.03. 23
i will be bound to pay it ten times o'er, | on 4.01.211
thou art not for the fashion of these times, AYL 2.03. 59
you are a thousand times a properer man | than 3.05. 51
upon a lie seven times remov'd (bear your body 5.04. 68 P
i love her ten times more than e'er i did. SHR 2.01.161
i'll not be tied to hours nor 'pointed times, 3.01. 19
one girth six times piec'd, and a woman's 3.02. 60 P
hound, | but twenty times so much upon my wife. 5.02. 73
generally is at all times good must of necessity AWW 1.01. 7 P
by being once lost, may be ten times found; 1.01.131 P
a man | might be a copy to these younger times; 1.02. 46
or four and twenty times the pilot's glass 2.01.165
wonder that hath shot out in our latter times. 2.03. 8 P
love make your fortunes twenty times above | her 2.03. 82
mightily some other times we drown our gain in 4.03. 67 P
of these most brisk and giddy–paced times. TN 2.04. 6
thou hast said to me a thousand times | thou 5.01.267
i witness to | the times that brought them in; WT 4.01. 12
are germane to him (though remov'd fifty times) 4.04.774 P
which waits upon worn times, hath something 5.01.142
the times conspire with you, | for he that JN 3.04.146
a purity, | to the yet unbegotten sin of times; 4.03. 54
the purest treasure mortal times afford | is R2 1.01.177
change their moons and bring their times about, 1.03.220
if thou deniest it twenty times, thou liest, 4.01. 38
away, fond woman, were he twenty times my son, 5.02.101
and groans | show minutes, times, and hours; 5.05. 58
three times they breath'd and three times did 1H4 1.03.102
they breath'd and three times did they drink, 1.03.102
i am eight times thrust through the doublet, 2.04.166 P
three times hath henry bullingbrook made head 3.01. 63
little, dic'd not above seven times — a week, 3.03. 16 P
money that i borrow'd — three or four times, 3.03. 18 P
ten times more dishonorable ragged than an old 4.02. 30 P
of broached mischief to the unborn times? 5.01. 21
the times are wild, contention, like a horse 2H4 1.01. 9
won, | came not till now to dignify the times, 1.01. 22
had three times slain th' appearance of the king 1.01.128
in these costermongers' times that true valor is 1.02.169 P
for his divisions, as the times do brawl, | /are 1.03. 70
repent at idle times as thou mayst and so 2.02.129 P
put not you on the visage of the times, | and be 2.03. 3
and ten times better than the nine worthies. 2.04.220 P
and see the revolution of the times | make 3.01. 46
and other times to see | the beachy girdle of 3.01. 49
figuring the natures /of the times deceas'd, 3.01. 81
and suffer the condition of these times | to lay 4.01. 99
and rotten times that you shall look upon, 4.04. 60
and golden times, and happy news of price. 5.03. 96
carry them here and there, jumping o'er times, H5 pr 29
three or four times. 2.03. 19 P
pertain | by custom, and the ordinance of times, 2.04. 83
and nym had ten times more valor than this 4.04. 70 P
comets, importing change of times and states, 1H6 1.01. 2
that now our loss might be ten times so much? 2.01. 53
at all times will you have my power alike? 2.01. 55
patience, good lady, wizards know their times. 2H6 1.04. 15
being call'd | a hundred times and oft'ner, in 2.01. 88
and had i twenty times so many foes, | and each 2.04. 60
and each of them had twenty times their power, 2.04. 61
though suffolk dare him twenty thousand times. 3.02.206
your loving uncle, twenty times his worth, 3.02.268
loather a hundred times to part than die. 3.02.355
thus is poor suffolk ten times banished, | once 3.02.357
by the king, and three times thrice by thee. 3.02.358
well, he shall be beheaded for it ten times. 4.07. 24 P
three times to–day i holp him to his horse, 5.03. 8
him to his horse, | three times bestrid him; 5.03. 9
and it hath pleas'd him that three times to–day 5.03. 18
three times did richard make a lane to me, | and 3H6 1.04. 9
o, ten times more, than tigers of hyrcania. 1.04.155
when this is known, then to divide the times: 2.05. 30
o heavy times, begetting such events! 2.05. 63
o bloody times! 2.05. 73
mine ten times so much. 2.05.112
now welcome more, and ten times more belov'd, 5.01.103
and twenty times made pause to sob and weep, R3 1.02.161
england, | and cited up a thousand heavy times, 1.04. 14
three times to–day my foot–cloth horse did 3.04. 84
from the corruption of abusing times | unto a 3.07.199
and all the ruins of distressful times 4.04.318
of ten times double gain of happiness. 4.04.324
misus'd ere us'd, by times ill–us'd /o'erpast. 4.04.396
urge the necessity and state of times, | and be 4.04.416
my heart is ten times lighter than my looks. 5.03. 3
ten times more ugly | than ever they were fair. H8 1.02.117
i'll make ye know your times of business. 2.02. 71
wife, | at all times to your will conformable; 2.04. 24
nature does require | her times of preservation, 3.02.147
the times and titles now are alter'd strangely 4.02.112
times to repair our nature | with comforting 5.01. 3
repose, and not for us | to waste these times. 5.01. 5
fire–drake did i hit three times on the head, 5.03. 44 P
and three times was his nose discharg'd against 5.03. 45 P
nestor, | instructed by the antiquary times; TRO 2.03.251
when many times the captive grecian falls, 5.03. 40
and at all times | to undercrest your good COR 1.09. 71
five times, martius, | i have fought with thee; 1.10. 7
the prayers of priests nor times of sacrifice, 1.10. 21
my grained ash an hundred times hath broke, 4.05.108
thou hast beat me out | twelve several times, 4.05.122
five times he hath return'd | bleeding to rome, TIT 1.01. 33

and have a thousand times more cause than he 5.03. 51
how many thousand times hath these poor lips, 5.03.167
five times in that ere once in our /five wits. ROM 1.04. 47
a thousand times good night! 2.02.154
a thousand times the worse, to want thy light. 2.02.155
ay, a thousand times. peter! 2.04.214 P
which ten times faster glides than the sun's 2.05. 5
with twenty hundred thousand times more joy 3.03.153
these times of woe afford no times to woo. 3.04. 8
these times of woe afford no times to woo. 3.04. 8
for sweet discourses in our times to come. 3.05. 53
him with above compare | so many thousand times? 3.05.239
his days and times are past, | and my reliances TIM 2.01. 21
lord, | at many times i brought in my accompts, 2.02.133
strange times, that weep with laughing, not with 4.03.486
have fear'd false times when you did feast: 4.03.513
at all times alike | men are not still the same; 5.01.121
how i have thought of this, and of these times, JC 1.02.164
cowards die many times before their deaths, 2.02. 32
how many times shall caesar bleed in sport, 3.01.114
man | that ever lived in the tide of times. 3.01.257
appear'd to me | two several times by night; 5.05. 18
weary sev'nnights, nine times nine, | shall he MAC 1.03. 22
that it was he in the times past which held you 3.01. 76
but cruel are the times when we are traitors, 4.02. 18
that you, at such times seeing me, never shall, HAM 1.05.173
full thirty times hath phoebus' cart gone round 3.02.155
about the world have times twelve thirties been, 3.02.158
we shall obey, were she ten times our mother. 3.02.333 P
for in the fatness of these pursy times | virtue 3.04.153
tears seven times salt | burn out the sense and 4.05.155
he hath bore me on his back a thousand times. 5.01.186 P
woe | fall ten times /treble on that cursed head 5.01.247
makes the world bitter to the best of our times; LR 1.02. 47 P
nine or ten times | i had thought t' have yerk'd OTH 1.02. 4
upon the world for four times seven years, and 1.03.312 P
my wayward husband hath a hundred times | woo'd 3.03.292
more tedious than the dial eightscore times? 3.04.175
o, a thousand, a thousand times. 4.01.192 P
the act of shame | a thousand times committed. 5.02.212
more impediments | than twenty times your stop. 5.02.264
seen her die twenty times upon far poorer moment ANT 1.02.142 P
being barber'd ten times o'er, goes to the feast 2.02.224
o times! 2.05. 18
many times, madam. 2.05.108
when you have well deserv'd ten times as much 2.06. 77
he thinks, being twenty times of better fortune, 4.02. 3
with five times so much conversation, i should CYM 1.04.103 P
hath the king | five times redeem'd from death. 1.05. 63
many times | doth ill deserve by doing well; 3.03. 53
if you, born in those latter times, | when wit's PER 1.ch. 11
best, and wrastle, | that these times can allow. TNK 2.05. 4
your cousin | has ten times more offended, for i 3.06.181
seen it approv'd, how many times i know not, but 4.03. 97 P
o great corrector of enormous times, | shaker of 5.01. 62
twenty times had been far better, | for there 5.02. 7
a hundred times. 5.02.109
and the bloody times | could not have brought STM II.C 66
she cries, and twenty times, "woe, woe!" VEN 833
and twenty echoes twenty times cry so. 834
where herself herself beheld | a thousand times, 1130
and sung by children in succeeding times. LUC 525
through the length of times he stands disgraced; 718
he ten times pines that pines beholding food, 1115
three times with sighs she gives her sorrow fire 1604
thee, | or ten times happier be it ten for one; SON 6. 8
ten times thyself were happier than thou art, 6. 9
art, | if ten of thine ten times refigur'd thee, 6.10
if all were minded so, the times should cease, 11. 7
this wish i have, then ten times happy me! 37.14
ten times more in worth | than those old nine 38. 9
tend | upon the hours and times of your desire? 57. 2
in thought control your times of pleasure, | or 58. 2
and yet to times in hope my verse shall stand, 60.13

TIMON 75 FR 0.0084 REL FR 63 V 12 P
the boys, | and critic timon laugh at idle toys! LLL 4.03.168
o, pray let's see't. for the lord timon, sir? TIM 1.01. 13
tender down | their services to lord timon. 1.01. 55
to show lord timon that mean eyes have seen 1.01. 93
lord timon, hear me speak. 1.01.110
most noble timon, call the man before thee. 1.01.113
this fellow here, lord timon, this thy creature, 1.01.116
therefore he will be, timon. 1.01.129
of nothing so much as that i am not like timon. 1.01.190 P
most honored timon, | it hath pleas'd the gods 1.02. 1
let me stay at thine apperil, timon. 1.02. 33
what a number of men eats timon, and he sees 'em 1.02. 40 P
will make thee and thy state look ill, timon. 1.02. 57 P
thou weep'st to make them drink, timon. 1.02.109 P
hail to thee, worthy timon, and to all | that of 1.02.122
honor, and fortunes, keep with you, lord timon! 1.02.229
thou giv'st so long, timon (i fear me), thou 1.02.241 P
steal but a beggar's dog | and give it timon, 2.01. 6
better than he, why, give my horse to timon, 2.01. 8
get on your cloak and haste you to lord timon; 2.01. 15
wing, | lord timon will be left a naked gull, 2.01. 31
this is to lord timon, this to alcibiades. 2.02. 83 P
if timon stay at home. 2.02. 91 P
aside, aside, here comes lord timon. 2.02.119 P
great timon! 2.02.168
noble, worthy, royal timon! 2.02.168
who, the lord timon? 3.02. 1 P
i was sending to use lord timon myself, these 3.02. 50 P
true, as you said, timon is shrunk indeed, | and 3.02. 61
my knowing, timon has been this lord's father, 3.02. 67
own part, | i never tasted timon in my life, 3.02. 77
timon in this should pay more than he owes; 3.04. 22
hated be | of timon man and all humanity! 3.06.105
timon will to the woods, where he shall find 4.01. 35
and grant, as timon grows, his hate may grow 4.01. 39
his semblable, yea, himself, timon disdains; 4.03. 22
how came the noble timon to this change? 4.03. 67
noble timon, | what friendship may i do thee? 4.03. 70
what is it, timon? 4.03. 72
i have but little gold of late, brave timon, 4.03. 91
i am thy friend, and pity thee, dear timon. 4.03. 98
ay, timon, and have cause. 4.03.103
why me, timon? 4.03.106
give us some gold, good timon; hast thou more? 4.03.133
more counsel with more money, bounteous timon. 4.03.167
farewell, timon! 4.03.169
perfumes, and have forgot | that ever timon was. 4.03.208
where liest a' nights, timon? 4.03.292
ay, timon. 4.03.326 P
then, timon, presently prepare thy grave; 4.03.377
eat, timon, and abhor /them. 4.03.397
'save thee, timon. 4.03.411 P
hail, worthy timon! 5.01. 55
it is vain that you would speak with timon; 5.01.116
promise to th' athenians | to speak with timon. 5.01.121
lord timon! 5.01.127
timon, | look out and speak to friends. 5.01.127
speak to them, noble timon. 5.01.130
worthy timon — 5.01.134
of none but such as you, and you of timon. 5.01.135
the senators of athens greet thee, timon. 5.01.136
of it own fall, restraining aid to timon, | and 5.01.148
therefore, timon — 5.01.167
countrymen, | let alcibiades know this of timon, 5.01.170
know this of timon, | that timon cares not. 5.01.171
then let him know, and tell him timon speaks it, 5.01.175
timon hath made his everlasting mansion | upon 5.01.215
sun, hide thy beams, timon hath done his reign. 5.01.223
we stand much hazard if they bring not timon. 5.02. 5
no talk of timon, nothing of him expect. 5.02. 14
"timon is dead, who hath outstretch'd his span: 5.03. 3
we woo | transformed timon to our city's love 5.04. 19
my noble general, timon is dead, | entomb'd upon 5.04. 65
here lie i, timon, who, alive, all living men 5.04. 72
dead | is noble timon, of whose memory 5.04. 80

TIMON'S 25 FR 0.0028 REL FR 20 V 5 P
and returns in peace | most rich in timon's nod. TIM 1.01. 62
one do i personate of lord timon's frame, | whom 1.01. 69
when thou art timon's dog, and these knaves 1.01.180
thou art going to lord timon's feast? 1.01.260
shall we in | and taste lord timon's bounty? 1.01.274
fool, i will go with you to lord timon's. 2.02. 89 P
who is not timon's? 2.02.166
head, sword, force, means, but is lord timon's? 2.02.167
that timon's fortunes 'mong his friends can sink 2.02.231
one of lord timon's men? 3.01. 5 P
now lord timon's happy hours are done and past, 3.02. 6 P
timon's money | has paid his men their wages. 3.02. 69
drinks | but timon's silver treads upon his lip, 3.02. 71
'tis deepest winter in lord timon's purse; 3.04. 14
and he wears jewels now of timon's gift, | for 3.04. 19
i know my lord hath spent of timon's wealth, 3.04. 26
one of lord timon's men. 3.04. 33 P
this is timon's last, | who, stuck and spangled 3.06. 90
know you the quality of lord timon's fury? 3.06.107 P
lord timon's mad. 3.06.119
yet do our hearts wear timon's livery, | that 4.02. 17
meet, for timon's sake | let's yet be fellows. 4.02. 24
feeling in itself | a lack of timon's aid, hath 5.01.147
man was riding | from alcibiades to timon's cave 5.02. 10
those enemies of timon's and mine own | whom you 5.04. 56

TIMOR 1 FR 0.0001 REL FR 1 V 0 P
/pene gelidus timor occupat artus: 2H6 4.01.117

TIMOROUS 9 FR 0.0010 REL FR 9 V 0 P
but, like a timorous thief, most fain would AWW 2.05. 81
bell, | sings heavy music to thy timorous soul, 1H6 4.02. 40
a little herd of england's timorous deer, 4.02. 46
ah, timorous wretch, | thou hast undone thyself, 3H6 1.01.231
but with his timorous dreams was still awak'd. R3 4.01. 84
do, with like timorous accent and dire yell | as OTH 1.01. 75
success i dare not | make any timorous question; TNK 1.03. 3
by me, | uncouple at the timorous flying hare, VEN 674
even so the timorous yelping of the hounds 881

TIMOROUSLY 1 FR 0.0001 REL FR 1 V 0 P
and timorously confess | the manner and the R3 3.05. 57

TIMOTHY 1 FR 0.0001 REL FR 1 V 0 P
why, timothy! TNK 3.05. 24

TINCT 4 FR 0.0004 REL FR 4 V 0 P
that knows the tinct and multiplying med'cine, AWW 5.03.102
/grained spots | as will /not leave their tinct. HAM 3.04. 91
med'cine hath | with his tinct gilded thee. ANT 1.05. 37
azure lac'd | with blue of heaven's own tinct. CYM 2.02. 23

TINCTURE 2 FR 0.0002 REL FR 2 V 0 P
you can bring | tincture or lustre in her lip, WT 3.02.205
a dye | as the perfumed tincture of the roses, SON 54. 6

TINCTURES 1 FR 0.0001 REL FR 1 V 0 P
and that great men shall press | for tinctures, JC 2.02. 89

TINDER 1 FR 0.0001 REL FR 1 V 0 P
strike on the tinder, ho! OTH 1.01.140

TINDERBOX 1 FR 0.0001 REL FR 0 V 1 P
i am glad i am so acquit of this tinderbox; WIV 1.03. 24 P

TINDER–LIKE 1 FR 0.0001 REL FR 0 V 1 P
hasty and tinder–like upon too trivial motion; COR 2.01. 50 P

TINE* *(also thyme, tiny)*

/TINE* 1 FR 0.0001 REL FR 0 V 1 P
set hyssop and weed up /tine, supply it with one OTH 1.03.322 P

TINE* 2 FR 0.0002 REL FR 2 V 0 P
when that i was and a little tine boy, | with TN 5.01.389
"he that has and a little tine wit — | with LR 3.02. 74

TINGLING 1 FR 0.0001 REL FR 0 V 1 P
of sleeping in the blood, a whoreson tingling. 2H4 1.02.113 P

TINKER 8 FR 0.0009 REL FR 4 V 4 P
tom snout, the tinker. MND 1.02. 61 P
snout, the tinker! 4.01.203 P
and now by present profession a tinker? SHR in.2. 21 P
indeed | and not a tinker nor christopher sly. in.2. 73
i can drink with any tinker in his own language 1H4 2.04. 19 P
i know you, y' are a tinker. TNK 3.05. 82
sirrah tinker, | stop no more holes but what you 3.05. 82
dii boni! | a tinker, damsel? 3.05. 84

TINKER'S 1 FR 0.0001 REL FR 0 V 1 P
and married a tinker's wife within a mile where WT 4.03. 97 P

TINKERS 3 FR 0.0003 REL FR 2 V 1 P
but to gabble like tinkers at this time of night TN 2.03. 88 P
if tinkers may have leave to live, | and bear WT 4.03. 19
sent from a sort of tinkers to the king. 2H6 3.02.277

TINSEL 1 FR 0.0001 REL FR 0 V 1 P
skirts, round underborne with a bluish tinsel; ADO 3.04. 22 P

TINY *(also tine*)*

TINY 2 FR 0.0002 REL FR 0 V 2 P
and any pretty little tiny kickshaws, tell 2H4 5.01. 28 P
welcome, my little tiny thief, and welcome 5.03. 57 P

TIP 4 FR 0.0004 REL FR 2 V 2 P
fear not, man, we'll tip thy horns with gold, ADO 5.04. 44
in love, i' faith, to the very tip of the nose. TRO 3.01.127 P
a piece of silver on the tip of your tongue, or TNK 4.03. 20 P
"so on the tip of his subduing tongue | all kind LC 120

TIPP'D 1 FR 0.0001 REL FR 0 V 1 P
staff more reverent than one tipp'd with horn. ADO 5.04.123 P

TIPPLING 1 FR 0.0001 REL FR 1 V 0 P
and keep the turn of tippling with a slave, | to ANT 1.04. 19

TIPS 1 FR 0.0001 REL FR 1 V 0 P
that tips with silver all these fruit–tree tops ROM 2.02.108

TIPSY 1 FR 0.0001 REL FR 1 V 0 P
"the riot of the tipsy bacchanals, | tearing the MND 5.01. 48

TIPTOE 3 FR 0.0003 REL FR 3 V 0 P
will stand a' tiptoe when this day is named, H5 4.03. 42
day | stands tiptoe on the misty mountain tops. ROM 3.05. 10
or to go tiptoe | before the street be foul? TNK 1.02. 57

TIR'D 16 FR 0.0018 REL FR 10 V 6 P
that, when gentlemen are tir'd, gives them a sob ERR 4.03. 25 P
fie, fie on all tir'd jades, on all mad masters, SHR 4.01. 1 P
first, know my horse is tir'd, my master and 4.01. 54 P
till our very pastime, tir'd out of breath, TN 3.04.138 P
gall'd, and tir'd by jauncing bullingbrook. R2 5.05. 94
again, and when thou hast tir'd thyself in base 1H4 2.04.250 P
though patience be a tir'd /mare, yet she will H5 2.01. 23 P
wants similes, truth tir'd with iteration, | as TRO 3.02.176
i am weary, yea, my memory is tir'd. COR 1.09. 91
and that to prove more fortunes | th' art tir'd, 4.05. 94
then should not we be tir'd with this ado. TIT 2.01. 98
life is a tedious one, | i have tir'd myself; CYM 3.06. 2
till fortune, tir'd with doing bad, | threw him PER 2.ch. 37
as the fleet–foot roe that's tir'd with chasing, VEN 561
tir'd with all these, for restful death i cry: SON 66. 1
tir'd with all these, from these would i be gone 66.13

TIRE* *(also attire, etc.)*

TIRE* 15 FR 0.0017 REL FR 11 V 4 P
if i had such a tire, this face of mine | were TGV 4.04.185
or any tire of venetian admittance. WIV 3.03. 58 P
and tire the hearer with a book of words. ADO 1.01.307
i like the new tire within excellently, if the 3.04. 13 P
wit's too hot, it speeds too fast, 'twill tire. LLL 2.01.119
true as truest horse, that yet would never tire, MND 3.01. 96
it is, "never tire." 3.01.101 P
as truest horse, that yet would never tire." 3.01.102
besides, i have stay'd | to tire your royalty. WT 1.02. 15
eagle | tire on the flesh of me and of my son! 3H6 1.01.269
which in the day of battle tire thee more | than R3 4.04.189
faults (with surplus) to tire in repetition. COR 1.01. 45 P
vesture of creation | does tire the /ingener. OTH 2.01. 65
having | rich tire about you, should at these PER 3.02. 22
till, like a jade, self–will himself doth tire. LUC 707

/TIRED* 1 FR 0.0001 REL FR 1 V 0 P
/which /tired /majesty /did /make /thee /offer: R2 4.01.178

TIRED* 10 FR 0.0011 REL FR 9 V 1 P
the ape his keeper, the tired horse his rider. LLL 4.02.127 P
he is as tedious | as a tired horse, a railing 1H4 3.01.158
the waves of tiber | did i the tired caesar. JC 1.02.115
than doth, within a dull, stale, tired bed, | go LR 1.02. 13
them, | and titan, tired in the midday heat, VEN 177
and in his will his willful eye he tired. LUC 417
so woe hath wearied woe, moan tired moan, | that 1363
to tell them all with one poor tired tongue. 1617
the dear repose for limbs with travel tired, SON 27. 2
the beast that bears me, tired with my woe, 50. 5

TIRES* 7 FR 0.0008 REL FR 7 V 0 P
as motion and long–during action tires | the LLL 4.03.303
goes all the day, | your sad tires in a mile–a. WT 4.03.126
he tires betimes that spurs too fast betimes; R2 2.01. 36
being allow'd his way, | self–mettle tires him. H8 1.01.134
then put my tires and mantles on him, whilst | i ANT 2.05. 22
tires with her beak on feathers, flesh, and bone VEN 56
set, | and you in grecian tires are painted new; SON 53. 8

TIREST 1 FR 0.0001 REL FR 1 V 0 P
be disedg'd by her | that now thou tirest on, CYM 3.04. 94

TIRE–VALIANT 1 FR 0.0001 REL FR 0 V 1 P
that becomes the ship–tire, the tire–valiant, or WIV 3.03. 57 P

/TIRING* 1 FR 0.0001 REL FR 0 V 1 P
to save the money that he spends in /tiring; ERR 2.02. 98 P

TIRING* 3 FR 0.0003 REL FR 2 V 1 P
the posts come tiring on, | and not a man of 2H4 in 37
care, | witness the tiring day and heavy night, TIT 5.02. 24
were my thoughts tiring when we encount'red. TIM 3.06. 4 P

TIRING–HOUSE 1 FR 0.0001 REL FR 0 V 1 P
this hawthorn brake our tiring–house, and we MND 3.01. 4 P

TIRRA–LYRA 1 FR 0.0001 REL FR 1 V 0 P
the lark, that tirra–lyra chaunts, | with heigh, WT 4.03. 9

TIRRITS 1 FR 0.0001 REL FR 0 V 1 P
afore i'll be in these tirrits and frights. 2H4 2.04.205 P

'TIS *(also 'tish)*

/'TIS 12 FR 0.0013 REL FR 7 V 5 P
/me /at /the /font, | /but /'tis /usurp'd. R2 4.01.257
/'tis /very /true, /my /grief /lies /all /within 4.01.295
/or /bad, /'tis /but /the /chance /of /war. TRO pr 31
/this /'tis: 1.03.315
do you think /'tis this? HAM 2.02.151
/why /then /'tis /none /to /you; 2.02.249 P
/'tis /too /narrow /for /your /mind. 2.02.252 P
/is /fine /in /love, /and /where /'tis /fine, 4.05.162
/arraign /her /first, /'tis /goneril. LR 3.06. 46 P
/'tis /so, /they /are /afoot. 4.03. 49
/as /'tis /said, /the /bastard /son /of 4.07. 88 P
/'tis /time /to /look /about, /the /powers /of 4.07. 91 P

'TIS 1508 FR 0.1704 REL FR 1192 V 316 P
'tis time | i should inform thee farther. TMP 1.02. 22
'tis far off — | and rather like a dream than 1.02. 44
for still 'tis beating in my mind, your reason 1.02.176
'tis a good dullness, | and give it way. 1.02.185
'tis a villain, sir, | i do not love to look on. 1.02.309
but, as 'tis, | we cannot miss him. 1.02.310
but 'tis gone. 1.02.395
but 'tis a spirit. 1.02.412
this speech, | were i but where 'tis spoken. 1.02.431
alive, | 'tis as impossible that he's undrown'd, 2.01.237
'tis true, my brother's daughter 's queen of 2.01.255
'tis best we stand upon our guard, | or that we 2.01.321
'tis fresh morning with me | when you are by at 3.01. 33

'tis a custom with him | i' th' afternoon to 3.02. 87
come to me, | and i'll be sworn 'tis true. 3.03. 26
with such love as 'tis now, the murkiest den, 4.01. 25
of this, | for 'tis a chronicle of day by day, 5.01.163
'tis new to thee. 5.01.184
now 'tis true, | i must be here confin'd by you, ep 3
'tis true; TGV 1.01. 25
'tis love you cavil at; i am not love. 1.01. 38
'tis threefold too little for carrying a letter 1.01.109
dear madam, 'tis a passing shame | that i 1.02. 17
now, trust me, 'tis an office of great worth, 1.02. 44
no, madam, 'tis too sharp. 1.02. 88
'tis a word or two | of commendations sent from 1.03. 52
you, gentle servant — 'tis very clerkly done. 2.01.108
'tis you that have the reason. 2.01.143 P
i'll warrant you, 'tis as well: 2.01.164 P
'tis dinner–time. 2.01.170 P
there 'tis. 2.03. 19 P
why, there 'tis; 2.03. 28 P
'tis indeed, madam, we thank the giver. 2.04. 35 P
i think 'tis no unwelcome news to you. 2.04. 81
'tis but her picture i have yet beheld, | and 2.04.209
'tis well that i get it so. 2.05. 41 P
'tis not unknown to thee that i have sought | to 3.01. 61
if she do frown, 'tis not in hate of you, | but 3.01. 96
if she do chide, 'tis not to have you gone, 3.01. 98
'tis so; 3.01.152
not a hair on 's head but 'tis a valentine. 3.01.192 P
nor who 'tis i love; 3.01.268 P
and yet 'tis a woman; 3.01.268 P
and yet 'tis a milkmaid; 3.01.269 P
yet 'tis not a maid, for she hath had gossips; 3.01.270 P
yet 'tis a maid, for she is her master's maid, 3.01.271 P
'tis an ill office for a gentleman, | especially 3.02. 40
trust me, i think 'tis almost day. 4.02.138 P
'tis a foul thing when a cur cannot keep himself 4.04. 9 P
for 'tis no trusting to yond foolish lout — 4.04. 66
'tis pity love should be so contrary; 4.04. 83
and take this shadow up, | for 'tis thy rival. 4.04.198
'tis true; 5.02. 13
'tis true; 5.02. 37
o, 'tis the curse in love, and still approv'd, 5.04. 43
here 'tis; this is it. 5.04. 91
'tis true. 5.04.110
'tis your penance but to hear | the story of 5.04.170
'tis your fault, 'tis your fault; WIV 1.01. 93 P
'tis your fault, 'tis your fault; 1.01. 93 P
'tis a good dog. 1.01. 94 P
but 'tis no matter; 1.01.180 P
'tis ready, sir, here in the porch. 1.04. 61 P
'tis a great charge to come under one body's 1.04. 98 P
pity me — 'tis not a soldier–like phrase — but 2.01. 12 P
'tis true; 2.01.134 P
'tis the heart, master page, 'tis here, 'tis 2.01.226 P
the heart, master page, 'tis here, 'tis here. 2.01.227 P
the heart, master page, 'tis here, 'tis here. 2.01.227 P
if she be otherwise, 'tis labor well bestow'd. 2.01.239 P
her into such a canaries as 'tis wonderful. 2.02. 61 P
for 'tis not good that children should know any 2.02.128 P
let them say 'tis grossly done, so it be fairly 2.02.142 P
'tis past the hour, sir, that sir hugh promis'd 2.03. 4 P
'tis true, master shallow. 2.03. 50 P
by gar, 'tis good; vell said. 2.03. 96 P
he will carry't — 'tis in his buttons — he 3.02. 69 P
'tis not so, i hope. 3.03.111 P
but 'tis most certain your husband's coming, 3.03.113 P
by gar, 'tis no the fashion of france; 3.03.172 P
'tis my fault, master page. i suffer for it. 3.03.218 P
by gar, i see 'tis an honest woman. 3.03.222 P
and tells me 'tis a thing impossible | i should 3.04. 9
and 'tis the very riches of thyself | that now i 3.04. 17
'slid, 'tis but venturing. 3.04. 24 P
'tis past eight already, sir. 3.05.132 P
this 'tis to be married! 3.05.142 P
this 'tis to have linen and buck–baskets! 3.05.142 P
'tis impossible he should; 3.05.145 P
'tis a playing–day, i see. 4.01. 9 P
'tis old, but true: 4.02.107
'tis unreasonable! 4.02.141 P
'tis a goodly credit for you. 4.02.189 P
'tis one of the best discretions of a oman as 4.04. 1 P
'tis well, 'tis well, no more. 4.04. 10
'tis well, 'tis well, no more. 4.04. 10
'tis painted about with the story of the 4.05. 7 P
'tis, 'tis his fortune. 4.05. 49 P
'tis, 'tis his fortune. 4.05. 49 P
and 'tis not convenient you should be cozen'd. 4.05. 81 P
but 'tis no matter; 5.03. 9 P
in state as wholesome as in state 'tis fit, 5.05. 59
but till 'tis one a' clock, | our dance of 5.05. 74
a jack–a–lent, when 'tis upon ill employment! 5.05.127 P
'tis time i were chok'd with a piece of toasted 5.05.138 P
and 'tis a postmaster's boy. 5.05.187 P
ay, be–gar, and 'tis a boy. 5.05.209 P
'tis so with me. MM 1.01. 81
claudio to prison? 'tis not so. 1.02. 66 P
nay, but i know 'tis so. 1.02. 67 P
yet still 'tis just. 1.02.123
act | freshly on me — 'tis surely for a name. 1.02.171
'tis true. 1.04. 30
though 'tis my familiar sin | with maids to seem 1.04. 31
fewness and truth, 'tis thus: 1.04. 39
'tis one thing to be tempted, escalus, | another 2.01. 17
'tis very pregnant, | the jewel that we find, we 2.01. 23
'tis for a good purpose. 2.01.148 P
he's sentenc'd; 'tis too late. 2.02. 55
now 'tis awake, | takes note of what is done, 2.02. 93
'tis wit in them, | but in the less foul 2.02.127
and 'tis | such sense that my sense breeds with 2.02.141
go to; 'tis well. away! 2.02.156
'tis meet so, daughter, but lest you do repent 2.03. 30
'tis pity of him. 2.03. 42
the devil's horn, | 'tis not the devil's crest. 2.04. 17
better please me | than to demand what 'tis. 2.04. 33
'tis all as easy | falsely to take away a life 2.04. 46
'tis set down so in heaven, but not in earth. 2.04. 50
o, 'tis the cunning livery of hell, | the 3.01. 94
thought | imagine howling — 'tis too horrible! 3.01.127

a bawd, | 'tis best that thou diest quickly. 3.01.150
think | what 'tis to cram a maw or clothe a back 3.02. 22
why, 'tis good; 3.02. 58 P
why, 'tis not amiss, pompey. 3.02. 63 P
be the due of a bawd, why, 'tis his right. 3.02. 67 P
'tis not possible. 3.02.124 P
'tis a secret must be lock'd within the teeth 3.02.134 P
'tis good; 4.01. 14
'tis well borne up. 4.01. 47
to bring you thus together 'tis no sin, | sith 4.01. 72
'tis now dead midnight, and by eight to–morrow 4.02. 64
o, 'tis an accident that heaven provides! 4.03. 77
'tis that he sent me of the duke's return. 4.03.138
for 'tis a physic | that's bitter to sweet end. 4.06. 7
'tis not impossible | but one, the wicked'st 5.01. 52
my lord, i know him, 'tis a meddling friar. 5.01.127
to find out this abuse, whence 'tis deriv'd. 5.01.247
'tis false. 5.01.290
'tis he should hear me speak. 5.01.294
'tis he, my lord. 5.01.325
'tis my deserving, and i do entreat it. 5.01.477
but we that know what 'tis to fast and pray, ERR 1.02. 51
"'tis dinner–time," quoth i: 2.01. 62
if thou art chang'd to aught, 'tis to an ass. 2.02.199
'tis true she rides me and i long for grass. 2.02.200
'tis so, i am an ass, else it could never be 2.02.201
by this i know 'tis made. 3.01.115
'tis double wrong, to truant with your bed, 3.02. 17
'tis holy sport to be a little vain, | when the 3.02. 27
sir, 'tis in grain, noah's flood could not do it 3.02.106 P
'tis time, i think, to trudge, pack, and be gone 3.02.153
and therefore 'tis high time that i were hence. 3.02.157
no, no, the bell, 'tis time that i were gone: 4.02. 53
why, 'tis a plain case: 4.03. 23 P
nay, 'tis for me to be patient: 4.04. 19 P
'tis so; 5.01. 10
'tis pity that thou liv'st | to walk where any 5.01. 27
'tis true, my liege, this ring i had of her. 5.01.278
'tis once, thou lovest, | and i will fit thee ADO 1.01.318
'tis certain so, the prince woos for himself. 2.01.174
speak, count, 'tis your cue. 2.01.305 P
'tis true indeed, so your daughter says. 2.03.127 P
of her love, 'tis very possible he'll scorn it, 2.03.179 P
'tis a truth, i can bear them witness; 2.03.231 P
'tis so, i cannot reprove it; 2.03.232 P
'tis even so. 3.02. 76 P
'tis very true. 3.03. 73 P
otherwise 'tis light, and not heavy. 3.04. 37 P
'tis almost five a' clock, cousin, 'tis time you 3.04. 52 P
five a' clock, cousin, 'tis time you were ready. 3.04. 52 P
and 'twere a thousand pound more than 'tis, for 3.05. 25 P
'tis well consented; 4.01.251
and 'tis not wisdom thus to second grief 5.01. 2
no, 'tis all men's office to speak patience | to 5.01. 27
come, 'tis no matter; 5.01.100
that eye my daughter lent her, 'tis most true. 5.04. 23
'tis no such matter. then you do not love me? 5.04. 82
i am resolved, 'tis but a three years' fast: LLL 1.01. 24
'tis won as towns with fire — so won, so lost. 1.01.146
since, but i think now 'tis not to be found; 1.02.112 P
'tis deadly sin to keep that oath, my lord, 2.01.105
'tis long of you that spur me with such 2.01.118
navarre and his book–men, for here 'tis abused. 2.01.227
'tis true indeed, the collusion holds in the 4.02. 42 P
'tis pretty; 4.02. 89 P
you'll not be perjur'd, 'tis a hateful thing; 4.03.155
o, 'tis the sun that maketh all things shine! 4.03.242
o, 'tis more than need. 4.03.285
but while 'tis spoke each turn away /her face. 5.02.148
'tis our will | that some plain man recount 5.02.176
much upon this 'tis; 5.02.472
and 'tis some policy | to have one show worse 5.02.512
you are deceived, 'tis not so. 5.02.541
'tis not so much worth; 5.02.558 P
most true, 'tis right; you were so, alisander. 5.02.569
alas, you see how 'tis — a little o'erparted. 5.02.584 P
'tis yours. 5.02.677 P
it is not friendly, 'tis not maidenly. MND 3.02.217
'tis partly my own fault, | which death, or 3.02.243
'tis no jest | that i do hate thee and love 3.02.280
'tis strange, my theseus, that these lovers 5.01. 1
lovers, to bed, 'tis almost fairy time. 5.01.364
what stuff 'tis made of, whereof it is born, | i MV 1.01. 4
i love thee, and 'tis my love that speaks — 1.01. 87
'tis not unknown to you, antonio, | how much i 1.01.122
three thousand ducats — 'tis a good round sum. 1.03.103
'tis vile, unless it may be quaintly ordered, 2.04. 6
'tis now but four of clock, we have two hours 2.04. 8
in faith, 'tis a fair hand, | and whiter than 2.04. 12
'tis good we do so. 2.04. 27
i am glad 'tis night, you do not look on me, 2.06. 34
why, 'tis an office of discovery, love, | and i 2.06. 43
'tis nine a' clock — our friends all stay for 2.06. 63
i speak too long, but 'tis to peize the time, 3.02. 22
and you shall see 'tis purchas'd by the weight, 3.02. 89
and then 'tis thought | thou'lt show thy mercy 4.01. 19
'tis mightiest in the mightiest, it becomes 4.01.188
here 'tis, most reverend doctor, here it is. 4.01.226
'tis very true. 4.01.250
i cannot find it, 'tis not in the bond. 4.01.262
'tis well you offer it behind her back, | the 4.01.293
'tis a day, | such as the day is when the sun is 5.01.125
'tis true, for those that she makes fair she AYL 1.02. 37 P
"'tis right," quoth he, "thus misery doth part 2.01. 51
and greasy citizens, | 'tis just the fashion. 2.01. 56
'tis a greek invocation, to call fools into a 2.05. 59 P
'tis but an hour ago since it was nine, | and 2.07. 24
and know what 'tis to pity and be pitied, | let 2.07.117
i' faith, coz, 'tis he. 3.02.216 P
'tis a word too great for any mouth of this 3.02.226 P
'tis he. slink by, and note him. 3.02.252 P
'tis a fault i will not change for your best 3.02.283 P
dowry of his wife, 'tis none of his own getting. 3.03. 55 P
'tis no matter; 3.03.106 P
'tis pretty, sure, and very probable, | that 3.05. 11
'tis not your inky brows, your black silk hair, 3.05. 46
'tis such fools as you | that makes the world 3.05. 52
'tis not her glass, but you, that flatters her, 3.05. 54

'tis at the tuft of olives here hard by. 3.05. 75
'tis but a peevish boy — yet he talks well — 3.05.110
his leg is but so so — and yet 'tis well; 3.05.119
why, 'tis good to be sad and say nothing. 4.01. 8 P
why then 'tis good to be a post. 4.01. 9 P
'tis but one cast away, and so, come death! 4.01.185 P
'tis no matter how it be in tune, so it make 4.02. 8 P
why, 'tis a boisterous and a cruel style, | a 4.03. 31
for 'tis | the royal disposition of that beast 4.03.116
but 'tis not i. 4.03.135
ay, i know who 'tis; 5.01. 8 P
nay, 'tis true. 5.02. 29 P
shepherd, tell this youth what 'tis to love. 5.02. 83
'tis like the howling of irish wolves against 5.02.109 P
'tis i must make conclusion | of these most 5.04.126
'tis hymen peoples every town, | high wedlock 5.04.143
'tis true that a good play needs no epilogue. ep 4 P
sirrah, go see what trumpet 'tis that sounds. SHR in.1. 74
'tis very true; in.1. 89
'tis much. in.2. 116
nay, then 'tis time to stir him from his trance. 1.01.177
ay, marry, am i, sir; and now 'tis plotted. 1.01.188
'tis hatch'd, and shall be so. 1.01.206
sirrah, come hither, 'tis no time to jest, | and 1.01.226
my lord, 'tis but begun. 1.01.252
'tis a very excellent piece of work, madam lady; 1.01.253 P
nay, 'tis no matter, sir, what he 'leges in 1.02. 28 P
tell me her father's name, and 'tis enough; 1.02. 94
'tis well; 1.02.171
gremio, 'tis now no time to vent our love; 1.02.178
'tis with cares. 2.01.238
father, 'tis thus: 2.01.290
'tis bargain'd 'twixt us twain, being alone, 2.01.304
i tell you 'tis incredible to believe | how much 2.01.306
'tis a world to see | how tame, when men and 2.01.311
'tis a match. 2.01.319
'tis age that nourisheth. 2.01.339
'tis deeds must win the prize, and he of both 2.01.342
'tis known my father hath no less | than three 2.01.377
'tis in my head to do my master good. 2.01.406
madam, 'tis now in tune. 3.01. 46
base is right, 'tis the base knave that jars. 3.01. 47
'tis some odd humor pricks him to this fashion; 3.02. 72
the morning wears, 'tis time we were at church. 3.02.111
'tis a groom indeed, | a grumbling groom, and 3.02.152
curster than she? why, 'tis impossible. 3.02.154
'tis like you'll prove a jolly surly groom, 3.02.213
this 'tis to feel a tale, not to hear a tale. 4.01. 63 P
and therefore 'tis call'd a sensible tale; 4.01. 64 P
'tis burnt, and so is all the meat. 4.01.161
reign, | and 'tis my hope to end successfully. 4.01.189
'tis charity to shew. 4.01.211
'tis death for any one in mantua | to come to 4.02. 81
'tis marvel, but that you are but newly come, 4.02. 86
'tis passing good, i prithee let me have it. 4.03. 18
i cannot tell, i fear 'tis choleric. 4.03. 22
fie, fie, 'tis lewd and filthy. 4.03. 65
why, 'tis a cockle or a walnut–shell, | a knack, 4.03. 66
'tis like /a demi–cannon. 4.03. 88
you are i' th' right, sir, 'tis for my mistress. 4.03.156 P
for 'tis the mind that makes the body rich; 4.03.172
let's see, i think 'tis now some seven a' clock, 4.03.187
i dare assure you, sir, 'tis almost two, | and 4.03.189
'tis well, and hold your own in any case | with 4.04. 6
'tis well, sir, that you hunted for yourself; 5.02. 55
'tis thought your deer does hold you at a bay. 5.02. 56
'tis ten to one it maim'd you /two outright. 5.02. 62
a match! 'tis done. 5.02. 74
'tis a good hearing when children are toward. 5.02.182
'tis a wonder, by your leave, she will be tam'd 5.02.189
father — o, that "had," how sad a passage 'tis! AWW 1.01. 18 P
'tis the best brine a maiden can season her 1.01. 48 P
my lord, | 'tis an unseason'd courtier; 1.01. 71
'tis too cold a companion; 1.01.132 P
be said in't, 'tis against the rule of nature. 1.01.135 P
'tis a commodity will lose the gloss with lying: 1.01.153 P
off with't while 'tis vendible; 1.01.155 P
ill, it eats drily, marry, 'tis a wither'd pear; 1.01.162 P
better, marry, yet 'tis a wither'd pear. 1.01.163 P
that i wish well. 'tis pity — 1.01.179
so 'tis reported, sir. 1.02. 3
nay, 'tis most credible; 1.02. 4
'tis my slowness that i do not, for i know you 1.03. 10 P
'tis not unknown to you, madam, i am a poor 1.03. 13 P
madam, 'tis not so well that i am poor, though 1.03. 16 P
'tis often seen | adoption strives with nature, 1.03.144
now to all sense 'tis gross: 1.03.172
tell me true, | but tell me then, 'tis so; 1.03.176
the gift doth stretch itself as 'tis receiv'd, 2.01. 4
'tis our hope, sir, | after well–ent'red 2.01. 5
'tis not his fault, the spark. 2.01. 25
o, 'tis brave wars! 2.01. 25
young" and "the next year" and "'tis too early." 2.01. 28
but, my good lord, 'tis thus: 2.01. 68
as 'tis with us that square our guess by shows; 2.01.150
'tis the rarest argument of wonder that hath 2.03. 7 P
and so 'tis. 2.03. 9 P
why, there 'tis, so say i too. 2.03. 15 P
nay, 'tis strange, 'tis very strange, that is 2.03. 28 P
'tis strange, 'tis very strange, that is the 2.03. 28 P
'tis only title thou disdain'st in her, the 2.03.117
'tis hard! 2.03.297
but hush, 'tis so. 2.03.300
of the wealth i owe, | nor dare i say 'tis mine; 2.05. 80
'tis bitter. 3.02. 76
'tis but the boldness of his hand, haply, 3.02. 77
as 'tis reported, for the king had married him 3.05. 53
'tis a hard bondage to become the wife | of a 3.05. 64
'tis a most gallant fellow. 3.05. 78
'tis pity he is not honest. 3.05. 82
a pox on't, let it go, 'tis but a drum. 3.06. 46 P
as we'll direct her how 'tis best to bear it. 3.07. 20
'tis not the many oaths that makes the truth, 4.02. 21
when you have spoken it, 'tis dead, and i am the 4.03. 12 P
here 'tis, here's a paper. 4.03.206 P
'fore whose throne 'tis needful, | ere i can 4.04. 3
i like him well, 'tis not amiss. 4.05. 68 P
velvet knows, but 'tis a goodly patch of velvet. 4.05. 96 P

'tis too late to pare her nails now. 5.02. 28 P
'tis past, my liege, | and i beseech your 5.03. 4
and inform him | so 'tis our will he should. 5.03. 27
he blushes, and 'tis hit. 5.03.195
lord, | 'tis but the shadow of a wife you see, 5.03.307
'tis not so sweet now as it was before. TN 1.01. 8
'tis thought among the prudent he would quickly 1.03. 32 P
ay, 'tis strong; 1.03.134 P
'tis a fair young man, and well attended. 1.05.102 P
'tis a gentleman here — a plague o' these 1.05.120 P
as a squash is before 'tis a peascod, or a 1.05.157 P
peascod, or a codling when 'tis almost an apple. 1.05.158 P
'tis with him in standing water, between boy and 1.05.158 P
took great pains to study it, and 'tis poetical. 1.05.194 P
'tis not that time of moon with me to make one 1.05.200 P
'tis in grain, sir, 'twill endure wind and 1.05.237 P
'tis beauty truly blent, whose red and white 1.05.239
if it be so, as 'tis, | poor lady, she were 2.02. 25
'tis not hereafter; 2.03. 47
'tis not the first time i have constrain'd one 2.03. 67 P
burn some sack, 'tis too late to go to bed now. 2.03.190 P
but 'tis that miracle and queen of gems | that 2.04. 85
'tis but fortune, all is fortune. 2.05. 23 P
'tis my lady. 2.05. 93 P
yellow stockings, and 'tis a color she abhors, 2.05.199 P
i understand you, sir. 'tis well begg'd. 3.01. 53 P
for 'tis a vulgar proof | that very oft we pity 3.01.124
why then methinks 'tis time to smile again. 3.01.126
you have not seen such a thing as 'tis. 3.02. 81 P
i am not weary, and 'tis long to night; 3.03. 21
'tis not for gravity to play at cherry-pit with 3.04.116 P
here, wear this jewel for me, 'tis my picture. 3.04.208
i do assure you, 'tis against my will. 3.04.311 P
and though 'tis wonder that enwraps me thus, 4.03. 3
that enwraps me thus, | yet 'tis not madness. 4.03. 4
what occasion now | reveals before 'tis ripe, 5.01.154
or say 'tis not your seal, not your invention. 5.01.333
but out of question 'tis maria's hand. 5.01.347
'tis grace indeed. WT 1.02.105
then 'tis very credent | thou mayst co-join with 1.02.142
that will strike | where 'tis predominant; 1.02.202
and 'tis pow'rful — think it — | from east, 1.02.202
'tis far gone, | when i shall gust it last. 1.02.218
if i then deny it, | 'tis none of mine. 1.02.267
opinion, and betimes, | for 'tis most dangerous. 1.02.298
say it be, 'tis true. 1.02.298
be intelligent to me, 'tis thereabouts: 1.02.378
but i am sure 'tis safer to | avoid what's grown 1.02.432
avoid what's grown than question how 'tis born. 1.02.433
he so troubles me, | 'tis past enduring. 2.01. 2
for 'tis polixenes | has made thee swell thus. 2.01. 61
will thereto add | 'tis pity she's not honest — 2.01. 68
'tis hop'd his sickness is discharg'd. 2.03. 11
'tis such as you, | that creep like shadows by 2.03. 33
here 'tis — commends it to your blessing. 2.03. 67
to your charge, | so like you, 'tis the worse. 2.03. 98
look to your babe, my lord, 'tis yours. 2.03.126
within this hour bring me word 'tis done | (and 2.03.136
save this bastard's life — for 'tis a bastard, 2.03.161
'tis good speed; 2.03.199
for honor, | 'tis a derivative from me to mine, 3.02. 44
though 'tis a saying, sir, not due to me. 3.02. 58
awake), i tell you | 'tis rigor and not law. 3.02.114
'tis like to be loud weather. 3.03. 11
if any where i have them, 'tis by the sea-side, 3.03. 67 P
'tis a lucky day, boy, and we'll do good deeds 3.03.138 P
time's news | be known when 'tis brought forth. 4.01. 27
'tis a sickness denying thee any thing; 4.02. 2 P
your resolution cannot hold when 'tis | oppos'd 4.04. 36
'tis well they are whisp'ring. 4.04.247 P
'tis in request, i can tell you. 4.04.290 P
'tis in three parts. 4.04.293 P
bear my part, you must know 'tis my occupation. 4.04.295 P
'tis time to part them. 4.04.344
which 'tis not fit you know, i not acquaint | my 4.04.412
i cannot say 'tis pity | she lacks instructions, 4.04.581
so 'tis said, sir — about his son, that should 4.04.766 P
he must know 'tis none of your daughter nor my 4.04.819 P
'tis your counsel | my lord should to the 5.01. 44
tells us | 'tis not a visitation fram'd, but 5.01. 91
'tis shrewdly ebb'd, | to say you have seen a 5.01.102
'tis strange | he thus should steal upon us. 5.01.114
but 'tis all one to me; 5.02.121 P
behold, and say 'tis well. 5.03. 20
and do not say 'tis superstition, that | i kneel 5.03. 43
for 'tis as easy | to make her speak as move. 5.03. 93
'tis time; 5.03. 99
yet sell your face for five pence and 'tis dear. JN 1.01.153
'tis too respective and too sociable | for your 1.01.188
o me, 'tis my mother. 1.01.220
'tis france, for england. 2.01.202
'tis not the rounder of your old-fac'd walls 2.01.259
it cannot be, thou dost but say 'tis so. 3.01. 6
'tis true, fair daughter, and this blessed day 3.01. 75
for then 'tis like i should forget myself. 3.04. 49
'tis strange to think how much king john hath 3.04.121
'tis wonderful | what may be wrought out of 3.04.178
breast, | and i do fearfully believe 'tis done, 4.02. 74
it is apparent foul play and 'tis shame | that 4.02. 93
'tis true — to hurt his master, no /man else. 4.03. 33
'tis not an hour since i left him well. 4.03.104
and now 'tis far too huge to be blown out | with 5.02. 86
'tis strange that death should sing. 5.07. 20
nay, 'tis in a manner done already, | for many 5.07. 89
'tis not the trial of a woman's war, | the R2 1.01. 48
he is our cousin's cousin, but 'tis doubt, 1.04. 20
'tis breath thou lack'st, and that breath wilt 2.01. 30
next | we will for ireland, and 'tis time, i 2.01.218
god, 'tis shame such wrongs are borne | in him, 2.01.238
or if it be, 'tis with false sorrow's eye, 2.02. 26
'tis nothing but conceit, my gracious lady. 2.02. 33
'tis nothing less: 2.02. 34
'tis in reversion that i do possess — | but 2.02. 38
'tis nameless woe, i wot. 2.02. 40
'tis better hope he is, | for his designs crave 2.02. 43
'tis too true, and that is worse, | the lord 2.02. 52
'tis not my meaning | to rase one title of your 2.03. 74
'tis thought the king is dead; 2.04. 7
'tis well that thou hast cause, | but thou 3.04. 19
is already, and depos'd | 'tis doubt he will be. 3.04. 69
'tis very true, you were in presence then, | and 4.01. 62
my lord, 'tis nothing. 5.02. 58
'tis nothing but some band that he is ent'red 5.02. 65
'tis full three months since i did see him last. 5.03. 2
if any plague hang over us, 'tis he. 5.03. 3
a woman, and thy aunt, great king, 'tis i. 5.03. 76
speak "pardon" as 'tis current in our land, 5.03.123
for 'tis a sign of love; 5.05. 65
if thou love me, 'tis time thou wert away. 5.05. 96
old, | and bootless 'tis to tell you we will go; 1H4 1.01. 29
why, hal, 'tis my vocation, hal, 'tis no sin for 1.02.104 P
'tis no sin for a man to labor in his vocation. 1.02.104 P
yea, but 'tis like that they will know us by our 1.02.174 P
and 'tis no little reason bids us speed, | to 1.03.283
o, 'tis our setter, i know his voice. 2.02. 51 P
the hill, 'tis going to the king's exchequer. 2.02. 55 P
lie, ye rogue, 'tis going to the king's tavern. 2.02. 56 P
'tis dangerous to take a cold, to sleep, to 2.03. 8 P
'tis like the forc'd gait of a shuffling nag. 3.01.133
welsh, | and 'tis no marvel he is so humorous. 3.01.230
neither, 'tis a woman's fault. 3.01.240 P
'tis the next way to turn tailor, or be 3.01.259 P
in the poop, but 'tis in the nose of thee. 3.03. 26 P
i say 'tis copper. 3.03.143 P
not like that paying back, 'tis a double labor. 3.03.179 P
do so, and 'tis well. 4.01. 12
'tis catching hither, even to our camp. 4.01. 30
sir john, 'tis more than time that i were there, 4.02. 54 P
i hope no less, yet needful 'tis to fear, | and, 4.04. 34
and 'tis but wisdom to make strong against him. 4.04. 39
'tis not well | that you and i should meet upon 5.01. 9
'tis a point of friendship. 5.01.122 P
'tis not due yet, i would be loath to pay him 5.01.127 P
well, 'tis no matter, honor pricks me on. 5.01.129 P
'tis insensible then? 5.01.137 P
deliver what you will, i'll say 'tis so. 5.02. 26
ay, hal, 'tis hot, 'tis hot. 5.03. 53 P
ay, hal, 'tis hot, 'tis hot. 5.03. 53 P
'tis more than time, and, my most noble lord, 2H4 1.01.187
it when he will, 'tis not a hair amiss yet. 1.02. 24 P
'tis no matter if i do halt, i have the wars for 1.02.245 P
'tis very true, lord bardolph, for indeed | it 1.03. 25
there 'tis, boy. 2.02. 93 P
'tis with my mind | as with the tide swell'd up 2.03. 62
peesel, be quiet, 'tis very late, i' faith. 2.04.161 P
'tis one a' clock, and past. 3.01. 34
'tis not ten years gone | since richard and 3.01. 57
certain, 'tis certain, very sure, very sure. 3.02. 36 P
'tis the more time thou wert us'd. 3.02.106 P
'tis gaultree forest, and't shall please your 4.01. 2
'tis well done. 4.01. 5
'tis very true, | and therefore be assur'd, my 4.01.217
'tis needful that the most immodest word | be 4.04. 70
'tis seldom when the bee doth leave her comb 4.04. 79
thee | will i to mine leave, as 'tis left to me. 4.05. 47
'tis call'd jerusalem, my noble lord. 4.05.234
'tis merry in hall when beards wags all, | and 5.03. 34
'tis true bred! 5.03. 67 P
'tis so. 5.03. 77 P
what office thou wilt in the land, 'tis thine. 5.03.124 P
but 'tis no matter, this poor show doth better, 5.05. 13 P
'tis "semper idem," for "obsque hoc nihil est." 5.05. 28 P
'tis /all in every part. 5.05. 29 P
'tis so indeed. 5.05. 30 P
know you what 'tis you speak? 5.05. 45
for 'tis your thoughts that now must deck our H5 pr 28
as 'tis ever common | that men are merriest when 1.02.271
'tis so strange, | that, though the truth of it 2.02.102
'tis meet we all go forth | to view the sick and 2.04. 21
well, 'tis not so, my lord high constable; 2.04. 41
in cases of defense 'tis best to weigh | the 2.04. 43
know | 'tis no sinister nor no awkward claim, 2.04. 85
'tis shame for us all. 3.02.109 P
so god sa' me, 'tis shame to stand still, it is 3.02.110 P
'tis certain he hath pass'd the river somme. 3.05. 1
why, 'tis a gull, a fool, a rogue, that now and 3.06. 67 P
though 'tis no wisdom to confess so much | unto 3.06.143
'tis a subject for a sovereign to reason on, and 3.07. 35 P
'tis midnight, i'll go arm myself. 3.07. 89 P
'tis a hooded valor, and when it appears, it 3.07.111 P
'tis not the first time you were overshot. 3.07.124 P
'tis true that we are in great danger, | the 4.01. 1
'tis good for men to love their present pains 4.01. 18
but i believe, as cold a night as 'tis, he could 4.01.114 P
'tis certain, every man that dies ill, the ill 4.01.186 P
come, 'tis a foolish saying. 4.01.202 P
and i know | 'tis not the balm, the sceptre, and 4.01.260
'tis positive against all exceptions, lords, 4.02. 25
'tis a fearful odds. 4.03. 5
'tis expressly against the law of arms. 4.07. 1 P
'tis as arrant a piece of knavery, mark you now, 4.07. 2 P
'tis certain there's not a boy left alive, and 4.07. 5 P
o, 'tis a gallant king! 4.07. 10 P
but 'tis all one, 'tis alike as my fingers is to 4.07. 29 P
one, 'tis alike as my fingers is to my fingers, 4.07. 30 P
'tis the gage of one that i should fight withal, 4.07.122 P
'tis a good silling, i warrant you, or i will 4.08. 71 P
'tis wonderful! 4.08.112
the interim, by rememb'ring you 'tis past. 5.pr. 43
'tis no matter for his swellings nor his 5.01. 16 P
'tis hereafter to know, but now to promise. 5.02.212 P
whoe'er helps thee, 'tis thou that must help me: 1H6 1.02.107
'tis the french dolphin sueth to thee thus. 1.02.112
open the gates, 'tis gloucester that calls. 1.03. 4
come, come, 'tis only i that must disgrace thee. 1.05. 8
'tis joan, not we, by whom the day is won; 1.06. 17
'tis sure they found some place | but weakly 2.01. 73
'tis thought, lord talbot, when the fight began, 2.02. 22
no, truly, 'tis more than manners will; 2.02. 54
'tis not for fear, but anger, that thy cheeks 2.04. 65
that whoso draws a sword, 'tis present death, 3.04. 39
'tis much, when sceptres are in children's hands 4.01.192
'tis but the short'ning of my life one day. 4.06. 37
'tis a mere french word; 4.07. 54
'tis said the stout parisians do revolt, | and 5.02. 2
i cry you mercy, 'tis but quid for quo. 5.03.109
my lords, and please you, 'tis not so, | i did 5.04. 10
'tis true, i gave a noble to the priest | the 5.04. 23
'tis known already that i am possess'd | with 5.04.138
for france, 'tis ours; 2H6 1.01.106
'tis not my speeches that you do mislike, | but 1.01.140
but 'tis my presence that doth trouble ye; 1.01.141
'tis known to you he is mine enemy; 1.01.148
'tis thine they give away, and not their own. 1.01.221
'tis his highness' pleasure | you do prepare to 1.02. 56
'tis but a base ignoble mind | that mounts no 2.01. 13
'tis like, my lord, you will not keep your hour. 2.01.177
'tis that they seek; 2.02. 75
'tis not his wont to be the hindmost man, | what 3.01. 2
'tis to be fear'd they all will follow him. 3.01. 30
now 'tis the spring, and weeds are 3.01. 31
'tis thought, my lord, that you took bribes of 3.01.104
why, 'tis well known that, whiles i was 3.01.124
'tis my special hope | that you will clear 3.01.139
'tis meet he be condemn'd by course of law. 3.01.237
'tis york that hath more reason for his death. 3.01.245
madam, 'tis true; 3.01.252
sleeping, or waking, 'tis no matter how, | so he 3.01.263
thrice-noble suffolk, 'tis resolutely spoke. 3.01.266
'tis meet that lucky ruler be employ'd — 3.01.291
'tis politicly done, | to send me packing with 3.01.341
say that he thrive, as 'tis great like he will, 3.01.379
'tis, my good lord. 3.02. 13
to-day, | if he be guilty, as 'tis published. 3.02. 17
that he is dead, good warwick, 'tis too true, 3.02.130
'tis like you would not feast him like a friend, 3.02.184
friend, | and 'tis well seen he found an enemy. 3.02.185
'tis like the commons, rude unpolish'd hinds, 3.02.271
'tis but surmis'd whiles thou art standing by, 3.02.347
'tis not the land i care for, wert thou thence; 3.02.359
so he had need, for 'tis threadbare. 4.02. 7 P
the bee stings, but i say, 'tis the bee's wax; 4.02. 82 P
but i say, 'tis true. 4.02.141
nay, 'tis too true; therefore he shall be king. 4.02.147
now show yourselves men, 'tis for liberty. 4.02.183
the mouth with a spear, and 'tis not whole yet. 4.07. 9 P
nothing but this; 'tis "bona terra, mala gens." 4.07. 56
and yield to mercy whilst 'tis offered you, | or 4.08. 12
clifford of cumberland, 'tis warwick calls! 5.02. 1
nobly, york, 'tis for a crown thou fight'st. 5.02. 16
but that 'tis shown ignobly and in treason. 5.02. 23
and while 'tis mine, | it shall be stony. 5.02. 50
'tis not enough our foes are this time fled, 5.03. 21
'tis not thy southern power | of essex, norfolk, 3H6 1.01.155
o, 'tis a fault too too unpardonable! 1.04.106
'tis beauty that doth oft make women proud, 1.04.128
'tis virtue that doth make them most admir'd, 1.04.130
'tis government that makes them seem divine, 1.04.132
methinks 'tis prize enough to be his son. 2.01. 20
'tis wondrous strange, the like yet never heard 2.01. 33
'tis love i bear thy glories make me speak. 2.01.158
'tis not my fault, | nor wittingly have i 2.02. 7
then 'twas my turn to fly, and now 'tis thine. 2.02.105
no, 'tis impossible he should escape; 2.06. 38
revoke that doom of mercy, for 'tis clifford, 2.06. 46
'tis but his policy to counterfeit, | because he 2.06. 65
no, harry, harry, 'tis no land of thine; 3.01. 15
an easy task, 'tis but to love a king. 3.02. 53
but stay thee, 'tis the fruits of love i mean. 3.02. 58
'tis better said than done, my gracious lord. 3.02. 90
'tis a happy thing | to be the father unto many 3.02.104
then 'tis but reason that i be releas'd | from 3.03.147
'tis not his new-made bride shall succor him, 3.03.207
alas, you know, 'tis far from hence to france; 4.01. 4
but the safer when 'tis back'd with france. 4.01. 41
'tis better using france than trusting france. 4.01. 42
'tis the lord hastings, the king's chiefest 4.03. 11
'tis the more honor, because more dangerous. 4.03. 15
stands, | 'tis to be doubted he would waken him. 4.03. 19
but wherefore stay we? 'tis no time to talk. 4.05. 24
'tis like that richmond with the rest shall down 4.06.100
till then, 'tis wisdom to conceal our meaning. 4.07. 60
for 'tis my right, | and henry but usurps the 4.07. 65
why then 'tis mine, if but by warwick's gift. 5.01. 35
'tis even so, yet you are warwick still. 5.01. 47
say you can swim, alas, 'tis but a while; 5.04. 29
'twas sin before, but now 'tis charity. 5.05. 76
'tis sin to flatter, "good" was little better: 5.06. 3
indeed 'tis true that henry told me of; 5.06. 69
'tis not the king that sends you to the tower; R3 1.01. 63
'tis she | that /tempers him to this extremity. 1.01. 64
'tis very grievous to be thought upon. 1.01.141
for 'tis thy presence that exhales this blood 1.02. 58
'tis figur'd in my tongue. 1.02.193
'tis more than you deserve; 1.02.222
'tis time to speak, my pains are quite forgot. 1.03.116
'tis done by me, and ends in "margaret." 1.03.238
and tell them 'tis the queen and her allies 1.03.329
'tis better, sir, than to be tedious. 1.04. 89 P
you may, sir, 'tis a point of wisdom. 1.04. 98 P
'tis no matter, let it go. 1.04.131 P
'tis a blushing shame-fac'd spirit that mutinies 1.04.137 P
/'zounds, 'tis even now at my elbow, persuading 1.04.145 P
'tis he that sends us to destroy you here. 1.04.243
relent? no: 'tis cowardly and womanish. 1.04.261
'tis death to me to be at enmity; 2.01. 61
in common worldly things 'tis call'd ungrateful 2.02. 91
it so, | 'tis more than we deserve or i expect. 2.03. 37
o, 'tis a perilous boy, | bold, quick, ingenious 3.01.154
'tis a vile thing to die, my gracious lord, 3.02. 62
protest, | was it so precious to me as 'tis now. 3.02. 80
'tis better with me now | than when thou met'st 3.02. 98
come, come, dispatch, 'tis bootless to exclaim. 3.04.102
at their beads, 'tis much to draw them thence, 3.07. 93
ha? am i king? 'tis so — but edward lives. 4.02. 14
'tis full of thy foul wrongs. 4.04.375
'tis thought that richmond is their admiral; 4.04.437
'tis said, my liege, in yorkshire are in arms. 4.04.519
ratcliffe, my lord, 'tis i. 5.03.209
'tis not yet near day. 5.03.220
why, then 'tis time to arm and give direction. 5.03.236
your choler question | what 'tis you go about: H8 1.01.131
count-cardinal | has done this, and 'tis well; 1.01.173
'tis his highness' pleasure | you shall to th' 1.01.206

let me say | 'tis but the fate of place, and the 1.02. 75
if he may | find mercy in the law, 'tis his; 1.02.212
i'm glad 'tis there. 1.03. 21
'tis time to give 'em physic, their diseases 1.03. 36
o, 'tis true; 1.03. 51
pledge it, madam, | for 'tis to such a thing — 1.04. 48
'tis likely, | by all conjectures: 2.01. 40
if the duke be guiltless, | 'tis full of woe; 2.01.140
'tis the cardinal; 2.01.161
'tis woeful. 2.01.167
'tis so; 2.02. 18
'tis most true | these news are every where; 2.02. 37
o, 'tis a tender place, and i must leave her. 2.02.143
bitter than | 'tis sweet at first t' acquire — 2.03. 9
'tis a sufferance panging | as soul and body's 2.03. 15
verily, | i swear, 'tis better to be lowly born, 2.03. 19
'tis strange. 2.03. 36
this burthen, 'tis too weak | ever to get a boy. 2.03. 43
there was a lady once ('tis an old story) | that 2.03. 90
'tis not well. 2.04.123
'tis a needful fitness | that we adjourn this 2.04.232
'tis not well, lords. 3.01.133
'tis so. | the cardinal! 3.02. 74
candle burns not clear, 'tis i must snuff it, 3.02. 96
'tis well said again, | and 'tis a kind of good 3.02.152
and 'tis a kind of good deed to say well, | and 3.02.153
'tis nobly spoken. 3.02.199
'tis so! 3.02.209
'tis th' accompt | of all that world of wealth i 3.02.210
'tis virtue. 3.02.333
o, 'tis a burden, cromwell, 'tis a burden | too 3.02.384
'tis a burden | too heavy for a man that hopes 3.02.384
i have, | to the last penny, 'tis the king's. 3.02.452
'tis all my business. 4.01. 4
'tis very true; 4.01. 6
'tis well. 4.01. 7
yes, 'tis the list | of those that claim their 4.01. 14
'tis the same: high steward. 4.01. 41
'tis now the king's, and call'd whitehall. 4.01. 97
but 'tis so lately alter'd that the old name 4.01. 98
too late, | 'tis like a pardon after execution. 4.02.121
'tis midnight, charles, | prithee to bed, and in 5.01. 72
'tis true; where is he, denny? 5.01. 82
'tis his aspect of terror. 5.01. 88
'tis a girl | promises boys hereafter. 5.01.165
'tis as like you | as cherry is to cherry. 5.01.168
now, | while 'tis hot, i'll put it to the issue. 5.01.176
'tis butts, | the king's physician. 5.02. 10
'tis he indeed. 5.02. 25
'tis well there's one above 'em yet. 5.02. 27
'tis his highness' pleasure | and our consent, 5.02. 87
i see your end, | 'tis my undoing. 5.02. 97
'tis a cruelty | to load a falling man. 5.02.111
'tis no counterfeit. 5.02.137
'tis the right ring, by heav'n! 5.02.138
'tis now too certain. 5.02.142
'tis as much impossible — | unless we sweep 'em 5.03. 12
as 'tis to make 'em sleep | on may–day morning, 5.03. 14
'tis ten to one this play can never please | all ep 1
so, 'tis clear, | they'll say 'tis naught; ep 4
so, 'tis clear, | they'll say 'tis naught; ep 5
for 'tis ill hap | if they hold when their ep 13
if she be fair, 'tis better for her; TRO 1.01. 67 P
and she were a blackamoor, 'tis all one to me. 1.01. 78 P
let paris bleed, 'tis but a scar to scorn; 1.01.111
'tis just to each of them; he is himself. 1.02. 71 P
for a brown favor (for so 'tis, i must confess) 1.02. 94 P
why, you know 'tis dimpled. 1.02.121 P
i'll be sworn 'tis true; 1.02.173 P
'tis troilus! 1.02.227 P
and 'tis this fever that keeps troy on foot, 1.03.135
'tis like a chime a–mending, with terms 1.03.159
'tis agamemnon right! 1.03.164
'tis nestor right. 1.03.170
sir, pardon, 'tis for agamemnon's ears. 1.03.248
'tis dry enough), will, with great speed of 1.03.329
why, 'tis most meet. 1.03.333
therefore 'tis meet achilles meet not hector. 1.03.357
'tis no matter, i shall speak as much as thou 2.01.111 P
dare | maintain — i know not what, 'tis trash. 2.01.126
i know not, 'tis put to lott'ry. 2.01.128
what's aught but as 'tis valued? 2.02. 52
as well wherein 'tis precious of itself | as in 2.02. 55
'tis mad idolatry | to make the service greater 2.02. 56
'tis our mad sister, i do know her voice. 2.02. 98
for 'tis a cause that hath no mean dependance 2.02.192
but, by my head, 'tis pride. 2.03. 88 P
'tis said he holds you well, and will be led 2.03.180
why, 'tis this naming of him does him harm. 2.03.228
here is a man — but 'tis before his face, | i 2.03.229
and 'tis a burthen | which i am proud to bear. 3.03. 36
'tis like he'll question me | why such 3.03. 42
'tis certain, greatness, once fall'n out with 3.03. 75
but 'tis not so with me, | fortune and i are 3.03. 87
'tis known, achilles, that you are in love 3.03.193
i know what 'tis to love, | and would, as i 4.03. 10
ay, ay, ay, ay, 'tis too plain a case. 4.04. 29 P
'tis troilus' fault. 4.04.143
'tis but early days. 4.05. 12
'tis he, i ken the manner of his gait, | he 4.05. 14
not, for you know 'tis true | that you are odd, 4.05. 43
i am your debtor, claim it when 'tis due. 4.05. 51
'tis done like hector. 4.05. 73
'tis agamemnon's wish, and great achilles | doth 4.05.152
'tis the old nestor. 4.05.201
no, yonder 'tis, | there where we see the lights 5.01. 67
well, well, 'tis done, 'tis past. 5.02. 97
well, well, 'tis done, 'tis past. 5.02. 97
o, 'tis true. 5.03. 13
o, 'tis fair play. 5.03. 43
hector, then 'tis wars. 5.03. 49
martius, 'tis true that you have lately told us, COR 1.01.227
'tis not four days gone | since i heard thence; 1.02. 6
lead on this preparation | whither 'tis bent. 1.02. 16
most likely 'tis for you; 1.02. 16
'tis sworn between us we shall ever strike 1.02. 35
i'll swear 'tis a very pretty boy. 1.03. 57 P
indeed la, 'tis a noble child. 1.03. 67 P
'tis not to save labor, nor that i want love. 1.03. 81 P
'tis done. 1.04. 2
'tis for the followers fortune widens them, 1.04. 44
o, 'tis martius! 1.04. 61
'tis not a mile; 1.06. 16
'tis not my blood | wherein thou seest me mask'd 1.08. 9
take't, 'tis yours. what is't? 1.09. 81
dries, 'tis time | it should be look'd to. 1.09. 93
learn how 'tis held, and what they are that must 1.10. 28
i pray you | ('tis south the city mills) bring 1.10. 31
why, 'tis no great matter; 2.01. 28 P
nay, 'tis true. 2.01.107 P
'tis right. 2.01.236
'tis most like he will. 2.01.241
'tis thought | that martius shall be consul. 2.01.260
but 'tis thought of every one coriolanus will 2.02. 3 P
'tis strongly wadg'd up in a blockhead; 2.03. 28 P
and 'twere to give again — but 'tis no matter. 2.03. 83 P
'tis a condition they account gentle. 2.03. 97 P
by his looks, methinks, | 'tis warm at 's heart. 2.03.152
no, 'tis his kind of speech, he did not mock us. 2.03.161
and this shall seem, as partly 'tis, their own, 2.03.262
for 'tis a sore upon us | you cannot tent 3.01.234
but now 'tis odds beyond arithmetic, | and 3.01.244
sir, 'tis fit | you make strong party, or defend 3.02. 93
i have; 'tis ready. 3.03. 10
say then; 'tis true, i ought so. 3.03. 62
women | 'tis fond to wail inevitable strokes, 4.01. 26
inevitable strokes, | as 'tis to laugh at 'em. 4.01. 27
city, | 'tis i that made thy widows; 4.04. 2
'tis an honester service than to meddle with thy 4.05. 47 P
and say "'tis true," i'd not believe them more 4.05.105
'tis, as it were, a parcel of their feast, and 4.05.215 P
'tis so, and as wars, in some sort, may be said 4.05.227 P
'tis he, 'tis he. 4.06. 11
'tis he, 'tis he. 4.06. 11
'tis aufidius, | who, hearing of our martius' 4.06. 42
'tis this slave — | go whip him 'fore the 4.06. 60
'tis true; 4.06.114
'tis no matter; 4.06.136
you guard like men, 'tis well. 5.02. 2
'tis a spell, you see, of much power. 5.02. 96 P
to infringe my vow | in the same time 'tis made? 5.03. 21
'tis the first time that ever | i was forc'd to 5.06.104
have writ your annals true, 'tis there | that, 5.06.113
'tis good, sir, you are very short with us; TIT 1.01.409
'tis thou, and those, that have dishonored me. 1.01.425
and make them know what 'tis to let a queen 1.01.454
'tis not the difference of a year or two | makes 2.01. 31
'tis policy and stratagem must do | that you 2.01.104
'tis thought you have a goodly gift in horning, 2.03. 67
'tis pity they should take him for a stag. 2.03. 71
'tis true, the raven doth not hatch a lark, 2.03.149
for 'tis not life that i have begg'd so long, 2.03.170
'tis present death i beg, and one thing more 2.03.173
if it be dark, how dost thou know 'tis he? 2.03.225
'tis not an hour since i left them there. 2.03.256
sweet huntsman — bassianus 'tis we mean — | do 2.03.269
shall i say 'tis so? 2.04. 33
whose souls is not corrupted as 'tis thought. 3.01. 9
why, 'tis no matter, man: 3.01. 33
'tis well, lavinia, that thou hast no hands, 3.01. 79
grandsire, 'tis ovid's metamorphosis, | my 4.01. 42
'tis sure enough, and you knew how, | but if you 4.01. 95
o, 'tis a verse in horace, i know it well, | i 4.02. 22
o lord, sir, 'tis a deed of policy. 4.02.148
ye draw home enough, and 'tis there straight. 4.03. 3
'tis you must dig with mattock and with spade, 4.03. 11
'tis he. 4.04. 42 P
'tis he the common people love so much; 4.04. 73
'tis sad titus calls. 5.02.121
since 'tis my father's mind | that i repair to 5.03. 1
'tis true, 'tis true, witness my knive's sharp 5.03. 63
'tis true, 'tis true, witness my knive's sharp 5.03. 63
'tis true, and therefore women, being the weaker ROM 1.01. 15 P
'tis all one; 1.01. 21 P
and 'tis known i am a pretty piece of flesh. 1.01. 29 P
'tis well thou art not fish; 1.01. 30 P
'tis the way | to call hers, exquisite, in 1.01.228
in penalty alike, and 'tis not hard, i think, 1.02. 2
both, | and pity 'tis you liv'd at odds so long. 1.02. 5
'tis since the earthquake now aleven years, 1.03. 23
and 'tis much pride | for fair without the fair 1.03. 89
in going to this mask, | but 'tis no wit to go. 1.04. 49
hands, and they unwash'd too, 'tis a foul thing. 1.05. 4 P
'tis gone, 'tis gone, 'tis gone. 1.05. 24
'tis gone, 'tis gone, 'tis gone. 1.05. 24
'tis gone, 'tis gone, 'tis gone. 1.05. 24
'tis not so much, 'tis not so much: 1.05. 34
'tis not so much, 'tis not so much: 1.05. 34
'tis since the nuptial of lucentio, | come 1.05. 35
'tis more, 'tis more. 1.05. 38
'tis more, 'tis more. 1.05. 38
'tis he, that villain romeo. 1.05. 64
why, uncle, 'tis a shame. 1.05. 82
marry, 'tis time. 1.05. 85
for 'tis in vain | to seek him here that means 2.01. 41
i am too bold, 'tis not to me she speaks. 2.02. 14
'tis but thy name that is my enemy; 2.02. 38
i will not fail, 'tis twenty year till then. 2.02.169
'tis almost morning, i would have thee gone — 2.02.176
'tis no less, i tell ye, for the bawdy hand of 2.04.112 P
ay, a scratch, a scratch, marry, 'tis enough. 3.01. 93
no, 'tis not so deep as a well, nor so wide as a 3.01. 96 P
nor so wide as a church–door, but 'tis enough, 3.01. 97 P
for 'tis a throne where honor may be crown'd 3.02. 93
'tis torture, and not mercy. 3.03. 29
'tis late; 3.03.172
'tis very late, she'll not come down to–night. 3.04. 5
'tis but the pale reflex of cynthia's brow; 3.05. 20
sir, 'tis an ill cook that cannot lick his own 4.02. 6 P
short in our provision, | 'tis now near night. 4.02. 39
the curfew–bell hath rung, 'tis three a' clock. 4.04. 4
good /faith, 'tis day. 4.04. 21
not a dump we, 'tis no time to play now. 4.05.109 P
o, 'tis a worthy lord. TIM 1.01. 9
'tis a good form. 1.01. 17
/gum, which /oozes | from whence 'tis nourish'd. 1.01. 22
'tis a good piece. 1.01. 28
so 'tis. this comes off well and excellent. 1.01. 29
'tis conceiv'd to scope. 1.01. 72
'tis common: 1.01. 89
'tis not enough to help the feeble up, | but to 1.01.107
will strain a little, | for 'tis a bond in men. 1.01.144
if i should pay you for't as 'tis extoll'd, | it 1.01.167
'tis rated | as those which sell would give; 1.01.168
what dost thou think 'tis worth? 1.01.213 P
'tis alcibiades, and some twenty horse, | all of 1.01.241
recanting goodness, sorry ere 'tis shown; 1.02. 17
does not become a man, 'tis much to blame. 1.02. 27
a precious comfort 'tis to have so many like 1.02.104 P
'tis pity bounty had not eyes behind, | that man 1.02.163
'tis yours, because you lik'd it. 1.02.212
so kind to heart, 'tis not enough to give; 1.02.219
no, 'tis to thyself. come away. 2.02. 53 P
'tis a spirit; 2.02.109 P
'tis all engag'd, some forfeited and gone, | and 2.02.146
a wrench — would all were well — 'tis pity — 2.02.209
their blood is cak'd, 'tis cold, it seldom flows 2.02.216
'tis lack of kindly warmth they are not kind; 2.02.217
give't these fellows | to whom 'tis instant due. 2.02.230
a noble gentleman 'tis, if he would not keep so 3.01. 22 P
upon my soul, 'tis true, sir. 3.02. 43
'tis deepest winter in lord timon's purse; 3.04. 14
'tis much deep, and it should seem by th' sum 3.04. 30
if 'twill not serve, 'tis not so base as you, 3.04. 58
'tis necessary he should die. 3.05. 2
kill, | what folly 'tis to hazard life for ill! 3.05. 37
but in defense, by mercy, 'tis most just. 3.05. 55
'tis inferr'd to us, | his days are foul and his 3.05. 72
'tis in few words, but spacious in effect: 3.05. 96
'tis honor with most lands to be at odds; 3.05.115
'tis so, be sure of it. 3.06. 55 P
here 'tis. 3.06.116 P
'tis, then, because thou dost not keep a dog, 4.03.200
'tis most just | that thou turn rascal; 4.03.216
'tis not well mended so, it is but botch'd; 4.03.285
true; for he bears it not about him, 'tis hid. 4.03.406 P
'tis his description. 4.03.409 P
'tis in the malice of mankind that he thus 4.03.452 P
look thee, 'tis so. 4.03.523
'tis said he gave unto | his steward a mighty 5.01. 7
'tis not amiss | we tender our loves to him in 5.01. 11
'tis thou that rig'st the bark and plough'st the 5.01. 50
marry, 'tis not monstrous in you, neither wish i 5.01. 88
'tis most nobly spoken. 5.04. 63
'tis just, | and it is very much lamented, JC 1.02. 54
i did mark | how he did shake — 'tis true, this 1.02.121
'tis very like, he hath the falling sickness. 1.02.254
'tis caesar that you mean; is it not, cassius? 1.03. 79
'tis cinna, i do know him by his gait, | he is a 1.03.132
but 'tis a common proof | that lowliness is 2.01. 21
'tis good. 2.01. 60
sir, 'tis your brother cassius at the door, 2.01. 70
'tis time to part. 2.01.193
caesar, 'tis strucken eight. 2.02.114
'tis furnish'd well with men, | and men are 3.01. 66
that we shall die we know, 'tis but the time, 3.01. 99
that i did love thee, caesar, o, 'tis true; 3.01.194
therefore 'tis certain he was not ambitious. 3.02.113
i found it in his closet, 'tis his will. 3.02.129
'tis good you know not that you are his heirs, 3.02.145
'tis not meet | they be alone. 4.03.125
bear with him, brutus, 'tis his fashion. 4.03.135
'tis better that the enemy seek us; 4.03.199
but 'tis not so. 5.01. 12
if not, 'tis true this parting was well made. 5.01.121
and when my face is cover'd, as 'tis now, 5.03. 44
'tis three a' clock, and, romans, yet ere night 5.03.109
but 'tis strange; MAC 1.03.122
if it were done, when 'tis done, then 'twere 1.07. 1
how tender 'tis to love the babe that milks me; 1.07. 55
i take't, 'tis later, sir. 2.01. 3
if you shall cleave to my consent, when 'tis, 2.01. 25
am afraid they have awak'd, | and 'tis not done; 2.02. 10
'tis the eye of childhood | that fears a painted 2.02. 51
but yet 'tis one. 2.03. 49
so bold to call, | for 'tis my limited service. 2.03. 52
'tis not for you to hear what i can speak: 2.03. 84
by th' clock 'tis day, | and yet dark night 2.04. 6
'tis unnatural, | even like the deed that's done 2.04. 10
'tis said, they eat each other. 2.04. 18
then 'tis most like | the sovereignty will fall 2.04. 29
'tis much he dares, | and, to that dauntless 3.01. 50
'tis safer to be that which we destroy | than by 3.02. 6
then 'tis he; 3.03. 9
'tis he. 3.03. 14
'tis banquo's then. 3.04. 13
'tis better thee without than he within. 3.04. 14
that is not often vouch'd, while 'tis a–making, 3.04. 33
while 'tis a–making, | 'tis given with welcome. 3.04. 34
'tis no other; 3.04. 96
harpier cries, "'tis time, 'tis time." 4.01. 3
harpier cries, "'tis time, 'tis time." 4.01. 3
now i see 'tis true, | for the blood–bolter'd 4.01.122
'tis two or three, my lord, that bring you word 4.01.141
things at once | 'tis hard to reconcile. 4.03.139
'tis call'd the evil: 4.03.146
put on with holy prayers, and 'tis spoken, | to 4.03.154
you may to me, and 'tis most meet you should. 5.01. 15 P
has light by her continually, 'tis her command. 5.01. 23 P
one — two — why then 'tis time to do't. 5.01. 36 P
we on | to give obedience where 'tis truly ow'd. 5.02. 26
'tis not needed yet. 5.03. 33
'tis his main hope; 5.04. 10
who (as 'tis thought) by self and violent hands 5.09. 36
'tis now strook twelf. HAM 1.01. 7
'tis bitter cold, | and i am sick at heart. 1.01. 8
horatio says 'tis but our fantasy, | and will 1.01. 23
'tis gone, and will not answer. 1.01. 52
'tis strange. 1.01. 64
'tis here! 1.01.141
'tis here! 1.01.141
'tis gone! 1.01.142
thou know'st 'tis common, all that lives must 1.02. 72
'tis not alone my inky cloak, /good mother, 1.02. 77

'tis sweet and commendable in your nature, 1.02. 87
of impious stubbornness, 'tis unmanly grief, 1.02. 94
fie, 'tis a fault to heaven, | a fault against 1.02.101
why, 'tis a loving and a fair reply. 1.02.121
'tis an unweeded garden | that grows to seed, 1.02.135
'tis very strange. 1.02.220
as i do live, my honor'd lord, 'tis true, | and 1.02.221
'tis in my memory lock'd, | and you yourself 1.03. 85
'tis told me, he hath very oft of late | given 1.03. 91
if it be so — as so 'tis put on me, | and that 1.03. 94
let's follow. 'tis not fit thus to obey him. 1.04. 88
'tis given out that, sleeping in my orchard, | a 1.05. 35
that he's mad, 'tis true, 'tis true 'tis pity, 2.02. 97
that he's mad, 'tis true, 'tis true 'tis pity, 2.02. 97
that he's mad, 'tis true, 'tis true 'tis pity, 2.02. 97
'tis true 'tis pity, | and pity 'tis 'tis true. 2.02. 98
'tis true 'tis pity, | and pity 'tis 'tis true. 2.02. 98
that i have positively said, "'tis so," | when 2.02.154
beast —" | 'tis not so, it begins with pyrrhus: 2.02.451 P
'tis well, i'll have thee speak out the rest of 2.02.521 P
'tis most true, | and he beseech'd me to entreat 3.01. 21
'tis too much prov'd — that with devotion's 3.01. 46
o, 'tis too true! 3.01. 48
whether 'tis nobler in the mind to suffer | the 3.01. 56
'tis a consummation | devoutly to be wish'd. 3.01. 62
nay, 'tis twice two months, my lord. 3.02.128 P
'tis brief, my lord. 3.02.153 P
most necessary 'tis that we forget | to pay 3.02.192
aye, nor 'tis not strange | that even our loves 3.02.200
for 'tis a question left us yet to prove, 3.02.202
'tis deeply sworn. 3.02.225
'tis a knavish piece of work, but what of that? 3.02.240 P
by th' mass and 'tis, like a camel indeed. 3.02.378 P
'tis now the very witching time of night, | when 3.02.388
'tis meet that some more audience than a mother, 3.03. 31
and oft 'tis seen the wicked prize itself | buys 3.03. 59
but 'tis not so above: 3.03. 60
and course of thought | 'tis heavy with him. 3.03. 84
alack, | i had forgot. 'tis so concluded on. 3.04.201
for 'tis the sport to have the enginer | hoist 3.04.206
o, 'tis most sweet | when in one line two crafts 3.04.209
you must translate, 'tis fit we understand them. 4.01. 2
/compounded it with dust, whereto 'tis kin. 4.02. 6
tell us where 'tis, that we may take it thence, 4.02. 7
and where 'tis so, th' offender's scourge is 4.03. 6
till i know 'tis done, | how e'er my haps, my 4.03. 67
'tis hamlet's character. 4.07. 51
why, 'tis found so. 5.01. 8 P
'tis e'en so, the hand of little employment hath 5.01. 69 P
lie out on't, sir, and therefore 'tis not yours; 5.01.123 P
'tis for the dead, not for the quick, therefore 5.01.126 P
'tis a quick lie, sir, 'twill away again from me 5.01.128 P
or, if 'a do not, 'tis no great matter there. 5.01.151 P
'tis dangerous when the baser nature comes 5.02. 60
the more gracious, for 'tis a vice to know him. 5.02. 84 P
'tis a chough, but, as i say, spacious in the 5.02. 87 P
your bonnet to his right use, 'tis for the head. 5.02. 92 P
no, believe me, 'tis very cold, the wind is 5.02. 95 P
if it be /now, 'tis not to come; 5.02.221 P
and 'tis our fast intent | to shake all cares LR 1.01. 38
'tis strange that from their cold'st neglect 1.01.254
'tis the infirmity of his age, yet he hath ever 1.01.293 P
'tis strange. 1.02.117 P
then 'tis like the breath of an unfee'd lawyer, 1.04.129 P
'tis not so. 1.04.229
'tis politic and safe to let him keep | at point 1.04.323
i know not, madam. 'tis too bad, too bad. 2.01. 96
'tis they have put him on the old man's death, 2.01. 99
sir, 'tis my occupation to be plain: 2.02. 92
for thee, friend, 'tis the /duke's pleasure, 2.02.152
i know 'tis from cordelia, | who hath most 2.02.166
'tis strange that they should so depart from 2.04. 1
'tis worse than murther | to do upon respect 2.04. 23
'tis on such ground and to such wholesome end 2.04.144
'tis not in thee | to grudge my pleasures, to 2.04.173
'tis hard, almost impossible. 2.04.242
'tis his own blame hath put himself from rest, 2.04.290
'tis best to give him way, he leads himself. 2.04.298
shut up your doors, my lord, 'tis a wild night, 2.04.308
'tis foul. 3.02. 24
harder than the stones whereof 'tis rais'd, 3.02. 64
this night — 'tis dangerous to be spoken; 3.03. 10 P
thou think'st 'tis much that this contentious 3.04. 6
so 'tis to thee; 3.04. 7
be contented, 'tis a naughty night to swim in. 3.04.110 P
ingrateful fox, 'tis he. 3.07. 28
'tis most ignobly done | to pluck me by the 3.07. 35
full oft 'tis seen, | our means secure us, and 4.01. 19
'tis poor mad tom. 4.01. 26
'tis the time's plague, when madmen lead the 4.01. 46
'tis from your sister. 4.02. 83
alack, 'tis he! 4.04. 1
'tis known before; 4.04. 22
how fearful | and dizzy 'tis, to cast one's eyes 4.06. 12
'tis a lie, i am not ague–proof. 4.06.105 P
not ha' bin zo long as 'tis by a vortnight. 4.06.239 P
for him 'tis well | that of thy death and 4.06.277
'tis wonder that thy life and wits at once | had 4.07. 40
madam, do you, 'tis fittest. 4.07. 42
'tis to be doubted, madam. 5.01. 6
'tis most convenient, pray go with us. 5.01. 36
'tis she is sub–contracted to this lord, | and i 5.03. 86
'tis past, and so am i. 5.03.165
th' hast spoken right, 'tis true. 5.03.174
and when 'tis told, o, that my heart would burst 5.03.183
'tis hot, it smokes, | it came even from the 5.03.224
'tis noble kent, your friend. 5.03.269
'tis true, my lords, he did. 5.03.276
'tis the curse of service; OTH 1.01. 35
'tis not long after | but i will wear my heart 1.01. 63
'tis better as it is. 1.02. 6
'tis yet to know — | which, when i know that 1.02. 19
'tis well i am found by you. 1.02. 47
judge me the world, if 'tis not gross in sense, 1.02. 72
on, | 'tis probable, and palpable to thinking. 1.02. 76
'tis true, most worthy signior; 1.02. 91
'tis oft with difference), yet do they all 1.03. 7
'tis a pageant | to keep us in false gaze. 1.03. 18
'tis certain then for cyprus. 1.03. 43
'tis in ourselves that we are thus or thus. 1.03.319 P
i am glad on't; 'tis a worthy governor. 2.01. 30
and give us truth who 'tis that is arriv'd. 2.01. 58
'tis one iago, ancient to the general. 2.01. 66
'tis my breeding | that gives me this bold show 2.01. 98
you say true, 'tis so indeed. 2.01.171 P
'tis so indeed. 2.01.175 P
'tis truly so. 2.01.179
with him? why, 'tis not possible. 2.01.220 P
she loves him, 'tis apt and of great credit. 2.01.287
'tis here; 2.01.311
'tis not yet ten o' th' clock. 2.03. 13 P
'tis a night of revels, the gallants desire it. 2.03. 43 P
'tis pride that pulls the country down, | /then 2.03. 95
his vice, | 'tis to his virtue a just equinox, 2.03.124
'tis pity of him. 2.03.125
'tis evermore /the prologue to his sleep. 2.03.129
and 'tis great pity that the noble moor | should 2.03.138
'tis monstrous. 2.03.217
'tis the soldiers' life | to have their balmy 2.03.257
for 'tis most easy | th' inclining desdemona to 2.03.339
/by /the /mass, 'tis morning; 2.03.378
'tis as i should entreat you wear your gloves, 3.03. 77
'tis something, nothing; 3.03.157
'twas mine, 'tis his, and has been slave to 3.03.158
nor shall not, whilst 'tis in my custody. 3.03.164
'tis not to make me jealious | to say my wife is 3.03.183
although 'tis fit that cassio have his place — 3.03.246
yet 'tis the plague /of great ones, 3.03.273
'tis destiny unshunnable, like death. 3.03.275
look, here 'tis. 3.03.313
i swear 'tis better to be much abus'd | than but 3.03.336
'tis a shrewd doubt, though it be but a dream, 3.03.429
now do i see 'tis true. 3.03.444
'tis gone. 3.03.446
with thy fraught, | for 'tis of aspics' tongues! 3.03.450
'tis done at your request. 3.03.474
and for me to say a soldier lies, 'tis stabbing. 3.04. 6 P
'tis a good hand, | a frank one. 3.04. 43
'tis true; 3.04. 69
'tis not a year or two shows us a man: 3.04.103
'tis she must do't; 3.04.107
'tis even so; 3.04.145
'tis but a little way that i can bring you, 3.04.199
'tis very good; i must be circumstanc'd. 3.04.201
if they do nothing, 'tis a venial slip; 4.01. 9
why then 'tis hers, my lord, and, being hers, 4.01. 12
o, 'tis the spite of hell, the fiend's arch–mock 4.01. 70
o, thou art wise; 'tis certain. 4.01. 74
(as 'tis the strumpet's plague | to beguile many 4.01. 96
'tis such another fitchew! 4.01.146 P
o, 'tis foul in her. 4.01.201 P
'tis lodovico — | this comes from the duke. 4.01.214
'tis very much, | make her amends; 4.01.243
'tis meet i should be us'd so, very meet. 4.02.107
'tis but his humor. 4.02.165
i cannot go to, man, nor 'tis not very well. 4.02.193 P
i tell you 'tis not very well. 4.02.196 P
'tis neither here nor there. 4.03. 59
for your labor, 'tis a wrong in your own world, 4.03. 81 P
'tis but a man gone. 5.01. 10
i know his gait, 'tis he. 5.01. 23
'tis he! 5.01. 31
'tis some mischance, the voice is very direful. 5.01. 38
'tis heavy night; 5.01. 42
he, he, 'tis he. 5.01. 98
'tis emilia. 5.02. 91
'tis like she comes to speak of cassio's death; 5.02. 92
'tis a strange truth. 5.02.189
'tis proper i obey him; 5.02.196
'tis pitiful; 5.02.210
'tis a notorious villain. 5.02.239
that same villain, | for 'tis a damned slave. 5.02.243
'tis not so now. 5.02.265
'tis a lost fear; 5.02.269
for, in my sense, 'tis happiness to die. 5.02.290
'tis thus: ANT 1.02. 97
let her not say 'tis i that keep you here, | i 1.03. 22
'tis sweating labor | to bear such idleness so 1.03. 93
as his own state and ours, 'tis to be chid — 1.04. 30
shalt thou have report | how 'tis abroad. 1.04. 36
peep forth, but 'tis as soon | taken as seen; 1.04. 53
'tis pity of him. 1.04. 71
'tis time we twain | did show ourselves i' th' 1.04. 73
o, 'tis treason! 1.05. 7
'tis well for thee, | that, being unseminar'd, 1.05. 10
him, | note him, good charmian, 'tis the man; 1.05. 54
where have you this? 'tis false. 2.01. 18
from egypt, 'tis | a space for farther travel. 2.01. 30
good enobarbus, 'tis a worthy deed, | and shall 2.02. 1
'tis not a time | for private stomaching. 2.02. 8
'tis spoken well. 2.02. 25
'tis noble spoken. 2.02. 98
for 'tis a studied, not a present thought, | by 2.02.137
but, be /away, 'tis noble. 2.03. 31
yet, if thou say antony lives, 'tis well, | or 2.05. 43
say 'tis not so, a province i will give thee, 2.05. 68
'tis no matter. 2.05.110
'tis true. 2.06.114 P
'tis a strange serpent. 2.07. 48 P
'tis so, and the tears of it are wet. 2.07. 49 P
in me 'tis villainy, | in thee't had been good 2.07. 74
'tis not my profit that does lead mine honor; 2.07. 76
seeks, and will not take when once 'tis offer'd, 2.07. 83
'tis a noble lepidus. 3.02. 6
like her? o isis! 'tis impossible. 3.03. 15
but 'tis no matter, thou shalt bring him to me 3.03. 46
before gave audience, | as 'tis reported, so. 3.06. 19
'tis done already, and the messenger gone. 3.06. 31
and 'tis said in rome | that photinus an eunuch 3.07. 13
'tis impossible | strange that his power should 3.07. 56
'tis easy to't, and there i will attend | what 3.10. 31
caesar, 'tis his schoolmaster, | an argument 3.12. 2
to try thy eloquence, now 'tis time; 3.12. 26
'tis your noblest course. 3.13. 78
'tis better playing with a lion's whelp | than 3.13. 94
and at this time most easy 'tis to do't: 3.13.144
'tis one of those odd tricks which sorrow shoots 4.02. 14
belike 'tis but a rumor. good night to you. 4.03. 5
'tis a brave army, | and full of purpose. 4.03. 11
'tis the god hercules, whom antony lov'd, | now 4.03. 16
content. 'tis strange. 4.03. 22
'tis well blown, lads. 4.04. 25
that was like a t, | but now 'tis made an h. 4.07. 8
'tis sport to maul a runner. 4.07. 14
bring thee word | straight how 'tis like to go. 4.12. 3
'tis thou | hast sold me to this novice, and my 4.12. 13
'tis well th' art gone, | if it be well to live; 4.12. 39
strik'st not me, 'tis caesar thou defeat'st. 4.14. 68
'tis said, man, and farewell. 4.14. 92
'tis the last service that i shall command you. 4.14.132
antony | should conquer antony, but woe 'tis so! 4.15. 17
'tis paltry to be caesar; 5.02. 2
'tis yours, and we, | your scutcheons and your 5.02.134
'tis exactly valued, | not petty things admitted 5.02.139
nay, 'tis most certain, iras. 5.02.214
howsoe'er 'tis strange, | or that the negligence CYM 1.01. 65
ring i hold dear as my finger, 'tis part of it. 1.04.133 P
in himself, 'tis much; 1.06. 79
but 'tis your graces | that from my mutest 1.06.115
'tis plate of rare device, and jewels | of rich 1.06.189
and, 'tis thought, one of leonatus' friends. 2.01. 37 P
'tis her breathing that | perfumes the chamber 2.02. 18
'tis mine, and this will witness outwardly, | as 2.02. 35
'tis gold | which buys admittance (oft it doth), 2.03. 67
and 'tis gold | which makes the true man kill'd 2.03. 70
'tis very like. 2.04. 36
and now 'tis up again. 2.04. 97
o, no, no, no, 'tis true. 2.04.106
and take your ring again, 'tis not yet won. 2.04.114
'tis true — nay, keep the ring — 'tis true. 2.04.123
'tis true — nay, keep the ring — 'tis true. 2.04.123
yet 'tis greater skill | in a true hate, to pray 2.05. 33
read, and tell me | how far 'tis thither. 3.02. 50
no, 'tis slander, | whose edge is sharper than 3.04. 33
fear not, 'tis empty of all things but grief. 3.04. 69
for 'tis commanded | i should do so. 3.04.125
i have already fit | ('tis in my cloak–bag) 3.04.169
'tis all the better, | your valiant britains 3.05. 19
'tis not sleepy business, | but must be look'd 3.05. 26
the cure whereof, my lord, | 'tis time must do. 3.05. 38
'tis certain she is fled. 3.05. 66
on them, knowing 'tis | a punishment or trial? 3.06. 10
'tis some savage hold. 3.06. 18
will play the cook and servant, 'tis our match. 3.06. 30
as 'tis no better reckon'd, but of those | who 3.06. 54
'tis almost night, you shall have better cheer 3.06. 66
for 'tis said a woman's fitness comes by fits. 4.01. 5 P
'tis the ninth hour o' th' morn. 4.02. 30
i partly know him, 'tis | cloten, the son o' th' 4.02. 64
not these many years, and yet | i know 'tis he. 4.02. 67
well, 'tis done. 4.02.161
'tis wonder | that an invisible instinct should 4.02.176
'tis true. 4.02.256
but 'tis not so. 4.02.299
'tis gone. 4.02.312
'tis he and cloten. 4.02.324
o, 'tis pregnant, pregnant! 4.02.325
and bring me word how 'tis with her. 4.03. 1
'tis strange. 4.03. 37
'tis enough | that, britain, i have kill'd thy 5.01. 19
'tis their fresh supplies. 5.02. 16
'tis strange he hides him in fresh cups, soft 5.03. 71
'tis thought the old man and his sons were 5.03. 85
so 'tis reported; 5.03. 87
if of my freedom 'tis the main part, take | no 5.04. 16
and though | 'tis not so dear, yet 'tis a life; 5.04. 23
and though | 'tis not so dear, yet 'tis a life; 5.04. 23
no care of yours it is, you know 'tis ours. 5.04.100
'tis still a dream, or else such stuff as madmen 5.04.145
'tis now the time | to ask of whence you are. 5.05. 15
which read and not expounded, 'tis decreed, | as PER 1.01. 57
my lord, 'tis done. 1.01.158
'tis time to fear when tyrants seems to kiss. 1.02. 79
'tis dangerous. 1.03. 3 P
o, 'tis too true. 1.04. 32
bots on't, 'tis come at last, and 'tis turn'd to 2.01.118 P
come at last, and 'tis turn'd to a rusty armor. 2.01.118 P
'tis now your honor, daughter, to entertain 2.02. 14
'tis more by fortune, lady, than my merit. 2.03. 12
'tis very true. 2.04. 16
tied | her to her chamber, that 'tis impossible. 2.05. 9
'tis well, mistress, your choice agrees with 2.05. 18
'tis the king's subtilty to have my life. 2.05. 44
trouble you so early, | 'tis not our husbandry. 3.02. 20
'tis most strange | nature should be so 3.02. 24
'tis known, i ever | have studied physic; 3.02. 31
'tis of some wrack. 3.02. 51
'tis like a coffin, sir. 3.02. 52
what e'er it be, | 'tis wondrous heavy. 3.02. 53
'tis a good constraint of fortune it belches 3.02. 55
'tis so, my lord. 3.02. 56
how close 'tis caulk'd and /bitum'd! 3.02. 56
sea she lies in, yet the end | must be as 'tis. 3.03. 12
'tis but a blow, which never shall be known. 4.01. 2
come, come, i know 'tis good for you. 4.01. 44
'tis not our bringing up of poor bastards — as 4.02. 13 P
and care in us | at whose expense 'tis done. 4.03. 46
so, 'tis the better for you that your resorters 4.06. 23 P
your honor knows what 'tis to say well enough. 4.06. 31 P
'tis well bethought. 5.01. 44
sir, 'tis the governor of meteline, | who, 5.01.219
'tis most certain. 5.03. 20
'tis not this | i did begin to speak of. TNK 1.02. 34
'tis in our power | (unless we fear that apes 1.02. 42
too, for 'tis not scissor'd just | to such a 1.02. 54
with mind assur'd | 'tis bad he goes about? 1.02. 98
'tis in motion, | the intelligence of state came 1.02.105
'tis right — those, those. | they are not dead? 1.04. 23
'tis pity they are in prison, and 'twere pity 2.01. 22 P
'tis too true, arcite. 2.02. 46
certainly | 'tis a main goodness, cousin, that 2.02. 63
'tis most true, two souls | put in two noble 2.02. 64
'tis like a beast, methinks. 2.02. 99
to tell the world 'tis but a gaudy shadow | that 2.02.103

'tis call'd narcissus, madam. 2.02.119
'tis a rare one. 2.02.153
'tis a benefit, | a mercy i must thank 'em for; 2.03. 1
'tis but a chiding. 2.03. 27
yes, 'tis a question | to me that know not. 2.03. 61
wrastling and running. — 'tis a pretty fellow. 2.03. 67
'tis odds | he never will affect me. 2.04. 1
this afternoon to ride, but 'tis a rough one. 2.05. 46
'tis your passion | that thus mistakes, the 3.01. 48
'tis now well–nigh morning; 3.02. 2
hark, 'tis a wolf! 3.02. 4
'tis a lusty meat. 3.03. 27
a pretty brown wench 'tis. 3.03. 39
'tis justice. 3.06. 15
'tis the duke's, | and, to say true, i stole it. 3.06. 54
no, no, 'tis well. 3.06. 86
'tis to me | a thing as soon to die as thee to 3.06.158
'tis worse to me than begging | to take my life 3.06.266
no, sir, not well: | 'tis too true, she is mad. 4.01. 46
'tis likely. 4.01. 51
'tis true. 4.01.115
'tis, love! 4.01.118
'tis up! 4.01.147
'tis pity love should be so tyrannous. 4.02.146
'tis a sore life they have i' th' tother place, 4.03. 31 P
'tis not an engraff'd madness, but a most thick 4.03. 48 P
but that's all one, 'tis nothing to our purpose. 5.02. 32
'tis true, | for there, i will assure you, we 5.02. 76
'tis a sweet one, | and will perfume me finely 5.02. 88
yet sometime 'tis not so, but alters to | the 5.03. 47
'tis the latest thing | i shall be glad of, 5.04. 29
but such a vessel 'tis that floats but for | the 5.04. 83
'tis done. 5.04. 94
'tis strange if none be here — and, if he will ep 7
'tis in vain, i see, to stay ye; ep 9
if the tale we have told | (for 'tis no other) ep 13
breed sore eyes and 'tis enough to infect the STM II.C 10 P
'tis a sin | which oft th' apostle did forewarn II.C 93
boy, | 'tis but a kiss i beg, why art thou coy? VEN 96
son and canst not feel | what 'tis to love? 202
gone, | and 'tis your fault i am bereft him so. 381
'tis much to borrow, and i will not owe it; 411
owl (night's herald) shrieks, 'tis very late; 531
though the rose have prickles, yet 'tis pluck'd! 574
and now 'tis dark, and going i shall fall." 719
she says, "'tis so," they answer all, "'tis so," 851
so," they answer all, "'tis so," | and would say 851
she tells them 'tis a causeless fantasy | and 897
"'tis not my fault, the boar provok'd my tongue, 1003
'tis he, foul creature, that hath done thee 1005
"'tis true, 'tis true, thus was adonis slain: 1111
"'tis true, 'tis true, thus was adonis slain: 1111
and so 'tis thine, but know, it is as good | to 1181
thou art the next of blood, and 'tis thy right. 1184
what terror 'tis! LUC 453
'tis thou that execut'st the traitor's treason; 877
'tis thou that spurn'st at right, at law, at 880
sometime 'tis mad and too much talk affords. 1106
'tis double death to drown in ken of shore, | he 1114
'tis honor to deprive dishonor'd life, | the one 1186
'tis but a part of sorrow that we hear: 1328
for now 'tis stale to sigh, to weep, and groan. 1362
for 'tis a meritorious fair design | to chase 1692
she utters this, "he, he, fair lords, 'tis he, 1721
i owed her, and 'tis mine that she hath kill'd." 1803
but cannot be, | beauty brag, but 'tis not she, PHT 63
my body is the frame wherein 'tis held, | and SON 24. 3
'tis not enough that through the cloud thou 34. 5
'tis thee (myself) that for myself i praise, 62.13
you prais'd, i say, "'tis so, 'tis true," | and 85. 9
say, "'tis so, 'tis true," | and to the most of 85. 9
'tis with so dull a cheer | that leaves look 97.13
alas, 'tis true i have gone here and there, 110. 1
o, 'tis the first, 'tis flatt'ry in my seeing, 114. 9
o, 'tis the first, 'tis flatt'ry in my seeing, 114. 9
'tis the lesser sin | that mine eye loves it and 114.13
'tis better to be vile than vile esteemed, 121. 1
but 'tis my heart that loves what they despise, 141. 3
assuage, | 'tis promis'd in the charity of age. LC 70

TIS *(also this)*
TIS 2 FR 0.0002 REL FR 2 V 0 P
what's tis? what's tis? ROM 1.05.142
what's tis? what's tis? 1.05.142

'TISH *(also 'tis)*
'TISH 4 FR 0.0004 REL FR 0 V 4 P
by chrish law, 'tish ill done! H5 3.02. 88 P
o, 'tish ill done, 'tish ill done; 3.02. 92 P
o, 'tish ill done, 'tish ill done; 3.02. 93 P
by my hand, 'tish ill done! 3.02. 93 P

TISICK 3 FR 0.0003 REL FR 0 V 3 P
i was before master tisick, the debuty, t' other 2H4 2.04. 85 P
a whoreson tisick, a whoreson rascally tisick so TRO 5.03.101 P
a whoreson rascally tisick so troubles me, and 5.03.101 P

TISSUE 1 FR 0.0001 REL FR 1 V 0 P
in her pavilion — cloth of gold, of tissue — ANT 2.02.199

TITAN 5 FR 0.0005 REL FR 3 V 2 P
didst thou never see titan kiss a dish of butter 1H4 2.04.120 P
kiss a dish of butter, pitiful–hearted titan, 2.04.121 P
plains, | let titan rise as early as he dare, TRO 5.10. 25
to the greedy touch | of common–kissing titan, CYM 3.04.163
and titan, tired in the midday heat, | with VEN 177

TITANIA 9 FR 0.0010 REL FR 9 V 0 P
ill met by moonlight, proud titania. MND 2.01. 60
how canst thou thus for shame, titania, | glance 2.01. 74
why should titania cross her oberon? 2.01.119
juice, | i'll watch titania when she is asleep, 2.01.177
there sleeps titania sometime of the night, 2.01.253
i wonder if titania be awak'd; 3.02. 1
titania wak'd, and straightway lov'd an ass. 3.02. 34
now, my titania, wake you, my sweet queen. 4.01. 75
titania, music call, and strike more dead | than 4.01. 81

/TITAN'S 1 FR 0.0001 REL FR 1 V 0 P
reflect on rome as /titan's rays on earth, | and TIT 1.01.226

TITAN'S 2 FR 0.0002 REL FR 2 V 0 P
yet do thy cheeks look red as titan's face TIT 2.04. 31
from forth day's path and titan's /fiery wheels. ROM 2.03. 4

/TITHE 2 FR 0.0002 REL FR 1 V 1 P
the /tithe of a hair was never lost in my house 1H4 3.03. 57 P
a slave that is not twentith part the /tithe HAM 3.04. 97

TITHE 3 FR 0.0003 REL FR 3 V 0 P
priest | shall tithe or toll in our dominions; JN 3.01.154
every tithe soul, 'mongst many thousand dismes, TRO 2.02. 19
to take prerogative and tithe of knees | from STM III 9

TITHED 1 FR 0.0001 REL FR 1 V 0 P
by decimation, and a tithed death, | if thy TIM 5.04. 31

TITHE–PIG'S 1 FR 0.0001 REL FR 1 V 0 P
and sometime comes she with a tithe–pig's tail ROM 1.04. 79

TITHE'S 1 FR 0.0001 REL FR 1 V 0 P
our corn's to reap, for yet our tithe's to sow. MM 4.01. 75

TITHE–WOMAN 1 FR 0.0001 REL FR 0 V 1 P
find no fault with the tithe–woman if i were the AWW 1.03. 85 P

TITHING 2 FR 0.0002 REL FR 0 V 2 P
who is whipt from tithing to tithing, and LR 3.04.134 P
who is whipt from tithing to tithing, and 3.04.134 P

TITINIUS' 2 FR 0.0002 REL FR 2 V 0 P
come, cassius' sword, and find titinius' heart. JC 5.03. 90
titinius' face is upward. 5.03. 93

TITINIUS 17 FR 0.0019 REL FR 17 V 0 P
"give me some drink, titinius," | as a sick girl JC 1.02.127
let /lucilius and titinius guard our door. 4.02. 52
lucilius and titinius, bid the commanders 4.03.139
come in, titinius. 4.03.163
good night, titinius. 4.03.232
stand fast, titinius; we must out and talk. 5.01. 22
o, look, titinius, look, the villains fly! 5.03. 1
look, look, titinius, | are those my tents where 5.03. 12
titinius, if thou lovest me, | mount thou my 5.03. 14
regard titinius, | and tell me what thou not'st 5.03. 21
titinius is enclosed round about | with horsemen 5.03. 28
now, titinius! 5.03. 31
it is but change, titinius; 5.03. 51
seek him, titinius, whilst i go to meet | the 5.03. 73
lo yonder, and titinius mourning it. 5.03. 92
brave titinius! 5.03. 96
why, now thou diest as bravely as titinius, 5.04. 10

/TITLE 1 FR 0.0001 REL FR 1 V 0 P
/i /have /no /name, /no /title, | /no, /not R2 4.01.255

TITLE 106 FR 0.0119 REL FR 95 V 11 P
of craft, | of disobedience, or unduteous title, WIV 5.05.227
sith that the justice of your title to him MM 4.01. 73
may be i go under that title because i am merry. ADO 2.01.205 P
think you of a worse title, and i will fit her 3.02.111 P
as an appertinent title to your old time, which LLL 1.02. 16 P
crowns, | to have his title live in aquitaine; 2.01.145
a title to phoebe, to luna, to the moon. 4.02. 38
yield | thy crazed title to my certain right. MND 1.01. 92
tell me once more what title thou dost bear: MV 2.09. 35
o that i had a title good enough to keep his 3.01. 13 P
a title for a maid of all titles the worst. SHR 1.02.130
bride | and seal the title with a lovely kiss! 3.02.123
may lawfully make title to as much love as she AWW 1.03.103 P
'tis only title thou disdain'st in her, the 2.03.117
by what /it is should go, | not by the title. 2.03.131
to which title age cannot bring thee. 2.03.199 P
is to be a great part of your title, which is 2.04. 26 P
am proof against that title and what shame else WT 4.04.840 P
produce | a will that bars the title of thy son. JN 2.01.192
let us hear them speak | whose title they admit, 2.01.200
to verify our title with their lives. 2.01.277
john, to stop arthur's title in the whole, 2.01.562
having so great a title | to be more prince, as 4.01. 10
pomp, | to guard a title that was rich before, 4.02. 10
good hap, | add an immortal title to your crown! R2 1.01. 24
barely in title, not in revenues. 2.01.226
and i must find that title in your tongue, 2.03. 72
meaning | to rase one title of your honor out. 2.03. 75
only to be brief | left i his title out. 3.03. 11
and therefore lost that title of respect | which 1H4 1.03. 8
my brother mortimer doth stir | about his title, 2.03. 82
chief majority | and military title capital 3.02.110
and withal to pry | into his title, the which we 4.03.104
a borrowed title hast thou bought too dear. 5.03. 23
make claim and title to the crown of france. H5 1.02. 68
to /fine his title with some shows of truth, 1.02. 72
king pepin's title and hugh capet's claim, 1.02. 87
to hold in right and title of the female; 1.02. 89
the farced title running 'fore the king, | the 4.01.263
in whom the title rested, were suppress'd. 1H6 2.05. 92
france, | and not have title of an earldom here. 3.03. 26
either accept the title thou usurp'st, | of 5.04.151
deliver up my title in the queen | to your most 2H6 1.01. 12
your grace's title shall be multiplied. 1.02. 73
am i a queen in title and in style, | and must 1.03. 48
myself | in craving your opinion of my title, 2.02. 4
long, | or sell my title for a glorious grave. 3.01. 92
well he can, | under the title of john mortimer. 3.01.359
myself | the title of this most renowned duke, 5.01.176
will you we show our title to the crown? 3H6 1.01.102
what title hast thou, traitor, to the crown? 1.01.104
king henry, be thy title right or wrong, | lord 1.01.159
sits, | write up his title with usurping blood. 1.01.169
whose father bears the title of a king | (as if 2.02.140
hadst thou been meek, our title still had slept, 2.02.160
whiles warwick tells his title, smooths the 3.01. 48
and me — | the lustful edward's title buried — 3.02.129
but now mischance hath trod my title down, | and 3.03. 8
york, | usurps the regal title and the seat | of 3.03. 28
but if your title to the crown be weak, | as may 3.03.145
majesty | to raise my state to title of a queen, 4.01. 68
but as this title honors me and mine, | so your 4.01. 72
forget | our title to the crown and only claim 4.07. 46
why shall we fight if you pretend no title? 4.07. 57
sorrow | as i had title in thy noble husband! R3 2.02. 48
late he died that might have kept that title, 3.01. 99
then i salute you with this royal title — 3.07.239
the lord protect him from that kingly title! 4.01. 19
in love | than is the doting title of a mother; 4.04.300
under what title shall i woo for thee, | that 4.04.340
to vail the title, as her mother doth. 4.04.348
but how long shall that title "ever" last? 4.04.350
a proper title of a peace, and purchas'd | at a H8 1.01. 98
how grounded he his title to the crown | upon 1.02.144
have you limbs | to bear that load of title? 2.03. 39
to which title | a thousand pound a year, annual 2.03. 63
to give up willingly that noble title | your 3.01.140
this good man (few of you deserve that title), 5.02.173
where gentry, title, wisdom, | cannot conclude COR 3.01.144
plead my successive title with your swords. TIT 1.01. 4
perfection which he owes | without that title. ROM 2.02. 47
have you that charitable title from thousands, TIM 1.02. 91 P
and give them title, knee, and approbation 4.03. 37
that he may never more false title plead, | nor 4.03.154
and with his former title greet macbeth. MAC 1.02. 65
all–hail'd me 'thane of cawdor,' by which title, 1.05. 8 P
wear thou thy wrongs, | the title is affeer'd! 4.03. 34
now does he feel his title | hang loose about 5.02. 20
the devil himself could not pronounce a title 5.07. 8
whose age had charms in it, whose title more, LR 5.03. 48
let the drum strike, and prove my title thine. 5.03. 81
my parts, my title, and my perfect soul | shall OTH 1.02. 31
now to that name my courage prove my title! ANT 5.02.288
you may wear her in title yours; CYM 1.04. 88 P
first, sir, i pray, | what is your title? PER 5.01.203
sensually subdu'd | we lose our human title. TNK 1.01.233
and a fellow | false as thy title to her. 2.02.172
lover, | and have as just a title to her beauty, 2.02.180
if a good title, | i am persuaded this question, 3.01.112
by title paedagogus, that let fall | the birch 3.05.110
best loves me | and has the truest title in't, 5.01.159
and garland | to crown the question's title. 5.03. 17
the title of a kingdom may be tried | out of 5.03. 33
whose title is as momentary | as to us death is 5.04. 17
to /'cide this title is impanelled | a quest of SON 46. 9
o, what a happy title do i find, | happy to have 92.11

/TITLED 1 FR 0.0001 REL FR 1 V 0 P
his merit, | as amply /titled as achilles' is, TRO 2.03.193

TITLED 1 FR 0.0001 REL FR 1 V 0 P
titled goddess, | and worth it, with addition! AWW 4.02. 2

TITLE–LEAF 1 FR 0.0001 REL FR 1 V 0 P
yea, this man's brow, like to a title–leaf, 2H4 1.01. 60

TITLELESS 1 FR 0.0001 REL FR 1 V 0 P
he was a kind of nothing, titleless, | till he COR 5.01. 13

TITLE–PAGE 1 FR 0.0001 REL FR 1 V 0 P
as in a title–page, your worth in arms, | were PER 2.03. 4

TITLERS 1 FR 0.0001 REL FR 1 V 0 P
and | the two bold titlers at this instant are TNK 5.03. 83

TITLE'S 3 FR 0.0003 REL FR 3 V 0 P
my title's good, and better far than his. 3H6 1.01.130
i know not what to say, my title's weak. 1.01.134
for since the cardinal fell that title's lost. H8 4.01. 96

/TITLES 1 FR 0.0001 REL FR 0 V 1 P
/all /thy /other /titles /thou /hast /given LR 1.04.149 P

TITLES 27 FR 0.0030 REL FR 24 V 3 P
in all his dressings, caracts, titles, forms, MM 5.01. 56
titles; LLL 4.01. 83 P
a title for a maid of all titles the worst. SHR 1.02.130
bad as those | that vulgars give bold'st titles; WT 2.01. 94
which sways usurpingly these several titles, JN 1.01. 13
her bridal bed and make her rich | in titles, 2.01.492
all the titles of good fellowship come to you! 1H4 2.04.278 P
than those proud titles thou hast won of me. 5.04. 79
of his true titles to some certain dukedoms, H5 1.01. 87
soul | with opening titles miscreate, whose 1.02. 16
a net | than amply to imbar their crooked titles 1.02. 94
will go out | with titles blown from adulation? 4.01.254
him that thou magnifi'st with all these titles 1H6 4.07. 75
an earl, | although in glorious titles he excel. 5.05. 38
princes have but their titles for their glories, R3 1.04. 78
so that between their titles and low name 1.04. 82
the times and titles now are alter'd strangely H8 4.02.112
honor and lordship are my titles. TRO 3.01. 17 P
great lords, be as your titles witness, TIT 5.01. 5
his mansion and his titles, in a place | from MAC 4.02. 7
but had his titles by tenantius, whom | he CYM 1.01. 31
borne | as i wear mine, are titles but of scorn. 5.02. 7
in a field | that their crowns' titles tried. TNK 3.01. 22
show | bravely about the titles of two kingdoms. 4.02.145
thou grand decider | of dusty and old titles, 5.01. 64
fast, | thy smoothing titles to a ragged name, LUC 892
stars | of public honor and proud titles boast, SON 25. 2

TITTLES 1 FR 0.0001 REL FR 0 V 1 P
for tittles? LLL 4.01. 83 P

TITTLE–TATTLING *(also tiddle taddle)*
TITTLE–TATTLING 1 FR 0.0001 REL FR 0 V 1 P
but you must be tittle–tattling before all our WT 4.04.246 P

/TITUS' 1 FR 0.0001 REL FR 1 V 0 P
/the /innocent | /becomes /not /titus' /brother. TIT 3.02. 57

TITUS' 6 FR 0.0006 REL FR 6 V 0 P
to tremble under titus' threat'ning look. TIT 1.01.134
for good lord titus' innocence in all, | whose 1.01.437
too, | upon a just survey take titus' part, 1.01.446
calm thee, and bear the faults of titus' age, 4.04. 29
the villain is alive in titus' house, | and as 5.03.123
go, go into old titus' sorrowful house, | and 5.03.142

TITUS 46 FR 0.0052 REL FR 43 V 3 P
when your young nephew titus lost his leg. TN 5.01. 63
titus /lartius, thou | shalt see me once more COR 1.01.239
and titus lartius, a most valiant roman, | these 1.02. 14
your lord and titus lartius are set down before 1.03. 98 P
advance, brave titus! 1.04. 25
then, valiant titus, take | convenient numbers 1.05. 11
of warriors, | how is't with titus lartius? 1.06. 33
you, titus lartius, | must to corioles back. 1.09. 75
deliver him, titus. 1.09. 89
titus lartius writes they fought together, but 2.01.127 P
of the volsces and | to send for titus lartius, 2.02. 38
to rome, | renowned titus, flourishing in arms. TIT 1.01. 38
thine, | thy noble brother titus and his sons, 1.01. 50
titus, unkind and careless of thine own, | why 1.01. 86
victorious titus, rue the tears i shed, | a 1.01.105
thrice–noble titus, spare my first–born son! 1.01.120
in peace and honor live lord titus long! 1.01.157
long live lord titus, my beloved brother, 1.01.169
titus andronicus, the people of rome, | whose 1.01.179
titus, thou shalt obtain and ask the empery. 1.01.201
good | that noble–minded titus means to thee! 1.01.209
titus andronicus, for thy favors done | to us in 1.01.234
and for an onset, titus, to advance | thy name 1.01.238
thanks, noble titus, father of my life! 1.01.253
lord titus, by your leave, this maid is mine. 1.01.276
ay, noble titus, and resolv'd withal | to do 1.01.278
no, titus, no, the emperor needs her not, | nor 1.01.299
titus, when wert thou wont to walk alone, 1.01.339
o titus, see! 1.01.341

no, noble titus, but entreat of thee | to pardon 1.01.362
renowmed titus, more than half my soul — 1.01.373
rome, | this noble gentleman, lord titus here, 1.01.415
rise, titus, rise, my empress hath prevail'd. 1.01.459
titus, i am incorporate in rome, | a roman now 1.01.462
be it so, titus, and gramercy too. 1.01.495
titus, prepare thy aged eyes to weep, | or, if 3.01. 59
good titus, dry thine eyes. 3.01.138
titus andronicus, my lord the emperor | sends 3.01.150
let marcus, lucius, or thyself, old titus, | or 3.01.152
but, titus, i have touch'd thee to the quick; 4.04. 36
titus, i am come to talk with thee. 5.02. 16
'tis sad titus calls. 5.02.121
the feast is ready which the careful titus 5.03. 21
now judge what /cause had titus to revenge 5.03.125
well met, good morrow, titus and hortensius. TIM 3.04. 1
put in now, titus. 3.04. 84 P
TO *(also t'*)*
/TO 176 FR 0.0199 REL FR 152 V 24 P
TO 19938 FR 2.2537 REL FR 15661 V 4277 P
TOAD 17 FR 0.0019 REL FR 13 V 4 P
which, like the toad, ugly and venomous, | wears AYL 2.01. 13
never hung poison on a fouler toad. R3 1.02.147
thee curse this poisonous bunch–back'd toad. 1.03.245
bottled spider, that foul bunch–back'd toad! 4.04. 81
thou toad, thou toad, where is thy brother 4.04.145
thou toad, thou toad, where is thy brother 4.04.145
a cat, a fitchook, a toad, a lezard, an owl, a TRO 5.01. 61 P
as loathsome as a toad | amongst the fair–fac'd TIT 4.02. 67
good soul, had as lieve see a toad, a very toad, ROM 2.04.203 P
had as lieve see a toad, a very toad, as see him 2.04.203 P
some say the lark and loathed toad change eyes; 3.05. 31
engenders the black toad and adder blue, | the TIM 4.03.181
toad! 4.03.373
toad, that under cold stone | days and nights MAC 4.01. 6
tom, that eats the swimming frog, the toad, the LR 3.04.130 P
i had rather be a toad | and live upon the vapor OTH 3.03.270
were it toad, or adder, spider, | 'twould move CYM 4.02. 90
TOADS 9 FR 0.0010 REL FR 7 V 2 P
all the charms | of sycorax, toads, beetles, TMP 1.02.340
to eat adders' heads, and toads carbonado'd. WT 4.04.265 P
and heavy–gaited toads lie in their way, | doing R2 3.02. 15
as venom toads, or lizards' dreadful stings. 3H6 2.02.138
than i can wish to wolves — to spiders, toads, R3 1.02. 19
man, as i do hate the engend'ring of toads. TRO 2.03.159 P
ten thousand swelling toads, as many urchins, TIT 2.03.101
or keep it as a cestern for foul toads | to knot OTH 4.02. 61
or toads infect fair founts with venom mud? LUC 850
TOAD–SPOTTED 1 FR 0.0001 REL FR 1 V 0 P
below thy foot, | a most toad–spotted traitor. LR 5.03.139
TOADSTOOL 1 FR 0.0001 REL FR 0 V 1 P
toadstool! learn me the proclamation. TRO 2.01. 21 P
//TO–AND–FRO–CONFLICTING
1 FR 0.0001 REL FR 1 V 0 P
/the //to–and–fro–conflicting /wind /and /rain. LR 3.01. 11
TOAST 3 FR 0.0003 REL FR 1 V 2 P
go fetch me a quart of sack — put a toast in't. WIV 3.05. 3 P
it will toast cheese, and it will endure cold as H5 2.01. 9 P
to harbor fled, | or made a toast for neptune. TRO 1.03. 45
TOASTED 3 FR 0.0003 REL FR 0 V 3 P
i were chok'd with a piece of toasted cheese. WIV 5.05.139 P
his breath stinks with eating toasted cheese. 2H6 4.07. 12 P
peace, this piece of toasted cheese will do't. LR 4.06. 89 P
TOASTING–IRON 1 FR 0.0001 REL FR 1 V 0 P
or i'll so maul you and your toasting–iron JN 4.03. 99
TOASTS 1 FR 0.0001 REL FR 0 V 1 P
as rheumatic as two dry toasts, you cannot one 2H4 2.04. 57 P
TOASTS–AND–BUTTER
1 FR 0.0001 REL FR 0 V 1 P
i press'd me none but such toasts–and–butter, 1H4 4.02. 21 P
TO–BE–PITIED 1 FR 0.0001 REL FR 1 V 0 P
such to–be–pitied and o'er–wrested seeming | he TRO 1.03.157
TOBY 35 FR 0.0039 REL FR 4 V 31 P
by my troth, sir toby, you must come in earlier TN 1.03. 4 P
sir toby belch! how now, sir toby belch? 1.03. 44 P
sir toby belch! how now, sir toby belch? 1.03. 44 P
i'll ride home to–morrow, sir toby. 1.03. 89 P
faith, i'll home to–morrow, sir toby. 1.03.105 P
go thy way, if sir toby would leave drinking, 1.05. 27 P
sir toby will be sworn that i am no fox, but he 1.05. 79 P
sir toby, madam, your kinsman. 1.05.105 P
good sir toby! 1.05.122 P
sir toby, i must be round with you. 2.03. 95 P
nay, good sir toby. 2.03.103 P
sir toby, there you lie. 2.03.107
sweet sir toby, be patient for to–night. 2.03.131 P
do theirs — to ask for my kinsman toby — 2.05. 55 P
toby approaches; 2.05. 61 P
and does not toby take you a blow o' the lips 2.05. 67 P
saying, "cousin toby, my fortunes, having cast 2.05. 69 P
read politic authors, i will baffle sir toby, i 2.05.162 P
this is a dear manikin to you, sir toby. 3.02. 53 P
where's my cousin toby? 3.04. 61 P
no worse man than sir toby to look to me! 3.04. 65 P
sir toby, my lady prays you to have a care of 3.04. 92 P
get him to say his prayers, good sir toby, get 3.04.118 P
o good sir toby, hold! here come the officers. 3.04.319 P
hold, toby, on thy life i charge thee hold! 4.01. 45
i'll call sir toby the whilst. 4.02. 3 P
bonos dies, sir toby: 4.02. 12 P
send one presently to sir toby. 5.01.173 P
and has given sir toby a bloody coxcomb too. 5.01.176 P
that i did, i was set on to do't by sir toby. 5.01.186 P
here comes sir toby halting — you shall hear 5.01.192 P
o, he's drunk, sir toby, an hour agone; 5.01.198 P
i'll help you, sir toby, because we'll be 5.01.204 P
to frown | upon sir toby and the lighter people; 5.01.339
myself and toby | set this device against 5.01.359
TOBY'S 1 FR 0.0001 REL FR 1 V 0 P
the letter at sir toby's great importance, | in TN 5.01.363
TOD 1 FR 0.0001 REL FR 0 V 1 P
tods, every tod yields pound and odd shilling; WT 4.03. 33 P
//TO–DAY 2 FR 0.0002 REL FR 2 V 0 P
//to–day /might /i, /hanging /on /hotspur's 2H4 2.03. 44
/i /am /not /in /the /giving /vein //to–day. R3 4.02.116
TO–DAY 168 FR 0.0190 REL FR 142 V 26 P
coward that hath drunk so much sack as i to–day? TMP 3.02. 28 P
what hallowing and what stir is this to–day? TGV 5.04. 13
i shall see her to–day. WIV 1.04.155 P
how now, sir hugh, no school to–day? 4.01. 10 P
me, hath any body inquir'd for me here to–day? MM 4.01. 17 P
i swear i will not die to–day for any man's 4.03. 59 P
for thence will not i to–day. 4.03. 63 P
pray, | are penitent for your default to–day. ERR 1.02. 52
husband, i'll dine above with you to–day, | and 2.02.207
i have not din'd to–day. 3.01. 40
nor to–day here you must not, come again when 3.01. 41
if thou hadst been dromio to–day in my place, 3.01. 46
is that the chain you promis'd me to–day? 4.03. 47
rage, | is a mad tale he told to–day at dinner, 4.03. 88
my wife is in a wayward mood to–day, | and will 4.04. 4
face | revel and feast it at my house to–day, 4.04. 62
say, wherefore didst thou lock me forth to–day? 4.04. 95
when as your husband all in rage to–day | came 4.04.137
had hoisted sail and put to sea to–day. 5.01. 21
he, and my sister | to–day did dine together: 5.01.208
which of you two did dine with me to–day? 5.01.370
that kitchen'd me for you to–day at dinner: 5.01.416
what was it you told me of to–day, that your ADO 2.03. 90 P
as to be a dutchman to–day, a frenchman 3.02. 33 P
to–day to marry with my brother's daughter? 5.04. 37
well, lords, to–day we shall have our dispatch; LLL 4.01. 5
i do dine to–day at the father's of a certain 4.02.153 P
i'll find a fairer face not wash'd to–day. 4.03.269
that you to–day promis'd to tell me of? MV 1.01.121
away, | for we must measure twenty miles to–day. 3.04. 84
sent for to determine this, | come here to–day. 4.01.107
to–day my lord of amiens and myself | did steal AYL 2.01. 29
and twice to–day pick'd out the dullest scent. SHR in.1. 24
what raiment will your honor wear to–day? in.2. 4
i know you think to dine with me to–day, | and 3.02.185
i must away to–day, before night come. 3.02.190
do what thou canst, i will not go to–day, | no, 3.02.208
she eat no meat to–day, nor none shall eat; 4.01.197
i will not go to–day, and ere i do, | it shall 4.03.194
i can well observe | to–day in our young lords; AWW 1.02. 33
i saw the man to–day, if man he be. 5.03.203
youth of the count's was to–day with my lady, TN 2.03.132 P
to–day, my lord; 5.01. 94
i should have given't you to–day morning. 5.01.287 P
behind | but such a day to–morrow as to–day, WT 1.02. 64
offer, | who but to–day hammered of this design, 2.02. 47
you look pale to–day. JN 4.01. 28
once more to–day well met, distemper'd lords! 4.03. 21
farewell, my blood, which if to–day thou shed, R2 1.03. 57
let not to–morrow then ensue to–day; 2.01.197
to–day, as i came by, i called there — | but i 2.02. 94
to–day, to–day, unhappy day, too late, 3.02. 71
to–day, to–day, unhappy day, too late, 3.02. 71
to–day will i set forth, to–morrow you. 1H4 2.03.116
says she, "how many hast thou kill'd to–day?" 2.04.106 P
i am a rogue if i drunk to–day. 2.04.152 P
the earl of westmerland set forth to–day, | with 3.02.170
your uncle worcester's horses came but to–day, 4.03. 21
and that no man might draw short breath to–day 5.02. 48
the lord of stafford dear to–day hath bought 5.03. 7
death hath not strook so fat a deer to–day, 5.04.107
if thou embowel me to–day, i'll give you leave 5.04.111 P
three knights upon our party slain to–day, | a 5.05. 6
his valors shown upon our crests to–day | have 5.05. 29
god, and not we, hath safely fought to–day. 2H4 4.02.121
he is not there to–day, he dines in london. 4.04. 51
your highness bade me ask for it to–day. H5 2.02. 63
not to–day, o lord, | o, not to–day, think not 4.01.292
o, not to–day, think not upon the fault | my 4.01.293
that our french gallants shall to–day draw out, 4.02. 22
fight valiantly to–day! 4.03. 12
those men in england | that do not work to–day! 4.03. 18
for he to–day that sheds his blood with me 4.03. 61
but why wear you your leek to–day? 5.01. 2 P
but i will make you to–day a squire of low 5.01. 36 P
this brawl to–day, | grown to this faction in 1H6 2.04.124
if i to–day die not with frenchmen's rage, 4.06. 34
death been french, then death had died to–day. 4.07. 28
duke humphrey has done a miracle to–day. 2H6 2.01.157
say we intend to try his grace to–day, | if he 3.02. 16
storm | than any thou canst conjure up to–day; 5.01.199
as i intend, clifford, to thrive to–day, | it 5.02. 17
three times to–day i holp him to his horse, 5.03. 8
now, by my sword, well hast thou fought to–day; 5.03. 15
and it hath pleas'd him that three times to–day 5.03. 18
a thousand men have broke their fasts to–day 3H6 2.02.127
saw you the king to–day, my lord of derby? R3 1.03. 30
why looks your grace so heavily to–day? 1.04. 1
who slew to–day a riotous gentleman | lately 2.01.101
to–day the lords you /talk'd of are beheaded. 3.02. 91
to–day shalt thou behold a subject die | for 3.03. 3
his face | by any livelihood he show'd to–day? 3.04. 55
three times to–day my foot–cloth horse did 3.04. 84
to–day at pomfret bloodily were butcher'd, | and 3.04. 90
that it may be to–day read o'er in paul's. 3.06. 3
who saw the sun to–day? 5.03.277
the sun will not be seen to–day, | the sky doth 5.03.282
not shine to–day? 5.03.285
five have i slain to–day in stead of him. 5.04. 12
to–day the french, | all clinquant, all in gold, H8 1.01. 18
to–day he puts forth | the tender leaves of 3.02.352
what news, aeneas, from the field to–day? TRO 1.01.108
hark what good sport is out of town to–day. 1.01.113
is as a virtue fix'd, to–day was mov'd: 1.02. 5
he'll lay about him to–day, i can tell them that 1.02. 56 P
who said he came hurt home to–day? 1.02.215 P
i think he went not forth to–day. 1.02.220 P
i take to–day a wife, and my election | is led 2.02. 61
sweet lord, who's a–field to–day? 3.01.134 P
i would fain have arm'd to–day, but my nell 3.01.136 P
i long to hear how they sped to–day. 3.01.142 P
unarm, unarm, and do not fight to–day. 5.03. 3
now, young man, meanest thou to fight to–day? 5.03. 29
youth, | i am to–day i' th' vein of chivalry. 5.03. 32
i'll stand to–day for thee and me and troy. 5.03. 36
troilus, i would not have you fight to–day. 5.03. 50
than the cur achilles, and will not arm to–day; 5.04. 15 P
who hath done to–day | mad and fantastic 5.05. 37
i reak not though i end my life to–day. 5.06. 26
to–morrow, to–day, presently; COR 4.05.214 P
you have pray'd well to–day. 5.04. 55
be chosen with proclamations to–day, | to–morrow TIT 1.01.190
his philomel must lose her tongue to–day, | thy 2.03. 43
jove shield your husband from his hounds to–day! 2.03. 70
saw you him to–day? ROM 1.01.116
i pray, | that thou consent to marry us to–day. 2.03. 64
have you got leave to go to shrift to–day? 2.05. 66
lucullus you — i hunted with his honor to–day; TIM 2.02.189 P
but wherefore art not in thy shop to–day? JC 1.01. 27
you | what hath proceeded worthy note to–day. 1.02.181
tell us what hath chanc'd to–day | that caesar 1.02.217
whether caesar will come forth to–day or no; 2.01.194
augurers | may hold him from the capitol to–day. 2.01.201
you shall not stir out of your house to–day. 2.02. 9
they would not have you to stir forth to–day. 2.02. 38
if he should stay at home to–day for fear. 2.02. 43
do not go forth to–day; 2.02. 50
and he shall say you are not well to–day. 2.02. 53
and tell them that i will not come to–day. 2.02. 62
i will not come to–day. 2.02. 64
hath begg'd that i will stay at home to–day. 2.02. 82
remember that you call on me to–day; 2.02.122
i wish your enterprise to–day may thrive. 3.01. 13
he wish'd to–day our enterprise might thrive. 3.01. 16
this tongue had not offended so to–day, | if 5.01. 46
if you dare fight to–day, come to the field; 5.01. 65
the gods to–day stand friendly, that we may, 5.01. 93
goes the king hence to–day? MAC 2.03. 53
from the first corse till he that died to–day, HAM 1.02.105
no jocund health that denmark drinks to–day, 1.02.125
sir, you have show'd to–day your valiant strain, LR 5.03. 40
did i to–day | see cassio wipe his beard with. OTH 3.03.438
antonio's beard, | i would not shave't to–day. ANT 2.02. 8
if fortune be not ours to–day, it is | because 4.04. 4
that thou couldst see my wars to–day, and 4.04. 16
we'll spill the blood | that has to–day escap'd. 4.08. 4
he hath fought to–day | as if a god, in hate of 4.08. 24
their preparation is to–day by sea, | we please 4.10. 1
your highness, | i will from hence to–day. CYM 1.01. 80
what i have lost to–day at bowls i'll win 2.01. 49 P
we'll hunt no more to–day, nor seek for danger 4.02.162
to–day how many would have given their honors 5.03. 66
let the plough play to–day, i'll tickle't out TNK 2.03. 28
not far, sir. | are there such games to–day?' 2.03. 64
glister with new fire, or be | to–day extinct. 5.01. 70
which but to–day by feeding is allay'd, SON 56. 3
although to–day thou fill | thy hungry eyes even 56. 5
kind is my love to–day, to–morrow kind, | still 105. 5
TODPOLE *(also tadpole)*
TODPOLE 1 FR 0.0001 REL FR 0 V 1 P
frog, the toad, the todpole, the wall–newt, and LR 3.04.130 P
TODS 1 FR 0.0001 REL FR 0 V 1 P
every 'leven wether tods, every tod yields pound WT 4.03. 32 P
TOE 15 FR 0.0017 REL FR 12 V 3 P
cry "so, so," | each one, tripping on his toe, TMP 4.01. 46
from toe to crown he'll fill our skins with 4.01.233
the fourth turn'd on the toe, and down he fell. LLL 5.02.114
his brains turn o' th' toe like a parish–top. TN 1.03. 42 P
or the other plays the rogue with my great toe. 2H4 1.02.245 P
he is all the mother's, from the top to toe. R3 3.01.156
the manner of his gait, | he rises on the toe. TRO 4.05. 15
think, | you, the great toe of this assembly? COR 1.01.155
i the great toe! why the great toe? 1.01.156
i the great toe! why the great toe? 1.01.156
and fill me from the crown to the toe topful MAC 1.05. 42
eye of newt and toe of frog, | wool of bat and 4.01. 14
from top to toe? HAM 1.02.228
so pick'd that the toe of the peasant comes so 5.01.140 P
the man that makes his toe | what he his heart LR 3.02. 31
/TOES 1 FR 0.0001 REL FR 0 V 1 P
ere /your grandsires had nails /on /their /toes, TRO 2.01.106 P
TOES 2 FR 0.0002 REL FR 1 V 1 P
shoes, or such shoes as my toes look through the SHR in.2. 12 P
ladies that have their toes | unplagu'd with ROM 1.05. 16
TOFORE *(also afore, before, 'fore)*
TOFORE 2 FR 0.0002 REL FR 2 V 0 P
obscure precedence that hath tofore been sain. LLL 3.01. 82
o, would thou wert as thou tofore hast been! TIT 3.01.293
/TOGE 1 FR 0.0001 REL FR 1 V 0 P
why in this woolvish /toge should i stand here COR 2.03.115
/TOGED 1 FR 0.0001 REL FR 1 V 0 P
wherein the /toged consuls can propose | as OTH 1.01. 25
/TOGETHER 1 FR 0.0001 REL FR 1 V 0 P
/the /loud /trumpet /blowing /them /together; 2H4 4.01.120
TOGETHER 278 FR 0.0314 REL FR 201 V 77 P
come, | i'll manacle thy neck and feet together. TMP 1.02.462
they fell together all, as by consent; 2.01.203
draw together; 2.01.294
confin'd together | in the same fashion as you 5.01. 7
hath sever'd us, | and brought us thus together? 5.01.188
and that set together is "noddy." TGV 1.01.115 P
now you have taken the pains to set it together, 1.01.117 P
we have convers'd and spent our hours together, 2.04. 63
and keep place together than the hundred psalms WIV 2.01. 62 P
let's consult together against this greasy 2.01.107 P
but i would be loath to turn them together. 2.01.186 P
let us knog our prains together to be revenge on 3.01.119 P
and as idle as she may hang together, for want 3.02. 13 P
and our revolted wives share damnation together. 3.02. 40 P
after, we'll a–birding together. 3.03.231 P
hearts, what ado here is to bring you together! 4.05.125 P
we two must go together. 5.03. 4 P
let us withdraw together, | and we may soon our MM 1.01. 81
that offend that way but for ten year together, 2.01.239 P
you say seven years together? 2.01.263 P
to bring you thus together 'tis no sin, | sith 4.01. 72
help us, sirrah, we'll pluck a crow together. ERR 3.01. 83
last too long | if it were chain'd together, and 4.01. 26
he, and my sister | to–day did dine together: 5.01.208
where balthazar and i did dine together. 5.01.223
then all together | they fell upon me, bound me, 5.01.246
there left me and my man, both bound together, 5.01.249
children, | which accidentally are met together. 5.01.362
your hand, leonato, we will go together. ADO 1.01.160 P
presently call the rest of the watch together, 3.03. 29 P
thus did she an hour together trans–shape thy 5.01.170 P

for them all together, which maintain'd so 5.02. 62 P
park, which, put together, is in manner and form LLL 1.01.208 P
the treason and you go in peace away together. 4.03.190
love keep little company together now–a–days. MND 3.01.144 P
were met together to rehearse a play | intended 3.02. 11
so we grew together, | like to a double cherry, 3.02.208
i wonder of their being here together. 4.01.131
get your apparel together, good strings to your 4.02. 36 P
and all their minds transfigur'd so together, 5.01. 24
and they have conspir'd together. MV 2.05. 22 P
that in a gondilo were seen together | lorenzo 2.08. 8
where every something, being blent together, 3.02.181
that do converse and waste the time together, 3.04. 12
we turn'd o'er many books together. 4.01.157 P
being ever from their cradles bred together, AYL 1.01.108 P
we still have slept together, | rose at an 1.03. 73
at an instant, learn'd, play'd, eat together, 1.03. 74
and get our jewels and our wealth together, 1.03.134
but come thy ways, we'll go along together, 2.03. 66
to bring the ewes and the rams together, and to 3.02. 79 P
i'll rhyme you so eight years together, dinners 3.02. 96 P
will but join you together as they join wainscot 3.03. 87 P
sweet youth, i pray you chide a year together, 3.05. 64
which together is, abandon the society of this 5.01. 50 P
the very wrath of love, and they will together. 5.02. 40 P
to–morrow meet me all together. 5.02.112 P
when earthly things made even | atone together. 5.04.110
you and you are sure together, | as the winter 5.04.135
but we may blow our nails together, and fast it SHR 1.01.108 P
how the young folks lay their heads together! 1.02.139 P
and where two raging fires meet together, | they 2.01.132
we have 'greed so well together | that upon 2.01.297
i have seen them in the church together, god 5.01. 41 P
believe me, sir, they butt together well. 5.02. 39
they may jowl horns together like any deer i' AWW 1.03. 54 P
that dare leave two together, fare you well. 2.01. 98
of color, weight, and heat, pour'd all together, 2.03.119
is of a mingled yarn, good and ill together: 4.03. 72 P
to remain with me till they meet together. 4.05. 87 P
yes, being kept together and put to use. TN 3.01. 50 P
oxen and wain–ropes cannot hale them together. 3.02. 60 P
every thing adheres together, that no dram of a 3.04. 78 P
sir toby, because we'll be dress'd together. 5.01.205 P
they were train'd together in their childhoods; WT 1.01. 22 P
that they have seem'd to be together, though 1.01. 29 P
one so great and so forlorn | may hold together. 2.02. 21
and together with the dam | commit them to the 2.03. 95
together working with thy jealousies | (fancies 3.02.180
ten thousand years together, naked, fasting, 3.02.211
nature crush the sides o' th' earth together, 4.04.478
whose fresh complexion and whose heart together 4.04.574
make me to think so twenty years together! 5.03. 71
go together, | you precious winners all; 5.03.130
together with that pale, that white–fac'd shore, JN 2.01. 23
and link'd together | with all religious 3.01.228
cousin, go draw our puissance together. 3.01.339
faithful loves, | sticking together in calamity. 3.04. 67
was not so resolv'd when last we spake together. R2 2.03. 29
days, | and hardly kept our countrymen together, 2.04. 2
so two together weeping make one woe. 5.01. 86
and urg'd it twice together, did he not? 5.04. 5
with a dozen of them two hours together. 1H4 2.04.165 P
within that space you may have drawn together 3.01. 88
two napkins tack'd together and thrown over the 4.02. 43 P
the special head of all the land together: 4.04. 28
the douglas and the hotspur both together | are 5.01.116
he should draw his several strengths together, 2H4 1.03. 76
you'll pay me all together? 2.01.160 P
did feast together, and in two year after | were 3.01. 59
let's drink together friendly and embrace, 4.02. 63
i trust, lords, we shall lie to–night together. 4.02. 97
when means and lavish manners meet together, | o 4.04. 64
of society that they flock together in consent, 5.01. 70 P
by the mass, you'll crack a quart together, ha, 5.03. 62 P
we must to france together; H5 2.01. 91 P
treason and murther ever kept together, | as two 2.02.105
shall join together at the latter day and cry 4.01.137 P
knight, | collect them all together at my tent. 4.01.287
field | we kept together in our chivalry!" 4.06. 19
when alanson and myself were down together, i 4.07.155 P
not all together. 1H6 2.01. 29
together with the pitiful complaints | of such 4.01. 57
go cheerfully together and digest | your angry 4.01.167
come, side by side, together live and die, | and 4.05. 54
and all together, with the duke of suffolk, 2H6 1.01.168
join we together, for the public good, | in what 1.01.199
mine, | and, having both together heav'd it up, 1.02. 13
we'll both together lift our heads to heaven, 1.02. 14
then, father salisbury, kneel we together, | and 2.02. 59
ay, all of you have laid your heads together — 3.01.165
have seen him whipt three market–days together. 4.02. 58 P
there's an army gather'd together in smithfield. 4.06. 11 P
them lay their heads together to surprise me. 4.08. 59 P
the last day | knit earth and heaven together! 5.02. 42
should notwithstanding join our lights together, 3H6 2.01. 37
yet let us all together to our troops, | and 2.03. 49
so shalt thou sinow both these lands together, 2.06. 91
them sever'd | whom god hath join'd together; 4.01. 22
to sunder them that yoke so well together. 4.01. 23
we'll yoke together like a double shadow | to 4.06. 49
who gave his blood to lime the stones together, 5.01. 84
lately splinter'd, knit, and join'd together, R3 2.02.118
to me, | and we will both together to the tower, 3.02. 32
and mark how well the sequel hangs together: 3.06. 4
kind sister, thanks, we'll enter all together. 4.01. 11
by god's fair ordinance conjoin together! 5.05. 31
in their embracement, as they grew together, H8 1.01. 10
and the limbs | of this great sport together, as 1.01. 47
cardinal's malice and his potency | together; 1.01.106
two women plac'd together makes cold weather. 1.04. 22
whereupon we are | now present here together: 2.04.203
together with all famous colleges | almost in 3.02. 66
name of thrift, | does he rake this together? 3.02.110
and ever may your highness yoke together | (as i 3.02.150
all that world of wealth i have drawn together 3.02.211
thee and all thy best parts bound together) 3.02.258
music of the kingdom, | together sung te deum. 4.01. 92
come, you and i must walk a turn together; 5.01. 93
i should have ta'en some pains to bring together 5.01.119
will be father, godfather, and all together. 5.03. 38 P
come go we then together. TRO 1.01.116
general | to call together all his state of war. 2.03.260
i have taken such pain to bring you together, 3.02.200 P
down another, and together | die in the fall. 3.03. 86
and your bounties shall | concur together, 4.05.274
rump and potato finger, tickles /these together! 5.02. 56 P
and all troy on thee, | fall all together. 5.03. 62
wind, to wind, there turn and change together. 5.03.110
blood, | together with his mangled myrmidons, 5.05. 33
so, so, we draw together. 5.05. 44
sweet honey and sweet notes together fail. 5.10. 44
you have fought together? COR 1.01.232
upon him a' we'nsday half an hour together; 1.03. 59 P
by th' blood we have shed together, by th' vows 1.06. 57
titus lartius writes they fought together, but 2.01.127 P
we are not to stay all together, but to come by 2.03. 41 P
meal and bran together | he throws without 3.01.320
friends, | i' th' war do grow together; 3.02. 43
well, let us go together. 4.03. 52 P
whose meal and exercise | are still together, 4.04. 15
we have been down together in my sleep, 4.05.124
and the drops | that we have bled together. 5.01. 11
whereto we are bound, together with thy victory, 5.03.108
but we will drink together; 5.03.203
call all your tribes together, praise the gods, 5.05. 2
together with the seal a' th' senate, what | we 5.06. 82
together with the terror of the place — | as in ROM 4.03. 38
i saw them speak together. TIM 1.01. 62
we must needs dine together. 1.01.164
lucius! | what, do we meet together? 3.04. 3
come, bring in all together! 3.06. 47 P
together with the common /lag of people — what 3.06. 80 P
take wealth and lives together, | do, /villains, 4.03.433
together with a recompense more fruitful | than 5.01.150
th' infected forth, | but kill not all together. 5.04. 44
write them together, yours is as fair a name; JC 1.02.144
prevent, | let antony and caesar fall together. 2.01.161
we, like friends, will straightway go together. 2.02.127
stand fast together, lest some friend of 3.01. 87
the very last time we shall speak together: 5.01. 98
know'st that we two went to school together; 5.05. 26
as two spent swimmers that do cling together MAC 1.02. 8
there are two lodg'd together. 2.02. 23
readiness, | and meet i' th' hall together. 2.03.134
was it not yesterday we spoke together? 3.01. 73
of nature's /germains tumble all together, 4.01. 59
now we'll together, and the chance of goodness 4.03.136
together with that fair and warlike form | in HAM 1.01. 47
have heaven and earth together demonstrated 1.01.124
on him | together with remembrance of ourselves. 1.02. 7
together with all forms, moods, /shapes of grief 1.02. 82
two nights together had these gentlemen, 1.02.196
let us go in together, | and still your fingers 1.05.186
nay, come, let's go together. 1.05.190
go to your rest, at night we'll feast together. 2.02. 84
you know sometimes he walks four hours together 2.02.160
lack of wit, together with most weak hams; 2.02.200 P
did not together pluck such envy from him | as 4.07. 74
frenchman gave you, bring you in fine together, 4.07.133
pray you let us /hit together; LR 1.01.303 P
ay, two hours together. 1.02.155 P
call my train together! 1.04.253
combine together 'gainst the enemy; 5.01. 29
their lips that their breaths embrac'd together. OTH 2.01.260 P
i found them close together | at blow and thrust 2.03.237
and didst contract and purse thy brow together, 3.03.113
i do entreat that we may sup together. 4.01.262
yes, you have seen cassio and she together. 4.02. 3
your words and performances are no kin together. 4.02.183 P
i know they are in rome together, | looking for ANT 2.01. 19
caesar and antony shall well greet together: 2.01. 39
would we had spoke together! 2.02.164
matter to mine ear, | the good and bad together: 2.05. 55
then is caesar and he for ever knit together. 2.06.115 P
tie their friendship together will be the very 2.06.121 P
we should serve with horse and mares together, 3.07. 7
wisdom and fortune combating together, | if that 3.13. 79
my womb, | together with my brave egyptians all, 3.13.164
and all of you clapp'd up together in | an 4.02. 17
to camp this host, we all would sup together, 4.08. 33
and earth may strike their sounds together, 4.08. 38
they cast their caps up and carouse together 4.12. 12
they do not go together. 4.15. 47
we could not stall together | in the whole world 5.01. 39
crush him together rather than unfold | his CYM 1.01. 26
hath charg'd you should not speak together. 1.01. 83
they were again together; 1.01.151
i would they were in afric both together, 1.01.167
her beauty and her brain go not together. 1.02. 30 P
nay, come, let's go together. 1.02. 40 P
his father and i were soldiers together, to whom 1.04. 26 P
sir, we have known together in orleance. 1.04. 35 P
had been pity you should have been put together, 1.04. 40 P
winner of her honor, | together with your ring; 2.04. 54
together with | the natural bravery of your isle 3.01. 17
together with the adornment of my qualities. 3.05.136 P
and for two nights together | have made the 3.06. 2
in them both, | mingle their spurs together. 4.02. 58
and mighty, rotting | together, have one dust, 4.02.247
and a british ensign wave | friendly together. 5.05.481
we'll mingle our bloods together in the earth, PER 1.02.113
/coigns | which the world together joins, | is 3.ch. 18
together with my practice, made familiar | to me 3.02. 34
come, we will leave his honor and her together. 4.06. 65 P
when my maiden priests are met together | before 5.01.242
fought out together where death's self was TNK 1.03. 40
and the enjoying of our griefs together. 2.02. 60
that our fortunes | were twin'd together. 2.02. 64
the gall of hazard, so they grow together, 2.02. 66
and here being thus together, | we are an 2.02. 78
they howl'd many together, | and then they /fed 3.02. 18
o state of nature, fail together in me, | since 3.02. 31
in, which being glu'd together | makes morris, 3.05.119
let 's die together, at one instant, duke. 3.06.177
stand both together: 4.02. 50
proud lady and a proud city–wife howl together! 4.03. 52 P
and then we'll sleep together? 5.02.110
true, and pumpions together. STM II.C 16 P
were never four such lamps together mix'd, | had VEN 489
their lips together glued, fall to the earth. 546
like milk and blood being mingled both together, 902
then join they all together, | like many clouds 971
cost | the death of all, and all together lost. LUC 147
"all which together, like a troubled ocean, 589
crabbed age and youth cannot live together: PP 12. 1
itself confounded, | saw division grow together, PHT 42
as truth and beauty shall together thrive | if SON 14.11

TOIL* 34 FR 0.0038 REL FR 32 V 2 P
is there more toil? TMP 1.02.242
whose spirits toil in frame of villainies. ADO 4.01.189
they have pitch'd a toil: LLL 4.03. 2 P
scarce show a harvest of their heavy toil; 4.03.323
unapt to toil and trouble in the world, | but SHR 5.02.166
this toil of ours should be a work of thine; JN 2.01. 93
after such bloody toil, we bid good night, | and 5.05. 6
when i was dry with rage and extreme toil, 1H4 1.03. 31
of indigent faint souls past corporal toil, | a H5 1.01. 16
so service shall with steeled sinews toil, | and 2.02. 36
winding up days with toil, and nights with sleep 4.01.279
your faithful service, and your toil in war; 1H6 3.04. 21
and did my brother bedford toil his wits, | to 2H6 1.01. 83
forespent with toil, as runners with a race, | i 3H6 2.03. 1
glories, | an outward honor for an inward toil, R3 1.04. 79
not us'd to toil, did almost sweat to bear | the H8 1.01. 24
of their observant toil the enemies' weight — TRO 1.03.203
here shall miss, our toil shall strive to mend. ROM pr 14
i am the drudge, and toil in your delight; 2.05. 75
stop thy unhallowed toil, vile montague! 5.03. 54
double, double, toil and trouble; MAC 4.01. 10
double, double, toil and trouble; 4.01. 20
double, double, toil and trouble; 4.01. 35
of me, as if you would drive me into a toil? HAM 3.02.347 P
another antony | in her strong toil of grace. ANT 5.02.348
the toil o' th' war, | a pain that only seems to CYM 3.03. 49
i am weak with toil, yet strong in appetite. 3.06. 37
so puts himself unto the shipman's toil, | with PER 1.03. 23
bootless toil must recompense itself | with its TNK 1.01.153
such most | that, sweating in an honorable toil, 1.02. 33
weary with toil, i haste me to my bed, | the SON 27. 1
the one by toil, the other to complain | how far 28. 7
the other to complain | how far i toil, still 28. 8
in sequent toil all forwards do contend. 60. 4

TOIL'D 3 FR 0.0003 REL FR 3 V 0 P
and, toil'd with works of war, retir'd himself R2 4.01. 96
soul, | who like a brother toil'd in my affairs, 2H4 3.01. 62
and all the rest forgot for which he toil'd. SON 25.12

TOILED 1 FR 0.0001 REL FR 1 V 0 P
and now have toiled their unbreathed memories MND 5.01. 74

TOILING 2 FR 0.0002 REL FR 1 V 1 P
i am toiling in a pitch — pitch that defiles — LLL 4.03. 2 P
air | but toiling desperately to find it out — 3H6 3.02.178

TOILS* 2 FR 0.0002 REL FR 2 V 0 P
lions with toils, and men with flatterers; JC 2.01.206
so nightly toils the subject of the land, | and HAM 1.01. 72

TOKEN 32 FR 0.0036 REL FR 28 V 4 P
give her no token but stones, for she's as hard TGV 1.01.140 P
it seems you lov'd not her, /to leave her token: 4.04. 74
to pinch her by the hand, and, on that token, WIV 4.06. 44
say, by this token, i desire his company | at MM 4.03.139
either send the chain, or send me by some token. ERR 4.01. 56
in token of which duty, if he please, | my hand SHR 5.02.178
him not | by any token of presumptuous suit, AWW 1.03.198
may token to the future our past deeds. 4.02. 63
send forth your amorous token for fair maudlin. 5.03. 68
help, that by this token | i would relieve her. 5.03. 85
this token serveth for a flag of truce | betwixt 1H6 3.01.138
you again, | no loving token to his majesty? 5.03.181
go, by this token. R3 4.02. 79
car | gives token of a goodly day to–morrow. 5.03. 21
ay, a token from troilus. TRO 1.02.280 P
by the same token, you are a bawd. 1.02.281 P
a token from her daughter, my fair love, | both 5.01. 40
give me some token for the surety of it. 5.02. 60
in token of the which, | my noble steed, known COR 1.09. 60
thy glove, | or any token of thine honor else, TIM 5.04. 50
send | thy token of reprieve. LR 5.03.250
but she so loves the token | (for he conjur'd OTH 3.03.293
this is some token from a newer friend; 3.04.181
this is some minx's token, and i must take out 4.01.153 P
i never gave him token. 5.02. 61
an antique token | my father gave my mother. 5.02.216
and say | some nobler token i have kept apart ANT 5.02.168
sweet, keep it as my token. TNK 1.01.217
/void'st of honor | that ev'r bore gentle token! 3.01. 37
me, great mars, | some token of thy pleasure. 5.01. 61
i give thee thanks | for this fair token, which 5.01.133
woes, | corrupted blood some watery token shows, LUC 1748

TOKEN'D 1 FR 0.0001 REL FR 1 V 0 P
on our side like the token'd pestilence, | where ANT 3.10. 9

TOKENS 14 FR 0.0015 REL FR 11 V 3 P
are there no other tokens | between you 'greed MM 4.01. 40
free, | for the lord's tokens on you do i see. LLL 5.02.423
no, they are free that gave these tokens to us. 5.02.424
the meaning or moral of his signs and tokens. SHR 4.04. 80 P
oaths, tokens, and all these engines of lust, AWW 3.05. 19 P
tokens and letters which she did re–send, | and 3.06.115
do you not read some tokens of my son | in the JN 1.01. 87
that all their eyes may bear those tokens home 2H4 4.02. 64
presume | to send such peevish tokens to a king. 1H6 5.03.186
see how with signs and tokens she can scrowl. TIT 2.04. 5
when the most mighty gods by tokens send | such JC 1.03. 55
admit no messengers, receive no tokens. HAM 2.02.144
his belief in her renown | with tokens thus, and CYM 5.05.203
palamon in their mouths and appear with tokens, TNK 4.03. 92 P

/TOLD 3 FR 0.0003 REL FR 3 V 0 P
/could /not /at /that /time | /have /told /me, R3 4.02.101
/because /a /bard /of /ireland /told /me /once 4.02.106
/told /the /most /piteous /tale /of /lear /and LR 5.03.215

TOLD 249 FR 0.0281 REL FR 172 V 77 P
told thee no lies, made thee no mistakings, TMP 1.02.248
as i told thee before, i am subject to a tyrant, 3.02. 42
why, as i told thee, 'tis a custom with him | i' 3.02. 87
methought the billows spoke, and told me of it; 3.03. 96

i thought to have told thee of it, but i fear'd 4.01.168
i told you, sir, they were red–hot with drinking 4.01.171
this is the gentleman i told your ladyship | had TGV 2.04. 87
i tell you what launce, his man, told me: 4.02. 75 P
you heard what this knave told me, did you not? WIV 2.01.169 P
yes, and you heard what the other told me? 2.01.171 P
i could have told you more. 2.01.224 P
when i have told you that, i have told you all. 2.02.220 P
when i have told you that, i have told you all. 2.02.220 P
marry, as i told you before, john and robert, be 3.03. 9 P
i ha' told them over and over, they lack no 3.03. 18 P
i told you, sir, my daughter is dispos'd of. 3.04. 70
say the woman told me so. 4.05. 51 P
sir, as you told me you had appointed? 5.01. 14 P
they kept very good diet, as i told you — MM 2.01.112 P
see this come to pass, say pompey told you so. 2.01.243 P
i told you: 4.02.115 P
you have told me too many of him already, sir, 4.03.167 P
this gentleman told somewhat of my tale — 5.01. 84
there was a friar told me of this man. 5.01.479
ay, ay, he told his mind upon mine ear. ERR 2.01. 48
to her, told me what privy marks i had about me, 3.02.141 P
and told thee to what purpose and what end. 4.01. 97
rage, | is a mad tale he told to–day at dinner, 4.03. 88
what i told you then | i hope i shall have 5.01.375
her mother hath many times told me so. ADO 1.01.105 P
hath the fellow any wit that told you this? 1.02. 17 P
daughter, remember what i told you. 2.01. 66 P
will you not tell me who told you so? 2.01.125 P
i told him, and i think i told him true, that 2.01.215 P
i told him, and i think i told him true, that 2.01.215 P
that danc'd with her told her she is much 2.01.237 P
she told me, not thinking i had been myself, 2.01.242 P
will you look to those things i told you of? 2.01.337 P
i think i told your lordship a year since, how 2.02. 12 P
what was it you told me of to–day, that your 2.03. 90 P
a pretty jest your daughter told /us /of. 2.03.135 P
the old man's daughter told us all. 5.01.178 P
life, for i was told you were in a consumption. 5.04. 96 P
how many is one thrice told? LLL 1.02. 39 P
i told you: my lord. 4.01.101
many, | the measure then of one is eas'ly told. 5.02.190
when she's dispos'd, | told our intents before; 5.02.467
even so: my tale is told. 5.02.720
i told him of your stealth unto this wood. MND 3.02.310
my lord, fair helen told me of their stealth, 4.01.160
but all the story of the night told over, | and 5.01. 23
that have i told my love, | in glory of my 5.01. 46
you shall see it will fall pat as i told you. 5.01.187 P
the iron tongue of midnight hath told twelve. 5.01.363
for the which, as i told you, antonio shall be MV 1.03. 4 P
i had forgot — three months — you told me so. 1.03. 67
his wife who wins me by that means i told you, 2.01. 19
is not gold, | often have you heard that told; 2.07. 66
who told me, in the narrow seas that part | the 2.08. 28
i thought upon antonio when he told me, | and 2.08. 31
bassanio told him he would make some speed | of 2.08. 37
i freely told you all the wealth i had | ran in 3.02.254
and then i told you true. 3.02.256
when i told you | my state was nothing, i should 3.02.258
i should then have told you | that i was worse 3.02.259
and, when the tale is told, bid her be judge 4.01.276
i would have told you of good wrastling, which AYL 1.02.110 P
i would thou hadst told me of another father. 1.02.230
you told me you salute not at the court but you 3.02. 48 P
i have been told so of many; 3.02.343 P
i told him, of as good as he, so he laugh'd and 3.04. 37 P
my friends told me as much, and i thought no 4.01.183 P
hortensio, have you told him all her faults? SHR 1.02.186
'twas told me you were rough and coy and sullen, 2.01.243
"hic ibat," as i told you before, "simois," i am 3.01. 31 P
i told you, i, he was a frantic fool, | hiding 3.02. 12
i told him that your father was at venice, | and 4.04. 15
sir, this is the gentleman i told you of. 4.04. 20
i told you your son was well belov'd in padua. 5.01. 25 P
hath told the thievish minutes how they pass, AWW 2.01.166
i have told my neighbor how you have been 3.05. 14 P
they told me that your name was fontibell. 4.02. 1
my mother told me just how he would woo, | as if 4.02. 69
i have told your lordship already: 4.03.105 P
and say a soldier, dian, told thee this: 4.03.227
her | with an importing visage, and she told me, 5.03.136
i told him you were sick; TN 1.05.140 P
i told him you were asleep; 1.05.142 P
h'as been told so; 1.05.147 P
she never told her love, | but let concealment, 2.04.110
maria once told me she did affect me, and i have 2.05. 24 P
since when, my watch hath told me, toward my 5.01.162
me, it was she | first told me thou wast mad. 5.01.349
he hath not told us of the captain yet. 5.01.381
he must be told on't, and he shall. WT 2.02. 29
i told her so, my lord, | on your displeasure's 2.03. 44
it was told me i should be rich by the fairies. 3.03.117 P
have i not told thee how i was cozen'd by the 4.04.251 P
i told you what would come of this. 4.04.447
how often have i told you 'twould be thus! 4.04.474
told him i heard them talk of a farthel and i 5.02.115 P
were it but told you, should be hooted at | like 5.03.116
and told me hubert should put out mine eyes, | i JN 4.01. 69
done, | this act is as an ancient tale new told, 4.02. 18
for when you should be told they do prepare, 4.02.114
told of a many thousand warlike french | that 4.02.199
that villain hubert told me he did live. 5.01. 42
till i have told this slander of his blood | how R2 1.01.113
my lord, you told me you would tell the rest, 5.02. 1
and told him of those triumphs held at oxford. 5.03. 14
for now the devil that told me i did well | says 5.05.115
and shape of likelihood the news was told; 1H4 1.01. 58
it holds current that i told you yesternight: 2.01. 54 P
four, hal, i told thee four. 2.04.198 P
these nine in buckrom that i told thee of — 2.04.212 P
so i told him, my lord, and i said i heard your 3.03.105 P
met me on the way and told me i had unloaded all 4.02. 36 P
i told him gently of our grievances, | of his 5.02. 36
he told me that rebellion had bad luck, | and 2H4 1.01. 41
and would have told him half his troy was burnt; 1.01. 73
whereby i told thee they were ill for a green 2.01. 97 P
and told him there were five more sir johns, and 2.04. 5 P
it, and told john a' gaunt he beat his own name, 3.02.324 P
peace, | but, as i told my lord of westmerland, 4.02. 32
i was told that by one that knows him better H5 3.07.104 P
marry, he told me so himself, and he said he 3.07.107 P
he hath not told his thought to the king? 4.01. 99 P
occasions | at eltam place i told your majesty. 1H6 3.01.155
been his mother, thou couldst have better told. 2H6 2.01. 79
father, the duke hath told the truth; 2.02. 28
i think i should have told your grace's tale. 3.01. 44
birth | and told me that by water i should die: 4.01. 35
stab poniards in our flesh till all were told, 3H6 2.01. 98
you told not how henry the sixt hath lost | all 3.03. 89
i told your majesty as much before: 3.03.179
indeed 'tis true that henry told me of; 5.06. 69
and says a wizard told him that by g | his issue R3 1.01. 56
told the sad story of my father's death, | and 1.02.160
who told me how the poor soul did forsake | the 2.01.110
who told me, when we both lay in the field 2.01.112
for my good uncle gloucester | told me the king, 2.01.115
and when my uncle told me so, he wept, | and 2.02. 21
i prithee, pretty york, who told thee this? 2.02. 23
if 'twere not she, i cannot tell who told me. 2.04. 31
my grandam told me he was murd'red there. 2.04. 34
i now repent i told the pursuivant, | as too 3.01.145
when dighton thus told on, "we smothered | the 3.04. 88
an honest tale speeds best being plainly told. 4.03. 17
your highness told me i should post before. 4.04.358
is colder /tidings, yet they must be told. 4.04.455
i told my lord the duke, by th' devil's 4.04.534
i told your grace they would talk anon. H8 1.02.178
i have told him | what, and how true, thou art; 1.04. 49
i told ye all, | when we first put this 3.02.415
well, i have told you enough of this. 5.02.138
cousin, i told you a thing yesterday, think on't TRO 1.01. 13 P
this shall be told our lovers, lord aeneas. 1.02.170 P
let him be told so, lest perchance he think | we 1.03.284
wherein | you told how diomed, a whole week by 2.03. 81
martius, 'tis true that you have lately told us, 4.01. 10
which told me they had beat you to your trenches COR 1.01.227
could you not have told him | as you were 1.06. 40
you have told them home, | and, by my troth, you 2.03.176
if you had told as many lies in his behalf as 4.02. 48
they told me, here, at dead time of the night, 5.02. 24 P
no sooner had they told this hellish tale, | but TIT 2.03. 99
but straight they told me they would bind me 2.03.105
and told the moor he should not choose | but 2.03.106
and when i told the empress of this sport, | she 4.03. 75
many a story hath he told to thee, | and bid 5.01.118
and as i told you, my young lady bid me inquire 5.03.164
things that, to hear them told, have made me ROM 2.04.163 P
he told me paris should have married juliet. 4.01. 86
i have told more of you to myself than you can 5.03. 78
i have told my lord of you, he is coming down to TIM 1.02. 92 P
often i ha' din'd with him, and told him on't, 3.01. 1 P
i ha' told him on't, but i could ne'er get him 3.01. 24 P
while they have told their money, and let out 3.01. 28 P
thou wast told thus; 3.05.106
and, as i told you, he put it by once; 4.03.214
brutus | hath told you caesar was ambitious; JC 1.02.238 P
you have forgot the will i told you of. 3.02. 78
two truths are told, | as happy prologues to the 3.02.238
it is a tale | told by an idiot, full of sound MAC 1.03.127
you told us of some suit, what is't, laertes? 5.05. 27
'tis told me, he hath very oft of late | given HAM 1.02. 43
before my daughter told me — what might you, 1.03. 91
of these we told him, | and there did seem in 2.02.134
which i have told thee of my father's death. 3.01. 17
i have told you what i have seen and heard; 3.02. 77
but that i told him, the /revengive gods LR 1.02.174 P
i told him of the army that was landed; 2.01. 45
i told him you were coming; 4.02. 4
and told me i had turn'd the wrong side out. 4.02. 5
and told me i had the white hairs in my beard 4.02. 9
they told me i was every thing. 4.06. 97 P
that eye that told you so look'd but a–squint. 4.06.104 P
and when 'tis told, o, that my heart would burst 5.03. 72
from first to last | told him our pilgrimage. 5.03.183
i have told thee often, and i retell thee again 5.03.197
hour of five till the bell have told eleven. OTH 1.03.365 P
and when i told thee he was of my counsel | /in 2.02. 10 P
she told her, while she kept it, | 'twould make 3.03.111
you have told me she hath receiv'd them and 3.04. 58
ay, 'twas he that told me on her first. 4.02.188 P
i told him what i thought, and told no more 5.02.147
and told no more | than what he found himself 5.02.176
you told a lie, an odious, damned lie; 5.02.176
still, and our ills told us | is as our earing. 5.02.180
so fulvia told me. ANT 1.02.110
but next day | i told him of myself, which was 1.03. 75
my news | i might have told hereafter. 2.02. 78
i have told him lepidus was grown too cruel, 3.05. 22
sir, as i told you always: 3.06. 32
thou wouldst have told this tale for virtue, not CYM 1.02. 29 P
who told you of this stranger? 1.06.143
you may then revolve what tales i have told you 2.01. 40 P
my fault being nothing (as i have told you oft) 3.03. 14
two beggars told me | i could not miss my way. 3.03. 65
his wife, | his riddle told not, lost his life. 3.06. 8
convey, | which might not what by me is told. PER 1.ch. 38
sir, | if you have told diana's altar true, 3.ch. 57
some of thebes have told 's | they are sisters' 5.03. 17
what /was't /that /prisoner told me | when i TNK 1.04. 15
you have told me | that i was palamon, and you 1.04. 21
this is the duke, a–hunting as i told you. 2.02.185
i half suspected | what you told me. 3.06.108
now for this charm that i told you of, you must 4.01. 48
a man | of eighty winters — this i told them — 4.03. 19 P
has this advice i told you done any good upon 5.01.108
i told her, presently, and kiss'd her twice. 5.02. 1
then she told me | she would watch with me 5.02. 6
i have told my last hour; 5.02. 8
if the tale we have told | (for 'tis no other) 5.04. 92
'twere no error if i told you all you were in ep 12
sometime he trots, as if he told the steps, STM II.C 95
are they not quickly told, and quickly gone? VEN 277
as if they heard the woeful words she told; 520
peace," quoth lucrece, "if it should be told, 1126
see sad sights moves more than hear them told, LUC 1284
their face their manners most expressly told: 1324
and age in love, loves not to have years told. 1397
she told him stories to delight his /ear; PP 1.12
she told the youngling how god mars did try her, 4. 5
this told, i joy, but then no longer glad, | i 11. 3
old, | so is my love still telling what is told. SON 45.13
than think that we before have heard them told. 76.14
and age in love loves not t' have years told. 123. 8
138.12

TOLDST 6 FR 0.0006 REL FR 6 V 0 P
and toldst me of a mistress, and a dinner, | for ERR 2.02. 18
thou toldst me they were stol'n unto this wood; MND 2.01.191
thou toldst me thou didst hold him in thy hate. OTH 1.01. 7
he says thou toldst him that his wife was false. 5.02.173
thou toldst me, when we came from horse, the CYM 3.04. 1
but that thou toldst me thou wouldst hunt the VEN 614

TOLEDO 1 FR 0.0001 REL FR 1 V 0 P
him at his asking | the archbishopric of toledo, H8 2.01.164

TOLERABLE 2 FR 0.0002 REL FR 0 V 2 P
watch to babble and to talk, is most tolerable, ADO 3.03. 36 P
thou didst make tolerable vent of thy travel; AWW 2.03.202 P

TOLL* 3 FR 0.0003 REL FR 2 V 1 P
me a son–in–law in a fair, and toll for this. AWW 5.03.148 P
priest | shall tithe or toll in our dominions; JN 3.01.154
the country cocks do crow, the clocks do toll, H5 4.pr. 15

TOLLING* 2 FR 0.0002 REL FR 2 V 0 P
bell, | rememb'red tolling a departing friend. 2H4 1.01.103
bee, tolling from every flower | /the /virtuous 4.05. 74

/TOM 3 FR 0.0003 REL FR 1 V 2 P
/fiend /haunts /poor /tom /in /the /voice /of /a LR 3.06. 29 P
/tom, /away! 3.06.110
/fiends /have /been /in /poor /tom /at /once: 4.01. 59 P

TOM 19 FR 0.0021 REL FR 5 V 14 P
his nail | and tom bears logs into the hall LLL 5.02.914
tom snout, the tinker. MND 1.02. 61 P
good tom drum, lend me a handkercher. AWW 5.03.321 P
i prithee, tom, beat cut's saddle, put a few 1H4 2.01. 5 P
call them all by their christen names, as tom, 2.04. 8 P
and here, tom, take all the money that i have. 2H6 2.03. 76 P
melancholy, with a sigh like tom o' bedlam. LR 1.02.136 P
poor tom! 2.03. 20
fathom and half, fathom and half! poor tom! 3.04. 38 P
a spirit, a spirit! he says his name's poor tom. 3.04. 43 P
who gives any thing to poor tom? 3.04. 51 P
do poor tom some charity, whom the foul fiend 3.04. 60 P
poor tom, that eats the swimming frog, the toad, 3.04.129 P
tom will throw his head at them. 3.06. 64 P
trundle–tail, | tom will make him weep and wail, 3.06. 71
poor tom, thy horn is dry. 3.06. 75 P
'tis poor mad tom. 4.01. 26
poor tom hath been scar'd out of his good wits. 4.01. 57 P
give me thy arm; | poor tom shall lead thee. 4.01. 79

TOMB 49 FR 0.0055 REL FR 47 V 2 P
o, in a tomb where never scandal slept, | save ADO 5.01. 70
invention, | hang her an epitaph upon her tomb, 5.01.284
not erect in this age his own tomb ere he dies, 5.02. 78 P
hang thou there upon the tomb, | praising her 5.03. 9
songs of woe, | round about her tomb they go. 5.03. 15
i'll meet thee, pyramus, at ninny's tomb." MND 3.01. 97
"ninus' tomb," man. 3.01. 98 P
lovers think no scorn | to meet at ninus' tomb, 5.01.138
wilt thou at ninny's tomb meet me straightway? 5.01.202
this is old ninny's tomb. where is my love? 5.01.263
a tomb | must cover thy sweet eyes. 5.01.328
lies richer in your thoughts than on his tomb. AWW 1.02. 49
mere word's a slave | debosh'd on every tomb, on 2.03.138
where dust and damn'd oblivion is the tomb | of 2.03.140
so went he suited to his watery tomb. TN 5.01.234
and by the honorable tomb he swears | that R2 3.03.105
thou map of honor, thou king richard's tomb, 5.01. 12
for in his tomb lie my affections, | and with 2H4 5.02.124
my dread lord, to your great–grandsire's tomb, H5 1.02.103
their chiefest temple i'll erect | a tomb, 1H6 2.02. 13
shall all thy mother's hopes lie in one tomb? 4.05. 34
is all thy comfort shut in gloucester's tomb? 2H6 3.02. 78
and hang thee o'er my tomb when i am dead. 4.10. 68
and cried, "a crown, or else a glorious tomb! 3H6 1.04. 16
may have a tomb of orphants' tears wept on him! H8 3.02.399
hath not a tomb so evident as a chair | t' extol COR 4.07. 52
andronicus, stain not thy tomb with blood! TIT 1.01.116
lo at this tomb my tributary tears | i render 1.01.159
traitors, away, he rests not in this tomb. 1.01.349
till we with trophies do adorn thy tomb. 1.01.388
for by my fathers' reverent tomb i vow | they 2.03.296
the earth that's nature's mother is her tomb; ROM 2.03. 9
so low, | as one dead in the bottom of a tomb. 3.05. 56
how if, when i am laid into the tomb, | i wake 4.03. 30
poor living corse, clos'd in a dead man's tomb! 5.02. 30
merciful, | open the tomb, lay me with juliet. 5.03. 73
but then a noise did scare me from the tomb, 5.03.262
anon comes one with light to ope the tomb, | and 5.03.283
what's on this tomb | i cannot read; TIM 5.03. 5
which is not tomb enough and continent | to hide HAM 4.04. 64
i would divorce me from thy /mother's tomb, LR 2.04.131
with female fairies will his tomb be haunted, CYM 4.02.217
the tomb where grief should sleep, can breed me PER 1.02. 5
slain, | he might be buried in a tomb so simple, VEN 244
or who is he so fond will be the tomb, | of his SON 3. 7
it is but as a tomb | which hides your life, and 17. 3
when others would give life and bring a tomb. 83.12
making their tomb the womb wherein they grew? 86. 4
thee | to make him much outlive a gilded tomb, 101.11

TOMB'D 1 FR 0.0001 REL FR 1 V 0 P
thy unus'd beauty must be tomb'd with thee, SON 4.13

TOMBE 1 FR 0.0001 REL FR 0 V 1 P
heureux que je tombe entre les mains d'un H5 4.04. 56 P

TOMBLESS 1 FR 0.0001 REL FR 1 V 0 P
urn, | tombless, with no remembrance over them. H5 1.02.229

TOMBOYS 1 FR 0.0001 REL FR 1 V 0 P
with tomboys hir'd with that self exhibition CYM 1.06.122

/TOMBS 1 FR 0.0001 REL FR 1 V 0 P
gilded /tombs do worms infold. MV 2.07. 69

TOMBS 4 FR 0.0004 REL FR 4 V 0 P
lives, | live regist'red upon our brazen tombs, LLL 1.01. 2
upon them, fit to open | these dead men's tombs. ROM 5.03.201
statues, tombs, and stories | his victories, his VEN 1013
tyrants' crests and tombs of brass are spent. SON 107.14

TO–MORROW 252 FR 0.0284 REL FR 179 V 73 P

to–morrow, may it please you, don alphonso TGV 1.03. 39
to–morrow be in readiness to go — | excuse it 1.03. 70
to–morrow thou must go. 1.03. 75
gone to seek his dog, which to–morrow, by his 4.02. 78 P
let him be sent for to–morrow, eight a' clock, WIV 3.03.198 P
i do invite you to–morrow morning to my house to 3.03.229 P
you now remembrance to–morrow on the lousy knave 3.03.239 P
the duke himself will be to–morrow at court, and 4.03. 2 P
claudio | be executed by nine to–morrow morning. MM 2.01. 34
is it your will claudio shall die to–morrow? 2.02. 7
he must die to–morrow. 2.02. 82
to–morrow? 2.02. 83
your brother dies to–morrow; 2.02.105
i will bethink me. come again to–morrow. 2.02.144
well; come to me to–morrow. 2.02.155
at what hour to–morrow | shall i attend your 2.02.159
as i do think, to–morrow. 2.03. 16
your partner, as i hear, must die to–morrow, 2.03. 37
must die to–morrow? 2.03. 40
answer me to–morrow, | or, by the affection that 2.04.167
make with speed, | to–morrow you set on. 3.01. 60
i abhor to name, | or else thou diest to–morrow. 3.01.102
be ready, claudio, for your death to–morrow. 3.01.106
hopes that are fallible, to–morrow you must die; 3.01.169 P
canst thou tell if claudio die to–morrow, or no? 3.02.170 P
will not be alter'd, claudio must die to–morrow. 3.02.208 P
to–morrow morning are to die claudio and 4.02. 7 P
will help you to–morrow in your execution. 4.02. 22 P
provide your block and your axe to–morrow, four 4.02. 53 P
and by eight to–morrow | thou must be made 4.02. 64
for claudio yet, | but he must die to–morrow? 4.02. 93
the duke comes home to–morrow — nay, dry your 4.03.127
but they say the duke will be here to–morrow. 4.03.155 P
and that to–morrow you will bring it home. ERR 3.01. 5
to–morrow, my lord. ADO 2.01.357 P
for to–morrow night we would have it at the lady 2.03. 86 P
why, every day to–morrow. 3.01.101
which is the best to furnish me to–morrow. 3.01.103
to be a dutchman to–day, a frenchman to–morrow, 3.02. 34 P
means your lordship to be married to–morrow? 3.02. 89 P
if you love her then, to–morrow wed her; 3.02.115 P
not marry her, to–morrow in the congregation, 3.02.124 P
for the wedding being there to–morrow, there is 3.03. 93 P
to–morrow morning come you to my house, | and 5.01.286
to–morrow then i will expect your coming, 5.01.296
until to–morrow morning, lords, farewell. 5.01.328
farewell, my lords, we look for you to–morrow. 5.01.329
think not on him till to–morrow. 5.04.127 P
to–morrow you shall have a sight of them. LLL 2.01.165
to–morrow shall we visit you again. 2.01.176
i will come to your worship to–morrow morning. 3.01.160 P
steal forth thy father's house to–morrow night; MND 1.01.164
me | to–morrow truly will i meet with thee. 1.01.178
to–morrow night, when phoebe doth behold | her 1.01.209
then to the wood will he to–morrow night 1.01.247
and desire you, to con them by to–morrow night; 1.02.100 P
and will to–morrow midnight solemnly | dance in 4.01. 88
of flesh | to–morrow to my bloody creditor. MV 3.03. 34
and to–morrow the wrastling is. AYL 1.01. 94 P
what, you wrastle to–morrow before the new duke? 1.01.120 P
to–morrow, sir, i wrastle for my credit, and he 1.01.126 P
if he come to–morrow, i'll give him his payment. 1.01.160 P
let your wedding be to–morrow; 5.02. 14 P
they shall be married to–morrow; 5.02. 42 P
the more shall i to–morrow be at the height of 5.02. 45 P
why then to–morrow i cannot serve your turn for 5.02. 48 P
to set her before your eyes to–morrow, human as 5.02. 67 P
for if you will be married to–morrow, you shall; 5.02. 73 P
to–morrow meet me all together. 5.02.112 P
i marry woman, and i'll be married to–morrow. 5.02.114 P
man, and you shall be married to–morrow. 5.02.116 P
you, and you shall be married to–morrow. 5.02.118 P
to–morrow is the joyful day, audrey, to–morrow 5.03. 1 P
day, audrey, to–morrow will we be married. 5.03. 1 P
them all, | to–morrow i intend to hunt again. SHR in.1. 29
and if i die to–morrow, this is hers, | if 2.01.361
you know to–morrow is the wedding–day. 3.01. 84
no, nor to–morrow — not till i please myself. 3.02.209
tailor, i'll pay thee for thy gown to–morrow, 4.03.166
be gone to–morrow, and be sure of this, | what i AWW 1.03.255
to–morrow, | i'll to the wars, she to her single 2.03.295
to–morrow to th' field. 3.01. 23
'a will be here to–morrow, or i am deceiv'd by 4.05. 82 P
i'll ride home to–morrow, sir toby. TN 1.03. 89 P
faith, i'll home to–morrow, sir toby. 1.03.105 P
if that the youth will come this way to–morrow, 1.05.305
to–morrow, sir. best first go see your lodging. 3.03. 20
it shall be done to–morrow morning if i live. 3.04.103 P
and i beseech you come again to–morrow. 3.04.210
well, come again to–morrow. 3.04.216
sir, that's to–morrow. WT 1.02. 10
very sooth, to–morrow. 1.02. 17
behind | but such a day to–morrow as to–day, 1.02. 64
to–morrow morning let us meet him then. JN 4.03. 18
as i, | to try the fair adventure of to–morrow. 5.05. 22
let not to–morrow then ensue to–day; R2 2.01.197
to–morrow next | we will for ireland, and 'tis 2.01.217
come on, our queen, to–morrow must we part. 2.01.222
where shall we take a purse to–morrow, jack? 1H4 1.02. 98 P
lads, to–morrow morning by four a' clock early, 1.02.124 P
have bespoke supper to–morrow night in eastcheap 1.02.130 P
good sweet honey lord, ride with us to–morrow. 1.02.161 P
and meet me to–morrow night in eastcheap, there 1.02.192 P
to–day will i set forth, to–morrow you. 2.03.116
but to–morrow, francis; 2.04. 65 P
watch to–night, pray to–morrow. 2.04.277 P
be horribly chid to–morrow when thou comest to 2.04.373 P
to thee | that i will by to–morrow dinner–time 2.04.515
to–morrow, cousin percy, you and i | and my good 3.01. 82
meet me to–morrow in the temple hall | at two 3.03.199
let it be seen to–morrow in the battle | which 4.03. 13
to–morrow, good sir michael, is a day | wherein 4.04. 8
you leave to powder me and eat me too to–morrow. 5.04.112 P
or to know thy face to–morrow, or to take note 2H4 2.02. 14 P
money a' thursday, shalt have a cap to–morrow. 2.04.275 P
to say thus, some good thing comes to–morrow. 4.02. 84
to–morrow shall you bear our full intent | back H5 2.04.114
to–morrow shall you know our mind at full. 2.04.140
to–morrow for the march are we address'd. 3.03. 58
and on to–morrow bid them march away. 3.06.172
some of them will fall to–morrow, i hope. 3.07. 72 P
i will trot to–morrow a mile, and my way shall 3.07. 80 P
nor will do none to–morrow. 3.07.101 P
then shall we find to–morrow they have only 3.07.153 P
ever thou come to me and say, after to–morrow, 4.01.214 P
and to–morrow the king himself will be a clipper 4.01.228 P
and say, "to–morrow is saint crispian." 4.03. 46
rage, | to–morrow i shall die with mickle age. 1H6 4.06. 35
and warwick | to sup with me to–morrow night. 2H6 1.04. 80
to–morrow toward london back again, | to look 2.01.197
meet me to–morrow in saint george's field, | you 5.01. 46
to–morrow then belike shall be the day, | if 3H6 4.03. 7
to–morrow, or next day, they will be here. R3 2.04. 3
and summon him to–morrow to the tower | to sit 3.01.172
for we to–morrow hold divided councils, 3.01.179
to–morrow are let blood at pomfret castle, | and 3.01.183
to–morrow then i judge a happy day. 3.04. 6
to–morrow, in my judgment, is too sudden, | for 3.04. 43
lord, | to visit him to–morrow or next day. 3.07. 60
to–morrow may it please you to be crown'd? 3.07.242
to–morrow then we will attend your grace, | and 3.07.244
will i lie to–night — | but where to–morrow? 5.03. 8
no delay, | for, lords, to–morrow is a busy day. 5.03. 18
car | gives token of a goodly day to–morrow. 5.03. 21
stir with the lark to–morrow, gentle norfolk. 5.03. 56
saddle white surrey for the field to–morrow. 5.03. 64
lest leaden slumber peize me down to–morrow, 5.03.105
let me sit heavy on thy soul to–morrow! 5.03.118
let me sit heavy in thy soul to–morrow, | i that 5.03.131
to–morrow in the battle think on me, | and fall 5.03.134
let me sit heavy in thy soul to–morrow, | rivers 5.03.139
to–morrow in the battle think on me, | and fall 5.03.162
and, to–morrow, they | made britain india: H8 1.01. 20
the tender leaves of hopes, to–morrow blossoms, 3.02.353
to–morrow morning to the council–board | he be 5.01. 51
and will to–morrow with his trumpet call, TRO 1.03.277
to–morrow morning call some knight to arms 2.01.124
achilles will not to the field to–morrow. 2.03.162
to–morrow | we must with all our main of power 2.03.261
and you take leave till to–morrow morning — 3.02.141 P
withal bring word if hector will to–morrow | be 3.03. 34
now shall we see to–morrow — | an act that very 3.03.130
he must fight singly to–morrow with hector, and 3.03.247 P
if to–morrow be a fair day, by aleven of the 3.03.295 P
with every joint a wound, and that to–morrow! 4.01. 30
this white beard, i'd fight with thee to–morrow. 4.05.209
to–morrow do i meet thee, fell as death; 4.05.269
which with my scimitar i'll cool to–morrow. 5.01. 2
i will not meet with you to–morrow night. 5.02. 73
to–morrow will i wear it on my helm, | and 5.02. 93
to–morrow, to–day, presently; COR 4.05.214 P
we will before the walls of rome to–morrow | set 5.03. 1
to–morrow yield up rule, resign my life, | and TIT 1.01.191
to–morrow, and it please your majesty | to hunt 1.01.492
thy purpose marriage, send me word to–morrow, ROM 2.02.144
to–morrow will i send. 2.02.153
what a' clock to–morrow | shall i send to thee? 2.02.167
ask for me to–morrow, and you shall find me a 3.01. 98 P
i will, and know her mind early to–morrow; 3.04. 10
my lord, i would that thursday were to–morrow. 3.04. 29
we'nsday is to–morrow; 4.01. 90
to–morrow night look that thou lie alone, | let 4.01. 91
i'll have this knot knit up to–morrow morning. 4.02. 24
as you think fit to furnish me to–morrow? 4.02. 35
nurse, go with her, we'll to church to–morrow. 4.02. 37
paris, to prepare up him | against to–morrow. 4.02. 46
as are behoofeful for our state to–morrow. 4.03. 8
shall i be married then to–morrow morning? 4.03. 22
you'll be sick to–morrow | for this night's 4.04. 7
your company to–morrow to hunt with him, and has TIM 1.02.187 P
it will be seen to–morrow. 5.01.186
will you dine with me to–morrow? JC 1.02.290 P
to–morrow, if you please to speak with me, | i 1.02.304
comes caesar to the capitol to–morrow? 1.03. 36
send word to you he would be there to–morrow. 1.03. 38
say, the senators to–morrow | mean to establish 1.03. 85
is not to–morrow, boy, the /ides of march? 2.01. 40
early to–morrow will we rise, and hence. 4.03.230
to–morrow, as he purposes. MAC 1.05. 60
but we'll take to–morrow. 3.01. 22
but of that to–morrow, | when therewithal we 3.01. 32
to–morrow | we'll hear ourselves again. 3.04. 30
i will to–morrow | (and betimes i will) to the 3.04.131
to–morrow, and to–morrow, and to–morrow, 5.05. 19
to–morrow, and to–morrow, and to–morrow, 5.05. 19
to–morrow, and to–morrow, and to–morrow, 5.05. 19
him, friends, we'll hear a play to–morrow. HAM 2.02.535 P
we'll ha't to–morrow night. 2.02.540 P
"to–morrow is saint valentine's day, | all in 4.05. 48
to–morrow shall i beg leave to see your kingly 4.07. 44 P
our troops set forth to–morrow, stay with us; LR 4.05. 16
and they are ready | to–morrow, or at further 5.03. 53
we will have more of this to–morrow. OTH 1.03.372 P
to–morrow with your earliest | let me have 2.03. 7
to–morrow dinner then? 3.03. 58
why then to–morrow night, /or tuesday morn; 3.03. 60
kill me to–morrow, let me live to–night! 5.02. 80
but i will hope | of better deeds to–morrow. ANT 1.01. 62
to–morrow, caesar, | i shall be furnish'd to 1.04. 76
know that to–morrow the last of many battles 4.01. 11
to–morrow, soldier, | by sea and land i'll fight 4.02. 4
perchance to–morrow | you'll serve another 4.02. 27
i hope well of to–morrow, and will lead you 4.02. 42
brother, good night; to–morrow is the day. 4.03. 1
and if to–morrow | our navy thrive, i have an 4.03. 9
to–morrow, | before the sun shall see 's, we'll 4.08. 2
i must aboard to–morrow. CYM 1.06.199
but not away to–morrow! 1.06.204
the roman, comes to milford–haven | to–morrow. 3.04.143
a fair daughter, and to–morrow is her birthday, PER 2.01.108 P
to–morrow all for speeding do their best. 2.03.115
shall have him here to–morrow with his best ruff 4.02.102 P
at it, and swore he would see her to–morrow. 4.02.109 P
'twill take form, the heats are gone to–morrow. TNK 1.01.152
tickle't out | of the jades' tails to–morrow. 2.03. 29
clap her aboard to–morrow night and stow her, 2.03. 32
and this night, or to–morrow, he shall love me. 2.04. 33
to–morrow, by the sun, to do observance | to 2.05. 50
is truss'd up in a trice | to–morrow morning; 3.04. 18
i'll find him out to–morrow." 4.01. 69
that you must lose your head to–morrow morning, 4.01. 77
i'll bring it to–morrow. 4.01.109
besides, my father must be hang'd to–morrow, 5.02. 80
tell me, love's master, shall we meet to–morrow? VEN 585
no, to–morrow he intends | to hunt the boar with 587
if thou encounter with the boar to–morrow. 672
quoth she, "and come again to–morrow." PP 14. 5
for why, she sight, and bade me come to–morrow. 14.24
night to–night, and length thyself to–morrow. 14.30
to–morrow sharp'ned in his former might. SON 56. 4
to–morrow see again, and do not kill | the 56. 7
kind is my love to–day, to–morrow kind, | still 105. 5

TO–MORROW'S 3 FR 0.0003 REL FR 3 V 0 P
let us consult upon to–morrow's business. R3 5.03. 45
to–morrow's vengeance on the head of richard. 5.03.206
from my great purpose in to–morrow's battle. TRO 5.01. 38

TO–MORROW'T 1 FR 0.0001 REL FR 1 V 0 P
be patient, to–morrow't shall be mended, | and SHR 4.01.176

/TOM'S 1 FR 0.0001 REL FR 0 V 1 P
/cries /in /tom's /belly /for /two /white LR 3.06. 30 P

TOM'S 7 FR 0.0008 REL FR 2 V 5 P
punk, as tib's rush for tom's forefinger, as a AWW 2.02. 23 P
tom's a–cold — o, do de, do de, do de. LR 3.04. 58 P
tom's a–cold. 3.04. 83 P
have been tom's food for seven long year. 3.04.139
poor tom's a–cold. 3.04.147 P
tom's a–cold. 3.04.173 P
poor tom's a–cold. i cannot daub it further. 4.01. 52

TOMYRIS 1 FR 0.0001 REL FR 1 V 0 P
exploit | as scythian tomyris by cyrus' death. 1H6 2.03. 6

TON* 2 FR 0.0002 REL FR 1 V 1 P
impossible d'echapper la force de ton bras? H5 4.04. 16 P
is that a ton of moys? 4.04. 22

TONGEUS *(also tongues)*

TONGEUS 1 FR 0.0001 REL FR 0 V 1 P
dat de tongeus of de mans is be full of deceits: H5 5.02.119 P

TONGS 1 FR 0.0001 REL FR 0 V 1 P
let's have the tongs and the bones. MND 4.01. 29 P

TONGU'D 1 FR 0.0001 REL FR 1 V 0 P
false italian | (as poisonous tongu'd as handed) CYM 3.02. 5

/TONGUE 1 FR 0.0001 REL FR 1 V 0 P
/with /mine /own /tongue /deny /my /sacred R2 4.01.209

TONGUE 434 FR 0.0490 REL FR 367 V 67 P
fie, what a spendthrift is he of his tongue! TMP 2.01. 24
for she had a tongue with a tang, | would cry to 2.02. 50
my man–monster hath drown'd his tongue in sack. 3.02. 12 P
trinculo, keep a good tongue in your head. 3.02. 35 P
thou liv'st, keep a good tongue in thy head. 3.02.112 P
(although they want the use of tongue) a kind 3.03. 38
no tongue! 4.01. 59
for fear thou shouldst lose thy tongue. TGV 2.03. 46 P
where should i lose my tongue? 2.03. 47 P
fie, fie, unreverend tongue, to call her bad, 2.06. 14
that man that hath a tongue, i say is no man, 3.01.104
man, | if with his tongue he cannot win a woman. 3.01.105
of her tongue she cannot, for that's writ down 3.01.349 P
peace–a your tongue. — speak–a your tale. WIV 1.04. 81 P
mock–water, in our english tongue, is valor, 2.03. 60 P
mercy in vienna | live in thy tongue and heart. MM 1.01. 45
tongue far from heart — play with all virgins 1.04. 33
you could not with more tame a tongue desire it; 2.02. 46
let it not sound a thought upon your tongue 2.02.140
whilst my invention, hearing not my tongue, 2.04. 3
i have no tongue but one; 2.04.139
that bear in them one and the self–same tongue, 2.04.173
can tie the gall up in the slanderous tongue? 3.02.188
the tongue of isabel. 4.03.107
her maiden loss, | how might she tongue me! 4.04. 25
out | most audible, even from his proper tongue, 5.01.408
so that my arrant, due unto my tongue, | i thank ERR 2.01. 72
be not thy tongue thy own shame's orator: 3.02. 10
my tongue, though not my heart, shall have his 4.02. 18
heart prays for him, though my tongue do curse. 4.02. 28
good now, hold thy tongue. 4.04. 21 P
hast thou so crack'd and splitted my poor tongue 5.01.309
a bird of my tongue is better than a beast of ADO 1.01.139 P
i would my horse had the speed of your tongue, 1.01.142 P
signior benedick's tongue in count john's mouth, 2.01. 11 P
a husband, if thou be so shrewd of thy tongue. 2.01. 19 P
dish i love not, i cannot endure my lady tongue. 2.01.275 P
sound as a bell, and his tongue is the clapper, 3.02. 13 P
for what his heart thinks, his tongue speaks. 3.02. 14 P
what pace is this that thy tongue keeps? 3.04. 93 P
and men are only turn'd into tongue, and trim 4.01.320 P
indeed | as i dare take a serpent by the tongue. 5.01. 90
there's a double tongue, there's two tongues." 5.01.169 P
"— on pain of losing her tongue." LLL 1.01.124 P
one who the music of his own vain tongue | doth 1.01.166
father's wit and my mother's tongue assist me! 1.02. 95 P
which his fair tongue, conceit's expositor, 2.01. 72
his tongue, all impatient to speak and not see, 2.01.238
by adding a tongue which i know will not lie. 2.01.253
well learned is that tongue that well can thee 4.02.112
heaven's praise with such an earthly tongue." 4.02.118
thought can think, nor tongue of mortal tell." 4.03. 40
love's tongue proves dainty bacchus gross in 4.03.336
his discourse peremptory, his tongue filed, his 5.01. 10 P
what, was your vizard made without a tongue? 5.02.242
you have a double tongue within your mask, | and 5.02.245
a blister on his sweet tongue, with my heart, 5.02.335
it were a fault to snatch words from my tongue. 5.02.382
nor to the motion of a schoolboy's tongue, | nor 5.02.403
sweet lord longaville, rein thy tongue. 5.02.656 P
for the news i bring | is heavy in my tongue. 5.02.719
a heavy heart bears not a humble tongue. 5.02.737
and the world's large tongue | proclaims you for 5.02.842
it, never in the tongue | of him that makes it; 5.02.862
my tongue should catch your tongue's sweet MND 1.01.189
you spotted snakes with double tongue, | thorny 2.02. 9
tie up my lover's tongue, bring him silently. 3.01.201
for with doubler tongue | than thine, thou 3.02. 72
tear | impatient answers from my gentle tongue? 3.02.287

like to lysander sometime frame thy tongue; 3.02.360
is not able to taste, his tongue to conceive, 4.01.213 P
i read as much as from the rattling tongue | of 5.01.102
tongue, lose thy light, | moon, take thy flight, 5.01.304
tongue, not a word! 5.01.342
the iron tongue of midnight hath told twelve. 5.01.363
luck | now to scape the serpent's tongue, | we 5.01.433
shalt not know the sound of thine own tongue. MV 1.01.109
in a neat's tongue dried and a maid not vendible 1.01.112
i have ne'er a tongue in my head, well! 2.02.157 P
tears exhibit my tongue. 2.03. 10 P
albeit i'll swear that i do know your tongue. 2.06. 27
and yet a maiden hath no tongue but thought — 3.02. 8
there is no power in the tongue of man | to 4.01.241
other had pull'd out thy tongue for saying so. AYL 1.01. 61 P
what passion hangs these weights upon my tongue? 1.02.257
let me see wherein | my tongue hath wrong'd him; 2.07. 84
cry "holla" to /thy tongue, i prithee; 3.02.244 P
and faster than his tongue | did make offense, 3.05.116
answer, unless you take her without her tongue. 4.01.173 P
that flattering tongue of yours won me. 4.01.184 P
if that an eye may profit by a tongue, | then 4.03. 83
do, | with soft low tongue and lowly courtesy, SHR in.1. 114
and make her bear the penance of her tongue? 1.01. 89
but i will charm him first to keep his tongue. 1.01.209
renown'd in padua for her scolding tongue. 1.02.100
and do you tell me of a woman's tongue, | that 1.02.207
the one as famous for a scolding tongue, | as is 1.02.252
in his tongue. 2.01.215
whose tongue? 2.01.216
what, with my tongue in your tail? 2.01.218
to my teeth, my tongue to the roof of my mouth, 4.01. 7 P
to tame a shrew and charm her chattering tongue. 4.02. 58
my tongue will tell the anger of my heart, | or 4.03. 77
and at this time | his tongue obey'd his hand. AWW 1.02. 41
only sin | and hellish obstinacy tie thy tongue, 1.03.180
for many a man's tongue shakes out his master's 2.04. 24 P
i find my tongue is too foolhardy, but my heart 4.01. 28 P
creatures, not daring the reports of my tongue. 4.01. 31 P
truth that e'er thine own tongue was guilty of. 4.01. 33 P
tongue, i must put you into a butter–woman's 4.01. 41 P
i understand thee, and can speak thy tongue. 4.01. 75 P
durst make too bold a herald of my tongue; 5.03. 46
when my tongue blabs, then let mine eyes not see TN 1.02. 63
thy tongue, thy face, thy limbs, actions, and 1.05.292
that methought her eyes had lost her tongue, 2.02. 20
let thy tongue tang arguments of state; 2.05.150 P
let thy tongue /tang with arguments of state; 3.04. 70 P
a reverend carriage, a slow tongue, in the habit 3.04. 73 P
refuse it not, it hath no tongue to vex you; 3.04.209
that very envy and the tongue of loss | cried 5.01. 58
there is no tongue that moves, none, none i' th' WT 1.02. 20
if i prove honey–mouth'd, let my tongue blister; 2.02. 31
tell her, emilia, | i'll use that tongue i have. 2.02. 50
a callat | of boundless tongue, who late hath 2.03. 92
to be hang'd, | that wilt not stay her tongue. 2.03.110
is as bitter | upon thy tongue as in my thought. 5.01. 19
obtain'd your eye, | will have your tongue too. 5.01.106
face, | the accent of his tongue affecteth him. JN 1.01. 86
he gives the bastinado with his tongue; 2.01.463
there is no tongue hath power to curse him right 3.01.183
how can the law forbid my tongue to curse? 3.01.190
france, thou mayst hold a serpent by the tongue, 3.01.258
oath to oath, | thy tongue against thy tongue. 3.01.265
oath to oath, | thy tongue against thy tongue. 3.01.265
till this time my tongue did ne'er pronounce, 3.01.307
bell | did with his iron tongue and brazen mouth 3.03. 38
and make reply | without a tongue, using conceit 3.03. 50
o, that my tongue were in the thunder's mouth! 3.04. 38
not have believ'd him — no tongue but hubert's. 4.01. 70
is this your promise? go to, hold your tongue. 4.01. 96
let me not hold my tongue, let me not, hubert; 4.01. 99
or, hubert, if you will, cut out my tongue, | so 4.01.100
i, as one that am the tongue of these | to sound 4.02. 47
but this from rumor's tongue | i idly heard — 4.02.123
and can give audience | to any tongue, speak it 4.02.140
whose tongue soe'er speaks false, | not truly 4.03. 91
my tongue shall hush again this storm of war, 5.01. 20
the scope | and warrant limited unto my tongue. 5.02.123
drums, and let the tongue of war | plead for our 5.02.164
art my friend that know'st my tongue so well. 5.06. 8
me | that any accent breaking from thy tongue 5.06. 14
what my tongue speaks, my right drawn sword may R2 1.01. 46
ere my tongue | shall wound my honor with such 1.01.190
within my mouth you have enjail'd my tongue, 1.03.166
which robs my tongue from breathing native 1.03.173
whereto thy tongue a party–verdict gave. 1.03.234
but you gave leave to my unwilling tongue 1.03.245
for my heart disdained that my tongue | should 1.04. 12
this tongue that runs so roundly in thy head 2.01.122
his tongue is now a stringless instrument, 2.01.149
ere't be disburdened with a liberal tongue. 2.01.229
and i must find that title in your tongue, 2.03. 72
whose double tongue may with a mortal touch 3.02. 21
discomfort guides my tongue | and bids me speak 3.02. 65
than can my care–tun'd tongue deliver him! 3.02. 92
my tongue hath but a heavier tale to say. 3.02.197
wounds me with the flatteries of his tongue. 3.02.216
that e'er this tongue of mine | that laid the 3.03.133
how dares thy harsh rude tongue sound this 3.04. 74
i know your daring tongue | scorns to unsay what 4.01. 8
the heavy accent of thy moving tongue, | and in 5.01. 47
no joyful tongue gave him his welcome home, 5.02. 29
my tongue cleave to my roof within my mouth, 5.03. 31
and if i were thy nurse, thy tongue to teach, 5.03.113
thine eye begins to speak, set thy tongue there; 5.03.125
what my tongue dares not, that my heart shall 5.05. 97
a son who is the theme of honor's tongue, 1H4 1.01. 81
whose tongue shall ask me for one penny cost 1.03. 91
no more but one tongue for all those wounds, 1.03. 96
forbade my tongue to speak of mortimer, | but i 1.03.220
tying thine ear to no tongue but thine own! 1.03.238
you /eel–skin, you dried neat's tongue, you 2.04.245 P
well, | and gave the tongue a helpful ornament, 3.01.123
for thy tongue | makes welsh as sweet as ditties 3.01.205
trimm'd up your praises with a princely tongue, 5.02. 56
than i, that have not well the gift of tongue, 5.02. 77

and cold hand of death | lies on my tongue. 5.04. 85
is apter than thy tongue to tell thy arrand. 2H4 1.01. 69
but priam found the fire ere he his tongue, 1.01. 74
see what a ready tongue suspicion hath! 1.01. 84
the tongue offends not that reports his death, 1.01. 97
and his tongue | sounds ever after as a sullen 1.01.101
pray god his tongue be hotter! 1.02. 35 P
i have no tongue, sir. 2.02.163 P
into the harsh and boist'rous tongue of war? 4.01. 49
and your tongue divine | to a loud trumpet and a 4.01. 51
and not a tongue of them all speaks any other 4.03. 19 P
deliver'd o'er to the voice, the tongue, which 4.03.101 P
studies his companions | like a strange tongue, 4.04. 69
if my tongue cannot entreat you to acquit me, ep 18 P
my tongue is weary, when my legs are too, i will ep 33 P
he hath a killing tongue and a quiet sword; H5 3.02. 34 P
confess it brokenly with your english tongue. 5.02.106 P
for these fellows of infinite tongue, that can 5.02.156 P
will hang upon my tongue like a new–married wife 5.02.179 P
but thy speaking of my tongue, and i thine, most 5.02.191 P
our tongue is rough, coz, and my condition is 5.02.286 P
and yet thy tongue will not confess thy error. 1H6 2.04. 67
among which terms he us'd his lavish tongue 2.05. 47
which obloquy set bars before my tongue, | else 2.05. 49
plantagenet, i see, must hold his tongue, | lest 3.01. 61
the envious barking of your saucy tongue 3.04. 33
this fellow here, with envious carping tongue, 4.01. 90
fell banning hag, enchantress, hold thy tongue! 5.03. 42
hast not a tongue? 5.03. 68
'confounds the tongue and makes the senses rough 5.03. 71
so york must sit, and fret, and bite his tongue, 2H6 1.01.230
this knave's tongue begins to double. 2.03. 91
sharp buckingham unburthens with his tongue 3.01.156
but that my heart accordeth with my tongue, 3.01.269
shall my name with slander's tongue be wounded, 3.02. 68
how often have i tempted suffolk's tongue | (the 3.02.114
a dreadful oath, sworn with a solemn tongue! 3.02.158
were there a serpent seen, with forked tongue, 3.02.259
my tongue should stumble in mine earnest words, 3.02.316
and therefore shall it charm thy riotous tongue. 4.01. 64
suffolk's imperial tongue is stern and rough, 4.01.121
he that speaks with the tongue of an enemy be a 4.02.171 P
this tongue hath parley'd unto foreign kings 4.07. 77
he has a familiar under his tongue, he speaks 4.07.108 P
be as free as heart can wish or tongue can tell. 4.07.125 P
and let thy tongue be equal with thy heart. 5.01. 89
and bite thy tongue, that slanders him with 3H6 1.04. 47
whose tongue more poisons than the adder's tooth 1.04.112
some dreadful story hanging on thy tongue? 2.01. 44
nor can my tongue unload my heart's great 2.01. 81
i prithee give no limits to my tongue, | i am a 2.02.119
that clifford's manhood lies upon his tongue. 2.02.125
for, well i wot, thou hast thy mother's tongue. 2.02.134
to let thy tongue detect thy base–born heart? 2.02.143
and his ill–boding tongue no more shall speak. 2.06. 59
mine eyes with tears | and stops my tongue, 3.03. 14
and with my tongue | to tell the passion of my 3.03. 61
peace, willful boy, or i will charm your tongue. 5.05. 31
lip, a bonny eye, a passing pleasing tongue; R3 1.01. 94
fairer than tongue can name thee, let me have 1.02. 81
i was provoked by her sland'rous tongue, | that 1.02. 97
my tongue could never learn sweet smoothing word 1.02.168
heart sues, and prompts my tongue to speak. 1.02.170
'tis figur'd in my tongue. 1.02.193
have i a tongue to doom my brother's death, 2.01.103
and shall that tongue give pardon to a slave? 2.01.104
alive, | i give a sparing limit to my tongue. 3.07.194
that my woe–wearied tongue is still and mute. 4.04. 18
my tongue should to thy ears not name my boys 4.04.231
and every tongue brings in a several tale, | and 5.03.194
no discerner | durst wag his tongue in censure. H8 1.01. 33
some life, | which action's self was tongue to. 1.01. 42
you can speak the french tongue; 1.04. 57
every tongue speaks 'em, | and every true heart 2.02. 38
self, hath sent | one general tongue unto us: 2.02. 95
she | so good a lady that no tongue could ever 2.03. 3
if my actions | were tried by ev'ry tongue, 3.01. 35
a strange tongue makes my cause more strange, 3.01. 45
to taint that honor every good tongue blesses, 3.01. 55
hath a witchcraft | over the king in 's tongue. 3.02. 19
better | have burnt that tongue than said so. 3.02.254
th' archbishop | is the king's hand and tongue, 5.01. 38
and think with wagging of your tongue to win me; 5.02.162
like your grace | to let my tongue excuse all. 5.02.184
had as lieve helen's golden tongue had commended TRO 1.02.105 P
the greekish ears | to his experienc'd tongue, 1.03. 68
from the tongue of roaring typhon dropp'd, 1.03.160
i shall cut out your tongue. 2.01.110 P
sweet, bid me hold my tongue, | for in this 3.02.129
he wears his tongue in 's arms. 3.03.270 P
o, these encounterers, so glib of tongue, | that 4.05. 58
speaking /in deeds, and deedless in his tongue, 4.05. 98
our steed the leg, the tongue our trumpeter, COR 1.01.117
more than i know the sound of martius' tongue 1.06. 26
i cannot bring | my tongue to such a pace. 2.03. 51
at once pluck out | the multitudinous tongue; 3.01.156
put not your worthy rage into your tongue; 3.01.240
his breast forges, that his tongue must vent, 3.01.257
such words that are but roted in | your tongue, 3.02. 56
i | with my base tongue give to my noble heart 3.02.100
a beggar's tongue | make motion through my lips, 3.02.117
or never trust to what my tongue can do | i' th' 3.02.136
in | thy lying tongue both numbers, i would say 3.03. 72
but your favor is well appear'd by your tongue. 4.03. 9 P
be your country's pleader, your good tongue, 5.01. 36
coward, that thund'rest with thy tongue, | and TIT 2.01. 58
his philomel must lose her tongue to–day, | thy 2.03. 43
more | that womanhood denies my tongue to tell. 2.03.174
so now go tell, and if thy tongue can speak, 2.04. 1
who 'twas that cut thy tongue and ravish'd thee. 2.04. 2
she hath no tongue to call, nor hands to wash, 2.04. 7
lest thou shouldst detect /him, cut thy tongue. 2.04. 27
fair philomela, why, she but lost her tongue, 2.04. 38
harmony | which that sweet tongue hath made, 2.04. 49
nor tongue to tell me who hath mart'red thee. 3.01.107
had she a tongue to speak, now would she say 3.01.144
yet should both ear and heart obey my tongue. 4.04. 99

they cut thy sister's tongue, and ravish'd her, 5.01. 92
but to torment you with my bitter tongue! 5.01.150
both her sweet hands, her tongue, and that more 5.02.175
and that more dear | than hands or tongue, her 5.02.176
and prompt me that my tongue may utter forth 5.03. 12
they ravish'd her, and cut away her tongue, 5.03. 57
when with his solemn tongue he did discourse 5.03. 81
and make her airy tongue more hoarse than /mine, ROM 2.02.162
what early tongue so sweet saluteth me? 2.03. 32
air, and let rich /music's tongue | unfold the 2.06. 27
and, swifter than his tongue, | his /agile arm 3.01.165
and every tongue that speaks | but romeo's name 3.02. 32
blister'd be thy tongue | for such a wish! 3.02. 90
poor my lord, what tongue shall smooth thy name, 3.02. 98
hold your tongue, | good prudence, smatter with 3.05.170
or to dispraise my lord with that same tongue 3.05.237
ties up my tongue and will not let me speak. 4.05. 32
he speaks the common tongue | which all men TIM 1.01.174
i would my tongue could rot them off! 4.03.365
that speak'st with every tongue | to every 4.03.388
be as a cantherizing to the root o' th' tongue, 5.01.133
i hear a tongue shriller than all the music JC 1.02. 16
ay, and that tongue of his that bade the romans 1.02.125
vouchsafe good morrow from a feeble tongue. 2.01.313
set a huge mountain 'tween my heart and tongue! 2.04. 7
to beg the voice and utterance of my tongue) | a 3.01.261
and put a tongue | in every wound of caesar, 3.02.228
this tongue had not offended so to–day, | if 5.01. 46
once, for brutus' tongue | hath almost ended his 5.05. 39
and chastise with the valor of my tongue | all MAC 1.05. 27
welcome in your eye, | your hand, your tongue; 1.05. 65
tongue nor heart | cannot conceive nor name thee 2.03. 64
present him eminence both with eye and tongue: 3.02. 31
toe of frog, | wool of bat and tongue of dog, 4.01. 15
let not your ears despise my tongue for ever, 4.03.201
with mine eyes, | and braggart with my tongue! 4.03.231
thou com'st to use thy tongue; 5.05. 28
accursed be that tongue that tells me so, | for 5.08. 17
but break my heart, for i must hold my tongue. HAM 1.02.159
give it an understanding, but no tongue. 1.02.249
give thy thoughts no tongue, | nor any 1.03. 59
how prodigal the soul | lends the tongue vows. 1.03.117
who this had seen, with tongue in venom steep'd, 2.02.510
for murther, though it have no tongue, will 2.02.593
soldier's, scholar's, eye, tongue, sword, | th' 3.01.151
pronounc'd it to you, trippingly on the tongue, 3.02. 2 P
no, let the candied tongue lick absurd pomp, 3.02. 60
my tongue and soul in this be hypocrites — 3.02.397
come, come, you answer with an idle tongue. 3.04. 11
go, go, you question with a wicked tongue. 3.04. 12
that thou dar'st wag thy tongue | in noise so 3.04. 39
that skull had a tongue in it, and could sing 5.01. 75 P
not possible to understand in another tongue? 5.02.126 P
sure my love's | more ponderous than my tongue. LR 1.01. 78
and such a tongue | that i am glad i have not, 1.01.231
yes, forsooth, i will hold my tongue; 1.04.195 P
look'd black upon me, strook me with her tongue, 2.04.160
and that thy tongue some say of breeding 5.03.144
lips | as of her tongue she oft bestows on me, OTH 2.01.101
she puts her tongue a little in her heart, | and 2.01.106
had tongue at will, and yet was never loud, 2.01.149
i had rather have this tongue cut from my mouth 2.03.221
with cassio, mistress. go to, charm your tongue. 5.02.183
i will not charm my tongue; 5.02.184
speak to me home, mince not the general tongue; ANT 1.02.105
you shall never | have tongue to charge me with. 2.02. 83
i see it in my motion, have it not in my tongue; 2.03. 14
repent that e'er thy tongue | hath so betray'd 2.07. 77
and mine own tongue | spleets what it speaks; 2.07.123
her tongue will not obey her heart, nor can 3.02. 47
nor can | her heart inform her tongue — the 3.02. 48
dull of tongue, and dwarfish. 3.03. 16
this is but a custom in your tongue; CYM 1.04.138 P
that from my mutest conscience to my tongue 1.06.116
we'll try with tongue too. 2.03. 15 P
man, thy tongue | may take off some extremity, 3.04. 16
whose tongue | outvenoms all the worms of nile, 3.04. 34
talk thy tongue weary, speak. 3.04.112
lolling the tongue with slaught'ring — having 5.03. 8
such stuff as madmen | tongue and brain not; 5.04.146
picture, which by his tongue being made, | and 5.05.175
by thine own tongue thou art condemn'd, and must 5.05.298
then give my tongue like leave to love my head. PER 1.01.108
peace, peace, and give experience tongue. 1.02. 37
how durst thy tongue move anger to our face? 1.02. 54
to give my tongue that heat to ask your help; 2.01. 75
resolve your angry father if my tongue | did 2.05. 68
thou still make good | the tongue o' th' world. TNK 1.01.227
he has a tongue will tame tempests, | and make 2.03. 16
he speaks, his tongue | sounds like a trumpet. 4.02.112
a piece of silver on the tip of your tongue, or 4.03. 21 P
said, impatience chokes her pleading tongue, VEN 217
when it is barr'd the aidance of the tongue. 330
quoth she, "hast thou a tongue? 427
and every tongue more moving than your own, 776
"'tis not my fault, the boar provok'd my tongue, 1003
"my tongue cannot express my grief for one, 1069
whose tongue is music now? 1077
thinks he that her husband's shallow tongue — LUC 78
will not my tongue be mute, my frail joints 227
first like a trumpet doth his tongue begin | to 470
thy sug'red tongue to bitter wormwood taste; 893
my tongue shall utter all, mine eyes like 1076
with untun'd tongue she hoarsely calls her maid, 1214
with soft slow tongue, true mark of modesty, 1220
to give her so much grief, and not a tongue. 1463
i'll tune thy woes with my lamenting tongue, 1465
and from her tongue "can lurk" from "cannot" 1537
to tell them all with one poor tired tongue. 1617
my bloody judge forbod my tongue to speak, | no 1648
more than "he" her poor tongue could not speak, 1718
hath serv'd a dumb arrest upon his tongue, | who 1780
i smiling credit her false–speaking tongue, PP 1. 7
o, love's best habit's in a soothing tongue, 1.11
well learned is that tongue that well can thee 5. 8
heaven's praise with such an earthly tongue. 5.14
tell, | smooth not thy tongue with filed talk, 18. 8

on th' ear, | to teach my tongue to be so long. 18.52
young, | and truth in every shepherd's tongue, 19.18
scorn'd, like old men of less truth than tongue, SON 17.10
more than that tongue that more hath more 23.12
and in my tongue | thy sweet beloved name no 89. 9
that tongue that tells the story of thy days 95. 5
the owner's tongue doth publish every where. 102. 4
therefore, like her, i sometime hold my tongue, 102.13
to know my shames and praises from your tongue; 112. 6
that every tongue says beauty should look so. 127.14
simply i credit her false-speaking tongue; 138. 7
wound me not with thine eye but with thy tongue, 139. 3
chiding that tongue that, ever sweet, | was us'd 145. 6
"so on the tip of his subduing tongue | all kind LC 120

TONGUELESS 4 FR 0.0004 REL FR 4 V 0 P
one good deed dying tongueless | slaughters a WT 1.02. 92
even from the tongueless caverns of the earth, R2 1.01.105
turkish mute, shall have a tongueless mouth, H5 1.02.232
what tongueless blocks were they! R3 3.07. 42

TONGUE'S 7 FR 0.0008 REL FR 6 V 1 P
but to jig off a tune at the tongue's end, LLL 3.01. 12 P
and your tongue's sweet air | more tuneable than MND 1.01.183
tongue should catch your tongue's sweet melody. 1.01.189
and now my tongue's use is to me no more | than R2 1.03.161
when the tongue's office should be prodigal | to 1.03.256
a hundred words | of thy tongue's uttering, yet ROM 2.02. 59
are mine ears with thy tongue's tune delighted, SON 141. 5

TONGUES *(also tongeus)*

TONGUES 81 FR 0.0091 REL FR 66 V 15 P
who with cloven tongues | do hiss me into TMP 2.02. 13
th' harmony of their tongues hath into bondage 3.01. 41
have you the tongues? TGV 4.01. 33
all hearts in love use their own tongues. ADO 2.01.177
out of all eyes, tongues, minds, and injuries. 4.01.243
"nay," said i, "he hath the tongues." 5.01.166 P
there's a double tongue, there's two tongues." 5.01.170 P
"done to death by slanderous tongues | was the 5.03. 3
not utt'red by base sale of chapmen's tongues. LLL 2.01. 16
when tongues speak sweetly, then they name her 3.01.166
lend me the flourish of all gentle tongues — 4.03.234
the tongues of mocking wenches are as keen | as 5.02.256
finds tongues in trees, books in the running AYL 2.01. 16
and you that will not, hold your tongues. 2.05. 30 P
tongues i'll hang on every tree, | that shall 3.02.127
beasts, which in all tongues are call'd fools. 5.04. 37 P
that time in the tongues that i have in fencing, TN 1.03. 92 P
the injury of tongues in courts and kingdoms WT 1.02.338
deserv'd | all tongues to talk their bitt'rest. 3.02.216
clamor your tongues, and not a word more. 4.04.247 P
abortives, presages, and tongues of heaven, JN 3.04.158
the utterance of a brace of tongues | must needs 4.01. 97
deed, which both our tongues held vild to name. 4.02.241
war, | the bitter clamor of two eager tongues, R2 1.01. 49
but they say the tongues of dying men | enforce 2.01. 5
whilst all tongues cried, "god save /thee, 5.02. 11
minutes capons, and clocks the tongues of bawds, 1H4 1.02. 8 P
i do defy | the tongues of soothers, but a 4.01. 7
upon my tongues continual slanders ride, | the 2H4 in 6
from rumor's tongues | they bring smooth in 39
a whole school of tongues in this belly of mine, 4.03. 18 P
turn the sands into eloquent tongues, and my H5 3.07. 34 P
that the tongues of men are full of deceits? 5.02.117 P
touch of them than in the tongues of the french 5.02.277 P
women are shrewd tempters with their tongues. 1H6 1.02.123
we go to use our hands, and not our tongues. R3 1.03.351
my conscience hath a thousand several tongues, 5.03.193
tongues spit their duties out, and cold hearts H8 1.02. 61
if i am | traduc'd by ignorant tongues, which 1.02. 72
and allay those tongues | that durst disperse it 2.01.152
carry gentle peace | to silence envious tongues. 3.02.446
none stands under more calumnious tongues | than 5.01.112
all tongues speak of him, and the bleared sights COR 2.01.205
that for their tongues to be silent and not 2.02. 30 P
we are to put our tongues into those wounds and 2.03. 7 P
giving him our own voices with our own tongues; 2.03. 45 P
or had you tongues to cry | against the 2.03.204
ask but mock, bestow | your su'd-for tongues? 2.03.208
the people, | the tongues o' th' common mouth. 3.01. 22
them now, | and straight disclaim their tongues? 3.01. 35
the palace full of tongues, of eyes, and ears; TIT 2.01.127
tribunes with their tongues doom men to death. 3.01. 47
or shall we bite our tongues, and in dumb shows 3.01.131
let us that have our tongues | plot some device 3.01.133
ease their stomachs with their bitter tongues. 3.01.233
how silver-sweet sound lovers' tongues by night, ROM 2.02.165
the mouths, the tongues, the eyes, and hearts of TIM 4.03.261
why do we hold our tongues, | that most may MAC 2.03.119
tyrant, whose sole name blisters our tongues, 4.03. 12
hands, and tongues applaud it to the clouds, HAM 4.05.108
and delays as many | as there are tongues, are 4.07.121
himself, there are no tongues else for 's turn. 5.02.184 P
when slanders do not live in tongues; LR 3.02. 89
had i your tongues and eyes, i'ld use them so 5.03.259
with thy fraught, | for 'tis of aspics' tongues! OTH 3.03.450
will speak, | though tongues were out of use. 5.01.110
give to a gracious message | an host of tongues, ANT 2.05. 87
hoo, hearts, tongues, /figures, scribes, bards, 3.02. 16
and their tongues rot | that speak against us! 3.07. 15
and will to ears and tongues | be theme and CYM 3.01. 3
with speechless tongues and semblance pale, PER 1.01. 36
our tongues and sorrows to sound deep our woes 1.04. 13
till tongues | fetch breath that may proclaim 1.04. 14
here | that ruder tongues distinguish villager, TNK 3.05.104
"if love have lent you twenty thousand tongues, VEN 775
grief hath two tongues, and never woman yet 1007
to sland'rous tongues and wretched hateful days? LUC 161
all tongues (the voice of souls) give thee that SON 69. 3
but those same tongues that give thee so thine 69. 6
and tongues to be your being shall rehearse, 81.11
have eyes to wonder, but lack tongues to praise. 106.14

TONGUE-TIED 12 FR 0.0013 REL FR 12 V 0 P
and tongue-tied simplicity | in least speak most MND 5.01.104
tongue-tied our queen? speak you. WT 1.02. 27
since you are tongue-tied and so loath to speak, 1H6 2.04. 25
and give my tongue-tied sorrows leave to speak. 3H6 3.03. 22
you might haply think | tongue-tied ambition, R3 3.07.145
if so then, be not tongue-tied; 4.04.132
and cupid grant all tongue-tied maidens here TRO 3.02.210
they vanish tongue-tied in their guiltiness. JC 1.01. 62
and art made tongue-tied by authority, | and SON 66. 9
to make me tongue-tied, speaking of your fame. 80. 4
my tongue-tied muse in manners holds her still, 85. 1
my tongue-tied patience with too much disdain, 140. 2

//TO-NIGHT 2 FR 0.0002 REL FR 2 V 0 P
/what /will /hap /more //to-night, /safe /scape LR 3.06.114
//to-night, /my /lord? OTH 1.03.278

/TO-NIGHT 2 FR 0.0002 REL FR 1 V 1 P
refrain /to-night, | and that shall lend a kind HAM 3.04.165
of a stranger that's come to court /to-night? CYM 2.01. 33 P

TO-NIGHT 191 FR 0.0216 REL FR 142 V 49 P
this, be sure, to-night thou shalt have cramps, TMP 1.02.325
let it be to-night, | for, now they are 3.03. 14
i say, to-night. no more. 3.03. 17
gentlemen, i have dream'd to-night; WIV 3.03.161 P
once to-night | give my sweet nan this ring. 3.04. 99
to-night at herne's oak, just 'twixt twelve and 4.06. 19
the matter will be known to-night, or never. 5.01. 10 P
knave ford, on whom to-night i will be reveng'd, 5.01. 28 P
thou shalt eat a posset to-night at my house, 5.05.171 P
for he to-night shall lie with mistress ford. 5.05.245
with angelo to-night shall lie | his old MM 3.02.278
his company | at mariana's house to-night. 4.03.140
i will not harbor in this town to-night. ERR 3.02.149
is there any ships puts forth to-night? 4.03. 35 P
that the bark expedition put forth to-night, and 4.03. 38 P
i will not stay to-night for all the town: 4.04.157
i know we shall have revelling to-night; ADO 1.01.320
i too, and he swore he would marry her to-night. 2.01.170 P
go but with me to-night, you shall see her 3.02.112 P
if i see any thing to-night why i should not 3.02.123 P
there to-morrow, there is a great coil to-night. 3.03. 94 P
but know that i have to-night woo'd margaret, 3.03.145 P
marry, sir, our watch to-night, excepting your 3.05. 30 P
and sing it to her bones, sing it to-night. 5.01.285
expect your coming, | to-night i take my leave. 5.01.297
to-night i'll mourn with hero. 5.01.330
they not, think you, hang themselves to-night? LLL 5.02.270
boyet, prepare, i will away to-night. 5.02.727
the king doth keep his revels here to-night; MND 2.01. 18
the prince his master will be here to-night. MV 1.02.126 P
for i do feast to-night | my best esteem'd 2.02.171
nay, but i bar to-night, you shall not gauge me 2.02.199
you shall not gauge me | by what we do to-night. 2.02.200
the jew to sup to-night with my new master the 2.04. 18 P
will you prepare you for this masque to-night? 2.04. 22
rest, | for i did dream of money-bags to-night. 2.05. 18
i have no mind of feasting forth to-night; 2.05. 37
no masque to-night, the wind is come about, 2.06. 64
than to be under sail, and gone to-night. 2.06. 68
we'll away to-night, | and be a day before our 4.02. 2
do you intend to stay with me to-night? SHR in.1. 81
there is a lord will hear you play to-night; in.1. 93
is't possible you will away to-night? 3.02.189
night she slept not, nor to-night she shall not; 4.01.198
the now-born brief, | and be perform'd to-night. AWW 2.03.180
madam, my lord will go away to-night, | a very 2.04. 39
will she away to-night? 2.05. 22 P
given order for our horses, and to-night, | when 2.05. 25
and this gentle maid | to eat with us to-night, 3.05. 98
emboss'd him, you shall see his fall to-night; 3.06.100 P
why then to-night | let us assay our plot, which 3.07. 43
we shall not then have his company to-night? 4.03. 28 P
i have to-night dispatch'd sixteen businesses, a 4.03. 85 P
have letters that my son will be here to-night. 4.05. 86 P
sweet sir toby, be patient for to-night. TN 2.03.131 P
you | shall bear along impawn'd, away to-night! WT 1.02.436
he took good rest to-night; 2.03. 10
madam — he hath not slept to-night, commanded 2.03. 31
he tells us arthur is deceas'd to-night. JN 4.02. 85
whom they say is kill'd to-night | on your 4.02.165
my lord, they say five moons were seen to-night; 4.02.182
i did not think to be so sad to-night | as this 5.05. 15
keep good quarter and good care to-night; 5.05. 20
gadshill lies to-night in rochester. 1H4 1.02.129 P
i will set forward to-night. 2.03. 35 P
watch to-night, pray to-morrow. 2.04.277 P
worcester is stol'n away to-night. 2.04.358 P
we'll to sutton co'fil' to-night. 4.02. 3 P
we'll fight with him to-night. 4.03. 1
good cousin, be advis'd, stir not to-night. 4.03. 5
yea, or to-night. 4.03. 14
to-night, say i. 4.03. 15
where lay the king to-night? 2H4 2.01.168
bestow himself to-night in his true colors, and 2.02.170 P
i must a dozen mile to-night. 3.02.290 P
i trust, lords, we shall lie to-night together. 4.02. 97
cock and pie, sir, you shall not away to-night. 5.01. 1 P
and uncle exeter, | we will aboard to-night. H5 2.02. 71
to-night in harfleu will we be your guest; 3.03. 57
the armor that i saw in your tent to-night, are 3.07. 70 P
that, being captain of the watch to-night, | did 1H6 2.01. 61
hath at least five frenchmen died to-night. 2.02. 9
i did dream to-night | the duke was dumb and 2H6 3.02. 31
for you shall sup with jesu christ to-night. 5.01.214
more than the infant that is born to-night. R3 2.01. 72
and at northampton they do rest to-night. 2.04. 2
here will i lie to-night — | but where 5.03. 7
it, | and so god give you quiet rest to-night! 5.03. 43
i will not sup to-night. 5.03. 48
shadows to-night | have strook more terror to 5.03.216
charles, i will play no more to-night, | my H8 5.01. 56
what exploit's in hand? where sups he to-night? TRO 3.01. 81 P
my brother troilus lodges there to-night. 4.01. 43
hast not slept to-night? 4.02. 32 P
to-night all friends. 4.05.270
there diomed doth feast with him to-night, | who 4.05.280
i'll heat his blood with greekish wine to-night, 5.01. 1
augurer tells me we shall have news to-night. COR 2.01. 2 P
i will make my very house reel to-night. 2.01.111 P
therefore it is decreed | he dies to-night. 3.01.288
i dreamt a dream to-night. ROM 1.04. 50
that which thou hast heard me speak to-night. 2.02. 87
thee, | i have no joy of this contract to-night, 2.02.117
what satisfaction canst thou have to-night? 2.02.126
our romeo hath not been in bed to-night. 2.03. 42
came he not home to-night? 2.04. 2
'tis very late, she'll not come down to-night. 3.04. 5
to-night she's mewed up to her heaviness. 3.04. 11
i'll not to bed to-night; 4.02. 42
i pray thee leave me to myself to-night, | for i 4.03. 2
i will hence to-night. 5.01. 26
well, juliet, i will lie with thee to-night. 5.01. 34
what cursed foot wanders this way to-night, | to 5.03. 19
how oft to-night | have my old feet stumbled at 5.03.121
alas, my liege, my wife is dead to-night; 5.03.210
i dreamt of a silver basin and ew'r to-night. TIM 3.01. 7 P
will you sup with me to-night, casca? JC 1.02.288 P
but never till to-night, never till now, | did i 1.03. 9
and what men to-night | have had resort to you; 2.01.275
heaven nor earth have been at peace to-night. 2.02. 1
she dreamt to-night she saw my statue, | which, 2.02. 76
he lies to-night within seven leagues of rome. 3.01.286
i dreamt to-night that i did feast with caesar, 3.03. 1
prepare to lodge their companies to-night. 4.03.140
as in thy red rays thou dost sink to-night, | so 5.03. 61
within my tent his bones to-night shall lie, 5.05. 78
the king comes here to-night. MAC 1.05. 31
my dearest love, | duncan comes here to-night. 1.05. 59
and noble hostess, | we are your guest to-night. 1.06. 25
to-night we hold a solemn supper, sir, | and 3.01. 14
the moment on't, for't must be done to-night, 3.01.130
if it find heaven, must find it out to-night. 3.01.141
ay, madam, but returns again to-night. 3.02. 2
be bright and jovial among your guests to-night. 3.02. 28
it will be rain to-night. 3.03. 16
do we but find the tyrant's power to-night, 5.06. 7
what, has this thing appear'd again to-night? HAM 1.01. 21
let us impart what we have seen to-night | unto 1.01.169
hold you the watch to-night? 1.02.225
i will watch to-night, | perchance 'twill walk 1.02.241
and whatsomever else shall hap to-night, | give 1.02.248
the king doth wake to-night and takes his rouse, 1.04. 8
never make known what you have seen to-night. 1.05.144
there is a play to-night before the king, | one 3.02. 75
ah, mine own lord, what have i seen to-night! 4.01. 5
delay it not, i'll have him hence to-night. 4.03. 55
i think our father will hence to-night. LR 1.01.285 P
and the king gone to-night? 1.02. 24
the duke be here to-night? 2.01. 14
my worthy arch and patron, comes to-night. 2.01. 59
faith, he to-night hath boarded a land carract. OTH 1.02. 50
we lack'd your counsel and your help to-night. 1.03. 51
you must away to-night. 1.03.277
the lieutenant to-night watches on the court of 2.01.217 P
watch you to-night; 2.01.264 P
good michael, look you to the guard to-night. 2.03. 1
not to-night, good iago, i have very poor and 2.03. 33 P
i have drunk but one cup to-night — and that 2.03. 39 P
with that which he hath drunk to-night already, 2.03. 49
to desdemona hath to-night carous'd | potations 2.03. 53
have i to-night fluster'd with flowing cups, 2.03. 58
which till to-night | i ne'er might say before. 2.03.235
i have been to-night exceedingly well cudgell'd; 2.03.365 P
shall't be to-night at supper? 3.03. 57
no, not to-night. 3.03. 57
/an' you'll come to supper to-night, you may; 4.01.159 P
rot, and perish, and be damn'd to-night, for she 4.01.181 P
to-night | i do entreat that we may sup together 4.01.261
prithee to-night | lay on my bed my 4.02.104
he sups to-night with a harlotry, and thither 4.02.233 P
that song to-night | will not go from my mind; 4.03. 30
go know of cassio where he supp'd to-night. 5.01.117
have you pray'd to-night, desdemon? 5.02. 25
kill me to-morrow, let me live to-night! 5.02. 80
what sport to-night? ANT 1.01. 47
to-night we'll wander through the streets and 1.01. 53
and most of our fortunes to-night, shall be — 1.02. 45 P
and to-night i'll force | the wine peep through 3.13.189
let's to-night | be bounteous at our meal. 4.02. 9
well, my good fellows, wait on me to-night. 4.02. 20
tend me to-night; 4.02. 24
tend me to-night two hours, i ask no more, | and 4.02. 32
to greet your lord with writing, do't to-night. CYM 1.06.206
lost to-day at bowls i'll win to-night of him. 2.01. 49 P
this chanc'd to-night. PER 3.02. 77
nay, certainly to-night, | for look how fresh 3.02. 78
to-night, to-night. 4.02.104 P
to-night, to-night. 4.02.104 P
i'll bring home some to-night. 4.02.144 P
she told me | she would watch with me to-night, TNK 5.02. 9
short night to-night, and length thyself PP 14.30

TOO *(also t'*)*

/TOO 7 FR 0.0008 REL FR 3 V 4 P
cut off the heads of /too fast growing sprays, R2 3.04. 34
/'tis /too /narrow /for /your /mind. HAM 2.02.253 P
/my /lord — /hercules /and /his /load /too. 2.02.362 P
more of his purchases, and /double /ones /too, 5.01.109 P
/and /ladies, /too, /they /will /not /let /me LR 1.04.154 P
/are /o' /th' /commission, | /sit /you /too. 3.06. 39
/to /amplify /too /much, /would /make /much 5.03.207

TOO 1344 FR 0.1519 REL FR 972 V 372 P
for thou wast a spirit too delicate | to act her TMP 1.02.272
lest too light winning | make the prize light. 1.02.452
make not too rash a trial of him, for | he's 1.02.468
what if he had said "widower aeneas" too? 2.01. 80 P
he hath rais'd the wall, and houses too. 2.01. 88 P
my son is lost and (in my rate) she too, | who 2.01.110
and women too, but innocent and pure; 2.01.156
you | must be so too, if heed me; 2.01.220
the man i' th' moon's too slow — till new-born 2.01.249
(and that a strange one too) which did awake me. 2.01.318
this is a scurvy tune too; 2.02. 55 P
keep him tame, i will not take too much for him; 2.02. 77 P
hath into bondage | brought my too diligent ear. 3.01. 42
but i prattle | something too wildly, and my 3.01. 58
out o' your wits, and hearing too? 3.02. 79 P
after a little time | i'll beat him too. 3.02. 86
i cannot too much muse | such shapes, such 3.03. 36
your swords are now too massy for your strengths 3.03. 67
if i have too austerely punish'd you, | your 4.01. 1
do not give dalliance | too much the rein. 4.01. 52
be not too late. 4.01.133
here's too small a pasture for such store of TGV 1.01. 99 P
'tis threefold too little for carrying a letter 1.01.109

it is too heavy for so light a tune. 1.02. 81
no, madam, 'tis too sharp. 1.02. 88
you, minion, are too saucy. 1.02. 89
nay, now you are too flat, | and mar the concord 1.02. 90
and mar the concord with too harsh a descant: 1.02. 91
i see things too, although you judge i wink. 1.02.136
well — you'll still be too forward. 2.01. 11 P
and yet i was last chidden for being too slow. 2.01. 12 P
perchance you think too much of so much pains? 2.01.112
ay, sir, and done too — for this time. 2.04. 30 P
too low a mistress for so high a servant. 2.04.106
but too mean a servant | to have a look of such 2.04.107
and i will help thee to prefer her too: 2.04.157
o, but i love his lady too too much, | and 2.04.205
o, but i love his lady too too much, | and 2.04.205
ay, and what i do too. 2.05. 29 P
than for all the favors | which (all too much) i 3.01.162
out with that too; 3.01.338 P
"item, she is too liberal." 3.01.348 P
but silvia is too fair, too true, too holy, | to 4.02. 5
but silvia is too fair, too true, too holy, | to 4.02. 5
but silvia is too fair, too true, too holy, | to 4.02. 5
little, | unless i flatter with myself too much. 4.04.188
what? that my leg is too long? 5.02. 4
no, that it is too little. 5.02. 5
than plural faith, which is too much by one. 5.04. 52
ay, and rato–lorum too; WIV 1.01. 8 P
ay, you spake in latin then too: 1.01.180 P
his thefts were too open; 1.03. 25 P
who even now gave me good eyes too, examin'd my 1.03. 60 P
she bears the purse too; 1.03. 68 P
by my trot, i tarry too long. 1.04. 62 P
she is given too much to allicholy and musing; 1.04.153 P
and my good man too. 2.01.103 P
a man may be too confident. 2.01.186 P
page hath her hearty commendations to you too; 2.02. 96 P
she is too bright to be look'd against. 2.02.244 P
which now are too too strongly embattled against 2.02.250 P
which now are too too strongly embattled against 2.02.250 P
better three hours too soon than a minute too 2.02.312 P
three hours too soon than a minute too late. 2.02.313 P
by gar, he deceive me too. 3.01.124 P
he is of too high a region, he knows too much. 3.02. 73 P
he is of too high a region, he knows too much. 3.02. 74 P
he's too big to go in there. what shall i do? 3.03.134 P
buck, and of the season too, it shall appear. 3.03.159 P
you wrong yourself too much. 3.03.167 P
be–gar nor i too; there is no–bodies. 3.03.213 P
among five thousand, and five hundred too. 3.03.221 P
he doth object i am too great of birth, | and 3.04. 4
come, we stay too long. 4.01. 85 P
there's her thrumm'd hat and her muffler too. 4.02. 79 P
and talks of the basket too, howsoever he hath 4.02. 92 P
do, | wives may be merry, and yet honest too: 4.02.105
so say i too, sir. 4.02.128 P
so think i too. 4.04. 25 P
things to have spoken with her too from him. 4.05. 40 P
cozen'd, for i have been cozen'd and beaten too. 4.05. 94 P
that's good too; 5.02. 8 P
ay, and an ox too; both the proofs are extant. 5.05.120 P
and leave you your jealousies too, i pray you. 5.05.132 P
am i ridden with a welsh goat too? 5.05.137 P
i am too sure of it; MM 1.02. 72 P
they had gone down too, but that a wise burgher 1.02.100 P
from too much liberty, my lucio, liberty: 1.02.125
with character too gross is writ on juliet. 1.02.155
i do fear — too dreadful; 1.03. 34
which, i think, is a very ill house too. 2.01. 67 P
ear, you might have your action of slander too. 2.01.181 P
lest i might be too rash. 2.02. 9
you are too cold. 2.02. 45
he's sentenc'd; 'tis too late. 2.02. 55
you are too cold. 2.02. 56
too late? 2.02. 57
nay, women are frail too. 2.04.124
thou art too noble to conserve a life | in base 3.01. 87
thought | imagine howling — 'tis too horrible! 3.01.127
and furr'd with fox and lambskins too, to 3.02. 8 P
sir, we take him to be a thief too, sir, for we 3.02. 16 P
bawd is he doubtless, and of antiquity too; 3.02. 68 P
something too crabbed that way, friar. 3.02. 98 P
it is too general a vice, and severity must cure 3.02. 99 P
he would be drunk too, that let me inform you. 3.02.128 P
or you imagine me too unhurtful an opposite. 3.02.165 P
it is not my consent, | but my entreaty too. 4.01. 67
if it be too little for your thief, your true 4.02. 44 P
if it be too big for your thief, your thief 4.02. 45 P
tell him he must awake, and that quickly too. 4.03. 31 P
you have told me too many of him already, sir, 4.03.167 P
the benefit of silence, would thou wert so too! 5.01.191 P
then is your cause gone too. 5.01.300
away with those giglets too, and with the other 5.01.347 P
say you will be mine, | he is my brother too. 5.01.493
too soon | we came aboard. ERR 1.01. 60
lest that your goods too soon be confiscate: 1.02. 2
rather approach'd too late: 1.02. 43
so plainly, i could too well feel his blows; 2.01. 52 P
but, too unruly deer, he breaks the pale, | and 2.01.100
get a sconce for my head, and insconce it too, 2.02. 38 P
for two — and sound ones too. 2.02. 91 P
as take from me thyself and not me too. 2.02.129
come, come, antipholus, we dine too late. 2.02.219
for such store, | when one is one too many? 3.01. 35
faith, no, he comes too late, | and so tell your 3.01. 49
here's too much "out upon thee!" 3.01. 78
wild, and yet, too, gentle; 3.01.110
i will discharge my bond, and thank you too. 4.01. 13
belike you thought our love would last too long 4.01. 25
and i, to blame, have held him here too long. 4.01. 47
she is too big, i hope, for me to compass. 4.01.111
nay, he's a thief too: 4.02. 59
choose, | for forty ducats is too much to lose. 4.03. 96
go bind this man, for he is frantic too. 4.04.113
yes, that you did, sir, and forswore it too. 5.01. 24
bind dromio too, and bear them to my house. 5.01. 35
and in assemblies too. 5.01. 60
you tax signior benedick too much, but he'll be ADO 1.01. 46 P
and a good soldier too, lady. 1.01. 53 P
you embrace your charge too willingly. 1.01.103 P
faith, methinks she's too low for a high praise, 1.01.171 P
for a high praise, too brown for a fair praise, 1.01.172 P
fair praise, and too little for a great praise; 1.01.172 P
i look for an earthquake too then. 1.01.273 P
but lest my liking might too sudden seem, | i 1.01.314
the one is too like an image and says nothing, 2.01. 8 P
and the other too like my lady's eldest son, 2.01. 9 P
in faith, she's too curst. 2.01. 20 P
too curst is more than curst. 2.01. 21 P
horns" — but to a cow too curst he sends none. 2.01. 23 P
so, by being too curst, god will send you no 2.01. 25 P
if the prince be too important, tell him there 2.01. 71 P
so did i too, and he swore he would marry her 2.01.169 P
the rod had been made, and the garland too, for 2.01.228 P
and have cleft his club to make the fire too. 2.01.254 P
your grace is too costly to wear every day. 2.01.328 P
hence a just sevennight, and a time too brief, 2.01.360 P
and a time too brief, too, to have all things 2.01.360 P
and you too, gentle hero? 2.01.374 P
they say too that she will rather die than give 2.03.226 P
no, truly, ursula, she is too disdainful, | i 3.01. 34
that would i know too. 3.02. 64 P
(for she has been too long a–talking of), the 3.02.103 P
the word is too good to paint out her wickedness 3.02.109 P
that were a punishment too good for them, if 3.03. 4 P
art not thou thyself giddy with the fashion too, 3.03.141 P
indeed, neighbor, he comes too short of you. 3.05. 41 P
i never tempted her with word too large, | but, 4.01. 52
o, one too much by thee! 4.01.129
hath drops too few to wash her clean again, 4.01.141
and salt too little which may season give | to 4.01.142
are only turn'd into tongue, and trim ones too. 4.01.321 P
make those that do offend you suffer too. 5.01. 40
i doubt we should have been too young for them. 5.01.119 P
shall i not find a woodcock too? 5.01.157 P
this learned constable is too cunning to be 5.01.228 P
master signior leonato, and the sexton too. 5.01.258 P
thou and i are too wise to woo peaceably. 5.02. 72 P
very ill too. 5.02. 92 P
there will i leave you too, for here comes one 5.02. 94 P
subscribe to your deep oaths, and keep it too. LLL 1.01. 23
and make a dark night too of half the day — 1.01. 45
o, these are barren tasks, too hard to keep, 1.01. 47
or, having sworn too hard–a–keeping oath, 1.01. 65
too much to know is to know nought but fame; 1.01. 92
so you, to study now it is too late, | climb 1.01.108
it is so varied too, for it was proclaim'd 1.01.294 P
i am in love too. 1.02. 75 P
as i have read, sir, and the best of them too. 1.02. 85 P
for prisoners to be too silent in their words, 1.02.163 P
cupid's butt–shaft is too hard for hercules' 1.02.176 P
and therefore too much odds for a spaniard's 1.02.177 P
is a sharp wit match'd with too blunt a will, 2.01. 49
and much too little of that good i saw | is my 2.01. 62
the roof of this court is too high to be yours, 2.01. 92 P
welcome to the wide fields too base to be mine. 2.01. 93 P
but pardon me, i am too sudden bold; 2.01.107
your wit's too hot, it speeds too fast, 'twill 2.01.119
your wit's too hot, it speeds too fast, 'twill 2.01.119
you do the king my father too much wrong, | and 2.01.153
you are too hard for me. 2.01.258
and keep not too long in one tune, but a snip 3.01. 21 P
you are too swift, sir, to say so. 3.01. 61
she's too hard for you at pricks, sir, challenge 4.01.138
i fear too much rubbing. 4.01.139
and thank you too; 4.02.161 P
sir, i do invite you too, you shall not say me 4.02.164 P
and mine too, good lord! 4.03. 91
berowne, and longaville, | were lovers too! 4.03.122
too bitter is thy jest. 4.03.172
passes praise, then praise too short doth blot. 4.03.237
her feet were much too dainty for such tread! 4.03.275
your stomachs are too young, | and abstinence 4.03.290
eyes, | and study too, the causer of your vow. 4.03.307
and win them too; 4.03.369
he is too picked, too spruce, too affected, too 5.01. 12 P
he is too picked, too spruce, too affected, too 5.01. 13 P
too spruce, too affected, too odd as it were, 5.01. 13 P
spruce, too affected, too odd as it were, too 5.01. 13 P
too odd as it were, too peregrinate, as i may 5.01. 14 P
and of great import indeed too — but let that 5.01.101 P
ay, and a shrowd unhappy gallows too. 5.02. 12
but, rosaline, you have a favor too? 5.02. 30
nay, i have verses too, i thank berowne; 5.02. 34
the numbers true, and, were the numb'ring too, 5.02. 35
the letter is too long by half a mile. 5.02. 54
and change you favors too, so shall your loves 5.02.134
my face is but a moon, and clouded too. 5.02.203
'a can carve too, and lisp; 5.02.323
is exceeding fantastical, too too vain, too too 5.02.529 P
is exceeding fantastical, too too vain, too too 5.02.529 P
fantastical, too too vain, too too vain: 5.02.529 P
fantastical, too too vain, too too vain: 5.02.529 P
for it stands too right. 5.02.565
his leg is too big for hector's. 5.02.639 P
coming too short of thanks | for my great suit 5.02.738
a time methinks too short | to make a 5.02.788
you must be purged too, your sins are rack'd, 5.02.818
that's too long for a play. 5.02.878
o cross! too high to be enthrall'd to /low. MND 1.01.136
o spite! too old to be engag'd to young. 1.01.138
and i may hide my face, let me play thisby too. 1.02. 52 P
let me play the lion too. 1.02. 70 P
and you should do it too terribly, you would 1.02. 74 P
tempt not too much the hatred of my spirit, 2.01.211
you do impeach your modesty too much, | to leave 2.01.214
auditor, | an actor too perhaps, if i see cause. 3.01. 80
i shall desire you of more acquaintance too. 3.01.189 P
i took him sleeping — that is finish'd too — 3.02. 38
in blood, plunge in the deep, | and kill me too. 3.02. 49
do, | but you must join in souls to mock me too? 3.02.150
if thou say so, withdraw, and prove it too. 3.02.255
to strike me, spurn me, nay, to kill me too. 3.02.313
you are too officious | in her behalf that 3.02.330
do not fret yourself too much in the action, 4.01. 13 P
yea, and the best person too; 4.02. 11 P
but by ten words, my lord, it is too long, 5.01. 63
ay, and wall too. 5.01.350 P
what harm a wind too great might do at sea. MV 1.01. 24
you have too much respect upon the world. 1.01. 74
wherein my time something too prodigal | hath 1.01.129
as sick that surfeit with too much as they that 1.02. 6 P
to spet on thee again, to spurn thee too. 1.03.131
virgins of our clime | have lov'd it too. 2.01. 11
thou art too wild, too rude, and bold of voice 2.02.181
thou art too wild, too rude, and bold of voice 2.02.181
why, there they show | something too liberal. 2.02.185
in themselves, good sooth, are too too light. 2.06. 42
in themselves, good sooth, are too too light. 2.06. 42
it were too gross | to rib her cerecloth in the 2.07. 50
i have too griev'd a heart | to take a tedious 2.07. 76
he came too late, the ship was under sail, | but 2.08. 6
and well said too; 2.09. 37
too long a pause for that which you find there. 2.09. 53
yes, other men have ill luck too. 3.01. 97 P
i speak too long, but 'tis to peize the time, 3.02. 22
i feel too much thy blessing; 3.02.113
you | even at that time i may be married too. 3.02.194
and so did mine too, as the matter falls; 3.02.202
this comes too near the praising of myself, 3.04. 22
that is done too, sir, only "cover" is the word. 3.05. 51 P
nay, but ask my opinion too of that. 3.05. 85
shylock, the world thinks, and i think so too, 4.01. 17
proceeding, | that indirectly, and directly too, 4.01.359
but we'll outface them, and outswear them too. 4.02. 17
you give your wife too unkind a cause of grief; 5.01.175
that begg'd it, and indeed | deserv'd it too; 5.01.181
my clerk hath some good comforts too for you. 5.01.289
come, elder brother, you are too young in this. AYL 1.01. 53 P
indeed there is fortune too hard for nature, 1.02. 48 P
our natural wits too dull to reason of such 1.02. 53 P
alas, he is too young! 1.02.153 P
your spirits are too bold for your years. 1.02.173 P
thy words are too precious to be cast away upon 1.03. 4 P
i was too young that time to value her, | but 1.03. 71
she is too subtile for thee, and her smoothness, 1.03. 77
thy sum of more | to that which had too /much." 2.01. 49
your praise is come too swiftly home before you. 2.03. 9
seek, | but at fourscore it is too late a week; 2.03. 74
he is too disputable for my company. 2.05. 35 P
sav'd, a world too wide | for his shrunk shank, 2.07.160
you have too courtly a wit for me, i'll rest. 3.02. 70 P
and more, too, for some of them had in them more 3.02.164 P
narrow–mouth'd bottle, either too much at once, 3.02.201 P
'tis a word too great for any mouth of this 3.02.226 P
fashion sake, i thank you too for your society. 3.02.256 P
foot can fall, he thinks himself too soon there. 3.02.328 P
one that knew courtship too well, for there he 3.02.346 P
so ordinary that the whippers are in love too. 3.02.404 P
life, | i think she means to tangle my eyes too! 3.05. 44
and i'll employ thee too. 3.05. 96
to make me sad — and to travel for it too! 4.01. 29 P
then, can one desire too much of a good thing? 4.01.123 P
yet heard too much of phebe's cruelty. 4.03. 38
there is too great testimony in your complexion 4.03.169 P
why do you speak too, "why blame you me to love 5.02.106 P
and you may avoid that too, with an if. 5.04. 98 P
seeing too much sadness hath congeal'd your SHR in.2. 132
she's too rough for me. 1.01. 55
and me too, good lord! 1.01. 67
why, and i trust i may go too, may i not? 1.01.102
the better for him, would i were so too! 1.01.238
but th' art too much my friend, | and i'll not 1.02. 63
take your paper too, | and let me have them very 1.02.150
you are too blunt, go to it orderly. 2.01. 45
let us that are poor petitioners speak too. 2.01. 72
too light for such a swain as you to catch, 2.01.204
come, you wasp, i' faith you are too angry. 2.01.209
no cock of mine, you crow too like a craven. 2.01.227
now, by saint george, i am too young for you. 2.01.236
fiddler, forbear, you grow too forward, sir. 3.01. 1
patience, good katherine, and baptista too. 3.02. 21
is it new and old too? how may that be? 3.02. 32 P
i stay too long from her. 3.02.110
i fear it is too choleric a meat. 4.03. 19
ay, but the mustard is too hot a little. 4.03. 25
when you are gentle, you shall have one too, 4.03. 71
and she to him, to stay him not too long, | i am 4.04. 30
tell me, sweet kate, and tell me truly too, 4.05. 28
better once than never, for never too late. 5.01.150
ay, and a kind one too. 5.02. 83
i would your duty were as foolish too. 5.02.126
too little payment for so great a debt. 5.02.154
they are virtues and traitors too. AWW 1.01. 43 P
i do affect a sorrow indeed, but i have it too. 1.01. 54 P
heart too capable | of every line and trick of 1.01. 95
'tis too cold a companion; 1.01.132 P
father's moral parts | mayst thou inherit too! 1.02. 22
i, after him, do after him wish too, | since i 1.02. 64
"too young" and "the next year" and "'tis too 2.01. 28
young" and "the next year" and "'tis too early." 2.01. 28
yourself within the list of too cold an adieu. 2.01. 52 P
that we with thee | may spend our wonder too, or 2.01. 89
why, there 'tis, so say i too. 2.03. 15 P
before i speak, too threat'ningly replies. 2.03. 81
you are too young, too happy, and too good, | to 2.03. 96
you are too young, too happy, and too good, | to 2.03. 96
you are too young, too happy, and too good, | to 2.03. 96
you are too old, sir; 2.03.196 P
let it satisfy you, you are too old. 2.03.197 P
what i dare too well do, i dare not do. 2.03.200 P
believing thee a vessel of too great a burthen. 2.03.205 P
do not plunge thyself too far in anger, lest 2.03.211 P
by the misprising of a maid too virtuous | for 3.02. 31
there's nothing here that is too good for him 3.02. 80
lady, | the fellow has a deal of that too much, 3.02. 90
it is | a charge too heavy for my strength, but 3.03. 4
he is too good and fair for death and me, | whom 3.04. 16
of her worth, | that he does weigh too light. 3.04. 32
she is too mean | to have her name repeated. 3.05. 60
lest, reposing too far in his virtue, which he 3.06. 14 P
to buy his will, it would not seem too dear, 3.07. 27
have of late knock'd too often at my door. 4.01. 28 P
i find my tongue is too foolhardy, but my heart 4.01. 29 P
they cannot be too sweet for the king's tartness 4.03. 82 P

fare ye well, sir, i am for france too. 4.03.329 P
which i take to be too little for pomp to enter. 4.05. 51 P
may, but the many will be too chill and tender, 4.05. 53 P
'tis too late to pare her nails now. 5.02. 29 P
oil and fire, too strong for reason's force, 5.03. 7
durst make too bold a herald of my tongue; 5.03. 46
but love that comes too late, | like a 5.03. 57
vanity, | having vainly fear'd too little. 5.03.123
your reputation comes too short for my daughter, 5.03.176 P
but thou art too fine in thy evidence, therefore 5.03.268 P
enough to drink in, and so be these boots too; TN 1.03. 12 P
and you too, sir. 1.03. 48 P
he seems to have a foreknowledge of that too, 1.05.143 P
i see you what you are, you are too proud; 1.05.250
not too fast! 1.05.293
mine eye too great a flatterer for my mind. 1.05.309
not i, | it is too hard a knot for me t' untie! 2.02. 41
there's a testril of me too. 2.03. 33 P
well enough if he be dispos'd, and so do i too. 2.03. 82 P
anne, and ginger shall be hot i' th' mouth too. 2.03.118 P
i have't in my nose too. 2.03.163 P
i was ador'd once too. 2.03.181 P
burn some sack, 'tis too late to go to bed now. 2.03.191 P
too old, by heaven. 2.04. 29
too well what love women to men may owe; 2.04.105
and all the brothers too — and yet i know not. 2.04.121
so could i too. 2.05.183 P
i'll make one too. 2.05.207 P
do not then walk too open. 3.03. 37
i speak too loud. 3.04. 4
i have said too much unto a heart of stone, 3.04.201
stone, | and laid mine honor too unchary on't. 3.04.202
that my most jealious and too doubtful soul 4.03. 27
little faith, though thou hast too much fear. 5.01.171
and has given sir toby a bloody coxcomb too. 5.01.176 P
father — | such a sebastian was my brother too; 5.01.233
you pay a great deal too dear for what's given WT 1.01. 17 P
to make us say, | "this is put forth too truly." 1.02. 14
you, sir, | charge him too coldly. 1.02. 30
too hot, too hot! 1.02.108
too hot, too hot! 1.02.108
prove | (as /ornament oft does) too dangerous. 1.02.158
and i | play too, but so disgrac'd a part, whose 1.02.188
himself, will have | all that are his so too. 1.02.356
me a mirror | which shows me mine chang'd too; 1.02.382
nay, hated too, worse than the great'st 1.02.423
so that there be not | too much hair there, but 2.01. 10
i know't too well. 2.01. 55
of me, yet you | have too much blood in him. 2.01. 58
lady, | no court in europe is too good for thee, 2.02. 3
in himself too mighty, | and in his parties, his 2.03. 20
it, if thou hast | the ordering of the mind too, 2.03.106
our wife, and one | of us too much belov'd. 3.02. 4
i have too much believ'd mine own suspicion. 3.02.151
lace, lest my heart, cracking it, | break too! 3.02.174
thy jealousies | (fancies too weak for boys, too 3.02.181
boys, too green and idle | for girls of nine), o 3.02.181
thou canst not speak too much, i have deserv'd 3.02.215
i have show'd too much | the rashness of a woman 3.02.220
remember you of my own lord, | who is lost too. 3.02.231
best haste, and go not | too far i' th' land; 3.03. 11
thou'rt like to have | a lullaby too rough. 3.03. 55
not enough consider'd (as too much i cannot), to 4.02. 18 P
gallows and knock are too powerful on the 4.03. 28 P
i'll be with you at your sheep-shearing too. 4.03.120 P
the ord'ring your affairs, | to sing them too. 4.04.140
o doricles, | your praises are too large. 4.04.147
than herself, | too noble for this place. 4.04.159
i think so too; 4.04.172
i love a ballad but even too well, if it be 4.04.188 P
the feast, but they come not too late now. 4.04.236 P
is it true too, think you? 4.04.282 P
lay it by too. another. 4.04.285 P
me too; let me go thither. 4.04.302
mind (if it be not too rough for some that know 4.04.330 P
here has been too much homely foolery already. 4.04.332 P
is it not too far gone? 4.04.344
and this my neighbor too? 4.04.370
thou art too base | to be /acknowledg'd. 4.04.418
worthy enough a herdsman, yea, him too, | that 4.04.435
all, every word, yea, and his son's pranks too; 4.04.700 P
but that death is too soft for him, say i. 4.04.779 P
all deaths are too few, the sharpest too easy. 4.04.780 P
all deaths are too few, the sharpest too easy. 4.04.780 P
true, too true, my lord. 5.01. 12
obtain'd your eye, | will have your tongue too. 5.01.106
amity too, of your brave father, whom | (though 5.01.136
and hath he too | expos'd this paragon to th' 5.01.152
my liege, | your eye hath too much youth in't. 5.01.225
my lord, your sorrow was too sore laid on, 5.03. 49
if she pertain to life let her speak too. 5.03.113
'tis too respective and too sociable | for your JN 1.01.188
'tis too respective and too sociable | for your 1.01.188
hast thou conspired with thy brother too, | that 1.01.241
some bastards too. 2.01.279
and your lips too, for i am well assur'd | that 2.01.534
thou art perjur'd too, | and sooth'st up 3.01.120
and for mine too: 3.01.185
is all too wanton and too full of gawds | to 3.03. 36
is all too wanton and too full of gawds | to 3.03. 36
too well, too well i feel | the different plague 3.04. 59
too well i feel | the different plague of each 3.04. 59
you hold too heinous a respect of grief. 3.04. 90
too fairly, hubert, for so foul effect. 4.01. 38
found it too precious-princely for a grave. 4.03. 40
i am too high-born to be propertied, | to be a 5.02. 79
and now 'tis far too huge to be blown out | with 5.02. 86
the dolphin is too willful-opposite, | and will 5.02.124
he is prepar'd, and reason too he should — 5.02.130
we hold our time too precious to be spent | with 5.02.161
if they miscarry, we miscarry too. 5.04. 3
it is too late, the life of all his blood | is 5.07. 1
too good to be so, and too bad to live, | since R2 1.01. 40
too good to be so, and too bad to live, | since 1.01. 40
deep malice makes too deep incision. 1.01.155
i am too old to fawn upon a nurse, | too far in 1.03.170
a nurse, | too far in years to be a pupil now. 1.03.171
after our sentence plaining comes too late. 1.03.175
and all too soon, i fear, the king shall rue. 1.03.205
say | i was too strict to make mine own away; 1.03.244
i have too few to take my leave of you, | when 1.03.255
with too great a court | and liberal largess, 1.04. 43
pray god we may make haste and come too late! 1.04. 64
then all too late comes counsel to be heard, 2.01. 27
he tires betimes that spurs too fast betimes; 2.01. 36
and thou, too careless patient as thou art, 2.01. 97
to crop at once a too long withered flower. 2.01.134
york is too far gone with grief, | or else he 2.01.184
and living too, for now his son is duke. 2.01.225
madam, your majesty is too much sad. 2.02. 1
'tis too true, and that is worse, | the lord 2.02. 52
i should to plashy too, | but time will not 2.02.120
the noble duke hath been too much abused. 2.03.137
with too much urging your pernicious lives, 3.01. 4
he means, my lord, that we are too remiss, 3.02. 33
one day too late, i fear me, noble lord, | hath 3.02. 67
to-day, to-day, unhappy day, too late, 3.02. 71
we'll serve him too, and be his fellow so. 3.02. 99
too well, too well thou tell'st a tale so ill. 3.02.121
too well, too well thou tell'st a tale so ill. 3.02.121
cousin, i am too young to be your father, 3.03.204
what you will have, i'll give, and willing too, 3.03.206
that look too lofty in our commonwealth: 3.04. 35
with too much riches it confound itself; 3.04. 60
though being all too base | to stain the temper 4.01. 28
woman, do not so, | to make my end too sudden. 5.01. 17
half, | it is too little, helping him to all; 5.01. 61
the cheapest of us is ten groats too dear. 5.05. 68
thou sayest well, and it holds well too, for the 1H4 1.02. 30 P
and yet he talk'd wisely, and in the street too. 1.02. 87 P
yea, but i doubt they will be too hard for us. 1.02.181 P
my blood hath been too cold and temperate, 1.03. 1
and that same greatness too which our own hands 1.03. 12
sir, your presence is too bold and peremptory, 1.03. 17
one that hath abundance of charge too — god 2.01. 58 P
when a jest is so forward, and afoot too! 2.02. 47 P
unsorted, and your whole plot too light for the 2.03. 13 P
and crack'd crowns, | and pass them current too. 2.03. 94
kate, | whither i go, thither shall you go too; 2.03.115
of all cowards, i say, and a vengeance too! 2.04.115 P
nether-stocks, and mend them and foot them too. 2.04.117 P
you rogue, here's lime in this sack too. 2.04.124 P
ay, and mark thee too, jack. 2.04.210 P
you are lions too, you ran away upon instinct, 2.04.299 P
well, he is there too, and one mordake, and a 2.04.357 P
home without boots, and in foul weather too! 3.01. 67
in faith, my lord, you are too willful-blame, 3.01.175
she'll be a soldier too, she'll to the wars. 3.01.193
these swelling heavens | i am too perfect in, 3.01.200
come, kate, i'll have your song too. 3.01.245 P
little | more than a little is by much too much. 3.02. 73
thou doest, and do it with unwash'd hands too. 3.03.184 P
you strain too far. 4.01. 75
he shall be welcome too. 4.01. 94
more than time that i were there, and you too, 4.02. 55 P
they are exceeding poor and bare, too beggarly. 4.02. 69 P
he is, sir john. i fear we shall stay too long. 4.02. 77 P
swore him assistance, and perform'd it too. 4.03. 65
that lie too heavy on the commonwealth, | cries 4.03. 80
we find | too indirect for long continuance. 4.03.105
thence, | who with them was a rated sinew too, 4.04. 17
i fear the power of percy is too weak | to wage 4.04. 19
and so i hear he doth account me too; 5.01. 95
to spend that shortness basely were too long 5.02. 82
a borrowed title hast thou bought too dear. 5.03. 23
i am as hot as molten lead, and as heavy too. 5.03. 34 P
harry, withdraw thyself, thou bleedest too much. 5.04. 2
not i, my lord, unless i did bleed too. 5.04. 4
we breathe too long. 5.04. 15
they did me too much injury | that ever said i 5.04. 51
a kingdom for it was too small a bound, | but 5.04. 90
you leave to powder me and eat me too to-morrow. 5.04.112 P
hot termagant scot had paid me scot and lot too. 5.04.114 P
how if he should counterfeit too and rise? 5.04.123 P
bear worcester to the death and vernon too. 5.05. 14
you are too great to be by me gainsaid, | your 2H4 1.01. 91
your spirit is too true, your fears too certain. 1.01. 92
your spirit is too true, your fears too certain. 1.01. 92
that art a guard too wanton for the head | which 1.01.148
of our youth, i must confess, are wags too. 1.02.177 P
they have a good thing, to make it too common. 1.02.216 P
a penny, you are too impatient to bear crosses. 1.02.225 P
but if without him we be thought too feeble, 1.03. 19
my judgment is we should not step too far 1.03. 20
wert an honest man, thyself and the money too. 2.01. 86 P
sir john, you loiter here too long, being you 2.01.186 P
my friend —, i could be sad, and sad indeed too. 2.02. 43 P
be not too familiar with poins, for he misuses 2.02.127 P
the room where they supp'd is too hot, they'll 2.04. 14 P
i' faith, you have drunk too much canaries, and 2.04. 26 P
angel about him, but the devil blinds him too. 2.04.336 P
of the ocean | too wide for neptune's hips; 3.01. 51
and i would have done any thing indeed too, and 3.02. 18 P
have done any thing indeed too, and roundly too. 3.02. 18 P
in faith, sir, and it is well said indeed too. 3.02. 69 P
no man's too good to serve 's prince, and let it 3.02.236 P
all too confident | to give admittance to a 4.01.150
you are too shallow, hastings, much too shallow, 4.02. 50
you are too shallow, hastings, much too shallow, 4.02. 50
and some about him have too lavishly | wrested 4.02. 57
my lord, | and let our army be discharged too. 4.02. 92
thine's too heavy to mount. 4.03. 56 P
thine's too thick to shine. 4.03. 58 P
cowards, which some of us should be too, but for 4.03. 95 P
i stay too long by thee, i weary thee. 4.05. 93
might make them look | too near unto my state. 4.05.212
argument | is all too heavy to admit much talk. 5.02. 24
i'll be your father and your brother too. 5.02. 57
the mass, i have drunk too much sack at supper. 5.03. 13 P
my little tiny thief, and welcome indeed too. 5.03. 58 P
if you be not too much cloy'd with fat meat, our ep 26 P
my tongue is weary, when my legs are too, i will ep 33 P
wildness, mortified in him, | seem'd to die too; H5 1.01. 27
says that you savor too much of your youth, 1.02.250
and — pauca, there's enough too! 2.01. 79
thou wilt not, why then be enemies with me too. 2.01.104 P
that's mercy, but too much security. 2.02. 44
so may your highness, and yet punish too. 2.02. 48
your too much love and care of me | are heavy 2.02. 52
you are too much mistaken in this king. 2.04. 30
witness our too much memorable shame | when 2.04. 53
here, | to whom expressly i bring greeting too. 2.04.112
the knocks are too hot; 3.02. 4 P
the humor of it is too hot, that is the very 3.02. 5 P
for our losses, his exchequer is too poor; 3.06.130 P
the muster of his kingdom too faint a number; 3.06.131 P
and his kinsman too. 4.01. 59 P
your reproof is something too round, i should be 4.01.203 P
and what have kings, that privates have not too, 4.01.238
let life be short, else shame will be too long. 4.05. 23
with /mistful eyes, or they will issue too. 4.06. 34
as it pleases his grace, and his majesty too! 4.07.109 P
and out of doubt and out of question too, and 5.01. 46 P
alas, she hath from france too long been chas'd, 5.02. 38
when articles too nicely urg'd be stood on. 5.02. 94
yet i love thee too. 5.02.152 P
in the latter end, and she must be blind too. 5.02.314 P
king henry the fift, too famous to live long! 1H6 1.01. 6
christ's mother helps me, else i were too weak. 1.02.106
then have i substance too. 2.03. 49
within the temple hall we were too loud, | the 2.04. 3
in sign whereof i pluck a white rose too. 2.04. 58
you see what mischief, and what murther too, 3.01.115
and there will we be too, ere it be long, | or 3.02. 75
and me, my lord, grant me the combat too. 4.01. 79
it is too late, i cannot send them now. 4.04. 1
was by york and talbot | too rashly plotted. 4.04. 3
too late comes rescue, he is ta'en or slain; 4.04. 42
o, too much folly is it, well i wot, | to hazard 4.06. 32
somewhat too sudden, sirs, the warning is, | but 5.02. 14
my ancient incantations are too weak, | and hell 5.03. 27
and hell too strong for me to buckle with: 5.03. 28
but there remains a scruple in that too; 5.03. 93
hanging is too good. 5.04. 33
take her away, for she hath liv'd too long, | to 5.04. 34
my lord of gloucester, now ye grow too hot: 2H6 1.01.137
what, is't too short? 1.02. 12
thy wife too? 1.03. 19 P
too true, and bought his climbing very dear. 2.01. 98
now thou dost penance too. 2.04. 20
art thou gone too? 2.04. 87
and too well given | to dream on evil or to work 3.01. 72
gloucester, know that thou art come too soon, 3.01. 95
in great affairs, | too full of foolish pity; 3.01.225
be poisonous too, and kill thy forlorn queen. 3.02. 77
that he is dead, good warwick, 'tis too true, 3.02.130
nay, 'tis too true; therefore he shall be king. 4.02.147
fire, and, if you can, burn down the tower too. 4.06. 15 P
and work in their shirt too, as myself, for 4.07. 52 P
in any case, be not too rough in terms, | for he 4.09. 44
that ever was broach'd, and beard thee too. 4.10. 38 P
that is too much presumption on thy part; 5.01. 38
lords, | and be you silent and attentive too, 3H6 1.01.122
thou hast spoke too much already; get thee gone. 1.01.258
i am too mean a subject for thy wrath, | be thou 1.03. 19
o, 'tis a fault too too unpardonable! 1.04.106
o, 'tis a fault too too unpardonable! 1.04.106
to thee | as now i reap at thy too cruel hand! 1.04.166
o, speak no more, for i have heard too much. 2.01. 48
this too much lenity | and harmful pity must be 2.02. 9
why, that's my fortune too, therefore i'll stay. 2.02. 76
and reason too: 2.02. 93
for margaret my queen, and clifford too, | have 2.05. 16
thy father gave thee life too soon, | and hath 2.05. 92
and hath bereft thee of thy life too late. 2.05. 93
and what makes robbers bold but too much lenity? 2.06. 22
for gloucester's dukedom is too ominous. 2.06.107
i know i am too mean to be your queen, | and yet 3.02. 97
queen, | and yet too good to be your concubine. 3.02. 98
my eye's too quick, my heart o'erweens too much, 3.02.144
my eye's too quick, my heart o'erweens too much, 3.02.144
yea, brother richard, are you offended too? 4.01. 19
and you too, somerset and montague, | speak 4.01. 27
nay, whom they shall obey, and love thee too, 4.01. 79
yea, brother of clarence, art thou here too? 4.03. 41
my brother was too careless of his charge. 4.06. 86
the gates are open, let us enter too. 5.01. 60
give more strength to that which hath too much, 5.04. 9
untutor'd lad, thou art too malapert. 5.05. 32
o, kill me too! 5.05. 41
hold, richard, hold, for we have done too much. 5.05. 43
no doubt, no doubt, and so shall clarence too, R3 1.01.129
then god grant me too | thou mayst be damned for 1.02.102
with all my heart, and much it joys me too, | to 1.02.219
a bachelor, and a handsome stripling too: 1.03.100
i have too long borne | your blunt upbraidings 1.03.102
i do remember them too well: 1.03.117
i am too childish-foolish for this world. 1.03.141
she hath had too much wrong, and i repent | my 1.03.306
i was too hot to do somebody good | that is too 1.03.310
good | that is too cold in thinking of it now. 1.03.311
for false forswearing and for murther too. 1.04.202
that came too lag to see him buried. 2.01. 91
and i, unjustly too, must grant it you. 2.01.126
ay, sir, it is too true, god help the while! 2.03. 8
now be nearest | will touch us all too near, if 2.03. 26
a parlous boy! go to, you are too shrewd. 2.04. 35
you are too senseless-obstinate, my lord, | too 3.01. 44
my lord, | too ceremonious and traditional. 3.01. 45
too late he died that might have kept that title 3.01. 99
it is too heavy for your grace to wear. 3.01.120
be thou so too, and so break off the talk, | and 3.01.177
and supper too, although thou know'st it not. 3.02.122
to-morrow, in my judgment, is too sudden, | for 3.04. 43
for i, too fond, might have prevented this. 3.04. 81
as too triumphing, how mine enemies | to-day at 3.04. 89
which since you come too late of our intent, 3.05. 69
so say we too, but not by edward's wife; 3.07.178
i had a richard too, and thou didst kill him; 4.04. 44
i had a rutland too, thou /holp'st to kill him. 4.04. 45
thou hadst a clarence too, and richard kill'd 4.04. 46
you speak too bitterly. 4.04.181
plain and not honest is too harsh a style. 4.04.360
your reasons are too shallow and too quick. 4.04.361

your reasons are too shallow and too quick. 4.04.361
o no, my reasons are too deep and dead — | too 4.04.362
too deep and dead, poor infants, in their graves 4.04.363
look that my staves be sound, and not too heavy. 5.03. 65
but on thy side i may not be too forward, | lest 5.03. 94
they may believe, | may here find truth too. H8 pr 9
the madams too, | not us'd to toil, did almost 1.01. 23
or else you suffer | too hard an exclamation. 1.02. 52
i am much too venturous | in tempting of your 1.02. 54
whereof | we cannot feel too little, hear too 1.02.128
we cannot feel too little, hear too much. 1.02.128
and, by'r lady, | held current music too. 1.03. 47
your lordship is a guest too. 1.03. 51
o, very mad, exceeding mad, in love too; 1.04. 28
i fear, too much. 1.04.101
earl surrey was sent thither, and in haste too, 2.01. 43
employment, | and far enough from court too. 2.01. 49
too many curses on their heads | that were the 2.01.138
to confirm this too, | cardinal campeius is 2.01.159
we are too open here to argue this; 2.01.168
wife | has crept too near his conscience. 2.02. 17
conscience | has crept too near another lady. 2.02. 18
these sad thoughts that work too much upon him. 2.02. 57
ye are too bold. 2.02. 70
have, too, a woman's heart, which ever yet 2.03. 28
this burthen, 'tis too weak | ever to get a boy. 2.03. 43
could | come pat betwixt too early and too late 2.03. 84
come pat betwixt too early and too late | for 2.03. 84
or made it not mine too? 2.04. 29
and prove it too, against mine honor aught — 2.04. 39
woman, much too weak | t' oppose your cunning. 2.04.106
way to sorrow — | you have too much, good lady; 3.01. 57
both of his truth and him (which was too far), 3.01. 65
me his bed already, | his love, too long ago! 3.01.120
have ever come too short of my desires, | yet 3.02.170
o my lord, | press not a falling man too far! 3.02.333
a load would sink a navy — too much honor. 3.02.383
too heavy for a man that hopes for heaven! 3.02.385
not to let | thy hopeful service perish too. 3.02.419
that i can tell you too. 4.01. 24
o my good lord, that comfort comes too late, 4.02.120
i must to him too, | before he go to bed. 5.01. 8
from your affairs | i hinder you too long. 5.01. 54
my mind's not on't, you are too hard for me. 5.01. 57
i hope i am not too late, and yet the gentleman 5.02. 1
and at the door too, like a post with packets. 5.02. 32
which reformation must be sudden too, | my noble 5.02. 55
are a little, | by your good favor, too sharp; 5.02.109
do. | remember your bold life too. 5.02.120
this is too much. | forbear for shame, my lords. 5.02.120
'tis now too certain. 5.02.142
they are too thin and base to hide offenses. 5.02.160
they grow still too; 5.03. 68
my noble gossips, y' have been too prodigal. 5.04. 12
you must stay the cooling too, or ye may chance TRO 1.01. 26 P
it is too starv'd a subject for my sword. 1.01. 93
i know the cause too. 1.02. 55 P
i can tell them that too. 1.02. 58 P
what, is he angry too? 1.02. 59 P
then troilus should have too much: 1.02.101 P
is too flaming a praise for a good complexion. 1.02.103 P
did her eyes run o'er too? 1.02.147 P
been a green hair, i should have laugh'd too. 1.02.153 P
is't not a gallant man too, is't not? 1.02.213 P
and that's one of the chiefest of them too. 1.02.267 P
lose their names, and so should justice too! 1.03.118
but he already is too insolent; 1.03.368
a great deal of your wit, too, lies in your 2.01. 98 P
what, with me too, thersites? 2.01.103 P
we are too well acquainted with these answers, 2.03.113
my lord, you feed too much on this dislike. 2.03.225
i am too courtly and thou too cunning. 3.01. 28 P
i am too courtly and thou too cunning. 3.01. 28 P
sounding destruction, or some joy too fine, 3.02. 23
fine, | too subtile, potent, tun'd too sharp in 3.02. 24
tun'd too sharp in sweetness | for the capacity 3.02. 24
but she'll bereave you a' th' deeds too, if she 3.02. 56 P
what too curious dreg espies my sweet lady in 3.02. 65 P
nay, i'll give my word for her too. 3.02.109 P
grown | too headstrong for their mother. 3.02.123
ay, and good next day too. 3.03. 69
out with fortune, | must fall out with men too. 3.03. 76
the love that lean'd on them as slippery too, 3.03. 85
that's my mind too. good morrow, lord aeneas. 4.01. 7
you are too bitter to your country–woman. 4.01. 68
night hath been too brief. 4.02. 11
you bring me to do — and then you flout me too. 4.02. 26
let me embrace too. 4.04. 15 P
ay, ay, ay, ay, 'tis too plain a case. 4.04. 29 P
what, and from troilus too? 4.04. 31
thou art too gentle and too free a man. 4.05.139
thou art too gentle and too free a man. 4.05.139
thou art too brief. 4.05.237
with too much blood and too little brain, these 5.01. 48 P
with too much blood and too little brain, these 5.01. 48 P
if with too much brain and too little blood they 5.01. 49 P
too much brain and too little blood they do, 5.01. 50 P
and you too, diomed, | keep hector company an 5.01. 80
and i have a rheum in mine eyes too, and such an 5.03.104 P
i'll be ta'en too, | or bring him off. 5.06. 24
i am a bastard too, i love bastards. 5.07. 16 P
but they think we are too dear. COR 1.01. 19 P
they shall know we have strong arms too. 1.01. 61 P
he is grown | too proud to be so valiant. 1.01.259
thy exercise hath been too violent for | a 1.05. 15
come i too late? 1.06. 24
come i too late? 1.06. 27
too modest are you; 1.09. 53
your abilities are too infant–like for doing 2.01. 37 P
menenius, you are known well enough too. 2.01. 46 P
hasty and tinder–like upon too trivial motion; 2.01. 51 P
follows it that i am known well enough too? 2.01. 64 P
this character, if i be known well enough too? 2.01. 65 P
so do i too, if it be not too much. 2.01.122 P
so do i too, if it be not too much. 2.01.122 P
and 'twas time for him too, i'll warrant him 2.01.129 P
and mountainous error be too highly heap'd | for 2.03.120
you show too much of that | for which the people 3.01. 52

his nature is too noble for the world; 3.01.254
the harm of unscann'd swiftness, will (too late) 3.01.311
the other course | will prove too bloody; 3.01.326
ay, and burn too. 3.02. 24
come, you have been too rough, something too 3.02. 25
you have been too rough, something too rough; 3.02. 25
you are too absolute, | though therein you can 3.02. 39
though therein you can never be too noble, | but 3.02. 40
and thou art too full | of the wars' surfeits to 4.01. 45
you shall stay too. 4.02. 15
nay, but thou shalt stay too. 4.02. 23
then thou dwell'st with daws too? 4.05. 44 P
ay, and for an assault too. 4.05.171 P
he was ever too hard for him; 4.05.184 P
he was too hard for him, directly to say the 4.05.185 P
given, he might have boil'd and eaten him too. 4.05.189 P
the senators and patricians love him too; 4.07. 30
wife, his child, | and this brave fellow too: 5.01. 30
i have sate too long. 5.03.131
made my heart | too great for what contains it. 5.06.103
lest then the people, and patricians too, | upon TIT 1.01.445
be it so, titus, and gramercy too. 1.01.495
would you had hit it too! 2.01. 97
somewhat too early for new–married ladies. 2.02. 15
away, for thou hast stay'd us here too long. 2.03.181
then all too late i bring this fatal writ, | the 2.03.264
give me a sword, i'll chop off my hands too, 3.01. 72
and yet dear too, because i bought mine own. 3.01.199
she loves thee, boy, too well to do thee harm. 4.01. 6
too like the sire for ever being good. 5.01. 50
rapine and murther, you are welcome too. 5.02. 83
tell him the emperor and the empress too | feast 5.02.127
fie, publius, fie, thou art too much deceiv'd. 5.02.155
but soft, methinks i do digress too much, 5.03.116
be found, | being one too many by my weary self, ROM 1.01.128
doth add more grief to too much of mine own. 1.01.189
she is too fair, too wise, wisely too fair, | to 1.01.221
she is too fair, too wise, wisely too fair, | to 1.01.221
she is too fair, too wise, wisely too fair, | to 1.01.221
and too soon marr'd are those so early made. 1.02. 13
susan is with god, | she was too good for me. 1.03. 20
and stint thou too, i pray thee, nurse, say i. 1.03. 58
i am too sore enpierced with his shaft | to soar 1.04. 19
too great oppression for a tender thing. 1.04. 24
it is too rough, | too rude, too boist'rous, and 1.04. 25
too rude, too boist'rous, and it pricks like 1.04. 26
too rude, too boist'rous, and it pricks like 1.04. 26
supper is done, and we shall come too late. 1.04.105
i fear, too early, for my mind misgives | some 1.04.106
one or two men's hands, and they unwash'd too, 1.05. 4 P
we cannot be here and there too. 1.05. 14 P
and quench the fire, the room is grown too hot. 1.05. 28
beauty too rich for use, for earth too dear! 1.05. 47
beauty too rich for use, for earth too dear! 1.05. 47
good pilgrim, you do wrong your hand too much, 1.05. 97
have not saints lips, and holy palmers too? 1.05.101
too early seen unknown, and known too late! 1.05.139
too early seen unknown, and known too late! 1.05.139
nay, i'll conjure too. 2.01. 6
this field–bed is too cold for me to sleep. 2.01. 40
i am too bold, 'tis not to me she speaks. 2.02. 14
or if thou thinkest i am too quickly won, | i'll 2.02. 95
in truth, fair montague, i am too fond, | and 2.02. 98
it is too rash, too unadvis'd, too sudden, | too 2.02.118
it is too rash, too unadvis'd, too sudden, | too 2.02.118
it is too rash, too unadvis'd, too sudden, | too 2.02.118
too like the lightning, which doth cease to be 2.02.119
dream, | too flattering–sweet to be substantial. 2.02.141
a hare that is hoar | is too much for a score, 2.04.138
and thou must stand by too and suffer every 2.04.155 P
too swift arrives as tardy as too slow. 2.06. 15
too swift arrives as tardy as too slow. 2.06. 15
as much to him, else is his thanks too much. 2.06. 23
i have it, | and soundly too. 3.01.108
which too untimely here did scorn the earth. 3.01.118
too familiar | is my dear son with such sour 3.03. 6
well, we'nsday is too soon, | a' thursday let it 3.04. 19
o, now i would they had chang'd voices too, 3.05. 32
now, by saint peter's church and peter too, | he 3.05.116
child, | but now i see this one is one too much, 3.05.166
you are too hot. 3.05.175
i am too young, i pray you pardon me." 3.05.186
and from my soul too, else beshrew them both. 3.05.227
which, too much minded by herself alone, | may 4.01. 13
/pretty too! what say you, james soundpost? 4.05.136 P
what, paris too? 5.03.144
and paris too. 5.03.156
a great suspicion. stay the friar too. 5.03.187
and she, too desperate, would not go with me, 5.03.263
and i for winking at your discords too | have 5.03.294
and all the madness is, he cheers them up too. TIM 1.02. 42 P
here's that which is too weak to be a sinner, 1.02. 58
feasts are too proud to give thanks to the gods. 1.02. 61
wrong, you bate too much of your own merits. 1.02.206
for if i should be brib'd too, there would be 1.02.239 P
is't not your business too? 2.02. 10
it is; and yours too, isidore? 2.02. 11
though you hear now (too late), yet now's a time 2.02.143
ay, too well. 3.02. 63
and now ventidius is wealthy too, | whom he 3.03. 3
and, sir, philotus too! 3.04. 6
tell him that, he knows you are too diligent. 3.04. 40 P
you undergo too strict a paradox, | striving to 3.05. 24
he has made too much plenty with /'em. 3.05. 66
i am sick of that grief too, as i understand how 3.06. 17 P
take thy physic first — thou too — and thou; 3.06.100
take thou that too, with multiplying bans! 4.01. 34
when man's worst sin is, he does too much good! 4.02. 39
i know thee too, and more than that i know thee 4.03. 58
what, a knave too? 4.03.238
they mock'd thee for too much curiosity; 4.03.302 P
a plague on thee, thou art too bad to curse! 4.03.360
both too, and women's sons. 4.03.414 P
doubt and suspect, alas, are plac'd too late; 4.03.512
i must serve him so too: 5.01. 20
when we may profit meet, and come too late. 5.01. 42
toward thee forgetfulness too general gross; 5.01.144
who, like a boar too savage, doth root up | his 5.01.165

so do you too, where you perceive them thick. JC 1.01. 71
you bear too stubborn and too strange a hand 1.02. 35
you bear too stubborn and too strange a hand 1.02. 35
a lean and hungry look, | he thinks too much; 1.02.195
why, for that too. 1.02.225 P
why, for that too. 1.02.227 P
i could tell you more news too. 1.02.285 P
or else the world, too saucy with the gods, 1.03. 12
i think we are too bold upon your rest. 2.01. 86
he is welcome too. 2.01. 95
our course will seem too bloody, caius cassius, 2.01.162
and too impatiently stamp'd with your foot. 2.01.244
impatience | which seem'd too much enkindled; 2.01.249
what, brutus, are you stirr'd so early too? 2.02.110
and cassius too. 3.01. 84
your brother too must die; consent you, lepidus? 4.01. 2
do not presume too much upon my love, | i may do 4.03. 63
when i spoke that, i was ill–temper'd too. 4.03.116
and my heart too. 4.03.118
i cannot drink too much of brutus' love. 4.03.162
i trouble thee too much, but thou art willing. 4.03.259
not stingless too? 5.01. 35
o yes, and soundless too; 5.01. 36
he bears too great a mind. 5.01.112
o cassius, brutus gave the word too early, | who 5.03. 5
advantage on octavius, | took it too eagerly. 5.03. 7
o, he lights too. 5.03. 31
farewell to thee too, strato. 5.05. 33
but all's too weak; MAC 1.02. 15
and thane of cawdor too; went it not so? 1.03. 87
it is too full o' th' milk of human kindness 1.05. 17
take thee that too. 2.01. 5
to the heat of deeds too cold breath gives. 2.01. 61
but this place is too cold for hell. 2.03. 16 P
i think, being too strong for him, though he 2.03. 39 P
too cruel any where. 2.03. 88
if thou canst nod, speak too. 3.04. 69
ay, and since too, murthers have been perform'd 3.04. 76
have been perform'd | too terrible for the ear. 3.04. 77
and the right valiant banquo walk'd too late, 3.06. 5
men must not walk too late. 3.06. 7
ay, and wisely too; 3.06. 14
thou art too like the spirit of banquo; 4.01.112
to fright you thus methinks i am too savage; 4.02. 70
fell cruelty, | which is too nigh your person. 4.02. 72
o, relation! | too nice, and yet too true. 4.03.174
o, relation! | too nice, and yet too true. 4.03.174
well too. 4.03.177
my children too? 4.03.211
and i must be from thence! | my wife kill'd too? 4.03.213
if he scape, | heaven forgive him too! 4.03.235
things, | whose hearts are absent too. 5.04. 14
my soul is too much charg'd | with blood of 5.08. 5
not so, my lord, i am too much in the sun. HAM 1.02. 67
o, that this too too sallied flesh would melt, 1.02.129
o, that this too too sallied flesh would melt, 1.02.129
winds of heaven | visit her face too roughly. 1.02.142
if with too credent ear you list his songs, | or 1.03. 30
too oft before their buttons be disclos'd, | and 1.03. 40
i stay too long — but here my father comes. 1.03. 52
habit, that too much o'er–leavens | the form of 1.04. 29
but there is, horatio, | and much offense too. 1.05.137
instantly to visit | my too much changed son. 2.02. 36
friends, my thanks are too dear a halfpenny. 2.02.274 P
you, guildenstern, and you too — at each ear a 2.02.382 P
seneca cannot be too heavy, nor plautus too 2.02.400 P
cannot be too heavy, nor plautus too light, for 2.02.401 P
he finds him | striking too short at greeks. 2.02.469
this is too long. 2.02.498 P
'tis too much prov'd — that with devotion's 3.01. 46
o, 'tis too true! 3.01. 48
to a nunn'ry, go, and quickly too. 3.01.139 P
nor do not saw the air too much with your hand, 3.02. 4 P
be not too tame neither, but let your own 3.02. 16 P
some quantity of barren spectators to laugh too, 3.02. 42 P
and the queen too, and that presently. 3.02. 48 P
something too much of this. 3.02. 74
faith, i must leave thee, love, and shortly too; 3.02.173
the lady doth protest too much, methinks. 3.02.230 P
o my lord, if my duty be too bold, my love is 3.02.348 P
my duty be too bold, my love is too unmannerly. 3.02.349 P
this fear, | which now goes too free–footed. 3.03. 26
him his pranks have been too broad to bear with, 3.04. 2
thou find'st to be too busy is some danger. 3.04. 33
of thinking too precisely on th' event — | a 4.04. 41
let him bless thee too. 4.06. 8 P
finding ourselves too slow of sail, we put on a 4.06. 17 P
yet are they much too light for the /bore of the 4.06. 26 P
too slightly timber'd for so /loud /a /wind, 4.07. 22
yet needful too, for youth no less becomes | the 4.07. 78
to a plurisy, | dies in his own too much. 4.07.118
too much of water hast thou, poor ophelia, | and 4.07.185
ay, my lord, and of calves'–skins too. 5.01.115 P
'twere to consider too curiously, to consider so 5.01.205 P
importing denmark's health and england's too, 5.02. 21
this is too heavy; let me see another. 5.02.264
it is the pois'ned cup, it is too late. 5.02.292
the point envenom'd too! 5.02.321
and our affairs from england come too late. 5.02.368
only she comes too short, that i profess LR 1.01. 72
he hath now cast her off appears too grossly. 1.01.291 P
let me hire him too, here's my coxcomb. 1.04. 95 P
you are too much of late i' th' frown. 1.04.190 P
by what yourself too late have said and done, 1.04.207
woe, that too late repents! 1.04.257
well, you may fear too far. 1.04.328
safer than trust too far. 1.04.328
all vengeance comes too short | which can pursue 2.01. 88
i know not, madam. 'tis too bad, too bad. 2.01. 96
i know not, madam. 'tis too bad, too bad. 2.01. 96
sir, i am too old to learn. 2.02.127
show too bold malice | against the grace and 2.02.130
till night, my lord, and all night too. 2.02.135
o sides, you are too tough! 2.04.197
duke | instantly know, and of that letter too. 3.03. 22
the tyranny of the open night's too rough | for 3.04. 2
o, i have ta'en | too little care of this! 3.04. 33
one side will mock another; th' other too. 3.07. 71

treasons to us, | who is too good to pity thee. 3.07. 90
madman and beggar too. 4.01. 30
her cock, a buoy | almost too small for sight. 4.06. 20
too well, too well. 4.06. 66
too well, too well. 4.06. 66
"ay," and "no" too, was no good divinity. 4.06.100 P
my life will be too short, | and every measure 4.07. 2
and that's true too. 5.02. 11
and we'll talk with them too — | who loses and 5.03. 14
(alack, too weak the conflict to support!) 5.03.198
he'll strike, and quickly too. 5.03.286
it is too true an evil; OTH 1.01.160
i think this tale would win my daughter too. 1.03.171
venetian be not too hard for my wits and all the 1.03.356 P
/ear | that he is too familiar with his wife. 1.03.396
in faith, too much; 2.01.103
it is too much of joy. 2.01.197
to anger cassio, either by speaking too loud, or 2.01.268 P
now i do love her too, | not out of absolute 2.01.291
(for i fear cassio with my night–cap too), 2.01.307
and that was craftily qualified too — and 2.03. 40 P
with flowing cups, | and they watch too. 2.03. 59
he held them sixpence all too dear, | with that 2.03. 91
and so do i too, lieutenant. 2.03.108 P
come, you are too severe a moraler. 2.03.299 P
in thy thought | too hideous to be shown. 3.03.108
i think so too. 3.03.126
you of your pardon | for too much loving you. 3.03.213
let me be thought too busy in my fears | (as 3.03.253
your napkin is too little; 3.03.287
one is too poor, too weak for my revenge. 3.03.443
one is too poor, too weak for my revenge. 3.03.443
she is protectress of her honor too; 4.01. 14
ay, too gentle. 4.01.194 P
you have lost him, | /why, i have lost him too. 4.02. 47
yet could i bear that too, well, very well; 4.02. 56
/faith, i have heard too much; 4.02.182 P
it is so too. 4.03.100
and have you mercy too! 5.02. 58
it is too late. 5.02. 83
she was too fond of her most filthy bargain. 5.02.157
discontented paper, | found in his pocket too; 5.02.315
of one that lov'd not wisely but too well; 5.02.344
he comes too short of that great property ANT 1.01. 58
and let her die too, and give him a worse! 1.02. 65 P
but the letters too | of many our contriving 1.02.181
tempt him not so too far; 1.03. 11
you are too indulgent. 1.04. 16
till which encounter, | it is my business too. 1.04. 80
you think of him too much. 1.05. 6
which not wanted | shrowdness of policy too — i 2.02. 69
i grieving grant | did you too much disquiet. 2.02. 70
vacancy, | had gone to gaze on cleopatra too, 2.02.217
good will is show'd, though't come too short, 2.05. 8
rogue, thou hast liv'd too long. 2.05. 73
brought from rome | are all too dear for me. 2.05.105
i think so too. 2.06.120 P
of it own color too. 2.07. 47 P
place, note well, | may make too great an act. 3.01. 13
acquire too high a fame when him we serve's away 3.01. 15
he wail'd, | believe't — till i weep too. 3.02. 59
for the most part, too, they are foolish that 3.03. 31
i have told him lepidus was grown too cruel, 3.06. 32
thou knew'st too well | my heart was to thy 3.11. 56
caesar, thou hast subdu'd | his judgment too. 3.13. 37
our sever'd navy too | have knit again, and 3.13.170
and thou art honest too. 4.02. 15
of me | as when mine empire was your fellow too, 4.02. 22
you take me in too dolorous a sense, | for i 4.02. 39
nay, i'll help too. | what's this for? 4.04. 5
retire, we have engag'd ourselves too far. 4.07. 1
we'ld fight there too. 4.10. 4
the truth, and i am come, | i dread, too late. 4.14.127
too late, good diomed. call my guard, i prithee. 4.14.128
she's dead too, our sovereign. 4.15. 69
what, of death too, | that rids our dogs of 5.02. 41
very many, men and women too. 5.02.250 P
nay, i will take thee too: 5.02.312
too slow a messenger. 5.02.321
o, sir, you are too sure an augurer; 5.02.334
he that hath lost her too; CYM 1.01. 11
princess is a thing | too bad for bad report; 1.01. 17
to air yourself, | such parting were too petty. 1.01.111
had been something too fair and too good for any 1.04. 71 P
something too fair and too good for any lady in 1.04. 71 P
your ring may be stol'n too: 1.04. 90 P
to bar your offense herein too, i durst attempt 1.04.112 P
a great deal abus'd in too bold a persuasion, 1.04.114 P
you call it) deserve more — a punishment too. 1.04.119 P
it came in too suddenly, let it die as it was 1.04.120 P
ducats are yours, so is your diamond too. 1.04.151 P
her humor, shall be assur'd | to taste of too. 1.05. 82
i am bound to wonder, i am bound | to pity too. 1.06. 82
and yet of moment too, for it concerns: 1.06.182
you are cock and capon too, and you crow, cock, 2.01. 23 P
we'll try with tongue too. 2.03. 15 P
the exile of her minion is too new, | she hath 2.03. 41
you lay out too much pains | for purchasing but 2.03. 87
besides, thou wert too base | to be his groom. 2.03.126
search for a jewel that too casually | hath left 2.03.141
your mother too. 2.03.152
or is't not | too dull for your good wearing? 2.04. 41
the stone's too hard to come by. 2.04. 46
did outsell her gift, | and yet enrich'd it too. 2.04.103
here, take this too, | it is a basilisk unto 2.04.106
use the sword of caesar | hath too much mangled, 3.01. 56
hath prevail'd | on thy too ready hearing? 3.02. 6
madam, 's enough for you — and too much too. 3.02. 69
madam, 's enough for you — and too much too. 3.02. 69
thou art too slow to do thy master's bidding 3.04. 97
do thy master's bidding | when i desire it too. 3.04. 98
us, for | we have been too slight in sufferance. 3.05. 35
by him that made the tailor, not be fit too? 4.01. 4 P
whose rudeness | answer'd my steps too loud. 4.02.215
that is my bed too, lads, and there i'll lie. 4.04. 52
i know he'll quickly fly my friendship too. 5.03. 62
took heel to do't, | and yet died too! 5.03. 68
of meat, depart reeling with too much drink; 5.04.161 P

sorry that you have paid too much, and sorry 5.04.162 P
too much, and sorry that you are paid too much; 5.04.163 P
the brain the heavier for being too light, the 5.04.164 P
for being too light, the purse too light, being 5.04.165 P
there be some of them too that die against their 5.04.202 P
yet death | will seize the doctor too. 5.05. 30
he was too good to be | where ill men were, and 5.05.158
all too soon i shall, | unless thou wouldst 5.05.169
in that he spake too far. 5.05.309
not too hot. 5.05.321
i am too blunt and saucy: 5.05.325
you are my father too, and did relieve me | to 5.05.400
let them be joyful too, | for they shall taste 5.05.402
'twould braid yourself too near for me to tell PER 1.01. 93
whose arm seems far too short to hit me here. 1.02. 8
'gainst whom i am too little to contend, | since 1.02. 17
and justly too, i think, you fear the tyrant, 1.02.103
o, 'tis too true. 1.04. 32
air | were all too little to content and please, 1.04. 35
thought nought too curious, are ready now | to 1.04. 43
for comfort is too far for us to expect. 1.04. 59
because he should have swallow'd me too, and 2.01. 39 P
then i'll turn craver too, and so i shall scape 2.01. 88 P
awhile, | yon knight doth sit too melancholy, 2.03. 54
come, gentlemen, we sit too long on trifles, 2.03. 92
loud music is too harsh for ladies' heads, 2.03. 97
sir, here's a lady that wants breathing too, 2.03.100
princes, it is too late to talk of love, | and 2.03.112
and she is fair too, is she not? 2.05. 35
nay, come, your hands and lips must seal it too; 2.05. 85
here is a thing too young for such a place, 3.01. 15
a passport too! 3.02. 66
they were too rough | that threw her in the sea. 3.02. 79
thy /lone bosom | inflame too nicely, nor let 4.01. 6
we lost too much money this mart by being too 4.02. 4 P
too much money this mart by being too wenchless. 4.02. 5 P
ay, and better too; 4.02. 37 P
whom thou hast pois'ned too. 4.03. 10
earlier too, sir, if now i be one. 4.06. 76 P
as cold as a snowball, saying his prayers too. 4.06.140 P
could he speak, | would own a name too dear. 4.06.179
'twould be too tedious to repeat, | but the main 5.01. 28
and too ambitious, to aspire to him, | weak as TNK pr 23
and his love too, who is a servant for | the 1.01. 89
know o' th' earth | must know the centre too; 1.01.115
sav'd too, | speaking it truly? 1.02. 48
with him | my poor chin too, for 'tis not 1.02. 54
who made too proud the bed, took leave o' th' 1.03. 52
'tis too true, arcite. 2.02. 46
i saw her too. 2.02.161
and me too, | even when you please, of life. 2.02.224
my lord, for you | i have this charge too — 2.02.260
the windows are too open. 2.02.262
the matter's too far driven between him | and 2.03. 43
she must see the duke, and she must dance too. 2.03. 45
and yet he had a cousin, fair as he too; 2.04. 16
that were too cruel. 2.05. 41
i hope too wise for that, sir. 2.05. 64
that way he takes | i purpose is my way too. 2.06. 18
yea | (we challenge too), the bank of any nymph, 3.01. 8
but if it did, yours is too tart, sweet cousin. 3.03. 26
the marshal's sister | had her share too, as i 3.03. 37
you are now too foul; 3.03. 51
i am very cold, and all the stars are out too, 3.04. 1
if we have pleas'd /thee too | and have done as 3.05.142
i have put you | to too much pains, sir. 3.06. 18
that too much, fair cousin, | is but a debt to 3.06. 18
is't not too heavy? 3.06. 56
is not this piece too strait? 3.06. 86
we shall find | too many hours to die in, gentle 3.06.112
nay then i'll in too. 3.06.201
are you content too, princes? 3.06.279
i cannot, sir, they are both too excellent: 3.06.286
half his own heart, set in too, that i hope 4.01. 14
your daughter's, | whose pardon is procur'd too; 4.01. 21
no, sir, not well: | 'tis too true, she is mad. 4.01. 46
i guess he is a prince too, | and, if it may be, 4.02. 91
must these men die too? 4.02.112
he's as fantastical, too, as ever he may go upon 4.03. 14 P
i did think so too, and would account | i had a 4.03. 66 P
the breath of tigers, yea, the fierceness too, 5.01. 40
goddess of it grant, she gives | victory too. 5.01. 72
can he write and read too? 5.02. 57
do you think so too? 5.02. 93
my palamon | i hope will grow too, finely, | now 5.02. 95
they are. | you bear a charge there too. 5.02.101
and shall we kiss too? 5.02.108
his race | should show i' th' world too godlike. 5.03.118
than all women, | i should and would die too. 5.03.144
laid down, | you have sold 'em too too cheap. 5.04. 15
laid down, | you have sold 'em too too cheap. 5.04. 15
part is play'd, and, though it were too short, 5.04.102
should so much come too short of your great STM II.C 124
if they burn too, i'll quench them with my tears VEN 192
a wild bird being tam'd with too much handling, 560
say, | the text is old, the orator too green, 806
not to believe, and yet too credulous: 986
"it shall be sparing, and too full of riot, 1147
it shall be merciful, and too severe, | and most 1155
did instigate | his all too timeless speed, if LUC 44
save sometime too much wonder of his eye, 95
charm, | doth too too oft betake him to retire, 174
charm, | doth too too oft betake him to retire, 174
her twinkling handmaids too (by him defil'd) 787
their father was too weak, and they too strong, 865
their father was too weak, and they too strong, 865
with too much labor drowns for want of skill. 1099
sometime 'tis mad and too much talk affords. 1106
this is too curious–good, this blunt and ill: 1300
and both she thinks too long with her remaining. 1572
and my laments would be drawn out too long | to 1616
my woe too sensible thy passion maketh | more 1678
that thou shalt lend me | comes all too late, 1686
which she too early and too late hath spill'd." 1801
which she too early and too late hath spill'd." 1801
he rose and ran away, ah, fool too froward! PP 4.14
bright orient pearl, alack, too timely shaded! 10. 3
kill'd too soon by death's sharp sting! 10. 4

hie thee, | for methinks thou stays too long. 12.12
were i with her, the night would post too soon, 14.25
wiser head, | neither too young nor yet unwed. 18. 6
and then too late she will repent | that thus 18.27
but soft, enough — too much, i fear — | lest 18.49
thyself thy foe, to thy sweet self too cruel. SON 1. 8
for thou art much too fair | to be death's 6.13
and summer's lease hath all too short a date; 18. 4
sometime too hot the eye of heaven shines, | and 18. 5
or some fierce thing replete with too much rage, 23. 3
too excellent | for every vulgar paper to 38. 3
from me far off, with others all too near. 61.14
knife, | too base of thee to be remembered. 74.12
how far a modern quill doth come too short, 83. 7
farewell, thou art too dear for my possessing, 87. 1
and i by this will be a gainer too, | for, 88. 9
lest i (too much profane) should do it wrong, 89.11
in my love's veins thou hast too grossly dy'd. 99. 5
so dost thou too, and therein dignified. 101. 4
lose all, and more, by paying too much rent, 125. 6
my tongue–tied patience with too much disdain, 140. 2
love is too young to know what conscience is, 151. 1
is me, too early i attended | a youthful suit — LC 78

/TOOK 2 FR 0.0002 REL FR 1 V 1 P
/you /mercy, /i /took /you /for /a //join–stool. LR 3.06. 52 P
/ay, /sir, /she /took /them, /read /them /in /my 4.03. 11

TOOK 171 FR 0.0193 REL FR 134 V 37 P
took pains to make thee speak, taught thee each TMP 1.02.354
i took him to be kill'd with a thunder–stroke. 2.02.108 P
what is't that you | took up so gingerly? TGV 1.02. 70
serv'd me, when i took my leave of madam silvia. 4.04. 35 P
be thou asham'd that i have took upon me | such 5.04.105
they took me on their shoulders; WIV 3.05.100 P
upon my life then, you took the wrong. 5.05.189 P
i think so, when i took a boy for a girl. 5.05.191 P
if he took you a box o' th' ear, you might have MM 2.01.180 P
and he that might the vantage best have took 2.02. 74
most just law | now took your brother's life, 2.04. 53
the body | that took away the match from isabel, 5.01.211
hath homely age th' alluring beauty took | from ERR 2.01. 89
me, | and therewithal took measure of my body. 4.03. 9
into my house, and took perforce | my ring away. 4.03. 94
came to my house, and took away my ring — | the 4.04.138
he took this place for sanctuary, | and it shall 5.01. 94
day | a most outrageous fit of madness took him, 5.01.139
wars, and took | deep scars to save thy life; 5.01.192
slave, | forsooth, took on him as a conjurer, 5.01.243
by force took dromio and my son from them, | and 5.01.353
i took no more pains for those thanks than you ADO 2.03.250 P
"i took no more pains for those thanks than you 2.03.259 P
those thanks than you took pains to thank me" — 2.03.260 P
may say they are not the men you took them for. 3.03. 47 P
hand | took up a beggar's issue at my gates, 4.01.132
country girl that i took in the park with the LLL 1.02.117 P
you took the moon at full, but now she's changed 5.02.214
by jove, i always took three threes for nine. 5.02.495 P
a certain aim he took | at a fair vestal throned MND 2.01.157
i took him sleeping — that is finish'd too — 3.02. 38
woman, she is indeed more than i took her for. MV 3.05. 42 P
that took some pains in writing, he begg'd mine, 5.01.182
so was i when your highness took his dukedom, AYL 1.03. 59
instead of her, from whom i took two cods and, 2.04. 52 P
advis'd, he took some care | to get her cunning SHR 1.01.186
this mad–brain'd bridegroom took him such a cuff 3.02.163
he took the bride about the neck | and kiss'd 3.02.177
proffers not took reap thanks for their reward. AWW 2.01.147
i took this lark for a bunting. 2.05. 6 P
do so ever, though i took him at 's prayers. 2.05. 41 P
richest eyes, whose words all ears took captive, 5.03. 17
the last that e'er i took her leave at court, 5.03. 79
alas, i took great pains to study it, and 'tis TN 1.05.194 P
he might have took his answer long ago. 1.05.263
some hour before you took me from the breach of 2.01. 22 P
she took the ring of me, i'll none of it. 2.02. 12 P
the lady olivia's father took much delight in. 2.04. 12 P
answer'd in repaying | what we took from them, 3.03. 34
that took the phoenix and her fraught from candy 5.01. 61
we took him for a coward, but he's the very 5.01.181 P
he took good rest to–night; WT 2.03. 10
he straight declin'd, droop'd, took it deeply, 2.03. 14
and the thing she took to quench it | she would 4.04. 61
took something good | to make a perfect woman, 5.01. 14
shepherd's daughter (so he then took her to be), 5.02.118 P
for the king's son took me by the hand, and 5.02.140 P
from thy admiring daughter took the spirits, 5.03. 41
fall the bones that took the pains for me!), JN 1.01. 78
th' advantage of his absence took the king, 1.01.102
and took it on his death | that this my mother's 1.01.110
who, as you say, took pains to get this son, 1.01.121
may know wherefore we took the sacrament, | and 5.02. 6
hotspur took | mordake earl of fife and eldest 1H4 1.01. 70
which harry percy here at holmedon took, | were, 1.03. 24
took it in snuff — and still he smil'd and 1.03. 41
those mouthed wounds, which valiantly he took, 1.03. 97
me no more ado but took all their seven points 2.04.201 P
you took occasion to be quickly wooed | to gripe 5.01. 56
he was so bruis'd | that the pursuers took him. 5.05. 22
took fire and heat away | from the best–temper'd 2H4 1.01.114
in his flight, | stumbling in fear, was took. 1.01.131
prince, and you took it like a sensible lord. 1.02.196 P
and a famous true subject took him. 4.03. 64 P
where is the crown? who took it from my pillow? 4.05. 57
basis by | took stand for idle speculation — H5 4.02. 31
for had you been as i took you for, i made no 4.08. 55 P
o no, he lives, but is took prisoner, | and lord 1H6 1.01.145
most of the rest slaughter'd or took likewise. 1.01.147
and he first took exceptions at this badge, 4.01.105
pardon me, i took ye for my lord protector. 2H6 1.03. 11 P
my lord, that you took bribes of france, | and, 3.01.104
view, | i took a costly jewel from my neck, | a 3.02.106
that dread king that took our state upon him, 3.02.154
thy mother took into her blameful bed | some 3.02.212
for suddenly a grievous sickness took him, 3.02.370
we took him setting of boys' copies. 4.02. 88 P
kent, | took odds to combat a poor famish'd man. 4.10. 44
i took an oath that he should quietly reign. 3H6 1.02. 15
being not took | before a true and lawful 1.02. 22
ay, this is he that took king henry's chair, 1.04. 97

they took his head, and on the gates of york 2.01. 65
but when he took a beggar to his bed, | and 2.02.154
and go we, brothers, to the man that took him, 3.02.121
i took him for the plainest harmless creature R3 3.05. 25
and thus i took the vantage of those few: 3.07. 37
upon this french going out, took he upon him H8 1.01. 73
by commission and main power, took 'em from me, 2.02. 6 P
hence i took a thought | this was a judgment on 2.04.194
can watch you for telling how i took the blow — TRO 1.02.269 P
the seas and winds, old wranglers, took a truce, 2.02. 75
prisoner call'd antenor, | yesterday took; 3.03. 19
a murrain on't! i took this for silver. COR 1.05. 3 P
death's stamp, | where it did mark, it took; 2.02.108
took from you | th' apprehension of his present 2.03.223
with fire, and took | what lay before them. 4.06. 78
i took him; 5.06. 30
and took some pride | to do myself this wrong; 5.06. 36
and from her bosom took the enemy's point, TIT 5.03.111
'a was a merry man — took up the child. ROM 1.03. 40
then have my lips the sin that they have took. 1.05.108
very well took, i' faith, wisely, wisely. 2.04.125 P
vault, | and presently took post to tell it you. 5.01. 21
we took this mattock and this spade from him, 5.03.185
potion, which so took effect | as i intended, 5.03.244
perchance some single vantages you took, | when TIM 2.02.129
your words have took such pains as if they 3.05. 26
as i took note of the place, it cannot be far 5.01. 1
been often dropp'd | where i have took them up. JC 2.01. 50
withal | a woman that lord brutus took to wife. 2.01.293
therefore i took your hands, but was indeed 3.01.218
and took his voice who should be prick'd to die 4.01. 16
advantage on octavius, | took it too eagerly. 5.03. 7
for him, though he took up my legs sometime, yet MAC 2.03. 40 P
by self and violent hands | took off her life; 5.09. 37
he took me by the wrist, and held me hard, HAM 2.01. 84
which done, she took the fruits of my advice; 2.02.145
'a took my father grossly, full of bread, | with 3.03. 80
i took thee for thy better. 3.04. 32
this three years i have took note of it: 5.01.139 P
summon'd up their meiny, straight took horse, LR 2.04. 35
france, that dowerless took | our youngest born, 2.04.212
they took from me the use of mine own house, 3.03. 3 P
that thing you speak of, | i took it for a man; 4.06. 78
my name, have in my name | took their discharge. 5.03.105
took once a pliant hour, and found good means OTH 1.03.151
i took you for that cunning whore of venice 4.02. 89
i took by th' throat the circumcised dog, | and 5.02.355
our will is antony be took alive; ANT 4.06. 2
purposes, and, being royal, | took her own way. 5.02.337
of issue, took such sorrow | that he quit being, CYM 1.01. 37
could make him the receiver of, which he took, 1.01. 44
they took thee for their mother, | and every day 3.03.104
tear, took pity | from most true wretchedness. 3.04. 60
suit he wore when he took leave of my lady and 3.05.126 P
to have begg'd or bought what i have took. 3.06. 47
and though you took his life, as being our foe, 4.02.250
took heel to do't, | and yet died too! 5.03. 67
lent not me her aid, | but took me in my throes, 5.04. 44
for you a mortal mineral, which, being took, 5.05. 50
and one | that had a royal lover, took his hint, 5.05.172
this king unto him took a peer, | who died and PER 1.ch. 21
with whom the father liking took, | and her to 1.ch. 25
took some displeasure at him, at least he judg'd 1.03. 20
took it in rage, though calm'd have given't 2.01.132
made too proud the bed, took leave o' th' moon TNK 1.03. 52
i, that took possession | first with mine eye of 2.02.167
each took | a several land. 3.01. 1
food took i none these two days — | sipp'd some 3.02. 26
this way the stag took. 3.05. 95
took toy at this, and fell to what disorder 5.04. 66
when he was by, the birds such pleasure took, VEN 1101
quoth he, "she took me kindly by the hand, | and LUC 253
lay, | then white as lawn, the roses took away. 259
from her tongue "can lurk" from "cannot" took: 1537
sword, | swearing, unless i took all patiently, 1641
betwixt mine eye and heart a league is took, SON 47. 1
how careful was i, when i took my way, | each 48. 1
save what is had or must from you be took. 75.12
hand | the fairest votary took up that fire, 154. 5
which from love's fire took heat perpetual, 154.10
TOOK'ST 2 FR 0.0002 REL FR 2 V 0 P
off thine | by wond'ring how thou took'st it. AWW 2.01. 90
thou took'st a beggar, wouldst have made my CYM 1.01.141
/TOOK'T 1 FR 0.0001 REL FR 1 V 0 P
the best hint was given him, he not /took't, ANT 3.04. 9
TOOK'T 3 FR 0.0003 REL FR 2 V 1 P
fan, i took't upon mine honor thou hadst it not. WIV 2.02. 13 P
anon | he gave his nose and took't away again, 1H4 1.03. 39
and, to th' advantage, i, being here, took't up. OTH 3.03.312
TOOL 4 FR 0.0004 REL FR 2 V 2 P
indian with the great tool come to court, the H8 5.03. 34 P
draw thy tool, here comes /two of the house of ROM 1.01. 31 P
the bavian, with long tail and eke long tool, TNK 3.05.132
but this no slaughter–house no tool imparteth, LUC 1039
TOOLS 3 FR 0.0003 REL FR 3 V 0 P
sirs, take you to your tools. TIT 4.03. 6
some coiner with his tools | made me a CYM 2.05. 5
work | more plentiful than tools to do't — 5.03. 9
TOOTH 23 FR 0.0026 REL FR 20 V 3 P
a forted residence 'gainst the tooth of time MM 5.01. 12
poisons more deadly than a mad dog's tooth. ERR 5.01. 70
thy tooth is not so keen, | because thou art not AYL 2.07.177
or an old trot with ne'er a tooth in her head, SHR 1.02. 80 P
the better whilst i have a tooth in my head. AWW 2.03. 42 P
doth set my pugging tooth an edge, | for a quart WT 4.03. 7
or ethiopian's tooth, or the fann'd snow that's 4.04.364
sweet, sweet, sweet poison for the age's tooth, JN 1.01.213
paw, | a fasting tiger safer by the tooth, 3.01.260
fell sorrow's tooth doth never rankle more R2 1.03.302
veriest varlet that ever chew'd with a tooth. 1H4 2.02. 24 P
dog | shall flesh his tooth on every innocent. 2H4 4.05.132
tongue more poisons than the adder's tooth! 3H6 1.04.112
his venom tooth will rankle to the death. R3 1.03.290
'twas full two years ere i could get a tooth. 2.04. 29
lord sands, | your colt's tooth is not cast yet? H8 1.03. 48
still sweet love is food for fortune's tooth. TRO 4.05.293
malice | remains in danger of her former tooth. MAC 3.02. 15
scale of dragon, tooth of wolf, | witch's mummy, 4.01. 22
how sharper than a serpent's tooth it is | to LR 1.04.288
black or white, | tooth that poisons if it bite; 3.06. 67
by treason's tooth bare–gnawn and canker–bit, 5.03.122
and, being troubled with a raging tooth, | i OTH 3.03.414
TOOTHACHE 5 FR 0.0005 REL FR 1 V 4 P
i have the toothache. ADO 3.02. 21 P
what? sigh for the toothache? 3.02. 26 P
yet is this no charm for the toothache. 3.02. 70 P
that could endure the toothache patiently, 5.01. 36
sir, he that sleeps feels not the toothache; CYM 5.04.173 P
TOOTH'D 2 FR 0.0002 REL FR 2 V 0 P
my lowing follow'd through | tooth'd briers, TMP 4.01.180
"had i been tooth'd like him, i must confess, VEN 1117
TOOTH–DRAWER 1 FR 0.0001 REL FR 0 V 1 P
ay, and worn in the cap of a tooth–drawer. LLL 5.02.618 P
TOOTHPICK 2 FR 0.0002 REL FR 1 V 1 P
just like the brooch and the toothpick, which AWW 1.01.158 P
he and his toothpick at my worship's mess, | and JN 1.01.190
TOOTHPICKER 1 FR 0.0001 REL FR 0 V 1 P
i will fetch you a toothpicker now from the ADO 2.01.266 P
TOO–TIMELY 1 FR 0.0001 REL FR 1 V 0 P
youths must wither | like a too–timely spring. TNK 2.02. 28
/TOP* 4 FR 0.0004 REL FR 2 V 2 P
/that /cry /out /on /the /top /of /question, HAM 2.02.340 P
from my lowest note to /the /top /of my compass; 3.02.367 P
edmund the base | shall /top th' legitimate. LR 1.02. 21
/make /much /more, | /and /top /extremity. 5.03.208
TOP* 55 FR 0.0062 REL FR 45 V 10 P
admir'd miranda, | indeed the top of admiration! TMP 3.01. 38
play'd truant, and whipt top, i knew not what WIV 5.01. 25 P
you be | if he, which is the top of judgment, MM 2.02. 76
in itself, | that skins the vice o' th' top. 2.02.136
he meant to take the present time by the top, ADO 1.02. 15 P
at the charge–house on the top of the mountain? LLL 5.01. 83 P
a red–hipp'd humble–bee on the top of a thistle; MND 4.01. 12 P
we will, fair queen, up to the mountain's top, 4.01.109
vailing her high top lower than her ribs | to MV 1.01. 28
with age | and high top bald with dry antiquity: AYL 4.03.105
and bow'd his eminent top to their low ranks, AWW 1.02. 43
let's take the instant by the forward top; 5.03. 39
is not big enough to bear | a schoolboy's top. WT 2.01.103
this is the very top, | the heighth, the crest, JN 4.03. 45
than had i seen the vaulty top of heaven 5.02. 52
he is walk'd up to the top of the hill, i'll go 1H4 2.02. 8 P
who take the ruffian /billows by the top, 2H4 3.01. 22
with mine own picture on the top on't (colevile 4.03. 49 P
discourse, i prithee, on this turret's top. 1H6 1.04. 26
thyself | from top of honor to disgrace's feet? 2H6 1.02. 49
though standing naked on a mountain top, | where 3.02.336
they use to write it on the top of letters; 4.02.100 P
as on a mountain top the cedar shows | that 5.01.205
the raven rook'd her on the chimney's top, | and 3H6 5.06. 47
our aery buildeth in the cedar's top | and R3 1.03.263
he is all the mother's, from the top to toe. 3.01.156
which, to the spire and top of praises vouch'd, COR 1.09. 24
finger and his thumb as one would set up a top. 4.05.153 P
now climbeth tamora olympus' top, | safe out of TIT 2.01. 1
chase, | and climb the highest promontory top. 2.02. 22
which labor'd after him to the mountain's top TIM 1.01. 86
baby–brow the round | and top of sovereignty? MAC 4.01. 89
a devil more damn'd | in evils to top macbeth. 4.03. 57
from top to toe? HAM 1.02.228
in such matters cried in the top of mine — an 2.02.439 P
blow, with flaming top | stoops to his base, and 2.02.475
they fool me to the top of my bent. 3.02.384 P
secrecy, | unpeg the basket on the house's top, 3.04.193
of heaven fall | on her ingrateful top! LR 2.04.163
when shall i come to th' top of that same hill? 4.06. 1
cassio did top her; OTH 5.02.136
my competitor | in top of all design, my mate in ANT 5.01. 43
whose top to climb | is certain falling, or so CYM 3.03. 47
when from the mountain top pisanio show'd thee, 3.06. 5
that by the top doth take the mountain pine 4.02.175
without his top? 4.02.354
a withered branch, that's only green at top; PER 2.02. 43
know that our griefs are risen to the top, | and 2.04. 23
i shall sleep like a top else. TNK 3.04. 26
top the bowling! 4.01.148
up to the top, boy! 4.01.150
he turns ye like a top. 5.02. 50
and the top o'erstraw'd | with sweets that shall VEN 1143
now stand you on the top of happy hours, | and SON 16. 5
this said, in top of rage the lines she rents, LC 55
TOPAS 16 FR 0.0018 REL FR 0 V 16 P
make him believe thou art sir topas the curate, TN 4.02. 2 P
to him, sir topas. 4.02. 17 P
sir topas the curate, who comes to visit 4.02. 21 P
sir topas, sir topas, good sir topas, go to my 4.02. 23 P
sir topas, sir topas, good sir topas, go to my 4.02. 23 P
topas, sir topas, good sir topas, go to my lady. 4.02. 23 P
sir topas, never was man thus wrong'd. 4.02. 28 P
good sir topas, do not think i am mad; 4.02. 29 P
as hell, sir topas. 4.02. 35 P
i am not mad, sir topas, i say to you this house 4.02. 40 P
sir topas, sir topas! 4.02. 61 P
sir topas, sir topas! 4.02. 61 P
my most exquisite sir topas! 4.02. 62 P
sir topas! 4.02. 98 P
god buy you, good sir topas. 4.02.101 P
sir, in this enterlude — one sir topas, sir, 5.01.372 P
TOP–BRANCH 1 FR 0.0001 REL FR 1 V 0 P
whose top–branch overpeer'd jove's spreading 3H6 5.02. 14
TOPFUL 2 FR 0.0002 REL FR 2 V 0 P
now that their souls are topful of offense. JN 3.04.180
and fill me from the crown to the toe topful MAC 1.05. 42
TOP–GALLANT 1 FR 0.0001 REL FR 1 V 0 P
which to the high top–gallant of my joy | must ROM 2.04.190
TOPLESS 1 FR 0.0001 REL FR 1 V 0 P
agamemnon, | thy topless deputation he puts on, TRO 1.03.152
TOPMAST 4 FR 0.0004 REL FR 3 V 1 P
down with the topmast! TMP 1.01. 34 P
on the topmast, | the yards and boresprit, would 1.02.199
and montague our topmast; 3H6 5.04. 14
boats, | but suck them up to th' topmast. CYM 3.01. 22
TOPP'D 4 FR 0.0004 REL FR 4 V 0 P
so far he topp'd /my thought, | that i, in HAM 4.07. 88
behold her topp'd? OTH 3.03.396
but like to groves, being topp'd, they higher PER 1.04. 9
that could have topp'd the peace, as now you STM II.C 64
TOPPING 1 FR 0.0001 REL FR 0 V 1 P
and topping all others in boasting. COR 2.01. 20 P
TOPPLE 3 FR 0.0003 REL FR 3 V 0 P
though castles topple on their warders' heads; MAC 4.01. 56
and the deficient sight | topple down headlong. LR 4.06. 24
did seem to rend, | and all to topple. PER 3.02. 17
TOPPLES 2 FR 0.0002 REL FR 2 V 0 P
then slip i from her bum, down topples she, MND 2.01. 53
and topples down | steeples and moss–grown 1H4 3.01. 31
TOP–PROUD 1 FR 0.0001 REL FR 1 V 0 P
but this top–proud fellow, | whom from the flow H8 1.01.151
TOPS 11 FR 0.0012 REL FR 11 V 0 P
to wag their high tops and to make no noise MV 4.01. 76
he fires the proud tops of the eastern pines R2 3.02. 42
where rude misgoverned hands from windows' tops 5.02. 5
have we mow'd down in tops of all their pride! 3H6 5.07. 4
made trees, | and the mountain tops that freeze, H8 3.01. 4
towers, whose wanton tops do buss the clouds, TRO 4.05.220
tips with silver all these fruit–tree tops — ROM 2.02.108
day | stands tiptoe on the misty mountain tops. 3.05. 10
who /am no more but as the tops of trees, PER 1.02. 30
that cedar tops and hills seem burnish'd gold. VEN 858
flatter the mountain tops with sovereign eye, SON 33. 2
TOPSAIL 1 FR 0.0001 REL FR 0 V 1 P
take in the topsail. TMP 1.01. 6 P
TOPSY–TURVY 1 FR 0.0001 REL FR 1 V 0 P
help | we shall o'erturn it topsy–turvy down. 1H4 4.01. 82
TORCH 20 FR 0.0022 REL FR 20 V 0 P
shall be paid | till hymen's torch be lighted; TMP 4.01. 97
here dies the dusky torch of mortimer, | chok'd 1H6 2.05.122
by thrusting out a torch from yonder tower, 3.02. 23
this is the happy wedding torch | that joineth 3.02. 26
the burning torch in yonder turret stands. 3.02. 30
follow his torch, he goes to calchas' tent. TRO 5.01. 85
stand where the torch may not discover us. 5.02. 5
give me a torch, i am not for this ambling; ROM 1.04. 11
a torch for me. 1.04. 35
give me thy torch, boy. 5.03. 1
what, with a torch? 5.03. 21
what torch is yond, that vainly lends his light 5.03.125
is the place, there where the torch doth burn. 5.03.171
since the torch is out, | lie down and stray no ANT 4.14. 46
a burning torch that's turned upside down; PER 2.02. 32
whereat a waxen torch forthwith he lighteth, LUC 178
"fair torch, burn out thy light, and lend it not 190
the wind wars with his torch to make him stay, 311
puffs forth another wind that fires the torch. 315
are by his flaming torch dimm'd and controll'd. 448
TORCH–BEARER 4 FR 0.0004 REL FR 4 V 0 P
i am provided of a torch–bearer. MV 2.04. 23
fair jessica shall be my torch–bearer. 2.04. 39
descend, for you must be my torch–bearer. 2.06. 40
to be to thee this night a torch–bearer | and ROM 3.05. 14
TORCH–BEARERS 1 FR 0.0001 REL FR 1 V 0 P
we have not spoke us yet of torch–bearers. MV 2.04. 5
TORCHER 1 FR 0.0001 REL FR 1 V 0 P
bring | their fiery torcher his diurnal ring, AWW 2.01.162
TORCHES 10 FR 0.0011 REL FR 9 V 1 P
heaven doth with us as we with torches do, | not MM 1.01. 32
good morrow, masters, put your torches out. ADO 5.03. 24
sav'd me a thousand marks in links and torches, 1H4 3.03. 43 P
o, she doth teach the torches to burn bright! ROM 1.05. 44
more torches here! 1.05.125
did flame and burn | like twenty torches join'd; JC 1.03. 17
torches, torches! LR 2.01. 32
torches, torches! 2.01. 32
desire you | to burn this night with torches. ANT 4.02. 41
"torches are made to light, jewels to wear, VEN 163
TORCHLIGHT 1 FR 0.0001 REL FR 1 V 0 P
statilius show'd the torchlight, but, my lord, JC 5.05. 2
TORCH–STAVES 1 FR 0.0001 REL FR 1 V 0 P
candlesticks, | with torch–staves in their hand; H5 4.02. 46
TORE 6 FR 0.0006 REL FR 4 V 2 P
she tore the letter into a thousand halfpence; ADO 2.03.140 P
to see how the bear tore out his shoulder–bone, WT 3.03. 95 P
i tore them from their bonds, and cried aloud, JN 3.04. 70
i tore it from the traitor's bosom, king; R2 5.03. 55
but through his teeth, as if the name he tore. LUC 1787
she perus'd, sigh'd, tore, and gave the flood, LC 44
TORMENT 33 FR 0.0037 REL FR 26 V 7 P
forget | from what a torment i did free thee? TMP 1.02.251
best know'st | what torment i did find thee in; 1.02.287
it was a torment | to lay upon the damn'd, which 1.02.289
and to torment me | for bringing wood in slowly. 2.02. 15
do not torment me! o! 2.02. 56 P
do not torment me, prithee. 2.02. 71 P
all torment, trouble, wonder, and amazement 5.01.104
torment me for my love's forgetfulness! TGV 2.02. 12
and why not death, rather than living torment? 3.01.170
that's her torment. ADO 2.03.126 P
a sport of it, and torment the poor lady worse. 2.03.157 P
grove | till i torment thee for this injury. MND 2.01.147
o happy torment, when my torturer | doth teach MV 3.02. 37
you, | what ever torment you do put me to. JN 4.01. 83
house of york | is as a fury to torment my soul; 3H6 1.03. 31
torment myself to catch the english crown; 3.02.179
and from that torment i will free myself, | or 3.02.180
seize on him, furies, take him unto torment!" R3 1.04. 57
weep, | to chide my fortune, and torment myself? 2.02. 35
for thee, | god knows, in torment and in agony. 4.04.164
but to torment you with my bitter tongue! TIT 5.01.150
sent to me, | to be a torment to mine enemies? 5.02. 42
what devil art thou that dost torment me thus? ROM 3.02. 43
wert the ass, thy dullness would torment thee, TIM 4.03.332 P
and be a thwart disnatur'd torment to her. LR 1.04.283
is silliness to live, when to live is torment; OTH 1.03.308 P
any cunning cruelty | that can torment him much, 5.02.334
which will then be a torment to her contempt. CYM 3.05.139 P
each errant step beside is torment. TNK 3.02. 34
gain | but torment that it cannot cure his pain. LUC 861
o absence, what a torment wouldst thou prove, SON 39. 9
me, | knowing thy heart torment me with disdain, 132. 2
a torment thrice threefold thus to be crossed. 133. 8
TORMENTA 1 FR 0.0001 REL FR 1 V 0 P
si fortuna me tormenta, spero contenta. 2H4 5.05. 96
TORMENTE 1 FR 0.0001 REL FR 1 V 0 P

"si fortune me tormente, sperato me contento." 2H4 2.04.181
TORMENTED 1 FR 0.0001 REL FR 1 V 0 P
whipt and tormented and — god–den, good fellow. ROM 1.02. 56
TORMENTETH 1 FR 0.0001 REL FR 1 V 0 P
how want of love tormenteth? VEN 202
TORMENTING 2 FR 0.0002 REL FR 2 V 0 P
unless it be while some tormenting dream R3 1.03.225
when i to sulph'rous and tormenting flames HAM 1.05. 3
TORMENTORS 1 FR 0.0001 REL FR 1 V 0 P
these words hereafter thy tormentors be! R2 2.01.136
/TORMENTS 1 FR 0.0001 REL FR 1 V 0 P
/thou /torments /me /ere /i /come /to /hell! R2 4.01.270
TORMENTS 11 FR 0.0012 REL FR 10 V 1 P
the spirit torments me! o! TMP 2.02. 64 P
for that which now torments me to rehearse: TGV 4.01. 26
a world of torments though i should endure, | i LLL 5.02.353
what studied torments, tyrant, hast for me? WT 3.02.175
i grieve to hear what torments you endur'd, 1H6 1.04. 57
the loss of those three lords torments my heart; 3H6 1.01.270
by hell and all hell's torments, | i will not TRO 5.02. 43
torments him so, that he will sure run mad. ROM 2.04. 5
torments will ope your lips. OTH 5.02.305
to utter that | which torments me to conceal. CYM 5.05.142
much, torments us with defect | of that we have: LUC 151
TORMENT'ST 1 FR 0.0001 REL FR 1 V 0 P
enough, sweet suffolk, thou torment'st thyself, 2H6 3.02.329
TORN 16 FR 0.0018 REL FR 15 V 1 P
our loving lawful, and our faith not torn. LLL 4.03.281
bedabbled with the dew and torn with briers, | i MND 3.02.443
his arm | the lioness had torn some flesh away, AYL 4.03.147
he was torn to pieces with a bear. WT 5.02. 63 P
from my own windows torn my household coat, R2 3.01. 24
have torn their souls by turning them from us, 3.03. 83
france should have torn and rent my very heart 2H6 1.01.126
broke be my sword, my arms torn and defac'd, 4.01. 42
may do, | not being torn a–pieces, we have done. H8 5.03. 76
a thought of added honor torn from hector. TRO 4.05.145
though thy tackle's torn, | thou show'st a noble COR 4.05. 61
is torn from forth that pretty hollow cage, TIT 3.01. 84
shrikes like mandrakes' torn out of the earth, ROM 4.03. 47
i'll set it down | he's torn to pieces. TNK 3.02. 18
o, from thy cheeks my image thou hast torn, LUC 1762
and new faith torn | in vowing new hate after SON 152. 3
/TORRENT 1 FR 0.0001 REL FR 1 V 0 P
/there | /by /the /rough /torrent /of /occasion, 2H4 4.01. 72
TORRENT 2 FR 0.0002 REL FR 1 V 1 P
the torrent roar'd, and we did buffet it | with JC 1.02.107
but use all gently, for in the very torrent, HAM 3.02. 6 P
TORRENTS 1 FR 0.0001 REL FR 1 V 0 P
torrents whose roaring tyranny and power | i' TNK 1.03. 38
TORTERING *(also torturing)*
TORTERING 1 FR 0.0001 REL FR 1 V 0 P
some never–heard–of tortering pain for them. TIT 2.03.285
TORTIVE 1 FR 0.0001 REL FR 1 V 0 P
tortive and errant from his course of growth. TRO 1.03. 9
TORTOISE 2 FR 0.0002 REL FR 2 V 0 P
come, thou tortoise, when? TMP 1.02.316
and in his needy shop a tortoise hung, | an ROM 5.01. 42
/TORTUR'D 1 FR 0.0001 REL FR 1 V 0 P
/swells /with /silence /in /the /tortur'd /soul. R2 4.01.298
TORTUR'D 3 FR 0.0003 REL FR 2 V 1 P
grow to you, and our parting is a tortur'd body. AWW 2.01. 36 P
how have the hours rack'd and tortur'd me, TN 5.01.219
i tortur'd | above the felon or what trespass 2H6 3.01.131
TORTURE 33 FR 0.0037 REL FR 31 V 2 P
i will take him, then torture my wife, pluck the WIV 3.02. 40 P
refuse me, hate me, torture me to death! ADO 4.01.184
that same berowne i'll torture ere i go. LLL 5.02. 60
i'll plague him, i'll torture him. MV 3.01.117 P
extended | with vildest torture, let my life be AWW 2.01.174
on thy soul's peril and thy body's torture, WT 2.03.181
what old or newer torture | must i receive, 3.02.177
turning dispiteous torture out of door? JN 4.01. 34
let hell want pains enough to torture me. 4.03.138
stake, | that so her torture may be shortened. 1H6 5.04. 58
you go about to torture me in vain. 2H6 2.01.143
and torture him with grievous ling'ring death. 3.02.247
from thee to die were torture more than death. 3.02.401
o, torture me no more, i will confess. 3.03. 11
of what thou wast | to torture thee the more, R3 4.04.108
on pain of torture, from those bloody hands ROM 1.01. 86
this torture should be roar'd in dismal hell. 3.02. 44
walls, | but purgatory, torture, hell itself. 3.03. 18
'tis torture, and not mercy. 3.03. 29
than on the torture of the mind to lie | in MAC 3.02. 21
if thou dost slander her and torture me, | never OTH 3.03.368
the time, the place, the torture, o, enforce it! 5.02.369
he may at pleasure whip, or hang, or torture, ANT 3.13.150
so it must be, for now | all length is torture; 4.14. 46
we'll enforce it from thee | by a sharp torture. CYM 4.03. 12
answer would be death | drawn on with torture. 4.04. 14
bitter torture shall | winnow the truth from 5.05.133
thou'lt torture me to leave unspoken that 5.05.139
that | which, to be spoke, would torture thee. 5.05.140
that what was life | in him seem'd torture. TNK 5.01.115
and that deep torture may be call'd a hell, LUC 1287
do in consent shake hands to torture me, | the SON 28. 6
is't not enough to torture me alone, | but slave 133. 3
TORTURED 1 FR 0.0001 REL FR 1 V 0 P
say he be taken, rack'd, and tortured, | i know 2H6 3.01.376
TORTURER 2 FR 0.0002 REL FR 2 V 0 P
when my torturer | doth teach me answers for MV 3.02. 37
i play the torturer by small and small | to R2 3.02.198
TORTURERS 1 FR 0.0001 REL FR 1 V 0 P
thou, king, send out | for torturers ingenious; CYM 5.05.215
TORTURES 5 FR 0.0005 REL FR 2 V 3 P
he calls for the tortures. AWW 4.03.120 P
he shall have, the tortures he shall feel, will WT 4.04.769 P
deep, with erebus and tortures vile also. 2H4 2.04.158 P
you did devise | strange tortures for offenders, 2H6 3.01.122
while we devise fell tortures for thy faults. 3H6 2.06. 72
TORTUREST 1 FR 0.0001 REL FR 0 V 1 P
thou torturest me, tubal. MV 3.01.120 P
TORTURING *(also tortering)*
TORTURING 2 FR 0.0002 REL FR 2 V 0 P
play | to ease the anguish of a torturing hour? MND 5.01. 37
torturing convulsions from his globy eyes | had TNK 5.01.113

TORYNE 2 FR 0.0002 REL FR 2 V 0 P
cut the ionian sea, | and take in toryne? ANT 3.07. 23
caesar has taken toryne. 3.07. 55
TOSS 5 FR 0.0005 REL FR 3 V 2 P
tut, tut, good enough to toss, food for powder, 1H4 4.02. 65 P
i will toss the rogue in a blanket. 2H4 2.04.222 P
on which i'll toss the flow'r–de–luce of france. 2H6 5.01. 11
back do i toss these treasons to thy head, LR 5.03.147
did the sea toss up upon our shore this chest. PER 3.02. 50
TOSS'D 8 FR 0.0009 REL FR 8 V 0 P
such a deal of spleen | as you are toss'd with. 1H4 2.03. 79
soldiers should have toss'd me on their pikes, 3H6 1.01.244
and often up and down my sons were toss'd | for R3 2.04. 58
must not be toss'd and turn'd to me in words, TIM 2.01. 26
lost, | by waves from coast to coast is toss'd. PER 2.ch. 34
huge a billow, sir, | as toss'd it upon shore. 3.02. 59
thou hadst been toss'd from wrong to injury, 5.01.130
arm, | is madly toss'd between desire and dread; LUC 171
TOSSEL 1 FR 0.0001 REL FR 0 V 1 P
a sore eye, thou tossel of a prodigal's purse, TRO 5.01. 32 P
TOSSETH 1 FR 0.0001 REL FR 1 V 0 P
lucius, what book is that she tosseth so? TIT 4.01. 41
TOSSING 2 FR 0.0002 REL FR 2 V 0 P
your mind is tossing on the ocean, | there where MV 1.01. 8
after your late tossing on the breaking seas? R2 3.02. 3
TOSS–POTS 1 FR 0.0001 REL FR 1 V 0 P
with toss–pots still had drunken heads, | for TN 5.01.403
TO'T 120 FR 0.0135 REL FR 79 V 41 P
fall to't, yarely, or we run ourselves aground. TMP 1.01. 3 P
it is a hint | that wrings mine eyes to't. 1.02.135
what say you to't, sir john? WIV 2.02.251 P
and i will provoke him to't, or let him wag. 2.03. 70 P
sir, in my poor opinion, they will to't then. MM 2.01.233 P
in such a one as, you consenting to't, | would 3.01. 70
he puts transgression to't. 3.02. 95 P
one fruitful meal would set me to't. 4.03.154 P
the warrant's for yourself; take heed to't. 5.01. 83
now i come to't, my lord. 5.01.194
but shall we dance, if they desire us to't? LLL 5.02.145
and we ought to look to't. MND 3.01. 33 P
and thou wert best look to't; AYL 1.01.148 P
free for a husband, and then have to't afresh. SHR 1.01.139 P
but if you have a stomach, to't a' god's name; 1.02.194
and thy mind stand to't, boy, steal away bravely AWW 2.01. 29
here it is, and all that belongs to't. 2.02. 36 P
o lord, sir! — nay, put me to't, i warrant you. 2.02. 48 P
well to a whipping, if you were but bound to't. 2.02. 56 P
the danger is in standing to't. 3.02. 41 P
i am the caitiff that do hold him to't; 3.02.114
nay, good my lord, put him to't. 3.06. 1 P
why, if you have a stomach, to't, monsieur: 3.06. 64 P
while i was speaking, oft was fasten'd to't. 5.03. 82
he knows i am no maid, and he'll swear to't; 5.03.290
and i can cut the mutton to't. TN 1.03.122 P
that defense thou hast, betake thee to't. 3.04.220 P
come on, to't. 3.04.309 P
i will help you to't. 4.02.113 P
tougher, brother, | than you can put us to't. WT 1.02. 16
and love as mine), | without ripe moving to't? 1.02.332
seen't or been an instrument | to vice you to't, 1.02.416
it is a curse | he cannot be compell'd to't) 2.03. 89
to fear as i have purpose | to put you to't. 4.04.153
here's the midwive's name to't, one mistress 4.04.269 P
do, and be witness to't. 4.04.369
friends unknown, you shall bear witness to't: 4.04.384
as cruel for thee | as thou art tender to't. 4.04.441
that title and what shame else belongs to't. 4.04.841 P
bed of majesty again | with a sweet fellow to't? 5.01. 34
manner how she came to't bravely confess'd and 5.02. 85 P
pembroke, look to't. JN 1.01. 30
sirrah, look to't, i' faith i will, i' faith. 2.01.140
look to't. 4.01. 7
will 'a stand to't? 2H4 2.01. 4 P
therefore captains had need look to't. 2.04.150 P
look to't in time, | she'll hamper thee, and 2H6 1.03.144
protector, see to't well, protect yourself. 2.01. 52
pray look to't; H8 1.02.101
their clothes are after such a pagan cut to't, 1.03. 14
now, what mov'd me to't, | i will be bold with 2.04.168
give heed to't: 2.04.170
do no more offices of life to't than | the grave 2.04.191
my amen to't! 3.02. 45
out of the pain you suffer'd, gave no ear to't. 4.02. 8
and if there be | no great offense belongs to't, 5.01. 12
th' other's not come to't. TRO 1.02. 84 P
tell me another tale when th' other's come to't. 1.02. 85 P
hector, what say you to't? 2.02. 7
that's to't indeed, sir. 3.01. 30 P
what say you to't? 3.03.292 P
alone | till accident or purpose bring you to't. 4.05.262
what say you to't? COR 1.01.146
tullus aufidius, that will put you to't. 1.01.229
look to't; 1.04. 40
put them not to't. 2.02.141
we do, sir, tell us what hath brought you to't. 2.03. 64 P
custom calls me to't. 2.03.117
would unclog my heart | of what lies heavy to't. 4.02. 48
we stood to't in good time. is this menenius? 4.06. 10
assault thy country than to tread | (trust to't, 5.03.124
and to't they go like lightning, for, ere i ROM 3.01.172
look to't, think on't, i do not use to jest. 3.05.189
trust to't, bethink you, i'll not be forsworn. 3.05.195
so fall to't: TIM 1.02. 70
and show'd what necessity belong'd to't, and yet 3.02. 13 P
my lord, you have my voice to't; 3.05. 1
we shall to't presently. 3.06. 35 P
with thy smile | than hew to't with thy sword. 5.04. 46
stand to't. MAC 3.03. 15
listen, but speak not to't. 4.01. 89
look to't, i charge you. HAM 1.03.135
your daughter may conceive, friend, look to't. 2.02.186 P
we'll e'en to't like /french falc'ners — fly at 2.02.429 P
young men will do't, if they come to't, | by 4.05. 60
to't again, come. 5.01. 49 P
to't. 5.01. 54 P
i came to't that day that our last king hamlet 5.01.143 P
so guildenstern and rosencrantz go to't. 5.02. 56
you will to't, sir, really. 5.02.126 P

to acknowledge him, that now i am braz'd to't. LR 1.01. 11 P
should win your displeasure to entreat me to't. 2.02.113 P
should tear this hand | for lifting food to't? 3.04. 16
the wren goes to't, and the small gilded fly 4.06.112
to't, luxury, pell–mell, for i lack soldiers. 4.06.117
the fitchew nor the soiled horse goes to't 4.06.122
thy friendly hand | put strength enough to't. 4.06.231
o gentle lady, do not put me to't, | for i am OTH 2.01.118
with my personal eye | will i look to't. 2.03. 6
any music that may not be heard, to't again; 3.01. 16 P
look to't. 3.03.200
far | (prick'd to't by foolish honesty and love) 3.03.412
and will upon the instant put thee to't: 3.03.471
most veritable, therefore look to't well. 3.04. 76
for that he dares us to't. ANT 3.07. 29
'tis easy to't, and there i will attend | what 3.10. 31
love we rise betime, | and go to't with delight. 4.04. 21
fight, | follow me close, i'll bring you to't. 4.04. 34
if you will make't an action, call witness to't. CYM 2.03.151
if't be summer news, | smile to't before; 3.04. 13
here is a path to't; 3.06. 18
bid the captains look to't. 4.02.344
i mov'd her to't, | having receiv'd the 5.05.342
your honor and your goodness teach me to't PER 3.03. 26
did you go to't so young? 4.06. 74 P
may | be wish'd upon thy head, i cry amen to't! TNK 1.04. 3
and, as i have a soul, i'll nail thy life to't! 2.02.213
i am gladder | i have so good meat to't. 3.03. 22
then take my life, i'll woo thee to't. 3.06.156
which perish'd should | go to't unsentenc'd. 5.01.157
TOTAL 2 FR 0.0002 REL FR 1 V 1 P
soon bring his particulars therein to a total. TRO 1.02.114 P
head to foot | now is he total gules, horridly HAM 2.02.457
TOTALLY 1 FR 0.0001 REL FR 0 V 1 P
no; he doth but mistake the truth totally. TMP 2.01. 58 P
T'OTHER 1 FR 0.0001 REL FR 1 V 0 P
and his page a' t'other side, that handful of LLL 4.01.147
TOTHER 1 FR 0.0001 REL FR 0 V 1 P
'tis a sore life they have i' th' tother place, TNK 4.03. 32 P
TOTTER'D *(also tatter'd, etc., tottered)*
TOTTER'D 2 FR 0.0002 REL FR 1 V 1 P
a hundred and fifty totter'd prodigals lately 1H4 4.02. 34 P
will be a totter'd weed, of small worth held: SON 2. 4
TOTTERED 2 FR 0.0002 REL FR 2 V 0 P
that from this castle's tottered battlements R2 3.03. 52
and puts apparel on my tottered loving, | to SON 26.11
TOTTERING 1 FR 0.0001 REL FR 1 V 0 P
than to be thirsty after tottering honor, | or PER 3.02. 40
TOTTERS* 2 FR 0.0002 REL FR 0 V 2 P
other two be brain'd like us, the state totters. TMP 3.02. 7 P
periwig–pated fellow tear a passion to totters, HAM 3.02. 10 P
TOTT'RING* 4 FR 0.0004 REL FR 3 V 1 P
which hung so tott'ring in the balance that i AWW 1.03.124 P
and wound our tott'ring colors clearly up, JN 5.05. 7
news, what news, in this our tott'ring state? R3 3.02. 37
and with our patience anger tott'ring fortune, TNK 5.04. 20
/TOUCH 2 FR 0.0002 REL FR 2 V 0 P
/a /touch, /a /touch, i do confess't. HAM 5.02.286
/a /touch, /a /touch, i do confess't. 5.02.286
TOUCH 124 FR 0.0140 REL FR 105 V 19 P
if thou beest stephano, touch me, and speak to TMP 2.02.100 P
which art but air, a touch, a feeling | of their 5.01. 21
o, touch me not, i am not stephano, but a cramp. 5.01.286 P
didst thou but know the inly touch of love, TGV 2.07. 18
with thee of some affairs | that touch me near, 3.01. 60
whose golden touch could soften steel and stones 3.02. 78
let go that rude uncivil touch, | thou friend of 5.04. 60
take but possession of her with a touch — | i 5.04.130
with trial–fire touch me his finger–end. WIV 5.05. 84
ay, touch him; there's the vein. MM 2.02. 70
my habit, no loss shall touch her by my company. 3.01.178 P
that no particular scandal once can touch | but 4.04. 27
who is as free from touch or soil with her | as 5.01.141
the gold bides still | that others touch and, ERR 2.01.111
that never touch well welcome to thy hand, 2.02.116
how dearly would it touch thee to the quick, 2.02.130
may, but i think they that touch pitch will be ADO 3.03. 57 P
and one day in a week to touch no food, | and LLL 1.01. 39
never durst poet touch a pen to write | until 4.03.343
salt /wave of the mediterraneum, a sweet touch, 5.01. 59 P
o brave touch! MND 3.02. 70
no maiden shame, | no touch of bashfulness? 3.02.286
and not one vessel scape the dreadful touch | of MV 3.02.270
sound, | or any air of music touch their ears, 5.01. 76
evils, age and hunger, | i will not touch a bit. AYL 2.07.133
as full of sanctity as the touch of holy bread. 3.04. 14 P
madam, before you touch the instrument, | to SHR 3.01. 64
and here she stands, touch her whoever dare, 3.02.233
sweet wench, they shall not touch thee, kate! 3.02.238
and not presume to touch a hair of my master's 4.01. 93 P
away, | and i expressly am forbid to touch it; 4.01.171
and so shall mine before you touch the meat. 4.03. 46
will deign to sip or touch one drop of it. 5.02.145
in the most bitter touch of sorrow that e'er i AWW 1.03.117 P
whose simple touch | is powerful to araise king 2.01. 75
that sings with piercing, do not touch my lord. 3.02.111
perceive in you so excellent a touch of modesty, TN 2.01. 13 P
and not worthy to touch fortune's fingers. 2.05.157 P
may be he will not touch young arthur's life, JN 3.04.160
i will not touch thine eye | for all the 4.01.121
so bold | or daring–hardy as to touch the lists, R2 1.03. 43
hands | that knows no touch to tune the harmony. 1.03.165
and shortly mean to touch our northern shore. 2.01.288
dar'd once to touch a dust of england's ground? 2.03. 91
whose double tongue may with a mortal touch 3.02. 21
where fadom–line could never touch the ground, 1H4 1.03.204
the lion will not touch the true prince. 2.04.272 P
instinct, you will not touch the true prince, no 2.04.300 P
of ten thousand men | must bide the touch; 4.04. 10
thus do the hopes we have in him touch ground 2H4 4.01. 17
touch her soft mouth, and march. H5 2.03. 58
define, | a little touch of harry in the night. 4.pr. 47
eloquence in a sugar touch of them than in the 5.02.277 P
o, tell me when my lips do touch his cheeks, 1H6 2.05. 39
for i will touch thee but with reverend hands. 5.03. 47
ready to starve, and dare not touch his own. 2H6 1.01.229
their touch affrights me as a serpent's sting. 3.02. 47
their softest touch as smart as lizards' stings! 3.02.325

no beast so fierce but knows some touch of pity. R3 1.02. 71
now be nearest | will touch us all too near, if 2.03. 26
to touch his growth nearer than he touch'd mine. 2.04. 25
yet touch this sparingly, as 'twere far off, 3.05. 93
ah, buckingham, now do i play the touch, | to 4.02. 8
madam, i have a touch of your condition, | that 4.04.158
his curses and his blessings | touch me alike; H8 2.02. 53
present state, | or touch of her good person? 2.04.156
your friend | some touch of your late business. 5.01. 13
fair lord aeneas, let me touch your hand; TRO 1.03.304
one touch of nature makes the whole world kin — 3.03.175
my father, | i know no touch of consanguinity; 4.02. 97
the drink you give me touch my palate adversely, COR 2.01. 56 P
dearest mother, and | my friends of noble touch; 4.01. 49
touch not the boy, he is of royal blood. TIT 5.01. 49
to smooth that rough touch with a tender kiss. ROM 1.05. 96
saints have hands that pilgrims' hands do touch, 1.05. 99
upon that hand, | that i might touch that cheek! 2.02. 25
if he will touch the estimate. but for that — TIM 1.01. 14
here is a touch; 1.01. 36
taste, touch, all, pleas'd from thy table rise; 1.02.126
is divident, touch them with several fortunes, 4.03. 5
o thou touch of hearts, | think thy slave man 4.03.389
in your speed, antonio, | to touch calphurnia; JC 1.02. 7
and touch thy instrument a strain or two? 4.03.257
foreign levy, nothing, | can touch him further. MAC 3.02. 26
he loves us not, | he wants the natural touch; 4.02. 9
but at his touch, | such sanctity hath heaven 4.03.143
than your particular demands will touch it. HAM 2.01. 12
i know no touch of it, my lord. 3.02.356 P
the sun no sooner shall the mountains touch, 4.01. 29
i'll touch my point | with this contagion, that, 4.07.146
touch me with noble anger, | and let not women's LR 2.04.276
might i but live to see thee in my touch, | i'ld 4.01. 23
no, they cannot touch me for /coining; 4.06. 83 P
rocks, /and hills whose /heads touch heaven, OTH 1.03.141
touch me not so near; 2.03.220
suit | wherein i mean to touch your love indeed, 3.03. 81
her patent to offend, for if it touch not you, 4.01.198 P
from any other foul unlawful touch | be not to 4.02. 84
to palestine for a touch of his nether lip. 4.03. 39 P
touch you the sourest points with sweetest terms ANT 2.02. 24
the party that should desire you to touch him, 2.02.246 P
thy thoughts | touch their effects in this: 5.02.330
a touch more rare | subdues all pangs, all fears CYM 1.01.135
this hand, whose touch | (whose every touch) 1.06.100
whose touch | (whose every touch) would force 1.06.101
that i might touch! 2.02. 16
to the greedy touch | of common–kissing titan, 3.04.162
heavens, | how deeply you at once do touch me! 4.03. 4
hind that shall | once touch my shoulder. 5.03. 78
that, knowing sin within, will touch the gate. PER 1.01. 80
prince pericles, touch not, upon thy life, | for 1.01. 87
but touch the ground for us no longer time TNK 1.01. 97
asprays do the fish, | subdue before they touch. 1.01.139
the schoolmaster, | keep touch, do you think? 2.03. 41
if he keep touch, he dies for't. 3.03. 53
fair and knightly strength to touch the pillar, 3.06.295
"touch but my lips with those fair lips of thine VEN 115
that dares not be so bold | to touch the fire, 402
and that i could not see, nor hear, nor touch, 440
or what fond beggar, but to touch the crown, LUC 216
in stead of love's coy touch, shall rudely tear 669
the tender nibbler would not touch the bait, PP 4.11
whose heavenly touch | upon the lute doth ravish 8. 5
the boy for trial needs would touch my breast; SON 153.10
TOUCH'D 56 FR 0.0063 REL FR 52 V 4 P
which touch'd | the very virtue of compassion in TMP 1.02. 26
till this day | saw i him touch'd with anger, so 4.01.145
spirits are not finely touch'd | but to fine MM 1.01. 35
if so your heart were touch'd with that remorse 2.02. 54
how seems he to be touch'd? 4.02.141 P
that opinion | that i am touch'd with madness. 5.01. 51
scope of justice, | my patience here is touch'd. 5.01.235
spake, or look'd, or touch'd, or carv'd to thee. ERR 2.02.118
of blood in him to be truly touch'd with love. ADO 3.02. 19 P
but, touch'd with humane gentleness and love, MV 4.01. 25
you touch'd my vein at first. AYL 2.07. 94
to be touch'd with so many giddy offenses as he 3.02.348 P
if love have touch'd you, nought remains but so, SHR 1.01.161
for her, they touch'd not any stranger sense. AWW 1.03.109 P
hearing your high majesty is touch'd | with that 2.01.110
that you have touch'd his queen | forbiddenly. WT 1.02.416
(which was as gross as ever touch'd conjecture, 2.01.176
he is touch'd | to th' noble heart. 3.02.221
our ship hath touch'd upon | the deserts of 3.03. 1
by his command | have i here touch'd sicilia, 5.01.139
majesty, which, being touch'd and tried, JN 3.01.100
life of all his blood | is touch'd corruptibly; 5.07. 2
beard the silver hand of peace hath touch'd, 2H4 4.01. 43
fluellen valiant | and, touch'd with choler, hot H5 4.07.180
yes, when his holy state is touch'd so near. 1H6 3.01. 58
the hungry cannibals | would not have touch'd, 3H6 1.04.153
to touch his growth nearer than he touch'd mine. R3 2.04. 25
touch'd you the bastardy of edward's children? 3.07. 4
the fairest hand i ever touch'd! H8 1.04. 75
i have touch'd the highest point of all my 3.02.223
he touch'd the ports desir'd, | and for an old TRO 2.02. 76
i am no more touch'd than all priam's sons; 2.02.126
why, there you touch'd the life of our design: 2.02.194
/these your white enchanting fingers touch'd, 3.01.151
had touch'd his spirit | and tried his COR 2.03.191
even when the navel of the state was touch'd, 3.01.123
lots to blanks | my name hath touch'd your ears: 5.02. 11
would not then have touch'd them for his life! TIT 2.04. 47
but, titus, i have touch'd thee to the quick; 4.04. 36
they have all been touch'd and found base metal, TIM 3.03. 6
seeing his reputation touch'd to death, | he did 3.05. 19
shall no man else be touch'd but only caesar? JC 2.01.154
what villain touch'd his body, that did stab 4.03. 20
he hath not touch'd you yet. MAC 4.03. 14
or by collateral hand | they find us touch'd, we HAM 4.05.208
not till he hears how antony is touch'd | with ANT 2.02.139
caesar is touch'd. 5.01. 33
i think the king | be touch'd at very heart. CYM 1.01. 10
with shame | (the first that ever touch'd him) 3.01. 25
down | some mortally, some slightly touch'd, 5.03. 10
with golden fruit, but dangerous to be touch'd; PER 1.01. 28
and what this fourteen years no razor touch'd, 5.03. 75
she touch'd no unknown baits, nor fear'd no LUC 103
to win his heart she touch'd him here and there PP 4. 7
heavenly touches ne'er touch'd earthly faces." SON 17. 8
"so many have, that never touch'd his hand, LC 141
TOUCHED 1 FR 0.0001 REL FR 1 V 0 P
say, | the barren, touched in this holy chase, JC 1.02. 8
/TOUCHES 1 FR 0.0001 REL FR 1 V 0 P
/it /touches /us, /as /france /invades /our LR 5.01. 25
TOUCHES 28 FR 0.0031 REL FR 25 V 3 P
from their abominable and beastly touches | i MM 3.02. 24
this touches me in reputation. ERR 4.01. 71
the night | become the touches of sweet harmony. MV 5.01. 57
with sweetest touches pierce your mistress' ear, 5.01. 67
he dies that touches any of this fruit | till i AYL 2.07. 98
hearts, | to have the touches dearest priz'd. 3.02.152
some lively touches of my daughter's favor. 5.04. 27
one of the prettiest touches of all, and that WT 5.02. 82 P
with linstock now the devilish cannon touches, H5 3.pr. 33
the earth sings when he touches it; 3.07. 16 P
touches me deeper than you can imagine. R3 1.01.112
it touches you, my lord, as much as me. 1.03.261
in our sister work | some touches of remorse? TRO 2.02.115
that touches this my first–born son and heir! TIT 4.02. 92
artificial strife | lives in these touches, TIM 1.01. 38
some good necessity | touches his friend, which 2.02.228
for mine's a suit | that touches caesar nearer. JC 3.01. 7
what touches us ourself shall be last serv'd. 3.01. 8
and we that have free souls, it touches us not. HAM 3.02.242 P
makes us tremble, | touches us not with pity. LR 5.03.233
the death of fulvia, with more urgent touches, ANT 1.02.180
swell with the touches of those flower–soft 2.02.210
what is ten hundred touches unto thee? VEN 519
touches so soft still conquer chastity. PP 4. 8
such heavenly touches ne'er touch'd earthly SON 17. 8
a loss in love that touches me more nearly. 42. 4
what strained touches rhetoric can lend, | thou, 82.10
nor tender feeling to base touches prone, | nor 141. 6
TOUCHETH 4 FR 0.0004 REL FR 3 V 1 P
upon advice, it toucheth us both, that we may SHR 1.01.115 P
the quarrel toucheth none but us alone, 1H6 4.01.118
where nothing can proceed that toucheth us R3 3.02. 23
than i | as far as toucheth my particular, | yet TRO 2.02. 9
TOUCHING 27 FR 0.0030 REL FR 21 V 6 P
our satisfaction have | touching that point. MM 1.01. 83
still | that others touch and, often touching, ERR 2.01.111
sir, the contempts thereof are as touching me. LLL 1.01.190 P
france was a little boy, as touching the hit it? 4.01.121 P
was a little wench, as touching the hit it. 4.01.124 P
and touching now the point of human skill, MND 2.02.119
which, touching but my gentle vessel's side, MV 1.01. 32
to treat of high affairs touching that time. JN 1.01.101
as touching france, to give a greater sum | than H5 1.01. 79
touching our person seek we no revenge, | but we 2.02.174
as partly touching or concerning the disciplines 3.02. 96 P
as touching the direction of the military 3.02.100 P
art reverent | touching thy spiritual function, 1H6 3.01. 50
and touching the duke of york, i will take my 2H6 2.03. 87 P
touching king henry's oath and your succession. 3H6 2.01.119
touching the jointure that your king must make, 3.03.136
what said northumberland as touching richmond? R3 5.03.271
rightly | touching the weal a' th' common, you COR 1.01.151
and, touching hers, make blessed my rude hand. ROM 1.05. 51
o insupportable and touching loss! JC 4.03.151
take hold of him | touching this dreaded sight, HAM 1.01. 25
please you, something touching the lord hamlet. 1.03. 89
touching this vision here, | it is an honest 1.05.137
he speak of comfort | touching the turkish loss, OTH 2.01. 32
history of my knowledge | touching her flight. CYM 3.05.100
do well | that on the touching of her lips i may PER 5.03. 42
see, | yet should i be in love by touching thee. VEN 438
TOUCHSTONE 4 FR 0.0004 REL FR 1 V 3 P
ay, be so, good touchstone. AYL 2.04. 19 P
you this shepherd's life, master touchstone? 3.02. 12 P
not a whit, touchstone. 3.02. 45 P
holding out gold that's by the touchstone tried; PER 2.02. 37
TOUGH 10 FR 0.0011 REL FR 5 V 5 P
demonstration of the working, my tough signior. LLL 1.02. 10 P
why tough signior? why tough signior? 1.02. 11 P
why tough signior? why tough signior? 1.02. 11 P
and i tough signior as an appertinent title to 1.02. 16 P
title to your old time, which we may name tough. 1.02. 17 P
and, now i fall, thy tough commixtures melts, 3H6 2.06. 6
o sides, you are too tough! LR 2.04.197
that would upon the rack of this tough world 5.03.315
a little man, but of a tough soul, seeming | as TNK 4.02.117
tough and nimble set, | which shows an active 4.02.125
TOUGHER 2 FR 0.0002 REL FR 2 V 0 P
we are tougher, brother, | than you can put us WT 1.02. 15
seen, | since hercules, a man of tougher sinews. TNK 2.05. 2
TOUGHNESS 1 FR 0.0001 REL FR 0 V 1 P
deserving with cables of perdurable toughness. OTH 1.03.338 P
TOURAINE 5 FR 0.0005 REL FR 5 V 0 P
to ireland, poictiers, anjou, touraine, maine, JN 1.01. 11
england and ireland, /anjou, touraine, maine, 2.01.152
for /anjou and fair touraine, maine, poictiers, 2.01.487
then do i give volquessen, touraine, maine, 2.01.527
the which at touraine, in saint katherine's 1H6 1.02.100
TOURNAMENTS 1 FR 0.0001 REL FR 1 V 0 P
there shall he practice tilts and tournaments, TGV 1.03. 30
TOURNEY 2 FR 0.0002 REL FR 0 V 2 P
of the world to just and tourney for her love. PER 2.01.110 P
why, wilt thou tourney for the lady? 2.01.144 P
TOURS 3 FR 0.0003 REL FR 3 V 0 P
blois, poictiers, and tours, are won away, 1H6 4.03. 45
so, in the famous ancient city tours, | in 2H6 1.01. 5
when in the city tours | thou ran'st a–tilt in 1.03. 50
TOUS 1 FR 0.0001 REL FR 0 V 1 P
fais la repetition de tous les mots que vous H5 3.04. 25 P
TOUT 3 FR 0.0003 REL FR 1 V 2 P
les seigneurs de france pour tout le monde. H5 3.04. 56 P
ici est dispose tout /a /cette /heure de couper 4.04. 35 P
o seigneur! le jour est perdu, tout est perdu! 4.05. 2
TOUZE *(also toze)*
TOUZE 1 FR 0.0001 REL FR 1 V 0 P
we'll touze you | joint by joint, but we will MM 5.01.311
/TOW 1 FR 0.0001 REL FR 1 V 0 P
th' strings, | and thou shouldst /tow me after. ANT 3.11. 58
/TOWARD 1 FR 0.0001 REL FR 1 V 0 P
/athenian /bay | /put /forth /toward /phrygia, TRO pr 7
TOWARD 107 FR 0.0121 REL FR 88 V 19 P
of the mountain foot | that leads toward mantua, TGV 5.02. 47
if he should intend this voyage toward my wife, WIV 2.01.182 P
which i will be thy adversary toward anne page. 2.03. 95 P
which sorrow is always toward ourselves, not MM 2.03. 32
to shun, | and yet run'st toward him still. 3.01. 13
in his love toward her ever most kind and 3.01.220 P
be consummate, and then go i toward arragon. ADO 3.02. 2 P
toward that shade i might behold address'd | the LLL 5.02. 92
what, a play toward? MND 3.01. 79
i have toward heaven breath'd a secret vow | to MV 3.04. 27
pardon, | i must away this night toward padua, 4.01.403
morning early will we both | fly toward belmont. 4.01.457
and sigh'd his soul toward the grecian tents, 5.01. 5
turning again toward childish treble, pipes AYL 2.07.162
there is sure another flood toward, and these 5.04. 35 P
husht, master, here's some good pastime toward; SHR 1.01. 68
and toward the education of your daughters, | i 2.01. 98
once more toward our father's. 4.05. 1
my father's bears more toward the market–place; 5.01. 9
and by all likelihood some cheer is toward. 5.01. 13
'tis a good hearing when children are toward. 5.02.182
wherein toward me my homely stars have fail'd AWW 2.05. 75
go thou toward home, where i will never come 2.05. 90
was a great argument of love in her toward you. TN 3.02. 12 P
the /clerestories toward the south north are as 4.02. 37 P
toward my grave | i have travell'd but two hours 5.01.162
thou dost guess of harm | is creeping toward me; WT 1.02.404
and ingratitude | to you and toward your friend, 3.02. 69
walk before toward the sea–side, go on the right 4.04.824 P
upon which errand | i now go toward him; 5.01.232
po, | it draws toward supper in conclusion so. JN 1.01.204
on toward callice, ho! 3.03. 73
away toward bury, to the dolphin there! 4.03.114
tell him toward swinstead, to the abbey there. 5.03. 8
set on toward swinstead. 5.03. 16
that arrows fled not swifter toward their aim 2H4 1.01.123
here's goodly stuff toward! 2.04.200 P
each hurries toward his home and sporting–place. 4.02.105
and now dispatch we toward the court, my lords, 4.03. 76
march to the bridge, it now draws toward night; H5 3.06.170
their wither'd hands hold up | toward heaven, to 4.01.300
there is more good toward you peradventure than 4.08. 4 P
now we bear the king | toward callice; 5.pr. 7
i met in travel toward his warlike father! 1H6 4.03. 36
to–morrow toward london back again, | to look 2H6 2.01.197
they are all in order, and march toward us. 4.02.188 P
march'd toward saint albons to intercept the 3H6 2.01.114
why, that is spoken like a toward prince. 2.02. 66
that they do hold their course toward tewksbury. 5.03. 19
/thence we look'd toward england, | and cited up R3 1.04. 13
toward /ludlow then, for we'll not stay behind. 2.02.154
with all speed post with him toward the north, 3.02. 17
what, shall we toward the tower? 3.02. 89
what, go you toward the tower? 3.02.118
hind'red, oft, | the passages made toward it. H8 2.04.166
i did steer | toward this remedy, whereupon we 2.04.202
the way of loyalty and truth | toward the king, 3.02.273
toward the king first, then his laws, in filling 5.02. 50
up here and see them as they pass toward ilion? TRO 1.02.178 P
could turn your eyes toward the napes of your COR 2.01. 39 P
your loving motion toward the common body | to 2.02. 53
love goes toward love as schoolboys from their ROM 2.02.156
love from love, toward school with heavy looks. 2.02.157
look, sir, here comes the lady toward my cell. 4.01. 17
all run | with open outcry toward our monument. 5.03.193
found time to use 'em toward a supply of money. TIM 2.02.192 P
and nature, as it grows again toward earth, | is 2.02.218
here's a noble feast toward. 3.06. 60 P
him of an intent | that's coming toward him. 5.01. 21
toward thee forgetfulness too general gross; 5.01.144
if it be aught toward the general good, | set JC 1.02. 85
up higher toward the north | he first presents 2.01.109
bending their expedition toward philippi. 4.03.170
let us toward the king. MAC 1.03.152
every thing | safe toward your love and honor. 1.04. 27
i see before me, | the handle toward my hand? 2.01. 34
i look'd toward birnan, and anon methought | the 5.05. 33
and now a wood | comes toward dunsinane. 5.05. 45
what might be toward, that this sweaty haste HAM 1.01. 77
my thoughts and wishes bend again toward france, 1.02. 55
father bears his son | do i impart toward you. 1.02.112
what if it tempt you toward the flood, my lord, 1.04. 69
come, sir, to draw toward an end with you. 3.04.216
what feast is toward in thine eternal cell, 5.02.365
while we | unburthen'd crawl toward death. LR 1.01. 41
we first address toward you, who with this king 1.01.190
man if there be any good meaning toward you. 1.02.173 P
have you heard of no likely wars toward, 'twixt 2.01. 10 P
o, how this mother swells up toward my heart! 2.04. 56
there is strange things toward, edmund, pray you 3.03. 19 P
but if /thy flight lay toward the roaring sea, 3.04. 10
and drive toward dover, friend, where thou shalt 3.06. 91
are gone with him toward dover, where they boast 3.07. 19
hence a mile or twain | i' th' way toward dover, 4.01. 43
do you hear aught, sir, of a battle toward? 4.06.209
with due course toward the isle of rhodes, OTH 1.03. 34
frank appearance | their purposes toward cyprus. 1.03. 39
to do, for i perceive | four feasts are toward. ANT 2.06. 73
toward peloponnesus are they fled. 3.10. 30
cold–hearted toward me? 3.13.158
no, but he fled forward still, toward your face. CYM 1.02. 16 P
the flame o' th' taper | bows toward her, and 2.02. 20
toward ephesus | turn our blown sails; PER 5.01.254
they would glance their eyes | toward my seat, TNK 5.03. 62
perverse it shall be where it shows most toward, VEN 1157
fell she on her back, fair queen, and toward: PP 4.13
no love toward others in that bosom sits | that SON 9.13
TOWARDLY 1 FR 0.0001 REL FR 0 V 1 P
thee always for a towardly prompt spirit — give TIM 3.01. 34 P
TOWARDS 70 FR 0.0079 REL FR 63 V 7 P
her deity | cutting the clouds towards paphos; TMP 4.01. 93
yet always bending | towards their project. 4.01.175
if you can carry her your desires towards her. WIV 1.01.237 P
him in his intent towards our wives are a yoke 2.01.175 P
was carried towards corinth, as we thought. ERR 1.01. 87

in your affection towards any of these princely MV 1.02. 34 P
there is some ill a–brewing towards my rest, 2.05. 17
the rather will i spare my praises towards him, AWW 2.01.103
towards florence is he? 3.02. 68
if the duke continue these favors towards you, TN 1.04. 1 P
will you walk towards him? 3.04.268 P
of you, and pace softly towards my kinsman's. WT 4.03.113 P
the manner of your bearing towards him, with 4.04.558
towards our assistance we do seize to us | the R2 2.01.160
quick is mine ear to hear of good towards him. 2.01.234
is coming towards me, and my inward soul | with 2.02. 11
set on towards london, cousin, is it so? 3.03.208
i towards the north, | where shivering cold and 5.01. 76
who, travelling towards york, | with much ado 5.05. 73
towards york shall bend you with your dearest 1H4 5.05. 36
myself and you, son harry, will towards wales, 5.05. 39
fly | towards fronting peril and oppos'd decay! 2H4 4.04. 66
king is now in progress towards saint albons, 2H6 1.04. 72
and bid them blow towards england's blessed 3.02. 90
with diamonds, | and threw it towards thy land. 3.02.108
that slily glided towards your majesty, | it 3.02.260
come, let's march towards london. 4.03. 18 P
mount you, my lord, towards berwick post amain. 3H6 2.05.128
i am inform'd that he comes towards london | to 4.04. 26
we'll forward towards warwick and his mates; 4.07. 82
and, lords, towards coventry bend we our course, 4.08. 58
brave warriors, march amain towards coventry. 4.08. 64
i will away towards barnet presently, | and bid 5.01.110
come now towards chertsey with your holy load, R3 1.02. 29
towards chertsey, noble lord? 1.02.225
the mayor towards guildhall hies him in all post 3.05. 73
and towards three or four a' clock | look for 3.05.101
away towards salisbury! 4.04.535
and towards london do they bend their power, 4.05. 17
take it from a heart that wishes towards you H8 1.01.103
nobility she has | carried herself towards me. 2.04.144
translate his malice towards you into love, COR 2.03.189
towards her deserved children is enroll'd | in 3.01.290
your love can do | for rome, towards martius. 5.01. 41
who leads towards rome a band of warlike goths, TIT 5.02.113
towards him i made, but he was ware of me, | and ROM 1.01.124
we have a trifling foolish banquet towards. 1.05.122
fiery–footed steeds, | towards phoebus' lodging; 3.02. 2
strike up the drum towards athens! TIM 4.03.169
go you down that way towards the capitol, | this JC 1.01. 63
know'st thou any harm's intended towards him? 2.04. 31
and shall continue our graces towards him. MAC 1.06. 30
towards his design | moves like a ghost. 2.01. 55
make we our march towards birnan. 5.02. 31
must arbitrate, | towards which advance the war. 5.04. 21
i look down towards his feet; OTH 5.02.286
it ripens towards it. ANT 2.07. 97
which towards you are most gentle, you shall 5.02.127
but yet heaven's bounty towards him might | be CYM 1.06. 78
and towards himself, his goodness forespent on 2.03. 59
have need | t' employ you towards this roman. 2.03. 63
the malice towards you to forgive you, live, 5.05.419
blind mole casts | copp'd hills towards heaven, PER 1.01.101
for it seems | you have been noble towards her. 5.01.263
now turn we towards your comforts. TNK 1.01.234
me your aid | and bend your spirits towards him. 5.01. 48
we come towards the gods, | young and unwapper'd 5.04. 9
towards thee i'll run, and give him leave to go. SON 51.14
as the waves make towards the pibbled shore, 60. 1
towards this afflicted fancy fastly drew, | and, LC 61

/TOWER 1 FR 0.0001 REL FR 1 V 0 P
/some /of /you, /convey /him /to /the /tower. R2 4.01.316

TOWER 61 FR 0.0069 REL FR 59 V 2 P
strong as a tower in hope, i cry amen. R2 1.03.102
the way | to julius caesar's ill–erected tower, 5.01. 2
you must to pomfret, not unto the tower. 5.01. 52
i'll to the tower with all the haste i can, | to 1H6 1.01.167
i am come to survey the tower this day; 1.03. 1
hath here distrain'd the tower to his use. 1.03. 61
and would have armor here out of the tower, | to 1.03. 67
bars | in yonder tower to overpeer the city, 1.04. 11
accursed tower! 1.04. 76
as well at london bridge as at the tower. 3.01. 23
by thrusting out a torch from yonder tower, 3.02. 23
of your honor from the tower to defend the city 2H6 4.05. 5 P
the rebels have assay'd to win the tower. 4.05. 8
fire, and, if you can, burn down the tower too. 4.06. 15 P
tell him i'll send duke edmund to the tower; 4.09. 38
the duke of somerset is in the tower. 5.01. 41
he is a traitor, let him to the tower, | and 5.01.134
see that he be convey'd unto the tower; 3H6 3.02.120
hence with him to the tower, let him not speak. 4.08. 57
and ten to one you'll meet him in the tower. 5.01. 46
/the tower, the tower. 5.05. 50
/the tower, the tower. 5.05. 50
i guess, | to make a bloody supper in the tower. 5.05. 85
this conduct to convey me to the tower. R3 1.01. 45
that you should be new christ'ned in the tower. 1.01. 50
'tis not the king that sends you to the tower; 1.01. 63
that made him send lord hastings to the tower, 1.01. 68
thou kill'dst my husband henry in the tower, 1.03.118
methoughts that i had broken from the tower 1.04. 9
your highness shall repose you at the tower; 3.01. 65
i do not like the tower, of any place. 3.01. 68
her | to meet you at the tower and welcome you. 3.01.139
what, will you go unto the tower, my lord? 3.01.140
i shall not sleep in quiet at the tower. 3.01.142
heart, | thinking on them, go i unto the tower. 3.01.150
and summon him to–morrow to the tower | to sit 3.01.172
to me, | and we will both together to the tower, 3.02. 32
what, shall we toward the tower? 3.02. 89
then was i going prisoner to the tower, | by the 3.02.100
what, go you toward the tower? 3.02.118
and started when he look'd upon the tower, | as 3.04. 85
now, for my life, she's wand'ring to the tower, 4.01. 3
no farther than the tower, and, as i guess, 4.01. 8
stay, yet look back with me unto the tower. 4.01. 97
tyrrel, i mean those bastards in the tower. 4.02. 75
the chaplain of the tower hath buried them, 4.03. 29
besides, the king's name is a tower of strength, 5.03. 12
think on the tower and me. 5.03.126
dream on thy cousins smothered in the tower. 5.03.146
his highness' pleasure | you shall to th' tower. H8 1.01.207
the king | is pleas'd you shall to th' tower, 1.01.213
as to the tower, i thought — i would have 1.02.194
you, | from hence you be committed to the tower, 5.02. 89
you be convey'd to th' tower a prisoner; 5.02.124
way of mercy | but i must needs to th' tower, my 5.02.128
receive him, | and see him safe i' th' tower. 5.02.132
up to the eastern tower, | whose height commands TRO 1.02. 2
paris, | from off the battlements of any tower, ROM 4.01. 78
nor stony tower, nor walls of beaten brass, JC 1.03. 93
"child rowland to the dark tower came, | his LR 3.04.182
the strongest castle, tower, and town, | the PP 18.17

/TOWER'D 1 FR 0.0001 REL FR 1 V 0 P
a /tower'd citadel, a pendant rock, | a forked ANT 4.14. 4

TOWER–HILL 1 FR 0.0001 REL FR 0 V 1 P
the tribulation of tower–hill or the limbs of H8 5.03. 62 P

TOWERS 5 FR 0.0005 REL FR 5 V 0 P
topples down | steeples and moss–grown towers. 1H4 3.01. 32
shall lay your stately and air–braving towers, 1H6 4.02. 13
yon towers, whose wanton tops do buss the clouds TRO 4.05.220
whose towers bore heads so high they kiss'd the PER 1.04. 24
when sometime lofty towers i see down rased, SON 64. 3

/TOWN 1 FR 0.0001 REL FR 1 V 0 P
/the /poor /distressed /lear's /i' /th' /town, LR 4.03. 38

TOWN 119 FR 0.0134 REL FR 95 V 24 P
be there bears i' th' town? WIV 1.01.287 P
which of you know ford of this town? 1.03. 36 P
the priest o' th' town commended him for a true 2.01.145 P
there is a gentlewoman in this town, her 2.02.191 P
slender, go you through the town to frogmore. 2.03. 75 P
old windsor way, and every way but the town way. 3.01. 7 P
there is a friend of mine come to town, tells me 4.05. 76 P
yokes | become the forest better than the town? 5.05.108
his life | according to the statute of the town, ERR 1.02. 6
till that, i'll view the manners of the town, 1.02. 12
what, will you walk with me about the town, 1.02. 22
they say this town is full of cozenage: 1.02. 97
as strange unto your town as to your talk, | who 2.02.149
all that, and a pair of stocks in the town? 3.01. 60
troth, your town is troubled with unruly boys. 3.01. 62
i will not harbor in this town to–night. 3.02.149
besides, i have some business in the town. 4.01. 35
i will not stay to–night for all the town: 4.04.157
against the laws and statutes of this town, 5.01.126
brought to this town by that most famous warrior 5.01.368
the gallants of the town are come to fetch you ADO 3.04. 97 P
for he carried the town gates on his back like a LLL 1.02. 71 P
and in the wood, a league without the town MND 1.01.165
me in the palace wood, a mile without the town, 1.02.102 P
ay, in the temple, in the town, the field, | you 2.01.238
i am fear'd in field and town. 3.02.398
as a wall'd town is more worthier than a village AYL 3.03. 59 P
'tis hymen peoples every town, | high wedlock 5.04.143
honor, and renown | to hymen, god of every town! 5.04.146
master, some show to welcome us to town. SHR 1.01. 47
hearing thy mildness prais'd in every town, 2.01.191
an old rusty sword ta'en out of the town armory, 3.02. 47 P
while he did bear my countenance in the town, 5.01.126
shall we go see the reliques of this town? TN 3.03. 19
feed your knowledge | with viewing of the town. 3.03. 42
that he did range the town to seek me out. 4.03. 7
love) | into the danger of this adverse town, 5.01. 84
when came he to this town? 5.01. 93
i'll bring you to a captain in this town, 5.01.254
bent | against the brows of this resisting town. JN 2.01. 38
we'll lay before this town our royal bones, 2.01. 41
his marches are expedient to this town, | his 2.01. 60
here | before the eye and prospect of your town, 2.01.208
in warlike march these greens before your town, 2.01.242
which here we came to spout against your town, 2.01.256
for him, and in his right, we hold this town. 2.01.268
weigh so even, | we hold our town for neither; 2.01.333
your sharpest deeds of malice on this town. 2.01.380
being wrong'd as we are by this peevish town, 2.01.402
shall rain their drift of bullets on this town. 2.01.412
this friendly treaty of our threat'ned town? 2.01.481
and this rich fair town | we make him lord of. 2.01.552
fire | our town of ciceter in gloucestershire, R2 5.06. 3
says up and down the town that her eldest son is 2H4 2.01.105 P
he heard of your grace's coming to town. 2.02.100 P
kin as the parish heckfers are to the town bull. 2.02.158 P
word to your master that i am yet come to town. 2.02.161 P
is old double of your town living yet? 3.02. 40 P
as many ways meet in one town; H5 1.02.208
i would have blowed up the town, so chrish save 3.02. 92 P
the town is beseech'd, and the trumpet call us 3.02.108 P
the town sounds a parley. 3.02.137 P
how yet resolves the governor of the town? 3.03. 1
take pity of your town and of your people, 3.03. 28
we yield our town and lives to thy soft mercy. 3.03. 48
let's leave this town, for they are hare–brain'd 1H6 1.02. 37
chief master gunner am i of this town, 1.04. 6
recover'd is the town of orleance. 1.06. 9
not out the bells aloud throughout the town? 1.06. 11
the middle centure of this cursed town. 2.02. 6
france, | either to get the town again, or die: 3.02. 79
as sure as in this late–betrayed town | great 3.02. 82
so sure i swear to get the town, or die. 3.02. 84
now will we take some order in the town, 3.02.126
might with a sally of the very town | be buckled 4.04. 4
have you not | beadles in your town, and things 2H6 2.01.134
let them be whipt through every market town, 2.01.155
away, and throughout every town | proclaim them 4.02.176
gates, | so york may overlook the town of york. 3H6 1.04.180
welcome, my lord, to this brave town of york. 2.02. 1
his soldiers lurking in the town about, | and 4.02. 15
for edward will defend the town and thee, | and 4.07. 38
warwick, wilt thou leave the town, and fight? 5.01.107
near to the town of leicester, as we learn. R3 5.02. 12
he is, my lord, and safe in leicester town, 5.05. 10
the first and happiest hearers of the town, | be H8 pr 24
hark what good sport is out of town to–day. TRO 1.01.113
for yonder walls, that pertly front your town, 4.05.219
go in and cheer the town. 5.03. 92
summon the town. COR 1.04. 7
call thither all the officers a' th' town, 1.05. 27
if we lose the field, | we cannot keep the town. 1.07. 5
the town is ta'en! 1.10. 1
for they had so vildly | yielded the town. 3.01. 11
all | than to take in a town with gentle words, 3.02. 59
/hate i, and my love's upon | this enemy town. 4.04. 24
for the defense of a town, our general is 4.05.170 P
your native town you enter'd like a post, | and 5.06. 49
i would not for the wealth of all this town ROM 1.05. 69
o, there is a nobleman in town, one paris, that 2.04.201 P
displant a town, reverse a prince's doom, | it 3.03. 59
and finding him, the searchers of the town, 5.02. 8
from thee | but nakedness, thou detestable town! TIM 4.01. 33
sound to this coward and lascivious town | our 5.04. 1
shall make their harbor in our town till we 5.04. 53
marcus luccicos, is not he in town? OTH 1.03. 44
the town is empty; 2.01. 53
the town will rise. 2.03.162
what, in a town of war, | yet wild, the people's 2.03.213
it so fell out) | the town might fall in fright. 2.03.232
iago, look with care about the town, | and 2.03.255
how silent is this town! 5.01. 64
was in debt, it went o' th' backside the town. CYM 1.02. 13 P
your grace is welcome to our town and us. PER 1.04.106
boult, spend thou that in the town. 4.02.137 P
and there i'll be, for our town, and here again, TNK 2.03. 48
now, when the credit of our town lay on it, 3.05. 56
young maids | of our town are in love with him, 4.01.126
the strongest castle, tower, and town, | the PP 18.17

TOWN–CRIER 1 FR 0.0001 REL FR 0 V 1 P
do, i had as live the town–crier spoke my lines. HAM 3.02. 3 P

TOWN'S 3 FR 0.0003 REL FR 0 V 3 P
bid my lieutenant peto meet me at town's end. 1H4 4.02. 9 P
and they are for the town's end, to beg during 5.03. 38 P
what call you the town's name where alexander H5 4.07. 12 P

TOWNS 28 FR 0.0031 REL FR 24 V 4 P
i better brook than flourishing peopled towns: TGV 5.04. 3
to admit no traffic to our adverse towns: ERR 1.01. 15
'tis won as towns with fire — so won, so lost. LLL 1.01.146
when adverse foreigners affright my towns | with JN 4.02.172
as i have bank'd their towns? 5.02.104
this have i rumor'd through the peasant towns 2H4 in 33
girding with grievous siege castles and towns; H5 1.02.152
to line and new repair our towns of war | with 2.04. 7
or the loss of those great towns | will make him 1H6 1.01. 63
quite, | except some petty towns of no import. 1.01. 91
what towns of any moment but we have? 1.02. 5
play on the lute, beholding the towns burn: 1.04. 96
razeth your cities, and subverts your towns, 2.03. 65
and see the cities and the towns defac'd | by 3.03. 45
cities, and seven walled towns of strength, 3.04. 7
have we not lost most part of all the towns, 5.04.108
no interest | in any of our towns of garrison. 5.04.168
thy sale of offices and towns in france, | if 2H6 1.03.135
you made in a day, my lord, whole towns to fly. 2.01.160
by means whereof the towns each day revolted? 3.01. 63
the lord say, which sold the towns in france; 4.07. 21 P
the giving up of some more towns in france. 4.07.133 P
and seiz'd upon their towns and provinces. 3H6 1.01.109
and in the towns, as they do march along, 2.02. 70
his chief followers lodge in towns about him, 4.03. 13
it is turn'd out of towns and cities for a R3 1.04.142 P
which was | to take in many towns ere (almost) COR 1.02. 24
come, march to wakes and fairs and market towns. LR 3.06. 75 P

TOWNSHIP 1 FR 0.0001 REL FR 0 V 1 P
am but a poor petitioner of our whole township. 2H6 1.03. 24 P

TOWNSMEN 2 FR 0.0002 REL FR 2 V 0 P
whose party do the townsmen yet admit? JN 2.01.361
here comes the townsmen on procession, | to 2H6 2.01. 66

TOW'R 5 FR 0.0005 REL FR 5 V 0 P
i nightly lodge her in an upper tow'r, | the key TGV 3.01. 35
would serve to scale another hero's tow'r, | so 3.01.119
my lord protector's hawks do tow'r so well; 2H6 2.01. 10
i dare adventure to be sent to th' tow'r. R3 1.03.115
well contented | to make your house our tow'r. H8 5.01.106

/TOW'RING 1 FR 0.0001 REL FR 1 V 0 P
/did /put /me | /into /a /tow'ring /passion. HAM 5.02. 80

TOW'RING 2 FR 0.0002 REL FR 2 V 0 P
a falcon, tow'ring in her pride of place, | was MAC 2.04. 12
which, like a falcon tow'ring in the skies, LUC 506

TOW'RS 8 FR 0.0009 REL FR 8 V 0 P
the cloud–capp'd tow'rs, the gorgeous palaces, TMP 4.01.152
heralds, from off our tow'rs we might behold, JN 2.01.325
how high thy glory tow'rs | when the rich blood 2.01.350
arms, | and like an eagle o'er his aery tow'rs, 5.02.149
nor are they such | that these great tow'rs, TIM 5.04. 25
to tow'rs and windows, yea, to chimney–tops, JC 1.01. 39
smear with dust their glitt'ring golden tow'rs; LUC 945
and from the tow'rs of troy there would appear 1382

TOY 19 FR 0.0021 REL FR 17 V 2 P
a toy, my liege, a toy; LLL 4.03.197
a toy, my liege, a toy; 4.03.197
even a toy in hand here, sir. AYL 3.03. 76 P
tut, a toy! SHR 2.01.402
a knack, a toy, a trick, a baby's cap. 4.03. 67
haply your eye shall light upon some toy | you TN 3.03. 44
and the rain, | a foolish thing was but a toy, 5.01.391
princes shall be certified | that for a toy, a 1H6 4.01.145
and being but a toy, which is no grief to give. R3 3.01.114
if no inconstant toy, nor womanish fear, | abate ROM 4.01.119
favor, | hold it a fashion and a toy in blood, HAM 1.03. 6
each toy seems prologue to some great amiss, 4.05. 18
think, | and no conception nor no jealious toy OTH 3.04.156
on my head no toy | but was her pattern, her TNK 1.03. 71
their mirth, and affliction a toy to jest at. 2.01. 35 P
took toy at this, and fell to what disorder 5.04. 66
disdain, | with leaden appetite, unapt to toy; VEN 34
to toy, to wanton, dally, smile, and jest, 106
or sells eternity to get a toy? LUC 214

TOYS 16 FR 0.0018 REL FR 15 V 1 P
as little by such toys as may be possible: TGV 1.02. 79
i do not like des toys. WIV 1.04. 44 P
silence, you aery toys! 5.05. 42
the boys, | and critic timon laugh at idle toys! LLL 4.03.168
these antic fables, nor these fairy toys. MND 5.01. 3
dreams are toys, | yet for this once, yea, WT 3.03. 39
any toys for your head | of the new'st and 4.04.319
james, | there's toys abroad; JN 1.01.232

shall we fall foul for toys? 2H4 2.04.169
and such-like toys as these | hath mov'd his R3 1.01. 60
all is but toys: MAC 2.03. 94
the very place puts toys of desperation, HAM 1.04. 75
when light-wing'd toys | of feather'd cupid seel OTH 1.03.268
immoment toys, things of such dignity | as we ANT 5.02.166
triumphs for nothing, and lamenting toys, | is CYM 4.02.193
show, | the tricks and toys that in them lurk, PP 18.39
TOZE *(also touze)*
TOZE 1 FR 0.0001 REL FR 0 V 1 P
i insinuate, /that toze from thee thy business, WT 4.04.735 P
TRACE* 13 FR 0.0014 REL FR 11 V 2 P
come, | as we do trace this alley up and down, ADO 3.01. 16
knight of his train, to trace the forests wild; MND 2.01. 25
son | can trace me in the tedious ways of art, 1H4 3.01. 47
now all my joy | trace the conjunction! H8 3.02. 45
unfortunate souls | that trace him in his line. MAC 4.01.153
why may not imagination trace the noble dust of HAM 5.01.203 P
is his mirror, and who else would trace him, his 5.02.119 P
of venice, whom i trace | for his quick hunting, OTH 2.01.303
the search so slow, | that could not trace them! CYM 1.01. 65
but no trace of him. 5.05. 12
i had as lief trace this good action with you TNK 1.01.102
or i am none | that draw i' th' sequent trace. 1.02. 60
and sweetly, by a figure, trace and turn, boys. 3.05. 21
TRACES 1 FR 0.0001 REL FR 1 V 0 P
her traces of the smallest spider web, | her ROM 1.04. 64
TRACK 1 FR 0.0001 REL FR 1 V 0 P
to dim his glory and to stain the track | of his R2 3.03. 66
TRACT 4 FR 0.0004 REL FR 4 V 0 P
and by the bright tract of his fiery car | gives R3 5.03. 20
the tract of ev'ry thing | would by a good H8 1.01. 40
bold, and forth on, | leaving no tract behind. TIM 1.01. 50
are | from his low tract and look another way: SON 7.12
TRACTABLE 6 FR 0.0006 REL FR 3 V 3 P
thou shalt find me tractable to any honest 1H4 3.03.172 P
if thou dost find him tractable to us, R3 3.01.174
to pass | this tractable obedience is a slave H8 1.02. 64
much more gentle, and altogether more tractable. TRO 2.03.150 P
that you will be more mild and tractable. TIT 1.01.470
not but i shall find them tractable enough. PER 4.06.199 P
/TRADE 1 FR 0.0001 REL FR 1 V 0 P
/him /where /most /trade /of /danger /rang'd; 2H4 1.01.174
TRADE 41 FR 0.0046 REL FR 20 V 21 P
a tapster is a good trade. WIV 1.03. 17 P
and west indies, and i will trade to them both. 1.03. 72 P
your place, you need not change your trade; MM 1.02.108 P
so. what trade are you of, sir? 2.01.197 P
what do you think of the trade, pompey? 2.01.225 P
is it a lawful trade? 2.01.226 P
the valiant heart's not whipt out of his trade. 2.01.256
thy sin's not accidental, but a trade. 3.01.148
is a more penitent trade than your bawd — he 4.02. 50 P
come on, bawd, i will instruct thee in my trade; 4.02. 55 P
all great doers in our trade, and are now "for 4.03. 19 P
since that the trade and profit of the city MV 3.03. 30
than hath been taught by any of my trade; SHR 3.01. 69
you should enter, if your trade be to her. TN 3.01. 75 P
some way of common trade, where subjects' feet R2 3.03.156
what trade art thou, feeble? 2H4 3.02.149 P
others, like merchants, venter trade abroad; H5 1.02.192
stands in the gap and trade of moe preferments, H8 5.01. 36
brethren and sisters of the hold-door trade, TRO 5.10. 51
enough to make a whore forswear her trade, | and TIM 4.03.134
believe him as an enemy, and give over my trade. 4.03.455 P
speak, what trade art thou? JC 1.01. 5
you, sir, what trade are you? 1.01. 9
but what trade art thou? answer me directly. 1.01. 12
a trade, sir, that i hope i may use with a safe 1.01. 13 P
what trade, thou knave? 1.01. 15
thou naughty knave, what trade? 1.01. 15
steep'd in the colors of their trade, their MAC 2.03.115
did you dare | to trade and traffic with macbeth 3.05. 4
have you any further trade with us? HAM 3.02.334 P
is so tann'd with his trade that 'a will keep 5.01.170 P
though they had been but two years o' th' trade. LR 2.02. 60 P
bad is the trade that must play fool to sorrow, 4.01. 38
hangs one that gathers sampire, dreadful trade! 4.06. 15
though in the trade of war i have slain men, OTH 1.02. 1
music, moody food | of us that trade in love. ANT 2.05. 2
be not a conscience to be us'd in every trade, PER 4.02. 12 P
neither is our profession any trade, it's no 4.02. 38 P
one, how long have you been at this trade? 4.06. 67 P
what trade, sir? 4.06. 68 P
i cannot be offended with my trade. 4.06. 70 P
TRADED 2 FR 0.0002 REL FR 2 V 0 P
and he, long traded in it, makes it seem | like JN 4.03.109
two traded pilots 'twixt the dangerous /shores TRO 2.02. 64
TRADE-FALL'N 1 FR 0.0001 REL FR 0 V 1 P
revolted tapsters, and ostlers trade-fall'n, the 1H4 4.02. 29 P
/TRADERS 1 FR 0.0001 REL FR 0 V 1 P
o /traders and bawds, how earnestly are you set TRO 5.10. 37 P
TRADERS 4 FR 0.0004 REL FR 2 V 2 P
peruse the traders, gaze upon the buildings, ERR 1.02. 13
marking th' embarked traders on the flood; MND 2.01.127
and traders riding to london with fat purses. 1H4 1.02.127 P
good traders in the flesh, set this in your TRO 5.10. 45 P
TRADES 4 FR 0.0004 REL FR 4 V 0 P
to the common ferry | which trades to venice. MV 3.04. 54
come home belov'd | of all the trades in rome. COR 3.02.134
the red pestilence strike all trades in rome, 4.01. 13
instruction, manners, mysteries, and trades, TIM 4.01. 18
TRADESMAN'S 1 FR 0.0001 REL FR 0 V 1 P
i meddle with no tradesman's matters, nor JC 1.01. 22 P
TRADESMEN 2 FR 0.0002 REL FR 1 V 1 P
it becomes none but tradesmen, and they often WT 4.04.723 P
than see | our tradesmen singing in their shops, COR 4.06. 8
TRADING 1 FR 0.0001 REL FR 0 V 1 P
it is like we shall have good trading that way. 1H4 2.04.365 P
TRADITION 3 FR 0.0003 REL FR 1 V 2 P
but the same tradition takes not away my blood, AYL 1.01. 47 P
tradition, form, and ceremonious duty, | for you R2 3.02.173
will you mock at an ancient tradition, /begun H5 5.01. 70 P
TRADITIONAL 1 FR 0.0001 REL FR 1 V 0 P
my lord, | too ceremonious and traditional. R3 3.01. 45
TRADUC'D 5 FR 0.0005 REL FR 5 V 0 P
a divulged shame, | traduc'd by odious ballads; AWW 2.01.172
if i am | traduc'd by ignorant tongues, which H8 1.02. 72
makes us traduc'd and tax'd of other nations. HAM 1.04. 18
turk | beat a venetian and traduc'd the state, OTH 5.02.354
he is already | traduc'd for levity, and 'tis ANT 3.07. 13
TRADUCEMENT 1 FR 0.0001 REL FR 1 V 0 P
worse than a theft, no less than a traducement, COR 1.09. 22
TRAFFIC 11 FR 0.0012 REL FR 8 V 3 P
for no kind of traffic | would i admit; TMP 2.01.149
to admit no traffic to our adverse towns: ERR 1.01. 15
a merchant of great traffic through the world, SHR 1.01. 12
my traffic is sheets; WT 4.03. 23 P
thanks, | because this is in traffic of a king. 1H6 5.03.164
is now the two hours' traffic of our stage; ROM pr 12
traffic confound thee, if the gods will not! TIM 1.01.237 P
if traffic do it, the gods do it. 1.01.238 P
did you dare | to trade and traffic with macbeth MAC 3.05. 4
despair to gain doth traffic oft for gaining, LUC 131
for having traffic with thyself alone, | thou of SON 4. 9
TRAFFICKERS 1 FR 0.0001 REL FR 1 V 0 P
do overpeer the petty traffickers | that cur'sy MV 1.01. 12
TRAFFIC'S 2 FR 0.0002 REL FR 1 V 1 P
which for traffic's sake | most of our city did. TN 3.03. 34
traffic's thy god, and thy god confound thee! TIM 1.01.239 P
TRAFFICS 1 FR 0.0001 REL FR 1 V 0 P
for since dishonor traffics with man's nature, TIM 1.01.158
TRAGEDIAN 1 FR 0.0001 REL FR 1 V 0 P
tut, i can counterfeit the deep tragedian, R3 3.05. 5
TRAGEDIANS 2 FR 0.0002 REL FR 0 V 2 P
h'as led the drum before the english tragedians. AWW 4.03.267 P
such delight in, the tragedians of the city. HAM 2.02.328 P
TRAGEDIES 2 FR 0.0002 REL FR 2 V 0 P
a den, | unless the gods delight in tragedies? TIT 4.01. 60
black stage for tragedies and murthers fell! LUC 766
TRAGEDY 10 FR 0.0011 REL FR 8 V 2 P
garter, it would have been a fine tragedy; MND 5.01.360 P
who on the french ground play'd a tragedy, H5 1.02.106
hand | that hath contriv'd this woeful tragedy! 1H6 1.04. 77
will not conclude their plotted tragedy. 2H6 3.01.153
even so suspicious is this tragedy. 3.02.194
upon, as if the tragedy | were play'd in jest by 3H6 2.03. 27
hate, | i live to look upon their tragedy. R3 3.02. 59
writ, | the complot of this timeless tragedy, TIT 2.03.265
best actors in the world, either for tragedy, HAM 2.02.396 P
for us, and for our tragedy, | here stooping to 3.02.149
TRAGIC 9 FR 0.0010 REL FR 9 V 0 P
deep | gave any tragic instance of our harm: ERR 1.01. 64
foretells the nature of a tragic volume. 2H4 1.01. 61
jades | that drag the tragic melancholy night; 2H6 4.01. 4
point | than can my ears that tragic history. 3H6 5.06. 28
to make an act of tragic violence. R3 2.02. 39
this is the tragic tale of philomel, | and TIT 4.01. 47
look on the tragic loading of this bed; OTH 5.02.363
of love, | as chorus to their tragic scene. PHT 52
or to turn white and sound at tragic shows; LC 308
TRAGICAL 5 FR 0.0005 REL FR 5 V 0 P
very tragical mirth." MND 5.01. 57
merry and tragical? 5.01. 58
and tragical, my noble lord, it is; 5.01. 66
why look you still so stern and tragical? 1H6 3.01.125
will prove as bitter, black, and tragical. R3 4.04. 7
//TRAGICAL-COMICAL-HISTORICAL-PASTORAL 1 FR 0.0001 REL FR 0 V 1 P
//tragical-comical-historical-pastoral, scene HAM 2.02.398 P
//TRAGICAL-HISTORICAL 1 FR 0.0001 REL FR 0 V 1 P
historical-pastoral, //tragical-historical, HAM 2.02.398 P
TRAIL 6 FR 0.0006 REL FR 5 V 1 P
if i cry out thus upon no trail, never trust me WIV 4.02.197 P
tail, | along the field i will the troyan trail. TRO 5.08. 22
trail your steel pikes. COR 5.06.150
of mine | hunts not the trail of policy so sure HAM 2.02. 47
how cheerfully on the false trail they cry! 4.05.110
this is an aspic's trail, and these fig leaves ANT 5.02.351
TRAIL'ST 1 FR 0.0001 REL FR 1 V 0 P
trail'st thou the puissant pike? H5 4.01. 40
TRAIN 30 FR 0.0034 REL FR 30 V 0 P
i invite your highness and your train | to my TMP 5.01.301
to bear my lady's train, lest the base earth TGV 2.04.159
o, train me not, sweet mermaid, with thy note, ERR 3.02. 45
and train our intellects to vain delight. LLL 1.01. 71
park, | and in her train there is a gentle lady: 3.01.165
would have the child | knight of his train, to MND 2.01. 25
was he met there? his train? camillo with him? WT 2.01. 33
what train? 5.01. 92
my best train | i have from your sicilian shores 5.01.163
to train ten thousand english to their side, JN 3.04.175
we did train him on, | and, his corruption being 1H4 5.02. 21
which of this princely train | call ye the 1H6 2.02. 34
we'll pull his plumes and take away his train, 3.03. 7
and here at hand the dolphin and his train 5.04.100
the very train of her worst wearing gown | was 2H6 1.03. 85
me seemeth good that, with some little train, R3 2.02.120
why with some little train, my lord of 2.02.123
honor's train | is longer than his foreskirt. H8 2.03. 97
a royal train, believe me. 4.01. 37
it, she that carries up the train | is that old 4.01. 51
you train me to offend you, get you in. TRO 5.03. 4
why are you sequest'red from all your train, TIT 2.03. 75
and all the rest look like a chidden train: JC 1.02.184
she begs, | a little to disquantity your train, LR 1.04.249
call my train together! 1.04.253
my train are men of choice and rarest parts, 1.04.263
she hath abated me of half my train; 2.04.159
to grudge my pleasures, to cut off my train, 2.04.174
dismissing half your train, come then to me. 2.04.204
he is attended with a desperate train, | and 2.04.305
TRAIN'D 13 FR 0.0014 REL FR 11 V 2 P
and tartars never train'd | to offices of tender MV 4.01. 32
you have train'd me like a peasant, obscuring AYL 1.01. 68 P
they were train'd together in their childhoods; WT 1.01. 22 P
for i was train'd up in the english court, 1H4 3.01.120
henry the fift he first train'd to the wars; 1H6 1.04. 79
and for that cause i train'd thee to my house. 2.03. 35
hath yok'd a nation strong, train'd up in arms. TIT 1.01. 30
i train'd thy brethren to that guileful hole, 5.01.104
he must be taught, and train'd, and bid go forth JC 4.01. 35
and, though train'd up thus meanly | i' th' cave CYM 3.03. 82
are) these twenty years | have i train'd up; 5.05.338
and by cleon train'd | in music's letters, who PER 4.ch. 7
being therein train'd | and of kind manage; TNK 5.04. 68
TRAINED 1 FR 0.0001 REL FR 1 V 0 P
that he was never trained up in arms. R3 5.03.272
TRAINING 3 FR 0.0003 REL FR 3 V 0 P
his training such | that he may furnish and H8 1.02.112
beseeching you | to give her princely training, PER 3.03. 16
i doubt not but thy training hath been noble. 4.06.112
TRAINS* 3 FR 0.0003 REL FR 3 V 0 P
so please you, let our trains | march by us, 2H4 4.02. 93
by many of these trains hath sought to win me MAC 4.03.118
as stars with trains of fire and dews of blood, HAM 1.01.117
/TRAITOR 1 FR 0.0001 REL FR 1 V 0 P
/i /find /myself /a /traitor /with /the /rest; R2 4.01.248
TRAITOR 138 FR 0.0156 REL FR 122 V 16 P
he's a traitor. TMP 1.02.461
put thy sword up, traitor, | who mak'st a show 1.02.470
unless i prove false traitor to myself. TGV 4.04.105
hath almost made me traitor to myself; ERR 3.02.162
a kissing traitor. how art thou prov'd judas? LLL 5.02.600 P
yet your mistrust cannot make me a traitor. AYL 1.03. 56
my father was no traitor. 1.03. 63
if she be a traitor, | why so am i. 1.03. 72
and graceless traitor to her loving lord? SHR 5.02.160
a traitor you do look like, but such traitors AWW 2.01. 96
more — she's a traitor, and camillo is | a WT 2.01. 89
thou, traitor, hast set on thy wife to this. 2.03.131
thou, old traitor, | i am sorry that by hanging 4.04.420
he doth espy | himself love's traitor. JN 2.01.507
thou art a traitor and a miscreant, | too good R2 1.01. 39
not light, | if i be traitor or unjustly fight! 1.01. 83
like a false traitor and injurious villain; 1.01. 91
and consequently, like a traitor coward, 1.01.102
a recreant and most degenerate traitor, | which 1.01.144
a traitor to my god, my king, and me — | and as 1.03. 24
that he is a traitor, foul and dangerous, | to 1.03. 39
a traitor to his god, his king, and him, | and 1.03.108
no, bullingbrook, if ever i were traitor, | my 1.03.201
because your lordship was proclaimed traitor. 2.03. 30
i wot your love pursues | a banish'd traitor. 2.03. 60
so when this thief, this traitor bullingbrook, 3.02. 47
and send | defiance to the traitor, and so die? 3.03.130
is a foul traitor to proud herford's king, | and 4.01.135
villain, traitor, slave! 5.02. 72
thou hast a traitor in thy presence there. 5.03. 40
the traitor lives, the true man's put to death. 5.03. 73
shall thy old dugs once more a traitor rear? 5.03. 90
by the lord, i'll be a traitor then, when thou 1H4 1.02.146 P
then | be emptied to redeem a traitor home? 1.03. 86
for the which | i do arrest thee, traitor, of 2H4 4.02.107
shall be still your name, a traitor your degree, 4.03. 7 P
unless to dub thee with the name of traitor. H5 2.02.120
an arrant traitor as any's in the universal 4.08. 9 P
i am no traitor. 4.08. 15 P
my liege, here is a villain and a traitor, that, 4.08. 25 P
condemn'd to die for treason, but no traitor; 1H6 2.04. 97
and i am louted by a traitor villain | and 4.03. 13
by forfeiting a traitor and a coward. 4.03. 27
all long of this vile traitor somerset. 4.03. 33
fact | did never traitor in the land commit. 2H6 1.03.174
doth any one accuse york for a traitor? 1.03.179
go, take hence that traitor from our sight, 2.03.100
and 'twixt each groan | say, "who's a traitor, 3.01.222
he's a villain and a traitor. 4.02.108 P
can speak french, and therefore he is a traitor. 4.02.167 P
join with the traitor, and they jointly swear 4.04. 52
why, buckingham, is the traitor cade surpris'd? 4.09. 8
the duke of somerset, whom he terms a traitor. 4.09. 30
cade that i have slain, that monstrous traitor? 4.10. 66
to heave the traitor somerset from hence, | and 5.01. 61
dar'st not, no, nor canst not rule a traitor. 5.01. 95
o monstrous traitor! 5.01.106
obey, audacious traitor, kneel for grace. 5.01.108
shall be the surety for their traitor father. 5.01.116
he is a traitor, let him to the tower, | and 5.01.134
i am thy king, and thou a false-heart traitor. 5.01.143
a subtle traitor needs no sophister. 5.01.191
thy father was a traitor to the crown. 3H6 1.01. 79
exeter, thou art a traitor to the crown, | in 1.01. 80
what title hast thou, traitor, to the crown? 1.01.104
durst the traitor breathe out so proud words? 4.01.112
forthwith that edward be pronounc'd a traitor, 4.06. 54
and take the great-grown traitor unawares. 4.08. 63
o passing traitor, perjur'd and unjust! 5.01.106
which, traitor, thou wouldst have me answer to. 5.05. 21
and like a traitor to the name of god | didst R3 1.04.205
thou art a traitor. 3.04. 75
here is the head of that ignoble traitor, | the 3.05. 22
he was the covert'st shelt'red traitor | that 3.05. 33
that the subtile traitor | this day had plotted, 3.05. 37
i would have had you heard | the traitor speak, 3.05. 57
reward to him that brings the traitor in? 4.04.516
what traitor hears me, and says not amen? 5.05. 22
a giant traitor! H8 1.02.199
by day and night, | he's traitor to th' height. 1.02.214
thou art a proud traitor, priest. 3.02.252
for me? | must i go like a traitor thither? 5.02.131
so, traitor, then she comes when she is thence. TRO 1.01. 31
troyan drab, and uses the traitor calchas' tent. 5.01. 97 P
o traitor diomed! 5.06. 6
turn thy false face, thou traitor, | and pay thy 5.06. 6
h'as spoken like a traitor, and shall answer COR 3.01.162
peremptory to dispatch | this viperous traitor. 3.01.285
for which you are a traitor to the people. 3.03. 66
how? traitor? 3.03. 67
call me their traitor, thou injurious tribune! 3.03. 69
but tell the traitor, in the highest degree | he 5.06. 84
"traitor"? how now? 5.06. 86
ay, traitor, martius! 5.06. 86
traitor, restore lavinia to the emperor. TIT 1.01.296
traitor, if rome have law, or we have power, 1.01.403
and vengeance on the traitor saturnine. 4.03. 35
that is because the traitor murderer lives. ROM 3.05. 84
let not a traitor live! JC 3.02.205 P
assisted by that most disloyal traitor, | the MAC 1.02. 52
was my father a traitor, mother? 4.02. 44 P
what is a traitor? 4.02. 46 P

every one that does so is a traitor, and must be 4.02. 49 P
he's a traitor. 4.02. 82
bridges, to course his own shadow for a traitor. LR 3.04. 58 P
death, traitor! 3.04. 70
seek out the traitor gloucester. 3.07. 3 P
go seek the traitor gloucester, | pinion him 3.07. 22
the traitor? 3.07. 27
hard, hard. o filthy traitor! 3.07. 32
so white, and such a traitor? 3.07. 37
if you do chance to hear of that blind traitor, 4.05. 37
thou old unhappy traitor, | briefly thyself 4.06.228
/durst thou support a publish'd traitor? 4.06.232
in the world /he /is | that names me traitor, 5.03. 98
that he is a manifold traitor, let him appear by 5.03.113 P
thy valor, and thy heart, thou art a traitor; 5.03.134
below thy foot, | a most toad–spotted traitor. 5.03.139
yet the traitor | stands in worse case of woe. CYM 3.04. 86
who call'd me traitor, mountaineer, and swore 4.02.120
what of him? he is | a banish'd traitor. 5.05.318
a banish'd man, | i know not how a traitor. 5.05.320
traitor, thou liest. PER 2.05. 55
traitor? 2.05. 55
ay, traitor. 2.05. 55
that calls me traitor, i return the lie. 2.05. 57
thou art a traitor, arcite, and a fellow | false TNK 2.02.171
traitor kinsman, | thou shouldst perceive my 3.01. 30
my love, would make thee | a confess'd traitor! 3.01. 35
as thou mak'st me, traitor! 3.03. 47
a bolder traitor never trod thy ground, | a 3.06.141
where this man calls me traitor, | let me say 3.06.160
so let me be most traitor, and ye please me. 3.06.167
and if she say "traitor," | i am a villain fit 3.06.170
who will obey a traitor? STM II.C 116
in their pure ranks his traitor eye encloses, LUC 73
thou ravisher, thou traitor, thou false thief, 888
comes all too late, yet let the traitor die, 1686

TRAITORLY 1 FR 0.0001 REL FR 0 V 1 P
but what talk we of these traitorly rascals, WT 4.04.791 P

TRAITOROUS 8 FR 0.0009 REL FR 7 V 1 P
with charles, alanson, and that traitorous rout. 1H6 4.01.173
myself | attach thee as a traitorous innovator, COR 3.01.174
thee never, nor thy traitorous haughty sons, TIT 1.01.302
the cruel father and his traitorous sons, | to 1.01.452
mortal revenge upon these traitorous goths, 4.01. 93
may this be borne as if his traitorous sons, 4.04. 53
witchcraft of his wits, with traitorous gifts — HAM 1.05. 43
to take upon your traitorous father are not fit LR 3.07. 8 P

TRAITOROUSLY 4 FR 0.0004 REL FR 2 V 2 P
you that have so traitorously discover'd the AWW 4.03.304 P
harmless richard was murthered traitorously. 2H6 2.02. 27
that good duke humphrey traitorously is murd'red 3.02.123
thou hast most traitorously corrupted the youth 4.07. 32 P

TRAITOR'S 11 FR 0.0012 REL FR 11 V 0 P
with a foul traitor's name stuff i thy throat, R2 1.01. 44
my gage | upon this overweening traitor's foot, 1.01.147
i am no traitor's uncle, and that word "grace" 2.03. 88
i tore it from the traitor's bosom, king; 5.03. 55
have thy head for this thy traitor's speech. 2H6 1.03.194
lo, i present your grace a traitor's head, | the 5.01. 66
i would prolong a while the traitor's life. 3H6 1.04. 52
off with the traitor's head, | and rear it in 2.06. 85
i have this day receiv'd a traitor's judgment, H8 2.01. 58
incurr'd a traitor's name, expos'd myself | from TRO 3.03. 6
'tis thou that execut'st the traitor's treason; LUC 877

TRAITORS' 5 FR 0.0005 REL FR 5 V 0 P
to come at traitors' calls and do them grace. R2 3.03.181
from treason's secret knife and traitors' rage 2H6 3.01.174
ingratitude, more strong than traitors' arms, JC 3.02.185
and with the brands fire the traitors' houses. 3.02.255
caesar, thou canst not die by traitors' hands, 5.01. 56

/TRAITORS 2 FR 0.0002 REL FR 2 V 0 P
/they /can /see /a /sort /of /traitors /here. R2 4.01.246
some guard /these /traitors to the block of 2H4 4.02.122

TRAITORS 54 FR 0.0061 REL FR 50 V 4 P
frown upon you | and justify you traitors. TMP 5.01.128
our doubts are traitors, | and makes us lose the MM 1.04. 77
aside the true folk, and let the traitors stay. LLL 4.03.209
thus do all traitors! AYL 1.03. 52
are sanctified and holy traitors to you. 2.03. 13
they are virtues and traitors too. AWW 1.01. 43 P
but such traitors | his majesty seldom fears. 2.01. 96
merely our own traitors. 4.03. 21 P
traitors! WT 2.03. 73
a nest of traitors! 2.03. 82
and all the rest revolted faction traitors? R2 2.02. 57
to oxford, or where e'er these traitors are. 5.03.141
two of the dangerous consorted traitors | that 5.06. 15
he calls us rebels, traitors, and will scourge 1H4 5.02. 39
the sum is paid, the traitors are agreed, | the H5 2.pr. 33
god, his grace is bold to trust these traitors. 2.02. 1
what noise is this? what traitors have we here? 1H6 1.03. 15
traitors have never other company. 2.01. 19
that thus we die, while remiss traitors sleep. 4.03. 29
lay hands upon these traitors and their trash. 2H6 1.04. 41
proclaim them traitors that are up with cade, 4.02.177
lord say, the traitors hateth thee, | therefore 4.04. 43
why, what a brood of traitors have we here! 5.01.141
we'll quickly rouse the traitors in the same. 3H6 5.01. 65
ye all | i am your better, traitors as ye are, 5.05. 36
o traitors, murtherers! 5.05. 52
friends suspect for traitors while thou liv'st, R3 1.03.222
and take deep traitors for thy dearest friends! 1.03.223
to warn false traitors from the like attempts. 3.05. 49
we must be brief when traitors brave the field. 4.03. 57
who hath descried the number of the traitors? 5.03. 9
abate the edge of traitors, gracious lord, 5.05. 35
a traitor, and shall answer | as traitors do. COR 3.01.163
traitors, avaunt! TIT 1.01.283
traitors, away, he rests not in this tomb. 1.01.349
that we may know the traitors and the truth! 4.01. 76
inhuman traitors, you constrain'd and forc'd. 5.02.177
writ, | but set them down horrible traitors. TIM 4.03.119
if not, the fates with traitors do contrive. JC 2.03. 16
they were traitors; honorable men! 3.02.153
is himself, marr'd as you see with traitors. 3.02.197
o traitors, villains! 3.02.201 P
have added slaughter to the sword of traitors. 5.01. 55
defiance, traitors, hurl we in your teeth. 5.01. 64
actions do not, | our fears do make us traitors. MAC 4.02. 4
but cruel are the times when we are traitors, 4.02. 18
and be all traitors that do so? 4.02. 48 P
and what confederacy have you with the traitors LR 3.07. 44
a plague upon you, murderers, traitors all! 5.03.270
traitors ensteep'd to enclog the guiltless keel, OTH 2.01. 70
men's vows are women's traitors. CYM 3.04. 54
what ignorant and mad malicious traitors | are TNK 3.06.132
we are certainly both traitors, both despisers 3.06.137
thus treason works ere traitors be espied. LUC 361

TRAITRESS 1 FR 0.0001 REL FR 1 V 0 P
a counsellor, a traitress, and a dear: AWW 1.01.170

TRAIT'ROUS 1 FR 0.0001 REL FR 1 V 0 P
the trait'rous warwick, with the men of bury, 2H6 3.02.240

/TRAJECT 1 FR 0.0001 REL FR 1 V 0 P
thee with imagin'd speed | unto the /traject, to MV 3.04. 53

TRAMMEL 1 FR 0.0001 REL FR 1 V 0 P
could trammel up the consequence, and catch MAC 1.07. 3

TRAMPLE 3 FR 0.0003 REL FR 3 V 0 P
which with usurping steps do trample thee. R2 3.02. 17
may hourly trample on their sovereign's head; 3.03.157
the calkins | did rather tell than trample; TNK 5.04. 56

/TRAMPLED 1 FR 0.0001 REL FR 1 V 0 P
/abject /rear, | /o'errun /and /trampled /on. TRO 3.03.163

TRAMPLING 2 FR 0.0002 REL FR 2 V 0 P
trampling contemptuously on thy disdain. TGV 1.02.109
proud, | adonis' trampling courser doth espy; VEN 261

/TRANC'D 1 FR 0.0001 REL FR 1 V 0 P
/sounded, | /and /there /i /left /him /tranc'd. LR 5.03.219

TRANCE 2 FR 0.0002 REL FR 2 V 0 P
nay, then 'tis time to stir him from his trance. SHR 1.01.177
both stood like old acquaintance in a trance, LUC 1595

TRANCES 1 FR 0.0001 REL FR 1 V 0 P
his hours of rest with restless trances, LUC 974

TRANIO 34 FR 0.0038 REL FR 31 V 3 P
tranio, since for the great desire i had | to SHR 1.01. 1
and therefore, tranio, for the time i study, 1.01. 17
gramercies, tranio, well dost thou advise. 1.01. 41
peace, tranio! 1.01. 72
hark, tranio, thou mayst hear minerva speak. 1.01. 84
o tranio, till i found it to be true, | i never 1.01.148
tranio, i burn, i pine, i perish, tranio, | if i 1.01.155
tranio, i burn, i pine, i perish, tranio, | if i 1.01.155
counsel me, tranio, for i know thou canst; 1.01.157
assist me, tranio, for i know thou wilt. 1.01.158
tranio, i saw her coral lips to move, | and with 1.01.174
ah, tranio, what a cruel father's he! 1.01.185
i have it, tranio. 1.01.189
thou shalt be master, tranio, in my stead; 1.01.202
tranio, at once | uncase thee; 1.01.206
tranio, be so, because lucentio loves, | and let 1.01.218
has my fellow tranio stol'n your clothes? 1.01.223 P
your fellow tranio here, to save my life, | puts 1.01.228
and not a jot of tranio in your mouth, | tranio 1.01.236
your mouth, | tranio is chang'd into lucentio. 1.01.237
when i am alone, why then i am tranio; 1.01.243
tranio, let's go. 1.01.245
well begun, tranio. 1.02.227
a–wooing, "priami," is my man tranio, "regia," 3.01. 35 P
tranio, you jest, but have you both forsworn me? 4.02. 48
he says so, tranio. 4.02. 53
and what of him, tranio? 4.02. 66
he was three years old, and his name is tranio. 5.01. 83 P
where is that damned villain tranio, | that 5.01.120
love | made me exchange my state with tranio, 5.01.125
what tranio did, myself enforc'd him to; 5.01.129
here, signior tranio, | this bird you aim'd at, 5.02. 49
o, o, petruchio, tranio hits you now. 5.02. 57
i thank thee for that gird, good tranio. 5.02. 58

TRANQUIL 1 FR 0.0001 REL FR 1 V 0 P
o now, for ever | farewell the tranquil mind! OTH 3.03.348

TRANQUILITY 1 FR 0.0001 REL FR 0 V 1 P
but with nobility and tranquility, burgomasters 1H4 2.01. 76 P

TRANSCENDENCE 1 FR 0.0001 REL FR 0 V 1 P
great power, great transcendence, which should AWW 2.03. 35 P

TRANSCENDS 1 FR 0.0001 REL FR 1 V 0 P
fame blows, that praise, sole pure, transcends. TRO 1.03.244

TRANSFERRED 1 FR 0.0001 REL FR 1 V 0 P
to this false plague are they now transferred. SON 137.14

TRANSFIGUR'D 1 FR 0.0001 REL FR 1 V 0 P
and all their minds transfigur'd so together, MND 5.01. 24

TRANSFIX 1 FR 0.0001 REL FR 1 V 0 P
time doth transfix the flourish set on youth, SON 60. 9

TRANSFORM 6 FR 0.0006 REL FR 2 V 4 P
lest he transform me to a piece of cheese! WIV 5.05. 82 P
transform me then, and to your pow'r i'll yield. ERR 3.02. 40
be sworn but love may transform me to an oyster, ADO 2.03. 24 P
beauty will sooner transform honesty from what HAM 3.01.111 P
and applause, transform ourselves into beasts! OTH 2.03.292 P
for shame, | transform us not to women. ANT 4.02. 36

TRANSFORMATION 6 FR 0.0006 REL FR 2 V 4 P
and how my transformation hath been wash'd and WIV 4.05. 96 P
misuse, | such beastly shameless transformation, 1H4 1.01. 44
a low transformation! 2H4 2.02.175 P
and the goodly transformation of jupiter there, TRO 5.01. 53 P
that seest not thy loss in transformation! TIM 4.03.345 P
have you heard | of hamlet's transformation; HAM 2.02. 5

TRANSFORMATIONS 1 FR 0.0001 REL FR 1 V 0 P
their transformations | were never for a piece WT 4.04. 31

TRANSFORM'D 7 FR 0.0008 REL FR 5 V 2 P
ear of the court, how i have been transform'd, WIV 4.05. 95 P
she had transform'd me to a curtal dog, and made ERR 3.02.146
i think he be transform'd into a beast, | for i AYL 2.07. 1
in shape and mind | transform'd and weak'ned? R2 5.01. 27
if the fat villain have not transform'd him ape. 2H4 2.02. 72 P
shall come again, transform'd to orient pearl, R3 4.04.322
him | the triple pillar of the world transform'd ANT 1.01. 12

TRANSFORMED 7 FR 0.0008 REL FR 7 V 0 P
i am transformed, master, am /not /i? ERR 2.02.195
dumaine transformed! LLL 4.03. 80
i sat, | to see a king transformed to a gnat! 4.03.164
take this transformed scalp | from off the head MND 4.01. 64
blush | to see me thus transformed to a boy. MV 2.06. 39
we woo | transformed timon to our city's love TIM 5.04. 19
transformed with their fear, who swore they saw JC 1.03. 24

TRANSGRESS'D 2 FR 0.0002 REL FR 0 V 2 P
that adam had left him before he transgress'd. ADO 2.01.252 P
experience and transgress'd against his valor, AWW 2.05. 11 P

TRANSGRESSED 1 FR 0.0001 REL FR 1 V 0 P
alone | upon his head that hath transgressed so; LUC 1481

TRANSGRESSES 1 FR 0.0001 REL FR 0 V 1 P
virtue that transgresses is but patch'd with sin TN 1.05. 48 P

TRANSGRESSING 2 FR 0.0002 REL FR 1 V 1 P
come, you transgressing slave, away. LLL 1.02.154 P
by pardoning rutland, my transgressing boy. R2 5.03. 96

TRANSGRESSION 9 FR 0.0010 REL FR 5 V 4 P
her true perfection, or my false transgression, TGV 2.04.197
he puts transgression to't. MM 3.02. 95 P
the flat transgression of a schoolboy, who, ADO 2.01.222 P
wilt thou make a trust a transgression? 2.01.225 P
the transgression is in the stealer. 2.01.226 P
for our rude transgression | some fair excuse. LLL 5.02.431
lay not my transgression to my charge | that art JN 1.01.256
why, such is love's transgression. ROM 1.01.185
feel | needs must i under my transgression bow, SON 120. 3

TRANSGRESSIONS 1 FR 0.0001 REL FR 1 V 0 P
their own transgressions partially they smother: LUC 634

TRANSLATE 9 FR 0.0010 REL FR 7 V 2 P
that can translate the stubbornness of fortune AYL 2.01. 19
make thee away, translate thy life into death, 5.01. 53 P
i can with ease translate it to my will; JN 2.01.513
wherefore do you so ill translate yourself | out 2H4 4.01. 47
did in great ilion thus translate him to me. TRO 4.05.112
translate his malice towards you into love, COR 2.03.189
force of honesty can translate beauty into his HAM 3.01.112 P
you must translate, 'tis fit we understand them. 4.01. 2
if like a lamb he could his looks translate! SON 96.10

TRANSLATED 5 FR 0.0005 REL FR 3 V 2 P
hath studied her /well, and translated her will, WIV 1.03. 49 P
the rest i'll give to be to you translated. MND 1.01.191
thou art translated. 3.01.119 P
fear, | and left sweet pyramus translated there; 3.02. 32
that in thee are seen | to truths translated, SON 96. 8

TRANSLATES 1 FR 0.0001 REL FR 1 V 0 P
slaves and servants | translates his rivals. TIM 1.01. 72

TRANSLATION 1 FR 0.0001 REL FR 1 V 0 P
a huge translation of hypocrisy, | vildly LLL 5.02. 51

TRANSMIGRATES 1 FR 0.0001 REL FR 0 V 1 P
the elements once out of it, it transmigrates. ANT 2.07. 45 P

TRANSMUTATION 1 FR 0.0001 REL FR 0 V 1 P
a card–maker, by transmutation a bear–herd, and SHR in.2. 20 P

TRANSPARENT 5 FR 0.0005 REL FR 4 V 1 P
through the transparent bosom of the deep, | as LLL 4.03. 30
transparent helena, nature shows art, | that MND 2.02.104
it hath bay windows transparent as barricadoes, TN 4.02. 36 P
like to the glorious sun's transparent beams, 2H6 3.01.353
die, | transparent heretics, be burnt for liars! ROM 1.02. 91

TRANSPORT 7 FR 0.0008 REL FR 7 V 0 P
and to transport him in the mind he is | were MM 4.03. 68
i shall not need transport my words by you, R2 2.03. 81
he cannot temp'rately transport his honors COR 2.01.224
when i came hither to transport the tidings, MAC 4.03.181
these dispositions which of late transport you LR 1.04.221
might not you | transport her purposes by word? 4.05. 20
which should transport me farthest from your SON 117. 8

TRANSPORTANCE 1 FR 0.0001 REL FR 1 V 0 P
and give me swift transportance to these fields TRO 3.02. 11

TRANSPORTATION 1 FR 0.0001 REL FR 1 V 0 P
to th' ports and coasts for transportation, STM II.C 76

TRANSPORTED 12 FR 0.0013 REL FR 11 V 1 P
being transported | and rapt in secret studies. TMP 1.02. 76
out of doubt he is transported. MND 4.02. 4 P
being transported by my jealousies | to bloody WT 3.02.158
my lord's almost so far transported that | he'll 5.03. 69
and the scene | is now transported, gentles, to H5 2.pr. 35
transported shall be at high festivals | before 1H6 1.06. 26
mean | shall be transported presently to france. 5.01. 40
you are transported by calamity | thither where COR 1.01. 75
thy letters have transported me beyond | this MAC 1.05. 56
transported with no worse nor better guard | but OTH 1.01.124
i was transported with your speech, and suffer'd TNK 1.01. 55
much unlike | you should be so transported, as 1.01.187

TRANSPORTING 2 FR 0.0002 REL FR 1 V 1 P
master's command transporting a sum of money, be H5 4.01.151 P
for costs and charges in transporting her! 2H6 1.01.134

TRANSPORTS 1 FR 0.0001 REL FR 1 V 0 P
transports his pois'ned shot, may miss our name, HAM 4.01. 43

TRANSPOSE 2 FR 0.0002 REL FR 2 V 0 P
love can transpose to form and dignity. MND 1.01.233
which you are, my thoughts cannot transpose: MAC 4.03. 21

TRANS–SHAPE 1 FR 0.0001 REL FR 0 V 1 P
she an hour together trans–shape thy particular ADO 5.01.170 P

TRANSYLVANIAN 1 FR 0.0001 REL FR 0 V 1 P
the poor transylvanian is dead that lay with the PER 4.02. 22 P

TRAP 4 FR 0.0004 REL FR 3 V 1 P
i will say "marry trap" with you, if you run the WIV 1.01.167 P
in that thou laidst a trap to take my life, | as 1H6 3.01. 22
weaves tedious snares to trap mine enemies. 2H6 3.01.340
or i fall into | the trap is laid for me! H8 5.01.142

TRAPP'D 2 FR 0.0002 REL FR 2 V 0 P
thy horses shall be trapp'd, | their harness SHR in.2. 41
you | four milk–white horses, trapp'd in silver. TIM 1.02.183

TRAPPINGS 3 FR 0.0003 REL FR 2 V 1 P
ay, sir, we are some of her trappings. TN 5.01. 9 P
these but the trappings and the suits of woe. HAM 1.02. 86
spur, | for rich caparisons or trappings gay? VEN 286

TRAPS 2 FR 0.0002 REL FR 2 V 0 P
some cupid kills with arrows, some with traps. ADO 3.01.106
and pretty traps to catch the petty thieves. H5 1.02.177

TRASH* 12 FR 0.0013 REL FR 10 V 2 P
and who | to trash for overtopping, new created TMP 1.02. 81
let it alone, thou fool, it is but trash. 4.01.224
lay hands upon these traitors and their trash. 2H6 1.04. 41
dare | maintain — i know not what, 'tis trash. TRO 2.01.126
what trash is rome? JC 1.03.108
for so much trash as may be grasped thus? 4.03. 26
from the hard hands of peasants their vile trash 4.03. 74
if this poor trash of venice, whom i trace | for OTH 2.01.303
who steals my purse steals trash; 3.03.157
i do suspect this trash | to be a party in this 5.01. 85
trash, trash; STM II.C 10 P

trash, trash; II.C 10 P
TRAVAIL 12 FR 0.0013 REL FR 11 V 1 P
now they are oppress'd with travail, they | will TMP 3.03. 15
thirty–three years have i but gone in travail ERR 5.01.401
but on this travail look for greater birth: ADO 4.01.213
is all our travail turn'd to this effect? 1H6 5.04.102
and | with gentle travail, to the gladding of H8 5.01. 71
i have had my labor for my travail; TRO 1.01. 70 P
as honor, loss of time, travail, expense, 2.02. 4
load our purposes | with what they travail for, TIM 5.01. 15
does fall in travail with her fear; PER 3.ch. 52
art, may yet appear | worth two hours' travail. TNK pr 29
(as if with grief or travail he had fainted), LUC 1543
deserves the travail of a worthier pen, | yet SON 79. 6
TRAVAIL'D 1 FR 0.0001 REL FR 1 V 0 P
have travail'd in the great show'r of your gifts TIM 5.01. 70
TRAVAILS 2 FR 0.0002 REL FR 2 V 0 P
obey our will, which travails in thy good; AWW 2.03.158
make swift the pangs | of my queen's travails! PER 3.01. 14
TRAVEL 36 FR 0.0040 REL FR 26 V 10 P
some rare noteworthy object in thy travel. TGV 1.01. 13
age, | in having known no travel in his youth. 1.03. 16
whither travel you? 4.01. 16
my youthful travel therein made me happy, | or 4.01. 34
for with long travel i am stiff and weary. ERR 1.02. 15
a soldier, a man of travel, that hath seen the LLL 5.01.108 P
are numb'red in the travel of one mile? 5.02.197
us, | maids as we are, to travel forth so far! AYL 1.03.109
would he not be a comfort to our travel? 1.03.131
here's a young maid with travel much oppressed, 2.04. 74
to make me sad — and to travel for it too! 4.01. 29 P
travel you far on, or are you at the farthest? SHR 4.02. 73
thou didst make tolerable vent of thy travel; AWW 2.03.203 P
will he travel higher, or return again into 4.03. 42 P
not three hours' travel from this very place. TN 1.02. 23
and after a demure travel of regard — telling 2.05. 53 P
but jealousy what might befall your travel, 3.03. 8
call it a travel that thou tak'st for pleasure. R2 1.03.262
the tediousness and process of my travel. 2.03. 12
if i travel but four foot by the squier further 1H4 2.02. 12 P
but to stand stain'd with travel, and sweating 2H4 5.05. 24 P
i met in travel toward his warlike father! 1H6 4.03. 36
late, not able to travel with her furr'd pack, 2H6 4.02. 47 P
blist'red breeches, and those types of travel, H8 1.03. 31
how chances it they travel? HAM 2.02.329 P
you have been talk'd of since your travel much, 4.07. 71
blest withal would have discredited your travel. ANT 1.02.155 P
from egypt, 'tis | a space for farther travel. 2.01. 31
what he learns by this | may prove his travel, CYM 3.05.103
therefore, my lord, go travel for a while, PER 1.02.106
and to tharsus | intend my travel, where i'll 1.02.116
does speak sufficiently he's gone to travel. 1.03. 13
sir, we are much indebted to your travel, | nor TNK 2.05. 30
where ever they shall travel, ever strangers 3.06.255
the dear repose for limbs with travel tired, SON 27. 2
and make me travel forth without my cloak, | to 34. 2
TRAVELL'D 8 FR 0.0009 REL FR 8 V 0 P
and he supposes me travell'd to poland — | for MM 1.03. 14
my grave | i have travell'd but two hours. TN 5.01.163
but as i travell'd hither through the land, | i JN 4.02.143
the reformation of our travell'd gallants, H8 1.03. 19
till it hath travell'd and is /mirror'd there TRO 3.03.110
i have watch'd and travell'd hard: LR 2.02.155
they have travell'd all the night? 2.04. 89
morn | hath travell'd on to age's steepy night, SON 63. 5
TRAVELLER 14 FR 0.0015 REL FR 6 V 8 P
and brave master shoe–tie the great traveller, MM 4.03. 17 P
is haunted | with a refined traveller of spain, LLL 1.01.163
speak of thee as the traveller doth of venice: 4.02. 95 P
tires | the sinowy vigor of the traveller. 4.03.304
a traveller! AYL 4.01. 21 P
farewell, monsieur traveller: 4.01. 33 P
you are a vagabond and no true traveller. AWW 2.03.260 P
a good traveller is something at the latter end 2.05. 28 P
now your traveller, | he and his toothpick at my JN 1.01.189
now spurs the lated traveller apace | to gain MAC 3.03. 6
from whose bourn | no traveller returns, puzzles HAM 3.01. 79
i was then a young traveller, rather shunn'd to CYM 1.04. 44 P
if we had of every nation a traveller, we should PER 4.02.113 P
welcomes to their cost | the galled traveller, TNK 3.05.129
TRAVELLER'S 1 FR 0.0001 REL FR 1 V 0 P
when it lies starkly in the traveller's bones. MM 4.02. 67
TRAVELLERS 5 FR 0.0005 REL FR 3 V 2 P
travellers ne'er did lie, | though fools at home TMP 3.03. 26
that all the travellers do fear so much. TGV 4.01. 6
a better place, but travellers must be content. AYL 2.04. 18 P
like pleasant travellers, to break a jest | upon SHR 4.05. 72
list if thou canst hear the tread of travellers. 1H4 2.02. 33 P
TRAVELLEST 1 FR 0.0001 REL FR 1 V 0 P
withal make known | which way thou travellest —
SHR 4.05. 51
TRAVELLING 5 FR 0.0005 REL FR 5 V 0 P
and travelling along this coast, i here am come LLL 5.02.554
gentleman that means | (travelling some journey) SHR in.1. 76
who, travelling towards york, | with much ado R2 5.05. 73
yet dark night strangles the travelling lamp. MAC 2.04. 7
it is | a cell of ignorance, travelling a–bed, CYM 3.03. 33
/TRAVEL'S 1 FR 0.0001 REL FR 1 V 0 P
thence | and portance in my /travel's history; OTH 1.03.139
TRAVEL'S 1 FR 0.0001 REL FR 1 V 0 P
way, | when what i seek (my weary travel's end) SON 50. 2
TRAVELS 7 FR 0.0008 REL FR 5 V 2 P
could all my travels warrant me they live. ERR 1.01.139
time travels in divers paces with divers persons AYL 3.02.308 P
indeed the sundry contemplation of my travels, 4.01. 18 P
way, | for honor travels in a strait so narrow, TRO 3.03.154
lord has /betook himself to unknown travels; PER 1.03. 34
us, | we with our travels will endeavor. 2.04. 56
rang'd, | like him that travels i return again, SON 109. 6
TRAVEL–TAINTED 1 FR 0.0001 REL FR 0 V 1 P
posts, and here, travel–tainted as i am, have, 2H4 4.03. 36 P
TRAVERS 3 FR 0.0003 REL FR 3 V 0 P
here comes my servant travers, who i sent | on 2H4 1.01. 28
now, travers, what good tidings comes with you? 1.01. 33
why should that gentleman that rode by travers 1.01. 55
TRAVERS'D 1 FR 0.0001 REL FR 1 V 0 P
power | have wander'd with our travers'd arms, TIM 5.04. 7
TRAVERSE 4 FR 0.0004 REL FR 0 V 4 P
to see thee foin, to see thee traverse, to see WIV 2.03. 25 P
and breaks them bravely, quite traverse, athwart AYL 3.04. 42 P
hold, wart, traverse! thas, thas, thas. 2H4 3.02.272 P
traverse, go, provide thy money. OTH 1.03.371 P
TRAY–TRIP 1 FR 0.0001 REL FR 0 V 1 P
shall i play my freedom at tray–trip, and become TN 2.05.190 P
TREACHEROUS 28 FR 0.0031 REL FR 27 V 1 P
a treacherous army levied, one midnight | fated TMP 1.02.128
treacherous man, | thou hast beguil'd my hopes! TGV 5.04. 63
and greedily devour the treacherous bait; ADO 3.01. 28
entrap thee by some treacherous device, and AYL 1.01.151 P
so much | to think my poverty is treacherous. 1.03. 65
even with a treacherous fine of all your lives, JN 5.04. 38
way, | doing annoyance to the treacherous feet, R2 3.02. 16
as may be hollowed in thy treacherous ear | from 4.01. 54
o loyal father of a treacherous son! 5.03. 60
and sav'd the treacherous labor of your son. 1H4 5.04. 57
which he fills | with treacherous crowns; H5 2.pr. 22
but o, the treacherous falstaff wounds my heart, 1H6 1.04. 35
sheep run not half so treacherous from the wolf, 1.05. 30
the treacherous manner of his mournful death, 2.02. 16
ay, like a dastard and a treacherous coward, 3H6 2.02.114
just | as i am subtle, false, and treacherous, R3 1.01. 37
and with thy treacherous blade | unrip'st the 1.04.206
hollow, treacherous, and full of guile | be he 2.01. 38
fie, treacherous hue, that will betray with TIT 4.02.117
or my true heart with treacherous revolt | turn ROM 4.01. 58
i am not treacherous. MAC 4.03. 18
remorseless, treacherous, lecherous, kindless HAM 2.02.581
the treacherous instrument is in /thy hand, 5.02.316
out, treacherous villain! LR 3.07. 87
o treacherous villains! OTH 5.01. 58
to write and read | be henceforth treacherous! CYM 4.02.317
why should a friend be treacherous? TNK 2.02.229
i was false, | yet never treacherous. 5.04. 93
TREACHEROUSLY 1 FR 0.0001 REL FR 1 V 0 P
and treacherously hast thou vanquish'd him, 3H6 2.01. 72
TREACHERS 1 FR 0.0001 REL FR 0 V 1 P
and treachers by spherical predominance; LR 1.02.123 P
TREACHERY 26 FR 0.0029 REL FR 24 V 2 P
without some treachery us'd to valentine. TGV 2.06. 32
without false vantage, or base treachery. 4.01. 29
those that betray them do no treachery. WIV 5.03. 22
he is compos'd and fram'd of treachery, | and ADO 5.01.249
lest that the treachery of the two fled hence WT 2.01.195
paying the fine of rated treachery | even with a JN 5.04. 37
on some known ground of treachery in him? R2 1.01. 11
what treachery is here! 5.02. 75
his sovereign's life to death and treachery. H5 2.02. 11
how were they lost? what treachery was us'd? 1H6 1.01. 68
no treachery, but want of men and money. 1.01. 69
and for thy treachery, what's more manifest? 3.01. 21
tears, | if talbot but survive thy treachery. 3.02. 37
o monstrous treachery! 4.01. 61
by treason, falsehood, and by treachery, | our 5.04.109
and wilt thou still be hammering treachery, | to 2H6 1.02. 47
to kings that fear their subjects' treachery? 3H6 2.05. 45
o, treachery! MAC 3.03. 17
what, you egg! | young fry of treachery! 4.02. 84
i am justly kill'd with mine own treachery. HAM 5.02.307
treachery! 5.02.312
hollowness, treachery, and all ruinous disorders LR 1.02.113 P
of gloucester's treachery, | and of the loyal 4.02. 6
this world with treachery and devise engines for OTH 4.02.216 P
men lose when they incline to treachery, | and TNK 3.01. 67
this treachery, like a most trusty lover, | i 3.06.150
TREAD 46 FR 0.0052 REL FR 41 V 5 P
and think'st it much to tread the ooze | of the TMP 1.02.252
pray you tread softly, that the blind mole may 4.01.194
in their so sacred paths he dares to tread | in WIV 4.04. 60
but what we do not see | we tread upon, and MM 2.01. 26
and the poor beetle, that we tread upon, | in 3.01. 78
guided by her foot (which is basest) doth tread. LLL 1.02.169 P
her feet were much too dainty for such tread! 4.03.275
to tread a measure with her on this grass. 5.02.185
to tread a measure with you on this grass. 5.02.187
when turtles tread, and rooks and daws, | and 5.02.905
green | for lack of tread are undistinguishable. MND 2.01.100
the groves may tread | even till the eastern 3.02.390
it no more merits | the tread of a man's foot. AWW 2.03.275
we tread | in warlike march these greens before JN 2.01.241
to tread down fair respect of sovereignty, | and 3.01. 58
o then tread down my need, and faith mounts up; 3.01.215
and wheresoe'er this foot of mine doth tread, 3.03. 62
but tread the stranger paths of banishment. R2 1.03.143
for on my heart they tread now whilst i live, 3.03.158
for accordingly | you tread upon my patience; 1H4 1.03. 4
list if thou canst hear the tread of travellers. 2.02. 33 P
and if we live, we live to tread on kings, | if 5.02. 85
by this heavenly ground i tread on, i must be 2H4 2.01.140 P
by her foot, that she may tread out the oath. H5 3.07. 95 P
to tread them with her tender–feeling feet. 2H6 2.04. 9
laugh, | and bid me be advised how i tread. 2.04. 36
and tread it under foot with all contempt, 5.01.209
and spies a far–off shore where he would tread, 3H6 3.02.136
tread on the sand, why, there you quickly sink; 5.04. 30
go tread the path that thou shalt ne'er return: R3 1.01.117
head below his knee, | and tread upon his neck. COR 1.03. 47
else | triumphantly tread on thy country's ruin, 5.03.116
march to assault thy country than to tread 5.03.123
'a shall not tread on me; 5.03.127
tread not upon him. 5.06.133
so shall no foot upon the churchyard tread, ROM 5.03. 5
when i shall tread upon the tyrant's head, | or MAC 4.03. 45
one woe doth tread upon another's heel, | so HAM 4.07.163
i will tread this unbolted villain into mortar, LR 2.02. 65 P
hark, the land bids me tread no more upon't, ANT 3.11. 1
i'll tread these flats. CYM 3.03. 11
you should tread a course | pretty and full of 3.04.146
shall make the gazer joy to see him tread. PER 2.01.159
to tread upon thy dukedom, and to be, | where TNK 3.06.254
teaching decrepit age to tread the measures; VEN 1148
maze, | that cannot tread the way out readily, LUC 1152
TREADING 2 FR 0.0002 REL FR 1 V 1 P
with many hundreds treading on his heels; JN 4.02.149
and the ground shrinks before his treading. COR 5.04. 20 P
TREADS 11 FR 0.0012 REL FR 10 V 1 P
the stairs, as he treads on them, kiss his feet. LLL 5.02.330
a kinder gentleman treads not the earth. MV 2.08. 35
horse with any that treads but on four /pasterns H5 3.07. 12 P
the shadow | which he treads on at noon. COR 1.01.261
april on the heel | of limping winter treads, ROM 1.02. 28
drinks | but timon's silver treads upon his lip, TIM 3.02. 71
himself the primrose path of dalliance treads, HAM 1.03. 50
she treads the path that she untreads again; VEN 908
the grass stoops not, she treads on it so light, 1028
the cock that treads them shall not know. PP 18.40
my mistress when she walks treads on the ground.
SON 130.12
TREAD'ST 1 FR 0.0001 REL FR 1 V 0 P
grass whereon thou tread'st the presence strow'd R2 1.03.289
TREASON 99 FR 0.0112 REL FR 86 V 13 P
treason, felony, | sword, pike, knife, gun, or TMP 2.01.161
some treason, masters; yet stand close. ADO 3.03.106 P
some certain treason. LLL 4.03.188
what makes treason here? 4.03.188
the treason and you go in peace away together. 4.03.190
'twas treason, he said. 4.03.192
flat treason 'gainst the kingly state of youth. 4.03.289
what treason there is mingled with your love. MV 3.02. 27
none but that ugly treason of mistrust, | which 3.02. 28
'tween snow and fire, as treason and my love. 3.02. 31
treason is not inherited, my lord, | or, if we AYL 1.03. 61
art here accused and arraigned of high treason, WT 3.02. 14 P
namely, to appeal each other of high treason. R2 1.01. 27
these terms of treason doubled down his throat. 1.01. 57
in gross rebellion and detested treason. 2.03.109
he makes upon my land | is dangerous treason. 3.03. 93
pains, | of capital treason we arrest you here. 4.01.151
treason, foul treason! 5.02. 72
treason, foul treason! 5.02. 72
shall i for love speak treason to thy face? 5.03. 44
the treason that my haste forbids me show. 5.03. 50
shall we buy treason? 1H4 1.03. 87
eyes, | for treason is but trusted like the fox, 5.02. 9
i do arrest thee, traitor, of high treason, 2H4 4.02.107
mowbray, | of capital treason i attach you both. 4.02.109
die, | if hell and treason hold their promises, H5 2.pr. 29
treason and murther ever kept together, | as two 2.02.105
in | wonder to wait on treason and on murther; 2.02.110
thee no instance why thou shouldst do treason, 2.02.119
i arrest thee of high treason, by the name of 2.02.145 P
i arrest thee of high treason, by the name of 2.02.147 P
i arrest thee of high treason, by the name of 2.02.149 P
at the discovery of most dangerous treason 2.02.162
this dangerous treason lurking in our way | to 2.02.186
but it is no english treason to cut french 4.01.227 P
i will give treason his payment into plows, i 4.08. 14 P
a most contagious treason come to light, look 4.08. 21 P
for treason executed in our late king's days? 1H6 2.04. 91
and, by his treason, stand'st not thou attainted 2.04. 92
condemn'd to die for treason, but no traitor; 2.04. 97
thou shalt rue this treason with thy tears, | if 3.02. 36
let no words, but deeds, revenge this treason! 3.02. 49
let him perceive how ill we brook his treason, 4.01. 74
by treason, falsehood, and by treachery, | our 5.04.109
because here is a man accused of treason. 2H6 1.03.177
that doth accuse his master of high treason. 1.03.182
hold, peter, hold! i confess, i confess treason. 2.03. 94 P
and in his simple show he harbors treason. 3.01. 54
from meaning treason to our royal person | as is 3.01. 70
i do arrest thee of high treason here. 3.01. 97
as i am clear from treason to my sovereign. 3.01.102
it shall be treason for any that calls me other 4.06. 5 P
of capital treason 'gainst the king and crown. 5.01.107
but that 'tis shown ignobly and in treason. 5.02. 23
and neither by treason nor hostility | to seek 3H6 1.01.199
when care, mistrust, and treason waits on him. 2.05. 54
and not bewray thy treason with a blush? 3.03. 97
thou and thy brother both shall buy this treason 5.01. 68
we speak no treason, man. R3 1.01. 90
that would with treason wound this fair land's 5.05. 39
is a kind of puppy | to th' old dam, treason), H8 1.01.176
i | arrest thee of high treason, in the name 1.01.201
have found him guilty of high treason. 2.01. 27
what treason were it to the ransack'd queen, TRO 2.02.150
manifest treason! COR 3.01.171
here lurks no treason, here no envy swells, TIT 1.01.153
treason, my lord! 1.01.284
and treats of tereus' treason and his rape — 4.01. 48
inspire me, that i may this treason find! 4.01. 67
complots of mischief, treason, villainies, 5.01. 65
i speak no treason. ROM 3.05.172
whilst bloody treason flourish'd over us. JC 3.02.192
who committed treason enough for god's sake, yet
MAC 2.03. 10 P
murther and treason! 2.03. 74
treason has done his worst; 3.02. 24
fortune's state would treason have pronounc'd. HAM 2.02.511
such love must needs be treason in my breast. 3.02.178
that treason can but peep to what it would, 4.05.125
treason! treason! 5.02.323
treason! treason! 5.02.323
in palaces, treason; LR 1.02.108 P
that this treason were not — or not i the 3.05. 12 P
edmund, i arrest thee | on capital treason, and, 5.03. 83
o treason of the blood! OTH 1.01.169
o, 'tis treason! ANT 1.05. 7
that are betray'd | do feel the treason sharply, CYM 3.04. 86
my punishment | itself, and all my treason: 5.05.335
beaten for loyalty | excited me to treason. 5.05.345
poison and treason are the hands of sin, | ay, PER 1.01.139
who either by public war or private treason 1.02.104
if in love be treason | in service of so TNK 3.06.161
till forging nature be condemn'd of treason, VEN 729
thus treason works ere traitors be espied. LUC 361
by their high treason is his heart misled, 369
with close–tongu'd treason and the ravisher! 770
'tis thou that execut'st the traitor's treason; 877
wrath, envy, treason, rape, and murther's rages, 909
guilty of treason, forgery, and shift, | guilty 920
my nobler part to my gross body's treason; SON 151. 6
TREASONABLE 1 FR 0.0001 REL FR 0 V 1 P
would close now, after his treasonable abuses! MM 5.01.343 P
TREASONOUS 3 FR 0.0003 REL FR 3 V 0 P
i do know | to be corrupt and treasonous. H8 1.01.156

say not treasonous. 1.01.156
pretense i fight | of treasonous malice. MAC 2.03.132
TREASON'S 4 FR 0.0004 REL FR 4 V 0 P
treason's true bed and yielder–up of breath. 2H4 4.02.123
from treason's secret knife and traitors' rage 2H6 3.01.174
by treason's tooth bare–gnawn and canker–bit, LR 5.03.122
life | /seeks to take off by treason's knife, PER 4.ch. 14
TREASONS 20 FR 0.0022 REL FR 18 V 2 P
is fit for treasons, stratagems, and spoils; MV 5.01. 85
and as in the common course of all treasons, we AWW 4.03. 22 P
that all the treasons for these eighteen years, R2 1.01. 95
confess thy treasons ere thou fly the realm; 1.03.198
then murthers, treasons, and detested sins, 3.02. 44
his treasons will sit blushing in his face, 3.02. 51
then treasons make me wish myself a beggar, 5.05. 33
and other devils that suggest by treasons | do H5 2.02.114
there minotaurs and ugly treasons lurk. 1H6 5.03.189
me, | nor store of treasons to augment my guilt. 2H6 3.01.169
my followers' base and ignominious treasons, 4.08. 64 P
to search the secret treasons of the world. 3H6 5.02. 18
the manner and the purpose of his treasons, R3 3.05. 58
and point by point the treasons of his master H8 1.02. 7
but treasons capital, confess'd and prov'd, MAC 1.03.115
that very frankly he confess'd his treasons, 1.04. 5
that made the overture of thy treasons to us, LR 3.07. 89
thy heinous, manifest, and many treasons, 5.03. 92
back do i toss these treasons to thy head, 5.03.147
yet at the first | i saw the treasons planted. ANT 1.03. 26
TREASURE 64 FR 0.0072 REL FR 59 V 5 P
think, no other treasure to give your followers; TGV 2.04. 44 P
and show thee all the treasure we have got; 4.01. 73
if so, our copper buys no better treasure. LLL 4.03.383
why then to thee, thou silver treasure house! MV 2.09. 34
thee, | for in baptista's keep my treasure is. SHR 1.02.118
now i see | she is your treasure, she must have 2.01. 32
to deck thy body with his ruffling treasure. 4.03. 60
i have writ my letters, casketed my treasure, AWW 2.05. 24
you waste the treasure of your time with a TN 2.05. 77 P
eyes, | have taken treasure from her lips — WT 5.01. 54
for all the treasure that thine uncle owes. JN 4.01.122
the purest treasure mortal times afford | is R2 1.01.177
meeter for your spirit, | this tun of treasure; H5 1.02.255
what treasure, uncle? 1.02.258
beat on a crown, the treasure of thy heart, 2H6 2.01. 20
omitting suffolk's exile, my soul's treasure? 3.02.382
beest death, i'll give thee england's treasure, 3.03. 2
for swallowing the treasure of the realm. 4.01. 74
our treasure seiz'd, our soldiers put to flight, 3H6 3.03. 36
his statutes cancell'd, and his treasure spent; 5.04. 79
and thither bear your treasure and your goods. R3 2.04. 69
th' interview | that swallowed so much treasure, H8 1.01.166
the several parcels of his plate, his treasure, 3.02.125
the treasure in this field achiev'd and city, COR 1.09. 33
her womb's increase | and treasure of my loins; 3.03.115
there to dispose this treasure in mine arms, TIT 4.02.173
the precious treasure of his eyesight lost. ROM 1.01.233
that now they are at fall, want treasure, cannot TIM 2.02.205
it is nois'd he hath a mass of treasure. 4.03.402 P
gods out of my misery | has sent thee treasure. 4.03.525
and having brought our treasure where we will, JC 4.01. 24
though the treasure | of nature's /germains MAC 4.01. 58
life | extorted treasure in the womb of earth, HAM 1.01.137
or your chaste treasure open | to his unmast'red 1.03. 31
judge of israel, what a treasure hadst thou! 2.02.403 P
what a treasure had he, my lord? 2.02.405 P
great egypt sends | this treasure of an oyster; ANT 1.05. 44
i will possess you of that ship and treasure. 3.11. 21
his chests and treasure | he has not with him. 4.05. 10
go, eros, send his treasure after; 4.05. 12
antony | hath after thee sent all thy treasure, 4.06. 20
the lock and ta'en | the treasure of her honor. CYM 2.02. 42
forget that rarest treasure of your cheek, 3.04.160
besides this treasure for a fee, | the gods PER 3.02. 74
he that will all the treasure know o' th' earth TNK 1.01.114
of this war | you are the treasure, and must 5.03. 31
that she will draw his lips' rich treasure dry. VEN 552
foul cank'ring rust the hidden treasure frets, 767
as full of fear | as one with treasure laden, 1022
"alas, poor world, what treasure hast thou lost! 1075
unlock'd the treasure of his happy state; LUC 16
and when great treasure is the meed proposed, 132
who fears sinking where such treasure lies?" 280
and scarce hath eyes his treasure to behold, 857
poor helpless help, the treasure stol'n away, 1056
where all the treasure of thy lusty days, | to SON 2. 6
treasure thou some place | with beauty's 6. 3
with beauty's treasure ere it be self–kill'd. 6. 4
be thy love, and thy love's use their treasure. 20.14
can bring him to his sweet up–locked treasure, 52. 2
stealing away the treasure of his spring; 63. 8
the filching age will steal his treasure; 75. 6
may detain, but not still keep, her treasure! 126.10
will will fulfill the treasure of thy love, | ay 136. 5
TREASURER 1 FR 0.0001 REL FR 1 V 0 P
this is my treasurer, let him speak, my lord, ANT 5.02.142
TREASURE'S 1 FR 0.0001 REL FR 1 V 0 P
my treasure's in the harbor; ANT 3.11. 11
TREASURES 4 FR 0.0004 REL FR 4 V 0 P
you must lay down the treasures of your body MM 2.04. 96
and given my treasures and my rights of thee 1H4 2.03. 45
and pour our treasures into foreign laps; OTH 4.03. 88
down the rich, enrich the poor with treasures; VEN 1150
TREASURIES 1 FR 0.0001 REL FR 1 V 0 P
sea | with sunken wrack and sumless treasuries. H5 1.02.165
TREASURY 6 FR 0.0006 REL FR 6 V 0 P
the pedlar's silken treasury and have pour'd it WT 4.04.350
all my treasury | is yet but unfelt thanks, R2 2.03. 60
attire | have cost a mass of public treasury. 2H6 1.03.131
the treasury of everlasting joy. 2.01. 18
heaven's eye, | and revel in lavinia's treasury. TIT 2.01.131
not how conceit may rob | the treasury of life, LR 4.06. 43
TREAT 1 FR 0.0001 REL FR 1 V 0 P
to treat of high affairs touching that time. JN 1.01.101
TREATIES 1 FR 0.0001 REL FR 1 V 0 P
i must | to the young man send humble treaties, ANT 3.11. 62
TREATISE 3 FR 0.0003 REL FR 3 V 0 P
i would have salv'd it with a longer treatise. ADO 1.01.315
hair | would at a dismal treatise rouse and stir MAC 5.05. 12
your treatise makes me like you worse and worse. VEN 774
TREATS 3 FR 0.0003 REL FR 2 V 1 P
good peter quince, say what the play treats on; MND 1.02. 9 P
will i apply that treats of happiness | by SHR 1.01. 19
and treats of tereus' treason and his rape — TIT 4.01. 48
TREATY 6 FR 0.0006 REL FR 5 V 1 P
this friendly treaty of our threat'ned town? JN 2.01.481
king our master | to this last costly treaty — H8 1.01.165
what good condition can a treaty find | i' th' COR 1.10. 6
we are convented | upon a pleasing treaty, and 2.02. 55
making a treaty where | there was a yielding — 5.06. 67
pompey, would ne'er have made this treaty. ANT 2.06. 83 P
/TREBLE 1 FR 0.0001 REL FR 1 V 0 P
woe | fall ten times /treble on that cursed head HAM 5.01.247
TREBLE 12 FR 0.0013 REL FR 10 V 2 P
double and treble admonition, and still forfeit MM 3.02.193 P
twice treble shame on angelo, | to weed my vice 3.02.269
double six thousand, and then treble that, MV 3.02.300
turning again toward childish treble, pipes AYL 2.07.162
let's hear. o fie, the treble jars. SHR 3.01. 39
the case of a treble hoboy was a mansion for him 2H4 3.02.326 P
england shall double gild his treble guilt, 4.05.128
any scath, | let him make treble satisfaction. TIT 5.01. 8
that twofold balls and treble sceptres carry. MAC 4.01.121
o, treble woe | fall ten times /treble on that HAM 5.01.246
and honor them | with treble ceremony — rather TNK 1.04. 8
the heart hath treble wrong | when it is barr'd VEN 329
TREBLED 1 FR 0.0001 REL FR 1 V 0 P
you | i would be trebled twenty times myself, MV 3.02.153
TREBLE–DATED 1 FR 0.0001 REL FR 1 V 0 P
and thou treble–dated crow, | that thy sable PHT 17
TREBLES 3 FR 0.0003 REL FR 3 V 0 P
which to do, | trebles thee o'er. TMP 2.01.221
why, our battalia trebles that account; R3 5.03. 11
the master calls, and trebles their confusion. PER 4.01. 64
TREBLE–SINEW'D 1 FR 0.0001 REL FR 1 V 0 P
i will be treble–sinew'd, hearted, breath'd, ANT 3.13.177
TREBONIUS 7 FR 0.0008 REL FR 6 V 1 P
is decius brutus and trebonius there? JC 1.03.148
this is trebonius. 2.01. 94
what, trebonius: 2.02.120
trust not trebonius; 2.03. 3 P
trebonius doth desire you to o'er–read | (at 3.01. 4
trebonius knows his time; 3.01. 25
last, not least in love, yours, good trebonius. 3.01.189
TREE* *(also three)*
TREE* 57 FR 0.0064 REL FR 44 V 13 P
i made of the bark of a tree with mine own hands TMP 2.02.123 P
if you prove a mutineer — the next tree! 3.02. 36 P
that in arabia | there is one tree, the phoenix' 3.03. 23
vat be all you, one, two, tree, four, come for? WIV 2.03. 22 P
two, tree hours for him, and he is no come. 2.03. 36 P
and there he blasts the tree, and takes the 4.04. 32
be, | to guide our measure round about the tree. 5.05. 79
dumaine is mine, as sure as bark on tree. LLL 5.02.285
the cuckoo then on every tree | mocks married 5.02.898
the cuckoo then on every tree | mocks married 5.02.907
but, poor old man, thou prun'st a rotten tree, AYL 2.03. 63
under the greenwood tree | who loves to lie with 2.05. 1
the duke will drink under this tree. 2.05. 32 P
orlando, carve on every tree | the fair, the 3.02. 9
peace, you dull fool, i found them on a tree. 3.02.115 P
truly, the tree yields bad fruit. 3.02.116 P
tongues i'll hang on every tree, | that shall 3.02.127
for look here what i found on a palm tree. 3.02.176 P
i found him under a tree, like a dropp'd acorn. 3.02.235 P
it may well be call'd jove's tree, when it drops 3.02.236 P
will you dispatch us here under this tree, or 3.03. 66 P
if then the tree may be known by the fruit, as 1H4 2.04.428 P
be known by the fruit, as the fruit by the tree, 2.04.429 P
the fewest roses are cropp'd from the tree 1H6 2.04. 41
a fall off of a tree. 2H6 2.01. 94
what, and wouldst climb a tree? 2.01. 96
top–branch overpeer'd jove's spreading tree, 3H6 5.02. 14
not like the fruit of such a goodly tree. 5.06. 52
that i love the tree from whence thou sprang'st, 5.07. 31
the royal tree hath left us royal fruit, | which R3 3.07.167
why, we take | from every tree, lop, bark, and H8 1.02. 96
i had none, | to bury so much gold under a tree, TIT 2.03. 2
hang him on this tree, | and by his side his 5.01. 47
now will he sit under a medlar tree, | and wish ROM 2.01. 34
nightly she sings on yond pomegranate tree. 3.05. 4
as i did sleep under this /yew tree here, | i 5.03.137
i have a tree, which grows here in my close, TIM 5.01.205
come hither, ere my tree hath felt the axe, 5.01.211
bid the tree | unfix his earth–bound root? MAC 4.01. 95
upon the next tree shall thou hang alive, | till 5.05. 38
which now, the fruit unripe, sticks on the tree, HAM 3.02.190
and by the happy hollow of a tree | escap'd the LR 2.03. 2
take the shadow of this tree | for your good 5.02. 1
"the poor soul sat /sighing by a sycamore tree, OTH 4.03. 40
i'll smell thee on the tree. 5.02. 15
then was i as a tree | whose boughs did bend CYM 3.03. 60
there like fruit, my soul, | till the tree die! 5.05.264
to taste the fruit of yon celestial tree | (or PER 1.01. 21
succeeding from so fair a tree | as your fair 1.01.114
yon little tree, yon blooming apricock! TNK 2.02.236
better lads nev'r danc'd | under green tree; 2.03. 39
give us but a tree or twain | for a maypole, and 3.05.144
the flow'r is fall'n, the tree descends. 5.01.169
the strong–neck'd steed, being tied unto a tree, VEN 263
"how like a jade he stood, tied to the tree, 391
like a green plum that hangs upon a tree, | and PP 10. 5
bird of loudest lay, | on the sole arabian tree, PHT 2
TREE'S 1 FR 0.0001 REL FR 1 V 0 P
his wonted sleep under a fresh tree's shade, 3H6 2.05. 49
TREES 31 FR 0.0035 REL FR 28 V 3 P
still climbing trees in the hesperides? LLL 4.03.338
when the sweet wind did gently kiss the trees MV 5.01. 2
the poet | did feign that orpheus drew trees, 5.01. 80
finds tongues in trees, books in the running AYL 2.01. 16
o rosalind, these trees shall be my books, | and 3.02. 5
should be hang'd and carv'd upon these trees? 3.02.173 P
i pray you mar no more trees with writing 3.02.259 P
are you he that hangs the verses on the trees, 3.02.392 P
there stands the castle, by yon tuft of trees, R2 2.03. 53
let's step into the shadow of these trees. 3.04. 25
their sweetest shade a grove of cypress trees! 2H6 3.02.323
howl'd, and hideous tempest shook down trees; 3H6 5.06. 46
their cheeks | like trees bedash'd with rain — R3 1.02.163
orpheus with his lute made trees, | and the H8 3.01. 3
the trees, though summer, yet forlorn and lean, TIT 2.03. 94
and on their skins, as on the bark of trees, 5.01.138
he hath hid himself among these trees | to be ROM 2.01. 30
under yond /yew trees lay thee all along, 5.03. 3
will these moist trees, | that have outliv'd the TIM 4.03.223
hear | that unicorns may be betray'd with trees, JC 2.01.204
have been known to move and trees to speak; MAC 3.04.122
bladed corn be lodg'd, and trees blown down; 4.01. 55
drops tears as fast as the arabian trees | their OTH 5.02.350
sheets, | the barks of trees thou brows'd. ANT 1.04. 66
the trees by th' way | should have borne men, 3.06. 46
with trees upon't that nod unto the world | and 4.14. 6
who /am no more but as the tops of trees, PER 1.02. 30
forceless flowers like sturdy trees support me; VEN 152
sing, | trees did grow and plants did spring; PP 20. 6
senseless trees they cannot hear thee, 20.21
when lofty trees i see barren of leaves, | which SON 12. 5
TREMBLE 39 FR 0.0044 REL FR 36 V 3 P
to besiege, and make his bold waves tremble, TMP 1.02.205
roar | that beasts shall tremble at thy din. 1.02.371
would entreat you, not to fear, not to tremble: MND 3.01. 41 P
may now perchance both quake and tremble here, 5.01.221
therefore tremble and depart. AYL 5.01. 57 P
blush, and tyranny | tremble at patience. WT 3.02. 32
even now i tremble | to think your father, by 4.04. 18
o, tremble! for you hear the lion roar. JN 2.01.294
but they will quake and tremble all this day. 3.01. 18
and make him tremble there? 5.01. 58
day, | but, self–affrighted, tremble at his sin. R2 3.02. 53
heavens were all on fire, the earth did tremble. 1H4 3.01. 23
such as my heart doth tremble to unfold: 2H6 2.01.162
but great men tremble when the lion roars, | and 3.01. 19
and made the forest tremble when they roar'd. 3H6 5.07. 12
what do you tremble? R3 1.02. 43
side, | tremble and start at wagging of a straw; 3.05. 7
and made to tremble | the region of my breast, H8 2.04.184
as if the world | were feverous and did tremble. COR 1.04. 61
to tremble under titus' threat'ning look. TIT 1.01.134
hands | tremble like aspen leaves upon a lute, 2.04. 45
makes my flesh tremble in their different ROM 1.05. 90
that, to hear them told, have made me tremble — 4.01. 86
it is the part of men to fear and tremble | when JC 1.03. 54
you are, | and make your bondmen tremble. 4.03. 44
that, and my firm nerves | shall never tremble. MAC 3.04.102
you tremble and look pale. HAM 1.01. 53
you that look pale, and tremble at this chance, 5.02.334
tremble, thou wretch | that hast within thee LR 3.02. 51
judgment of the heavens, that makes us tremble, 5.03.232
i tremble at it. OTH 4.01. 39 P
thief, | hear but my name, and tremble. CYM 4.02. 87
villain, be thy name, | i cannot tremble at it. 4.02. 90
good faith, | i tremble still with fear; 4.02.303
that thou wouldst tremble to receive thyself. PER 1.02. 69
i fear'd thy fortune, and my joints did tremble. VEN 642
so indeed, | that tremble at th' imagination? 668
forc'd it to tremble with her loyal fear! LUC 261
one would swear he saw them quake and tremble. 1393
TREMBLED 5 FR 0.0005 REL FR 5 V 0 P
trembled and shook; SHR 3.02.167
hath shook and trembled at th' ill neighborhood. H5 1.02.154
that tiber trembled underneath her banks | to JC 1.01. 45
that kings | have lipp'd, and trembled kissing. ANT 2.05. 30
by that you would have trembled to deny | a TNK 3.06.204
TREMBLES 9 FR 0.0010 REL FR 8 V 1 P
mark, how he trembles in his ecstasy! ERR 4.04. 51
hector trembles. LLL 5.02.687 P
me, and my inward soul | with nothing trembles; R2 2.02. 12
wretch | that trembles under his devouring paws; 3H6 1.03. 13
which of you trembles not that looks on me? R3 1.03.159
and virtue stoops and trembles at her frown; TIT 2.01. 11
the thing whereat it trembles by surmise. 2.03.219
here is a friar, that trembles, sighs, and weeps ROM 5.03.184
she trembles at his tale, | and on his neck her VEN 591
TREMBLEST 3 FR 0.0003 REL FR 3 V 0 P
thou tremblest, and the whiteness in thy cheek 2H4 1.01. 68
whose name and power | thou tremblest at, answer 2H6 1.04. 26
why tremblest thou? 3.02. 27
TREMBLING *(also trempling)*
TREMBLING 25 FR 0.0028 REL FR 22 V 3 P
thou wilt anon, i know it by thy trembling. TMP 2.02. 80 P
to enter into a quarrel with fear and trembling. ADO 2.03.195 P
nor on the birth | of trembling winter, the WT 4.04. 81
pale trembling coward, there i throw my gage, R2 1.01. 69
stand bare and naked, trembling at themselves? 3.02. 46
ran fearfully among the trembling reeds, | and 1H4 1.03.105
death, | trembling even at the name of mortimer. 1.03.144
therefore rouse up fear and trembling, and do 2H4 4.03. 14 P
and shakes his head, and trembling stands aloof, 2H6 1.01.227
the trembling lamb environed with wolves. 3H6 1.01.242
with trembling wings misdoubteth every bush; 5.06. 14
cries that with the very noise | i, trembling, R3 1.04. 61
cold fearful drops stand on my trembling flesh. 5.03.181
a trembling contribution! H8 1.02. 95
you have brought | a trembling upon rome, such COR 4.06.119
a chilling sweat o'erruns my trembling joints, TIT 2.03.212
if trembling i inhabit then, protest me | the MAC 3.04.104
and, trembling in her passion, calls it balm, VEN 27
thus stands she in a trembling ecstasy, | till, 895
but coward–like with trembling terror die. LUC 231
like to a new–kill'd bird she trembling lies; 457
marking what he tells | with trembling fear, as 511
to trembling clients be you mediators: 1020
pale cowards, marching on with trembling paces, 1391
thee befall'n, that thou dost trembling stand? 1599
TREMBLINGLY 1 FR 0.0001 REL FR 1 V 0 P
tremblingly she stood, | and on the sudden ANT 5.02.343
TREMOR 1 FR 0.0001 REL FR 1 V 0 P
i have tremor cordis on me; WT 1.02.110
TREMPLING *(also trembling)*
TREMPLING 1 FR 0.0001 REL FR 0 V 1 P
how full of chollors i am and trempling of mind! WIV 3.01. 12 P
TRENCH 1 FR 0.0001 REL FR 1 V 0 P
yea, but a little charge will trench him here, 1H4 3.01.111

TRENCHANT 1 FR 0.0001 REL FR 1 V 0 P
virgin's cheek | make soft thy trenchant sword; TIM 4.03.116
TRENCH'D 1 FR 0.0001 REL FR 1 V 0 P
upon the wide wound that the boar had trench'd VEN 1052
TRENCHED 2 FR 0.0002 REL FR 2 V 0 P
of love is as a figure | trenched in ice, which TGV 3.02. 7
with twenty trenched gashes on his head, | the MAC 3.04. 26
TRENCHER 8 FR 0.0009 REL FR 4 V 4 P
but he steps me to her trencher and steals her TGV 4.04. 9 P
the fire, | holding a trencher, jesting merrily? LLL 5.02.477
fed from my trencher, kneel'd down at the board, 2H6 4.01. 57
serve with thy trencher. COR 4.05. 49 P
he shift a trencher? ROM 1.05. 2 P
he scrape a trencher? 1.05. 2 P
more rais'd | than one which holds a trencher. TIM 1.01.120
as a morsel, cold upon | dead caesar's trencher; ANT 3.13.117
TRENCHER–FRIENDS 1 FR 0.0001 REL FR 1 V 0 P
you fools of fortune, trencher–friends, time's TIM 3.06. 96
TRENCHERING 1 FR 0.0001 REL FR 1 V 0 P
nor scrape trenchering, nor wash dish. TMP 2.02.183
TRENCHER–KNIGHT 1 FR 0.0001 REL FR 1 V 0 P
some mumble–news, some trencher–knight, some LLL 5.02.464
TRENCHERMAN 1 FR 0.0001 REL FR 0 V 1 P
he is a very valiant trencherman, he hath an ADO 1.01. 51 P
TRENCHERS 1 FR 0.0001 REL FR 1 V 0 P
there, take it to you, trenchers, cups, and all. SHR 4.01.165
TRENCHES 7 FR 0.0008 REL FR 7 V 0 P
talk'd | of sallies and retires, of trenches, 1H4 2.03. 51
it will not be, retire into your trenches. 1H6 1.05. 33
to their wives, | as they us to our trenches. COR 1.04. 42
i saw our party to their trenches driven, | and 1.06. 12
told me they had beat you to your trenches? 1.06. 40
witness these trenches made by grief and care, TIT 5.02. 23
and dig deep trenches in thy beauty's field, SON 2. 2
TRENCHING 1 FR 0.0001 REL FR 1 V 0 P
no more shall trenching war channel her fields, 1H4 1.01. 7
TRENT 5 FR 0.0005 REL FR 5 V 0 P
england, from trent and severn hitherto, | by 1H4 3.01. 73
the remnant northward lying off from trent. 3.01. 78
and here the smug and silver trent shall run 3.01.101
come, you shall have trent turn'd. 3.01.134
more famous yet 'twixt po and silver trent. TNK pr 12
TRES 4 FR 0.0004 REL FR 0 V 4 P
et tres /distingue seigneur d'angleterre. H5 4.04. 57 P
du monde, mon tres cher et devin deesse? 5.02.217 P
je vous supplie, mon tres puissant seigneur. 5.02.256 P
in french, notre tres cher fils henri, roi 5.02.339 P
TRESPASS 26 FR 0.0029 REL FR 26 V 0 P
it did base my trespass. TMP 3.03. 99
me, let me know my trespass | by its own visage. WT 1.02.265
of | (if any be) the trespass of the queen. 2.02. 61
paid down | more penitence than done trespass. 5.01. 4
a trespass that doth vex my grieved soul; R2 1.01.138
wilt thou not hide the trespass of thine own? 5.02. 89
my nephew's trespass may be well forgot, | it 1H4 5.02. 16
shall chide your trespass and return your mock H5 2.04.125
his trespass yet lives guilty in thy blood, 1H6 2.04. 94
above the felon or what trespass else. 2H6 3.01.132
i am so sorry for my trespass made | that, to 3H6 5.01. 92
o trespass sweetly urg'd! ROM 1.05.109
that not your trespass, but my madness speaks; HAM 3.04.146
your son and daughter found this trespass worth LR 2.04. 44
and yet his trespass, in our common reason OTH 3.03. 64
if e'er my will did trespass 'gainst his love, 4.02.152
i will forgive | the trespass thou hast done me, TNK 3.01. 77
so much come too short of your great trespass STM II.C 124
shalt have thy trespass cited up in rhymes, LUC 524
were | to view thy present trespass in another. 632
will cote my loathsome trespass in my looks. 812
and with my trespass never will dispense, | till 1070
and here in troy, for trespass of thine eye, 1476
words," quoth she, "shall fit the trespass best, 1613
this, | authorizing thy trespass with compare, SON 35. 6
but that your trespass now becomes a fee, | mine 120.13
/TRESPASSES 1 FR 0.0001 REL FR 1 V 0 P
/for /pilf'rings /and /most /common /trespasses LR 2.02.144
TRESPASSES 3 FR 0.0003 REL FR 3 V 0 P
to have him kill a king — poor trespasses, WT 3.02.189
his wife that's dead did trespasses to caesar; ANT 2.01. 40
shall raze you out o' th' book of trespasses TNK 1.01. 33
TRESSEL 1 FR 0.0001 REL FR 1 V 0 P
tressel and berkeley, go along with me. R3 1.02.221
TRESSES 5 FR 0.0005 REL FR 5 V 0 P
bind up those tresses. JN 3.04. 61
brandish your crystal tresses in the sky, | and 1H6 1.01. 3
not juno's mantle fairer than your tresses, TNK 1.01. 63
her careless tresses | a /wreath of bulrush 4.01. 83
before the golden tresses of the dead, | the SON 68. 5
TREY 1 FR 0.0001 REL FR 1 V 0 P
trey, blanch, and sweetheart, see, they bark at LR 3.06. 63
TREYS 1 FR 0.0001 REL FR 1 V 0 P
nay then two treys, and if you grow so nice, LLL 5.02.232
/TRIAL 2 FR 0.0002 REL FR 1 V 1 P
/want'st /thou /eyes /at /trial, /madam? LR 3.06. 24 P
/i'll /see /their /trial /first, /bring /in 3.06. 35
TRIAL 60 FR 0.0067 REL FR 49 V 11 P
make not too rash a trial of him, for | he's TMP 1.02.468
a trial, come. WIV 5.05. 88
he made trial of you only. MM 3.01.197 P
and put your trial in the villain's mouth 5.01.302
but let my trial be mine own confession. 5.01.372
they will scarcely believe this without trial. ADO 2.02. 41 P
days, | do challenge thee to trial of a man. 5.01. 66
least of thy sweet notice, bring her to trial. LLL 1.01.276 P
of your love | but that it bear this trial, and 5.02.803
then let us teach our trial patience, | because MND 1.01.152
acceptance, whose trial shall better publish his MV 4.01.165 P
eyes and gentle wishes go with me to my trial; AYL 1.02.187 P
all purity, all trial, all observance; 5.02. 98
too far in anger, lest thou hasten thy trial; AWW 2.03.212 P
make the trial of it in any constant question. TN 4.02. 48 P
so shall she have | a just and open trial. WT 2.03.205
and here beholding | his daughter's trial! 3.02.121
fleet | in dreadful trial of our kingdom's king! JN 2.01.286
in this hot trial more than we of france, 2.01.342
'tis not the trial of a woman's war, | the R2 1.01. 48
degree | or chivalrous design of knightly trial; 1.01. 81
i pray | your highness to assign our trial day. 1.01.151
order the trial, marshal, and begin. 1.03. 99
pawn, | engage it to the trial, if thou darest. 4.01. 56
pawn, | engage it to the trial, if thou dar'st. 4.01. 71
against aumerle we will enforce his trial. 4.01. 90
gage | till we assign you to your days of trial. 4.01.106
to keep him safely till his day of trial. 4.01.153
weak | to wage an instant trial with the king. 1H4 4.04. 20
this encounter, | if once they join in trial. 5.01. 85
suit, | before thou make a trial of her love? 1H6 5.03. 76
my use, | be brought against me at my trial day! 2H6 3.01.114
to keep, until your further time of trial. 3.01.138
bring me unto my trial when you will. 3.03. 8
peace | by this one bloody trial of sharp war. R3 5.02. 16
he is attach'd, | call him to present trial. H8 1.02.211
that wretch betray'd, | and without trial fell; 2.01.111
i had my trial, | and must needs say a noble one 2.01.118
have any goodness, | the trial just and noble. 2.02. 91
for if the trial of the law o'ertake ye, 3.01. 96
the duke of buckingham came from his trial. 4.01. 5
till further trial in those charges | which will 5.01.103
and our consent, for better trial of you, | from 5.02. 88
meant for his trial | and fair purgation to the 5.02.186
have record, trial did draw | bias and thwart, TRO 1.03. 14
combat, | yet in the trial much opinion dwells; 1.03.336
and therefore law shall scorn him further trial COR 3.01.267
only make trial what your love can do | for rome 5.01. 40
made it seem in the trial of his several friends TIM 3.06. 6 P
and like deceitful jades | sink in the trial. JC 4.02. 27
and it would come to immediate trial, if your HAM 5.02.168 P
my lord, the opposition of your person in trial. 5.02.172 P
and do but blow them to their trial, the bubbles 5.02.193 P
to his love, which stands | an honorable trial. ANT 1.03. 75
on them, knowing 'tis | a punishment or trial? CYM 3.06. 11
sir, | as i shall here make trial of my pray'rs, TNK 1.01.193
off | this great adventure to a second trial. 3.06.119
this trial is as 'twere i' th' night, and you 5.03. 19
him, | he takes for accidental things of trial; LUC 326
the boy for trial needs would touch my breast; SON 153.10
TRIAL–FIRE 1 FR 0.0001 REL FR 1 V 0 P
with trial–fire touch me his finger–end. WIV 5.05. 84
TRIALS 4 FR 0.0004 REL FR 4 V 0 P
thy vexations | were but my trials of thy love, TMP 4.01. 6
but the protractive trials of great jove | to TRO 1.03. 20
his comforts thrive, his trials well are spent. CYM 5.04.104
for none but such dare die in these just trials. TNK 3.06.105
TRIB *(also trip)*
TRIB 4 FR 0.0004 REL FR 0 V 4 P
trib, trib, fairies; WIV 5.04. 1 P
trib, trib, fairies; 5.04. 1 P
come, come, trib, trib. 5.04. 4 P
come, come, trib, trib. 5.04. 4 P
TRIBE 10 FR 0.0011 REL FR 8 V 2 P
cursed be my tribe | if i forgive him! MV 1.03. 51
tubal, a wealthy hebrew of my tribe, | will 1.03. 57
for suff'rance is the badge of all our tribe. 1.03.110
here comes another of the tribe; 3.01. 77 P
son | were in arabia, and thy tribe before him, COR 4.02. 24
him, | with six aufidiuses, or more, his tribe, 5.06.128
bed, | go to th' creating a whole tribe of fops, LR 1.02. 14
too hard for my wits and all the tribe of hell, OTH 1.03.357 P
the souls of all my tribe defend | from jealousy 3.03.175
threw a pearl away | richer than all his tribe; 5.02.348
TRIBES 3 FR 0.0003 REL FR 3 V 0 P
have you collected them by tribes? COR 3.03. 11
call all your tribes together, praise the gods, 5.05. 2
he insults o'er dull and speechless tribes: SON 107.12
TRIBULATION 1 FR 0.0001 REL FR 0 V 1 P
no audience but the tribulation of tower–hill or H8 5.03. 62 P
TRIBUNAL 2 FR 0.0002 REL FR 1 V 1 P
am going with my pigeons to the tribunal plebs, TIT 4.03. 93 P
i' th' market–place, on a tribunal silver'd, ANT 3.06. 3
TRIBUNE 13 FR 0.0014 REL FR 13 V 0 P
ill as you, and make me | your fellow tribune. COR 3.01. 52
as a consul, | nor yoke with him for tribune. 3.01. 57
let's hear our tribune; 3.01.192
call me their traitor, thou injurious tribune! 3.03. 69
the plebeians have got your fellow tribune, 5.04. 36
how fair the tribune speaks to calm my thoughts! TIT 1.01. 46
thanks, gentle tribune, noble brother marcus. 1.01.171
send thee by me, their tribune and their trust, 1.01.181
proud and ambitious tribune, canst thou tell? 1.01.202
no, foolish tribune, no; 1.01.343
the tribune and his nephews kneel for grace, | i 1.01.480
my gracious lord, no tribune hears you speak. 3.01. 32
to brave the tribune in his brother's hearing. 4.02. 36
TRIBUNES' 1 FR 0.0001 REL FR 1 V 0 P
if, by the tribunes' leave, and yours, good COR 3.01.280
TRIBUNES 42 FR 0.0047 REL FR 41 V 1 P
five tribunes to defend their vulgar wisdoms, COR 1.01.215
when we were chosen tribunes for the people — 1.01.254
tribunes for them!), 1.06. 43
where the dull tribunes, | that with the fusty 1.09. 6
we recommend to you, tribunes of the people, 2.02.151
and the tribunes | endue you with the people's 2.03.138
lay | a fault on us, your tribunes, that we 2.03.227
behold, these are the tribunes of the people, 3.01. 21
tribunes, give way, he shall to th' market–place 3.01. 31
should the people do with these bald tribunes? 3.01.164
tribunes! 3.01.185
you, tribunes | to th' people! 3.01.189
beseech you, tribunes, hear me but a word. 3.01.215
tribunes, withdraw a while. 3.01.225
o' th' best of them, yea, the two tribunes. 3.01.243
you worthy tribunes — 3.01.264
the noble tribunes are the people's mouths, 3.01.270
noble tribunes, | it is the humane way. 3.01.324
return to th' tribunes. 3.02. 36
away, the tribunes do attend you. 3.02.138
list to your tribunes. audience! peace, i say! 3.03. 40
and in the power of us the tribunes, we, | even 3.03.100
the gods preserve our noble tribunes! 3.03.143
and to pluck from them their tribunes for ever. 4.03. 24 P
worthy tribunes, | there is a slave, whom we 4.06. 37
the tribunes cannot do't for shame; 4.06.109
the tribunes are no soldiers, and their people 4.07. 31
a pair of tribunes that have wrack'd for rome 5.01. 16
of tribunes, such as you, | a sea and land full. 5.04. 54
tribunes, and me, a poor competitor. TIT 1.01. 63
people of rome, and people's tribunes here, | i 1.01.217
tribunes, i thank you, and this suit i make, 1.01.223
noble tribunes, stay! 3.01. 1
for these, tribunes, in the dust i write | my 3.01. 12
o reverent tribunes! 3.01. 23
the tribunes hear you not, no man is by, | and 3.01. 28
grave tribunes, once more i entreat of you — 3.01. 31
in some sort they are better than the tribunes, 3.01. 39
rome could afford no tribunes like to these. 3.01. 44
is soft as wax, tribunes more hard than stones; 3.01. 45
and tribunes with their tongues doom men to 3.01. 47
and to you the tribunes, | for this immediate CYM 3.07. 8
TRIBUTARIES 2 FR 0.0002 REL FR 2 V 0 P
what tributaries follow him to rome, | to grace JC 1.01. 33
were't twenty of the greatest tributaries | that ANT 3.13. 96
TRIBUTARY 7 FR 0.0008 REL FR 7 V 0 P
lo at this tomb my tributary tears | i render TIT 1.01.159
and make them blind with tributary tears; 3.01.269
spring, | your tributary drops belong to woe, ROM 3.02.103
king, | as england was his faithful tributary, HAM 5.02. 39
the dish, | poor tributary rivers as sweet fish. CYM 4.02. 36
to which love's eyes pays tributary gazes, | nor VEN 632
whereat each tributary subject quakes, | as when 1045
TRIBUTE 27 FR 0.0030 REL FR 19 V 8 P
th' king of naples | to give him annual tribute, TMP 1.02.113
of homage, and i know not how much tribute, 1.02.124
free thee from the tribute which thou payest, 2.01.293
redeem | the virgin tribute paid by howling troy MV 3.02. 56
take some remembrance of us, as a tribute, | not 4.01.422
and craves no other tribute at thy hands | but SHR 5.02.152
dispose, | subjected tribute to commanding love, JN 1.01.264
well, | and had the tribute of his supple knee, R2 1.04. 33
duer paid to the hearer than the turk's tribute. 2H4 3.02.308 P
swear | to pay him tribute and submit thyself, 1H6 5.04.130
head on his shoulders, unless he pay me tribute. 2H6 4.07.121 P
receive them then, the tribute that i owe, TIT 1.01.251
his majesty shall have tribute on me, the HAM 2.02.320 P
for the demand of our neglected tribute. 3.01.170
and i think | he'll grant the tribute, send th' CYM 2.04. 13
than have tidings | of any penny tribute paid. 2.04. 20
him | and his succession granted rome a tribute, 3.01. 8
come, there's no more tribute to be paid. 3.01. 34 P
why tribute? 3.01. 42 P
why should we pay tribute? 3.01. 42 P
his pocket, we will pay him tribute for light; 3.01. 44 P
else, sir, no more tribute, pray you now. 3.01. 45 P
romans did extort | this tribute from us, we 3.01. 48
thou com'st not, caius, now for tribute; 5.05. 69
promising | to pay our wonted tribute, from the 5.05.462
yet they | must yield their tribute there. TNK 1.03. 8
paying more slavish tribute than they owe. LUC 299
TRIBUTES 1 FR 0.0001 REL FR 1 V 0 P
"'look here what tributes wounded fancies sent LC 197
TRICE 5 FR 0.0005 REL FR 4 V 1 P
on a trice, so please you, | even in a dream, TMP 5.01.238
in a trice, | like to the old vice, | your need TN 4.02.123
should in this trice of time | commit a thing so LR 1.01.216
it sums up thousands in a trice. CYM 5.04.167 P
is truss'd up in a trice | to–morrow morning; TNK 3.04. 17
TRICK 53 FR 0.0060 REL FR 29 V 24 P
and i must use you | in such another trick. TMP 4.01. 37
by some sly trick blunt thurio's dull proceeding TGV 2.06. 41
nay, i remember the trick you serv'd me, when i 4.04. 35 P
didst thou ever see me do such a trick? 4.04. 39 P
in honest, civil, godly company, for this trick. WIV 1.01.182 P
that were a trick indeed! 2.02.112 P
/and i be serv'd such another trick, i'll have 3.05. 7 P
why would he for the momentary trick | be MM 3.01.113
the trick of it? 3.02. 52 P
was a mad fantastical trick of him to steal from 3.02. 92 P
my lord, i spoke it but according to the trick. 5.01.505 P
you always end with a jade's trick, i know you ADO 1.01.144 P
this can be no trick: 2.03.220 P
yet i have a trick | of the old rage. LLL 5.02.416
i see the trick an't; 5.02.460
smiles his cheek in years and knows the trick 5.02.465
and you serve me such another trick, never come AYL 4.01. 41 P
a knack, a toy, a trick, a baby's cap. SHR 4.03. 67
of every line and trick of his sweet favor. AWW 1.01. 96
a man that had this trick of melancholy /sold a 3.02. 8 P
put thyself into the trick of singularity. TN 2.05.151 P
put thyself into the trick of singularity"; 3.04. 71 P
yea, a very trick | for them to play at will. WT 2.01. 51
the trick of 's frown, his forehead, nay, the 2.03.101
are you in earnest, sir? i smell the trick on't. 4.04.643 P
he hath a trick of cordelion's face, | the JN 1.01. 85
soft, i know a trick worth two of that, i' faith 1H4 2.01. 36 P
what trick? 2.04.262 P
let's hear, jack, what trick hast thou now? 2.04.265 P
but chiefly a villainous trick of thine eye, and 2.04.404 P
up, | will have a wild trick of his ancestors. 5.02. 11
it was alway yet the trick of our english nation 2H4 1.02.214 P
war, which they trick up with new–tun'd oaths; H5 3.06. 76 P
at this instant | he bores me with some trick. H8 1.01.128
have got a speeding trick to lay down ladies. 1.03. 40
that trick of state | was a deep envious one. 2.01. 44
a juggling trick — to be secretly open. TRO 5.02. 24 P
some trick not worth an egg, shall grow dear COR 4.04. 21
the very trick on't. 4.06. 71
is it your trick to make me ope the door | that TIT 5.02. 10
this trick may chance to scath you. ROM 1.05. 84
as good a trick as ever hangman serv'd thief. TIM 2.02. 94 P
that for a fantasy and trick of fame | go to HAM 4.04. 61
but yet | it is our trick. 4.07.187
fine revolution, and we had the trick to see't. 5.01. 91 P
the trick of that voice i do well remember; LR 4.06.106
this is a trick to put me from my suit. OTH 3.04. 87
how comes this trick upon him? 4.02.129
is't not your trick? ANT 5.02. 75
to prince it much | beyond the trick of others. CYM 3.03. 86
this fellow has a vengeance trick o' th' hip. TNK 2.03. 70
him, tell her so, | for a trick that i know. 4.01.123
all these must be boys, | he has the trick on't; 4.01.132
TRICK'D 1 FR 0.0001 REL FR 1 V 0 P
gules, horridly trick'd | with blood of fathers, HAM 2.02.457
TRICKING 1 FR 0.0001 REL FR 1 V 0 P
us properties | and tricking for our fairies. WIV 4.04. 79

TRICKLING 1 FR 0.0001 REL FR 1 V 0 P
not, sweet queen, for trickling tears are vain. 1H4 2.04.391
TRICKS 34 FR 0.0038 REL FR 23 V 11 P
mad, and play'd | some tricks of desperation. TMP 1.02.210
do you put tricks upon 's with salvages and men 2.02. 58 P
and we will yet have more tricks with falstaff. WIV 3.03.191 P
plays such fantastic tricks before high heaven MM 2.02.121
that stands on tricks when i am undispos'd: ERR 1.02. 80
some tricks, some quillets, how to cheat the LLL 4.03.284
such tricks hath strong imagination, | that, if MND 5.01. 18
a thousand raw tricks of these bragging jacks, MV 3.04. 77
that teacheth tricks eleven and twenty long, SHR 4.02. 57
my horses be well look'd to, without any tricks. AWW 4.05. 59 P
if i put any tricks upon 'em, sir, they shall be 4.05. 60 P
they shall be jades' tricks, which are their own 4.05. 61 P
tricks he hath had in him, which gentlemen have. 5.03.239 P
of my lord's tricks and yours when you were boys WT 1.02. 61
these tardy tricks of yours will, on my life, 2H4 4.03. 28
but i, that am not shap'd for sportive tricks, R3 1.01. 14
abhor | this dilatory sloth and tricks of rome. H8 2.04.238
but in this point | all his tricks founder, and 3.02. 40
a red murrion a' thy jade's tricks! TRO 2.01. 20 P
and what needs /these tricks? 5.01. 13 P
you are never without your tricks; COR 2.03. 34 P
with twenty popish tricks and ceremonies, TIT 5.01. 76
there are no tricks in plain and simple faith; JC 4.02. 22
says she hears | there's tricks i' th' world, HAM 4.05. 5
that i, in forgery of shapes and tricks, | come 4.07. 89
his cases, his tenures, and his tricks? 5.01.100 P
these are unsightly tricks. LR 2.04.157
if such tricks as these strip you out of your OTH 2.01.171 P
a false disloyal knave | are tricks of custom; 3.03.122
'tis one of those odd tricks which sorrow shoots ANT 4.02. 14
of courts, of princes, of the tricks in war. CYM 3.03. 15
hath taught them scornful tricks, and such VEN 501
"this glove to wanton tricks | is not inur'd; LUC 320
show, | the tricks and toys that in them lurk, PP 18.39
TRICKSY 2 FR 0.0002 REL FR 2 V 0 P
my tricksy spirit! TMP 5.01.226
him, that for a tricksy word | defy the matter. MV 3.05. 69
TRIDENT 2 FR 0.0002 REL FR 2 V 0 P
waves tremble, | yea, his dread trident shake. TMP 1.02.206
he would not flatter neptune for his trident, COR 3.01.255
TRIED 24 FR 0.0027 REL FR 23 V 1 P
man, | not being tried and tutor'd in the world: TGV 1.03. 21
i have tried. ADO 5.02. 36 P
being ten times undervalued to tried gold? MV 2.07. 53
"the fire seven times tried this: 2.09. 63
seven times tried that judgment is, | that did 2.09. 64
in friendship | first tried our soldiership! AWW 1.02. 26
you had only in your silent judgment tried it, WT 2.01.171
pushes 'gainst our heart — the party tried, 3.02. 2
majesty, which, being touch'd and tried, JN 3.01.100
let this dissension first be tried by fight, 1H6 4.01.116
left i the court, to see this quarrel tried. 2H6 2.03. 53
to accuse it, and | disdainful to be tried by't: H8 2.04.123
if my actions | were tried by ev'ry tongue, 3.01. 35
touch'd his spirit | and tried his inclination; COR 2.03.192
not, | for he hath still been tried a holy man. ROM 4.03. 29
he might have tried lord lucius or lucullus; TIM 3.03. 2
but he's a tried and valiant soldier. JC 4.01. 28
that we have tried the utmost of our friends, 4.03.214
friends thou hast, and their adoption tried, HAM 1.03. 62
holding out gold that's by the touchstone tried; PER 2.02. 37
in a field | that their crowns' titles tried. TNK 3.01. 22
the title of a kingdom may be tried | out of 5.03. 33
who should say, "lo thus my strength is tried; VEN 280
are but dreams till their effects be tried, LUC 353
TRIER 1 FR 0.0001 REL FR 1 V 0 P
to say extremities was the trier of spirits, COR 4.01. 4
TRIES 1 FR 0.0001 REL FR 1 V 0 P
that mother tries a merciless conclusion | who, LUC 1160
TRIFLE 27 FR 0.0030 REL FR 19 V 8 P
but | for every trifle are they set upon me, TMP 2.02. 8
or some enchanted trifle to abuse me | (as late 5.01.112
alas, how love can trifle with itself! TGV 4.04.183
hang the trifle, woman! WIV 2.01. 46 P
here's a small trifle of wives! MV 2.02.161 P
we trifle time. 4.01.298
this ring, good sir, alas, it is a trifle! 4.01.430
but a trifle neither, in good faith, if the AWW 2.02. 34 P
mistress, | which he counts but a trifle. WT 5.01.224
"a trifle, a trifle." 1H4 2.04.108 P
"a trifle, a trifle." 2.04.108 P
a trifle, some eight–penny matter. 3.03.104 P
that for a trifle that was bought with blood! 1H6 4.01.150
i may perceive | these cardinals trifle with me; H8 2.04.237
come, lords, we trifle time away; 5.02.212
here, my lord, a trifle of our love. TIM 1.02.207
thing he ow'd, | as 'twere a careless trifle. MAC 1.04. 11
i fear'd he did but trifle | and meant to wrack HAM 2.01.109
and himself upbraids us | on every trifle. LR 1.03. 7
why i do trifle thus with his despair | is done 4.06. 33
that's but a trifle here. 5.03.296
thus would play and trifle with your reverence. OTH 1.01.132
(more than indeed belong'd to such a trifle), 5.02.228
is dead, or she's outpriz'd by a trifle. CYM 1.04. 81 P
else, never trifle, | but take our lives, duke. TNK 3.06.260
as one would think, for such a trifle. 4.03. 46 P
way, | each trifle under truest bars to thrust, SON 48. 2
TRIFLED 1 FR 0.0001 REL FR 1 V 0 P
this sore night | hath trifled former knowings. MAC 2.04. 4
TRIFLER 1 FR 0.0001 REL FR 1 V 0 P
away, | away, you trifler! 1H4 2.03. 90
TRIFLES 17 FR 0.0019 REL FR 13 V 4 P
dispense with trifles. WIV 2.01. 47 P
knacks, trifles, nosegays, sweetmeats — MND 1.01. 34
and sail upon the land | to fetch me trifles, 2.01.133
hence is it that we make trifles of terrors, AWW 2.03. 4 P
let him that makes but trifles of his eyes WT 2.03. 63
likewise a snapper–up of unconsider'd trifles. 4.03. 26 P
know | she prizes not such trifles as these are. 4.04.357
my father will grant precious things as trifles. 5.01.222
his tyranny for trifles, his own bastardy, | as R3 3.07. 9
plate, jewels, and such–like trifles — nothing TIM 3.02. 22 P
win us with honest trifles, to betray 's | in MAC 1.03.125
trifles light as air | are to the jealious OTH 3.03.322
that i some lady trifles have reserv'd, ANT 5.02.165
loss, so in our trifles | i still win of you. CYM 1.01.120
come, gentlemen, we sit too long on trifles, PER 2.03. 92
trifles, unwitnessed with eye or ear, | thy VEN 1023
but thou, to whom my jewels trifles are, | most SON 48. 5
TRIFLING 5 FR 0.0005 REL FR 4 V 1 P
but this is trifling, | and all the more it TMP 3.01. 79
if it were not for one trifling respect, i could WIV 2.01. 45 P
we have a trifling foolish banquet towards. ROM 1.05.122
when, for some trifling present, you have bid me TIM 2.02.136
for hamlet, and the trifling of his favor, HAM 1.03. 5
TRIGON 1 FR 0.0001 REL FR 0 V 1 P
and look whether the fiery trigon, his man, be 2H4 2.04.265 P
/TRILL'D 1 FR 0.0001 REL FR 1 V 0 P
/now /and /then /an /ample /tear /trill'd /down LR 4.03. 12
/TRIM* 1 FR 0.0001 REL FR 1 V 0 P
young abraham cupid, he that shot so /trim, ROM 2.01. 13
TRIM* 22 FR 0.0024 REL FR 20 V 2 P
where we, in all our trim, freshly beheld | our TMP 5.01.236
look | to have my pardon, trim it handsomely. 5.01.294
the ship is in her trim, the merry wind | blows ERR 4.01. 90
are only turn'd into tongue, and trim ones too. ADO 4.01.321 P
trim gallants, full of courtship and of state. LLL 5.02.363
a trim exploit, a manly enterprise, | to conjure MND 3.02.157
they come like sacrifices in their trim, | and 1H4 4.01.113
a trim reckoning! 5.01.135 P
but, by the mass, our hearts are in the trim; H5 4.03.115
our ladies | will have of these trim vanities! H8 1.03. 38
there's a trim rabble let in. 5.03. 71
o, this is trim! TRO 4.05. 33
come, come, thersites, help to trim my tent; 5.01. 45
camp, i give him, | with all his trim belonging; COR 1.09. 62
trim sport for them which had the doing of it. TIT 5.01. 96
go waken juliet, go and trim her up, | i'll go ROM 4.04. 25
early though't be, have on their riveted trim, ANT 4.04. 22
like one another's glass to trim them by; PER 1.04. 27
on death–beds blowing, | larks'–heels trim; TNK 1.01. 12
flowers are sweet, their colors fresh and trim, VEN 1079
when proud–pied april (dress'd in all his trim) SON 98. 2
yet their purpos'd trim | piec'd not his grace, LC 118
TRIMLY 1 FR 0.0001 REL FR 1 V 0 P
there a certain lord, neat, and trimly dress'd, 1H4 1.03. 33
/TRIMM'D 1 FR 0.0001 REL FR 1 V 0 P
/and /being /now /trimm'd /in /thine /own 2H4 1.03. 94
TRIMM'D 12 FR 0.0013 REL FR 11 V 1 P
part, | and i was trimm'd in madam julia's gown, TGV 4.04.161
bed | on purpose trimm'd up for semiramis. SHR in.2. 39
is supper ready, the house trimm'd, rushes 4.01. 46 P
that he had not so trimm'd and dress'd his land R2 3.04. 56
trimm'd up your praises with a princely tongue, 1H4 5.02. 56
trimm'd like a younker prancing to his love! 3H6 2.01. 24
do a vessel follow | that is new trimm'd, but H8 1.02. 80
cut her hands, and trimm'd her as thou sawest. TIT 5.01. 93
and cut, and trimm'd, and 'twas | trim sport for 5.01. 95
are | who, trimm'd in forms and visages of duty, OTH 1.01. 50
his banners sable, trimm'd with rich expense, PER 5.ch. 19
born, | and needy nothing trimm'd in jollity, SON 66. 3
TRIMMING 2 FR 0.0002 REL FR 2 V 0 P
detestable villain, call'st thou that trimming? TIT 5.01. 94
i found her trimming up the diadem | on her dead ANT 5.02.342
TRIMS 1 FR 0.0001 REL FR 1 V 0 P
and forget | your laborsome and dainty trims, CYM 3.04.164
TRINCULO 15 FR 0.0017 REL FR 1 V 14 P
for i am trinculo — be not afeard — thy good TMP 2.02.101 P
be not afeard — thy good friend trinculo. 2.02.102 P
if thou beest trinculo, come forth. 2.02.103 P
thou art very trinculo indeed! 2.02.105 P
trinculo, the king and all our company else 2.02.174 P
fellow trinculo, we'll fill him by and by again. 2.02.176 P
trinculo, keep a good tongue in your head. 3.02. 35 P
i will stand, and so shall trinculo. 3.02. 41 P
trinculo, if you trouble him any more in 's tale 3.02. 48 P
trinculo, run into no further danger. 3.02. 68 P
and trinculo and thyself shall be viceroys. 3.02.108 P
dost thou like the plot, trinculo? 3.02.109 P
come on, trinculo, let us sing. 3.02.120 P
put off that gown, trinculo. 4.01.227 P
and trinculo is reeling ripe. 5.01.279
TRINCULO'S 1 FR 0.0001 REL FR 0 V 1 P
if any be trinculo's legs, these are they. TMP 2.02.104 P
TRINCULOS 1 FR 0.0001 REL FR 0 V 1 P
can he vent trinculos? TMP 2.02.107 P
TRINKETS 3 FR 0.0003 REL FR 2 V 1 P
as if my trinkets had been hallow'd and brought WT 4.04.601 P
we'll see your trinkets here all forthcoming. 2H6 1.04. 53
get off your trinkets, you shall want nought. TNK 3.03. 52
TRIP *(also trib)*
TRIP 14 FR 0.0015 REL FR 11 V 3 P
and, as you trip, still pinch him to your time. WIV 5.05. 92
trip and go, my sweet, deliver this paper into LLL 4.02.140 P
in silence sad | trip we after night's shade. MND 4.01. 96
trip away; 5.01.421
trip, audrey, trip, audrey! i attend, i attend. AYL 5.01. 62 P
trip, audrey, trip, audrey! i attend, i attend. 5.01. 62 P
trip no further, pretty sweeting; TN 2.03. 42
that thine own trip shall be thine overthrow? 5.01.167
to trip the course of law and blunt the sword 2H4 5.02. 87
then trip him, that his heels may kick at heaven HAM 3.03. 93
these her women | can trip me, if i err, who CYM 5.05. 35
of tyre | are excellent in making ladies trip, PER 2.03.102
come, lass, let's trip it. TNK 3.05. 89
ear, | or like a fairy, trip upon the green, VEN 146
TRIPARTITE 1 FR 0.0001 REL FR 1 V 0 P
and our indentures tripartite are drawn, | which 1H4 3.01. 79
TRIPE 1 FR 0.0001 REL FR 1 V 0 P
how say you to a fat tripe finely broil'd? SHR 4.03. 20
TRIPE–VISAG'D 1 FR 0.0001 REL FR 0 V 1 P
thee what, thou damn'd tripe–visag'd rascal, and 2H4 5.04. 8 P
TRIPLE 4 FR 0.0004 REL FR 4 V 0 P
that do run | by the triple hecat's team | from MND 5.01.384
darling, | he bade me store up, as a triple eye, AWW 2.01.108
and set the triple crown upon his head — | that 2H6 1.03. 63
him | the triple pillar of the world transform'd ANT 1.01. 12
TRIPLE–TURN'D 1 FR 0.0001 REL FR 1 V 0 P
triple–turn'd whore! ANT 4.12. 13
TRIPLEX 1 FR 0.0001 REL FR 0 V 1 P
the triplex, sir, is a good tripping measure, or TN 5.01. 37 P
TRIPOLI 1 FR 0.0001 REL FR 1 V 0 P
rome, | and so to tripoli, if god lend me life. SHR 4.02. 76
TRIPOLIS 3 FR 0.0003 REL FR 1 V 2 P
he hath an argosy bound to tripolis, another to MV 1.03. 18 P
hath an argosy cast away, coming from tripolis. 3.01.101 P
from tripolis, from mexico, and england, | from 3.02.268
TRIPP'D 5 FR 0.0005 REL FR 2 V 3 P
orlando, that tripp'd up the wrastler's heels, AYL 3.02.212 P
by this we gather | you have tripp'd since. WT 1.02. 76
nor tripp'd neither, you base football player. LR 1.04. 86 P
is it two days since i tripp'd up thy heels, and 2.02. 29 P
flattering his displeasure, | tripp'd me behind; 2.02.119
TRIPPING 5 FR 0.0005 REL FR 4 V 1 P
cry "so, so," | each one, tripping on his toe, TMP 4.01. 46
sir, is a good tripping measure, or the bells of TN 5.01. 38 P
maids | like amazons come tripping after drums, JN 5.02.155
and all the greekish girls shall tripping sing, TRO 3.03.211
vow'd chaste life to keep | came tripping by, SON 154. 4
TRIPPINGLY 2 FR 0.0002 REL FR 1 V 1 P
after me, | sing, and dance it trippingly. MND 5.01.396
pronounc'd it to you, trippingly on the tongue, HAM 3.02. 2 P
TRIPS 1 FR 0.0001 REL FR 1 V 0 P
the earth, in love with thee, thy footing trips, VEN 722
/TRISTFUL 1 FR 0.0001 REL FR 1 V 0 P
god's sake, lords, convey my /tristful queen, 1H4 2.04.393
TRITON 1 FR 0.0001 REL FR 1 V 0 P
hear you this triton of the minnows? COR 3.01. 89
TRIUMPH 49 FR 0.0055 REL FR 43 V 6 P
art thou led in triumph? MM 3.02. 44 P
air, would i might triumph so! LLL 4.03.108
how will he triumph, leap, and laugh at it! 4.03.146
with pomp, with triumph, and with revelling. MND 1.01. 19
pack of you | that triumph thus upon my misery! SHR 4.03. 34
of twenty thousand men | did triumph in my face, R2 3.02. 77
should grace the triumph of great bullingbrook? 3.04. 99
when triumph is become an alehouse guest? 5.01. 15
into | for gay apparel 'gainst the triumph day. 5.02. 66
o, thou art a perpetual triumph, an everlasting 1H4 3.03. 41 P
on, | and rebels' arms triumph in massacres! 5.04. 14
france, triumph in thy glorious prophetess! 1H6 1.06. 8
let frantic talbot triumph for a while, | and 3.03. 5
or one that at a triumph, having vow'd | to try 5.05. 31
thou didst ride in triumph through the streets. 2H6 2.04. 14
which i will bear in triumph to the king, 4.10. 83
so triumph thieves upon their conquer'd booty, 3H6 1.04. 63
in thy sex | to triumph like an amazonian trull 1.04.114
mind | still ride in triumph over all mischance. 3.03. 18
room, | and triumph, henry, in thy day of doom. 5.06. 93
we have not yet set down this day of triumph. R3 3.04. 42
o harry's wife, triumph not in my woes! 4.04. 59
will triumph o'er my person, which i weigh not, H8 5.01.124
coffin'd home, | that weep'st to see me triumph? COR 2.01.177
but safer triumph is this funeral pomp, | that TIT 1.01.176
whom thou in triumph long | hast prisoner held, 2.01. 14
and in their triumph die, like fire and powder, ROM 2.06. 10
he /gone in triumph, and mercutio slain! 3.01.122
to see caesar, and to rejoice in his triumph. JC 1.01. 31 P
that comes in triumph over pompey's blood? 1.01. 51
bring him with triumph home unto his house. 3.02. 49
battle, | you are contented to be led in triumph 5.01.108
thus bray out | the triumph of his pledge. HAM 1.04. 12
fleet, every man put himself into triumph; OTH 2.02. 4 P
do /you triumph, roman? do you triumph? 4.01.118 P
do /you triumph, roman? do you triumph? 4.01.118 P
be thou sorry | to follow caesar in his triumph, ANT 3.13.136
thy deserving, | and blemish caesar's triumph. 4.12. 33
false–play'd my glory | unto an enemy's triumph. 4.14. 20
life in rome | would be eternal in our triumph. 5.01. 66
he'll lead me then in triumph? 5.02.109
are the knights ready to begin the triumph? PER 2.02. 1
to an honor'd triumph strangely furnished. 2.02. 53
him go, | rather than triumph in so false a foe. LUC 77
showing life's triumph in the map of death, 402
may blow, | air, would i might triumph so! PP 16.10
whilst i, whom fortune of such triumph bars, SON 25. 3
being had, to triumph, being lack'd, to hope. 52.14
doth tell my body that he may | triumph in love; 151. 8
TRIUMPHANT 13 FR 0.0014 REL FR 12 V 1 P
of color like the red rose on triumphant brier, MND 3.01. 94
england, bound in with the triumphant sea, R2 2.01. 61
which his triumphant father's hand had won. 2.01.181
like captives bound to a triumphant car. 1H6 1.01. 22
triumphant death, smear'd with captivity, 4.07. 3
and now to london with triumphant march, | there 3H6 2.06. 87
secure, | i would be so triumphant as i am? R3 3.02. 82
bound with triumphant garlands will i come | and 4.04.333
praise the gods, | and make triumphant fires! COR 5.05. 3
i'll bury thee in a triumphant grave. ROM 5.03. 83
she's a most triumphant lady, if report be ANT 2.02.184 P
shall set thee on triumphant chariots, and | put 3.01. 10
doth point out thee | as his triumphant prize. SON 151.10
TRIUMPHANTLY 3 FR 0.0003 REL FR 3 V 0 P
dance in duke theseus' house triumphantly, | and MND 4.01. 89
who are at hand, triumphantly displayed, | to JN 2.01.309
else | triumphantly tread on thy country's ruin, COR 5.03.116
TRIUMPH'D 3 FR 0.0003 REL FR 3 V 0 P
thus, | i never had triumph'd upon a scot. 1H4 5.03. 15
antony, | but antony's hath triumph'd on itself. ANT 4.15. 15
which triumph'd in that sky of his delight; LUC 12
TRIUMPHER 1 FR 0.0001 REL FR 1 V 0 P
gracious triumpher in the eyes of rome! TIT 1.01.170
TRIUMPHERATE 1 FR 0.0001 REL FR 1 V 0 P
that lepidus of the triumpherate | should be ANT 3.06. 28
TRIUMPHERS 1 FR 0.0001 REL FR 1 V 0 P
and enter in our ears like great triumphers | in TIM 5.01.196
TRIUMPHERY 1 FR 0.0001 REL FR 1 V 0 P
thou makest the triumphery, the corner–cap of LLL 4.03. 51
TRIUMPHING 4 FR 0.0004 REL FR 4 V 0 P
so ridest thou triumphing in my woe. LLL 4.03. 34
as too triumphing, how mine enemies | to–day at R3 3.04. 89
heart, and there | ride on the pants triumphing! ANT 4.08. 16
you might behold triumphing in their faces; LUC 1388
TRIUMPHS 13 FR 0.0014 REL FR 13 V 0 P
we will include all jars | with triumphs, mirth, TGV 5.04.161
do these justs and triumphs hold? R2 5.02. 52
and told him of those triumphs held at oxford. 5.03. 14
here's the heart that triumphs in their death, 3H6 2.04. 8
that we spend the time | with stately triumphs, 5.07. 43
are brought to rome | to beautify thy triumphs, TIT 1.01.110

and triumphs over chance in honor's bed. 1.01.178
all thy conquests, glories, triumphs, spoils, JC 3.01.149
triumphs for nothing, and lamenting toys, | is CYM 4.02.193
in honor of whose birth these triumphs are, PER 2.02. 5
being on shore, honoring of neptune's triumphs, 5.01. 17
the conquer'd triumphs, | the victor has the TNK 5.04.113
and stories | his victories, his triumphs, and VEN 1014
TRIUMVIRATE *(see triumpherate)*
TRIUMVIRI *(see triumphery)*
TRIVIAL 7 FR 0.0008 REL FR 5 V 2 P
make trivial price of serious things we have, AWW 5.03. 61
and yet we have but trivial argument, | more 2H6 3.01.241
but the respects thereof are nice and trivial, R3 3.07.175
hasty and tinder–like upon too trivial motion; COR 2.01. 51 P
i'll wipe away all trivial fond records, | all HAM 1.05. 99
when we debate | our trivial difference loud, we ANT 2.02. 21
importance of so slight and trivial a nature. CYM 1.04. 42 P
TROAT *(also throat)*
TROAT 1 FR 0.0001 REL FR 0 V 1 P
i will cut his troat in de park; WIV 1.04.108 P
TROD 14 FR 0.0015 REL FR 10 V 4 P
he trod the water, | whose enmity he flung aside TMP 2.01.116
any emperor that ever trod on neat's–leather. 2.02. 70 P
here's a maze trod indeed | through forth–rights 3.03. 2
this is as strange a maze as e'er men trod, 5.01.242
i have trod a measure, i have flatt'red a lady, AYL 5.04. 44 P
had you first died, and he been thus trod down, R2 2.03.126
ever his black shoe trod upon god's ground and H5 4.07.142 P
but now mischance hath trod my title down, | and 3H6 3.03. 8
would i had never trod this english earth, | or H8 3.01.143
say wolsey, that once trod the ways of glory, 3.02.435
but for thy sword and fortune, trod upon them —
TIM 4.03. 96
as proper men as ever trod upon neat's–leather JC 1.01. 25 P
i trod upon a worm against my will, | but i wept PER 4.01. 78
a bolder traitor never trod thy ground, | a TNK 3.06.141
TRODDEN 7 FR 0.0008 REL FR 5 V 2 P
if we walk not in the trodden paths, our very AYL 1.03. 14 P
keep my need up, and faith is trodden down! JN 3.01.216
though the camomile, the more it is trodden on, 1H4 2.04.400 P
this, | where stain'd nobility lies trodden on, 5.04. 13
the smallest worm will turn, being trodden on, 3H6 2.02. 17
a little fire is quickly trodden out, | which, 4.08. 7
murmur stay, | for misery is trodden on by many, VEN 707
TROIANT *(also troyan)*
TROIANT 1 FR 0.0001 REL FR 1 V 0 P
caesars and with cannibals | and troiant greeks? 2H4 2.04.167
/TROIEN 1 FR 0.0001 REL FR 1 V 0 P
/and /timbria, /helias, /chetas, /troien, | /and TRO pr 16
TROILUS' 3 FR 0.0003 REL FR 2 V 1 P
white hair that helen spied on troilus' chin. TRO 1.02.151 P
'tis troilus' fault. 4.04.143
go, go, my servant, take thou troilus' horse, 5.05. 1
TROILUS 87 FR 0.0098 REL FR 44 V 43 P
swimmer, troilus the first employer of pandars, ADO 5.02. 31 P
troilus methinks mounted the troyan walls, | and MV 5.01. 4
troilus had his brains dash'd out with a grecian AYL 4.01. 97 P
where's my spaniel troilus? SHR 4.01.150
sir, to bring a cressida to this troilus. TN 3.01. 52 P
let him to field, troilus, alas, hath none. TRO 1.01. 5
how now, prince troilus, wherefore not a–field? 1.01.105
troilus, by menelaus. 1.01.110
and there's troilus will not come far behind him 1.02. 57 P
let them take heed of troilus; 1.02. 58 P
who, troilus? 1.02. 60 P
troilus is the better man of the two. 1.02. 60 P
what, not between troilus and hector? 1.02. 63 P
well, i say troilus is troilus. 1.02. 66 P
well, i say troilus is troilus. 1.02. 66 P
no, nor hector is not troilus in some degrees. 1.02. 69 P
himself? alas, poor troilus, i would he were! 1.02. 72 P
well, troilus, well, i would my heart were in 1.02. 78 P
no, hector is not a better man than troilus. 1.02. 80 P
helen herself swore th' other day that troilus, 1.02. 93 P
then troilus should have too much: 1.02.101 P
tongue had commended troilus for a copper nose. 1.02.105 P
but to prove to you that helen loves troilus — 1.02.128 P
troilus will stand to the proof, if you'll prove 1.02.129 P
troilus! 1.02.131 P
they pass by, but mark troilus above the rest. 1.02.183 P
but mark troilus; 1.02.188 P
when comes troilus? 1.02.193 P
i'll show you troilus anon. 1.02.194 P
would i could see troilus now! 1.02.217 P
you shall see troilus anon. 1.02.217 P
i marvel where troilus is. 1.02.219 P
i marvel where troilus is. 1.02.224 P
hark, do you not hear the people cry "troilus"? 1.02.225 P
'tis troilus! 1.02.228 P
brave troilus, the prince of chivalry! 1.02.228 P
o brave troilus! 1.02.231 P
go thy way, troilus, go thy way! 1.02.236 P
i could live and die in the eyes of troilus. 1.02.243 P
be such a man as troilus than agamemnon and all 1.02.245 P
the greeks achilles, a better man than troilus. 1.02.248 P
ay, a token from troilus. 1.02.280 P
but more in troilus thousandfold i see | than in 1.02.284
now, youthful troilus, do not these high strains 2.02.113
paris and troilus, you have both said well, 2.02.163
to speak with paris from the prince troilus. 3.01. 39 P
most esteem'd friend, your brother troilus — 3.01. 64 P
how chance my brother troilus went not? 3.01.138 P
troilus shall be such to cressid as what envy 3.02. 95 P
truth can speak truest not truer than troilus. 3.02. 98 P
prince troilus, i have lov'd you night and day 3.02.114
world to come | approve their truth by troilus. 3.02.174
"as true as troilus" shall crown up the verse, 3.02.182
my brother troilus lodges there to–night. 4.01. 43
troilus had rather troy were borne to greece 4.01. 47
is not prince troilus here? 4.02. 47
must to thy father, and be gone from troilus. 4.02. 92 P
no soul so near me | as the sweet troilus. 4.02. 99
crown of falsehood, | if ever she leave troilus! 4.02.101
sobs and break my heart | with sounding troilus. 4.02.109
good my brother troilus, | tell you the lady 4.03. 3
altar, and thy brother troilus | a priest there 4.03. 8
o troilus, troilus! 4.04. 13
o troilus, troilus! 4.04. 13
what, and from troilus too? 4.04. 31
from troy and troilus. 4.04. 32
brother troilus! 4.04. 99
o, be not mov'd, prince troilus. 4.04.129
they call him troilus, and on him erect | a 4.05.108
aeneas, call my brother troilus to me, | and 4.05.154
at menelaus' tent, most princely troilus. 4.05.279
troilus, farewell! 5.02.107
may worthy troilus be half attached | with that 5.02.161
no, faith, young troilus, doff thy harness, 5.03. 31
good troilus, chide me for it. 5.03. 39
troilus, i would not have you fight to–day. 5.03. 50
roaring for troilus, who hath done to–day | mad 5.05. 37
troilus, thou coward troilus! 5.05. 43
troilus, thou coward troilus! 5.05. 43
troilus, thou coward troilus, show thy head! 5.06. 1
troilus, thou coward troilus, show thy head! 5.06. 1
troilus, i say, where's troilus? 5.06. 2
troilus, i say, where's troilus? 5.06. 2
troilus, i say, what, troilus! 5.06. 5
troilus, i say, what, troilus! 5.06. 5
yea, troilus? 5.06. 12
here manly hector faints, here troilus sounds, LUC 1486
TROILUSES 1 FR 0.0001 REL FR 0 V 1 P
let all constant men be troiluses, all false TRO 3.02.203 P
TROJAN *(see troiant, troyan, etc.)*
TROLL 1 FR 0.0001 REL FR 1 V 0 P
will you troll the catch | you taught me but TMP 3.02.117
TROLL–MY–DAMES 1 FR 0.0001 REL FR 0 V 1 P
i have known to go about with troll–my–dames. WT 4.03. 87 P
TROMPERIES 1 FR 0.0001 REL FR 0 V 1 P
langues des hommes sont pleines de tromperies. H5 5.02.116 P
TROMPERY *(also trumpery)*
TROMPERY 1 FR 0.0001 REL FR 0 V 1 P
i have sold all my trompery; WT 4.04.597 P
TROMPET *(also trumpet)*
TROMPET 1 FR 0.0001 REL FR 0 V 1 P
ish give over, the trompet sound the retreat. H5 3.02. 89 P
/TROOP 2 FR 0.0002 REL FR 2 V 0 P
/it /not /shame /thee /in /so /fair /a /troop R2 4.01.231
/troop /in /the /throngs /of /military /men; 2H4 4.01. 62
TROOP 26 FR 0.0029 REL FR 23 V 3 P
troop on. WIV 1.03.105 P
where is nan now, and her troop of fairies, and 5.03. 11 P
and at her heels a huge infectious troop | of ERR 5.01. 81
here and there, | troop home to churchyards. MND 3.02.382
the troop is past. AWW 3.05. 93
i, with a troop of florentines, will suddenly 3.06. 22 P
and like a jolly troop of huntsmen come | our JN 2.01.321
is not the lady constance in this troop? 2.01.540
having full scarce six thousand in his troop, 1H6 1.01.112
cade | oppose himself against a troop of kerns, 2H6 3.01.361
methought he bore him in the thickest troop | as 3H6 2.01. 13
by this at daintry, with a puissant troop. 5.01. 6
from troop to troop | went through the army, R3 5.03. 70
from troop to troop | went through the army, 5.03. 70
a noble troop of strangers, | for so they seem. H8 1.04. 53
saw you not even now a blessed troop | invite me 4.02. 87
find a way out | to let the troop pass fairly; 5.03. 85
yonder comes the troop. TRO 4.05. 64
but i beseech you, | what says the other troop? COR 1.01.204
there will the lovely roman ladies troop; TIT 2.01.113
unfurnish'd of her well–beseeming troop? 2.03. 56
all the large effects | that troop with majesty. LR 1.01.132
stratagem, to shoe | a troop of horse with felt. 4.06.185
here comes another troop to seek for you. OTH 1.02. 54
dreadful clap of thunder | break from the troop. TNK 3.06. 84
fever's end, | to this troop come thou not near. PHT 8
TROOPING 1 FR 0.0001 REL FR 1 V 0 P
so shows a snowy dove trooping with crows, | as ROM 1.05. 48
TROOPS 32 FR 0.0036 REL FR 31 V 1 P
in troops i have dispers'd them 'bout the isle. TMP 1.02.220
holy pilgrim, | but till the troops come by, | i AWW 3.05. 40
the troops are all scatter'd, and the commanders 4.03.132 P
this /unhair'd sauciness and boyish troops, JN 5.02.133
hath beaten down young hotspur and his troops, 2H4 in 25
from the best–temper'd courage in his troops, 1.01.115
our english troops retire, i cannot stay them; 1H6 1.05. 2
drives back our troops and conquers as she lists 1.05. 22
they did amongst the troops of armed men | leap 2.02. 24
and all the troops of english after him. 3.03. 32
your troops of horsemen with his bands of foot, 4.01.165
two mightier troops than that the dolphin led, 4.03. 7
it through the court with troops of ladies, 2H6 1.03. 77
and they have troops of soldiers at their beck? 3H6 1.01. 68
yet let us all together to our troops, | and 2.03. 49
some troops pursue the bloody–minded queen, 2.06. 33
and with his troops doth march amain to london, 4.08. 4
such troops of citizens to come to him, | his R3 3.07. 85
be the thronging troops that followed thee? 4.04. 96
or gild again the noble troops that waited H8 3.02.411
from our troops i stray'd | to gaze upon a TIT 5.01. 20
i'll cheer up | my discontented troops, and lay TIM 3.05.114
till he have brought thee up to yonder troops JC 5.03. 16
whether yond troops are friend or enemy. 5.03. 18
as honor, love, obedience, troops of friends, MAC 5.03. 25
our troops set forth to–morrow, stay with us; LR 4.05. 16
farewell the plumed troops and the big wars OTH 3.03.349
of heaven, | rais'd by your populous troops. ANT 3.06. 50
dido and her aeneas shall want troops, | and all 4.14. 53
away, boy, from the troops, and save thyself; CYM 5.02. 14
with prey, | make lanes in troops aghast. TNK 1.04. 19
to whose weak ruins muster troops of cares, | to LUC 720
TROP 1 FR 0.0001 REL FR 0 V 1 P
il est trop difficile, madame, comme je pense. H5 3.04. 27 P
TROPHIES 7 FR 0.0008 REL FR 7 V 0 P
till we with trophies do adorn thy tomb. TIT 1.01.388
they such | that these great tow'rs, trophies, TIM 5.04. 25
let no images | be hung with caesar's trophies. JC 1.01. 69
when down her weedy trophies and herself | fell HAM 4.07.174
tells him of trophies, statues, tombs, and VEN 1013
hung with the trophies of my lovers gone, | who SON 31.10
"'lo all these trophies of affections hot, | of LC 218
TROPHY 5 FR 0.0005 REL FR 4 V 1 P
on every grave | a lying trophy, and as oft is AWW 2.03.139
giving full trophy, signal, and ostent | quite H5 5.pr. 21
worn as a memorable trophy of predeceas'd valor, 5.01. 72 P
it more becomes a man | than gilt his trophy. COR 1.03. 40
no trophy, sword, nor hatchment o'er his bones, HAM 4.05.215
TROPICALLY 1 FR 0.0001 REL FR 0 V 1 P
tropically. HAM 3.02.237 P
TROT* *(also troth, truth)*
TROT* 11 FR 0.0012 REL FR 1 V 10 P
trot, trot. WIV 1.03. 7 P
trot, trot. 1.03. 7 P
by my trot, i tarry too long. 1.04. 62 P
by my trot, dere is no duke that the court is 4.05. 88 P
what say'st thou, trot? MM 3.02. 50 P
i prithee, who doth he trot withal? AYL 3.02.312 P
or an old trot with ne'er a tooth in her head, SHR 1.02. 79 P
bears your praises, who would trot as well, were H5 3.07. 77 P
i will trot to–morrow a mile, and my way shall 3.07. 80 P
trot like a servile footman all day long, | even TIT 5.02. 55
let him trot by. LR 3.04.100 P
TROTH *(also trot*, truth)*
/TROTH 5 FR 0.0005 REL FR 4 V 1 P
o wonderful, when devils tell the /troth! R3 1.02. 73
/no, /by /my /troth, /my /lord. 3.07. 43
/in /good /troth, /it /begins /so. TRO 3.01.114 P
/in /this /extant /moment, /faith /and /troth, 4.05.168
/by /my /troth, i am glad on't. OTH 4.01.238
TROTH 103 FR 0.0116 REL FR 36 V 67 P
warm, o' my troth! TMP 2.02. 34 P
mistress ford, by my troth, you are very well WIV 1.01.192 P
and, by my troth, i cannot abide the smell of 1.01.285 P
troth, sir, all is in his hands above. 1.04.144 P
troth, and i have a bag of money here troubles 2.02.171 P
troth, and your bum is the greatest thing about MM 2.01.217 P
troth, sir, she hath eaten up all her beef, and 3.02. 56 P
by my troth, isabel, i lov'd thy brother. 4.03.156 P
by my troth, i'll go with thee to the lane's end 4.03.177 P
by my troth, your town is troubled with unruly ERR 3.01. 62
by my troth, i speak my thought. ADO 1.01.224 P
by my troth, niece, thou wilt never get thee a 2.01. 18 P
troth, my lord, i have play'd the part of lady 2.01.213 P
by my troth, a pleasant–spirited lady. 2.01.341 P
by my troth, a good song. 2.03. 75 P
by my troth, my lord, i cannot tell what to 2.03. 99 P
by my troth, it is no addition to her wit, nor 2.03.233 P
troth, i think your other rebato were better. 3.04. 6 P
by my troth 's not so good, and i warrant your 3.04. 9 P
by my troth 's but a night–gown /in respect of 3.04. 18 P
by my troth, i am exceeding ill. 3.04. 53 P
by my troth, i am sick. 3.04. 72 P
no, by my troth, i have no moral meaning; 3.04. 79 P
sir, by my troth he is, as ever broke bread; 3.05. 38 P
and, by my troth, there's one meaning well 5.01.225 P
troth, no, no more than reason. 5.04. 77
study to break it and not break my troth. LLL 1.01. 66
by my troth, most pleasant. how both did fit it! 4.01.129
o' my troth, most sweet jests, most incony 4.01.142
you would for paradise break faith and troth, 4.03.141
for virtue's office never breaks men's troth. 5.02.350
by my life, my troth, | i never swore this lady 5.02.450
and to speak troth, i have forgot our way. MND 2.02. 36
one heart, one bed, two bosoms, and one troth. 2.02. 42
oath, | so then two bosoms and a single troth. 2.02. 50
good troth, you do me wrong (good sooth, you do) 2.02.129
fate o'errules, that, one man holding troth, | a 3.02. 92
by my troth, nerissa, my little body is a–weary MV 1.02. 1 P
by my troth, thou sayest true; AYL 1.02. 88 P
by my troth, i was seeking for a fool when i 3.02.285 P
by my troth, and in good earnest, and so god 4.01.188 P
by my troth, we that have good wits have much to 5.01. 11 P
by my troth, well met. 5.03. 8 P
by my troth, yes; 5.03. 39 P
by my troth, i take my young lord to be a very AWW 3.02. 3 P
by my troth, sir, if i were to live this present 4.03.160 P
by my troth, sir toby, you must come in earlier TN 1.03. 4 P
by my troth, i would not undertake her in this 1.03. 58 P
nay, by my troth, i know not; 2.03. 4 P
by my troth, the fool has an excellent breast. 2.03. 19 P
troth, sir, i can yield you none without words, 3.01. 23 P
by my troth, i'll tell thee, i am almost sick 3.01. 46 P
by my troth, thou hast an open hand. 4.01. 21 P
by my troth, sir, no; 5.01. 25 P
and, by my troth, i think thou lov'st me well. JN 3.03. 55
lo, by my troth, the instrument is cold, | and 4.01.103
now, by mine honor, by my life, by my troth, | i R2 5.02. 78
no, by my troth, not so much as will serve to be 1H4 1.02. 20 P
and violation of all faith and troth | sworn to 5.01. 70
for, by my troth, i do now remember the poor 2H4 2.02. 10 P
by my troth, this is the old fashion, you two 2.04. 55 P
but i do not love swaggering, by my troth. 2.04.104 P
by my troth, captain, these are very bitter 2.04.170 P
by my troth, i kiss thee with a most constant 2.04.269 P
by my troth, thou't set me a–weeping and thou 2.04.278 P
by my troth, welcome to london. 2.04.292 P
and so she is, by my troth. 2.04.304 P
by my troth, i was not there. 3.02. 39 P
by my troth, you like well and bear your years 3.02. 83 P
i am glad to see you, by my troth, master 3.02.192 P
by my troth, i care not; 3.02.234 P
no, by my troth, not long; H5 2.01. 32 P
by my troth, he'll yield the crow a pudding one 2.01. 87 P
by my troth, i will speak my conscience of the 4.01.118 P
no, by my troth, i did not mean such love. 3H6 3.02. 64
now, by my troth, if i had been rememb'red, | i R3 2.04. 23
by my troth and maidenhead, | i would not be a H8 2.03. 23
nay, good troth. 2.03. 33
yes, troth, and troth. you would not be a queen? 2.03. 34
yes, troth, and troth. you would not be a queen? 2.03. 34
i'll prove this troth with my three drops of TRO 1.03.301
by my troth, sweet /lord, thou hast a fine 3.01.107 P
by my troth, | i knew you not. 4.02. 45
a' my troth, i look'd upon him a' we'nsday half COR 1.03. 58 P
in troth, i think she would. 1.03.106 P
in troth, there's wondrous things spoke of him. 2.01.137 P
them home, | and, by my troth, you have cause. 4.02. 49
hard for him, directly to say the troth on't, 4.05.186 P
by my troth, it is well said; ROM 2.04.117 P
ay, /by my troth, the case may be amended. 4.05.100 P
bid her alight, | and her troth plight, | and LR 3.04.123
/good troth, i think thou wouldst not. OTH 4.03. 70
/by /my troth, i think i should, and undo't when 4.03. 71 P
loyall'st husband that did e'er plight troth. CYM 1.01. 96

good troth, | i have stol'n nought, nor would 3.06. 47
lord, | now fear is from me, i'll speak troth. 5.05.274
as i can remember, by my troth, | i never did PER 4.01. 73
by my troth, i think fame but stammers 'em, they TNK 2.01. 27 P
in troth, a very grievous punishment, as one 4.03. 45 P
love, | by holy human law, and common troth, LUC 571
thou smother'st honesty, thou murth'rest troth, 885
not know | the stained taste of violated troth; 1059
that shall prefer and undertake my troth.' LC 280
TROTH–PLIGHT 3 FR 0.0003 REL FR 2 V 1 P
that puts to | before her troth–plight: WT 1.02.278
directing, | is troth–plight to your daughter. 5.03.151
did you wrong, for you were troth–plight to her. H5 2.01. 19 P
TROTHS 1 FR 0.0001 REL FR 0 V 1 P
and by my two faiths and troths, my lord, i ADO 1.01.226 P
TROTS 4 FR 0.0004 REL FR 1 V 3 P
who time ambles withal, who time trots withal, AYL 3.02.310 P
he trots hard with a young maid between the 3.02.313 P
he trots the air; H5 3.07. 16 P
sometime he trots, as if he told the steps, VEN 277
TROTTING 2 FR 0.0002 REL FR 2 V 0 P
and great general | of trotting paritors — o my LLL 3.01.186
horse is arcite | trotting the stones of athens, TNK 5.04. 55
TROTTING–HORSE 1 FR 0.0001 REL FR 0 V 1 P
to ride on a bay trotting–horse over four–inch'd LR 3.04. 56 P
/TROUBLE 1 FR 0.0001 REL FR 1 V 0 P
/then /be /gone /and /trouble /you /no /more. R2 4.01.303
TROUBLE 79 FR 0.0089 REL FR 65 V 14 P
trouble us not. TMP 1.01. 18 P
alack, what trouble | was i then to you! 1.02.151
if you trouble him any more in 's tale, by this 3.02. 48 P
all torment, trouble, wonder, and amazement 5.01.104
this babble shall not henceforth trouble me. TGV 1.02. 95
meaning henceforth to trouble you no more. 2.01.119
come, trouble not yourself. WIV 3.04. 88
and i'll be gone, sir, and not trouble you. ERR 4.03. 70
that you would put me to this shame and trouble, 5.01. 14
leonato, are you come to meet your trouble? ADO 1.01. 97 P
never came trouble to my house in the likeness 1.01. 99 P
likeness of your grace, for trouble being gone, 1.01.100 P
home, and to trouble you with no more suit, MV 1.02.103 P
is it your dear friend that is thus in trouble? 3.02.291
i will not trouble you | as yet to question you AYL 2.07.171
unapt to toil and trouble in the world, | but SHR 5.02.166
o good antonio, forgive me your trouble. TN 2.01. 34 P
and part being prompted by your present trouble, 3.04.343
my stay, | to you a charge and trouble. WT 1.02. 26
are in sad talk, and we'll not trouble them. 4.04.311 P
o paulina, | we honor you with trouble; 5.03. 9
push) to trouble | your joys with like relation. 5.03.129
hal, i prithee trouble me no more with vanity; 1H4 1.02. 81 P
be happy, he will trouble you no more. 2H4 4.05.127
there was no need to trouble himself with any H5 2.03. 21 P
i'll never trouble you, if i may spy them. 1H6 1.04. 22
madam, i have been bold to trouble you; 2.03. 25
away, my masters, trouble us no more, | but join 3.01.144
to trouble and disturb the king and us? 4.01.127
but, madam, i must trouble you again, | no 5.03.180
but 'tis my presence that doth trouble ye; 2H6 1.01.141
lays, | and never mount to trouble you again. 1.03. 91
that henceforth he shall trouble us no more. 3.01.324
that living wrought me such exceeding trouble. 5.01. 70
for my part, i'll not trouble thee with words. 3H6 5.05. 5
and all the trouble thou hast turn'd me to? 5.05. 16
devil, for god's sake hence, and trouble us not, R3 1.02. 50
but you must trouble him with lewd complaints. 1.03. 61
i have not long to trouble thee. H8 4.02. 77
say his long trouble now is passing | out of 4.02.162
dear, trouble not yourself, the morn is cold. TRO 4.02. 1
trouble him not; 4.02. 3
i trouble you. 5.01. 68
my desire yet to trouble the poor with begging. COR 2.03. 69 P
of your voices, and so trouble you no farther. 2.03.109 P
stand, aufidius, | and trouble not the peace. 5.06.127
what should i don this robe and trouble you? TIT 1.01.189
one, | so trouble me no more, but get you gone. 1.01.367
away, and talk not, trouble us no more. 1.01.478
logs, | and never trouble peter for the matter. ROM 4.04. 19
i will be gone, sir, and not trouble ye. 5.03. 40
must he needs trouble me in't — hum! TIM 3.03. 1
o, sir, let it not trouble you. 3.06. 38 P
how dost thou pity him whom thou dost trouble? 4.03. 99
trouble him no further, thus you still shall 5.01.213
i turn the trouble of my countenance | merely JC 1.02. 38
good morrow, brutus, do we trouble you? 2.01. 87
i trouble thee too much, but thou art willing. 4.03.259
love that follows us sometime is our trouble, MAC 1.06. 11
for your pains, | and thank us for your trouble. 1.06. 14
i know this is a joyful trouble to you; 2.03. 48
double, double, toil and trouble; 4.01. 10
wing, | for a charm of pow'rful trouble, | like 4.01. 18
double, double, toil and trouble; 4.01. 20
double, double, toil and trouble; 4.01. 35
a mote it is to trouble the mind's eye. HAM 1.01.112
/gain–giving, as would perhaps trouble a woman. 5.02.216 P
degenerate bastard, i'll not trouble thee; LR 1.04.254
i will not trouble thee, my child; 2.04.219
sir, but trouble him not — his wits are gone. 3.06. 87
in, trouble him no more | till further settling. 4.07. 80
nor build yourself a trouble | out of his OTH 3.03.150
beseech you, sir, trouble yourself no further. 4.03. 1
trouble yourselves no further; ANT 2.04. 1
out too much pains | for purchasing but trouble. CYM 2.03. 88
where's hourly trouble for a minute's ease. PER 2.04. 44
that is the cause we trouble you so early, 3.02. 19
is twenty hundred kisses such a trouble?" VEN 522
and trouble deaf heaven with my bootless cries, SON 29. 3
TROUBLED 38 FR 0.0043 REL FR 33 V 5 P
bear with my weakness, my old brain is troubled. TMP 4.01.159
troth, your town is troubled with unruly boys. ERR 3.01. 62
else have been troubled with a pernicious suitor ADO 1.01.129 P
what if my house be troubled with a rat, | and i MV 4.01. 44
i will not long be troubled with you; AYL 1.01. 77 P
with pure love and troubled brain, he hath ta'en 4.03. 3 P
to mose in the chine, troubled with the lampass, SHR 3.02. 51 P
your husband, being troubled with a shrew, 5.02. 28
a woman mov'd is like a fountain troubled, 5.02.142
i would not by my will have troubled you, | but TN 3.03. 1
fresh expectation troubled not the land | with JN 4.02. 7
/doth show the mood of a much troubled breast, 4.02. 73
this fever, that hath troubled me so long, 5.03. 3
which, like the meteors of a troubled heaven, 1H4 1.01. 10
we will not now be troubled with reply. 5.01.113
of not marking, that i am troubled withal. 2H4 1.02.122 P
but i am troubled here with them myself; 2H6 4.05. 7
my mind was troubled with deep melancholy. 5.01. 34
and better 'twere you troubled him than france. 3H6 3.03.155
i'll strive with troubled thoughts to take a nap R3 5.03.104
my mind is troubled, like a fountain stirr'd, TRO 3.03.308
i have been troubled in my sleep this night, TIT 2.02. 9
troubled, confronted thus, and, for the extent 4.04. 3
east, | a troubled mind drive me to walk abroad, ROM 1.01.120
the troubled tiber chafing with her shores, JC 1.02.101
seest the heavens, as troubled with man's act, MAC 2.04. 5
as she is troubled with thick–coming fancies, 5.03. 38
and, being troubled with a raging tooth, | i OTH 3.03.414
says, is troubled | with the green–sickness. ANT 3.02. 5
that year indeed, he was troubled with a rheum; 3.02. 57
be you not troubled with the time, which drives 3.06. 82
troubled i am. TNK 1.01. 77
all the neighbor caves, as seeming troubled, VEN 830
light | to the disposing of her troubled brain, 1040
oft the eye mistakes, the brain being troubled. 1068
and cares, and troubled minds that wakes. LUC 126
"all which together, like a troubled ocean, 589
through which i may convey this troubled soul. 1176
TROUBLER 2 FR 0.0002 REL FR 2 V 0 P
on thee, the troubler of the poor world's peace! R3 1.03.220
me, | but, not to be a troubler of your peace, PER 5.01.151
TROUBLES 16 FR 0.0018 REL FR 14 V 2 P
and i have a bag of money here troubles me. WIV 2.02.172 P
not this, but troubles of the marriage–bed. ERR 2.01. 27
he so troubles me, | 'tis past enduring. WT 2.01. 1
which troubles oft the bed of blessed marriage, H5 5.02.364
i would his troubles likewise were expir'd, 1H6 2.05. 31
troubles the silver spring where england drinks. 2H6 4.01. 72
ely with richmond troubles me more near | than R3 4.03. 49
private, | full of sad thoughts and troubles. H8 2.02. 15
lute, wench, my soul grows sad with troubles. 3.01. 1
a whoreson rascally tisick so troubles me, and TRO 5.03.102 P
unnatural deeds | do breed unnatural troubles; MAC 5.01. 72
raze out the written troubles of the brain, 5.03. 42
but this troubles me. HAM 1.02.224
or to take arms against a sea of troubles, | and 3.01. 58
i'll show you those in troubles reign, | losing PER 2.ch. 7
mark the poor wretch, to overshut his troubles, VEN 680
TROUBLESOME 8 FR 0.0009 REL FR 6 V 2 P
i'll rather be unmannerly than troublesome. WIV 1.01.312 P
told, | and, in the last repeating, troublesome, JN 4.02. 19
times, | and be like them to percy troublesome. 2H4 2.03. 4
his pillow, | being so troublesome a bedfellow? 4.05. 22
well | how troublesome it sate upon my head. 4.05.186
you are strangely troublesome. H8 5.02.129
now th' art troublesome. COR 4.05. 16 P
the time is troublesome. CYM 4.03. 21
TROUBLEST 1 FR 0.0001 REL FR 1 V 0 P
thou troublest me, i am not in the vein. R3 4.02.118
TROUBLOUS 4 FR 0.0004 REL FR 4 V 0 P
my troublous dreams this night doth make me sad. 2H6 1.02. 22
but in this troublous time what's to be done? 3H6 2.01.159
so part we sadly in this troublous world, | to 5.05. 7
then, masters, look to see a troublous world. R3 2.03. 9
TROUGH 1 FR 0.0001 REL FR 1 V 0 P
your warm blood like wash and makes his trough R3 5.02. 9
TROUT 1 FR 0.0001 REL FR 0 V 1 P
for here comes the trout that must be caught TN 2.05. 22 P
TROUTS 1 FR 0.0001 REL FR 0 V 1 P
groping for trouts in a peculiar river. MM 1.02. 90 P
TROVATO 1 FR 0.0001 REL FR 1 V 0 P
con tutto /il core, ben trovato, may i say. SHR 1.02. 24
TROW 14 FR 0.0015 REL FR 10 V 4 P
who's there, i trow? WIV 1.04.132 P
what tempest, i trow, threw this whale (with so 2.01. 64 P
what means the fool, trow? ADO 3.04. 59 P
his heart, | and trow you what he call'd me? LLL 5.02.279
trow you who hath done this? AYL 3.02.179 P
and i trow this is his house. SHR 1.02. 4
trow you whither i am going? 1.02.164
we will for ireland, and 'tis time, i trow. R2 2.01.218
'twas time, i trow, to wake and leave our beds, 1H6 2.01. 41
now winchester will not submit, i trow, | or be 5.01. 56
deals with our cardinal, and, as i trow — H8 1.01.184
'twas no need, i trow, | to bid me trudge. ROM 1.03. 33
marry come up, i trow; 2.05. 62
what is the matter, trow? CYM 1.06. 47
TROWEL 1 FR 0.0001 REL FR 0 V 1 P
well said — that was laid on with a trowel. AYL 1.02.106 P
TROWEST 3 FR 0.0003 REL FR 3 V 0 P
trowest thou that e'er i'll look upon the world, 2H6 2.04. 38
why, trowest thou, warwick, | that clarence is 3H6 5.01. 85
than thou goest, | learn more than thou trowest, LR 1.04.122
/TROY* 5 FR 0.0005 REL FR 5 V 0 P
/in /troy, /there /lies /the /scene. TRO pr 1
/and /their /vow /is /made | /to /ransack /troy, pr 8
/bolts | /sperr /up /the /sons /of /troy. pr 19
/the /glory /of /our /troy /doth /this /day /lie 4.04.147
/how /troy /was /burnt /and /he /made /miserable TIT 3.02. 28
TROY* 85 FR 0.0096 REL FR 76 V 9 P
shall i sir pandarus of troy become, | and by my WIV 1.03. 75
he presents hector of troy; LLL 5.02.534 P
the worthy knight of troy. 5.02.881
the virgin tribute paid by howling troy | to the MV 3.02. 56
quoth she, | "why the grecians sacked troy? AWW 1.03. 71
ah, thou, the model where old troy did stand, R2 5.01. 11
and would have told him half his troy was burnt; 2H4 1.01. 73
thou art as valorous as hector of troy, worth 2.04.220 P
the time of night when troy was set on fire, 2H6 1.04. 17
his father's acts commenc'd in burning troy! 3.02.118
as the hope of troy | against the greeks that 3H6 2.01. 51
against the greeks that would have ent'red troy. 2.01. 52
could, | and, like a sinon, take another troy. 3.02.190
why should i war without the walls of troy, TRO 1.01. 2
he's one of the flowers of troy, i can tell you. 1.02.187 P
he's one o' th' soundest judgments in troy, 1.02.192 P
after seven years' siege yet troy walls stand, 1.03. 12
troy, yet upon his bases, had been down, | and 1.03. 75
and 'tis this fever that keeps troy on foot, 1.03.135
troy in our weakness stands, not in her strength 1.03.137
from troy. 1.03.214
or the men of troy | are ceremonious courtiers. 1.03.233
sir, you of troy, call you yourself aeneas? 1.03.245
he hears nought privately that comes from troy. 1.03.249
nor i from troy come not to whisper with him. 1.03.250
what troy means fairly shall be spoke aloud. 1.03.259
here in troy | a prince call'd hector — priam 1.03.260
midway between your tents and walls of troy, 1.03.278
if none, he'll say in troy when he retires, 1.03.281
will with a trumpet 'twixt our tents and troy 2.01.123
troy must not be, nor goodly ilion stand. 2.02.109
troy burns, or else let helen go. 2.02.112
if troy be not taken till these two undermine it 2.03. 8 P
fresh kings are come to troy; 2.03.261
helenus, antenor, and all the gallantry of troy. 3.01.136 P
when water–drops have worn the stones of troy, 3.02.186
i have abandon'd troy, left my possession, 3.03. 5
troy holds him very dear. 3.03. 19
whom troy hath still denied, but this antenor, 3.03. 22
know my mind, i'll fight no more 'gainst troy. 3.03. 56
brave hector's breast | and great troy shriking. 3.03.141
all the commerce that you have had with troy 3.03.205
in humane gentleness, | welcome to troy! 4.01. 22
troilus had rather troy were borne to greece 4.01. 47
borne to greece | than cressid borne from troy. 4.01. 48
i would not for half troy have you seen here. 4.02. 41
by priam and the general state of troy. 4.02. 67
i will not go from troy. 4.02.109
and is it true that i must go from troy? 4.04. 30
from troy and troilus. 4.04. 32
give with thy trumpet a loud note to troy, 4.05. 3
of this leg | all greek, and this all troy; 4.05.127
my well–fam'd lord of troy, no less to you. 4.05.173
me, of what honor was | this cressida in troy? 4.05.288
why, thou full dish of fool, from troy. 5.01. 9 P
so now, fair prince of troy, i bid good night. 5.01. 71
hector, by this, is arming him in troy; 5.02.183
i'll stand to–day for thee and me and troy. 5.03. 36
thou on him leaning, and all troy on thee, 5.03. 61
hark how troy roars! 5.03. 83
thou dost thyself and all our troy deceive. 5.03. 90
/young knave's sleeve of troy there in his helm. 5.04. 4 P
come, troy, sink down! 5.08. 11
great troy is ours, and our sharp wars are ended 5.09. 10
sit, gods, upon your thrones, and smile at troy! 5.10. 7
aye be call'd | go in to troy and say /there, 5.10. 17
and, in a word, | scare troy out of itself. 5.10. 21
to troy with comfort go; 5.10. 30
the self–same gods that arm'd the queen of troy TIT 1.01.136
or brought a faggot to bright–burning troy? 3.01. 69
and i have read that hecuba of troy | ran mad 4.01. 20
when subtile greeks surpris'd king priam's troy. 5.03. 84
the fatal engine in | that gives our troy, our 5.03. 87
did from the flames of troy upon his shoulder JC 1.02.113
by a halfpenny loaf a day, troy weight. STM II.C 7 P
of skillful painting, made for priam's troy, LUC 1367
and from the tow'rs of troy there would appear 1382
and from the walls of strong–besieged troy, 1429
with my tears quench troy that burns so long, 1468
this load of wrath that burning troy doth bear; 1474
and here in troy, for trespass of thine eye, 1476
troy had been bright with fame, and not with 1491
onward to troy with the blunt swains he goes, 1504
so did i tarquin, so my troy did perish. 1547
he finds means to burn his troy with water." 1561
TROYAN *(also troiant)*
/TROYAN 1 FR 0.0001 REL FR 1 V 0 P
/on /one /and /other /side, /troyan /and /greek, TRO pr 21
TROYAN 36 FR 0.0040 REL FR 31 V 5 P
hector was but a troyan in respect of this. LLL 5.02.636 P
unless you play the honest troyan, the poor 5.02.675 P
when the false troyan under sail was seen, | by MND 1.01.174
troilus methinks mounted the troyan walls, | and MV 5.01. 4
dost thou thirst, base troyan, | to have me fold H5 5.01. 19
base troyan, thou shalt die. 5.01. 31
love, | but prosper better than the troyan did. 1H6 5.05.106
each troyan that is master of his heart, | let TRO 1.01. 4
is among the greeks | a lord of troyan blood, 1.02. 13
this troyan scorns us, or the men of troy | are 1.03.233
peace, troyan, lay thy finger on thy lips! 1.03.240
that thou shalt know, troyan, he is awake, | he 1.03.255
i would not wish a drop of troyan blood | spent 2.02.197
would he were a troyan! 2.03.234
what wouldst thou of us, troyan? make demand. 3.03. 17
you have a troyan prisoner call'd antenor, 3.03. 18
t' invite the troyan lords after the combat | to 3.03.236
carrion weight, | a troyan hath been slain. 4.01. 73
this blended knight, half troyan and half greek. 4.05. 86
what troyan is that same that looks so heavy? 4.05. 95
were thy commixtion greek and troyan so | that 4.05.124
"this hand is grecian all, | and this is troyan; 4.05.126
interview | to the expecters of our troyan part; 4.05.156
i have, thou gallant troyan, seen thee oft, 4.05.183
there's many a greek and troyan dead | since 4.05.214
they say he keeps a troyan drab, and uses the 5.01. 96 P
how now, troyan? 5.02. 30
i cannot conjure, troyan. 5.02.125
that that same young troyan ass, that loves the 5.04. 6 P
now for thy whore, troyan! 5.04. 25 P
tell her i have chastis'd the amorous troyan, 5.05. 4
i do disdain thy courtesy, proud troyan. 5.06. 15
tail, | along the field i will the troyan trail. 5.08. 22
are like the troyan horse was stuff'd within PER 1.04. 93
stood many troyan mothers, sharing joy | to see LUC 1431
for every tear he falls a troyan bleeds; 1551
TROYANS' 2 FR 0.0002 REL FR 2 V 0 P
the troyans' trumpet. TRO 4.05. 64
the troyans' trumpet sound the like, my lord. 5.08. 16
TROYANS 10 FR 0.0011 REL FR 8 V 2 P
there are other troyans that thou dream'st not 1H4 2.01. 69 P
hector, in view of troyans and of greeks, TRO 1.03.273
for here the troyans taste our dear'st repute 1.03.337
thou art here but to thrash troyans, and thou 2.01. 46 P
cry, troyans, cry! 2.02. 97

cry, troyans! 2.02. 99
cry, troyans, cry! 2.02.101
cry, troyans, cry! 2.02.108
cry, troyans, cry! 2.02.111
as for her greeks and troyans suff'red death. 4.01. 75
TROY'S 2 FR 0.0002 REL FR 2 V 0 P
farewell, my hector, and my troy's true hope. 3H6 4.08. 25
here feelingly she weeps troy's painted woes, LUC 1492
TRUANT 14 FR 0.0015 REL FR 12 V 2 P
and though myself have been an idle truant, TGV 2.04. 64
since i pluck'd geese, play'd truant, and whipt WIV 5.01. 25 P
'tis double wrong, to truant with your bed, ERR 3.02. 17
hang him, truant! ADO 3.02. 18 P
words | that aged ears play truant at his tales, LLL 2.01. 74
but i will never be a truant, love, | till i 1H4 3.01.204
to my shame, | i have a truant been to chivalry, 5.01. 94
and chid his truant youth with such a grace | as 5.02. 62
faith, i have been a truant in the law, | and 1H6 2.04. 7
i am not such a truant since my coming, | as not H8 3.01. 43
with truant vows to her own lips he loves, | and TRO 1.03.270
a truant disposition, good my lord. HAM 1.02.169
i know you are no truant. 1.02.173
o truant muse, what shall be thy amends | for SON 101. 1
TRUCE 15 FR 0.0017 REL FR 15 V 0 P
then fair league and truce with thy true bed, ERR 2.02.145
with my vex'd spirits i cannot take a truce, JN 3.01. 17
and even before this truce, but new before, | no 3.01.233
parley, and base truce | to arms invasive? 5.01. 68
call'd for the truce of winchester and 1H6 2.04.118
this token serveth for a flag of truce | betwixt 3.01.138
i have a while given truce unto my wars, | to do 3.04. 3
that peaceful truce shall be proclaim'd in 5.04.117
and therefore take this compact of a truce, 5.04.163
excitements to the field, or speech for truce, TRO 1.03.182
who in /this dull and long–continued truce | is 1.03.262
the seas and winds, old wranglers, took a truce, 2.02. 75
sir, | during all question of the gentle truce; 4.01. 12
could not take truce with the unruly spleen | of ROM 3.01.157
till he take truce with her contending tears, VEN 82
TRUCKLE–BED 2 FR 0.0002 REL FR 1 V 1 P
his castle, his standing–bed and truckle–bed; WIV 4.05. 7 P
romeo, good night, i'll to my truckle–bed, ROM 2.01. 39
TRUDGE 6 FR 0.0006 REL FR 5 V 1 P
trudge! WIV 1.03. 82
that done, trudge with it in all haste, and 3.03. 13 P
'tis time, i think, to trudge, pack, and be gone ERR 3.02.153
that trudge betwixt the king and mistress shore. R3 1.01. 73
sirrah, trudge about | through fair verona, find ROM 1.02. 34
'twas no need, i trow, | to bid me trudge. 1.03. 34
/TRUE 5 FR 0.0005 REL FR 4 V 1 P
/'tis /very /true, /my /grief /lies /all /within R2 4.01.295
/rise /thus /nimbly /by /a /true /king's /fall. 4.01.318
/takes /false /shadows /for /true /substances. TIT 3.02. 80
/but /true /it /is, /from /france /there /comes LR 3.01. 30
/holds /it /true, /sir, /that /the /duke /of 4.07. 84 P
TRUE 849 FR 0.0959 REL FR 645 V 204 P
is not this true? TMP 1.02.267
true — save means to live. 2.01. 51 P
'tis true, my brother's daughter 's queen of 2.01.255
true. 2.01.271
swear upon that bottle to be thy true subject, 2.02.125 P
i profess with kind event | if i speak true! 3.01. 70
come to me, | and i'll be sworn 'tis true. 3.03. 26
look thou be true; 4.01. 51
a contract of true love to celebrate, | and some 4.01. 84
and help to celebrate | a contract of true love; 4.01.133
my true preserver, and a loyal sir | to him thou 5.01. 69
if these be true spies which i wear in my head, 5.01.259 P
these men, my lords, | then say if they be true. 5.01.268
now 'tis true, | i must be here confin'd by you, ep 3
'tis true; TGV 1.01. 25
true; and thy master a shepherd. 1.01. 83 P
true, sir; 2.01. 81 P
here is my hand for my true constancy; 2.02. 8
ay, so true love should do: 2.02. 17
her true perfection, or my false transgression, 2.04.197
but tell me true, will't be a match? 2.05. 34 P
but silvia is too fair, too true, too holy, | to 4.02. 5
when i protest true loyalty to her, | she twits 4.02. 7
and to your shadow will i make true love. 4.02.125
i am my master's true confirmed love; 4.04.103
but cannot be true servant to my master, 4.04.104
'tis true; 5.02. 13
true — from a gentleman to a fool. 5.02. 24
'tis true; 5.02. 37
thou counterfeit to thy true friend! 5.04. 53
'tis true. 5.04.110
is false, or as i despise one that is not true. WIV 1.01. 70 P
is this true, pistol? 1.01.159 P
of mine is dangerous — that is my true humor. 1.03.103 P
by me, thine own true knight, | by day or night, 2.01. 14
and this is true; 2.01.128 P
'tis true; 2.01.134 P
priest o' th' town commended him for a true man. 2.01.145 P
your worship says very true. 2.02. 48 P
is it not true, master page? 2.03. 41 P
'tis true, master shallow. 2.03. 50 P
little jack–a–lent, have you been true to us? 3.03. 28 P
true, master page. 3.03.168 P
may be he tells you true. 3.04. 11
'tis old, but true: 4.02.107
ay, but if it prove true, master page, have you 4.02.114 P
my intelligence is true, my jealousy is 4.02.148 P
as i am a true spirit, welcome! 5.05. 29 P
upon a true contract | i got possession of MM 1.02.145
may formally in person bear | like a true friar. 1.03. 48
'tis true. 1.04. 30
all this is true. 2.01.113 P
is this true? 2.01.173 P
come, tell me true, it shall be the better for 2.01.221 P
but with true prayers, | that shall be up at 2.02.151
falsely to take away a life true made | as to 2.04. 47
true. 2.04. 87
my false o'erweighs your true. 2.04.170
confessor to angelo, and i know this to be true; 3.01.167 P
is it true, think you? 3.02.105 P
urine is congeal'd ice, that i know to be true; 3.02.111 P
every true man's apparel fits your thief. 4.02. 43 P
your thief, your true man thinks it big enough; 4.02. 44 P
so every true man's apparel fits your thief. 4.02. 46 P
too many of him already, sir, if they be true; 4.03.168 P
if not true, none were enough. 4.03.168 P
till you have heard me in my true complaint 5.01. 24
than this is all as true as it is strange; 5.01. 44
nay, it is ten times true, for truth is truth 5.01. 45
it seems hid, | and hide the false seems true. 5.01. 67
o that it were as like as it is true! 5.01.104
mouth, what he doth know | is true and false; 5.01.156
as this is true, | let me in safety raise me 5.01.230
here comes the almanac of my true date: ERR 1.02. 41
then fair league and truce with thy true bed, 2.02.145
'tis true she rides me and i long for grass. 2.02.200
and true he swore, though yet forsworn he were. 4.02. 10
establish him in his true sense again, | and i 4.04. 48
mistress, upon my life, i tell you true; 5.01.180
'tis true, my liege, this ring i had of her. 5.01.278
man should do, for my simple true judgment? ADO 1.01.167 P
for an answer, if peradventure this be true. 1.02. 23 P
you should take true root but by the fair 1.03. 23 P
to tell you true, i counterfeit him. 2.01.116 P
and i think i told him true, that your grace had 2.01.216 P
lady, i think your blazon to be true, though, 2.01.297 P
'tis true indeed, so your daughter says. 2.03.127 P
it is very true. 2.03.153 P
she cannot be so much without true judgment — 3.01. 88
can this be true? 3.01.107
there's no true drop of blood in him to be truly 3.02. 18 P
are you good men and true? 3.03. 1 P
true, and they are to meddle with none but the 3.03. 33 P
by virtue of your office, to be no true man; 3.03. 51 P
'tis very true. 3.03. 73 P
and i will, like a true drunkard, utter all to 3.03.104 P
and bad thinking do not wrest true speaking, 3.04. 33 P
sir, they are spoken, and these things are true. 4.01. 67
"true"! o god! 4.01. 68
no, though he thought his accusation true. 4.01.233
was charg'd with nothing | but what was true, 5.01.105
in a false quarrel there is no true valor. 5.01.120 P
"true," said she, "a fine little one." 5.01.161 P
in the true course of all the question. 5.04. 6
that eye my daughter lent her, 'tis most true. 5.04. 23
say it is so, he is, in telling true — but so. LLL 1.01.225 P
for true it is, i was taken with jaquenetta, and 1.01.311 P
with jaquenetta, and jaquenetta is a true girl, 1.01.312 P
true. 1.02. 49 P
and how can that be true love, which is falsely 1.02.171 P
may | make tender of to thy true worthiness. 2.01.170
true, and i for a plantan; 3.01.108
true, true, and now you will be my purgation and 3.01.126 P
true, true, and now you will be my purgation and 3.01.126 P
(good my glass), take this for telling true: 4.01. 18
true, that thou art beauteous; 4.01. 61 P
'tis true indeed, the collusion holds in the 4.02. 42 P
that shall express my true love's fasting pain. 4.03.120
a true man, or a thief, that gallops so? 4.03.185
true, true, we are four. 4.03.207
true, true, we are four. 4.03.207
walk aside the true folk, and let the traitors 4.03.209
as true we are as flesh and blood can be. 4.03.211
whence doth spring the true promethean fire. 4.03.300
true wit! 5.01. 61 P
the numbers true, and, were the numb'ring too, 5.02. 35
true, out indeed. 5.02.165
madam, speak true. 5.02.364
it is not so, for how can this be true, | that 5.02.426
most true, 'tis right; you were so, alisander. 5.02.569
true, and it was enjoin'd him in rome for want 5.02.712 P
by being once false for ever to be true | to 5.02.773
i'll serve thee true and faithfully till then. 5.02.831
scornful lysander, true, he hath my love; MND 1.01. 95
the course of true love never did run smooth; 1.01.134
if then true lovers have been ever cross'd, | it 1.01.150
ask some tears in the true performing of it. 1.02. 25 P
draw not iron, for my heart | is true as steel. 2.01.197
i thought you lord of more true gentleness. 2.02.132
as true as truest horse, that yet would never 3.01. 96
o — "as true as truest horse, that yet would 3.01.102
bill, | the throstle with his note so true, 3.01.127
the sun was not so true unto the day | as he to 3.02. 50
o, once tell true; 3.02. 68
tell true, even for my sake! 3.02. 68
must perforce ensue | some true love turn'd, and 3.02. 91
true love turn'd, and not a false turn'd true. 3.02. 91
bearing the badge of faith to prove them true? 3.02.127
thou tak'st | true delight | in the sight | of 3.02.455
for it, | and will for evermore be true to it. 4.01.176
for if i tell you, i am /no true athenian. 4.02. 30 P
more strange than true. 5.01. 2
skill, | that is the true beginning of our end. 5.01.111
as minding to content you, | our true intent is. 5.01.114
it is not enough to speak, but to speak true. 5.01.121 P
not shafalus to procrus was so true. 5.01.198
true; and a goose for his discretion. 5.01.232 P
all the couples three | ever true in loving be; 5.01.408
true, madam; MV 1.02.117 P
and fair she is, if that mine eyes be true, 2.06. 54
and true she is, as she hath prov'd herself; 2.06. 55
therefore, like herself, wise, fair, and true, 2.06. 56
then be gleaned | from the true seed of honor? 2.09. 47
but it is true, without any slips of prolixity 3.01. 11 P
is it true, is it true? 3.01.102 P
is it true, is it true? 3.01.103 P
nay, that's true, that's very true. 3.01.125 P
nay, that's true, that's very true. 3.01.125 P
even as the flourish when true subjects bow | to 3.02. 49
the view, | chance as fair, and choose as true: 3.02.132
so, | as doubtful whether what i see be true, 3.02.147
is this true, nerissa? 3.02.208
and then i told you true. 3.02.256
but is it true, salerio? 3.02.266
when it is paid, bring your true friend along. 3.02.308
you have a noble and a true conceit | of godlike 3.04. 2
honor, | how true a gentleman you send relief, 3.04. 6
'tis very true. 4.01.250
with many vows of faith, | and ne'er a true one. 5.01. 20
are | to their right praise and true perfection! 5.01.108
most true, i have lost my teeth in your service. AYL 1.01. 82 P
'tis true, for those that she makes fair she 1.02. 37 P
by my troth, thou sayest true; 1.02. 88 P
deserv'd | high commendation, true applause, and 1.02.263
though in thy youth thou wast as true a lover 2.04. 26
we that are true lovers run into strange capers; 2.04. 54 P
true is it that we have seen better days, | and 2.07.120
sir, i am a true laborer: 3.02. 73 P
speak sad brow and true maid. 3.02.215 P
then there is no true lover in the forest, else 3.02.302 P
is it a true thing? 3.03. 18 P
not true in love? 3.04. 26 P
between the pale complexion of true love | and 3.04. 53
if you be a true lover, hence, and not a word; 4.03. 73 P
nay, 'tis true. 5.02. 29 P
not well cut, he would answer i spake not true: 5.04. 78 P
if sight and shape be true, | why then my love 5.04.120
hymen's bands, | if truth holds true contents. 5.04.130
this to be true, | i do engage my life. 5.04.165
you to a love, that your true faith doth merit; 5.04.188
as we do trust they'll end, in true delights. 5.04.198
if it be true that good wine needs no bush, 'tis ep 3 P
'tis true that a good play needs no epilogue. ep 4 P
as he shall think by our true diligence | he is SHR in.1. 70
'tis very true; in.1. 89
o tranio, till i found it to be true, | i never 1.01.148
to /change true rules for /odd inventions. 3.01. 81
why, thou say'st true, it is /a paltry cap, | a 4.03. 81
why, true, he means to make a puppet of thee. 4.03.104
this is true that i say; 4.03.149 P
right true it is, your son lucentio here | doth 4.04. 40
but is this true, or is it else your pleasure, 4.05. 71
for both our sakes, i would that word were true. 5.02. 15
but love, fair looks, and true obedience — 5.02.153
knew the true minute when | exception bid him AWW 1.02. 39
will repeat, | which men full true shall find: 1.03. 61
therefore tell me true, | but tell me then, 'tis 1.03.175
did ever in so true a flame of liking | wish 1.03.211
wherefore? tell true. 1.03.219
there do muster true gait, eat, speak, and move 2.01. 54 P
you are a vagabond and no true traveller. 2.03.260 P
then my dial goes not true. 2.05. 6 P
with true observance seek to eke out that 2.05. 74
attributed to the true and exact performer, i 3.06. 61 P
but the plain single vow that is vow'd true. 4.02. 22
which makes her story true, even to the point of 4.03. 56 P
i said — i will say true — "or thereabouts," 4.03.149 P
to live this present hour, i will tell true. 4.03.161 P
me, sirrah — but tell me true, i charge you, 5.03.234
true, madam, and, to comfort you with chance, TN 1.02. 8
as there is no true cuckold but calamity, so 1.05. 51 P
a mellifluous voice, as i am true knight. 2.03. 53 P
for such as i am, all true lovers are, | unstaid 2.04. 17
my part of death, no one so true | did share it. 2.04. 57
o, where | sad true lover never find my grave, 2.04. 65
in faith, they are as true of heart as we. 2.04.106
nay, but say true, does it work upon him? 2.05.195 P
one, it is with me as the very true sonnet is, 3.04. 23 P
but this — your true love for my master. 3.04.213
prove true, imagination, o, prove true, | that i 3.04.375
prove true, imagination, o, prove true, | that i 3.04.375
but tell me true, are you not mad indeed, or do 4.02.113 P
believe me, i am not, i tell thee true. 4.02.115 P
and, having sworn truth, ever will be true. 4.03. 33
that screws me from my true place in your favor, 5.01.123
if this be so, as yet the glass seems true, | i 5.01.265
and all those swearings keep as true in soul 5.01.270
yet were it true | to say this boy were like me. WT 1.02.134
were sin | as deep as that, though true. 1.02.284
say it be, 'tis true. 1.02.298
if i | had servants true about me, that bare 1.02.309
in my true opinion! 2.01. 37
all's true that is mistrusted. 2.01. 48
if this prove true, they'll pay for't. 2.01.146
me | to have her honor true than your suspicion, 2.01.160
i | do come with words as medicinal as true, 2.03. 37
to the faith and allegiance of a true subject, 3.02. 19 P
hath been as continent, as chaste, as true, | as 3.02. 34
that's true enough, | though 'tis a saying, sir, 3.02. 57
polixenes blameless, camillo a true subject, 3.02.133 P
very true, sir; 4.03.103 P
and the true blood which peeps fairly through't, 4.04.148
a–life, for then we are sure they are true. 4.04.261 P
is it true, think you? 4.04.266 P
very true, and but a month old. 4.04.267 P
the ballad is very pitiful, and as true. 4.04.281 P
is it true too, think you? 4.04.282 P
one of these is true: 4.04.575
true, too true, my lord. 5.01. 12
true, too true, my lord. 5.01. 12
my true paulina, | we shall not marry till thou 5.01. 81
your mother was most true to wedlock, prince, 5.01.124
this news, which is call'd true, is so like an 5.02. 28 P
most true, if ever truth were pregnant by 5.02. 30 P
thou art as honest a true fellow as any is in 5.02.157 P
a true gentleman may swear it in the behalf of 5.02.162 P
in right and true behalf | of thy deceased JN 1.01. 7
but whe'er i be as true begot or no, | that 1.01. 75
my bed was ever to thy son as true | as thine 2.01.124
i think | his father never was so true begot — 2.01.130
but this one word, whether thy tale be true. 3.01. 26
as true as i believe you think them false | that 3.01. 27
that give you cause to prove my saying true. 3.01. 28
'tis true, fair daughter, and this blessed day 3.01. 75
true love | between our kingdoms and our royal 3.01.231
a riot on the gentle brow | of true sincerity? 3.01.248
be your man, attend on you | with all true duty. 3.03. 73
but that which ends all counsel, true redress: 3.04. 24
grief, | like true, inseparable, faithful loves, 3.04. 66
if that be true, i shall see my boy again; 3.04. 78
for he that steeps his safety in true blood 3.04.147
i idly heard — if true or false i know not. 4.02.124
'tis true — to hurt his master, no /man else. 4.03. 33
nor tempt the danger of my true defense, | lest 4.03. 84
may this be possible? may this be true? 5.04. 21
since it is true | that i must die here and live 5.04. 28
whoever spoke it, it is true, my lord. 5.05. 19
should scape the true acquaintance of mine ear. 5.06. 15

services | and true subjection everlastingly.		5.07.105
us rue, | if england to itself do rest but true.		5.07.118
look what i speak, my life shall prove it true:	R2	1.01. 87
speak like a true knight, so defend thee heaven!		1.03. 34
lives or dies, true to king richard's throne,		1.03. 86
home, | for christian service and true chivalry,		2.01. 54
right, you say true:		2.01.145
and is not harry true?		2.01.192
now, afore god — god forbid i say true!		2.01.200
which for things true weeps things imaginary.		2.02. 27
'tis too true, and that is worse, | the lord		2.02. 52
it shall be still thy true love's recompense.		2.03. 49
and sends allegiance and true faith of heart		3.03. 37
as my true service shall deserve your love.		3.03.199
to breathe this news, yet what i say is true:		3.04. 82
his honor is as true | in this appeal as thou		4.01. 44
'tis very true, you were in presence then, | and		4.01. 62
and you can witness with me this is true.		4.01. 63
as false, by heaven, as heaven itself is true.		4.01. 64
world, | aumerle is guilty of my true appeal;		4.01. 79
then true noblesse would | learn him forbearance		4.01.119
have any resting for her true king's queen.		5.01. 6
the traitor lives, the true man's put to death.		5.03. 73
against them both my true joints bended be.		5.03. 98
ours of true zeal and deep integrity;		5.03.108
that mercy which true prayer ought to have.		5.03.110
mother well hath pray'd, and prove you true.		5.03.145
had not an ear to hear my true time broke.		5.05. 48
here is /a dear, a true industrious friend,	1H4	1.01. 62
by the lord, thou say'st true, lad.		1.02. 39 P
to a true man.		1.02.109 P
hears may be believ'd, that the true prince may		1.02.155 P
to prove that true | needs no more but one		1.03. 95
you say true.		1.03.250
true, who bears hard | his brother's death at		1.03.270
a share in our purchase, as i am a true man.		2.01. 92 P
a deed as drink to turn true man and to leave		2.02. 23 P
it when thieves cannot be true one to another!		2.02. 28 P
the thieves have bound the true men.		2.02. 93 P
as ever was laid, our friends true and constant:		2.03. 17 P
and if thou wilt not tell me all things true.		2.03. 88
should i turn upon the true prince?		2.04.270 P
the lion will not touch the true prince.		2.04.272 P
for a valiant lion, and thou for a true prince.		2.04.275 P
you will not touch the true prince, no, fie!		2.04.301 P
with it and swear it was the blood of true men.		2.04.311 P
swore the devil his true liegeman upon the cross		2.04.338 P
lad, thou sayest true, it is like we shall have		2.04.364 P
kind jack falstaff, true jack falstaff, valiant		2.04.476 P
never call a true piece of gold a counterfeit.		2.04.491 P
my masters, for a true face and good conscience.		2.04.501 P
in good sooth," and "as true as i live," and "as		3.01.249 P
i may for some things true, wherein my youth		3.02. 26
irregular, | find pardon on my true submission.		3.02. 28
now, as i am a true woman, holland of eight		3.03. 71 P
thou say'st true, hostess, and he slanders thee		3.03.131 P
so long as out of limit and true rule | you		4.03. 39
they tell thee true.		5.03. 6
but the true and perfect image of life indeed.		5.04.119 P
borne | betwixt our armies true intelligence.		5.05. 10
but what mean i | to speak so true at first?	2H4	in 28
smooth comforts false, worse than true wrongs.		in 40
that freely rend'red me these news for true.		1.01. 27
your spirit is too true, your fears too certain.		1.01. 92
twenty yards of satin (as i am a true knight),		1.02. 44 P
times that true valor is turn'd berrord;		1.02.169 P
'tis very true, lord bardolph, for indeed | it		1.03. 25
of wrenching the true cause the false way.		2.01.110 P
bestow himself to-night in his true colors, and		2.02.170 P
mass, thou say'st true.		2.04. 4 P
very true, sir, and i come to draw you out by		2.04.289 P
the part of a careful friend and a true subject,		2.04.322 P
if damn'd commotion so /appear'd | in his true,		4.01. 37
action | acquitted by a true substantial form		4.01.171
'tis very true, | and therefore be assur'd, my		4.01.217
and true obedience, of this madness cured,		4.02. 41
so much the worse, if your own rule be true.		4.02. 86
treason's true bed and yielder-up of breath.		4.02.123
and a famous true subject took him.		4.03. 64 P
the manner and true order of the fight | this		4.04.100
which my most inward true and duteous spirit		4.05.147
my father, | the quarrel of a true inheritor.		4.05.168
and grant it may with thee in true peace live!		4.05.219
'tis true bred!		5.03. 67 P
and a true lover of the holy church.	H5	1.01. 23
of his true titles to some certain dukedoms,		1.01. 87
of the true line and stock of charles the great,		1.02. 71
but there's a saying very old and true, | "if		1.02.166
true;		2.02. 29
and true repentance | of all your dear offenses!		2.02.180
held | from him, the native and true challenger.		2.04. 95
directions in the true disciplines of the wars,		3.02. 72 P
i could make as true a boast as that, if i had a		3.07. 62 P
minding true things by what their mock'ries be.		4.pr. 53
'tis true that we are in great danger, | the		4.01. 1
when the true and aunchient prerogatifes and		4.01. 67 P
but the saying is true, "the empty vessel makes		4.04. 68 P
your majesty says very true.		4.07. 97 P
you say very true, scald knave, when god's will		5.01. 32 P
not, to say to thee that i shall die, is true;		5.02.151 P
by mine honor, in true english, i love thee,		5.02.221 P
her, that he will appear in his true likeness.		5.02.289 P
if conjure up love in her in his true likeness,		5.02.294 P
mars his true moving, even as in the heavens,	1H6	1.02. 1
and if thou vanquishest, thy words are true,		1.02. 96
that shall maintain what i have said is true,		2.04. 73
father's sake, | in honor of a true plantagenet,		2.05. 52
true;		2.05. 94
if richard will be true, not that alone | but		3.01.162
rise, richard, like a true plantagenet, | and		3.01.171
of foot, | and, like true subjects, sons of your		4.01.166
'tis true, i gave a noble to the priest | the		5.04. 23
you shall become true liegemen to his crown.		5.04.128
heat, | to conquer france, his true inheritance?	2H6	1.01. 82
true, madam, none at all.		1.04. 49
true, uncle.		2.01. 46
most true, forsooth;		2.01. 91
too true, and bought his climbing very dear.		2.01. 98
true; made the lame to leap and fly away.		2.01.158
me any scathe | so long as i am loyal, true, and		2.04. 63
madam, 'tis true;		3.01.252
than from true evidence of good esteem | he be		3.02. 21
that he is dead, good warwick, 'tis too true,		3.02.130
true nobility is exempt from fear:		4.01.129
true;		4.02. 16 P
but i say, 'tis true.		4.02.141
nay, 'tis too true; therefore he shall be king.		4.02.147
against thy oath and true allegiance sworn,		5.01. 20
and never live but true unto his liege!		5.01. 82
the first i warrant thee, if dreams prove true.		5.01.195
as i in justice and true right express it.		5.02. 25
that this is true, father, behold his blood.	3H6	1.01. 13
true, clifford, that's richard duke of york.		1.01. 83
not took | before a true and lawful magistrate		1.02. 23
so true men yield, with robbers so o'ermatch'd.		1.04. 64
if this news be true, | poor queen and son, your		3.01. 31
and you were sworn true subjects unto me;		3.01. 78
we are true subjects to the king, king edward.		3.01. 94
he knows the game; how true he keeps the wind!		3.02. 14
o, but impatience waiteth on true sorrow.		3.03. 42
upon thy conscience, | is edward your true king?		3.03.114
pass, | and henceforth i am thy true servitor.		3.03.196
itself | england is safe, if true within itself?		4.01. 40
and their true sovereign whom they must obey?		4.01. 78
but if you mind to hold your true obedience,		4.01.140
so god help montague as he proves true!		4.01.143
and be true king indeed, thou but the shadow.		4.03. 50
edward's fruit, true heir to th' english crown.		4.04. 24
true, my good lord, i know you for no less.		4.07. 22
farewell, my hector, and my troy's true hope.		4.08. 25
and, if the rest be true which i have heard,		5.06. 55
indeed 'tis true that henry told me of;		5.06. 69
and if king edward be as true and just | as i am	R3	1.01. 36
if thou please to hide in this true breast,		1.02.175
then never /was /man true.		1.02.195
or, if she be accus'd on true report, | bear		1.03. 27
and with my hand i seal my true heart's love.		2.01. 10
first, madam, i entreat true peace of you,		2.01. 63
love, charity, obedience, and true duty!		2.02.108
of us, | and the compact is firm and true in me.		2.02.133
ay, sir, it is too true, god help the while!		2.03. 8
and so leisurely | that, if his rule were true,		2.04. 20
to bar my master's heirs in true descent —		3.02. 54
be satisfied, dear god, with our true blood,		3.03. 22
france, | and, by true computation of the time,		3.05. 89
his hand — | true ornaments to know a holy man.		3.07. 99
true, noble prince.		4.02. 15
that edward still should live true noble prince!		4.02. 16
true — when avoided grace makes destiny:		4.04.219
bear her my true love's kiss;		4.04.430
o, true, good catesby.		4.04.449
so deal with him as i prove true to you.		4.04.497
true hope is swift and flies with swallow's		5.02. 23
thou — will our friends prove all true?		5.03.213
the true succeeders of each royal house, | by		5.05. 30
we bring | to make that only true we now intend,	H8	pr 21
and those of true condition, that your subjects		1.02. 19
o, 'tis true;		1.03. 51
true, they are so;		1.03. 62
'tis most true | these news are every where;		2.02. 37
speaks 'em, | and every true heart weeps for't.		2.02. 39
i have been to you a true and humble wife, | at		2.04. 23
and like her true nobility she has | carried		2.04.143
virtue finds no friends) a wife, a true one?		3.01.126
believe it, this is true.		3.02. 25
if what i now pronounce you have found true;		3.02.163
i have told him | what, and how true, thou art;		3.02.416
forgo | so good, so noble, and so true a master?		3.02.423
'tis very true;		4.01. 6
for virtue and true beauty of the soul, | for		4.02.144
'tis true; where is he, denny?		5.01. 82
with a true heart | and brother-love i do it.		5.02.205
man, those joyful tears show thy true /heart.		5.02.208
as true thou tell'st me, when i say i love her,	TRO	1.01. 60
true, he was so;		1.02. 55 P
to say the truth, true and not true.		1.02. 97 P
to say the truth, true and not true.		1.02. 97 P
that's true, make no question of that.		1.02.160 P
i'll be sworn 'tis true;		1.02.173 P
reproof of chance | lies the true proof of men:		1.03. 34
good arms, strong joints, true swords, and,		1.03.238
troy, | to rouse a grecian that is true in love.		1.03.279
true, the purpose is perspicuous as substance,		1.03.324
than adders to the voice | of any true decision.		2.02.173
be true to my lord;		3.02.105 P
who shall be true to us, | when we are so		3.02.124
but alas, | i am as true as truth's simplicity,		3.02.169
true swains in love shall in the world to come		3.02.173
as true as steel, as plantage to the moon, | as		3.02.177
"as true as troilus" shall crown up the verse,		3.02.182
tell me, noble diomed — faith, tell me true,		4.01. 52
you'll be so true to him, to be false to him.		4.02. 55 P
and is it true that i must go from troy?		4.04. 30
hear me, love. be thou but true of heart —		4.04. 58
i true? how now? what wicked deem is this?		4.04. 59
i speak not "be thou true" as fearing thee,		4.04. 62
but "be thou true," say i, to fashion in | my		4.04. 65
be thou true, | and i will see thee.		4.04. 66
but i'll be true.		4.04. 69
but yet be true.		4.04. 74
o heavens, "be true" again?		4.04. 74
my lord, will you be true?		4.04.101
the moral of my wit | is "plain and true";		4.04.108
not, for you know 'tis true | that you are odd,		4.05. 43
the youngest son of priam, a true knight, | not		4.05. 96
o, 'tis true.		5.03. 13
nor you, my brother, with your true sword drawn,		5.03. 56
true indeed!	COR	1.01. 79 P
"true is it, my incorporate friends," quoth he,		1.01.130
martius, 'tis true that you have lately told us,		1.01.227
in earnest, it's true;		1.03. 95 P
this is true, on mine honor, and so i pray go		1.03.100 P
true sword to sword, i'll potch at him some way,		1.10. 15
nay, 'tis true.		2.01.107 P
you, and not without his true purchasing.		2.01.140 P
the gods grant them true!		2.01.141 P
true? pow, waw.		2.01.142 P
true?		2.01.143 P
i'll be sworn they are true.		2.01.143 P
him manifests the true knowledge he has in their		2.02. 13 P
than as guided | by your own true affections,		2.03.231
and in true fear | they gave us our demands."		3.01.134
your dishonor | mangles true judgment, and		3.01.158
true, | the people are the city.		3.01.198
say then; 'tis true, i ought so.		3.03. 62
thou old and true menenius, | thy tears are		4.01. 21
true, so i am.		4.05. 28 P
and say "'tis true," i'd not believe them more		4.05.105
but is this true, sir?		4.06.101
'tis true;		4.06.114
to have | this true which they so seem to fear.		4.06.151
i am one that, telling true under him, must say		5.02. 32 P
and my true lip | hath virgin'd it e'er since.		5.03. 47
aufidius, though i cannot make true wars, | i'll		5.03.190
friend, | art thou certain this is true?		5.04. 44
if you have writ your annals true, 'tis there		5.06.113
tears of true joy for his return to rome.	TIT	1.01. 76
sweet mercy is nobility's true badge.		1.01.119
sith true nobility | warrants these words in		1.01.271
own, | my true betrothed love, and now my wife?		1.01.406
'tis true, the raven doth not hatch a lark,		2.03.149
his napkin, with /his true tears all bewet,		3.01.146
of me, | as true a dog as ever fought at head.		5.01.102
'tis true, 'tis true, witness my knive's sharp		5.03. 63
'tis true, 'tis true, witness my knive's sharp		5.03. 63
of age, | grave witnesses of true experience,		5.03. 78
of that true hand that fought rome's quarrel out		5.03.102
who drown'd their enmity in my true tears, | and		5.03.107
house, | and as he is to witness, this is true.		5.03.124
face, | the last true duties of thy noble son!		5.03.155
'tis true, and therefore women, being the weaker	ROM	1.01. 15 P
is to himself (i will not say how true) | but to		1.01.148
wert so happy by thy stay | to hear true shrift.		1.01.159
in bed asleep, while they do dream things true.		1.04. 52
true, i talk of dreams, | which are the children		1.04. 96
for i ne'er saw true beauty till this night.		1.05. 53
i'll prove more true | than those that have		2.02.100
sweet montague, be true.		2.02.137
plants, herbs, stones, and their true qualities;		2.03. 16
revolts from true birth, stumbling on abuse.		2.03. 20
that last is true — the sweeter rest was mine.		2.03. 43
'warrant thee, my man's as true as steel.		2.04.198
but my true love is grown to such excess | i		2.06. 33
prince, as thou art true, | for blood of ours,		3.01.148
affection makes him false, he speaks not true.		3.01.177
bold, | think true love acted simple modesty.		3.02. 16
give this ring to my true knight, | and bid him		3.02.142
and usest none in that true use indeed | which		3.03.124
or my true heart with treacherous revolt | turn		4.01. 58
and art | could to no issue of true honor bring.		4.01. 65
to cross my obsequies and true love's rite?		5.03. 20
o true apothecary!		5.03.119
a cup clos'd in my true love's hand?		5.03.161
but the true ground of all these piteous woes		5.03.180
their spring, their head, their true descent,		5.03.218
lay | the noble paris and true romeo dead.		5.03.259
be set | as that of true and faithful juliet.		5.03.302
but where there is true friendship, there needs	TIM	1.02. 18
i'll tell you true, i'll call to you.		1.02.217
you tell me true.		2.02.154
is't true? can 't be?		2.02.203
(prithee be not sad, | thou art true and honest;		2.02.221
upon my soul, 'tis true, sir.		3.02. 43
true, as you said, timon is shrunk indeed, | and		3.02. 61
most true, he does.		3.04. 18
most true; the law shall bruise 'em.		3.05. 4
true; for he bears it not about him, 'tis hid.		4.03.406 P
is no time so miserable but a man may be true.		4.03.457 P
had i a steward | so true, so just, and now so		4.03.491
but tell me true | (for i must ever doubt,		4.03.506
does the rumor hold for true that he's | so full		5.01. 3
a just and true report that goes of his having.		5.01. 16
true:		5.01. 43
for each true word, a blister, and each false		5.01.132
i did mark | how he did shake — 'tis true, this	JC	1.02.121
do the players in the theatre, i am no true man.		1.02.261 P
but if you would consider the true cause | why		1.03. 62
for i can give his humor the true bent, | and i		2.01.210
you have said, and show yourselves true romans.		2.01.223
you are my true and honorable wife, | as dear to		2.01.288
if this were true, then should i know this		2.01.291
that will be thaw'd from the true quality | with		3.01. 41
of this untrod state | with all true faith.		3.01.137
that i did love thee, caesar, o, 'tis true;		3.01.194
have all true rites and lawful ceremonies.		3.01.241
most true.		3.02.239
make your vaunting true, | and it shall please		4.03. 52
now as you are a roman tell me true.		4.03.187
if not, 'tis true this parting was well made.		5.01.121
my life | i found no man but he was true to me.		5.05. 35
that thou hast prov'd lucilius' saying true.		5.05. 59
what, can the devil speak true?	MAC	1.03.107
true, worthy banquo!		1.04. 54
so please you, it is true;		1.05. 34
true, my lord.		3.01.114
flaws and starts | (imposters to true fear)		3.04. 63
now i see 'tis true, | for the blood-bolter'd		4.01.122
o, relation! | too nice, and yet too true.		4.03.174
let our just censures | attend the true event,		5.04. 15
without the sensible and true avouch | of mine	HAM	1.01. 57
form of the thing, each word made true and good,		1.02.210
as i do live, my honor'd lord, 'tis true, | and		1.02.221
to thine own self be true, | and it must follow,		1.03. 78
that you have ta'en these tenders for true pay,		1.03.106
mad call i it, for, to define true madness,		2.02. 93
that he's mad, 'tis true, 'tis true 'tis pity,		2.02. 97
that he's mad, 'tis true, 'tis true 'tis pity,		2.02. 97
'tis true 'tis pity, | and pity 'tis 'tis true.		2.02. 98
that's very true, my lord.		2.02.180 P
o, most true, she is a strumpet.		2.02.236 P
but your news is not true.		2.02.239 P
him on to some confession | of his true state.		3.01. 10
'tis most true, | and he beseech'd me to entreat		3.01. 21
o, 'tis too true!		3.01. 48

there the action lies | in his true nature, and 3.03. 62
or but a sickly part of one true sense | could 3.04. 80
then what i have to do | will want true color — 3.04.130
to my sick soul, as sin's true nature is, | each 4.05. 17
the chaste unsmirched brow | of my true mother. 4.05.121
speak | like a good child and a true gentleman. 4.05.149
and rareness as, to make true diction of him, 5.02.118 P
in my true heart | i find she names my very deed LR 1.01. 70
so young, my lord, and true. 1.01.107
me still remain | the true blank of thine eye. 1.01.159
my mind as generous, and my shape as true, | as 1.02. 8
they'll have me whipt for speaking true; 1.04.183 P
if it be true, all vengeance comes too short 2.01. 88
but, for true need — | you heavens, give me 2.04.270
true, boy. come bring us to this hovel. 3.02. 78
true to tell thee, | the grief hath craz'd my 3.04.169
true or false, it hath made thee earl of 3.05. 17 P
is the guess of their true strength and forces, 5.01. 52
and that's true too. 5.02. 11
th' hast spoken right, 'tis true. 5.03.174
'tis true, my lords, he did. 5.03.276
it is too true an evil; OTH 1.01.160
'tis true, most worthy signior; 1.02. 91
away this old man's daughter, | it is most true; 1.03. 79
true i have married her; 1.03. 79
i know not if't be true, | but i, for mere 1.03.388
how? is this true? 2.01. 25
nay, it is true, or else i am a turk: 2.01.114
you say true, 'tis so indeed. 2.01.171 P
though true advantage never present itself; 2.01.244 P
shall come into no true taste again but by the 2.01.275 P
it's true, good lieutenant. 2.03.105 P
is not this true? 2.03.135
he's never any thing but your true servant. 3.03. 9
now do i see 'tis true. 3.03.444
but my noble moor | is true of mind, and made of 3.04. 27
'tis true; 3.04. 69
/i' /faith! is't true? 3.04. 75
prithee say true. 4.01.124 P
for, if she be not honest, chaste, and true, 4.02. 17
your wife, my lord; your true | and loyal wife. 4.02. 34
upon her, | that true hearts cannot bear it. 4.02.117
is that true? 4.02.222 P
o, she was heavenly true! 5.02.135
/nay, had she been true, | if heaven would make 5.02.143
than what he found himself was apt and true. 5.02.177
nay, stare not, masters, it is true indeed. 5.02.188
so come my soul to bliss, as i speak true; 5.02.250
who tells me true, though in his tale lie death, ANT 1.02. 98
why should i think you can be mine, and true 1.03. 27
and give true evidence to his love, which stands 1.03. 74
and have my learning from some true reports 2.02. 47
is this true? 2.02.180 P
be it art or hap, | he hath spoken true. 2.03. 34
all men's faces are true, whatsome'er their 2.06. 97 P
but there is never a fair woman has a true face. 2.06. 99 P
true, sir, she was the wife of caius marcellus. 2.06.110 P
'tis true. 2.06.114 P
the news is true, my lord: 3.07. 54
mock not, enobarbus, | i tell you true. 4.06. 25
o sovereign mistress of true melancholy, | the 4.09. 12
not live to wear | all your true followers out. 4.14.134
may well be laugh'd at, | yet it is true, sir. CYM 1.01. 67
if it be a sin to make a true election, she is 1.02. 27 P
if this be true | (as i have such a heart that 1.06.129
ears | must not in haste abuse), if it be true, 1.06.131
which makes the true man kill'd and saves the 2.03. 71
nay, sometime hangs both thief and true man. 2.03. 72
wrought, | since the true life on't was — 2.04. 76
this is true; 2.04. 76
o, no, no, no, 'tis true. 2.04.106
very true, | and so i hope he came by't. 2.04.117
'tis true — nay, keep the ring — 'tis true. 2.04.123
'tis true — nay, keep the ring — 'tis true. 2.04.123
yet 'tis greater skill | in a true hate, to pray 2.05. 34
then, true pisanio, | who long'st like me to see 3.02. 52
true honest men being heard, like false aeneas, 3.04. 58
tear, took pity | from most true wretchedness. 3.04. 61
sirrah, is this letter true? 3.05.106 P
not be a villain, but do me true service, 3.05.109 P
and true preferment shall tender itself to thee. 3.05.154 P
come, and be true. 3.05.156 P
for true to thee | were to prove false, which i 3.05.157
i will never be | to him that is most true. 3.05.159
no wonder, | when rich ones scarce tell true. 3.06. 12
'tis true. 4.02.256
i dare be bound he's true and shall perform 4.03. 18
not true, to be true. 4.03. 42
not true, to be true. 4.03. 42
you have no true debitor and creditor but it; 5.04.168 P
further to boast were neither true nor modest, 5.05. 18
diligent, | so tender over his occasions, true, 5.05. 87
he, true knight, | no lesser of her honor 5.05.186
most worthy prince, as yours, is true guiderius; 5.05.358
if this be true which makes me pale to read it? PER 1.01. 75
if it be true that i interpret false, | then 1.01.124
show'dst a subject's shine, i a true prince'. 1.02.124
o, 'tis too true. 1.04. 32
is not this true? 1.04. 50
'tis very true. 2.04. 16
a more content in course of true delight | than 3.02. 39
thou say'st true. 4.02. 13 P
thou sayest true, there's two unwholesome, a' 4.02. 21 P
thou sayest true, i' faith, so they must: 4.02.126 P
this borrowed passion stands for true old woe; 4.04. 24
sir, | if you have told diana's altar true, 5.03. 17
yet most quaint, | and sweet thyme true; TNK 1.01. 6
for pity's sake and true gentility's, | hear and 1.01. 25
it is true; 1.01.148
tied, weav'd, entangled, with so true, so long, 1.03. 42
that the true love 'tween maid and maid may be 1.03. 81
it can appear to me report is a true speaker. 2.01. 6 P
'tis too true, arcite. 2.02. 46
'tis most true, two souls | put in two noble 2.02. 64
seen so young a man so noble | (if he say true) 2.05. 19
with the mind and sword | of a true gentleman. 3.01. 57
like true lovers, | cast yourselves in a body 3.05. 19
'tis the duke's, | and, to say true, i stole it. 3.06. 55
virtuous, | the true decider of all injuries, 3.06.153
for, to say true, your cousin | has ten times 3.06.180
no, sir, not well: | 'tis too true, she is mad. 4.01. 46
prettiest posies — "thus our true love's tied," 4.01. 90
'tis true. 4.01.115
"i will be true, my stars, my fate," etc. 4.03. 57
true worshippers of mars, whose spirit in you 5.01. 35
which | is true love's merit, and bless me with 5.01.128
being laid unto | mine innocent true heart, arms 5.01.134
'tis true, | for there, i will assure you, we 5.02. 76
true, and pumpions together. STM II.C 16 P
before god, that's as true as the gospel. II.C 88 P
faith, 'a says true. II.C 141 P
these mine eyes, true leaders to their queen, VEN 503
that sometime true news, sometime false doth 658
rich preys make true men thieves; 724
but true sweet beauty liv'd and died with him. 1080
"'tis true, 'tis true, thus was adonis slain: 1111
"'tis true, 'tis true, thus was adonis slain: 1111
true valor still a true respect should have; LUC 201
true valor still a true respect should have; 201
the sight which makes supposed terror true. 455
his true respect will prison false desire, | and 642
and my true eyes have never practic'd how | to 748
of that true type hath tarquin rifled me. 1050
i will not wrong thy true affection so, | to 1060
true grief is fond and testy as a child, | who 1094
true sorrow then is feelingly suffic'd | when 1112
tune our heart-strings to true languishment. 1141
with soft slow tongue, true mark of modesty, 1220
her grief, but not her grief's true quality. 1313
such harmless creatures have a true respect | to 1347
we will revenge the death of this true wife." 1841
mild as a dove, but neither true nor trusty, PP 7. 2
each kiss her oaths of true love swearing! 7. 8
assured trust, | and in thy suit be humble true; 18.20
"how true a twain | seemeth this concordant one! PHT 45
let those repair | that are either true or fair; 66
if the true concord of well-tuned sounds, | by SON 8. 5
and your true rights be term'd a poet's rage, 17.11
o, let me, true in love, but truly write, | and 21. 9
to find where your true image pictur'd lies, 24. 6
love, my love, that thou mayst true love call, 40. 3
so true a fool is love that in your will 57.13
mine own true love that doth my rest defeat, 61.11
no shape so true, no truth of such account, 62. 6
seek | roses of shadow, since his rose is true? 67. 8
seen, | without all ornament, itself and true, 68.10
o, lest your true love may seem false in this, 72. 9
in true plain words by thy true-telling friend; 82.12
say, "'tis so, 'tis true," | and to the most of 85. 9
so shall i live, supposing thou art true, | like 93. 1
truths translated, and for true things deem'd. 96. 8
"fair," "kind," and "true" is all my argument, 105. 9
"kind," and "true" varying to other words, | and 105.10
"kind," and "true" have often liv'd alone, 105.13
can yet the lease of my true love control, 107. 3
which hath not figur'd to thee my true spirit? 108. 2
alas, 'tis true i have gone here and there, 110. 1
most true it is that i have look'd on truth 110. 5
my most true mind thus maketh mine untrue. 113.14
or whether shall i say mine eye saith true, 114. 3
let me not to the marriage of true minds | admit 116. 1
to be diseas'd ere that there was true needing. 118. 8
but thence i learn, and find the lesson true, 118.13
now i find true | that better is by evil still 119. 9
my deepest sense, how hard true sorrow hits, 120.10
i will be true, despite thy scythe and thee. 123.14
a true soul | when most impeach'd stands least 125.13
in things right true my heart and eyes have 137.13
which have no correspondence with true sight, 148. 2
denote | love's eye is not so true as all men's: 148. 8
o, how can love's eye be true, | that is so 148. 9
to make me give the lie to my true sight, | and 150. 3
which many legions of true hearts had warm'd, 154. 6
and, true to bondage, would not break from LC 34
than the true gouty landlord which doth owe them 140
be, | where neither party is nor true nor kind: 186
"'o, pardon me, in that my boast is true: 246

TRUE-ANOINTED 1 FR 0.0001 REL FR 1 V 0 P
seat | of england's true-anointed lawful king. 3H6 3.03. 29

TRUE-BEGOTTEN 1 FR 0.0001 REL FR 0 V 1 P
o heavens, this is my true-begotten father, who, MV 2.02. 35 P

TRUE-BORN 2 FR 0.0002 REL FR 2 V 0 P
though banish'd, yet a true-born englishman. R2 1.03.309
let him that is a true-born gentleman | and 1H6 2.04. 27

TRUE-BRED 3 FR 0.0003 REL FR 1 V 2 P
she's a beagle, true-bred, and one that adores TN 2.03.179 P
i know them to be as true-bred cowards as ever 1H4 1.02.184 P
o, true-bred! COR 1.01.243

TRUE-DERIVED 1 FR 0.0001 REL FR 1 V 0 P
times | unto a lineal true-derived course. R3 3.07.200

TRUE-DEVOTED 1 FR 0.0001 REL FR 1 V 0 P
a true-devoted pilgrim is not weary | to measure TGV 2.07. 9

TRUE-DISPOSING 1 FR 0.0001 REL FR 1 V 0 P
o upright, just, and true-disposing god, | how R3 4.04. 55

TRUE-DIVINING 1 FR 0.0001 REL FR 1 V 0 P
to prove thou hast a true-divining heart, TIT 2.03.214

TRUE-FIX'D 1 FR 0.0001 REL FR 1 V 0 P
of whose true-fix'd and resting quality | there JC 3.01. 61

TRUE-HEARTED 3 FR 0.0003 REL FR 2 V 1 P
in warwickshire i have true-hearted friends, 3H6 4.08. 9
i swear he is true-hearted, and a soul | none H8 5.01.154
and the noble and true-hearted kent banish'd! LR 1.02.116 P

TRUE-LOVE 8 FR 0.0009 REL FR 8 V 0 P
with twenty odd-conceited true-love knots: TGV 2.07. 46
heart | as when thy lady and thy true-love died, 4.03. 20
thou dost wake, | do it for thy true-love take; MND 2.02. 28
and wash him fresh again with true-love tears. R2 5.01. 10
ere i was ware, | my true-love passion; ROM 2.02.104
"how should i your true-love know | from another HAM 4.05. 23
the ground did not go | with true-love showers." 4.05. 40
"who sees his true-love in her naked bed, VEN 397

TRUE-LOVE'S 2 FR 0.0002 REL FR 2 V 0 P
laid the love-juice on some true-love's sight. MND 3.02. 89
o, stay and hear, your true-love's coming, TN 2.03. 40

TRUE-MEANT 1 FR 0.0001 REL FR 1 V 0 P
infinite distance | from his true-meant design. MM 1.04. 55

TRUEPENNY 1 FR 0.0001 REL FR 1 V 0 P
art thou there, truepenny? HAM 1.05.150

TRUER 17 FR 0.0019 REL FR 12 V 5 P
you have spoken truer than you purpos'd. TMP 2.01. 20 P
but truer stars did govern proteus' birth: TGV 2.07. 74
it is not truer he is angelo | than this is all MM 5.01. 43
there are no faces truer than those that are so ADO 1.01. 27 P
than beauteous, truer than truth itself, have LLL 4.01. 63 P
nothing truer; MND 3.02.280
beguiles the truer office of mine eyes? AWW 5.03.305
far truer spoke than meant. 2H6 3.01.183
shall for thy love kill a far truer love; R3 1.02.190
he hath a lady, wiser, fairer, truer, | than TRO 1.03.275
truth can speak truest not truer than troilus. 3.02. 98 P
there was never a truer rhyme. 4.04. 21 P
never man | sigh'd truer breath; COR 4.05.115
nev'r did poor steward wear a truer grief | for TIM 4.03.480
and i the truer, | so to be false with her. CYM 1.05. 43
nothing truer. TNK 1.02. 79
that lover never yet made sigh | truer than i. 5.01.126

TRUER-HEARTED 1 FR 0.0001 REL FR 0 V 1 P
but an honester and truer-hearted man — well, 2H4 2.04.384 P

TRUEST 14 FR 0.0015 REL FR 12 V 2 P
as true as truest horse, that yet would never MND 3.01. 96
o — "as true as truest horse, that yet would 3.01.102
i trust to take of truest thisby sight. 5.01.275
for the truest poetry is the most feigning, and AYL 3.03. 19 P
and what truth can speak truest not truer than TRO 3.02. 98 P
the best, and truest; TIM 4.03.290
since that the truest issue of thy throne | by MAC 4.03.106
and he is one | the truest manner'd, such a holy CYM 1.06.166
never say hereafter | but i am truest speaker. 5.05.376
and here the bracelet of the truest princess 5.05.416
as i have serv'd her truest, worthiest, | as i TNK 3.06.165
best loves me | and has the truest title in't, 5.01.159
with sweets that shall the truest sight beguile; VEN 1144
way, | each trifle under truest bars to thrust, SON 48. 2

TRUE-TELLING 1 FR 0.0001 REL FR 1 V 0 P
in true plain words by thy true-telling friend; SON 82.12

/TRUIE 1 FR 0.0001 REL FR 0 V 1 P
vomissement, et la /truie lavee au bourbier." H5 3.07. 65 P

TRULL 4 FR 0.0004 REL FR 4 V 0 P
am sure i scar'd the dolphin and his trull, 1H6 2.02. 28
to triumph like an amazonian trull | upon their 3H6 1.04.114
and let my spleenful sons this trull deflow'r. TIT 2.03.191
and gives his potent regiment to a trull | that ANT 3.06. 95

TRULLS 1 FR 0.0001 REL FR 1 V 0 P
our brags | were crak'd of kitchen trulls, or CYM 5.05.177

/TRULY 1 FR 0.0001 REL FR 0 V 1 P
/truly, /and /i /hold /ambition /of /so /airy HAM 2.02.261 P

TRULY 179 FR 0.0202 REL FR 91 V 88 P
truly, sir, i think you'll hardly win her. TGV 1.01.133 P
i do as truly suffer | as e'er i did commit. 5.04. 76
truly i will not go first; WIV 1.01.309 P
truly la! 1.01.309 P
truly, mine host, i must turn away some of my 1.03. 4 P
truly, an honest gentleman; 1.04.163 P
and truly master page is an honest man. 2.02.116 P
and truly she deserves it, for if there be a 2.02.120 P
truly, sir, to see your wife. is she at home? 3.02. 11 P
truly, for mine own part, i would little or 3.04. 62 P
but truly he is very courageous mad about his 4.01. 4 P
truly, i thought there had been one number more, 4.01. 23 P
truly, i am so glad you have nobody here. 4.02. 18 P
yes, truly; MM 1.04. 3
truly, officer, because he hath some offenses in 2.01.185 P
truly, sir, i am a poor fellow that would live. 2.01.223 P
truly, sir, in my poor opinion, they will to't 2.01.233 P
for truly, sir, for your kindness, i owe you a 4.02. 58 P
if i read it not truly, my ancient skill 4.02.155 P
truly, sir, i would desire you to clap into your 4.03. 41 P
but yet most truly will i speak: 5.01. 37
truly the lady fathers herself. ADO 1.01.110 P
i had not a hard heart, for truly i love none. 1.01.127 P
i pray thee tell me truly how thou lik'st her. 1.01.178 P
and truly i hold it a sin to match in my kinred. 2.01. 64 P
no, truly, ursula, she is too disdainful, | i 3.01. 34
and truly i'll devise some honest slanders | to 3.01. 84
of blood in him to be truly touch'd with love. 3.02. 19 P
truly, by your office, you may, but i think they 3.03. 56 P
truly, i would not hang a dog by my will, much 3.03. 63 P
but truly, for mine own part, if it were as 3.05. 20 P
that you have in her, bid her answer truly. 4.01. 75
to make you answer truly to your name. 4.01. 79
no, truly, not, although, until last night, | i 4.01.148
they were never so truly turn'd over and over as 5.02. 35 P
no, truly, but in friendly recompense. 5.04. 83
very reverent sport, truly, and done in the LLL 4.02. 1 P
truly, master holofernes, the epithites are 4.02. 8 P
me | to-morrow truly will i meet with thee. MND 1.01.178
truly, a peck of provender; 4.01. 31 P
i swear, | i cannot truly say how i came here. 4.01.148
but, as i think — for truly would i speak, 4.01.149
truly, the moon shines with a good grace. 5.01.267 P
and so it is, truly, and very notably discharg'c 5.01.360 P
yes, truly, for look you, the sins of the father MV 3.05. 1 P
a' good cheer, for truly i think you are damn'd. 3.05. 5 P
truly then i fear you are damn'd both by father 3.05. 15 P
truly, the more to blame he; 3.05. 21 P
and truly, when he dies, thou shalt be his heir; AYL 1.02. 18 P
most truly limn'd and living in your face, | be 2.07.194
living in your face, | be truly welcome hither. 2.07.195
truly, shepherd, in respect of itself, it is a 3.02. 13 P
no, truly. 3.02. 34 P
truly, thou art damn'd, like an ill-roasted egg 3.02. 37 P
truly, the tree yields bad fruit. 3.02.116 P
something and for no passion truly any thing, as 3.02.414 P
truly, i would the gods had made thee poetical. 3.03. 15 P
no, truly; 3.03. 19 P
i do, truly; 3.03. 25 P
no, truly, unless thou wert hard-favor'd; 3.03. 29 P
truly, and to cast away honesty upon a foul slut 3.03. 35 P
truly, she must be given, or the marriage is not 3.03. 69 P
if you will see a pageant truly play'd | between 3.04. 52
truly, young gentlemen, though there was no 5.03. 34 P
tell me, sweet kate, and tell me truly too, SHR 4.05. 28
work in me for thine avail, | to tell me truly. AWW 1.03.185

had you not lately an intent — speak truly — 1.03.218
truly, madam, if god have lent a man any manners 2.02. 8 P
i may truly say it is a novelty to the world. 2.03. 20 P
truly, she's very well indeed, but for two 2.04. 8 P
and truly, as i hope to live. 4.03.128 P
ever a friend whose thoughts more truly labor 4.04. 17
truly, fortune's displeasure is but sluttish if 5.02. 6 P
'tis beauty truly blent, whose red and white TN 1.05.239
truly, sir, and pleasure will be paid, one time 2.04. 70 P
truly, sir, the better for my foes and the worse 5.01. 12 P
truly, madam, he holds belzebub at the stave's 5.01.284 P
to make us say, | "this is put forth too truly." WT 1.02. 14
we have always truly serv'd you, and beseech' 2.03.148
tyrant, his innocent babe truly begotten, and 3.02.134 P
to pay that duty which you truly owe | to him JN 2.01.247
do amiss | is not amiss when it is truly done; 3.01.271
tongue soe'er speaks false, | not truly speaks; 4.03. 92
who speaks not truly, lies. 4.03. 92
speak truly on thy knighthood and thy oath, | as R2 1.03. 14
me — | and as i truly fight, defend me heaven! 1.03. 25
me — | and as i truly fight, defend me heaven! 1.03. 41
to demand that truly which thou wouldest truly 1H4 1.02. 5 P
that truly which thou wouldest truly know. 1.02. 5 P
if a man should speak truly, little better than 1.02. 94 P
saint nicholas as truly as a man of falsehood 2.01. 65 P
shrewsbury, | as i am truly given to understand, 4.04. 11
if like a christian thou hadst truly borne 5.05. 9
i have serv'd your worship truly, sir, this 2H4 5.01. 47 P
the service that i truly did his life | hath 5.02. 7
line, | in every branch truly demonstrative; H5 2.04. 89
"as duly, but not as truly, | as bird doth sing 3.02. 18
i tell thee truly, herald, | i know not if the 4.07. 83
and never changes, but keeps his course truly. 5.02.164 P
and i thine, most truly falsely, must needs be 5.02.191 P
more truly now may this be verified, | for none 1H6 1.02. 32
no, truly, 'tis more than manners will; 2.02. 54
i'll see it truly done, my lord of york. 2H6 3.01.330
he that is truly dedicate to war | hath no 5.02. 37
so thrive i, as i truly swear the like! R3 2.01. 11
truly, the hearts of men are full of fear. 2.03. 38
truly, gentlemen, | a bloody tyrant and a 5.03.245
yes, truly is he, and condemn'd upon't. H8 2.01. 8
succeeding, truly pitying | my father's loss, 2.01.112
my lord of norfolk, as you are truly noble, | as 3.02.289
never so truly happy, my good cromwell; 3.02.377
with th' king, and truly | a worthy friend. 4.01.109
god shall be truly known, and those about her 5.04. 36
truly, lady, no. TRO 3.01. 54 P
make devils of cherubins, they never see truly. 3.02. 70 P
than grateful | to us that give you truly. COR 1.09. 55
and truly i think if all our wits were to issue 2.03. 21 P
be that you seem, truly your country's friend, 3.01.217
it is so, sir. truly, i have forgot you. 4.03. 3 P
yes, mercy, if you report him truly. 5.04. 25 P
nay, truly, sir, i could never say grace in all TIT 4.03.100 P
love then lies | not truly in their hearts, but ROM 2.03. 68
truly it were an ill thing to be off'red to any 2.04.169 P
no, truly, sir, not a penny. 2.04.183 P
none | can truly say he gives if he receives. TIM 1.02. 11
he's truly valiant that can wisely suffer | the 3.05. 31
truly, sir, in respect of a fine workman, i am JC 1.01. 10 P
truly, sir, all that i live by is with the awl: 1.01. 21 P
truly, sir, to wear out their shoes, to get 1.01. 29 P
and tell me truly what thou think'st of him. 1.02.214
ay, and truly, you were best. 3.03. 12 P
man directly and briefly, wisely and truly: 3.03. 16 P
your name, sir, truly. 3.03. 26 P
truly, my name is cinna. 3.03. 27 P
what i am truly | is thine and my poor country's MAC 4.03.131
we on | to give obedience where 'tis truly ow'd. 5.02. 26
/shapes of grief, | that can /denote me truly. HAM 1.02. 83
lord, i do not know, | but truly i do fear it. 2.01. 83
he truly found | it was against your highness. 2.02. 64
and truly in my youth i suff'red much extremity 2.02.189 P
ay, truly, for the power of beauty will sooner 3.01.110 P
truly to speak, and with no addition, | we go to 4.04. 17
all this can i | truly deliver. 5.02.386
to serve him truly that will put me in trust, to LR 1.04. 14 P
i shall serve you, sir, | truly, however else. 2.01.117
no, truly. 4.06. 4
tell me but truly, but then speak the truth, 5.01. 8
nor all masters | cannot be truly follow'd. OTH 1.01. 44
truly, i think they are. 1.01.168
as truly as to heaven | i do confess the vices 1.03.122
'tis truly so. 2.01.179
for if he be not one that truly loves you, 3.03. 48
truly, /an obedient lady: 4.01.248
heaven doth truly know it. 4.02. 38
heaven truly knows that thou art false as hell. 4.02. 39
truly, i have him; ANT 5.02.245 P
truly, she makes a very good report o' th' worm; 5.02.254 P
but truly, these same whoreson devils do the 5.02.275 P
his virtue | by her election may be truly read, CYM 1.01. 53
it shall safe be kept, | and truly yielded you. 1.06.210
him hourly to your ear | as truly as he moves. 3.04.151
(the handmaids of all women, or, more truly, 3.04.156
to perform it directly and truly, i would think 3.05.113 P
should meet, if pisanio have mapp'd it truly. 4.01. 2 P
serve truly; 4.02.373
her honor confident | than i did truly find her, 5.05.188
sav'd too, | speaking it truly? TNK 1.02. 49
speak truly: 2.02.191
thee | and take thy life, i deal but truly. 2.02.203
the birthright of this beauty | truly pertains 3.06. 32
them, | that truly noble prince pirithous, 4.01. 13
yes, truly, can i. 4.01.107
i will, sir, | and truly what i think. 4.02. 73
they knew, | and him by oath they truly honored: LUC 410
o, let me, true in love, but truly write, | and SON 21. 9
the wrinkles which thy glass will truly show, 77. 5
thou, truly fair, wert truly sympathiz'd | in 82.11
wert truly sympathiz'd | in true plain words by 82.11
and truly not the morning sun of heaven | better 132. 5

TRUMP 5 FR 0.0005 REL FR 5 V 0 P
whilst any trump did sound, or drum struck up, 1H6 1.04. 80
when fame shall in our islands sound her trump, TRO 3.03.210
proclaim our honors, lords, with trump and drum. TIT 1.01.275
what means that trump? how now? TIM 1.02.115
the neighing steed and the shrill trump, | the OTH 3.03.351

TRUMPERY *(also trompery)*

TRUMPERY 1 FR 0.0001 REL FR 1 V 0 P
the trumpery in my house, go bring it hither, TMP 4.01.186

TRUMPET *(also trompet)*

/TRUMPET 2 FR 0.0002 REL FR 2 V 0 P
/and /the /loud /trumpet /blowing /them 2H4 4.01.120
/sound, /trumpet! LR 5.03.109

TRUMPET 59 FR 0.0066 REL FR 54 V 5 P
contrary, to be the trumpet of his own virtues, ADO 5.02. 85 P
the trumpet sounds, be mask'd; the maskers come. LLL 5.02.157
if they but hear perchance a trumpet sound, | or MV 5.01. 75
your husband is at hand, i hear his trumpet. 5.01.122
sirrah, go see what trumpet 'tis that sounds. SHR in.1. 74
my red–look'd anger be | the trumpet any more. WT 2.02. 33
be thou the trumpet of our wrath, | and sullen JN 1.01. 27
some trumpet summon hither to the walls | these 2.01.198
our trumpet call'd you to this gentle parle — 2.01.205
what lusty trumpet thus doth summon us? 5.02.117
but the summons of the appellant's trumpet. R2 1.03. 4
through brazen trumpet send the breath of parley 3.03. 33
wind | doth play the trumpet to his purposes, 1H4 5.01. 4
the trumpet sounds retrait, the day is our. 5.04.159
divine | to a loud trumpet and a point of war? 2H4 4.01. 52
and the trumpet call us to the breach, and we H5 3.02.108 P
i will the banner from a trumpet take, | and use 4.02. 61
take a trumpet, herald, | ride thou unto the 4.07. 56
now, when the angry trumpet sounds alarum, | and 2H6 5.02. 3
now let the general trumpet blow his blast, 5.02. 43
sound trumpet, edward shall be here proclaim'd. 3H6 4.07. 69
go, trumpet, to the walls, and sound a parle. 5.01. 16
the trumpet sounds, be copious in exclaims. R3 4.04.135
what trumpet? look, menelaus. TRO 1.03.213
i bring a trumpet to awake his ear, | to set his 1.03.251
trumpet, blow /loud, | send thy brass voice 1.03.256
he bade me take a trumpet, | and to this purpose 1.03.263
and will to–morrow with his trumpet call, 1.03.277
will with a trumpet 'twixt our tents and troy 2.01.123
pride is his own glass, his own trumpet, his own 2.03.155 P
hark, hector's trumpet! 4.04.140
give with thy trumpet a loud note to troy, 4.05. 3
thou, trumpet, there's my purse. 4.05. 6
no trumpet answers. 4.05. 12
the troyans' trumpet. 4.05. 64
ho! bid my trumpet sound! 5.03. 13
the troyans' trumpet sound the like, my lord. 5.08. 16
go sound thy trumpet in the market–place; COR 1.05. 26
then, dreadful trumpet, sound the general doom, ROM 3.02. 67
that such a hideous trumpet calls to parley MAC 2.03. 82
the cock, that is the trumpet to the morn, HAM 1.01.150
the kettle–drum and trumpet thus bray out | the 1.04. 11
been lodg'd | till the last trumpet; 5.01.230
cups, | and let the kettle to the trumpet speak, 5.02.275
speak, | the trumpet to the cannoneer without, 5.02.276
let the trumpet sound | for him that brought it. LR 5.01. 41
art armed, gloucester, let the trumpet sound. 5.03. 90
call by the trumpet; 5.03. 99
let the trumpet sound, | and read out this. 5.03.107
him appear by the third sound of the trumpet. 5.03.114 P
why he appears | upon this call o' th' trumpet. 5.03.119
storm of fortunes | may trumpet to the world. OTH 1.03.250
i know his trumpet. 2.01.178 P
excellent good. what trumpet is that same? 4.01.213
so tart a favor | to trumpet such good tidings! ANT 2.05. 39
he must not live to trumpet forth my infamy, PER 1.01.145
he speaks, his tongue | sounds like a trumpet. TNK 4.02.113
first like a trumpet doth his tongue begin | to LUC 470
sole arabian tree, | herald sad and trumpet be, PHT 3

TRUMPET–CLANGOR 1 FR 0.0001 REL FR 1 V 0 P
roar'd the sea, and trumpet–clangor sounds. 2H4 5.05. 40

TRUMPETER 2 FR 0.0002 REL FR 2 V 0 P
go to the gates of burdeaux, trumpeter, | summon 1H6 4.02. 1
our steed the leg, the tongue our trumpeter, COR 1.01.117

TRUMPETERS 2 FR 0.0002 REL FR 1 V 1 P
in us, to be trumpeters of our unlawful intents? AWW 4.03. 27 P
trumpeters, | with brazen din blast you the ANT 4.08. 35

TRUMPET'S 4 FR 0.0004 REL FR 3 V 1 P
spurr'd their coursers at the trumpet's sound; 3H6 5.07. 9
what trumpet's that? TIM 1.01.240
will fare so harshly o' th' trumpet's sound; 3.06. 35 P
what trumpet's that? LR 2.04.182

TRUMPETS' 2 FR 0.0002 REL FR 2 V 0 P
'larums, neighing steeds, and trumpets' clang? SHR 1.02.206
with harsh–resounding trumpets' dreadful bray, R2 1.03.135

/TRUMPETS 1 FR 0.0001 REL FR 1 V 0 P
/twice /then /the /trumpets /sounded, | /and LR 5.03.218

TRUMPETS 30 FR 0.0034 REL FR 26 V 4 P
and bid them bring the trumpets to the gate. MM 4.05. 9
twice have the trumpets sounded; 4.06. 12
you may know by their trumpets. AWW 3.05. 9 P
the king's coming, i know by his trumpets. 5.02. 52 P
shall braying trumpets and loud churlish drums, JN 3.01.303
sound, trumpets, and set forward, combatants. R2 1.03.117
us, and let the trumpets sound | while we return 1.03.121
the trumpets have sounded twice. 2H4 5.05. 2 P
then let the trumpets sound | the tucket sonance H5 4.02. 34
sound, trumpets, alarum to the combatants! 2H6 2.03. 92
sound drum and trumpets, and to london all, 5.03. 32
sound drums and trumpets, and the king will fly. 3H6 1.01.118
but sound the trumpets, and about our task. 2.01.200
sound trumpets! 2.02.173
sound drums and trumpets! 5.07. 45
a flourish, trumpets! R3 4.04.149
sound drums and trumpets boldly and cheerfully. 5.03.269
the trumpets sound; H8 4.01. 36
hark, the trumpets sound; 5.03. 82
we fear, | w' have frighted with our trumpets; ep 4
/loud /the /taborins, let the trumpets blow, TRO 4.05.275
when drums and trumpets shall | i' th' field COR 1.09. 42
hark, the trumpets. 2.01.157 P
the trumpets, sackbuts, psalteries, and fifes, 5.04. 49
why do the emperor's trumpets flourish thus? TIT 4.02. 49
the trumpets show the emperor is at hand. 5.03. 16
make all our trumpets speak, give them all MAC 5.06. 9
hark, the duke's trumpets! LR 2.01. 79
trumpets, speak! 5.03.151
these drums, these trumpets, flutes! ANT 2.07.131

TRUMPET–TONGU'D 1 FR 0.0001 REL FR 1 V 0 P
will plead like angels, trumpet–tongu'd, against MAC 1.07. 19

TRUNCHEON 4 FR 0.0004 REL FR 3 V 1 P
the marshal's truncheon, nor the judge's robe, MM 2.02. 61
they would truncheon you out for taking their 2H4 2.04.142 P
thy leg a stick compared with this truncheon; 2H6 4.10. 49
mars | beck'ning with fiery truncheon my retire, TRO 5.03. 53

TRUNCHEONERS 1 FR 0.0001 REL FR 0 V 1 P
far some forty truncheoners draw to her succor, H8 5.03. 52 P

TRUNCHEON'S 1 FR 0.0001 REL FR 1 V 0 P
within his truncheon's length, whilst they, HAM 1.02.204

TRUNDLE–TAIL 1 FR 0.0001 REL FR 1 V 0 P
or /lym, | or bobtail /tike or trundle–tail, LR 3.06. 70

TRUNK 20 FR 0.0022 REL FR 17 V 3 P
was | the ivy which had hid my princely trunk, TMP 1.02. 86
press, coffer, chest, trunk, well, vault, but he WIV 4.02. 61 P
would bark your honor from that trunk you bear, MM 3.01. 71
"with a trunk sleeve" — SHR 4.03.141 P
that lies enclosed in this trunk which you WT 1.02.435
dost thou converse with that trunk of humors, 1H4 2.04.449 P
wings is flown | from this bare wither'd trunk. 2H4 4.05.229
my ransom is this frail and worthless trunk; H5 3.06.154
to tell my love unto his dumb deaf trunk, | and 2H6 3.02.144
leaving thy trunk for crows to feed upon. 4.10. 84
until my misshap'd trunk that bears this head 3H6 3.02.170
honor'd mould | wherein this trunk was fram'd, COR 5.03. 23
and make his dead trunk pillow to our lust. TIT 2.03.130
near | to shed obsequious tears upon this trunk. 5.03.152
and that the trunk may be discharg'd of breath ROM 5.01. 63
thy banish'd trunk be found in our dominions, LR 1.01.177
they are in a trunk, | attended by my men. CYM 1.06.196
send your trunk to me, it shall safe be kept, 1.06.209
to th' trunk again, and shut the spring of it. 2.02. 47
soft ho, what trunk is here? 4.02.353

TRUNKS 4 FR 0.0004 REL FR 4 V 0 P
infuse themselves | into the trunks of men. MV 4.01.133
are empty trunks o'erflourish'd by the devil. TN 3.04.370
lie like pawns lock'd up in chests and trunks, JN 5.02.141
of wreakful heaven, whose bare unhoused trunks, TIM 4.03.229

TRUNK–WORK 1 FR 0.0001 REL FR 0 V 1 P
this has been some stair–work, some trunk–work, WT 3.03. 74 P

TRUSS'D 1 FR 0.0001 REL FR 1 V 0 P
is truss'd up in a trice | to–morrow morning; TNK 3.04. 17

/TRUST 1 FR 0.0001 REL FR 1 V 0 P
/what /trust /is /in /these /times? 2H4 1.03.100

TRUST 180 FR 0.0203 REL FR 144 V 36 P
brother | awak'd an evil nature, and my trust, TMP 1.02. 93
as great | as my trust was, which had indeed no 1.02. 96
now, trust me, 'tis an office of great worth, TGV 1.02. 44
now trust me, madam, it came hardly off; 2.01.109
no, trust me, she is peevish, sullen, froward, 3.01. 68
and, proteus, we dare trust you in this kind, 3.02. 56
trust me, i think 'tis almost day. 4.02.137 P
i am sorry i must never trust thee more, | but 5.04. 69
mistress page, trust me, i was going to your WIV 2.01. 33 P
and, trust me, i was coming to you. 2.01. 35 P
trust me, i thought on her. she'll fit it. 2.01.160 P
he will trust his wife, he will not be jealous. 2.02.301 P
i will rather trust a fleming with my butter, 2.02.302 P
trust me, a good knot. 3.02. 51 P
go in, gentlemen, but, trust me, we'll mock him. 3.03.228 P
upon no trail, never trust me when i open again. 4.02.197 P
trust me, he beat him most pitifully. 4.02.201 P
and i trust it will grow to a most prosperous MM 3.01.260 P
trust not my holy order | if i pervert your 4.03.147
and, on my trust, a man that never yet | did, as 5.01.147
now trust me, were it not against our laws, ERR 1.01.142
how dar'st thou trust | so great a charge from 1.02. 60
and will not lightly trust the messenger, | that 4.04. 5
no, trust me, sir, nor i. 5.01.303
i would scarce trust myself, though i had sworn ADO 1.01.195 P
any, i will do myself the right to trust none; 1.01.244 P
niece, i trust you will be rul'd by your father. 2.01. 50 P
eye negotiate for itself, | and trust no agent; 2.01.179
wilt thou make a trust a transgression? 2.01.225 P
upon this, i will never trust my expectation. 2.03.212 P
if you dare not trust that you see, confess not 3.02.119 P
trust not my reading, nor my observations, 4.01.165
trust not my age, | my reverence, calling, nor 4.01.167
o, never will i trust to speeches penn'd, | nor LLL 5.02.402
your oath i will not trust, but go with speed 5.02.794
to trust the opportunity of night | and the ill MND 2.01.217
i'll not trust your word. 3.02.268
i will not trust you, i, | nor longer stay in 3.02.340
trust me, sweet, | out of this silence yet i 5.01. 99
i trust to take of truest thisby sight. 5.01.275
and i no question make | to have it of my trust, MV 1.01.185
to please his grandam, never trust me more. 2.02.197
or be not frantic | (as i do trust i am not), AYL 1.03. 50
let it suffice thee that i trust thee not. 1.03. 55
as we do trust they'll end, in true delights. 5.04.198
trust me, i take him for the better dog. SHR in.1. 25
why, and i trust i may go too, may i not? 1.01.102
"hic est /sigeia tellus," i trust you not, "hic 3.01. 43 P
but thus, i trust, you will not marry her. 3.02.115
if he be credulous, and trust my tale, | i'll 4.02. 67
why, sir, i trust i may have leave to speak, 4.03. 73
then never trust me if i be afeard. 5.02. 17
love all, trust a few, | do wrong to none. AWW 1.01. 64
more to know could not be more to trust — 2.01.206
trust him not in matter of heavy consequence; 2.05. 44 P
upon oath, never trust my judgment in any thing. 3.06. 32 P
first, give me trust, the count he is my husband 3.07. 8
i will never trust a man again for keeping his 4.03.144 P
you never had a servant to whose trust | your 4.04. 15
bid him turn you out of doors, never trust me. TN 2.03. 74 P
if i do not, never trust me, take it how you 2.03.188 P
never trust me then; 3.02. 58 P
me | to any other trust but that i am mad | or 4.03. 15
a servant grafted in my serious trust | and WT 1.02.246
if therefore you dare trust my honesty, | that 1.02.434
wish'd to see you sorry, now | i trust i shall. 2.01.124
when i feel and see her no farther trust her; 2.01.136
if she dares trust me with her little babe, 2.02. 35

commit me for committing honor — trust it, | he 2.03. 49
more than man | and after that trust to thee. 4.04.536
and trust, his sworn brother, a very simple 4.04.595 P
i will trust you. 4.04.824 P
be drunk, not being a tall fellow, trust me not. 5.02.172 P
which trust accordingly, kind citizens, | and JN 2.01.231
i trust we shall, | if not fill up the measure 2.01.555
i trust i may not trust thee, for thy word | is 3.01. 7
i trust i may not trust thee, for thy word | is 3.01. 7
trust not those cunning waters of his eyes, 4.03.107
some honest christian trust me with a gage — R2 4.01. 83
good brother, we shall thrive, i trust. 1H4 1.03.300
and so far will i trust thee, gentle kate. 2.03.112
shalt have charge and sovereign trust herein. 3.02.161
to lay so dangerous and dear a trust | on any 4.01. 34
you have deceiv'd our trust, | and made us doff 5.01. 11
we will not trust our eyes | without our ears: 5.04.136
misuse the tenor of thy kinsman's trust? 5.05. 5
i trust, lords, we shall lie to–night together. 2H4 4.02. 97
god, his grace is bold to trust these traitors. H5 2.02. 1
trust none; 2.03. 50
to see it, i will never trust his word after. 4.01.195 P
you'll never trust his word after! 4.01.201 P
upon the which, i trust, | shall witness live in 4.03. 96
no prophet will i trust, if she prove false. 1H6 1.02.150
ne'er trust me then; 2.02. 48
i trust ere long to choke thee with thine own, 3.02. 46
what is the trust or strength of foolish man? 3.02.112
that will not trust thee but for profit's sake? 3.03. 63
so farewell, talbot, i'll no longer trust thee. 3.03. 84
his false hopes, the trust of england's honor, 4.04. 20
i trust the ghost of talbot is not there. 5.02. 16
farewell, my lord, trust not the kentish rebels. 2H6 4.04. 57
trust nobody, for fear you /be betray'd. 4.04. 58
the trust i have is in mine innocence, | and 4.04. 59
in them i trust, for they are soldiers, | witty, 3H6 1.02. 42
and trust not simple henry nor his oaths. 1.02. 59
trust me, my lord, all hitherto goes well, | the 4.02. 1
(for trust not him that hath once broken faith), 4.04. 30
is put unto the trust of richard gloucester, | a R3 1.03. 12
live well endeavors to trust to himself and live 1.04.143 P
to trust the mock'ry of unquiet slumbers. 3.02. 27
but i trust | my absence doth neglect no great 3.04. 23
but i'll not trust thee. 4.04.491
hear | (this was his gentleman in trust) of him H8 1.02.125
they that my trust must grow to, live not here. 3.01. 89
(if you please | to trust us in your business), 3.01.173
and trust to me, ulysses, | our imputation shall TRO 1.03.338
i will no more trust him when he leers than i 5.01. 89 P
in faith i will lo, never trust me else. 5.02. 59
trust ye? COR 1.01.181
side | they have plac'd their men of trust? 1.06. 52
vaward are the /antiates, | of their best trust; 1.06. 54
or never trust to what my tongue can do | i' th' 3.02.136
assault thy country than to tread | (trust to't, 5.03.124
send thee by me, their tribune and their trust, TIT 1.01.181
a goodly lady, trust me, of the hue | that i 1.01.261
i'll trust by leisure him that mocks me once, 1.01.301
i see thou wilt not trust the air | with secrets 4.02.169
but trust me, gentleman, i'll prove more true ROM 2.02.100
there's no trust, | no faith, no honesty in men, 3.02. 85
and trust me, love, in my eye so do you; 3.05. 58
trust to't, bethink you, i'll not be forsworn. 3.05.195
if i may trust the flattering truth of sleep, 5.01. 1
i wonder men dare trust themselves with men. TIM 1.02. 43
so fond, | to trust man on his oath or bond; 1.02. 65
i'll trust to your conditions, be whores still. 4.03.140
trust not the physician, | his antidotes are 4.03.431
trust not trebonius; JC 2.03. 3 P
these skipping kerns to trust their heels, | but MAC 1.02. 30
a gentleman on whom i built | an absolute trust. 1.04. 14
he's here in double trust: 1.07. 12
ride, | and damn'd all those that trust them! 4.01.139
night, | to desperation turn my trust and hope, HAM 3.02.218
whom i will trust as i will adders fang'd, 3.04.203
to serve him truly that will put me in trust, to LR 1.04. 14 P
safer than trust too far. 1.04.328
thee, would the reposal | of any trust, virtue, 2.01. 69
natures of such deep trust we shall much need; 2.01.115
i will lay trust upon thee; 3.05. 24 P
if not, i'll ne'er trust medicine. 5.03. 96
trust to thy single virtue, for thy soldiers, 5.03.103
from hence trust not your daughters' minds | by OTH 1.01.170
the trust, the office i do hold of you, | not 1.03.118
a man he is of honesty and trust. 1.03.284
i fear the trust othello puts him in, | on some 2.03.126
madam, i trust not so. ANT 1.05. 7
not fight by sea, | trust not to rotten planks. 3.07. 62
have entertainment, but | no honorable trust. 4.06. 17
none about caesar trust but proculeius. 4.15. 48
my resolution and my hands i'll trust, | none 4.15. 49
antony | did tell me of you, bade me trust you, 5.02. 13
of no more trust | than love that's hir'd! 5.02.154
hah? | no harm, i trust, is done? CYM 1.01.161
leave her in such honor as you have trust in, 1.04.152 P
and will not trust one of her malice with | a 1.05. 35
upon him accordingly, as you value your trust — 1.06. 24 P
that thy lady hath of thee | deserves thy trust, 1.06.158
their tenure good, i trust. 2.04. 36
pray you trust me here, | i'll rob none but 4.02. 14
tells us life's but breath, to trust it error. PER 1.01. 46
his seal'd commission, left in trust with me, 1.03. 12
thyself) | than i will trust a sickly appetite, TNK 1.03. 89
do, maids will not so easily | trust men again. 2.06. 21
so priam's trust false sinon's tears doth LUC 1560
not daring trust the office of mine eyes. PP 14.16
serve always with assured trust, | and in thy 18.19
so i, for fear of trust, forget to say | the SON 23. 5
from hands of falsehood, in sure wards of trust! 48. 4
to trust those tables that receive thee more: 122.12
savage, extreme, rude, cruel, not to trust, 129. 4
o, love's best habit is in seeming trust, | and 138.11

TRUSTED 11 FR 0.0012 REL FR 9 V 2 P

who should be trusted, when one's right hand TGV 5.04. 67
i am trusted with a muzzle and enfranchis'd with ADO 1.03. 32 P
it, | my ventures are not in one bottom trusted, MV 1.01. 42
let no such man be trusted. 5.01. 88
i have trusted thee, camillo, | with all the WT 1.02.235
eyes, | for treason is but trusted like the fox, 1H4 5.02. 9
by the false faith of him whom most i trusted; R3 5.01. 17
let him in nought be trusted | for speaking H8 2.04.136
that, trusted home, | might yet enkindle you MAC 1.03.120
no man's life was to be trusted with them. 2.03.105
worm is not to be trusted but in the keeping of ANT 5.02.265 P

TRUSTER 1 FR 0.0001 REL FR 1 V 0 P

to make it truster of your own report | against HAM 1.02.172

TRUSTERS' 1 FR 0.0001 REL FR 1 V 0 P

your knives, | and cut your trusters' throats! TIM 4.01. 10

TRUSTING 6 FR 0.0006 REL FR 6 V 0 P

for 'tis no trusting to yond foolish lout — TGV 4.04. 66
when saucy trusting of the cozen'd thoughts AWW 4.04. 23
(not trusting to this halting legate here, JN 5.02.174
and but in purged judgment trusting neither? H5 2.02.136
'tis better using france than trusting france. 3H6 4.01. 42
to be deceiv'd, | that have no use for trusting. ANT 5.02. 15

TRUSTLESS 1 FR 0.0001 REL FR 1 V 0 P

borne by the trustless wings of false desire, LUC 2

/TRUSTS 1 FR 0.0001 REL FR 0 V 1 P

/he's /mad /that /trusts /in /the /tameness /of LR 3.06. 18 P

TRUSTS 3 FR 0.0003 REL FR 3 V 0 P

a man is well holp up that trusts to you: ERR 4.01. 22
he that trusts to you, | where he should find COR 1.01.170
there's never a one of you but trusts a knave TIM 5.01. 93

TRUSTY 21 FR 0.0023 REL FR 19 V 2 P

adieu, trusty pompey. MM 3.02. 77 P
a trusty villain, sir, that very oft, | when i ERR 1.02. 19
the trusty thisby, coming first by night, | did MND 5.01.140
and finds his trusty thisby's mantle slain; 5.01.145
and, like limander, am i trusty still. 5.01.196
come, trusty sword, | come, blade, my breast 5.01.343
my trusty servant, well approv'd in all, | here SHR 1.01. 7
your ancient, trusty, pleasant servant grumio. 1.02. 47
at some great and trusty business in a main AWW 3.06. 15 P
stay yet another day, thou trusty welshman. R2 2.04. 5
but for our trusty brother–in–law and the abbot, 5.03.137
given, | like to a trusty squire did run away; 1H6 4.01. 23
our trusty friend, unless i be deceiv'd. 3H6 4.07. 41
use careful watch, choose trusty /sentinels. R3 5.03. 54
"for i must bear thee to a trusty goth, | who, TIT 5.01. 34
farewell, be trusty, and i'll quit thy pains. ROM 2.04.192
this trusty servant | shall pass between us. LR 4.02. 18
your trusty and most valiant servitor, | with OTH 1.03. 40
this treachery, like a most trusty lover, | i TNK 3.06.150
mild as a dove, but neither true nor trusty, PP 7. 2
for of the two the trusty knight was wounded 15.11

TRUTH *(also trot*, troth)*

/TRUTH 1 FR 0.0001 REL FR 1 V 0 P

/in /twelve, | /found /truth /in /all /but /one; R2 4.01.171

TRUTH 346 FR 0.0391 REL FR 276 V 70 P

like one | who having into truth, by telling of TMP 1.02.100
no; he doth but mistake the truth totally. 2.01. 58 P
the truth you speak doth lack some gentleness, 2.01.138
scarce think | their eyes do offices of truth, 5.01.156
for truth hath better deeds than words to grace TGV 2.02. 18
then speak the truth by her; 2.04.151
wrong, | to bear a hard opinion of his truth: 2.07. 81
one, lady, if you knew his pure heart's truth, 4.02. 88
witness good bringing up, fortune, and truth: 4.04. 69
hear the truth of it: WIV 1.04. 76 P
in truth, sir, and she is pretty, and honest, 1.04.139 P
would have gone to the truth of his words; 2.01. 61 P
do you think there is truth in them? 2.01.172 P
yes, in truth. 2.02.104 P
age | this tale of herne the hunter for a truth. 4.04. 38
and till he tell the truth, | let the supposed 4.04. 61
the truth being known, | we'll all present 4.04. 63
hear the truth of it. 5.05.220
the truth is, she and i (long since contracted) 5.05.223
away! let's go learn the truth of it. MM 1.02. 81 P
and yet, to say the truth, i had as lief have 1.02.133 P
fewness and truth, 'tis thus: 1.04. 39
she (having the truth of honor in her) hath made 3.01.164 P
that appears not foul in the truth of my spirit. 3.01.206 P
there is scarce truth enough alive to make 3.02.226 P
i would say the truth, but to accuse him so, 4.06. 2
for truth is truth | to th' end of reck'ning. 5.01. 45
for truth is truth | to th' end of reck'ning. 5.01. 45
to make the truth appear where it seems hid, 5.01. 66
confess the truth, and say by whose advice 5.01.113
as there is sense in truth, and truth in virtue, 5.01.226
as there is sense in truth, and truth in virtue, 5.01.226
against my soul's pure truth, why labor you, ERR 3.02. 37
is, | i long to know the truth hereof at large. 4.04.143
but she tells to your highness simple truth! 5.01.211
my lord, in truth, thus far i witness with him: 5.01.255
appear such seeming truth of hero's disloyalty, ADO 2.02. 48 P
they have the truth of this from hero; 2.03.222 P
'tis a truth, i can bear them witness; 2.03.231 P
why, you speak truth. 3.01. 59
and never gives to truth and virtue that | which 3.01. 69
yes, in truth it is, sir. 3.05. 7 P
what authority and show of truth | can cunning 4.01. 35
these princes hold | against her maiden truth. 4.01.164
if they speak but truth of her, | these hands 4.01.190
it, for in most comely truth thou deservest it. 5.02. 7 P
signior leonato, truth it is, good signior, 5.04. 21
pore upon a book | to seek the light of truth, LLL 1.01. 75
while truth the while | doth falsely blind the 1.01. 75
i suffer for the truth, sir; 1.01.311 P
was there with him, if i have heard a truth. 2.01. 65
it is so, truth is truth. 4.01. 48
it is so, truth is truth. 4.01. 48
truth itself, that thou art lovely. 4.01. 61 P
than beauteous, truer than truth itself, have 4.01. 63 P
ay, in truth, my lord; 5.02.362
the naked truth of it is, i have no shirt; 5.02.710 P
or rather do i not in plainest truth | tell you MND 2.01.200
and yet, to say the truth, reason and love keep 3.01.143 P
so born, | in their nativity all truth appears. 3.02.125
when truth kills truth, o devilish–holy fray! 3.02.129
when truth kills truth, o devilish–holy fray! 3.02.129
but wonder on till truth make all things plain. 5.01.128
the truth is so; 5.01.162
no, in truth, sir, he should not. 5.01.184 P
in truth, i know it is a sin to be a mocker, but MV 1.02. 57 P
truth will come to light; 2.02. 79 P
a man's son may, but in the end truth will out. 2.02. 80 P
to be brief, the very truth is that the jew, 2.02.132 P
promise me life, and i'll confess the truth. 3.02. 34
the seeming truth which cunning times put on 3.02.100
it must appear | that malice bears down truth. 4.01.214
even so void is your false heart of truth. 5.01.189
thou, if the truth of thy love to me were so AYL 1.02. 13 P
thee | to the last gasp, with truth and loyalty. 2.03. 70
nay certainly there is no truth in him. 3.04. 20 P
if there be truth in sight, you are my daughter. 5.04.118
if there be truth in sight, you are my rosalind. 5.04.119
hymen's bands, | if truth holds true contents. 5.04.130
come go along and see the truth hereof, | for SHR 4.05. 75
i, madam, and i speak the truth the next way: AWW 1.03. 58 P
it is the show and seal of nature's truth, 1.03.132
thy tongue, | that truth should be suspected. 1.03.181
i will tell truth, by grace itself i swear. 1.03.220
faith, if the learned should speak truth of it. 2.02. 35 P
this had been truth, sir. 2.04. 31 P
thirds and uses a known truth to pass a thousand 2.05. 30 P
ay, surely, mere the truth, i know his lady. 3.05. 55
this is the first truth that e'er thine own 4.01. 32 P
'tis not the many oaths that makes the truth, 4.02. 21
now will i charge you in the band of truth, 4.02. 56
thereabouts," set down, for i'll speak truth. 4.03.150 P
he's very near the truth in this. 4.03.151 P
a truth's a truth, the rogues are marvellous 4.03.156 P
that you would think truth were a fool. 4.03.254 P
whose nature sickens but to speak a truth. 5.03.207
i have spoke the truth. 5.03.230
know, | to make the even truth in pleasure flow. 5.03.326
by maidhood, honor, truth, and every thing, | i TN 3.01.150
i have one heart, one bosom, and one truth, 3.01.158
and, having sworn truth, ever will be true. 4.03. 33
the honor of my parents, | i have utt'red truth; WT 1.02.443
relish a truth like us, inform yourselves | we 2.01.167
credulity will not | come up to th' truth. 2.01.193
as i take it, | if the good truth were known. 2.01.199
suddenly will have | the truth of this appear. 2.03.201
(those of your fact are so), so past all truth; 3.02. 85
hast thou read truth? 3.02.138
there is no truth at all i' th' oracle. 3.02.140
whom i proclaim a man of truth, of mercy; 3.02.157
thou didst speak but well | when most the truth; 3.02.233
disliken | the truth of your own seeming, that 4.04.653
thou speak'st truth: 5.01. 55
if ever truth were pregnant by circumstance. 5.02. 30 P
but for the certain knowledge of that truth | i JN 1.01. 61
but truth is truth. 1.01.105
but truth is truth. 1.01.105
madam, by chance, but not by truth; 1.01.169
ill, | the truth is then most done not doing it. 3.01.273
and mak'st an oath the surety for thy truth 3.01.282
the truth thou art unsure | to swear, swears 3.01.283
makes sound opinion sick, and truth suspected, 4.02. 26
that thou for truth giv'st out are landed here? 4.02.130
foreknowing that the truth will fall out so. 4.02.154
and truth of all this realm | is fled to heaven; 4.03.144
that i must die here and live hence by truth? 5.04. 29
both to defend my loyalty and truth | to god, my R2 1.03. 19
truth hath a quiet breast. 1.03. 96
you never shall, so help you truth and god, 1.03.183
for they breathe truth that breathe their words 2.01. 8
yet best beseeming me to speak the truth. 4.01.116
the truth of what we are | shows us but this. 5.01. 19
i am in parliament pledge for his truth | and 5.02. 44
if they speak more or less than truth, they are 1H4 2.04.171 P
is not the truth the truth? 2.04.230 P
is not the truth the truth? 2.04.230 P
said he would swear truth out of england but he 2.04.306 P
coz, to shame the devil | by telling truth: 3.01. 58
tell truth and shame the devil. 3.01. 58
while you live, tell truth and shame the devil! 3.01. 61
there's neither faith, truth, nor womanhood in 3.03.110 P
nor no more truth in thee than in a drawn fox, 3.03.113 P
there's no room for faith, truth, nor honesty in 3.03.154 P
if speaking truth | in this fine age were not 4.01. 1
and the shirt, to say the truth, stol'n from my 4.02. 45 P
and hold'st it fear or sin | to speak a truth. 2H4 1.01. 96
i hear for certain and dare speak the truth, 1.01.188
i knew of this before, but, to speak truth, 1.01.210
well, the truth is, sir john, you live in great 1.02.136 P
say of wax, my growth would approve the truth. 1.02.159 P
the truth is, i am only old in judgment and 1.02.191 P
she hath been in good case, and the truth is, 2.01.106 P
yea, in truth, my lord. 2.01.117 P
you, is as red as any rose, in good truth law! 2.04. 25 P
you are both, i' good truth, as rheumatic as two 2.04. 57 P
yea, in very truth, do i, and 'twere an aspen 2.04.108 P
in very truth, sir, i had as live be hang'd, sir 3.02.222 P
if truth and upright innocency fail me, | i'll 5.02. 39
let king cophetua know the truth thereof. 5.03.102
i speak the truth. 5.03.117
pistol speaks nought but truth. 5.05. 38
suits not in native colors with the truth; H5 1.02. 17
to /fine his title with some shows of truth, 1.02. 72
though in pure truth it was corrupt and naught, 1.02. 73
though the truth of it stands off as gross | as 2.02.103
in good truth, the poet makes a most excellent 3.06. 37 P
for thou art fram'd of the firm truth of valor. 4.03. 14
yes, verily and in truth you shall take it, or i 5.01. 61 P
dare no man answer in a case of truth? 1H6 2.04. 2
then say at once if i maintain'd the truth; 2.04. 5
the truth appears so naked on my side | that any 2.04. 20
if he suppose that i have pleaded truth, | from 2.04. 29
but dare maintain the party of the truth, 2.04. 32
then for the truth and plainness of the case, 2.04. 46
fear, as witnessing | the truth on our side. 2.04. 64
ay, sharp and piercing, to maintain his truth, 2.04. 70
long since we were resolved of your truth, 3.04. 20
to say the truth, this fact was infamous | and 4.01. 30
when stubbornly he did repugn the truth | about 4.01. 94
to say the truth, it is your policy | to save 5.04.159
father, the duke hath told the truth; 2H6 2.02. 28
the truth and innocence of this poor fellow, 2.03.103
i say no more than truth, so help me god! 3.01.120
in thy face i see | the map of honor, truth, and 3.01.203
and, to speak truth, thou deserv'st no less. 4.03. 10 P

but, to conclude with truth, | their weapons 3H6 2.01.128
tell me for truth the measure of his love | unto 3.03.120
with my talk and tears | (both full of truth) i 3.03.159
suggest but truth to my divining thoughts, 4.06. 69
in sign of truth, i kiss your highness' hand. 4.08. 26
and thus i seal my truth, and bid adieu. 4.08. 29
to say the truth, so judas kiss'd his master, 5.07. 33
but thus his simple truth must be abus'd | with R3 1.03. 52
methinks the truth should live from age to age, 3.01. 76
they, for their truth, might better wear their 3.02. 92
shalt thou behold a subject die | for truth, for 3.03. 4
in saying so you shall but say the truth. 3.07.238
but where (to say the truth) i do not know. 4.03. 30
he said the truth, and what said surrey then? 5.03.273
they may believe, | may here find truth too. H8 pr 9
to rank our chosen truth with such a show | as pr 18
on my soul, i'll speak but truth. 1.02.177
accusers, | that never knew what truth meant. 2.01.105
but that slander, sir, | is found a truth now; 2.01.154
no, in truth. 2.03. 39
foe, and think not | at all a friend to truth. 2.04. 84
yea, as much | as you have done my truth. 2.04. 98
truth loves open dealing. 3.01. 39
if you speak truth, for their poor mistress' 3.01. 47
your late censure | both of his truth and him 3.01. 65
of gravity and learning, | in truth i know not. 3.01. 74
that in the way of loyalty and truth | toward 3.02.272
innocence arise | when the king knows my truth. 3.02.302
thou hast forc'd me | (out of thy honest truth) 3.02.430
made me, | with thy religious truth and modesty, 4.02. 74
thy truth and thy integrity is rooted | in us, 5.01.114
the good i stand on is my truth and honesty. 5.01.122
ever | the justice and the truth o' th' question 5.01.130
you are a sectary, | that's the plain truth. 5.02.106
none think flattery, for they'll find 'em truth. 5.04. 16
truth shall nurse her, | holy and heavenly 5.04. 28
peace, plenty, love, truth, terror, | that were 5.04. 47
i speak no more than truth. TRO 1.01. 64 P
faith, to say truth, brown and not brown. 1.02. 96 P
to say the truth, true and not true. 1.02. 97 P
hector's opinion | is this in way of truth; 2.02.189
serve your turn, that shall it not, in truth la! 3.01. 75 P
can say worst shall be a mock for his truth, and 3.02. 97 P
and what truth can speak truest not truer than 3.02. 97 P
that my integrity and truth to you | might be 3.02.165
and simpler than the infancy of truth. 3.02.170
world to come | approve their truth by troilus. 3.02.174
wants similes, truth tir'd with iteration, | as 3.02.176
/yet, after all comparisons of truth | (as 3.02.180
if i be false, or swerve a hair from truth, 3.02.184
a hateful truth. 4.04. 31
i with great truth catch mere simplicity; 4.04.104
with truth and plainness i do wear mine bare. 4.04.106
fear not my truth: 4.04.107
doth that grieve thee? | o withered truth! 5.02. 46
shall i not lie in publishing a truth? 5.02.119
in truth la, go with me, and i'll tell you COR 1.03. 89 P
though thou speakest truth, | methinks thou 1.06. 13
let him alone, | he did inform the truth. 1.06. 42
be too highly heap'd | for truth to o'erpeer. 2.03.121
of no allowance to your bosom's truth. 3.02. 57
do't, | lest i surcease to honor mine own truth, 3.02.121
and power i' th' truth a' th' cause. 3.03. 18
and, to say the truth, so did very many of us. 4.06.142 P
the commons' ears, | will vouch the truth of it. 5.06. 5
him, and i pawn'd | mine honor for his truth; 5.06. 21
that we may know the traitors and the truth! TIT 4.01. 76
are, | that my report is just and full of truth. 5.03.115
now have you heard the truth, what say you, 5.03.128
and, to say truth, verona brags of him | to be a ROM 1.05. 67
in truth, fair montague, i am too fond, | and 2.02. 98
this is the truth, or let benvolio die. 3.01.175
that is no slander, sir, which is a truth, | and 4.01. 33
if i may trust the flattering truth of sleep, 5.01. 1
religion to the gods, peace, justice, truth, TIM 4.01. 16
speak truth, y' are honest men. 5.01. 77
and to speak truth of caesar, | i have not known JC 2.01. 19
to be afeard to tell greybeards the truth? 2.02. 67
then like a roman bear the truth i tell: 4.03.188
i' th' name of truth, | are ye fantastical, or MAC 1.03. 52
me earnest of success, | commencing in a truth? 1.03.133
to you they have show'd some truth. 2.01. 21
if there come truth from them — | as upon thee, 3.01. 6
my thoughts | to thy good truth and honor. 4.03.117
and delight | no less in truth than life. 4.03.130
you, but can perceive no truth in your report. 5.01. 2 P
of the fiend | that lies like truth. 5.05. 43
and of the truth herein | this present object HAM 1.01.155
give me up the truth. 1.03. 98
your bait of falsehood take this carp of truth, 2.01. 60
the sun doth move, | doubt truth to be a liar, 2.02.118
i will find | where truth is hid, though it were 2.02.158
will you ha' the truth an't? 5.01. 23 P
thy truth then be thy dow'r! LR 1.01.108
an honest mind and plain, he must speak truth! 2.02. 99
be simple–answer'd, for we know the truth. 3.07. 43
all my reports go with the modest truth, | nor 4.07. 5
tell me but truly, but then speak the truth, 5.01. 8
i will maintain | my truth and honor firmly. 5.03.101
and give us truth who 'tis that is arriv'd. OTH 2.01. 58
thou dost deliver more or less than truth, 2.03.219
to speak the truth | shall nothing wrong him. 2.03.223
which lead directly to the door of truth | will 3.03.407
with nought but truth. 4.02.185 P
let him confess a truth. 5.02. 68
she said so; i must needs report the truth. 5.02.128
'tis a strange truth. 5.02.189
with such full license as both truth and malice ANT 1.02.108
truth is, that fulvia, | to have me out of egypt 2.02. 94
that truth should be silent i had almost forgot. 2.02.108 P
hath sent | me to proclaim the truth, and i am 4.14.126
speak the truth, seleucus. 5.02.144
do here pronounce | by th' very truth of it, i CYM 2.03.108
being so near the truth as i will make them, 2.04. 62
truth, where semblance; 2.04.109
she's punish'd for her truth, and undergoes, 3.02. 7
upon the love and truth and vows which i | have 3.02. 12
that place them on the truth of girls and boys. 5.05.107
torture shall | winnow the truth from falsehood. 5.05.134
time of both this truth shall ne'er convince, PER 1.02.123
a /palace | for the crown'd truth to dwell in. 5.01.122
that, | for truth can never be confirm'd enough, 5.01.201
may you well descry | a figure of truth, of 5.03. 92
for, to say truth, it were an endless thing, TNK pr 22
love is all truth, lust full of forged lies. VEN 804
then, gentle shadow (truth i must confess), | i 1001
then where is truth, if there be no self–trust? LUC 158
"when truth and virtue have to do with thee, | a 911
to unmask falsehood and bring truth to light, 940
to hide the truth of this false night's abuses. 1075
such signs of truth in his plain face she spied, 1532
when my love swears that she is made of truth, PP 1. 1
the truth i shall not know, but live in doubt, 2.13
young, | and truth in every shepherd's tongue, 19.18
beauty, truth, and rarity, | grace in all PHT 53
truth may seem, but cannot be, | beauty brag, 62
but 'tis not she, | truth and beauty buried be. 64
art | as truth and beauty shall together thrive SON 14.11
scorn'd, like old men of less truth than tongue, 17.10
take all my comfort of thy worth and truth. 37. 4
where thou art forc'd to break a twofold truth: 41.12
for truth proves thievish for a prize so dear. 48.14
by that sweet ornament which truth doth give! 54. 2
that shall vade, by verse distills your truth. 54.14
brow, | feeds on the rarities of nature's truth, 60.11
no shape so true, no truth of such account, 62. 6
skill, | and simple truth miscall'd simplicity, 66.11
utt'ring bare truth, even so as foes commend. 69. 4
i | than niggard truth would willingly impart: 72. 8
for thy neglect of truth in beauty dy'd? 101. 2
both truth and beauty on my love depends; 101. 3
"truth needs no color with his color fix'd, 101. 6
beauty no pencil, beauty's truth to lay; 101. 7
most true it is that i have look'd on truth 110. 5
is not, | to put fair truth upon so foul a face? 137.12
when my love swears that she is made of truth, 138. 1
on both sides thus is simple truth suppress'd. 138. 8
at randon from the truth vainly express'd; 147.12
oaths of thy love, thy truth, thy constancy, 152.10
eye, | to swear against the truth so foul a lie! 152.14
did livery falseness in a pride of truth. LC 105

TRUTH'S 7 FR 0.0008 REL FR 5 V 2 P
a truth's a truth, the rogues are marvellous AWW 4.03.156 P
justice | for truth's sake and his conscience, H8 3.02.397
at be thy country's, | thy god's, and truth's; 3.02.448
but alas, | i am as true as truth's simplicity, TRO 3.02.169
(as truth's authentic author to be cited), | "as 3.02.181
truth's a dog must to kennel, he must be whipt LR 1.04.111 P
thy end is truth's and beauty's doom and date. SON 14.14

TRUTHS 7 FR 0.0008 REL FR 5 V 2 P
i hope here be truths. MM 2.01.127 P
why, very well then; i hope here be truths. 2.01.133 P
the instruments of darkness tell us truths, MAC 1.03.124
two truths are told, | as happy prologues to the 1.03.127
truths would be tales, | where now half tales be ANT 2.02.133
be tales, | where now half tales be truths. 2.02.134
that in thee are seen | to truths translated, SON 96. 8

TRY 95 FR 0.0107 REL FR 73 V 22 P
bring her to try with main–course. TMP 1.01. 35 P
some to the wars, to try their fortune there; TGV 1.03. 8
i will try thee. tell me this: who begot thee? 3.01.293 P
come, fool, come; try me in thy paper. 3.01.299 P
i will lay a plot to try that, and we will yet WIV 3.03.190 P
we'll try that; 4.02. 94 P
a thief or two | guiltier than him they try. MM 2.01. 21
and try your penitence, if it be sound, | or 2.03. 22
to try her gracious fortune with lord angelo, 5.01. 76
try all the friends thou hast in ephesus; ERR 1.01.152
well, i will marry one day, but to try. 2.01. 42
that's a question; how shall we try it? 5.01.422
well, as time shall try: ADO 1.01.260 P
now follow, if thou dar'st, to try whose right, MND 3.02.336
follow my voice; we'll try no manhood here. 3.02.412
go forth, | try what my credit can in venice do. MV 1.01.180
you lead me to the caskets | to try my fortune. 2.01. 24
i will try confusions with him. 2.02. 37 P
to come in disguis'd against me to try a fall. AYL 1.01.126 P
do, to try with him the strength of my youth. 1.02.171 P
you shall try but one fall. 1.02.204 P
i would try, if i could cry "hem" and have him. 1.03. 19 P
you will try in time, in despite of a fall. 1.03. 24 P
examines all such offenders, and let time try. 4.01.200 P
i'll try how you can sol, fa, and sing it. SHR 1.02. 17
that i'll try. 2.01.219
if he were living, i would try him yet. AWW 1.02. 72
your honor | but give me leave to try success, 1.03.247
what i can do can do no hurt to try, | since you 2.01.134
sweet practicer, thy physic i will try, | that 2.01.185
i knew in what particular action to try him. 3.06. 18 P
tastes, though it be dish'd | for me to try how. WT 3.02. 73
that please some, try all, both joy and terror 4.01. 1
and try whether i am not now a gentleman born. 5.02.133 P
as i, | to try the fair adventure of to–morrow. JN 5.05. 22
then, dear my liege, mine honor let me try; R2 1.01.184
now shall he try his friends that flatter'd him. 2.02. 85
this, | if he may be repeal'd to try his honor. 4.01. 85
side, | try fortune with him in a single fight. 1H4 5.01.100
let the end try the man. 2H4 2.02. 47 P
all our loves, | first let them try themselves. 2.03. 56
and spoke it on purpose to try my patience. 2.04.308 P
we ready are to try our fortunes | to the last 4.02. 43
to try with it, as with an enemy | that had 4.05.166
can try it out with all unspotted soldiers. H5 4.01.160 P
but first, to try her skill, | reignier, stand 1H6 1.02. 60
my courage try by combat, if thou dar'st, | and 1.02. 89
presently we'll try; 1.02.149
and then we'll try what these dastard frenchmen 1.04.111
fools, | to try if that our own be ours or no. 3.02. 63
charms, | and try if they can gain your liberty. 5.03. 32
having vow'd | to try his strength, forsaketh 5.05. 32
my lord of york, try what your fortune is. 2H6 3.01.309
some, | and try your hap against the irishmen? 3.01.314
say we intend to try his grace to–day, | if he 3.02. 16
lords, give us leave. i'll try this widow's wit. 3H6 3.02. 33
touch, | to try if thou be current gold indeed. R3 4.02. 9
ye | power as he was a councillor to try him, H8 5.02.178
would try him to the utmost had ye mean, | which 5.02.181
let me go and try. TRO 3.02.147
come, try upon yourselves what you have seen me. COR 3.01.224
i'll try whether my old wit be in request | with 3.01.250
those whose great power must try him — even 3.03. 80
you | are singled forth to try thy experiments. TIT 2.03. 69
for i'll try if they can lick their fingers. ROM 4.02. 3 P
how canst thou try them so? 4.02. 5
and try the argument of hearts by borrowing, TIM 2.02.178
for by these | shall i try friends. 2.02.183
honorable lord did but try us this other day. 3.06. 3 P
of his | has been but a try for his friends? 5.01. 9
there shall i try, | in my oration, how the JC 3.01.292
night | we shall try fortune in a second fight. 5.03.110
of no woman born, | yet i will try the last. MAC 5.08. 32
how may we try it further? HAM 2.02.159
we will try it. 2.02.167
and who in want a hollow friend doth try, 3.02.208
try what repentance can. 3.03. 65
ape, | to try conclusions in the basket creep, 3.04.195
plot | whereon the numbers cannot try the cause, 4.04. 63
or ice try whither your costard or my ballow be LR 4.06.241 P
it pleas'd heaven | to try me with affliction, OTH 4.02. 48
and what may follow, | to try a larger fortune. ANT 2.06. 34
i'll try you on the shore. 2.07.126
to try thy eloquence, now 'tis time; 3.12. 26
try thy cunning, thidias, | make thine own edict 3.12. 31
i will try the forces | of these thy compounds CYM 1.05. 18
to try the vigor of them, and apply | allayments 1.05. 21
to try your taking of a false report, which hath 1.06.173
we'll try with tongue too. 2.03. 15 P
cry out for service, | try many, all good; 4.02.373
try honor's cause; PER 2.04. 41
i would not, | should i try death by dozens. TNK 3.02. 25
she told the youngling how god mars did try her, PP 11. 3
what though she strive to try her strength, 18.31
grind | on newer proof, to try an older friend, SON 110.11

T'S 2 FR 0.0002 REL FR 0 V 2 P
her u's, and her t's, and thus makes she her TN 2.05. 87 P
her c's, her u's, and her t's: why that? 2.05. 89 P

TU 3 FR 0.0003 REL FR 1 V 2 P
alice, tu as ete en angleterre, et tu bien H5 3.04. 1 P
ete en angleterre, et tu bien parles le langage. 3.04. 1 P
et tu, brute? — then fall, caesar! JC 3.01. 77

TUA 1 FR 0.0001 REL FR 1 V 0 P
"lux tua vita mihi." PER 2.02. 21

TUAE 1 FR 0.0001 REL FR 1 V 0 P
dii faciant laudis summa sit ista tuae! 3H6 1.03. 48

TUB 2 FR 0.0002 REL FR 1 V 1 P
up all her beef, and she is herself in the tub. MM 3.02. 57 P
desire, that tub | both fill'd and running — CYM 1.06. 48

TUBAL 9 FR 0.0010 REL FR 2 V 7 P
tubal, a wealthy hebrew of my tribe, | will MV 1.03. 57
how now, tubal! 3.01. 79 P
i thank thee, good tubal, good news, good news! 3.01.106 P
thou torturest me, tubal. 3.01.120 P
go, tubal, fee me an officer; 3.01.125 P
go, tubal, and meet me at our synagogue; 3.01.129 P
go, good tubal, at our synagogue, tubal. 3.01.130 P
go, good tubal, at our synagogue, tubal. 3.01.130 P
i have heard him swear | to tubal and to chus, 3.02.285

/TUB–FAST 1 FR 0.0001 REL FR 1 V 0 P
youth | to the /tub–fast and the diet. TIM 4.03. 88

TUBS 1 FR 0.0001 REL FR 1 V 0 P
season the slaves | for tubs and baths, bring TIM 4.03. 87

TUCK 2 FR 0.0002 REL FR 0 V 2 P
dismount thy tuck, be yare in thy preparation, TN 3.04.224 P
sheath, you bowcase, you vile standing tuck — 1H4 2.04.248 P

TUCKET 1 FR 0.0001 REL FR 1 V 0 P
the tucket sonance and the note to mount; H5 4.02. 35

TUESDAY 8 FR 0.0009 REL FR 5 V 3 P
but tuesday night last gone, in 's garden–house, MM 5.01.229
night, which he forswore on tuesday morning. ADO 5.01.168 P
as a pancake for shrove tuesday, a morris for AWW 2.02. 24 P
and most dissolutely spent on tuesday morning; 1H4 1.02. 35 P
i sent | on tuesday last to listen after news. 2H4 1.01. 29
on tuesday last, | a falcon, tow'ring in her MAC 2.04. 11
why then to–morrow night, /or tuesday morn; OTH 3.03. 60
on tuesday noon, or night; 3.03. 61

TUFFS 1 FR 0.0001 REL FR 1 V 0 P
soit qui mal y pense" write | in em'rald tuffs, WIV 5.05. 70

TUFT 3 FR 0.0003 REL FR 3 V 0 P
'tis at the tuft of olives here hard by. AYL 3.05. 75
behind the tuft of pines i met them; WT 2.01. 34
there stands the castle, by yon tuft of trees, R2 2.03. 53

TUG 4 FR 0.0004 REL FR 4 V 0 P
myself and fortune | tug for the time to come. WT 4.04.497
and england now is left | to tug and scamble, JN 4.03.146
i mean to tug it and to cuff you soundly. 1H6 1.03. 48
tug him away. ANT 3.13.102

TUGG'D 2 FR 0.0002 REL FR 2 V 0 P
as one that grasp'd | and tugg'd for life, and 2H6 3.02.173
so weary with disasters, tugg'd with fortune, MAC 3.01.111

TUGGING 1 FR 0.0001 REL FR 1 V 0 P
both tugging to be victors, breast to breast, 3H6 2.05. 11

TUITION 1 FR 0.0001 REL FR 0 V 1 P
to the tuition of god. ADO 1.01.281 P

TULLUS' 1 FR 0.0001 REL FR 1 V 0 P
shalt see me once more strike at tullus' face. COR 1.01.240

TULLUS 8 FR 0.0009 REL FR 7 V 1 P
tullus aufidius, that will put you to't. COR 1.01.229
tullus aufidius, is he within your walls? 1.04. 13
within these three hours, tullus, | alone i 1.08. 7
tullus aufidius then had made new head? 3.01. 1
your noble tullus aufidius /will appear well in 4.03. 34 P
if, tullus, | not yet thou know'st me, and, 4.05. 54
tullus aufidius, | the second name of men, obeys 4.06.124
o tullus! 5.06.131

TULLY 1 FR 0.0001 REL FR 1 V 0 P
and bandetto slave | murder'd sweet tully; 2H6 4.01.136

TULLY'S 1 FR 0.0001 REL FR 1 V 0 P
read to thee | sweet poetry and tully's orator. TIT 4.01. 14

TUMBLE 8 FR 0.0009 REL FR 8 V 0 P
with that they all did tumble on the ground, LLL 5.02.115
to tumble down thy husband and thyself | from 2H6 1.02. 48
ready with every nod to tumble down | into the R3 3.04.100
as you threw caps up will he tumble down, | and COR 4.06.135

lust, | and tumble me into some loathsome pit, TIT 2.03.176
of nature's /germains tumble all together, MAC 4.01. 59
is not | amiss to tumble on the bed of ptolomy, ANT 1.04. 17
be sure | you tumble with audacity and manhood, TNK 3.05. 36
TUMBLED 6 FR 0.0006 REL FR 5 V 1 P
side, | or as a little snow, tumbled about, JN 3.04.176
now phaeton hath tumbled from his car, | and 3H6 1.04. 33
subtle ground, | i have tumbled past the throw; COR 5.02. 21
"quoth she, 'before you tumbled me, | you HAM 4.05. 62
i saw the porpas how he bounc'd and tumbled? PER 2.01. 24 P
he tumbled down upon his /nemean hide, | and TNK 1.01. 68
TUMBLER'S 1 FR 0.0001 REL FR 1 V 0 P
and wear his colors like a tumbler's hoop! LLL 3.01.188
TUMBLES 2 FR 0.0002 REL FR 1 V 1 P
'a plays and tumbles, driving the poor fry PER 2.01. 30 P
how't tumbles! TNK 3.04. 5
TUMBLING 3 FR 0.0003 REL FR 3 V 0 P
which | lie tumbling in my barefoot way, and TMP 2.02. 11
my aunts, | while we lie tumbling in the hay. WT 4.03. 12
into the tumbling billows of the main. R3 1.04. 20
TUMBLING–TRICK 1 FR 0.0001 REL FR 0 V 1 P
a christmas gambold, or a tumbling–trick? SHR in.2. 138 P
TUMULT 4 FR 0.0004 REL FR 3 V 1 P
hostility and civil tumult reigns | between my JN 4.02.247
here's a goodly tumult! 2H4 2.04.204 P
what hath broach'd this tumult but thy pride? 3H6 2.02.159
who, peeping forth this tumult to behold, | are LUC 447
TUMULT'S 2 FR 0.0002 REL FR 2 V 0 P
what tumult's in the heavens? 1H6 1.04. 98
what tumult's this? 3.01. 74
TUMULTUOUS 4 FR 0.0004 REL FR 4 V 0 P
and in this seat of peace tumultuous wars R2 4.01.140
nought rests for me in this tumultuous strife 1H6 1.03. 70
why, what tumultuous clamor have we here? 2H6 3.02.239
now here a period of tumultuous broils. 3H6 5.05. 1
TUN 2 FR 0.0002 REL FR 1 V 1 P
an old fat man, a tun of man is thy companion. 1H4 2.04.448 P
meeter for your spirit, | this tun of treasure; H5 1.02.255
TUN'D 5 FR 0.0005 REL FR 4 V 1 P
his lecture will be done ere you have tun'd. SHR 3.01. 23
who had even tun'd his bounty to sing happiness AWW 4.03. 9 P
and with an accent tun'd in self–same key TRO 1.03. 53
tun'd too sharp in sweetness | for the capacity 3.02. 24
o, you are well tun'd now! OTH 2.01.199
TUN–DISH 1 FR 0.0001 REL FR 0 V 1 P
for filling a bottle with a tun–dish. MM 3.02.172 P
/TUNE 3 FR 0.0003 REL FR 3 V 0 P
this /tune goes manly. MAC 4.03.235
/town, | /who /sometime, /in /his /better /tune, LR 4.03. 39
and gallops to the /tune of "light a' love." TNK 5.02. 54
TUNE 63 FR 0.0071 REL FR 39 V 24 P
i' th' state | to what tune pleas'd his ear, TMP 1.02. 85
this is a very scurvy tune to sing at a man's 2.02. 44 P
this is a scurvy tune too; 2.02. 55 P
that's not the tune. 3.02.124
this is the tune of our catch, play'd by the 3.02.126 P
that i might sing it, madam, to a tune: TGV 1.02. 77
best sing it to the tune of "light o' love." 1.02. 80
it is too heavy for so light a tune. 1.02. 81
keep tune there still, so you will sing it out. 1.02. 86
and yet methinks i do not like this tune. 1.02. 87
to their instruments | tune a deploring dump — 3.02. 84
let's tune, and to it lustily a while. 4.02. 25
how, out of tune on the strings? 4.02. 60 P
notes | tune my distresses and record my woes. 5.04. 6
hundred psalms to the tune of "green–sleeves." WIV 2.01. 63 P
let it thunder to the tune of "green–sleeves," 5.05. 19 P
what say'st thou to this tune, matter, and MM 3.02. 48 P
why, how now? do you speak in the sick tune? ADO 3.04. 42 P
i am out of all other tune, methinks. 3.04. 43 P
neither serve for the writing nor the tune. LLL 1.02.114 P
but to jig off a tune at the tongue's end, 3.01. 12 P
and keep not too long in one tune, but a snip 3.01. 21 P
a gig, | and profound salomon to tune a jig, 4.03.166
thou bring'st me out of tune. AYL 3.02.248 P
'tis no matter how it be in tune, so it make 4.02. 8 P
i' faith, and both in a tune, like two gipsies 5.03. 14 P
you'll leave his lecture when i am in tune? SHR 3.01. 24
that will be never, tune your instrument. 3.01. 25
madam, my instrument's in tune. 3.01. 38
spit in the hole, man, and tune again. 3.01. 40
madam, 'tis now in tune. 3.01. 46
out o' tune, sir! TN 2.03.113 P
seek him out, and play the tune the while. 2.04. 14
how dost thou like this tune? 2.04. 20
if it be aught to the old tune, my lord, | it is 5.01.108
here's one to a very doleful tune, how a WT 4.04.262 P
one and goes to the tune of "two maids wooing a 4.04.289 P
we had the tune on't a month ago. 4.04.294 P
his pettitoes till he had both tune and words, 4.04.607 P
hands | that knows no touch to tune the harmony. R2 1.03.165
whose dismal tune bereft my vital pow'rs; 2H6 3.02. 41
why, but he is not in this tune, is he? TRO 3.03.300
but /he's out of tune thus. 3.03.301 P
it may stand with the tune of your voices that i COR 2.03. 85 P
it is the lark that sings so out of tune, ROM 3.05. 27
this is a sleepy tune. JC 4.03.267
to th' self–same tune and words. who's here? MAC 1.03. 88
age dotes on, only got the tune of the time and, HAM 5.02.190 P
cassio, | my advocation is not now in tune. OTH 3.04.123
then murther's out of tune, | and sweet revenge 5.02.115
which to the tune of flutes kept stroke, and ANT 2.02.195
and scald rhymers | ballad 's out a' tune. 5.02.216
come on, tune. CYM 2.03. 14 P
for notes of sorrow out of tune are worse | than 4.02.241
the tune of imogen! 5.05.238
the fingers of the pow'rs above do tune | the 5.05.466
as your fair self, doth tune us otherwise. PER 1.01.115
melodious discord, heavenly tune harsh sounding, VEN 431
yet from mine ear the tempting tune is blown; 778
the little birds that tune their morning's joy LUC 1107
shall tune our heart–strings to true 1141
i'll tune thy woes with my lamenting tongue, 1465
are mine ears with thy tongue's tune delighted, SON 141. 5
TUNEABLE 2 FR 0.0002 REL FR 2 V 0 P
air | more tuneable than lark to shepherd's ear MND 1.01.184
a cry more tuneable | was never hollow'd to, nor 4.01.124
TUNED 2 FR 0.0002 REL FR 2 V 0 P
voice was propertied | as all the tuned spheres, ANT 5.02. 84
and wish her lays were tuned like the lark. PP 14.18
TUNERS 1 FR 0.0001 REL FR 0 V 1 P
/phantasimes, these new tuners of accent! ROM 2.04. 29 P
TUNES 9 FR 0.0010 REL FR 4 V 5 P
he sings several tunes faster than you'll tell WT 4.04.184 P
ballads and all men's ears grew to his tunes. 4.04.186 P
him that he use no scurrilous words in 's tunes. 4.04.214 P
made on you all and sung to filthy tunes, let a 1H4 2.02. 46 P
and sung those tunes to the overscutch'd 2H4 3.02.316 P
a stiff tempest, | as loud and to as many tunes. H8 4.01. 73
for to a pretty ear she tunes her tale. VEN 74
"your tunes entomb | within your hollow swelling LUC 1121
stern, sad tunes to change their kinds; 1147
TUNING 1 FR 0.0001 REL FR 1 V 0 P
feast–finding minstrels, tuning my defame, LUC 817
TUNIS 9 FR 0.0010 REL FR 4 V 5 P
fair daughter claribel to the king of tunis. TMP 2.01. 72 P
tunis was never grac'd before with such a 2.01. 75 P
she was of carthage, not of tunis. 2.01. 83 P
this tunis, sir, was carthage. 2.01. 84 P
as when we were at tunis at the marriage of your 2.01. 98 P
she that is queen of tunis; 2.01.246
true, my brother's daughter 's queen of tunis, 2.01.255
keep in tunis, | and let sebastian wake." 2.01.259
voyage | did claribel her husband find at tunis, 5.01.209
TUNS 2 FR 0.0002 REL FR 1 V 1 P
whale (with so many tuns of oil in his belly) WIV 2.01. 65 P
drawn tuns of blood out of thy country's breast, COR 4.05. 99
TUPPING 1 FR 0.0001 REL FR 1 V 0 P
an old black ram | is tupping your white ewe. OTH 1.01. 89
TURBAN'D 1 FR 0.0001 REL FR 1 V 0 P
where a malignant and a turban'd turk | beat a OTH 5.02.353
TURBANDS 1 FR 0.0001 REL FR 1 V 0 P
and keep their impious turbands on without CYM 3.03. 6
TURBULENCE 1 FR 0.0001 REL FR 1 V 0 P
for i have dreamt | of bloody turbulence, and TRO 5.03. 11
TURBULENT 3 FR 0.0003 REL FR 3 V 0 P
froth | the turbulent surge shall cover; TIM 5.01.218
of quiet | with turbulent and dangerous lunacy? HAM 3.01. 4
't 'as been a turbulent and stormy night. PER 3.02. 4
TURD *(also third)*
TURD 1 FR 0.0001 REL FR 0 V 1 P
if there be one or two, i shall make–a the turd. WIV 3.03.237 P
TURF 6 FR 0.0006 REL FR 5 V 1 P
a good lustre of conceit in a turf of earth; LLL 4.02. 88 P
one turf shall serve as pillow for us both, MND 2.02. 41
love, | who you saw sitting by me on the turf, AYL 3.04. 49
were better than a churlish turf of france. H5 4.01. 15
dead and gone, | at his head a grass–green turf, HAM 4.05. 31
by the battle, ditch'd, and wall'd with turf, CYM 5.03. 14
TURFY 1 FR 0.0001 REL FR 1 V 0 P
thy turfy mountains, where live nibbling sheep, TMP 4.01. 62
TURK 17 FR 0.0019 REL FR 10 V 7 P
when thou shalt lack, | base phrygian turk! WIV 1.03. 88
and you be not turn'd turk, there's no more ADO 3.04. 57 P
why, she defies me, | like turk to christian. AYL 4.03. 33
whipt, or i would send them to th' turk, to make AWW 2.03. 88 P
turk gregory never did such deeds in arms as i 1H4 5.03. 45 P
constantinople and take the turk by the beard? H5 5.02.209 P
the turk, that two and fifty kingdoms hath, 1H6 4.07. 73
eclipse, | nose of turk and tartar's lips, MAC 4.01. 29
if the rest of my fortunes turn turk with me — HAM 3.02.276 P
and in woman out–paramour'd the turk. LR 3.04. 92 P
consider | th' importancy of cyprus to the turk, OTH 1.03. 20
that, as it more concerns the turk than rhodes, 1.03. 22
we must not think the turk is so unskillful | to 1.03. 27
so let the turk of cyprus us beguile, | we lose 1.03.210
let the turk with a most mighty preparation makes 1.03.221 P
nay, it is true, or else i am a turk: 2.01.114
where a malignant and a turban'd turk | beat a 5.02.353
TURKEY 2 FR 0.0002 REL FR 2 V 0 P
fine linen, turkey cushions boss'd with pearl, SHR 2.01.353
sure | to have my wife as jealous as a turkey. TNK 2.03. 30
TURKEY–COCK 2 FR 0.0002 REL FR 0 V 2 P
contemplation makes a rare turkey–cock of him. TN 2.05. 31 P
why, here he comes, swelling like a turkey–cock. H5 5.01. 14 P
TURKEY–COCKS 1 FR 0.0001 REL FR 0 V 1 P
matter for his swellings nor his turkey–cocks. H5 5.01. 17 P
TURKEYS 1 FR 0.0001 REL FR 0 V 1 P
the turkeys in my pannier are quite starv'd. 1H4 2.01. 26 P
TURKIS 1 FR 0.0001 REL FR 0 V 1 P
it was my turkis, i had it of leah when i was a MV 3.01.121 P
TURKISH 9 FR 0.0010 REL FR 8 V 1 P
desk | that's cover'd o'er with turkish tapestry ERR 4.01.104
this is the english, not the turkish court, 2H4 5.02. 47
like turkish mute, shall have a tongueless mouth H5 1.02.232
yet do they all confirm | a turkish fleet, and OTH 1.03. 8
the turkish preparation makes for rhodes, | so 1.03. 14
a segregation of the turkish fleet: 2.01. 10
if that the turkish fleet | be not enshelter'd 2.01. 17
he speak of comfort | touching the turkish loss, 2.01. 32
the mere perdition of the turkish fleet, every 2.02. 3 P
TURK'S 1 FR 0.0001 REL FR 0 V 1 P
duer paid to the hearer than the turk's tribute. 2H4 3.02.308 P
TURKS 7 FR 0.0008 REL FR 7 V 0 P
from stubborn turks, and tartars never train'd MV 4.01. 32
christian cross | against black pagans, turks, R2 4.01. 95
peace shall go sleep with turks and infidels, 4.01.139
think you we are turks or infidels? R3 3.05. 41
the desperate tempest hath so bang'd the turks, OTH 2.01. 21
the turks are drown'd. 2.01.202
are we turn'd turks, and to ourselves do that 2.03.170
TURLYGOD 1 FR 0.0001 REL FR 1 V 0 P
poor turlygod! LR 2.03. 20
TURMOIL 1 FR 0.0001 REL FR 1 V 0 P
as after much turmoil | a blessed soul doth in TGV 2.07. 37
TURMOILED 1 FR 0.0001 REL FR 1 V 0 P
who would live turmoiled in the court | and may 2H6 4.10. 16
/TURN 3 FR 0.0003 REL FR 3 V 0 P
/nay, /if /i /turn /mine /eyes /upon /myself, R2 4.01.247
/would /turn /their /own /perfection /to /abuse 2H4 2.03. 27
/of /death, | /women /will /all /turn /monsters. LR 3.07.102
TURN 285 FR 0.0322 REL FR 222 V 63 P
prithee do not turn me about, my stomach is not TMP 2.02.114 P
by this hand, i'll turn my mercy out o' doors, 3.02. 70 P
a turn or two i'll walk | to still my beating 4.01.162
of wine is, or i'll turn you out of my kingdom. 4.01.251 P
if you turn not, you will return the sooner. TGV 2.02. 4
wife | and turn her out to who will take her in: 3.01. 77
a cloak as long as thine will serve the turn? 3.01.131
why, any cloak will serve the turn, my lord. 3.01.134
so long that going will scarce serve the turn. 3.01.379 P
i have a sonnet that will serve the turn | to 3.02. 92
host, i must turn away some of my followers. WIV 1.03. 4 P
page, i shall turn your head out of my door. 1.04.124 P
toward my wife, i would turn her loose to him; 2.01.182 P
but i would be loath to turn them together. 2.01.186 P
turn another into the register of your own, that 2.02.187 P
for he swears he'll turn me away. 3.03. 32 P
therefore no more turn me to him, sweet nan. 3.04. 2
will back descend | and turn him to no pain; 5.05. 86
pinch him, and burn him, and turn him about, 5.05.101
will none but herne the hunter serve your turn? 5.05.104
turn you the key, and know his business of him; MM 1.04. 8
gentle my lord, turn back. 2.02.143
good my lord, turn back. 2.02.145
you will turn good husband now, pompey, you will 3.02. 70 P
a feather will turn the scale. 4.02. 31 P
you have occasion to use me for your own turn, 4.02. 57 P
sir, for your kindness, i owe you a good turn. 4.02. 59 P
we in your motion turn, and you may move us. ERR 3.02. 24
to a curtal dog, and made me turn i' th' wheel. 3.02.146
hath he not reason to turn back an hour in a day 4.02. 62
in my heart to stay here still, and turn witch. 4.04.156 P
but i hope you have no intent to turn husband, ADO 1.01.193 P
to turn all beauty into thoughts of harm, | and 4.01.107
if he be, he knows how to turn his girdle. 5.01.142 P
this maid will not serve your turn, sir. LLL 1.01.298 P
this maid will serve my turn, sir. 1.01.299 P
first and second cause will not serve my turn; 1.02.178 P
god of rhyme, for i am sure i shall turn sonnet. 1.02.184 P
o, but for my love, day would turn to night! 4.03.229
but while 'tis spoke each turn away /her face. 5.02.148
let us confess and turn it to a jest. 5.02.390
we will turn it finely off, sir; 5.02.510
of mirth, | turn melancholy forth to funerals: MND 1.01. 14
and thence from athens turn away our eyes, | to 1.01.218
horse, hound, hog, bear, fire, at every turn. 3.01.111
this wood, i have enough to serve mine owe turn. 3.01.151 P
make mouths upon me when i turn my back, | wink 3.02.238
a mote will turn the balance, which pyramus, 5.01.318 P
the hebrew will turn christian, he grows kind. MV 1.03.178
may turn by fortune from the weaker hand: 2.01. 34
turn up on your right hand at the next turning, 2.02. 41 P
at the very next turning, turn of no hand, but 2.02. 43 P
but turn down indirectly to the jew's house. 2.02. 44 P
be match'd, unless the devil himself turn jew. 3.01. 78 P
for your bliss, | turn you where your lady is, 3.02.137
the world | could turn so much the constitution 3.02.246
and turn two mincing steps | into a manly stride 3.04. 67
why, shall we turn to men? 3.04. 78
grace of wit will shortly turn into silence, and 3.05. 44 P
if the scale do turn | but in the estimation of 4.01.330
and when i break that oath, let me turn monster. AYL 1.02. 22 P
and turn his merry note | unto the sweet bird's 2.05. 3
if it do come to pass | that any man turn ass, 2.05. 51
or turn thou no more | to seek a living in our 3.01. 7
do this expediently, and turn him going. 3.01. 18
twice did he turn his back, and purpos'd so; 4.03.127
to–morrow i cannot serve your turn for rosalind? 5.02. 49 P
for learning and behavior | fit for her turn, SHR 1.02.169
she is not for your turn, the more my grief. 2.01. 63
now, kate, i am a husband for your turn, | for 2.01.272
it skills not much, we'll fit him to our turn — 3.02.132
coming down the hill, | will serve the turn. 4.02. 62
this young maid might do her | a shrewd turn, if AWW 3.05. 68
the cutting of my garments would serve the turn, 4.01. 47 P
me this other day to turn him out a' th' band. 4.03.199 P
my niece till his brains turn o' th' toe like a TN 1.03. 41 P
malvolio and bid him turn you out of doors, 2.03. 74 P
is, that it cannot but turn him into a notable 2.05.203 P
then, my best blood turn | to an infected jelly, WT 1.02.417
turn then my freshest reputation to | a savor 1.02.420
great apollo | turn all to th' best! 3.01. 15
i turn my glass, and give my scene such growing 4.01. 16
would sing her song and dance her turn; 4.04. 58
if | his going i could frame to serve my turn, 4.04.509
knows how that may turn back to my advancement? 4.04.835 P
turn, good lady, | our perdita is found. 5.03.120
then turn your forces from this paltry siege, JN 2.01. 54
turn face to face and bloody point to point; 2.01.390
town, | turn thou the mouth of thy artillery, 2.01.403
nay, rather turn this day out of the week, 3.01. 87
burn thee up, and thou shalt turn | to ashes, 3.01.344
there end thy brave, and turn thy face in peace; 5.02.159
now, thomas mowbray, do i turn to thee, | and R2 1.01. 35
o, let my sovereign turn away his face, | and 1.01.111
and then thus i turn me from my country's light, 1.03.176
york | hath power enough to serve our turn. 3.02. 90
and i will turn thy falsehood to thy heart, 4.01. 39
then give me leave that /i may turn the key, 5.03. 36
a deed as drink to turn true man and to leave 1H4 2.02. 23 P
should i turn upon the true prince? 2.04.269 P
'tis the next way to turn tailor, or be 3.01.259 P
may turn the tide of fearful faction, | and 4.01. 67
the clouds | to turn and wind a fiery pegasus, 4.01.109
it pleas'd your majesty to turn your looks | of 5.01. 30
and wouldst thou turn our offers contrary? 5.05. 4
i will turn diseases to commodity. 2H4 1.02.248 P
hen, if her feathers turn back in any show of 2.04.100 P
weight of a hair will turn scales between their 2.04.254 P
out of your revenge and turn all to a merriment, 2.04.298 P
now doth it turn and ebb back to the sea, 5.02.131
turn him to any cause of policy, | the gordian H5 1.01. 45
for your own reasons turn into your bosoms, | as 2.02. 82
turn head, and stop pursuit; 2.04. 69
turn thee back, | and tell thy king i do not 3.06.139
turn the sands into eloquent tongues, and my 3.07. 34 P
may as well go about to turn the sun to ice with 4.01.200 P
soldiers' heads | and turn them out of service. 4.03.119
so did he turn and over suffolk's neck | he 4.06. 24
well, bawd i'll turn, | and something lean to 5.01. 85
back will stoop, a black beard will turn white, 5.02.160 P
wars | will turn unto a peaceful comic sport, 1H6 2.02. 45

thy mirth shall turn to moan. 2.03. 44
turn not thy scorns this way, plantagenet. 2.04. 77
i'll turn my part thereof into thy throat. 2.04. 79
o, turn the edged sword another way, | strike 3.03. 52
done like a frenchman — turn and turn again! 3.03. 85
done like a frenchman — turn and turn again! 3.03. 85
and no way canst thou turn thee for redress, 4.02. 25
turn on the bloody hounds with heads of steel, 4.02. 51
and turn again unto the warlike french. 5.02. 3
peace be amongst them if they turn to us, | else 5.02. 6
will nothing turn your unrelenting hearts? 5.04. 59
what, dost thou turn away and hide thy face? 2H6 3.02. 74
shore, | or turn our stern upon a dreadful rock? 3.02. 91
so shouldst thou either turn my flying soul, 3.02.397
means to dress the commonwealth, and turn it, 4.02. 5 P
steel, if thou turn the edge, or cut not out the 4.10. 56 P
all will revolt from me and turn to him. 3H6 1.01.151
turn this way, henry, and regard them not. 1.01.189
followers to the eager foe | turn back and fly, 1.04. 4
foes, | but never once again turn back and fly. 2.01.185
the smallest worm will turn, being trodden on, 2.02. 17
then 'twas my turn to fly, and now 'tis thine. 2.02.105
then none but i shall turn his jest to sorrow. 3.03.261
and to my brother turn my blushing cheeks. 5.01. 99
clarence, thy turn is next, and then the rest, 5.06. 90
but first i'll turn yon fellow in his grave, R3 1.02.260
ah, gentle villain, do not turn away! 1.03.162
and turn you all your hatred now on me? 1.03.189
when ever buckingham doth turn his hate | upon 2.01. 32
ere from this war thou turn a conqueror, | or i 4.04.185
men | to turn their own points in their masters' 5.01. 24
i doubt not but his friends will turn to us. 5.02. 19
they turn to vicious forms, ten times more ugly H8 1.02.117
sacred person — in god's name | turn me away; 2.04. 42
my drops of tears | i'll turn to sparks of fire. 2.04. 73
you turn the good we offer into envy. 3.01.113
ye turn me into nothing! 3.01.114
come, you and i must walk a turn together; 5.01. 93
by some that hate me | (god turn their hearts! 5.02. 15
"do my lord of canterbury | a shrewd turn, and 5.02.211
we turn not back the silks upon the merchant, TRO 2.02. 69
that shall not serve your turn, that shall it 3.01. 74 P
which seems the wound to kill, | doth turn o ho! 3.01.123
malice and malice fac'd with wit turn him to? 5.01. 58 P
wind, to wind, there turn and change together. 5.03.110
turn thy false face, thou traitor, | and pay thy 5.06. 6
turn, slave, and fight. 5.07. 13 P
there is a word will priam turn to stone, | make 5.10. 18
virgilia, turn thy solemnness out a' door, and COR 1.03.107 P
o that you could turn your eyes toward the napes 2.01. 39 P
i know not where to turn. 2.01.181
made the coward | turn terror into sport; 2.02.105
to say he'll turn your current in a ditch, | and 3.01. 96
the which shall turn you to no further harm 3.01.282
for you, the city, thus i turn my back; 3.03.134
straight | and make my misery serve thy turn. 4.05. 88
and turn the dregs of it upon this varlet here 5.02. 77 P
that brought her for this high good turn so far? TIT 1.01.397
ay, so the turn were served. 2.01. 96
milk thou suck'st from her did turn to marble, 2.03.144
my hand will serve the turn. 3.01.164
about, | that i may turn me to each one of you, 3.01.277
at such a bay, by turn to serve our lust. 4.02. 42
can never turn the swan's black legs to white, 4.02.102
fair, | and tarry with him till i turn again. 5.02.141
now is my turn to speak. 5.03.119
how, turn thy back and run? ROM 1.01. 35 P
turn thee, benvolio, look upon thy death. 1.01. 67
turn giddy, and be holp by backward turning; 1.02. 47
such falsehood, then turn tears to /fires; 1.02. 89
more light, you knaves, and turn the tables up; 1.05. 27
pray — grant thou, lest faith turn to despair. 1.05.104
turn back, dull earth, and find thy centre out. 2.01. 2
to turn your households' rancor to pure love. 2.03. 92
that thou hast done me, therefore turn and draw. 3.01. 67
and, as he fell, did romeo turn and fly. 3.01.174
heart with treacherous revolt | turn to another, 4.01. 59
turn from their office to black funeral: 4.05. 85
i must serve my turn | out of mine own. TIM 2.01. 20
why should it thrive and turn to nutriment 3.01. 58
i'll look you out a good turn, servilius. 3.02. 60
matrons, turn incontinent! 4.01. 3
as we do turn our backs | from our companion 4.02. 8
'tis most just | that thou turn rascal; 4.03.217
i'll meet you at the turn. 5.01. 47
i turn the trouble of my countenance | merely JC 1.02. 38
that you have no such mirrors as will turn 1.02. 56
cassius or caesar never shall turn back, | for i 3.01. 21
and turn preordinance and first decree | into 3.01. 38
his name out of his heart, and turn him going. 3.03. 34 P
then take we down his load, and turn him off 4.01. 25
the proof of it will turn to redder drops. 5.01. 49
hold then my sword, and turn away thy face, 5.05. 47
are regist'red where every day i turn | the leaf MAC 1.03.151
turn, hell-hound, turn! 5.08. 3
turn, hell-hound, turn! 5.08. 3
with this regard their currents turn awry, | and HAM 3.01. 86
night, | to desperation turn my trust and hope, 3.02.218
if the rest of my fortunes turn turk with me — 3.02.276 P
but, o, what form of prayer | can serve my turn? 3.03. 52
with weight | /till our scale turn the beam. 4.05.158
i am to do a /good turn for them. 4.06. 22 P
himself, there are no tongues else for 's turn. 5.02.184 P
shall our abode | make with you by due turn. LR 1.01.135
and on the sixt to turn thy hated back | upon 1.01.175
turn all her mother's pains and benefits | to 1.04.286
i'ld turn it all | to thy suggestion, plot, and 2.01. 72
and turn their halcyon beaks | with every gale 2.02. 78
smile once more, turn thy wheel! 2.02.173
of a corn cry woe, | and turn his sleep to wake. 3.02. 34
my wits begin to turn. 3.02. 67
this cold night will turn us all to fools and 3.04. 78 P
shouldst have said, "good porter, turn the key." 3.07. 64
turn out that eyeless villain; 3.07. 96
lest my brain turn, and the deficient sight 4.06. 23
and turn our impress'd lances in our eyes 5.03. 50
i follow him to serve my turn upon him. OTH 1.01. 42
so will i turn her virtue into pitch, | and out 2.03.360
when i shall turn the business of my soul | to 3.03.181
ay, you did wish that i would make her turn. 4.01.252
sir, she can turn, and turn; 4.01.253
sir, she can turn, and turn; 4.01.253
and yet go on | and turn again; 4.01.254
turn thy complexion there, | patience, thou 4.02. 62
i pray you turn the key and keep our counsel. 4.02. 94
this sight would make him do a desperate turn, 5.02.207
now turn | the office and devotion of their view ANT 1.01. 4
i prithee turn aside, and weep for her, | then 1.03. 76
and keep the turn of tippling with a slave, | to 1.04. 19
for what good turn? 2.05. 58
for the best turn i' th' bed. 2.05. 59
and kindly creatures | turn all to serpents! 2.05. 79
turn your displeasure that way, for our faults 3.04. 34
with all their sixty, fly and turn the rudder. 3.10. 3
i turn you not away, but, like a master 4.02. 30
turn from me then that noble countenance, 4.14. 85
i'll fetch a turn about the garden, pitying CYM 1.01. 81
all gold and silver rather turn to dirt, | as 3.06. 53
testiness, shall turn all into my commendations. 4.01. 21 P
then i'll turn craver too, and so i shall scape PER 2.01. 88 P
word, nor did ill turn | to any living creature. 4.01. 75
fram'd this piece, she meant thee a good turn; 4.02.140 P
i think you'll turn a child again. 4.03. 4
and to her father turn our thoughts again, 5.ch. 12
pray you turn your eyes upon me. 5.01.101
toward ephesus | turn our blown sails; 5.01.255
name | of pericles to rage the city turn, | that 5.03. 97
now turn we towards your comforts. TNK 1.01.234
us to an eddy | where we should turn or drown; 1.02. 11
and sweetly, by a figure, trace and turn, boys. 3.05. 21
before i turn, let me embrace thee, cousin; 5.01. 31
mars's drum | and turn th' alarm to whispers; 5.01. 81
not physick'd by respect might turn our blood STM III 13
thirst for drink than she for this good turn. VEN 92
now which way shall she turn? 253
shalt thou see the dew-bedabbled wretch | turn, 704
whereat her tears began to turn their tide, 979
the sweets we wish for turn to loathed sours LUC 867
and turn the giddy round of fortune's wheel; 952
nothing could be used to turn them both to gain, PP 15.10
for sweetest things turn sourest by their deeds; SON 94.13
but if thou catch thy hope, turn back to me, 143.11
if thou turn back and my loud crying still. 143.14
or to turn white and sound at tragic shows; LC 308

TURNBULL 1 FR 0.0001 REL FR 0 V 1 P
the feats he hath done about turnbull street, 2H4 3.02.306 P

TURNCOAT 1 FR 0.0001 REL FR 0 V 1 P
then is courtesy a turncoat. ADO 1.01.124 P

TURNCOATS 1 FR 0.0001 REL FR 1 V 0 P
predominate his smoke, | and be no turncoats; TIM 4.03.144

/TURN'D 1 FR 0.0001 REL FR 1 V 0 P
/turn'd /her | /to /foreign /casualties, /gave LR 4.03. 43

TURN'D 103 FR 0.0116 REL FR 71 V 32 P
to think o' th' teen that i have turn'd you to, TMP 1.02. 64
and all be turn'd to barnacles, or to apes 4.01.248
the young and tender wit | is turn'd to folly, TGV 1.01. 48
i have turn'd away my other guests; WIV 4.03. 10 P
turn'd my daughter into /green; 5.05.201 P
she would have made hercules have turn'd spit, ADO 2.01.253 P
and now is he turn'd ortography — his words are 2.03. 20 P
o day untowardly turn'd! 3.02.131 P
well, and you be not turn'd turk, there's no 3.04. 57 P
compliment, and men are only turn'd into tongue, 4.01.320 P
were never so truly turn'd over and over as my 5.02. 35 P
when they are catch'd, | as wit turn'd fool; LLL 5.02. 70
the fourth turn'd on the toe, and down he fell. 5.02.114
of the fairest dames | that ever turn'd their — 5.02.161
"that /ever turn'd their eyes to mortal views! 5.02.163
turn'd her obedience (which is due to me) | to MND 1.01. 37
that he hath turn'd a heaven unto a hell! 1.01.207
must perforce ensue | some true love turn'd, and 3.02. 91
true love turn'd, and not a false turn'd true. 3.02. 91
we turn'd o'er many books together. MV 4.01.156 P
their savage eyes turn'd to a modest gaze, | by 5.01. 78
many a fair year though hero had turn'd nun, if AYL 4.01.101 P
a fool, | and turn'd into the extremity of love. 4.03. 23
"art thou god to shepherd turn'd, | that a 4.03. 40
a pair of old breeches thrice turn'd; SHR 3.02. 44 P
you, that have turn'd off a first so noble wife, AWW 5.03.220
that instant was i turn'd into a hart, | and my TN 1.01. 20
being so long absent, or to be turn'd away — is 1.05. 17 P
quickly the wrong side may be turn'd outward! 3.01. 13 P
yond gull malvolio is turn'd heathen, a very 3.02. 70 P
was a woman and was turn'd into a cold fish for WT 4.04.279 P
which we, god knows, have turn'd another way, JN 2.01.549
or turn'd an eye of doubt upon my face, | as bid 4.02.233
to be as true-bred cowards as ever turn'd back; 1H4 1.02.184 P
and on my face he turn'd an eye of death, 1.03.143
this house is turn'd upside down since robin 2.01. 10 P
father's beard is turn'd white with the news. 2.04.359 P
i had rather hear a brazen canstick turn'd, | or 3.01.129
come, you shall have trent turn'd. 3.01.134
this house is turn'd bawdy-house, they pick 3.03. 98 P
the fortune of the day quite turn'd from him, 5.05. 18
sir john umfrevile turn'd me back | with joyful 2H4 1.01. 34
all the rest | turn'd on themselves, like dull 1.01.118
the shame | of those that turn'd their backs, 1.01.130
times that true valor is turn'd berrord; 1.02.169 P
have you turn'd him out a' doors? 2.04.212 P
them, is turn'd into a justice-like servingman. 5.01. 68 P
that i have turn'd away my former self; 5.05. 58
of his | hath turn'd his balls to gun-stones, H5 1.02.282
turn'd away the fat knight with the great belly 4.07. 47 P
the cities turn'd into a maid; 5.02.321 P
o, were mine eyeballs into bullets turn'd, 1H6 4.07. 79
is all our travail turn'd to this effect? 5.04.102
news, i think, hath turn'd your weapon's edge; 2H6 2.01.176
on my knees thou mayst be turn'd to hobnails. 4.10. 59 P
at this sight | my heart is turn'd to stone; 5.02. 50
these words have turn'd my hate to love, | and i 3H6 3.03.199
seat, | and turn'd my captive state to liberty, 4.06. 3
and all the trouble thou hast turn'd me to? 5.05. 16
it is turn'd out of towns and cities for a R3 1.04.141 P
hath turn'd my feigned prayer on my head, | and 5.01. 21
ships, | and turn'd crown'd kings to merchants. TRO 2.02. 83
unplausive eyes are bent, why turn'd on him? 3.03. 43
unless she said, "my mind is now turn'd whore." 5.02.114
my throat of war be turn'd, | which quier'd with COR 3.02.112
he turn'd me about with his finger and his thumb 4.05.152 P
me, and turn'd weeping out | to beg relief among TIT 5.03.105
the law, | and turn'd that black word "death" to ROM 3.03. 27
must not be toss'd and turn'd to me in words, TIM 2.01. 26
turn to nutriment | when he is turn'd to poison? 3.01. 59
speak, caesar is turn'd to hear. JC 1.02. 17
is not the leaf turn'd down | where i left 4.03.273
myself have to mine own turn'd enemy. 5.03. 2
turn'd wild in nature, broke their stalls, flung MAC 2.04. 16
and, with his head over his shoulder turn'd, HAM 2.01. 94
whe'er he has not turn'd his color and has tears 2.02.519 P
imperious caesar, dead and turn'd to clay, 5.01.213
the foul practice | hath turn'd itself on me. 5.02.318
and told me i had turn'd the wrong side out. LR 4.02. 9
whom love hath turn'd almost the wrong side out, OTH 2.03. 52
are we turn'd turks, and to ourselves do that 2.03.170
no, my heart is turn'd to stone; 4.01.182 P
that turn'd your wit the seamy side without, 4.02.146
she turn'd to folly, and she was a whore. 5.02.132
of the world, | art turn'd the greatest liar. ANT 1.03. 39
my part, i am sorry it is turn'd to a drinking. 2.06.103 P
air, and then | have turn'd mine eye and wept. CYM 1.03. 22
here the leaf's turn'd down | where philomele 2.02. 45
loss, the most coldest that ever turn'd up ace. 2.03. 2 P
of the loyal leonatus, | all turn'd to heresy? 3.04. 82
to have turn'd my leaping time into a crutch, 4.02.200
it is a day turn'd strangely. 5.02. 17
which could have turn'd | a distaff to a lance, 5.03. 33
that some, turn'd coward | but by example (o, a 5.03. 35
his merits due, | being all to dolors turn'd? 5.04. 80
come at last, and 'tis turn'd to a rusty armor. PER 2.01.119 P
that with thy power hast turn'd | green neptune TNK 5.01. 49
the night of sorrow now is turn'd to day: VEN 481
mine eyes are turn'd to fire, my heart to lead: 1072
and turn'd it thus, "it cannot be, i find, | but LUC 1539
and whether that my angel be turn'd fiend, PP 2. 9
three beauteous springs to yellow autumn turn'd SON 104. 5
and whether that my angel be turn'd fiend 144. 9

TURNED 5 FR 0.0005 REL FR 5 V 0 P
like far-off mountains turned into clouds. MND 4.01.188
rank, | in end of autumn turned to the rams, MV 1.03. 81
my life should sail | are turned to one thread, JN 5.07. 54
i am the turned forth, be it known to you, TIT 5.03.109
a burning torch that's turned upside down; PER 2.02. 32

TURNETH 1 FR 0.0001 REL FR 1 V 0 P
work like the spring that turneth wood to stone, HAM 4.07. 20

TURNING 28 FR 0.0031 REL FR 18 V 10 P
any ill, i will leave them at the next turning. ADO 2.01.154 P
feet, humor it with turning up your eyelids, LLL 3.01. 13 P
for jove, | turning mortal for thy love." 4.03.118
turn up on your right hand at the next turning, MV 2.02. 42 P
next turning, but at the next turning of all, on 2.02. 42 P
marry, at the very next turning, turn of no hand 2.02. 43 P
turning his face, he put his hand behind him, 2.08. 47
but, turning these jests out of service, let us AYL 1.03. 25 P
turning again toward childish treble, pipes 2.07.162
and for turning away, let summer bear it out. TN 1.05. 20 P
turning with splendor of his precious eye | the JN 3.01. 79
turning dispiteous torture out of door? 4.01. 34
have torn their souls by turning them from us, R2 3.03. 83
he, from the one side to the other turning, 5.02. 18
turning your books to graves, your ink to blood, 2H4 4.01. 50
turning the word to sword and life to death. 4.02. 10
of other, | turning past evils to advantages. 4.04. 78
turning th' accomplishment of many years | into H5 pr 30
twelve and one, ev'n at the turning o' th' tide; 2.03. 13 P
and on your head | turning the widows' tears, 2.04.106
which is the moral of it, that she is turning, 3.06. 34 P
turn giddy, and be holp by backward turning; ROM 1.02. 47
turning his side to the dew-dropping south. 1.04.103
this ensign here of mine was turning back; JC 5.03. 3
hell gate, he should have old turning the key. MAC 2.03. 2 P
by turning o'er authorities, i have, | together PER 3.02. 33
eyes are grey, and bright, and quick in turning; VEN 140
for jove, | turning mortal for thy love." PP 16.18

TURNIPS 1 FR 0.0001 REL FR 1 V 0 P
th' earth, | and bowl'd to death with turnips! WIV 3.04. 87

/TURNS 1 FR 0.0001 REL FR 1 V 0 P
/bishop | /turns /insurrection /to /religion. 2H4 1.01.201

TURNS 60 FR 0.0067 REL FR 58 V 2 P
a slave, that still an end turns me to shame! TGV 4.04. 62
by the immoderate use | turns to restraint. MM 1.02.128
meet a sergeant, 'a turns back for very fear. ERR 4.02. 56
so turns she every man the wrong side out, | and ADO 3.01. 68
how giddily 'a turns about all the hot-bloods 3.03.131 P
their counsel turns to passion, which before 5.01. 23
catch | the other turns to a mirth-moving jest, LLL 2.01. 71
her favor turns the fashion of the days, | for 4.03.258
sin, | thus purifies itself and turns to grace. 5.02.776
turns to a crow | when thou hold'st up thy hand. MND 3.02.142
turns into yellow gold his salt green streams. 3.02.393
turns them to shapes and gives to aery nothing 5.01. 16
turns to a wild of nothing, save of joy MV 3.02.182
she's apt to learn and thankful for good turns. SHR 2.01.165
he that is giddy thinks the world turns round. 5.02. 20
"he that is giddy thinks the world turns round": 5.02. 26
to the great sender turns a sour offense, AWW 5.03. 59
oft good turns | are shuffled off with such TN 3.03. 15
turns to the sourest and most deadly hate. R2 3.02.136
and hate turns one or both | to worthy danger 5.01. 67
turns head against the lion's armed jaws, | and, 1H4 3.02.102
and turns the force of them upon thyself. 2H6 3.02.332
and turns the sun to shade — alas, alas! R3 1.03.265
the eldest son of fortune, | turns what he list. H8 2.02. 21
is like that mirth fate turns to sudden sadness. TRO 1.01. 40
for speculation turns not to itself, | till it 3.03.109
look how thy eye turns pale! 5.03. 81
o world, thy slippery turns! COR 4.04. 12
hand, and turns up the white o' th' eye to his 4.05.196 P
news is coming | that turns their countenances. 4.06. 60
he turns away. 5.03.168
certain snatch or so | would serve your turns. TIT 2.01. 96
and strike, brave boys, and take your turns; 2.01.129
soft, so busily she turns the leaves! 4.01. 45
virtue itself turns vice, being misapplied, ROM 2.03. 21

who, all as hot, turns deadly point to point, 3.01.160
becomes thy friend, | and turns it to exile: 3.03.140
milky heart, | it turns in less than two nights? TIM 3.01. 55
it almost turns my dangerous nature wild. 4.03.492
whereto the climber–upward turns his face; JC 2.01. 23
round, | he then unto the ladder turns his back, 2.01. 25
abroad, and turns our swords | in our own proper 5.03. 95
i," | the cloudy messenger turns me his back, MAC 3.06. 41
itself, | she turns to favor and to prettiness. HAM 4.05.189
arrant whore, | ne'er turns the key to th' poor. LR 2.04. 53
the knave turns fool that runs away, | the fool 2.04. 84
most large | in his abominations, turns you off, ANT 3.06. 94
spare your arithmetic, never count the turns. CYM 2.04.142
sword | that does good turns to th' world; TNK 1.01. 49
the soldier in | the cranks and turns of thebes? 1.02. 28
he turns ye like a top. 5.02. 50
pay, | he winks, and turns his lips another way. VEN 90
"my uncontrolled tide | turns not, but swells LUC 646
thy honey turns to gall, thy joy to grief! 889
"thy secret pleasure turns to open shame, | thy 890
while with a joyless smile she turns away | the 1711
now see what good turns eyes for eyes have done: SON 24. 9
and each doth good turns now unto the other: 47. 2
and all things turns to fair that eyes can see! 95.12
and therefore from my face she turns my foes, 139.11
TURN'ST 2 FR 0.0002 REL FR 2 V 0 P
ah, now thou turn'st away thy face for shame! TIT 2.04. 28
thou turn'st my /eyes into my /very soul, | and HAM 3.04. 89
TURPH 1 FR 0.0001 REL FR 1 V 0 P
and peter turph, and henry pimpernell, | and SHR in.2. 94
TURPITUDE 2 FR 0.0002 REL FR 2 V 0 P
minds sway'd by eyes are full of turpitude. TRO 5.02.112
when my turpitude | thou dost so crown with gold ANT 4.06. 32
TURQUOISE *(see turkis)*
TURRET 1 FR 0.0001 REL FR 1 V 0 P
the burning torch in yonder turret stands. 1H6 3.02. 30
TURRET'S 1 FR 0.0001 REL FR 1 V 0 P
discourse, i prithee, on this turret's top. 1H6 1.04. 26
TURRETS 3 FR 0.0003 REL FR 3 V 0 P
from forth blue clouds | the mason'd turrets, TNK 5.01. 55
left their round turrets destitute and pale. LUC 441
as heaven (it seem'd) to kiss the turrets bow'd. 1372
TURTLE 7 FR 0.0008 REL FR 7 V 0 P
o slow–wing'd turtle, shall a buzzard take thee? SHR 2.01.207
ay, for a turtle, as he takes a buzzard. 2.01.208
i, an old turtle, | will wing me to some WT 5.03.132
moon, | as sun to day, as turtle to her mate, TRO 3.02.178
phoenix and the turtle fled | in a mutual flame PHT 23
was seen | 'twixt this turtle and his queen: 31
that the turtle saw his right | flaming in the 34
TURTLE–DOVES 1 FR 0.0001 REL FR 1 V 0 P
like to a pair of loving turtle–doves | that 1H6 2.02. 30
TURTLE'S 1 FR 0.0001 REL FR 1 V 0 P
and the turtle's loyal breast | to eternity doth PHT 57
TURTLES 5 FR 0.0005 REL FR 3 V 2 P
twenty lascivious turtles ere one chaste man. WIV 2.01. 81 P
we'll teach him to know turtles from jays. 3.03. 42 P
will these turtles be gone? LLL 4.03.208
when turtles tread, and rooks and daws, | and 5.02.905
so turtles pair | that never mean to part. WT 4.04.154
TUSCAN 2 FR 0.0002 REL FR 2 V 0 P
gentlemen that mean to see | the tuscan service, AWW 1.02. 14
i'll to the tuscan wars, and never bed her. 2.03.273
/TUSH 1 FR 0.0001 REL FR 1 V 0 P
/tush, never tell me! OTH 1.01. 1
TUSH 21 FR 0.0023 REL FR 18 V 3 P
tush, i may as well say the fool's the fool. ADO 3.03.123 P
tush, tush, man, never fleer and jest at me; 5.01. 58
tush, tush, man, never fleer and jest at me; 5.01. 58
tush, fear not, man, we'll tip thy horns with 5.04. 44
tush, none but minstrels like of sonneting! LLL 4.03.156
tush, gremio; SHR 1.01.126 P
tush, tush, fear boys with bugs. 1.02.210
tush, tush, fear boys with bugs. 1.02.210
tush, man, mortal men, mortal men. 1H4 4.02. 67 P
tush, that was but his fancy, blame him not. 1H6 4.01.178
tush, that's a wooden thing! 5.03. 89
tush, women have been captivate ere now. 5.03.107
tush, my good lord, this superficial tale | is 5.05. 10
tush, man, abodements must not now affright us. 3H6 4.07. 13
he answer'd, "tush, | it can do me no damage"; H8 1.02.182
tush, tush! COR 3.02. 45
tush, tush! 3.02. 45
tush, i will stir about, | and all things shall ROM 4.02. 39
tush, thou art deceiv'd. 5.01. 29
tush, tush, 'twill not appear. HAM 1.01. 30
tush, tush, 'twill not appear. 1.01. 30
TUSHES 2 FR 0.0002 REL FR 2 V 0 P
whose tushes never sheath'd he whetteth still, VEN 617
and whom he strikes his crooked tushes slay. 624
TUSK 1 FR 0.0001 REL FR 1 V 0 P
sheath'd unaware the tusk in his soft groin. VEN 1116
TUT 37 FR 0.0041 REL FR 26 V 11 P
tut, man, i mean thou'lt lose the flood, and, in TGV 2.03. 41 P
tut, a pin! this shall be answer'd. WIV 1.01.114 P
tut, sir; 2.01.224 P
tut, a toy! SHR 2.01.402
tut, i like it not. 3.01. 79
tut, she's a lamb, a dove, a fool to him! 3.02.157
tut, fear not me. 4.04. 13
tut, there's life in't, man. TN 1.03.111 P
tut, tut! R2 2.03. 86
tut, tut! 2.03. 86
tut, our horses they shall not see — i'll tie 1H4 1.02.177 P
tut, there are other troyans that thou dream'st 2.01. 69 P
tut, never fear me, i am as vigilant as a cat to 4.02. 58 P
tut, tut, good enough to toss, food for powder, 4.02. 65 P
tut, tut, good enough to toss, food for powder, 4.02. 65 P
tut, i came not to hear this. 4.03. 89
tut, i have the best armor of the world. H5 3.07. 1 P
tut, holy joan was his defensive guard. 1H6 2.01. 49
tut, tut, here is a mannerly forbearance. 2.04. 19
tut, tut, here is a mannerly forbearance. 2.04. 19
tut, this was nothing but an argument | that he 2H6 1.02. 32
tut, these are petty faults to faults unknown, 3.01. 64
tut, when struck'st thou one blow in the field? 4.07. 79 P
tut, that's a foolish observation. 3H6 2.06.108
tut, were it farther off, i'll pluck it down. 3.02.195
tut, tut, my lord, we will not stand to prate; R3 1.03.349
tut, tut, my lord, we will not stand to prate; 1.03.349
tut, i can counterfeit the deep tragedian, 3.05. 5
tut, tut, thou art all ice, thy kindness freezes 4.02. 22
tut, tut, thou art all ice, thy kindness freezes 4.02. 22
tut, lucius, this was but a deed of charity | to TIT 5.01. 89
tut, i have work enough for you to do. 5.02.150
tut, i have lost myself, i am not here: ROM 1.01.197
tut, man, one fire burns out another's burning, 1.02. 45
tut, you saw her fair, none else being by, 1.02. 94
tut, dun's the mouse, the constable's own word. 1.04. 40
tut, i am in their bosoms, and i know JC 5.01. 7
/TUTOR 1 FR 0.0001 REL FR 1 V 0 P
/give /sorrow /leave /a /while /to /tutor /me R2 4.01.166
TUTOR 15 FR 0.0017 REL FR 11 V 4 P
what, i say, | my foot my tutor? TMP 1.02.470
he being her pupil, to become her tutor. TGV 2.01.138
now therefore would i have thee to my tutor 3.01. 84
wast, | the tutor and the feeder of my riots. 2H4 5.05. 62
for thee | to tutor thee in stratagems of war, 1H6 4.05. 2
ah, tutor, look where bloody clifford comes! 3H6 1.03. 2
have in mine elbows, an asinico may tutor thee. TRO 2.01. 44 P
heaven bless thee from a tutor, and discipline 2.03. 29 P
fam'd be thy tutor, and thy parts of nature 2.03.242
indeed i was their tutor to instruct them. TIT 5.01. 98
and yet thou wilt tutor me from quarrelling! ROM 3.01. 29 P
but let your own discretion be your tutor. HAM 3.02. 17 P
(unless we fear that apes can tutor 's) to | be TNK 1.02. 43
thy eyes' shrowd tutor, that hard heart of thine VEN 500
"o time, thou tutor both to good and bad, LUC 995
TUTOR'D 5 FR 0.0005 REL FR 4 V 1 P
man, | not being tried and tutor'd in the world: TGV 1.03. 21
for their sons are well tutor'd by you, and LLL 4.02. 74 P
and hath been tutor'd in the rudiments | of many AYL 5.04. 31
learning and good letters peace hath tutor'd, 2H4 4.01. 44
then gave i her (so tutor'd by my art) | a ROM 5.03.243
TUTORS 5 FR 0.0005 REL FR 5 V 0 P
for vainer hours, and tutors not so careful. TMP 1.02.174
of beauty's tutors have enrich'd you with? LLL 4.03.320
and tell them both, | these are their tutors. SHR 2.01.110
i will say of it, | it tutors nature. TIM 1.01. 37
when nobles are their tailors' tutors; LR 3.02. 83
TUTTO 1 FR 0.0001 REL FR 1 V 0 P
con tutto /il core, ben trovato, may i say. SHR 1.02. 24
TU–WHIT 2 FR 0.0002 REL FR 2 V 0 P
sings the staring owl, | "tu–whit, tu–who!" LLL 5.02.918
sings the staring owl, | "tu–whit, tu–who!" 5.02.927
TU–WHO 2 FR 0.0002 REL FR 2 V 0 P
sings the staring owl, | "tu–whit, tu–who!" LLL 5.02.918
sings the staring owl, | "tu–whit, tu–who!" 5.02.927
TWAIN *(also tway)*
TWAIN 48 FR 0.0054 REL FR 46 V 2 P
duke of milan | and his brave son being twain. TMP 1.02.439
go with me | to bless this twain, that they may 4.01.104
to save a head, | to cleave a heart in twain. MM 3.01. 62
did he not send you twain? LLL 5.02. 48
i remit both twain. 5.02.459
wall, and lovers twain | at large discourse, MND 5.01.150
stay, | nor rest be interposer 'twixt us twain. MV 3.02.327
'tis bargain'd 'twixt us twain, being alone, SHR 2.01.304
what have we twain forgot? WT 4.04.660
can arbitrate this cause betwixt us twain; R2 1.01. 50
twice saying "pardon" doth not pardon twain, 5.03.134
than can yourself yourself in twain divide. 1H6 4.05. 49
was broke in twain (by whom i have forgot, | but 2H6 1.02. 26
we twain will go into his highness' tent. 5.01. 55
you twain, of all the rest, | are near to 3H6 4.01.135
as wedged with a sigh, would rive in twain, TRO 1.01. 35
and in the imitation of these twain — | who, as 1.03.185
to fight, | let mars divide eternity in twain, 2.03.245
he? no! she'll none of him. they two are twain. 3.01.102 P
forbids | a gory emulation 'twixt us twain. 4.05.123
thou and my bosom henceforth shall be twain. ROM 3.05.240
than with that hand that cut thy youth in twain 5.03. 99
of the night | for a dark hour or twain. MAC 3.01. 27
and never come mischance between us twain! HAM 3.02.228
o hamlet, thou hast cleft my heart in twain. 3.04.156
thou wilt o'ertake us hence a mile or twain | i' LR 4.01. 42
general curse | which twain have brought her to. 4.06.207
of my soul, you twain | rule in this realm, and 5.03.320
and pure grief | shore his old thread in twain. OTH 5.02.206
such a mutual pair | and such a twain can do't, ANT 1.01. 38
'tis time we twain | did show ourselves i' th' 1.04. 73
his soldiership | is twice the other twain; 2.01. 35
wars 'twixt you twain would be | as if the world 3.04. 30
multitudes, | could not outpeer these twain. CYM 3.06. 86
seats we came, | our parents and us twain, 5.04. 70
cleaving his conscience into twain and doing TNK 1.03. 46
arcite is the lower of the twain; 2.01. 50 P
give us but a tree or twain | for a maypole, and 3.05.144
love keeps his revels where there are but twain; VEN 123
and one for int'rest, if thou wilt have twain. 210
his face seems twain, each several limb is 1067
as if between them twain there were no strife, LUC 405
to live or die which of the twain were better, 1154
so they loved as love in twain | had the essence PHT 25
"how true a twain | seemeth this concordant one! 45
let me confess that we two must be twain, SON 36. 1
and that thou teachest how to make one twain, 39.13
both find each other, and i lose both twain, 42.11
TWANG'D 1 FR 0.0001 REL FR 0 V 1 P
with a swaggering accent sharply twang'd off, TN 3.04.180 P
TWANGLING 2 FR 0.0002 REL FR 2 V 0 P
sometimes a thousand twangling instruments TMP 3.02.137
did call me rascal fiddler | and twangling jack, SHR 2.01.158
/'TWAS 2 FR 0.0002 REL FR 2 V 0 P
whether /'twas pride, | which out of daily COR 4.07. 37
/finding | /who /'twas /that /so /endur'd, /with LR 5.03.212
'TWAS 170 FR 0.0192 REL FR 128 V 42 P
'twas a sweet marriage, and we prosper well in TMP 2.01. 73 P
'twas you we laugh'd at. 2.01.176 P
o, 'twas a din to fright a monster's ear, | to 2.01.314
'twas of his nephew proteus, your son. TGV 1.03. 3
quoth i, "'twas i did the thing you wot of." 4.04. 27 P
'twas ariadne passioning | for theseus' perjury 4.04.167
by these gloves, then 'twas he. WIV 1.01.165 P
'twas a good sensible fellow — well. 2.01.147 P
i knew not what 'twas to be beaten till lately. 5.01. 26 P
'twas a commandement to command the captain and MM 1.02. 12 P
sith 'twas my fault to give the people scope, 1.03. 35
sir — 'twas in the bunch of grapes, where 2.01.128 P
'twas never merry world since, of two usuries, 3.02. 5 P
"it is not so, nor 'twas not so, but indeed, god ADO 1.01.217 P
'twas the boy that stole your meat, and you'll 2.01.199 P
no, 'twas the vane on the house. 3.03.129 P
'twas bravely done, if you bethink you of it. 5.01.270
'twas not a haud credo, 'twas a pricket. LLL 4.02. 12 P
'twas not a haud credo, 'twas a pricket. 4.02. 12 P
the deer was not a haud credo, 'twas a pricket. 4.02. 20 P
that, 'twas a pricket that the princess kill'd. 4.02. 48 P
'twas treason, he said. 4.03.192
unfold to any one | which casket 'twas i chose; MV 2.09. 11
i think 'twas made of atalanta's heels. AYL 3.02.276 P
'twas just the difference | betwixt the constant 3.05.122
her old gloves were on, but 'twas her hands; 4.03. 26
'twas i; 4.03.135
'twas where you woo'd the gentlewoman so well. SHR in.1. 85
i think 'twas soto that your honor means. in.1. 88
he, | although i think 'twas in another sense — 1.01.215
'twas told me you were rough and coy and sullen, 2.01.243
'twas a commodity lay fretting by you; 2.01.328
patience, i pray you, 'twas a fault unwilling. 4.01.156
i tell thee, kate, 'twas burnt and dried away, 4.01.170
'twas i won the wager, though you hit the white, 5.02.186
'twas pretty, though a plague, | to see him AWW 1.01. 92
'twas a good lady, 'twas a good lady. 4.05. 13 P
'twas a good lady, 'twas a good lady. 4.05. 13 P
'twas mine, 'twas helen's, | whoever gave it you 5.03.104
'twas mine, 'twas helen's, | whoever gave it you 5.03.104
confess 'twas hers, and by what rough 5.03.107
by jove, if ever i knew man, 'twas you. 5.03.287
and then 'twas fresh in murmur (as, you know, TN 1.02. 32
'twas very good, i' faith. 2.03. 24 P
i knew 'twas i, for many do call me fool. 2.05. 81 P
'twas never merry world | since lowly feigning 3.01. 98
"be not afraid of greatness": 'twas well writ. 3.04. 39 P
i know not what 'twas but distraction. 5.01. 68
'twas a fear | which oft infects the wisest: WT 1.02.261
that thou betrayedst polixenes, 'twas nothing — 3.02.185
'twas nothing to geld a codpiece of a purse; 4.04.610 P
who says it was, he lies, i say 'twas not. JN 1.01.276
why, 'twas my care, | and what loss is it to be R2 3.02. 95
and yet not so, for with a kiss 'twas made. 5.01. 75
'twas where the madcap duke his uncle kept — 1H4 1.03.244
the sugar thou gavest me, 'twas a pennyworth, 2.04. 59 P
'sblood, 'twas time to counterfeit, or that hot 5.04.113 P
that if we wrought out life 'twas ten to one, 2H4 1.01.182
to me — 'twas no longer ago than wed'sday last, 2.04. 86 P
ha, 'twas a merry night. 3.02.198 P
abide carnation — 'twas a color he never lik'd. H5 2.03. 33 P
'twas i indeed thou promisedst to strike, | and 4.08. 41
'twas time, i trow, to wake and leave our beds, 1H6 2.01. 41
'twas full of darnel; 3.02. 44
'twas neither charles nor yet the duke i nam'd, 5.04. 77
sweet aunt, be quiet, 'twas against her will. 2H6 1.03.143
'twas men i lack'd, and you will give them me; 3.01.345
axe, | but will suspect 'twas he that made the 3.02.190
now, by my /faith, lords, 'twas a glorious day. 5.03. 29
'twas by rebellion against his king. 3H6 1.01.133
then, seeing 'twas he that made you to depose, 1.02. 26
but 'twas ere i was born. 1.03. 39
but whether 'twas the coldness of the king, 2.01.122
or whether 'twas report of her success, | or 2.01.125
'twas odds, belike, when valiant warwick fled: 2.01.148
'twas you that kill'd young rutland, was it not? 2.02. 98
then 'twas my turn to fly, and now 'tis thine. 2.02.105
'twas not your valor, clifford, drove me thence. 2.02.107
when he was made a shriver, 'twas for shift. 3.02.108
'twas i that gave the kingdom to thy brother. 5.01. 34
'twas sin before, but now 'tis charity. 5.05. 76
but 'twas thy beauty that provoked me. R3 1.02.180
'twas i that stabb'd young edward — | but 'twas 1.02.181
but 'twas thy heavenly face that set me on. 1.02.182
o, 'twas the foulest deed to slay that babe, 1.03.182
no, he'll say 'twas done cowardly when he wakes. 1.04.101 P
'twas full two years ere i could get a tooth. 2.04. 29
'twas said they saw but one, and no discerner H8 1.01. 32
queen his aunt | (for 'twas indeed his color, 1.01.178
the duke | said, 'twas the fear indeed, and that 1.02.158
and that 'twas dangerous for /him | to ruminate 1.02.179
service was suff'rance, 'twas not voluntary; TRO 2.01. 95 P
if you'll avouch 'twas wisdom paris went — | as 2.02. 84
me, | 'twas not my purpose thus to beg a kiss. 3.02.137
'twas to bring this greek | to calchas' house, 4.01. 37
'twas one's that lov'd me better than you will. 5.02. 89
or whether his fall enrag'd him, or how 'twas, COR 1.03. 64 P
and 'twas time for him too, i'll warrant him 2.01.129 P
'twas never my desire yet to trouble the poor 2.03. 69 P
'twas from the canon. 3.01. 90
gratis, as 'twas us'd | sometime in greece — 3.01.114
'twas you incens'd the rabble; 4.02. 33
when i said banish him, i said 'twas pity. 4.06.140
i minded him how royal 'twas to pardon | when it 5.01. 18
he said 'twas folly, | for one poor grain or two 5.01. 26
'twas very faintly he said, "rise"; 5.01. 66
who 'twas that cut thy tongue and ravish'd thee. TIT 2.04. 2
'twas her two sons that murdered bassianus; 5.01. 91
and 'twas | trim sport for them which had the 5.01. 95
not i, 'twas chiron and demetrius: 5.03. 56
and they, 'twas they, that did her all this 5.03. 58
'twas no need, i trow, | to bid me trudge. ROM 1.03. 33
when 'twas a little prating thing — o, there is 2.04.200 P
for 'twas your heaven she should be advanc'd, 4.05. 72
'twas due on forfeiture, my lord, six weeks TIM 2.02. 30
he did behoove his anger, ere 'twas spent, | as 3.05. 22
'twas time and griefs | that fram'd him thus. 5.01.122
him a crown — yet 'twas not a crown neither, JC 1.02.237 P
a crown neither, 'twas one of these coronets — 1.02.238 P
'twas on a summer's evening, in his tent, | that 3.02.172
'twas a rough night. MAC 2.03. 61
sir, a' monday morning, 'twas then indeed. HAM 2.02.388 P
not the million, 'twas caviary to the general, 2.02.436 P
i chiefly lov'd, 'twas aeneas' /tale to dido, 2.02.446 P
'twas of some estate. 5.01.221

'twas her brother that, in pure kindness to his LR 2.04.125 P
'twas this flesh begot | those pelican daughters 3.04. 74
'twas he inform'd against him, | and quit the 4.02. 92
'twas yet some comfort, | when misery could 4.06. 62
how didst thou know 'twas she? OTH 1.01.165
she swore, in faith 'twas strange, 'twas passing 1.03.160
in faith 'twas strange, 'twas passing strange; 1.03.160
'twas pitiful, 'twas wondrous pitiful. 1.03.161
'twas pitiful, 'twas wondrous pitiful. 1.03.161
i do believe 'twas he. 3.03. 40
'twas mine, 'tis his, and has been slave to 3.03.158
he thought 'twas witchcraft — but i am much to 3.03.211
i gave her such a one; 'twas my first gift. 3.03.436
for 'twas that hand that gave away my heart. 3.04. 45
an old thing 'twas, but it express'd her fortune 4.03. 29
'twas i that kill'd her. 5.02.130
ay, 'twas he that told me on her first. 5.02.147
'twas merry when | you wager'd on your angling; ANT 2.05. 15
and 'twas i | that the mad brutus ended. 3.11. 37
'twas a shame no less | than was his loss, to 3.13. 10
took, | as we do air, fast as 'twas minist'red, CYM 1.01. 45
'twas a contention in public, which may, without 1.04. 54 P
last night 'twas on mine arm; 2.03.146
i am absolute | 'twas very cloten. 4.02.107
'twas but a bolt of nothing, shot at nothing, 4.02.300
'twas leonatus' jewel, | whom thou didst banish; 5.05.143
'twas at a feast — o, would | our viands had 5.05.155
leonatus, and | be villainy less than 'twas! 5.05.225
the more of you 'twas felt, the more it shap'd 5.05.346
'twas a fitment for | the purpose i then 5.05.409
'twas we that made up this garment through the PER 2.01.148 P
this was well ask'd, 'twas so well perform'd. 2.03. 99
'twas very strange. 2.04. 13
'twas helicanus then. 5.03. 53
'twas /flavina. TNK 1.03. 54
'twas possible | they might have been recovered. 1.04. 26
o, 'twas a studied punishment, a death | beyond 2.03. 4
'twas an excellent dance, and for a preface, | i 3.05.150
i might well perceive | 'twas one that sung, and 4.01. 58
'twas thy power | to put life into dust: 5.01.109
'twas well done. 5.02. 7
'twas very ill done then. 5.02. 13
'twas ever likely: 5.03. 68
no posterity, | 'twas not their infirmity, | it PHT 60
why, 'twas beautiful and hard, | whereto his LC 211

TWAY *(also twain)*

TWAY 1 FR 0.0001 REL FR 0 V 1 P
full fain heard some question 'tween you tway. H5 3.02.119 P

TWEAKS 1 FR 0.0001 REL FR 1 V 0 P
tweaks me by the nose, gives me the lie i' th' HAM 2.02.574

'TWEEN *(also between)*

'TWEEN 20 FR 0.0022 REL FR 18 V 2 P
well be amity and life | 'tween snow and fire, MV 3.02. 31
pale and common drudge | 'tween man and man; 3.02.104
meet his grace just distance 'tween our armies. 2H4 4.01.224
full fain heard some question 'tween you tway. H5 3.02.119 P
where his grace stands, 'tween two clergymen! R3 3.07. 95
whiles that lavinia 'tween her stumps doth hold TIT 5.02.182
set a huge mountain 'tween my heart and tongue! JC 2.04. 7
never come such division 'tween our souls! 4.03.235
wear | and stand a comma 'tween their amities, HAM 5.02. 42
tribe of fops, | got 'tween asleep and wake? LR 1.02. 15
my daughters | got 'tween the lawful sheets. 4.06.116
that profit's yet to come 'tween me and you. OTH 2.03. 10
being an abstract 'tween his lust and him. ANT 3.06. 61
make distinction | of place 'tween high and low. CYM 4.02.249
'tween man and man they weigh not every stamp; 5.04. 24
that the true love 'tween maid and maid may be TNK 1.03. 81
that are inserted 'tween her mind and eye become 4.03. 79 P
but that | he kept him 'tween his legs, on his 5.04. 76
the iron bit he crusheth 'tween his teeth, VEN 269
'tween frozen conscience and hot burning will, LUC 247

TWELF 4 FR 0.0004 REL FR 4 V 0 P
"o' the twelf day of december" — TN 2.03. 84
'tis now strook twelf. HAM 1.01. 7
upon the platform 'twixt aleven and twelf | i'll 1.02.251
i think it lacks of twelf. 1.04. 3

TWELFTH *(see twelf)*

TWELVE *(also twelf)*

/TWELVE 2 FR 0.0002 REL FR 2 V 0 P
/but /he, /in /twelve, | /found /truth /in /all R2 4.01.170
/i, /in /twelve /thousand, /none. 4.01.171

TWELVE 42 FR 0.0047 REL FR 30 V 12 P
twelve year since, miranda, twelve year since, TMP 1.02. 53
twelve year since, miranda, twelve year since, 1.02. 53
till | thou hast howl'd away twelve winters. 1.02.296
as a cannon will shoot point-blank twelve score. WIV 3.02. 34 P
at herne's oak, just 'twixt twelve and one, 4.06. 19
to stay for me at church, 'twixt twelve and one, 4.06. 49
the windsor bell hath strook twelve; 5.05. 1 P
may in the sworn twelve have a thief or two MM 2.01. 20
the clock hath strucken twelve upon the bell: ERR 1.02. 45
out at your window betwixt twelve and one? ADO 4.01. 84
there stay until the twelve celestial signs LLL 5.02.797
the iron tongue of midnight hath told twelve. MND 5.01.363
three months from twelve; MV 1.03.104
and let it be more than alcides' twelve. SHR 1.02.256
two galliasses | and twelve tight galleys. 2.01.379
of the three but jumps twelve foot and a half by WT 4.04.339 P
and thou shalt have twelve thousand fighting men R2 3.02. 70
but this our purpose now is twelve month old, 1H4 1.01. 28
age of this present twelve a' clock at midnight. 2.04. 94 P
know his death will be a march of twelve score. 2.04.547 P
some twelve days hence | our general forces at 3.02.177
would have clapp'd i' th' clout at twelve score, 2H4 3.02. 46 P
'a parted ev'n just between twelve and one, ev'n H5 2.03. 12 P
stole a lute-case, bore it twelve leagues, and 3.02. 43 P
twelve cities, and seven walled towns of 1H6 3.04. 7
in which assault we lost twelve hundred men; 4.01. 24
seven earls, twelve barons, and twenty reverend 2H6 1.01. 8
thou hast beat me out | twelve several times, COR 4.05.122
we would muster all | from twelve to seventy, 4.05.129
now, by my maidenhead at twelve year old, | i ROM 1.03. 2
and from nine till twelve | is /three long hours 2.05. 10
if there sit twelve women at the table, let a TIM 3.06. 78 P
and she goes down at twelve. MAC 2.01. 3
about the world have times twelve thirties been, HAM 3.02.158
he hath laid on twelve for nine, and it would 5.02.167 P
for that i am some twelve or fourteen moonshines LR 1.02. 5
will fashion to fall out between twelve and one) OTH 4.02.236 P
at a breakfast, and but twelve persons there; ANT 2.02.180 P
hold by land, | and our twelve thousand horse. 3.07. 59
one twelve moons more she'll wear diana's livery PER 2.05. 10
my twelve months are expir'd, and tyrus stands 3.03. 2
whose twelve strong labors crown his memory, TNK 3.06.176

TWELVEMONTH 14 FR 0.0015 REL FR 13 V 1 P
i have this twelvemonth been her bedfellow. ADO 4.01.149
a twelvemonth shall you spend, and never rest, LLL 5.02.821
a twelvemonth and a day | i'll mark no words 5.02.827
you shall this twelvemonth term from day to day 5.02.850
a twelvemonth? 5.02.870
i'll jest a twelvemonth in an hospital. 5.02.871
come, sir, it wants a twelvemonth an' a day, 5.02.877
have discontinued school | above a twelvemonth. MV 3.04. 76
him dead or living | within this twelvemonth, or AYL 3.01. 7
a she-lamb of a twelvemonth to a crooked-pated, 3.02. 81 P
of a count | that died some twelvemonth since, TN 1.02. 37
but i shall laugh at this a twelvemonth hence, R3 3.02. 57
a twelvemonth longer let me entreat you | to PER 2.04. 45
that for this twelvemonth she'll not undertake 2.05. 3

TWELVEMONTH'S 1 FR 0.0001 REL FR 1 V 0 P
at the twelvemonth's end | i'll change my black LLL 5.02.833

TWELVEPENCE 1 FR 0.0001 REL FR 0 V 1 P
hold, there is twelvepence for you, and i pray H5 4.08. 63 P

TWENTITH 2 FR 0.0002 REL FR 2 V 0 P
or the division of the twentith part | of one MV 4.01.329
a slave that is not twentith part the /tithe HAM 3.04. 97

TWENTY 170 FR 0.0192 REL FR 134 V 36 P
twenty consciences, | that stand 'twixt me and TMP 2.01.278
fading moment's mirth | with twenty watchful, TGV 1.01. 31
twenty to one then he is shipp'd already, | and 1.01. 72
why, lady, love hath twenty pair of eyes. 2.04. 95
as rich in having such a jewel | as twenty seas, 2.04.170
with twenty thousand soul-confirming oaths. 2.06. 16
with twenty odd-conceited true-love knots: 2.07. 46
if he were twenty sir john falstaffs, he shall WIV 1.01. 2 P
i have seen sackerson loose twenty times, and 1.01.295 P
i will find you twenty lascivious turtles ere 2.01. 80 P
good even and twenty, good master page! 2.01.196 P
i had myself twenty angels given me this morning 2.02. 72 P
this boy will carry a letter twenty mile, as 3.02. 33 P
though twenty thousand worthier come to crave 4.04. 90
and twenty glow-worms shall our lanthorns be, 5.05. 78
his cudgel, and twenty pounds of money, which 5.05.113 P
had he twenty heads to tender down | on twenty MM 2.04.180
heads to tender down | on twenty bloody blocks, 2.04.181
not once, nor twice, but twenty times you have. ERR 3.02.172
twenty years | have i been patron to antipholus, 5.01.327
for she'll be up twenty times a night, and there ADO 2.03.131 P
not one wise man among twenty that will praise 5.02. 74 P
i am compar'd to twenty thousand fairs. LLL 5.02. 37
twenty adieus, my frozen muscovits. 5.02.265
i can easier teach twenty what were good to be MV 1.02. 16 P
than to be one of the twenty to follow mine own 1.02. 17 P
marry him, i should marry twenty husbands. 1.02. 63 P
i have sent twenty out to seek for you. 2.06. 66
you | i would be trebled twenty times myself, 3.02.153
twenty merchants, | the duke himself, and the 3.02.279
flesh | than twenty times the value of the sum 3.02.287
gold | to pay the petty debt twenty times over. 3.02.307
and twenty of these puny lies i'll tell, | that 3.04. 74
away, | for we must measure twenty miles to-day. 3.04. 84
my blood, were there twenty brothers betwixt us. AYL 1.01. 48 P
so near our public court as twenty miles, | thou 1.03. 44
ay, and twenty such. 4.01.119 P
five and twenty, sir. 5.01. 19 P
i would not lose the dog for twenty pound. SHR in.1. 21
plays, | and twenty caged nightingales do sing. in.2. 36
and twenty more such names and men as these, in.2. 95
and in possession twenty thousand crowns. 2.01.122
and twangling jack, with twenty such vild terms, 2.01.158
that teacheth tricks eleven and twenty long, 4.02. 57
remember me | near twenty years ago in genoa, 4.04. 4
twenty crowns. 5.02. 70
twenty crowns! 5.02. 71
hound, | but twenty times so much upon my wife. 5.02. 73
add | unto their losses twenty thousand crowns, 5.02.113
or four and twenty times the pilot's glass AWW 2.01.165
love make your fortunes twenty times above | her 2.03. 82
that twenty such rude boys might tend upon | and 3.02. 82
plenty, | then come kiss me, sweet and twenty; TN 2.03. 51
and grew a twenty years removed thing | while 5.01. 89
hath made me four and twenty nosegays for the WT 4.03. 41 P
brought to bed of twenty money-bags at a burthen 4.04.263 P
make me to think so twenty years together! 5.03. 71
no! not these twenty years. 5.03. 84
each substance of a grief hath twenty shadows, R2 2.02. 14
but now the blood of twenty thousand men | did 3.02. 76
is not the king's name twenty thousand names? 3.02. 85
if thou deniest it twenty times, thou liest, 4.01. 38
breast, | to answer twenty thousand such as you. 4.01. 59
away, fond woman, were he twenty times my son, 5.02.101
ten thousand bold scots, two and twenty knights, 1H4 1.01. 68
hourly any time this two and twenty years, and 2.02. 16 P
and money lent you, four and twenty pound. 3.03. 74 P
of the age of two and twenty or threreabouts! 3.03.189 P
take it for thy labor, and if it make twenty, 4.02. 8 P
and when he was not six and twenty strong, 4.03. 56
have sent me two and twenty yards of satin (as i 2H4 1.02. 44 P
to five and twenty thousand men of choice, | and 1.03. 11
whether our present five and twenty thousand 1.03. 16
what, is the king but five and twenty thousand? 1.03. 68
thee, sir john, let it be but twenty nobles. 2.01.153 P
that's to make him eat twenty of his words. 2.02.137 P
and there are twenty weak and wearied posts 2.04.356
until four hundred one and twenty years | after H5 1.02. 57
by french fathers | had twenty years been made. 2.04. 62
will go to hazard with me for twenty prisoners? 3.07. 85 P
the french may lay twenty french crowns to one 4.01.225 P
and of all other men | but five and twenty. 4.08.106
by three and twenty thousand of the french | was 1H6 1.01.113
twelve barons, and twenty reverend bishops, | i 2H6 1.01. 8
and had i twenty times so many foes, | and each 2.04. 60
and each of them had twenty times their power, 2.04. 61
his paly lips | with twenty thousand kisses, and 3.02.142
though suffolk dare him twenty thousand times. 3.02.206
your loving uncle, twenty times his worth, 3.02.268
he that made us pay one and twenty fifteens, and 4.07. 22 P
she is hard by with twenty thousand men; 3H6 1.02. 51
five men to twenty! 1.02. 71
will but amount to five and twenty thousand, 2.01.181
than to accomplish twenty golden crowns! 3.02.152
and twenty times made pause to sob and weep, R3 1.02.161
was wont to hold me but while one tells twenty. 1.04.119 P
gold were as good as twenty orators, | and will, 4.02. 38
now, | he would kiss you twenty with a breath. H8 1.04. 30
a jewel, has hung twenty years | about his neck, 2.02. 31
wife in this obedience | upward of twenty years, 2.04. 36
twenty of the dog-days now reign in 's nose; 5.03. 41 P
he never saw three and twenty. TRO 1.02.235 P
within thine eyes sate twenty thousand deaths, COR 3.03. 70
romans, of five and twenty valiant sons, | half TIT 1.01. 79
and buried one and twenty valiant sons, 1.01.195
for two and twenty sons i never wept, | because 3.01. 10
and that would she for twenty thousand more. 4.02. 45
with twenty popish tricks and ceremonies, 5.01. 76
and for my tidings gave me twenty kisses. 5.01.120
some five and twenty years, and then we mask'd. ROM 1.05. 37
in thine eye | than twenty of their swords! 2.02. 72
i will not fail, 'tis twenty year till then. 2.02.169
were lustier than he is, and twenty such jacks; 2.04.151 P
it beats as it would fall in twenty pieces. 2.05. 49
some twenty of them fought in this black strife, 3.01.178
and all those twenty could but kill one life. 3.01.179
with twenty hundred thousand times more joy 3.03.153
sirrah, go hire me twenty cunning cooks. 4.02. 2
and if you had the strength | of twenty men, it 5.01. 79
'tis alcibiades, and some twenty horse, | all of TIM 1.01.241
my former sum, | which makes it five and twenty. 2.01. 3
if i would sell my horse and buy twenty moe 2.01. 7
let no assembly of twenty be without a score of 3.06. 77 P
gifts, | expecting in return twenty for one? 4.03.510
did flame and burn | like twenty torches join'd; JC 1.03. 17
he that cuts off twenty years of life | cuts off 3.01.101
with twenty trenched gashes on his head, | the MAC 3.04. 26
with twenty mortal murthers on their crowns, 3.04. 80
why, i can buy me twenty at any market. 4.02. 40
at him while my father liv'd, give twenty, forty HAM 2.02.365 P
two thousand souls and twenty thousand ducats 4.04. 25
see | the imminent death of twenty thousand men, 4.04. 60
lien you i' th' earth three and twenty years. 5.01.174 P
ends | than twenty silly-ducking observants LR 2.02.103
not a nose among twenty but can smell him that's 2.04. 70 P
i entreat you | to bring but five and twenty; 2.04.248
what, must i come to you | with five and twenty? 2.04.254
thy fifty yet doth double five and twenty, | and 2.04.259
what need you five and twenty? 2.04.261
make thee known, | though i lost twenty lives. OTH 5.02.166
more impediments | than twenty times your stop. 5.02.264
i have seen her die twenty times upon far poorer ANT 1.02.142 P
ay, madam, twenty several messengers. 1.05. 62
were't twenty of the greatest tributaries | that 3.13. 96
he thinks, being twenty times of better fortune, 4.02. 3
of better fortune, | he is twenty men to one. 4.02. 4
some twenty years. CYM 1.01. 62
and this her son | cannot take two from twenty, 2.01. 55
and this twenty years | this rock and these 3.03. 69
are now each one the slaughter-man of twenty. 5.03. 49
are) these twenty years | have i train'd up; 5.05.337
twenty to one, he'll come to speak to her, | and TNK 2.03. 14
twenty to one, is truss'd up in a trice 3.04. 17
take twenty, domine. — how does my sweet heart? 3.05.148
i can sing twenty more. 4.01.106
not so few last night | as twenty to dispatch. 4.01.138
his age some five and twenty. 4.02.116
twenty times had been far better, | for there 5.02. 7
he'll dance the morris twenty mile an hour, 5.02. 51
and twenty strike of oats, but he'll ne'er have 5.02. 65
and twenty? 5.02.109
ay, and twenty. 5.02.109
ten kisses short as one, one long as twenty: VEN 22
is twenty hundred kisses such a trouble?" 522
were beauty under twenty locks kept fast, | yet 575
"if love have lent you twenty thousand tongues, 775
she cries, and twenty times, "woe, woe!" 833
and twenty echoes twenty times cry so. 834
and twenty echoes twenty times cry so. 834
breach do i accuse thee, | when i break twenty? SON 152. 6

TWENTY-FIVE 1 FR 0.0001 REL FR 0 V 1 P
last expedition, twenty-five wounds upon him. COR 2.01.153 P

TWENTY-NINE 1 FR 0.0001 REL FR 0 V 1 P
i have known thee these twenty-nine years, come 2H4 2.04.383 P

TWENTY-ONE 1 FR 0.0001 REL FR 1 V 0 P
were i but twenty-one, | your father's image is WT 5.01.126

TWENTY-SEVEN 1 FR 0.0001 REL FR 0 V 1 P
now it's twenty-seven; COR 2.01.155 P

TWENTY-SIX 2 FR 0.0002 REL FR 2 V 0 P
of our redemption | four hundred twenty-six; H5 1.02. 61
there lie dead | one hundred twenty-six; 4.08. 83

TWENTY-THREE 2 FR 0.0002 REL FR 2 V 0 P
methoughts i did recoil | twenty-three years, WT 1.02.155
twenty-three days | they have been absent. 2.03.198

'TWERE 135 FR 0.0152 REL FR 104 V 31 P
could control thee, | if now 'twere fit to do't. TMP 1.02.441
or, as 'twere perfum'd by a fen. 2.01. 49 P
if 'twere a kibe, | 'twould put me to my slipper 2.01.276
'twere best pound you. TGV 1.01.103 P
'twere good, i think, your lordship sent him 1.03. 29
'twere good you knock'd him. 2.04. 7 P
'twere false, if i should speak it; 4.02.106
if 'twere a substance, you would sure deceive it 4.02.126
'twere pity two such friends should be long foes 5.04.118
'twere better for you if it were known in WIV 1.01.118 P
there is, as 'twere, a tender, a kind of tender, 1.01.208 P
of us, 'twere all alike | as if we had them not. MM 1.01. 34
i will, as 'twere a brother of your order, 1.03. 44
i would tell what 'twere to be a judge, | and 2.02. 69
and 'twere the cheaper way. 2.04.105
and with no face, as 'twere, outfacing me, ERR 5.01.245
it worse, and 'twere such a face as yours were. ADO 1.01.137 P
yea, and 'twere a thousand pound more than 'tis, 3.05. 24 P
'twere good yours did; LLL 4.03.268

i will roar you and 'twere any nightingale. MND 1.02. 83 P
into this place, 'twere pity on my life. 5.01.226
and 'twere as easy | for you to laugh and leap, MV 1.01. 48
'twere damnation | to think so base a thought; 2.07. 49
'twere good you do so much for charity. 4.01.261
and 'twere to me i should be mad at it. 5.01.176
would 'twere done! SHR 1.01.254 P
'twere well for kate and better for myself. 3.02.120
'twere good methinks to steal our marriage, 3.02.140
and better 'twere that both of us did fast, 4.01.173
'twere deadly sickness or else present death. 4.03. 14
'twere good he were school'd. 4.04. 9
imagine 'twere the right vincentio. 4.04. 12
'twere all one | that i should love a bright AWW 1.01. 85
right, as 'twere a man assur'd of a — 2.03. 17 P
king, who, so ennobled, | is as 'twere born so. 2.03.173
better 'twere | i met the ravin lion when he 3.02.116
better 'twere | that all the miseries which 3.02.118
'twere as good a deed as to drink when a man's TN 2.03.126 P
yet, if 'twere so, | she could not sway her 4.03. 16
request, although | 'twere needful i denied it. WT 1.02. 23
to sigh, as 'twere | the mort o' th' deer — o, 1.02.117
(for in an act of this importance 'twere | most 2.01.181
then 'twere past all doubt | you'd call your 2.03. 81
would wish | this youth should say 'twere well, 4.04.102
stand and read | as 'twere my daughter's eyes; 4.04.174
my dignity would last | but till 'twere known! 4.04.476
forgiveness, | as 'twere i' th' father's person; 4.04.550
or else 'twere hard luck, being in so 5.02.147 P
therefore 'twere reason you had manners now. JN 4.03. 31
as 'twere to banish their affects with him. R2 1.04. 30
your pernicious lives, | for 'twere no charity; 3.01. 5
'twere no good part | to take on me to keep and 5.01. 97
and 'twere not as good deed as drink to break 1H4 2.01. 29 P
and 'twere not as good a deed as drink to turn 2.02. 22 P
i would 'twere bed–time, hal, and all well. 5.01.125 P
'twere best he did. 5.02. 3
come, and 'twere not for thy humors, there's not 2H4 2.01.148 P
in very truth, do i, and 'twere an aspen leaf. 2.04.108 P
had the wit, 'twere better than your dukedom. 4.03. 86 P
i am the sorrier, would 'twere otherwise! 5.02. 32
and 'twere more honor some were away. H5 3.07. 75 P
'twere not amiss | he were created knight for 2H6 5.01. 76
think you 'twere prejudicial to his crown? 3H6 1.01.144
'twere pity they should lose their father's 3.02. 31
and better 'twere you troubled him than france. 3.03.155
and 'twere pity | to sunder them that yoke so 4.01. 22
that all were well, | so 'twere not long of him; 4.07. 32
'twere childish weakness to lament or fear. 5.04. 38
why, 'twere perpetual shame. 5.04. 51
judge | what 'twere to lose it and be miserable! R3 1.03.257
though 'twere to buy a world of happy days — 1.04. 6
there were crept | (as 'twere in scorn of eyes) 1.04. 31
if 'twere not she, i cannot tell who told me. 2.04. 34
to age, | as 'twere retail'd to all posterity, 3.01. 77
yet touch this sparingly, as 'twere far off, 3.05. 93
i would 'twere something that would fret the H8 3.02.105
as 'twere in love's particular, be more | to me, 3.02.189
o yes, and 'twere a cloud in autumn. TRO 1.02.126 P
he will weep you an' 'twere a man born in april. 1.02.174 P
up in his tears an' 'twere a nettle against may. 1.02.175 P
and doth boil | (as 'twere from forth us all) a 1.03.350
must /tarre the mastiffs on, as 'twere a bone. 1.03.390
and 'twere dark you'd close sooner. 3.02. 48 P
'twere better she were kiss'd in general. 4.05. 21
'twere a concealment | worse than a theft, no COR 1.09. 21
lives of men, as if | 'twere a perpetual spoil; 2.02.120
and 'twere to give again — but 'tis no matter. 2.03. 83 P
'twere well | we let the people know't. 3.01. 82
who twin, as 'twere, in love | unseparable, 4.04. 15
and 'twere my cause, i should go hang myself. TIT 2.04. 9
or 'twere as good he were | as living here and ROM 3.05.224
certain as your waiting, | 'twere sure enough. TIM 3.04. 48
as 'twere a knell unto our master's fortunes, 4.02. 26
habit on | to castigate thy pride, 'twere well; 4.03.240
would 'twere so! 4.03.392
'twere best he speak no harm of brutus here! JC 3.02. 68
thing he ow'd, | as 'twere a careless trifle. MAC 1.04. 11
done, then 'twere well | it were done quickly. 1.07. 1
to know my deed, 'twere best not know myself. 2.02. 70
they should find | what 'twere to kill a father; 3.06. 20
state, | have we, as 'twere with a defeated joy, HAM 1.02. 10
take you, as 'twere, some distant knowledge of 2.01. 13
as 'twere a thing a little soil'd /wi' /th' 2.01. 40
that he, as 'twere by accident, may here 3.01. 30
is, to hold, as 'twere, the mirror up to nature: 3.02. 22 P
'twere good you let him know, | for who, that's 3.04.188
'twere good she were spoken with, for she may 4.05. 14
cry to be heard, as 'twere from heaven to earth, 4.05.217
bad performance, | 'twere better not assay'd; 4.07.152
it to the ground, as if 'twere cain's jaw–bone, 5.01. 77 P
'twere to consider too curiously, to consider so 5.01.205 P
it is very sultry — as 'twere — i cannot tell 5.02.101 P
cannot but feel this wrong as 'twere their own; OTH 1.02. 97
were now to die, | 'twere now to be most happy; 2.01.190
if 'twere no other — 4.02.168
'twere pregnant they should square between ANT 2.01. 45
but better 'twere | thou fell'st into my fury, 4.12. 40
and 'twere good | you lean'd unto his sentence CYM 1.01. 77
it, 'twere a paper lost | as offer'd mercy is. 1.03. 3
if you but said so, 'twere as deep with me. 2.03. 91
to leave you in your madness, 'twere my sin; 2.03. 99
if 'twere made | comparative for your virtues, 2.03.128
'twere not amiss to keep our door hatch'd. PER 4.02. 33 P
believe me, 'twere best i did give o'er. 5.01.166
in prison, and 'twere pity they should be out. TNK 2.01. 22 P
sigh, martyr'd as 'twere i' th' deliverance, 2.01. 41 P
what 'twere to filch affection from another! 2.02.210
'twere wrong else. 2.05. 61
do bear thy yoke | as 'twere a wreath of roses, 5.01. 96
one, a woman, | and women 'twere they wrong'd. 5.01.107
this trial as 'twere i' th' night, and you 5.03. 19
dancing as 'twere to th' music | his own hoofs 5.04. 59
and 'twere no error if i told you all you were STM II.C 95
should step as 'twere up to my country's head III 7
as 'twere encouraging the greeks to fight, LUC 1402

/TWICE 3 FR 0.0003 REL FR 3 V 0 P
/to /bid /aeneas /tell /the /tale /twice /o'er TIT 3.02. 27
/once /or /twice /she /heav'd /the /name /of LR 4.03. 25
/twice /then /the /trumpets /sounded, | /and 5.03.218

TWICE 74 FR 0.0083 REL FR 60 V 14 P
and "go," | and breathe twice, and cry "so, so," TMP 4.01. 45
me, and return | or ere your pulse twice beat. 5.01.103
the island, one dear son | shall i twice lose. 5.01.177
but twice, or thrice, was "proteus" written down TGV 1.02.114
lo, here in one line is his name twice writ, 1.02.120
was mine and not mine twice or thrice in that 3.01.356 P
ask'd them once or twice what they had in their WIV 3.05.102 P
twice treble shame on angelo, | to weed my vice MM 3.02.269
of precept, he did show me | the way twice o'er. 4.01. 40
ere twice the sun hath made his journal greeting 4.03. 88
twice have the trumpets sounded; 4.06. 12
ere the ships could meet by twice five leagues, ERR 1.01.100
not once, nor twice, but twenty times you have. 3.02.172
a victory is twice itself when the achiever ADO 1.01. 8 P
he hath twice or thrice cut cupid's bow–string, 3.02. 10 P
twice sod simplicity, bis coctus! LLL 4.02. 22 P
you chide at him, offending twice as much. 4.03.130
twice to your visor, and half once to you. 5.02.227
wouldst thou have a serpent sting thee twice? MV 4.01. 69
it is twice blest: 4.01.186
it for him in the court, | yea, twice the sum. 4.01.210
twice did he turn his back, and purpos'd so; AYL 4.03.127
and twice to–day pick'd out the dullest scent. SHR in.1. 24
and twice as much, what e'er thou off'rest next. 2.01.380
ere twice the horses of the sun shall bring AWW 2.01.161
ere twice in murk and occidental damp | moist 2.01.163
have i twice said well? WT 1.02. 90
i have spoke to th' purpose twice: 1.02.106
bolted | by th' northern blasts twice o'er. 4.04.365
for once or twice | i was about to speak, and 4.04.442
for she hath privately twice or thrice a day, 5.02.105 P
twice fifteen thousand hearts of england's breed JN 2.01.275
till twice five summers have enrich'd our fields R2 1.03.141
and much more, much more than twice all this, 3.01. 28
twice for one step i'll groan, the way being 5.01. 91
twice saying "pardon" doth not pardon twain, 5.03.134
he spake it twice, | and urg'd it twice together 5.04. 4
and urg'd it twice together, did he not? 5.04. 5
such as had been ask'd twice on the banes, such 1H4 4.02. 17 P
and i cannot once or twice in a quarter bear out 2H4 5.01. 48 P
i have been merry twice and once ere now. 5.03. 39 P
the trumpets have sounded twice. 5.05. 2 P
who twice a day their wither'd hands hold up H5 4.01.299
at their dead masters, | killing them twice. 4.07. 81
and galling at this gentleman twice or thrice. 5.01. 74 P
o, twice my father, twice am i thy son! 1H6 4.06. 6
o, twice my father, twice am i thy son! 4.06. 6
and twice by awkward wind from england's bank 2H6 3.02. 83
but buckler with thee blows, twice two for one. 3H6 1.04. 50
cock | hath twice done salutation to the morn, R3 5.03.210
i twice five hundred, and their friends to piece COR 2.03.212
and nobly named so, twice being censor, | was 2.03.244
thou art a fool to bid me farewell twice. TIM 1.01.263
all our service | in every point twice done, and MAC 1.06. 15
touching this dreaded sight, twice seen of us; HAM 1.01. 25
thus twice before, and jump at this dead hour, 1.01. 65
them, for they say an old man is twice a child. 2.02.385 P
nay, 'tis twice two months, my lord. 3.02.128 P
five and twenty, | and thou art twice her love. LR 2.04.260
to follow in a house where twice so many | have 2.04.262
his soldiership | is twice the other twain; ANT 2.01. 35
that's twice. 2.07. 62
i'll make a journey twice as far, t' enjoy | a CYM 2.04. 43
was carried | from off our coast, twice beaten; 3.01. 26
(such as i can) twice o'er, i'll weep and sigh, 4.02.392
"two boys, an old man (twice a boy), a lane, 5.03. 57
pericles | come not home in twice six moons, PER 3.ch. 31
doth appear, | to make the world twice rich. 3.02.102
i had rather than twice the worth of her she had 4.06. 1 P
i told her, presently, and kiss'd her twice. TNK 5.02. 6
that twice she doth begin ere once she speaks. LUC 567
and twice desire, yer it be day, | that which PP 18.29
you should live twice, in it and in my rhyme. SON 17.14
but thou art twice forsworn, to me love swearing 152. 2

TWICE–TOLD 1 FR 0.0001 REL FR 1 V 0 P
life is as tedious as a twice–told tale | vexing JN 3.04.108

TWIGGEN 1 FR 0.0001 REL FR 0 V 1 P
i'll beat the knave into a twiggen bottle. OTH 2.03.148 P

TWIGS 5 FR 0.0005 REL FR 4 V 1 P
having bound up the threat'ning twigs of birch, MM 1.03. 24
are lim'd with the twigs that threatens them. AWW 3.05. 24 P
i must go look my twigs. he shall be caught. 3.06.107
give some supportance to the bending twigs. R2 3.04. 32
with hair, | put forth disorder'd twigs; H5 5.02. 44

TWILIGHT 1 FR 0.0001 REL FR 1 V 0 P
in me thou seest the twilight of such day | as SON 73. 5

'TWILL 69 FR 0.0078 REL FR 47 V 22 P
burns, | 'twill weep for having wearied you. TMP 3.01. 19
'twill be this hour ere i have done weeping; TGV 2.03. 1 P
well, sir, then 'twill be dry. ERR 2.02. 59 P
i tell you, 'twill sound harshly in her ears. 4.04. 7
'twill be heavier soon by the weight of a man. ADO 3.04. 26 P
wit's too hot, it speeds too fast, 'twill tire. LLL 2.01.119
put up this — 'twill be thine another day. 4.01.107
priscian a little scratch'd, 'twill serve. 5.01. 29 P
a twelvemonth an' a day, | and then 'twill end. 5.02.878
be god's sonties, 'twill be a hard way to hit. MV 2.02. 45 P
'twill be recorded for a precedent, | and many 4.01.220
'twill be a good way; AYL 1.01. 93 P
and after one hour more 'twill be eleven, | and 2.07. 25
shut that, and 'twill out at the key–hole; 4.01.163 P
'twill fly with the smoke out at the chimney. 4.01.164 P
'twill bring you gain, or perish on the seas. SHR 2.01.329
and 'twill be supper–time ere you come there. 4.03.190
'twill be two days ere i shall see you, so | i AWW 2.05. 70
these three hours 'twill be time enough to go 4.01. 24 P
that thou art so inhuman — 'twill not prove so; 5.03.116
in grain, sir, 'twill endure wind and weather. TN 1.05.237 P
o, 'twill be admirable! 2.03.171 P
i dare lay any money 'twill be nothing yet. 3.04.396 P
this is fairy gold, boy, and 'twill prove so. WT 3.03.123 P
forward, for 'twill be | two long days' journey, JN 4.03. 19
'twill make me think the world is full of rubs, R2 3.04. 4
'twill be two a' clock ere they come from the 2H4 5.05. 3 P
'twill make them cool in zeal unto your grace. 2H6 3.01.177
'twill go hard with you. 4.02.101 P
mass, 'twill be sore law then, for he was thrust 4.07. 8 P
o margaret, thus 'twill be, and thou, poor soul, 3H6 3.01. 53
'twill grieve your grace my sons should call you 3.02.100
i fear, i fear 'twill prove a giddy world. R3 2.03. 5
and so 'twill do | with some men else, that 3.02. 65
it reaches far, and where 'twill not extend, H8 1.01.111
'twill require | a strong faith to conceal it. 2.01.144
'twill be much | both for your honor better and 3.01. 94
i know 'twill stir him strongly; 3.02.218
'twill not, sir thomas lovell, take't of me — 5.01. 30
and say 'twill do, i know within a while | all ep 12
'twill make us proud to be his servant, paris! TRO 3.01.155
'twill be his death, 'twill be his bane, he 4.02. 92 P
'twill be his death, 'twill be his bane, he 4.02. 93 P
'twill be deliver'd back on good condition. COR 1.10. 2
i think 'twill serve, if he | can thereto frame 3.02. 96
'twill vex thy soul to hear what i shall speak: TIT 5.01. 62
'twill fill your stomachs, please you eat of it. 5.03. 29
as a church–door, but 'tis enough, 'twill serve. ROM 3.01. 97 P
if 'twill not serve, 'tis not so base as you, TIM 3.04. 58
tush, tush, 'twill not appear. HAM 1.01. 30
watch to–night, | perchance 'twill walk again. 1.02.242
lie, sir, 'twill away again from me to you. 5.01.128 P
'twill not be seen in him there, there the men 5.01.154 P
duke's to blame in this, 'twill be ill taken. LR 2.02.159
let us withdraw, 'twill be a storm. 2.04.287
/faith, that's with watching, 'twill away again. OTH 3.03.285
o, pardon me; 'twill do me good to walk. 4.03. 2
'twill out, 'twill out! 5.02.219
'twill out, 'twill out! 5.02.219
know | if 'twill tie up thy discontented sword, ANT 2.06. 6
'twill be naught, | but let it be. 3.05. 22
'twill not be lost. CYM 2.03.148
i fear 'twill be reveng'd. 4.02.154
see if 'twill teach us to forget our own? PER 1.04. 3
'twill hardly come out. 2.01.117 P
now 'twill take form, the heats are gone TNK 1.01.152
'twill disturb us, | we shall have time enough. 3.03. 15
'twill be known. 4.01. 31
by cocklight, | 'twill never thrive else. 4.01.113

TWILLED 1 FR 0.0001 REL FR 1 V 0 P
thy banks with pioned and twilled brims, | which TMP 4.01. 64

/TWIN 1 FR 0.0001 REL FR 1 V 0 P
her inkle, silk, /twin with the rubied cherry, PER 5.ch. 8

TWIN 3 FR 0.0003 REL FR 3 V 0 P
and i, | and the twin dromio, all were taken up; ERR 5.01.351
is not more twin | than these two creatures. TN 5.01.223
and exercise | are still together, who twin, as COR 4.04. 15

TWIN–BORN 1 FR 0.0001 REL FR 1 V 0 P
twin–born with greatness, subject to the breath H5 4.01.234

TWIN–BROTHER 1 FR 0.0001 REL FR 0 V 1 P
opinions, here's the twin–brother of thy letter; WIV 2.01. 72 P

TWIN'D 3 FR 0.0003 REL FR 3 V 0 P
that our fortunes | were twin'd together. TNK 2.02. 64
and curl'd, thick twin'd like ivy/–tods, | not 4.02.104
some twin'd about her thigh to make her stay. VEN 873

TWINE 2 FR 0.0002 REL FR 2 V 0 P
flow in grief, | the smallest twine may lead me. ADO 4.01.250
let me twine | mine arms about that body, where COR 4.05.106

TWINING 1 FR 0.0001 REL FR 1 V 0 P
and from her twining arms doth urge releasing. VEN 256

TWINK 2 FR 0.0002 REL FR 2 V 0 P
ay, with a twink. TMP 4.01. 43
oath, | that in a twink she won me to her love. SHR 2.01.310

TWINKLE 1 FR 0.0001 REL FR 1 V 0 P
to twinkle in their spheres till they return. ROM 2.02. 17

TWINKLED 1 FR 0.0001 REL FR 0 V 1 P
in the firmament twinkled on my bastardizing. LR 1.02.133 P

TWINKLING 5 FR 0.0005 REL FR 4 V 1 P
at first i did adore a twinkling star, | but now TGV 2.06. 9
i'll take my leave of the jew in the twinkling. MV 2.02.168 P
streams, | twinkling another counterfeited beam, 1H6 5.03. 63
and with thy twinkling eyes look right and TNK 3.05.117
her twinkling handmaids too (by him defil'd) LUC 787

TWINN'D 4 FR 0.0004 REL FR 4 V 0 P
we were as twinn'd lambs that did frisk i' th' WT 1.02. 67
twinn'd brothers of one womb, | whose TIM 4.03. 3
though he had twinn'd with me, both at a birth, OTH 2.03.212
the fiery orbs above and the twinn'd stones CYM 1.06. 35

TWINNING 1 FR 0.0001 REL FR 1 V 0 P
her twinning cherries shall their sweetness fall TNK 1.01.178

TWINS 6 FR 0.0006 REL FR 6 V 0 P
of such a burthen male, twins both alike. ERR 1.01. 55
to him one of the other twins was bound, 1.01. 81
those twins of learning that he rais'd in you, H8 4.02. 58
when vantage like a pair of twins appear'd, ANT 3.10. 12
mind nurse equal | to these so diff'ring twins. TNK 1.03. 33
shall we two exercise, like twins of honor, 2.02. 18

TWIRE 1 FR 0.0001 REL FR 1 V 0 P
when sparkling stars twire not, thou /gild'st SON 28.12

TWIST 2 FR 0.0002 REL FR 2 V 0 P
that thou began'st to twist so fine a story? ADO 1.01.311
and resolution like | a twist of rotten silk, COR 5.06. 95

TWISTED 3 FR 0.0003 REL FR 3 V 0 P
thread | that ever spider twisted from her womb JN 4.03.128
like a poor prisoner in his twisted gyves, | and ROM 2.02.179
hair, | with twisted metal amorously impleach'd, LC 205

TWIT 2 FR 0.0002 REL FR 2 V 0 P
age, | and twit with cowardice a man half dead? 1H6 3.02. 55
hath he not twit our sovereign lady here | with 2H6 3.01.178

TWITS 1 FR 0.0001 REL FR 1 V 0 P
she twits me with my falsehood to my friend; TGV 4.02. 8

TWITTING 1 FR 0.0001 REL FR 1 V 0 P
and there's for twitting me with perjury. 3H6 5.05. 40

'TWIXT *(also betwixt)*

'TWIXT 80 FR 0.0090 REL FR 75 V 5 P
the time 'twixt six and now | must by us both be TMP 1.02.240
'twixt which regions | there is some space. 2.01.256
that stand 'twixt me and milan, candied be they, 2.01.279
and 'twixt the green sea and the azur'd vault 5.01. 43
'twixt eight and nine is the hour, master /brook WIV 3.05.130 P
at herne's oak, just 'twixt twelve and one, 4.06. 19
to stay for me at church, 'twixt twelve and one, 4.06. 49
of business 'twixt you and your poor brother. MM 1.04. 71
but that i am | at war 'twixt will and will not. 2.02. 33
jars | 'twixt thy seditious countrymen and us, ERR 1.01. 12
stay, | nor rest be interposer 'twixt us twain. MV 3.02.327

vows | 'twixt the souls of friend and friend; AYL 3.02.134
why, this' a heavy chance 'twixt him and you, SHR 1.02. 46
'twixt such friends as we | few words suffice; 1.02. 65
'tis bargain'd 'twixt us twain, being alone, 2.01.304
for private quarrel 'twixt your duke and him, 4.02. 84
'twixt me and one baptista's daughter here. 4.02.119
one that fixes | no bourn 'twixt his and mine, WT 1.02.134
him | 'twixt his unkindness and his kindness: 4.04.552
that 'twixt heaven and earth | might thus have 5.01.132
the lands and waters 'twixt your throne and his 5.01.144
the noble combat that 'twixt joy and sorrow was 5.02. 73 P
set armed discord 'twixt these perjur'd kings! JN 3.01.111
like heralds 'twixt two dreadful battles set: 4.02. 78
o, when the last accompt 'twixt heaven and earth 4.02.216
a twofold marriage — 'twixt my crown and me, R2 5.01. 72
let me unkiss the oath 'twixt thee and me; 5.01. 74
and 'twixt his finger and his thumb he held | a 1H4 1.03. 37
making such difference 'twixt wake and sleep 3.01.216
which salique, as i said, 'twixt /elbe and sala, H5 1.02. 52
his bleeding sword 'twixt england and fair 5.02.355
so be there 'twixt your kingdoms such a spousal, 5.02.362
some words there grew 'twixt somerset and me; 1H6 2.05. 46
i will weep, and 'twixt each groan | say, "who's 2H6 3.01.221
my state, 'twixt cade and york distress'd, 4.09. 31
'twixt guynes and arde — | i was then present, H8 1.01. 7
/a marriage 'twixt the duke of orleance and 2.04.175
'twixt his stretch'd footing and the scaffolage, TRO 1.03.156
will with a trumpet 'twixt our tents and troy 2.01.123
two traded pilots 'twixt the dangerous /shores 2.02. 64
a free determination | 'twixt right and wrong; 2.02.171
that 'twixt his mental and his active parts 2.03.174
forbids | a gory emulation 'twixt us twain. 4.05.123
he wav'd indifferently 'twixt doing them neither COR 2.02. 17 P
confusion | may enter 'twixt the gap of both, 3.01.111
dreamt of encounters 'twixt thyself and me; 4.05.123
whilst | 'twixt you there's difference; 5.06. 17
their fatal points, | and 'twixt them rushes; ROM 3.01.167
'twixt my extremes and me this bloody knife 4.01. 62
dear divorce | 'twixt natural /son and /sire! TIM 4.03.382
the people 'twixt philippi and this ground | do JC 4.03.204
will fill up the time | 'twixt this and supper. MAC 3.01. 25
upon the platform 'twixt aleven and twelf | i'll HAM 1.02.251
and they shall hear and judge 'twixt you and me. 4.05.206
and the bond crack'd 'twixt son and father. LR 1.02.109 P
toward, 'twixt the dukes of cornwall and albany? 2.01. 11 P
with mutual cunning) 'twixt albany and cornwall; 3.01. 21
'twixt two extremes of passion, joy and grief, 5.03.199
and it is thought abroad that 'twixt my sheets OTH 1.03.387
i cannot, 'twixt the heaven and the main, 2.01. 3
is there division 'twixt my lord and cassio? 4.01.231
no midway | 'twixt these extremes at all. ANT 3.04. 20
wars 'twixt you twain would be | as if the world 3.04. 30
which can distinguish 'twixt | the fiery orbs CYM 1.06. 34
spectacles so precious | 'twixt fair and foul? 1.06. 38
'twixt two such shes would chatter this way, and 1.06. 40
of miles may we well rid | 'twixt hour and hour? 3.02. 68
one score 'twixt sun and sun, | madam, 's enough 3.02. 68
to weep 'twixt clock and clock? 3.04. 42
nobler sir ne'er liv'd | 'twixt sky and ground. 5.05.146
wide difference | 'twixt amorous and villainous. 5.05.195
it hath been a shield | 'twixt me and death" — PER 2.01.127
more famous yet 'twixt po and silver trent. TNK pr 12
'twixt crimson shame and anger ashy-pale. VEN 76
and set dissension 'twixt the son and sire, 1160
then must the love be great 'twixt thee and me, PP 8. 3
was seen | 'twixt this turtle and his queen: PHT 31
as 'twixt a miser and his wealth is found: SON 75. 4
million'd accidents | creep in 'twixt vows, and 115. 6
a storm | as oft 'twixt may and april is to see, LC 102

/TWO 7 FR 0.0008 REL FR 4 V 3 P

'tis ten to one it maim'd you two outright. SHR 5.02. 62
/a /deep /well | /that /owes /two /buckets, R2 4.01.185
wept like /two children in their deaths' sad R3 4.03. 8
tool, here comes /two of the house of montagues. ROM 1.01. 32 P
with /two provincial roses on my raz'd shoes, HAM 3.02.276 P
/in /tom's /belly /for /two /white /herring. LR 3.06. 31 P
palates who, not yet /two /summers younger, PER 1.04. 39

TWO 639 FR 0.0722 REL FR 423 V 216 P

set her two courses off to sea again! TMP 1.01. 49 P
at least two glasses. 1.02.240
and after two days | i will discharge thee. 1.02.298
i'll free thee | within two days for this. 1.02.422
we two, my lord, | will guard your person while 2.01.196
four legs and two voices; 2.02. 89 P
o stephano, two neapolitans scap'd! 2.02.113 P
fair encounter | of two most rare affections! 3.01. 75
if th' other two be brain'd like us, the state 3.02. 6 P
a turn or two i'll walk | to still my beating 4.01.162
two of these fellows you | must know and own, 5.01.274
'tis a word or two | of commendations sent from TGV 1.03. 52
please you deliberate a day or two. 1.03. 73
sir valentine and servant! to you two thousand. 2.01.100 P
where have you been these two days loitering? 4.04. 44
hast no faith left now, unless thou'dst two, 5.04. 50
'twere pity two such friends should be long foes 5.04.118
in mill-sixpences, and two edward shovel-boards, WIV 1.01.155 P
that cost me two shilling and two pence a-piece 1.01.156 P
me two shilling and two pence a-piece of yead 1.01.157 P
two yards, and more. 1.03. 40 P
indeed i am in the waist two yards about; 1.03. 42 P
by gar, i will cut all his two stones; 1.04.112 P
puts into the press, when he would put us two. 2.01. 79 P
shall i vouchsafe your worship a word or two? 2.02. 41 P
two thousand, fair woman, and i'll vouchsafe 2.02. 42 P
vat be all you, one, two, tree, four, come for? 2.03. 22 P
witness that me have stay six or seven, two, 2.03. 36 P
if your husbands were dead, you two would marry. 3.02. 15 P
be sure of that — two other husbands. 3.02. 16 P
send him by your two men to datchet-mead. 3.03.132 P
there is one, i shall make two in the company. 3.03.234 P
if there be one or two, i shall make-a the turd. 3.03.236 P
jest how my father stole two geese out of a pen, 3.04. 40 P
to sir john falstaff from my two mistresses. 3.04.110 P
two. 4.01. 22 P
afflicted, we two will still be the ministers. 4.02.218 P
and let us two devise to bring him thither. 4.04. 27
sight, | we two in great amazedness will fly; 4.04. 56
from the two parties, forsooth. 4.05.105 P
we two must go together. 5.03. 4 P
he promis'd to meet me two hours since, and he MM 1.02. 75 P
within two hours. 1.02.193
may in the sworn twelve have a thief or two 2.01. 20
before your good honor two notorious benefactors 2.01. 50 P
sir, we had but two in the house, which at that 2.01. 91 P
and having but two in the dish (as i said), 2.01.100 P
in ransom and free pardon | are of two houses: 2.04.112
my business is a word or two with claudio. 3.01. 48
'twas never merry world since, of two usuries, 3.02. 5 P
that he was begot between two stock-fishes. 3.02.109 P
find, within these two days he will be here. 4.02.198 P
she became | a joyful mother of two goodly sons: ERR 1.01. 50
my wife, not meanly proud of two such boys, 1.01. 58
and we discovered | two ships from far, making 1.01. 92
sure, luciana, it is two a' clock. 2.01. 3
nay, he's at two hands with me, and that my two 2.01. 45 P
hands with me, and that my two ears can witness. 2.01. 46 P
for two — and sound ones too. 2.02. 91 P
for if we two be one, and thou play false, | i 2.02.142
in ephesus i am but two hours old, | as strange 2.02.148
it was two ere i left him, and now the clock 4.02. 54
two hundred ducats. 4.04.134
but he, i thank him, gnaw'd in two my cords: 5.01.290
i see two husbands, or mine eyes deceive me. 5.01.332
that bore thee at a burthen two fair sons. 5.01.344
these two antipholus', these two so like, | and 5.01.358
these two antipholus', these two so like, | and 5.01.358
and these two dromios, one in semblance — 5.01.359
which of you two did dine with me to-day? 5.01.370
and by my two faiths and troths, my lord, i ADO 1.01.226 P
he'll but break a comparison or two on me, which 2.01.147 P
and i, with your two helps, will so practice on 2.01.382 P
or in the shape of two countries at once, as a 3.02. 34 P
and then the two bears will not bite one another 3.02. 78 P
us go sit here upon the church-bench till two, 3.03. 89 P
two of them did, the prince and claudio, but the 3.03.154 P
and two men ride of a horse, one must ride 3.05. 37 P
have indeed comprehended two aspicious persons, 3.05. 46 P
would the two princes lie, and claudio lie, 4.01.152
two of them have the very bent of honor, | and 4.01.186
hath had losses, and one that hath two gowns, 4.02. 85 P
he shall kill two of us, and men indeed; 5.01. 80
lik'd to have had our two noses snapp'd off with 5.01.115 P
noses snapp'd off with two old men without teeth 5.01.116 P
there's a double tongue, there's two tongues." 5.01.169 P
two of my brother's men bound? 5.01.210 P
it doth amount to one more than two. LLL 1.02. 47 P
and study three years in two words, the dancing 1.02. 53 P
or the three, or the two, or one of the four. 1.02. 79 P
two hot sheeps, marry. 2.01.219
with two pitch-balls stuck in her face for eyes; 3.01.197
/saw, two; 4.01. 70 P
you two are book-men: 4.02. 34
yes, for her two eyes. 4.03. 10 P
not by two that i know. 4.03. 50
the sheep: the other two concludes it — o,u. 5.01. 56 P
nay then two treys, and if you grow so nice, 5.02.232
she is two months on her way. 5.02.672 P
hear the dialogue that the two learned men have 5.02.886 P
one heart, one bed, two bosoms, and one troth. MND 2.02. 42
two bosoms interchained with an oath, | so then 2.02. 49
oath, | so then two bosoms and a single troth. 2.02. 50
make it two more; 3.01. 25 P
but there is two hard things: 3.01. 47 P
then will two at once woo one; 3.02.118
your vows to her and me, put in two scales, 3.02.132
is all the counsel that we two have shar'd, 3.02.198
we, hermia, like two artificial gods, | have 3.02.203
two lovely berries moulded on one stem; 3.02.211
so, with two seeming bodies but one heart, | two 3.02.212
two of the first, /like coats in heraldry, | due 3.02.213
two of both kinds makes up four. 3.02.438
had rather have a handful or two of dried peas. 4.01. 37 P
i know you two are rival enemies. 4.01.142
and there is two or three lords and ladies more 4.02. 16 P
now is the moon used between the two neighbors. 5.01.206 P
here come two noble beasts in, a man and a lion. 5.01.217 P
a bergomask dance between two of our company? 5.01.354 P
we two will leave you, but at dinner-time | i MV 1.01. 70
well, keep me company but two years moe, | thou 1.01.108
his reasons are as two grains of wheat hid in 1.01.116 P
two grains of wheat hid in two bushels of chaff; 1.01.116 P
god defend me from these two! 1.02. 53 P
within these two months, that's a month before 1.03.157
of clock, we have two hours | to furnish us. 2.04. 8
a sealed bag, two sealed bags of ducats, | of 2.08. 18
and jewels, two stones, two rich and precious 2.08. 20
two stones, two rich and precious stones, 2.08. 20
head i came to woo, | but i go away with two. 2.09. 76
gone, cost me two thousand ducats in frankford! 3.01. 84 P
two thousand ducats in that, and other precious, 3.01. 86 P
tarry, pause a day or two | before you hazard, 3.02. 1
i would detain you here some month or two 3.02. 9
like one of two contending in a prize, | that 3.02.141
there is a monast'ry two miles off, | and there 3.04. 31
i'll prove the prettier fellow of the two, | and 3.04. 64
and turn two mincing steps | into a manly stride 3.04. 67
if two gods should play some heavenly match, 3.05. 79
match, | and on the wager lay two earthly women, 3.05. 80
two things provided more, that for this favor 4.01.386
in christ'ning shalt thou have two godfathers: 4.01.398
grant me two things, i pray you, | not to deny 4.01.423
nor master would take aught | but the two rings. 5.01.184
or go to bed now, being two hours to day. 5.01.303
daughter, and never two ladies lov'd as they do. AYL 1.01.112 P
which of the two was daughter of the duke, 1.02.269
then there were two cousins laid up, when the 1.03. 7 P
instead of her, from whom i took two cods and, 2.04. 52 P
is like th' encounter of two dog-apes; 2.05. 27 P
oppress'd with two weak evils, age and hunger, 2.07.132
and we two will rail against our mistress the 3.02.278 P
for these two hours, rosalind, i will leave thee 4.01.177 P
alas, dear love, i cannot lack thee two hours! 4.01.179 P
by two a' clock i will be with thee again. 4.01.180 P
two a' clock is your hour? 4.01.186 P
is it not past two a' clock? 4.03. 1 P
when from the first to last betwixt us two 4.03.139
any thing so sudden but the fight of two rams, 5.02. 31 P
here come two of the banish'd duke's pages. 5.03. 5 P
and both in a tune, like two gipsies on a horse. 5.03. 15 P
let me have audience for a word or two. 5.04.151
voyage | is but for two months victuall'd. 5.04.192
of you | to pardon me yet for a night or two; SHR in.2. 119
(for aught i see) two and thirty, a peep out? 1.02. 33 P
have as many diseases as two and fifty horses. 1.02. 81 P
he that has the two fair daughters? 1.02.221
no, sir, but hear i do that he hath two: 1.02.251
and where two raging fires meet together, | they 2.01.132
besides two thousand ducats by the year | of 2.01.369
two thousand ducats by the year of land! 2.01.372
besides two galliasses | and twelve tight 2.01.378
d sol re, one cliff, two notes have i; 3.01. 77
with two broken points; 3.02. 48 P
which hath two letters for her name fairly set 3.02. 61 P
sir, at the farthest for a week or two, | but 4.02. 74
i confess two sleeves. 4.03.142 P
i dare assure you, sir, 'tis almost two, | and 4.03.189
as those two eyes become that heavenly face? 4.05. 32
what if a man bring him a hundred pound or two, 5.01. 22 P
have at you for a /bitter jest or two! 5.02. 45
we three are married, but you two are sped. 5.02.185
within /t' /one year it will make itself two, AWW 1.01.147 P
put such difference betwixt their two estates; 1.03.112 P
that dare leave two together, fare you well. 2.01. 98
eye, | safer than mine own two, more dear. 2.01.109
i did think thee, for two ordinaries, to be a 2.03.201 P
by mine honor, if i were but two hours younger, 2.03.253 P
she's very well indeed, but for two things. 2.04. 8 P
what two things? 2.04. 10 P
'twill be two days ere i shall see you, so | i 2.05. 70
news within between two soldiers and my young 3.02. 34 P
and clap upon you two or three probable lies. 3.06. 98 P
here he comes, to beguile two hours in a sleep, 4.01. 22 P
his wife some two months since fled from his 4.03. 47 P
lodowick, and gratii, two hundred fifty each; 4.03.164 P
vaumond, bentii, two hundred fifty each; 4.03.165 P
left cheek is a cheek of two pile and a half, 4.05. 97 P
so, neither, but i am resolv'd on two points — TN 1.05. 22 P
two faults, madonna, that drink and good counsel 1.05. 43 P
as, item, two lips, indifferent red; 1.05.247 P
item, two grey eyes, with lids to them; 1.05.247 P
i will plant you two, and let the fool make a 2.03.173 P
to him, lad, some two thousand strong, or so. 3.02. 54 P
whisper o'er a couplet or two of most sage saws. 3.04.378 P
must have an ounce or two of this malapert blood 4.01. 44 P
your four negatives make your two affirmatives, 5.01. 22 P
sir, may put you in mind — one, two, three. 5.01. 39 P
my grave | i have travell'd but two hours. 5.01.163
one face, one voice, one habit, and two persons, 5.01.216
an apple, cleft in two, is not more twin | than 5.01.223
is not more twin | than these two creatures. 5.01.224
two lads that thought there was no more behind WT 1.02. 63
was not my lord | the verier wag o' th' two? 1.02. 66
we two will walk, my lord, | and leave you to 1.02.172
did expect my hence departure | two days ago. 1.02.451
lest that the treachery of the two fled hence 2.01.195
begin some speech, her eyes | became two spouts; 3.03. 26
they have scar'd away two of my best sheep, 3.03. 65 P
i have seen two such sights, by sea and by land! 3.03. 83 P
a race or two of ginger, but that i may beg; 4.03. 47 P
one of these two must be necessities, | which 4.04. 38
nuptial, which | we two have sworn shall come. 4.04. 51
goes to the tune of "two maids wooing a man." 4.04.289 P
i will bring these two moles, these blind ones, 4.04.836 P
did you see the meeting of the two kings? 5.02. 40 P
and then the two kings call'd my father brother; 5.02.141 P
which now the manage of two kingdoms must | with JN 1.01. 37
him, | and if my legs were two such riding-rods, 1.01.140
o, two such silver currents when they join | do 2.01.441
and two such shores to two such streams made one 2.01.443
and two such shores to two such streams made one 2.01.443
two such controlling bounds shall you be, kings, 2.01.444
to these two princes, if you marry them. 2.01.445
so | as doth the fury of two desperate men, 3.01. 32
like heralds 'twixt two dreadful battles set: 4.02. 78
for 'twill be | two long days' journey, lords, 4.03. 20
where these two christian armies might combine 5.02. 37
king john did fly an hour or two before | the 5.05. 17
war, | the bitter clamor of two eager tongues, R2 1.01. 49
for mowbray and myself are like two men | that 1.03. 48
two kinsmen digg'd their graves with weeping 3.03.169
didst send two of thy men | to execute the noble 4.01. 81
so two together weeping make one woe. 5.01. 86
off, | of our two cousins coming into london. 5.02. 3
my lord, some two days since i saw the prince, 5.03. 13
father, and these two beget | a generation of 5.05. 7
two of the dangerous consorted traitors | that 5.06. 15
ten thousand bold scots, two and twenty knights, 1H4 1.01. 68
well, for two of them, i know them to be as 1.02.183 P
have a gammon of bacon and two razes of ginger, 2.01. 24 P
i think it be two a' clock. 2.01. 33 P
soft, i know a trick worth two of that, i' faith 2.01. 37 P
hourly any time this two and twenty years, and 2.02. 16 P
the prince and poins be not two arrant cowards, 2.02.100 P
i must leave you within these two hours. 2.03. 36
o lord, i would it had been two! 2.04. 60 P
with a dozen of them two hours together. 2.04.165 P
if there were not two or three and fifty upon 2.04.187 P
past praying for, i have pepper'd two of them. 2.04.192 P
two i am sure i have paid, two rogues in buckrom 2.04.192 P
sure i have paid, two rogues in buckrom suits. 2.04.192 P
what, four? thou saidst but two even now. 2.04.197 P
so, two more already. 2.04.213 P
eleven buckrom men grown out of two. 2.04.220 P
we two saw you four set on four and bound them, 2.04.253 P
then did we two set on you four, and, with a 2.04.255 P
there are two gentlemen | have in this robbery 2.04.519
indeed, my lord, i think it be two a' clock. 2.04.525
item, sack, two gallons ... 5s.8d.. 2.04.537 P
i'll away within these two hours, and so come in 3.01.261 P
with fire any time this two and thirty years, 3.03. 47 P
yea, two and two, newgate fashion. 3.03. 90 P
yea, two and two, newgate fashion. 3.03. 90 P

of the age of two and twenty or threereabouts! 3.03.189 P
temple hall | at two /a' clock in the afternoon; 3.03.200
and the half shirt is two napkins tack'd 4.02. 43 P
i have two boys | seek percy and thyself about 5.04. 31
two stars keep not their motion in one sphere, 5.04. 65
but now two paces of the vilest earth | is room 5.04. 91
'a should have sent me two and twenty yards of 2H4 1.02. 43 P
by the lord, i take but two shirts out with me, 1.02.209 P
seven groats and two pence. 1.02.235 P
good people, bring a rescue or two. 2.01. 56 P
and those two things i confess i cannot help. 2.02. 68 P
eyes, and methought he had made two holes in the 2.02. 82 P
put on two leathern jerkins and aprons, and wait 2.02.171 P
there were two honors lost, yours and your son's 2.03. 16
and they will put on two of our jerkins and 2.04. 16 P
you two never meet but you fall to some discord. 2.04. 55 P
i' good truth, as rheumatic as two dry toasts, 2.04. 57 P
discharge upon her, sir john, with two bullets. 2.04.114 P
god's light, with two points on your shoulder? 2.04.133 P
what's a joint of mutton or two in a whole lent? 2.04.347 P
and in two year after | were they at wars. 3.01. 59
here come two of sir john falstaff's men, as i 3.02. 53 P
here is two more call'd than your number, you 3.02.188 P
i'll make him a philosopher's two stones to me. 3.02.330 P
revives two greater in the heirs of life; 4.01.198
which is four terms, or two actions, and 'a 5.01. 80 P
i take it there's but two ways, either to utter 5.03.110 P
there hath been a man or two kill'd about her. 5.04. 6 P
'twill be two a' clock ere they come from the 5.05. 3 P
walls | are now confin'd two mighty monarchies, H5 pr 20
six thousand and two hundred good esquires; 1.01. 14
for never two such kingdoms did contend 1.02. 24
come, shall i make you two friends? 2.01. 90 P
as two yoke–devils sworn to either's purpose, 2.02.106
it is now two a' clock; 3.07.156
and i have built | two chauntries, where the sad 4.01.301
his ransom he will give you two hundred crowns. 4.04. 46 P
would fain see the man, that hath but two legs, 4.07.162 P
as man and wife, being two, are one in love, 5.02.361
between two hawks, which flies the higher pitch, 1H6 2.04. 11
between two dogs, which hath the deeper mouth, 2.04. 12
between two blades, which bears the better 2.04. 13
between two horses, which doth bear him best, 2.04. 14
between two girls, which hath the merriest eye 2.04. 15
that two such noble peers as ye should jar! 3.01. 70
two mightier troops than that the dolphin led, 4.03. 7
who two hours since | i met in travel toward his 4.03. 35
two talbots, winged through the lither sky, | in 4.07. 21
the turk, that two and fifty kingdoms hath, 4.07. 73
that divided was | into two parties, is now 5.02. 12
and those two counties i will undertake | your 5.03.158
to change two dukedoms for a duke's fair 2H6 1.01.219
till suffolk gave two dukedoms for his daughter. 1.03. 87
two pulls at once — | his lady banish'd, and a 2.03. 41
there's two of you, the devil make a third, 3.02.303
even thus two friends condemn'd | embrace, and 3.02.353
what, think you much to pay two thousand crowns, 4.01. 18
they have been up these two days. 4.02. 2 P
by her he had two children at one birth. 4.02.139
head, and bring them both upon two poles hither. 4.07.112 P
call hither to the stake my two brave bears, 5.01.144
but buckler with thee blows, twice two for one. 3H6 1.04. 50
if this right hand would buy two hours' life 2.06. 80
nay then whip me; he'll rather give her two. 3.02. 28
brothers, you muse what chat we two have had. 3.02.109
tell a pedigree | of threescore and two years — 3.03. 93
and do expect him here some two hours hence. 5.01. 10
two of thy name, both dukes of somerset, | have 5.01. 73
two cliffords, as the father and the son, | and 5.07. 7
son, | and two northumberlands — two braver men 5.07. 8
two braver men | ne'er spurr'd their coursers at 5.07. 8
with them, the two brave bears, warwick and 5.07. 10
and entertain a score or two of tailors | to R3 1.02.256
that scarce some two days since were worth a 1.03. 81
if two such murtherers as yourselves came to you 1.04.259
but now two mirrors of his princely semblance 2.02. 51
and pluck'd two crutches from my feeble hands, 2.02. 58
for god sake let not us two stay at home; 2.02.147
that he could gnaw a crust at two hours old; 2.04. 28
'twas full two years ere i could get a tooth. 2.04. 29
some day or two | your highness shall repose you 3.01. 64
iniquity, | i moralize two meanings in one word. 3.01. 83
besides, he says there are two councils kept; 3.02. 12
and stand between two churchmen, good my lord — 3.07. 48
he is within, with two right reverend fathers, 3.07. 61
but meditating with two deep divines; 3.07. 75
where his grace stands, 'tween two clergymen! 3.07. 95
two props of virtue for a christian prince, | to 3.07. 96
and reverend looker–on of two fair queens. 4.01. 30
please you; | but i had rather kill two enemies. 4.02. 71
two deep enemies, | foes to my rest and my sweet 4.02. 72
a mother only mock'd with two fair babes; 4.04. 87
where be thy two sons? 4.04. 93
my damned son that thy two sweet sons smother'd. 4.04.134
which now, two tender bedfellows for dust, | thy 4.04.385
those that come to see | only a show or two, and H8 pr 10
away their shilling | richly in two short hours. pr 13
those suns of glory, those two lights of men, 1.01. 6
the two kings, | equal in lustre, were now best, 1.01. 28
is but merely | a fit or two o' th' face — but 1.03. 7
were but now confessor | to one or two of these! 1.04. 16
two women plac'd together makes cold weather. 1.04. 22
two equal men. 2.02.107
the two great cardinals | wait in the presence. 3.01. 16
upon my soul, two reverend cardinal virtues; 3.01.103
what two reverend bishops | were those that went 4.01. 99
cromwell, her two hands, and she | sleep in 5.01. 31
sir, you speak of two | the most remark'd i' th' 5.01. 32
you shall have | two noble partners with you, 5.02.202
the running banquet of two beadles that is to 5.03. 66 P
marshalsea shall hold ye play these two months. 5.03. 86
to take their ease, | and sleep an act or two; ep 3
troilus is the better man of the two. TRO 1.02. 61 P
"here's but two and fifty hairs on your chin — 1.02.157 P
"two and fifty hairs," quoth he, "and one white. 1.02.160 P
cut, | bounding between the two moist elements, 1.03. 41
as stuff for these two to make paradoxes. 1.03.184
in this | are dogg'd with two strange followers. 1.03.364

two curs shall tame each other; 1.03.389
two traded pilots 'twixt the dangerous /shores 2.02. 64
troy be not taken till these two undermine it, 2.03. 8 P
he? no! she'll none of him. they two are twain. 3.01.101 P
we two, that with so many thousand sighs | did 4.04. 39
and too little brain, these two may run mad, but 5.01. 49 P
diomed, | keep hector company an hour or two. 5.01. 81
but if i tell how these two did //co–act, 5.02.118
no space of earth shall sunder our two hates. 5.10. 27
some two months hence my will shall here be made 5.10. 52
you two are old men: COR 2.01. 13 P
poor in, that you two have not in abundance? 2.01. 17 P
do you two know how you are censur'd here in the 2.01. 21 P
meeting two such wealsmen as you are (i cannot 2.01. 54 P
one i' th' neck, and two i' th' thigh — there's 2.01.151 P
there's in all two worthy voices begg'd. 2.03. 80 P
for your voices bear | of wounds two dozen odd; 2.03.128
aches | to know, when two authorities are up, 3.01.109
o' th' best of them, yea, the two tribunes. 3.01.243
i may be heard, i would crave a word or two, 3.01.281
reports the volsces with two several powers 4.06. 39
for one poor grain or two, to leave unburnt 5.01. 27
for one poor grain or two? 5.01. 28
if the emperor's court can feast two brides, TIT 1.01.489
'tis not the difference of a year or two | makes 2.01. 31
i have been broad awake two hours and more. 2.02. 17
these two have 'ticed me hither to this place: 2.03. 92
two of thy whelps, fell curs of bloody kind, 2.03.281
and made thy body bare | of her two branches, 2.04. 18
for two and twenty sons i never wept, | because 3.01. 10
that shall distill from these two ancient /urns, 3.01. 17
to rescue my two brothers from their death, 3.01. 49
to ransom my two nephews from their death; 3.01.172
here are the heads of thy two noble sons, | and 3.01.236
see thy two sons' heads, | thy warlike hand, thy 3.01.254
for these two heads do seem to speak to me, 3.01.271
two may keep counsel when the third's away. 4.02.144
'twas her two sons that murdered bassianus; 5.01. 91
confederate with the queen and her two sons; 5.01.108
when, for his hand, he had his two sons' heads, 5.01.115
myself, | set deadly enmity between two friends, 5.01.131
provide thee two proper palfreys, black as jet, 5.02. 50
know you these two? 5.02.153
two of her brothers were condemn'd to death, 5.02.173
and make two pasties of your shameful heads, 5.02.189
two households, both alike in dignity, | in fair ROM pr 1
from forth the fatal loins of these two foes | a pr 5
is now the two hours' traffic of our stage; pr 12
let two more summers wither in their pride, 1.02. 10
being thus frighted, swears a prayer or two, 1.04. 87
manners shall lie all in one or two men's hands, 1.05. 4 P
his son was but a ward two years ago. 1.05. 40
my lips, two blushing pilgrims, ready stand | to 1.05. 95
two of the fairest stars in all the heaven, 2.02. 15
two such opposed kings encamp them still | in 2.03. 27
rests, one, two, and the third in your bosom: 2.04. 22 P
two, two: a shirt and a smock. 2.04.103 P
two, two: a shirt and a smock. 2.04.103 P
say, | "two may keep counsel, putting one away"? 2.04.197
alone | till holy church incorporate two in one. 2.06. 37
nay, and there were two such, we should have 3.01. 15 P
for who is living, if those two are gone? 3.02. 68
we'll keep no great ado — a friend or two, 3.04. 23
death | thou shalt continue two and forty hours, 4.01.105
dead, | who here hath lain this two days buried. 5.03.176
and has sent your honor two brace of greyhounds. TIM 1.02.188 P
with two stones moe than 's artificial one. 2.02.111 P
milky heart, | it turns in less than two nights? 3.01. 55
if after two days' shine athens contain thee, 3.05.100
if you had sent but two hours before — 3.06. 45 P
have i once liv'd to see two honest men? 5.01. 56
but two in company; 5.01.106
if where thou art two villains shall not be, 5.01.109
by two of their most reverend senate, greet thee 5.01.129
there's two or three of us have seen strange JC 1.03.138
some two months hence, up higher toward the 2.01.109
we /are two lions litter'd in one day, | and i 2.02. 46
that one of two bad ways you must conceit me, 3.01.192
love, and be friends, as two such men should be, 4.03.131
and touch thy instrument a strain or two? 4.03.257
on our former ensign | two mighty eagles fell, 5.01. 80
are yet two romans living such as these? 5.03. 98
appear'd to me | two several times by night; 5.05. 18
thou know'st that we two went to school together 5.05. 26
as two spent swimmers that do cling together MAC 1.02. 8
two truths are told, | as happy prologues to the 1.03.127
his two chamberlains | will i with wine and 1.07. 63
when we have mark'd with blood those sleepy two 1.07. 75
there are two lodg'd together. 2.02. 23
malcolm and donalbain, the king's two sons, 2.04. 25
in pious rage the two delinquents tear, | that 3.06. 12
'tis two or three, my lord, that bring you word 4.01.141
i have two nights watch'd with you, but can 5.01. 1 P
one — two — why then 'tis time to do't. 5.01. 36 P
our story, | what we have two nights seen. HAM 1.01. 33
but two months dead! 1.02.138
nay, not so much, not two. 1.02.138
two nights together had these gentlemen, 1.02.196
make thy two eyes, like stars, start from their 1.05. 17
and sure i am two men there is not living | to 2.02. 20
sweet gertrude, leave us two, | for we have 3.01. 28
will you two help to hasten them? 3.02. 50 P
looks, and my father died within 's two hours. 3.02.127 P
nay, 'tis twice two months, my lord. 3.02.128 P
o heavens, die two months ago, and not forgotten 3.02.130 P
the counterfeit presentment of two brothers. 3.04. 54
letters seal'd, and my two schoolfellows, | whom 3.04.202
when in one line two crafts directly meet. 3.04.210
lean beggar is but variable service, two dishes, 4.03. 24 P
two thousand souls and twenty thousand ducats 4.04. 25
ere we were two days old at sea, a pirate of 4.06. 15 P
o, for two special reasons, | which may to you, 4.07. 9
two months since | here was a gentleman of 4.07. 81
that's two of his weapons — but well. 5.02.146 P
with my two daughters' dow'rs digest the third; LR 1.01.128
ay, two hours together. 1.02.155 P
i have not seen him this two days. 1.04. 72 P

this fellow has banish'd two on 's daughters, 1.04.102 P
would i had two coxcombs and two daughters! 1.04.105 P
would i had two coxcombs and two daughters! 1.04.105 P
thou shalt have more | than two tens to a score. 1.04.127
give me an egg, and i'll give thee two crowns. 1.04.156 P
what two crowns shall they be? 1.04.157 P
and eat up the meat, the two crowns of the egg. 1.04.159 P
is it two days since i tripp'd up thy heels, and 2.02. 29 P
though they had been but two years o' th' trade. 2.02. 60 P
should many people under two commands | hold 2.04.241
that will with two pernicious daughters join 3.02. 22
below, methought his eyes | were two full moons; 4.06. 70
repair those violent harms that my two sisters 4.07. 27
we two alone will sing like birds i' th' cage; 5.03. 9
'twixt two extremes of passion, joy and grief, 5.03.199
if fortune brag of two she lov'd and hated, 5.03.281
moor are /now making the beast with two backs. OTH 1.01.117 P
and mine, two hundred! 1.03. 4
two things are to be done: 2.03.382
world | the sun to course two hundred compasses, 3.04. 71
'tis not a year or two shows us a man: 3.04.103
two or three groan. 5.01. 42
my leg is cut in two. 5.01. 72
a word or two before you go. 5.02.338
equality of two domestic powers | breed ANT 1.03. 47
you'll win two days upon me. 2.04. 9
here they might take two thieves kissing. 2.06. 96 P
that have my heart parted betwixt two friends 3.06. 77
tend me to–night two hours, i ask no more, | and 4.02. 32
two other sons, who in the wars o' th' time CYM 1.01. 35
he had two sons (if this be worth your hearing, 1.01. 57
which i had set | betwixt two charming words, 1.03. 35
and by such two that would by all likelihood 1.04. 50 P
fetch my gold and have our two wagers recorded. 1.04.167 P
been thief–stol'n, | as my two brothers, happy! 1.06. 6
'twixt two such shes would chatter this way, and 1.06. 40
two creatures heartily. 1.06. 83
and this her son | cannot take two from twenty, 2.01. 55
one, two, three: 2.02. 51
them) were two winking cupids | of silver, each 2.04. 89
make pastime with us a day or two, or longer. 3.01. 78 P
content — yet not | that we two are asunder; 3.02. 32
oft) | but that two villains, whose false oaths 3.03. 66
feast, | to him the other two shall minister, 3.03. 76
at three and two years old, i stole these babes, 3.03.101
old servant, | i have not seen these two days. 3.05. 55
and for two nights together | have made the 3.06. 2
two beggars told me | i could not miss my way. 3.06. 8
thou blazon'st | in these two princely boys! 4.02.171
he, with two striplings (lads more like to run 5.03. 19
a narrow lane, an old man, and two boys! 5.03. 52
"two boys, an old man (twice a boy), a lane, 5.03. 57
thou hast created | a mother and two brothers. 5.04.125
but i will prove that two on 's are as good | as 5.05.311
these two young gentlemen, that call me father 5.05.328
two of the sweet'st companions in the world. 5.05.349
i have got two worlds by't. 5.05.374
thy lopp'd branches point | thy two sons forth; 5.05.455
how they may be, and yet in two, | as you will PER 1.01. 70
heirs | may the two latter darken and expend; 3.02. 29
when you caught hurt in parting two that fought; 4.01. 87
thou sayest true, there's two unwholesome, a' 4.02. 21 P
art, may yet appear | worth two hours' travail. TNK pr 29
they two have cabin'd | in many as dangerous as 1.03. 35
mean time, look tenderly to the two prisoners. 2.01. 19 P
o, never | shall we two exercise, like twins of 2.02. 18
of noble minds) | in us two here shall perish; 2.02. 53
i see two comforts rising, two mere blessings, 2.02. 58
i see two comforts rising, two mere blessings, 2.02. 58
most true, two souls | put in two noble bodies, 2.02. 64
two souls | put in two noble bodies, let 'em 2.02. 65
is there record of any two that lov'd | better 2.02.112
two such steeds might well | be by a pair of 3.01. 20
food took i none these two days — | sipp'd some 3.02. 26
i'll tell you | after a draught or two more. 3.03. 19
or two, or three, or ten. 3.03. 36
i'll come again some two hours hence and bring 3.03. 49
up with a course or two, and tack about, boys! 3.04. 10
gallants of war, | by one, by two, by three–a. 3.05. 62
with him bring | two swords and two good armors. 3.06. 3
with him bring | two swords and two good armors. 3.06. 3
like meeting of two tides, fly strongly from us, 3.06. 30
can these two live, | and have the agony of love 3.06.218
and in their funeral songs for these two cousins 3.06.248
or the sweet compassion | of those two ladies; 4.01. 12
there is at least two hundred now with child by 4.01.129
he'll tickle't up | in two hours, if his hand be 4.01.139
two such young handsome men | shall never fall 4.02. 3
that, having two fair gauds of equal sweetness, 4.02. 53
two greater and two better never yet | made 4.02. 62
two greater and two better never yet | made 4.02. 62
your two contending lovers are return'd, | and 4.02. 66
show | bravely about the titles of two kingdoms. 4.02.145
out of two i should | choose one, and pray for 5.01.152
he of the two pretenders that best loves me 5.01.158
some two hundred bottles, | and twenty strike of 5.02. 64
but this poor petticoat and two coarse smocks. 5.02. 84
he whom the gods | do of the two know best, i 5.03. 39
and | the two bold titlers at this instant are 5.03. 83
two emulous philomels beat the ear o' th' night 5.03.124
on one | that two must needs be blind for't! 5.03.146
a day or two | let us look sadly, and give grace 5.04.124
two strengthless doves will draw me through the VEN 153
showed like two silver doves that sit a–billing. 366
her two blue windows faintly she upheaveth, 482
the crystal tide that from her two cheeks fair 957
grief hath two tongues, and never woman yet 1007
and yet," quoth she, "behold two adons dead! 1070
sun and sharp air | lurk'd like two thieves, to 1086
where lo, two lamps burnt out in darkness lies; 1128
two glasses, where herself herself beheld | a 1129
to those two armies that would let him go, LUC 76
conclusion | who, having two sweet babes, when 1161
why her two suns were cloud–eclipsed so, | nor 1224
that two red fires in both their faces blazed; 1353
it doth divide | in two slow rivers, that the 1738
two loves i have, of comfort and despair, | that PP 2. 1
that like two spirits do suggest me still: 2. 2

for of the two the trusty knight was wounded 15.11
but in one, | two distincts, division none: PHT 27
double name | neither two nor one was called. 40
let me confess that we two must be twain, SON 36. 1
in our two loves there is but one respect, 36. 5
the other two, slight air and purging fire, 45. 1
of four, with two alone | sinks down to death, 45. 7
which parts the shore where two contracted new 56.10
as those two /mourning eyes become thy face. 132. 9
two loves i have of comfort and despair, | which 144. 1
which like two spirits do suggest me still: 144. 2
but why of two oaths' breach do i accuse thee, 152. 5

TWO-AND-TWENTY 1 FR 0.0001 REL FR 0 V 1 P
of nineteen and two–and–twenty hunt this weather WT 3.03. 64 P

TWOFOLD 6 FR 0.0006 REL FR 5 V 1 P
doth with a twofold vigor lift me up | to reach R2 1.03. 71
you violate | a twofold marriage — 'twixt my 5.01. 72
sherris–sack hath a twofold operation in it. 2H4 4.03. 96 P
that twofold balls and treble sceptres carry. MAC 4.01.121
and what's in prayer but this twofold force, HAM 3.03. 48
where thou art forc'd to break a twofold truth: SON 41.12

TWO-HAND 1 FR 0.0001 REL FR 1 V 0 P
come with thy two–hand sword. 2H6 2.01. 45

TWO-HEADED 1 FR 0.0001 REL FR 1 V 0 P
now, by two–headed janus, | nature hath fram'd MV 1.01. 50

TWO-LEGG'D 1 FR 0.0001 REL FR 0 V 1 P
poor old jack, then am i no two–legg'd creature. 1H4 2.04.188 P

TWOPENCE 2 FR 0.0002 REL FR 0 V 2 P
pass his word for twopence that you are no fool. TN 1.05. 81 P
would not be in some of your coats for twopence. 4.01. 31 P

TWOPENCES 1 FR 0.0001 REL FR 0 V 1 P
you do not all show like gilt twopences to me, 2H4 4.03. 51 P

TWOS 2 FR 0.0002 REL FR 1 V 1 P
and will by twos and threes at several posterns WT 1.02.438
he stands, by ones, by twos, and by threes. COR 2.03. 42 P

'TWOULD 30 FR 0.0034 REL FR 21 V 9 P
'twere a kibe, | 'twould put me to my slipper; TMP 2.01.277
'twould be my tyranny to strike and gall them MM 1.03. 36
i knew 'twould be a bald conclusion. ERR 2.02.108 P
at an earthquake, 'twould mend the lottery well; AWW 1.03. 87 P
'twould not do. 4.01. 51 P
if my heart were great, | 'twould burst at this. 4.03.331
how often have i told you 'twould be thus! WT 4.04.474
'twould drink the cup and all. H5 1.01. 20
'twould prove the verity of certain words H8 1.02.159
stone a–rolling, | 'twould fall upon ourselves. 5.02.140
'twould not become him, his own's better. TRO 1.02. 91 P
and 'twould, you'd carry half. 2.03.219 P
there were wit in this head, and 'twould out — 3.03.256 P
if it were at liberty, 'twould sure southward. COR 2.03. 29 P
midnight sleep, | by jove, 'twould be my mind! 3.01. 86
sit in gold, his eye | red as 'twould burn rome; 5.01. 64
'twould anger him | to raise a spirit in his ROM 2.01. 23
i scorn thy meat, 'twould choke me; TIM 1.02. 38 P
for 'twould have anger'd any heart alive | to MAC 3.06. 15
that he cried out 'twould be a sight indeed | if HAM 4.07. 99
often 'twould say, | "the fiend, the fiend!" LR 4.06. 78
life, 'twould not ha' bin zo long as 'tis by a 4.06.239 P
'twould make her amiable, and subdue my father OTH 3.04. 59
to do antonius good, | but 'twould offend him; ANT 3.01. 26
poison, 'twould appear | by external swelling; 5.02.345
or adder, spider, | 'twould move me sooner. CYM 4.02. 91
'twould braid yourself too near for me to tell PER 1.01. 93
'twould be too tedious to repeat, | but the main 5.01. 28
'twould bring us to an eddy | where we should TNK 1.02. 10
i knew 'twould be so. 4.01. 28

TYBALT 46 FR 0.0052 REL FR 42 V 4 P
in the instant came | the fiery tybalt, with his ROM 1.01.109
signior valentio and his cousin tybalt; 1.02. 70 P
tybalt, the kinsman to old capulet, | hath sent 2.04. 6
and is he a man to encounter tybalt? 2.04. 17 P
why, what is tybalt? 2.04. 18 P
tybalt, the reason that i have to love thee 3.01. 62
tybalt, you rat–catcher, will you walk? 3.01. 75 P
tybalt, mercutio, the prince expressly hath 3.01. 88
hold, tybalt! 3.01. 90
stain'd | with tybalt's slander — tybalt, that 3.01.112
here comes the furious tybalt back again. 3.01.121
now, tybalt, take the "villain" back again 3.01.125
the citizens are up, and tybalt slain. 3.01.133
tybalt, that murtherer, which way ran he? 3.01.138
there lies that tybalt. 3.01.139
tybalt, my cousin! 3.01.146
tybalt, here slain, whom romeo's hand did slay! 3.01.152
the unruly spleen | of tybalt deaf to peace, but 3.01.158
and with the other sends | it back to tybalt, 3.01.163
an envious thrust from tybalt hit the life | of 3.01.168
life | of stout mercutio, and then tybalt fled; 3.01.169
could draw to part them, was stout tybalt slain; 3.01.173
romeo slew tybalt, romeo must not live. 3.01.181
what the law should end, | the life of tybalt. 3.01.186
o tybalt, tybalt, the best friend i had! 3.02. 61
o tybalt, tybalt, the best friend i had! 3.02. 61
o courteous tybalt, honest gentleman, | that 3.02. 62
and is tybalt dead? 3.02. 65
tybalt is gone, and romeo banished, | romeo that 3.02. 69
my husband lives that tybalt would have slain, 3.02.105
"tybalt is dead, and romeo banished." 3.02.112
is father, mother, tybalt, romeo, juliet, | all 3.02.123
love, | an hour but married, tybalt murdered, 3.03. 66
and tybalt calls, and then on romeo cries, | and 3.03.101
hast thou slain tybalt? 3.03.116
tybalt would kill thee, | but thou slewest 3.03.137
would kill thee, | but thou slewest tybalt: 3.03.138
look you, she lov'd her kinsman tybalt dearly, 3.04. 3
two, | for hark you, tybalt being slain so late, 3.04. 24
dram | that he shall soon keep tybalt company; 3.05. 91
bed | in that dim monument where tybalt lies. 3.05.201
where bloody tybalt, yet but green in earth, 4.03. 42
and pluck the mangled tybalt from his shroud, 4.03. 52
stay, tybalt, stay! 4.03. 57
tybalt, liest thou there in thy bloody sheet? 5.03. 97
for whom, and not for tybalt, juliet pin'd. 5.03.236

TYBALT'S 10 FR 0.0011 REL FR 10 V 0 P
my reputation stain'd | with tybalt's slander — ROM 3.01.112
o god, did romeo's hand shed tybalt's blood? 3.02. 71
and tybalt's dead that would have slain my 3.02.106
some word there was, worser than tybalt's death, 3.02.108
tybalt's death | was woe enough if it had ended 3.02.114
when she said, "tybalt's dead," | thy father or 3.02.118
but with a rearward following tybalt's death, 3.02.121
weeping and wailing over tybalt's corse. 3.02.128
immoderately she weeps for tybalt's death, | and 4.01. 6
stol'n marriage–day | was tybalt's dooms–day, 5.03.234

TYBALTS 1 FR 0.0001 REL FR 1 V 0 P
"banished," | hath slain ten thousand tybalts. ROM 3.02.114

TYBURN 1 FR 0.0001 REL FR 1 V 0 P
the shape of love's tyburn that hangs up LLL 4.03. 52

TYING 4 FR 0.0004 REL FR 3 V 1 P
tying thine ear to no tongue but thine own! 1H4 1.03.238
easily endures not article | tying him to aught; COR 2.03.197
with another for tying his new shoes with old ROM 3.01. 28 P
tying her duty, beauty, wit, and fortunes | in OTH 1.01.135

TYMBRIA *(see timbria)*

TYPE 3 FR 0.0003 REL FR 3 V 0 P
thy father bears the type of king of naples, 3H6 1.04.121
the high imperial type of this earth's glory. R3 4.04.245
of that true type hath tarquin rifled me. LUC 1050

TYPES 1 FR 0.0001 REL FR 1 V 0 P
blist'red breeches, and those types of travel, H8 1.03. 31

TYPHON 1 FR 0.0001 REL FR 1 V 0 P
from the tongue of roaring typhon dropp'd, TRO 1.03.160

TYPHON'S 1 FR 0.0001 REL FR 1 V 0 P
with all his threat'ning band of typhon's brood, TIT 4.02. 94

TYRANNICAL 2 FR 0.0002 REL FR 2 V 0 P
him home, that he affects | tyrannical power. COR 3.03. 2
and to wind | yourself into a power tyrannical, 3.03. 65

/TYRANNICALLY 1 FR 0.0001 REL FR 0 V 1 P
/and /are /most /tyrannically /clapp'd /for't. HAM 2.02.341 P

/TYRANNIZE 1 FR 0.0001 REL FR 1 V 0 P
/is /left /to /tyrannize /upon /my /breast, TIT 3.02. 8

TYRANNIZE 3 FR 0.0003 REL FR 3 V 0 P
is as a fiend confin'd to tyrannize | on JN 5.07. 47
on him that thus doth tyrannize o'er me. TIT 4.03. 20
when most unseen, then most doth tyrannize. LUC 676

TYRANNOUS 14 FR 0.0015 REL FR 14 V 0 P
but it is tyrannous | to use it like a giant. MM 2.02.108
which he corrects, then were he tyrannous, | but 4.02. 84
thoughts | that tyrannous heart can think? TN 3.01.120
fear you his tyrannous passion more, alas, WT 2.03. 28
let us be clear'd | of being tyrannous, since we 3.02. 5
the tyrannous and bloody act is done, | the most R3 4.03. 1
should be so tyrannous and rough in proof! ROM 1.01.170
that lend a tyrannous and a damned light | to HAM 2.02.460
and let this tyrannous night take hold upon you, LR 3.04.151
crown and hearted throne | to tyrannous hate! OTH 3.03.449
and like the tyrannous breathing of the north CYM 1.03. 36
i knew him tyrannous, and tyrants' /fears PER 1.02. 84
'tis pity love should be so tyrannous. TNK 4.02.146
thou art as tyrannous, so as thou art, | as SON 131. 1

/TYRANNY 1 FR 0.0001 REL FR 1 V 0 P
/eyes /are /cloy'd /with /view /of /tyranny. TIT 3.02. 55

TYRANNY 36 FR 0.0040 REL FR 34 V 2 P
whether the tyranny be in his place, | or in his MM 1.02.163
'twould be my tyranny to strike and gall them 1.03. 36
of spirit, | the very tyranny and rage of his. MV 4.01. 13
her heart but the tyranny of her sorrows takes AWW 1.01. 50 P
something savors | of tyranny, and will ignoble WT 2.03.120
blush, and tyranny | tremble at patience. 3.02. 31
thy tyranny, | together working with thy 3.02.179
and waste for churlish winter's tyranny. 2H4 1.03. 62
a deep demeanor in great sorrow | that tyranny, 4.05. 85
that hast by tyranny these many years | wasted 1H6 2.03. 40
was nothing less than bloody tyranny. 2.05.100
the period of thy tyranny approacheth. 4.02. 17
to scorn, | anon, from thy insulting tyranny, 4.07. 19
heard of, | that england was defam'd by tyranny. 2H6 3.01.123
happy, | and prove the period of their tyranny, 3.01.149
upon thy eyeballs murderous tyranny | sits in 3.02. 49
king | and lofty, proud, encroaching tyranny, 4.01. 96
insulting tyranny begins to jut | upon the R3 2.04. 51
his tyranny for trifles, his own bastardy, | as 3.07. 9
bruis'd underneath the yoke of tyranny, | thus 5.02. 2
the last was i that felt thy tyranny. 5.03.168
best of my flesh, | forgive my tyranny; COR 5.03. 43
even at thy teat thou hadst thy tyranny; TIT 2.03.145
in pleasing smiles such murderous tyranny. 2.03.267
that part of tyranny that i do bear | i can JC 1.03. 99
so let high–sighted tyranny range on, | till 2.01.118
tyranny is dead! 3.01. 78
great tyranny, lay thou thy basis sure, | for MAC 4.03. 32
boundless intemperance | in nature is a tyranny; 4.03. 67
that fled the snares of watchful tyranny, 5.09. 33
fond bondage in the oppression of aged tyranny, LR 1.02. 50 P
the tyranny of the open night's too rough | for 3.04. 2
child, | for thy escape would teach me tyranny, OTH 1.03.197
torrents whose roaring tyranny and power | i' TNK 1.03. 38
making it subject to the tyranny | of mad VEN 737
alas, why, fearing of time's tyranny, | might i SON 115. 9

TYRANT 57 FR 0.0064 REL FR 50 V 7 P
a plague upon the tyrant that i serve! TMP 2.02.162
as i told thee before, i am subject to a tyrant, 3.02. 42
there, tyrant, there! 4.01.257
/by /the /lord, thou art a tyrant to say so. WIV 3.03. 61 P
you seem'd of late to make the law a tyrant, MM 2.04.114
guides me most, | i'll prove a tyrant to him. 2.04.169
this would make mercy swear and play the tyrant. 3.02.195 P
as being a profess'd tyrant to their sex? ADO 1.01.169 P
what is pyramus? a lover, or a tyrant? MND 1.02. 22 P
the rest — yet my chief humor is for a tyrant. 1.02. 28 P
from tyrant duke unto a tyrant brother. AYL 1.02.288
from tyrant duke unto a tyrant brother. 1.02.288
mark how the tyrant writes. 4.03. 39
live you the marble–breasted tyrant still. TN 5.01.124
i'll not call you tyrant; WT 2.03.116
were i a tyrant, | where were her life? 2.03.122
a true subject, leontes a jealous tyrant, his 3.02.134 P
what studied torments, tyrant, hast for me? 3.02.175
but, o thou tyrant! 3.02.207
ay me, this tyrant fever burns me up, | and will JN 5.03. 14
is thought with child by the stern tyrant war, 2H4 in 14
we are no tyrant, but a christian king, | unto H5 1.02.241
and beauty, that the tyrant oft reclaims, 2H6 5.02. 54
to prove him tyrant this reason may suffice, 3H6 3.03. 71
and force the tyrant from his seat by war. 3.03.206
that excellent grand tyrant of the earth | that R3 4.04. 52
gentlemen, | a bloody tyrant and a homicide; 5.03.246
if you do sweat to put a tyrant down, | you 5.03.255
you sleep in peace, the tyrant being slain; 5.03.256
if i confess much, you will play the tyrant. TRO 3.02.119
revenge | upon the thracian tyrant in his tent TIT 1.01.138
i will show myself a tyrant: ROM 1.01. 21 P
beautiful tyrant! 3.02. 75
and why should caesar be a tyrant then? JC 1.03.103
this caesar was a tyrant. 3.02. 69
(from whom this tyrant holds the due of birth) MAC 3.06. 25
this tyrant, whose sole name blisters our 4.03. 12
with an untitled tyrant bloody–sceptred, | when 4.03.104
the tyrant has not batter'd at their peace? 4.03.178
what does the tyrant? 5.02. 11
we learn no other but the confident tyrant 5.04. 8
thou liest, abhorred tyrant, with my sword 5.07. 10
tyrant, show thy face! 5.07. 14
and underwrit, | "here may you see the tyrant." 5.08. 27
so, as a painted tyrant, pyrrhus stood | /and, HAM 2.02.480
the tyrant custom, most grave senators, | hath OTH 1.03.229
how fine this tyrant | can tickle where she CYM 1.01. 84
and justly too, i think, you fear the tyrant, PER 1.02.103
a most unbounded tyrant, whose successes | makes TNK 1.02. 63
to call the fiercest tyrant from his rage, | and 5.01. 78
which the hot tyrant stains, and soon bereaves, VEN 797
"hard–favor'd tyrant, ugly, meagre, lean, 931
or tyrant folly lurk in gentle breasts? LUC 851
session interdict | every fowl of tyrant wing, PHT 10
mightier way | make war upon this bloody tyrant, SON 16. 2
and i, a tyrant, have no leisure taken | to 120. 7
forgot | am of myself, all tyrant for thy sake? 149. 4

TYRANT'S 10 FR 0.0011 REL FR 9 V 1 P
this is ercles' vein, a tyrant's vein; MND 1.02. 40 P
but, to prevent the tyrant's violence | (for 3H6 4.04. 29
he fail'd | his presence at the tyrant's feast, MAC 3.06. 22
the whole space that's in the tyrant's grasp, 4.03. 36
when i shall tread upon the tyrant's head, | or 4.03. 45
for that i saw the tyrant's power afoot. 4.03.185
do we but find the tyrant's power to–night, 5.06. 7
the tyrant's people on both sides do fight, 5.07. 25
when misery could beguile the tyrant's rage, LR 4.06. 63
th' great, | thou art past the tyrant's stroke; CYM 4.02.265

TYRANTS' 2 FR 0.0002 REL FR 2 V 0 P
tyrannous, and tyrants' /fears | decrease not, PER 1.02. 84
when tyrants' crests and tombs of brass are SON 107.14

TYRANTS 10 FR 0.0011 REL FR 10 V 0 P
ears | and plant in tyrants mild humility. LLL 4.03.346
swearing that we | are mere usurpers, tyrants, AYL 2.01. 61
should be called tyrants, butchers, murtherers! 3.05. 14
for how can tyrants safely govern home, | unless 3H6 3.03. 69
tyrants themselves wept when it was reported. R3 1.03.184
the law, | and none but tyrants use it cruelly. TIM 3.05. 9
therein, ye gods, you tyrants do defeat; JC 1.03. 92
a foe to tyrants, and my country's friend. 5.04. 5
'tis time to fear when tyrants seems to kiss. PER 1.02. 79
dwell | will play the tyrants to the very same, SON 5. 3

TYRE 24 FR 0.0027 REL FR 22 V 2 P
young prince of tyre, you have at large received PER 1.01. 1
young prince of tyre, | though by the tenor of 1.01.110
we hate the prince | of tyre, and thou must kill 1.01.156
tyre, i now look from thee then, and to tharsus 1.02.115
so this is tyre, and this the court. 1.03. 1 P
here comes the lords of tyre. 1.03. 9 P
you shall not need, my fellow peers of tyre, 1.03. 10
peace to the lords of tyre! 1.03. 29
as friends to antioch, we may feast in tyre. 1.03. 39
we have heard your miseries as far as tyre, 1.04. 88
desire, | /sends /word of all that haps in tyre: 2.ch. 22
a gentleman of tyre, my name, pericles, | my 2.03. 81
names himself pericles, | a gentleman of tyre, 2.03. 87
and i have heard you knights of tyre | are 2.03.101
a letter that she loves the knight of tyre! 2.05. 43
at last from tyre, | fame answering the most 3.ch. 21
of helicanus would set on | the crown of tyre, 3.ch. 28
brief, he must hence depart to tyre: 3.ch. 39
gentle mariner, | alter thy course for tyre. 3.01. 75
imagine pericles arriv'd at tyre, | welcom'd and 4.ch. 1
our vessel is of tyre, in it the king, | a man 5.01. 23
i am pericles of tyre; 5.01.204
i here confess myself the king of tyre, | who, 5.03. 2
you have heard me say, when i did fly from tyre, 5.03. 50

TYRIAN 2 FR 0.0002 REL FR 2 V 0 P
my hangings all of tyrian tapestry; SHR 2.01.349
from whence | lysimachus our tyrian ship espies, PER 5.ch. 18

TYRREL 8 FR 0.0009 REL FR 8 V 0 P
his name, my lord, is tyrrel. R3 4.02. 40
is thy name tyrrel? 4.02. 66
james tyrrel, and your most obedient subject. 4.02. 67
tyrrel, i mean those bastards in the tower. 4.02. 75
hark, come hither, tyrrel. 4.02. 78
kind tyrrel, am i happy in thy news? 4.03. 24
and buried, gentle tyrrel? 4.03. 28
come to me, tyrrel, soon, /at after–supper, 4.03. 31

TYRUS 5 FR 0.0005 REL FR 5 V 0 P
the men of tyrus on the head | of helicanus PER 3.ch. 26
cleon, for the babe | cannot hold out to tyrus. 3.01. 79
and tyrus stands | in a litigious peace. 3.03. 2
she was of tyrus the king's daughter, | on whom 4.04. 36
our son and daughter shall in tyrus reign. 5.03. 82

UBIQUE 1 FR 0.0001 REL FR 1 V 0 P
hic et ubique? HAM 1.05.156

UDDERS 1 FR 0.0001 REL FR 1 V 0 P
shade | a lioness, with udders all drawn dry, AYL 4.03.114

UDGE *(also judge)*

UDGE 1 FR 0.0001 REL FR 0 V 1 P
so got udge me, that is a virtuous mind. WIV 1.01.185 P

'UD'S *(also god's*, got's, 'od's*)*

/'UD'S 1 FR 0.0001 REL FR 0 V 1 P
for all the whole world — /'ud's /pity, who OTH 4.03. 75 P

UGLIER 2 FR 0.0002 REL FR 2 V 0 P
and as with age his body uglier grows, | so his TMP 4.01.191
the uglier seem the clouds that in it fly. R2 1.01. 42

UGLIEST 1 FR 0.0001 REL FR 1 V 0 P
where hateful death put on his ugliest mask | to 2H4 1.01. 66

UGLY 30 FR 0.0034 REL FR 30 V 0 P
i am as ugly as a bear; MND 2.02. 94

none but that ugly treason of mistrust, | which MV 3.02. 28
which, like the toad, ugly and venomous, | wears AYL 2.01. 13
this news hath made thee a most ugly man. JN 3.01. 37
ugly, and sland'rous to thy mother's womb, 3.01. 44
there is not yet so ugly a fiend of hell | as 4.03.123
by breaking through the foul and ugly mists | of 1H4 1.02.202
had not been here to dress the ugly form | of 2H4 4.01. 39
who like a foul and ugly witch doth limp | so H5 4.pr. 21
see how the ugly witch doth bend her brows, | as 1H6 5.03. 34
there minotaurs and ugly treasons lurk. 5.03.189
whose ugly and unnatural aspect | may fright the R3 1.02. 23
affrights thee with a hell of ugly devils! 1.03.226
so full of fearful dreams, of ugly sights, 1.04. 3
what sights of ugly death within /my eyes! 1.04. 23
ten times more ugly | than ever they were fair. H8 1.02.117
how ugly night comes breathing at his heels; TRO 5.08. 6
striving to make an ugly deed look fair. TIM 3.05. 25
banish usury, | that makes the senate ugly! 3.05. 99
is not more ugly to the thing that helps it HAM 3.01. 51
fault, | how ugly didst thou in cordelia show! LR 1.04.267
a daily beauty in his life | that makes me ugly; OTH 5.01. 20
thy face, to me | thou wouldst appear most ugly. ANT 2.05. 97
being an ugly monster, | 'tis strange he hides CYM 5.03. 70
"hard–favor'd tyrant, ugly, meagre, lean, VEN 931
who bids them still consort with ugly night, 1041
quick–shifting antics, ugly in her eyes. LUC 459
"misshapen time, copesmate of ugly night, 925
with slow sad gait descended | to ugly hell, 1082
to ride | with ugly rack on his celestial face, SON 33. 6
ULCER 2 FR 0.0002 REL FR 2 V 0 P
pourest in the open ulcer of my heart | her eyes TRO 1.01. 53
but to the quick of th' ulcer: HAM 4.07.123
ULCEROUS 3 FR 0.0003 REL FR 3 V 0 P
she, whom the spittle–house and ulcerous sores TIM 4.03. 40
all swoll'n and ulcerous, pitiful to the eye, MAC 4.03.151
it will but skin and film the ulcerous place, HAM 3.04.147
ULYSSES' 1 FR 0.0001 REL FR 0 V 1 P
yarn she spun in ulysses' absence did but fill COR 1.03. 83 P
ULYSSES 21 FR 0.0023 REL FR 19 V 2 P
nestor, | deceive more slily than ulysses could, 3H6 3.02.189
that as ulysses and stout diomede | with sleight 4.02. 19
should be shut up, hear what ulysses speaks. TRO 1.03. 58
thou great, and wise, to hear ulysses speak. 1.03. 69
most wisely hath ulysses here discover'd | the 1.03.138
the nature of the sickness found, ulysses, 1.03.140
who, as ulysses says, opinion crowns | with an 1.03.186
what says ulysses? 1.03.311
and trust to me, ulysses, | our imputation shall 1.03.338
now, ulysses, i begin to relish thy advice, 1.03.386
there's ulysses and old nestor, whose wit was 2.01.104 P
ulysses, /enter /you. 2.03.141
here is ulysses, | i'll interrupt his reading. 3.03. 92
how now, ulysses? 3.03. 94
this is not strange, ulysses. 3.03.102
i know your favor, lord ulysses, well. 4.05.213
i shall forestall thee, lord ulysses, thou! 4.05.230
my lord ulysses, tell me, i beseech you, | in 4.05.277
and that same dog–fox, ulysses, is not prov'd 5.04. 11 P
in ajax and ulysses, o, what art | of LUC 1394
but the mild glance that sly ulysses lent 1399
'UM *(also 'em, them)*
'UM 1 FR 0.0001 REL FR 1 V 0 P
which if they have as i will leave 'um them, H5 4.03.124
UMBER 1 FR 0.0001 REL FR 1 V 0 P
and with a kind of umber smirch my face; AYL 1.03.112
UMBER'D 1 FR 0.0001 REL FR 1 V 0 P
each battle sees the other's umber'd face. H5 4.pr. 9
UMBRA 1 FR 0.0001 REL FR 0 V 1 P
gelida quando /pecus /omne sub umbra ruminat —
LLL 4.02. 94 P
UMBRAGE 1 FR 0.0001 REL FR 0 V 1 P
and who else would trace him, his umbrage, HAM 5.02.119 P
UMFREVILE 1 FR 0.0001 REL FR 1 V 0 P
sir john umfrevile turn'd me back | with joyful 2H4 1.01. 34
UMPEER 3 FR 0.0003 REL FR 3 V 0 P
wrong | have chose as umpeer of their mutiny. LLL 1.01.169
let me be umpeer in this doubtful strife. 1H6 4.01.151
me this bloody knife | shall play the umpeer, ROM 4.01. 63
UMPIRE 2 FR 0.0002 REL FR 2 V 0 P
just death, kind umpire of men's miseries, 1H6 2.05. 29
i think | theseus cannot be umpire to himself, TNK 1.03. 45
UMPIRES 1 FR 0.0001 REL FR 0 V 1 P
there is three umpires in this matter, as i WIV 1.01.137 P
UN *(also oon)*
UN 1 FR 0.0001 REL FR 0 V 1 P
un peu, madame. H5 3.04. 3 P
UNABLE 6 FR 0.0006 REL FR 6 V 0 P
to my heart, | making both it unable for itself, MM 2.04. 21
come, come, you froward and unable worms! SHR 5.02.169
is numb | (unable to support this lump of clay), 1H6 2.05. 14
when sapless age and weak unable limbs | should 4.05. 4
love that makes breath poor, and speech unable: LR 1.01. 60
if wars, we are unable to resist. PER 1.04. 84
UNACCOMMODATED 1 FR 0.0001 REL FR 0 V 1 P
unaccommodated man is no more but such a poor,
LR 3.04.106 P
UNACCOMPANIED 1 FR 0.0001 REL FR 1 V 0 P
honor must | not unaccompanied invest him only, MAC 1.04. 40
UNACCUSTOM'D 5 FR 0.0005 REL FR 5 V 0 P
broil, | and set this unaccustom'd fight aside. 1H6 3.01. 93
what unaccustom'd cause procures her hither? ROM 3.05. 67
shall give him such an unaccustom'd dram | that 3.05. 90
and all this day an unaccustom'd spirit | lifts 5.01. 4
the unaccustom'd terror of this night, | and the JC 2.01.199
UNACHING 1 FR 0.0001 REL FR 1 V 0 P
show them th' unaching scars which i should hide COR 2.02.148
UNACQUAINTED 3 FR 0.0003 REL FR 3 V 0 P
him, | and kiss the lips of unacquainted change, JN 3.04.166
remote, | and follow unacquainted colors here? 5.02. 32
as new into the world, strange, unacquainted. TRO 3.03. 12
UNACTED 1 FR 0.0001 REL FR 1 V 0 P
the fault unknown is as a thought unacted. LUC 527
UNACTIVE 1 FR 0.0001 REL FR 1 V 0 P
i' th' midst a' th' body, idle and unactive, COR 1.01. 99
UNADVIS'D 4 FR 0.0004 REL FR 4 V 0 P
i have unadvis'd | deliver'd you a paper that i TGV 4.04.122
lest unadvis'd you stain your swords with blood. JN 2.01. 45
why, boy, although our mother, unadvis'd, | gave TIT 2.01. 38
it is too rash, too unadvis'd, too sudden, | too ROM 2.02.118
UNADVISED 3 FR 0.0003 REL FR 3 V 0 P
thou unadvised scold, i can produce | a will JN 2.01.191
this harness'd masque and unadvised revel, 5.02.132
and friend to friend gives unadvised wounds, LUC 1488
UNADVISEDLY 1 FR 0.0001 REL FR 1 V 0 P
men shall deal unadvisedly sometimes, | which R3 4.04.292
UNAGREEABLE 1 FR 0.0001 REL FR 1 V 0 P
the time is unagreeable to this business. TIM 2.02. 40
UNANEL'D 1 FR 0.0001 REL FR 1 V 0 P
of my sin, | unhous'led, disappointed, unanel'd, HAM 1.05. 77
UNANSWER'D 1 FR 0.0001 REL FR 1 V 0 P
but your petition | is yet unanswer'd. WT 5.01.229
UNAPPEAS'D 1 FR 0.0001 REL FR 1 V 0 P
bones, | that so the shadows be not unappeas'd, TIT 1.01.100
UNAPPROVED 1 FR 0.0001 REL FR 1 V 0 P
lies, | what unapproved witness dost thou bear! LC 53
UNAPT 6 FR 0.0006 REL FR 6 V 0 P
unapt to toil and trouble in the world, | but SHR 5.02.166
temperate, | unapt to stir at these indignities, 1H4 1.03. 2
i am a soldier and unapt to weep | or to exclaim 1H6 5.03.133
the morning, are unapt | to give or to forgive; COR 5.01. 52
disdain, | with leaden appetite, unapt to toy; VEN 34
unapt for tender smell, or speedy flight, | make LUC 695
UNAPTNESS 1 FR 0.0001 REL FR 1 V 0 P
and that unaptness made your minister | thus to TIM 2.02.131
UNARM 7 FR 0.0008 REL FR 7 V 0 P
call here my varlet, i'll unarm again. TRO 1.01. 1
i must woo you | to help unarm our hector. 3.01.150
unarm, unarm, and do not fight to–day. 5.03. 3
unarm, unarm, and do not fight to–day. 5.03. 3
unarm, sweet hector. 5.03. 25
unarm thee, go, and doubt thou not, brave boy, 5.03. 35
unarm, eros, the long day's task is done, | and ANT 4.14. 35
UNARM'D 8 FR 0.0009 REL FR 7 V 1 P
/to french and welsh he leaves his back unarm'd, 2H4 1.03. 79
unarm'd, and unresolv'd to beat them back. R3 4.04.436
courtiers as free, as debonair, unarm'd, | as TRO 1.03.235
lords after the combat | to see us here unarm'd. 3.03.237
valorous hector to come unarm'd to my tent, and 3.03.275 P
doth long to see unarm'd the valiant hector. 4.05.153
i am unarm'd, forgo this vantage, greek. 5.08. 9
have in them | a sense to know a man unarm'd, TNK 3.02. 16
UNARMED 1 FR 0.0001 REL FR 1 V 0 P
to melt | and drop upon our bare unarmed heads. 2H4 2.04.365
UNARMS 1 FR 0.0001 REL FR 0 V 1 P
at your own house, there he unarms him. TRO 1.02.274 P
UNASK'D 1 FR 0.0001 REL FR 1 V 0 P
begg'd for that which thou unask'd shalt have. VEN 102
UNASSAILABLE 1 FR 0.0001 REL FR 1 V 0 P
but one | that unassailable holds on his rank, JC 3.01. 69
UNASSAIL'D 1 FR 0.0001 REL FR 1 V 0 P
it grieves my soul to leave thee unassail'd. 2H6 5.02. 18
UNATTAINTED 1 FR 0.0001 REL FR 1 V 0 P
and with unattainted eye | compare her face with ROM 1.02. 85
UNATTEMPTED 1 FR 0.0001 REL FR 1 V 0 P
my palm, | but for my hand, as unattempted yet, JN 2.01.591
UNATTENDED 1 FR 0.0001 REL FR 1 V 0 P
your constancy | hath left you unattended. MAC 2.02. 66
UNAUSPICIOUS *(also inauspicious)*
UNAUSPICIOUS 1 FR 0.0001 REL FR 1 V 0 P
to whose ingrate and unauspicious altars | my TN 5.01.113
UNAUTHORIZ'D 1 FR 0.0001 REL FR 1 V 0 P
an unauthoriz'd kiss! OTH 4.01. 2
UNAVOIDED 4 FR 0.0004 REL FR 4 V 0 P
must suffer, | and unavoided is the danger now, R2 2.01.268
of death, | a terrible and unavoided danger; 1H6 4.05. 8
the world, | whose unavoided eye is murtherous. R3 4.01. 55
all unavoided is the doom of destiny. 4.04.218
UNAWARE 2 FR 0.0002 REL FR 2 V 0 P
whereat amaz'd as one that unaware | hath VEN 823
sheath'd unaware the tusk in his soft groin. 1116
UNAWARES *(also unwares)*
/UNAWARES 1 FR 0.0001 REL FR 1 V 0 P
like vassalage at /unawares encount'ring | the TRO 3.02. 38
UNAWARES 4 FR 0.0004 REL FR 4 V 0 P
hath wrought this hellish mischief unawares, 1H6 3.02. 39
at unawares may beat down edward's guard, | and
3H6 4.02. 23
his guard | or by his foe surpris'd at unawares; 4.04. 9
and take the great–grown traitor unawares. 4.08. 63
UNBACK'D 2 FR 0.0002 REL FR 2 V 0 P
at which, like unback'd colts, they prick'd TMP 4.01.176
when lo the unback'd breeder, full of fear, VEN 320
UNBAK'D 1 FR 0.0001 REL FR 0 V 1 P
have made all the unbak'd and doughy youth of a AWW 4.05. 3 P
UNBANDED 1 FR 0.0001 REL FR 0 V 1 P
hose should be ungarter'd, your bonnet unbanded,
AYL 3.02.379 P
UNBAR 1 FR 0.0001 REL FR 1 V 0 P
death, who is the key | t' unbar these locks. CYM 5.04. 8
UNBARB'D 1 FR 0.0001 REL FR 1 V 0 P
must i go show them my unbarb'd sconce? COR 3.02. 99
UNBASHFUL 1 FR 0.0001 REL FR 1 V 0 P
nor did not with unbashful forehead woo | the AYL 2.03. 50
UNBATED 3 FR 0.0003 REL FR 3 V 0 P
his tedious measures with the unbated fire MV 2.06. 11
you may choose | a sword unbated, and in a /pass HAM 4.07.138
is in /thy hand, | unbated and envenom'd. 5.02.317
UNBATTERED 1 FR 0.0001 REL FR 1 V 0 P
or else my sword with an unbattered edge | i MAC 5.07. 19
UNBECOMING 1 FR 0.0001 REL FR 1 V 0 P
in our great feast, | and all–thing unbecoming. MAC 3.01. 13
UNBEFITTING 1 FR 0.0001 REL FR 1 V 0 P
as love is full of unbefitting strains, | all LLL 5.02.760
UNBEGOT 1 FR 0.0001 REL FR 1 V 0 P
strike | your children yet unborn and unbegot, R2 3.03. 88
UNBEGOTTEN 1 FR 0.0001 REL FR 1 V 0 P
a purity, | to the yet unbegotten sin of times; JN 4.03. 54
UNBELIEVED 1 FR 0.0001 REL FR 1 V 0 P
woe, | as i, thus wrong'd, hence unbelieved go! MM 5.01.119
UNBEND 1 FR 0.0001 REL FR 1 V 0 P
you do unbend your noble strength, to think | so MAC 2.02. 42
UNBENT 2 FR 0.0002 REL FR 2 V 0 P
to be unbent when thou hast ta'en thy stand, CYM 3.04.108
a brow unbent, that seem'd to welcome woe, LUC 1509
UNBEWAIL'D 1 FR 0.0001 REL FR 1 V 0 P
things to destiny | hold unbewail'd their way. ANT 3.06. 85
UNBID 1 FR 0.0001 REL FR 1 V 0 P
o unbid spite, is sportful edward come? 3H6 5.01. 18
UNBIDDEN 1 FR 0.0001 REL FR 1 V 0 P
unbidden guests | are often welcomest when they 1H6 2.02. 55
UNBIND 2 FR 0.0002 REL FR 2 V 0 P
unbind my hands, i'll pull them off myself, SHR 2.01. 4
unbind my sons, reverse the doom of death, | and TIT 3.01. 24
UNBITTED 1 FR 0.0001 REL FR 0 V 1 P
motions, our carnal stings, /our unbitted lusts; OTH 1.03.331 P
UNBLESS 1 FR 0.0001 REL FR 1 V 0 P
dost beguile the world, unbless some mother. SON 3. 4
UNBLESS'D 1 FR 0.0001 REL FR 0 V 1 P
every inordinate cup is unbless'd, and the OTH 2.03.307 P
UNBLEST 2 FR 0.0002 REL FR 2 V 0 P
dear lies dead, | and your unblest fate hies. OTH 5.01. 34
or let me know | why mine own barber is unblest, TNK 1.02. 53
UNBLOODIED 1 FR 0.0001 REL FR 1 V 0 P
although the kite soar with unbloodied beak? 2H6 3.02.193
/UNBLOWN 1 FR 0.0001 REL FR 1 V 0 P
my /unblown flow'rs, new–appearing sweets! R3 4.04. 10
UNBODIED 1 FR 0.0001 REL FR 1 V 0 P
aim | and that unbodied figure of the thought TRO 1.03. 16
UNBOLT 2 FR 0.0002 REL FR 2 V 0 P
mine uncle down, | he shall unbolt the gates. TRO 4.02. 3
i will unbolt to you. TIM 1.01. 51
UNBOLTED 1 FR 0.0001 REL FR 0 V 1 P
i will tread this unbolted villain into mortar, LR 2.02. 66 P
/UNBONNETED 1 FR 0.0001 REL FR 1 V 0 P
/keep /their /fur /dry, /unbonneted /he /runs, LR 3.01. 14
UNBONNETED 1 FR 0.0001 REL FR 1 V 0 P
and my demerits | may speak, unbonneted, to as OTH 1.02. 23
UNBOOKISH 1 FR 0.0001 REL FR 1 V 0 P
and his unbookish jealousy must /conster | poor OTH 4.01.101
UNBORN 10 FR 0.0011 REL FR 10 V 0 P
never so much as in a thought unborn | did i AYL 1.03. 51
yet again methinks | some unborn sorrow, ripe in R2 2.02. 10
strike | your children yet unborn and unbegot, 3.03. 88
the children yet unborn | shall feel this day as 4.01.322
of broached mischief to the unborn times? 1H4 5.01. 21
and some are yet ungotten and unborn | that H5 1.02.287
all cause unborn, could never be the native | of COR 3.01.129
in /states unborn and accents yet unknown! JC 3.01.113
the unborn event | i do commend to your content;
PER 4.ch. 45
and lovers yet unborn shall bless my ashes. TNK 3.06.283
UNBOSOM 1 FR 0.0001 REL FR 1 V 0 P
their several counsels they unbosom shall | to LLL 5.02.141
UNBOUND 3 FR 0.0003 REL FR 2 V 1 P
now am i dromio, and his man, unbound. ERR 5.01.291
and unbound the rest, and then come in the other
1H4 2.04.182 P
this precious book of love, this unbound lover, ROM 1.03. 87
UNBOUNDED 2 FR 0.0002 REL FR 2 V 0 P
he was a man | of an unbounded stomach, ever H8 4.02. 34
a most unbounded tyrant, whose successes | makes
TNK 1.02. 63
UNBOW'D 1 FR 0.0001 REL FR 1 V 0 P
crown, and bend | the dukedom yet unbow'd (alas,
TMP 1.02.115
UNBOWED 1 FR 0.0001 REL FR 1 V 0 P
eye, | and passeth by with stiff unbowed knee, 2H6 3.01. 16
UNBRAC'D 1 FR 0.0001 REL FR 1 V 0 P
lord hamlet, with his doublet all unbrac'd, | no HAM 2.01. 75
UNBRACED 2 FR 0.0002 REL FR 2 V 0 P
and, thus unbraced, casca, as you see, | have JC 1.03. 48
to walk unbraced and suck up the humors | of the 2.01.262
UNBRAIDED 1 FR 0.0001 REL FR 0 V 1 P
has he any unbraided wares? WT 4.04.203 P
UNBREATHED 1 FR 0.0001 REL FR 1 V 0 P
and now have toiled their unbreathed memories MND 5.01. 74
UNBRED 1 FR 0.0001 REL FR 1 V 0 P
for fear of which, hear this, thou age unbred: SON 104.13
UNBREECH'D 1 FR 0.0001 REL FR 1 V 0 P
and saw myself unbreech'd | in my green velvet WT 1.02.155
UNBRIDLED 2 FR 0.0002 REL FR 2 V 0 P
this is not well, rash and unbridled boy, | to AWW 3.02. 28
my thoughts were like unbridled children grown TRO 3.02.122
/UNBROKE 1 FR 0.0001 REL FR 1 V 0 P
/keep /all /vows /unbroke /are /made /to /thee! R2 4.01.215
UNBROKEN 1 FR 0.0001 REL FR 1 V 0 P
thy worthy, manly heart, be yet unbroken, | give TNK 5.04. 88
UNBRUIS'D 3 FR 0.0003 REL FR 2 V 1 P
my kinsman, live unbruis'd and love my cousin. ADO 5.04.111 P
with unhack'd swords, and helmets all unbruis'd, JN 2.01.254
to go rove with one | that's yet unbruis'd. COR 4.01. 47
/UNBRUISED 1 FR 0.0001 REL FR 1 V 0 P
/fresh /and /yet /unbruised /greeks /do /pitch TRO pr 14
UNBRUISED 1 FR 0.0001 REL FR 1 V 0 P
but where unbruised youth with unstuff'd brain ROM 2.03. 37
UNBUCKLE 2 FR 0.0002 REL FR 0 V 2 P
unbuckle, unbuckle. WT 4.04.647 P
unbuckle, unbuckle. 4.04.647 P
UNBUCKLES 1 FR 0.0001 REL FR 1 V 0 P
he that unbuckles this, till we do please | to ANT 4.04. 12
UNBUCKLING 1 FR 0.0001 REL FR 1 V 0 P
unbuckling helms, fisting each other's throat, COR 4.05.125
UNBUILD 1 FR 0.0001 REL FR 1 V 0 P
to unbuild the city, and to lay all flat. COR 3.01.197
UNBURDEN *(see unburthen, etc.)*
UNBURIED 3 FR 0.0003 REL FR 3 V 0 P
as the dead carcasses of unburied men | that do COR 3.03.122
why suffer'st thou thy sons, unburied yet, | to TIT 1.01. 87
"traitor," | i am a villain fit to lie unburied. TNK 3.06.171
UNBURNT 1 FR 0.0001 REL FR 1 V 0 P
to leave unburnt | and still to nose th' offense COR 5.01. 27
UNBURTHEN 1 FR 0.0001 REL FR 1 V 0 P
to unburthen all my plots and purposes | how to MV 1.01.133
UNBURTHEN'D 1 FR 0.0001 REL FR 1 V 0 P
while we | unburthen'd crawl toward death. LR 1.01. 41
UNBURTHENS 1 FR 0.0001 REL FR 1 V 0 P
sharp buckingham unburthens with his tongue 2H6 3.01.156
UNBUTTON 1 FR 0.0001 REL FR 0 V 1 P
come, unbutton here. LR 3.04.109 P
UNBUTTON'D 1 FR 0.0001 REL FR 0 V 1 P
your bonnet unbanded, your sleeve unbutton'd, AYL 3.02.379 P
UNBUTTONING 1 FR 0.0001 REL FR 0 V 1 P
of old sack, and unbuttoning thee after supper, 1H4 1.02. 3 P
UNCANDIED 1 FR 0.0001 REL FR 1 V 0 P

set down in ice, which, by hot grief uncandied, TNK 1.01.107
UNCAPABLE *(also incapable)*
UNCAPABLE 2 FR 0.0002 REL FR 1 V 1 P
uncapable of pity, void and empty | from any MV 4.01. 5
why, by making him uncapable of othello's place: OTH 4.02.229 P
UNCAPE 1 FR 0.0001 REL FR 0 V 1 P
so, now uncape. WIV 3.03.165 P
UNCASE 1 FR 0.0001 REL FR 1 V 0 P
tranio, at once | uncase thee; SHR 1.01.207
UNCASING 1 FR 0.0001 REL FR 0 V 1 P
you not see pompey is uncasing for the combat? LLL 5.02.701 P
UNCAUGHT 2 FR 0.0002 REL FR 2 V 0 P
not in this land shall he remain uncaught; LR 2.01. 57
smiling from | the world's great snare uncaught? ANT 4.08. 18
UNCERTAIN *(also incertain, etc.)*
UNCERTAIN 11 FR 0.0012 REL FR 9 V 2 P
the uncertain glory of an april day, | which now TGV 1.03. 85
uncertain life, and sure death. AWW 2.03. 18 P
be not uncertain, | for, by the honor of my WT 1.02.441
take horse, | uncertain of the issue any way. 1H4 1.01. 61
the friends you have nam'd uncertain, the time 2.03. 12 P
and then marry her — | uncertain way of gain! R3 4.02. 63
great son, | the end of war's uncertain; COR 5.03.141
the people will remain uncertain whilst | 'twixt 5.06. 16
doth sustain | in life's uncertain voyage, i TIM 5.01.202
uncertain favor! CYM 3.03. 64
ill, | th' uncertain sickly appetite to please. SON 147. 4
UNCERTAINLY 1 FR 0.0001 REL FR 1 V 0 P
her woe, | her certain sorrow writ uncertainly. LUC 1311
UNCERTAINTY 3 FR 0.0003 REL FR 3 V 0 P
until i know this sure uncertainty, | i'll ERR 2.02.185
arms, | which now we hold at much uncertainty. 1H4 1.03.299
and here remain with your uncertainty! COR 3.03.124
UNCHAIN 1 FR 0.0001 REL FR 1 V 0 P
unchain your spirits now with spelling charms, 1H6 5.03. 31
UNCHANGING 1 FR 0.0001 REL FR 1 V 0 P
but that thy face is vizard-like, unchanging, 3H6 1.04.116
UNCHARGE 1 FR 0.0001 REL FR 1 V 0 P
but even his mother shall uncharge the practice, HAM 4.07. 67
UNCHARGED 1 FR 0.0001 REL FR 1 V 0 P
/descend, and open your uncharged ports. TIM 5.04. 55
UNCHARITABLY *(also incharitable)*
UNCHARITABLY 1 FR 0.0001 REL FR 1 V 0 P
uncharitably with me have you dealt, | and R3 1.03.274
UNCHARM'D 1 FR 0.0001 REL FR 1 V 0 P
love's weak childish bow she lives uncharm'd. ROM 1.01.211
UNCHARY 1 FR 0.0001 REL FR 1 V 0 P
stone, | and laid mine honor too unchary on't. TN 3.04.202
UNCHASTE 4 FR 0.0004 REL FR 3 V 1 P
a bloody fire, | kindled with unchaste desire, WIV 5.05. 96
thinks himself made in the unchaste composition. AWW 4.03. 18 P
no unchaste action, or dishonored step, | that LR 1.01.228
away he posts | with unchaste purpose, and with CYM 5.05.284
UNCHECK'D 2 FR 0.0002 REL FR 1 V 1 P
yet it lives there uncheck'd that antonio hath a MV 3.01. 2 P
in their rough power | has uncheck'd theft. TIM 4.03.444
UNCHEERFUL 1 FR 0.0001 REL FR 1 V 0 P
at time, at tarquin, and uncheerful night, | in LUC 1024
UNCHILDED 1 FR 0.0001 REL FR 1 V 0 P
city he | hath widowed and unchilded many a one,
COR 5.06.151
UNCIVIL *(also incivil)*
UNCIVIL 8 FR 0.0009 REL FR 6 V 2 P
much to do | to keep them from uncivil outrages. TGV 5.04. 17
let go that rude uncivil touch, | thou friend of 5.04. 60
you would not give means for this uncivil rule. TN 2.03.123 P
this is as uncivil as strange. 3.04.253 P
sway | in this uncivil and unjust extent 4.01. 53
you uncivil lady, | to whose ingrate and 5.01.112
should so with civil and uncivil arms | be R2 3.03.102
th' uncivil kerns of ireland are in arms, | and 2H6 3.01.310
UNCLAIM'D 1 FR 0.0001 REL FR 1 V 0 P
like a wild goose flies, | unclaim'd of any man. AYL 2.07. 87
UNCLASP 6 FR 0.0006 REL FR 6 V 0 P
and in her bosom i'll unclasp my heart, | and ADO 1.01.323
and now i will unclasp a secret book, | and to 1H4 1.03.188
and wide unclasp the tables of their thoughts TRO 4.05. 60
unclasp, unclasp: PER 2.03.106
unclasp, unclasp: 2.03.106
unclasp thy mystery. TNK 5.01.172
UNCLASP'D 2 FR 0.0002 REL FR 2 V 0 P
i have unclasp'd | to thee the book even of my TN 1.04. 13
to my kingly guest | unclasp'd my practice, quit WT 3.02.167
UNCLE 186 FR 0.0210 REL FR 158 V 28 P
my brother and thy uncle, call'd antonio — | i TMP 1.02. 66
thy false uncle — | dost thou attend me? 1.02. 77
my uncle can tell you good jests of him. WIV 3.04. 38 P
pray you, uncle, tell mistress anne the jest how 3.04. 39 P
father stole two geese out of a pen, good uncle. 3.04. 41 P
your father and my uncle hath made motions. 3.04. 63 P
duke menaphon, your most renowned uncle. ERR 5.01.369
he hath an uncle here in messina will be very ADO 1.01. 18 P
with a good leg and a good foot, uncle, and 2.01. 14 P
no, uncle, i'll none. 2.01. 63 P
i have a good eye, uncle, i can see a church by 2.01. 82 P
i cry you mercy, uncle. by your grace's pardon. 2.01.339 P
just cause, being her uncle and her guardian. 2.03.166 P
help, uncle! 4.01.113
uncle! 4.01.114
you must come to your uncle, yonder's old coil 5.02. 95 P
why then your uncle and the prince and claudio 5.04. 75
when jacob graz'd his uncle laban's sheep — MV 1.03. 71
less belov'd of her uncle than his own daughter, AYL 1.01.111 P
if my uncle, thy banish'd father, had banish'd 1.02. 9 P
thy banish'd father, had banish'd thy uncle, the 1.02. 10 P
and here detain'd by her usurping uncle | to 1.02.274
me, uncle? 1.03. 42
(as i do trust i am not), then, dear uncle, 1.03. 50
to seek my uncle in the forest of arden. 1.03.107
an old religious uncle of mine taught me to 3.02.344 P
of many desperate studies by his uncle, | whom 5.04. 32
i am cressid's uncle, | that dare leave two AWW 2.01. 97
rebuke the usurpation | of thy unnatural uncle, JN 2.01. 10
sh' adulterates hourly with thine uncle john, 3.01. 56
knee i beg, go not to arms | against mine uncle. 3.01.309
uncle, i needs must pray that thou mayst lose; 3.01.332
and thy uncle will | as dear be to thee as thy 3.03. 3
i doubt | my uncle practices more harm to me. 4.01. 20
for all the treasure that thine uncle owes. 4.01.122
your uncle must not know but you are dead. 4.01.127
good uncle, let this end where it begun; R2 1.01.158
uncle, even in the glasses of thine eyes | i see 1.03.208
why, uncle, thou hast many years to live. 1.03.225
and, uncle, bid him so. 1.03.247
how fares our noble uncle lancaster? 2.01. 71
whereof our uncle gaunt did stand possess'd. 2.01.162
why, uncle, what's the matter? 2.01.186
our uncle york lord governor of england; 2.01.220
uncle, for god's sake speak comfortable words. 2.02. 76
harry, how fares your uncle? 2.03. 23
my noble uncle! 2.03. 82
my gracious uncle — 2.03. 85
grace me no grace, nor uncle me no uncle. 2.03. 87
grace me no grace, nor uncle me no uncle. 2.03. 87
i am no traitor's uncle, and that word "grace" 2.03. 88
my gracious uncle, let me know my fault, | on 2.03.106
and, noble uncle, i beseech your grace | look on 2.03.115
he should have found his uncle gaunt a father 2.03.127
an offer, uncle, that we will accept, | but we 2.03.162
uncle, you say the queen is at your house, | for 3.01. 36
thanks, gentle uncle. 3.01. 42
i know my uncle york | hath power enough to 3.02. 89
scroop, where lies our uncle with his power? 3.02.192
your uncle york is join'd with bullingbrook, 3.02.200
mistake not, uncle, further than you should. 3.03. 15
i know it, uncle, and oppose not myself 3.03. 18
uncle, give me your hands; 3.03.202
what is the matter, uncle? 5.03. 46
good uncle, help to order several powers | to 5.03.140
uncle, farewell, and, cousin, adieu! 5.03.144
kind uncle york, the latest news we hear | is 5.06. 1
here comes your uncle. 1H4 1.03.130
'twas where the madcap duke his uncle kept — 1.03.244
his uncle york — where i first bow'd my knee 1.03.245
good uncle, tell your tale — i have done. 1.03.256
uncle, adieu! 1.03.301
is there not my father, my uncle, and myself? 2.03. 24 P
and uncle worcester — a plague upon it! 3.01. 5
your uncle worcester's horses came but to-day, 4.03. 21
my father and my uncle and myself | did give him 4.03. 54
rated mine uncle from the council-board, | in 4.03. 99
and in the morning early shall mine uncle 4.03.110
my uncle is return'd, | deliver up my lord of 5.02. 27
uncle, what news? 5.02. 29
send for him, good uncle. H5 1.02. 2
what treasure, uncle? 1.02.258
uncle of exeter, | enlarge the man committed 2.02. 39
my lord of westmerland, and uncle exeter, | we 2.02. 70
come, uncle exeter, | go you and enter harflew; 3.03. 51
use mercy to them all for us, dear uncle. 3.03. 54
lives he, good uncle? 4.06. 4
go you with me, uncle of exeter. 4.07.183
here, uncle exeter, fill this glove with crowns, 4.08. 57
what prisoners of good sort are taken, uncle? 4.08. 75
go, uncle exeter, | and brother clarence, and 5.02. 83
ay, noble uncle, thus ignobly us'd, | your 1H6 2.05. 35
therefore, good uncle, for my father's sake, 2.05. 51
but now thy uncle is removing hence, | as 2.05.104
o uncle, would some part of my young years 2.05.107
pray, uncle gloucester, mitigate this strife. 3.01. 88
fie, uncle beauford, i have heard you preach 3.01.127
o loving uncle, kind duke of gloucester, | how 3.01.142
and those occasions, uncle, were of force: 3.01.156
is this the lord talbot, uncle gloucester, 3.04. 13
letter | sent from our uncle duke of burgundy. 4.01. 49
what? doth my uncle burgundy revolt? 4.01. 64
marry, uncle, for i always thought | it was both 5.01. 11
marriage, uncle? 5.01. 21
and you, good uncle, banish all offense. 5.05. 96
uncle, how now? 2H6 1.01. 53
uncle of winchester, i pray read on. 1.01. 56
thanks, uncle winchester, | gloucester, york, 1.01. 68
or hath mine uncle beauford and myself, | with 1.01. 88
ay, uncle, we will keep it, if we can; 1.01.107
uncle, what shall we say to this in law? 1.03.203
good uncle, hide such malice; 2.01. 25
faith, holy uncle, would't were come to that! 2.01. 37
true, uncle. 2.01. 46
why, how now, uncle gloucester? 2.01. 48
ah, uncle humphrey, in thy face i see | the map 3.01.202
go call our uncle to our presence straight. 3.02. 15
proceed no straiter 'gainst our uncle gloucester 3.02. 20
where is our uncle? 3.02. 28
your loving uncle, twenty times his worth, 3.02.268
be great, | i doubt not, uncle, of our victory. 3H6 1.02. 72
the king mine uncle is to blame for it. R3 2.02. 13
for my good uncle gloucester | told me the king, 2.02. 20
and when my uncle told me so, he wept, | and 2.02. 23
think you my uncle did dissemble, grandam? 2.02. 31
my uncle rivers talk'd how i did grow | more 2.04. 11
"ay," quoth my uncle gloucester, | "small herbs 2.04. 12
my uncle grew so fast | that he could gnaw a 2.04. 27
no, uncle, but our crosses on the way | have 3.01. 4
say, uncle gloucester, if our brother come, 3.01. 61
what say you, uncle? 3.01. 80
i thank you, gentle uncle. 3.01.102
i pray you, uncle, give me this dagger. 3.01.110
of my kind uncle, that i know will give, | and 3.01.113
uncle, your grace knows how to bear with him. 3.01.127
uncle, my brother mocks both you and me: 3.01.129
to mitigate the scorn he gives his uncle, | he 3.01.133
marry, my uncle clarence' angry ghost. 3.01.144
indeed, and by their uncle cozen'd | of comfort, 4.04.223
tell her thou mad'st away her uncle clarence, 4.04.281
her uncle rivers, ay (and for her sake!), 4.04.282
or shall i say her uncle? 4.04.338
madam, your uncle pandarus. TRO 1.02. 38 P
good morrow, uncle pandarus. 1.02. 42 P
this morning, uncle. 1.02. 46 P
can helenus fight, uncle? 1.02.222 P
adieu, uncle. 1.02.277 P
to bring, uncle? 1.02.279 P
well, uncle, what folly i commit, i dedicate to 3.02.102 P
then, sweet my lord, i'll call mine uncle down, 4.02. 2
it is your uncle. 4.02. 20
go hang yourself, you naughty mocking uncle! 4.02. 25
good uncle, go and see. 4.02. 35
tell me, sweet uncle, what's the matter? 4.02. 81 P
good uncle, i beseech you, on my knees /i 4.02. 88 P
i will not, uncle. 4.02. 96
shall thy good uncle, and thy brother lucius, TIT 3.01.122
good uncle marcus, see how swift she comes. 4.01. 3
sweet aunt, | and, madam, if my uncle marcus go, 4.01. 27
and, uncle, so will i, and if i live. 4.01.112
case, | to see thy noble uncle thus distract? 4.03. 26
matter of brawl betwixt my uncle and one of the 4.03. 94 P
pledges | unto my father and my uncle marcus, 5.01.164
uncle marcus, since 'tis my father's mind | that 5.03. 1
good uncle, take you in this barbarous moor, 5.03. 4
sirs, help our uncle to convey him in. 5.03. 15
but, uncle, draw you near | to shed obsequious 5.03.151
my noble uncle, do you know the cause? ROM 1.01.143
mine uncle capulet, his wife, and daughters; 1.02. 68 P
uncle, this is a montague, our foe; 1.05. 61
why, uncle, 'tis a shame. 1.05. 82
his uncle siward, and the good macduff. MAC 5.02. 2
you, worthy uncle, | shall with my cousin, your 5.06. 2
writ | to norway, uncle of young fortinbras — HAM 1.02. 28
have mourn'd longer — married with my uncle, 1.02.151
o my prophetic soul! | my uncle? 1.05. 41
upon my secure hour thy uncle stole, | with 1.05. 61
so, uncle, there you are. 1.05.110
makes vow before his uncle never more | to give 2.02. 70
very strange, for my uncle is king of denmark, 2.02.363 P
the murther of my father | before mine uncle. 2.02.596
the very comment of thy soul | observe my uncle. 3.02. 80
i scarce did know you, uncle; OTH 5.02.201
uncle, i must come forth. 5.02.254
cassibelan, thine uncle | (famous in caesar's CYM 3.01. 5
our uncle creon. TNK 1.02. 62
UNCLEAN 5 FR 0.0005 REL FR 2 V 3 P
and, fairy-like, to pinch the unclean knight; WIV 4.04. 58
slut were to put good meat into an unclean dish. AYL 3.03. 36 P
for where an unclean mind carries virtuous AWW 1.01. 42 P
that has fall'n into the unclean fishpond of her 5.02. 20 P
where civil blood makes civil hands unclean. ROM pr 4
UNCLEANLINESS 1 FR 0.0001 REL FR 0 V 1 P
adultery, and all uncleanliness there. MM 2.01. 81 P
UNCLEANLY 5 FR 0.0005 REL FR 3 V 2 P
courtesy would be uncleanly if courtiers were AYL 3.02. 50 P
than tar, the very uncleanly flux of a cat. 3.02. 68 P
uncleanly scruples! JN 4.01. 7
th' uncleanly savors of a slaughter-house, | for 4.03.112
so pure | /but /some uncleanly apprehensions OTH 3.03.139
UNCLEANNESS 2 FR 0.0002 REL FR 2 V 0 P
give up your body to such sweet uncleanness | as MM 2.04. 54
with your uncleanness that which is divine; LUC 193
UNCLE-FATHER 1 FR 0.0001 REL FR 0 V 1 P
but my uncle-father and aunt-mother are deceiv'd
HAM 2.02.376 P
UNCLE'S 10 FR 0.0011 REL FR 6 V 4 P
cupid at the flight, and my uncle's fool, ADO 1.01. 40 P
and moreover i will go with thee to thy uncle's. 5.02.104 P
there is none of my uncle's marks upon you. AYL 3.02.369 P
my uncle's will in this respect is mine. JN 2.01.510
o me, my uncle's spirit is in these stones. 4.03. 9
as far as calice, to mine uncle's head?" R2 4.01. 13
this is his uncle's teaching; 1H4 1.01. 96
i could have given my uncle's grace a flout, R3 2.04. 24
your uncle's word and my firm faith. TRO 3.02.107 P
good night, but go not to my uncle's bed — HAM 3.04.159
UNCLES 9 FR 0.0010 REL FR 9 V 0 P
uncles of gloucester and of winchester, | the 1H6 3.01. 65
sir john and sir hugh mortimer, mine uncles, 3H6 1.02. 62
my uncles both are slain in rescuing me; 1.04. 2
thine uncles and myself | have in our armors 5.07. 16
king | had virtuous uncles to protect his grace. R3 2.03. 21
i want more uncles here to welcome me. 3.01. 6
those uncles which you want were dangerous; 3.01. 12
i fear no uncles dead. 3.01.146
or he that slew her brothers and her uncles? 4.04.339
UNCLEW 1 FR 0.0001 REL FR 1 V 0 P
as 'tis extoll'd, | it would unclew me quite. TIM 1.01.168
UNCLOG 1 FR 0.0001 REL FR 1 V 0 P
it would unclog my heart | of what lies heavy COR 4.02. 47
UNCOIN'D 1 FR 0.0001 REL FR 0 V 1 P
take a fellow of plain and uncoin'd constancy, H5 5.02.153 P
UNCOLTED 1 FR 0.0001 REL FR 0 V 1 P
liest, thou art not colted, thou art uncolted. 1H4 2.02. 39 P
UNCOMELINESS 1 FR 0.0001 REL FR 0 V 1 P
and well-behav'd reproof to all uncomeliness, WIV 2.01. 59 P
UNCOMFORTABLE 1 FR 0.0001 REL FR 1 V 0 P
uncomfortable time, why cam'st thou now | to ROM 4.05. 60
UNCOMPASSIONATE 1 FR 0.0001 REL FR 1 V 0 P
could penetrate her uncompassionate sire; TGV 3.01.233
UNCOMPREHENSIVE 1 FR 0.0001 REL FR 1 V 0 P
finds bottom in th' uncomprehensive depth, TRO 3.03.198
UNCONFINABLE 1 FR 0.0001 REL FR 0 V 1 P
why, thou unconfinable baseness, it is as much WIV 2.02. 21 P
UNCONFIRM'D 1 FR 0.0001 REL FR 0 V 1 P
that shows thou art unconfirm'd. ADO 3.03.117 P
UNCONFIRMED 1 FR 0.0001 REL FR 0 V 1 P
unlettered, or ratherest unconfirmed fashion, to LLL 4.02. 18 P
UNCONQUER'D 2 FR 0.0002 REL FR 1 V 1 P
man, | of an invincible unconquer'd spirit! 1H6 4.02. 32
because the unconquer'd soul of cade is fled. 2H6 4.10. 64 P
UNCONQUERED 1 FR 0.0001 REL FR 1 V 0 P
blue, | a pair of maiden worlds unconquered, LUC 408
UNCONSIDER'D 2 FR 0.0002 REL FR 1 V 1 P
likewise a snapper-up of unconsider'd trifles. WT 4.03. 26 P
your pity, | but th' unconsider'd soldier? TNK 1.02. 31
UNCONSIDERED 1 FR 0.0001 REL FR 1 V 0 P
love | not unconsidered leave your honor nor H8 1.02. 15
UNCONSTANT *(also inconstant)*
UNCONSTANT 4 FR 0.0004 REL FR 3 V 1 P
unconstant womankind! SHR 4.02. 14
make such unconstant children of ourselves, | as JN 3.01.243
for i will henceforth be no more unconstant. 3H6 5.01.102
such unconstant starts are we like to have from LR 1.01.300 P
UNCONSTRAIN'D 1 FR 0.0001 REL FR 1 V 0 P
suppose, my lords, he did it unconstrain'd, 3H6 1.01.143
UNCONSTRAINED 2 FR 0.0002 REL FR 2 V 0 P
will you with free and unconstrained soul | give ADO 4.01. 24
playing patient sports in unconstrained gyves? LC 242

UNCONTEMN'D 1 FR 0.0001 REL FR 1 V 0 P
of the peers | have uncontemn'd gone by him, or H8 3.02. 10
UNCONTROLL'D 1 FR 0.0001 REL FR 1 V 0 P
his golden uncontroll'd enfranchisement, | more R2 1.03. 90
UNCONTROLLED 2 FR 0.0002 REL FR 2 V 0 P
his batt'red shield, his uncontrolled crest, VEN 104
quoth he, "my uncontrolled tide | turns not, but LUC 645
UNCORRECTED 1 FR 0.0001 REL FR 1 V 0 P
wanting the scythe withal, uncorrected, rank, H5 5.02. 50
UNCOUNTED 1 FR 0.0001 REL FR 1 V 0 P
that the blunt monster with uncounted heads, 2H4 in 18
UNCOUPLE 3 FR 0.0003 REL FR 3 V 0 P
uncouple in the western valley, let them go. MND 4.01.107
uncouple here and let us make a bay, | and wake TIT 2.02. 3
by me, | uncouple at the timorous flying hare, VEN 674
UNCOURTEOUS 1 FR 0.0001 REL FR 1 V 0 P
upon some stubborn and uncourteous parts | we TN 5.01.361
UNCOUTH 3 FR 0.0003 REL FR 2 V 1 P
if this uncouth forest yield any thing savage, i AYL 2.06. 6 P
i am surprised with an uncouth fear, | a TIT 2.03.211
"what uncouth ill event | hath thee befall'n, LUC 1598
UNCOVER 1 FR 0.0001 REL FR 0 V 1 P
uncover, dogs, and lap! TIM 3.06. 85 P
UNCOVER'D 3 FR 0.0003 REL FR 1 V 2 P
then, with public accusation, uncover'd slander, ADO 4.01.305 P
pole | than stand uncover'd to the vulgar groom. 2H6 4.01.128
to answer with thy uncover'd body this extremity LR 3.04.102 P
UNCOVERED 1 FR 0.0001 REL FR 1 V 0 P
is, | /in thy best robes, uncovered on the bier, ROM 4.01.110
UNCROPPED 1 FR 0.0001 REL FR 1 V 0 P
if thou beest yet a fresh uncropped flower, AWW 5.03.327
UNCROSS'D 1 FR 0.0001 REL FR 1 V 0 P
makes him fine, | yet keeps his book uncross'd. CYM 3.03. 26
UNCROWN 2 FR 0.0002 REL FR 2 V 0 P
and therefore i'll uncrown him ere't be long. 3H6 3.03.232
and therefore i'll uncrown him ere't be long." 4.01.111
UNCTION 2 FR 0.0002 REL FR 2 V 0 P
lay not that flattering unction to your soul, HAM 3.04.145
i bought an unction of a mountebank, | so mortal 4.07.141
UNCTIOUS 1 FR 0.0001 REL FR 1 V 0 P
with liquorish draughts | and morsels unctious, TIM 4.03.195
UNCUCKOLDED 1 FR 0.0001 REL FR 0 V 1 P
sorrow to behold a foul knave uncuckolded; ANT 1.02. 73 P
UNCURABLE *(also incurable)*
UNCURABLE 2 FR 0.0002 REL FR 2 V 0 P
betime, | before the wound do grow uncurable; 2H6 3.01.286
uncurable discomfit | reigns in the hearts of 5.02. 86
UNCURBABLE 1 FR 0.0001 REL FR 1 V 0 P
so much uncurbable her garboils, caesar, | made ANT 2.02. 67
UNCURBED 1 FR 0.0001 REL FR 1 V 0 P
therefore with frank and with uncurbed plainness H5 1.02.244
UNCURLS 1 FR 0.0001 REL FR 1 V 0 P
my fleece of woolly hair that now uncurls, TIT 2.03. 34
UNCURRENT 3 FR 0.0003 REL FR 2 V 1 P
are shuffled off with such uncurrent pay; TN 3.03. 16
with what encounter so uncurrent i | have WT 3.02. 49
god your voice, like a piece of uncurrent gold, HAM 2.02.428 P
UNCURSE 1 FR 0.0001 REL FR 1 V 0 P
again uncurse their souls, their peace is made R2 3.02.137
UNDAUNTED 4 FR 0.0004 REL FR 4 V 0 P
his soldiers, spying his undaunted spirit, | "a 1H6 1.01.127
undaunted spirit in a dying breast! 3.02. 99
her valiant courage and undaunted spirit | (more 5.05. 70
for thy undaunted mettle should compose MAC 1.07. 73
UNDEAF 1 FR 0.0001 REL FR 1 V 0 P
my death's sad tale may yet undeaf his ear. R2 2.01. 16
/UNDECK 1 FR 0.0001 REL FR 1 V 0 P
/t' /undeck /the /pompous /body /of /a /king; R2 4.01.250
UNDEEDED 1 FR 0.0001 REL FR 1 V 0 P
an unbattered edge | i sheathe again undeeded. MAC 5.07. 20
/UNDER 4 FR 0.0004 REL FR 4 V 0 P
/you /that /here /are /under /our /arrest, R2 4.01.158
/that /every /day /under /his /household /roof 4.01.282
/gasping /for /life /under /great /bullingbrook, 2H4 1.01.208
/have /since /miscarried /under /bullingbrook. 4.01.127
UNDER 291 FR 0.0329 REL FR 199 V 92 P
under my burthen groan'd, which rais'd in me TMP 1.02.156
the mariners all under hatches stowed, | who, 1.02.230
i saw him beat the surges under him, | and ride 2.01.115
my best way is to creep under his gaberdine; 2.02. 38 P
i hid me under the dead moon–calf's gaberdine 2.02.111 P
now is the jerkin under the line. 4.01.236 P
under the blossom that hangs on the bough. 5.01. 94
find the mariners asleep | under the hatches. 5.01. 99
and (how we know not) all clapp'd under hatches, 5.01.231
it stands under thee indeed. TGV 2.05. 31 P
bear it | under a cloak that is of any length. 3.01.130
under the color of commending him, | i have 4.02. 3
gentleman–like dogs, under the duke's table. 4.04. 18 P
a great charge to come under one body's hand. WIV 1.04. 99 P
be a giantess, and lie under mount pelion. 2.01. 80 P
if he come under my hatches, i'll never to sea 2.01. 92 P
oaths, under the shelter of your honor! 2.02. 28 P
but stand under the adoption of abominable terms 2.02.295 P
cut and long–tail, under the degree of a squire. 3.04. 46 P
what's brought to pass under the profession of 4.02.175 P
i spy a great peard under his muffler. 4.02.194 P
as many diseases under her roof as come to — MM 1.02. 46 P
if i could speak so wisely under an arrest, i 1.02.131 P
else would stand under grievous imposition, as 1.02.188 P
under whose heavy sense your brother's life 1.04. 65
under your good correction, i have seen | when, 2.02. 10
under your sentence? 2.04. 37
that is, were i under the terms of death, | th' 2.04.100
and an express command, under penalty, to 4.02.166 P
herself (almost at fainting under | the pleasing ERR 1.01. 45
there's nothing situate under heaven's eye | but 2.01. 16
horse to hire," let them signify under my sign, ADO 1.01.267 P
as thou say'st thou art, born under saturn) 1.03. 11 P
or under your arm, like a lieutenant's scarf? 2.01.190 P
it may be i go under that title because i am 2.01.205 P
was a star danc'd, and under that was i born. 2.01.335 P
stand thee close then under this penthouse, for 3.03.103 P
not guiltless here | under some biting error. 4.01.170
to those that wring under the load of sorrow, 5.01. 28
as under privilege of age to brag | what i have 5.01. 60
i would bend under any heavy weight | that he'll 5.01.277
sir, which indeed is not under white and black, 5.01.304 P
no, i was not born under a rhyming planet, nor i 5.02. 40 P
thoughts, master, are mask'd under such colors. LLL 1.02. 93 P
their daughters profit very greatly under you. 4.02. 76 P
under pardon, sir, what are the contents? 4.02.100 P
him with thy bird–bolt under the left pap. 4.03. 24 P
under the cool shade of a sycamore | i thought 5.02. 89
not so, sir, under correction, sir, i hope it is 5.02.489
under correction, sir, we know whereuntil it 5.02.493 P
the ship is under sail, and here she comes amain 5.02.546
when the false troyan under sail was seen, | by MND 1.01.174
match'd in mouth like bells, | each under each. 4.01.124
became his surety and seal'd under for another. MV 1.02. 83 P
her foot, | unless she do it under this excuse, 2.04. 36
this is the penthouse under which lorenzo 2.06. 1
desire no more delight | than to be under sail, 2.06. 68
why, man, i saw bassanio under sail, | with him 2.08. 1
he came too late, the ship was under sail, | but 2.08. 6
why sweat they under burthens? 4.01. 95
his brother, gain nothing under him but growth, AYL 1.01. 14 P
under an oak whose antique root peeps out | upon 2.01. 31
the thrifty hire i sav'd under your father, 2.03. 39
under the greenwood tree | who loves to lie with 2.05. 1
the duke will drink under this tree. 2.05. 32 P
under the shade of melancholy boughs, | lose and 2.07.111
i found him under a tree, like a dropp'd acorn. 3.02.235 P
and under that habit play the knave with him. 3.02.296 P
will you dispatch us here under this tree, or 3.03. 65 P
breeding, be married under a bush like a beggar? 3.03. 84 P
object did present itself | under an old oak, 4.03.104
a bush, under which bush's shade | a lioness, 4.03.113
and under the presentation of that he shoots his 5.04.107 P
in his waning age | set foot under thy table. SHR 2.01.402
how her horse fell and she under her horse; 4.01. 74 P
wants, | he does it under name of perfect love; 4.03. 12
somebody in this city under my countenance. 5.01. 39 P
under whose practices he hath persecuted time AWW 1.01. 14 P
and keep thy friend | under thy own life's key. 1.01. 67
parolles, you were born under a charitable star. 1.01.190 P
under mars, i. 1.01.192 P
i especially think, under mars. 1.01.193 P
why under mars? 1.01.194 P
wars hath so kept you under that you must needs 1.01.195 P
under that you must needs be born under mars. 1.01.196 P
speak, and move under the influence of the most 2.01. 54 P
of lust, are not the things they go under. 3.05. 20 P
under my poor instructions yet must suffer 4.04. 27
would not have knaves thrive long under /her? 5.02. 32 P
both suffer under this complaint we bring, | and 5.03.163
he be, under the degree of my betters, and yet i TN 1.03.118 P
leg, it was form'd under the star of a galliard. 1.03.133 P
were we not born under taurus? 1.03.138 P
how he jets under his advanc'd plumes! 2.05. 31 P
that suffers under probation: 2.05.130 P
under your hard construction must i sit, | to 3.01.115
the men are not yet cold under water, nor the WT 3.03.105 P
far that i have eyes under my service which look 4.02. 35 P
as i am, litter'd under mercury, was likewise a 4.03. 25 P
fifty times) shall all come under the hangman; 4.04.775 P
shadowing their right under your wings of war. JN 2.01. 14
boy, | under whose warrant i impeach thy wrong, 2.01.116
but as we, under /god, are supreme head, | so 3.01.155
head, | so under him that great supremacy, 3.01.156
but in despair die under their black weight. 3.01.297
under whose conduct came those pow'rs of france 4.02.129
under the dolphin. 4.02.131
me, cousin, for i was amaz'd | under the tide; 4.02.138
me, | have stoop'd my neck under your injuries, R2 3.01. 19
king | shall falter under foul rebellion's arms. 3.02. 26
but when from under this terrestrial ball | he 3.02. 41
these differences shall all rest under gage 4.01. 86
under whose colors he had fought so long. 4.01.100
your differences shall all rest under gage 4.01.105
tell me, gentle friend, | how went he under him? 5.05. 82
under whose blessed cross | we are impressed and 1H4 1.01. 20
the moon, under whose countenance we steal. 1.02. 29 P
wherein you range under this subtile king! 1.03.169
spleen, | to fight against me under percy's pay, 3.02.126
under whose government come they along? 4.01. 19
arm | that he shall shrink under my courtesy. 5.02. 74
and stiff | under the hoofs of vaunting enemies, 5.03. 42
under the smile of safety wounds the world; 2H4 in 10
fell | under the wrath of noble hotspur's sword, in 30
under the conduct of young lancaster | and 1.01.134
like strengthless hinges, buckle under life, 1.01.141
the great, | under the canopies of costly state, 3.01. 13
and laid his love and life under my foot, | yea, 3.01. 63
let me have him to sit under, he's like to be a 3.02.122 P
ta'en up, | under the counterfeited zeal of god, 4.02. 27
i am, sir, under the king, in some authority. 5.03.111 P
under which king, besonian? speak, or die. 5.03.113
under king harry. 5.03.114
his contemplation | under the veil of wildness, H5 1.01. 64
under this conjuration speak, my lord; 1.02. 29
under the sweet shade of your government. 2.02. 28
digt himself four yard under the countermines. 3.02. 62 P
look you, under your correction, there is not 3.02.120 P
return into london under the form of a soldier. 3.06. 69 P
to re–answer, his pettiness would bow under. 3.06.129 P
under what captain serve you? 4.01. 93 P
under sir /thomas erpingham. 4.01. 94 P
under his master's command transporting a sum of 4.01.151 P
who serv'st thou under? 4.07.147 P
under captain gower, my liege. 4.07.148 P
what your highness suffer'd under that shape, i 4.08. 53 P
under the correction of bragging be it spoken, i 5.02.138 P
under my feet i stamp thy cardinal's hat; 1H6 1.03. 49
burns under feigned ashes of forg'd love, | and 3.01.189
under the lordly monarch of the north, | appear, 5.03. 6
out of the powerful regions under earth, | help 5.03. 11
thou shalt be plac'd as viceroy under him, | and 5.04.131
a spirit rais'd from depth of under ground, 2H6 1.02. 79
under the wings of our protector's grace, 1.03. 38
still | under the surly gloucester's governance? 1.03. 47
under the countenance and confederacy | of lady 2.01.164
raising up wicked spirits from under ground, 2.01.170
well he can, | under the title of john mortimer. 3.01.359
under the which is writ, "invitis nubibus." 4.01. 99
honorable, and there was he born, under a hedge; 4.02. 51 P
with him, he has a familiar under his tongue, he 4.07.108 P
and tread it under foot with all contempt, 5.01.209
wretch | that trembles under his devouring paws; 3H6 1.03. 13
his wonted sleep under a fresh tree's shade, 2.05. 49
under this thick–grown brake we'll shroud 3.01. 1
this way, | under the color of his usual game, 4.05. 11
under whose shade the ramping lion slept, 5.02. 13
which, in his nonage, council under him, | and, R3 2.03. 13
under what title shall i woo for thee, | that 4.04.340
under our tents i'll play the ease–dropper, | to 5.03.221
under pretense to see the queen his aunt | (for H8 1.01.177
i shall perish | under device and practice. 1.01.204
but am bold'ned | under your promis'd pardon. 1.02. 56
whom after under the /confession's seal | he 1.02.164
and under your fair conduct | crave leave to 1.04. 70
no, not for all the riches under heaven. 2.03. 35
remember | how under my oppression i did reek 2.04.209
consent proceeded | under your hands and seals. 2.04.223
the cardinal | cannot stand under them. 3.02. 3
my high–blown pride | at length broke under me, 3.02.362
know | there's none stands under more calumnious 5.01.112
shade thy person | under their blessed wings! 5.01.161
all that stand about him are under the line, 5.03. 43 P
in safety | under his own vine what he plants, 5.04. 34
a more temperate fire under the pot of her eyes. TRO 1.02.146 P
and flies fled under shade, why then the thing 1.03. 51
yet go we under our opinion still | that we have 1.03.382
here the voluntary, and you as under an impress. 2.01. 97 P
an engine | not portable, lie under this report: 2.03.135
would i were as deep under the earth as i am 4.02. 82 P
senate, who | (under the gods) keep you in awe, COR 1.01.187
can brook to be commanded | under cominius. 1.01.263
and sore blows | for sinking under them. 2.01.253
as weeds before | a vessel under sail, so men 2.02.106
under the canopy. 4.05. 38 P
under the canopy? 4.05. 39 P
with the spleen | of all the under fiends. 4.05. 92
i am one that, telling true under him, must say 5.02. 32 P
but still subsisting | under your great command. 5.06. 73
to tremble under titus' threat'ning look. TIT 1.01.134
i had none, | to bury so much gold under a tree, 2.03. 2
under their sweet shade, aaron, let us sit, 2.03. 16
under your patience, gentle emperess, | 'tis 2.03. 66
hither march amain, under conduct | of lucius, 4.04. 65
sitting in the sun under the dove–house wall. ROM 1.03. 27
under love's heavy burthen do i sink. 1.04. 22
now will he sit under a medlar tree, | and wish 2.01. 34
i was hurt under your arm. 3.01.103 P
under yond /yew trees lay thee all along, 5.03. 3
as i did sleep under this /yew tree here, | i 5.03.137
sir, your jewel | hath suffered under praise. TIM 1.01.165
and what hast thou there under thy cloak, pretty 3.01. 14 P
like those that under hot ardent zeal would set 3.03. 32 P
then, under favor, pardon me | if i speak like a 3.05. 40
under that's above me. 4.03.292
and we petty men | walk under his huge legs, and JC 1.02.137
rome | under these hard conditions as this time 1.02.174
shall rome stand under one man's awe? 2.01. 52
here, under leave of brutus and the rest | (for 3.02. 81
here is the will, and under caesar's seal: 3.02.240
gold, | to groan and sweat under the business, 4.01. 22
i stand and crouch | under your testy humor? 4.03. 46
under your pardon. 4.03.213
canopy most fatal, under which | our army lies, 5.01. 87
but under heavy judgment bears that life | which MAC 1.03.110
fatal entrance of duncan | under my battlements. 1.05. 40
and under him | my genius is rebuk'd, as it is 3.01. 54
times past which held you | so under fortune, 3.01. 77
think | that, had he duncan's sons under his key 3.06. 18
our suffering country | under a hand accurs'd! 3.06. 49
that under cold stone | days and nights has 4.01. 6
as oft as any passions under heaven | that does HAM 2.01.102
bear, | to grunt and sweat under a weary life, 3.01. 76
under the which he shall not choose but fall; 4.07. 65
all simples that have virtue | under the moon, 4.07.145
this villain of mine comes under the prediction; LR 1.02.109 P
with my mother under the dragon's tail, and my 1.02.129 P
tail, and my nativity was under ursa major, so 1.02.130 P
yours | though i condemn not, yet, under pardon, 1.04.342
under th' allowance of your great aspect, 2.02.106
approach, thou beacon to this under globe, 2.02.163
house | should many people under two commands 2.04.241
that under covert and convenient seeming | has 3.02. 56
that hath laid knives under his pillow, and 3.04. 54 P
thought t' have yerk'd him here under the ribs. OTH 1.02. 5
under a compelling occasion, let women die. ANT 1.02.137 P
to such whose places under us require, | our 1.02.195
my better cunning faints | under his chance. 2.03. 36
prevail | under the service of a child as soon 3.13. 24
antony, | and put yourself under his shroud, 3.13. 71
under the earth. 4.03. 13
she hath sold me, and i fall | under this plot. 4.12. 49
this lamentable divorce under her colors are CYM 1.04. 20 P
now canopied | under these windows, white and 2.02. 22
seek | for further satisfying, under her breast 2.04.134
my youth i spent | much under him; 3.01. 70
they come | under the conduct of bold jachimo, 4.02.340
fled, | under the covering of a careful night, PER 1.02. 81
in the cheapest country under the cope, shall 4.06.123 P
and make him cry from under ground, "o, fan TNK pr 18
under the shadow of his sword may cool us; 1.01. 92
some say, | groan under such a mast'ry. 1.01.231
of their ladies, | like tall ships under sail; 2.02. 12
our fiery horses | like proud seas under us! 2.02. 20
better lads nev'r danc'd | under green tree; 2.03. 39
and there's a rock lies watching under water; 3.04. 6
up, and under me | i had a right good horse. 3.06. 76
to all the under world the loves and fights | of 4.02. 24
never fainting | under the weight of arms; 4.02.130
not halting under crimes | many and stale. 5.04. 10
rein, | under her other was the tender boy, VEN 32
were beauty under twenty locks kept fast, | yet 575
under whose sharp fangs on his back doth lie 663
but in one minute's fight brings beauty under; 746
under whose simple semblance he hath fed | upon 795
on, | under whose brim the gaudy sun would peep; 1088
her lily hand her rosy cheek lies under, LUC 386
still | under what color he commits this ill. 476

under that color am i come to scale | thy 481
so under his insulting falchion lies | harmless 509
like a white hind under the gripe's sharp claws, 543
which bleeding under pyrrhus' proud foot lies. 1449
adonis made | under an osier growing by a brook, PP 6. 5
by her, | under a myrtle shade began to woo him. 11. 2
head, each under eye | doth homage to his SON 7. 2
way, | each trifle under truest bars to thrust, 48. 2
my use, | and under thee their poesy disperse. 78. 4
feel | needs must i under my transgression bow, 120. 3
falls | under the blow of thralled discontent, 124. 7
me | under that bond that him as fast doth bind. 134. 8
works under you, and to your audit comes | their LC 230
UNDERBEAR 1 FR 0.0001 REL FR 1 V 0 P
alone which i alone | am bound to underbear. JN 3.01. 65
UNDERBEARING 1 FR 0.0001 REL FR 1 V 0 P
and patient underbearing of his fortune, | as R2 1.04. 29
UNDERBORNE 1 FR 0.0001 REL FR 0 V 1 P
skirts, round underborne with a bluish tinsel; ADO 3.04. 21 P
UNDERCREST 1 FR 0.0001 REL FR 1 V 0 P
at all times | to undercrest your good addition COR 1.09. 72
UNDER–FOOT 1 FR 0.0001 REL FR 1 V 0 P
off with that bable, throw it under–foot. SHR 5.02.122
/UNDERGO 1 FR 0.0001 REL FR 1 V 0 P
/how /able /such /a /work /to /undergo, | /to 2H4 1.03. 54
UNDERGO 16 FR 0.0018 REL FR 12 V 4 P
back, | than you should such dishonor undergo, TMP 3.01. 27
death, | would i not undergo for one calm look? TGV 5.04. 42
worth | to undergo such ample grace and honor, MM 1.01. 23
their blood | to undergo such maiden pilgrimage; MND 1.01. 75
that my ability may undergo | and nobleness WT 2.03.164
change your purpose | but undergo this flight: 4.04.543
much danger do i undergo for thee. JN 4.01.133
is't not i | that undergo this charge? 5.02.100
it be | that you a world of curses undergo, 1H4 1.03.164
i will not undergo this sneap without reply. 2H4 2.01.122 P
than for us to undergo any difficulty impos'd. TRO 3.02. 80 P
you undergo too strict a paradox, | striving to TIM 3.05. 24
romans | to undergo with me an enterprise | of JC 1.03.123
pure as grace, | as infinite as man may undergo, HAM 1.04. 34
of my speeches, and would undergo what's spoken,
CYM 1.04.141 P
undergo those employments wherein i should have 3.05.110 P
UNDERGOES 2 FR 0.0002 REL FR 1 V 1 P
thee plainly, claudio undergoes my challenge, ADO 5.02. 57 P
she's punish'd for her truth, and undergoes, CYM 3.02. 7
UNDERGOING 1 FR 0.0001 REL FR 1 V 0 P
which rais'd in me | an undergoing stomach, to TMP 1.02.157
UNDERGONE 1 FR 0.0001 REL FR 1 V 0 P
some kinds of baseness | are nobly undergone; TMP 3.01. 3
UNDERHAND 2 FR 0.0002 REL FR 1 V 1 P
and have by underhand means labor'd to dissuade
AYL 1.01.140 P
by underhand corrupted foul injustice, | if that R3 5.01. 6
UNDER–HANGMAN 1 FR 0.0001 REL FR 1 V 0 P
to be styl'd | the under–hangman of his kingdom, CYM 2.03.130
UNDER–HONEST 1 FR 0.0001 REL FR 1 V 0 P
say we think him over–proud | and under–honest, TRO 2.03.124
UNDERLINGS 1 FR 0.0001 REL FR 1 V 0 P
but in ourselves, that we are underlings. JC 1.02.141
UNDERMINE 3 FR 0.0003 REL FR 1 V 2 P
before you, will undermine you and blow you up. AWW 1.01.119 P
humor, | have hired me to undermine the duchess,
2H6 1.02. 98
troy be not taken till these two undermine it, TRO 2.03. 8 P
UNDERMINERS 1 FR 0.0001 REL FR 0 V 1 P
poor virginity from underminers and blowers–up! AWW 1.01.120 P
UNDERNEATH 15 FR 0.0017 REL FR 14 V 1 P
yea, and text underneath, "here dwells benedick ADO 5.01.183 P
him, | and underneath that consecrated roof, TN 4.03. 25
afoot, | come underneath the yoke of government.
2H4 4.04. 10
the strawberry grows underneath the nettle, H5 1.01. 60
if underneath the standard of the french | she 1H6 2.01. 23
keeping them prisoner underneath /her wings. 5.03. 57
for underneath an alehouse' paltry sign, | the 2H6 5.02. 67
so, underneath the belly of their steeds, | that 3H6 2.03. 20
bruis'd underneath the yoke of tyranny, | thus R3 5.02. 2
i heard a child cry underneath a wall. TIT 5.01. 24
underneath the grove of sycamore | that westward
ROM 1.01.121
underneath whose arm | an envious thrust from 3.01.167
that tiber trembled underneath her banks | to JC 1.01. 45
and groaning underneath this age's yoke, | have 1.02. 61
which underneath thy black all–hiding cloak LUC 801
UNDER–PEEP 1 FR 0.0001 REL FR 1 V 0 P
bows toward her, and would under–peep her lids, CYM 2.02. 20
UNDERPRIZING 1 FR 0.0001 REL FR 1 V 0 P
doth wrong this shadow | in underprizing it, so MV 3.02.128
UNDERPROP 3 FR 0.0003 REL FR 3 V 0 P
what munition sent, | to underprop this action? JN 5.02. 99
here am i left to underprop his land, | who, R2 2.02. 82
which of them both should underprop her fame. LUC 53
UNDER–SKINKER 1 FR 0.0001 REL FR 0 V 1 P
even now into my hand by an under–skinker, one 1H4 2.04. 24 P
/UNDERSTAND 2 FR 0.0002 REL FR 1 V 1 P
/understand /more /clear, | /what's /past /and TRO 4.05.165
/how /dost /thou /understand /the /scripture? HAM 5.01. 36 P
UNDER–STAND 1 FR 0.0001 REL FR 0 V 1 P
why, stand–under and under–stand is all one. TGV 2.05. 32 P
UNDERSTAND 99 FR 0.0112 REL FR 57 V 42 P
do you understand me? TMP 2.01.268
what an ass art thou! i understand thee not. TGV 2.05. 24 P
now let us understand. WIV 1.01.136 P
three umpires in this matter, as i understand: 1.01.138 P
do you understand me? 1.01.209 P
nay, but understand me. 1.01.212 P
and the boy never need to understand any thing; 2.02.127 P
for i must let you understand i think myself in 2.02.165 P
o, understand my drift. 2.02.242 P
but this i can let you understand, the greater MM 3.02.136 P
i am made to understand that you have lent him 3.02.240 P
to make you understand this in a manifested 4.02.159 P
beshrew his hand, i scarce could understand it. ERR 2.01. 49
doubtfully, that i could scarce understand them. 2.01. 54 P
wants wit in all one word to understand. 2.02.151
i understand thee not. 4.03. 22 P
i understand you not, my griefs are double. LLL 5.02.752
and by these badges understand the king. 5.02.754
for you must understand he goes but to see a MND 3.01. 90 P
i understand not what you mean by this. 3.02.236
good man is to have you understand me that he is
MV 1.03. 16 P
i understand, moreover, upon the rialto, he hath 1.03. 19 P
but there the duke was given to understand 2.08. 7
but lest you should not understand me well — 3.02. 7
i pray thee understand a plain man in his plain 3.05. 57 P
"your grace shall understand that at the receipt 4.01.150 P
secretly to understand that your younger brother AYL 1.01.124 P
hand, | and let me all your fortunes understand. 2.07.200
i am. what must we understand by this? 4.03. 94
you understand me? SHR 1.01.235
you understand me. 1.02.148
sir, understand you this of me, in sooth: 1.02.257
you understand me, sir? 4.02.110
this by the way i let you understand: 4.02.116
how understand we that? AWW 1.01. 60 P
counsel and understand what advice shall thrust 1.01.209 P
not much employment for you. you understand me? 2.02. 69 P
we understand it, and thank heaven for you. 2.03. 65
though you understand it not yourselves, no 4.01. 3 P
for we must not seem to understand him, unless 4.01. 5 P
i understand thee, and can speak thy tongue. 4.01. 74 P
my suit, as i do understand, you know, | and 5.03.160
he takes on him to understand so much, and TN 1.05.141 P
i would not understand it. 1.05.267
i understand you, sir. 'tis well begg'd. 3.01. 53 P
my legs do better understand me, sir, than i 3.01. 79 P
than i understand what you mean by bidding me 3.01. 80 P
i think most understand | bohemia stays here WT 1.02.229
you speak a language that i understand not. 3.02. 80
i understand the business, i hear it. 4.04.670 P
dost thou understand me? JN 3.03. 63
the winking of authority | to understand a law; 4.02.212
but thou didst understand me by my signs, | and 4.02.237
the chopping french we do not understand. R2 5.03.124
let me understand you then, | speak it in welsh. 1H4 3.01.117
i understand thy looks. 3.01.198
i understand thy kisses, and thou mine, | and 3.01.202
shrewsbury, | as i am truly given to understand, 4.04. 11
and we understand him well, | how he comes o'er H5 1.02.266
pistol, i do partly understand your meaning. 3.06. 50 P
sauf votre honneur, me understand well. 5.02.131 P
kate, dost thou understand thus much english? 5.02.193 P
as more at large your grace shall understand. 2H6 2.01.173
and, as i further have to understand, | is new 3H6 4.04. 10
this speak i, lords, to let you understand, | if 5.04. 33
and you shall understand from me her mind. R3 4.04.429
travel, | and understand again like honest men, H8 1.03. 32
the king | shall understand it presently. 5.02. 10
to men that understand you, words and weakness. 5.02.107
friend, we understand not one another; TRO 3.01. 27 P
you understand me not that tell me so. 5.10. 11
i understand thee well, and be thou sure, | when COR 4.07. 17
i understand her signs. TIT 3.01.143
how shall i understand you? TIM 1.01. 51
that i may make his lordship understand 2.02. 42
grief too, as i understand how all things go. 3.06. 17 P
i understand thee: 4.03.316 P
you seem to understand me, | by each at once her MAC 1.03. 43
you do not understand yourself so clearly | as HAM 1.03. 96
i do not well understand that. 3.02.350 P
you must translate, 'tis fit we understand them. 4.01. 2
we would not understand what was most fit, | but 4.01. 20
i understand you not, my lord. 4.02. 22 P
not possible to understand in another tongue? 5.02.125 P
the contents, as in part i understand them, are LR 1.02. 42 P
beseech you | to understand my purposes aright, 1.04.239
"inform'd" them? dost thou understand me, man? 2.04. 99
i do not understand. OTH 1.02. 52
and let ourselves again but understand | that, 1.03. 21
i understand a fury in your words, | /but /not 4.02. 32
dost understand the word? 5.02.153
sir, you shall understand what hath befall'n, 5.02.307
i understand not, madam. ANT 5.02. 75
me directly to understand you have prevail'd, i CYM 1.04.159 P
me, for | i yet not understand the case myself. 2.03. 75
"here | give to understand, | if e'er this PER 3.02. 68
i understand you not. 4.02.122
and "then let be," and no man understand me? TNK 3.05. 10
understand you she ever affected any man ere she 4.03. 62 P
UNDERSTANDETH 1 FR 0.0001 REL FR 0 V 1 P
who understandeth thee not, loves thee not. LLL 4.02. 99 P
UNDERSTANDING 20 FR 0.0022 REL FR 12 V 8 P
their understanding | begins to swell, and the TMP 5.01. 79
you, fortune hath convey'd to my understanding; MM 3.01.185 P
or, for thy more sweet understanding, a woman. LLL 1.01.264 P
understanding that the curate and your sweet 5.01.113 P
seconded with the forward child, understanding, AYL 3.03. 14 P
or, to thy better understanding, diest; 5.01. 52 P
i speak as my understanding instructs me and as WT 1.01. 19 P
taken | by any understanding pate but thine? 1.02.223
is, i am only old in judgment and understanding; 2H4 1.02.192 P
or nicely charge your understanding soul | with H5 1.02. 15
kate, my wooing is fit for thy understanding. 5.02.122 P
i think /his understanding is bereft. 3H6 2.06. 60
will leave us never an understanding friend. H8 pr 22
had thought i had had men of some understanding 5.02.170
an understanding simple and unschool'd: HAM 1.02. 97
give it an understanding, but no tongue. 1.02.249
him | so much from th' understanding of himself, 2.02. 9
i speak in understanding: LR 4.05. 28
and marrow of my understanding laid upon ye, TNK 3.05. 6
but want the understanding where to use it. 3.06.216
UNDERSTANDINGS 1 FR 0.0001 REL FR 0 V 1 P
hast thou no understandings for thy cases and WIV 4.01. 70 P
UNDERSTANDS 5 FR 0.0005 REL FR 2 V 3 P
my staff understands me. TGV 2.05. 27 P
i'll but lean, and my staff understands me. 2.05. 30 P
i say nothing to him, for he understands not me, MV 1.02. 69 P
now i perceive the devil understands welsh, 1H4 3.01.229
me, | and, for he understands you are in arms, TIT 5.01.158
UNDERSTAND'ST 1 FR 0.0001 REL FR 1 V 0 P
but there's more in me than thou understand'st. TRO 4.05.240
UNDERSTOOD 14 FR 0.0015 REL FR 7 V 7 P
constable is too cunning to be understood. ADO 5.01.228 P
nor understood none neither, sir. LLL 5.01.151 P
how blow? how blow? speak to be understood. 5.02.294
when a man's verses cannot be understood, nor a AYL 3.03. 12 P
one, and not to be understood without bloody AWW 2.03.190 P
but to answer you as you would be understood, he 4.03.107 P
but by bad courses may be understood | that R2 2.01.213
are hardly attain'd, and hardly understood. 2H6 1.04. 71
you are well understood to be a perfecter giber COR 2.01. 81 P
but those that understood him smil'd at one JC 1.02.282 P
augures and understood relations have | by MAC 3.04.123
but since my landing i have understood | your PER 1.03. 33
petitions are not | without gifts understood, TNK 1.03. 15
aptly understood | in bloodless white and the LC 200
UNDER'T 2 FR 0.0002 REL FR 1 V 1 P
whether there be a scar under't or no, the AWW 4.05. 96 P
innocent flower, | but be the serpent under't. MAC 1.05. 66
UNDERTA'EN 1 FR 0.0001 REL FR 1 V 0 P
what you have underta'en to do in 's absence. WT 3.02. 78
UNDERTAKE 47 FR 0.0053 REL FR 31 V 16 P
how with my honor i may undertake | a journey to
TGV 2.07. 6
then you must undertake to slander him. 3.02. 38
you'll undertake her no more? WIV 3.05.125 P
i will in the interim undertake one of hercules' ADO 2.01.364 P
child or pupil, undertake your bien venuto; LLL 4.02.157 P
well — i will undertake it. MND 1.02. 90 P
and undertake the teaching of the maid: SHR 1.01.192
liking, | will undertake to woo curst katherine, 1.02.183
his name and credit shall you undertake, | and 4.02.107
you hear him so confidently undertake to do. AWW 3.06. 20 P
by the hand of a soldier, i will undertake it. 3.06. 72 P
so confidently seems to undertake this business, 3.06. 87 P
should move me to undertake the recovery of this 4.01. 34 P
will you undertake to betray the florentine? 4.03.292 P
i would not undertake her in this company. TN 1.03. 58 P
but, would you undertake another suit, | i had 3.01.108
unless you undertake that with me which with as 3.04.249 P
king, and undertake to be | her advocate to th' WT 2.02. 36
sir, to undertake the business for us, here is 4.04.806 P
so well, that what you bid me undertake, JN 3.03. 56
"the purpose you undertake is dangerous" — why,
1H4 2.03. 7 P
"the purpose you undertake is dangerous, the 2.03. 11 P
i'll undertake to make thee henry's queen, | to 1H6 5.03.117
and those two counties i will undertake | your 5.03.158
and will they undertake to do me good? 2H6 1.02. 77
and never will i undertake the thing | wherein 3H6 2.06.101
i'll undertake to land them on our coast, | and 3.03.205
sleep | to undertake the death of all the world, R3 1.02.123
the deed you undertake is damnable. 1.04.192
upon my life, my lord, i'll undertake it, | and 5.03. 42
i'll undertake may see away their shilling H8 pr 12
this shall i undertake, and 'tis a burthen TRO 3.03. 36
him, and undertake to bring him | where he shall COR 3.01.322
but on mine honor dare i undertake | for good TIT 1.01.436
then is it likely thou wilt undertake | a thing ROM 4.01. 73
and that he means | no more to undertake it, i HAM 4.07. 63
what would you undertake | to show yourself 4.07.124
terror of his spirit | that dares not undertake; LR 4.02. 13
and do undertake | this present wars against the OTH 1.03.233
the virtuous desdemona to undertake for me. 2.03.330 P
lordship should undertake every companion that CYM 2.01. 26 P
wherefore then | didst undertake it? 3.04.102
are | full weak to undertake our wars against 3.07. 5
received | the danger of the task you undertake. PER 1.01. 2
that for this twelvemonth she'll not undertake 2.05. 3
boast, | and will undertake all these to teach. 4.06.185
that shall prefer and undertake my troth.' LC 280
UNDERTAKER 3 FR 0.0003 REL FR 1 V 2 P
nay, if you be an undertaker, i am for you. TN 3.04.318 P
and for cassio, let me be his undertaker. OTH 4.01.211 P
pow'r and press you forth | our undertaker! TNK 1.01. 74
UNDERTAKES 4 FR 0.0004 REL FR 3 V 1 P
or undertakes them with a most christian–like ADO 2.03.191 P
the task he undertakes | is numb'ring sands and R2 2.02.145
nicholas vaux, | who undertakes you to your end. H8 2.01. 97
all the fair hopes of what he undertakes, | and TNK 4.02. 99
UNDERTAKE'T 1 FR 0.0001 REL FR 1 V 0 P
i'll undertake't. COR 5.01. 47
UNDERTAKING 5 FR 0.0005 REL FR 3 V 2 P
me | for undertaking so unstaid a journey? TGV 2.07. 60
is virtuous to be constant in any undertaking. MM 3.02.226 P
which holy undertaking with most austere AWW 4.03. 49 P
evident | that your free undertaking cannot miss WT 2.02. 42
to come alone, either he so undertaking, | or CYM 4.02.142
UNDERTAKINGS 3 FR 0.0003 REL FR 2 V 1 P
as well my undertakings as your counsels, | but TRO 2.02.131
nothing but our undertakings, when we vow to 3.02. 77 P
and leads the will to desperate undertakings HAM 2.01.101
UNDERTOOK 5 FR 0.0005 REL FR 5 V 0 P
ordered, | and better in my mind not undertook. MV 2.04. 7
i undertook it, | vanquish'd thereto by the fair AWW 5.03.132
liege, | who undertook to sit and watch by you. 2H4 4.05. 52
ten years are spent since first he undertook TIT 1.01. 31
the death of cassio to be undertook | by OTH 5.02.311
UNDERVALU'D 1 FR 0.0001 REL FR 1 V 0 P
nothing undervalu'd | to cato's daughter, MV 1.01.165
UNDERVALUED 1 FR 0.0001 REL FR 1 V 0 P
being ten times undervalued to tried gold? MV 2.07. 53
UNDERWENT 1 FR 0.0001 REL FR 1 V 0 P
off | by him for whom these shames ye underwent?
1H4 1.03.179
UNDERWRIT 1 FR 0.0001 REL FR 1 V 0 P
are, | painted upon a pole, and underwrit, MAC 5.08. 26
UNDERWRITE 1 FR 0.0001 REL FR 1 V 0 P
and underwrite in an observing kind | his TRO 2.03.128
UNDER–WROUGHT 1 FR 0.0001 REL FR 1 V 0 P
that thou hast under–wrought his lawful king, JN 2.01. 95
UNDESCRIED 1 FR 0.0001 REL FR 1 V 0 P
fear eyes over) to shipboard | get undescried. WT 4.04.655
UNDESERV'D 3 FR 0.0003 REL FR 2 V 1 P
this is hard and undeserv'd measure, my lord. AWW 2.03.257 P
comfort, to be us'd | in undeserv'd extremes. JN 4.01.107
and undeserv'd reproach to him allotted | that LUC 824
UNDESERVED 2 FR 0.0002 REL FR 2 V 0 P
none presume | to wear an undeserved dignity. MV 2.09. 40
some undeserved fault | i'll find about the SHR 4.01.199
UNDESERVER 2 FR 0.0002 REL FR 1 V 1 P

the undeserver may sleep when the man of action 2H4 2.04.376 P
great graces | heap'd upon me, poor undeserver, H8 3.02.175
UNDESERVERS 1 FR 0.0001 REL FR 1 V 0 P
and mart your offices for gold | to undeservers. JC 4.03. 12
UNDESERVING 2 FR 0.0002 REL FR 2 V 0 P
favors | done to me (undeserving as i am), | my TGV 3.01. 7
days) | in courtesy gives undeserving praise. LLL 5.02.366
UNDETERMIN'D 1 FR 0.0001 REL FR 1 V 0 P
of men, | in undetermin'd differences of kings. JN 2.01.355
UNDID 2 FR 0.0002 REL FR 1 V 1 P
to dance for your sake, kate, why, you undid me: H5 5.02.133 P
which they did cool, | and what they undid did. ANT 2.02.205
UNDINTED 1 FR 0.0001 REL FR 1 V 0 P
edges and bear back | our targes undinted. ANT 2.06. 39
UNDISCERNIBLE 1 FR 0.0001 REL FR 1 V 0 P
guiltiness, | to think i can be undiscernible, MM 5.01.368
UNDISCOVER'D 3 FR 0.0003 REL FR 2 V 1 P
continuing, this mystery remain'd undiscover'd. WT 5.02.120 P
the enemy, | and undiscover'd come to me again, 2H6 3.01.369
the undiscover'd country, from whose bourn | no HAM 3.01. 78
UNDISHONORED 1 FR 0.0001 REL FR 1 V 0 P
bed, | i live dis–stain'd, thou undishonored. ERR 2.02.146
UNDISPOS'D 1 FR 0.0001 REL FR 1 V 0 P
that stands on tricks when i am undispos'd: ERR 1.02. 80
UNDISTINGUISHABLE
2 FR 0.0002 REL FR 2 V 0 P
green | for lack of tread are undistinguishable. MND 2.01.100
these things seem small and undistinguishable, 4.01.187
UNDISTINGUISH'D *(also indistinguish'd)*
UNDISTINGUISH'D 1 FR 0.0001 REL FR 1 V 0 P
as often shriking undistinguish'd woe, | in LC 20
UNDIVIDABLE 1 FR 0.0001 REL FR 1 V 0 P
strange to me, | that, undividable incorporate, ERR 2.02.122
UNDIVIDED 1 FR 0.0001 REL FR 1 V 0 P
twain, | although our undivided loves are one: SON 36. 2
UNDIVULG'D 1 FR 0.0001 REL FR 1 V 0 P
thence | against the undivulg'd pretense i fight MAC 2.03.131
UNDIVULGED 1 FR 0.0001 REL FR 1 V 0 P
wretch | that hast within thee undivulged crimes LR 3.02. 52
/UNDO 1 FR 0.0001 REL FR 1 V 0 P
/now /mark /me /how /i /will /undo /myself: R2 4.01.203
UNDO 31 FR 0.0035 REL FR 20 V 11 P
damn'd, which sycorax | could not again undo. TMP 1.02.291
to vex claudio, to undo hero, and kill leonato. ADO 2.02. 29 P
to bind me, or undo me — one of them. 5.04. 20
our states are forfeit, seek not to undo us. LLL 5.02.425
i will undo | this hateful imperfection of her MND 4.01. 62
discover that which shall undo the florentine. AWW 4.01. 73
that quaffing and drinking will undo you. TN 1.03. 14 P
if you will not undo what you have done, that is 2.01. 37 P
would do that | which should undo more doing; WT 1.02.312
if you look for a good speech now, you undo me, 2H4 ep 4 P
best, | do or undo, as if ourself were here. 2H6 3.01.196
being scribbled o'er, should undo a man? 4.02. 81 P
shall do and undo as him pleaseth best. 3H6 2.06.105
him with a scruple | that will undo her. H8 2.01.159
this love will undo us all. TRO 3.01.110 P
honest neighbors, | will you undo yourselves? COR 1.01. 63
adore, | this petty brabble will undo us all. TIT 2.01. 62
that which thou canst not undo. 4.02. 74
a little part, and undo a great deal of honor! TIM 3.02. 48 P
speak by the card, or equivocation will undo us. HAM 5.01.138 P
so distribution should undo excess, | and each LR 4.01. 70
pray you undo this button. 5.03.310
good, | she shall undo her credit with the moor. OTH 2.03.359
undo that prayer, by crying out as loud, | "o, ANT 3.04. 17
what | can it not do, and undo? CYM 2.03. 73
wilt thou undo the worth thou art unpaid for, 5.05.307
spacious world, | i'd give it to undo the deed. PER 4.03. 6
the god priapus, and undo a whole generation. 4.06. 4 P
under the cope, shall undo a whole household, 4.06.124 P
she's born to undo us. 4.06.149 P
like ivy/–tods, | not to undo with thunder. TNK 4.02.105
UNDOES 2 FR 0.0002 REL FR 0 V 2 P
to follow it and undoes description to do it. WT 5.02. 58 P
my womb, my womb, my womb undoes me. 2H4 4.03. 22 P
UNDOING 6 FR 0.0006 REL FR 4 V 2 P
a man's tongue shakes out his master's undoing. AWW 2.04. 24 P
france, | undoing all, as all had never been! 2H6 1.01.103
to the mere undoing | of all the kingdom. H8 3.02.329
i see your end, | 'tis my undoing. 5.02. 97
my master's bounty by | th' undoing of yourself. ANT 5.02. 44
is merely to the undoing of poor prentices, for STM II.C 8 P
/UNDONE* 1 FR 0.0001 REL FR 1 V 0 P
then are we all /undone; 1H4 5.02. 3
UNDONE* 61 FR 0.0069 REL FR 37 V 24 P
that a man is never undone till he be hang'd, TGV 2.05. 5 P
sir, we are undone; 4.01. 5
y' are overthrown, y' are undone for ever! WIV 3.03. 95 P
you are undone. 3.03.110 P
i am undone! the knight is here. 4.02. 41 P
assist me, knight, i am undone! 4.05. 91 P
i am undone! 4.05. 92 P
she is wrong'd, she is sland'red, she is undone. ADO 4.01.313 P
but antonio is certainly undone. MV 3.01.124 P
with mine enemy, i have undone three tailors, i AYL 5.04. 46 P
now we are undone and brought to nothing. SHR 5.01. 43 P
o, i am undone! 5.01. 68 P
i am undone! 5.01. 68 P
him, forswear him, or else we are all undone. 5.01.111 P
i am undone! AWW 1.01. 84
undone, and forfeited to cares for ever! 2.03.267
she hath recover'd the king, and undone me. 3.02. 20 P
you are undone, captain, all but your scarf; 4.03.323 P
a seducer flourishes, and a poor maid is undone. 5.03.146 P
even here undone! WT 4.04.441
sir, | you have undone a man of fourscore three, 4.04.453
undone, undone! 4.04.460
undone, undone! 4.04.460
o, we are undone, both we and ours for ever! 1H4 2.02. 86 P
hang ye, gorbellied knaves, are ye undone? 2.02. 88 P
i am undone by his going, i warrant you, he's an 2H4 2.01. 23 P
my old dame will be undone now for one to do her 3.02.112 P
thou hast undone thyself, thy son, and me, | and 3H6 1.01.232
this paper has undone me. H8 3.02.210
the man's undone for ever, for if hector break TRO 3.03.258 P
we cannot, sir, we are undone already. COR 1.01. 64
it him, and leaves nothing undone that may fully 2.02. 20 P
we are all undone, unless | the noble man have 4.06.107
yet he hath left undone | that which shall break 4.07. 24
o gentle aaron, we are all undone! TIT 4.02. 55
thou hast undone our mother. 4.02. 75
and therein, hellish dog, thou hast undone her. 4.02. 77
we are undone, lady, we are undone! ROM 3.02. 38
we are undone, lady, we are undone! 3.02. 38
are we undone, cast off, nothing remaining? TIM 4.02. 2
low by his own heart, | undone by goodness! 4.02. 38
seek to thrive | by that which has undone thee; 4.03.211
for his undone lord than mine eyes for you. 4.03.481
some worthy cause to wish | things done undone; JC 4.02. 9
dost fear to do | than wishest should be undone. MAC 1.05. 25
what's done cannot be undone. 5.01. 68 P
wish th' estate o' th' world were now undone. 5.05. 49
i cannot wish the fault undone, the issue of it LR 1.01. 17 P
best conscience | is not to leave't undone, but OTH 3.03.204
o, i am spoil'd, undone by villains! 5.01. 54
alas, he is betray'd and i undone! 5.02. 76
lie they upon thy hand, | and be undone by 'em! ANT 2.05.106
better to leave undone, than by our deed 3.01. 14
we are all undone. CYM 4.02.123
if by which time our secret be undone, | this PER 1.01.117
why /are you foolish? can it be undone? 4.03. 1
deep a cunning, | may be outworn, never undone. TNK 1.03. 44
lo, cousin, lo, our folly has undone us. 3.06.107
gone — she's done, | and undone in an hour. 4.01.125
spun, | a bottom great wound up, greatly undone. STM III 21
and then my little heart were quite undone, | in VEN 783
UNDO'T 1 FR 0.0001 REL FR 0 V 1 P
i think i should, and undo't when i had /done't. OTH 4.03. 71 P
UNDOUBTED 4 FR 0.0004 REL FR 4 V 0 P
rest | unquestion'd welcome and undoubted blest. AWW 2.01.208
and till it be undoubted, we do lock | our JN 2.01.369
brave burgundy, undoubted hope of france, | stay 1H6 3.03. 41
/renown'd | for hardy and undoubted champions; 3H6 5.07. 6
UNDOUBTEDLY 1 FR 0.0001 REL FR 1 V 0 P
undoubtedly | was fashion'd to much honor. H8 4.02. 49
UNDOUBTFUL 1 FR 0.0001 REL FR 0 V 1 P
of lord angelo, came not to an undoubtful proof. MM 4.02.137 P
UNDREAM'D 1 FR 0.0001 REL FR 1 V 0 P
to unpath'd waters, undream'd shores, most WT 4.04.567
UNDRESS 1 FR 0.0001 REL FR 1 V 0 P
madam, undress you and come now to bed. SHR in.2. 117
UNDRESSED 1 FR 0.0001 REL FR 0 V 1 P
his inclination, after his undressed, unpolished LLL 4.02. 16 P
UNDROWN'D 2 FR 0.0002 REL FR 2 V 0 P
alive, | 'tis as impossible that he's undrown'd, TMP 2.01.237
i have no hope | that he's undrown'd. 2.01.239
UNDUTEOUS 1 FR 0.0001 REL FR 1 V 0 P
of craft, | of disobedience, or unduteous title, WIV 5.05.227
UNDUTIFUL 1 FR 0.0001 REL FR 1 V 0 P
i know my duty, you are all undutiful. 3H6 5.05. 33
/UNE 1 FR 0.0001 REL FR 0 V 1 P
and vetch me in my closet /une /boite /en verd, WIV 1.04. 45 P
UNE 2 FR 0.0002 REL FR 0 V 2 P
je reciterai une autre fois ma lecon ensemble: H5 3.04. 57 P
c'est assez pour une fois: allons–nous a diner. 3.04. 61 P
UNEAR'D 1 FR 0.0001 REL FR 1 V 0 P
for where is she so fair whose unear'd womb SON 3. 5
UNEARNED 1 FR 0.0001 REL FR 1 V 0 P
if we have unearned luck | now to scape the MND 5.01.432
UNEARTHED 1 FR 0.0001 REL FR 1 V 0 P
havoc in vast field | unearthed skulls proclaim, TNK 5.01. 52
UNEARTHLY 1 FR 0.0001 REL FR 1 V 0 P
solemn, and unearthly | it was i' th' off'ring! WT 3.01. 7
UNEASINESS 1 FR 0.0001 REL FR 1 V 0 P
that sits in heart–grief and uneasiness | under H5 2.02. 27
UNEASY 4 FR 0.0004 REL FR 3 V 1 P
but this swift business | i must uneasy make, TMP 1.02.452
i think it not uneasy to get the cause of my WT 4.02. 49 P
cribs, | upon uneasy pallets stretching thee, 2H4 3.01. 10
uneasy lies the head that wears a crown. 3.01. 31
UNEATH 1 FR 0.0001 REL FR 1 V 0 P
uneath may she endure the flinty streets, | to 2H6 2.04. 8
UNEDUCATED 1 FR 0.0001 REL FR 0 V 1 P
his undressed, unpolished, uneducated, unpruned,
LLL 4.02. 17 P
UNEFFECTUAL 1 FR 0.0001 REL FR 1 V 0 P
near, | and gins to pale his uneffectual fire. HAM 1.05. 90
UNELECTED 1 FR 0.0001 REL FR 1 V 0 P
of his choler, | and pass'd him unelected. COR 2.03.199
UNEQUAL 5 FR 0.0005 REL FR 5 V 0 P
of these times | to lay a heavy and unequal hand 2H4 4.01.100
a poor earl's daughter is unequal odds, | and 1H6 5.05. 34
to shape my legs of an unequal size, | to 3H6 3.02.159
unequal match'd, | pyrrhus at priam drives, in HAM 2.02.471
me for what you make me do | seems much unequal.
ANT 2.05.101
UNEVEN 7 FR 0.0008 REL FR 5 V 2 P
in most uneven and distracted manner. MM 4.04. 3 P
did fly, | that fallen am i in dark uneven way, MND 3.02.417
all is uneven, | and every thing is left at six R2 2.02.121
these high wild hills and rough uneven ways 2.03. 4
for more uneven and unwelcome news | came from
1H4 1.01. 50
eight yards of uneven ground is threescore and 2.02. 25 P
uneven is the course, i like it not. ROM 4.01. 5
UNEXAMIN'D 1 FR 0.0001 REL FR 1 V 0 P
untainted, unexamin'd, free, at liberty. R3 3.06. 9
UNEXECUTED 1 FR 0.0001 REL FR 1 V 0 P
leave unexecuted | your own renowned knowledge,
ANT 3.07. 44
UNEXPECTED 2 FR 0.0002 REL FR 2 V 0 P
by how much unexpected, by so much | we must JN 2.01. 80
all unwarily | devoured by the unexpected flood. 5.07. 64
UNEXPERIENC'D 1 FR 0.0001 REL FR 0 V 1 P
and thou return unexperienc'd to thy grave. SHR 4.01. 83 P
UNEXPERIENT 1 FR 0.0001 REL FR 1 V 0 P
that th' unexperient gave the tempter place, LC 318
UNEXPRESSIVE 1 FR 0.0001 REL FR 1 V 0 P
the fair, the chaste, and unexpressive she. AYL 3.02. 10
UNFAIR 1 FR 0.0001 REL FR 1 V 0 P
same, | and that unfair which fairly doth excel: SON 5. 4
UNFAITHFUL 1 FR 0.0001 REL FR 0 V 1 P
chosen out of the gross band of the unfaithful; AYL 4.01.195 P
UNFALLIBLE *(also infallible)*
UNFALLIBLE 1 FR 0.0001 REL FR 1 V 0 P
my words, | for they are certain and unfallible. 1H6 1.02. 59
UNFAM'D 1 FR 0.0001 REL FR 1 V 0 P
whose life were ill bestow'd, or death unfam'd, TRO 2.02.159
UNFASHIONABLE 1 FR 0.0001 REL FR 1 V 0 P
and that so lamely and unfashionable | that dogs R3 1.01. 22
UNFASTEN 1 FR 0.0001 REL FR 1 V 0 P
enemy, | he doth unfasten so and shake a friend, 2H4 4.01.207
UNFATHER'D 2 FR 0.0002 REL FR 2 V 0 P
unfather'd heirs and loathly births of nature. 2H4 4.04.122
it might for fortune's bastard be unfather'd, SON 124. 2
UNFATHERED 1 FR 0.0001 REL FR 1 V 0 P
me | but hope of orphans and unfathered fruit, SON 97.10
UNFEAR'D 1 FR 0.0001 REL FR 1 V 0 P
whose successes | makes heaven unfear'd, and TNK 1.02. 64
UNFED 1 FR 0.0001 REL FR 1 V 0 P
how shall your houseless heads and unfed sides, LR 3.04. 30
UNFEE'D 1 FR 0.0001 REL FR 0 V 1 P
then 'tis like the breath of an unfee'd lawyer, LR 1.04.129 P
UNFEELING 4 FR 0.0004 REL FR 4 V 0 P
unfeeling fools can with such wrongs dispense: ERR 2.01.103
this is no answer, thou unfeeling man, | to MV 4.01. 63
and dull unfeeling barren ignorance | is made my R2 1.03.168
and with my fingers feel his hand unfeeling. 2H6 3.02.145
UNFEIGNED 3 FR 0.0003 REL FR 3 V 0 P
and here i take the like unfeigned oath, | never SHR 4.02. 32
i come, in kindness and unfeigned love, | first, 3H6 3.03. 51
so much his friend, ay, his unfeigned friend, 3.03.202
UNFEIGNEDLY 4 FR 0.0004 REL FR 2 V 2 P
i most unfeignedly beseech your lordship to make
AWW 2.03.244 P
from love, | for i do love her most unfeignedly. JN 2.01.526
your hand, | and what you do, do it unfeignedly. R3 2.01. 22
this present stood unfeignedly on the same terms TNK 4.03. 68 P
UNFELLOW'D 1 FR 0.0001 REL FR 0 V 1 P
on him by them, in his meed he's unfellow'd. HAM 5.02.142 P
UNFELT 4 FR 0.0004 REL FR 4 V 0 P
all my treasury | is yet but unfelt thanks, R2 2.03. 61
and for unfelt imaginations | they often feel a R3 1.04. 80
to show an unfelt sorrow is an office | which MAC 2.03.136
o unfelt sore, crest–wounding private scar! LUC 828
UNFENCED 1 FR 0.0001 REL FR 1 V 0 P
even till unfenced desolation | leave them as JN 2.01.386
UNFILIAL 1 FR 0.0001 REL FR 1 V 0 P
if this be so, a wrong | something unfilial. WT 4.04.406
UNFILL'D 2 FR 0.0002 REL FR 1 V 1 P
i hate it as an unfill'd can. TN 2.03. 6 P
the veins unfill'd, our blood is cold, and then COR 5.01. 51
UNFINISH'D 4 FR 0.0004 REL FR 4 V 0 P
the chain unfinish'd made me stay thus long. ERR 3.02.168
deform'd, unfinish'd, sent before my time | into R3 1.01. 20
the other, though unfinish'd, yet so famous, H8 4.02. 61
"who wears a garment shapeless and unfinish'd? VEN 415
UNFIRM *(also infirm)*
UNFIRM 4 FR 0.0004 REL FR 4 V 0 P
our fancies are more giddy and unfirm, | more TN 2.04. 33
so is the unfirm king | in three divided, and 2H4 1.03. 73
being loose, unfirm, with digging up of graves, ROM 5.03. 6
the sway of earth | shakes like a thing unfirm? JC 1.03. 4
UNFIT 10 FR 0.0011 REL FR 10 V 0 P
you 'mongst men | being most unfit to live. TMP 3.03. 58
unfit to live, or die; MM 4.03. 64
though time seem so adverse and means unfit. AWW 5.01. 26
jest withal, | but far unfit to be a sovereign. 3H6 3.02. 92
and thou unfit for any place, but hell. R3 1.02.109
i am unfit for state and majesty. 3.07.205
unfit for other life, compell'd by hunger | and H8 1.02. 34
you'll find a most unfit time to disturb him. 2.02. 60
thought | unfit to hear moral philosophy. TRO 2.02.167
very ill at ease, | unfit for mine own purposes. OTH 3.03. 33
UNFITNESS 1 FR 0.0001 REL FR 1 V 0 P
when i have show'd th' unfitness — how now, LR 1.04.333
UNFIX 3 FR 0.0003 REL FR 3 V 0 P
his friends | that, plucking to unfix an enemy, 2H4 4.01.206
whose horrid image doth unfix my hair | and make
MAC 1.03.135
bid the tree | unfix his earth–bound root? 4.01. 96
UNFLEDG'D 3 FR 0.0003 REL FR 3 V 0 P
in those unfledg'd days was my wife a girl; WT 1.02. 78
of each new–hatch'd, unfledg'd courage. HAM 1.03. 65
we poor unfledg'd | have never wing'd from view CYM 3.03. 27
/UNFOLD 1 FR 0.0001 REL FR 1 V 0 P
/are /wrong'd /and /would /unfold /our /griefs, 2H4 4.01. 77
UNFOLD 31 FR 0.0035 REL FR 30 V 1 P
and i to /ford shall eke unfold | how falstaff, WIV 1.03. 96
of government the properties to unfold | would MM 1.01. 3
to th' observer doth thy history | fully unfold. 1.01. 29
time | unfold the evil which is here wrapp'd up 5.01.117
helen, to you our minds we will unfold: MND 1.01.208
never to unfold to any one | which casket 'twas MV 2.09. 10
unfold to us some warlike resistance. AWW 1.01.116 P
o, then unfold the passion of my love, TN 1.04. 24
i charge thee by thy reverence | here to unfold, 5.01.152
men | i will unfold some causes of your deaths: R2 3.01. 7
the worst is worldly loss thou canst unfold. 3.02. 94
still unfold | the acts commenced on this ball 2H4 in 4
and justly and religiously unfold | why the law H5 1.02. 10
unfold it. 3.06.117
such as my heart doth tremble to unfold: 2H6 2.01.162
did | when he to madding dido would unfold | his 3.02.117
tongue | unfold the imagin'd happiness that both ROM 2.06. 28
that you unfold to me, yourself, your half, JC 2.01.274
i shall unfold to thee, as we are going, | to 2.01.330
england, and unfold | his message ere he come, MAC 3.06. 46
nay, answer me. stand and unfold yourself. HAM 1.01. 2
thy serious hearing | to what i shall unfold. 1.05. 6
i could a tale unfold whose lightest word 1.05. 15
time shall unfold what plighted cunning hides, LR 1.01.280
o /heaven, that such companions thou'dst unfold, OTH 4.02.141
and, besides, the moor | may unfold me to him; 5.01. 21
crush him together rather than unfold | his CYM 1.01. 26
i shall unfold equal discourtesy | to your best 2.03. 96
for mine own part unfold a dangerous speech, 5.05.313
for they their guilt with weeping will unfold, LUC 754
and there we will unfold | to creatures stern, 1146
UNFOLDED 4 FR 0.0004 REL FR 2 V 2 P
eye upon my follies, as you hear them unfolded, WIV 2.02.186 P
to what purpose have you unfolded this to me? 2.02.218 P
his contrary proceedings | are all unfolded; H8 3.02. 27

must i be unfolded | with one that i have bred? ANT 5.02.170
UNFOLDETH 1 FR 0.0001 REL FR 1 V 0 P
mine own escape unfoldeth to my hope, | whereto TN 1.02. 19
UNFOLDING* 3 FR 0.0003 REL FR 2 V 1 P
look, th' unfolding star calls up the shepherd. MM 4.02.203 P
to my unfolding lend your prosperous ear, | and OTH 1.03.244
blest, | by new unfolding his imprison'd pride. SON 52.12
UNFOLDS 3 FR 0.0003 REL FR 3 V 0 P
in a spleen, unfolds both heaven and earth; MND 1.01.146
of good and bad, that makes and unfolds error, WT 4.01. 2
sees and knows more, much more, than he unfolds. OTH 3.03.243
UNFOOL 1 FR 0.0001 REL FR 0 V 1 P
page, have you any way then to unfool me again? WIV 4.02.115 P
UNFORC'D 2 FR 0.0002 REL FR 1 V 1 P
this gentle and unforc'd accord of hamlet | sits HAM 1.02.123
(as it is a most pregnant and unforc'd position) OTH 2.01.236 P
UNFORFEITED 1 FR 0.0001 REL FR 1 V 0 P
are wont | to keep obliged faith unforfeited! MV 2.06. 7
UNFORTIFIED 1 FR 0.0001 REL FR 1 V 0 P
a heart unfortified, or mind impatient, | an HAM 1.02. 96
UNFORTUNATE *(also infortunate)*
UNFORTUNATE 10 FR 0.0011 REL FR 7 V 3 P
of rosalind, i am that he, that unfortunate he. AYL 3.02.395 P
your unfortunate son, bertram." AWW 3.02. 26 P
at them, | howe'er unfortunate i miss'd my aim. 1H6 1.04. 4
the more that henry was unfortunate. 3H6 3.03.118
how more unfortunate than all living women | are COR 5.03. 97
day sent to me, i was so unfortunate a beggar. TIM 3.06. 43 P
and all unfortunate souls | that trace him in MAC 4.01.152
a poor unfortunate beggar. LR 4.06. 68
where is this rash and most unfortunate man? OTH 5.02.283
he said he was gentle, but unfortunate; CYM 4.02. 39
UNFORTUNATELY 1 FR 0.0001 REL FR 1 V 0 P
and in her haste unfortunately spies | the foul VEN 1029
UNFOUGHT 1 FR 0.0001 REL FR 1 V 0 P
if they march along | unfought withal, but i H5 3.05. 12
UNFREQUENTED 2 FR 0.0002 REL FR 2 V 0 P
this shadowy desert, unfrequented woods, | i TGV 5.04. 2
and many unfrequented plots there are, | fitted TIT 2.01.115
UNFRIENDED 3 FR 0.0003 REL FR 3 V 0 P
unguided and unfriended, often prove | rough and TN 3.03. 10
unfriended, new adopted to our hate, | dow'r'd LR 1.01.203
and charge me live to comfort this unfriended, TNK 5.03.141
UNFRIENDLY 1 FR 0.0001 REL FR 1 V 0 P
th' unfriendly elements | forgot thee utterly, PER 3.01. 57
UNFRUITFUL 1 FR 0.0001 REL FR 1 V 0 P
but in the midst of his unfruitful prayer, LUC 344
UNFURNISH 1 FR 0.0001 REL FR 1 V 0 P
that which may | unfurnish me of reason. WT 5.01.123
UNFURNISH'D 5 FR 0.0005 REL FR 5 V 0 P
steal both his | and leave itself unfurnish'd. MV 3.02.126
see | but empty lodgings and unfurnish'd walls, R2 1.02. 68
but that the scot on his unfurnish'd kingdom H5 1.02.148
unfurnish'd of her well–beseeming troop? TIT 2.03. 56
we shall be much unfurnish'd for this time. ROM 4.02. 10
UNGAIN'D 2 FR 0.0002 REL FR 2 V 0 P
men prize the thing ungain'd more than it is. TRO 1.02.289
ungain'd, beseech; 1.02.293
UNGALLED 2 FR 0.0002 REL FR 2 V 0 P
rout | against your yet ungalled estimation, ERR 3.01.102
strooken deer go weep, | the hart ungalled play, HAM 3.02.272
UNGARTER'D 2 FR 0.0002 REL FR 0 V 2 P
you chid at sir proteus for going ungarter'd! TGV 2.01. 73 P
then your hose should be ungarter'd, your bonnet AYL 3.02.378 P
UNGART'RED 1 FR 0.0001 REL FR 1 V 0 P
ungart'red, and down–gyved to his ankle, | pale HAM 2.01. 77
UNGENITUR'D 1 FR 0.0001 REL FR 0 V 1 P
this ungenitur'd agent will unpeople the MM 3.02.174 P
UNGENTLE 12 FR 0.0013 REL FR 12 V 0 P
vicious, ungentle, foolish, blunt, unkind, ERR 4.02. 21
study | to seem despiteful and ungentle to you. AYL 5.02. 80
for this ungentle business, | put on thee by my WT 3.03. 34
to th' fearful usage | (at least ungentle) of 5.01.154
to crush our old limbs in ungentle steel. 1H4 5.01. 13
by us you us'd us so | as that ungentle gull, 5.01. 60
ungentle queen, to call him gentle suffolk! 2H6 3.02.290
or strike, ungentle death! 3H6 2.03. 6
what stern ungentle hands | hath lopp'd and TIT 2.04. 16
was, | you star'd upon me with ungentle looks. JC 2.01.242
for caesar cannot /live | to be ungentle. ANT 5.01. 60
though most ungentle fortune | have plac'd me in PER 4.06. 96
UNGENTLENESS 1 FR 0.0001 REL FR 1 V 0 P
youth, you have done me much ungentleness, | to AYL 5.02. 77
UNGENTLY 3 FR 0.0003 REL FR 3 V 0 P
why speaks my father so ungently? TMP 1.02.445
when was my lord so much ungently temper'd | to TRO 5.03. 1
y' have ungently, brutus, | stole from my bed; JC 2.01.237
UNGIRD 1 FR 0.0001 REL FR 0 V 1 P
i prithee now ungird thy strangeness and tell me TN 4.01. 15 P
UNGODLY 1 FR 0.0001 REL FR 1 V 0 P
let not the hours of this ungodly day | wear out JN 3.01.109
UNGOR'D 1 FR 0.0001 REL FR 1 V 0 P
president of peace | to /keep my name ungor'd. HAM 5.02.250
UNGOT 1 FR 0.0001 REL FR 1 V 0 P
touch or soil with her | as she from one ungot. MM 5.01.142
UNGOTTEN 1 FR 0.0001 REL FR 1 V 0 P
and some are yet ungotten and unborn | that H5 1.02.287
UNGOVERN'D 5 FR 0.0005 REL FR 5 V 0 P
such as the fury of ungovern'd youth | thrust TGV 4.01. 43
how much the estate is green and yet ungovern'd. R3 2.02.127
and all good men of this ungovern'd isle. 3.07.110
ungovern'd youth, to wail it /in their age; 4.04.392
lest his ungovern'd rage dissolve the life LR 4.04. 19
UNGRACIOUS 8 FR 0.0009 REL FR 7 V 1 P
ungracious wretch, | fit for the mountains and TN 4.01. 47
"grace" | in an ungracious mouth is but profane. R2 2.03. 89
swearest thou, ungracious boy? 1H4 2.04.445 P
and there cut off thy most ungracious head, 2H6 4.10. 82
nor i, ungracious, speak unto myself | for him, R3 2.01.128
peace, you ungracious clamors! TRO 1.01. 89
do not, as some ungracious pastors do, | show me HAM 1.03. 47
with this ungracious paper strike the sight | of LR 4.06.276
UNGRATEFUL *(also ingrate, ingrateful)*
UNGRATEFUL 7 FR 0.0008 REL FR 7 V 0 P
most ungrateful maid! MND 3.02.195
in common worldly things 'tis call'd ungrateful R3 2.02. 91
war | into the bowels of ungrateful rome, | like COR 4.05.130
oft | for his ungrateful country done the like. TIT 4.01.111
shaken with sorrows in ungrateful rome. 4.03. 17
man | when he looks out in an ungrateful shape! TIM 3.02. 73
not to be held ungrateful to her goodness — TNK 4.01. 22
UNGRAVELY 1 FR 0.0001 REL FR 1 V 0 P
which most gibingly, ungravely, he did fashion COR 2.03.225
UNGROWN 2 FR 0.0002 REL FR 2 V 0 P
i did look for | of such an ungrown warrior. 1H4 5.04. 23
me, | no fisher but the ungrown fry forbears; VEN 526
UNGUARDED 3 FR 0.0003 REL FR 3 V 0 P
to her unguarded nest the weasel (scot) | comes H5 1.02.170
you and i perform upon | th' unguarded duncan? MAC 1.07. 70
the back door open | of the unguarded hearts, CYM 5.03. 46
UNGUEM 1 FR 0.0001 REL FR 0 V 1 P
o, i smell false latin, "dunghill" for unguem. LLL 5.01. 79 P
UNGUIDED 2 FR 0.0002 REL FR 2 V 0 P
unguided and unfriended, often prove | rough and TN 3.03. 10
th' unguided days | and rotten times that you 2H4 4.04. 59
UNHACK'D 2 FR 0.0002 REL FR 2 V 0 P
with unhack'd swords, and helmets all unbruis'd, JN 2.01.254
to part with unhack'd edges and bear back | our ANT 2.06. 38
UNHAIR 1 FR 0.0001 REL FR 1 V 0 P
i'll unhair thy head, | thou shalt be whipt with ANT 2.05. 64
/UNHAIR'D 1 FR 0.0001 REL FR 1 V 0 P
this /unhair'd sauciness and boyish troops, JN 5.02.133
/UNHALLOW'D 1 FR 0.0001 REL FR 1 V 0 P
from this /unhallow'd and blood–stained hole? TIT 2.03.210
UNHALLOW'D 1 FR 0.0001 REL FR 1 V 0 P
state holy or unhallow'd, what of that? 1H6 3.01. 59
UNHALLOWED 10 FR 0.0011 REL FR 10 V 0 P
why, thou unreverend and unhallowed friar, MM 5.01.305
and, whilst thou layest in thy unhallowed dam, MV 4.01.136
let never day nor night unhallowed pass, | but 2H6 2.01. 83
and bid that strumpet, your unhallowed dam, TIT 5.02.190
away, inhuman dog, unhallowed slave! 5.03. 14
stop thy unhallowed toil, vile montague! ROM 5.03. 54
would set me free from this unhallowed place, PER 4.06.100
and die, unhallowed thoughts, before you blot LUC 192
lies, | to be admir'd of lewd unhallowed eyes. 392
so his unhallowed haste her words delays, | and 552
UNHAND 1 FR 0.0001 REL FR 1 V 0 P
unhand me, gentlemen. HAM 1.04. 84
UNHANDLED 2 FR 0.0002 REL FR 2 V 0 P
herd, | or race of youthful and unhandled colts, MV 5.01. 72
has left the cause o' th' king unhandled, and H8 3.02. 58
UNHANDSOME 4 FR 0.0004 REL FR 2 V 2 P
were she other than she is, she were unhandsome, ADO 1.01.175 P
but it is no more unhandsome than to see the AYL ep 2 P
to bring a slovenly unhandsome corse | betwixt 1H4 1.03. 44
emilia, | i was (unhandsome warrior as i am) OTH 3.04.151
UNHANG'D 1 FR 0.0001 REL FR 0 V 1 P
lives not three good men unhang'd in england, 1H4 2.04.131 P
UNHAPPIED 1 FR 0.0001 REL FR 1 V 0 P
by you unhappied and disfigured clean; R2 3.01. 10
UNHAPPILY 5 FR 0.0005 REL FR 4 V 1 P
unhappily, even so. MM 1.02.156
you, cardinal, | i should judge now unhappily. H8 1.04. 89
though nothing sure, yet much unhappily. HAM 4.05. 13
the effects he writes of succeed unhappily, /as LR 1.02.144 P
jollity, | and purest faith unhappily forsworn, SON 66. 4
UNHAPPINESS 2 FR 0.0002 REL FR 1 V 1 P
often dreamt of unhappiness and wak'd herself ADO 2.01.345 P
the view, | and that be heir to his unhappiness! R3 1.02. 25
UNHAPP'LY 1 FR 0.0001 REL FR 1 V 0 P
happ'ly that name of "chaste" unhapp'ly set LUC 8
UNHAPPY 41 FR 0.0046 REL FR 38 V 3 P
and now am i, unhappy messenger, | to plead for TGV 4.04. 99
law, | have some unhappy passenger in chase. 5.04. 15
o miserable, unhappy that i am! 5.04. 28
unhappy were you, madam, ere i came; 5.04. 29
by thy approach thou mak'st me most unhappy. 5.04. 31
o me unhappy! 5.04. 84
fair sister | to her unhappy brother claudio? MM 1.04. 20
why "her unhappy brother"? 1.04. 21
unhappy claudio! 4.03.121
in quest of them (unhappy), ah, lose myself. ERR 1.02. 40
o most unhappy day! 4.04.123
o most unhappy strumpet! 4.04.124
ay, and a shrowd unhappy gallows too. LLL 5.02. 12
i am th' unhappy subject of these quarrels. MV 5.01.238
o unhappy youth, | come not within these doors! AYL 2.03. 16
thou seest we are not all alone unhappy: 2.07.136
but be thou arm'd for some unhappy words. SHR 2.01.139
a shrewd knave and an unhappy. AWW 4.05. 63 P
as chaste, as true, | as i am now unhappy; WT 3.02. 35
kings are no less unhappy, their issue not being 4.02. 26 P
again of dear sicilia | and that unhappy king, 4.04.512
to–day, to–day, unhappy day, too late, R2 3.02. 71
and then it was when the unhappy king | (whose 1H4 1.03.148
ay me, unhappy, | to be a queen, and crown'd 2H6 3.02. 70
and cry, "o clarence, my unhappy son!"? R3 2.02. 4
edward's unhappy sons do bid thee flourish. 5.03.153
i am the most unhappy woman living. H8 3.01.147
the unhappy sons of old andronicus, | brought TIT 2.03.250
accurs'd, unhappy, wretched, hateful day! ROM 4.05. 43
unhappy fortune! 5.02. 17
unhappy that i am, i cannot heave | my heart LR 1.01. 91
thou old unhappy traitor, | briefly thyself 4.06.228
o unhappy girl! OTH 1.01.163
i have very poor and unhappy brains for drinking 2.03. 34 P
i am most unhappy in the loss of it. 3.04.102
a most unhappy one. 4.01.232
a more unhappy lady, | if this division chance, ANT 3.04. 12
unhappy was the clock | that strook the hour! CYM 5.05.153
already, | and make a conquest of unhappy me, PER 1.04. 69
must be the sacrifice | to my unhappy beauty? TNK 4.02. 64
comparing him to that unhappy guest | whose deed LUC 1565
UNHARDENED 1 FR 0.0001 REL FR 1 V 0 P
of strong prevailment in unhardened youth. MND 1.01. 35
UNHARD'NED 1 FR 0.0001 REL FR 1 V 0 P
yet unhard'ned in | the crimes of nature — let TNK 1.02. 2
UNHATCH'D* 2 FR 0.0002 REL FR 1 V 1 P
dubb'd with unhatch'd rapier and on carpet TN 3.04.235 P
or some unhatch'd practice | made demonstrable OTH 3.04.141
UNHEARD 4 FR 0.0004 REL FR 4 V 0 P
then let the worst unheard fall on your head. JN 4.02.136
as cominius is return'd, | unheard — what then? COR 5.01. 43
if she perform, | she shall not sue unheard. ANT 3.12. 24
is as a whisper in the ears of death, | unheard. PER 3.01. 10
UNHEARTS 1 FR 0.0001 REL FR 1 V 0 P
lip | and hum at good cominius much unhearts me. COR 5.01. 49
UNHEEDFUL 2 FR 0.0002 REL FR 2 V 0 P
unheedful vows may heedfully be broken, | and he TGV 2.06. 11
his gloss of former honor | by this unheedful, 1H6 4.04. 7
UNHEEDFULLY 1 FR 0.0001 REL FR 1 V 0 P
ay, madam, so you stumble not unheedfully. TGV 1.02. 3
UNHEEDY 1 FR 0.0001 REL FR 1 V 0 P
wings, and no eyes, figure unheedy haste; MND 1.01.237
UNHELPFUL 1 FR 0.0001 REL FR 1 V 0 P
gloucester's case | with sad unhelpful tears, 2H6 3.01.218
UNHIDDEN 1 FR 0.0001 REL FR 1 V 0 P
the severals and unhidden passages | of his true H5 1.01. 86
UNHOLY 4 FR 0.0004 REL FR 4 V 0 P
hence, | to keep me from a most unholy match, TGV 4.03. 30
which was your shame, by this unholy braggart, COR 5.06.118
show, | but mere /implorators of unholy suits, HAM 1.03.129
and heavy well–a–day | in her unholy service. PER 4.04. 50
UNHOP'D 1 FR 0.0001 REL FR 1 V 0 P
mine such as fill my heart with unhop'd joys. 3H6 3.03.172
UNHOPEFULLEST 1 FR 0.0001 REL FR 0 V 1 P
is not the unhopefullest husband that i know. ADO 2.01.377 P
UNHORSE 1 FR 0.0001 REL FR 1 V 0 P
that | he would unhorse the lustiest challenger. R2 5.03. 19
UNHOSPITABLE *(also inhospitable)*
UNHOSPITABLE 1 FR 0.0001 REL FR 1 V 0 P
often prove | rough and unhospitable. TN 3.03. 11
UNHOUSED 2 FR 0.0002 REL FR 2 V 0 P
of wreakful heaven, whose bare unhoused trunks, TIM 4.03.229
i would not my unhoused free condition | put OTH 1.02. 26
UNHOUS'LED 1 FR 0.0001 REL FR 1 V 0 P
sin, | unhous'led, disappointed, unanel'd, | no HAM 1.05. 77
UNHURTFUL 1 FR 0.0001 REL FR 0 V 1 P
or you imagine me too unhurtful an opposite. MM 3.02.165 P
UNICORN 2 FR 0.0002 REL FR 1 V 1 P
wert thou the unicorn, pride and wrath would TIM 4.03.336 P
slaughter, | to tame the unicorn and lion wild, LUC 956
UNICORNS 2 FR 0.0002 REL FR 2 V 0 P
now i will believe | that there are unicorns; TMP 3.03. 22
hear | that unicorns may be betray'd with trees, JC 2.01.204
UNIMPROVED 1 FR 0.0001 REL FR 1 V 0 P
fortinbras, | of unimproved mettle hot and full, HAM 1.01. 96
UNINHABITABLE *(also inhabitable)*
UNINHABITABLE 1 FR 0.0001 REL FR 0 V 1 P
uninhabitable, and almost inaccessible — TMP 2.01. 38 P
UNINTELLIGENT 1 FR 0.0001 REL FR 0 V 1 P
your senses (unintelligent of our insufficience) WT 1.01. 14 P
/UNION* 2 FR 0.0002 REL FR 2 V 0 P
and in the cup an /union shall he throw, HAM 5.02.272
is /thy /union here? 5.02.326
UNION* 3 FR 0.0003 REL FR 3 V 0 P
the union of your bed with weeds so loathly TMP 4.01. 21
seeming parted, | but yet an union in partition, MND 3.02.210
this union shall do more than battery can | to JN 2.01.446
UNIONS 1 FR 0.0001 REL FR 1 V 0 P
by unions married, do offend thine ear, | they SON 8. 6
UNITE 6 FR 0.0006 REL FR 6 V 0 P
unite | your troops of horsemen with his bands 1H6 4.01.164
soul, | if sympathy of love unite our thoughts. 2H6 1.01. 23
we will unite the white rose and the red. R3 5.05. 19
if you will now unite in your complaints, | and H8 3.02. 1
our hands | unite comutual in most sacred bands. HAM 3.02.160
should again unite | his favor with the radiant CYM 5.05.474
UNITED 5 FR 0.0005 REL FR 5 V 0 P
marrying, | to give our hearts united ceremony. WIV 4.06. 51
that done, dissever your united strengths, | and JN 2.01.388
our peace will, like a broken limb united, 2H4 4.01.220
in, | that the united vessel of their blood, 4.04. 44
you peers, continue this united league. R3 2.01. 2
UNITY 8 FR 0.0009 REL FR 6 V 2 P
you see, there is such unity in the proofs. WT 5.02. 32 P
allies, | and make me happy in your unity. R3 2.01. 31
the unity the king my husband made | thou hadst 4.04.379
the unity and married calm of states | quite TRO 1.03.100
delight, | if there be rule in unity itself, 5.02.141
universal peace, confound | all unity on earth. MAC 4.03.100
if i were bound to divine of this unity, i would ANT 2.06.116 P
these contraries such unity do hold | only to LUC 1558
UNIVERSAL *(also versal)*
UNIVERSAL 14 FR 0.0015 REL FR 11 V 3 P
why, universal plodding poisons up | the nimble LLL 4.03.301
eyes, | hearing applause and universal shout, MV 3.02.143
this wide and universal theatre | presents more AYL 2.07.137
could have seen't, the woe had been universal. WT 5.02. 92 P
a largess universal, like the sun, | his liberal H5 4.pr. 43
the greatest admiration in the universal world, 4.01. 66 P
arrant traitor as any's in the universal world, 4.08. 10 P
and appetite, an universal wolf | (so doubly TRO 1.03.121
power), | must make perforce an universal prey, 1.03.123
crown'd | sole monarch of the universal earth. ROM 3.02. 94
appear, | have you not made an universal shout, JC 1.01. 44
uproar the universal peace, confound | all unity MAC 4.03. 99
under his shroud, | the universal landlord. ANT 3.13. 72
the time of universal peace is near. 4.06. 4
UNIVERSE 2 FR 0.0002 REL FR 2 V 0 P
dark | fills the wide vessel of the universe. H5 4.pr. 3
for nothing this wide universe i call, | save SON 109.13
UNIVERSITIES 1 FR 0.0001 REL FR 1 V 0 P
some to the studious universities. TGV 1.03. 10
UNIVERSITY 2 FR 0.0002 REL FR 0 V 2 P
son and my servant spend all at the university. SHR 5.01. 70 P
you play'd once i' th' university, you say? HAM 3.02. 99 P
UNJOINTED 1 FR 0.0001 REL FR 1 V 0 P
this bald unjointed chat of his, my lord, | i 1H4 1.03. 65
UNJUST 25 FR 0.0028 REL FR 19 V 6 P
and now i must be as unjust to thurio: TGV 4.02. 2
for theseus' perjury and unjust flight; 4.04.168
his unjust unkindness (that in all reason should MM 3.01.240 P

the duke's unjust | thus to retort your manifest 5.01.300
"unjust"? 5.01.313
so that, in this unjust divorce of us, | fortune ERR 1.01.104
thirdly, they have verified unjust things; ADO 5.01.218 P
oft our displeasures, to ourselves unjust, AWW 5.03. 63
in this uncivil and unjust extent | against thy TN 4.01. 53
is the time that the unjust man doth thrive. WT 4.04.674 P
as true | in this appeal as thou art all unjust, R2 4.01. 45
power | did gage them both in an unjust behalf 1H4 1.03.173
thou art an unjust man in saying so. 3.03.129 P
never soldiers, but discarded unjust servingmen, 4.02. 28 P
the north, | finding his usurpation most unjust, 1H6 2.05. 68
o passing traitor, perjur'd and unjust! 3H6 5.01.106
a false-hearted rogue, a most unjust knave. TRO 5.01. 89 P
say my request's unjust, | and spurn me back; COR 5.03.164
my lord, you are unjust, and more than so, | in TIT 1.01.292
quarrels unjust against the good and loyal, MAC 4.03. 83
no; but unjust | if thou pursue that sight. TNK 2.02.192
and justly thus controls his thoughts unjust: LUC 189
both which, as servitors to the unjust, | so 285
unless thy lady prove unjust, | press never thou PP 18.21
but wherefore says she not she is unjust? SON 138. 9
UNJUSTICE *(also injustice)*
UNJUSTICE 1 FR 0.0001 REL FR 1 V 0 P
and blazoning our unjustice every where? TIT 4.04. 18
UNJUSTLY 9 FR 0.0010 REL FR 8 V 1 P
no sin | to cozen him that would unjustly win. AWW 4.02. 76
not light, | if i be traitor or unjustly fight! R2 1.01. 83
which salique land the french unjustly gloze H5 1.02. 40
and i, unjustly too, must grant it you. R3 2.01.126
which, as thou know'st, unjustly must be spilt. 3.03. 23
you charge me most unjustly. OTH 4.02.184 P
knows | thou didst unjustly banish me; CYM 3.03.100
and i know your office | unjustly is achiev'd. TNK 3.01.112
and by this chaste blood so unjustly stained, LUC 1836
UNKENNEL 2 FR 0.0002 REL FR 1 V 1 P
i'll warrant we'll unkennel the fox. WIV 3.03.163 P
guilt | do not itself unkennel in one speech, HAM 3.02. 81
UNKEPT 1 FR 0.0001 REL FR 0 V 1 P
more properly, stays me here at home unkept; AYL 1.01. 8 P
UNKIND 30 FR 0.0034 REL FR 30 V 0 P
unkind julia, | as in revenge of thy ingratitude TGV 1.02.106
thou, that hast no unkind mate to grieve thee, ERR 2.01. 38
vicious, ungentle, foolish, blunt, unkind, 4.02. 21
you are unkind, demetrius; MND 3.02.162
you give your wife too unkind a cause of grief; MV 5.01.175
thou art not so unkind | as man's ingratitude; AYL 2.07.175
fie, fie, unknit that threat'ning unkind brow, SHR 5.02.136
none can be call'd deform'd but the unkind. TN 3.04.368
"my lady is unkind, perdie." 4.02. 75
unkind remembrance! JN 5.06. 12
have forg'd against yourself | by unkind usage, 1H4 5.01. 69
but more, when envy breeds unkind division: 1H6 4.01.193
nor set no footing on this unkind shore"? 2H6 3.02. 87
assure yourselves, will never be unkind. 4.09. 19
but an unkind self, that itself will leave | to TRO 3.02.149
titus, unkind and careless of thine own, | why TIT 1.01. 86
what hast thou done, unnatural and unkind? 5.03. 48
ah, what an unkind hour | is guilty of this ROM 5.03.145
we were not all unkind, nor all deserve | the TIM 5.04. 21
rich gifts wax poor when givers prove unkind. HAM 3.01.100
bid them farewell, cordelia, though unkind, LR 1.01.260
to such a lowness but his unkind daughters. 3.04. 71
between him and my lord | an unkind breach; OTH 4.01.225
speedily | from our kind air, to them unkind, TNK 1.04. 38
"ay me," quoth venus, "young, and so unkind, VEN 187
she had not brought forth thee, but died unkind. 204
she puts on outward strangeness, seems unkind: 310
that you were once unkind befriends me now, SON 120. 1
sake, | so him i lose through my unkind abuse. 134.12
let no unkind, no fair beseechers kill; 135.13
UNKINDEST 4 FR 0.0004 REL FR 2 V 2 P
for it is the unkindest tied that ever any man TGV 2.03. 38 P
what's the unkindest tide? 2.03. 39 P
th' unkindest beast more kinder than mankind. TIM 4.01. 36
this was the most unkindest cut of all; JC 3.02.183
UNKINDLY 6 FR 0.0006 REL FR 5 V 1 P
but why unkindly didst thou leave me so? MND 3.02.183
good master, take it not unkindly, pray, | that SHR 3.01. 57
lastly, myself unkindly banished, | the gates TIT 5.03.104
hope it remains not unkindly with your lordship TIM 3.06. 36 P
resolv'd | if brutus so unkindly knock'd or no; JC 3.02.180
i take it much unkindly | that thou, iago, who OTH 1.01. 1
/UNKINDNESS 1 FR 0.0001 REL FR 1 V 0 P
/his /own /unkindness, | /that /stripp'd /her LR 4.03. 42
UNKINDNESS 23 FR 0.0026 REL FR 18 V 5 P
i hope we shall drink down all unkindness. WIV 1.01.197 P
but thy unkindness shall his death draw out | to MM 2.04.166
his unjust unkindness (that in all reason should 3.01.240 P
unkindness blunts it more than marble hard. ERR 2.01. 93
take no unkindness of his hasty words. SHR 4.03.167
is there any unkindness between my lord and you, AWW 2.05. 32 P
him | 'twixt his unkindness and his kindness: WT 4.04.552
have, | and thy unkindness be like crooked age, R2 2.01.133
tears as salt as sea, through thy unkindness. 2H6 3.02. 96
friend, grief-shot | with his unkindness? COR 5.01. 45
that nature being sick of man's unkindness TIM 4.03.176
in this i bury all unkindness, cassius. JC 4.03.159
who may i rather challenge for unkindness | than MAC 3.04. 41
as a very pretense and purpose of unkindness. LR 1.04. 71 P
she hath tied | sharp-tooth'd unkindness, like a 2.04.135
i tax not you, you elements, with unkindness; 3.02. 16
i am) | arraigning his unkindness with my soul; OTH 3.04.152
unkindness may do much, | and his unkindness may 4.02.159
much, | and his unkindness may defeat my life, 4.02.160
we see how mortal an unkindness is to them; ANT 1.02.134 P
to mend the hurt that his unkindness marr'd: VEN 478
for if you were by my unkindness shaken | as i SON 120. 5
wrong | that thy unkindness lays upon my heart, 139. 2
/UNKING'D 1 FR 0.0001 REL FR 1 V 0 P
/save /king /henry, /unking'd /richard /says, R2 4.01.220
UNKING'D 1 FR 0.0001 REL FR 1 V 0 P
by | think that i am unking'd by bullingbrook, R2 5.05. 37
UNKINGLIKE 1 FR 0.0001 REL FR 1 V 0 P
than they, must needs | appear unkinglike. CYM 3.05. 7
UNKISS 1 FR 0.0001 REL FR 1 V 0 P
let me unkiss the oath 'twixt thee and me; R2 5.01. 74
UNKISS'D 1 FR 0.0001 REL FR 0 V 1 P
therefore i will depart unkiss'd. ADO 5.02. 54 P
/UNKNIT 1 FR 0.0001 REL FR 1 V 0 P
/marcus, /unknit /that //sorrow-wreathen /knot; TIT 3.02. 4
UNKNIT 3 FR 0.0003 REL FR 3 V 0 P
fie, fie, unknit that threat'ning unkind brow, SHR 5.02.136
will you again unknit | this churlish knot of 1H4 5.01. 15
and not unknit himself | the noble knot he made. COR 4.02. 31
UNKNOWING 1 FR 0.0001 REL FR 1 V 0 P
and let me speak to /th' yet unknowing world HAM 5.02.379
UNKNOWN 48 FR 0.0054 REL FR 39 V 9 P
'tis not unknown to thee that i have sought | to TGV 3.01. 61
employ'd and pain'd | your unknown sovereignty! MM 5.01.387
plead on /her part some cause to you unknown; ERR 3.01. 91
you, | to make it wander in an unknown field? 3.02. 38
/that he, unknown to me, should be in debt. 4.02. 48
this shame derives itself from unknown loins"? ADO 4.01.135
bodies forth | the forms of things unknown, the MND 5.01. 15
'tis not unknown to you, antonio, | how much i MV 1.01.122
my affection hath an unknown bottom, like the AYL 4.01.208 P
to whom my father is not all unknown, | and were SHR 1.02.239
nor is your firm resolve unknown to me, | in the 2.01. 92
'tis not unknown to you, madam, i am a poor AWW 1.03. 13 P
we should submit ourselves to an unknown fear. 2.03. 6 P
"to the unknown belov'd, this, and my good TN 2.05. 90 P
his happier affairs may be, are to me unknown; WT 4.02. 30 P
you bid | these unknown friends to 's welcome, 4.04. 65
and, friends unknown, you shall bear witness 4.04.384
or the profound seas hides | in unknown fadoms, 4.04.491
and for the world, familiar to us and unknown, H5 3.07. 37 P
my worth unknown, no loss is known in me. 1H6 4.05. 23
tut, these are petty faults to faults unknown, 2H6 3.01. 64
for divers unknown reasons, i beseech you, R3 1.02.217
nobles were committed | is all unknown to me, my 2.04. 48
apprehended here immediately | th' unknown ajax. TRO 3.03.125
our business is not unknown to th' senate; COR 1.01. 57 P
and the end of it | unknown to the beginning. 3.01.327
too early seen unknown, and known too late! ROM 1.05.139
in /states unborn and accents yet unknown! JC 3.01.113
the posture of your blows are yet unknown; 5.01. 33
tell me, thou unknown power — MAC 4.01. 69
i am yet | unknown to woman, never was forsworn, 4.03.126
whether aught, to us unknown, afflicts him thus, HAM 2.02. 17
things standing thus unknown, shall i leave 5.02.345
wast not bound to answer | an unknown opposite. LR 5.03.154
comfort like to this | succeeds in unknown fate. OTH 2.01.193
is not to leave't undone, but keep't unknown. 3.03.204
being done unknown, | i should have found it ANT 2.07. 78
blest beams, remaining | so long a poor unknown. CYM 4.04. 43
and thus, unknown, | pitied nor hated, to the 5.01. 27
as a lion's whelp shall, to himself unknown, 5.04.139 P
as a lion's whelp shall, to himself unknown, 5.05.436 P
unknown to you, unsought, were clipt about 5.05.451
lord has /betook himself to unknown travels; PER 1.03. 34
of that rich jewel he should keep unknown | from LUC 34
she touch'd no unknown baits, nor fear'd no 103
the fault unknown is as a thought unacted. 527
whose worth's unknown, although his highth be SON 116. 8
that i have frequent been with unknown minds, 117. 5
UNLAC'D 1 FR 0.0001 REL FR 1 V 0 P
quoth she, "the warlike god unlac'd me," | as if PP 11. 7
UNLACE 1 FR 0.0001 REL FR 1 V 0 P
matter | that you unlace your reputation thus, OTH 2.03.194
UNLAID 2 FR 0.0002 REL FR 2 V 0 P
ghost unlaid forbear thee! CYM 4.02.278
shed | to keep his bed of blackness unlaid ope, PER 1.02. 89
UNLAWFUL 11 FR 0.0012 REL FR 8 V 3 P
i have been an unlawful bawd time out of mind, MM 4.02. 15 P
eye | stray'd his affection in unlawful love — ERR 5.01. 51
count solicits her | in the unlawful purpose. AWW 3.05. 70
in us, to be trumpeters of our unlawful intents? 4.03. 27 P
those that think it is unlawful business | i am WT 5.03. 96
as doth a ruler with unlawful oaths, | or one 1H6 5.05. 30
to threaten me with death is most unlawful. R3 1.04.188
by her, in his unlawful bed, he got | this 3.07.190
from any other foul unlawful touch | be not to OTH 4.02. 84
my suit and repent my unlawful solicitation; 4.02.198 P
and all the unlawful issue that their lust ANT 3.06. 7
UNLAWFULLY 3 FR 0.0003 REL FR 2 V 1 P
the law than my son should be unlawfully born. MM 3.01.191 P
unlawfully made drunk with innocent blood! R3 4.04. 30
how? unlawfully? OTH 5.02. 70
UNLEARN'D 2 FR 0.0002 REL FR 2 V 0 P
but in thy fortunes am unlearn'd and strange. TIM 4.03. 57
should frame them | to royalty unlearn'd, honor CYM 4.02.178
UNLEARNED 3 FR 0.0003 REL FR 2 V 1 P
i will prove those verses to be very unlearned, LLL 4.02.158 P
how shall they credit | a poor unlearned virgin, AWW 1.03.240
unlearned in the world's false subtilties. SON 138. 4
/UNLESS 1 FR 0.0001 REL FR 0 V 1 P
/unless /the /poet /and /the /player /went /to HAM 2.02.355 P
UNLESS 166 FR 0.0187 REL FR 123 V 43 P
can have no note, unless the sun were post — TMP 2.01.248
in the dark | out of my way, unless he bid 'em; 2.02. 7
is despair, | unless i be reliev'd by prayer, ep 16
concerns | unless it have a false interpreter. TGV 1.02. 75
unless you have a codpiece to stick pins on. 2.07. 56
unless it be to think that she is by, | and feed 3.01.176
unless i look on silvia in the day, | there is 3.01.180
unless the next word that thou speak'st | have 3.01.239
unless i prove false traitor to myself. 4.04.105
little, | unless i flatter with myself too much. 4.04.188
hours, | unless it be to come before their time, 5.01. 5
hast no faith left now, unless thou'dst two, 5.04. 50
unless he know some strain in me that i know not WIV 2.01. 87 P
receiv'd none, unless experience be a jewel — 2.02.204 P
die, sir john — unless you go out disguis'd. 4.02. 67 P
unless you have the grace by your fair prayer MM 1.04. 69
you wot of, unless they kept very good diet, as 2.01.111 P
unless a thousand marks be levied | to quit the ERR 1.01. 21
unless i spake, or look'd, or touch'd, or carv'd 2.02.118
us by our names, | unless it be by inspiration? 2.02.167
and sure (unless you send some present help) 5.01.176
unless the fear of death doth make me dote, | i 5.01.195
him so ill-well, unless you were the very man. ADO 2.01.117 P
unless i might have another for working-days. 2.01.327 P
unless it be a fancy that he hath to strange 3.02. 32 P
unless he have a fancy to this foolery, as it 3.02. 37 P
nothing, unless you render her again. 4.01. 29
sheep, sweet lamb, unless we feed on your lips. LLL 2.01.220
faith, unless you play the honest troyan, the 5.02.675 P
unless you can find sport in their intents, MND 5.01. 79
unless you may be won by some other sort than MV 1.02.103 P
diana, unless i be obtain'd by the manner of my 1.02.107 P
'tis vile, unless it may be quaintly ordered, 2.04. 6
her foot, | unless she do it under this excuse, 2.04. 36
be match'd, unless the devil himself turn jew. 3.01. 78 P
not sick, my lord, unless it be in mind, | nor 3.02.234
it be in mind, | nor well, unless in mind. 3.02.235
unless bellario, a learned doctor, | whom i have 4.01.105
to do it, | unless he live until he be a man. 5.01.283
unless you could teach me to forget a banish'd AYL 1.02. 5 P
no, truly, unless thou wert hard-favor'd; 3.03. 29 P
answer, unless you take her without her tongue. 4.01.173 P
will never have her unless thou entreat for her. 4.03. 72 P
you, | unless you were of gentler, milder mould. SHR 1.01. 60
unless you will accompany me thither. 1.02.106
words | than you — unless you were a scholar, 1.02.158
unless her prayers, whom heaven delights to hear AWW 3.04. 27
to understand him, unless some one among us, 4.01. 5 P
finger, | unless she gave it to yourself in bed, 5.03.110
already, unless thou canst say they are married. 5.03.267 P
unless thou tell'st me where thou hadst this 5.03.283
i think, unless you see canary put me down. TN 1.03. 82 P
unless you laugh and minister occasion to him, 1.05. 86 P
unless, perchance, you come to me again | to 1.05.281
unless the master were the man. 1.05.294
unless it be to report your lord's taking of 2.02. 10 P
unless you do redeem it by some laudable attempt 3.02. 28 P
unless you undertake that with me which with as 3.04.249 P
unless he take the course that you have done — WT 2.03. 48
unless another, | as like hermione as is her 5.01. 73
unless thou let his silver water keep | a JN 2.01.339
his head, | unless he do submit himself to rome. 3.01.194
for him, | unless you call it good to pity him, R2 2.01.236
unless you please to enter in the castle, | and 2.03.160
unless he do profane, steal, or usurp. 3.03. 81
my mouth, | unless a pardon ere i rise or speak. 5.03. 32
unless hours were cups of sack, and minutes 1H4 1.02. 7 P
unless you call three fingers in the ribs bare. 4.02. 73 P
unless a brother should a brother dare | to 5.02. 53
thee, | unless thou yield thee as my prisoner. 5.03. 10
not i, my lord, unless i did bleed too. 5.04. 4
unless a woman should be made an ass and a beast 2H4 2.01. 37 P
not find a ground to root upon | unless on you. 3.01. 92
unless some dull and favorable hand | will 4.05. 2
unless you give me your doublet and stuff me out 5.05. 81 P
unless already 'a be kill'd with your hard ep 30 P
unless to dub thee with the name of traitor. H5 2.02.120
unless the dolphin be in presence here, | to 2.04.111
peasant, unless thou give me crowns, brave 4.04. 38
thee in french, unless it be to laugh at me. 5.02.186 P
unless my study and my books be false, | the 1H6 2.04. 56
unless thou wert more loyal than thou art. 2H6 3.01. 96
unless it were a bloody murtherer, | or foul 3.01.128
unless lord suffolk straight be done to death, 3.02.244
unless i find him guilty, he shall not die. 4.02. 96 P
biting statutes, unless his teeth be pull'd out. 4.07. 17 P
unless you be possess'd with devilish spirits 4.07. 75
head on his shoulders, unless he pay me tribute. 4.07.121 P
unless by robbing of your friends and us. 4.08. 40
unless he seek to thrust you out perforce. 3H6 1.01. 34
unless plantagenet, duke of york, be king, | and 1.01. 40
york cannot speak unless he wear a crown. 1.04. 93
queen, | unless the adage must be verified, 1.04.126
ne'er shall dine unless thou yield the crown. 2.02.128
i fear her not, unless she chance to fall. 3.02. 24
unless my hand and strength could equal them. 3.02.145
unless abroad they purchase great alliance? 3.03. 70
disdain, | unless the lady bona quit his pain. 3.03.128
unless thou rescue him from foul despair? 3.03.215
too, | unless they seek for hatred at my hands; 4.01. 80
unless our halberds did shut up his passage. 4.03. 20
our trusty friend, unless i be deceiv'd. 4.07. 41
unless to see my shadow in the sun | and descant R3 1.01. 26
unless it be while some tormenting dream 1.03.225
i will not rise, unless your highness hear me. 2.01. 98
unless thou couldst put on some other shape 4.04.286
unless for that, my liege, i cannot guess. 4.04.474
unless for that he comes to be your liege, | you 4.04.475
unless i have mista'en his colors much | (which 5.03. 35
unless we sweep 'em from the door with cannons H8 5.03. 13
so do all men, unless th' are drunk, sick, or TRO 1.02. 17 P
i took the blow — unless it swell past hiding, 1.02.269 P
unless the fiddler apollo get his sinews to make 3.03.303 P
unless she said, "my mind is now turn'd whore." 5.02.114
nothing at all, unless that this were she. 5.02.135
ache in my bones that, unless a man were curs'd, 5.03.105 P
unless, by not so doing, our good city | cleave COR 3.02. 27
to thy shame, unless | it be to do thee service. 4.05.100
all undone, unless | the noble man have mercy. 4.06.107
unless by using means i lame the foot | of our 4.07. 7
vain, | unless his noble mother and his wife — 5.01. 71
breeds, | unless the nightly owl or fatal raven; TIT 2.03. 97
unless some fit or frenzy do possess her; 4.01. 17
a den, | unless the gods delight in tragedies? 4.01. 60
unless thou swear to me my child shall live. 5.01. 68
unless good counsel may the cause remove. ROM 1.01.142
no hare, sir, unless a hare, sir, in a lenten 2.04.132 P
unless philosophy can make a juliet, | displant 3.03. 58
not i, unless the breath of heart-sick groans 3.03. 72
unless that husband send it me from heaven | by 3.05.207
unless thou tell me how i may prevent it. 4.01. 51
hands, | unless thou bring'st them with thee. JC 5.01. 57
never is o'ertook | unless the deed go with it. MAC 4.01.146
unless things mortal move them not at all, HAM 2.02.516
unless she drown'd herself in her own defense? 5.01. 6 P
be a maid long, unless things be cut shorter. LR 1.05. 52
than a spinster — unless the bookish theoric, OTH 1.01. 24
unless self-charity be sometimes a vice, | and 2.03.202
at all, unless you repute yourself such a loser. 2.03.271 P
unless his abode be ling'red here by some 4.02.225 P
not so, unless it had been the fall of an ass, CYM 1.02. 36 P
proceeded | (unless thou think'st me devilish), 1.05. 16

portends | (unless my sins abuse my divination) 4.02.351
unless a man would marry a gallows and beget 5.04.198 P
true nor modest, | unless i add, we are honest. 5.05. 19
i shall, | unless thou wouldst grieve quickly. 5.05.170
unless thou say prince pericles is dead. PER 1.01.164
to be got now–a–days unless thou canst fish 2.01. 69 P
even in his throat — unless it be the king — 2.05. 56
convey, | unless your thoughts went on my way. 4.ch. 50
unless you play the /pious innocent | and for an 4.03. 17
power | (unless we fear that apes can tutor 's) TNK 1.02. 43
not his kinsmen | in blood unless in quality. 1.02. 79
unless by th' tail | and with thy teeth thou 3.05. 49
unless the earth with thy increase be fed? VEN 170
it, | unless it be a boar, and then i chase it; 410
unless thou couldst return to make amends? LUC 961
he, | 'unless thou yoke thy liking to my will, 1633
sword, | swearing, unless i took all patiently, 1641
unless thy lady prove unjust, | press never thou PP 18.21
noon, | unlook'd on diest unless thou get a son. SON 7.14
me, | unless thou take that honor from thy name. 36.12
o none, unless this miracle have might, | that 65.13
unless you would devise some virtuous lie, | to 72. 5
unless my nerves were brass or hammered steel. 120. 4
shown, | unless this general evil they maintain: 121.13

UNLESSON'D 1 FR 0.0001 REL FR 1 V 0 P
is an unlesson'd girl, unschool'd, unpractic'd, MV 3.02.159

UNLETTER'D 1 FR 0.0001 REL FR 1 V 0 P
his companies unletter'd, rude, and shallow, H5 1.01. 55

UNLETTERED 3 FR 0.0003 REL FR 1 V 2 P
"that unlettered small–knowing soul" — LLL 1.01.250 P
untrained, or rather unlettered, or ratherest 4.02. 18 P
and, like unlettered clerk, still cry "amen" SON 85. 6

UNLICENS'D 1 FR 0.0001 REL FR 1 V 0 P
why (as it were unlicens'd of your loves) | he PER 1.03. 16

UNLICK'D 1 FR 0.0001 REL FR 1 V 0 P
or an unlick'd bear–whelp | that carries no 3H6 3.02.161

UNLIKE 17 FR 0.0019 REL FR 17 V 0 P
not impossible | that which but seems unlike; MM 5.01. 52
not unlike, sir, that may be. LLL 2.01.208
how much unlike art thou to portia! MV 2.09. 56
how much unlike my hopes and my deservings! 2.09. 57
wife, | and sent you hither so unlike yourself? SHR 3.02.104
himself | unlike the ruler of a commonweal. 2H6 1.01.189
how proud, how peremptory, and unlike himself? 3.01. 8
not much | unlike young men, whom aristotle TRO 2.02.166
not unlike, | each way, to better yours. COR 3.01. 48
this accident is not unlike my dream, | belief OTH 1.01.142
how much unlike art thou mark antony! ANT 1.05. 35
but the gods made you | (unlike all others) CYM 1.06.178
so follow, to be most unlike our courtiers, | as 5.04.136
done is more | unlike than this thou tell'st. 5.05.354
though much unlike | you should be so TNK 1.01.186
so strangely, so unlike a noble kinsman, | to 2.02.190
boar, | unlike myself thou hear'st me moralize, VEN 712

UNLIKELY 4 FR 0.0004 REL FR 4 V 0 P
to ambition, they do plot | unlikely wonders: R2 5.05. 19
and more unlikely | than to accomplish twenty 3H6 3.02.151
this is unlikely: COR 4.06. 72
the one doth flatter thee in thoughts unlikely, VEN 989

UNLIMITED 1 FR 0.0001 REL FR 0 V 1 P
scene individable, or poem unlimited; HAM 2.02.400 P

UNLINEAL 1 FR 0.0001 REL FR 1 V 0 P
thence to be wrench'd with an unlineal hand, MAC 3.01. 62

UNLINK'D 1 FR 0.0001 REL FR 1 V 0 P
suddenly, | seeing orlando, it unlink'd itself, AYL 4.03.111

UNLIVED 1 FR 0.0001 REL FR 1 V 0 P
where shall i live now lucrece is unlived? LUC 1754

UNLOAD 2 FR 0.0002 REL FR 2 V 0 P
to you duke humphrey must unload his grief, 2H6 1.01. 76
nor can my tongue unload my heart's great 3H6 2.01. 81

UNLOADED 1 FR 0.0001 REL FR 0 V 1 P
and told me i had unloaded all the gibbets and 1H4 4.02. 36 P

UNLOADING 1 FR 0.0001 REL FR 1 V 0 P
and at thy tent is now | unloading of his mules. ANT 4.06. 23

UNLOADS 1 FR 0.0001 REL FR 1 V 0 P
riches but a journey, | and death unloads thee. MM 3.01. 28

UNLOCK 4 FR 0.0004 REL FR 3 V 1 P
climb o'er the house to unlock the little gate. LLL 1.01.109
this, | and instantly unlock my fortunes here. MV 2.09. 52
i'll frush it and unlock the rivets all, | but TRO 5.06. 29
her night–gown upon her, unlock her closet, take MAC 5.01. 6 P

UNLOCK'D 2 FR 0.0002 REL FR 2 V 0 P
means, | lie all unlock'd to your occasions. MV 1.01.139
unlock'd the treasure of his happy state; LUC 16

UNLOOK'D 6 FR 0.0006 REL FR 5 V 1 P
how much unlook'd for is this expedition! JN 2.01. 79
and all unlook'd for from your highness' mouth. R2 1.03.155
if not, honor comes unlook'd for, and there's an 1H4 5.03. 60 P
age, | but by some unlook'd accident cut off! R3 1.03.213
noon, | unlook'd on diest unless thou get a son. SON 7.14
bars, | unlook'd for joy in that i honor most. 25. 4

UNLOOK'D–FOR 5 FR 0.0005 REL FR 5 V 0 P
us, | to this unlook'd–for, unprepared pomp. JN 2.01.560
and all the unlook'd–for issue of their bodies 3H6 3.02.131
who should that be? belike unlook'd–for friends. 5.01. 14
ah, sirrah, this unlook'd–for sport comes well. ROM 1.05. 29
o unlook'd–for evil, | when virtue is profan'd LUC 846

UNLOOS'D 1 FR 0.0001 REL FR 1 V 0 P
there must i be unloos'd, although not there H8 2.04.148

UNLOOSE 6 FR 0.0006 REL FR 6 V 0 P
to unloose this tied–up justice when you pleas'd MM 1.03. 32
the gordian knot of it he will unloose, H5 1.01. 46
york, unloose thy long–imprisoned thoughts, 2H6 5.01. 88
shall from your neck unloose his amorous fold, TRO 3.03.223
a–twain | which are t' intrinse t' unloose; LR 2.02. 75
they scatter and unloose it from their bond, LUC 136

UNLOV'D 2 FR 0.0002 REL FR 2 V 0 P
(but miserable most, to love unlov'd)? MND 3.02.234
which, left unshown, | is often left unlov'd. ANT 3.06. 53

UNLOVING 1 FR 0.0001 REL FR 1 V 0 P
him, | which argued thee a most unloving father. 3H6 2.02. 25

UNLUCKILY 7 FR 0.0008 REL FR 5 V 2 P
who put unluckily into this bay | against the ERR 5.01.125
run, | and not unluckily against the bias. SHR 4.05. 25
my third comfort | (starr'd most unluckily) is WT 3.02. 99
if like an ill venture it come unluckily home, i 2H4 ep 11 P
so unluckily | that we have had no time to move ROM 3.04. 1
how unluckily it happ'ned that i should purchase TIM 3.02. 46 P
and things unluckily charge my fantasy. JC 3.03. 2

UNLUCKY 4 FR 0.0004 REL FR 4 V 0 P
the king | so long in his unlucky irish wars 1H4 5.01. 53
brought hither in a most unlucky hour, | to find TIT 2.03.251
all | the unlucky manage of this fatal brawl: ROM 3.01.143
when you shall these unlucky deeds relate, OTH 5.02.341

UNMADE 1 FR 0.0001 REL FR 1 V 0 P
do now, | taking the measure of an unmade grave. ROM 3.03. 70

UNMAKE 2 FR 0.0002 REL FR 2 V 0 P
and that their fitness now | does unmake you. MAC 1.07. 54
that she may make, unmake, do what she list, OTH 2.03.346

UNMANLY 5 FR 0.0005 REL FR 5 V 0 P
york, | and die in bands for this unmanly deed! 3H6 1.01.186
never so ridiculous | (nay, let 'em be unmanly), H8 1.03. 4
a poor unmanly melancholy sprung | from change TIM 4.03.203
of impious stubbornness, 'tis unmanly grief, HAM 1.02. 94
he cannot | be so unmanly as to leave me here. TNK 2.06. 19

UNMANN'D* 2 FR 0.0002 REL FR 2 V 0 P
hood my unmann'd blood, bating in my cheeks, ROM 3.02. 14
what? quite unmann'd in folly? MAC 3.04. 72

UNMANNER'D 2 FR 0.0002 REL FR 2 V 0 P
you heedless joltheads and unmanner'd slaves! SHR 4.01.166
unmanner'd dog! R3 1.02. 39

UNMANNERLY 13 FR 0.0014 REL FR 9 V 4 P
for reading my letter — an unmannerly slave, TGV 3.01.383 P
i'll rather be unmannerly than troublesome. WIV 1.01.312 P
being so full of unmannerly sadness in his youth MV 1.02. 50 P
should — | this apish and unmannerly approach, JN 5.02.131
he call'd them untaught knaves, unmannerly, | to 1H4 1.03. 43
even he escapes not | language unmannerly; H8 1.02. 27
i were unmannerly to take you out | and not to 1.04. 95
if i have us'd myself unmannerly, | you know i 3.01.176
highness' pardon, | my haste made me unmannerly. 4.02.105
limbs, | unmannerly intruder as thou art! TIT 2.03. 65
their daggers | unmannerly breech'd with gore. MAC 2.03.116
my duty be too bold, my love is too unmannerly. HAM 3.02.349 P
be kent unmannerly | when lear is mad. LR 1.01.145

UNMARRIED 2 FR 0.0002 REL FR 2 V 0 P
that die unmarried, ere they can behold | bright WT 4.04.123
us, | and which is heaviest, palamon, unmarried. TNK 2.02. 29

UNMASK 4 FR 0.0004 REL FR 4 V 0 P
my husband bids me, now i will unmask. MM 5.01.206
enough | if she unmask her beauty to the moon. HAM 1.03. 37
to unmask falsehood and bring truth to light, LUC 940
unmask, dear dear, this moody heaviness, | and 1602

UNMAST'RED 1 FR 0.0001 REL FR 1 V 0 P
treasure open | to his unmast'red importunity. HAM 1.03. 32

UNMATCHABLE 4 FR 0.0004 REL FR 2 V 2 P
exquisite, and unmatchable beauty — i pray you TN 1.05.170 P
and this, so sole and unmatchable, | shall give JN 4.03. 52
their mastiffs are of unmatchable courage. H5 3.07.141 P
thee, is | noble, courageous, high unmatchable, ANT 2.03. 21

UNMATCH'D 2 FR 0.0002 REL FR 2 V 0 P
an excellent | and unmatch'd wit and judgment; H8 2.04. 47
that unmatch'd form and stature of blown youth HAM 3.01.159

UNMATCHED 3 FR 0.0003 REL FR 3 V 0 P
against whose fury and unmatched force | the JN 1.01.265
love, | duty, and zeal to your unmatched mind, TIM 4.03.516
to praise the clear unmatched red and white LUC 11

UNMEASURABLE 2 FR 0.0002 REL FR 1 V 1 P
and that, i hope, is an unmeasurable distance. WIV 2.01.104 P
whose womb unmeasurable and infinite breast TIM 4.03.178

UNMEET 6 FR 0.0006 REL FR 6 V 0 P
a creature unprepar'd, unmeet for death; MM 4.03. 67
any man with me convers'd | at hours unmeet, or ADO 4.01.182
vow, alack, for youth unmeet, | youth so apt to LLL 4.03.111
force, | that york is most unmeet of any man. 2H6 1.03.164
i'll tell thee, suffolk, why i am unmeet: 1.03.165
from thy /thorn, | vow, alack, for youth unmeet, PP 16.13

UNMELLOWED 1 FR 0.0001 REL FR 1 V 0 P
his head unmellowed, but his judgment ripe; TGV 2.04. 70

UNMERCIFUL 1 FR 0.0001 REL FR 1 V 0 P
unmerciful lady as you are, i'm none. LR 3.07. 33

UNMERITABLE 2 FR 0.0002 REL FR 2 V 0 P
my desert | unmeritable shuns your high request. R3 3.07.155
this is a slight unmeritable man, | meet to be JC 4.01. 12

UNMERITING 1 FR 0.0001 REL FR 0 V 1 P
then you should discover a brace of unmeriting, COR 2.01. 44 P

UNMINDED 1 FR 0.0001 REL FR 1 V 0 P
and low, | a poor unminded outlaw sneaking home, 1H4 4.03. 58

UNMINDFUL 1 FR 0.0001 REL FR 1 V 0 P
thou com'st thither — dull unmindful villain, R3 4.04.445

UNMINGLED 2 FR 0.0002 REL FR 2 V 0 P
and take unmingled thence that drop again, ERR 2.02.127
by itself | lies rich in virtue and unmingled. TRO 1.03. 30

UNMITIGABLE 1 FR 0.0001 REL FR 1 V 0 P
ministers, | and in her most unmitigable rage, TMP 1.02.276

UNMITIGATED 1 FR 0.0001 REL FR 0 V 1 P
uncover'd slander, unmitigated rancor — o god, ADO 4.01.305 P

UNMIX'D 1 FR 0.0001 REL FR 1 V 0 P
volume of my brain, | unmix'd with baser matter. HAM 1.05.104

UNMOAN'D 1 FR 0.0001 REL FR 1 V 0 P
our fatherless distress was left unmoan'd, R3 2.02. 64

UNMOV'D 1 FR 0.0001 REL FR 1 V 0 P
patience unmov'd! ERR 2.01. 32

UNMOVED 1 FR 0.0001 REL FR 1 V 0 P
unmoved, cold, and to temptation slow, | they SON 94. 4

/UNMOVING 1 FR 0.0001 REL FR 1 V 0 P
scorn | to point his slow /unmoving finger at! OTH 4.02. 55

UNMUSICAL 1 FR 0.0001 REL FR 1 V 0 P
a name unmusical to the volscians' ears, | and COR 4.05. 58

UNMUZZLE 1 FR 0.0001 REL FR 0 V 1 P
ay, marry, now unmuzzle your wisdom. AYL 1.02. 70 P

UNMUZZLED 1 FR 0.0001 REL FR 1 V 0 P
and baited it with all th' unmuzzled thoughts TN 3.01.119

/UNNATURAL 1 FR 0.0001 REL FR 1 V 0 P
/of /how /unnatural /and /bemadding /sorrow LR 3.01. 38

UNNATURAL 38 FR 0.0043 REL FR 35 V 3 P
i do forgive thee, | unnatural though thou art. TMP 5.01. 79
and he did render him the most unnatural | that AYL 4.03.122
might so do, | for well i know he was unnatural. 4.03.124
a most unworthy and unnatural lord | can do no WT 2.03.113
rebuke the usurpation | of thy unnatural uncle, JN 2.01. 10
attire, | and every thing that seems unnatural. H5 5.02. 62
behold the wounds, the most unnatural wounds, 1H6 3.03. 50
it was both impious and unnatural | that such 5.01. 12
seeing thou hast prov'd so unnatural a father! 3H6 1.01.218
erroneous, mutinous, and unnatural, | this 2.05. 90
that clarence is so harsh, so blunt, unnatural, 5.01. 86
whose ugly and unnatural aspect | may fright the R3 1.02. 23
thy deeds inhuman and unnatural | provokes this 1.02. 60
unnatural | provokes this deluge most unnatural. 1.02. 61
it is a quarrel most unnatural, | to be reveng'd 1.02.134
a most unnatural and faithless service. H8 2.01.123
like an unnatural dam | should now eat up her COR 3.01.291
tell me not | wherein i seem unnatural; 5.03. 84
down, and this unnatural scene | they laugh at. 5.03.184
what hast thou done, unnatural and unkind? TIT 5.03. 48
nest | of death, contagion, and unnatural sleep. ROM 5.03.152
'tis unnatural, | even like the deed that's done MAC 2.04. 10
unnatural deeds | do breed unnatural troubles; 5.01. 71
unnatural deeds | do breed unnatural troubles; 5.01. 72
revenge his foul and most unnatural murther. HAM 1.05. 25
but this most foul, strange, and unnatural. 1.05. 28
firm bosom, | let me be cruel, not unnatural; 3.02.395
hear | of carnal, bloody, and unnatural acts, 5.02.381
her offense | must be of such unnatural degree LR 1.01.219
unnatural, detested, brutish villain! 1.02. 76 P
opposite i stood | to his unnatural purpose, in 2.01. 50
no, you unnatural hags, | i will have such 2.04.278
edmund, i like not this unnatural dealing. 3.03. 1 P
most savage and unnatural! 3.03. 7 P
rank, | foul disproportions, thoughts unnatural. OTH 3.03.233
that death's unnatural that kills for loving. 5.02. 42
receive us | for barbarous and unnatural revolts CYM 4.04. 6
and though you call my course unnatural, | you PER 4.03. 36

UNNATURALLY 1 FR 0.0001 REL FR 1 V 0 P
my son, | whom i unnaturally shall disinherit. 3H6 1.01.193

/UNNATURALNESS 1 FR 0.0001 REL FR 0 V 1 P
/as /of /unnaturalness /between /the /child /and LR 1.02.144 P

UNNECESSARILY 1 FR 0.0001 REL FR 1 V 0 P
that can prate | as amply and unnecessarily | as TMP 2.01.264

UNNECESSARY 3 FR 0.0003 REL FR 2 V 1 P
who in unnecessary action swarm | about our H5 4.02. 27
thou whoreson zed, thou unnecessary letter! LR 2.02. 64 P
age is unnecessary. 2.04.155

UNNEIGHBORLY 1 FR 0.0001 REL FR 1 V 0 P
league, | and not to spend it so unneighborly! JN 5.02. 39

UNNERVED 1 FR 0.0001 REL FR 1 V 0 P
of his fell sword | th' unnerved father falls. HAM 2.02.474

UNNOBLE 1 FR 0.0001 REL FR 1 V 0 P
offended reputation, | a most unnoble swerving. ANT 3.11. 50

UNNOTED 3 FR 0.0003 REL FR 3 V 0 P
till their own scorn return to them unnoted AWW 1.02. 34
and with such sober and unnoted passion | he did TIM 3.05. 21
gnats are unnoted wheresoe'er they fly, | but LUC 1014

UNNUMB'RED 2 FR 0.0002 REL FR 2 V 0 P
the skies are painted with unnumb'red sparks, JC 3.01. 63
that on th' unnumb'red idle pebble chafes, LR 4.06. 21

UNOWED 1 FR 0.0001 REL FR 1 V 0 P
the unowed interest of proud swelling state. JN 4.03.147

UNPACK 1 FR 0.0001 REL FR 1 V 0 P
must, like a whore, unpack my heart with words, HAM 2.02.585

UNPAID 3 FR 0.0003 REL FR 3 V 0 P
yet there remains unpaid | a hundred thousand LLL 2.01.133
she should that duty leave unpaid to you | which CYM 3.05. 48
wilt thou undo the worth thou art unpaid for, 5.05.307

UNPAID–FOR 1 FR 0.0001 REL FR 1 V 0 P
prouder than rustling in unpaid–for silk: CYM 3.03. 24

UNPANG'D 1 FR 0.0001 REL FR 1 V 0 P
grief | cull forth, as unpang'd judgment can, TNK 1.01.169

UNPARAGON'D 2 FR 0.0002 REL FR 1 V 1 P
either your unparagon'd mistress is dead, or CYM 1.04. 80 P
rubies unparagon'd, | how dearly they do't! 2.02. 17

UNPARALLEL'D 3 FR 0.0003 REL FR 3 V 0 P
woman, she you kill'd | would be unparallel'd. WT 5.01. 16
whence men have read | his fame unparallel'd, COR 5.02. 16
in thy possession lies | a lass unparallel'd. ANT 5.02.316

UNPARDONABLE 1 FR 0.0001 REL FR 1 V 0 P
o, 'tis a fault too too unpardonable! 3H6 1.04.106

UNPARTIAL *(also impartial)*

UNPARTIAL 1 FR 0.0001 REL FR 1 V 0 P
in the unpartial judging of this business. H8 2.02.106

UNPATH'D 1 FR 0.0001 REL FR 1 V 0 P
dedication of yourselves | to unpath'd waters, WT 4.04.567

UNPAV'D 1 FR 0.0001 REL FR 0 V 1 P
nor the voice of unpav'd eunuch to boot, can CYM 2.03. 30 P

UNPAY 1 FR 0.0001 REL FR 0 V 1 P
and unpay the villainy you have done with her. 2H4 2.01.119 P

UNPEACEABLE 1 FR 0.0001 REL FR 0 V 1 P
away, unpeaceable dog, or i'll spurn thee hence! TIM 1.01.270 P

UNPEG 1 FR 0.0001 REL FR 1 V 0 P
secrecy, | unpeg the basket on the house's top, HAM 3.04.193

UNPEOPLE 4 FR 0.0004 REL FR 3 V 1 P
agent will unpeople the province with continency MM 3.02.174 P
first shall war unpeople this my realm; 3H6 1.01.126
a several greeting, | or i'll unpeople egypt. ANT 1.05. 78
shall quite unpeople her | of liegers for her CYM 1.05. 79

/UNPEOPLED 1 FR 0.0001 REL FR 1 V 0 P
oath, | to let you enter his /unpeopled house. LLL 2.01. 88

UNPEOPLED 3 FR 0.0003 REL FR 3 V 0 P
for it is unpeopled? AYL 3.02.126
walls, | unpeopled offices, untrodden stones? R2 1.02. 69
bare and unpeopled in this fearful flood. LUC 1741

UNPERCEIV'D 1 FR 0.0001 REL FR 1 V 0 P
mire | and unperceiv'd fly with the filth away, LUC 1010

UNPERFECT *(also imperfect)*

UNPERFECT 1 FR 0.0001 REL FR 1 V 0 P
as an unperfect actor on the stage, | who with SON 23. 1

UNPERFECTNESS 1 FR 0.0001 REL FR 0 V 1 P
one unperfectness shows me another, to make me OTH 2.03.297 P

UNPICK'D 1 FR 0.0001 REL FR 0 V 1 P
night, and we must hence and leave it unpick'd. 2H4 2.04.368 P

UNPIN 2 FR 0.0002 REL FR 2 V 0 P
prithee unpin me — have grace and favor /in OTH 4.03. 21
no, unpin me here. 4.03. 34

UNPINK'D 1 FR 0.0001 REL FR 1 V 0 P
gabr'el's pumps were all unpink'd i' th' heel; SHR 4.01.133

UNPITIED 4 FR 0.0004 REL FR 3 V 1 P
and your deliverance with an unpitied whipping, MM 4.02. 13 P
property | of what i spoke, unpitied let me die, AWW 2.01.188
at hand, | ensues his piteous and unpitied end. R3 4.04. 74
hence, | therefore be deaf to my unpitied folly, ANT 1.03. 98

UNPITIFULLY 1 FR 0.0001 REL FR 0 V 1 P
he beat him most unpitifully, methought. WIV 4.02.203 P
UNPLAGU'D 1 FR 0.0001 REL FR 1 V 0 P
unplagu'd with corns will walk /a /bout with you ROM 1.05. 17
UNPLAUSIVE 1 FR 0.0001 REL FR 1 V 0 P
question me | why such unplausive eyes are bent, TRO 3.03. 43
UNPLEASANT'ST 1 FR 0.0001 REL FR 1 V 0 P
here are a few of the unpleasant'st words | that MV 3.02.251
UNPLEASED 1 FR 0.0001 REL FR 1 V 0 P
love | than my unpleased eye see your courtesy. R2 3.03.193
UNPLEASING 6 FR 0.0006 REL FR 6 V 0 P
o word of fear, | unpleasing to a married ear! LLL 5.02.902
o word of fear, | unpleasing to a married ear! 5.02.911
full of unpleasing blots and sightless stains, JN 3.01. 45
harsh rude tongue sound this unpleasing news? R2 3.04. 74
despiteful tidings, o unpleasing news! R3 4.01. 36
straining harsh discords and unpleasing sharps. ROM 3.05. 28
UNPLUCK'D 1 FR 0.0001 REL FR 1 V 0 P
a virgin flow'r, | must grow alone, unpluck'd. TNK 5.01.168
UNPOLICIED 1 FR 0.0001 REL FR 1 V 0 P
hear thee call great caesar ass | unpolicied! ANT 5.02.308
UNPOLISH'D 2 FR 0.0002 REL FR 2 V 0 P
you loggerheaded and unpolish'd grooms! SHR 4.01.125
'tis like the commons, rude unpolish'd hinds, 2H6 3.02.271
UNPOLISHED 1 FR 0.0001 REL FR 0 V 1 P
after his undressed, unpolished, uneducated, LLL 4.02. 17 P
UNPOLLUTED 1 FR 0.0001 REL FR 1 V 0 P
and from her fair and unpolluted flesh | may HAM 5.01.239
UNPOSSESS'D 1 FR 0.0001 REL FR 1 V 0 P
the empire unpossess'd? R3 4.04.470
UNPOSSESSING 1 FR 0.0001 REL FR 1 V 0 P
"thou unpossessing bastard, dost thou think, LR 2.01. 67
UNPOSSIBLE *(also impossible)*
UNPOSSIBLE 1 FR 0.0001 REL FR 1 V 0 P
proportionable to the enemy | is all unpossible. R2 2.02.126
UNPRACTIC'D 3 FR 0.0003 REL FR 3 V 0 P
is an unlesson'd girl, unschool'd, unpractic'd, MV 3.02.159
night, | and skilless as unpractic'd infancy. TRO 1.01. 12
like an unpractic'd swimmer plunging still, LUC 1098
UNPREGNANT 2 FR 0.0002 REL FR 2 V 0 P
me quite, makes me unpregnant | and dull to all MM 4.04. 20
like john–a–dreams, unpregnant of my cause, HAM 2.02.568
UNPREMEDITATED 1 FR 0.0001 REL FR 1 V 0 P
possible, | and i will answer unpremeditated; 1H6 1.02. 88
UNPREPAR'D 3 FR 0.0003 REL FR 3 V 0 P
a creature unprepar'd, unmeet for death; MM 4.03. 67
when men are unprepar'd and look not for it. R3 3.02. 63
being unprepar'd, | our will became the servant MAC 2.01. 17
UNPREPARED 2 FR 0.0002 REL FR 2 V 0 P
us, | to this unlook'd–for, unprepared pomp. JN 2.01.560
i would not kill thy unprepared spirit, | no, OTH 5.02. 31
UNPRESS'D 1 FR 0.0001 REL FR 1 V 0 P
have i my pillow left unpress'd in rome, ANT 3.13.106
UNPREVAILING 1 FR 0.0001 REL FR 1 V 0 P
pray you throw to earth | this unprevailing woe, HAM 1.02.107
UNPREVENTED 1 FR 0.0001 REL FR 1 V 0 P
being unprevented, to your timeless grave. TGV 3.01. 21
UNPRIZABLE 2 FR 0.0002 REL FR 1 V 1 P
of, | for shallow draught and bulk unprizable, TN 5.01. 55
so your brace of unprizable estimations, the one CYM 1.04. 90 P
UNPRIZ'D 1 FR 0.0001 REL FR 1 V 0 P
can buy this unpriz'd precious maid of me. LR 1.01.259
UNPROFITABLE 6 FR 0.0006 REL FR 6 V 0 P
your suit's unprofitable; MM 5.01.455
come, come, no more of this unprofitable chat. 1H4 3.01. 62
dowry, | some petty and unprofitable dukedoms. H5 3.pr. 31
and unprofitable | seem to me all the uses of HAM 1.02.133
favor's chang'd | with this unprofitable woe! PER 4.01. 25
unprofitable sounds, weak arbitrators! LUC 1017
UNPROFITED 1 FR 0.0001 REL FR 1 V 0 P
bounds, | rather than make unprofited return. TN 1.04. 22
UNPROPER *(also improper)*
UNPROPER 1 FR 0.0001 REL FR 1 V 0 P
that nightly lie in those unproper beds | which OTH 4.01. 68
UNPROPERLY 1 FR 0.0001 REL FR 1 V 0 P
and unproperly | show duty as mistaken all this COR 5.03. 54
UNPROPORTION'D 1 FR 0.0001 REL FR 1 V 0 P
nor any unproportion'd thought his act. HAM 1.03. 60
UNPROVIDE 1 FR 0.0001 REL FR 0 V 1 P
her body and beauty unprovide my mind again. OTH 4.01.206 P
UNPROVIDED 7 FR 0.0008 REL FR 5 V 2 P
come, | now sadder, that you come so unprovided.
SHR 3.02. 99
i am heinously unprovided. 1H4 3.03.190 P
then if they die unprovided, no more is the king H5 4.01.173 P
to haste thus fast, to find us unprovided. 3H6 5.04. 63
fear you the boar, and go so unprovided? R3 3.02. 73
sword he charges home | my unprovided body, LR 2.01. 52
i yet am unprovided | of a pair of bases. PER 2.01.160
UNPROVIDENT *(also improvident)*
UNPROVIDENT 1 FR 0.0001 REL FR 1 V 0 P
to any, | who for thyself art so unprovident. SON 10. 2
UNPROVOKES 1 FR 0.0001 REL FR 0 V 1 P
lechery, sir, it provokes, and unprovokes: MAC 2.03. 29 P
UNPRUN'D 1 FR 0.0001 REL FR 1 V 0 P
her fruit–trees all unprun'd, her hedges ruin'd, R2 3.04. 45
UNPRUNED 2 FR 0.0002 REL FR 1 V 1 P
unpolished, uneducated, unpruned, untrained, or LLL 4.02. 17 P
the merry cheerer of the heart, | unpruned dies; H5 5.02. 42
UNPUBLISH'D 1 FR 0.0001 REL FR 1 V 0 P
all you unpublish'd virtues of the earth, LR 4.04. 16
UNPURGED 1 FR 0.0001 REL FR 1 V 0 P
and tempt the rheumy and unpurged air | to add JC 2.01.266
UNPURPOS'D 1 FR 0.0001 REL FR 1 V 0 P
services are all | but accidents unpurpos'd. ANT 4.14. 84
UNQUALITED 1 FR 0.0001 REL FR 1 V 0 P
speak to him, | he's unqualited with very shame. ANT 3.11. 44
UNQUEEN'D 1 FR 0.0001 REL FR 1 V 0 P
although unqueen'd, yet like | a queen, and H8 4.02.171
UNQUESTIONABLE 1 FR 0.0001 REL FR 0 V 1 P
an unquestionable spirit, which you have not; AYL 3.02.374 P
UNQUESTION'D 2 FR 0.0002 REL FR 2 V 0 P
and leaves unquestion'd | matters of needful MM 1.01. 54
rest | unquestion'd welcome and undoubted blest. AWW 2.01.208
UNQUIET 8 FR 0.0009 REL FR 7 V 1 P
unquiet meals make ill digestions, | thereof the ERR 5.01. 74
you lie by portia's side | with an unquiet soul. MV 3.02.306
the wish would make else an unquiet house. 4.01.294
you may thank th' unquiet time for your quiet 2H4 1.02.150 P
but that the scambling and unquiet time | did H5 1.01. 4
accursed and unquiet wrangling days, | how many R3 2.04. 55
to trust the mock'ry of unquiet slumbers. 3.02. 27
makes such unquiet, that the ship | should house PER 2.ch. 31
UNQUIETLY 1 FR 0.0001 REL FR 1 V 0 P
one minded like the weather, most unquietly. LR 3.01. 2
UNQUIETNESS 2 FR 0.0002 REL FR 1 V 1 P
for a fool that betroths himself to unquietness? ADO 1.03. 48 P
and certainly in strange unquietness. OTH 3.04.133
UNRAISED 1 FR 0.0001 REL FR 1 V 0 P
the flat unraised spirits that hath dar'd | on H5 pr 9
UNRAK'D 1 FR 0.0001 REL FR 1 V 0 P
fires thou find'st unrak'd and hearths unswept, WIV 5.05. 44
UNREAD 1 FR 0.0001 REL FR 1 V 0 P
the wise and fool, the artist and unread, | the TRO 1.03. 24
UNREADY 2 FR 0.0002 REL FR 2 V 0 P
how now, my lords? what, all unready so? 1H6 2.01. 39
unready? ay, and glad we scap'd so well. 2.01. 40
UNREAL 2 FR 0.0002 REL FR 2 V 0 P
with what's unreal thou co–active art, | and WT 1.02.141
unreal mock'ry, hence! MAC 3.04.106
UNREASONABLE 4 FR 0.0004 REL FR 3 V 1 P
'tis unreasonable! WIV 4.02.141 P
what man is there so much unreasonable, | if you MV 5.01.203
unreasonable creatures feed their young, | and 3H6 2.02. 26
acts /denote | the unreasonable fury of a beast. ROM 3.03.111
UNREASONABLY 1 FR 0.0001 REL FR 0 V 1 P
fie, you confine yourself most unreasonably. COR 1.03. 76 P
UNREASON'D 1 FR 0.0001 REL FR 1 V 0 P
leave that unreason'd. TNK 1.02. 98
UNRECALLING 1 FR 0.0001 REL FR 1 V 0 P
and ever let his unrecalling crime | have time LUC 993
UNRECLAIMED 1 FR 0.0001 REL FR 1 V 0 P
fiery mind, | a savageness in unreclaimed blood, HAM 2.01. 34
UNRECONCIL'D 1 FR 0.0001 REL FR 1 V 0 P
crime | unreconcil'd as yet to heaven and grace, OTH 5.02. 27
UNRECONCILIABLE 1 FR 0.0001 REL FR 1 V 0 P
unreconciliable, should divide | our equalness ANT 5.01. 47
UNRECOUNTED 1 FR 0.0001 REL FR 1 V 0 P
and may be left | to some ears unrecounted. H8 3.02. 48
UNRECURING 1 FR 0.0001 REL FR 1 V 0 P
deer | that hath receiv'd some unrecuring wound. TIT 3.01. 90
UNREGARDED 1 FR 0.0001 REL FR 1 V 0 P
lame, | and unregarded age in corners thrown. AYL 2.03. 42
UNREGIST'RED 1 FR 0.0001 REL FR 1 V 0 P
hours, | unregist'red in vulgar fame, you have ANT 3.13.119
UNRELENTING 3 FR 0.0003 REL FR 3 V 0 P
will nothing turn your unrelenting hearts? 1H6 5.04. 59
arm | of unrelenting clifford and the queen; 3H6 2.01. 58
to them | as unrelenting flint to drops of rain. TIT 2.03.141
UNREMOVABLE 1 FR 0.0001 REL FR 1 V 0 P
how unremovable and fix'd he is | in his own LR 2.04. 93
UNREMOVABLY 1 FR 0.0001 REL FR 1 V 0 P
his discontents are unremovably | coupled to TIM 5.01.224
UNREPRIEVABLE 1 FR 0.0001 REL FR 1 V 0 P
to tyrannize | on unreprievable condemned blood.
JN 5.07. 48
UNRESISTED 1 FR 0.0001 REL FR 1 V 0 P
fear | is almost chok'd by unresisted lust. LUC 282
UNRESOLV'D 1 FR 0.0001 REL FR 1 V 0 P
unarm'd, and unresolv'd to beat them back. R3 4.04.436
UNRESPECTED 2 FR 0.0002 REL FR 2 V 0 P
for all the day they view things unrespected, SON 43. 2
show, | they live unwoo'd, and unrespected fade, 54.10
UNRESPECTIVE 2 FR 0.0002 REL FR 2 V 0 P
with iron–witted fools | and unrespective boys; R3 4.02. 29
viands | we do not throw in unrespective sieve, TRO 2.02. 71
UNREST 8 FR 0.0009 REL FR 8 V 0 P
witnessing storms to come, woe, and unrest. R2 2.04. 22
rest thy unrest on england's lawful earth, R3 4.04. 29
you sleeping safe, they bring to you unrest; 5.03.320
and so repose, sweet gold, for their unrest, TIT 2.03. 8
but let her rest in her unrest a while. 4.02. 31
ay, so i fear, the more is my unrest. ROM 1.05.120
that blow did bail it from the deep unrest | of LUC 1725
care, | and frantic mad with evermore unrest; SON 147.10
UNRESTOR'D 1 FR 0.0001 REL FR 1 V 0 P
he say he lent me | some shipping unrestor'd. ANT 3.06. 27
UNRESTRAINED 1 FR 0.0001 REL FR 1 V 0 P
frequent, | with unrestrained loose companions, R2 5.03. 7
UNREVENG'D 2 FR 0.0002 REL FR 2 V 0 P
enemies, | whose deaths are yet unreveng'd. 1H4 5.03. 43
she shall not strike dame eleanor unreveng'd. 2H6 1.03.147
UNREVEREND 3 FR 0.0003 REL FR 3 V 0 P
fie, fie, unreverend tongue, to call her bad, TGV 2.06. 14
why, thou unreverend and unhallowed friar, MM 5.01.305
ay, thou unreverend boy, | sir robert's son! JN 1.01.227
UNREVERENT 4 FR 0.0004 REL FR 4 V 0 P
see not your bride in these unreverent robes, SHR 3.02.112
run thy head from thy unreverent shoulders. R2 2.01.123
unreverent gloucester! 1H6 3.01. 49
lift up for peace, and your unreverent knees, STM II.C 110
UNREVERS'D 1 FR 0.0001 REL FR 1 V 0 P
(which, unrevers'd, stands in effectual force) TGV 3.01.225
UNREWARDED 1 FR 0.0001 REL FR 0 V 1 P
wit shall not go unrewarded while i am king of TMP 4.01.242 P
UNRIGHTEOUS 1 FR 0.0001 REL FR 1 V 0 P
ere yet the salt of most unrighteous tears | had HAM 1.02.154
UNRIGHTFUL 1 FR 0.0001 REL FR 1 V 0 P
knowest the way | to plant unrightful kings, R2 5.01. 63
UNRIPE 4 FR 0.0004 REL FR 4 V 0 P
which now, the fruit unripe, sticks on the tree, HAM 3.02.190
upon thy tempting lip | shows thee unripe; VEN 128
measure my strangeness with my unripe years; 524
but whether unripe years did want conceit, | or PP 4. 9
UNRIP'ST 1 FR 0.0001 REL FR 1 V 0 P
unrip'st the bowels of thy sov'reign's son. R3 1.04.207
UNRIVALL'D 1 FR 0.0001 REL FR 1 V 0 P
plead a new state in thy unrivall'd merit, | to TGV 5.04.144
UNROLL 1 FR 0.0001 REL FR 1 V 0 P
even as an adder when she doth unroll | to do TIT 2.03. 35
UNROLL'D 1 FR 0.0001 REL FR 0 V 1 P
the shearers prove sheep, let me be unroll'd, WT 4.03.122 P
/UNROOF'D 1 FR 0.0001 REL FR 1 V 0 P
the rabble should have first /unroof'd the city COR 1.01.218
UNROOSTED 1 FR 0.0001 REL FR 1 V 0 P
unroosted | by thy dame partlet here. WT 2.03. 75
UNROOT 1 FR 0.0001 REL FR 1 V 0 P
grow in my requital | as nothing can unroot you. AWW 5.01. 6
UNROUGH 1 FR 0.0001 REL FR 1 V 0 P
and many unrough youths that even now | protest MAC 5.02. 10
UNRULY 16 FR 0.0018 REL FR 14 V 2 P
the mean is drown'd with /your unruly bass. TGV 1.02. 93
in the current) made it more violent and unruly. MM 3.01.243 P
but, too unruly deer, he breaks the pale, | and ERR 2.01.100
troth, your town is troubled with unruly boys. 3.01. 62
a sceptre snatch'd with an unruly hand | must be JN 3.04.135
phaeton, | wanting the manage of unruly jades. R2 3.03.179
which like unruly children make their sire 3.04. 30
make way, unruly woman! 5.02.110
by the imprisoning of unruly wind | within her 1H4 3.01. 29
could not take truce with the unruly spleen | of ROM 3.01.157
there's not a whittle in th' unruly camp | but i TIM 5.01.180
the night has been unruly. MAC 2.03. 54
but therewithal the unruly waywardness that LR 1.01.298 P
sits, | banning his boist'rous and unruly beast; VEN 326
"unruly blasts wait on the tender spring, LUC 869
when winds breathe sweet, unruly though they be.
LC 103
UNSAFE 4 FR 0.0004 REL FR 3 V 1 P
no incredulous or unsafe circumstance — what TN 3.04. 80 P
these dangerous, unsafe lunes i' th' king, WT 2.02. 28
unsafe the while, that we | must lave our honors MAC 3.02. 32
let's think't unsafe | to come in to the cry OTH 5.01. 43
UNSALLIED 1 FR 0.0001 REL FR 1 V 0 P
yet as pure | as the unsallied lily, i protest, LLL 5.02.352
UNSALUTED 1 FR 0.0001 REL FR 1 V 0 P
noble mother of the world | leave unsaluted. COR 5.03. 50
UNSANCTIFIED 3 FR 0.0003 REL FR 3 V 0 P
in no place so unsanctified | where such as thou MAC 4.02. 81
she should in ground unsanctified been lodg'd HAM 5.01.229
the post unsanctified | of murtherous lechers; LR 4.06.274
UNSATIATE *(also insatiate)*
UNSATIATE 1 FR 0.0001 REL FR 1 V 0 P
th' unsatiate greediness of his desire, | and R3 3.07. 7
UNSATISFIED 6 FR 0.0006 REL FR 6 V 0 P
but that one half which is unsatisfied, | we LLL 2.01.138
and think we think ourselves unsatisfied, | till 1H4 1.03.287
and though he were unsatisfied in getting H8 4.02. 55
o, wilt thou leave me so unsatisfied? ROM 2.02.125
me and my cause aright | to the unsatisfied. HAM 5.02.340
that satiate yet unsatisfied desire, that tub CYM 1.06. 48
UNSAVORY 5 FR 0.0005 REL FR 4 V 1 P
thou hast the most unsavory /similes and art 1H4 1.02. 79 P
unsavory news! but how made he escape? 3H6 4.06. 80
come, bitter conduct, come, unsavory guide! ROM 5.03.116
all viands that i eat do seem unsavory, PER 2.03. 31
find sweet beginning, but unsavory end; VEN 1138
UNSAY 3 FR 0.0003 REL FR 3 V 0 P
that fair again unsay. MND 1.01.181
scorns to unsay what once it hath delivered. R2 4.01. 9
impeach | what then he said, so he unsay it now. 1H4 1.03. 76
UNSAY'T 1 FR 0.0001 REL FR 1 V 0 P
i'll have more, or else unsay't; H8 5.01.175
UNSCALABLE 1 FR 0.0001 REL FR 1 V 0 P
in | with oaks unscalable and roaring waters, CYM 3.01. 20
UNSCANN'D 1 FR 0.0001 REL FR 1 V 0 P
it shall find | the harm of unscann'd swiftness, COR 3.01.311
UNSCARR'D 2 FR 0.0002 REL FR 2 V 0 P
so she may live unscarr'd of bleeding slaughter, R3 4.04.210
and let the unscarr'd braggarts of the war TIM 4.03.161
UNSCHOOL'D 2 FR 0.0002 REL FR 2 V 0 P
is an unlesson'd girl, unschool'd, unpractic'd, MV 3.02.159
an understanding simple and unschool'd: HAM 1.02. 97
/UNSCISSOR'D 1 FR 0.0001 REL FR 1 V 0 P
/unscissor'd shall this hair of mine remain, PER 3.03. 29
UNSCORCH'D 1 FR 0.0001 REL FR 1 V 0 P
not sensible of fire, remain'd unscorch'd. JC 1.03. 18
UNSCOUR'D 1 FR 0.0001 REL FR 1 V 0 P
penalties | which have, like unscour'd armor, MM 1.02.167
UNSCRATCH'D 1 FR 0.0001 REL FR 1 V 0 P
to save unscratch'd your city's threat'ned JN 2.01.225
/UNSEAL 1 FR 0.0001 REL FR 1 V 0 P
manners, to /unseal | their grand commission; HAM 5.02. 17
UNSEAL 3 FR 0.0003 REL FR 3 V 0 P
unseal this letter soon; MV 5.01.275
presently | he did unseal them, and the first he H8 3.02. 79
love thee much — | let me unseal the letter. LR 4.05. 22
UNSEAL'D 1 FR 0.0001 REL FR 1 V 0 P
are words and poor conditions, but unseal'd — AWW 4.02. 30
UNSEAM'D 1 FR 0.0001 REL FR 1 V 0 P
till he unseam'd him from the nave to th' chops, MAC 1.02. 22
UNSEARCH'D 1 FR 0.0001 REL FR 1 V 0 P
and leave you not a man–of–war unsearch'd. TIT 4.03. 22
UNSEASONABLE 4 FR 0.0004 REL FR 3 V 1 P
i can, at any unseasonable instant of the night, ADO 2.02. 16 P
being urged at a time unseasonable. JN 4.02. 20
like an unseasonable stormy day, | which makes R2 3.02.106
his bow | to strike a poor unseasonable doe. LUC 581
UNSEASONABLY 2 FR 0.0002 REL FR 1 V 1 P
it curvets unseasonably. AYL 3.02.245 P
we come unseasonably; TNK 1.01.168
UNSEASON'D 2 FR 0.0002 REL FR 1 V 1 P
embold'ned me to this unseason'd intrusion; WIV 2.02.168 P
my lord, | 'tis an unseason'd courtier; AWW 1.01. 71
UNSEASONED 1 FR 0.0001 REL FR 1 V 0 P
and these unseasoned hours perforce must add 2H4 3.01.105
/UNSECONDED 1 FR 0.0001 REL FR 1 V 0 P
/second /to /none, /unseconded /by /you, | /to 2H4 2.03. 34
UNSECRET 1 FR 0.0001 REL FR 1 V 0 P
to us, | when we are so unsecret to ourselves? TRO 3.02.125
UNSEDUC'D 1 FR 0.0001 REL FR 0 V 1 P
if she remain unseduc'd, you not making it CYM 1.04.161 P
UNSEEING 2 FR 0.0002 REL FR 2 V 0 P
i should have scratch'd out your unseeing eyes, TGV 4.04.204
when to unseeing eyes thy shade shines so! SON 43. 8
UNSEEMING 1 FR 0.0001 REL FR 1 V 0 P
in so unseeming to confess receipt | of that LLL 2.01.155
UNSEEMLY 1 FR 0.0001 REL FR 1 V 0 P
unseemly woman in a seeming man, | and ROM 3.03.112
/UNSEEN 2 FR 0.0002 REL FR 2 V 0 P
/the /other /down, /unseen, /and /full /of R2 4.01.187
/are /merely /shadows /to /the /unseen /grief 4.01.297
UNSEEN 22 FR 0.0024 REL FR 21 V 1 P
o jest unseen, inscrutable; TGV 2.01.135

here can i sit alone, unseen of any, | and to 5.04. 4
there to find his fellow forth | (unseen, ERR 1.02. 38
leaves the wind, | all unseen, can passage find; LLL 4.03.104
here, | unseen, unvisited, much to our shame. 5.02.358
he wears his honor in a box unseen, | that hugs AWW 2.03.279
theirs only, | that would unseen be wicked? WT 1.02.292
then thieves and robbers range abroad unseen R2 3.02. 39
by night, | unseen, yet crescive in his faculty. H5 1.01. 66
leap to these arms untalk'd of and unseen! ROM 3.02. 7
we'll so bestow ourselves that, seeing unseen, HAM 3.01. 32
corruption, mining all within, | infects unseen. 3.04.149
apprehension kills | the unseen good old man. 4.01. 12
you had then left unseen a wonderful piece of ANT 1.02.153 P
when most unseen, then most doth tyrannize. LUC 676
be, | to have their unseen sin remain untold; 753
her spite | against the unseen secrecy of night: 763
"o unseen shame, invisible disgrace! 827
himself behind | was left unseen, save to the 1426
leaves the wind | all unseen gan passage find, PP 16. 6
stealing unseen to west with this disgrace: SON 33. 8
urge, | as to prevent our maladies unseen, | we 118. 3
UNSEMINAR'D 1 FR 0.0001 REL FR 1 V 0 P
that, being unseminar'd, thy freer thoughts ANT 1.05. 11
UNSENTENC'D 1 FR 0.0001 REL FR 1 V 0 P
which perish'd should | go to't unsentenc'd. TNK 5.01.157
UNSEPARABLE *(also inseparable)*
UNSEPARABLE 1 FR 0.0001 REL FR 1 V 0 P
in love | unseparable, shall within this hour, COR 4.04. 16
UNSERVICEABLE 1 FR 0.0001 REL FR 0 V 1 P
six thousand, but very weak and unserviceable. AWW 4.03.131 P
UNSET 1 FR 0.0001 REL FR 1 V 0 P
hours, | and many maiden gardens, yet unset, SON 16. 6
UNSETTLE 2 FR 0.0002 REL FR 2 V 0 P
to go, my lord, | his wits begin t' unsettle. LR 3.04.162
let not my sense unsettle | lest i should drown, TNK 3.02. 29
UNSETTLED 7 FR 0.0008 REL FR 7 V 0 P
and the best comforter | to an unsettled fancy, TMP 5.01. 59
therefore am i found | so much unsettled. AWW 2.05. 63
he something seems unsettled. WT 1.02.147
dost think i am so muddy, so unsettled, | to 1.02.325
and all th' unsettled humors of the land, | rash JN 2.01. 66
as to rectify | what is unsettled in the king. H8 2.04. 64
is in expectation, | yet quaking and unsettled. TNK 5.03.106
UNSEVER'D 1 FR 0.0001 REL FR 1 V 0 P
say | honor and policy, like unsever'd friends, COR 3.02. 42
UNSEX 1 FR 0.0001 REL FR 1 V 0 P
that tend on mortal thoughts, unsex me here, MAC 1.05. 41
UNSHAK'D 2 FR 0.0002 REL FR 2 V 0 P
holds on his rank, | unshak'd of motion; JC 3.01. 70
keep unshak'd | that temple, thy fair mind, that CYM 2.01. 63
UNSHAKEN 2 FR 0.0002 REL FR 2 V 0 P
wild river break, | and stand unshaken yours. H8 3.02.199
tree, | but fall unshaken when they mellow be. HAM 3.02.191
UNSHAPED 1 FR 0.0001 REL FR 1 V 0 P
yet the unshaped use of it doth move | the HAM 4.05. 8
UNSHAPES 1 FR 0.0001 REL FR 1 V 0 P
this deed unshapes me quite, makes me unpregnant
MM 4.04. 20
UNSHEATH'D 1 FR 0.0001 REL FR 1 V 0 P
there is not now a rebel's sword unsheath'd, 2H4 4.04. 86
UNSHEATHE 3 FR 0.0003 REL FR 3 V 0 P
unsheathe your sword, and dub him presently. 3H6 2.02. 59
unsheathe your sword, good father; 2.02. 80
then, executioner, unsheathe thy sword. 2.02.123
UNSHEATHED 1 FR 0.0001 REL FR 1 V 0 P
harmful knife, that thence her soul unsheathed; LUC 1724
UNSHORN 1 FR 0.0001 REL FR 1 V 0 P
like unshorn velvet on that termless skin, LC 94
/UNSHOUT 1 FR 0.0001 REL FR 1 V 0 P
/unshout the noise that banish'd martius! COR 5.05. 4
UNSHOWN 1 FR 0.0001 REL FR 1 V 0 P
ostentation of our love, which, left unshown, ANT 3.06. 52
UNSHRINKING 1 FR 0.0001 REL FR 1 V 0 P
in the unshrinking station where he fought, MAC 5.09. 8
UNSHRUBB'D 1 FR 0.0001 REL FR 1 V 0 P
crown | my bosky acres and my unshrubb'd down,
TMP 4.01. 81
UNSHUNNABLE 1 FR 0.0001 REL FR 1 V 0 P
'tis destiny unshunnable, like death. OTH 3.03.275
UNSHUNN'D 1 FR 0.0001 REL FR 0 V 1 P
your powder'd bawd, an unshunn'd consequence; MM 3.02. 60 P
UNSIFTED 1 FR 0.0001 REL FR 1 V 0 P
girl, | unsifted in such perilous circumstance. HAM 1.03.102
UNSIGHTLY 1 FR 0.0001 REL FR 1 V 0 P
these are unsightly tricks. LR 2.04.157
UNSINOW'D 1 FR 0.0001 REL FR 1 V 0 P
which may to you, perhaps, seem much unsinow'd,
HAM 4.07. 10
UNSISTING 1 FR 0.0001 REL FR 1 V 0 P
that wounds th' unsisting postern with these MM 4.02. 89
UNSKILLFUL 5 FR 0.0005 REL FR 3 V 2 P
his filching was like an unskillful singer, he WIV 1.03. 26 P
and, though unskillful, why not ned and i | for 3H6 5.04. 19
though it makes the unskillful laugh, cannot but HAM 3.02. 25 P
we must not think the turk is so unskillful | to OTH 1.03. 27
unskillful in the world's false forgeries. PP 1. 4
UNSKILLFULLY 1 FR 0.0001 REL FR 0 V 1 P
therefore you speak unskillfully; MM 3.02.147 P
UNSLIPPING 1 FR 0.0001 REL FR 1 V 0 P
to knit your hearts | with an unslipping knot, ANT 2.02.126
UNSMIRCHED 1 FR 0.0001 REL FR 1 V 0 P
between the chaste unsmirched brow | of my true HAM 4.05.120
UNSOIL'D 1 FR 0.0001 REL FR 1 V 0 P
my unsoil'd name, th' austereness of my life, MM 2.04.155
UNSOLICITED 2 FR 0.0002 REL FR 2 V 0 P
unsolicited | i left no reverend person in this H8 2.04.220
to effect, | there's not a god left unsolicited. TIT 4.03. 61
UNSORTED 1 FR 0.0001 REL FR 0 V 1 P
have nam'd uncertain, the time itself unsorted, 1H4 2.03. 12 P
UNSOUGHT 3 FR 0.0003 REL FR 3 V 0 P
to find, yet loath to leave unsought | or that, ERR 1.01.135
sought is good, but given unsought is better. TN 3.01.156
unknown to you, unsought, were clipt about CYM 5.05.451
UNSOUND 1 FR 0.0001 REL FR 1 V 0 P
lest that it make me so unsound a man | as to TN 3.04.350
UNSOUNDED 3 FR 0.0003 REL FR 3 V 0 P
forsake unsounded deeps to dance on sands. TGV 3.02. 80
a man | unsounded yet and full of deep deceit. 2H6 3.01. 57
let my unsounded self, suppos'd a fool, | now LUC 1819
UNSPEAK 1 FR 0.0001 REL FR 1 V 0 P
direction, and | unspeak mine own detraction; MAC 4.03.123
UNSPEAKABLE 5 FR 0.0005 REL FR 3 V 2 P
impos'd | than i to speak my griefs unspeakable: ERR 1.01. 32
you have an unspeakable comfort of your young WT 1.01. 34 P
neighbors, is grown into an unspeakable estate. 4.02. 40 P
forget | the least of these unspeakable deserts, TIT 1.01.256
had titus to revenge | these wrongs unspeakable, 5.03.126
UNSPEAKING 1 FR 0.0001 REL FR 1 V 0 P
or his description | prov'd us unspeaking sots. CYM 5.05.178
UNSPHERE 1 FR 0.0001 REL FR 1 V 0 P
you would seek t' unsphere the stars with oaths, WT 1.02. 48
UNSPOKE 1 FR 0.0001 REL FR 1 V 0 P
which often leaves the history unspoke | that it LR 1.01.236
UNSPOKEN 1 FR 0.0001 REL FR 1 V 0 P
thou'lt torture me to leave unspoken that CYM 5.05.139
UNSPOTTED 7 FR 0.0008 REL FR 6 V 1 P
can try it out with all unspotted soldiers. H5 4.01.161 P
yes, my good lord, a pure unspotted heart, 1H6 5.03.182
a heart unspotted is not easily daunted. 2H6 3.01.100
a most unspotted lily shall she pass | to th' H8 5.04. 61
but my unspotted fire of love to you. PER 1.01. 53
that my unspotted youth must now be soil'd TNK 4.02. 59
for collatine's dear love be kept unspotted: LUC 821
/UNSQUAR'D 1 FR 0.0001 REL FR 1 V 0 P
like a chime a–mending, with terms /unsquar'd, TRO 1.03.159
UNSTABLE 1 FR 0.0001 REL FR 1 V 0 P
and give way the while | to unstable slightness. COR 3.01.148
UNSTAID 2 FR 0.0002 REL FR 2 V 0 P
me | for undertaking so unstaid a journey? TGV 2.07. 60
are, | unstaid and skittish in all motions else, TN 2.04. 18
UNSTAIN'D 3 FR 0.0003 REL FR 3 V 0 P
do plainly give you out an unstain'd shepherd, WT 4.04.149
to live an unstain'd wife to my sweet love. ROM 4.01. 88
for unstain'd thoughts do seldom dream on evil; LUC 87
UNSTAINED 4 FR 0.0004 REL FR 4 V 0 P
hand, | but with a heart full of unstained love. JN 2.01. 16
th' unstained sword that you have us'd to bear, 2H4 5.02.114
stalks, | and gazeth on her yet unstained bed. LUC 366
and thou present'st a pure unstained prime. SON 70. 8
UNSTANCH'D 1 FR 0.0001 REL FR 0 V 1 P
a nutshell and as leaky as an unstanch'd wench. TMP 1.01. 48 P
UNSTANCHED 1 FR 0.0001 REL FR 1 V 0 P
stifle the villain whose unstanched thirst 3H6 2.06. 83
UNSTATE 2 FR 0.0002 REL FR 1 V 1 P
i would unstate myself to be in a due resolution LR 1.02. 99 P
unstate his happiness and be stag'd to th' show ANT 3.13. 30
UNSTAYED 1 FR 0.0001 REL FR 1 V 0 P
in wholesome counsel to his unstayed youth? R2 2.01. 2
UNSTEADFAST 1 FR 0.0001 REL FR 1 V 0 P
loud | on the unsteadfast footing of a spear. 1H4 1.03.193
UNSTOOPING 1 FR 0.0001 REL FR 1 V 0 P
the unstooping firmness of my upright soul. R2 1.01.121
UNSTRINGED 1 FR 0.0001 REL FR 1 V 0 P
me no more | than an unstringed viol or a harp, R2 1.03.162
UNSTUFF'D 1 FR 0.0001 REL FR 1 V 0 P
but where unbruised youth with unstuff'd brain ROM 2.03. 37
UNSUBSTANTIAL *(also insubstantial)*
UNSUBSTANTIAL 2 FR 0.0002 REL FR 2 V 0 P
i believe | that unsubstantial death is amorous, ROM 5.03.103
then, | thou unsubstantial air that i embrace: LR 4.01. 7
UNSUITABLE 2 FR 0.0002 REL FR 0 V 2 P
richly suited, but unsuitable — just like the AWW 1.01.157 P
will now be so unsuitable to her disposition, TN 2.05.201 P
/UNSUITING 1 FR 0.0001 REL FR 1 V 0 P
grief | (a passion most /unsuiting such a man), OTH 4.01. 77
UNSULLIED *(see unsallied)*
UNSUNN'D 1 FR 0.0001 REL FR 1 V 0 P
that i thought her | as chaste as unsunn'd snow. CYM 2.05. 13
UNSUR'D 1 FR 0.0001 REL FR 1 V 0 P
tie | thy now unsur'd assurance to the crown, JN 2.01.471
/UNSURE 1 FR 0.0001 REL FR 1 V 0 P
/an /habitation /giddy /and /unsure | /hath /he 2H4 1.03. 89
UNSURE 5 FR 0.0005 REL FR 5 V 0 P
what's to come is still unsure. TN 2.03. 49
the truth thou art unsure | to swear, swears JN 3.01.283
thoughts speculative their unsure hopes relate, MAC 5.04. 19
exposing what is mortal and unsure | to all that HAM 4.04. 51
out of his scattering and unsure observance. OTH 3.03.151
UNSUSPECTED 2 FR 0.0002 REL FR 2 V 0 P
to her, | and unsuspected court her by herself. SHR 1.02.137
the dangerous and unsuspected hastings. R3 3.05. 23
UNSWAYABLE 1 FR 0.0001 REL FR 1 V 0 P
known before | but to be rough, unswayable, and COR 5.06. 25
UNSWAY'D 2 FR 0.0002 REL FR 2 V 0 P
is the sword unsway'd? R3 4.04.469
who leaves unsway'd the likeness of a man, | thy SON 141.11
UNSWEAR 2 FR 0.0002 REL FR 2 V 0 P
unswear faith sworn, and on the marriage–bed JN 3.01.245
you well assur'd, | no more than he'll unswear. OTH 4.01. 31
UNSWEPT 3 FR 0.0003 REL FR 3 V 0 P
fires thou find'st unrak'd and hearths unswept, WIV 5.05. 44
the dust on antique time would lie unswept, COR 2.03.119
bright in these contents | than unswept stone, SON 55. 4
UNSWORN 1 FR 0.0001 REL FR 1 V 0 P
you are yet unsworn. MM 1.04. 9
UNTAINTED 7 FR 0.0008 REL FR 6 V 1 P
is your brother sav'd, your honor untainted, the MM 3.01.254 P
stronger breastplate than a heart untainted! 2H6 3.02.232
the untainted virtue of your years | hath not R3 3.01. 7
untainted, unexamin'd, free, at liberty. 3.06. 9
her body's stain her mind untainted clears, LUC 1710
and blood untainted still doth red abide, 1749
him in thy course untainted do allow | for SON 19.11
UNTALK'D 1 FR 0.0001 REL FR 1 V 0 P
leap to these arms untalk'd of and unseen! ROM 3.02. 7
UNTANGLE 1 FR 0.0001 REL FR 1 V 0 P
o time, thou must untangle this, not i, | it is TN 2.02. 40
UNTANGLED 1 FR 0.0001 REL FR 1 V 0 P
which, once untangled, much misfortune bodes. ROM 1.04. 91
UNTASTED 1 FR 0.0001 REL FR 1 V 0 P
an unwholesome dish, | are like to rot untasted. TRO 2.03.121
UNTAUGHT 5 FR 0.0005 REL FR 5 V 0 P
where their untaught love | must needs appear MM 2.04. 29
he call'd them untaught knaves, unmannerly, | to 1H4 1.03. 43
us'd to command, untaught to plead for favor. 2H6 4.01.122
o thou untaught! ROM 5.03.214
them | to royalty unlearn'd, honor untaught, CYM 4.02.178
UNTEMPERING 1 FR 0.0001 REL FR 0 V 1 P
the poor and untempering effect of my visage. H5 5.02.224 P
UNTENDER 2 FR 0.0002 REL FR 2 V 0 P
so young, and so untender? LR 1.01.106
thou that paper to me with | a look untender? CYM 3.04. 12
UNTENDER'D 1 FR 0.0001 REL FR 1 V 0 P
which, by thee, lately | is left untender'd. CYM 3.01. 10
UNTENT 1 FR 0.0001 REL FR 1 V 0 P
untent his person and share th' air with us? TRO 2.03.168
UNTENTED 1 FR 0.0001 REL FR 1 V 0 P
th' untented woundings of a father's curse LR 1.04.300
UNTHANKFUL 1 FR 0.0001 REL FR 1 V 0 P
as high in the air as this unthankful king, | as 1H4 1.03.136
UNTHANKFULNESS 4 FR 0.0004 REL FR 3 V 1 P
else thou diest in thine unthankfulness, and AWW 1.01.211 P
that you take with unthankfulness his doing. R3 2.02. 90
o rude unthankfulness! ROM 3.03. 24
or pay you with unthankfulness in thought, | be PER 1.04.102
UNTHINK 1 FR 0.0001 REL FR 1 V 0 P
to unthink your speaking | and to say so no more H8 2.04.104
UNTHOUGHT 1 FR 0.0001 REL FR 0 V 1 P
i leave my duty a little unthought of, and speak TN 5.01.310 P
UNTHOUGHT–OF 1 FR 0.0001 REL FR 1 V 0 P
and your unthought–of harry chance to meet. 1H4 3.02.141
UNTHOUGHT–ON 1 FR 0.0001 REL FR 1 V 0 P
but as th' unthought–on accident is guilty | to WT 4.04.538
UNTHREAD 1 FR 0.0001 REL FR 1 V 0 P
unthread the rude eye of rebellion, | and JN 5.04. 11
UNTHRIFT 3 FR 0.0003 REL FR 2 V 1 P
and with an unthrift love did run from venice, MV 5.01. 16
thou ever know unthrift that was belov'd after TIM 4.03.311 P
look what an unthrift in the world doth spend SON 9. 9
UNTHRIFTS 2 FR 0.0002 REL FR 2 V 0 P
and given away | to upstart unthrifts? R2 2.03.122
o, none but unthrifts: SON 13.13
UNTHRIFTY 5 FR 0.0005 REL FR 4 V 1 P
in the fearful guard | of an unthrifty knave, MV 1.03.176
our absence makes us unthrifty to our knowledge.
WT 5.02.111 P
can no man tell me of my unthrifty son? R2 5.03. 1
o, much i fear some ill unthrifty thing. ROM 5.03.136
unthrifty loveliness, why dost thou spend | upon SON 4. 1
UNTIE 7 FR 0.0008 REL FR 6 V 1 P
untie the spell. TMP 5.01.253
i prithee, sister kate, untie my hands. SHR 2.01. 21
not i, | it is too hard a knot for me t' untie! TN 2.02. 41
that wisdom knits not, folly may easily untie. TRO 2.03.102 P
though you untie the winds, and let them fight MAC 4.01. 52
this knot intrinsicate | of life at once untie. ANT 5.02.305
or a speaking such | as sense cannot untie. CYM 5.04.148
UNTIED 2 FR 0.0002 REL FR 1 V 1 P
your sleeve unbutton'd, your shoe untied, and AYL 3.02.380 P
deep, | untied i still my virgin knot will keep. PER 4.02.147
UNTIL 80 FR 0.0090 REL FR 76 V 4 P
there he must stay until the officer | arise to MM 4.02. 90
will not show my face | until my husband bid me. 5.01.170
until i know this sure uncertainty, | i'll ERR 2.02.185
where would you had remain'd until this time, 4.04. 66
and never rise until my tears and prayers | have 5.01.115
no, truly, not, although, until last night, | i ADO 4.01.148
bear her in hand until they come to take hands, 4.01.304 P
until to–morrow morning, lords, farewell. 5.01.328
until the goose came out of door, | and stayed LLL 3.01. 91
until the goose came out of door, | staying the 3.01. 97
until his ink were temp'red with love's sighs: 4.03.344
there stay until the twelve celestial signs 5.02.797
things growing are not ripe until their season, MND 2.02.117
now, until the break of day, | through this 5.01.401
until confirm'd, sign'd, ratified by you. MV 3.02.148
for, wooing here until i sweat again, | and 3.02.203
and manage of my house | until my lord's return. 3.04. 26
here, | until her husband and my lord's return. 3.04. 30
shines brightly as a king | until a king be by, 5.01. 95
ne'er come in your bed | until i see the ring! 5.01.191
to do it, | unless he live until he be a man. 5.01.283
or, if not so, until the sun be set. SHR in.2. 120
any man, | until the elder sister first be wed. 1.02.261
nothing in france, until he have no wife! AWW 3.02. 79
nothing in france, until he has no wife! 3.02.100
not knowing them until we know their grave. 5.03. 62
sir, to have held my peace until | you had drawn WT 1.02. 28
let him be, | until a time may serve. 2.03. 22
do not shun her | until you see her die again, 5.03.106
kings of our fear, until our fears, resolv'd, JN 2.01.371
better other's happiness | until the heavens, R2 1.01. 23
which else would post until it had return'd 1.01. 56
until thou bid me joy | by pardoning rutland, my 5.03. 95
piece by piece, | until i meet the king. 1H4 5.03. 28
will not go off until they hear you speak. 2H4 4.02.100
land | until four hundred one and twenty years H5 1.02. 57
since i came to france | until this instant. 4.07. 56
england ne'er had a king until his time: 1H6 1.01. 8
wear, | until it wither with me to my grave, 2.04.110
and so farewell until i meet thee next. 2.04.113
face, | until thy head be circled with the same. 2H6 1.02. 10
but fear not thou, until thy foot be snar'd, 2.04. 56
to keep, until your further time of trial. 3.01.138
to rage | until the golden circuit on my head, 3.01.352
until they hear the order of his death. 3.02.129
lie, | until the queen his mistress bury it. 4.01.143
until a power be rais'd to put them down. 4.04. 40
defer the spoil of the city until night; 4.07.134 P
thither, | until his army be dismiss'd from him. 4.09. 40
bed, | until that act of parliament be repeal'd 3H6 1.01.249
rest | until the white rose that i wear be dy'd 1.02. 33
until i be resolv'd | where our right valiant 2.01. 9
king, | had slipp'd our claim until another age. 2.02.162
now, lords, take leave until we meet again, 2.03. 42
until my misshap'd trunk that bears this head 3.02.170
he shall never wake until the great judgment day R3 1.04.103 P
and if i live until i be a man, | i'll win our 3.01. 91
farewell, until we meet again in heaven. 3.03. 26
i swear | i will not dine until i see the same. 3.04. 77
die | until your lordship came to see his end, 3.05. 53
this so far, until | it forg'd him some design, H8 1.02.180
i am hush'd until our city be afire, | and then COR 5.03.181
there let them bide until we have devis'd | some TIT 2.03.284

the east, | until his very downfall in the sea; 5.02. 57
stir not until the signal. JC 5.01. 26
macbeth shall never vanquish'd be until | great MAC 4.01. 92
theme | until my eyelids will no longer wag. HAM 5.01.267
forbear his presence until some little time hath LR 1.02.161 P
until their greater pleasures first be known 5.03. 2
until some half hour past, when i was arm'd. 5.03.194
that he which is was wish'd, until he were; ANT 1.04. 42
until | of many thousand kisses the poor last 4.15. 19
service, doctor, | until i send for thee. CYM 1.05. 45
lov'd, | continu'd so, until we thought he died. 5.05.380
and until then your entertain shall be | as doth PER 1.01.119
until our stars that frown lend us a smile. 1.04.108
set purpose let his armor rust | until this day, 2.02. 55
haply so long until | the follow'd make pursuit? TNK 1.02. 51
until her husband's welfare she did hear; LUC 263
until live's composition be recured | by those SON 45. 9
UNTIMBER'D 1 FR 0.0001 REL FR 1 V 0 P
boat | whose weak untimber'd sides but even now TRO 1.03. 43
UNTIMELY 27 FR 0.0030 REL FR 27 V 0 P
here, | in weeping after this untimely bier. R2 5.06. 52
of york | my father came untimely to his death? 3H6 3.03.187
how sweet a plant have you untimely cropp'd! 5.05. 62
th' untimely fall of virtuous lancaster. R3 1.02. 4
it, | prodigious, and untimely brought to light, 1.02. 22
die in his youth by like untimely violence! 1.03.200
untimely storms makes men expect a dearth. 2.03. 35
untimely smoth'red in their dusky graves. 4.04. 70
an untimely ague | stay'd me a prisoner in my H8 1.01. 4
breast | by some vile forfeit of untimely death. ROM 1.04.111
which too untimely here did scorn the earth. 3.01.118
death lies on her like an untimely frost | upon 4.05. 28
whose untimely death | banish'd the new-made 5.03.234
here untimely lay | the noble paris and true 5.03.258
th' untimely emptying of the happy throne, | and MAC 4.03. 68
was from his mother's womb | untimely ripp'd. 5.08. 16
what we mean to do | and what's untimely done, HAM 4.01. 40
i bleed apace, | untimely comes this hurt. LR 3.07. 98
o untimely death! 4.06.250
son | by your untimely claspings with your child PER 1.01.128
so neither for my sake should fall untimely. TNK 4.02. 69
but some untimely thought did instigate | his LUC 43
by her untimely tears, her husband's love, | by 570
have heard the cause of my untimely death, 1178
and his untimely frenzy thus awaketh: 1675
untimely breathings, sick and short assays, 1720
rose, fair flower, untimely pluck'd, soon vaded, PP 10. 1
UNTIRABLE 1 FR 0.0001 REL FR 1 V 0 P
were, | to an untirable and continuate goodness; TIM 1.01. 11
UNTIR'D 2 FR 0.0002 REL FR 2 V 0 P
hath he so long held out with me untir'd, | and R3 4.02. 44
do, | with untir'd spirits and formal constancy. JC 2.01.227
UNTITLED 1 FR 0.0001 REL FR 1 V 0 P
with an untitled tyrant bloody-sceptred, | when MAC 4.03.104
/UNTO 1 FR 0.0001 REL FR 1 V 0 P
/we /are /denied /access /unto /his /person 2H4 4.01. 78
UNTO 470 FR 0.0531 REL FR 443 V 27 P
remember | a time before we came unto this cell? TMP 1.02. 39
come unto these yellow sands, | and then take 1.02.375
expos'd unto the sea (which hath requit it) 3.03. 71
some whirlwind bear | unto a ragged, fearful, TGV 1.02.118
me, i have writ your letter | unto the secret, 2.01.105
her love himself to write unto her lover." 2.01.168
i must unto the road, to disembark | some 2.04.187
for love of you, not hate unto my friend, | hath 3.01. 46
friends | unto a youthful gentleman of worth, 3.01.107
/an heir, and /near allied unto the duke. 4.01. 47
who, in my mood, i stabb'd unto the heart. 4.01. 49
we talk on | often resort unto this gentlewoman? 4.02. 74
good will | i bear unto the banish'd valentine, 4.03. 15
your message done, hie home unto my chamber, 4.04. 88
then | she's fled unto that peasant valentine; 5.02. 35
at my depart | i gave this unto julia. 5.04. 97
falstaff have committed disparagements unto you, WIV 1.01. 32 P
he'll speak like an anthropophaginian unto thee. 4.05. 10 P
rate, | cannot amount unto a hundred marks, ERR 1.01. 24
born, and wed | unto a woman, happy but for me, 1.01. 37
grant | did but convey unto our fearful minds 1.01. 67
had fast'ned him unto a small spare mast, | such 1.01. 79
what, wilt thou flout me thus unto my face, 1.02. 91
so that my arrant, due unto my tongue, | i thank 2.01. 72
as strange unto your town as to your talk, | who 2.02.149
known unto these, and to myself disguis'd? 2.02.214
bear me forthwith unto his creditor, | and, 4.04.120
complain unto the duke of this indignity. 5.01.113
egeon, speak, | and speak unto the same aemilia! 5.01.346
now in great haste, as it may appear unto you. ADO 3.05. 51 P
and given way unto this course of fortune, | by 4.01.157
and do all rites | that appertain unto a burial. 4.01.208
love | is very much unto the prince and claudio, 4.01.246
now, unto thy bones good night! 5.03. 22
containing her affection unto benedick. 5.04. 90
all liberal reason i will yield unto. LLL 2.01.167
the party /writing to the person written unto: 4.02.135 P
consider what you first did swear unto: 4.03.287
will advance | unto his several mistress, which 5.02.124
yield my virgin patent up | unto his lordship, MND 1.01. 81
my right of her | i do estate unto demetrius. 1.01. 98
that he hath turn'd a heaven unto a hell! 1.01.207
thou toldst me they were stol'n unto this wood; 2.01.191
i mean, that my heart unto yours /is knit, | so 2.02. 47
the sun was not so true unto the day | as he to 3.02. 50
but that my nails can reach unto thine eyes. 3.02.298
save that, in love unto demetrius, | i told him 3.02.309
i told him of your stealth unto this wood. 3.02.310
so, good night unto you all. 5.01.436
may by me be done, | and i am prest unto it; MV 1.01.160
yes, shylock, i will seal unto this bond. 1.03.171
nor will not. come bring me unto my chance. 2.01. 43
i hope, an old man, shall frutify unto you — 2.02.134 P
thee with imagin'd speed | unto the /traject, to 3.04. 53
venice, confiscate | unto the state of venice. 4.01.312
state, | which humbleness may drive unto a fine. 4.01.372
to render it | upon his death unto the gentleman 4.01.384
unto his son lorenzo and his daughter. 4.01.390
three thousand ducats, due unto the jew, | we 4.01.411
him, if thou canst, | unto antonio's house. 4.01.454
and so riveted with faith unto your flesh. 5.01.169
his ring away | unto the judge that begg'd it, 5.01.180
if i could add a lie unto a fault, | i would 5.01.186
"be it known unto all men by these presents." AYL 1.02.123 P
i should have given him tears unto entreaties, 1.02.238
from tyrant duke unto a tyrant brother. 1.02.288
his merry note | unto the sweet bird's throat, 2.05. 4
unto the green holly, | most friendship is 2.07.180
committing me unto my brother's love, | who led 4.03.144
love, | who led me instantly unto his cave, 4.03.145
unto the shepherd youth | that he in sport doth 4.03.155
but sup them well, and look unto them all, SHR in.1. 28
it would seem strange unto him when he wak'd. in.1. 43
observ'd in noble ladies | unto their lords, by in.1. 112
ay, and the time seems thirty unto me, | being in.2. 114
that none shall have access unto bianca | till 1.02.127
any, freely give unto /you this young scholar, 2.01. 79 P
your daughter, | unto bianca, fair and virtuous. 2.01. 91
i will unto venice | to buy apparel 'gainst the 2.01.314
"hic est," son unto vincentio of pisa, "/sigeia 3.01. 32 P
heart | unto a mad-brain rudesby full of spleen, 3.02. 10
to me she's married, not unto my clothes. 3.02.117
faith, he is gone unto the taming-school. 4.02. 54
beggars that come unto my father's door | upon 4.03. 4
much good do it unto thy gentle heart! 4.03. 51
love, | will we return unto thy father's house, 4.03. 53
i say unto thee, i bid thy master cut out the 4.03.126 P
go take it up unto thy master's use. 4.03.157
kate, we will unto your father's | even in these 4.03.169
him, | and bring our horses unto long-lane end; 4.03.185
at the last | unto the wished haven of my bliss. 5.01.128
assurance | let's each one send unto his wife, 5.02. 66
me them soundly forth unto their husbands. 5.02.104
add | unto their losses twenty thousand crowns, 5.02.113
that before you, and next unto high heaven, | i AWW 1.03.193
that so seriously he does address himself unto? 3.06. 96 P
'a will betray us all unto ourselves: 4.01. 92
off, | but give thyself unto my sick desires, 4.02. 35
good youth, address thy gait unto her, | be not TN 1.04. 15
i have said too much unto a heart of stone, 3.04.201
but when i came unto my beds, | with hey ho, etc 5.01.401
their death appear (unto | our shame perpetual). WT 3.02.237
quarters of a mile hence, unto whom i was going. 4.03. 81 P
and son unto the king, whom heavens directing, 5.03.150
madam, i'll follow you unto the death. JN 1.01.154
been forward first | to speak unto this city: 2.01.483
a grave unto a soul, | holding th' eternal 3.04. 17
or add another hue | unto the rainbow, or with 4.02. 14
and, like a shifted wind unto a sail, | it makes 4.02. 23
the heighth, the crest, or crest unto the crest, 4.03. 46
thyself, | and /gripple thee unto a pagan shore, 5.02. 36
the scope | and warrant limited unto my tongue. 5.02.123
add proof unto mine armor with thy prayers, R2 1.03. 73
stoop | unto the sovereign mercy of the king; 2.03.157
be it known unto you | i do remain as neuter. 2.03.158
gives in your weakness strength unto your foe, 3.02.181
my wretchedness unto a row of /pins, | they will 3.04. 26
and his pure soul unto his captain christ, 4.01. 99
you must to pomfret, not unto the tower. 5.01. 52
bring me my boots, i will unto the king. 5.02. 84
his answer was, he would unto the stews, | and 5.03. 16
unto my mother's prayers i bend my knee. 5.03. 97
this prison where i live unto the world; 5.05. 2
they jar | their watches on unto mine eyes, the 5.05. 52
send danger from the east unto the west, | so 1H4 1.03.195
start away, | and lend no ear unto my purposes. 1.03.217
first bow'd my knee | unto this king of smiles, 1.03.246
i say unto you again, you are a shallow, 2.03. 14 P
me | directly unto this question that i ask. 2.03. 86
cry | hath followed certain men unto this house. 2.04.508
a rendezvous, a home to fly unto, | if that the 4.01. 57
what may the king's whole battle reach unto? 4.01.129
daughter, | give even way unto my rough affairs; 2H4 2.03. 2
as with the tide swell'd up unto his height, 2.03. 63
very smooth, like unto the sign of the leg, and 2.04.249 P
hours perforce must add | unto your sickness. 3.01.106
we would, dear lords, unto the holy land. 3.01.108
your part, bullcalf, grow till you come unto it. 3.02.252 P
unto your grace do i in chief address | the 4.01. 31
you, | discharge your powers unto their several 4.02. 61
word, | and thereupon i drink unto your grace. 4.02. 68
give that which gave thee life unto the worms, 4.05.116
tears, | the moist impediments unto my speech, 4.05.139
were, | i spake unto this crown as having sense, 4.05.157
might make them look | too near unto my state. 4.05.212
unto the lodging where i first did swound? 4.05.233
and drink unto /thee, leman mine, | and a merry 5.03. 47
him whose wrongs gives edge unto the swords H5 1.02. 27
so do the kings of france unto this day. 1.02. 90
let the inheritance | descend unto the daughter. 1.02.100
unto whose grace our passion is as subject | as 1.02.242
and hides a sword, from hilts unto the point, 2.pr. 9
then, | unto southampton do we shift our scene. 2.pr. 42
for i shall sutler be | unto the camp, and 2.01.112
and sworn unto the practices of france | to kill 2.02. 90
ordinance of times, | unto the crown of france. 2.04. 84
once more unto the breach, dear friends, once 3.01. 1
th' athversary — you may discuss unto the duke, 3.02. 61 P
so much | unto an enemy of craft and vantage, 3.06.144
presented them unto the gazing moon | so many 4.pr. 27
of color | unto the weary and all-watched night; 4.pr. 38
discuss unto me, art thou officer, | or art thou 4.01. 37
discuss the same in french unto him. 4.04. 29 P
expound unto me, boy. 4.04. 58
ride thou unto the horsemen on yond hill. 4.07. 57
patches will i get unto these cudgell'd scars, 5.01. 88
unto our brother france, and to our sister, 5.02. 2
majesties | unto this bar and royal interview, 5.02. 27
stars | that have consented unto henry's death: 1H6 1.01. 5
unto the french the dreadful judgment day | so 1.01. 29
aid, | unto his dastard foemen is betray'd. 1.01.144
open the gates unto the lord protector, | or 1.03. 27
speak unto talbot, nay, look up to him. 1.04. 89
you all consented unto salisbury's death, | for 1.05. 34
now have i paid my vow unto his soul; 2.02. 7
wars | will turn unto a peaceful comic sport, 2.02. 45
it, | and therefore frame the law unto my will. 2.04. 9
we sent unto the temple, unto his chamber, | and 2.05. 19
we sent unto the temple, unto his chamber, | and 2.05. 19
or aught intend'st to lay unto my charge, | do 3.01. 4
give | that doth belong unto the house of york, 3.01.164
torch | that joineth roan unto her countrymen, 3.02. 27
hecate, | but unto thee, alanson, and the rest. 3.02. 65
their powers are marching unto paris-ward. 3.03. 30
i have a while given truce unto my wars, | to do 3.04. 3
got | first to my god and next unto your grace. 3.04. 12
but i'll unto his majesty, and crave | i may 3.04. 41
from callice, | to haste unto your coronation, 4.01. 10
gather strength and march unto him straight. 4.01. 73
trumpeter, | summon their general unto the wall. 4.02. 2
yield up his life unto a world of odds. 4.04. 25
now thou art come unto a feast of death, | a 4.05. 7
they humbly sue unto your excellence | to have a 5.01. 4
and call'd unto a cardinal's degree? 5.01. 29
and turn again unto the warlike french. 5.02. 3
success unto our valiant general, | and 5.02. 8
why, what concerns his freedom unto me? 5.03.116
what answer makes your grace unto my suit? 5.03.150
royal name, | as deputy unto that gracious king, 5.03.161
is betroth'd | unto another lady of esteem. 5.05. 27
do, | because he is near kinsman unto charles. 5.05. 45
for henry, son unto a conqueror, | is likely to 5.05. 73
margaret, daughter unto reignier king of naples, 2H6 1.01. 47 P
unto the poor king reignier, whose large style 1.01.111
nay more, an enemy unto you all, | and no great 1.01.149
let's make haste away, and look unto the main. 1.01.208
unto the main? 1.01.209
burnt | unto the prince's heart of calydon. 1.01.235
anjou and maine both given unto the french! 1.01.236
as to vouchsafe one glance unto the ground. 1.02. 16
next time i'll keep my dreams unto myself, | and 1.02. 53
you do prepare to ride unto saint albons, 1.02. 57
york | was rightful heir unto the english crown 1.03.184
as i have read, laid claim unto the crown, | and 2.02. 40
anne, | my mother, being heir unto the crown, 2.02. 44
sole daughter unto lionel duke of clarence; 2.02. 50
from thence, unto the place of execution. 2.03. 6
the reverent care i bear unto my lord | made me 3.01. 34
all health unto my gracious sovereign! 3.01. 82
all happiness unto my lord the king! 3.01. 93
but mightier crimes are laid unto your charge, 3.01.134
'twill make them cool in zeal unto your grace. 3.01.177
are up | and put the englishmen unto the sword. 3.01.284
bank | drove back again unto my native clime? 3.02. 84
but left that hateful office unto thee. 3.02. 93
to tell my love unto his dumb deaf trunk, | and 3.02.144
mischance unto my state by suffolk's means. 3.02.284
him, | thou wilt but add increase unto my wrath. 3.02.292
to signify unto his majesty | that cardinal 3.02.368
bring me unto my trial when you will. 3.03. 8
that lays strong siege unto this wretch's soul, 3.03. 22
lord | unto the daughter of a worthless king, 4.01. 81
his body will i bear unto the king. 4.01.145
reign, | for i am rightful heir unto the crown. 4.02.131
i have a suit unto your lordship. 4.07. 3 P
giving up of normandy unto mounsieur basimecu, 4.07. 28 P
be it known unto thee by these presence, even 4.07. 29 P
this tongue hath parley'd unto foreign kings 4.07. 77
ambassadors from the king | unto the commons, 4.08. 8
unto all they meet. 4.08. 46
than you should stoop unto a frenchman's mercy. 4.08. 48
him, | and he that brings his head unto the king 4.08. 66
a mean | to reconcile you all unto the king. 4.08. 69
or unto death, to do my country good. 4.09. 43
as all things shall redound unto your good. 4.09. 47
thee headlong by the heels | unto a dunghill, 4.10. 81
end, | the king hath yielded unto thy demand: 5.01. 40
york doth present himself unto your highness. 5.01. 59
and never live but true unto his liege! 5.01. 82
me | that bows unto the grave with mickle age. 5.01.174
hast thou not sworn allegiance unto me? 5.01.179
it is great sin to swear unto a sin, | but 5.01.182
to aspire unto the crown and reign as king. 3H6 1.01. 53
do right unto this princely duke of york, | or i 1.01.166
what wrong is this unto the prince your son! 1.01.176
be thou a prey unto the house of york, | and die 1.01.185
and i unto the sea, from whence i came. 1.01.209
and giv'n unto the house of york such head | as 1.01.233
to entail him and his heirs unto the crown, 1.01.235
i'll write unto them and entreat them fair; 1.01.271
you, edward, shall unto my lord cobham, | with 1.02. 40
with downright payment show'd unto my father. 1.04. 32
what would your grace have done unto him now? 1.04. 65
to every good | as the antipodes are unto us, 1.04.135
the king unto the queen; 2.01.137
make war with him that climb'd unto their nest, 2.02. 31
fault, | and long hereafter say unto his child, 2.02. 36
would bring white hairs unto a quiet grave. 2.05. 40
did, | giving no ground unto the house of york, 2.06. 16
but set his murth'ring knife unto the root 2.06. 49
and you were sworn true subjects unto me; 3.01. 78
the king's, | to go with us unto the officers. 3.01. 98
and what he will, i humbly yield unto. 3.01.101
therefore i came unto your majesty. 3.02. 41
and that is more than i will yield unto. 3.02. 96
a happy thing | to be the father unto many sons. 3.02.105
see that he be convey'd unto the tower; 3.02.120
where i must take like seat unto my fortune, 3.03. 10
the measure of his love | unto our sister bona. 3.03.121
these from our king unto your majesty. 3.03.165
scales | unto the brother of your loving bride. 4.01. 53
king, | and not be tied unto his brother's will. 4.01. 66
what answer makes king lewis unto our letters? 4.01. 91
then, gentle clarence, welcome unto warwick, 4.02. 6
duke edward be convey'd | unto my brother, 4.03. 53
i'll hence forthwith unto the sanctuary, | to 4.04. 31
my fear to hope, my sorrows unto joys, | at our 4.06. 4
for now we owe allegiance unto henry. 4.07. 19
both him and all his brothers unto reason. 4.07. 34
and fearless minds climb soonest unto crowns. 4.07. 62
brave montgomery, and thanks unto you all. 4.07. 77
have sold their lives unto the house of york, 5.01. 74
and next his throat unto the butcher's knife. 5.06. 9
the duty that i owe unto your majesty | i seal 5.07. 28
brother, farewell, i will unto the king, | and R3 1.01.107
good time of day unto my gracious lord! 1.01.122

as much unto my good lord chamberlain! 1.01.123
by marrying her which i must reach unto. 1.01.159
is put unto the trust of richard gloucester, | a 1.03. 12
good time of day unto your royal grace! 1.03. 18
who is it that complains unto the king | that i, 1.03. 43
i lay unto the grievous charge of others. 1.03.325
write of, | unto the kingdom of perpetual night. 1.04. 47
seize on him, furies, take him unto torment!" 1.04. 57
their verdict up | unto the frowning judge? 1.04.185
treacherous, and full of guile | be he unto me! 2.01. 39
is this thy vow unto my sickly heart. 2.01. 42
i, ungracious, speak unto myself | for him, poor 2.01.128
o, they did urge it still unto the king! 2.01.138
i'll resign unto your grace | the seal i keep, 2.04. 70
of york | unto his princely brother presently? 3.01. 34
where it seems best unto your royal self. 3.01. 63
what, will you go unto the tower, my lord? 3.01.140
heart, | thinking on them, go i unto the tower. 3.01.150
go, fellow, go, return unto thy lord, | bid him 3.02. 19
have signified the same | unto the citizens, who 3.05. 60
which stretch'd unto their servants, daughters, 3.05. 82
have any time recourse unto the princes. 3.05.109
i'll signify so much unto him straight. 3.07. 70
times | unto a lineal true–derived course. 3.07.200
stay, yet look back with me unto the tower. 4.01. 97
gold | will tempt unto a close exploit of death? 4.02. 35
well, look unto it. 4.02. 87
unto the dignity and height of fortune, | the 4.04.244
sweetly in force unto her fair live's end. 4.04.351
in dorsetshire sent out a boat | unto the shore, 4.04.523
any good | that i myself have done unto myself? 5.03.188
go, gentlemen, every man unto his charge. 5.03.307
self, hath sent | one general tongue unto us: H8 2.02. 95
whom once more i present unto your highness. 2.02. 97
here, | before you all, appeal unto the pope, 2.04.119
back her appeal | she intends unto his holiness. 2.04.236
remember me | in all humility unto his highness. 4.02.161
the king's further pleasure | be known unto us. 5.02.126
a scantling | of good or bad unto the general, TRO 1.03.342
i say unto you, what he hath done famously, he COR 1.01. 36 P
unto the appetite and affection common | of the 1.01.104
when you speak best unto the purpose, it is not 2.01. 86 P
to brag unto them, "thus i did, and thus!" 2.02.147
enforce his pride, | and his old hate unto you; 2.03.220
"thou liest" unto thee with a voice as free | as 3.03. 73
and cowardly nobles gave way unto your clusters, 4.06.122
time, | and power, unto itself most commendable, 4.07. 51
the gods be good unto us! 5.04. 30 P
such a case the gods will not be good unto us. 5.04. 32 P
being banish'd for't, he came unto my hearth, 5.06. 29
shall join | to thrust the lie unto him. 5.06.109
rome, be as just and gracious unto me | as i am TIT 1.01. 60
these that i bring unto their latest home, 1.01. 83
birds | be unto us as is a nurse's song | of 2.03. 28
bind me here | unto the body of a dismal yew, 2.03.107
and shall she carry this unto her grave? 2.03.127
sirs, drag them from the pit unto the prison, 2.03.283
yet plead i must, | and bootless unto them. 3.01. 36
and swear unto my soul to right your wrongs. 3.01.278
aaron, what shall i say unto the empress? 4.02.128
i made unto the noise, when soon i heard | the 5.01. 25
pledges | unto my father and my uncle marcus, 5.01.164
till he be brought unto the empress' face | for 5.03. 7
let rome herself be bane unto herself, | and she 5.03. 73
out, | and sent her enemies unto the grave. 5.03.103
by giving liberty unto thine eyes: ROM 1.01.227
faith, i can tell her age unto an hour. 1.03. 11
heaven | unto the white–upturned wond'ring eyes 2.02. 29
i protest unto thee — 2.04.172 P
either withdraw unto some private place, | or 3.01. 51
bed, | which heavy sorrow makes them apt unto. 3.03.157
to follow this fair corse unto her grave. 4.05. 93
iron crow, and bring it straight | unto my cell. 5.02. 22
his time, | unto the rigor of severest law. 5.03.269
unto his honor has my lord's meat in him; TIM 3.01. 57
all these | owes their estates unto him. 3.03. 5
as 'twere a knell unto our master's fortunes, 4.02. 26
eye, i will present | my honest grief unto him; 4.03.470
'tis said he gave unto | his steward a mighty 5.01. 7
what have you now to present unto him? 5.01. 17
and strain what other means is left unto us | in 5.01.227
what said he when he came unto himself? JC 1.02.262
things | unto the climate that they point upon. 1.03. 32
submitting me unto the perilous night; 1.03. 47
of fear and warning | unto some monstrous state. 1.03. 71
round, | he then unto the ladder turns his back, 2.01. 25
unto bad causes swear | such creatures as men 2.01.131
and unpurged air | to add unto his sickness? 2.01.267
tell him, so please him come unto this place, 3.01.140
bring him with triumph home unto his house. 3.02. 49
it as a rich legacy | unto their issue. 3.02.137
bills | unto the legions on the other side. 5.02. 2
thou never com'st unto a happy birth, | but 5.03. 70
and bring us word unto octavius' tent | how 5.04. 31
by this vile conquest shall attain unto. 5.05. 38
home, | might yet enkindle you unto the crown, MAC 1.03.121
recommends itself | unto our gentle senses. 1.06. 3
i'll spend | unto a dismal and a fatal end. 3.05. 21
other, | as it doth well appear unto our state, HAM 1.01.101
unto our climatures and countrymen. 1.01.125
what we have seen to–night | unto young hamlet, 1.01.170
unto the voice and yielding of that body 1.03. 23
grapple them unto thy soul with hoops of steel, 1.03. 63
had witchcraft in't, he grew unto his seat, 4.07. 85
creature native and indued | unto that element. 4.07.180
had thought, by making this well known unto you,
LR 1.04.205
the wretch that thou hast blown unto the worst 4.01. 8
reveal'd myself unto him, | until some half hour 5.03.193
stir hither, i shall seem to notify unto her. OTH 3.01. 29 P
power of caesar, and | his power unto octavia. ANT 2.02.143
he's bound unto octavia. 2.05. 58
unto her | he gave the stablishment of egypt, 3.06. 8
stop their nose | that kneel'd unto the buds. 3.13. 40
like boys unto a muss, kings would start forth 3.13. 91
man, | commend unto his lips thy /favoring hand. 4.08. 23
with trees upon't that nod unto the world | and 4.14. 6
false–play'd my glory | unto an enemy's triumph. 4.14. 20
what thou wouldst do | is done unto thy hand; 4.14. 29
a ditch in egypt | be gentle grave unto me! 5.02. 58
herself | unto a poor but worthy gentleman. CYM 1.01. 7
of most stepmothers, | evil–ey'd unto you. 1.01. 72
you lean'd unto his sentence with what patience 1.01. 78
i would thou grew'st unto the shores o' th' 1.03. 1
take this too, | it is a basilisk unto mine eye, 2.04.107
but unto us it is | a cell of ignorance, 3.03. 32
more it shap'd | unto my end of stealing them. 5.05.347
this king unto him took a peer, | who died and PER 1.ch. 21
that ministers a potion unto me | that thou 1.02. 68
he would depart, i'll give some light unto you. 1.03. 17
so puts himself unto the shipman's toil, | with 1.03. 23
i come | with message unto princely pericles, 1.03. 32
unto thy value i will mount myself | upon a 2.01.157
here, with a cup that's /stor'd unto the brim — 2.03. 50
not me | unto a stranger knight to be so bold. 2.03. 67
wishing it so much blood unto your life. 2.03. 77
these knights unto their several lodgings! 2.03.109
reign, | we thus submit unto — our sovereign. 2.04. 39
whom if you find, and win unto return, | you 2.04. 52
i came unto your court for honor's cause, | and 2.05. 61
at ephesus, | unto diana there 's a votaress. 4.ch. 4
your ears unto your eyes i'll reconcile. 4.04. 22
your principal made known unto you who i am? 4.06. 82 P
it nips me unto list'ning, and thick slumber 5.01.234
unto the helmeted bellona use them | and pray TNK 1.01. 75
been labor'd so long with ye, milk'd unto ye, 3.05. 4
i meet him | and unto him i utter learned things 3.05. 14
o theseus, | if unto neither thou show mercy. 3.06.173
and implore | her power unto our party. 5.01. 76
tyrant from his rage, | and weep unto a girl; 5.01. 79
which being laid unto | mine innocent true heart 5.01.133
and give grace unto | the funeral of arcite, in 5.04.125
to your comforts, | but charter'd unto them? STM II.C 138
sick–thoughted venus makes amain unto him, | and
VEN 5
be | that thou should think it heavy unto thee? 156
the strong–neck'd steed, being tied unto a tree, 263
he looks upon his love, and neighs unto her, 307
as they were mad, unto the wood they hie them, 323
sorrow to shepherds, woe unto the birds, | gusts 455
what is ten hundred touches unto thee? 519
that lends embracements unto every stranger. 790
to grow unto himself was his desire, | and so 1180
for then is tarquin brought unto his bed, LUC 120
divine, | unto a view so false will not incline, 292
now is he come unto the chamber door | that 337
unto a greater uproar tempts his veins. 427
for those thine eyes betray thee unto mine. 483
thee | unto the base bed of some rascal groom, 671
"my honor i'll bequeath unto the knife | that 1184
poor lucrece' cheeks unto her maid seem so | as 1217
her contrite sighs unto the clouds bequeathed 1727
the night so pack'd, i post unto my pretty; PP 14.21
alas, it was a spite | unto the silly damsel! 15. 8
and each doth good turns now unto the other: SON 47. 2
for feasts of love i have been call'd unto, LC 181

UNTOLD 3 FR 0.0003 REL FR 3 V 0 P
do our longing stay | to hear the rest untold. PER 5.03. 84
be, | to have their unseen sin remain untold; LUC 753
then in the number let me pass untold, | though SON 136. 9

UNTO'T 3 FR 0.0003 REL FR 3 V 0 P
of neither on the start | can woman me unto't. AWW 3.02. 51
you have added worth unto't and lustre, | and TIM 1.02.149
which whilst it was mine had annex'd unto't | a ANT 4.14. 17

UNTOUCH'D 2 FR 0.0002 REL FR 2 V 0 P
untouch'd or slightly handled in discourse. R3 3.07. 19
and, by my honor, | depart untouch'd. JC 3.01.142

UNTOWARD 2 FR 0.0002 REL FR 2 V 0 P
then hast thou taught hortensio to be untoward. SHR 4.05. 79
what means this scorn, thou most untoward knave?
JN 1.01.243

UNTOWARDLY 1 FR 0.0001 REL FR 0 V 1 P
o day untowardly turn'd! ADO 3.02.131 P

UNTRADED 1 FR 0.0001 REL FR 1 V 0 P
mock not /that /i affect th' untraded /oath, TRO 4.05.178

UNTRAIN'D 1 FR 0.0001 REL FR 1 V 0 P
daughter, | my wit untrain'd in any kind of art. 1H6 1.02. 73

UNTRAINED 1 FR 0.0001 REL FR 0 V 1 P
unpruned, untrained, or rather unlettered, or LLL 4.02. 17 P

UNTREAD 2 FR 0.0002 REL FR 2 V 0 P
where is the horse that doth untread again | his MV 2.06. 10
we will untread the steps of damned flight, JN 5.04. 52

UNTREADS 1 FR 0.0001 REL FR 1 V 0 P
she treads the path that she untreads again; VEN 908

UNTREASUR'D 1 FR 0.0001 REL FR 1 V 0 P
they found the bed untreasur'd of their mistress AYL 2.02. 7

UNTRIED 1 FR 0.0001 REL FR 1 V 0 P
o'er sixteen years and leave the growth untried WT 4.01. 6

UNTRIMM'D 1 FR 0.0001 REL FR 1 V 0 P
by chance or nature's changing course untrimm'd:
SON 18. 8

UNTRIMMED 1 FR 0.0001 REL FR 1 V 0 P
here | in likeness of a new untrimmed bride. JN 3.01.209

UNTROD 1 FR 0.0001 REL FR 1 V 0 P
thorough the hazards of this untrod state | with JC 3.01.136

UNTRODDEN 1 FR 0.0001 REL FR 1 V 0 P
walls, | unpeopled offices, untrodden stones? R2 1.02. 69

UNTROUBLED 1 FR 0.0001 REL FR 1 V 0 P
quiet untroubled soul, awake, awake! R3 5.03.157

UNTRUE 7 FR 0.0008 REL FR 7 V 0 P
forestall our sport, to make us thus untrue? LLL 5.02.473
if it appear not plain and prove untrue, AWW 5.03.317
shall find but bloody safety, and untrue. JN 3.04.148
but when to my good lord i prove untrue, | i'll CYM 1.05. 86
that you for love speak well of me untrue, | my SON 72.10
my most true mind thus maketh mine untrue. 113.14
"for further i could say, 'this man's untrue,' LC 169

UNTRUSSING 1 FR 0.0001 REL FR 0 V 1 P
marry, this claudio is condemn'd for untrussing. MM 3.02.179 P

UNTRUTH 1 FR 0.0001 REL FR 1 V 0 P
god | (so my untruth had not provok'd him to it) R2 2.02.101

UNTRUTHS 3 FR 0.0003 REL FR 2 V 1 P
moreover, they have spoken untruths; ADO 5.01.216 P
i' th' presence | he would say untruths, and be H8 4.02. 38
let all untruths stand by thy stained name, TRO 5.02.179

UNTUCK'D 1 FR 0.0001 REL FR 1 V 0 P
for some, untuck'd, descended her sheav'd hat, LC 31

UNTUN'D 4 FR 0.0004 REL FR 4 V 0 P
son | knows not my feeble key of untun'd cares? ERR 5.01.311
so rous'd up with boist'rous untun'd drums, R2 1.03.134
th' untun'd and jarring senses, o, wind up | of LR 4.07. 15
with untun'd tongue she hoarsely calls her maid, LUC 1214

UNTUNE 1 FR 0.0001 REL FR 1 V 0 P
take but degree away, untune that string, | and TRO 1.03.109

UNTUNEABLE 2 FR 0.0002 REL FR 1 V 1 P
mine, | for they are harsh, untuneable, and bad. TGV 3.01.209
in the ditty, yet the note was very untuneable. AYL 5.03. 36 P

UNTUTOR'D 5 FR 0.0005 REL FR 5 V 0 P
her blameful bed | some stern, untutor'd churl; 2H6 3.02.213
untutor'd lad, thou art too malapert. 3H6 5.05. 32
thou speak'st like /him's untutor'd to repeat: PER 1.04. 74
that she might think me some untutor'd youth, PP 1. 3
that she might think me some untutor'd youth, SON 138. 3

UNTWIND 1 FR 0.0001 REL FR 1 V 0 P
gaping wounds | untwind the sisters three! 2H4 2.04.199

UNTWINE 1 FR 0.0001 REL FR 1 V 0 P
untwine | his perishing root with the increasing CYM 4.02. 59

UNURG'D 2 FR 0.0002 REL FR 2 V 0 P
when thou unurg'd wouldst vow | that never words
ERR 2.02.113
a voluntary zeal and an unurg'd faith | to your JN 5.02. 10

UNUS'D 4 FR 0.0004 REL FR 4 V 0 P
and godlike reason | to fust in us unus'd. HAM 4.04. 39
thy unus'd beauty must be tomb'd with thee, SON 4.13
end, | and kept unus'd, the user so destroys it: 9.12
then can i drown an eye (unus'd to flow) | for 30. 5

UNUSED 2 FR 0.0002 REL FR 2 V 0 P
eyes, | albeit unused to the melting mood, OTH 5.02.349
that to my use it might unused stay | from hands SON 48. 3

UNUSUAL 6 FR 0.0006 REL FR 6 V 0 P
it claudio was beheaded | at an unusual hour? MM 5.01.458
monument, | some comet or unusual prodigy? SHR 3.02. 96
these your unusual weeds to each part of you WT 4.04. 1
strange, unusual blood, | when man's worst sin TIM 4.02. 38
he hath been in unusual pleasure, and | sent MAC 2.01. 13
that guard and most unusual vigilance | does not LR 2.03. 4

UNVALUED 2 FR 0.0002 REL FR 2 V 0 P
of pearl, | inestimable stones, unvalued jewels, R3 1.04. 27
he may not, as unvalued persons do, | carve for HAM 1.03. 19

UNVANQUISH'D 1 FR 0.0001 REL FR 1 V 0 P
shall i, for lucre of the rest unvanquish'd, 1H6 5.04.141

UNVARNISH'D 1 FR 0.0001 REL FR 1 V 0 P
i will a round unvarnish'd tale deliver | of my OTH 1.03. 90

UNVEIL 1 FR 0.0001 REL FR 1 V 0 P
do thoughts unveil in their dumb cradles. TRO 3.03.200

UNVENERABLE 1 FR 0.0001 REL FR 1 V 0 P
for ever | unvenerable be thy hands, if thou WT 2.03. 78

UNVEX'D 1 FR 0.0001 REL FR 1 V 0 P
heaven, | and with a blessed and unvex'd retire, JN 2.01.253

UNVIOLATED 1 FR 0.0001 REL FR 1 V 0 P
of suspect | th' unviolated honor of your wife. ERR 3.01. 88

UNVIRTUOUS 1 FR 0.0001 REL FR 0 V 1 P
hearts the poor unvirtuous fat knight shall be WIV 4.02.217 P

UNVISITED 1 FR 0.0001 REL FR 1 V 0 P
here, | unseen, unvisited, much to our shame. LLL 5.02.358

UNVULNERABLE *(also invulnerable)*

UNVULNERABLE 1 FR 0.0001 REL FR 1 V 0 P
that thou mayst prove | to shame unvulnerable, COR 5.03. 73

UNWAPPER'D 1 FR 0.0001 REL FR 1 V 0 P
young and unwapper'd, not halting under crimes TNK 5.04. 10

UNWARES *(also unawares)*

UNWARES 1 FR 0.0001 REL FR 1 V 0 P
whom in this conflict i, unwares, have kill'd. 3H6 2.05. 62

UNWARILY 1 FR 0.0001 REL FR 1 V 0 P
were in the washes all unwarily | devoured by JN 5.07. 63

UNWASH'D 3 FR 0.0003 REL FR 1 V 2 P
another lean unwash'd artificer | cuts off his JN 4.02.201
thou doest, and do it with unwash'd hands too. 1H4 3.03.184 P
one or two men's hands, and they unwash'd too, ROM 1.05. 4 P

/UNWATCH'D 1 FR 0.0001 REL FR 1 V 0 P
madness in great ones must not /unwatch'd go. HAM 3.01.188

UNWEARIED 1 FR 0.0001 REL FR 1 V 0 P
the best–condition'd and unwearied spirit | in MV 3.02.293

UNWEAVES 1 FR 0.0001 REL FR 1 V 0 P
now she unweaves the web that she hath wrought:
VEN 991

UNWED 2 FR 0.0002 REL FR 2 V 0 P
this servitude makes you to keep unwed. ERR 2.01. 26
wiser head, | neither too young nor yet unwed. PP 18. 6

UNWEDGEABLE 1 FR 0.0001 REL FR 1 V 0 P
bolt | splits the unwedgeable and gnarled oak MM 2.02.116

UNWEEDED 1 FR 0.0001 REL FR 1 V 0 P
'tis an unweeded garden | that grows to seed, HAM 1.02.135

UNWEIGH'D 1 FR 0.0001 REL FR 0 V 1 P
what an unweigh'd behavior hath this flemish WIV 2.01. 23 P

UNWEIGHING 1 FR 0.0001 REL FR 0 V 1 P
a very superficial, ignorant, unweighing fellow. MM 3.02.139 P

UNWELCOME 6 FR 0.0006 REL FR 6 V 0 P
i think 'tis no unwelcome news to you. TGV 2.04. 81
for more uneven and unwelcome news | came from
1H4 1.01. 50
yet the first bringer of unwelcome news | hath 2H4 1.01.100
i fear | we shall be much unwelcome. TRO 4.01. 46
such welcome and unwelcome things at once | 'tis MAC 4.03.138
lest jealousy, that sour unwelcome guest, VEN 449

UNWEPT 2 FR 0.0002 REL FR 2 V 0 P
unmoan'd, | your widow–dolor likewise be unwept!
R3 2.02. 65
we had died as they do, ill old men, unwept, TNK 2.02.109

UNWHIPT 1 FR 0.0001 REL FR 1 V 0 P
thee undivulged crimes | unwhipt of justice! LR 3.02. 53

UNWHOLESOME 10 FR 0.0011 REL FR 6 V 4 P
with raven's feather from unwholesome fen | drop
TMP 1.02.322
we'll use this unwholesome humidity, this gross WIV 3.03. 40 P
and that's but unwholesome food, they say. H5 2.03. 57 P
yea, like fair fruit in an unwholesome dish, TRO 2.03.120
you are they | that made the air unwholesome, COR 4.06.130
thick and unwholesome in /their thoughts and HAM 4.05. 82
to my wit, do not think it so unwholesome. OTH 4.01.120 P
thou sayest true, there's two unwholesome, a' PER 4.02. 21 P
let their exhal'd unwholesome breaths make sick LUC 779
unwholesome weeds take root with precious 870

/UNWIELDY 1 FR 0.0001 REL FR 1 V 0 P

/and /this /unwieldy /sceptre /from /my /hand, R2 4.01.205
UNWIELDY 2 FR 0.0002 REL FR 2 V 0 P
in stiff unwieldy arms against thy crown; R2 3.02.115
dead, | unwieldy, slow, heavy, and pale as lead. ROM 2.05. 17
UNWILLING 10 FR 0.0011 REL FR 9 V 1 P
which i was much unwilling to proceed in, | but TGV 2.01.106
unwilling i agreed. ERR 1.01. 60
patience, i pray you, 'twas a fault unwilling. SHR 4.01.156
but you gave leave to my unwilling tongue R2 1.03.245
care, but rather, because i am unwilling, and, 2H4 3.02.224 P
if he be leaden, icy, cold, unwilling, | be thou R3 3.01.176
unwilling to outlive the good that did it; H8 4.02. 60
this beauteous combat, willful and unwilling, VEN 365
threw unwilling light | upon the wide wound that 1051
as each unwilling portal yields him way, LUC 309
UNWILLINGLY 6 FR 0.0006 REL FR 6 V 0 P
if thou neglect'st or dost unwillingly | what i TMP 1.02.368
writ, | but (since unwillingly) take them again. TGV 2.01.123
the ring, | and how unwillingly i left the ring, MV 5.01.196
creeping like snail | unwillingly to school. AYL 2.07.147
back, not following | my leash unwillingly. WT 4.04.466
i have, and most unwillingly, of late | heard H8 5.01. 97
UNWILLINGNESS 3 FR 0.0003 REL FR 3 V 0 P
which i with some unwillingness pronounce: R2 1.03.149
with dull unwillingness to repay a debt, | which R3 2.02. 92
and i with all unwillingness will go. 4.01. 57
UNWIND 2 FR 0.0002 REL FR 2 V 0 P
therefore, as you unwind her love from him, TGV 3.02. 51
stand for your own, unwind your bloody flag, H5 1.02.101
UNWIP'D 1 FR 0.0001 REL FR 1 V 0 P
which unwip'd we found | upon their pillows. MAC 2.03.103
UNWISE 3 FR 0.0003 REL FR 3 V 0 P
be not ta'en tardy by unwise delay. R3 4.01. 51
o /good but most unwise patricians! COR 3.01. 91
never mind | was to be so unwise, to be so kind. TIM 2.02. 6
UNWISELY 2 FR 0.0002 REL FR 2 V 0 P
unwisely, not ignobly, have i given. TIM 2.02.174
when collatine unwisely did not let | to praise LUC 10
UNWISH'D 1 FR 0.0001 REL FR 1 V 0 P
why, now thou hast unwish'd five thousand men; H5 4.03. 76
UNWISHED 1 FR 0.0001 REL FR 1 V 0 P
whose unwished yoke | my soul consents not to MND 1.01. 81
UNWITNESSED 1 FR 0.0001 REL FR 1 V 0 P
trifles, unwitnessed with eye or ear, | thy VEN 1023
UNWITTED 1 FR 0.0001 REL FR 1 V 0 P
but now | (as if some planet had unwitted men), OTH 2.03.182
/UNWITTINGLY 1 FR 0.0001 REL FR 1 V 0 P
if i /unwittingly, or in my rage, | have aught R3 2.01. 57
UNWITTINGLY 1 FR 0.0001 REL FR 1 V 0 P
there (on my conscience, put unwittingly)? H8 3.02.123
UNWONTED 2 FR 0.0002 REL FR 1 V 1 P
this is unwonted | which now came from him. TMP 1.02.498
awakens me with this unwonted putting–on, MM 4.02.116 P
UNWOO'D 1 FR 0.0001 REL FR 1 V 0 P
they live unwoo'd, and unrespected fade, | die SON 54.10
UNWORTHIER 1 FR 0.0001 REL FR 1 V 0 P
me, | miss that which one unworthier may attain, MV 2.01. 37
UNWORTHIEST 3 FR 0.0003 REL FR 3 V 0 P
th' unworthiest shows as fairly in the mask. TRO 1.03. 84
if i profane with my unworthiest hand | this ROM 1.05. 93
that, in my regard, | of the unworthiest siege. HAM 4.07. 76
UNWORTHILY 2 FR 0.0002 REL FR 2 V 0 P
err, | and so, unworthily, disgrace the man | (a TGV 3.01. 29
leg, | which i have done, because, unworthily, 1H6 4.01. 16
UNWORTHINESS 5 FR 0.0005 REL FR 5 V 0 P
at mine unworthiness, that dare not offer | what TMP 3.01. 77
sorts, and songs compos'd | to her unworthiness. AWW 3.07. 41
gentle all | behold, as may unworthiness define, H5 4.pr. 46
thou fraught the court | with thy unworthiness, CYM 1.01.127
if thy unworthiness rais'd love in me, | more SON 150.13
UNWORTHY 39 FR 0.0044 REL FR 33 V 6 P
a passing shame | that i (unworthy body as i am) TGV 1.02. 18
to see how much he is unworthy so good a lady. ADO 2.03.208 P
me leave, | unworthy as i am, to follow you. MND 2.01.207
god made, a poor unworthy brother of yours, with AYL 1.01. 33 P
the cost of princes on unworthy shoulders? 2.07. 76
and the most unworthy of her you call rosalind, 4.01.193 P
her | as one unworthy all the former favors SHR 4.02. 30
proud scornful boy, unworthy this good gift, AWW 2.03.151
what angel shall | bless this unworthy husband? 3.04. 26
rinaldo, | to this unworthy husband of his wife. 3.04. 30
a most unworthy and unnatural lord | can do no WT 2.03.113
unworthy thee — if ever, henceforth, thou 4.04.437
devise a name | so slight, unworthy, and JN 3.01.150
dar'd | on this unworthy scaffold to bring forth H5 pr 10
or lay these bones in an unworthy urn, 1.02.228
french, | he left me proudly, as unworthy fight. 1H6 4.07. 43
i am unworthy to be henry's wife. 5.03.122
i unworthy am | to woo so fair a dame to be his 5.03.123
if somerset be unworthy of the place, | let york 2H6 1.03.105
unworthy though thou art, i'll cope with thee, 3.02.230
relent, | that were unworthy to behold the same? 4.04. 18
that didst unworthy slaughter upon others. R3 1.02. 88
man, unworthy now | to be thy lord and master. H8 3.02.413
but thieves unworthy of a thing so stol'n, TRO 2.02. 94
as thou unworthy to be call'd her servant. 4.04.125
to my poor unworthy notice, | he mock'd us when COR 2.03.158
unworthy brother, and unworthy sons! TIT 1.01.346
unworthy brother, and unworthy sons! 1.01.346
dog | and little mouse, every unworthy thing, ROM 3.03. 31
unworthy as she is, that we have wrought | so 3.05.144
that patient merit of th' unworthy takes, | when HAM 3.01. 73
you now, how unworthy a thing you make of me! 3.02.363 P
i hold him to be unworthy of his place that does OTH 2.03.101 P
in) | bestow'd his lips on that unworthy place, ANT 3.13. 84
goodness the hugeness of your unworthy thinking. CYM 1.04.145 P
i am unworthy for her schoolmaster. PER 2.05. 40
do you think me | unworthy of her sight? TNK 2.02.192
your servant | (your most unworthy creature) but 2.05. 40
lord | of that unworthy wife that greeteth thee, LUC 1304
UNWRUNG 1 FR 0.0001 REL FR 0 V 1 P
the gall'd jade winch, our withers are unwrung. HAM 3.02.243 P
UNYIELDING 1 FR 0.0001 REL FR 1 V 0 P
remove your siege from my unyielding heart, | to VEN 423
UNYOK'D 2 FR 0.0002 REL FR 2 V 0 P
uphold | the unyok'd humor of your idleness, 1H4 1.02.196
like youthful steers unyok'd, they take their 2H4 4.02.103
UNYOKE 2 FR 0.0002 REL FR 1 V 1 P
unyoke this seizure and this kind regreet? JN 3.01.241
ay, tell me that, and unyoke. HAM 5.01. 52 P
/UP 11 FR 0.0012 REL FR 11 V 0 P
stones with lime and hair knit /up /in /thee. MND 5.01.191
/my /griefs, /whilst /you /mount /up /on /high. R2 4.01.189
/your /cares /set /up /do /not /pluck /my /cares 4.01.195
/the /gentle /archbishop /of /york /is /up 2H4 1.01.189
/word, /rebellion, /it /had /froze /them /up, 1.01.199
/a /kingdom /down | /and /set /another /up), 1.03. 50
/thou /provok'st /thyself /to /cast /him /up. 1.03. 96
/now /thou /wouldst /eat /thy /dead /vomit /up, 1.03. 99
/sirs, /take /up /the /corse. R3 1.02.225
/bolts | /sperr /up /the /sons /of /troy. TRO pr 19
/will /in /concealment /wrap /me /up /awhile; LR 4.03. 52
UP 1114 FR 0.1259 REL FR 891 V 223 P
stomach, to bear up | against what should ensue. TMP 1.02.157
thou call'dst me up at midnight to fetch dew 1.02.228
side–stitches, that shall pen thy breath up; 1.02.326
put thy sword up, traitor, | who mak'st a show 1.02.470
my spirits, as in a dream, are all bound up. 1.02.487
look, he's winding up the watch of his wit, by 2.01. 12 P
ay, or very falsely pocket up his report. 2.01. 68 P
would, with themselves, shut up my thoughts. 2.01.192
all the infections that the sun sucks up | from 2.02. 1
some thousands of these logs, and pile them up, 3.01. 10
burnt up those logs that you are enjoin'd to 3.01. 17
therefore bear up and board 'em. 3.02. 2 P
sea | hath caus'd to belch up you; 3.03. 56
are all knit up | in their distractions. 3.03. 89
lifted up their noses | as they smelt music. 4.01.177
there dancing up to th' chins, that the foul 4.01.183
shorten up their sinews | with aged cramps, and 4.01.259
and by the spurs pluck'd up | the pine and cedar 5.01. 47
what is't that you | took up so gingerly? TGV 1.02. 70
to take a paper up that i let fall. 1.02. 71
if you respect them, best to take them up. 1.02.131
nay, i was taken up for laying them down; 1.02.132
here's my mother's breath up and down. 2.03. 29 P
the more thou dam'st it up, the more it burns: 2.07. 24
no, girl, i'll knit it up in silken strings, 2.07. 45
to cast up, with a pair of anchoring hooks, 3.01.118
but neither bended knees, pure hands held up, 3.01.231
one that i brought up of a puppy; 4.04. 3 P
"hang him up," says the duke. 4.04. 22 P
didst thou see me heave up my leg and make water 4.04. 37 P
witness good bringing up, fortune, and truth: 4.04. 69
come, shadow, come, and take this shadow up, 4.04.197
look up; 5.04. 87 P
did seem to scorch me up like a burning–glass! WIV 1.03. 67 P
does he not hold up his head, as it were, and 1.04. 29 P
and to be up early and down late; 1.04.101 P
up with your fights; 2.02.136
go take up these clothes here quickly. 3.03.146 P
up, gentlemen, you shall see sport anon. 3.03.168 P
come hither, william; hold up your head; come. 4.01. 17 P
hold up your head. 4.01. 19 P
ford, your sorrow hath eaten up my sufferance. 4.02. 1 P
what shall i do? i'll creep up into the chimney. 4.02. 55 P
run up, sir john. 4.02. 79 P
go up, i'll bring linen for him straight. 4.02.100 P
come, come, take it up. 4.02.111 P
will you take up your wive's clothes? 4.02.141 P
woman, a fat woman, gone up into his chamber. 4.05. 12 P
come up into my chamber. 4.05.127 P
i say, time wears, hold up your head and mince. 5.01. 7 P
said, | raise up the organs of her fantasy, 5.05. 51
i pray you come, hold up the jest no higher. 5.05.105
place, | or in his eminence that fills it up, MM 1.02.164
having bound up the threat'ning twigs of birch, 1.03. 24
law, | setting it up to fear the birds of prey, 2.01. 2
do you your office, or give up your place, | and 2.02. 13
that shall be up at heaven and enter there | ere 2.02.152
give up your body to such sweet uncleanness | as 2.04. 54
sick for, ere i'ld yield | my body up to shame. 2.04.104
brother | by yielding up thy body to my will, 2.04.164
on twenty bloody blocks, he'ld yield them up, 2.04.181
this wrong'd maid to stead up your appointment, 3.01.250 P
it lies much in your holding up. 3.01.261 P
sir, she hath eaten up all her beef, and she is 3.02. 56 P
can tie the gall up in the slanderous tongue? 3.02.188
'tis well borne up. 4.01. 47
as fast lock'd up in sleep as guiltless labor 4.02. 66
he is call'd up. 4.02. 91
but here nurs'd up and bred, one that is a 4.02.130 P
look, th' unfolding star calls up the shepherd. 4.02.203 P
at the gates, | there to give up their pow'r. 4.03.132
unfold the evil which is here wrapp'd up | in 5.01.117
and all probation will make up full clear, 5.01.157
wife as strongly | as words could make up vows; 5.01.228
hold up your hands, say nothing; 5.01.438
stand up, i say. 5.01.455
give up your keys. 5.01.462
i bought, and brought up to attend my sons. ERR 1.01. 57
and in our sight they three were taken up | by 1.01.110
beg thou, or borrow, to make up the sum, | and 1.01.153
and wander up and down to view the city. 1.02. 31
"hang up thy mistress! 2.01. 67
the gold i gave to dromio is laid up | safe at 2.02. 1
a man is well holp up that trusts to you: 4.01. 22
/one whose hard heart is button'd up with steel; 4.02. 34
he that sets up his rest to do more exploits 4.03. 27 P
were not my doors lock'd up, and i shut out? 4.04. 70
and all the conduits of my blood froze up, | yet 5.01.314
and i, | and the twin dromio, all were taken up; 5.01.351
he set up his bills here in messina, and ADO 1.01. 39 P
that she brought me up, i likewise give her most 1.01.239 P
pen and hang me up at the door of a 1.01.253 P
so deliver i up my apes, and away to saint peter 2.01. 47 P
here's his dry hand up and down. 2.01.118 P
as being forsaken, or to bind him up a rod, as 2.01.219 P
whose estimation do you mightily hold up — to a 2.02. 25 P
he hath ta'en th' infection. hold it up. 2.03.122 P
for she'll be up twenty times a night, and there 2.03.131 P
come, | as we do trace this alley up and down, 3.01. 16
thee | to bind our loves up in a holy band; 3.01.114
be any matter of weight chances, call up me. 3.03. 85 P
'a goes up and down like a gentleman. 3.03.126 P
call up the right master constable. 3.03.166 P
commodity, being taken up of these men's bills. 3.03.178 P
for thee i'll lock up all the gates of love, 4.01.105
come thus to light, | smother her spirits up. 4.01.112
dost thou look up? 4.01.119
hand | took up a beggar's issue at my gates, 4.01.132
which was before barr'd up with ribs of iron! 4.01.151
blood of mine, | nor age so eat up my invention, 4.01.194
we have been up and down to seek thee, for we 5.01.122 P
pluck up, my heart, and be sad. 5.01.203 P
's | than this for whom we rend'red up this woe. 5.03. 33
strike up, pipers. 5.04.128 P
about surrender up of aquitaine | to her LLL 1.01.137
take away this villain, shut him up. 1.02.153 P
let me not be pent up, sir; 1.02.155 P
now, madam, summon up your dearest spirits; 2.01. 1
we will give up our right in aquitaine, | and 2.01.139
it, i'll repay it back, | or yield up aquitaine. 2.01.159
humor it with turning up your eyelids, sigh a 3.01. 13 P
as if you snuff'd up love by smelling love; 3.01. 16 P
boyet, you can carve, | break up this capon. 4.01. 56
sweet, put up this — 'twill be thine another 4.01.107
shape of love's tyburn that hangs up simplicity. 4.03. 52
three fools lack'd me fool to make up the mess. 4.03.203
why, universal plodding poisons up | the nimble 4.03.301
as would be cramm'd up in a sheet of paper, 5.02. 7
tell | how many inches doth fill up one mile. 5.02.193
this fellow pecks up wit as pigeons pease, | and 5.02.315
shut | my woeful self up in a mourning house, 5.02.808
to flatter up these powers of mine with rest, 5.02.814
the sudden hand of death close up mine eye! 5.02.815
stir up the athenian youth to merriments, MND 1.01. 12
ere i will yield my virgin patent up | unto his 1.01. 80
or else the law of athens yields you up | (which 1.01.119
the jaws of darkness do devour it up: 1.01.148
have suck'd up from the sea | contagious fogs; 2.01. 89
the nine men's morris is fill'd up with mud, 2.01. 98
die, | and for her sake do i rear up her boy; 2.01.136
herb), | i'll make her render up her page to me. 2.01.185
i will walk up and down here, and i will sing, 3.01.122 P
tie up my lover's tongue, bring him silently. 3.01.201
turns to a crow | when thou hold'st up thy hand. 3.02.143
to conjure tears up in a poor maid's eyes | with 3.02.158
in hermia's love i yield you up my part; 3.02.165
wink each at other, hold the sweet jest up; 3.02.239
then stir demetrius up with bitter wrong; 3.02.361
up and down, up and down, | i will lead them up 3.02.396
up and down, up and down, | i will lead them up 3.02.396
up and down, | i will lead them up and down; 3.02.397
goblin, lead them up and down. 3.02.399
and sleep, that sometimes shuts up sorrow's eye, 3.02.435
two of both kinds makes up four. 3.02.438
we will, fair queen, up to the mountain's top, 4.01.109
no doubt they rose up early to observe | the 4.01.132
i pray you all, stand up. 4.01.141
i cannot instantly raise up the gross | of full MV 1.03. 55
he stuck them up before the fulsome ewes, | who 1.03. 86
"for the heavens, rouse up a brave mind," says 2.02. 12 P
turn up on your right hand at the next turning, 2.02. 41 P
pray you, sir, stand up. 2.02. 81 P
own part, as i have set up my rest to run away, 2.02.103 P
and it shall please you to break up this, it 2.04. 10 P
lock up my doors, and when you hear the drum 2.05. 29
clamber not you up to the casements then, | nor 2.05. 31
we have been up and down to seek him. 3.01. 76 P
you can the getting up of the negro's belly; 3.05. 38 P
to fill up your grace's request in my stead. 4.01.160 P
even he that had held up the very life | of my 5.01.214
and thou shalt hear how he will shake me up. AYL 1.01. 28 P
only in the world i fill up a place, which may 1.02.191 P
down, and that which here stands up | is but a 1.02.250
then there were two cousins laid up, when the 1.03. 7 P
to fright the animals and to kill them up | in 2.01. 62
and having that do choke their service up | even 2.03. 61
orlando, that tripp'd up the wrastler's heels, 3.02.212 P
i will fetch up your goats, audrey. 3.03. 2 P
did make offense, his eye did heal it up. 3.05.117
and by him seal up thy mind, | whether that thy 4.03. 58
brief, i recover'd him, bound up his wound, 4.03.150
and how was that ta'en up? 5.04. 48 P
when seven justices could not take up a quarrel, 5.04. 99 P
then take him up, and manage well the jest. SHR in.1. 45
take him up gently and to bed with him, | and in.1. 72
sheer ale, score me up for the lying'st knave in in.2. 24 P
bed | on purpose trimm'd up for semiramis. in.2. 39
maid, | nor no such men as you have reckon'd up, in.2. 92
vincentio's son, brought up in florence, | it 1.01. 14
why will you mew her up, | signior baptista, for 1.01. 87
began to scold and raise up such a storm | that 1.01.172
and therefore has he closely mew'd her up, 1.01.183
brought up as best becomes a gentlewoman. 1.02. 87
have i not heard the sea, puff'd up with winds, 1.02.201
was ever match clapp'd up so suddenly? 2.01.325
and help to dress your sister's chamber up. 3.01. 83
book, | and as he stoop'd again to take it up, 3.02.162
"now take them up," quoth he, "if any list." 3.02.165
but then up farther, and as far as rome, | and 4.02. 75
pluck up thy spirits, look cheerfully upon me. 4.03. 38
eat it up all, hortensio, if thou lovest me. 4.03. 50
what, up and down carv'd like an apple–tart? 4.03. 89
sleeves should be cut out, and sew'd up again, 4.03.146 P
go take it up unto thy master's use. 4.03.157
take up my mistress' gown for thy master's use! 4.03.158 P
take up my mistress' gown to his master's use! 4.03.162
i have brought him up ever since he was three 5.01. 82 P
my banket is to close our stomachs up | after 5.02. 9
would stir it up where it wanted rather than AWW 1.01. 9 P
if knowledge could be set up against mortality. 1.01. 31 P
before you, will undermine you and blow you up. 1.01.119 P
military policy how virgins might blow up men? 1.01.122 P
blown down, man will quicklier be blown up. 1.01.124 P
whose baser stars do shut us up in wishes, 1.01.183
till honor be bought up, and no sword worn | but 2.01. 32
i'll see thee to stand up. 2.01. 62
and that at my bidding you could so stand up. 2.01. 65
he bade me store up, as a triple eye, | safer 2.01.108
since you set up your rest 'gainst remedy. 2.01.135

disdain'st in her, the which | i can build up. 2.03.118
that dost in vile misprision shackle up | my 2.03.152
yet art thou good for nothing but taking up, and 2.03.207 P
why dost thou garter up thy arms a' this fashion 2.03.250 P
i pray you, sir, put it up again. 4.03.216 P
virginity and devours up all the fry it finds. 4.03.221 P
hath brought me up to be your daughter's dower, 4.04. 19
to stop up the displeasure he hath conceiv'd 4.05. 75 P
with his lord, | nor hold him up with hopes: TN 1.05.304
to be a–bed after midnight is to be up betimes, 2.03. 2 P
but i know, to be up late is to be up late. 2.03. 5 P
but i know, to be up late is to be up late. 2.03. 5 P
to be up after midnight and to go to bed then, 2.03. 7 P
lady have not call'd up her steward malvolio and 2.03. 73 P
we did keep time, sir, in our catches. sneck up! 2.03. 94 P
frown the while, and perchance wind up my watch, 2.05. 60 P
o ay, make up that. he is now at a cold scent. 2.05.121 P
i have his horse to take up the quarrel. 3.04.292 P
put up your sword. 3.04.312
pray, sir, put your sword up, if you please. 3.04.321 P
come, my young soldier, put up your iron; 4.01. 39 P
fruitless pranks | this ruffian hath botch'd up, 4.01. 56
fear not, cesario, take thy fortunes up, | be 5.01.148
time as long again | would be fill'd up, my WT 1.02. 4
how she holds up the neb! 1.02.183
all other circumstances | made up to th' deed), 2.01.179
credulity will not | come up to th' truth. 2.01.193
to lock up honesty | and honor from th' access 2.02. 9
take up the bastard, | take't up, i say; 2.03. 76
take up the bastard, | take't up, i say; 2.03. 77
tak'st up the princess by that forced baseness 2.03. 79
take it up straight. 2.03.135
take it up. 2.03.183
(thus by apollo's great divine seal'd up) 3.01. 19
break up the seals, and read. 3.02.131
as nature | will bear up with this exercise, so 3.02.241
i'll take it up for pity — yet i'll tarry till 3.03. 76 P
chafes, how it rages, how it takes up the shore! 3.03. 89 P
look thee here, take up, take up, boy; 3.03.116 P
look thee here, take up, take up, boy; 3.03.116 P
up with't, keep it close. 3.03.124 P
so grieving | that he shuts up himself — 4.01. 19
poor lowly maid, | most goddess–like prank'd up. 4.04. 10
to see his work, so noble, | vildly bound up? 4.04. 22
lift up your countenance, as it were the day 4.04. 49
come on. strike up. 4.04.161
come, strike up. 4.04.165
from me are pack'd and lock'd | up in my heart, 4.04.359
lift up thy looks. 4.04.479
strive to qualify, | and bring him up to liking. 4.04.533
for my visitation shall i | hold up before him? 4.04.556
let me pocket up my pedlar's excrement. 4.04.713 P
dear, look up. 5.01.215
there was casting up of eyes, holding up of 5.02. 46 P
was casting up of eyes, holding up of hands, 5.02. 47 P
grief from you as he | will piece up in himself. 5.03. 56
i'll fill your grave up. 5.03.101
that holds in chase mine honor up and down? JN 1.01.223
and stir them up against a mightier task. 2.01. 55
they shoot but calm words folded up in smoke, 2.01.229
save in aspect, hath all offense seal'd up; 2.01.250
have we ramm'd up our gates against the world. 2.01.272
up higher to the plain, where we'll set forth 2.01.295
know him in us, that here hold up his right. 2.01.364
for this match made up | her presence would have 2.01.541
we will heal up all, | for we'll create young 2.01.550
shall, | if not fill up the measure of her will, 2.01.556
but the huge firm earth | can hold it up. 3.01. 73
and our oppression hath made up this league. 3.01.106
art perjur'd too, | and sooth'st up greatness. 3.01.121
well, ruffian, i must pocket up these wrongs, 3.01.200
o then tread down my need, and faith mounts up; 3.01.215
keep my need up, and faith is trodden down! 3.01.216
hands | to clap this royal bargain up of peace, 3.01.235
france, i am burn'd up with inflaming wrath, | a 3.01.340
thy rage shall burn thee up, and thou shalt turn 3.01.344
philip, make up. 3.02. 5
which else runs tickling up and down the veins, 3.03. 44
bind up those tresses. 3.04. 61
bind up your hairs. 3.04. 68
grief fills the room up of my absent child, 3.04. 93
lies in his bed, walks up and down with me, 3.04. 94
makes nice of no vild hold to stay him up. 3.04.138
of all his people, and freeze up their zeal, 3.04.150
still and anon cheer'd up the heavy time, 4.01. 47
should move you to mew up | your tender kinsman, 4.02. 57
your highness should deliver up your crown. 4.02.152
whereon he says | i shall yield up my crown, let 4.02.157
your sword is bright, sir, put it up again. 4.03. 79
put up thy sword betime, | or i'll so maul you 4.03. 98
the ocean, | enough to stifle such a villain up. 4.03.133
how easy dost thou take all england up | from 4.03.142
thus have i yielded up into your hand | the 5.01. 1
it was my breath that blew this tempest up, 5.01. 17
and wild amazement hurries up and down | the 5.01. 35
bosom, and fill up | her enemies' ranks — i 5.02. 28
this show'r, blown up by tempest of the soul, 5.02. 50
lift up thy brow, renowned salisbury, | and with 5.02. 54
therefore thy threat'ning colors now wind up, 5.02. 73
war, | that, like a lion fostered up at hand, 5.02. 75
lie like pawns lock'd up in chests and trunks, 5.02.141
ripping up the womb | of your dear mother 5.02.152
strike up the drums, and let the tongue of war 5.02.164
strike up our drums, to find this danger out. 5.02.179
ay me, this tyrant fever burns me up, | and will 5.03. 14
up once again! 5.04. 2
and wound our tott'ring colors clearly up, 5.05. 7
the day shall not be up so soon as i, | to try 5.05. 21
bosom | that all my bowels crumble up to dust. 5.07. 31
and against this fire | do i shrink up. 5.07. 34
much strength | as to take up mine honor's pawn, R2 1.01. 74
i take it up, and by that sword i swear | which 1.01. 78
cousin, throw up your gage, do you begin. 1.01.186
doth with a twofold vigor lift me up | to reach 1.03. 71
rouse up thy youthful blood, be valiant and live 1.03. 83
civil wounds plough'd up with neighbors' sword; 1.03.128
which so rous'd up with boist'rous untun'd drums 1.03.134
a harp, | or like a cunning instrument cas'd up, 1.03.163
gentlemen, go muster up your men, | and meet me 2.02.118
but let thy spiders, that suck up thy venom, 3.02. 14
and all your northern castles yielded up, | and 3.02.201
up, cousin, up, your heart is up, i know, | thus 3.03.194
up, cousin, up, your heart is up, i know, | thus 3.03.194
up, cousin, up, your heart is up, i know, | thus 3.03.194
go bind thou up young dangling apricocks, 3.04. 29
is full of weeds, her fairest flowers chok'd up, 3.04. 44
that seem'd in eating him to hold him up, | are 3.04. 51
are pluck'd up root and all by bullingbrook, | i 3.04. 52
bagot, forbear, thou shalt not take it up. 4.01. 30
stirr'd up by god, thus boldly for his king. 4.01.133
yet look up, behold, | that you in pity may 5.01. 8
is not my teeming date drunk up with time? 5.02. 91
an' never will i rise up from the ground | till 5.02.116
rise up, good aunt. 5.03. 92
good aunt, stand up. 5.03.111
nay, do not say "stand up"; 5.03.111
say "pardon" first, and afterwards "stand up." 5.03.112
good aunt, stand up. 5.03.129
thy seat is up on high, | whilst my gross flesh 5.05.111
hath yielded up his body to the grave; 5.06. 21
and bristle up | the crest of youth against your 1H4 1.01. 98
to smother up his beauty from the world, | that, 1.02.199
who strook this heat up after i was gone? 1.03.139
days, | or fill up chronicles in time to come, 1.03.171
and pluck up drowned honor by the locks, | so he 1.03.205
deliver them up without their ransom straight, 1.03.260
neighbor mugs, we'll call up the gentlemen. 2.01. 45 P
they are up already, and call for eggs and 2.01. 59 P
prey on her, for they ride up and down on her, 2.01. 82 P
he is walk'd up to the top of the hill, i'll go 2.02. 8 P
have you any levers to lift me up again, being 2.02. 34 P
his industry is up stairs and down stairs, his 2.04.100 P
and grief, it blows a man up like a bladder. 2.04.332 P
that runs a' horseback up a hill perpendicular 2.04.343 P
hang me up by the heels for a rabbit–sucker or a 2.04.436 P
well as another man, a plague on my bringing up! 2.04.497 P
thee behind the arras, the rest walk up above. 2.04.501 P
i'll have the current in this place damm'd up, 3.01.100
and runs me up | with like advantage on the 3.01.107
for i was train'd up in the english court, 3.01.120
in reckoning up the several devils' names | that 3.01.155
the skipping king, he ambled up and down, | with 3.02. 60
of him, | to fill the mouth of deep defiance up, 3.02.116
mortimer, | capitulate against us, and are up. 3.02.120
to engross up glorious deeds on my behalf; 3.02.148
account | that he shall render every glory up, 3.02.150
when thou ran'st up gadshill in the night to 3.03. 38 P
it is all fill'd up with guts and midriff. 3.03.155 P
will stand to it, you will not pocket up wrong. 3.03.163 P
on his /altar sit | up to the ears in blood. 4.01.117
to fill up the rooms of them as have bought out 4.02. 32 P
of my cousin vernon's are not yet come up. 4.03. 20
who, never so tame, so cherish'd and lock'd up, 5.02. 10
return'd, | deliver up my lord of westmerland. 5.02. 28
trimm'd up your praises with a princely tongue, 5.02. 56
can lift your blood up with persuasion. 5.02. 78
up and away! 5.03. 28
i beseech your majesty make up, | lest your 5.04. 5
hold up thy head, vile scot, or thou art like 5.04. 39
or thou art like | never to hold it up again! 5.04. 40
make up to clifton, i'll to sir nicholas gawsey. 5.04. 58
and deliver him | up to his pleasure, ransomless 5.05. 28
sides of his poor jade | up to the rowel–head, 2H4 1.01. 46
from whence with life he never more sprung up. 1.01.111
a man is through with them in honest taking up, 1.02. 40 P
you follow the young prince up and down, like 1.02.163 P
may hold up head without northumberland? 1.03. 17
perforce a third | must take up us. 1.03. 73
mare, if i have any vantage of ground to get up. 2.01. 79 P
soul, and she says up and down the town that her 2.01.105 P
horse, | are march'd up to my lord of lancaster, 2.01.174
are to take soldiers up in counties as you go. 2.01.187 P
have /made /a /shift /to eat up thy holland. 2.02. 22 P
look to see his father | bring up his powers; 2.03. 14
as with the tide swell'd up unto his height, 2.03. 63
call him up, drawer. 2.04.101 P
alas, put up your naked weapons, put up your 2.04.206 P
your naked weapons, put up your naked weapons. 2.04.207 P
and begin to patch up thine old body for heaven? 2.04.233 P
and giddy /mast | seal up the ship–boy's eyes, 3.01. 19
a number of shadows fill up the muster–book. 3.02.134 P
holds his infant up | and hangs resolv'd 4.01.210
you have ta'en up, | under the counterfeited 4.02. 26
to this monstrous form | to hold our safety up. 4.02. 35
and heir from heir shall hold his quarrel up 4.02. 48
west, north, south, or, like a school broke up, 4.02.104
strike up our drums, pursue the scatt'red stray; 4.02.120
therefore rouse up fear and trembling, and do 4.03. 14 P
who, great and puff'd up with this retinue, doth 4.03.111 P
haunch of winter sings | the lifting up of day. 4.04. 93
my sovereign lord, cheer up yourself, look up. 4.04.113
my sovereign lord, cheer up yourself, look up. 4.04.113
i pray you take me up, and bear me hence | into 4.04.131
for this they have engrossed and pil'd up | the 4.05. 70
my death | thou hast seal'd up my expectation. 4.05.103
up, vanity! 4.05.119
most renown'd, | hast eat thy bearer up." 4.05.164
till his face be like a wet cloak ill laid up. 5.01. 85 P
a son | that would deliver up his greatness so 5.02.111
rouse up revenge from ebon den with fell 5.05. 37
his hours fill'd up with riots, banquets, sports H5 1.01. 56
they would hold up this salique law | to bar 1.02. 91
the civil citizens kneading up the honey, | the 1.02.199
nym, show thy valor, and put up your sword. 2.01. 44 P
for i can take, and pistol's cock is up, | and 2.01. 52
the first stroke, i'll run him up to the hilts, 2.01. 64 P
prithee put up. 2.01.104 P
by treasons | do botch and bungle up damnation 2.02.115
but he that temper'd thee, bade thee stand up, 2.02.118
boy, bristle thy courage up; 2.03. 5
up in the air, crown'd with the golden sun, 2.04. 58
take up the english short, and let them know 2.04. 72
deliver up the crown, and to take mercy | on the 2.04.103
or close the wall up with our english dead. 3.01. 2
stiffen the sinews, /conjure up the blood, 3.01. 7
and bend up every spirit | to his full height. 3.01. 16
up to the breach, you dogs! 3.02. 20 P
for it is plain pocketing up of wrongs. 3.02. 51 P
weak stomach, and therefore i must cast it up. 3.02. 53 P
by cheshu, i think 'a will plow up all, if there 3.02. 63 P
i would have blowed up the town, so chrish save 3.02. 91 P
the gates of mercy shall be all shut up, | and 3.03. 10
spirt up so suddenly into the clouds | and 3.05. 8
up, princes, and, with spirit of honor edged 3.05. 38
war, which they trick up with new–tun'd oaths; 3.06. 76 P
and i will take up that with "give the devil his 3.07.116 P
knights, | with busy hammers closing rivets up, 4.pr. 13
break up their drowsy grave, and newly move 4.01. 22
he could wish himself in thames up to the neck; 4.01.115 P
winding up days with toil, and nights with sleep 4.01.279
who twice a day their wither'd hands hold up 4.01.299
the sun doth gild our armor, up, my lords! 4.02. 1
and draw their honors reeking up to heaven, 4.03.101
let us on heaps go offer up our lives. 4.05. 18
to smother up the english in our throngs, | if 4.05. 20
thrice up again, and fighting; 4.06. 5
upon these words i came and cheer'd him up. 4.06. 20
came into mine eyes | and gave me up to tears. 4.06. 32
troyan, | to have me fold up parca's fatal web? 5.01. 20
our fertile france, put up her lovely visage? 5.02. 37
i cannot so conjure up the spirit of love in her 5.02.288 P
if conjure up love in her in his true likeness, 5.02.293 P
son, and from her blood raise up | issue to me, 5.02.348
he ne'er lift up his hand but conquered. 1H6 1.01. 16
in stead of gold, we'll offer up our arms, 1.01. 46
is roan yielded up? 1.01. 65
here had the conquest fully been seal'd up, | if 1.01.130
break up the gates, i'll be your warrantize. 1.03. 13
here by the cheeks i'll drag thee up and down. 1.03. 51
whilst any trump did sound, or drum struck up, 1.04. 80
speak unto talbot, nay, look up to him. 1.04. 89
join'd, | a holy prophetess new risen up, | is 1.04.102
go, go, cheer up thy hungry–starved men; 1.05. 16
and dare not take up arms like gentlemen. 3.02. 70
therefore stand up, and for these good deserts 3.04. 25
yield up his life unto a world of odds. 4.04. 25
hang up your ensigns, let your drums be still, 5.04.174
charge, | among the people gather up a tenth. 5.05. 93
deliver up my title in the queen | to your most 2H6 1.01. 12
wounds | deliver'd up again with peaceful words? 1.01.122
mine, | and, having both together heav'd it up, 1.02. 13
seal up your lips, and give no words but mum; 1.02. 89
spirits walk, and ghosts break up their graves, 1.04. 19
away with them, let them be clapp'd up close, 1.04. 50
make up no factious numbers for the matter, | in 2.01. 39
had not your man put up the fowl so suddenly, 2.01. 44
raising up wicked spirits from under ground, 2.01.170
ere thou go, | give up thy staff. 2.03. 23
give up your staff, sir, and the king his realm. 2.03. 31
and, in thy closet pent up, rue my shame, | and 2.04. 24
mail'd up in shame, with papers on my back, 2.04. 31
and with your best endeavor have stirr'd up | my 3.01.163
and as the dam runs lowing up and down, 3.01.214
to signify that rebels there are up | and put 3.01.283
i will stir up in england some black storm 3.01.349
rear up his body, wring him by the nose. 3.02. 34
that want their leader, scatter up and down, 3.02.126
and he but naked, though lock'd up in steel, 3.02.234
and cry out for thee to close up mine eyes, | to 3.02.395
hold up thy hand, make signal of thy hope. 3.03. 28
close up his eyes, and draw the curtain close, 3.03. 32
the duke of suffolk muffled up in rags? 4.01. 46
now will i dam up this thy yawning mouth | for 4.01. 73
vain, | as hating thee, /are rising up in arms; 4.01. 93
the commons here in kent are up in arms, | and 4.01.100
they have been up these two days. 4.02. 2 P
merry world in england since gentlemen came up. 4.02. 9 P
been so well brought up that i can write my name 4.02.106 P
rise up sir john mortimer. 4.02.120 P
with a staff, but that my puissance holds it up. 4.02.164 P
proclaim them traitors that are up with cade, 4.02.177
be hang'd up for example at their doors. 4.02.180
to my majesty for giving up of normandy unto 4.07. 28 P
are my chests fill'd up with extorted gold? 4.07. 99
go to cheapside and take up commodities upon our 4.07.127 P
about the giving up of some more towns in france 4.07.133 P
up fish street! 4.08. 1 P
fling up his cap, and say, "god save his majesty 4.08. 15
o, i could hew up rocks and fight with flint, 5.01. 24
rise up a knight. 5.01. 78
here is a hand to hold a sceptre up, | and with 5.01.102
storm | than any thou canst conjure up to–day; 5.01.199
cheer'd up the drooping army, and himself, 3H6 1.01. 6
best, | the proudest he that holds up lancaster, 1.01. 46
i'll plant plantagenet, root him up who dares. 1.01. 48
proud, | can set the duke up in despite of me. 1.01.158
sits, | write up his title with usurping blood. 1.01.169
no, if i digg'd up thy forefathers' graves | and 1.03. 27
and hung their rotten coffins up in chains, | it 1.03. 28
the sands are numb'red that makes up my life, 1.04. 25
for raging wind blows up incessant showers, 1.04.145
body | might in the ground be closed up in rest! 2.01. 76
and burns me up with flames that tears would 2.01. 84
i cheer'd them up with justice of our cause, 2.01.133
and he that throws not up his cap for joy 2.01.196
then strike up drums. 2.01.204
my lord, cheer up your spirits, our foes are 2.02. 56
blood, | the noble gentleman gave up the ghost. 2.03. 22
day, | how many days will finish up the year, 2.05. 28
any life be left in thee, | throw up thine eye! 2.05. 85
to shrink mine arm up like a wither'd shrub, 3.02.156
unless our halberds did shut up his passage. 4.03. 20
what, fear not, man, but yield me up the keys, 4.07. 37
drummer, strike up, and let us march away. 4.07. 50
those will i muster up; 4.08. 11
shalt stir up in suffolk, norfolk, and in kent, 4.08. 12
in oxfordshire shalt muster up thy friends. 4.08. 18
confess who set thee up and pluck'd thee down, 5.01. 26
the stones together, | and set up lancaster. 5.01. 85
thy very beams will dry those vapors up, | for 5.03. 12
strike up the drum, cry "courage!" 5.03. 24
must by the roots be hewn up yet ere night. 5.04. 69
for bearing arms, for stirring up my subjects, 5.05. 15
thought of them would have stirr'd up remorse, 5.05. 64

whose envious gulf did swallow up his life. 5.06. 25
our bruised arms hung up for monuments, | our R3 1.01. 6
into this breathing world, scarce half made up, 1.01. 21
this day should clarence closely be mew'd up 1.01. 38
george be pack'd with post–horse up to heaven. 1.01.146
what black magician conjures up this fiend | to 1.02. 34
as thou dost swallow up this good king's blood, 1.02. 66
take up the sword again, or take up me. 1.02.183
take up the sword again, or take up me. 1.02.183
well, well, put up your sword. 1.02.196
and for his meed, poor lord, he is mewed up. 1.03.138
no sleep close up that deadly eye of thine, 1.03.224
wrath | hath in eternal darkness folded up. 1.03.268
he is frank'd up to fatting for his pains — 1.03.313
england, | and cited up a thousand heavy times, 1.04. 14
what lawful quest have given their verdict up 1.04.184
and often up and down my sons were toss'd | for 2.04. 58
arm | is like a blasted sapling, wither'd up; 3.04. 69
at lower end of the hall, hurl'd up their caps, 3.07. 35
go, go up to the leads, the lord mayor knocks. 3.07. 55
the son of clarence have i pent up close, | his 4.03. 36
strike up the drum. 4.04.180
up to some scaffold, there to lose their heads. 4.04.243
stirr'd up by dorset, buckingham, and morton, 4.04.467
i'll muster up my friends and meet your grace 4.04.488
march on, march on, since we are up in arms, 4.04.528
my son george stanley is frank'd up in hold; 4.05. 3
up with my tent! 5.03. 7
up with the tent! 5.03. 14
went through the army, cheering up the soldiers. 5.03. 71
bind up my wounds! 5.03.177
your friends are up and buckle on their armor. 5.03.211
that he was never trained up in arms. 5.03.272
call up lord stanley, bid him bring his power. 5.03.290
bulk | take up the rays o' th' beneficial sun, H8 1.01. 56
he makes up the file | of all the gentry; 1.01. 75
bosom up my counsel, | you'll find it wholesome. 1.01.112
grosser quality, is cried up | for our best act. 1.02. 84
his end, | goodness and he fill up one monument! 2.01. 94
then give my charge up to sir nicholas vaux, 2.01. 96
than to be perk'd up in a glist'ring grief | and 2.03. 21
have your mouth fill'd up | before you open it. 2.03. 87
me, and so give me up | to the sharp'st kind of 2.04. 43
break up the court! 2.04.241
guilty | to give up willingly that noble title 3.01.140
again, there is sprung up | an heretic, an 3.02.101
you | to render up the great seal presently 3.02.229
it, she that carries up the train | is that old 4.01. 51
i think) flew up, and had their faces | been 4.01. 74
stock, sir thomas, | i wish it grubb'd up now. 5.01. 23
stand up, good canterbury! 5.01.113
give me thy hand, stand up; 5.01.115
stand close up, or i'll make your head ache. 5.03. 88
you i' th' chamblet, get up o' th' rail, | i'll 5.03. 89
lady | heaven ever laid up to make parents happy 5.04. 7
stand up, lord. 5.04. 9
that mould up such a mighty piece as this is, 5.04. 26
up to the eastern tower, | whose height commands TRO 1.02. 2
helen was not up, was she? 1.02. 49 P
hector was gone, but helen was not up. 1.02. 50 P
and i'll spring up in his tears an' 'twere a 1.02.175 P
shall we stand up here and see them as they pass 1.02.178 P
and the minds of all | should be shut up, hear 1.03. 58
hand of greece | should hold up high in brass, 1.03. 64
an universal prey, | and last eat up himself. 1.03.124
that hath to this maturity blown up | in rank 1.03.317
whose grossness little characters sum up; 1.03.325
come safe off, | we'll dress him up in voices; 1.03.381
draught–oxen, and make you plough up the wars. 2.01.107 P
reason which denies | the yielding of her up? 2.02. 25
now to deliver her possession up | on terms of 2.02.152
blood | than to make up a free determination 2.02.170
he that is proud eats up himself. 2.03.154 P
and how his silence drinks up his applause! 2.03.201
"as true as troilus" shall crown up the verse, 3.02.182
troy, | and blind oblivion swallow'd cities up, 3.02.187
ajax goes up and down the field, asking for 3.03.244 P
why, 'a stalks up and down like a peacock — a 3.03.251 P
would drink up | the lees and dregs of a flat 4.01. 62
hark, there's one up. 4.02. 18
we must give up to diomedes' hand | the lady 4.02. 65
a robber's haste | crams his rich thiev'ry up, 4.04. 43
to them, | he fumbles up into a loose adieu; 4.04. 46
or my heart will be blown up by /th' /root. 4.04. 54 P
what, are you up here, ho? speak! 5.02. 1
that cause sets up, with and against itself, 5.02.143
they set me up, in policy, that mongril cur, 5.04. 12 P
to close the day up, hector's life is done. 5.08. 8
daily to chain up and restrain the poor. COR 1.01. 84 P
if the wars eat us not up, they will; 1.01. 85 P
yet i can make my audit up, that all | from me 1.01.144
before 's, for the remove | bring up your army; 1.02. 29
again, and over and over he comes, and up again; 1.03. 62 P
our walls | rather than they shall pound us up; 1.04. 17
sword | and, when it bows, stand'st up. 1.04. 54
slaves, | ere yet the fight be done, pack up. 1.05. 8
revenge | wrench up thy power to th' highest. 1.08. 11
fury, shall lift up | their rotten privilege and 1.10. 22
set up the bloody flag against all patience, and 2.01. 75 P
nay, my good soldier, up; 2.01.171
are smother'd up, leads fill'd, and ridges 2.01.211
for once we stood up about the corn, he himself 2.03. 15 P
'tis strongly wadg'd up in a blockhead; 2.03. 28 P
as cause had call'd you up, have held him to; 2.03.194
aches | to know, when two authorities are up, 3.01.109
myself | take up a brace o' th' best of them, 3.01.243
an unnatural dam | should now eat up her own! 3.01.292
when one but of my ordinance stood up | to speak 3.02. 12
and schoolboys' tears take up | the glasses of 3.02.116
you, poor gentleman, take up some other station; 4.05. 29 P
finger and his thumb as one would set up a top. 4.05.153 P
hand, and turns up the white o' th' eye to his 4.05.196 P
sir, his crest up again and the man in blood, 4.05.210 P
shall have the drum strook up this afternoon. 4.05.215 P
as you threw caps up will he tumble down, | and 4.06.135
o, stand up blest! 5.03. 52
and cry, "be blest | for making up this peace!" 5.03.140
but kneels and holds up hands for fellowship, 5.03.175
and hale him up and down, all swearing, if | the 5.04. 37
he has betray'd your business, and given up, 5.06. 91
masters all, be quiet, | put up your swords. 5.06.134
take him up. 5.06.147
hath yok'd a nation strong, train'd up in arms. TIT 1.01. 30
to–morrow yield up rule, resign my life, | and 1.01.191
clear up, fair queen, that cloudy countenance; 1.01.263
openly, | and basely put it up without revenge? 1.01.433
take up this good old man, and cheer the heart 1.01.457
stand up. 1.01.485
for shame, put up. 2.01. 53
the hunt is up, the /morn is bright and grey, 2.02. 1
take it up, i pray thee, | and give the king 2.03. 46
andronicus himself did take it up. 2.03.294
in bootless prayer have they been held up, | and 3.01. 75
herbs as these | are meet for plucking up, and 3.01.178
o, here i lift this one hand up to heaven, | and 3.01.206
the closing up of our most wretched eyes. 3.01.262
why lifts she up her arms in sequence thus? 4.01. 37
sooner this sword shall plough thy bowels up. 4.02. 87
and bring you up | to be a warrior and command a 4.02.179
to take up a matter of brawl betwixt my uncle 4.03. 93 P
can you with a grace deliver up a supplication? 4.03.107 P
kiss his foot, then deliver up your pigeons, and 4.03.111 P
then i have brought up a neck to a fair end. 4.04. 48 P
to save my boy, to nourish and bring him up, 5.01. 84
oft have i digg'd up dead men from their graves, 5.01.135
for up and down she doth resemble thee. 5.02.107
put up your swords, you know not what you do. ROM 1.01. 65
put up thy sword, | or manage it to part these 1.01. 68
shuts up his windows, locks fair daylight out, 1.01.139
shut up in prison, kept without my food, | whipt 1.02. 55
up. 1.02. 72 P
'a was a merry man — took up the child. 1.03. 40
the guests are come, supper serv'd up, you 1.03.101 P
love, wherein thou stickest | up to the ears. 1.04. 43
more light, you knaves, and turn the tables up; 1.05. 27
name | i conjure only but to raise up him. 2.01. 29
full soon the canker death eats up that plant. 2.03. 30
that runs lolling up and down to hide his bable 2.04. 92 P
to catch my death with jauncing up and down! 2.05. 52
marry come up, i trow; 2.05. 62
now comes the wanton blood up in your cheeks, 2.05. 70
excess | i cannot sum up sum of half my wealth. 2.06. 34
gentle mercutio, put thy rapier up. 3.01. 84
the citizens are up, and tybalt slain. 3.01.133
up, sir, go with me; 3.01.139
to woe, | which you, mistaking, offer up to joy. 3.02.104
take up those cords. 3.02.132
hang up philosophy! 3.03. 57
stand up; 3.03. 75
stand up, stand up, stand, and you be a man. 3.03. 88
stand up, stand up, stand, and you be a man. 3.03. 88
and now falls on her bed, and then starts up, 3.03.100
to–night she's mewed up to her heaviness. 3.04. 11
ho, daughter, are you up? 3.05. 64
is she not down so late, or up so early? 3.05. 66
like death when he shuts up the day of life; 4.01.101
i'll have this knot knit up to–morrow morning. 4.02. 24
why, i am glad on't, this is well, stand up. 4.02. 28
go thou to juliet, help to deck up her. 4.02. 41
paris, to prepare up him | against to–morrow. 4.02. 45
and let the nurse this night sit up with you, 4.03. 10
that almost freezes up the heat of life. 4.03. 16
go waken juliet, go and trim her up, | i'll go 4.04. 25
the county paris hath set up his rest | that you 4.05. 6
in your bed, | he'll fright you up, i' faith. 4.05. 11
revive, look up, or i will die with thee! 4.05. 20
ties up my tongue and will not let me speak. 4.05. 32
dry up your tears, and stick your rosemary | on 4.05. 79
faith, we may put up our pipes and be gone. 4.05. 96 P
honest good fellows, ah, put up, put up, | for 4.05. 98
honest good fellows, ah, put up, put up, | for 4.05. 98
pray you put up your dagger, and put out your 4.05.121 P
you with an iron wit, and put up my iron dagger. 4.05.124 P
were thinly scattered, to make up a show. 5.01. 48
seal'd up the doors and would not let us forth, 5.02. 11
being loose, unfirm, with digging up of graves, 5.03. 6
o, here | will i set up my everlasting rest, 5.03.110
run to the capulets, | raise up the montagues; 5.03.178
what misadventure is so early up, | that calls 5.03.188
for thou art early up | to see thy son and heir 5.03.208
seal up the mouth of outrage for a while, | till 5.03.216
letter he desires | to those have shut him up, TIM 1.01. 98
'tis not enough to help the feeble up, | but to 1.01.107
and all the madness is, he cheers them up too. 1.02. 42 P
sweet instruments hung up in cases that keeps 1.02. 99 P
and at that instant like a babe sprung up. 1.02.111
men | upon whose age we void it up again | with 1.02.138
in all shapes that man goes up and down in from 2.02.113 P
you do yourselves but wrong to stir me up, | let 3.04. 53
i'll cheer up | my discontented troops, and lay 3.05.113
put up thy gold. 4.03.108
hold up, you sluts, | your aprons mountant. 4.03.135
be strong in whore, allure him, burn him up, 4.03.142
strike up the drum towards athens! 4.03.169
dry up thy marrows, vines, and plough–torn leas, 4.03.193
were all the wealth i have shut up in thee, 4.03.279
and may diseases lick up their false bloods! 4.03.532
too savage, doth root up | his country's peace. 5.01.165
have you climb'd up to walls and battlements, JC 1.01. 38
hands, and threw up their sweaty night–caps, and 1.02.245 P
held up his left hand, which did flame and burn 1.03. 16
besides — i ha' not since put up my sword — 1.03. 19
men, all in fire, walk up and down the streets. 1.03. 25
set this up with wax | upon old brutus' statue. 1.03.145
i found | this paper, thus seal'd up, and i am 2.01. 37
been often dropp'd | where i have took them up. 2.01. 50
i have been up this hour, awake all night. 2.01. 88
up higher toward the north | he first presents 2.01.109
we all stand up against the spirit of caesar, 2.01.167
do, | stir up their servants to an act of rage, 2.01.176
to walk unbraced and suck up the humors | of the 2.01.262
hast conjur'd up | my mortified spirit. 2.01.323
graves have yawn'd and yielded up their dead; 2.02. 18
say, | "break up the senate till another time, 2.02. 98
revels long a–nights, | is notwithstanding up. 2.02.117
hence! wilt thou lift up olympus? 3.01. 74
our hands in caesar's blood | up to the elbows, 3.01.107
let him go up into the public chair, | we'll 3.02. 63
noble antony, go up. 3.02. 64
and, in his mantle muffling up his face, | even 3.02.187
let me not stir you up | to such a sudden flood 3.02.210
were an antony | would ruffle up your spirits, 3.02.228
take up the body. 3.02.256
them, | by them shall make a fuller number up, 4.03.208
canst thou hold up thy heavy eyes awhile, | and 4.03.256
when think you that the sword goes up again? 5.01. 52
the storm is up, and all is on the hazard. 5.01. 68
our army lies, ready to give up the ghost. 5.01. 88
till he have brought thee up to yonder troops 5.03. 16
yet, countrymen! o, yet, hold up your heads! 5.04. 1
so mix'd in him that nature might stand up | and 5.05. 74
to mine, | and thrice again, to make up nine. MAC 1.03. 36
peace, the charm's wound up. 1.03. 37
scarcely more | than would make up his message. 1.05. 37
stop up th' access and passage to remorse, 1.05. 44
only look up clear: 1.05. 71
old, | and the late dignities heap'd up to them, 1.06. 19
could trammel up the consequence, and catch 1.07. 3
and bend up | each corporal agent to this 1.07. 79
hostess, and shut up | in measureless content. 2.01. 16
sleep that knits up the ravell'd sleave of care, 2.02. 34
for him, though he took up my legs sometime, yet 2.03. 40 P
up, up, and see | the great doom's image! 2.03. 77
up, up, and see | the great doom's image! 2.03. 77
as from your graves rise up, and walk like 2.03. 79
that will ravin up | thine own live's means! 2.04. 28
be my oracles as well, | and set me up in hope? 3.01. 10
lord, as will fill up the time | 'twixt this and 3.01. 24
night, | scarf up the tender eye of pitiful day, 3.02. 47
waves | confound and swallow navigation up; 4.01. 54
come, sisters, cheer we up his sprites, | and 4.01.127
enow to beat the honest men and hang up them. 4.02. 58 P
then, alas, | do i put up that womanly defense, 4.02. 78
me, and wisdom | to offer up a weak, poor, 4.03. 16
and your maids could not fill up | the cestern 4.03. 62
scotland hath foisons to fill up your will | of 4.03. 88
them lie | till famine and the ague eat them up. 5.05. 4
there | shark'd up a list of lawless resolutes, HAM 1.01. 98
break we our watch up, and, by my advice, | let 1.01.168
methought | it lifted up it head and did address 1.02.216
o yes, my lord, he wore his beaver up. 1.02.230
give me up the truth. 1.03. 98
and marble jaws | to cast thee up again. 1.04. 51
and tormenting flames | must render up myself. 1.05. 4
whose lightest word | would harrow up thy soul, 1.05. 16
grow not instant old, | but bear me /stiffly up. 1.05. 95
and thrice his head thus waving up and down, 2.01. 90
being of so young days brought up with him, 2.02. 11
and here give up ourselves, in the full bent, 2.02. 30
"run barefoot up and down, threat'ning the 2.02.505
a blanket, in the alarm of fear caught up — 2.02.509
is, to hold, as 'twere, the mirror up to nature: 3.02. 22 P
then i'll look up. 3.03. 50
up, sword, and know thou a more horrid hent: 3.03. 88
my words fly up, my thoughts remain below: 3.03. 97
you go not till i set you up a glass | where you 3.04. 19
life in excrements, | start up and stand an end. 3.04.122
we'll call up our wisest friends | and let them 4.01. 38
sir, that soaks up the king's countenance, his 4.02. 15 P
nose him as you go up the stairs into the lobby. 4.03. 36 P
and botch the words up fit to their own thoughts 4.05. 10
"then up he rose and donn'd his clo'es, | and 4.05. 52
o heat, dry up my brains! 4.05.155
all things else | you mainly were stirr'd up. 4.07. 9
and, mermaid–like, awhile they bore her up, 4.07.176
they hold up adam's profession. 5.01. 31 P
all their quantity of love | make up my sum. 5.01.271
woo't drink up eisel, eat a crocadile? 5.01.276
up from my cabin, | my sea–gown scarf'd about me 5.02. 12
folded the writ up in the form of th' other, 5.02. 51
take up the bodies. 5.02.401
sir, | election makes not up in such conditions. LR 1.01.206
upon, | be it lawful i take up what's cast away. 1.01.253
now, gods, stand up for bastards! 1.02. 22
why so earnestly seek you to put up that letter? 1.02. 28
cut the egg i' th' middle and eat up the meat, 1.04.159 P
dry up in her the organs of increase, | and from 1.04.279
is it two days since i tripp'd up thy heels, and 2.02. 29 P
those contents | they summon'd up their meiny, 2.04. 35
o, how this mother swells up toward my heart! 2.04. 56
shut up your doors. 2.04.304
shut up your doors, my lord, 'tis a wild night, 2.04.308
take up thy master; 3.06. 92
take up, take up, | and follow me, that will to 3.06. 95
take up, take up, | and follow me, that will to 3.06. 95
would have buoy'd up | and quench'd the stelled 3.07. 60
give me thy sword. a peasant stand up thus? 3.07. 80
would stretch thy spirits up into the air. 4.02. 23
you do climb up it now. look how we labor. 4.06. 2
look up a–height, the shrill–gorg'd lark so far 4.06. 58
do but look up. 4.06. 59
up — so. 4.06. 65
bring up the brown bills. 4.06. 91 P
thee i'll rake up, the post unsanctified | of 4.06.274
how stiff is my vild sense | that i stand up, 4.06.280
o, wind up | of this child–changed father! 4.07. 15
the enemy's in view, draw up your powers. 5.01. 51
person, | the which immediacy may well stand up, 5.03. 65
look up, my lord. 5.03.313
call up her father. OTH 1.01. 67
call up all my people! 1.01.141
call up my brother. 1.01.175
keep up your bright swords, for the dew will 1.02. 59
a turkish fleet, and bearing up to cyprus. 1.03. 8
and with a greedy ear | devour up my discourse. 1.03.150
take up this mangled matter at the best; 1.03.173
or sow lettuce, set hyssop and weed up /tine, 1.03.322 P
to get his place and to plume up my will | in 1.03.393
look if my gentle love be not rais'd up! 2.03.250
that he hath devoted and given up himself to the 2.03.316 P
hound that hunts, but one that fills up the cry. 2.03.364 P
then put up your pipes in your bag, for i'll 3.01. 19 P
prithee keep up thy quillets. 3.01. 23 P

as if thou then hadst shut up in thy brain 3.03.114
such a seeming | to seel her father's eyes up, 3.03.210
for sure he fills it up with great ability — 3.03.247
and, to th' advantage, i, being here, took't up. 3.03.312
i see, /sir, you are eaten up with passion; 3.03.391
as if he pluck'd up kisses by the roots | that 3.03.423
yield up, o love, thy crown and hearted throne 3.03.448
a capable and wide revenge | swallow them up. 3.03.460
witness that here iago doth give up | the 3.03.465
and shut myself up in some other course, | to 3.04.121
each syllable that breath made up between them. 4.02. 5
but there, where i have garner'd up my heart, 4.02. 57
the which my current runs | or else dries up: 4.02. 60
cheeks, | that would to cinders burn up modesty, 4.02. 75
i yet persuaded to put up in peace what already 4.02.179 P
sweetest innocent | that e'er did lift up eye. 5.02.200
the world to weet | we stand up peerless. ANT 1.01. 40
and life, stands up | for the main soldier; 1.02.190
(though daintily brought up) with patience more 1.04. 60
tie up the libertine in a field of feasts, 2.01. 23
were't not that we stand up against them all, 2.01. 44
divisions, and bind up | the petty difference, 2.01. 48
but pray you stir no embers up. 2.02. 13
but | you patch'd up your excuses. 2.02. 56
in alexandria you | did pocket up my letters; 2.02. 73
and then when poisoned hours had bound me up 2.02. 90
she purs'd up his heart upon the river of cydnus 2.02.187 P
and, as i draw them up, | i'll think them every 2.05. 13
on his hook, which he | with fervency drew up. 2.05. 18
know | if 'twill tie up thy discontented sword, 2.06. 6
the sighs of octavia blow the fire up in caesar, 2.06.127 P
and that slain men | should solder up the rift. 3.04. 32
so the poor third is up, till death enlarge his 3.05. 12 P
he hath given his empire | up to a whore, who 3.06. 67
give up yourself merely to chance and hazard, 3.07. 47
then have courtesy, so she | will yield us up. 3.13. 16
and all of you clapp'd up together in | an 4.02. 17
an absolute hope | our landmen will stand up. 4.03. 11
and snatch 'em up, as we take hares, behind: 4.07. 13
they cast their caps up and carouse together 4.12. 12
and hoist thee up to the shouting plebeians! 4.12. 34
patient octavia plough thy visage up | with her 4.12. 38
take me up. 4.14.138
help me, my women — we must draw thee up. 4.15. 30
the strong–wing'd mercury should fetch thee up, 4.15. 35
whilst he stood up and spoke, | he was my master 5.01. 7
if thou pleasest not, | i yield thee up my life. 5.01. 12
which shackles accidents and bolts up change, 5.02. 6
shall they hoist me up, | and show me to the 5.02. 55
pyramides my gibbet, | and hang me up in chains! 5.02. 62
you lie up to the hearing of the gods! 5.02. 95
i found her trimming up the diadem | on her dead 5.02.342
take up her bed, | and bear her women from the 5.02.356
you the keys | that lock up your restraint. CYM 1.01. 74
and cere up my embracements from a next | with 1.01.116
away with her, | and pen her up. 1.01.153
on cats and dogs, | then afterward up higher; 1.05. 39
more than the locking up the spirits a time, 1.05. 41
thou tak'st up | thou know'st not what; 1.05. 60
jack–an–apes must take me up for swearing, as if 2.01. 4 P
and i must go up and down like a cock that 2.01. 21 P
leaf's turn'd down | where philomele gave up. 2.02. 46
loss, the most coldest that ever turn'd up ace. 2.03. 2 P
i am glad i was up so late, for that's the 2.03. 33 P
late, for that's the reason i was up so early. 2.03. 34 P
if she be up, i'll speak with her; 2.03. 64
yield up | their deer to th' stand o' th' 2.03. 69
and now 'tis up again. 2.04. 97
boats, | but suck them up to th' topmast. 3.01. 22
up to yond hill, | your legs are young; 3.03. 10
but up to th' mountains! 3.03. 73
and, though train'd up thus meanly | i' th' cave 3.03. 82
the game is up. 3.03.107
that didst set up my disobedience 'gainst the 3.04. 88
my horse is tied up safe; 4.01. 22 P
being scarce made up, | i mean, to man, he had 4.02.109
the senate hath stirr'd up the confiners | and 4.02.337
where was he | that could stand up his parallel, 5.04. 54
din | express impatience, lest you stir up mine. 5.04.112
it sums up thousands in a trice. 5.04.167 P
are) these twenty years | have i train'd up; 5.05.338
built up this city for his chiefest seat, | the PER 1.ch. 18
him, | for flattery is the bellows blows up sin, 1.02. 39
how dares the plants look up to heaven, from 1.02. 55
throws down one mountain to cast up a higher. 1.04. 6
those mothers who, to nousle up their babes, 1.04. 42
the great ones eat up the little ones. 2.01. 29 P
bells, steeple, church, and parish up again. 2.01. 43 P
a man throng'd up with cold, my veins are chill, 2.01. 73
but, master, i'll go draw up the net. 2.01. 93 P
'twas we that made up this garment through the 2.01.149 P
him, | a fire from heaven came and shrivell'd up 2.04. 9
dives, | so up and down the poor ship drives. 3.ch. 50
honor, | or tie my pleasure up in silken bags, 3.02. 41
did the sea toss up upon our shore this chest. 3.02. 50
did the sea cast it up? 3.02. 57
so, up with it. 3.02. 62
our wonder, and sets up | your fame for ever. 3.02. 96
the gods | make up the rest upon you! 3.03. 5
blessed in your care | in bringing up my child. 3.03. 32
then give you up to the mask'd neptune and | the 3.03. 36
'tis not our bringing up of poor bastards — as 4.02. 13 P
as i think, i have brought up some eleven — 4.02. 14 P
our youths we could pick up some pretty estate, 4.02. 32 P
comfort you, men must feed you, men stir you up. 4.02. 92 P
out her beauty stirs up the lewdly inclin'd. 4.02.144 P
marry, hang her up for ever! 4.06.137 P
marry, come up, my dish of chastity with 4.06.150 P
that he have his. call up some gentlemen. 5.01. 6
stand up. TNK 1.01. 35
pray stand up, | your grief is written in your 1.01.109
pray stand up. 1.01.205
your advice | is cried up with example. 1.02. 13
have patiently | laid up my hour to come. 2.02. 6
night and stow her, | and all's made up again. 2.03. 33
provide him necessaries and pack my clothes up, 2.06. 32
come up to me! 3.01. 71
up with a course or two, and tack about, boys! 3.04. 10
is truss'd up in a trice | to–morrow morning; 3.04. 17
at length | i fling my cap up; 3.05. 17
draw up the company. where's the taborer? 3.05. 23
ira, nec ignis" — | strike up, and lead her in. 3.05. 89
at whose great feet i offer up my penner. 3.05.124
i spurr'd hard to come up, and under me | i had 3.06. 76
he'll tickle't up | in two hours, if his hand be 4.01.138
'tis up! 4.01.147
up to the top, boy! 4.01.150
yet i may bind those wounds up, that must open 4.02. 1
snatch up the goodly boy and set him by him, | a 4.02. 17
they shall stand in fire up to the nav'l, and in 4.03. 43 P
up to the nav'l, and in ice up to th' heart, and 4.03. 43 P
and ill lodging, | but i'll kiss him up again. 5.02. 98
the peace wherein you have till now grown up STM II.C 65
let me set up before your thoughts, good friends II.C 90
lift against the peace | lift up for peace, and II.C 110
give up yourself to form, obey the magistrate, II.C 146
should step as 'twere up to my country's head III 7
spun, | a bottom great wound up, greatly undone. III 21
the steed is stalled up, and even now | to tie VEN 39
hold up thy head, | look in mine eyeballs, there 118
with one fair hand she heaveth up his hat, | her 351
and careless lust stirs up a desperate courage, 556
this canker that eats up love's tender spring, 656
dries up his oil to lend the world his light. 756
from his moist cabinet mounts up on high, | and 854
wreath'd up in fatal folds just in his way, 879
till, cheering up her senses all dismay'd, | she 896
so she at these sad signs draws up her breath, 929
and there, all smoth'red up, in shade doth sit, 1035
a purple flow'r sprung up, check'red with white, 1168
when heavy sleep had clos'd up mortal eyes. LUC 163
and therein heartens up his servile powers, 295
stuff up his lust, as minutes fill up hours; 297
stuff up his lust, as minutes fill up hours; 297
this said, his guilty hand pluck'd up the latch, 358
his drumming heart cheers up his burning eye, 435
wounding itself to death, rise up and fall, 466
shalt have thy trespass cited up in rhymes, 524
dead–killing eye | he rouseth up himself, and 541
shame folded up in blind concealing night, 675
"the aged man that coffers up his gold | is 855
of foes, | to eat up errors by opinion bred, 937
"madam, ere i was up," replied the maid, | "the 1277
here folds she up the tenure of her woe, | her 1310
wagg'd up and down, and from his lips did fly 1406
thin winding breath, which purl'd up to the sky. 1407
which seem'd to swallow up his sound advice, 1409
to jump up higher seem'd, to mock the mind. 1414
head declin'd, and voice damm'd up with woe, 1661
what he breathes out his breath drinks up again. 1666
this windy tempest, till it blow up rain, | held 1788
scarce had the sun dried up the dewy morn, | and PP 6. 1
the gracious light | lifts up his burning head, SON 7. 2
and summer's green all girded up in sheaves 12. 7
i summon up remembrance of things past, | i sigh 30. 2
thee have i not lock'd up in any chest, | save 48. 9
praise cannot be so thy praise | to tie up envy, 70.12
death's second self, that seals up all in rest. 73. 8
your shallowest help will hold me up afloat, 80. 9
but when your countenance fill'd up his line, 86.13
growth | a vengeful canker eat him up to death. 99.13
drink up the monarch's plague, this flattery? 114. 2
and my great mind most kingly drinks it up: 114.10
that level | at my abuses reckon up their own; 121.10
thy pyramids built up with newer might | to me 123. 2
inheritors of this excess, | eat up thy charge? 146. 8
hand | the fairest votary took up that fire, 154. 5
but yield them up where i myself must render: LC 221

UP'ARD *(also upward)*

UP'ARD 2 FR 0.0002 REL FR 0 V 2 P
i felt to his knees, and so up'ard and up'ard, H5 2.03. 25 P
i felt to his knees, and so up'ard and up'ard, 2.03. 25 P

UPBRAID *(also braid*)*

UPBRAID 9 FR 0.0010 REL FR 9 V 0 P
prudence, who | should not upbraid our course. TMP 2.01.287
fool, | i did upbraid her and fall out with her. MND 4.01. 50
a man | as to upbraid you with those kindnesses TN 3.04.351
and i had many living to upbraid | my gain of it 2H4 4.05.192
and did upbraid me with my father's death; 1H6 2.05. 48
as well they may upbraid me with my crown, 4.01.156
false maids in love, | upbraid my falsehood! TRO 3.02.191
help, yet do not | upbraid 's with our distress. COR 5.01. 35
now minutely revolts upbraid his faith–breach; MAC 5.02. 18

UPBRAIDED 5 FR 0.0005 REL FR 4 V 1 P
desert) | hath oftentimes upbraided me withal: ERR 3.01.113
crown as having sense, | and thus upbraided it: 2H4 4.05.158
none of the french upbraided or abus'd in H5 3.06.111 P
tongue, | upbraided me about the rose i wear, 1H6 4.01. 91
knife and traitors' rage | be thus upbraided, 2H6 3.01.175

UPBRAIDINGS *(also obbraidings)*

UPBRAIDINGS 2 FR 0.0002 REL FR 2 V 0 P
say'st his meat was sauc'd with thy upbraidings: ERR 5.01. 73
your blunt upbraidings and your bitter scoffs. R3 1.03.103

UPBRAIDS 3 FR 0.0003 REL FR 3 V 0 P
the clock upbraids me with the waste of time. TN 3.01.130
and himself upbraids us | on every trifle. LR 1.03. 6
how he upbraids iago, that he made him | brave OTH 5.02.325

UP–CAST 1 FR 0.0001 REL FR 0 V 1 P
when i kiss'd the jack upon an up–cast, to be CYM 2.01. 2 P

UP–FILL 1 FR 0.0001 REL FR 1 V 0 P
i must up–fill this osier cage of ours | with ROM 2.03. 7

UPHEAVETH 1 FR 0.0001 REL FR 1 V 0 P
her two blue windows faintly she upheaveth, VEN 482

UPHOARDED 1 FR 0.0001 REL FR 1 V 0 P
or if thou hast uphoarded in thy life | extorted HAM 1.01.136

UPHOLD 6 FR 0.0006 REL FR 6 V 0 P
lord | most honorably doth uphold his word. LLL 5.02.449
we will alone uphold | without th' assistance of JN 3.01.157
and will a while uphold | the unyok'd humor of 1H4 1.02.195
do you uphold and maintain in your speeches, TIT 5.02. 72
born to uphold creation in that honor | first TNK 1.01. 82
which husbandry in honor might uphold | against SON 13.10

UPHOLDETH 1 FR 0.0001 REL FR 1 V 0 P
that which upholdeth him that thee upholds, JN 3.01.315

UPHOLDING 1 FR 0.0001 REL FR 0 V 1 P
for upholding the nice fashion of your country H5 5.02.273 P

UPHOLDS 4 FR 0.0004 REL FR 4 V 0 P
that which upholdeth him that thee upholds, JN 3.01.315
in spite of spite, alone upholds the day. 5.04. 5
while life upholds this arm, | this arm upholds 3H6 3.03.106
arm, | this arm upholds the house of lancaster. 3.03.107

UPLIFT 2 FR 0.0002 REL FR 2 V 0 P
and hammers, shall | uplift us to the view. ANT 5.02.211
your low–laid son our godhead will uplift. CYM 5.04.103

UPLIFTED 4 FR 0.0004 REL FR 4 V 0 P
for your strengths, | and will not be uplifted. TMP 3.03. 68
and with uplifted arms is safe arriv'd | at R2 2.02. 50
how were i then uplifted! TRO 3.02.168
there would be hands uplifted in my right; MAC 4.03. 42

UP–LOCKED 1 FR 0.0001 REL FR 1 V 0 P
can bring him to his sweet up–locked treasure, SON 52. 2

UPMOST 1 FR 0.0001 REL FR 1 V 0 P
but when he once attains the upmost round, | he JC 2.01. 24

/UPON 18 FR 0.0020 REL FR 16 V 2 P
rock, | which being violently borne /upon, | our ERR 1.01.102
/if /thy /offenses /were /upon /record, | /would R2 4.01.230
/all /of /you /that /stand /and /look /upon /me 4.01.237
/nay, /if /i /turn /mine /eyes /upon /myself, 4.01.247
/so /many /blows /upon /this /face /of /mine, 4.01.278
/model, | /consent /upon /a /sure /foundation, 2H4 1.03. 52
/that /threw'st /dust /upon /his /goodly /head 1.03.103
/to /look /upon /the /hideous /god /of /war 2.03. 35
/own /life /hung /upon /the /staff /he /threw), 4.01.124
/a /general /voice | /cried /hate /upon /him; 4.01.135
/upon /the /stroke /of /ten. R3 4.02.112
/is /left /to /tyrannize /upon /my /breast, TIT 3.02. 8
/such /violent /hands /upon /her /tender /life. 3.02. 22
/with /her /sorrow, /mesh'd /upon /her /cheeks. 3.02. 38
thou /pouts /upon thy fortune and thy love. ROM 3.03.144
/we'll /wait /upon /you. HAM 2.02.266 P
/i /mean, /my /head /upon /your /lap? 3.02.114 P
/you /lie /down /and /rest /upon /the /cushions? LR 3.06. 34

UPON 1832 FR 0.2070 REL FR 1479 V 353 P
methinks he hath no drowning mark upon him, his TMP 1.01. 29 P
a plague upon this howling! 1.01. 36 P
study, | the government i cast upon my brother, 1.02. 75
to the present business | which now's upon 's; 1.02.137
i find my zenith doth depend upon | a most 1.02.181
met again | and are upon the mediterranean float 1.02.234
deep, | to run upon the sharp wind of the north, 1.02.254
it was a torment | to lay upon the damn'd, which 1.02.290
got by the devil himself | upon thy wicked dam, 1.02.320
and sure it waits upon | some god o' th' island. 1.02.389
wrack, | this music crept by me upon the waters, 1.02.392
may know if you remain upon this island, | and 1.02.424
hast put thyself | upon this island as a spy, to 1.02.456
the air breathes upon us here most sweetly. 2.01. 47 P
surges under him, | and ride upon their backs. 2.01.116
sees a crown | dropping upon thy head. 2.01.209
and look how well my garments sit upon me, 2.01.272
no better than the earth he lies upon, | if he 2.01.281
upon mine honor, sir, i heard a humming | (and 2.01.317
'tis best we stand upon our guard, | or that we 2.01.321
but | for every trifle are they set upon me, 2.02. 8
do you put tricks upon 's with salvages and men 2.02. 58 P
now prosper works upon thee. 2.02. 81 P
i escap'd upon a butt of sack which the sailors 2.02.121 P
i'll swear upon that bottle to be thy true 2.02.125 P
a plague upon the tyrant that i serve! 2.02.162
and pile them up, | upon a sore injunction. 3.01. 11
they say there's but five upon this isle: 3.02. 5 P
mercy upon us! 3.02.132 P
open and show riches | ready to drop upon me, 3.02.142
else falls | upon your heads — is nothing but 3.03. 81
must | bestow upon the eyes of this young couple 4.01. 40
sir, | the white cold virgin snow upon my heart 4.01. 55
who with thy saffron wings upon my flow'rs 4.01. 78
done | some wanton charm upon this man and maid, 4.01. 95
and increasing, | hourly joys be still upon you! 4.01.108
monster, come put some lime upon your fingers, 4.01.245 P
to work mine end upon their senses that | this 5.01. 53
and as the morning steals upon the night, 5.01. 65
i here could pluck his highness' frown upon you 5.01.127
hours since | were wrack'd upon this shore; 5.01.137
who most strangely | upon this shore (where you 5.01.161
upon some book i love i'll pray for thee. TGV 1.01. 20
stomach on your meat, | and not upon your maid. 1.02. 69
thus will i fold them one upon another; 1.02.125
them | upon some other pawn for fealty. 2.04. 91
upon a homely object love can wink. 2.04. 98
i wait upon his pleasure. 2.04.117
we'll both attend upon your ladyship. 2.04.121
and sleep, | upon the very naked name of love. 2.04.142
thee, | because thou seest me dote upon my love. 2.04.173
of, | to furnish me upon my longing journey. 2.07. 85
upon mine honor, he shall never know | that i 3.01. 48
upon advice, hath drawn my love from her, | and, 3.01. 73
i pray thee let me feel thy cloak upon me. 3.01.136
is by, | and feed upon the shadow of perfection. 3.01.177
the day, | there is no day for me to look upon. 3.01.181
o, i have fed upon this woe already, | and now 3.01.221
with them, upon her knees, her humble self, 3.01.228
have some malignant power upon my life; 3.01.240
grace | let me not live to look upon your grace. 3.02. 21
upon this warrant shall you have access | where 3.02. 60
say that upon the altar of her beauty | you 3.02. 72
we'll wait upon your grace till after supper, 3.02. 95
mortal thing | upon the dull earth dwelling. 4.02. 52
upon whose grave thou vow'dst pure chastity. 4.03. 21
company, | upon whose faith and honor i repose. 4.03. 26
but think upon my grief, a lady's grief, | and 4.03. 28
say) one that takes upon him to be a dog indeed, 4.04. 12 P
than he, to take a fault upon me that he did, i 4.04. 14 P
i will not look upon your master's lines; 4.04.128
to think upon her woes i do protest | that i 4.04.144
i weep myself to think upon thy words. 4.04.175
with me | upon the rising of the mountain foot 5.02. 46
be thou asham'd that i have took upon me | such 5.04.105
i dare thee but to breathe upon my love. 5.04.131
silver, is her grandsire upon his death's–bed WIV 1.01. 51 P
will afterwards ork upon the cause with as great 1.01.145 P
it to alice shortcake upon all–hallowmas last, a 1.01.204 P
i will marry her upon any reasonable demands. 1.01.225 P

will you, upon good dowry, marry her? 1.01.238 P
do a greater thing than that, upon your request, 1.01.240 P
heaven may decrease it upon better acquaintance, 1.01.247 P
i hope, upon familiarity will grow more content. 1.01.249 P
you are my man, go wait upon my cousin shallow. 1.01.272 P
a sword, and it shall bite upon my necessity. 2.01.131 P
i have grated upon my good friends for three 2.02. 7 P
fan, i took't upon mine honor thou hadst it not. 2.02. 13 P
you stand upon your honor! 2.02. 20 P
i never knew a woman so dote upon a man; 2.02.103 P
to press with so little preparation upon you. 2.02.157 P
sir john, as you have one eye upon my follies, 2.02.186 P
out upon you! 3.03.103 P
and throw foul linen upon him, as if it were 3.03.131 P
i mine, to build upon a foolish woman's promise. 3.05. 41 P
and to call "horum," — fie upon you! 4.01. 68 P
if i cry out thus upon no trail, never trust me 4.02.197 P
discretions of a oman as ever i did look upon. 4.04. 2 P
that likewise have we thought upon, and thus: 4.04. 47
upon a sudden, | as falstaff, she, and i are 4.04. 52
upon their sight, | we two in great amazedness 4.04. 55
a jack–a–lent, when 'tis upon ill employment! 5.05.127 P
upon my life then, you took the wrong. 5.05.189 P
forced marriage would have brought upon her. 5.05.230
proper as to waste | thyself upon thy virtues, MM 1.01. 31
and so great a figure | be stamp'd upon it. 1.01. 50
i'll wait upon your honor. 1.01. 83
why then all the dukes fall upon the king. 1.02. 3 P
upon a true contract | i got possession of 1.02.145
a more strict restraint | upon the sisterhood, 1.04. 5
upon his place, | and with full line of his 1.04. 55
you censure him, | and pull'd the law upon you. 2.01. 16
but what we do not see | we tread upon, and 2.01. 26
i do lean upon justice, sir, and do bring in 2.01. 48 P
good master froth, look upon his honor; 2.01.148 P
i'll be suppos'd upon a book, his face is the 2.01.155 P
thou wicked varlet, now, what's come upon thee. 2.01.190 P
not find you before me again upon any complaint 2.01.246 P
kneel down before him, hang upon his gown; 2.02. 44
why do you put these sayings upon me? 2.02.133
let it not sound a thought upon your tongue 2.02.140
and feast upon her eyes? 2.02.178
appears, | accountant to the law upon that pain. 2.04. 86
and the poor beetle, that we tread upon, | in 3.01. 78
at that place call upon me, and dispatch with 3.01.266 P
thief too, sir, for we have found upon him, sir, 3.02. 17 P
must, upon a warranted need, give him a better 3.02.143 P
i am bound to call upon you, and i pray you your 3.02.158 P
much upon this riddle runs the wisdom of the 3.02.228 P
much upon this time have i promis'd here to meet 4.01. 17 P
may be i will call upon you anon for some 4.01. 23 P
there have i made my promise upon the heavy 4.01. 34
heavy | middle of the night to call upon him. 4.01. 35
that stays upon me, whose persuasion is | i come 4.01. 46
millions of false eyes | are stuck upon thee. 4.01. 60
and most contrarious /quests | upon thy doings; 4.01. 62
she'll take the enterprise upon her, father, 4.01. 65
fie upon him, he will discredit our mystery. 4.02. 28 P
upon the very siege of justice | lord angelo 4.02. 98
if any thing fall to you upon this, more than 4.02.178 P
is the axe upon the block, sirrah? 4.03. 37 P
and very near upon | the duke is ent'ring; 4.06. 14
vail your regard | upon a wrong'd — i would 5.01. 21
condemn'd upon the act of fornication | to lose 5.01. 70
upon his mere request, | being come to knowledge 5.01.152
nor heard from her, | upon my faith and honor. 5.01.224
have well determin'd | upon these slanderers. 5.01.259
speak not you to him till we call upon you. 5.01.286 P
lay bolts enough upon him. 5.01.346 P
thou hast, | rely upon it till my tale be heard, 5.01.365
like pow'r divine, | hath look'd upon my passes. 5.01.370
prince, | no longer session hold upon my shame, 5.01.371
go fetch him hither, let me look upon him. 5.01.469
upon mine honor, thou shalt marry her. 5.01.518
at length the sun, gazing upon the earth, ERR 1.01. 88
peruse the traders, gaze upon the buildings, 1.02. 13
please you, i'll meet with you upon the mart, 1.02. 27
the clock hath strucken twelve upon the bell: 1.02. 45
my mistress made it one upon my cheek: 1.02. 46
for she will /score your fault upon my pate: 1.02. 65
i have some marks of yours upon my pate: 1.02. 82
some of my mistress' marks upon my shoulders: 1.02. 83
upon my life, by some device or other | the 1.02. 95
ay, ay, he told his mind upon mine ear. 2.01. 48
i thank him, i bare home upon my shoulders: 2.01. 73
earnest, | upon what bargain do you give it me? 2.02. 25
you, | your sauciness will jest upon my love, 2.02. 28
it seems thou want'st breaking, out upon thee, 3.01. 77
here's too much "out upon thee!" 3.01. 78
and dwell upon your grave when you are dead; 3.01.104
for slander lives upon succession, | for ever 3.01.105
but to spite my wife) | upon mine hostess there. 3.01.119
o, sir, upon her nose, all o'er embellish'd with 3.02.134 P
consider how it stands upon my credit. 4.01. 68
whilst upon me the guilty doors were shut, | and 4.04. 63
ring — | the ring i saw upon his finger now — 4.04.139
upon what cause? 5.01.123
mistress, upon my life, i tell you true; 5.01.180
day, great duke, she shut the doors upon me, 5.01.204
then all together | they fell upon me, bound me, 5.01.247
o lord, he will hang upon him like a disease; ADO 1.01. 86 P
i look'd upon her with a soldier's eye, | that 1.01.298
and there heard it agreed upon that the prince 1.03. 62 P
we'll wait upon your lordship. 1.03. 75 P
blessing i am at him upon my knees every morning 2.01. 28 P
huddling jest upon jest with such impossible 2.01.245 P
impossible conveyance upon me that i stood like 2.01.245 P
as in a sanctuary, and people sin upon purpose, 2.01.259 P
away myself for you, and dote upon the exchange. 2.01.309 P
then down upon her knees she falls, weeps, sobs, 2.03.146 P
if he do not dote on her upon this, i will never 2.03.211 P
so much as you may take upon a knive's point and 2.03.254 P
a bed | as ever beatrice shall couch upon? 3.01. 46
let us go sit here upon the church–bench till 3.03. 89 P
fie upon thee, art not asham'd? 3.04. 28 P
i'll wait upon them, i am ready. 3.05. 56 P
upon mine honor, | myself, my brother, and this 4.01. 88
not every earthly thing | cry shame upon her? 4.01.121
upon the instant that she was accus'd, | shall 4.01.215
when he shall hear she died upon his words, 4.01.223
and that count claudio did mean, upon his words, 4.02. 54 P
and upon the grief of this suddenly died. 4.02. 63 P
as shall be prov'd upon thee by good witness. 4.02. 79 P
yet bend not all the harm upon yourself; 5.01. 39
nay, never lay thy hand upon thy sword, | i fear 5.01. 54
my villainy they have upon record, which i had 5.01.240 P
the lady is dead upon mine and my master's false 5.01.242 P
treachery, | and fled he is upon this villainy. 5.01.250
penance your invention | can lay upon my sin; 5.01.274
invention, | hang her an epitaph upon her tomb, 5.01.284
pray you examine him upon that point. 5.01.313 P
hang thou there upon the tomb, | praising her 5.03. 9
her | upon the error that you heard debated. 5.04. 3
i think he thinks upon the savage bull. 5.04. 43
which is the lady i must seize upon? 5.04. 53
by this good day, i yield upon great persuasion, 5.04. 95 P
lives, | live regist'red upon our brazen tombs, LLL 1.01. 2
he throws upon the gross world's baser slaves; 1.01. 30
as, painfully to pore upon a book | to seek the 1.01. 74
the eye indeed | by fixing it upon a fairer eye, 1.01. 81
the manor–house, sitting with her upon the form, 1.01.207 P
which, i mean, i walk'd upon: 1.01.239 P
nothing, master moth, but what they look upon. 1.02.163 P
this, "by, in, and without," upon the instant: 3.01. 41 P
you must send the ass upon the horse, for he is 3.01. 54 P
hereby, upon the edge of yonder coppice, | a 4.01. 9
king cophetua set eye upon the pernicious and 4.01. 66 P
shall i come upon thee with an old saying, that 4.01.119 P
and delivered upon the mellowing of occasion. 4.02. 70 P
to those fresh morning drops upon the rose, | as 4.03. 26
eye | dares look upon the heaven of her brow, 4.03.223
advance your standards, and upon them, lords; 4.03.364
world) sometime to lean upon my poor shoulder, 5.01.103 P
withal | upon the next occasion that we meet, 5.02.143
(those clouds removed) upon our watery eyne. 5.02.206
upon mine honor, no. 5.02.439
much upon this 'tis; 5.02.472
squier, | and laugh upon the apple of her eye? 5.02.475
you leer upon me, do you? 5.02.480
upon that day either prepare to die | for MND 1.01. 86
upon this spotted and inconstant man. 1.01.110
or else it stood upon the choice of friends — 1.01.139
i frown upon him; yet he loves me still. 1.01.194
i | upon faint primrose beds were wont to lie, 1.01.215
fairy queen, | to dew her orbs upon the green. 2.01. 9
and sail upon the land | to fetch me trifles, 2.01.132
since once i sat upon a promontory, | and heard 2.01.149
it fell upon a little western flower, | before 2.01.166
dote | upon the next live creature that it sees. 2.01.172
the next thing then she waking looks upon | (be 2.01.179
of hell, | to die upon the hand i love so well. 2.01.244
prove | more fond on her than she upon her love; 2.01.266
for i upon this bank will rest my head. 2.02. 40
upon thy eyes i throw | all the power this charm 2.02. 78
nay, i can gleek upon occasion. 3.01.146 P
the summer still doth tend upon my state; 3.01.155
come wait upon him; 3.01.197
that work for bread upon athenian stalls, | were 3.02. 10
durst thou have look'd upon him being awake? 3.02. 69
so hung upon with love, so fortunate | (but 3.02.233
make mouths upon me when i turn my back, | wink 3.02.238
for fear lest day should look their shames upon, 3.02.385
come sit thee down upon this flow'ry bed, 4.01. 1
i have an exposition of sleep come upon me. 4.01. 39 P
i beg the law, the law, upon his head. 4.01.155
gaud | which in my childhood i did dote upon; 4.01.168
this fellow doth not stand upon points. 5.01.118 P
in nativity, | shall upon their children be. 5.01.414
antonio | is sad to think upon his merchandise. MV 1.01. 40
estate | upon the fortune of this present year: 1.01. 44
you have too much respect upon the world. 1.01. 74
the men that ever my foolish eyes look'd upon, 1.02.118 P
whiles we shut the gate upon one wooer, another 1.02.133
moreover, upon the rialto, he hath a third at 1.03. 19 P
if i can catch him once upon the hip, | i will 1.03. 46
you neither lend nor borrow | upon advantage. 1.03. 70
dog, | and spet upon my jewish gaberdine, | and 1.03.112
that did void your rheum upon my beard | and 1.03.117
of doves that i would bestow upon your worship, 2.02.136 P
which doth offer to swear upon a book, i shall 2.02.159 P
in hate, to feed upon | the prodigal christian. 2.05. 14
stamp'd in gold, but that's insculp'd upon; 2.07. 57
she hath the stones upon her, and the ducats." 2.08. 22
i thought upon antonio when he told me, | and 2.08. 31
out upon it, old carrion! 3.01. 35 P
that was us'd to come so smug upon the mart: 3.01. 47 P
the curse never fell upon our nation till now, i 3.01. 85 P
why, thou loss upon loss! 3.01. 92 P
out upon her! 3.01.120 P
me choose, | for as i am, i live upon the rack. 3.02. 25
upon the rack, bassanio! 3.02. 26
ay, but i fear you speak upon the rack, | where 3.02. 32
sand, wear yet upon their chins | the beards of 3.02. 84
gambols with the wind | upon supposed fairness, 3.02. 94
your fortune stood upon the caskets there, | and 3.02.201
for you shall hence upon your wedding–day. 3.02.311
my love and some necessity | now lays upon you. 3.04. 35
of the father are to be laid upon the children; 3.05. 2 P
the sins of my mother should be visited upon me. 3.05. 14 P
how every fool can play upon the word! 3.05. 43 P
upon your charter and your city's freedom! 4.01. 39
you may as well go stand upon the beach | and 4.01. 71
if you deny me, fie upon your law! 4.01.101
upon my power i may dismiss this court, | unless 4.01.104
rain from heaven | upon the place beneath. 4.01.186
my deeds upon my head! 4.01.206
i pray you let me look upon the bond. 4.01.225
shall i lay perjury upon my soul? 4.01.229
which here appeareth due upon the bond. 4.01.249
to render it | upon his death unto the gentleman 4.01.384
my lord bassanio upon more advice | hath sent 4.02. 6
a willow in her hand | upon the wild sea–banks, 5.01. 11
how sweet the moonlight sleeps upon this bank! 5.01. 54
the world like cutler's poetry | upon a knife, 5.01.150
a thing stuck on with oaths upon your finger, 5.01.168
you see my finger | hath not the ring upon it, 5.01.188
my soul upon the forfeit, that your lord | will 5.01.252
in, | and charge us there upon inter'gatories, 5.01.298
it was upon this fashion bequeath'd me by will AYL 1.01. 1 P
begin you to grow upon me? 1.01. 85 P
is there yet another dotes upon rib–breaking? 1.02.142 P
what passion hangs these weights upon my tongue? 1.02.257
grounded upon no other argument | but that the 1.02.279
are too precious to be cast away upon curs, 1.03. 5 P
cousin, thrown upon thee in holiday foolery; 1.03. 13 P
o, a good wish upon you! 1.03. 24 P
is my doom | which i have pass'd upon her; 1.03. 84
if you outstay the time, upon mine honor, | and 1.03. 88
and do not seek to take your change upon you, 1.03.102
a gallant curtle–axe upon my thigh, | a 1.03.117
which when it bites and blows upon my body 2.01. 8
upon the brook that brawls along this wood, | to 2.01. 32
upon that poor and broken bankrupt there?" 2.01. 57
weeping and commenting | upon the sobbing deer. 2.01. 66
we'll light upon some settled low content. 2.03. 68
a lover | as ever sigh'd upon a midnight pillow. 2.04. 27
i was in love i broke my sword upon a stone, and 2.04. 47 P
shepherd's passion | is much upon my fashion. 2.04. 61
if you like upon report | the soil, the profit, 2.04. 97
and take upon command what help we have | that 2.07.125
make an extent upon his house and lands. 3.01. 17
but upon the fairest boughs, | or at every 3.02.135
should be hang'd and carv'd upon these trees? 3.02.173 P
of the forest, like fringe upon a petticoat. 3.02.336 P
hangs odes upon hawthorns and elegies on 3.02.361 P
he seems to have the quotidian of love upon him. 3.02.365 P
there is none of my uncle's marks upon you. 3.02.369 P
this way will i take upon me to wash your liver 3.02.422 P
to cast away honesty upon a foul slut were to 3.03. 35 P
falls not the axe upon the humbled neck | but 3.05. 5
lean upon a rush, | the cicatrice and capable 3.05. 22
why look you so upon me? 3.05. 70 P
a scatt'red smile, and that i'll live upon. 3.05.104
make the doors upon a woman's wit, and it will 4.01.162 P
do well to set the deer's horns upon his head, 4.02. 5 P
an instrument, and play false strains upon thee? 4.03. 68 P
and here upon his arm | the lioness had torn 4.03.146
and cried, in fainting, upon rosalind. 4.03.149
was old sir rowland's will i estate upon you, 5.02. 11 P
faithful shepherd — | look upon him, love him; 5.02. 82
found the quarrel was upon the seventh cause. 5.04. 50 P
upon a lie seven times remov'd (bear your body 5.04. 68 P
he cried upon it at the merest loss, | and twice SHR in.1. 23
in sweet clothes, rings put upon his fingers, in.1. 38
upon my life, i am a lord indeed | and not a in.2. 72
door, | and rail upon the hostess of the house, in.2. 86
know now, upon advice, it toucheth us both, that 1.01.115 P
i bade the rascal knock upon your gate, | and 1.02. 37
think scolding would do little good upon him. 1.02.109 P
i met, | upon agreement from us to his liking, 1.02.182
request, | that, upon knowledge of my parentage, 2.01. 95
together | that upon sunday is the wedding–day. 2.01.298
i should be arguing still upon that doubt. 3.01. 55
upon my life, petruchio means but well, 3.02. 22
how he left her with the horse upon her, how he 4.01. 76 P
for then she never looks upon her lure. 4.01.192
look that you take upon you as you should; 4.02.109
door | upon entreaty have a present alms, | if 4.03. 5
a dish that i do love to feed upon. 4.03. 24
pack of you | that triumph thus upon my misery! 4.03. 34
pluck up thy spirits, look cheerfully upon me. 4.03. 38
sew'd up again, and that i'll prove upon thee, 4.03.147 P
i, upon some agreement | me shall you find ready 4.04. 33
you saw my master wink and laugh upon you? 4.04. 75 P
to break a jest | upon the company you overtake? 4.05. 73
knavery, to take upon you another man's name. 5.01. 36 P
hound, | but twenty times so much upon my wife. 5.02. 73
understand what advice shall thrust upon thee, AWW 1.01.210 P
no note upon my parents, his all noble. 1.03.157
daughter and mother | so strive upon your pulse. 1.03.169
adore | the sun, that looks upon his worshipper, 1.03.206
upon thy certainty and confidence | what dar'st 2.01.169
blessing upon your vows, and in your bed | find 2.03. 91
both my revenge and hate | loosing upon thee, in 2.03.165
favor of the king | smile upon this contract, 2.03.178
feast | shall more attend upon the coming space, 2.03.181
thou not the privilege of antiquity upon thee — 2.03.209 P
created for men to breathe themselves upon thee. 2.03.256 P
in every thing i wait upon his will. 2.04. 54
holy seems the quarrel | upon your grace's part; 3.01. 5
why, he will look upon his boot and sing, mend 3.02. 6 P
think upon patience. 3.02. 48
"when thou canst get the ring upon my finger, 3.02. 57 P
the duke will lay upon him all the honor | that 3.02. 71
that twenty such rude boys might tend upon | and 3.02. 82
that ride upon the violent speed of fire, | fly 3.02.109
love and credence | upon thy promising fortune. 3.03. 3
and fortune play upon thy prosperous helm | as 3.03. 7
that barefoot plod i the cold ground upon, 3.04. 6
i thank you, and will stay upon your leisure. 3.05. 45
with the divine forfeit of his soul upon oath, 3.06. 32 P
to charge in with our horse upon our own wings, 3.06. 49 P
but with an invention and clap upon you two or three 3.06. 98 P
but i shall lose the grounds i work upon. 3.07. 3
when you sally upon him, speak what terrible 4.01. 2 P
worthy blame laid upon him for shaking off so 4.03. 6 P
a plague upon him! 4.03.116 P
upon my reputation and credit and as i hope to 4.03.133 P
rotten and sound, upon my life, amounts not to 4.03.166 P
upon my knowledge, he is, and lousy. 4.03.194 P
nay, look not so upon me; 4.03.195 P
or it is upon a file with the duke's other 4.03.204 P
a pox upon him for me, he's more and more a cat. 4.03.264 P
i am yours | upon your will to suffer. 4.04. 30
if i put any tricks upon 'em, sir, they shall be 4.05. 60 P
that my lord your son was upon his return home, 4.05. 70 P
from the report that goes upon your goodness, 5.01. 13
out upon thee, knave! 5.02. 48 P
dost thou put upon me at once both the office of 5.02. 48 P
though my revenges were high bent upon him | and 5.03. 10
at first | i stuck my choice upon her, ere my 5.03. 45
her leave at court, | i saw upon her finger. 5.03. 80
come, or sent it us | upon her great disaster. 5.03.112
"upon his many protestations to marry me when 5.03.139 P

why do you look so strange upon your wife?		5.03.168
lay a more noble thought upon mine honor | than		5.03.180
ask him upon his oath, if he does think | he had		5.03.185
sir, much like | the same upon your finger.		5.03.226
sound | that breathes upon a bank of violets,	TN	1.01. 6
to a strong mast that liv'd upon the sea;		1.02. 14
gate, | and call upon my soul within the house;		1.05.269
that upon the least occasion more mine eyes will		2.01. 41 P
eye | hath stay'd upon some favor that it loves.		2.04. 24
the parts that fortune hath bestow'd upon her,		2.04. 83
and some have greatness thrust upon 'em.		2.05.146 P
nay, but say true, does it work upon him?		2.05.195 P
and he will smile upon her, which will now be so		2.05.201 P
nay, and thou pass upon me, i'll no more with		3.01. 42 P
servingman than ever she bestow'd upon me.		3.02. 7 P
sir, upon the oaths of judgment and reason.		3.02. 14 P
build me thy fortunes upon the basis of valor.		3.02. 33 P
haply your eye shall light upon some toy | you		3.03. 44
i sent for thee upon a sad occasion.		3.04. 18 P
"and some have greatness thrust upon them."		3.04. 45 P
if this were play'd upon a stage now, i could		3.04.127 P
well, and god have mercy upon one of our souls!		3.04.167 P
he may have mercy upon mine, but my hope is		3.04.168 P
set upon aguecheek a notable report of valor,		3.04.191 P
meditate the while upon some horrid message for		3.04.199 P
deny, | that honor, sav'd, may upon asking give?		3.04.212
but in conclusion put strange speech upon me.		5.01. 67
three months this youth hath tended upon me,		5.01. 99
you drew your sword upon me without cause, | but		5.01.188
you throw a strange regard upon me, and by that		5.01.212
i should my tears let fall upon your cheek,		5.01.240
my father had a mole upon his brow.		5.01.242
he upon some action | is now in durance, at		5.01.275
to frown | upon sir toby and the lighter people;		5.01.339
here were presuppos'd | upon thee in the letter.		5.01.351
practice hath most shrewdly pass'd upon thee;		5.01.352
upon some stubborn and uncourteous parts | we		5.01.361
and some have greatness thrown upon them."		5.01.371 P
of what may chance | or breed upon our absence,	WT	1.02. 12
slaughters a thousand waiting upon that.		1.02. 93
still virginalling | upon his palm?		1.02.126
whose foundation | is pil'd upon his faith, and		1.02.430
in those foundations which i build upon, | the		2.01.101
did lack than i, my lord, | upon this ground;		2.01.159
i'll take't upon me.		2.02. 30
upon mine honor, i | will stand betwixt you and		2.02. 63
of my revenges that way | recoil upon me:		2.03. 20
leave me, | and think upon my bidding.		2.03.207
so forcing faults upon hermione, | i little like		3.01. 16
and my near'st of kin | cry fie upon my grave!		3.02. 54
if i shall be condemn'd | upon surmises (all		3.02.112
you here shall swear upon this sword of justice,		3.02.124
upon a barren mountain, and still winter | in		3.02.212
upon them shall | the causes of their death		3.02.236
our ship hath touch'd upon | the deserts of		3.03. 1
we have in hand are angry, | and frown upon 's.		3.03. 6
i'll not be long before | i call upon thee.		3.03. 9
or death, upon the earth | of its right father.		3.03. 45
now take upon me, in the name of time, | to use		4.01. 3
my service which look upon his removedness;		4.02. 36 P
me, and these detestable things put upon me.		4.03. 63 P
out upon him!		4.03.101 P
have taken | the shapes of beasts upon them.		4.04. 27
liv'd, upon | this day she was both pantler,		4.04. 55
that wear upon your virgin branches yet | your		4.04.115
not a word, a word, we stand upon our manners.		4.04.164
but i have it | upon his own report, and i		4.04.170
moon | upon the water as he'll stand and read		4.04.173
if young doricles | do light upon her, she shall		4.04.179
a fish that appear'd upon the coast on we'nsday		4.04.276 P
the self–same sun that shines upon his court		4.04.444
yea, | to die upon the bed my father died, | to		4.04.455
why look you so upon me?		4.04.462
cast your good counsels | upon his passion.		4.04.496
but o, the thorns we stand upon!		4.04.585
the sun looking with a southward eye upon him,		4.04.790 P
i will but look upon the hedge and follow you.		4.04.825 P
is as bitter | upon thy tongue as in my thought.		5.01. 19
may drop upon his kingdom and devour | incertain		5.01. 28
i might have look'd upon my queen's full eyes,		5.01. 53
'tis strange | he thus should steal upon us.		5.01.115
which waits upon worn times, hath something		5.01.142
your throne and his | measur'd to look upon you;		5.01.145
the heaven sets spies upon us, will not have		5.01.203
upon which errand | i now go toward him;		5.01.231
not | that which my daughter came to look upon,		5.03. 13
excels what ever yet you look'd upon | or hand		5.03. 16
the very life seems warm upon her lip.		5.03. 66
the ruddiness upon her lip is wet;		5.03. 81
strike all that look upon with marvel.		5.03.100
pour your graces | upon my daughter's head!		5.03.123
least they desire (upon this push) to trouble		5.03.129
in vain, said many | a prayer upon her grave.		5.03.141
look upon my brother.		5.03.147
world, | upon the right and party of her son?	JN	1.01. 34
or no, | that still i lay upon my mother's head,		1.01. 76
upon his death–bed he by will bequeath'd | his		1.01.109
me | upon good friday and ne'er broke his fast.		1.01.235
upon thy cheek lay i this zealous kiss | as seal		2.01. 19
lo upon thy wish | our messenger chatillion is		2.01. 50
o'er | did never float upon the swelling tide		2.01. 74
a rape | upon the maiden virtue of the crown.		2.01. 98
look here upon thy brother geffrey's face:		2.01. 99
of him | as great alcides' /shows upon an ass.		2.01.144
now shame upon you, whe'er she does or no!		2.01.167
a plague upon her!		2.01.190
made | for bloody power to rush upon your peace.		2.01.221
is most divinely vow'd upon the right | of him		2.01.237
play | upon the dancing banners of the french,		2.01.308
i'd play incessantly upon these jades, | even		2.01.385
and pell–mell | make work upon ourselves, for		2.01.407
look upon the years | of lewis the dolphin and		2.01.424
and all that we upon this side the sea | (except		2.01.488
well, | made to run even upon even ground,		2.01.576
since kings break faith upon commodity, | gain,		2.01.597
what means that hand upon that breast of thine?		3.01. 21
thou ever strong upon the stronger side!		3.01.117
to brag and stamp and swear | upon my party!		3.01.123
bidding me depend | upon thy stars, thy fortune,		3.01.126
and raise the power of france upon his head,		3.01.193
upon which better part our pray'rs come in, | if		3.01.293
upon thy wedding–day?		3.01.300
upon my knee i beg, go not to arms | against		3.01.308
o, upon my knee, | made hard with kneeling, i do		3.01.309
i will denounce a curse upon his head.		3.01.319
of peace | must by the hungry now be fed upon.		3.03. 10
i will not keep this form upon my head | when		3.04.101
she looks upon them with a threat'ning eye.		3.04.120
and he that stands upon a slipp'ry place | makes		3.04.137
plainly denouncing vengeance upon john.		3.04.159
i strike my foot | upon the bosom of the ground,		4.01. 3
speak a word, | nor look upon the iron angerly.		4.01. 81
and look'd upon, i hope, with cheerful eyes.		4.02. 2
as patches set upon a little breach | discredit		4.02. 32
the streets | do prophesy upon it dangerously.		4.02.186
haste | had falsely thrust upon contrary feet,		4.02.198
frowns | more upon humor than advis'd respect.		4.02.214
or turn'd an eye of doubt upon my face, | as bid		4.02.233
comment that my passion made | upon thy feature,		4.02.264
upon my soul —		4.03.125
and heaven itself doth frown upon the land.		4.03.159
up, | upon your stubborn usage of the pope;		5.01. 18
well, | upon your oath of service to the pope,		5.01. 23
shall we, upon the footing of our land, | send		5.01. 66
upon our sides it never shall be broken.		5.02. 8
defense | cries out upon the name of salisbury!		5.02. 19
march | upon her gentle bosom, and fill up | her		5.02. 28
weep | upon the spot of this enforced cause —		5.02. 30
to feast upon whole thousands of the french.		5.02.178
with me, | upon the altar at saint edmundsbury,		5.04. 18
i will upon all hazards well believe | thou art		5.06. 7
death, having prey'd upon the outward parts,		5.07. 15
you are born | to set a form upon that indigest		5.07. 26
drawn with a pen | upon a parchment, and against		5.07. 33
of my pow'r, | as i upon advantage did remove,		5.07. 62
spar'd, | shall wait upon your father's funeral.		5.07. 98
speak | my body shall make good upon this earth,	R2	1.01. 37
upon his bad life to make all this good, | that		1.01. 99
in my debt, | upon remainder of a dear account,		1.01.130
my gage | upon this overweening traitor's foot,		1.01.147
despite of death that lives upon my grave, | to		1.01.168
it, | at coventry upon saint lambert's day.		1.01.199
you, cousin herford, upon pain of life, | till		1.03.140
breathe i against thee, upon pain of life.		1.03.153
i am too old to fawn upon a nurse, | too far in		1.03.170
nor never look upon each other's face, | nor		1.03.185
thy son is banish'd upon good advice, | whereto		1.03.233
consuming means, soon preys upon itself.		2.01. 39
the pleasure that some fathers feed upon | is my		2.01. 79
but basely yielded upon compromise | that which		2.01.253
we see the wind sit sore upon our sails, | and		2.01.265
which rightly gaz'd upon | show nothing but		2.02. 18
looking awry upon your lord's departure, | find		2.02. 21
march | so many miles upon her peaceful bosom,		2.03. 93
it stands your grace upon to do him right.		2.03.138
thy friends are fled to wait upon thy foes,		2.04. 23
whilst you have fed upon my signories,		3.01. 22
for joy | to stand upon my kingdom once again.		3.02. 5
throw death upon thy sovereign's enemies.		3.02. 22
side, | for time hath set a blot upon my pride.		3.02. 81
make war upon their spotted souls for this!		3.02.134
for god's sake let us sit upon the ground | and		3.02.155
southern gentlemen in arms | upon his party.		3.02.203
with some few private friends upon this coast.		3.03. 4
we march | upon the grassy carpet of this plain.		3.03. 50
that every stride he makes upon my land | is		3.03. 92
so with civil and uncivil arms | be rush'd upon!		3.03.103
that stands upon your royal grandsire's bones,		3.03.106
i live, | and buried once, why not upon my head?		3.03.159
as thus to drop them still upon one place,		3.03.166
cousin, stand forth, and look upon that man.		4.01. 7
and spit upon him whilst i say he lies, | and		4.01. 75
prove | that ever fell upon this cursed earth.		4.01.147
mounted upon a hot and fiery steed, | which his		5.02. 8
darted their desiring eyes | upon his visage,		5.02. 15
but dust was thrown upon his sacred head,		5.02. 30
mount thee upon his horse, | spur post, and get		5.02.111
for ever will i walk upon my knees, | and never		5.03. 93
look upon his face:		5.03.100
clamorous groans, which strike upon my heart,		5.05. 56
to look upon my sometimes royal master's face.		5.05. 75
hand | upon my head and all this famous land.		5.06. 36
upon whose dead corpse' there was such misuse,	1H4	1.01. 43
supper, and sleeping upon benches after noon,		1.02. 4 P
thou hast done much harm upon me, hal, god		1.02. 92 P
will they adventure upon the exploit themselves,		1.02.172 P
have no sooner achiev'd but we'll set upon them.		1.02.173 P
for accordingly | you tread upon my patience;		1.03. 4
breathless and faint, leaning upon my sword,		1.03. 32
upon agreement, of swift severn's flood, | who		1.03.103
did set forth | upon his irish expedition;		1.03.150
the crown | upon the head of this forgetful man,		1.03.161
but out upon this half–fac'd fellowship!		1.03.208
a plague upon it, it is in gloucestershire —		1.03.243
i smell it. upon my life, it will do well.		1.03.277
a plague upon you both!		2.02. 20 P
a plague upon it when thieves cannot be true one		2.02. 27 P
a plague upon you all!		2.02. 29 P
why dost thou bend thine eyes upon the earth,		2.03. 42
that beads of sweat have stood upon thy brow,		2.03. 58
they take it already upon their salvation, that		2.04. 9 P
i'll be sworn upon all the books in england, i		2.04. 49 P
and says to his wife, "fie upon this quiet life!		2.04.104 P
be not forgot upon the face of the earth, then		2.04.129 P
a plague upon such backing!		2.04.151 P
a hundred upon poor four of us.		2.04.162 P
we four set upon some dozen —		2.04.174 P
some six or seven fresh men set upon us —		2.04.181 P
not two or three and fifty upon poor old jack,		2.04.187 P
what, upon compulsion?		2.04.236 P
i would give no man a reason upon compulsion, i.		2.04.240 P
should i turn upon the true prince?		2.04.269 P
you are lions too, you ran away upon instinct,		2.04.300 P
his true liegeman upon the cross of a welsh hook		2.04.338 P
yes, jack, upon instinct.		2.04.355 P
i grant ye, upon instinct.		2.04.356 P
father and examine me upon the particulars of my		2.04.377 P
the devil rides upon a fiddlestick.		2.04.487 P
and uncle worcester — a plague upon it!		3.01. 5
shed | upon the parting of your wives and you.		3.01. 94
a stain | upon the beauty of all parts besides,		3.01.186
one that no persuasion can do good upon.		3.01.197
down, | and rest your gentle head upon her lap,		3.01.212
thy face but i think upon hell–fire and dives		3.03. 31 P
look upon his face;		3.03. 77 P
no man so potent breathes upon the ground | but		4.01. 11
we may boldly spend upon the hope of what | /is		4.01. 54
look big | upon the maidenhead of our affairs.		4.01. 59
whence | the eye of reason may pry in upon us.		4.01. 72
was poor, | upon the naked shore at ravenspurgh,		4.03. 77
cries out upon abuses, seems to weep | over his		4.03. 81
that you and i should meet upon such terms | as		5.01. 10
love | that are misled upon your cousin's part,		5.01.105
all his offenses live upon my head | and on his		5.02. 20
o, would the quarrel lay upon our heads, | and		5.02. 47
too long | if life did ride upon a dial's point,		5.02. 83
what honor dost thou seek | upon my head?		5.03. 3
thus, | i never had triumph'd upon a scot.		5.03. 15
shot here, here's no scoring but upon the pate.		5.03. 31 P
or is it fantasy that plays upon our eyesight?		5.04.135
reward valor bear the sin upon their own heads.		5.04.150 P
i'll take it upon my death, i gave him this		5.04.151 P
three knights upon our party slain to–day, | a		5.05. 6
other offenders we will pause upon.		5.05. 15
and all his men | upon the foot of fear, fled		5.05. 20
his valors shown upon our crests to–day | have		5.05. 29
upon my tongues continual slanders ride, | the	2H4	in 6
wav'ring multitude, | can play upon it.		in 20
upon mine honor, for a silken point | i'll give		1.01. 53
the horse he rode on, and, upon my life, | spoke		1.01. 58
upon enforcement flies with greatest speed, | so		1.01.120
to frown upon th' enrag'd northumberland!		1.01.152
gentleman in hand, and then stand upon security!		1.02. 37 P
taking up, then they must stand upon security.		1.02. 41 P
but i hope he that looks upon me will take me		1.02.166 P
can peep out his head but i am thrust upon it.		1.02.213 P
upon the power and puissance of the king.		1.03. 9
our present musters grow upon the file | to five		1.03. 10
you, he's an infinitive thing upon my score.		2.01. 24 P
him, fellow, wherefore hang'st thou upon him?		2.01. 68
didst swear to me upon a parcel–gilt goblet,		2.01. 86 P
a sea–coal fire, upon wednesday in wheeson week,		2.01. 88 P
practic'd upon the easy–yielding spirit of this		2.01.114 P
being upon hasty employment in the king's		2.01.127 P
i must wait upon my good lord here, i thank you,		2.01.184 P
very hardly, upon such a subject.		2.02. 44 P
says he, that takes upon him not to conceive.		2.02.114 P
shall we steal upon them, ned, at supper?		2.02.158 P
and wait upon him at his table as drawers.		2.02.172 P
it stuck upon him as the sun | in the grey vault		2.03. 18
to rain upon remembrance with mine eyes, | that		2.03. 59
to venture upon the charg'd chambers bravely —		2.04. 51 P
cup of sack, do you discharge upon mine hostess.		2.04.112 P
i will discharge upon her, sir john, with two		2.04.114 P
for taking their names upon you before you have		2.04.143 P
he lives upon mouldy stew'd pruins and dried		2.04.146 P
with the boys, and jumps upon join'd–stools, and		2.04.247 P
there is another indictment upon thee, for		2.04.343 P
to melt | and drop upon our bare unarmed heads.		2.04.365
cribs, | upon uneasy pallets stretching thee,		3.01. 10
wilt thou upon the high and giddy /mast | seal		3.01. 18
which should not find a ground to root upon		3.01. 91
upon my soul, my lord, | the powers that you		3.01. 99
for /'s apparel is built upon his back, and the		3.02.144 P
his back, and the whole frame stands upon pins.		3.02.144 P
in the king's affairs upon his coronation–day,		3.02.182 P
head fantastically carv'd upon it with a knife.		3.02.311 P
upon or near the rate of thirty thousand.		4.01. 22
lay a heavy and unequal hand | upon our honors?		4.01.101
upon mine honor, all too confident | to give		4.01.150
of what conditions we shall stand upon?		4.01.163
peace | upon such large terms and so absolute		4.01.184
absolute | as our conditions shall consist upon,		4.01.185
with speed redress'd, | upon my soul they shall.		4.02. 60
and rotten times that you shall look upon,		4.04. 60
most immodest word | be look'd upon and learnt,		4.04. 71
set me the crown upon my pillow here.		4.05. 5
he alt'red much upon the hearing it.		4.05. 13
why doth the crown lie there upon his pillow,		4.05. 21
depending | hath fed upon the body of my father;		4.05.159
well | how troublesome it sate upon my head.		4.05.186
falls upon thee in a more fairer sort;		4.05.200
upon thy sight | my worldly business makes a		4.05.229
which cannot look more hideously upon me | than		5.02. 12
than a joint burden laid upon us all.		5.02. 55
forget | so great indignities you laid upon me?		5.02. 69
i will leer upon him as 'a comes by, and do but		5.05. 6 P
or rather swaying more upon our part | than	H5	1.01. 73
upon our spiritual convocation | and in regard		1.01. 76
the french embassador upon that instant | crav'd		1.01. 91
i'll wait upon you, and i long to hear it.		1.01. 98
the sin upon my head, dread sovereign!		1.02. 97
you are their heir, you sit upon their throne;		1.02.117
who will make road upon us | with all advantages		1.02.138
make boot upon the summer's velvet buds, | which		1.02.194
and all things thought upon | that may with		1.02.305
as dogs upon their masters, worrying you.		2.02. 83
was | that wrought upon thee so preposterously		2.02.112
with flowers, and smile upon his finger's end, i		2.03. 15 P
'a saw a flea stick upon bardolph's nose, and 'a		2.03. 41 P
thus comes the english with full power upon us,		2.04. 1
fatal and neglected english | upon our fields.		2.04. 14
the kindred of him hath been flesh'd upon us;		2.04. 50
upon the hempen tackle ship–boys climbing;		3.pr. 8
but think | you stand upon the rivage and behold		3.pr. 14
in the slips, | /straining upon the start.		3.01. 32
and upon this charge | cry, "god for harry,		3.01. 33
upon my particular knowledge of his directions.		3.02. 78 P
upon th' enraged soldiers in their spoil, | as		3.03. 25
your naked infants spitted upon pikes, | whiles		3.03. 38
on, and sickness growing | upon our soldiers, we		3.03. 56
like roping icicles | upon our houses' thatch,		3.05. 24
snow | upon the valleys whose low vassal seat		3.05. 51
the alps doth spit and void his rheum upon.		3.05. 52

go down upon him, you have power enough, | and 3.05. 53
that stands upon the rolling restless stone — 3.06. 29
look you, is fixed upon a spherical stone, which 3.06. 35 P
now we speak upon our cue, and our voice is 3.06.123 P
i thought upon one pair of english legs | did 3.06.149
i hope they will not come upon us now. 3.06.168
tent to–night, are those stars or suns upon it? 3.07. 70 P
upon his royal face there is no note | how dread 4.pr. 35
men to love their present pains | upon example; 4.01. 19
his leek about his pate | upon saint davy's day. 4.01. 55
even as men wrack'd upon a sand, that look to be 4.01. 97 P
some upon their wives left poor behind them, 4.01.139 P
poor behind them, some upon the debts they owe, 4.01.140 P
they owe, some upon their children rawly left. 4.01.140 P
merchandise do sinfully miscarry upon the sea, 4.01.148 P
should be impos'd upon his father that sent him; 4.01.150 P
man that dies ill, the ill upon his own head, 4.01.187 P
upon the king! 4.01.230
that beats upon the high shore of this world — 4.01.265
think not upon the fault | my father made in 4.01.293
though we upon this mountain's basis by | took 4.02. 30
gold, | nor care i who doth feed upon my cost; 4.03. 25
that fought with us upon saint crispin's day. 4.03. 67
upon the which, i trust, | shall witness live in 4.03. 96
he gives you, upon his knees, a thousand thanks, 4.04. 59 P
throngs, | if any order might be thought upon. 4.05. 21
gashes | that bloodily did yawn upon his face. 4.06. 14
upon these words i came and cheer'd him up. 4.06. 20
no scorn to wear the leek upon saint tavy's day. 4.07.103 P
his black shoe trod upon god's ground and his 4.07.142 P
seen, | heave him away upon your winged thoughts 5.pr. 8
even now | you may imagine him upon blackheath; 5.pr. 16
tradition, /begun upon an honorable respect, and 5.01. 71 P
and rank femetary | doth root upon, while that 5.02. 46
which i am sure will hang upon my tongue like a 5.02.179 P
now fie upon my false french! 5.02.220 P
of beauty, can do no more spoil upon my face. 5.02.231 P
upon that i kiss your hand, and i call you my 5.02.251 P
upon a wooden coffin we attend, | and death's 1H6 1.01. 19
french | was round encompassed, and set upon. 1.01.114
late did he shine upon the english side; 1.02. 3
now we are victors, upon us he smiles. 1.02. 4
food, | do rush upon us as their hungry prey. 1.02. 28
she takes upon her bravely at first dash. 1.02. 71
hence, | then will i think upon a recompense. 1.02.116
or dagger, henceforward, upon pain of death. 1.03. 79 P
when others sleep upon their quiet beds, 2.01. 6
upon the which, that every one may read, | shall 2.02. 14
and stands upon the honor of his birth, | if he 2.04. 28
till you conclude that he upon whose side | the 2.04. 40
pole, | will i upon thy party wear this rose. 2.04.123
this day, in argument upon a case, | some words 2.05. 45
out of hand, | and set upon our boasting enemy. 3.02.103
and made me almost yield upon my knees. 3.03. 80
lord bishop, set the crown upon his head. 4.01. 1
"i have, upon especial cause, | mov'd with 4.01. 55
of such as your oppression feeds upon, 4.01. 58
conceit | to set a gloss upon his bold intent, 4.01.103
o, think upon the conquest of my father, | my 4.01.148
but if you frown upon this proffer'd peace, 4.02. 9
upon no christian soul but english talbot. 4.02. 30
a plague upon that villain somerset, | that thus 4.03. 9
and york as fast upon your grace exclaims, 4.04. 30
upon my death the french can little boast; 4.05. 24
upon my blessing i command thee go. 4.05. 36
i will attend upon your lordship's leisure. 5.01. 55
as plays the sun upon the glassy streams, 5.03. 62
hand, | and set a precious crown upon thy head, 5.03.119
upon thy princely warrant, i descend | to give 5.03.143
upon condition i may quietly | enjoy mine own, 5.03.153
place barrels of pitch upon the fatal stake, 5.04. 57
beams | upon the country where you make abode; 5.04. 88
upon condition thou wilt swear | to pay him 5.04.129
stand'st thou aloof upon comparison? 5.04.150
and humbly now upon my bended knee, | in sight 2H6 1.01. 10
fist, | nor wear the diadem upon his head, 1.01.246
and smooth my way upon their headless necks; 1.02. 65
it is enough, i'll think upon the questions. 1.02. 82
and set the triple crown upon his head — | that 1.03. 63
in execution | upon offenders hath exceeded law, 1.03.133
he did vow upon his knees he would be even with 1.03.199 P
o lord, have mercy upon me! 1.03.215 P
safer shall he be upon the sandy plains | than 1.04. 36
lay hands upon these traitors and their trash. 1.04. 41
a pretty plot, well chosen to build upon! 1.04. 56
safer shall he be upon the sandy plains | than 1.04. 68
as it were, upon my man's instigation, to prove 2.03. 85 P
trowest thou that e'er i'll look upon the world, 2.04. 38
to think upon my pomp shall be my hell. 2.04. 41
no, it will hang upon my richest robes, | and 2.04.108
look, | immediately he was upon his knee, | that 3.01. 11
upon my life, began her devilish practices; 3.01. 46
the envious load that lies upon his heart; 3.01.157
i know no pain they can inflict upon him | will 3.01.377
upon thy eyeballs murderous tyranny | sits in 3.02. 49
look not upon me, for thine eyes are wounding. 3.02. 51
was i for this nigh wrack'd upon the sea, | and 3.02. 82
shore, | or turn our stern upon a dreadful rock? 3.02. 91
back, | i stood upon the hatches in the storm; 3.02.103
and comment then upon his sudden death. 3.02.133
to drain | upon his face an ocean of salt tears, 3.02.143
that dread king that took our state upon him, 3.02.154
laid | upon the life of this thrice–famed duke. 3.02.157
of bury, | set all upon me, mighty sovereign. 3.02.241
and threefold vengeance tend upon your steps! 3.02.304
a plague upon them! 3.02.309
and turns the force of them upon thyself. 3.02.332
that thou mightst think upon these by the seal, 3.02.344
i'll give a thousand pound to look upon him. 3.03. 13
look with a gentle eye upon this wretch! 3.03. 20
god, to shoot forth thunder | upon these paltry, 4.01.105
and sooner dance upon a bloody pole | than stand 4.01.127
and turn it, and set a new nap upon it. 4.02. 6 P
and here, sitting upon london stone, i charge 4.06. 2 P
i have thought upon it, it shall be so. 4.07. 13 P
head, and bring them both upon two poles hither. 4.07.112 P
and take up commodities upon our bills? 4.07.127 P
and so god's curse light upon you all! 4.08. 32 P
leaving thy trunk for crows to feed upon. 4.10. 84
upon thine honor, is he prisoner? 5.01. 42
upon mine honor, he is prisoner. 5.01. 43
and that i'll write upon thy burgonet, | might i 5.01.200
bear, | so bear i thee upon my manly shoulders; 5.02. 63
and seiz'd upon their towns and provinces. 3H6 1.01.109
to my blade | shall rust upon my weapon, till 1.03. 51
forth | a bird that will revenge upon you all; 1.04. 36
so triumph thieves upon their conquer'd booty, 1.04. 63
come make him stand upon this molehill here 1.04. 67
trull | upon their woes whom fortune captivates! 1.04.115
upon my soul, the hearers will shed tears; 1.04.161
my soul to heaven, my blood upon your heads! 1.04.168
think but upon the wrong he did us all, | and 1.04.173
i bear | upon my target three fair shining suns. 2.01. 40
sweet duke of york, our prop to lean upon, | now 2.01. 68
upon our foes, | but never once again turn back 2.01.184
not he that sets his foot upon her back. 2.02. 16
for grace, | and set thy diadem upon my head, 2.02. 82
of my big–swoll'n heart | upon that clifford, 2.02.112
that clifford's manhood lies upon his tongue. 2.02.125
if thou deny, their blood upon thy head, | for 2.02.129
and look upon, as if the tragedy | were play'd 2.03. 27
brother | to execute the like upon thyself — 2.04. 10
to sit upon a hill, as i do now, | to carve out 2.05. 23
the windy tempest of my heart | upon thy wounds, 2.05. 87
let's seize upon him. 3.01. 23
why linger we? let us lay hands upon him. 3.01. 26
like one that stands upon a promontory | and 3.02.135
i'll make my heaven to dream upon the crown, 3.02.168
now, warwick, tell me, even upon thy conscience, 3.03.113
my love, forbear to fawn upon their frowns. 4.01. 75
and when the lion fawns upon the lamb, | the 4.08. 49
so other foes may set upon our backs. 5.01. 61
and, richard, do not frown upon my faults, | for 5.01.101
i seal upon the lips of this sweet babe. 5.07. 29
and all the clouds that low'r'd upon our house R3 1.01. 3
this armed guard | that waits upon your grace? 1.01. 43
upon what cause? 1.01. 46
'tis very grievous to be thought upon. 1.01.141
and spurn upon thee, beggar, for thy boldness. 1.02. 42
that didst unworthy slaughter upon others. 1.02. 88
that laid their guilt upon my guiltless 1.02. 98
his better doth not breathe upon the earth. 1.02.140
stroke, | and humbly beg the death upon my knee. 1.02.178
upon my life, she finds (although i cannot) 1.02.253
a plague upon you all! 1.03. 58
against thee, are all fall'n upon thee; 1.03.179
exceeding those that i can wish upon thee, | o, 1.03.217
foul shame upon you, you have all mov'd mine. 1.03.248
we wait upon your grace. 1.03.322
well thought upon, i have it here about me. 1.03.343
my cabin tempted me to walk | upon the hatches. 1.04. 13
along | upon the giddy footing of the hatches, 1.04. 17
a thousand men that fishes gnaw'd upon; 1.04. 25
death | to gaze upon these secrets of the deep? 1.04. 35
what we will do, we do upon command. 1.04.193
to hurl upon their heads that break his law. 1.04.200
protest, | upon my part shall be inviolable. 2.01. 27
buckingham doth turn his hate | upon your grace, 2.01. 33
we wait upon your grace. 2.01.141
to jut | upon the innocent and aweless throne. 2.04. 52
make war upon themselves, brother to brother, 2.04. 62
is it upon record, or else reported 3.01. 72
upon record, my gracious lord. 3.01. 74
thou know'st our reasons urg'd upon the way; 3.01.160
upon the stroke of four. 3.02. 5
forward | upon his party for the gain thereof; 3.02. 47
hate, | i live to look upon their tragedy. 3.02. 59
for they account his head upon the bridge. 3.02. 70
i'll wait upon your lordship. 3.02.112
i'll wait upon your lordship. 3.02.123
now margaret's curse is fall'n upon our heads, 3.03. 15
had you not come upon your cue, my lord, 3.04. 26
upon my body with their hellish charms? 3.04. 62
and started when he look'd upon the tower, | as 3.04. 85
thee | that ever wretched age hath look'd upon. 3.04.105
that breath'd upon the earth a christian; 3.05. 26
i guess, | upon the like devotion as yourselves, 4.01. 9
for it stands me much upon | to stop all hopes 4.02. 58
are they that i would have thee deal upon: 4.02. 74
mine issue of your blood upon your daughter. 4.04.298
then tell me, what makes he upon the seas? 4.04.473
are they not now upon the western shore, 4.04.481
him, they came from buckingham | upon his party. 4.04.526
which they upon the adverse faction want. 5.03. 13
upon my life, my lord, i'll undertake it, | and 5.03. 42
let us consult upon to–morrow's business. 5.03. 45
so long sund'red friends should dwell upon. 5.03.100
think upon grey, and let thy soul despair! 5.03.141
think upon vaughan, and with guilty fear | let 5.03.142
what, myself upon myself? 5.03.186
upon the stroke of four. 5.03.235
enforcement of the time | forbids to dwell upon, 5.03.239
god and our good cause fight upon our side; 5.03.240
the sky doth frown and low'r upon our army. 5.03.283
heaven | that frowns on me looks sadly upon him. 5.03.287
advance our standards, set upon our foes. 5.03.348
upon them! 5.03.351
slave, i have set my life upon a cast, | and i 5.04. 9
smile heaven upon this fair conjunction, | that 5.05. 20
that long have frown'd upon their enmity! 5.05. 21
i'll say | a man may weep upon his wedding–day. H8 pr 32
did almost sweat to bear | the pride upon them, 1.01. 25
nor call'd upon | for high feats done to th' 1.01. 60
upon this french going out, took he upon him 1.01. 73
upon this french going out, took he upon him 1.01. 73
a charge as little honor | he meant to lay upon; 1.01. 78
lo you, my lord, | the net has fall'n upon me! 1.01.203
for, upon these taxations, | the clothiers all, 1.02. 30
by oath he menac'd | revenge upon the cardinal. 1.02.138
he his title to the crown | upon our fail? 1.02.145
the part my father meant to act upon | th' 1.02.195
that's clapp'd upon the court gate. 1.03. 18
of beauty | shall shine at full upon them. 1.04. 60
and so his peers upon this evidence | have found 2.01. 26
't has done, upon the premises, but justice; 2.01. 63
hour | of my long weary life is come upon me. 2.01.133
that so long have slept upon | this bold bad man 2.02. 42
these sad thoughts that work too much upon him. 2.02. 57
so much the more | must pity drop upon her. 2.03. 18
fie, fie, fie upon | this compell'd fortune! 2.03. 86
let the foul'st contempt | shut door upon me, 2.04. 43
more | upon this business my appearance make 2.04.133
yea, upon mine honor, | i free you from't. 2.04.157
out upon ye! 3.01. 99
upon my soul, two reverend cardinal virtues; 3.01.103
once | the burthen of my sorrows fall upon ye. 3.01.111
woe upon ye | and all such false professors! 3.01.114
or felt the flatteries that grow upon it! 3.01.144
shipwrack'd upon a kingdom, where no pity, | no 3.01.149
we, good lady, | upon what cause, wrong you? 3.01.156
stops on a sudden, looks upon the ground, | then 3.02.114
time | to think upon the part of business which 3.02.145
and with his deed did crown | his word upon you. 3.02.156
havings, to bestow | my bounties upon you. 3.02.160
for your great graces | heap'd upon me, poor 3.02.175
upon the daring huntsman that has gall'd him; 3.02.207
else | this talking lord can lay upon my credit, 3.02.265
and bears his blushing honors thick upon him; 3.02.354
the noble troops that waited | upon my smiles. 3.02.412
his overthrow heap'd happiness upon him; 4.02. 64
bright faces | cast thousand beams upon me, like 4.02. 89
would have some pity | upon my wretched women, 4.02.140
whiles here he liv'd | upon this naughty earth? 5.01.138
along, | how earnestly he cast his eyes upon me! 5.02. 12
lay all the weight ye can upon my patience, | i 5.02.101
stone a–rolling, | 'twould fall upon ourselves. 5.02.140
that rail'd upon me till her pink'd porringer 5.03. 48 P
to make parents happy | may hourly fall upon ye! 5.04. 8
upon this land a thousand thousand blessings, 5.04. 19
i cannot fight upon this argument; TRO 1.01. 92
and she takes upon her to spy a white hair on 1.02.139 P
look well upon him, niece. 1.02.232 P
upon my back, to defend my belly, upon my wit, 1.02.260 P
to defend my belly, upon my wit, to defend my 1.02.260 P
to defend my wiles, upon my secrecy, to defend 1.02.261 P
boats dare sail | upon her /patient breast, 1.03. 36
troy, yet upon his bases, had been down, | and 1.03. 75
grecian tents do stand | hollow upon this plain, 1.03. 80
him patroclus | upon a lazy bed the livelong day 1.03.147
the plague of greece upon thee, thou mongrel 2.01. 12 P
nay, look upon him. 2.01. 59 P
but yet you look not well upon him, for, 2.01. 63 P
tenor of the proclamation, and he rails upon me. 2.01. 91 P
we turn not back the silks upon the merchant, 2.02. 69
upon our joint and several dignities. 2.02.193
as smiles upon the forehead of this action | for 2.02.205
but it is no matter, thyself upon thyself! 2.03. 27 P
draw emulous factions and bleed to death upon. 2.03. 74 P
and this noble state | to call upon him. 2.03.110
why will he not upon our fair request | untent 2.03.167
not for the worth that hangs upon our quarrel. 2.03.207
you depend upon him, i mean. 3.01. 4 P
sir, i do depend upon the lord. 3.01. 5 P
you depend upon a notable gentleman; 3.01. 6 P
i will make a complimental assault upon him, for 3.01. 40 P
if you do, our melancholy upon your head! 3.01. 69 P
like to a strange soul upon the stygian banks 3.02. 9
all, | lay negligent and loose regard upon him. 3.03. 41
as when his virtues, aiming upon others, | heat 3.03.100
an act that very chance doth throw upon him — 3.03.131
a plague upon antenor! 4.02. 76 P
a plague upon antenor! 4.02. 87 P
to this valiant greek | comes fast upon. 4.03. 3
fie, fie upon her! 4.05. 54
aeneas | consent upon the order of their fight, 4.05. 90
hector would have them fall upon him thus. 4.05.137
thy hand upon that match. 4.05.270
who neither looks upon the heaven nor earth, 4.05.281
you look upon that sleeve, behold it well. 5.02. 69
the venom'd vengeance ride upon our swords, 5.03. 47
lay hold upon him, priam, hold him fast, | he is 5.03. 59
you, | upon the love you bear me, get you in. 5.03. 78
his beam, | upon the pashed corses of the kings 5.05. 10
he is my prize, i will not look upon. 5.06. 10
a retire upon our grecian part. 5.08. 15
sit, gods, upon your thrones, and smile at troy! 5.10. 7
thus proudly /pight upon our phrygian plains, 5.10. 24
general food at first | which you do live upon; COR 1.01.132
no, | than is the coal of fire upon the ice, 1.01.173
upon your favors swims with fins of lead, | and 1.01.180
it will in time | win upon power, and throw 1.01.220
by th' ears, and he | upon my party, i'd revolt, 1.01.234
martius, | attend upon cominius to these wars. 1.01.237
i'll lean upon one crutch, and fight with t' 1.01.242
singularity, he goes | upon this present action. 1.01.279
head below his knee, | and tread upon his neck. 1.03. 47
and hear a drum than look upon his schoolmaster. 1.03. 56 P
i look'd upon him a' we'nsday half an hour 1.03. 58 P
who upon the sudden | clapp'd to their gates. 1.04. 50
and shut your gates upon 's. 1.07. 6
i have some wounds upon me, and they smart | to 1.09. 28
and stand upon my common part with those | that 1.09. 39
the blood upon your visage dries, 'tis time | it 1.09. 93
were it | at home, upon my brother's guard, even 1.10. 25
hasty and tinder–like upon too trivial motion; 2.01. 51 P
last expedition, twenty–five wounds upon him. 2.01.154 P
i doubt not but | our rome will cast upon thee. 2.01.202
but they | upon their ancient malice will forget 2.01.228
and handkerchers, | upon him as he pass'd; 2.01.265
know not why, they hate upon no better a ground. 2.02. 11 P
we are convented | upon a pleasing treaty, and 2.02. 55
and look'd upon things precious as they were 2.02.125
you must desire them | to think upon you. 2.03. 56
think upon me? 2.03. 56
summon'd | to meet anon, upon your approbation. 2.03.144
nature | would think upon you for your voices, 2.03.188
thinking upon his services, took from you | th' 2.03.223
shall prompt them, to make road | upon 's again. 3.01. 6
that of all things upon the earth he hated 3.01. 14
upon the part o' th' people, in whose power | we 3.01.209
lay hands upon him, | and bear him to the rock. 3.01.221
come, try upon yourselves what you have seen me. 3.01.224
lay hands upon him. 3.01.226
for 'tis a sore upon us | you cannot tent 3.01.234

than spend a fawn upon 'em | for the inheritance 3.02. 67
as i hear, more strong | than are upon you yet. 3.02.141
for such faults | as shall be prov'd upon you? 3.03. 47
think | upon the wounds his body bears, which 3.03. 50
can show /for rome | her enemies' marks upon me. 3.03.111
thou hast years upon thee, and thou art too full 4.01. 45
i sup upon myself, | and so shall starve with 4.02. 50
and hope to come upon them in the heat of their 4.03. 18 P
/hate i, and my love's upon | this enemy town. 4.04. 23
rages | upon our territories, and have already 4.06. 77
and | to melt the city leads upon your pates, 4.06. 82
stood so much | upon the voice of occupation and 4.06. 97
you have brought | a trembling upon rome, such 4.06.119
and not a hair upon a soldier's head | which 4.06.133
and then | we pout upon the morning, are unapt 5.01. 52
to my request, | and then i'll set upon him. 5.01. 58
like to a bowl upon a subtle ground, | i have 5.02. 20
and swound for what's to come upon thee. 5.02. 67 P
turn the dregs of it upon this varlet here — 5.02. 77 P
the blame | may hang upon your hardness, 5.03. 91
throats are sentenc'd, and stay upon execution. 5.04. 8 P
which my sinews shall be stretch'd upon him — 5.06. 44
who wears my stripes impress'd upon him, that 5.06.107
tread not upon him. 5.06.133
and with our swords, upon a pile of wood, TIT 1.01.128
revenge | upon the thracian tyrant in his tent 1.01.138
to quit the bloody wrongs upon her foes. 1.01.141
i am not bid to wait upon this bride. 1.01.338
even thou hast strook upon my crest, | and with 1.01.364
the greeks upon advice did bury ajax | that slew 1.01.379
too, | upon a just survey take titus' part, 1.01.446
upon her wit doth earthly honor wait, | and 2.01. 10
and gold, | to wait upon this new-made empress. 2.01. 20
and that my sword upon thee shall approve, | and 2.01. 35
dangerous | it is to jet upon a prince's right? 2.01. 64
should drive upon thy new-transformed limbs, 2.03. 64
this minion stood upon her chastity, | upon her 2.03.124
upon her nuptial vow, her loyalty, | and with 2.03.125
upon whose leaves are drops of new-shed blood 2.03.200
upon his bloody finger he doth wear | a precious 2.03.226
doth shine upon the dead man's earthy cheeks, 2.03.229
upon the north side of this pleasant chase; 2.03.255
emperor, upon my feeble knee | i beg this boon, 2.03.288
death, | that end upon them should be executed. 2.03.303
hands | tremble like aspen leaves upon a lute, 2.04. 45
in summer's drought i'll drop upon thee still, 3.01. 19
faint-hearted boy, arise and look upon her. 3.01. 65
for now i stand as one upon a rock, | environ'd 3.01. 93
upon a gath'red lily almost withered. 3.01.113
that woe is me to think upon thy woes, | more 3.01.239
an enemy, | and would usurp upon my wat'ry eyes, 3.01.268
there is enough written upon this earth | to 4.01. 84
mortal revenge upon these traitorous goths, 4.01. 93
than foemen's marks upon his batt'red shield, 4.01.127
got, | he dies upon my scimitar's sharp point, 4.02. 91
i blush to think upon this ignomy. 4.02.115
look how the black slave smiles upon the father, 4.02.120
i stray'd | to gaze upon a ruinous monastery, 5.01. 21
did fix mine eye | upon the wasted building, 5.01. 23
with this, my weapon drawn, i rush'd upon him, 5.01. 37
near | to shed obsequious tears upon this trunk. 5.03.152
these sorrowful drops upon thy blood/-stain'd 5.03.154
turn thee, benvolio, look upon thy death. ROM 1.01. 67
of all the days of the year, upon that day; 1.03. 25
"yea," quoth he, "dost thou fall upon thy face? 1.03. 41
and yet i warrant it had upon it brow | a bump 1.03. 52
"yea," quoth my husband, "fall'st upon thy face? 1.03. 55
i was your mother much upon these years | that 1.03. 72
it seems she hangs upon the cheek of night | as 1.05. 45
see how she leans her cheek upon her hand! 2.02. 23
o that i were a glove upon that hand, | that i 2.02. 24
clouds, | and sails upon the bosom of the air. 2.02. 32
it is my soul that calls upon my name. 2.02.164
sleep dwell upon thine eyes, peace in thy breast 2.02.186
lo here upon thy cheek the stain doth sit | of 2.03. 75
hand of the dial is now upon the prick of noon. 2.04.113 P
out upon you, what a man are you! 2.04.114 P
now is the sun upon the highmost hill | of this 2.05. 9
so smile the heavens upon this holy act, | that 2.06. 1
of a tavern, claps me his sword upon the table, 3.01. 7 P
for thou wilt lie upon the wings of night, 3.02. 18
whiter than new snow upon a raven's back. 3.02. 19
upon his brow shame is asham'd to sit; 3.02. 92
and smilest upon the stroke that murders me. 3.03. 23
and fall upon the ground, as i do now, | taking 3.03. 69
/lives, | by doing damned hate upon thyself? 3.03.118
a pack of blessings light upon thy back, 3.03.141
it, | that romeo should, upon receipt thereof, 3.05. 98
upon his body that hath slaughter'd him! 3.05.102
stratagems | upon so soft a subject as myself! 3.05.210
to move the heavens to smile upon my state, 4.03. 4
that did spit his body | upon a rapier's point. 4.03. 57
upon the sweetest flower of all the field. 4.05. 29
the heavens do low'r upon you for some ill; 4.05. 94
contempt and beggary hangs upon thy back; 5.01. 71
so shall no foot upon the churchyard tread, 5.03. 5
upon thy life i charge thee, | what e'er thou 5.03. 25
fly hence and leave me, think upon these gone, 5.03. 60
thee, youth, | put not another sin upon my head, 5.03. 62
breath, | hath had no power yet upon thy beauty: 5.03. 93
bliss be upon you! 5.03.124
fear comes upon me. 5.03.135
with instruments upon them, fit to open | these 5.03.200
see what a scourge is laid upon your hate, 5.03.292
upon the heels of my presentment, sir. TIM 1.01. 27
upon his good and gracious nature hanging, 1.01. 56
i have upon a high and pleasant hill | feign'd 1.01. 63
those men | upon whose age we void it up again 1.02.138
before me now | would one day stamp upon me. 1.02.144
there would be none left to rail upon thee, and 1.02.239 P
awak'd by great occasion | to call upon his own, 2.02. 22
lords, keep on, | i'll wait upon you instantly. 2.02. 35
a plague upon him, dog! 2.02. 49 P
especially upon bare friendship without security 3.01. 42 P
upon my soul, 'tis true, sir. 3.02. 43
drinks | but timon's silver treads upon his lip, 3.02. 71
must i take th' cure upon me? 3.03. 12
then they could smile, and fawn upon his debts, 3.04. 51
tear me, take me, and the gods fall upon you! 3.04. 99
fortune to lie heavy | upon a friend of mine, 3.05. 11
and set quarrelling | upon the head of valor; 3.05. 28
all | my honor to you, upon his good returns. 3.05. 81
and let out | their coin upon large interest — 3.05.107
upon that were my thoughts tiring when we 3.06. 4 P
i pray you, upon what? 3.06. 57 P
meat cool ere we can agree upon the first place; 3.06. 68 P
i feel't upon my bones. 3.06.119
let me look back upon thee. 4.01. 1
but for thy sword and fortune, trod upon them — 4.03. 96
or dost thou not, heaven's curse upon thee! 4.03.132
paint till a horse may mire upon your face: 4.03.148
that numberless upon me stuck as leaves | do on 4.03.263
to me, thou mightst have hit upon it here. 4.03.347 P
the plague of company light upon thee! 4.03.352 P
would thou wert clean enough to spit upon! 4.03.359
let us make the assay upon him. 4.03.403 P
what vilder thing upon the earth than friends, 4.03.463
second masters, | upon their first lord's neck. 4.03.506
upon the beached verge of the salt flood, | who 5.01.216
dead, | entomb'd upon the very hem o' th' sea, 5.04. 66
not walk | upon a laboring day without the sign JC 1.01. 4
men as ever trod upon neat's-leather have gone 1.01. 25 P
upon neat's-leather have gone upon my handiwork. 1.01. 26 P
run to your houses, fall upon your knees, | pray 1.01. 53
fellow, come from the throng, look upon caesar. 1.02. 21
trouble of my countenance | merely upon myself. 1.02. 39
for once, upon a raw and gusty day, | the 1.02.100
upon the word, | accoutred as i was, i plunged 1.02.104
did from the flames of troy upon his shoulder 1.02.113
upon what meat doth this our caesar feed | that 1.02.149
till then, my noble friend, chew upon this: 1.02.171
as this time | is like to lay upon us. 1.02.175
who glaz'd upon me, and went surly by, | without 1.03. 21
drawn | upon a heap a hundred ghastly women, 1.03. 23
sit | even at noon-day upon the market-place, 1.03. 27
things | unto the climate that they point upon. 1.03. 32
set this up with wax | upon old brutus' statue. 1.03.146
upon the next encounter yields him ours. 1.03.156
i think we are too bold upon your rest. 2.01. 86
the morning comes upon 's. 2.01.221
was, | you star'd upon me with ungentle looks. 2.01.242
and could it work so much upon your shape | as 2.01.253
and upon my knees | i charm you, by my once 2.01.270
fierce fiery warriors fight upon the clouds | in 2.02. 19
of war, | which drizzled blood upon the capitol; 2.02. 21
let me, upon my knee, prevail in this. 2.02. 54
the heart of brutus earns to think upon! 2.02.129
o constancy, be strong upon my side, | set a 2.04. 6
and drawing days out, that men stand upon. 3.01.100
if then thy spirit look upon us now, | shall it 3.01.195
upon this hope, that you shall give me reasons 3.01.221
a curse shall light upon the limbs of men; 3.01.262
nay, press not so upon me, stand far off. 3.02.167
he comes upon a wish. 3.02.266
upon condition publius shall not live, | who is 4.01. 4
have mind upon your health; 4.03. 36
do not presume too much upon my love, | i may do 4.03. 63
upon what sickness? 4.03.152
antony | come down upon us with a mighty power, 4.03.169
the deep of night is crept upon our talk, | and 4.03.226
layest thou thy leaden mace upon my boy, | that 4.03.268
it comes upon me. 4.03.278
on | upon the left hand of the even field. 5.01. 17
upon the right hand i, keep thou the left. 5.01. 18
to set | upon one battle all our liberties. 5.01. 75
is not that he that lies upon the ground? 5.03. 57
night hangs upon mine eyes, my bones would rest, 5.05. 41
turn away thy face, | while i do run upon it. 5.05. 48
upon the heath. MAC 1.01. 6
villainies of nature | do swarm upon him) from 1.02. 12
and fix'd his head upon our battlements. 1.02. 23
so they | doubly redoubled strokes upon the foe. 1.02. 38
night nor day | hang upon his penthouse lid; 1.03. 20
her choppy finger laying | upon her skinny lips. 1.03. 45
why | upon this blasted heath you stop our way 1.03. 77
new honors come upon him, | like our strange 1.03.144
worthy macbeth, we stay upon your leisure. 1.03.148
think upon what hath chanc'd; 1.03.153
we will establish our estate upon | our eldest, 1.04. 37
but here, upon this bank and /shoal of time, 1.07. 6
hors'd | upon the sightless couriers of the air, 1.07. 23
letting "i dare not" wait upon "i would," | like 1.07. 44
what cannot you and i perform upon | th' 1.07. 69
what not put upon | his spungy officers, who 1.07. 70
our griefs and clamor roar | upon his death? 1.07. 79
a heavy summons lies like lead upon me, | and 2.01. 6
would spend it in some words upon that business, 2.01. 23
my drink is ready, | she strike upon the bell. 2.01. 32
which unwip'd we found | upon their pillows. 2.03.104
nor our strong sorrow | upon the foot of motion. 2.03.125
which puts upon them | suspicion of the deed. 2.04. 26
like | the sovereignty will fall upon macbeth. 2.04. 30
as upon thee, macbeth, their speeches shine — 3.01. 7
let your highness | command upon me, to the 3.01. 16
ay, my good lord. our time does call upon 's. 3.01. 36
when first they put the name of king upon me, 3.01. 57
upon my head they plac'd a fruitless crown, 3.01. 60
i'll call upon you straight; 3.01.139
there's blood upon thy face. 3.04. 13
his absence, sir, | lays blame upon his promise. 3.04. 43
upon a thought | he will again be well. 3.04. 54
stand not upon the order of your going, | but go 3.04.118
upon the corner of the moon | there hangs a 3.05. 23
king, upon his aid | to wake northumberland and 3.06. 30
and wears upon his baby-brow the round | and top 4.01. 88
for the blood-bolter'd banquo smiles upon me, 4.01.123
seize upon fife, give to th' edge o' th' sword 4.01.151
but float upon a wild and violent sea | each way 4.02. 21
my pretty cousin, | blessing upon you! 4.02. 26
when i shall tread upon the tyrant's head, | or 4.03. 45
fear not yet | to take upon you what is yours. 4.03. 70
thee, | oft'ner upon her knees than on her feet, 4.03.110
these evils thou repeat'st upon thyself | hath 4.03.112
the taints and blames i laid upon myself, | for 4.03.124
my first false speaking | was this upon myself. 4.03.131
what, man, ne'er pull your hat upon your brows; 4.03.208
throw her night-gown upon her, unlock her closet 5.01. 6 P
her very guise, and, upon my life, fast asleep. 5.01. 20 P
all annoyance, | and still keep eyes upon her. 5.01. 77
like a giant's robe | upon a dwarfish thief. 5.02. 22
of woman | shall e'er have power upon thee." 5.03. 7
perilous stuff | which weighs upon the heart? 5.03. 45
that struts and frets his hour upon the stage, 5.05. 25
as i did stand my watch upon the hill, | i 5.05. 32
upon the next tree shall thou hang alive, | till 5.05. 38
we | shall take upon 's what else remains to do, 5.06. 5
i see lives, the gashes | do better upon them. 5.08. 3
painted upon a pole, and underwrit, | "here may 5.08. 26
and what needful else | that calls upon us, by 5.09. 38
you come most carefully upon your hour. HAM 1.01. 6
upon whose influence neptune's empire stands 1.01.119
like a guilty thing | upon a fearful summons. 1.01.149
to-night | unto young hamlet, for, upon my life, 1.01.170
last | upon his will i seal'd my hard consent. 1.02. 60
indeed, my lord, it followed hard upon. 1.02.179
in all, | i shall not look upon his like again. 1.02.188
deliver, | upon the witness of these gentlemen, 1.02.194
my lord, upon the platform where we watch. 1.02.213
and fix'd his eyes upon you? 1.02.233
upon the platform 'twixt aleven and twelf | i'll 1.02.251
grace, | occasion smiles upon a second leave. 1.03. 54
end, | like quills upon the fearful porpentine. 1.05. 20
upon a wretch whose natural gifts were poor | to 1.05. 51
upon my secure hour thy uncle stole, | with 1.05. 61
upon my sword. 1.05.147
indeed, upon my sword, indeed. 1.05.148
and lay your hands again upon my sword. 1.05.158
no hat upon his head, his stockins fouled, 2.01. 76
upon our first, he sent out to suppress | his 2.02. 61
read, | answer, and think upon this business. 2.02. 82
or look'd upon this love with idle sight, | what 2.02.138
upon my honor — 2.02.394 P
a clout upon that head | where late the diadem 2.02.506
upon whose property and most dear life | a 2.02.570
let the doors be shut upon him, that he may play 3.01.131 P
ay, my lord, they stay upon your patience. 3.02.107 P
upon the talk of the pois'ning? 3.02.289 P
surely bar the door upon your own liberty if you 3.02.338 P
will you play upon this pipe? 3.02.351 P
you would play upon me, you would seem to know 3.02.364 P
you fret me, /yet you cannot play upon me. 3.02.372 P
safe | that live and feed upon your majesty. 3.03. 10
that spirit upon whose weal depends and rests 3.03. 14
liege, | i'll call upon you ere you go to bed, 3.03. 34
look here upon this picture, and on this, | the 3.04. 53
and waits upon the judgment, and what judgment 3.04. 70
son, | upon the heat and flame of thy distemper 3.04.123
do not look upon me, | lest with this piteous 3.04.127
conceit upon her father. 4.05. 45
upon my life, lamord. 4.07. 92
one woe doth tread upon another's heel, | so 4.07.163
upon what ground? 5.01.160 P
now pile your dust upon the quick and dead, 5.01.251
i will fight with him upon this theme | until my 5.01.266
i pray thee, good horatio, wait upon him. 5.01.293
does it not, think thee, stand me now upon — 5.02. 63
set me the stoups of wine upon that table. 5.02.267
mine and my father's death come not upon thee, 5.02.330
but since, so jump upon this bloody question, 5.02.375
and /the fee bestow | upon the foul disease. LR 1.01.164
sixt to turn thy hated back | upon our kingdom. 1.01.176
thee and thy virtues here i seize upon, | be it 1.01.252
all this done | upon the gad? 1.02. 26
blasts and fogs upon thee! 1.04.299
upon his party 'gainst the duke of albany? 2.01. 26
in cunning i must draw my sword upon you. 2.01. 29
riotous knights | that tended upon my father? 2.01. 95
keep peace, upon your lives! 2.02. 48
a plague upon your epileptic visage! 2.02. 81
goose, /and i had you upon sarum plain, | i'ld 2.02. 83
to strike at me, upon his misconstruction, 2.02.117
and put upon him such a deal of man | that 2.02.120
to do upon respect such violent outrage. 2.04. 24
look'd black upon me, strook me with her tongue, 2.04.160
most serpent-like, upon the very heart. 2.04.161
art not asham'd to look upon this beard? 2.04.193
and dare upon the warrant of my note | commend a 3.01. 18
and let this tyrannous night take hold upon you, 3.04.151
i will lay trust upon thee; 3.05. 24 P
red burning spits | come hizzing in upon 'em — 3.06. 16
i have o'erheard a plot of death upon him. 3.06. 89
we are bound to take upon your traitorous father 3.07. 8 P
though well we may not pass upon his life 3.07. 24
upon these eyes of thine i'll set my foot. 3.07. 68
if you did wear a beard upon your chin, | i'ld 3.07. 76
throw this slave | upon the dunghill. 3.07. 97
in my fancy pluck | upon my hateful life. 4.02. 86
the fishermen, that /walk upon the beach, 4.06. 17
upon the crown o' th' cliff, what thing was that 4.06. 67
how yond justice rails upon yond simple thief. 4.06.152 P
and when i have stol'n upon these son-in-laws, 4.06.186
lay hand upon him. 4.06.188
seek him out | upon the english party. 4.06.250
a plot upon her virtuous husband's life, | and 4.06.272
but i am bound | upon a wheel of fire, that mine 4.07. 46
o, look upon me, sir, | and hold your hand in 4.07. 56
lord, | you know the goodness i intend upon you: 5.01. 7
and take upon 's the mystery of things | as if 5.03. 16
upon such sacrifices, my cordelia, | the gods 5.03. 20
if none appear to prove upon thy person | thy 5.03. 91
my sickness grows upon me. 5.03.105
the lists of the army will maintain upon edmund, 5.03.111 P
why he appears | upon this call o' th' trumpet. 5.03.119
best spirits are bent | to prove upon thy heart, 5.03.141
and | to lay the blame upon her own despair, 5.03.255
a plague upon you, murderers, traitors all! 5.03.270
that would upon the rack of this tough world 5.03.315
i follow him to serve my turn upon him. OTH 1.01. 42
but i will wear my heart upon my sleeve | for 1.01. 64
upon malicious /bravery dost thou come | to 1.01.100
or put upon you what restraint or grievance 1.02. 15
the goodness of the night upon you, friends! 1.02. 35
lay hold upon him, if he do resist | subdue him 1.02. 80
side, | upon some present business of the state, 1.02. 90

conjur'd to this effect, | he wrought upon her. 1.03.106
but let your sentence | even fall upon my life. 1.03.120
upon this hint i spake: 1.03.166
my life upon her faith! 1.03.294
i have look'd upon the world for four times 1.03.311 P
if it hath ruffian'd so upon the sea, | what 2.01. 7
for do but stand upon the foaming shore, | the 2.01. 11
o, fie upon thee, slanderer! 2.01.113
ay, smile upon her, do; 2.01.169 P
for the command, i'll lay't upon you. 2.01.265 P
and practicing upon his peace and quiet | even 2.01.310
general, that upon certain tidings now arriv'd, 2.02. 2 P
if i can fasten but one cup upon him, | with 2.03. 48
he dies upon his motion. 2.03.174
him with determin'd sword | to execute upon him. 2.03.228
we'll wait upon your lordship. 3.02. 6
or feed upon such nice and waterish diet, | or 3.03. 15
be a toad | and live upon the vapor of a dungeon 3.03.271
i have a pain upon my forehead, here. 3.03.284
but with a little act upon the blood | burn like 3.03.328
or woe upon thy life! 3.03.366
up kisses by the roots | that grew upon my lips; 3.03.424
and will upon the instant put thee to't: 3.03.471
it is a monster | begot upon itself, born on 3.04.162
away, | and laid good 'scuses upon your ecstasy; 4.01. 79
so hangs, and lolls, and weeps upon me; 4.01.139 P
or did the letters work upon his blood | and 4.01.275
upon my knee, what doth your speech import? 4.02. 31
most goodly book, | made to write "whore" upon? 4.02. 72
thrown such despite and heavy terms upon her, 4.02.116
could not have laid such terms upon his callet. 4.02.121
how comes this trick upon him? 4.02.129
o fie upon them! 4.02.145
jealousies, | throwing restraint upon us; 4.03. 90
i pray you look upon her. 5.01.108
o, fie upon thee, strumpet! 5.01.121
as i? /fough, fie upon thee! 5.01.123
but that i did proceed upon just grounds | to 5.02.138
upon my soul, a lie, a wicked lie. 5.02.181
fie, | your sword upon a woman? 5.02.224
look in upon me then and speak with me, | or, 5.02.257
did itself sustain | upon a soldier's thigh. 5.02.261
that he made him | brave me upon the watch, 5.02.326
but this, | killing myself, to die upon a kiss. 5.02.359
and seize upon the fortunes of the moor, | for 5.02.366
and devotion of their view | upon a tawny front; ANT 1.01. 6
we will not look upon him. go with us. 1.02. 87
italy, | upon the first encounter, drave them. 1.02. 94
he stays upon your will. 1.02.115
her die twenty times upon far poorer moment. 1.02.142 P
which commits some loving act upon her, she hath 1.02.144 P
the great and all his dignities | upon his son, 1.02.189
that keep you here, | i have no power upon you; 1.03. 23
as have not thrived | upon the present state, 1.03. 52
upon your sword | sit laurel victory, and smooth 1.03. 99
body, | like to a vagabond flag upon the stream, 1.04. 45
his brother /warr'd upon him, although i think 2.01. 41
our lives upon to use our strongest hands. 2.01. 51
your wife and brother | made wars upon me, and 2.02. 43
sir, | he fell upon me, ere admitted, then; 2.02. 75
strange courtesies and great | of late upon me. 2.02.155
time calls upon 's. 2.02.157
purs'd up his heart upon the river of cydnus. 2.02.187 P
the city cast | her people out upon her; 2.02.214
upon her landing, antony sent to her, | invited 2.02.219
you'll win two days upon me. 2.04. 9
of gold, and hail | rich pearls upon thee. 2.05. 46
fie upon "but yet"! 2.05. 51
the most infectious pestilence upon thee! 2.05. 61
lie they upon thy hand, | and be undone by 'em! 2.05.105
this 'greed upon, | to part with unhack'd edges 2.06. 37
i saw you last, | there's a change upon you. 2.06. 53
what counts harsh fortune casts upon my face, 2.06. 54
upon the slime and ooze scatters his grain, 2.07. 22
that stands upon the swell at the full of tide, 3.02. 49
herod of jewry dare not look upon you | but when 3.03. 3
caesar and lepidus have made wars upon pompey. 3.05. 4 P
upon his own appeal, seizes him. 3.05. 11 P
why have you stol'n upon us thus? 3.06. 42
i have eyes upon him, | and his affairs come to 3.06. 62
our fortune lies | upon this jump. 3.08. 6
the breeze upon her, like a cow in /june — 3.10. 14
i have myself resolv'd upon a course | which has 3.11. 9
o, | i follow'd that i blush to look upon. 3.11. 12
tell him he wears the rose | of youth upon him; 3.13. 21
the scars upon your honor, therefore, he | does 3.13. 58
fortunes you should make a staff | to lean upon; 3.13. 69
as a morsel, cold upon | dead caesar's trencher; 3.13.116
that i were | upon the hill of basan, to outroar 3.13.127
may seem to spend his fury | upon himself. 4.06. 10
when men revolted shall upon record | bear 4.09. 8
the poisonous damp of night dispunge upon me, 4.09. 13
our foot | upon the hills adjoining to the city 4.10. 5
for when i am reveng'd upon my charm, | i have 4.12. 16
the shirt of nessus is upon me; 4.12. 43
have by their brave instruction got upon me | a 4.14. 98
his death's upon him, but not dead. 4.15. 7
kisses the poor last | i lay upon thy lips. 4.15. 21
shall acquire no honor | demuring upon me. 4.15. 29
and i wore my life | to spend upon his haters. 5.01. 9
upon his peril, that i have reserv'd | to myself 5.02.143
our care and pity is so much upon you, | that we 5.02.188
and these fig leaves | have slime upon them, 5.02.352
as th' aspic leaves | upon the caves of nile. 5.02.353
no grave upon the earth shall clip in it | a 5.02.359
i'll place it | upon this fairest prisoner. CYM 1.01.123
he takes his part | to draw upon an exile. 1.01.166
how long a fool you were upon the ground. 1.02. 24 P
she shines not upon fools, lest the reflection 1.02. 32 P
but | to look upon him, till the diminution | of 1.03. 18
bore, upon importance of so slight and trivial a 1.04. 41 P
but upon my mended judgment (if i offend /not to 1.04. 46 P
(and upon warrant of bloody affirmation) his to 1.04. 59 P
know strange fowl light upon neighboring ponds. 1.04. 89 P
if you make your voyage upon her and give me 1.04.158 P
flattering rascal, upon him | will i first work. 1.05. 27
reflect upon him accordingly, as you value your 1.06. 24 P
the twinn'd stones | upon the number'd beach, 1.06. 36
had i this cheek | to bathe my lips upon; 1.06.100
in your despite, upon your purse — revenge it. 1.06.135
when i kiss'd the jack upon an up–cast, to be 2.01. 2 P
is it fit i went to look upon him? 2.01. 42 P
o sleep, thou ape of death, lie dull upon her, 2.02. 31
or look upon our romans, whose remembrance | is 2.04. 14
they are people such | that mend upon the world. 2.04. 26
is one of the fairest that i have look'd upon. 2.04. 32
you do remember | this stain upon her? 2.04.139
like egg–shells mov'd upon their surges, crack'd 3.01. 28
all color here | did put the yoke upon 's; 3.01. 51
upon the love and truth and vows which i | have 3.02. 12
hate her, nay indeed, | to be reveng'd upon her. 3.05. 79
she said upon a time (the bitterness of it i now 3.05.133 P
with that suit upon my back will i ravish her; 3.05.137 P
weariness | can snore upon the flint, when resty 3.06. 34
which now is growing upon thy shoulders, shall 4.01. 16 P
upon their faces. 4.02.285
these herblets shall, which we upon you strew. 4.02.287
come on, away, apart upon our knees. 4.02.288
bed | with the defunct, or sleep upon the dead. 4.02.358
my queen | upon a desperate bed, and in a time 4.03. 6
that they will waste their time upon our note, 4.04. 20
i am asham'd | to look upon the holy sun, to 4.04. 41
grin like lions | upon the pikes o' th' hunters. 5.03. 39
not now be stol'n, you have locks upon you; 5.04. 1
longer exercise | upon a valiant race thy harsh 5.04. 83
upon your never–withering banks of flow'rs. 5.04. 98
this tablet lay upon his breast, wherein | our 5.04.109
be directed by some that take upon them to know, 5.04.180 P
or to take upon yourself that which i am sure 5.04.181 P
that diamond upon your finger, say | how came it 5.05.137
upon a time — unhappy was the clock | that 5.05.153
which then he wore | upon his honor'd finger, to 5.05.184
and throw stones, cast mire upon me, set | the 5.05.222
think that you are upon a rock, and now | throw 5.05.262
upon my lady's missing, came to me | with his 5.05.275
stole these children | upon my banishment; 5.05.342
guiderius had | upon his neck a mole, a sanguine 5.05.364
who hath upon him still that natural stamp. 5.05.366
see, | posthumus anchors upon imogen; 5.05.393
great jupiter, upon his eagle back'd, | appear'd 5.05.427
but being play'd upon before your time, | hell PER 1.01. 84
prince pericles, touch not, upon thy life, | for 1.01. 87
he flatters you, makes war upon your life. 1.02. 45
griefs as you yourself do lay upon yourself. 1.02. 66
we have descried, upon our neighboring shore, 1.04. 60
may see the sea hath cast upon your coast — 2.01. 56
hath made the ball | for them to play upon, 2.01. 61
thy value i will mount myself | upon a courser, 2.01.158
and the device he bears upon his shield | is a 2.02. 19
and the device he bears upon his shield | is an 2.02. 25
/to place upon the volume of your deeds, | as in 2.03. 3
these cates resist me, he not thought upon. 2.03. 29
and after shipwrack driven upon this shore. 2.03. 85
your love and your affections | upon a stranger? 2.05. 78
ship, upon whose deck | the seas–toss'd pericles 3.ch. 59
and thou that hast | upon the winds command, 3.01. 3
/ooze, | where, for a monument upon thy bones, 3.01. 61
lay the babe | upon the pillow. 3.01. 68
our lodgings, standing bleak upon the sea, 3.02. 14
did the sea toss up upon our shore this chest. 3.02. 50
a good constraint of fortune it belches upon us. 3.02. 55
huge a billow, sir, | as toss'd it upon shore. 3.02. 59
the gods | make up the rest upon you! 3.03. 5
which the people's prayers still fall upon you, 3.03. 19
the gods revenge it upon me and mine | to the 3.03. 24
shall as a carpet hang upon thy grave | while 4.01. 16
i trod upon a worm against my will, | but i wept 4.01. 78
they will but please themselves upon her, | not 4.01.100
sore terms we stand upon with the gods will be 4.02. 34 P
you have fortunes coming upon you. 4.02.116 P
slaughter | the sun and moon ne'er look'd upon! 4.03. 3
make raging battery upon shores of flint." 4.04. 43
fie, fie upon her, she's able to freeze the god 4.06. 3 P
now the pox upon her green–sickness for me! 4.06. 13 P
you that your resorters stand upon sound legs. 4.06. 24 P
not see thee, or else look friendly upon thee. 4.06. 89 P
if put upon you, make the judgment good | that 4.06. 93
a curse upon him, die he like a thief, | that 4.06.114
upon what ground is his distemperature? 5.01. 27
/is now upon | the leavy shelter that abuts 5.01. 50
but there is something glows upon my cheek, 5.01. 95
pray you turn your eyes upon me. 5.01.101
lest this great sea of joys rushing upon me 5.01.192
and thick slumber | hangs upon mine eyes. 5.01.235
thither, | and do upon mine altar sacrifice. 5.01.241
shall we refresh us, sir, upon your shore, | and 5.01.256
upon this coast, i warrant you. 5.03. 20
morn this lady was | thrown upon this shore. 5.03. 23
he tumbled down upon his /nemean hide, | and TNK 1.01. 68
your sorrow beats so ardently upon me | that it 1.01.126
their sweetness fall | upon thy tasteful lips, 1.01.179
haste, | i stamp this kiss upon thy currant lip. 1.01.216
or to be fond upon | another's way of speech, 1.02. 46
all the good that may | be wish'd upon thy head, 1.04. 3
i will assure upon my daughter at the day of my 2.01. 8 P
chanc'd to name you here, upon the old business. 2.01. 17 P
from all that fortune can inflict upon us, | i 2.02. 57
will't not do | rarely upon a skirt, wench? 2.02.130
us, i disclaim | if thou once think upon her! 2.02.174
upon his oath and life, must he set foot | upon 2.02.246
and life, must he set foot | upon this kingdom. 2.02.247
wicked, all my sins | could never pluck upon me. 2.03. 7
feed | upon the sweetness of a noble beauty, 2.03. 11
run | swifter than wind upon a field of corn, 2.03. 77
upon my soul, a proper man! 2.05. 16
wait well, sir, | upon your mistress. 2.05. 52
thou | so little dream'st upon my fortune that 3.01. 24
you are going now to gaze upon my mistress, 3.01.117
you are going now to look upon a sun | that 3.01.120
for emily, upon my life! 3.03. 42
now, now, it beats upon it — now, now, now! 3.04. 7
and marrow of my understanding laid upon ye, 3.05. 6
some country sport, upon my life, sir. 3.05. 97
the birch upon the breeches of the small ones, 3.05.111
right and straight | upon this mighty morr— — 3.05.118
when we are arm'd | and both upon our guards, 3.06. 29
you charg'd | upon the left wing of the enemy, 3.06. 75
put thyself | upon thy present guard — 3.06.122
upon their lives; but with their banishments. 3.06.214
to tread upon thy dukedom, and to be, | where 3.06.254
look upon 'em, | and, if you can love, end this 3.06.277
who loses, yet i'll weep upon his bier. 3.06.308
upon their knees | begg'd with such handsome 4.01. 8
too, as ever he may go upon 's legs, for in the 4.03. 14 P
take upon you, young sir her friend, the name of 4.03. 76 P
her attention, for this her mind beats upon; 4.03. 79 P
what godlike power | hast thou not power upon? 5.01. 90
i never practiced | upon man's wife, nor would 5.01.101
this advice i told you done any good upon her? 5.02. 1
long time his eye | will dwell upon his object; 5.03. 49
upon my my right side still i wore thy picture, 5.03. 73
mounted upon a steed that emily | did first 5.04. 49
yet stay a while, | and let me look upon ye. ep 4
you would have us upon th' hip, would you? STM II.C 18 P
but we will show no mercy upon the strangers. II.C 19 P
look what you do offend you cry upon, | that is II.C 61
upon this promise did he raise his chin, | like VEN 85
"the tender spring upon thy tempting lip | shows 127
ear, | or like a fairy, trip upon the green, 146
can thy right hand seize love upon thy left? 158
"upon the earth's increase why shouldst thou 169
or what great danger dwells upon my suit? 206
upon his compass'd crest now stand on end; | his 272
he looks upon his love, and neighs unto her, 307
whose beams upon his hairless face are fix'd, 487
like lawn being spread upon the blushing rose, 590
whose blood upon the fresh flowers being shed 665
"by this, poor wat, far off upon a hill, 697
so to so, | for love can comment upon every woe. 714
semblance he hath fed | upon fresh beauty, 796
leaves love upon her back, deeply distress'd. 814
on shore | gazing upon a late embarked friend, 818
upon the wide wound that the boar had trench'd 1052
upon his hurt she looks so steadfastly, | that 1063
he ran upon the boar with his sharp spear, | who 1112
she looks upon his lips, and they are pale, 1123
which in round drops upon their whiteness stood. 1170
upon the world dim darkness doth display, | and LUC 118
now stole upon the time the dead of night, 162
might have excuse to work upon his wife, | as in 235
his hand, that yet remains upon her breast 463
this said, he sets his foot upon the light, 673
upon my cheeks what helpless shame i feel." 756
the stain upon his silver down will stay. 1012
fly, | but eagles gaz'd upon with every eye. 1015
these means, as frets upon an instrument, 1140
gazing upon the greeks with little lust. 1384
ranks began | to break upon the galled shore, 1440
alone | upon his head that hath transgressed so; 1481
so should my shame still rest upon record, | and 1643
which seems to weep upon the tainted place, 1746
hath serv'd a dumb arrest upon his tongue, | who 1780
this said, he strook his hand upon his breast, 1842
touch | upon the lute doth ravish human sense; PP 8. 6
her stand she takes upon a steep–up hill. 9. 5
like a green plum that hangs upon a tree, | and 10. 5
there will we sit upon the rocks, | and see the 19. 5
as it fell upon a day, | in the merry month of 20. 1
so lively shown, | made me think upon mine own. 20.18
thou spend | upon thyself thy beauty's legacy? SON 4. 2
mightier way | make war upon this bloody tyrant, 16. 2
cries, | and look upon myself and curse my fate, 29. 4
upon the farthest earth remov'd from thee, | for 44. 6
tend | upon the hours and times of your desire? 57. 2
his, | and, proud of many, lives upon his gains? 67.12
o, if (i say) you look upon this verse, | when i 71. 9
and hang more praise upon deceased i | than 72. 7
upon those boughs which shake against the cold, 73. 3
whilst i alone did call upon thy aid, | my verse 79. 1
whilst he upon your soundless deep doth ride, 80.10
so thy great gift, upon misprision growing, 87.11
upon thy side against myself i'll fight, | and 88. 3
upon thy part i can set down a story | of faults 88. 6
fault, | and i will comment upon that offense; 89. 2
so ill, | to set a form upon desired change, 89. 6
stay, | for it depends upon that love of thine. 92. 4
which vulgar scandal stamp'd upon my brow, | for 112. 2
if this be error and upon me proved, | i never 116.13
repay, | forgot upon your dearest love to call, 117. 3
what thou dost foist upon us that is old, | and 123. 6
upon that blessed wood whose motion sounds 128. 2
be, | looking with pretty ruth upon my pain. 132. 4
is not, | to put fair truth upon so foul a face? 137.12
wrong | that thy unkindness lays upon my heart, 139. 2
dost thou upon thy fading mansion spend? 146. 6
then, soul, live thou upon thy servant's loss, 146. 9
on whom frown'st thou that i do fawn upon? 149. 6
spend | revenge upon myself with present moan? 149. 8
upon her head a platted hive of straw, | which LC 8
threw, | upon whose weeping margent she was set, 39
so slides he down upon his grained bat, | and 64
wind | upon his lips their silken parcels hurls. 87
"small show of man was yet upon his chin, | his 92
blood | that we must curb it upon others' proof, 163
"and long upon these terms i held my city, 176
her eye | upon the moment did her force subdue, 248

UPON'T 28 FR 0.0031 REL FR 23 V 5 P

out upon't! WIV 1.04.165 P
they do you wrong to put you so oft upon't. MM 2.01.266 P
i have ta'en a due and wary note upon't. 4.01. 37
and i'll be sworn upon't that he loves her, ADO 5.04. 85
my life upon't, young though thou art, thine eye TN 2.04. 23
sowter will cry upon't for all this, though it 2.05.123 P
to bide upon't: WT 1.02.242
that forced baseness | which he has put upon't! 2.03. 80
for the creatures | of prey that keep upon't. 3.03. 13
yes, truly is he, and condemn'd upon't. H8 2.01. 8
be sworn and sworn upon't she never shrouded any TRO 2.03. 33 P
if he be put upon't, and that's as easy | as to COR 2.01.256
do not stand upon't. 2.02.150
"i pray, sir" — plague upon't! 2.03. 50
o, may diseases only work upon't! TIM 3.01. 60
sleep upon't, | and let the foes quietly cut 3.05. 43

nought | but even the mere necessities upon't. 4.03.376
th' amazement of mine eyes | that look'd upon't. MAC 2.04. 20
forth paper, fold it, write upon't, read it, 5.01. 7 P
fie upon't, foh! HAM 2.02.587
it hath the primal eldest curse upon't, | a 3.03. 37
i think upon't, i think — i smell't — o OTH 5.02.191
hark, the land bids me tread no more upon't, ANT 3.11. 1
with trees upon't that nod unto the world | and 4.14. 6
will you rhyme upon't, | and vent it for a CYM 5.03. 55
the good gods | throw their best eyes upon't! PER 3.01. 37
set't down, let's look upon't. 3.02. 51
out upon't! TNK 2.04. 5

UPPER 6 FR 0.0006 REL FR 5 V 1 P
i nightly lodge her in an upper tow'r, | the key TGV 3.01. 35
at upper end o' th' table, now i' th' middle; WT 4.04. 59
and let my griefs frown on the upper hand. R3 4.04. 37
the upper germany, can dearly witness, | yet H8 5.02. 65
set at upper end o' th' table; COR 4.05.192 P
down, | but keep the hills and upper regions. JC 5.01. 3

UP–PRICK'D 1 FR 0.0001 REL FR 1 V 0 P
his ears up–prick'd, his braided hanging mane VEN 271

UPREAR 1 FR 0.0001 REL FR 1 V 0 P
and this my hand against myself uprear, | to SON 49.11

UPREAR'D 2 FR 0.0002 REL FR 2 V 0 P
in the arm | that was uprear'd to execution. 2H4 4.01.212
his hair uprear'd, his nostrils stretch'd with 2H6 3.02.171

UPREARED 1 FR 0.0001 REL FR 1 V 0 P
whose high, upreared, and abutting fronts | the H5 pr 21

UPRIGHT 23 FR 0.0026 REL FR 22 V 1 P
and time | goes upright with his carriage. TMP 5.01. 3
as upright as the cedar. LLL 4.03. 87
meet | the lord bassanio live an upright life, MV 3.05. 74
o wise and upright judge! 4.01.250
o upright judge! mark, jew: o learned judge! 4.01.313
o jew! an upright judge, a learned judge! 4.01.323
the unstooping firmness of my upright soul. R2 1.01.121
throne, | a loyal, just, and upright gentleman. 1.03. 87
were enough noble to be upright judge | of noble 4.01.118
away, you whoreson upright /rabbit, away! 2H4 2.02. 85 P
if truth and upright innocency fail me, | i'll 5.02. 39
know your grace to be a man | just and upright; 1H6 3.01. 95
seen | him caper upright like a wild morisco, 2H6 3.01.365
look, look, it stands upright, | like lime–twigs 3.03. 15
with whom /an upright zeal to right prevails 3H6 5.01. 78
and i believe will never stand upright | till R3 3.02. 39
o upright, just, and true–disposing god, | how 4.04. 55
upright he held it, lords, that held it last. TIT 1.01.200
and set them upright at their dear friends' door 5.01.136
in purity of manhood stand upright | and say, TIM 4.03. 14
all beneath the moon | would i not leap upright. LR 4.06. 27
or knife, or poison, | some upright justicer! CYM 5.05.214
anon he rears upright, curvets, and leaps, | as VEN 279

UPRIGHTEOUSLY 1 FR 0.0001 REL FR 0 V 1 P
that you may most uprighteously do a poor MM 3.01.200 P

UPRIGHTNESS 1 FR 0.0001 REL FR 1 V 0 P
so i do affy | in thy uprightness and integrity, TIT 1.01. 48

UPRISE 2 FR 0.0002 REL FR 2 V 0 P
that gives sweet tidings of the sun's uprise? TIT 3.01.159
o sun, thy uprise shall i see no more, | fortune ANT 4.12. 18

UPROAR 4 FR 0.0004 REL FR 4 V 0 P
an uproar, i dare warrant, | begun through 1H6 3.01. 74
th' event to th' teeth, are all in uproar, | and H8 1.02. 36
uproar the universal peace, confound | all unity MAC 4.03. 99
unto a greater uproar tempts his veins. LUC 427

UPROARS 2 FR 0.0002 REL FR 2 V 0 P
commotions, uproars, with a general taint | of H8 5.02. 63
rome, | by uproars sever'd, as a flight of fowl TIT 5.03. 68

UP–ROUS'D 1 FR 0.0001 REL FR 1 V 0 P
thou art up–rous'd with some distemp'rature; ROM 2.03. 40

UPSHOOT 1 FR 0.0001 REL FR 1 V 0 P
will she get the upshoot by cleaving the /pin. LLL 4.01.136

UPSHOT 2 FR 0.0002 REL FR 1 V 1 P
with any safety this sport /t' the upshot. TN 4.02. 71 P
and, in this upshot, purposes mistook | fall'n HAM 5.02.384

UPSIDE 2 FR 0.0002 REL FR 1 V 1 P
this house is turn'd upside down since robin 1H4 2.01. 10 P
a burning torch that's turned upside down; PER 2.02. 32

UP–SPRING 1 FR 0.0001 REL FR 1 V 0 P
wassail, and the swagg'ring up–spring reels; HAM 1.04. 9

UP–STARING 1 FR 0.0001 REL FR 1 V 0 P
with hair up–staring (then like reeds, not hair) TMP 1.02.213

UPSTART 2 FR 0.0002 REL FR 2 V 0 P
and given away | to upstart unthrifts? R2 2.03.122
i think this upstart is old talbot's ghost, | he 1H6 4.07. 87

UPSWARM'D 1 FR 0.0001 REL FR 1 V 0 P
of heaven and him | have here upswarm'd them. 2H4 4.02. 30

UP–TILL 1 FR 0.0001 REL FR 1 V 0 P
forlorn, | lean'd her breast up–till a thorn, PP 20.10

UPWARD *(also up'ard)*
11 FR 0.0012 REL FR 8 V 3 P
i have liv'd fourscore years and upward; WIV 3.01. 56 P
and a spaniard from the hip upward, no doublet. ADO 3.02. 36 P
what upward lies | the street should see as she LLL 4.03.276
thus far our fortune keeps an upward course, 3H6 5.03. 1
wife in this obedience | upward of twenty years, H8 2.04. 36
whom thy upward face | hath to the marbled TIM 4.03.190
titinius' face is upward. JC 5.03. 93
or else climb upward | to what they were before. MAC 4.02. 24
but the great one that goes upward, let him draw LR 2.04. 74 P
fourscore and upward, not an hour more nor less; 4.07. 60
and from th' extremest upward of thy head | to 5.03.137

UPWARDS 1 FR 0.0001 REL FR 0 V 1 P
she shall be buried with her face upwards. ADO 3.02. 68 P

URCHINFIELD 1 FR 0.0001 REL FR 1 V 0 P
lord talbot of goodrig and urchinfield, | lord 1H6 4.07. 64

URCHINS 3 FR 0.0003 REL FR 3 V 0 P
urchins | shall, for that vast of night that TMP 1.02.326
growth, we'll dress | like urchins, ouphes, and WIV 4.04. 50
ten thousand swelling toads, as many urchins, TIT 2.03.101

URCHIN–SHOWS 1 FR 0.0001 REL FR 1 V 0 P
fright me with urchin–shows, pitch me i' th' TMP 2.02. 5

URCHIN–SNOUTED 1 FR 0.0001 REL FR 1 V 0 P
"but this foul, grim, and urchin–snouted boar, VEN 1105

URG'D 30 FR 0.0034 REL FR 28 V 2 P
she hath urg'd her height, | and with her MND 3.02.291
i cannot speak to her, yet she urg'd conference. AYL 1.02.258
patience once more, whiles our compact is urg'd: 5.04. 5
which was so strongly urg'd past my defense. JN 1.01.258
you urg'd me as a judge, but i had rather | you R2 1.03.237
being ne'er so little urg'd, another way | to 5.01. 64
and urg'd it twice together, did he not? 5.04. 5
and when i urg'd the ransom once again | of my 1H4 1.03.141
life | did hear a challenge urg'd more modestly, 5.02. 52
what i have done my safety urg'd me to; 5.05. 11
that self bill is urg'd | which in th' eleventh H5 1.01. 1
mitigation of this bill | urg'd by the commons? 1.01. 71
which you before so urg'd, lies in his answer. 5.02. 76
when articles too nicely urg'd be stood on. 5.02. 94
which i never use till urg'd, nor never break 5.02.145 P
well urg'd, my lord of warwick; 1H6 3.01.151
which haply by much company might be urg'd; R3 2.02.137
thou know'st our reasons urg'd upon the way; 3.01.160
then he was urg'd to tell my tale again: 3.07. 31
on the contrary | urg'd on the examinations, H8 2.01. 16
i urg'd our old acquaintance, and the drops COR 5.01. 10
a word ill urg'd to one that is so ill! ROM 1.01.203
o trespass sweetly urg'd! 1.05.109
was, and urg'd withal | your high displeasure; 3.01.154
nay, urg'd extremely for't, and show'd what TIM 3.02. 12 P
decius, well urg'd. JC 2.01.155
i urg'd you further; 2.01.243
discovery, but your haste | is now urg'd on you. LR 5.01. 54
"what have you urg'd that i cannot reprove? VEN 787
and to his protestation urg'd the rest, | who, LUC 1844

/URGE 2 FR 0.0002 REL FR 2 V 0 P
/urge /it /no /more, /my /lord /northumberland. R2 4.01.271
/dost /thou /urge /the /name /of /hands, | /to TIT 3.02. 26

URGE 34 FR 0.0038 REL FR 32 V 2 P
urge not my father's anger, eglamour, | but TGV 4.03. 27
i urge this childhood proof, | because what MV 1.01.144
modesty | to urge the thing held as a ceremony? 5.01.206
this, | and urge her to a present answer back. AWW 2.02. 64
that right in peace which here we urge in war, JN 2.01. 47
urge them while their souls | are capable of 2.01.475
done, | doth lay it open to urge on revenge. 4.03. 38
urge doubts to them that fear. R2 2.01.299
then if you urge me farther than to say "do you H5 5.02.127 P
urge it no more, lest that, in stead of words, 3H6 1.01. 98
to urge his hatred more to clarence | with lies R3 1.01.147
days, | which here you urge to prove us enemies, 1.03.145
urge neither charity nor shame to me. 1.03.273
how canst thou urge god's dreadful law to us, 1.04.209
o, they did urge it still unto the king! 2.01.138
urge his hateful luxury | and bestial appetite 3.05. 80
urge the necessity and state of times, | and be 4.04.416
and urge the king | to do me this last right. H8 4.02.157
face to face, | and freely urge against me. 5.02. 83
he knows not | what i can urge against him. COR 4.07. 19
careful to observe, | therefore i urge thy oath; TIT 5.01. 78
by that god he swears, | to that i'll urge him: 5.01. 81
i should not urge it half so faithfully. TIM 3.02. 41
urge it no more | on height of our displeasure. 3.05. 85
many my near occasions did urge me to put off; 3.06. 11 P
what, urge you your petitions in the street? JC 3.01. 11
urge me no more, i shall forget myself; 4.03. 35
i should not urge thy duty past thy might; 4.03.261
my brother never | did urge me in his act. ANT 2.02. 46
urge it thou: 3.13.151
urge it home, brave lady. TNK 3.06.233
and from her twining arms doth urge releasing. VEN 256
keen, | with eager compounds we our palate urge, SON 118. 2
then, gentle cheater, urge not my amiss, | lest 151. 3

URGED 1 FR 0.0001 REL FR 1 V 0 P
being urged at a time unseasonable. JN 4.02. 20

URGENT 2 FR 0.0002 REL FR 2 V 0 P
please your highness | to take the urgent hour. WT 1.02.465
the death of fulvia, with more urgent touches, ANT 1.02.180

URGES 1 FR 0.0001 REL FR 1 V 0 P
allow the compliment | which very manners urges. LR 5.03.235

URGEST 2 FR 0.0002 REL FR 2 V 0 P
for, as thou urgest justice, be assur'd | thou MV 4.01.315
why urgest thou so oft young arthur's death? JN 4.02.204

URGETH 2 FR 0.0002 REL FR 2 V 0 P
but she with vehement prayers urgeth still LUC 475
extremity still urgeth such extremes. 1337

URGING 11 FR 0.0012 REL FR 9 V 2 P
with urging helpless patience would relieve me; ERR 2.01. 39
for urging it the second time to me. 2.02. 46
in bed he slept not for my urging it; 5.01. 63
at board he fed not for my urging it; 5.01. 64
besides her urging of her wrack at sea — 5.01.360
with too much urging your pernicious lives, R2 3.01. 4
use till urg'd, nor never break for urging. H5 5.02.146 P
the urging of that word "judgment" hath bred a R3 1.04.107 P
sin upon my head, | by urging me to fury: ROM 5.03. 63
forewarn us of, urging obedience to authority, STM II.C 94
urging the worser sense for vantage still; LUC 249

URINAL 1 FR 0.0001 REL FR 0 V 1 P
shine through you like the water in an urinal, TGV 2.01. 39 P

/URINALS 1 FR 0.0001 REL FR 0 V 1 P
i will knog your /urinals about your knave's WIV 3.01. 88 P

URINALS 1 FR 0.0001 REL FR 0 V 1 P
i will knog his urinals about his knave's WIV 3.01. 14 P

URINE 3 FR 0.0003 REL FR 1 V 2 P
when he makes water his urine is congeal'd ice, MM 3.02.110 P
sings i' th' nose, | cannot contain their urine: MV 4.01. 50
marry, sir, nose–painting, sleep, and urine. MAC 2.03. 28 P

URN 5 FR 0.0005 REL FR 5 V 0 P
or lay these bones in an unworthy urn, H5 1.02.228
in an urn more precious | than the rich–jewell'd 1H6 1.06. 24
corse that ever herald | did follow to his urn. COR 5.06.144
to urn their ashes, nor to take th' offense | of TNK 1.01. 44
to this urn let those repair | that are either PHT 65

/URNS 1 FR 0.0001 REL FR 1 V 0 P
that shall distill from these two ancient /urns, TIT 3.01. 17

URNS 1 FR 0.0001 REL FR 1 V 0 P
urns and odors bring away, | vapors, sighs, TNK 1.05. 1

URSA 1 FR 0.0001 REL FR 0 V 1 P
and my nativity was under ursa major, so that it LR 1.02.130 P

URSLEY 1 FR 0.0001 REL FR 1 V 0 P
and tell her i and ursley | walk in the orchard, ADO 3.01. 4

URSULA 7 FR 0.0008 REL FR 4 V 3 P
ursula, bring my picture there. TGV 4.04.117
now, ursula, when beatrice doth come, | as we do ADO 3.01. 15
no, truly, ursula, she is too disdainful, | i 3.01. 34
good ursula, wake my cousin beatrice, and desire 3.04. 1 P
to dress me, good coz, good meg, good ursula. 3.04. 99 P
margaret, and ursula | are much deceiv'd, for 5.04. 78
and this to old mistress ursula, whom i have 2H4 1.02.240 P

U'S 2 FR 0.0002 REL FR 0 V 2 P
these be her very c's, her u's, and her t's, and TN 2.05. 87 P
her c's, her u's, and her t's: why that? 2.05. 89 P

US *(also 's*)*

/US 16 FR 0.0018 REL FR 14 V 2 P
a pretty jest your daughter told /us /of. ADO 2.03.135 P
/before /you /said, | "/let /us /make /head." 2H4 1.01.168
/let /us /on! 1.03. 85
/now, "/o /earth, /yield /us /that /king /again, 1.03.106
/those /men /that /most /have /done /us /wrong. 4.01. 79
/and /charg'd /us /from /his /soul /to /love R3 1.04.237
diomed, and our antenor | deliver'd to /us; TRO 4.02. 63
/let /us /make /ready /straight. 4.04.144
/let /us /address /to /tend /on /hector's /heels 4.04.146
/preserve /just /so /much /strength /in /us TIT 3.02. 2
/melody, | /came /here /to /make /us /merry! 3.02. 65
/but /that /between /us /we /can /kill /a /fly 3.02. 77
thus conscience does make cowards /of /us /all, HAM 3.01. 82
/let /us /deal /justly. LR 3.06. 40 P
/the /stars /above /us, /govern /our /conditions 4.03. 33
/it /touches /us, /as /france /invades /our 5.01. 25

US 1735 FR 0.1961 REL FR 1430 V 305 P
trouble us not. TMP 1.01. 18 P
"mercy on us!" 1.01. 60
wherefore did they not | that hour destroy us? 1.02.139
in few, they hurried us aboard a bark, | bore us 1.02.144
bore us some leagues to sea, where they prepared 1.02.145
there they hoist us, | to cry to th' sea, that 1.02.148
us, | to cry to th' sea, that roar'd to us; 1.02.149
sighing back again, | did us but loving wrong. 1.02.151
appointed | master of this design, did give us, 1.02.163
now | must by us both be spent most preciously. 1.02.241
my slave, who never | yields us kind answer. 1.02.309
wood, and serves in offices | that profit us. 1.02.313
fetch us in fuel, and be quick, thou'rt best, 1.02.366
few in millions | can speak like us. 2.01. 8
the air breathes upon us here most sweetly. 2.01. 47 P
to and importun'd otherwise | by all of us, and 2.01.130
it is foul weather in us all, good sir, | when 2.01.142
go sleep, and hear us. 2.01.190 P
shall that claribel | measure us back to naples? 2.01.259
then let us both be sudden. 2.01.306
and margery, | but none of us car'd for kate; 2.02. 49
if th' other two be brain'd like us, the state 3.02. 6 P
i am full of pleasure, | let us be jocund. 3.02.117
come on, trinculo, let us sing. 3.02.120 P
mercy upon us! 3.02.132 P
give us kind keepers, heavens! what were these? 3.03. 20
each putter–out of five for one will bring us 3.03. 48
done little better than play'd the jack with us. 4.01.198 P
our skins with pinches, | make us strange stuff. 4.01.234
some heavenly power guide us | out of this 5.01.105
give us particulars of thy preservation, | how 5.01.135
how thou hast met us here, whom three hours 5.01.136
is she the goddess that hath sever'd us, | and 5.01.187
hath sever'd us, | and brought us thus together? 5.01.188
let us not burthen our remembrances with | a 5.01.199
chalk'd forth the way | which brought us hither. 5.01.204
and all of us, ourselves, | when no man was his 5.01.212
o, look, sir, look, sir, here is more of us. 5.01.216
now let us take our leave. TGV 1.01. 56
lord, lord! to see what folly reigns in us! 1.02. 15
well, let us go. 1.02.129
sir thurio, give us leave, i pray, a while, | we 3.01. 1
let us into the city presently | to sort some 3.02. 90
stand, sir, and throw us that you have about ye. 4.01. 3
tell us this: have you any thing to take to? 4.01. 40
know, then, that some of us are gentlemen, 4.01. 42
say "ay" and be the captain of us all: 4.01. 63
come, go with us, we'll bring thee to our crews, 4.01. 72
how now, sir proteus, are you crept before us? 4.02. 18
then to silvia let us sing, | that silvia is 4.02. 49
to her let us garlands bring. 4.02. 53
being nimble–footed, he hath outrun us, | but 5.03. 7
come, let us go, we will include all jars | with 5.04.160
well, let us see honest master page. WIV 1.01. 66 P
now let us understand. 1.01.136 P
let us command to know that of your mouth, or of 1.01.227 P
puts into the press, when he would put us two. 2.01. 79 P
what doth he think of us? 2.01. 83 P
go in with us and see. 2.01.166 P
master page, will you go with us? 2.01.197 P
will you go with us to behold it? 2.01.206 P
heaven forgive you, and all of us, i pray — 2.02. 57 P
give us leave, drawer. 2.02.159 P
we have some salt of our youth in us, we are the 2.03. 48 P
let us wag then. 2.03. 97 P
pray you let us not be laughing–stocks to other 3.01. 85 P
have you make–a de sot of us, ha, ha? 3.01.116 P
he has made us his vlouting–stog. 3.01.117 P
and let us knog our prains together to be 3.01.119 P
little jack–a–lent, have you been true to us? 3.03. 28 P
i think, in the way of waste, attempt us again. 4.02.212 P
wives | yet once again (to make us public sport) 4.04. 13
and let us two devise to bring him thither. 4.04. 27
that falstaff at that oak shall meet with us, 4.04. 42
go get us properties | and tricking for our 4.04. 78
let us about it. 4.04. 80 P
what are they? let us know. 4.05. 42 P
oak | of herne the hunter, let us not forget. 5.05. 76
are now so sure that nothing can dissolve us. 5.05.224
good husband, let us every one go home, | and 5.05.241
call hither, | i say, bid come before us angelo. MM 1.01. 15
what figure of us think you he will bear? 1.01. 16
heaven doth with us as we with torches do, | not 1.01. 32
for if our virtues | did not go forth of us, 1.01. 34
how it goes with us, and do look to know | what 1.01. 57
let us withdraw together, | and we may soon our 1.01. 81
heaven grant us its peace, but not the king of 1.02. 4 P
there's not a soldier of us all, that, in the 1.02. 14 P
there went but a pair of shears between us. 1.02. 28 P
make us pay down for our offense by weight | the 1.02.121
hide our love | till time had made them for us. 1.02.153
and makes us lose the good we oft might win, 1.04. 78

ay, but yet | let us be keen, and rather cut a		2.01. 5
and forgive us all!		2.01. 37
is a more respected person than any of us all.		2.01.166 P
is that temptation that doth goad us on | to sin		2.02.181
nay, call us ten times frail, | for we are soft		2.04.128
let him be call'd before us.		3.02.205 P
come, let us go, | our corn's to reap, for yet		4.01. 74
and to deliver us from devices hereafter, which		4.04. 12 P
shall then have no power to stand against us.		4.04. 14 P
other of our friends | will greet us here anon.		4.05. 13
you must walk by us on our other hand;		5.01. 17
a scandalous breath to fall | on him so near us?		5.01.123
give us some seats.		5.01.165
the duke's in us;		5.01.295
is this the man | that you did tell us of?		5.01.325
and now, dear maid, be you as free to us.		5.01.388
so bring us to our palace, where we'll show		5.01.538
jars | 'twixt thy seditious countrymen and us,	ERR	1.01. 12
and left the ship, then sinking–ripe, to us.		1.01. 77
dispers'd those vapors that offended us, | and		1.01. 89
two ships from far, making amain to us, | of		1.01. 92
not now | worthily term'd them merciless to us!		1.01. 99
so that, in this unjust divorce of us, | fortune		1.01.104
fortune had left to both of us alike | what to		1.01.105
at length, another ship had seiz'd on us, | and,		1.01.112
good sister, let us dine, and never fret;		2.01. 6
but soft, who wafts us yonder?		2.02.109 P
how can she thus then call us by our names,		2.02.166
suck our breath, or pinch us black and blue.		2.02.192
good signior angelo, you must excuse us all,		3.01. 1
go bid them let us in.		3.01. 30
you'll let us in, i hope?		3.01. 54
if a crow help us in, sirrah, we'll pluck a crow		3.01. 83
and let us to the tiger all to dinner;		3.01. 95
make us /but believe | (being compact of credit)		3.02. 21
(being compact of credit) that you love us;		3.02. 22
though others have the arm, show us the sleeve:		3.02. 23
we in your motion turn, and you may move us.		3.02. 24
if every one knows us, and we know none, | 'tis		3.02.152
some blessed power deliver us from hence!		4.03. 44
will shake her chain, and fright us with it.		4.03. 76
avaunt, thou witch! come, dromio, let us go.		4.03. 79
away, they'll kill us.		4.04.146
here this night, they will surely do us no harm.		4.04.152 P
you saw they speak us fair, give us gold:		4.04.152 P
you saw they speak us fair, give us gold:		4.04.152 P
let us come in, that we may bind him fast, | and		5.01. 40
met us again, and madly bent on us | chas'd us		5.01.152
us again, and madly bent on us | chas'd us away;		5.01.152
us again, and madly bent on us | chas'd us away;		5.01.153
and here the abbess shuts the gates on us, | and		5.01.156
us, | and will not suffer us to fetch him out,		5.01.157
and that is false thou dost report to us.		5.01.179
the pains | to go with us into the abbey here,		5.01.395
error | have suffer'd wrong, go keep us company,		5.01.399
come go with us, we'll look to that anon.		5.01.413
prays some occasion may detain us longer.	ADO	1.01.150 P
jack, to tell us cupid is a good hare–finder and		1.01.184 P
in practice let us put it presently.		1.01.328
come, let us thither, this may prove food to my		1.03. 65 P
let us to the great supper, their cheer is the		1.03. 71 P
come let us to the banquet.		2.01.171 P
claudio, the time shall not go dully by us.		2.01.364 P
i pray thee get us some excellent music;		2.03. 85 P
my daughter tells us all.		2.03.133 P
let us send her to call him in to dinner.		2.03.218 P
say that thou overheardst us, | and bid her		3.01. 6
bear thee well in it, and leave us alone.		3.01. 13
how if the nurse be asleep and will not hear us?		3.03. 68 P
let us go sit here upon the church–bench till		3.03. 89 P
let us obey you to go with us.		3.03.175 P
let us obey you to go with us.		3.03.176 P
god help us, it is a world to see!		3.05. 35 P
come, let us go.		4.01.111
the virtue that possession would not show us		4.01.221
nay, do not quarrel with us, good old man.		5.01. 50
with quarrelling, | some of us would lie low.		5.01. 52
he shall kill two of us, and men indeed;		5.01. 80
and shall, or some of us will smart for it.		5.01.109
as we do the minstrels, draw to pleasure us.		5.01.129 P
the old man's daughter told us all.		5.01.178 P
dead, | and she alone is heir to both of us.		5.01.290
give us the swords, we have bucklers of our own.		5.02. 18 P
assist our moan, | help us to sigh and groan,		5.03. 17
thanks to you all, and leave us.		5.03. 28
come let us hence, and put on other weeds, | and		5.03. 30
familiar, | and to the chapel let us presently.		5.04. 71
and then grace us in the disgrace of death;	LLL	1.01. 3
keen edge, | and make us heirs of all eternity.		1.01. 7
necessity will make us all forsworn | three		1.01.149
god grant us patience!		1.01.195 P
as the style shall give us cause to climb in the		1.01.199 P
which | one part of aquitaine is bound to us,		2.01.135
and such barren plants are set before us, that		4.02. 28
those parts that do fructify in us more than he.		4.02. 29
a soul feminine saluteth us.		4.02. 81 P
god amend us, god amend!		4.03. 74
sweet lords, sweet lovers, o, let us embrace!		4.03.210
/let us once lose our oaths to find ourselves,		4.03.358
therefore let us devise | some entertainment for		4.03.369
from the park let us conduct them thither;		4.03.371
that will be time, and may by us be fitted.		4.03.379
for what is inward between us, let it pass.		5.01. 97 P
are they | that charge their breath against us?		5.02. 88
but what, but what, come they to visit us?		5.02.119
but shall we dance, if they desire us to't?		5.02.145
let us complain to them what fools were here,		5.02.302
should be presented at our tent to us.		5.02.307
a mess of russians left us but of late.		5.02.361
they did not bless us with one happy word.		5.02.370
we were descried, they'll mock us now downright.		5.02.389
let us confess and turn it to a jest.		5.02.390
soft, let us see — | write "lord have mercy on		5.02.418
write "lord have mercy on us" on those three:		5.02.419
no, they are free that gave these tokens to us.		5.02.424
our states are forfeit, seek not to undo us.		5.02.425
teach us, sweet madam, for our rude		5.02.431
forestall our sport, to make us thus untrue?		5.02.473
you cannot beg us, sir, i can assure you, sir,		5.02.490
berowne, they will shame us;		5.02.511
hath much deformed us, fashioning our humors		5.02.757
and what in us hath seem'd ridiculous — | as		5.02.759
presence of loose love | put on by us, if, in		5.02.767
look into these faults, | suggested us to make.		5.02.770
ever to be true | to those that make us both —		5.02.774
minute of the hour, | grant us your loves.		5.02.788
then let us teach our trial patience, | because	MND	1.01.152
place the sharp athenian law | cannot pursue us.		1.01.163
farewell, sweet playfellow, pray thou for us;		1.01.220
and that were enough to hang us all.		1.02. 77 P
that would hang us, every mother's son.		1.02. 78 P
would have no more discretion but to hang us;		1.02. 81 P
therefore the winds, piping to us in vain, | as		2.01. 88
and see our moonlight revels, go with us;		2.01.141
we'll rest us, hermia, if you think it good,		2.02. 37
one turf shall serve as pillow for us both,		2.02. 41
with /yourselves, to bring in (god shield us!)		3.01. 30 P
chid the hasty–footed time | for parting us — o		3.02.201
with us | these couples shall eternally be knit.		4.01.180
away with us to athens.		4.01.184
the duke was here, and bid us follow him?		4.01.195
and he did bid us follow to the temple.		4.01.197
a paramour is, god bless us, a thing of naught.		4.02. 14 P
let us hear, sweet bottom.		4.02. 33 P
more than to us | wait in your royal walks, your		5.01. 30
his discretion, and let us listen to the moon.		5.01.237 P
he for a man, god warr'nt us;		5.01.320 P
she for a woman, god bless us.		5.01.320 P
will we, | which by us shall blessed be;		5.01.404
then let us say you are sad | because you are	MV	1.01. 47
if it please you to dine with us.		1.03. 32 P
the rate of usance here with us in venice.		1.03. 45
and let us make incision for your love, | to		2.01. 6
disguise us at my lodging, and return | all in		2.04. 2
we have not spoke us yet of torch–bearers.		2.04. 5
of clock, we have two hours | to furnish us.		2.04. 9
under which lorenzo | desir'd us to make stand.		2.06. 2
our masquing mates by this time for us stay.		2.06. 59
i pray thee let us go and find him out | and		2.08. 51
but tell us, do you hear whether antonio have		3.01. 42 P
if you prick us, do we not bleed?		3.01. 64 P
if you tickle us, do we not laugh?		3.01. 65 P
if you poison us, do we not die?		3.01. 66 P
and if you wrong us, shall we not revenge?		3.01. 66 P
let us all ring fancy's knell.		3.02. 70
stay, | nor rest be interposer 'twixt us twain.		3.02.327
that strangers have | with us in venice, if it		3.03. 28
see our husbands | before they think of us.		3.04. 59
shall they see us?		3.04. 59
my coach, which stays for us | at the park–gate;		3.04. 82
nay, you need not fear us, lorenzo, launcelot		3.05. 31 P
i will anon, first let us go to dinner.		3.05. 86
bring us the letters; call the messenger.		4.01.110
of justice, none of us | should see salvation.		4.01.199
and that same prayer doth teach us all to render		4.01.201
take some remembrance of us, as a tribute, | not		4.01.422
and ceremoniously let us prepare | some welcome		5.01. 37
let us go in, | and charge us there upon		5.01.297
in, | and charge us there upon inter'gatories,		5.01.298
my blood, were there twenty brothers betwixt us.	AYL	1.01. 49 P
let us sit and mock the good huswife fortune		1.02. 31 P
nature hath given us wit to flout at fortune,		1.02. 45 P
which he will put on us, as pigeons feed their		1.02. 93 P
yet tell us the manner of the wrastling.		1.02.112 P
let us now stay and see it.		1.02.147 P
ay, my liege, so please you give us leave.		1.02.157 P
let us go thank him, and encourage him.		1.02.240
he calls us back.		1.02.252
out of service, let us talk in good earnest.		1.03. 26 P
fly, | whither to go, and what to bear with us,		1.03.101
alas, what danger will it be to us, | maids as		1.03.108
way | to hide us from pursuit that will be made		1.03.136
come, shall we go and kill us venison?		2.01. 21
yond man | if he for gold will give us any food;		2.04. 65
bring us where we may rest ourselves and feed.		2.04. 73
and thou shalt have to pay for it of us.		2.04. 93
more than your force move us to gentleness.		2.07.103
give us some music, and, good cousin, sing.		2.07.173
and would you have us kiss tar?		3.02. 63 P
shepherd, let us make an honorable retreat,		3.02.160 P
your features, lord warrant us! what features?		3.03. 5 P
me in this place of the forest and to couple us.		3.03. 45 P
well, the gods give us joy!		3.03. 47 P
will you dispatch us here under this tree, or		3.03. 65 P
o, come, let us remove, | the sight of lovers		3.04. 56
bring us to this sight, and you shall say | i'll		3.04. 58
will spit, and for lovers lacking (god warn us!)		4.01. 77 P
sister, you shall be the priest, and marry us.		4.01.125 P
pray thee marry us.		4.01.127 P
why now, as fast as she can marry us.		4.01.134 P
when from the first to last betwixt us two		4.03.139
good sir, go with us.		4.03.178 P
in this forest let us do those ends | that here		5.04.170
have endur'd shrewd days and nights with us,		5.04.173
here let us breathe and haply institute | a	SHR	1.01. 8
ashore, | we could at once put us in readiness,		1.01. 43
master, some show to welcome us to town.		1.01. 47
from all such devils, good lord deliver us!		1.01. 66
upon advice, it toucheth us both, that we may		1.01.116 P
since this bar in law makes us friends, it shall		1.01.136 P
i met, | upon agreement from us to his liking,		1.02.182
what, this gentleman will out–talk us all.		1.02.246
that you are the man | must stead us all, and me		1.02.264
let us that are poor petitioners speak too.		2.01. 72
let specialties be therefore drawn between us,		2.01.126
signior petruchio, will you go with us, | or		2.01.166
'tis bargain'd 'twixt us twain, being alone,		2.01.304
"hic steterat priami," take heed he hear us not,		3.01. 44 P
and tell us what occasion of import | hath all		3.02.102
love concerneth us to add | her father's liking,		3.02.128
let us entreat you stay till after dinner.		3.02.198
and better 'twere that both of us did fast,		4.01.173
come, tailor, let us see these ornaments;		4.03. 61
come, tailor, let us see't.		4.03. 86
to feast and sport us at thy father's house.		4.03.183
go call my men, and let us straight to him,		4.03.184
which way thou travellest — if along with us,		4.05. 51
chance to need thee at home, therefore leave us.		5.01. 3 P
packing, with a witness, to deceive us all!		5.01.118 P
unfold to us some warlike resistance.	AWW	1.01.116 P
whose baser stars do shut us up in wishes,		1.01.183
must think, which never | returns us thanks.		1.01.186
the fated sky | gives us free scope, only doth		1.01.218
that the florentine will move us | for speedy		1.02. 6
and would seem | to have us make denial.		1.02. 9
long, | but on us both did haggish age steal on,		1.02. 29
haggish age steal on, | and wore us out of act.		1.02. 30
our blood to us, this to our blood is born.		1.03.131
breeds | a native slip to us from foreign seeds.		1.03.146
o my sweet lord, that you will stay behind us!		2.01. 24
now, fair one, does your business follow us?		2.01. 99
when our most learned doctors leave us, and		2.01.116
as 'tis with us that square our guess by shows;		2.01.150
but most it is presumption in us when | the help		2.01.151
should indeed give us a further use to be made		2.03. 35 P
dream | we, poising us in her defective scale,		2.03.154
know | it is in us to plant thine honor where		2.03.156
i pray you make us friends, i will pursue the		2.05. 13 P
and all the honors that can fly from us | shall		3.01. 20
look, he has spied us.		3.05. 90 P
and this gentle maid | to eat with us to–night,		3.05. 98
it nothing steads us | to chide him from our		3.07. 41
why then to–night | let us assay our plot, which		3.07. 44
unless some one among us, whom we must produce		4.01. 5 P
linsey–woolsey hast thou to speak to us again?		4.01. 12 P
he must think us some band of strangers i' th'		4.01. 14 P
'a will betray us all unto ourselves:		4.01. 92
ay, so you serve us | till we serve you;		4.02. 17
ourselves, | and mock us with our bareness.		4.02. 20
is it not meant damnable in us, to be trumpeters		4.03. 26 P
sometimes we make us comforts of our losses!		4.03. 65 P
our waggon is prepar'd, and time revives us.		4.04. 34
let us go see your son, i pray you.		4.05.102 P
what good speed | our means will make us means.		5.01. 35
come, or sent it us | upon her great disaster.		5.03.111
let us from point to point this story know, | to		5.03.325
your gentle hands lend us, and take our hearts.		ep 6
thou hast spoke for us, madonna, as if thy	TN	1.05.112 P
give us the place alone, we will hear this		1.05.218 P
let us therefore eat and drink.		2.03. 13 P
possess us, possess us, tell us something of him		2.03.138 P
possess us, possess us, tell us something of him		2.03.138 P
us, possess us, tell us something of him.		2.03.138 P
though our silence be drawn from us with cars,		2.05. 63 P
come bring us, bring us where he is.		3.02. 84 P
come bring us, bring us where he is.		3.02. 84 P
i pray you let us satisfy our eyes | with the		3.03. 22
might well have given us bloody argument.		3.03. 32
out of breath, prompt us to have mercy on him;		3.04.139 P
what's that to us? the time goes by; away!		3.04.364
both form and suit, | you come to fright us.		5.01.236
if nothing lets to make us happy both | but this		5.01.249
he hath not told us of the captain yet.		5.01.381
wherein our entertainment shall shame us:	WT	1.01. 8 P
though they cannot praise us, as little accuse		1.01. 15 P
they cannot praise us, as little accuse us.		1.01. 16 P
no sneaping winds at home, to make us say,		1.02. 13
tougher, brother, | than you can put us to't.		1.02. 16
if you first sinn'd with us, and that with us		1.02. 84
us, and that with us | you did continue fault,		1.02. 84
and that you slipp'd not | with any but with us.		1.02. 86
how thou lov'st us, show in our brother's		1.02.174
if you would seek us, | we are yours i' th'		1.02.177
a sickness | which puts some of us in distemper,		1.02.385
let us avoid.		1.02.462
of these days, and then you'ld wanton with us,		2.01. 18
pray you sit by us, | and tell 's a tale.		2.01. 22
relish a truth like us, inform yourselves | we		2.01.167
come follow us, | we are to speak in public;		2.01.196
for this business | will raise us all.		2.01.198
beseech your highness, give us better credit.		2.03.147
serv'd you, and beseech' | so to esteem of us;		2.03.149
as thou art liegeman to us, that thou carry		2.03.174
as by strange fortune | it came to us, i do in		2.03.180
as it hath been to us rare, pleasant, speedy,		3.01. 13
our wife, and one | of us too much belov'd.		3.02. 4
let us be clear'd | of being tyrannous, since we		3.02. 4
thou shalt accompany us to the place, where we		4.02. 47 P
for it is | a way to make us better friends,		4.04. 66
on, | and bid us welcome to your sheep–shearing,		4.04. 69
you weary those that refresh us.		4.04.335 P
come on, | contract us 'fore these witnesses.		4.04.390
follow us to the court.		4.04.432
things known betwixt us three, i'll write you		4.04.560
omit | nothing may give us aid.		4.04.625
fortune speed us!		4.04.667
sure the gods do this year connive at us, and we		4.04.677 P
let us to the king.		4.04.707 P
and they often give us soldiers the lie, but we		4.04.724 P
steel, therefore they do not give us the lie.		4.04.726 P
your worship had like to have given us one, if		4.04.727 P
to undertake the business for us, here is that		4.04.807 P
let's before, as he bids us.		4.04.829 P
he was provided to do us good.		4.04.830 P
we shall not marry till thou bid'st us.		5.01. 82
sudden, tells us | 'tis not a visitation fram'd,		5.01. 90
'tis strange | he thus should steal upon us.		5.01.115
of something wildly | by us perform'd before.		5.01.130
the heaven sets spies upon us, will not have		5.01.203
should chase us with my father, pow'r no jot		5.01.217
our absence makes us unthrifty to our knowledge.		5.02.111 P
come, follow us;		5.02.174 P
and here justified | by us, a pair of kings.		5.03.146
lead us from hence, where we may leisurely		5.03.152
now say, chatillion, what would france with us?	JN	1.01. 1
our strong possession and our right for us.		1.01. 39
if old sir robert did beget us both, | and were		1.01. 80
why, what a madcap hath heaven lent us here!		1.01. 84
james gurney, wilt thou give us leave a while?		1.01.230
let us hear them speak | whose title they admit,		2.01.199
who is it that hath warn'd us to the walls?		2.01.201
for our advantage — therefore hear us first:		2.01.206
but on the sight of us, your lawful king, | who		2.01.222
and let us in — your king, whose labor'd		2.01.232

when i have said, make answer to us both. 2.01.235
then tell us, shall your city call us lord, | in 2.01.263
then tell us, shall your city call us lord, | in 2.01.263
at mine hostess' door, | teach us some fence! 2.01.290
know him in us, that here hold up his right. 2.01.364
in us, that are our own great deputy, | and bear 2.01.365
hear us, great kings! 2.01.416
the sea | (except this city now by us besieg'd) 2.01.489
it likes us well, young princes; 2.01.533
go we, as well as haste will suffer us, | to 2.01.559
let us go; 3.04.182
our suit | that you have bid us ask his liberty, 4.02. 63
he tells us arthur is deceas'd to-night. 4.02. 85
hand and seal | witness against us to damnation! 4.02.218
to-morrow morning let us meet him then. 4.03. 18
the king hath dispossess'd himself of us. 4.03. 23
there, tell the king, he may inquire us out. 4.03.115
let us, my liege, to arms. 5.01. 73
to give us warrant from the hand of heaven, 5.02. 66
what lusty trumpet thus doth summon us? 5.02.117
we grant thou canst outscold us. 5.02.160
how goes the day with us? o, tell me, hubert. 5.03. 1
and tempt us not to bear above our power! 5.06. 38
straight let us seek, or straight we shall be 5.07. 79
o, let us pay the time but needful woe, | since 5.07.110
nought shall make us rue, | if england to itself 5.07.117
which then our leisure would not let us hear, R2 1.01. 5
we thank you both, yet one but flatters us, | as 1.01. 25
can arbitrate this cause betwixt us twain; 1.01. 50
it must be great that can inherit us | so much 1.01. 85
then let us take a ceremonious leave | and 1.03. 50
withdraw with us, and let the trumpets sound 1.03.121
and make us wade even in our kinred's blood: 1.03.138
or complot any ill | 'gainst us, our state, our 1.03.190
by this time, had the king permitted us, | one 1.03.194
the revenue whereof shall furnish us | for our 1.04. 46
towards our assistance we do seize to us | the 2.01.160
bid him repair to us to ely house | to see this 2.01.216
for he is just and always loved us well. 2.01.221
inform, | merely in hate, 'gainst any of us all, 2.01.243
will the king severely prosecute | 'gainst us, 2.01.245
nay, let us share thy thoughts, as thou dost 2.01.273
for us to levy power | proportionable to the 2.02.124
will the hateful commons perform for us, 2.02.138
us, | except like curs to tear us all to pieces. 2.02.139
will you go along with us? 2.02.140
your presence makes us rich, most noble lord. 2.03. 63
but we must win your grace to go with us | to 2.03.163
shall see us rising in our throne, the east, 3.02. 50
they break their faith to god as well as us. 3.02.101
for god's sake let us sit upon the ground | and 3.02.155
show us the hand of god | that hath dismiss'd us 3.03. 77
that hath dismiss'd us from our stewardship, 3.03. 78
have torn their souls by turning them from us, 3.03. 83
till they have fretted us a pair of graves 3.03.167
for do we must what force will have us do. 3.03.207
i'll lay | a plot shall show us all a merry day. 4.01.334
here let us rest, if this rebellious earth 5.01. 5
the truth of what we are | shows us but this. 5.01. 20
part us, northumberland: 5.01. 76
banish us both, and send the king with me. 5.01. 83
if any plague hang over us, 'tis he. 5.03. 3
withdraw yourselves, and leave us here alone. 5.03. 28
tell us how near is danger | that we may arm us 5.03. 47
is danger | that we may arm us to encounter it. 5.03. 48
the cheapest of us is ten groats too dear. 5.05. 68
and he hath brought us smooth and welcome news. 1H4 1.01. 66
but come yourself with speed to us again, | for 1.01.105
let not us that are squires of the night's body 1.02. 24 P
let us be diana's foresters, gentlemen of the 1.02. 25 P
for the fortune of us that are the moon's men 1.02. 31 P
good sweet honey lord, ride with us to-morrow. 1.02.161 P
'tis like that they will know us by our horses, 1.02.174 P
yea, but i doubt they will be too hard for us. 1.02.182 P
fat rogue will tell us when we meet at supper, 1.02.188 P
provide us all things necessary, and meet me 1.02.191 P
you have good leave to leave us. 1.03. 20
send us your prisoners, or you will hear of it. 1.03.124
unhappy king | (whose wrongs in us god pardon!) 1.03.149
and 'tis no little reason bids us speed, | to 1.03.283
till he hath found a time to pay us home. 1.03.288
to make us strangers to his looks of love. 1.03.290
why, they will allow us ne'er a jordan, and then 2.01. 19 P
there's enough to make us all. 2.02. 58 P
from your encounter, then they light on us. 2.02. 62 P
'zounds, will they not rob us? 2.02. 65 P
jesus bless us! 2.02. 82 P
they hate us youth. 2.02. 85 P
my masters, let us share, and then to horse 2.02. 98 P
there be four of us here have ta'en a thousand 2.04.158 P
taken from us it is: 2.04.161 P
a hundred upon poor four of us. 2.04.162 P
some six or seven fresh men set upon us — 2.04.181 P
come, tell us your reason; 2.04.233 P
done in fight, and persuaded us to do the like. 2.04.308 P
power, | as is appointed us, at shrewsbury. 3.01. 85
here come our wives, and let us take our leave. 3.01.189
lords, give us leave, the prince of wales and i 3.02. 1
mortimer, | capitulate against us, and are up. 3.02.120
yet doth he give us bold advertisement | that 4.01. 36
on, | to see how fortune is dispos'd to us, 4.01. 38
your father's sickness is a maim to us. 4.01. 42
whence | the eye of reason may pry in upon us. 4.01. 72
the powers of us may serve so great a day. 4.01.132
come let us take a muster speedily. 4.01.133
i can tell you, looks for us all, we must away 4.02. 56 P
to-morrow in the battle | which of us fears. 4.03. 14
some of us love you well, and even those some 4.03. 34
quality, | but stand against us like an enemy. 4.03. 37
and in conclusion drove us to seek out | this 4.03.102
king | dismiss his power he means to visit us, 4.04. 37
and made us doff our easy robes of peace, | to 5.01. 12
you swore to us, | and you did swear that oath 5.01. 41
hand, | forgot your oath to us at doncaster, 5.01. 58
and being fed by us you us'd us so | as that 5.01. 59
and being fed by us you us'd us so | as that 5.01. 59
troth | sworn to us in your younger enterprise. 5.01. 71
yield, | rebuke and dread correction wait on us, 5.01.111
and god befriend us, as our cause is just! 5.01.120
the king should keep his word in loving us. 5.02. 5
he will suspect us still, and find a time | to 5.02. 6
on, | and, his corruption being ta'en from us, 5.02. 22
he calls us rebels, traitors, and will scourge 5.02. 39
with haughty arms this hateful name in us. 5.02. 40
if die, brave death, when princes die with us! 5.02. 86
of war, | and by that music let us all embrace, 5.02. 98
some of us never shall | a second time do such a 5.02. 99
o, this boy | lends mettle to us all! 5.04. 24
for the hour is come | to end the one of us, and 5.04. 69
brother, let us to the highest of the field, 5.04.160
have taught us how to cherish such high deeds 5.05. 30
let us not leave till all our own be won. 5.05. 44
not the capacities of us that are young, you do 2H4 1.02.174 P
to us no more, nay, not so much, lord bardolph, 1.03. 69
perforce a third | must take up us. 1.03. 73
and come against us in full puissance, | need 1.03. 77
it may chance cost some of us our lives, for he 2.01. 11 P
telling us she had a good dish of prawns, 2.01. 96 P
instruct us, boy, what dream, boy? 2.02. 88 P
nay, they will be kin to us, or they will fetch 2.02.117 P
of the wise sit in the clouds and mock us. 2.02.143 P
this virtuous gentlewoman to close with us. 2.04.327 P
then let us meet them like necessities; 3.01. 93
and that same word even now cries out on us. 3.01. 94
god send us peace! 3.02.293 P
let us sway on and face them in the field. 4.01. 24
what well-appointed leader fronts us here? 4.01. 25
now) | hath put us in these ill-beseeming arms, 4.01. 84
and to us all | that feel the bruises of the 4.01. 97
but he hath forc'd us to compel this offer, 4.01.145
to us and /to our purposes confin'd | we come 4.01.173
to us the speaker in his parliament, | to us th' 4.02. 18
to us th' /imagin'd voice of god himself, | the 4.02. 19
crowd us and crush us to this monstrous form 4.02. 34
crowd us and crush us to this monstrous form 4.02. 34
let our trains | march by us, that we may peruse 4.02. 94
our news shall go before us to his majesty, 4.03. 78
and cowards, which some of us should be too, but 4.03. 95 P
and pause us, till these rebels, now afoot, 4.04. 9
let us withdraw into the other room. 4.05. 18
will't please your grace to go along with us? 4.05. 19
depart the chamber, leave us here alone. 4.05. 90
well, peace be with him that hath made us heavy! 5.02. 25
peace be with us, lest we be heavier! 5.02. 26
than a joint burden laid upon us all. 5.02. 55
and let us choose such limbs of noble counsel 5.02.135
be | as things acquainted and familiar to us, 5.02.139
let us take any man's horses, the laws of 5.03.135 P
and let us, ciphers to this great accompt, | on H5 pr 17
was like, and had indeed against us pass'd, 1.01. 3
if it pass against us, | we lose the better half 1.01. 7
given to the church, | would they strip from us; 1.01. 11
than cherishing th' exhibiters against us; 1.01. 74
task our thoughts, concerning us and france. 1.02. 6
or should, or should not, bar us in our claim; 1.02. 12
of what your reverence shall incite us to. 1.02. 20
who will make road upon us | with all advantages 1.02.138
who hath been still a giddy neighbor to us; 1.02.145
let us be worried, and our nation lose | the 1.02.219
may't please your majesty to give us leave 1.02.237
uncurbed plainness | tell us the dolphin's mind. 1.02.245
we are glad the dolphin is so pleasant with us, 1.02.259
how he comes o'er us with our wilder days, | not 1.02.267
yea, strike the dolphin blind to look on us. 1.02.280
for we have now no thought in us but france, 1.02.302
let us condole the knight, for, lambkins, we 2.01.127
think you not that the pow'rs we bear with us 2.02. 15
we carry not a heart with us from hence | that 2.02. 21
not wish | success and conquest to attend on us. 2.02. 24
o, let us yet be merciful. 2.02. 47
swallow'd, and digested, | appear before us? 2.02. 57
the mercy that was quick in us but late, | by 2.02. 79
of france | to kill us here in hampton. 2.02. 91
no less for bounty bound to us | than cambridge 2.02. 92
the enterprise whereof | shall be to you as us, 2.02.183
let us deliver | our puissance into the hand of 2.02.189
let us to france, like horse-leeches, my boys, 2.03. 55
thus comes the english with full power upon us, 2.04. 1
and more than carefully it us concerns | to 2.04. 2
it fits us then to be as provident | as fear may 2.04. 11
as fear may teach us out of late examples | left 2.04. 12
it is most meet we arm us 'gainst the foe; 2.04. 15
and let us do it with no show of fear, | no, 2.04. 23
the kindred of him hath been flesh'd upon us; 2.04. 50
strain | that haunted us in our familiar paths. 2.04. 52
and let us fear | the native mightiness and fate 2.04. 63
for us, we will consider of this further. 2.04.113
dispatch us with all speed, lest that our king 2.04.141
show us here | the mettle of your pasture; 3.01. 26
let us swear | that you are worth your breeding, 3.01. 27
and the trumpet call us to the breach, and we 3.02.108 P
'tis shame for us all. 3.02.110 P
proud of destruction, | defy us to our worst; 3.03. 5
returns us that his powers are yet not ready 3.03. 46
enter our gates, dispose of us and ours, | for 3.03. 49
use mercy to them all for us, dear uncle. 3.03. 54
withal, my lord, | let us not live in france; 3.05. 3
let us quit all, | and give our vineyards to a 3.05. 3
shall a few sprays of us, | the emptying of our 3.05. 5
let us not hang like roping icicles | upon our 3.05. 23
our madams mock at us, and plainly say | our 3.05. 28
they bid us to the english dancing-schools, 3.05. 32
fear, | and for achievement offer us his ransom. 3.05. 60
prince dolphin, you shall stay with us in roan. 3.05. 64
be patient, for you shall remain with us. 3.05. 66
and quickly bring us word of england's fall. 3.05. 68
i hope they will not come upon us now. 3.06.168
and for the world, familiar to us and unknown, 3.07. 37 P
for our bad neighbor makes us early stirrers, 4.01. 6
outward consciences | and preachers to us all, 4.01. 9
that we should dress us fairly for our end. 4.01. 10
to the king wipes the crime of it out of us. 4.01.133 P
ay, he said so, to make us fight cheerfully; 4.01.192 P
let it be a quarrel between us, if you live. 4.01.205 P
twenty french crowns to one they will beat us, 4.01.226 P
let us our lives, our souls, | our debts, our 4.01.230
let us but blow on them, | the vapor of our 4.02. 23
a very little little let us do, | and all is 4.02. 33
god's arm strike with us! 4.03. 5
that fears his fellowship to die with us. 4.03. 39
that fought with us upon saint crispin's day. 4.03. 67
and will with all expedience charge on us. 4.03. 70
which likes me better than to wish us one. 4.03. 77
fly — | and time hath worn us into slovenry. 4.03.114
the french might have a good prey of us, if he 4.04. 76 P
let us die! 4.05. 11
disorder, that hath spoil'd us, friend us now! 4.05. 17
disorder, that hath spoil'd us, friend us now! 4.05. 17
let us on heaps go offer up our lives. 4.05. 18
if they will fight with us, bid them come down, 4.07. 58
o, give us leave, great king, | to view the 4.07. 81
and not to us, but to thy arm alone, | ascribe 4.08.107
this acknowledgment, | that god fought for us. 4.08.120
yes, my conscience, he did us great good. 4.08.121 P
and bless us with her former qualities. 5.02. 67
council presently | to sit with us once more, 5.02. 80
go with the princes, or stay here with us? 5.02. 91
yet leave our cousin katherine here with us: 5.02. 95
heralds, wait on us. 1H6 1.01. 45
now we are victors, upon us he smiles. 1.02. 4
faintly besiege us one hour in a month. 1.02. 8
food, | do rush upon us as their hungry prey. 1.02. 28
bastard of orleance, thrice welcome to us. 1.02. 47
back, you lords, and give us leave a while. 1.02. 70
leave off delays, and let us raise the siege. 1.02.146
they may vex us with shot or with assault. 1.04. 13
let us look in, the sight will much delight thee 1.04. 62
o lord, have mercy on us, wretched sinners! 1.04. 70
chance is this that suddenly hath cross'd us? 1.04. 72
they call'd us for our fierceness english dogs, 1.05. 25
is ent'red into orleance | in spite of us, or 1.05. 37
to celebrate the joy that god hath given us. 1.06. 14
come in, and let us banquet royally, | after 1.06. 30
let us have knowledge at the court of guard. 2.01. 4
artois, | wallon, and picardy are friends to us, 2.01. 10
let us resolve to scale their flinty bulwarks. 2.01. 27
that, if it chance the one of us do fail, | the 2.01. 31
didst thou at first, to flatter us withal, 2.01. 51
us withal, | make us partakers of a little gain, 2.01. 52
judge you, my lord of warwick, then between us. 2.04. 10
ah, thou shalt find us ready for thee still; 2.04.104
and know us by these colors for thy foes, | for 2.04.105
come, let us four to dinner. 2.04.132
henry, | pity the city of london, pity us! 3.01. 77
away, my masters, trouble us no more, | but join 3.01.144
dare ye come forth and meet us in the field? 3.02. 61
belike your lordship takes us then for fools, 3.02. 62
away, captains, let's get us from the walls, 3.02. 71
courageous bedford, let us now persuade you. 3.02. 93
burgundy | to leave the talbot and to follow us. 3.03. 20
nor should that nation boast it so with us, 3.03. 23
brave duke, thy friendship makes us fresh. 3.03. 86
now let us on, my lords, and join our powers, 3.03. 90
the quarrel toucheth none but us alone, 4.01.118
betwixt ourselves let us decide it then. 4.01.119
to trouble and disturb the king and us? 4.01.127
and let us not forgo | that for a trifle that 4.01.149
so let us still continue peace, and love. 4.01.161
be humble to us, call my sovereign yours, | and 4.02. 6
on us thou canst not enter but by death; 4.02. 18
and they shall find dear deer of us, my friends. 4.02. 54
and left us to the rage of france his sword. 4.06. 3
antic death, which laugh'st us here to scorn, 4.07. 18
during the life, let us not wrong it dead. 4.07. 50
peace be amongst them if they turn to us, | else 5.02. 6
most of all these reasons bindeth us | in our 5.05. 60
they please us well. 2H6 1.01. 63
come, let us in, and with all speed provide | to 1.01. 73
and greatness of his place be grief to us, | yet 1.01.173
to us, | yet let us watch the haughty cardinal; 1.01.174
behooves it us to labor for the realm. 1.01.182
i go. come, nell, thou wilt ride with us? 1.02. 59
so i pray you go in god's name, and leave us. 1.04. 10 P
and let us to our work. 1.04. 12 P
you, madam, shall with us. 1.04. 51
good fellow, tell us here the circumstance, 2.01. 72
well, for this night we will repose us here; 2.01.196
in sight of god and us, your guilt is great; 2.03. 2
and god in justice hath reveal'd to us | the 2.03.102
come, fellow, follow us for thy reward. 2.03.105
with her that hateth thee and hates us all, 2.04. 52
man, | what e'er occasion keeps him from us now. 3.01. 3
knee, | disdaining duty that to us belongs. 3.01. 17
the care you have of us | to mow down thorns 3.01. 66
the welfare of us all | hangs on the cutting 3.01. 80
he'll wrest the sense and hold us here all day. 3.01.186
world, | to rid us from the fear we have of him. 3.01.234
that henceforth he shall trouble us no more. 3.01.324
when from thy shore the tempest beat us back, 3.02.102
to free us from his father's wrathful curse, | i 3.02.155
curtain close, | and let us all to meditation. 3.03. 33
normans thorough thee | disdain to call us lord, 4.01. 88
therefore come you with us and let him go. 4.01.141
for our enemies shall /fall before us, inspir'd 4.02. 35 P
they are all in order, and march toward us. 4.02.188 P
we will have the mayor's sword borne before us. 4.03. 14 P
thee, | therefore away with us to killingworth. 4.04. 44
come, margaret, god, our hope, will succor us. 4.04. 55
he that made us pay one and twenty fifteens, and 4.07. 21 P
nay, he nods at us, as who should say, i'll be 4.07. 94 P
for with these borne before us, in stead of 4.07.135 P
quake, | shake he his weapon at us and pass by. 4.08. 18
unless by robbing of your friends and us. 4.08. 40
doth york intend no harm to us | that thus he 5.01. 56
and will that thou henceforth attend on us. 5.01. 80
nay, do not fright us with an angry look. 5.01.126
of one or both of us the time is come. 5.02. 13
enemy way, and to secure us | by what we can, 5.02. 76
let us pursue him ere the writs go forth. 5.03. 26
all, | and more such days as these to us befall! 5.03. 33
by words or blows here let us win our right. 3H6 1.01. 37
hath made us by-words to our enemies. 1.01. 42
parliament | let us assail the family of york. 1.01. 65

art thou against us, duke of exeter? 1.01.147
how hast thou injur'd both thyself and us! 1.01.179
come, cousin, let us tell the queen these news. 1.01.182
about that which concerns your grace and us: 1.02. 8
the army of the queen mean to besiege us. 1.02. 64
to every good | as the antipodes are unto us, 1.04.135
think but upon the wrong he did us all, | and 1.04.173
i think it cites us, brother, to the field, 2.01. 34
god and saint george for us! 2.01.204
ay, good my lord, and leave us to our fortune. 2.02. 75
by him that made us all, i am resolv'd | that 2.02.124
and that thy summer bred us no increase, | we 2.02.164
our ranks are broke, and ruin follows us. 2.03. 10
bootless is flight, they follow us with wings, 2.03. 12
yet let us all together to our troops, | and 2.03. 49
and call them pillars that will stand to us; 2.03. 51
for death doth hold us in pursuit. 2.05.127
breathe we, lords, good fortune bids us pause, 2.06. 31
that nothing sung but death to us and ours. 2.06. 57
and he nor sees nor hears us what we say. 2.06. 63
why linger we? let us lay hands upon him. 3.01. 26
and you must be contented | to go along with us; 3.01. 68
the king's, | to go with us unto the officers. 3.01. 98
lords, give us leave. i'll try this widow's wit. 3.02. 33
of england, worthy margaret, | sit down with us. 3.03. 2
and if thou fail us, all our hope is done. 3.03. 33
now, sister, let us hear your firm resolve. 3.03.129
warwick, this is some post to us or thee. 3.03.162
dare he presume to scorn us in this manner? 3.03.178
if king lewis vouchsafe to furnish us | with 3.03.203
let us be back'd with god, and with the seas, 4.01. 43
now, brother richard, will you stand by us? 4.01.145
now therefore let us hence, and lose no hour, 4.01.148
the common people by numbers swarm to us. 4.02. 2
for us to do | but march to london with our 4.03. 60
come therefore let us fly while we may fly, | if 4.04. 34
fly, | if warwick take us we are sure to die. 4.04. 35
but let us hence, my sovereign, to provide | a 4.06. 87
rest, | yet thus far fortune maketh us amends, 4.07. 2
tush, man, abodements must not now affright us. 4.07. 13
in, | for hither will our friends repair to us. 4.07. 15
drummer, strike up, and let us march away. 4.07. 50
and once again proclaim us king of england. 4.08. 53
the gates are open, let us enter too. 5.01. 60
doubt | will issue out again and bid us battle. 5.01. 63
for warwick was a bug that fear'd us all. 5.02. 2
and, as we hear, march on to fight with us. 5.03. 9
shelves and rocks that threaten us with wrack. 5.04. 23
if case some one of you would fly from us, 5.04. 34
to haste thus fast, to find us unprovided. 5.04. 63
bring forth the gallant, let us hear him speak. 5.05. 12
sirrah, leave us to ourselves, we must confer. 5.06. 6
"o, jesus bless us, he is born with teeth!" 5.06. 75
i know it pleaseth neither of us well. R3 1.01.113
that makes us wretched by the death of thee 1.02. 18
devil, for god's sake hence, and trouble us not, 1.02. 50
days, | which here you urge to prove us enemies, 1.03.145
to pray for them that have done scath to us. 1.03.316
tell them that god bids us do good for evil: 1.03.334
of york and lancaster, | that had befall'n us. 1.04. 16
when he opens his purse to give us our reward, 1.04.129 P
offended us you have not, but the king. 1.04.178
how canst thou urge god's dreadful law to us, 1.04.209
provoke us hither now to slaughter thee. 1.04.225
ay, millstones, as he lesson'd us to weep. 1.04.240
'tis he that sends us to destroy you here. 1.04.243
if ever any grudge were lodg'd between us; 2.01. 66
good grandam, tell us, is our father dead? 2.02. 1
why do you look on us, and shake your head, 2.02. 5
and call us orphans, wretches, castaways, | if 2.02. 6
all of us have cause | to wail the dimming of 2.02.101
i hope the king made peace with all of us, | and 2.02.132
for god sake let not us two stay at home; 2.02.147
now be nearest | will touch us all too near, if 2.03. 26
would long ere this have met us on the way. 3.01. 21
not | to tell us whether they will come or no! 3.01. 23
if thou dost find him tractable to us, 3.01.174
talk, | and give us notice of his inclination; 3.01.178
at crosby house, there shall you find us both. 3.01.190
come, let us sup betimes, that afterwards | we 3.01.199
where nothing can proceed that toucheth us 3.02. 23
pursues | were to incense the boar to follow us, 3.02. 29
where he shall see the boar will use us kindly. 3.02. 33
to hear her prayer for them, as now for us! 3.03. 20
come, grey, come, vaughan, let us here embrace. 3.03. 25
god and our /innocence defend and guard us! 3.05. 20
safety, | enforc'd us to this execution? 3.05. 46
may | misconster us in him and wail his death. 3.05. 61
marry, god defend his grace should say us nay! 3.07. 81
and pardon us the interruption | of thy devotion 3.07.102
the royal tree hath left us royal fruit, | which 3.07.167
and make (no doubt) us happy by his reign. 3.07.170
if not to bless us and the land withal, | yet to 3.07.197
come, let us to our holy work again. 3.07.246
who meets us here? 4.01. 1
a hell–hound that doth hunt us all to death: 4.04. 48
thy womb let loose to chase us to our graves. 4.04. 54
i doubt not but his friends will turn to us. 5.02. 19
let us survey the vantage of the ground. 5.03. 15
let us consult upon to–morrow's business. 5.03. 45
in brief — for so the season bids us be — 5.03. 87
god give us leisure for these rites of love! 5.03.101
make us thy ministers of chastisement, | that we 5.03.113
let us be lead within thy bosom, richard, | and 5.03.147
had rather have us win than him they follow: 5.03.244
march on, join bravely, let us to it pell–mell; 5.03.312
if we be conquered, let men conquer us, | and 5.03.332
inspire us with the spleen of fiery dragons! 5.03.350
if it please you, we may now withdraw us. 5.05. 11
fled | that in submission will return to us, 5.05. 17
will leave us never an understanding friend. H8 pr 22
/'a gives us note | the force of his own merit 1.01. 63
the peace between the french and us not values 1.01. 88
let be call'd before us | that gentleman of 1.02. 4
arise, and take place by us. 1.02. 10
half your suit | never name to us; 1.02. 11
you that are blam'd for it alike with us, | know 1.02. 39
sit by us, you shall hear | (this was his 1.02.124
his period, | to sheathe his knife in us. 1.02.210
if none, | let him not seek't of us. 1.02.213
a hand as fruitful as the land that feeds us; 1.03. 56
then we shall have 'em | talk us to silence. 1.04. 45
good angels keep it from us! 2.01.142
crack'd the league | between us and the emperor 2.02. 25
and free us from his slavery. 2.02. 43
or this imperious man will work us all | from 2.02. 46
my lord, you'll bear us company? 2.02. 58
reverend sir, into our kingdom, | use us and it. 2.02. 77
i would your grace would give us but an hour 2.02. 79
self, hath sent | one general tongue unto us: 2.02. 95
your rage mistakes us. 3.01.101
pray think us | those we profess, peacemakers, 3.01.166
for us (if you please | to trust us in your 3.01.172
(if you please | to trust us in your business), 3.01.173
(though now the time | gives way to us) i much 3.02. 16
it, say withal | if you are bound to us, or no. 3.02.165
forward, | and dare us with his cap, like larks. 3.02.282
about the giving–back the great seal to us, 3.02.347
good sir, speak it to us. 4.01. 61
you may command us, sir. 4.01.117
repose, and not for us | to waste these times. 5.01. 4
bring him to us. 5.01. 83
have mov'd us and our council, that you shall 5.01.100
that you shall | this morning come before us, 5.01.101
you a brother of us, | it fits we thus proceed, 5.01.106
thy truth and thy integrity is rooted | in us, 5.01.115
and your appeal to us | there make before them. 5.01.151
want of wisdom, you, that best should teach us, 5.02. 48
the king's further pleasure | be known unto us. 5.02.126
in daily thanks, that gave us such a prince, 5.02.150
tool come to court, the women so besiege us? 5.03. 35 P
he stands there like a mortar–piece to blow us. 5.03. 46 P
is it matter new to us | that we come short of TRO 1.03. 10
slanderer, he imitation calls, | he pageants us. 1.03.151
a mint, | to match us in comparisons with dirt, 1.03.194
this troyan scorns us, or the men of troy | are 1.03.233
yourself shall feast with us before you go, 1.03.308
a nursery of like evil, | to overbulk us all. 1.03.320
and doth boil | (as 'twere from forth us all) a 1.03.350
let us, like merchants, first show foul wares, 1.03.358
to guard a thing not ours nor worth to us | (had 2.02. 22
let us pay betimes | a moi'ty of that mass of 2.02.106
our fire–brand brother, paris, burns us all. 2.02.110
and jove forbid there should be done amongst us 2.02.127
foes, | and fame in time to come canonize us, 2.02.202
let him show us a cause. 2.03. 88 P
untent his person and share th' air with us? 2.03.168
a whoreson dog, that shall palter with us thus! 2.03.233
nay, this shall not hedge us out, we'll hear you 3.01. 60 P
you shall not bob us out of our melody. 3.01. 68 P
this love will undo us all. 3.01.111 P
let us to priam's hall | to greet the warriors. 3.01.148
'twill make us proud to be his servant, paris! 3.01.155
what he shall receive of us in duty | gives us 3.01.156
gives us more palm in beauty than we have, | yea 3.01.157
enough than for us to undergo any difficulty 3.02. 80 P
praise us as we are tasted, allow us as we prove 3.02. 90 P
us as we are tasted, allow us as we prove. 3.02. 91 P
who shall be true to us, | when we are so 3.02.124
what wouldst thou of us, troyan? make demand. 3.03. 17
they will almost | give us a prince of blood, a 3.03. 26
bear him, | and bring us cressid hither; 3.03. 31
calchas shall have | what he requests of us. 3.03. 32
what says achilles? would he aught with us? 3.03. 57
lords after the combat | to see us here unarm'd. 3.03.237
or, if you please, | haste there before us. 4.01. 41
let us cast away nothing, for we may live to 4.04. 21 P
and scants us with a single famish'd kiss, 4.04. 47
kindly, | for it is parting from us. 4.04. 61
come kiss, and let us part. 4.04. 98
i am not warm yet, let us fight again. 4.05.118
forbids | a gory emulation 'twixt us twain. 4.05.123
great agamemnon comes to meet us here. 4.05.159
but, by great mars, the captain of us all, 4.05.198
when we have here her base and pillar by us. 4.05.212
i pray you let us see you in the field; 4.05.266
patroclus, let us feast him to the height. 5.01. 3
stand where the torch may not discover us. 5.02. 5
you are moved, prince, let us depart, i pray, 5.02. 36
this fault in us i find, | the error of our eye 5.02.109
take heed, the quarrel's most ominous to us. 5.07. 21 P
be sent | to pray achilles see us at our tent. 5.09. 8
if in his death the gods have us befriended, 5.09. 9
let us kill him, and we'll have corn at our own COR 1.01. 10 P
what authority surfeits /on would relieve us. 1.01. 17 P
if they would yield us but the superfluity while 1.01. 17 P
we might guess they reliev'd us humanely; 1.01. 19 P
the leanness that afflicts us, the object of our 1.01. 20 P
let us revenge this with our pikes, ere we 1.01. 22 P
care for us? 1.01. 79 P
they ne'er car'd for us yet. 1.01. 80 P
suffer us to famish, and their store–houses 1.01. 80 P
if the wars eat us not up, they will; 1.01. 85 P
and there's all the love they bear us. 1.01. 86 P
martius, 'tis true that you have lately told us, 1.01.227
where i know | our greatest friends attend us. 1.01.245
made doubt but rome was ready | to answer us. 1.02. 19
to your bands, | let us alone to guard corioles. 1.02. 27
you'll find | th' have not prepar'd for us. 1.02. 30
'tis sworn between us we shall ever strike 1.02. 35
come, you shall go with us. 1.03. 86 P
true, on mine honor, and so i pray go with us. 1.03.101 P
solemnness out a' door, and go along with us. 1.03.108 P
now, mars, i prithee make us quick in work, 1.04. 10
our walls | rather than they shall pound us up; 1.04. 17
they fear us not, but issue forth their city. 1.04. 23
they do disdain us much beyond our thoughts, 1.04. 26
to their wives, | as they us to our trenches. 1.04. 42
and you shall | divide in all with us. 1.06. 87
our guider, come, to th' roman camp conduct us. 1.07. 7
than grateful | to us that give you truly. 1.09. 55
as to us, to all the world, that caius martius 1.09. 59
where, ere we do repose us, we will write | to 1.09. 74
send us to rome | the best, with whom we may 1.09. 76
the city, i mean of us a' th' right–hand file? 2.01. 22 P
and carry with us ears and eyes for th' time, 2.01.269
and make us think | rather our state's defective 2.02. 49
i know they do attend us. 2.02.160
for if he show us his wounds and tell us his 2.03. 6 P
if he show us his wounds and tell us his deeds, 2.03. 6 P
so, if he tell us his noble deeds, we must also 2.03. 8 P
and to make us no better thought of, a little 2.03. 14 P
stuck not to call us the many–headed multitude. 2.03. 16 P
wherein every one of us has a single honor, in 2.03. 44 P
we do, sir, tell us what hath brought you to't. 2.03. 63 P
he mock'd us when he begg'd our voices. 2.03.159
certainly, | he flouted us downright. 2.03.160
no, 'tis his kind of speech, he did not mock us. 2.03.161
not one amongst us, save yourself, but says | he 2.03.162
save yourself, but says | he us'd us scornfully. 2.03.163
he should have show'd us | his marks of merit, 2.03.163
lay | a fault on us, your tribunes, that we 2.03.227
lay the fault on us. 2.03.234
ay, spare us not. 2.03.235
by mingling them with us, the honor'd number, 3.01. 72
measles | which we disdain should tetter us, yet 3.01. 79
and in true fear | they gave us our demands." 3.01.135
or let us stand to our authority, | or let us 3.01.207
us stand to our authority, | or let us lose it. 3.01.208
leave us to cure this cause. 3.01.234
for 'tis a sore upon us | you cannot tent 3.01.234
come, sir, along with us. 3.01.236
country | were to us all that do't and suffer it 3.01.301
come, go with us, speak fair. 3.02. 70
pray you let us go. 3.02.142
if he evade us there, | enforce him with his 3.03. 2
there which looks | with us to break his neck. 3.03. 30
answer to us. 3.03. 61
and in the power of us the tribunes, we, | even 3.03.100
let a guard | attend us through the city. 3.03.141
that thou mayst hear of us | and we of thee; 4.01. 39
let us seem humbler after it is done | than when 4.02. 4
they have ta'en note of us; keep on your way. 4.02. 10
well, let us go together. 4.03. 52 P
it cannot be | the volsces dare break with us. 4.06. 49
him | against us brats with no less confidence 4.06. 93
if he could burn us all into one coal, | we have 4.06.137
and, to say the truth, so did very many of us. 4.06.143 P
the gods be good to us! 4.06.153 P
thou art preparing fire for us; 5.02. 71 P
the sorrow that delivers us thus chang'd | makes 5.03. 39
you have said you will not grant us any thing; 5.03. 87
may hang upon your hardness, therefore hear us. 5.03. 91
thou barr'st us | our prayers to the gods, which 5.03.104
nay, go not from us thus. 5.03.131
volsces whom you serve, you might condemn us, 5.03.134
let us shame him with our knees. 5.03.169
come, let us go. 5.03.177
yet give us our dispatch. 5.03.180
come enter with us. 5.03.206
the gods be good unto us! 5.04. 30 P
such a case the gods will not be good unto us. 5.04. 32 P
to break our necks, they respect not us. 5.04. 34 P
the same intent wherein | you wish'd us parties, 5.06. 13
our levies, answering us | with our own charge, 5.06. 66
his last offenses to us | shall have judicious 5.06.125
let us entreat by honor of his name, | whom TIT 1.01. 39
give us the proudest prisoner of the goths, 1.01. 96
favors done | to us in our election this day, 1.01.235
romans, let us go; 1.01.273
but let us give him burial as becomes, | give 1.01.347
he is not with himself, let us withdraw. 1.01.368
dear father, soul and substance of us all — 1.01.374
'tis good, sir, you are very short with us; 1.01.409
away, and talk not, trouble us no more. 1.01.478
adore, | this petty brabble will undo us all. 2.01. 62
uncouple here and let us make a bay, | and wake 2.02. 3
come on then, horse and chariots let us have, 2.02. 18
under their sweet shade, aaron, let us sit, 2.03. 16
let us sit down and mark their yellowing noise; 2.03. 20
birds | be unto us as is a nurse's song | of 2.03. 28
i pray you let us hence, | and let her joy her 2.03. 82
let not this wasp outlive, us both to sting. 2.03.132
away, for thou hast stay'd us here too long. 2.03.181
this is the hole where aaron bid us hide him. 2.03.186
do this and purchase us thy lasting friends." 2.03.275
come let us go, and make thy father blind, | for 2.04. 52
let us that have our tongues | plot some device 3.01.133
to make us wonder'd at in time to come. 3.01.135
be that heart that forc'd us to this shift! 4.01. 72
of lucius, | he hath some message to deliver us. 4.02. 2
lords, was't not a happy star | led us to rome, 4.02. 33
a lord | basely insinuate and send us gifts. 4.02. 38
come let us go and pray to all the gods | for 4.02. 46
pray to the devils, the gods have given us over. 4.02. 48
then sit we down and let us all consult. 4.02.132
for it is you that puts us to our shifts. 4.02.176
it highly us concerns | by day and night t' 4.03. 27
come, marcus, let us go. publius, follow me. 4.03.121
now, good fellow, wouldst thou speak with us? 4.04. 39
but he will not entreat his son for us. 4.04. 94
be bold in us, we'll follow where thou lead'st, 5.01. 13
what wouldst thou have us do, andronicus? 5.02. 92
well hast thou lesson'd us, this shall we do. 5.02.110
madam, depart at pleasure, leave us here. 5.02.145
tell us, old man, how shall we be employ'd? 5.02.149
i fear the emperor means no good to us. 5.03. 10
go fetch them hither to us presently. 5.03. 59
tell us what sinon hath bewitch'd our ears, | or 5.03. 85
have we done aught amiss, show us wherein, | and 5.03.129
from the place where you behold us pleading, 5.03.130
come, and learn of us | to melt in showers; 5.03.160
quarrel is between our masters and us their men. ROM 1.01. 19 P
let us take the law of our sides, let them begin 1.01. 38 P
do you bite your thumb at us, sir? 1.01. 44 P
do you bite your thumb at us, sir? 1.01. 46 P
being black, puts us in mind they hide the fair. 1.01.231
but let them measure us by what they will, 1.04. 9
this wind you talk of blows us from ourselves: 1.04.104
lie, | that in thy likeness thou appear to us! 2.01. 21
i pray, | that thou consent to marry us to–day. 2.03. 64
o, let us hence, i stand on sudden haste. 2.03. 93
you gave us the counterfeit fairly last night. 2.04. 45 P
come between us, good benvolio, my wits faints. 2.04. 67 P

that after–hours with sorrow chide us not! 2.06. 2
romeo shall thank thee, daughter, for us both. 2.06. 22
and but one word with one of us? 3.01. 39 P
what, dost thou make us minstrels? 3.01. 46 P
and thou make minstrels of us, look to hear 3.01. 47 P
here all eyes gaze on us. 3.01. 53
why the dev'l came you between us? 3.01.103 P
this doth not so, for she divideth us. 3.05. 30
since arm from arm that voice doth us affray, 3.05. 33
doth she not give us thanks? 3.05.142
we scarce thought us blest | that god had lent 3.05.164
that god had lent us but this only child, | but 3.05.165
for though /fond nature bids us all lament, 4.05. 82
what will you give us? 4.05.113 P
and you re us and fa us, you note us. 4.05.120 P
and you re us and fa us, you note us. 4.05.120 P
and you re us and fa us, you note us. 4.05.120 P
seal'd up the doors and would not let us forth, 5.02. 11
our own precedent passions do instruct us | what TIM 1.01.133
pray entertain them, give them guide to us. 1.01.243
pray you let us in. 1.01.255
my lord, you take us even at the best. 1.02.152
he commands us to provide, and give great gifts, 1.02.192
hang him, he'll abuse us. 2.02. 48 P
ay, would they serv'd us! 2.02. 93 P
and i think | one business does command us all; 3.04. 4
if wrongs be evils and enforce us kill, | what 3.05. 36
'tis inferr'd to us, | his days are foul and his 3.05. 72
honorable lord did but try us this other day. 3.06. 3 P
one day he gives us diamonds, next day stones. 3.06.120
o, the fierce wretchedness that glory brings us! 4.02. 30
give us some gold, good timon; hast thou more? 4.03.133
hadst thou like us from our first swath 4.03.252
let us make the assay upon him. 4.03.403 P
if he care not for't, he will supply us easily; 4.03.404 P
the malice of mankind that he thus advises us, 4.03.453 P
us, not to have us thrive in our mystery. 4.03.453 P
let us first see peace in athens. 4.03.456 P
it will show honestly in us, | and is very 5.01. 13
beseech your honor | to make it known to us. 5.01. 90
bring us to his cave. 5.01.119
bring us to him, | and /chance it as it may. 5.01.125
and send forth us to make their sorrowed render, 5.01.149
therefore so please thee to return with us, 5.01.159
let us return, | and strain what other means is 5.01.226
and strain what other means is left unto us | in 5.01.227
force, | and made us speak like friends. 5.02. 9
though thou abhorr'dst in us our human griefs, 5.04. 75
men, | and keep us all in servile fearfulness. JC 1.01. 75
he is a dreamer, let us leave him. pass. 1.02. 24
as this time | is like to lay upon us. 1.02.175
casca will tell us what the matter is. 1.02.189
tell us what hath chanc'd to–day | that caesar 1.02.217
tell us the manner of it, gentle casca. 1.02.234
send | such dreadful heralds to astonish us. 1.03. 56
our yoke and sufferance show us womanish. 1.03. 84
two or three of us have seen strange sights. 1.03.138
to pompey's porch, where you shall find us. 1.03.147
and that which would appear offense in us, | his 1.03.158
let us go, | for it is after midnight, and ere 1.03.162
and let us swear our resolution. 2.01.113
spur but our own cause | to prick us to redress? 2.01.124
i think he will stand very strong with us. 2.01.142
let us not leave him out. 2.01.143
o, let us have him, for his silver hairs | will 2.01.144
silver hairs | will purchase us a good opinion, 2.01.145
let us not break with him, | for he will never 2.01.150
may well stretch so far | as to annoy us all; 2.01.160
nay, we will all of us be there to fetch him. 2.01.212
vow | which did incorporate and make us one, 2.01.273
what touches us ourself shall be last serv'd. 3.01. 8
and leave us, publius, lest that the people, 3.01. 92
rushing on us, should do your age some mischief. 3.01. 93
and let us bathe our hands in caesar's blood 3.01.106
so often shall the knot of us be call'd | the 3.01.117
beg not your death of us. 3.01.164
if then thy spirit look upon us now, | shall it 3.01.195
so, | but what compact mean you to have with us? 3.01.215
it shall advantage more than do us wrong. 3.01.242
you shall not in your funeral speech blame us, 3.01.245
prepare the body then, and follow us. 3.01.253
we will be satisfied! let us be satisfied! 3.02. 1
stay ho, and let us hear mark antony. 3.02. 62
sake | he finds himself beholding to us all. 3.02. 67
peace, let us hear what antony can say. 3.02. 71
peace ho, let us hear him. 3.02. 72
you shall read us the will, caesar's will. 3.02.148
then i, and you, and all of us fell down, 3.02.191
whilst bloody treason flourish'd over us. 3.02.192
and in this mood will give us any thing. 3.02.267
and let us presently go sit in council, | how 4.01. 45
let us do so; 4.01. 48
(which should perceive nothing but love from us) 4.02. 44
nothing but love from us) | let us not wrangle. 4.02. 45
shall one of us, | that struck the foremost man 4.03. 21
and bring messala with you | immediately to us. 4.03.142
antony | come down upon us with a mighty power, 4.03.169
'tis better that the enemy seek us; 4.03.199
for they have grudg'd us contribution. 4.03.206
they mean to warn us at philippi here, 5.01. 5
if arguing make us sweat, | the proof of it will 5.01. 48
hands, | who to philippi here consorted us. 5.01. 82
and downward look on us | as we were sickly prey 5.01. 85
of some high powers | that govern us below. 5.01.107
not be in our camp, | lest it discomfort us. 5.03.106
and come, young cato, let us to the field. 5.03.107
and bring us word unto octavius' tent | how 5.04. 31
our enemies have beat us to the pit. 5.05. 23
in ourselves | than tarry till they push us. 5.05. 25
according to his virtue let us use him, | with 5.05. 76
and, to conclude, | the victory fell on us. MAC 1.02. 58
and oftentimes, to win us to our harm, | the 1.03.123
the instruments of darkness tell us truths, 1.03.124
win us with honest trifles, to betray 's | in 1.03.125
let us toward the king. 1.03.152
let us speak | our free hearts each to other. 1.03.154
to enverness, | and bind us further to you. 1.04. 43
whose care is gone before to bid us welcome: 1.04. 57

the love that follows us sometime is our trouble 1.06. 11
how you shall bid god 'ield us for your pains, 1.06. 13
for your pains, | and thank us for your trouble. 1.06. 14
his spur, hath holp him | to his home before us. 1.06. 24
th' attempt, and not the deed, | confounds us. 2.02. 11
one cried, "god bless us!" 2.02. 24
say "amen," | when they did say "god bless us!" 2.02. 27
so, it will make us mad. 2.02. 31
a little water clears us of this deed; 2.02. 64
lest occasion call us | and show us to be 2.02. 67
occasion call us | and show us to be watchers. 2.02. 68
hid in an auger–hole, may rush and seize us? 2.03.122
let us meet | and question this most bloody 2.03.127
fears and scruples shake us. 2.03.129
fortune | shall keep us both the safer. 2.03.139
and let us not be dainty of leave–taking, | but 2.03.144
shall have cause of state | craving us jointly. 3.01. 34
bring them before us. 3.01. 47
you made it known to us. 3.01. 83
off, | grapples you to the heart and love of us, 3.01.105
shall, my lord, | perform what you command us. 3.01.126
these terrible dreams | that shake us nightly. 3.02. 19
but who did bid thee join with us? 3.03. 1
then stand with us. 3.03. 4
give us a light there, ho! 3.03. 9
highness | to grace us with your royal company? 3.04. 44
on their crowns, | and push us from our stools. 3.04. 81
be, | and overcome us like a summer's cloud, 3.04.110
actions do not, | our fears do make us traitors. 4.02. 4
he loves us not, | he wants the natural touch; 4.02. 8
let us seek out some desolate shade, and there 4.03. 1
let us rather | hold fast the mortal sword, and 4.03. 2
remove | the means that makes us strangers! 4.03.163
gracious england hath | lent us good siward, and 4.03.190
let's make us med'cines of our great revenge 4.03.214
god, god, forgive us all! 5.01. 75
we, in our country's purge, | each drop of us. 5.02. 29
royal preparation | makes us hear something. 5.03. 58
what wood is this before us? 5.04. 3
host, and make discovery | err in report of us. 5.04. 7
that will with due decision make us know | what 5.04. 17
let us be beaten, if we cannot fight. 5.06. 8
we have met with foes | that strike beside us. 5.07. 29
that palter with us in a double sense, | that 5.08. 20
your several loves, | and make us even with you. 5.09. 28
and what needful else | that calls upon us, by 5.09. 38
whom we invite to see us crown'd at scone. 5.09. 41
touching this dreaded sight, twice seen of us; HAM 1.01. 25
with us to watch the minutes of this night, 1.01. 27
while, | and let us once again assail your ears, 1.01. 31
down, | and let us hear barnardo speak of this. 1.01. 34
king, | whose image even but now appear'd to us, 1.01. 81
but to recover of us, by strong hand | and terms 1.01.102
let us impart what we have seen to–night | unto 1.01.169
this spirit, dumb to us, will speak to him. 1.01.171
and that it us befitted | to bear our hearts in 1.02. 2
he hath not fail'd to pester us with message 1.02. 22
you told us of some suit, what is't, laertes? 1.02. 43
woe, and think of us | as of a father, for, let 1.02.107
i pray thee stay with us, go not to wittenberg. 1.02.119
makes us traduc'd and tax'd of other nations. 1.04. 18
they clip us drunkards, and with swinish phrase 1.04. 19
angels and ministers of grace defend us! 1.04. 39
my lord, come from the grave | to tell us this. 1.05.126
for your desire to know what is between us, 1.05.139
let us go in together, | and still your fingers 1.05.186
whether aught, to us unknown, afflicts him thus, 2.02. 17
you | to show us so much gentry and good will 2.02. 22
as to expend your time with us a while | for the 2.02. 23
might, by the sovereign power you have of us, 2.02. 27
it likes us well, | and at our more considered 2.02. 80
mad let us grant him then, and now remains 2.02.100
come give us a taste of your quality, come, a 2.02.431 P
sweet gertrude, leave us two, | for we have 3.01. 28
off this mortal coil, | must give us pause. 3.01. 67
and makes us rather bear those ills we have, 3.01. 80
we are arrant knaves, believe none of us. 3.01.128 P
you need not tell us what lord hamlet said, | we 3.01.179
we have reform'd that indifferently with us, 3.02. 37 P
will 'a tell us what this show meant? 3.02.143 P
for us, and for our tragedy, | here stooping to 3.02.149
make us again count o'er ere love be done! 3.02.162
for 'tis a question left us yet to prove, 3.02.202
and never come mischance between us twain! 3.02.228
and we that have free souls, it touches us not. 3.02.242 P
have you any further trade with us? 3.02.334 P
nor stands it safe with us | to let his madness 3.03. 1
we will haste us. 3.03. 26
bestow this place on us a little while. 4.01. 4
it had been so with us had we been there. 4.01. 13
to all, | to you yourself, to us, to every one. 4.01. 15
it will be laid to us, whose providence | should 4.01. 17
tell us where 'tis, that we may take it thence, 4.02. 7
my lord, you must tell us where the body is, and 4.02. 25 P
where the body is, and go with us to the king. 4.02. 26 P
bring him before us. 4.03. 15
we fat all creatures else to fat us, and we fat 4.03. 22 P
and thy free awe | pays homage to us — thou 4.03. 62
if that his majesty would aught with us, | we 4.04. 5
sure he that made us with such large discourse, 4.04. 36
gave us not | that capability and godlike reason 4.04. 37
and godlike reason | to fust in us unus'd. 4.04. 39
or by collateral hand | they find us touch'd, we 4.05.208
be you content to lend your patience to us, 4.05.211
of very warlike appointment gave us chase. 4.06. 17 P
leave us. 4.07. 42
of time and means | may fit us to our shape. 4.07.150
speak by the card, or equivocation will undo us. 5.01.138 P
let them throw | millions of acres on us, till 5.01.281
let us know | our indiscretion sometime serves 5.02. 7
our indiscretion sometime serves us well | when 5.02. 8
and that should learn us | there's a divinity 5.02. 9
give us the foils. 5.02.254
ears are senseless that should give us hearing, 5.02.369
let us haste to hear it, | and call the noblest 5.02.386
it did always seem so to us; LR 1.01. 3 P
(since now we will divest us both of rule, 1.01. 49
which of you shall we say doth love us most, 1.01. 51

thou hast sought to make us break our /vow — 1.01.168
when she was dear to us, we did hold her so, 1.01.196
is queen of us, of ours, and our fair france. 1.01.257
prescribe not us our duty. 1.01.276
say of what most nearly appertains to us both. 1.01.284 P
next month with us. 1.01.287 P
pray you let us /hit together; 1.01.303 P
this last surrender of his will but offend us. 1.01.306 P
why brand they us | with base? 1.02. 9
our fortunes from us till our oldness cannot 1.02. 48 P
you where you shall hear us confer of this, and 1.02. 91 P
in the sun and moon portend no good to us. 1.02.104 P
disorders follow us disquietly to our graves. 1.02.114 P
gross crime or other | that sets us all at odds. 1.03. 5
and himself upbraids us | on every trifle. 1.03. 6
what wouldst thou with us? 1.04. 12 P
or they impose, this usage, | coming from us. 2.04. 27
let us withdraw, 'twill be a storm. 2.04.287
true, boy. come bring us to this hovel. 3.02. 78
this contentious storm | invades us to the skin; 3.04. 7
cold night will turn us all to fools and madmen. 3.04. 78 P
sirrah, come on; go along with us. 3.04.179 P
posts shall be swift and intelligent betwixt us. 3.07. 12 P
pinion him like a thief, bring him before us. 3.07. 23
that made the overture of thy treasons to us, 3.07. 89
that thy strange mutations make us hate thee, 4.01. 11
our means secure us, and our mere defects 4.01. 20
we to th' gods, | they kill us for their sport. 4.01. 37
thou wilt o'ertake us hence a mile or twain | i' 4.01. 42
marvel our mild husband | not met us on the way. 4.02. 2
this trusty servant | shall pass between us. 4.02. 19
he arrives he moves | all hearts against us. 4.05. 11
our troops set forth to–morrow, stay with us; 4.05. 16
let us see. 4.06.258
leave, gentle wax, and, manners, blame us not: 4.06.259
sister, you'll go with us? 5.01. 34
'tis most convenient, pray go with us. 5.01. 36
he that parts us shall bring a brand from heaven 5.03. 22
from heaven, | and fire us hence like foxes. 5.03. 23
flesh and fell, | ere they shall make us weep! 5.03. 25
pleasant vices | make instruments to plague us: 5.03.172
judgment of the heavens, that makes us tremble, 5.03.232
makes us tremble, | touches us not with pity. 5.03.233
great thing of us forgot! 5.03.237
and vain is it | that we present us to him. 5.03.295
for us, we will resign, | during the life of 5.03.299
'tis a pageant | to keep us in false gaze. OTH 1.03. 19
write from us to him, post–post–haste. dispatch! 1.03. 46
so let the turk of cyprus us beguile, | we lose 1.03.210
natures would conduct us to most prepost'rous 1.03.329 P
let us be conjunctive in our revenge against him 1.03.367 P
and give us truth who 'tis that is arriv'd. 2.01. 58
let us to the castle. 2.01.201
our general cast us thus early for the love of 2.03. 14 P
who let us not therefore blame. 2.03. 15 P
/god forgive us our sins! 2.03.112 P
it be a sin | when violence assails us. 2.03.204
no name to be known by, let us call thee devil! 2.03.282 P
o yes, and went between us very oft. 3.03.100
even then this forked plague is fated to us 3.03.276
let us be wary, let us hide our loves"; 3.03.420
let us be wary, let us hide our loves"; 3.03.420
above, | you elements that clip us round about, 3.03.464
/heaven bless us! 3.04. 81
'tis not a year or two shows us a man: 3.04.103
they eat us hungerly, and when they are full 3.04.105
and when they are full | they belch us. 3.04.106
o, heaven forgive us! 4.02. 88
your attempt, and he shall fall between us. 4.02.239 P
jealousies, | throwing restraint upon us; 4.03. 90
or say they strike us, | or scant our former 4.03. 90
that they do | when they change us for others? 4.03. 97
then let them use us well; 4.03.102
the ills we do, their ills instruct us so. 4.03.103
it makes us, or it mars us, think on that, | and 5.01. 4
it makes us, or it mars us, think on that, | and 5.01. 4
as you shall prove us, praise us. 5.01. 66
as you shall prove us, praise us. 5.01. 66
you must forsake this room and go with us. 5.02.330
speak not to us. ANT 1.01. 55
we will not look upon him. go with us. 1.02. 87
still, and our ills told us | is as our earing. 1.02.110
what our contempts doth often hurl from us, | we 1.02.123
more urgent touches, | do strongly speak to us; 1.02.181
friends in rome | petition us at home. 1.02.183
to such whose places under us require, | our 1.02.195
let us go. 1.03.101
it hath been taught us from the primal state 1.04. 41
which the wise pow'rs | deny us for our good; 2.01. 7
but let us rear | the higher our opinion, that 2.01. 35
but how the fear of us | may cement their 2.01. 47
that which combin'd us was most great, and let 2.02. 18
great, and let not | a leaner action rend us. 2.02. 19
what hoop should hold us staunch from edge to 2.02.115
of us must pompey presently be sought, | or else 2.02.158
presently be sought, | or else he seeks out us. 2.02.159
let us, lepidus, | not lack your company. 2.02.168
let us go. 2.02.242
music, moody food | of us that trade in love. 2.05. 2
have we | our written purposes before us sent, 2.06. 4
let us know | if 'twill tie up thy discontented 2.06. 5
thou canst not fear us, pompey, with thy sails; 2.06. 24
be pleas'd to tell us | (for this is from the 2.06. 29
may be written | and seal'd between us. 2.06. 59
cup us till the world go round, | cup us till 2.07.117
go round, | cup us till the world go round! 2.07.118
the wild disguise hath almost | antick'd us all. 2.07.125
is set | betwixt us as the cement of our love, 3.02. 29
why have you stol'n upon us thus? 3.06. 42
his ministers | of us and those that love you. 3.06. 89
best of comfort, | and ever welcome to us. 3.06. 90
regiment to a trull | that noises it against us. 3.06. 96
if not denounc'd against us, why should not we 3.07. 5
and their tongues rot | that speak against us! 3.07. 16
for that he dares us to't. 3.07. 29
then have courtesy, so she | will yield us up. 3.13. 16
as many, sir, as caesar has, | or needs not us. 3.13. 50
for us, you know, | whose he is, we are, and 3.13. 51

of caesar's shall | bear us an arrant to him. 3.13.104
our clear judgments, make us | adore our errors, 3.13.113
for shame, | transform us not to women. 4.02. 36
let us score their backs, | and snatch 'em up, 4.07. 12
awake, sir, awake, speak to us. 4.09. 28
let us bear him | to th' court of guard; 4.09. 30
adjoining to the city | shall stay with us — 4.10. 6
there is left us | ourselves to end ourselves. 4.14. 21
bid that welcome | which comes to punish us, and 4.14.137
house of death | ere death dare come to us? 4.15. 82
fashion, | and make death proud to take us. 4.15. 88
what art thou that dar'st | appear thus to us? 5.01. 5
that nature must compel us to lament | our most 5.01. 29
but you gods will give us | some faults to make 5.01. 32
gods will give us | some faults to make us men. 5.01. 33
she soon shall know of us, by some of ours, 5.01. 57
by some mortal stroke | she do defeat us; 5.01. 65
and with your speediest bring us what she says, 5.01. 67
the record of what injuries you did us, | though 5.02.118
good queen, let us entreat you. 5.02.158
dispose you as | yourself shall give us counsel. 5.02.187
and hammers, shall | uplift us to the view. 5.02.211
saucy lictors | will catch at us like strumpets, 5.02.215
quick comedians | extemporally will stage us, 5.02.217
leave us to ourselves, and make yourself some CYM 1.01.155
i would they had not come between us. 1.02. 22 P
you'll go with us? 1.02. 38 P
where each of us fell in praise of our country 1.04. 57 P
let us leave here, gentlemen. 1.04. 99 P
conditions, let us have articles betwixt us. 1.04.156 P
conditions, let us have articles betwixt us. 1.04.157 P
pray let us follow 'em. 1.04.172 P
and to expound | his beastly mind to us, he hath 1.06.153
some dozen romans of us and your lord | (the 1.06.185
towards himself, his goodness forespent on us, 2.03. 59
to your mistress, | attend the queen and us; 2.03. 62
that cures us both. 2.03.104
now say, what would augustus caesar with us? 3.01. 1
we have yet many among us can gripe as hard as 3.01. 40 P
caesar can hide the sun from us with a blanket, 3.01. 43 P
romans did extort | this tribute from us, we 3.01. 48
make pastime with us a day or two, or longer. 3.01. 78 P
if you seek us afterwards in other terms, you 3.01. 79 P
you shall find us in our salt-water girdle. 3.01. 79 P
if you beat us out of it, it is yours; 3.01. 80 P
thus | draws us a profit from all things we see; 3.03. 18
but unto us it is | a cell of ignorance, 3.03. 32
we'll even | all that good time will give us. 3.04.182
but it honors us | that we have given him cause. 3.05. 18
it fits us therefore ripely | our chariots and 3.05. 22
that it would be thus | hath made us forward. 3.05. 29
nor to us hath tender'd | the duty of the day. 3.05. 31
she /looks us like | a thing more made of malice 3.05. 32
call her before us, for | we have been too 3.05. 34
prithee, fair youth, | think us no churls; 3.06. 64
means he not us? 4.02. 64
with his own single hand he'ld take us in, 4.02.121
the law | protects not us; 4.02.126
to let an arrogant piece of flesh threat us, 4.02.127
might break out and swear | he'ld fetch us in; 4.02.141
would seek us through | and put us to our answer 4.02.160
seek us through | and put us to our answer. 4.02.161
what cloten's being here to us portends, | or 4.02.182
us portends, | or what his death will bring us. 4.02.183
let us bury him, | and not protract with 4.02.231
and let us, polydore, though now our voices 4.02.235
may seem to those | which chance to find us. 4.02.332
he'll then instruct us of this body. 4.02.360
inform us of thy fortunes, for it seems | they 4.02.361
friends, | the boy hath taught us manly duties. 4.02.397
let us | find out the prettiest daisied plot we 4.02.397
he's preferr'd | by thee to us, and he shall be 4.02.401
withdraw, | and meet the time as it seeks us. 4.03. 33
we fear not | what can from italy annoy us, but 4.03. 34
the noise is round about us. 4.04. 1
let us from it. 4.04. 1
nay, what hope | have we in hiding us? 4.04. 4
must or for britains slay us or receive us | for 4.04. 5
must or for britains slay us or receive us | for 4.04. 5
revolts | during their use, and slay us after. 4.04. 7
we'll higher to the mountains, there secure us. 4.04. 8
may drive us to a render | where we have liv'd, 4.04. 11
time nothing becoming you, | nor satisfying us. 4.04. 16
nothing routs us but | the villainy of our fears 5.02. 12
seats we came, | our parents and us twain, 5.04. 70
the holy eagle | stoop'd, as to foot us. 5.04.116
let us with care perform his great behest. 5.04.122
had it gone with us, | we should not, when the 5.05. 76
he eyes us not, forbear. 5.05.124
he, i am sure | he would have spoke to us. 5.05.126
hearing us praise our loves of italy | for 5.05.161
or his description | prov'd us unspeaking sots. 5.05.178
you holp us, sir, | as you did mean indeed to be 5.05.422
who tells us life's but breath, to trust it PER 1.01. 46
as your fair self, doth tune us otherwise. 1.01.115
who attends us there? 1.01.150
let none disturb us. 1.02. 1
and keep your mind, till you return to us, 1.02. 35
all leave us else; 1.02. 48
lading's in our haven, | and then return to us. 1.02. 50
helicanus, thou | hast mov'd us. 1.02. 51
desire it, | commended to our master, not to us; 1.03. 37
my dionyza, shall we rest us here, | and by 1.04. 1
see if 'twill teach us to forget our own? 1.04. 3
for comfort is too far for us to expect. 1.04. 59
vessels with their power | to beat us down, the 1.04. 68
white flags display'd, they bring us peace, 1.04. 72
and come to us as favorers, not as foes. 1.04. 73
your grace is welcome to our town and us. 1.04.106
until our stars that frown lend us a smile. 1.04.108
poor men that were cast away before us even now. 2.01. 19 P
what pitiful cries they made to us to help them, 2.01. 21 P
that makes us scan | the outward habit by the 2.02. 56
but if the prince do live, let us salute him, 2.04. 27
and be resolved he lives to govern us, | or, 2.04. 31
funeral, | and leave us to our free election. 2.04. 33
and since lord helicane enjoineth us, | we with 2.04. 55
then you love us, we you, and we'll clasp hands: 2.04. 57
why do you make us love your goodly gifts | and 3.01. 23
pardon us, sir; 3.01. 51 P
with us at sea it hath been still observ'd, and 3.01. 51 P
a good constraint of fortune it belches upon us. 3.02. 55
live, and make | us weep to hear your fate, fair 3.02.103
and aesculapius guide us! 3.02.110
mortally, | yet glance full wond'ringly on us. 3.03. 7
we cannot but obey | the powers above us. 3.03. 10
the gods will be strong with us for giving o'er. 4.02. 35 P
pray you, will you go with us? 4.02.150 P
and care in us | at whose expense 'tis done. 4.03. 45
or she'll disfurnish us of all our cavalleria, 4.06. 12 P
well, there's for you, leave us. 4.06. 45 P
she's born to undo us. 4.06.149 P
seeing this goodly vessel ride before us, | i 5.01. 18
let us beseech you | that for our gold we may 5.01. 55
come, let us leave her, | and the gods make her 5.01. 78
no, nor look'd on us. 5.01. 80
the holy gods as loud | as thunder threatens us. 5.01.199
shall we refresh us, sir, upon your shore, | and 5.01.256
riding, her fortunes brought the maid aboard us, 5.03. 11
shall tack about | and something do to save us. TNK pr 27
play do not keep | a little dull time from us, pr 31
be advocate | for us and our distresses! 1.01. 32
he will not suffer us to burn their bones, | to 1.01. 43
give us the bones | of our dead kings, that we 1.01. 49
under the shadow of his sword may cool us; 1.01. 92
key — like such a woman | as any of us three; 1.01. 95
lend us a knee; 1.01. 96
but touch the ground for us no longer time 1.01. 97
take hands, | let us be widows to our woes; 1.01.166
delay | commends us to a famishing hope. 1.01.167
and at the banks of /aulis meet us with | the 1.01.212
let us leave the city | thebes and the temptings 1.02. 3
'twould bring us to an eddy | where we should 1.02. 10
in him, he brings not | a jot of terror to us. 1.02. 95
tell us | when we know all ourselves, and let us 1.02.114
and let us follow | the becking of our chance. 1.02.115
if | you stay to see of us such spinsters, we 1.03. 23
the mounted heavens | view us their mortal herd, 1.04. 5
their lives concern us | much more than thebes 1.04. 32
rather have 'em | prisoners to us than death. 1.04. 37
they would not make us their object. 2.01. 52 P
leave 'em all behind us | like lazy clouds, 2.02. 13
our fiery horses | like proud seas under us! 2.02. 20
and deck the temples of those gods that hate us; 2.02. 23
palamon, | those hopes are prisoners with us. 2.02. 26
here age must find us, | and which is heaviest, 2.02. 28
no issue know us; 2.02. 32
of noble minds) | in us two here shall perish; 2.02. 53
from all that fortune can inflict upon us, | i 2.02. 57
to keep us from corruption of worse men. 2.02. 72
might, like women, | woo us to wander from. 2.02. 76
no hard oppressor | dare take this from us; 2.02. 85
no surfeits seek us; 2.02. 86
a wife might part us lawfully, or business, 2.02. 89
quarrels consume us, envy of ill men | crave our 2.02. 90
chances, | were we from hence, would sever us. 2.02. 95
had not the loving gods found this place for us, 2.02.108
possible our friendship | should ever leave us. 2.02.115
and all the ties between us, i disclaim | if 2.02.173
hold? | what should ail us? 2.03. 37
by any means | before the ladies see us, and do 2.03. 57
driven to | when fifteen once has found us! 2.04. 7
let us not, | having our ancient reputation with 3.03. 10
us not, | having our ancient reputation with us, 3.03. 11
'twill disturb us, | we shall have time enough. 3.03. 15
let us alone, sir. 3.05. 31
give us but a tree or twain | for a maypole, and 3.05.144
like meeting of two tides, fly strongly from us, 3.06. 30
lo, cousin, lo, our folly has undone us. 3.06.107
then all the world will scorn us, | and say we 3.06.115
thou shalt have pity of us both, o theseus, | if 3.06.172
as thou art just, thy noble ear against us; 3.06.174
the powers of all women will be with us. 3.06.194
before us that are here, can force his cousin 3.06.294
themselves, thither they go — jupiter bless us! 4.03. 36 P
let us put it in execution; 4.03.100 P
their swelling incense | to those above us. 5.01. 5
now that cannot finish | till one of us expire. 5.01. 19
let us go. 5.01. 68
let us rise | and bow before the goddess. 5.01.135
for the purpose that will venture | to marry us, 5.02. 79
sooner than such, to give us nectar with 'em, 5.04. 12
o'er us the victors have | fortune, whose title 5.04. 16
is as momentary | as to us death is certain. 5.04. 18
a grain of honor | they not o'erweigh us. 5.04. 19
let us bid farewell; 5.04. 19
commend us to her. 5.04. 35
what | hath wak'd us from our dream? 5.04. 48
that we should things desire which do cost us 5.04.110
a day or two | let us look sadly, and give grace 5.04.125
heavenly charmers, | what things you make of us! 5.04.132
let us be thankful | for that which is, and with 5.04.134
let's go off, | and bear us like the time. 5.04.137
a better, to prolong | your old loves to us. ep 17
you know they grow in dung — have infected us, STM II.C 13 P
you would have us upon th' hip, would you? II.C 18 P
sin | which oft th' apostle did forewarn us of, II.C 94
let's us do as we may be done by. II.C 141 P
"you hurt my hand with wringing, let us part, VEN 421
light | do summon us to part and bid good night. 534
much, torments us with defect | of that we have: LUC 151
soul that late complained | her wrongs to us, 1840
all our pleasure known to us poor swains, | all PP 17.29
plains, | all our evening sport from us is fled, 17.31
even for this, let us divided live, | and our SON 39. 5
what thou dost foist upon us that is old, | and 123. 6
by blunting us to make our wits more keen. LC 161
strong, | must for your victory us all congest, 258

USAGE 12 FR 0.0013 REL FR 10 V 2 P
comptible, even to the least sinister usage. TN 1.05.176 P
but this most cruel usage of your queen | (not WT 2.03.117
too | expos'd this paragon to th' fearful usage 5.01.153
up, | upon your stubborn usage of the pope; JN 5.01. 18
have forg'd against yourself | by unkind usage, 1H4 5.01. 69
yet, if this servile usage once offend, | go, 1H6 5.03. 58
hands | he hath good usage and great liberty, 3H6 4.05. 6
pleads your fair usage, and to diomed | you TRO 4.04.119
princely shall be thy usage every way. TIT 1.01.266
mightst deserve, or they impose, this usage, LR 2.04. 26
be a little angry for my so rough usage; CYM 4.01. 20 P
ye | now usage like to princes and to friends. TNK 3.06.306

USANCE 2 FR 0.0002 REL FR 2 V 0 P
the rate of usance here with us in venice. MV 1.03. 45
and take no doit | of usance for my moneys, and 1.03.141

USANCES 1 FR 0.0001 REL FR 1 V 0 P
have rated me | about my moneys and my usances. MV 1.03.108

/US'D 1 FR 0.0001 REL FR 1 V 0 P
/again, /and /must /be /us'd | /with /checks /as LR 1.03. 19

US'D 74 FR 0.0083 REL FR 61 V 13 P
i have us'd thee | (filth as thou art) with TMP 1.02.345
without some treachery us'd to valentine. TGV 2.06. 32
kindly for thy mistress' sake | that us'd me so; 4.04.203
strangely, for he hath not us'd it before. MM 4.02.117 P
till i have us'd the approved means i have, ERR 5.01.103
the which he hath us'd so long and never paid ADO 5.01.310 P
that was us'd to come so smug upon the mart: MV 3.01. 46 P
him | he us'd as creatures of another place, AWW 1.02. 42
thy pains not us'd must by thyself be paid. 2.01.146
fiend is rough, and will not be roughly us'd. TN 3.04.111 P
your greatness | hath not been us'd to fear. WT 4.04. 18
and better us'd, would make her sainted spirit 5.01. 57
comfort, to be us'd | in undeserv'd extremes. JN 4.01.106
whom he hath us'd rather for sport than need) 5.02.175
and where it would not, i have us'd my credit. 1H4 1.02. 55 P
yea, and so us'd it that, were it not here 1.02. 57 P
the scourge of greatness to be us'd on it, | and 1.03. 11
and being fed by us you us'd us so | as that 5.01. 59
'tis the more time thou wert us'd. 2H4 3.02.106 P
th' unstained sword that you have us'd to bear, 5.02.114
his eyes are humbler than they us'd to be. H5 4.07. 67
how were they lost? what treachery was us'd? 1H6 1.01. 68
ay, noble uncle, thus ignobly us'd, | your 2.05. 35
among which terms he us'd his lavish tongue 2.05. 47
means | us'd intercession to obtain a league, 5.04.148
man, | there to be us'd according to your state. 2H6 2.04. 95
and shall i then be us'd reproachfully? 2.04. 97
according to that state you shall be us'd. 2.04. 99
us'd to command, untaught to plead for favor. 4.01.122
thou hast caus'd printing to be us'd, and, 4.07. 36 P
sometime they have us'd with fearful flight, 3H6 2.02. 30
for that thou hast | misus'd ere us'd, by times R3 4.04.396
all several sins, all us'd in each degree, 5.03.198
not us'd to toil, did almost sweat to bear | the H8 1.01. 24
whose tenor | was, were he evil us'd, he would 1.02.207
if i have us'd myself unmannerly, | you know i 3.01.176
dead, good wench, | let me be us'd with honor; 4.02.168
they were us'd to bend, | to send their smiles TRO 3.03. 71
to come as humbly as they us'd to creep | to 3.03. 73
he us'd me kindly. COR 1.09. 83
save yourself, but says | he us'd us scornfully. 2.03.163
gratis, as 'twas us'd | sometime in greece — 3.01.114
and o'erbear | what they are us'd to bear? 3.01.249
straight, he hath been us'd | ever to conquer, 3.03. 25
you were us'd | to say extremities was the trier 4.01. 3
you were us'd to load me | with precepts that 4.01. 9
of egall justice, us'd in such contempt? TIT 4.04. 4
for worse than philomel you us'd my daughter, 5.02.194
friendly conference, | as he hath us'd of old. JC 4.02. 18
the rest is labor, which is not us'd for you. MAC 1.04. 44
of his own chamber, and us'd their very daggers, 1.07. 76
trail of policy so sure | as it hath us'd to do, HAM 2.02. 48
do you hear, let them be well us'd, for they are 2.02.523 P
i have us'd it, nuncle, e'er since thou mad'st LR 1.04.172 P
to see't, | that going shall be us'd with feet. 3.02. 94
they have us'd | their dearest action in the OTH 1.03. 84
this only is the witchcraft i have us'd. 1.03.169
knavery's plain face is never seen till us'd. 2.01.312
is a good familiar creature, if it be well us'd; 2.03.310 P
'tis meet i should be us'd so, very meet. 4.02.107
that he hath us'd thee. 5.02. 70
we have us'd our throats in egypt. ANT 2.06.134 P
we | have us'd to conquer standing on the earth, 3.07. 65
towards him might | be us'd more thankfully. CYM 1.06. 79
/be /my so us'd a guest as not an hour | in the PER 1.02. 3
he asks of you that never us'd to beg. 2.01. 62
be not a conscience to be us'd in every trade, 4.02. 11 P
faith, very little. love has us'd you kindly. TNK 3.06. 67
what would you think | to be thus us'd? STM II.C 139
how tarquin must be us'd, read it in me: LUC 1195
a brook where adon us'd to cool his spleen. PP 6. 6
and their gross painting might be better us'd SON 82.13
the hardest knife ill us'd doth lose his edge. 95.14
ever sweet, | was us'd in giving gentle doom, 145. 7

/USE 2 FR 0.0002 REL FR 2 V 0 P
/we /would /give /much /to /use /violent /thefts TRO 5.03. 21
/must /wither, | /and /come /to /deadly /use. LR 4.02. 36

USE 350 FR 0.0395 REL FR 254 V 96 P
use your authority. TMP 1.01. 23 P
else o' th' earth | let liberty make use of; 1.02.493
riches, poverty, | and use of service, none; 2.01.152
no use of metal, corn, or wine, or oil; 2.01.154
lungs that they always use to laugh at nothing. 2.01.174 P
use such vigilance | as when they are fresh. 3.03. 16
(although they want the use of tongue) a kind 3.03. 38
and i must use you | in such another trick. 4.01. 36
didst thou, alonso, use me and my daughter; 5.01. 72
name) | made use and fair advantage of his days; TGV 2.04. 68
some necessaries that i needs must use, | and 2.04.188
if not, to compass her i'll use my skill. 2.04.214
base men, that use them to so base effect! 2.07. 73
when would you use it? pray, sir, tell me that. 3.01.123
i'll use thee kindly for thy mistress' sake 4.04.202
mind, | and will not use a woman lawlessly. 5.03. 14
how use doth breed a habit in a man! 5.04. 1
for though love use reason for his precisian, he WIV 2.01. 5 P
use your art of wooing; 2.02.235 P
i will use her as the key of the cuckoldly 2.02.274 P
pray you use your patience in good time. 3.01. 81 P
sure they sleep, he hath no use of them. 3.02. 32 P
we'll use this unwholesome humidity, this gross 3.03. 40 P
you use me well, master ford, do you? 3.03.202 P
there they always use to discharge their 4.02. 57 P
devise but how you'll use him when he comes, 4.04. 26

fairies use flow'rs for their charactery. 5.05. 73
use me as you will. 5.05.163 P
the glory of a creditor, | both thanks and use. MM 1.01. 40
so every scope by the immoderate use | turns to 1.02.127
their children's sight | for terror, not to use, 1.03. 26
he (to give fear to use and liberty, | which 1.04. 62
that do nothing but use their abuses in common 2.01. 42 P
but it is tyrannous | to use it like a giant. 2.02.109
officer | would use his heaven for thunder, 2.02.113
and his use was to put a ducat in her clack–dish 3.02.126 P
though my chance is now | to use it for my time. 3.02.218
if not, use him for the present and dismiss him. 4.02. 25 P
you have occasion to use me for your own turn, 4.02. 57 P
i familiarly sometimes | do use you for my fool, ERR 2.02. 27
and you use these blows long, i must get a 2.02. 36 P
when were you wont to use my sister thus? 2.02.153
for her wealth's sake use her with more kindness 3.02. 6
and i know not what use to put her to but to 3.02. 96 P
you use this dalliance to excuse | your breach 4.01. 48
hath scar'd thy husband from the use of wits. 5.01. 86
left, | my dull deaf ears a little use to hear: 5.01.317
go you with me, and i will use your skill. ADO 1.02. 26 P
can you make no use of your discontent? 1.03. 38 P
i make all use of it, for i use it only. 1.03. 39 P
i make all use of it, for i use it only. 1.03. 39 P
all hearts in love use their own tongues. 2.01.177
he lent it me awhile, and i gave him use for it, 2.01.279 P
use it for my love some other way than swearing 4.01.326 P
wilt thou use thy wit? 5.01.124 P
if you use them, margaret, you must put in the 5.02. 20 P
him lie, | and i will use him for my minstrelsy. LLL 1.01.176
you have in that forsworn the use of eyes, | and 4.03.306
use me but as your spaniel; MND 2.01.205
with me) | than to be used as you use your dog? 2.01.210
but i should use thee worse, | for thou, i fear, 3.02. 45
in show, | you would not use a gentle lady so; 3.02.152
she should not use a long one for such a pyramus 5.01.316 P
i do never use it. MV 1.03. 70
and all for use of that which is mine own. 1.03.113
or "good launcelot /gobbo, use your legs, take 2.02. 5 P
say amen, | use all the observance of civility, 2.02.195
notwithstanding, use your pleasure; 3.02.320 P
and use thou all th' endeavor of a man | in 3.04. 48
you may as well use question with the wolf | why 4.01. 73
you | make no moe offers, use no farther means, 4.01. 81
mules, | you use in abject and in slavish parts, 4.01. 92
it is still her use | to let the wretched man 4.01.268
so he will let me have | the other half in use, 4.01.383
therefore use thy discretion — i had as lief AYL 1.01.146 P
to burn the lodging where you use to lie, | and 2.03. 23
which she did use as she was writing of it, | it 4.03. 10
yet to good wine they do use good bushes; ep 5 P
talk, | music and poesy use to quicken you, SHR 1.01. 36
and paint your face, and use you like a fool. 1.01. 65
you use your manners discreetly in all kind of 1.01.242
was it fit for a servant to use his master so, 1.02. 32 P
bid them use them well. 2.01.110
go take it up unto thy master's use. 4.03.157
take up my mistress' gown for thy master's use! 4.03.159 P
take up my mistress' gown to his master's use! 4.03.162
able for thine enemy | rather in power than use, AWW 1.01. 66
a good husband, and use him as he uses thee. 1.01.214 P
use a more spacious ceremony to the noble lords; 2.01. 50 P
give us a further use to be made than alone the 2.03. 36 P
power and father's voice | i have to use. 2.03. 55
give me leave to use | the help of mine own eyes 2.03.107
held, can serve the world for no honest use; 4.03.307 P
that can such sweet use make of what they hate, 4.04. 22
i put you to | the use of your own virtues, for 5.01. 16
night, and with more haste | than is his use. 5.01. 24
sir, use the carp as you may, for he looks like 5.02. 22 P
that are fools, let them use their talents. TN 1.05. 15 P
their thread with bones, | do use to chaunt it. 2.04. 46
yes, being kept together and put to use. 3.01. 50 P
gentle ones that will use the devil himself with 4.02. 33 P
which i had recommended to his use | not half an 5.01. 91
(these petty brands | that calumny doth use — o WT 2.01. 72
should a like language use to all degrees, | and 2.01. 85
tell her, emilia, | i'll use that tongue i have. 2.02. 50
speedy, | the time is worth the use on't. 3.01. 14
this exercise, so long | i daily vow to use it. 3.02.242
upon me, in the name of time, | to use my wings. 4.01. 4
forewarn him that he use no scurrilous words in 4.04.213 P
and what i saw, to my good use i rememb'red. 4.04.604 P
use our commission in his utmost force. JN 3.03. 11
if heaven be pleas'd that you must use me ill, 4.01. 55
though to no use but still to look on you! 4.01.102
all things that you should use to do me wrong 4.01.117
to safety, and return, | for i must use thee. 4.02.159
and from his holiness use all your power | to 5.01. 6
since i must lose the use of all deceit? 5.04. 27
to dark dishonor's use thou shalt not have. R2 1.01.169
and now my tongue's use is to me no more | than 1.03.161
if not, i'll use the advantage of my power, 3.03. 42
hath surpris'd | to his own use he keeps, and 1H4 1.01. 94
when we need | your use and counsel, we shall 1.03. 21
but do not use it oft, let me entreat you. 3.01.174
aspect | as cloudy men use to their adversaries, 3.02. 83
i make as good use of it as many a man doth of a 3.03. 29 P
i rather of his absence make this use: 4.01. 76
a good wit will make use of any thing. 2H4 1.02.247 P
as, one for superfluity, and another for use! 2.02. 18 P
but do you use me thus, ned? 2.02.138 P
things that are mouldy lack use. 3.02.108 P
silence, i will not use many words with you. 3.02.288 P
our men more perfect in the use of arms, | our 4.01.153
sack commences it and sets it in act and use. 4.03.116 P
comes to no further use | but to be known and 4.04. 72
yea, davy, i will use him well. 5.01. 30 P
use his men well, davy, for they are arrant 5.01. 31 P
i then did use the person of your father, | the 5.02. 73
that you use the same | with the like bold, just 5.02.115
acquit me, will you command me to use my legs? ep 19 P
days, | not measuring what use we made of them. H5 1.02.268
thou have practic'd on me, for thy use — | may 2.02. 99
use lenity, sweet chuck! 3.02. 25
i shall think you do not use me with that 3.02.127 P
affability as in discretion you ought to use me, 3.02.128 P
use mercy to them all for us, dear uncle. 3.03. 54
would desire the duke to use his good pleasure, 3.06. 55 P
thou mak'st use of any thing. 3.07. 65 P
yet do i not use my horse for my mistress, or 3.07. 67 P
from a trumpet take, | and use it for my haste. 4.02. 62
downright oaths, which i never use till urg'd, 5.02.145 P
i'll use to carry thee out of this place. 1H6 1.03. 43
hath here distrain'd the tower to his use. 1.03. 61
not to wear, handle, or use any sword, weapon, 1.03. 78 P
use no entreaty, for it is in vain. 5.04. 85
not the worse in that i pray | you use her well. 2H6 2.04. 82
the king, | or any groat i hoarded to my use, 3.01.113
they use to write it on the top of letters; 4.02.100 P
dost thou use to write thy name? 4.02.102 P
any thing i have | is his to use, so somerset 5.01. 53
shall be the war that henry means to use. 3H6 1.01. 73
made impudent with use of evil deeds, | i would 1.04.117
and in that quarrel use it to the death. 2.02. 65
lords, use her /honorably. 3.02.123
ay, edward will use women honorably. 3.02.124
while i use further conference with warwick. 3.03.111
kingdom, | that know not how to use embassadors, 4.03. 36
wife, | nor how to use your brothers brotherly, 4.03. 38
the sun shines hot, and, if we use delay, | cold 4.08. 60
use means for her recovery. 5.05. 45
we go to use our hands, and not our tongues. R3 1.03.351
where he shall see the boar will use us kindly. 3.02. 33
for tender princes — use my babies well! 4.01.102
but that still use of grief makes wild grief 4.04.230
use careful watch, choose trusty /sentinels. 5.03. 54
conscience is but a word that cowards use, 5.03.309
reverend sir, into our kingdom, | use us and it. H8 2.02. 77
to use our utmost studies in your service. 3.01.174
glad your grace has made that right use of it. 3.02.386
make use now, and provide | for thine own future 3.02.420
her wonted greatness, | to use so rude behavior. 4.02.103
persuasions to the contrary | fail not to use, 5.01.148
respect him, | take him, and use him well; 5.02.189
he is a gouty briareus, many hands and no use, TRO 1.02. 29 P
if thou use to beat me, i will begin at thy heel 2.01. 47 P
to use between your strangeness and his pride, 3.03. 45
are | most /abject in regard, and dear in use! 3.03.128
nay, we must use expostulation kindly, | for it 4.04. 60
grecian, thou dost not use me courteously, | to 4.04.121
i charge thee use her well, even for my charge; 4.04.126
be happy that my arms are out of use; 5.06. 16
lay aside their ruth | and let me use my sword, COR 1.01.198
you see how he intends to use the people. 2.02.155
but yet a brain that leads my use of anger | to 3.02. 30
were fit for thee to use as they to claim, | in 3.02. 83
so use it | that my revengeful services may 4.05. 88
your soldiers use him as the grace 'fore meat, 4.07. 3
i were here, he would use me with estimation. 5.02. 52 P
or more, his tribe, | to use my lawful sword! 5.06.129
state, | will use you nobly and your followers. TIT 1.01.260
away with her, and use her as you will; 2.03.166
up, | and they have serv'd me to effectless use. 3.01. 76
but i will use the axe. 3.01.185
did you not use his daughter very friendly? 4.02. 40
hither | to use as you think needful of the man. 5.01. 39
beauty too rich for use, for earth too dear! ROM 1.05. 47
ay, pilgrim, lips that they must use in pray'r. 1.05.102
to breathe such vows as lovers use to swear, 2.pr. 10
aught so good but, strain'd from that fair use, 2.03. 19
suffer every knave to use me at his pleasure! 2.04.155 P
i saw no man use you at his pleasure; 2.04.157 P
and, as you shall use me hereafter, dry–beat the 3.01. 79 P
therefore use none. 3.01.194
o friar, the damned use that word in hell; 3.03. 47
and usest none in that true use indeed | which 3.03.124
look to't, think on't, i do not use to jest. 3.05.189
he were | as living here and you no use of him. 3.05.225
to juliet's grave, for there must i use thee. 5.01. 86
a ring that i must use | in dear employment — 5.03. 31
giver a return exceeding | all use of quittance. TIM 1.01.280
my lord, that you would once use our hearts, 1.02. 85 P
living, should we ne'er have use for 'em; 1.02. 98 P
men and men's fortunes could i frankly use | as 2.02.179
have found time to use 'em toward a supply of 2.02.192 P
way) | to them to use your signet and your name, 2.02.201
great and instant occasion to use fifty talents, 3.01. 18 P
and canst use the time well, if the time use 3.01. 36 P
use the time well, if the time use thee well. 3.01. 37 P
to supply his instant use with so many talents. 3.02. 35 P
i was sending to use lord timon myself, these 3.02. 50 P
me so far as to use mine own words to him? 3.02. 58 P
carriage, | had his necessity made use of me, 3.02. 82
the law, | and none but tyrants use it cruelly. 3.05. 9
they love thee not that use thee; 4.03. 84
make use of thy salt hours, season the slaves 4.03. 86
thou dost affect my manners, and dost use them. 4.03.199
here is no use for gold. 4.03.290
people | the deed of saying is quite out of use. 5.01. 26
vacant lie, | for thy best use and wearing. 5.01.143
that mine own use invites me to cut down, | and 5.01.206
that thou wilt use the wars as thy redress | and 5.04. 51
city, | and i will use the olive with my sword: 5.04. 82
that i hope i may use with a safe conscience, JC 1.01. 13 P
or did use | to stale with ordinary oaths my 1.02. 72
as they use to do the players in the theatre, i 1.02.260 P
in a roman you do want, | or else you use not. 1.03. 59
o caesar, these things are beyond all use, | and 2.02. 25
blood and destruction shall be so in use, | and 3.01.265
which, out of use and stal'd by other men, 4.01. 38
i'll use you for my mirth, yea, for my laughter, 4.03. 49
of your philosophy you make no use, | if you 4.03.145
according to his virtue let us use him, | with 5.05. 76
inch | ten thousand dollars to our general use. MAC 1.02. 62
knock at my ribs, | against the use of nature? 1.03.137
not to their mould | but with the aid of use. 1.03.146
going, | and such an instrument i was to use. 2.01. 43
is the initiate fear that wants hard use: 3.04.142
thou com'st to use thy tongue; 5.05. 28
if thou hast any sound, or use of voice, | speak HAM 1.01.128
the need we have to use you did provoke | our 2.02. 3
madam, i swear i use no art at all. 2.02. 96
but farewell it, for i will use no art. 2.02. 99
knight shall use his foil and target, the lover 2.02.321 P
lord, i will use them according to their desert. 2.02.527 P
use every man after his desert, and who shall 2.02.529 P
use them after your own honor and dignity — the 2.02.531 P
hand, thus, but use all gently, for in the very 3.02. 5 P
i will speak /daggers to her, but use none. 3.02.396
that to the use of actions fair and good | he 3.04.163
for use almost can change the stamp of nature, 3.04.168
yet the unshaped use of it doth move | the 4.05. 8
sir, | what is the reason that you use me thus? 5.01.289
/put your bonnet to his right use, 'tis for the 5.02. 92 P
the queen desires you to use some gentle 5.02.206 P
can you make no use of nothing, nuncle? LR 1.04.131 P
i would you would make use of your good wisdom 1.04.219
see thy other daughter will use thee kindly, for 1.05. 14 P
wherein we must have use of your advice. 2.01.121
our businesses, | which craves the instant use. 2.01.128
why dost thou use me thus? i know thee not. 2.02. 11 P
your father's dog, | you should not use me so. 2.02.137
they took from me the use of mine own house, 3.03. 3 P
thou hotly lusts to use her in that kind | for 4.06.162
use me well, | you shall have ransom. 4.06.191
salt, | to use his eyes for garden water–pots, 4.06.196
we'll use | his countenance for the battle, 5.01. 62
so to use them | as we shall find their merits 5.03. 43
i'ld use them so | that heaven's vault should 5.03.259
men do their broken weapons rather use | than OTH 1.03.174
adieu, brave moor, use desdemona well. 1.03.291
wit, | the one's for use, the other useth it. 2.01.130
i have use for it. 3.03.319
is it his use? 4.01.274
then let them use us well; 4.03.102
will speak, | though tongues were out of use. 5.01.110
but my full heart | remains in use with you. ANT 1.03. 44
our lives upon to use our strongest hands. 2.01. 51
sirrah, mark, we use | to say the dead are well. 2.05. 32
antony will use his affection where it is; 2.06.130 P
use me well in't. 3.02. 25
having made use of him in the wars 'gainst 3.05. 7 P
to be deceiv'd, | that have no use for trusting. 5.02. 15
make your best use of this. 5.02.203
whose use the sword of caesar | hath too much CYM 3.01. 55
yet use thee not so hardly | as prouder livers 3.03. 8
and my end | can make good use of either. 3.05. 64
i should have cause to use thee with a serious 3.05.111 P
use like note and words, | save that euriphile 4.02.237
and unnatural revolts | during their use, and 4.04. 7
going, but such as wink and will not use them. 5.04.187 P
should have the best use of eyes to see the way 5.04.189 P
did begin | was with long use account'd no sin. PER 1.ch. 30
as houses are defil'd for want of use, | they 1.04. 37
we give, and therein may | use honor with you. 3.01. 26
to use one language in each several clime 4.04. 6
more virginal fencing, will you use him kindly? 4.06. 58 P
boult, take her away, use her at thy pleasure. 4.06.141 P
i will use | my utmost skill in his recovery, 5.01. 75
unto the helmeted bellona use them | and pray TNK 1.01. 75
then like men use 'em. 1.04. 28
let that one say so, | and use thy freedom; 2.02.198
and somewhat better than your rank i'll use you. 2.05. 43
do | what he will with me, so he use me kindly, 2.06. 29
for use me so he shall, or i'll proclaim him, 2.06. 30
y'ave seen me use my sword | against th' advice 3.01. 59
no, no, we'll use no horses. 3.06. 59
but use your gauntlets though. 3.06. 64
but want the understanding where to use it. 3.06.216
order it | fitting the persons that must use it. 4.02.151
make use of time, let not advantage slip, VEN 129
dainties to taste, fresh beauty for the use, 164
so thou wilt buy, and pay, and use good dealing, 514
but gold that's put to use more gold begets." 768
teaching them thus to use it in the fight, LUC 62
"so then he hath it when he cannot use it, | and 862
who, mad that sorrow should his use control, 1781
as if the boy should use like loving charms; PP 11. 8
fawn'd on him before | use his company no more. 20.48
how much more praise deserv'd thy beauty's use, SON 2. 9
why dost thou use | so great a sum of sums, yet 4. 7
that use is not forbidden usury, | which happies 6. 5
be thy love, and thy love's use their treasure. 20.14
who heaven itself for ornament doth use, | and 21. 3
and that to my use it might unused stay | from hands 48. 3
my verse | as every alien pen hath got my use, 78. 3
knowing a better spirit doth use your name, 80. 2
the dedicated words which writers use | of their 82. 3
if thou wouldst use the strength of all thy 96.12
thou canst not then use rigor in my jail: 133.12
thou usurer, that put'st forth all to use, | and 134.10
use power with power and slay me not by art. 139. 4

USED 8 FR 0.0009 REL FR 6 V 2 P

this civil war of wits were much better used LLL 2.01.226
with me) | than to be used as you use your dog? MND 2.01.210
now is the moon used between the two neighbors. 5.01.206 P
for discipline ought to be used. H5 3.06. 56 P
if friend or foe, let him be gently used. 3H6 2.06. 45
the people were not used | to be spoke to but by R3 3.07. 29
that nothing could be used to turn them both to PP 15.10
thee, | which used lives th' executor to be. SON 4.14

USEFUL 2 FR 0.0002 REL FR 2 V 0 P

or useful servingman and instrument | to any JN 5.02. 81
thou hast worn | most useful for thy country. ANT 4.14. 80

USELESS 2 FR 0.0002 REL FR 2 V 0 P

brains, | now useless, /boil'd within thy skull! TMP 5.01. 60
and useless barns the harvest of his wits; LUC 859

USER 1 FR 0.0001 REL FR 1 V 0 P

end, | and kept unus'd, the user so destroys it: SON 9.12

USES 20 FR 0.0022 REL FR 9 V 11 P

sweet are the uses of adversity, | which, like AYL 2.01. 12
he uses his folly like a stalking–horse, and 5.04.106 P
a good husband, and use him as he uses thee. AWW 1.01.215 P
lies three thirds and uses a known truth to pass 2.05. 29 P
she uses me with a more exalted respect than any TN 2.05. 26 P
her lucrece, with which she uses to seal. 2.05. 93 P
olivia, and in my sight she uses thee kindly. 3.04.156 P
creatures of note for mercy–lacking uses. JN 4.01.120
made her serve your uses both in purse and in 2H4 2.01.116 P
this davy serves you for good uses, he is your 5.03. 10 P
troyan drab, and uses the traitor calchas' tent. TRO 5.01. 96 P
hand, thus — but tell him | my uses cry to me; TIM 2.01. 20

seem to me all the uses of this world! HAM 1.02.134
most pitiful ambition in the fool that uses it. 3.02. 45 P
to what base uses we may return, horatio! 5.01.202 P
a corner in the thing i love | for others' uses. OTH 3.03.273
/god me such uses send, | not to pick bad from 4.03.104
all valiant uses | (the food and nourishment of TNK 2.02. 51
shall we make worthy uses of this place | that 2.02. 69
and to those gentle uses gave me life. 2.05. 7
USEST 5 FR 0.0005 REL FR 3 V 2 P
thy friend, as thou usest him, and thy sworn TN 3.04.169 P
which is as much as to say, as thou usest him, 2H4 2.02.132 P
ay, but thou usest to forswear thyself. 3H6 5.05. 75
and usest none in that true use indeed | which ROM 3.03.124
i cannot blame thee for my love thou usest, SON 40. 6
USETH 4 FR 0.0004 REL FR 4 V 0 P
gull, the cuckoo's bird, | useth the sparrow; 1H4 5.01. 61
keeps | and useth it to patronage his theft. 1H6 3.01. 48
and decay | it useth an enforced ceremony. JC 4.02. 21
wit, | the one's for use, the other useth it. OTH 2.01.130
USHER 2 FR 0.0002 REL FR 2 V 0 P
no sun shall ever usher forth mine honors, | or H8 3.02.410
of antony | should have an army for an usher, ANT 3.06. 44
USHERING *(see hushering)*
USHERS 2 FR 0.0002 REL FR 1 V 1 P
these are the ushers of martius: COR 2.01.158 P
nor that full star that ushers in the even SON 132. 7
USING 8 FR 0.0009 REL FR 7 V 1 P
being members of my occupation, using painting, MM 4.02. 38 P
reply | without a tongue, using conceit alone, JN 3.03. 50
using the names of men in stead of men, | like 2H4 1.03. 57
spoils, | using no other weapon but his name. 1H6 2.01. 81
'tis better using france than trusting france. 3H6 4.01. 42
for well using me? 4.06. 9
unless by using means i lame the foot | of our COR 4.07. 7
using those thoughts which should indeed have MAC 3.02. 10
USQUE 1 FR 0.0001 REL FR 1 V 0 P
quo usque tandem? here is a woman wanting. TNK 3.05. 38
USUAL 6 FR 0.0006 REL FR 6 V 0 P
where is our usual manager of mirth? MND 5.01. 35
and bid the main flood bate his usual height; MV 4.01. 72
of man | after his studies or his usual pain? SHR 3.01. 12
this way, | under the color of his usual game, 3H6 4.05. 11
first, it was usual with him — every day | it H8 1.02.132
and usual slips | as are companions noted and HAM 2.01. 22
USUALLY 2 FR 0.0002 REL FR 1 V 1 P
men about thee that usually talk of a noun and a 2H6 4.07. 39 P
but he does usually, | so all men do, from hence MAC 3.03. 12
USURER 9 FR 0.0010 REL FR 6 V 3 P
he was wont to call me usurer, let him look to MV 3.01. 48 P
bless me from marrying a usurer! WT 4.04.268 P
thou art a most pernicious usurer, | froward by 1H6 3.01. 17
which, like a usurer, abound'st in all, | and ROM 3.03.123
i think no usurer but has a fool to his servant; TIM 2.02. 98 P
age for his white beard, | he is an usurer. 4.03.113
the usurer hangs the cozener. LR 4.06.163
profitless usurer, why dost thou use | so great SON 4. 7
thou usurer, that put'st forth all to use, | and 134.10
USURER'S 2 FR 0.0002 REL FR 0 V 2 P
about your neck, like an usurer's chain? ADO 2.01.189 P
how a usurer's wife was brought to bed of twenty WT 4.04.263 P
USURERS' 3 FR 0.0003 REL FR 0 V 3 P
poor rogues, and usurers' men, bawds between TIM 2.02. 60 P
are you three usurers' men? 2.02. 96 P
put in a cauldron of lead and usurers' grease, TNK 4.03. 37 P
USURERS 3 FR 0.0003 REL FR 1 V 2 P
make edicts for usury, to support usurers; COR 1.01. 82 P
you three serve three usurers? TIM 2.02. 92 P
when usurers tell their gold i' th' field, | and LR 3.02. 91
USURIES 2 FR 0.0002 REL FR 1 V 1 P
'twas never merry world since, of two usuries, MM 3.02. 6 P
did you but know the city's usuries, | and felt CYM 3.03. 45
USURING 2 FR 0.0002 REL FR 2 V 0 P
is this the balsom that the usuring senate TIM 3.05.109
if not a usuring kindness, and, as rich men deal 4.03.509
USURP 20 FR 0.0022 REL FR 17 V 3 P
thou dost here usurp | the name thou ow'st not, TMP 1.02.454
and usurp the beggary he was never born to. MM 3.02. 93 P
and in that kind swears you do more usurp | than AYL 2.01. 27
i know the boy will well usurp the grace, SHR in.1. 131
if i do not usurp myself, i am. TN 1.05.186 P
certain, if you are she, you do usurp yourself; 1.05.187 P
alack, thou dost usurp authority. JN 2.01.118
thou and thine usurp | the dominations, 2.01.175
unless he do profane, steal, or usurp. R2 3.03. 81
of that proud man that did usurp his back? 5.05. 89
doth but usurp the sacred name of knight, 1H6 4.01. 40
nor shall proud lancaster usurp my right, | nor 2H6 1.01.244
henry had none, but did usurp the place. 3H6 1.02. 25
not to the beast that would usurp their den. 2.02. 12
because thy father henry did usurp, | and thou 3.03. 79
and all the pleasures you usurp are mine. R3 1.03.172
thou didst usurp my place, and dost thou not 4.04.109
not | usurp the just proportion of my sorrow? 4.04.110
an enemy, | and would usurp upon my wat'ry eyes, TIT 3.01.268
death may usurp on nature many hours, | and yet PER 3.02. 82
USURPATION 3 FR 0.0003 REL FR 3 V 0 P
and to rebuke the usurpation | of thy unnatural JN 2.01. 9
flood | hath left a witness'd usurpation. 2H4 1.01. 63
the north, | finding his usurpation most unjust, 1H6 2.05. 68
/USURP'D 1 FR 0.0001 REL FR 1 V 0 P
/me /at /the /font, | /but /'tis /usurp'd. R2 4.01.257
USURP'D 12 FR 0.0013 REL FR 11 V 1 P
both | but this my masculine usurp'd attire, TN 5.01.250
set apart | to him and his usurp'd authority. JN 3.01.160
who usurp'd the crown | of charles the duke of H5 1.02. 69
titles | usurp'd from you and your progenitors. 1.02. 95
is prisoner to the foe, his state usurp'd, | his 3H6 5.04. 77
and seek their ruin that usurp'd our right? 5.06. 73
world's shame, grave's due by life usurp'd, R3 4.04. 27
profan'd, dishonor'd, and the third usurp'd. 4.04.367
thy crown, usurp'd, disgrac'd his kingly glory. 4.04.371
hath endur'd so long, | he but usurp'd his life. LR 5.03.318
defeat thy favor with an usurp'd beard. OTH 1.03.341 P
since sweating lust on earth usurp'd his name, VEN 794
USURPED 1 FR 0.0001 REL FR 1 V 0 P
to pluck him headlong from the usurped throne. R2 5.01. 65
USURPER 7 FR 0.0008 REL FR 6 V 1 P
who is it thou dost call usurper, france? JN 2.01.120
tenth, | who was sole heir to the usurper capet, H5 1.02. 78
that he was, and that the king was an usurper. 2H6 1.03. 32 P
crown | and that your majesty was an usurper. 1.03.185
and calls your grace usurper, openly, | and vows 4.04. 30
father meant to act upon | th' usurper richard, H8 1.02.196
who like a foul usurper went about | from this LUC 412
USURPER'S 2 FR 0.0002 REL FR 2 V 0 P
father, tear the crown from the usurper's head. 3H6 1.01.114
behold where stands | th' usurper's cursed head: MAC 5.09. 21
USURPERS 2 FR 0.0002 REL FR 2 V 0 P
swearing that we | are mere usurpers, tyrants, AYL 2.01. 61
for though usurpers sway the rule a while, | yet 3H6 3.03. 76
USURPING 15 FR 0.0017 REL FR 14 V 1 P
usurping ivy, brier, or idle moss, | who, all ERR 2.02.178
it mourns that painting /and usurping hair LLL 4.03.255
and here detain'd by her usurping uncle | to AYL 1.02.274
have deserv'd it, in usurping his spurs so long. AWW 4.03.103 P
excuse it is to beat usurping down. JN 2.01.119
let me make answer: thy usurping son. 2.01.121
that strumpet fortune, that usurping john! 3.01. 61
which with usurping steps do trample thee. R2 3.02. 17
i do, thou most usurping proditor, | and not 1H6 1.03. 31
the crown, | in following this usurping henry. 3H6 1.01. 81
sits, | write up his title with usurping blood. 1.01.169
increase, | we set the axe to thy usurping root; 2.02.165
the wretched, bloody, and usurping boar, | that R3 5.02. 7
fall | the usurping helmets of our adversaries; 5.03.112
who first rais'd head against usurping richard, H8 2.01.108
USURPINGLY 1 FR 0.0001 REL FR 1 V 0 P
which sways usurpingly these several titles, JN 1.01. 13
USURPS 6 FR 0.0006 REL FR 6 V 0 P
which now the house of lancaster usurps, | i vow 3H6 1.01. 23
york, | usurps the regal title and the seat | of 3.03. 28
my right, | and henry but usurps the diadem. 4.07. 66
property | on wholesome life usurps immediately. HAM 3.02.260
services are due, | /a fool usurps my /bed. LR 4.02. 28
upon the blushing rose, | usurps her cheek; VEN 591
USURP'ST 3 FR 0.0003 REL FR 3 V 0 P
either accept the title thou usurp'st, | of 1H6 5.04.151
and thou usurp'st my father's right and mine. 3H6 5.05. 37
what art thou that usurp'st this time of night, HAM 1.01. 46
USURY 4 FR 0.0004 REL FR 3 V 1 P
make edicts for usury, to support usurers; COR 1.01. 82 P
banish your dotage, banish usury, | that makes TIM 3.05. 98
that use is not forbidden usury, | which happies SON 6. 5
like usury, applying wet to wet, | or monarch's LC 40
UT 2 FR 0.0002 REL FR 1 V 1 P
ut, re, sol, la, mi, fa. LLL 4.02.100 P
lord, | c fa ut, that loves with all affection. SHR 3.01. 76
UTENSIL 1 FR 0.0001 REL FR 0 V 1 P
every particle and utensil labell'd to my will: TN 1.05.246 P
UTENSILS 1 FR 0.0001 REL FR 1 V 0 P
he has brave utensils (for so he calls them) TMP 3.02. 96
UTILITY 1 FR 0.0001 REL FR 1 V 0 P
burs, | losing both beauty and utility; H5 5.02. 53
UTIS 1 FR 0.0001 REL FR 0 V 1 P
by the mass, here will be old utis, it will be 2H4 2.04. 19 P
UTMOST 20 FR 0.0022 REL FR 18 V 2 P
for that's the utmost of his pilgrimage. MM 2.01. 36
much your chain weighs to the utmost charect, ERR 4.01. 28
what they weigh, even to the utmost scruple — ADO 5.01. 93
even to the utmost syllable of your worthiness. AWW 3.06. 71 P
even till that utmost corner of the west JN 2.01. 29
use our commission in his utmost force. 3.03. 11
the very utmost bound | of all our fortunes. 1H4 4.01. 51
now possess'd | the utmost man of expectation, 2H4 1.03. 65
now he weighs time | even to the utmost grain; H5 2.04.138
six or seven thousand is their utmost power. R3 5.03. 10
to use our utmost studies in your service. H8 3.01.174
would try him to the utmost had ye mean, | which 5.02.181
though he perform | to th' utmost of a man, and COR 1.01.268
a lawful form | (in peace), to his utmost peril. 3.01.324
back, that's the utmost of your having, back! . 5.02. 57 P
that we have tried the utmost of our friends, JC 4.03.214
given to captivity me and my utmost hopes, | i OTH 4.02. 51
my butt | and very sea–mark of my utmost sail. 5.02.268
i will use | my utmost skill in his recovery, PER 5.01. 76
when as thy love hath cast his utmost sum, SON 49. 3
UTTER* 41 FR 0.0046 REL FR 31 V 10 P
backward voice is to utter foul speeches and to TMP 2.02. 91 P
my duty pricks me on to utter that | which, else TGV 3.01. 8
my father's grave | did utter forth a voice. MM 3.01. 86
i now begin with grief and shame to utter. 5.01. 96
i'll utter what my sorrow gives me leave. ERR 1.01. 35
i will, like a true drunkard, utter all to thee. ADO 3.03.105 P
i charge you on your souls to utter it. 4.01. 14 P
in language | without offense to utter them. 4.01. 98
sweet breath as will utter a brace of words. LLL 5.02.523 P
nor garlic, for we are to utter sweet breath; MND 4.02. 43 P
as the dog jew did utter in the streets. MV 2.08. 14
am i or that or this for what he'll utter, AWW 5.03.208
then didst thou utter, | "i am yours for ever." WT 1.02.104
as swiftly followed as | i mean to utter it; 1.02.410
a meddler, | that doth utter all men's ware–a. 4.04.323
lady, you utter madness, and not sorrow. JN 3.04. 43
thou wilt not utter what thou dost not know, 1H4 2.03.111
o for breath to utter what is like thee! 2.04.246 P
light in thy face, the son of utter darkness. 3.03. 37 P
it there's but two ways, either to utter them, 2H4 5.03.111 P
pistol, utter more to me, and withal devise 5.03.133 P
the utter loss of all the realm of france. 1H6 5.04.112
dame | (had i sufficient skill to utter them) 5.05. 13
disgrace, | and utter ruin of the house of york. 3H6 1.01.254
words | i've heard him utter to his son–in–law, H8 1.02.136
to no creature living but | to me should utter, 1.02.167
and the words i utter | let none think flattery, 5.04. 15
what i think, i utter, and spend my malice in my COR 2.01. 53 P
but let them hear what fearful words i utter. TIT 5.02.168
and prompt me that my tongue may utter forth 5.03. 12
steel, | nor can i utter all our bitter grief, 5.03. 89
utter your gravity o'er a gossip's bowl, | for ROM 3.05.174
may be mov'd | by that which he will utter? JC 3.01.235
more grief to hide, than hate to utter love. HAM 2.01.116
utter my thoughts? OTH 3.03.136
as both truth and malice | have power to utter. ANT 1.02.109
graces speak | that which none else can utter. 2.02.130
i am glad to be constrain'd to utter that CYM 5.05.141
i meet him | and unto him i utter learned things TNK 3.05. 14
we have, as learned authors utter, wash'd a tile 3.05. 40
my tongue shall utter all, mine eyes like LUC 1076
UTTERANCE* 7 FR 0.0008 REL FR 6 V 1 P
me and as mine honesty puts it to utterance. WT 1.01. 20 P
the utterance of a brace of tongues | must needs JN 4.01. 97
with all the gracious utterance thou hast R2 3.03.125
to beg the voice and utterance of my tongue) | a JC 3.01.261
action, nor utterance, nor the power of speech 3.02.222
the list, | and champion me to th' utterance! MAC 3.01. 71
perforce, | behooves me keep at utterance. CYM 3.01. 72
UTTER'D 6 FR 0.0006 REL FR 4 V 2 P
i have drunk poison whiles he utter'd it. ADO 5.01.246
on certain speeches utter'd | by th' bishop of H8 2.04.172
of coriolanus | should not be utter'd feebly. COR 2.02. 83
behalf as you have utter'd words in your own, 5.02. 25 P
and utter'd such a deal of stinking breath JC 1.02.246 P
what he hath utter'd i have writ my sister; LR 1.04.331
UTTERED 4 FR 0.0004 REL FR 4 V 0 P
and yield your dead, | till death be uttered, ADO 5.03. 20
by, | which holds but till thy news be uttered, JN 5.07. 56
to be done | than out of anger can be uttered. 1H4 1.01.107
all this, uttered | with gentle breath, calm ROM 3.01.155
UTTERETH 1 FR 0.0001 REL FR 1 V 0 P
and say she uttereth piercing eloquence; SHR 2.01.176
UTTERING 2 FR 0.0002 REL FR 2 V 0 P
uttering such dulcet and harmonious breath MND 2.01.151
a hundred words | of thy tongue's uttering, yet ROM 2.02. 59
UTTERLY 10 FR 0.0011 REL FR 8 V 2 P
why then you are utterly sham'd, and he's but a WIV 4.02. 42 P
reverence, a whoremaster, that i utterly deny. 1H4 2.04.470 P
that strength of speech is utterly denied me. 2H4 4.05.217
either to quell the dolphin utterly, | or bring 1H6 1.01.163
in those territories | is utterly bereft you: 2H6 3.01. 85
i utterly abhor, yea, from my soul | refuse you H8 2.04. 81
ay, utterly | grow from the king's acquaintance, 3.01.160
now antony | must leave her utterly. ANT 2.02.233
th' unfriendly elements | forgot thee utterly, PER 3.01. 58
i am sotted, | utterly lost. TNK 4.02. 46
UTTERMOST 8 FR 0.0009 REL FR 7 V 1 P
in making question of my uttermost | than if you MV 1.01.156
that shall be rack'd, even to the uttermost, 1.01.181
even to the uttermost, as i please, in words. SHR 4.03. 80
my live, and my living, and my uttermost power. H5 3.06. 9 P
fight, | so be it, either to the uttermost, | or TRO 4.05. 91
by the eight hour; is that the uttermost? JC 2.01.213
be that the uttermost, and fail not then. 2.01.214
suit | and seek to effect it to my uttermost. OTH 3.04.167
UTTERS 7 FR 0.0008 REL FR 4 V 3 P
and utters it again when god doth please. LLL 5.02.316
without book and utters it by great swarths; TN 2.03.149 P
he utters them as he had eaten ballads and all WT 4.04.184 P
lo, lo, lo, lo, what modicums of wit he utters! TRO 2.01. 69 P
law | is death to any he that utters them. ROM 5.01. 67
what stuff she utters! TNK 5.02. 68
she utters this, "he, he, fair lords, 'tis he, LUC 1721
UTT'RANCE 3 FR 0.0003 REL FR 2 V 1 P
he has a merit | to choke it in the utt'rance. COR 4.07. 49
and break my utt'rance, even in the time | when TIT 5.03. 91
cannot i command to any utt'rance of harmony. HAM 3.02.361 P
UTT'RED 6 FR 0.0006 REL FR 4 V 2 P
if this were so, so were it utt'red. ADO 1.01.215 P
not utt'red by base sale of chapmen's tongues. LLL 2.01. 16
the honor of my parents, i | have utt'red truth; WT 1.02.443
'a utt'red as prave words at the pridge as you H5 3.06. 63 P
these were her words, utt'red with mild disdain: 3H6 4.01. 98
it is not madness | that i have utt'red. HAM 3.04.142
UTT'RING 2 FR 0.0002 REL FR 2 V 0 P
for sportive words and utt'ring foolish things. LUC 1813
utt'ring bare truth, even so as foes commend. SON 69. 4
VACANCY 4 FR 0.0004 REL FR 4 V 0 P
before, | no int'rim, not a minute's vacancy, TN 5.01. 95
you, | that you do bend your eye on vacancy, HAM 3.04.117
he fill'd | his vacancy with his voluptuousness, ANT 1.04. 26
whistling to th' air, which, but for vacancy, 2.02.216
VACANT 6 FR 0.0006 REL FR 6 V 0 P
war–thoughts | have left their places vacant, in ADO 1.01.302
stuffs out his vacant garments with his form; JN 3.04. 97
who, with a body fill'd and vacant mind, | gets H5 4.01.269
i weigh not, | being of those virtues vacant. H8 5.01.125
on special dignities, which vacant lie, | for TIM 5.01.142
the vacant leaves thy mind's imprint will bear, SON 77. 3
VACATION 1 FR 0.0001 REL FR 0 V 1 P
with lawyers in the vacation; AYL 3.02.331 P
VADE *(also fade, etc.)*
VADE 1 FR 0.0001 REL FR 1 V 0 P
when that shall vade, by verse distills your SON 54.14
VADED 4 FR 0.0004 REL FR 4 V 0 P
rose, fair flower, untimely pluck'd, soon vaded, PP 10. 1
pluck'd in the bud, and vaded in the spring! 10. 2
lost, vaded, broken, dead within an hour. 13. 6
found, | as vaded gloss no rubbing will refresh, 13. 8
VADETH 1 FR 0.0001 REL FR 1 V 0 P
good, | a shining gloss that vadeth suddenly, PP 13. 2
VAGABOND 4 FR 0.0004 REL FR 3 V 1 P
you are a vagabond and no true traveller. AWW 2.03.259 P
i shall stand condemn'd | a wandering vagabond, R2 2.03.120
vagabond exile, fleaing, pent to linger | but COR 3.03. 89
body, | like to a vagabond flag upon the stream, ANT 1.04. 45
VAGABONDS 1 FR 0.0001 REL FR 1 V 0 P
a sort of vagabonds, rascals, and runaways, | a R3 5.03.316
VAGARY 1 FR 0.0001 REL FR 0 V 1 P
but they are now in a most extravagant vagary. TNK 4.03. 73 P
VAGRAM *(also fragrant)*
VAGRAM 1 FR 0.0001 REL FR 1 V 0 P
in pabylon — | and a thousand vagram posies. WIV 3.01. 25
VAGROM 1 FR 0.0001 REL FR 0 V 1 P
you shall comprehend all vagrom men; ADO 3.03. 25 P
VAIL 9 FR 0.0010 REL FR 9 V 0 P
vail your regard | upon a wrong'd — i would MM 5.01. 20
then vail your stomachs, for it is no boot, SHR 5.02.176
gan vail his stomach and did grace the shame 2H4 1.01.129
that france must vail her lofty–plumed crest 1H6 5.03. 25
to vail the title, as her mother doth. R3 4.04.348
even with the vail and dark'ning of the sun, TRO 5.08. 7
if he have power, | then vail your ignorance; COR 3.01. 98
did vail their crowns to his supremacy; PER 2.03. 42
and constant pen | vail to her mistress dian; 4.ch. 29

VAIL'D 1 FR 0.0001 REL FR 1 V 0 P
she vail'd her eyelids, who like sluices stopp'd VEN 956
VAILED 1 FR 0.0001 REL FR 1 V 0 P
do not for ever with thy vailed lids | seek for HAM 1.02. 70
/VAILING 1 FR 0.0001 REL FR 1 V 0 P
are angels /vailing clouds, or roses blown. LLL 5.02.297
VAILING 1 FR 0.0001 REL FR 1 V 0 P
vailing her high top lower than her ribs | to MV 1.01. 28
VAILLANT 1 FR 0.0001 REL FR 0 V 1 P
le plus brave, vaillant, et tres /distingue H5 4.04. 57 P
VAILS* 2 FR 0.0002 REL FR 1 V 1 P
there are certain condolements, certain vails. PER 2.01.151 P
he vails his tail that, like a falling plume, VEN 314
VAIN 92 FR 0.0104 REL FR 87 V 5 P
but in vain, | mars's hot minion is return'd TMP 4.01. 97
i will not hear thy vain excuse, | but, as thou TGV 3.01.168
my father would enforce me marry | vain thurio, 4.03. 17
their names | by vain though apt affection. MM 1.04. 48
an idle plume, | which the air beats for vain. 2.04. 12
i will open my lips in vain, or discover his 3.01.193 P
seals of love, but seal'd in vain, seal'd in 4.01. 6
of love, but seal'd in vain, seal'd in vain. 4.01. 6
'tis holy sport to be a little vain, | when the ERR 3.02. 27
there's no man is so vain | that would refuse so 3.02.180
and train our intellects to vain delight. LLL 1.01. 71
all delights are vain, but that most vain 1.01. 72
delights are vain, but that most vain | which, 1.01. 72
therefore this article is made in vain, | or 1.01.139
one who the music of his own vain tongue | doth 1.01.166
for as it would ill become me to be vain, 4.02. 30
and his general behavior vain, ridiculous, and 5.01. 12 P
o vain petitioner! 5.02.207
is exceeding fantastical, too too vain, too too 5.02.529 P
fantastical, too too vain, too too vain: 5.02.529 P
all wanton as a child, skipping and vain, 5.02.761
therefore the winds, piping to us in vain, | as MND 2.01. 88
ox hath therefore stretch'd his yoke in vain, 2.01. 93
i know i love in vain, strive against hope; AWW 1.03.201
and yet she writes, | pursuit would be but vain. 3.04. 25
honor on my part, | against your vain assault. 4.02. 51
to sleep, and leave thy vain bibble babble. TN 4.02. 96 P
the want of which vain dew | perchance shall dry WT 2.01.109
and have, in vain, said many | a prayer upon her 5.03.140
word | is but the vain breath of a common man. JN 3.01. 8
for all in vain comes counsel to his ear. R2 2.01. 4
words are scarce, they are seldom spent in vain, 2.01. 7
if heart's presages be not vain, | we three here 2.02.142
infusing him with self and vain conceit, | as if 3.02.166
again | to alter this, for counsel is but vain. 3.02.214
how these vain weak nails | may tear a passage 5.05. 19
not, sweet queen, for trickling tears are vain. 1H4 2.04.391
the push | of every beardless vain comparative, 3.02. 67
but he did long in vain. 2H4 2.03. 14
if any rebel or vain spirit of mine | did with 4.05.171
my lord chief justice, speak to that vain man. 5.05. 44
it, | since his addiction was to courses vain, H5 1.01. 54
by a vain, giddy, shallow, humorous youth, 2.04. 28
we may as bootless spend our vain command | upon 3.03. 24
use no entreaty, for it is in vain. 1H6 5.04. 85
you go about to torture me in vain. 2H6 2.01.143
but all in vain are these mean obsequies, | and 3.02.146
against the senseless winds shall grin in vain, 4.01. 77
whose dreadful swords were never drawn in vain, 4.01. 92
your oath, my lord, is vain and frivolous. 3H6 1.02. 27
in vain thou speak'st, poor boy; 1.03. 21
but all in vain, they had no heart to fight, 2.01.135
poor painted queen, vain flourish of my fortune! R3 1.03.240
i call'd thee then vain flourish of my fortune; 4.04. 82
to this | by a vain prophecy of nicholas henton. H8 1.02.147
vain pomp and glory of this world, i hate ye! 3.02.365
so that all hope is vain, | unless his noble COR 5.01. 70
lose not so noble a friend on vain suppose, TIT 1.01.440
kneel in the streets and beg for grace in vain. 1.01.455
i pour'd forth tears in vain | to save your 2.03.163
o noble father, you lament in vain: 3.01. 27
for they have fought for rome, and all in vain; 3.01. 73
for hands to do rome service is but vain. 3.01. 80
in delay | we waste our lights in vain, /like ROM 1.04. 45
idle brain, | begot of nothing but vain fantasy, 1.04. 98
for 'tis in vain | to seek him here that means 2.01. 41
him her resort, | myself have spoke in vain. TIM 1.01.128
you breathe in vain. 3.05. 59
in vain? 3.05. 59
it is vain that you would speak with timon; 5.01.116
stay not, all's in vain. 5.01.184
we speak in vain. 5.01.190
and our vain blows malicious mockery. HAM 1.01.146
apollo, king, | thou swear'st thy gods in vain. LR 1.01.161
o vain fool! 4.02. 61
and vain is it | that we present us to him. 5.03.294
not with vain thanks, but with acceptance OTH 3.03.470
but (o vain boast!) 5.02.264
it is in vain, he will not speak to you. PER 5.01. 41
and, good now, | no more of these vain parleys; TNK 3.03. 10
'tis in vain, i see, to stay ye; ep 9
but all in vain, good queen, it will not be; VEN 607
the kiss i gave you is bestow'd in vain, | and 771
and all in vain you strive against the stream, 772
"in vain i rail at opportunity, | at time, at LUC 1023
night, | in vain i cavil with mine infamy, | in 1025
in vain i spurn at my confirm'd despite: 1026
"in vain," quoth she, "i live, and seek in vain 1044
and seek in vain | some happy mean to end a 1044
but, wretched as he is, he strives in vain, 1665
beauty is but a vain and doubtful good, | a PP 13. 1
ah, thought i, thou mourn'st in vain! 20.19
VAINER 1 FR 0.0001 REL FR 1 V 0 P
can, that have more time | for vainer hours, and TMP 1.02.174
VAINGLORIES 1 FR 0.0001 REL FR 0 V 1 P
what needs these feasts, pomps, and vainglories? TIM 1.02.243 P
VAINGLORY 3 FR 0.0003 REL FR 1 V 2 P
a woman (i dare say without vainglory) | never H8 3.01.127
th' combat, he'll break't himself in vainglory. TRO 3.03.259 P
for it is not vainglory for a man and his glass CYM 4.01. 7 P
VAINLY 12 FR 0.0013 REL FR 12 V 0 P
or vainly comes th' admired princess hither. LLL 1.01.140
vanity, | having vainly fear'd too little. AWW 5.03.123
our cannons' malice vainly shall be spent JN 2.01.251
which vainly i suppos'd the holy land. 2H4 4.05.238
but benefit no further | than vainly longing. H8 1.02. 81
yond, that vainly lends his light | to grubs and ROM 5.03.125
arms, and breath'd | our sufferance vainly. TIM 5.04. 8
tile, | we have been fatuus, and labored vainly. TNK 3.05. 41
yes, but all | was vainly labor'd in me; 3.06. 79
thus vainly thinking that she thinks me young, PP 1. 5
thus vainly thinking that she thinks me young, SON 138. 5
at randon from the truth vainly express'd; 147.12
VAINNESS 2 FR 0.0002 REL FR 2 V 0 P
more in a man | than lying, vainness, babbling, TN 3.04.355
being free from vainness and self-glorious pride H5 5.pr. 20
VAIS *(see vois)*
VALANC'D 1 FR 0.0001 REL FR 0 V 1 P
why, thy face is valanc'd since i saw thee last; HAM 2.02.423 P
VALANCE *(see valens)*
VALDES 1 FR 0.0001 REL FR 1 V 0 P
roguing thieves serve the great pirate valdes, PER 4.01. 96
VALE 9 FR 0.0010 REL FR 9 V 0 P
person | comes this way to the melancholy vale, ERR 5.01.120
great is his comfort in this earthly vale, 2H6 2.01. 68
two lights of men, | met in the vale of andren. H8 1.01. 7
whose height commands as subject all the vale, TRO 1.02. 3
a barren detested vale you see it is; TIT 2.03. 93
no vast obscurity or misty vale, | where bloody 5.02. 36
or for i am declin'd | into the vale of years OTH 3.03.266
mountain pine | and make him stoop to th' vale. CYM 4.02.176
a plaintful story from a sist'ring vale, | my LC 2
VALENCE 1 FR 0.0001 REL FR 1 V 0 P
great earl of washford, waterford, and valence, 1H6 4.07. 63
VALENS 1 FR 0.0001 REL FR 1 V 0 P
pearl, | valens of venice gold in needle-work; SHR 2.01.354
VALENTINE 59 FR 0.0066 REL FR 55 V 4 P
sweet valentine, adieu! TGV 1.01. 11
for i will be thy beadsman, valentine. 1.01. 18
and thither will i bring thee, valentine. 1.01. 55
how his companion, youthful valentine, | attends 1.03. 26
or two | of commendations sent from valentine, 1.03. 53
sir valentine and servant! to you two thousand. 2.01.100 P
sir valentine, your father is in good health: 2.04. 50
for valentine, i need not cite him to it. 2.04. 85
why, valentine, what braggadism is this? 2.04.164
methinks my zeal to valentine is cold, | and 2.04.203
julia i lose, and valentine i lose: 2.06. 19
find i by their loss — | for valentine, myself; 2.06. 22
and valentine i'll hold an enemy, | aiming at 2.06. 29
without some treachery us'd to valentine. 2.06. 32
who, all enrag'd, will banish valentine; 2.06. 38
but, valentine being gone, i'll quickly cross 2.06. 40
know, worthy prince, sir valentine, my friend, 3.01. 10
forbid | sir valentine her company and my court; 3.01. 27
adieu, my lord, sir valentine is coming. 3.01. 50
sir valentine, whither away so fast? 3.01. 51
not a hair on 's head but 'tis a valentine. 3.01.192 P
valentine? 3.01.193 P
friend valentine, a word. 3.01.205
no, valentine. 3.01.211
no valentine indeed, for sacred silvia. 3.01.212
no, valentine. 3.01.214
no valentine, if silvia have forsworn me. 3.01.215
but valentine, if he be ta'en, must die. 3.01.234
go, sirrah, find him out. come, valentine. 3.01.261
o my dear silvia! hapless valentine! 3.01.262
you | now valentine is banish'd from her sight. 3.02. 2
and worthless valentine shall be forgot. 3.02. 10
she did, my lord, when valentine was here. 3.02. 27
to make the girl forget | the love of valentine, 3.02. 30
the best way is to slander valentine | with 3.02. 31
but say this weed her love from valentine, | it 3.02. 49
much | as you in worth dispraise sir valentine. 3.02. 55
to hate young valentine and love my friend. 3.02. 65
already have i been false to valentine, | and 4.02. 1
yet valentine thy friend | survives, to whom, 4.02.108
i likewise hear that valentine is dead. 4.02.112
good will | i bear unto the banish'd valentine, 4.03. 15
sir eglamour, i would to valentine, | to mantua, 4.03. 22
then | she's fled unto that peasant valentine; 5.02. 35
o valentine, this i endure for thee! 5.03. 15
withdraw thee, valentine: 5.04. 18
o, heaven be judge how i love valentine, | whose 5.04. 36
valentine! 5.04. 61
forgive me, valentine; 5.04. 74
to a man disgrac'd, | banished valentine. 5.04.124
sir valentine! 5.04.124
sir valentine, i care not for her, i; 5.04.132
ancestry, | i do applaud thy spirit, valentine, 5.04.140
sir valentine, | thou art a gentleman and well 5.04.145
saint valentine is past; MND 4.01.139
caius and valentine! TIT 5.02.151
caius and valentine, lay hands on them. 5.02.158
mercutio and his brother valentine; ROM 1.02. 67 P
i a maid at your window, | to be your valentine. HAM 4.05. 51
VALENTINE'S 3 FR 0.0003 REL FR 3 V 0 P
sir valentine's page; TGV 1.02. 38
kind, | because we know, on valentine's report, 3.02. 57
"to-morrow is saint valentine's day, | all in HAM 4.05. 48
VALENTINUS' 1 FR 0.0001 REL FR 1 V 0 P
/is /it mine /eye, or valentinus' praise, | her TGV 2.04.196
VALENTINUS 1 FR 0.0001 REL FR 1 V 0 P
time | with valentinus in the emperor's court; TGV 1.03. 67
VALENTIO 1 FR 0.0001 REL FR 0 V 1 P
signior valentio and his cousin tybalt; ROM 1.02. 69 P
VALENTIUS 1 FR 0.0001 REL FR 1 V 0 P
give the like notice | to valentius, rowland, MM 4.05. 8
VALERIA 3 FR 0.0003 REL FR 3 V 0 P
madam, the lady valeria is come to visit you. COR 1.03. 26
tell valeria | we are fit to bid her welcome. 1.03. 43
and hangs on dian's temple — dear valeria! 5.03. 67
VALERIUS 2 FR 0.0002 REL FR 2 V 0 P
outrun us, | but moyses and valerius follow him. TGV 5.03. 8
valerius! TNK 1.02. 83
VALES 1 FR 0.0001 REL FR 1 V 0 P
to the vales, | and hold our best advantage. ANT 4.11. 3
/VALIANT 3 FR 0.0003 REL FR 3 V 0 P
/became /the /accents /of /the /valiant; 2H4 2.03. 25
/in /england /the /most /valiant /gentleman. 4.01.130
/be /honest, | /i /never /yet /was /valiant. LR 5.01. 24
VALIANT 154 FR 0.0174 REL FR 115 V 39 P
i'll not serve him, he is not valiant. TMP 3.02. 24 P
i would my valiant master would destroy thee. 3.02. 46
valiant, wise, remorseful, well accomplish'd: TGV 4.03. 13
the valiant heart's not whipt out of his trade. MM 2.01.256
thou'rt by no means valiant, | for thou dost 3.01. 15
he is a very valiant trencherman, he hath an ADO 1.01. 51 P
to be overmaster'd with a piece of valiant dust? 2.01. 61 P
and i take him to be valiant. 2.03.188 P
he is now as valiant as hercules that only tells 4.01.321 P
this aspect of mine | hath fear'd the valiant; MV 2.01. 9
wherefore are you gentle, strong, and valiant? AYL 2.03. 6
this is call'd the reproof valiant. 5.04. 79 P
the fourth, the reproof valiant; 5.04. 94 P
our virginity, though valiant in the defense, AWW 1.01.116 P
yes, my lord, and of very valiant approof. 2.05. 3 P
great in knowledge, and accordingly valiant. 2.05. 9 P
i know th' art valiant, and to the possibility 3.06. 82 P
well divulg'd, free, learn'd, and valiant, | and TN 1.05.260
good, and valiant. 3.04.149 P
on't, and i thought he had been valiant, and so 3.04.284 P
thou little valiant, great in villainy! JN 3.01.116
my lord, your valiant kinsman, faulconbridge, 5.03. 5
up thy youthful blood, be valiant and live. R2 1.03. 83
blood-stained with these valiant combatants. 1H4 1.03.107
darest thou be so valiant as to play the coward 2.04. 47 P
why, thou knowest i am as valiant as hercules; 2.04.270 P
i for a valiant lion, and thou for a true prince 2.04.274 P
true jack falstaff, valiant jack falstaff, and 2.04.476 P
jack falstaff, and therefore more valiant, being 2.04.477 P
in strange concealments, valiant as a lion, 3.01.165
more active, valiant, or more valiant, young, 5.01. 90
more active, valiant, or more valiant, young, 5.01. 90
the spirits | of valiant shirley, stafford, 5.04. 41
then i see | a very valiant rebel of the name. 5.04. 62
ah, you whoreson little valiant villain, you! 2H4 2.04.209 P
thou wilt be as valiant as the wrathful dove or 3.02.159 P
hereof comes it that prince harry is valiant, 4.03.117 P
sherris, that he is become very hot and valiant. 4.03.122 P
awake remembrance of these valiant dead, | and H5 1.02.115
by an irishman, a very valiant gentleman, i' 3.02. 67 P
decoct their cold blood to such valiant heat? 3.05. 20
conscience he is as valiant a man as mark antony 3.06. 13 P
i know him to be valiant. 3.07.103 P
a valiant and most expert gentleman. 3.07.129 P
island of england breeds very valiant creatures; 3.07.140 P
say, that's a valiant flea that dare eat his 3.07.145 P
fame, | of parents good, of fist most valiant. 4.01. 46
those that leave their valiant bones in france, 4.03. 98
for i do know fluellen valiant | and, touch'd 4.07.179
where valiant talbot above human thought 1H6 1.01.121
i girt thee with the valiant sword of york: 3.01.170
becomes it thee to taunt his valiant age, | and 3.02. 54
dying prince, | the valiant duke of bedford. 3.02. 87
grief | that such a valiant company are fled. 3.02.125
valiant and virtuous, full of haughty courage, 4.01. 35
there thou stand'st, a breathing valiant man, 4.02. 31
so should we save a valiant gentleman | by 4.03. 26
where is valiant john? 4.07. 2
valiant lord talbot, earl of shrewsbury, 4.07. 61
success unto our valiant general, | and 5.02. 8
her valiant courage and undaunted spirit | (more 5.05. 70
but wherefore weeps warwick, my valiant son? 2H6 1.01.115
valiant i am. 4.02. 53 P
'a must needs, for beggary is valiant. 4.02. 55 P
the people liberal, valiant, active, wealthy, 4.07. 63
hold, valiant clifford! 3H6 1.04. 51
and where's that valiant crook-back prodigy, 1.04. 75
that valiant clifford with his rapier's point 1.04. 80
where our right valiant father is become. 2.01. 10
his name that valiant duke hath left with thee; 2.01. 89
o valiant lord, the duke of york is slain! 2.01.100
'twas odds, belike, when valiant warwick fled: 2.01.148
king edward, valiant richard, montague, | stay 2.01.198
more, | as priam was for all his valiant sons. 2.05.120
where is the post that came from valiant oxford? 5.01. 1
and said, "commend me to my valiant brother." 5.02. 42
methinks a woman of this valiant spirit | should 5.04. 39
be valiant, and give signal to the fight. 5.04. 82
what valiant foemen, like to autumn's corn, 5.07. 3
young, valiant, wise, and (no doubt) right royal R3 1.02.244
and rice ap thomas, with a valiant crew, | and 4.05. 15
be valiant, and speed well! 5.03.102
to their skill, and to their fierceness valiant, TRO 1.01. 8
less valiant than the virgin in the night, | and 1.01. 11
he is as valiant as the lion, churlish as the 1.02. 20 P
you scurvy valiant ass! 2.01. 45 P
so to be valiant, is no praise at all. 2.02.145
a spur to valiant and magnanimous deeds, | whose 2.02.200
yours, | you valiant offspring of great priamus. 2.02.207
ajax, you are as strong, as valiant, as wise, no 2.03.149 P
this thrice worthy and right valiant lord 2.03.190
know the whole world, he is as valiant — 2.03.232
i humbly desire the valiant ajax to invite the 3.03.274 P
a tick in a sheep than such a valiant ignorance. 3.03.312 P
a valiant greek, aeneas, take his hand, 4.01. 8
health to you, valiant sir, | during all 4.01. 11
for her delivery to this valiant greek | comes 4.03. 2
doth long to see unarm'd the valiant hector. 4.05.153
most gentle and most valiant hector, welcome! 4.05.227
he is grown | too proud to be so valiant. COR 1.01.259
you), | and titus lartius, a most valiant roman, 1.02. 14
then, valiant titus, take | convenient numbers 1.05. 11
officious, and not valiant, you have sham'd me 1.08. 14
who resists | are mock'd for valiant ignorance, 4.06.104
bearing his valiant sons | in coffins from the TIT 1.01. 34
romans, of five and twenty valiant sons, | half 1.01. 79
for valiant doings in their country's cause? 1.01.113
and buried one and twenty valiant sons, 1.01.195
a valiant son-in-law thou shalt enjoy, | one fit 1.01.311
th' effects of sorrow for his valiant sons, 4.04. 30
move is to stir, and to be valiant is to stand; ROM 1.01. 9 P
the valiant paris seeks you for his love. 1.03. 74
he's truly valiant that can wisely suffer | the TIM 3.05. 31
women are more valiant | that stay at home, if 3.05. 47
why, let the war receive't in valiant gore, 3.05. 83
right, | base noble, old young, coward valiant. 4.03. 30
thou valiant mars! 4.03.383
the valiant never taste of death but once. JC 2.02. 33

brutus is noble, wise, valiant, and honest; 3.01.126
thy master is a wise and valiant roman, | i 3.01.138
and, my valiant casca, yours; 3.01.188
as he was valiant, i honor him; 3.02. 26 P
but he's a tried and valiant soldier. 4.01. 28
o valiant cousin, worthy gentleman! MAC 1.02. 24
he is full so valiant, | and in his 1.04. 54
and the right valiant banquo walk'd too late, 3.06. 5
that lesser hate him | do call it valiant fury; 5.02. 14
in which our valiant hamlet | (for so this side HAM 1.01. 84
all bands of law, | to our most valiant brother. 1.02. 25
sir, you have show'd to–day your valiant strain, LR 5.03. 40
your trusty and most valiant servitor, | with OTH 1.03. 40
here comes brabantio and the valiant moor. 1.03. 47
valiant othello, we must straight employ you 1.03. 48
and to his honors and his valiant parts | did i 1.03.253
thanks you, the valiant of /this warlike isle, 2.01. 43
i thank you, valiant cassio. 2.01. 87
if thou be'st valiant (as they say base men 2.01.215 P
pleasure, our noble and valiant general, that 2.02. 1 P
the same indeed, a very valiant fellow. 5.01. 52
i am not valiant neither, | but every puny 5.02.243
the valiant caesar! ANT 1.05. 69
antony | is valiant, and dejected, and by starts 4.12. 7
thou teachest me, o valiant eros, what | i 4.14. 96
thou mayst be valiant in a better cause, | but CYM 3.04. 72
your valiant britains have their wishes in it. 3.05. 20
ere clean it o'erthrow nature, makes it valiant. 3.06. 20
a very valiant britain, and a good, | that here 4.02.369
longer exercise | upon a valiant race thy harsh 5.04. 83
prithee, valiant youth, | deny't again. 5.05.289
all valiant uses | (the food and nourishment of TNK 2.02. 51
their valiant temper | men lose when they 3.01. 66
as thou art valiant, for thy cousin's soul, 3.06.175
you valiant and strong–hearted enemies, | you 5.01. 8
and makes her absence valiant, not her might. LC 245

VALIANTLY 5 FR 0.0005 REL FR 3 V 2 P
those mouthed wounds, which valiantly he took, 1H4 1.03. 97
world, but keeps the bridge most valiantly, with H5 3.06. 11 P
fight valiantly to–day! 4.03. 12
o, he smiles valiantly. TRO 1.02.124 P
a roman by a roman | valiantly vanquish'd. ANT 4.15. 58

VALIANTNESS 1 FR 0.0001 REL FR 1 V 0 P
thy valiantness was mine, thou suck'st it from COR 3.02.129

VALIDITY 5 FR 0.0005 REL FR 5 V 0 P
whose high respect and rich validity | did lack AWW 5.03.192
there, | of what validity and pitch soe'er, TN 1.01. 12
more validity, | more honorable state, more ROM 3.03. 33
memory, | of violent birth, but poor validity, HAM 3.02.189
no less in space, validity, and pleasure, | than LR 1.01. 81

VALLEY 3 FR 0.0003 REL FR 3 V 0 P
uncouple in the western valley, let them go. MND 4.01.107
of 's frown, his forehead, nay, the valley, WT 2.03.101
this valley fits the purpose passing well. TIT 2.03. 84

VALLEY–FOUNTAIN 1 FR 0.0001 REL FR 1 V 0 P
in a cold valley–fountain of that ground; SON 153. 4

VALLEYS 4 FR 0.0004 REL FR 4 V 0 P
the stars, i see, will kiss the valleys first; WT 5.01.206
snow | upon the valleys whose low vassal seat H5 3.05. 51
i'll meet you in the valleys. CYM 3.03. 78
the pleasures prove | that hills and valleys, PP 19. 3

VALOR *(also valure)*

VALOR 106 FR 0.0119 REL FR 65 V 41 P
and even with such–like valor men hang and drown TMP 3.03. 59
so full of valor that they smote the air | for 4.01.172
what says she to my valor? TGV 5.02. 19
in our english tongue, is valor, bully. WIV 2.03. 61 P
he is of a noble strain, of approv'd valor, and ADO 2.01.379 P
for shape, for bearing, argument, and valor, 3.01. 96
is melted into cur'sies, valor into compliment, 4.01.319 P
in a false quarrel there is no true valor. 5.01.120 P
adieu, valor, rust, rapier, be still, drum, for LLL 1.02.181 P
most rude melancholy, valor gives thee place. 3.01. 68
for valor, is not love a hercules, | still 4.03.337
speed, | when cowardice pursues and valor flies. MND 2.01.234
this lion is a very fox for his valor. 5.01.231 P
for his valor cannot carry his discretion, and 5.01.233 P
discretion, i am sure, cannot carry his valor; 5.01.236 P
composition that your valor and fear makes in AWW 1.01.203 P
experience and transgress'd against his valor, 2.05. 11 P
dignity that his valor hath here acquir'd for 4.03. 69 P
what his valor, honesty, and expertness in wars; 4.03.177 P
his reputation with the duke, and to his valor; 4.03.249 P
to awake your dormouse valor, to put fire in TN 3.02. 20 P
some laudable attempt either of valor or policy. 3.02. 29 P
and't be any way, it must be with valor, for 3.02. 31 P
build me thy fortunes upon the basis of valor. 3.02. 34 P
commendation with woman than report of valor. 3.02. 38 P
set upon aguecheek a notable report of valor, 3.04.192 P
purposely on others, to taste their valor. 3.04.244 P
are like to find him in the proof of his valor. 3.04.266 P
whose valor plucks dead lions by the beard; JN 2.01.138
oath, | as so defend thee heaven and thy valor! R2 1.03. 15
to prove by god's grace, and my body's valor, 1.03. 37
i espy | virtue with valor couched in thine eye. 1.03. 98
there's no more valor in that poins than in a 1H4 2.02.101 P
the better part of valor is discretion, in the 5.04.120 P
that should reward valor bear the sin upon their 5.04.150 P
times that true valor is turn'd berrord; 2H4 1.02.169 P
but rebuke and check was the reward of valor. 4.03. 32 P
in my pure and immaculate valor, taken sir john 4.03. 38 P
and this valor comes of sherris. 4.03.113 P
good corporal nym, show thy valor, and put up H5 2.01. 43 P
and of buxom valor, hath, by cruel fate, | and 3.06. 26
'tis a hooded valor, and when it appears, it 3.07.111 P
there is much care and valor in this welshman. 4.01. 84
the vapor of our valor will o'erturn them. 4.02. 24
for thou art fram'd of the firm truth of valor. 4.03. 14
he is as full of valor as of kindness, 4.03. 15
mark then abounding valor in our english: 4.03.104
had ten times more valor than this roaring devil 4.04. 70 P
worn as a memorable trophy of predecess'd valor, 5.01. 72 P
only this proof i'll of thy valor make, | in 1H6 1.02. 94
where is my strength, my valor, and my force? 1.05. 1
young talbot's valor makes me smile at thee. 4.07. 4
his valor, coin, and people, in the wars? 2H6 1.01. 79
by my valor, the most complete champion that 4.10. 55 P
any, am vanquish'd by famine, not by valor. 4.10. 75 P
but by circumstance | the name of valor. 5.02. 40
what valor were it, when a cur doth grin, | for 3H6 1.04. 56
and ten to one is no impeach of valor. 1.04. 60
'twas not your valor, clifford, drove me thence. 2.02.107
with what his valor did enrich his wit, | his R3 3.01. 85
humors that his valor is crush'd into folly, his TRO 1.02. 23 P
and at this sport | sir valor dies; 1.03.176
that knows his valor, and knows not his fear, 1.03.268
what propugnation is in one man's valor | to 2.02.136
valor and pride excel themselves in hector, 4.05. 79
even in the faith of valor, to appear | this 5.03. 69
bastard in mind, bastard in valor, in every 5.07. 18 P
mutiners, | your valor puts well forth; COR 1.01.251
it is held | that valor is the chiefest virtue, 2.02. 84
wherein they show'd | most valor, spoke not for 3.01.127
strength i did | contend against thy valor. 4.05.113
thou hast done a deed whereat valor will weep. 5.06.132
of wax, | digressing from the valor of a man; ROM 3.03.127
fear, | abate thy valor in the acting it. 4.01.120
and set quarrelling | upon the head of valor; TIM 3.05. 28
which indeed | is valor misbegot, and came into 3.05. 29
to revenge is no valor, but to bear. 3.05. 39
if there be | such valor in the bearing, what 3.05. 46
how full of valor did he bear himself | in the 3.05. 64
often | drowns him and takes his valor prisoner. 3.05. 68
and to steel with valor | the melting spirits of JC 2.01.121
honor for his valor; 3.02. 28 P
no sooner justice had, with valor arm'd, MAC 1.02. 29
and chastise with the valor of my tongue | all 1.05. 27
to be the same in thine own act and valor | as 1.07. 40
he hath a wisdom that doth guide his valor | to 3.01. 52
we put on a compell'd valor, and in the grapple HAM 4.06. 18 P
no marvel, you have so bestirr'd your valor. LR 2.02. 53 P
thy valor, and thy heart, thou art a traitor; 5.03.134
(i mean purpose, courage, and valor), this night OTH 4.02.214 P
when valor /preys /on reason, | it eats the ANT 3.13.198
comfort, and tenfold | for thy good valor. 4.07. 16
not caesar's valor hath o'erthrown antony, | but 4.15. 14
our valor is to chase what flies. CYM 3.03. 42
there shall she see my valor, which will then be 3.05.139 P
though valor | becomes thee well enough. 4.02.155
valor | that wildly grows in them but yields a 4.02.179
men know | more valor in me than my habits show. 5.01. 30
i never saw such valor. TNK 3.06. 74
before that flew | the lightning of your valor. 3.06. 85
by valor, | by all the chaste nights i have ever 3.06.199
and when he's angry, then a settled valor | (not 4.02.100
as if she ever meant to /crown his valor. 4.02.109
knights must kindle | their valor at your eye. 5.03. 30
put fear to valor, courage to the coward. VEN 1158
true valor still a true respect should have; LUC 201

VALOROUS *(also falorous)*

VALOROUS 4 FR 0.0004 REL FR 0 V 4 P
thou art as valorous as hector of troy, worth 2H4 2.04.219 P
dale, a most furious knight and valorous enemy. 4.03. 39 P
the most brave, valorous, and thrice–worthy H5 4.04. 62 P
ajax to invite the /most valorous hector to come TRO 3.03.274 P

VALOROUSLY 1 FR 0.0001 REL FR 0 V 1 P
and i'll pay't as valorously as i may, that sall H5 3.02.117 P

VALOR'S 7 FR 0.0008 REL FR 7 V 0 P
and these assume but valor's excrement | to MV 3.02. 87
erects | thy noble deeds as valor's monuments. 1H6 3.02.120
so | doth valor's show and valor's worth divide TRO 1.03. 46
doth valor's show and valor's worth divide | in 1.03. 46
my valor's poison'd | with only suff'ring stain COR 1.10. 17
and in my temper soft'ned valor's steel! ROM 3.01.115
(like valor's minion) carv'd out his passage MAC 1.02. 19

VALORS 1 FR 0.0001 REL FR 1 V 0 P
his valors shown upon our crests to–day | have 1H4 5.05. 29

VALUATION 2 FR 0.0002 REL FR 2 V 0 P
but our valuation shall be such | that every 2H4 4.01.187
of your lives you set | so slight a valuation, CYM 4.04. 49

VALU'D 2 FR 0.0002 REL FR 2 V 0 P
being valu'd thus: H5 1.01. 11
we never valu'd this poor seat of england, | and 1.02.269

VALUE 29 FR 0.0032 REL FR 27 V 2 P
i found thee of more value | than stamps in gold WIV 3.04. 15
leaves unquestion'd | matters of needful value. MM 1.01. 55
lack'd and lost, | why then we rack the value; ADO 4.01.220
eyesight, and did value me | above this world; LLL 5.02.445
of thrice three times the value of this bond. MV 1.03.159
and weigh thy value with an even hand. 2.07. 25
and courteous breath), | gifts of rich value. 2.09. 91
than twenty times the value of the sum | that he 3.02.287
state, | thou hast not left the value of a cord; 4.01.366
there's more depends on this than on the value. 4.01.434
what talk you of the posy or the value? 5.01.151
i was too young that time to value her, | but AYL 1.03. 71
of much less value is my company | than your R2 2.03. 19
gifts, | her beauty, and the value of her dower, 1H6 5.01. 44
how much more is his life in value with him! H8 5.02.143
to us | (had it our name) the value of one ten, TRO 2.02. 23
but value dwells not in particular will, | it 2.02. 53
rome must know | the value of her own. COR 1.09. 21
he remember | a kinder value of the people than 2.02. 59
some better than his value — on the moment TIM 1.01. 79
things of like value differing in the owners 1.01.170
of mine hath buried | thoughts of great value, JC 1.02. 50
you less know how to value her desert | than she LR 2.04.139
be weigh'd rather by her value than his own, CYM 1.04. 15 P
upon him accordingly, as you value your trust — 1.06. 24 P
that it did strive | in workmanship and value, 2.04. 74
unto thy value i will mount myself | upon a PER 2.01.157
seated in a chariot | of an inestimable value, 2.04. 8
i purchase cheaply, | as i do rate your value. TNK 5.03.114

VALUED 11 FR 0.0012 REL FR 11 V 0 P
thy substance, valued at the highest rate, ERR 1.01. 23
us, | although not valued to the money's worth. LLL 2.01.136
be valued 'gainst your wive's commandement. MV 4.01.451
our business valued, some twelve days hence 1H4 3.02.177
by still dispraising praise valued with you, 5.02. 59
the queen is valued thirty thousand strong, 3H6 5.03. 14
what's aught but as 'tis valued? TRO 2.02. 52
the valued file | distinguishes the swift, the MAC 3.01. 94
beyond what can be valued, rich or rare, | no LR 1.01. 57
that he, so slightly valued in his messenger, 2.02.146
'tis exactly valued, | not petty things admitted ANT 5.02.139

VALUELESS 1 FR 0.0001 REL FR 1 V 0 P
being touch'd and tried, | proves valueless. JN 3.01.101

VALUE'S 1 FR 0.0001 REL FR 1 V 0 P
the prejudice of disparity, value's shortness, TNK 5.03. 88

VALUES 6 FR 0.0006 REL FR 5 V 1 P
are either rich or poor | as fancy values them; MM 2.02.151
her wit | values itself so highly that to her ADO 3.01. 53
the peace between the french and us not values H8 1.01. 88
it values not your asking. 2.03. 52
appears not which of the dukes he values most, LR 1.01. 5 P
of rich and exquisite form, their values great, CYM 1.06.190

VALUING 1 FR 0.0001 REL FR 1 V 0 P
valuing of her — why, she, o, she is fall'n ADO 4.01.139

VALURE *(also valor)*

VALURE 3 FR 0.0003 REL FR 3 V 0 P
if that thy valure stand on sympathy, | there is R2 4.01. 33
as full of valure as of royal blood! 5.05.113
wit, | his wit set down to make his valure live. R3 3.01. 86

VAMBRACE 1 FR 0.0001 REL FR 1 V 0 P
and in my vambrace put my withered brawns, | and TRO 1.03.297

VAN *(see vant)*

VANE 3 FR 0.0003 REL FR 2 V 1 P
if speaking, why, a vane blown with all winds; ADO 3.01. 66
no, 'twas the vane on the house. 3.03.129 P
what vane? LLL 4.01. 95

VANGUARD *(see vaward)*

VANISH 6 FR 0.0006 REL FR 4 V 2 P
rogues, hence, avaunt, vanish like hailstones; WIV 1.03. 81
keep some state in thy exit, and vanish. LLL 5.02.594 P
ah, would the scandal vanish with my life, | how R2 2.01. 67
they vanish tongue–tied in their guiltiness. JC 1.01. 62
go, vanish into air, away! OTH 3.01. 20 P
vanish, or i shall give thee thy deserving, ANT 4.12. 32

VANISH'D 13 FR 0.0014 REL FR 10 V 3 P
they vanish'd strangely. TMP 3.03. 40
there is a proclamation that you are vanish'd. TGV 3.01.218 P
and so the lion vanish'd. MND 5.01.271 P
and so he vanish'd. R3 1.04. 52
a gentler judgment vanish'd from his lips — ROM 3.03. 10
whither are they vanish'd? MAC 1.03. 80
made themselves air, into which they vanish'd. 1.05. 5 P
in haste away | and vanish'd from our sight. HAM 1.02.220
there vanish'd in the sunbeams, which portends CYM 4.02.350
and in the beams o' th' sun | so vanish'd; 5.05.473
runs, and chides his vanish'd loath'd delight. LUC 742
and moan th' expense of many a vanish'd sight; SON 30. 8
king | are vanishing, or vanish'd out of sight, 63. 7

VANISHED 1 FR 0.0001 REL FR 1 V 0 P
see | the face of caesar, they are vanished. JC 2.02. 12

VANISHEST 2 FR 0.0002 REL FR 2 V 0 P
now i have taken heart thou vanishest. JC 4.03.287
if thus thou vanishest, thou tell'st the world ANT 5.02.297

VANISHETH 1 FR 0.0001 REL FR 1 V 0 P
her lips, so vanisheth | as smoke from aetna, LUC 1041

VANISHING 1 FR 0.0001 REL FR 1 V 0 P
beauties whereof now he's king | are vanishing, SON 63. 7

VANITIES 7 FR 0.0008 REL FR 7 V 0 P
and some few vanities that make him light; R2 3.04. 86
i can no longer brook thy vanities. 1H4 5.04. 74
and you shall find his vanities forespent | were H5 2.04. 36
what had he | to do in these fierce vanities? H8 1.01. 54
our ladies | will have of these trim vanities! 1.03. 38
nor my wishes | more worth than empty vanities; 2.03. 69
thy violent vanities can never last. LUC 894

VANITY 22 FR 0.0024 REL FR 17 V 5 P
of this young couple | some vanity of mine art. TMP 4.01. 41
o heaven, the vanity of wretched fools! MM 5.01.164
appear when there is no need of such vanity. ADO 3.03. 22 P
fall, | shall /tax my fears of little vanity, AWW 5.03.122
o vanity of sickness! JN 5.07. 13
where doth the world thrust forth a vanity — R2 2.01. 24
light vanity, insatiate cormorant, | consuming 2.01. 38
hal, i prithee trouble me no more with vanity; 1H4 1.02. 82 P
that father ruffian, that vanity in years? 2.04.454 P
here's no vanity! 5.03. 33 P
of thee | if i were much in love with vanity! 5.04.106
up, vanity! 2H4 4.05.119
in me | hath proudly flow'd in vanity till now; 5.02.130
that end, | as matching to his youth and vanity, H5 2.04.130
prince, | to stay him from the fall of vanity; R3 3.07. 97
what did this vanity | but minister H8 1.01. 85
o heavy lightness, serious vanity, | misshapen ROM 1.01.178
so light is vanity. 2.06. 20
what a sweep of vanity comes this way! TIM 1.02.132
and take vanity the puppet's part against the LR 2.02. 36 P
not the world's mass of vanity could make me. OTH 4.02.164
that woo the wills of men to vanity | i see TNK 2.02.101

VANQUISH 2 FR 0.0002 REL FR 2 V 0 P
should make a start o'er seas and vanquish you? 2H6 4.08. 43
fear, ere wildness | vanquish my staider senses. CYM 3.04. 10

VANQUISH'D 14 FR 0.0015 REL FR 13 V 1 P
have vanquish'd the resistance of her youth, ADO 4.01. 46
vanquish'd thereto by the fair grace and speech AWW 5.03.133
"thou maiden youth, be vanquish'd by a maid!" 1H6 4.07. 38
sorrow and grief have vanquish'd all my powers; 2H6 2.01.179
and, vanquish'd as i am, i yield to thee, | or 2.01.180
that never fear'd any, am vanquish'd by famine, 4.10. 75 P
and treacherously hast thou vanquish'd him, 3H6 2.01. 72
for hand to hand he would have vanquish'd thee. 2.01. 73
than traitors' arms, | quite vanquish'd him. JC 3.02.186
macbeth shall never vanquish'd be until | great MAC 4.01. 92
thou art not vanquish'd, | but cozen'd and LR 5.03.154
a roman by a roman | valiantly vanquish'd. ANT 4.15. 58
our men be vanquish'd ere they do resist, | and PER 1.02. 27
like a thousand vanquish'd men in bloody fight! PP 17.24

VANQUISHED 5 FR 0.0005 REL FR 5 V 0 P
with wit, | or else a wit by folly vanquished. TGV 1.01. 35
came to the field and vanquished his foes. 1H6 3.02. 96
i am vanquished. 3.03. 78
the fearful french, whom you late vanquished, 2H6 4.08. 42
the coward captive vanquished doth yield | to LUC 75

VANQUISHER 2 FR 0.0002 REL FR 2 V 0 P
so he might | be call'd your vanquisher. COR 3.01. 17
of fortinbras, | had he been vanquisher; HAM 1.01. 93

VANQUISHEST 1 FR 0.0001 REL FR 1 V 0 P
and if thou vanquishest, thy words are true, 1H6 1.02. 96

VANT 1 FR 0.0001 REL FR 1 V 0 P

plant those that have revolted in the vant, ANT 4.06. 8
VANTAGE 42 FR 0.0047 REL FR 40 V 2 P
and with the vantage of mine own excuse | hath TGV 1.03. 82
without false vantage, or base treachery. 4.01. 29
and when the doctor spies his vantage ripe, | to WIV 4.06. 43
and he that might the vantage best have took MM 2.02. 74
where you may have such vantage on the duke, 4.06. 11
though thou wouldst deny, denies thee vantage. 5.01.413
way as fairly rank'd | (if not with vantage) as MND 1.01.102
love, | and be my vantage to exclaim on you. MV 3.02.174
into, | and watch our vantage in this business. SHR 3.02.144
have turn'd another way, | to our own vantage. JN 2.01.550
but little vantage shall i reap thereby; R2 1.03.218
o happy vantage of a kneeling knee! 5.03.132
mare, if i have any vantage of ground to get up. 2H4 2.01. 79 P
if they get ground and vantage of the king, 2.03. 53
am i, | till time and vantage crave my company. 2.03. 68
so much | unto an enemy of craft and vantage, H5 3.06.144
sleep, | had the forehand and vantage of a king. 4.01.280
you fled for vantage, every one will swear; 1H6 4.05. 28
yet you have all the vantage of her wrong. R3 1.03.309
and thus i took the vantage of those few: 3.07. 37
all for our vantage. 5.02. 22
let us survey the vantage of the ground. 5.03. 15
i am unarm'd, forgo this vantage, greek. TRO 5.08. 9
to run, | lead'st first to win some vantage. COR 1.01.160
observe and answer | the vantage of his anger. 2.03.260
that leads my use of anger | to better vantage. 3.02. 31
therefore at your vantage, | ere he express 5.06. 53
but the norweyan lord, surveying vantage, | with MAC 1.02. 31
line the rebel | with hidden help and vantage, 1.03.113
buttress, nor coign of vantage, but this bird 1.06. 7
should o'erhear | the speech, of vantage. HAM 3.03. 33
which now to claim my vantage doth invite me. 5.02.390
take vantage, heavy eyes, not to behold | this LR 2.02.171
and as many to th' vantage as would store the OTH 4.03. 84 P
which serve not for his vantage, he shakes off, ANT 3.07. 33
when vantage like a pair of twins appear'd, 3.10. 12
be assur'd, madam, | with his next vantage. CYM 1.03. 24
for my vantage, excellent; 5.05.198
there you have | a vantage o'er me, but enjoy't TNK 3.01.122
but having thee at vantage (wondrous dread!) VEN 635
urging the worser sense for vantage still; LUC 249
i do, | doing thee vantage, double-vantage me. SON 88.12
VANTAGES 5 FR 0.0005 REL FR 5 V 0 P
to match with her that brings no vantages. 2H6 1.01.131
it is war's prize to take all vantages, | and 3H6 1.04. 59
god forbid that, for he'll take vantages. 3.02. 25
perchance some single vantages you took, | when TIM 2.02.129
who lets go by no vantages that may | prefer you CYM 2.03. 45
VAPIANS 1 FR 0.0001 REL FR 0 V 1 P
of the vapians passing the equinoctial of TN 2.03. 23 P
VAPOR 10 FR 0.0011 REL FR 10 V 0 P
vows are but breath, and breath a vapor is; LLL 4.03. 66
like the south | borne with black vapor, doth 2H4 2.04.364
the vapor of our valor will o'erturn them. H5 4.02. 24
be hid | and in the vapor of my glory smother'd. R3 3.07.164
be a toad | and live upon the vapor of a dungeon OTH 3.03.271
a vapor sometime like a bear or lion, | a ANT 4.14. 3
be enclouded, | and forc'd to drink their vapor. 5.02.213
kill'd | was melted like a vapor from her sight, VEN 1166
my vow was breath, and breath a vapor is, | then PP 3. 9
/exhal'st this vapor vow, in thee it is: 3.11
VAPOROUS 2 FR 0.0002 REL FR 2 V 0 P
but make haste, | the vaporous night approaches. MM 4.01. 57
"o hateful, vaporous, and foggy night! LUC 771
VAPORS 12 FR 0.0013 REL FR 10 V 2 P
dispers'd those vapors that offended us, | and ERR 1.01. 89
mists | of vapors that did seem to strangle him. 1H4 1.02.203
and dull and crudy vapors which environ it, 2H4 4.03. 98 P
for smoke and dusky vapors of the night, | am 1H6 2.02. 27
thy very beams will dry those vapors up, | for 3H6 5.03. 12
cap-and-knee slaves, vapors, and minute-jacks! TIM 3.06. 97
but a foul and pestilent congregation of vapors. HAM 2.02.303 P
bring away, | vapors, sighs, darken the day; TNK 1.05. 2
like misty vapors when they blot the sky, VEN 184
again | as from a furnace, vapors doth he send; 274
blow these pitchy vapors from their biding, LUC 550
and let thy musty vapors march so thick | that 782
VAPOR-VOW 1 FR 0.0001 REL FR 1 V 0 P
my earth dost shine, | exhal'st this vapor-vow; LLL 4.03. 68
VAP'ROUS 1 FR 0.0001 REL FR 1 V 0 P
the moon | there hangs a vap'rous drop profound, MAC 3.05. 24
VARA *(also fery, vary*, very)*
VARA 1 FR 0.0001 REL FR 1 V 0 P
no, sir, but it is vara fine, | for every one LLL 5.02.487
VARIABLE 7 FR 0.0008 REL FR 6 V 1 P
and so variable | as the dog jew did utter in MV 2.08. 13
and ridges hors'd | with variable complexions, COR 2.01.212
lest that thy love prove likewise variable. ROM 2.02.111
different | with variable objects shall expel HAM 3.01.172
and your lean beggar is but variable service, 4.03. 23 P
sheets, | whiles he is vaulting variable ramps, CYM 1.06.134
variable passions throng her constant woe, | as VEN 967
VARIANCE 1 FR 0.0001 REL FR 0 V 1 P
prove the immediate author of their variance. ANT 2.06.129 P
VARIATION 3 FR 0.0003 REL FR 2 V 1 P
horse, | stain'd with the variation of each soil 1H4 1.01. 64
and inconstant, and mutability, and variation; H5 3.06. 35 P
so far from variation or quick change? SON 76. 2
VARIATIONS 1 FR 0.0001 REL FR 0 V 1 P
save the phrase is a little variations. H5 4.07. 18 P
VARIED 4 FR 0.0004 REL FR 2 V 2 P
it is so varied too, for it was proclaim'd LLL 1.01.294 P
the epithites are sweetly varied, like a scholar 4.02. 9 P
roll | to every varied object in his glance; 5.02.765
melodious bird it sung | sweet varied notes, TIT 3.01. 86
VARIES 1 FR 0.0001 REL FR 1 V 0 P
but fortune, mov'd, | varies again; PER 3.ch. 47
VARIEST 1 FR 0.0001 REL FR 0 V 1 P
for thou variest no more from picking of purses 1H4 2.01. 50 P
VARIETY 2 FR 0.0002 REL FR 2 V 0 P
her, nor custom stale | her infinite variety. ANT 2.02.235
making them red and pale with fresh variety — VEN 21
VARLD *(also orld, vorld, world)*
VARLD 1 FR 0.0001 REL FR 0 V 1 P
i vill not for the varld i shall leave behind. WIV 1.04. 64 P
VARLET *(also varlot, etc.)*
VARLET 20 FR 0.0022 REL FR 4 V 16 P
shall eke unfold | how falstaff, varlet vile, WIV 1.03. 97
hang him, dishonest varlet! 4.02.102 P
varlet, thou liest! MM 2.01.167 P
thou liest, wicked varlet! 2.01.167 P
o thou varlet! 2.01.174 P
thou seest, thou wicked varlet, now, what's come 2.01.190 P
thou art to continue now, thou varlet, thou art 2.01.191 P
thou naughty varlet! ADO 4.02. 72 P
i am the veriest varlet that ever chew'd with a 1H4 2.02. 24 P
and tell me now, thou naughty varlet, tell me, 2.04.432 P
a good varlet, a good varlet, a very good varlet 2H4 5.03. 12 P
a good varlet, a good varlet, a very good varlet 5.03. 12 P
a good varlet, a very good varlet, sir john. 5.03. 13 P
a good varlet. 5.03. 14 P
call here my varlet, i'll unarm again. TRO 1.01. 1
that dissembling abominable varlet, diomed, has 5.04. 2 P
turn the dregs of it upon this varlet here — COR 5.02. 77 P
what a brazen-fac'd varlet art thou, to deny LR 2.02. 28 P
out, varlet, from my sight! 2.04.187
thou precious varlet, | my tailor made them not. CYM 4.02. 83
VARLETS 2 FR 0.0002 REL FR 0 V 2 P
prove it before these varlets here, thou MM 2.01. 86 P
away, varlets! 2H4 2.01. 46 P
VARLETTO 1 FR 0.0001 REL FR 0 V 1 P
speak well of them, varletto. WIV 4.05. 65 P
VARLOT *(also varlet, etc.)*
VARLOT 3 FR 0.0003 REL FR 1 V 2 P
montez /a cheval! my horse, varlot lackey! ha! H5 4.02. 2
thou art said to be achilles' male varlot. TRO 5.01. 15 P
male varlot, you rogue! what's that? 5.01. 16 P
VARLOTRY 1 FR 0.0001 REL FR 1 V 0 P
up, | and show me to the shouting varlotry | of ANT 5.02. 56
VARLOTS 2 FR 0.0002 REL FR 1 V 1 P
say again, where didst thou leave these varlots? TMP 4.01.170
all incontinent varlots! TRO 5.01. 98 P
VARNISH 3 FR 0.0003 REL FR 2 V 1 P
they are both the varnish of a complete man. LLL 1.02. 43 P
beauty doth varnish age, as if new born, | and 4.03.240
and set a double varnish on the fame | the HAM 4.07.132
VARNISH'D 3 FR 0.0003 REL FR 3 V 0 P
to gaze on christian fools with varnish'd faces; MV 2.05. 33
and ruin of the times | to be new varnish'd? 2.09. 49
but only painted, like his varnish'd friends? TIM 4.02. 36
VARRIUS 3 FR 0.0003 REL FR 3 V 0 P
i thank thee, varrius, thou hast made good haste MM 4.05. 11
my gentle varrius! 4.05. 13
till a lethe'd dullness — how now, varrius! ANT 2.01. 27
VARRO 3 FR 0.0003 REL FR 3 V 0 P
to varro and to isidore | he owes nine thousand, TIM 2.01. 1
good even, varro. what, | you come for money? 2.02. 9
the like to you, kind varro. 3.04. 2
VARRO'S 1 FR 0.0001 REL FR 1 V 0 P
one varro's servant, my good lord — TIM 2.02. 27
VARRUS 2 FR 0.0002 REL FR 2 V 0 P
varrus and claudio! JC 4.03.244
varrus! 4.03.289
VARY* *(also fery, vara, very)*
VARY* 4 FR 0.0004 REL FR 2 V 2 P
once more i'll mark how love can vary wit. LLL 4.03. 98
it sall be vary gud, gud feith, gud captens bath H5 3.02.102 P
of the lamb, vary deserv'd praise on my palfrey. 3.07. 32 P
with every gale and vary of their masters, LR 2.02. 79
VARYING 5 FR 0.0005 REL FR 5 V 0 P
varying in subjects as the eye doth roll | to LLL 5.02.764
and with his varying childness cures in me WT 1.02.170
goes to and back, /lackeying the varying tide, ANT 1.04. 46
darkling stand | the varying shore o' th' world! 4.15. 11
"kind," and "true" varying to other words, | and SON 105.10
VASSAL 21 FR 0.0023 REL FR 19 V 2 P
dam's god, setebos, | and make a vassal of him. TMP 1.02.374
that i, your vassal, have employ'd and pain'd MM 5.01.386
"that shallow vassal" — LLL 1.01.253 P
have commiseration on thy heroical vassal! 4.01. 64 P
bows not his vassal head and, strooken blind, 4.03.220
i | his servant live, and will his vassal die. AWW 1.03.159
but such a one, thy vassal, whom i know | is 2.01.199
that lift your vassal hands against my head, R2 3.03. 89
thou that art like enough, through vassal fear, 1H4 3.02.124
and make me as the poorest vassal is | that doth 2H4 4.05.175
upon the valleys whose low vassal seat | the H5 3.05. 51
should die | by such a lowly vassal as thyself. 2H6 4.01.111
o, vassal! miscreant! LR 1.01.161
she never come, | to make my heart her vassal. ANT 2.06. 56
pray you tell him | i am his fortune's vassal, 5.02. 29
who, being born your vassal, | am something CYM 5.05.113
force the king | to be his subject's vassal, and TNK 5.01. 84
thing | from vassal actors can be wip'd away; LUC 608
and yet the duteous vassal scarce is gone; 1360
being your vassal bound to stay your leisure. SON 58. 4
thy proud heart's slave and vassal wretch to be: 141.12
VASSALAGE 2 FR 0.0002 REL FR 2 V 0 P
like vassalage at /unawares encount'ring | the TRO 3.02. 38
to whom in vassalage | thy merit hath my duty SON 26. 1
VASSALS 7 FR 0.0008 REL FR 7 V 0 P
god's vassals drop and die; H5 3.02. 8
presumptuous vassals, are you not asham'd | with 1H6 4.01.125
erroneous vassals, the great king of kings R3 1.04.195
but when your carters or your waiting vassals 2.01.122
who was wont | to call them woollen vassals, COR 3.02. 9
obdurate vassals fell exploits effecting, | in LUC 429
let thy thoughts, low vassals to thy state" — 666
VAST 16 FR 0.0018 REL FR 15 V 1 P
for that vast of night that they may work, | all TMP 1.02.327
one sees more devils than vast hell can hold; MND 5.01. 9
shook hands, as over a vast; WT 1.01. 30 P
and vast confusion waits, | as doth a raven on a JN 4.03.152
not let it forth | to find the empty, vast, and R3 1.04. 39
send | o'er the vast world to seek a single man, COR 4.01. 42
forc'd in the ruthless, vast, and gloomy woods? TIT 4.01. 53
no vast obscurity or misty vale, | where bloody 5.02. 36
as that vast shore /wash'd with the farthest sea ROM 2.02. 83
with his great attraction | robs the vast sea; TIM 4.03.437
taught thee to make vast neptune weep for aye 5.04. 78
wherein of antres vast and deserts idle, | rough OTH 1.03.140
in that vast tennis-court, hath made the ball PER 2.01. 60
the god of this great vast, rebuke these surges, 3.01. 1
whose havoc in vast field | unearthed skulls TNK 5.01. 51
vast sin-concealing chaos! LUC 767
VASTIDITY 1 FR 0.0001 REL FR 1 V 0 P
/though all the world's vastidity you had, | to MM 3.01. 68
VASTLY 1 FR 0.0001 REL FR 1 V 0 P
vastly stood | bare and unpeopled in this LUC 1740
VASTY 5 FR 0.0005 REL FR 5 V 0 P
the hyrcanian deserts and the vasty wilds | of MV 2.07. 41
i can call spirits from the vasty deep. 1H4 3.01. 52
this cockpit hold | the vasty fields of france? H5 pr 12
world, | he might return to vasty tartar back, 2.02.123
for whom this hungry war | opens his vasty jaws; 2.04.105
VAT *(see fat*, etc.)*
VAT *(also wat*, what)*
VAT 9 FR 0.0010 REL FR 0 V 9 P
vat is you sing? WIV 1.04. 44 P
do intend vat i speak? 1.04. 46 P
vat is in my closet? 1.04. 67 P
vat is the clock, jack? 2.03. 3 P
vat be all you, one, two, tree, four, come for? 2.03. 22 P
mock-vater? vat is dat? 2.03. 59 P
clapper-de-claw? vat is dat? 2.03. 66 P
i cannot tell vat is dat; 4.05. 86 P
i know vat i have to do. adieu. 5.03. 5 P
VAUDEMONT 2 FR 0.0002 REL FR 2 V 0 P
jacques chatillion, rambures, vaudemont, H5 3.05. 43
beaumont and marle, vaudemont and lestrake. 4.08.100
VAUGHAN 7 FR 0.0008 REL FR 7 V 0 P
and with them sir thomas vaughan, prisoners. R3 2.04. 43
and so falls it out | with rivers, vaughan, grey 3.02. 65
come, grey, come, vaughan, let us here embrace. 3.03. 25
th' adulterate hastings, rivers, vaughan, grey, 4.04. 69
where is the gentle rivers, vaughan, grey? 4.04.147
vaughan, and all that have miscarried | by 5.01. 5
think upon vaughan, and with guilty fear | let 5.03.142
VAULT 17 FR 0.0019 REL FR 16 V 1 P
and 'twixt the green sea and the azur'd vault TMP 5.01. 43
well, vault, but he hath an abstract for the WIV 4.02. 61 P
and in a dark and dankish vault at home | there ERR 5.01.248
him as the sun | in the grey vault of heaven, 2H4 2.03. 19
spoke, | which sounded like a cannon in a vault, 3H6 5.02. 44
thou shall be borne to that same ancient vault ROM 4.01.111
shall i not then be stifled in the vault, | to 4.03. 33
as in a vault, an ancient receptacle, | where 4.03. 39
i saw her laid low in her kindred's vault, | and 5.01. 20
this vault a feasting presence full of light. 5.03. 86
go with me to the vault. 5.03.131
came i to take her from her kindred's vault, 5.03.254
threat'ned me with death, going in the vault, 5.03.276
and therewithal | came to this vault to die, and 5.03.290
the mere lees | is left this vault to brag of. MAC 2.03. 96
use them so | that heaven's vault should crack. LR 5.03.260
and the bear's, | and vault to every thing! TNK 1.01. 54
VAULTAGES 1 FR 0.0001 REL FR 1 V 0 P
that caves and womby vaultages of france | shall H5 2.04.124
VAULTED* 2 FR 0.0002 REL FR 2 V 0 P
and vaulted with such ease into his seat | as if 1H4 4.01.107
to see this vaulted arch and the rich crop | of CYM 1.06. 33
VAULTING *(also vauting)*
VAULTING 3 FR 0.0003 REL FR 3 V 0 P
the pretty vaulting sea refus'd to drown me, 2H6 3.02. 94
but only | vaulting ambition, which o'erleaps MAC 1.07. 27
sheets, | whiles he is vaulting variable ramps, CYM 1.06.134
VAULTS 2 FR 0.0002 REL FR 2 V 0 P
seek sweet safety out | in vaults and prisons, JN 5.02.143
when our vaults have wept | with drunken spilth TIM 2.02.159
VAULTY 4 FR 0.0004 REL FR 4 V 0 P
and put my eyeballs in thy vaulty brows, | and JN 3.04. 30
than had i seen the vaulty top of heaven 5.02. 52
the vaulty heaven so high above our heads. ROM 3.05. 22
and in her vaulty prison stows the day. LUC 119
VAUMOND 1 FR 0.0001 REL FR 0 V 1 P
mine own company, chitopher, vaumond, bentii, AWW 4.03.165 P
/VAUNT* 1 FR 0.0001 REL FR 1 V 0 P
/leaps /o'er /the /vaunt /and /firstlings /of TRO pr 27
VAUNT* 2 FR 0.0002 REL FR 2 V 0 P
that meaner men should vaunt | that golden hap LUC 41
vaunt in their youthful sap, at height decrease, SON 15. 7
VAUNT-COURIERS 1 FR 0.0001 REL FR 1 V 0 P
vaunt-couriers of oak-cleaving thunderbolts, LR 3.02. 5
VAUNTED 1 FR 0.0001 REL FR 1 V 0 P
she vaunted 'mongst her minions t' other day, 2H6 1.03. 84
VAUNTER 1 FR 0.0001 REL FR 1 V 0 P
alas, you know i am no vaunter, i; TIT 5.03.113
VAUNTING 3 FR 0.0003 REL FR 3 V 0 P
and stiff | under the hoofs of vaunting enemies, 1H4 5.03. 42
nym, rouse thy vaunting veins; H5 2.03. 4
make your vaunting true, | and it shall please JC 4.03. 52
VAUNTINGLY 1 FR 0.0001 REL FR 1 V 0 P
heard thee say, and vauntingly thou spak'st it, R2 4.01. 36
VAUNTS 2 FR 0.0002 REL FR 2 V 0 P
heir, | and such high vaunts of his nobility, 2H6 3.01. 50
arm, arm, my lord, the foe vaunts in the field. R3 5.03.288
VAUTING *(also vaulting)*
VAUTING 1 FR 0.0001 REL FR 0 V 1 P
or by vauting into my saddle with my armor on my
H5 5.02.137 P
VAUVADO 1 FR 0.0001 REL FR 0 V 1 P
boskos vauvado. AWW 4.01. 74 P
VAUX 2 FR 0.0002 REL FR 2 V 0 P
whither goes vaux so fast? what news, i prithee? 2H6 3.02.367
then give my charge up to sir nicholas vaux, H8 2.01. 96
VAWARD 5 FR 0.0005 REL FR 4 V 1 P
and since we have the vaward of the day, | my MND 4.01.105
and we that are in the vaward of our youth, i 2H4 1.02.176 P
on my knee i beg | the leading of the vaward. H5 4.03.131
he, being in the vaward, plac'd behind | with 1H6 1.01.132
their bands i' th' vaward are the /antiates, COR 1.06. 53
VEAL* 2 FR 0.0002 REL FR 2 V 0 P
"veal," quoth the dutchman. is not veal a calf? LLL 5.02.247
"veal," quoth the dutchman. is not veal a calf? 5.02.247
/VEDE 1 FR 0.0001 REL FR 1 V 0 P
che non te /vede, che non te /prechia. LLL 4.02. 98
VEGETIVES 1 FR 0.0001 REL FR 1 V 0 P
the blest infusions | that dwells in vegetives, PER 3.02. 36
VEHEMENCE 1 FR 0.0001 REL FR 0 V 1 P
with most petitionary vehemence, tell me who it AYL 3.02.190 P
VEHEMENCY 3 FR 0.0003 REL FR 2 V 1 P
apply well to the vehemency of your affection, WIV 2.02.238 P

that with such vehemency he should pursue MM 5.01.109
and with what vehemency | th' occasion shall H8 5.01.148
VEHEMENT 6 FR 0.0006 REL FR 6 V 0 P
well | their loud applause and aves vehement; MM 1.01. 70
though not for me, yet for your vehement oaths, MV 5.01.155
by long and vehement suit i was seduc'd | to JN 1.01.254
friends, | and by their vehement instigation, R3 3.07.139
with any strong or vehement importunity; OTH 3.03.251
but she with vehement prayers urgeth still LUC 475
VEHEMENTLY *(see fehemently)*
VEHOR 1 FR 0.0001 REL FR 1 V 0 P
calm these fits, | per stygia, per manes vehor. TIT 2.01.135
VEIL 8 FR 0.0009 REL FR 7 V 1 P
pluck the borrow'd veil of modesty from the WIV 3.02. 41 P
to do it, | he says, to veil full purpose. MM 4.06. 4
give me my veil. TN 1.05.165
his contemplation | under the veil of wildness, H5 1.01. 64
that now are dimm'd with death's black veil. 3H6 5.02. 16
bed, | throw over her the veil of infamy. R3 4.04.209
"bonnet nor veil henceforth no creature wear! VEN 1081
where beauty's veil doth cover every blot, | and SON 95.11
VEIL'D 4 FR 0.0004 REL FR 4 V 0 P
to keep your great pretenses veil'd till when COR 1.02. 20
our veil'd dames | commit the war of white and 2.01.215
if i have veil'd my look, | i turn the trouble JC 1.02. 37
and, veil'd in them, did win whom he would maim. LC 312
VEILED 1 FR 0.0001 REL FR 1 V 0 P
but like a cloistress she will veiled walk, TN 1.01. 27
VEILING 1 FR 0.0001 REL FR 1 V 0 P
the beauteous scarf | veiling an indian beauty; MV 3.02. 99
/VEIN 1 FR 0.0001 REL FR 1 V 0 P
/i /am /not /in /the /giving /vein //to–day. R3 4.02.116
VEIN 15 FR 0.0017 REL FR 12 V 3 P
ay, touch him; there's the vein. MM 2.02. 70
i am glad to see you in this merry vein. ERR 2.02. 20
the fellow finds his vein, | and, yielding to 4.04. 80
pick out five such, take each one in his vein. LLL 5.02.545
this is ercles' vein, a tyrant's vein; MND 1.02. 40 P
this is ercles' vein, a tyrant's vein; 1.02. 40 P
there is no following her in this fierce vein. 3.02. 82
you touch'd my vein at first. AYL 2.07. 94
the blood of malice in a vein of league, | and JN 5.02. 38
and i will do it in king cambyses' vein. 1H4 2.04.387 P
and now to paris in this conquering vein, | all 1H6 4.07. 95
thou troublest me, i am not in the vein. R3 4.02.118
o, this is well. he rubs the vein of him. TRO 2.03.200
youth, | i am to–day i' th' vein of chivalry. 5.03. 32
her blue blood chang'd to black in every vein, LUC 1454
/VEINS 1 FR 0.0001 REL FR 1 V 0 P
/begin /to /stop | /our /very /veins /of /life. 2H4 4.01. 66
VEINS 31 FR 0.0035 REL FR 31 V 0 P
to do me business in the veins o' th' earth TMP 1.02.255
only my blood speaks to you in my veins, | and MV 3.02.176
told you all the wealth i had | ran in my veins: 3.02.255
and that those veins | did verily bear blood? WT 5.03. 64
whose veins bound richer blood than lady blanch? JN 2.01.431
within the scorched veins of one new burn'd. 3.01.278
which else runs tickling up and down the veins, 3.03. 44
whiles warm life plays in that infant's veins, 3.04.132
yea, on his part i'll empty all these veins, 1H4 1.03.133
courage that renowned them | runs in your veins; H5 1.02.119
nym, rouse thy vaunting veins; 2.03. 4
scarce blood enough in all their sickly veins 4.02. 20
than drops of blood were in my father's veins. 3H6 1.01. 97
from cold and empty veins where no blood dwells. R3 1.02. 59
grow in the veins of actions highest rear'd, TRO 1.03. 6
for every false drop in her bawdy veins, | a 4.01. 70
the strongest nerves and small inferior veins COR 1.01.138
the veins unfill'd, our blood is cold, and then 5.01. 51
with purple fountains issuing from your veins — ROM 1.01. 85
when presently through all thy veins shall run 4.01. 95
have a faint cold fear thrills through my veins, 4.03. 15
as will disperse itself through all the veins 5.01. 61
and here | my bluest veins to kiss — a hand ANT 2.05. 29
nor | the azur'd harebell, like thy veins; CYM 4.02.222
horse was stuff'd within | with bloody veins, PER 1.04. 94
a man throng'd up with cold, my veins are chill, 2.01. 73
than admiration he admired | her azure veins, LUC 419
unto a greater uproar tempts his veins. 427
whose ranks of blue veins, as his hand did scale 440
beggar'd of blood to blush through lively veins, SON 67.10
in my love's veins thou hast too grossly dy'd. 99. 5
VELL *(also well*)*
VELL 2 FR 0.0002 REL FR 0 V 2 P
vell? WIV 1.04. 78 P
by gar, 'tis good; vell said. 2.03. 96 P
VELURE 1 FR 0.0001 REL FR 0 V 1 P
and a woman's crupper of velure, which hath two SHR 3.02. 61 P
VELUTUS 1 FR 0.0001 REL FR 1 V 0 P
sicinius velutus, and i know not — 'sdeath, COR 1.01.217
VELVET 18 FR 0.0020 REL FR 8 V 10 P
as there may between the lists and the velvet. MM 1.02. 30 P
and thou the velvet — thou art good velvet; 1.02. 31 P
and thou the velvet — thou art good velvet; 1.02. 32 P
pil'd, as thou art pil'd, for a french velvet. 1.02. 34 P
of all, | a whitely wanton with a velvet brow, LLL 3.01.196
through the velvet leaves the wind, | all unseen 4.03.103
left and abandoned of his velvet /friends: AYL 2.01. 50
was moulded on a porringer — | a velvet dish. SHR 4.03. 65
a silken doublet, a velvet hose, a scarlet cloak 5.01. 67 P
lord your son with a patch of velvet on 's face. AWW 4.05. 95 P
there be a scar under't or no, the velvet knows, 4.05. 96 P
velvet knows, but 'tis a goodly patch of velvet. 4.05. 97 P
officers about me, in my branch'd velvet gown; TN 2.05. 48 P
saw myself unbreech'd | in my green velvet coat, WT 1.02.156
horse, and he frets like a gumm'd velvet. 1H4 2.02. 2 P
make boot upon the summer's velvet buds, | which H5 1.02.194
through the velvet leaves the wind | all unseen PP 16. 5
like unshorn velvet on that termless skin, LC 94
VELVET–GUARDS 1 FR 0.0001 REL FR 1 V 0 P
to velvet–guards and sunday–citizens. 1H4 3.01.256
VENDIBLE 2 FR 0.0002 REL FR 1 V 1 P
a neat's tongue dried and a maid not vendible. MV 1.01.112
off with't while 'tis vendible; AWW 1.01.155 P

VENECHIA *(also venice)*
/VENECHIA 2 FR 0.0002 REL FR 2 V 0 P
/venechia, /venechia, | che non te /vede, che LLL 4.02. 97
/venechia, /venechia, | che non te /vede, che 4.02. 97
VENERABLE 4 FR 0.0004 REL FR 4 V 0 P
set down your venerable burthen, | and let him AYL 2.07.167
methought did promise | most venerable worth, TN 3.04.363
and such again | as venerable nestor, hatch'd in TRO 1.03. 65
and that most venerable man which i | did call CYM 2.05. 3
VENEREAL 1 FR 0.0001 REL FR 1 V 0 P
no, madam, these are no venereal signs. TIT 2.03. 37
VENETIAN 9 FR 0.0010 REL FR 6 V 3 P
or any tire of venetian admittance. WIV 3.03. 58 P
in your father's time, a venetian, a scholar and MV 1.02.113 P
is alighted at your gate | a young venetian, one 2.09. 87
what, and my old venetian friend salerio? 3.02.219
yet in such rule that the venetian law | cannot 4.01.178
and /a super–subtle venetian be not too hard for OTH 1.03.356 P
hath kill'd a young venetian | call'd roderigo. 5.02.112
of your fault be known | to the venetian state. 5.02.337
turk | beat a venetian and traduc'd the state, 5.02.354
VENETIANS 1 FR 0.0001 REL FR 0 V 1 P
talking on the sea–bank with certain venetians, OTH 4.01.134 P
VENEYS *(also venue)*
VENEYS 1 FR 0.0001 REL FR 0 V 1 P
fence (three veneys for a dish of stew'd prunes) WIV 1.01.284 P
VENGE 8 FR 0.0009 REL FR 8 V 0 P
the best way is to venge my gloucester's death. R2 1.02. 36
dolphin i am coming on | to venge me as i may, H5 1.02.292
crave | i may have liberty to venge this wrong, 1H6 3.04. 42
richard, i bear thy name, i'll venge thy death, 3H6 2.01. 87
would none but i might venge my cousin's death! ROM 3.05. 86
these our nether crimes | so speedily can venge! LR 4.02. 80
but | it is an office of the gods to venge it, CYM 1.06. 92
with swift pursuit to venge this wrong of mine, LUC 1691
VENGEANCE 55 FR 0.0062 REL FR 48 V 7 P
rarer action is | in virtue than in vengeance. TMP 5.01. 28
mother, and this my father — a vengeance on't! TGV 2.03. 19 P
vengeance of jinny's case! WIV 4.01. 62 P
did woo me, | that could do no vengeance to me." AYL 4.03. 48
a vengeance on your crafty withered hide! SHR 2.01.404
so, without | my present vengeance taken. WT 1.02.281
for present vengeance, | take it on her. 2.03. 22
and vengeance for't | not dropp'd down yet. 3.02.201
what wit can make heavy and vengeance bitter; 4.04.773 P
plainly denouncing vengeance upon john. JN 3.04.159
will rain hot vengeance on offenders' heads. R2 1.02. 8
that it shall render vengeance and revenge 4.01. 67
of all cowards, i say, and a vengeance too! 1H4 2.04.114 P
thou art only mark'd | for the hot vengeance, 3.02. 10
stand sore charged for the wasteful vengeance H5 1.02.283
war is his beadle, war is his vengeance; 4.01.169 P
will cry for vengeance at the gates of heaven. 1H6 5.04. 53
and threefold vengeance tend upon your steps! 2H6 3.02.304
bosoms of our part | hot coals of vengeance! 5.02. 36
and every drop cries vengeance for his death 3H6 1.04.148
for vengeance comes along with them. 2.05.134
and they shall feel the vengeance of my wrath. 4.01. 82
excused | for doing worthy vengeance on thyself, R3 1.02. 87
for he holds vengeance in his hand, | to hurl 1.04.199
and that same vengeance doth he hurl on thee 1.04.201
to–morrow's vengeance on the head of richard. 5.03.206
paris should do some vengeance on the greeks. TRO 2.02. 73
after this, the vengeance on the whole camp! 2.03. 18 P
the venom'd vengeance ride upon our swords, 5.03. 47
is arming, weeping, cursing, vowing vengeance. 5.05. 31
but he's vengeance proud, and loves not the COR 2.02. 5 P
what the vengeance, | could he not speak 'em 3.01.261
wit | to villainy and vengeance consecrate, TIT 2.01.121
vengeance is in my heart, death in my hand, 2.03. 38
come, | this vengeance on me had they executed: 2.03.113
and vengeance on the traitor saturnine. 4.03. 35
i'll speak no more but "vengeance rot you all!" 5.01. 58
by working wreakful vengeance on thy foes. 5.02. 32
'cause they take vengeance of such kind of men. 5.02. 63
we will have vengeance for it, fear thou not. ROM 3.05. 87
can vengeance be pursued further than death? 5.03. 55
pause, | a roused vengeance sets him new a–work, HAM 2.02.488
all vengeance comes too short | which can pursue LR 2.01. 88
vengeance! 2.04. 95
the winged vengeance overtake such children. 3.07. 66
if you see vengeance — 3.07. 72
arise, black vengeance, from the hollow hell! OTH 3.03.447
o, vengeance, vengeance! CYM 2.05. 8
o, vengeance, vengeance! 2.05. 8
you | should have ta'en vengeance on my faults, 5.01. 8
strook | me, wretch, more worth your vengeance. 5.01. 11
to withhold the vengeance that they had in store PER 2.04. 4
as wakes my vengeance and revenge for 'em. TNK 1.01. 58
such a vengeance | that, were i old and wicked, 2.03. 5
this fellow has a vengeance trick o' th' hip. 2.03. 70
VENGEANCES 1 FR 0.0001 REL FR 1 V 0 P
all the stor'd vengeances of heaven fall | on LR 2.04.162
VENGEFUL 3 FR 0.0003 REL FR 3 V 0 P
but here's a vengeful sword, rusted with ease, 2H6 3.02.198
jet, | to hale thy vengeful waggon swift away, TIT 5.02. 51
growth | a vengeful canker eat him up to death. SON 99.13
VENI 1 FR 0.0001 REL FR 0 V 1 P
and he it was that might rightly say, veni, vidi LLL 4.01. 67 P
VENIAL 1 FR 0.0001 REL FR 1 V 0 P
if they do nothing, 'tis a venial slip; OTH 4.01. 9
VENICE *(also venechia)*
VENICE 44 FR 0.0049 REL FR 34 V 10 P
cupid have not spent all his quiver in venice, ADO 1.01.272 P
speak of thee as the traveller doth of venice: LLL 4.02. 96 P
of nothing, more than any man in all venice. MV 1.01.115 P
go forth, | try what my credit can in venice do. 1.01.180
the rate of usance here with us in venice. 1.03. 45
why, all the boys in venice follow him, | crying 2.08. 23
in my company to venice that swear he cannot 3.01.114 P
for, were he out of venice, i can make what 3.01.128 P
what's the news from venice? 3.02.238
wife, | and then away to venice to your friend; 3.02.304
that strangers have | with us in venice, if it 3.03. 28
to the common ferry | which trades to venice. 3.04. 54
there is no force in the decrees of venice. 4.01.102

this strict court of venice | must needs give 4.01.204
there is no power in venice | can alter a decree 4.01.218
/no, not for venice. 4.01.230
lands and goods | are, by the laws of venice, 4.01.311
venice, confiscate | unto the state of venice. 4.01.312
it is enacted in the laws of venice, | if it be 4.01.348
the dearest ring in venice will i give you, 4.01.435
and with an unthrift love did run from venice, 5.01. 16
i will unto venice | to buy apparel 'gainst the SHR 2.01.314
i will to venice, sunday comes apace. 2.01.322
pearl, | valens of venice gold in needle–work; 2.01.354
your ships are stay'd at venice, and the duke, 4.02. 83
i told him that your father was at venice, | and 4.04. 15
and there at venice gave | his body to that R2 4.01. 97
this is venice; OTH 1.01.105
a noble ship of venice | hath seen a grievous 2.01. 22
i have brought you from venice. 2.01.264 P
if this poor trash of venice, whom i trace | for 2.01.303
and a little more wit, return again to venice. 2.03.369 P
in venice they do let /god see the pranks | they 3.03.202
either from venice, or some unhatch'd practice 3.04.141
i warrant, something from venice. 4.01.214
the duke and the senators of venice greet you. 4.01.217
my lord, this would not be believ'd in venice, 4.01.242
i obey the mandate, | and will return to venice. 4.01.260
i took you for that cunning whore of venice 4.02. 89
the messengers of venice stays the meat. 4.02.170
commission come from venice to depute cassio in 4.02.221 P
othello and desdemona return again to venice. 4.02.223 P
i know a lady in venice would have walk'd 4.03. 38 P
what, of venice? 5.01. 91
VENISON 7 FR 0.0008 REL FR 4 V 3 P
i thank you for my venison, master shallow. WIV 1.01. 80 P
i wish'd your venison better, it was ill kill'd. 1.01. 82 P
come, we have a hot venison pasty to dinner. 1.01.195 P
come, shall we go and kill us venison? AYL 2.01. 21
the venison first shall be the lord o' th' feast CYM 3.03. 75
that of coward hares, hot goats, and venison! 4.04. 37
venison. TNK 3.03. 27
VENIT 1 FR 0.0001 REL FR 0 V 1 P
videsne quis venit? LLL 5.01. 30 P
VENOM 19 FR 0.0021 REL FR 18 V 1 P
the venom clamors of a jealous woman | poisons ERR 5.01. 69
thy reason, dear venom, give thy reason. TN 3.02. 2 P
and yet partake no venom (for his knowledge | is WT 2.01. 41
to whose venom sound | the open ear of youth R2 2.01. 19
which live like venom where no venom else | but 2.01.157
which live like venom where no venom else | but 2.01.157
but let thy spiders, that suck up thy venom, 3.02. 14
mingled with venom of suggestion | (as, force 2H4 4.04. 45
the venom of such looks we fairly hope | have H5 5.02. 18
as venom toads, or lizards' dreadful stings. 3H6 2.02.138
his venom tooth will rankle to the death. R3 1.03.290
anointed let me be with deadly venom, | and die 4.01. 61
you shall digest the venom of your spleen JC 4.03. 47
hath nature that in time will venom breed, | no MAC 3.04. 29
has thirty–one | swelt'red venom sleeping got, 4.01. 8
who this had seen, with tongue in venom steep'd, HAM 2.02.510
then, venom, to thy work. 5.02.322
so applied, | his venom in effect is purified. LUC 532
or toads infect fair founts with venom mud? 850
VENOM'D 6 FR 0.0006 REL FR 6 V 0 P
to the soul with slander's venom'd spear, | the R2 1.01.171
or any creeping venom'd thing that lives! R3 1.02. 20
the venom'd vengeance ride upon our swords, TRO 5.03. 47
the gilded newt and eyeless venom'd worm, | with TIM 4.03.182
if he by chance escape your venom'd stuck, | our HAM 4.07.161
'gainst venom'd sores the only sovereign plaster VEN 916
VENOM'D–MOUTH'D 1 FR 0.0001 REL FR 1 V 0 P
this butcher's cur is venom'd–mouth'd, and i H8 1.01.120
VENOMOUS 5 FR 0.0005 REL FR 5 V 0 P
which, like the toad, ugly and venomous, | wears AYL 2.01. 13
with venomous wights she stays | as tediously as TRO 4.02. 12
a younger man's, | and venomous to thine eyes. COR 4.01. 23
the venomous malice of my swelling heart! TIT 5.03. 13
poor venomous fool, | be angry, and dispatch. ANT 5.02.305
/VENOMOUSLY 1 FR 0.0001 REL FR 1 V 0 P
/things /sting | /his /mind /so /venomously, LR 4.03. 46
VENOMOUSLY 1 FR 0.0001 REL FR 1 V 0 P
storm, venomously | wilt thou spet all thyself? PER 3.01. 7
VENT 20 FR 0.0022 REL FR 12 V 8 P
where thou didst vent thy groans | as fast as TMP 1.02.280
can he vent trinculos? 2.02.107 P
gremio, 'tis now no time to vent our love; SHR 1.02.178
thou didst make tolerable vent of thy travel; AWW 2.03.202 P
i prithee vent thy folly somewhere else, | thou TN 4.01. 10
vent my folly! 4.01. 12 P
vent my folly! 4.01. 13 P
and tell me what i shall vent to my lady. 4.01. 16 P
shall i vent to her that thou art coming? 4.01. 17 P
the vent of hearing when loud rumor speaks? 2H4 in 2
they vent reproaches | most bitterly on you as H8 1.02. 23
then we shall ha' means to vent | our musty COR 1.01.225
his breast forges, that his tongue must vent, 3.01.257
sprightly, /waking, audible, and full of vent. 4.05.223 P
or, whilst i can vent clamor from my throat, LR 1.01.165
there is a vent of blood, and something blown; ANT 5.02.349
none abroad so wholesome as that you vent. CYM 1.02. 4 P
you rhyme upon't, | and vent it for a mock'ry? 5.03. 56
free vent of words love's fire doth assuage, VEN 334
to make more vent for passage of her breath, LUC 1040
VENTAGES 1 FR 0.0001 REL FR 0 V 1 P
govern these ventages with your fingers and HAM 3.02.357 P
VENTED 2 FR 0.0002 REL FR 2 V 0 P
these shreds | they vented their complainings, COR 1.01.209
cold and sickly | he vented /them, most narrow ANT 3.04. 8
VENTER *(also venture)*
VENTER 4 FR 0.0004 REL FR 4 V 0 P
and confidence | what dar'st thou venter? AWW 2.01.170
rode on, and, upon my life, | spoke at a venter. 2H4 1.01. 59
others, like merchants, venter trade abroad; H5 1.02.192
being ireful, on the lion he will venter. VEN 628
VENTIDIUS 11 FR 0.0012 REL FR 11 V 0 P
noble ventidius! TIM 1.01. 99
o, by no means, | honest ventidius. 1.02. 9
go to ventidius. 2.02.220
ventidius lately | buried his father, by whose 2.02.222
and now ventidius is wealthy too, | whom he 3.03. 3

has ventidius and lucullus denied him, | and 3.03. 8
hark, ventidius. ANT 2.02. 16
say to ventidius i would speak with him. 2.03. 32
o, come, ventidius, | you must to parthia. 2.03. 41
noble ventidius, | whilst yet with parthian 3.01. 5
thou hast, ventidius, that | without the which a 3.01. 27
VENTRICLE 1 FR 0.0001 REL FR 0 V 1 P
these are begot in the ventricle of memory, LLL 4.02. 68 P
VENT'RING 2 FR 0.0002 REL FR 2 V 0 P
out of hope are compass'd oft with vent'ring, VEN 567
so that in vent'ring ill we leave to be | the LUC 148
VENTS 3 FR 0.0003 REL FR 3 V 0 P
the which he vents | in mangled forms. AYL 2.07. 41
look how thy wounds do bleed at many vents! TRO 5.03. 82
through little vents and crannies of the place LUC 310
VENTUR'D 6 FR 0.0006 REL FR 6 V 0 P
entreaties, | ere he should thus have ventur'd. AYL 1.02.239
one, | and yet we ventur'd for the gain propos'd 2H4 1.01.183
i have ventur'd, | like little wanton boys that H8 3.02.358
and i myself have ventur'd | to speak my mind of 5.01. 40
say i ventur'd | to set him free? TNK 2.04. 30
i have ventur'd for him, | and out i have 2.06. 2
VENTURE *(also venter)*
VENTURE 30 FR 0.0034 REL FR 24 V 6 P
to thee, | that i may venture to depart alone. TGV 4.03. 36
believe me, sir, had i such venture forth, | the MV 1.01. 15
this was a venture, sir, that jacob serv'd for, 1.03. 91
some month or two | before you venture for me. 3.02. 10
part, | and venture madly on a desperate mart. SHR 2.01.327
i'll venture so much of my hawk or hound, | but 5.02. 72
i'd venture | the well-lost life of mine on his AWW 1.03.247
not wonder how thou dar'st venture to be drunk, WT 5.02.171 P
i am afraid, and yet i'll venture it. JN 4.03. 5
and, prince of wales, so dare we venture thee, 1H4 5.01.101
and since we are o'erset, venture again. 2H4 1.01.185
to venture upon the charg'd chambers bravely — 2.04. 51 P
a whole merchant's venture of burdeaux stuff in 2.04. 63 P
but to the purpose, and so to the venture. ep 7 P
which if like an ill venture it come unluckily ep 11 P
lov'dst plums well, that wouldst venture so. 2H6 2.01. 99
held for certain | the king will venture at it. H8 2.01.156
if it do, | i'll venture one; have at him! 2.02. 84
and venture maidenhead for't, and so would you 2.03. 25
little england | you'ld venture an emballing. 2.03. 47
i will venture | to /stale't a little more. COR 1.01. 91
he had rather venture all his limbs for honor 2.02. 80
thy personal venture in the rebels' fight, | his MAC 1.03. 91
hear | (if you dare venture in your own behalf) LR 4.02. 20
i should venture purgatory for't. OTH 4.03. 77 P
in, the blood we venture | should be as for our TNK 1.02.109
i'll be hang'd though, | if he dare venture. 2.03. 72
i'll venture, | and in some poor disguise be 2.03. 78
where there is a path of ground i'll venture, 2.06. 33
blind priest for the purpose that will venture 5.02. 78
VENTURED 2 FR 0.0002 REL FR 2 V 0 P
knew that we ventured on such dangerous seas 2H4 1.01.181
you, | yet have i ventured to come seek you out, LR 3.04.152
VENTURES 6 FR 0.0006 REL FR 5 V 1 P
might make me fear | misfortune to my ventures, MV 1.01. 21
it, | my ventures are not in one bottom trusted, 1.01. 42
fourth for england, and other ventures he hath, 1.03. 21 P
hath all his ventures fail'd? 3.02.267
current when it serves, | or lose our ventures. JC 4.03.224
with diseas'd ventures | that play with all CYM 1.06.123
VENTURING 1 FR 0.0001 REL FR 0 V 1 P
'slid, 'tis but venturing. WIV 3.04. 25 P
VENTUROUS 5 FR 0.0005 REL FR 5 V 0 P
i have a venturous fairy that shall seek | the MND 4.01. 35
more venturous or desperate than this. 1H6 2.01. 45
i will reward you for this venturous deed. 2H6 3.02. 9
prime of manhood daring, bold, and venturous; R3 4.04.171
i am much too venturous | in tempting of your H8 1.02. 54
VENUE *(also veneys)*
VENUE 1 FR 0.0001 REL FR 0 V 1 P
a sweet touch, a quick venue of wit — snip, LLL 5.01. 59 P
VENUS' 9 FR 0.0010 REL FR 9 V 0 P
head, | by the simplicity of venus' doves, | by MND 1.01.171
o, ten times faster venus' pigeons fly | to seal MV 2.06. 5
by venus' hand i swear, | no man alive can love TRO 4.01. 23
why then, for venus' sake, give me a kiss | when 4.05. 49
your quondam wife swears still by venus' glove. 4.05.179
so he were like him, and by venus' side. VEN 180
open'd their mouths to swallow venus' liking. 248
so glides he in the night from venus' eye, 816
in that white intituled | from venus' doves, LUC 58
VENUS 24 FR 0.0027 REL FR 21 V 3 P
if venus or her son, as thou dost know, | do now TMP 4.01. 87
are more intemperate in your blood | than venus, ADO 4.01. 60
then was venus like her mother, for her father LLL 2.01.256
as yonder venus in her glimmering sphere. MND 3.02. 61
shine as gloriously | as the venus of the sky. 3.02.107
same wicked bastard of venus that was begot of AYL 4.01.211 P
saturn and venus this year in conjunction! 2H4 2.04.263 P
bright star of venus, fall'n down on the earth, 1H6 1.02.144
with him, the mortal venus, the heart-blood of TRO 3.01. 32 P
as red as mars his heart | inflam'd with venus. 5.02.165
madam, though venus govern your desires, TIT 2.03. 30
speak to my gossip venus one fair word, | one ROM 2.01. 11
for venus smiles not in a house of tears. 4.01. 8
and think | what venus did with mars. ANT 1.05. 18
o'er-picturing that venus where we see | the 2.02.200
the shrine of venus or straight-pight minerva, CYM 5.05.164
to the goddess venus | commend we our proceeding TNK 5.01. 74
can that be, when | venus i have said is false? 5.04. 45
the powerful venus well hath grac'd her altar, 5.04.105
sick-thoughted venus makes amain unto him, | and VEN 5
"ay me," quoth venus, "young, and so unkind, 187
venus salutes him with this fair good morrow: 859
this solemn sympathy poor venus noteth, | over 1057
venus, with adonis sitting by her, | under a PP 11. 1
VENUTO 3 FR 0.0003 REL FR 1 V 2 P
child or pupil, undertake your bien venuto; LLL 4.02.157 P
alla nostra casa ben venuto, molto honorato SHR 1.02. 25 P
it so, | petruchio, i shall be your ben venuto. 1.02.280
VER* *(also for, vor)*
VER* 4 FR 0.0004 REL FR 1 V 3 P
it is no matter–a ver dat. WIV 1.04.115 P
this ver, the spring; LLL 5.02.891 P
ver, begin. 5.02.893 P
primrose, first-born child of ver, | merry TNK 1.01. 7
VERB 1 FR 0.0001 REL FR 0 V 1 P
thee that usually talk of a noun and a verb, and 2H6 4.07. 39 P
VERBA 2 FR 0.0002 REL FR 0 V 2 P
pauca verba; sir john, good worts. WIV 1.01.120 P
pauca verba. LLL 4.02.165 P
/VERBAL 1 FR 0.0001 REL FR 1 V 0 P
/made /she /no /verbal /question? LR 4.03. 24
VERBAL 3 FR 0.0003 REL FR 3 V 0 P
in a sweet verbal brief, it did concern | your AWW 5.03.137
to forget a lady's manners | by being so verbal; CYM 2.03.106
troubled, | make verbal repetition of her moans; VEN 831
VERBATIM 1 FR 0.0001 REL FR 1 V 0 P
verbatim to rehearse the method of my pen. 1H6 3.01. 13
VERBOSITY 1 FR 0.0001 REL FR 0 V 1 P
out the thread of his verbosity finer than the LLL 5.01. 16 P
VERD 1 FR 0.0001 REL FR 0 V 1 P
and vetch me in my closet /une /boite /en verd, WIV 1.04. 46 P
VERDICT 7 FR 0.0008 REL FR 6 V 1 P
giving my verdict on the white rose side. 1H6 2.04. 48
must your bold verdict enter talk with lords?" 3.01. 63
what lawful quest have given their verdict up R3 1.04.184
carries | the due o' th' verdict with it. H8 5.01.131
is't a verdict? COR 1.01. 11 P
and by their verdict is determined | the clear SON 46.11
"but quickly on this side the verdict went: LC 113
VERDON 1 FR 0.0001 REL FR 1 V 0 P
lord strange of blackmere, lord verdon of alton, 1H6 4.07. 65
VERDOUR 1 FR 0.0001 REL FR 1 V 0 P
and as they last, their verdour still endure, VEN 507
VERDURE 2 FR 0.0002 REL FR 2 V 0 P
trunk, | and suck'd my verdure out on't. TMP 1.02. 87
losing his verdure, even in the prime, | and all TGV 1.01. 49
VERE* *(also where)*
VERE* 4 FR 0.0004 REL FR 1 V 3 P
vere is dat knave rugby? WIV 1.04. 55 P
vere is mine host de jarteer? 4.05. 83 P
vere is mistress page? 5.05.204 P
doom | my elder brother, the lord aubrey vere, 3H6 3.03.102
VERGE 8 FR 0.0009 REL FR 8 V 0 P
stood on th' extremest verge of the swift brook, AYL 2.01. 42
or here or elsewhere to the furthest verge R2 1.01. 93
head, | and yet, /incaged in so small a verge, 2.01.102
we will make fast within a hallow'd verge. 2H6 1.04. 22
o, would to god that the inclusive verge | of R3 4.01. 58
upon the beached verge of the salt flood, | who TIM 5.01.216
nature in you stands on the very verge | of his LR 2.04.147
are now within a foot | of th' extreme verge. 4.06. 26
VERGES 3 FR 0.0003 REL FR 0 V 3 P
goodman verges, sir, speaks a little /off the ADO 3.05. 9 P
are odorous — palabras, neighbor verges. 3.05. 17 P
well said, i' faith, neighbor verges. 3.05. 36 P
VERIER 2 FR 0.0002 REL FR 1 V 1 P
was not my lord | the verier wag o' th' two? WT 1.02. 66
there are verier knaves desire to live, for all CYM 5.04.200 P
VERIEST 4 FR 0.0004 REL FR 3 V 1 P
were he the veriest antic in the world. SHR in.1. 101
i think thou hast the veriest shrew of all. 5.02. 64
i am the veriest varlet that ever chew'd with a 1H4 2.02. 24 P
but yield me to the veriest hind that shall CYM 5.03. 77
VERIFIED 6 FR 0.0006 REL FR 5 V 1 P
thirdly, they have verified unjust things; ADO 5.01.218 P
more truly now may this be verified, | for none 1H6 1.02. 32
then i perceive that will be verified | henry 5.01. 30
queen, | unless the adage must be verified, 3H6 1.04.126
i see, is verified | of thee, which says thus, H8 5.02.209
for i have ever verified my friends | (of whom COR 5.02. 17
VERIFY 2 FR 0.0002 REL FR 1 V 1 P
to verify our title with their lives. JN 2.01.277
i will verify as much in his beard. H5 3.02. 71 P
VERILY 14 FR 0.0015 REL FR 10 V 4 P
there was a noise, | that's verily. TMP 2.01.321
he did, i think verily he had been hang'd for't; TGV 4.04. 15 P
i verily did think | that her old gloves were on AYL 4.03. 25
verily, i speak it in the freedom of my WT 1.01. 11 P
i may not, verily. 1.02. 45
verily? 1.02. 46
verily, | you shall not go; 1.02. 49
a lady's "verily" is | as potent as a lord's. 1.02. 50
by your dread "verily," | one of them you shall 1.02. 55
and that those veins | did verily bear blood? 5.03. 65
yes, verily and in truth you shall take it, or i H5 5.01. 61 P
verily, | i swear, 'tis better to be lowly born, H8 2.03. 18
verily, i do not jest with you; COR 1.03. 92 P
verily i think so, | a right good creature, more TNK 5.04. 33
VERITABLE 1 FR 0.0001 REL FR 1 V 0 P
most veritable, therefore look to't well. OTH 3.04. 76
VERITE 1 FR 0.0001 REL FR 0 V 1 P
sauf votre honneur, en verite, vous prononcez H5 3.04. 37 P
VERITIES 1 FR 0.0001 REL FR 1 V 0 P
why, by the verities on thee made good, | may MAC 3.01. 8
VERITY 11 FR 0.0012 REL FR 7 V 4 P
find | by every syllable a faithful verity. MM 4.03.126
in verity you did, my bones bears witness, ERR 4.04. 77
nor a horse-stealer, but for his verity in love, AYL 3.04. 23 P
from point, to the full arming of the verity. AWW 4.03. 62 P
that the verity of it is in strong suspicion. WT 5.02. 28 P
'twould prove the verity of certain words H8 1.02.159
with all the size that verity | would without COR 5.02. 18
as justice, verity, temp'rance, stableness, MAC 4.03. 92
but, in the verity of extolment, i take him to HAM 5.02.116 P
sir, in good faith, in sincere verity, | under LR 2.02.105
and, to say verity, and not to fable, | we are a TNK 3.05.105
VERMILION 1 FR 0.0001 REL FR 1 V 0 P
nor praise the deep vermilion in the rose, SON 98.10
VERMIN 1 FR 0.0001 REL FR 0 V 1 P
how to prevent the fiend, and to kill vermin. LR 3.04.159 P
VERNON 5 FR 0.0005 REL FR 5 V 0 P
my cousin vernon, welcome, by my soul! 1H4 4.01. 86
but there is mordake, vernon, lord harry percy, 4.04. 24
bear worcester to the death and vernon too. 5.05. 14
good master vernon, it is well objected; 1H6 2.04. 43
good master vernon, i am bound to you | that you 2.04.128
VERNON'S 1 FR 0.0001 REL FR 1 V 0 P
of my cousin vernon's are not yet come up. 1H4 4.03. 20
VEROLLUS 1 FR 0.0001 REL FR 0 V 1 P
who, monsieur verollus? PER 4.02.106 P
VERONA 17 FR 0.0019 REL FR 16 V 1 P
to verona. TGV 4.01. 17
myself was from verona banished | for practicing 4.01. 45
verona, for a while i take my leave | to see my SHR 1.02. 1
how do you all at verona? 1.02. 22 P
gale | blows you to padua here from old verona? 1.02. 49
born in verona, old /antonio's son. 1.02.190
i am a gentleman of verona, sir, | that, hearing 2.01. 47
in fair verona, where we lay our scene, | from ROM pr 2
trudge about | through fair verona, find those 1.02. 35
with all the admired beauties of verona. 1.02. 84
here in verona, ladies of esteem, | are made 1.03. 70
verona brags of him | to be a virtuous and 1.05. 67
hath | forbid this bandying in verona streets. 3.01. 89
here from verona art thou banished. 3.03. 15
there is no world without verona walls, | but 3.03. 17
news from verona! 5.01. 12
that whiles verona by that name is known, 5.03.300
VERONA'S 2 FR 0.0002 REL FR 2 V 0 P
and made verona's ancient citizens | cast by ROM 1.01. 92
verona's summer hath not such a flower. 1.03. 77
VERONESA 1 FR 0.0001 REL FR 1 V 0 P
a veronesa, michael cassio, | lieutenant to the OTH 2.01. 26
VERSAL *(also universal)*
VERSAL 1 FR 0.0001 REL FR 0 V 1 P
looks as pale as any clout in the versal world. ROM 2.04.206 P
VERSE 32 FR 0.0036 REL FR 24 V 8 P
run smoothly in the even road of a blank verse, ADO 5.02. 34 P
let me hear a staff, a stanze, a verse; LLL 4.02.104
i'll give you a verse to this note, that i made AYL 2.05. 46 P
hang there, my verse, in witness of my love, 3.02. 1
and could not bear themselves without the verse, 3.02.170 P
verse, and therefore stood lamely in the verse. 3.02.171 P
then god buy you, and you talk in blank verse. 4.01. 32 P
come, but one verse. TN 2.04. 7
thus your verse | flow'd with her beauty once. WT 5.01.101
"as true as troilus" shall crown up the verse, TRO 3.02.182
for we may live to have need of such a verse. 4.04. 22 P
what verse for it? 5.10. 40 P
o, 'tis a verse in horace, i know it well, | i TIT 4.02. 22
ay, just — a verse in horace, right, you have 4.02. 24
it stains the glory in that happy verse | which TIM 1.01. 16
thy verse swells with stuff so fine and smooth 5.01. 84
freely, or the /blank verse shall halt for't. HAM 2.02.325 P
who will believe my verse in time to come | if SON 17. 1
my love shall in my verse ever live young. 19.14
muse | stirr'd by a painted beauty to his verse, 21. 2
that pour'st into my verse | thine own sweet 38. 2
that shall vade, by verse distills your truth. 54.14
and yet to times in hope my verse shall stand, 60.13
o, if (i say) you look upon this verse, | when i 71. 9
why is my verse so barren of new pride? 76. 1
and found such fair assistance in my verse | as 78. 2
aid, | my verse alone had all thy gentle grace, 79. 2
your monument shall be my gentle verse, | which 81. 9
was it the proud full sail of his great verse, 86. 1
by night | giving him aid, my verse astonished. 86. 8
and more, much more than in my verse can sit, 103.13
therefore my verse, to constancy confin'd, | one 105. 7
VERSES 20 FR 0.0022 REL FR 5 V 15 P
he writes verses, he speaks holiday, he smells WIV 3.02. 68 P
as horace says in his — what, my soul, verses? LLL 4.02.102 P
but to return to the verses: 4.02.150 P
i will prove those verses to be very unlearned, 4.02.158 P
nay, i have verses too, i thank berowne; 5.02. 34
some thousand verses of a faithful lover. 5.02. 50
with faining voice verses of faining love, | and MND 1.01. 31
this is the very false gallop of verses; AYL 3.02.113 P
didst thou hear these verses? 3.02.163 P
in them more feet than the verses would bear. 3.02.166 P
the feet might bear the verses. 3.02.168 P
you mar no moe of my verses with reading them 3.02.261 P
are you he that hangs the verses on the trees, 3.02.392 P
when a man's verses cannot be understood, nor a 3.03. 12 P
he writes brave verses, speaks brave words, 3.04. 41 P
if you would put me to verses, or to dance for H5 5.02.132 P
him, | by magic verses have contriv'd his end? 1H6 1.01. 27
tear him for his bad verses, tear him for his JC 3.03. 30 P
for his bad verses, tear him for his bad verses. 3.03. 31 P
for to no other pass my verses tend | than of SON 103.11
VERSING 1 FR 0.0001 REL FR 1 V 0 P
playing on pipes of corn and versing love | to MND 2.01. 67
VERT *(see verd)*
VERY *(also fery, vara, vary*)*
/VERY 10 FR 0.0011 REL FR 9 V 1 P
/when /i /do /see /the /very /book /indeed R2 4.01.274
/'tis /very /true, /my /grief /lies /all /within 4.01.295
/begin /to /stop | /our /very /veins /of /life. 2H4 4.01. 66
/and /very /well /appointed, /as /i /thought, 3H6 2.01.113
very like, /very /like. stay'd it long? HAM 1.02.236
/for /the /very /substance /of /the /ambitious 2.02.258 P
thou turn'st my /eyes into my /very soul, | and 3.04. 89
/but /i /am /very /sorry, /good /horatio, 5.02. 75
straight to my sister | to hold my /very course. LR 1.03. 26
/very /well. 4.07. 23
VERY 839 FR 0.0948 REL FR 457 V 382 P
o, the cry did knock | against my very heart. TMP 1.02. 9
touch'd | the very virtue of compassion in thee, 1.02. 27
come, | the very minute bids thee ope thine ear. 1.02. 37
the very rats | instinctively have quit it. 1.02.147
ay, or very falsely pocket up his report. 2.01. 68 P
very well. 2.01.140
very foul. 2.01.143
will you laugh me asleep, for i am very heavy? 2.01.189 P
a very ancient and fish-like smell; 2.02. 26 P
this is a very scurvy tune to sing at a man's 2.02. 44 P
thou art very trinculo indeed! 2.02.105 P
this good light, this is a very shallow monster! 2.02.144 P
a very weak monster! 2.02.145 P
the very instant that i saw you, did | my heart 3.01. 64
here on this grass-plot, in this very place, 4.01. 73
at the farthest | in the very end of harvest! 4.01.115
that i am prospero and that very duke | which 5.01.159
very like; 5.01.265
indeed a sheep doth very often stray, | and if TGV 1.01. 74
the letter, very orderly, having nothing but the 1.01.123 P

you, gentle servant — 'tis very clerkly done.		2.01.108
it goes, | i writ at random, very doubtfully.		2.01.111
the lines are very quaintly writ, | but (since		2.01.122
the kind of the launces have this very fault.		2.03. 2 P
he is a stone, a very pibble stone, and has no		2.03. 10 P
and sleep, | upon the very naked name of love.		2.04.142
in earnest, they parted very fairly in jest.		2.05. 13 P
this very night;		3.01.124
gentleman, | especially against his very friend.		3.02. 41
so false that he grieves my very heart–strings.		4.02. 62 P
i am very loath to be your idol, sir;		4.02.128
marry | vain thurio, whom my very soul /abhors.		4.03. 17
him | that with his very heart despiseth me?		4.04. 94
dead | if i in thought felt not her very sorrow.		4.04.172
and now it is about the very hour | that silvia		5.01. 2
humor on me — that is the very note of it.	WIV	1.01.168 P
ford, by my troth, you are very well met.		1.01.192 P
the very point of it — to mistress anne page.		1.01.223 P
i am very well.		1.01.268 P
'em, they are very ill–favor'd rough things.		1.01.298 P
and the very yea and the no is, the french		1.04. 93 P
you look very ill.		2.01. 36 P
why, this is the very same:		2.01. 82 P
the very hand;		2.01. 82 P
the very words.		2.01. 83 P
are a yoke of his discarded men — very rogues,		2.01.176 P
your worship says very true.		2.02. 48 P
he's a very jealousy man.		2.02. 89 P
she leads a very frampold life with him, good		2.02. 90 P
you, wherein i must very much lay open mine own		2.02.184 P
very well, sir, proceed.		2.02.190 P
you prescribe to yourself very preposterously.		2.02.240 P
ay, dat is very good, excellant.		3.01. 99 P
pray you do so, she's a very tattling woman.		3.03. 91 P
and 'tis the very riches of thyself | that now i		3.04. 17
very ill–favoredly, master /brook.		3.05. 67 P
but truly he is very courageous mad about his		4.01. 4 P
you are a very simplicity oman;		4.01. 30 P
she says that the very same man that beguil'd		4.05. 36 P
which, at the very instant of falstaff's and our		5.03. 14 P
the duke is very strangely gone from hence;	MM	1.04. 50
by those that know the very nerves of state,		1.04. 53
angelo, a man whose blood | is very snow–broth;		1.04. 58
'tis very pregnant, | the jewel that we find, we		2.01. 23
which, i think, is a very ill house too.		2.01. 66 P
house, which at that very distant time stood, as		2.01. 91 P
they are not china dishes, but very good dishes.		2.01. 94 P
master froth here, this very man, having eaten		2.01.101 P
and (as i say) paying for them very honestly;		2.01.102 P
very well;		2.01.106 P
why, very well;		2.01.109 P
you wot of, unless they kept very good diet, as		2.01.112 P
why, very well then —		2.01.114 P
why, very well;		2.01.127 P
why, very well then; i hope here be truths.		2.01.133 P
ay, sir, very well.		2.01.150 P
she's very near her hour.		2.02. 16
ay, my good lord, a very virtuous maid, | and to		2.02. 20
mine were the very cipher of a function, | to		2.02. 39
that respites me a life whose very comfort | is		2.03. 41
and very welcome.		3.01. 49
a very superficial, ignorant, unweighing fellow.		3.02.139 P
the very stream of his life, and the business he		3.02.142 P
and the prisoner the very debt of your calling.		3.02.250 P
very well met, and well come.		4.01. 26
upon the very siege of justice | lord angelo		4.02. 98
we have very oft awak'd him, as if to carry him		4.02.150 P
for he this very day receives letters of strange		4.02.200 P
very ready, sir.		4.03. 38 P
talk offend you, we'll have very little of it.		4.03.178 P
and very near upon | the duke is ent'ring;		4.06. 14
my very worthy cousin, fairly met!		5.01. 1
a saucy friar, | a very scurvy fellow.		5.01.136
in very good time.		5.01.285 P
the very mercy of the law cries out | most		5.01.407
we do condemn thee to the very block | where		5.01.414
that very hour, and in the self–same inn, | a	ERR	1.01. 53
had not their /bark been very slow of sail;		1.01.116
this very day a syracusian merchant | is		1.02. 3
a trusty villain, sir, that very oft, | when i		1.02. 19
for even her very words | didst thou deliver to		2.02.163
me, but that she, being a very beastly creature,		3.02. 88 P
a very reverent body:		3.02. 90 P
meet a sergeant, 'a turns back for very fear.		4.02. 56
time is a very bankrout and owes more than he's		4.02. 58
of very reverent reputation, sir, | of credit		5.01. 5
he is very near by this, he was not three	ADO	1.01. 3 P
here in messina will be very much glad of it.		1.01. 19 P
he is a very valiant trencherman, he hath an		1.01. 51 P
very easily possible.		1.01. 75 P
you love her, for the lady is very well worthy.		1.01.222 P
he is very busy about it.		1.02. 3 P
a very forward march–chick!		1.03. 56 P
he is of a very melancholy disposition.		2.01. 5 P
him so ill–well, unless you were the very man.		2.01.118 P
he is the prince's jester, a very dull fool;		2.01.137 P
you are very near my brother in his love.		2.01.163 P
my very visor began to assume life and scold		2.01.241 P
bring them to see this the very night before the		2.02. 45 P
his words are a very fantastical banquet, just		2.03. 20 P
o, very well, my lord.		2.03. 41
why, these are very crotchets that he speaks —		2.03. 56
it is very true.		2.03.153 P
of her love, 'tis very possible he'll scorn it,		2.03.179 P
he is a very proper man.		2.03.182 P
before god! and, in my mind, very wise.		2.03.185 P
if low, an agot very vildly cut;		3.01. 65
'tis very true.		3.03. 73 P
two of them have the very bent of honor, | and		4.01.186
love | is very much unto the prince and claudio,		4.01.246
a very even way, but no such friend.		4.01.264 P
manner accus'd, in this very manner refus'd, and		4.02. 62 P
but what was true, and very full of proof.		5.01.105
so, though very many have been beside their wit.		5.01.127 P
i have deceiv'd even your very eyes.		5.01.232 P
very ominous endings.		5.02. 39 P
very ill.		5.02. 90 P
very ill too.		5.02. 92 P
the world was very guilty of such a ballet some	LLL	1.02.111 P
i do affect the very ground (which is base)		1.02.167 P
salomon so seduced, and he had a very good wit.		1.02.175 P
if my observation (which very seldom lies), | by		2.01.228
ass upon the horse, for he is very slow–gaited.		3.01. 55 P
love's whip, | a very beadle to a humorous sigh,		3.01.175
very reverent sport, truly, and done in the		4.02. 1 P
their daughters profit very greatly under you.		4.02. 75 P
ay, sir, and very learned.		4.02.103 P
done this in the fear of god, very religiously;		4.02.148 P
i will prove those verses to be very unlearned,		4.02.158 P
there is the very remuneration i had of thy		5.01. 73 P
my familiar, i do assure ye, very good friend;		5.01. 96 P
the very all of all is — but, sweet heart, i do		5.01.109 P
good neighbor, faith, and a very good bowler;		5.02.583 P
and often, at his very loose, decides | that		5.02.742
a very good piece of work, i assure you, and a	MND	1.02. 13 P
bowl, | in very likeness of a roasted crab,		2.01. 48
that very time i saw (but thou couldst not)		2.01.155
lysander riddles very prettily.		2.02. 53
and he is a very paramour for a sweet voice.		4.02. 12 P
very tragical mirth."		5.01. 57
and thisby, | did whisper often, very secretly.		5.01.160
a very gentle beast, and of a good conscience.		5.01.227 P
the very best at a beast, my lord, that e'er i		5.01.229 P
this lion is a very fox for his valor.		5.01.231 P
so it is, truly, and very notably discharg'd.		5.01.360 P
your worth is very dear in my regard.	MV	1.01. 62
when, i am very sure, | if they should speak,		1.01. 97
very vildly in the morning, when he is sober,		1.02. 86 P
one among them but i dote on his very absence,		1.02.110 P
the neck of my heart, says very wisely to me,		2.02. 14 P
certainly the jew is the very devil incarnation,		2.02. 27 P
marry, at the very next turning, turn of no hand		2.02. 43 P
forbid, the boy was the very staff of my age, my		2.02. 66 P
boy was the very staff of my age, my very prop.		2.02. 67 P
my master's a very jew.		2.02.104 P
to be brief, the very truth is that the jew,		2.02.132 P
in very brief, the suit is impertinent to myself		2.02.137 P
that is the very defect of the matter, sir.		2.02.143 P
the old proverb is very well parted between my		2.02.149 P
but stay the very riping of the time;		2.08. 40
they call the place, a very dangerous flat, and		3.01. 5 P
i am very glad of it.		3.01.116 P
nay, that's true, that's very true.		3.01.125 P
love | had been the very sum of my confession.		3.02. 36
and swearing till my very /roof was dry | with		3.02.204
leave, | i bid my very friends and countrymen,		3.02.223
my creditors grow cruel, my estate is very low,		3.02.317 P
it is very meet | the lord bassanio live an		3.05. 73
of spirit, | the very tyranny and rage of his.		4.01. 13
at the receipt of your letter i am very sick,		4.01.151 P
'tis very true.		4.01.250
"nearest his heart," those are the very words.		4.01.254
thou hast contrived against the very life | of		4.01.360
sir, you are very welcome to our house.		5.01.139
even he that had held up the very life | of my		5.01.214
o, sir, very well; here in your orchard.	AYL	1.01. 41 P
she makes honest she makes very ill–favoredly.		1.02. 39 P
paths, our very petticoats will catch them.		1.03. 15 P
her very silence, and her patience | speak to		1.03. 78
else are they very wretched.		2.04. 68
of life, | i will your very faithful feeder be,		2.04. 99
eye, | says very wisely, "it is ten a' clock.		2.07. 22
he that a fool doth very wisely hit | doth very		2.07. 53
fool doth very wisely hit | doth very foolishly,		2.07. 54
sea, | till that the weary very means do ebb?		2.07. 73
that it is solitary, i like it very well;		3.02. 16 P
that it is private, it is a very vild life.		3.02. 17 P
good breeding or comes of a very dull kindred.		3.02. 30 P
than tar, the very uncleanly flux of a cat.		3.02. 68 P
this is the very false gallop of verses;		3.02.113 P
very well. what would you?		3.02.298 P
you are very well met.		3.03. 74 P
i am very glad to see you.		3.03. 75 P
his very hair is of the dissembling color.		3.04. 7 P
the very ice of chastity is in them.		3.04. 17 P
'tis pretty, sure, and very probable, | that		3.05. 11
not very well, but i have met him oft, | and he		3.05.106
it is a pretty youth — not very pretty — | but		3.05.113
he is not very tall — yet for his years he's		3.05.118
i'll write to him a very taunting letter, | and		3.05.134
to me now, and i were your very very rosalind?		4.01. 70 P
to me now, and i were your very very rosalind?		4.01. 70 P
very good orators, when they are out, they will		4.01. 75 P
so" is good, very good, very excellent good;		5.01. 27 P
so" is good, very good, very excellent good;		5.01. 27 P
they are in the very wrath of love, and they		5.02. 40 P
in the ditty, yet the note was very untuneable.		5.03. 36 P
here comes a pair of very strange beasts, which		5.04. 37 P
i like him very well.		5.04. 53 P
by my faith, he is very swift and sententious.		5.04. 62 P
'tis very true;	SHR	in.1. 89
o yes, my lord, but very idle words, | for		in.2. 83
comedy, | for so your doctors hold it very meet,		in.2. 131
for to cunning men | i will be very kind, and		1.01. 98
though her father be very rich, any man is so		1.01.124 P
any man is so very a fool to be married to hell?		1.01.124 P
'tis a very excellent piece of work, madam lady;		1.01.253 P
promise thee she shall be rich, | and very rich.		1.02. 63
o, very well, i have perus'd the note.		1.02.144
you, sir, i'll have them very fairly bound —		1.02.145
too, | and let me have them very well perfum'd;		1.02.151
/neighbor, this is a gift very grateful, i am		2.01. 76 P
you are very welcome, sir.		2.01.105
and sullen, | and now i find report a very liar;		2.01.244
for such an injury would vex a very saint,		3.02. 28
a monster, a very monster in apparel, and not		3.02. 70 P
why, he's a devil, a devil, a very fiend.		3.02.155
and i, seeing this, came thence for very shame,		3.02.180
soon hot, my very lips might freeze to my teeth,		4.01. 6 P
that feed'st me with the very name of meat.		4.03. 32
you are very sensible, and yet you miss my sense		5.02. 18
very well mended. kiss him for that, good widow.		5.02. 25
a very mean meaning.		5.02. 31
the king very lately spoke of him admiringly and	AWW	1.01. 29 P
consumes itself to the very paring, and so dies		1.01.142 P
i was very late more near her than i think she		1.03.106 P
it was this very sword entrench'd it.		2.01. 44 P
is very sequent to your whipping;		2.02. 54 P
you would answer very well to a whipping, if you		2.02. 55 P
that's it i would have said, the very same.		2.03. 25 P
'tis strange, 'tis very strange, that is the		2.03. 28 P
very hand of heaven.		2.03. 31 P
good, very good, it is so then.		2.03.265 P
good, very good, let it be conceal'd awhile.		2.03.265 P
she's very merry, but yet she is not well;		2.04. 3 P
but thanks be given, she's very well, and wants		2.04. 4 P
if she be very well, what does she ail that		2.04. 6 P
what does she ail that she's not very well?		2.04. 7 P
truly, she's very well indeed, but for two		2.04. 8 P
title, which is within a very little of nothing.		2.04. 27 P
a very serious business calls on him.		2.04. 40
yes, my lord, and of very valiant approof.		2.05. 3 P
you, my lord, he is very great in knowledge, and		2.05. 8 P
he, sir, 's a good workman, a very good tailor.		2.05. 19 P
my haste is very great.		2.05. 77
take my young lord to be a very melancholy man.		3.02. 4 P
a very tainted fellow, and full of wickedness.		3.02. 87
this very day, | great mars, i put myself into		3.03. 8
find him, which you shall see this very night.		3.06.106 P
you, interpreter, you must seem very politic.		4.01. 21 P
it must be a very plausive invention that		4.01. 26 P
remembrance to this very instant disaster of his		4.03.110 P
six thousand, but very weak and unserviceable.		4.03.131 P
scatter'd, and the commanders very poor rogues,		4.03.133 P
he's very near the truth in this.		4.03.151 P
foolish idle boy, but for all that very ruttish.		4.03.215 P
was very honest in the behalf of the maid;		4.03.218 P
such pestiferous reports of men very nobly held,		4.03.306 P
and i were not a very coward, i'd compel it of		4.03.321 P
with very much content, my lord, and i wish it		4.05. 78 P
not three hours' travel from this very place.	TN	1.02. 23
and so is now, or was so very late;		1.02. 30
that will allow me very worth his service.		1.02. 59
he's a very fool and a prodigal.		1.03. 24 P
my very walk should be a jig.		1.03.129 P
apt, in good faith, very apt.		1.05. 26 P
think they have thee do very oft prove fools;		1.05. 34 P
of very ill manner:		1.05.153 P
he is very well–favor'd and he speaks very		1.05.160 P
very well–favor'd and he speaks very shrewishly.		1.05.160 P
i am very comptible, even to the least sinister		1.05.175 P
and yet (by the very fangs of malice i swear) i		1.05.183 P
else would i very shortly see thee there.		2.01. 46
thou wast in very gracious fooling last night,		2.03. 22 P
'twas very good, i' faith.		2.03. 24 P
very sweet and contagious, i' faith.		2.03. 55 P
of her, she is very willing to bid you farewell.		2.03.100 P
i can write very like my lady your niece;		2.03.159 P
it gives a very echo to the seat | where love is		2.04. 21
being once display'd, doth fall that very hour.		2.04. 39
changeable taffata, for thy mind is a very opal.		2.04. 75 P
these be her very c's, her u's, and her t's, and		2.05. 87 P
her very phrases!		2.05. 91 P
i will be point–devise the very man.		2.05.163 P
words are very rascals since bonds disgrac'd		3.01. 21 P
a vulgar proof | that very oft we pity enemies.		3.01.125
malvolio is turn'd heathen, a very renegado;		3.02. 70 P
he's coming, madam, but in very strange manner.		3.04. 8 P
one, it is with me as the very true sonnet is,		3.04. 23 P
why, this is very midsummer madness.		3.04. 56 P
his very genius hath taken the infection of the		3.04.129 P
pleasure and his penance, till our very pastime,		3.04.138 P
very brief, and to exceeding good sense — less.		3.04.158 P
you may have very fit occasion for't;		3.04.173 P
my remembrance is very free and clear from any		3.04.227 P
derives itself out of a very /competent injury;		3.04.247 P
man, he's a very devil, i have not seen such a		3.04.273 P
a very dishonest paltry boy, and more a coward		3.04.385 P
very wittily said to a niece of king gorboduc,		4.02. 13 P
that very envy and the tongue of loss | cried		5.01. 58
a coward, but he's the very devil incardinate.		5.01.181 P
i very well agree with you in the hopes of him;	WT	1.01. 37 P
very sooth, to–morrow.		1.02. 17
then 'tis very credent | thou mayst co–join with		1.02.142
yea, a very trick | for them to play at will.		2.01. 51
the very thought of my revenges that way		2.03. 19
the very mould and frame of hand, nail, finger.		2.03.103
like very sanctity, she did approach | my cabin		3.03. 23
a very pretty barne!		3.03. 70 P
a pretty one, a very pretty one:		3.03. 71 P
away with thee the very services thou hast done;		4.02. 16 P
no more, whose very naming punishes me with the		4.02. 21 P
they say, that from very nothing, and beyond the		4.02. 38 P
(three–man song–men all, and very good ones),		4.03. 42 P
horseman's coat, it hath seen very hot service.		4.03. 68 P
very true, sir;		4.03.103 P
y' are very welcome.		4.04.108
down, or a very pleasant thing indeed and sung		4.04.189 P
here's one to a very doleful tune, how a		4.04.262 P
very true, and but a month old.		4.04.267 P
the ballad is very pitiful, and as true.		4.04.281 P
this is a merry ballad, but a very pretty one.		4.04.286 P
very nobly | have you deserv'd.		4.04.517
bosom there, | and speak his very heart.		4.04.564
you know, | prosperity's the very bond of love,		4.04.573
his sworn brother, a very simple gentleman!		4.04.596 P
very wisely, puppies!		4.04.706 P
father's image is so hit in you | (his very air)		5.01.128
good father's speed, | will come on very slowly.		5.01.211
king and camillo were very notes of admiration.		5.02. 11 P
their dumbness, language in their very gesture;		5.02. 14 P
the very life seems warm upon her lip.		5.03. 66
made whole | with very easy arguments of love,	JN	1.01. 36
the very spirit of plantagenet!		1.01.167
king john, this is the very sum of all:		2.01.151
made | will give her sadness very little cure.		2.01.546
men, | which in the very meeting fall, and die.		3.01. 33
for very little pains | will bring this labor to		3.02. 9
my friend, | he is a very serpent in my way,		3.03. 61
with this same very iron to burn them out.		4.01.124
this is the very top, | the heighth, the crest,		4.03. 45
i do suspect thee very grievously.		4.03.134
we cannot deal but with the very hand | of stern		5.02. 22
beshrew thy very heart!		5.05. 14

show me the very wound of this ill news; 5.06. 21
the dolphin rages at our very heels. 5.07. 80
we see the very wrack that we must suffer, | and R2 2.01.267
hath very much beguil'd | the tediousness and 2.03. 11
thy very beadsmen learn to bend their bows | of 3.02.116
the news is very fair and good, my lord: 3.03. 5
amongst much other talk, that very time, | i 4.01. 14
well | the very time aumerle and you did talk. 4.01. 61
'tis very true, you were in presence then, | and 4.01. 62
you would have thought the very windows spake, 5.02. 12
these were his very words. 5.04. 3
in the very heat | and pride of their contention 1H4 1.01. 59
amongst a grove the very straightest plant, 1.01. 82
i mark'd him not, and yet he talk'd very wisely, 1.02. 86 P
to break the pate on thee, i am a very villain. 2.01. 30 P
an excellent plot, very good friends. 2.03. 19 P
you shall see now in very sincerity of fear and 2.03. 30 P
i have sounded the very base–string of humility. 2.04. 6 P
divided it | into three limits very equally: 3.01. 72
and in that very line, harry, standest thou, 3.02. 85
infect | the very life–blood of our enterprise, 4.01. 29
a perilous gash, a very limb lopp'd off — | and 4.01. 43
we read | the very bottom and the soul of hope, 4.01. 50
the very list, the very utmost bound | of all 4.01. 51
the very utmost bound | of all our fortunes. 4.01. 51
marry, and shall, and very willingly. 5.02. 33
shadows thou hast met | and not the very king. 5.04. 31
then i see | a very valiant rebel of the name. 5.04. 62
very well, my lord, very well. 2H4 1.02.120 P
very well, my lord, very well. 1.02.120 P
your means are very slender, and your waste is 1.02.140 P
'tis very true, lord bardolph, for indeed | it 1.03. 25
very hardly, upon such a subject. 2.02. 44 P
i am in good name and fame with the very best. 2.04. 76 P
yea, in very truth, do i, and 'twere an aspen 2.04.108 P
peesel, be quiet, 'tis very late, i' faith. 2.04.161 P
my troth, captain, these are very bitter words. 2.04.170 P
a good grace, and wears his boots very smooth, 2.04.249 P
very true, sir, and i come to draw you out by 2.04.289 P
forth | shall bring this prize in very easily. 3.01.101
the same sir john, the very same. 3.02. 29 P
and the very same day did i fight with one 3.02. 31 P
certain, 'tis certain, very sure, very sure. 3.02. 36 P
certain, 'tis certain, very sure, very sure. 3.02. 36 P
are surely, and ever were, very commendable. 3.02. 71 P
it comes of accommodo, very good, a good phrase. 3.02. 72 P
it is very just. 3.02. 81 P
you like well and bear your years very well. 3.02. 84 P
very singular good, in faith, well said, sir 3.02.108 P
in faith, well said, sir john, very well said. 3.02.109 P
thou art a very ragged wart. 3.02.141 P
in very truth, sir, i had as live be hang'd, sir 3.02.222 P
so — very well, go to, very good, exceeding 3.02.273 P
very well, go to, very good, exceeding good. 3.02.274 P
'a was the very genius of famine, yet lecherous 3.02.314 P
the dove, and very blessed spirit of peace, 4.01. 46
in very ample virtue of his father, | to hear 4.01.161
lack | the very instruments of chastisement, 4.01.215
'tis very true, | and therefore be assur'd, my 4.01.217
the very opener and intelligencer | between the 4.02. 20
you wish me health in very happy season, | for i 4.02. 79
speeded hither with the very extremest inch of 4.03. 35 P
sherris, that he is become very hot and valiant. 4.03.122 P
fits | are with his highness very ordinary. 4.04.115
the very latest counsel | that ever i shall 4.05.182
for, by my faith, it very well becomes you. 5.02. 50
and strook me in my very seat of judgment; 5.02. 80
a good varlet, a very good varlet, sir john. 5.03. 12 P
very well. 5.04. 31 P
followers | shall all be very well provided for, 5.05. 99
be it known to you, as it is very well, i was ep 8 P
within this wooden o the very casques | that did H5 pr 13
yea, at that very moment, | consideration like 1.01. 27
liege | is in the very may–morn of his youth, 1.02.120
but there's a saying very old and true, | "if 1.02.166
he is very sick, and would to bed. 2.01. 82 P
faith, he's very ill. 2.01. 85 P
that knew'st the very bottom of my soul, | that 2.02. 97
to suck, to suck, the very blood to suck! 2.03. 56
is too hot, that is the very plain–song of it. 3.02. 5 P
by an irishman, a very valiant gentleman, i' 3.02. 67 P
there is very excellent services committed at 3.06. 3 P
i think in my very conscience he is as valiant a 3.06. 13 P
very good. 3.06. 60 P
but it is very well; 3.06. 65 P
duke of exeter has very gallantly maintain'd the 3.06. 91 P
of th' athversary hath been very great, 3.06. 98 P
have at the very eye of that proverb with "a pox 3.07.119 P
island of england breeds very valiant creatures; 3.07.140 P
a very little little let us do, | and all is 4.02. 33
your majesty says very true. 4.07. 97 P
you say very true, scald knave, when god's will 5.01. 32 P
whose very shores look pale | with envy of each 5.02.350
my lord, methinks, is very long in talk. 1H6 1.02.118
pranks, | as very infants prattle of thy pride. 3.01. 16
and the very parings of our nails | shall pitch 3.01.102
might with a sally of the very town | be buckled 4.04. 4
chaste, and immaculate in very thought, | whose 5.04. 51
france should have torn and rent my very heart 2H6 1.01.126
the very train of her worst wearing gown | was 1.03. 85
yet, by your leave, the wind was very high, 2.01. 3
too true, and bought his climbing very dear. 2.01. 98
i think he hath a very fair warning. 4.06. 10 P
and hell, have through the very middest of you! 4.08. 61 P
that with the very shaking of their chains 5.01.145
to see this sight, it irks my very soul. 3H6 2.02. 6
and in the very pangs of death he cried, | like 2.03. 17
with fiery eyes sparkling for very wrath, | and 2.05.131
the widow likes it not, for she looks very sad. 3.02.110
me, | he's very likely now to fall from him, 3.03.209
at my depart, these were his very words: 4.01. 92
our scouts have found the adventure very easy; 4.02. 18
thy very beams will dry those vapors up, | for 5.03. 12
'tis very grievous to be thought upon. R3 1.01.141
when he shall split thy very heart with sorrow, 1.03.299
such hideous cries that with the very noise | i, 1.04. 60
news, | that this same very day your enemies, 3.02. 49
your very worshipful and loving friends, | and 3.07.138
that anne, my wife, is very grievous sick; 4.02. 51
for queen, a very caitiff crown'd with care; 4.04.101
about, | and left thee but a very prey to time, 4.04.106
below, | even of your metal, of your very blood; 4.04.302
write to me very shortly, | and you shall 4.04.428
my soul is very jocund | in the remembrance of 5.03.232
ye see | the very persons of our noble story H8 pr 26
them, that their very labor | was to them as a 1.01. 25
that such a keech can with his very bulk | take 1.01. 55
i do pronounce him in that very shape | he shall 1.01.196
these very words | i've heard him utter to his 1.02.135
directly | their very noses had been councillors 1.03. 9
the very thought of this fair company | clapp'd 1.04. 8
o, very mad, exceeding mad, in love too; 1.04. 28
a very fresh fish here — fie, fie, fie upon 2.03. 86
very well, my liege. 2.04.210
'tis very true; 4.01. 6
i'm very sorry | to sit here at this present, 5.02. 43
they say he is a very man per se and stands TRO 1.02. 15 P
why, he is very young, and yet will he, within 1.02.115 P
achilles! a drayman, a porter, a very camel. 1.02.249 P
do set | the very wings of reason to his heels 2.02. 44
rude, in sooth, in good sooth, very rude. 3.01. 56 P
says my sweet queen, my very very sweet queen? 3.01. 79 P
says my sweet queen, my very very sweet queen? 3.01. 79 P
in love, i' faith, to the very tip of the nose. 3.01.127 P
my weakness draws | my very soul of counsel! 3.02.133
troy holds him very dear. 3.03. 19
a very horse, | that has he knows not what. 3.03.126
an act that very chance doth throw upon him — 3.03.131
he's grown a very land–fish, languageless, a 3.03.263 P
make cressid's name the very crown of falsehood, 4.02.100
of my love | is as the very centre of the earth, 4.02.104
and very courtly counsel. 4.05. 22
from heart of very heart, great hector, welcome. 4.05.171
and make distinct the very breach whereout 4.05.245
a scurvy railing knave, a very filthy rogue. 5.04. 29 P
as if that /luck, in very spite of cunning, 5.05. 41
he's a very dog to the commonalty. COR 1.01. 28 P
very well, and could be content to give him good 1.01. 32 P
i'll swear 'tis a very pretty boy. 1.03. 58 P
following the fliers at the very heels, | with 1.04. 49
o'er them aufidius, | their very heart of hope. 1.06. 55
advanc'd and darts, | we prove this very hour. 1.06. 62
for a very little thief of occasion will rob you 2.01. 28 P
i know you can do very little alone, for your 2.01. 35 P
our very priests must become mockers if they 2.01. 84 P
i will make my very house reel to–night. 2.01.111 P
a curse begin at very root on 's heart, | that 2.01.185
i have lived | to see inherited my very wishes 2.01.199
us, yet sought | the very way to catch them. 3.01. 80
helps, are very poisonous | where the disease is 3.01.220
very well. 3.03. 22
i am so dishonor'd that the very hour | you take 3.03. 60
peace is a very apoplexy, lethargy, mull'd, deaf 4.05.223 P
we have record that very well it can, | and 4.06. 50
the very trick on't. 4.06. 71
and, to say the truth, so did very many of us. 4.06.143 P
very well. | could he say less? 5.01. 21
you know the very road into his kindness, | and 5.01. 59
'twas very faintly he said, "rise"; 5.01. 66
push'd out your gates the very defender of them, 5.02. 39 P
a very little | i have yielded to. 5.03. 16
'tis good, sir, you are very short with us; TIT 1.01.409
will beget | a very excellent piece of villainy. 2.03. 7
my sight is very dull, what e'er it bodes. 2.03.195
a very fatal place it seems to me. 2.03.202
doth fat me with the very thoughts of it! 3.01.203
did you not use his daughter very friendly? 4.02. 40
but metal, marcus, steel to the very back, | yet 4.03. 48
the east, | until his very downfall in the sea; 5.02. 57
life i did, | i do repent it from my very soul. 5.03.190
that "marry" is the very theme | i came to talk ROM 1.03. 63
nay, he's a flower, in faith, a very flower. 1.03. 78
this is that very mab | that plats the manes of 1.04. 88
the very pin of his heart cleft with the blind 2.04. 15 P
the very butcher of a silk button, a duellist, a 2.04. 23 P
a gentleman of the very first house, of the 2.04. 24 P
"by jesu, a very good blade! 2.04. 30 P
a very tall man! 2.04. 30 P
a very good whore!" 2.04. 30 P
nay, i am the very pink of courtesy. 2.04. 57 P
thy wit is a very bitter sweeting, it is a most 2.04. 79 P
very well took, i' faith, wisely, wisely. 2.04.125 P
an old hare hoar, | is very good meat in lent; 2.04.136
they say, it were a very gross kind of behavior, 2.04.166 P
to any gentlewoman, and very weak dealing. 2.04.170 P
had as lieve see a toad, a very toad, as see him 2.04.203 P
my very friend, hath got this mortal hurt | in 3.01.110
hie you, make haste, for it grows very late. 3.03.164
'tis very late, she'll not come down to–night. 3.04. 5
it is so very late that we | may call it early 3.04. 34
beshrow my very heart, | i think you are happy 3.05.221
on thursday, sir? the time is very short. 4.01. 1
and that very night | shall romeo bear thee 4.01.116
is it not very like | the horrible conceit of 4.03. 36
he outgoes | the very heart of kindness. TIM 1.01.275
furor brevis est," | but yond man is very angry. 1.02. 29
o, he's the very soul of bounty! 1.02.209
he is very often like a knight; 2.02.111 P
flaminius, you are very respectively welcome, 3.01. 8 P
athens, thy very bountiful good lord and master? 3.01. 10 P
he is my very good friend, and an honorable 3.02. 1 P
there was very little honor show'd in't. 3.02. 19 P
virtuous lord, my very exquisite friend. 3.02. 29 P
and let his very breath whom thou'lt observe 4.03.212
and is very likely to load our purposes | with 5.01. 14
promising is the very air o' th' time; 5.01. 22
surprise me to the very brink of tears. 5.01.156
dead, | entomb'd upon the very hem o' th' sea, 5.04. 66
and it is very much lamented, brutus, | that you JC 1.02. 55
and therefore are they very dangerous. 1.02.210
he was very loath to lay his fingers off it. 1.02.242 P
'tis very like, he hath the falling sickness. 1.02.254
a very pleasing night to honest men. 1.03. 43
myself | even in the aim and very flash of it. 1.03. 52
i think he will stand very strong with us. 2.01.142
and you are come in very happy time | to bear my 2.02. 60
and very wisely threat before you sting. 5.01. 38
as this very day | was cassius born. 5.01. 71
resolv'd | to meet all perils very constantly. 5.01. 91
the very last time we shall speak together: 5.01. 98
all the other, | and the very ports they blow, MAC 1.03. 15
very gladly. 1.03.155
that very frankly he confess'd his treasons, 1.04. 5
of his own chamber, and us'd their very daggers, 1.07. 76
fear | the very stones prate of my whereabout, 2.01. 58
that it did, sir, i' the very throat on me; 2.03. 38 P
is stopp'd, the very source of it is stopp'd. 2.03. 99
this is the very painting of your fear; 3.04. 60
the very firstlings of my heart shall be | the 4.01.147
this is her very guise, and, upon my life, fast 5.01. 19 P
health, | i would applaud thee to the very echo, 5.03. 53
such was the very armor he had on | when he the HAM 1.01. 60
i am very glad to see you. 1.02.167
'tis very strange. 1.02.220
nay, very pale. 1.02.233
very like, /very /like. stay'd it long? 1.02.236
he hath very oft of late | given private time to 1.03. 91
the air bites shrowdly, it is very cold. 1.04. 1
the very place puts toys of desperation, 1.04. 75
marry, well said, very well said. 2.01. 6
ay, very well, my lord. 2.01. 16
but, if't be he i mean, he's very wild, 2.01. 18
very good, my lord. 2.01. 48
this is the very ecstasy of love, | whose 2.01. 99
have found | the very cause of hamlet's lunacy. 2.02. 49
it may be, very like. 2.02.152
that's very true, my lord. 2.02.180 P
much extremity for love — very near this. 2.02.190 P
on fortune's /cap we are not the very button. 2.02.229 P
it is not very strange, for my uncle is king of 2.02.363 P
sweet, and by very much more handsome than fine. 2.02.445 P
very well. 2.02.545 P
indeed | the very faculties of eyes and ears. 2.02.566
words, | and fall a–cursing, like a very drab, 2.02.586
a play | have by the very cunning of the scene 2.02.590
as he is very potent with such spirits, | abuses 2.02.602
i am very proud, revengeful, ambitious, with 3.01.123 P
but use all gently, for in the very torrent, 3.02. 5 P
fellow tear a passion to totters, to very rags, 3.02. 10 P
and the very age and body of the time his form 3.02. 23 P
even with the very comment of thy soul | observe 3.02. 79
is extant, and written in very choice italian. 3.02.263 P
himself, and now reigns here | a very, very — 3.02.284
and now reigns here | a very, very — pajock. 3.02.284
very well, my lord. 3.02.288 P
i did very well note him. 3.02.290 P
very like a whale. 3.02.382 P
'tis now the very witching time of night, | when 3.02.388
the body of contraction plucks | the very soul, 3.04. 47
this is the very coinage of your brain, | this 3.04.137
bodiless creation ecstasy | is very cunning in. 3.04.139
o'er whom his very madness, like some ore 4.01. 25
a pirate of very warlike appointment gave us 4.06. 16 P
it warms the very sickness in my heart | that i 4.07. 55
a very riband in the cap of youth, | yet needful 4.07. 77
the very same. 4.07. 92
there lives within the very flame of love | a 4.07.114
love, did love, | methought it was very sweet, 5.01. 62
the very conveyances of his lands will scarcely 5.01.110 P
it was that very day that young hamlet was born 5.01.147 P
very strangely, they say. 5.01.157 P
that is laertes, a very noble youth. mark. 5.01.224
i thank your lordship, it is very hot. 5.02. 94 P
no, believe me, 'tis very cold, the wind is 5.02. 95 P
yet methinks it is very /sultry and hot /for my 5.02. 98 P
my lord, it is very sultry — as 'twere — i 5.02.100 P
excellent differences, of very soft society, and 5.02.108 P
in faith, are very dear to fancy, very 5.02.151 P
dear to fancy, very responsive to the hilts, 5.02.151 P
delicate carriages, and of very liberal conceit. 5.02.153 P
very well, my lord. 5.02.260
a hit, a very palpable hit. 5.02.281
heart | i find she names my very deed of love; LR 1.01. 71
his very opinion in the letter. 1.02. 75 P
any further delay than this very evening. 1.02. 93 P
a very honest–hearted fellow, and as poor as the 1.04. 19 P
curiosity than as a very pretense and purpose of 1.04. 70 P
though thou didst produce | my very character), 2.01. 72
death | were very pregnant and potential spirits 2.01. 76
it pleas'd the king his master very late | to 2.02.116
being the very fellow which of late | display'd 2.04. 40
nature in you stands on the very verge | of his 2.04.147
most serpent–like, upon the very heart. 2.04.161
skies | gallow the very wanderers of the dark, 3.02. 44
he sought my life, | but lately, very late. 3.04.168
bring me but to the very brim of it, | and i'll 4.01. 75
i am a very foolish fond old man, | fourscore 4.07. 59
our very loving sister, well bemet. 5.01. 20
methought thy very gait did prophesy | a royal 5.03.176
assume a semblance | that very dogs disdain'd; 5.03.189
allow the compliment | which very manners urges. 5.03.235
no, my good lord, i am the very man — 5.03.287
very bootless. 5.03.295
now, very now, an old black ram | is tupping OTH 1.01. 88
yet do i hold it very stuff o' th' conscience 1.02. 2
this very night at one another's heels; 1.02. 42
we are very sorry for't. 1.03. 73
my very noble and approv'd good masters: 1.03. 77
the very head and front of my offending | hath 1.03. 80
to th' very moment that he bade me tell it; 1.03.133
subdu'd | even to the very quality of my lord. 1.03.251
pilot | of very expert and approv'd allowance; 2.01. 49
justly put on the vouch of very malice itself? 2.01.146 P
very good; 2.01.174 P
very nature will instruct her in it and compel 2.01.234 P
a knave very voluble; 2.01.238 P
sir, he's rash and very sudden in choler, and 2.01.272 P
i have very poor and unhappy brains for drinking 2.03. 33 P
the very elements of this warlike isle, | have i 2.03. 57
why, very well then; 2.03.118 P
i am very ill at ease, | unfit for mine own 3.03. 32
o yes, and went between us very oft. 3.03.100
i am very sorry that you are not well. 3.03.289
from his very arm | puff'd his own brother — 3.04.136

'tis very good; i must be circumstanc'd. 3.04.201
they have it very oft that have it not. 4.01. 17
i am a very villain else. 4.01.125 P
for i would very fain speak with you. 4.01.167 P
very good. 4.01.209 P
i am very glad to see you, signior; 4.01.220
'tis very much, | make her amends; 4.01.243
very obedient. 4.01.256
head, | steep'd me in poverty to the very lips, 4.02. 50
yet could i bear that too, well, very well; 4.02. 56
i should make very forges of my cheeks, | that 4.02. 74
'tis meet i should be us'd so, very meet. 4.02.107
well, go to; very well. 4.02.191 P
very well! 4.02.192 P
i cannot go to, man, nor 'tis not very well. 4.02.193 P
very well. 4.02.195 P
i tell you 'tis not very well. 4.02.196 P
a very handsome man. 4.03. 36
'tis some mischance, the voice is very direful. 5.01. 38
the same indeed, a very valiant fellow. 5.01. 52
some bloody passion shakes your very frame. 5.02. 44
it is the very error of the moon, | she comes 5.02.109
my butt | and very sea–mark of my utmost sail. 5.02.268
is i would — | o, my oblivion is a very antony, ANT 1.03. 90
very necessity of this thought, that i, | your 2.02. 58
the very dice obey him, | and in our sports my 2.03. 34
together will be the very strangler of their 2.06.121 P
the ptolomies' pyramises are very goodly things; 2.07. 35 P
pompey gives him, else he is a very epicure. 2.07. 52 P
a very fine one. o, how he loves caesar! 3.02. 7
he's very knowing, | i do perceive't. 3.03. 23
of the world is lost | with very ignorance, we 3.10. 7
my very hairs do mutiny; 3.11. 13
speak to him, | he's unqualited with very shame. 3.11. 44
and what thou think'st his very action speaks 3.12. 35
upon me, | that life, a very rebel to my will, 4.09. 14
loose | beguil'd me to the very heart of loss. 4.12. 29
very force entangles | itself with strength. 4.14. 48
a grief that /smites | my very heart at root. 5.02.105
very many, men and women too. 5.02.250 P
no longer than yesterday, a very honest woman — 5.02.251 P
truly, she makes a very good report o' th' worm; 5.02.255 P
very good. 5.02.269 P
i think the king | be touch'd at very heart. CYM 1.01. 10
i am very glad on't. 1.01.164
we had very many there could behold the sun with 1.04. 11 P
but even the very middle of my heart | is warm'c 1.06. 27
you're very welcome. 1.06.210
first, a very excellent good conceited thing; 2.03. 17 P
do here pronounce | by th' very truth of it, i 2.03.108
your very goodness and your company | o'erpays 2.04. 9
'tis very like. 2.04. 36
very true, | and so i hope he came by't. 2.04.117
the very devils cannot plague them better. 2.05. 35
that she held the very garment of posthumus in 3.05.135 P
this is the very description of their 4.01. 24 P
i am very sick. 4.02. 5
i am not very sick, | since i can reason of it. 4.02. 13
i am absolute | 'twas very cloten. 4.02.107
our very eyes | are sometimes like our judgments 4.02.301
last night the very gods show'd me a vision | (i 4.02.346
a very valiant britain, and a good, | that here 4.02.369
thou dost approve thyself the very same; 4.02.380
a very drudge of nature's, have subdu'd me | in 5.02. 5
very oft importun'd me | to temper poisons for 5.05.249
'twas very strange. PER 2.04. 13
'tis very true. 2.04. 16
sir, my daughter thinks very well of you, | ay, 2.05. 37
the very principals did seem to rend, | and all 3.02. 16
and he went to bed to her very description. 4.02.101 P
to me | the very doors and windows savor vilely. 4.06.110
justify in knowledge | she is thy very princess. 5.01.218
i threw her overboard with these very arms. 5.03. 19
the very lees of such (millions of rates) TNK 1.04. 29
it is the very emblem of a maid; 2.02.137
and art | a very thief in love, a chaffy lord, 3.01. 41
i am very cold, and all the stars are out too, 3.04. 1
i am very hungry: 3.04. 11
even the very plum–broth | and marrow of my 3.05. 5
faith, very little. love has us'd you kindly. 3.06. 67
methinks this armor's very like that, arcite, 3.06. 70
that was a very good one, and that day, | i well 3.06. 72
i do not think she was very well, for, now | you 4.01. 36
her, but this very day | i ask'd her questions, 4.01. 37
a fool, | an innocent, and i was very angry. 4.01. 41
o, a very fine one! 4.01.105
do, very /rearly, i must be abroad else, | to 4.01.110
his face a prince | (his very looks so say him), 4.02. 78
in troth, a very grievous punishment, as one 4.03. 45 P
hand will honor | the very powers that love 'em. 5.01. 7
o, very much! 5.02. 2
'twas very ill done then. 5.02. 13
yet very well, sir. 5.02. 36
he's a very fair one. 5.02. 46
he dances very finely, very comely, | and, for a 5.02. 48
he dances very finely, very comely, | and, for a 5.02. 48
a very fair hand, and casts himself th' accounts 5.02. 58
very well. 5.02. 61
an offense, | which crav'd that very time. 5.03. 64
ev'n very here | i sund'red you. 5.04. 99
and nothing but the very smell were left me, VEN 441
owl (night's herald) shrieks, 'tis very late; 531
now is she in the very lists of love, | her 595
the very eyes of men through loop–holes thrust, LUC 1383
dwell | will play the tyrants to the very same, SON 5. 3
review | the very part was consecrate to thee: 74. 6
at first the very worst of fortune's might; 90.12
thee, | and, thou away, the very birds are mute; 97.12
i must each day say o'er the very same, 108. 6
a bliss in proof, and prov'd, /a very woe, 129.11
that in the very refuse of thy deeds | there is 150. 6
VESPER'S 1 FR 0.0001 REL FR 1 V 0 P
these signs, | they are black vesper's pageants. ANT 4.14. 8
VESSEL 36 FR 0.0040 REL FR 27 V 9 P
a brave vessel | (who had, no doubt, some noble TMP 1.02. 6
betid to any creature in the vessel | which thou 1.02. 31
in the foaming brine, and quit the vessel; 1.02.211
in that perish'd vessel the dowry of his sister. MM 3.01.217 P
"for jaquenetta (so is the weaker vessel called) LLL 1.01.273 P
swain, i keep her as a vessel of thy law's fury, 1.01.274 P
a vessel of our country richly fraught. MV 2.08. 30
and not one vessel scape the dreadful touch | of 3.02.270
but i must comfort the weaker vessel, as doublet AYL 2.04. 6 P
believing thee a vessel of too great a burthen. AWW 2.03.205 P
a baubling vessel was he captain of, | for TN 5.01. 54
i never saw a vessel of like sorrow, | so fill'd WT 3.03. 21
to her need i have | a vessel rides fast by, but 4.04.501
and that must be you, you are the weaker vessel, 2H4 2.04. 60 P
weaker vessel, as they say, the emptier vessel. 2.04. 61 P
can a weak empty vessel bear such a huge full 2.04. 62 P
in, | that the united vessel of their blood, 4.04. 44
dark | fills the wide vessel of the universe. H5 4.pr. 3
"the empty vessel makes the greatest sound." 4.04. 69 P
do a vessel follow | that is new trimm'd, but H8 1.02. 79
as weeds before | a vessel under sail, so men COR 2.02.106
tackle's torn, | thou show'st a noble vessel. 4.05. 62
that nature's fragile vessel doth sustain | in TIM 5.01.201
now is that noble vessel full of grief, | that JC 5.05. 13
put rancors in the vessel of my peace | only for MAC 3.01. 66
as well to see the vessel that's come in | as to OTH 2.01. 37
if to preserve this vessel for my lord | from 4.02. 83
no vessel can peep forth, but 'tis as soon ANT 1.04. 53
these competitors, | are in thy vessel. 2.07. 71
kiss'd your sails, | to make your vessel nimble. CYM 2.04. 29
from this most bravest vessel of the world 4.02.319
their vessel shakes | on neptune's billow; PER 3.ch. 44
a tempest, which his mortal vessel tears, | and 4.04. 30
seeing this goodly vessel ride before us, | i 5.01. 18
our vessel is of tyre, in it the king, | a man 5.01. 23
but such a vessel 'tis that floats but for | the TNK 5.04. 83
VESSEL'S 1 FR 0.0001 REL FR 1 V 0 P
which, touching but my gentle vessel's side, MV 1.01. 32
VESSELS 6 FR 0.0006 REL FR 5 V 1 P
and therefore women, being the weaker vessels, ROM 1.01. 16 P
if i would broach the vessels of my love, | and TIM 2.02.177
your vessels and your spells provide, | your MAC 3.05. 18
strike the vessels ho! ANT 2.07. 97
stuff'd the hollow vessels with their power | to PER 1.04. 67
sails that must these vessels port even where TNK 5.01. 29
VESTAL 8 FR 0.0009 REL FR 8 V 0 P
certes she did, the kitchen vestal scorn'd you. ERR 4.04. 75
he took | at a fair vestal throned by /the west, MND 2.01.158
her vestal livery is but sick and green, | and ROM 2.02. 8
lips, | who, even in pure and vestal modesty, 3.03. 38
want will perjure | the ne'er–touch'd vestal. ANT 3.12. 31
see again, | a vestal livery will i take me to, PER 3.04. 10
this is my last | of vestal office; TNK 5.01.150
"thou makest the vestal violate her oath, | thou LUC 883
VESTALS 2 FR 0.0002 REL FR 1 V 1 P
shall 's go hear the vestals sing? PER 4.05. 7 P
love–lacking vestals and self–loving nuns, VEN 752
VESTMENTS 2 FR 0.0002 REL FR 2 V 0 P
do their gay vestments his affections bait? ERR 2.01. 94
nor sight of priests in holy vestments bleeding, TIM 4.03.126
VESTURE 5 FR 0.0005 REL FR 5 V 0 P
should from her vesture chance to steal a kiss, TGV 2.04.160
but whilst this muddy vesture of decay | doth MV 5.01. 64
on him put | the napless vesture of humility, COR 2.01.234
you but behold | our caesar's vesture wounded? JC 3.02.196
and in th' essential vesture of creation | does OTH 2.01. 64
VETCH *(also fetch)*
VETCH 1 FR 0.0001 REL FR 0 V 1 P
pray you go and vetch me in my closet /une WIV 1.04. 45 P
VETCHES *(see fetches*)*
VEUX 1 FR 0.0001 REL FR 0 V 1 P
ma foi, je ne veux point que vous abaissez votre H5 5.02.254 P
VEX 19 FR 0.0021 REL FR 16 V 3 P
stayest thou to vex me here? TGV 4.04. 61
enough to misuse the prince, to vex claudio, to ADO 2.02. 28 P
for such an injury would vex a very saint, SHR 3.02. 28
refuse it not, it hath no tongue to vex you; TN 3.04.209
a trespass that doth vex my grieved soul; R2 1.01.138
vex not yourself, nor strive not with your 2.01. 3
bushy and green, i will not vex your souls — 3.01. 2
they may vex us with shot or with assault. 1H6 1.04. 13
not all these lords do vex me half so much | as 2H6 1.03. 75
if so thou think'st, vex him with eager words. 3H6 2.06. 68
the lord help, | they vex me past my patience. H8 2.04.131
a sight to vex the father's soul withal. TIT 5.01. 52
'twill vex thy soul to hear what i shall speak: 5.01. 62
to vex thee. TIM 4.03.236
vex not his ghost. LR 5.03.314
vex not his prescience, be attentive. ANT 1.02. 21 P
to vex her i will execute in the clothes that CYM 3.05.142 P
thou canst not vex me with inconstant mind, SON 92. 9
more than enough am i that vex thee still, | to 135. 3
VEXATION 11 FR 0.0012 REL FR 10 V 1 P
you, | it would be much vexation to your age. TGV 3.01. 16
full of vexation come i, with complaint MND 1.01. 22
but as the fierce vexation of a dream. 4.01. 69
my lord, you do me most insupportable vexation. AWW 2.03.231 P
to appoint myself in this vexation, sully | the WT 1.02.326
vexation almost stops my breath, | that sund'red 1H6 4.03. 41
your children were vexation to your youth, | but R3 4.04.305
give him deserv'd vexation. COR 3.03.140
joy, | yet throw such /changes of vexation on't, OTH 1.01. 72
sir, | harm not yourself with your vexation, | i CYM 1.01.134
the deep vexation of his inward soul | hath LUC 1779
VEXATIONS 2 FR 0.0002 REL FR 2 V 0 P
all thy vexations | were but my trials of thy TMP 4.01. 5
of grief, and those repeated | vexations of it! CYM 1.06. 5
VEX'D 13 FR 0.0014 REL FR 10 V 3 P
sir, i am vex'd; TMP 4.01.158
he's shrewdly vex'd at something. AWW 3.05. 89 P
whose passage, vex'd with thy impediment, JN 2.01.336
with my vex'd spirits i cannot take a truce, 3.01. 17
is with a kind of colic pinch'd and vex'd | by 1H4 3.01. 28
he's vex'd at something. H8 3.02.104
but the little finger | of this man to be vex'd? 5.02.142
being vex'd, a sea nourish'd with loving tears. ROM 1.01.192
i am so vex'd that every part about me quivers. 2.04.161 P
is my poor heart, so for a kinsman vex'd. 3.05. 95
he was met even now | as mad as the vex'd sea, LR 4.04. 2
i am not vex'd more at any thing in th' earth; CYM 2.01. 17 P
that is so vex'd with watching and with tears? SON 148.10
VEXED 2 FR 0.0002 REL FR 2 V 0 P
the nobility are vexed, whom we see have sided COR 4.02. 2
vexed i am | of late with passions of some JC 1.02. 39
VEXES 1 FR 0.0001 REL FR 0 V 1 P
tom some charity, whom the foul fiend vexes. LR 3.04. 61 P
VEXEST 1 FR 0.0001 REL FR 0 V 1 P
how vexest thou this man! TN 4.02. 25 P
VEXETH 1 FR 0.0001 REL FR 1 V 0 P
when grief and blood ill–temper'd vexeth him? JC 4.03.115
VEXING 1 FR 0.0001 REL FR 1 V 0 P
tale | vexing the dull ear of a drowsy man; JN 3.04.109
VHEREFORE *(also wherefore)*
VHEREFORE 1 FR 0.0001 REL FR 0 V 1 P
vherefore vill you not meet–a me? WIV 3.01. 80 P
VIA *(also fia)*
VIA 6 FR 0.0006 REL FR 3 V 3 P
go to, via! WIV 2.02.153 P
yet a kind of insinuation, as it were in via, in LLL 4.02. 14 P
via, goodman dull! 5.01.149 P
with his finger and his thumb, | cried, "via! 5.02.112
via! les eaux et terre. H5 4.02. 4
amount to five and twenty thousand, | why, via! 3H6 2.01.182
VIAGE *(also voyage)*
VIAGE 1 FR 0.0001 REL FR 1 V 0 P
arm you, i pray you, to this speedy viage, | for HAM 3.03. 24
/VIAL 1 FR 0.0001 REL FR 1 V 0 P
the /vial once more. PER 3.02. 90
VIAL 5 FR 0.0005 REL FR 5 V 0 P
one vial full of edward's sacred blood, | one R2 1.02. 17
take thou this vial, being then in bed, | and ROM 4.01. 93
come, vial. 4.03. 20
stole, | with juice of cursed hebona in a vial, HAM 1.05. 62
make sweet some vial; SON 6. 3
VIALS 4 FR 0.0004 REL FR 4 V 0 P
and from your sacred vials pour your graces WT 5.03.122
one, | were as seven vials of his sacred blood, R2 1.02. 12
where be the sacred vials thou shouldst fill ANT 1.03. 63
heavy cheers, | sacred vials fill'd with tears, TNK 1.05. 5
VIAND 1 FR 0.0001 REL FR 1 V 0 P
still cupboarding the viand, never bearing COR 1.01.100
VIANDS 8 FR 0.0009 REL FR 8 V 0 P
since | they have left their viands behind; TMP 3.03. 41
their palates | be season'd with such viands"? MV 4.01. 97
his viands sparkling in a golden cup, | his body 3H6 2.05. 52
nor the remainder viands | we do not throw in TRO 2.02. 70
some wine, within there, and our viands! ANT 3.11. 73
o, would | our viands had been poison'd, or at CYM 5.05.156
all viands that i eat do seem unsavory, PER 2.03. 31
night, i will be here | with wholesome viands; TNK 3.01. 84
VICAR 4 FR 0.0004 REL FR 3 V 1 P
that you'll procure the vicar | to stay for me WIV 4.06. 48
i'll to the vicar. 4.06. 52
oliver martext, the vicar of the next village, AYL 3.03. 43 P
and swore | as if the vicar meant to cozen him. SHR 3.02.168
/VICE* 3 FR 0.0003 REL FR 1 V 2 P
there is no /vice so simple but assumes | some MV 3.02. 81
him once, and 'a come but within my /vice — 2H4 2.01. 22 P
if it do not, it is a /vice in her ears, which CYM 2.03. 29 P
VICE* 52 FR 0.0058 REL FR 41 V 11 P
well, your old vice still: TGV 3.01.284 P
all ages smack of this vice, and he | to die MM 2.02. 5
there is a vice that most i do abhor, | and most 2.02. 29
in itself, | that skins the vice o' th' top. 2.02.136
of your brother | a merriment than a vice. 2.04.116
wilt thou be made a man out of my vice? 3.01.137
maw or clothe a back | from such a filthy vice; 3.02. 23
it is too general a vice, and severity must cure 3.02. 99 P
in good sooth, the vice is of a great kindred; 3.02.101 P
on angelo, | to weed my vice and let his grow! 3.02.270
craft against vice i must apply. 3.02.277
when vice makes mercy, mercy's so extended, 4.02.112
apparel vice like virtue's harbinger; ERR 3.02. 12
you must put in the pikes with a vice, and they ADO 5.02. 21 P
vice you should have spoke, | for virtue's LLL 5.02.349
and on that vice in him will my revenge find TN 2.03.153 P
or any taint of vice whose strong corruption 3.04.356
in a trice, | like to the old vice, | your need 4.02.124
seen't or been an instrument | to vice you to't, WT 1.02.416
shall be | to say there is no vice but beggary. JN 2.01.596
the pudding in his belly, that reverent vice, 1H4 2.04.453 P
subject we old men are to this vice of lying! 2H4 3.02.304 P
your air of france | hath blown that vice in me. H5 3.06.152
and with a virtuous visor hide deep vice! R3 2.02. 28
thus, like the formal vice, iniquity, | i 3.01. 82
so smooth he daub'd his vice with show of virtue 3.05. 29
what a vice were it in ajax now — TRO 2.03.235
alas, it is my vice, my fault: 4.04.102
brother, you have a vice of mercy in you, 5.03. 37
what vice is that? 5.03. 39
help in his nature, you account a vice in him. COR 1.01. 42 P
virtue itself turns vice, being misapplied, ROM 2.03. 21
and vice sometime by action dignified. 2.03. 22
all the particulars of vice so grafted | that, MAC 4.03. 51
of your precedent lord, a vice of kings, | a HAM 3.04. 98
times | virtue itself of vice must pardon beg, 3.04.154
the more gracious, for 'tis a vice to know him. 5.02. 84 P
and do but see his vice, | 'tis to his virtue a OTH 2.03.123
unless self–charity be sometimes a vice, | and 2.03.202
she holds it a vice in her goodness not to do 2.03.321 P
that lov'st to make thine honesty a vice! 3.03.376
did you perceive how he laugh'd at his vice? 4.01.171 P
it is a great price | for a small vice. 4.03. 70
it is not caesar's natural vice to hate | /our ANT 1.04. 2
there's no motion | that tends to vice in man, CYM 2.05. 21
for even to vice | they are not constant, but 2.05. 29
one vice but of a minute old, for one | not half 2.05. 31
for vice repeated is like the wand'ring wind, PER 1.01. 96
in vice their law's their will; 1.01.103
honesty, but yet defil'd | with inward vice: LUC 1546
if he be addict to vice, | quickly him they will PP 20.41
for canker vice the sweetest buds doth love, SON 70. 7
VICEGERENT 1 FR 0.0001 REL FR 0 V 1 P
"great deputy, the welkin's vicegerent, and sole LLL 1.01.220 P
VICEROY 2 FR 0.0002 REL FR 2 V 0 P
thou shalt be plac'd as viceroy under him, | and 1H6 5.04.131
as to be call'd but viceroy of the whole? 5.04.143
VICEROYS 1 FR 0.0001 REL FR 0 V 1 P
and trinculo and thyself shall be viceroys. TMP 3.02.108 P
VICE'S 2 FR 0.0002 REL FR 1 V 1 P

so shall my virtue be his vice's bawd, | an' he R2 5.03. 67
and now is this vice's dagger become a squire, 2H4 3.02.319 P
VICES 14 FR 0.0015 REL FR 10 V 4 P
here follow her vices. TGV 3.01.321 P
o villain, that set this down among her vices! 3.01.334 P
fie, these filthy vices! MM 2.04. 42
that any of these bolder vices wanted | less WT 3.02. 55
his vices, you would say; 4.03. 91 P
vices, i would say, sir. 4.03. 94 P
corrupt and tainted with a thousand vices, 1H6 5.04. 45
shall have more vices than it had before, | more MAC 4.03. 47
tatter'd clothes /small vices do appear; LR 4.06.164
as duteous to the vices of thy mistress | as 4.06.253
and of our pleasant vices | make instruments to 5.03.171
to heaven | i do confess the vices of my blood, OTH 1.03.123
when thus thy vices bud before thy spring? LUC 604
what a mansion have those vices got | which for SON 95. 9
VICI 1 FR 0.0001 REL FR 0 V 1 P
it was that might rightly say, veni, vidi, vici; LLL 4.01. 68 P
VICIOUS 9 FR 0.0010 REL FR 9 V 0 P
vicious, ungentle, foolish, blunt, unkind, ERR 4.02. 21
to fill the world with vicious qualities. 1H6 5.04. 35
they turn to vicious forms, ten times more ugly H8 1.02.117
praise his most vicious strain, | and call it TIM 4.03.213
that for some vicious mole of nature in them, HAM 1.04. 24
that you make known | it is no vicious blot, LR 1.01.227
the dark and vicious place where thee he got 5.03.173
though i perchance am vicious in my guess | (as OTH 3.03.145
it had been vicious | to have mistrusted her; CYM 5.05. 65
VICIOUSNESS 1 FR 0.0001 REL FR 1 V 0 P
but when we in our viciousness grow hard | (o ANT 3.13.111
VICT'LERS 1 FR 0.0001 REL FR 0 V 1 P
all vict'lers do so. 2H4 2.04.346 P
/VICTOR 1 FR 0.0001 REL FR 1 V 0 P
/if /your /father /had /been /victor /there, 2H4 4.01.132
VICTOR 7 FR 0.0008 REL FR 7 V 0 P
and tell me who is victor, york or warwick? 3H6 5.02. 6
or do you purpose | a victor shall be known? TRO 4.05. 67
although the victor, we submit to caesar, | and CYM 5.05.460
conquer'd triumphs, | the victor has the loss; TNK 5.04.114
a captive victor that hath lost in gain, LUC 730
art with arms contending was victor of the day, PP 15.13
either not assail'd, or victor being charg'd, SON 70.10
VICTORESS 1 FR 0.0001 REL FR 1 V 0 P
and she shall be sole victoress, caesar's caesar R3 4.04.336
VICTORIES 6 FR 0.0006 REL FR 6 V 0 P
disgrac'd me in my happy victories, | sought to 1H4 4.03. 97
ere long | to be presented, by your victories, 1H6 4.01.172
laid open all your victories in scotland, | your R3 3.07. 15
ages love | security, i'll pawn my victories, TIM 3.05. 80
and stories | his victories, his triumphs, and VEN 1014
after a thousand victories once foil'd, | is SON 25.10
VICTORIOUS 14 FR 0.0015 REL FR 14 V 0 P
shall that victorious hand be feebled here, JN 5.02.146
this is a stem | of that victorious stock; H5 2.04. 63
victorious talbot, pardon my abuse. 1H6 2.03. 67
welcome, brave captain and victorious lord! 3.04. 16
brave york, salisbury, and victorious warwick, 2H6 1.01. 86
and so to arms, victorious father, | to quell 5.01.211
and so do i, victorious prince of york. 3H6 1.01. 21
now are our brows bound with victorious wreaths, R3 1.01. 5
blest his three sons with his victorious arm, 1.04.236
and your arms be prais'd, victorious friends; 5.05. 1
hail, rome, victorious in thy mourning weeds! TIT 1.01. 70
victorious titus, rue the tears i shed, | a 1.01.105
o, bless me here with thy victorious hand, 1.01.163
where rather i'll expect victorious life | than ANT 4.02. 43
VICTOR'S 3 FR 0.0003 REL FR 3 V 0 P
see | justice design the victor's chivalry. R2 1.01.203
you are the victor's meed, the price and garland TNK 5.03. 16
his victor's wreath | even then fell off his 5.04. 79
VICTORS 9 FR 0.0010 REL FR 8 V 1 P
open your gates and give the victors way. JN 2.01.324
now we are victors, upon us he smiles. 1H6 1.02. 4
rewards | as victors wear at the olympian games. 3H6 2.03. 53
both tugging to be victors, breast to breast, 2.05. 11
slaves, | the strides /they victors made: CYM 5.03. 43
they would have look'd had they been victors, TNK 2.01. 33 P
o'er us the victors have | fortune, whose title 5.04. 16
thou dead, both die, and both shall victors be." LUC 1211
as victors of my silence cannot boast; SON 86.11
VICTOR–SWORD 1 FR 0.0001 REL FR 1 V 0 P
/despite thy victor–sword and fire–new fortune, LR 5.03.133
VICTORY 55 FR 0.0062 REL FR 48 V 7 P
a victory is twice itself when the achiever ADO 1.01. 8 P
ten proofs to one that blood hath the victory. 2.03.165 P
the conclusion is victory; LLL 4.01. 75 P
horns upon his head, for a branch of victory. AYL 4.02. 5 P
and victory, with little loss, doth play | upon JN 2.01.307
the day, | and kiss him with a glorious victory. 2.01.394
lift me up | to reach at victory above my head, R2 1.03. 72
i run before king harry's victory, | who in a 2H4 in 23
this had been cheerful after victory. 4.02. 88
and death's dishonorable victory | we with our 1H6 1.01. 20
royally, | after this golden day of victory. 1.06. 31
yet heavens have glory for this victory! 3.02.117
saint george and victory! 4.06. 1
heart with proud desire | of bold–fac'd victory. 4.06. 12
this monument of the victory will i bear, and 2H6 4.03. 11 P
god on our side, doubt not of victory. 4.08. 52
iden, farewell, and be proud of thy victory. 4.10. 72 P
when i return with victory /from the field 3H6 1.01.261
be great, | i doubt not, uncle, of our victory. 1.02. 72
and either victory, or else a grave. 2.02.174
breasts, | for yet is hope of life and victory. 2.03. 55
to whom god will, there be the victory! 2.05. 15
then am i sure of victory. 4.01.147
the harder match'd, the greater victory: 5.01. 70
saint george and victory! 5.01.113
and we are grac'd with wreaths of victory. 5.03. 2
enemies | and promise them success and victory. R3 4.04.194
fortune and victory sit on thy helm! 5.03. 79
when i should mount with wings of victory. 5.03.106
that we may praise thee in the victory! 5.03.114
sleep, | dream of success and happy victory! 5.03.165
came to my tent and cried on victory. 5.03.231
richmond and victory! 5.03.270
victory sits on our helms. 5.03.351
shall be done | to him that victory commands? TRO 4.05. 66
brings 'a victory in his pocket? COR 2.01.123 P
whereto we are bound, together with thy victory, 5.03.108
you have won a happy victory to rome; 5.03.186
tears | he whin'd and roar'd away your victory, 5.06. 97
the tears have got small victory by that, | for ROM 4.01. 30
they | put on my brows this wreath of victory, JC 5.03. 82
and, to conclude, | the victory fell on us. MAC 1.02. 58
if you have victory, let the trumpet sound | for LR 5.01. 41
upon your sword | sit laurel victory, and smooth ANT 1.03.100
and our advantage serves | for a fair victory. 4.07. 12
why so sadly | greet you our victory? CYM 5.05. 24
guest, | to whom this wreath of victory i give, PER 2.03. 10
now you may take him | drunk with his victory. TNK 1.01.158
and in his rolling eyes sits victory, | as if 4.02.108
goddess of it grant, she gives | victory too. 5.01. 72
give me the victory of this question, which | is 5.01.127
and "victory!" 5.03. 93
victory!" 5.03. 93
with bruised arms and wreaths of victory. LUC 110
strong, | must for your victory us all congest, LC 258
VICTRESS *(see victoress)*
VICTUAL 2 FR 0.0002 REL FR 1 V 1 P
you had musty victual, and he hath holp to eat ADO 1.01. 50 P
i must go victual orleance forthwith. 1H6 1.05. 14
VICTUALERS *(see vict'lers)*
VICTUALL'D 1 FR 0.0001 REL FR 1 V 0 P
voyage | is but for two months victuall'd. AYL 5.04.192
VICTUALS 4 FR 0.0004 REL FR 2 V 2 P
i am one that am nourish'd by my victuals, and TGV 2.01.174 P
to live in the mean time, and eat your victuals. H5 5.01. 34 P
but that it eats our victuals, i should think CYM 3.06. 40
how tastes your victuals? TNK 3.03. 24
VIDELICET 5 FR 0.0005 REL FR 2 V 3 P
videlicet, he came, /saw, and overcame: LLL 4.01. 69 P
and thus she means, videlicet — MND 5.01.323 P
not any man died in his own person, videlicet, AYL 4.01. 97 P
such a house of sale," | videlicet, a brothel, HAM 2.01. 59
videlicet, the way of flesh — you have me? TNK 5.02. 35
VIDEO 1 FR 0.0001 REL FR 0 V 1 P
video, et gaudeo. LLL 5.01. 31 P
VIDES 1 FR 0.0001 REL FR 1 V 0 P
tam lentus vides? TIT 4.01. 82
VIDESNE 1 FR 0.0001 REL FR 0 V 1 P
videsne quis venit? LLL 5.01. 30 P
VIDI 1 FR 0.0001 REL FR 0 V 1 P
it was that might rightly say, veni, vidi, vici; LLL 4.01. 67 P
VIE* 5 FR 0.0005 REL FR 4 V 1 P
mort /dieu, ma vie! H5 3.05. 11
gardez ma vie, et je vous donnerai deux cents 4.04. 42 P
mort dieu, ma vie! 4.05. 3
wants stuff | to vie strange forms with fancy; ANT 5.02. 98
paphos might with the crow | vie feathers white. PER 4.ch. 33
VIED 1 FR 0.0001 REL FR 1 V 0 P
and kiss on kiss | she vied so fast, protesting SHR 2.01.309
VIENNA 10 FR 0.0011 REL FR 4 V 6 P
if any in vienna be of worth | to undergo such MM 1.01. 22
mortality and mercy in vienna | live in thy 1.01. 44
in the suburbs of vienna must be pluck'd down. 1.02. 95 P
my absolute power and place here in vienna, 1.03. 13
here in vienna, sir. 2.01.194 P
nor it shall not be allow'd in vienna. 2.01.229 P
if this law hold in vienna ten year, i'll rent 2.01.241 P
as any in vienna, on my word. 5.01.268 P
this state | made me a looker–on here in vienna, 5.01.317
play is the image of a murther done in vienna. HAM 3.02.239 P
/VIEW 2 FR 0.0002 REL FR 2 V 0 P
/that /in /common /view | /he /may /surrender; R2 4.01.155
/eyes /are /cloy'd /with /view /of /tyranny. TIT 3.02. 55
VIEW 86 FR 0.0097 REL FR 83 V 3 P
and would not force the letter to my view! TGV 1.02. 54
sometimes the beam of her view gilded my foot, WIV 1.03. 61 P
ay, as the glasses where they view themselves, MM 2.04.125
to deliver his head in the view of angelo? 4.02.167 P
till that, i'll view the manners of the town, ERR 1.02. 12
and wander up and down to view the city. 1.02. 31
doth move me | on the first view to say, to MND 3.01.141
her charmed eye release | from monster's view, 3.02.377
now | for princes to come view fair portia. MV 2.07. 43
come forth to view | the issue of th' exploit. 3.02. 59
i view the fight than thou that mak'st the fray. 3.02. 62
"you that choose not by the view, | chance as 3.02.131
to view with hollow eye and wrinkled brow | an 4.01.270
greater than shows itself at the first view | to AWW 2.05. 68
and the first view shall kill | all repetition. 5.03. 21
heat, | shall not behold her face at ample view; TN 1.01. 26
she made good view of me; 2.02. 19
master's death and in the view of the shepherd; WT 5.02. 70 P
have i not hideous death within my view, JN 5.04. 22
here in the view of men | i will unfold some R2 3.01. 6
to view the sick and feeble parts of france; H5 2.04. 22
the king himself is rode to view their battle. 4.03. 2
to view the field in safety, and dispose | of 4.07. 82
me, | if i demand, before this royal view, 5.02. 32
lords, view these letters full of bad mischance. 1H6 1.01. 89
i can, | to view th' artillery and munition, 1.01.168
one, | and view the frenchmen how they fortify. 1.04. 61
view the letter | sent from our uncle duke of 4.01. 48
my earnest–gaping sight of thy land's view, | i 2H6 3.02.105
and even with this i lost fair england's view, 3.02.110
enter his chamber, view his breathless corpse, 3.02.132
come hither, gracious sovereign, view this body. 3.02.149
o, let me view his visage, being dead, | that 5.01. 69
even to affright thee with the view thereof. 5.01.207
for richard, in the view of many lords, 3H6 1.01.138
and, if thou canst for blushing, view this face, 1.04. 46
may fright the hopeful mother at the view, | and R3 1.02. 24
if thou delight to view thy heinous deeds, 1.02. 53
then you lost | the view of earthly glory. H8 1.01. 14
nought rebell'd, | order gave each thing view; 1.01. 44
fair conduct | crave leave to view these ladies, 1.04. 71
which when the people | had the full view of, 4.01. 71
hector, in view of troyans and of greeks, TRO 1.03.273
to behold his visage, | even to my full of view. 3.03.241
i have with exact view perus'd thee, hector, 4.05.232
as i would buy thee, view thee limb by limb. 4.05.238
but gives all gaze and bent of amorous view | on 4.05.282
they lie in view, but have not spoke as yet. COR 1.04. 4
but then aufidius was within my view, | and 1.09. 85
and i' th' consul's view | slew three opposers. 2.02. 93
alas that love, so gentle in his view, | should ROM 1.01.169
alas that love, whose view is muffled still, 1.01.171
which /on more view of many, mine, being one, 1.02. 32
who else would soar above the view of men, | and JC 1.01. 74
that, on the view and knowing of these contents, HAM 5.02. 44
bodies | high on a stage be placed to the view, 5.02.378
the enemy's in view, draw up your powers. LR 5.01. 51
i never did like molestation view | on the OTH 2.01. 16
the office and devotion of their view | upon a ANT 1.01. 5
and do invite you to my sister's view, | whither 2.02.167
the sight and could not | endure a further view. 3.10. 17
and hammers, shall | uplift us to the view. 5.02.211
a pudency so rosy the sweet view on't | might CYM 2.05. 11
have never wing'd from view o' th' nest, nor 3.03. 28
should tread a course | pretty and full of view; 3.04.147
enticeth thee to view | her countless glory, PER 1.01. 30
gives heaven countless eyes to view men's acts, 1.01. 73
or never more to view nor day nor light. 2.05. 17
the mounted heavens | view us their mortal herd, TNK 1.04. 5
for they were a mark | worth a god's view. 1.04. 21
wistly to view | how she came stealing to the VEN 343
which seen, her eyes /as murd'red with the view, 1031
so at his bloody view her eyes are fled | into 1037
divine, | unto a view so false will not incline, LUC 292
heedfully doth view | the sight which makes 454
were | to view thy present trespass in another. 632
the president whereof in lucrece view, 1261
presents /thy shadow to my sightless view, SON 27.10
their images i lov'd i view in thee, | and thou 31.13
for all the day they view things unrespected, 43. 2
return of love, more blest may be the view; 56.12
parts of thee that the world's eye doth view 69. 1
there, | and made myself a motley to the view, 110. 2
who in despite of view is pleas'd to dote; 141. 4
no marvel then though i mistake my view, | the 148.11
sometimes they do extend | their view right on; LC 26
VIEW'D 6 FR 0.0006 REL FR 6 V 0 P
the saddest spectacle that e'er i view'd. 3H6 2.01. 67
he did unseal them, and the first he view'd, H8 3.02. 79
this day was view'd in open as his queen, 3.02.404
crystals, where they view'd each other's sorrow, VEN 963
which tarquin view'd in her fair face's field, LUC 72
glass fell wherein they view'd their faces. 1526
VIEWEST 2 FR 0.0002 REL FR 1 V 1 P
the ebon–colored ink which here thou viewest, LLL 1.01.243 P
in thy glass and tell the face thou viewest, SON 3. 1
VIEWETH 1 FR 0.0001 REL FR 1 V 0 P
the sun with one eye vieweth all the world. 1H6 1.04. 84
/VIEWING 1 FR 0.0001 REL FR 1 V 0 P
/over /your /woes /again /by /viewing /mine: R3 4.04. 39
VIEWING 4 FR 0.0004 REL FR 4 V 0 P
feed your knowledge | with viewing of the town. TN 3.03. 42
happiest youth, viewing his progress through, 2H4 3.01. 54
in viewing o'er the rest o' th' self–same day, MAC 1.03. 94
face remains alive that's worth the viewing? VEN 1076
VIEWLESS 1 FR 0.0001 REL FR 1 V 0 P
to be imprison'd in the viewless winds | and MM 3.01.123
VIEWS 3 FR 0.0003 REL FR 3 V 0 P
ever turn'd their — backs — to mortal views!" LLL 5.02.161
"that /ever turn'd their eyes to mortal views! 5.02.163
holds disputation with each thing she views, LUC 1101
VIGIL 1 FR 0.0001 REL FR 1 V 0 P
will yearly on the vigil feast his neighbors, H5 4.03. 45
VIGILANCE 3 FR 0.0003 REL FR 3 V 0 P
use such vigilance | as when they are fresh. TMP 3.03. 16
shall henry's conquest, bedford's vigilance, 2H6 1.01. 96
that guard and most unusual vigilance | does not LR 2.03. 4
VIGILANT 3 FR 0.0003 REL FR 2 V 1 P
me, i am as vigilant as a cat to steal cream. 1H4 4.02. 58 P
sirs, take your places and be vigilant. 1H6 2.01. 1
the kingly–crowned head, the vigilant eye, | the COR 1.01.115
VIGITANT 1 FR 0.0001 REL FR 0 V 1 P
be vigitant, i beseech you. ADO 3.03. 94 P
VIGOR 13 FR 0.0014 REL FR 13 V 0 P
their infancy again | and have no vigor in them. TMP 1.02.486
with all her double vigor, art and nature, MM 2.02.183
that since have felt the vigor of his rage. ERR 4.04. 78
tires | the sinowy vigor of the traveller. LLL 4.03.304
the grappling vigor and rough frown of war | is JN 3.01.104
doth with a twofold vigor lift me up | to reach R2 1.03. 71
and, for thy vigor, | bull–bearing milo his TRO 2.03.246
high birth, vigor of bone, desert in service, 3.03.172
myself, | the vigor and the picture of my youth: TIT 4.02.108
and with a sudden vigor it doth /posset | and HAM 1.05. 68
to try the vigor of them, and apply | allayments CYM 1.05. 21
force, | or sentencing for aye their vigor dumb, TNK 1.01.195
now nature cares not for thy mortal vigor, VEN 953
/VILD 4 FR 0.0004 REL FR 4 V 0 P
/and /goodness /to /the /vild /seem /vild, LR 4.02. 38
/and /goodness /to /the /vild /seem /vild, 4.02. 38
/quickly /down /to /tame /these /vild /offenses, 4.02. 47
in this /vild world? ANT 5.02.314
VILD 35 FR 0.0039 REL FR 34 V 1 P
but thy vild race | (though thou didst learn) TMP 1.02.358
what a world of vild ill–favor'd faults | looks WIV 3.04. 32
vild worm, thou wast o'erlook'd even in thy 5.05. 83
the vild conclusion | i now begin with grief and MM 5.01. 95
still did i tell him it was vild and bad. ERR 5.01. 67
and a rabble more | of vild confederates. 5.01.237
o, kiss me through the hole of this vild wall! MND 5.01.200
since lion vild hath here deflow'r'd my dear; 5.01.292
that it is private, it is a very vild life. AYL 3.02. 17 P
and twangling jack, with twenty such vild terms, SHR 2.01.158
o vild, | intolerable, not to be endur'd! 5.02. 93
but o, how vild an idol proves this god! TN 3.04.365
herself | but with her most vild principal — WT 2.01. 92
and by the merit of vild gold, dross, dust, JN 3.01.165
will, | in the vild prison of afflicted breath. 3.04. 19
makes nice of no vild hold to stay him up. 3.04.138
your vild intent must needs seem horrible. 4.01. 95
deed, which both our tongues held vild to name. 4.02.241
great men oft die by vild besonians: 2H6 4.01.134
shall be oddly pois'd | in this vild action, for TRO 1.03.340
him vild, that was your garland. COR 1.01.184
and for that vild fault | two of her brothers TIT 5.02.172

"when we for recompense have prais'd the vild, TIM 1.01. 15
is strange | and can make vild things precious. LR 3.02. 71
is grown so vild | that it doth hate what gets 3.04.145
out, vild jelly! 3.07. 83
how stiff is my vild sense | that i stand up, 4.06.279
silence those whom this vild brawl distracted. OTH 2.03.256
why, say they are vild and false, | as where's 3.03.136
my speech should fall into such vild success 3.03.222
throw your vild guesses in the devil's teeth, 3.04.184
o, thy vild lady! ANT 4.14. 22
o thou vild one! CYM 1.01.143
i know you are more clement than vild men, | who 5.04. 18
her knowledge only | in killing creatures vild, 5.05.252

VILDER 1 FR 0.0001 REL FR 1 V 0 P
what vilder thing upon the earth than friends, TIM 4.03.463

VILDEST 4 FR 0.0004 REL FR 4 V 0 P
extended | with vildest torture, let my life be AWW 2.01.174
the wildest savagery, the vildest stroke, | that JN 4.03. 48
for vildest things | become themselves in her, ANT 2.02.237
this vile world, with vildest worms to dwell: SON 71. 4

VILDLY 13 FR 0.0014 REL FR 7 V 6 P
in my forehead, and let me be vildly painted, ADO 1.01.264 P
if low, an agot very vildly cut; 3.01. 65
times good night — i tell this tale vildly, i 3.03.148 P
vildly compiled, profound simplicity. LLL 5.02. 52
their shallow shows and prologue vildly penn'd, 5.02.305
very vildly in the morning, when he is sober, MV 1.02. 86 P
he is sober, and most vildly in the afternoon, 1.02. 87 P
to see his work, so noble, | vildly bound up? WT 4.04. 22
doth it not show vildly in me to desire small 2H4 2.02. 6 P
how vildly did you speak of me /even now before 2.04.301 P
against the volsces for they had so vildly COR 3.01. 10
ha, ha! how vildly doth this cynic rhyme! JC 4.03.133
in your duller britain operate | most vildly; CYM 5.05.198

/VILE 1 FR 0.0001 REL FR 1 V 0 P
you /vile abominable tents, | thus proudly TRO 5.10. 23

VILE 82 FR 0.0092 REL FR 72 V 10 P
no, we detest such vile base practices. TGV 4.01. 71
shall eke unfold | how falstaff, varlet vile, WIV 1.03. 97
was wrought by nature, not by vile offense, ERR 1.01. 34
'a has been a vile thief this seven year; ADO 3.03.126 P
confess'd the vile encounters they have had | a 4.01. 93
i never knew man hold vile stuff so dear. LLL 4.03.272
o vile! 4.03.276
things base and vile, holding no quantity, MND 1.01.232
wake when some vile thing is near. 2.02. 34
word | is that vile name to perish on my sword! 2.02.107
vile thing, let loose; 3.02.260
doth present | wall, that vile wall, which did 5.01.132
which lion vile with bloody mouth did stain. 5.01.143
'tis vile, unless it may be quaintly ordered, MV 2.04. 6
and the vile squealing of the wry-neck'd fife, 2.05. 30
wicked sir oliver, audrey, a most vile martext. AYL 5.01. 6 P
that dost in vile misprision shackle up | my AWW 2.03.152
i his lady, | i would poison that vile rascal. 3.05. 84
should be | in such a love so vile a lout as he. JN 2.01.509
so it be new, there's no respect how vile — R2 2.01. 25
and but for these vile guns | he would himself 1H4 1.03. 63
pismires, when i hear | of this vile politician, 1.03.241
sheath, you bowcase, you vile standing tuck — 2.04.247 P
princely privilege | with vile participation. 3.02. 87
hold up thy head, vile scot, or thou art like 5.04. 39
neither in gold nor silver, but in vile apparel, 2H4 1.02. 18 P
and keeping such vile company as thou art hath 2.02. 49 P
deep, with erebus and tortures vile also. 2.04.158 P
why li'st thou with the vile | in loathsome beds 3.01. 15
that must strike sail to spirits of vile sort! 5.02. 18
let vultures vile seize on his lungs also! 5.03.139
o viper vile! H5 2.01. 46
o braggard vile and damned furious wight! 2.01. 60
is not so vile a sin | as self-neglecting. 2.04. 74
cut | with edge of penny cord and vile reproach. 3.06. 48
with four or five most vile and ragged foils 4.pr. 50
be he ne'er so vile, | this day shall gentle his 4.03. 62
the manner of thy vile outrageous crimes, | that 1H6 3.01. 11
scoff on, vile fiend and shameless courtezan! 3.02. 45
with other vile and ignominious terms: 4.01. 97
all long of this vile traitor somerset. 4.03. 33
to be a queen in bondage is more vile | than is 5.03.112
wicked and vile, and so her death concludes. 5.04. 16
o, let the vile world end, | and the premised 2H6 5.02. 40
falsely to draw me in these vile suspects. R3 1.03. 88
'tis a vile thing to die, my gracious lord, 3.02. 62
i bade the vile owl go learn me the tenor of the TRO 2.01. 90 P
and in that paste let their vile heads be bak'd. TIT 5.02.200
breast | by some vile forfeit of untimely death. ROM 1.04.111
for nought so vile that on the earth doth live 2.03. 17
o calm, dishonorable, vile submission! 3.01. 73
where are the vile beginners of this fray? 3.01.141
vile earth, to earth resign, end motion here, 3.02. 59
was ever book containing such vile matter | so 3.02. 83
in what vile part of this anatomy | doth my name 3.03.106
stop thy unhallowed toil, vile montague! 5.03. 54
to illuminate | so vile a thing as caesar! JC 1.03.111
bed | to dare the vile contagion of the night, 2.01.265
who is here so vile that will not love his 3.02. 32 P
for i can raise no money by vile means. 4.03. 71
from the hard hands of peasants their vile trash 4.03. 74
when your vile daggers | hack'd one another in 5.01. 39
not how, | but i do find it cowardly and vile, 5.01.103
by this vile conquest shall attain unto. 5.05. 38
whom the vile blows and buffets of the world MAC 3.01.108
most lazar-like, with vile and loathsome crust, HAM 1.05. 72
ophelia" — that's an ill phrase, a vile phrase, 2.02.111 P
a vile phrase, "beautified" is a vile phrase. 2.02.111 P
hence, and this vile deed | we must with all our 4.01. 30
o thou vile king, | give me my father! 4.05.116
hence, vile instrument! CYM 3.04. 73
if neglection | should therein make me vile, the PER 3.03. 21
the sooner her vile thoughts to stead, 4.ch. 41
and we must | be vile or disobedient — not his TNK 1.02. 78
then my digression is so vile, so base, | that LUC 202
post hither, this vile purpose to prevent? 220
that what is vile shows like a virtuous deed. 252
"think but how vile a spectacle it were | to 631
how comes it then, vile opportunity, | being so 895
the world that i am fled | from this vile world, SON 71. 4
'tis better to be vile than vile esteemed, 121. 1
'tis better to be vile than vile esteemed, 121. 1

VILE-CONCLUDED 1 FR 0.0001 REL FR 1 V 0 P
war | to a most base and vile-concluded peace. JN 2.01.586

VILE-DRAWING 1 FR 0.0001 REL FR 1 V 0 P
till this advantage, this vile-drawing bias, JN 2.01.577

VILELY 3 FR 0.0003 REL FR 1 V 2 P
am i not fall'n away vilely since this last 1H4 3.03. 1 P
my lord, he speaks most vilely of you, like a 3.03.107 P
to me | the very doors and windows savor vilely. PER 4.06.110

VILENESS 1 FR 0.0001 REL FR 1 V 0 P
vileness is so: AWW 2.03.129

VILEST 1 FR 0.0001 REL FR 1 V 0 P
but now two paces of the vilest earth | is room 1H4 5.04. 91

VILL *(also will*, woll)*

VILL 9 FR 0.0010 REL FR 0 V 9 P
dat i vill not for the varld i shall leave WIV 1.04. 64 P
by gar, i vill kill de jack priest; 1.04.117 P
de herring is no dead so as i vill kill him. 2.03. 12 P
jack, i vill tell you how i vill kill him. 2.03. 13 P
jack, i vill tell you how i vill kill him. 2.03. 14 P
by gar, me vill cut his ears. 2.03. 64 P
me, for, by gar, me vill have it. 2.03. 69 P
by gar, me vill kill de priest, for he speak for 2.03. 82 P
vherefore vill you not meet-a me? 3.01. 80 P

VILLAGE 6 FR 0.0006 REL FR 3 V 3 P
the vicar of the next village, who hath promis'd AYL 3.03. 44 P
a wall'd town is more worthier than a village, 3.03. 59 P
come, go /we in procession to the village; H5 4.08.113
well that i will not part with a village of it; 5.02.174 P
the early village cock | hath twice done R3 5.03.209
why they are so, but, like to village curs, H8 2.04.160

VILLAGER 2 FR 0.0002 REL FR 2 V 0 P
brutus had rather be a villager | than to repute JC 1.02.172
here | that ruder tongues distinguish villager, TNK 3.05.104

VILLAGERY 1 FR 0.0001 REL FR 1 V 0 P
he | that frights the maidens of the villagery, MND 2.01. 35

VILLAGES 4 FR 0.0004 REL FR 3 V 1 P
frighting her pale-fac'd villages with war | and R2 2.03. 94
knee, | met him in boroughs, cities, villages, 1H4 4.03. 69
there be nothing compell'd from the villages; H5 3.06.110 P
poor pelting villages, sheep-cotes, and mills, LR 2.03. 18

VILLAIN 251 FR 0.0283 REL FR 174 V 77 P
'tis a villain, sir, | i do not love to look on. TMP 1.02.309
villain, forbear. TGV 3.01.202 P
o villain, that set this down among her vices! 3.01.333 P
peace, villain. 4.01. 39
set down the basket, villain! WIV 4.02.116 P
they are gone but to meet the duke, villain, do 4.05. 71 P
hue and cry, villain, go! 4.05. 90 P
fly, run, hue and cry, villain! 4.05. 91 P
thou thyself art a wicked villain, despite of MM 1.02. 26 P
to call him villain, and then to glance from him 5.01.309
hark how the villain would close now, after his 5.01.342 P
a trusty villain, sir, that very oft, | when i ERR 1.02. 19
the villain is o'erraught of all my money. 1.02. 96
horn-mad, thou villain! 2.01. 58
is the thousand marks i gave thee, villain?" 2.01. 65
villain, thou didst deny the gold's receipt, 2.02. 17
villain, thou liest, for even her very words 2.02.163
but here's a villain that would face me down 3.01. 6
o villain, thou hast stol'n both mine office and 3.01. 44
to adriana, villain, hie thee straight: 4.01.102
five hundred ducats, villain, for a rope? 4.04. 13
thou whoreson, senseless villain! 4.04. 24 P
din'd at home? thou villain, what sayest thou? 4.04. 68
dissembling villain, thou speak'st false in both 4.04.100
out on thee, villain, wherefore dost thou mad me 4.04.126
thou art a villain to impeach me thus: 5.01. 29
i dare, and do defy thee for a villain. 5.01. 32
brought one pinch, a hungry lean-fac'd villain, 5.01.238
not be denied but i am a plain-dealing villain. ADO 1.03. 32 P
if i do not take pity of her, i am a villain; 2.03.263 P
who hath indeed, most like a liberal villain, 4.01. 92
is 'a not approv'd in the height a villain, that 4.01.301 P
don john, the prince's brother, was a villain. 4.02. 40 P
write down prince john a villain. 4.02. 41 P
perjury, to call a prince's brother villain. 4.02. 42 P
o villain! 4.02. 56 P
no, thou villain, thou art full of piety, as 4.02. 78 P
you are a villain. 5.01.145 P
i desire nothing but the reward of a villain. 5.01.244 P
which is the villain? 5.01.259
no, not so, villain, thou beliest thyself. 5.01.265
villain, thou shalt fast for thy offenses ere LLL 1.02.146 P
take away this villain, shut him up. 1.02.153 P
why, villain, thou must know first. 3.01.159 P
their "eyes," villain, their "eyes." 5.02.162 P
here, villain, drawn and ready. where art thou? MND 3.02.402
the villain is much lighter-heel'd than i; 3.02.415
is like a villain with a smiling cheek, | a MV 1.03.100
the villain jew with outcries rais'd the duke, 2.08. 4
wilt thou lay hands on me, villain? AYL 1.01. 55 P
i am no villain; 1.01. 56 P
and he is thrice a villain that says such a 1.01. 58 P
more villain thou. 3.01. 15
villain, i say, knock me here soundly. SHR 1.02. 8
villain, i say, knock me at this gate, | and rap 1.02. 11
now, knock when i bid you, sirrah villain! 1.02. 19
a senseless villain! 1.02. 36
you whoreson villain! 4.01.155
villain, not for thy life! 4.03.158 P
lay hands on the villain. 5.01. 38 P
what, you notorious villain, didst thou never 5.01. 52 P
o fine villain! 5.01. 66 P
o villain, he is a sailmaker in bergamo. 5.01. 77 P
tell me, thou villain, where is my son lucentio? 5.01. 89 P
o monstrous villain! 5.01.109 P
where is that damned villain tranio, | that 5.01.120
here comes the little villain. TN 2.05. 13 P
"thou kill'st me like a rogue and a villain." 3.04.163 P
sweet villain! WT 1.02.136
that false villain | whom i employ'd was 2.01. 48
should a villain say so, | the most replenish'd 2.01. 78
so, | the most replenish'd villain in the world, 2.01. 79
in the world, | he were as much more villain: 2.01. 80
would i knew the villain, | i would land-damn 2.01.142
thou dar'st not say so, villain, for thy life. JN 3.01.132
avaunt, thou hateful villain, get thee gone! 4.03. 77
i am no villain. 4.03. 78
second a villain and a murtherer? 4.03.102
the ocean, | enough to stifle such a villain up. 4.03.133
that villain hubert told me he did live. 5.01. 42
a monk, i tell you, a resolved villain, | whose 5.06. 29
call him a slanderous coward, and a villain, R2 1.01. 61
like a false traitor and injurious villain; 1.01. 91
it issues from the rancor of a villain, | a 1.01.143
villain, traitor, slave! 5.02. 72
life, by my troth, | i will appeach the villain. 5.02. 79
hence, villain! 5.02. 86
villain, i'll make thee safe. 5.03. 41
it was, villain, ere thy hand did set it down. 5.03. 54
villain, thy own hand yields thy death's 5.05.106
and i do not, i am a villain, i'll be damn'd for 1H4 1.02. 96 P
an' i do not, call me villain and baffle me. 1.02.101 P
is the most omnipotent villain that ever cried 1.02.109 P
to break the pate on thee, i am a very villain. 2.01. 30 P
o villain, thy lips are scarce wip'd since thou 2.04.153 P
seven, by these hilts, or i am a villain else. 2.04.206 P
o villain, thou stolest a cup of sack eighteen 2.04.314 P
any other injuries but these, i am a villain. 3.03.162 P
ah, thou honeysuckle villain! 2H4 2.01. 51 P
and look if the fat villain have not transform'd 2.02. 71 P
ah, you whoreson little valiant villain, you! 2.04.209 P
ah, villain! 2.04.221 P
strook thy mother, thou paper-fac'd villain! 5.04. 10 P
ish a villain, and a basterd, and a knave, and a H5 3.02.123 P
he is a craven and a villain else, and't please 4.07.133 P
is as arrant a villain and a jack sauce, as ever 4.07.141 P
how now, sir? you villain! 4.08. 11 P
my liege, here is a villain and a traitor, that, 4.08. 25 P
villain, thou knowest the law of arms is such 1H6 3.04. 38
a plague upon that villain somerset, | that thus 4.03. 9
and i am louted by a traitor villain | and 4.03. 13
my witness, i am falsely accus'd by the villain. 2H6 1.03.189 P
base dunghill villain and mechanical, | i'll 1.03.193
it made me laugh to see the villain run. 2.01.152
this villain here, | being captain of a pinnace, 4.01.106
here's a villain! 4.02. 89 P
he's a villain and a traitor. 4.02.108 P
stand, villain, stand, or i'll fell thee down. 4.02.115 P
villain, thy father was a plasterer, | and thou 4.02.132
ah, villain, thou wilt betray me, and get a 4.10. 26 P
stifle the villain whose unstanched thirst 3H6 2.06. 83
i am determined to prove a villain | and hate R3 1.01. 30
villain, thou know'st nor law of god nor man: 1.02. 70
a murth'rous villain, and so still thou art. 1.03.133
ah, gentle villain, do not turn away! 1.03.162
the devil" — there the villain stopp'd; 4.03. 16
thou com'st thither — dull unmindful villain, 4.04.445
i am a villain; 5.03.191
and every tale condemns me for a villain. 5.03.195
it is the prettiest villain, she fetches her TRO 3.02. 33 P
die i a villain then! 4.04. 83
blow, villain, till thy sphered bias cheek 4.05. 8
whoremasterly villain with the sleeve back to 5.04. 7 P
insolent villain! COR 5.06.129
what, villain boy, | barr'st me my way in rome? TIT 1.01.290
what villain was it spake that word? 1.01.359
villain, what hast thou done? 4.02. 73
villain, i have done thy mother. 4.02. 76
who should find them but the empress' villain? 4.03. 74
why, villain, art not thou the carrier? 4.03. 87
go drag the villain hither by the hair, | nor 4.04. 56
villain, thou mightst have been an emperor. 5.01. 30
peace, villain, peace!" 5.01. 33
o detestable villain, call'st thou that trimming 5.01. 94
show me a villain that hath done a rape, | and i 5.02. 94
the villain is alive in titus' house, | and as 5.03.123
thou villain capulet! — hold me not, let me go. ROM 1.01. 79
a villain that is hither come in spite | to 1.05. 62
'tis he, that villain romeo. 1.05. 64
it fits when such a villain is a guest. 1.05. 75
thou art a villain. 3.01. 61
villain am i none; 3.01. 64
go, villain, fetch a surgeon. 3.01. 94
a rogue, a villain, that fights by the book of 3.01.102 P
take the "villain" back again | that late thou 3.01.125
a /damned saint, an honorable villain! 3.02. 79
but wherefore, villain, didst thou kill my 3.02.100
that villain cousin would have kill'd my husband 3.02.101
as that the villain lives which slaughter'd him. 3.05. 79
what villain, madam? 3.05. 80
that same villain romeo. 3.05. 80
villain and he be many miles asunder. 3.05. 81
condemned villain, i do apprehend thee. 5.03. 56
your lordship's a goodly villain. TIM 3.03. 27 P
needs | stand for a villain in thine own work? 5.01. 38
remain assur'd | that he's a made-up villain. 5.01. 98
wouldst not reside | but where one villain is, 5.01.111
what villain touch'd his body, that did stab JC 4.03. 20
thou li'st, thou shag-ear'd villain! MAC 4.02. 83
i would not be the villain that thou think'st 4.03. 35
geese, villain? 5.03. 13
thou bloodier villain | than terms can give thee 5.08. 7
o villain, villain, smiling, damned villain! HAM 1.05.106
o villain, villain, smiling, damned villain! 1.05.106
o villain, villain, smiling, damned villain! 1.05.106
that one may smile, and smile, and be a villain! 1.05.108
there's never a villain dwelling in all denmark 1.05.123
who calls me villain, breaks my pate across, 2.02.572
bloody, bawdy villain! 2.02.580
treacherous, lecherous, kindless villain! 2.02.581
a villain kills my father, and for that | i, his 3.03. 76
sole son, do this same villain send | to heaven. 3.03. 77
a murtherer and a villain! 3.04. 96
o villain, villain! LR 1.02. 75 P
o villain, villain! 1.02. 75 P
abhorred villain! 1.02. 76 P
unnatural, detested, brutish villain! 1.02. 77 P
abominable villain! 1.02. 78 P
this villain of mine comes under the prediction; 1.02.109 P
find out this villain, edmund, it shall lose 1.02.114 P
some villain hath done me wrong. 1.02.165 P
now, edmund, where's the villain? 2.01. 37
where is the villain, edmund? 2.01. 41
o strange and fast'ned villain! 2.01. 77

all ports i'll bar, the villain shall not scape; 2.01. 80
i will tread this unbolted villain into mortar, 2.02. 66 P
villain, thou shalt find — 3.07. 34
my villain! 3.07. 78
out, treacherous villain! 3.07. 87
turn out that eyeless villain; 3.07. 96
villain, take my purse: 4.06.246
a serviceable villain, | as duteous to the vices 4.06.252
thou art a villain. OTH 1.01.118
and what's he then that says i play the villain? 2.03.336
how am i then a villain, | to counsel cassio to 2.03.348
villain, be sure thou prove my love a whore; 3.03.359
i am a very villain else. 4.01.125 P
i will be hang'd if some eternal villain, | some 4.02.130
villain, thou diest! 5.01. 23
o, villain that i am! 5.01. 29
o wretched villain! 5.01. 41
o murd'rous slave! o villain! 5.01. 61
disprove this villain, if thou be'st a man. 5.02.172
thou'rt not such a villain. 5.02.174
precious villain! 5.02.235
'tis a notorious villain. 5.02.239
i'll after that same villain, | for 'tis a 5.02.242
where is that viper? bring the villain forth. 5.02.285
o villain! 5.02.313
roderigo meant t' have sent this damned villain; 5.02.316
remains the censure of this hellish villain, 5.02.368
if thou say so, villain, | thou kill'st thy ANT 2.05. 26
horrible villain, or i'll spurn thine eyes 2.05. 63
i am alone the villain of the earth, | and feel 4.06. 29
slave, soulless villain, dog! 5.02.157
the villain would not stand me. CYM 1.02. 14 P
thou then look'dst like a villain; 3.04. 48
some villain, | ay, and singular in his art, 3.04.120
villain, | where is thy lady? 3.05. 81
close villain, | i'll have this secret from thy 3.05. 85
all–worthy villain! 3.05. 94
if thou wouldst not be a villain, but do me true 3.05.109 P
even there, thou villain posthumus, will i kill 3.05.132 P
those runagates, that villain | hath mock'd me. 4.02. 62
some villain mountainers? 4.02. 71
thou art a robber, | a law–breaker, a villain. 4.02. 75
thou villain base, | know'st me not by my 4.02. 80
cloten, thou villain. 4.02. 88
cloten, thou double villain, be thy name, | i 4.02. 89
that caus'd a lesser villain than myself, | a 5.05.219
every villain | be call'd posthumus leonatus, 5.05.223
for if a king bid a man be a villain, he's bound PER 1.03. 8 P
bewitch'd my daughter, and thou art | a villain. 2.05. 50
hold, villain! 4.01. 92 P
o villain leonine! 4.03. 9
and having wooed | a villain to attempt it, who 5.01.173
man that hates his country, | a branded villain! TNK 2.02.200
a chaffy lord, | nor worth the name of villain! 3.01. 42
"traitor," | i am a villain fit to lie unburied. 3.06.171
he's a villain then. 3.06.264
the homely villain cur'sies to her low, | and, LUC 1338
/VILLAINIES 1 FR 0.0001 REL FR 1 V 0 P
being thus benetted round with /villainies — HAM 5.02. 29
VILLAINIES 5 FR 0.0005 REL FR 4 V 1 P
whose spirits toil in frame of villainies. ADO 4.01.189
and given me notice of their villainies. 2H6 3.01.370
complots of mischief, treason, villainies, TIT 5.01. 65
end, the villainies of man will set him clear. TIM 3.03. 30 P
to that | the multiplying villainies of nature MAC 1.02. 11
VILLAIN–LIKE 2 FR 0.0002 REL FR 2 V 0 P
that names me traitor, villain–like he lies. LR 5.03. 98
that kill'd thy daughter — villain–like, i lie CYM 5.05.218
VILLAINOUS 27 FR 0.0030 REL FR 8 V 19 P
or to apes | with foreheads villainous low. TMP 4.01.249
i shall not only receive this villainous wrong, WIV 2.02.294 P
compound of villainous smell that ever offended 3.05. 92 P
more than the villainous inconstancy of man's 4.05.108 P
hath spoke most villainous speeches of the duke. MM 5.01.264 P
a secret and villainous contriver against me his AYL 1.01.144 P
one so young and so villainous this day living. 1.01.154 P
whose villainous saffron would have made all the AWW 4.05. 2 P
this villainous saltpetre should be digg'd | out 1H4 1.03. 60
this be the most villainous house in all london 2.01. 14 P
but roguery to be found in villainous man, yet a 2.04.125 P
a villainous coward! 2.04.127 P
there's villainous news abroad. 2.04.333 P
but chiefly a villainous trick of thine eye, and 2.04.404 P
wherein villainous, but in all things? 2.04.458 P
that villainous abominable misleader of youth, 2.04.462 P
company, villainous company, hath been the spoil 3.03. 10 P
and here is come to do some villainous shame ROM 5.03. 52
no villainous bounty yet hath pass'd my heart; TIM 2.02.173
that's villainous, and shows a most pitiful HAM 3.02. 44 P
my cue is villainous melancholy, with a sigh LR 1.02.135 P
o villainous! OTH 1.03.311 P
villainous thoughts, roderigo! 2.01.260 P
a closet lock and key of villainous secrets; 4.02. 22
the moor's abus'd by some most villainous knave, 4.02.139
villainous whore! 5.02.229
wide difference | 'twixt amorous and villainous. CYM 5.05.195
VILLAINOUSLY 2 FR 0.0002 REL FR 1 V 1 P
my lord, most villainously, believe it. MM 5.01.149
most villainously; TN 3.02. 75 P
VILLAIN'S 8 FR 0.0009 REL FR 5 V 3 P
and put your trial in the villain's mouth MM 5.01.302
i like not fair terms and a villain's mind. MV 1.03.179
i'll slit the villain's nose, that would have SHR 5.01.131 P
bardolph, cut me off the villain's head, throw 2H4 2.01. 47 P
away an honest man for a villain's accusation. 2H6 1.03.202 P
proceed thus rashly in the villain's death, R3 3.05. 43
feast | whereat a villain's not a welcome guest. TIM 3.06.103
always a villain's office, or a fool's. 4.03.237
VILLAINS' 2 FR 0.0002 REL FR 1 V 1 P
cut the villains' throats! 1H4 2.02. 83 P
cut both the villains' throats; 2H6 4.01. 20
/VILLAINS 2 FR 0.0002 REL FR 2 V 0 P
do, /villains, do, since you protest to do't. TIM 4.03.434
/fools /do /those /villains /pity /who /are LR 4.02. 54
VILLAINS 45 FR 0.0050 REL FR 32 V 13 P
these are the villains | that all the travellers TGV 4.01. 5
but precise villains they are, that i am sure of MM 2.01. 54 P
for when rich villains have need of poor ones, ADO 3.03.113 P
defend but god should go before such villains! 4.02. 20 P
and she is dead, slander'd to death by villains, 5.01. 88
villain that says such a father begot villains. AYL 1.01. 59 P
some villains of my court | are of consent and 2.02. 2
you villains, when? SHR 4.01.144
how durst you, villains, bring it from the 4.01.163
o villains, vipers, damn'd without redemption! R2 3.02.129
the stony–hearted villains know it well enough. 1H4 2.02. 26 P
villains! 2.02.103 P
they are villains and the sons of darkness. 2.04.172 P
and the villains march wide betwixt the legs, as 4.02. 40 P
these villains will make the word as odious as 2H4 2.04.148 P
villains, answer you so the lord protector? 1H6 1.03. 8
ah, barbarous villains! 2H6 4.04. 15
butchers and villains! 3H6 5.05. 61
villains, set down the corse, or, by saint paul, R3 1.02. 36
albeit they were flesh'd villains, bloody dogs, 4.03. 6
the news, | for villains mark'd with rape. TIT 4.02. 9
and so i leave you both — like bloody villains. 4.02. 17
stay, murtherous villains, will you kill your 4.02. 88
o barbarous, beastly villains like thyself! 5.01. 97
villains, forbear, we are the empress' sons. 5.02.162
o villains, chiron and demetrius! 5.02.169
villains, for shame you could not beg for grace. 5.02.179
hark, villains, i will grind your bones to dust, 5.02.186
of twenty be without a score of villains. TIM 3.06. 77 P
that, by killing of villains, | thou wast born 4.03.106
all villains that do stand by thee are pure. 4.03.361
kept were knaves, to serve in meat to villains. 4.03.478
rid me these villains from your companies; 5.01.101
if where thou art two villains shall not be, 5.01.109
they were villains, murderers. JC 3.02.155 P
o traitors, villains! 3.02.201 P
villains! 5.01. 39
o, look, titinius, look, the villains fly! 5.03. 1
and stars, as if we were villains on necessity, LR 1.02.122 P
o, i am spoil'd, undone by villains! OTH 5.01. 54
o me, lieutenant! what villains have done this? 5.01. 56
o treacherous villains! 5.01. 58
i cry you mercy. here's cassio hurt by villains. 5.01. 69
oft) | but that two villains, whose false oaths CYM 3.03. 66
any thing | that's due to all the villains past, 5.05.212
VILLAIN–SLAVE 1 FR 0.0001 REL FR 1 V 0 P
tell me, thou villain–slave, where are my R3 4.04.144
VILLAINY 52 FR 0.0058 REL FR 34 V 18 P
villainy! WIV 1.04. 68 P
i will consent to act any villainy against him, 2.01. 98 P
villainy, take your rapier. 2.03. 16 P
pinch him for his villainy! 5.05.100
is not in his wit but in his villainy, for he ADO 2.01.140 P
it possible that any villainy should be so dear? 3.03.110 P
it were possible any villainy should be so rich; 3.03.113 P
did deceive them, but chiefly by my villainy, 3.03.158 P
save this of hers, fram'd by thy villainy! 5.01. 71
my villainy? 5.01. 72
my villainy they have upon record, which i had 5.01.239 P
treachery, | and fled he is upon this villainy. 5.01.250
there's villainy abroad; LLL 1.01.188 P
the villainy you teach me, i will execute, and MV 3.01. 71 P
ay, there's the villainy. SHR 4.03.144 P
but i will in to be reveng'd for this villainy. 5.01.136 P
he hath out–villain'd villainy so far, that the AWW 4.03.273 P
bears not one, | let villainy itself forswear't. WT 1.02.361
thou little valiant, great in villainy! JN 3.01.116
aspect, | finding thee fit for bloody villainy, 4.02.225
eyes, | for villainy is not without such rheum, 4.03.108
wherein crafty, but in villainy? 1H4 2.04.458 P
poor jack falstaff do in the days of villainy? 3.03.166 P
and unpay the villainy you have done with her. 2H4 2.01.119 P
their villainy goes against my weak stomach, and H5 3.02. 52 P
clouds | of headly murther, spoil, and villainy. 3.03. 32
and thus i clothe my naked villainy | with odd R3 1.03.335
are, | fitted by kind for rape and villainy. TIT 2.01.116
wit | to villainy and vengeance consecrate, 2.01.121
will beget | a very excellent piece of villainy. 2.03. 7
o, how this villainy | doth fat me with the very 3.01.202
shall i endure this monstrous villainy? 4.04. 51
sprinkles in your faces | your reeking villainy. TIM 3.06. 93
in our cursed natures | but direct villainy. 4.03. 20
o villainy! HAM 5.02.311
o mistress, villainy hath made mocks with love! OTH 5.02.151
villainy, villainy, villainy! 5.02.190
villainy, villainy, villainy! 5.02.190
villainy, villainy, villainy! 5.02.190
upon't, i think — i smell't — o villainy! 5.02.191
i'll kill myself for grief — | o villainy! 5.02.193
villainy! 5.02.193
this wretch hath part confess'd his villainy. 5.02.296
in me 'tis villainy, | in thee't had been good ANT 2.07. 74
husband, shall be thought | put on for villainy; CYM 3.04. 56
that is, what villainy soe'er i bid thee do, to 3.05.112 P
routs us but | the villainy of our fears. 5.02. 13
the geck and scorn | o' th' other's villainy? 5.04. 68
by villainy | i got this ring. 5.05.142
leonatus, and | be villainy less than 'twas! 5.05.225
no visor does become black villainy | so well as PER 4.04. 44
and villainy assured | beyond its power there's TNK 1.02. 64
VILLIAGO 1 FR 0.0001 REL FR 1 V 0 P
it in london streets, | crying "villiago!" 2H6 4.08. 46
VILLIANDA 1 FR 0.0001 REL FR 0 V 1 P
cargo, cargo, cargo, villianda par corbo, cargo. AWW 4.01. 66 P
VINAIGRE 1 FR 0.0001 REL FR 0 V 1 P
mort du vinaigre! is not this helen? AWW 2.03. 44 P
VINCENTIO 17 FR 0.0019 REL FR 12 V 5 P
the world, | vincentio, come of the bentivolii; SHR 1.01. 13
of pisa, sir, son to vincentio. 2.01.103
must get a father, call'd — suppos'd vincentio; 2.01.408
"hic est," son unto vincentio of pisa, "/sigeia 3.01. 32 P
our turn — | and he shall be vincentio of pisa, 3.02.133
my tale, | i'll make him glad to seem vincentio, 4.02. 68
minola, | as if he were the right vincentio. 4.02. 70
among them know you one vincentio? 4.02. 96
fortunes | that you are like to sir vincentio. 4.02.106
imagine 'twere the right vincentio. 4.04. 12
my name is call'd vincentio, my dwelling pisa, 4.05. 55
let me embrace with old vincentio, | and wander 4.05. 68
mine old master vincentio! 5.01. 43 P
thou never see thy /master's father, vincentio? 5.01. 53 P
and heir to the lands of me, signior vincentio. 5.01. 86 P
i dare swear this is the right vincentio. 5.01.100 P
lucentio, | right son to the right vincentio, 5.01.115
VINCENTIO'S 2 FR 0.0002 REL FR 2 V 0 P
vincentio's son, brought up in florence, | it SHR 1.01. 14
part, | and be in padua here vincentio's son, 1.01.195
VINCERE 1 FR 0.0001 REL FR 1 V 0 P
"aio /te, aeacida, romanos vincere posse." 2H6 1.04. 62
VINDICATIVE 1 FR 0.0001 REL FR 1 V 0 P
action | is more vindicative than jealous love. TRO 4.05.107
VINE 9 FR 0.0010 REL FR 9 V 0 P
thou art an elm, my husband, i a vine, | whose ERR 2.02.174
her vine, the merry cheerer of the heart, H5 5.02. 41
arms, like to a withered vine | that droops his 1H6 2.05. 11
in safety | under his own vine what he plants, H8 5.04. 34
shall then be his, and like a vine grow to him. 5.04. 49
come, thou monarch of the vine, | plumpy bacchus ANT 2.07.113
his perishing root with the increasing vine. CYM 4.02. 60
the vine shall grow, but we shall never see it; TNK 2.02. 43
for one sweet grape who will the vine destroy? LUC 215
VINEGAR 3 FR 0.0003 REL FR 1 V 2 P
and other of such vinegar aspect | that they'll MV 1.01. 54
i warrant there's vinegar and pepper in't. TN 3.04.144 P
coming in to borrow a mess of vinegar, telling 2H4 2.01. 95 P
VINES 4 FR 0.0004 REL FR 4 V 0 P
vines with clust'ring bunches growing, | plants TMP 4.01.112
spoil'd your summer fields and fruitful vines, R3 5.02. 8
dry up thy marrows, vines, and plough–torn leas, TIM 4.03.193
love | the vines of france and milk of burgundy LR 1.01. 84
VINEWED'ST *(see whinid'st)*
VINEYARD 5 FR 0.0005 REL FR 5 V 0 P
bourn, bound of land, tilth, vineyard, none; TMP 2.01.153
thy pole–clipt vineyard, | and thy sea–marge, 4.01. 68
whose western side is with a vineyard back'd; MM 4.01. 29
and to that vineyard is a planched gate, | that 4.01. 30
which from the vineyard to the garden leads; 4.01. 33
VINEYARDS 2 FR 0.0002 REL FR 2 V 0 P
and give our vineyards to a barbarous people. H5 3.05. 4
and all our vineyards, fallows, meads, and 5.02. 54
VIOL 2 FR 0.0002 REL FR 2 V 0 P
me no more | than an unstringed viol or a harp, R2 1.03.162
you are a fair viol, and your sense the strings; PER 1.01. 81
VIOLA 3 FR 0.0003 REL FR 3 V 0 P
and say, "thrice welcome, drowned viola!" TN 5.01.241
and died that day when viola from her birth 5.01.244
do cohere and jump | that i am viola — which to 5.01.253
VIOLATE 6 FR 0.0006 REL FR 6 V 0 P
till thou didst seek to violate | the honor of TMP 1.02.347
(which god defend a knight should violate!) R2 1.03. 18
bad men, you violate | a twofold marriage — 5.01. 71
honor, ne'er before | did violate so itself. ANT 3.10. 23
and with oath to violate | my lady's honor. CYM 5.05.284
"thou makest the vestal violate her oath, | thou LUC 883
VIOLATED 2 FR 0.0002 REL FR 2 V 0 P
of violated vows | 'twixt the souls of friend AYL 3.02.133
not know | the stained taste of violated troth; LUC 1059
VIOLATES 1 FR 0.0001 REL FR 1 V 0 P
down | that violates the smallest branch herein. LLL 1.01. 21
VIOLATION 4 FR 0.0004 REL FR 4 V 0 P
in double violation | of sacred chastity and of MM 5.01.404
but by | the violation of my faith, and then WT 4.04.477
and violation of all faith and troth | sworn to 1H4 5.01. 70
into the hand | of hot and forcing violation? H5 3.03. 21
VIOL–DE–GAMBOYS 1 FR 0.0001 REL FR 0 V 1 P
he plays o' th' viol–de–gamboys, and speaks TN 1.03. 26 P
VIOLENCE 20 FR 0.0022 REL FR 18 V 2 P
and blown with restless violence round about MM 3.01.124
lest your justice | prove violence, in the which WT 2.01.128
they will by violence tear him from your palace, 2H6 3.02.246
and when the king comes, offer him no violence, 3H6 1.01. 33
but, to prevent the tyrant's violence | (for 4.04. 29
die in his youth by like untimely violence! R3 1.03.200
to make an act of tragic violence. 2.02. 39
that seal | you ask with such a violence, the H8 3.02.246
me, | but, as it seems, did violence on herself. ROM 5.03.264
majestical, | to offer it the show of violence, HAM 1.01.144
say so, | nor shall you do my ear that violence, 1.02.171
the violence of either grief or joy | their own 3.02.196
i pray you pass with your best violence; 5.02.298
my downright violence and storm of fortunes OTH 1.03.249
mark me with what violence she first lov'd the 2.01.222 P
it be a sin | when violence assails us. 2.03.204
or merry, | the violence of either thee becomes, ANT 1.05. 60
the violence of action hath made you reek as a CYM 1.02. 2 P
my parentage, | you would not do me violence. PER 5.01.100
that breaking out in hideous violence | would STM II.C 132
/VIOLENT 3 FR 0.0003 REL FR 3 V 0 P
/we /would /give /much /to /use /violent /thefts TRO 5.03. 21
/such /violent /hands /upon /her /tender /life. TIT 3.02. 22
/what /violent /hands /can /she /lay /on /her 3.02. 25
VIOLENT 40 FR 0.0045 REL FR 34 V 6 P
and to these violent proceedings all my WIV 3.02. 43 P
in the current) made it more violent and unruly. MM 3.01.243 P
that ride upon the violent speed of fire, | fly AWW 3.02.109
as his person's mighty, | must it be violent; WT 1.02.454
his gorge, his sides, | with violent hefts. 2.01. 45
the violent carriage of it | will clear or end 3.01. 17
i am scalded with my violent motion | and spleen JN 5.07. 49
for violent fires soon burn out themselves; R2 2.01. 34
womb, | although ye hale me to a violent death. 1H6 5.04. 64
but him out–live, and die a violent death. 2H6 1.04. 31
but him out–live, and die a violent death." 1.04. 60
some violent hands were laid on humphrey's life! 3.02.138
i do believe that violent hands were laid | upon 3.02.156
by violent swiftness that which we run at, | and H8 1.01.142
thy exercise hath been too violent for | a COR 1.05. 15
of unmeriting, proud, violent, testy magistrates 2.01. 44 P
very poisonous | where the disease is violent. 3.01.221
the violent fit a' th' time craves it as physic 3.02. 33
is almost mature for the violent breaking out. 4.03. 26 P
and, in a violent popular ignorance, given your 5.02. 40 P
i pray thee do on them some violent death, TIT 5.02.108
death, | they have been violent to me and mine. 5.02.109
these violent delights have violent ends, | and ROM 2.06. 9
these violent delights have violent ends, | and 2.06. 9
th' expedition of my violent love | outrun the MAC 2.03.110
but float upon a wild and violent sea | each way 4.02. 21

where violent sorrow seems | a modern ecstasy. 4.03.169
by self and violent hands | took off her life; 5.09. 36
love, | whose violent property fordoes itself, HAM 2.01.100
of violent birth, but poor validity, | which now 3.02.189
and he most violent author | of his own just 4.05. 80
as make your bouts more violent to that end — 4.07.158
to do upon respect such violent outrage. LR 2.04. 24
repair those violent harms that my two sisters 4.07. 27
it was a violent commencement in her, and thou OTH 1.03.344 P
were parted | with foul and violent tempest. 2.01. 34
even so my bloody thoughts, with violent pace, 3.03.457
never was waves nor wind more violent, | and PER 4.01. 59
thy violent vanities can never last. LUC 894
as through an arch the violent roaring tide 1667
VIOLENTETH 1 FR 0.0001 REL FR 1 V 0 P
and violenteth in a sense as strong | as that TRO 4.04. 4
VIOLENTLY 5 FR 0.0005 REL FR 3 V 2 P
rock, | which being violently borne /upon, | our ERR 1.01.102
thou art violently carried away from grace, 1H4 2.04.446 P
to what you would | thus violently redress. COR 3.01.219
of breath | as violently as hasty powder fir'd ROM 5.01. 64
where, if you violently proceed against him, LR 1.02. 83 P
VIOLENT'ST 1 FR 0.0001 REL FR 1 V 0 P
can | no more atone than violent'st contrariety. COR 4.06. 73
VIOLET 9 FR 0.0010 REL FR 8 V 1 P
it is i | that, lying by the violet in the sun, MM 2.02.165
where oxlips and the nodding violet grows, MND 2.01.250
the lily, | to throw a perfume on the violet, JN 4.02. 12
the violet smells to him as it doth to me; H5 4.01.102 P
blood, | a violet in the youth of primy nature, HAM 1.03. 7
as gentle | as zephyrs blowing below the violet, CYM 4.02.172
set | gloss on the rose, smell to the violet. VEN 936
when i behold the violet past prime, | and sable SON 12. 3
the forward violet thus did i chide: 99. 1
VIOLETS 9 FR 0.0010 REL FR 8 V 1 P
when daisies pied and violets blue | and LLL 5.02.894
sound | that breathes upon a bank of violets, TN 1.01. 6
violets, dim, | but sweeter than the lids of WT 4.04.120
who are the violets now | that strew the green R2 5.02. 46
i would give you some violets, but they wither'd HAM 4.05.184 P
fair and unpolluted flesh | may violets spring! 5.01.240
the violets, cowslips, and the primeroses, CYM 1.05. 83
the purple violets, and marigolds | shall as a PER 4.01. 15
these blue–vein'd violets whereon we lean VEN 125
VIPER 4 FR 0.0004 REL FR 4 V 0 P
o viper vile! H5 2.01. 46
where is this viper | that would depopulate the COR 3.01.262
where is that viper? bring the villain forth. OTH 5.02.285
i am no viper, yet i feed | on mother's flesh PER 1.01. 64
VIPEROUS 3 FR 0.0003 REL FR 3 V 0 P
civil dissension is a viperous worm | that gnaws 1H6 3.01. 72
peremptory to dispatch | this viperous traitor. COR 3.01.285
of the grave | this viperous slander enters. CYM 3.04. 39
VIPERS 3 FR 0.0003 REL FR 1 V 2 P
o villains, vipers, damn'd without redemption! R2 3.02.129
why, they are vipers. TRO 3.01.132 P
is love a generation of vipers? 3.01.133 P
VIR 1 FR 0.0001 REL FR 0 V 1 P
but vir /sapit qui pauca loquitur. LLL 4.02. 80 P
VIRAGO *(see firago)*
VIRGILIA 1 FR 0.0001 REL FR 0 V 1 P
prithee, virgilia, turn thy solemnness out a' COR 1.03.107 P
VIRGIN 41 FR 0.0046 REL FR 31 V 10 P
o, if a virgin, | and your affection not gone TMP 1.02.448
sir, | the white cold virgin snow upon my heart 4.01. 55
hail, virgin, if you be, as those cheek–roses MM 1.04. 16
the night, | those that slew thy virgin knight, ADO 5.03. 13
was no damsel neither, sir, she was a virgin. LLL 1.01.293 P
is so varied too, for it was proclaim'd virgin. 1.01.295 P
but, damosella virgin, was this directed to you? 4.02.127 P
and, by this virgin palm now kissing thine, | i 5.02.806
than that which withering on the virgin thorn MND 1.01. 77
ere i will yield my virgin patent up | unto his 1.01. 80
noble sort | would so offend a virgin and extort 3.02.160
what says the silver with her virgin hue? MV 2.07. 22
redeem | the virgin tribute paid by howling troy 3.02. 56
a poor virgin, sir, an ill–favor'd thing, sir, AYL 5.04. 57 P
young budding virgin, fair, and fresh, and sweet SHR 4.05. 37
and there was never virgin /got till virginity AWW 1.01.128 P
for't a little, though therefore i die a virgin. 1.01.134 P
he that hangs himself is a virgin; 1.01.138 P
of sorrow that e'er i heard virgin exclaim in, 1.03.118 P
how shall they credit | a poor unlearned virgin, 1.03.240
i will bestow some precepts of this virgin 3.05.100
that wear upon your virgin branches yet | your WT 4.04.115
ros'd over with the virgin crimson of modesty, H5 5.02.296 P
employ thee then, sweet virgin, for our good. 1H6 3.03. 16
a maid, | a virgin, and his servant, say to him. 5.03.178
hath been | a virgin from her tender infancy, 5.04. 50
and yet, forsooth, she is a virgin pure. 5.04. 83
yet a virgin, | a most unspotted lily shall she H8 5.04. 60
less valiant than the virgin in the night, | and TRO 1.01. 11
or the virgin voice | that babies lull asleep! COR 3.02.114
yet here she is allow'd her virgin crants, | her HAM 5.01.232
and on her virgin honor will not break it. PER 2.05. 12
you say she's a virgin? 4.02. 41 P
deep, | untied i still my virgin knot will keep. 4.02.147
house, but for this virgin that doth prop it, 4.06.119
thy name, my most kind virgin? 5.01.140
this blushing virgin, should take manhood to her TNK 2.02.258
to this lady, | this bright young virgin. 2.05. 35
beheld thing maculate — look on thy virgin, 5.01.145
these brave knights, and i, a virgin flow'r, 5.01.167
desire | was sleeping by a virgin hand disarm'd. SON 154. 8
VIRGINAL 3 FR 0.0003 REL FR 1 V 2 P
tears virginal | shall be to me even as the dew 2H6 5.02. 52
old women, the virginal palms of your daughters, COR 5.02. 43 P
pray you, without any more virginal fencing, PER 4.06. 57 P
VIRGINALLING 1 FR 0.0001 REL FR 1 V 0 P
still virginalling | upon his palm? WT 1.02.125
VIRGINALS 1 FR 0.0001 REL FR 1 V 0 P
play o' th' virginals? TNK 3.03. 34
VIRGIN'D 1 FR 0.0001 REL FR 1 V 0 P
and my true lip | hath virgin'd it e'er since. COR 5.03. 48
VIRGINITIES 1 FR 0.0001 REL FR 0 V 1 P
how now? how a dozen of virginities? PER 4.06. 20 P
VIRGINITY 28 FR 0.0031 REL FR 7 V 21 P
master /george page, which is pretty virginity. WIV 1.01. 46 P
claudio, | if i would yield him my virginity, MM 3.01. 97
her youth, | and made defeat of her virginity — ADO 4.01. 47
if it were, i deny her virginity; LLL 1.01.296 P
place | with the rich worth of your virginity. MND 2.01.219
are you meditating on virginity? AWW 1.01.110 P
man is enemy to virginity; 1.01.112 P
but he assails, and our virginity, though 1.01.115 P
bless our poor virginity from underminers and 1.01.120 P
virginity being blown down, man will quicklier 1.01.123 P
commonwealth of nature to preserve virginity. 1.01.127 P
loss of virginity is rational increase, and 1.01.127 P
never virgin /got till virginity was first lost. 1.01.129 P
virginity, by being once lost, may be ten times 1.01.130 P
speak on the part of virginity is to accuse your 1.01.136 P
virginity murthers itself, and should be buried 1.01.139 P
virginity breeds mites, much like a cheese, 1.01.141 P
besides, virginity is peevish, proud, idle, made 1.01.144 P
virginity, like an old courtier, wears her cap 1.01.156 P
and your virginity, your old virginity, is like 1.01.160 P
and your virginity, your old virginity, is like 1.01.160 P
not my virginity yet /... | there shall your 1.01.165
who is a whale to virginity and devours up all 4.03.221 P
if he does think | he had not my virginity. 5.03.186
convert o' th' instant, green virginity! TIM 4.01. 7
her age, with warrant of her virginity, and cry, PER 4.02. 59 P
crack the glass of her virginity, and make the 4.06.142 P
bed, and for the sake | of clear virginity, be TNK 1.01. 31
VIRGINIUS 2 FR 0.0002 REL FR 2 V 0 P
was it well done of rash virginius | to slay his TIT 5.03. 36
i am as woeful as virginius was, | and have a 5.03. 50
VIRGIN–KNOT 1 FR 0.0001 REL FR 1 V 0 P
if thou dost break her virgin–knot before | all TMP 4.01. 15
VIRGIN–LIKE 1 FR 0.0001 REL FR 1 V 0 P
this act, and look'st | so virgin–like without? CYM 3.02. 22
VIRGIN'S 3 FR 0.0003 REL FR 3 V 0 P
a man, | to force a spotless virgin's chastity, 2H6 5.01.186
let not the virgin's cheek | make soft thy TIM 4.03.115
my virgin's faith has fled me; TNK 4.02. 46
VIRGINS 9 FR 0.0010 REL FR 5 V 4 P
far from heart — play with all virgins so. MM 1.04. 33
i swear | the best–regarded virgins of our clime MV 2.01. 10
military policy how virgins might blow up men? AWW 1.01.122 P
that you were made of is metal to make virgins. 1.01.130 P
/diana /no queen of virgins, that would suffer 1.03.114 P
your fresh fair virgins and your flow'ring H5 3.03. 14
of beguiling virgins with the broken seals of 4.01.163 P
virgins and boys, mid–age and wrinkled /eld, TRO 2.02.104
giving our holy virgins to the stain | of TIM 5.01.173
VIRGIN–VIOLATOR 1 FR 0.0001 REL FR 1 V 0 P
thief, | an hypocrite, a virgin–violator, | is MM 5.01. 41
VIRGO'S 1 FR 0.0001 REL FR 1 V 0 P
good boy, in virgo's lap; TIT 4.03. 65
VIRTUE 205 FR 0.0231 REL FR 163 V 42 P
touch'd | the very virtue of compassion in thee, TMP 1.02. 27
thy mother was a piece of virtue, and | she said 1.02. 56
rarer action is | in virtue than in vengeance. 5.01. 28
the gentleman | is full of virtue, bounty, worth TGV 3.01. 65
you, a sweet virtue in a maid with clean hands. 3.01.278 P
a special virtue; 3.01.312 P
to be slow in words is a woman's only virtue. 3.01.334 P
out with't, and place it for her chief virtue. 3.01.336 P
to make a virtue of necessity | and live as we 4.01. 60
we would have thrust virtue out of our hearts by WIV 5.05.147 P
(whom i believe to be most strait in virtue) MM 2.01. 9
some rise by sin, and some by virtue fall; 2.01. 38
from thee — even from thy virtue. 2.02.161
that doth goad us on | to sin in loving virtue. 2.02.182
i know your virtue hath a license in't, | which 2.04.145
the deed so far, | that it becomes a virtue. 3.01.135
hath made an assay of her virtue to practice his 3.01.163 P
virtue is bold, and goodness never fearful. 3.01.208 P
calumny | the whitest virtue strikes. 3.02.187
to know, | grace to stand, and virtue go; 3.02.264
as there is sense in truth, and truth in virtue, 5.01.226
i have confess'd her, and i know her virtue. 5.01.527
her sober virtue, years, and modesty, | plead on ERR 3.01. 90
can virtue hide itself? ADO 2.01.122 P
and never gives to truth and virtue that | which 3.01. 69
you may suspect him, by virtue of your office, 3.03. 51 P
as modest evidence | to witness simple virtue? 4.01. 38
hero, | hero itself can blot out hero's virtue. 4.01. 82
the virtue that possession would not show us 4.01.221
but no man's virtue nor sufficiency | to be so 5.01. 29
of all that virtue love for virtue loved; LLL 2.01. 57
of all that virtue love for virtue loved; 2.01. 57
by virtue thou enforcest laughter — thy silly 3.01. 75 P
the virtue of your eye must break my oath. 5.02.348
you nickname virtue; 5.02.349
your virtue is my privilege. MND 2.01.220
and all the faith, the virtue of my heart, | the 4.01.169
some mark of virtue on his outward parts. MV 3.02. 82
silence bestows that virtue on it, madam. 5.01.101
if you had known the virtue of the ring, | or 5.01.199
shall see thy virtue witness'd every where. AYL 3.02. 8
ripe, and that's the right virtue of the medlar. 3.02.120 P
a fault i will not change for your best virtue. 3.02.284 P
virtue is no horn–maker; 4.01. 63 P
much virtue in if. 5.04.103 P
your patience and your virtue well deserves it; 5.04.187
virtue and that part of philosophy | will i SHR 1.01. 18
happiness | by virtue specially to be achiev'd. 1.01. 20
admire | this virtue and this moral discipline, 1.01. 30
obedience, | her new–built virtue and obedience. 5.02.118
good must of necessity hold his virtue to you, AWW 1.01. 8 P
thy blood and virtue | contend for empire in 1.01. 62
fear makes in you is a virtue of a good wing, 1.01.204 P
thou dislik'st | of virtue for the name. 2.03.124
where great additions swell 's, and virtue none, 2.03.127
virtue and she | is her own dower; 2.03.143
of your birth and virtue gives you heraldry. 2.03.262 P
reposing too far in his virtue, which he hath 3.06. 14 P
drunkenness is his best virtue, for he will be 4.03.255 P
i pray you yet | (since you lack virtue, i will 5.03.222
virtue that transgresses is but patch'd with sin TN 1.05. 48 P
and sin that amends is but patch'd with virtue. 1.05. 49 P
good my mouse of virtue, answer me. 1.05. 63 P
virtue is beauty, but the beauteous evil | are 3.04.369
does, for calumny will sear | virtue itself), WT 2.01. 74
there's no virtue whipt out of the court. 4.03. 91 P
unroll'd, and my name put in the book of virtue! 4.03.122 P
that must be | i' th' virtue of your daughter. 4.04.387
a rape | upon the maiden virtue of the crown. JN 2.01. 98
if zealous love should go in search of virtue, 2.01.428
such as she is, in beauty, virtue, birth, | is 2.01.432
my virtue then shall be | to say there is no 2.01.595
o that there were some virtue in my tears, 5.07. 44
i espy | virtue with valor couched in thine eye. R2 1.03. 98
there is no virtue like necessity. 1.03.278
so shall my virtue be his vice's bawd, | an' he 5.03. 67
the virtue of this jest will be the 1H4 1.02.186 P
is there no virtue extant? 2.04.119 P
for, harry, i see virtue in his looks. 2.04.428 P
i speak it, there is virtue in that falstaff; 2.04.430 P
ornament, | a virtue that was never seen in you. 3.01.124
if thou wert any way given to virtue, i would 3.03. 34 P
virtue is of so little regard in these 2H4 1.02.168 P
grant that, my poor virtue, grant that. 2.04. 46 P
in very ample virtue of his father, | to hear 4.01.161
he needs not, it is no hidden virtue in him. H5 3.07.109 P
virtue he had, deserving to command; 1H6 1.01. 9
but if she have forgot | honor and virtue, and 2H6 2.01.191
virtue is chok'd with foul ambition, | and 3.01.143
virtue is not regarded in handicrafts–men. 4.02. 10 P
'tis virtue that doth make them most admir'd, 3H6 1.04.130
that love which virtue begs and virtue grants. 3.02. 63
that love which virtue begs and virtue grants. 3.02. 63
hath plac'd thy beauty's image and thy virtue. 3.03. 64
the untainted virtue of your years | hath not R3 3.01. 7
so smooth he daub'd his vice with show of virtue 3.05. 29
in peace, | your bounty, virtue, fair humility; 3.07. 17
two props of virtue for a christian prince, | to 3.07. 96
garter, blemish'd, pawn'd his knightly virtue; 4.04.370
the rough brake | that virtue must go through. H8 1.02. 76
by whose virtue, | the court of rome commanding, 2.02.103
since virtue finds no friends) a wife, a true 3.01.126
'tis virtue. 3.02.333
that christendom shall ever speak his virtue. 4.02. 63
for virtue and true beauty of the soul, | for 4.02.144
and, by that virtue, no man dare accuse you. 5.02. 85
by virtue of that ring, i take my cause | out of 5.02.134
more covetous of wisdom and fair virtue | than 5.04. 24
whose patience | is as a virtue fix'd, to–day TRO 1.02. 5
there is no man hath a virtue that he hath not a 1.02. 24 P
learning, gentleness, virtue, youth, liberality, 1.02.254 P
by itself | lies rich in virtue and unmingled. 1.03. 30
let not virtue seek | remuneration for the thing 3.03.169
but we in silence hold this virtue well — 4.01. 78
which he is, even to the altitude of his virtue. COR 1.01. 40 P
your virtue is | to make him worthy whose 1.01.174
it is held | that valor is the chiefest virtue, 2.02. 84
who lack not virtue, no, nor power, but that 3.01. 73
the virtue of your name | is not here passable. 5.02. 12
the imperial seat, to virtue consecrate, | to TIT 1.01. 14
patron of virtue, rome's best champion, 1.01. 65
of my joys, | sweet cell of virtue and nobility, 1.01. 93
and virtue stoops and trembles at her frown; 2.01. 11
virtue itself turns vice, being misapplied, ROM 2.03. 21
as in grateful virtue i am bound | to your free TIM 1.02. 5
for his right noble mind, illustrious virtue, 3.02. 80
for pity is the virtue of the law, | and none 3.05. 8
'gainst the stream of virtue they may strive, 4.01. 27
and by thy virtue | set them into confounding 4.03.390
i know that virtue to be in you, brutus, | as JC 1.02. 90
will change to virtue and to worthiness. 1.03.160
not stain | the even virtue of our enterprise, 2.01.133
which, by the right and virtue of my place, | i 2.01.269
my heart laments that virtue cannot live | out 2.03. 13
according to his virtue let us use him, | with 5.05. 76
with this strange virtue, | he hath a heavenly MAC 4.03.156
cautel doth besmirch | the virtue of his will, HAM 1.03. 16
virtue itself scapes not calumnious strokes. 1.03. 38
but virtue, as it never will be moved, | though 1.05. 53
for virtue cannot so /inoculate our old stock 3.01.116 P
to show virtue her feature, scorn her own image, 3.02. 22 P
calls virtue hypocrite, takes off the rose 3.04. 42
to flaming youth let virtue be as wax | and melt 3.04. 84
forgive me this my virtue, | for in the fatness 3.04.152
times | virtue itself of vice must pardon beg, 3.04.154
bed — | assume a virtue, if you have it not. 3.04.160
burn out the sense and virtue of mine eye! 4.05.156
my virtue or my plague, be it either which — 4.07. 13
collected from all simples that have virtue 4.07.144
this but as an essay or taste of my virtue. LR 1.02. 45 P
would the reposal | of any trust, virtue, or 2.01. 69
whose virtue and obedience doth this instant 2.01.113
and thou simular of virtue | that art incestuous 3.02. 54
that minces virtue, and does shake the head | to 4.06.120
trust to thy single virtue, for thy soldiers, 5.03.103
friends shall taste | the wages of their virtue, 5.03.304
signior, | if virtue no delighted beauty lack, OTH 1.03.289
so fond, but it is not in my virtue to amend it. 1.03.318 P
virtue? 1.03.319 P
his vice, | 'tis to his virtue a just equinox, 2.03.124
prizes the virtue that appears in cassio, | and 2.03.134
so will i turn her virtue into pitch, | and out 2.03.360
where virtue is, these are more virtuous. 3.03.186
and the big wars | that makes ambition virtue! 3.03.350
the devil their virtue tempts, and they tempt 4.01. 8
whose solid virtue | the shot of accident nor 4.01.266
whose virtue and whose general graces speak ANT 2.02.129
and ambition | (the soldier's virtue) rather 3.01. 23
let not the piece of virtue which is set 3.02. 28
o infinite virtue, com'st thou smiling from 4.08. 17
and his virtue | by her election may be truly CYM 1.01. 52
she holds her virtue still, and i my mind. 1.04. 64 P
thou wouldst have told this tale for virtue, not 1.06.143
such assaults | as would take in some virtue. 3.02. 9
that did attend themselves and had the virtue 3.06. 83
let his virtue join | with my request, which 5.05. 88
therein | he was as calm as virtue) he began 5.05.174
the temple | of virtue was she; 5.05.221
the king | of every virtue gives renown to men! PER 1.01. 14
i'll show the virtue i have borne in arms. 2.01.145
virtue and cunning were endowments greater 3.02. 27
much less in blood than virtue, yet a princess 4.03. 7
thou art a piece of virtue, and | i doubt not 4.06.111

virtue /preserv'd from fell destruction's blast, 5.03. 89
this is virtue | of no respect in thebes. TNK 1.02. 35
mark how his virtue, like a hidden sun, | breaks 2.05. 23
more by virtue. | you are modest, cousin. 3.06. 81
their virtue lost, wherein they late excell'd, VEN 1131
within whose face beauty and virtue strived LUC 52
when virtue bragg'd, beauty would blush for 54
virtue would stain that o'er with silver white. 56
then virtue claims from beauty beauty's red, 59
which virtue gave the golden age to gild | their 60
this dying virtue, this surviving shame, | whose 223
he did complain him, | and talk'd of virtue: 846
evil, | when virtue is profan'd in such a devil! 847
sing, | what virtue breeds iniquity devours: 872
"when truth and virtue have to do with thee, | a 911
but, for their virtue only is their show, | they SON 54. 9
and maiden virtue rudely strumpeted, | and right 66. 6
he lends thee virtue, and he stole that word 79. 9
you still shall live (such virtue hath my pen) 81.13
grow, | if thy sweet virtue answer not thy show! 93.14
prove | the constancy and virtue of your love. 117.14
love is my sin, and thy dear virtue hate, | hate 142. 1
VIRTUE'S 12 FR 0.0013 REL FR 12 V 0 P
apparel vice like virtue's harbinger; ERR 3.02. 12
the only soil of his fair virtue's gloss, | if LLL 2.01. 47
if virtue's gloss will stain with any soil, | is 2.01. 48
for virtue's office never breaks men's troth. 5.02.350
and thy fair virtue's force (perforce) doth move MND 3.01.140
that they take place when virtue's steely bones AWW 1.01.103
whereof the root was fix'd in virtue's ground, 3H6 3.03.125
and fame's eternal date, for virtue's praise! TIT 1.01.168
inter | his noble nephew here in virtue's nest, 1.01.376
he lives in fame, that died in virtue's cause. 1.01.390
argued by beauty's red and virtue's white; LUC 65
watch of woes, sin's pack-horse, virtue's snare! 928
/VIRTUES 1 FR 0.0001 REL FR 1 V 0 P
so our /virtues | lie in th' interpretation of COR 4.07. 49
VIRTUES 53 FR 0.0060 REL FR 40 V 13 P
for several virtues | have i lik'd several women TMP 3.01. 42
"item, she hath many nameless virtues." TGV 3.01.317 P
that's as much as to say "bastard virtues," that 3.01.318 P
close at the heels of her virtues. 3.01.322 P
proper as to waste | thyself upon thy virtues, MM 1.01. 31
for if our virtues | did not go forth of us, 1.01. 33
to a man, stuff'd with all honorable virtues. ADO 1.01. 57 P
together trans-shape thy particular virtues, yet 5.01.171 P
to be the trumpet of his own virtues, as i am to 5.02. 86 P
fairer than that word, | of wondrous virtues. MV 1.01.163
i might in virtues, beauties, livings, friends, 3.02.156
but that the people praise her for her virtues, AYL 1.02.280
your virtues, gentle master, | are sanctified 2.03. 12
thy virtues spoke of, and thy beauty sounded, SHR 2.01.192
they are virtues and traitors too. AWW 1.01. 43 P
our virtues would be proud, if our faults whipt 4.03. 72 P
if they were not cherish'd by our virtues. 4.03. 74 P
i put you to | the use of your own virtues, for 5.01. 16
is it a world to hide virtues in? TN 1.03.132 P
them when they have approv'd their virtues. WT 4.02. 28 P
good sir, for which of his virtues it was, but 4.03. 89 P
whilest i remember | her and her virtues, i 5.01. 7
bethink thee on her virtues that surmount, 1H6 5.03.191
her virtues, graced with external gifts, | do 5.05. 3
and high note's | ta'en of your many virtues, H8 2.03. 60
upon my soul, two reverend cardinal virtues; 3.01.103
you wrong your virtues | with these weak women's 3.01.168
in brass, their virtues | we write in water. 4.02. 45
i weigh not, | being of those virtues vacant. 5.01.125
is, | with all the virtues that attend the good, 5.04. 27
all) a man distill'd | out of our virtues, who TRO 1.03.351
yet all his virtues, | not virtuously on his own 2.03.117
the clearer, /ajax, and your virtues the fairer. 2.03.154 P
as when his virtues, aiming upon others, | heat 3.03.100
nor play at subtile games — fair virtues all, 4.04. 87
like the virtues | which our divines lose by 'em COR 2.03. 57
lord saturnine, whose virtues will, i hope, TIT 1.01.225
many for many virtues excellent, | none but for ROM 2.03. 13
i am an humble suitor to your virtues; TIM 3.05. 7
(setting his fate aside) | of comely virtues; 3.05. 15
that his virtues | will plead like angels, MAC 1.07. 18
his virtues else, be they as pure as grace, | as HAM 1.04. 33
so shall i hope your virtues | will bring him to 3.01. 39
thee and thy virtues here | i seize upon, | be it LR 1.01.252
all you unpublish'd virtues of the earth, 4.04. 16
them gather | their several virtues and effects. CYM 1.05. 23
if 'twere made | comparative for your virtues, 2.03.129
they are made | than they are to their virtues, 2.04.112
with other virtues, which i'll keep from boast, PER 4.06.184
and ignorance | the virtues of the great ones? TNK 2.02.107
honor'd her fair birthday with your virtues, 2.05. 36
in another, | by your own virtues infinite — 3.06.199
having these virtues, | i think he might be 5.02. 55
/VIRTUOUS 1 FR 0.0001 REL FR 1 V 0 P
from every flower | /the /virtuous /sweets, 2H4 4.05. 75
VIRTUOUS 104 FR 0.0117 REL FR 78 V 26 P
a virtuous gentlewoman, mild and beautiful! TGV 4.04.180
so got udge me, that is a virtuous mind. WIV 1.01.185 P
the modest wife, the virtuous creature, that 4.02.130 P
ay, my good lord, a very virtuous maid, | and to MM 2.02. 20
as the flow'r, | corrupt with virtuous season. 2.02.167
but this virtuous maid | subdues me quite. 2.02.184
course, as it is virtuous to be constant in any 3.02.225 P
she is a virtuous and a reverend lady: ERR 5.01.134
another virtuous, yet i am well; ADO 2.03. 28 P
virtuous, or i'll never cheapen her; 2.03. 31 P
and (out of all suspicion) she is virtuous. 2.03.160 P
and virtuous; 2.03.232 P
but always hath been just and virtuous | in any 5.01.302
that are vow-fellows with this virtuous duke? LLL 2.01. 38
said | becomes a virtuous bachelor and a maid, MND 2.02. 59
whose liquor hath this virtuous property, | to 3.02.367
your father was ever virtuous, and holy men at MV 1.02. 27 P
wilt show more bright and seem more virtuous AYL 1.03. 81
why are you virtuous? 2.03. 5
and my rosalind is virtuous. 4.01. 64 P
to deck his fortune with his virtuous deeds. SHR 1.01. 16
daughter | call'd katherina, fair and virtuous? 2.01. 43
your daughter, | unto bianca, fair and virtuous. 2.01. 91
to this most patient, sweet, and virtuous wife. 3.02.195
an unclean mind carries virtuous qualities, AWW 1.01. 42 P
whose aged honor cites a virtuous youth, | did 1.03.210
to each of you one fair and virtuous mistress 2.03. 57
if she be | all that is virtuous — save what 2.03.122
from lowest place /when virtuous things proceed, 2.03.125
by the misprising of a maid too virtuous | for 3.02. 31
death of the most virtuous gentlewoman that ever 4.05. 9 P
a virtuous maid, the daughter of a count | that TN 1.02. 36
yet i suppose him virtuous, know him noble, | of 1.05.258
dost thou think, because thou art virtuous, 2.03.115 P
thou virtuous dolphin, alter not the doom JN 3.01.311
and yet there is a virtuous man whom i have 1H4 2.04.417 P
as a gentleman need to be, virtuous enough: 3.03. 15 P
these rebels, they offend none but the virtuous. 3.03.191 P
make curtsy and say nothing, he is virtuous. 2H4 2.01.125 P
come, you virtuous ass, you bashful fool, must 2.02. 75 P
of me /even now before this honest, virtuous, 2.04.302 P
thee wrong this virtuous gentlewoman to close 2.04.326 P
his new-come champion, virtuous joan of /aire, 1H6 2.02. 20
the virtuous lady, countess of auvergne, | with 2.02. 38
o my good lords, and virtuous henry, | pity the 3.01. 76
valiant and virtuous, full of haughty courage, 4.01. 35
as, liking of the lady's virtuous gifts, | her 5.01. 43
virtuous and holy, chosen from above, | by 5.04. 39
command, i mean, of virtuous chaste intents, 5.05. 20
against my king and nephew, virtuous henry, | be 2H6 1.02. 20
that virtuous prince, the good duke humphrey. 2.02. 74
the duke is virtuous, mild, and too well given 3.01. 72
and let my sovereign, virtuous henry, | command 5.01. 48
i'll leave my son my virtuous deeds behind, 3H6 2.02. 49
vouchsafe to grant | that virtuous lady bona, 3.03. 56
son edward, she is fair and virtuous, 3.03.245
your grace hath still been fam'd for virtuous, 4.06. 26
and now may seem as wise as virtuous | by spying 4.06. 27
we say the king | is wise and virtuous, and his R3 1.01. 91
th' untimely fall of virtuous lancaster. 1.02. 4
o, he was gentle, mild, and virtuous! 1.02.104
a virtuous and a christian-like conclusion — 1.03.315
and with a virtuous visor hide deep vice! 2.02. 28
king | had virtuous uncles to protect his grace. 2.03. 21
would this virtuous prince | take on his grace 3.07. 78
virtuous and fair, royal and gracious. 4.04.205
virtuous and holy, be thou conqueror! 5.03.128
and fearing he would rise (he was so virtuous), H8 2.02.127
was a fool — | for he would needs be virtuous. 2.02.132
what though i know her virtuous | and well 3.02. 97
of the archbishop's, | the virtuous cranmer. 4.01.105
beseeching him to give her virtuous breeding — 4.02.134
o virtuous fight, | when right with right wars TRO 3.02.171
(which i beseech you call a virtuous sin) 4.04. 81
account me the more virtuous that i have not COR 2.03. 94 P
no, though it were as virtuous to lie as to live 5.02. 26 P
let it be virtuous to be obstinate. 5.03. 26
in a bad quarrel slain a virtuous son. TIT 1.01.342
him | to be a virtuous and well-govern'd youth. ROM 1.05. 68
and a good lady, and a wise and virtuous. 1.05.114
i warrant, a virtuous — where is your mother? 2.05. 57
commend me to thy honorable virtuous lord, my TIM 3.02. 28 P
if his occasion were not virtuous, | i should 3.02. 40
takes virtuous copies to be wicked; 3.03. 32 P
a good and virtuous nature may recoil | in an MAC 4.03. 19
the will of my most seeming virtuous queen. HAM 1.05. 46
a plot upon her virtuous husband's life, | and LR 4.06.272
morning i will beseech the virtuous desdemona to OTH 2.03.330 P
is that she will to virtuous desdemona | procure 3.01. 35
where virtue is, these are more virtuous. 3.03.186
you | that by your virtuous means i may again 3.04.111
his to be more fair, virtuous, wise, chaste, CYM 1.04. 60 P
the piece of tender air, thy virtuous daughter, 5.05.446
a most virtuous princess. PER 2.05. 34
then, as you are as virtuous as fair, | resolve 2.05. 67
i'll do any thing now that is virtuous, but i am 4.05. 8 P
of such a virtuous greatness that this lady, TNK 2.02.257
be'st, | as thou art spoken, great and virtuous, 3.06.152
in a deed so virtuous | the powers of all women 3.06.193
that what is vile shows like a virtuous deed. LUC 252
where like a virtuous monument she lies, | to be 391
with virtuous wish would bear your living SON 16. 7
unless you would devise some virtuous lie, | to 72. 5
and prove thee virtuous, though thou art 88. 4
VIRTUOUSLY 5 FR 0.0005 REL FR 4 V 1 P
which since i know they virtuously are plac'd, TGV 4.03. 38
i was as virtuously given as a gentleman need to 1H4 3.03. 14 P
not virtuously on his own part beheld, | do in TRO 2.03.118
we are so virtuously bound — TIM 1.02.226
they that mean virtuously, and yet do so, | the OTH 4.01. 7
VISAG'D 1 FR 0.0001 REL FR 1 V 0 P
arcite is gently visag'd; TNK 5.03. 41
VISAGE 35 FR 0.0039 REL FR 32 V 3 P
whose settled visage and deliberate word | nips MM 3.01. 89
and satisfy the deputy with the visage | of 4.03. 75
show your knave's visage, with a pox to you! 5.01.353 P
behold | her silver visage in the wat'ry glass, MND 1.01.210
o, how mine eyes do loathe his visage now! 4.01. 79
looks in her | with an importing visage, and she AWW 5.03.136
bears in his visage no great presage of cruelty. TN 3.02. 65 P
me, let me know my trespass | by its own visage. WT 1.02.266
court | hides not his visage from our cottage, 4.04.445
darted their desiring eyes | upon his visage, R2 5.02. 15
put not you on the visage of the times, | and be 2H4 2.03. 3
our fertile france, put up her lovely visage? H5 5.02. 37
the poor and untempering effect of my visage. 5.02.224 P
o, let me view his visage, being dead, | that 2H6 5.01. 69
for him, | there's more in't than fair visage. H8 3.02. 88
to talk with him, and to behold his visage, TRO 3.03.240
the blood upon your visage dries, 'tis time | it COR 1.09. 93
give me a case to put my visage in, | a visor ROM 1.04. 29
a most importunate aspect, | a visage of demand; TIM 2.01. 29
dark enough | to mask thy monstrous visage? JC 2.01. 81
eye, | nor the dejected havior of the visage, HAM 1.02. 81
that from her working all the visage wann'd, 2.02.554
that with devotion's visage | and pious action 3.01. 46
mercy | but to confront the visage of offense? 3.03. 47
mass, | with heated visage, as against the doom; 3.04. 50
with her nails | she'll flea thy wolvish visage. LR 1.04.308
a plague upon your epileptic visage! 2.02. 81
i saw othello's visage in his mind, | and to his OTH 1.03.252
that was as fresh | as dian's visage, is now 3.03.387
patient octavia plough thy visage up | with her ANT 4.12. 38
manly courage | are bedfellows in his visage. TNK 5.03. 44
and from the forlorn world his visage hide, SON 33. 7
which fortified her visage from the sun, LC 9
for on his visage was in little drawn | what 90
yet showed his visage by that cost more dear, 96
VISAGES 5 FR 0.0005 REL FR 5 V 0 P
with visages display'd, to talk and greet. LLL 5.02.144
there are a sort of men whose visages | do cream MV 1.01. 88
with bleared visages, come forth to view | the 3.02. 59
are | who, trimm'd in forms and visages of duty, OTH 1.01. 50
end | the visages of bridegrooms we'll put on TNK 5.04.127
VISCOUNT 1 FR 0.0001 REL FR 1 V 0 P
the viscount rochford — one of her highness' H8 1.04. 93
/VISIBLE 1 FR 0.0001 REL FR 1 V 0 P
/the /heavens /do /not /their /visible /spirits LR 4.02. 46
VISIBLE 4 FR 0.0004 REL FR 4 V 0 P
though fortune, visible an enemy, | should chase WT 5.01.216
thou visible god, | that sold'rest close TIM 4.03.386
yet cannot hold this visible shape, my knave. ANT 4.14. 14
that though his actions were not visible, yet CYM 3.04.149
VISIBLY 1 FR 0.0001 REL FR 1 V 0 P
thoughts | are visibly character'd and engrav'd, TGV 2.07. 4
VISION 16 FR 0.0018 REL FR 14 V 2 P
this is a most majestic vision, and | harmonious TMP 4.01.118
and, like the baseless fabric of this vision, 4.01.151
if this prove | a vision of the island, one dear 5.01.176
is this a vision? WIV 3.05.139 P
shall seem a dream and fruitless vision, | and MND 3.02.371
i have had a most rare vision. 4.01.205 P
(for to a vision so apparent rumor | cannot be WT 1.02.270
which by a vision sent to her from heaven 1H6 1.02. 52
and in a vision full of majesty | will'd me to 1.02. 79
it was a vision fair and fortunate. JC 2.02. 84
art thou not, fatal vision, sensible | to MAC 2.01. 36
touching this vision here, | it is an honest HAM 1.05.137
last night the very gods show'd me a vision | (i CYM 4.02.346
the vision | which i made known to lucius, ere 5.05.467
/i bless thee for thy vision, and will offer PER 5.03. 69
nor his own vision holds what it doth catch; SON 113. 8
VISIONS 3 FR 0.0003 REL FR 3 V 0 P
my oberon, what visions have i seen! MND 4.01. 76
slumb'red here | while these visions did appear. 5.01.426
wife hath dreamt, thy mother hath had visions, TRO 5.03. 63
VISIT 60 FR 0.0067 REL FR 50 V 10 P
we'll visit caliban my slave, who never | yields TMP 1.02.308
i leave them, while i visit | young ferdinand, 3.03. 91
and i likewise will visit thee with mine. TGV 1.01. 60
visit by night your lady's chamber-window | with 3.02. 82
well, i will visit her, tell her so. WIV 3.05. 49 P
of your order, | visit both prince and people; MM 1.03. 45
i come to visit the afflicted spirits | here in 2.03. 4
dear sir, ere long i'll visit you again. 3.01. 46
i am going to visit the prisoner. fare you well. 3.02.258 P
and soon at supper-time i'll visit you, | and ERR 3.02.174
and claudio promis'd by this hour | to visit me. ADO 5.04. 14
i will visit thee at the lodge. LLL 1.02.135 P
to-morrow shall we visit you again. 2.01.176
but what, but what, come they to visit us? 5.02.119
we came to visit you, and purpose now | to lead 5.02.343
visit the speechless sick and still converse 5.02.851
rest, | but we will visit you at supper-time. MV 2.02.206
visit his countrymen, and banquet them? SHR 1.01.197
not i, believe me, thus i'll visit her. 3.02.114
i am to padua, there to visit | a son of mine, 4.05. 56
curate, who comes to visit malvolio the lunatic. TN 4.02. 21 P
to visit bohemia on the like occasion whereon my WT 1.01. 1 P
please your ladyship | to visit the next room, 2.02. 45
peril and on mine, | she should not visit you. 2.03. 46
once a day i'll visit | the chapel where they 3.02.238
heirs of your kingdoms, my poor house to visit, 5.03. 6
with all good speed at plashy visit me. R2 1.02. 66
to entreat your majesty to visit him. 1.04. 56
come, gentlemen, let's all go visit him. 1.04. 63
king | dismiss his power he means to visit us, 1H4 4.04. 37
at your return visit our house, let our old 2H4 3.02.294 P
and there will i visit master robert shallow, 4.03.129 P
to visit her poor castle where she lies, | that 1H6 2.02. 41
i'll sort some other time to visit you. 2.03. 27
lord, | to visit him to-morrow or next day. R3 3.07. 60
patience, | i may not suffer you to visit them, 4.01. 16
the king's request that i would visit you, | who H8 4.02.116
i prithee, diomed, visit me no more. TRO 5.02. 74
madam, the lady valeria is come to visit you. COR 1.03. 26
you must go visit the good lady that lies in. 1.03. 77 P
speedy strength, and visit her with my prayers; 1.03. 78 P
of rome, | or rudely visit them in parts remote, 4.05.142
senate | newly alighted, and come to visit you. TIM 1.02.175
if i thrive well, i'll visit thee again. 4.03.170
are the ruddy drops | that visit my sad heart. JC 2.01.290
and thither will i straight to visit him; 3.02.265
they could be content | to visit other places, 5.01. 9
winds of heaven | visit her face too roughly. HAM 1.02.142
'twixt aleven and twelf | i'll visit you. 1.02.252
before you visit him, to make inquire | of his 2.01. 4
and i beseech you instantly to visit | my too 2.02. 35
to visit you, my lord, no other occasion. 2.02.271 P
you know not why we came to visit you? LR 2.01.118
this, | that thou, vouchsafing here to visit me, ANT 5.02.160
my lord, when last i went to visit her, | she CYM 3.05. 45
there will i visit cleon, for the babe | cannot PER 3.01. 78
my cousin gave his faith | to visit me again, TNK 3.06. 2
come, i'll go visit 'em. 4.02.152
and has done this long hour, to visit you. 5.02. 42
see) | some present speed to come and visit me. LUC 1307
VISITATING 1 FR 0.0001 REL FR 1 V 0 P
lords | lie blist'ring 'fore the visitating sun, TNK 1.01.146
VISITATION 17 FR 0.0019 REL FR 13 V 4 P
this visitation shows it. TMP 3.01. 32
to understand that you have lent him visitation. MM 3.02.241 P
nothing but peace and gentle visitation. LLL 5.02.179
nothing but peace and gentle visitation. 5.02.181
in loving visitation was with me a young doctor MV 4.01.153 P
to pay bohemia the visitation which he justly WT 1.01. 6 P
what color for my visitation shall i | hold up 4.04.555
tells us | 'tis not a visitation fram'd, but 5.01. 91
surge, | and in the visitation of the winds, 2H4 3.01. 21
my god, | deferr'd the visitation of my friends. R3 3.07.107

to whisper wolsey), here makes visitation — H8 1.01.179
your queen | desires your visitation, and to be 5.01.167
sentinels, | to give thee nightly visitation. TRO 4.04. 73
nothing at this time but my visitation; TIM 5.01. 18
your visitation shall receive such thanks | as HAM 2.02. 25
is it a free visitation? 2.02.275 P
this visitation | is but to whet thy almost 3.04.110
VISITATIONS 1 FR 0.0001 REL FR 1 V 0 P
i take all and your several visitations | so TIM 1.02.218
VISITED 9 FR 0.0010 REL FR 6 V 3 P
these lords are visited; LLL 5.02.422
by day's approach look to be visited. MND 3.02.430
the sins of my mother should be visited upon me. MV 3.05. 14 P
kept in a dark house, visited by the priest, TN 5.01.342
death of hermione, visited that remov'd house. WT 5.02.106 P
thy sins are visited in this poor child, | the JN 2.01.179
whole | ere he by sickness had been visited, 1H4 4.01. 26
impieties for the which they are now visited. H5 4.01.176 P
my head, | the good patricians must be visited, COR 2.01.196
VISITING 5 FR 0.0005 REL FR 5 V 0 P
my father gave me | for visiting your highness. WT 5.01.163
and i | are come from visiting his majesty. R3 1.03. 32
we lay by | our appertainings, visiting of him. TRO 2.03. 80
me, | here in this city visiting the sick, | and ROM 5.02. 7
left remarkable | beneath the visiting moon. ANT 4.15. 68
VISITINGS 1 FR 0.0001 REL FR 1 V 0 P
that no compunctious visitings of nature | shake MAC 1.05. 45
VISITOR 1 FR 0.0001 REL FR 0 V 1 P
the visitor will not give him o'er so. TMP 2.01. 11 P
VISITORS 2 FR 0.0002 REL FR 2 V 0 P
and honor from th' access of gentle visitors. WT 2.02. 10
this confluence, this great flood of visitors. TIM 1.01. 42
VISITS 3 FR 0.0003 REL FR 3 V 0 P
it seldom visits sorrow; TMP 2.01.195
all places that the eye of heaven visits | are R2 1.03.275
for forth he goes, and visits all his host, H5 4.pr. 32
VISOR 13 FR 0.0014 REL FR 6 V 7 P
my visor is philemon's roof, within the house is ADO 2.01. 96 P
why then your visor should be thatch'd. 2.01. 98 P
ladies follow her, and but one visor remains. 2.01.157 P
my very visor began to assume life and scold 2.01.241 P
twice to your visor, and half once to you. LLL 5.02.227
to countenance william visor of woncote against 2H4 5.01. 39 P
is many complaints, davy, against that visor. 5.01. 41 P
that visor is an arrant knave, on my knowledge. 5.01. 41 P
and with a virtuous visor hide deep vice! R3 2.02. 28
case to put my visage in, | a visor for a visor! ROM 1.04. 30
case to put my visage in, | a visor for a visor! 1.04. 30
day | that i have worn a visor and could tell 1.05. 22
no visor does become black villainy | so well as PER 4.04. 44
VITA 1 FR 0.0001 REL FR 1 V 0 P
"lux tua vita mihi." PER 2.02. 21
VITAE 1 FR 0.0001 REL FR 1 V 0 P
"integer vitae, scelerisque purus, | non eget TIT 4.02. 20
VITAL 4 FR 0.0004 REL FR 3 V 1 P
and then the vital commoners and inland petty 2H4 4.03.109 P
and let not bardolph's vital thread be cut H5 3.06. 47
whose dismal tune bereft my vital pow'rs; 2H6 3.02. 41
thy rose, | i cannot give it vital growth again, OTH 5.02. 14
VITEMENT 1 FR 0.0001 REL FR 0 V 1 P
j'ai gagne deux mots d'anglois vitement. H5 3.04. 14 P
/VITRUVIO 1 FR 0.0001 REL FR 0 V 1 P
the lady widow of /vitruvio; ROM 1.02. 66 P
VIVA 1 FR 0.0001 REL FR 1 V 0 P
desir'd | to him brought viva voce to his face; H8 2.01. 18
VIVANT 1 FR 0.0001 REL FR 1 V 0 P
o dieu vivant! H5 3.05. 5
VIVE 1 FR 0.0001 REL FR 1 V 0 P
heard these islanders shout out | "vive le roi!" JN 5.02.104
VIVES *(see fives)*
VIVO 1 FR 0.0001 REL FR 1 V 0 P
"in hac spe vivo." PER 2.02. 44
VIXEN 1 FR 0.0001 REL FR 1 V 0 P
she was a vixen when she went to school; MND 3.02.324
/VIZ 1 FR 0.0001 REL FR 0 V 1 P
many pair of silk stockings thou hast, /viz., 2H4 2.02. 15 P
VIZAMENTS 1 FR 0.0001 REL FR 0 V 1 P
take your vizaments in that. WIV 1.01. 39 P
VIZARD 5 FR 0.0005 REL FR 5 V 0 P
what, was your vizard made without a tongue? LLL 5.02.242
and would afford my speechless vizard half. 5.02.246
where? when? what vizard? why demand you this? 5.02.386
then, that vizard, that superfluous case | that 5.02.387
tongue, | nor never come in vizard to my friend, 5.02.404
VIZARDED 2 FR 0.0002 REL FR 2 V 0 P
for they must all be mask'd and vizarded) | that WIV 4.06. 40
degree being vizarded, | th' unworthiest shows TRO 1.03. 83
VIZARD-LIKE 1 FR 0.0001 REL FR 1 V 0 P
but that thy face is vizard-like, unchanging, 3H6 1.04.116
VIZARDS 7 FR 0.0008 REL FR 4 V 3 P
i'll go buy them vizards. WIV 4.04. 70
or ever but in vizards show their faces? LLL 5.02.271
which of the vizards was it that you wore? 5.02.385
i have vizards for you all; 1H4 1.02.128 P
our vizards we will change after we leave them; 1.02.178 P
case ye, case ye, on with your vizards. 2.02. 53 P
and make our faces vizards to our hearts, MAC 3.02. 34
VLOUTING-STOCKS 1 FR 0.0001 REL FR 0 V 1 P
are wise and full of gibes and vlouting-stocks, WIV 4.05. 80 P
VLOUTING-STOG 1 FR 0.0001 REL FR 0 V 1 P
he has made us his vlouting-stog. WIV 3.01.117 P
VOCATION 4 FR 0.0004 REL FR 1 V 3 P
why, hal, 'tis my vocation, hal, 'tis no sin for 1H4 1.02.104 P
'tis no sin for a man to labor in his vocation. 1.02.105 P
will'd me to leave my base vocation | and free 1H6 1.02. 80
and yet it is said, labor in thy vocation; 2H6 4.02. 16 P
VOCATIVE *(see focative)*
VOCATIVO 1 FR 0.0001 REL FR 0 V 1 P
o — vocativo, o. WIV 4.01. 52 P
VOCATUR 1 FR 0.0001 REL FR 0 V 1 P
neighbor vocatur "nebor"; LLL 5.01. 23 P
VOCE 1 FR 0.0001 REL FR 1 V 0 P
desir'd | to him brought viva voce to his face; H8 2.01. 18
VOIC'D 1 FR 0.0001 REL FR 1 V 0 P
minion, whom the world | voic'd so regardfully? TIM 4.03. 82
/VOICE 3 FR 0.0003 REL FR 2 V 1 P
/for /all /the /country /in /a /general /voice 2H4 4.01.134
/of /author's /pen /or /actor's /voice, /but TRO pr 24
/poor /tom /in /the /voice /of /a /nightingale. LR 3.06. 29 P
VOICE 168 FR 0.0190 REL FR 133 V 35 P
i should know that voice; TMP 2.02. 87 P
his forward voice now is to speak well of his 2.02. 90 P
his backward voice is to utter foul speeches and 2.02. 91 P
would quickly learn to know him by his voice. TGV 4.02. 89
style, and the hardest voice of her behavior (to WIV 1.03. 47 P
let me have thy voice in my behalf. 1.04.156 P
implore her, in my voice, that she make friends MM 1.02.180
it is a man's voice. 1.04. 7
i (now the voice of the recorded law) 2.04. 61
my father's grave | did utter forth a voice. 3.01. 86
i remember you, sir, by the sound of your voice; 5.01.328 P
but tell me yet, dost thou not know my voice? ERR 5.01.301
not know my voice! 5.01.308
tax not so bad a voice | to slander music any ADO 2.03. 44
and i pray god his bad voice bode no mischief. 2.03. 81 P
lightning bears, thy voice his dreadful thunder, LLL 4.02.115
the voice of all the gods | make heaven drowsy 4.03.341
with faining voice verses of faining love, | and MND 1.01. 31
but in this kind, wanting your father's voice, 1.01. 54
my ear should catch your voice, my eye your eye, 1.01.188
i'll speak in a monstrous little voice, "thisne! 1.02. 52 P
i will aggravate my voice so that i will roar 1.02. 82 P
but hark, a voice! 3.01. 86
follow my voice; we'll try no manhood here. 3.02.412
and he is a very paramour for a sweet voice. 4.02. 12 P
i see a voice! 5.01.192
art too wild, too rude, and bold of voice — MV 2.02.181
but, being season'd with a gracious voice, 3.02. 76
the change of man and boy | with a reed voice, 3.04. 67
of the duke only, 'gainst all other voice: 4.01.356
that is the voice, | or i am much deceiv'd, of 5.01.110
blind man knows the cuckoo, | by the bad voice! 5.01.113
and in my voice most welcome shall you be. AYL 2.04. 87
my voice is ragged, i know i cannot please you. 2.05. 15 P
for his shrunk shank, and his big manly voice, 2.07.161
which are the only prologues to a bad voice? 5.03. 13 P
voice, gait, and action of a gentlewoman. SHR in.1. 132
whom both sovereign power and father's voice | i AWW 2.03. 54
knows he not thy voice? 4.01. 9 P
a mellifluous voice, as i am true knight. TN 2.03. 53 P
without any mitigation or remorse of voice? 2.03. 91 P
my matter hath no voice, lady, but to your own 3.01. 88 P
none, | nor know i you by voice or any feature. 3.04.353
to him in thine own voice, and bring me word how 4.02. 66 P
one face, one voice, one habit, and two persons, 5.01.216
and the ear-deaf'ning voice o' th' oracle, | kin WT 3.01. 9
which cannot hear a lady's feeble voice, | which JN 3.04. 41
crow, | thinking this voice an armed englishman; 5.02.145
o, 'tis our setter, i know his voice. 1H4 2.02. 51 P
is not your voice broken, your wind short, your 2H4 1.02.182 P
for my voice, i have lost it with hallowing and 1.02.189 P
rumor doth double, like the voice and echo, 3.01. 97
to us th' /imagin'd voice of god himself, | the 4.02. 19
which, deliver'd o'er to the voice, the tongue, 4.03.101 P
my voice shall sound as you do prompt mine ear, 5.02.119
hath got the voice in hell for excellence; H5 2.02.113
go speak, the duke will hear thy voice; 3.06. 46
speak upon our cue, and our voice is imperial: 3.06.123 P
my brother gloucester's voice? 4.01.307
never know so full a voice issue from so empty a 4.04. 67 P
happily a woman's voice may do some good, | when 5.02. 93
for thy voice is music and thy english broken; 5.02.244 P
that, having neither the voice nor the heart of 5.02.287 P
lieutenant, is it you whose voice i hear? 1H6 1.03. 16
well didst thou, richard, to suppress thy voice; 4.01.182
the hollow passage of my poison'd voice, | by 5.04.121
lords, with one cheerful voice welcome my love. 2H6 1.01. 36
their hands, and crying with loud voice, | "jesu 1.01.160
oft | myself have heard a voice to call him so. 2.01. 92
boy, that with his grumbling voice | was wont to 3H6 1.04. 76
thy voice is thunder, but thy looks are humble. R3 1.04.167
my voice is now the king's, my looks mine own. 1.04.168
but that i'll give my voice on richard's side 3.02. 53
and in the duke's behalf i'll give my voice, 3.04. 19
i mean, your voice for crowning of the king. 3.04. 28
so many miseries have craz'd my voice | that my 4.04. 17
further gone in this than by | a single voice, H8 1.02. 70
what warlike voice, | and to what end is this? 1.04. 50
your scruple to the voice of christendom. 2.02. 87
and the voice is now | only about her coronation 3.02.405
well, the voice goes, madam: 4.02. 11
the common voice, i see, is verified | of thee, 5.02.209
eyes, her hair, her cheek, her gait, her voice, TRO 1.01. 54
opinion crowns | with an imperial voice — many 1.03.187
which with one voice | call agamemnon head and 1.03.221
send thy brass voice through all these lazy 1.03.257
'tis our mad sister, i do know her voice. 2.02. 98
have ears more deaf than adders to the voice 2.02.172
in second voice we'll not be satisfied, | we 2.03.140
they that have the voice of lions and the act of 3.02. 88 P
like an arch, reverb'rate | the voice again, or, 3.03.121
crack my clear voice with sobs and break my 4.02.108
be divided | by any voice or order of the field? 4.05. 70
to take that course by your consent and voice, 5.03. 74
i shall lack voice: COR 2.02. 82
your good voice, sir, what say you? 2.03. 78 P
and cannot go without any honest man's voice. 2.03.133 P
tribunes | endue you with the people's voice. 2.03.139
make them of no more voice | than dogs, that are 2.03.215
you against the grain | to voice him consul. 2.03.234
people give | one that speaks thus their voice? 3.01.119
or the virgin voice | that babies lull asleep! 3.02.114
that being pass'd for consul with full voice, 3.03. 59
"thou liest" unto thee with a voice as free | as 3.03. 73
and suffer'd me by th' voice of slaves to be 4.05. 77
stood so much | upon the voice of occupation and 4.06. 97
stand | a special party, have by common voice, TIT 1.01. 21
i know | the common voice do cry it shall be so. 5.03.140
lies my consent and fair according voice. ROM 1.02. 19
this, by his voice, should be a montague. 1.05. 54
o, for a falc'ner's voice, | to lure this 2.02.158
since arm from arm that voice doth us affray, 3.05. 33
this same should be the voice of friar john. 5.02. 2
they answer, in a joint and corporate voice, TIM 2.02.204
my lord, you have my voice to't; 3.05. 1
crack the lawyer's voice, | that he may never 4.03.153
casca, by your voice. JC 1.03. 41
is there no voice more worthy than my own, | to 3.01. 49
your voice shall be as strong as any man's | in 3.01.177
to beg the voice and utterance of my tongue) | a 3.01.261
shall in these confines with a monarch's voice 3.01.272
and took his voice who should be prick'd to die 4.01. 16
methought i heard a voice cry, "sleep no more! MAC 2.02. 32
my voice is in my sword, thou bloodier villain 5.08. 7
if thou hast any sound, or use of voice, | speak HAM 1.01.128
of reason to the dane | and lose your voice. 1.02. 45
unto the voice and yielding of that body 1.03. 23
than the main voice of denmark goes withal. 1.03. 28
give every man thy ear, but few thy voice, 1.03. 68
pray god your voice, like a piece of uncurrent 2.02.427 P
a broken voice, an' his whole function suiting 2.02.556
when you have the voice of the king himself for 3.02.341 P
and there is much music, excellent voice, in 3.02.368 P
honor | i have a voice and president of peace 5.02.249
lights | on fortinbras, he has my dying voice. 5.02.356
from his mouth whose voice will draw /on more, 5.02.392
methinks thy voice is alter'd, and thou speak'st LR 4.06. 7
i know that voice. 4.06. 95
the trick of that voice i do well remember; 4.06.106
her voice was ever soft, | gentle, and low, an 5.03.273
most reverend signior, do you know my voice? OTH 1.01. 93
and hath in his effect a voice potential | as 1.02. 13
of effects, throws a more safer voice on you. 1.03.226 P
and let me find a charter in your voice | t' 1.03.245
let her have your voice. 1.03.260
the voice of cassio! iago keeps his word. 5.01. 28
'tis some mischance, the voice is very direful. 5.01. 38
out, and alas, that was my lady's voice. 5.02.119
his voice was propertied | as all the tuned ANT 5.02. 83
nor the voice of unpav'd eunuch to boot, can CYM 2.03. 30 P
for thy relief nor my voice for thy preferment. 3.05.115 P
the snatches in his voice, | and burst of 4.02.105
hairs, i have drawn her picture with my voice. PER 4.02. 95 P
voice and favor! 5.03. 13
the voice of dead thaisa! 5.03. 34
sport, | i heard a voice, a shrill one; TNK 4.01. 56
i have no voice, sir, to confirm her that way! 5.02. 15
you that have voice and credit with the number, STM II.C 51
ill-nurtur'd, crooked, churlish, harsh in voice, VEN 134
thy mermaid's voice hath done me double wrong: 429
against the welkin volleys out his voice; 921
rejoice, | and flatters her it is adonis' voice. 978
her voice is stopp'd, her joints forget to bow, 1061
with her own white fleece her voice controll'd LUC 678
head declin'd, and voice damm'd up with woe, 1661
lightning seems, thy voice his dreadful thunder, PP 5.11
all tongues (the voice of souls) give thee that SON 69. 3
my spirits t' attend this double voice accorded, LC 3
VOICES 54 FR 0.0061 REL FR 44 V 10 P
four legs and two voices; TMP 2.02. 89 P
will hum about mine ears, and sometime voices, 3.02.138
hands, our sides, voices, and minds | had been MND 3.02.207
god buy you, and god mend your voices! AYL 5.03. 41 P
in voices well divulg'd, free, learn'd, and TN 1.05.260
boys, with women's voices, | strive to speak big R2 3.02.113
and some ten voices cried, "god save king R3 3.07. 36
in christian kingdoms) | have their free voices. H8 2.02. 93
it stands agreed, | i take it, by all voices: 5.02.123
come safe off, | we'll dress him up in voices; TRO 1.03.381
sir, the people | must have their voices; COR 2.02.140
once if he do require our voices, we ought not 2.03. 1 P
are you all resolv'd to give your voices? 2.03. 36 P
giving him our own voices with our own tongues; 2.03. 45 P
there's in all two worthy voices begg'd. 2.03. 81 P
the tune of your voices that i may be consul, i 2.03. 86 P
and therefore give you our voices heartily. 2.03.105 P
i will make much of your voices, and so trouble 2.03.109 P
most sweet voices! 2.03.112
here come moe voices. 2.03.125
your voices? 2.03.126
for your voices i have fought; 2.03.126
watch'd for your voices; 2.03.127
for your voices bear | of wounds two dozen odd; 2.03.127
for your voices have | done many things, some 2.03.129
your voices? 2.03.130
worthy voices! 2.03.137 P
he has our voices, sir. 2.03.156
he mock'd us when he begg'd our voices. 2.03.159
but by your voices, will not so permit me; 2.03.169
your voices therefore." 2.03.170
here was "i thank you for your voices, thank you 2.03.171
voices, thank you, | your most sweet voices. 2.03.172
now you have left your voices, | i have no 2.03.172
childish friendliness | to yield your voices? 2.03.176
your voices might | be curses to yourselves? 2.03.184
nature | would think upon you for your voices, 2.03.188
i'll have five hundred voices of that sound. 2.03.211
have i had children's voices? 3.01. 30
must these have voices, that can yield them now, 3.01. 34
when, both your voices blended, the great'st 3.01.103
my reasons, | more worthier than their voices. 3.01.120
of all the voices that we have procur'd | set 3.03. 9
if you submit you to the people's voices, 3.03. 44
he tumble down, | and pay you for your voices. 4.06.136
y' are goodly things, you voices! 4.06.146
here, | i ask your voices and your suffrages: TIT 1.01.218
with voices and applause of every sort, 1.01.230
o, now i would they had chang'd voices too, ROM 3.05. 32
and buy men's voices to commend our deeds. JC 2.01.146
whose voices i desire aloud with mine: MAC 5.09. 24
of bedlam beggars, who, with roaring voices, LR 2.03. 14
though now our voices | have got the mannish CYM 4.02.235
abysm i throw all care | of others' voices, that SON 112.10
VOID 11 FR 0.0012 REL FR 10 V 1 P
and void of all profanation in the world that MM 2.01. 55 P
that did void your rheum upon my beard | and MV 1.03.117
pity, void and empty | from any dram of mercy. 4.01. 5
even so void is your false heart of truth. 5.01.189
the alps doth spit and void his rheum upon. H5 3.05. 52
us, bid them come down, | or void the field; 4.07. 59
which makes me hope you are not void of pity. 2H6 4.07. 64
device | by this alliance to make void my suit. 3H6 3.03.142
those men | upon whose age we void it up again TIM 1.02.138
i'll get me to a place more void, and there JC 2.04. 37

with these hands | void of appointment, that TNK 3.01. 40
'VOIDED *(also avoided)*
'VOIDED 1 FR 0.0001 REL FR 1 V 0 P
men i' th' world | i would have 'voided thee; COR 4.05. 82
VOIDING 1 FR 0.0001 REL FR 1 V 0 P
how in our voiding lobby hast thou stood | and 2H6 4.01. 61
/VOID'ST 1 FR 0.0001 REL FR 1 V 0 P
the /void'st of honor | that ev'r bore gentle TNK 3.01. 36
VOIS 1 FR 0.0001 REL FR 0 V 1 P
/o, /je /m'en vois a la cour — la grande WIV 1.04. 52 P
VOKE *(also folk)*
VOKE 1 FR 0.0001 REL FR 0 V 1 P
gentleman, go your gait, and let poor voke pass. LR 4.06.238 P
VOLABLE *(also voluble)*
VOLABLE 1 FR 0.0001 REL FR 1 V 0 P
a most acute juvenal, volable and free of grace! LLL 3.01. 66
VOLANT 1 FR 0.0001 REL FR 0 V 1 P
le cheval volant, the pegasus, chez les narines H5 3.07. 14 P
VOLIVORCO 1 FR 0.0001 REL FR 0 V 1 P
oscorbidulchos volivorco. AWW 4.01. 79 P
VOLLEY 4 FR 0.0004 REL FR 3 V 1 P
a fine volley of words, gentlemen, and quickly TGV 2.04. 33 P
off, | when with a volley of our needless shot, JN 5.05. 5
of england gives | this warlike volley. HAM 5.02.352
/bear as loud | as his strong sides can volley. ANT 2.07.112
VOLLEYS 1 FR 0.0001 REL FR 1 V 0 P
against the welkin volleys out his voice; VEN 921
VOLQUESSEN 1 FR 0.0001 REL FR 1 V 0 P
then do i give volquessen, touraine, maine, JN 2.01.527
VOLSCE 2 FR 0.0002 REL FR 2 V 0 P
he that retires, i'll take him for a volsce, COR 1.04. 28
for i cannot, | being a volsce, be that i am. 1.10. 5
VOLSCES 18 FR 0.0020 REL FR 17 V 1 P
the news is, sir, the volsces are in arms. COR 1.01.224
have lately told us, | the volsces are in arms. 1.01.228
the volsces have much corn; 1.01.249
children from a bear, the volsces shunning him. 1.03. 31
the volsces have an army forth; 1.03. 96 P
spies of the volsces | held me in chase, that i 1.06. 18
not outward, which of you | but is four volsces? 1.06. 78
having determin'd of the volsces and | to send 2.02. 37
so then the volsces stand but as at first, 3.01. 4
against the volsces for they had so vildly 3.01. 10
to thee particularly, and to all the volsces, 4.05. 66
reports the volsces with two several powers 4.06. 39
it cannot be | the volsces dare break with us. 4.06. 49
let the volsces | plough rome and harrow italy, 5.03. 33
aufidius, and you volsces, mark, for we'll 5.03. 92
thereby to destroy | the volsces whom you serve, 5.03.134
while the volsces | may say, "this mercy we have 5.03.136
cut me to pieces, volsces, men and lads, | stain 5.06.111
VOLSCIAN 5 FR 0.0005 REL FR 4 V 1 P
a note from the volscian state to find you out COR 4.03. 11 P
and shows good husbandry for the volscian state, 4.07. 22
my remission lies | in volscian breasts. 5.02. 85
you must report to th' volscian lords, how 5.03. 3
this fellow had a volscian to his mother; 5.03.178
VOLSCIANS' 1 FR 0.0001 REL FR 1 V 0 P
a name unmusical to the volscians' ears, | and COR 4.05. 58
VOLSCIANS 4 FR 0.0004 REL FR 3 V 1 P
i hope to see romans as cheap as volscians. COR 4.05.233 P
martius should be join'd /wi' /th' volscians — 4.06. 89
the volscians are dislodg'd, and martius gone. 5.04. 41
i | /flutter'd your volscians in corioles. 5.06.115
VOLTEMAND 2 FR 0.0002 REL FR 2 V 0 P
you, good cornelius, and you, voltemand, | for HAM 1.02. 34
say, voltemand, what from our brother norway? 2.02. 59
VOLUBILITY 2 FR 0.0002 REL FR 1 V 1 P
a word, | then i'll commend her volubility, SHR 2.01.175
sir, with such volubility, that you would think AWW 4.03.254 P
VOLUBLE *(also volable)*
VOLUBLE 4 FR 0.0004 REL FR 3 V 1 P
if voluble and sharp discourse be marr'd, ERR 2.01. 92
so sweet and voluble is his discourse. LLL 2.01. 76
a knave very voluble; OTH 2.01.238 P
in a fever, and deifies alone | voluble chance; TNK 1.02. 67
VOLUME 11 FR 0.0012 REL FR 11 V 0 P
shall draw this brief into as huge a volume. JN 2.01.103
he should have had a volume of farewells; R2 1.04. 18
foretells the nature of a tragic volume. 2H4 1.01. 61
them) | would make a volume of enticing lines, 1H6 5.05. 14
piece | will bear the knave by th' volume. COR 3.03. 33
read o'er the volume of young paris' face, | and ROM 1.03. 81
and what obscur'd in this fair volume lies 1.03. 85
within the volume of which time i have seen MAC 2.04. 2
live | within the book and volume of my brain, HAM 1.05.103
i' th' world's volume | our britain seems as of CYM 3.04.137
/to place upon the volume of your deeds, | as in PER 2.03. 3
VOLUMES 4 FR 0.0004 REL FR 3 V 1 P
me | from mine own library with volumes that | i TMP 1.02.167
volumes of report | run with these false and MM 4.01. 60
write, pen, for i am for whole volumes in folio. LLL 1.02.185 P
small pricks | to their subsequent volumes) TRO 1.03.344
VOLUMNIA 1 FR 0.0001 REL FR 1 V 0 P
this volumnia | is worth of consuls, senators, COR 5.04. 52
VOLUMNIUS 6 FR 0.0006 REL FR 6 V 0 P
come hither, good volumnius; list a word. JC 5.05. 15
why, this, volumnius: 5.05. 16
nay, i am sure it is, volumnius. 5.05. 21
thou seest the world, volumnius, how it goes; 5.05. 22
good volumnius, | thou know'st that we two went 5.05. 25
farewell to you, and you, and you, volumnius. 5.05. 31
VOLUNTARIES 1 FR 0.0001 REL FR 1 V 0 P
land, | rash, inconsiderate, fiery voluntaries, JN 2.01. 67
VOLUNTARY 12 FR 0.0013 REL FR 6 V 6 P
bars me the right of voluntary choosing. MV 2.01. 16
put themselves into voluntary exile with him, AYL 1.01.101 P
thy voluntary oath | lives in this bosom, dearly JN 3.03. 23
but, heav'n be thank'd, it is but voluntary. 5.01. 29
we swear | a voluntary zeal and an unurg'd faith 5.02. 10
i serve here voluntary. TRO 2.01. 94 P
service was suff'rance, 'twas not voluntary; 2.01. 96 P
no man is beaten voluntary. 2.01. 96 P
ajax was here the voluntary, and you as under an 2.01. 97 P
giving myself a voluntary wound | here, in the JC 2.01.300
suit, | or voluntary dotage of some mistress, OTH 4.01. 27
that thou wilt be a voluntary mute to my design. CYM 3.05.153 P
VOLUPTUOUSLY 1 FR 0.0001 REL FR 0 V 1 P
country than one voluptuously surfeit out of COR 1.03. 25 P
VOLUPTUOUSNESS 2 FR 0.0002 REL FR 2 V 0 P
there's no bottom, none, | in my voluptuousness. MAC 4.03. 61
he fill'd | his vacancy with his voluptuousness, ANT 1.04. 26
VOMISSEMENT 1 FR 0.0001 REL FR 0 V 1 P
"le chien est retourne a son propre vomissement, H5 3.07. 64 P
/VOMIT 1 FR 0.0001 REL FR 1 V 0 P
/now /thou /wouldst /eat /thy /dead /vomit /up, 2H4 1.03. 99
VOMIT 4 FR 0.0004 REL FR 3 V 1 P
woes, | but like a drunkard must i vomit them. TIT 3.01.231
your hollander a vomit ere the next pottle can OTH 2.03. 84 P
oppos'd, | should make desire vomit emptiness, CYM 1.06. 45
drunken desire must vomit his receipt | ere he LUC 703
VOMITS 1 FR 0.0001 REL FR 1 V 0 P
whom their o'ercloyed country vomits forth | to R3 5.03.318
VOR' *(also warn)*
VOR' 1 FR 0.0001 REL FR 0 V 1 P
keep out, che vor' ye, or ice try whither your LR 4.06.240 P
VOR *(also for, ver*)*
VOR 2 FR 0.0002 REL FR 0 V 2 P
by gar, me dank you vor dat. WIV 2.03. 90 P
come, no matter vor your foins. LR 4.06.245 P
VORLD *(also orld, varld, world)*
VORLD 1 FR 0.0001 REL FR 0 V 1 P
by gar, he is de coward jack priest of de vorld; WIV 2.03. 32 P
VORTNIGHT *(also fortnight)*
VORTNIGHT 1 FR 0.0001 REL FR 0 V 1 P
not ha' bin zo long as 'tis by a vortnight. LR 4.06.239 P
VOTARESS 1 FR 0.0001 REL FR 1 V 0 P
at ephesus, | unto diana there 's a votaress. PER 4.ch. 4
VOTARIES 2 FR 0.0002 REL FR 1 V 1 P
who are the votaries, my loving lords, | that LLL 2.01. 37
berowne is one of the votaries with the king, 4.02.137 P
VOTARIST 2 FR 0.0002 REL FR 1 V 1 P
no, gods, i am no idle votarist; TIM 4.03. 27
desdemona would half have corrupted a votarist. OTH 4.02.187 P
VOTARISTS 1 FR 0.0001 REL FR 1 V 0 P
the sisterhood, the votarists of saint clare. MM 1.04. 5
VOTARY 4 FR 0.0004 REL FR 3 V 1 P
counsel thee | that art a votary to fond desire? TGV 1.01. 52
you are already love's firm votary | and cannot 3.02. 58
i am a votary; LLL 5.02.883 P
hand | the fairest votary took up that fire, SON 154. 5
VOTRE 9 FR 0.0010 REL FR 0 V 9 P
et vous aussi; votre serviteur. TN 3.01. 72 P
sauf votre honneur, en verite, vous prononcez H5 3.04. 37 P
sauf votre honneur, d' elbow. 3.04. 48 P
tout /a /cette /heure de couper votre gorge. 4.04. 36 P
oui, vraiment, sauf votre grace, ainsi dit–il. 5.02.112 P
sauf votre honneur, me understand well. 5.02.131 P
donc votre est france et vous etes mienne. 5.02.183 P
sauf votre honneur, le francois que vous parlez, 5.02.188 P
que vous abaissez votre /grandeur en baisant la 5.02.254 P
VOT'RESS 2 FR 0.0002 REL FR 2 V 0 P
his mother was a vot'ress of my order, | and, in MND 2.01.123
moon, | and the imperial vot'ress passed on, 2.01.163
VOUCH 12 FR 0.0013 REL FR 10 V 2 P
my vouch against you, and my place i' th' state, MM 2.04.156
what can you vouch | against him, signior lucio? 5.01.323
fain would steal | what law does vouch mine own. AWW 2.05. 82
and make my vouch as strong | as shore of rock. H8 1.01.157
(which, i dare vouch, is more than that he hath, COR 3.01.298
the commons' ears, | will vouch the truth of it. 5.06. 5
he that would vouch it in any place but here. TIT 1.01.360
will /his vouchers vouch him no more of his HAM 5.01.108 P
i therefore vouch again | that with some OTH 1.03.103
to vouch this is no proof, | without more wider 1.03.106
vouch with me, heaven, i therefore beg it not 1.03.261
did justly put on the vouch of very malice 2.01.146 P
VOUCH'D 5 FR 0.0005 REL FR 4 V 1 P
as many vouch'd rarieties are. TMP 2.01. 61 P
a certainty, vouch'd from our cousin austria, AWW 1.02. 5
which, to the spire and top of praises vouch'd, COR 1.09. 24
the feast is sold | that is not often vouch'd, MAC 3.04. 33
our master mars | /hath vouch'd his oracle, and TNK 5.04.107
VOUCHER 1 FR 0.0001 REL FR 1 V 0 P
here's a voucher, | stronger than ever law could CYM 2.02. 39
VOUCHERS 2 FR 0.0002 REL FR 0 V 2 P
his fines, his double vouchers, his recoveries. HAM 5.01.105 P
will /his vouchers vouch him no more of his 5.01.108 P
VOUCHES 2 FR 0.0002 REL FR 2 V 0 P
a man that never yet | did, as he vouches, MM 5.01.148
that does appear, | their needless vouches? COR 2.03.117
VOUCHING 1 FR 0.0001 REL FR 0 V 1 P
this gentleman at that time vouching (and upon CYM 1.04. 58 P
/VOUCHSAF'D 1 FR 0.0001 REL FR 1 V 0 P
or | /vouchsaf'd to think he had partners. ANT 1.04. 8
VOUCHSAF'D 1 FR 0.0001 REL FR 1 V 0 P
but that you have vouchsaf'd, | with your WT 5.03. 4
VOUCHSAFE *(also voutsafe)*
VOUCHSAFE 52 FR 0.0058 REL FR 46 V 6 P
vouchsafe my pray'r | may know if you remain TMP 1.02.423
vouchsafe me yet your picture for my love, | the TGV 4.02.120
vouchsafe me, for my meed, but one fair look: 5.04. 23
shall i vouchsafe your worship a word or two? WIV 2.02. 40 P
fair woman, and i'll vouchsafe thee the hearing. 2.02. 42 P
vouchsafe a word, young sister, but one word. MM 3.01.151
most mighty duke, vouchsafe me speak a word: ERR 5.01.283
vouchsafe to take the pains | to go with us into 5.01.394
you thither, my lord, if you'll vouchsafe me. ADO 3.02. 4 P
vouchsafe to read the purpose of my coming, LLL 2.01.109
heavenly spirits, vouchsafe | not to behold" — 5.02.166
vouchsafe to show the sunshine of your face, 5.02.201
vouchsafe, bright moon, and these thy stars, to 5.02.205
then in our measure do but vouchsafe one change. 5.02.209
the music plays, vouchsafe some motion to it. 5.02.216
our ears vouchsafe it. 5.02.217
will you vouchsafe with me to change a word? 5.02.238
that she vouchsafe me audience for one word. 5.02.313
vouchsafe it then. 5.02.344
that you vouchsafe | in your rich wisdom to 5.02.731
sweet majesty, vouchsafe me — 5.02.879 P
behold, the french amaz'd vouchsafe a parle, JN 2.01.226
vouchsafe awhile to stay, | and i shall show you 2.01.416
do | what you in wisdom still vouchsafe to say. 2.01.523
our pray'rs come in, | if thou vouchsafe them. 3.01.294
king, | if you vouchsafe me hearing and respect. 1H4 4.03. 31
vouchsafe to those that have not read the story, H5 5.pr. 1
will you vouchsafe to teach a soldier terms, 5.02. 99
lord, thou wouldst vouchsafe | to visit her poor 1H6 2.02. 40
vouchsafe | to give me hearing what i shall 3.01. 27
lady, vouchsafe to listen what i say. 5.03.103
that lady margaret do vouchsafe to come | to 5.05. 89
as to vouchsafe one glance unto the ground. 2H6 1.02. 16
if thou vouchsafe to grant | that virtuous lady 3H6 3.03. 55
vouchsafe, at our request, to stand aside, 3.03.110
if king lewis vouchsafe to furnish us | with 3.03.203
vouchsafe, divine perfection of a woman, | of R3 1.02. 75
vouchsafe, defus'd infection of /a man, | of 1.02. 78
vouchsafe to wear this ring. 1.02.201
if your back | cannot vouchsafe this burthen, H8 2.03. 43
vouchsafe to speak my thanks and my obedience, 2.03. 71
my lord, will you vouchsafe me a word? TRO 3.01. 59 P
vouchsafe my labor, and long live your lordship! TIM 1.01.152
vouchsafe me a word, it does concern you near. 1.02.177
vouchsafe good morrow from a feeble tongue. JC 2.01.313
if brutus will vouchsafe that antony | may 3.01.130
if your lordship would vouchsafe the answer. HAM 5.02.169 P
knees i beg | that you'll vouchsafe me raiment, LR 2.04.156
o, vouchsafe, | with that thy rare green eye — TNK 5.01.143
"vouchsafe, thou wonder, to alight thy steed, VEN 13
next, vouchsafe t' afford | (if ever, love, thy LUC 1305
not once vouchsafe to hide my will in thine? SON 135. 6
VOUCHSAFED 2 FR 0.0002 REL FR 0 V 2 P
to your own most pregnant and vouchsafed ear. TN 3.01. 89 P
"odors," "pregnant," and "vouchsafed"; 3.01. 90 P
VOUCHSAFES 1 FR 0.0001 REL FR 0 V 1 P
her with musics, but she vouchsafes no notice. CYM 2.03. 40 P
VOUCHSAFING 1 FR 0.0001 REL FR 1 V 0 P
this, | that thou, vouchsafing here to visit me, ANT 5.02.160
VOUDRAIS 1 FR 0.0001 REL FR 0 V 1 P
je ne voudrais prononcer ces mots devant les H5 3.04. 55 P
VOUS 22 FR 0.0024 REL FR 1 V 21 P
dieu vous garde, monsieur. TN 3.01. 71 P
et vous aussi; votre serviteur. 3.01. 72 P
de tous les mots que vous m'avez appris des a H5 3.04. 26 P
vous prononcez les mots aussi droit que les 3.04. 37 P
n'avez vous deja oublie ce que je vous ai 3.04. 42 P
vous deja oublie ce que je vous ai enseigne? 3.04. 42 P
non, je reciterai a vous promptement: 3.04. 44 P
qui vous la? 4.01. 35
je pense que vous etes le gentilhomme de bonne 4.04. 2 P
il me commande a vous dire que vous faites vous 4.04. 34 P
commande a vous dire que vous faites vous pret; 4.04. 34 P
commande a vous dire que vous faites vous pret; 4.04. 34 P
o, je vous supplie, pour l'amour de dieu, me 4.04. 40 P
ma vie, et je vous donnerai deux cents ecus. 4.04. 42 P
pour les ecus que vous /lui promettez, il est 4.04. 51 P
il est content a vous donner la liberte, le 4.04. 52 P
sur mes genoux /je vous donne mille 4.04. 54 P
et quand vous avez le possession de moi — let 5.02.182 P
donc votre est france et vous etes mienne. 5.02.184 P
sauf votre honneur, le francois que vous parlez, 5.02.188 P
ma foi, je ne veux point que vous abaissez votre 5.02.254 P
excusez–moi, je vous supplie, mon tres puissant 5.02.256 P
VOUTSAFE *(also vouchsafe)*
VOUTSAFE 4 FR 0.0004 REL FR 2 V 2 P
i beseech you now, will you voutsafe me, look H5 3.02. 95 P
that you voutsafe your rest here in our court HAM 2.02. 13
good my lord, voutsafe me a word with you. 3.02.296 P
o, then voutsafe me but this loving thought: SON 32. 9
/VOW* 2 FR 0.0002 REL FR 2 V 0 P
/and /their /vow /is /made | /to /ransack /troy, TRO pr 7
thou hast sought to make us break our /vow — LR 1.01.168
VOW* 89 FR 0.0100 REL FR 78 V 11 P
more abstenious, | or else good night your vow! TMP 4.01. 54
or else, by jove i vow, | i should have TGV 4.04.203
her reputation, her marriage vow, and a thousand WIV 2.02.249 P
by the vow of mine order i warrant you, if my MM 4.02.169 P
my poor self, | i am combined by a sacred vow, 4.03.144
when thou unurg'd wouldst vow | that never words ERR 2.02.113
and break it with a deep–divorcing vow? 2.02.138
doth noise abroad, navarre hath made a vow, LLL 2.01. 22
my vow was earthly, thou a heavenly love; 4.03. 64
vow, alack, for youth unmeet, | youth so apt to 4.03.111
hold it sin | to break the vow i am engaged in. 4.03.176
eyes, | and study too, the causer of your vow. 4.03.307
o, we have made a vow to study, lords, | and in 4.03.315
and in that vow we have forsworn our books. 4.03.316
this field shall hold me, and so hold your vow: 5.02.345
to death, or to a vow of single life. MND 1.01.121
look when i vow, i weep; 3.02.124
to vow, and swear, and superpraise my parts, 3.02.153
i have toward heaven breath'd a secret vow | to MV 3.04. 27
she made me vow | that i should neither sell, 4.01.442
and here i firmly vow | never to woo her more, SHR 4.02. 28
henceforth i vow it shall be so for me. 4.05. 15
she thought, i dare vow for her, they touch'd AWW 1.03.109 P
with sainted vow my faults to have amended. 3.04. 7
success will be, my lord, but the attempt i vow. 3.06. 81 P
but the plain single vow that is vow'd true. 4.02. 22
for i by vow am so embodied yours, | that she 5.03.173
therefore draw, for the supportance of his vow. TN 3.04.300 P
this exercise, so long | i daily vow to use it. WT 3.02.242
but it does fulfill my vow; 4.04.486
o, let thy vow | first made to heaven, first be JN 3.01.265
breathless excellence | the incense of a vow, a 4.03. 67
excellence | the incense of a vow, a holy vow, 4.03. 67
son, | now by /my sceptre's awe i make a vow, R2 1.01.118
two men | that vow a long and weary pilgrimage. 1.03. 49
ere break the smallest parcel of this vow. 1H4 3.02.159
and when he heard him swear and vow to god | he 4.03. 60
steps me a little higher than his vow | made to 4.03. 75
your grace, that he keep his vow and his oath. H5 4.07.139 P
then keep thy vow, sirrah, when thou meet'st the 4.07.144 P
now have i paid my vow unto his soul; 1H6 2.02. 7
vow, burgundy, by honor of thy house, | prick'd 3.02. 77
he did vow upon his knees he would be even with 2H6 1.03.199 P
what instance gives lord warwick for his vow? 3.02.159
who can be bound by any solemn vow | to do a 5.01.184
i vow by heaven these eyes shall never close. 3H6 1.01. 24
fault, | nor wittingly have i infring'd my vow. 2.02. 8
here on my knee i vow to god above | i'll never 2.03. 29
and in this vow do chain my soul to thine! 2.03. 34

and here, to pledge my vow, i give my hand. 3.03.250
give me assurance with some friendly vow, | that 4.01.141
for he hath made a solemn vow | never to lie and 4.03. 4
to the name of god | didst break that vow, and R3 1.04.206
is this thy vow unto my sickly heart. 2.01. 42
your mother lives a witness to his vow — | and 3.07.180
but our undertakings, when we vow to weep seas, TRO 3.02. 77 P
honor or go or stay, | my major vow lies here; 5.01. 44
it is the purpose that makes strong the vow, 5.03. 23
shall i be tempted to infringe my vow | in the COR 5.03. 20
do, and vow to heaven and to his highness | that TIT 1.01.474
upon her nuptial vow, her loyalty, | and with 2.03.125
for by my fathers' reverent tomb i vow | they 2.03.296
the vow is made. 3.01.279
therefore thou shalt vow | by that same god, 5.01. 81
and in that vow | do i live dead that live to ROM 1.01.223
lady, by yonder blessed moon i vow, | that tips 2.02.107
exchange of thy love's faithful vow for mine. 2.02.127
we met, we woo'd, and made exchange of vow, 2.03. 62
and that great vow | which did incorporate and JC 2.01.272
that it went hand in hand even with the vow | i HAM 1.05. 49
makes vow before his uncle never more | to give 2.02. 70
if sanctimony and a frail vow betwixt an erring OTH 1.03.355 P
if i do vow a friendship, i'll perform it | to 3.03. 21
in the due reverence of a sacred vow | i here 3.03.461
that remains loyal to his vow, and your CYM 3.02. 46 P
if your vow stand, shall curse me and my beauty, TNK 3.06.247
and vow that lover never yet made sigh | truer 5.01.125
decay, | the impious breach of holy wedlock vow; LUC 809
that he may vow, in that sad hour of mine, 1179
and kiss'd the fatal knife, to end his vow; 1843
and that deep vow which brutus made before, | he 1847
my vow was earthly, thou a heavenly love; PP 3. 7
my vow was breath, and breath a vapor is, | then 3. 9
/exhal'st this vapor vow, in thee it is: 3.11
vow, alack, for youth unmeet, | youth, so apt to 16.13
for thee, against myself i'll vow debate, | for SON 89.13
this i do vow and this shall ever be: 123.13
till now did ne'er invite, nor never vow. LC 182
vow, bond, nor space, | in thee hath neither 264

VOW'D 17 FR 0.0019 REL FR 15 V 2 P
when you have vow'd, you must not speak with men MM 1.04. 10
this is the hand which, with a vow'd contract, 5.01.209
and where that you have vow'd to study, lords, LLL 4.03.292
to be | of heavenly oaths, vow'd with integrity. 5.02.356
i have vow'd to jaquenetta to hold the plough 5.02.883 P
but the plain single vow that is vow'd true. AWW 4.02. 22
thine, as he vow'd to thee in thine ear, 4.03.231 P
is most divinely vow'd upon the right | of him JN 2.01.237
i vow'd, base knight, when i did meet thee next, 1H6 4.01. 14
a triumph, having vow'd | to try his strength, 5.05. 31
and you both have vow'd revenge | on him, his 3H6 1.01. 55
kiss, | as if they vow'd some league inviolable. 2.01. 30
that love which thou hast vow'd to cherish; ROM 3.03.129
or vow'd her maidenhead | to a young handsome TNK 2.04. 13
beauty, | thus let me seal my vow'd faith. 2.05. 39
take to thy grace | me thy vow'd soldier, who do 5.01. 95
many nymphs that vow'd chaste life to keep SON 154. 3

VOW'DST 1 FR 0.0001 REL FR 1 V 0 P
upon whose grave thou vow'dst pure chastity. TGV 4.03. 21

VOWED 6 FR 0.0006 REL FR 6 V 0 P
never faith could hold, if not to beauty vowed! LLL 4.02.106
do him good, | so mighty are his vowed enemies. 2H6 3.01.220
but both of you were vowed duke humphrey's foes, 3.02.182
my lord and sovereign and thy vowed friend, | i 3H6 3.03. 50
this by the eye of cynthia hath she vowed, | and PER 2.05. 11
never faith could hold, if not to beauty vowed: PP 5. 2

VOWEL 1 FR 0.0001 REL FR 1 V 0 P
and that bare vowel i shall poison more | than ROM 3.02. 46

VOWELS 1 FR 0.0001 REL FR 0 V 1 P
the last of the five vowels, if "you" repeat LLL 5.01. 53 P

VOW-FELLOWS 1 FR 0.0001 REL FR 1 V 0 P
that are vow-fellows with this virtuous duke? LLL 2.01. 38

VOWING 3 FR 0.0003 REL FR 2 V 1 P
vowing more than the perfection of ten, and TRO 3.02. 86 P
is arming, weeping, cursing, vowing vengeance. 5.05. 31
in vowing new hate after new love bearing. SON 152. 4

/VOWS 1 FR 0.0001 REL FR 1 V 0 P
/god /keep /all /vows /unbroke /are /made /to R2 4.01.215

VOWS 71 FR 0.0080 REL FR 67 V 4 P
whose vows are, that no bed-right shall be paid TMP 4.01. 96
unheedful vows may heedfully be broken, | and he TGV 2.06. 11
should be full-fraught with serviceable vows. 3.02. 70
when to her beauty i commend my vows, | she bids 4.02. 9
that hast deceiv'd so many with thy vows? 4.02. 98
swallow'd his vows whole, pretending in her MM 3.01.226 P
wife as strongly | as words could make up vows; 5.01.228
he cries for you, and vows, if he can take you, ERR 5.01.182
vows for thee broke deserve not punishment. LLL 4.03. 61
vows are but breath, and breath a vapor is; 4.03. 66
by all the vows that ever men have broke | (in MND 1.01.175
and vows so born, | in their nativity all truth 3.02.124
these vows are hermia's. 3.02.130
your vows to her and me, put in two scales, 3.02.132
the sisters' vows, the hours that we have spent, 3.02.199
stealing her soul with many vows of faith, | and MV 5.01. 19
of violated vows | 'twixt the souls of friend AYL 3.02.133
me, | for i am falser than vows made in wine. 3.05. 73
blessing upon your vows, and in your bed | find AWW 2.03. 91
i prithee do not strive against my vows. 4.02. 14
a widower, his vows are forfeited to me, and my 5.03.142 P
you give away heaven's vows, and those are mine; 5.03.171
for still we prove | much in our vows, but TN 2.04.118
even for the vows | we made each other but so 5.01.214
you put me off with limber vows; WT 1.02. 47
this is a match, | and made between 's by vows. 5.03.138
with all religious strength of sacred vows. JN 3.01.229
it is religion that doth make vows kept, | but 3.01.279
therefore thy later vows, against thy first, 3.01.288
thy humble servant vows obedience | and humble 1H6 3.01.166
my vows are equal partners with thy vows. 3.02. 85
my vows are equal partners with thy vows. 3.02. 85
for your captain is brave, and vows reformation. 2H6 4.02. 65 P
and vows to crown himself in westminster. 4.04. 31
to entertain my vows of thanks and praise! 4.09. 14
lord clifford vows to fight in thy defense. 3H6 1.01.160
cuts off the ceremonious vows of love | and R3 5.03. 98
my vows and prayers | yet are the king's; H8 2.01. 88
words, vows, gifts, tears, and love's full TRO 1.02.282
with truant vows to her own lips he loves, | and 1.03.270
strangles our dear vows | even in the birth of 4.04. 37
if souls guide vows, if vows be sanctimonies, 5.02.139
if souls guide vows, if vows be sanctimonies, 5.02.139
the gods are deaf to hot and peevish vows; 5.03. 16
vow, | but vows to every purpose must not hold; 5.03. 24
by th' vows | we have made to endure friends, COR 1.06. 57
and vows revenge as spacious as between | the 4.06. 68
to breathe such vows as lovers use to swear, ROM 2.pr. 10
slink all away, leave their false vows with him, TIM 4.02. 11
by all your vows of love, and that great vow JC 2.01.272
lord, | with almost all the holy vows of heaven. HAM 1.03.114
how prodigal the soul | lends the tongue vows. 1.03.117
do not believe his vows, for they are brokers, 1.03.127
that suck'd the honey of his /music vows, | now 3.01.156
makes marriage vows | as false as dicers' oaths, 3.04. 44
vows, to the blackest devil! 4.05.132
"let our reciprocal vows be rememb'red. LR 4.06.262 P
to be entangled with those mouth-made vows, ANT 1.03. 30
the vows of women | of no more bondage be to CYM 2.04.110
upon the love and truth and vows which i | have 3.02. 12
men's vows are women's traitors. 3.04. 54
your goodness teach me to't | without your vows. PER 3.03. 27
if such vows | stand for express will, all the TNK 3.06.228
dismiss your vows, your feigned tears, your VEN 425
that now he vows a league, and now invasion. LUC 287
vows for thee broke deserve not punishment. PP 3. 4
million'd accidents | creep in 'twixt vows, and SON 115. 6
for all my vows are oaths but to misuse thee, 152. 7
knew vows were ever brokers to defiling, LC 173
pity | and be not of my holy vows afraid. 179
all vows and consecrations giving place. 263

VOX 1 FR 0.0001 REL FR 0 V 1 P
have it as it ought to be, you must allow vox. TN 5.01.296 P

VOYAGE *(also viage)*

VOYAGE 22 FR 0.0024 REL FR 12 V 10 P
in one voyage | did claribel her husband find at TMP 5.01.208
and, in losing the flood, lose thy voyage, and, TGV 2.03. 42 P
and, in losing thy voyage, lose thy master, and, 2.03. 43 P
lose the tide, and the voyage, and the master, 2.03. 50 P
if he should intend this voyage toward my wife, WIV 2.01.182 P
to persia, and want guilders for my voyage: ERR 4.01. 4
now that will make a voyage with him to the ADO 1.01. 82 P
as from a voyage, rich with merchandise. MND 2.01.134
dry as the remainder biscuit | after a voyage, AYL 2.07. 40
for thy loving voyage | is but for two months 5.04.191
my determinate voyage is mere extravagancy. TN 2.01. 11 P
it that always makes a good voyage of nothing. 2.04. 78 P
i mean, she is the list of my voyage. 3.01. 77 P
as might have drawn one to a longer voyage) 3.03. 7
i'll make a voyage to the holy land, | to wash R2 5.06. 49
have got by the late voyage is but merely | a H8 1.03. 6
doth sustain | in life's uncertain voyage, i TIM 5.01.202
all the voyage of their life | is bound in JC 4.03.220
as /checking at his voyage, and that he means HAM 4.07. 62
if you make your voyage upon her and give me CYM 1.04.158 P
he will repent the breadth of his great voyage, PER 4.01. 36
she would serve after a long voyage at sea. 4.06. 44 P

VOYAGES 2 FR 0.0002 REL FR 2 V 0 P
increas'd | by prosperous voyages i often made ERR 1.01. 40
like fragments in hard voyages, became | the CYM 5.03. 44

VRAIMENT 2 FR 0.0002 REL FR 0 V 2 P
oui, vraiment, sauf votre grace, ainsi dit-il. H5 5.02.112 P
oui, vraiment. 5.02.267 P

VULCAN 3 FR 0.0003 REL FR 2 V 1 P
a good hare-finder and vulcan a rare carpenter? ADO 1.01.185 P
as black as vulcan in the smoke of war. TN 5.01. 53
of parallels, as like as vulcan and his wife; TRO 1.03.168

VULCAN'S 3 FR 0.0003 REL FR 3 V 0 P
were it a casque compos'd by vulcan's skill, TRO 5.02.170
better than he have worn vulcan's badge. TIT 2.01. 89
imaginations are as foul | as vulcan's stithy. HAM 3.02. 84

/VULGAR 1 FR 0.0001 REL FR 1 V 0 P
/he /that /buildeth /on /the /vulgar /heart. 2H4 1.03. 90

VULGAR 23 FR 0.0026 REL FR 19 V 4 P
the day, | a vulgar comment will be made of it; ERR 3.01.100
which the base vulgar do call three. LLL 1.02. 48 P
which to annothanize in the vulgar — o base and 4.01. 68 P
in the vulgar — o base and obscure vulgar! 4.01. 69 P
troth, most sweet jests, most incony vulgar wit! 4.01.142
abandon — which is in the vulgar leave — the AYL 5.01. 48 P
for 'tis a vulgar proof | that very oft we pity TN 3.01.124
leave them as naked as the vulgar air. JN 2.01.387
of men, | so stale and cheap to vulgar company, 1H4 3.02. 41
so do our vulgar drench their peasant limbs | in H5 4.07. 77
talk like the vulgar sort of market men | that 1H6 3.02. 4
pole | than stand uncover'd to the vulgar groom. 2H6 4.01.128
five tribunes to defend their vulgar wisdoms, COR 1.01.215
throngs, and puff | to win a vulgar station; 2.01.215
and is no less apparent | to th' vulgar eye, 4.07. 21
and drive away the vulgar from the streets; JC 1.01. 70
common | as any the most vulgar thing to sense, HAM 1.02. 99
be thou familiar, but by no means vulgar: 1.03. 61
most sure and vulgar; LR 4.06.210
hours, | unregist'red in vulgar fame, you have ANT 3.13.119
excellent | for every vulgar paper to rehearse? SON 38. 4
care, | art left the prey of every vulgar thief. 48. 8
which vulgar scandal stamp'd upon my brow, | for 112. 2

VULGARLY 1 FR 0.0001 REL FR 1 V 0 P
nobleman, | so vulgarly and personally accus'd, MM 5.01.160

VULGARS 1 FR 0.0001 REL FR 1 V 0 P
bad as those | that vulgars give bold'st titles; WT 2.01. 94

VULGO 1 FR 0.0001 REL FR 0 V 1 P
castiliano vulgo! TN 1.03. 43 P

VULNERABLE 1 FR 0.0001 REL FR 1 V 0 P
let fall thy blade on vulnerable crests, | i MAC 5.08. 11

VULTUR 1 FR 0.0001 REL FR 1 V 0 P
whose vultur thought doth pitch the price so VEN 551

VULTURE 5 FR 0.0005 REL FR 5 V 0 P
while the vulture of sedition | feeds in the 1H6 4.03. 47
to ease the gnawing vulture of thy mind, | by TIT 5.02. 31
be | that vulture in you to devour so many | as MAC 4.03. 74
tied | sharp-tooth'd unkindness, like a vulture, LR 2.04.135
her sad behavior feeds his vulture folly, | a LUC 556

VULTURES 2 FR 0.0002 REL FR 2 V 0 P
let vultures gripe thy guts! WIV 1.03. 85
let vultures vile seize on his lungs also! 2H4 5.03.139

VURTHER *(also further)*

VURTHER 1 FR 0.0001 REL FR 0 V 1 P
chill not let go, zir, without vurther /cagion. LR 4.06.235 P

W' *(also we)*

W' 2 FR 0.0002 REL FR 2 V 0 P
we fear, | w' have frighted with our trumpets; H8 ep 4
all the expected good w' are like to hear | for ep 8

WAD *(also would)*

WAD 1 FR 0.0001 REL FR 0 V 1 P
i wad full fain heard some question 'tween you H5 3.02.118 P

WADDLED 1 FR 0.0001 REL FR 1 V 0 P
she could have run and waddled all about; ROM 1.03. 37

WADE 3 FR 0.0003 REL FR 3 V 0 P
wade to the market-place in frenchmen's blood, JN 2.01. 42
and make us wade even in our kinred's blood: R2 1.03.138
stepp'd in so far that, should i wade no more, MAC 3.04.136

WADED 2 FR 0.0002 REL FR 0 V 2 P
how she waded through the dirt to pluck him off SHR 4.01. 78 P
leave of them, for their joy waded in tears. WT 5.02. 46 P

WADG'D *(also wedg'd)*

WADG'D 1 FR 0.0001 REL FR 0 V 1 P
'tis strongly wadg'd up in a blockhead; COR 2.03. 28 P

WAFER-CAKES 1 FR 0.0001 REL FR 1 V 0 P
oaths are straws, men's faiths are wafer-cakes, H5 2.03. 51

WAFT* 6 FR 0.0006 REL FR 6 V 0 P
and waft her love | to come again to carthage. MV 5.01. 11
than now the english bottoms have waft o'er JN 2.01. 73
i charge thee waft me safely cross the channel. 2H6 4.01.115
come, suffolk, i must waft thee to thy death. 4.01.116
shall waft them over with our royal fleet. 3H6 3.03.253
away with her, and waft her hence to france. 5.07. 41

WAFTAGE 2 FR 0.0002 REL FR 2 V 0 P
a ship you sent me to, to hire waftage. ERR 4.01. 95
upon the stygian banks | staying for waftage. TRO 3.02. 10

WAFTER 1 FR 0.0001 REL FR 1 V 0 P
but with an angry wafter of your hand | gave JC 2.01.246

WAFTING 1 FR 0.0001 REL FR 1 V 0 P
wafting his eyes to th' contrary and falling | a WT 1.02.372

WAFTS 2 FR 0.0002 REL FR 1 V 1 P
but soft, who wafts us yonder? ERR 2.02.109 P
whom fortune with her ivory hand wafts to her, TIM 1.01. 70

WAFTURE *(see wafter)*

WAG 18 FR 0.0020 REL FR 8 V 10 P
why, wag! TGV 5.04. 86 P
let them wag; WIV 1.03. 7 P
here, boys, here, here! shall we wag? 2.01.230 P
and i will provoke him to't, or let him wag. 2.03. 71 P
let us wag then. 2.03. 97 P
stroke his beard, | and, sorrow wag, cry "hem!" ADO 5.01. 16
making the bold wag by their praises bolder. LLL 5.02.108
to wag their high tops and to make no noise MV 4.01. 76
was not my lord | the verier wag o' th' two? WT 1.02. 66
and i prithee, sweet wag, when thou art a king, 1H4 1.02. 16 P
marry then, sweet wag, when thou art king, let 1.02. 23 P
how now, how now, mad wag? 1.02. 44 P
but i prithee, sweet wag, shall there be gallows 1.02. 59 P
how now, mad wag? 4.02. 50 P
no discerner | durst wag his tongue in censure. H8 1.01. 33
he, that dares most, but wag his finger at thee. 5.02.166
that thou dar'st wag thy tongue | in noise so HAM 3.04. 39
theme | until my eyelids will no longer wag. 5.01.267

WAG'D 3 FR 0.0003 REL FR 3 V 0 P
and | he wag'd me with his countenance as if | i COR 5.06. 39
but he hath wag'd | new wars 'gainst pompey; ANT 3.04. 3
his taints and honors | wag'd equal with him. 5.01. 31

WAGE 7 FR 0.0008 REL FR 6 V 1 P
the aweless lion could not wage the fight, | nor JN 1.01.266
weak | to wage an instant trial with the king. 1H4 4.04. 20
but as /a pawn | to wage against thine enemies, LR 1.01.156
choose | to wage against the enmity o' th' air, 2.04.209
and gain | to wake and wage a danger profitless. OTH 1.03. 30
ay, and to wage this battle at pharsalia, ANT 3.07. 31
i will wage against your gold, gold to it. CYM 1.04.132 P

WAGER 20 FR 0.0022 REL FR 16 V 4 P
of he or adrian, for a good wager, first begins TMP 2.01. 28 P
done. the wager? 2.01. 32 P
i'll hold thee any wager, | when we are both MV 3.04. 62
match, | and on the wager lay two earthly women, 3.05. 80
shall win the wager which we will propose. SHR 5.02. 69
content. what's the wager? 5.02. 70
the wager thou hast won, and i will add | unto 5.02.112
nay, i will win my wager better yet, | and show 5.02.116
'twas i won the wager, though you hit the white, 5.02.186
yonder comes news: a wager they have met. COR 1.04. 1
in fine together, | and wager o'er your heads. HAM 4.07.134
we'll make a solemn wager on your cunnings — 4.07.155
you that 'a has laid a great wager on your head. 5.02.102 P
and will this brother's wager frankly play. 5.02.253
cousin hamlet, | you know the wager? 5.02.260
i durst, my lord, to wager she is honest; OTH 4.02. 12
but i make my wager rather against your CYM 1.04.110 P
th' arabian bird, and i | have lost the wager. 1.06. 18
chamber nothing saves | the wager you have laid. 2.04. 95
we have a maid in meteline, i durst wager, PER 5.01. 43

WAGER'D 3 FR 0.0003 REL FR 2 V 1 P
sir, hath wager'd with him six barbary horses, HAM 5.02.147 P
'twas merry when | you wager'd on your angling; ANT 2.05. 16
and wager'd with him | pieces of gold 'gainst CYM 5.05.182

WAGERS 2 FR 0.0002 REL FR 1 V 1 P
fetch my gold and have our two wagers recorded. CYM 1.04.167 P
i have heard of riding wagers, | where horses 3.02. 71

WAGES 12 FR 0.0013 REL FR 7 V 5 P
thou for wages followest thy master, thy master TGV 1.01. 91 P
master, thy master for wages follows not thee: 1.01. 91 P
she is her master's maid, and serves for wages. 3.01.272 P
and ere we have thy youthful wages spent, AYL 2.03. 67
and we will mend thy wages. 2.04. 94
our praises are our wages. WT 1.02. 94
sir, do you mean to stop any of william's wages, 2H4 5.01. 24 P
that they may have their wages duly paid 'em, H8 4.02.150
timon's money | has paid his men their wages. TIM 3.02. 70
friends shall taste | the wages of their virtue, LR 5.03.304
hast done, | home art gone, and ta'en thy wages. CYM 4.02.261
nor the commodity wages not with the danger; PER 4.02. 31 P

WAGG'D 1 FR 0.0001 REL FR 1 V 0 P
wagg'd up and down, and from his lips did fly LUC 1406

WAGGING 5 FR 0.0005 REL FR 4 V 1 P
side, | tremble and start at wagging of a straw; R3 3.05. 7
and think with wagging of your tongue to win me; H8 5.02.162
it is not worth the wagging of your beards, and COR 2.01. 87 P
below the violet, | not wagging his sweet head; CYM 4.02.173
arcite, | even in the wagging of a wanton leg, TNK 2.02. 15
WAGGISH 2 FR 0.0002 REL FR 2 V 0 P
as waggish boys in game themselves forswear, MND 1.01.240
woman it pretty self) into a waggish courage, CYM 3.04.157
WAGGLING 1 FR 0.0001 REL FR 0 V 1 P
i know you by the waggling of your head. ADO 2.01.115 P
WAGGON 3 FR 0.0003 REL FR 3 V 0 P
our waggon is prepar'd, and time revives us. AWW 4.04. 34
frighted, thou let'st fall | from dis's waggon! WT 4.04.118
jet, | to hale thy vengeful waggon swift away, TIT 5.02. 51
WAGGONER 3 FR 0.0003 REL FR 3 V 0 P
and then i'll come and be thy waggoner, | and TIT 5.02. 48
film, | her waggoner a small grey–coated gnat, ROM 1.04. 67
such a waggoner | as phaeton would whip you to 3.02. 2
WAGGON–SPOKES 1 FR 0.0001 REL FR 1 V 0 P
her waggon–spokes made of long spinners' legs, ROM 1.04. 62
WAGGON–WHEEL 1 FR 0.0001 REL FR 1 V 0 P
and by thy waggon–wheel | trot like a servile TIT 5.02. 54
WAGS 4 FR 0.0004 REL FR 3 V 1 P
thus we may see," quoth he, "how the world wags. AYL 2.07. 23
of our youth, i must confess, are wags too. 2H4 1.02.177 P
'tis merry in hall when beards wags all, | and 5.03. 34
for well i wot the empress never wags | but in TIT 5.02. 87
WAGTAIL 1 FR 0.0001 REL FR 0 V 1 P
spare my grey beard, you wagtail? LR 2.02. 67 P
/WAIL 1 FR 0.0001 REL FR 1 V 0 P
/that /not /only /giv'st | /me /cause /to /wail, R2 4.01.301
WAIL 24 FR 0.0027 REL FR 24 V 0 P
since to wail friends lost | is not by much so LLL 5.02.749
shapes of grief, more than himself, to wail, R2 2.02. 22
my lord, wise men ne'er sit and wail their woes, 3.02.178
woes, | but presently prevent the ways to wail; 3.02.179
and none but women left to wail the dead. 1H6 1.01. 51
and can do nought but wail her darling's loss, 2H6 3.01.216
lords, wise men ne'er sit and wail their loss, 3H6 5.04. 1
mayst thou live to wail thy children's death, R3 1.03.203
it were lost sorrow to wail one that's lost. 2.02. 11
who shall hinder me to wail and weep, | to chide 2.02. 34
cause | to wail the dimming of our shining star; 2.02.102
may | misconster us in him and wail his death. 3.05. 61
ungovern'd youth, to wail it /in their age; 4.04.392
old barren plants, to wail it with their age. 4.04.394
women | 'tis fond to wail inevitable strokes, COR 4.01. 26
that hath ta'en her hence to make me wail, ROM 4.05. 31
but wail his fall | who i myself struck down. MAC 3.01.121
what i believe, i'll wail, | what know, believe; 4.03. 8
trundle–tail, | tom will make him weep and wail, LR 3.06. 71
to wail his death who lives and must not die VEN 1017
who buys a minute's mirth to wail a week? LUC 213
have time to wail th' abusing of his time. 994
the world will wail thee like a makeless wife, SON 9. 4
and with old woes new wail my dear time's waste; 30. 4
WAIL'D 3 FR 0.0003 REL FR 3 V 0 P
no evil lost is wail'd when it is gone. ERR 4.02. 24
what willingly he did confound he wail'd, ANT 3.02. 58
mine, | and only must be wail'd by collatine." LUC 1799
WAILFUL 1 FR 0.0001 REL FR 1 V 0 P
lime to tangle her desires | by wailful sonnets, TGV 3.02. 69
WAILING 8 FR 0.0009 REL FR 7 V 1 P
my mother weeping, my father wailing, my sister TGV 2.03. 7 P
away with these disgraceful wailing robes! 1H6 1.01. 86
wailing our losses, whiles the foe doth rage, 3H6 2.03. 26
but none can help our harms by wailing them. R3 2.02.103
weeping and wailing over tybalt's corse. ROM 3.02.128
she, marking them, begins a wailing note, | and VEN 835
an humble gait, calm looks, eyes wailing still, LUC 1508
that she hath thee, is of my wailing chief, | a SON 42. 3
WAILS 3 FR 0.0003 REL FR 3 V 0 P
for joyful mother, one that wails the name; R3 4.04. 99
had she no lover there | that wails her absence? TRO 4.05.289
like to a bankrout beggar wails his case: LUC 711
WAIN* *(also wean)*
WAIN* 2 FR 0.0002 REL FR 1 V 1 P
charles' wain is over the new chimney, and yet 1H4 2.01. 2 P
and i the rather wain me from despair | for love 3H6 4.04. 17
WAIN–ROPES 1 FR 0.0001 REL FR 0 V 1 P
i think oxen and wain–ropes cannot hale them TN 3.02. 59 P
WAINSCOT 1 FR 0.0001 REL FR 0 V 1 P
but join you together as they join wainscot; AYL 3.03. 87 P
WAIST 15 FR 0.0017 REL FR 9 V 6 P
now in the waist, the deck, in every cabin, | i TMP 1.02.197
indeed i am in the waist two yards about; WIV 1.03. 42 P
his neck will come to your waist — a cord, sir. MM 3.02. 40 P
as a german from the waist downward, all slops, ADO 3.02. 35 P
and your waist, mistress, were as slender as my LLL 4.01. 49
maids' girdles for your waist should be fit. 4.01. 50
a gait, a state, a brow, a breast, a waist, | a 4.03.183
stones, | that as a waist doth girdle you about, JN 2.01.217
hal, i was not an eagle's talent in the waist, i 1H4 2.04.330 P
my means were greater and my waist /slenderer. 2H4 1.02.143 P
who now is girdled with a waist of iron | and 1H6 4.03. 20
and buckle in a waist most fathomless | with TRO 2.02. 30
then you live about her waist, or in the middle HAM 2.02.232 P
down from the waist they are centaurs, | though LR 4.06.124
and girdle with embracing flames the waist | of LUC 6
/WAIT 1 FR 0.0001 REL FR 0 V 1 P
/we'll /wait /upon /you. HAM 2.02.266 P
WAIT 67 FR 0.0075 REL FR 54 V 13 P
i wait upon his pleasure. TGV 2.04.117
we'll wait upon your grace till after supper, 3.02. 95
o'ernight | that wait for execution in the morn. 4.02.133
i must wait on myself, must i? WIV 1.01.201 P
i will wait on him, fair mistress anne. 1.01.263 P
you are my man, go wait upon my cousin shallow. 1.01.271 P
i'll wait upon your honor. MM 1.01. 83
i have stomach, and wait for no man's leisure; ADO 1.03. 15 P
we'll wait upon your lordship. 1.03. 75 P
i'll wait upon them, i am ready. 3.05. 56 P
and wait the season, and observe the times, LLL 5.02. 63
dance, | nor never more in russian habit wait. 5.02.401
come wait upon him; MND 3.01.197
more than to us | wait in your royal walks, your 5.01. 31
not i, but my affairs, have made you wait. MV 2.06. 22
wait you on him, i charge you, as becomes, SHR 1.01.233
well, i must wait, | and watch withal, for, but 3.01. 61
in every thing i wait upon his will. AWW 2.04. 54
wait on me home, i'll make sport with thee. 5.03.322 P
and then my soul shall wait on thee to heaven, JN 5.07. 72
spar'd, | shall wait upon your father's funeral. 5.07. 98
thy friends are fled to wait upon thy foes, R2 2.04. 23
yield, | rebuke and dread correction wait on us, 1H4 5.01.111
to be worn in my cap than to wait at my heels. 2H4 1.02. 16 P
wait close, i will not see him. 1.02. 57 P
i must wait upon my good lord here, i thank you, 2.01.184 P
and wait upon him at his table as drawers. 2.02.172 P
i'll wait upon you, and i long to hear it. H5 1.01. 98
in | wonder to wait on treason and on murther; 2.02.110
the maiden cities you talk of may wait on her; 5.02.327 P
heralds, wait on us. 1H6 1.01. 45
where be these warders, that they wait not here? 1.03. 3
we wait upon your grace. R3 1.03.322
we wait upon your grace. 2.01.141
i'll wait upon your lordship. 3.02.112
i'll wait upon your lordship. 3.02.123
the two great cardinals | wait in the presence. H8 3.01. 17
your grace must wait till you be call'd for. 5.02. 7
they would shame to make me | wait else at door, 5.02. 17
wait like a lousy footboy | at chamber–door? 5.02.174
i purpose not to wait on fortune till | these COR 5.03.119
i am not bid to wait upon this bride. TIT 1.01.338
upon her wit doth earthly honor wait, | and 2.01. 10
and gold, | to wait upon this new–made emperess. 2.01. 20
to wait, said i? 2.01. 21
i must hence to wait; ROM 1.03.103 P
wait attendance | till you hear further from me. TIM 1.01.161
lords, keep on, | i'll wait upon you instantly. 2.02. 35
of timon's gift, | for which i wait for money. 3.04. 20
we wait for certain money here, sir. 3.04. 46
come home to me, and i will wait for you. JC 1.02.306
substances | you wait on nature's mischief! MAC 1.05. 50
letting "i dare not" wait upon "i would," | like 1.07. 44
now good digestion wait on appetite, | and 3.04. 37
i pray thee, good horatio, wait upon him. HAM 5.01.293
we'll wait upon your lordship. OTH 3.02. 6
well, my good fellows, wait on me to–night. ANT 4.02. 20
will not wait pinion'd at your master's court, 5.02. 53
or death, | i wait the sharpest blow, antiochus. PER 1.01. 55
for he's no man on whom perfections wait | that, 1.01. 79
evermore attending, | new joy wait on you! 5.03.102
wait well, sir, | upon your mistress. TNK 2.05. 51
respect and reason, wait on wrinkled age! LUC 275
"unruly blasts wait on the tender spring, 869
thy heinous hours wait on them as their pages. 910
i am to wait, though waiting so be hell, | not SON 58.13
for summer and his pleasures wait on thee, | and 97.11
WAITED 7 FR 0.0008 REL FR 7 V 0 P
lo, whilest i waited on my tender lambs, | and 1H6 1.02. 76
how often hast thou waited at my cup, | fed from 2H6 4.01. 56
stood | and duly waited for my coming forth? 4.01. 62
or gild again the noble troops that waited H8 3.02.411
ay, marry, will we, sir, and we'll be waited on. TIT 4.01.122
i am to blame to be thus waited for. JC 2.02.119
it shall be waited on with jealousy, | find VEN 1137
WAITETH 1 FR 0.0001 REL FR 1 V 0 P
o, but impatience waiteth on true sorrow. 3H6 3.03. 42
WAITING 6 FR 0.0006 REL FR 5 V 1 P
see | cold wisdom waiting on superfluous folly. AWW 1.01.105
slaughters a thousand waiting upon that. WT 1.02. 93
with my humor as well as waiting in the court, i 1H4 1.02. 70 P
but when your carters or your waiting vassals R3 2.01.122
ay, | if money were as certain as your waiting, TIM 3.04. 47
i am to wait, though waiting so be hell, | not SON 58.13
WAITING–GENTLEWOMAN 4 FR 0.0004 REL FR 1 V 3 P
my apparel and make him my waiting–gentlewoman? ADO 2.01. 35 P
of margaret, the waiting–gentlewoman to hero. 2.02. 13 P
yet i can read waiting–gentlewoman in the scape. WT 3.03. 73 P
and talk so like a waiting–gentlewoman | of guns 1H4 1.03. 55
//WAITING–WOMEN 1 FR 0.0001 REL FR 0 V 1 P
/possesses /chambermaids /and //waiting–women. LR 4.01. 63 P
WAITING–WOMEN 1 FR 0.0001 REL FR 1 V 0 P
by all diana's waiting–women yond, | and by TRO 5.02. 91
WAITS 12 FR 0.0013 REL FR 11 V 1 P
and sure it waits upon | some god o' th' island. TMP 1.02.389
the wealth i have waits on my consent, and my WIV 3.02. 77 P
when biondello comes, he waits on thee, | but i SHR 1.01.208
which waits upon worn times, hath something WT 5.01.142
and vast confusion waits, | as doth a raven on a JN 4.03.152
when care, mistrust, and treason waits on him. 3H6 2.05. 54
this armed guard | that waits upon your grace? R3 1.01. 43
who waits there? H8 5.02. 4
who waits there? 5.02. 39
and waits upon the judgment, and what judgment HAM 3.04. 70
danger deviseth shifts, wit waits on fear. VEN 690
for greatest scandal waits on greatest state. LUC 1006
WAK'D 20 FR 0.0022 REL FR 16 V 4 P
that, if i then had wak'd after long sleep, TMP 3.02.139
me, that when i wak'd | i cried to dream again. 3.02.142
at my command | have wak'd their sleepers, op'd, 5.01. 49
i am wak'd with it when i sleep, rais'd with it ERR 4.04. 34 P
of unhappiness and wak'd herself with laughing. ADO 2.01.345 P
titania wak'd, and straightway lov'd an ass. MND 3.02. 34
that, when he wak'd, of force she must be ey'd. 3.02. 40
it would seem strange unto him when he wak'd. SHR in.1. 43
or when you wak'd, so wak'd as if you slept. in.2. 80
or when you wak'd, so wak'd as if you slept. in.2. 80
majesty, | it were but necessary you were wak'd, 2H6 3.02.261
trembling, wak'd, and for a season after | could R3 1.04. 61
wak'd by the lark, hath rous'd the ribald crows, TRO 4.02. 9
throat, | and wak'd half dead with nothing. COR 4.05.126
if our father would sleep till i wak'd him, you LR 1.02. 52 P
in the contriving of lust, and wak'd to do it. 3.04. 90 P
to have their balmy slumbers wak'd with strife. OTH 2.03.258
been born a dog | than answer my wak'd wrath! 3.03.363
when i wak'd, i found | this label on my bosom, CYM 5.05.429
what | hath wak'd us from our dream? TNK 5.04. 48
/WAKE 1 FR 0.0001 REL FR 1 V 0 P
o, if i /wake, shall i not be distraught, ROM 4.03. 49
WAKE 54 FR 0.0061 REL FR 47 V 7 P
keep in tunis, | and let sebastian wake." TMP 2.01.260
did'st not wake you? 2.01.312
my horns are his horns, whether i wake or sleep. TGV 1.01. 80 P
he will not wake. MM 4.02. 68
peace, and let the child wake her with crying, ADO 3.03. 70 P
good ursula, wake my cousin beatrice, and desire 3.04. 1 P
gentlemen both, we will not wake your patience. 5.01.102
what thou seest when thou dost wake, | do it for MND 2.02. 27
wake when some vile thing is near. 2.02. 34
when they next wake, all this derision | shall 3.02.370
now, my titania, wake you, my sweet queen. 4.01. 75
go, bid the huntsmen wake them with their horns. 4.01.138
come ho, and wake diana with a hymn, | with MV 5.01. 66
set on you | to wake our peace, which in our R2 1.03.132
making such difference 'twixt wake and sleep 1H4 3.01.216
is well, keep it so, wake not a sleeping wolf. 2H4 1.02.153 P
to wake a wolf is as bad as smell a fox. 1.02.155 P
'twas time, i trow, to wake and leave our beds, 1H6 2.01. 41
watch thou, and wake when others be asleep, | to 2H6 1.01.249
he shall never wake until the great judgment day R3 1.04.103 P
sleep, richmond, sleep in peace and wake in joy. 5.03.150
therefore best | not wake him in his slumber. H8 1.01.122
let's sit down quiet | for fear we wake her; 4.02. 82
and wake him to the answer, think you? TRO 1.03.332
this, i presume, will wake him. 2.02.213
and wake the emperor and his lovely bride, | and TIT 2.02. 4
i do dream, would all my wealth would wake me! 2.04. 13
if i do wake, some planet strike me down, | that 2.04. 14
the dam will wake and if she wind ye once; 4.01. 97
i wake before the time that romeo | come to ROM 4.03. 31
i needs must wake her. 4.05. 9
i must needs wake you. 4.05. 13
within this three hours will fair juliet wake. 5.02. 25
i will not do thee so much wrong to wake thee. JC 4.03.270
that they did wake each other. MAC 2.02. 21
wake duncan with thy knocking! 2.02. 71
aid | to wake northumberland and warlike siward, 3.06. 31
the king doth wake to–night and takes his rouse, HAM 1.04. 8
tribe of fops, | got 'tween asleep and wake? LR 1.02. 15
"sleep till i wake him, you should enjoy half 1.02. 55 P
of a corn cry woe, | and turn his sleep to wake. 3.02. 34
please your majesty | that we may wake the king? 4.07. 17
and gain | to wake and wage a danger profitless. OTH 1.03. 30
hark, the drums | demurely wake the sleepers. ANT 4.09. 30
speak softly, wake her not. 5.02.320
i'll wake mine eyeballs /out first. CYM 3.04.101
even when i wake, it is | without me, as within 4.02.306
dream as i have done, | wake, and find nothing. 5.04.129
wake, my mistress! 5.05.233
will he not wake, and in a desp'rate rage | post LUC 219
to wake the morn and sentinel the night, | to 942
if thou wake, he cannot sleep; PP 20.52
thee watch i, whilst thou dost wake elsewhere, SON 61.13
for his advantage still did wake and sleep. LC 123
WAKEFIELD 1 FR 0.0001 REL FR 1 V 0 P
after the bloody fray at wakefield fought, 3H6 2.01.107
WAKEN 4 FR 0.0004 REL FR 4 V 0 P
stands, | 'tis to be doubted he would waken him. 3H6 4.03. 19
which here we waken to our country's good, | the R3 3.07.124
ay, | i ask, that i might waken reverence, | and TRO 1.03.227
go waken juliet, go and trim her up, | i'll go ROM 4.04. 25
WAKEN'D 3 FR 0.0003 REL FR 2 V 1 P
because he hath waken'd thy dog that hath lain ROM 3.01. 26 P
may the winds blow till they have waken'd death! OTH 2.01.186
did softly press the rushes ere he waken'd | the CYM 2.02. 13
WAKENED 1 FR 0.0001 REL FR 1 V 0 P
but shoot not at me in your wakened hate: SON 117.12
WAKES 20 FR 0.0022 REL FR 16 V 4 P
and retails his wares | at wakes and wassails, LLL 5.02.318
what angel wakes me from my flow'ry bed? MND 3.01.129
sleep when he wakes? MV 1.01. 85
and brave attendants near him when he wakes, SHR in.1. 40
procure me music ready when he wakes, | to make in.1. 50
him, | and each one to his office when he wakes. in.1. 73
he haunts wakes, fairs, and bear–baitings. WT 4.03.102 P
no, he'll say 'twas done cowardly when he wakes. R3 1.04.102 P
soft, he wakes. 1.04.158 P
drums in his ear, at which he starts and wakes, ROM 1.04. 86
she wakes, and i entreated her come forth | and 5.03.260
and wakes it now to look so green and pale | at MAC 1.07. 37
come, march to wakes and fairs and market towns. LR 3.06. 74 P
he wakes, speak to him. 4.07. 41
she wakes. OTH 5.02. 22
as wakes my vengeance and revenge for 'em. TNK 1.01. 58
and wakes the morning, from whose silver breast VEN 855
and cares, and troubled minds that wakes. LUC 126
while lust and murder wakes to stain and kill. 168
she wakes her heart by beating on her breast, 759
/WAKEST 1 FR 0.0001 REL FR 1 V 0 P
"/sleepest /or /wakest /thou, /jolly /shepherd? LR 3.06. 41
/WAKING 2 FR 0.0002 REL FR 1 V 1 P
it's sprightly, /waking, audible, and full of COR 4.05.222 P
an' he and i | will watch thy /waking, and that ROM 4.01.116
WAKING 22 FR 0.0024 REL FR 21 V 1 P
what? art thou waking? TMP 2.01.209
wink'st | whiles thou art waking. 2.01.217
sleeping or waking, mad or well–advis'd? ERR 2.02.213
the next thing then she waking looks upon | (be MND 2.01.179
take his own, | in your waking shall be shown. 3.02.460
shall reply amazedly, | half sleep, half waking; 4.01.147
with oaths kept waking, and with brawling fed; SHR 4.03. 10
our own love waking cries to see what's done, AWW 5.03. 65
for ne'er was dream | so like a waking. WT 3.03. 19
sleeping or waking, must i still prevail, | or 1H6 2.01. 56
by day, by night, waking and in my dreams, | in 2H6 1.01. 26
sleeping, or waking, 'tis no matter how, | so he 3.01.263
thou shalt be waking while i shed thy blood, 3.02.227
sleeping and waking, o, defend me still! R3 5.03.117
my lord sands, you are one will keep 'em waking; H8 1.04. 23
hath ever since kept hector fasting and waking. TRO 1.02. 36 P
so early waking — what with loathsome smells, ROM 4.03. 46
all alone, | at the prefixed hour of her waking, 5.03.253
waking? LR 1.04.229
from forth dull sleep by dreadful fancy waking, LUC 450

thy part | to keep thy sharp woes waking, 1136
in sleep a king, but waking no such matter. SON 87.14
WAK'ST 5 FR 0.0005 REL FR 5 V 0 P
in thy eye that shall appear | when thou wak'st, MND 2.02. 33
when thou wak'st, let love forbid | sleep his 2.02. 80
when thou wak'st, if she be by, | beg of her for 3.02.108
when thou wak'st, | thou tak'st | true delight 3.02.453
now, when thou wak'st, with thine own fool's 4.01. 84
WALES 34 FR 0.0038 REL FR 26 V 8 P
of whom thy father, prince of wales, was first. R2 2.01.172
came | a post from wales loaden with heavy news, 1H4 1.01. 37
and that same sword–and–buckler prince of wales, 1.03.230
that though i be but prince of wales, yet i am 2.04. 10 P
you, prince of wales! 2.04.139 P
and he of wales that gave amamon the bastinado 2.04.336 P
chides the banks of england, scotland, wales, 3.01. 44
all westward, wales beyond the severn shore, 3.01. 75
the prince of wales and i | must have some 3.02. 1
son, | the nimble–footed madcap prince of wales, 4.01. 95
against the bosom of the prince of wales. 4.01.121
indeed his king) to be engag'd in wales, | there 4.03. 95
the prince of wales, lord john of lancaster, 4.04. 29
the prince of wales doth join with all the world 5.01. 86
and, prince of wales, so dare we venture thee, 5.01.101
the prince of wales stepp'd forth before the 5.02. 45
the prince of wales from such a field as this, 5.04. 12
it is the prince of wales that threatens thee, 5.04. 42
i am the prince of wales, and think not, percy, 5.04. 63
reign | of harry percy and the prince of wales. 5.04. 67
myself and you, son harry, will towards wales, 5.05. 39
is return'd with some discomfort from wales. 2H4 1.02.104 P
and harry prince of wales | are near at hand. 2.01.134
comes the king back from wales, my noble lord? 2.01.176 P
king nearest his father, harry prince of wales, 2.02.120 P
o jesu, are you come from wales? 2.04.293 P
the prince of wales, where is he? 4.05. 53
that black name, edward, black prince of wales; H5 2.04. 56
great–uncle edward the plack prince of wales, as 4.07. 94 P
first, edward the black prince, prince of wales; 2H6 2.02. 11
edward thy son, that now is prince of wales, R3 1.03.198
for edward our son, that was prince of wales, 1.03.199
at pembroke or at /ha'rford–west in wales. 4.05. 10
th' way | tell me how wales was made so happy as CYM 3.02. 60
/WALK 1 FR 0.0001 REL FR 1 V 0 P
the fishermen, that /walk upon the beach, LR 4.06. 17
WALK 127 FR 0.0143 REL FR 89 V 38 P
a turn or two i'll walk | to still my beating TMP 4.01.162
to walk alone, like one that had the pestilence; TGV 2.01. 21 P
when you walk'd, to walk like one of the lions; 2.01. 28 P
walk hence with that | and manage it against 3.01.248
and, as we walk along, i dare be bold | with our 5.04.162
i pray you, sir, walk in. WIV 1.01.281 P
i had rather walk here, i thank you. 1.01.282 P
bottle, or a thief to walk my ambling gelding, 2.02.304 P
as well say i love to walk by the counter–gate, 3.03. 77 P
come, come, walk in the park. 3.03.224 P
walk round about an oak, with great ragg'd horns 4.04. 31
in deep of night to walk by this herne's oak. 4.04. 40
my shoulders for the fellow of this walk — and 5.05. 26 P
will't please you walk aside? MM 4.01. 58
come, we will walk. 4.05. 12
you must walk by us on our other hand; 5.01. 17
what, will you walk with me about the town, ERR 1.02. 22
let him walk from whence he came, lest he catch 3.01. 37
where i will walk till thou return to me. 3.02.151
pleaseth you walk with me down to his house, | i 4.01. 12
liv'st | to walk where any honest men resort. 5.01. 28
will you walk in to see their gossiping? 5.01.420
lady, will you walk about with your friend? ADO 2.01. 86 P
so you walk softly, and look sweetly, and say 2.01. 88 P
and say nothing, i am yours for the walk, and 2.01. 89 P
for the walk, and especially when i walk away. 2.01. 90 P
my lord, will you walk? dinner is ready. 2.03.210 P
and tell her i and ursley | walk in the orchard, 3.01. 5
old signior, walk aside with me, i have studied 3.02. 71 P
than those that walk and wot not what they are. LLL 1.01. 91
and, as i am a gentleman, betook myself to walk: 1.01.235 P
to see him walk before a lady and to bear her 4.01.145
walk aside the true folk, and let the traitors 4.03.209
i will walk up and down here, and i will sing, MND 3.01.122 P
talk with you, walk with you, and so following; MV 1.03. 36 P
if you would walk in absence of the sun. 5.01.128
if we walk not in the trodden paths, our very AYL 1.03. 14 P
say thou wilt walk; SHR in.2. 40
gentle sir, methinks you walk like a stranger. 2.01. 86 P
we will go walk a little in the orchard, | and 2.01.111
o, let me see thee walk. 2.01.256
you may go walk, and give me leave a while; 3.01. 59
there will we mount, and thither walk on foot. 4.03.186
but like a cloistress she will veiled walk, TN 1.01. 27
my very walk should be a jig. 1.03.129 P
malvolio's coming down this walk. 2.05. 16 P
sir, does walk about the orb like the sun, it 3.01. 38 P
i do not without danger walk these streets. 3.03. 25
do not then walk too open. 3.03. 37
will you walk towards him? 3.04.268 P
we two will walk, my lord, | and leave you to WT 1.02.172
the spirits o' th' dead | may walk again. 3.03. 17
i can stand and walk. 4.03.112 P
walk before toward the sea–side, go on the right 4.04.824 P
who dares not stir by day must walk by night, JN 1.01.172
why, here walk i in the black brow of night, 5.06. 17
for ever will i walk upon my knees, | and never R2 5.03. 93
the receipt of fern–seed, we walk invisible. 1H4 2.01. 87 P
ned poins and i will walk lower. 2.02. 61 P
we'll walk afoot a while, and ease our legs. 2.02. 79 P
thee behind the arras, the rest walk up above. 2.04.500 P
i do here walk before thee like a sow that hath 2H4 1.02. 11 P
if you would walk off, i would prick your guts a H5 2.01. 57 P
should with his lion gait walk the whole world, 2.02.122
and spirits walk, and ghosts break up their 2H6 1.04. 19
me leave | in this close walk to satisfy myself 2.02. 3
who from my cabin tempted me to walk | upon the R3 1.04. 12
as i walk thither, | i'll tell ye more. H8 4.01.116
affairs that walk | (as they say spirits do) at 5.01. 13
come, you and i must walk a turn together; 5.01. 93
prithee let's walk. 5.01.116
sirrah, walk off. TRO 3.02. 6
walk here i' th' orchard, i'll bring her 3.02. 16 P
will you walk in, my lord? 3.02. 60 P
will you walk in, my lord? 3.02. 99 P
walk into her house. 4.03. 5
please you walk in, my lords. 4.03. 12
lady, give me your hand, and, as we walk, | to 4.04.138
will you walk on, my lord? 4.05.291
did see and hear, devise, instruct, walk, feel, COR 1.01.102
titus, when wert thou wont to walk alone, TIT 1.01.339
east, | a troubled mind drive me to walk abroad, ROM 1.01.120
with corns will walk /a /bout with you. 1.05. 17
tybalt, you rat–catcher, will you walk? 3.01. 75 P
or walk in thievish ways, or bid me lurk | where 4.01. 79
well, i will walk myself | to county paris, to 4.02. 44
pray you walk near, i'll speak with you anon. TIM 2.02.123
you ought not walk | upon a laboring day without JC 1.01. 3
and we petty men | walk under his huge legs, and 1.02.137
men, all in fire, walk up and down the streets. 1.03. 25
this disturbed sky | is not to walk in. 1.03. 40
to walk unbraced and suck up the humors | of the 2.01.262
think you to walk forth? 2.02. 8
then walk we forth, even to the market–place, 3.01.108
to walk abroad and recreate yourselves. 3.02.251
hear not my steps, which /way /they walk, for MAC 2.01. 57
from your graves rise up, and walk like sprites, 2.03. 79
hence to th' palace gate | make it their walk. 3.03. 14
men must not walk too late. 3.06. 7
which, they say, your spirits oft walk in death, HAM 1.01.138
watch to–night, | perchance 'twill walk again. 1.02.242
and with a larger teder may he walk | than may 1.03.125
wherein the spirit held his wont to walk. 1.04. 6
doom'd for a certain term to walk the night, 1.05. 10
let her not walk i' th' sun. 2.02.184 P
will you walk out of the air, my lord? 2.02.206 P
ophelia, walk you here. 3.01. 42
sir, i will walk here in the hall. 5.02.173 P
does lear walk thus? LR 1.04.227
will't please your highness walk? 4.07. 82
cassio, walk hereabout; OTH 3.04.165
o, pardon me; 'twill do me good to walk. 4.03. 2
will you walk, sir? | o, desdemona! 4.03. 4
well, do it, and be brief, i will walk by. 5.02. 30
or does he walk? ANT 1.05. 20
walk; 4.03. 17
yet i'll move him | to walk this way. CYM 1.01.104
pray walk awhile. 1.01.176
walk with me; 5.05.119
in the day's glorious walk or peaceful night, PER 1.02. 4
walk with leonine, the air is quick there, | and 4.01. 27
leonine, take her by the arm, walk with her. 4.01. 29
walk, and be cheerful once again, reserve | that 4.01. 39
walk half an hour, leonine, at the least. 4.01. 45
pray walk softly, do not heat your blood. 4.01. 48
the sun grows high, let's walk in. TNK 2.02.148
o'er whom /thy fingers walk with gentle gait, SON 128.11
/WALK'D 1 FR 0.0001 REL FR 1 V 0 P
/you /knew /he /walk'd /o'er /perils, /on /an 2H4 1.01.170
WALK'D 21 FR 0.0023 REL FR 14 V 7 P
when you walk'd, to walk like one of the lions; TGV 2.01. 27 P
when he would have walk'd ten mile afoot to see ADO 2.03. 15 P
which, i mean, i walk'd upon: LLL 1.01.239 P
the street should see as she walk'd overhead. 4.03.277
were i the ghost that walk'd, i'ld bid you mark WT 5.01. 63
be such | as, walk'd your first queen's ghost, 5.01. 80
over whose acres walk'd those blessed feet 1H4 1.01. 25
he is walk'd up to the top of the hill, i'll go 2.02. 8 P
his lordship is walk'd forth into the orchard. 2H4 1.01. 4
he's walk'd the way of nature, | and to our 5.02. 4
i had | that walk'd about me every minute while; 1H6 1.04. 54
that hast so long walk'd hand in hand with time. TRO 4.05.203
for my part, i have walk'd about the streets, JC 1.03. 46
at supper | you suddenly arose and walk'd about, 2.01.239
and the right valiant banquo walk'd too late, MAC 3.06. 5
when was it she last walk'd? 5.01. 3 P
those which have walk'd in their sleep who have 5.01. 60 P
thrice he walk'd | by their oppress'd and HAM 1.02.202
a lady in venice would have walk'd barefoot to OTH 4.03. 38 P
in his livery | walk'd crowns and crownets; ANT 5.02. 91
"to see his face the lion walk'd along | behind VEN 1093
WALKED 2 FR 0.0002 REL FR 2 V 0 P
orders grey, | as he forth walked on his way" — SHR 4.01.146
say, | when i have walked like a private man, TIT 4.04. 75
WALKING 14 FR 0.0015 REL FR 9 V 5 P
walking in a thick–pleach'd alley in mine ADO 1.02. 9 P
than to fern–seed for your walking invisible. 1H4 2.01. 89 P
walking with thee in the night betwixt tavern 3.03. 43 P
this ruin'd band | walking from watch to watch, H5 4.pr. 30
with walking once about the quadrangle, | i come 2H6 1.03.153
side, | so early walking did i see your son. ROM 1.01.123
there is no stir or walking in the streets; JC 1.03.127
forth the adder, | and that craves wary walking. 2.01. 15
agitation, besides her walking and other actual MAC 5.01. 11 P
life's but a walking shadow, a poor player, 5.05. 24
look, here comes a walking fire. LR 3.04.114 P
that done, i will be walking on the works; OTH 3.02. 3
he's walking in the garden — thus, and spurns ANT 3.05. 16
to school, may we perceive | walking in thebes! TNK 1.02. 15
WALKING–STAFF 1 FR 0.0001 REL FR 1 V 0 P
wood, | my sceptre for a palmer's walking–staff, R2 3.03.151
WALKS 26 FR 0.0029 REL FR 23 V 3 P
speak softly, yonder, as i think, he walks. ERR 5.01. 9
hop in his walks and gambol in his eyes; MND 3.01.165
more than to us | wait in your royal walks, your 5.01. 31
yonder, sir, he walks. MV 2.02.174
comes the countess, now heaven walks on earth. TN 5.01. 97
lies in his bed, walks up and down with me, JN 3.04. 94
how wildly then walks my estate in france! 4.02.128
leaves the print of blood where e'er it walks. 4.03. 26
and lards the lean earth as he walks along. 1H4 2.02.109
court | and may enjoy such quiet walks as these? 2H6 4.10. 17
and so he walks, insulting o'er his prey, | and 3H6 1.03. 14
my parks, my walks, my manors that i had, | even 5.02. 24
when he walks, he moves like an engine, and the COR 5.04. 18 P
the forest walks are wide and spacious, | and TIT 2.01.114
and so let's leave her to her silent walks. 2.04. 8
fourscore to thirteen, this spirit walks in. TIM 2.02.114 P
poverty, | walks, like contempt, alone. 4.02. 15
that her wide walks encompass'd but one man? JC 1.02.155
moreover, he hath left you all his walks, | his 3.02.247
thy spirit walks abroad, and turns our swords 5.03. 95
walks o'er the dew of yon high eastward hill. HAM 1.01.167
you know sometimes he walks four hours together 2.02.160
at curfew, and walks /till /the first cock; LR 3.04.116 P
the curtains being close, about he walks, LUC 367
be absent from thy walks, and in my tongue | thy SON 89. 9
my mistress when she walks treads on the ground. 130.12
WALK'ST 1 FR 0.0001 REL FR 1 V 0 P
as if thou never walk'st further than finsbury. 1H4 3.01.252
WALL 63 FR 0.0071 REL FR 43 V 20 P
he hath rais'd the wall, and houses too. TMP 2.01. 88 P
out at the postern by the abbey wall; TGV 5.01. 9
hung by th' wall | so long that nineteen zodiacs MM 1.02.167
when icicles hang by the wall | and dick the LLL 5.02.912
we must have a wall in the great chamber; MND 3.01. 62 P
the story) did talk through the chink of a wall. 3.01. 64 P
you can never bring in a wall. 3.01. 65 P
some man or other must present wall; 3.01. 67 P
or some rough–cast about him, to signify wall; 3.01. 69 P
rough–cast, doth present | wall, that vile wall, 5.01.132
doth present | wall, that vile wall, which did 5.01.132
moonshine, wall, and lovers twain | at large 5.01.150
that i, one /snout by name, present a wall; 5.01.156
and such a wall, as i would have you think, 5.01.157
this stone doth show | that i am that same wall; 5.01.162
pyramus draws near the wall. silence! 5.01.169 P
and thou, o wall, o sweet, o lovely wall, | that 5.01.174
and thou, o wall, o sweet, o lovely wall, | that 5.01.174
thou wall, o wall, o sweet and lovely wall, 5.01.176
thou wall, o wall, o sweet and lovely wall, 5.01.176
thou wall, o wall, o sweet and lovely wall, 5.01.176
thanks, courteous wall; 5.01.178
o wicked wall, through whom i see no bliss! 5.01.180
the wall, methinks, being sensible, should curse 5.01.182 P
enter now, and i am to spy her through the wall. 5.01.186 P
o wall, full often hast thou heard my moans, 5.01.188
o, kiss me through the hole of this vild wall! 5.01.200
thus have i, wall, my part discharged so; 5.01.204
and, being done, thus wall away doth go. 5.01.205
ay, and wall too. 5.01.350 P
you, the wall is down that parted their fathers. 5.01.351 P
builds in the weather on the outward wall, MV 2.09. 29
and though that nature with a beauteous wall TN 1.02. 48
within this wall of flesh | there is a soul JN 3.03. 20
the wall is high, and yet will i leap down. 4.03. 1
sea, | which serves it in the office of a wall, R2 2.01. 47
a little pin | bores thorough his castle wall, 3.02.170
shall be a wall sufficient to defend | our H5 1.02.141
or close the wall up with our english dead. 3.01. 2
trumpeter, | summon their general unto the wall. 1H6 4.02. 2
to wall thee from the liberty of flight; 4.02. 24
on a brick wall have i climb'd into this garden, 2H6 4.10. 7 P
wert thou environ'd with a brazen wall 3H6 2.04. 4
see how the surly warwick mans the wall! 5.01. 17
so that the ram that batters down the wall, TRO 1.03.206
no better than picture–like to hang by th' wall, COR 1.03. 11 P
i heard a child cry underneath a wall. TIT 5.01. 24
i pried me through the crevice of a wall, | when 5.01.114
i will take the wall of any man or maid of ROM 1.01. 12 P
a weak slave, for the weakest goes to the wall. 1.01. 14 P
the weaker vessels, are ever thrust to the wall; 1.01. 16 P
i will push montague's men from the wall, and 1.01. 17 P
from the wall, and thrust his maids to the wall. 1.01. 18 P
sitting in the sun under the dove–house wall. 1.03. 27
he ran this way and leapt this orchard wall. 2.01. 5
behind the abbey wall | within this hour my man 2.04.187
o thou wall | that girdles in those wolves, dive TIM 4.01. 1
th' athenians both within and out that wall! 4.01. 38
how has the ass broke the wall, that thou art 4.03.349 P
should patch a wall t' expel the /winter's flaw! HAM 5.01.216
mortar, and daub the wall of a jakes with him. LR 2.02. 66 P
(rude ram, to batter such an ivory wall!), LUC 464
have batter'd down her consecrated wall, | and 723
WALL'D 4 FR 0.0004 REL FR 3 V 1 P
a lady wall'd about with diamonds! LLL 5.02. 3
as a wall'd town is more worthier than a village AYL 3.03. 59 P
in a wall'd prison, packs and sects of great LR 5.03. 18
by the battle, ditch'd, and wall'd with turf, CYM 5.03. 14
WALLED 1 FR 0.0001 REL FR 1 V 0 P
cities, and seven walled towns of strength, 1H6 3.04. 7
WALLET 1 FR 0.0001 REL FR 1 V 0 P
time hath, my lord, a wallet at his back, TRO 3.03.145
WALLETS 1 FR 0.0001 REL FR 1 V 0 P
throats had hanging at 'em | wallets of flesh? TMP 3.03. 46
WALL–EY'D 2 FR 0.0002 REL FR 2 V 0 P
that ever wall–ey'd wrath or staring rage JN 4.03. 49
say, wall–ey'd slave, whither wouldst thou TIT 5.01. 44
WALL–NEWT 1 FR 0.0001 REL FR 0 V 1 P
toad, the todpole, the wall–newt, and the water; LR 3.04.130 P
WALLON 2 FR 0.0002 REL FR 2 V 0 P
a base wallon, to win the dolphin's grace, 1H6 1.01.137
wallon, and picardy are friends to us, | this 2.01. 10
WALLOW 2 FR 0.0002 REL FR 2 V 0 P
or wallow naked in december snow | by thinking R2 1.03.298
fields | where i may wallow in the lily–beds TRO 3.02. 12
WALL'S 2 FR 0.0002 REL FR 2 V 0 P
and through wall's chink, poor souls, they are MND 5.01.133
i kiss the wall's hole, not your lips at all. 5.01.201
WALLS 61 FR 0.0069 REL FR 57 V 4 P
i never came within these abbey walls, | nor ERR 5.01.266
lord, when walls are so willful to hear without MND 5.01.208 P
troilus methinks mounted the troyan walls, | and MV 5.01. 4
within rich pisa walls, as any one | old signior SHR 2.01.367
some trumpet summon hither to the walls | these JN 2.01.198
who is it that hath warn'd us to the walls? 2.01.201
their iron indignation 'gainst your walls; 2.01.212
fire, | to make a shaking fever in your walls, 2.01.228
craves harborage within your city walls. 2.01.234
'tis not the rounder of your old–fac'd walls 2.01.259
as we will ours, against these saucy walls, 2.01.404
see | but empty lodgings and unfurnish'd walls, R2 1.02. 68
as if this flesh which walls about our life 3.02.167
and that all the walls | with painted imagery 5.02. 15
of this hard world, my ragged prison walls; 5.05. 21
is the only drinking, and for thy walls, a 2H4 2.01.144 P
suppose within the girdle of these walls | are H5 pr 19

their most reverend heads dash'd to the walls; 3.03. 37
girdled with maiden walls that war hath /never 5.02.322 P
the walls they'll tear down than forsake the 1H6 1.02. 40
in iron walls they deem'd me not secure; 1.04. 49
advance our waving colors on the walls, 1.06. 1
or soldier you perceive | near to the walls, by 2.01. 3
leap o'er the walls for refuge in the field. 2.02. 25
like peasant footboys do they keep the walls, 3.02. 69
away, captains, let's get us from the walls, 3.02. 71
here will i sit before the walls of roan | and 3.02. 91
at your father's castle walls | we'll crave a 5.03.129
climbing my walls in spite of me the owner, 2H6 4.10. 35
go, trumpet, to the walls, and sound a parle. 3H6 5.01. 16
within the guilty closure of thy walls | richard R3 3.03. 11
catesby, o'erlook the walls. 3.05. 17
whom envy hath immur'd within your walls — 4.01. 99
why should i war without the walls of troy, TRO 1.01. 2
after seven years' siege yet troy walls stand, 1.03. 12
midway between your tents and walls of troy, 1.03.278
it, the walls will stand till they fall of 2.03. 9 P
for yonder walls, that pertly front your town, 4.05.219
that hunger broke stone walls, that dogs must COR 1.01.206
tullus aufidius, is he within your walls? 1.04. 13
we'll break our walls | rather than they shall 1.04. 16
tullus, | alone i fought in your corioles walls, 1.08. 8
reechy neck, | clamb'ring the walls to eye him; 2.01.210
we will before the walls of rome to–morrow | set 5.03. 1
lives not this day within the city walls. TIT 1.01. 26
ye white–lim'd walls! 4.02. 98
the orchard walls are high and hard to climb, ROM 2.02. 63
love's light wings did i o'erperch these walls, 2.02. 66
there is no world without verona walls, | but 3.03. 17
threat'ning sword | against the walls of athens. TIM 5.01.167
these walls of ours | were not erected by their 5.04. 22
have you climb'd up to walls and battlements, JC 1.01. 38
nor stony tower, nor walls of beaten brass, 1.03. 93
hang out our banners on the outward walls, | the MAC 5.05. 1
the walls is thine. LR 5.03. 76
heavens hold firm | the walls of thy dear honor; CYM 2.01. 63
and, for i am richer than to hang by th' walls, 3.04. 52
through crystal walls each little mote will peep LUC 1251
and from the walls of strong–besieged troy, 1429
left | a liquid prisoner pent in walls of glass, SON 5.10
painting thy outward walls so costly gay? 146. 4
WALNUT 1 FR 0.0001 REL FR 0 V 1 P
search'd a hollow walnut for his wive's leman." WIV 4.02.164 P
WALNUT–SHELL 1 FR 0.0001 REL FR 1 V 0 P
why, 'tis a cockle or a walnut–shell, | a knack, SHR 4.03. 66
WALTER 13 FR 0.0014 REL FR 10 V 3 P
nicholas, philip, walter, sugarsop, and the rest SHR 4.01. 90 P
sir walter blunt, new lighted from his horse, 1H4 1.01. 63
did sir walter see | on holmedon's plains. 1.01. 69
welcome, sir walter blunt; 4.03. 32
not so, sir walter; 4.03.107
sir walter blunt. 5.03. 32 P
like not such grinning honor as sir walter hath. 5.03. 59 P
the other, walter whitmore, is thy share. 2H6 4.01. 14
my name is walter whitmore. 4.01. 31
gualtier or walter, which it is, i care not. 4.01. 38
sir walter herbert, a renowned soldier, | sir R3 4.05. 12
and /you, sir walter herbert — stay with me. 5.03. 28
john duke of norfolk, walter lord /ferrers, 5.05. 13
WALTER'S 1 FR 0.0001 REL FR 1 V 0 P
and walter's dagger was not come from sheathing; SHR 4.01.135
WAN* *(also won)*
WAN* 4 FR 0.0004 REL FR 4 V 0 P
ay me, poor man, how pale and wan he looks! ERR 4.04.108
so shaken as we are, so wan with care, | find we 1H4 1.01. 1
a feast, | and wan by rareness such solemnity. 3.02. 59
why doth your highness look so pale and wan? TIT 2.03. 90
WAN'D 1 FR 0.0001 REL FR 1 V 0 P
of love, | salt cleopatra, soften thy wan'd lip! ANT 2.01. 21
WAND 2 FR 0.0002 REL FR 1 V 1 P
is as white as a lily and as small as a wand. TGV 2.03. 21 P
and on the pieces of the broken wand | were 2H6 1.02. 28
WANDER 24 FR 0.0027 REL FR 22 V 2 P
and wander up and down to view the city. ERR 1.02. 31
you, | to make it wander in an unknown field? 3.02. 38
and so am i, | and here we wander in illusions: 4.03. 43
how now, spirit, whither wander you? MND 2.01. 1
flood, thorough fire, | i do wander every where, 2.01. 6
therefore he gives them good leave to wander. AYL 1.01.104 P
how now, wit, whither wander you? 1.02. 56 P
and wander we to see thy honest son, | who will SHR 4.05. 69
and when i wander here and there, | i then do WT 4.03. 17
of world | i wander from the jewels that i love. R2 1.03.270
where e'er i wander, boast of this i can, 1.03.308
with cain go wander thorough shades of night, 5.06. 43
that we may wander o'er this bloody field | to H5 4.07. 72
thou mayest not wander in that labyrinth, 1H6 5.03.188
madam, you wander from the good we aim at. H8 3.01.138
planets | in evil mixture to disorder wander, TRO 1.03. 95
i have no will to wander forth of doors, | yet JC 3.03. 3
to–night we'll wander through the streets and ANT 1.01. 53
safe mayst thou wander, safe return again! CYM 3.05.105
i may wander | from east to occident, cry out 4.02.371
might, like women, | woo us to wander from. TNK 2.02. 76
sits sin, to seize the souls that wander by him. LUC 882
't may be again, to make me wander thither: PP 14.10
"wander," a word for shadows like myself, | as 14.11
WANDER'D 2 FR 0.0002 REL FR 2 V 0 P
as he in penance wander'd through the forest; TGV 5.02. 38
power | have wander'd with our travers'd arms, TIM 5.04. 7
WANDERER 2 FR 0.0002 REL FR 2 V 0 P
i am that merry wanderer of the night. MND 2.01. 43
welcome, wanderer. 2.01.247
WANDERERS 1 FR 0.0001 REL FR 1 V 0 P
skies | gallow the very wanderers of the dark, LR 3.02. 44
WANDERING 4 FR 0.0004 REL FR 4 V 0 P
a grain, a dust, a gnat, a wandering hair, | any JN 4.01. 92
i shall stand condemn'd | a wandering vagabond, R2 2.03.120
return, thou wandering lord! 1H6 3.03. 76
face | rul'd like a wandering planet over me, 2H6 4.04. 16
WANDERS 1 FR 0.0001 REL FR 1 V 0 P
what cursed foot wanders this way to–night, | to ROM 5.03. 19
WAND–LIKE 1 FR 0.0001 REL FR 1 V 0 P
her stature to an inch, as wand–like straight, PER 5.01.109
WAND'RED 5 FR 0.0005 REL FR 5 V 0 P
and the heedful slave | is wand'red forth, in ERR 2.02. 3
us, | one of our souls had wand'red in the air, R2 1.03.195
my youth | hath faulty wand'red and irregular, 1H4 3.02. 27
scatter'd, | and he himself wand'red away alone, R3 4.04.512
steed, | and wand'red hither to an obscure plot, TIT 2.03. 77
WAND'REST 1 FR 0.0001 REL FR 1 V 0 P
shall death brag thou wand'rest in his shade, SON 18.11
WAND'RING 16 FR 0.0018 REL FR 14 V 2 P
what is thisby? a wand'ring knight? MND 1.02. 45 P
fair love, you faint with wand'ring in the wood; 2.02. 35
approach, ghosts, wand'ring here and there, 3.02.381
compass soon, | swifter than the wand'ring moon. 4.01. 98
to cast thy wand'ring eyes on every stale, SHR 3.01. 90
whilst we were wand'ring with the antipodes, R2 3.02. 49
by phoebus, he, "that wand'ring knight so fair." 1H4 1.02. 15 P
to find the empty, vast, and wand'ring air, R3 1.04. 39
then came wand'ring by | a shadow like an angel, 1.04. 52
now, for my life, she's wand'ring to the tower, 4.01. 3
let it be call'd the wild and wand'ring flood, TRO 1.01.102
the wand'ring prince and dido once enjoyed, TIT 2.03. 22
conjures the wand'ring stars and makes them HAM 5.01.256
for vice repeated is like the wand'ring wind, PER 1.01. 96
in thy weak hive a wand'ring wasp hath crept, LUC 839
it is the star to every wand'ring bark, | whose SON 116. 7
WANDS 1 FR 0.0001 REL FR 1 V 0 P
the skillful shepherd pill'd me certain wands, MV 1.03. 84
WANE 2 FR 0.0002 REL FR 1 V 1 P
light of discretion, that he is in the wane; MND 5.01.254 P
as fast as thou shalt wane, so fast thou grow'st SON 11. 1
WANED 1 FR 0.0001 REL FR 1 V 0 P
my waned state for henry's regal crown. 3H6 4.07. 4
/WANES 1 FR 0.0001 REL FR 1 V 0 P
o, methinks, how slow | this old moon /wanes! MND 1.01. 4
/WANING 1 FR 0.0001 REL FR 1 V 0 P
i seek not to wax great by others' /waning, | or 2H6 4.10. 20
WANING 5 FR 0.0005 REL FR 5 V 0 P
beautiful | than any woman in this waning age. SHR in.2. 63
and in his waning age | set foot under thy table 2.01.401
i lurk'd, | to watch the waning of mine enemies. R3 4.04. 4
with honor, wealth, and ease, in waning age; LUC 142
who hast by waning grown, and therein show'st SON 126. 3
WANN'D 1 FR 0.0001 REL FR 1 V 0 P
that from her working all the visage wann'd, HAM 2.02.554
/WANNY 1 FR 0.0001 REL FR 1 V 0 P
lips and cheeks shall fade | to /wanny ashes, ROM 4.01.100
/WANT 1 FR 0.0001 REL FR 1 V 0 P
/want /our /hands | /and /cannot /passionate TIT 3.02. 5
WANT 150 FR 0.0169 REL FR 124 V 26 P
scape being drunk, for want of wine. TMP 2.01.147
and much less take | what i shall die to want. 3.01. 79
and what does else want credit, come to me, 3.03. 25
(although they want the use of tongue) a kind 3.03. 38
bring a corollary, | rather than want a spirit. 4.01. 58
scarcity and want shall shun you, | ceres' 4.01.116
now i want | spirits to enforce, art to enchant, ep 13
when you look'd sadly, it was for want of money: TGV 2.01. 30 P
or else for want of idle time, could not again 2.01.166
and duty never yet did want his meed. 2.04.112
because myself do want my servants' fortune. 3.01.147
as we do in our quality much want — 4.01. 56
want no money, sir john, you shall want none. WIV 2.02.258 P
want no money, sir john, you shall want none. 2.02.258 P
want no mistress ford, master /brook, you shall 2.02.260 P
ford, master /brook, you shall want none. 2.02.261 P
as she may hang together, for want of company. 3.02. 14 P
why yet there want not many that do fear | in 4.04. 39
you of such things | that want no ear but yours. MM 4.03.105
who, all for want of pruning, with intrusion ERR 2.02.179
to persia, and want guilders for my voyage: 4.01. 4
be /ingenious, they shall want no instruction; LLL 4.02. 79 P
where nothing wants that want itself doth seek. 4.03.233
it was enjoin'd him in rome for want of linen; 5.02.713 P
belike for want of rain; MND 1.01.130
the human mortals want their winter here; 2.01.101
by so much is a horn more precious than to want. AYL 3.03. 63 P
let them want nothing that my house affords. SHR in.1. 104
to want the bridegroom when the priest attends 3.02. 5
he cannot want the best | that shall attend his AWW 1.01. 72
whose want, and whose delay, is strew'd with 2.04. 44
and i shall lose my life for want of language. 4.01. 70
sir, for want of other idleness, i'll bide your TN 1.05. 64 P
the want of which vain dew | perchance shall dry WT 2.01.109
not to have had thee than thus to want thee. 4.02. 13 P
i shall there have money, or any thing i want. 4.03. 82 P
that you may know you shall not want — one word 4.04.594
and she again wants nothing, to name want, | if JN 2.01.435
want, | if want it be not that she is not he. 2.01.436
order in so fierce a cause, | doth want example. 3.04. 13
must needs want pleading for a pair of eyes. 4.01. 98
let hell want pains enough to torture me. 4.03.138
i live with bread like you, feel want, | taste R2 3.02.175
tears show their love, but want their remedies. 3.03.203
had, | it adds more sorrow to my want of joy; 3.04. 16
and what i want it boots not to complain. 3.04. 18
i am press'd to death through want of speaking! 3.04. 72
the poor abuses of the time want countenance. 1H4 1.02.156 P
my soul | want mercy if i do not join with him. 1.03.132
i want work." 2.04.105 P
rage, | defect of manners, want of government, 3.01.182
his present want | seems more than we shall find 4.01. 44
and never yet did insurrection want | such 5.01. 79
only, we want a little personal strength; 2H4 4.04. 8
what you want in meat, we'll have in drink, but 5.03. 28 P
and yet my sky shall not want. H5 3.07. 73 P
have lost, or do not learn for want of time, 5.02. 57
whose want gives growth to th' imperfections 5.02. 69
no treachery, but want of men and money. 1H6 1.01. 69
they want their porridge and their fat 1.02. 9
good morrow, gallants, want ye corn for bread? 3.02. 41
because you want the grace that others have, 5.04. 46
and choke the herbs for want of husbandry. 2H6 3.01. 33
i shall not want false witness to condemn me, 3.01.168
policy, | but yet we want a color for his death. 3.01.236
an angry hive of bees | that want their leader, 3.02.126
by, | as one that surfeits thinking on a want. 3.02.348
be witness that no want of resolution in me, but 4.08. 62 P
nor should thy prowess want praise and esteem, 5.02. 22
the want thereof makes thee abominable. 3H6 1.04.133
that, though i want a kingdom, yet in marriage 4.01.121
ay, therein clarence shall not want his part. 4.06. 57
o, welcome, oxford, for we want thy help. 5.01. 66
my blood, my want of strength, my sick heart 5.02. 8
and want love's majesty | to strut before a R3 1.01. 16
why wither not the leaves that want their sap? 2.02. 42
i want more uncles here to welcome me. 3.01. 6
those uncles which you want were dangerous; 3.01. 12
the noble isle doth want /her proper limbs; 3.07.125
which they upon the adverse faction want. 5.03. 13
for want of means, poor rats, had hang'd 5.03.331
i blush, | it is to see a nobleman want manners. H8 3.02.308
i had rather want those than my head. 3.02.309
out of which frailty | and want of wisdom, you, 5.02. 48
'tis not to save labor, nor that i want love. COR 1.03. 81 P
teach the people — which time shall not want, 2.01.255
and safeguard | of what that want might ruin. 3.02. 69
a thousand times the worse, to want thy light. ROM 2.02.155
but much of grief shows still some want of wit. 3.05. 73
if i want gold, steal but a beggar's dog | and TIM 2.01. 5
and usurers' men, bawds between gold and want! 2.02. 60 P
that now they are at fall, want treasure, cannot 2.02.205
he cannot want for money. 3.02. 8 P
he cannot want fifty — five hundred talents. 3.02. 38
sides, | the want that makes him /lean. 4.03. 13
the want whereof doth daily make revolt | in my 4.03. 92
the mere want of gold, and the falling–from of 4.03.400 P
we are not thieves, but men that much do want. 4.03.415
your greatest want is, you want much of meat. 4.03.416
your greatest want is, you want much of meat. 4.03.416
why should you want? 4.03.417
want? 4.03.421
why want? 4.03.421
an alteration of honor has desp'rate want made! 4.03.462
of life | that should be in a roman you do want, JC 1.03. 58
who cannot want the thought, how monstrous | it MAC 3.06. 8
and who in want a hollow friend doth try, HAM 3.02.208
then what i have to do | will want true color — 3.04.130
if for i want that glib and oily art | to speak LR 1.01.224
but even for want of that for which i am richer 1.01.230
well are worth the want that you have wanted. 1.01.279
/nor crumb, | weary of all, shall want some. 1.04.199
/you are much more /attax'd for want of wisdom 1.04.343
i have no way, and therefore want no eyes; 4.01. 18
if your will want not, time and place will be 4.06.264 P
now for want of these requir'd conveniences, her OTH 2.01.231 P
give me the addition | whose want even kills me. 4.01.105
and did want | of what i was i' th' morning; ANT 2.02. 76
wherefore my father should revengers want, 2.06. 11
but want will perjure | the ne'er–touch'd vestal 3.12. 30
dido and her aeneas shall want troops, | and all 4.14. 53
thou shouldst neither want my means for thy CYM 3.05.114 P
the want is but to put those pow'rs in motion 4.03. 31
who find in my exile the want of breeding, | the 4.04. 26
you come in faint for want of meat, depart 5.04.161 P
there are none want eyes to direct them the way 5.04.185 P
if heaven slumber while their creatures want, PER 1.04. 16
as houses are defil'd for want of use, | they 1.04. 37
they are now starv'd for want of exercise; 1.04. 38
but what i am, want teaches me to think on: 2.01. 72
have, | wherein we are not destitute for want, 5.01. 57
feast's solemnity | shall want till your return. TNK 1.01.222
peril and want contending, they have skiff'd 1.03. 37
and what | you want at any time, let me but know 2.05. 55
get off your trinkets, you shall want nought. 3.03. 52
which cannot want due mercy, i beg first. 3.06.209
but want the understanding where to use it. 3.06.216
there shall want no bravery. 4.02.154
how want of love tormenteth? VEN 202
that golden hap which their superiors want. LUC 42
the thing we have, and all for want of wit, 153
swelling on either side to want his bliss; 389
with too much labor drowns for want of skill. 1099
but whether unripe years did want conceit, | or PP 4. 9
crowns be scant, | no man will supply thy want. 20.36
yet eyes this cunning want to grace their art, SON 24.13
how can my muse want subject to invent | while 38. 1
want nothing that the thought of hearts can mend 69. ?
no want of conscience hold it that i call | her 151.13
lets not bounty fall | where want cries some, LC 42
WANTED 8 FR 0.0009 REL FR 7 V 1 P
wanted the modesty | to urge the thing held as a MV 5.01.205
stir it up where it wanted rather than lack it AWW 1.01. 9 P
that any of these bolder vices wanted | less WT 3.02. 55
being wanted, he may be more wond'red at | by 1H4 1.02.201
he wanted pikes to set before his archers; 1H6 1.01.116
shame, that they wanted cunning in excess, TIM 5.04. 28
well are worth the want that you have wanted. LR 1.01.279
which not wanted | shrowdness of policy too — i ANT 2.02. 68
WANTETH 6 FR 0.0006 REL FR 6 V 0 P
there wanteth but a mean to fill your song. TGV 1.02. 92
another would fly swift, but wanteth wings; 1H6 1.01. 75
there wanteth now our brother gloucester here R3 2.01. 43
who wanteth food and will not say he wants it, PER 1.04. 11
but poorly rich, so wanteth in his store, | that LUC 97
a swallowing gulf that even in plenty wanteth. 557
WANTING 27 FR 0.0030 REL FR 27 V 0 P
who, wanting guilders to redeem their lives, ERR 1.01. 8
but in this kind, wanting your father's voice, MND 1.01. 54
have | that to your wanting may be minist'red. AYL 2.07.126
in ross and willoughby, wanting your company, R2 2.03. 10
phaeton, | wanting the manage of unruly jades. 3.03.179
for if of joy, being altogether wanting, | it 3.04. 13
wanting the scythe withal, uncorrected, rank, H5 5.02. 50
were our tears wanting to this funeral, | these 1H6 1.01. 82
whilst such a worthy leader, wanting aid, | unto 1.01.143
the other lords, like lions wanting food, | do 1.02. 27
wherein thy counsel and consent is wanting. 3H6 2.06.102
wanting his manage, and they will almost | give TRO 3.03. 25
only | there's one thing wanting, which i doubt COR 2.01.201
or, wanting strength to do thee so much good, TIT 2.03.238
talk, | wanting a hand to give/'t that accord? 5.02. 18
than death prorogued, wanting of thy love. ROM 2.02. 78
or, wanting that, with tears distill'd by moans. 5.03. 15
as the moon does, by wanting light to give: TIM 4.03. 68
he that is robb'd, not wanting what is stol'n, OTH 3.03.342
and, wanting breath to speak, help me with tears PER 1.04. 19

so sorrow, wanting form, | is press'd with TNK 1.01.108
couple then, | and see what's wanting. 3.05. 33
quo usque tandem? here is a woman wanting. 3.05. 38
let no due be wanting; 5.01. 5
wanting the spring that those shrunk pipes had LUC 1455
may make seem bare, in wanting words to show it, SON 26. 6
the cause of this fair gift in me is wanting, 87. 7
/WANTON 2 FR 0.0002 REL FR 2 V 0 P
/and /with /our /surfeiting /and /wanton /hours 2H4 4.01. 55
/with /wanton /paris /sleeps — /and /that's TRO pr 10
WANTON 75 FR 0.0084 REL FR 70 V 5 P
done | some wanton charm upon this man and maid, TMP 4.01. 95
dare you presume to harbor wanton lines? TGV 1.02. 42
nay then the wanton lies; my face is black. 5.02. 10
lord, lord, your worship's a wanton! WIV 2.02. 56 P
the wanton stings and motions of the sense; MM 1.04. 59
not to knit my soul to an approved wanton. ADO 4.01. 44
of all, | a whitely wanton with a velvet brow, LLL 3.01.196
o, rhymes are guards on wanton cupid's hose: 4.03. 56
passing fair | playing in the wanton air: 4.03.102
all wanton as a child, skipping and vain, 5.02.761
tarry, rash wanton! am not i thy lord? MND 2.01. 63
and the quaint mazes in the wanton green | for 2.01. 99
and grow big–bellied with the wanton wind; 2.01.129
which /make such wanton gambols with the wind MV 3.02. 93
for do but note a wild and wanton herd, | or 5.01. 71
and hang it round with all my wanton pictures. SHR in.1. 47
which seem to move and wanton with her breath, in.2. 52
lays down his wanton siege before her beauty, AWW 3.07. 18
and boarded her i' th' wanton way of youth. 5.03.211
nicely with words may quickly make them wanton. TN 3.01. 15 P
with that word might make my sister wanton. 3.01. 20 P
how now, you wanton calf, | art thou my calf? WT 1.02.126
of these days, and then you'ld wanton with us, 2.01. 18
is all too wanton and too full of gawds | to JN 3.03. 36
a cock'red silken wanton, brave our fields, 5.01. 70
four lagging winters and four wanton springs R2 1.03.214
we make woe wanton with this fond delay, | once 5.01.101
which he, young wanton and effeminate boy, 5.03. 10
she bids you on the wanton rushes lay you down, 1H4 3.01.211
wanton as youthful goats, wild as young bulls. 4.01.103
king, | what with the injuries of a wanton time, 5.01. 50
that art a guard too wanton for the head | which 2H4 1.01.148
yea, every idle, nice, and wanton reason, 4.01.189
lascivious, wanton, more than well beseems | a 1H6 3.01. 19
books | than wanton dalliance with a paramour. 5.01. 23
now, | the wanton edward, and the lusty george? 3H6 1.04. 74
for matching more for wanton lust than honor, 3.03.210
to strut before a wanton ambling nymph; R3 1.01. 17
made prize and purchase of his wanton eye, 3.07.187
and how sleek and wanton | ye appear in every H8 3.02.241
like little wanton boys that swim on bladders, 3.02.359
and the weak wanton cupid | shall from your neck TRO 3.03.222
her wanton spirits look out | at every joint and 4.05. 56
towers, whose wanton tops do buss the clouds, 4.05.220
their nicely gawded cheeks to th' wanton spoil COR 2.01.217
to wanton with this queen, | this goddess, this TIT 2.01. 21
now comes the wanton blood up in your cheeks, ROM 2.05. 70
gossamers | that idles in the wanton summer air, 2.06. 19
wanton in fullness, seek to hide themselves | in MAC 1.04. 34
but, sir, such wanton, wild, and usual slips HAM 2.01. 22
pinch wanton on your cheek, call you his mouse, 3.04.183
i am sure you make a wanton of me. 5.02.299
as flies to wanton boys are we to th' gods, LR 4.01. 36
of feather'd cupid seel with wanton dullness OTH 1.03.269
he hath not yet made wanton the night with her; 2.03. 16 P
arch–mock, | to lip a wanton in a secure couch, 4.01. 71
but not so citizen a wanton as | to seem to die CYM 4.02. 8
come away, or i'll fetch th' with a wanton. PER 2.01. 17 P
arcite, | even in the wagging of a wanton leg, TNK 2.02. 15
arcite) almost wanton | with my captivity. 2.02. 96
thou art wanton. 2.02.146
and fling my wanton arms | in at her window! 2.02.237
tame tempests, | and make the wild rocks wanton. 2.03. 17
just such another wanton ganymede | set /jove 4.02. 15
not wanton white, but such a manly color | next 4.02.124
whose youth, like wanton boys through bonfires, 5.01. 86
into whose port | ne'er ent'red wanton sound) to 5.01.148
to toy, to wanton, dally, smile, and jest, VEN 106
bewitching like the wanton mermaids' songs, 777
mine ears, that to your wanton talk attended, 809
nor could she moralize his wanton sight, | more LUC 104
"this glove to wanton tricks | is not inur'd; 320
wanton modesty! 401
passing fair, | playing in the wanton air. PP 16. 4
bearing the wanton burthen of the prime, | like SON 97. 7
WANTONLY 1 FR 0.0001 REL FR 1 V 0 P
hang on such thorns, and play as wantonly, SON 54. 7
/WANTONNESS 1 FR 0.0001 REL FR 1 V 0 P
excess | as gravity's revolt to /wantonness. LLL 5.02. 74
WANTONNESS 7 FR 0.0008 REL FR 5 V 2 P
the spirit of wantonness is sure scar'd out of WIV 4.02.209 P
the sun with /cold | than thee with wantonness. 4.04. 8
would be as sad as night, | only for wantonness. JN 4.01. 16
hope, | so much misconstrued in his wantonness. 1H4 5.02. 68
while pride is fasting in his wantonness! TRO 3.03.137
and make your wantonness /your ignorance. HAM 3.01.145 P
some say thy fault is youth, some wantonness, SON 96. 1
WANTON'S 1 FR 0.0001 REL FR 1 V 0 P
and yet no farther than a wanton's bird, | that ROM 2.02.177
WANTONS 4 FR 0.0004 REL FR 3 V 1 P
or shall we play the wantons with our woes | and R2 3.03.164
let wantons light of heart | tickle the ROM 1.04. 35
with a stick, and cried, "down, wantons, down!" LR 2.04.125 P
play'd with her breath — | o modest wantons! LUC 401
WANTS 45 FR 0.0050 REL FR 36 V 9 P
and he wants wit that wants resolved will | to TGV 2.06. 12
and he wants wit that wants resolved will | to 2.06. 12
it, that it wants matter to prevent so gross WIV 5.05.136 P
he wants advice. MM 4.02.146 P
no, sir, i think the meat wants that i have. ERR 2.02. 55 P
wants wit in all one word to understand. 2.02.151
if he be sad, he wants money. ADO 3.02. 20 P
where nothing wants that want itself doth seek. LLL 4.03.233
come, sir, it wants a twelvemonth an' a day, 5.02.877
a bill of properties, such as our play wants. MND 1.02.106 P
yet, to supply the ripe wants of my friend, MV 1.03. 63
supply your present wants, and take no doit | of 1.03.140
and that he that wants money, means, and content AYL 3.02. 25 P
though bride and bridegroom wants | for to SHR 3.02.246
you know there wants no junkets at the feast. 3.02.248
that which spites me more than all these wants, 4.03. 11
she's very well, and wants nothing i' th' world; AWW 2.04. 4 P
(who wants but something to be a reasonable man) WT 4.04.605 P
and she again wants nothing, to name want, | if JN 2.01.435
gold, | and send them after to supply our wants, R2 1.04. 51
alive, | if salisbury wants mercy at thy hands! 1H6 1.04. 86
it is, and wants but nomination. R3 3.04. 5
what his high hatred would effect wants not | a H8 1.01.107
is, a fair young maid that yet wants baptism, 5.02.196
wants similes, truth tir'd with iteration, | as TRO 3.02.176
for your wants, | your suffering in this dearth, COR 1.01. 66
wants not spirit | to say he'll turn your 3.01. 95
we to be baited | with one that wants her wits? 4.02. 44
he wants nothing of a god but eternity and a 5.04. 23 P
chiron, thy years wants wit, thy wits wants edge TIT 2.01. 26
thy years wants wit, thy wits wants edge, | and 2.01. 26
if you did know, my lord, my master's wants — TIM 2.02. 29
in some sort these wants of mine are crown'd, 2.02.181
but in the mean time he wants less, my lord. 3.02. 39
is the initiate fear that wants hard use: MAC 3.04.142
he loves us not, | he wants the natural touch; 4.02. 9
o god, a beast, that wants discourse of reason, HAM 1.02.150
and wants not buzzers to infect his ear | with 4.05. 90
the life | that wants the means to lead it. LR 4.04. 20
nature wants stuff | to vie strange forms with ANT 5.02. 97
there wants no diligence in seeking him, | and CYM 4.03. 20
who wanteth food and will not say he wants it, PER 1.04. 11
sir, here's a lady that wants breathing too, 2.03.100
grown so low | and crestfall'n with my wants. TNK 3.06. 7
who nothing wants to answer her but cries, | and LUC 1459
/WANT'ST 1 FR 0.0001 REL FR 0 V 1 P
/want'st /thou /eyes /at /trial, /madam? LR 3.06. 23 P
WANT'ST 7 FR 0.0008 REL FR 6 V 1 P
look what thou want'st shall be sent after thee. TGV 1.03. 74
it seems thou want'st breaking, out upon thee, ERR 3.01. 77
thou want'st a rough pash and the shoots that i WT 1.02.128
and if thou want'st a cord, the smallest thread JN 4.03.127
if thou want'st any thing, and wilt not call, 2H4 5.03. 55 P
why art thou old, and want'st experience? 2H6 5.01.171
find what thou want'st by free and offer'd light TIM 5.01. 45
WANT–WIT 1 FR 0.0001 REL FR 1 V 0 P
and such a want–wit sadness makes of me, | that MV 1.01. 6
WAPPEN'D 1 FR 0.0001 REL FR 1 V 0 P
is it | that makes the wappen'd widow wed again; TIM 4.03. 39
/WAR 8 FR 0.0009 REL FR 7 V 1 P
/you /cast /th' /event /of /war, /my /noble 2H4 1.01.166
/yes, /if /this /present /quality /of /war — 1.03. 36
/to /look /upon /the /hideous /god /of /war 2.03. 35
/but /rather /show /a /while /like /fearful /war 4.01. 63
/ministers /and /instruments | /of /cruel /war. TRO pr 5
/or /bad, /'tis /but /the /chance /of /war. pr 31
/and /war /and /lechery /confound /all! 2.03. 75 P
whereto i am going, | greater than any /war. TNK 1.01.172
WAR 261 FR 0.0295 REL FR 239 V 22 P
sea and the azur'd vault | set roaring war; TMP 5.01. 44
war with good counsel, set the world at nought; TGV 1.01. 68
ill, when you talk of war. 5.02. 16
thus, what with the war, what with the sweat, MM 1.02. 82 P
but that i am | at war 'twixt will and will not. 2.02. 33
herein you war against your reputation, | and ERR 3.01. 86
arm'd and reverted, making war against her heir. 3.02.124 P
is a kind of merry war betwixt signior benedick ADO 1.01. 62 P
that war against your own affections | and the LLL 1.01. 9
this civil war of wits were much better used 2.01.226
war, death, or sickness did lay siege to it, MND 1.01.142
some war with rere–mice for their leathren wings 2.02. 4
such war of white and red within her cheeks! SHR 4.05. 30
and time it is, when raging war is /done, | to 5.02. 2
to offer war where they should kneel for peace, 5.02.162
equal fortune, and continue | a braving war. AWW 1.02. 3
/with his cicatrice, an emblem of war, here on 2.01. 43 P
that dwell in't jades, | therefore to th' war! 2.03.285
you heard | the fundamental reasons of this war, 3.01. 2
of thine to the event | of the none–sparing war? 3.02.105
that from the bloody course of war | my dearest 3.04. 8
it was a disaster of war that caesar himself 3.06. 52 P
had the whole theoric of war in the knot of his 4.03.142 P
what say you to his expertness in war? 4.03.265 P
i bring no overture of war, no taxation of TN 1.05.209 P
as black as vulcan in the smoke of war. 5.01. 53
the proud control of fierce and bloody war, | to JN 1.01. 17
here have we war for war and blood for blood, 1.01. 19
here have we war for war and blood for blood, 1.01. 19
shadowing their right under your wings of war. 2.01. 14
swords | in such a just and charitable war. 2.01. 36
that right in peace which here we urge in war, 2.01. 47
if that war return | from france to england, 2.01. 89
walls | can hide you from our messengers of war, 2.01.260
from a resolv'd and honorable war | to a most 2.01.585
the grappling vigor and rough frown of war | is 3.01.104
war, war, no peace! 3.01.113
war, war, no peace! 3.01.113
peace is to me a war. 3.01.113
and like a civil war set'st oath to oath, | thy 3.01.264
doth dogged war bristle his angry crest, | and 4.03.149
my tongue shall hush again this storm of war, 5.01. 20
away, and glister like the god of war | when he 5.01. 54
up, | and tame the savage spirit of wild war, 5.02. 74
sweat in this business and maintain this war? 5.02.102
before i drew this gallant head of war, | and 5.02.113
is well prepar'd | to whip this dwarfish war, 5.02.135
drums, and let the tongue of war | plead for our 5.02.164
with purpose presently to leave this war. 5.07. 86
'tis not the trial of a woman's war, | the R2 1.01. 48
hither | thus plated in habiliments of war, 1.03. 28
we will ourself in person to this war, | and, 1.04. 42
herself | against infection and the hand of war, 2.01. 44
in war was never lion rag'd more fierce, | in 2.01.173
eight tall ships, three thousand men of war, 2.01.286
with signs of war about his aged neck. 2.02. 74
keeps good old york there with his men of war? 2.03. 52
frighting her pale–fac'd villages with war | and 2.03. 94
enjoy, | the other to enjoy by rage and war. 2.04. 14
make war upon their spotted souls for this! 3.02.134
how some have been depos'd, some slain in war, 3.02.157
to open | the purple testament of bleeding war; 3.03. 94
and, toil'd with works of war, retir'd himself 4.01. 96
no more shall trenching war channel her fields, 1H4 1.01. 7
the edge of war, like an ill–sheathed knife, 1.01. 17
my sovereign liege, | but by the chance of war; 1.03. 95
thy spirit within thee hath been so at war, 2.03. 56
and to the fire–ey'd maid of smoky war | all hot 4.01.114
here, | when he was personal in the irish war. 4.03. 88
unknit | this churlish knot of all–abhorred war? 5.01. 16
sound all the lofty instruments of war, | and by 5.02. 97
is thought with child by the stern tyrant war, 2H4 in 14
into the harsh and boist'rous tongue of war? 4.01. 49
divine | to a loud trumpet and a point of war? 4.01. 52
court, | whereon this hydra son of war is born, 4.02. 38
doth the man of war stay all night, sir? 5.01. 29 P
that war, or peace, or both at once, may be | as 5.02.138
list his discourse of war, and you shall hear H5 1.01. 43
how you awake our sleeping sword of war — | we 1.02. 22
we doubt not of a fair and lucky war, | since 2.02.184
the signs of war advance! 2.02.192
to line and new repair our towns of war | with 2.04. 7
(though war nor no known quarrel were in 2.04. 17
and collected, | as were a war in expectation. 2.04. 20
on the poor souls for whom this hungry war 2.04.104
but when the blast of war blows in our ears, 3.01. 5
of grosser blood, | and teach them how to war. 3.01. 25
is not according to the disciplines of the war; 3.02. 59 P
or concerning the disciplines of the war, the 3.02. 97 P
both in the disciplines of war, and in the 3.02.129 P
as to tell you i know the disciplines of war; 3.02.140 P
what is it then to me, if impious war, | arrayed 3.03. 15
and this they con perfitly in the phrase of war, 3.06. 75 P
war is his beadle, war is his vengeance; 4.01.169 P
war is his beadle, war is his vengeance; 4.01.169 P
with maiden walls that war hath /never ent'red. 5.02.322 P
that never war advance | his bleeding sword 5.02.354
gall — | nor men nor money hath he to make war. 1H6 1.02. 17
one that still motions war and never peace, 1.03. 63
and prosperous be thy life in peace and war! 2.05.114
and peace, no war, befall thy parting soul! 2.05.115
your faithful service, and your toil in war; 3.04. 21
stands with the snares of war to tangle thee. 4.02. 22
for thee | to tutor thee in stratagems of war, 4.05. 2
free from oppression or the stroke of war, | my 5.03.155
to ease your country of distressful war | and 5.04.126
your deeds of war, and all our counsel die? 2H6 1.01. 97
rather than bloody war shall cut them short, 4.04. 12
wilt thou go dig a grave to find out war, | and 5.01.169
thus war hath given thee peace, for thou art 5.02. 29
o war, thou son of hell, | whom angry heavens do 5.02. 33
he that is truly dedicate to war | hath no 5.02. 37
shall be the war that henry means to use. 3H6 1.01. 73
first shall war unpeople this my realm; 1.01.126
in dreadful war mayst thou be overcome, | or 1.01.187
thou take an oath | to cease this civil war, and 1.01.197
i shall be, if i claim by open war. 1.02. 19
with aid of soldiers to this needful war. 2.01.147
were he as famous and as bold in war | as he is 2.01.155
make war with him that climb'd unto their nest, 2.02. 31
this battle fares like to the morning's war, 2.05. 1
so is the equal poise of this fell war. 2.05. 13
whiles lions war and battle for their dens, 2.05. 74
and let our hearts and eyes, like civil war, 2.05. 77
smooth the frowns of war with peaceful looks. 2.06. 32
and force the tyrant from his seat by war. 3.03.206
me, | but dreadful war shall answer his demand. 3.03.259
behalf | go levy men, and make prepare for war; 4.01.131
crown, | as likely to be blest in peace and war; 4.06. 35
shut | but in the night or in the time of war. 4.07. 36
not mutinous in peace, yet bold in war; 4.08. 10
to bend the fatal instruments of war | against 5.01. 87
grim–visag'd war hath smooth'd his wrinkled R3 1.01. 9
though not by war, by surfeit die your king, 1.03.196
that you will war with god by murd'ring me? 1.04.253
make war upon themselves, brother to brother, 2.04. 62
your discipline in war, wisdom in peace, | your 3.07. 16
or with the clamorous report of war | thus will 4.04.153
ere from this war thou turn a conqueror, | or i 4.04.185
which she shall purchase with still–lasting war. 4.04.344
peace | by this one bloody trial of sharp war. 5.02. 16
of bloody strokes and mortal–staring war. 5.03. 90
by all the laws of war y' are privileg'd. H8 1.04. 52
like rams | in the old time of war, would shake 4.01. 78
why should i war without the walls of troy, TRO 1.01. 2
and, like as there were husbandry in war, 1.02. 7
factious feasts, rails on our state of war, 1.03.191
count wisdom as no member of the war, 1.03.198
in hot digestion of this cormorant war — 2.02. 6
curse depending on those that war for a placket. 2.03. 20 P
"bring action hither, this cannot go to war." 2.03.136
general | to call together all his state of war. 2.03.260
in that i'll war with you. 3.02.171
they think my little stomach to the war | and 3.03.220
and tempt not yet the brushes of the war. 5.03. 34
have, you curs, | that like nor peace nor war? COR 1.01.169
to a cruel war i sent him, from whence he 1.03. 13 P
he gives my son the whole name of the war. 2.01.135 P
dames | commit the war of white and damask in 2.01.216
for the world | than camels in their war, who 2.01.251
when by and by the din of war gan pierce | his 2.02.115
being press'd to th' war, | even when the navel 3.01.122
being i' th' war, | their mutinies and revolts, 3.01.125
ordinance stood up | to speak of peace or war. 3.02. 13
friends, | i' th' war do grow together; 3.02. 43
companionship in peace | with honor, as in war, 3.02. 50
my throat of war be turn'd, | which quier'd with 3.02.112
shows of peace, | and not our streets with war! 3.03. 37
and pouring war | into the bowels of ungrateful 4.05.129
let me have war, say i, it exceeds peace as far 4.05.221 P
caius martius was | a worthy officer i' th' war, 4.06. 30
and with the deepest malice of the war | destroy 4.06. 41

austerity and garb | as he controll'd the war; 4.07. 45
silk, never admitting | counsel a' th' war; 5.06. 96
though /chance of war hath wrought this change TIT 1.01.264
brood, | nor great alcides, nor the god of war, 4.02. 95
and with revengeful war | take wreak on rome for 4.03. 33
this to apollo, this to the god of war: 4.04. 15
he might have died in war. TIM 3.05. 74
why, let the war receive't in valiant gore, 3.05. 83
for law is strict, and war is nothing more. 3.05. 84
then what should war be? 4.03. 62
and let the unscarr'd braggarts of the war 4.03.161
of contumelious, beastly, mad–brain'd war, 5.01.174
nor all deserve | the common stroke of war. 5.04. 22
make war breed peace, make peace stint war, make 5.04. 83
make war breed peace, make peace stint war, make 5.04. 83
than that poor brutus, with himself at war, JC 1.02. 46
in ranks and squadrons and right form of war, 2.02. 20
their infants quartered with the hands of war; 3.01.268
cry "havoc," and let slip the dogs of war, 3.01.273
as they would make | war with mankind. MAC 2.04. 18
king that he | prepares for some attempt of war. 3.06. 39
must arbitrate, | towards which advance the war. 5.04. 21
fight, | the noble thanes do bravely in the war, 5.07. 26
and foreign mart for implements of war, | why HAM 1.01. 74
the soldiers' music and the rite of war | speak 5.02.399
with th' ancient of war on our proceeding. LR 5.01. 32
i hold you but a subject of this war, | not as a 5.03. 60
by th' law of war thou wast not bound to answer 5.03.153
horribly stuff'd with epithites of war, | /and, OTH 1.01. 14
though in the trade of war i have slain men, 1.02. 1
hath made the flinty and steel /couch of war 1.03.230
behind, | a moth of peace, and he go to the war, 1.03.256
what, in a town of war, | yet wild, the people's 2.03.213
pride, pomp, and circumstance of glorious war! 3.03.354
that o'er the files and musters of the war ANT 1.01. 3
but soon that war had end, and the time's state 1.02. 91
whose better issue in the war from italy, | upon 1.02. 93
servant, making peace or war | as thou affects. 1.03. 70
name strikes more | than could his war resisted. 1.04. 55
have donn'd his helm | for such a petty war. 2.01. 34
was theme for you — you were the word of war. 2.02. 44
it raises the greater war between him and his 2.07. 9 P
that magical word of war, we have effected; 3.01. 31
i'll raise the preparation of a war | shall 3.04. 26
hearing that you prepar'd for war, acquainted 3.06. 58
are levying | the kings o' th' earth for war. 3.06. 68
an eunuch and your maids | manage this war. 3.07. 15
a charge we bear i' th' war, | and, as the 3.07. 16
no practice had | in the brave squares of war; 3.11. 40
though you fled | from that great face of war, 3.13. 5
determine this great war in single fight! 4.04. 37
o, wither'd is the garland of the war, | the 4.15. 64
friend and companion in the front of war, | the 5.01. 44
see | how hardly i was drawn into this war, 5.01. 74
nor like to be) | that this will prove a war; CYM 2.04. 17
war and confusion | in caesar's name pronounce i 3.01. 65
of courts, of princes, of the tricks in war. 3.03. 15
the toil o' th' war, | a pain that only seems to 3.03. 49
from whence he moves | his war for britain. 3.05. 26
the disorder's such | as war were hoodwink'd. 5.02. 16
turn'd coward | but by example (o, a sin in war, 5.03. 36
than we | that draw his knives i' th' war. 5.03. 73
sir, the chance of war, the day | was yours by 5.05. 75
never was a war did cease | (ere bloody hands 5.05.484
and with /th' /ostent of war will look so huge, PER 1.02. 25
he flatters you, makes war upon your life. 1.02. 45
who either by public war or private treason 1.02.104
bid him that we, whom flaming war doth scorch, TNK 1.01. 91
and be more costly than | your suppliants' war! 1.01.133
hard, and harsher | than strife or war could be. 1.02. 26
peace be to you | as i pursue this war! 1.03. 25
by th' helm of mars, i saw them in the war, 1.04. 17
at misery | and bear the chance of war yet. 2.02. 3
(better the red–ey'd god of war nev'r /ware), 2.02. 21
the hand of war hurts none here, nor the seas 2.02. 87
and there he met with brave gallants of war, 3.05. 61
know, of this war | you are the treasure, and 5.03. 30
now, | even by the stern and direful god of war, VEN 98
o, what a war of looks was then between them! 355
"it shall be cause of war and dire events, | and 1159
this silent war of lilies and of roses, | which LUC 71
make war against proportion'd course of time; 774
afar, | how he in peace is wounded, not in war. 831
sweets with sweets war not, joy delights in joy. SON 8. 2
and all in war with time for love of you, | as 15.13
mightier way | make war upon this bloody tyrant, 16. 2
such civil war is in my love and hate, | that i 35.12
mine eye and heart are at a mortal war, | how to 46. 1
when wasteful war shall statues overturn, | and 55. 5
WARBLE 3 FR 0.0003 REL FR 1 V 2 P
warble, child, make passionate my sense of LLL 3.01. 1 P
come, warble, come. AYL 2.05. 37 P
the well–tun'd warble of her nightly sorrow, LUC 1080
WARBLING 2 FR 0.0002 REL FR 2 V 0 P
both warbling of one song, both in one key, | as MND 3.02.206
song by rote, | to each word a warbling note. 5.01.398
WARD 18 FR 0.0020 REL FR 8 V 10 P
come, from thy ward, | for i can here disarm TMP 1.02.472
drive her then from the ward of her purity, her WIV 2.02.248 P
there not men in your ward sufficient to serve MM 2.01.267 P
have any thing to say to me, come to my ward; 4.03. 63 P
for the best ward of mine honor is rewarding my LLL 3.01.132 P
his majesty's command, to whom i am now in ward,
AWW 1.01. 5 P
say this to him, | he's beat from his best ward. WT 1.02. 33
thou knowest my old ward: 1H4 2.04.195 P
may be the deputy's wife of the ward to thee. 3.03.115 P
i know, ere they will have me go to ward, 2H6 5.01.112
god will in justice ward you as his soldiers; R3 5.03.254
a woman, a man knows not at what ward you lie. TRO 1.02.259 P
if i cannot ward what i would not have hit, i 1.02.267 P
his son was but a ward two years ago. ROM 1.05. 40
the father should be as ward to the son, and the LR 1.02. 73 P
seat, and in that motion might | omit a ward, or TNK 5.03. 63
each one by him enforc'd retires his ward; LUC 303
prison my heart in thy steel bosom's ward, | but SON 133. 9
WARDED 1 FR 0.0001 REL FR 1 V 0 P
tell him it was a hand that warded him | from TIT 3.01.194
WARDEN 1 FR 0.0001 REL FR 0 V 1 P
i must have saffron to color the warden pies; WT 4.03. 45 P
/WARDER* 1 FR 0.0001 REL FR 1 V 0 P
/when /the /king /did /throw /his /warder /down 2H4 4.01.123
WARDER* 2 FR 0.0002 REL FR 2 V 0 P
stay, the king hath thrown his warder down. R2 1.03.118
that memory, the warder of the brain, | shall be MAC 1.07. 65
WARDERS' 1 FR 0.0001 REL FR 1 V 0 P
though castles topple on their warders' heads; MAC 4.01. 56
WARDERS 1 FR 0.0001 REL FR 1 V 0 P
where be these warders, that they wait not here? 1H6 1.03. 3
WARDROBE 5 FR 0.0005 REL FR 2 V 3 P
look what a wardrobe here is for thee! TMP 4.01.223 P
the strachy married the yeoman of the wardrobe. TN 2.05. 40 P
whereof the hangman hath no lean wardrobe. 1H4 1.02. 73 P
and silken dalliance in the wardrobe lies; H5 2.pr. 2
or as the wardrobe which the robe doth hide, SON 52.10
WARDROP 1 FR 0.0001 REL FR 1 V 0 P
i'll murder all his wardrop, piece by piece, 1H4 5.03. 27
/WARDS 1 FR 0.0001 REL FR 0 V 1 P
/in /which /there /are /many /confines, /wards, HAM 2.02.246 P
WARDS 5 FR 0.0005 REL FR 3 V 2 P
it | to lock it in the wards of covert bosom, MM 5.01. 10
how thirty at least he fought with, what wards, 1H4 1.02.189 P
and at all these wards i lie, at a thousand TRO 1.02.263 P
that were ne'er acquainted with their wards TIM 3.03. 37
from hands of falsehood, in sure wards of trust! SON 48. 4
WARE* *(also wore)*
/WARE* 1 FR 0.0001 REL FR 1 V 0 P
(better the red–ey'd god of war nev'r /ware), TNK 2.02. 21
WARE* 9 FR 0.0010 REL FR 4 V 5 P
ware pencils /ho! LLL 5.02. 43
thou speak'st wiser than thou art ware of. AYL 2.04. 57 P
i shall ne'er be ware of mine own wit till i 2.04. 58 P
were big enough for the bed of ware in england, TN 3.02. 48 P
come, you'll do him wrong ere you are ware. TRO 4.02. 55 P
the bull has the game, ware horns ho! 5.07. 12 P
last | that ware the imperial diadem of rome, TIT 1.01. 6
towards him i made, but he was ware of me, | and ROM 1.01.124
but that thou overheardst, ere i was ware, | my 2.02.103
WARE–A 1 FR 0.0001 REL FR 1 V 0 P
a meddler, | that doth utter all men's ware–a. WT 4.04.323
WARES 3 FR 0.0003 REL FR 2 V 1 P
and retails his wares | at wakes and wassails, LLL 5.02.317
has he any unbraided wares? WT 4.04.203 P
let us, like merchants, first show foul wares, TRO 1.03.358
WARILY 2 FR 0.0002 REL FR 1 V 1 P
warily | i stole into a neighbor thicket by, LLL 5.02. 93
they that ride so, and ride not warily, fall H5 3.07. 57 P
/WARLIKE 1 FR 0.0001 REL FR 1 V 0 P
/there /disgorge | /their /warlike /fraughtage. TRO pr 13
WAR–LIKE 1 FR 0.0001 REL FR 0 V 1 P
generally allow'd for your many war–like, WIV 2.02.228 P
WARLIKE 61 FR 0.0069 REL FR 58 V 3 P
unfold to us some warlike resistance. AWW 1.01.117 P
these warlike principles | do not throw from you 2.01. 1
where the warlike smalus, | that noble honor'd WT 5.01.157
in warlike march these greens before your town, JN 2.01.242
told of a many thousand warlike french | that 4.02.199
and flesh his spirit in a warlike soil, 5.01. 71
rather for sport than need) | is warlike john; 5.02.176
head, | and by the buried hand of warlike gaunt, R2 3.03.109
the noble westmerland, and warlike blunt, | and 1H4 4.04. 30
then should the warlike harry, like himself, H5 pr 5
invoke his warlike spirit, | and your 1.02.104
if thou receive me for thy warlike mate. 1H6 1.02. 92
ne'er heard i of a warlike enterprise | more 2.01. 44
princely train | call ye the warlike talbot, for 2.02. 35
the reason mov'd these warlike lords to this 2.05. 70
warlike and martial talbot, burgundy | enshrines 3.02.118
to burdeaux, warlike duke! 4.03. 22
i break my warlike word; 4.03. 31
i met in travel toward his warlike father! 4.03. 36
till with thy warlike sword, despite of fate, 4.06. 8
quicken'd with youthful spleen and warlike rage, 4.06. 13
and turn again unto the warlike french. 5.02. 3
that dims the honor of this warlike isle! 2H6 1.01.125
whose warlike ears could never brook retreat, 3H6 1.01. 5
so fled his enemies my warlike father; 2.01. 19
who look'd full gently on his warlike queen, 2.01.123
nor when thy warlike father, like a child, R3 1.02.159
thou didst crown his warlike brows with paper, 1.03.174
a good direction, warlike sovereign. 5.03.302
what warlike voice, | and to what end is this? H8 1.04. 50
you brace of warlike brothers, welcome hither. TRO 4.05.175
the warlike service he has done, consider; COR 3.03. 49
they are in a most warlike preparation, and hope 4.03. 17 P
now, by the gods that warlike goths adore, TIT 2.01. 61
thy warlike hand, thy mangled daughter here, 3.01.255
is warlike lucius general of the goths? 4.04. 69
emperor requests a parley | of warlike lucius, 4.04.102
to pluck proud lucius from the warlike goths. 4.04.110
who leads towards rome a band of warlike goths, 5.02.113
welcome, ye warlike goths; 5.03. 27
aid | to wake northumberland and warlike siward, MAC 3.06. 31
with ten thousand warlike men | already at a 4.03.134
before my body | i throw my warlike shield. 5.08. 33
together with that fair and warlike form | in HAM 1.01. 47
th' imperial jointress to this warlike state, 1.02. 9
a pirate of very warlike appointment gave us 4.06. 16 P
what warlike noise is this? 5.02.349
of england gives | this warlike volley. 5.02.352
since thy outside looks so fair and warlike, LR 5.03.143
for that it stands not in such warlike brace, OTH 1.03. 24
lieutenant to the warlike moor othello, | is 2.01. 27
thanks you, the valiant of /this warlike isle, 2.01. 43
the very elements of this warlike isle, | have i 2.03. 57
look'st like him that knows a warlike charge. ANT 4.04. 19
which to shake off | becomes a warlike people, CYM 3.01. 52
like warlike as the wolf for what we eat; 3.03. 41
i sit and tell | the warlike feats i have done, 3.03. 90
face | the livery of the warlike maid appears, TNK 4.02.106
fearing some hard news from the warlike band LUC 255
quoth she, "the warlike god embrac'd me," | and PP 11. 5
quoth she, "the warlike god unlac'd me," | as if 11. 7
WARM 48 FR 0.0054 REL FR 36 V 12 P
warm, o' my troth! TMP 2.02. 34 P
this sensible warm motion to become | a kneaded MM 3.01.119
by order of law a furr'd gown to keep him warm; 3.02. 8 P
your cake here is warm within: ERR 3.01. 71
when i am warm, he cools me with beating. 4.04. 33 P
that if he have wit enough to keep himself warm, ADO 1.01. 68 P
why should a man, whose blood is warm within, MV 1.01. 83
go to thy cold bed, and warm thee. SHR in.1. 10 P
balm his foul head in warm distilled waters, in.1. 48
yes, keep you warm. 2.01.266
a fire, and they are coming after to warm them. 4.01. 5 P
but i with blowing the fire shall warm myself; 4.01. 10 P
whilst thou li'st warm at home, secure and safe; 5.02.151
even with such life of majesty (warm life, | as WT 5.03. 35
the very life seems warm upon her lip. 5.03. 66
o, she's warm! 5.03.109
whiles warm life plays in that infant's veins, JN 3.04.132
full warm of blood, of mirth, of gossiping. 5.02. 59
on the banes, such a commodity of warm slaves, 1H4 4.02. 17 P
for maids, well summer'd and warm kept, are like
H5 5.02.308 P
i fear me you but warm the starved snake, | who, 2H6 3.01.343
shall, whiles thy head is warm and new cut off, 3H6 5.01. 55
swills your warm blood like wash and makes his R3 5.02. 9
he's not yet through warm. TRO 2.03.222 P
i am not warm yet, let us fight again. 4.05.118
by his looks, methinks, | 'tis warm at 's heart. COR 2.03.152
alas, a crimson river of warm blood, | like to a TIT 2.04. 22
in winter with warm tears i'll melt the snow, 3.01. 20
o, take this warm kiss on thy pale cold lips, 5.03.153
had she affections and warm youthful blood, ROM 2.05. 12
thy lips are warm. 5.03.167
and juliet bleeding, warm, and newly dead, | who 5.03.175
and juliet, dead before, | warm and new kill'd. 5.03.197
chamberlain, | will put thy shirt on warm? TIM 4.03.223
heaven's benediction com'st | to the warm sun! LR 2.02.162
if only to go warm were gorgeous, | why, nature 2.04.268
wear'st, | which scarcely keeps thee warm. 2.04.270
go to thy bed, and warm thee. 3.04. 48 P
keep thee warm. 3.04.174
or feed on nourishing dishes, or keep you warm, OTH 3.03. 78
yet with parthian blood thy sword is warm, | the ANT 3.01. 6
but it would warm his spirits | to hear from me 3.13. 69
come put it on, keep thee warm. PER 2.01. 79 P
my brother's heart, and warm it to some pity, TNK 1.01.128
sun that shines from heaven shines but warm, VEN 193
welcomes the warm approach of sweet desire; 386
the warm effects which she in him finds missing 605
and see thy blood warm when thou feel'st it cold SON 2.14
WAR–MAN 1 FR 0.0001 REL FR 0 V 1 P
the sweet war–man is dead and rotten, sweet LLL 5.02.660 P
WAR–MARK'D 1 FR 0.0001 REL FR 1 V 0 P
which doth most consist | of war–mark'd footmen,
ANT 3.07. 44
WARM'D 9 FR 0.0010 REL FR 8 V 1 P
warm'd and cool'd by the same winter and summer,
MV 3.01. 63 P
were he not warm'd with ale, | this were a bed SHR in.1. 32
snakes, in my heart–blood warm'd, that sting my R2 3.02.131
it warm'd thy father's heart with proud desire 1H6 4.06. 11
my work hath yet not warm'd me. COR 1.05. 17
they were living, warm'd themselves on thine! TIT 5.03.168
middle of my heart | is warm'd by th' rest — CYM 1.06. 28
view on't | might well have warm'd old saturn; 2.05. 12
which many legions of true hearts had warm'd, SON 154. 6
WARMED 2 FR 0.0002 REL FR 2 V 0 P
not one whose flame my heart so much as warmed,
LC 191
what breast so cold that is not warmed here? 292
WARMER 2 FR 0.0002 REL FR 1 V 1 P
they were warmer that got this than the poor WT 3.03. 75 P
state, and wish | that warmer days would come. CYM 2.04. 6
WARMING 1 FR 0.0001 REL FR 0 V 1 P
excellent sherris is the warming of the blood, 2H4 4.03.103 P
WARMING–PAN 1 FR 0.0001 REL FR 0 V 1 P
his sheets, and do the office of a warming–pan. H5 2.01. 84 P
WARMS 3 FR 0.0003 REL FR 2 V 1 P
that sun that warms you here shall shine on me, R2 1.03.145
but the sherris warms it, and makes it course 2H4 4.03.106 P
it warms the very sickness in my heart | that i HAM 4.07. 55
WARMTH 6 FR 0.0006 REL FR 4 V 2 P
but what warmth is there in your affection MV 1.02. 33 P
no warmth, no /breath shall testify thou livest; ROM 4.01. 98
'tis lack of kindly warmth they are not kind; TIM 2.02.217
from the loath'd warmth whereof deliver me, and LR 4.06.267 P
come then, and take the last warmth of my lips. ANT 5.02.291
nature awakes, | a warmth /breathes out of her. PER 3.02. 93
WARN *(also vor')*
WARN 5 FR 0.0005 REL FR 4 V 1 P
will spit, and for lovers lacking (god warn us!) AYL 4.01. 77 P
and sent to warn them to his royal presence. R3 1.03. 39
and soothe the devil that i warn thee from? 1.03.297
to warn false traitors from the like attempts. 3.05. 49
they mean to warn us at philippi here, JC 5.01. 5
WARN'D 5 FR 0.0005 REL FR 4 V 1 P
who is it that hath warn'd us to the walls? JN 2.01.201
be warn'd by me then: H5 3.07. 56 P
look to it well, and say you are well warn'd. 1H6 2.04.103
his grace not being warn'd thereof before: R3 3.07. 86
but say i warn'd ye; H8 3.01.109
WARNING 15 FR 0.0017 REL FR 9 V 6 P
the deputy, sir, he has given him warning. MM 3.02. 35 P
walls are so willful to hear without warning. MND 5.01.209 P
third, dull lead, with warning all as blunt, MV 2.07. 8
the worst is this, that, at so slender warning, SHR 4.04. 60
as a beacon gives warning to all the rest of 2H4 4.03.108 P
hark, hark, the dolphin's drum, a warning bell, 1H6 4.02. 39
somewhat too sudden, sirs, the warning is, | but 5.02. 14
i think he hath a very fair warning. 2H6 4.06. 10 P
and to be on foot at an hour's warning. COR 4.03. 45 P
the boy gives warning, something doth approach. ROM 5.03. 18
i come to observe, i give thee warning on't. TIM 1.02. 34
no counsel, take no warning by my coming. 3.01. 26 P
to make them instruments of fear and warning JC 1.03. 70
awake the god of day, and at his warning, HAM 1.01.152
bell | give warning to the world that i am fled SON 71. 3
WARNINGS 2 FR 0.0002 REL FR 2 V 0 P
our hearts receive your warnings. AWW 2.01. 22
these does she apply for warnings and portents JC 2.02. 80
WARNS 1 FR 0.0001 REL FR 1 V 0 P

a bell | that warns my old age to a sepulchre. ROM 5.03.207
WARP 5 FR 0.0005 REL FR 3 V 2 P
from which we would not have you warp. MM 1.01. 14
though thou the waters warp, | thy sting is not AYL 2.07.187
shrunk panel, and like green timber warp, warp. 3.03. 89 P
shrunk panel, and like green timber warp, warp. 3.03. 89 P
methinks | my favor here begins to warp. WT 1.02.365
/WARP'D 1 FR 0.0001 REL FR 1 V 0 P
/whose /warp'd /looks /proclaim | /what /store LR 3.06. 53
WARP'D 2 FR 0.0002 REL FR 2 V 0 P
which warp'd the line of every other favor, AWW 5.03. 49
in me, | since thy best props are warp'd! TNK 3.02. 32
WARPED 1 FR 0.0001 REL FR 1 V 0 P
for such a warped slip of wilderness | ne'er MM 3.01.141
WAR–PROOF 1 FR 0.0001 REL FR 1 V 0 P
whose blood is fet from fathers of war–proof! H5 3.01. 18
'WARRANT 1 FR 0.0001 REL FR 1 V 0 P
'warrant thee, my man's as true as steel. ROM 2.04.198
WARRANT *(also warr'nt)*
/WARRANT 2 FR 0.0002 REL FR 2 V 0 P
/cracking /the /strong /warrant /of /an /oath, R2 4.01.235
/fruit | /hope /gives /not /so /much /warrant, 2H4 1.03. 40
WARRANT 179 FR 0.0202 REL FR 84 V 95 P
i'll warrant him for drowning, though the ship TMP 1.01. 46 P
no, i warrant you, i will not adventure my 2.01.187 P
ay, lord, she will become thy bed, i warrant, 3.02.104
of five for one will bring us | good warrant of. 3.03. 49
i warrant you, sir, | the white cold virgin snow 4.01. 54
i'll warrant you, 'tis as well: TGV 2.01.164 P
his worth is warrant for his welcome hither, 2.04.102
of love, | warrant me welcome to my proteus. 2.07. 71
upon this warrant shall you have access | where 3.02. 60
i warrant you, my lord — more grace than boy. 5.04.166
armigero, in any bill, warrant, quittance, or WIV 1.01. 10 P
but, i warrant you, the women have so cried and 1.01.296 P
and, i warrant you, no tell–tale nor no 1.04. 12 P
i warrant he hath a thousand of these letters, 2.01. 74 P
i warrant thee, nobody hears — mine own people, 2.02. 50 P
i warrant you, coach after coach, letter after 2.02. 65 P
and so rushling, i warrant you, in silk and gold 2.02. 67 P
and, i warrant you, they could never get an 2.02. 70 P
and, i warrant you, they could never get her so 2.02. 74 P
but, i warrant you, all is one with her. 2.02. 77 P
i warrant you, he's the man should fight with 3.01. 68 P
i warrant. what, robin, i say! 3.03. 4 P
i warrant thee, if i do not act it, hiss me. 3.03. 38 P
i warrant you, buck, and of the season too, it 3.03.158 P
i'll warrant we'll unkennel the fox. 3.03.163 P
she'll make you amends, i warrant you. 3.05. 47 P
"hang–hog" is latin for bacon, i warrant you. 4.01. 48 P
with the warrant of womanhood and the witness of 4.02.207 P
i'll warrant they'll have him publicly sham'd, 4.02.220 P
i warrant they would whip me with their fine 4.05. 99 P
yes, i warrant; 4.05.110 P
how things go, and, i warrant, to your content. 4.05.122 P
thou'rt a three–pil'd piece, i warrant thee. MM 1.02. 32 P
i warrant it is; 1.02.172 P
the provost hath | a warrant for 's execution. 1.04. 74
nay, i'll not warrant that; 2.04. 59
look, here's the warrant, claudio, for thy death 4.02. 63
and show'd him a seeming warrant for it; 4.02.152 P
claudio, whom here you have warrant to execute, 4.02.157 P
by the vow of mine order i warrant you, if my 4.02.169 P
i warrant your honor. 5.01. 82
he sends a warrant | for my poor brother's head. 5.01.102
had you a special warrant for the deed? 5.01.459
minds | a doubtful warrant of immediate death, ERR 1.01. 68
could all my travels warrant me they live. 1.01.139
i warrant, her rags and the tallow in them will 3.02. 98 P
money, | to warrant thee, as i am 'rested for. 4.04. 3
here's that, i warrant you, will pay them all. 4.04. 10
head at so long a breathing, but i warrant thee, ADO 2.01.363 P
i'll make her come, i warrant you, presently. 3.01. 14
she's limed, i warrant you. 3.01.104
i warrant one that knows him not. 3.02. 64 P
wonder not till further warrant. 3.02.112 P
be made bring deformed forth, i warrant you. 3.03.173 P
a commodity in question, i warrant you. 3.03.179 P
so good, and i warrant your cousin will say so. 3.04. 9 P
we will spare for no wit, i warrant you. 3.05. 61 P
which with experimental seal doth warrant | the 4.01.166
than that which maiden modesty doth warrant, 4.01.179
and, i'll warrant you, for the love of beatrice. 5.01.195 P
hath wisdom's warrant and the help of school, LLL 5.02. 71
thou mayst, i warrant. MV 4.02. 15
no, i warrant your grace, you shall not entreat AYL 1.02.205 P
it, which i warrant she is apter to do than to 3.02.388 P
your features, lord warrant us! what features? 3.03. 5 P
th' shoulder, but i'll warrant him heart–whole. 4.01. 49 P
i warrant you, with pure love and troubled brain 4.03. 3 P
i warrant you we will play our part | as he SHR in.1. 69
and other books, good ones, i warrant ye. 1.02.170
i warrant him, petruchio is kated. 3.02.245
i warrant you. 4.04. 8
o lord, sir! — nay, put me to't, i warrant you. AWW 2.02. 48 P
no, sir, i warrant you. 4.01. 10 P
sport royal, i warrant you. TN 2.03.172 P
that's me, i warrant you. 2.05. 79 P
i warrant thou art a merry fellow and car'st for 3.01. 26 P
no, i warrant you, he will not hear of godliness 3.04.121 P
i warrant there's vinegar and pepper in't. 3.04.143 P
ay, is't! i warrant him. do but read. 3.04.146 P
i shall incur to pass it, | having no warrant. WT 2.02. 56
which is enough, i'll warrant, | as this world 2.03. 72
heart that way, and that he knew, i warrant him. 4.03.108 P
i warrant you. 4.04.698 P
a great man, i'll warrant; 4.04.752 P
boy, | under whose warrant i impeach thy wrong, JN 2.01.116
there's law and warrant, lady, for my curse. 3.01.184
i hope your warrant will bear out the deed. 4.01. 6
i warrant i love you more than you do me. 4.01. 31
he show'd his warrant to a friend of mine. 4.02. 70
by slaves that take their humors for a warrant 4.02.209
to give us warrant from the hand of heaven, 5.02. 66
the scope | and warrant limited unto my tongue. 5.02.123
i warrant they have made peace with bullingbrook R2 3.02.127
to go to bed with a candle, i warrant thee. 1H4 2.01. 44 P
hanging of thy nether lip, that doth warrant me. 2.04.405 P
i warrant you, that man is not alive | might so 3.01.171
i am undone by his going, i warrant you, he's an 2H4 2.01. 23 P
i warrant you, as common as the way between 2.02.167 P
and your color, i warrant you, is as red as any 2.04. 25 P
masters, how i shake, look you, i warrant you. 2.04.106 P
murder, i warrant now. 2.04.206 P
no, i warrant you. 2.04.341 P
she shall have whipping cheer, i warrant her. 5.04. 5 P
that is well, i warrant you, when time is serve. H5 3.06. 66 P
you shall find, i warrant you, that there is no 4.01. 70 P
i warrant you, you shall find the ceremonies of 4.01. 71 P
the maps of the orld, i warrant you sall find, 4.07. 24 P
i warrant it is to knight you, captain. 4.08. 1 P
treason his payment into plows, i warrant you. 4.08. 14 P
and, i warrant you, it is the better for you. 4.08. 66 P
'tis a good silling, i warrant you, or i will 4.08. 71 P
father, i warrant you, take you no care, | i'll 1H6 1.04. 21
and that my fainting words do warrant death. 2.05. 95
an uproar, i dare warrant, | begun through 3.01. 74
upon thy princely warrant, i descend | to give 5.03.143
beside, his wealth doth warrant a liberal dower, 5.05. 46
fear not that, i warrant thee. 2H6 4.03. 17 P
they come, i'll warrant they'll make it good. 5.01.122
the first i warrant thee, if dreams prove true. 5.01.195
then i'll warrant you all your lands, | and if 3H6 3.02. 21
we are, my lord, and come to have the warrant, R3 1.03.341
not to kill him, having a warrant, but to be 1.04.110 P
him, from the which no warrant can defend me. 1.04.111 P
but nothing /spake in warrant from himself. 3.07. 33
i warrant you, my lord. 5.03. 57
here is a warrant from | the king t' attach lord H8 1.01.216
you have christian warrant for 'em, and no doubt 3.02.244
paris is dirt to him, and i warrant helen, to TRO 1.02.238 P
no, i warrant you, the fool's will shame it. 2.01. 87 P
we fear to warrant in our native place! 2.02. 96
o, i warrant, how he mammock'd it! COR 1.03. 65 P
to th' pot, i warrant him. 1.04. 47
'twas time for him too, i'll warrant him that; 2.01.129 P
ay, i warrant you, and not without his true 2.01.139 P
on the sudden, | i warrant him consul. 2.01.222
where you should but hunt | with modest warrant. 3.01.274
a noble fellow, i warrant him. 5.02.109 P
i warrant you, madam, we will make that sure. TIT 2.03.133
i warrant you, sir, let me alone. 4.03.114 P
president, and lively warrant | for me, most 5.03. 44
i warrant, and i should live a thousand years, ROM 1.03. 46
and yet i warrant it had upon it brow | a bump 1.03. 52
i warrant you, i dare draw as soon as another 2.04.158 P
man, but, i'll warrant you, when i say so, she 2.04.205 P
but, i'll warrant him, as gentle as a lamb. 2.05. 44 P
and, i warrant, a virtuous — where is your 2.05. 57
i am pepper'd, i warrant, for this world. 3.01. 99 P
and all things shall be well, i warrant thee, 4.02. 40
fast, i warrant her, she. 4.05. 1
sleep for a week, for the next night, i warrant, 4.05. 5
a gift, i warrant. TIM 3.01. 6 P
royal cheer, i warrant you. 3.06. 49 P
there's warrant in that theft | which steals MAC 2.03.145
i warrant your honor. HAM 3.02. 15 P
i'll warrant she'll tax him home, | and, as you 3.03. 29
and dare upon the warrant of my note | commend a LR 3.01. 18
of arts inhibited and out of warrant. OTH 1.02. 79
i warrant thee. 2.01.283 P
and, i'll warrant her, full of game. 2.03. 19 P
i warrant it grieves my husband | as if the 3.03. 3
emilia here, | i give thee warrant of thy place. 3.03. 20
i warrant, something from venice. 4.01.214
it is but so, i warrant. 4.02.168
i warrant you, madam. ANT 3.03. 48
thou shalt | go back, i warrant thee; 5.02.156
(and upon warrant of bloody affirmation) his to CYM 1.04. 59 P
an ancient soldier | (an honest one, i warrant), 5.03. 16
i warrant you, madam. PER 4.01. 46
her age, with warrant of her virginity, and cry, 4.02. 58 P
with shame which is her way to go with warrant. 4.02.128 P
i warrant you, mistress, thunder shall not so 4.02.142 P
what my thoughts | did warrant me was likely. 5.01.134
upon this coast, i warrant you. 5.03. 20
i warrant her, she'll do the rarest gambols. TNK 3.05. 75
i warrant you. 3.06. 62
i'll warrant thee, i'll strike home. 3.06. 68
i'll warrant ye he had not so few last night 4.01.137
i'll warrant you within these three or four days 5.02.104
discern | authority for sin, warrant for blame, LUC 620
WARRANTED 4 FR 0.0004 REL FR 2 V 2 P
must, upon a warranted need, give him a better MM 3.02.143 P
and by other warranted testimony. AWW 2.05. 5 P
shall, is warranted | by a commission from the H8 2.04. 91
of goodness | be like our warranted quarrel! MAC 4.03.137
WARRANTETH 1 FR 0.0001 REL FR 1 V 0 P
that warranteth by law to be thy privilege. 1H6 5.04. 61
WARRANTING 1 FR 0.0001 REL FR 1 V 0 P
shall | by warranting moonlight corslet thee — TNK 1.01.177
WARRANTISE 1 FR 0.0001 REL FR 1 V 0 P
there is such strength and warrantise of skill SON 150. 7
WARRANTIZE 1 FR 0.0001 REL FR 1 V 0 P
break up the gates, i'll be your warrantize. 1H6 1.03. 13
WARRANT'S 2 FR 0.0002 REL FR 1 V 1 P
for look you, the warrant's come. MM 4.03. 42 P
the warrant's for yourself; take heed to't. 5.01. 83
WARRANTS 3 FR 0.0003 REL FR 3 V 0 P
an assurance | that my remembrance warrants. TMP 1.02. 46
are well express'd | by all external warrants), MM 2.04.137
warrants these words in princely courtesy. TIT 1.01.272
WARRANTY 3 FR 0.0003 REL FR 3 V 0 P
and from your love i have a warranty | to MV 1.01.132
have been as far enlarg'd | as we have warranty. HAM 5.01.227
but with such general warranty of heaven | as i OTH 5.02. 60
/WARR'D 1 FR 0.0001 REL FR 1 V 0 P
his brother /warr'd upon him, although i think ANT 2.01. 41
WARR'D 1 FR 0.0001 REL FR 1 V 0 P
wars hath not wasted it, for warr'd he hath not, R2 2.01.252
WARREN 1 FR 0.0001 REL FR 0 V 1 P
him here as melancholy as a lodge in a warren. ADO 2.01.215 P
WARRENER 1 FR 0.0001 REL FR 0 V 1 P
he hath fought with a warrener. WIV 1.04. 27 P
/WARRING 1 FR 0.0001 REL FR 1 V 0 P
face | to be oppos'd against the /warring winds? LR 4.07. 31
WARRIOR 13 FR 0.0014 REL FR 13 V 0 P
to this town by that most famous warrior, | duke ERR 5.01.368
your buskin'd mistress and your warrior love, MND 2.01. 71
this infant warrior, in his enterprises 1H4 3.02.113
i did look for | of such an ungrown warrior. 5.04. 23
to feast so great a warrior in my house. 1H6 2.03. 82
and, worthy warrior, welcome to our tents. TRO 4.05.200
thou art my warrior, | i /holp to frame thee. COR 5.03. 62
a nobler man, a braver warrior, | lives not this TIT 1.01. 25
you up | to be a warrior and command a camp. 4.02.180
o my fair warrior! OTH 2.01.182
emilia, | i was (unhandsome warrior as i am) 3.04.151
kiss it, my warrior; ANT 4.08. 24
the painful warrior famoused for /fight, | after SON 25. 9
WARRIORS 16 FR 0.0018 REL FR 16 V 0 P
and a head | of gallant warriors, noble 1H4 4.04. 26
to new–store france with bastard warriors. H5 3.05. 31
and my kind kinsman, warriors all, adieu! 4.03. 10
we are but warriors for the working–day; 4.03.109
france were no place for henry's warriors, | nor 1H6 3.03. 22
we english warriors wot not what it means. 4.07. 55
and when the hardiest warriors did retire, 3H6 1.04. 14
brave warriors, clifford and northumberland, 1.04. 66
why then it sorts, brave warriors. let's away. 2.01.209
brave warriors, march amain towards coventry. 4.08. 64
of so high a courage, | and warriors faint! 5.04. 51
let us to priam's hall | to greet the warriors. TRO 3.01.149
flower of warriors, | how is't with titus COR 1.06. 32
yet welcome, warriors; 2.01.189
approved warriors, and my faithful friends, | i TIT 5.01. 1
fierce fiery warriors fight upon the clouds | in JC 2.02. 19
WARR'NT *(also warrant)*
/WARR'NT 2 FR 0.0002 REL FR 2 V 0 P
i /warr'nt, good creature, wheresoe'er she is, AWW 3.05. 66
i'll /warr'nt you, fear me not. HAM 3.04. 6
WARR'NT 2 FR 0.0002 REL FR 1 V 1 P
he for a man, god warr'nt us; MND 5.01.320 P
i warr'nt it will. HAM 1.02.242
WARR'ST 2 FR 0.0002 REL FR 2 V 0 P
apart, | warr'st thou with a woman's heart?" AYL 4.03. 45
warr'st thou 'gainst athens? TIM 4.03.103
WAR'S 10 FR 0.0011 REL FR 9 V 1 P
gracing the scroll that tells of this war's loss JN 2.01.348
it is war's prize to take all vantages, | and 3H6 1.04. 59
i long till edward fall by war's mischance, 3.03.254
that caius martius | wears this war's garland; COR 1.09. 60
bastard children than war's a destroyer of men. 4.05.225 P
great son, | the end of war's uncertain; 5.03.141
have you dream'd of late of this war's purpose? CYM 4.02.345
must feel war's blow, who spares not innocence: PER 1.02. 93
is't said this war's afoot? TNK 1.02.104
mars his sword nor war's quick fire shall burn SON 55. 7
WARS' 1 FR 0.0001 REL FR 1 V 0 P
full | of the wars' surfeits to go rove with one COR 4.01. 46
WARS 143 FR 0.0161 REL FR 104 V 39 P
some to the wars, to try their fortune there; TGV 1.03. 8
long since thy husband serv'd me in my wars, ERR 5.01.161
when i bestrid thee in the wars, and took | deep 5.01.192
signior mountanto return'd from the wars or no? ADO 1.01. 31 P
how many hath he kill'd and eaten in these wars? 1.01. 43 P
he hath done good service, lady, in these wars. 1.01. 49 P
is, | saying i lik'd her ere i went to wars. 1.01.305
entire sum | disbursed by my father in his wars. LLL 2.01.131
telling the bushes that thou look'st for wars, MND 3.02.408
the wars hath so kept you under that you must AWW 1.01.195 P
o, 'tis brave wars! 2.01. 25
most admirable! i have seen those wars. 2.01. 26
i'll to the tuscan wars, and never bed her. 2.03.273
to th' wars! 2.03.275
to th' wars, my boy, to th' wars! 2.03.278
to th' wars, my boy, to th' wars! 2.03.278
wars is no strife | to the dark house and the 2.03.291
i'll to the wars, she to her single sorrow. 2.03.296
in the mean time, what hear you of these wars? 4.03. 38 P
what his valor, honesty, and expertness in wars; 4.03.178 P
in the wars, and that may you be bold to say in TN 1.05. 12 P
heart, | and fought the holy wars in palestine, JN 2.01. 4
your breath first kindled the dead coal of wars 5.02. 83
to deck our soldiers for these irish wars. R2 1.04. 62
now for our irish wars: 2.01.155
wars hath not wasted it, for warr'd he hath not, 2.01.252
more hath he spent in peace than they in wars. 2.01.255
he hath not money for these irish wars, | his 2.01.259
how shall we do for money for these wars? 2.02.104
and in this seat of peace tumultuous wars 4.01.140
and heard thee murmur tales of iron wars, 1H4 2.03. 48
we must all to the wars, and thy place shall be 2.04.544 P
she'll be a soldier too, she'll to the wars. 3.01.193
so long in his unlucky irish wars | that all in 5.01. 53
is there not wars? 2H4 1.02. 73 P
if i do halt, i have the wars for my color, and 1.02.246 P
o yet, for god's sake, go not to these wars! 2.03. 9
thou art going to the wars, and whether i shall 2.04. 66 P
and in two year after | were they at wars. 3.01. 60
and were these inward wars once out of hand, 3.01.107
come, thou shalt go to the wars in a gown. 3.02.184 P
therefore let our proportions for these wars H5 1.02.304
directions in the true disciplines of the wars, 3.02. 72 P
expedition and knowledge in th' aunchiant wars, 3.02. 78 P
disciplines of the pristine wars of the romans. 3.02. 81 P
the disciplines of the war, the roman wars, in 3.02. 97 P
and the weather, and the wars, and the king, and 3.02.106 P
that now and then goes to the wars, to grace 3.06. 68 P
prerogatifes and laws of the wars is not kept. 4.01. 68 P
but to examine the wars of pompey the great, you 4.01. 69 P
you shall find the ceremonies of the wars, and 4.01. 72 P
some, making the wars their bulwark, that have 4.01.164 P
every soldier in the wars do as every sick man 4.01.178 P
is good knowledge and literatured in the wars. 4.07.150 P
and /swear i got them in the gallia wars. 5.01. 89
he was thinking of civil wars when he got me; 5.02.226 P
one would have ling'ring wars with little cost; 1H6 1.01. 74
days, | since i have entered into these wars. 1.02.132
henry the fift he first train'd to the wars; 1.04. 79
then i see our wars | will turn unto a peaceful 2.02. 44
i have a while given truce unto my wars, | to do 3.04. 3

such as were grown to credit by the wars; 4.01. 36
if he miscarry, farewell wars in france! 4.03. 16
of all his wars within the realm of france? 4.07. 71
or we will plague thee with incessant wars. 5.04.154
his valor, coin, and people, in the wars? 2H6 1.01. 79
they shall have wars, and pay for their 3H6 4.01.114
and we shall have more wars before't be long. 4.06. 91
times, | during the wars of york and lancaster, R3 1.04. 15
my princely father, then had wars in france, 3.05. 88
and dangerous success of bloody wars, | as i 4.04.237
for this | is nam'd, your wars in france. H8 1.02. 60
more pangs and fears than wars or women have; 3.02.370
draught–oxen, and make you plough up the wars. TRO 2.01.107 P
when right with right wars who shall be most 3.02.172
we have had pelting wars since you refus'd | the 4.05.267
lechery, still wars and lechery, nothing else 5.02.195 P
hector, then 'tis wars. 5.03. 49
troy is ours, and our sharp wars are ended. 5.09. 10
if the wars eat us not up, they will; COR 1.01. 85 P
i'd revolt, to make | only my wars with him. 1.01.235
martius, | attend upon cominius to these wars. 1.01.237
the present wars devour him! 1.01.258
the threshold till my lord return from the wars. 1.03. 75 P
doubt prevailing, and to make it brief wars. 1.03.100 P
i'll leave the foe | and make my wars on you. 1.04. 40
let him be made an overture for th' wars! 1.09. 46
he has been bred i' th' wars | since 'a could 3.01.318
if it be honor in your wars to seem | the same 3.02. 46
tullus aufidius /will appear well in these wars, 4.03. 34 P
of these fair edifices 'fore my wars | have i 4.04. 3
'tis so, and as wars, in some sort, may be said 4.05.227 P
the wars for my money! 4.05.232 P
and stick i' th' wars | like a great sea–mark, 5.03. 73
to wait on fortune till | these wars determine. 5.03.120
has cluck'd thee to the wars, and safely home 5.03.163
aufidius, though i cannot make true wars, | i'll 5.03.190
with bloody passage led your wars even to | the 5.06. 75
from weary wars against the barbarous goths, TIT 1.01. 28
sleep in peace, slain in your country's wars! 1.01. 91
and welcome, nephews, from successful wars, 1.01.172
in dangerous wars whilst you securely slept; 3.01. 3
that thou wilt use the wars as thy redress | and TIM 5.04. 51
what should the wars do with these jigging fools JC 4.03.137
that was and is the question of these wars. HAM 1.01.111
you from the polack wars, and you from england, 5.02.376
have you heard of no likely wars toward, 'twixt LR 2.01. 10 P
with such loud reason to the cyprus wars OTH 1.01.150
this present wars against the ottomites. 1.03.234
follow thou the wars; 1.03.340 P
our wars are done. 2.01. 20
our wars are done; 2.01.202
(save that they say the wars must make example 3.03. 65
farewell the plumed troops and the big wars 3.03.349
dinner, and will make | no wars without–doors. ANT 2.01. 13
your wife and brother | made wars upon me, and 2.02. 43
and make the wars alike against my stomach, 2.02. 50
could not with graceful eyes attend those wars 2.02. 60
that the men might go to wars with the women! 2.02. 66 P
to have me out of egypt, made wars here; 2.02. 95
who does i' th' wars more than his captain can 3.01. 21
but he hath wag'd | new wars 'gainst pompey; 3.04. 4
wars 'twixt you twain would be | as if the world 3.04. 30
caesar and lepidus have made wars upon pompey. 3.05. 4 P
made use of him in the wars 'gainst pompey, 3.05. 7 P
thou hast forespoke my being in these wars, 3.07. 3
that thou couldst see my wars to–day, and 4.04. 16
novice, and my heart | makes only wars on thee. 4.12. 15
eye beck'd forth my wars and call'd them home, 4.12. 26
i made these wars for egypt, and the queen, 4.14. 15
who in the wars o' th' time | died with their CYM 1.01. 35
full weak to undertake our wars against | the 3.07. 5
and in a time | when fearful wars point at me; 4.03. 7
these present wars shall find i love my country, 4.03. 43
if in your country wars you chance to die, 4.04. 51
here they stand martyrs, slain in cupid's wars; PER 1.01. 38
if wars, we are unable to resist. 1.04. 84
go to the wars, would you? 4.06.171 P
you were at wars when she the grave enrich'd, TNK 1.03. 51
by all you love most — wars, and this sweet 3.06.203
for musicians, | and sing the wars of theseus. 4.01.134
forgiven | is safer wars than ever you can make, STM II.C 112
the wind wars with his torch to make him stay, LUC 311

WART 13 FR 0.0014 REL FR 1 V 12 P
have not your worship a wart above your eye? WIV 1.04.147 P
we had an hour's talk of that wart. 1.04.152 P
worship more of the wart the next time we have 1.04.159 P
mole in my neck, the great wart on my left arm, ERR 3.02.143 P
thomas wart! 2H4 3.02.136 P
is thy name wart? 3.02.139 P
thou art a very ragged wart. 3.02.141 P
i would wart might have gone, sir. 3.02.163 P
here's wart, you see what a ragged appearance it 3.02.260 P
hold, wart, traverse! thas, thas, thas. 3.02.272 P
well said, i' faith, wart, th' art a good scab. 3.02.276 P
alas, poor chin! many a wart is richer. TRO 1.02.141 P
the burning zone, | make ossa like a wart! HAM 5.01.283

WAR–THOUGHTS 1 FR 0.0001 REL FR 1 V 0 P
and that war–thoughts | have left their places ADO 1.01.301

WART'S 1 FR 0.0001 REL FR 0 V 1 P
put me a caliver into wart's hand, bardolph. 2H4 3.02.270 P

WAR–WEARIED 1 FR 0.0001 REL FR 1 V 0 P
drops bloody sweat from his war–wearied limbs, 1H6 4.04. 18

WARWICK 165 FR 0.0186 REL FR 164 V 1 P
go call the earls of surrey and of warwick; 2H4 3.01. 1
warwick! gloucester! clarence! 4.05. 48
find him, my lord of warwick, chide him hither. 4.05. 62
where is my lord of warwick? 4.05.231
my lord of warwick! 4.05.231
good morrow, cousin warwick, good morrow. 5.02. 20
warwick and talbot, salisbury and gloucester, H5 4.03. 54
my lord of warwick, and my brother gloucester, 4.07.170
follow, good cousin warwick. 4.07.175
my lord of warwick, here is — praised be god 4.08. 20 P
warwick, and huntington, go with the king, | and 5.02. 85
judge you, my lord of warwick, then between us. 1H6 2.04. 10
york, | i will not live to be accounted warwick. 2.04.120
well urg'd, my lord of warwick; 3.01.151
o warwick, warwick, i foresee with grief | the 5.04.111
o warwick, warwick, i foresee with grief | the 5.04.111
buckingham, somerset, | salisbury, and warwick; 2H6 1.01. 70
brave york, salisbury, and victorious warwick, 1.01. 86
but wherefore weeps warwick, my valiant son? 1.01.115
warwick, my son, the comfort of my age, | thy 1.01.190
so god help warwick, as he loves the land | and 1.01.205
that maine which by main force warwick did win, 1.01.210
salisbury and warwick are no simple peers. 1.03. 74
ambitious warwick, let thy betters speak. 1.03.109
all in this presence are thy betters, warwick. 1.03.111
warwick may live to be the best of all. 1.03.112
peace, headstrong warwick! 1.03.175
invite my lords of salisbury and warwick | to 1.04. 79
now, my good lords of salisbury and warwick, 2.02. 1
my heart assures me that the earl of warwick 2.02. 78
richard shall live to make the earl of warwick 2.02. 81
that he is dead, good warwick, 'tis too true, 3.02.130
what instance gives lord warwick for his vow? 3.02.159
why, warwick, who should do the duke to death? 3.02.179
what dares not warwick, if false suffolk dare 3.02.203
the trait'rous warwick, with the men of bury, 3.02.240
come, warwick, come, good warwick, go with me, 3.02.298
come, warwick, come, good warwick, go with me, 3.02.298
the princely warwick, and the nevils all, 4.01. 91
bid salisbury and warwick come to me. 5.01.147
if you oppose yourselves to match lord warwick. 5.01.156
why, warwick, hath thy knee forgot to bow? 5.01.161
clifford of cumberland, 'tis warwick calls! 5.02. 1
warwick is hoarse with calling thee to arms. 5.02. 7
hold, warwick; 5.02. 14
what says lord warwick? 5.03. 27
assist me then, sweet warwick, and i will, | for 3H6 1.01. 28
dares stir a wing if warwick shake his bells. 1.01. 47
back'd by the power of warwick, that false peer, 1.01. 52
and warwick shall disprove it. 1.01. 89
no, warwick, i remember it to my grief, | and, 1.01. 93
i send thee, warwick, such a messenger | as 1.01. 99
my lord of warwick, hear but one word: 1.01.170
not for myself, lord warwick, but my son, | whom 1.01.192
the earl of warwick and the duke enforc'd me. 1.01.229
warwick is chancellor and the lord of callice, 1.01.238
and whet on warwick to this enterprise. 1.02. 37
let noble warwick, cobham, and the rest, | whom 1.02. 56
great lord of warwick, if we should recompt 2.01. 96
o warwick, warwick, that plantagenet, | which 2.01.101
o warwick, warwick, that plantagenet, | which 2.01.101
where is the duke of norfolk, gentle warwick? 2.01.142
'twas odds, belike, when valiant warwick fled: 2.01.148
i know it well, lord warwick, blame me not. 2.01.157
why, therefore warwick came to seek you out, 2.01.166
ay, now methinks i hear great warwick speak. 2.01.186
if warwick bid him stay. 2.01.188
lord warwick, on thy shoulder will i lean, | and 2.01.189
a band of thirty thousand men | comes warwick, 2.02. 69
how now, long–tongu'd warwick, dare you speak? 2.02.102
if that be right which warwick says is right, 2.02.131
ah, warwick, why hast thou withdrawn thyself? 2.03. 14
clangor heard from far, | "warwick, revenge! 2.03. 19
o warwick, i do bend my knee with thine, | and 2.03. 33
brother, give me thy hand, and gentle warwick, 2.03. 44
nay, warwick, single out some other chase, | for 2.04. 12
fled, | and warwick rages like a chafed bull. 2.05.126
come, york and richard, warwick and the rest, 2.06. 29
from whence shall warwick cut the sea to france, 2.06. 89
even as thou wilt, sweet warwick, let it be; 2.06. 99
warwick, as ourself, | shall do and undo as him 2.06.104
the great commanding warwick | /is thither gone 3.01. 29
for warwick is a subtle orator, | and lewis a 3.01. 33
warwick, to give: 3.01. 42
whiles warwick tells his title, smooths the 3.01. 48
our earl of warwick, edward's greatest friend. 3.03. 45
welcome, brave warwick! 3.03. 46
bona, hear me speak | before you answer warwick. 3.03. 66
then warwick disannuls great john of gaunt, 3.03. 81
why, warwick, canst thou speak against thy liege 3.03. 95
no, warwick, no; 3.03.106
while i use further conference with warwick. 3.03.111
now, warwick, tell me, even upon thy conscience, 3.03.113
then, warwick, thus: 3.03.134
deceitful warwick, it was thy device | by this 3.03.141
peace, impudent and shameless warwick, | proud 3.03.156
warwick, this is some post to us or thee. 3.03.162
smiles at her news, while warwick frowns at his. 3.03.168
warwick, what are thy news? 3.03.171
warwick, these words have turn'd my hate to love 3.03.199
but, warwick, | thou and oxford, with five 3.03.233
therefore delay not, give thy hand to warwick, 3.03.246
how could he stay till warwick made return? 4.01. 5
well as lewis of france or the earl of warwick, 4.01. 11
they are but lewis and warwick, i am edward, 4.01. 15
and warwick, doing what you gave in charge, | is 4.01. 32
what if both lewis and warwick be appeas'd | by 4.01. 34
but what said warwick to these injuries? 4.01.107
but say, is warwick friends with margaret? 4.01.115
you that love me and warwick, follow me. 4.01.123
clarence and somerset both gone to warwick? 4.01.127
are near to warwick by blood and by alliance: 4.01.136
tell me if you love warwick more than me? 4.01.137
till we meet warwick with his foreign pow'r. 4.01.149
then, gentle clarence, welcome unto warwick, 4.02. 6
for warwick and his friends, god and saint 4.02. 29
till warwick or himself be quite suppress'd. 4.03. 6
the day, | if warwick be so near as men report. 4.03. 8
if warwick knew in what estate he stands, | 'tis 4.03. 18
why, warwick, when we parted, | thou call'dst me 4.03. 30
yet, warwick, in despite of all mischance, | of 4.03. 43
loss of some pitch'd battle against warwick? 4.04. 4
warwick may lose, that now hath won the day. 4.04. 15
but, madam, where is warwick then become? 4.04. 25
fly, | if warwick take us we are sure to die. 4.04. 35
but, warwick, after god, thou set'st me free, 4.06. 16
warwick, although my head still wear the crown, 4.06. 23
no, warwick, thou art worthy of the sway, | to 4.06. 32
warwick and clarence, give me both your hands. 4.06. 38
that he consents, if warwick yield consent, 4.06. 46
we'll forward towards warwick and his mates; 4.07. 82
as we may, we'll meet both thee and warwick. 4.07. 86
course, | where peremptory warwick now remains. 4.08. 59
the drum your honor hears marcheth from warwick. 5.01. 13
see how the surly warwick mans the wall! 5.01. 17
now, warwick, wilt thou ope the city–gates, 5.01. 21
down, | call warwick patron, and be penitent? 5.01. 27
and, weakling, warwick takes his gift again, 5.01. 37
and henry is my king, warwick his subject. 5.01. 38
and, gallant warwick, do but answer this: 5.01. 40
alas, that warwick had no more forecast, | but, 5.01. 42
'tis even so, yet you are warwick still. 5.01. 47
come, warwick, take the time, kneel down, kneel 5.01. 48
"wind–changing warwick now can change no more." 5.01. 57
thou wilt, if warwick call. 5.01. 80
father of warwick, know you what this means? 5.01. 81
why, trowest thou, warwick, | that clarence is 5.01. 85
and so, proud–hearted warwick, i defy thee, 5.01. 98
what, warwick, wilt thou leave the town, and 5.01.107
yes, warwick, edward dares, and leads the way. 5.01.112
for warwick was a bug that fear'd us all. 5.02. 2
and tell me who is victor, york or warwick? 5.02. 6
and who durst smile when warwick bent his brow? 5.02. 22
ah, warwick, warwick, wert thou as we are, | we 5.02. 29
ah, warwick, warwick, wert thou as we are, | we 5.02. 29
ah, warwick! 5.02. 40
and to the latest gasp cried out for warwick, 5.02. 41
with a groan, | "o, farewell, warwick!" 5.02. 47
for warwick bids you all farewell, to meet in 5.02. 49
say warwick was our anchor; 5.04. 13
them, the two brave bears, warwick and montague, 5.07. 10
poor clarence did forsake his father, warwick, R3 1.03.134
was my great father–in–law, renowned warwick, 1.04. 49
the mighty warwick and did fight for me? 2.01.111
besides, he hates me for my father warwick, 4.01. 85

WARWICK'S 13 FR 0.0014 REL FR 13 V 0 P
my father, being the earl of warwick's man, 3H6 2.05. 65
heavens grant that warwick's words bewitch him 3.03.112
proveth edward's love and warwick's honesty. 3.03.180
that only warwick's daughter shall be thine. 3.03.248
your king and warwick's, and must have my will. 4.01. 16
young prince edward marries warwick's daughter. 4.01.117
for i will hence to warwick's other daughter, 4.01.120
fell warwick's brother, and by that our foe. 4.04. 12
shield thee from warwick's frown, | and pray 4.05. 28
why then 'tis mine, if but by warwick's gift. 5.01. 35
but warwick's king is edward's prisoner. 5.01. 39
that warwick's bones may keep thine company. 5.02. 4
for then i'll marry warwick's youngest daughter. R3 1.01.153

WARWICKSHIRE 3 FR 0.0003 REL FR 2 V 1 P
what a devil dost thou in warwickshire? 1H4 4.02. 51 P
say, if thou dar'st, proud lord of warwickshire, 2H6 3.02.201
in warwickshire i have true–hearted friends, 3H6 4.08. 9

WAR–WORN 1 FR 0.0001 REL FR 1 V 0 P
investing lank–lean cheeks and war–worn coats, H5 4.pr. 26

WARY 11 FR 0.0012 REL FR 10 V 1 P
i have ta'en a due and wary note upon't. MM 4.01. 37
abroad, therefore it behooves men to be wary. WT 4.04.254 P
but yet be wary in thy studious care. 1H6 2.05. 97
take heed, be wary how you place your words, 3.02. 3
the day is broke, be wary, look about. ROM 3.05. 40
forth the adder, | and that craves wary walking. JC 2.01. 15
be wary then, best safety lies in fear: HAM 1.03. 43
and you, the judges, bear a wary eye. 5.02.279
that hold their honors in a wary distance, | the OTH 2.03. 56
let us be wary, let us hide our loves"; 3.03.420
love, be of thyself so wary | as i, not for SON 22. 9

/WAS 27 FR 0.0030 REL FR 24 V 3 P
/not /that /name /was /given /me /at /the /font, R2 4.01.256
/was /this /face /the /face | /that /every /day 4.01.281
/was /this /the /face | /that, /like /the /sun, 4.01.283
/follies, | /that /was /at /last //out–fac'd /by 4.01.286
/for /when /i /was /a /king /my /flatterers 4.01.306
/it /was /your /presurmise | /that /in /the 2H4 1.01.168
/you /were /advis'd /his /flesh /was /capable 1.01.172
/than /that /being /which /was /like /to /be? 1.01.179
/before /he /was /what /thou /wouldst /have /him 1.03. 93
/he /was /the /mark /and /glass, /copy /and 2.03. 31
/was /force /perforce /compell'd /to /banish 4.01.114
/when /there /was /nothing /could /have /stay'd 4.01.121
/the /earl /of /herford /was /reputed /then 4.01.129
then never /was /man true. R3 1.02.195
/when /last /i /was /at /exeter, | /the /mayor 4.02.103
/and /censorinus /that /was /so /surnam'd, | and COR 2.03.243
/how /troy /was /burnt /and /he /made /miserable TIT 3.02. 28
/sir, /it /was /a /black //ill–favor'd /fly, 3.02. 66
/there /was /for /a /while /no /money /bid /for HAM 2.02.354 P
/his /personal /return /was /most /requir'd /and LR 4.03. 6 P
/it /seem'd /she /was /a /queen | /over /her 4.03. 13
/was /this /before /the /king /return'd? 4.03. 37
/that /the /duke /of /cornwall /was /so /slain? 4.07. 85 P
/be /honest, | /i /never /yet /was /valiant. 5.01. 24
/whilst /i | /was /big /in /clamor, /came /there 5.03.209
/but /who /was /this? 5.03.219
tears, that his wound wept, /was drench'd. VEN 1054

WAS 2416 FR 0.2731 REL FR 1801 V 615 P
thy father was the duke of milan and | a prince TMP 1.02. 54
thy mother was a piece of virtue, and | she said 1.02. 56
and thy father | was duke of milan, and his only 1.02. 58
through all the signories it was the first, 1.02. 71
ear, that now he was | the ivy which had hid my 1.02. 85
as great | as my trust was, which had indeed no 1.02. 96
he did believe | he was indeed the duke, out o' 1.02.103
man) my library | was dukedom large enough: 1.02.110
confederates | (so dry he was for sway) wi' th' 1.02.112
which was, that he, in lieu o' th' premises, 1.02.123
alack, what trouble | was i then to you! 1.02.152
who was so firm, so constant, that this coil 1.02.207
not hair), | was the first man that leapt; 1.02.214
but was not this nigh shore? 1.02.216
who with age and envy | was grown into a hoop? 1.02.259
thou hast. where was she born? speak. tell me. 1.02.260
o, was she so? 1.02.261
from argier, | thou know'st, was banish'd; 1.02.266
this blue–ey'd hag was hither brought with child 1.02.269
with child, | and here was left by th' sailors. 1.02.270
as thou report'st thyself, was then her servant, 1.02.271
then was this island | (save for the son that 1.02.281
it was a torment | to lay upon the damn'd, which 1.02.289
it was mine art, | when i arriv'd and heard thee 1.02.291

that you have, | which first was mine own king; 1.02.342
gallant which thou seest | was in the wrack; 1.02.415
"temperance" was a delicate wench. 2.01. 44 P
tunis was never grac'd before with such a 2.01. 75 P
she was of carthage, not of tunis. 2.01. 83 P
this tunis, sir, was carthage. 2.01. 84 P
that "sort" was well fish'd for. 2.01.105 P
what a blow was there given! 2.01.180 P
sure it was the roar | of a whole herd of lions. 2.01.315
there was a noise, | that's verily. 2.01.320
were i in england now (as once i was) and had 2.02. 28 P
with mine own hands since i was cast ashore. 2.02.123 P
i was the man i' th' moon, when time was. 2.02.138 P
i was the man i' th' moon, when time was. 2.02.139 P
was there ever man a coward that hath drunk so 3.02. 27 P
this was well done, my bird. 4.01.184
thy brother was a furtherer in the act. 5.01. 73
and myself present | as i was sometime milan. 5.01. 86
very duke | which was thrust forth of milan, who 5.01.160
this shore (where you were wrack'd) was landed, 5.01.161
was milan thrust from milan, that his issue 5.01.205
found a wife | where he himself was lost; 5.01.211
all of us, ourselves, | when no man was his own. 5.01.213
business more than nature | was ever conduct of. 5.01.244
his mother was a witch, and one so strong | that 5.01.269
ass | was i to take this drunkard for a god, 5.01.297
or else my project fails, | which was to please. ep 13
love, | for he was more than over shoes in love. TGV 1.01. 24
twice, or thrice, was "proteus" written down: 1.02.114
nay, i was taken up for laying them down; 1.02.132
what sad talk was that | wherewith my brother 1.03. 1
he said that proteus, your son, was meet; 1.03. 12
and yet i was last chidden for being too slow. 2.01. 12 P
when you fasted, it was presently after dinner; 2.01. 28 P
when you look'd sadly, it was for want of money: 2.01. 29 P
you never saw her since she was deform'd. 2.01. 63 P
i was in love with my bed. 2.01. 81 P
which i was much unwilling to proceed in, | but 2.01.106
excellent device, was there ever heard a better, 2.01.139
nay, i was rhyming; 2.01.143 P
come; come away, man — i was sent to call thee. 2.03. 55 P
was this the idol that you worship so? 2.04.144
when i was sick, you gave me bitter pills, | and 2.04.149
fire, | bears no impression of the thing it was. 2.04.202
cold, | and that i love him not as i was wont: 2.04.204
him so, | when she for thy repeal was suppliant, 3.01.236
it was the son of thy grandmother. 3.01.296 P
it was eve's legacy, and cannot be ta'en from 3.01.338 P
she was mine and not mine twice or thrice in 3.01.355 P
she did, my lord, when valentine was here. 3.02. 27
for orpheus' lute was strung with poets' sinews, 3.02. 77
i was. 4.01. 24
i was, and held me glad of such a doom. 4.01. 32
myself was from verona banished | for practicing 4.01. 45
by my halidom, i was fast asleep. 4.02.135 P
i was sent to deliver him as a present to 4.04. 6 P
with the smell before, knew it was crab, and 4.04. 23 P
marry, she says your dog was a cur, and tells 4.04. 48 P
the other squirrel was stol'n from me by the 4.04. 55 P
well, | she, in my judgment, was as fair as you; 4.04.151
how tall was she? 4.04.157
part, | and i was trimm'd in madam julia's gown, 4.04.161
o, sir, i find her milder than she was, | and 5.02. 2
him he knew well, and guess'd that it was she, 5.02. 39
she, | but, being mask'd, he was not sure of it; 5.02. 40
patrick's cell this even, and there she was not. 5.02. 42
where is the gentleman that was with her? 5.03. 6
fall | and leave no memory of what it was! 5.04. 10
free, | all that was mine in silvia i give thee. 5.04. 83
which, out of my neglect, was never done. 5.04. 90 P
i wish'd your venison better, it was ill kill'd. WIV 1.01. 83 P
i heard say he was outrun on cotsall. 1.01. 90 P
and being fap, sir, was, as they say, cashier'd; 1.01.178 P
he was gotten in drink. 1.03. 22 P
his filching was like an unskillful singer, he 1.03. 25 P
i was then frugal of my mirth. 2.01. 27 P
page, trust me, i was going to your house. 2.01. 33 P
and, trust me, i was coming to you. 2.01. 35 P
she was in his company at page's house; 2.01.235 P
as my mother was, the first hour i was born. 2.02. 38
as my mother was, the first hour i was born. 2.02. 38
of what quality was your love then? 2.02.214 P
what a taking was he in when your husband ask'd 3.03.180 P
when your husband ask'd who was in the basket! 3.03.181 P
wealth | was the first motive that i woo'd thee, 3.04. 14
but that the shore was shelvy and shallow — a 3.05. 15 P
i was thrown into the ford; 3.05. 36 P
good heart, that was not her fault. 3.05. 38 P
i was at her house the hour she appointed me. 3.05. 64 P
while i was there. 3.05. 80 P
there was the rankest compound of villainous 3.05. 91 P
it was a miracle to scape suffocation. 3.05.117 P
(when i was more than half stew'd in grease, 3.05.118 P
he is a better scholar than i thought he was. 4.01. 81 P
of none but him, and swears he was carried out, 4.02. 31 P
there was one convey'd out of my house yesterday 4.02.145 P
stand, | in him that was of late an heretic, 4.04. 9
there was, mine host, an old fat woman even now 4.05. 24 P
ay, marry, was it, mussel-shell, what would you 4.05. 28 P
was there a wise woman with thee? 4.05. 58 P
ay, that there was, mine host, one that hath 4.05. 59 P
for it neither, but was paid for my learning. 4.05. 61 P
i was beaten myself into all the colors of the 4.05.115 P
and i was like to be apprehended for the witch 4.05.116 P
i was three or four times in the thought they 5.05.121 P
to him (for all he was in woman's apparel) i 5.05.192 P
and i had appointed, and yet it was not anne, 5.05.199 P
where there was no proportion held in love. 5.05.222
i think thou never wast where grace was said. MM 1.02. 19 P
and carried to prison was worth five thousand of 1.02. 61 P
and he was ever precise in promise-keeping. 1.02. 75 P
whose house, sir, was (as they say) pluck'd down 2.01. 64 P
what was done to elbow's wife, that he hath 2.01.116 P
come me to what was done to her. 2.01.117 P
what was done to elbow's wife, once more? 2.01.139 P
once, sir? there was nothing done to her once. 2.01.141 P
yet to come that she was ever respected with man 2.01.168 P
she was respected with him before he married 2.01.170 P
respected with her before i was married to her? 2.01.175 P
if ever i was respected with her, or she with me 2.01.176 P
most offenseful act | was mutually committed? 2.03. 27
then was your sin of heavier kind than his. 2.03. 28
was affianc'd to her /by oath, and the nuptial 3.01.213 P
her brother frederick was wrack'd at sea, having 3.01.216 P
of two usuries, the merriest was put down, and 3.02. 6 P
is the world as it was, man? 3.02. 50 P
it was a mad fantastical trick of him to steal 3.02. 92 P
and usurp the beggary he was never born to. 3.02. 93 P
they say this angelo was not made by man and 3.02.104 P
that he was begot between two stock-fishes. 3.02.109 P
for women, he was not inclin'd that way. 3.02.122 P
and his use was to put a ducat in her clack-dish 3.02.126 P
sir, i was an inward of his. 3.02.130 P
a shy fellow was the duke, and i believe i know 3.02.131 P
wise? why, no question but he was. 3.02.138 P
mistress kate keepdown was with child by him in 3.02.199 P
pray you, sir, of what disposition was the duke? 3.02.231 P
what pleasure was he given to? 3.02.234 P
i have heard it was ever his manner to do so. 4.02.134 P
and say it was the desire of the penitent to be 4.02.176 P
as well acquainted here as i was in our house of 4.03. 1 P
marry, then ginger was not much in request, for 4.03. 7 P
i was once before him for getting a wench with 4.03.169 P
but i was fain to forswear it. 4.03.172 P
of a sisterhood) | was sent to by my brother; 5.01. 73
how i replied | (for this was of much length) — 5.01. 95
being come to knowledge that there was complaint 5.01.153
my lord, i do confess i ne'er was married, | and 5.01.184
he was drunk then, my lord, it can be no better. 5.01.188 P
once thou swor'st was worth the looking on; 5.01.208
a vow'd contract, | was fast belock'd in thine; 5.01.210
and five years since there was some speech of 5.01.217
which was broke off, | partly for that her 5.01.218
for that her reputation was disvalued | in 5.01.221
and was the duke a fleshmonger, a fool, and a 5.01.333 P
i was, my lord. 5.01.376
as i was then | advertising and holy to your 5.01.382
maid, | it was the swift celerity of his death, 5.01.394
how came it claudio was beheaded | at an unusual 5.01.457
it was commanded so. 5.01.458
no, my good lord; it was by private message. 5.01.460
i thought it was a fault, but knew it not, | yet 5.01.463
there was a friar told me of this man. 5.01.479
may witness that my end | was wrought by nature, ERR 1.01. 34
in syracusa was i born, and wed | unto a woman, 1.01. 36
from whom my absence was not six months old 1.01. 44
me, | and soon, and safe, arrived where i was. 1.01. 48
and, which was strange, the one so like the 1.01. 51
a mean woman was delivered | of such a burthen 1.01. 54
and this it was (for other means was none): 1.01. 75
and this it was (for other means was none): 1.01. 75
to him one of the other twins was bound, 1.01. 81
i, | fixing our eyes on whom our care was fix'd, 1.01. 84
was carried towards corinth, as we thought. 1.01. 87
our helpful ship was splitted in the midst; 1.01.103
was carried with more speed before the wind, 1.01.109
and, knowing whom it was their hap to save, 1.01.113
that by misfortunes was my life prolong'd, | to 1.01.119
me | that his attendant — so his case was like, 1.01.127
my charge was but to fetch you from the mart 1.02. 74
my house was at the phoenix? 2.02. 11
which, i hope, thou felt'st i was displeas'd. 2.02. 19
was there ever any man thus beaten out of season 2.02. 47
but your reason was not substantial, why there 2.02.104 P
the time was once, when thou unurg'd wouldst vow 2.02.113
what, was i married to her in my dream? 2.02.182
there was blow for blow. 3.01. 56
in debating which was best, we shall part with 3.01. 67
call'd me dromio, swore i was assur'd to her, 3.02.141 P
then swore he that he was a stranger here. 4.02. 9
tell me, was he arrested on a band? 4.02. 49
it was two ere i left him, and now the clock 4.02. 54
goes in the calve's-skin that was kill'd for the 4.03. 19 P
that i was sent for nothing but a rope! 4.04. 91
i knew he was not in his perfect wits. 5.01. 42
sad, | and much different from the man he was; 5.01. 46
it was the copy of our conference: 5.01. 62
alone, it was the subject of my theme; 5.01. 65
still did i tell him it was vild and bad. 5.01. 67
and thereof came it that the man was mad. 5.01. 68
thou say'st his meat was sauc'd with thy 5.01. 73
could witness it, for he was with me then, | who 5.01.220
outfacing me, | cries out, i was possess'd. 5.01.246
that he din'd not at home, but was lock'd out. 5.01.256
within this hour i was his bondman, sir, | but 5.01.289
and i was ta'en for him, and he for me, | and 5.01.388
he was not three leagues off when i left him. ADO 1.01. 3 P
there was none such in the army of any sort. 1.01. 33 P
he's return'd, and as pleasant as ever he was. 1.01. 38 P
for a perfumer, as i was smoking a musty room, 1.03. 58 P
was not count john here at supper? 2.01. 1 P
that i was disdainful, and that i had my good 2.01.129 P
well, this was signior benedick that said so. 2.01.131 P
had been myself, that i was the prince's jester, 2.01.243 P
jester, that i was duller than a great thaw, 2.01.244 P
me, i was born to speak all mirth and no matter. 2.01.330 P
mother cried, but then there was a star danc'd, 2.01.335 P
was a star danc'd, and under that was i born. 2.01.335 P
have known when there was no music with him but 2.03. 13 P
he was wont to speak plain and to the purpose 2.03. 18 P
the fraud of men was ever so, | since summer 2.03. 72
men was ever so, | since summer first was leavy. 2.03. 73
what was it you told me of to-day, that your 2.03. 90 P
your niece beatrice was in love with signior 2.03. 91 P
there was never counterfeit of passion came so 2.03.104 P
when she had writ it, and was reading it over, 2.03.136 P
the conference was sadly borne; 2.03.221 P
and when was he wont to wash his face? 3.02. 56 P
and thought they margaret was hero? 3.03.153 P
but the devil my master knew she was margaret; 3.03.155 P
would meet her as he was appointed next morning 3.03.160 P
piece of lechery that ever was known in the 3.03.168 P
yet benedick was such another, and now is he 3.04. 87 P
what man was he talk'd with you yesternight 4.01. 83
and mine that i was proud on, mine so much 4.01.137
so much | that i myself was to myself not mine, 4.01.138
which was before barr'd up with ribs of iron! 4.01.151
upon the instant that she was accus'd, | shall 4.01.215
would not show us | whiles it was ours. 4.01.222
happy hour, i was about to protest i lov'd you. 4.01.283 P
don john, the prince's brother, was a villain. 4.02. 40 P
flat burglary as ever was committed. 4.02. 50 P
hero was in this manner accus'd, in this very 4.02. 62 P
for there was never yet philosopher | that could 5.01. 35
she was charg'd with nothing | but what was true 5.01.104
was charg'd with nothing | but what was true, 5.01.105
him another staff, this last was broke cross. 5.01.139 P
god saw him when he was hid in the garden. 5.01.180 P
did he not say my brother was fled? 5.01.204 P
who i believe was pack'd in all this wrong, 5.01.299
no, by my soul, she was not, | nor knew not what 5.01.300
no, i was not born under a rhyming planet, nor i 5.02. 40 P
tongues | was the hero that here lies. 5.03. 4
did i not tell you she was innocent? 5.04. 1
but margaret was in some fault for this, 5.04. 4
and when i liv'd, i was your other wife, | and 5.04. 60
life, for i was told you were in a consumption. 5.04. 96 P
when i was wont to think no harm all night, LLL 1.01. 44
and give him light that it was blinded by. 1.01. 83
what say you, lords? why, this was quite forgot. 1.01.141
manner of it is, i was taken with the manner. 1.01.202 P
i was seen with her in the manor-house, sitting 1.01.206 P
it was proclaim'd a year's imprisonment to be 1.01.287 P
i was taken with none, sir, i was taken with a 1.01.289 P
taken with none, sir, i was taken with a damsel. 1.01.289 P
well, it was proclaim'd damsel. 1.01.291 P
this was no damsel neither, sir, she was a 1.01.292 P
was no damsel neither, sir, she was a virgin. 1.01.292 P
is so varied too, for it was proclaim'd virgin. 1.01.294 P
i was taken with a maid. 1.01.296 P
for true it is, i was taken with jaquenetta, and 1.01.311 P
he was a man of good carriage, great carriage, 1.02. 70 P
and he was in love. 1.02. 72 P
who was sampson's love, my dear moth? 1.02. 76 P
it was so, sir, for she had a green wit. 1.02. 89 P
the world was very guilty of such a ballet some 1.02.111 P
yet was sampson so tempted, and he had an 1.02.173 P
yet was salomon so seduced, and he had a very 1.02.174 P
grace | as nature was in making graces dear, 2.01. 10
students at that time | was there with him, if i 2.01. 65
how needless was it then | to ask the question? 2.01.116
it was well done of you to take him at his word. 2.01.217
i was as willing to grapple as he was to board. 2.01.218
i was as willing to grapple as he was to board. 2.01.218
then was venus like her mother, for her father 2.01.256
by saying that a costard was broken in a shin. 3.01.106
me, how was there a costard broken in a shin? 3.01.111 P
i, costard, running out, that was safely within, 3.01.116
was that the king that spurr'd his horse so hard 4.01. 1
i know not, but i think it was not he. 4.01. 3
whoe'er 'a was, 'a show'd a mounting mind. 4.01. 4
if wounding, then it was to show my skill, 4.01. 28
and he it was that might rightly say, veni, vidi 4.01. 67 P
that was a man when king pippen of france was a 4.01.120 P
man when king pippen of france was a little boy, 4.01.120 P
that was a woman when queen guinover of britain 4.01.123 P
queen guinover of britain was a little wench, as 4.01.123 P
the deer was, as you know, sanguis, in blood, 4.02. 3 P
i assure ye it was a buck of the first head. 4.02. 10 P
i said the deer was not a haud credo, 'twas a 4.02. 20 P
your wit | what was a month old at cain's birth, 4.02. 35
the moon was a month old when adam was no more. 4.02. 39
the moon was a month old when adam was no more. 4.02. 39
it was given me by costard, and sent me from don 4.02. 91 P
ovidius naso was the man. 4.02.123 P
but, damosella virgin, was this directed to you? 4.02.128 P
my vow was earthly, thou a heavenly love; 4.03. 64
an amber-color'd raven was well noted. 4.03. 86
all, | that he was fain to seal on cupid's name. 5.02. 9
that was the way to make his godhead wax, | for 5.02. 10
what was sent to you from fair dumaine? 5.02. 47
swore | a better speech was never spoke before. 5.02.110
what, was your vizard made without a tongue? 5.02.242
this pert berowne was out of count'nance quite. 5.02.272
the king was weeping-ripe for a good word. 5.02.274
dumaine was at my service, and his sword: 5.02.276
my servant straight was mute. 5.02.277
and longaville was for my service born. 5.02.284
which of the vizards was it that you wore? 5.02.385
madam, i was. 5.02.434
i was, fair madam. 5.02.435
here was a consent, | knowing aforehand of our 5.02.460
but i hope i was perfect. 5.02.558 P
the world i liv'd, i was the world's commander; 5.02.562
world i liv'd, i was the world's commander" — 5.02.568
and when he was a babe, a child, a shrimp, 5.02.590
well follow'd: judas was hang'd on an elder. 5.02.606 P
hector was but a troyan in respect of this. 5.02.636 P
i think hector was not so clean-timber'd. 5.02.638 P
when he breathed, he was a man. 5.02.662 P
and it was enjoin'd him in rome for want of 5.02.712 P
of breath — your gentleness | was guilty of it. 5.02.736
yet, since love's argument was first on foot, 5.02.747
was not that hector? 5.02.880
but either it was different in blood — MND 1.01.135
when the false troyan under sail was seen, | by 1.01.174
he hail'd down oaths that he was only mine; 1.01.243
this was lofty! 1.02. 39 P
swear | a merrier hour was never wasted there. 2.01. 57
his mother was a vot'ress of my order, | and, in 2.01.123
wherefore was i to this keen mockery born? 2.02.123
what a dream was here! 2.02.147
then, what it was that next came in her eye, 3.02. 2
while she was in her dull and sleeping hour, | a 3.02. 8
the sun was not so true unto the day | as he to 3.02. 50
i am as fair now as i was erewhile. 3.02.274
i was never curst; 3.02.300
she was a vixen when she went to school; 3.02.324
was wont to swell like round and orient pearls, 4.01. 54
methought i was enamor'd of an ass. 4.01. 77
came this night | that i sleeping here was found 4.01.101
i was with hercules and cadmus once, | when in a 4.01.112
a cry more tuneable | was never hollow'd to, nor 4.01.125

our intent | was to be gone from athens, where 4.01.152
my lord, | was i betrothed ere i /saw hermia; 4.01.172
do not you think | the duke was here, and bid us 4.01.195
past the wit of man to say what dream it was. 4.01.206 P
methought i was — there is no man can tell what 4.01.208 P
methought i was, and methought i had — but man 4.01.209 P
nor his heart to report, what my dream was. 4.01.214 P
and it was play'd | when i from thebes came last 5.01. 50
his speech was like a tangled chain; 5.01.125 P
not shafalus to procrus was so true. 5.01.198
no — which was the fairest dame | that liv'd, 5.01.293
your father was ever virtuous, and holy men at MV 1.02. 27 P
swore he would pay him again when he was able. 1.02. 81 P
yes, yes, it was bassanio — as i think, so was 1.02.115 P
it was bassanio — as i think, so was he call'd. 1.02.115 P
look'd upon, was the best deserving a fair lady. 1.02.118 P
your worship was the last man in our mouths. 1.03. 60
this jacob from our holy abram was | (as his 1.03. 72
ay, he was the third — 1.03. 74
when the work of generation was | between these 1.03. 82
this was a way to thrive, and he was blest; 1.03. 89
this was a way to thrive, and he was blest; 1.03. 89
this was a venture, sir, that jacob serv'd for, 1.03. 91
was this inserted to make interest good? 1.03. 94
forbid, the boy was the very staff of my age, my 2.02. 66 P
i am launcelot, your boy that was, your son that 2.02. 85 P
was not that letter from fair jessica? 2.04. 28
your worship was wont to tell me i could do 2.05. 8 P
then it was not for nothing that my nose fell 2.05. 24 P
that year on ash we'nsday was four year in th' 2.05. 26 P
so rich a gem | was set in worse than gold. 2.07. 55
he came too late, the ship was under sail, | but 2.08. 6
but there the duke was given to understand 2.08. 7
alive, iwis, | silver'd o'er, and so was this. 2.09. 69
sweet, | to show how costly summer was at hand, 2.09. 94
for his own part, knew the bird was fledge, and 3.01. 29 P
that was us'd to come so smug upon the mart: 3.01. 46 P
he was wont to call me usurer, let him look to 3.01. 47 P
he was wont to lend money for a christian cur'sy 3.01. 49 P
it was my turkis, i had it of leah when i was a 3.01.121 P
turkis, i had it of leah when i was a bachelor. 3.01.121 P
but now i was the lord | of this fair mansion, 3.02.167
and swearing till my very /roof was dry | with 3.02.204
my purpose was not to have seen you here, | but 3.02.227
i was a gentleman; 3.02.255
you shall see | how much i was a braggart: 3.02.258
when i told you | my state was nothing, i should 3.02.259
have told you | that i was worse than nothing; 3.02.260
when i was with him i have heard him swear | to 3.02.284
i was always plain with you, and so now i speak 3.05. 3 P
in loving visitation was with me a young doctor 4.01.153 P
my mind was never yet more mercenary. 4.01.418
good sir, this ring was given me by my wife, 4.01.441
for, as i hear, he was much bound for you. 5.01.137
whose posy was | for all the world like cutler's 5.01.148
i was enforc'd to send it after him, | i was 5.01.216
him, | i was beset with shame and courtesy, | my 5.01.217
there you shall find that portia was the doctor, 5.01.269
it was upon this fashion bequeath'd me by will AYL 1.01. 1 P
he was my father, and he is thrice a villain 1.01. 57 P
was not charles, the duke's wrastler, here to 1.01. 89 P
by mine honor, but i was bid to come for you. 1.02. 60 P
and swore by his honor the mustard was naught. 1.02. 65 P
pancakes were naught and the mustard was good, 1.02. 66 P
was good, and yet was not the knight forsworn. 1.02. 67 P
no more was this knight, swearing by his honor, 1.02. 77 P
the little wit that fools have was silenc'd, the 1.02. 89 P
well said — that was laid on with a trowel. 1.02.106 P
i heard breaking of ribs was sport for ladies. 1.02.139 P
there is but one sham'd that was never gracious; 1.02.188 P
and all the world was of my father's mind. 1.02.236
which of the two was daughter of the duke, 1.02.269
of the duke, | that here was at the wrastling? 1.02.270
so was i when your highness took his dukedom, 1.03. 59
so was i when your highness banish'd him. 1.03. 60
my father was no traitor. 1.03. 63
it was your pleasure and your own remorse. 1.03. 70
i was too young that time to value her, | but 1.03. 71
at whom so oft | your grace was wont to laugh, 2.02. 9
son) | of him i was about to call his father — 2.03. 21
when i was at home, i was in a better place, but 2.04. 17 P
when i was at home, i was in a better place, but 2.04. 17 P
when i was in love i broke my sword upon a stone 2.04. 46 P
here was he merry, hearing of a song. 2.07. 4
'tis but an hour ago since it was nine, | and 2.07. 24
of many parts | by heavenly synod was devis'd, 3.02.150
i was seven of the nine days out of the wonder 3.02.174 P
i was never so berhym'd since pythagoras' time, 3.02.176 P
since pythagoras' time, that i was an irish rat, 3.02.177 P
he was furnish'd like a hunter. 3.02.245 P
there was no thought of pleasing you when she 3.02.266 P
thought of pleasing you when she was christen'd. 3.02.267 P
i was seeking for a fool when i found you. 3.02.285 P
me to speak, who was in his youth an inland man, 3.02.345 P
he was to imagine me his love, his mistress; 3.02.407 P
of love to a living humor of madness, which was, 3.02.419 P
poet, honest ovid, was among the goths. 3.03. 8 P
your chestnut was ever the only color. 3.04. 11 P
you have heard him swear downright he was. 3.04. 29 P
"was" is not "is." 3.04. 30 P
he ask'd me of what parentage i was. 3.04. 37 P
disdainful shepherdess | that was his mistress. 3.04. 51
silvius, the time was that i hated thee; 3.05. 92
thy company, which erst was irksome to me, | i 3.05. 95
bounds | that the old carlot once was master of. 3.05.108
there was a pretty redness in his lip, | a 3.05.120
in all this time there was not any man died in 4.01. 96 P
and being taken with the cramp was drown'd; 4.01.104 P
foolish chroniclers of that age found it was — 4.01.105 P
bastard of venus that was begot of thought, 4.01.212 P
sir, it was i. 4.02. 2 P
the horn, | it was a crest ere thou wast born; 4.02. 14
which she did use as she was writing of it, | it 4.03. 10
why, and where | this handkercher was stain'd. 4.03. 97
approach the man | and found it was his brother, 4.03.120
might so do, | for well i know he was unnatural. 4.03.124
i do not shame | to tell you what i was, since 4.03.136
a body would think this was well counterfeited! 4.03.166 P
this was not counterfeit, there is too great 4.03.169 P
complexion that it was a passion of earnest. 4.03.170 P
faith, the priest was good enough, for all the 5.01. 3 P
all the revenue that was old sir rowland's will 5.02. 11 P
there was never any thing so sudden but the 5.02. 30 P
i have, since i was three year old, convers'd 5.02. 60 P
it was a lover and his lass, | with a hey, and a 5.03. 16
hey nonino, | how that a life was but a flower, 5.03. 28
though there was no great matter in the ditty, 5.03. 35 P
in the ditty, yet the note was very untuneable. 5.03. 35 P
methought he was a brother to your daughter. 5.04. 29
and how was that ta'en up? 5.04. 48 P
and found the quarrel was upon the seventh cause 5.04. 49 P
me word, if i said his beard was not cut well, 5.04. 71 P
was not cut well, he was in the mind it was: 5.04. 71 P
was not cut well, he was in the mind it was: 5.04. 72 P
if i sent him word again, it was not well cut, 5.04. 73 P
if again, it was not well cut, he disabled my 5.04. 75 P
if again, it was not well cut, he would answer i 5.04. 77 P
if again, it was not well cut, he would say i 5.04. 79 P
how oft did you say his beard was not well cut? 5.04. 83 P
was converted | both from his enterprise and 5.04.161
part | was aptly fitted and naturally perform'd. SHR in.1. 87
we'll show thee io as she was a maid, | and how in.2. 54
maid, | and how she was beguiled and surpris'd, in.2. 55
as lively painted as the deed was done. in.2. 56
she was the fairest creature in the world, | and in.2. 66
as dear | as anna to the queen of carthage was: 1.01.154
sacred and sweet was all i saw in her. 1.01.176
ashore | i kill'd a man and fear i was descried. 1.01.232
was it fit for a servant to use his master so, 1.02. 31 P
be she as foul as was florentius' love, | as old 1.02. 69
if that be jest, then all the rest was so. 2.01. 22
was ever gentleman thus griev'd as i? 2.01. 37
was ever match clapp'd up so suddenly? 2.01.325
i am your neighbor, and was suitor first. 2.01.334
far | to know the cause why music was ordain'd! 3.01. 10
was it not to refresh the mind of man | after 3.01. 11
for sure aeacides | was ajax, call'd so from his 3.01. 53
i told you, i, he was a frantic fool, | hiding 3.02. 12
and seem'd to ask him sops as he was drinking. 3.02.176
such a mad marriage never was before. 3.02.182
of all mad matches never was the like. 3.02.242
was ever man so beaten? 4.01. 2 P
was ever man so ray'd? 4.01. 3 P
was ever man so weary? 4.01. 3 P
she was, good curtis, before this frost; 4.01. 22 P
and this cuff was but to knock at your ear, and 4.01. 65 P
heard in how miry a place, how she was bemoil'd, 4.01. 75 P
the horses ran away, how her bridle was burst; 4.01. 81 P
here, sir — as foolish as i was before. 4.01.128
nathaniel's coat, sir, was not fully made, | and 4.01.132
there was no link to color peter's hat, | and 4.01.134
and walter's dagger was not come from sheathing; 4.01.135
"it was the friar of orders grey, | as he forth 4.01.145
the meat was well, if you were so contented. 4.01.169
why, this was moulded on a porringer — | a 4.03. 64
i told him that your father was at venice, | and 4.04. 15
i told you your son was well belov'd in padua. 5.01. 25 P
him up ever since he was three years old, and 5.01. 82 P
whose skill was almost as great as his honesty; AWW 1.01. 19 P
he was famous, sir, in his profession, and it 1.01. 26 P
and it was his great right to be so — gerard de 1.01. 27 P
he was excellent indeed, madam. 1.01. 28 P
he was skillful enough to have liv'd still, if 1.01. 30 P
was this gentlewoman the daughter of gerard de 1.01. 36 P
what was he like? 1.01. 81
and there was never virgin /got till virginity 1.01.128 P
never virgin /got till virginity was first lost. 1.01.129 P
it was formerly better, marry, yet 'tis a 1.01.162 P
when he was predominant. 1.01.197 P
when he was retrograde, i think rather. 1.01.198 P
of the time, and was | discipled of the bravest. 1.02. 27
when it was out — "let me not live," quoth he, 1.02. 58
he was much fam'd. 1.02. 71
"was this fair face the cause," quoth she, 1.03. 70
done, done fond, | was this king priam's joy?" 1.03. 73
i was very late more near her than i think she 1.03.106 P
alone she was, and did communicate to herself 1.03.107 P
her matter was, she lov'd your son. 1.03.110 P
she said, was no goddess, that had put such 1.03.111 P
even so it was with me when i was young. 1.03.128
even so it was with me when i was young. 1.03.128
that your dian | was both herself and love, o, 1.03.213
this was your motive | for paris, was it? speak. 1.03.230
this was your motive | for paris, was it? speak. 1.03.231
which was the great'st | of his profession, that 1.03.243
it was this very sword entrench'd it. 2.01. 44 P
gerard de narbon was my father, | in what he did 2.01.101
late | was in my nobler thoughts most base, is 2.03.171
sir, was profitable, and much fool may you find 2.04. 35 P
i have, sir, as i was commanded from you, 2.05. 54
prepar'd i was not | for such a business; 2.05. 61
i have no mind to isbel since i was at court. 3.02. 12 P
for my part, i only hear your son was run away. 3.02. 44 P
he was my son, | but i do wash his name out of 3.02. 66
haply, | which his heart was not consenting to. 3.02. 78
who was with him? 3.02. 83
parolles, was it not? 3.02. 85
not, i am the cause | his death was so effected. 3.02.116
there was excellent command — to charge in with 3.06. 48 P
that was not to be blam'd in the command of the 3.06. 51 P
it was a disaster of war that caesar himself 3.06. 52 P
he was first smok'd by the old lord lafew. 3.06.103 P
though my estate be fall'n, i was well born, 3.07. 4
truth that e'er thine own tongue was guilty of. 4.01. 33 P
of my beard, and to say it was in stratagem. 4.01. 49 P
or to drown my clothes, and say i was stripp'd. 4.01. 52 P
they told me that your name was fontibell. 4.02. 1
and now you should be as your mother was | when 4.02. 9
your mother was | when your sweet self was got. 4.02. 10
she then was honest. 4.02. 11
i was compell'd to her, but i love thee | by 4.02. 15
was faithfully confirm'd by the rector of the 4.03. 58 P
the last was the greatest, but that i have not 4.03. 91 P
gallant militarist — that was his own phrase — 4.03.141 P
'a was a botcher's prentice in paris, from 4.03.185 P
paris, from whence he was whipt for getting the 4.03.186 P
was very honest in the behalf of the maid; 4.03.218 P
have suspected an ambush where i was taken? 4.03.302 P
time was, i did him a desired office, | dear 4.04. 5
to whose trust | your business was more welcome. 4.04. 16
your son was misled with a snipt-taffata fellow 4.05. 1 P
it was the death of the most virtuous 4.05. 8 P
sir, she was the sweet marjorom of the sallet, 4.05. 16 P
and i was about to tell you, since i heard of 4.05. 68 P
that my lord your son was upon his return home, 4.05. 70 P
i was thinking with what manners i might safely 4.05. 88 P
was i, in sooth? 5.02. 44 P
and i was the first that lost thee. 5.02. 44 P
and our esteem | was made much poorer by it; 5.03. 2
was in mine eye | the dust that did offend it. 5.03. 54
helen, that's dead, | was a sweet creature; 5.03. 78
hers it was not. 5.03. 80
while i was speaking, oft was fasten'd to't. 5.03. 82
while i was speaking, oft was fasten'd to't. 5.03. 82
this ring was mine, and, when i gave it helen, 5.03. 83
you to take it so, | the ring was never hers. 5.03. 89
in florence was it from a casement thrown me, 5.03. 93
noble she was, and thought | i stood engag'd; 5.03. 95
if you shall prove | this ring was ever hers, 5.03.125
her bed in florence, | where yet she never was. 5.03.127
to marry me when his wife was dead, i blush to 5.03.140 P
the life of helen, lady, | was foully snatch'd. 5.03.154
lord, | and was a common gamester to the camp. 5.03.188
what ring was yours, i pray you? 5.03.225
know you this ring? this ring was his of late. 5.03.227
and this was it i gave him, being a-bed. 5.03.228
my lord, i do confess the ring was hers. 5.03.231
he lov'd her, for indeed he was mad for her, and 5.03.260 P
yet i was in that credit with them at that time 5.03.262 P
this ring you say was yours? 5.03.270
it was not given me, nor i did not buy it. 5.03.272
it was not lent me neither. 5.03.273
this ring was mine, i gave it his first wife. 5.03.279
o my good lord, when i was like this maid, | i 5.03.309
'tis not so sweet now as it was before. TN 1.01. 8
that instant was i turn'd into a hart, | and my 1.01. 20
well, for i was bred and born | not three hours' 1.02. 22
he was a bachelor then. 1.02. 29
and so is now, or was so very late; 1.02. 30
leg, it was form'd under the star of a galliard. 1.03.133 P
i can tell thee where that saying was born, of 1.05. 10 P
look you, sir, such a one i was this present. 1.05.234 P
my father was that sebastian of messaline, whom 2.01. 17 P
the breach of the sea was my sister drown'd. 2.01. 22 P
sir, though it was said she much resembled me, 2.01. 25 P
me, was yet of many accounted beautiful; 2.01. 26 P
youth of the count's was to-day with my lady, 2.03.132 P
i was ador'd once too. 2.03.181 P
who was it? 2.04. 10
was not this love indeed? 2.04.115
cressida was a beggar. 3.01. 55 P
since lowly feigning was call'd compliment. 3.01. 99
this was a great argument of love in her toward 3.02. 11 P
grand-jurymen since before noah was a sailor. 3.02. 17 P
this was look'd for at your hand, and this was 3.02. 23 P
look'd for at your hand, and this was balk'd. 3.02. 24 P
even such and so | in favor was my brother, and 3.04.381
sir topas, never was man thus wrong'd. 4.02. 28 P
and i say there was never man thus abus'd. 4.02. 47 P
fool, there was never man so notoriously abus'd; 4.02. 87 P
yet there he was, and there i found this credit, 4.03. 6
it was besmear'd | as black as vulcan in the 5.01. 52
a baubling vessel was he captain of, | for 5.01. 54
antonio never yet was thief or pirate, | though 5.01. 74
a wrack past hope he was. 5.01. 79
town, | drew to defend him when he was beset; 5.01. 85
that i did, i was set on to do't by sir toby. 5.01.185 P
sebastian was my father — | such a sebastian 5.01.232
father — | such a sebastian was my brother too; 5.01.233
i was preserv'd to serve this noble count. 5.01.256
me, it was she | first told me thou wast mad. 5.01.348
how with a sportful malice it was follow'd | may 5.01.365
i was one, sir, in this enterlude — one sir 5.01.372 P
when that i was and a little tine boy, | with 5.01.389
and the rain, | a foolish thing was but a toy, 5.01.391
on crutches ere he was born desire yet their WT 1.01. 40 P
two lads that thought there was no more behind 1.02. 63
was not my lord | the verier wag o' th' two? 1.02. 65
what we chang'd | was innocence for innocence; 1.02. 69
in those unfledg'd days was my wife a girl; 1.02. 78
my last good deed was to entreat his stay; 1.02. 97
what was my first? 1.02. 98
that was when | three crabbed months had sour'd 1.02.101
how like, methought, i then was to this kernel, 1.02.159
was this taken | by any understanding pate but 1.02.222
i were willful-negligent, | it was my folly; 1.02.256
i play'd the fool, it was my negligence, | not 1.02.257
infection | that e'er was heard or read! 1.02.424
there was a man — 2.01. 29
was he met there? his train? camillo with him? 2.01. 33
camillo was his help in this, his pandar. 2.01. 46
whom i employ'd was pre-employ'd by him: 2.01. 49
(which was as gross as ever touch'd conjecture, 2.01.176
this child was prisoner to the womb and is | by 2.02. 57
is rotten | as ever oak or stone was sound. 2.03. 91
solemn, and unearthly | it was i' th' off'ring! 3.01. 8
so surpris'd my sense, | that i was nothing. 3.01. 11
came to your court, how i was in your grace, 3.02. 47
from an infant, freely, | that it was yours. 3.02. 71
know of it | is that camillo was an honest man; 3.02. 74
the emperor of russia was my father. 3.02.119
for ne'er was dream | so like a waking. 3.03. 18
time collect myself and thought | this was so, 3.03. 39
to me for help and said his name was antigonus, 3.03. 96 P
name of mercy, when was this, boy? 3.03.103 P
it was told me i should be rich by the fairies. 3.03.117 P
pass | the same i am, ere ancient'st order was, 4.01. 10
was likewise a snapper-up of unconsider'd 4.03. 25 P
o that ever i was born! 4.03. 50 P
quarters of a mile hence, unto whom i was going. 4.03. 81 P
what manner of fellow was he that robb'd you? 4.03. 84 P
sir, for which of his virtues it was, but he was 4.03. 89 P
but he was certainly whipt out of the court. 4.03. 89 P
sweet sir, much better than i was: 4.03.111 P

upon | this day she was both pantler, butler, 4.04. 56
driven snow, | cypress black as e'er was crow, 4.04.219
i was promis'd them against the feast, but they 4.04.235 P
i not told thee how i was cozen'd by the way and 4.04.251 P
how a usurer's wife was brought to bed of twenty 4.04.263 P
it was thought she was a woman and was turn'd 4.04.278 P
it was thought she was a woman and was turn'd 4.04.279 P
she was a woman and was turn'd into a cold fish 4.04.279 P
sooth, when i was young, | and handed love as 4.04.347
you do, i was wont | to load my she with knacks. 4.04.348
swain seems to wash | the hand was fair before! 4.04.367
force and knowledge | more than was ever man's, 4.04.375
i was not much afeard; 4.04.442
for once or twice | i was about to speak, and 4.04.443
that knew'st this was the prince, and wouldst 4.04.459
what i was, i am: 4.04.464
means i saw whose purse was best in picture, and 4.04.603 P
might have pinch'd a placket, it was senseless; 4.04.610 P
indeed brother-in-law was the farthest off you 4.04.703 P
he was provided to do us good. 4.04.829 P
which was so much | that heirless it hath made 5.01. 9
so his successor | was like to be the best. 5.01. 49
she shall not be so young | as was your former, 5.01. 79
nor was not to be equall'd" — thus your verse 5.01.101
there was not full a month | between their 5.01.117
your mother was most true to wedlock, prince, 5.01.124
to your court | whiles he was hast'ning (in the 5.01.189
she was more worth such gazes | than what you 5.01.226
i was by at the opening of the farthel, heard 5.02. 3 P
there was speech in their dumbness, language in 5.02. 13 P
then have you lost a sight which was to be seen, 5.02. 42 P
there was casting up of eyes, holding up of 5.02. 46 P
he was torn to pieces with a bear. 5.02. 63 P
the child were even then lost when it was found. 5.02. 72 P
'twixt joy and sorrow was fought in paulina! 5.02. 73 P
another elevated that the oracle was fulfill'd. 5.02. 75 P
dignity of this act was worth the audience of 5.02. 79 P
of kings and princes, for by such was it acted. 5.02. 80 P
was when, at the relation of the queen's death 5.02. 84 P
who was most marble there chang'd color; 5.02. 90 P
this other day, because i was no gentleman born. 5.02.129 P
but i was a gentleman born before my father; 5.02.139 P
and there was the first gentleman-like tears 5.02.144 P
for she was as tender | as infancy and grace. 5.03. 26
hermione was not so much wrinkled, nothing | so 5.03. 28
my lord, your sorrow was too sore laid on, 5.03. 49
let him that was the cause of this have pow'r 5.03. 54
already — | what was he that did make it? 5.03. 63
when she was young, you woo'd her; 5.03.108
i give heaven thanks i was not like to thee! JN 1.01. 83
when this same lusty gentleman was got. 1.01.108
that this my mother's son was none of his; 1.01.111
my father's land, as was my father's will. 1.01.115
and if she did play false, the fault was hers, 1.01.118
sir, | than was his will to get me, as i think. 1.01.133
be the hour by night or day | when i was got, 1.01.166
or day | when i was got, sir robert was away! 1.01.166
well shot, | and i am i, howe'er i was begot. 1.01.175
a foot of honor better than i was, | but many a 1.01.182
madam, i was not old sir robert's son; 1.01.233
who was it, mother? 1.01.250
king richard cordelion was thy father. 1.01.253
by long and vehement suit i was seduc'd | to 1.01.254
which was so strongly urg'd past my defense. 1.01.258
your fault was not your folly; 1.01.262
but say thou didst not well | when i was got, 1.01.272
who says it was, he lies, i say 'twas not. 1.01.276
that geffrey was thy elder brother born, | and 2.01.104
england was geffrey's right, | and this is 2.01.105
my bed was ever to thy son as true | as thine 2.01.124
thy son as true | as thine was to thy husband, 2.01.125
i think | his father never was so true begot — 2.01.130
i was never so bethump'd with words | since i 2.01.466
cool and congeal again to what it was. 2.01.479
that i did so when i was first assur'd. 2.01.535
gave the sound of words | was deep-sworn faith, 3.01.231
will | as dear be to thee as thy father was. 3.03. 4
my name is constance, i was geffrey's wife, 3.04. 46
there was not such a gracious creature born. 3.04. 81
yet i remember, when i was in france, | young 4.01. 14
is it my fault that i was geffrey's son? 4.01. 22
nay, you may think my love was crafty love, 4.01. 53
your highness pleas'd) | was once superfluous. 4.02. 4
and that high royalty was ne'er pluck'd off; 4.02. 5
pomp, | to guard a title that was rich before, 4.02. 10
than did the fault before it was so patch'd. 4.02. 34
indeed we fear'd his sickness was past cure. 4.02. 86
indeed we heard how near his death he was 4.02. 87
was | before the child himself felt he was sick. 4.02. 88
preparation | was levied in the body of a land. 4.02.112
me, cousin, for i was amaz'd | under the tide; 4.02.137
made | upon thy feature, for my rage was blind, 4.02.264
which was embounded in this beauteous clay, 4.03.137
it was my breath that blew this tempest up, 5.01. 17
again | after they heard young arthur was alive? 5.01. 38
by some damn'd hand was robb'd and ta'en away. 5.01. 41
be glorified | as to my ample hope was promised 5.02.112
supply, | that was expected by the dolphin here, 5.03. 10
this news was brought to richard but even now. 5.03. 12
for that my grandsire was an englishman, 5.04. 42
the sun of heaven, methought, was loath to set, 5.05. 1
who was he that said | king john did fly an hour 5.05. 16
when this was now a king, and now is clay? 5.07. 69
verge | that ever was surveyed by english eye, R2 1.01. 94
for that my sovereign liege was in my debt, 1.01.129
ah, gaunt, his blood was thine! 1.02. 22
die, | who was the model of thy father's life. 1.02. 28
say | i was too strict to make mine own away; 1.03.244
else | but that i was a journeyman to grief? 1.03.274
that england, that was wont to conquer others, 2.01. 65
son, | for that i was his father edward's son, 2.01.125
of whom thy father, prince of wales, was first. 2.01.172
in war was never lion rag'd more fierce, | in 2.01.173
in peace was never gentle lamb more mild, | than 2.01.174
than was that young and princely gentleman. 2.01.175
but when he frowned it was against the french, 2.01.178
was not gaunt just? 2.01.192
my lord, your son was gone before i came. 2.02. 86
he was — why, so go all which way it will! 2.02. 87
what was his reason? 2.03. 28
he was not so resolv'd when last we spake 2.03. 29
because your lordship was proclaimed traitor. 2.03. 30
as i was banish'd, i was banish'd herford, | but 2.03.113
as i was banish'd, i was banish'd herford, | but 2.03.113
wherefore was i born? 2.03.122
forth | of that sweet way i was in to despair! 3.02.205
what, was i born to this, that my sad look 3.04. 98
dead time when gloucester's death was plotted, 4.01. 10
where it was forged, with my rapier's point. 4.01. 40
but dust was thrown upon his sacred head, 5.02. 30
aumerle that was, | but that is lost for being 5.02. 41
his answer was, he would unto the stews, | and 5.03. 16
intended, or committed, was this fault? 5.03. 33
it was, villain, ere thy hand did set it down. 5.03. 54
was it not so? 5.04. 3
penury | persuades me i was better when a king; 5.05. 35
i was a poor groom of thy stable, king, | when 5.05. 72
so proud that bullingbrook was on his back! 5.05. 84
i was not made a horse, | and yet i bear a 5.05. 92
my liege, this haste was hot in question, | and 1H4 1.01. 34
news, | whose worst was that the noble mortimer, 1.01. 38
was by the rude hands of that welshman taken, 1.01. 41
upon whose dead corpse' there was such misuse, 1.01. 43
and shape of likelihood the news was told; 1.01. 58
for he was never yet a breaker of proverbs. 1.02.118 P
but i remember, when the fight was done, | when 1.03. 30
when i was dry with rage and extreme toil, 1.03. 31
he was perfumed like a milliner, | and 'twixt 1.03. 36
on earth | was parmaciti for an inward bruise, 1.03. 58
and that it was great pity, so it was, | this 1.03. 59
bruise, | and that it was great pity, so it was, 1.03. 59
who strook this heat up after i was gone? 1.03.139
was not he proclaim'd | by richard, that dead is 1.03.145
he was, i heard the proclamation. 1.03.147
and then it was when the unhappy king | (whose 1.03.148
the price of oats rose, it was the death of him. 2.01. 13 P
our plot is a good plot as ever was laid, our 2.03. 17 P
i never dealt better since i was a man; 2.04.169 P
speak, sirs, how was it? 2.04.173 P
my back and let drive at me, for it was so dark, 2.04.223 P
in kendal green when it was so dark thou couldst 2.04.232 P
as thou hast done, and then say it was in fight! 2.04.262 P
was it for me to kill the heir-apparent? 2.04.268 P
i was now a coward on instinct. 2.04.272 P
he would make you believe it was done in fight, 2.04.307 P
with it and swear it was the blood of true men. 2.04.311 P
when i was about thy years, hal, i was not an 2.04.329 P
hal, i was not an eagle's talent in the waist, i 2.04.330 P
here was sir john bracy from your father; 2.04.334 P
the front of heaven was full of fiery shapes 3.01. 14
i say the earth did shake when i was born. 3.01. 20
and i say the earth was not of my mind, | if you 3.01. 21
the front of heaven was full of fiery shapes, 3.01. 37
for i was train'd up in the english court, 3.01.120
ornament, | a virtue that was never seen in you. 3.01.124
not stir | but like a comet i was wond'red at, 3.02. 47
be seen, | he was but as the cuckoo is in june, 3.02. 75
as thou art to this hour was richard then | when 3.02. 94
and even as i was then is percy now. 3.02. 96
i was as virtuously given as a gentleman need to 3.03. 14 P
the /tithe of a hair was never lost in my house 3.03. 58 P
bardolph was shav'd and lost many a hair, and 3.03. 59 P
a hair, and i'll be sworn my pocket was pick'd. 3.03. 60 P
i was never call'd so in mine own house before. 3.03. 62 P
i know not how oft, that that ring was copper! 3.03. 84 P
yea, if he said my ring was copper. 3.03.142 P
thence | he was much fear'd by his physicians. 4.01. 24
his health was never better worth than now. 4.01. 27
and when he was not six and twenty strong, 4.03. 56
made to my father, while his blood was poor, 4.03. 76
here, | when he was personal in the irish war. 4.03. 88
whose power was in the first proportion, | and 4.04. 15
thence, | who with them was a rated sinew too, 4.04. 17
it was myself, my brother, and his son, | that 5.01. 39
and westmerland, that was engag'd, did bear it, 5.02. 43
i was not born a yielder, thou proud scot, | and 5.03. 11
a gallant knight he was, his name was blunt, 5.03. 20
a gallant knight he was, his name was blunt, 5.03. 20
a kingdom for it was too small a bound, | but 5.04. 90
did you not tell me this fat man was dead? 5.04.132
i grant you i was down and out of breath, and so 5.04.146 P
you i was down and out of breath, and so was he, 5.04.147 P
he was so bruis'd | that the pursuers took him. 5.05. 21
and that young harry percy's spur was cold. 2H4 1.01. 42
said he young harry percy's spur was cold? 1.01. 49
he was some hilding fellow that had stol'n | the 1.01. 57
and would have told him half his troy was burnt; 1.01. 73
for from his metal was his party steeled, 1.01.116
then was that noble worcester | so soon ta'en 1.01.125
in his flight, | stumbling in fear, was took. 1.01.131
sir, the water itself was a good healthy water, 1.02. 3 P
i was never mann'd with an agot till now, but i 1.02. 16 P
writ man ever since his father was a bachelor. 1.02. 27 P
he that was in question for the robb'ry? 1.02. 60 P
i heard say your lordship was sick, i hope your 1.02. 95 P
as i was then advis'd by my learned counsel in 1.02.134 P
lord, i was born about three of the clock in the 1.02.187 P
but it was alway yet the trick of our english 1.02.214 P
it was young hotspur's cause at shrewsbury. 1.03. 26
it was, my lord, who lin'd himself with hope, 1.03. 27
swear to me then, as i was washing thy wound, to 2.01. 91 P
didst thou not, when she was gone down stairs, 2.01. 99 P
me not, he was a fool that taught them me. 2.01.192 P
belike then my appetite was not princely got, 2.02. 9 P
althaea dreamt she was deliver'd of a fire-brand 2.02. 89 P
it was jove's case. 2.02.174 P
the time was, father, that you broke your word 2.03. 10
he was indeed the glass | wherein the noble 2.03. 21
so did your son, | he was so suff'red; 2.03. 57
better than i was. hem! 2.04. 30 P
"and was a worthy king." 2.04. 35 P
i was before master tisick, the debuty, t' other 2.04. 84 P
our minister, was by then — "neighbor quickly," 2.04. 88 P
which was an excellent good word before it was 2.04.149 P
an excellent good word before it was ill sorted; 2.04.150 P
you knew i was at your back, and spoke it on 2.04.307 P
since | this percy was the man nearest my soul, 3.01. 61
but which of you was by — | you, cousin nevil, 3.01. 65
i was once of clement's inn, where i think they 3.02. 14 P
by the mass, i was call'd any thing, and i would 3.02. 17 P
there was i, and little john doit of 3.02. 19 P
then was jack falstaff, now sir john, a boy, and 3.02. 24 P
court-gate, when 'a was a crack not thus high; 3.02. 31 P
by my troth, i was not there. 3.02. 39 P
i was prick'd well enough before, and you could 3.02.111 P
she was then a bona roba. 3.02.205 P
our watch-word was "hem, boys!" 3.02.217 P
i was then sir dagonet in arthur's show — there 3.02.280 P
show — there was a little quiver fellow, and 'a 3.02.281 P
when 'a was naked, he was for all the world like 3.02.310 P
he was for all the world like a fork'd redish, 3.02.310 P
'a was so forlorn, that his dimensions to any 3.02.312 P
'a was the very genius of famine, yet lecherous 3.02.313 P
case of a treble hoboy was a mansion for him, a 3.02.326 P
when ever yet was your appeal denied? 4.01. 88
in the arm | that was uprear'd to execution. 4.01.212
but rebuke and check was the reward of valor. 4.03. 31 P
it was more of his courtesy than your deserving. 4.03. 43 P
thy wish was father, harry, to that thought: 4.05. 92
for what in me was purchas'd | falls upon thee 4.05.199
by whose fell working i was first advanc'd, 4.05.206
was this easy? 5.02. 71
law, | whiles i was busy for the commonwealth, 5.02. 76
jest, | presume not that i am the thing i was, 5.05. 56
this that you heard was but a color. 5.05. 86 P
i was lately here in the end of a displeasing ep 8 P
which was never seen in such an assembly. ep 24 P
year of the last king's reign | was like, and H5 1.01. 3
never was such a sudden scholar made; 1.01. 32
it, | since his addiction was to courses vain, 1.01. 54
save that there was not time enough to hear, 1.01. 84
what was th' impediment that broke this off? 1.01. 90
law | was not devised for the realm of france; 1.02. 55
blithild, which was daughter to king clothair, 1.02. 67
though in pure truth it was corrupt and naught, 1.02. 73
who was the son | to lewis the emperor, and 1.02. 75
tenth, | who was sole heir to the usurper capet, 1.02. 78
grandmother, | was lineal of the lady ermengare, 1.02. 82
great | was re-united to the crown of france. 1.02. 85
this was a merry message. 1.02.298
nay, but the man that was his bedfellow, | whom 2.02. 8
never was monarch better fear'd and lov'd | than 2.02. 25
it was excess of wine that set him on, | and on 2.02. 42
the mercy that was quick in us but late, | by 2.02. 79
you know how apt our love was to accord | to 2.02. 86
and whatsoever cunning fiend it was | that 2.02.111
his finger's end, i knew there was but one way; 2.03. 15 P
for his nose was as sharp as a pen, and 'a 2.03. 16 P
i hop'd there was no need to trouble himself 2.03. 21 P
and up'ard, and all was as cold as any stone. 2.03. 25 P
but then he was rheumatic, and talk'd of the 2.03. 38 P
and 'a said it was a black soul burning in hell? 2.03. 41 P
shame | when cressy battle fatally was struck, 2.04. 54
and that was against a post when he was drunk. 3.02. 41 P
and that was against a post when he was drunk. 3.02. 41 P
who came off bravely, who was shot, who 3.06. 74 P
th' athversary was have possession of the pridge 3.06. 93 P
mine was not bridled. 3.07. 51 P
o then belike she was old and gentle, and you 3.07. 52 P
i was told that by one that knows him better 3.07.104 P
damnation than he was before guilty of those 4.01.175 P
dying, the time was blessedly lost wherein such 4.01.181 P
lost wherein such preparation was gain'd; 4.01.182 P
the beast liv'd, was kill'd with hunting him. 4.03. 94
from helmet to the spur all blood he was. 4.06. 6
carried away all that was in the king's tent; 4.07. 8 P
ay, he was porn at monmouth, captain gower. 4.07. 11 P
town's name where alexander the pig was born? 4.07. 13 P
i think alexander the great was born in macedon. 4.07. 19 P
his father was called philip of macedon, as i 4.07. 20 P
he was full of jests, and gipes, and knaveries, 4.07. 48 P
i was not angry since i came to france | until 4.07. 55
which he swore, as he was a soldier, he would 4.07.129 P
my liege, this was my glove, here is the fellow 4.08. 28 P
it was ourself thou didst abuse. 4.08. 49
here was a royal fellowship of death! 4.08.101
o god, thy arm was here; 4.08.106
was ever known so great and little loss, | on 4.08.110
it was in a place where i could not breed no 5.01. 10 P
he was thinking of civil wars when he got me; 5.02.225 P
therefore was i created with a stubborn outside, 5.02.226 P
he was a king blest of the king of kings. 1H6 1.01. 28
day | so dreadful will not be as was his sight. 1.01. 30
how were they lost? what treachery was us'd? 1.01. 68
wherein lord talbot was o'erthrown. 1.01.108
thousand of the french | was round encompassed, 1.01.114
the french exclaim'd, the devil was in arms; 1.01.125
and, whereas i was black and swart before, 1.02. 84
was mahomet inspired with a dove? 1.02.140
for him was i exchang'd and ransomed. 1.04. 29
in fine, redeem'd i was as i desir'd. 1.04. 34
i'll rear | than rhodope's /of memphis ever was. 1.06. 22
tut, holy joan was his defensive guard. 2.01. 49
duke of alanson, this was your default, | that, 2.01. 60
mine was secure. 2.01. 66
and so was mine, my lord. 2.01. 66
precinct | i was employ'd in passing to and fro, 2.01. 69
but weakly guarded, where the breach was made. 2.01. 74
for every drop of blood was drawn from him 2.02. 8
or else was wrangling somerset in th' error? 2.04. 6
false, | the argument you held was wrong in you; 2.04. 57
his grandfather was lionel duke of clarence, 2.04. 83
was not thy father, richard earl of cambridge, 2.04. 90
my father was attached, not attainted, 2.04. 96
and answer was return'd that he will come. 2.05. 20
reign, | before whose glory i was great in arms, 2.05. 24
that so he might recover what was lost. 2.05. 32
to pine, | was cursed instrument of his decease. 2.05. 58
discover more at large what cause that was, 2.05. 59
reason mov'd these warlike lords to this | was, 2.05. 71
body) | i was the next by birth and parentage; 2.05. 73
york, | marrying my sister that thy mother was, 2.05. 86
so fell that noble earl | and was beheaded. 2.05. 91
was nothing less than bloody tyranny. 2.05.100

that malice was a great and grievous sin; 3.01.128
fift | was in the mouth of every sucking babe, 3.01.196
lives | and as his father here was conqueror, 3.02. 81
town | great cordelion's heart was buried, | so 3.02. 83
was not the duke of orleance thy foe? 3.03. 69
and was he not in england prisoner? 3.03. 70
but when they heard he was thine enemy, | they 3.03. 71
when i was young (as yet i am not old), | i do 3.04. 17
a letter was deliver'd to my hands, | writ to 4.01. 11
i was six thousand strong | and that the french 4.01. 20
before we met, or that a stroke was given, 4.01. 22
this fact was infamous | and ill beseeming any 4.01. 30
when first this order was ordain'd, my lords, 4.01. 33
yet know, my lord, i was provok'd by him, | and 4.01.104
that for a trifle that was bought with blood! 4.01.150
tush, that was but his fancy, blame him not. 4.01.178
this expedition was by york and talbot | too 4.04. 2
but, if i bow, they'll say it was for fear. 4.05. 29
my age was never tainted with such shame. 4.05. 46
the life thou gav'st me first was lost and done, 4.06. 7
"young talbot was not born | to be the pillage 4.07. 40
whose life was england's glory, gallia's wonder. 4.07. 48
thought | it was both impious and unnatural 5.01. 12
army, that divided was | into two parties, is 5.02. 11
where i was wont to feed you with my blood, 5.03. 14
she was the first fruit of my bach'lorship. 5.04. 13
the morn that i was wedded to her mother. 5.04. 24
of his, | it was alanson that enjoy'd my love. 5.04. 73
for that | my tender youth was never yet attaint 5.05. 81
i have perform'd my task, and was espous'd; 2H6 1.01. 9
it was the pleasure of my lord the king. 1.01.138
and henry was well pleas'd | to change two 1.01.218
was broke in twain (by whom i have forgot, | but 1.02. 26
but, as i think, it was by th' cardinal), | and 1.02. 27
this was my dream, what it doth bode god knows. 1.02. 31
this was nothing but an argument | that he that 1.02. 32
that the duke of york was rightful heir to the 1.03. 26 P
the duke of york say he was rightful heir to the 1.03. 29 P
that my /master was? 1.03. 30 P
my master said that he was, and that the king 1.03. 31 P
that he was, and that the king was an usurper. 1.03. 31 P
as i was cause | your highness came to england, 1.03. 65
was better worth than all my father's lands, 1.03. 86
was it you? 1.03.139
yea, i it was, proud frenchwoman. 1.03.140
on his will | till paris was besieg'd, famish'd, 1.03.172
york | was rightful heir unto the english crown 1.03.184
crown | and that your majesty was an usurper. 1.03.185
the time of night when troy was set on fire, 1.04. 17
yet, by your leave, the wind was very high, 2.01. 3
ay indeed was he. 2.01. 76
but that in all my life, when i was a youth. 2.01. 97
next to whom | was john of gaunt, the duke of 2.02. 14
the fift was edmund langley, duke of york; 2.02. 15
the sixt was thomas of woodstock, duke of 2.02. 16
william of windsor was the seventh and last. 2.02. 17
harmless richard was murthered traitorously. 2.02. 27
earl of cambridge, who was | to edmund langley, 2.02. 45
she was heir | to roger earl of march, who was 2.02. 47
of march, who was the son | of edmund mortimer, 2.02. 48
ten is the hour that was appointed me | to watch 2.04. 6
yet so he rul'd, and such a prince he was, | as 2.04. 44
was made a wonder and a pointing–stock | to 2.04. 46
we know the time since he was mild and affable, 3.01. 9
look, | immediately he was upon his knee, | that 3.01. 11
as next the king he was successive heir, | and 3.01. 49
heard of, | that england was defam'd by tyranny. 3.01.123
'tis well known that, whiles i was protector, 3.01.124
pity was all the fault that was in me; 3.01.125
pity was all the fault that was in me; 3.01.125
the duke was dumb and could not speak a word. 3.02. 32
although the duke was enemy to him, | yet he 3.02. 57
and for myself, foe as he was to me, | might 3.02. 59
why then dame /margaret was ne'er thy joy. 3.02. 79
was i for this nigh wrack'd upon the sea, | and 3.02. 82
a heart it was, bound in with diamonds, | and 3.02.107
tugg'd for life, and was by strength subdu'd. 3.02.173
it cannot be but he was murd'red here, | the 3.02.177
nest | but may imagine how the bird was dead, 3.02.192
and noble stock | was graft with crab–tree slip, 3.02.214
and say it was thy mother that thou meant'st, 3.02.222
that he was the lord embassador | sent from a 3.02.276
but jove was never slain, as thou shalt be. 4.01. 49
i say, it was never merry world in england since 4.02. 8 P
my father was a mortimer — 4.02. 39 P
he was an honest man, and a good bricklayer. 4.02. 40 P
i knew her well, she was a midwife. 4.02. 43 P
she was indeed a pedlar's daughter, and sold 4.02. 45 P
the field is honorable, and there was he born, 4.02. 51 P
to a thing, and i was never mine own man since. 4.02. 83 P
villain, thy father was a plasterer, | and thou 4.02.132
and adam was a gardener. 4.02.134
to nurse, | was by a beggar–woman stol'n away, 4.02.143
for he was thrust in the mouth with a spear, and 4.07. 9 P
was ever feather so lightly blown to and fro as 4.08. 55 P
was ever king that joy'd an earthly throne | and 4.09. 1
no sooner was i crept out of my cradle | but i 4.09. 3
crept out of my cradle | but i was made a king, 4.09. 4
was never subject long'd to be a king | as i do 4.09. 5
think this word "sallet" was born to do me good; 4.10. 10 P
by the best blood that ever was broach'd, and 4.10. 38 P
this hand was made to handle nought but gold. 5.01. 7
my mind was troubled with deep melancholy. 5.01. 34
i was, an't like your majesty. 5.01. 72
run back and bite, because he was withheld, 5.01.152
wrong | but that he was bound by a solemn oath? 5.01.190
but still, where danger was, still there i met 5.03. 11
house, | so was his will in old feeble body. 5.03. 13
it was my inheritance, as the earldom was. 3H6 1.01. 78
it was my inheritance, as the earldom was. 1.01. 78
thy father was a traitor to the crown. 1.01. 79
/thy father was, as thou art, duke of york, 1.01.105
when i was crown'd i was but nine months old. 1.01.112
when i was crown'd i was but nine months old. 1.01.112
whose heir my father was, and i am his. 1.01.140
but 'twas ere i was born. 1.03. 39
what, was it you that would be england's king? 1.04. 70
voice | was wont to cheer his dad in mutinies? 1.04. 77
chair, | and this is he was his adopted heir. 1.04. 98
tears, | and say, "alas, it was a piteous deed!" 1.04.163
one that was a woeful looker–on | when as the 2.01. 45
when as the noble duke of york was slain, | your 2.01. 46
environed he was with many foes, | and stood 2.01. 50
by many hands your father was subdu'd, | but 2.01. 56
for by my scouts i was advertised | that she was 2.01.116
that she was coming with a full intent | to dash 2.01.117
he was lately sent | from your kind aunt, 2.01.145
and happy always was it for that son | whose 2.02. 47
i was adopted heir by his consent. 2.02. 88
'twas you that kill'd young rutland, was it not? 2.02. 98
helen of greece was fairer far than thou, 2.02.146
and ne'er was agamemnon's brother wrong'd | by 2.02.148
from london by the king was i press'd forth; 2.05. 64
was ever son so ru'd a father's death? 2.05.109
was ever father so bemoan'd his son? 2.05.110
was ever king so griev'd for subjects' woe? 2.05.111
more, | as priam was for all his valiant sons. 2.05.120
thy balm wash'd off wherewith thou was anointed. 3.01. 17
more than i seem, and less than i was born to; 3.01. 56
where did you dwell when i was king of england? 3.01. 74
i was anointed king at nine months old, | my 3.01. 76
lady's husband, sir richard grey, was slain, 3.02. 2
when he was made a shriver, 'twas for shift. 3.02.108
i was, i must confess, | great albion's queen in 3.03. 6
whose wisdom was a mirror to the wisest; 3.03. 84
the lord aubrey vere, | was done to death? 3.03.103
the more that henry was unfortunate. 3.03.118
that this his love was an /eternal plant, 3.03.124
whereof the root was fix'd in virtue's ground, 3.03.125
it was thy device | by this alliance to make 3.03.141
before thy coming, lewis was henry's friend. 3.03.143
matter of marriage was the charge he gave me, 3.03.258
i was the chief that rais'd him to the crown, 3.03.262
it was my will and grant, | and for this once my 4.01. 49
all confess | that i was not ignoble of descent, 4.01. 70
for i have heard that she was there in place. 4.01.103
guess'd, believe me, for that was my meaning. 4.05. 22
he was the author, thou the instrument. 4.06. 18
he was convey'd by richard, duke of gloucester, 4.06. 81
for hunting was his daily exercise. 4.06. 85
my brother was too careless of his charge. 4.06. 86
the king was slily finger'd from the deck! 5.01. 44
for warwick was a bug that fear'd us all. 5.02. 2
say warwick was our anchor; 5.04. 13
he was a man; 5.05. 56
'tis sin to flatter, "good" was little better: 5.06. 3
in my eye | where my poor young was lim'd, was 5.06. 17
eye | where my poor young was lim'd, was caught, 5.06. 17
what a peevish fool was that of crete | that 5.06. 18
yet, for all his wings, the fool was drown'd. 5.06. 20
for this, amongst the rest, was i ordain'd. 5.06. 58
and so i was, which plainly signified | that i 5.06. 76
this shoulder was ordain'd so thick to heave, 5.07. 23
was it not she, and that good man of worship, R3 1.01. 66
lord hastings was /to /her /for /his delivery? 1.01. 75
i was provoked by her sland'rous tongue, | that 1.02. 97
o, he was gentle, mild, and virtuous! 1.02.104
for he was fitter for that place than earth. 1.02.108
your beauty was the cause of that effect — 1.02.121
why, that was he. 1.02.142
for it was made | for kissing, lady, not for 1.02.171
that was in thy rage. 1.02.187
was ever woman in this humor woo'd? 1.02.227
was ever woman in this humor won? 1.02.228
king, | i was a pack–horse in his great affairs: 1.03.121
was not your husband | in margaret's battle at 1.03.128
i was; 1.03.167
and the most merciless, that e'er was heard of! 1.03.183
tyrants themselves wept when it was reported. 1.03.184
for edward our son, that was prince of wales, 1.03.199
thyself a queen, for me that was a queen, 1.03.201
when my son | was stabb'd with bloody daggers: 1.03.211
but i was born so high, | our aery buildeth in 1.03.262
and say poor margaret was a prophetess! 1.03.300
i was too hot to do somebody good | that is too 1.03.310
days — | so full of dismal terror was the time. 1.04. 7
what was your dream, my lord? 1.04. 8
tower | and was embark'd to cross to burgundy, 1.04. 10
o lord, methought what pain it was to drown! 1.04. 21
no, no, my dream was lengthen'd after life. 1.04. 43
my stranger soul | was my great father–in–law, 1.04. 49
could not believe but that i was in hell, | such 1.04. 62
it was wont to hold me but while one tells 1.04.118 P
that princely novice, was struck dead by thee? 1.04.222
is clarence dead? the order was revers'd. 2.01. 87
my brother kill'd no man, his fault was thought, 2.01.105
and yet his punishment was bitter death. 2.01.106
our fatherless distress was left unmoan'd, 2.02. 64
was never widow had so dear a loss. 2.02. 77
was never mother had so dear a loss. 2.02. 79
which with a bounteous hand was kindly lent; 2.02. 93
was crown'd in paris but at nine months old. 2.03. 17
for then this land was famously enrich'd | with 2.03. 19
and so was i. i'll bear you company. 2.03. 47
he was the wretched'st thing when he was young, 2.04. 18
he was the wretched'st thing when he was young, 2.04. 18
his nurse? why, she was dead ere thou wast born. 2.04. 33
but by his mother was perforce withheld. 3.01. 30
that julius caesar was a famous man; 3.01. 84
my grandam told me he was murd'red there. 3.01.145
york | was not incensed by his subtile mother 3.01.152
whereof the king my brother was possess'd. 3.01.196
protest, | was it so precious to me as 'tis now. 3.02. 80
then was i going prisoner to the tower, | by the 3.02.100
death, | and i in better state than e'er i was. 3.02.104
richard the second here was hack'd to death; 3.03. 12
my lord of ely, when i was last in holborn, | i 3.04. 31
he was the covert'st shelt'red traitor | that 3.05. 33
which by the sign thereof was termed so. 3.05. 79
time, | found that the issue was not his begot; 3.05. 90
for yesternight by catesby was it sent me; 3.06. 6
the precedent was full as long a–doing, | and 3.06. 7
his answer was, the people were not used | to be 3.07. 29
then he was urg'd to tell my tale again: 3.07. 31
for first was he contract to lady lucy — | your 3.07.179
come, madam, come, i in all haste was sent. 4.01. 56
when scarce the blood was well wash'd from his 4.01. 67
i look'd on richard's face, | this was my wish: 4.01. 71
but with his timorous dreams was still awak'd. 4.01. 84
king, | when richmond was a little peevish boy. 4.02. 97
that ever yet this land was guilty of. 4.03. 3
when didst thou sleep when such a deed was done? 4.04. 24
queen, | the presentation of but what i was; 4.04. 84
a grievous burthen was thy birth to me, | tetchy 4.04.168
to me, | tetchy and wayward was thy infancy; 4.04.169
i will confess she was not edward's daughter. 4.04.211
no doubt the murd'rous knife was dull and blunt 4.04.227
till it was whetted on thy stone–hard heart | to 4.04.228
i never was nor never will be false. 4.04.493
i wish'd might fall on me when i was found 5.01. 14
sorrow, | remember margaret was a prophetess." 5.01. 27
is my beaver easier than it was? 5.03. 50
nor cheer of mind that i was wont to have. 5.03. 74
when i was mortal, my anointed body | by thee 5.03.124
body | by thee was punched full of deadly holes. 5.03.125
i that was wash'd to death with fulsome wine, 5.03.132
the first was i that help'd thee to the crown; 5.03.167
the last was i that felt thy tyranny. 5.03.168
that he was never trained up in arms. 5.03.272
he was in the right, and so indeed it is. 5.03.275
i was then present, saw them salute on horseback H8 1.01. 8
the whole time | i was my chamber's prisoner. 1.01. 13
men might say | till this time pomp was single, 1.01. 15
their very labor | was to them as a painting. 1.01. 26
now this masque | was cried incomparable; 1.01. 27
enough, got credit, | that bevis was believ'd. 1.01. 38
some life, | which action's self was tongue to. 1.01. 42
all was royal; 1.01. 42
all this was ord'red by the good discretion | of 1.01. 50
storm that follow'd, was | a thing inspir'd, and 1.01. 90
whereby his suit was granted | ere it was ask'd 1.01.186
his suit was granted | ere it was ask'd — but 1.01.187
but when the way was made | and pav'd with gold, 1.01.187
who was enroll'd 'mongst wonders, and when we, 1.02.119
shall hear | (this was his gentleman in trust) 1.02.125
first, it was usual with him — every day | it 1.02.132
he was brought to this | by a vain prophecy of 1.02.146
what was that henton? 1.02.148
demand | what was the speech among the londoners 1.02.154
which, being believ'd, | it was much like to do. 1.02.182
oath, whose tenor | was, were he evil us'd, he 1.02.207
for i was spoke to, with sir henry guilford 1.03. 66
was he mad, sir? 1.04. 27
yes indeed was i. 2.01. 6
that was he | that fed him with his prophecies? 2.01. 22
but all | was either pitied in him or forgotten. 2.01. 29
when he was brought again to th' bar, to hear 2.01. 31
he was stirr'd | with such an agony he sweat 2.01. 32
sure he does not, | he never was so womanish. 2.01. 38
earl surrey was sent thither, and in haste too, 2.01. 43
that trick of state | was a deep envious one. 2.01. 45
hither, i was lord high constable | and duke of 2.01.102
being distress'd, was by that wretch betray'd, 2.01.110
for it grows again | fresher than e'er it was, 2.01.155
was not one doctor pace | in this man's place 2.02.121
yes, he was. 2.02.122
was he not held a learned man? 2.02.123
and fearing he would rise (he was so virtuous), 2.02.127
he was a fool — | for he would needs be 2.02.131
it was a gentle business, and becoming | the 2.03. 54
there was a lady once ('tis an old story) | that 2.03. 90
when was the hour | i ever contradicted your 2.04. 27
gave notice | he was from thence discharg'd? 2.04. 34
father, was reputed for | a prince most prudent, 2.04. 45
was reckon'd one | the wisest prince that there 2.04. 48
i took a thought | this was a judgment on me, 2.04.195
so deep suspicion, where all faith was meant. 3.01. 53
both of his truth and him (which was too far), 3.01. 65
i was set at work | among my maids, full little, 3.01. 74
lily, | that once was mistress of the field, and 3.01.152
a noble spirit | as yours was put into you, ever 3.01.170
wherein was read | how that the cardinal did 3.02. 31
a heed | was in his countenance. 3.02. 81
how innocent i was | from any private malice in 3.02.267
"ego et rex meus" | was still inscrib'd; 3.02.315
this day was view'd in open as his queen, 3.02.404
there was the weight that pull'd me down. 3.02.407
to which | she was often cited by them, but 4.01. 29
of all these learned men she was divorc'd, | and 4.01. 32
since which she was remov'd to kimmalton, 4.01. 34
how was it? 4.01. 60
child of honor, cardinal wolsey, | was dead? 4.02. 7
he was a man | of an unbounded stomach, ever 4.02. 33
simony was fair play; 4.02. 36
his own opinion was his law. 4.02. 37
he was never | (but where he meant to ruin) 4.02. 39
his promises were, as he then was, mighty; 4.02. 41
of his own body he was ill, and gave | the 4.02. 43
undoubtedly | was fashion'd to much honor. 4.02. 50
from his cradle | he was a scholar, and a ripe 4.02. 51
were unsatisfied in getting | (which was a sin), 4.02. 56
yet in bestowing, madam, | he was most princely: 4.02. 57
may know | i was a chaste wife to my grave. 4.02.170
said i for this, the girl was like to him? 5.01.174
that was sent to me from the council pray'd me 5.02. 2
and the end | was ever to do well; 5.02. 72
was it discretion, lords, to let this man, 5.02.172
why, what a shame was this? 5.02.176
ye | power as he was a councillor to try him, 5.02.178
what was purpos'd | concerning his imprisonment 5.02.184
concerning his imprisonment was rather | (if 5.02.185
and three times was his nose discharg'd against 5.03. 45 P
there was a haberdasher's wife of small wit near 5.03. 46 P
the hope o' th' strond, where she was quarter'd. 5.03. 53 P
pibbles, that i was fain to draw mine honor in, 5.03. 57 P
the devil was amongst 'em, i think, surely. 5.03. 58 P
saba was never | more covetous of wisdom and 5.04. 23
star–like rise as great in fame as she was, 5.04. 46
i was about to tell thee — when my heart, | as TRO 1.01. 34
is as a virtue fix'd, to–day was mov'd: 1.02. 5
before the sun rose he was harness'd light, 1.02. 8
what was his cause of anger? 1.02. 11
was hector arm'd and gone ere ye came to ilium? 1.02. 48 P
helen was not up, was she? 1.02. 49 P

helen was not up, was she? 1.02. 49 P
hector was gone, but helen was not up. 1.02. 50 P
hector was gone, but helen was not up. 1.02. 50 P
e'en so; hector was stirring early. 1.02. 51 P
was he angry? 1.02. 53 P
true, he was so; 1.02. 55 P
but there was such laughing! 1.02.142 P
but there was a more temperate fire under the 1.02.146 P
at what was all this laughing? 1.02.149 P
what was his answer? 1.02.156 P
but there was such laughing! 1.02.165 P
that she was never yet that ever knew | love got 1.02.290
one that was a man | when hector's grandsire 1.03.291
him that my lady | was fairer than his grandam, 1.03.299
your last service was suff'rance, 'twas not 2.01. 95 P
ajax was here the voluntary, and you as under an 2.01. 96 P
whose wit was mouldy ere /your grandsires had 2.01.105 P
since the first sword was drawn about this 2.02. 18
it was thought meet | paris should do some 2.02. 72
i was advertis'd their great general slept, 2.02.211
but it was a strong composure a fool could 2.03. 99 P
why was my cressid then so hard to win? 3.02.116
but i was won, my lord, | with the first glance 3.02.117
i was much rapt in this, | and apprehended here 3.03.123
virtue seek | remuneration for the thing it was; 3.03.170
i was sent for to the king, but why, i know not. 4.01. 36
how now? what's the matter? who was here? 4.02. 78 P
there was never a truer rhyme. 4.04. 21 P
the first was menelaus' kiss, this, mine; 4.05. 32
he was a soldier good, | but, by great mars, the 4.05.197
me, of what honor was | this cressida in troy? 4.05.287
she was belov'd, /she /lov'd; 4.05.292
i will have this. whose was it? 5.02. 87
come, tell me whose it was. 5.02. 88
whose was it? 5.02. 90
my soul | of every syllable that here was spoke. 5.02.117
was cressid here? 5.02.125
she was not, sure. 5.02.126
most sure she was. 5.02.126
nor mine, my lord; cressid was here but now. 5.02.128
be rule in unity itself, | this was not she. 5.02.142
when was my lord so much ungently temper'd | to 5.03. 1
it be, | great hector was as good a man as he. 5.09. 6
can be content to say it was for his country, he COR 1.01. 38 P
there was a time when all the body's members 1.01. 96
your most grave belly was deliberate, | not rash 1.01.128
it was an answer. how apply you this? 1.01.147
and call him noble, that was now your hate; 1.01.183
him vild, that was your garland. 1.01.184
that meat was made for mouths, that the gods 1.01.207
was ever man so proud as is this martius? 1.01.252
we never yet made doubt but rome was ready | to 1.02. 18
our aim, which was | to take in many towns ere 1.02. 23
when yet he was but tender-bodied and the only 1.03. 6 P
that it was no better than picture-like to hang 1.03. 11 P
was pleas'd to let him seek danger where he was 1.03. 12 P
him seek danger where he was like to find fame. 1.03. 13 P
at first hearing he was a man-child than now in 1.03. 16 P
that i was forc'd to wheel | three or four miles 1.06. 19
as merry as when our nuptial day was done | and 1.06. 31
that was the whip of your bragg'd progeny | thou 1.08. 12
but then aufidius was within my view, | and 1.09. 85
he was wont to come home wounded. 2.01.119 P
every gash was an enemy's grave. 2.01.155 P
it was his word. 2.01.237
but yet my caution was more pertinent | than the 2.02. 63
and for his meed | was brow-bound with the oak. 2.02. 98
from face to foot | he was a thing of blood, 2.02.109
whose every motion | was tim'd with dying cries. 2.02.110
spirit | requick'ned what in flesh was fatigate, 2.02.117
to the people, there was never a worthier man. 2.03. 38 P
here was "i thank you for your voices, thank you 2.03.171
was not this mockery? 2.03.173
power, | but was a petty servant to the state, 2.03.178
he was your enemy, ever spake against | your 2.03.179
son, | who after great hostilius here was king; 2.03.240
twice being censor, | was his great ancestor. 2.03.245
lord, and that it was which caus'd | our swifter 3.01. 2
when corn was given them gratis, you repin'd, 3.01. 43
why this was known before. 3.01. 46
this was my speech, and i will speak't again — 3.01. 62
they know the corn | was not our recompense, 3.01.121
even when the navel of the state was touch'd, 3.01.123
when what's not meet, but what must be, was law, 3.01.167
is not then respected | for what before it was. 3.01.306
who was wont | to call them woollen vassals, 3.02. 8
thy valiantness was mine, thou suck'st it from 3.02.129
got on the antiates | was ne'er distributed. 3.03. 5
to say extremities was the trier of spirits, 4.01. 4
that when the sea was calm all boats alike 4.01. 6
after it is done | than when it was a-doing. 4.02. 5
was not a man my father? 4.02. 18
yet, martius, that was much. 4.05.147
by his face that there was something in him. 4.05.154 P
but i thought there was more in him than i could 4.05.158 P
here's he that was wont to thwack our general, 4.05.178 P
general," but he was always good enough for him. 4.05.182 P
he was ever too hard for him; 4.05.183 P
he was too hard for him, directly to say the 4.05.185 P
and but one half of what he was yesterday; 4.05.198 P
caius martius was | a worthy officer i' th' war, 4.06. 29
rome, such as was never | s' incapable of help. 4.06.119
to his banishment, yet it was against our will. 4.06.145 P
first he was | a noble servant to them, but he 4.07. 35
of those chances | which he was lord of; 4.07. 41
he hath said | which was sometime his general, 5.01. 2
he was a kind of nothing, titleless, | till he 5.01. 13
'twas to pardon | when it was less expected. 5.01. 19
it was a bare petition of a state | to one whom 5.01. 20
his answer to me was, | he could not stay to 5.01. 24
he was not taken well, he had not din'd: 5.01. 50
i was hardly mov'd to come to thee; 5.02. 72 P
this man, aufidius, | was my belov'd in rome; 5.02. 93
i say to you, as i was said to, "away!" 5.02.107 P
their latest refuge | was to send him; 5.03. 12
honor'd mould | wherein this trunk was fram'd, 5.03. 23
"the man was noble, | but with his last attempt 5.03.145
i was mov'd withal. 5.03.194
and a butterfly, yet your butterfly was a grub. 5.04. 12 P
there was it — | for which my sinews shall be 5.06. 43
but there to end | where he was to begin, and 5.06. 65
making a treaty where | there was a yielding — 5.06. 68
first time that ever | i was forc'd to scold. 5.06.105
which was your shame, by this unholy braggart, 5.06.118
son, that was the last | that ware the imperial TIT 1.01. 5
was never scythia half so barbarous. 1.01.131
(when goths were goths and tamora was queen), 1.01.140
was none in rome to make a stale | but saturnine 1.01.304
what villain was it spake that word? 1.01.359
let not young mutius then, that was thy joy, 1.01.382
that what we did was mildly as we might, 1.01.475
lucrece was not more chaste | than this lavinia, 2.01.108
and after conflict such as was suppos'd | the 2.03. 21
presently | with horns, as was actaeon's, and 2.03. 63
so long, | poor i was slain when bassianus died. 2.03.171
now | was i a child to fear i know not what. 2.03.221
o tamora, was ever heard the like? 2.03.276
tamora, was it you? 2.03.293
whose youth was spent | in dangerous wars whilst 3.01. 2
this was thy daughter. 3.01. 63
my grief was at the height before thou cam'st, 3.01. 70
it was my dear, and he that wounded her | hath 3.01. 91
tell him it was a hand that warded him | from 3.01.194
ay, when my father was in rome she did. 4.01. 7
ay, more there was; 4.01. 39
and rape, i fear, was root of thy annoy. 4.01. 49
ravish'd and wrong'd as philomela was, | forc'd 4.01. 52
what roman lord it was durst do the deed; 4.01. 62
that shone so brightly when this boy was got, 4.02. 90
his wife but yesternight was brought to bed; 4.02.153
this was the sport, my lord. 4.03. 71
was ever seen | an emperor in rome thus 4.04. 1
man, | that lucius' banishment was wrongfully, 4.04. 76
whose name was once our terror, now our comfort, 5.01. 10
this was but a deed of charity | to that which 5.01. 89
why, she was wash'd, and cut, and trimm'd, and 5.01. 95
indeed i was their tutor to instruct them. 5.01. 98
even when their sorrows almost was forgot, | and 5.01.137
was it well done of rash virginius | to slay his 5.03. 36
hand, | because she was enforc'd, stain'd, and 5.03. 38
it was, andronicus. 5.03. 39
i am as woeful as virginius was, | and have a 5.03. 50
what, was she ravish'd? tell who did the deed. 5.03. 53
of this was tamora delivered, | the issue of an 5.03.120
and talk of them when he was dead and gone. 5.03.166
her life was beastly and devoid of pity, | and, 5.03.199
right glad i am he was not at this fray. ROM 1.01.117
towards him i made, but he was ware of me, | and 1.01.124
was that my father that went hence so fast? 1.01.162
it was. what sadness lengthens romeo's hours? 1.01.163
what fray was here? 1.01.173
susan is with god, | she was too good for me. 1.03. 20
and she was wean'd — i never shall forget it — 1.03. 24
'a was a merry man — took up the child. 1.03. 40
i was your mother much upon these years | that 1.03. 72
the game was ne'er so fair, and i am /done. 1.04. 39
well, what was yours? 1.04. 51
his son was but a ward two years ago. 1.05. 40
but that thou overheardst, ere i was ware, | my 2.02.103
that last is true — the sweeter rest was mine. 2.03. 43
laura to his lady was a kitchen wench (marry, 2.04. 39 P
good mercutio, my business was great, and in 2.04. 49 P
was i with you there for the goose? 2.04. 74 P
for i was come to the whole depth of my tale, 2.04. 99 P
have found him than he was when you sought him. 2.04.121 P
sir, what saucy merchant was this, that was so 2.04.145 P
was this, that was so full of his ropery? 2.04.146 P
i was hurt under your arm. 3.01.103 P
bid him bethink | how nice the quarrel was, and 3.01.154
could draw to part them, was stout tybalt slain; 3.01.173
not romeo, prince, he was mercutio's friend; 3.01.184
was ever book containing such vile matter | so 3.02. 83
he was not born to shame: 3.02. 91
o, what a beast was i to chide at him! 3.02. 95
some word there was, worser than tybalt's death, 3.02.108
death | was woe enough if it had ended there; 3.02.115
go get thee to thy love as was decreed, | ascend 3.03.146
it was the nightingale, and not the lark, | that 3.05. 2
believe me, love, it was the nightingale. 3.05. 5
it was the lark, the herald of the morn, | no 3.05. 6
for it was bad enough before their spite. 4.01. 31
o, weraday, that ever i was born! 4.05. 15
lies, | flower as she was, deflowered by him. 4.05. 37
never was seen so black a day as this. 4.05. 53
the most you sought was her promotion, | for 4.05. 71
in my lips | that i reviv'd and was an emperor. 5.01. 9
so that my speed to mantua there was stay'd. 5.02. 12
the letter was not nice but full of charge, | of 5.02. 18
him talk of juliet, | to think it was so? 5.03. 81
in twain | to sunder his that was thine enemy? 5.03.100
as he was coming from this churchyard's side. 5.03.186
romeo, there dead, was husband to that juliet, 5.03.231
stol'n marriage-day | was tybalt's dooms-day, 5.03.234
john, | was stayed by accident, and yesternight 5.03.251
for never was a story of more woe | than this of 5.03.309
ceremony was but devis'd at first | to set a TIM 1.02. 15
which was not half so beautiful and kind; 1.02.148
never mind | was to be so unwise, to be so kind. 2.02. 6
when he was poor, | imprison'd, and in scarcity 2.02.224
ago one of his men was with the lord lucullus to 3.02. 11 P
necessity belong'd to't, and yet was denied. 3.02. 13 P
what a strange case was that! 3.02. 17 P
there was very little honor show'd in't. 3.02. 19 P
what a wicked beast was i to disfurnish myself 3.02. 44 P
i was sending to use lord timon myself, these 3.02. 50 P
i was the first man | that e'er received gift 3.03. 16
this was my lord's best hope, now all are fled, 3.03. 35
i wonder on't, he was wont to shine at seven. 3.04. 10
sum | your master's confidence was above mine, 3.04. 31
in like manner was i in debt to my importunate 3.06. 13 P
sent to borrow of me, that my provision was out. 3.06. 16 P
day sent to me, i was so unfortunate a beggar. 3.06. 43 P
i see them now, then was a blessed time. 4.03. 79
i was directed hither. 4.03.198
perfumes, and have forgot | that ever timon was. 4.03.208
i, that i was | no prodigal. 4.03.277
know unthrift that was belov'd after his means? 4.03.311 P
when man was wish'd to love his enemies! 4.03.466
surely, this man | was born of woman. 4.03.494
why, i was writing of my epitaph; 5.01.185
this man was riding | from alcibiades to timon's 5.02. 9
and show of love as i was wont to have. JC 1.02. 34
i was born free as caesar, so were you; 1.02. 97
accoutred as i was, i plunged in | and bade him 1.02.105
he had a fever when he was in spain, | and when 1.02.119
and when the fit was on him, i did mark | how he 1.02.120
but it was fam'd with more than with one man? 1.02.153
there was a brutus once that would have brook'd 1.02.159
why, there was a crown offer'd him; 1.02.221 P
what was the second noise for? 1.02.224
they shouted thrice; what was the last cry for? 1.02.226
was the crown offer'd him thrice? 1.02.228
it was mere foolery, i did not mark it. 1.02.236 P
he was very loath to lay his fingers off it. 1.02.242 P
and foam'd at mouth, and was speechless. 1.02.253 P
the common herd was glad he refus'd the crown, 1.02.264 P
their worships to think it was his infirmity. 1.02.271 P
but, for mine own part, it was greek to me. 1.02.284 P
there was more foolery yet, if i could remember 1.02.287 P
he was quick mettle when he went to school. 1.02.296
the tarquin drive when he was call'd a king. 2.01. 54
and when i ask'd you what the matter was, | you 2.01.241
withal | hoping it was but an effect of humor, 2.01.250
it was a vision fair and fortunate. 2.02. 84
caesar was ne'er so much your enemy | as that 2.02.112
that i was constant cimber should be banish'd, 3.01. 72
caesar was mighty, bold, royal, and loving. 3.01.127
hands, but was indeed | sway'd from the point, 3.01.218
why, and wherein, caesar was dangerous. 3.01.222
brutus' love to caesar was no less than his. 3.02. 19 P
as he was fortunate, i rejoice at it; 3.02. 25 P
as he was valiant, i honor him; 3.02. 26 P
but, as he was ambitious, i slew him. 3.02. 26 P
his glory not extenuated, wherein he was worthy; 3.02. 39 P
this caesar was a tyrant. 3.02. 69
brutus | hath told you caesar was ambitious; 3.02. 78
if it were so, it was a grievous fault, | and 3.02. 79
he was my friend, faithful and just to me; 3.02. 85
but brutus says he was ambitious, | and brutus 3.02. 86
yet brutus says he was ambitious, | and brutus 3.02. 93
was this ambition? 3.02. 97
yet brutus says he was ambitious, | and sure he 3.02. 98
therefore 'tis certain he was not ambitious. 3.02.113
for brutus, as you know, was caesar's angel. 3.02.181
this was the most unkindest cut of all; 3.02.183
o, what a fall was there, my countrymen! 3.02.190
here was a caesar! 3.02.252
because i knew the man, was slighted off. 4.03. 5
was that done like cassius? 4.03. 77
he was but a fool that brought | my answer back. 4.03. 84
when i spoke that, i was ill-temper'd too. 4.03.116
this was an ill beginning of the night. 4.03.234
i was sure your lordship did not give it me. 4.03.254
it was well done, and thou shalt sleep again; 4.03.264
i was not born to die on brutus' sword. 5.01. 58
as this very day | was cassius born. 5.01. 72
witness that against my will | (as pompey was) 5.01. 74
if not, why then this parting was well made. 5.01.118
if not, 'tis true this parting was well made. 5.01.121
this ensign here of mine was turning back; 5.03. 3
my sight was ever thick; 5.03. 21
no, this was he, messala, | but cassius is no 5.03. 59
my life | i found no man but he was true to me. 5.05. 35
this was the noblest roman of them all: 5.05. 68
his life was gentle, and the elements | so mix'd 5.05. 73
up | and say to all the world, "this was a man!" 5.05. 75
who was the thane lives yet, | but under heavy MAC 1.03.109
whether he was combin'd | with those of norway, 1.03.111
my dull brain was wrought | with things 1.03.149
he was a gentleman on whom i built | an absolute 1.04. 13
of my ingratitude even now | was heavy on me. 1.04. 16
was the hope drunk | wherein you dress'd 1.07. 35
i would, while it was smiling in my face, | have 1.07. 56
thou marshal'st me the way that i was going, 2.01. 42
going, | and such an instrument i was to use. 2.01. 43
gouts of blood, | which was not so before. 2.01. 47
it was the owl that shriek'd, the fatal bellman, 2.02. 3
who was it that thus cried? 2.02. 41
was it so late, friend, ere you went to bed, 2.03. 22
say, the earth | was feverous, and did shake. 2.03. 61
no man's life was to be trusted with them. 2.03.105
was by a mousing owl hawk'd at, and kill'd. 2.04. 13
yet it was said | it should not stand in thy 3.01. 3
as it is said | mark antony's was by caesar. 3.01. 56
was it not yesterday we spoke together? 3.01. 73
it was, so please your highness. 3.01. 74
that it was he in the times past which held you 3.01. 76
both of you | know banquo was your enemy. 3.01.114
all harms, | was never call'd to bear my part, 3.05. 8
the gracious duncan | was pitied of macbeth; 3.06. 4
marry, he was dead. 3.06. 4
monstrous | it was for malcolm and for donalbain 3.06. 9
was not that nobly done? 3.06. 14
his flight was madness. 4.02. 3
not | whether it was his wisdom or his fear. 4.02. 5
was my father a traitor, mother? 4.02. 44 P
ay, that he was. 4.02. 45 P
blisters our tongues, | was once thought honest; 4.03. 13
thy royal father | was a most sainted king; 4.03.109
i am yet | unknown to woman, never was forsworn, 4.03.126
scarcely have coveted what was mine own, | at no 4.03.127
my first false speaking | was this upon myself. 4.03.131
men | already at a point, was setting forth. 4.03.135
which was to my belief witness'd the rather, 4.03.184
when was it she last walk'd? 5.01. 2 P
was he not born of woman? 5.03. 4
all is confirm'd, my lord, which was reported. 5.03. 31
wherefore was that cry? 5.05. 15
what's he | that was not born of woman? 5.07. 3
macduff was from his mother's womb | untimely 5.08. 15
he only liv'd but till he was a man, | the which 5.09. 6
such was the very armor he had on | when he the HAM 1.01. 60
us, | was, as you know, by fortinbras of norway, 1.01. 82
a moi'ty competent | was gaged by our king, 1.01. 91

that was and is the question of these wars. 1.01.111
was sick almost to doomsday with eclipse. 1.01.120
it was about to speak, when the cock crew. 1.01.147
so excellent a king, that was, to this, 1.02.139
i think it was to /see my mother's wedding. 1.02.178
i saw him once, 'a was a goodly king. 1.02.186
'a was a man, take him for all in all, | i shall 1.02.187
but where was this? 1.02.212
his beard was grisl'd, no? 1.02.239
it was, as i have seen it in his life, | a sable 1.02.240
hamlet, what /a falling–off was there | from me, 1.05. 47
whose love was of that dignity | that it went 1.05. 48
thus was i, sleeping, by a brother's hand | of 1.05. 74
spite, | that ever i was born to set it right! 1.05.189
'a this — 'a does — what was i about to say? 2.01. 49
by the mass, i was about to say something. 2.01. 50
there was 'a gaming, there o'ertook in 's rouse, 2.01. 56
my lord, as i was sewing in my closet, | lord 2.01. 74
nor the inward man | resembles that it was. 2.02. 7
he truly found | it was against your highness. 2.02. 65
and impotence | was falsely borne in hand, sends 2.02. 67
me not at first, 'a said i was a fishmonger. 2.02.188 P
my lord, there was no such stuff in my thoughts. 2.02.311 P
in reputation and profit, was better both ways. 2.02.330 P
same estimation they did when i was in the city? 2.02.335 P
when roscius was an actor in rome — 2.02.391 P
know, "it came to pass, as most like it was" — 2.02.418
speak me a speech once, but it was never acted, 2.02.435 P
was never acted, or, if it was, not above once; 2.02.435 P
'twas caviary to the general, but it was — as i 2.02.437 P
which was declining on the milky head | of 2.02.478
and most dear life | a damn'd defeat was made. 2.02.571
this was sometime a paradox, but now the time 3.01.113 P
i was the more deceiv'd. 3.01.119 P
it lack'd form a little, | was not like madness. 3.01.164
both at the first and now, was and is, to hold, 3.02. 21 P
since my dear soul was mistress of her choice 3.02. 63
did i, my lord, and was accounted a good actor. 3.02.100 P
i was kill'd i' th' capitol; 3.02.103 P
it was a brute part of him to kill so capital a 3.02.105 P
this realm dismantled was | of jove himself, and 3.02.282
and, as you said, and wisely was it said, | 'tis 3.03. 30
ay, lady, it was my word. 3.04. 30
see what a grace was seated on this brow: 3.04. 55
this was your husband. 3.04. 63
nor sense to ecstasy was ne'er so thrall'd | but 3.04. 74
who was in life a foolish prating knave. 3.04.215
but so much was our love, | we would not 4.01. 19
we would not understand what was most fit, | but 4.01. 20
they say the owl was a baker's daughter. 4.05. 42 P
"his beard was as white as snow, | /all flaxen 4.05.195
as white as snow, | /all flaxen was his pole, 4.05.196
th' embassador that was bound for england — if 4.06. 11 P
months since | here was a gentleman of normandy: 4.07. 82
laertes, was your father dear to you? 4.07.107
was he a gentleman? 5.01. 32 P
'a was the first that ever bore arms. 5.01. 33 P
love, did love, | methought it was very sweet, 5.01. 62
methought there — a — was nothing — a — meet 5.01. 64
one that was a woman, sir, but, rest her soul, 5.01.135 P
it was that very day that young hamlet was born 5.01.147 P
was that very day that young hamlet was born — 5.01.147 P
ay, marry, why was he sent into england? 5.01.149 P
why, because 'a was mad. 5.01.150 P
whose was it? 5.01.175 P
a whoreson mad fellow's it was. 5.01.176 P
whose do you think it was? 5.01.177 P
this same skull, sir, was, sir, yorick's skull, 5.01.181 P
alexander died, alexander was buried, alexander 5.01.209 P
of that loam whereto he was converted might they 5.01.211 P
her death was doubtful, | and, but that great 5.01.227
in my heart there was a kind of fighting | that 5.02. 4
king, | as england was his faithful tributary, 5.02. 39
how was this seal'd? 5.02. 47
why, even in that was heaven ordinant. 5.02. 48
which was the model of that danish seal; 5.02. 50
the next day | was our sea–fight, and what to 5.02. 54
and what to this was sequent | thou knowest 5.02. 54
roughly awake, i here proclaim was madness. 5.02.232
for he was likely, had he been put on, | to have 5.02.397
saucily to the world before he was sent for, yet LR 1.01. 22 P
before he was sent for, yet was his mother fair, 1.01. 22 P
mother fair, there was good sport at his making, 1.01. 23 P
when she was dear to us, we did hold her so, 1.01.196
she, whom even but now was your /best object, 1.01.214
it was not brought me, my lord; 1.02. 59 P
tail, and my nativity was under ursa major, so 1.02.130 P
a bond | the child was bound to th' father; 2.01. 48
was he not companion with the riotous knights 2.01. 94
yes, madam, he was of that consort. 2.01. 97
it was my duty, sir. 2.01.106
you in a plain accent was a plain knave, which 2.02.111 P
what was th' offense you gave him? 2.02.114
king | for him attempting who was self–subdued, 2.02.122
king, | on whose employment i was sent to you. 2.02.129
the night before there was no purpose in them 2.04. 3
ere i was risen from the place that showed | my 2.04. 29
for there was never yet fair woman but she made 3.02. 35 P
since i was man, | such sheets of fire, such 3.02. 45
his word was still, 'fie, foh, and fum, | i 3.04.183
it was not altogether your brother's evil 3.05. 5 P
i have serv'd you ever since i was a child; 3.07. 73
it was he | that made the overture of thy 3.07. 88
then edgar was abus'd. 3.07. 91
i am worse than e'er i was. 4.01. 26
yet my mind | was then scarce friends with him. 4.01. 35
i told him of the army that was landed; 4.02. 4
his answer was, "the worse." 4.02. 6
where was his son when they did take his eyes? 4.02. 88
he was met even now | as mad as the vex'd sea, 4.04. 1
it was great ignorance, gloucester's eyes being 4.05. 9
what thing was that | which parted from you? 4.06. 67
it was some fiend; 4.06. 72
"ay," and "no" too, was no good divinity. 4.06.100 P
they told me i was every thing. 4.06.104 P
what was thy cause? 4.06.109
son | was kinder to his father than my daughters 4.06.115
eyeless head of thine was first fram'd flesh 4.06.227
was this a face | to be oppos'd against the 4.07. 30
i was forbid it. 5.01. 47
until some half hour past, when i was arm'd. 5.03.194
i was contracted to them both; 5.03.229
yet edmund was belov'd! 5.03.240
her voice was ever soft, | gentle, and low, an 5.03.273
i kill'd the slave that was a–hanging thee. 5.03.275
and what was he? OTH 1.01. 18
so was i bid report here to the state | by 1.03. 15
it was my hint to speak — such was my process 1.03.142
was my hint to speak — such was my process — 1.03.142
if she confess that she was half the wooer, 1.03.176
that the bruis'd heart was pierced through the 1.03.219
it was a violent commencement in her, and thou 1.03.344 P
she never yet was foolish that was fair, | for 2.01.136
she never yet was foolish that was fair, | for 2.01.136
she that was ever fair, and never proud, | had 2.01.148
had tongue at will, and yet was never loud, 2.01.149
she that in wisdom never was so frail | to 2.01.154
she was a wight (if ever such /wight were) — 2.01.158
yes, that i did; but that was but courtesy. 2.01.256 P
so much was his pleasure should be proclaim'd. 2.02. 7 P
and that was craftily qualified too — and 2.03. 40 P
"king stephen was and–a worthy peer, | his 2.03. 89
he was a wight of high renown, | and thou art 2.03. 93
when i came back | (for this was brief), i found 2.03.237
what was he that you follow'd with your sword? 2.03.284 P
love shall grow stronger than it was before. 2.03.325 P
was not that cassio parted from my wife? 3.03. 37
and when i told thee he was of my counsel | /in 3.03.111
this was her first remembrance from the moor. 3.03.291
next night well, fed well, was free and merry; 3.03.340
/her name, that was as fresh | as dian's visage, 3.03.386
nay, this was but his dream. 3.03.427
a handkerchief | (i am sure it was your wive's) 3.03.438
if it be that, or any /that was hers, | it 3.03.440
i think the sun where he was born | drew all 3.04. 30
she was a charmer, and could almost read | the 3.04. 57
and it was dy'd in mummy which the skillful 3.04. 74
i was (unhandsome warrior as i am) | arraigning 3.04.151
indeed, sweet love, i was coming to your house. 3.04.171
and i was going to your lodging, cassio. 3.04.172
she was here even now; 4.01.132 P
i was the other day talking on the sea–bank with 4.01.133 P
i was a fine fool to take it. 4.01.150 P
was that mine? 4.01.174 P
faith, that was not so well; 4.01.273
was this fair paper, this most goodly book, 4.02. 71
such as she said my lord did say i was. 4.02.119
some such squire he was | that turn'd your wit 4.02.145
it was his bidding; 4.03. 15
she was in love, and he she lov'd prov'd mad, 4.03. 27
lies slain here, cassio, | was my dear friend. 5.01.102
what malice was between you? 5.01.102
so sweet was ne'er so fatal. 5.02. 20
the noise was high. 5.02. 93
she comes more nearer earth than she was wont, 5.02.110
out, and alas, that was my lady's voice. 5.02.119
you /heard her say herself, it was not i. 5.02.127
she turn'd to folly, and she was a whore. 5.02.132
she was false as water. 5.02.134
art rash as fire to say | that she was false. 5.02.135
o, she was heavenly true! 5.02.135
that she was false to wedlock? 5.02.142
my husband say she was false? 5.02.152
she was too fond of her most filthy bargain. 5.02.157
he says thou toldst him that his wife was false. 5.02.173
than what he found himself was apt and true. 5.02.177
but did you ever tell him she was false? 5.02.178
o, she was foul! 5.02.200
thy match was mortal to him, and pure grief 5.02.205
it was a handkerchief, an antique token | my 5.02.216
moor, she was chaste; 5.02.249
it was a sword of spain, the ice–brook's temper 5.02.253
that's he that was othello; here i am. 5.02.284
o thou othello, that was once so good, | fall'n 5.02.291
by that handkerchief | that was my wive's? 5.02.320
the watch, whereon it came | that i was cast; 5.02.327
for he was great of heart. 5.02.361
was he not here? ANT 1.02. 80
he was dispos'd to mirth, but on the sudden | a 1.02. 82
o, never was there queen | so mightily betrayed! 1.03. 24
you sued staying, | then was the time for words; 1.03. 34
eternity was in our lips and eyes, | bliss in 1.03. 35
our parts so poor | but was a race of heaven. 1.03. 37
the primal state | that he which is was wish'd, 1.04. 42
when thou once | was beaten from modena, where 1.04. 57
was borne so like a soldier, that thy cheek | so 1.04. 70
the ground, i was | a morsel for a monarch; 1.05. 30
i would have spoke | was beastly /dumb'd by him. 1.05. 50
what, was he sad, or merry? 1.05. 50
of hot and cold, he was nor sad nor merry. 1.05. 52
he was not sad, for he would shine on those 1.05. 55
he was not merry, | which seem'd to tell them 1.05. 56
when i was green in judgment, cold in blood, 1.05. 74
that which combin'd us was most great, and let 2.02. 18
and their contestation | was theme for you — 2.02. 44
and did want | of what i was i' th' morning; 2.02. 77
which was as much | as to have ask'd him pardon. 2.02. 78
this was but as a fly by an eagle; 2.02.181 P
the poop was beaten gold, | purple the sails, 2.02.192
true, sir, she was the wife of caius marcellus. 2.06.110 P
that year indeed, he was troubled with a rheum; 3.02. 57
madam, | she was a widow — 3.03. 27
when the best hint was given him, he not /took't 3.04. 9
i have told him lepidus was grown too cruel, 3.06. 32
to come thus was i not constrain'd, but did it 3.06. 56
while he was yet in rome, | his power went out 3.07. 75
my heart was to thy rudder tied by th' strings, 3.11. 57
i was of late as petty to his ends | as is the 3.12. 8
'twas a shame no less | than was his loss, to 3.13. 11
mine honor was not yielded, | but conquer'd 3.13. 61
what's her name, | since she was cleopatra? 3.13. 99
harping on what i am, | not what he knew i was. 3.13.143
of me | as when mine empire was your fellow too, 4.02. 22
i had a wound here that was like a t, | but now 4.07. 7
it was a king's. 4.08. 27
this last day was | a shrewd one to 's. 4.09. 4
bad a prayer as his | was never yet for sleep. 4.09. 27
whose bosom was my crownet, my chief end, | like 4.12. 27
the boar of thessaly | was never so emboss'd. 4.13. 3
say that the last i spoke was "antony," | and 4.13. 8
which whilst it was mine had annex'd unto't | a 4.14. 17
the last she spake | was "antony, most noble 4.14. 30
it was divided | between her heart and lips. 4.14. 32
not be purg'd, she sent you word she was dead; 4.14.124
serv'd, who best was worthy | best to be serv'd. 5.01. 6
he was my master, and i wore my life | to spend 5.01. 8
me to thee, as i was to him | i'll be to caesar; 5.01. 10
see | how hardly i was drawn into this war, 5.01. 74
i dreamt there was an emperor antony. 5.02. 76
his face was as the heav'ns, and therein stuck 5.02. 79
his voice was propertied | as all the tuned 5.02. 83
and shake the orb, | he was as rattling thunder. 5.02. 86
for his bounty, | there was no winter in't; 5.02. 87
an /autumn it was | that grew the more by 5.02. 87
think you there was or might be such a man | as 5.02. 93
who was last with them? 5.02.338
this was his basket. 5.02.340
his father | was call'd sicilius, who did join CYM 1.01. 29
gentleman, our theme, deceas'd | as he was born. 1.01. 40
who to my father was a friend, to me | known but 1.01. 98
look here, love, | this diamond was my mother's. 1.01.112
his steel was in debt, it went o' th' backside 1.02. 12 P
what was the last | that he spake to thee? 1.03. 4
it was his queen, his queen! 1.03. 5
and that was all? 1.03. 8
he was then of a crescent note, expected to 1.04. 2 P
speak of him when he was less furnish'd than now 1.04. 8 P
i was glad i did atone my countryman and you. 1.04. 38 P
sir, i was then a young traveller, rather 1.04. 43 P
is mended) my quarrel was not altogether slight. 1.04. 47 P
we, with manners, ask what was the difference? 1.04. 52 P
it was much like an argument that fell out last 1.04. 56 P
being so far provok'd as i was in france, i 1.04. 67 P
came in too suddenly, let it die as it was born, 1.04.121 P
i was going, sir, | to give him welcome. 1.06. 54
when he was here, | he did incline to sadness, 1.06. 61
that others do | (i was about to say) enjoy your 1.06. 91
or she that bore you was no queen, and you 1.06.127
was there ever man had such luck? 2.01. 1 P
as slippery as the gordian knot was hard! 2.02. 34
i am glad i was up so late, for that's the 2.03. 33 P
late, for that's the reason i was up so early. 2.03. 34 P
it was thy master's. 2.03.142
was caius lucius in the britain court | when you 2.04. 37
he was expected then, | but not approach'd. 2.04. 38
sparkles this stone as it was wont, or is't not 2.04. 40
sweet stoneness which | was mine in britain, for 2.04. 45
but profess | had that was well worth watching), 2.04. 68
it was hang'd | with tapestry of silk and silver 2.04. 68
wrought, | since the true life on't was — 2.04. 76
the cutter | was as another nature, dumb; 2.04. 84
for this was stol'n. 2.04.120
was i know not where | when i was stamp'd. 2.05. 4
was i know not where | when i was stamp'd. 2.05. 5
be theme and hearing ever) was in this britain, 3.01. 4
him) he was carried | from off our coast, twice 3.01. 25
the fam'd cassibelan, who was once at point | (o 3.01. 30
kingdom is stronger than it was at that time; 3.01. 35 P
our ancestor was that mulmutius which | ordain'd 3.01. 54
who was the first of britain which did put | his 3.01. 59
th' way | tell me how wales was made so happy as 3.02. 60
and my report was once | first with the best of 3.03. 57
and when a soldier was the theme, my name | was 3.03. 59
was the theme, my name | was not far off. 3.03. 60
then was i as a tree | whose boughs did bend 3.03. 60
cymbeline | i was confederate with the romans. 3.03. 68
came from horse, the place | was near at hand. 3.04. 2
jay of italy | (whose mother was her painting) 3.04. 50
is not there, who was indeed | the riches of it. 3.04. 70
to you | which daily she was bound to proffer. 3.05. 49
when was she miss'd? 3.05. 90
even before, i was | at point to sink for food. 3.06. 16
who was made by him that made the tailor, not be 4.01. 3 P
he said he was gentle, but unfortunate; 4.02. 39
was that it was for not being such a smile; 4.02. 53
was that it was for not being such a smile; 4.02. 53
this cloten was a fool, an empty purse, | there 4.02.113
fool, an empty purse, | there was no money in't. 4.02.114
though his /humor | was nothing but mutation, ay 4.02.133
he was a queen's son, boys, | and though he came 4.02.244
came our enemy, remember | he was paid for that. 4.02.246
our foe was princely, | and though you took his 4.02.249
for so i thought i was a cave–keeper, | and cook 4.02.298
which he said was precious | and cordial to me, 4.02.326
speaks that sometime | it was a worthy building. 4.02.355
or who was he | that (otherwise than noble 4.02.363
this was my master, | a very valiant britain, 4.02.368
the day that she was missing he was here; 4.03. 17
the day that she was missing he was here; 4.03. 17
my master since | i wrote him imogen was slain. 4.03. 37
for all was lost | but that the heavens fought; 5.03. 3
that the strait pass was damm'd | with dead men 5.03. 11
where was this lane? 5.03. 13
this was strange chance. 5.03. 51
preserv'd the britains, was the romans' bane." 5.03. 58
there was a fourth man, in a silly habit, | that 5.03. 86
my throes, | that from me was posthumus ripp'd, 5.04. 45
when once he was mature for man, | in britain 5.04. 52
in britain where was he | that could stand up 5.04. 53
with marriage wherefore was he mock'd, | to be 5.04. 58
his birth, and in | our temple was he married. 5.04.106
his celestial breath | was sulphurous to smell; 5.04.115
married your royalty, was wife to your place, 5.05. 39
did confess | was as a scorpion to her sight, 5.05. 45
eyes | were not in fault, for she was beautiful; 5.05. 63
that it was folly in me, thou mayst say, | and 5.05. 67
chance of war, the day | was yours by accident. 5.05. 76
we should not, when the blood was cool, have 5.05. 77
that sweet rosy lad | who died, and was fidele. 5.05.122
unhappy was the clock | that strook the hour! 5.05.153
it was in rome — accurs'd | the mansion where! 5.05.154
he was too good to be | where ill men were, and 5.05.158
and was the best of all | amongst the rar'st of 5.05.159
therein | he was as calm as virtue) he began 5.05.174

where i was taught | of your chaste daughter the 5.05.193
the temple | of virtue was she; 5.05.221
if | that box i gave you was not thought by me 5.05.241
dreading that her purpose | was of more danger, 5.05.254
most like i did, for i was dead. 5.05.259
my boys, | there was our error. 5.05.260
o, she was naught; 5.05.271
and long of her it was | that we meet here so 5.05.271
if i discover'd not which way she was gone, | it 5.05.277
way she was gone, | it was my instant death. 5.05.278
he was a prince. 5.05.291
great king, a subject who | was call'd belarius. 5.05.317
your pleasure was my /mere offense, my 5.05.334
that i suffer'd | was all the harm i did. 5.05.336
my breeding was, sir, as | your highness knows. 5.05.339
he, sir, was lapp'd | in a most curious mantle, 5.05.360
a sanguine star, | it was a mark of wonder. 5.05.365
it was wise nature's end in the donation, | to 5.05.367
call'd me brother, | when i was but your sister; 5.05.377
that i was he, | speak, jachimo. 5.05.410
never was a war did cease | (ere bloody hands 5.05.484
to sing a song that old was sung, | from ashes PER 1.ch. 1
did begin | was with long use account'd no sin. 1.ch. 30
and what was first but fear what might be done, 1.02. 14
her face was to mine eye beyond all wonder; 1.02. 75
bethought what was past, what might succeed. 1.02. 83
i perceive he was a wise fellow and had good 1.03. 4 P
all poverty was scorn'd, and pride so great, 1.04. 30
are like the troyan horse was stuff'd within 1.04. 93
and that in tharsus was not best | longer for 2.ch. 25
what a drunken knave was the sea to cast thee in 2.01. 57 P
and though it was mine own, part of my heritage, 2.01.123
worth, | for it was sometime target to a king; 2.01.137
which tells /me in that glory once he was; 2.03. 38
was by the rough seas reft of ships and men, 2.03. 84
so, this was well ask'd, 'twas so well perform'd 2.03. 99
glory, | when he was seated in a chariot | of an 2.04. 7
his greatness was no guard | to bar heaven's 2.04. 14
to this world | that ever was prince's child. 3.01. 31
her burying, | she was the daughter of a king. 3.02. 73
dead, | who was by good appliance recovered. 3.02. 86
for she was born at sea, i have nam'd so, here 3.03. 13
that i was shipp'd at sea i well remember, 3.04. 5
when i was born, the wind was north. 4.01. 51
when i was born, the wind was north. 4.01. 51
when was this? 4.01. 57
when i was born. 4.01. 58
never was waves nor wind more violent, | and 4.01. 59
alack that leonine was so slack, so slow! 4.02. 64
fault | to scape his hands where i was to die. 4.02. 75
there was a spaniard's mouth wat'red, and he 4.02. 99 P
whilest ours was blurted at and held a mawkin 4.03. 34
she was of tyrus the king's daughter, | on whom 4.04. 36
marina was she call'd, and at her birth, 4.04. 38
this was a goodly person, | till the disaster 5.01. 36
my derivation was from ancestors | who stood 5.01. 90
was it not thus? 5.01. 98
yet i was mortally brought forth, and am | no 5.01.104
my dearest wife was like this maid, and such a 5.01.107
which was when i perceiv'd thee — that thou 5.01.127
what my thoughts | did warrant me was likely. 5.01.134
name | was given me by one that had some power, 5.01.148
call'd marina | for i was born at sea. 5.01.156
my mother was the daughter of a king, | who died 5.01.157
of a king, | who died the minute i was born, 5.01.158
what was thy mother's name? 5.01.200
than | to say my mother's name was thaisa? 5.01.210
thaisa was my mother, who did end | the minute i 5.01.211
my purpose was for tharsus, there to strike 5.01.252
she at tharsus | was nurs'd with cleon, who at 5.03. 8
early in blustering morn this lady was | thrown 5.03. 22
and call'd marina | for she was yielded there. 5.03. 48
where shall be shown you all was found with her; 5.03. 66
i was transported with your speech, and suffer'd TNK 1.01. 55
king capaneus was your lord. 1.01. 59
wreath | was then nor thresh'd nor blasted; 1.01. 65
o, my petition was | set down in ice, which, by 1.01.106
and power | i' th' least of these was dreadful, 1.03. 39
out together where death's self was lodg'd; 1.03. 40
i was acquainted | once with a time when i 1.03. 49
at parting) when our count | was each aleven. 1.03. 54
what she lik'd | was then of me approv'd, what 1.03. 65
on my head no toy | but was her pattern, her 1.03. 72
why, it was a note | whereon her spirits would 1.03. 76
that was a fair boy certain, but a fool | to 2.02.120
never till now i was in prison, arcite. 2.02.132
you have told me | that i was palamon, and you 2.02.186
lady, | if ever thou hast felt what sorrow was, 2.02.276
i, seeing, thought he was a goodly man; 2.04. 8
but in my heart was palamon, and there, | lord, 2.04. 17
fairer spoken | was never gentleman. 2.04. 21
that knew me | would say it was my best piece; 2.05. 14
his mother was a wondrous handsome woman, | his 2.05. 20
dirge, | and tell to memory my death was noble, 2.06. 16
there was a time | when young men went a–hunting 3.03. 39
i say again, | that sigh was breath'd for emily. 3.03. 44
in manners this was false position. 3.05. 51
"there was three fools fell out about an howlet: 3.05. 67
the one said it was an owl, | the other he said 3.05. 68
he said nay, | the third he said it was a hawk, 3.05. 70
me, i was grown so low | and crestfall'n with my 3.06. 6
that was a very good one, and that day, | i well 3.06. 72
yes, but all | was vainly labor'd in me; 3.06. 79
if i fall, curse me, and say i was a coward, 3.06.104
this is the man | was begg'd and banish'd, this 3.06.143
that oath was rashly made, and in your anger, 3.06.227
was nothing said of me | concerning the escape 4.01. 1
came home before the business | was fully ended. 4.01. 5
means he escap'd, which was your daughter's, 4.01. 20
how was it ended? 4.01. 25
was she well? 4.01. 34
was she in health? 4.01. 34
i do not think she was very well, for, now | you 4.01. 36
and she answered me | so far from what she was, 4.01. 39
a fool, | an innocent, and i was very angry. 4.01. 41
either this was her love to palamon, | or fear 4.01. 49
as i late was angling | in the great lake that 4.01. 52
sedges, | as patiently i was attending sport, 4.01. 55
by the fishermen, | i saw it was your daughter. 4.01. 65
and between | ever was "palamon, fair palamon," 4.01. 81
palamon," | and "palamon was a tall young man." 4.01. 82
the place | was knee–deep where she sat; 4.01. 83
narcissus was a sad boy, but a heavenly. 4.02. 32
o' my conscience, | was never soldier's friend. 4.02. 88
the burden on't was "down–a, down–a," and penn'd 4.03. 11 P
i was once, sir, in great hope she had fix'd her 4.03. 64 P
that what was life | in him seem'd torture. 5.01.114
and i | believ'd it was his, for she swore it 5.01.117
i | believ'd it was his, for she swore it was, 5.01.117
he was kept down with hard meat and ill lodging, 5.02. 97
lose the noblest sight | that ev'r was seen. 5.02.100
darkness, which ever was | the dam of horror, 5.03. 22
that the cry | was general "a palamon!"; 5.03. 81
half–sights saw | that arcite was no babe. 5.03. 96
so charm'd me that methought alcides was | to 5.03.119
for he that was thus good | encount'red yet his 5.03.122
i heard she was not well; 5.04. 26
i was false, | yet never treacherous. 5.04. 92
i was as dearly sorry | as glad of arcite; 5.04.129
(for to that honest purpose it was meant ye), ep 14
rein, | under her other was the tender boy, VEN 32
so soon was she along as he was down, | each 43
so soon was she along as he was down, | each 43
obeyed, | yet was he servile to my coy disdain. 112
controlling what he was controlled with. 270
his love, perceiving how he was enrag'd, | grew 317
grew kinder, and his fury was assuag'd. 318
o, what a sight it was, wistly to view | how she 343
but now her cheek was pale, and by and by | it 347
now was she just before him as he sat, | and 349
o, what a war of looks was then between them! 355
but now i liv'd, and life was death's annoy, 497
but now i died, and death was lively joy. 498
was it not white? 643
her song was tedious and outwore the night, 841
it was not she that call'd him all to naught: 993
"how much a fool was i | to be of such a weak 1015
whereat she leaps, that was but late forlorn. 1026
no flow'r was nigh, no grass, herb, leaf, or 1055
when he was by, the birds such pleasure took, 1101
"'tis true, 'tis true, thus was adonis slain: 1111
kill'd | was melted like a vapor from her sight, 1166
quoth she, "this was thy father's guise — 1177
to grow unto himself was his desire, | and so 1180
"here was thy father's bed, here in my breast; 1183
well was he welcom'd by the roman dame, | within LUC 51
this heraldry in lucrece' face was seen, 64
of either's color was the other queen, | proving 66
without the bed her other fair hand was, | on 393
dead, | by thy bright beauty was it newly bred. 490
for it was lent thee all that brood to kill. 627
of mine | as i ere this was pure to collatine. 826
their father was too weak, and they too strong, 865
when tarquin did, but he was stay'd by thee. 917
but when i fear'd, i was a loyal wife: 1048
but thou shalt know thy int'rest was not bought 1067
"my body or my soul, which was the dearer, 1163
whose love of either to myself was nearer, 1165
how was i overseen that thou shalt see it! 1206
"madam, ere i was up," replied the maid, | "the 1277
myself was stirring ere the break of day, | and 1280
of day, | and ere i rose was tarquin gone away. 1281
groom, god wot, it was defect | of spirit, life, 1345
such sweet observance in this work was had, 1385
some high, some low, the painter was so nice; 1412
for much imaginary work was there, | conceit 1422
himself behind | was left unseen, save to the 1426
of what she was, no semblance did remain. 1453
the painter was no god to lend her those, | and 1461
saying, some shape in sinon's was abus'd: 1529
that she concludes the picture was belied. 1533
"mine enemy was strong, my poor self weak | (and 1646
that was not forc'd, that never was inclin'd 1657
that never was inclin'd | to accessary yieldings 1657
for she that was thy lucrece, now attend me: 1682
"that life was mine which thou hast here 1752
glass, | that i no more can see what once i was! 1764
yet sometime "tarquin" was pronounced plain, 1786
say | he weeps for her, for she was only mine, 1798
"woe, woe," quoth collatine, "she was my wife, 1802
he with the romans was esteemed so | as seely 1811
my vow was earthly, thou a heavenly love; PP 3. 7
my vow was breath, and breath a vapor is, | then 3. 9
hot was the day, she hotter that did look | for 6. 7
"o jove," quoth she, "why was not i a flood?" 6.14
was this a lover, or a lecher whether? 7.17
fair was the morn when the fair queen of love, 9. 1
in my thigh," quoth she, "here was the sore." 9.12
it was a lording's daughter, the fairest one of 15. 1
long was the combat doubtful, that love with 15. 5
alas, it was a spite | unto the silly damsel! 15. 7
more mickle was the pain, | that nothing could 15. 9
two the trusty knight was wounded with disdain: 15.11
art with arms contending was victor of the day, 15.13
love, whose month was ever may, | spied a 16. 2
where her faith was firmly fix'd in love, 17. 7
/lass, thy like ne'er was | for a sweet content, 17.33
ditty, | that to hear it was great pity. 20.12
number there in love was slain. PHT 28
distance and no space was seen | 'twixt this 30
either was the other's mine. 36
property was thus appalled, | that the self was 37
thus appalled, | that the self was not the same; 38
double name | neither two nor one was called. 40
not their infirmity, | it was married chastity. 61
bereft, | nor it nor no remembrance what it was: SON 5.12
but out, alack, he was but one hour mine, | the 33.11
all mine was thine, before thou hadst this more. 40. 4
how careful was i, when i took my way, | each 48. 1
eye, | when love converted from the thing it was 49. 7
since mind at first in character was done! 59. 8
to show false art what beauty was of yore. 68.14
for slander's mark was ever yet the fair; 70. 2
consum'd with that which it was nourish'd by. 73.12
review | the very part was consecrate to thee: 74. 6
thrive and i be cast away, | the worst was this: 80.14
my love was my decay. 80.14
was it the proud full sail of his great verse, 86. 1
was it his spirit, by spirits taught to write 86. 5
i was not sick of any fear from thence: 86.12
and yet this time remov'd was summer's time, 97. 5
our love was new, and then but in the spring, 102. 5
when i was wont to greet it with my lays, | as 102. 6
mend, | to mar the subject that before was well? 103.10
ere you were born was beauty's summer dead. 104.14
o, never say that i was false of heart, | though 109. 1
best," | when i was certain o'er incertainty, 115.11
to be diseas'd ere that there was true needing. 118. 8
therefore to give them from me was i bold, | to 122.11
no, it was builded far from accident; 124. 5
in the old age black was not counted fair, | or 127. 1
swear to thy blind soul that i was thy will, 136. 2
ever sweet, | was us'd in giving gentle doom, 145. 7
desire | was sleeping by a virgin hand disarm'd. 154. 8
threw, | upon whose weeping margent she was set, LC 39
a youthful suit — it was to gain my grace — 79
abide, | she was new lodg'd and newly deified. 84
for on his visage was in little drawn | what 90
what largeness thinks in paradise was sawn. 91
"small show of man was yet upon his chin, | his 92
stood in doubt | if best were as it was, or best 98
for maiden–tongu'd he was, and thereof free; 100
him, was he such a storm | as oft 'twixt may and 101
did in freedom stand | and was my own fee–simple 144
that's to ye sworn to none was ever said, | for 180
harm have i done to them, but ne'er was harmed, 194
kept hearts in liveries, but mine own was free, 195
"'lo this device was sent me from a nun, | or 232
for she was sought by spirits of richest coat, 236

/WASH 3 FR 0.0003 REL FR 3 V 0 P
/mine /own /tears /i /wash /away /my /balm, R2 4.01.207
/of /you, /with /pilate, /wash /your /hands, 4.01.239
/and /water /cannot /wash /away /your /sin. 4.01.242

WASH 53 FR 0.0060 REL FR 41 V 12 P
nor scrape trenchering, nor wash dish. TMP 2.02.183
"item, she can wash and scour." TGV 3.01.311 P
and i wash, wring, brew, bake, scour, dress meat WIV 1.04. 96 P
i would i could wash myself of the buck! 3.03.157 P
and when was he wont to wash his face? ADO 3.02. 56 P
hath drops too few to wash her clean again, 4.01.141
i take upon me to wash your liver as clean as a AYL 3.02.422 P
he went but forth to wash him in the hellespont 4.01.103 P
please your mightiness to wash your hands? SHR in.2. 76
come, kate, and wash, and welcome heartily. 4.01.154
son, | but i do wash his name out of my blood, AWW 3.02. 67
sir toby, i will wash off gross acquaintance, i TN 2.05.162 P
gilt of this opportunity you let time wash off, 3.02. 25 P
how prettily th' young swain seems to wash | the WT 4.04.366
no longer than we well could wash our hands | to JN 3.01.234
yet, to wash your blood | from off my hands, R2 3.01. 5
can wash the balm off from an anointed king; 3.02. 55
and wash him fresh again with true–love tears. 5.01. 10
to wash this blood off from my guilty hand. 5.06. 50
go wash thy face, and draw the action. 2H4 2.01.149 P
his bed, wash every mote out of his conscience; H5 4.01.179 P
water in wye cannot wash your majesty's welsh 4.07.106 P
and wash away thy country's stained spots. 1H6 3.03. 57
this place | to wash away my woeful monuments. 2H6 3.02.342
boy, | and i with tears do wash the blood away. 3H6 1.04.158
thy tears would wash this cold congealed blood 5.02. 37
bestride the rock, the tide will wash you off, 5.04. 31
would i wash my hands | of this most grievous R3 1.04.272
for i myself have many tears to wash | hereafter 4.04.389
your warm blood like wash and makes his trough 5.02. 9
i will go wash; COR 1.09. 68
would i | wash my fierce hand in 's heart. 1.10. 27
bid them wash their faces, | and keep their 2.03. 60
and wash their hands in bassianus' blood. TIT 2.03. 45
go home, call for sweet water, wash thy hands. 2.04. 6
she hath no tongue to call, nor hands to wash, 2.04. 7
wash they his wounds with tears? ROM 3.02.130
wilt thou wash him from his grave with tears? 3.05. 70
stoop then, and wash. JC 3.01.111
and wash this filthy witness from your hand. MAC 2.02. 44
will all great neptune's ocean wash this blood 2.02. 57
wash your hands, put on your night–gown, look 5.01. 62 P
neptune's salt wash and tellus' orbed ground, HAM 3.02.156
in the sweet heavens | to wash it white as snow? 3.03. 46
wash me in steep–down gulfs of liquid fire! OTH 5.02.280
it's monstrous labor when i wash my brain | and ANT 2.07. 99
tears | wash the congealment from your wounds, 4.08. 10
but it is tidings | to wash the eyes of kings. 5.01. 28
these surges, | which wash both heaven and hell; PER 3.01. 2
he swears | never to wash his face, nor cut his 4.04. 28
wash your foul minds with tears, and those same STM II.C 108
to wash the foul face of the sluttish ground, VEN 983
my blood shall wash the slander of mine ill; LUC 1207

/WASH'D 1 FR 0.0001 REL FR 1 V 0 P
as that vast shore /wash'd with the farthest sea ROM 2.02. 83

WASH'D 27 FR 0.0030 REL FR 21 V 6 P
for then she need not be wash'd and scour'd. TGV 3.01.313 P
transformation hath been wash'd and cudgell'd, WIV 4.05. 97 P
a marble to her tears, is wash'd with them, but MM 3.01.230 P
no faces truer than those that are so wash'd. ADO 1.01. 27 P
of her foulness, | wash'd it with tears? 4.01.154
for fear their colors should be wash'd away. LLL 4.03.267
i'll find a fairer face not wash'd to–day. 4.03.269
if so, my eyes are oft'ner wash'd than hers. MND 2.02. 93
clear | as morning roses newly wash'd with dew; SHR 2.01.173
which, wash'd away, shall scour my shame with it 1H4 3.02.137
have wash'd his knife | with gentle eye–drops. 2H4 4.05. 86
may this be wash'd in lethe and forgotten? 5.02. 72
that what you speak is in your conscience wash'd H5 1.02. 31
sand, that look to be wash'd off the next tide. 4.01. 98 P
that wash'd his father's fortunes forth of 3H6 2.02.157
thy balm wash'd off wherewith thou was anointed. 3.01. 17
scarce the blood was well wash'd from his hands R3 4.01. 67
i that was wash'd to death with fulsome wine, 5.03.132
for that i have not wash'd | my nose that bled, COR 1.09. 47
why, she was wash'd, and cut, and trimm'd, and TIT 5.01. 95
hath wash'd thy sallow cheeks for rosaline! ROM 2.03. 70
sit | of an old tear that is not wash'd off yet. 2.03. 76

father, with wash'd eyes | cordelia leaves you. LR 1.01.268
(ere bloody hands were wash'd) with such a peace CYM 5.05.485
wash'd me from shore to shore, and left /me PER 2.01. 6
them, they ne'er come but i look to be wash'd. 2.01. 26 P
have, as learned authors utter, wash'd a tile, TNK 3.05. 40
WASHER 1 FR 0.0001 REL FR 0 V 1 P
or his laundry — his washer and his wringer. WIV 1.02. 5 P
WASHES 7 FR 0.0008 REL FR 5 V 2 P
floods, | pale in her anger, washes all the air, MND 2.01.104
these lincoln washes have devoured them; JN 5.06. 41
were in the washes all unwarily | devoured by 5.07. 63
dozen of scots at a breakfast, washes his hands, 1H4 2.04.104 P
her furr'd pack, she washes bucks here at home. 2H6 4.02. 48 P
washes it off, and sprinkles in your faces TIM 3.06. 92
and from the ladder–tackle washes off | a PER 4.01. 60
WASHFORD 1 FR 0.0001 REL FR 1 V 0 P
great earl of washford, waterford, and valence, 1H6 4.07. 63
WASHING* *(also swashing)*
WASHING* 6 FR 0.0006 REL FR 2 V 4 P
mightst lie drowning | the washing of ten tides! TMP 1.01. 58
i am half afraid he will have need of washing, WIV 3.03.183 P
swear to me then, as i was washing thy wound, to 2H4 2.01. 91 P
washing with kindly tears his gentle cheeks, 4.05. 83
gregory, remember thy washing blow. ROM 1.01. 63 P
action with her, to seem thus washing her hands. MAC 5.01. 29 P
WASP 4 FR 0.0004 REL FR 4 V 0 P
come, you wasp, i' faith you are too angry. SHR 2.01.209
who knows not where a wasp does wear his sting? 2.01.213
let not this wasp outlive, us both to sting. TIT 2.03.132
in thy weak hive a wand'ring wasp hath crept, LUC 839
WASPISH 3 FR 0.0003 REL FR 3 V 0 P
by the stern brow and waspish action | which she AYL 4.03. 9
if i be waspish, best beware my sting. SHR 2.01.210
yea, for my laughter, | when you are waspish. JC 4.03. 50
WASPISH–HEADED 1 FR 0.0001 REL FR 1 V 0 P
her waspish–headed son has broke his arrows, TMP 4.01. 99
WASP'S 1 FR 0.0001 REL FR 0 V 1 P
with honey, set on the head of a wasp's nest; WT 4.04.784 P
WASPS 3 FR 0.0003 REL FR 3 V 0 P
injurious wasps, to feed on such sweet honey TGV 1.02.103
is goads, thorns, nettles, tails of wasps), WT 1.02.329
there be moe wasps that buzz about his nose H8 3.02. 55
WASP–STUNG 1 FR 0.0001 REL FR 1 V 0 P
what a wasp–stung and impatient fool | art thou 1H4 1.03.236
WASSAIL 3 FR 0.0003 REL FR 2 V 1 P
a wassail candle, my lord, all tallow; 2H4 1.02.158 P
will i with wine and wassail so convince, | that MAC 1.07. 64
keeps wassail, and the swagg'ring up–spring HAM 1.04. 9
/WASSAILS 1 FR 0.0001 REL FR 1 V 0 P
antony, | leave thy lascivious /wassails. ANT 1.04. 56
WASSAILS 1 FR 0.0001 REL FR 1 V 0 P
and retails his wares | at wakes and wassails, LLL 5.02.318
/WAS'T 1 FR 0.0001 REL FR 1 V 0 P
what /was't /that /prisoner told me | when i TNK 1.04. 21
WAS'T 26 FR 0.0029 REL FR 22 V 4 P
or blessed was't we did? TMP 1.02. 61
was't well done? 5.01.240
you, sir, was't not the wise woman of brainford? WIV 4.05. 26 P
was't not at hallowmas, master froth? MM 2.01.124 P
was't not to this end | that thou began'st to ADO 1.01.310
was't you he rescu'd? AYL 4.03.133
was't you that did so oft contrive to kill him? 4.03.134
when was't before? WT 1.02. 90
nor was't much | thou wouldst have poison'd good 3.02.187
thou gavest me, 'twas a pennyworth, was't not? 1H4 2.04. 59 P
was't i? 2H6 1.03.140
was't you that revell'd in our parliament, | and 3H6 1.04. 71
whose was't? TRO 5.02. 71
was't we? COR 4.06.121
lords, was't not a happy star | led us to rome, TIT 4.02. 32
ay, marry, was't, and he put it by thrice, every JC 1.02.229 P
what beast was't then | that made you break this MAC 1.07. 47
was't not the way? 3.03. 19
who was't came by? 4.01.140
what devil was't | that thus hath cozen'd you at HAM 3.04. 76
a norman, was't? 4.07. 90
was't hamlet wrong'd laertes? 5.02.233
my being in egypt, caesar, | what was't to you? ANT 2.02. 36
what was't | that mov'd pale cassius to conspire 2.06. 14
this yellow jachimo, in an hour — was't not? CYM 2.05. 14
was't so? PER 4.01. 51
/WAST 1 FR 0.0001 REL FR 0 V 1 P
/given /away, /that /thou /wast /born /with. LR 1.04.150 P
WAST 80 FR 0.0090 REL FR 62 V 18 P
for then thou wast not | out three years old. TMP 1.02. 40
of virtue, and | she said thou wast my daughter; 1.02. 57
o, a cherubin | thou wast that did preserve me. 1.02.153
for thou wast a spirit too delicate | to act her 1.02.272
therefore wast thou | deservedly confin'd into 1.02.360
what is this maid with whom thou wast at play? 5.01.185
jove, thou wast a bull for thy europa, love set WIV 5.05. 3 P
worm, thou wast o'erlook'd even in thy birth. 5.05. 83
i think thou never wast where grace was said. MM 1.02. 18 P
wast thou e'er contracted to this woman? 5.01.375
wast thou mad, | that thus so madly thou didst ERR 2.02. 11
thou wast ever an obstinate heretic in the ADO 1.01.234 P
why ever wast thou lovely in my eyes? 4.01.130
a sigh, thou wast the proper'st man in italy. 5.01.172 P
be as thou wast wont to be; MND 4.01. 71
see as thou wast wont to see. 4.01. 72
though in thy youth thou wast as true a lover AYL 2.04. 26
wast ever in court, shepherd? 3.02. 33 P
why, if thou never wast at court, thou never 3.02. 40 P
the horn, | it was a crest ere thou wast born; 4.02. 14
a fair name. wast born i' the forest here? 5.01. 22 P
i think thou wast created for men to breathe AWW 2.03.255 P
where thou | wast shot at with fair eyes, to be 3.02.107
thou wast in very gracious fooling last night, TN 2.03. 22 P
me, it was she | first told me thou wast mad. 5.01.349
that the oracle | gave hope thou wast in being, WT 5.03.127
for thou wast got i' th' way of honesty. JN 1.01.181
created to be aw'd by man, | wast born to bear? R2 5.05. 92
come, come, i know thou wast set on to this. 2H4 2.01.152 P
so, i did not think thou wast within hearing. 2.04.309 P
approach me, and thou shalt be as thou wast, 5.05. 61
thou wast installed in that high degree. 1H6 4.01. 17
be packing therefore, thou that wast a knight; 4.01. 46
that thou thyself wast born in bastardy; 2H6 3.02.223
wast thou ordain'd, dear father, | to lose thy 5.02. 45
mock thee, clifford, swear as thou wast wont. 3H6 2.06. 76
ay, thou wast born to be a plague to men. 5.05. 28
shall rue the hour that ever thou wast born. 5.06. 43
hadst thou in thy head when thou wast born, | to 5.06. 53
thou wast provoked by thy bloody mind, | that R3 1.02. 99
thou wast the cause, and most accurs'd effect. 1.02.120
and so wast thou, lord hastings, when my son 1.03.210
thou that wast seal'd in thy nativity | the 1.03.228
whom thou wast sworn to cherish and defend. 1.04.208
his nurse? why, she was dead ere thou wast born. 2.04. 33
cousin, thou wast not wont to be so dull. 4.02. 17
a dream of what thou wast, a garish flag | to be 4.04. 88
having no more but thought of what thou wast 4.04.107
what, art thou devout? wast thou in prayer? TRO 2.03. 35 P
thou wast a soldier | even to /cato's wish, not COR 1.04. 56
thou wast the prettiest babe that e'er i nurs'd. ROM 1.03. 60
god pardon sin! wast thou with rosaline? 2.03. 44
if e'er thou wast thyself and these woes thine, 2.03. 77
thou wast never with me for any thing when thou 2.04. 75 P
any thing when thou wast not there for the goose 2.04. 76 P
for whose dear sake thou wast but lately dead: 3.03.136
go, thou wast born a bastard, and thou't die a TIM 2.02. 84 P
thou wast whelp'd a dog, and thou shalt famish a 2.02. 86 P
thou wast born to conquer my country. 4.03.107
thou wast told thus; 4.03.214
when thou wast in thy gilt and thy perfume, they 4.03.301 P
here wast thou bay'd, brave hart, | here didst JC 3.01.204
thou wast the forest to this hart, | and this 3.01.207
thou wast born of woman. MAC 5.07. 11
thou wast a pretty fellow when thou hadst no LR 1.04.191 P
wast thou not charg'd at peril — 3.07. 52
night | against my fire, and wast thou fain, 4.07. 37
by th' law of war thou wast not bound to answer 5.03.153
more worthy heaven | than thou wast worthy her. OTH 5.02.161
when thou wast here above the ground, i was | a ANT 1.05. 30
him repent | thou wast not made his daughter, 3.13.135
euriphile, | thou wast their nurse; CYM 3.03.104
pisanio show'd thee, | thou wast within a ken. 3.06. 6
thou that wast born at sea, buried at tharsus, PER 5.01.196
wast near to make the male | to thy sex captive, TNK 1.01. 80
thee into | the bound thou wast o'erflowing, at 1.01. 84
thou wast begot, to get it is thy duty. VEN 168
and wast afeard to scratch her wicked foe, LUC 1035
where thou wast wont to rest thy weary head, 1621
thou wast not to this end from me derived. 1755
WASTE 51 FR 0.0057 REL FR 46 V 5 P
part of it, i'll waste | with such discourse as, TMP 5.01.303
but wherefore waste i time to counsel thee TGV 1.01. 51
but i am now about no waste; WIV 1.03. 43 P
i think, in the way of waste, attempt us again. 4.02.212 P
are not thine own so proper as to waste MM 1.01. 30
of the law, | and you but waste your words. 2.02. 72
having waste ground enough, | shall we desire to 2.02.169
fire, | consume away in sighs, waste inwardly. ADO 3.01. 78
never did mockers waste more idle breath. MND 3.02.168
than if you had made waste of all i have. MV 1.01.157
to one that i would have him help to waste | his 2.05. 50
that do converse and waste the time together, 3.04. 12
waste no time in words, | but get thee gone. 3.04. 54
and willingly could waste my time in it. AYL 2.04. 95
and we will nothing waste till you return. 2.07.134
you waste the treasure of your time with a TN 2.05. 77 P
the clock upbraids me with the waste of time. 3.01.130
the waste is no whit lesser than thy land. R2 2.01.103
which waste of idle hours hath quite thrown down 3.04. 66
i wasted time, and now doth time waste me; 5.05. 49
means are very slender, and your waste is great. 2H4 1.02.141 P
and waste for churlish winter's tyranny. 1.03. 62
out, | may waste the memory of the former days. 4.05.215
that makes such waste in brief mortality. H5 1.02. 28
fell feats | enlink'd to waste and desolation? 3.03. 18
repose, and not for us | to waste these times. H8 5.01. 5
she hath, and in that sparing /makes huge waste; ROM 1.01.218
in delay | we waste our lights in vain, /like 1.04. 45
how much salt water thrown away in waste, | to 2.03. 71
still in motion | of raging waste? TIM 2.01. 4
so shall he waste his means, weary his soldiers, JC 4.03.200
in the dead waste and middle of the night, HAM 1.02.198
were nothing but to waste night, day, and time; 2.02. 89
to have th' expense and waste of his revenues. LR 2.01.100
high supper–time, and the night grows to waste. OTH 4.02.243 P
store to do't, | and they have earn'd the waste. ANT 4.01. 16
that they will waste their time upon our note, CYM 4.04. 20
on life, and ling'ring, | by inches waste you. 5.05. 52
i might | waste it for you like taper–light. PER 1.ch. 16
and waste the time, which looks for other revels 2.03. 93
thus time we waste, and long leagues make short; 4.04. 1
our richest balms, | rather than niggard, waste; TNK 1.04. 32
she says, "this night i'll waste in sorrow, VEN 583
and waste huge stones with little water–drops. LUC 959
and, tender chorl, mak'st waste in niggarding: SON 1.12
but beauty's waste hath in the world an end, 9.11
and with old woes new wail my dear time's waste; 30. 4
thy dial how thy precious minutes waste; 77. 2
cannot contain | commit to these waste /blanks, 77.10
which proves more short than waste or ruining? 125. 4
th' expense of spirit in a waste of shame | is 129. 1
WASTED 19 FR 0.0021 REL FR 16 V 3 P
then he hath wasted it. ERR 2.01. 90
swear | a merrier hour was never wasted there. MND 2.01. 57
now the wasted brands do glow, | whilst the 5.01.375
wars hath not wasted it, for warr'd he hath not, R2 2.01.252
i wasted time, and now doth time waste me; 5.05. 49
/yet youth, the more it is wasted, the sooner it 1H4 2.04.401 P
and his quick wit wasted in giving reckonings; 2H4 1.02.171 P
the king hath wasted all his rods | on late 4.01.213
i, but my lungs are wasted so | that strength of 4.05.216
tyranny these many years | wasted our country, 1H6 2.03. 41
would he were wasted, marrow, bones, and all, 3H6 3.02.125
did fix mine eye | upon the wasted building, TIT 5.01. 23
sir, march is wasted fifteen days. JC 2.01. 59
till now some nine moons wasted, they have us'd OTH 1.03. 84
i have wasted myself out of my means. 4.02.185 P
being wasted in such time–beguiling sport." VEN 24
beauty within itself should not be wasted. 130
are on the sudden wasted, thaw'd, and done, | as 749
when in the chronicle of wasted time | i see SON 106. 1
WASTEFUL 9 FR 0.0010 REL FR 8 V 1 P
the burthen of lean and wasteful learning, the AYL 3.02.323 P
to garnish, | is wasteful and ridiculous excess. JN 4.02. 16
bullingbrook | hath seiz'd the wasteful king. R2 3.04. 55
stand sore charged for the wasteful vengeance H5 1.02.283
swill'd with the wild and wasteful ocean. 3.01. 14
i have retir'd me to a wasteful cock | and set TIM 2.02.162
breach in nature | for ruin's wasteful entrance; MAC 2.03.114
where wasteful time debateth with decay | to SON 15.11
when wasteful war shall statues overturn, | and 55. 5
WASTES 4 FR 0.0004 REL FR 4 V 0 P
run o'er | in seeming to augment it wastes it? H8 1.01.145
and wastes | the lamps of night in revel; ANT 1.04. 4
that thou among the wastes of time must go, SON 12.10
give my love fame faster than time wastes life, 100.13
WASTING 4 FR 0.0004 REL FR 4 V 0 P
my wasting lamps some fading glimmer left, | my ERR 5.01.316
eyes, like lamps whose wasting oil is spent, 1H6 2.05. 8
defac'd | by wasting ruin of the cruel foe. 3.03. 46
poor wasting monuments of lasting moans. LUC 798
WAT* *(also vat, what)*
WAT* 4 FR 0.0004 REL FR 1 V 3 P
pardonnez–moi, i cannot tell wat is "like me." H5 5.02.108 P
i cannot tell wat is dat. 5.02.177 P
i cannot tell wat is /baiser en anglish. 5.02.262 P
"by this, poor wat, far off upon a hill, VEN 697
/WATCH 1 FR 0.0001 REL FR 1 V 0 P
/to /watch — /poor /perdu! LR 4.07. 34
WATCH 121 FR 0.0136 REL FR 95 V 26 P
look, he's winding up the watch of his wit, by TMP 2.01. 12 P
you take your rest, | and watch your safety. 2.01.198
to watch, like one that fears robbing; TGV 2.01. 24 P
i'll go watch. WIV 1.04. 7 P
ford's brothers watch the door with pistols, 4.02. 52 P
in them, being chosen for the prince's watch. ADO 3.03. 6 P
and fit man for the constable of the watch; 3.03. 23 P
presently call the rest of the watch together, 3.03. 29 P
for, for the watch to babble and to talk, is 3.03. 35 P
than talk, we know what belongs to a watch. 3.03. 38 P
for indeed the watch ought to offend no man, and 3.03. 81 P
i pray you watch about signior leonato's door, 3.03. 92 P
marry, sir, our watch to–night, excepting your 3.05. 30 P
our watch, sir, have indeed comprehended two 3.05. 45 P
you must call forth the watch that are their 4.02. 34 P
let the watch come forth. 4.02. 37 P
also, the watch heard them talk of one deformed. 5.01.307 P
frame, | and never going aright, being a watch, LLL 3.01.192
and i to sigh for her, to watch for her, | to 3.01.200
juice, | i'll watch titania when she is asleep, MND 2.01.177
the self–same way with more advised watch | to MV 1.01.142
as i will watch the aim, or to find both | or 1.01.150
for wives, | i'll watch as long for you then. 2.06. 24
watch me like argus, | if you do not, if i be 5.01.230
couching, head on ground, with cat–like watch, AYL 4.03.115
pedascule, i'll watch you better yet. SHR 3.01. 50
and watch withal, for, but i be deceiv'd, | our 3.01. 62
doth watch bianca's steps so narrowly, | 'twere 3.02.139
into, | and watch our vantage in this business. 3.02.144
that is, to watch her, as we watch these kites 4.01.195
as we watch these kites | that bate and beat and 4.01.195
and, in conclusion, she shall watch all night, 4.01.205
to watch the night in storms, the day in cold, 5.02.150
and perchance wind up my watch, or play with my TN 2.05. 60 P
since when, my watch hath told me, toward my 5.01.162
hence, and watch. JN 4.01. 5
that i might sit all night and watch with you. 4.01. 30
to watch the fearful bending of thy knee, R2 3.03. 73
and beat our watch and rob our passengers, 5.03. 9
watches on unto mine eyes, the outward watch, 5.05. 52
watch to–night, pray to–morrow. 1H4 2.04.277 P
with a most monstrous watch is at the door. 2.04.483 P
the sheriff and all the watch are at the door, 2.04.489 P
no, i will sit and watch here by the king. 2H4 4.05. 20
biggen bound | snores out the watch of night. 4.05. 28
liege, | who undertook to sit and watch by you. 4.05. 52
the secret whispers of each other's watch. H5 4.pr. 7
this ruin'd band | walking from watch to watch, 4.pr. 30
this ruin'd band | walking from watch to watch, 4.pr. 30
what watch the king keeps to maintain the peace, 4.01.283
since they, so few, watch such a multitude. 1H6 1.01.161
now do thou watch, for i can stay no longer. 1.04. 18
constrain'd to watch in darkness, rain, and cold 2.01. 7
improvident soldiers, had your watch been good, 2.01. 58
that, being captain of the watch to–night, | did 2.01. 61
and that we find the slothful watch but weak, 3.02. 7
presently, | and then do execution on the watch. 3.02. 35
to us, | yet let us watch the haughty cardinal; 2H6 1.01.174
watch thou, and wake when others be asleep, | to 1.01.249
me | to watch the coming of my punish'd duchess. 2.04. 7
i lurk'd, | to watch the waning of mine enemies. R3 4.04. 4
use careful watch, choose trusty /sentinels. 5.03. 54
give me a watch. 5.03. 63
bid my guard watch; 5.03. 76
nay, i'll watch you for that; TRO 1.02.266 P
i can watch you for telling how i took the blow 1.02.268 P
yea, watch | his /pettish /lines, his ebbs, /his 2.03.129
therefore i'll watch him | till he be dieted to COR 5.01. 56
the measure done, i'll watch her place of stand, ROM 1.05. 50
care keeps his watch in every old man's eye, 2.03. 35
but look thou stay not till the watch be set, 3.03.148
either be gone before the watch be set, | or by 3.03.167
an' he and i | will watch thy /waking, and that 4.01.116
but i will watch you from such watching now. 4.04. 12
o lord, they fight! i will go call the watch. 5.03. 71
stay not to question, for the watch is coming. 5.03.158
is the county's page that rais'd the watch? 5.03.279
on him, | and then i ran away to call the watch. 5.03.285
recounts most horrid sights seen by the watch. JC 2.02. 16
you, we will stand and watch your pleasure. 4.03.249
whose howl's his watch, thus with his stealthy MAC 2.01. 54
and near approaches | the subject of our watch. 3.03. 8
as i did stand my watch upon the hill, | i 5.05. 32
the rivals of my watch, bid them make haste. HAM 1.01. 13
with us to watch the minutes of this night, 1.01. 27
with martial stalk hath he gone by our watch. 1.01. 66
why this same strict and most observant watch 1.01. 71

the source of this our watch, and the chief head 1.01.106
figure | comes armed through our watch, so like 1.01.110
break we our watch up, and, by my advice, | let 1.01.168
marcellus and barnardo, on their watch, | in the 1.02.197
and i with them the third night kept the watch, 1.02.208
my lord, upon the platform where we watch. 1.02.213
hold you the watch to–night? 1.02.225
i will watch to–night, | perchance 'twill walk 1.02.241
thence to a watch, thence into a weakness, 2.02.148
for some must watch, while some must sleep, 3.02.273
follow her close, give her good watch, i pray 4.05. 74
good gertrude, set some watch over your son. 5.01.296
at this odd–even and dull watch o' th' night, OTH 1.01.123
watch you to–night; 2.01.264 P
welcome, iago; we must to the watch. 2.03. 12 P
and he's to watch. 2.03. 54
with flowing cups, | and they watch too. 2.03. 59
platform, masters, come, let's set the watch. 2.03.120
he'll watch the horologe a double set | if drink 2.03.130
here's a goodly watch indeed! 2.03.160
good night, lieutenant, i must to the watch. 2.03.334 P
rest, | i'll watch him tame, and talk him out of 3.03. 23
if you will watch his going thence (which i will 4.02.235 P
what ho! no watch? no passage? murther, murther! 5.01. 37
that he made him | brave me upon the watch, 5.02.326
soldiers, have careful watch. ANT 4.03. 7
to lie in watch there and to think on him? CYM 3.04. 41
she told me | she would watch with me to–night, TNK 5.02. 9
for my sick heart commands mine eyes to watch. VEN 584
base watch of woes, sin's pack–horse, virtue's LUC 928
and they that watch see time how slow it creeps. 1575
my heart doth charge the watch; PP 14.14
whilst i, my sovereign, watch the clock for you, SON 57. 6
for thee watch i, whilst thou dost wake 61.13
WATCH–CASE 1 FR 0.0001 REL FR 1 V 0 P
couch | a watch–case or a common 'larum–bell? 2H4 3.01. 17
WATCH'D 19 FR 0.0021 REL FR 17 V 2 P
been the longest night | that e'er i watch'd, TGV 4.02.140
do not fly, i think we have watch'd you now. WIV 5.05.103
but being watch'd that it may still go right! LLL 3.01.193
i have watch'd so long | that i am dog–weary, SHR 4.02. 59
bent upon him | and watch'd the time to shoot. AWW 5.03. 11
for sleeping england long time have i watch'd, R2 2.01. 77
in thy faint slumbers i by thee have watch'd, 1H4 2.03. 47
and even these three days have i watch'd | if i 1H6 1.04. 16
beldam, i think we watch'd you at an inch. 2H6 1.04. 42
lord buckingham, methinks you watch'd her well. 1.04. 55
so help me god, as i have watch'd the night, 3.01.110
and watch'd him how he singled clifford forth. 3H6 2.01. 12
have in our armors watch'd the winter's night, 5.07. 17
you must be watch'd ere you be made tame, must TRO 3.02. 43 P
watch'd for your voices; COR 2.03.127
for all the frosty nights that i have watch'd, TIT 3.01. 5
i have watch'd ere now | all night for lesser ROM 4.04. 9
i have two nights watch'd with you, but can MAC 5.01. 1 P
i have watch'd and travell'd hard: LR 2.02.155
WATCH–DOGS 1 FR 0.0001 REL FR 1 V 0 P
the watch–dogs bark! TMP 1.02.383
WATCHERS 2 FR 0.0002 REL FR 2 V 0 P
and made them watchers of mine own heart's TGV 2.04.135
occasion call us | and show us to be watchers. MAC 2.02. 68
WATCHES 5 FR 0.0005 REL FR 2 V 3 P
they jar | their watches on unto mine eyes, the R2 5.05. 52
at all these wards i lie, at a thousand watches. TRO 1.02.264 P
say one of your watches. 1.02.265 P
my father watches: LR 2.01. 20
the lieutenant to–night watches on the court of OTH 2.01.218 P
WATCHFUL 11 FR 0.0012 REL FR 11 V 0 P
fading moment's mirth | with twenty watchful, TGV 1.01. 31
then, in despite of brooded watchful day, | i JN 3.03. 52
and like the watchful minutes to the hour, 4.01. 46
of slumber open wide | to many a watchful night, 2H4 4.05. 25
by their watchful fires | sit patiently and inly H5 4.pr. 23
but praying, to enrich his watchful soul. R3 3.07. 77
to thee i do commend my watchful soul | ere i 5.03.115
cry mercy, lords and watchful gentlemen, | that 5.03.224
the providence that's in a watchful state TRO 3.03.196
what watchful cares do interpose themselves JC 2.01. 98
that fled the snares of watchful tyranny, MAC 5.09. 33
WATCHING 11 FR 0.0012 REL FR 9 V 2 P
watching breeds leanness, leanness is all gaunt. R2 2.01. 78
cheeks are pale for watching for your good. 2H6 4.07. 85
swell past hiding, and then it's past watching. TRO 1.02.270 P
be sick to–morrow | for this night's watching. ROM 4.04. 8
but i will watch you from such watching now. 4.04. 12
benefit of sleep and do the effects of watching! MAC 5.01. 11 P
/faith, that's with watching, 'twill away again. OTH 3.03.285
but profess | had that was well worth watching), CYM 2.04. 68
by watching, weeping, tendance, kissing, to 5.05. 53
and there's a rock lies watching under water; TNK 3.04. 6
that is so vex'd with watching and with tears? SON 148.10
WATCHINGS 1 FR 0.0001 REL FR 0 V 1 P
you, though it cost me ten nights' watchings. ADO 2.01.372 P
WATCHINS 2 FR 0.0002 REL FR 0 V 2 P
made my brother arthur watchins sergeant safe's STM II.C 43 P
thy good worship for my brother arthur watchins. II.C 59 P
WATCHMAN 3 FR 0.0003 REL FR 2 V 1 P
speak like an ancient and most quiet watchman, ADO 3.03. 40 P
this good lesson keep | as watchman to my heart. HAM 1.03. 46
to play the watchman ever for thy sake. SON 61.12
WATCHMEN 2 FR 0.0002 REL FR 2 V 0 P
the special watchmen of our english weal, | i 1H6 3.01. 66
let's see if other watchmen | do hear what we do ANT 4.03. 17
WATCH–ORDS 1 FR 0.0001 REL FR 0 V 1 P
and when i give the watch–ords, do as i pid you. WIV 5.04. 3 P
WATCH–WORD 2 FR 0.0002 REL FR 1 V 1 P
our watch–word was "hem, boys!" 2H4 3.02.217 P
which gives the watch–word to his hand full soon LUC 370
/WATER 4 FR 0.0004 REL FR 4 V 0 P
/other /down, /unseen, /and /full /of /water: R2 4.01.187
/and /water /cannot /wash /away /your /sin. 4.01.242
/and /yet /salt /water /blinds /them /not /so 4.01.245
/the /holy /water /from /her /heavenly /eyes, LR 4.03. 30
WATER 137 FR 0.0154 REL FR 92 V 45 P
though every drop of water swear against it, TMP 1.01. 59
some food we had, and some fresh water, that | a 1.02.160
wouldst give me | water with berries in't, and 1.02.334
rather new dy'd than stain'd with salt water. 2.01. 65 P
he trod the water, | whose enmity he flung aside 2.01.116
well — i am standing water. 2.01.221
when the butt is out, we will drink water — not 3.02. 2 P
shine through you like the water in an urinal, TGV 2.01. 39 P
the water nectar, and the rocks pure gold. 2.04.171
which with an hour's heat | dissolves to water, 3.02. 8
up my leg and make water against a gentlewoman's 4.04. 38 P
thy impatience, throw cold water on thy choler. WIV 2.03. 85 P
so throwing him into the water will do him a 3.03.183 P
and excuse his throwing into the water, and give 3.03.195 P
run through fire and water for such a kind heart 3.04.103 P
for the water swells a man; 3.05. 16 P
let me pour in some sack to the thames water; 3.05. 22 P
mad about his throwing into the water. 4.01. 5 P
that when he makes water his urine is congeal'd MM 3.02.110 P
i am fain to dine and sup with water and bran; 4.03.153 P
i to the world am like a drop of water, | that ERR 1.02. 35
fall | a drop of water in the breaking gulf, 2.02.126
that's a fault that water will mend. 3.02.105 P
mine ears as profitless | as water in a sieve. ADO 5.01. 5
you shall fast a week with bran and water. LLL 1.01.301 P
thou now requests but moonshine in the water. 5.02.208
your kindred hath made my eyes water ere now. MND 3.01.194 P
i must confess, | made mine eyes water; 5.01. 69
cast on no water. SHR 4.01. 20 P
some water here! 4.01.149
shall i have some water? 4.01.153
no more than a fish loves water. AWW 3.06. 85 P
and water once a day her chamber round | with TN 1.01. 28
not so much as make water but in a sink–a–pace. 1.03.130 P
'tis with him in standing water, between boy and 1.05.159 P
sir, with salt water, though i seem to drown her 2.01. 30 P
carry his water to th' wise woman. 3.04.102 P
would have shed water out of fire ere done't; WT 3.02.193
the men are not yet cold under water, nor the 3.03.105 P
moon | upon the water as he'll stand and read 4.04.173
forty thousand fadom above water, and sung this 4.04.277 P
mine eyes (caught the water though not the fish) 5.02. 83 P
being as like | as rain to water, or devil to JN 2.01.128
unless thou let his silver water keep | a 2.01.339
thyself, | put but a little water in a spoon, 4.03.131
not all the water in the rough rude sea | can R2 3.02. 54
terror than the elements | of fire and water, 3.03. 56
be he the fire, i'll be the yielding water; 3.03. 58
will she hold out water in foul way? 1H4 2.01. 84 P
for there will be a world of water shed | upon 3.01. 93
you giant, what says the doctor to my water? 2H4 1.02. 2 P
sir, the water itself was a good healthy water, 1.02. 3 P
the water itself was a good healthy water, but, 1.02. 4 P
can sodden water, | a drench for sur–rein'd H5 3.05. 18
elements of earth and water never appear in him, 3.07. 22 P
all the water in wye cannot wash your majesty's 4.07.106 P
glory is like a circle in the water, | which 1H6 1.02.133
by water shall he die, and take his end. 2H6 1.04. 33
"by water shall he die, and take his end." 1.04. 65
smooth runs the water where the brook is deep, 3.01. 53
birth | and told me that by water i should die: 4.01. 35
and if thine eyes can water for his death, | i 3H6 1.04. 82
lad, | with tearful eyes add water to the sea, 5.04. 8
i speak, | ye see i drink the water of my eye. 5.04. 75
see | the water swell before a boist'rous storm. R3 2.03. 44
to th' water side i must conduct your grace; H8 2.01. 95
fall away | like water from ye, never found 2.01.130
in brass, their virtues | we write in water. 4.02. 46
more dregs than water, if my /fears have eyes. TRO 3.02. 67 P
when th' have said as false | as air, as water, 3.02.192
clear again, that i might water an ass at it! 3.03.311 P
that our best water brought by conduits hither, COR 2.03.242
look thee, here's water to quench it. 5.02. 72 P
gods, | sith priest and holy water are so near, TIT 1.01.323
more water glideth by the mill | than wots the 2.01. 85
go home, call for sweet water, wash thy hands. 2.04. 6
what fool hath added water to the sea? 3.01. 68
as frozen water to a starved snake. 3.01.251
for all the water in the ocean | can never turn 4.02.101
how much salt water thrown away in waste, | to ROM 2.03. 71
which with sweet water nightly i will dew, | or, 5.03. 14
and rich. here is a water, look ye. TIM 1.01. 18
honest water, which ne'er left man i' th' mire. 1.02. 59
mine eyes cannot hold out water, methinks. 1.02.107 P
she's e'en setting on water to scald such 2.02. 69 P
smoke and lukewarm water | is your perfection. 3.06. 89
we cannot live on grass, on berries, water, | as 4.03.422
can you eat roots and drink cold water? 5.01. 74
of sorrow stand in thine, | began to water. JC 3.01.285
the earth hath bubbles, as the water has, | and MAC 1.03. 79
go get some water, | and wash this filthy 2.02. 43
a little water clears us of this deed; 2.02. 64
cast | the water of my land, find her disease, 5.03. 51
too much of water hast thou, poor ophelia, | and HAM 4.07.185
here lies the water; 5.01. 15 P
if the man go to this water and drown himself, 5.01. 16 P
but if the water come to him and drown him, he 5.01. 18 P
trade that 'a will keep out water a great while, 5.01.171 P
while, and your water is a sore decayer of your 5.01.172 P
when brewers mar their malt with water; LR 3.02. 82
toad, the todpole, the wall–newt, and the water; 3.04.130 P
mane, | seems to cast water on the burning bear, OTH 2.01. 14
have i none | but what should go by water. 4.02.104
she was false as water. 5.02.134
live in an onion that should water this sorrow. ANT 1.02.170 P
vials thou shouldst fill | with sorrowful water? 1.03. 64
like a burnish'd throne, | burnt on the water. 2.02.192
the water which they beat to follow faster, | as 2.02.196
you have done well by water. 2.06. 86 P
nor what i have done by water. 2.06. 90 P
and makes it indistinct | as water is in water. 4.14. 11
and makes it indistinct | as water is in water. 4.14. 11
his steeds to water at those springs | on CYM 2.03. 22
my tears that fall | prove holy water on thee! 5.05.269
chiding a nativity | as fire, air, water, earth, PER 3.01. 33
and humming water must o'erwhelm thy corpse, 3.01. 63
diamonds | of a most praised water doth appear, 3.02.101
and almost breathless swim | in this deep water. TNK pr 25
the one of th' other may be said to water 1.03. 58
i come in | to bring him water in a morning, 2.04. 22
i none these two days — | sipp'd some water. 3.02. 27
and there's a rock lies watching under water; 3.04. 6
she bathes in water, yet her fire must burn. VEN 94
shone like the moon in water seen by night. 492
desire, | as air and water do abate the fire. 654
for stones dissolv'd to water do convert. LUC 592
and grave, like water that doth eat in steel, 755
his eye drops fire, no water thence proceeds; 1552
he finds means to burn his troy with water." 1561
but that, so much of earth and water wrought, SON 44.11
so that myself bring water for my stain. 109. 8
the sea, all water, yet receives rain still, 135. 9
love's fire heats water, water cools not love. 154.14
love's fire heats water, water cools not love. 154.14
roses | that flame through water which their hue LC 287
eyes | what rocky heart to water will not wear? 291
of burning blushes, or of weeping water, | or 304
WATER–COLORS 1 FR 0.0001 REL FR 1 V 0 P
want | such water–colors to impaint his cause, 1H4 5.01. 80
//WATER–DROPS 1 FR 0.0001 REL FR 1 V 0 P
/to /melt /myself /away /in //water–drops! R2 4.01.262
WATER–DROPS 3 FR 0.0003 REL FR 3 V 0 P
when water–drops have worn the stones of troy, TRO 3.02.186
and let not women's weapons, water–drops, LR 2.04.277
and waste huge stones with little water–drops. LUC 959
WATERED 1 FR 0.0001 REL FR 1 V 0 P
he watered his new plants with dews of flattery, COR 5.06. 22
WATER–FLIES 2 FR 0.0002 REL FR 1 V 1 P
poor world is pest'red with such water–flies, TRO 5.01. 34 P
and let the water–flies | blow me into abhorring ANT 5.02. 59
WATER–FLOWERS 1 FR 0.0001 REL FR 1 V 0 P
thousand fresh water–flowers of several colors, TNK 4.01. 85
WATER–FLOWING 1 FR 0.0001 REL FR 1 V 0 P
my mercy dried their water–flowing tears; 3H6 4.08. 43
WATER–FLY 1 FR 0.0001 REL FR 1 V 0 P
dost know this water–fly? HAM 5.02. 82
WATERFORD 1 FR 0.0001 REL FR 1 V 0 P
great earl of washford, waterford, and valence, 1H6 4.07. 63
WATER–GALLS 1 FR 0.0001 REL FR 1 V 0 P
these water–galls in her dim element | foretell LUC 1588
WATERING 1 FR 0.0001 REL FR 0 V 1 P
and when you breathe in your watering, they cry 1H4 2.04. 16 P
WATERISH 1 FR 0.0001 REL FR 1 V 0 P
or feed upon such nice and waterish diet, | or OTH 3.03. 15
WATER–POTS 1 FR 0.0001 REL FR 1 V 0 P
salt, | to use his eyes for garden water–pots, LR 4.06.196
WATER–RATS 1 FR 0.0001 REL FR 0 V 1 P
there be land–rats and water–rats, water–thieves MV 1.03. 23 P
WATER–RUGS 1 FR 0.0001 REL FR 1 V 0 P
shoughs, water–rugs, and demi–wolves are clipt MAC 3.01. 93
/WATERS 1 FR 0.0001 REL FR 1 V 0 P
what dreadful noise of /waters in /my ears! R3 1.04. 22
WATERS 32 FR 0.0036 REL FR 27 V 5 P
you have | put the wild waters in this roar, TMP 1.02. 2
wrack, | this music crept by me upon the waters, 1.02.392
stabs | kill the still–closing waters, as 3.03. 64
command these fretting waters from your eyes MM 4.03.146
enrobe the roaring waters with my silks, | and, MV 1.01. 34
and then there is the peril of waters, winds, 1.03. 25 P
mark me now, now will i raise the waters. 2.02. 49 P
doth an inland brook | into the main of waters. 5.01. 97
though thou the waters warp, | thy sting is not AYL 2.07.187
balm his foul head in warm distilled waters, SHR in.1. 48
i still pour in the waters of my love | and lack AWW 1.03.203
nay, i am for all waters. TN 4.02. 63 P
as wind, as waters, false | as dice are to be WT 1.02.132
dedication of yourselves | to unpath'd waters, 4.04.567
the lands and waters 'twixt your throne and his 5.01.144
trust not those cunning waters of his eyes, JN 4.03.107
commend these waters to those baby eyes | that 5.02. 56
whilst on the earth i rain | my waters — on the R2 3.03. 60
as fierce | as waters to the sucking of a gulf. H5 2.04. 10
those waters from me which i would have stopp'd, 4.06. 29
is that by sudden floods and fall of waters R3 4.04.510
the bounded waters | should lift their bosoms TRO 1.03.111
whose rage doth rend | like interrupted waters, COR 3.01.248
and cast you, with the waters that you loose, LR 1.04.303
or swell the curled waters 'bove the main, 3.01. 6
call her winds and waters sighs and tears; ANT 1.02.148 P
in | with oaks unscalable and roaring waters, CYM 3.01. 20
a man whom both the waters and the wind, | in PER 2.01. 59
garment through the rough seams of the waters. 2.01.150 P
if fires be hot, knives sharp, or waters deep, 4.02.146
fair nymph | that feeds the lake with waters, or TNK 4.01. 87
than humble banks can go to law with waters 5.03. 99
WATER–SPANIEL 1 FR 0.0001 REL FR 0 V 1 P
she hath more qualities than a water–spaniel, TGV 3.01.272 P
WATER–STANDING 1 FR 0.0001 REL FR 1 V 0 P
and many an orphan's water–standing eye — | men 3H6 5.06. 40
WATER–THIEVES 1 FR 0.0001 REL FR 0 V 1 P
and water–rats, water–thieves and land–thieves, MV 1.03. 23 P
WATERTON 1 FR 0.0001 REL FR 1 V 0 P
sir john norbery, sir robert waterton, and R2 2.01.284
WATER–WALLED 1 FR 0.0001 REL FR 1 V 0 P
that water–walled bulwark, still secure | and JN 2.01. 27
WATERWORK 1 FR 0.0001 REL FR 0 V 1 P
or the german hunting in waterwork, is worth a 2H4 2.01.145 P
WATERY 6 FR 0.0006 REL FR 6 V 0 P
(those clouds removed) upon our watery eyne. LLL 5.02.206
the watery kingdom, whose ambitious head | spets MV 2.07. 44
shall in despite enforce a watery eye. SHR in.1. 128
so went he suited to his watery tomb. TN 5.01.234
that i, being govern'd by the watery moon, | may R3 2.02. 69
woes, | corrupted blood some watery token shows, LUC 1748
WAT'RED 1 FR 0.0001 REL FR 0 V 1 P
there was a spaniard's mouth wat'red, and he PER 4.02.100 P
WAT'RISH 1 FR 0.0001 REL FR 1 V 0 P
not all the dukes of wat'rish burgundy | can buy LR 1.01.258
WAT'RY 18 FR 0.0020 REL FR 17 V 1 P
th' sky, | whose wat'ry arch and messenger am i, TMP 4.01. 71
unwholesome humidity, this gross wat'ry pumpion. WIV 3.03. 41 P
lord of the wide world and wild wat'ry seas, ERR 2.01. 21
behold | her silver visage in the wat'ry glass, MND 1.01.210
quench'd in the chaste beams of the wat'ry moon, 2.01.162
the moon methinks looks with a wat'ry eye; 3.01.198
be the stream | and wat'ry death–bed for him. MV 3.02. 47

nine changes of the wat'ry star hath been | the WT 1.02. 1
back the envious siege | of wat'ry neptune, is R2 2.01. 63
be, | when that the wat'ry palates taste indeed TRO 3.02. 21
an enemy, | and would usurp upon my wat'ry eyes, TIT 3.01.268
her collars of the moonshine's wat'ry beams, ROM 1.04. 65
and having thrown him from your wat'ry grave, PER 2.01. 10
and from their wat'ry empire recollect | all 2.01. 50
and now this pale swan in her wat'ry nest LUC 1611
face | of that black blood a wat'ry rigol goes, 1745
and the firm soil win of the wat'ry main, SON 64. 7
"this said, his wat'ry eyes he did dismount, LC 281
WAUL *(see wawl)*
WAV'D 2 FR 0.0002 REL FR 1 V 1 P
he wav'd indifferently 'twixt doing them neither COR 2.02. 17 P
then wav'd his handkerchief? CYM 1.03. 6
/WAVE 1 FR 0.0001 REL FR 0 V 1 P
now, by the salt /wave of the mediterraneum, a LLL 5.01. 58 P
WAVE 11 FR 0.0012 REL FR 11 V 0 P
i wish you | a wave o' th' sea, that you might WT 4.04.141
let our bloody colors wave! 3H6 2.02.173
minded, | wave thus to express his disposition, COR 1.06. 74
in our ages see | their banners wave again. 3.01. 8
who marks the waxing tide grow wave by wave, TIT 3.01. 95
who marks the waxing tide grow wave by wave, 3.01. 95
which he did wave against my throat, i have CYM 4.02.150
their friends | o'erborne i' th' former wave. 5.03. 48
a roman and a british ensign wave | friendly 5.05.480
like a dive–dapper peering through a wave, | who VEN 86
the hairs, who wave like feath'red wings. 306
WAVED 1 FR 0.0001 REL FR 1 V 0 P
horns welk'd and waved like the /enridged sea. LR 4.06. 71
WAVER 1 FR 0.0001 REL FR 1 V 0 P
thou almost mak'st me waver in my faith | to MV 4.01.130
WAVERER 1 FR 0.0001 REL FR 1 V 0 P
but come, young waverer, come go with me, | in ROM 2.03. 89
WAVERING 4 FR 0.0004 REL FR 4 V 0 P
more longing, wavering, sooner lost and worn, TN 2.04. 34
and that is the wavering commons, for their love R2 2.02.129
in france, amongst a fickle, wavering nation. 1H6 4.01.138
and nice affections wavering stood in doubt | if LC 97
WAVES 21 FR 0.0023 REL FR 21 V 0 P
to besiege, and make his bold waves tremble, TMP 1.02.205
you have, and kiss'd, | the wild waves whist: 1.02.378
bold head | 'bove the contentious waves he kept, 2.01.119
spread o'er the silver waves thy golden hairs, ERR 3.02. 48
i saw him hold acquaintance with the waves | so TN 1.02. 16
tempests are kind and salt waves fresh in love. 3.04.384
whom the blind waves and surges have devour'd. 5.01.229
and spend her strength with overmatching waves. 3H6 1.04. 21
gust, | command an argosy to stem the waves. 2.06. 36
as good to chide the waves as speak them fair. 5.04. 24
the brothers | more than with ruthless waves, 5.04. 36
so from the waves of tiber | did i the tired JC 1.02.114
though the yesty waves | confound and swallow MAC 4.01. 53
action | it waves you to a more removed ground, HAM 1.04. 61
it waves me forth again, i'll follow it. 1.04. 68
it waves me still. — | go on, i'll follow thee. 1.04. 78
lost, | by waves from coast to coast is toss'd. PER 2.ch. 34
never was waves nor wind more violent, | and 4.01. 59
till the wild waves will have him seen no more, VEN 819
whose waves to imitate the battle sought | with LUC 1438
like as the waves make towards the pibbled shore SON 60. 1
WAVE–WORN 1 FR 0.0001 REL FR 1 V 0 P
th' shore, that o'er his wave–worn basis bowed, TMP 2.01.121
WAVING 8 FR 0.0009 REL FR 8 V 0 P
even as the waving sedges play with wind. SHR in.2. 53
advance our waving colors on the walls, 1H6 1.06. 1
and stands colossus–wise, waving his beam, TRO 5.05. 9
and with his hat, thus waving it in scorn, | "i COR 2.03.167
more learned than the ears), waving thy head, 3.02. 77
and, waving our red weapons o'er our heads, JC 3.01.109
and thrice his head thus waving up and down, HAM 2.01. 90
glove or hat or handkerchief | still waving, as CYM 1.03. 12
WAV'RING 1 FR 0.0001 REL FR 1 V 0 P
the still–discordant wav'ring multitude, | can 2H4 in 19
WAW 1 FR 0.0001 REL FR 0 V 1 P
true? pow, waw. COR 2.01.142 P
WAWL 1 FR 0.0001 REL FR 1 V 0 P
time that we smell the air | we wawl and cry. LR 4.06.180
WAX* 31 FR 0.0035 REL FR 26 V 5 P
break the neck of the wax, and every one give LLL 4.01. 59
that was the way to make his godhead wax, | for 5.02. 10
to whom you are but as a form in wax | by him MND 1.01. 49
too, | since i nor wax nor honey can bring home, AWW 1.02. 65
by your leave, wax. TN 2.05. 92 P
life, | which bleeds away even as a form of wax JN 5.04. 24
if i did say of wax, my growth would approve the 2H4 1.02.159 P
our /thighs pack'd with wax, our mouths with 4.05. 76
old i do wax, and from my weary limbs | honor is H5 5.01. 84
face will wither, a full eye will wax hollow; 5.02.162 P
kate, the elder i wax, the better i shall appear 5.02.229 P
spent, | wax dim, as drawing to their exigent; 1H6 2.05. 9
the bee stings, but i say, 'tis the bee's wax; 2H6 4.02. 82 P
i seek not to wax great by others' /waning, | or 4.10. 20
have wrought the easy–melting king like wax. 3H6 2.01.171
as red as fire? nay then, her wax must melt. 3.02. 51
a stone is soft as wax, tribunes more hard than TIT 3.01. 45
if the winds rage, doth not the sea wax mad, 3.01.222
as all the world — why, he's a man of wax. ROM 1.03. 76
thy noble shape is but a form of wax, 3.03.126
but moves itself | in a wide sea of wax. TIM 1.01. 47
the character i'll take with wax; 5.03. 6
which | with wax i brought away, whose soft 5.04. 68
set this up with wax | upon old brutus' statue. JC 1.03.145
rich gifts wax poor when givers prove unkind. HAM 3.01.100
to flaming youth let virtue be as wax | and melt 3.04. 84
leave, gentle wax, and, manners, blame us not: LR 4.06.259
good wax, thy leave. CYM 3.02. 35
what wax so frozen but dissolves with temp'ring, VEN 565
ill, | no more than wax shall be accounted evil, LUC 1245
softer than wax, and yet as iron rusty: PP 7. 4
WAX'D 2 FR 0.0002 REL FR 2 V 0 P
of his wished light | the seas wax'd calm, and ERR 1.01. 91
ay, but the days are wax'd shorter with him. TIM 3.04. 11
WAXED 2 FR 0.0002 REL FR 2 V 0 P
them | as if but now they waxed pale for woe: TGV 3.01.230
age | man–ent'red thus, he waxed like a sea, COR 2.02. 99
WAXEN* 11 FR 0.0012 REL FR 11 V 0 P
which, like a waxen image 'gainst a fire, TGV 2.04.201
with rounds of waxen tapers on their heads, WIV 4.04. 51
and waxen in their mirth, and neeze, and swear MND 2.01. 56
and for night–tapers crop their waxen thighs 3.01.169
in women's waxen hearts to set their forms! TN 2.02. 30
point, | that it may enter mowbray's waxen coat, R2 1.03. 75
mouth, | not worshipp'd with a waxen epitaph. H5 1.02.233
art thou like the adder waxen deaf? 2H6 3.02. 76
whereat a waxen torch forthwith he lighteth, LUC 178
for men have marble, women waxen, minds, | and 1240
from lips new waxen pale begins to blow | the 1663
WAXES 3 FR 0.0003 REL FR 3 V 0 P
ah, sirrah, by my fay, it waxes late, | i'll to ROM 1.05.126
in thews and /bulk, but, as this temple waxes, HAM 1.03. 12
he waxes desperate with /imagination. 1.04. 87
WAXETH 1 FR 0.0001 REL FR 1 V 0 P
loseth his pride, and never waxeth strong. VEN 420
WAXING 1 FR 0.0001 REL FR 1 V 0 P
who marks the waxing tide grow wave by wave, TIT 3.01. 95
WAX–RED 1 FR 0.0001 REL FR 1 V 0 P
slips, | set thy seal manual on my wax–red lips. VEN 516
/WAY 6 FR 0.0006 REL FR 4 V 2 P
/you /that /way; LLL 5.02.931 P
/we /this /way. 5.02.931 P
/but /teachest /me /the /way | /how /to /lament R2 4.01.301
/we /see /which /way /the /stream /of /time 2H4 4.01. 70
hear not my steps, which /way /they walk, for MAC 2.01. 57
/and /tears | /were /like /a /better /way: LR 4.03. 19
WAY 608 FR 0.0687 REL FR 463 V 145 P
out of our way, i say. TMP 1.01. 27 P
'tis a good dullness, | and give it way. 1.02.186
pity move my father | to be inclin'd my way! 1.02.448
no hope, that way, is | another way so high a 2.01.240
way, is | another way so high a hope that even 2.01.241
in the dark | out of my way, unless he bid 'em; 2.02. 7
which | lie tumbling in my barefoot way, and 2.02. 11
my best way is to creep under his gaberdine; 2.02. 38 P
i prithee now lead the way without any more 2.02.173 P
o brave monster! lead the way. 2.02.188 P
for it is you that have chalk'd forth the way 5.01.203
have given it you, but i, being in the way, TGV 1.02. 39
how could he see his way to seek out you? 2.04. 94
alas, the way is wearisome and long. 2.07. 8
gone, | and this way comes he with it presently, 3.01. 42
how and which way i may bestow myself | to be 3.01. 87
the best way is to slander valentine | with 3.02. 31
words | can no way change you to a milder form, 5.04. 56
nay, pray you lead the way. WIV 1.01.305 P
and ask of doctor caius' house which is the way; 1.02. 2 P
he is something peevish that way; 1.04. 14 P
anne page for my master in the way of marriage. 1.04. 84 P
i can tell you that by the way, i praise heaven 1.04.141 P
i think the best way were to entertain him with 2.01. 67 P
sort, as they say) but in the way of honesty; 2.02. 74 P
which way have you look'd for master caius, that 3.01. 3 P
the pittie–ward, the park–ward — every way; 3.01. 6 P
old windsor way, and every way but the town way. 3.01. 6 P
old windsor way, and every way but the town way. 3.01. 6 P
old windsor way, and every way but the town way. 3.01. 7 P
desire you you will also look that way. 3.01. 9 P
yonder he is coming, this way, sir hugh. 3.01. 27 P
from frogmore, over the stile, this way. 3.01. 33 P
and i will one way or other make you amends. 3.01. 87 P
nay, keep your way, little gallant; 3.02. 1 P
on my consent, and my consent goes not that way. 3.02. 78 P
let me stop this way first. 3.03.164 P
which way should he go? 4.02. 46 P
page, have you any way then to unfool me again? 4.02.115 P
i think, in the way of waste, attempt us again. 4.02.212 P
there is no better way than that they spoke of. 4.04. 16
if he be amaz'd, he will every way be mock'd. 5.03. 19 P
that we may bring you something on the way. MM 1.01. 61
hang all that offend that way but for ten year 2.01.238 P
for i am that way going to temptation, | where 2.02.158
teach her the way. 2.04. 19
admit no other way to save his life | (as i 2.04. 88
and 'twere the cheaper way. 2.04.105
come your way, sir. 3.02. 11 P
which is the way? 3.02. 51 P
something too crabbed that way, friar. 3.02. 98 P
and woman after this downright way of creation. 3.02.105 P
for women, he was not inclin'd that way. 3.02.122 P
but shall you on your knowledge find this way? 4.01. 36
of precept, he did show me | the way twice o'er. 4.01. 40
let me have way, my lord, | to find this 5.01.238
that's the way; for women are light at midnight. 5.01.279 P
but as an intent | that perish'd by the way. 5.01.453
road, | and if the wind blow any way from shore, ERR 3.02.148
be in debt and theft, and a sergeant in the way, 4.02. 61
on purpose shut the doors against his way. 4.03. 91
my way is now to hie home to his house, | and 4.03. 92
person | comes this way to the melancholy vale, 5.01.120
by th' way we met | my wife, her sister, and a 5.01.235
but keep your way a' god's name, i have done. ADO 1.01.142 P
which way looks he? 1.03. 53 P
if i can cross him any way, i bless myself every 1.03. 68 P
can cross him any way, i bless myself every way. 1.03. 68 P
i shall lessen god's sending that way, for it is 2.01. 22 P
you must wear it one way, for the prince hath 2.01.191 P
the most peaceable way for you, if you do take a 3.03. 58 P
and given way unto this course of fortune, | by 4.01.157
is there any way to show such friendship? 4.01.263 P
a very even way, but no such friend. 4.01.264 P
for my love some other way than swearing by it. 4.01.326 P
master constable, you go not the way to examine; 4.02. 33 P
yea, marry, that's the eftest way; 4.02. 36 P
good morrow, masters — each his several way. 5.03. 29
ay, our way to be gone. LLL 2.01.258
the way is but short, away! 3.01. 56 P
as it were in via, in way, of explication; 4.02. 14 P
accidentally, or by the way of progression, hath 4.02.139 P
we are much out a' th' way. 4.03. 74
fair love, strewing her way with flowers. 4.03.377
that is the way to make an offense gracious, 5.01.139 P
that was the way to make his godhead wax, | for 5.02. 10
she is two months on her way. 5.02.673 P
why, that's the way to choke a gibing spirit, 5.02.858
no, madam, we will bring you on your way. 5.02.873
my fortunes every way as fairly rank'd | (if not MND 1.01.101
well — go thy way. 2.01.146
and to speak troth, i have forgot our way. 2.02. 36
ay, that way goes the game. 3.02.289
astray | as one come not within another's way. 3.02.359
did fly, | that fallen am i in dark uneven way, 3.02.417
now, go thy way. 3.02.428
him, | and by the way let's recount our dreams. 4.01.199
they'll not show their teeth in way of smile MV 1.01. 55
the self–same way with more advised watch | to 1.01.142
to shoot another arrow that self way | which you 1.01.148
this was a way to thrive, and he was blest; 1.03. 89
to speak to lady afterward | in way of marriage; 2.01. 42
i pray you, which is the way to master jew's? 2.02. 34 P
i pray you, which is the way to master jew's? 2.02. 40 P
be god's sonties, 'twill be a hard way to hit. 2.02. 45 P
in my life | to woo a maid in way of marriage; 2.09. 13
you here, | but meeting with salerio by the way, 3.02.228
you drop manna in the way | of starved people. 5.01.294
'twill be a good way; AYL 1.01. 94 P
devise the fittest time and safest way | to hide 1.03.135
that is the way to make her scorn you still. 2.04. 22
and little reaks to find the way to heaven | by 2.04. 81
the "why" is plain as way to parish church: 2.07. 52
and this way will i take upon me to wash your 3.02.422 P
and by the way you shall tell me where in the 3.02.431 P
well, go your way to her (for i see love hath 4.03. 69 P
my way is to conjure you, and i'll begin with ep 11 P
iwis it is not half way to her heart; SHR 1.01. 62
while i make way from hence to save my life. 1.01.234
you, which is the readiest way | to the house of 1.02.219
and through the instrument my pate made way, 2.01.154
the door is open, sir, there lies your way; 3.02.210
on the proudest he | that stops my way in padua. 3.02.235
orders grey, | as he forth walked on his way" — 4.01.146
knows not which way to stand, to look, to speak, 4.01.185
another way i have to man my haggard, | to make 4.01.193
this way the coverlet, another way the sheets. 4.01.202
this way the coverlet, another way the sheets. 4.01.202
this is a way to kill a wife with kindness, 4.01.208
this by the way i let you understand: 4.02.116
signior baptista, shall i lead the way? 4.04. 69
withal make known | which way thou travellest — 4.05. 51
think him a great way fool, soly a coward; AWW 1.01.101
i, madam, and i speak the truth the next way: 1.03. 59 P
slay | in common sense, sense saves another way. 2.01.178
his valor, and my state that way is dangerous, 2.05. 11 P
you | that presently you take your way for home, 2.05. 64
lost our labor, they are gone a contrary way. 3.05. 8 P
is this the way? 3.05. 37
hark you, they come this way. 3.05. 38
let him have his way. 3.06. 2 P
he can come no other way but by this 4.01. 1 P
the sacrament on't, how and which way you will. 4.03.137 P
be for the flow'ry way that leads to the broad 4.05. 54 P
brightest beams | distracted clouds give way, so 5.03. 35
and boarded her i' th' wanton way of youth. 5.03.211
as a bristle may enter, in way of thy excuse. TN 1.05. 3 P
well, go thy way, if sir toby would leave 1.05. 27 P
will you hoist sail, sir? here lies your way. 1.05.202 P
if that the youth will come this way to–morrow, 1.05.305
i will drop in his way some obscure epistles of 2.03.155 P
cannot recover your niece, i am a foul way out. 2.03.185 P
there lies your way, due west. 3.01.134
and't be any way, it must be with valor, for 3.02. 30 P
there is no way but this, sir andrew. 3.02. 39 P
which way is he, in the name of sanctity? 3.04. 84 P
prithee hold thy peace, this is not the way. 3.04.108 P
no way but gentleness — gently, gently. 3.04.110 P
give them way till he take leave, and presently 3.04.198 P
i'll go another way to work with him; 4.01. 33 P
of the soul, and no way approve his opinion. 4.02. 55 P
then lead the way, good father, and heavens so 4.03. 34
if thou inclin'st that way, thou art a coward, WT 1.02.243
how near, | which way to be prevented, if to be; 1.02.405
never | saw i men scour so on their way. 2.01. 35
the very thought of my revenges that way 2.03. 19
or in act or will | that way inclining, hard'ned 3.02. 52
not move the gods | to look that way thou wert. 3.02.214
home, home, the next way. 3.03.125 P
come, good boy, the next way home. 3.03.127 P
go you the next way with your findings; 3.03.128 P
i am false of heart that way, and that he knew, 4.03.108 P
shall i bring thee on the way? 4.03.114 P
jog on, jog on, the foot–path way, | and merrily 4.03.123
accident, | should pass this way as you did. 4.04. 20
nor in a way so chaste, since my desires | run 4.04. 33
for it is | a way to make us better friends, 4.04. 66
fear, my doricles, | you woo'd me the false way. 4.04.151
i was cozen'd by the way and lost all my money? 4.04.252 P
there is no other way but to tell the king she's 4.04.688 P
so must thy grave | give way to what's seen now! 5.01. 98
meets he on the way | the father of this seeming 5.01.190
therefore follow me | and mark what way i make. 5.01.233
our country manners give our betters way. JN 1.01.156
for thou wast got i' th' way of honesty. 1.01.181
open your gates and give the victors way. 2.01.324
is the young dolphin every way complete: 2.01.433
which we, god knows, have turn'd another way, 2.01.549
my friend, | he is a very serpent in my way, 3.03. 61
i have a way to win their loves again. 4.02.168
and lose my way | among the thorns and dangers 4.03.140
and send him word by me which way you go. 5.03. 7
to think | i come one way of the plantagenets. 5.06. 11
the best way is to venge my gloucester's death. R2 1.02. 36
farewell, my liege, now no way can i stray; 1.03.206
save back to england, all the world's my way. 1.03.207
imagine it | to lie that way thou goest, not 1.03.287
come, come, my son, i'll bring thee on thy way; 1.03.304
how far brought you high herford on his way? 1.04. 2
but to the next high way, and there i left him. 1.04. 4
direct not him whose way himself will choose, 2.01. 29
he was — why, so go all which way it will! 2.02. 87
i | know how or which way to order these affairs 2.02.109
making the hard way sweet and delectable. 2.03. 7
but i bethink me what a weary way | from 2.03. 8
weary lords | shall make their way seem short, 2.03. 17

arms, | be his own carver and cut out his way, 2.03.144
and heavy–gaited toads lie in their way, | doing 3.02. 15
forth | of that sweet way i was in to despair! 3.02.205
or i'll be buried in the king's high way, | some 3.03.155
some way of common trade, where subjects' feet 3.03.156
that know the strong'st and surest way to get. 3.03.201
this way the king will come, this is the way 5.01. 1
this is the way | to julius caesar's ill–erected 5.01. 1
which knowest the way | to plant unrightful 5.01. 62
another way | to pluck him headlong from the 5.01. 64
go count thy way with sighs, i mine with groans. 5.01. 89
so longest way shall have the longest moans. 5.01. 90
for one step i'll groan, the way being short, 5.01. 91
and piece the way out with a heavy heart. 5.01. 92
make way, unruly woman! 5.02.110
march all one way and be no more oppos'd 1H4 1.01. 15
take horse, | uncertain of the issue any way. 1.01. 61
to do him wrong or any way impeach | what then 1.03. 75
and that is the next way to give poor jades the 2.01. 9 P
will she hold out water in foul way? 2.01. 84 P
it is like we shall have good trading that way. 2.04.365 P
but in the way of bargain, mark ye me, | i'll 3.01.137
'tis the next way to turn tailor, or be 3.01.259 P
if thou wert any way given to virtue, i would 3.03. 33 P
a mad fellow met me on the way and told me i had 4.02. 36 P
king | have any way your good deserts forgot, 4.03. 46
rebellion lay in his way, and he found it. 5.01. 28 P
posted day and night | to meet you on the way, 5.01. 36
if he do come in my way, so; 5.03. 57 P
cousin westmerland, | our duty this way lies; 5.04. 16
my lord, i overrode him on the way, | and he is 2H4 1.01. 30
he ask'd the way to chester, and of him | i did 1.01. 39
so | he seem'd in running to devour the way, 1.01. 47
man | the aptest way for safety and revenge. 1.01.213
you should have been well on your way to york. 2.01. 67
of wrenching the true cause the false way. 2.01.111 P
as common as the way between saint albons and 2.02.167 P
daughter, | give even way unto my rough affairs; 2.03. 2
that makes a still–stand, running neither way. 2.03. 64
's prince, and let it go which way it will, he 3.02.237 P
this door is open, he is gone this way. 4.05. 55
he's walk'd the way of nature, | and to our 5.02. 4
your father) | i gave bold way to my authority, 5.02. 82
this dangerous treason lurking in our way | to H5 2.02.186
not now | but every rub is smoothed on our way. 2.02.188
his finger's end, i knew there was but one way; 2.03. 16 P
the roman wars, in the way of argument, look you 3.02. 97 P
and such another neighbor | stand in our way. 3.06.158
and my way shall be pav'd with english faces. 3.07. 81 P
so, for fear i should be fac'd out of my way. 3.07. 83 P
'fore the king | seems to prepare his way. 5.pr. 13
for one fair french maid that stands in my way. 5.02.319 P
the maid that stood in the way for my wish shall 5.02.327 P
for my wish shall show me the way to my will. 5.02.328 P
then how, or which way, should they first break 1H6 2.01. 71
no further of the case, | how or which way. 2.01. 73
turn not thy scorns this way, plantagenet. 2.04. 77
no way to that, for weakness, which she ent'red. 3.02. 25
o, turn the edged sword another way, | strike 3.03. 52
and no way canst thou turn thee for redress, 4.02. 25
a knight, | and will not any way dishonor me. 5.03.102
and smooth my way upon their headless necks; 2H6 1.02. 65
my lord protector will come this way by and by, 1.03. 2 P
god, and the good wine in thy master's way. 2.03. 96 P
go, lead the way, i long to see my prison. 2.04.110
looking the way her harmless young one went, 3.01.215
this way fall i to death. 3.02.412
this way for me. 3.02.412
my sword make way for me, for here is no staying 4.08. 59 P
and defense | to give the enemy way, and to 5.02. 76
turn this way, henry, and regard them not. 3H6 1.01.189
now sways it this way, like a mighty sea 2.05. 5
now sways it that way, like the self–same sea 2.05. 7
no way to fly, nor strength to hold out flight. 2.06. 24
one way or other, she is for a king, | and she 3.02. 87
saying, he'll lade it dry to have his way: 3.02.139
seeking a way, and straying from the way, | not 3.02.176
seeking a way, and straying from the way, | not 3.02.176
myself, | or hew my way out with a bloody axe. 3.02.181
why then, let's on our way in silent sort. 4.02. 28
/comes hunting this way to disport himself. 4.05. 8
that if about this hour he make this way, 4.05. 10
this way, my lord, for this way lies the game. 4.05. 14
this way, my lord, for this way lies the game. 4.05. 14
nay, this way, man, see where the huntsmen stand 4.05. 15
yes, warwick, edward dares, and leads the way. 5.01.112
will thither straight, for willingness rids way, 5.03. 21
work thou the way — and that /shall execute. 5.07. 25
i'll tell you what, i think it is our way, | if R3 1.01. 78
the readiest way to make the wench amends | is 1.01.155
why then give way, dull clouds, to my quick 1.03.195
for, by the way, i'll sort occasion, | as index 2.02.148
the weary way hath made you melancholy. 3.01. 3
uncle, but our crosses on the way | have made it 3.01. 4
would long ere this have met us on the way. 3.01. 21
thou know'st our reasons urg'd upon the way; 3.01.160
his gracious pleasure any way therein. 3.04. 17
my son | in your behalf, to meet you on the way. 4.01. 50
and then marry her — | uncertain way of gain! 4.02. 63
this /is not the way | to win your daughter. 4.04.284
there is no other way, | unless thou couldst put 4.04.285
when thou mayest tell thy tale the nearest way? 4.04.461
if by the way they be not fought withal. 4.05. 18
whose grace | chalks successors their way, nor H8 1.01. 60
the force of his own merit makes his way — | a 1.01. 64
a full hot horse, who being allow'd his way, 1.01.133
but when the way was made | and pav'd with gold, 1.01.187
men of his way should be most liberal, | they 1.03. 61
our breach of duty this way | is business of 2.02. 68
i would not be a young count in your way | for 2.03. 41
pray you keep your way; 2.04.129
or | laid any scruple in your way which might 2.04.151
the region of my breast, which forc'd such way, 2.04.185
seek me out, and that way i am wife in, | out 3.01. 38
we come not by the way of accusation | to taint 3.01. 54
nor to betray you any way to sorrow — | you 3.01. 56
the way of our profession is against it; 3.01.157
(though now the time | gives way to us) i much 3.02. 16
him, how he coasts | and hedges his own way. 3.02. 39
is there no way to cure this? 3.02.216
yet i know | a way, if it take right, in spite 3.02.219
that in the way of loyalty and truth | toward 3.02.272
found thee a way, out of his wrack, to rise in; 3.02.437
gentlemen, ye shall go my way, which | is to th' 4.01.114
thomas, y' are a gentleman | of mine own way; 5.01. 28
they shall no more prevail than we give way to. 5.01.143
i am glad | i came this way so happily; 5.02. 9
course of my authority | might go one way, and 5.02. 71
is there no other way of mercy | but i must 5.02.127
and find a way out | to let the troop pass 5.03. 84
make way there for the princess. 5.03. 87
lead the way, lords, | ye must all see the queen 5.04. 72
go thy way, hector! TRO 1.02.200 P
go thy way, troilus, go thy way! 1.02.235 P
go thy way, troilus, go thy way! 1.02.236 P
making their way | with those of nobler bulk! 1.03. 36
hector's opinion | is this in way of truth; 2.02.189
i do beseech you, as in way of taste, | to give 3.03. 13
i will lead the way. 3.03. 54
take the instant way, | for honor travels in a 3.03.153
if you give way, | or /hedge aside from the 3.03.157
aleven of the clock it will go one way or other. 3.03.296 P
here lies our way. 4.01. 80
hand, | and by the way possess thee what she is. 4.04.112
which way would hector have it? 4.05. 71
make cruel way | through ranks of greekish youth 4.05.184
oppos'd to hinder me, should stop my way, | /but 5.03. 57
th' effect doth operate another way. 5.03.109
you must in no way say he is covetous. COR 1.01. 42 P
state, whose course will on | the way it takes, 1.01. 70
from them to you, | and no way from yourselves. 1.01.154
youth with comeliness pluck'd all gaze his way; 1.03. 7 P
true sword to sword, i'll potch at him some way, 1.10. 15
give way there, and go on! 2.01.193
i had rather be their servant in my way | than 2.01.203
make way, they are coming. 2.02. 36 P
consent of one direct way should be at once to 2.03. 23 P
which way do you judge my wit would fly? 2.03. 25 P
why that way? 2.03. 30 P
tribunes, give way, he shall to th' market–place 3.01. 31
not unlike, | each way, to better yours. 3.01. 49
where you are bound, you must inquire your way, 3.01. 54
laid falsely | i' th' plain way of his merit. 3.01. 61
us, yet sought | the very way to catch them. 3.01. 80
and give way the while | to unstable slightness. 3.01.147
this is the way to kindle, not to quench. 3.01.196
that is the way to lay the city flat, | to bring 3.01.203
noble tribunes, | it is the humane way. 3.01.325
not martius, we'll proceed | in our first way. 3.01.332
hast not the soft way which, thou dost confess, 3.02. 82
tongue can do | i' th' way of flattery further. 3.02.137
chance | that starts i' th' way before thee. 4.01. 37
they have ta'en note of us; keep on your way. 4.02. 10
if he give me way, | i'll do his country service 4.04. 25
and have already | o'erborne their way, consum'd 4.06. 78
and cowardly nobles gave way unto your clusters, 4.06.122
fall down, and knee | the way into his mercy. 5.01. 6
into his kindness, | and cannot lose your way. 5.01. 60
you know the way home again. 5.02. 97 P
gave him way | in all his own desires; 5.06. 31
after your way his tale pronounc'd shall bury 5.06. 57
romans, make way! TIT 1.01. 64
make way to lay them by their bretheren. 1.01. 89
princely shall be thy usage every way. 1.01.266
what, villain boy, | barr'st me my way in rome? 1.01.291
this way, or not at all, stand you in hope. 2.01.119
horse will follow where the game | makes way, 2.02. 24
this way to death my wretched sons are gone, 3.01. 98
then which way shall i find revenge's cave? 3.01.270
kinsmen, this is the way. 4.03. 1
ravish a maid, or plot the way to do it, 5.01.129
'tis the way | to call hers, exquisite, in ROM 1.01.228
he ran this way and leapt this orchard wall. 2.01. 5
hie you to church, i must another way, | to 2.05. 72
soul | is but a little way above our heads, 3.01.127
which way ran he that kill'd mercutio? 3.01.137
tybalt, that murtherer, which way ran he? 3.01.138
and light thee on thy way to mantua. 3.05. 15
what cursed foot wanders this way to–night, | to 5.03. 19
lead, boy, which way? 5.03.168
let it flow this way, my good lord. TIM 1.02. 54
flow this way? 1.02. 55 P
what a sweep of vanity comes this way! 1.02.132
bold | (for that i knew it the most general way) 2.02.200
his debts, | and make a clear way to the gods. 3.04. 76
i will fear to catch it, and give way. 4.03.353 P
you that way and you this; 5.01.106
and do you now strew flowers in his way, | that JC 1.01. 50
go you down that way towards the capitol, | this 1.01. 63
that way towards the capitol, | this way will i. 1.01. 64
stand you directly in antonio's way | when he 1.02. 3
which is a great way growing on the south, 2.01.107
and this way have you well expounded it. 2.02. 91
security gives way to conspiracy. 2.03. 7 P
come hither, fellow; which way hast thou been? 2.04. 21
brutus, | he draws mark antony out of the way. 3.01. 26
him, | i spurn thee like a cur out of my way. 3.01. 46
either led or driven, as we point the way; 4.01. 23
must i give way and room to your rash choler? 4.03. 39
you wrong me every way; 4.03. 55
upon this blasted heath you stop our way | with MAC 1.03. 77
down, or else o'erleap, | for in my way it lies. 1.04. 50
of human kindness | to catch the nearest way. 1.05. 18
thoughts that nature | gives way to in repose! 2.01. 9
thou marshal'st me the way that i was going, 2.01. 42
that go the primrose way to th' everlasting 2.03. 19 P
and our safest way | is to avoid the aim. 2.03.142
was't not the way? 3.03. 19
i hear it by the way; 3.04.129
for mine own good | all causes shall give way. 3.04.135
of my thumbs, | something wicked this way comes. 4.01. 45
float upon a wild and violent sea | each way, 4.02. 22
that way are they coming. 5.02. 6
my way of life | is fall'n into the sear, the 5.03. 22
have lighted fools | the way to dusty death. 5.05. 23
that way the noise is. 5.07. 14
this way, my lord, the castle's gently rend'red: 5.07. 24
show me the steep and thorny way to heaven, HAM 1.03. 48
and that in way of caution — i must tell you, 1.03. 95
he seem'd to find his way without his eyes, 2.01. 95
but in the beaten way of friendship, what make 2.02.270 P
we coted them on the way, and hither are they 2.02.317 P
that certain players | we o'erraught on the way; 3.01. 17
will bring him to his wonted way again, | to 3.01. 40
his affections do not that way tend, | nor what 3.01.162
they bear the mandate — they must sweep my way, 3.04.204
i will /give you way for these your letters, 4.06. 32
nothing, neither way. 5.02.301
t' avert your liking a more worthier way | than LR 1.01.211
fled this way, sir, when by no means he could — 2.01. 42
that wouldst be a bawd in way of good service, 2.02. 20 P
resolve me with all modest haste which way 2.04. 25
not gone yet, if the wild geese fly that way. 2.04. 47 P
'tis best to give him way, he leads himself. 2.04.298
in which your pain | that way, i'll this — he 3.01. 54
of him, entreat for him, or any way sustain him. 3.03. 5 P
o, that way madness lies, let me shun that! 3.04. 21
this way, my lord. 3.04.175
that nature thus gives way to loyalty, something 3.05. 3 P
of his wits have given way to his impatience. 3.06. 4 P
at gates, and let him smell | his way to dover. 3.07. 94
you cannot see your way. 4.01. 17
i have no way, and therefore want no eyes; 4.01. 18
hence a mile or twain | i' th' way toward dover, 4.01. 43
know'st thou the way to dover? 4.01. 55
marvel our mild husband | not met us on the way. 4.02. 2
our wishes on the way | may prove effects. 4.02. 14
one way i like this well, | but being widow, and 4.02. 83
another way, | the news is not so tart. 4.02. 86
half way down | hangs one that gathers sampire, 4.06. 14
but have you never found my brother's way | to 5.01. 10
thou dost make thy way | to noble fortunes. 5.03. 29
this sword of mine shall give them instant way 5.03.150
some one way, some another. OTH 1.01.176
gone | is the next way to draw new mischief on. 1.03.205
do it a more delicate way than drowning. 1.03.354 P
of drowning thyself, it is clean out of the way. 1.03.359 P
when these /mutualities so marshal the way, hard 2.01.261 P
best judgment collied, | assays to lead the way. 2.03.207
ay, that's the way; 2.03.387
devise a mean to draw the moor | out of the way, 3.01. 38
speak, is't out o' th' way? 3.04. 80
there is no other way: 3.04.107
i pray you bring me on the way a little, | and 3.04.197
'tis but a little way that i can bring you, 3.04.199
nay, that's not your way. 4.01.186 P
nor send you out o' th' way? 4.02. 7
do kill the other, | every way makes my gain. 5.01. 14
i have made my way through more impediments 5.02.263
no way but this, | killing myself, to die upon a 5.02.358
in each thing give him way, cross him in nothing ANT 1.03. 9
thou teachest like a fool: the way to lose him. 1.03. 10
yet must antony | no way excuse his foils, when 1.04. 24
how lesser enmities may give way to greater. 2.01. 43
but small to greater matters must give way. 2.02. 11
your way is shorter, | my purposes do draw me 2.04. 7
though he be painted one way like a gorgon, 2.05.116
way like a gorgon, | the other way 's a mars. 2.05.117
show 's the way, sir. 2.06. 81
show me which way. 2.07. 69
at the full of tide, | and neither way inclines. 3.02. 50
of the stars give light | to thy fair way! 3.02. 66
turn your displeasure that way, for our faults 3.04. 34
the trees by th' way | should have borne men, 3.06. 46
things to destiny | hold unbewail'd their way. 3.06. 85
quite forgo | the way which promises assurance, 3.07. 46
six kings already | show me the way of yielding. 3.10. 34
the world, that i | have lost my way for ever. 3.11. 4
some friends that will | sweep your way for you. 3.11. 17
i will seek | some way to leave him. 3.13.200
it will determine one way; 4.03. 2
this way — well said. 4.04. 28
may frame herself | to th' way she's forc'd to. 5.01. 56
make way there! caesar! 5.02.111
why, that's the way | to fool their preparation, 5.02.224
woman should not do but in the way of honesty — 5.02.253 P
a way there, a way for caesar! 5.02.333
a way there, a way for caesar! 5.02.333
purposes, and, being royal, | took her own way. 5.02.337
no guess in knowledge | which way they went. CYM 1.01. 61
yet i'll move him | to walk this way. 1.01.104
past hope, and in despair, that way past grace. 1.01.137
fie, you must give way. 1.01.158
thief, or a (that way) accomplish'd courtier, 1.04. 92 P
for this time is ended, | take your own way. 1.05. 31
'twixt two such shes would chatter this way, and 1.06. 40
is there no way for men to be, but women | must 2.05. 1
and by th' way | tell me how wales was made so 3.02. 59
accessible is none but milford way. 3.02. 82
two beggars told me | i could not miss my way. 3.06. 9
fidele's sickness | did make my way long forth. 4.02.149
yes, sir, to milford–haven, which is the way? 4.02.291
this way, the romans | must or for britains slay 4.04. 4
gan to look | the way that they did, and to grin 5.03. 38
chickens, the way which they /stoop'd eagles; 5.03. 42
for thou art a way, | i think, to liberty; 5.04. 3
you, sir, you know not which way you shall go. 5.04.176 P
want eyes to direct them the way i am going, but 5.04.186 P
best use of eyes to see the way of blindness! 5.04.189 P
i am sure hanging's the way of winking. 5.04.190 P
if i discover'd not which way she was gone, | it 5.05.277
thus ready for the way of life or death, | i PER 1.01. 54
ground's the lowest, and we are half way there. 1.04. 78
knave was the sea to cast thee in our way! 2.01. 58 P
show | can any way speak in his just commend; 2.02.,49
convey, | unless your thoughts went on my way. 4.ch. 50
with shame which is her way to go with warrant. 4.02.127 P
there's no way to be rid on't but by the way to 4.06. 15 P
no way to be rid on't but by the way to the pox. 4.06. 16 P
peevish baggage would but give way to customers. 4.06. 19 P
persever in that clear way thou goest, | and the 4.06.106
will you not go the way of womenkind? 4.06.149 P
it is not good to cross him, give him way. 5.01.230
sir, lead 's the way. 5.03. 84

am going, and never yet | went i so willing way. TNK 1.01.104
or to be fond upon | another's way of speech, 1.02. 47
yours this way. 1.05. 13
either way, i am happy: 2.03. 22
woman, | his face, methinks, goes that way. 2.05. 21
go lead the way; 2.05. 59
that way he takes | i purpose is my way too. 2.06. 17
that way he takes | i purpose is my way too. 2.06. 18
to clear his own way with the mind and sword 3.01. 56
so which way now? 3.02. 32
the best way is, the next way to a grave; 3.02. 33
the best way is, the next way to a grave; 3.02. 33
this way the stag took. 3.05. 95
lives, invent a way | safer than banishment. 3.06.217
love that tells close offices | the foulest way, 5.01.123
you should observe her ev'ry way. 5.02. 14
i have no voice, sir, to confirm her that way! 5.02. 15
yes, in the way of cure. 5.02. 19
first, by your leave, | i' th' way of honesty. 5.02. 20
cure her first this way; 5.02. 22
her mood inclining that way that i spoke of, 5.02. 34
videlicet, the way of flesh — you have me? 5.02. 35
yours to command i' th' way of honesty. 5.02. 71
from her, | but still preserve her in this way. 5.02.106
(for 'tis no other) any way content ye | (for to ep 13
to give the smooth and dexter way to me | that STM III 11
pay, | he winks, and turns his lips another way. VEN 90
now which way shall she turn? 253
mov'd, he strikes, what e'er is in his way, 623
turn, and return, indenting with the way; 704
having lost the fair discovery of her way. 828
and as she runs, the bushes in the way, | some 871
wreath'd up in fatal folds just in his way, 879
this way she runs, and now she will no further, 905
as each unwilling portal yields him way, LUC 309
if thou deny, then force must work my way, | for 513
he learn'd to sin, and thou didst teach the way? 630
some dark deep desert, seated from the way, 1144
at gaze, | wildly determining which way to fly, 1150
maze, | that cannot tread the way out readily, 1152
pausing for means to mourn some newer way. 1365
are | from his low tract and look another way: SON 7.12
but wherefore do not you a mightier way | make 16. 1
to let base clouds o'ertake me in my way, 34. 3
injurious distance should not stop my way, | for 44. 2
how careful was i, when i took my way, | each 48. 1
how heavy do i journey on the way, | when what i 50. 1
content, | to put the by–past perils in her way? LC 158
WAYLAID 1 FR 0.0001 REL FR 0 V 1 P
rob those men that we have already waylaid; 1H4 1.02.163 P
WAYLAY 1 FR 0.0001 REL FR 0 V 1 P
"i will waylay thee going home, where if it be TN 3.04.159 P
/WAYS 4 FR 0.0004 REL FR 2 V 2 P
fairies, be gone, and be /all /ways away. MND 4.01. 41
from her shall read the perfect /ways of honor, H8 5.04. 37
come your /ways. PER 4.06.129 P
come, mistress, come your /ways with me. 4.06.152 P
WAYS 78 FR 0.0088 REL FR 44 V 34 P
come on your ways. TMP 2.02. 82 P
shall step by step attend | you and your ways, 3.03. 79
and, for the ways are dangerous to pass, | i do TGV 4.03. 24
go your ways, and ask of doctor caius' house WIV 1.02. 1 P
sir — i pray come a little nearer this ways. 2.02. 45 P
your worship come a little nearer this ways. 2.02. 49 P
go thy ways. 2.02.138 P
say, if money go before, all ways do lie open. 2.02.169 P
go your ways and play, go. 4.01. 79 P
come your ways, sir, come. MM 3.02. 80 P
come your ways, sir, come. 3.02. 84 P
when blood is nipp'd and ways be /foul, | then LLL 5.02.916
well, you are gone both ways. MV 3.05. 18 P
it must appear in other ways than words, 5.01.140
in summer, where the ways are fair enough. 5.01.264
but come your ways. AYL 1.02.209 P
but come thy ways, we'll go along together, 2.03. 66
ay, go your ways, go your ways; 4.01.182 P
ay, go your ways, go your ways; 4.01.182 P
i will kill thee a hundred and fifty ways: 5.01. 57 P
jades, on all mad masters, and all foul ways! SHR 4.01. 2 P
petruchio, go thy ways, the field is won. 4.05. 23
well, go thy ways, old lad, for thou shalt ha't. 5.02.181
now go thy ways, thou hast tam'd a curst shrow. 5.02.188
nay, come your ways. AWW 2.01. 93
nay, come your ways; 2.01. 94
go thy ways, i begin to be a–weary of thee, and 4.05. 56 P
go thy ways, let my horses be well look'd to, 4.05. 58 P
if it were yours by none of all these ways, 5.03.275
come thy ways, signior fabian. TN 2.05. 1 P
these high wild hills and rough uneven ways R2 2.03. 4
woes, | but presently prevent the ways to wail; 3.02.179
go thy ways, old jack, die when thou wilt; 1H4 2.04.127 P
son | can trace me in the tedious ways of art, 3.01. 47
the oldest sins the newest kind of ways? 2H4 4.05.126
by what by–paths and indirect crook'd ways | i 4.05.184
i take it there's but two ways, either to utter 5.03.110 P
as many arrows loosed several ways | come to one
H5 1.02.207
as many ways meet in one town; 1.02.208
i know no ways to mince it in love, but directly 5.02.126 P
that we do make our entrance several ways; 1H6 2.01. 30
go thy ways, kate. H8 2.04.134
and to prepare the ways | you have for dignities 3.02.328
say wolsey, that once trod the ways of glory, 3.02.435
come your ways, come your ways; TRO 3.02. 44 P
come your ways, come your ways; 3.02. 45 P
sir, those cold ways, | that seem like prudent COR 3.01.219
strength and weakness — thine own ways: 4.05.140
but go thy ways, go give that changing piece TIT 1.01.309
go thy ways, wench, serve god. ROM 2.05. 44 P
or walk in thievish ways, or bid me lurk | where 4.01. 79
that one of two bad ways you must conceit me, JC 3.01.192
deeds must not be thought | after these ways; MAC 2.02. 31
more suffer, and more sundry ways than ever, 4.03. 48
of each several crime, | acting it many ways. 4.03. 97
come your ways. HAM 1.03.135
in reputation and profit, was better both ways. 2.02.331 P
go thy ways to a nunn'ry. 3.01.129 P
come your ways. LR 2.02. 39 P
the ways are dangerous. 4.05. 17
there are more ways to recover the general again OTH 2.03.272 P
ruffian know | i have many other ways to die; ANT 4.01. 5
conclusions infinite | of easy ways to die. 5.02.356
go thy ways, good mariner, | i'll bring the body PER 3.01. 80
come your ways, my masters. 4.02. 40 P
come your ways, follow me. 4.02.145 P
go thy ways. 4.06. 65 P
come your ways. 4.06.125 P
come your ways, i say. 4.06.130 P
any of these ways are yet better than this; 4.06.177
come your ways. 4.06.200 P
a thousand differing ways to one sure end. TNK 1.05. 14
we are young and yet desire the ways of honor, 2.02. 73
her, | if he be noble arcite — thousand ways! 2.02.255
go thy ways, i'll remember thee, i'll fit thee! 3.05. 58
a thousand ways he seeks | to mend the hurt that VEN 477
a thousand spleens bear her a thousand ways, 907
and to her will frame all thy ways, | spare not PP 18.13
WAYWARD 14 FR 0.0015 REL FR 13 V 1 P
fie, fie, how wayward is this foolish love, TGV 1.02. 57
my wife is in a wayward mood to–day, | and will ERR 4.04. 4
account of her life to a clod of wayward marl? ADO 2.01. 62 P
this wimpled, whining, purblind, wayward boy, LLL 3.01.179
words | to wayward sickliness and age in him. R2 2.01.142
from wayward sickness and no grounded malice. R3 1.03. 29
to me, | tetchy and wayward was thy infancy; 4.04.169
since this same wayward girl is so reclaim'd. ROM 4.02. 47
you have done | hath been but for a wayward son,
MAC 3.05. 11
my wayward husband hath a hundred times | woo'd
OTH 3.03.292
is now again thwarting /the wayward seas, PER 4.04. 10
though wayward fortune did malign my state, | my 5.01. 89
view | how she came stealing to the wayward boy! VEN 344
who wayward once, his mood with nought agrees.
LUC 1095
WAYWARDER 1 FR 0.0001 REL FR 0 V 1 P
the wiser, the waywarder. AYL 4.01.161 P
WAYWARDNESS 1 FR 0.0001 REL FR 0 V 1 P
the unruly waywardness that infirm and choleric LR 1.01.298 P
WE *(also w')*
/WE 39 FR 0.0044 REL FR 36 V 3 P
WE 3530 FR 0.3990 REL FR 2874 V 656 P
WEAK 121 FR 0.0136 REL FR 105 V 16 P
although this lord of weak remembrance, this TMP 2.01.232
a very weak monster! 2.02.145 P
by whose aid | (weak masters though ye be) i 5.01. 41
made wit with musing weak, heart sick with TGV 1.01. 69
this weak impress of love is as a figure 3.02. 6
smoth'red in errors, feeble, shallow, weak, ERR 3.02. 35
highly that to her | all matter else seems weak. ADO 3.01. 54
their sense thus weak, lost with their fears MND 3.02. 27
have no more strength than her weak /prays. 3.02.250
bond, for i perceive | a weak bond holds you. 3.02.268
and this weak and idle theme, | no more yielding 5.01.427
deserving | were but a weak disabling of myself. MV 2.07. 30
oppress'd with two weak evils, age and hunger, AYL 2.07.132
why are our bodies soft, and weak, and smooth, SHR 5.02.165
our strength as weak, our weakness past compare, 5.02.174
though valiant in the defense, yet is weak. AWW 1.01.116 P
speak | his powerful sound within an organ weak; 2.01.176
in a most weak — 2.03. 33 P
my heart is heavy, and mine age is weak; 3.04. 41
six thousand, but very weak and unserviceable. 4.03.131 P
one of thy kin has a most weak pia mater. TN 1.05.115 P
and our weak spirits ne'er been higher rear'd WT 1.02. 72
thy jealousies | (fancies too weak for boys, too 3.02.181
with that same weak wind which enkindled it. JN 5.02. 87
out of the weak door of our fainting land. 5.07. 78
who, weak with age, cannot support myself. R2 2.02. 83
because my power is weak and all ill left; 2.03.154
weak men must fall, for heaven still guards the 3.02. 62
off, my gracious lord, | than this weak arm. 3.02. 65
how these vain weak nails | may tear a passage 5.05. 19
i hold as little counsel with weak fear | as you 1H4 4.03. 11
i fear the power of percy is too weak | to wage 4.04. 19
studied as to remember so weak a composition. 2H4 2.02. 8 P
can a weak empty vessel bear such a huge full 2.04. 62 P
'a has, that show a weak mind and an able body, 2.04.251 P
and there are twenty weak and wearied posts 2.04.356
seeds | and weak beginning lie intreasured. 3.01. 85
is held from falling with so weak a wind | that 4.05. 99
and weak age | of indigent faint souls past H5 1.01. 15
which, of a weak and niggardly projection, 2.04. 46
their villainy goes against my weak stomach, and 3.02. 53 P
kneeling at our feet but a weak and worthless 3.06.133 P
my army but a weak and sickly guard; 3.06.155
be confin'd within the weak list of a country's 5.02.270 P
the english army is grown weak and faint; 1H6 1.01.158
christ's mother helps me, else i were too weak. 1.02.106
it cannot be this weak and writhled shrimp 2.03. 23
kind keepers of my weak decaying age, | let 2.05. 1
weak shoulders, overborne with burthening grief, 2.05. 10
and that we find the slothful watch but weak, 3.02. 7
to beat assailing death from his weak /legions; 4.04. 16
when sapless age and weak unable limbs | should 4.05. 4
my ancient incantations are too weak, | and hell 5.03. 27
till henry be more weak and i more strong. 2H6 5.01. 31
i know not what to say, my title's weak. 3H6 1.01.134
and weak we are and cannot shun pursuit. 2.03. 13
but if your title to the crown be weak, | as may 3.03.145
which are so weak of courage and in judgment 4.01. 12
and, often but attended with weak guard, 4.05. 7
why, i, in this weak piping time of peace, R3 1.01. 24
the king is sickly, weak, and melancholy, | and 1.01.136
if my weak oratory | can from his mother win the 3.01. 37
by sick interpreters (once weak ones) is | not H8 1.02. 82
this burthen, 'tis too weak | ever to get a boy. 2.03. 43
woman, much too weak | t' oppose your cunning. 2.04.106
be their business | with me, a poor weak woman, 3.01. 20
(more near my life, i fear), with my weak wit, 3.01. 72
your virtues | with these weak women's fears. 3.01.169
boat | whose weak untimber'd sides but even now TRO 1.03. 43
and the weak wanton cupid | shall from your neck 3.03.222
or brew it to a weak and colder palate, | the 4.04. 7
to flame in, with such weak breath as this? COR 5.02. 46 P
that shows thee a weak slave, for the weakest ROM 1.01. 13 P
arm'd, | from love's weak childish bow she lives 1.01.211
within the infant rind of this weak flower 2.03. 23
to any gentlewoman, and very weak dealing. 2.04.170 P
here's that which is too weak to be a sinner, TIM 1.02. 58
i am glad that my weak words | have struck but JC 1.02.176
therein, ye gods, you make the weak most strong; 1.03. 91
make a mighty fire | begin it with weak straws. 1.03.108
if these be motives weak, break off betimes, 2.01.116
your weak condition to the raw cold morning. 2.01.236
how weak a thing | the heart of woman is! 2.04. 39
but all's too weak; MAC 1.02. 15
me, and wisdom | to offer up a weak, poor, 4.03. 16
holding a weak supposal of our worth, | or HAM 1.02. 18
lack of wit, together with most weak hams; 2.02.200 P
i pray you, father, being weak, seem so. LR 2.04.201
a poor, infirm, weak, and despis'd old man; 3.02. 20
(alack, too weak the conflict to support!) 5.03.198
shall play the god | with his weak function. OTH 2.03.348
nor from mine own weak merits will i draw | the 3.03.187
one is too poor, too weak for my revenge. 3.03.443
the jove of power make me most weak, most weak,
ANT 3.04. 29
the jove of power make me most weak, most weak, 3.04. 29
and that | my sword, made weak by my affection, 3.11. 67
mine eyes are weak. CYM 2.02. 3
i speak not out of weak surmises, but from proof 3.04. 23 P
so divine | that cravens my weak hand. 3.04. 78
i am weak with toil, yet strong in appetite. 3.06. 37
are | full weak to undertake our wars against 3.07. 5
weak as we are, and almost breathless swim | in TNK pr 24
now, alack, weak sister, | i must no more 1.03. 86
know, weak cousin, | i love emilia, and in that 3.06.125
was i | to be of such a weak and silly mind, VEN 1016
the strongest body shall it make most weak, 1145
my will is strong, past reason's weak removing: LUC 243
such shadows are the weak brain's forgeries, 460
in his hold–fast foot the weak mouse panteth. 555
to whose weak ruins muster troops of cares, | to 720
in thy weak hive a wand'ring wasp hath crept, 839
their father was too weak, and they too strong, 865
unprofitable sounds, weak arbitrators! 1017
the weak oppress'd, th' impression of strange 1242
"mine enemy was strong, my poor self weak | (and 1646
but through his lips do throng | weak words, so 1784
such childish humor from weak minds proceeds; 1825
youth is hot and bold, age is weak and cold, PP 12. 7
th' offender's sorrow lends but weak relief | to SON 34.11
is strength'ned, though more weak in seeming, 102. 1
weak sights their sickly radiance do amend; LC 214
WEAK–BUILT 1 FR 0.0001 REL FR 1 V 0 P
though weak–built hopes persuade him to LUC 130
WEAKEN 1 FR 0.0001 REL FR 1 V 0 P
dirt, | to weaken /or discredit our exposure, TRO 1.03.195
WEAKENS 4 FR 0.0004 REL FR 4 V 0 P
either his notion weakens, his discernings | are LR 1.04.228
with drugs or minerals | that weakens motion. OTH 1.02. 75
which some will say | weakens his price, and TNK 5.04. 52
strength's abundance weakens his own heart, | so SON 23. 4
WEAKER 14 FR 0.0015 REL FR 10 V 4 P
have i means much weaker | than you may call to TMP 5.01.146
"for jaquenetta (so is the weaker vessel called) LLL 1.01.272 P
may turn by fortune from the weaker hand: MV 2.01. 34
or charles, or something weaker, masters thee. AYL 1.02.260
but i must comfort the weaker vessel, as doublet 2.04. 6 P
and that must be you, you are the weaker vessel, 2H4 2.04. 60 P
valiant, | but i am weaker than a woman's tear, TRO 1.01. 9
rais'd only that the weaker sort may wish | good COR 4.06. 70
and therefore women, being the weaker vessels, ROM 1.01. 16 P
your grace has laid the odds a' th' weaker side. HAM 5.02.261
strong enobarb | is weaker than the wine, and ANT 2.07.123
you between, | and save poor me, the weaker. PER 4.01. 90
our kinsman | (then weaker than your eyes) laid TNK 1.01. 67
(and far the weaker with so strong a fear), | my LUC 1647
WEAKEST 5 FR 0.0005 REL FR 4 V 1 P
the weakest kind of fruit | drops earliest to MV 4.01.115
oft does them by the weakest minister: AWW 2.01.137
such things as might offend the weakest spleen TRO 2.02.128
a weak slave, for the weakest goes to the wall. ROM 1.01. 13 P
conceit in weakest bodies strongest works, HAM 3.04.114
WEAK–HEARTED 1 FR 0.0001 REL FR 1 V 0 P
far | than my weak–hearted enemies dare offer. H8 3.02.390
WEAK–HING'D 1 FR 0.0001 REL FR 1 V 0 P
accusation | than your own weak–hing'd fancy) WT 2.03.119
WEAKLING 2 FR 0.0002 REL FR 2 V 0 P
and, weakling, warwick takes his gift again, 3H6 5.01. 37
myself a weakling, do not then ensnare me; LUC 584
WEAKLY 4 FR 0.0004 REL FR 3 V 1 P
i will not adventure my discretion so weakly. TMP 2.01.188 P
sure they found some place | but weakly guarded, 1H6 2.01. 74
then you are weakly made; H8 2.03. 40
are weakly fortress'd from a world of harms. LUC 28
WEAK–MADE 1 FR 0.0001 REL FR 1 V 0 P
make weak–made women tenants to their shame. LUC 1260
WEAK'NED 2 FR 0.0002 REL FR 2 V 0 P
in shape and mind | transform'd and weak'ned? R2 5.01. 27
weak'ned with grief, being now enrag'd with 2H4 1.01.144
WEAKNESS 28 FR 0.0031 REL FR 26 V 2 P
my father's loss, the weakness which i feel, TMP 1.02.488
bear with my weakness, my old brain is troubled. 4.01.159
but only he, | owe and succeed thy weakness. MM 2.04.123
whose weakness, married to thy /stronger state, ERR 2.02.175
woo | the means of weakness and debility; AYL 2.03. 51
our strength as weak, our weakness past compare,
SHR 5.02.174
amaz'd me more | than i dare blame my weakness.
AWW 2.01. 85
it is but weakness | to bear the matter thus — WT 2.03. 1
to bear the matter thus — mere weakness. 2.03. 2
weakness possesseth me, and i am faint. JN 5.03. 17
gives in your weakness strength unto your foe, R2 3.02.181
shall repent his folly, see his weakness, and H5 3.06.124 P
no way to that, for weakness, which she ent'red. 1H6 3.02. 25
'twere childish weakness to lament or fear. 3H6 5.04. 38
bear with her weakness, which i think proceeds R3 1.03. 28
who grieves much for your weakness, and by me H8 4.02.117
to men that understand you, words and weakness. 5.02.107
troy in our weakness stands, not in her strength TRO 1.03.137
from my weakness draws | my very soul of counsel 3.02.132

know'st | thy country's strength and weakness — COR 4.05.140
i think it is the weakness of mine eyes | that JC 4.03.276
thence to a watch, thence into a weakness, HAM 2.02.148
perhaps, | out of my weakness and my melancholy, 2.02.601
and dare not task my weakness with any more. OTH 2.03. 42 P
o noble weakness! ANT 5.02.344
labor through, | our gain but life and weakness. TNK 1.02. 12
with cold–pale weakness numbs each feeling part: VEN 892
with mine own weakness being best acquainted, SON 88. 5
WEAL 16 FR 0.0018 REL FR 16 V 0 P
we do no further ask | than whereupon our weal, JN 4.02. 65
counts it your weal he have his liberty. 4.02. 66
and sit at chiefest stern of public weal. 1H6 1.01.177
the special watchmen of our english weal, | i 3.01. 66
roan | and will be partner of your weal or woe. 3.02. 92
tends to god's glory and my country's weal. 5.01. 27
rightly | touching the weal a' th' common, you COR 1.01.151
that you bear | i' th' body of the weal; 2.03.181
innovator, | a foe to th' public weal. 3.01.175
brief sounds determine my weal or woe. ROM 3.02. 51
to foresee, | smells from the general weal. TIM 4.03.160
ere humane statute purg'd the gentle weal; MAC 3.04. 75
meet we the med'cine of the sickly weal, | and 5.02. 27
that spirit upon whose weal depends and rests HAM 3.03. 14
which, in the tender of a wholesome weal, LR 1.04.211
thy weal and woe are both of them extremes; VEN 987
WEAL–BALANC'D 1 FR 0.0001 REL FR 1 V 0 P
by cold gradation and weal–balanc'd form, | we MM 4.03.100
WEALD *(see wild*)*
WEALSMEN 1 FR 0.0001 REL FR 0 V 1 P
meeting two such wealsmen as you are (i cannot COR 2.01. 54 P
WEALTH 76 FR 0.0086 REL FR 67 V 9 P
well of his wealth; but of himself, so, so. TGV 1.02. 13
faults than hairs, and more wealth than faults." 3.01.354 P
"and more wealth than faults." 3.01.367 P
then know that i have little wealth to lose. 4.01. 11
the wealth i have waits on my consent, and my WIV 3.02. 76 P
in this kind for the wealth of windsor castle. 3.03.217 P
expense, | i seek to heal it only by his wealth. 3.04. 6
albeit i will confess thy father's wealth | was 3.04. 13
our wealth increas'd | by prosperous voyages i ERR 1.01. 39
if you did wed my sister for her wealth, | then 3.02. 5
his word might bear my wealth at any time. 5.01. 8
hath he not lost much wealth by wrack of sea? 5.01. 49
for it is all the wealth that he hath left to be ADO 1.01. 70 P
to love, to wealth, to pomp, i pine and die, LLL 1.01. 31
for all the wealth that ever i did see, | i 4.03.147
i freely told you all the wealth i had | ran in MV 3.02.254
wilt thou show the whole wealth of thy wit in an 3.05. 56 P
to let the wretched man outlive his wealth, | to 4.01.269
and yet, thy wealth being forfeit to the state, 4.01.365
for half thy wealth, it is antonio's; 4.01.370
finger, for the wealth | that the world masters. 5.01.173
i once did lend my body for his wealth, | which, 5.01.249
and get our jewels and our wealth together, AYL 1.03.134
leaving his wealth and ease | a stubborn will to 2.05. 52
wife | (as wealth is burthen of my wooing dance) SHR 1.02. 68
help thee to a wife | with wealth enough, and 1.02. 86
a merchant of incomparable wealth. 4.02. 98
honor and wealth from me. AWW 2.03.144
i am not worthy of the wealth i owe, | nor dare 2.05. 79
that hubert, for the wealth of all the world, JN 4.01.130
bound them, and were masters of their wealth. 1H4 2.04.254 P
good | to set the exact wealth of all our states 4.01. 46
beside, his wealth doth warrant a liberal dower, 1H6 5.05. 46
to choose for wealth and not for perfect love. 5.05. 50
having neither subject, wealth, nor diadem. 2H6 4.01. 82
have i affected wealth or honor? 4.07. 98
or gather wealth, i care not with what envy. 4.10. 21
i have not been desirous of their wealth, | nor 3H6 4.08. 44
which ever yet | affected eminence, wealth, H8 2.03. 29
what piles of wealth hath he accumulated | to 3.02.107
of all that world of wealth i have drawn 3.02.211
of gleaning all the land's wealth into one, 3.02.284
with such a costly loss of wealth and friends. TRO 4.01. 61
would half my wealth | would buy this for a lie! COR 4.06.159
i do dream, would all my wealth would wake me! TIT 2.04. 13
i would not for the wealth of all this town ROM 1.05. 69
excess | i cannot sum up sum of half my wealth. 2.06. 34
honest fools lay out their wealth on curtsies. TIM 1.02.235
but i would not, for the wealth of athens, i had 3.02. 51 P
me, | i would have put my wealth into donation, 3.02. 83
who cannot keep his wealth must keep his house. 3.03. 41
i know my lord hath spent of timon's wealth, 3.04. 26
the latest of my wealth i'll share amongst you. 4.02. 23
who would not wish to be from wealth exempt, 4.02. 31
hadst thou wealth again, | rascals should have't 4.03.217
were all the wealth i have shut up in thee, 4.03.279
take wealth and lives together, | do, /villains, 4.03.433
and whilst this poor wealth lasts | to entertain 4.03.488
that you had power and wealth | to requite me by 4.03.521
even such heaps and sums of love and wealth | as 5.01.152
good and loyal, | destroying them for wealth. MAC 4.03. 84
this is th' imposthume of much wealth and peace, HAM 4.04. 27
pow'r that made me, | i tell you all her wealth. LR 1.01.208
or if there were wealth enough for the /purchase CYM 1.04. 83 P
either of honor, office, wealth, and calling, STM III 15
what priceless wealth the heavens had him lent LUC 17
is but to nurse the life | with honor, wealth, 142
honor for wealth, and oft that wealth doth cost 146
and oft that wealth doth cost | the death of all 146
thy sweet love rememb'red such wealth brings, SON 29.13
for whether beauty, birth, or wealth, or wit, 37. 5
to show what wealth she had | in days long since 67.13
as 'twixt a miser and his wealth is found: 75. 4
some in their wealth, some in their body's force 91. 2
richer than wealth, prouder than garments' cost, 91.10
those impediments stand forth | of wealth, of LC 270
WEALTHIEST 1 FR 0.0001 REL FR 1 V 0 P
and therein wealthiest | that i protest i simply AWW 2.03. 66
WEALTHILY 2 FR 0.0002 REL FR 2 V 0 P
seas, | i come to wive it wealthily in padua; SHR 1.02. 75
if wealthily, then happily in padua. 1.02. 76
WEALTH'S 1 FR 0.0001 REL FR 1 V 0 P
then for her wealth's sake use her with more ERR 3.02. 6
WEALTHY 12 FR 0.0013 REL FR 12 V 0 P
and see my wealthy andrew /dock'd in sand, MV 1.01. 27
tubal, a wealthy hebrew of my tribe, | will 1.03. 57
night | did jessica steal from the wealthy jew, 5.01. 15
oath, | i will be married to a wealthy widow, SHR 4.02. 37
her dowry wealthy, and of worthy birth; 4.05. 65
and all the wealthy kingdoms of the west, 2H6 1.01.154
the people liberal, valiant, active, wealthy, 4.07. 63
yet not so wealthy as an english yeoman. 3H6 1.04.123
i am wealthy in my friends. TIM 2.02.184
and now ventidius is wealthy too, | whom he 3.03. 3
the wealthy curled /darlings of our nation, OTH 1.02. 68
of corn, | curling the wealthy ears, never flew. TNK 2.03. 78
WEAN *(also wain*)*
WEAN 2 FR 0.0002 REL FR 2 V 0 P
take all and wean it, it may prove an ox. LLL 5.02.250
people's hearts, and wean them from themselves. TIT 1.01.211
WEAN'D 1 FR 0.0001 REL FR 1 V 0 P
and she was wean'd — i never shall forget it — ROM 1.03. 24
WEAPON 28 FR 0.0031 REL FR 18 V 10 P
with this stick, | and make thy weapon drop. TMP 1.02.474
mine host of de jarteer to measure our weapon. WIV 1.04.119 P
nay, good master parson, keep in your weapon. 3.01. 74 P
draw forth thy weapon, we are beset with thieves SHR 3.02.236
not what mischief he does, if his weapon be out. 2H4 2.01. 15 P
so that skill in the weapon is nothing without 4.03.113 P
handle, or use any sword, weapon, or dagger, 1H6 1.03. 78 P
spoils, | using no other weapon but his name. 2.01. 81
men, | forbidden late to carry any weapon, 3.01. 79
take away his weapon. 2H6 2.03. 95 P
quake, | shake he his weapon at us and pass by. 4.08. 18
to my blade | shall rust upon my weapon, till 3H6 1.03. 51
ah, kill me with thy weapon, not with words! 5.06. 26
what, would you have my weapon, little lord? R3 3.01.122
and with thy weapon nothing dar'st perform! TIT 2.01. 59
wherefore stand'st thou with thy weapon drawn? 3.01. 48
with this, my weapon drawn, i rush'd upon him, 5.01. 37
my naked weapon is out. ROM 1.01. 33 P
i had, my weapon should quickly have been out. 2.04.158 P
sir, for /his weapon, but in the imputation laid HAM 5.02.141 P
what's his weapon? 5.02.144 P
his body — horse to ride, and weapon to wear; LR 3.04.137
take you this weapon | which i have /here OTH 5.02.239
i have another weapon in this chamber; 5.02.252
thou hast no weapon, and perforce must suffer. 5.02.256
behold, i have a weapon; 5.02.259
this did i fear, but thought he had no weapon; 5.02.360
bent, or a sharp weapon | in a soft sheath; TNK 5.03. 42
WEAPON'D 1 FR 0.0001 REL FR 1 V 0 P
be not afraid though you do see me weapon'd; OTH 5.02.266
WEAPON'S 1 FR 0.0001 REL FR 1 V 0 P
news, i think, hath turn'd your weapon's edge; 2H6 2.01.176
/WEAPONS 1 FR 0.0001 REL FR 1 V 0 P
/that /their /weapons /only | /seem'd /on /our 2H4 1.01.197
WEAPONS 38 FR 0.0043 REL FR 26 V 12 P
mine eyes open'd, | i saw their weapons drawn. TMP 2.01.320
let's draw our weapons. 2.01.322
host hath had the measuring of their weapons, WIV 2.01.208 P
what weapons is he? 3.01. 30 P
no weapons, sir. 3.01. 31 P
it appears so by his weapons. 3.01. 71 P
vice, and they are dangerous weapons for maids. ADO 5.02. 22 P
mounsieur, get you your weapons in your hand, MND 4.01. 11 P
with the same food, hurt with the same weapons, MV 3.01. 61 P
alas, put up your naked weapons, put up your 2H4 2.04.207 P
your naked weapons, put up your naked weapons. 2.04.207 P
'a breaks words, and keeps whole weapons. H5 3.02. 36 P
his weapons holy saws of sacred writ, | his 2H6 1.03. 58
you put sharp weapons in a madman's hands. 3.01.347
your wrathful weapons drawn | here in our 3.02.237
mark'd for the gallows, lay your weapons down, 4.02.123
and if words will not, then our weapons shall. 5.01.140
their weapons like to lightning came and went; 3H6 2.01.129
empale him with your weapons round about, | in TRO 5.07. 5
weapons, weapons, weapons! COR 3.01.184
weapons, weapons, weapons! 3.01.184
weapons, weapons, weapons! 3.01.184
masters, lay down your weapons. 3.01.329
sent by me | the goodliest weapons of his armory TIT 4.02. 11
and sends them weapons wrapp'd about with lines 4.02. 27
throw your mistempered weapons to the ground, ROM 1.01. 87
draw, benvolio, beat down their weapons. 3.01. 86
and, waving our red weapons o'er our heads, JC 3.01.109
but swords i smile at, weapons laugh to scorn, MAC 5.07. 12
that's two of his weapons — but well. HAM 5.02.146 P
weapons? arms? what's the matter here? LR 2.02. 47 P
and let not women's weapons, water–drops, 2.04.277
get weapons, ho! OTH 1.01.181
command with years | than with your weapons. 1.02. 61
men do their broken weapons rather use | than 1.03.174
one comes in his shirt, with light and weapons. 5.01. 47
he has no weapons, | he cannot run, the jingling TNK 3.02. 13
to see their youthful sons bright weapons wield, LUC 1432
/WEAR 4 FR 0.0004 REL FR 3 V 1 P
brooch and the toothpick, which /wear not now. AWW 1.01.158 P
though happily her careless /wear) i followed TNK 1.03. 73
harden lust, though marble /wear with raining. LUC 560
thy glass will show thee how thy beauties /wear, SON 77. 1
WEAR 200 FR 0.0226 REL FR 146 V 54 P
if these be true spies which i wear in my head, TMP 5.01.259 P
wear out thy youth with shapeless idleness. TGV 1.01. 8
what compass will you wear your farthingale?" 2.07. 51
how shall i fashion me to wear a cloak? 3.01.135
i'll wear a boot, to make it somewhat rounder. 5.02. 6
of troy become, | and by my side wear steel? WIV 1.03. 76
does he not wear a great round beard, like a 1.04. 20 P
impression of keen whips i'ld wear as rubies, MM 2.04.101
indeed will i not, pompey, it is not the wear. 3.02. 75 P
deny | this chain which now you wear so openly. ERR 5.01. 17
one man but he will wear his cap with suspicion? ADO 1.01.198 P
thy neck into a yoke, wear the print of it, and 1.01.201 P
what fashion will you wear the garland of? 2.01.188 P
you must wear it one way, for the prince hath 2.01.191 P
your grace is too costly to wear every day. 2.01.329 P
let her wear it out with good counsel. 2.03.201 P
impossible, she may wear her heart out first. 2.03.203 P
a child his new coat and forbid him to wear it. 3.02. 7 P
no, pray thee, good meg, i'll wear this. 3.04. 8 P
i'll wear none but this. 3.04. 12 P
god give me joy to wear it, for my heart is 3.04. 24 P
not seen enough, you should wear it in your cap. 3.04. 71 P
win me and wear me, let him answer me. 5.01. 82
dost thou wear thy wit by thy side? 5.01.126 P
'a shall wear nothing handsome about him. 5.04.104 P
and wear his colors like a tumbler's hoop! LLL 3.01.188
hold, rosaline, this favor thou shalt wear, 5.02.130
come on then, wear the favors most in sight. 5.02.136
pardon me, sir, this jewel did she wear, | and 5.02.456
weeds of athens he doth wear: MND 2.02. 71
to wear away this long age of three hours 5.01. 33
wear prayer–books in my pocket, look demurely, MV 2.02.192
none presume | to wear an undeserved dignity. 2.09. 40
sand, wear yet upon their chins | the beards of 3.02. 84
making them lightest that wear most of it. 3.02. 91
two, | and wear my dagger with the braver grace, 3.04. 65
me your gloves, i'll wear them for your sake, 4.01.426
that you would wear it till your hour of death, 5.01.153
the clerk will ne'er wear hair on 's face that 5.01.158
gentleman, | wear this for me; AYL 1.02.246
with weeping tears, "wear these for my sake." 2.04. 53 P
motley's the only wear. 2.07. 34
i earn that i eat, get that i wear, owe no man 3.02. 74 P
look you lisp and wear strange suits; 4.01. 34 P
his leather skin and horns to wear. 4.02. 11
take thou no scorn to wear the horn, | it was a 4.02. 13
me to see thee wear thy heart in a scarf! 5.02. 20 P
suit, | and ask him what apparel he will wear; SHR in.1. 60
what raiment will your honor wear to–day? in.2. 4
ne'er ask me what raiment i'll wear, for i have in.2. 8 P
who knows not where a wasp does wear his sting? 2.01.213
could i repair what she will wear in me, | as i 3.02.118
time, | and gentlewomen wear such caps as these. 4.03. 70
what 'cerns it you if i wear pearl and gold? 5.01. 75 P
virtue of a good wing, and i like the wear well. AWW 1.01.205 P
it will wear the surplice of humility over the 1.03. 94 P
for they wear themselves in the cap of the time; 2.01. 53 P
day and night | must wear your spirits low; 5.01. 2
one, | to wear your gentle limbs in my affairs, 5.01. 4
i have seen her wear it, and she reckon'd it 5.03. 90
i am sure i saw her wear it. 5.03. 91
as much to say as i wear not motley in my brain. TN 1.05. 57 P
here, wear this jewel for me, 'tis my picture. 3.04.208
certain, or forswear to wear iron about you. 3.04.252 P
that wear upon your virgin branches yet | your WT 4.04.115
will they wear their plackets where they should 4.04.243 P
this ungodly day | wear out the /day in peace; JN 3.01.110
thou wear a lion's hide! 3.01.128
creature pluck a glove | and wear it as a favor, R2 5.03. 18
and for his sake wear the detested blot | of 1H4 1.03.162
so he that doth redeem her thence might wear 1.03.206
geese, i'll never wear hair on my face more. 2.04.139 P
son, | when i will wear a garment all of blood, 3.02.135
to all those | that wear those colors on them. 5.04. 27
smoothy–pates do now wear nothing but high shoes 2H4 1.02. 38 P
put the fashion on | and wear it in my heart. 5.02. 53
they could never wear such heavy head–pieces. H5 3.07.138 P
do not you wear your dagger in your cap that day 4.01. 56 P
gage of thine, and i will wear it in my bonnet; 4.01.208 P
this will i also wear in my cap. 4.01.213 P
it yearns me not if men my garments wear; 4.03. 26
takes no scorn to wear the leek upon saint 4.07.102 P
i wear it for a memorable honor; 4.07.104
as he was a soldier, he would wear if alive, i 4.07.129 P
wear thou this favor for me and stick it in thy 4.07.153 P
i by bargain should | wear it myself. 4.07.175
it to in change promis'd to wear it in his cap. 4.08. 30 P
and wear it for an honor in thy cap | till i do 4.08. 59
but why wear you your leek to–day? 5.01. 1 P
i will be so bold as to wear it in my cap till i 5.01. 12 P
i wear out my suit. 5.02.128 P
and thou shalt wear me, if thou wear me, better 5.02.232 P
and thou shalt wear me, if thou wear me, better 5.02.233 P
your several dwelling–places, and not to wear, 1H6 1.03. 77 P
i'll find friends to wear my bleeding roses, 2.04. 72
these my friends in spite of thee shall wear. 2.04.106
hate, | will i for ever and my faction wear, 2.04.109
pole, | will i upon thy party wear this rose. 2.04.123
in your behalf still will i wear the same. 2.04.130
disgracing of these colors that i wear | in 3.04. 29
or whether that such cowards ought to wear 4.01. 28
tongue, | upbraided me about the rose i wear, 4.01. 91
i see no reason, if i wear this rose, | that any 4.01.152
fist, | nor wear the diadem upon his head, 2H6 1.01.246
in this place most master wear no breeches, 1.03.146
as thus | to name the several colors we do wear. 2.01.126
i wear no knife to slaughter sleeping men, | but 3.02.197
thou oughtst not to let thy horse wear a cloak, 4.07. 50 P
the realm shall not wear a head on his shoulders 4.07.120 P
but thou shalt wear it as a herald's coat, | to 4.10. 70
staff, | this day i'll wear aloft my burgonet, 5.01.204
think | how sweet a thing it is to wear a crown, 3H6 1.02. 29
until the white rose that i wear be dy'd | even 1.02. 33
york cannot speak unless he wear a crown. 1.04. 93
and yet be seen to wear a woman's face? 1.04.140
you that are king, though he do wear the crown, 2.02. 90
rewards | as victors wear at the olympian games. 2.03. 53
i wear the willow garland for his sake. 3.03.228
i'll wear the willow garland for his sake." 4.01.100
but henry now shall wear the english crown, 4.03. 49
warwick, although my head still wear the crown, 4.06. 23
his head by nature fram'd to wear a crown, | his 4.06. 72
the king, | to be her men and wear her livery. R3 1.01. 80
vouchsafe to wear this ring. 1.02.201
wear both of them, for both of them are thine. 1.02.205
it is too heavy for your grace to wear. 3.01.120
till richard wear the garland of the realm. 3.02. 40
how? wear the garland? dost thou mean the crown? 3.02. 41
might better wear their heads | than some that 3.02. 92
some that have accus'd them wear their hats. 3.02. 93
but shall we wear these glories for a day? 4.02. 5
wear it, enjoy it, and make much of it. 5.05. 7
a glist'ring grief | and wear a golden sorrow. H8 2.03. 22
to wear our mortal state to come with her, 2.04.229
which i feel | i am not worthy yet to wear. 4.02. 92
a man may wear it on both sides, like a leather TRO 3.03.264 P
wear this sleeve. 4.04. 70
with truth and plainness i do wear mine bare. 4.04.106

to–morrow will i wear it on my helm, | and 5.02. 93
stand fast, and wear a castle on thy head! 5.02.187
you wear out a good wholesome forenoon in COR 2.01. 69 P
dear, | such eyes the widows in corioles wear, 2.01.178
whose double bosoms seems to wear one heart, 4.04. 13
upon his bloody finger he doth wear | a precious TIT 2.03.226
sick and green, | and none but fools do wear it; ROM 2.02. 9
will ne'er wear out the everlasting flint; 2.06. 17
but i'll be hang'd, sir, if he wear your livery. 3.01. 57
that hath new robes | and may not wear them. 3.02. 31
accept it and wear it, | kind my lord. TIM 1.02.170
and e'en as if your lord should wear rich jewels 3.04. 23
his outsides, to wear them like his raiment, 3.05. 33
yet do our hearts wear timon's livery, | that 4.02. 17
wear them, betray with them. 4.03.147
thy flatterers yet wear silk, drink wine, lie 4.03.206
nev'r did poor steward wear a truer grief | for 4.03.480
sir, to wear out their shoes, to get myself into JC 1.01. 29 P
and he shall wear his crown by sea and land, 1.03. 87
i know where i will wear this dagger then; 1.03. 89
chose out, brave caius, | to wear a kerchief! 2.01.315
but i shame | to wear a heart so white. MAC 2.02. 62
who wear our health but sickly in his life, 3.01.106
all things foul would wear the brows of grace, 4.03. 23
wear thou thy wrongs, | the title is affeer'd! 4.03. 33
or wear it on my sword, yet my poor country 4.03. 46
slave, and i will wear him | in my heart's core, HAM 3.02. 72
nay then let the dev'l wear black, for i'll have 3.02.129 P
you may wear your rue with a difference. 4.05.183 P
as peace should still her wheaten garland wear 5.02. 41
follow him, thou must needs wear my coxcomb. LR 1.04.104 P
foppish, | and know not how their wits to wear, 1.04.168
that such a slave as this should wear a sword, 2.02. 72
fathers that wear rags | do make their children 2.04. 48
his body — horse to ride, and weapon to wear; 3.04.137
if you did wear a beard upon your chin, | i'ld 3.07. 76
wear this; 4.02. 21
this great world | shall so wear out to nought. 4.06.135
and we'll wear out, | in a wall'd prison, packs 5.03. 17
after | but i will wear my heart upon my sleeve OTH 1.01. 64
'tis as i should entreat you wear your gloves, 3.03. 77
wear your eyes thus, not jealious nor secure. 3.03.198
wear thy good rapier bare, and put it home. 5.01. 2
sir, you may not live to wear | all your true ANT 4.14.133
lips that power, | thus would i wear them out. 4.15. 40
although they wear their faces to the bent | of CYM 1.01. 13
for my sake wear this: 1.01.121
you may wear her in title yours; 1.04. 88 P
must wear the print of his remembrance on't, 2.03. 43
if you could wear a mind | dark as your fortune 3.04.143
from this time forth | i wear it as your enemy. 3.05. 14
for i wear not | my dagger in my mouth. 4.02. 78
borne | as i wear mine, are titles but of scorn. 5.02. 7
twelve moons more she'll wear diana's livery; PER 2.05. 10
wear the girlond | with joy that you have won. TNK 5.03.130
"torches are made to light, jewels to wear, VEN 163
o, never let their crimson liveries wear! 506
"bonnet nor veil henceforth no creature wear! 1081
and wear their brave state out of memory: SON 15. 8
that wear this world out to the ending doom. 55.12
whose bare outbragg'd the web it seem'd to wear;
LC 95
eyes | what rocky heart to water will not wear? 291

WEAR–A 1 FR 0.0001 REL FR 1 V 0 P
head | of the new'st and fin'st, fin'st wear–a? WT 4.04.320

WEARER 2 FR 0.0002 REL FR 2 V 0 P
were purchas'd by the merit of the wearer! MV 2.09. 43
jupiter, | were i the wearer of antonio's beard, ANT 2.02. 7

WEARERS 1 FR 0.0001 REL FR 1 V 0 P
them) and the reverence | of the grave wearers. WT 3.01. 6

WEARIED 6 FR 0.0006 REL FR 5 V 1 P
burns, | 'twill weep for having wearied you. TMP 3.01. 19
of love have you wearied your parishioners AYL 3.02.156 P
faint quittance, wearied and outbreath'd, | to 2H4 1.01.108
and there are twenty weak and wearied posts 2.04.356
she like a wearied lamb lies panting there; LUC 737
so woe hath wearied woe, moan tired moan, | that 1363

WEARIES 2 FR 0.0002 REL FR 2 V 0 P
it wearies me, you say it wearies you; MV 1.01. 2
it wearies me, you say it wearies you; 1.01. 2

WEARIEST 1 FR 0.0001 REL FR 1 V 0 P
the weariest and most loathed worldly life MM 3.01.128

WEARILY 1 FR 0.0001 REL FR 1 V 0 P
you look wearily. TMP 3.01. 32

WEARINESS 5 FR 0.0005 REL FR 4 V 1 P
who am myself attach'd with weariness | to th' TMP 3.03. 5
i had thought weariness durst not have attach'd 2H4 2.02. 2 P
weariness | can snore upon the flint, when resty CYM 3.06. 33
bed, | intending weariness with heavy sprite; LUC 121
besides, of weariness he did complain him, | and 845

/WEARING 1 FR 0.0001 REL FR 0 V 1 P
/that /many /wearing /rapiers /are /afraid /of HAM 2.02.343 P

WEARING 16 FR 0.0018 REL FR 11 V 5 P
why, he comes in like a perjure, wearing papers. LLL 4.03. 46
wearing thy hearer in thy mistress' praise, AYL 2.04. 38
thing in him by wearing his apparel neatly. AWW 4.03.146 P
you have obscur'd | with a swain's wearing, and WT 4.04. 9
laughter the wearing out of six fashions, which 2H4 5.01. 79 P
be you contented, wearing now the garland, | to 5.02. 84
wearing the crown of france, till satisfied H5 1.02. 80
did grow, wearing leeks in their monmouth caps, 4.07. 99 P
the very train of her worst wearing gown | was 2H6 1.03. 85
the jest may remain, after the wearing, soly ROM 2.04. 63 P
with a tailor for wearing his new doublet before 3.01. 27 P
lord, | you mend the jewel by the wearing it. TIM 1.01.172
vacant lie, | for thy best use and wearing. 5.01.143
emilia, | give me my nightly wearing, and adieu. OTH 4.03. 16
or is't not | too dull for your good wearing? CYM 2.04. 41
we will nothing pay | for wearing our own noses. 3.01. 14

WEARISOME 3 FR 0.0003 REL FR 3 V 0 P
alas, the way is wearisome and long. TGV 2.07. 8
draws out our miles and makes them wearisome, R2 2.03. 5
on the way | hath made it tedious, wearisome, R3 3.01. 5

WEARS 45 FR 0.0050 REL FR 29 V 16 P
i say, time wears, hold up your head and mince. WIV 5.01. 7 P
lamentation, which she yet wears for his sake; MM 3.01.229 P
he wears his faith but as the fashion of his hat ADO 1.01. 75 P
see that the fashion wears out more apparel than 3.03.140 P
i know him, 'a wears a lock. 3.03.170 P
they say he wears a key in his ear and a lock 5.01.308 P
and that 'a wears next his heart for a favor. LLL 5.02.714 P
wears yet a precious jewel in his head; AYL 2.01. 14
the morning wears, 'tis time we were at church. SHR 3.02.111
an old courtier, wears her cap out of fashion, AWW 1.01.156 P
he wears his honor in a box unseen, | that hugs 2.03.279
a ring the county wears, | that downward hath 3.07. 22
an elder than herself, so wears she to him; TN 2.04. 30
he that wears her like her medal hanging | about WT 1.02.307
as clear | as friendship wears at feasts, keep 1.02.344
are rich, but he wears them not handsomely. 4.04.749 P
the more it is wasted, the sooner it wears. 1H4 2.04.402 P
did give him that same royalty he wears, | and 4.03. 55
a good grace, and wears his boots very smooth, 2H4 2.04.248 P
uneasy lies the head that wears a crown. 3.01. 31
and he that wears the crown immortally | long 4.05.143
thee, constable, my mistress wears his own hair. H5 3.07. 60 P
not, | in that he wears the badge of somerset. 1H6 4.01.177
plies her hard, and much rain wears the marble. 3H6 3.02. 50
who wears his wit in his belly and his guts in TRO 2.01. 73 P
he wears his tongue in 's arms. 3.03.270 P
that caius martius | wears this war's garland; COR 1.09. 60
who wears my stripes impress'd upon him, that 5.06.107
it wears, sir, as it grows. TIM 1.01. 3
and he wears jewels now of timon's gift, | for 3.04. 19
and wears upon his baby–brow the round | and top
MAC 4.01. 88
sting thy father's life | now wears his crown. HAM 1.05. 40
the light and careless livery that it wears 4.07. 79
should wear a sword, | who wears no honesty. LR 2.02. 73
hah, ha, he wears cruel garters. 2.04. 7 P
at legs, then he wears wooden nether–stocks. 2.04. 10 P
wears out his time, much like his master's ass, OTH 1.01. 47
tell him he wears the rose | of youth upon him; ANT 3.13. 20
my brother wears thee not the one half so well CYM 4.02.202
whom, o goddess, | wears yet thy silver livery. PER 5.03. 7
the worth that learned charity aye wears. 5.03. 94
he wears a well–steel'd axe, the staff of gold. TNK 4.02.115
about his head he wears the winner's oak, | and 4.02.137
"who wears a garment shapeless and unfinish'd? VEN 415
for with the nightly linen that she wears | he LUC 680

WEAR'ST 4 FR 0.0004 REL FR 3 V 1 P
so thou the garland wear'st successively. 2H4 4.05.201
soldier, why wear'st thou that glove in thy cap? H5 4.07.120 P
than all the complete armor that thou wear'st! R3 4.04.190
nature needs not what thou gorgeous wear'st, LR 2.04.269

/WEARY 3 FR 0.0003 REL FR 2 V 1 P
o jupiter, how /weary are my spirits! AYL 2.04. 1 P
from which even here i slip my /weary head, R3 4.04.112
how /weary, stale, flat, and unprofitable | seem HAM 1.02.133

WEARY 89 FR 0.0100 REL FR 81 V 8 P
you sunburn'd sicklemen, of august weary, | come TMP 4.01.134
moment's mirth | with twenty watchful, weary, TGV 1.01. 31
my tales of love were wont to weary you; 2.04.126
a true–devoted pilgrim is not weary | to measure 2.07. 9
stream, | and make a pastime of each weary step, 2.07. 35
not to be weary with you, he's in prison. MM 1.04. 25
town, | dies ere the weary sun set in the west. ERR 1.02. 7
for with long travel i am stiff and weary. 1.02. 15
tell her, we measure them by weary steps. LLL 5.02.194
how many weary steps | of many weary miles you 5.02.195
steps | of many weary miles you have o'ergone 5.02.196
rest, | but seek the weary beds of people sick. 5.02.822
o weary night, o long and tedious night, | abate MND 3.02.431
never so weary, never so in woe, | bedabbled 3.02.442
snores, | all with weary task foredone. 5.01.374
not for my spirits, if my legs were not weary. AYL 2.04. 3 P
sea, | till that the weary very means do ebb? 2.07. 73
who after me hath many a weary step | limp'd in 2.07.130
i am weary of you. 3.02.284 P
i will weary you then no longer with idle 5.02. 51 P
was ever man so weary? SHR 4.01. 3 P
i am not weary, and 'tis long to night; TN 3.03. 21
i know, sir, we weary you. WT 4.04.333 P
you weary those that refresh us. 4.04.335 P
the stumbling night did part our weary pow'rs? JN 5.05. 18
two men | that vow a long and weary pilgrimage. R2 1.03. 49
the sullen passage of thy weary steps | esteem 1.03.265
but i bethink me what a weary way | from 2.03. 8
by this the weary lords | shall make their way 2.03. 16
his weary joints would gladly rise, i know, 5.03.105
patience is stale, and i am weary of it. 5.05.103
so far afoot, i shall be weary, love. 1H4 2.03. 84
before god, i am exceeding weary. 2H4 2.02. 1 P
weary of solid firmness, melt itself | into the 3.01. 48
the king is weary | of dainty and such picking 4.01.195
hand | will whisper music to my weary spirit. 4.05. 3
i stay too long by thee, i weary thee. 4.05. 93
my tongue is weary, when my legs are too, i will ep 33 P
of color | unto the weary and all–watched night; H5 4.pr. 38
and from my weary limbs | honor is cudgell'd. 5.01. 84
he fighteth as one weary of his life. 1H6 1.02. 26
art thou not weary, john? 4.06. 27
warwick, | let me embrace thee in my weary arms.
3H6 2.03. 45
and still, as you are weary of this weight, R3 1.02. 31
the weary way hath made you melancholy. 3.01. 3
the weary sun hath made a golden set, | and by 5.03. 19
these famish'd beggars weary of their lives, 5.03.329
hour | of my long weary life is come upon me. H8 2.01.133
weary and old with service, to the mercy | of a 3.02.363
is come to lay his weary bones among ye; 4.02. 22
lov'd you night and day | for many weary months. TRO 3.02.115
i am weary, yea, my memory is tir'd. COR 1.09. 91
word, i also am | longer to live most weary, and 4.05. 95
from weary wars against the barbarous goths, TIT 1.01. 28
be found, | being one too many by my weary self, ROM 1.01.128
on | the dashing rocks thy sea–sick weary bark! 5.03.118
kingdoms to my friends, | and ne'er be weary. TIM 1.02.221
i'm weary of this charge, the gods can witness. 3.04. 25
but life, being weary of these worldly bars, JC 1.03. 96
so shall he waste his means, weary his soldiers, 4.03.200
weary sev'nnights, nine times nine, | shall he MAC 1.03. 22
so weary with disasters, tugg'd with fortune, 3.01.111
bear, | to grunt and sweat under a weary life, HAM 3.01. 76
put on what weary negligence you please, | you LR 1.03. 12
/nor crumb, | weary of all, shall want some. 1.04.199
all weary and o'erwatch'd, | take vantage, heavy 2.02.170
they are weary? 2.04. 88
o weary reck'ning! OTH 3.04.176
talk thy tongue weary, speak. CYM 3.04.112
i am throughly weary. 3.06. 36
for want, | but weary for the staleness. PER 5.01. 58
weary of this world's light, have to themselves TNK 1.01.143
i wish his weary soul that falls may win it. 3.06.100
or morn or weary even? VEN 495
"look, the world's comforter, with weary gait, 529
hot, faint, and weary, with her hard embracing, 559
each envious brier his weary legs do scratch, 705
lo here the gentle lark, weary of rest, | from 853
and asks the weary caitiff for his master, | and 914
thus weary of the world, away she hies, | and 1189
fair, | ere he arrive his weary noontide prick, LUC 781
the weary time she cannot entertain, | for now 1361
so sober–sad, so weary, and so mild | (as if 1542
and time doth weary time with her complaining; 1570
where thou wast wont to rest thy weary head, 1621
but when from highmost pitch, with weary car, SON 7. 9
weary with toil, i haste me to my bed, | the 27. 1
way, | when what i seek (my weary travel's end) 50. 2
keep open | my heavy eyelids to the weary night? 61. 2

WEASAND *(see wezand)*

WEASEL 6 FR 0.0006 REL FR 3 V 3 P
out of a song, as a weasel sucks eggs. AYL 2.05. 13 P
a weasel hath not such a deal of spleen | as you 1H4 2.03. 78
to her unguarded nest the weasel (scot) | comes H5 1.02.170
methinks it is like a weasel. HAM 3.02.379 P
it is back'd like a weasel. 3.02.380 P
saucy, and | as quarrellous as the weasel; CYM 3.04.159

WEASELS 1 FR 0.0001 REL FR 1 V 0 P
night–wand'ring weasels shriek to see him there; LUC 307

/WEATHER 1 FR 0.0001 REL FR 1 V 0 P
/no /enemy | /but /winter /and /rough /weather. AYL 2.05. 45

WEATHER 33 FR 0.0037 REL FR 21 V 12 P
they are louder than the weather, or our office. TMP 1.01. 37 P
it is foul weather in us all, good sir, | when 2.01.142
fowl weather? 2.01.143
bush nor shrub to bear off any weather at all. 2.02. 19 P
true root but by the fair weather that you make ADO 1.03. 24 P
fair weather after you! LLL 1.02.144 P
many can brook the weather that love not the 4.02. 33
builds in the weather on the outward wall, MV 2.09. 29
see | no enemy | but winter and rough weather. AYL 2.05. 8
sure together, | as the winter to foul weather. 5.04.136
for, considering the weather, a taller man than SHR 4.01. 10 P
in grain, sir, 'twill endure wind and weather. TN 1.05.238 P
'tis like to be loud weather. WT 3.03. 11
nineteen and two–and–twenty hunt this weather? 3.03. 65 P
both roaring louder than the sea or weather. 3.03.102 P
little better, extremity of weather continuing, 5.02.119 P
not without a storm, | pour down thy weather. JN 4.02.109
and make fair weather in your blust'ring land. 5.01. 21
we'll make foul weather with despised tears; R2 3.03.161
home without boots, and in foul weather too! 1H4 3.01. 67
fie, this is hot weather, gentlemen. 2H4 3.02. 92 P
the day is hot, and the weather, and the wars, H5 3.02.106 P
amiss to cool a man's stomach this hot weather. 2H6 4.10. 9 P
but i must make fair weather yet a while, | till 5.01. 30
two women plac'd together makes cold weather. H8 1.04. 22
mine honor keeps the weather of my fate. TRO 5.03. 26
who's there, besides foul weather? LR 3.01. 1
one minded like the weather, most unquietly. 3.01. 2
nay, my leaves, | and left me bare to weather. CYM 3.03. 64
to touch the fire, the weather being cold? VEN 402
like many clouds consulting for foul weather. 972
no cloudy show of stormy blust'ring weather LUC 115
youth like summer morn, age like winter weather,
PP 12. 3

WEATHER–BEATEN 1 FR 0.0001 REL FR 1 V 0 P
him | bootless home and weather–beaten back. 1H4 3.01. 66

WEATHER–BITTEN 1 FR 0.0001 REL FR 0 V 1 P
stands by like a weather–bitten conduit of many WT 5.02. 55 P

WEATHERCOCK 3 FR 0.0003 REL FR 2 V 1 P
on a man's face, or a weathercock on a steeple! TGV 2.01.136
where had you this pretty weathercock? WIV 3.02. 18 P
what weathercock? LLL 4.01. 95

WEATHER–FENDS 1 FR 0.0001 REL FR 1 V 0 P
in the line–grove which weather–fends your cell; TMP 5.01. 10

WEATHERS 1 FR 0.0001 REL FR 1 V 0 P
whose honesty till now | endur'd all weathers. WT 5.01.195

WEAV'D *(also woven)*

WEAV'D 2 FR 0.0002 REL FR 2 V 0 P
be't when they weav'd the sleided silk | with PER 4.ch. 21
their knot of love | tied, weav'd, entangled, TNK 1.03. 42

//WEAV'D–UP 1 FR 0.0001 REL FR 1 V 0 P
/must /i /ravel /out | /my //weav'd–up /follies? R2 4.01.229

WEAVE 2 FR 0.0002 REL FR 2 V 0 P
and the free maids that weave their thread with TN 2.04. 45
proclaim that i can sing, weave, sew, and dance, PER 4.06.183

WEAVER 5 FR 0.0005 REL FR 0 V 5 P
answer as i call you. nick bottom, the weaver. MND 1.02. 17 P
i pyramus am not pyramus, but bottom the weaver. 3.01. 21 P
that will draw three souls out of one weaver? TN 2.03. 59 P
i would i were a weaver, i could sing psalms, or 1H4 2.04.133 P
and smith the weaver — 2H6 4.02. 28 P

WEAVER'S 1 FR 0.0001 REL FR 0 V 1 P
i fear not goliah with a weaver's beam, because WIV 5.01. 22 P

WEAVERS 2 FR 0.0002 REL FR 2 V 0 P
the spinsters, carders, fullers, weavers, who, H8 1.02. 33
ha, boys, heigh for the weavers! TNK 2.03. 49

WEAVES 2 FR 0.0002 REL FR 2 V 0 P
weaves tedious snares to trap mine enemies. 2H6 3.01.340
this weaves itself perforce into my business. LR 2.01. 15

WEAVING 1 FR 0.0001 REL FR 1 V 0 P
weaving spiders, come not here; MND 2.02. 20

WEB 12 FR 0.0013 REL FR 8 V 4 P
the web of our life is of a mingled yarn, good AWW 4.03. 71 P
eyes | blind with the pin and web but theirs, WT 1.02.291
troyan, | to have me fold up parca's fatal web? H5 5.01. 20
spider | whose deadly web ensnareth thee about? R3 1.03.242
but spider–like | out of his self–drawing web, H8 1.01. 63
drawing their massy irons and cutting the web! TRO 2.03. 17 P
her traces of the smallest spider web, | her ROM 1.04. 64
he gives the web and the pin, /squinies the eye, LR 3.04.117 P
with as little a web as this will i ensnare as OTH 2.01.168 P

there's magic in the web of it. 3.04. 69
now she unweaves the web that she hath wrought: VEN 991
whose bare outbragg'd the web it seem'd to wear; LC 95

WE'D 1 FR 0.0001 REL FR 0 V 1 P
we'd find no fault with the tithe–woman if i AWW 1.03. 84 P

WED 38 FR 0.0043 REL FR 34 V 4 P
for thurio, he intends, shall wed his daughter; TGV 2.06. 39
in syracusa was i born, and wed | unto a woman, ERR 1.01. 36
if you did wed my sister for her wealth, | then 3.02. 5
if you love her then, to–morrow wed her; ADO 3.02.115 P
in the congregation, where i should wed, there 3.02.125 P
that he would wed me, or else die my lover. LLL 5.02.447
but i will wed thee in another key, | with pomp, MND 1.01. 18
me in this case, | if i refuse to wed demetrius. 1.01. 64
or else to wed demetrius, as he would, | or on 1.01. 88
are april when they woo, december when they wed; AYL 4.01.148 P
or else, refusing me, to wed this shepherd; 5.04. 22
nor ne'er wed woman, if you be not she. 5.04.124
wooing that would thoroughly woo her, wed her, SHR 1.01.144 P
it is, | i would not wed her for a mine of gold. 1.02. 92
any man, | until the elder sister first be wed. 1.02.261
if she deny to wed, i'll crave the day | when i 2.01.179
regard, | to wish me wed to one half lunatic, 2.01.287
who woo'd in haste, and means to wed at leisure. 3.02. 11
yet never means to wed where he hath woo'd. 3.02. 17
a bright particular star | and think to wed it, AWW 1.01. 87
that you come | not to woo honor, but to wed it, 2.01. 15
your bed | find fairer fortune, if you ever wed! 2.03. 92
you are one of those | would have him wed again. WT 5.01. 24
that noble title | your master wed me to. H8 3.01.141
that i must wed | ere he that should be husband ROM 3.05.118
to answer, "i'll not wed, i cannot love; 3.05.185
but, and you will not wed, i'll pardon you. 3.05.187
is it | that makes the wappen'd widow wed again; TIM 4.03. 39
none wed the second but who kill'd the first. HAM 3.02.180
so think thou wilt no second husband wed, | but 3.02.214
you tumbled me, | you promis'd me to wed.'" 4.05. 63
happily, when i shall wed, | that lord whose LR 1.01.100
tells me here, she'll wed the stranger knight, PER 2.05. 16
it pleaseth me so well that i will see you wed, 2.05. 92
no better choice, and think me rarely to wed. 5.01. 69
did wed | at pentapolis the fair thaisa. 5.03. 3
if she refuse me, yet my grave will wed me, TNK 3.06.284
the joys in bed, | one woman would another wed. PP 18.48

WEDDED 18 FR 0.0020 REL FR 17 V 1 P
but, were you wedded, you would bear some sway. ERR 2.01. 28
is she wedded or no? LLL 2.01.211
to theseus must be wedded, and you come | to MND 2.01. 72
shall the pairs of faithful lovers be | wedded, 4.01. 92
now, | that shall be woo'd and wedded in a day. SHR 4.02. 51
i have wedded her, not bedded her, and sworn to AWW 3.02. 21 P
if, one by one, you wedded all the world, | or, WT 5.01. 13
thy daughter shall be wedded to my king, | whom 1H6 5.03.137
the morn that i was wedded to her mother. 5.04. 24
and wedded be thou to the hags of hell, | for 2H6 4.01. 79
heart | than when i first my wedded mistress saw COR 4.05.117
of thy parts, | and thou art wedded to calamity. ROM 3.03. 3
death is my heir, | my daughter he hath wedded. 4.05. 39
she's wedded, | her husband banish'd, she CYM 1.01. 7
a foolish suitor to a wedded lady | that hath 1.06. 2
why did you throw your wedded lady /from you? 5.05.261
euriphile | (whom for the theft i wedded), stole 5.05.341
my wedded lord, i ne'er shall see again, | a PER 3.04. 9

WEDDING 17 FR 0.0019 REL FR 11 V 6 P
wooing, wedding, and repenting, is as a scotch ADO 2.01. 73 P
the wedding, mannerly–modest, as a measure, full 2.01. 76 P
the very night before the intended wedding — 2.02. 46 P
door, for the wedding being there to–morrow, 3.03. 93 P
gone, i say, | i will not to wedding with thee. AYL 3.03.105
let your wedding be to–morrow; 5.02. 13 P
wedding is great juno's crown, | o blessed bond 5.04.141
thou offer'st fairly to thy brothers' wedding: 5.04.167
and have prepar'd great store of wedding cheer, SHR 3.02.186
and every officer his wedding garment on? 4.01. 48 P
since, wedding it, there is such length in grief R2 5.01. 94
this is the happy wedding torch | that joineth 1H6 3.02. 26
our wedding cheer to a sad burial feast; ROM 4.05. 87
i think it was to /see my mother's wedding. HAM 1.02.178
where's my wedding gown? TNK 4.01.109
content, | if we shall keep our wedding there. 5.02. 76
and will perfume me finely against the wedding. 5.02. 89

WEDDING–BED 2 FR 0.0002 REL FR 2 V 0 P
my grave is like to be my wedding–bed. ROM 1.05.135
cords, come, nurse, i'll to my wedding–bed, 3.02.136

WEDDING–DAY 14 FR 0.0015 REL FR 12 V 2 P
ent'red, even the night before her wedding–day. ADO 3.02.114 P
this wedding–day | perhaps is but prolong'd, 4.01.253
and the duchess, on his wedding–day at night. MND 1.02. 7 P
perchance till after theseus' wedding–day. 2.01.139
for you shall hence upon your wedding–day. MV 3.02.311
i must dance barefoot on her wedding–day, | and SHR 2.01. 33
together | that upon sunday is the wedding–day. 2.01.298
venice | to buy apparel 'gainst the wedding–day. 2.01.315
you know to–morrow is the wedding–day. 3.01. 84
why, sir, you know this is your wedding–day. 3.02. 97
upon thy wedding–day? JN 3.01.300
i'll say | a man may weep upon his wedding–day. H8 pr 32
prepare her, wife, against this wedding–day. ROM 3.04. 32
the night before thy wedding–day | hath death 4.05. 35

WEDDING–DOW'R 1 FR 0.0001 REL FR 1 V 0 P
then let her beauty be her wedding–dow'r, | for TGV 3.01. 78

WEDDING–RING 1 FR 0.0001 REL FR 1 V 0 P
and from my false hand cut the wedding–ring, ERR 2.02.137

WEDDING–SHEETS 1 FR 0.0001 REL FR 1 V 0 P
to–night | lay on my bed my wedding–sheets — OTH 4.02.105

WEDG'D *(also wadg'd)*

WEDG'D 1 FR 0.0001 REL FR 1 V 0 P
where a finger | could not be wedg'd in more. H8 4.01. 58

WEDGED 1 FR 0.0001 REL FR 1 V 0 P
as wedged with a sigh, would rive in twain, TRO 1.01. 35

WEDGES 2 FR 0.0002 REL FR 2 V 0 P
wedges of gold, great anchors, heaps of pearl, R3 1.04. 26
blunt wedges rive hard knots; TRO 1.03.316

WEDLOCK 11 FR 0.0012 REL FR 10 V 1 P
she kneels and prays | for happy wedlock hours. MV 5.01. 32
as pigeons bill, so wedlock would be nibbling. AYL 3.03. 81 P
every town, | high wedlock then be honored. 5.04.144
your mother was most true to wedlock, prince, WT 5.01.124
your father's wife did after wedlock bear him; JN 1.01.117
for what is wedlock forced, but a hell, | an age 1H6 5.05. 62
joy, | to him forthwith in holy wedlock bands. 3H6 3.03.243
my bond to wedlock or my love and duty, H8 2.04. 40
that she was false to wedlock? OTH 5.02.142
our life, this daring deed | of fate in wedlock. TNK 1.01.165
decay, | the impious breach of holy wedlock vow; LUC 809

WEDLOCK–HYMN 1 FR 0.0001 REL FR 1 V 0 P
whiles a wedlock–hymn we sing, | feed yourselves AYL 5.04.137

WEDNESDAY *(also wed'sday, we'nsday)*

WEDNESDAY 6 FR 0.0006 REL FR 4 V 2 P
"fair sir, you spet on me on wednesday last, MV 1.03.126
on wednesday next we solemnly proclaim | our R2 4.01.319
on wednesday next our council we | will hold at 1H4 1.01.103
on wednesday next, harry, you shall set forward, 3.02.173
he that died a' wednesday. 5.01.136 P
a sea–coal fire, upon wednesday in wheeson week, 2H4 2.01. 88 P

WED'SDAY 1 FR 0.0001 REL FR 0 V 1 P
'twas no longer ago than wed'sday last, i' good 2H4 2.04. 86 P

WED'ST 1 FR 0.0001 REL FR 1 V 0 P
and, when thou wed'st, let sorrow haunt thy bed; R3 4.01. 73

WEED* 22 FR 0.0024 REL FR 21 V 1 P
but say this weed her love from valentine, | it TGV 3.02. 49
on angelo, | to weed my vice and let his grow! MM 3.02.270
to weed this wormwood from your fructful brain, LLL 5.02.847
skin, | weed wide enough to wrap a fairy in; MND 2.01.256
provided that you weed your better judgments AYL 2.07. 45
which i have sworn to weed and pluck away. R2 2.03.167
he cannot so precisely weed this land | as his 2H4 4.01.203
thus may we gather honey from the weed, | and H5 4.01. 11
so one by one we'll weed them all at last, | and 2H6 1.03. 99
he's a rank weed, sir thomas, | and we must root H8 5.01. 52
with what contempt he wore the humble weed, COR 2.03.221
no funeral rite, nor man in mourning weed, | no TIT 5.03.196
and duller shouldst thou be than the fat weed HAM 1.05. 32
or sow lettuce, set hyssop and weed up /tine, OTH 1.03.322 P
o thou weed! 4.02. 67
i will rob tellus of her weed | to strow thy PER 4.01. 13
they bid thee crop a weed, thou pluck'st a VEN 946
flow'r was nigh, no grass, herb, leaf, or weed, 1055
spots and stains love's modest snow–white weed. LUC 196
will be a totter'd weed, of small worth held: SON 2. 4
the same, | and keep invention in a noted weed, 76. 6
meet, | the basest weed outbraves his dignity: 94.12

WEEDED 1 FR 0.0001 REL FR 1 V 0 P
word thou hast spoke hath weeded from my heart COR 4.05.102

WEEDER–OUT 1 FR 0.0001 REL FR 1 V 0 P
a weeder–out of his proud adversaries, | a R3 1.03.122

WEEDING 1 FR 0.0001 REL FR 1 V 0 P
weeds the corn and still lets grow the weeding. LLL 1.01. 96

WEEDS* 46 FR 0.0052 REL FR 46 V 0 P
the union of your bed with weeds so loathly TMP 4.01. 21
fit me with such weeds | as may beseem some TGV 2.07. 42
(the needful bits and curbs to headstrong weeds) MM 1.03. 20
come let us hence, and put on other weeds, | and ADO 5.03. 30
he weeds the corn and still lets grow the LLL 1.01. 96
hard lodging and thin weeds | nip not the gaudy 5.02.801
weeds of athens he doth wear: MND 2.02. 71
in this town, | where lie my maiden weeds; TN 5.01.255
and let me see thee in thy woman's weeds. 5.01.273
these your unusual weeds to each part of you WT 4.04. 1
the noisome weeds which without profit suck R2 3.04. 38
is full of weeds, her fairest flowers chok'd up, 3.04. 44
the weeds which his broad–spreading leaves did 3.04. 50
most subject is the fattest soil to weeds, | and 2H4 4.04. 54
'tis the spring, and weeds are shallow–rooted; 2H6 3.01. 31
for what doth cherish weeds but gentle air? 3H6 2.06. 21
tell him, my mourning weeds are laid aside, 3.03.229
him," quoth she, "my mourning weeds are done, 4.01.104
herbs have grace, great weeds do grow apace." R3 2.04. 13
sweet flow'rs are slow and weeds make haste. 2.04. 15
you said that idle weeds are fast in growth: 3.01.103
to see great hector in his weeds of peace, | to TRO 3.03.239
as weeds before | a vessel under sail, so men COR 2.02.105
with a proud heart he wore his humble weeds. 2.03.153
hail, rome, victorious in thy mourning weeds! TIT 1.01. 70
away with slavish weeds and servile thoughts! 2.01. 18
me, | and, were they but attired in grave weeds, 3.01. 43
with baleful weeds and precious–juiced flowers. ROM 2.03. 8
which late i noted | in tatt'red weeds, with 5.01. 39
to dew the sovereign flower and drown the weeds. MAC 5.02. 30
thou mixture rank, of midnight weeds collected, HAM 3.02.257
and do not spread the compost on the weeds | to 3.04.151
than settled age his sables and his weeds, 4.07. 80
there, on the pendant boughs her crownet weeds 4.07.172
and all the idle weeds that grow | in our LR 4.04. 5
these weeds are memories of those worser hours; 4.07. 7
then we bring forth weeds | when our quick winds ANT 1.02.109
wild wood–leaves and weeds i ha' strew'd his CYM 4.02.390
me | of these italian weeds and suit myself | as 5.01. 23
scars and bare weeds | the gain o' th' TNK 1.02. 15
as corn o'ergrown by weeds, so heedful fear | is LUC 281
unwholesome weeds take root with precious 870
to thy fair flower add the rank smell of weeds: SON 69.12
lilies that fester smell far worse than weeds. 94.14
weeds among weeds, or flowers with flowers 124. 4
weeds among weeds, or flowers with flowers 124. 4

WEEDY 1 FR 0.0001 REL FR 1 V 0 P
when down her weedy trophies and herself | fell HAM 4.07.174

WEEK* 31 FR 0.0035 REL FR 20 V 11 P
i sit at ten pounds a week. WIV 1.03. 8 P
they have had my /house a week at command. 4.03. 10 P
she'll burn a week longer than the whole world. ERR 3.02.100 P
this week he hath been heavy, sour, sad, | and 5.01. 45
my lord, if they were but a week married, they ADO 2.01.353 P
and one day in a week to touch no food, | and LLL 1.01. 39
you shall fast a week with bran and water. 1.01.301 P
no penance, but 'a must fast three days a week. 1.02.130 P
o that i knew he were but in by th' week! 5.02. 61
seek, | but at fourscore it is too late a week; AYL 2.03. 74
as though she bid me stay by her a week; SHR 2.01.178
sir, at the farthest for a week or two, | but 4.02. 74
a man's favor and for a week escape a great deal AWW 3.06. 92 P
presence i'll adventure | the borrow of a week. WT 1.02. 39
thee i can | but shorten thy life one week. 4.04.422
nay, rather turn this day out of the week, JN 3.01. 87
it would be argument for a week, laughter for a 1H4 2.02. 95 P
dic'd not above seven times — a week, went to a 3.03. 16 P
upon wednesday in wheeson week, when the prince 2H4 2.01. 89 P
and each hour's joy wrack'd with a week of teen. R3 4.01. 96
that had not half a week to go, like rams | in H8 4.01. 77
you told how diomed, a whole week by days, | did TRO 4.01. 10
the man must not be hang'd till the next week. TIT 4.03. 83 P
delay this marriage for a month, a week, | or, ROM 3.05.199
sleep for a week, for the next night, i warrant, 4.05. 5
task | does not divide the sunday from the week, HAM 1.01. 76
a kind of week or snuff that will abate it, 4.07.115
keep a week away? OTH 3.04.173
if one of mean affairs | may plod it in a week, CYM 3.02. 51
i did not think a week could have restor'd | my TNK 3.06. 5
who buys a minute's mirth to wail a week? LUC 213

WEEKE 2 FR 0.0002 REL FR 2 V 0 P
weeke, weeke! TIT 4.02.146
weeke, weeke! 4.02.146

WEEKLY 1 FR 0.0001 REL FR 0 V 1 P
whom i have weekly sworn to marry since i 2H4 1.02.241 P

WEEK'S 1 FR 0.0001 REL FR 1 V 0 P
but the whole week's not fair | if any day it TNK 3.01. 65

WEEKS 7 FR 0.0008 REL FR 6 V 1 P
continue in it five weeks without changing. TMP 2.01.184 P
cain's birth, that's not five weeks old as yet? LLL 4.02. 35
and raught not to five weeks when he came to 4.02. 40
full fourteen weeks before the course of time. JN 1.01.113
so many weeks ere the poor fools will ean, | so 3H6 2.05. 36
on forfeiture, my lord, six weeks | and past. TIM 2.02. 30
love alters not with his brief hours and weeks, SON 116.11

WEEN 1 FR 0.0001 REL FR 1 V 0 P
ween you of better luck, | i mean in perjur'd H8 5.01.135

WEENING 1 FR 0.0001 REL FR 1 V 0 P
weening to redeem | and have install'd me in the 1H6 2.05. 88

/WEEP 3 FR 0.0003 REL FR 3 V 0 P
i for a clarence /weep, so doth not she; R3 2.02. 83
/i /for /an /edward /weep, so do not they. 2.02. 85
/mov'd, | /doth /weep /to /see /his /grandsire's TIT 4.01. 49

WEEP 186 FR 0.0210 REL FR 167 V 19 P
he does hear me, | and that he does i weep. TMP 1.02.435
burns, | 'twill weep for having wearied you. 3.01. 19
i am a fool | to weep at what i am glad of. 3.01. 74
wherefore weep you? 3.01. 76
to weep, like a young wench that had buried her TGV 2.01. 23 P
to that i'll speak, to that i'll sigh and weep; 4.02.122
and at that time i made her weep agood, | for i 4.04.165
i weep myself to think upon thy words. 4.04.175
but when they weep and kneel, | all their MM 1.04. 81
before high heaven | as makes the angels weep; 2.02.122
i'll weep what's left away, and weeping die. ERR 2.01.115
a fool, | to put the finger in the eye and weep, 2.02.204
much better is it to weep at joy than to joy at ADO 1.01. 28 P
yea, and i will weep a while longer. 4.01.256 P
thou shin'st in every tear that i do weep, | no LLL 4.03. 32
my tears for glasses, and still make me weep. 4.03. 38
look when i vow, i weep; MND 3.02.124
him to thee as he is, i must blush and weep, and AYL 1.01.157 P
now weep for him, then spit at him; 3.02.417 P
never talk to me, i will weep. 3.04. 1 P
but have i not cause to weep? 3.04. 4 P
good cause as one would desire, therefore weep. 3.04. 6 P
i will weep for nothing, like diana in the 4.01.153 P
and at that sight shall sad apollo weep, | so SHR in.2. 59
talk not to me, i will go sit and weep, | till i 2.01. 35
go, girl, i cannot blame thee now to weep, | for 3.02. 27
going, madam, weep o'er my father's death anew; AWW 1.01. 3 P
destroy our friends and after weep their dust; 5.03. 64
mine eyes smell onions, i shall weep anon. 5.03.320
true lover never find my grave, | to weep there! TN 2.04. 66
do not weep, good fools, | there is no cause. WT 2.01.118
in bohemia, | there weep and leave it crying; 3.03. 32
weep i cannot, | but my heart bleeds; 3.03. 51
no inch farther, | but milk my ewes, and weep. 4.04.450
him, and will weep | my date of life out for his JN 4.03.105
i must withdraw and weep | upon the spot of this 5.02. 29
more than your lord's departure weep not — more R2 2.02. 25
i weep for joy | to stand upon my kingdom once 3.02. 4
shouldst please me better wouldst thou weep. 3.04. 20
i could weep, madam, would it do you good. 3.04. 21
tongue, | and in compassion weep the fire out, 5.01. 48
weep thou for me in france, i for thee here; 5.01. 87
weep not, sweet queen, for trickling tears are 1H4 2.04.391
seems to weep | over his /country's wrongs, and 4.03. 81
what wouldst thou think of me if i should weep? 2H4 2.02. 53 P
of thy lovers, and they weep for thy death; 4.03. 13 P
yet weep that harry's dead, and so will i, | but 5.02. 59
when thousands weep more than did laugh at it. H5 1.02.296
i will weep for thee; 2.02.140
what, will you have them weep our horses' blood? 4.02. 12
of eyes, | to weep their intermissive miseries. 1H6 1.01. 88
mad ire and wrathful fury makes me weep, | that 4.03. 28
i am a soldier and unapt to weep | or to exclaim 5.03.133
his fortunes i will weep, and 'twixt each groan 2H6 3.01.221
think therefore on revenge and cease to weep. 4.04. 3
but who can cease to weep and look on this? 4.04. 4
wouldst have me weep? 3H6 1.04.144
i should not for my life but weep with him, | to 1.04.170
i cannot weep; 2.01. 79
to weep is to make less the depth of grief: 2.01. 85
i, that did never weep, now melt with woe | that 2.03. 46
weep, wretched man; 2.05. 76
i'll bear thee hence, where i may weep my fill. 2.05.113
we will not from the helm to sit and weep, | but 5.04. 21
and twenty times made pause to sob and weep, R3 1.02.161
bid gloucester think /of this, and he will weep. 1.04.239
ay, millstones, as he lesson'd us to weep. 1.04.240
why do /you weep so oft, and beat your breast, 2.02. 3
who shall hinder me to wail and weep, | to chide 2.02. 34
these babes for clarence weep, /and /so /do /i; 2.02. 84

for me to joy and weep their gain and loss; 2.04. 59
so dear i lov'd the man that i must weep. 3.05. 24
then haply will she weep. 4.04.273
and make poor england weep in streams of blood! 5.05. 37
i'll say | a man may weep upon his wedding–day. H8 pr 32
me | and dare be bold to weep for buckingham, 2.01. 72
sir, | i am about to weep; 2.04. 70
no friends, no hope, no kindred weep for me, 3.01.150
nay, and you weep | i am fall'n indeed. 3.02.375
weep what it foresaw | in hector's wrath. TRO 1.02. 10
he will weep you an' 'twere a man born in april. 1.02.173 P
but our undertakings, when we vow to weep seas, 3.02. 78 P
i'll go in and weep. 4.02.105
your eyes, half out, weep out at pandar's fall; 5.10. 48
or if you cannot weep, yet give some groans, 5.10. 49
i could weep, | and i could laugh; COR 2.01.183
come, let's not weep. 4.01. 54
constrains them weep and shake with fear and 5.03.100
thou hast done a deed whereat valor will weep. 5.06.132
when i do weep, they humbly at my feet | receive TIT 3.01. 41
receive my tears, and seem to weep with me, 3.01. 42
titus, prepare thy aged eyes to weep, | or, if 3.01. 59
when heaven doth weep, doth not the earth 3.01.221
to weep with them that weep doth ease some deal, 3.01.244
to weep with them that weep doth ease some deal, 3.01.244
while i stand by and weep to hear him speak. 5.03. 95
no, coz, i rather weep. ROM 1.01.183
all this is comfort, wherefore weep i then? 3.02.107
yet let me weep for such a feeling loss. 3.05. 74
loss, but not the friend | which you weep for. 3.05. 76
i cannot choose but ever weep the friend. 3.05. 77
then weep no more. 3.05. 88
come weep with me, past hope, past /cure, past 4.01. 45
and weep ye now, seeing she is advanc'd | above 4.05. 73
nightly shall be to strew thy grave and weep. 5.03. 17
why dost thou weep? TIM 2.02.175
what, dost thou weep? 4.03.482
strange times, that weep with laughing, not with 4.03.486
taught thee to make vast neptune weep for aye 5.04. 78
banks, and weep your tears | into the channel, JC 1.01. 58
get thee apart and weep. 3.01.282
as caesar lov'd me, i weep for him; 3.02. 25 P
o, now you weep, and i perceive you feel | the 3.02.193
what weep you when you but behold | our caesar's 3.02.195
o, i could weep | my spirit from mine eyes! 4.03. 99
if he were dead, you'ld weep for him; MAC 4.02. 61 P
shade, and there | weep our sad bosoms empty. 4.03. 2
or he to /hecuba, | that he should weep for her? HAM 2.02.560
why, let the strooken deer go weep, | the hart 3.02.271
i cannot choose but weep to think they would lay 4.05. 69 P
woo't weep, woo't fight, woo't fast, woo't tear 5.01.275
breeches, "then they for sudden joy did weep, LR 1.04.175
you think i'll weep: 2.04.282
no, i'll not weep. 2.04.283
a hundred thousand flaws | or ere i'll weep. 2.04.286
no, i will weep no more. 3.04. 17
trundle–tail, | tom will make him weep and wail, 3.06. 71
if thou wilt weep my fortunes, take my eyes. 4.06.176
i pray weep not. 4.07. 70
flesh and fell, | ere they shall make us weep! 5.03. 25
do deeds to make heaven weep, all earth amaz'd; OTH 3.03.371
and she can weep, sir, weep; 4.01.254
and she can weep, sir, weep; 4.01.254
why do you weep? 4.02. 42
i cannot weep, nor answers have i none | but 4.02.103
do not weep, do not weep. alas the day! 4.02.124
do not weep, do not weep. alas the day! 4.02.124
would it not make one weep? 4.02.127
go in, and weep not; 4.02.171
i must weep, | but they are cruel tears. 5.02. 20
thing becomes — to chide, to laugh, | to weep; ANT 1.01. 50
i prithee turn aside, and weep for her, | then 1.03. 76
will caesar weep? 3.02. 50
he wail'd, | believe't — till i weep too. 3.02. 59
to make his followers weep. 4.02. 24
look, they weep, | and i, an ass, am onion–ey'd. 4.02. 34
nay, weep not, gentle eros, there is left us 4.14. 21
thee, cleopatra, and | weep for my pardon. 4.14. 45
that i may say | the gods themselves do weep! 5.02.300
o lady, weep no more, lest i give cause | to be CYM 1.01. 93
of those that weep this lamentable divorce under 1.04. 19 P
to weep 'twixt clock and clock? 3.04. 42
i'll weep, and word it with thee; 4.02.240
(such as i can) twice o'er, i'll weep and sigh, 4.02.392
deep our woes | into the air, our eyes to weep, PER 1.04. 14
live, and make | us weep to hear your fate, fair 3.02.103
to weep that you live as ye do makes pity in 4.02.119 P
why do you weep? 5.01.176
is like to be, | that thus hath made me weep. 5.01.185
demanded that, | she would sit still and weep. 5.01.189
weep ere you fail; TNK 1.01. 95
and we cannot weep | when our friends don their 1.03. 18
the fair–ey'd maids shall weep our banishments, 2.02. 37
who loses, yet i'll weep upon his bier. 3.06.308
weep not, till they weep blood. 4.02.148
weep not, till they weep blood. 4.02.148
poor wench, go weep, for whosoever wins | loses 4.02.155
tyrant from his rage, | and weep unto a girl; 5.01. 79
then would adonis weep; VEN 1090
but as the earth doth weep, the sun being set, LUC 1226
which makes the maid weep like the dewy night. 1232
their gentle sex to weep are often willing, 1237
if thou dost weep for grief of my sustaining, 1272
for now 'tis stale to sigh, to weep, and groan. 1362
which seems to weep upon the tainted place, 1746
then son and father weep with equal strife | who 1791
weep with equal strife | who should weep most, 1792
i weep for thee, and yet no cause i have, | for PP 10. 7
with sighs so deep procures to weep, | in 17.21
if thou sorrow, he will weep; 20.51
the world will be thy widow and still weep, SON 9. 5
and weep afresh love's long since cancell'd woe, 30. 7
but weep to have that which it fears to lose. 64.14
to make the weeper laugh, the laugher weep, | he LC 124
though reason weep and cry, 'it is thy last.' 168
to blush at speeches rank, to weep at woes, | or 307

WEEPER 1 FR 0.0001 REL FR 1 V 0 P
to make the weeper laugh, the laugher weep, | he LC 124

WEEPING 69 FR 0.0078 REL FR 62 V 7 P
weeping again the king my father's wrack, | this TMP 1.02.391
'twill be this hour ere i have done weeping; TGV 2.03. 2 P
my mother weeping, my father wailing, my sister 2.03. 6 P
should not the shoe speak a word for weeping; 2.03. 25 P
weeping before for what she saw must come, | and ERR 1.01. 71
i'll weep what's left away, and weeping die. 2.01.115
i know | your weeping sister is no wife of mine, 3.02. 42
is it to weep at joy than to joy at weeping! ADO 1.01. 28 P
he will prove the weeping philosopher when he MV 1.02. 49 P
all the beholders take his part with weeping. AYL 1.02.132 P
first, for his weeping into the needless stream: 2.01. 46
weeping and commenting | upon the sobbing deer. 2.01. 65
giving her them again, said with weeping tears, 2.04. 53 P
i am not prone to weeping, as our sex | commonly WT 2.01.108
to bed wi' th' sun | and with him rises weeping. 4.04.106
leontes opening his free arms and weeping | his 4.04.548
the last leave of thee takes my weeping eye. R2 1.02. 74
thy sun sets weeping in the lowly west, 2.04. 21
so weeping, smiling, greet i thee, my earth, 3.02. 10
kinsmen digg'd their graves with weeping eyes. 3.03.169
and i could sing, would weeping do me good, 3.04. 22
seen, | in the remembrance of a weeping queen. 3.04.107
and send the hearers weeping to their beds. 5.01. 45
so two together weeping make one woe. 5.01. 86
when weeping made you break the story off, | of 5.02. 2
here, | in weeping after this untimely bier. 5.06. 52
a naked subject to the weeping clouds | and 2H4 1.03. 61
makes me from wond'ring fall to weeping joys, 2H6 1.01. 34
i would be blind with weeping, sick with groans, 3.02. 62
beauty hath, and made them blind with weeping. R3 1.02.166
that dear saint which then i weeping follow'd — 4.01. 69
that reigns in galled eyes of weeping souls, 4.04. 53
they shall be praying nuns, not weeping queens; 4.04.202
and bid her wipe her weeping eyes withal. 4.04.278
great achilles | is arming, weeping, cursing, TRO 5.05. 31
if that i could for weeping, you should hear — COR 4.02. 13
he cares not for your weeping. 5.03.156
man, | and here my brother, weeping at my woes; TIT 3.01.100
she is the weeping welkin, i the earth: 3.01.226
me, and turn'd weeping out | to beg relief among 5.03.105
o lord, i cannot speak to him for weeping, | my 5.03.174
weeping and wailing over tybalt's corse. ROM 3.02.128
blubb'ring and weeping, weeping and blubb'ring. 3.03. 87
blubb'ring and weeping, weeping and blubb'ring. 3.03. 87
evermore weeping for your cousin's death? 3.05. 69
or a harlot for her weeping, | or a dog that TIM 1.02. 66
that weep with laughing, not with weeping! 4.03.486
weeping as fast as they stream forth thy blood, JC 3.01.201
soul, his eyes are red as fire with weeping. 3.02.115
and herself | fell in the weeping brook. HAM 4.07.175
i have full cause of weeping, but this heart LR 2.04.284
doth that bode weeping? OTH 4.03. 59
and sinon's weeping | did scandal many a holy CYM 3.04. 59
by watching, weeping, tendance, kissing, to 5.05. 53
here stands a lord, and there a lady weeping; PER 1.04. 47
here she comes weeping for her only mistress' 4.01. 11
i am great with woe, and shall deliver weeping. 5.01.106
nurse lychorida hath oft | delivered weeping. 5.01.160
their weeping mothers, | following the dead–cold TNK 4.02. 4
had ta'en his last leave of the weeping morn, VEN 2
drink tears, that thou provok'st such weeping? 949
the spots whereof could weeping purify, | her LUC 685
for they their guilt with weeping will unfold, 754
seems to point her out where she sits weeping, 1087
many a dry drop seem'd a weeping tear, | shed 1375
to drown /one woe, one pair of weeping eyes. 1680
herds stands weeping, flocks all sleeping, PP 17.27
threw, | upon whose weeping margent she was set, LC 39
of burning blushes, or of weeping water, | or 304

WEEPINGLY 1 FR 0.0001 REL FR 1 V 0 P
their kind acceptance weepingly beseech'd, LC 207

WEEPING–RIPE 2 FR 0.0002 REL FR 2 V 0 P
the king was weeping–ripe for a good word. LLL 5.02.274
what, weeping–ripe, my lord northumberland? 3H6 1.04.172

WEEPINGS 1 FR 0.0001 REL FR 1 V 0 P
yet the incessant weepings of my wife, | weeping ERR 1.01. 70

WEEPS 41 FR 0.0046 REL FR 36 V 5 P
my sweet mistress | weeps when she sees me work, TMP 3.01. 12
well, he weeps on. TGV 2.03. 26 P
then down upon her knees she falls, weeps, sobs, ADO 2.03.147 P
than the bell rings and the widow weeps. 5.02. 80 P
and when she weeps, weeps every little flower, MND 3.01.199
and when she weeps, weeps every little flower, 3.01.199
poor girl, she weeps. SHR 2.01. 24
he weeps like a wench that had shed her milk. AWW 4.03.107 P
his mother shames him so, poor boy, he weeps. JN 2.01.166
which for things true weeps things imaginary. R2 2.02. 27
my daughter weeps, she'll not part with you, 1H4 3.01.192
the blood weeps from my heart when i do shape, 2H4 4.04. 58
but wherefore weeps warwick, my valiant son? 2H6 1.01.115
the silly owner of the goods | weeps over them, 1.01.226
for henry weeps that thou dost live so long. 3.02.121
she weeps, and says her henry is depos'd; 3H6 3.01. 45
see how my sword weeps for the poor king's death 5.06. 63
she for an edward weeps, and so do i; R3 2.02. 82
speaks 'em, | and every true heart weeps for't. H8 2.02. 39
my heart weeps to see him | so little of his 3.02.335
look, the good man weeps! 5.01.152
perchance she weeps because they kill'd her TIT 3.01.114
see how my wretched sister sobs and weeps. 3.01.137
o, she says nothing, sir, but weeps and weeps, ROM 3.03. 99
o, she says nothing, sir, but weeps and weeps, 3.03. 99
immoderately she weeps for tybalt's death, | and 4.01. 6
is a friar, that trembles, sighs, and weeps. 5.03.184
it weeps, it bleeds, and each new day a gash MAC 4.03. 40
'a weeps for what is done. HAM 4.01. 27
so hangs, and lolls, and weeps upon me; OTH 4.01.139 P
she weeps. 4.01.244
octavia weeps | to part from rome; ANT 3.02. 3
weeps she still, say'st thou? CYM 1.05. 46
and now she weeps, and now she fain would speak, VEN 221
that laughs and weeps, and all but with a breath 414
justice is feasting while the widow weeps, LUC 906
as the dank earth weeps at thy languishment, 1130
one justly weeps, the other takes in hand | no 1235
"lo here weeps hecuba, here priam dies, | here 1485
here feelingly she weeps troy's painted woes, 1492
let no mourner say | he weeps for her, for she 1798

WEEP'ST 7 FR 0.0008 REL FR 5 V 2 P
why weep'st thou, man? TGV 2.03. 35 P
aumerle, thou weep'st, my tender–hearted cousin! R2 3.03.160
coffin'd home, | that weep'st to see me triumph? COR 2.01.177
girl, thou weep'st not so much for his death, ROM 3.05. 78
thou weep'st to make them drink, timon. TIM 1.02.109 P
out, strumpet! weep'st thou for him to my face? OTH 5.02. 77
thou weep'st, and speak'st. CYM 5.05.352

WEEP'T 1 FR 0.0001 REL FR 0 V 1 P
if he do, sure he cannot weep't back again. ANT 2.06.106 P

WEET *(also wit)*

WEET 1 FR 0.0001 REL FR 1 V 0 P
the world to weet | we stand up peerless. ANT 1.01. 39

/WEIGH 1 FR 0.0001 REL FR 1 V 0 P
/undergo, | /to /weigh /against /his /opposite; 2H4 1.03. 55

WEIGH 42 FR 0.0047 REL FR 39 V 3 P
good sir, weigh | our sorrow with our comfort. TMP 2.01. 8
we cannot weigh our brother with ourself. MM 2.02.126
go to, sir, you weigh equally; 4.02. 30 P
and what they weigh, even to the utmost scruple ADO 5.01. 93
you, she shall ne'er weigh more reasons in her 5.01.207 P
indeed i weigh not you, and therefore light. LLL 5.02. 26
you weigh me not? o, that's you care not for me. 5.02. 27
weigh oath with oath, and you will nothing weigh MND 3.02.131
oath with oath, and you will nothing weigh. 3.02.131
and me, put in two scales, | will even weigh; 3.02.133
and weigh thy value with an even hand. MV 2.07. 25
are there balance here to weigh | the flesh? 4.01.255
to those | that weigh their pains in sense, and AWW 1.01.225
defective scale, | shall weigh thee to the beam; 2.03.155
let every word weigh heavy of her worth, | that 3.04. 31
of her worth, | that he does weigh too light. 3.04. 32
i prize it | as i weigh grief, which i would WT 3.02. 43
while they weigh so even, | we hold our town for JN 2.01.332
her dowry shall weigh equal with a queen; 2.01.486
thing the purpose must weigh with the folly. 2H4 2.02.176 P
that thou no more wilt weigh my eyelids down, 3.01. 7
you are right justice, and you weigh this well, 5.02.102
in cases of defense 'tis best to weigh | the H5 2.04. 43
weigh it but with the grossness of this age, R3 3.01. 46
i weigh it lightly, were it heavier. 3.01.121
and weigh thee down to ruin, shame, and death! 5.03.148
they that must weigh out my afflictions, | they H8 3.01. 88
will triumph o'er my person, which i weigh not, 5.01.124
weigh you the worth and honor of a king | so TRO 2.02. 26
weigh him well, | and that which looks like 4.05. 81
but your people, | i love them as they weigh — COR 2.02. 74
counterpoise, | and make him weigh with her. TIM 1.01.146
i weigh my friend's affection with mine own. 1.02.216
weigh but the crime with this. 3.05. 58
than their offense can weigh down by the dram; 5.01.151
weigh them, it is as heavy; JC 1.02.146
then weigh what loss your honor may sustain | if HAM 1.03. 29
weigh what convenience both of time and means 4.07.149
to, but weigh | what it is worth embrac'd. ANT 2.06. 32
'tween man and man they weigh not every stamp; CYM 5.04. 24
come weigh, my hearts, cheerly! TNK 4.01.146
to weigh how once i suffered in your crime. SON 120. 8

/WEIGH'D 1 FR 0.0001 REL FR 1 V 0 P
/i /have /in /equal /balance /justly /weigh'd 2H4 4.01. 67

WEIGH'D 17 FR 0.0019 REL FR 15 V 2 P
weigh'd between loathness and obedience, at TMP 2.01.131
he would have weigh'd thy brother by himself, MM 5.01.111
if that the injuries be justly weigh'd | that TN 5.01.367
their fortunes both are weigh'd. R2 3.04. 84
what four thron'd ones could have weigh'd | such H8 1.01. 11
i weigh'd the danger which my realms stood in 2.04.198
bound together) | weigh'd not a hair of his. 3.02.259
commit my cause in balance to be weigh'd. TIT 1.01. 55
from whence at first she weigh'd her anchorage, 1.01. 73
but in that crystal scales let there be weigh'd ROM 1.02. 96
the interim having weigh'd it, let us speak MAC 1.03.154
these are portable, | with other graces weigh'd. 4.03. 90
his greatness weigh'd, his will is not his own, HAM 1.03. 17
'tis so, th' offender's scourge is weigh'd, 4.03. 6
for /equalities are so weigh'd, that curiosity LR 1.01. 6 P
wherein he must be weigh'd rather by her value CYM 1.04. 15 P
might equal yours, if both were justly weigh'd. PER 5.01. 88

WEIGHING 5 FR 0.0005 REL FR 4 V 1 P
others paying | than by self–offenses weighing. MM 3.02.266
was my negligence, | not weighing well the end; WT 1.02.258
looks upon me will take me without weighing, and 2H4 1.02.167 P
weighing the youthful season of the year. JC 2.01.108
in equal scale weighing delight and dole, HAM 1.02. 13

WEIGHS 9 FR 0.0010 REL FR 9 V 0 P
how much your chain weighs to the utmost charect ERR 4.01. 28
wheresoe'er she is, | her heart weighs sadly. AWW 3.05. 67
and with that odds he weighs king richard down. R2 3.04. 89
now he weighs time | even to the utmost grain; H5 2.04.137
merits pois'd, each weighs no less nor more, TRO 4.01. 66
perilous stuff | which weighs upon the heart? MAC 5.03. 45
how heavy weighs my lord! ANT 4.15. 32
case | weighs not the dust and injury of age, SON 108.10
whose white weighs down the airy scale of praise LC 226

WEIGH'ST 1 FR 0.0001 REL FR 1 V 0 P
and weigh'st thy words before thou giv'st them OTH 3.03.119

/WEIGHT 1 FR 0.0001 REL FR 1 V 0 P
/give /this /heavy /weight /from /off /my /head, R2 4.01.204

WEIGHT 47 FR 0.0053 REL FR 39 V 8 P
make us pay down for our offense by weight | the MM 1.02.121
seeming as burdened | with lesser weight, but ERR 1.01.108
but were we burd'ned with like weight of pain, 2.01. 36
and there be any matter of weight chances, call ADO 3.03. 85 P
'twill be heavier soon by the weight of a man. 3.04. 26 P
i would bend under any heavy weight | that he'll 5.01.277
the plea of no less weight | than aquitaine, a LLL 2.01. 7
and you shall see 'tis purchas'd by the weight, MV 3.02. 89
have | a weight of carrion flesh than to receive 4.01. 41
me not with the full weight that i love thee. AYL 1.02. 9 P

and yet as heavy as my weight should be. SHR 2.01.205
of color, weight, and heat, pour'd all together, AWW 2.03.119
but in despair die under their black weight. JN 3.01.297
not with the empty hollowness, but weight. R2 1.02. 59
stoop with oppression of their prodigal weight; 3.04. 31
i need no more weight than mine own bowels. 1H4 5.03. 35 P
lend to this weight such lightness with their 2H4 1.01.122
the weight of a hair will turn scales between 2.04.253 P
him, of some things of weight | that task our H5 1.02. 5
merit, | according to the weight and worthiness. 2.02. 35
which in weight to re–answer, his pettiness 3.06.128 P
i mean, in bearing weight of government, | while 3H6 4.06. 51
thou art no atlas for so great a weight; 5.01. 36
and heave it shall some weight, or break my back 5.07. 24
and still, as you are weary of this weight, R3 1.02. 31
suddenly an answer | in such a point of weight, H8 3.01. 71
there was the weight that pull'd me down. 3.02.407
lay all the weight ye can upon my patience, | i 5.02.101
of their observant toil the enemies' weight — TRO 1.03.203
might be affronted with the match and weight 3.02.166
scruple | of her contaminated carrion weight, 4.01. 72
love, | so much by weight hate i her diomed. 5.02.168
thy madness shall be paid with weight | /till HAM 4.05.157
the weight of this sad time we must obey, LR 5.03.324
it shall be full of poise and difficult weight, OTH 3.03. 82
though thou deny me a matter of more weight; ANT 1.02. 69 P
we do bear | so great weight in his lightness. 1.04. 25
o happy horse, to bear the weight of antony! 1.05. 21
the weight we must convey with 's will permit, 3.01. 36
gone into heaviness, | that makes the weight. 4.15. 34
and you bear it | as answering to the weight. 5.02.102
how much the quantity, the weight as much, | as CYM 4.02. 17
upon this mighty morr— — of mickle weight — TNK 3.05.118
never fainting | under the weight of arms; 4.02.130
by a halfpenny loaf a day, troy weight. STM II.C 7 P
once set on ringing, with his own weight goes; LUC 1494
plods /dully on, to bear that weight in me, | as SON 50. 6

WEIGHTIER 3 FR 0.0003 REL FR 3 V 0 P
in weightier things you'll say a beggar nay. R3 3.01.119
to your ear | much weightier than this work. H8 5.01. 18
contain thee, | attend our weightier judgment. TIM 3.05.101

WEIGHTLESS 1 FR 0.0001 REL FR 1 V 0 P
that light and weightless down | perforce must 2H4 4.05. 33

WEIGHTS 2 FR 0.0002 REL FR 2 V 0 P
what passion hangs these weights upon my tongue? AYL 1.02.257
from whose so many weights of baseness cannot CYM 3.05. 88

WEIGHTY 13 FR 0.0014 REL FR 13 V 0 P
sufficeth my reasons are both good and weighty. SHR 1.01.248
made me acquainted with a weighty cause | of 4.04. 26
did look no better to that weighty charge. 1H6 2.01. 62
this weighty business will not brook delay, 2H6 1.01.170
with thy confederates in this weighty cause. 1.02. 86
what counsel give you in this weighty cause? 3.01.289
with lies well steel'd with weighty arguments, R3 1.01.148
now | that bear a weighty and a serious brow, H8 pr 2
this secret is so weighty, 'twill require | a 2.01.144
there ye shall meet about this weighty business. 2.02.139
how you stand minded in the weighty difference 3.01. 58
words cannot carry | authority so weighty. 3.02.234
the common eye | for sundry weighty reasons. MAC 3.01.125

WEIRD 6 FR 0.0006 REL FR 5 V 1 P
the weird sisters, hand in hand, | posters of MAC 1.03. 32
before, these weird sisters saluted me, and 1.05. 8 P
i dreamt last night of the three weird sisters: 2.01. 20
as the weird women promis'd, and i fear | thou 3.01. 2
(and betimes i will) to the weird sisters. 3.04.132
saw you the weird sisters? 4.01.136

WELCOM'D 5 FR 0.0005 REL FR 4 V 1 P
from home, welcom'd home with it when i return; ERR 4.04. 36 P
her sister katherine welcom'd you withal? SHR 3.01. 3
welcom'd all, serv'd all; WT 4.04. 57
tyre, | welcom'd and settled to his own desire. PER 4.ch. 2
well was he welcom'd by the roman dame, | within LUC 51

/WELCOME 1 FR 0.0001 REL FR 1 V 0 P
/but /that's /no /welcome. TRO 4.05.165

WELCOME 378 FR 0.0427 REL FR 326 V 52 P
thee and thy company i bid | a hearty welcome. TMP 5.01.111
welcome, my friends all! 5.01.125
welcome, sir; 5.01.165
welcome him then according to his worth — TGV 2.04. 83
welcome, dear proteus! 2.04.100
confirm his welcome with some special favor. 2.04.101
his worth is warrant for his welcome hither, 2.04.102
you are welcome to a worthless mistress. 2.04.113
that you are welcome? 2.04.115
once more, new servant, welcome; 2.04.118
launce, by mine honesty, welcome to /milan. 2.05. 1 P
not thyself, sweet youth, for i am not welcome. 2.05. 4 P
nor never welcome to a place till some certain 2.05. 5 P
shot be paid and the hostess say "welcome." 2.05. 7 P
of love, | warrant me welcome to my proteus. 2.07. 71
your grace is welcome to a man disgrac'd, 5.04.123
wife, bid these gentlemen welcome. WIV 1.01.194 P
such /brooks are welcome to me, that o'erflows 2.02.151 P
you're welcome. 2.02.158 P
he's welcome. 3.01. 28 P
as i am a true spirit, welcome! 5.05. 29 P
y' are welcome; MM 2.02. 26
come in, the wish deserves a welcome. 3.01. 45
and very welcome. 3.01. 49
welcome, how agreed? 4.01. 64
welcome, father. 4.02. 72
gave healthful welcome to their shipwrack'd ERR 1.01.114
that never touch well welcome to thy hand, 2.02.116
answer my good will and your good welcome here. 3.01. 20
your dainties cheap, sir, and your welcome dear. 3.01. 21
a table full of welcome makes scarce one dainty 3.01. 23
and welcome more common, for that's nothing but 3.01. 25
cheer and great welcome makes a merry feast. 3.01. 26
here is neither cheer, sir, nor welcome: 3.01. 66
at the door, master, bid them welcome hither. 3.01. 68
and to that end, sir, i will welcome you. 4.04. 17
let me bid you welcome, my lord, being ADO 1.01.154 P
welcome, signior, you are almost come to part 5.01.113 P
and therefore welcome the sour cup of prosperity LLL 1.01.313 P
fair princess, welcome to the court of navarre. 2.01. 90
you back again, and "welcome" i have not yet. 2.01. 91 P
and welcome to the wide fields too base to be 2.01. 93 P
you shall be welcome, madam, to my court. 2.01. 95
i will be welcome then — conduct me thither. 2.01. 96
mean time receive such welcome at my hand | as 2.01.168
o, you are welcome, sir, adieu. 2.01.213
farewell to me, sir, and welcome to you. 2.01.214
welcome, pure wit! 5.02.484
welcome, marcade, | but that thou interruptest 5.02.716
welcome, wanderer. MND 2.01.247
welcome, good robin. 4.01. 46
have broke off, | not paying me a welcome. 5.01. 99
out of this silence yet i pick'd a welcome; 5.01.100
i could bid the fift welcome with so good heart MV 1.02.127 P
then farewell heat, and welcome frost! 2.07. 75
lorenzo and salerio, welcome hither, | if that 3.02.220
int'rest here | have power to bid you welcome. 3.02.222
friends and countrymen, | sweet portia, welcome. 3.02.224
so do i, my lord, | they are entirely welcome. 3.02.225
nerissa, cheer yond stranger, bid her welcome. 3.02.237
bid your friends welcome, show a merry cheer — 3.02.312
you are welcome, take your place. 4.01.170
this deed will be well welcome to lorenzo. 4.02. 4
some welcome for the mistress of the house. 5.01. 38
dear lady, welcome home! 5.01.113
you are welcome home, my lord. 5.01.132
give welcome to my friend; 5.01.133
sir, you are very welcome to our house. 5.01.139
grieve not you, you are welcome notwithstanding. 5.01.239
antonio, you are welcome, | and i have better 5.01.273
and in my voice most welcome shall you be. AYL 2.04. 87
sit down and feed, and welcome to our table. 2.07.105
welcome. 2.07.167
welcome, fall to. 2.07.171
living in your face, | be truly welcome hither. 2.07.195
man, | thou art right welcome as thy /master is. 2.07.198
good my lord, bid him welcome. 5.04. 40 P
o my dear niece, welcome thou art to me! 5.04.147
even daughter, welcome, in no less degree. 5.04.148
welcome, young man; 5.04.166
now, fellows, you are welcome. SHR in.1. 79
and give them friendly welcome every one. in.1. 103
master, some show to welcome us to town. 1.01. 47
house and ply his book, welcome his friends, 1.01.196
y' are welcome, sir, and he, for your good sake. 2.01. 61
i know him well; you are welcome for his sake. 2.01. 70
welcome, good cambio. 2.01. 84 P
i may have welcome 'mongst the rest that woo, 2.01. 96
you are very welcome, sir. 2.01.105
you are passing welcome, | and so i pray you all 2.01.112
you are welcome, sir. 3.02. 88
welcome home, grumio! 4.01.106 P
welcome, you; 4.01.111 P
are those" — | sit down, kate, and welcome. 4.01.142
come, kate, and wash, and welcome heartily. 4.01.154
you are welcome. 4.02. 72
welcome! 4.04. 70
i think i shall command your welcome here; 5.01. 12
my fair bianca, bid my father welcome, | while i 5.02. 4
while i with self–same kindness welcome thine. 5.02. 5
feast with the best, and welcome to my house. 5.02. 8
you are welcome all. 5.02. 48
welcome to paris. AWW 1.02. 22
welcome, count, | my son's no dearer. 1.02. 75
rest | unquestion'd welcome and undoubted blest. 2.01.208
welcome shall they be; 3.01. 19
y' are welcome, gentlemen. 3.02. 91
lord the king, | we'll be before our welcome. 4.04. 14
to whose trust | your business was more welcome. 4.04. 16
the bitter past, more welcome is the sweet. 5.03.334
welcome, ass. now let's have a catch. TN 2.03. 18 P
your misdemeanors, you are welcome to the house; 2.03. 99 P
o, welcome, father! 5.01.150
and say, "thrice welcome, drowned viola!" 5.01.241
thou lov'st us, show in our brother's welcome; WT 1.02.174
you bid | these unknown friends to 's welcome, 4.04. 65
on, | and bid us welcome to your sheep–shearing, 4.04. 69
sir, welcome. 4.04. 70
you're welcome, sir. 4.04. 72
be to you both, | and welcome to our shearing! 4.04. 77
y' are very welcome. 4.04.108
pleas'd with madness, | do bid it welcome. 4.04.485
most dearly welcome! 5.01.130
welcome hither, | as is the spring to th' earth. 5.01.151
embrace him, love him, give him welcome hither. JN 2.01. 11
i give you welcome with a powerless hand, | but 2.01. 15
welcome before the gates of angiers, duke. 2.01. 17
let them be welcome then, we are prepar'd. 2.01. 83
and will not let me welcome this good news. 5.03. 15
and welcome home again discarded faith. 5.04. 12
and what hear there for welcome but my groans? R2 1.02. 70
return with welcome home from banishment. 1.03.212
why i should welcome such a guest as grief, 2.02. 7
welcome, my lords. 2.03. 59
nor friends, nor foes, to me welcome you are: 2.03.170
more welcome is the stroke of death to me | than 3.01. 31
welcome, my lord. 3.02. 63
welcome, harry. 3.03. 20
his noble cousin is right welcome hither, | and 3.03.122
welcome, bullingbrook!" 5.02. 17
no joyful tongue gave him his welcome home, 5.02. 29
welcome, my son! 5.02. 46
welcome, my lord, what is the news? 5.06. 5
and he hath brought us smooth and welcome news. 1H4 1.01. 66
shillings and sixpence," and "you are welcome," 2.04. 26 P
welcome, jack, where hast thou been? 2.04.113 P
my cousin vernon, welcome, by my soul! 4.01. 86
pray god my news be worth a welcome, lord. 4.01. 87
he shall be welcome too. 4.01. 94
welcome, sir walter blunt; 4.03. 32
home, | my father gave him welcome to the shore; 4.03. 59
welcome, ancient pistol. 2H4 2.04.111 P
by my troth, welcome to london. 2.04.292 P
light flesh and corrupt blood, thou art welcome. 2.04.295 P
welcome, good sir john. 3.02. 84 P
your good worship is welcome. 3.02. 91 P
did with the least affection of a welcome | give 4.05.172
kind master bardolph, and welcome, my tall 5.01. 58 P
myself | to welcome the condition of the time, 5.02. 11
wags all, | and welcome merry shrove–tide. 5.03. 35
honest bardolph, welcome. 5.03. 55 P
welcome, my little tiny thief, and welcome 5.03. 57 P
my little tiny thief, and welcome indeed too. 5.03. 57 P
why, here it is, welcome these pleasant days! 5.03.141
would the peaceful city quit, | to welcome him! H5 5.pr. 34
now welcome, kate; 5.02.357
bastard of orleance, thrice welcome to us. 1H6 1.02. 47
and he is welcome. what? is this the man? 2.03. 14
welcome, high prince, the mighty duke of york! 3.01.176
welcome, brave duke, thy friendship makes us 3.03. 86
welcome, brave captain and victorious lord! 3.04. 16
to bid his young son welcome to his grave? 4.03. 40
welcome, brave earl, into our territories! 5.03.146
welcome, queen margaret, | i can express no 2H6 1.01. 17
lords, with one cheerful voice welcome my love. 1.01. 36
well said, my masters, and welcome all. 1.04. 13 P
welcome is banishment, welcome were my death. 2.03. 14
welcome is banishment, welcome were my death. 2.03. 14
welcome, lord somerset. what news from france? 3.01. 83
welcome, my lord, to this brave town of york. 3H6 2.02. 1
welcome, brave warwick! 3.03. 46
then, gentle clarence, welcome unto warwick, 4.02. 6
welcome unto warwick, | and welcome, somerset! 4.02. 7
but welcome, sweet clarence, my daughter shall 4.02. 12
welcome, sir john! but why come you in arms? 4.07. 42
o, welcome, oxford, for we want thy help. 5.01. 66
now welcome more, and ten times more belov'd, 5.01.103
welcome, good clarence, this is brother–like. 5.01.105
well are you welcome to /the open air. R3 1.01.124
welcome destruction, blood, and massacre! 2.04. 53
welcome, sweet prince, to london, to your 3.01. 1
welcome, dear cousin, my thoughts' sovereign, 3.01. 2
i want more uncles here to welcome me. 3.01. 6
welcome, my lord. what, will our mother come? 3.01. 25
her | to meet you at the tower and welcome you. 3.01.139
welcome, my lord! 3.07. 56
the aid | of buckingham to welcome them ashore. 4.04.439
your wives shall welcome home the conquerors; 5.03.260
a general welcome from his grace | salutes ye H8 1.04. 1
first, good company, good wine, good welcome, 1.04. 6
y' are welcome, my fair guests. 1.04. 35
this, to confirm my welcome, | and to you all 1.04. 37
good lord chamberlain, | go, give 'em welcome: 1.04. 57
and once more | i show'r a welcome on ye. 1.04. 63
welcome all! 1.04. 63
you're welcome, | most learned reverend sir, 2.02. 75
and once more in mine arms i bid him welcome, 2.02. 98
that cranmer is return'd with welcome, 3.02.400
you go, | and find the welcome of a noble foe. TRO 1.03.309
the welcome ever smiles, | and farewell goes out 3.03.168
in humane gentleness, | welcome to troy! 4.01. 22
now, by anchises' life, | welcome indeed! 4.01. 23
welcome, sir diomed! 4.04.109
most dearly welcome to the greeks, sweet lady. 4.05. 18
achilles bids you welcome. 4.05. 25
that give a coasting welcome ere it comes, | and 4.05. 59
as welcome as to one | that would be rid of such 4.05.163
from heart of very heart, great hector, welcome. 4.05.171
you brace of warlike brothers, welcome hither. 4.05.175
and, worthy warrior, welcome to our tents. 4.05.200
well, welcome, welcome! 4.05.210
well, welcome, welcome! 4.05.210
most gentle and most valiant hector, welcome! 4.05.227
that this great soldier may his welcome know. 4.05.276
welcome, brave hector, welcome, princes all. 5.01. 70
welcome, brave hector, welcome, princes all. 5.01. 70
good night and welcome, both /at /once, to those 5.01. 77
tell valeria | we are fit to bid her welcome. COR 1.03. 44
welcome to rome, renowned coriolanus! 2.01.166
welcome to rome, renowned coriolanus! 2.01.167
o, welcome home; 2.01.181
and welcome, general, and y' are welcome all. 2.01.182
and welcome, general, and y' are welcome all. 2.01.182
welcome! 2.01.184
yet welcome, warriors; 2.01.189
welcome home. 3.01. 20
you will be welcome with this intelligence, 4.03. 29 P
most welcome! 4.05.147
repeal him with the welcome of his mother. 5.05. 5
cry, "welcome, ladies, welcome!" 5.05. 6
cry, "welcome, ladies, welcome!" 5.05. 6
welcome, ladies, | welcome! 5.05. 6
welcome, ladies, | welcome! 5.05. 7
most welcome! 5.06. 8
you are most welcome home. 5.06. 60
and with loud 'larums welcome them to rome. TIT 1.01.147
and welcome, nephews, from successful wars, 1.01.172
welcome, aemilius, what's the news from rome? 5.01.155
come down and welcome me to this world's light; 5.02. 33
i am, therefore come down and welcome me. 5.02. 43
welcome, dread fury, to my woeful house; 5.02. 82
rapine and murther, you are welcome too. 5.02. 83
but welcome as you are: 5.02. 91
welcome, my lord; 5.03. 26
welcome, dread queen; 5.03. 26
welcome, ye warlike goths; 5.03. 27
welcome, lucius; 5.03. 27
and welcome, all. 5.03. 28
among the store | one more, most welcome, makes ROM 1.02. 23
my house and welcome on their pleasure stay. 1.02. 37
welcome, gentlemen! 1.05. 16
welcome, gentlemen! 1.05. 21
you are welcome, gentlemen! 1.05. 25
welcome then. 3.03. 80
come, death, and welcome! 3.05. 24
welcome from mantua! 5.02. 3
painting is welcome. TIM 1.01.156
most welcome, sir! 1.01.247
right welcome, sir! 1.01.253
more welcome are ye to my fortunes | than my 1.02. 19
o, apemantus, you are welcome. 1.02. 23
you shall not make me welcome. 1.02. 24
th' art an athenian, therefore welcome. 1.02. 36 P

they're welcome all, let 'em have kind 1.02.128
music, make their welcome! 1.02.129
they are fairly welcome. 1.02.176
o, none so welcome. 1.02.217
you are very respectively welcome, sir. 3.01. 8 P
welcome, good brother. 3.04. 7
bless them, and to nothing are they welcome. 3.06. 84 P
feast | whereat a villain's not a welcome guest. 3.06.103
thine ears (like tapsters that bade welcome) 4.03.215
nothing living but thee, thou shalt be welcome. 4.03.356 P
he is welcome hither. JC 2.01. 94
he is welcome too. 2.01. 95
they are all welcome. 2.01. 97
and such suffering souls | that welcome wrongs; 2.01.131
welcome, publius. 2.02.109
but here comes antony. welcome, mark antony! 3.01.147
welcome, good messala. 4.03.163
shall be as welcome to the ears of brutus | as 5.03. 77
welcome hither! MAC 1.04. 27
whose care is gone before to bid us welcome: 1.04. 57
bear welcome in your eye, | your hand, your 1.05. 64
to make society | the sweeter welcome, we will 3.01. 42
at first | and last, the hearty welcome. 3.04. 2
but in best time | we will require her welcome. 3.04. 6
friends, | for my heart speaks they are welcome. 3.04. 8
while 'tis a–making, | 'tis given with welcome. 3.04. 34
may kindly say | our duties did his welcome pay. 4.01.132
such welcome and unwelcome things at once | 'tis 4.03.138
my ever gentle cousin, welcome hither. 4.03.161
welcome, horatio, welcome, good marcellus. HAM 1.01. 20
welcome, horatio, welcome, good marcellus. 1.01. 20
and therefore as a stranger give it welcome. 1.05.165
welcome, dear rosencrantz and guildenstern! 2.02. 1
welcome, my good friends! 2.02. 58
most welcome home! 2.02. 85
he that plays the king shall be welcome — his 2.02.319 P
gentlemen, you are welcome to elsinore. 2.02.370 P
then, th' appurtenance of welcome is fashion and 2.02.371 P
you are welcome; 2.02.375 P
you are welcome, masters, welcome all. 2.02.421 P
you are welcome, masters, welcome all. 2.02.421 P
welcome, good friends. 2.02.422 P
masters, you are all welcome. 2.02.429 P
you are welcome to elsinore. 2.02.547 P
you are welcome. 3.02.313 P
your lordship is right welcome back to denmark. 5.02. 81
your graces are right welcome. LR 2.01.129
whose welcome i perceiv'd had poison'd mine — 2.04. 39
you yet, nor am provided | for your fit welcome. 2.04.233
thou shalt meet | both welcome and protection. 3.06. 92
welcome then, | thou unsubstantial air that i 4.01. 6
welcome, my lord! 4.02. 1
/you are welcome hither. 5.03.290
the worser welcome; OTH 1.01. 95
welcome, gentle signior, | we lack'd your 1.03. 50
good ancient, you are welcome. 2.01. 96
welcome, mistress. 2.01. 96
welcome, iago; we must to the watch. 2.03. 12 P
welcome to cyprus. 4.01.221
you are welcome, sir, to cyprus. 4.01.263
your honor is most welcome. 4.03. 4
welcome, my good alexas. ANT 1.05. 66
welcome to rome. 2.02. 28
welcome from egypt, sir. 2.02.171 P
to sicily and did find | her welcome friendly. 2.06. 46
enobarbus, welcome! 2.07. 86
welcome hither! 3.06. 78
welcome to rome, | nothing more dear to me. 3.06. 85
best of comfort, | and ever welcome to us. 3.06. 90
welcome, lady. 3.06. 90
welcome, dear madam. 3.06. 91
sister, welcome. 3.06. 97
good morrow to thee, welcome. 4.04. 18
bid that welcome | which comes to punish us, and 4.14.136
all strange and terrible events are welcome, 4.15. 3
o, come, come, come, | and welcome, welcome! 4.15. 38
o, come, come, come, | and welcome, welcome! 4.15. 38
thanks, good sir, | you're kindly welcome. CYM 1.06. 14
you are as welcome, worthy sir, as i | have 1.06. 29
i was going, sir, | to give him welcome. 1.06. 55
you're very welcome. 1.06.210
welcome, sir. 2.04. 29
thou art welcome, caius. 3.01. 68
his majesty bids you welcome. 3.01. 77 P
all the remain is "welcome!" 3.01. 85
boys, bid him welcome. 3.06. 68
and such a welcome as i'ld give to him | (after 3.06. 72
most welcome! 3.06. 73
to th' owl and morn to th' lark less welcome. 3.06. 93
most welcome, bondage! 5.04. 3
lord thaliard from antiochus is welcome. PER 1.03. 30
welcome is peace, if he on peace consist; 1.04. 83
your grace is welcome to our town and us. 1.04.106
which welcome we'll accept; 1.04.107
and flap–jacks, and thou shalt be welcome. 2.01. 83 P
to say you're welcome were superfluous. 2.03. 2
with me? and welcome. happy day, my lords. 2.04. 22
thou art the rudeliest welcome to this world 3.01. 30
welcome, fair one! 5.01. 65
they are welcome. TNK 4.01. 18
and reverend welcome to her princely guest, LUC 90
a brow unbent, that seem'd to welcome woe, 1509
for she doth welcome daylight with her ditty, PP 14.19
makes summer's welcome thrice more wish'd, more SON 56.14
then give me welcome, next my heaven the best, 110.13

WELCOMER 1 FR 0.0001 REL FR 1 V 0 P
farewell, thou woeful welcomer of glory! R3 4.01. 89

WELCOMES 9 FR 0.0010 REL FR 8 V 1 P
pence, thou shalt have five thousand welcomes. TGV 2.05. 10 P
to greet me with premeditated welcomes; MND 5.01. 94
his free arms and weeping | his welcomes forth; WT 4.04.549
a hundred thousand welcomes! COR 2.01.183
a thousand welcomes! 4.05.145
post, | and had no welcomes home, but he returns 5.06. 50
to set a gloss on faint deeds, hollow welcomes, TIM 1.02. 16
spouse, that welcomes to their cost | the galled TNK 3.05.128
welcomes the warm approach of sweet desire; VEN 386

WELCOMEST 1 FR 0.0001 REL FR 1 V 0 P
guests | are often welcomest when they are gone. 1H6 2.02. 56

WE'LD 2 FR 0.0002 REL FR 2 V 0 P
/shoal of time, | we'ld jump the life to come. MAC 1.07. 7
we'ld fight there too. ANT 4.10. 4

WELFARE 6 FR 0.0006 REL FR 6 V 0 P
we have been praying for our husbands' welfare, MV 5.01.114
the welfare of us all | hangs on the cutting 2H6 3.01. 80
nor how to study for the people's welfare, | nor 3H6 4.03. 39
that have preserv'd her welfare in my blood, TIT 5.03.110
until her husband's welfare she did hear; LUC 263
and, sick of welfare, found a kind of meetness SON 118. 7

WELK'D 1 FR 0.0001 REL FR 1 V 0 P
horns welk'd and waved like the /enridged sea. LR 4.06. 71

WELKIN 16 FR 0.0018 REL FR 13 V 3 P
by welkin and her star! WIV 1.03. 92
by thy favor, sweet welkin, i must sigh in thy LLL 3.01. 67
ear of caelo, the sky, the welkin, the heaven, 4.02. 5 P
the starry welkin cover thou anon | with MND 3.02.356
thy hounds shall make the welkin answer them SHR in.2. 45
but shall we make the welkin dance indeed? TN 2.03. 57 P
are and what you would are out of my welkin — i 3.01. 58 P
sir page, | look on me with your welkin eye. WT 1.02.136
but stay'd and made the western welkin blush, JN 5.05. 2
with | king cerberus, and let the welkin roar. 2H4 2.04.168
amaze the welkin with your broken staves! R3 5.03.341
or with our sighs we'll breathe the welkin dim, TIT 3.01.211
threat'ning the welkin with his big–swoll'n face 3.01.223
she is the weeping welkin, i the earth: 3.01.226
against the welkin volleys out his voice; VEN 921
doth yet in his fair welkin once appear, | till LUC 116

WELKIN'S 3 FR 0.0003 REL FR 2 V 1 P
that the sea, mounting to th' welkin's cheek, TMP 1.02. 4
"great deputy, the welkin's vicegerent, and sole LLL 1.01.219 P
(as loud as thine) rattle the welkin's ear, JN 5.02.172

/WE'LL 2 FR 0.0002 REL FR 1 V 1 P
/we'll /wait /upon /you. HAM 2.02.266 P
but in our orbs /we'll live so round and safe, PER 1.02.122

WE'LL 345 FR 0.0390 REL FR 262 V 83 P
we'll visit caliban my slave, who never | yields TMP 1.02.308
fellow trinculo, we'll fill him by and by again. 2.02.176 P
we'll not run, monsieur monster. 3.02. 18 P
lead, monster, we'll follow. 3.02.150 P
why then we'll make exchange: TGV 2.02. 6
we'll both attend upon your ladyship. 2.04.121
we'll wait upon your grace till after supper, 3.02. 95
if not, we'll make you sit, and rifle you. 4.01. 4
peace! we'll hear him. 4.01. 9
we'll have him. sirs, a word. 4.01. 38
we'll do thee homage and be rul'd by thee, 4.01. 64
come, go with us, we'll bring thee to our crews, 4.01. 72
come, we'll have you merry: 4.02. 30 P
we'll follow him that's fled — | the thicket is 5.03. 10
daughter, carry the wine in, we'll drink within. WIV 1.01.188 P
go, and we'll have a posset for't soon at night, 1.04. 8 P
we'll use this unwholesome humidity, this gross 3.03. 40 P
we'll teach him to know turtles from jays. 3.03. 42 P
i'll warrant we'll unkennel the fox. 3.03.163 P
go in, gentlemen, but, trust me, we'll mock him. 3.03.228 P
after, we'll a–birding together. 3.03.230 P
we'll come dress you straight. 4.02. 82 P
we'll try that; 4.02. 94 P
we'll leave a proof, by that which we will do, 4.02.104
of their growth, we'll dress | like urchins, 4.04. 49
being known, | we'll all present ourselves; 4.04. 64
we'll couch i' th' castle–ditch till we see the 5.02. 1 P
we'll betray him finely. 5.03. 20 P
sir, we'll bring you to windsor, to one master 5.05.165 P
talk offend you, we'll have very little of it. MM 4.03.178 P
my lord, we'll do it throughly. 5.01.259
we'll touze you | joint by joint, but we will 5.01.311
sit you down, | we'll borrow place of him. 5.01.362
palace, where we'll show | what's yet behind, 5.01.538
help us in, sirrah, we'll pluck a crow together. ERR 3.01. 83
we'll mend our dinner here. 4.03. 59
come go with us, we'll look to that anon. 5.01.413
we'll draw cuts for the senior, till then, lead 5.01.423
we'll wait upon your lordship. ADO 1.03. 75 P
we'll fit the /hid–fox with a pennyworth. 2.03. 42
come, balthasar, we'll hear that song again. 2.03. 43
come, we'll obey you. 3.03.180 P
we'll be friends first. 4.01.297 P
we'll talk with margaret, | how her acquaintance 5.01.331
fear not, man, we'll tip thy horns with gold, 5.04. 44
we'll have dancing afterward. 5.04.120 P
and come here by chance, | we'll not be nice; LLL 5.02.219
we'll rest us, hermia, if you think it good, MND 2.02. 37
follow my voice; we'll try no manhood here. 3.02.412
three, | we'll hold a feast in great solemnity. 4.01.185
we'll none of that: 5.01. 46
we'll make our leisures to attend on yours. MV 1.01. 68
we'll play with them the first boy for a 3.02.213 P
we'll see our husbands | before they think of us 3.04. 58
we'll away to–night, | and be a day before our 4.02. 2
but we'll outface them, and outswear them too. 4.02. 17
we'll have a swashing and a martial outside, AYL 1.03.120
but come thy ways, we'll go along together, 2.03. 66
we'll light upon some settled low content. 2.03. 68
we'll lead you thither. 4.03.161
we'll begin these rites, | as we do trust 5.04.197
we'll have thee to a couch, | softer and sweeter SHR in.2. 37
we'll show thee io as she was a maid, | and how in.2. 54
well, we'll see't. in.2. 142 P
it skills not much, we'll fit him to our turn — 3.02.132
we'll overreach the greybeard, gremio, | the 3.02.145
and for this night we'll fast for company. 4.01.177
we'll pass the business privately and well. 4.04. 57
come, kate, we'll to bed. 5.02.184
cheek for ever, | we'll ne'er come there again." AWW 2.03. 72
we'll strive to bear it for your worthy sake 3.03. 5
we'll take your offer kindly. 3.05.101
we'll make you some sport with the fox ere we 3.06.102 P
as we'll direct her how 'tis best to bear it. 3.07. 20
in such a scarre | that we'll forsake ourselves. 4.02. 39
marry, we'll search. 4.03.202 P
we'll see what may be done, so you confess 4.03.246 P
lord the king, | we'll be before our welcome. 4.04. 14
had, and here we'll stay | to see our widower's 5.03. 69
we'll sift this matter further. 5.03.124
we'll once more hear orsino's embassy. TN 1.05.166
to anger him we'll have the bear again, and we 2.05. 9 P
we'll call thee at the cubiculo. go. 3.02. 52 P
come, we'll have him in a dark room and bound. 3.04.135 P
we'll whisper o'er a couplet or two of most sage 3.04.378 P
sir toby, because we'll be dress'd together. 5.01.204 P
and we'll strive to please you every day. 5.01.408
we'll part the time between 's then; WT 1.02. 18
stay, | we'll thwack him hence with distaffs. 1.02. 37
th' offenses we have made you do we'll answer, 1.02. 83
a lucky day, boy, and we'll do good deeds on't. 3.03.138 P
we'll buy the other things anon. 4.04.274 P
we'll have this song out anon by ourselves. 4.04.309 P
are in sad talk, and we'll not trouble them. 4.04.311 P
we'll none on't. 4.04.332 P
thou shalt), we'll bar thee from succession, 4.04.429
we'll make an instrument of this; 4.04.624
we'll be thy good masters. 5.02.174 P
we'll lay before this town our royal bones, JN 2.01. 41
where we'll set forth | in best appointment all 2.01.295
down our just–borne arms | we'll put these down, 2.01.346
for we'll create young arthur duke of britain 2.01.551
we'll calm the duke of norfolk, you your son. R2 1.01.159
we'll serve him too, and be his fellow so. 3.02. 99
we'll make foul weather with despised tears; 3.03.161
madam, we'll play at bowls. 3.04. 3
madam, we'll dance. 3.04. 6
madam, we'll tell tales. 3.04. 10
we'll keep him here, then what is that to him? 5.02.100
have no sooner achiev'd but we'll set upon them. 1H4 1.02.173 P
he does, he does, we'll be reveng'd on him. 1.03.291
neighbor mugs, we'll call up the gentlemen. 2.01. 44 P
we'll walk afoot a while, and ease our legs. 2.02. 79 P
we'll jure ye, faith. 2.02. 91 P
keep close, we'll read it at more advantage. 2.04.542 P
by this our book is drawn, we'll but seal, | and 3.01.265
we'll to sutton co'fil' to–night. 4.02. 3 P
we'll fight with him to–night. 4.03. 1
we'll withdraw a while. 4.03.107
come, it grows late, we'll to bed. 2H4 2.04.276 P
what you want in meat, we'll have in drink, but 5.03. 28 P
we'll ride all night. 5.03.131 P
france being ours, we'll bend it to our awe, H5 1.02.224
or there we'll sit, | ruling in large and ample 1.02.225
we'll chide this dolphin at his father's door. 1.02.308
on, and we'll digest | th' abuse of distance; 2.pr. 31
we'll not offend one stomach with our play. 2.pr. 40
and we'll be all three sworn brothers to france. 2.01. 12 P
we'll yet enlarge that man, | though cambridge, 2.02. 57
we'll give them present audience. 2.04. 67
beyond the river we'll encamp ourselves, | and 3.06.171
besides, we'll cut the throats of those we have, 4.07. 63
out of our demands, | and we'll consign thereto. 5.02. 90
my lord of burgundy, we'll take your oath, | and 5.02.371
in stead of gold, we'll offer up our arms, 1H6 1.01. 46
by my consent, we'll even let them alone. 1.02. 44
what she says i'll confirm. we'll fight it out. 1.02.128
presently we'll try; 1.02.149
or we'll burst them open, if that you come not 1.03. 28
gloucester, we'll meet to thy cost, be sure: 1.03. 82
and then we'll try what these dastard frenchmen 1.04.111
we'll follow them with all the power we have. 2.02. 33
stones, we'll fall to it with our teeth. 3.01. 89 P
and rulers over roan, | therefore we'll knock. 3.02. 12
and once again we'll sleep secure in roan. 3.02. 19
we'll pull his plumes and take away his train, 3.03. 7
we'll set thy statue in some holy place, | and 3.03. 14
father's castle walls | we'll crave a parley, to 5.03.130
well, go to, we'll have no bastards live, 5.04. 70
we'll quickly hoise duke humphrey from his seat. 2H6 1.01.169
we'll both together lift our heads to heaven, 1.02. 14
we'll see these things effected to the full. 1.02. 84
we'll hear more of your matter before the king. 1.03. 35 P
so one by one we'll weed them all at last, | and 1.03. 99
come, somerset, we'll see thee sent away. 1.03.220 P
we'll see your trinkets here all forthcoming. 1.04. 53
your grace, we'll take her from the sheriff. 2.04. 17
we'll have the lord say's head for selling the 4.02.160 P
no, no, and therefore we'll have his head. 4.02.173 P
we'll follow cade, we'll follow cade! 4.08. 33 P
we'll follow cade, we'll follow cade! 4.08. 33 P
we'll follow the king and clifford. 4.08. 53 P
we'll devise a mean | to reconcile you all unto 4.08. 68
we'll bait thy bears to death, | and manacle the 5.01.148
we'll all assist you; he that flies shall die. 3H6 1.01. 30
come, we'll after them. 1.01.256
she shall not need, we'll meet her in the field. 1.02. 65
we'll never leave till we have hewn thee down, 2.02.168
no, wrangling woman, we'll no longer stay, 2.02.176
this thick–grown brake we'll shroud ourselves, 3.01. 1
forbear awhile, we'll hear a little more. 3.01. 27
we'll yoke together like a double shadow | to 4.06. 49
forthwith we'll send him hence to brittany, 4.06. 97
and we'll debate | by what safe means the crown 4.07. 51
we grow stronger, then we'll make our claim; 4.07. 59
we'll forward towards warwick and his mates; 4.07. 82
as we may, we'll meet both thee and warwick. 4.07. 86
we'll quickly rouse the traitors in the same. 5.01. 65
no, we'll reason with him. R3 1.04.160 P
toward /ludlow then, for we'll not stay behind. 2.02.154
kind sister, thanks, we'll enter all together. 4.01. 11
you have now a broken banket, but we'll mend it. H8 1.04. 61
no, we'll no bullens. 3.02. 89
and so we'll leave you to your meditations | how 3.02.345
come safe off, | we'll dress him up in voices; TRO 1.03.381
overhold his price so much, | we'll none of him; 2.03.134
in second voice we'll not be satisfied, | we 2.03.140
we'll consecrate the steps that ajax makes 2.03.183
shall not hedge us out, we'll hear you sing, 3.01. 60 P
you draw backward, we'll put you i' th' fills. 3.02. 45 P
we'll execute your purpose, and put on | a form 3.03. 50
on, lord, we'll follow you. 4.01. 50
we'll not commend what we intend to sell. 4.01. 79
we'll answer it: 4.05.147
we'll forth and fight, | do deeds worth praise, 5.03. 92
kill him, and we'll have corn at our own price. COR 1.01. 10 P

intend to do, which now we'll show 'em in deeds. 1.01. 59 P
we'll break our walls | rather than they shall 1.04. 16
stand fast, we'll beat them to their wives, | as 1.04. 41
'gainst yourself you be incens'd, we'll put you 1.09. 56
we'll inform them | of our proceedings here on 2.02.158
we'll surety him. 3.01.177
we'll hear no more. 3.01.306
we'll attend you there; 3.01.330
not martius, we'll proceed | in our first way. 3.01.331
come, come, we'll prompt you. 3.02.106
and we'll no further. 4.02. 1
well, well, we'll leave you. 4.02. 43
for we'll | hear nought from rome in private. 5.03. 92
we'll meet them, | and help the joy. 5.04. 61
we'll deliver you | of your great danger. 5.06. 13
but if we live we'll be as sharp with you. TIT 1.01.410
with horn and hound we'll give your grace bon 1.01.494
or with our sighs we'll breathe the welkin dim, 3.01.211
ay, marry, will we, sir, and we'll be waited on. 4.01.122
be bold in us, we'll follow where thou lead'st, 5.01. 13
gregory, on my word, we'll not carry coals. ROM 1.01. 1 P
i mean, and we be in choler, we'll draw. 1.01. 3 P
we'll have no cupid hoodwink'd with a scarf, 1.04. 4
we'll measure them a measure and be gone. 1.04. 10
dun, we'll draw thee from the mire | /of /this 1.04. 41
we'll to dinner thither. 2.04.140 P
we'll keep no great ado — a friend or two, 3.04. 23
therefore we'll have some half a dozen friends, 3.04. 27
nurse, go with her, we'll to church to–morrow. 4.02. 37
come, we'll in here, tarry for the mourners, and 4.05.145 P
we'll bear, with your lordship. TIM 1.01.177
we'll share a bounteous time | in different 1.01.254
so soon as dinner's done, we'll forth again, 2.02. 14
believe't that we'll do any thing for gold. 4.03.150
what we can do, we'll do, to do you service. 5.01. 75
we'll leave you, brutus, | and, friends, JC 2.01.221
we'll send mark antony to the senate–house, 2.02. 52
we'll bring him to his house | with shouts and 3.02. 52
go up into the public chair, | we'll hear him. 3.02. 64
we'll hear the will. read it, mark antony. 3.02.138
read the will, we'll hear it, antony. 3.02.147
we'll hear him, we'll follow him, we'll die with 3.02.208 P
we'll hear him, we'll follow him, we'll die with 3.02.208 P
hear him, we'll follow him, we'll die with him. 3.02.208 P
we'll mutiny. 3.02.231
we'll burn the house of brutus. 3.02.231
most noble caesar! we'll revenge his death. 3.02.243
we'll burn his body in the holy place, | and 3.02.254
we'll along ourselves, and meet them at philippi 4.03.225
if we do meet again, we'll smile indeed; 5.01.120
to the sticking place, | and we'll not fail. MAC 1.07. 61
but we'll take to–morrow. 3.01. 22
anon we'll drink a measure | the table round. 3.04. 11
to–morrow | we'll hear ourselves again. 3.04. 31
come, we'll to sleep. 3.04.141
we'll answer. 4.01. 61
now we'll together, and the chance of goodness 4.03.136
at least we'll die with harness on our back. 5.05. 51
we'll have thee, as our rarer monsters are, 5.08. 25
we'll teach you to drink /deep ere you depart. HAM 1.02.175
then we'll shift our ground. 1.05.156
and at our more considered time we'll read, 2.02. 81
go to your rest, at night we'll feast together. 2.02. 84
we'll e'en to't like /french falc'ners — fly at 2.02.429 P
we'll have a speech straight. 2.02.430 P
him, friends, we'll hear a play to–morrow. 2.02.535 P
we'll ha't to–morrow night. 2.02.540 P
we'll so bestow ourselves that, seeing unseen, 3.01. 32
we'll call up our wisest friends | and let them 4.01. 38
we'll put on those shall praise your excellence, 4.07.131
we'll make a solemn wager on your cunnings — 4.07.155
we'll put the matter to the present push. 5.01.295
and you lie, sirrah, we'll have you whipt. LR 1.04.181 P
knave, you reverent braggart, | we'll teach you. 2.02.127
we'll set thee to school to an ant, to teach 2.04. 67 P
we'll no more meet, no more see one another. 2.04.220
we'll go to supper i' th' morning. 3.06. 84 P
we'll use | his countenance for the battle, 5.01. 62
so we'll live, | and pray, and sing, and tell 5.03. 11
and we'll talk with them too — | who loses and 5.03. 14
and we'll wear out, | in a wall'd prison, packs 5.03. 17
we'll see 'em starv'd first. 5.03. 25
at nine i' th' morning here we'll meet again. OTH 1.03.279
we'll wait upon your lordship. 3.02. 6
to–night we'll wander through the streets and ANT 1.01. 53
we'll know all our fortunes. 1.02. 44 P
will e'en but kiss octavia, and we'll follow. 2.04. 3
give me mine angle, we'll to th' river; 2.05. 10
we'll speak with thee at sea. 2.06. 25
we'll feast each other ere we part, and let's 2.06. 60
we'll to our ship, | away, my thetis! 3.07. 59
do so, we'll speak to them, and to–night i'll 3.13.189
we'll beat 'em into bench–holes. 4.07. 9
we'll spill the blood | that has to–day escap'd. 4.08. 3
souls do couch on flowers, we'll hand in hand, 4.14. 51
good sirs, take heart, | we'll bury him; 4.15. 86
we'll hear him what he says. 5.01. 51
now, noble charmian, we'll dispatch indeed, 5.02.230
we'll try with tongue too. CYM 2.03. 15 P
we'll talk of that hereafter. 3.02. 66
soft, soft, we'll no defense, | obedient as the 3.04. 79
but we'll even | all that good time will give us 3.04.181
cave, we'll browse on that | whilst what we have 3.06. 38
boys, we'll go dress our hunt. 3.06. 89
we'll mannerly demand thee of thy story, | so 3.06. 91
in the cave, | we'll come to you after hunting. 4.02. 2
we'll leave you for this time, go in, and rest. 4.02. 43
we'll not be long away. 4.02. 44
we'll hunt no more to–day, nor seek for danger 4.02.162
we'll speak it then. 4.02.242
go fetch him, | we'll say our song whilst. 4.02.254
we'll enforce it from thee | by a sharp torture. 4.03. 11
we'll slip you for a season, but our jealousy 4.03. 22
we'll higher to the mountains, there secure us. 4.04. 8
thou art my brother, so we'll hold thee ever. 5.05.399
we'll learn our freeness of a son–in–law: 5.05.421
of great jupiter | our peace we'll ratify; 5.05.483
this mercy shows we'll joy in such a son; PER 1.01.118
we'll mingle our bloods together in the earth, 1.02.113
and we'll pray for you. 1.04. 98
which welcome we'll accept; 1.04.107
go home, and we'll have flesh for /holidays, 2.01. 81 P
we'll sure provide. 2.01.162 P
if in the world he live, we'll seek him out; 2.04. 29
if in his grave he rest, we'll find him there; 2.04. 30
then you love us, we you, and we'll clasp hands: 2.04. 57
we'll bring your grace e'en to the edge a' th' 3.03. 35
we'll have no more gentlemen driven away. 4.06.129 P
yet nothing we'll omit | that bears recovery's 5.01. 53
we'll celebrate their nuptials, and ourselves 5.03. 80
we'll see how near art can come near their TNK 2.02.149
we'll see the sports, then every man to 's 2.03. 55
the sports | once ended, we'll perform. 2.03. 59
that's no matter, | we'll argue that hereafter. 3.03. 5
ladies, sit down, we'll stay it. 3.05. 99
out, | we'll make thee laugh and all this rout. 3.05.147
no, no, we'll use no horses. 3.06. 59
and all we'll dance an antic 'fore the duke, 4.01. 75
we'll to bed then. 5.02. 86
nay, we'll go with you, | i will not lose the 5.02.102
come, sweet, we'll go to dinner, | and then 5.02.107
go to dinner, | and then we'll play at cards. 5.02.108
and then we'll sleep together? 5.02.110
we'll follow cheerfully. 5.04. 39
the visages of bridegrooms we'll put on | and 5.04.127
we'll hear the earl of surrey. STM II.C 31 P
we'll hear both. II.C 33 P
we'll not hear my lord of surrey, no, no, no, no II.C 38 P
we'll be rul'd by you, master more, if you'll II.C 142 P

WELL* *(also vell)*

/WELL* 18 FR 0.0020 REL FR 16 V 2 P

he hath studied her /well, and translated her WIV 1.03. 49 P
/yet /i /well /remember | /the /favors /of R2 4.01.167
/well /then, /amen. 4.01.173
/is /this /golden /crown /like /a /deep /well 4.01.184
/and /very /well /appointed, /as /i /thought, 3H6 2.01.113
/well, /but /what's /a' /clock? R3 4.02.111
/well, /let /it /strike. 4.02.112
/their /loving /well /compos'd /with /gift /of TRO 4.04. 77
i humbly thank you, well, /well, /well. HAM 3.01. 91
i humbly thank you, well, /well, /well. 3.01. 91
and purpose not, since what i /well intend, LR 1.01.225
if but as /well i other accents borrow, | that 1.04. 1
/well, /sir, /the /poor /distressed /lear's /i' 4.03. 38
/well, /sir, /i'll /bring /you /to /our /master 4.03. 50
/very /well. 4.07. 23
/fare /you /well, /sir. 4.07. 94 P
/or /well /or /ill, /as /this /day's /battle's 4.07. 96
free of speech, sings, plays, and dances /well; OTH 3.03.185

WELL* 2282 FR 0.2579 REL FR 1542 V 740 P

well demanded, wench; TMP 1.02.139
thou hast slept well, | awake! 1.02.305
thou hast done well, fine ariel! 1.02.495
well, i have done. but yet — 2.01. 26
marriage, and we prosper well in our return. 2.01. 73 P
that "sort" was well fish'd for. 2.01.105 P
very well. 2.01.140
i do well believe your highness, and did it to 2.01.172 P
well — i am standing water. 2.01.221
can rule naples | as well as he that sleeps; 2.01.263
and look how well my garments sit upon me, 2.01.272
well, here's my comfort. 2.02. 45 P
voice now is to speak well of his friend; 2.02. 90 P
well drawn, monster, in good sooth! 2.02.147 P
it would become me | as well as it does you; 3.01. 29
well, let him go. 3.03. 10
honest lord, | thou hast said well; 3.03. 35
temper'd, may as well | wound the loud winds, or 3.03. 62
well! i conceive. 4.01. 50
well. 4.01. 56
well done! 4.01.142
this was well done, my bird. 4.01.184
if i did think, sir, i were well awake, | i'ld 5.01.229
was't well done? 5.01.240
be cheerful | and think of each thing well. 5.01.251
to the elements | be free, and fare thou well! 5.01.319
a silly answer, and fitting well a sheep. TGV 1.01. 81 P
well, i perceive i must be fain to bear with you 1.01.120 P
well, sir, here is for your pains. 1.01.131 P
well of his wealth; but of himself, so, so. 1.02. 13
well, let us go. 1.02.129
i have consider'd well his loss of time, | and 1.03. 19
i know it well. 1.03. 28
well hast thou advis'd; 1.03. 34
and that thou mayst perceive how well i like it, 1.03. 35
well — you'll still be too forward. 2.01. 11 P
sir, i know that well enough. 2.01. 50 P
she is not so fair as (of you) well favor'd. 2.01. 52 P
no, boy, but as well as i can do them. 2.01. 92 P
well — i guess the sequel; 2.01.116
i'll warrant you, 'tis as well: 2.01.164 P
well, he weeps on. 2.03. 26 P
well, i kiss her; 2.03. 28 P
well, i will go. 2.03. 59 P
well then i'll double your folly. 2.04. 21 P
i know it well, sir; 2.04. 31 P
i know it well, sir; 2.04. 43 P
and not without desert so well reputed. 2.04. 57
a son that well deserves | the honor and regard 2.04. 59
you know him well? 2.04. 61
well, sir — this gentleman is come to me | with 2.04. 78
your friends are well and have them much 2.04.123
when it stands well with him, it stands well 2.05. 22 P
stands well with him, it stands well with her. 2.05. 23 P
'tis well that i get it so. 2.05. 41 P
that fits as well as "tell me, good my lord, 2.07. 50
i know it well, my lord, and sure the match 3.01. 63
well, your old vice still: 3.01.284 P
well, that fault may be mended with a breakfast. 3.01.325 P
well, the best is, she hath no teeth to bite. 3.01.344 P
well, proceed. 3.01.352 P
well, i'll have her; 3.01.369 P
will well become such sweet–complaining 3.02. 85
to sort some gentlemen well skill'd in music. 3.02. 91
at saint gregory's well. 4.02. 84
but since your falsehood shall become you well 4.02.129
valiant, wise, remorseful, well accomplish'd: 4.03. 13
i like thee well, | and will employ thee in some 4.04. 40
she lov'd me well deliver'd it to me. 4.04. 73
because methinks that she lov'd you as well | as 4.04. 79
well, give her that ring and therewithal | this 4.04. 85
almost as well as i do know myself. 4.04.143
when she did think my master lov'd her well, 4.04.150
but well, when i discourse of love and peace. 5.02. 17
that you are well deriv'd. 5.02. 23
him he knew well, and guess'd that it was she, 5.02. 39
they love me well; 5.04. 16
thou art a gentleman and well deriv'd, | take 5.04.146
dozen white louses do become an old coat well; WIV 1.01. 20 P
it agrees well, passant. 1.01. 20 P
well, let us see honest master page. 1.01. 66 P
i am glad to see your worships well. 1.01. 79 P
ford, by my troth, you are very well met. 1.01.193 P
ay — i think my cousin meant well. 1.01.257 P
i am very well. 1.01.268 P
i love the sport well, but i shall as soon 1.01.290 P
well, sir. 1.02. 6 P
said i well, bully hector? 1.03. 11 P
well, sirs, i am almost out at heels. 1.03. 31 P
well, heaven send anne page no worse fortune! 1.04. 32 P
i doubt he be not well, that he comes not home. 1.04. 41 P
sir, the maid loves you, and all shall be well. 1.04.121 P
well, thereby hangs a tale. 1.04.149 P
but for you — well — go to. 1.04.154 P
well; 1.04.155 P
well, farewell, i am in great haste now. 1.04.161 P
for i know anne's mind as well as another does. 1.04.164 P
well — i do then; 2.01. 40 P
well — i will find you twenty lascivious 2.01. 80 P
well, i hope it be not so. 2.01.109 P
if i do find it — well. 2.01.143 P
'twas a good sensible fellow — well. 2.01.147 P
shalt have egress and regress — said i well? 2.01.218 P
well, i will look further into't, and i have a 2.01.237 P
if she be otherwise, 'tis labor well bestow'd. 2.01.240 P
well, on. mistress ford, you say — 2.02. 47 P
well; mistress ford, what of her? 2.02. 54 P
well — heaven forgive you, and all of us, i 2.02. 56 P
why, you say well. 2.02. 94 P
fare thee well, commend me to them both. 2.02.131 P
very well, sir, proceed. 2.02.190 P
well, sir. 2.02.193 P
would it apply well to the vehemency of your 2.02.238 P
amaimon sounds well; 2.02.297 P
lucifer, well; 2.02.297 P
barbason, well; 2.02.298 P
he has pray his pible well, dat he is no come. 2.03. 7 P
will it do well? 2.03. 79 P
said i well? 2.03. 89 P
said i well? 2.03. 95 P
fery well; what is it? 3.01. 51 P
this is well! 3.01.117 P
well, i will smite his noddles. pray you follow. 3.01.125 P
well met, mistress page. whither go you? 3.02. 9 P
well, i will take him, then torture my wife, 3.02. 40 P
well met, master ford. 3.02. 50 P
well, fare you well. 3.02. 84 P
well, fare you well. 3.02. 84 P
become nothing else, nor that well neither. 3.03. 60 P
thou mightst as well say i love to walk by the 3.03. 77 P
well, heaven knows how i love you, and you shall 3.03. 80 P
you use me well, master ford, do you? 3.03.202 P
well, i promis'd you a dinner. 3.03.223 P
as well as i love any woman in gloucestershire. 3.04. 43 P
well, i must of another errand to sir john 3.04.109 P
well, /and i be serv'd such another trick, i'll 3.05. 6 P
well, she laments, sir, for it, that it would 3.05. 43 P
well, i will visit her, tell her so. 3.05. 49 P
well, be gone; i will not miss her. 3.05. 55 P
i like his money well. 3.05. 58 P
well, on went he for a search, and away went i 3.05.105 P
well, i will proclaim myself what i am. 3.05.143 P
well, what is your accusative case? 4.01. 43 P
chest, trunk, well, vault, but he hath an 4.02. 61 P
indeed, master ford, this is not well indeed. 4.02.126 P
well said, brazen–face! 4.02.135 P
by my fidelity, this is not well, master ford; 4.02.153 P
well, he's not here i seek for. 4.02.158 P
'tis well, 'tis well, no more. 4.04. 10
'tis well, 'tis well, no more. 4.04. 10
a spirit, and well you know | the superstitious 4.04. 35
well, let it not be doubted but he'll come, 4.04. 44
the children must | be practic'd well to this, 4.04. 66
that slender, though well landed, is an idiot; 4.04. 86
the doctor is well money'd, and his friends 4.04. 88
speak well of them, varletto. 4.05. 64 P
fare you well. 4.05. 82 P
well, if my wind were but long enough /to /say 4.05.102 P
one of you does not serve heaven well, that you 4.05.125 P
well, husband your device; 4.06. 52
the white will decipher her well enough. 5.02. 10 P
is dark, light and spirits will become it well. 5.02. 12 P
fare you well, sir. 5.03. 6 P
well said, fairy hugh. 5.05.131 P
well, i am your theme. 5.05.161 P
well, what remedy? 5.05.236
well, i will muse no further. 5.05.239
so fare you well. MM 1.01. 58
though it do well, i do not relish well | their 1.01. 69
i do not relish well | their loud applause and 1.01. 69
once more fare you well. 1.01. 72
i thank you. fare you well. 1.01. 75
relish the petition well that prays for peace. 1.02. 16 P
well; 1.02. 27 P
well, well; 1.02. 60 P
well, well; 1.02. 60 P
well; what has he done? 1.02. 87 P
and discourse, | and well she can persuade. 1.02.186
as well for the encouragement of the like, which 1.02.187 P
well; 2.01. 37
well; 2.01. 51 P
your honor, i know not well what they are; 2.01. 53 P
this comes off well. here's a wise officer. 2.01. 57 P
i will detest myself also, as well as she, that 2.01. 75 P

very well; 2.01.106 P
why, very well; 2.01.109 P
why, very well then — 2.01.114 P
why, very well; 2.01.127 P
why, very well then; i hope here be truths. 2.01.133 P
well, sir, what did this gentleman to her? 2.01.146 P
ay, sir, very well. 2.01.150 P
nay, i beseech you mark it well. 2.01.151 P
well, i do so. 2.01.152 P
well; 2.01.211 P
so for this time, pompey, fare you well. 2.01.251 P
fare you well. 2.01.275 P
up your place, | and you shall well be spar'd. 2.02. 14
well; 2.02. 22
well; what's your suit? 2.02. 28
well; the matter? 2.02. 33
well, believe this, | no ceremony that to great 2.02. 58
ay, well said. 2.02. 89
that's well said. 2.02.109
fare you well. 2.02.142
well; come to me to–morrow. 2.02.155
go to; 'tis well. away! 2.02.156
i think it well; 2.04.130
one (as you are well express'd | by all external 2.04.136
if you think well to carry this as you may, the 3.01.256 P
fare you well, good father. 3.01.268 P
well, then imprison him. 3.02. 66 P
but wheresoever, i wish him well. 3.02. 91 P
lord angelo dukes it well in his absence; 3.02. 94 P
he does well in't. 3.02. 96 P
it is well allied; 3.02.102 P
sir, my name is lucio, well known to the duke. 3.02.159 P
of his proceeding, it shall become him well; 3.02.256 P
i am going to visit the prisoner. fare you well. 3.02.259 P
and well could wish | you had not found me here 4.01. 10
very well met, and well come. 4.01. 26
very well met, and well come. 4.01. 26
'tis well borne up. 4.01. 47
well, go, prepare yourself. 4.02. 69
i am as well acquainted here as i was in our 4.03. 1 P
this reprobate till he were well inclin'd, | and 4.03. 74
thou knowest not the duke so well as i do; 4.03.161 P
well; you'll answer this one day. fare ye well. 4.03.163 P
well; you'll answer this one day. fare ye well. 4.03.164 P
rest you well. 4.03.176 P
well; 4.04. 15 P
i shall, sir. fare you well. 4.04. 18 P
it shall be speeded well. 4.05. 10
well; 5.01.150
well, my lord. 5.01.183 P
well, my lord. 5.01.192 P
but stir not you till you have well determin'd 5.01.258
well, angelo, your evil quits you well. 5.01.496
well, angelo, your evil quits you well. 5.01.496
well, syracusian; ERR 1.01. 28
well, i will marry one day, but to try. 2.01. 42
so plainly, i could too well feel his blows; 2.01. 53 P
well, sir, i thank you. 2.02. 49 P
well, sir, then 'twill be dry. 2.02. 59 P
well, sir, learn to jest in good time — there's 2.02. 64 P
that never touch well welcome to thy hand, 2.02.116
but i should know her as well as she knows me. 2.02.202
dromio, play the porter well. 2.02.211
luce — luce, thou hast answer'd him well. 3.01. 53
well strook! 3.01. 56
well, i'll break in: go borrow me a crow. 3.01. 80
but she will well excuse | why at this time the 3.01. 92
shame hath a bastard fame, well managed; 3.02. 19
i, then well i know | your weeping sister is no 3.02. 41
i know it well, sir. 3.02.166
you are a merry man, sir, fare you well. 3.02.178
a man is well holp up that trusts to you: 4.01. 22
well, sir, i will. have you the chain about you? 4.01. 42
well, officer, arrest him at my suit. 4.01. 69
where is thy master, dromio? is he well? 4.02. 31
that runs counter, and yet draws dry–foot well; 4.02. 39
i know not at whose suit he is arrested well; 4.02. 44
well, sir, there rest in your foolery. 4.03. 34 P
well met, well met, master antipholus. 4.03. 45
well met, well met, master antipholus. 4.03. 45
and, yielding to him, humors well his frenzy. 4.04. 81
why look you strange on me? you know me well. 5.01.296
but for the stuffing — well, we are all mortal. ADO 1.01. 59 P
well, you are a rare parrot–teacher. 1.01.138 P
you love her, for the lady is very well worthy. 1.01.222 P
well, if ever thou dost fall from this faith, 1.01.255 P
well, as time shall try: 1.01.260 P
well, you will temporize with the hours. 1.01.274 P
they show well outward. 1.02. 8 P
well then, go you into hell. 2.01. 42 P
well, niece, i trust you will be rul'd by your 2.01. 50 P
well, niece, i hope to see you one day fitted 2.01. 57 P
well, i would you did like me. 2.01.100 P
i know you well enough, you are signior antonio. 2.01.112 P
wit out of the "hundred merry tales" — well, 2.01.130 P
i am sure you know him well enough. 2.01.133 P
you know me well, i am he. 2.01.162 P
well, i'll be reveng'd as i may. 2.01.209 P
your grace may well say i have lost it. 2.01.281 P
is neither sad, nor sick, nor merry, nor well; 2.01.294 P
one woman is fair, yet i am well; 2.03. 27 P
another is wise, yet i am well; 2.03. 28 P
another virtuous, yet i am well; 2.03. 28 P
o, very well, my lord. 2.03. 41
well, a horn for my money, when all's done. 2.03. 60 P
no, faith, thou sing'st well enough for a shift. 2.03. 77 P
bait the hook well, this fish will bite. 2.03.108 P
she doth well. 2.03.178 P
well, i am sorry for your niece. 2.03.198 P
well, we will hear further of it by your 2.03.205 P
i love benedick well, and i could wish he would 2.03.207 P
you have no stomach, signior, fare you well. 2.03.256 P
bear thee well in it, and leave us alone. 3.01. 13
well, every one /can master a grief but he that 3.02. 28 P
i think he holds you well, and in dearness of 3.02. 98 P
o plague right well prevented! 3.02.133 P
well, give them their charge, neighbor dogberry. 3.03. 7 P
well, for your favor, sir, why, give god thanks, 3.03. 19 P
well, you are to call at all the alehouses, and 3.03. 42 P
well, sir. 3.03. 49 P
well, masters, good night. 3.03. 84 P
well, masters, we hear our charge. 3.03. 88 P
tush, i may as well say the fool's the fool. 3.03.123 P
well. 3.04. 5 P
well, and you be not turn'd turk, there's no 3.04. 57 P
well said, i' faith, neighbor verges. 3.05. 35 P
well, god's a good man; 3.05. 36 P
drink some wine ere you go; fare you well. 3.05. 53 P
is my lord well, that he doth speak so wide? 4.01. 62
but fare thee well, most foul, most fair! 4.01.103
the proudest of them shall well hear of it. 4.01.192
this well carried shall on her behalf | change 4.01.210
and if it sort not well, you may conceal her, 4.01.240
'tis well consented; 4.01.251
i do love nothing in the world so well as you — 4.01.267 P
for me to say i lov'd nothing so well as you, 4.01.271 P
well, stand aside. 4.02. 30 P
well, fare you well, my lord. 5.01. 48
well, fare you well, my lord. 5.01. 48
well, all is one. 5.01. 49
that dare as well answer a man indeed | as i 5.01. 89
well, i will meet you, so i may have good cheer. 5.01.151 P
sir, your wit ambles well, it goes easily. 5.01.158 P
fare you well, boy, you know my mind. 5.01.185 P
by my troth, there's one meaning well suited. 5.01.225 P
i wish your worship well. 5.01.324 P
deserve well at my hands by helping me to the 5.02. 2 P
well, i will call beatrice to you, who i think 5.02. 23 P
fare you well now. 5.02. 46 P
fare you well. 5.03. 28
well, i am glad that all things sorts so well. 5.04. 7
well, i am glad that all things sorts so well. 5.04. 7
well, daughter, and you gentlewomen all, 5.04. 10
i had well hop'd thou wouldst have denied 5.04.112 P
term, | which i hope well is not enrolled there; LLL 1.01. 38
which i hope well is not enrolled there. 1.01. 46
as thus — to study where i well may dine, 1.01. 61
how well he's read, to reason against reading! 1.01. 94
proceeded well, to stop all good proceeding! 1.01. 95
well, say i am, why should proud summer boast 1.01.102
well, sit you out; go home, berowne; adieu. 1.01.110
how well this yielding rescues thee from shame! 1.01.118
for well you know here comes in embassy | the 1.01.134
well, sir, be it as the style shall give us 1.01.199 P
this is not so well as i look'd for, but the 1.01.279 P
well, it was proclaim'd damsel. 1.01.291 P
she deserves well. 1.02.119 P
fare you well. 1.02.132 P
well, sir, i hope when i do it i shall do it on 1.02.148 P
well, if ever i do see the merry days of 1.02.159 P
well fitted in arts, glorious in arms; 2.01. 45
nothing becomes him ill that he would well. 2.01. 46
breast, | and go well satisfied to france again. 2.01.152
a gallant lady. monsieur, fare you well. 2.01.196
it was well done of you to take him at his word. 2.01.217
a message well sympathiz'd — a horse to be 3.01. 51 P
to sell a bargain well is as cunning as fast and 3.01.103
o, my good knave costard, exceedingly well met! 3.01.143 P
well, i will do it, sir; fare you well. 3.01.156 P
well, i will do it, sir; fare you well. 3.01.156 P
well, i will love, write, sigh, pray, sue, groan 3.01.204
well, lords, to–day we shall have our dispatch; 4.01. 5
kill, | and shooting well is then accounted ill. 4.01. 25
well then i am the shooter. 4.01.114
a mark marvellous well shot, for they both did 4.01.130
for their sons are well tutor'd by you, and 4.02. 74 P
it is well. 4.02. 89 P
well learned is that tongue that well can thee 4.02.112
is that tongue that well can thee commend, | all 4.02.112
marvellous well for the pen. 4.02.152 P
well, "set thee down, sorrow!" 4.03. 3 P
well prov'd, wit! 4.03. 5 P
well prov'd again a' my side! 4.03. 7 P
well, i do nothing in the world but lie, and lie 4.03. 11 P
well, she hath one a' my sonnets already: 4.03. 14 P
an amber–color'd raven was well noted. 4.03. 86
sighs reek from you, noted well your passion. 4.03.138
and beauty's crest becomes the heavens well. 4.03.252
men of peace, well encount'red. 5.01. 34 P
the word is well cull'd, chose, sweet, and apt, 5.01. 93 P
hiss, you may cry, "well done, hercules, now 5.01.138 P
well bandied both, a set of wit well played. 5.02. 29
well bandied both, a set of wit well played. 5.02. 29
that well by heart hath conn'd his embassage. 5.02. 98
third he caper'd, and cried, "all goes well." 5.02.113
and they, well mock'd, depart away with shame. 5.02.156
well run, dice! 5.02.233
well, better wits have worn plain statute–caps. 5.02.281
mock them still, as well known as disguis'd. 5.02.301
and were you well advis'd? 5.02.434
well said, old mocker. 5.02.549
well follow'd: judas was hang'd on an elder. 5.02.606 P
well, befall what will befall, | i'll jest a 5.02.870
might well have made our sport a comedy. 5.02.876
know of your youth, examine well your blood, MND 1.01. 68
i am, my lord, as well deriv'd as he, | as well 1.01. 99
as well deriv'd as he, | as well possess'd; 1.01.100
which i could well | beteem them from the 1.01.130
well, proceed. 1.02. 57 P
well — i will undertake it. 1.02. 90 P
well — go thy way. 2.01.146
of hell, | to die upon the hand i love so well. 2.01.244
fare thee well, nymph. 2.01.245
now all is well. 2.02. 25
such separation as may well be said | becomes a 2.02. 58
but fare you well; 2.02.131
then i well perceive you are not nigh: 2.02.155
i have a device to make all well. 3.01. 16 P
well; 3.01. 23 P
well; 3.01. 47 P
if that may be, then all is well. 3.01. 72 P
master mustardseed, i know your patience well. 3.01.192 P
i pray thee, tell me then that he is well. 3.02. 77
our sex, as well as i, may chide you for it, 3.02.218
this sport, well carried, shall be chronicled. 3.02.240
but fare ye well; 3.02.243
for well i wot | thou run'st before me, shifting 3.02.422
have his mare again, and all shall be well. 3.02.463
jove shield thee well for this! 5.01.178
it is well; 5.01.236 P
well roar'd, lion. 5.01.265 P
well run, thisby. 5.01.266 P
well shone, moon. 5.01.267 P
well mous'd, lion. 5.01.269 P
this palpable–gross play hath well beguil'd 5.01.367
fare ye well, | we leave you now with better MV 1.01. 58
you look not well, signior antonio, | you have 1.01. 73
fare ye well a while, | i'll end my exhortation 1.01.103
well, we will leave you then till dinner–time. 1.01.105
well, keep me company but two years moe, | thou 1.01.108
fare you well! i'll grow a talker for this gear. 1.01.110
well, tell me now what lady is the same | to 1.01.119
you know me well, and herein spend but time | to 1.01.153
good sentences, and well pronounc'd. 1.02. 10 P
they would be better if well follow'd. 1.02. 11 P
i remember him well, and i remember him worthy 1.02.120 P
three thousand ducats — well. 1.03. 1 P
for three months — well. 1.03. 3 P
antonio shall become bound — well. 1.03. 6 P
well then, your bond; 1.03. 68
well, shylock, shall we be beholding to you? 1.03.105
well then, it now appears you need my help. 1.03.114
well, the most courageous fiend bids me pack. 2.02. 10 P
well, my conscience, hanging about the neck of 2.02. 13 P
he had a kind of taste — well, my conscience 2.02. 18 P
"conscience," say i, "you counsel well." 2.02. 21 P
"fiend," say i, "you counsel well." 2.02. 22 P
poor man and, god be thank'd, well to live. 2.02. 53 P
well, let his father be what 'a will, we talk of 2.02. 54 P
well, old man, i will tell you news of your son. 2.02. 77 P
well, well; 2.02.102 P
well, well; 2.02.102 P
i know thee well, thou hast obtain'd thy suit. 2.02.144
the old proverb is very well parted between my 2.02.149 P
thou speak'st it well. 2.02.152
i have ne'er a tongue in my head, well! 2.02.157 P
well, if fortune be a woman, she's a good wench 2.02.166 P
like one well studied in a sad ostent | to 2.02.196
well, we shall see your bearing. 2.02.198
but fare you well, | i have some business. 2.02.203
but fare thee well, there is a ducat for thee, 2.03. 4
well, thou shalt see, thy eyes shall be thy 2.05. 1
well, jessica, go in. 2.05. 51
fare you well, your suit is cold." 2.07. 73
marry, well rememb'red. 2.08. 26
and well said too; 2.09. 37
well, but to my choice: 2.09. 49
you knew, none so well, none so well as you, of 3.01. 24 P
knew, none so well, none so well as you, of my 3.01. 24 P
but lest you should not understand me well — 3.02. 7
there may as well be amity and life | 'tween 3.02. 30
well then, confess and live. 3.02. 35
if you be well pleas'd with this, | and hold 3.02.135
that thinks he hath done well in people's eyes, 3.02.142
it be in mind, | nor well, unless in mind. 3.02.235
his reason well i know: 3.03. 21
well, jailer, on. 3.03. 35
so fare you well till we shall meet again. 3.04. 40
and am well pleas'd | to wish it back on you. 3.04. 43
fare you well, jessica. 3.04. 44
well, you are gone both ways. 3.05. 17 P
e'en as many as could well live one by another. 3.05. 22 P
well, i'll set you forth. 3.05. 90
you may as well go stand upon the beach | and 4.01. 71
you may as well use question with the wolf | why 4.01. 73
you may as well forbid the mountain pines | to 4.01. 75
you may as well do any thing most hard, | as 4.01. 78
i am arm'd and well prepar'd. 4.01.264
give me your hand, bassanio, fare you well! 4.01.265
'tis well you offer it behind her back, | the 4.01.293
give me leave to go from hence, | i am not well. 4.01.396
he is well paid that is well satisfied, | and i, 4.01.415
he is well paid that is well satisfied, | and i, 4.01.415
and therein do account myself well paid. 4.01.417
i wish you well, and so i take my leave. 4.01.420
and know how well i have deserv'd this ring, 4.01.446
well, peace be with you! 4.01.448
this deed will be well welcome to lorenzo. 4.02. 4
fair sir, you are well o'erta'en. 4.02. 5
did young lorenzo swear he lov'd her well, 5.01. 18
no more than i am well acquitted of. 5.01.138
know him i shall, i am well sure of it. 5.01.229
therefore be well advis'd | how you do leave me 5.01.234
well, do you so; 5.01.236
well, while i live i'll fear no other thing | so 5.01.306
my brother, on his blessing, to breed me well; AYL 1.01. 4 P
o, sir, very well; here in your orchard. 1.01. 41 P
well, sir, get you in. 1.01. 76 P
without some broken limb shall acquit him well. 1.01.128 P
brook such disgrace well as he shall run into, 1.01.134 P
well, i will forget the condition of my estate, 1.02. 15 P
well said — that was laid on with a trowel. 1.02.106 P
well, the beginning, that is dead and buried. 1.02.117 P
fare you well! pray heaven i be deceiv'd in you! 1.02.197 P
beseech your grace, i am not yet well breath'd. 1.02.218 P
but fare thee well, thou art a gallant youth. 1.02.229
sir, you have well deserv'd. 1.02.242
ay. fare you well, fair gentleman. 1.02.248
sir, you have wrastled well, and overthrown 1.02.254
have with you. fare you well. 1.02.256
sir, fare you well. 1.02.283
fare you well. 1.02.286
why should i not? doth he not deserve well? 1.03. 37 P
how well in thee appears | the constant service 2.03. 56
cannot recompense me better | than to die well, 2.03. 76
well, this is the forest of arden. 2.04. 15 P
well then, if ever i thank any man, i'll thank 2.05. 25 P
well, i'll end the song. 2.05. 31 P
well said! 2.06. 13 P
his youthful hose, well sav'd, a world too wide 2.07.160
well, push him out of doors, | and let my 3.01. 15
that it is solitary, i like it very well; 3.02. 16 P
it is in the fields, it pleaseth me well; 3.02. 18 P
a spare life, look you, it fits my humor well; 3.02. 20 P

it may well be call'd jove's tree, when it drops		3.02.236 P
to see such a sight, it well becomes the ground.		3.02.242 P
very well. what would you?		3.02.298 P
detect the lazy foot of time as well as a clock.		3.02.304 P
one that knew courtship too well, for there he		3.02.346 P
you, deserves as well a dark house and a whip as		3.02.401 P
well, i am not fair, and therefore i pray the		3.03. 33 P
well, prais'd be the gods for thy foulness!		3.03. 40 P
well, the gods give us joy!		3.03. 47 P
well, that is the dowry of his wife, 'tis none		3.03. 55 P
sir oliver martext, you are well met.		3.03. 65 P
you are very well met.		3.03. 74 P
of another, for he is not like to marry me well;		3.03. 92 P
and not being well married, it will be a good		3.03. 92 P
well; and what of him?		3.04. 51
fare you well.		3.05. 63
but since that thou canst talk of love so well,		3.05. 94
not very well, but i have met him oft, | and he		3.05.106
'tis but a peevish boy — yet he talks well —		3.05.110
yet words do well | when he that speaks them		3.05.111
his leg is but so so — and yet 'tis well;		3.05.119
well, in her person, i say i will not have you.		4.01. 91 P
well, time is the old justice that examines all		4.01.199 P
and it would do well to set the deer's horns		4.02. 4 P
well, shepherd, well, | this is a letter of your		4.03. 19
well, shepherd, well, | this is a letter of your		4.03. 19
well, go your way to her (for i see love hath		4.03. 69 P
and well he might so do, | for well i know he		4.03.123
might so do, | for well i know he was unnatural.		4.03.124
a body would think this was well counterfeited!		4.03.166 P
you tell your brother how well i counterfeited.		4.03.167 P
well then, take a good heart and counterfeit to		4.03.173 P
why, thou say'st well.		5.01. 30 P
so fare you well;		5.02.121 P
well met, honest gentleman.		5.03. 7 P
by my troth, well met.		5.03. 8 P
i like him very well.		5.04. 53 P
if i said his beard was not cut well, he was in		5.04. 71 P
if i sent him word again, it was not well cut,		5.04. 73 P
if again, it was not well cut, he disabled my		5.04. 75 P
if again, it was not well cut, he would answer i		5.04. 77 P
if again, it was not well cut, he would say i		5.04. 79 P
how oft did you say his beard was not well cut?		5.04. 84 P
ends | that here were well begun and well begot;		5.04.171
ends | that here were well begun and well begot;		5.04.171
your patience and your virtue well deserves it;		5.04.187
i charge thee, tender well my hounds | (brach	SHR	in.1. 16
but sup them well, and look unto them all,		in.1. 28
then take him up, and manage well the jest.		in.1. 45
'twas where you woo'd the gentlewoman so well.		in.1. 85
well, you are come to me in happy time, | the		in.1. 90
tears, | an onion will do well for such a shift,		in.1. 126
i know the boy will well usurp the grace,		in.1. 131
presence | may well abate the over–merry spleen,		in.1. 137
well, bring our lady hither to our sight, | and		in.2. 74
marry, i fare well, for here is cheer enough.		in.2. 101
i know it well. what must i call her?		in.2. 108
well, we'll see't.		in.2. 142 P
my trusty servant, well approv'd in all, | here		1.01. 7
gramercies, tranio, well dost thou advise.		1.01. 41
because i know you well and love you well,		1.01. 53
because i know you well and love you well,		1.01. 53
well said, master, mum, and gaze your fill.		1.01. 73
be lucentio, | because so well i love lucentio.		1.01.217
and rap me well, or i'll knock your knave's pate		1.02. 12
well, was it fit for a servant to use his master		1.02. 31 P
whom would to god i had well knock'd at first,		1.02. 34
knock me well, and knock me soundly"?		1.02. 41 P
not her, | and he knew my deceased father well.		1.02.102
a' my word, and she knew him as well as i do,		1.02.108 P
baptista as a schoolmaster | well seen in music,		1.02.134
o, very well, i have perus'd the note.		1.02.144
too, | and let me have them very well perfum'd;		1.02.151
and you are well met, signior hortensio.		1.02.163
and by good fortune i have lighted well | on		1.02.167
her turn, well read in poetry | and other books,		1.02.169
'tis well;		1.02.171
so said, so done, is well.		1.02.185
well begun, tranio.		1.02.227
then well one more may fair bianca have;		1.02.243
sir, you say well, and well you do conceive,		1.02.269
sir, you say well, and well you do conceive,		1.02.269
i do, | so well i know my duty to my elders.		2.01. 7
and now i well perceive | you have but jested		2.01. 19
son, | a man well known throughout all italy.		2.01. 69
i know him well; you are welcome for his sake.		2.01. 70
by report | i know him well.		2.01.105
bid them use them well.		2.01.110
you knew my father well, and in him me, | left		2.01.116
ay, when the special thing is well obtain'd,		2.01.128
well mayst thou woo, and happy be thy speed!		2.01.138
well, go with me and be not so discomfited.		2.01.163
well have you heard, but something hard of		2.01.183
well ta'en, and like a buzzard.		2.01.206
well aim'd of such a young one.		2.01.235
thy beauty that doth make me like thee well,		2.01.274
how but well, sir?		2.01.282
how but well?		2.01.282
we have 'greed so well together | that upon		2.01.297
that "only" came well in.		2.01.363
and may not young men die as well as old?		2.01.391
well, gentlemen, | i am thus resolv'd:		2.01.392
well, i must wait, | and watch withal, for, but		3.01. 61
upon my life, petruchio means but well,		3.02. 22
and yet i come not well.		3.02. 88
not so well apparell'd | as i wish you were.		3.02. 89
as you shall well be satisfied with all.		3.02.109
'twere well for kate and better for myself.		3.02.120
the meat was well, if you were so contented.		4.01.169
lov'd /none in the world so well as lucentio.		4.02. 13
well, sir, to do you courtesy, | this will i do,		4.02. 91
i like it well, good grumio, fetch it me.		4.03. 21
i love thee well in that thou lik'st it not.		4.03. 83
you bid me make it orderly and well, | according		4.03. 94
well, sir, in brief, the gown is not for me.		4.03.155
well, come, my kate, we will unto your father's		4.03.169
and well we may come there by dinner–time.		4.03.188
'tis well, and hold your own in any case | with		4.04. 6
you, | signior baptista, of whom i hear so well.		4.04. 37
plainness and your shortness please me well.		4.04. 39
we'll pass the business privately and well.		4.04. 57
it likes me well.		4.04. 62
well, forward, forward!		4.05. 24
and now by law, as well as reverent age, | i may		4.05. 60
well, petruchio, this has put me in heart.		4.05. 77
i told you your son was well belov'd in padua.		5.01. 25 P
is not this well?		5.01.149
down, | for now we sit to chat as well as eat.		5.02. 11
very well mended. kiss him for that, good widow.		5.02. 25
believe me, sir, they butt together well.		5.02. 39
'tis well, sir, that you hunted for yourself;		5.02. 55
well, i say no;		5.02. 65
should well agree with our external parts?		5.02.168
well, go thy ways, old lad, for thou shalt ha't.		5.02.181
i know not what he shall — god send him well!	AWW	1.01.176
that i wish well. 'tis pity —		1.01.179
that wishing well had not a body in't, | which		1.01.181
virtue of a good wing, and i like the wear well.		1.01.205 P
it well may serve | a nursery to our gentry, who		1.02. 15
than in haste, | hath well compos'd thee.		1.02. 21
he had the wit which i can well observe | to–day		1.02. 32
which, followed well, would demonstrate them now		1.02. 47
well, sir.		1.03. 15 P
madam, 'tis not so well that i am poor, though		1.03. 16 P
at an earthquake, 'twould mend the lottery well;		1.03. 88 P
well, now.		1.03. 98 P
that done, laugh well at me.		2.01. 87
that dare leave two together, fare you well.		2.01. 98
my father, | in what he did profess, well found.		2.01.102
i must not hear thee, fare thee well, kind maid!		2.01.145
spoke, unpitied let me die, | and well deserv'd.		2.01.189
you would answer very well to a whipping, if you		2.02. 55 P
o lord, sir! — why, there't serves well again.		2.02. 62 P
just, you say well; so would i have said.		2.03. 19 P
you say well.		2.03. 39 P
peruse them well.		2.03. 61
i know her well;		2.03.113
that you are well restor'd, my lord, i'm glad.		2.03.147
lord and master did well to make his recantation		2.03.186 P
what i dare too well do, i dare not do.		2.03.200 P
so, my good window of lettice, fare thee well!		2.03.214 P
well, i shall be wiser.		2.03.223 P
well, thou hast a son shall take this disgrace		2.03.235 P
well, i must be patient, there is no fettering		2.03.236 P
my mother greets me kindly. is she well?		2.04. 1 P
she is not well, but yet she has her health.		2.04. 2 P
she's very merry, but yet she is not well;		2.04. 3 P
but thanks be given, she's very well, and wants		2.04. 4 P
but yet she is not well.		2.04. 5 P
if she be very well, what does she ail that		2.04. 6 P
what does she ail that she's not very well?		2.04. 7 P
truly, she's very well indeed, but for two		2.04. 8 P
a good knave, i' faith, and well fed.		2.04. 38
o, i know him well, i, sir, he, sir, 's a good		2.05. 18 P
fare you well, my lord, and believe this of me:		2.05. 42 P
yes, i do know him well, and common speech		2.05. 52
well, what would you say?		2.05. 78
you know your places well;		3.01. 21
this is not well, rash and unbridled boy, | to		3.02. 28
her, | i could have well diverted her intents,		3.04. 21
well, diana, take heed of this french earl.		3.05. 11 P
i like him well.		3.05. 81
lose our drum! well.		3.05. 88 P
well, we cannot greatly condemn our success.		3.06. 55 P
if you speed well in it, the duke shall both		3.06. 69 P
though my estate be fall'n, i was well born,		3.07. 4
for you have show'd me that which well approves		3.07. 13
well, that's set down.		4.03.147 P
well, that's set down.		4.03.155 P
well, that's set down.		4.03.174 P
well, is this captain in the duke of florence's		4.03.192 P
our interpreter does it well.		4.03.209 P
half won is match well made;		4.03.225
match, and well make it;		4.03.225
only to seem to deserve well, and to beguile the		4.03.299 P
coward, i'd compel it of you, but fare you well.		4.03.322 P
fare ye well, sir, i am for france too.		4.03.328 P
that you may well perceive i have not wrong'd		4.04. 1
when briers shall have leaves as well as thorns,		4.04. 32
all's well that ends well!		4.04. 35
all's well that ends well!		4.04. 35
go thy ways, let my horses be well look'd to,		4.05. 58 P
i like him well, 'tis not amiss.		4.05. 68 P
all's well that ends well yet, | though time		5.01. 25
all's well that ends well yet, | though time		5.01. 25
and you shall find yourself to be well thank'd,		5.01. 36
well, call him hither, | we are reconcil'd, and		5.03. 20
he looks well on't.		5.03. 31
well excus'd.		5.03. 55
that you are well acquainted with yourself,		5.03.106
the heavens have thought well on thee, lafew,		5.03.150
all yet seems well, and if it end so meet, | the		5.03.333
all is well ended, if this suit be won, | that		ep 2
madam, well, for i was bred and born | not three	TN	1.02. 22
fare you well, gentlemen.		1.03. 60 P
but it becomes /me well enough, does't not?		1.03.100 P
it does indifferent well in a /dun–color'd stock		1.03.135 P
it shall become thee well to act my woes.		1.04. 26
prosper well in this, | and thou shalt live as		1.04. 38
he that is well hang'd in this world needs to		1.05. 5 P
well, god give them wisdom that have it;		1.05. 14 P
well, go thy way, if sir toby would leave		1.05. 26 P
well, sir, for want of other idleness, i'll bide		1.05. 64 P
with leasing, for thou speak'st well of fools!		1.05. 98 P
'tis a fair young man, and well attended.		1.05.103 P
well, it's all one.		1.05.129 P
for besides that it is excellently well penn'd,		1.05.174 P
is't not well done?		1.05.235 P
in voices well divulg'd, free, learn'd, and		1.05.260
above my fortunes, yet my state is well:		1.05.278
fare you well!		1.05.282
"above my fortunes, yet my state is well:		1.05.290
well, let it be.		1.05.298
fare ye well at once;		2.01. 39 P
by'r lady, sir, and some dogs will catch well.		2.03. 62 P
ay, he does well enough if he be dispos'd, and		2.03. 81 P
i think it well, my lord.		2.04. 35
too well what love women to men may owe;		2.04.105
thy smiles become thee well.		2.05.176 P
i understand you, sir. 'tis well begg'd.		3.01. 53 P
and to do that well craves a kind of wit.		3.01. 61
youth's a rare courtier — "rain odors," well.		3.01. 87 P
might well have given us bloody argument.		3.03. 32
and suits well for a servant with my fortunes.		3.04. 6
"be not afraid of greatness": 'twas well writ.		3.04. 39 P
well, jove, not i, is the doer of this, and he		3.04. 82 P
"fare thee well, and god have mercy upon one of		3.04.166 P
well, come again to–morrow.		3.04.216
fare thee well!		3.04.216
i'll ride your horse as well as i ride you.		3.04.291 P
he will bear you easily, and reins well.		3.04.324 P
i know your favor well, | though now you have no		3.04.329
take him away, he knows i know him well.		3.04.331
well held out, i' faith!		4.01. 5 P
you are well flesh'd!		4.01. 39 P
well, i'll put it on, and i will dissemble		4.02. 4 P
am not tall enough to become the function well,		4.02. 7 P
the knave counterfeits well; a good knave.		4.02. 19 P
well said, master parson.		4.02. 27 P
fare thee well.		4.02. 57 P
fare thee well.		4.02. 60 P
i would we were well rid of this knavery.		4.02. 67 P
as ever thou wilt deserve well at my hand, help		4.02. 80 P
i am as well in my wits, fool, as thou art.		4.02. 88 P
but as well!		4.02. 89 P
i tell thee i am as well in my wits as any man		4.02.106 P
for though my soul disputes well with my sense,		4.03. 9
if you mean well, | now go with me and with this		4.03. 22
i know thee well; how dost thou, my good fellow?		5.01. 10 P
well, i will be so much a sinner to be a		5.01. 34 P
that face of his i do remember well, | yet, when		5.01. 51
at the stave's end as well as a man in his case		5.01.285 P
look then to be well edified when the fool		5.01.290 P
benefit of my senses as well as your ladyship.		5.01.305 P
on, | to think me as well a sister as a wife,		5.01.317
well, grant it then, | and tell me, in the		5.01.334
i very well agree with you in the hopes of him;	WT	1.01. 37 P
tell him you are sure | all in bohemia's well;		1.02. 31
well said, hermione.		1.02. 33
have i twice said well?		1.02. 90
fertile bosom, | and well become the agent;		1.02.114
to my heart, as well | my chamber–councils,		1.02.236
was my negligence, | not weighing well the end;		1.02.258
and it is caught | of you that yet are well.		1.02.387
a sickness caught of me, and yet i well?		1.02.398
you may as well | forbid the sea for to obey the		1.02.426
i know't too well.		2.01. 55
you, my lords, | look on her, mark her well;		2.01. 65
have i done well?		2.01.187
well done, my lord.		2.01.188
well;		2.02. 16
as well as one so great and so forlorn | may		2.02. 20
being well arriv'd from delphos, are both landed		2.03.196
thou didst speak but well | when most the truth;		3.02.232
blossom, speed thee well!		3.03. 46
well may i get aboard!		3.03. 57
youth are forgiven you, you're well to live.		3.03.121 P
now may be | in fair bohemia, and remember well,		4.01. 21
bouget, | then my account i well may give, | and		4.03. 21
i know this man well;		4.03. 95 P
then fare thee well, i must go buy spices for		4.03.116 P
well you fit our ages | with flow'rs of winter.		4.04. 78
would wish | this youth should say 'twere well,		4.04.102
i love a ballad but even too well, if it be		4.04.188 P
'tis well they are whisp'ring.		4.04.247 P
it becomes thy oath full well, | thou to me thy		4.04.300
and you shall pay well for 'em.		4.04.314 P
i cannot speak | so well, nothing so well;		4.04.381
i cannot speak | so well, nothing so well;		4.04.381
well, my lord, | if you may please to think i		4.04.520
i am a poor fellow, sir. i know ye well enough.		4.04.639 P
well;		4.04.707 P
well, give me the moi'ty.		4.04.812 P
holy | than to rejoice the former queen is well?		5.01. 30
this hour, he had pair'd | well with this lord;		5.01.117
as beauty, | that you might well enjoy her.		5.01.215
you are well met, sir.		5.02.128 P
sovereign sir, | i did not well, i meant well.		5.03. 3
sovereign sir, | i did not well, i meant well.		5.03. 3
so her dead likeness, i do well believe,		5.03. 15
behold, and say 'tis well.		5.03. 20
that is well known — and, as i think, one	JN	1.01. 60
but that i am as well begot, my liege | (fair		1.01. 77
mine eye hath well examined his parts, | and		1.01. 89
well, sir, by this you cannot get my land;		1.01. 97
i like thee well.		1.01.148
near or far off, well won is still well shot,		1.01.174
near or far off, well won is still well shot,		1.01.174
well, now can i make any joan a lady.		1.01.184
sir robert could do well — marry, to confess —		1.01.236
who lives and dares but say thou didst not well		1.01.271
before angiers well met, brave austria.		2.01. 1
well, then to work!		2.01. 37
o, well did he become that lion's robe, | that		2.01.141
that hangs above our heads, | i like it well.		2.01.398
it likes us well, young princes;		2.01.533
for i am well assur'd | that i did so when i was		2.01.534
go we, as well as haste will suffer us, | to		2.01.559
the world, who of itself is peized well, | made		2.01.575
well, whiles i am a beggar, i will rail, | and		2.01.593
be well advis'd, tell o'er thy tale again.		3.01. 5
well, ruffian, i must pocket up these wrongs,		3.01.200
o, be remov'd from him, and answer well!		3.01.218
no longer than we well could wash our hands | to		3.01.234
well then, france shall rue.		3.01.325
yet i love thee well, | and, by my troth, i		3.03. 54
and, by my troth, i think thou lov'st me well.		3.03. 55
so well, that what you bid me undertake,		3.03. 56
well, i'll not say what i intend for thee.		3.03. 68
madam, fare you well, | i'll send those powers		3.03. 69
courage and comfort! all shall yet go well.		3.04. 4
what can go well, when we have run so ill?		3.04. 5
well could i bear that england had this praise,		3.04. 15
too well, too well i feel | the different plague		3.04. 59

too well i feel | the different plague of each 3.04. 59
fare you well! 3.04. 99
well, see to live; 4.01.121
when workmen strive to do better than well, 4.02. 28
to overbear it, and we are all well pleas'd, 4.02. 37
what you would have reform'd that is not well, 4.02. 44
and well shall you perceive how willingly | i 4.02. 45
once more to–day well met, distemper'd lords! 4.03. 21
'tis not an hour since i left him well. 4.03.104
i left him well. 4.03.139
on this ascension–day, remember well, | upon 5.01. 22
i know | our party may well meet a prouder foe. 5.01. 79
that ever fury breath'd, | the youth says well. 5.02.128
and is well prepar'd | to whip this dwarfish war 5.02.134
fare thee well! 5.02.160
well; 5.05. 20
of thine affairs, as well as thou of mine? 5.06. 5
i will upon all hazards well believe | thou art 5.06. 7
art my friend that know'st my tongue so well. 5.06. 8
myself, well mounted, hardly have escap'd. 5.06. 42
he sees | ourselves well sinewed to our defense. 5.07. 88
us, | as well appeareth by the cause you come: R2 1.01. 26
i do turn to thee, | and mark my greeting well; 1.01. 36
a brace of draymen bid god speed him well, | and 1.04. 32
well, he is gone, and with him go these thoughts 1.04. 37
for he is just and always loved us well. 2.01.221
well, lords, the duke of lancaster is dead. 2.01.224
well furnished by the duke of britain | with 2.01.285
and well met, gentlemen. 2.02. 41
well, somewhat we must do. 2.02.116
well, i will for refuge straight to bristow 2.02.135
well, we may meet again. 2.02.149
well, well, i see the issue of these arms. 2.03.152
well, well, i see the issue of these arms. 2.03.152
so fare you well, | unless you please to enter 2.03.159
as well assured richard their king is dead. 2.04. 17
needs must i like it well; 3.02. 4
they break their faith to god as well as us. 3.02.101
too well, too well thou tell'st a tale so ill. 3.02.121
too well, too well thou tell'st a tale so ill. 3.02.121
thou chid'st me well. 3.02.188
our fair appointments may be well perus'd. 3.03. 53
for well we know no hand of blood and bone | can 3.03. 79
would not this ill do well? 3.03.170
well, well, i see | i talk but idlely, and you 3.03.170
well, well, i see | i talk but idlely, and you 3.03.170
well you deserve; 3.03.200
they well deserve to have | that know the 3.03.200
'tis well that thou hast cause, | but thou 3.04. 19
i do remember well | the very time aumerle and 4.01. 60
well have you argued, sir, and, for your pains, 4.01.150
well, bear you well in this new spring of time, 5.02. 50
well, bear you well in this new spring of time, 5.02. 50
your mother well hath pray'd, and prove you true 5.03.145
for now the devil that told me i did well | says 5.05.115
forgot, | right noble is thy merit, well i wot. 5.06. 18
well, how then? come, roundly, roundly. 1H4 1.02. 22 P
thou sayest well, and it holds well too, for the 1.02. 30 P
thou sayest well, and it holds well too, for the 1.02. 30 P
well, thou hast call'd her to a reckoning many a 1.02. 49 P
well, hal, well, and in some sort it jumps with 1.02. 69 P
hal, well, and in some sort it jumps with my 1.02. 69 P
with my humor as well as waiting in the court, i 1.02. 70 P
thou didst well, for wisdom cries out in the 1.02. 88 P
well then, once in my days i'll be a madcap. 1.02.142 P
why, that's well said. 1.02.144 P
well, come what will, i'll tarry at home. 1.02.145 P
well, god give thee the spirit of persuasion and 1.02.152 P
well, for two of them, i know them to be as 1.02.183 P
well, i'll go with thee. 1.02.191 P
he durst as well have met the devil alone | as 1.03.116
creep | of that same noble prelate well belov'd, 1.03.267
i smell it. upon my life, it will do well. 1.03.277
in faith, it is exceedingly well aim'd. 1.03.282
well, i doubt not but to die a fair death for 2.02. 13 P
the stony–hearted villains know it well enough. 2.02. 27 P
well, we leave that to the proof. 2.02. 69 P
my lord, i could be well contented to be there, 2.03. 2 P
well, i will back him straight. 2.03. 71
well, do not then, for since you love me not, 2.03. 97
for i well believe | thou wilt not utter what 2.03.110
well, breathe a while, and then to it again, and 2.04.249 P
the lord, i knew ye as well as he that made ye. 2.04.267 P
well, that rascal hath good mettle in him, he 2.04.349 P
well, he is there too, and one mordake, and a 2.04.356 P
well, thou wilt be horribly chid to–morrow when 2.04.373 P
well, and the fire of grace be not quite out of 2.04.383 P
well, here is my leg. 2.04.388 P
well, here i am set. 2.04.438 P
if i become not a cart as well as another man, a 2.04.497 P
one of them is well known, my gracious lord, | a 2.04.510
this oily rascal is known as well as paul's. 2.04.526 P
i can speak english, lord, as well as you, | for 3.01.119
to the harp | many an english ditty lovely well, 3.01.122
i cried "hum," and "well, go to," | but mark'd 3.01.156
exceedingly well read, and profited | in strange 3.01.164
well, i am school'd: 3.01.188
excuse | as well as i am doubtless i can purge 3.02. 20
well, i'll repent, and that suddenly, while i am 3.03. 4 P
or four times, liv'd well and in good compass, 3.03. 19 P
go to, i know you well enough. 3.03. 64 P
i love him well, he is an honest man. 3.03. 93 P
where shall i find one that can steal well? 3.03.188 P
well, god be thank'd for these rebels, they 3.03.190 P
well said, my noble scot! 4.01. 1
do so, and 'tis well. 4.01. 12
for well you know we of the off'ring side | must 4.01. 69
yet all goes well, yet all our joints are whole. 4.01. 83
they'll fill a pit as well as better. 4.02. 66 P
well, to the latter end of a fray and the 4.02. 78 P
you do not counsel well, | you speak it out of 4.03. 6
and i dare well maintain it with my life, | if 4.03. 9
some of us love you well, and even those some 4.03. 34
and well we know the king | knows at what time 4.03. 52
(who is, if every owner were well plac'd, 4.03. 94
doubt not, my lord, they shall be well oppos'd. 4.04. 33
'tis not well | that you and i should meet upon 5.01. 9
this is not well, my lord, this is not well. 5.01. 14
this is not well, my lord, this is not well. 5.01. 14
i could be well content | to entertain the lag 5.01. 23
we love our people well, even those we love 5.01.104
i would 'twere bed–time, hal, and all well. 5.01.125 P
well, 'tis no matter, honor pricks me on. 5.01.129 P
my nephew's trespass may be well forgot, | it 5.02. 16
than i, that have not well the gift of tongue, 5.02. 77
no, i know this face full well. 5.03. 19
well, if percy be alive, i'll pierce him. 5.03. 56 P
well said, hal! 5.04. 75 P
fare thee well, great heart! 5.04. 87
why may not he rise as well as i? 5.04.126 P
a gentleman well bred and of good name, | that 2H4 1.01. 26
having been well, that would have made me sick, 1.01.138
being sick, have (in some measure) made me well. 1.01.139
well, he may sleep in security, for he hath the 1.02. 45 P
well, god mend him! 1.02.109 P
very well, my lord, very well. 1.02.120 P
very well, my lord, very well. 1.02.120 P
well, the truth is, sir john, you live in great 1.02.136 P
well, i am loath to gall a new–heal'd wound. 1.02.147 P
but since all is well, keep it so, wake not a 1.02.153 P
well, god send the prince a better companion! 1.02.199 P
well, the king hath sever'd you. 1.02.203 P
well, i cannot last ever, but it was alway yet 1.02.213 P
well, be honest, be honest, and god bless your 1.02.221 P
fare you well! 1.02.226 P
i well allow the occasion of our arms, | but 1.03. 5
you should have been well on your way to york. 2.01. 67
john, i am well acquainted with your manner of 2.01.109 P
well, you shall have it, though i pawn my gown. 2.01.158 P
i hope, my lord, all's well. 2.01.170 P
by this light, i am well spoke on, i can hear it 2.02. 65 P
well, there is sixpence to preserve thee. 2.02. 95 P
well, my lord. 2.02. 99 P
well, thus we play the fools with the time, and 2.02.142 P
fare you well; 2.02.165 P
why, that's well said; 2.04. 31 P
"you are an honest woman, and well thought on, 2.04. 92 P
a good pantler, 'a would 'a' chipp'd bread well. 2.04.238 P
and 'a plays at quoits well, and eats cunger and 2.04.245 P
i dress myself handsome till thy return — well, 2.04.280 P
if my heart be not ready to burst — well, sweet 2.04.380 P
well, fare thee well. 2.04.382 P
well, fare thee well. 2.04.382 P
but an honester and truer–hearted man — well, 2.04.384 P
and truer–hearted man — well, fare thee well. 2.04.384 P
these letters | and well consider of them. 3.01. 3
john a' gaunt lov'd him well, and betted much 3.02. 45 P
he greets me well, sir. 3.02. 63 P
it is well said, in faith, sir, and it is well 3.02. 68 P
in faith, sir, and it is well said indeed too. 3.02. 68 P
you like well and bear your years very well. 3.02. 83 P
you like well and bear your years very well. 3.02. 84 P
i am glad to see you well, good master robert 3.02. 85 P
it well befits you should be of the peace. 3.02. 89 P
singular good, in faith, well said, sir john, 3.02.109 P
in faith, well said, sir john, very well said. 3.02.109 P
i was prick'd well enough before, and you could 3.02.111 P
do it, sir, you can do it, i commend you well. 3.02.147 P
well said, good woman's tailor! 3.02.158 P
well said, courageous feeble! 3.02.158 P
well, master shallow, deep, master shallow. 3.02.161 P
doth she hold her own well? 3.02.205 P
ha, sir john, said i well? 3.02.213 P
well said, th' art a good fellow. 3.02.239 P
go to, well. 3.02.245 P
so — very well, go to, very good, exceeding 3.02.274 P
well said, i' faith, wart, th' art a good scab. 3.02.275 P
these fellows woll do well, master shallow. 3.02.287 P
fare you well, gentlemen both, i thank you. 3.02.289 P
fare you well, gentle gentlemen. 3.02.299 P
well, i'll be acquainted with him if i return, 3.02.328 P
'tis well done. 4.01. 5
well, by my will we shall admit no parley. 4.01.157
for full well he knows | he cannot so precisely 4.01.202
marshal, | if we do now make our atonement well, 4.01.219
you are well encount'red here, my cousin mowbray 4.02. 1
whose dangerous eyes may well be charm'd asleep 4.02. 39
i like them all, and do allow them well, | and 4.02. 54
i know it will well please them. 4.02. 71
well then, colevile is your name, a knight is 4.03. 5 P
fare you well, falstaff. 4.03. 84
our substitutes in absence well invested, | and 4.04. 6
nothing but well to thee, thomas of clarence. 4.04. 19
his temper therefore must be well observ'd. 4.04. 36
from him, give him air, he'll straight be well. 4.04.116
and i myself know well | how troublesome it sate 4.05.185
and by whose power i well might lodge a fear 4.05.207
yea, davy, i will use him well. 5.01. 30 P
use his men well, davy, for they are arrant 5.01. 32 P
well conceited, davy. about thy business, davy. 5.01. 36 P
exceeding well, his cares are now all ended. 5.02. 3
well, peace be with him that hath made us heavy! 5.02. 25
well, you must now speak sir john falstaff fair, 5.02. 33
for, by my faith, it very well becomes you. 5.02. 50
you are right justice, and you weigh this well, 5.02.102
well said, davy. 5.03. 9 P
well said, master silence. 5.03. 49 P
well, of sufferance comes ease. 5.04. 25 P
very well. 5.04. 31 P
followers | shall all be very well provided for, 5.05. 99
be it known to you, as it is very well, i was ep 8 P
a hundred almshouses right well supplied; H5 1.01. 17
then doth it well appear the salique law | was 1.02. 54
she hath herself not only well defended | but 1.02.159
purpose, and be all well borne | without defeat. 1.02.212
now are we well resolv'd, and by god's help 1.02.222
now are we well prepar'd to know the pleasure 1.02.234
and we understand him well, | how he comes o'er 1.02.266
fare you well. 1.02.297
well met, corporal nym. 2.01. 1 P
there must be conclusions — well, i cannot tell 2.01. 24 P
i have an humor to knock you indifferently well. 2.01. 55 P
well, then that/'s the humor of't. 2.01.116 P
since we are well persuaded | we carry not a 2.02. 20
well, the fuel is gone that maintain'd that fire 2.03. 43 P
how well supplied with noble counsellors, | how 2.04. 33
well, 'tis not so, my lord high constable; 2.04. 41
his argument as well as any military man in the 3.02. 80 P
the duke of exeter doth love thee well. 3.06. 22
it is well. 3.06. 58 P
but it is very well; 3.06. 65 P
what he has spoke to me, that is well, i warrant 3.06. 65 P
well then, i know thee. 3.06.115
go bid thy master well advise himself. 3.06.159
and so, montjoy, fare you well. 3.06.162
you are as well provided of both as any prince 3.07. 9 P
your mistress bears well. 3.07. 45 P
me well, which is the prescript praise and 3.07. 46 P
bears your praises, who would trot as well, were 3.07. 77 P
"ill will never said well." 3.07.113 P
well plac'd. 3.07.118 P
you may as well say, that's a valiant flea that 3.07.145 P
it sorts well with your fierceness. 4.01. 63 P
there are few die well that die in a battle; 4.01.142 P
if these men do not die well, it will be a black 4.01.144 P
you may as well go about to turn the sun to ice 4.01.199 P
thou dar'st as well be hang'd. 4.01.218 P
well, i will do it, though i take thee in the 4.01.219 P
keep thy word; fare thee well. 4.01.221 P
and so fare thee well; 4.03.126
well have we done, thrice–valiant countrymen, 4.06. 1
if you mark alexander's life well, harry of 4.07. 32 P
life is come after it indifferent well, for 4.07. 33 P
it is not well done, mark you now, to take the 4.07. 42 P
fare ye well. 5.01. 79 P
well, bawd i'll turn, | and something lean to 5.01. 85
well then: 5.02. 75
sauf votre honneur, me understand well. 5.02.131 P
for i love france so well that i will not part 5.02.173 P
nay, it will please him well, kate; 5.02.248 P
for maids, well summer'd and warm kept, are like 5.02.307 P
and may our oaths well kept and prosp'rous be! 5.02.374
and he may well in fretting spend his gall — 1H6 1.02. 16
i know thee well, though never seen before. 1.02. 67
well, let them practice and converse with 2.01. 25
unready? ay, and glad we scap'd so well. 2.01. 40
as far as i could well discern | for smoke and 2.02. 26
well then, alone (since there's no remedy) | i 2.02. 57
for soldiers' stomachs always serve them well. 2.03. 80
and on my side it is so well apparell'd, | so 2.04. 22
good master vernon, it is well objected; 2.04. 43
well, well, come on, who else? 2.04. 55
well, well, come on, who else? 2.04. 55
well, i'll find friends to wear my bleeding 2.04. 72
look to it well, and say you are well warn'd. 2.04.103
look to it well, and say you are well warn'd. 2.04.103
well, i will lock his counsel in my breast, 2.05.118
more than well beseems | a man of thy profession 3.01. 19
as well at london bridge as at the tower. 3.01. 23
well, duke of gloucester, i will yield to thee; 3.01.134
well urg'd, my lord of warwick; 3.01.151
sir, as well as you dare patronage | the envious 3.04. 32
well, miscreant, i'll be there as soon as you, 3.04. 44
methinks you do not well | to bear with their 4.01.128
as well they may upbraid me with my crown, 4.01.156
well didst thou, richard, to suppress thy voice; 4.01.182
for i protest we are well fortified, | and 4.02. 19
if thou retire, the dolphin, well appointed, 4.02. 21
these eyes, that see thee now well colored, 4.02. 37
o, too much folly is it, well i wot, | to hazard 4.06. 32
well, my good lord, and as the only means | to 5.01. 8
i shall be well content with any choice | tends 5.01. 26
thou shalt well perceive | that neither in birth 5.01. 58
your grace shall well and quietly enjoy. 5.03.159
and yet methinks i could be well content | to be 5.03.165
well, go to, we'll have no bastards live, 5.04. 70
i think she knows not well | (there were so many 5.04. 80
you do not well in obstinacy | to cavil in the 5.04.155
they please us well. 2H6 1.01. 63
and henry was well pleas'd | to change two 1.01.218
well, so it stands; 1.02.104
well said, my masters, and welcome all. 1.04. 13 P
see you well guerdon'd for these good deserts. 1.04. 46
lord buckingham, methinks you watch'd her well. 1.04. 55
a pretty plot, well chosen to build upon! 1.04. 56
well, to the rest: 1.04. 63
my lord protector's hawks do tow'r so well; 2.01. 10
no more than well becomes | so good a quarrel 2.01. 27
protector, see to't well, protect yourself. 2.01. 52
mass, thou lov'dst plums well, that wouldst 2.01. 99
in my opinion yet thou seest not well. 2.01.104
why, that's well said. what color is my gown of? 2.01.109
thou mightst as well have known all our names, 2.01.125
well, sir, we must have you find your legs. 2.01.144 P
well, for this night we will repose us here; 2.01.196
fear not, neighbor, you shall do well enough. 2.03. 61 P
thump? then see thou thump thy master well. 2.03. 84 P
well, i will be there. 2.04. 73
not the worse in that i pray | you use her well. 2.04. 82
well hath your highness seen into this duke; 3.01. 42
and too well given | to dream on evil or to work 3.01. 72
well, suffolk, thou shalt not see me blush | nor 3.01. 98
it serves you well, my lord, to say so much. 3.01.119
why, 'tis well known that, whiles i was 3.01.124
the ancient proverb will be well effected: 3.01.170
and well such losers may have leave to speak. 3.01.185
say you consent, and censure well the deed, 3.01.275
well, nobles, well; 3.01.341
well, nobles, well; 3.01.341
yet be well assur'd | you put sharp weapons in a 3.01.346
to make commotion, as full well he can, | under 3.01.358
why, that's well said. 3.02. 8
is all things well, | according as i gave 3.02. 11
but well forewarning wind | did seem to say, 3.02. 85
friend, | and 'tis well seen he found an enemy. 3.02.185
well could i curse away a winter's night, 3.02.335
i will repeal thee, or, be well assur'd, 3.02.349
well, i say, it was never merry world in england 4.02. 7 P
i knew her well, she was a midwife. 4.02. 43 P
i have been so well brought up that i can write 4.02.105 P
well, seeing gentle words will not prevail, 4.02.174
well, he shall be beheaded for it ten times. 4.07. 24 P
and it be but for pleading so well for his life. 4.07.107 P
for they lov'd well when they were alive. 4.07.131 P

and show'd how well you love your prince and		4.09. 16
and sends the poor well pleased from my gate.		4.10. 23
look on me well.		4.10. 38 P
york, if thou meanest well, i greet thee well.		5.01. 14
york, if thou meanest well, i greet thee well.		5.01. 14
even of the bonny beast he lov'd so well.		5.02. 12
but if we haply scape | (as well we may, if not		5.02. 80
now, by my sword, well hast thou fought to–day;		5.03. 15
well, lords, we have not got that which we have:		5.03. 20
well hast thou spoken, cousin, be it so.	3H6	1.01. 66
hadst thou but lov'd him half so well as i, | or		1.01.220
how well resembles it the prime of youth,		2.01. 23
i know it well, lord warwick, blame me not.		2.01.157
full well hath clifford play'd the orator,		2.02. 43
for, well i wot, thou hast thy mother's tongue.		2.02.134
the one his purple blood right well resembles,		2.05. 99
well, if you be a king crown'd with content,		3.01. 66
lands, | which we in justice cannot well deny,		3.02. 5
your highness shall do well to grant her suit;		3.02. 8
well, jest on, brothers.		3.02.116
well, say there is no kingdom then for richard;		3.02.146
i'll play the orator as well as nestor,		3.02.188
i like it well that our fair queen and mistress		3.03.167
yes, i accept her, for she well deserves it,		3.03.249
as well as lewis of france or the earl of		4.01. 11
yet hasty marriage seldom proveth well.		4.01. 18
to sunder them that yoke so well together.		4.01. 23
for this one speech lord hastings well deserves		4.01. 47
and yet methinks your grace hath not done well		4.01. 51
well, i will arm me, being thus forewarn'd.		4.01.113
trust me, my lord, all hitherto goes well, | the		4.02. 1
we, well cover'd with the night's black mantle,		4.02. 22
well guess'd, believe me, for that was my		4.05. 22
for well using me?		4.06. 9
be thou sure, i'll well requite thy kindness,		4.06. 10
well have we pass'd and now repass'd the seas,		4.07. 5
are well foretold that danger lurks within.		4.07. 12
as being well content with that alone.		4.07. 24
the good old man would fain that all were well,		4.07. 31
then fare you well, for i will hence again, | i		4.07. 48
for well i wot that henry is no soldier.		4.07. 83
men well inclin'd to hear what thou command'st;		4.08. 16
and thou, brave oxford, wondrous well belov'd,		4.08. 17
that, to deserve well at my brother's hands, | i		5.01. 93
but at last | i well might hear, delivered with		5.02. 46
be well assur'd | her faction will be full as		5.03. 16
for well i wot ye blaze to burn them out.		5.04. 71
and see our gentle queen how well she fares.		5.05. 89
and his noble queen | well strook in years, fair	R3	1.01. 92
i know it pleaseth neither of us well.		1.01.113
well, your imprisonment shall not be long, | i		1.01.114
well are you welcome to /the open air.		1.01.124
with lies well steel'd with weighty arguments,		1.01.148
well, well, put up your sword.		1.02.196
well, well, put up your sword.		1.02.196
would all were well!		1.03. 40
i do remember them too well:		1.03.117
were you well serv'd, you would be taught your		1.03.249
to serve me well, you all should do me duty,		1.03.250
o, serve me well, and teach yourselves that duty		1.03.252
marry, as for clarence, he is well repaid;		1.03.312
so do i ever — being well advis'd;		1.03.317
well thought upon, i have it here about me.		1.03.343
fare you well.		1.04. 99 P
that means to live well endeavors to trust to		1.04.143 P
i am his brother and i love him well.		1.04.227
well, i'll go hide the body in some hole | till		1.04.280
i would to god all strifes were well compounded.		2.01. 75
children, peace, the king doth love you well.		2.02. 17
as well the fear of harm, as harm apparent, | in		2.02.130
no doubt shall then, and till then, govern well.		2.03. 15
come, come, we fear the worst; all will be well.		2.03. 31
all may be well;		2.03. 36
well, madam, and in health.		2.04. 40
to me | as well i tender you and all of yours!		2.04. 72
well, my dread lord — so must i call you now.		3.01. 97
well, let them rest.		3.01.157
well then, no more but this:		3.01.169
well, catesby, ere a fortnight make me older,		3.02. 60
i know they do, and i have well deserv'd it.		3.02. 71
well met, my lord, i am glad to see your honor.		3.02.108
i thank his grace, i know he loves me well;		3.04. 14
his lordship knows me well and loves me well.		3.04. 30
his lordship knows me well and loves me well.		3.04. 30
for i myself am not so well provided | as else i		3.04. 44
there's some conceit or other likes him well,		3.04. 49
well, well, he was the covert'st shelt'red		3.05. 33
well, well, he was the covert'st shelt'red		3.05. 33
and your good graces both have well proceeded,		3.05. 48
that you might well have signified the same		3.05. 59
words shall serve | as well as i had seen, and		3.05. 63
which well appeared in his lineaments, | being		3.05. 91
if you thrive well, bring them to baynard's		3.05. 98
where you shall find me well accompanied | with		3.05. 99
and mark how well the sequel hangs together:		3.06. 4
and if you plead as well for them | as i can say		3.07. 52
of time, | will well become the seat of majesty,		3.07.169
trivial, | all circumstances well considered.		3.07.176
as well we know your tenderness of heart | and		3.07.210
daughter, well met.		4.01. 5
right well, dear madam.		4.01. 15
scarce the blood was well wash'd from his hands		4.01. 67
for tender princes — use my babies well!		4.01.102
well, be it so.		4.02. 45
well, let that rest. dorset is fled to richmond.		4.02. 85
well, look unto it.		4.02. 87
o thou well skill'd in curses, stay awhile,		4.04.116
no, by the holy rood, thou know'st it well,		4.04.166
well then, who dost thou mean shall be her king?		4.04.265
nor none so bad but well may be reported.		4.04.458
well, as you guess?		4.04.466
as i by friends am well advertised, | sir edward		4.04.499
well, hie thee to thy lord;		4.05. 19
well, all's one for that.		5.03. 8
much | (which well i am assur'd i have not done)		5.03. 36
be valiant, and speed well!		5.03.102
fool, of thyself speak well;		5.03.192
shall be well winged with our chiefest horse.		5.03.300
courageous richmond, well hast thou acquit thee.		5.05. 3
here | may (if they think it well) let fall a	H8	pr 6
good morrow, and well met.		1.01. 1
well, we shall then know more, and buckingham		1.01.118
only to show his pomp as well in france | as		1.01.163
count–cardinal | has done this, and 'tis well;		1.01.173
which i do well, for i am sure the emperor		1.01.185
o my lord aburga'ny, fare you well!		1.01.211
things done well | and with a care exempt		1.02. 88
noble benefits shall prove | not well dispos'd,		1.02.116
if i know you well, | you were the duke's		1.02.171
well said, lord sands, | your colt's tooth is		1.03. 47
well said, my lord.		1.04. 30
you do well, lord.		1.04. 87
for, with all the care i had, i saw well chosen,		2.02. 2 P
well, let him have them:		2.02. 10
well met, my lord chamberlain.		2.02. 12
there is hope | all will be well.		2.03. 56
i have perus'd her well;		2.03. 75
desire the court, as well | for your own quiet,		2.04. 62
his grace | hath spoken well and justly;		2.04. 65
'tis not well.		2.04.123
(well worthy the best heir o' th' world) should		2.04.196
i then did feel full sick, and yet not well —		2.04.205
very well, my liege.		2.04.210
'tis not well, lords.		3.01.133
though i know her virtuous | and well deserving?		3.02. 98
it may well be, | there is a mutiny in 's mind.		3.02.119
you have said well.		3.02.149
you cause) my doing well | with my well saying!		3.02.151
you cause) my doing well | with my well saying!		3.02.152
'tis well said again, | and 'tis a kind of good		3.02.152
and 'tis a kind of good deed to say well, | and		3.02.153
so fare you well, my little good lord cardinal.		3.02.349
why, well;		3.02.376
y' are well met once again.		4.01. 1
'tis well.		4.01. 7
well worth the seeing.		4.01. 61
as well as i am able.		4.01. 62
if well, he stepp'd before me happily | for my		4.02. 10
well, the voice goes, madam:		4.02. 11
i hope she will deserve well — and a little		4.02.136
and, let me tell you, it will ne'er be well —		5.01. 29
charles, good night. | well, sir, what follows?		5.01. 79
all's not well.		5.01. 88
and be well contented | to make your house our		5.01.105
'tis well there's one above 'em yet.		5.02. 27
and the end | was ever to do well;		5.02. 72
well, well, my lords, respect him, | take him,		5.02.188
well, well, my lords, respect him, | take him,		5.02.188
respect him, | take him, and use him well;		5.02.189
we may as well push against powle's as stir 'em.		5.03. 16
well, i have told you enough of this.	TRO	1.01. 13 P
well, she look'd yesternight fairer than ever i		1.01. 32 P
were not somewhat darker than helen's — well,		1.01. 42 P
well, i say troilus is troilus.		1.02. 66 P
well, the gods are above, time must friend or		1.02. 77 P
well, troilus, well, i would my heart were in		1.02. 78 P
troilus, well, i would my heart were in her body		1.02. 78 P
love an addle egg as well as you love an idle		1.02.133 P
well, cousin, i told you a thing yesterday,		1.02.170 P
yes, he'll fight indifferent well.		1.02.223 P
look well upon him, niece.		1.02.232 P
well, well.		1.02.250 P
well, well.		1.02.250 P
well, well!		1.02.251 P
well, well!		1.02.251 P
fare ye well, good niece.		1.02.276 P
well, and how?		1.03.320
nay, but regard him well.		2.01. 61 P
well! why, so i do.		2.01. 62 P
but yet you look not well upon him, for,		2.01. 63 P
well, go to, go to.		2.01. 93 P
as well wherein 'tis precious of itself | as in		2.02. 55
as well my undertakings as your counsels, | but		2.02.131
well may we fight for her whom, we know well,		2.02.161
well may we fight for her whom, we know well,		2.02.161
paris and troilus, you have both said well,		2.02.163
we are too well acquainted with these answers,		2.03.113
'tis said he holds you well, and will be led		2.03.180
o, this is well. he rubs the vein of him.		2.03.200
well said, my lord! well, you say so in fits.		3.01. 57 P
well said, my lord! well, you say so in fits.		3.01. 57 P
well, sweet queen, you are pleasant with me.		3.01. 62 P
well, i'll make 's excuse.		3.01. 90 P
well, uncle, what folly i commit, i dedicate to		3.02.102 P
but, though i lov'd you well, i woo'd you not,		3.02.126
well know they what they speak that speak so		3.02.152
fare ye well, with all my heart.		3.03.299 P
we know each other well.		4.01. 31
he merits well to have her that doth seek her,		4.01. 56
and you as well to keep her, that defend her,		4.01. 59
but we in silence hold this virtue well —		4.01. 78
i charge thee use her well, even for my charge;		4.04.126
weigh him well, | and that which looks like		4.05. 81
his blows are well dispos'd. there, ajax!		4.05.116
she's well, but bade me not commend her to you.		4.05.180
well, welcome, welcome!		4.05.210
i know your favor, lord ulysses, well.		4.05.213
henceforth guard thee well, | for i'll not kill		4.05.253
well said, adversity!		5.01. 12 P
you look upon that sleeve, behold it well.		5.02. 69
now she sharpens. well said, whetstone!		5.02. 75 P
well, well, 'tis done, 'tis past.		5.02. 97
well, well, 'tis done, 'tis past.		5.02. 97
and that shall be divulged well | in characters		5.02.163
o, well fought, my youngest brother!		5.06. 12
fare thee well.		5.06. 19
i like thy armor well;		5.06. 28
very well, and could be content to give him good	COR	1.01. 32 P
you may as well | strike at the heaven with your		1.01. 67
well, i'll hear it, sir;		1.01. 93 P
well, sir, what answer made the belly?		1.01.106
i may make the belly smile | as well as speak —		1.01.110
well, what then?		1.01.122
ay, sir, well, well.		1.01.142
ay, sir, well, well.		1.01.142
whereof they say | the city is well stor'd.		1.01.190
mutiners, | your valor puts well forth;		1.01.251
aims, | in whom already he's well grac'd, cannot		1.01.264
besides, if things go well, | opinion that so		1.01.270
i thank your ladyship; well, good madam.		1.03. 54 P
fare you well then.		1.03.106 P
well, then farewell.		1.03.111 P
fare you well.		1.05. 17
well fought;		1.06. 1
truth, | methinks thou speak'st not well.		1.06. 14
well might they fester 'gainst ingratitude,		1.09. 30
o, well begg'd!		1.09. 87
well, sir.		2.01. 15 P
well, well, sir, well.		2.01. 27 P
well, well, sir, well.		2.01. 27 P
well, well, sir, well.		2.01. 27 P
menenius, you are known well enough too.		2.01. 46 P
your worships have deliver'd the matter well,		2.01. 58 P
follows it that i am known well enough too?		2.01. 63 P
this character, if i be known well enough too?		2.01. 65 P
come, sir, come, we know you well enough.		2.01. 66 P
you are well understood to be a perfecter giber		2.01. 81 P
are well pleas'd | to make thee consul.		2.02.132
and might well | be taken from the people.		2.02.145
well then, i pray, your price a' th' consulship?		2.03. 73 P
fare you well.		2.03.150
that hath beside well in his person wrought | to		2.03.246
well, no more.		3.01. 74
'twere well | we let the people know't.		3.01. 82
well, on to th' market–place.		3.01.112
well, well, no more of that.		3.01.115
well, well, no more of that.		3.01.115
resting well assur'd | they ne'er did service		3.01.121
well, what then?		3.01.130
he shall well know | the noble tribunes are the		3.01.269
i would have had you put your power well on		3.02. 17
well said, noble woman!		3.02. 31
well, what then? what then?		3.02. 36
well, i will do't;		3.02.101
well, i must do't.		3.02.110
well, mildly be it then. mildly!		3.02.145
very well.		3.03. 22
well, here he comes.		3.03. 30
well, say. peace ho!		3.03. 41
well, well, no more.		3.03. 57
well, well, no more.		3.03. 57
but since he hath | serv'd well for rome —		3.03. 83
my wife, my mother, | i'll do well yet.		4.01. 21
you wot well | my hazards still have been your		4.01. 27
fare ye well!		4.01. 44
o, y' are well met.		4.02. 11
well, well, we'll leave you.		4.02. 43
well, well, we'll leave you.		4.02. 43
i know you well, sir, and you know me.		4.03. 1 P
but your favor is well appear'd by your tongue.		4.03. 9 P
you have well sav'd me a day's journey.		4.03. 12 P
the day serves well for them now.		4.03. 31 P
tullus aufidius /will appear well in these wars,		4.03. 34 P
sir, heartily well met, and most glad of your		4.03. 48 P
well, let us go together.		4.03. 52 P
the feast smells well, but i | appear not like a		4.05. 5
his friends | blush that the world goes well,		4.06. 5
all's well;		4.06. 16
the gods have well prevented it, and rome | sits		4.06. 36
we have record that very well it can, | and		4.06. 50
i understand thee well, and be thou sure, | when		4.07. 17
very well. | could he say less?		5.01. 21
well, and say that martius | return me, as		5.01. 41
rome, after the measure | as you intended well.		5.01. 47
he was not taken well, he had not din'd:		5.01. 50
you guard like men, 'tis well.		5.02. 2
you have pray'd well to–day.		5.04. 55
presents well worthy rome's imperious lord:	TIT	1.01.250
full well, andronicus, | agree these deeds with		1.01.305
well, bury him, and bury me the next.		1.01.386
full well shalt thou perceive how much i dare.		2.01. 44
full well i wot the ground of all this grudge.		2.01. 48
this valley fits the purpose passing well.		2.03. 84
gave thee life when well he might have slain		2.03.159
well could i leave our sport to sleep a while.		2.03.197
fear not thy sons, they shall do well enough.		2.03.305
'tis well, lavinia, that thou hast no hands,		3.01. 79
brother, well i wot, | thy napkin cannot drink a		3.01.139
she loves thee, boy, too well to do thee harm.		4.01. 6
my grandsire, well advis'd, hath sent by me		4.02. 10
need, | you may be armed and appointed well:		4.02. 16
o, 'tis a verse in horace, i know it well, | i		4.02. 22
but were our witty empress well afoot, | she		4.02. 29
well, more or less, or ne'er a whit at all,		4.02. 53
well, god give her good rest!		4.02. 63
the midwife and the nurse well made away, | then		4.02.167
well, well, i made thee miserable | what time i		4.03. 18
well, well, i made thee miserable | what time i		4.03. 18
o, well said, lucius!		4.03. 64
well, let my deeds be witness of my worth:		5.01.103
i am not mad, i know thee well enough.		5.02. 21
that i know thee well | for our proud empress,		5.02. 25
well are you fitted, had you but a moor.		5.02. 85
for well i wot the empress never wags | but in		5.02. 87
well shalt thou know her by thine own proportion		5.02.106
well hast thou lesson'd us, this shall we do.		5.02.110
because i would be sure to have all well, | to		5.03. 31
was it well done of rash virginius | to slay his		5.03. 36
for well i know | the common voice do cry it		5.03.139
thy grandsire lov'd thee well.		5.03.161
'tis well thou art not fish;	ROM	1.01. 30 P
well, sir.		1.01. 57 P
well, in that hit you miss:		1.01.208
and, in strong proof of chastity well arm'd,		1.01.210
but montague is bound as well as i, | in penalty		1.02. 1
she shall scant show well that now seems best.		1.02. 99
well, susan is with god, | she was too good for		1.03. 19
that shall she, marry, i remember it well.		1.03. 22
well, think of marriage now;		1.03. 69
and we mean well in going to this mask, | but		1.04. 48
well, what was yours?		1.04. 51
ah, sirrah, this unlook'd–for sport comes well.		1.05. 29
well said, my hearts!		1.05. 86
well, do not swear.		2.02.116

but if thou meanest not well, | i do beseech 2.02.150
encamp them still | in man as well as herbs, 2.03. 28
she knew well | thy love did read by rote that 2.03. 87
why then is my pump well flower'd. 2.04. 60 P
and is it not then well serv'd in to a sweet 2.04. 81 P
thou what thou art, by art as well as by nature, 2.04. 90 P
by my troth, it is well said; 2.04.117 P
you say well. 2.04.124 P
yea, is the worst well? 2.04.125 P
very well took, i' faith, wisely, wisely. 2.04.125 P
this afternoon, sir? well, she shall be there. 2.04.185 P
well, sir, my mistress is the sweetest lady — 2.04.199 P
well, you have made a simple choice, you know 2.05. 38 P
i' faith, i am sorry that thou art not well. 2.05. 53
well, peace be with you, sir, here comes my man. 3.01. 56
no, 'tis not so deep as a well, nor so wide as a 3.01. 96 P
will you speak well of him that kill'd your 3.02. 96
romeo | to comfort you, i wot well where he is. 3.02.139
how well my comfort is reviv'd by this! 3.03.165
well, we were born to die. 3.04. 4
well, we'nsday is too soon, | a' thursday let it 3.04. 19
well, get you gone, a' thursday be it then. 3.04. 30
madam, i am not well. 3.05. 68
well, girl, thou weep'st not so much for his 3.05. 78
and joy comes well in such a needy time. 3.05.105
well, well, thou hast a careful father, child, 3.05.107
well, well, thou hast a careful father, child, 3.05.107
well, thou hast comforted me marvellous much. 3.05.230
well, he may chance to do some good on her. 4.02. 13
why, i am glad on't, this is well, stand up. 4.02. 28
and all things shall be well, i warrant thee, 4.02. 40
well, i will walk myself | to county paris, to 4.02. 44
which, well thou knowest, is cross and full of 4.03. 5
mass, and well said, a merry whoreson, ha! 4.04. 20
ill | that you run mad, seeing that she is well. 4.05. 76
she's not well married that lives married long, 4.05. 77
up, | for well you know this is a pitiful case. 4.05. 99
is my father well? 5.01. 14
again, | for nothing can be ill if she be well. 5.01. 16
then she is well and nothing can be ill: 5.01. 17
well, juliet, i will lie with thee to–night. 5.01. 34
one, a friend, and one that knows you well. 5.03.123
i do remember well where i should be, | and 5.03.149
i am glad y' are well. TIM 1.01. 1
ay, that's well known; 1.01. 3
so 'tis. this comes off well and excellent. 1.01. 29
as well of glib and slipp'ry creatures as | of 1.01. 53
would be well express'd | in our condition. 1.01. 76
yet you do well | to show lord timon that mean 1.01. 92
well; 1.01. 99
him | a gentleman that well deserves a help, 1.01.102
fare you well. 1.01.108
well; what further? 1.01.120
well fare you, gentleman; 1.01.163
but you well know, | things of like value 1.01.169
well mock'd. 1.01.173
wrought he not well that painted it? 1.01.197 P
not so well as plain–dealing, which will not 1.01.211 P
fare thee well, fare thee well. 1.01.262
fare thee well, fare thee well. 1.01.262
he keeps his tides well. 1.02. 56 P
else i should tell him well (i' faith, i should) 1.02.161
well, would i were gently put out of office 1.02.201
do so, my friends. see them well entertain'd. 2.02. 44
may catch a wrench — would all were well — 2.02.209
his health is well, sir. 3.01. 12 P
i am right glad that his health is well, sir; 3.01. 13 P
and canst use the time well, if the time use 3.01. 37 P
use the time well, if the time use thee well. 3.01. 37 P
but thou art wise, and thou know'st well enough 3.01. 40 P
fare thee well. 3.01. 45 P
fare thee well, commend me to thy honorable 3.02. 28 P
ay, too well. 3.02. 63
well met, good morrow, titus and hortensius. 3.04. 1
these debts may well be call'd desperate ones, 3.04.101 P
ever at the best, hearing well of your lordship. 3.06. 27 P
i know thee well; 4.03. 56
why, fare thee well; 4.03.100
well, more gold — what then? 4.03.149
if i thrive well, i'll visit thee again. 4.03.170
if i hope well, i'll never see thee more. 4.03.171
yes, thou spok'st well of me. 4.03.173
habit on | to castigate thy pride, 'twere well; 4.03.240
'tis not well mended so, it is but botch'd; 4.03.285
look you, i love you well, i'll give you gold, 5.01.100
well, sir, i will; 5.01.168
that's well spoke. 5.01.193
i like this well, he will return again. 5.01.204
these well express in thee thy latter spirits: 5.04. 74
cannot see yourself | so well as by reflection, JC 1.02. 68
i would not, cassius, yet i love him well. 1.02. 82
as well as i do know your outward favor. 1.02. 91
well, honor is the subject of my story: 1.02. 92
we both have fed as well, and we can both 1.02. 98
both | endure the winter's cold as well as he; 1.02. 99
sound them, it doth become the mouth as well; 1.02.145
he is a noble roman, and well given. 1.02.197
i can as well be hang'd as tell the manner of it 1.02.235 P
fare you well. 1.02.286 P
well, brutus, thou art noble; 1.02.308
a common slave — you know him well by sight — 1.03. 15
well, i will hie, | and so bestow these papers 1.03.150
need of him, | you have right well conceited. 1.03.162
decius, well urg'd. 2.01.155
meet, | mark antony, so well belov'd of caesar, 2.01.156
may well stretch so far | as to annoy us all; 2.01.159
who rated him for speaking well of pompey; 2.01.216
he loves me well, and i have given him reasons; 2.01.219
i am not well in health, and that is all. 2.01.257
but withal | a woman well reputed, cato's 2.01.295
danger knows full well | that caesar is more 2.02. 44
and he shall say you are not well to–day. 2.02. 53
mark antony shall say i am not well, | and, for 2.02. 55
and this way have you well expounded it. 2.02. 91
mark well metellus cimber; 2.03. 3 P
yes, bring me word, boy, if thy lord look well, 2.04. 13
prithee listen well; 2.04. 17
fare you well. 3.01. 14
i could be well mov'd, if i were as you; 3.01. 58
'tis furnish'd well with men, | and men are 3.01. 66
not love caesar dead | so well as brutus living; 3.01.134
i know that we shall have him well to friend. 3.01.143
fare thee well! 3.01.150
and that they know full well | that gave me 3.02.219
he greets me well. 4.02. 6
i do know you well. 4.02. 42
vaunting true, | and it shall please me well. 4.03. 53
therein our letters do not well agree; 4.03.176
well, to our work alive. 4.03.196
every thing is well. 4.03.236
it was well done, and thou shalt sleep again; 4.03.264
well; then i shall see thee again? 4.03.284
three and thirty wounds | be well aveng'd; 5.01. 54
if not, why then this parting was well made. 5.01.118
if not, 'tis true this parting was well made. 5.01.121
these tidings will well comfort cassius. 5.03. 54
the last of all the romans, fare thee well! 5.03. 99
so fare you well at once, for brutus' tongue 5.05. 39
give me your hand first. fare you well, my lord. 5.05. 49
for brave macbeth (well he deserves that name), MAC 1.02. 16
so well thy words become thee as thy wounds, 1.02. 43
but he rides well, | and his great love, sharp 1.06. 22
done, then 'twere well | it were done quickly. 1.07. 1
all's well. 2.01. 19
well contented. 2.03.134
threescore and ten i can remember well, | within 2.04. 1
well, i will thither. 2.04. 36
well, may you see things well done there: 2.04. 37
well, may you see things well done there: 2.04. 37
made good, | may they not be my oracles as well, 3.01. 9
well then, now | have you consider'd of my 3.01. 74
after life's fitful fever he sleeps well. 3.02. 23
well, let's away, and say how much is done. 3.03. 22
gentlemen, rise, his highness is not well. 3.04. 51
upon a thought | he will again be well. 3.04. 55
fear) would well become | a woman's story at a 3.04. 63
he has borne all things well, and i do think 3.06. 17
and that well might | advise him to a caution, 3.06. 43
o, well done! 4.01. 39
you have lov'd him well; 4.03. 13
fare thee well, lord, | i would not be the 4.03. 34
fare thee well, | these evils thou repeat'st 4.03.111
well, more anon. 4.03.140
why, well. 4.03.177
well too. 4.03.177
they were well at peace when i did leave 'em. 4.03.179
well, well, well. 5.01. 57 P
well, well, well. 5.01. 57 P
well, well, well. 5.01. 57 P
near birnan wood | shall we well meet them; 5.02. 6
well, march we on | to give obedience where 'tis 5.02. 25
well, say, sir. 5.05. 31
fare you well. 5.06. 6
they say he parted well, and paid his score, 5.09. 18
well, good night. HAM 1.01. 11
well, sit we down, | and let us hear barnardo 1.01. 33
compact | well ratified by law and heraldy, 1.01. 87
other, | as it doth well appear unto our state, 1.01.101
well may it sort that this portentous figure 1.01.109
i am glad to see you well. 1.02.160
so fare you well. 1.02.250
all is not well, | i doubt some foul play. 1.02.254
and remember well | what i have said to you. 1.03. 84
marry, well bethought. 1.03. 90
fare thee well at once! 1.05. 88
well said, old mole, canst work i' th' earth so 1.05.162
as "well, well, we know," or "we could, and if 1.05.176
as "well, well, we know," or "we could, and if 1.05.176
marry, well said, very well said. 2.01. 6
marry, well said, very well said. 2.01. 6
ay, very well, my lord. 2.01. 16
in part him — but," you may say, "not well. 2.01. 17
god buy ye, fare ye well. 2.01. 66
well, my lord. 2.01. 70
well, we shall sift him. 2.02. 58
it likes us well, | and at our more considered 2.02. 80
this business is well ended. 2.02. 85
well, god–a–mercy. 2.02.172 P
excellent well, you are a fishmonger. 2.02.174 P
fare you well, my lord. 2.02.218 P
well be with you, gentlemen! 2.02.380 P
and no more, | the which he loved passing well." 2.02.408
i have a daughter that i love passing well. 2.02.412 P
i am glad to see thee well. 2.02.422 P
an excellent play, well digested in the scenes, 2.02.439 P
my lord, well spoken, with good accent and good 2.02.466 P
'tis well, i'll have thee speak out the rest of 2.02.521 P
my lord, will you see the players well bestow'd? 2.02.523 P
do you hear, let them be well us'd, for they are 2.02.523 P
very well. 2.02.545 P
did he receive you well? 3.01. 10
i humbly thank you, well, /well, /well. 3.01. 91
my honor'd lord, you know right well you did, 3.01. 96
for wise men know well enough what monsters you 3.01.138 P
i have heard of your paintings, well enough. 3.01.142 P
it shall do well; 3.01.176
journeymen had made men, and not made them well, 3.02. 34 P
whose blood and judgment are so well co–meddled, 3.02. 69
well, my lord, | if 'a steal aught the whilst 3.02. 87
meet what i would have well and it destroy! 3.02.221
very well, my lord. 3.02.288 P
i did very well note him. 3.02.290 P
i do not well understand that. 3.02.350 P
fare you well, my liege, | i'll call upon you 3.03. 33
all may be well. 3.03. 72
and will answer well | the death i gave him. 3.04.176
well, god dild you! 4.05. 42 P
i hope all will be well. 4.05. 68 P
and for my means, i'll husband them so well, 4.05.139
rain'd many a tear" — | fare you well, my dove! 4.05.168 P
it well appears. 4.07. 5
and they can well on horseback, but this gallant 4.07. 84
i know him well. 4.07. 93
i like thy wit well, in good faith. 5.01. 45 P
the gallows does well; 5.01. 46 P
but how does it well? 5.01. 46 P
it does well to those that do ill. 5.01. 46 P
argal, the gallows may do well to thee. 5.01. 49 P
thou pray'st not well. 5.01.259
and thou'lt mouth, | i'll rant as well as thou. 5.01.284
our indiscretion sometime serves us well | when 5.02. 8
well, sir? 5.02.135 P
but to know a man well were to know himself. 5.02.139 P
that's two of his weapons — but well. 5.02.146 P
/'a does well to commend it himself, there are 5.02.183 P
she well instructs me. 5.02.208 P
very well, my lord. 5.02.260
this likes me well. 5.02.265
well, again. 5.02.281
shall to my bosom | be as well neighbor'd, LR 1.01.119
fare thee well, king; 1.01.180
love well our father; 1.01.271
and well are worth the want that you have wanted 1.01.279
well may you prosper! 1.01.282
when my dimensions are as well compact, | my 1.02. 7
well then, | legitimate edgar, i must have your 1.02. 15
well, my legitimate, if this letter speed | and 1.02. 19
i do not well know, my lord. 1.02. 79 P
slack of former services, | you shall do well; 1.03. 10
well, madam. 1.03. 21
he says, my lord, your /daughter is not well. 1.04. 51 P
of kindness appears as well in the general 1.04. 61 P
no more of that, i have noted it well. 1.04. 75 P
had thought, by making this well known unto you, 1.04.205
well, you may fear too far. 1.04.328
striving to better, oft we mar what's well. 1.04.346
well, well, th' event. 1.04.348
well, well, th' event. 1.04.348
you may do then in time. fare you well, sir. 2.01. 13 P
now quit you well. 2.01. 30
from my sister | been well inform'd of them, and 2.01.102
whose disposition, all the world well knows, 2.02.153
for that question, thou'dst well deserv'd it. 2.04. 65 P
well, my good lord, i have inform'd them so. 2.04. 98
no, but not yet, may be he is not well: 2.04.105
i would have all well betwixt you. 2.04.120
i could as well be brought | to knee his throne, 2.04.213
is this well spoken? 2.04.236
is it not well? 2.04.238
old man and 's people | cannot be well bestow'd. 2.04.289
'tis a wild night, | my regan counsels well. 2.04.309
consider him well. 3.04.103 P
though well we may not pass upon his life 3.07. 24
conceive, and fare thee well. 4.02. 24
one way i like this well, | but being widow, and 4.02. 83
so fare you well. 4.05. 36
fare thee well. 4.05. 40
in it a jewel | well worth a poor man's taking. 4.06. 29
now fare ye well, good sir. 4.06. 32
now, fellow, fare thee well. 4.06. 41
too well, too well. 4.06. 66
too well, too well. 4.06. 66
o, well flown, bird! 4.06. 91 P
the trick of that voice i do well remember; 4.06.106
i remember thine eyes well enough. 4.06.136 P
i know thee well enough, thy name is gloucester. 4.06.177
use me well, | you shall have ransom. 4.06.191
well pray you, father. 4.06.219
i know thee well; 4.06.252
for him 'tis well | that of thy death and 4.06.277
our very loving sister, well bemet. 5.01. 20
why, fare thee well, i will o'erlook thy paper. 5.01. 50
your valiant strain, | and fortune led you well. 5.03. 41
person, | the which immediacy may well stand up, 5.03. 65
lady, i am not well, else i should answer | from 5.03. 73
she is not well, convey her to my tent. 5.03.106
what safe and nicely i might well delay | by 5.03.145
well thought on. 5.03.251
on their lords, | do well thrive by them; OTH 1.01. 53
'tis well i am found by you. 1.02. 47
he bears the sentence well that nothing bears 1.03.212
adieu, brave moor, use desdemona well. 1.03.291
he holds me well, | the better shall my purpose 1.03.390
as well to see the vessel that's come in | as to 2.01. 37
is he well shipp'd? 2.01. 47
but that he's well and will be shortly here. 2.01. 90
well prais'd! how if she be black and witty? 2.01.131
ay, well said, whisper. 2.01.167 P
well kiss'd! 2.01.175 P
o, you are well tun'd now! 2.01.199
honey, you shall be well desir'd in cyprus, | i 2.01.204
desdemona, | once more, well met at cyprus. 2.01.212
well. 2.01.271 P
that cassio loves her, i do well believe't; 2.01.286
well — happiness to their sheets! 2.03. 29 P
i could well wish courtesy would invent some 2.03. 34 P
well, /god's above all; 2.03.102 P
i can stand well enough, and i speak well enough 2.03.115 P
can stand well enough, and i speak well enough. 2.03.116 P
excellent well. 2.03.117 P
why, very well then; 2.03.118 P
it were well | the general were put in mind of 2.03.131
i do love cassio well; 2.03.143
all's well /now, sweeting; 2.03.252
why, but you are now well enough. 2.03.294 P
is a good familiar creature, if it be well us'd; 2.03.310 P
i have well approv'd it, sir. i drunk! 2.03.312 P
you advise me well. 2.03.326 P
i have been to–night exceedingly well cudgell'd; 2.03.365 P
does't not go well? 2.03.374
well, sir, we will not. 3.01. 14 P
but all will sure be well. 3.01. 42
well, my good lord, i'll do't. 3.02. 4
him long, and be you well assur'd | he shall in 3.03. 11
well, do your discretion. 3.03. 34
jealious | to say my wife is fair, feeds well, 3.03.184
look to your wife, observe her well with cassio, 3.03.197
i know our country disposition well: 3.03.201
why do you speak so faintly? | are you not well? 3.03.283
it hard, within this hour | it will be well. 3.03.287
i am very sorry that you are not well. 3.03.289
i slept the next night well, fed well, was free 3.03.340
i slept the next night well, fed well, was free 3.03.340
lord on his behalf, and hope all will be well. 3.04. 20 P

well, my good lady. 3.04. 34
well, my good lord. 3.04. 35
most veritable, therefore look to't well. 3.04. 76
well, well. 3.04.183
well, well. 3.04.183
i like the work well; 3.04.189
he hath, my lord, but be you well assur'd, | no 4.01. 30
ply desdemona well, and you are sure on't. 4.01.106
go to, well said, well said. 4.01.114
go to, well said, well said. 4.01.114
have you scor'd me? well. 4.01.126 P
well, i must leave her company. 4.01.144 P
well, i may chance to see you; 4.01.166 P
but you shall make all well. 4.01.225
faith, that was not so well; 4.01.273
yet could i bear that too, well, very well; 4.02. 56
yet could i bear that too, well, very well; 4.02. 56
all things shall be well. 4.02.171
well, go to; very well. 4.02.191 P
well, go to; very well. 4.02.191 P
very well! 4.02.192 P
i cannot go to, man, nor 'tis not very well. 4.02.193 P
very well. 4.02.195 P
i tell you 'tis not very well. 4.02.196 P
well; 4.02.218 P
he speaks well. 4.03. 37
i might do't as well i' th' dark. 4.03. 67
then let them use us well; 4.03.102
o, that's well said: 5.01. 98
behold her well; 5.01.108
well, do it, and be brief, i will walk by. 5.02. 30
you have done well, | that men must lay their 5.02.169
well, thou dost best. 5.02.306
of one that lov'd not wisely but too well; 5.02.344
well, if you were but an inch of fortune better ANT 1.02. 59 P
well, what worst? 1.02. 94
fare thee well awhile. 1.02.111
be, she makes a show'r of rain as well as jove. 1.02.151 P
i am quickly ill, and well, | so antony loves. 1.03. 72
that you know well. 1.03. 89
kill me when they do not | eye well to you. 1.03. 97
'tis well for thee, | that, being unseminar'd, 1.05. 10
i shall do well: 2.01. 8
caesar and antony shall well greet together: 2.01. 39
and shall become you well, to entreat your 2.02. 2
if we compose well here, to parthia. 2.02. 15
'tis spoken well. 2.02. 25
your /reproof | were well deserv'd of rashness. 2.02.122
to be glad that matters are so well digested. 2.02.176 P
you stay'd well by't in egypt. 2.02.176 P
or my reporter devis'd well for her. 2.02.189 P
as well a woman with an eunuch play'd | as with 2.05. 5
as well as i can, madam. 2.05. 7
but well and free, | if thou so yield him, there 2.05. 27
first, madam, he is well. 2.05. 31
sirrah, mark, we use | to say the dead are well. 2.05. 33
well, go to, i will. 2.05. 36
if not well, | thou shouldst come like a fury 2.05. 39
yet, if thou say antony lives, 'tis well, | or 2.05. 43
madam, he's well. 2.05. 46
well said. 2.05. 46
and am well studied for a liberal thanks, 2.06. 47
well, i know not | what counts harsh fortune 2.06. 53
well met here. 2.06. 56
well, | and well am like to do, for i perceive 2.06. 71
and well am like to do, for i perceive | four 2.06. 72
when you have well deserv'd ten times as much 2.06. 77
you have done well by water. 2.06. 86 P
i am not so well as i should be; 2.07. 30 P
hast thou drunk well? 2.07. 65
i should have found it afterwards well done, 2.07. 79
i could well forbear't. 2.07. 98
a lower place, note well, | may make too great 3.01. 12
use me well in't. 3.02. 25
farewell, my dearest sister, fare thee well! 3.02. 39
fare thee well! 3.02. 41
sir, look well to my husband's house; and — 3.02. 45
look upon you | but when you are well pleas'd. 3.03. 4
all may be well enough. 3.03. 47
well; is it, is it? 3.07. 4
well, i could reply: 3.07. 6
which might have well becom'd the best of men, 3.07. 26
your ships are not well mann'd, | your mariners 3.07. 34
well, well, away! 3.07. 66
well, well, away! 3.07. 66
well i know the man. 3.07. 78
been what he knew himself, it had gone well. 3.10. 26
well then, sustain me. o! 3.11. 45
thou knew'st too well | my heart was to thy 3.11. 56
the loyalty well held to fools does make | our 3.13. 42
we will yet do well. 3.13.187
woo't thou fight well? 4.02. 7
well said, come on. 4.02. 8
you have serv'd me well, | and kings have been 4.02. 12
well, my good fellows, wait on me to–night. 4.02. 20
i hope well of to–morrow, and will lead you 4.02. 42
fare you well. 4.03. 2
well, sir, good night. 4.03. 6
it signs well, does it not? 4.03. 14
well, well, | we shall thrive now. 4.04. 8
well, well, | we shall thrive now. 4.04. 8
is not this buckled well? 4.04. 11
'tis well blown, lads. 4.04. 25
this way — well said. 4.04. 28
fare thee well, dame, what e'er becomes of me. 4.04. 29
then, antony — but now — well, on. 4.04. 38
'tis well th' art gone, | if it be well to live; 4.12. 39
'tis well th' art gone, | if it be well to live; 4.12. 40
let the world see | his nobleness well acted, 5.02. 45
i cannot project mine own cause so well | to 5.02.121
puppet, shall be shown | in rome as well as i. 5.02.209
well, get thee gone, farewell. 5.02.278
so fare thee well! 5.02.314
approach ho, all's not well; caesar's beguil'd. 5.02.323
what work is here, charmian? is this well done? 5.02.325
it is well done, and fitting for a princess 5.02.326
or that the negligence may well be laugh'd at, CYM 1.01. 66
i do well believe you. 1.01. 67
well, my lord. 1.02. 41 P
well done, well done. 1.05. 82
well done, well done. 1.05. 82
fare thee well, pisanio; 1.05. 84
what, dear sir, | thus raps you? are you well? 1.06. 51
thanks, madam, well. 1.06. 52
continues well my lord? his health, beseech you? 1.06. 56
well, madam. 1.06. 57
such boil'd stuff | as well might poison poison. 1.06.126
all's well, sir. 1.06.179
and hated | for being preferr'd so well. 2.03.131
i'll be reveng'd. | "his mean'st garment"! well. 2.03.156
all is well yet. 2.04. 39
but profess | had that was well worth watching), 2.04. 68
to be believ'd | of one persuaded well of. 2.04.132
view on't | might well have warm'd old saturn; 2.05. 12
how many /score of miles may we well rid 3.02. 67
well corresponding | with your stiff age; 3.03. 31
many times | doth ill deserve by doing well; 3.03. 54
as honest, then | my purpose would prove well. 3.04.119
at court, | and that will well confirm it. 3.04.127
well then, here's the point: 3.04.153
well, madam, we must take a short farewell, 3.04.185
fare you well. 3.05. 15
well, my good lord. 3.05.116 P
well encounter'd! 3.06. 65
the lines of my body are as well drawn as his; 4.01. 9 P
you are not well. 4.02. 1
so sick i am not, yet i am not well; 4.02. 7
well or ill, | i am bound to you. 4.02. 45
howsoe'er, | my brother hath done well. 4.02.147
though valor | becomes thee well enough. 4.02.156
well, 'tis done. 4.02.161
my brother wears thee not the one half so well 4.02.202
thy name well fits thy faith; 4.02.381
i will not say | thou shalt be so well master'd, 4.02.383
well, i will find him; 5.03. 73
hath my poor boy done aught but well, | whose 5.04. 35
his comforts thrive, his trials well are spent. 5.04.104
if you be ready for that, you are well cook'd. 5.04.154 P
well may you, sir, | remember me at court, where 5.05.192
as well descended as thyself, and hath | more of 5.05.303
a dangerous speech, | though haply well for you. 5.05.314
he would have well becom'd this place, and 5.05.406
well, | my peace we will begin. 5.05.458
well, my lord, since you have given me leave to PER 1.02.101
well, i perceive he was a wise fellow and had 1.03. 3 P
well, i perceive | i shall not be hang'd now, 1.03. 25
how well this honest mirth becomes their labor! 2.01. 95
not well. 2.01. 98
he loves you well that holds his life of you. 2.02. 22
which can as well inflame as it can kill. 2.02. 35
he well may be a stranger, for he comes | to an 2.02. 52
address'd, | will well become a soldier's dance. 2.03. 95
since they love men in arms as well as beds. 2.03. 98
so, this was well ask'd, 'twas so well perform'd 2.03. 99
this was well ask'd, 'twas so well perform'd. 2.03. 99
thanks, gentlemen, to all, all have done well; 2.03.107
so, | they are well dispatch'd; 2.05. 15
'tis well, mistress, your choice agrees with 2.05. 18
i like that well. 2.05. 19
well, i do commend her choice, | and will no 2.05. 21
sir, my daughter thinks very well of you, | ay, 2.05. 37
ay, so well, that you must be her master, | and 2.05. 38
it pleaseth me so well that i will see you wed, 2.05. 92
o, you say well. 3.02. 20
well said, well said. 3.02. 87
well said, well said. 3.02. 87
that i was shipp'd at sea i well remember, 3.04. 5
well, i will go, | but yet i have no desire to 4.01. 42
good sooth, it show'd well in you. 4.01. 88
come, other sorts offend as well as we. 4.02. 36 P
as well as we! 4.02. 37 P
she has a good face, speaks well, and has 4.02. 47 P
well, follow me, my masters, you shall have your 4.02. 53 P
you shall fare well, you shall have the 4.02. 79 P
well, well, as for him, he brought his disease 4.02.110 P
well, well, as for him, he brought his disease 4.02.110 P
well, if we had of every nation a traveller, we 4.02.113 P
one, i like the manner of your garments well. 4.02.134 P
'ad been a kindness | becoming well thy /fact. 4.03. 12
well, well, | of all the faults beneath the 4.03. 19
well, well, | of all the faults beneath the 4.03. 19
you not your child well loving, yet i find | it 4.03. 37
villainy | so well as soft and tender flattery. 4.04. 45
well, i had rather than twice the worth of her 4.06. 1 P
your honor knows what 'tis to say well enough. 4.06. 31 P
well, call forth, call forth. 4.06. 33 P
well, there's for you, leave us. 4.06. 45 P
did not think | thou couldst have spoke so well, 4.06.103
fare thee well, thou art a piece of virtue, and 4.06.111
well, i will see what i can do for thee. 4.06.192 P
you wish me well. 5.01. 16
'tis well bethought. 5.01. 44
were i well assur'd | came of a gentle kind and 5.01. 67
well, speak on. 5.01.154
well, where were you bred? 5.01.163
well, my companion friends, | if this but answer 5.01.237
to my just belief, | i'll well remember you. 5.01.239
you shall do well | that on the touching of her 5.03. 41
in helicanus may you well descry | a figure of 5.03. 91
in reverend cerimon there well appears | the 5.03. 93
much money gi'n, | if they stand sound and well; TNK pr 3
/ev'ry innocent wots well, comes in | like old 1.03. 79
well, we will talk more of this when the 2.01. 12 P
they eat well, look merrily, discourse of many 2.01. 38 P
well, agree then. 2.02.152
might not a man well lose himself and love her? 2.02.155
well, sir, | take your own time. come, boys. 2.03. 68
well i could have wrestled, | the best men 2.03. 75
and well have hollow'd | to a deep cry of dogs; 2.05. 11
he's well got sure. 2.05. 24
if you deserve well, sir, i shall soon see't. 2.05. 42
wait well, sir, | upon your mistress. 2.05. 51
and that, methinks, is not so well; 2.06. 23
two such steeds might well | be by a pair of 3.01. 20
you have been well advertis'd | how much i dare; 3.01. 58
place, which well | might justify your manhood; 3.01. 63
kinsman, you might as well | speak this, and act 3.01. 69
well, sir, i'll pledge you. 3.03. 16
she did so; well, sir? 3.03. 31
"well hail'd, well hail'd, you jolly gallants! 3.05. 63
"well hail'd, well hail'd, you jolly gallants! 3.05. 63
well, sir, go forward, we will edify. 3.05. 98
think either, | well done, a noble recompense. 3.06. 24
i am well and lusty, choose your arms. 3.06. 45
that's well said. 3.06. 49
day, | i well remember, you outdid me, cousin; 3.06. 73
no, no, 'tis well. 3.06. 86
i dare as well | die as discourse or sleep. 3.06.128
look to thine own well, arcite. 3.06.131
thy prison — | think well what that deserves; 3.06.140
set in too, that i hope | all shall be well. 4.01. 15
was she well? 4.01. 34
i do not think she was very well, for, now | you 4.01. 36
well, sir? 4.01. 44
not well? 4.01. 45
no, sir, not well: | 'tis too true, she is mad. 4.01. 45
when i might well perceive | 'twas one that sung 4.01. 57
thou hast well describ'd him. 4.02. 89
yes, they are well. 4.02.121
being so few and well dispos'd, they show 4.02.122
you speak well. 5.01. 30
if well inspir'd, this battle shall confound 5.01.166
'twas well done. 5.02. 7
for well she knew | what hour my fit would take 5.02. 9
yet very well, sir. 5.02. 36
very well. 5.02. 61
honor in their kind | which sometime show well, 5.03. 13
well, well then, at your pleasure. 5.03. 34
well, well then, at your pleasure. 5.03. 34
i heard she was not well; 5.04. 26
sir, she's well restor'd, | and to be married 5.04. 27
and, though it were too short, | he did it well; 5.04.103
the powerful venus well hath grac'd her altar, 5.04.105
or how can well that proclamation sound | when STM II.C 117
the kiss shall be thine own as well as mine. VEN 117
yet mayst thou well be tasted. 128
foreknowing well, if there he came to lie, | why 245
fair fall the wit that can so well defend her! 472
to sell myself i can be well contented, | so 513
whose precious taste her thirsty lips well knew, 543
bids him farewell, and look well to her heart, 580
they that thrive well take counsel of their 640
and now his grief may be compared well | to one 701
a nurse's song ne'er pleas'd her babe so well. 974
resembling well his pale cheeks and the blood 1169
an expir'd date, cancell'd ere well begun: LUC 26
well was he welcom'd by the roman dame, | within 51
fee, | he gratis comes, and thou art well apaid, 914
as well to hear as grant what he hath said. 915
"well, well, dear collatine, thou shalt not know 1058
"well, well, dear collatine, thou shalt not know 1058
to imitate thee well, against my heart | will 1137
for more it is than i can well express, | and 1286
which heartless peasants did so well resemble, 1392
well learned is that tongue that well can thee PP 5. 8
is that tongue that well can thee commend, | all 5. 8
fare well i could not, for i supp'd with sorrow. 14. 6
liked of her master as well as well might be, 15. 2
liked of her master as well as well might be, 15. 2
worthy blame, | as well as fancy, partial might. 18. 4
halt — | but plainly say thou lov'st her well, 18.11
neither, | simple were so well compounded: PHT 44
when every private widow well may keep, | by SON 9. 7
wind, | or say with princes if it shall go well, 14. 7
let them say more that like of hearsay well, | i 21.13
for no man well of such a salve can speak | that 34. 7
lascivious grace, in whom all ill well shows, 40.13
thy beauty and thy years full well befits, | for 41. 3
not blame your pleasure, be it ill or well. 58.14
that you for love speak well of me untrue, | my 72.10
to love that well, which thou must leave ere 73.14
well might show | how far a modern quill doth 83. 6
queen | the basest jewel will be well esteem'd, 96. 6
mend, | to mar the subject that before was well? 103.10
for what care i who calls me well or ill, | so 112. 3
mine eye well knows what with his gust is 114.11
all this the world well knows, yet none knows 129.13
yet none knows well | to shun the heaven that 129.13
yet well i know | that music hath a far more 130. 9
for well thou know'st to my dear doting heart 131. 3
let it then as well beseem thy heart | to mourn 132.10
my love well knows | her pretty looks have been 139. 9
then love doth well denote | love's eye is not 148. 7
lest eyes well seeing thy foul faults should 148.14
this brand she quenched in a cool well by, 154. 9
"well could he ride, and often men would say, LC 106
with wit well blazon'd, smil'd or made some moan 217
have emptied all their fountains in my well, 255

WELL–ACCOMPLISH'D 1 FR 0.0001 REL FR 1 V 0 P
the young dumaine, a well–accomplish'd youth, LLL 2.01. 56

WELL–ACQUAINTED 1 FR 0.0001 REL FR 1 V 0 P
me | as if i were their well–acquainted friend, ERR 4.03. 2

WELL–A–DAY *(also welliday, weraday)*

WELL–A–DAY 4 FR 0.0004 REL FR 1 V 3 P
o well–a–day, mistress ford, having an honest WIV 3.03. 99 P
well–a–day that you were sir! TN 4.02.108 P
when, well–a–day, we could scarce help ourselves PER 2.01. 22 P
his daughter's woe and heavy well–a–day | in her 4.04. 49

WELL–ADVIS'D 1 FR 0.0001 REL FR 1 V 0 P
sleeping or waking, mad or well–advis'd? ERR 2.02.213

WELL–ADVISED 1 FR 0.0001 REL FR 1 V 0 P
hath any well–advised friend proclaim'd | reward R3 4.04.515

WELL–A–NEAR 1 FR 0.0001 REL FR 1 V 0 P
and well–a–near | does fall in travail with her PER 3.ch. 51

WELL–APPARELL'D 1 FR 0.0001 REL FR 1 V 0 P
feel | when well–apparell'd april on the heel ROM 1.02. 27

//WELL–APPOINTED 1 FR 0.0001 REL FR 1 V 0 P
/york /is /up | /with //well–appointed /pow'rs. 2H4 1.01.190

WELL–APPOINTED 2 FR 0.0002 REL FR 2 V 0 P
what well–appointed leader fronts us here? 2H4 4.01. 25
seen | the well–appointed king at /hampton pier H5 3.pr. 4

WELL–ARMED 1 FR 0.0001 REL FR 1 V 0 P

where they boast | to have well–armed friends. LR 3.07. 20
WELL–BEHAV'D 1 FR 0.0001 REL FR 0 V 1 P
such orderly and well–behav'd reproof to all WIV 2.01. 59 P
WELL–BELOV'D 1 FR 0.0001 REL FR 1 V 0 P
how well–belov'd | and daily graced by the TGV 1.03. 57
WELL–BELOVED 2 FR 0.0002 REL FR 2 V 0 P
my learn'd and well–beloved servant, cranmer, H8 2.04.239
through this the well–beloved brutus stabb'd, JC 3.02.176
WELL–BESEEMING 2 FR 0.0002 REL FR 2 V 0 P
shall now, in mutual well–beseeming ranks, 1H4 1.01. 14
unfurnish'd of her well–beseeming troop? TIT 2.03. 56
WELL–BORN 1 FR 0.0001 REL FR 1 V 0 P
as many and as well–born bloods as those — JN 2.01.278
WELL–BREATH'D 1 FR 0.0001 REL FR 1 V 0 P
and on thy well–breath'd horse keep with thy VEN 678
WELL–CHOSEN 1 FR 0.0001 REL FR 1 V 0 P
and his well–chosen bride. 3H6 4.01. 7
WELL–CONTENTED 1 FR 0.0001 REL FR 1 V 0 P
if thou survive my well–contented day, | when SON 32. 1
WELL–DEALING 1 FR 0.0001 REL FR 1 V 0 P
to merchants, our well–dealing countrymen, | who
ERR 1.01. 7
WELL–DEFENDED 1 FR 0.0001 REL FR 1 V 0 P
yet hath wrong'd | your well–defended honor, you
MM 5.01.402
WELL–DERIVED 1 FR 0.0001 REL FR 1 V 0 P
my son corrupts a well–derived nature | with his AWW 3.02. 88
WELL–DESERVED 1 FR 0.0001 REL FR 1 V 0 P
you to a long and well–deserved bed; AYL 5.04.190
WELL–DESERVING 3 FR 0.0003 REL FR 3 V 0 P
law, | whereof you are a well–deserving pillar, MV 4.01.239
is not his heir a well–deserving son? R2 2.01.194
so much land | to any well–deserving friend; 1H4 3.01.136
WELL–DISPOSED 1 FR 0.0001 REL FR 1 V 0 P
you lose a thousand well–disposed hearts, | and R2 2.01.206
WELL–DIVIDED 1 FR 0.0001 REL FR 1 V 0 P
o well–divided disposition! ANT 1.05. 53
WELL–DOING 1 FR 0.0001 REL FR 1 V 0 P
or he his manage by th' well–doing steed. LC 112
WELL–EDUCATED 1 FR 0.0001 REL FR 0 V 1 P
define, define, well–educated infant. LLL 1.02. 94 P
WELL–ENT'RED 1 FR 0.0001 REL FR 1 V 0 P
after well–ent'red soldiers, to return | and AWW 2.01. 6
WELL–EXPERIENC'D 1 FR 0.0001 REL FR 1 V 0 P
from a well–experienc'd archer hits the mark PER 1.01.162
WELL–FAM'D 1 FR 0.0001 REL FR 1 V 0 P
my well–fam'd lord of troy, no less to you. TRO 4.05.173
WELL–FAVOR'D 5 FR 0.0005 REL FR 1 V 4 P
not so fair, boy, as well–favor'd. TGV 2.01. 49 P
for the which his wife seems to me well–favor'd. WIV 2.02.273 P
to be a well–favor'd man is the gift of fortune, ADO 3.03. 14 P
he is very well–favor'd and he speaks very TN 1.05.160 P
those wicked creatures yet do look well–favor'd LR 2.04.256
WELL–FAVORED 1 FR 0.0001 REL FR 1 V 0 P
you are well–favored, and your looks foreshow PER 4.01. 85
WELL–FOUGHTEN 1 FR 0.0001 REL FR 1 V 0 P
as in this glorious and well–foughten field | we H5 4.06. 18
WELL–FOUND 2 FR 0.0002 REL FR 2 V 0 P
and last general | in our well–found successes, COR 2.02. 44
to such a well–found wonder as thy worth, | for TNK 2.05. 27
WELL–GOVERN'D 1 FR 0.0001 REL FR 1 V 0 P
him | to be a virtuous and well–govern'd youth. ROM 1.05. 68
WELL–GRACED 1 FR 0.0001 REL FR 1 V 0 P
after a well–graced actor leaves the stage, R2 5.02. 24
WELL–HALLOW'D 1 FR 0.0001 REL FR 1 V 0 P
my rightful hand in a well–hallow'd cause. H5 1.02.293
WELLIDAY *(also well–a–day, weraday)*
WELLIDAY 1 FR 0.0001 REL FR 0 V 1 P
o welliday, lady, if he be not hewn now, we H5 2.01. 36 P
WELL–KNIT 1 FR 0.0001 REL FR 0 V 1 P
o well–knit sampson! LLL 1.02. 73 P
WELL–KNOWN 1 FR 0.0001 REL FR 1 V 0 P
need i thus | my well–known body to anatomize 2H4 in 21
WELL–LABORING 1 FR 0.0001 REL FR 1 V 0 P
whose well–laboring sword | had three times 2H4 1.01.127
WELL–LEARNED 1 FR 0.0001 REL FR 1 V 0 P
with reverend fathers and well–learned bishops. R3 3.05.100
WELL–LIKING 1 FR 0.0001 REL FR 1 V 0 P
well–liking wits they have — gross gross, fat LLL 5.02.268
WELL–LOST 1 FR 0.0001 REL FR 1 V 0 P
the well–lost life of mine on his grace's cure AWW 1.03.248
WELL–MEANING 1 FR 0.0001 REL FR 1 V 0 P
my brother gloucester, plain well–meaning soul, R2 2.01.128
WELL–MEANT 1 FR 0.0001 REL FR 1 V 0 P
not from edward's well–meant honest love, | but 3H6 3.03. 67
WELL–MINDED 1 FR 0.0001 REL FR 1 V 0 P
well–minded clarence, be thou fortunate! 3H6 4.08. 27
WELL–NIGH 3 FR 0.0003 REL FR 2 V 1 P
one that is well–nigh worn to pieces with age to WIV 2.01. 21 P
they swore that you were well–nigh dead for me. ADO 5.04. 81
'tis now well–nigh morning; TNK 3.02. 2
WELL–NOTED 1 FR 0.0001 REL FR 1 V 0 P
in this the antique and well–noted face | of JN 4.02. 21
WELL–ORDER'D 1 FR 0.0001 REL FR 1 V 0 P
there is a law in each well–order'd nation | to TRO 2.02.180
WELL–PAID 1 FR 0.0001 REL FR 1 V 0 P
how, with his banners and his well–paid ranks, ANT 3.01. 32
WELL–PAINTED 3 FR 0.0003 REL FR 3 V 0 P
concerning this, sir — o well–painted passion! OTH 4.01.257
well–painted idol, image dull and dead, | statue VEN 212
to this well–painted piece is lucrece come, | to LUC 1443
WELL–PRACTIC'D 1 FR 0.0001 REL FR 1 V 0 P
to your well–practic'd wise directions. 2H4 5.02.121
WELL–PROPORTION'D
1 FR 0.0001 REL FR 1 V 0 P
his well–proportion'd beard made rough and 2H6 3.02.175
WELL–PROPORTIONED
1 FR 0.0001 REL FR 1 V 0 P
life | in limning out a well–proportioned steed, VEN 290
WELL–REFINED 1 FR 0.0001 REL FR 1 V 0 P
affords | in polish'd form of well–refined pen. SON 85. 8
//WELL–REMEMB'RED
1 FR 0.0001 REL FR 1 V 0 P
/noble /and /right //well–rememb'red /father's? 2H4 4.01.110
WELL–REPUTED 1 FR 0.0001 REL FR 1 V 0 P
weeds | as may beseem some well–reputed page. TGV 2.07. 43
WELL–RESPECTED 1 FR 0.0001 REL FR 1 V 0 P
my life, | if well–respected honor bid me on, 1H4 4.03. 10

WELLS 3 FR 0.0003 REL FR 3 V 0 P
to dive like buckets in concealed wells, | to JN 5.02.139
make wells and niobes of the maids and wives, TRO 5.10. 19
clear wells spring not, sweet birds sing not, PP 17.25
WELL–SAILING 1 FR 0.0001 REL FR 1 V 0 P
well–sailing ships and bounteous winds have PER 4.04. 17
WELL/–SEEMING 1 FR 0.0001 REL FR 1 V 0 P
misshapen chaos of well/–seeming forms, ROM 1.01.179
WELL–SEEMING 1 FR 0.0001 REL FR 0 V 1 P
her combinate–husband, this well–seeming angelo.
MM 3.01.223 P
WELL–SKILL'D 1 FR 0.0001 REL FR 1 V 0 P
the well–skill'd workman this mild image drew LUC 1520
WELL–SPOKEN 3 FR 0.0003 REL FR 3 V 0 P
as of a knight well–spoken, neat, and fine; TGV 1.02. 10
to entertain these fair well–spoken days, | i am R3 1.01. 29
for clarence is well–spoken, and perhaps | may 1.03.347
WELL–STEEL'D 2 FR 0.0002 REL FR 2 V 0 P
our rages, | struck with our well–steel'd darts. TNK 2.02. 51
he wears a well–steel'd axe, the staff of gold. 4.02.115
WELL–TOOK 1 FR 0.0001 REL FR 1 V 0 P
time, we thank you for your well–took labor. HAM 2.02. 83
WELL–TUN'D 2 FR 0.0002 REL FR 2 V 0 P
replying shrilly to the well–tun'd horns, | as TIT 2.03. 18
the well–tun'd warble of her nightly sorrow, LUC 1080
WELL–TUNED 1 FR 0.0001 REL FR 1 V 0 P
if the true concord of well–tuned sounds, | by SON 8. 5
WELL–WARRANTED 1 FR 0.0001 REL FR 1 V 0 P
and you, my noble and well–warranted cousin, MM 5.01.254
WELL–WEIGHING 1 FR 0.0001 REL FR 0 V 1 P
not possible with well–weighing sums of gold to AWW 4.03.179 P
WELL–WILLER 1 FR 0.0001 REL FR 1 V 0 P
is blown abroad, help me, thy poor well–willer, TNK 3.05.116
WELL–WILLERS 1 FR 0.0001 REL FR 0 V 1 P
and i beseech you be rul'd by your well–willers. WIV 1.01. 71 P
WELL–WISH'D 1 FR 0.0001 REL FR 1 V 0 P
the general subject to a well–wish'd king | quit MM 2.04. 27
WELL–WON 1 FR 0.0001 REL FR 1 V 0 P
on me, my bargains, and my well–won thrift, MV 1.03. 50
WELSH 20 FR 0.0022 REL FR 9 V 11 P
between sir hugh the welsh priest and caius the WIV 2.01.201 P
gallia and gaul, french and welsh, soul–curer 3.01. 98 P
her troop of fairies, and the welsh devil /hugh? 5.03. 12 P
heavens defend me from that welsh fairy, lest he 5.05. 81 P
am i ridden with a welsh goat too? 5.05.137 P
i am not able to answer the welsh flannel; 5.05.162 P
true liegeman upon the cross of a welsh hook — 1H4 2.04.338 P
i think there's no man speaks better welsh. 3.01. 49
let me understand you then, | speak it in welsh. 3.01.118
my wife can speak no english, i no welsh. 3.01.191
that pretty welsh | which thou pourest down from 3.01.198
makes welsh as sweet as ditties highly penn'd, 3.01.206
now i perceive the devil understands welsh, 3.01.229
ye thief, and hear the lady sing in welsh. 3.01.234 P
to the welsh lady's bed. 3.01.242 P
/to french and welsh he leaves his back unarm'd, 2H4 1.03. 79
against the welsh, himself and harry monmouth; 1.03. 83
for i am welsh, you know, good countryman. H5 4.07.105
wash your majesty's welsh plood out of your pody 4.07.107 P
and henceforth let a welsh correction teach you 5.01. 78 P
WELSHMAN 6 FR 0.0006 REL FR 4 V 2 P
butter, parson hugh the welshman with my cheese,
WIV 2.02.303 P
stay yet another day, thou trusty welshman. R2 2.04. 5
was by the rude hands of that welshman taken, 1H4 1.01. 41
no, i am a welshman. H5 4.01. 51 P
there is much care and valor in this welshman. 4.01. 84
you cannot guess wherefore the welshman comes.
R3 4.04.476
WELSHMEN 5 FR 0.0005 REL FR 4 V 1 P
for all the welshmen, hearing thou wert dead, R2 3.02. 73
we learn | the welshmen are dispers'd, and 3.03. 2
the welshmen did good service in a garden where H5 4.07. 98 P
amongst the loving welshmen canst procure, 3H6 2.01.180
and buckingham, back'd with the hardy welshmen,
R3 4.03. 47
WELSHWOMEN 1 FR 0.0001 REL FR 1 V 0 P
by those welshwomen done as may not be | without
1H4 1.01. 45
WEN 1 FR 0.0001 REL FR 0 V 1 P
i do allow this wen to be as familiar with me as 2H4 2.02.106 P
WENCH 70 FR 0.0079 REL FR 41 V 29 P
a nutshell and as leaky as an unstanch'd wench. TMP 1.01. 48 P
well demanded, wench; 1.02.139
no, wench, it eats and sleeps and hath such 1.02.413
foolish wench, | to th' most of men this is a 1.02.480
"temperance" was a delicate wench. 2.01. 44 P
like a young wench that had buried her grandam; TGV 2.01. 23 P
but tell me, wench, how will the world repute me 2.07. 59
what need a man care for a stock with a wench, 3.01.310 P
o, to him, to him, wench! MM 2.02.124
once before him for getting a wench with child. 4.03.169 P
i know a wench of excellent discourse, | pretty ERR 3.01.109
sir, she's the kitchen wench and all grease, and 3.02. 95 P
here she comes in the habit of a light wench; 4.03. 52 P
as much to say, "god make me a light wench." 4.03. 55 P
with a wench. LLL 1.01.262 P
sir, i confess the wench. 1.01.283 P
a year's imprisonment to be taken with a wench. 1.01.288 P
to love, so am i in love with a base wench. 1.02. 59 P
and that's great marvel, loving a light wench. 1.02.124 P
queen guinover of britain was a little wench, as 4.01.124 P
so do not you, for you are a light wench. 5.02. 25
and, to begin, wench — so god help me, law! 5.02.414
the honest troyan, the poor wench is cast away. 5.02.676 P
be a woman, she's a good wench for this gear. MV 2.02.166 P
that wench is stark mad or wonderful froward. SHR 1.01. 69
now, by the world, it is a lusty wench! 2.01.160
what said the wench when he rose again? 3.02.166
fear not, sweet wench, they shall not touch thee 3.02.238
i knew a wench married in an afternoon as she 4.04. 99 P
why, there's a wench! 5.02.180
he weeps like a wench that had shed her milk. AWW 4.03.107 P
what, wench! TN 1.03. 42 P
before me, she's a good wench. 2.03.178 P
excellent wench, say i. 2.05.109 P
i could marry this wench for this device — 2.05.182 P
sun himself a fair hot wench in flame–color'd 1H4 1.02. 10 P

not my hostess of the tavern a most sweet wench? 1.02. 40 P
humors, there's not a better wench in england. 2H4 2.01.149 P
god send the wench no worse fortune! 2.02.140 P
not born | to be the pillage of a giglot wench." 1H6 4.07. 41
the readiest way to make the wench amends | is R3 1.01.155
take thy lute, wench, my soul grows sad with H8 3.01. 1
when the brown wench | lay kissing in your arms, 3.02.295
good wench, let's sit down quiet | for fear we 4.02. 81
she is going, wench. pray, pray. 4.02. 99
when i am dead, good wench, | let me be us'd 4.02.167
thou must be gone, wench, thou must be gone; TRO 4.02. 90 P
he lov'd me — o false wench! 5.02. 70
bear thou my hand, sweet wench, between thy TIT 3.01.282
that same pale hard–hearted wench, that rosaline ROM 2.04. 4
laura to his lady was a kitchen wench (marry, 2.04. 40 P
go thy ways, wench, serve god. 2.05. 45 P
array, | but, like a mishaved and sullen wench, 3.03.143
a good wench, give it me. OTH 3.03.313
o ill–starr'd wench, | pale as thy smock! 5.02.272
royal wench! ANT 2.02.226
hath | one daughter, and a full–grown wench, PER 4.ch. 16
that's a good wench! TNK 2.02.124
canst not thou work such flowers in silk, wench? 2.02.127
will't not do | rarely upon a skirt, wench? 2.02.130
take a new lesson out, and be a good wench. 2.03. 35
and so would any young wench, o' my conscience, 2.04. 12
a pretty brown wench 'tis. 3.03. 39
yes, wench, we know him. 4.01.117
wench, it must be. 4.02.148
poor wench, go weep, for whosoever wins | loses 4.02.155
why, a day's journey, wench. 5.02. 73
what shall we do there, wench? 5.02. 74
he that has | lov'd a young handsome wench then, ep 6
know, gentle wench, it small avails my mood; LUC 1273
WENCHES' 2 FR 0.0002 REL FR 1 V 1 P
grew so in love with the wenches' song, that he WT 4.04.606 P
no heretics burn'd, but wenches' suitors; LR 3.02. 84
WENCHES 25 FR 0.0028 REL FR 14 V 11 P
dost thou conjure for wenches, that thou call'st ERR 3.01. 34
and thereof comes that the wenches say, "god 4.03. 53 P
ergo, light wenches will burn. 4.03. 57 P
do you hear, my mad wenches? LLL 2.01.257
these betray nice wenches that would be betray'd 3.01. 23 P
light wenches may prove plagues to men forsworn; 4.03.382
arm, wenches, arm! 5.02. 82
the tongues of mocking wenches are as keen | as 5.02.256
farewell, mad wenches, you have simple wits. 5.02.264
this gallant pins the wenches on his sleeve; 5.02.321
nor bite the lip, as angry wenches will, | nor SHR 2.01.248
in the between but getting wenches with child, WT 3.03. 62 P
wenches, i'll buy for you both. 4.04.312 P
a dance which the wenches say is a gallimaufry 4.04.328 P
you see, my good wenches, how men of merit are 2H4 2.04.375 P
farewell, good wenches, if i be not sent away 2.04.377 P
and then, when they marry, they get wenches. 4.03. 94 P
alas, poor wenches, where are now your fortunes?
H8 3.01.148
three or four wenches, where i stood, cried, JC 1.02.271 P
prithee, how many boys and wenches must i have?
ANT 1.02. 36 P
and /ye know what wenches, ha? TNK 2.03. 39
what pushes are we wenches driven to | when 2.04. 6
me, and then condemn me for't, some wenches, 2.06. 14
to the wenches | we have known in our days! 3.03. 28
ye have danc'd rarely, wenches. 3.05.159
WENCHING 1 FR 0.0001 REL FR 0 V 1 P
what's become of the wenching rogues? TRO 5.04. 33 P
WENCHLESS 1 FR 0.0001 REL FR 0 V 1 P
too much money this mart by being too wenchless.
PER 4.02. 5 P
WENCH–LIKE 1 FR 0.0001 REL FR 1 V 0 P
and do not play in wench–like words with that CYM 4.02.230
WENCH'S 1 FR 0.0001 REL FR 0 V 1 P
stabb'd with a white wench's black eye, run ROM 2.04. 14 P
WEND 3 FR 0.0003 REL FR 3 V 0 P
wend you with this letter. MM 4.03.145
hopeless and helpless doth egeon wend, | but to ERR 1.01.157
and back to athens shall the lovers wend | with MND 3.02.372
WE'NSDAY *(also wednesday, wed'sday)*
WE'NSDAY 8 FR 0.0009 REL FR 5 V 3 P
sixpence that i had a' we'nsday last | to pay ERR 1.02. 55
that year on ash we'nsday was four year in th' MV 2.05. 26 P
upon the coast on we'nsday the fourscore of WT 4.04.276 P
i look'd upon him a' we'nsday half an hour COR 1.03. 59 P
on we'nsday next — | but soft, what day is this ROM 3.04. 17
well, we'nsday is too soon, | a' thursday let it 3.04. 19
we'nsday is to–morrow; 4.01. 90
on we'nsday morn. OTH 3.03. 61
/WENT 2 FR 0.0002 REL FR 1 V 1 P
/jove /sometime /went /disguis'd, /and /why /not 2H6 4.01. 48
/and /the /player /went /to /cuffs /in /the HAM 2.02.355 P
WENT 108 FR 0.0122 REL FR 74 V 34 P
proper a man as ever went on four legs cannot TMP 2.02. 61 P
all this service | have i done since i went. 5.01.226
of his blind brothers and sisters went to it. TGV 4.04. 4 P
i am glad he went not in himself; WIV 1.04. 49 P
well, on went he for a search, and away went i 3.05.105 P
for a search, and away went i for foul clothes. 3.05.106 P
went you not to her yesterday, sir, as you told 5.01. 13 P
i went to her, master /brook, as you see, like a 5.01. 15 P
i went to her in /white and cried "mum," and she 5.05.197 P
how chance you went not with master slender? 5.05.217 P
why went you not with master doctor, maid? 5.05.219
that went to sea with the ten commandements, but
MM 1.02. 8 P
there went but a pair of shears between us. 1.02. 27 P
of the lady, and good words went with her name. 3.01.211 P
i went | to this pernicious caitiff deputy — 5.01. 87
gather the sequel by that went before. ERR 1.01. 95
if you went in pain, master, this knave would go 3.01. 65
he that went, like a base–viol, in a case of 4.03. 23 P
whilst to take order for the wrongs i went, 5.01.146
and he not coming thither, | i went to seek him. 5.01.225
conflict four of his five wits went halting off, ADO 1.01. 66 P
when you went onward on this ended action, | i 1.01.297
is, | saying i lik'd her ere i went to wars. 1.01.305
don john had made, away went claudio enrag'd; 3.03.159 P
see, see, here comes the man we went to seek. 5.01.110

she was a vixen when she went to school; MND 3.02.324
who went with him to search bassanio's ship. MV 2.08. 5
and wheresoe'er we went, like juno's swans, AYL 1.03. 75
swans, | still we went coupled and inseparable. 1.03. 76
wherein went he? 3.02.221 P
he went but forth to wash him in the hellespont 4.01.103 P
went they not quickly, i should die with SHR 3.02.241
in an afternoon as she went to the garden for 4.04.100 P
for but a month ago i went from hence, | and TN 1.02. 31
and when she went away now, "let this fellow be 3.04. 76 P
my brother, and he went | still in this fashion, 3.04.381
so went he suited to his watery tomb. 5.01.234
they that went on crutches ere he was born WT 1.01. 39 P
i do feel it gone, | but know not how it went. 3.02. 96
since last i went to france to fetch his queen. R2 1.01.131
tell me, gentle friend, | how went he under him? 5.05. 82
week, went to a bawdy–house not above once in a 1H4 3.03. 16 P
so went on, | foretelling this same time's 2H4 3.01. 77
never went with his forces into france | but H5 1.02.147
bosom, if ever man went to arthur's bosom. 2.03. 10 P
and went away and it had been any christom child 2.03. 11 P
pride went before, ambition follows him. 2H6 1.01.180
looking the way her harmless young one went, 3.01.215
(in whose time boys went to span–counter for 4.02.157 P
their weapons like to lightning came and went; 3H6 2.01.129
whose father for his hoarding went to hell? 2.02. 48
went all afoot in summer's scalding heat, | that 5.07. 18
when that my mother went with child | of that R3 3.05. 86
from troop to troop | went through the army, 5.03. 71
which went | beyond all man's endeavors. H8 3.02.168
when you went | ambassador to the emperor, you 3.02.317
were those that went on each side of the queen? 4.01.100
so went to bed; 4.02. 24
who were those went by? TRO 1.02. 1
i think he went not forth to–day. 1.02.220 P
if you'll avouch 'twas wisdom paris went — | as 2.02. 84
how chance my brother troilus went not 3.01.138 P
the cry went once on thee, | and still it might, 3.03.184
was that my father that went hence so fast? ROM 1.01.162
who were the motives that you first went out; TIM 5.04. 27
when went there by an age since the great flood JC 1.02.152
he was quick mettle when he went to school. 1.02.296
a lion, | who glaz'd upon me, and went surly by, 1.03. 21
sure | it did not lie there when i went to bed. 2.01. 38
thy lord look well, | for he went sickly forth; 2.04. 14
know'st that we two went to school together; 5.05. 26
and thane of cawdor too; went it not so? MAC 1.03. 87
was it so late, friend, ere you went to bed, 2.03. 22
and went further, which is now | our point of 3.01. 84
since his majesty went into the field, i have 5.01. 4 P
that it went hand in hand even with the vow | i HAM 1.05. 49
for out a' doors he went without their helps, 2.01. 96
no, i went round to work, | and my young 2.02.139
since he went into france i have been in 5.02.210 P
so out went the candle, and we were left LR 1.04.217 P
never lack'd gold, and yet went never gay, OTH 2.01.150
went he hence now? 3.03. 51
o yes, and went between us very oft. 3.03.100
he went hence but now; 3.04.132
since he went from egypt, 'tis | a space for ANT 2.01. 30
his power went out in such distractions as 3.07. 76
and went to jewry on | affairs of antony, there 4.06. 11
no guess in knowledge | which way they went. CYM 1.01. 61
was in debt, it went o' th' backside the town. 1.02. 12 P
if she went before others i have seen, as that 1.04. 72 P
is it fit i went to look upon him? 2.01. 42 P
my lord, when last i went to visit her, | she 3.05. 45
how long is't since she went to milford–haven? 3.05.148 P
he went hence even now. 4.02.189
they went hence so soon as they were born. 5.04.126
i went to antioch, | where, as thou know'st, PER 1.02. 70
convey, | unless your thoughts went on my way. 4.ch. 50
and he went to bed to her very description. 4.02.100 P
and a poet never went | more famous yet 'twixt TNK pr 11
am going, and never yet | went i so willing way. 1.01.104
since first we went to school, may we perceive 1.02. 14
was a time | when young men went a–hunting, and 3.03. 40
in which you swore i went beyond all women, 3.06.206
as he thus went counting | the flinty pavement, 5.04. 58
who like a foul usurper went about | from this LUC 412
girl, when went" (and there she stay'd | till 1275
since from thee going he went willful–slow, SON 51.13
"but quickly on this side the verdict went: LC 113

WENT'ST 3 FR 0.0003 REL FR 3 V 0 P

went'st not thou to her for a purse of ducats? ERR 4.04. 87
art then forsaken, as thou went'st forlorn! 3H6 3.01. 54
joy | than thou went'st forth in lamentation. ROM 3.03.154

WEPT 34 FR 0.0038 REL FR 25 V 9 P

i have inly wept, | or should have spoke ere TMP 5.01.200
a jew would have wept to have seen our parting; TGV 2.03. 11 P
look you, wept herself blind at my parting. 2.03. 13 P
that i have wept a hundred several times. 4.04.145
mistress, moved therewithal, | wept bitterly; 4.04.171
lady beatrice, have you wept all this while? ADO 4.01.255 P
for the which she wept heartily and said she 5.01.174 P
neighbors believe she wept for the death of a MV 3.01. 10 P
that it seem'd sorrow wept to take leave of them WT 5.02. 45 P
and so i am sure my heart wept blood. 5.02. 89 P
and so we wept; 5.02.144 P
that it may be thought i have wept, for i must 1H4 2.04.386 P
and when with grief he wept, | the ruthless 3H6 2.01. 60
when my father york and edward wept | to hear R3 1.02.156
tyrants themselves wept when it was reported. 1.03.184
northumberland, then present, wept to see it. 1.03.186
and when my uncle told me so, he wept, | and 2.02. 23
you wept not for our father's death; 2.02. 62
wept like /two children in their deaths' sad 4.03. 8
god witness with me, i have wept for thine. 4.04. 60
may have a tomb of orphants' tears wept on him! H8 3.02.399
for two and twenty sons i never wept, | because TIT 3.01. 10
death, | and let me say (that never wept before) 3.01. 25
return so much, i have shook my head, and wept; TIM 2.02.137
when our vaults have wept | with drunken spilth 2.02.159
when that the poor have cried, caesar hath wept; JC 3.02. 91
and he wept | when at philippi he found brutus ANT 3.02. 55
air, and then | have turn'd mine eye and wept. CYM 1.03. 22
upon a worm against my will, | but i wept for't. PER 4.01. 79
we wept after her hearse, | and yet we mourn. 4.03. 41
eat them) | the brine they wept at killing 'em. TNK 1.03. 22
and then she wept, and sung again, and sigh'd, 4.01. 92
white | with purple tears, that his wound wept, VEN 1054
her eyes are mad that they have wept till now. 1062

WERADAY *(also well–a–day, wellday)*

WERADAY 2 FR 0.0002 REL FR 2 V 0 P

ah, weraday, he's dead, he's dead, he's dead! ROM 3.02. 37
o, weraday, that ever i was born! 4.05. 15

/WERE 14 FR 0.0015 REL FR 13 V 1 P

/were born to see so sad an hour as this, JN 5.02. 26
/were /they /not /mine? R2 4.01.168
/if /thy /offenses /were /upon /record, | /would 4.01.230
/o, /that /i /were /a /mockery /king /of /snow, 4.01.260
/my /flatterers | /were /then /but /subjects; 4.01.307
/you /will, /so /i /were /from /your /sights. 4.01.315
/you /were /advis'd /his /flesh /was /capable 2H4 1.01.172
/were /you /not /restor'd | /to /all /the /duke 4.01.108
/prayers /and /love | /were /set /on /herford, 4.01.136
/flattering /myself /as /if /it /were /the /moor TIT 3.02. 72
/were /it /not /that /i /have /bad /dreams. HAM 2.02.255 P
how e'er my haps, my joys /were ne'er /begun. 4.03. 68
/and /tears | /were /like /a /better /way: LR 4.03. 19
/to /know | /what /guests /were /in /her /eyes, 4.03. 21

WERE 1698 FR 0.1919 REL FR 1257 V 441 P

though the ship were no stronger than a nutshell TMP 1.01. 47 P
play (as thou say'st) were we heav'd thence, 1.02. 62
new created | the creatures that were mine, i 1.02. 82
the which this story | were most impertinent. 1.02.138
more momentary | and sight–outrunning were not; 1.02.203
those are pearls that were his eyes: 1.02.399
this speech, | were i but where 'tis spoken. 1.02.431
being, as they were, drench'd in the sea, hold 2.01. 62 P
we were talking that our garments seem now as 2.01. 97 P
now as fresh as when we were at tunis at the 2.01. 98 P
you were kneel'd to and importun'd otherwise 2.01.129
and were the king on't, what would i do? 2.01.146
can have no note, unless the sun were post — 2.01.248
she that from whom | we all were sea–swallow'd, 2.01.251
say this were death | that now hath seiz'd them, 2.01.260
why, they were no worse | than now they are. 2.01.261
what a sleep were this | for your advancement! 2.01.267
my brother's servants | were then my fellows, 2.01.274
if he were that which now he's like — that's 2.01.282
were i in england now (as once i was) and had 2.02. 27 P
he were a brave monster indeed if they were set 3.02. 10 P
monster indeed if they were set in his tail. 3.02. 11 P
give us kind keepers, heavens! what were these? 3.03. 20
when we were boys, | who would believe that 3.03. 43
who would believe that there were mountaineers, 3.03. 44
or that there were such men | whose heads stood 3.03. 46
thy vexations | were but my trials of thy love, 4.01. 6
son, in a mov'd sort, | as if you were dismay'd; 4.01.147
(as i foretold you) were all spirits, and | are 4.01.149
told you, sir, they were red–hot with drinking, 4.01.171
mine would, sir, were i human. 5.01. 20
but you, my brace of lords, were i so minded, 5.01.126
hours since | were wrack'd upon this shore; 5.01.137
o heavens, that they were living both in naples, 5.01.149
that they were, i wish | myself were mudded in 5.01.150
i wish | myself were mudded in that oozy bed 5.01.151
upon this shore (where you were wrack'd) was 5.01.161
i prophesied, if a gallows were on land, | this 5.01.217
if i did think, sir, i were well awake, | i'ld 5.01.229
we were dead of sleep, | and (how we know not) 5.01.230
of sounds, all horrible, | we were awak'd; 5.01.235
even in a dream, were we divided from them, 5.01.239
from them, | and were brought moping hither. 5.01.240
ground be overcharg'd, you were best stick her. TGV 1.01.101 P
but, were i you, he never should be mine. 1.02. 11
it were a shame to call her back again, | and 1.02. 51
i would it were, | that you might kill your 1.02. 67
ay; and melodious were it, would you sing it. 1.02. 83
nay, would i were so ang'red with the same. 1.02.101
then tell me, whither were i best to send him? 1.03. 24
you were wont, when you laugh'd, to crow like a 2.01. 26 P
for, without you were so simple, none else would 2.01. 37 P
had the lights they were wont to have when you 2.01. 71 P
i would you were set, so your affection would 2.01. 85 P
i would it were no worse. 2.01.163 P
it is no matter if the tied were lost; 2.03. 37 P
man, if the river were dry, i am able to fill it 2.03. 52 P
if the wind were down, i could drive the boat 2.03. 53 P
my tales of love were wont to weary you; 2.04.126
as twenty seas, if all their sand were pearl, 2.04.170
and sure the match | were rich and honorable; 3.01. 64
child, | nor fearing me as if i were her father; 3.01. 71
that's monstrous. o, that that were out! 3.01.365 P
what, were you banish'd thence? 4.01. 23
why, ne'er repent it, if it were done so. 4.01. 30
but were you banish'd for so small a fault? 4.01. 31
this fellow were a king for our wild faction! 4.01. 37
are you sadder than you were before? 4.02. 54 P
ay, i would i were deaf; 4.02. 64 P
indeed, to be, as it were, a dog at all things. 4.04. 13 P
when all our pageants of delight were play'd, 4.04.159
mine | were full as lovely as is this of hers; 4.04.186
if this fond love were not a blinded god? 4.04.196
and, were there sense in his idolatry, | my 4.04.200
unhappy were you, madam, ere i came; 5.04. 29
were man | but constant, he were perfect; 5.04.110
were man | but constant, he were perfect; 5.04.111
if he were twenty sir john falstaffs, he shall WIV 1.01. 2 P
o' my life, if i were young again, the sword 1.01. 40 P
it were a goot motion if we leave our pribbles 1.01. 54 P
better for you if it were known in counsel. 1.01.118 P
would i were young for your sake, mistress anne! 1.01.260 P
his thefts were too open; 1.03. 25 P
does he not hold up his head, as it were, and 1.04. 29 P
if it were not for one trifling respect, i could 2.01. 44 P
i think the best way were to entertain him with 2.01. 67 P
were they his men? 2.01.177 P
marry, were they. 2.01.178 P
you were good soldiers and tall fellows; 2.02. 11 P
that were a jest indeed! 2.02.111 P
that were a trick indeed! 2.02.112 P
you were wont to be a follower, but now you are 3.02. 2 P
i think, if your husbands were dead, you two 3.02. 14 P
i would thy husband were dead. 3.03. 50 P
see what thou wert, if fortune thy foe were not, 3.03. 65 P
than a thousand pound he were out of the house. 3.03.124 P
linen upon him, as if it were going to bucking; 3.03.131 P
you were best meddle with buck–washing. 3.03.155 P
of the same strain were in the same distress. 3.03.186 P
/and the bottom were as deep as hell, i should 3.05. 13 P
and, as it were, spoke the prologue of our 3.05. 74 P
what? while you were there? 3.05. 79 P
were call'd forth by their mistress to carry me 3.05. 98 P
they were nothing but about mistress anne page, 4.05. 46 P
to know if it were my master's fortune to have 4.05. 47 P
fine wits till i were as crestfall'n as a dried 4.05.100 P
if my wind were but long enough /to /say /my 4.05.102 P
you were also, jupiter, a swan for the love of 5.05. 6 P
four times in the thought they were not fairies, 5.05.122 P
of all rhyme and reason, that they were fairies. 5.05.126 P
'tis time i were chok'd with a piece of toasted 5.05.138 P
would i were hang'd la, else! 5.05.181 P
his /givings–out were of an infinite distance MM 1.04. 54
at that very distant time stood, as it were, in 2.01. 92 P
a one and such a one were past cure of the thing 2.01.110 P
where were you born, friend? 2.01.193 P
mine were the very cipher of a function, | to 2.02. 39
if so your heart were touch'd with that remorse 2.02. 54
i had your potency, | and you were isabel! 2.02. 68
why, all the souls that were were forfeit once, 2.02. 73
why, all the souls that were were forfeit once, 2.02. 73
were he my kinsman, brother, or my son, | it 2.02. 81
when men were fond, i smil'd and wond'red how. 2.02.186
i would do more than that, if more were needful. 2.03. 9
it were as good | to pardon him that hath from 2.04. 42
soul, | were equal poise of sin and charity. 2.04. 68
and that there were | no earthly mean to save 2.04. 94
that is, were i under the terms of death, | th' 2.04.100
better it were a brother died at once, | than 2.04.106
were not you then as cruel as the sentence 2.04.109
age, | but as it were an after–dinner's sleep, 3.01. 33
o, were it but my life, | i'd throw it down for 3.01.103
if it were damnable, he being so wise, | why 3.01.112
what a merit were it in death to take this poor 3.01.231 P
him, he were as good go a mile on his errand. 3.02. 37 P
that we were all, as some would seem to be, 3.02. 38
i would the duke we talk of were return'd again. 3.02.173 P
would he were return'd! 3.02.178 P
lips away, | that so sweetly were forsworn, 4.01. 2
being a murtherer, though he were my brother. 4.02. 62
were he meal'd with that | which he corrects, 4.02. 83
which he corrects, then were he tyrannous, | but 4.02. 84
were you sworn to the duke, or to the deputy? 4.02.182 P
one would think it were mistress overdone's own 4.03. 2 P
in request, for the old women were all dead. 4.03. 8 P
transport him in the mind he is | were damnable. 4.03. 69
this reprobate till he were well inclin'd, | and 4.03. 74
danger that might come | if he were known alive? 4.03. 86
if not true, none were enough. 4.03.168 P
you were not bid to speak. 5.01. 78
o that it were as like as it is true! 5.01.104
one that i would were here, friar lodowick. 5.01.125
were testimonies against his worth and credit 5.01.244
would he were here, my lord, for he indeed 5.01.250
those, for their parents were exceeding poor, ERR 1.01. 56
leagues, | we were encount'red by a mighty rock, 1.01.101
and in our sight they three were taken up | by 1.01.110
my life, | and happy were i in my timely death, 1.01.138
now trust me, were it not against our laws, 1.01.142
but, were you wedded, you would bear some sway. 2.01. 28
but were we burd'ned with like weight of pain, 2.01. 36
have denied that before you were so choleric. 2.02. 66 P
vow | that never words were music to thine ear, 2.02.114
shouldst thou but hear i were licentious, | and 2.02.131
when were you wont to use my sister thus? 2.02.153
if the skin were parchment, and the blows you 3.01. 13
were parchment, and the blows you gave were ink, 3.01. 13
say so, master, if your garments were thin. 3.01. 70
and therefore 'tis high time that i were hence. 3.02.157
last too long | if it were chain'd together, and 4.01. 26
and true he swore, though yet forsworn he were. 4.02. 10
and yet would herein others' eyes were worse: 4.02. 26
no, no, the bell, 'tis time that i were gone: 4.02. 53
as if time were in debt! 4.02. 57
me | as if i were their well–acquainted friend, 4.03. 2
and then were you hind'red by the sergeant to 4.03. 39 P
i would i were senseless, sir, that i might not 4.04. 25 P
whilst upon me the guilty doors were shut, | and 4.04. 63
were not my doors lock'd up, and i shut out? 4.04. 70
perdie, your doors were lock'd, and you shut out 4.04. 71
but i confess, sir, that we were lock'd out. 4.04. 99
i long that we were safe and sound aboard. 4.04.150
it seems his sleeps were hind'red by thy railing 5.01. 71
say'st his sports were hind'red by thy brawls: 5.01. 77
goldsmith there, were he not pack'd with her, 5.01.219
if he were mad, he would not plead so coldly. 5.01.273
for lately we were bound as you are now. 5.01.294
and i, | and the twin dromio, all were taken up; 5.01.351
no, and he were, i would burn my study. ADO 1.01. 80 P
were you in doubt, sir, that you ask'd her? 1.01.106 P
signior benedick, no, for then were you a child. 1.01.107 P
it worse, and 'twere such a face as yours were. 1.01.137 P
can afford her, that were she other than she is, 1.01.174 P
were she other than she is, she were unhandsome, 1.01.174 P
cousin, and she were not possess'd with a fury, 1.01.191 P
if this were so, so were it utt'red. 1.01.215 P
if this were so, so were it utt'red. 1.01.215 P
were thus much overheard by a man of mine. 1.02. 10 P
would the cook were a' my mind! 1.03. 73 P
he were an excellent man that were made just in 2.01. 6 P
were an excellent man that were made just in the 2.01. 6 P
him so ill–well, unless you were the very man. 2.01.118 P
if her breath were as terrible as her 2.01.248 P
her terminations, there were no living near her, 2.01.249 P
though she were endow'd with all that adam had 2.01.251 P
i were but little happy, if i could say how much 2.01.307 P
out a' question, you were born in a merry hour. 2.01.333 P
she were an excellent wife for benedick. 2.01.351 P
my lord, if they were but a week married, they 2.01.353 P
ladies, sigh no more, | men were deceivers ever, 2.03. 63
it were good that benedick knew of it by some 2.03.154 P

and he should, it were an alms to hang him. 2.03.158 P
were it good, think you? 2.03.172 P
did not think i should live till i were married. 2.03.244 P
and therefore certainly it were not good | she 3.01. 57
it were a better death than die with mocks, 3.01. 79
i could say she were worse; 3.02.110 P
yea, or else it were pity but they should suffer 3.03. 2 P
nay, that were a punishment too good for them, 3.03. 4 P
rather ask if it were possible any villainy 3.03.112 P
troth, i think your other rebato were better. 3.04. 6 P
excellently, if the hair were a thought browner; 3.04. 14 P
five a' clock, cousin, 'tis time you were ready. 3.04. 53 P
as, god help, i would desire they were, but, in 3.05. 11 P
mine own part, if i were as tedious as a king, i 3.05. 21 P
all you that see her, that she were a maid, | by 4.01. 39
thought i thy spirits were stronger than thy 4.01.125
lady, were you her bedfellow last night? 4.01.147
it were as possible for me to say i lov'c 4.01.270 P
o that i were a man! 4.01.303 P
unmitigated rancor — o god, that i were a man! 4.01.306 P
o that i were a man for his sake! 4.01.317 P
o that he were here to write me down as ass! 4.02. 75 P
being young, or what would do | were i not old. 5.01. 62
how you were brought into the orchard and saw me 5.01.237 P
that were impossible — but i pray you both, 5.01.280
they were never so truly turn'd over and over as 5.02. 34 P
i'll hold my mind were she an ethiope. 5.04. 38
and when you lov'd, you were my other husband. 5.04. 61
they swore that you were almost sick for me. 5.04. 80
they swore that you were well–nigh dead for me. 5.04. 81
life, for i was told you were in a consumption. 5.04. 96 P
if it were, i deny her virginity; LLL 1.01.296 P
or, if it were, it would neither serve for the 1.02.113 P
no, sir, that were fast and loose; 1.02.157 P
in oath | were all address'd to meet you, gentle 2.01. 83
were my lord so, his ignorance were wise, 2.01.102
were my lord so, his ignorance were wise, 2.01.102
you will the sooner, that i were away, | for 2.01.112
were not his requests so far | from reason's 2.01.149
one for herself, to desire that were a shame. 2.01.200
this civil war of wits were much better used 2.01.226
methought all his senses were lock'd in his eye, 2.01.242
their own worth from where they were glass'd, 2.01.244
were still at odds, being but three. 3.01. 85
were still at odds, being but three. 3.01. 90
were still at odds, being but three. 3.01. 96
though argus were her eunuch and her guard. 3.01.199
your waist, mistress, were as slender as my wit, 4.01. 49
comes so smoothly off, so obscenely as it were, 4.01.143
yet a kind of insinuation, as it were in via, in 4.02. 14 P
facere, as it were, replication, or rather 4.02. 15 P
ostentare, to show, as it were, his inclination, 4.02. 16 P
he hath not eat paper, as it were; 4.02. 25 P
so were there a patch set on learning, to see 4.02. 31
those thoughts to me were oaks, to thee like 4.02.108
not care a pin, if the other three were in. 4.03. 18 P
whom jove would swear | juno but an ethiop were, 4.03.116
berowne, and longaville, | were lovers too! 4.03.122
one, her hairs were gold, crystal the other's 4.03.140
you were born to do me shame. 4.03.200
we cannot cross the cause why we were born; 4.03.214
a wife of such wood were felicity. 4.03.245
o, if the streets were paved with thine eyes, 4.03.274
her feet were much too dainty for such tread! 4.03.275
until his ink were temp'red with love's sighs: 4.03.344
then fools you were these women to forswear, 4.03.352
spruce, too affected, too odd as it were, too 5.01. 13 P
and the heavens were so pleas'd that thou wert 5.01. 75 P
and sudden breaking out of mirth, as it were, i 5.01.115 P
and if my face were but as fair as yours, | my 5.02. 32
but as fair as yours, | my favor were as great: 5.02. 33
the numbers true, and, were the numb'ring too, 5.02. 35
too, | i were the fairest goddess on the ground. 5.02. 36
o that your face were not so full of o's! 5.02. 45
the chain were longer and the letter short? 5.02. 56
o that i knew he were but in by th' week! 5.02. 61
you were best call it "daughter–beamed eyes." 5.02.172
they were all in lamentable cases! 5.02.273
let us complain to them what fools were here, 5.02.302
and wonder what they were, and to what end 5.02.304
we four indeed confronted were with four | in 5.02.367
it were a fault to snatch words from my tongue. 5.02.382
we were descried, they'll mock us now downright. 5.02.389
were not you here but even now, disguis'd? 5.02.433
and were you well advis'd? 5.02.434
when you then were here, | what did you whisper 5.02.435
sir, it were pity you should get your living by 5.02.496 P
most true, 'tis right; you were so, alisander. 5.02.569
or, if there were a sympathy in choice, | war, MND 1.01.141
o, were favor so, | /yours /would i catch, fair 1.01.186
were the world mine, demetrius being bated, 1.01.190
would that fault were mine! 1.01.201
i | upon faint primrose beds were wont to lie, 1.01.215
you were best to call them generally, man by man 1.02. 2 P
and that were enough to hang us all. 1.02. 76 P
what beard were i best to play it in? 1.02. 90 P
and here my mistress. would that he were gone! 2.01. 59
thou toldst me they were stol'n unto this wood; 2.01.191
we should be woo'd, and were not made to woo. 2.01.242
come hither as a lion, it were pity of my life. 3.01. 43 P
"if i were fair, thisby, i were only thine." 3.01.103
"if i were fair, thisby, i were only thine." 3.01.103
were met together to rehearse a play | intended 3.02. 11
if you were civil and knew courtesy, | you would 3.02.147
if you were men, as men you are in show, | you 3.02.151
his eyes were green as leeks. 5.01.335
or, as it were, the pageants of the sea, | do MV 1.01. 11
if your miseries were in the same abundance as 1.02. 4 P
if to do were as easy as to know what were good 1.02. 12 P
do were as easy as to know what were good to do, 1.02. 12 P
easier teach twenty what were good to be done, 1.02. 16 P
when laban and himself were compremis'd | that 1.03. 78
all the eanlings which were streak'd and pied 1.03. 79
parti–color'd lambs, and those were jacob's. 1.03. 88
this were kindness. 1.03.143
no, that were pity. 2.02.200
his words were "farewell, mistress!" 2.05. 45
deserving | were but a weak disabling of myself. 2.07. 30
it were too gross | to rib her cerecloth in the 2.07. 50
that in a gondilo were seen together | lorenzo 2.08. 8
duke | they were not with bassanio in his ship. 2.08. 11
and wish'd in silence that it were not his. 2.08. 32
you were best to tell antonio what you hear, 2.08. 33
and offices | were not deriv'd corruptly, and 2.09. 42
were purchas'd by the merit of the wearer! 2.09. 43
i would she were as lying a gossip in that as 3.01. 8 P
i would my daughter were dead at my foot, and 3.01. 88 P
would she were hears'd at my foot, and the 3.01. 89 P
for, were he out of venice, i can make what 3.01.127 P
that were a kind of bastard hope indeed; 3.05. 13 P
we were christians enow before, e'en as many as 3.05. 21 P
in six thousand ducats | were in six parts, and 4.01. 86
if she were by to hear you make the offer. 4.01.289
i would she were in heaven, so she could 4.01.291
would he were gelt that had it, for my part, 5.01.144
you were to blame, i must be plain with you, 5.01.166
why, i were best to cut my left hand off, | and 5.01.177
were you the doctor, and i knew you not? 5.01.280
were you the clerk that is to make me cuckold? 5.01.281
but were the day come, i should wish it dark 5.01.304
till i were couching with the doctor's clerk. 5.01.305
my blood, were there twenty brothers betwixt us. AYL 1.01. 48 P
mistress of, and would you yet /i were merrier? 1.02. 4 P
of thy love to me were so righteously temper'd 1.02. 13 P
were you made the messenger? 1.02. 59 P
that swore by his honor they were good pancakes, 1.02. 64 P
it, the pancakes were naught and the mustard was 1.02. 66 P
by my knavery (if i had it) then i were. 1.02. 75 P
strength that i have, i would it were with you. 1.02.195 P
i would i were invisible, to catch the strong 1.02.211 P
were i my father, coz, would i do this? 1.02.231
then there were two cousins laid up, when the 1.03. 7 P
were it not better, | because that i am more 1.03.114
not for my spirits, if my legs were not weary. 2.04. 2 P
but if thy love were ever like to mine — | as 2.04. 28
my fortunes were more able to relieve her; 2.04. 77
o that i were a fool! 2.07. 42
if that you were the good sir rowland's son, 2.07.191
as you have whisper'd faithfully you were, | and 2.07.192
but were i not the better part made mercy, | i 3.01. 2
would be uncleanly if courtiers were shepherds. 3.02. 50 P
ay, but the feet were lame and could not bear 3.02.169 P
there were none principal, they were all like 3.02.353 P
they were all like one another as halfpence are, 3.02.353 P
what were his marks? 3.02.372 P
upon a foul slut were to put good meat into an 3.03. 36 P
a man may, if he were of a fearful heart, 3.03. 48 P
but i were better to be married of him than of 3.03. 90 P
your sorrow and my grief | were both extermin'd. 3.05. 89
why, that were covetousness. 3.05. 91
he said mine eyes were black and my hair black, 3.05.130
to me now, and i were your very very rosalind? 4.01. 70 P
nay, you were better speak first, and when you 4.01. 73 P
and when you were gravell'd for lack of matter, 4.01. 74 P
that should you if i were your mistress, or i 4.01. 83 P
could not love me | were man as rare as phoenix. 4.03. 17
verily did think | that her old gloves were on, 4.03. 26
whose boughs were moss'd with age | and high top 4.03.104
i would i were at home. 4.03.161
thereby that grapes were made to eat and lips to 5.01. 35 P
that would i, were i of all kingdoms king. 5.04. 10
to have her and death were both one thing. 5.04. 17
but when the parties were met themselves, one of 5.04.100 P
power, which were on foot | in his own conduct, 5.04.156
to /them again | that were with him exil'd. 5.04.165
ends | that here were well begun and well begot; 5.04.171
if i were a woman i would kiss as many of you as ep 18 P
if echo were as fleet, | i would esteem him SHR in.1. 26
were he not warm'd with ale, | this were a bed in.1. 32
this were a bed but cold to sleep so soundly. in.1. 33
what think you, if he were convey'd to bed, in.1. 37
were he the veriest antic in the world. in.1. 101
yet would you say ye were beaten out of door, in.2. 85
these, | which never were, nor no man ever saw. in.2. 96
you, | unless you were of gentler, milder mould. 1.01. 60
but if it were, doubt not her care should be 1.01. 63
the better for him, would i were so too! 1.01.238
that were my state far worser than it is, | i 1.02. 91
as firmly as yourself were still in place, | yea 1.02.156
words | than you — unless you were a scholar, 1.02.158
such a life, with such a wife, were strange! 1.02.193
i would i were as sure of a good dinner. 1.02.217
and were his daughter fairer than she is, | she 1.02.240
i knew you at the first | you were a moveable. 2.01.197
'twas told me you were rough and coy and sullen, 2.01.243
it were impossible i should speed amiss. 2.01.283
your father were a fool | to give thee all, and 2.01.400
methinks he looks as though he were in love; 3.01. 88
not so well apparell'd | as i wish you were. 3.02. 90
were it better i should rush in thus: 3.02. 91
first were we sad, fearing you would not come, 3.02. 98
tedious it were to tell, and harsh to hear — 3.02.105
the morning wears, 'tis time we were at church. 3.02.111
were it not that my fellow schoolmaster | doth 3.02.138
now, were not i a little pot and soon hot, my 4.01. 5 P
and gabr'el's pumps were all unpink'd i' th' 4.01.133
there were none fine but adam, rafe, and gregory 4.01.136
the rest were ragged, old, and beggarly, | yet, 4.01.137
the meat was well, if you were so contented. 4.01.169
minola, | as if he were the right vincentio. 4.02. 70
genoa, | where we were lodgers at the pegasus. 4.04. 5
'twere good he were school'd. 4.04. 9
they're busy within, you were best knock louder. 5.01. 14 P
for both our sakes, i would that word were true. 5.02. 15
would say your head and butt were head and horn. 5.02. 41
i would your duty were as foolish too. 5.02.126
would for the king's sake he were living! AWW 1.01. 22 P
i would it were not notorious. 1.01. 36 P
o, were that all! 1.01. 79
that you were made of is metal to make virgins. 1.01.129 P
parolles, you were born under a charitable star. 1.01.190 P
nor bitterness | were in his pride or sharpness; 1.02. 37
if they were, | his equal had awak'd them, and 1.02. 37
who were below him | he us'd as creatures of 1.02. 41
would i were with him! 1.02. 52
home, | i quickly were dissolved from my hive, 1.02. 66
if he were living, i would try him yet. 1.02. 72
what they are, there were no fear in marriage, 1.03. 51 P
fault with the tithe–woman if i were the parson. 1.03. 85 P
his might only where qualities were level; 1.03.114 P
such were our faults, or then we thought them 1.03.135
catalogue of those | that were enwombed mine. 1.03.144
would you were — | so that my lord your son 1.03.161
so that my lord your son were not my brother — 1.03.162
or were you both our mothers, | i care no more 1.03.163
i do for heaven, | so i were not his sister. 1.03.165
my friends were poor, but honest, so's my love. 1.03.195
as notes whose faculties inclusive were | more 1.03.226
inclusive were | more than they were in note. 1.03.227
to say precisely, were not for the court; 2.02. 12 P
you were lately whipt, sir, as i think. 2.02. 50 P
well to a whipping, if you were but bound to't. 2.02. 55 P
my mouth no more were broken than these boys', 2.03. 60
and they were sons of mine, i'd have them whipt, 2.03. 86 P
i would it were hell–pains for thy sake, and my 2.03.232 P
and he were double and double a lord. 2.03.239 P
by mine honor, if i were but two hours younger, 2.03.253 P
you were beaten in italy for picking a kernel 2.03.258 P
in yourself, sir, or were you taught to find me? 2.04. 34 P
miseries which nature owes | were mine at once. 3.02.120
though there were no further danger known but 3.05. 27 P
if he were honester | he were much goodlier. 3.05. 79
if he were honester | he were much goodlier. 3.05. 80
were i his lady, | i would poison that vile 3.05. 83
it were fit you knew him, lest, reposing too far 3.06. 13 P
which were the greatest obloquy i' th' world 4.02. 44
which were the greatest obloquy i' th' world 4.02. 48
if they were not cherish'd by our virtues. 4.03. 74 P
there, if they were more than they can commend. 4.03. 81 P
sir, if i were to live this present hour, i will 4.03.160 P
or whether he thinks it were not possible with 4.03.179 P
that you would think truth were a fool. 4.03.254 P
and i were not a very coward, i'd compel it of 4.03.321 P
where but women were that had receiv'd so much 4.03.327 P
if my heart were great, | 'twould burst at this. 4.03.330
so you were a knave at his service indeed. 4.05. 29 P
my good lord, you were the first that found me! 5.02. 42 P
though my revenges were high bent upon him | and 5.03. 10
if i were so, | he might have bought me at a 5.03.189
if it were yours by none of all these ways, 5.03.275
it is perchance that you yourself were saved. TN 1.02. 6
that were hard to compass, | because she will 1.02. 44
were we not born under taurus? 1.03.137 P
make your excuse wisely, you were best. 1.05. 30 P
i told him you were sick; 1.05.140 P
i told him you were asleep; 1.05.142 P
think his mother's milk were scarce out of him. 1.05.161 P
i heard you were saucy at my gates, and allow'd 1.05.197 P
were you sent hither to praise me? 1.05.249 P
but, if you were the devil, you are fair. 1.05.251
though you were crown'd | the nonpareil of 1.05.253
unless the master were the man. 1.05.294
it were a bad recompense for your love, to lay 2.01. 6 P
were you not ev'n now with the countess olivia? 2.02. 1 P
'tis, | poor lady, she were better love a dream. 2.02. 26
man, | as it might be, perhaps, were i a woman, 2.04.108
would they were blanks, rather than fill'd with 3.01.104
i would you were as i would have you be! 3.01.142
although the sheet were big enough for the bed 3.02. 47 P
if he were open'd and you find so much blood in 3.02. 61 P
but, were my worth as is my conscience firm, 3.03. 17
that, were i ta'en here, it would scarce be 3.03. 28
your ladyship were best to have some guard about 3.04. 12 P
if this were play'd upon a stage now, i could 3.04.127 P
and looks pale, as if a bear were at his heels. 3.04.295 P
caves, | where manners ne'er were preach'd! 4.01. 49
in't, and i would i were the first that ever 4.02. 5 P
though ignorance were as dark as hell; 4.02. 46 P
i would we were well rid of this knavery. 4.02. 67 P
may be conveniently deliver'd, i would he were, 4.02. 69 P
well–a–day that you were, sir! 4.02.108 P
i had rather than forty pound i were at home. 5.01.177 P
his eyes were set at eight i' th' morning. 5.01.199 P
were you a woman, as the rest goes even, | i 5.01.239
and in such forms which here were presuppos'd 5.01.350
they were train'd together in their childhoods; WT 1.01. 22 P
and embrac'd, as it were, from the ends of 1.01. 31 P
if there were no other excuse why they should 1.01. 43 P
were there necessity in your request, although 1.02. 22
which to hinder | were (in your love) a whip to 1.02. 25
to tell he longs to see his son were strong; 1.02. 34
my lord's tricks and yours when you were boys. 1.02. 61
you were pretty lordings then? 1.02. 62
we were, fair queen, | two lads that thought 1.02. 62
we were as twinn'd lambs that did frisk i' th' 1.02. 67
o, would her name were grace! 1.02. 99
but were they false | as o'er–dy'd blacks, as 1.02.131
yet were it true | to say this boy were like me. 1.02.134
yet were it true | to say this boy were like me. 1.02.135
my lord, | if ever i were willful–negligent, 1.02.255
which to reiterate were sin | as deep as that, 1.02.283
were my wive's liver | infected as her life, she 1.02.304
which draught to me were cordial. 1.02.318
and speak to me as if | i were a baby still. 2.01. 6
in the world, | he were as much more villain: 2.01. 80
as i take it, | if the good truth were known. 2.01.199
if | the cause were not in being — part o' th' 2.03. 3
i can hook to me — say that she were gone, 2.03. 7
by combat make her good, so were i | a man, the 2.03. 61
were i a tyrant, | where were her life? 2.03.122
were i a tyrant, | where were her life? 2.03.123
as you were past all shame | (those of your fact 3.02. 84
o that he were alive, and here beholding | his 3.02.120
thy by–gone fooleries were but spices of it. 3.02.184
i would there were no age between ten and 3.03. 59 P
they were warmer that got this than the poor 3.03. 75 P
were never for a piece of beauty rarer, | nor in 4.04. 32
as it were the day | of celebration of that 4.04. 49
as if you were a feasted one and not | the 4.04. 63
no more than were i painted i would wish | this 4.04.101
i should leave grazing, were i of your flock, 4.04.109
some stretch–mouth'd rascal would, as it were, 4.04.197 P
sings 'em over as they were gods or goddesses: 4.04.208 P
you would think a smock were a she–angel, he so 4.04.209 P

if i were not in love with mopsa, thou shouldst 4.04.231 P
and five or six honest wives that were present. 4.04.270 P
love or bounty, you were straited | for a reply, 4.04.354
that, were i crown'd the most imperial monarch, 4.04.372
were i the fairest youth | that ever made eye 4.04.373
i would your spirit were easier for advice, | or 4.04.505
now were i happy if | his going i could frame to 4.04.508
appointed, as if | the scene you play were mine. 4.04.593
if i thought it were a piece of honesty to 4.04.680 P
what were more holy | than to rejoice the former 5.01. 29
were i the ghost that walk'd, i'ld bid you mark 5.01. 63
were i but twenty-one, | your father's image is 5.01.126
bear no credit, | were not the proof so nigh. 5.01.180
from his liking, | where you were tied in duty; 5.01.213
you, sir, were you present at this relation? 5.02. 1 P
we were all commanded out of the chamber; 5.02. 6 P
in the king and camillo were very notes of 5.02. 11 P
not say if th' importance were joy or sorrow; 5.02. 18 P
if ever truth were pregnant by circumstance. 5.02. 30 P
such distraction that they were to be known by 5.02. 48 P
daughter, as if that joy were now become a loss, 5.02. 51 P
to expose the child were even then lost when it 5.02. 71 P
you were best say these robes are not gentlemen 5.02.131 P
would i were dead but that methinks already — 5.03. 62
were it but told you, should be hooted at | like 5.03.116
gap of time since first | we were dissever'd. 5.03.155
and were our father, and this son like him, | o JN 1.01. 81
and if he were, he came into the world | full 1.01.112
then, if he were my brother's, | my brother 1.01.125
him, | and if my legs were two such riding-rods, 1.01.140
and, to his shape, were heir to all this land, 1.01.144
now, by this light, were i to get again, | madam 1.01.259
eyes, these brows, were moulded out of his; 2.01.100
i would that i were low laid in my grave, | i am 2.01.164
were harbor'd in their rude circumference. 2.01.262
sirrah, were i at home, | at your den, sirrah, 2.01.290
of peace, | heaven knows they were besmear'd and 3.01.236
if this same were a churchyard where we stand, 3.03. 40
though that my death were adjunct to my act, 3.03. 57
o, that my tongue were in the thunder's mouth! 3.04. 38
i am not mad, i would to heaven i were! 3.04. 48
if i were mad, i should forget my son, | or 3.04. 57
son, | or madly think a babe of clouts were he. 3.04. 58
if but a dozen french | were there in arms, they 3.04.174
so i were out of prison and kept sheep, | i 4.01. 17
and i would to heaven | i were your son, so you 4.01. 24
in sooth, i would you were a little sick, | that 4.01. 29
that there were but a mote in yours, | a grain, 4.01. 91
all this while | you were disguis'd. 4.01.126
you were crown'd before, | and that high royalty 4.02. 4
to this effect, before you were new crown'd, 4.02. 35
my lord, they say five moons were seen to-night; 4.02.182
that were embattailed and rank'd in kent. 4.02.200
e'er you think, good words, i think, were best. 4.03. 28
when we were happy we had other names. 5.04. 8
o that there were some virtue in my tears, 5.07. 44
were in the washes all unwarily | devoured by 5.07. 63
were i tied to run afoot | even to the frozen R2 1.01. 63
were he my brother, nay, my kingdom's heir, | as 1.01.116
we were not born to sue, but to command, | which 1.01.196
one, | were as seven vials of his sacred blood, 1.02. 12
no, bullingbrook, if ever i were traitor, | my 1.03.201
and say, what store of parting tears were shed? 1.04. 5
as were our england in reversion his, | and he 1.04. 35
my life, | how happy then were my ensuing death! 2.01. 68
it were a shame to let this land by lease; 2.01.110
dear | as harry duke of herford, were he here. 2.01.144
his hands were guilty of no kinred blood, | but 2.01.182
were i but now lord of such hot youth | as when 2.03. 99
whilst we were wand'ring with the antipodes, 3.02. 49
as if the world were all dissolv'd to tears, 3.02.108
walls about our life | were brass impregnable; 3.02.168
o that i were as great | as is my grief, or 3.03.136
i would my skill were subject to thy curse. 3.04.103
i would he were the best | in all this presence 4.01. 31
now, by my soul, i would it were this hour. 4.01. 42
'tis very true, you were in presence then, | and 4.01. 62
presence | were enough noble to be upright judge 4.01.118
that were some love, but little policy. 5.01. 84
away, fond woman, were he twenty times my son, 5.02.101
and if i were thy nurse, thy tongue to teach, 5.03.113
these were his very words. 5.04. 3
o would the deed were good! 5.05.114
whose arms were moulded in their mother's womb, 1H4 1.01. 23
which fourteen hundred years ago were nail'd 1.01. 26
unless hours were cups of sack, and minutes 1.02. 7 P
were it not here apparent that thou art heir 1.02. 57 P
a commodity of good names were to be bought. 1.02. 83 P
o, if men were to be sav'd by merit, what hole 1.02.107 P
what hole in hell were hot enough for him? 1.02.108 P
if all the year were playing holidays, | to 1.02.204
you were about to speak. 1.03. 22
were, as he says, not with such strength denied 1.03. 25
by heaven, methinks it were an easy leap, | to 1.03.201
no, ye fat chuffs, i would your store were here! 2.02. 89 P
'zounds, and i were now by this rascal, i could 2.03. 22 P
i would i were a weaver, i could sing psalms, or 2.04.133 P
i am a rogue if i were not at half-sword with a 2.04.164 P
no, no, they were not bound. 2.04.177 P
you rogue, they were bound, every man of them, 2.04.178 P
as we were sharing, some six or seven fresh men 2.04.180 P
if there were not two or three and fifty upon 2.04.187 P
seven? why, there were but four even now. 2.04.203 P
'zounds, and i were at the strappado, or all the 2.04.236 P
if reasons were as plentiful as blackberries, i 2.04.239 P
bound them, and were masters of their wealth. 2.04.254 P
than in myself, were to say more than i know. 2.04.467 P
the heavens were all on fire, the earth did 3.01. 23
were strangely clamorous to the frighted fields. 3.01. 39
several devils' names | that were his lackeys. 3.01.156
on his helm | would they were multitudes, and on 3.02.143
'sblood, i would my face were in your belly! 3.03. 49 P
'sblood, and he were here, i would cudgel him 3.03. 86 P
if there were any thing in thy pocket but 3.03.157 P
if thy pocket were enrich'd with any other 3.03.161 P
o, i could wish this tavern were my drum! 3.03.206
in this fine age were not thought flattery, 4.01. 2
were it good | to set the exact wealth of all 4.01. 45
it were not good, for therein should we read 4.01. 49
than if the earl were here, for men must think, 4.01. 79
o that glendower were come! 4.01.124
sores, and such as indeed were never soldiers, 4.02. 27 P
'tis more than time that i were there, and you 4.02. 55 P
would to god | you were of our determination! 4.03. 33
(who is, if every owner were well plac'd, 4.03. 94
we were the first and dearest of your friends. 5.01. 33
when yet you were in place and in account 5.01. 37
but with nimble wing | we were enforc'd, for 5.01. 65
to spend that shortness basely were too long 5.02. 82
if it were so, i might have let alone | the 5.04. 53
thy name in arms were now as great as mine! 5.04. 70
of thee | if i were much in love with vanity! 5.04.106
if the man were alive and would deny it, 'zounds 5.04.152 P
get me but a wife in the stews, i were mann'd, 2H4 1.02. 54 P
were it worse than the name of rebellion can 1.02. 77 P
why, sir, did i say you were an honest man? 1.02. 80 P
when there were matters against you for your 1.02.132 P
i would it were otherwise, i would my means were 1.02.142 P
i would my means were greater and my waist 1.02.143 P
would to god my name were not so terrible to the 1.02.218 P
i were better to be eaten to death with a rust 1.02.218 P
i told thee they were ill for a green wound? 2.01. 97 P
and those that were thy peach-color'd once, or 2.02. 16 P
when you were more /endear'd to it than now, 2.03. 11
there were two honors lost, yours and your son's 2.03. 16
and told him there were five more sir johns, and 2.04. 6 P
and captains were of my mind, they would 2.04.142 P
o, if this were seen, | the happiest youth, 3.01. 53
and in two year after | were they at wars. 3.01. 60
that i and greatness were compell'd to kiss), 3.01. 74
and were these inward wars once out of hand, 3.01.107
you were call'd lusty shallow then, cousin. 3.02. 16 P
where the bona /robas were and had the best of 3.02. 23 P
good phrases are surely, and ever were, very 3.02. 71 P
mouldy, it is time you were spent. 3.02.117 P
it were superfluous, for /'s apparel is built 3.02.143 P
dimensions to any thick sight were /invisible. 3.02.313 P
whistle, and sware they were his fancies or his 3.02.318 P
or if there were, it not belongs to you. 4.01. 96
that, were our royal faiths martyrs in love, 4.01.191
how deep you were within the books of god? 4.02. 17
i were simply the most active fellow in europe. 4.03. 21 P
some few hours | were thine without offense, and 4.05.102
and dead almost, my liege, to think you were, 4.05.156
if i were saw'd into quantities, i should make 5.01. 62 P
if the deed were ill, | be you contented, 5.02. 83
o the lord, that sir john were come! 5.04. 11 P
as it were, to ride day and night, and not to 5.05. 20 P
as if there were nothing else to be done but to 5.05. 26 P
and yet that were but light payment, to dance ep 19 P
you would desire the king were made a prelate; H5 1.01. 40
do, | were all thy children kind and natural! 2.pr. 19
did you wrong, for you were troth-plight to her. 2.01. 19 P
those that were your father's enemies | have 2.02. 29
would i were with him, wheresome'er he is, 2.03. 7 P
felt them, and they were as cold as any stone; 2.03. 24 P
'a did, and said they were dev'ls incarnate. 2.03. 31 P
war nor no known quarrel were in question) | but 2.04. 17
and collected, | as were a war in expectation. 2.04. 20
were busied with a whitsun morris-dance; 2.04. 25
were but the outside of the roman brutus, 2.04. 37
were it the mistress court of mighty europe; 2.04.133
whose limbs were made in england, show us here 3.01. 26
would i were in an alehouse in london, i would 3.02. 12 P
look you, he were my brother, i would desire the 3.06. 54 P
learn you by rote where services were done — at 3.06. 72 P
good to bruise an injury till it were full ripe. 3.06.122 P
who when they were in health, i tell thee, 3.06.148
would it were day! 3.07. 2 P
from the earth, as if his entrails were hairs; 3.07. 13 P
and 'twere more honor some were away. 3.07. 75 P
as well, were some of your brags dismounted. 3.07. 77 P
would i were able to load him with his desert! 3.07. 79 P
but i would it were morning, for i would fain be 3.07. 83 P
'tis not the first time you were overshot. 3.07.124 P
would it were day! 3.07.130 P
were better than a churlish turf of france. 4.01. 15
and so i would he were, and i by him, at all 4.01.116 P
by him, at all adventures, so we were quit here. 4.01.116 P
then i would he were here alone; 4.01.121 P
who to disobey were against all proportion of 4.01.146 P
him that escapes, it were not sin to think that, 4.01.183 P
be angry with you, if the time were convenient. 4.01.204 P
were enow | to purge this field of such a 4.02. 28
think themselves accurs'd they were not here; 4.03. 65
when alanson and myself were down together, i 4.07.155 P
five hundred were but yesterday dubb'd knights. 4.08. 86
were now the general of our gracious empress, 5.pr. 30
it were, my lord, a hard condition for a maid to 5.02.298 P
if henry were recall'd to life again, | these 1H6 1.01. 66
how were they lost? what treachery was us'd? 1.01. 68
were our tears wanting to this funeral, | these 1.01. 82
enclosed were they with their enemies. 1.01.136
christ's mother helps me, else i were too weak. 1.02.106
yet saint philip's daughters, were like thee. 1.02.143
great fear of my name 'mongst them were spread 1.04. 50
bed, | ready they were to shoot me to the heart. 1.04. 56
o, would i were to die with salisbury! 1.05. 38
that one day bloom'd and fruitful were the next. 1.06. 7
i tell you, madam, were the whole frame here, 2.03. 54
your roof were not sufficient to contain't. 2.03. 56
within the temple hall we were too loud, | the 2.04. 3
were growing time once ripened to my will. 2.04. 99
i would his troubles likewise were expir'd, 2.05. 31
in whom the title rested, were suppress'd. 2.05. 92
beside, i fear me, if thy thoughts were sifted, 3.01. 24
if i were covetous, ambitious, or perverse, | as 3.01. 29
my lord, it were your duty to forbear. 3.01. 52
and those occasions, uncle, were of force: 3.01.156
they that of late were daring with their scoffs 3.02.113
france were no place for henry's warriors, | nor 3.03. 22
long since we were resolved of your truth, 3.04. 20
now, sir, to you, that were so hot at sea, 3.04. 28
and that the french were almost ten to one, 4.01. 21
were there surpris'd and taken prisoners. 4.01. 26
knights of the garter were of noble birth, 4.01. 34
such as were grown to credit by the wars; 4.01. 36
and should (if i were worthy to be judge) | be 4.01. 42
by your espials were discovered | two mightier 4.03. 6
of horsemen, that were levied for this siege! 4.03. 11
doth stop my cornets, were in talbot's place! 4.03. 25
how now, sir william, whither were you sent? 4.04. 12
o, were mine eyeballs into bullets turn'd, 4.07. 79
it were enough to fright the realm of france! 4.07. 82
were but his picture left amongst you here, | it 4.07. 83
i were best to leave him, for he will not hear. 5.03. 83
the christian prince, king henry, were he here. 5.03.172
think she knows not well | (there were so many) 5.04. 81
if you do censure me by what you were, | not 5.05. 97
all, | these counties were the keys of normandy. 2H6 1.01.114
for, were there hope to conquer them again, | my 1.01.117
as stout and proud as he were lord of all, 1.01.187
were plac'd the heads of edmund duke of somerset 1.02. 29
that chair where kings and queens were crown'd, 1.02. 38
were i a man, a duke, and next of blood, | i 1.02. 63
gold cannot come amiss, were she a devil. 1.02. 92
that were a state fit for his holiness. 1.03. 64
if they were known, as the suspect is great, 1.03.136
his words were these: 1.03.183
say, man, were these thy words? 1.03.186
as we were scouring my lord of york's armor. 1.03.192 P
were it not good your grace could fly to heaven? 2.01. 17
faith, holy uncle, would't were come to that! 2.01. 37
welcome is banishment, welcome were my death. 2.03. 14
i am come hither, as it were, upon my man's 2.03. 85 P
why, yet thy scandal were not wip'd away, | but 2.04. 65
or, if he were not privy to those faults, | yet, 3.01. 47
and lowly words were ransom for their fault. 3.01.127
unless it were a bloody murtherer, | or foul 3.01.128
ah, that my fear were false, ah, that it were! 3.01.193
ah, that my fear were false, ah, that it were! 3.01.193
best, | do or undo, as if ourself were here. 3.01.196
believe me, lords, were none more wise than i — 3.01.231
but, in my mind, that were no policy: 3.01.238
an empty eagle were set | to guard the chicken 3.01.248
not resolute, except so much were done, | for 3.01.267
by staying there so long till all were lost. 3.01.299
were almost like a sharp-quill'd porpentine; 3.01.363
o that it were to do! 3.02. 3
for it is known we were but hollow friends? 3.02. 66
some violent hands were laid on humphrey's life! 3.02.138
what were it but to make my sorrow greater? 3.02.148
i do believe that violent hands were laid | upon 3.02.156
the least of all these signs were probable. 3.02.178
but both of you were vowed duke humphrey's foes, 3.02.182
were there a serpent seen, with forked tongue, 3.02.259
majesty, | it were but necessary you were wak'd, 3.02.261
majesty, | it were but necessary you were wak'd, 3.02.261
but you, my lord, were glad to be employ'd, | to 3.02.273
as if duke humphrey's ghost | were by his side; 3.02.374
what were it else | but like a pleasant slumber 3.02.389
to die by thee were but to die in jest, | from 3.02.400
from thee to die were torture more than death. 3.02.401
by thee anjou and maine were sold to france. 4.01. 86
whose dreadful swords were never drawn in vain, 4.01. 92
o that i were a god, to shoot forth thunder 4.01.104
relent, | that were unworthy to behold the same? 4.04. 18
ah, were the duke of suffolk now alive, | these 4.04. 41
them about matters they were not able to answer. 4.07. 42 P
for they lov'd well when they were alive. 4.07.131 P
he were created knight for his good service. 5.01. 77
you were best to go to bed and dream again, | to 5.01.196
were by the swords of common soldiers slain. 3H6 1.01. 9
than drops of blood were in my father's veins. 1.01. 97
and thine | were not revenge sufficient for me; 1.03. 26
and were i strong, i would not shun their fury. 1.04. 24
what valor were it, when a cur doth grin, | for 1.04. 56
were shame enough to shame thee, wert thou not 1.04.120
stab poniards in our flesh till all were told, 2.01. 98
were brought me of your loss and his depart. 2.01.110
for in the marches here we heard you were, 2.01.140
were he as famous and as bold in war | as he is 2.01.155
then, clifford, were thy heart as hard as steel, 2.01.201
were it not pity that this goodly boy | should 2.02. 34
ah, what a shame were this! 2.02. 39
a wisp of straw were worth a thousand crowns 2.02.144
were play'd in jest by counterfeiting actors? 2.03. 28
would i were dead, if god's good will were so; 2.05. 19
would i were dead, if god's good will were so; 2.05. 19
methinks it were a happy life | to be no better 2.05. 21
pass'd over to the end they were created, 2.05. 39
what a life were this! 2.05. 41
that led calm henry, though he were a king, | as 2.06. 34
old, | my father and my grandfather were kings; 3.01. 77
and you were sworn true subjects unto me; 3.01. 78
for we were subjects but while you were king. 3.01. 81
for we were subjects but while you were king. 3.01. 81
to henry, | if he were seated as king edward is. 3.01. 96
it were dishonor to deny it her. 3.02. 9
it were no less, but yet i'll make a pause. 3.02. 10
would he were wasted, marrow, bones, and all, 3.02.125
wishing his foot were equal with his eye, | and 3.02.137
tut, were it farther off, i'll pluck it down. 3.02.195
but were he dead, | yet here prince edward 3.03. 72
for i were loath | to link with him that were 3.03.114
to link with him that were not lawful chosen. 3.03.115
nay, mark how lewis stamps as he were nettled. 3.03.169
at my depart, these were his very words: 4.01. 92
these were her words, utt'red with mild disdain: 4.01. 98
were but a feigned friend to our proceedings. 4.02. 11
my lords, we were forewarned of your coming, 4.07. 17
the good old man would fain that all were well, 4.07. 31
to keep that oath were more impiety | than 5.01. 90
blood, | were lik'ned oft to kingly sepulchres; 5.02. 20
ah, what a shame, ah, what a fault were this! 5.04. 12
did not offend, nor were not worthy blame, | if 5.05. 54
blame, | if this foul deed were by to equal it. 5.05. 55
"good gloucester" and "good devil" were alike, 5.06. 4
blast his harvest, /and your head were laid, 5.07. 21
one) | were best to do it secretly alone. R3 1.01.100
were it to call king edward's widow sister, | i 1.01.109
thanks | that were the cause of my imprisonment. 1.01.128
too, | for they that were your enemies are his, 1.01.130

then say they were not slain. 1.02. 89
i would i were, to be reveng'd on thee. 1.02.133
would it were mortal poison for thy sake! 1.02.145
would they were basilisks, to strike thee dead! 1.02.150
i would they were, that i might die at once; 1.02.151
if he were dead, what would betide on me? 1.03. 6
would all were well! 1.03. 40
scarce some two days since were worth a noble. 1.03. 81
you may deny that you were not the mean | of my 1.03. 89
ere you were queen, ay, or your husband king, 1.03.120
grey | were factious for the house of lancaster; 1.03.127
and, rivers, so were you. 1.03.128
i would to god my heart were flint, like 1.03.139
should enjoy, were you this country's king — 1.03.151
were you snarling all before i came, | ready to 1.03.187
rivers and dorset, you were standers–by, | and 1.03.209
were you well serv'd, you would be taught your 1.03.249
where eyes did once inhabit, there were crept 1.04. 30
which of you, if you were a prince's son, 1.04.257
me, | as you would beg, were you in my distress. 1.04.266
if ever any grudge were lodg'd between us; 2.01. 66
i would to god all strifes were well compounded. 2.01. 75
if that our noble father were alive? 2.02. 7
it were lost sorrow to wail one that's lost. 2.02. 11
were never orphans had so dear a loss. 2.02. 78
better it were they all came by his father, | or 2.03. 23
or by his father there were none at all; 2.03. 24
and were they to be rul'd, and not to rule, 2.03. 29
marry, we were sent for to the justices. 2.03. 46
and so leisurely | that, if his rule were true, 2.04. 20
the nobles were committed | is all unknown to me 2.04. 47
and often up and down my sons were toss'd | for 2.04. 58
those uncles which you want were dangerous; 3.01. 12
but they were none. 3.01. 16
but say, my lord, it were not regist'red, 3.01. 75
ay, gentle cousin, were it light enough. 3.01.117
i weigh it lightly, were it heavier. 3.01.121
and, as it were far off, sound thou lord 3.01.170
pursues | were to incense the boar to follow us, 3.02. 29
were jocund, and suppos'd their states were sure 3.02. 84
jocund, and suppos'd their states were sure, 3.02. 84
as else i would be, were the day prolong'd. 3.04. 45
for, were he, he had shown it in his looks. 3.04. 57
to–day at pomfret bloodily were butcher'd, | and 3.04. 90
as if thou were distraught and mad with terror? 3.05. 4
fee for which i plead | were for myself — and 3.05. 97
the people were not used | to be spoke to but by 3.07. 29
what tongueless blocks were they! 3.07. 42
happy were england, would this virtuous prince 3.07. 78
first, if all obstacles were cut away, | and 3.07.156
away, | and that my path were even to the crown, 3.07.157
and much i need to help you, were there need: 3.07.166
that must round my brow | were red–hot steel, to 4.01. 60
gold were as good as twenty orators, | and will, 4.02. 38
albeit they were flesh'd villains, bloody dogs, 4.03. 6
their lips were four red roses on a stalk, 4.03. 12
think that thy babes were sweeter than they were 4.04.120
that thy babes were sweeter than they were, 4.04.120
should be branded, if that right were right, 4.04.141
lo at their birth good stars were opposite. 4.04.216
no, to their lives ill friends were contrary. 4.04.217
my babes were destin'd to a fairer death, | if 4.04.220
till that my nails were anchor'd in thine eyes; 4.04.232
than ever you /or yours by me were harm'd! 4.04.239
your children were vexation to your youth, | but 4.04.305
what were i best to say? 4.04.337
on the banks | if they were his assistants, yea 4.04.524
those that were the means to help him; 5.03.249
i would these dewy tears were from the ground. 5.03.284
of our noble story | as they were living. H8 pr 27
their dwarfish pages were | as cherubins, all 1.01. 22
equal in lustre, were now best, now worst, | as 1.01. 29
and they were ratified | as he cried, "thus let 1.01.170
his fears were that the interview betwixt 1.01.180
and could wish he were | something mistaken in't 1.01.194
ten times more ugly | than ever they were fair. 1.02.118
habits put the graces | that once were his, and 1.02.123
you were the duke's surveyor, and lost your 1.02.172
whose tenor | was, were he evil us'd, he would 1.02.207
sir thomas, | whither were you a–going? 1.03. 50
o that your lordship were but now confessor | to 1.04. 15
i would i were, | they should find easy penance. 1.04. 16
i were unmannerly to take you out | and not to 1.04. 95
were you there? 2.01. 5
any malice in your heart | were hid against me, 2.01. 81
curses on their heads | that were the authors. 2.01.139
they were young and handsome, and of the best 2.02. 3 P
when they were ready to set out for london, a 2.02. 4 P
our mistress' sorrows we were pitying. 2.03. 53
say, | are you not stronger than you were? 2.03.100
to love, although i knew | he were mine enemy? 2.04. 31
whether our daughter were legitimate, 2.04.180
her male issue | or died where they were made, 2.04.193
if my actions | were tried by ev'ry tongue, 3.01. 35
think | his contemplation were above the earth, 3.02.131
the which | you were now running o'er. 3.02.139
all were woven | so strangely in one piece. 4.01. 80
were those that went on each side of the queen? 4.01.100
his promises were, as he then was, mighty; 4.02. 41
yes, good griffith, | i were malicious else. 4.02. 48
and though he were unsatisfied in getting 4.02. 55
would you were half so honest! 5.02.117
would i were fairly out on't! 5.02.144
you were ever good at sudden commendations, 5.02.157
her succor, which were the hope o' th' strond, 5.03. 52 P
that were the servants to this chosen infant, 5.04. 48
and her hair were not somewhat darker than TRO 1.01. 41 P
there were no more comparison between the women! 1.01. 42 P
and she were /not kin to me, she would be as 1.01. 75 P
i care not and she were a blackamoor, 'tis all 1.01. 77 P
better at home, if "would i might" were "may." 1.01.114
who were those went by? 1.02. 1
and, like as there were husbandry in war, 1.02. 7
when were you at ilium? 1.02. 45 P
what were you talking of when i came? 1.02. 47 P
that were we talking of, and of his anger. 1.02. 52 P
himself? alas, poor troilus, i would he were! 1.02. 72 P
would 'a were himself! 1.02. 77 P
well, i would my heart were in her body. 1.02. 79 P
had i a sister were a grace, or a daughter a 1.02.236 P
which were such | as agamemnon and the hand of 1.03. 62
were his brain as barren | as banks of libya 1.03.327
were he not proud, we all should share with him. 1.03.367
and it were better parch in afric sun | than in 1.03.369
if he were foil'd, | why then we do our main 1.03.371
were not that a botchy core? 2.01. 6 P
'a were as good crack a fusty nut with no kernel 2.01.101 P
were i alone to pass the difficulties, | and had 2.02.139
what treason were it to the ransack'd queen, 2.02.150
none so noble | whose life were ill bestow'd, or 2.02.159
were it not glory that we more affected | than 2.02.195
would it were otherwise: 2.03. 4 P
that were to enlard his fat–already pride, | and 2.03.195
and all men were of my mind — 2.03.215 P
would he were a troyan! 2.03.234
what a vice were it in ajax now — 2.03.235
if he were proud — 2.03.236
nestor, were your days | as green as ajax', and 2.03.253
so short, as if she were fray'd with a spirit. 3.02. 32 P
my thoughts were like unbridled children grown 3.02.122
how were i then uplifted! 3.02.168
as if he were forgot, and, princes all, | lay 3.03. 40
they were us'd to bend, | to send their smiles 3.03. 71
as if his foot were on brave hector's breast 3.03.140
as who should say there were wit in this head, 3.03.255 P
the fountain of your mind were clear again, that 3.03.310 P
troilus had rather troy were borne to greece 4.01. 47
would he were knock'd i' th' head! 4.02. 34
would i were as deep under the earth as i am 4.02. 82 P
'twere better she were kiss'd in general. 4.05. 21
it were no match, your nail against his horn. 4.05. 46
were thy commixtion greek and troyan so | that 4.05.124
to an ass, were nothing, he is both ass and ox; 5.01. 59 P
to an ox, were nothing, /he /is both ox and ass. 5.01. 60 P
me /not what i would be if i were not thersites, 5.01. 64 P
be the louse of a lazar, so i were not menelaus. 5.01. 66 P
nothing at all, unless that this were she. 5.02.135
were it a casque compos'd by vulcan's skill, 5.02.170
ache in my bones that, unless a man were curs'd, 5.03.105 P
were i the general, thou shouldst have my office 5.06. 4
us but the superfluity while it were wholesome, COR 1.01. 18 P
would all the rest were so! 1.01. 54 P
they said they were an–hungry; 1.01.205
and were i any thing but what i am, | i would 1.01.231
were half to half the world by th' ears, and he 1.01.233
when we were chosen tribunes for the people — 1.01.254
ere (almost) rome | should know we were afoot. 1.02. 25
if my son were my husband, i should freelier 1.03. 2 P
"come on, you cowards, you were got in fear, 1.03. 33
got in fear, | though you were born in rome!" 1.03. 34
come, i would your cambric were sensible as your 1.03. 85 P
as big as thou art, | were not so rich a jewel. 1.04. 56
as if the world | were feverous and did tremble. 1.04. 61
yonder, | that does appear as he were flea'd? 1.06. 22
could wish | you were conducted to a gentle bath 1.06. 63
if any such be here | (as it were sin to doubt) 1.06. 68
were he the butcher of my son, he should | be 1.09. 88
i would i were a roman, for i cannot, | being a 1.10. 4
where i find him, were it | at home, upon my 1.10. 24
some of the best of 'em were hereditary hangmen. 2.01. 93 P
and the moon, were she earthly, no nobler — 2.01. 98 P
him | were slily crept into his human powers, 2.01.220
were he to stand for consul, never would he 2.01.232
not confess so much were a kind of ingrateful 2.02. 31 P
to report otherwise were a malice that, giving 2.02. 32 P
sun | when the alarum were struck than idly sit 2.02. 76
and look'd upon things precious as they were 2.02.125
to be ingrateful were to make a monster of the 2.03. 10 P
i think if all our wits were to issue out of one 2.03. 21 P
but if it were at liberty, 'twould sure 2.03. 29 P
why either were you ignorant to see't, | or, 2.03.174
you not have told him | as you were lesson'd: 2.03.177
as you were fore–advis'd, had touch'd his spirit 2.03.191
of the same house publius and quintus were, 2.03.241
this mutiny were better put in hazard | than 2.03.256
you speak a' th' people | as if you were a god, 3.01. 81
were i as patient as the midnight sleep, | by 3.01. 85
what must be, was law, | then were they chosen; 3.01.168
we were establish'd | the people's magistrates. 3.01.200
in whose power | we were elected theirs, martius 3.01.210
i would they were barbarians, as they are, 3.01.237
i would they were a–bed! 3.01.260
i would they were in tiber! 3.01.261
to eject him hence | were but one danger, and to 3.01.286
country | were to us all that do't and suffer it 3.01.301
if it were so — 3.01.314
you had not show'd them how ye were dispos'd 3.02. 22
were fit for thee to use as they to claim, | in 3.02. 83
as she speaks, why, their hearts were yours; 3.02. 87
yet, were there but this single plot to lose, 3.02.102
you were us'd | to say extremities was the trier 4.01. 3
you were us'd to load me | with precepts that 4.01. 9
resume that spirit when you were wont to say, 4.01. 16
i would my son | were in arabia, and thy tribe 4.02. 24
he had so, looking as it were — would i were 4.05.157 P
would i were hang'd but i thought there was more 4.05.158 P
here within as if he were son and heir to mars; 4.05.192 P
which friends, sir, as it were, durst not (look 4.05.207 P
'tis, as it were, a parcel of their feast, and 4.05.216 P
the people, which before | were in wild hurry. 4.06. 4
and so would do, | were he more angry at it. 4.06. 15
which were inshell'd when martius stood for rome 4.06. 45
if he were putting to my house the brand | that 4.06.115
obeys his points | as if he were his officer. 4.06.126
i ever said we were i' th' wrong when we 4.06.154 P
no, though it were as virtuous to lie as to live 5.02. 26 P
if thy captain knew i were here, he would use me 5.02. 51 P
but stand | as if a man were author of himself, 5.03. 36
if it were so that our request did tend | to 5.03.132
were you in my stead, would you have heard | a 5.03.192
i dare be sworn you were; 5.03.194
son, | were gracious in the eyes of royal rome, TIT 1.01. 11
and if thy sons were ever dear to thee, | o, 1.01.107
for king and commonweal | were piety in thine, 1.01.115
(when goths were goths and tamora was queen), 1.01.140
andronicus, would thou were shipp'd to hell, 1.01.206
hue | that i would choose were i to choose anew. 1.01.262
were gracious in those princely eyes of thine, 1.01.429
the cause were known to them it most concerns, 2.01. 50
ay, so the turn were served. 2.01. 96
nor me, so i were one. 2.01.102
horns, | as if a double hunt were heard at once, 2.03. 19
when with a happy storm they were surpris'd, 2.03. 23
and if she do, i would i were an eunuch. 2.03.128
were it not for shame, | well could i leave our 2.03.196
how these were they that made away his brother. 2.03.208
by my soul, were there worse end than death, 2.03.302
me, | and, were they but attired in grave weeds, 3.01. 43
if there were reason for these miseries, | then 3.01.219
i think she means that there were more than one 4.01. 38
i say, my lord, that if i were a man, | their 4.01.107
but were our witty empress well afoot, | she 4.02. 29
and from your womb where you imprisoned were 4.02.124
you were as good to shoot against the wind. 4.03. 58
as who would say, in rome no justice were. 4.04. 20
they have wish'd that lucius were their emperor. 4.04. 77
that, were his heart | almost impregnable, his 4.04. 97
that both mine eyes were rainy like to his; 5.01.117
if there be devils, would i were a devil, | to 5.01.147
it were convenient you had such a devil. 5.02. 90
two of her brothers were condemn'd to death, 5.02.173
and if your highness knew my heart, you were. 5.03. 34
were they that murd'red our emperor's brother, 5.03. 98
and they it were that ravished our sister. 5.03. 99
their fell faults our brothers were beheaded, 5.03.100
o, were the sum of these that i should pay 5.03.158
when they were living, warm'd themselves on 5.03.168
ev'n with all my heart | would i were dead, so 5.03.173
speak, nephew, were you by when it began? ROM 1.01.105
here were the servants of your adversary, | and 1.01.106
while we were interchanging thrusts and blows, 1.01.113
were of an age. 1.03. 19
my lord and you were then at mantua — | nay, i 1.03. 28
were not i thine only nurse, | i would say thou 1.03. 67
now since last yourself and i | were in a mask? 1.05. 33
that were some spite. 2.01. 27
and wish his mistress were that kind of fruit 2.01. 35
o, romeo, that she were, o that she were | an 2.01. 37
that she were, o that she were | an open/–arse, 2.01. 37
o that she knew she were! 2.02. 11
what if her eyes were there, they in her head? 2.02. 18
birds would sing and think it were not night. 2.02. 22
o that i were a glove upon that hand, | that i 2.02. 24
so romeo would, were he not romeo call'd, 2.02. 45
my life were better ended by their hate, | than 2.02. 77
and yet i would it were to give again. 2.02.129
i would i were thy bird. 2.02.182
would i were sleep and peace, so sweet to rest! 2.02.187
thou and these woes were all for rosaline. 2.03. 78
take him down, and 'a were lustier than he is, 2.04.151 P
they say, it were a very gross kind of behavior, 2.04.166 P
truly it were an ill thing to be off'red to any 2.04.169 P
but old folks — many feign as they were dead, 2.05. 16
nay, and there were two such, we should have 3.01. 15 P
and i were so apt to quarrel as thou art, any 3.01. 31 P
men's eyes were made to look, and let them gaze; 3.01. 54
it were a grief, so brief to part with thee. 3.03.174
well, we were born to die. 3.04. 4
my lord, i would that thursday were to–morrow. 3.04. 29
i would the fool were married to her grave! 3.05.140
or 'twere as good he were | as living here and 3.05.224
meagre were his looks, | sharp misery had worn 5.01. 40
and old cakes of roses | were thinly scattered, 5.01. 48
suspecting that we both were in a house | where 5.02. 9
it thee, | so fearful were they of infection. 5.02. 16
a most incomparable man, breath'd, as it were, TIM 1.01. 10
all those which were his fellows but of late — 1.01. 78
heavens, that i were a lord! 1.01.227 P
if i were a huge man, i should fear to drink at 1.02. 49 P
so they were bleeding new, my lord, there's no 1.02. 78 P
all those flatterers were thine enemies then, 1.02. 81 P
they were the most needless creatures living, 1.02. 97 P
would i were gently put out of office | before i 1.02.201
put out of office | before i were forc'd out! 1.02.202
would we were all discharg'd! 2.02. 12
were it all yours to give it in a breath, | how 2.02.153
give it in a breath, | how quickly were it gone! 2.02.154
may catch a wrench — would all were well — 2.02.209
if his occasion were not virtuous, | i should 3.02. 40
that were ne'er acquainted with their wards 3.03. 37
ay, | if money were as certain as your waiting, 3.04. 47
world | when sects and factions were newly born. 3.05. 30
were a sufficient briber for his life. 3.05. 61
if there were no foes, that were enough | to 3.05. 69
no foes, that were enough | to overcome him. 3.05. 69
upon that were my thoughts tiring when we 3.06. 4 P
for, were your godheads to borrow of men, men 3.06. 74 P
there were no suns to borrow of. 4.03. 70
burthens of the dead — some that were hang'd, 4.03.146
were i like thee, i'd throw away myself. 4.03.219
were all the wealth i have shut up in thee, 4.03.279
that the whole life of athens were in this! 4.03.281
if not, i would it were. 4.03.286
would poison were obedient and knew my mind! 4.03.296 P
spots of thy kindred were jurors on thy life; 4.03.341 P
all thy safety were remotion and thy defense 4.03.342 P
thou be, that were not subject to a beast? 4.03.343 P
all | i kept were knaves, to serve in meat to 4.03.478
hearing you were retir'd, your friends fall'n 5.01. 59
shall to thee blot out what wrongs were theirs, 5.01.153
whom, though in general part we were oppos'd, 5.02. 7
when thy first griefs were but a mere conceit, 5.04. 14
we were not all unkind, nor all deserve | the 5.04. 21
ours | were not erected by their hands from whom 5.04. 23
who were the motives that you first went out; 5.04. 27
for those that were, it is not square to take 5.04. 36
were i a common laughter, or did use | to stale JC 1.02. 72
i was born free as caesar, so were you; 1.02. 97
would he were fatter! 1.02.198
yet if my name were liable to fear, | i do not 1.02.199
why, you were with him, were you not? 1.02.219 P
why, you were with him, were you not? 1.02.219 P
if i were brutus now and he were cassius, | he 1.02.314
if i were brutus now and he were cassius, | he 1.02.314

and there were drawn | upon a heap a hundred 1.03. 22
he were no lion, were not romans hinds. 1.03.106
he were no lion, were not romans hinds. 1.03.106
i would it were my fault to sleep so soundly. 2.01. 4
not erebus itself were dim enough | to hide thee 2.01. 84
and that were much he should, for he is given 2.01.188
brutus is wise, and, were he not in health, | he 2.01.258
i should not need, if you were gentle brutus. 2.01.279
am i yourself | but, as it were, in sort or 2.01.283
if this were true, then should i know this 2.01.291
would you were not sick! 2.01.315
besides, it were a mock | apt to be render'd, 2.02. 96
i could be well mov'd, if i were as you; 3.01. 58
stare, cry out, and run, | as it were doomsday. 3.01. 98
or else were this a savage spectacle. 3.01.223
are so full of good regard | that were you, 3.01.225
had you rather caesar were living, and die all 3.02. 23 P
and die all slaves, than that caesar were dead, 3.02. 24 P
if it were so, it was a grievous fault, | and 3.02. 79
if i were dispos'd to stir | your hearts and 3.02.121
they were traitors; honorable men! 3.02.153
they were villains, murderers. 3.02.155 P
but were i brutus, | and brutus antony, there 3.02.226
there were an antony | would ruffle up your 3.02.227
ay, and truly, you were best. 3.03. 12 P
by the gods, this speech were else your last. 4.03. 14
downward look on us | as we were sickly prey. 5.01. 86
i must report they were | as cannons overcharg'd MAC 1.02. 36
were such things here as we do speak about? 1.03. 83
were poor and single business to contend 1.06. 16
if it were done, when 'tis done, then 'twere 1.07. 1
done, then 'twere well | it were done quickly. 1.07. 2
when you durst do it, then you were a man; 1.07. 49
to be more than what you were, you would | be so 1.07. 50
if a man were porter of hell gate, he should 2.03. 1 P
sir, we were carousing till the second cock; 2.03. 24 P
our chimneys were blown down, and, as they say, 2.03. 55
their hands and faces were all badg'd with blood 2.03.102
so were their daggers, which unwip'd we found 2.03.103
they star'd and were distracted; 2.03.104
they were suborned. 2.04. 24
how you were borne in hand, how cross'd, the 3.01. 80
in his life, | which in his death were perfect. 3.01.107
to feed were best at home; 3.04. 34
is ceremony, | meeting were bare without it. 3.04. 36
were the grac'd person of our banquo present, 3.04. 40
that when the brains were out, the man would die 3.04. 78
would he were here! 3.04. 90
no more, | returning were as tedious as go o'er. 3.04.137
that were the slaves of drink and thralls of 3.06. 13
or else climb upward | to what they were before. 4.02. 25
if he were dead, you'ld weep for him; 4.02. 61 P
it were a good sign that i should quickly have a 4.02. 62 P
to do worse to you were fell cruelty, | which is 4.02. 71
such | a stanchless avarice that, were i king, 4.03. 78
they were well at peace when i did leave 'em. 4.03.179
a rumor | of many worthy fellows that were out, 4.03.183
were on the quarry of these murther'd deer | to 4.03.206
i cannot but remember such things were, | that 4.03.222
things were, | that were most precious to me. 4.03.223
sinful macduff, | they were all strook for thee! 4.03.225
were i from dunsinane away and clear, | profit 5.03. 61
were they not forc'd with those that should be 5.05. 5
treatise rouse and stir | as life were in't. 5.05. 13
wish th' estate o' th' world were now undone. 5.05. 49
i would the friends we miss were safe arriv'd. 5.09. 1
or ere those shoes were old | with which she HAM 1.02.147
would the night were come! 1.02.255
upon a wretch whose natural gifts were poor | to 1.05. 51
were nothing but to waste night, day, and time; 2.02. 89
though it were hid indeed | within the centre. 2.02.158
then i would you were so honest a man. 2.02.176 P
were you not sent for? 2.02.274 P
you were sent for, and there is a kind of 2.02.278 P
direct with me, whether you were sent for or no! 2.02.288 P
my lord, we were sent for. 2.02.292 P
even those you were wont to take such delight in 2.02.327 P
one said there were no sallets in the lines to 2.02.441 P
after your death you were better have a bad 2.02.525 P
of such things that it were better my mother had 3.01.122 P
we shall obey, were she ten times our mother. 3.02.333 P
were thicker than itself with brother's blood, 3.03. 44
and would it were not so, you are my mother. 3.04. 16
'twere good she were spoken with, for she may 4.05. 14
lord, | and, as the world were now but to begin, 4.05.104
ere we were two days old at sea, a pirate of 4.06. 15 P
all things else | you mainly were stirr'd up. 4.07. 9
they were given me by claudio. 4.07. 40
that were wont to set the table on a roar? 5.01.190 P
sweet lord, if your lordship were at leisure, i 5.02. 89 P
but to know a man well were to know himself. 5.02.140 P
what paper were you reading? LR 1.02. 30 P
if the matter were good, my lord, i durst swear 1.02. 63 P
were good, my lord, i durst swear it were his; 1.02. 64 P
respect of that, i would fain think it were not. 1.02. 65 P
and stars, as if we were villains on necessity, 1.02.121 P
that ceremonious affection as you were wont. 1.04. 59 P
sirrah, you were best take my coxcomb. 1.04. 97 P
when were you wont to be so full of songs, 1.04.170 P
which else were shame, that then necessity 1.04.213
out went the candle, and we were left darkling. 1.04.217 P
if a man's brains were in 's heels, were't not 1.05. 8 P
death | were very pregnant and potential spirits 2.01. 76
no marvel then, though he were ill affected: 2.01. 98
smile you my speeches, as i were a fool? 2.02. 82
why, madam, if i were your father's dog, | you 2.02.136
if only to go warm were gorgeous, | why, nature 2.04.268
fire in a wild field were like an old lecher's 3.04.111 P
that this treason were not — or not i the 3.05. 13 P
i told him you were coming; 4.02. 5
below, methought his eyes | were two full moons; 4.06. 70
hairs in my beard ere the black ones were there. 4.06. 98 P
were all thy letters suns, i could not see. 4.06.140
it were a delicate stratagem, to shoe | a troop 4.06.184
better i were distract, | so should my thoughts 4.06.281
would i were assur'd | of my condition! 4.07. 55
mystery of things | as if we were god's spies; 5.03. 17
who were the opposites of this day's strife; 5.03. 42
that were the most, if he should husband you. 5.03. 70
had my purse | as if the strings were thine, OTH 1.01. 3
were i the moor, i would not be iago. 1.01. 57
you were best go in. 1.02. 30
if she in chains of magic were not bound, 1.02. 65
were it my cue to fight, i should have known it 1.02. 83
for they were parted | with foul and violent 2.01. 33
she was a wight (if ever such /wight were) — 2.01.158
would they were clyster–pipes for your sake! 2.01.177 P
if it were now to die, | 'twere now to be most 2.01.189
the which there were no expectation of our 2.01.280 P
it were well | the general were put in mind of 2.03.131
were well | the general were put in mind of it. 2.03.132
it were an honest action to say | so to the moor 2.03.141
worthy montano, you were wont to be civil; 2.03.190
even as again they were | when you yourself did 2.03.238
grieves my husband | as if the cause were his. 3.03. 4
my lord and you again | as friendly as you were. 3.03. 7
as if there were some monster in thy thought 3.03.107
it were not for your quiet nor your good, | nor 3.03.152
you cannot, if my heart were in your hand, | nor 3.03.163
that her jesses were my dear heart–strings, 3.03.261
would i were satisfied! 3.03.390
it were a tedious difficulty, i think, | to 3.03.397
were they as prime as goats, as hot as monkeys, 3.03.403
he lies there, were to lie in mine own throat. 3.04. 13 P
it were enough | to put him to ill thinking. 3.04. 28
to lose't or give't away were such perdition 3.04. 67
the worms were hallowed that did breed the silk, 3.04. 73
it is not lost; but what and if it were? 3.04. 83
know him | were he in favor as in humor alter'd. 3.04.125
whilst you were here o'erwhelmed with your grief 4.01. 76
as it were; 4.01.137 P
he might he is not, | i would to heaven he were! 4.01.272
will speak, | though tongues were out of use. 5.01.110
o, i were damn'd beneath all depth in hell | but 5.02.137
peace, you were best. 5.02.161
if you were but an inch of fortune better than i ANT 1.02. 59 P
it were pity to cast them away for nothing, 1.02.138 P
if there were no more women but fulvia, then had 1.02.165 P
shouldst know | there were a heart in egypt. 1.03. 41
that he which is was wish'd, until he were; 1.04. 42
jupiter, | were i the wearer of antonio's beard, 2.02. 7
were we before our armies, and to fight, | i 2.02. 26
was theme for you — you were the word of war. 2.02. 44
quite | were to remember that the present need 2.02.101
your /reproof | were well deserv'd of rashness. 2.02.122
that | the winds were love–sick with them; 2.02.194
the oars were silver, | which to the tune of 2.02.194
so half my egypt were submerg'd and made | a 2.05. 94
when caesar and your brother were at blows, 2.06. 44
if i were bound to divine of this unity, i would 2.06.116 P
would it were all, | that it might go on wheels! 2.07. 92
he were the worse for that, were he a horse; 3.02. 52
he were the worse for that, were he a horse; 3.02. 52
that were excusable, that, and thousands more 3.04. 2
better i were not yours | than /yours so 3.04. 23
in chairs of gold | were publicly enthron'd. 3.06. 5
till we perceiv'd both how you were wrong led 3.06. 80
mares together, | the horse were merely lost; 3.07. 8
you did know | how much you were my conqueror, 3.11. 66
you were half blasted ere i knew you; 3.13.105
nay, you were a fragment | of cneius pompey's — 3.13.117
o, that i were | upon the hill of basan, to 3.13.126
and to proclaim it civilly were like | a 3.13.129
when my good stars, that were my former guides, 3.13.145
for when mine hours | were nice and lucky, men 3.13.179
rebukable | and worthy shameful check it were, 4.04. 31
it, were it carbuncled | like holy phoebus' car. 4.08. 28
wishers were ever fools — o, come, come, come, 4.15. 37
it were for me | to throw my sceptre at the 4.15. 75
his delights | were dolphin–like, they show'd 5.02. 89
realms and islands were | as plates dropp'd from 5.02. 91
but if there be, nor ever were one such, | it's 5.02. 96
an antony were nature's piece 'gainst fancy, 5.02. 99
from their nursery | were stol'n, and to this CYM 1.01. 60
were you but riding forth to air yourself, 1.01.110
to air yourself, | such parting were too petty. 1.01.111
would i were | a neat–herd's daughter, and my 1.01.148
they were again together; 1.01.151
they were parted | by gentlemen at hand. 1.01.163
i would they were in afric both together, 1.01.167
if my shirt were bloody, then to shift it. 1.02. 5 P
how long a fool you were upon the ground. 1.02. 24 P
his father and i were soldiers together, to whom 1.04. 26 P
or if there were wealth enough for the /purchase 1.04. 83 P
it were fit | that all the plagues of hell 1.06.110
to know if your affiance | were deeply rooted, 1.06.164
if | you were inspir'd to do those duties which 2.03. 50
hairs above thee, | were they all made such men. 2.03.136
i would i were so sure | to win the king as i am 2.04. 1
in the britain court | when you were there? 2.04. 38
home, i grant | we were to question farther; 2.04. 52
them) were two winking cupids | of silver, each 2.04. 89
as hell can hold, | were there no more but it. 2.04.141
did extort | this tribute from us, we were free. 3.01. 48
thy mind to her is now as low as were | thy 3.02. 10
learn'd indeed were that astronomer | that knew 3.02. 27
false aeneas, | were in his time thought false; 3.04. 59
but if i were as wise as honest, then | my 3.04.118
that though his actions were not visible, yet 3.04.149
i would these garments were come. 3.05.133 P
for true to thee | were to prove false, which i 3.05.158
i were best not call; 3.06. 19
victuals, i should think | here were a fairy. 3.06. 41
were you a woman, youth, | i should woo hard, 3.06. 68
were it toad, or adder, spider, | 'twould move 4.02. 90
his voice, | and burst of speaking, were as his. 4.02.106
you were as flow'rs, now wither'd; 4.02.286
or if not, | nothing to be were better. 4.02.368
the disorder's such | as war were hoodwink'd. 5.02. 16
thought the old man and his sons were angels. 5.03. 85
he brags his service | as if he were of note. 5.03. 94
country's cause | fell bravely and were slain, 5.04. 72
they went hence so soon as they were born. 5.04.126
but a man that were to sleep your sleep, and a 5.04.173 P
so should i, if i were one. 5.04.203 P
i would we were all of one mind, and one mind 5.04.203 P
there were desolation of jailers and gallowses! 5.04.204 P
further to boast were neither true nor modest, 5.05. 18
wet cheeks | were present when she finish'd. 5.05. 36
the evils she hatch'd were not effected; 5.05. 60
mine eyes | were not in fault, for she was 5.05. 63
he was too good to be | where ill men were, and 5.05.159
our brags | were crak'd of kitchen trulls, or 5.05.177
dian had hot dreams, | and she alone were cold; 5.05.181
the wrongs he did me | were nothing prince–like; 5.05.293
arms alone, | they were not born for bondage. 5.05.306
i you brothers, | when we were so indeed. 5.05.378
were clipt about | with this most tender air. 5.05.451
which | we were dissuaded by our wicked queen, 5.05.463
a war did cease | (ere bloody hands were wash'd) 5.05.485
as from thence | sorrow were ever ras'd, and PER 1.01. 17
were not this glorious casket stor'd with ill. 1.01. 77
then were it certain you were not so bad | as 1.01.125
then were it certain you were not so bad | as 1.01.125
how many worthy princes' bloods were shed | to 1.02. 88
why (as it were unlicens'd of your loves) | he 1.03. 16
that were to blow at fire in hope to quench it, 1.04. 4
their tables were stor'd full, to glad the sight 1.04. 28
air | were all too little to content and please, 1.04. 35
of the poor men that were cast away before us 2.01. 19 P
if the good king simonides were of my mind — 2.01. 43 P
for if all your beggars were whipt, i would wish 2.01. 92 P
were my fortunes equal to my desires, i could 2.01.111 P
to say you're welcome were superfluous. 2.03. 2
were more than you expect, or more than's fit, 2.03. 5
for though | this king were great, his greatness 2.04. 14
i do | protest my ears were never better fed 2.05. 27
virtue and cunning were endowments greater 3.02. 27
they were too rough | that threw her in the sea. 3.02. 79
we were never so much out of creatures. 4.02. 6 P
thousand chequins were as pretty a proportion to 4.02. 26 P
such a maidenhead were no cheap thing, if men 4.02. 60 P
no cheap thing, if men were as they have been. 4.02. 61 P
were i chief lord of all this spacious world, 4.03. 5
shall see a rose, and she were a rose indeed, if 4.06. 35 P
were you a gamester at five, or at seven? 4.06. 74 P
if you were born to honor, show it now; 4.06. 92
our profession as it were to stink afore the 4.06.135 P
and if she were a thornier piece of ground than 4.06.144 P
were i well assur'd | came of a gentle kind and 5.01. 67
might equal yours, if both were justly weigh'd. 5.01. 88
where were you bred? 5.01.115
what were thy friends? 5.01.125
griefs might equal mine, | if both were opened. 5.01.132
what were thy friends? 5.01.139
where were you born? 5.01.154
well, where were you bred? 5.01.163
where were you bred? 5.01.169
were it to woo my daughter, for it seems | you 5.01.262
now do i long to hear how you were found, | how 5.03. 56
for, to say truth, it were an endless thing, TNK pr 22
you were that time fair; 1.01. 62
if that you were | the ground–piece of some 1.01.121
it to some pity, | though it were made of stone. 1.01.129
sun, | and were good kings when living. 1.01.147
i' th' aid o' th' current were almost to sink, 1.02. 8
jump | as they are, here were to be strangers, 1.02. 41
yet to be neutral to him were dishonor; 1.02.100
were he | a quarter carrier of that honor which 1.02.107
be as for our health, which were not spent, 1.02.110
you were at wars when she the grave enrich'd, 1.03. 51
she (i sigh and spoke of) were things innocent, 1.03. 60
if i were ripe for your persuasion, you | have 1.03. 91
for they were a mark | worth a god's view. 1.04. 20
been taken | when their last hurts were given, 1.04. 26
i would i were really that i am deliver'd to be. 2.01. 7 P
"remember what your fathers were, and conquer!" 2.02. 36
that our fortunes | were twin'd together. 2.02. 64
were we at liberty, | a wife might part us 2.02. 88
chances, | were we from hence, would sever us. 2.02. 95
were there not maids enough? 2.02.121
or were they all hard–hearted? 2.02.122
me | that i was palamon, and you were arcite. 2.02.186
as her bright eyes shine on ye, would i were, 2.02.234
were i at liberty, i would do things | of such a 2.02.256
such a vengeance | that, were i old and wicked, 2.03. 6
where were you bred you know it not? 2.03. 63
that were too cruel. 2.05. 41
that were a shame, sir, | while i have horses. 2.05. 53
you have a servant | that, if i were a woman, 2.05. 63
signs | of prisonment were off me and this hand 3.01. 32
you were call'd | a good knight and a bold. 3.01. 64
compell'd bears, would fly | were they not tied. 3.01. 69
no matter, would it were perpetual night, | and 3.02. 3
it was a hawk, | and her bells were cut away." 3.05. 71
would you were so in all, sir! 3.06. 20
we were not bred to talk, man. 3.06. 28
that were a cruel wisdom! 3.06.242
if one of them were dead, as one must, are you 3.06.273
childishly, | so sillily, as if she were a fool, 4.01. 40
were here a mortal woman, and had in her | the 4.02. 10
i were a beast and i'ld call it good sport. 4.03. 52 P
were there aught in me which strove to show 5.01. 20
none — would not, | had i kenn'd all that were. 5.01.100
of mine eyes | were i to lose one — they are 5.01.155
i hope she's pleas'd, | her signs were gracious. 5.01.173
pardon me, | if i were there, i'ld wink. 5.03. 18
if i were by, | i might do hurt, for they would 5.03. 60
were they metamorphis'd | both into one — o, 5.03. 84
there were no woman | worth so compos'd a man! 5.03. 85
part is play'd, and, though it were too short, 5.04.102
there such fellows liv'd when you were babes, STM II.C 63
if i told you all you were in arms 'gainst god. II.C 95
were not all appropriate to your comforts, | but II.C 137
wishing her cheeks were gardens full of flowers, VEN 65
so they were dew'd with such distilling showers. 66
but when her lips were ready for his pay, | he 89
"were i hard–favor'd, foul, or wrinkled old, 133
thou pause, for then i were not for thee, | but 137
smooth moist hand, were it with thy hand felt, 143
so he were like him, and by venus' side. 180
me, | and were i not immortal, life were done, 197
me, | and were i not immortal, life were done, 197
what were thy lips the worse for one poor kiss? 207

love made those hollows, if himself were slain, 243
as they were mad, unto the wood they hie them, 323
though i were dumb, yet his proceedings teach 406
or were i deaf, thy outward parts would move 435
move | each part in me that were but sensible: 436
"say that the sense of feeling were bereft me, 439
and nothing but the very smell were left me, 441
for on the grass she lies as she were slain, 473
were never four such lamps together mix'd, | had 489
were beauty under twenty locks kept fast, | yet 575
as if another chase were in the skies. 696
stealing moulds from heaven that were divine, 730
and then my little heart were quite undone, | in 783
more than his eyes were open'd to the light. LUC 105
or were he not my dear friend, this desire 234
as if between them twain there were no strife, 405
if ever man were mov'd with woman's moans, | be 587
"think but how vile a spectacle it were | to 631
"were tarquin night, as he is but night's child, 785
to live or die which of the twain were better, 1154
kill myself," quoth she, "alack, what were it, 1156
when both were kept for heaven and collatine? 1166
why her two suns were cloud–eclipsed so, | nor 1224
about him were a press of gaping faces, | which 1408
cheeks with chops and wrinkles were disguis'd, 1452
of rich–built ilion, that the skies were sorry, 1524
her oaths, her tears, and all were jestings. PP 7.12
and wish her lays were tuned like the lark. 14.18
were i with her, the night would post too soon, 14.25
jove would swear | juno but an ethiope were, 16.16
were kisses all the joys in bed, | one woman 18.47
if that the world and love were young, | and 19.17
fortune smil'd, | thou and i were both beguil'd. 20.28
flattering, | "pity but he were a king!" 20.40
but in them it were a wonder. PHT 32
neither, | simple were so well compounded: 44
own deep–sunken eyes | were an all–eating shame, SON 2. 8
this were to be new made when thou art old, 2.13
then were not summer's distillation left | a 5. 9
beauty's effect with beauty were bereft, | nor 5.11
ten times thyself were happier than thou art, 6. 9
if all were minded so, the times should cease, 11. 7
o that you were yourself! 13. 1
then you were | /yourself again after yourself's 13. 6
if it were fill'd with your most high deserts? 17. 2
but were some child of yours alive that time, 17.13
were it not thy sour leisure gave sweet leave 39.10
if the dull substance of my flesh were thought, 44. 1
self so self–loving were iniquity. 62.12
before these bastard signs of fair were born, 68. 3
the right of sepulchres, were shorn away, | to 68. 6
their thoughts (although their eyes were kind) 69.11
they were but sweet, but figures of delight, 98.11
were it not sinful then, striving to mend, | to 103. 9
for as you were when first your eye i ey'd, 104. 2
ere you were born was beauty's summer dead. 104.14
pity me then, and wish i were renew'd, | whilst 111. 8
t' anticipate | the ills that were not, grew to 118.10
that you were once unkind befriends me now, 120. 1
unless my nerves were brass or hammered steel. 120. 4
for if you were by my unkindness shaken | as i 120. 5
thee | were to import forgetfulness in me. 122.14
if my dear love were but the child of state, 124. 1
or if it were, it bore not beauty's name; 127. 2
if i might teach thee wit, better it were, 140. 5
stood in doubt | if best were as it was, or best LC 98
"his qualities were beauteous as his form, | for 99
not his grace, but were all grac'd by him. 119
"many there were that did his picture get | to 134
saw how deceits were gilded in his smiling, 172
knew vows were ever brokers to defiling, 173
whose sights till then were levell'd on my face, 282
/WERE'T 1 FR 0.0001 REL FR 1 V 0 P
/were't /my /fitness | /to /let /these /hands LR 4.02. 63
WERE/'T 1 FR 0.0001 REL FR 1 V 0 P
win the moor, were/'t to renounce his baptism, OTH 2.03.343
WERE'T 15 FR 0.0017 REL FR 14 V 1 P
were't not affection chains thy tender days | to TGV 1.01. 3
were't not for laughing, i should pity him. 1H4 2.02.110
were't not all one, an empty eagle were set | to 2H6 3.01.248
and were't not madness then, | to make the fox 3.01.252
were't not a shame that, whilst you live at jar, 4.08. 41
were't not that by great preservation | we live R3 3.05. 36
what were't worth to know | the secret of your H8 2.03. 50
who, were't so, | would have inform'd for MAC 1.05. 32
were in 's heels, were't not in danger of kibes? LR 1.05. 8 P
were't good? OTH 5.02. 94
were't not that we stand up against them all, ANT 2.01. 44
were't twenty of the greatest tributaries | that 3.13. 96
were't he, i am sure | he would have spoke to us CYM 5.05.125
this business, were't one eye | against another, TNK 5.01. 21
were't aught to me i bore the canopy, | with my SON 125. 1
WERT 97 FR 0.0109 REL FR 62 V 35 P
what wert thou, if the king of naples heard thee TMP 1.02.432
thou wert but a lost monster. 4.01.203 P
i see what thou wert, if fortune thy foe were WIV 3.03. 65 P
the benefit of silence, would thou wert so too! MM 5.01.190 P
o that thou wert not, poor distressed soul! ERR 4.04. 59
thou wert immured, restrained, captivated, bound LLL 3.01.124 P
were so pleas'd that thou wert but my bastard, 5.01. 76 P
what wert thou | till this madman show'd thee? 5.02.337
and thou wert a lion, we would do so. 5.02.624
that, | if thou wert near a lewd interpreter! MV 3.04. 80
wert thou not my brother, i would not take this AYL 1.01. 59 P
and thou wert best look to't; 1.01.147 P
now, if thou wert a poet, i might have some hope 3.03. 26 P
no, truly, unless thou wert hard–favor'd; 3.03. 29 P
religion than if thou wert indeed my rosalind; 4.01.197 P
if, biondello, thou wert come ashore, | we could SHR 1.01. 42
then thou wert best say that i am not lucentio. 5.01.103 P
thou wert best set thy lower part where thy nose AWW 2.03.251 P
thou wert as witty a piece of eve's flesh as any TN 1.05. 27 P
ignorant by age, | or thou wert born a fool. WT 2.01.174
not move the gods | to look that way thou wert. 3.02.214
it cannot be, and if thou wert his mother. JN 2.01.131
if thou that bid'st me be content wert grim, 3.01. 43
thou wert better gall the devil, salisbury. 4.03. 95
deposing thee before thou wert possess'd, R2 2.01.107
why, cousin, wert thou regent of the world, | it 2.01.109
wert thou not brother to great edward's son, 2.01.121
for all the welshmen, hearing thou wert dead, 3.02. 73
that thou wert cause of noble gloucester's death 4.01. 37
"i would thou wert the man | that would divorce 5.04. 8
of thy stable, king, | when thou wert king; 5.05. 73
if thou love me, 'tis time thou wert away. 5.05. 96
much honor that thou wert not with me in this 1H4 2.04. 21 P
years ago, and wert taken with the manner, and 2.04.315 P
if thou wert any way given to virtue, i would 3.03. 33 P
thou art altogether given over, and wert indeed, 3.03. 36 P
why didst thou tell me that thou wert a king? 5.03. 24
if thou wert sensible of courtesy, | i should 5.04. 94
thou tak'st leave, thou wert better be hang'd. 2H4 1.02. 89 P
marry, if thou wert an honest man, thyself and 2.01. 85 P
'tis the more time thou wert us'd. 3.02.106 P
i would thou wert a man's tailor, that thou 3.02.164 P
thou wert better thou hadst strook thy mother, 5.04. 9 P
how wert thou handled, being prisoner? 1H6 1.04. 24
yet tell'st thou not how thou wert entertain'd. 1.04. 38
why didst thou say, of late thou wert despis'd? 2.05. 42
o, wert thou for myself! 5.03.187
when thou wert regent for our sovereign, | have 2H6 1.01.197
since thou wert king — as who is king but thou? 1.03.123
where wert thou born? 2.01. 80
and look thyself be faultless, thou wert best. 2.01.185
than when thou wert protector to thy king. 2.03. 27
unless thou wert more loyal than thou art. 3.01. 96
'tis not the land i care for, wert thou thence; 3.02.359
enough to shame thee, wert thou not shameless. 3H6 1.04.120
either that is thine, or else thou wert not his. 2.01. 94
wert thou environ'd with a brazen wall. 2.04. 4
ay, but thou talk'st as if thou wert a king. 3.01. 59
ah, warwick, warwick, wert thou as we are, | we 5.02. 29
wert thou not banished on pain of death? R3 1.03.166
wert thou an oracle to tell me so, | i'd not TRO 4.05.252
wert thou the devil, and wor'st it on thy horn, 5.02. 95
wert thou the hector | that was the whip of your COR 1.08. 11
titus, when wert thou wont to walk alone, TIT 1.01.339
o, would thou wert as thou tofore hast been! 3.01.293
lavinia, wert thou thus surpris'd, sweet girl? 4.01. 51
i would thou wert so happy by thy stay | to hear ROM 1.01.158
wert thou as far | as that vast shore /wash'd 2.02. 82
wert thou as young as i, juliet thy love, | an 3.03. 65
now, apemantus (if thou wert not sullen), | i TIM 1.02.236
for thy part, i do wish thou wert a dog, | that 4.03. 55
courtier be again, | wert thou not beggar. 4.03.242
if thou wert the lion, the fox would beguile 4.03.328 P
if thou wert the lamb, the fox would eat thee; 4.03.329 P
if thou wert the fox, the lion would suspect 4.03.330 P
when peradventure thou wert accus'd by the ass; 4.03.331 P
if thou wert the ass, thy dullness would torment 4.03.332 P
if thou wert the wolf, thy greediness would 4.03.334 P
wert thou the unicorn, pride and wrath would 4.03.336 P
wert thou a bear, thou wouldst be kill'd by the 4.03.338 P
wert thou a horse, thou wouldst be seiz'd by the 4.03.339 P
wert thou a leopard, thou wert germane to the 4.03.340 P
thou a leopard, thou wert germane to the lion, 4.03.340 P
would thou wert clean enough to spit upon! 4.03.359
o, if thou wert the noblest of thy strain, JC 5.01. 59
if thou wert my fool, nuncle, i'ld have thee LR 1.05. 41 P
thou wert better in a grave than to answer with 3.04.101 P
wert thou a man, | thou wouldst have mercy on me ANT 5.02.174
if thou wert honorable, | thou wouldst have told CYM 1.06.142
wert thou the son of jupiter, and no more | but 2.03.125
besides, thou wert too base | to be his groom. 2.03.126
thou wert dignified enough, | even to the point 2.03.127
would thou wert as i am, and i a man, | my heart VEN 369
"but o, what banquet wert thou to the taste, 445
and for a woman wert thou first created, | till SON 20. 9
i grant thou wert not married to my muse, | and 82. 1
wert truly sympathiz'd | in true plain words by 82.11
WEST 34 FR 0.0038 REL FR 31 V 3 P
go thou with her to the west end of the wood; TGV 5.03. 9
they shall be my east and west indies, and i WIV 1.03. 71 P
town, | dies ere the weary sun set in the west. ERR 1.02. 7
and by east from the west corner of thy LLL 1.01.246 P
by east, west, north, and south, i spread my 5.02.563
he took | at a fair vestal throned by /the west, MND 2.01.158
west of this place, down in the neighbor bottom, AYL 4.03. 78
there lies your way, due west. TN 3.01.134
think it — | from east, west, north, and south. WT 1.02.203
even till that utmost corner of the west JN 2.01. 29
by east and west let france and england mount 2.01.381
we from the west will send destruction | into 2.01.409
thy sun sets weeping in the lowly west, R2 2.04. 21
send danger from the east unto the west, | so 1H4 1.03.195
i, from the orient to the drooping west 2H4 in 3
west of this forest, scarcely off a mile, | in 4.01. 19
they take their courses | east, west, north, 4.02.104
and all the wealthy kingdoms of the west, 2H6 1.01.154
they should serve their sovereign in the west? R3 4.04.485
here's a lord — come knights from east to west, TRO 2.03.263
but it is not known | whether for east or west. COR 1.02. 10
of one skull, they would fly east, west, north, 2.03. 22 P
as phaeton would whip you to the west, | and ROM 3.02. 3
the west yet glimmers with some streaks of day; MAC 3.03. 5
this heavy–headed revel east and west | makes us HAM 1.04. 17
the world | even from the east to th' west! OTH 4.02.144
from the spungy south to this part of the west, CYM 4.02.349
from south to west on wing soaring aloft, 5.05.471
cymbeline, | which shines here in the west. 5.05.476
for when the west wind courts her gently, | how TNK 2.02.138
his day's hot task hath ended in the west; VEN 530
stealing unseen to west with this disgrace: SON 33. 8
such day | as after sunset fadeth in the west, 73. 6
even | doth half that glory to the sober west, 132. 8
WESTERLY 1 FR 0.0001 REL FR 1 V 0 P
is this wind westerly that blows? PER 4.01. 50
WESTERN 10 FR 0.0011 REL FR 10 V 0 P
the sun begins to gild the western sky, | and TGV 5.01. 1
whose western side is with a vineyard back'd; MM 4.01. 29
it fell upon a little western flower, | before MND 2.01.166
uncouple in the western valley, let them go. 4.01.107
"from the east to western inde, | no jewel is AYL 3.02. 88
but stay'd and made the western welkin blush, JN 5.05. 2
sun, | ere he attain his easeful western bed: 3H6 5.03. 6
on the western coast | rideth a puissant navy; R3 4.04.433
are they not now upon the western shore, 4.04.481
upon him) from the western isles | of kerns and MAC 1.02. 12
/WESTMERLAND 1 FR 0.0001 REL FR 1 V 0 P
/but, /my /most /noble /lord /of /westmerland, 2H4 4.01. 59
WESTMERLAND 31 FR 0.0035 REL FR 28 V 3 P
me hear | of you, my gentle cousin westmerland, 1H4 1.01. 31
the earl of westmerland set forth to–day, | with 3.02.170
this to my lord of westmerland. 3.03.196
the earl of westmerland, seven thousand strong, 4.01. 88
my good lord of westmerland, i cry you mercy! 4.02. 52 P
the noble westmerland, and warlike blunt, | and 4.04. 30
return'd, | deliver up my lord of westmerland. 5.02. 28
defy him by the lord of westmerland. 5.02. 31
and westmerland, that was engag'd, did bear it, 5.02. 43
my lord of westmerland, lead him to his tent. 5.04. 8
come, cousin westmerland, | our duty this way 5.04. 15
and my cousin westmerland | towards york shall 5.05. 35
and westmerland and stafford fled the field; 2H4 1.01. 18
conduct of young lancaster | and westmerland. 1.01.135
commend me to my cousin westmerland. 1.02.227 P
this to the earl of westmerland, and this to old 1.02.240 P
the duke of lancaster and westmerland; 1.03. 82
i think it is my lord of westmerland. 4.01. 26
say on, my lord of westmerland, in peace, | what 4.01. 29
then take, my lord of westmerland, this schedule 4.01.166
here is return'd my lord of westmerland. 4.01.222
peace, | but, as i told my lord of westmerland, 4.02. 32
to you, my noble lord of westmerland. 4.02. 72
call in the powers, good cousin westmerland. 4.03. 25
westmerland? 4.04. 80
o westmerland, thou art a summer bird, | which 4.04. 91
my lord of westmerland, and uncle exeter, | we H5 2.02. 70
my cousin westmerland? 4.03. 19
rather proclaim it, westmerland, through my host 4.03. 34
be patient, gentle earl of westmerland. 3H6 1.01. 61
and that the lord of westmerland shall maintain. 1.01. 88
WESTMINSTER 6 FR 0.0006 REL FR 6 V 0 P
my lord of westminster, be it your charge | to R2 4.01.152
the grand conspirator, abbot of westminster, 5.06. 19
the king your father is at westminster, | and 2H4 2.04.355
in the cathedral church of westminster, | and in 2H6 1.02. 37
and vows to crown himself in westminster. 4.04. 31
come, madam, you must straight to westminster, R3 4.01. 31
WESTMORELAND *(see westmerland)*
WESTWARD 4 FR 0.0004 REL FR 3 V 1 P
there's scarce a maid westward but she sings it. WT 4.04.290 P
all westward, wales beyond the severn shore, 1H4 3.01. 75
that westward rooteth from this city side, | so ROM 1.01.122
yond same star that's westward from the pole HAM 1.01. 36
WESTWARD–HO 1 FR 0.0001 REL FR 1 V 0 P
then westward–ho! TN 3.01.134
WET 22 FR 0.0024 REL FR 18 V 4 P
eye, | who hath cause to wet the grief on't. TMP 2.01.128
the property of rain is to wet and fire to burn; AYL 3.02. 26 P
that this distempered messenger of wet, | the AWW 1.03.151
the ruddiness upon her lip is wet; WT 5.03. 81
to the wet //sea–boy in an hour so rude, | and 2H4 3.01. 27
till his face be like a wet cloak ill laid up. 5.01. 85 P
nor let the rain of heaven wet this place | to 2H6 3.02.341
and wet my cheeks with artificial tears, | and 3H6 3.02.184
that all the standers–by had wet their cheeks R3 1.02.162
and wet his grave with my repentant tears) | i 1.02.215
when the rain came to wet me once, and the wind LR 4.06.101 P
be your tears wet? 4.07. 70
'tis so, and the tears of it are wet. ANT 2.07. 49 P
err, who with wet cheeks | were present when she CYM 5.05. 35
rain, being in't, | knows neither wet nor dry. TNK 1.01.121
long have rain'd, making her cheeks all wet, VEN 83
sighs dry her cheeks, tears make them wet again. 966
for every little grief to wet his eyes; 1179
even so the maid with swelling drops gan wet LUC 1228
is it for fear to wet a widow's eye | that thou SON 9. 1
she was set, | like usury, applying wet to wet, LC 40
she was set, | like usury, applying wet to wet, 40
WETHER 2 FR 0.0002 REL FR 1 V 1 P
i am a tainted wether of the flock, | meetest MV 4.01.114
every 'leven wether tods, every tod yields pound WT 4.03. 32 P
WETHER'S 1 FR 0.0001 REL FR 1 V 0 P
no deal, | my wether's bell rings doleful knell, PP 17.18
WETS 1 FR 0.0001 REL FR 1 V 0 P
"look, look how list'ning priam wets his eyes, LUC 1548
WETTING 1 FR 0.0001 REL FR 0 V 1 P
that's more to me than my wetting; TMP 4.01.211 P
WEZAND 1 FR 0.0001 REL FR 1 V 0 P
a stake, | or cut his wezand with thy knife. TMP 3.02. 91
WHALE 8 FR 0.0009 REL FR 3 V 5 P
i trow, threw this whale (with so many tuns of WIV 2.01. 64 P
who is a whale to virginity and devours up all AWW 4.03.220 P
till that his passions, like a whale on ground, 2H4 4.04. 40
like scaling sculls | before the belching whale; TRO 5.05. 23
or like a whale? HAM 3.02.381 P
very like a whale. 3.02.382 P
rich misers to nothing so fitly as to a whale: PER 2.01. 30 P
the belching whale | and humming water must 3.01. 62
WHALE'S 1 FR 0.0001 REL FR 1 V 0 P
to show his teeth as white as whale's bone; LLL 5.02.332
WHALES 1 FR 0.0001 REL FR 0 V 1 P
such whales have i heard on a' th' land, who PER 2.01. 32 P
WHARF 1 FR 0.0001 REL FR 1 V 0 P
weed | that roots itself in ease on lethe wharf, HAM 1.05. 33
WHARFS 1 FR 0.0001 REL FR 1 V 0 P
perfume hits the sense | of the adjacent wharfs. ANT 2.02.213
WHAT *(also vat, wat*)*
/WHAT 41 FR 0.0046 REL FR 35 V 6 P
WHAT 4793 FR 0.5418 REL FR 3635 V 1158 P
WHAT–DO–YE–CALL 1 FR 0.0001 REL FR 0 V 1 P
you shall read it in what–do–ye–call there. AWW 2.03. 22 P
WHATEVER 2 FR 0.0002 REL FR 1 V 1 P
whatever fortune stays him from his word. SHR 3.02. 23
and whatever praises itself but in the deed, TRO 2.03.156 P
/WHAT'S 4 FR 0.0004 REL FR 4 V 0 P
/ay, /what's /a' /clock? R3 4.02.109
/well, /but /what's /a' /clock? 4.02.111
/what's /past /and /what's /to /come /is TRO 4.05.166

/what's /past /and /what's /to /come /is 4.05.166
WHAT'S 349 FR 0.0394 REL FR 227 V 122 P
an act | whereof what's past is prologue, what TMP 2.01.253
what's the matter? 2.01.309
what's the matter? 2.02. 57 P
the mistress which i serve quickens what's dead, 3.01. 6
worth | what's dearest to the world! 3.01. 39
thy thoughts i cleave to. what's thy pleasure? 4.01.165
what's the matter? TGV 2.03. 34 P
what's the unkindest tide? 2.03. 39 P
now tell me, proteus, what's your will with me? 3.01. 3
what's here? 3.01.137
what's here? 3.01.150
what's next? 3.01.363 P
what's your will? 4.02. 92
what's the matter? 5.04. 86 P
what's the matter, woman? WIV 2.01. 43 P
what's your will? 2.02.158 P
what's the matter? 3.03. 93 P
what's the matter, good mistress page? 3.03. 97 P
why, alas, what's the matter? 3.03.105 P
we do not know what's brought to pass under the 4.02.175 P
what's the news with you? MM 1.02. 85 P
but what's his offense? 1.02. 89 P
what's to do here, thomas tapster? 1.02.112 P
what's thy offense, claudio? 1.02.134 P
what's open made to justice, | that justice 2.01. 21
how now, sir, what's your name? 2.01. 45 P
and what's the matter? 2.01. 46 P
thou wicked varlet, now, what's come upon thee. 2.01.190 P
what's your name, master tapster? 2.01.213 P
what's a' clock, think you? 2.01.276 P
now, what's the matter, provost? 2.02. 6
what's your will? 2.02. 26
well; what's your suit? 2.02. 28
what's this? 2.02.162
what's this? 2.02.162
i am the provost. what's your will, good friar? 2.03. 2
what's yet in this | that bears the name of life 3.01. 38
now, sister, what's the comfort? 3.01. 54
what's your will, father? 3.01.175 P
reakless, and fearless of what's past, present, 4.02.144 P
how now, abhorson? what's the news with you? 4.03. 39 P
what's he? 5.01.467
what's mine is yours, and what is yours is mine. 5.01.537
where we'll show | what's yet behind, that/'s 5.01.539
i'll weep what's left away, and weeping die. ERR 2.01.115
in good time, sir: what's that? 2.02. 57 P
what's her name? 3.02.108 P
bred, | and what's a fever but a fit of madness? 5.01. 76
shall we go prove what's to be done? ADO 1.03. 73 P
what's he? 2.01.132 P
to be whipt? what's his fault? 2.01.221 P
what's the matter? 3.02. 87 P
why, what's the matter? 3.02.101 P
thirdly, i ask thee what's their offense; 5.01.221 P
what's your offense? 5.01.229 P
but what's your will? 5.04. 26
why, what's the matter, | that you have such a 5.04. 40
to whom he sends, and what's his embassy: LLL 2.01. 3
what's her name in the cap? 2.01.209
"what's the price of this inkle?" 3.01.138 P
what's your will, sir? what's your will? 4.01. 52
what's your will, sir? what's your will? 4.01. 52
what's your dark meaning, mouse, of this light 5.02. 19
thanks, good egeus. what's the news with thee? MND 1.01. 21
what's this to my lysander? 3.02. 62
what's your will? 4.01. 21
friend launcelot, what's the news? MV 2.04. 9
what's here? 2.09. 54
what's that good for? 3.01. 52 P
and what's his reason? 3.01. 58 P
so — and i know not what's spent in the search. 3.01. 91 P
what's the news from venice? 3.02.238
seek to soften that — than which what's harder? 4.01. 79
a quarrel ho already! what's the matter? 5.01.146
charles, what's the new news at the new court? AYL 1.01. 96 P
what's the news? 1.02. 97 P
derive it from our friends, | what's that to me? 1.03. 63
are mere usurpers, tyrants, and what's worse, 2.01. 61
why, what's the matter? 2.03. 16
what's that "ducdame"? 2.05. 58 P
what's that? 4.01. 58 P
what's here? SHR in.1. 31
what's that, i pray? 1.01.119 P
perhaps you mark'd not what's the pith of all. 1.01.166
pray what's the news? 1.01.224 P
how now, what's the matter? 1.02. 20 P
why, what's a moveable? 2.01.197
if she and i be pleas'd, what's that to you? 2.01.303
mistress, what's your opinion of your sister? 3.02.243
what's that to thee? 4.01. 70 P
what's this? 4.01.160
what's this? 4.03. 88
why, sir, what's your conceit in that? 4.03.160
what's he that knocks as he would beat down the 5.01. 16 P
how now, what's the matter? 5.01. 71 P
content. what's the wager? 5.02. 70
what's pity? AWW 1.01.180 P
what's he comes here? 1.02. 17
what's in "mother," | that you start at it? 1.03.141
what's the matter, | that this distempered 1.03.150
what's the matter, sweet heart? 2.03.268 P
what's his will else? 2.04. 47
what's his name? 3.05. 57
wherefore, what's the instance? 4.01. 40 P
what's his brother, the other captain dumaine? 4.03.282 P
what's he? 4.03.285 P
what's your will? 5.01. 17
our own love waking cries to see what's done, 5.03. 65
what's she? TN 1.02. 35
what's that to th' purpose? 1.03. 21 P
what's that? 1.03. 50 P
wherefore, sweetheart? what's your metaphor? 1.03. 71 P
but what's your jest? 1.03. 75 P
what's a drunken man like, fool? 1.05.130 P
what's to come is still unsure. 2.03. 49
and what's her history? 2.04.109
what's to do? 3.03. 18
why, what's the matter? does he rave? 3.04. 10
what's that to us? the time goes by; away! 3.04.364
what's the matter? 5.01. 59
what's the matter? 5.01.174 P
a great deal too dear for what's given freely. WT 1.01. 17 P
with what's unreal thou co–active art, | and 1.02.141
avoid what's grown than question how 'tis born. 1.02.433
what's gone and what's past help | should be 3.02.222
what's gone and what's past help | should be 3.02.222
what's within, boy? 3.03.118 P
king | and through him what's nearest to him, 4.04.522
what's i' th' farthel? 4.04.754 P
so must thy grave | give way to what's seen now! 5.01. 98
what's that to thee? JN 5.06. 4
brief then; and what's the news? 5.06. 18
and what's thy quarrel? R2 1.03. 33
why, uncle, what's the matter? 2.01.186
good morrow, carriers, what's a' clock? 1H4 2.01. 32 P
come, what's the issue? 2.04. 91 P
what's a' clock, francis? 2.04. 96 P
why, you whoreson round man, what's the matter? 2.04.140 P
what's the matter? 2.04.157 P
what's the matter! 2.04.158 P
what's the matter? 2.04.488 P
what's that? 3.01.243 P
what's he that goes there? 2H4 1.02. 58 P
how now, whose mare's dead? what's the matter? 2.01. 43 P
what's the news, my lord? 2.01.167 P
what's the matter? 2.01.181 P
the blood ere one can say, "what's this?" 2.04. 28 P
what's a joint of mutton or two in a whole lent? 2.04.346 P
how now, what's the matter? 2.04.370 P
what's the matter? 2.04.386 P
what's your name, sir? 4.03. 1 P
what's he? H5 3.07.106 P
what's to say? 4.02. 32
what's he that wishes so? 4.03. 18
how now, how now, what's the matter? 4.08. 19 P
how now, what's the matter? 4.08. 24 P
what's past and what's to come she can descry. 1H6 1.02. 57
what's past and what's to come she can descry. 1.02. 57
but what's that pucelle whom they term so pure? 2.01. 20
and for thy treachery, what's more manifest? 3.01. 21
what's here? 4.01. 55
what's yours? 2H6 1.03. 20 P
what's here? 1.03. 20 P
tell me, sirrah, what's my name? 2.01.115
what's his name? 2.01.117
what's thine own name? 2.01.121
sirrah, what's thy name? 2.03. 80 P
sirs, what's a' clock? 2.04. 5
what's more dangerous than this fond affiance! 3.01. 74
for what's more miserable than discontent? 3.01.201
what's the matter, suffolk? 3.02. 28
and ask him what's the reason of these arms. 4.09. 37
but in this troublous time what's to be done? 3H6 2.01.159
what's he approacheth boldly to our presence? 3.03. 44
thou seest what's pass'd, go fear thy king 3.03.226
what's worse than murtherer, that i may name it? 5.05. 58
but what's the matter, clarence, may i know? R3 1.01. 51
how now, lord stanley, what's the news? 4.02. 46
what's that? H8 1.04. 49
what's the cause? 2.02. 15
what's the need? 2.04. 2
what's this? 3.02.220
but i beseech you, what's become of katherine, 4.01. 22
what's the matter? 5.01. 10
what's that, butts? 5.02. 20
what's that? what's that? TRO 1.02. 41 P
what's that? what's that? 1.02. 41 P
what's your affairs, i pray you? 1.03.247
how now, thersites, what's the matter, man? 2.01. 56
ay, what's the matter? 2.01. 58 P
so i do. what's the matter? 2.01. 60 P
what's the quarrel? 2.01. 89 P
what's aught but as 'tis valued? 2.02. 52
come, what's agamemnon? 2.03. 43 P
then tell me, patroclus, what's achilles? 2.03. 45 P
then tell me, i pray thee, what's thersites? 2.03. 47 P
what's his excuse? 2.03.163
what's all the doors open here? 4.02. 19 P
what's the matter? 4.02. 42 P
how now, what's the matter? 4.02. 43 P
how now, what's the matter? 4.02. 58
how now? what's the matter? who was here? 4.02. 78 P
tell me, sweet uncle, what's the matter? 4.02. 81 P
o the gods! what's the matter? 4.02. 84 P
on my knees /i /beseech /you, what's the matter? 4.02. 89 P
thou crusty batch of nature, what's the news? 5.01. 5
male varlot, you rogue! what's that? 5.01. 16 P
what's become of the wenching rogues? 5.04. 32 P
what's the matter, you dissentious rogues, COR 1.01.164
what's the matter, | that in these several 1.01.184
what's their seeking? 1.01.188
presume to know | what's done i' th' capitol; 1.01.192
here. what's the matter? 1.01.223
what's the matter? 2.01.259
deeds express | what's like to be their words: 3.01.133
when what's not meet, but what must be, was law, 3.01.167
then he speaks | what's in his heart, and that 3.03. 29
what's the news in rome? 4.03. 10 P
what's thy name? 4.05. 54
say, what's thy name? 4.05. 59
what's thy name? 4.05. 62
directitude? what's that? 4.05.209 P
what's the news? what's the news? 4.06. 84
what's the news? what's the news? 4.06. 84
what's the matter? 5.02. 59 P
and swound for what's to come upon thee. 5.02. 67 P
what's this? 5.03. 56
what's the news? 5.04. 39
gramercy, lovely lucius. what's the news? TIT 4.02. 7
what's here? 4.02. 18
what's this but libelling against the senate, 4.04. 17
welcome, aemilius, what's the news from rome? 5.01.155
what's he that now is going out of door? ROM 1.05.130
what's he that follows here, that would not 1.05.132
what's tis? what's tis? 1.05.142
what's tis? what's tis? 1.05.142
what's montague? 2.02. 40
what's in a name? 2.02. 43
what's your will? 3.03. 78
what's here? 5.03.161
what's she, if i be a dog? TIM 1.01.201 P
yes, mine's three thousand crowns; what's yours? 3.04. 28
what's that? 3.05. 62
how do you? what's the news? 3.06. 52 P
what's to be thought of him? 5.01. 2
what's on this tomb | i cannot read; 5.03. 5
what's to do? JC 2.01.326
what's the matter? 4.03.118
how now? what's the matter? 4.03.129
what's the matter? MAC 2.03. 65
what's the business, | that such a hideous 2.03. 81
what's done, is done. 3.02. 12
what's to be done? 3.02. 44
what's your grace's will? 4.01.135
what's the disease he means? 4.03.146
what's the newest grief? 4.03.174
what's done cannot be undone. 5.01. 68 P
what's the boy malcolm? 5.03. 3
what's your gracious pleasure? 5.03. 30
what's he | that was not born of woman? 5.07. 2
what's more to do, | which would be planted 5.09. 30
and now, laertes, what's the news with you? HAM 1.02. 42
farewell! how now, ophelia, what's the matter? 2.01. 71
what's hecuba to him, or he to /hecuba, | that 2.02.559
like a gulf, doth draw | what's near it with it. 3.03. 17
and what's in prayer but this twofold force, 3.03. 48
now, mother, what's the matter? 3.04. 8
what's the matter now? 3.04. 13
repent what's past, avoid what is to come, | and 3.04.150
what we mean to do | and what's untimely done, 4.01. 40
what's that, my lord? 5.01.196 P
what's his weapon? 5.02.144 P
upon, | be it lawful i take up what's cast away. LR 1.01.253
what's that? 1.04. 29 P
what's the matter, sir? 1.04.295
striving to better, oft we mar what's well. 1.04.346
how now, what's the matter? part! 2.02. 44 P
weapons? arms? what's the matter here? 2.02. 47 P
what's he that hath so much thy place mistook 2.04. 12
what's he? 3.04.126
sir, speed you: what's your will? 4.06.208
what's he that speaks for edmund earl of 5.03.125
and what's to come of my despised time | is OTH 1.01.161
now? what's the business? 1.03. 13
why? what's the matter? 1.03. 58
what's the matter, lieutenant? 2.03.146 P
what's the matter | that you unlace your 2.03.193
and what's he then that says i play the villain? 2.03.336
how now, good cassio, what's the news with you? 3.04.109
what's the matter? 4.01. 49
and what's the news, good cousin lodovico? 4.01.219
good madam, what's the matter with my lord? 4.02. 98
what's the matter? 5.01. 50
i will so. what's the matter? 5.02. 47
what's best to do? 5.02. 95
what's the matter with thee now? 5.02.105
what's your pleasure, sir? ANT 1.02.131 P
what's the matter? 1.03. 18
what's your highness' pleasure? 1.05. 8
what's amiss, | may it be gently heard. 2.02. 19
what's else to say? 2.07. 58
what's antony? the god of jupiter. 3.02. 10
what's thy passion? 3.10. 5
what's your name? 3.13. 72
with the hand of she here — what's her name, 3.13. 98
nay, i'll help too. | what's this for? 4.04. 6
what's the noise? 4.14.104
and then, what's brave, what's noble, | let's 4.15. 86
and then, what's brave, what's noble, | let's 4.15. 86
what's thy name? 5.02. 11
but what's the matter? CYM 1.01. 3
what's his name and birth? 1.01. 27
what's that? 1.04.117 P
of my speeches, and would undergo what's spoken, 1.04.141 P
what's your lordship's pleasure? 2.03. 80
what's worse, | must curtsy at the censure. 3.03. 54
what's the matter? 3.04. 10
it from the queen, | what's in't is precious. 3.04.189
her judgment | that what's else rare is chok'd; 3.05. 77
our stomachs | will make what's homely savory; 3.06. 33
what's the matter, sir? 3.06. 41
what's your name? 3.06. 59
what's thy name? 4.02. 87
what's thy interest | in this sad wrack? 4.02.365
of what's past, is, and to come, the discharge. 5.04.168 P
think more and more | what's best to ask. 5.05.110
what's thy name? 5.05.117
what's that to him? 5.05.136
what's this, cornelius? 5.05.248
good fellow, what's that? PER 2.01. 53 P
and what's | the sixt and last, the which the 2.02. 39
what's here? 2.05. 42
what's dumb in show i'll plain with speech. 3.ch. 14
what's that? 3.02. 49
what's here? 3.02. 63
what's her price, boult? 4.02. 50 P
how now, what's the matter? 4.06.131 P
what's your request? deliver you for all. TNK 1.01. 38
small winds shake him. | but what's the matter? 1.02. 89
why, what's the matter, man? 2.02.133
couple then, | and see what's wanting. 3.05. 33
and reduce what's now out of square in her into 4.03. 95 P
to buy you i have lost what's dearest to me 5.03.112
for what's a sorry parsnip to a good heart? STM II.C 9 P
for day hath nought to do what's done by night." LUC 1092
but what's so blessed–fair that fears no blot? SON 92.13
what's in the brain that ink may character 108. 1
what's new to speak, what now to register, 108. 3
what's sweet to do, to do will aptly find: LC 88
WHATSOE'ER 5 FR 0.0005 REL FR 5 V 0 P
and bear his charge of wooing, whatsoe'er. SHR 1.02.215
why, rude companion, whatsoe'er thou be, | i 2H6 4.10. 31

king, | and whatsoe'er you will employ me in, R3 1.01.108
but, whatsoe'er thou tak'st me for, i'm sure H8 5.02.163
sons | to back thy quarrels, whatsoe'er they be. TIT 2.03. 54
WHATSOEVER 14 FR 0.0015 REL FR 6 V 8 P
but whatsoever i have merited, either in my mind WIV 2.02.202 P
before me again upon any complaint whatsoever; MM 2.01.246 P
"whatsoever you may hear to the contrary, let 4.02.120 P
am sure i do not — and whatsoever a man denies, ERR 5.01.306 P
him, and whatsoever comes athwart his affection ADO 2.02. 6 P
me, | in all my lands and leases whatsoever. SHR 2.01.125
as any man in illyria, whatsoever he be, under TN 1.03.117 P
"youth, whatsoever thou art, thou art but a 3.04.147 P
and whatsoever cunning fiend it was | that H5 2.02.111
/chattels, and whatsoever, and to be | out of H8 3.02.343
as if that whatsoever god who leads him | were COR 2.01.219
thy life, | that whatsoever i did bid thee do, JC 5.03. 39
and he's another, whatsoever he be. CYM 2.01. 40 P
till whatsoever star that guides my moving SON 26. 9
WHATSOME'ER 2 FR 0.0002 REL FR 1 V 1 P
whatsome'er he is, | he's bravely taken here. AWW 3.05. 51
faces are true, whatsome'er their hands are. ANT 2.06. 97 P
WHATSOMEVER 1 FR 0.0001 REL FR 1 V 0 P
and whatsomever else shall hap to-night, | give HAM 1.02.248
WHAT-YE-CALL'T 1 FR 0.0001 REL FR 0 V 1 P
good even, good master what-ye-call't; AYL 3.03. 73 P
WHEAT 8 FR 0.0009 REL FR 3 V 5 P
bounteous lady, thy rich leas | of wheat, rye, TMP 4.01. 61
lark to shepherd's ear | when wheat is green, MND 1.01.185
are as two grains of wheat hid in two bushels of MV 1.01.116 P
sir, shall we sow the hade land with wheat? 2H4 5.01. 15 P
with red wheat, davy. 5.01. 16 P
a cake out of the wheat must tarry the grinding. TRO 1.01. 15 P
mildews the white wheat, and hurts the poor LR 3.04.118 P
then, to send | measures of wheat to rome. ANT 2.06. 37
WHEATEN 3 FR 0.0003 REL FR 3 V 0 P
as peace should still her wheaten garland wear HAM 5.02. 41
your wheaten wreath | was then nor thresh'd nor TNK 1.01. 64
let him | take off my wheaten garland, or else 5.01.160
WHEEL 21 FR 0.0023 REL FR 16 V 5 P
to a curtal dog, and made me turn i' th' wheel. ERR 3.02.146
mock the good huswife fortune from her wheel, AYL 1.02. 32 P
turn'd, | or a dry wheel grate on the axle-tree, 1H4 3.01.130
not this nave of a wheel have his ears cut off? 2H4 2.04.255 P
and giddy fortune's furious fickle wheel, | that H5 3.06. 27
and she is painted also with a wheel, to signify 3.06. 33 P
my thoughts are whirled like a potter's wheel, 1H6 1.05. 19
my mind exceeds the compass of her wheel. 3H6 4.03. 47
attend me where i wheel; TRO 5.07. 2
that i was forc'd to wheel | three or four miles COR 1.06. 19
present me | death on the wheel, or at wild 3.02. 2
all the spokes and /fellies from her wheel, HAM 2.02.495
or it is a massy wheel, | fix'd on the summit of 3.03. 17
o, how the wheel becomes it! 4.05.172 P
smile once more, turn thy wheel! LR 2.02.173
go thy hold when a great wheel runs down a hill, 2.04. 72 P
but i am bound | upon a wheel of fire, that mine 4.07. 46
the wheel is come full circle, i am here. 5.03.175
that the false huswife fortune break her wheel, ANT 4.15. 44
so, had it been a carbuncle | of phoebus' wheel; CYM 5.05.190
and turn the giddy round of fortune's wheel; LUC 952
WHEEL'D 1 FR 0.0001 REL FR 1 V 0 P
whilst the wheel'd seat | of fortunate caesar, ANT 4.14. 75
WHEELING 1 FR 0.0001 REL FR 1 V 0 P
in an extravagant and wheeling stranger | of OTH 1.01.136
WHEELS 6 FR 0.0006 REL FR 4 V 2 P
then may i set the world on wheels, when she can TGV 3.01.315 P
what, at the wheels of caesar? MM 3.02. 44 P
day, | before the wheels of phoebus, round about ADO 5.03. 26
what wheels? WT 3.02.176
from forth day's path and titan's /fiery wheels. ROM 2.03. 4
would it were all, | that it might go on wheels! ANT 2.07. 93
WHE'ER *(also whe'r, whether, whither*)*
/WHE'ER 1 FR 0.0001 REL FR 1 V 0 P
/whe'er she is as rough | as are the swelling SHR 1.02. 73
WHE'ER 14 FR 0.0015 REL FR 12 V 2 P
whe'er thou beest he or no, | or some enchanted TMP 5.01.111
but whe'er i be as true begot or no, | that JN 1.01. 75
now shame upon you, whe'er she does or no! 2.01.167
look whe'er the wither'd elder hath not his pole 2H4 2.04.258 P
that they will guard you, whe'er you will or no, 2H6 3.02.265
can i make men live, whe'er they will or no? 3.03. 10
yet know, whe'er you accept our suit or no, R3 3.07.214
back, | to bear her burthen whe'er i will or no, 3.07.229
see whe'er their basest metal be not mov'd; JC 1.01. 61
look whe'er he have not crown'd dead cassius! 5.03. 97
go on, | and see whe'er brutus be alive or dead, 5.04. 30
look whe'er he has not turn'd his color and has HAM 2.02.519 P
and whe'er he run or fly they know not whether; VEN 304
whether we are mended, or whe'er better they, SON 59.11
WHEESON *(also whitsun)*
WHEESON 1 FR 0.0001 REL FR 0 V 1 P
a sea-coal fire, upon wednesday in wheeson week, 2H4 2.01. 89 P
WHEEZING *(see whissing)*
WHELK'D *(see welk'd)*
WHELKS 1 FR 0.0001 REL FR 0 V 1 P
his face is all bubukles, and whelks, and knobs, H5 3.06.103 P
WHELM 1 FR 0.0001 REL FR 1 V 0 P
she is my prize, or ocean whelm them all! WIV 2.02.137
WHELP 8 FR 0.0009 REL FR 5 V 3 P
a freckled whelp, hag-born) not honor'd with | a TMP 1.02.283
thee as i fear the roaring of the lion's whelp. 1H4 3.03.147 P
hill | stood smiling to behold his lion's whelp H5 1.02.109
how the young whelp of talbot's, raging wood, 1H6 4.07. 35
'tis better playing with a lion's whelp | than ANT 3.13. 94
"when as a lion's whelp shall, to himself CYM 5.04.138 P
"when as a lion's whelp shall, to himself 5.05.435 P
thou, leonatus, art the lion's whelp; 5.05.443
WHELP'D 1 FR 0.0001 REL FR 0 V 1 P
thou wast whelp'd a dog, and thou shalt famish a TIM 2.02. 86 P
WHELPED 1 FR 0.0001 REL FR 1 V 0 P
a lioness hath whelped in the streets, | and JC 2.02. 17
WHELPS 2 FR 0.0002 REL FR 2 V 0 P
dogs, | now, like to whelps, we crying run away. 1H6 1.05. 26
two of thy whelps, fell curs of bloody kind, TIT 2.03.281
/WHEN 23 FR 0.0026 REL FR 23 V 0 P
from lowest place /when virtuous things proceed, AWW 2.03.125
/when /i /do /see /the /very /book /indeed R2 4.01.274
/for /when /i /was /a /king /my /flatterers 4.01.306
/when /we /mean /to /build, | /we /first /survey 2H4 1.03. 41
/and /when /we /see /the /figure /of /the /house 1.03. 43
/they /that, /when /richard /liv'd, /would /have 1.03.101
/when /through /proud /london /he /came /sighing 1.03.104
/all /our /griefs | (/when /time /shall /serve) 4.01. 74
/when /we /are /wrong'd /and /would /unfold /our 4.01. 77
/when /there /was /nothing /could /have /stay'd 4.01.121
/when /the /king /did /throw /his /warder /down 4.01.123
/when /last /i /was /at /exeter, | /the /mayor R3 4.02.103
/when /rank /thersites /opes /his /mastic /jaws, TRO 1.03. 73
/who, /when /my /heart, /all /mad /with /misery, TIT 3.02. 9
/when /thy /poor /heart /beats /with /outrageous 3.02. 13
/and /thou /shalt /read /when /mine /begin /to 3.02. 85
/as /flatteries, /when /they /are /seen /abus'd. LR 1.03. 20
/when /we /our /betters /see /bearing /our /woes 3.06.102
/when /grief /hath /mates, /and /bearing 3.06.107
/when /that /which /makes /me /bend /makes /the 3.06.109
/and /thyself /bewray | /when /false /opinion, 3.06.112
/when /i /am /known /aright, /you /shall /not 4.03. 53
you are a spirit, i know; /when did you die? 4.07. 48
WHEN 2223 FR 0.2512 REL FR 1796 V 427 P
when the sea is. TMP 1.01. 16 P
when i have deck'd the sea with drops full salt, 1.02.155
o' th' earth | when it is bak'd with frost. 1.02.256
when i arriv'd and heard thee, that made gape 1.02.292
come, thou tortoise, when? 1.02.316
when thou cam'st first, | thou strok'st me and 1.02.332
when thou didst not, savage, | know thine own 1.02.355
curtsied when you have, and kiss'd, | the wild 1.02.377
when every grief is entertain'd that's offer'd, 2.01. 16
are now as fresh as when we put them on first in 2.01. 70 P
seem now as fresh as when we were at tunis at 2.01. 98 P
when i wore it at your daughter's marriage? 2.01.106 P
the sore, | when you should bring the plaster. 2.01.140
in us all, good sir, | when you are cloudy. 2.01.143
when it doth, | it is a comforter. 2.01.195
be of as little memory | when he is earth'd, 2.01.234
and when i rear my hand, do you the like, | to 2.01.295
when they will not give a doit to relieve a lame 2.02. 31 P
i was the man i' th' moon, when time was. 2.02.139 P
when 's god's asleep, he'll rob his bottle. 2.02.151 P
my sweet mistress | weeps when she sees me work, 3.01. 12
my labors, | most /busil'est when i do it. 3.01. 15
when this burns, | 'twill weep for having 3.01. 18
morning with me | when you are by at night. 3.01. 34
when the butt is out, we will drink water — not 3.02. 1 P
drink, servant-monster, when i bid thee. 3.02. 8 P
when that's gone, | he shall drink nought but 3.02. 65
which, when he has a house, he'll deck withal. 3.02. 97
me, that when i wak'd | i cried to dream again. 3.02.142
when prospero is destroy'd. 3.02.146
use such vigilance | as when they are fresh. 3.03. 17
when we were boys, | who would believe that 3.03. 43
when i shall think or phoebus' steeds are 4.01. 30
when i presented ceres, | i thought to have told 4.01.167
i did say so, | when first i rais'd the tempest. 5.01. 6
neptune, and do fly him | when he comes back; 5.01. 36
and when i have requir'd | some heavenly music 5.01. 51
there i couch when owls do cry. 5.01. 90
when did you lose your daughter? 5.01.152
i chose her when i could not ask my father | for 5.01.190
all of us, ourselves, | when no man was his own. 5.01.213
and bravely rigg'd as when | we first put out to 5.01.224
till when, be cheerful | and think of each thing 5.01.250
even as i would, when i to love begin. TGV 1.01. 10
think on thy proteus, when thou, happ'ly, seest 1.01. 12
in thy happiness | when thou dost meet good hap; 1.01. 15
when willingly i would have had her here! 1.02. 61
when inward joy enforc'd my heart to smile! 1.02. 63
you were wont, when you laugh'd, to crow like a 2.01. 26 P
when you walk'd, to walk like one of the lions; 2.01. 27 P
when you fasted, it was presently after dinner; 2.01. 28 P
when you look'd sadly, it was for want of money: 2.01. 29 P
that, when i look on you, i can hardly think you 2.01. 31 P
were wont to have when you chid at sir proteus 2.01. 72 P
and when it's writ, for my sake read it over, 2.01.130
she, when she hath made you write to yourself? 2.01.152 P
when possibly i can, i will return. 2.02. 3
and when that hour o'erslips me in the day 2.02. 9
when you have done, we look to hear from you. 2.04.120
when i was sick, you gave me bitter pills, | and 2.04.149
but when i look on her perfections, | there is 2.04.211
when it stands well with him, it stands well 2.05. 22 P
and when the flight is made to one so dear, | of 2.07. 12
but when his fair course is not hindered, | he 2.07. 27
if proteus like your journey when you come, | no 2.07. 65
no matter who's displeas'd when you are gone: 2.07. 66
pray heav'n he prove so when you come to him! 2.07. 79
but when i call to mind your gracious favors 3.01. 6
haply when they have judg'd me fast asleep, 3.01. 25
when would you use it? pray, sir, tell me that. 3.01.123
him so, | when she for thy repeal was suppliant, 3.01.236
with a wench, when she can knit him a stock? 3.01.310 P
on wheels, when she can spin for her living. 3.01.316 P
she did, my lord, when valentine was here. 3.02. 27
when i protest true loyalty to her, | she twits 4.02. 7
when to her beauty i commend my vows, | she bids 4.02. 9
not a whit, when it jars so. 4.02. 67 P
heart | as when thy lady and thy true-love died, 4.03. 20
when will you go? 4.03. 42
when a man's servant shall play the cur with him 4.04. 1 P
when three or four of his blind brothers and 4.04. 3 P
'tis a foul thing when a cur cannot keep himself 4.04. 10 P
serv'd me, when i took my leave of madam silvia. 4.04. 35 P
when didst thou see me heave up my leg and make 4.04. 37 P
this ring i gave him when he parted from me, 4.04. 97
when she did think my master lov'd her well, 4.04.150
when all our pageants of delight were play'd, 4.04.159
ill, when you talk of war. 5.02. 16
but well, when i discourse of love and peace. 5.02. 17
but better indeed, when you hold /your peace. 5.02. 18
she needs not, when she knows it cowardice. 5.02. 21
that flies her fortune when it follows her. 5.02. 50
and me, when he approacheth to your presence. 5.04. 32
when women cannot love where they're belov'd! 5.04. 44
when proteus cannot love where he's belov'd! 5.04. 45
when one's right hand | is perjured to the bosom 5.04. 67
when she is able to overtake seventeen years old WIV 1.01. 53 P
remember what i did when you made me drunk, yet 1.01.171 P
when we are married and have more occasion to 1.01.248 P
tester i'll have in pouch when thou shalt lack, 1.03. 87
puts into the press, when he would put us two. 2.01. 78 P
or money in his purse, when he looks so merrily. 2.01.191 P
and when mistress bridget lost the handle of her 2.02. 12 P
of them all (when the court lay at windsor) 2.02. 61 P
pay all, go to bed when she list, rise when she 2.02.119 P
go to bed when she list, rise when she list, all 2.02.119 P
like a shadow flies when substance love pursues, 2.02.207
when i have told you that, i have told you all. 2.02.220 P
about his knave's costard when i have good 3.01. 14 P
sing madrigals — | when as i sat in pabylon — 3.01. 24
in the brew-house, and when i suddenly call you, 3.03. 11 P
be gone, and come when you are call'd. 3.03. 19 P
a taking was he in when your husband ask'd who 3.03.180 P
should i have been when i had been swell'd! 3.05. 17 P
(when i was more than half stew'd in grease, 3.05.118 P
i like not when a woman has a great peard. 4.02.193 P
upon no trail, never trust me when i open again. 4.02.197 P
devise but how you'll use him when he comes, 4.04. 26
and in this shape when you have brought him 4.04. 45
when slender sees his time | to take her by the 4.06. 36
and when the doctor spies his vantage ripe, | to 4.06. 43
when you see your time, take her by the hand, 5.03. 2 P
me into the pit, and when i give the watch-ords, 5.04. 3 P
when gods have hot backs, what shall poor men do 5.05. 11 P
a jack-a-lent, when 'tis upon ill employment! 5.05.127 P
when need you tell me that? 5.05.190 P
i think so, when i took a boy for a girl. 5.05.190 P
when night-dogs run, all sorts of deer are 5.05.238
a thirsty evil, and when we drink we die. MM 1.02.130
when she will play with reason and discourse, 1.02.185
unloose this tied-up justice when you pleas'd: 1.03. 32
when evil deeds have their permissive pass, 1.03. 38
when you have vow'd, you must not speak with men 1.04. 10
and let him learn to know, when maidens sue, 1.04. 80
but when they weep and kneel, | all their 1.04. 81
when i, that censure him, do so offend, | let 2.01. 29
night in russia | when nights are longest there. 2.01.135
correction, i have seen | when, after execution, 2.02. 11
i show it most of all when i show justice; 2.02.100
have authority | when judges steal themselves. 2.02.176
when men were fond, i smil'd and wond'red how. 2.02.186
when must he die? 2.03. 16
when i would pray and think, i think and pray 2.04. 1
when, i beseech you? 2.04. 39
to appear most bright | when it doth tax itself; 2.04. 79
and when thou art old and rich, | thou hast 3.01. 36
finds a pang as great | as when a giant dies. 3.01. 80
the law by th' nose, | when he would force it? 3.01.109
it is certain that when he makes water his urine 3.02.110 P
have you to say | when you depart from him, but, 4.01. 68
when it lies starkly in the traveller's bones. 4.02. 67
seldom when | the steeled jailer is the friend 4.02. 86
celerity, | when it is borne in high authority. 4.02.111
when vice makes mercy, mercy's so extended, 4.02.112
difficulties are but easy when they are known. 4.02.205 P
of despair, | when it is least expected. 4.03.111
alack, when once our grace we have forgot, 4.04. 33
when it deserves, with characters of brass, | a 5.01. 11
and when you have | a business for yourself, 5.01. 80
a time | when i'll depose i had him in mine arms 5.01.198
when i perceive your grace, like pow'r divine, 5.01.369
who should have died when claudio lost his head 5.01.488
yet this my comfort, when your words are done, ERR 1.01. 26
oft, | when i am dull with care and melancholy, 1.02. 20
that stands on tricks when i am undispos'd: 1.02. 80
time is their master, and when they see time, 2.01. 8
look when i serve him so, he takes it /ill. 2.01. 12
we bid be quiet when we hear it cry; 2.01. 35
when i desir'd him to come home to dinner, | he 2.01. 60
what answer, sir? when spake i such a word? 2.02. 13
when the sun shines, let foolish gnats make 2.02. 30
but creep in crannies, when he hides his beams: 2.02. 31
when in the why and the wherefore is neither 2.02. 48
when thou unurg'd wouldst vow | that never words 2.02.113
when were you wont to use my sister thus? 2.02.153
my wife is shrewish when i keep not hours: 3.01. 2
for such store, | when one is one too many? 3.01. 35
sir, i'll tell you when, and you'll tell me 3.01. 39
here you must not, come again when you may. 3.01. 41
have at you with another, that's — when? 3.01. 52
ay, when fowls have no feathers, and fish have 3.01. 79
and dwell upon your grave when you are dead; 3.01.104
when the sweet breath of flattery conquers 3.02. 28
gaze when you should, and that will clear your 3.02. 57
when in the streets he meets such golden gifts. 3.02.183
no evil lost is wail'd when it is gone. 4.02. 24
that, when gentlemen are tir'd, gives them a sob 4.03. 25 P
when i am cold, he heats me with beating; 4.04. 32 P
when i am warm, he cools me with beating. 4.04. 33 P
i am wak'd with it when i sleep, rais'd with it 4.04. 34 P
with it when i sleep, rais'd with it when i sit, 4.04. 35 P
driven out of doors with it when i go from home, 4.04. 36 P
from home, welcom'd home with it when i return; 4.04. 36 P
i think, when he hath lam'd me, i shall beg with 4.04. 38 P
when as your husband all in rage to-day | came 4.04.137
when he demean'd himself rough, rude, and wildly 5.01. 88
when thou didst make him master of thy bed, | to 5.01.163
when i bestrid thee in the wars, and took | deep 5.01.192
he had, my lord, and when he ran in here, 5.01.258
he was not three leagues off when i left him. ADO 1.01. 4 P
is twice itself when the achiever brings home 1.01. 8 P
but when you depart from me, sorrow abides and 1.01.101 P
when you went onward on this ended action, | i 1.01.297
and when i have heard it, what blessing brings 1.03. 6 P
i must be sad when i have cause, and smile at no 1.03. 13 P
eat when i have stomach, and wait for no man's 1.03. 15 P
sleep when i am drowsy, and tend on no man's 1.03. 16 P
laugh when i am merry, and claw no man in his 1.03. 17 P
for the walk, and especially when i walk away. 2.01. 90 P
i may say so when i please. 2.01. 92 P
and when please you to say so? 2.01. 93 P
when i like your favor, for god defend the lute 2.01. 94 P
keep him out of my sight when the dance is done! 2.01.109 P

when i know the gentleman, i'll tell him what 2.01.144 P
she is never sad but when she sleeps, and not 2.01.343 P
county claudio, when mean you to go to church? 2.01.355 P
much another man is a fool when he dedicates his 2.03. 8 P
i have known when there was no music with him 2.03. 12 P
i have known when he would have walk'd ten mile 2.03. 15 P
well, a horn for my money, when all's done. 2.03. 61 P
this says she now when she is beginning to write 2.03.130 P
o, when she had writ it, and was reading it over 2.03.136 P
be, when they hold one an opinion of another's 2.03.215 P
when i said i would die a bachelor, i did not 2.03.242 P
now, ursula, when beatrice doth come, | as we do 3.01. 15
when i do name him, let it be thy part | to 3.01. 18
when are you married, madam? 3.01.100
and when was he wont to wash his face? 3.02. 56 P
bears will not bite one another when they meet. 3.02. 78 P
i know not that, when he knows what i know. 3.02. 91 P
show you enough, and when you have seen more, 3.02.121 P
so will you say when you have seen the sequel. 3.02.134 P
let that appear when there is no need of such 3.03. 21 P
if he will not stand when he is bidden, he is 3.03. 31 P
not hear her lamb when it baes will never answer 3.03. 71 P
it baes will never answer a calf when he bleats. 3.03. 72 P
for when rich villains have need of poor ones, 3.03.113 P
as they say, "when the age is in, the wit is out 3.05. 34 P
when he shall hear she died upon his words, 4.01.223
of his soul, | than when she liv'd indeed. 4.01.230
when he should groan, | patch grief with 5.01. 16
to be so moral when he shall endure | the like 5.01. 30
you dare, with what you dare, and when you dare. 5.01.147 P
god saw him when he was hid in the garden. 5.01.180 P
but when shall we set the savage bull's horns on 5.01.181 P
what a pretty thing man is when he goes in his 5.01.199 P
how you disgrac'd her when you should marry her. 5.01.239 P
to specify, when time and place shall serve, 5.01.256 P
that when i note another man like him | i may 5.01.260
nor knew not what she did when she spoke to me, 5.01.301
beatrice, wouldst thou come when i call'd thee? 5.02. 42 P
yea, signior, and depart when you bid me. 5.02. 44 P
upon the tomb, | praising her when i am /dumb. 5.03. 10
and when i send for you, come hither masked. 5.04. 12
when he would play the noble beast in love. 5.04. 47
and when i liv'd, i was your other wife, | and 5.04. 60
and when you lov'd, you were my other husband. 5.04. 61
when after that the holy rites are ended, | i'll 5.04. 68
when, spite of cormorant devouring time, | th' LLL 1.01. 4
when i was wont to think no harm all night, 1.01. 44
dine, | when i to /feast expressly am forbid; 1.01. 62
when mistresses from common sense are hid; 1.01. 64
the spring is near when green geese are 1.01. 97
and when it hath the thing it hunteth most, 1.01.145
the time when? 1.01.235 P
when beasts most graze, birds best peck, and men 1.01.236 P
so much for the time when. 1.01.238 P
what sign is it when a man of great spirit grows 1.02. 1 P
sir, i hope when i do it i shall do it on a full 1.02.148 P
when she did starve the general world beside 2.01. 11
when would you have it done, sir? 3.01.154 P
i shall know, sir, when i have done it. 3.01.158 P
when tongues speak sweetly, then they name her 3.01.166
when, for fame's sake, for praise, an outward 4.01. 32
when they strive to be | lords o'er their lords? 4.01. 37
that was a man when king pippen of france was a 4.01.120 P
that was a woman when queen guinover of britain 4.01.123 P
when it comes so smoothly off, so obscenely as 4.01.143
the moon was a month old when adam was no more. 4.02. 39
not to five weeks when he came to fivescore. 4.02. 40
when their fresh rays have smote | the night of 4.03. 27
what will berowne say when that he shall hear 4.03.143
when shall you see me write a thing in rhyme, 4.03.179
when shall you hear that i | will praise a hand, 4.03.181
for when would you, my lord, or you, or you, 4.03.295
then when ourselves we see in ladies' eyes, 4.03.312
for when would you, my liege, or you, or you, 4.03.317
when the suspicious head of theft is stopp'd. 4.03.333
and when love speaks, the voice of all the gods 4.03.341
speak "dout," fine, when he should say "doubt"; 5.01. 20 P
"det," when he should pronounce "debt" — 5.01. 21 P
are so surely caught, when they are catch'd, 5.02. 69
as fool'ry in the wise, when wit doth dote, 5.02. 76
when lo, to interrupt my purpos'd rest, | toward 5.02. 91
therefore change favors, and, when they repair, 5.02.292
and utters it again when god doth please. 5.02.316
that, when he plays at tables, chides the dice 5.02.326
when they are thirsty, fools would fain have 5.02.372
when we greet, | with eyes best seeing, heaven's 5.02.374
where? when? what vizard? why demand you this? 5.02.386
when you then were here, | what did you whisper 5.02.435
when she shall challenge this, you will reject 5.02.438
despise me when i break this oath of mine. 5.02.441
to make my lady laugh when she's dispos'd, 5.02.466
die when you will, a smock shall be your shroud. 5.02.479
when great things laboring perish in their birth 5.02.520
"when in the world i liv'd, i was the world'i 5.02.562
"when in the world i liv'd, i was the world's 5.02.568
and when he was a babe, a child, a shrimp, 5.02.590
when he breathed, he was a man. 5.02.662 P
since when, i'll be sworn, he wore none but a 5.02.713 P
come when the king doth to my lady come; 5.02.829
when daisies pied and violets blue | and 5.02.894
when shepherds pipe on oaten straws | and merry 5.02.903
when turtles tread, and rooks and daws, | and 5.02.905
when icicles hang by the wall | and dick the 5.02.912
when blood is nipp'd and ways be /foul, | then 5.02.916
when all aloud the wind doth blow | and coughing 5.02.921
when roasted crabs hiss in the bowl, | then 5.02.925
when the false troyan under sail was seen, | by MND 1.01.174
lark to shepherd's ear | when wheat is green, 1.01.185
when wheat is green, when hawthorn buds appear. 1.01.185
when phoebe doth behold | her silver visage in 1.01.209
and when this hail some heat from hermia felt, 1.01.244
smile | when i a fat and bean–fed horse beguile, 2.01. 45
and when she drinks, against her lips i bob, 2.01. 49
when thou hast stolen away from fairy land, 2.01. 65
when we have laugh'd to see the sails conceive 2.01.128
juice, | i'll watch titania when she is asleep, 2.01.177
spirit, | for i am sick when i do look on thee. 2.01.212
and i am sick when i look not on you. 2.01.213
that | it is not night when i do see your face, 2.01.221
when all the world is here to look on me? 2.01.226
run when you will; 2.01.230
speed, | when cowardice pursues and valor flies. 2.01.234
but do it when the next thing he espies | may be 2.01.262
what thou seest when thou dost wake, | do it for 2.02. 27
in thy eye that shall appear | when thou wak'st, 2.02. 33
wake when some vile thing is near. 2.02. 34
say i — | and then end life when i end loyalty! 2.02. 63
when thou wak'st, let love forbid | sleep his 2.02. 80
so awake when i am gone, | for i must now to 2.02. 82
when at your hands did i deserve this scorn? 2.02.124
we must leave the killing out, when all is done. 3.01. 14 P
when you have spoken your speech, enter into 3.01. 74 P
and when she weeps, weeps every little flower, 3.01.199
when i did him at this advantage take, | an 3.02. 16
when they him spy, | as wild geese that the 3.02. 19
when in that moment (so it came to pass) 3.02. 33
that, when he wak'd, of force she must be ey'd. 3.02. 40
when his love he doth espy, | let her shine as 3.02.105
when thou wak'st, if she be by, | beg of her for 3.02.108
look when i vow, i weep; 3.02.124
when truth kills truth, o devilish–holy fray! 3.02.129
i had no judgment when to her i swore. 3.02.134
turns to a crow | when thou hold'st up thy hand. 3.02.143
when i am sure you hate me with your hearts. 3.02.154
when we have chid the hasty–footed time | for 3.02.200
make mouths upon me when i turn my back, | wink 3.02.238
o, when she is angry, she is keen and shrewd! 3.02.323
she was a vixen when she went to school; 3.02.324
when they next wake, all this derision | shall 3.02.370
when i come where he calls, then he is gone. 3.02.414
when thou wak'st, | thou tak'st | true delight 3.02.453
when i had at my pleasure taunted her, | and she 4.01. 57
swain, | that he awaking when the other do, 4.01. 66
now, when thou wak'st, with thine own fool's 4.01. 84
when in a wood of crete they bay'd the bear 4.01.113
judge when you hear. 4.01.127
parted eye, | when every thing seems double. 4.01.190
when my cue comes, call me, and i will answer. 4.01.200 P
when i from thebes came last a conqueror. 5.01. 51
which, when i saw rehears'd, i must confess, 5.01. 68
be amiss, | when simpleness and duty tender it. 5.01. 83
one lion may, when many asses do. 5.01.153 P
o night, which ever art when day is not! 5.01.171
lord, when walls are so willful to hear without 5.01.208 P
when lion rough in wildest rage doth roar. 5.01.222
for when the players are all dead, there need 5.01.356 P
would blow me to an ague when i thought | what MV 1.01. 23
good signiors both, when shall we laugh? 1.01. 66
say, when? 1.01. 66
sleep when he wakes? 1.01. 85
and when i ope my lips let no dog bark!" 1.01. 94
when, i am very sure, | if they should speak, 1.01. 97
day ere you find them, and when you have them, 1.01.117 P
in my school–days, when i had lost one shaft, 1.01.140
prove the weeping philosopher when he grows old, 1.02. 49 P
swore he would pay him again when he was able. 1.02. 81 P
very vildly in the morning, when he is sober, 1.02. 86 P
most vildly in the afternoon, when he is drunk. 1.02. 87 P
when he is best, he is a little worse than a man 1.02. 88 P
a little worse than a man, and when he is worst, 1.02. 89 P
when jacob graz'd his uncle laban's sheep — 1.03. 71
when laban and himself were compremis'd | that 1.03. 78
when the work of generation was | between these 1.03. 82
for when did friendship take | a breed for 1.03.133
yea, mock the lion when 'a roars for prey, | to 2.01. 30
than i have of my face when i /last saw him. 2.02. 98 P
doors, and when you hear the drum | and the vile 2.05. 29
when you shall please to play the thieves for 2.06. 23
i thought upon antonio when he told me, | and 2.08. 31
when they do choose, | they have the wisdom by 2.09. 80
turkis, i had it of leah when i was a bachelor. 3.01.121 P
when my torturer | doth teach me answers for 3.02. 37
even as the flourish when true subjects bow | to 3.02. 49
when he did redeem | the virgin tribute paid by 3.02. 55
which when you part from, lose, or give away, 3.02.172
but when this ring | parts from this finger, 3.02.183
and when your honors mean to solemnize | the 3.02.192
lady, | when i did first impart my love to you, 3.02.253
when i told you | my state was nothing, i should 3.02.258
when i was with him i have heard him swear | to 3.02.284
when it is paid, bring your true friend along. 3.02.308
when we are both accoutered like young men, 3.04. 63
all my whole device | when i am in my coach, 3.04. 82
thus when i shun scylla, your father, i fall 3.05. 16 P
and others, when the bagpipe sings i' th' nose, 4.01. 49
when they are fretten with the gusts of heaven; 4.01. 77
show likest god's | when mercy seasons justice. 4.01.197
when it is paid according to the tenure. 4.01.235
and, when the tale is told, bid her be judge 4.01.276
you take my house when you do take the prop 4.01.375
when you do take the means whereby i live. 4.01.377
i pray you know me when we meet again; 4.01.419
and when she put it on, she made me vow | that i 4.01.442
when the sweet wind did gently kiss the trees 5.01. 2
i am never merry when i hear sweet music. 5.01. 69
when the moon shone, we did not see the candle. 5.01. 92
sweetly as the lark | when neither is attended; 5.01.103
when every goose is cackling, would be thought 5.01.105
a day, | such as the day is when the sun is hid. 5.01.126
you swore to me, when i did give /it you, | that 5.01.152
when nought would be accepted but the ring, 5.01.197
when i am absent, then lie with my wife. 5.01.285
beg, when that is spent? AYL 1.01. 75 P
and truly, when he dies, thou shalt be his heir; 1.02. 18 P
i will, and when i break that oath, let me turn 1.02. 21 P
when nature hath made a fair creature, may she 1.02. 43 P
nature, when fortune makes nature's natural the 1.02. 49 P
be better supplied when i have made it empty. 1.02.192 P
when the one should be lam'd with reasons and 1.03. 7 P
so was i when your highness took his dukedom, 1.03. 59
so was i when your highness banish'd him. 1.03. 60
and seem more virtuous | when she is gone. 1.03. 82
what shall i call thee when thou art a man? 1.03.123
which when it bites and blows upon my body 2.01. 8
when what is comely | envenoms him that bears it 2.03. 14
when service should in my old limbs lie lame, 2.03. 41
when service sweat for duty, not for meed! 2.03. 58
when i was at home, i was in a better place, but 2.04. 17 P
when i was in love i broke my sword upon a stone 2.04. 46 P
and when a man thanks me heartily, methinks i 2.05. 27 P
when i did hear | the motley fool thus moral on 2.07. 28
when that i say the city–woman bears | the cost 2.07. 75
when such a one as she, such is her neighbor? 2.07. 78
what did he when thou saw'st him? 3.02.220 P
and when shalt thou see him again? 3.02.223 P
call'd jove's tree, when it drops /such fruit. 3.02.236 P
when i think, i must speak. 3.02.249 P
thought of pleasing you when she was christen'd. 3.02.266 P
i was seeking for a fool when i found you. 3.02.285 P
when a man's verses cannot be understood, nor a 3.03. 12 P
yes, when he is in — but i think he is not in. 3.04. 27 P
of fathers, when there is such a man as orlando? 3.04. 38 P
and when that time comes, | afflict me with thy 3.05. 32
sell when you can, you are not for all markets. 3.05. 60
when he that speaks them pleases those that hear 3.05.112
and when you were gravell'd for lack of matter, 4.01. 73 P
very good orators, when they are out, they will 4.01. 75 P
ay, but when? 4.01.133 P
orlando, men are april when they woo, december 4.01.147 P
are april when they woo, december when they wed; 4.01.148 P
maids are may when they are maids, but the sky 4.01.148 P
maids, but the sky changes when they are wives. 4.01.149 P
and i will do that when you are dispos'd to be 4.01.155 P
hyen, and that when thou art inclin'd to sleep. 4.01.156 P
when last the young orlando parted from you | he 4.03. 98
watch, | when that the sleeping man should stir; 4.03.116
when from the first to last betwixt us two 4.03.139
many will swoon when they do look on blood. 4.03.158
when he had a desire to eat a grape, would open 5.01. 33 P
would open his lips when he put it into his 5.01. 34 P
to sound when he show'd me your handkercher? 5.02. 26 P
cries it out, when your brother marries aliena, 5.02. 63 P
when birds do sing, hey ding a ding, ding, 5.03. 20
and you say you will have her, when i bring her. 5.04. 9
i knew when seven justices could not take up a 5.04. 98 P
but when the parties were met themselves, one of 5.04. 99 P
when earthly things made even | atone together. 5.04.109
for my kind offer, when i make curtsy, bid me ep 22 P
and brave attendants near him when he wakes, SHR in.1. 40
it would seem strange unto him when he wak'd. in.1. 43
procure me music ready when he wakes, | to make in.1. 50
and when he says he is, say that he dreams, in.1. 64
him, | and each one to his office when he wakes. in.1. 73
when they do homage to this simple peasant. in.1. 135
or when you wak'd, so wak'd as if you slept. in.2. 80
when with his knees he kiss'd the cretan strond. 1.01.170
when biondello comes, he waits on thee, | but i 1.01.208
when i am alone, why then i am tranio; 1.01.243
now, knock when i bid you, sirrah villain! 1.02. 19
as thunder when the clouds in autumn crack. 1.02. 96
when did she cross thee with a bitter word? 2.01. 28
ay, when the special thing is well obtain'd, 2.01.128
when, with a most impatient devilish spirit, 2.01.151
and woo her with some spirit when she comes. 2.01.169
i'll crave the day | when i shall ask the banes, 2.01.180
when i shall ask the banes, and when be married. 2.01.180
it is my fashion when i see a crab. 2.01.229
to see | how tame, when men and women are alone, 2.01.312
and when in music we have spent an hour, | your 3.01. 7
you'll leave his lecture when i am in tune? 3.01. 24
to want the bridegroom when the priest attends 3.02. 5
when will be be here? 3.02. 39 P
when he stands where i am and sees you there. 3.02. 40 P
when i should bid good morrow to my bride | and 3.02.122
when the priest | should ask if katherine should 3.02.158
what said the wench when he rose again? 3.02.166
of you all shall find when he comes home. 4.01. 88 P
why, when, i say? 4.01.143
you villains, when? 4.01.144
when you are gentle, you shall have one too, 4.03. 71
but sun it is not, when you say it is not; 4.05. 19
and time it is, when raging war is /done, | to 5.02. 2
to come at first when he doth send for her, 5.02. 68
and when she is froward, peevish, sullen, sour, 5.02.157
when they are bound to serve, love, and obey. 5.02.164
'tis a good hearing when children are toward. 5.02.182
but a harsh hearing when women are froward. 5.02.183
that they take place when virtue's steely bones AWW 1.01.103
when he was predominant. 1.01.197 P
when he was retrograde, i think rather. 1.01.198 P
why you go so much backward when you fight. 1.01.200 P
is running away, when fear proposes the safety. 1.01.202 P
when thou hast leisure, say thy prayers; 1.01.212 P
when thou hast none, remember thy friends. 1.01.213 P
our slow designs when we ourselves are dull. 1.01.219
as when thy father and myself in friendship 1.02. 25
knew the true minute when | exception bid him 1.02. 39
when it was out — "let me not live," quoth he, 1.02. 58
deservings, when of ourselves we publish them. 1.03. 6 P
even so it was with me when i was young. 1.03.128
when i said "a mother," | methought you saw a 1.03.140
a poor unlearned virgin, when the schools, 1.03.240
to wed it, when | the bravest questant shrinks. 2.01. 15
when our most learned doctors leave us, and 2.01.116
a senseless help when help past sense we deem. 2.01.124
judgment shown, | when judges have been babes; 2.01.139
when miracles have by the great'st been denied. 2.01.141
but most it is presumption in us when | the help 2.01.151
when you put off that with such contempt? 2.02. 6 P
when we should submit ourselves to an unknown 2.03. 5 P
and virtuous mistress | fall, when love please! 2.03. 58
when rather from our acts we them derive | than 2.03.136
when i consider | what great creation and what 2.03.168
when i lose thee again, i care not; 2.03.206 P
when i should take possession of the bride, 2.05. 26
when better fall, for your avails they fell. 3.01. 22
see what he writes, and when he means to come. 3.02. 10 P
"when thou canst get the ring upon my finger, 3.02. 57 P
i will entreat you, when you see my son, | to 3.02. 92
i met the ravin lion when he roar'd | with sharp 3.02.117
when haply he shall hear that she is gone, | he 3.04. 35
adversaries, when we bring him to our own tents. 3.06. 27 P
when your lordship sees the bottom of /his 3.06. 35 P
deal of discoveries, but when you find him out, 3.06. 93 P

when his disguise and he is parted, tell me what 3.06.104 P
over–pay and pay again | when i have found it. 3.07. 17
when you sally upon him, speak what terrible 4.01. 2 P
when you are dead, you should be such a one | as 4.02. 7
your mother was | when your sweet self was got. 4.02. 10
but when you have our roses, | you barely leave 4.02. 18
you believe my oaths | when i did love you ill? 4.02. 27
when midnight comes, knock at my chamber–window; 4.02. 54
when you have conquer'd my yet maiden bed, 4.02. 57
when back again this ring shall be deliver'd; 4.02. 60
he had sworn to marry me | when his wife's dead; 4.02. 72
therefore i'll lie with him | when i am buried. 4.02. 73
when you have spoken it, 'tis dead, and i am the 4.03. 12 P
"when he swears oaths, bid him drop gold, and 4.03.223
who pays before, but not when he does owe it. 4.03.230
when saucy trusting of the cozen'd thoughts 4.04. 23
when briers shall have leaves as well as thorns, 4.04. 32
of as able body as when he number'd thirty. 4.05. 81 P
you, when i have held familiarity with fresher 5.02. 3 P
when oil and fire, too strong for reason's force 5.03. 7
this ring was mine, and, when i gave it helen, 5.03. 83
but when i had subscrib'd | to mine own fortune, 5.03. 96
to marry me when his wife was dead, i blush to 5.03.140 P
o my good lord, when i was like this maid, | i 5.03.309
"when from my finger you can get this ring | and 5.03.312
o, when mine eyes did see olivia first, TN 1.01. 18
how will she love when the rich golden shaft 1.01. 34
when liver, brain, and heart, | these sovereign 1.01. 36
lie rich when canopied with bow'rs. 1.01. 40
when you, and those poor number saved with you, 1.02. 10
when my tongue blabs, then let mine eyes not see 1.02. 63
when did i see thee so put down? 1.03. 81 P
for i myself am best | when least in company. 1.04. 38
peascod, or a codling when 'tis almost an apple. 1.05.158 P
deliver, when the courtesy of it is so fearful. 1.05.207 P
last night, when thou spok'st of pigrogromitus, 2.03. 23 P
why, this is the best fooling, when all is done. 2.03. 30 P
good a deed as to drink when a man's a–hungry, 2.03.126 P
to die, even when they to perfection grow! 2.04. 41
that when the image of it leaves him he must run 2.05.194 P
and yet, when wit and youth is come to harvest, 3.01.132
and when she went away now, "let this fellow be 3.04. 75 P
yet, when i saw it last, it was besmear'd | as 5.01. 52
when your young nephew titus lost his leg. 5.01. 63
town, | drew to defend him when he was beset; 5.01. 85
when came he to this town? 5.01. 93
since when, my watch hath told me, toward my 5.01.162
be | when time hath sow'd a grizzle on thy case? 5.01.165
and died that day when viola from her birth 5.01.244
so it skills not much when they are deliver'd. 5.01.288 P
to be well edified when the fool delivers the 5.01.290 P
but when we know the grounds and authors of it, 5.01.353
when that is known and golden time convents, | a 5.01.382
but when in other habits you are seen, 5.01.387
when that i was and a little tine boy, | with 5.01.389
but when i came to man's estate, | with hey ho, 5.01.393
but when i came, alas, to wive, | with hey ho, 5.01.397
but when i came unto my beds, | with hey ho, etc 5.01.401
thanks a while, | and pay them when you part. WT 1.02. 10
when at bohemia | you take my lord, i'll give 1.02. 39
so you shall pay your fees | when you depart, 1.02. 54
my lord's tricks and yours when you were boys. 1.02. 61
when was't before? 1.02. 90
when? 1.02.100
that was when | three crabbed months had sour'd 1.02.101
hold, | when you cast out, it still came home. 1.02.214
'tis far gone, | when i shall gust it last. 1.02.219
provided that, when he's remov'd, your highness 1.02.335
i met him | with customary compliment, when he, 1.02.371
when you have said she's goodly, come between 2.01. 75
when you shall come to clearer knowledge, that 2.01. 97
when you shall know your mistress | has deserv'd 2.01.119
than when i feel and see her no farther trust 2.01.136
pure innocence | persuades when speaking fails. 2.02. 40
when she will take the rein i let her run, | but 2.03. 51
when the oracle | (thus by apollo's great divine 3.01. 18
last — o lords, | when i have said, cry "woe!" 3.02.200
faults i make, when i shall come to know them, 3.02.219
thou didst speak but well | when most the truth; 3.02.233
a thing to talk on when thou art dead and rotten 3.03. 81 P
name of mercy, when was this, boy? 3.03.103 P
they are never curst but when they are hungry. 3.03.131 P
time's news | be known when 'tis brought forth. 4.01. 27
say to me, when saw'st thou the prince florizel, 4.02. 25 P
are in losing them when they have approv'd their 4.02. 28 P
when daffadils begin to peer, | with heigh, the 4.03. 1
and when i wander here and there, | i then do 4.03. 17
when the kite builds, look to lesser linen. 4.03. 23 P
when my good falcon made her flight across | thy 4.04. 15
your resolution cannot hold when 'tis | oppos'd 4.04. 36
daughter, when my old wife liv'd, upon | this 4.04. 55
when you speak, sweet, | i'ld have you do it 4.04.136
when you sing, | i'ld have you buy and sell so; 4.04.137
when you do dance, i wish you | a wave o' th' 4.04.140
when you are going to bed? 4.04.244 P
sooth, when i was young, | and handed love as 4.04.347
this hour, i have liv'd | to die when i desire. 4.04.462
when he shall miss me (as, in faith, i mean not 4.04.494
much as this old man does when the business is 4.04.821 P
shall be when your first queen's again in breath 5.01. 83
the other, when she has obtain'd your eye, 5.01.105
know'st | he dies to me again when talk'd of. 5.01.120
sure | when i shall see this gentleman, thy 5.01.121
she is, | when once she is my wife. 5.01.209
the child were even then lost when it was found. 5.02. 72 P
was when, at the relation of the queen's death 5.02. 84 P
now it coldly stands), when first i woo'd her! 5.03. 36
lady, | dear queen, that ended when i but began, 5.03. 45
when she was young, you woo'd her; 5.03.108
my gracious liege, when that my father liv'd, JN 1.01. 95
when this same lusty gentleman was got. 1.01.108
be the hour by night or day | when i was got, 1.01.166
and when my knightly stomach is suffic'd, | why 1.01.191
but say thou didst not well | when i was got, 1.01.272
and they shall say, when richard me begot, | if 1.01.274
when living blood doth in these temples beat, 2.01.108
when i have said, make answer to us both. 2.01.235
that did display them when we first march'd 2.01.320
when the rich blood of kings is set on fire! 2.01.351
the king of england, when we know the king. 2.01.363
and when that we have dash'd them to the ground, 2.01.405
o, two such silver currents when they join | do 2.01.441
that i did so when i was first assur'd. 2.01.535
when his fair angels would salute my palm, | but 2.01.590
fight | but when her humorous ladyship is by 3.01.119
when law can do no right, | let it be lawful 3.01.185
do amiss | is not amiss when it is truly done; 3.01.271
when such profound respects do pull you on. 3.01.318
when gold and silver becks me to come on. 3.03. 13
what can go well, when we have run so ill? 3.04. 5
when i shall meet him in the court of heaven | i 3.04. 87
my head | when there is such disorder in my wit. 3.04.102
when fortune means to men most good, | she looks 3.04.119
o sir, when he shall hear of your approach, | if 3.04.162
when i strike my foot | upon the bosom of the 4.01. 2
yet i remember, when i was in france, | young 4.01. 14
when your head did but ache, | i knit my 4.01. 41
when workmen strive to do better than well, 4.02. 28
and when it breaks, i fear will issue thence 4.02. 80
for when you should be told they do prepare, 4.02.114
when adverse foreigners affright my towns | with 4.02.172
and when they talk of him, they shake their 4.02.188
when perchance it frowns | more upon humor than 4.02.213
o, when the last accompt 'twixt heaven and earth 4.02.216
a pause | when i spake darkly what i purposed, 4.02.232
or, when he doom'd this beauty to a grave, 4.03. 39
of war | when he intendeth to become the field. 5.01. 55
when we were happy we had other names. 5.04. 8
when english measure backward their own ground 5.05. 3
off, | when with a volley of our needless shot, 5.05. 5
he is more patient | than when you left him; 5.07. 12
when this was now a king, and now is clay? 5.07. 69
he will the rather do it when he sees 5.07. 87
but when it first did help to wound itself. 5.07.114
and when i mount, alive may i not light, | if i R2 1.01. 82
when, harry? 1.01.162
when? 1.01.162
who, when they see the hour's ripe on earth, 1.02. 7
for sorrow ends not when it seemeth done. 1.02. 61
i look'd when some of you should say | i was too 1.03.243
when the tongue's office should be prodigal | to 1.03.256
my heart will sigh when i miscall it so, | which 1.03.263
doth never rankle more | than when he bites, but 1.03.303
what said our cousin when you parted with him? 1.04. 10
when time shall call him home from banishment, 1.04. 21
whereto, when they shall know what men are rich, 1.04. 49
but when he frowned it was against the french, 2.01.178
you promis'd, when you parted with the king, 2.02. 2
was not so resolv'd when last we spake together. 2.03. 29
lord of such hot youth | as when brave gaunt, 2.03.100
and when they from thy bosom pluck a flower, 3.02. 19
that when the searching eye of heaven is hid 3.02. 37
but when from under this terrestrial ball | he 3.02. 41
so when this thief, this traitor bullingbrook, 3.02. 47
when such a sacred king should hide his head! 3.03. 9
when their thund'ring shock | at meeting tears 3.03. 56
when he perceives the envious clouds are bent 3.03. 65
when my poor heart no measure keeps in grief; 3.04. 8
when our sea–walled garden, the whole land, | is 3.04. 43
say, where, when, and how, | /cam'st thou by 3.04. 79
in that dead time when gloucester's death was 4.01. 10
when he is return'd, | against aumerle we will 4.01. 89
when triumph is become an alehouse guest? 5.01. 15
when weeping made you break the story off, | of 5.02. 2
mine honor lives when his dishonor dies, | or my 5.03. 70
penury | persuades me i was better when a king; 5.05. 35
how sour sweet music is | when time is broke, 5.05. 43
of thy stable, king, | when thou wert king; 5.05. 73
how it ern'd my heart when i beheld | in london 5.05. 76
when bullingbrook rode on roan barbary, | that 5.05. 78
when all athwart there came | a post from wales 1H4 1.01. 36
i prithee, sweet wag, when thou art a king, as, 1.02. 16 P
sweet wag, when thou art king, let not us that 1.02. 23 P
gallows standing in england when thou art king? 1.02. 60 P
do not thou, when thou art king, hang a thief. 1.02. 62 P
i'll be a traitor then, when thou art king. 1.02.146 P
and when they have the booty, if you and i do 1.02.164 P
fat rogue will tell us when we meet at supper, 1.02.188 P
that, when he please again to be himself, 1.02.200
but when they seldom come, they wish'd for come, 1.02.206
when this loose behavior i throw off | and pay 1.02.208
redeeming time when men think least i will. 1.02.217
when we need | your use and counsel, we shall 1.03. 20
but i remember, when the fight was done, | when 1.03. 30
when i was dry with rage and extreme toil, 1.03. 31
who therewith angry, when it next came there, 1.03. 40
when they have lost and forfeited themselves? 1.03. 88
took, | when on the gentle severn's sedgy bank, 1.03. 98
and when i urg'd the ransom once again | of my 1.03.141
and then it was when the unhappy king | (whose 1.03.148
but i will find him when he lies asleep, | and 1.03.221
to you | when you are better temper'd to attend. 1.03.235
pismires, when i hear | of this vile politician, 1.03.240
when you and he came back from ravenspurgh — 1.03.248
"look when his infant fortune came to age" | and 1.03.253
when time is ripe, which will be suddenly, 1.03.294
ay, when, canst tell? 2.01. 39 P
a plague upon it when thieves cannot be true one 2.02. 27 P
when a jest is so forward, and afoot too! 2.02. 46 P
when thou need'st him, there thou shalt find him 2.02. 71 P
and start so often when thou sit'st alone? 2.03. 43
such as we see when men restrain their breath 2.03. 61
and when i am a' horseback, i will swear | i 2.03.101
and when i am king of england i shall command 2.04. 13 P
scarlet, and when you breathe in your watering, 2.04. 16 P
ask me when thou wilt, and thou shalt have it. 2.04. 62 P
or indeed, francis, when thou wilt. 2.04. 67 P
go thy ways, old jack, die when thou wilt; 2.04.128 P
men in kendal green when it was so dark thou 2.04.232 P
again, and when thou hast tir'd thyself in base 2.04.250 P
faith, i ran when i saw others run. 2.04.302 P
when i was about thy years, hal, i was not an 2.04.329 P
chid to–morrow when thou comest to thy father. 2.04.374 P
i say the earth did shake when i was born. 3.01. 20
but will they come when you do call for them? 3.01. 54
natural scope | when you come 'cross his humor, 3.01.170
these two hours, and so come in when ye will. 3.01.261 P
so when he had occasion to be seen, | he was but 3.02. 74
when it shines seldom in admiring eyes; 3.02. 80
when i from france set foot at ravenspurgh, 3.02. 95
son, | when i will wear a garment all of blood, 3.02.135
and that shall be the day, when e'er it lights, 3.02.138
when thou ran'st up gadshill in the night to 3.03. 37 P
knows at what time to promise, when to pay. 4.03. 53
and when he was not six and twenty strong, 4.03. 56
and when he heard him swear and vow to god | he 4.03. 60
now when the lords and barons of the realm 4.03. 66
here, | when he was personal in the irish war. 4.03. 88
when yet you were in place and in account 5.01. 37
but how if honor prick me off when i come on? 5.01.130 P
if die, brave death, when princes die with us! 5.02. 86
fair | when the intent of bearing them is just. 5.02. 88
when that this body did contain a spirit, | a 5.04. 89
to counterfeit dying, when a man thereby liveth, 5.04.118 P
when he saw | the fortune of the day quite 5.05. 17
the vent of hearing when loud rumor speaks? 2H4 in 2
god may finish it when he will, 'tis not a hair 1.02. 23 P
you would not come when i sent for you. 1.02.106 P
when there were matters against you for your 1.02.132 P
when the prince broke thy head for liking his 2.01. 89 P
didst thou not, when she was gone down stairs, 2.01. 98 P
of linen with thee when thou keepest not racket 2.02. 20 P
when you were more /endear'd to it than now, 2.03. 11
when your own percy, when my heart's dear harry, 2.03. 12
when your own percy, when my heart's dear harry, 2.03. 12
"when arthur first in court" — empty the jordan 2.04. 33 P
i am the worse when one says swagger. 2.04.104 P
since when, i pray you, sir? 2.04.132 P
when wilt thou leave fighting a' days and 2.04.231 P
thou't forget me when i am gone. 2.04.277 P
me, as you did when you ran away by gadshill. 2.04.306 P
when tempest of commotion, like the south 2.04.363
undeserver may sleep when the man of action is 2.04.376 P
when richard, with his eye brimful of tears, 3.01. 67
court–gate, when 'a was a crack not thus high; 3.02. 30 P
that is, when a man is, as they say, 3.02. 77 P
or when a man is being whereby 'a may be thought 3.02. 78 P
nobody to do any thing about her when i am gone, 3.02.231 P
mile–end green, when i lay at clement's inn — i 3.02.279 P
when 'a was naked, he was for all the world like 3.02.310 P
when ever yet was your appeal denied? 4.01. 88
better show'd with you | when that your flock, 4.02. 5
when every thing is ended, then you come. 4.03. 27
and, when you come to court, stand my good lord 4.03. 82 P
and then, when they marry, they get wenches. 4.03. 93 P
when you perceive his blood inclin'd to mirth; 4.04. 38
the blood weeps from my heart when i do shape, 4.04. 58
upon, | when i am sleeping with my ancestors. 4.04. 61
for when his headstrong riot hath no curb, 4.04. 62
when rage and hot blood are his counsellors, 4.04. 63
when means and lavish manners meet together, | o 4.04. 64
'tis seldom when the bee doth leave her comb 4.04. 79
and, when they stand against you, may they fall 4.04. 95
when thou dost pinch thy bearer, thou dost sit 4.05. 29
when we withdrew, my liege, we left it here. 4.05. 58
into revolt | when gold becomes her object! 4.05. 66
when, like the bee, tolling from every flower 4.05. 74
when that my care could not withhold thy riots, 4.05.134
what wilt thou do when riot is thy care? 4.05.135
god witness with me, when i here came in, | and 4.05.149
able to speak for himself, when a knave is not. 5.01. 46 P
year, | when flesh is cheap and females dear, 5.03. 19
'tis merry in hall when beards wags all, | and 5.03. 34
when pistol lies, do this, and fig me like | the 5.03.118
when thou dost hear i am as i have been, 5.05. 60
my tongue is weary, when my legs are too, i will ep 33 P
think, when we talk of horses, that you see them H5 pr 26
that, when he speaks, | the air, a charter'd 1.01. 47
when the man dies, let the inheritance | descend 1.02. 99
when all her chevalry hath been in france, | and 1.02.157
when we have match'd our rackets to these balls, 1.02.261
that men are merriest when they are from home. 1.02.272
when i do rouse me in my throne of france. 1.02.275
when thousands weep more than did laugh at it. 1.02.296
but when time shall serve, there shall be smiles 2.01. 6 P
and when i cannot live any longer, i will do as 2.01. 15 P
shall we stretch our eye | when capital crimes, 2.02. 56
shame | when cressy battle fatally was struck, 2.04. 54
most spend their mouths when what they seem to 2.04. 70
and when you find him evenly deriv'd | from his 2.04. 91
but when the blast of war blows in our ears, 3.01. 5
and that was against a post when he was drunk. 3.02. 41 P
when there is more better opportunity to be 3.02.138 P
what is't to me, when you yourselves are cause, 3.03. 19
when down the hill he holds his fierce career? 3.03. 23
for i am sure, when he shall see our army, 3.05. 58
that is well, i warrant you, when time is serve. 3.06. 66 P
for when /lenity and cruelty play for a kingdom, 3.06.112 P
who when they were in health, i tell thee, 3.06.148
when i bestride him, i soar, i am a hawk; 3.07. 15 P
the earth sings when he touches it; 3.07. 16 P
'tis a hooded valor, and when it appears, it 3.07.111 P
time | when creeping murmur and the poring dark 4.pr. 2
and when the mind is quick'ned, out of doubt, 4.01. 20
when the true and aunchient prerogatifes and 4.01. 67 P
yet, when they stoop, they stoop with the like 4.01.107 P
therefore, when he sees reason of fears, as we 4.01.108 P
a heavy reckoning to make, when all those legs, 4.01.135 P
of any thing, when blood is their argument? 4.01.143 P
not their death when they purpose their services 4.01.158 P
but when our throats are cut, he may be ransom'd 4.01.193 P
thou, when thou command'st the beggar's knee, 4.01.256
will stand a' tiptoe when this day is named, 4.03. 42
thy vow, sirrah, when thou meet'st the fellow. 4.07.144 P
when alanson and myself were down together, i 4.07.154 P
when, without stratagem, | but in plain shock 4.08.108
say very true, scald knave, when god's will is. 5.01. 32 P
when you take occasions to see leeks hereafter, 5.01. 55 P
when articles too nicely urg'd be stood on. 5.02. 94
kate, when france is mine and i am yours, then 5.02.175 P
and at night, when you come into your closet, 5.02.198 P
he was thinking of civil wars when he got me; 5.02.226 P
that, when i come to woo ladies, i fright them. 5.02.228 P
my lord, when they see not what they do. 5.02.302 P

when at their mothers' moist'ned eyes babes 1H6 1.01. 49
me, | when he sees me go back one foot or fly. 1.02. 21
when i have chased all thy foes from hence, 1.02.115
as who should say, "when i am dead and gone, 1.04. 93
when they shall hear how we have play'd the men. 1.06. 16
in memory of her when she is dead, | her ashes, 1.06. 23
when others sleep upon their quiet beds, 2.01. 6
'tis thought, lord talbot, when the fight began, 2.02. 22
when arm in arm they both came swiftly running, 2.02. 29
when ladies crave to be encount'red with. 2.02. 46
for when a world of men | could not prevail with 2.02. 48
guests | are often welcomest when they are gone. 2.02. 56
and when you have done so, bring the keys to me. 2.03. 2
o, tell me when my lips do touch his cheeks, 2.05. 39
long after this, when henry the fift 2.05. 82
when they are cloy'd | with long continuance in 2.05.105
which giveth many wounds when one will kill. 2.05.110
yes, when his holy state is touch'd so near. 3.01. 58
it be said, "speak, sirrah, when you should; 3.01. 62
nails | shall pitch a field when we are dead. 3.01.103
when gloucester says the word, king henry goes, 3.01.183
now, quiet soul, depart when heaven please, 3.02.110
when death doth close his tender-dying eyes, 3.03. 48
when talbot hath set footing once in france 3.03. 64
but when they heard he was thine enemy, | they 3.03. 71
when i was young (as yet i am not old), | i do 3.04. 17
when thou shalt see i'll meet thee to thy cost. 3.04. 43
i vow'd, base knight, when i did meet thee next, 4.01. 14
when, but in all, i was six thousand strong 4.01. 20
when first this order was ordain'd, my lords, 4.01. 33
when stubbornly he did repugn the truth | about 4.01. 94
when for so slight and frivolous a cause | such 4.01.112
when foreign princes shall be certified | that 4.01.144
much, when sceptres are in children's hands; 4.01.192
but more, when envy breeds unkind division: 4.01.193
when sapless age and weak unable limbs | should 4.05. 4
that basely fled when noble talbot stood. 4.05. 17
when from the dolphin's crest thy sword struck 4.06. 10
fly, to revenge my death when i am dead; 4.06. 30
when he perceiv'd me shrink and on my knee, 4.07. 5
but when my angry guardant stood alone, 4.07. 9
curse, miscreant, when thou com'st to the stake. 5.03. 44
that, when thou com'st to kneel at henry's feet, 5.03.194
mother gave thee, when thou suck'dst her breast, 5.04. 28
or else, when thou didst keep my lambs a-field, 5.04. 30
although you break it when your pleasure serves. 5.04.164
so, now dismiss your army when ye please; 5.04.173
lordings, farewell, and say, when i am gone, | i 2H6 1.01.145
when thou wert regent for our sovereign, | have 1.01.197
a day will come when york shall claim his own, 1.01.239
and, when i spy advantage, claim the crown, 1.01.242
watch thou, and wake when others be asleep, | to 1.01.249
when i imagine ill | against my king and nephew, 1.02. 19
when from saint albons we do make return, 1.02. 83
when in the city tours | thou ran'st a-tilt in 1.03. 50
and when i did correct him for his fault the 1.03.198 P
the time of night when troy was set on fire, 1.04. 17
the time when screech-owls cry and ban-dogs howl 1.04. 18
marry, when thou dar'st. 2.01. 38
when such strings jar, what hope of harmony? 2.01. 55
but that in all my life, when i was a youth. 2.01. 97
than when thou wert protector to thy king. 2.03. 27
when i am dead and gone, | may honorable peace 2.03. 37
when thou didst ride in triumph through the 2.04. 14
and when i start, the envious people laugh, 2.04. 35
when every one will give the time of day, | he 3.01. 14
small curs are not regarded when they grin, 3.01. 18
but great men tremble when the lion roars, | and 3.01. 19
and when he please to make commotion, | 'tis to 3.01. 29
the fox barks not when he would steal the lamb. 3.01. 55
binds the wretch and beats it when it strays, 3.01.211
when from thy shore the tempest beat us back, 3.02.102
and when the dusky sky began to rob | my 3.02.104
did | when he to madding dido would unfold | his 3.02.117
his eyeballs further out than when he lived, 3.02.169
but when i swear, it is irrevocable. 3.02.294
bring me unto my trial when you will. 3.03. 8
therefore, when merchant-like i sell revenge, 4.01. 41
and thought thee happy when i shook my head? 4.01. 55
when i have feasted with queen margaret? 4.01. 58
and when i am king, as king i will be — 4.02. 69 P
became a bricklayer when he came to age. 4.02.145
but then are we in order when we are most out of 4.02.189 P
not read, thou hast hang'd them, when, indeed, 4.07. 45 P
when honester men than thou go in their hose and 4.07. 50 P
when have i aught exacted at your hands, | /but 4.07. 69
tut, when struck'st thou one blow in the field? 4.07. 79 P
if when you make your pray'rs, | god should be 4.07.114
lord, when shall we go to cheapside and take up 4.07.126 P
for they lov'd well when they were alive. 4.07.131 P
retreat or parley when i command them kill? 4.08. 4 P
time, when i have been dry and bravely marching, 4.10. 13 P
and hang thee o'er my tomb when i am dead. 4.10. 68
now, when the angry trumpet sounds alarum, | and 5.02. 3
and when the king comes, offer him no violence, 3H6 1.01. 33
but when the duke is slain, they'll quickly fly. 1.01. 69
when i was crown'd i was but nine months old. 1.01.112
when i return with victory /from the field 1.01.261
france | when as the enemy hath been ten to one; 1.02. 74
my days, | and when i give occasion of offense, 1.03. 44
and when the hardiest warriors did retire, 1.04. 14
so cowards fight when they can fly no further, 1.04. 40
what valor were it, when a cur doth grin, | for 1.04. 56
when he might spurn him with his foot away? 1.04. 58
and when the rage allays, the rain begins. 1.04.146
when as the noble duke of york was slain, | your 2.01. 46
and when with grief he wept, | the ruthless 2.01. 60
and when came george from burgundy to england? 2.01.143
'twas odds, belike, when valiant warwick fled: 2.01.148
and when thou fail'st (as god forbid the hour!) 2.01.190
the queen hath best success when you are absent. 2.02. 74
since when, his oath is broke; 2.02. 89
when you and i met at saint albons last, | your 2.02.103
but when he took a beggar to his bed, | and 2.02.154
but when we saw our sunshine made thy spring, 2.02.163
when dying clouds contend with growing light, 2.05. 2
they prosper best of all when i am thence. 2.05. 18
when this is known, then to divide the times: 2.05. 30
when care, mistrust, and treason waits on him. 2.05. 54
in hewing rutland when his leaves put forth, 2.06. 48
when clifford cannot spare his friends an oath. 2.06. 78
where did you dwell when i was king of england? 3.01. 74
me again, | obeying with my wind when i do blow, 3.01. 86
blow, | and yielding to another when it blows, 3.01. 87
no more than when my daughters call thee mother. 3.02.101
when he was made a shriver, 'twas for shift. 3.02.108
when nature brought him to the door of death? 3.03.105
when i have heard your king's desert recounted, 3.03.132
but the safer when 'tis back'd with france. 4.01. 41
why, warwick, when we parted, | thou call'dst me 4.03. 30
when you disgrac'd me in my embassade | then i 4.03. 32
when i have fought with pembroke and his fellows 4.03. 54
a pleasure as incaged birds | conceive, when, 4.06. 13
for choosing me when clarence is in place. 4.06. 31
but when the fox hath once got in his nose, 4.07. 25
when we grow stronger, then we'll make our claim 4.07. 59
and when the morning sun shall raise his car 4.07. 80
and when the lion fawns upon the lamb, | the 4.08. 49
what is the body when the head is off? 5.01. 41
nay, when? 5.01. 49
than jephthah when he sacrific'd his daughter. 5.01. 91
and who durst smile when warwick bent his brow? 5.02. 22
thou been kill'd when first thou didst presume, 5.06. 35
hadst thou in thy head when thou wast born, | to 5.06. 53
and made the forest tremble when they roar'd. 5.07. 12
when as he meant all harm. 5.07. 34
yea, richard, when i know; R3 1.01. 52
why, this it is, when men are rul'd by women: 1.01. 62
when they are gone, then must i count my gains. 1.01.162
/stand thou when i command. 1.02. 39
o wonderful, when devils tell the /troth! 1.02. 73
more wonderful, when angels are so angry. 1.02. 74
when my father york and edward wept | to hear 1.02.156
when black-fac'd clifford shook his sword at him 1.02.158
nor when thy warlike father, like a child, 1.02.159
son | to be your comforter when he is gone. 1.03. 10
when have i injur'd thee? 1.03. 56
when done thee wrong? 1.03. 56
when thou didst crown his warlike brows with 1.03.174
tyrants themselves wept when it was reported. 1.03.184
when my son | was stabb'd with bloody daggers: 1.03.210
look when he fawns he bites; 1.03.289
and when he bites, | his venom tooth will rankle 1.03.289
when he shall split thy very heart with sorrow, 1.03.299
and seem a saint, when most i play the devil. 1.03.337
when you have done, repair to crosby place. 1.03.344
drop millstones, when fools' eyes fall tears. 1.03.352
no, he'll say 'twas done cowardly when he wakes. 1.04.101 P
remember our reward when the deed's done. 1.04.123 P
when he opens his purse to give us our reward, 1.04.129 P
when thou hast broke it in such dear degree? 1.04.210
when gallant-springing brave plantagenet, | that 1.04.221
when that our princely father york | blest his 1.04.235
doth, when he delivers you | from this earth's 1.04.247
and when i have my meed, i will away, | for this 1.04.282
when ever buckingham doth turn his hate | upon 2.01. 32
when i have most need to employ a friend, | and 2.01. 36
/god, | when i am cold in love to you or yours. 2.01. 40
when oxford had me down, he rescued me, | and 2.01.113
told me, when we both lay in the field | frozen 2.01.115
but when your carters or your waiting vassals 2.01.122
look'd pale when they did hear of clarence' 2.01.137
and when my uncle told me so, he wept, | and 2.02. 23
why grow the branches when the root is gone? 2.02. 41
that grieves me when i see my shame in him. 2.02. 54
so stood the state when henry the sixt | was 2.03. 16
when clouds are seen, wise men put on their 2.03. 32
when great leaves fall, then winter is at hand; 2.03. 33
when the sun sets, who doth not look for night? 2.03. 34
he was the wretched'st thing when he was young, 2.04. 18
and look when i am king, claim thou of me | the 3.01.194
when men are unprepar'd and look not for it. 3.02. 63
lords at pomfret, when they rode from london, 3.02. 83
than when thou met'st me last where now we meet. 3.02. 99
and when i met this holy man | the men you talk 3.02.116
when she exclaim'd on hastings, you, and i, 3.03. 16
for standing by when richard stabb'd her son. 3.03. 17
in god's name speak, when is the royal day? 3.04. 3
my lord of ely, when i was last in holborn, | i 3.04. 31
when that he bids good morrow with such spirit. 3.04. 50
and started when he look'd upon the tower, | as 3.04. 85
when that my mother went with child | of that 3.05. 86
when such ill dealing must be seen in thought. 3.06. 14
and when /mine oratory drew /to /an end, | i bid 3.07. 20
which when i saw, i reprehended them, | and 3.07. 27
when he had done, some followers of mine own, 3.07. 34
when holy and devout religious men | are at 3.07. 92
even when you please, for you will have it so. 3.07.243
when he that is my husband now | came to me as i 4.01. 65
when scarce the blood was well wash'd from his 4.01. 67
o, when, i say, i look'd on richard's face, 4.01. 70
and, when thou wed'st, let sorrow haunt thy bed; 4.01. 73
king, | when richmond was a little peevish boy. 4.02. 97
when dighton thus told on, "we smothered | the 4.03. 17
when thou shalt tell the process of their death. 4.03. 32
we must be brief when traitors brave the field. 4.03. 57
when didst thou sleep when such a deed was done? 4.04. 24
when didst thou sleep when such a deed was done? 4.04. 24
when holy harry died, and my sweet son. 4.04. 25
true — when avoided grace makes destiny: 4.04.219
and when this arm of mine hath chastised | the 4.04.331
when thou com'st thither — dull unmindful 4.04.445
when thou mayest tell thy tale the nearest way? 4.04.461
when they should serve their sovereign in the 4.04.485
i wish'd might fall on me when i was found 5.01. 14
"when he," quoth she, "shall split thy heart 5.01. 26
when i should mount with wings of victory. 5.03.106
when i was mortal, my anointed body | by thee 5.03.124
stay'd me a prisoner in my chamber when | those H8 1.01. 5
beheld them when they lighted, how they clung 1.01. 9
when these suns | (for so they phrase 'em) by 1.01. 33
and proofs as clear as founts in july when | we 1.01.154
but when the way was made | and pav'd with gold, 1.01.187
when these so noble benefits shall prove | not 1.02.115
who was enroll'd 'mongst wonders, and when we, 1.02.119
for when they hold 'em, you would swear directly 1.03. 8
when he was brought again to th' bar, to hear 2.01. 31
and when old time shall lead him to his end, 2.01. 93
when i came hither, i was lord high constable 2.01.102
when they once perceive | the least rub in your 2.01.128
and when you would say something that is sad, 2.01.135
for when the king once heard it, out of anger 2.01.150
when they were ready to set out for london, a 2.02. 4 P
that when the greatest stroke of fortune falls 2.02. 35
when was the hour | i ever contradicted your 2.04. 27
i will, when you are humble; 2.04. 74
when you are call'd, return. 2.04.130
to village curs, | bark when their fellows do: 2.04.161
oppression i did reek | when i first mov'd you. 2.04.210
that freeze, | bow themselves when he did sing. 3.01. 5
and to that woman (when she has done most) | yet 3.01.136
that little thought, when she set footing here, 3.01.183
when did he regard | the stamp of nobleness in 3.02. 11
but, my lord, | when returns cranmer? 3.02. 63
when the brown wench | lay kissing in your arms, 3.02.295
innocence arise | when the king knows my truth. 3.02.302
when you went | ambassador to the emperor, you 3.02.317
and, when he thinks, good easy man, full surely 3.02.356
and when he falls, he falls like lucifer, 3.02.371
when he has run his course and sleeps in 3.02.398
and when i am forgotten, as i shall be, | and 3.02.432
and more and richer, when he strains that lady. 4.01. 46
which when the people | had the full view of, 4.01. 70
when by the archbishop of canterbury | she had 4.01. 86
when it comes, | cranmer will find a friend will 4.01.106
when i shall dwell with worms, and my poor name 4.02.126
when i am dead, good wench, | let me be us'd 4.02.167
nor shall not, when my fancy's on my play. 5.01. 60
when we first put this dangerous stone a-rolling 5.02.139
when i might see from far some forty 5.03. 51 P
still, when suddenly a file of boys behind 'em, 5.03. 55 P
when they pass back from the christening. 5.03. 74
of bombards, when | ye should do service. 5.03. 81
shall this lady, | when she has so much english. 5.04. 14
but as when | the bird of wonder dies, the 5.04. 39
(when heaven shall call her from this cloud of 5.04. 44
me | that when i am in heaven i shall desire 5.04. 67
if they hold when their ladies bid 'em clap. ep 14
and when fair cressid comes into my thoughts — TRO 1.01. 30
so, traitor, then she comes when she is thence. 1.01. 31
i was about to tell thee — when my heart, | as 1.01. 34
i have (as when the sun doth light a-scorn) 1.01. 37
when i do tell thee there my hopes lie drown'd, 1.01. 49
as true thou tell'st me, when i say i love her, 1.01. 60
when with your blood you daily paint her thus. 1.01. 91
when were you at ilium? 1.02. 45 P
what were you talking of when i came? 1.02. 47 P
tell me another tale when th' other's come to't. 1.02. 85 P
when comes troilus? 1.02.193 P
knew | love got so sweet as when desire did sue. 1.02.291
but when the splitting wind | makes flexible the 1.03. 49
when that the general is not like the hive | to 1.03. 81
but when the planets | in evil mixture to 1.03. 94
o, when degree is shak'd, | which is the ladder 1.03.101
this chaos, when degree is suffocate, | follows 1.03.125
and when he speaks, | 'tis like a chime 1.03.158
hands shall strike | when fitness calls them on, 1.03.202
a blush | modest as morning when she coldly eyes 1.03.229
but when they would seem soldiers, they have 1.03.237
if none, he'll say in troy when he retires, 1.03.281
that was a man | when hector's grandsire suck'd. 1.03.292
when thou art forth in the incursions, thou 2.01. 29 P
i will hold my peace when achilles' /brach bids 2.01.114 P
when helenus beholds | a grecian and his sword, 2.02. 42
when we have soil'd them, nor the remainder 2.02. 70
or sword to draw, | when helen is defended; 2.02.158
that ajax makes | when they go from achilles. 2.03.184
and add more coals to cancer when he burns 2.03.196
ay, sir, when he goes before me. 3.01. 3 P
be, | when that the wat'ry palates taste indeed 3.02. 21
when they charge on heaps | the enemy flying. 3.02. 28
but our undertakings, when we vow to weep seas, 3.02. 77 P
to us, | when we are so unsecret to ourselves? 3.02.125
when right with right wars who shall be most 3.02.172
when their rhymes, | full of protest, of oath 3.02.174
when time is old /and hath forgot itself, | when 3.02.185
when water-drops have worn the stones of troy, 3.02.186
when th' have said as false | as air, as water, 3.02.191
which when they fall, as being slippery standers 3.03. 84
as when his virtues, aiming upon others, | heat 3.03.100
when fame shall in our islands sound her trump, 3.03.210
even then when they sit idly in the sun. 3.03.233
music will be in him when hector has knock'd out 3.03.302 P
but when i meet you arm'd, as black defiance 4.01. 13
/but when contention and occasion meet, | by 4.01. 17
and to his hand when i deliver her, | think it 4.03. 7
when shall we see again? 4.04. 57
and you this glove. when shall i see you? 4.04. 71
when we will tempt the frailty of our powers, 4.04. 96
when i am hence, | i'll answer to my lust, and 4.04.131
me a kiss | when helen is a maid again and his. 4.05. 50
i am your debtor, claim it when 'tis due. 4.05. 51
when thou hast hung /thy advanced sword i' th' 4.05.188
when that a ring of greeks have /hemm'd thee in, 4.05.193
when we have here her base and pillar by us. 4.05.212
no more trust him when he leers than i will a 5.01. 89 P
he leers than i will a serpent when he hisses. 5.01. 90 P
like brabbler the hound, but when he performs, 5.01. 92 P
borrows of the moon when diomed keeps his word. 5.01. 94 P
when was my lord so much ungently temper'd | to 5.03. 1
when many times the captive grecian falls, 5.03. 40
and when we have our armors buckled on, | the 5.03. 46
till when, go seek thy fortune. 5.06. 19
and when i have the bloody hector found, 5.07. 4
like fathers, | when you curse them as enemies. COR 1.01. 78
there was a time when all the body's members 1.01. 96
when we were chosen tribunes for the people — 1.01.254
to keep your great pretenses veil'd till when 1.02. 20
when yet he was but tender-bodied and the only 1.03. 5 P
when youth with comeliness pluck'd all gaze his 1.03. 7 P
when for a day of kings' entreaties a mother 1.03. 8 P
when she did suckle hector, look'd not lovelier 1.03. 41
than hector's forehead when it spit forth blood 1.03. 42
after a gilded butterfly, and when he caught it, 1.03. 61 P

his senseless sword | and, when it bows, 1.04. 54
me clip ye | in arms as sound as when i woo'd, 1.06. 30
as merry as when our nuptial day was done | and 1.06. 31
her blood, | when she does praise me grieves me. 1.09. 15
when drums and trumpets shall | i' th' field 1.09. 42
when steel grows soft as the parasite's silk, 1.09. 45
and when my face is fair, you shall perceive 1.09. 69
when i find the ass in compound with the major 2.01. 58 P
when you are hearing a matter between party and 2.01. 72 P
when you speak best unto the purpose, it is not 2.01. 86 P
the people, when he shall stand for his place. 2.01.148 P
at some time when his soaring insolence | shall 2.01.254
when blows have made me stay, i fled from words. 2.02. 72
sun | when the alarum were struck than idly sit 2.02. 76
when you now see | he had rather venture all his 2.02. 79
when tarquin made a head for rome, he fought 2.02. 88
when with his amazonian /chin he drove | the 2.02. 91
when he might act the woman in the scene, | he 2.02. 96
when by and by the din of war gan pierce | his 2.02.115
when | some certain of your brethren roar'd, and 2.03. 52
he mock'd us when he begg'd our voices. 2.03.159
when we granted that, | here was "i thank you 2.03.170
when he had no power, | but was a petty servant 2.03.177
in free contempt | when he did need your loves; 2.03.201
bruising to you | when he hath power to crush? 2.03.203
and presently, when you have drawn your number, 2.03.253
ready, when time shall prompt them, to make road 3.01. 5
when corn was given them gratis, you repin'd, 3.01. 43
when, both your voices blended, the great'st 3.01.103
aches | to know, when two authorities are up, 3.01.109
even when the navel of the state was touch'd, 3.01.123
when what's not meet, but what must be, was law, 3.01.167
and manhood is call'd foolery when it stands 3.01.245
when he did love his country, | it honor'd him. 3.01.303
rage, when it shall find | the harm of unscann'd 3.01.310
when one but of my ordinance stood up | to speak 3.02. 12
be too noble, | but when extremities speak. 3.02. 41
and when they hear me say, "it shall be so | i' 3.03. 13
and when such time they have begun to cry, | let 3.03. 19
this hint | when we shall hap to give't them. 3.03. 24
that when he speaks not like a citizen, | you 3.03. 53
that when the sea was calm all boats alike 4.01. 6
when most strook home, being gentle wounded, 4.01. 8
i shall be lov'd when i am lack'd. 4.01. 15
resume that spirit when you were wont to say, 4.01. 16
when i am forth, | bid me farewell, and smile. 4.01. 49
after it is done | than when it was a–doing. 4.02. 5
you had more beard when i last saw you, but your 4.03. 8 P
a man's wife is when she's fall'n out with her 4.03. 33 P
heart | than when i first my wedded mistress saw 4.05.117
but when they shall see, sir, his crest up again 4.05.210 P
but when goes this forward? 4.05.213 P
than when these fellows ran about the streets, 4.06. 28
which were inshell'd when martius stood for rome 4.06. 45
when you cast | your stinking greasy caps in 4.06.130
when i said banish him, i said 'twas pity. 4.06.140
said we were i' th' wrong when we banish'd him. 4.06.154 P
thought he would | when first i did embrace him; 4.07. 10
when he shall come to his account, he knows not 4.07. 18
hazard mine, | when e'er we come to our account. 4.07. 26
when, caius, rome is thine, | thou art poor'st 4.07. 56
'twas to pardon | when it was less expected. 5.01. 19
but when we have stuff'd | these pipes and these 5.01. 53
when you have push'd out your gates the very 5.02. 39 P
when she, poor hen, fond of no second brood, 5.03.162
when he walks, he moves like an engine, and the 5.04. 18 P
when we banish'd him, we respected not them; 5.04. 32 P
his stoutness | when he did stand for consul, 5.06. 27
when he had carried rome and that we look'd 5.06. 42
when he lies along, | after your way his tale 5.06. 56
my country's love | than when i parted hence, 5.06. 72
my lords, when you shall know (as in this rage, 5.06.135
(when goths were goths and tamora was queen), TIT 1.01.140
and when i do forget | the least of these 1.01.255
titus, when wert thou wont to walk alone, 1.01.339
as when the golden sun salutes the morn, | and, 2.01. 5
when every thing doth make a gleeful boast? 2.03. 11
when with a happy storm they were surpris'd, 2.03. 23
even as an adder when she doth unroll | to do 2.03. 35
and when they show'd me this abhorred pit, 2.03. 98
but when ye have the honey we desire, | let not 2.03.131
when did the tiger's young ones teach the dam? 2.03.142
that gave thee life when well he might have 2.03.159
so long, | poor i was slain when bassianus died. 2.03.171
when he by night lay bath'd in maiden blood. 2.03.232
when i do weep, they humbly at my feet | receive 3.01. 41
expecting ever when some envious surge | will in 3.01. 96
when i did name her brothers, then fresh tears 3.01.111
when they do hug him in their melting bosoms. 3.01.213
when heaven doth weep, doth not the earth 3.01.221
when will this fearful slumber have an end? 3.01.252
ay, when my father was in rome she did. 4.01. 7
and when he sleeps will she do what she list. 4.01.100
your lordships, /that, when ever you have need, 4.02. 15
that shone so brightly when this boy was got, 4.02. 90
lords, when we join in league | i am a lamb, but 4.02.136
two may keep counsel when the third's away. 4.02.144
then, when you come to pluto's region, | i pray 4.03. 13
marcus, loose when i bid. 4.03. 59
when publius shot, | the bull, being gall'd, 4.03. 71
and when you come to him, at the first approach 4.03.109 P
and when thou hast given it the emperor, | knock 4.03.118
say, | when i have walked like a private man, 4.04. 75
when as the one is wounded with the bait, | the 4.04. 92
when soon i heard | the crying babe controll'd 5.01. 25
who, when he knows thou art the empress' babe, 5.01. 35
and when i had it, drew myself apart, | and 5.01.112
when, for his hand, he had his two sons' heads, 5.01.115
and when i told the empress of this sport, | she 5.01.118
even when their sorrows almost was forgot, | and 5.01.137
and when thy car is loaden with their heads, | i 5.02. 53
and when thou find'st a man that's like thyself, 5.02. 99
and when it is thy hap | to find another that is 5.02.101
when he is here, even at thy solemn feast, | i 5.02.115
receive the blood, and when that they are dead, 5.02.197
when with his solemn tongue he did discourse 5.03. 81
when subtile greeks surpris'd king priam's troy. 5.03. 84
time | when it should move ye to attend me most, 5.03. 92
me, | for when no friends are by, men praise 5.03.118
and talk of them when he was dead and gone. 5.03.166
when they were living, warm'd themselves on 5.03.168
when i have fought with the men, i will be civil ROM 1.01. 22 P
speak, nephew, were you by when it began? 1.01.105
i aim'd so near when i suppos'd you lov'd. 1.01.205
only poor | that, when she dies, with beauty 1.01.216
feel | when well–apparell'd april on the heel 1.02. 27
when the devout religion of mine eye | maintains 1.02. 88
when it did taste the wormwood on the nipple 1.03. 30
thou wilt fall backward when thou hast more wit, 1.03. 42
thou wilt fall backward when thou comest to age, 1.03. 56
this is the hag, when maids lie on their backs, 1.04. 92
when good manners shall lie all in one or two 1.05. 3 P
it fits when such a villain is a guest. 1.05. 75
can i go forward when my heart is here? 2.01. 1
when king cophetua lov'd the beggar–maid! 2.01. 14
as maids call medlars, when they laugh alone. 2.01. 36
when he bestrides the lazy puffing clouds, | and 2.02. 31
may prove a beauteous flow'r when next we meet. 2.02.122
when and where and how | we met, we woo'd, and 2.03. 61
women may fall, when there's no strength in men. 2.03. 80
that, when the single sole of it is worn, the 2.04. 62 P
with me for any thing when thou wast not there 2.04. 75 P
romeo will be older when you have found him than 2.04.121 P
have found him than he was when you sought him. 2.04.121 P
for a score, | when it hoars ere it be spent. 2.04.139
when 'twas a little prating thing — o, there is 2.04.200 P
i'll warrant you, when i say so, she looks as 2.04.205 P
the clock strook nine when i did send the nurse; 2.05. 1
when thou hast breath | to say to me that thou 2.05. 31
must climb a bird's nest soon when it is dark. 2.05. 74
that, when he enters the confines of a tavern, 3.01. 5 P
him on the drawer, when indeed there is no need. 3.01. 9 P
else, when he is found, that hour is his last. 3.01.195
give me my romeo, and, when i shall die, | take 3.02. 21
when thou didst bower the spirit of a fiend | in 3.02. 81
when i, thy three–hours wife, have mangled it? 3.02. 99
why followed not, when she said, "tybalt's dead, 3.02.118
when theirs are dry, for romeo's banishment. 3.02.131
how should they when that wise men have no eyes? 3.03. 62
i will not marry yet, and when i do, i swear 3.05.121
when the sun sets, the earth doth drizzle dew, 3.05.126
that may be, sir, when i may be a wife. 4.01. 19
o, shut the door, and when thou hast done so, 4.01. 44
when presently through all thy veins shall run 4.01. 95
like death when he shuts up the day of life; 4.01.101
when the bridegroom in the morning comes | to 4.01.107
god knows when we shall meet again. 4.03. 14
how if, when i am laid into the tomb, | i wake 4.03. 30
"when griping griefs the heart doth wound, 4.05.126
when but love's shadows are so rich in joy! 5.01. 11
when my betossed soul | did not attend him as we 5.03. 76
how oft when men are at the point of death 5.03. 88
but when i came, some minute ere the time | of 5.03.257
"when we for recompense have prais'd the vild, TIM 1.01. 15
a picture, sir. when comes your book forth? 1.01. 26
when fortune in her shift and change of mood 1.01. 84
to shake off | my friend when he must need me. 1.01.101
when thou art timon's dog, and these knaves 1.01.180
when dinner's done, | show me this piece. 1.01.245
when all's spent, he'ld be cross'd then, and he 1.02.162
nor then silenc'd when | "commend me to your 2.01. 17
when every feather sticks in his own wing, 2.01. 30
when men come to borrow of your masters, they 2.02. 99 P
you took, | when my indisposition put you back, 2.02.130
when, for some trifling present, you have bid me 2.02.136
when i have | prompted you in the ebb of your 2.02.140
when all our offices have been oppress'd | with 2.02.158
when our vaults have wept | with drunken spilth 2.02.159
when every room | hath blaz'd with lights and 2.02.160
when the means are gone that buy this praise, 2.02.169
when he was poor, | imprison'd, and in scarcity 2.02.224
turn to nutriment | when he is turn'd to poison? 3.01. 59
and, when he's sick to death, let not that part 3.01. 61
time, when i might ha' shown myself honorable! 3.02. 45 P
man | when he looks out in an ungrateful shape! 3.02. 73
knew not what he did when he made man politic; 3.03. 28 P
when your false masters eat of my lord's meat? 3.04. 50
world | when sects and factions were newly born. 3.05. 30
were my thoughts tiring when we encount'red. 3.06. 4 P
i am sorry, when he sent to borrow of me, that 3.06. 15 P
when your lordship this other day sent to me, i 3.06. 42 P
when man's worst sin is, he does too much good! 4.02. 39
when gouty keepers of thee cannot stand. 4.03. 47
thou saw'st them, when i had prosperity. 4.03. 78
forgetting thy great deeds when neighbor states, 4.03. 95
when i have laid proud athens on a heap — 4.03.102
and thee after, when thou hast conquer'd! 4.03.105
be as a planetary plague when jove | will o'er 4.03.109
thy heels | and skip when thou point'st out? 4.03.225
when thou wast in thy gilt and thy perfume, they 4.03.301 P
when peradventure thou wert accus'd by the ass; 4.03.331 P
when i know not what else to do, i'll see thee 4.03.353 P
when there is nothing living but thee, thou 4.03.355 P
when man was wish'd to love his enemies! 4.03.466
have fear'd false times when you did feast: 4.03.513
when we may profit meet, and come too late. 5.01. 42
when the day serves, before black–corner'd night 5.01. 44
when crouching marrow in the bearer strong 5.04. 9
when thy first griefs were but a mere conceit, 5.04. 14
when they are in great danger, i recover them. JC 1.01. 24 P
and when you saw his chariot but appear, | have 1.01. 43
in antonio's way | when he doth run his course. 1.02. 4
when caesar says, "do this," it is perform'd. 1.02. 10
he had a fever when he was in spain, | and when 1.02.119
and when the fit was on him, i did mark | how he 1.02.120
when went there by an age since the great flood 1.02.152
when could they say, till now, that talk'd of 1.02.154
enough, | when there is in it but one only man. 1.02.157
what said he when he came unto himself? 1.02.262
when he perceiv'd the common herd was glad he 1.02.263 P
when he came to himself again, he said, if he 1.02.269 P
he was quick mettle when he went to school. 1.02.296
when all the sway of earth | shakes like a thing 1.03. 3
i have seen tempests when the scolding winds 1.03. 5
when these prodigies | do so conjointly meet, 1.03. 28
and when the cross blue lightning seem'd to open 1.03. 50
when the most mighty gods by tokens send | such 1.03. 55
when it serves | for the base matter to 1.03.109
when, lucius, when? 2.01. 5
when, lucius, when? 2.01. 5
when it is lighted, come and call me here. 2.01. 8
th' abuse of greatness is when it disjoins 2.01. 18
i have not known when his affections sway'd 2.01. 20
but when he once attains the upmost round, | he 2.01. 24
sure | it did not lie there when i went to bed. 2.01. 38
the tarquin drive when he was call'd a king. 2.01. 54
brow by night, | when evils are most free? 2.01. 79
when every drop of blood | that every roman 2.01.136
than caesar's arm | when caesar's head is off. 2.01.183
but when i tell him he hates flatterers | he 2.01.207
and when i ask'd you what the matter was, | you 2.01.241
when they shall see | the face of caesar, they 2.02. 11
when beggars die there are no comets seen; 2.02. 30
a necessary end, | will come when it will come. 2.02. 37
lest i be laugh'd at when i tell them so. 2.02. 70
i have, when you have heard what i can say; 2.02. 92
when caesar's wife shall meet with better dreams 2.02. 99
why i, that did love caesar when i strook him, 3.01.182
that mothers shall but smile when they behold 3.01.267
reasons, | when severally we hear them rendered. 3.02. 10
when it shall please my country to need my death 3.02. 46 P
when that the poor have cried, caesar hath wept; 3.02. 91
for when the noble caesar saw him stab, 3.02.184
what weep you when you but behold | our caesar's 3.02.195
when comes such another? 3.02.252
when love begins to sicken and decay | it useth 4.02. 20
but when they should endure the bloody spur, 4.02. 25
of yours hides wrongs, | and when you do them — 4.02. 41
shall i be frighted when a madman stares? 4.03. 40
yea, for my laughter, | when you are waspish. 4.03. 50
when caesar liv'd, he durst not thus have mov'd 4.03. 58
when marcus brutus grows so covetous | to lock 4.03. 79
when thou didst hate him worst, thou lovedst him 4.03.106
be angry when you will, it shall have scope; 4.03.108
when grief and blood ill–temper'd vexeth him? 4.03.115
when i spoke that, i was ill–temper'd too. 4.03.116
when that rash humor which my mother gave me 4.03.120
when you are over–earnest with your brutus, 4.03.122
i'll know his humor, when he knows his time. 4.03.136
how scap'd i killing when i cross'd you so? 4.03.150
and we must take the current when it serves, 4.03.223
when your vile daggers | hack'd one another in 5.01. 39
when think you that the sword goes up again? 5.01. 52
if not, when you have stomachs. 5.01. 66
and when my face is cover'd, as 'tis now, 5.03. 44
when you do find him, or alive or dead, | he 5.04. 24
when shall we three meet again? MAC 1.01. 1
when the hurly–burly's done, | when the battle's 1.01. 3
done, | when the battle's lost and won. 1.01. 4
and when he reads | thy personal venture in the 1.03. 90
when those that gave the thane of cawdor to me 1.03.119
that be | which the eye fears, when it is done, 1.04. 53
when i burnt in desire to question them further, 1.05. 3 P
and when goes hence? 1.05. 59
if it were done, when 'tis done, then 'twere 1.07. 1
when you durst do it, then you were a man; 1.07. 49
when duncan is asleep | (whereto the rather 1.07. 61
when in swinish sleep | their drenched natures 1.07. 67
when we have mark'd with blood those sleepy two 1.07. 75
yet when we can entreat an hour to serve, | we 2.01. 22
if you shall cleave to my consent, when 'tis, 2.01. 25
go bid thy mistress, when my drink is ready, 2.01. 31
when? 2.02. 16
say "amen," | when they did say "god bless us!" 2.02. 27
how is't with me, when every noise appalls me? 2.02. 55
and when we have our naked frailties hid, | that 2.03.126
which steals itself, when there's no mercy left. 2.03.146
entomb, | when living light should kiss it? 2.04. 10
when therewithal we shall have cause of state 3.01. 33
when first they put the name of king upon me, 3.01. 57
when all's done, | you look but on a stool. 3.04. 66
that when the brains were out, the man would die 3.04. 78
when now i think you can behold such sights, 3.04.113
your cheeks, | when mine is blanch'd with fear. 3.04.115
when our actions do not, | our fears do make us 4.02. 3
but cruel are the times when we are traitors, 4.02. 18
when we hold rumor | from what we fear, yet know 4.02. 19
when i shall tread upon the tyrant's head, | or 4.03. 45
so grafted | that, when they shall be open'd, 4.03. 52
when shalt thou see thy wholesome days again, 4.03.105
they were well at peace when i did leave 'em. 4.03.179
when i came hither to transport the tidings, 4.03.181
when was it she last walk'd? 5.01. 2 P
it, when none can call our pow'r to accompt? 5.01. 38 P
when all that is within him does condemn 5.02. 24
i am sick at heart | when i behold — seyton, i 5.03. 20
when yond same star that's westward from the HAM 1.01. 36
had on | when he the ambitious norway combated. 1.01. 61
so frown'd he once, when, in an angry parle, 1.01. 62
it was about to speak, when the cock crew. 1.01.147
not when i saw't. 1.02.239
when the blood burns, how prodigal the soul 1.03.116
when i to sulph'rous and tormenting flames 1.05. 3
so art thou to revenge, when thou shalt hear. 1.05. 7
when i had seen this hot love on the wing — 2.02.132
said, "'tis so," | when it prov'd otherwise? 2.02.155
why did ye laugh then, when i said, "man 2.02.313 P
same estimation they did when i was in the city? 2.02.335 P
when the wind is southerly i know a hawk from a 2.02.378 P
when roscius was an actor in rome — 2.02.390 P
is nearer to heaven than when i saw you last, by 2.02.426 P
of it especially when he speaks of priam's 2.02.447 P
when he lay couched in th' ominous horse, | hath 2.02.454
when she saw pyrrhus make malicious sport | in 2.02.513
when we would bring him on to some confession 3.01. 9
when we have shuffled off this mortal coil, 3.01. 66
when he himself might his quietus make | with a 3.01. 74
rich gifts wax poor when givers prove unkind. 3.01.100
i prithee, when thou seest that act afoot, 3.02. 78
dead, | when second husband kisses me in bed. 3.02.185
tree, | but fall unshaken when they mellow be. 3.02.191
but die thy thoughts when thy first lord is dead 3.02.215
when you have the voice of the king himself for 3.02.341 P
when churchyards yawn and hell itself /breathes 3.02.389

are mortis'd and adjoin'd, which, when it falls, 3.03. 20
yet what can it, when one can not repent? 3.03. 66
when he is fit and season'd for his passage? 3.03. 86
when he is drunk asleep, or in his rage, | or in 3.03. 89
when the compulsive ardure gives the charge, 3.04. 86
night, | and when you are desirous to be blest, 3.04.171
when in one line two crafts directly meet. 3.04.210
wind, when both contend | which is the mightier. 4.01. 7
when he needs what you have glean'd, it is but 4.02. 19 P
quarrel in a straw | when honor's at the stake. 4.04. 56
of this, but when they ask you what it means, 4.05. 46 P
when sorrows come, they come not single spies, 4.05. 78
but they wither'd all when my father died. 4.05.185 P
"horatio, when thou shalt have overlook'd this, 4.06. 13 P
beg leave to see your kingly eyes, when i shall, 4.07. 45 P
that we would do, | we should do when we would; 4.07.119
when in your motion you are hot and dry — | as 4.07.157
when down her weedy trophies and herself | fell 4.07.174
when these are gone, | the woman will be out. 4.07.188
in christian burial when she willfully seeks her 5.01. 1 P
and, when you are ask'd this question next, say 5.01. 58 P
"in youth, when i did love, did love, 5.01. 61
such–a–one's horse, when 'a /meant to beg it, 5.01. 85 P
shall my sister be | when thou liest howling. 5.01.242
when that her golden couplets are disclosed, 5.01.287
serves us well | when our deep plots do pall, 5.02. 9
'tis dangerous when the baser nature comes 5.02. 60
and when he's not himself does wrong laertes, 5.02.235
happily, when i shall wed, | that lord whose LR 1.01.100
be kent unmannerly | when lear is mad. 1.01.146
dread to speak | when power to flattery bows? 1.01.148
honor's bound, | when majesty falls to folly. 1.01.149
when she was dear to us, we did hold her so, 1.01.196
when it is mingled with regards that stands 1.01.239
when my dimensions are as well compact, | my 1.02. 7
when came you to this? 1.02. 58 P
the world, that when we are sick in fortune — 1.02.119 P
/come, /come, when saw you my father last? 1.02.152 P
when he returns from hunting, | i will not speak 1.03. 7
to fear judgment, to fight when i cannot choose, 1.04. 16 P
came not the slave back to me when i call'd him? 1.04. 52 P
duty cannot be silent when i think your highness 1.04. 65 P
when the lady brach may stand by th' fire and 1.04.112 P
when thou clovest thy /crown i' th' middle and 1.04.160 P
wit in thy bald crown when thou gav'st thy 1.04.163 P
when were you wont to be so full of songs, 1.04.170 P
thy mothers, for when thou gav'st them the rod, 1.04.173 P
wast a pretty fellow when thou hadst no need to 1.04.191 P
may not an ass know when the cart draws the 1.04.223 P
more hideous when thou show'st thee in a child 1.04.260
when she shall hear this of thee, with her nails 1.04.307
a fox, when one has caught her, | and such a 1.04.317
when i have show'd th' unfitness — how now, 1.04.333
fled this way, sir, when by no means he could — 2.01. 42
and when he saw my best alarum'd spirits, | bold 2.01. 53
when i dissuaded him from his intent, | and 2.01. 64
when he, compact, and flattering his displeasure 2.02.118
when a /man's overlusty at legs, then he wears 2.04. 9 P
my lord, when at their home | i did commend your 2.04. 27
let go thy hold when a great wheel runs down a 2.04. 72 P
when a wise man gives thee better counsel, give 2.04. 74 P
for form, | will pack when it begins to rain, 2.04. 80
we are not ourselves | when nature, being 2.04.108
did to the eels when she put 'em i' th' paste 2.04.123 P
will you wish on me, when the rash mood is on. 2.04.169
let shame come when it will, i do not call it. 2.04.226
mend when thou canst, be better at thy leisure, 2.04.229
look well–favor'd | when others are more wicked; 2.04.257
that when we have found the king — in which 3.01. 53
when priests are more in word than matter; 3.02. 81
when brewers mar their malt with water; 3.02. 82
when nobles are their tailors' tutors; 3.02. 83
when every case in law is right; 3.02. 87
when slanders do not live in tongues; 3.02. 89
when usurers tell their gold i' th' field, | and 3.02. 91
when i desir'd their leave that i might pity him 3.03. 2 P
the younger rises when the old doth fall. 3.03. 25
when the mind's free, | the body's delicate; 3.04. 11
fury of his heart, when the foul fiend rages, 3.04.131 P
i stumbled when i saw. 4.01. 19
the time's plague, when madmen lead the blind. 4.01. 46
when i inform'd him, then he call'd me sot, 4.02. 8
where was his son when they did take his eyes? 4.02. 88
and when your mistress hears thus much from you, 4.05. 34
when shall i come to th' top of that same hill? 4.06. 1
of life, when life itself | yields to the theft. 4.06. 43
when misery could beguile the tyrant's rage, 4.06. 63
when the rain came to wet me once, and the wind 4.06.100 P
when the thunder would not peace at my bidding, 4.06.102 P
when i do stare, see how the subject quakes. 4.06.108
when we are born, we cry that we are come | to 4.06.182
and when i have stol'n upon these son–in–laws, 4.06.186
be by, good madam, when we do awake him, | i 4.07. 22
when time shall serve, let but the herald cry, 5.01. 48
when thou dost ask me blessing, i'll kneel down 5.03. 10
about it, and write happy when th' hast done. 5.03. 35
and when 'tis told, o, that my heart would burst 5.03.183
until some half hour past, when i was arm'd. 5.03.194
i know when one is dead, and when one lives; 5.03.261
i know when one is dead, and when one lives; 5.03.261
for nought but provender, and when he's old, OTH 1.01. 48
and when they have lin'd their coats, | do 1.01. 53
for when my outward action doth demonstrate 1.01. 61
like timorous accent and dire yell | as when, by 1.01. 76
which, when i know that boasting is an honor, 1.02. 20
when, being not at your lodging to be found, 1.02. 45
when we consider | th' importancy of cyprus to 1.03. 19
when i did speak of some distressful stroke 1.03.157
when remedies are past, the griefs are ended 1.03.202
what cannot be preserv'd when fortune takes, 1.03.206
when light–wing'd toys | of feather'd cupid seel 1.03.268
is silliness to live, when to live is torment; 1.03.308 P
to die, when death is our physician. 1.03.309 P
when she is sated with his body, she will find 1.03.350 P
what ribs of oak, when mountains melt on them, 2.01. 8
i find it still, when i have /list to sleep. 2.01.104
when the blood is made dull with the act of 2.01.226 P
when these /mutualities so marshal the way, hard 2.01.261 P
and when she speaks, is it not an alarum to love 2.03. 26 P
it be a sin | when violence assails us. 2.03.204
when i came back | (for this was brief), i found 2.03.236
they were | when you yourself did part them. 2.03.239
when this advice is free i give, and honest, 2.03.337
when devils will the blackest sins put on, 2.03.351
and bring him jump when he may cassio find 2.03.386
when shall he come? 3.03. 67
time, | when i have spoke of you dispraisingly, 3.03. 72
let him come when he will; 3.03. 75
when i have a suit | wherein i mean to touch 3.03. 80
and when i love thee not, | chaos is come again. 3.03. 91
did michael cassio, when /you woo'd my lady, 3.03. 94
lik'st not that, | when cassio left my wife. 3.03.110
and when i told thee he was of my counsel | /in 3.03.111
when i shall turn the business of my soul | to 3.03.181
when i doubt, prove; 3.03.190
and when she seem'd to shake and fear your looks 3.03.207
plague is fated to us | when we do quicken. 3.03.277
lady, she'll run mad | when she shall lack it. 3.03.318
and bid me, when my fate would have me wiv'd, 3.04. 64
and when they are full | they belch us. 3.04.105
when it hath blown his ranks into the air, | and 3.04.135
we say lie on her, when they belie her. 4.01. 36 P
when he is gone, | i would on great occasion 4.01. 57
how long ago, and when | he hath, and is again 4.01. 85
he, when he hears of her, cannot restrain | from 4.01. 98
will not, come when you are next prepar'd for. 4.01.160 P
i think i should, and undo't when i had /done't. 4.03. 72 P
that they do | when they change us for others? 4.03. 97
when i have pluck'd thy rose, | i cannot give it 5.02. 13
be thus when thou art dead, and i will kill thee 5.02. 18
for you're fatal then | when your eyes roll so. 5.02. 38
when we shall meet at compt, | this look of 5.02.273
when you shall these unlucky deeds relate, 5.02.341
pays shame | when shrill–tongu'd fulvia scolds. ANT 1.01. 32
when such a mutual pair | and such a twain can 1.01. 37
sir, sometimes when he is not antony, | he comes 1.01. 57
no, you shall paint when you are old. 1.02. 19 P
when it concerns the fool or coward. 1.02. 96
forth weeds | when our quick winds lie still, 1.02.110
when it pleaseth their deities to take the wife 1.02.162 P
therein, that when old robes are worn out, there 1.02.164 P
when you sued staying, | then was the time for 1.03. 33
the last, best, | see when and where she died. 1.03. 62
since my becomings kill me when they do not 1.03. 96
foils, when we do bear | so great weight in his 1.04. 24
when thou once | was beaten from modena, where 1.04. 56
like the stag, when snow the pasture sheets, 1.04. 65
when thou wast here above the ground, i was | a 1.05. 30
born that day | when i forget to send to antony, 1.05. 64
when i was green in judgment, cold in blood, 1.05. 74
when we debate | our trivial difference loud, we 2.02. 20
when to sound your name | it not concern'd me. 2.02. 34
when rioting in alexandria you | did pocket up 2.02. 72
to lend me arms and aid when i requir'd them, 2.02. 88
and then when poisoned hours had bound me up 2.02. 90
you may, when you hear no more words of pompey, 2.02.104 P
time to wrangle in when you have nothing else to 2.02.106 P
when she first met mark antony, she purs'd up 2.02.186 P
holy priests | bless her when she is riggish. 2.02.239
no more but when to thee. 2.03. 25
thy lustre thickens | when he shines by. 2.03. 29
still of mine, | when it is all to nought; 2.03. 38
and when good will is show'd, though't come too 2.05. 8
'twas merry when | you wager'd on your angling; 2.05. 15
when your diver | did hang a salt–fish on his 2.05. 16
ill tidings tell | themselves when they be felt. 2.05. 88
when caesar and your brother were at blows, 2.06. 44
thee fight, | when i have envied thy behavior. 2.06. 75
when you have well deserv'd ten times as much 2.06. 77
and, when we are put off, fall to their throats: 2.07. 72
seeks, and will not take when once 'tis offer'd, 2.07. 83
it's monstrous labor when i wash my brain | and 2.07. 99
too high a fame when him we serve's away. 3.01. 15
when antony found julius caesar dead, | he cried 3.02. 54
wept | when at philippi he found brutus slain. 3.02. 56
look upon you | but when you are well pleas'd. 3.03. 4
but how, when antony is gone, | through whom i 3.03. 5
when perforce he could not | but pay me terms of 3.04. 6
when the best hint was given him, he not /took't 3.04. 9
when i shall pray, "o, bless my lord and husband 3.04. 16
when it appears to you where this begins, | turn 3.04. 33
when vantage like a pair of twins appear'd, 3.10. 12
we scorn her most when most she offers blows. 3.11. 74
when hither | he sends so poor a pinion of his 3.12. 3
when half to half the world oppos'd, he being 3.13. 9
oft | (when he hath mus'd of taking kingdoms in) 3.13. 83
of late, when i cried "ho!" 3.13. 90
but when we in our viciousness grow hard | (o 3.13.111
when my good stars, that were my former guides, 3.13.145
for when mine hours | were nice and lucky, men 3.13.178
when valor /preys /on reason, | it eats the 3.13.198
when one so great begins to rage, he's hunted 4.01. 7
of me | as when mine empire was your fellow too, 4.02. 22
when my turpitude | thou dost so crown with gold 4.06. 32
when men revolted shall upon record | bear 4.09. 8
for when i am reveng'd upon my charm, | i have 4.12. 16
that when the exigent should come, which now 4.14. 63
when i should see behind me | th' inevitable 4.14. 64
when i did make thee free, swor'st thou not then 4.14. 81
thou not then | to do this when i bade thee? 4.14. 82
when did she send thee? 4.14.119
for when she saw | (which never shall be found) 4.14.121
die when thou hast liv'd, | quicken with kissing 4.15. 38
when such a spacious mirror's set before him, 5.01. 34
you laugh when boys or women tell their dreams; 5.02. 74
but when he meant to quail and shake the orb, 5.02. 85
and, when we fall, | we answer others' merits in 5.02.177
and when thou hast done this chare, i'll give 5.02.231
you woo another wife, | when imogen is dead. CYM 1.01.114
o the gods! | when shall we see again? 1.01.124
good pisanio, | when shall we hear from him? 1.03. 23
you speak of him when he was less furnish'd than 1.04. 8 P
since when i have been debtor to you for 1.04. 36 P
when thou shalt bring me word she loves my son, 1.05. 49
but when to my good lord i prove untrue, | i'll 1.05. 86
when he was here, | he did incline to sadness, 1.06. 61
when i kiss'd the jack upon an up–cast, to be 2.01. 1 P
when a gentleman is dispos'd to swear, it is not 2.01. 10 P
you are most hot and furious when you win. 2.03. 6 P
save when command to your dismission tends, 2.03. 52
son, | when you have given good morning to your 2.03. 61
are men more order'd than when julius caesar 2.04. 21
in the britain court | when you were there? 2.04. 38
give me leave to spare when you shall find | you 2.04. 65
story | proud cleopatra, when she met her roman, 2.04. 70
was i know not where | when i was stamp'd. 2.05. 5
when julius caesar (whose remembrance yet 3.01. 2
when you above perceive me like a crow, | that 3.03. 12
should we speak of | when we are old as you? 3.03. 36
when we shall hear | the rain and wind beat dark 3.03. 36
and when a soldier was the theme, my name | was 3.03. 59
when on my three–foot stool i sit and tell | the 3.03. 89
thou toldst me, when we came from horse, the 3.04. 1
when thou seest him, | a little witness my 3.04. 65
when thou shalt be disedg'd by her | that now 3.04. 93
do thy master's bidding | when i desire it too. 3.04. 98
to be unbent when thou hast ta'en thy stand, 3.04.108
what comfort, when i am | dead to my husband? 3.04.129
my lord, when last i went to visit her, | she 3.05. 45
for when fools shall — | who is here? 3.05. 79
when was she miss'd? 3.05. 90
the same suit he wore when he took leave of my 3.05.126 P
on his dead body, and when my lust hath din'd 3.05.141 P
when from the mountain top pisanio show'd thee, 3.06. 5
no wonder, | when rich ones scarce tell true. 3.06. 12
when resty sloth | finds the down pillow hard. 3.06. 34
when we have supp'd, | we'll mannerly demand 3.06. 90
when i have slain thee with my proper hand, 4.02. 97
one half so well | as when thou grew'st thyself. 4.02.203
when flow'rs are none, | to winter–ground thy 4.02.228
is as good as ajax', | when neither are alive. 4.02.253
even when i wake, it is | without me, as within 4.02.306
when expect you them? 4.02.341
and when | with wild wood–leaves and weeds i ha' 4.02.389
and in a time | when fearful wars point at me; 4.03. 7
why gone, | nor when she purposes return. 4.03. 15
that when they hear their roman horses neigh, 4.04. 17
for three performers are the file when all | the 5.03. 30
when once he was mature for man, | in britain 5.04. 52
cloys his beak, | as when his god is pleas'd. 5.04.119
"when as a lion's whelp shall, to himself 5.04.138 P
and when from a stately cedar shall be lopp'd 5.04.140 P
wet cheeks | were present when she finish'd. 5.05. 36
time | (when she had fitted you with her craft), 5.05. 55
we should not, when the blood was cool, have 5.05. 77
call'd me brother, | when i was but your sister; 5.05.377
i you brothers, | when we were so indeed. 5.05.378
when shall i hear all through? 5.05.382
and when came you to serve our roman captive? 5.05.385
when i wak'd, i found | this label on my bosom, 5.05.429
"when as a lion's whelp shall, to himself 5.05.435 P
and when from a stately cedar shall be lopp'd 5.05.437 P
when wit's more ripe, accept my rhymes, | and PER 1.ch. 12
sin, | when what is done is like an hypocrite, 1.01.122
when signior sooth here does proclaim peace, 1.02. 44
'tis time to fear when tyrants seems to kiss. 1.02. 79
when all, for mine, if i may call offense, 1.02. 92
the which when any shall not gratify, | or pay 1.04.101
till when — the which i hope shall ne'er be 1.04.105
where when men been, there's seldom ease, | for 2.ch. 28
cries they made to us to help them, when, 2.01. 22 P
said not i as much when i saw the porpas how he 2.01. 23 P
me too, and when i had been in his belly, i 2.01. 40 P
which if you shall refuse, when i am dead, | for 2.01. 76
glory, | when he was seated in a chariot | of an 2.04. 7
when peers thus knit, a kingdom ever stands. 2.04. 58
when canst thou reach it? 3.01. 75
be't when they weav'd the sleided silk | with 4.ch. 21
or when she would with sharp needle wound | the 4.ch. 23
or when to th' lute | she sung, and made the 4.ch. 25
or when | she would with rich and constant pen 4.ch. 27
maid, | born in a tempest when my mother died, 4.01. 18
when he shall come and find | our paragon to all 4.01. 34
when i was born, the wind was north. 4.01. 51
when was this? 4.01. 57
when i was born. 4.01. 58
when you caught hurt in parting two that fought; 4.01. 87
is it a shame to get when we are old? 4.02. 29 P
when nature fram'd this piece, she meant thee a 4.02.139 P
when noble pericles shall demand his child? 4.03. 13
when she should do for clients her fitment, and 4.06. 5 P
thou not /say, when i did push thee back — 5.01.126
which was when i perceiv'd thee — that thou 5.01.127
when thou shalt kneel, and justify in knowledge 5.01.217
when my maiden priests are met together | before 5.01.242
with all my heart, and, when you come ashore, 5.01.260
when we with tears parted pentapolis, | the king 5.03. 38
you have heard me say, when i did fly from tyre, 5.03. 50
wife, when fame | had spread his cursed deed, 5.03. 95
than a dove's motion when the head's pluck'd off TNK 1.01. 98
sun, | and were good kings when living. 1.01.147
but when could grief | cull forth, as unpang'd 1.01.168
when her arms, | able to lock jove from a synod, 1.01.175
o, when | her twinning cherries shall their 1.01.177
i do bleed | when such i meet, and wish great 1.02. 21
when by mine own | i may be reasonably conceiv'd 1.02. 47
when | he broke his whipstock and exclaim'd 1.02. 85
when that his action's dregg'd with mind assur'd 1.02. 97
tell us | when we know all ourselves, and let us 1.02.115
cannot weep | when our friends don their helms, 1.03. 19
once with a time when i enjoy'd a playfellow; 1.03. 50
you were at wars when she the grave enrich'd, 1.03. 51
at parting) when our count | was each aleven. 1.03. 53
/prisoner told me | when i inquired their names? 1.04. 22
been taken | when their last hurts were given, 1.04. 26
talk more of this when the solemnity is past. 2.01. 12 P
when that shall be seen, i tender my consent. 2.01. 14 P
when the other presently gives it so sweet a 2.01. 42 P
for when the west wind courts her gently, | how 2.02.138
when the north comes near her, | rude and 2.02.140
out, | and leap the garden, when i see her next, 2.02.216
and me too, | even when you please, of life. 2.02.225
bold young men that, when he bids 'em charge, 2.02.249
driven to | when fifteen once has found us! 2.04. 7

when i come in | to bring him water in a morning 2.04. 21
when your servant | (your most unworthy creature 2.05. 39
when he considers more, this love of mine | will 2.06. 27
men lose when they incline to treachery, | and 3.01. 67
when you shall stretch yourself, and say but, 3.01. 87
when i spur | my horse, i chide him /not; 3.01.106
all's char'd when he is gone. 3.02. 21
save when my lids scour'd off their /brine. 3.02. 28
was a time | when young men went a–hunting, and 3.03. 40
and when you bark, do it with judgment. 3.05. 37
now, when the credit of our town lay on it, 3.05. 56
when he left me, | i did not think a week could 3.06. 4
make the world think, when it comes to hearing, 3.06. 11
when we are arm'd | and both upon our guards, 3.06. 28
when you charg'd | upon the left wing of the 3.06. 74
when i saw you charge first, | methought i heard 3.06. 82
when ye return, who wins i'll settle here; 3.06.307
o sir, when did you see her? 4.01. 33
sir, when did she sleep? 4.01. 35
when i might well perceive | 'twas one that sung 4.01. 57
when presently | she slipp'd away, and to the 4.01. 96
"when cynthia with her borrowed light," etc. 4.01.153
when he frowns | to seal his will with. 4.02. 86
and when he's angry, then a settled valor | (not 4.02.100
when he speaks, his tongue | sounds like a 4.02.112
still, | but, when he stirs, a tiger. 4.02.131
and when he smiles | he shows a lover, when he 4.02.135
he smiles | he shows a lover, when he frowns, a 4.02.136
heal'st with blood | the earth when it is sick, 5.01. 65
me what i would eat, and when i would kiss her. 5.02. 5
so, | and when your fit comes, fit her home, and 5.02. 11
ev'n when you will. 5.02. 87
are not prophets | when oft our fancies are. 5.03.103
can that be, when | venus i have said is false? 5.04. 44
when nought serv'd, | when neither curb would 5.04. 73
when neither curb would crack, girth break, nor 5.04. 74
there such fellows liv'd when you were babes, STM II.C 63
sound | when there is no addition but a rebel II.C 118
is, when the thread of hazard is once spun, | a III 20
but when her lips were ready for his pay, | he VEN 89
that thine may live, when thou thyself art dead; 172
like misty vapors when they blot the sky, 184
and when from thence he struggles to be gone, 227
look when a painter would surpass the life | in 289
when lo the unback'd breeder, full of fear, 320
when it is barr'd the aidance of the tongue. 330
but when the heart's attorney once is mute, 335
but when he saw his love, his youth's fair fee, 393
but, when his glutton eye so full hath fed, 399
when in his fresh array | he cheers the morn, 483
but then woos best when most his choice is 570
when he did frown, o, had she then gave over, 571
eyes like glow–worms shine when he doth fret, 621
when thou didst name the boar, not to dissemble, 641
"and when thou hast on foot the purblind hare, 679
when reason is the bawd to lust's abuse. 792
like soldiers when their captain once doth yield 893
when he hath ceas'd his ill–resounding noise, 919
who when he liv'd, his breath and beauty set 935
who is but drunken when she seemeth drown'd. 984
i felt a kind of fear | when as i met the boar, 999
as when the wind imprison'd in the ground, 1046
but when adonis liv'd, sun and sharp air 1085
to recreate himself when he hath song, | the 1095
"when he beheld his shadow in the brook, | the 1099
when he was by, the birds such pleasure took, 1101
and most deceiving when it seems most just; 1156
when collatine unwisely did not let | to praise LUC 10
when at collatium this false lord arrived, 50
when virtue bragg'd, beauty would blush for 54
when beauty boasted blushes, in despite | virtue 55
when shame assail'd, the red should fence the 63
and when great treasure is the meed proposed, 132
when shall he think to find a stranger just 159
just | when he himself himself confounds, 160
when heavy sleep had clos'd up mortal eyes. 163
when thou shalt charge me with so black a deed? 226
all orators are dumb when beauty pleadeth, 268
and when his gaudy banner is display'd, | the 272
but when a black–fac'd cloud the world doth 547
when thus thy vices bud before thy spring? 604
what dar'st thou not when once thou art a king? 606
when they in thee the like offenses prove. 613
when pattern'd by thy fault foul sin may say 629
when most unseen, then most doth tyrannize. 676
for there it revels, and when that decays, | the 713
evil, | when virtue is profan'd in such a devil! 847
"so then he hath it when he cannot use it, | and 862
thou blowest the fire when temperance is thaw'd, 884
"when wilt thou be the humble suppliant's friend 897
when wilt thou sort an hour great strifes to end 899
"when truth and virtue have to do with thee, | a 911
would else have come to me | when tarquin did, 917
but little stars may hide them when they list. 1008
but when i fear'd, i was a loyal wife: 1048
when lo the blushing morrow | lends light to all 1082
when with like semblance it is sympathiz'd. 1113
distress likes dumps when time is kept with 1127
when life is sham'd and death reproach's debtor. 1155
having two sweet babes, when death takes one, 1161
when the one pure, the other made divine? 1164
when both were kept for heaven and collatine? 1166
this plot of death when sadly she had laid, 1212
as winter meads when sun doth melt their snow. 1218
girl, when went" (and there she stay'd | till 1275
when more is felt than one hath power to tell. 1288
she hoards, to spend when he is by to hear her, 1318
when sighs and groans and tears may grace the 1319
when every part a part of woe doth bear. 1327
when, seely groom, god wot, it was defect | of 1345
when their brave hope, bold hector, march'd to 1430
when their glass fell wherein they view'd their 1526
which when her sad–beholding husband saw, 1590
and when the judge is robb'd, the prisoner dies. 1652
"and for my sake when i might charm thee so, 1681
when they had sworn to this advised doom, | they 1849
when my love swears that she is made of truth, PP 1. 1
when cytherea (all in love forlorn) | a longing 6. 3
drown'd | when as himself to singing he betakes. 8.12
fair was the morn when the fair queen of love, 9. 1
a flower that dies when first it gins to bud, 13. 3
when as thine eye hath chose the dame, | and 18. 1
and when thou com'st thy tale to tell, | smooth 18. 7
when time shall serve, be thou not slack | to 18.23
when craft hath taught her thus to say: 18.34
then, | when time with age shall them attaint. 18.46
when forty winters shall besiege thy brow, | and SON 2. 1
this were to be new made when thou art old, 2.13
see thy blood warm when thou feel'st it cold. 2.14
then how when nature calls thee to be gone, 4.11
lo in the orient when the gracious light | lifts 7. 1
but when from highmost pitch, with weary car, 7. 9
when every private widow well may keep, | by 9. 7
call thine, when thou from youth convertest. 11. 4
when i do count the clock that tells the time, 12. 1
when i behold the violet past prime, | and sable 12. 3
when lofty trees i see barren of leaves, | which 12. 5
breed, to brave him when he takes thee hence. 12.14
when your sweet issue your sweet form should 13. 8
when i consider every thing that grows | holds 15. 1
when i perceive that men as plants increase, 15. 5
when in eternal lines to time thou grow'st. 18.12
but when in thee time's furrows i behold, | then 22. 3
presume not on thy heart when mine is slain, 22.13
to work my mind, when body's work's expired; 27. 4
when day's oppression is not eas'd by night, 28. 3
and dost him grace when clouds do blot the 28.10
when sparkling stars twire not, thou /gild'st 28.12
when in disgrace with fortune and men's eyes, 29. 1
when to the sessions of sweet silent thought | i 30. 1
when that churl death my bones with dust shall 32. 2
the world may stain when heaven's sun staineth. 33.14
when thou thyself dost give invention light? 38. 8
sing, | when thou art all the better part of me? 39. 2
and what is't but mine own when i praise thee? 39. 4
when i am sometime absent from thy heart, | thy 41. 2
and when a woman woos, what woman's son | will 41. 7
when most i wink, then do mine eyes best see, 43. 1
but when i sleep, in dreams they look on thee, 43. 3
when to unseeing eyes thy shade shines so! 43. 8
when in dead night /thy fair imperfect shade 43.11
nights bright days when dreams do show thee me. 43.14
leap large lengths of miles when thou art gone, 44.10
for when these quicker elements are gone | in 45. 5
when that mine eye is famish'd for a look, | or 47. 3
how careful was i, when i took my way, | each 48. 1
when i shall see thee frown on my defects, 49. 2
when as thy love hath cast his utmost sum, 49. 3
against that time when thou shalt strangely pass 49. 5
eye, | when love converted from the thing it was 49. 7
when what i seek (my weary travel's end) | doth 50. 2
of my dull bearer, when from thee i speed: 51. 2
find, | when swift extremity can seem but slow? 51. 6
when summer's breath their masked buds discloses 54. 8
when that shall vade, by verse distills your 54.14
when wasteful war shall statues overturn, | and 55. 5
that, when they see | return of love, more blest 56.11
when you have bid your servant once adieu. 57. 8
but when my glass shows me myself indeed, 62. 9
when hours have drain'd his blood and fill'd his 63. 3
when his youthful morn | hath travell'd on to 63. 4
when i have seen by time's fell hand defaced 64. 1
when sometime lofty towers i see down rased, 64. 3
when i have seen the hungry ocean gain 64. 5
when i have seen such interchange of state, | or 64. 9
days, | when rocks impregnable are not so stout, 65. 7
when beauty liv'd and died as flowers do now, 68. 2
no longer mourn for me when i am dead | than you 71. 1
when i (perhaps) compounded am with clay, | do 71.10
thou mayst in me behold | when yellow leaves, or 73. 2
when that fell arrest | without all bail shall 74. 1
when thou reviewest this, thou dost review | the 74. 5
o, how i faint when i of you do write, | knowing 80. 1
or you survive when i in earth am rotten, | from 81. 2
when you entombed in men's eyes shall lie; 81. 8
when all the breathers of this world are dead; 81.12
yet when they have devis'd | what strained 82. 9
when others would give life and bring a tomb. 83.12
but when your countenance fill'd up his line, 86.13
when thou shalt be dispos'd to set me light, 88. 1
then hate me when thou wilt, if ever, now, | now 90. 1
do not, when my heart hath scap'd this sorrow, 90. 5
when other petty griefs have done their spite, 90.10
when in the least of them my life hath end; 92. 6
when proud–pied april (dress'd in all his trim) 98. 2
when i was wont to greet it with my lays, | as 102. 6
than when her mournful hymns did hush the night, 102.10
than when it hath my added praise beside. 103. 4
your own glass shows you when you look in it. 103.14
for as you were when first your eye i ey'd, 104. 2
when in the chronicle of wasted time | i see 106. 1
when tyrants' crests and tombs of brass are 107.14
even as when first i hallowed thy fair name. 108. 8
best," | when i was certain o'er incertainty, 115.11
love | which alters when it alteration finds, 116. 3
we sicken to shun sickness when we purge; 118. 4
fears, | still losing when i saw myself to win? 119. 4
and ruin'd love, when it is built anew, | grows 119.11
when not to be receives reproach of being, | and 121. 2
when most impeach'd stands least in thy control. 125.14
how oft, when thou, my music, music play'st 128. 1
with thy sweet fingers when thou gently sway'st 128. 3
my mistress when she walks treads on the ground. 130.12
when my love swears that she is made of truth, 138. 1
need'st thou wound with cunning when thy might 139. 7
as testy sick men, when their deaths be near, 140. 7
root pity in thy heart, that, when it grows, 142.11
but when she saw my woeful state, | straight in 145. 4
not, | when i against myself with thee partake? 149. 2
do i not think on thee when i forgot | am of 149. 3
when all my best doth worship thy defect, 149.11
breach do i accuse thee, | when i break twenty? 152. 6
when he again desires her, being sat, | her LC 66
and when in his fair parts she did abide, | she 83
when winds breathe sweet, unruly though they be. 103
for when we rage, advice is often seen | by 160
believ'd her eyes when they t' assail begun, 262
"'when thou impressest, what are precepts worth 267
when thou wilt inflame, | how coldly those 268
when he most burnt in heart–wish'd luxury, | he 314

WHENCE 88 FR 0.0099 REL FR 74 V 14 P
nought knowing | of whence i am, nor that i am TMP 1.02. 19
now tell me: how do all from whence you came? TGV 2.04.122
whence came you? 4.01. 18
whence come you? WIV 4.05.104 P
whence comes this restraint? MM 1.02.124
of whence are you? 3.02.216 P
to find out this abuse, whence 'tis deriv'd. 5.01.247
let him walk from whence he came, lest he catch ERR 3.01. 37
from whence, i think, you are come by miracle. 5.01.265
from whence doth spring the true promethean fire
LLL 4.03.300
from whence you have studied your questions. AYL 3.02.274 P
why, how now, dame, whence grows this insolence?
SHR 2.01. 23
whence are you, sir? 2.01. 67
lucentio is your name, of whence, i pray? 2.01.102
from whence thou cam'st, how tended on, but rest
AWW 2.01.207
in earth, from whence god send her quickly! 2.04. 13 P
whence honor but of danger wins a scar, | as oft 3.02.121
paris, from whence he was whipt for getting the 4.03.186 P
whence came you, sir? TN 1.05.177 P
i will conster to them whence you come; 3.01. 56 P
whence they gape and point | at your industrious JN 2.01.375
lie that way thou goest, not whence thou com'st. R2 1.03.287
from whence set forth in pomp | she came adorned 5.01. 78
from whence this stream through muddy passages 5.03. 62
from whence he intercepted did return | to be 1H4 1.03.151
now, harry, whence come you? 2.04.440 P
every loop from whence | the eye of reason may 4.01. 71
from whence with life he never more sprung up. 2H4 1.01.111
whence cometh this alarum, and the noise? 1H6 1.04. 99
from whence you spring by lineal descent. 3.01.165
they come to berwick, from whence they came. 2H6 2.01.156
his poor queen to france, from whence she came, 2.02. 25
and i unto the sea, from whence i came. 3H6 1.01.209
to tell thee whence thou cam'st, of whom deriv'd 1.04.119
thou not, knowing whence thou art extraught, 2.02.142
from whence that tender spray did sweetly spring 2.06. 50
from whence shall warwick cut the sea to france, 2.06. 89
fair queen, whence springs this deep despair? 3.03. 12
and blow it to the source from whence it came; 5.03. 11
that i love the tree from whence thou sprang'st, 5.07. 31
from whence this present day he is delivered? R3 1.01. 69
whence has he that? H8 1.01. 69
from whence, fragment? TRO 5.01. 8 P
a cruel war i sent him, from whence he return'd, COR 1.03. 14 P
from whence came | that ancus martius, numa's 2.03.238
whence are you? 4.05. 7 P
whence are you, sir? 4.05. 11 P
whence com'st thou? 4.05. 53
stay! whence are you? 5.02. 1
from whence? 5.02. 4
whence men have read | his fame unparallel'd, 5.02. 15
from whence at first she weigh'd her anchorage, TIT 1.01. 73
i know from whence this same device proceeds. 4.04. 52
could we but learn from whence his sorrows grow,
ROM 1.01.154
whence come you? 3.03. 78
/gum, which /oozes | from whence 'tis nourish'd. TIM 1.01. 22
dues? whence are you? 2.02. 17
as whence the sun gins his reflection MAC 1.02. 25
so from that spring whence comfort seem'd to 1.02. 27
whence cam'st thou, worthy thane? 1.02. 48
say from whence | you owe this strange 1.03. 75
whence is that knocking? 2.02. 54
in a place | from whence himself does fly? 4.02. 8
from whence though willingly i came to denmark HAM 1.02. 52
from whence i will fitly bring you to hear my LR 1.02.168 P
from whence ariseth this? OTH 2.03.169
o cassio, whence came this? 3.04.180
the devil's teeth, | from whence you have them. 3.04.185
whence are you? ANT 5.01. 51
from whence he moves | his war for britain. CYM 3.05. 25
upon our note, | to know from whence we are. 4.04. 21
'tis now the time | to ask of whence you are. 5.05. 16
my riches to the earth from whence they came; PER 1.01. 52
from whence | they have their nourishment? 1.02. 55
from whence an issue i might propagate, | are 1.02. 73
from whence we had our being and our birth. 1.02.114
now message must return from whence it came. 1.03. 35
to know for what he comes, and whence he comes, 1.04. 80
you'll remember from whence you had them. 2.01.152 P
we desire to know of him | of whence he is, his 2.03. 74
he desires to know of you of whence you are, 2.03. 80
from whence | lysimachus our tyrian ship espies, 5.ch. 17
us, | i made to it to know of whence you are. 5.01. 19
from whence come you, sir? TNK 4.02. 71
plunges | disroot his rider whence he grew, but 5.04. 75
from whence at pleasure thou mayst come and part
SON 48.12
whence didst thou steal thy sweet that smells, 99. 2
whence hast thou this becoming of things ill, 150. 5

WHENCESOEVER 1 FR 0.0001 REL FR 1 V 0 P
sent from my brother worcester, whencesoever. R2 2.03. 22

WHENSOEVER 2 FR 0.0002 REL FR 1 V 1 P
make up full clear, | whensoever he's convented. MM 5.01.158
now or whensoever, provided i be so able as now.
HAM 5.02.202 P

WHEN'T 1 FR 0.0001 REL FR 1 V 0 P
subject to, | when't pleas'd you to employ me. CYM 1.01.173

WHE'R (also whe'er, whether, whither*)

WHE'R 1 FR 0.0001 REL FR 1 V 0 P
good sir, say whe'r you'll answer me or no: ERR 4.01. 60

WHERE (also vere*)

/WHERE 9 FR 0.0010 REL FR 8 V 1 P
sweet, | whither away, or /where is thy abode? SHR 4.05. 38
/indeed | /where /all /my /sins /are /writ, /and R2 4.01.275
/where hotspur's father, old northumberland, 2H4 in 36
/would /lift /him /where /most /trade /of 1.01.174
/where /nothing /but /the /sound /of /hotspur's 2.03. 37
/is /fine /in /love, /and /where /'tis /fine, HAM 4.05.162
/look /where /he /stands /and /glares! LR 3.06. 23 P

/the /bedlam | /to /lead /him /where /he /would; 3.07.104
/where /i /could /not /be /honest, | /i /never 5.01. 23

WHERE 1400 FR 0.1582 REL FR 1168 V 232 P

where is the master, bos'n? TMP 1.01. 12 P
where they prepared | a rotten carcass of a butt 1.02.145
where once | thou call'dst me up at midnight to 1.02.227
thou hast. where was she born? speak. tell me. 1.02.260
where thou didst vent thy groans | as fast as 1.02.280
where should this music be? 1.02.388
this speech, | were i but where 'tis spoken. 1.02.431
where she, at least, is banish'd from your eye, 2.01.127
where lies that? 2.01.276
it did before, i know not where to hide my head. 2.02. 23 P
might scratch her where e'er she did itch. 2.02. 53
where the devil should he learn our language? 2.02. 66 P
in a rock by th' sea-side, where my wine is hid. 2.02.135 P
i prithee let me bring thee where crabs grow; 2.02.167
where should they be set else? 3.02. 10 P
where thou mayst knock a nail into his head. 3.02. 61
i'll not show him | where the quick freshes are. 3.02. 67
to me, where i shall have my music for nothing. 3.02.144 P
on this island | where man doth not inhabit — 3.03. 57
thy turfy mountains, where live nibbling sheep, 4.01. 62
where thou thyself dost air — the queen o' th' 4.01. 70
say again, where didst thou leave these varlots? 4.01.170
to bear this away where my hogshead of wine is, 4.01.251 P
where the bee sucks, there suck i, | in a 5.01. 88
where i have lost | (how sharp the point of this 5.01.137
mudded in that oozy bed | where my son lies. 5.01.152
upon this shore (where you were wrack'd) was 5.01.161
found a wife | where he himself was lost; 5.01.211
where, but even now, with strange and several 5.01.232
where we, in all our trim, freshly beheld | our 5.01.236
he is drunk now. where had he wine? 5.01.278
where should they | find this grand liquor that 5.01.279
and bestow your luggage where you found it. 5.01.299
where you shall take your rest | for this one 5.01.302
where i have hope to see the nuptial | of these 5.01.309
where | every third thought shall be my grave. 5.01.311
be in love — where scorn is bought with groans; TGV 1.01. 29
it will not lie where it concerns | unless it 1.02. 74
and drench'd me in the sea, where i am drown'd. 1.03. 79
i must, where is no remedy. 2.02. 2
where should i lose my tongue? 2.03. 47 P
where, for one shot of five pence, thou shalt 2.05. 9 P
but there i leave to love where i should love. 2.06. 18
where, if it please you, you may intercept him. 3.01. 43
where i thought the remnant of mine age | should 3.01. 74
advise me where i may have such a ladder. 3.01.122
himself would lodge where, senseless, they are 3.01.143
they should harbor where their lord should be." 3.01.149
where your good word cannot advantage him, 3.02. 42
where you with silvia may confer at large — 3.02. 61
where you may temper her by your persuasion | to 3.02. 64
love | will creep in service where it cannot go. 4.02. 20
i'll bring you where you shall hear music and 4.02. 31 P
where is launce? 4.02. 77 P
where meet we? 4.02. 84
pray you, where lies sir proteus? 4.02.136 P
to mantua, where i hear he makes abode; 4.03. 23
where shall i meet you? 4.03. 43
cell, | where i intend holy confession. 4.03. 44
where have you been these two days loitering? 4.04. 44
where thou shalt find me sad and solitary. 4.04. 89
to bring me where to speak with madam silvia. 4.04.109
see where she comes. 5.01. 7
where is the gentleman that was with her? 5.03. 6
when women cannot love where they're belov'd! 5.04. 44
when proteus cannot love where he's belov'd! 5.04. 45
where is that ring, boy? 5.04. 91
how now, simple, where have you been? WIV 1.01.200 P
why, look where he comes; 2.01.102 P
look where my ranting host of the garter comes. 2.01.189 P
by mistaking the place where i erected it. 2.02.217 P
i will bring thee where mistress anne page is, 2.03. 87 P
he promise to bring me where is anne page; 3.01.123 P
where had you this pretty weathercock? 3.02. 18 P
look where his master comes; 4.01. 9 P
where is it? 4.02. 59 P
no, nor no where else but in your brain. 4.02.159 P
where we may take him, and disgrace him for it. 4.04. 15
where be my horses? 4.05. 64 P
where is mine host? 4.05. 73 P
and at the dean'ry, where a priest attends, 4.06. 31
where is nan now, and her troop of fairies, and 5.03. 11 P
where fires thou find'st unrak'd and hearths 5.05. 44
go you, and where you find a maid | that, ere 5.05. 49
where i will desire thee to laugh at my wife, 5.05.171 P
where there was no proportion held in love. 5.05.222
look where he comes. MM 1.01. 24
i think thou never wast where grace was said. 1.02. 19 P
behold, behold, where madam mitigation comes! 1.02. 44 P
bear me to prison, where i am committed. 1.02.117
in idle price to haunt assemblies | where youth, 1.03. 10
where is the provost? 2.01. 32
grapes, where indeed you have a delight to sit, 2.01.129 P
where were you born, friend? 2.01.193 P
no, not for dwelling where you do. 2.01.247 P
way going to temptation, | where prayers cross. 2.02.159
where their untaught love | must needs appear 2.04. 29
ay, as the glasses where they view themselves, 2.04.125
that dost this habitation where thou keep'st 3.01. 10
to hear /them speak, where i may be conceal'd. 3.01. 52 P
where you shall be an everlasting leiger; 3.01. 58
ay, but to die, and go we know not where; 3.01.117
but where is he, think you? 3.02. 89 P
i know not where; 3.02. 90 P
where you shall find, within these two days he 4.02.198 P
at flavio's house, | and tell him where i stay. 4.05. 7
where you may have such vantage on the duke, 4.06. 11
to make the truth appear where it seems hid, 5.01. 66
your provost knows the place where he abides, 5.01.252
how! know you where you are? 5.01.291
where is the duke? 5.01.294
where i have seen corruption boil and bubble, 5.01.318
where is the provost? 5.01.345 P
the very block | where claudio stoop'd to death, 5.01.415
palace, where we'll show | what's yet behind, 5.01.538

me, | and soon, and safe, arrived where i was. ERR 1.01. 48
go bear it to the centaur, where we host, | and 1.02. 9
where have you left the money that i gave you? 1.02. 54
tell me, and dally not, where is the money? 1.02. 59
where is the gold i gave in charge to thee? 1.02. 70
where is the thousand marks thou hadst of me? 1.02. 81
how if your husband start some other where? 2.01. 30
"where is the thousand marks i gave thee, 2.01. 65
touch and, often touching, will | where gold; 2.01.112
for ever hous'd where it gets possession. 3.01.106
why, how now, dromio, where run'st thou so fast? 3.02. 71 P
where scotland? 3.02.119 P
where france? 3.02.122 P
where england? 3.02.125 P
where spain? 3.02.130 P
where america, the indies? 3.02.133 P
where stood belgia, the netherlands? 3.02.138 P
where i will walk till thou return to me. 3.02.151
that labor may you save; see where he comes. 4.01. 14
that is where we din'd, | where dowsabel did 4.01.109
where dowsabel did claim me for her husband: 4.01.110
ill-fac'd, worse bodied, shapeless every where; 4.02. 20
where is thy master, dromio? is he well? 4.02. 31
where would you had remain'd until this time, 4.04. 66
come, jailer, bring me where the goldsmith is, 4.04.142
liv'st | to walk where any honest men resort. 5.01. 28
see where they come, we will behold his death. 5.01.128
where balthazar and i did dine together. 5.01.223
where is that son | that floated with thee on 5.01.348
how now, brother, where is my cousin, your son? ADO 1.02. 1 P
where it is impossible you should take true root 1.03. 22 P
heavens, he shows me where the bachelors sit, 2.01. 48 P
see you where benedick hath hid himself? 2.03. 40
where honeysuckles, ripened by the sun, | forbid 3.01. 8
for look where beatrice, like a lapwing, runs 3.01. 24
where is but a humor or a worm. 3.02. 27 P
in the congregation, where i should wed, there 3.02.125 P
where his codpiece seems as massy as his club? 3.03.137 P
o, in a tomb where never scandal slept, | save 5.01. 70
as thus — to study where i well may dine, LLL 1.01. 61
or study where to meet some mistress fine, 1.01. 63
so, ere you find where light in darkness lies, 1.01. 78
then for the place where? 1.01.240 P
where, i mean, i did encounter that obscene and 1.01.241 P
but to the place where? 1.01.245 P
i know where it is situate. 1.02.137 P
(which is base) where her shoe (which is baser) 1.02.168 P
where now his knowledge must prove ignorance. 2.01.103
where that and other specialties are bound: 2.01.164
their own worth from where they were glass'd, 2.01.244
where is the bush | that we must stand and play 4.01. 7
a stand where you may make the fairest shoot. 4.01. 10
where fair is not, praise cannot mend the brow. 4.01. 17
where all those pleasures live that art would 4.02.110
the father's of a certain pupil of mine, where, 4.02.154 P
where i will prove those verses to be very 4.02.157 P
for none offend where all alike do dote. 4.03.124
where lies thy grief, o, tell me, good dumaine? 4.03.169
and, gentle longaville, where lies thy pain? 4.03.170
and where my liege's? 4.03.171
berowne, read it over. where hadst thou it? 4.03.193
where hadst thou it? 4.03.194
where several worthies make one dignity, | where 4.03.232
where nothing wants that want itself doth seek. 4.03.233
where is a book? 4.03.246
and where that you have vow'd to study, lords, 4.03.292
for where is any author in the world | teaches 4.03.308
and where we are, our learning likewise is. 4.03.311
where will you find men worthy enough to present 5.01.124 P
see where it comes! 5.02.337
where? when? what vizard? why demand you this? 5.02.386
where zeal strives to content, and the contents 5.02.517
(where i did meet thee once with helena | to do MND 1.01.166
where often you and i | upon faint primrose beds 1.01.214
so the boy love is perjur'd every where; 1.01.241
flood, thorough fire, | i do wander every where, 2.01. 6
yet mark'd i where the bolt of cupid fell. 2.01.165
where is lysander and fair hermia? 2.01.189
i know a bank where the wild thyme blows, 2.01.249
where oxlips and the nodding violet grows, 2.01.250
where is demetrius? 2.02.106
where i o'erlook | love's stories written in 2.02.121
alack, where are you? 2.02.153
of the great chamber window (where we play) open 3.01. 57 P
where shall we go? 3.01.163
where is he? 3.02. 62
look where thy love comes; 3.02.176
where art thou, proud demetrius? speak thou now. 3.02.401
here, villain, drawn and ready. where art thou? 3.02.402
where dost thou hide thy head? 3.02.406
when i come where he calls, then he is gone. 3.02.414
where art thou now? 3.02.425
was to be gone from athens, where we might, 4.01.152
where are these lads? where are these hearts? 4.02. 25 P
where are these lads? where are these hearts? 4.02. 25 P
where is our usual manager of mirth? 5.01. 35
where i have come, great clerks have purposed 5.01. 93
where i have seen them shiver and look pale, 5.01. 95
this is old ninny's tomb. where is my love? 5.01.263
ay, that left pap, | where heart doth hop. 5.01.299
there where your argosies with portly sail MV 1.01. 9
plucking the grass to know where sits the wind, 1.01. 18
i pray you have in mind where we must meet. 1.01. 71
a stage, where every man must play a part, | and 1.01. 78
where money is, and i no question make | to have 1.01.184
bonnet in germany, and his behavior every where. 1.02. 76 P
even there where merchants most do congregate, 1.03. 49
where phoebus' fire scarce thaws the icicles, 2.01. 5
but where thou art not known, why, there they 2.02.184
where is the horse that doth untread again | his 2.06. 10
fie, fie, gratiano, where are all the rest? 2.06. 62
where is my lady? 2.09. 85
where the carcasses of many a tall ship lie 3.01. 5 P
i often came where i did hear of her, but cannot 3.01. 81 P
rack, | where men enforced do speak any thing. 3.02. 33
tell me where is fancy bred, | or in the heart 3.02. 63
and fancy dies | in the cradle where it lies. 3.02. 69
for your bliss, | turn you where your lady is, 3.02.137

you see me, lord bassanio, where i stand, | such 3.02.149
where every something, being blent together, 3.02.181
and where thou now exacts the penalty, | which 4.01. 22
where is he? 4.01.145
thou know'st where i will tarry. 4.02. 18
grecian tents, | where cressid lay that night. 5.01. 6
where she kneels and prays | for happy wedlock 5.01. 31
sola! where, where? 5.01. 44 P
sola! where, where? 5.01. 44 P
in summer, where the ways are fair enough. 5.01.264
know you where you are, sir? AYL 1.01. 40 P
where will the old duke live? 1.01.113 P
where learn'd you that oath, fool? 1.02. 62 P
do, and here, where you are, they are coming to 1.02.115 P
where is this young gallant that is so desirous 1.02.200 P
and she believes, where ever they are gone, 2.02. 15
to burn the lodging where you use to lie, | and 2.03. 23
where none will sweat but for promotion, | and 2.03. 60
bring us where we may rest ourselves and feed. 2.04. 73
beast, | for i can no where find him like a man. 2.07. 2
if ever been where bells have knoll'd to church, 2.07.114
shall see thy virtue witness'd every where. 3.02. 8
where remains he? 3.02.222 P
where dwell you, pretty youth? 3.02.334 P
cony that you see dwell where she is kindled. 3.02.339 P
tell me where it is. 3.02.429 P
way you shall tell me where in the forest you 3.02.431 P
where ever sorrow is, relief would be: 3.05. 86
orlando, where have you been all this while? 4.01. 39 P
where in the purlieus of this forest stands | a 4.03. 76
why, and where | this handkercher was stain'd. 4.03. 96
o, i know where you are. 5.02. 29 P
where, meeting with an old religious man, 5.04.160
'twas where you woo'd the gentlewoman so well. SHR in.1. 85
where is my wife? in.2. 102
no profit grows where is no pleasure ta'en. 1.01. 39
sirrah, where have you been? 1.01.221
where have i been? 1.01.222 P
nay, how now, where are you? 1.01.222 P
than at home, | where small experience grows. 1.02. 52
and where two raging fires meet together, | they 2.01.132
ay, if the fool could find it where it lies. 2.01.212
who knows not where a wasp does wear his sting? 2.01.213
where did you study all this goodly speech? 2.01.262
where left we last? 3.01. 26
yet never means to wed where he hath woo'd. 3.02. 17
when he stands where i am and sees you there. 3.02. 40 P
come, where be these gallants? who's at home? 3.02. 87
but where is kate? 3.02. 92
where is my lovely bride? 3.02. 92
but where is kate? 3.02.110
where be these knaves? 4.01.120
where is nathaniel, gregory, philip? 4.01.122
where is the foolish knave i sent before? 4.01.127
"where is the life that late i led? 4.01.140
where are those" — | sit down, kate, and 4.01.141
where are my slippers? 4.01.153
where is the rascal cook? 4.01.162
where is he? 4.01.181 P
and i had thee in place where, thou shouldst 4.03.150 P
genoa, | where we were lodgers at the pegasus. 4.04. 5
where then do you know best | we be affied and 4.04. 48
good morrow, gentle mistress, where away? 4.05. 27
sir — see where he looks out of the window. 5.01. 55 P
tell me, thou villain, where is my son lucentio? 5.01. 89 P
how hast thou offended? | where is lucentio? 5.01.114
where is that damned villain tranio, | that 5.01.120
where is your sister, and hortensio's wife? 5.02.101
see where she comes, and brings your froward 5.02.119
to offer war where they should kneel for peace, 5.02.162
would stir it up where it wanted rather than AWW 1.01. 9 P
wanted rather than lack it where there is such 1.01. 10 P
for where an unclean mind carries virtuous 1.01. 41 P
extend his might only where qualities were level 1.03.113 P
where love's strong passion is impress'd in 1.03.133
with my love | for loving where you do; 1.03.209
but lend and give where she is sure to lose; 1.03.215
but riddle-like lives sweetly where she dies! 1.03.217
and most oft there | where most it promises; 2.01.143
where hope is coldest and despair most /fits. 2.01.144
where great additions swell 's, and virtue none, 2.03.127
where dust and damn'd oblivion is the tomb | of 2.03.140
it is in us to plant thine honor where | we 2.03.156
and what dole of honor | flies where you bid it, 2.03.170
best set thy lower part where thy nose stands. 2.03.252 P
italian fields | where noble fellows strike. 2.03.291
where are my other men, monsieur? 2.05. 89
where i will never come | whilst i can shake my 2.05. 90
where is my son, i pray you? 3.02. 51
court, where thou | wast shot at with fair eyes, 3.02.106
where death and danger dogs the heels of worth. 3.04. 15
hope your own grace will keep you where you are, 3.05. 26 P
where do the palmers lodge, i do beseech you? 3.05. 35
i will conduct you where you shall be lodg'd, 3.05. 41
i will bring you | where you shall host. 3.05. 94
where both not sin, and yet a sinful fact. 3.07. 47
i' th' stocks, or any where, so i may live. 4.03.244 P
have suspected an ambush where i was taken? 4.03.302 P
find out a country where but women were that had 4.03.326 P
my husband hies him home, where, heaven aiding, 4.04. 12
indeed he has no pace, but runs where he will. 4.05. 67 P
where the impression of mine eye infixing, 5.03. 47
where you have never come, or sent it us | upon 5.03.111
her bed in florence, | where yet she never was. 5.03.127
where did you buy it? or who gave it you? 5.03.271
where did you find it then? 5.03.274
thou tell'st me where thou hadst this ring, 5.03.283
where, like /arion on the dolphin's back, | i TN 1.02. 15
nay, either tell me where thou hast been, or i 1.05. 1 P
i can tell thee where that saying was born, of 1.05. 9 P
where, good mistress mary? 1.05. 11 P
where lies your text? 1.05.223 P
"o mistress mine, where are you roaming? 2.03. 39
make a third, where he shall find the letter; 2.03.174 P
a very echo to the seat | where love is thron'd. 2.04. 22
my poor corpse, where my bones shall be thrown. 2.04. 62
o, where | sad true lover never find my grave, 2.04. 64
be every thing and their intent every where, for 2.04. 77 P

a day–bed, where i have left olivia sleeping — 2.05. 48 P
"i may command where i adore, | but silence, 2.05.104
"i may command where i adore." 2.05.115 P
the orb like the sun, it shines every where. 3.01. 39 P
opinion, where you will hang like an icicle on a 3.02. 27 P
where shall i find you? 3.02. 51 P
look where the youngest wren of /nine comes. 3.02. 66 P
come bring us, bring us where he is. 3.02. 84 P
where is malvolio? 3.04. 7
home, where if it be thy chance to kill me" — 3.04.160 P
caves, | where manners ne'er were preach'd! 4.01. 49
where being apprehended, his false cunning 5.01. 86
where he sits crowned in his master's spite. 5.01.128
where goes cesario? 5.01.134
her, but direct thy feet | where thou and i, 5.01.169
deity in my nature | of here and every where. 5.01.228
in this town, | where lie my maiden weeds; 5.01.255
that will strike | where 'tis predominant; WT 1.02.202
to do a thing, where i the issue doubted, 1.02.259
may strike the dullest nostril | where i arrive, 1.02.422
i'll keep my stables where | i lodge my wife; 2.01.134
were i a tyrant, | where were her life? 2.03.123
some place | where chance may nurse or end it. 2.03.183
a day i'll visit | the chapel where they lie, 3.02.239
she did approach | my cabin where i lay; 3.03. 24
if any where i have them, 'tis by the sea–side, 3.03. 67 P
shalt accompany us to the place, where we will 4.02. 47 P
wife within a mile where my land and living lies 4.03. 98 P
and where some stretch–mouth'd rascal would, as 4.04.196 P
wear their plackets where they should bear their 4.04.243 P
for i must go | where it fits not you to know. 4.04.298
and lay me | where no priest shovels in dust. 4.04.458
i'll point you where you shall have such 4.04.526
highness, where you may | enjoy your mistress — 4.04.527
can but stay you | where you'll be loath to be. 4.04.572
where he is to behold him with flies blown to 4.04.790 P
consider'd, i'll bring you where he is aboard, 4.04.795 P
and on this stage | (where we offenders now) 5.01. 59
where the warlike smalus, | that noble honor'd 5.01.157
and my wife's, in safety | here, where we are. 5.01.168
from his liking, | where you were tied in duty; 5.01.213
ay, and make it manifest where she has liv'd, 5.03.114
me, mine own, | where hast thou been preserv'd? 5.03.124
where liv'd? 5.03.124
hence, where we may leisurely | each one demand, 5.03.152
where how he did prevail i shame to speak. JN 1.01.104
should say, "look where three–farthings goes!" 1.01.143
where is that slave, thy brother? 1.01.222
where is he, | that holds in chase mine honor up 1.01.222
where we'll set forth | in best appointment all 2.01.295
let it be so. say, where will you assault? 2.01.408
where should he find it fairer than in blanch? 2.01.427
where should he find it purer than in blanch? 2.01.429
where is she and her son? 2.01.543
o boy, then where art thou? 3.01. 34
where we do reign, we will alone uphold 3.01.157
where revenge did paint | the fearful difference 3.01.237
and being not done, where doing tends to ill, 3.01.272
there where my fortune lives, there my life dies 3.01.338
if this same were a churchyard where we stand, 3.03. 40
where but by chance a silver drop hath fall'n, 3.04. 63
and "where lies your grief?" 4.01. 48
where is that blood | that i have seen inhabit 4.02.106
o, where hath our intelligence been drunk? 4.02.116
where hath it slept? 4.02.117
where is my mother's care, | that such an army 4.02.117
leaves the print of blood where e'er it walks. 4.03. 26
where the jewel of life | by some damn'd hand 5.01. 40
and there | where honorable rescue and defense 5.02. 18
where these two christian armies might combine 5.02. 37
look where the holy legate comes apace, | to 5.02. 65
even on that altar where we swore to you | dear 5.04. 19
where i may think the remnant of my thoughts 5.04. 46
where is my prince, the dolphin? 5.05. 9
where /god he knows how we shall answer him; 5.07. 60
in your right spheres, | where be your pow'rs? 5.07. 75
where ever englishman durst set his foot. R2 1.01. 66
good uncle, let this end where it begun; 1.01.158
where shame doth harbor, even in mowbray's face. 1.01.195
where then, alas, may i complain myself? 1.02. 42
grief boundeth where /it falls, | not with the 1.02. 58
to seek out sorrow that dwells every where. 1.02. 72
know, | from where you do remain let paper show. 1.03.250
where it perceives it is but faintly borne. 1.03.281
where e'er i wander, boast of this i can, 1.03.308
where lies he? 1.04. 57
where words are scarce, they are seldom spent in 2.01. 7
where doth the world thrust forth a vanity — 2.01. 24
where will doth mutiny with wit's regard. 2.01. 28
which live like venom where no venom else | but 2.01.157
where nothing lives but crosses, cares, and 2.02. 79
where one on his side fights, thousands will fly 2.02.147
where is the earl of wiltshire? 3.02.122
where is bagot? 3.02.122
where is green? 3.02.123
where is the duke my father with his power? 3.02.143
no matter where — of comfort no man speak: 3.02.144
where fearing dying pays death servile breath. 3.02.185
scroop, where lies our uncle with his power? 3.02.192
where subjects' feet | may hourly trample on 3.03.156
base court, where kings grow base, | to come at 3.03.180
for night–owls shriek where mounting larks 3.03.183
say, where, when, and how, | /cam'st thou by 3.04. 79
fair sun which shows me where thou stand'st, | i 4.01. 35
where it was forged, with my rapier's point. 4.01. 40
ah, thou, the model where old troy did stand, 5.01. 11
where shivering cold and sickness pines the 5.01. 77
where did i leave? 5.02. 4
where rude misgoverned hands from windows' tops 5.02. 5
alack, poor richard, where rode he the whilst? 5.02. 22
where is the king? 5.03. 23
to oxford, or where e'er these traitors are. 5.03.141
but i will have them if i once know where. 5.03.143
this prison where i live unto the world; 5.05. 2
where no man never comes, but that sad dog 5.05. 70
where they did spend a sad and bloody hour, | as 1H4 1.01. 56
in cradle–clothes our children where they lay, 1.01. 88
my coin would stretch, and where it would not, i 1.02. 55 P
to god thou and i knew where a commodity of good 1.02. 82 P
where shall we take a purse to–morrow, jack? 1.02. 98 P
'zounds, where thou wilt, lad, i'll make one, 1.02.100 P
where fadom–line could never touch the ground, 1.03.204
'twas where the madcap duke his uncle kept — 1.03.244
where i first bow'd my knee | unto this king of 1.03.245
where you and douglas and our powers at once, 1.03.296
remov'd my horse, and tied him i know not where. 2.02. 12 P
ned, where are our disguises? 2.02. 74 P
where hast been, hal? 2.04. 3 P
welcome, jack, where hast thou been? 2.04.113 P
where is it, jack? where is it? 2.04.160 P
where is it, jack? where is it? 2.04.160 P
where is it? 2.04.161 P
i do not only marvel where thou spendest thy 2.04.398 P
tell me, where hast thou been this month? 2.04.432 P
where is he living, clipt in with the sea | that 3.01. 43
where, being but young, i framed to the harp 3.01.121
others would say, "where, which is bullingbrook? 3.02. 49
nor flesh, a man knows not where to have her. 3.03.128 P
thou or any man knows where to have me, thou 3.03.130 P
where shall i find one that can steal well? 3.03.187 P
should, | where now remains a sweet reversion, 4.01. 53
where is his son, | the nimble–footed madcap 4.01. 94
where the glutton's dogs lick'd his sores, and 4.02. 26 P
their poverty, i know not where they had that, 4.02. 70 P
where you did give a fair and natural light, 5.01. 18
where? 5.03. 17
have led my ragamuffins where they are pepper'd; 5.03. 36 P
this, | where stain'd nobility lies trodden on, 5.04. 13
who keeps the gate here ho? where is the earl? 2H4 1.01. 1
where hateful death put on his ugliest mask | to 1.01. 66
about it, you know where to find me. 1.02.243 P
where lay the king to–night? 2.01.168
where sups he? 2.02.146 P
the room where they supp'd is too hot, they'll 2.04. 13 P
where he doth nothing but roast malt–worms. 2.04.334 P
where i think they will talk of mad shallow yet. 3.02. 14 P
we knew where the bona /robas were and had the 3.02. 23 P
let me see, where is mouldy? 3.02.100 P
peace, stand aside, know you where you are? 3.02.120 P
falstaff, where have you been all this while? 4.03. 26
gloucester, | where is the prince your brother? 4.04. 13
but peace puts forth her olive every where. 4.04. 87
lo where it sits, | which god shall guard; 4.05. 43
the prince of wales, where is he? 4.05. 53
he came not through the chamber where we stay'd. 4.05. 56
where is the crown? who took it from my pillow? 4.05. 57
where is he that will not stay so long | till 4.05. 80
lo where he comes. 4.05. 89
where is my lord of warwick? 4.05.231
unto the lodging where i first did swound? 4.05.233
where are you, sir john? 5.01. 53 P
where it shall mingle with the state of floods, 5.02.132
you shall see my orchard, where, in an arbor, we 5.03. 1 P
"where is the life that late i led?" 5.03.140
you merry with fair katherine of france, where ep 29 P
where is my gracious lord of canterbury? H5 1.02. 1
where charles the great, having subdu'd the 1.02. 46
where some, like magistrates, correct at home; 1.02.191
where have they this mettle? 3.05. 15
where is montjoy the herald? 3.05. 36
learn you by rote where services were done — at 3.06. 71 P
where — o for pity! 4.pr. 49
not wish himself any where but where he is. 4.01.120 P
not wish himself any where but where he is. 4.01.120 P
i could not die any where so contented as in the 4.01.127 P
where they fear'd the death, they have borne 4.01.171 P
and where they would be safe, they perish. 4.01.172 P
where the sad and solemn priests | sing still 4.01.301
where is the king? 4.03. 1
a sweet retire | from off these fields, where, 4.03. 87
comes to him where in gore he lay insteeped, 4.06. 12
you the town's name where alexander the pig was 4.07. 12 P
think it is in macedon where alexander is porn. 4.07. 22 P
good service in a garden where leeks did grow, 4.07. 99 P
where is the number of our english dead? 4.08.102
where ne'er from france arriv'd more happy men. 4.08.126
where that his lords desire him to have borne 5.pr. 17
it was in a place where i could not breed no 5.01. 10 P
where your majesty demands, that the king of 5.02.336 P
where is it? 1H6 1.01. 33
where valiant talbot above human thought 1.01.121
here, there, and every where, enrag'd he slew. 1.01.124
to eltam will i, where the young king is, 1.01.170
where is the dolphin? 1.02. 66
my lord, where are you? 1.02.124
where be these warders, that they wait not here? 1.03. 3
where is best place to make our batt'ry next? 1.04. 65
where is my strength, my valor, and my force? 1.05. 1
wheel, | i know not where i am, nor what i do. 1.05. 20
but weakly guarded, where the breach was made. 2.01. 74
to visit her poor castle where she lies, | that 2.02. 41
and keep me on the side where still i am. 2.04. 54
now, somerset, where is your argument? 2.04. 59
where false plantagenet dare not be seen. 2.04. 74
but where is pucelle now? 3.02.121
nay, let it rest where it began at first. 4.01.121
remember where we are — | in france, amongst a 4.01.137
where i hope ere long | to be presented, by your 4.01.171
and now they meet where both their lives are 4.03. 38
where is john talbot? 4.06. 4
where is my other life? 4.07. 1
where is valiant john? 4.07. 2
o my dear lord, lo where your son is borne! 4.07. 17
see where he lies inhearsed in the arms | of the 4.07. 45
where i was wont to feed you with my blood, 5.03. 14
beams | upon the country where you make abode; 5.04. 88
arrive | where i may have fruition of her love. 5.05. 9
where reignier sooner will receive than give. 5.05. 47
and so conduct me where, from company, | i may 5.05.100
and in that chair where kings and queens were 2H6 1.02. 38
where henry and dame margaret kneel'd to me, 1.02. 39
where as the king and queen do mean to hawk. 1.02. 58
where are you there? 1.02. 68
sandy plains | than where castles mounted stand. 1.04. 37
plains | than where castles mounted stand." 1.04. 69
ay, where thou dar'st not peep. 2.01. 41
where wert thou born? 2.01. 80
where, as all you know, | harmless richard was 2.02. 26
where it best fits to be, in henry's hand. 2.03. 44
only convey me where thou art commanded. 2.04. 93
smooth runs the water where the brook is deep, 3.01. 53
where is our uncle? 3.02. 28
where are his talons? 3.02.196
where biting cold would never let grass grow, 3.02.337
for where thou art, there is the world itself, 3.02.362
and where thou art not, desolation. 3.02.364
where, from thy sight, i should be raging mad, 3.02.394
where death's approach is seen so terrible! 3.03. 6
where should he die? 3.03. 9
then show me where he is, | i'll give a thousand 3.03. 12
troubles the silver spring where england drinks. 4.01. 72
where we will have the mayor's sword borne 4.03. 13 P
hear me but speak, and bear me where you will. 4.07. 59
see where they come, i'll warrant they'll make 5.01.122
o, where is faith? 5.01.166
o, where is loyalty? 5.01.166
where shall it find a harbor in the earth? 5.01.168
and disorder wounds | where it should guard. 5.02. 33
we shall to london get, where you are lov'd, 5.02. 81
and where this breach now in our fortunes made 5.02. 82
but still, where danger was, still there i met 5.03. 11
but, noble as he is, look where he comes. 5.03. 14
my lords, look where the sturdy rebel sits, 3H6 1.01. 50
where i shall kneel to him that slew my father! 1.01.162
and over the chair of state, where now he sits, 1.01.168
ah, tutor, look where bloody clifford comes! 1.03. 2
stopp'd the passage where thy words should enter 1.03. 22
where are your mess of sons to back you now, 1.04. 73
with the rest, where is your darling, rutland? 1.04. 78
where our right valiant father is become. 2.01. 10
where your brave father breath'd his latest gasp 2.01.108
where is the duke of norfolk, gentle warwick? 2.01.142
where e'er it be, in heaven or in earth. 2.03. 43
i'll bear thee hence, where i may weep my fill. 2.05.113
for i have murthered where i should not kill. 2.05.122
in this self place where now we mean to stand. 3.01. 11
but, if thou be a king, where is thy crown? 3.01. 61
where did you dwell when i was king of england? 3.01. 74
here in this country where we now remain. 3.01. 75
go where you will, the king shall be commanded; 3.01. 92
and spies a far–off shore where he would tread, 3.02.136
my back, | where sits deformity to mock my body; 3.02.158
learn a while to serve | where kings command. 3.03. 6
where i must take like seat unto my fortune, 3.03. 10
and see where comes the breeder of my sorrow! 3.03. 43
where fame, late ent'ring at his heedful ears, 3.03. 63
where having nothing, nothing can he lose. 3.03.152
but see where somerset and clarence comes! 4.02. 3
to rest mistrustful where a noble heart | hath 4.02. 8
this is his tent, and see where stand his guard. 4.03. 23
but, madam, where is warwick then become? 4.04. 25
this way, man, see where the huntsmen stand. 4.05. 15
by living low, where fortune cannot hurt me, 4.06. 20
course, | where peremptory warwick now remains. 4.08. 59
where is the post that came from valiant oxford? 5.01. 1
where is the post that came from montague? 5.01. 5
where slept our scouts, or how are they seduc'd, 5.01. 19
o cheerful colors! see where oxford comes! 5.01. 58
and lo, where george of clarence sweeps along, 5.01. 76
it is, and lo where youthful edward comes! 5.05. 11
resign thy chair, and where i stand kneel thou, 5.05. 19
where is that devil's butcher, | hard–favor'd 5.05. 77
richard, where art thou? 5.05. 78
in my eye | where my poor young was lim'd, was 5.06. 17
where is he? R3 1.01.142
from cold and empty veins where no blood dwells. 1.02. 59
he is in heaven, where thou shalt never come. 1.02.106
ill rest betide the chamber where thou liest! 1.02.112
where is he? 1.02.144
where (after i have solemnly interr'd | at 1.02.213
that wrens make prey where eagles dare not perch 1.03. 70
warrant, | that we may be admitted where he is. 1.03.342
and, in the holes | where eyes did once inhabit, 1.04. 30
where art thou, keeper? give me a cup of wine. 1.04.161
where is the evidence that doth accuse me? 1.04.183
with hate in those where i expect most love! 2.01. 35
where every horse bears his commanding rein 2.02.128
where shall we sojourn till our coronation? 3.01. 62
where it seems best unto your royal self. 3.01. 63
then where you please, and shall be thought most 3.01. 66
where nothing can proceed that toucheth us 3.02. 23
and make pursuit where he did mean no chase. 3.02. 30
where he shall see the boar will use us kindly. 3.02. 33
come on, come on, where is your boar–spear, man? 3.02. 72
than when thou met'st me last where now we meet. 3.02. 99
where is my lord, the duke of gloucester? 3.04. 46
even where his raging eye or savage heart, 3.05. 83
where you shall find me well accompanied | with 3.05. 99
see where his grace stands, 'tween two clergymen 3.07. 95
i to my grave, where peace and rest lie with me! 4.01. 94
to richmond, in the parts where he abides. 4.02. 49
but where (to say the truth) i do not know. 4.03. 30
where is thy husband now? 4.04. 92
where be thy brothers? 4.04. 92
where be thy two sons? 4.04. 93
where be the bending peers that flattered thee? 4.04. 95
where be the thronging troops that followed thee 4.04. 96
with a golden crown | where should be branded, 4.04.141
me, thou villain–slave, where are my children? 4.04.144
toad, thou toad, where is thy brother clarence? 4.04.145
where is the gentle rivers, vaughan, grey? 4.04.147
where is kind hastings? 4.04.148
where in that nest of spicery they will breed 4.04.424
ratcliffe, thyself — or catesby — where is he? 4.04.441
where is thy power then, to beat him back? 4.04.479
where be thy tenants and thy followers? 4.04.480
where and what time your majesty shall please. 4.04.489
but tell me, where is princely richmond now? 4.05. 9
will i lie to–night — | but where to–morrow? 5.03. 8
where is lord stanley quarter'd, do you know? 5.03. 34
of england's chair, where he is falsely set; 5.03.251
it reaches far, and where 'twill not extend, H8 1.01.111
lo, where comes that rock | that i advise your 1.01.113
in that file | where others tell steps with me. 1.02. 43

their curses now | live where their prayers did; 1.02. 63
we should take root here where we sit, or sit 1.02. 87
where this is question'd send our letters, with 1.02. 99
his dews fall every where. 1.03. 57
where this heaven of beauty | shall shine at 1.04. 59
where to his accusations | he pleaded still not 2.01. 12
where you are liberal of your loves and counsels 2.01.126
found again | but where they mean to sink ye. 2.01.131
'tis most true | these news are every where; 2.02. 38
are mounted | where pow'rs are your retainers, 2.04.113
these ears (for, where i am robb'd and bound, 2.04.147
her male issue | or died where they were made, 2.04.193
so deep suspicion, where all faith was meant. 3.01. 53
alas, poor wenches, where are now your fortunes? 3.01.148
shipwrack'd upon a kingdom, where no pity, | no 3.01.149
employ'd you where high profits might come home, 3.02.158
and sleep in dull cold marble where no mention 3.02.433
off | from ampthill, where the princess lay — 4.01. 28
to kimmalton, | where she remains now sick. 4.01. 35
god save you, sir! where have you been broiling? 4.01. 56
where a finger | could not be wedg'd in more. 4.01. 57
paces | came to the altar, where she kneel'd, 4.01. 83
again | to york–place, where the feast is held. 4.01. 94
where the reverend abbot | with all his covent 4.02. 18
where eagerly his sickness | pursu'd him still, 4.02. 24
he was never | (but where he meant to ruin) 4.02. 40
spirits of peace, where are ye? 4.02. 83
'tis true; where is he, denny? 5.01. 82
you shall | this morning come before us, where, 5.01.101
where my chaff | and corn shall fly asunder; 5.01.110
body a' me, where is it? 5.02. 22
where, being but a private man again, | you 5.02. 90
the hope o' th' strond, where she was quarter'd. 5.03. 53 P
where are these porters? 5.03. 69
where ever the bright sun of heaven shall shine, 5.04. 50
between our ilium and where she /resides, | let TRO 1.01.101
where every flower | did, as a prophet, weep 1.02. 9
i marvel where troilus is. 1.02.219 P
i marvel where troilus is. 1.02.224 P
where? 1.02.227 P
where? 1.02.273 P
i will keep where there is wit stirring, and 2.01.118 P
or death unfam'd, | where helen is the subject. 2.02.160
where? 2.03. 40 P
where? 2.03. 40 P
o, where? 2.03. 40 P
where is achilles? 2.03. 76
what exploit's in hand? where sups he to–night? 3.01. 81 P
you must not know where he sups. 3.01. 86 P
fields | where i may wallow in the lily–beds 3.02. 12
tell you, they'll stick where they are thrown. 3.02.112 P
where is my wit? 3.02.151
is /mirror'd there | where it may see itself. 3.03.111
formed in th' applause | where th' are extended; 3.03.120
strait so narrow, | where one but goes abreast. 3.03.155
where he answers again, "because thou canst not 4.04. 18 P
where injury of chance | puts back leave–taking, 4.04. 33
where are my tears? 4.04. 53 P
nice conjecture | where thou wilt hit me dead? 4.05.251
i'll kill thee every where, yea, o'er and o'er. 4.05.256
yonder 'tis, | there where we see the lights. 5.01. 68
stand where the torch may not discover us. 5.02. 5
o beauty, where is thy faith? 5.02. 67
where reason can revolt | without perdition, and 5.02.144
where is my brother hector? 5.03. 7
there, and every where, he leaves and takes, 5.05. 26
where is this hector? 5.05. 44
attend me where i wheel; 5.07. 2
where go you | with bats and clubs? COR 1.01. 55
by calamity | thither where more attends you, 1.01. 76
where th' other instruments | did see and hear, 1.01.101
where he should find you lions, finds you hares; 1.01.171
where foxes, geese. 1.01.172
where i know | our greatest friends attend us. 1.01.244
of his bed where he would show most love. 1.03. 5 P
to let him seek danger where he was like to find 1.03. 13 P
a' th' town, | where they shall know our mind. 1.05. 28
where is that slave | which told me they had 1.06. 39
where is he? 1.06. 41
where is the enemy? 1.06. 47
where senators shall mingle tears with smiles; 1.09. 3
where great patricians shall attend and shrug, 1.09. 4
where ladies shall be frighted | and, gladly 1.09. 5
where the dull tribunes, | that with the fusty 1.09. 6
where, ere we do repose us, we will write | to 1.09. 74
for where | i thought to crush him in an equal 1.10. 13
where i find him, were it | at home, upon my 1.10. 24
where is he wounded? 2.01.143 P
where is he wounded? 2.01.146 P
where he hath won, | with fame, a name to 2.01.163
i know not where to turn. 2.01.181
his honors | from where he should begin and end, 2.01.225
death's stamp, | where it did mark, it took; 2.02.108
where he did | run reeking o'er the lives of men 2.02.118
where being three parts melted away with rotten 2.03. 31 P
together, but to come by him where he stands, by 2.03. 42 P
where? at the senate–house? 2.03.145
if you will pass | to where you are bound, you 3.01. 54
a mind | that shall remain a poison where it is; 3.01. 87
where /one part does disdain with cause, the 3.01.143
where gentry, title, wisdom, | cannot conclude 3.01.144
very poisonous | where the disease is violent. 3.01.221
where is this viper | that would depopulate the 3.01.262
do not cry havoc where you should but hunt 3.01.273
undertake to bring him | where he shall answer, 3.01.323
where if you bring not martius, we'll proceed 3.01.331
i would dissemble with my nature where | my 3.02. 62
nay, mother, | where is your ancient courage? 4.01. 3
devise with thee | where thou shalt rest, that 4.01. 39
if it be your will, | where great aufidius lies. 4.04. 8
where dwell'st thou? 4.05. 37 P
where is this fellow? 4.05. 50
where against | my grained ash an hundred times 4.05.107
where is he, hear you? 4.06. 17
before you punish him, where he heard this, 4.06. 53
where have you lurk'd, that you make doubt of it 5.04. 46
bid them repair to th' market–place, where i, 5.06. 3
but there to end | where he was to begin, and 5.06. 65
making a treaty where | there was a yielding — 5.06. 67
from where he circumscribed with his sword, TIT 1.01. 68
where is the emperor's guard? 1.01.283
bury him where you can, he comes not here. 1.01.354
and manners, to intrude where i am grac'd, | and 2.01. 27
and i have horse will follow where the game 2.02. 23
pit, | where never man's eye may behold my body: 2.03.177
this is the hole where aaron bid us hide him. 2.03.186
pit | where i espied the panther fast asleep. 2.03.194
we know not where you left them all alive, | but 2.03.257
where is my lord the king? 2.03.259
where is thy brother bassianus? 2.03.261
same pit | where we decreed to bury bassianus. 2.03.274
where is your husband? 2.04. 12
doth burn the heart to cinders where it is. 2.04. 37
where like a sweet melodious bird it sung 3.01. 85
where life hath no more interest but to breathe! 3.01.249
my aunt lavinia | follows me every where, i know 4.01. 2
ay, such a place there is where we did hunt | (o 4.01. 55
and from your womb where you imprisoned were 4.02.124
thinks, with jove in heaven, or some where else, 4.03. 41
and blazoning our unjustice every where? 4.04. 18
be bold in us, we'll follow where thou lead'st, 5.01. 13
but where the bull and cow are both milk–white, 5.01. 31
hole, | where the dead corpse of bassianus lay; 5.01.105
where they say he keeps | to ruminate strange 5.02. 5
where bloody murther or detested rape | can 5.02. 37
lo by thy side where rape and murder stands; 5.02. 45
bid him encamp his soldiers where they are. 5.02.126
from the place where you behold us pleading, 5.03.130
in fair verona, where we lay our scene, | from ROM pr 2
where civil blood makes civil hands unclean. pr 4
o, where is romeo? 1.01.116
where, underneath the grove of sycamore | that 1.01.121
then most sought where most might not be found, 1.01.127
see where he comes! 1.01.156
out of her favor where i am in love. 1.01.168
where shall we dine? 1.01.173
this is not romeo, he's some other where. 1.01.198
where i may read who pass'd that passing fair? 1.01.236
much less | to meet her new–beloved any where. 2.pr. 12
where and what time thou wilt perform the rite, 2.02.146
else would i tear the cave where echo lies, 2.02.161
and where the worser is predominant, | full soon 2.03. 29
and where care lodges, sleep will never lie; 2.03. 36
but where unbruised youth with unstuff'd brain 2.03. 37
my good son, but where hast thou been then? 2.03. 47
where on a sudden one hath wounded me | that's 2.03. 50
when and where and how | we met, we woo'd, and 2.03. 61
where the dev'l should this romeo be? 2.04. 1
any of you tell me where i may find the young 2.04.119 P
i warrant, a virtuous — where is your mother? 2.05. 57
where is my mother! 2.05. 58
why, she is within, | where should she be? 2.05. 59
an honest gentleman, | 'where is your mother?'" 2.05. 61
where is my page? 3.01. 94
where are the vile beginners of this fray? 3.01.141
for 'tis a throne where honor may be crown'd 3.02. 93
where is my father and my mother, nurse? 3.02.127
romeo | to comfort you, i wot well where he is. 3.02.139
heaven is here | where juliet lives, and every 3.03. 30
where is she? 3.03. 97
where thou shalt live till we can find a time 3.03.150
where that same banish'd runagate doth live, 3.05. 89
graze where you will, you shall not house with 3.05.188
bed | in that dim monument where tybalt lies. 3.05.201
ways, or bid me lurk | where serpents are; 4.01. 80
where all the kindred of the capulets lie. 4.01.112
see where she comes from shrift with merry look. 4.02. 15
now, my headstrong, where have you been gadding? 4.02. 16
where i have learnt me to repent the sin | of 4.02. 17
where for this many hundred years the bones | of 4.03. 40
where bloody tybalt, yet but green in earth, 4.03. 42
lies fest'ring in his shroud, where, as they say 4.03. 43
call peter, he will show thee where they are. 4.04. 17
where the infectious pestilence did reign, 5.02. 10
where is my lord? 5.03.148
i do remember well where i should be, | and 5.03.149
where is my romeo? 5.03.150
is the place, there where the torch doth burn. 5.03.171
where is the county's page that rais'd the watch 5.03.279
where be these enemies? 5.03.291
where thou hast feign'd him a worthy fellow. TIM 1.01.223 P
but where there is true friendship, there needs 1.02. 18
where be our men? 1.02.165
where he shall find | th' unkindest beast more 4.01. 35
where ever we shall meet, for timon's sake 4.02. 24
where liest a' nights, timon? 4.03.292
where feed'st thou a' days, apemantus? 4.03.293 P
where my stomach finds meat, or, rather, where i 4.03.294 P
stomach finds meat, or, rather, where i eat it. 4.03.295 P
where wouldst thou send it? 4.03.298 P
lie where the light foam of the sea may beat 4.03.378
where should he have this gold? 4.03.398 P
where? 4.03.408 P
suspect still comes where an estate is least. 4.03.514
the place, it cannot be far | where he abides. 5.01. 2
in a baser temple | than where swine feed! 5.01. 49
if where thou art two villains shall not be, 5.01.109
wouldst not reside | but where one villain is, 5.01.111
where is thy leather apron and thy rule? JC 1.01. 7
so do you too, where you perceive them thick. 1.01. 71
heard | where many of the best respect in rome 1.02. 59
three or four wenches, where i stood, cried, 1.02.272 P
i know where i will wear this dagger then; 1.03. 89
but, o grief, | where hast thou led me? 1.03.112
cinna, where haste you so? 1.03.133
praetor's chair, | where brutus may but find it; 1.03.144
to pompey's porch, where you shall find us. 1.03.147
been often dropp'd | where i have took them up. 2.01. 50
day | where wilt thou find a cavern dark enough 2.01. 80
and look where publius is come to fetch me. 2.02.108
where is metellus cimber? 3.01. 27
where is antony? 3.01. 96
where is he? 3.02.263
where do you dwell? 3.03. 7 P
where do i dwell? 3.03. 14 P
and having brought our treasure where we will, 4.01. 24
where is thy instrument? 4.03.239
not the leaf turn'd down | where i left reading? 4.03.274
are those my tents where i perceive the fire? 5.03. 13
and where i did begin, there shall i end; 5.03. 24
run, | where never roman shall take note of him. 5.03. 50
where did you leave him? 5.03. 55
what, pindarus? where art thou, pindarus? 5.03. 72
where, where, messala, doth his body lie? 5.03. 91
where, where, messala, doth his body lie? 5.03. 91
where is he? 5.04. 19
my master's man. strato, where is thy master? 5.05. 53
where the place? MAC 1.01. 6
where the norweyan banners flout the sky | and 1.02. 49
where hast thou been, sister? 1.03. 1
sister, where thou? 1.03. 3
pains | are regist'red where every day i turn 1.03.151
as a book, where men | may read strange matters. 1.05. 62
where they /most breed and haunt, i have 1.06. 9
where we lay, | our chimneys were blown down, 2.03. 54
too cruel any where. 2.03. 88
what should be spoken here, where our fate, 2.03.121
where we are, | there's daggers in men's smiles; 2.03.139
where is duncan's body? 2.04. 32
i will advise you where to plant yourselves, 3.01.128
where our desire is got without content; 3.02. 5
where? 3.04. 46
sir, can you tell | where he bestows himself? 3.06. 24
who chafes, who frets, or where conspirers are: 4.01. 91
where are they? 4.01.133
where are these gentlemen? 4.01.155
come bring me where they are. 4.01.156
where the flight | so runs against all reason. 4.02. 13
world — where to do harm | is often laudable, 4.02. 75
where is your husband? 4.02. 80
where such as thou mayst find him. 4.02. 82
perchance even there where i did find my doubts. 4.03. 25
stands scotland where it did? 4.03.164
where nothing, | but who knows nothing, is once 4.03.166
where sighs, and groans, and shrieks that rent 4.03.168
where violent sorrow seems | a modern ecstasy. 4.03.169
air, | where hearing should not latch them. 4.03.195
where is she now? 5.01. 42 P
we on | to give obedience where 'tis truly ow'd. 5.02. 26
where got'st thou that goose–look? 5.03. 12
for where there is advantage to be given, | both 5.04. 11
in the unshrinking station where he fought, 5.09. 8
behold where stands | th' usurper's cursed head: 5.09. 20
illume that part of heaven | where now it burns, HAM 1.01. 38
look where it comes again! 1.01. 40
lo where it comes again! 1.01.126
know | where we shall find him most convenient. 1.01.175
where, my lord? 1.02.185
where, as they had delivered, both in time, 1.02.209
but where was this? 1.02.212
my lord, upon the platform where we watch. 1.02.213
how, and who, what means, and where they keep, 2.01. 8
where did i leave? 2.01. 51
and bring these gentlemen where hamlet is. 2.02. 37
i will find | where truth is hid, though it were 2.02.158
but look where sadly the poor wretch comes 2.02.168
you more, for look where my abridgment comes. 2.02.420 P
rebellious to his arm, lies where it falls, 2.02.470
upon that head | where late the diadem stood, 2.02.507
may play the fool no where but in 's own house. 3.01.132 P
or confine him where | your wisdom best shall 3.01.186
of the knee | where thrift may follow fawning. 3.02. 62
where love is great, the littlest doubts are 3.02.171
where little fears grow great, great love grows 3.02.172
where joy most revels, grief doth most lament; 3.02.198
but, orderly to end where i begun, | our wills 3.02.210
i stand in pause where i shall first begin, 3.03. 42
where you may see the /inmost part of you. 3.04. 20
where every god did seem to set his seal | to 3.04. 61
o shame, where is thy blush? 3.04. 81
look where he goes, even now, out at the portal! 3.04.136
where is your son? 4.01. 3
where is he gone? 4.01. 23
tell us where 'tis, that we may take it thence, 4.02. 7
my lord, you must tell us where the body is, and 4.02. 25 P
and where 'tis so, th' offender's scourge is 4.03. 6
where the dead body is bestow'd, my lord, | we 4.03. 12
but where is he? 4.03. 13
at supper? where? 4.03. 18 P
not where he eats, but where 'a is eaten; 4.03. 19 P
not where he eats, but where 'a is eaten; 4.03. 19 P
where is polonius? 4.03. 32 P
where is the beauteous majesty of denmark? 4.05. 21
where is my swissers? 4.05. 98
where is this king? sirs, stand you all without. 4.05.113
where is my father? 4.05.129
and where th' offense is, let the great axe fall 4.05.219
these good fellows will bring thee where i am. 4.06. 27 P
my bow again, | but not where i have aim'd them. 4.07. 24
where it draws blood, no cataplasm so rare, 4.07.143
drown'd! o, where? 4.07.165
where be his quiddities now, his quillities, his 5.01. 99 P
where be your gibes now, your gambols, your 5.01.189 P
where i found, horatio — | ah, royal knavery! 5.02. 18
where is this sight? 5.02.362
where should we have our thanks? 5.02.372
extend | where nature doth with merit challenge? LR 1.01. 53
make such a stray | to match you where i hate; 1.01.210
thou losest here, a better where to find. 1.01.261
where is he? 1.02. 78 P
where, if you violently proceed against him, 1.02. 82 P
i will place you where you shall hear us confer 1.02. 91 P
if thou canst serve where thou dost stand 1.04. 5
where are his eyes? 1.04.227
intelligence is given where you are hid; 2.01. 21
but where is he? 2.01. 40
where is the villain, edmund? 2.01. 41
where may we set our horses? 2.02. 4 P
where is this daughter? 2.04. 58
where learn'd you this, fool? 2.04. 86 P
to follow in a house where twice so many | have 2.04.262
where is my lord of gloucester? 2.04.294
where is this straw, my fellow? 3.02. 69
but where the greater malady is fix'd, | the 3.04. 8

and bring you where both fire and food is ready. 3.04.153
seek out where thy father is, that he may be 3.05. 18 P
where is the patience now | that you so oft have 3.06. 58
where is the king my master? 3.06. 86
friend, where thou shalt meet | both welcome and 3.06. 91
advise the duke, where you are going, to a most 3.07. 9 P
where they boast | to have well–armed friends. 3.07. 19
where hast thou sent the king? 3.07. 50
where is thy lustre now? 3.07. 84
fellow, where goest? 4.01. 29
where was his son when they did take his eyes? 4.02. 88
where he arrives he moves | all hearts against 4.05. 10
set me where you stand. 4.06. 24
had he been where he thought, | by this had 4.06. 44
where have i been? 4.07. 51
where am i? 4.07. 51
nor i know not | where i did lodge last night. 4.07. 67
t' appear | where you shall hold your session. 5.03. 54
instant way | where they shall rest for ever. 5.03.151
the dark and vicious place where thee he got 5.03.173
where have you hid yourself? 5.03.180
where is your servant caius? 5.03.284
where each second | stood heir to th' first. OTH 1.01. 37
and wheeling stranger | of here and every where. 1.01.137
now, roderigo, | where didst thou see her? 1.01.163
know | where we may apprehend her and the moor? 1.01.177
foul thief, where hast thou stow'd my daughter? 1.02. 62
(as in these cases where the aim reports, | 'tis 1.03. 6
noble company | where most you owe obedience? 1.03.180
where shall we meet i' th' morning? 1.03.373 P
lo, where he comes! 2.01.181
where are they? 2.03. 45 P
where indeed they are most potent in potting; 2.03. 76 P
retire thee, go where thou art billeted. 2.03.380
i will bestow you where you shall have time | to 3.01. 54
where virtue is, these are more virtuous. 3.03.186
look where she comes: 3.03.277
look where he comes! 3.03.330
you know, sirrah, where lieutenant cassio lies? 3.04. 1 P
i dare not say he lies any where. 3.04. 3 P
go to! where lodges he? 3.04. 7 P
to tell you where he lodges, is to tell you 3.04. 8 P
you where he lodges, is to tell you where i lie. 3.04. 9 P
i know not where he lodges, and for me to devise 3.04. 11 P
where should i lose the handkerchief, emilia? 3.04. 23
i think the sun where he was born | drew all 3.04. 30
look where he comes. 3.04. 31
where, how, how oft, how long ago, and when | he 4.01. 85
before me! look where she comes. 4.01.145 P
but there, where i have garner'd up my heart, 4.02. 57
where either i must live or bear no life; 4.02. 58
where be these bloody thieves? 5.01. 63
go know of cassio where he supp'd to–night. 5.01.117
i know not where is that promethean heat | that 5.02. 12
heavenly, | it strikes where it doth love. 5.02. 22
where art thou? 5.02.105
where should othello go? 5.02.271
where is this rash and most unfortunate man? 5.02.283
where is that viper? bring the villain forth. 5.02.285
where a malignant and a turban'd turk | beat a 5.02.353
look where they come! ANT 1.01. 10
better than i, where would you choose it? 1.02. 60 P
where died she? 1.02.118
where is he? 1.03. 1
see where he is, who's with him, what he does. 1.03. 2
the last, best, | see when and where she died. 1.03. 62
where be the sacred vials thou shouldst fill 1.03. 63
modena, where thou slew'st | hirtius and pansa, 1.04. 57
where think'st thou he is now? 1.05. 19
caesar gets money where | he loses hearts. 2.01. 13
where have you this? 'tis false. 2.01. 18
be tales, | where now half tales be truths. 2.02.134
where lies he? 2.02.159
o'er–picturing that venus where we see | the 2.02.200
but she makes hungry | where most she satisfies; 2.02.237
high unmatchable, | where caesar's is not; 2.03. 22
antony will use his affection where it is; 2.06.130 P
move in't, are the holes where eyes should be, 2.07. 15 P
where is he now? 3.01. 34
where is the fellow? 3.03. 1
where? 3.03. 8
thou shalt bring him to me | where i will write. 3.03. 47
when it appears to you where this begins, | turn 3.04. 33
i' th' common show–place, where they exercise. 3.06. 12
where is he now? 3.06. 64
at pharsalia, | where caesar fought with pompey. 3.07. 32
the token'd pestilence, | where death is sure. 3.10. 10
in alexandria, where | i will oppose his fate. 3.13.168
where hast thou been, my heart? 3.13.172
grace grow where those drops fall, my hearty 4.02. 38
you | where rather i'll expect victorious life 4.02. 43
where their appointment we may best discover, 4.10. 8
where yond pine does stand | i shall discover 4.12. 1
where souls do couch on flowers, we'll hand in 4.14. 51
where is she? 4.14.119
bear me, good friends, where cleopatra bides, 4.14.131
heart | where mine his thoughts did kindle — 5.01. 46
where you shall see | how hardly i was drawn 5.01. 73
for kindness | where he for grace is kneel'd to. 5.02. 28
where art thou, death? 5.02. 46
fine this tyrant | can tickle where she wounds! CYM 1.01. 85
where air comes out, air comes in; 1.02. 3 P
where each of us fell in praise of our country 1.04. 57 P
commend me to the court where your lady is, with 1.04.128 P
instructions enter | where folly now possesses? 1.05. 48
return he cannot, nor | continue where he is. 1.05. 54
desire my man's abode where i did leave him: 1.06. 53
fold down the leaf where i have left. 2.02. 4
leaf's turn'd down | where philomele gave up. 2.02. 46
her bedchamber | (where i confess i slept not, 2.04. 67
let there be no honor | where there is beauty; 2.04.109
truth, where semblance; 2.04.109
love, | where there's another man. 2.04.110
of no more bondage be to where they are made 2.04.111
was i know not where | when i was stamp'd. 2.05. 4
where horses have been nimbler than the sands 3.02. 72
where i have liv'd at honest freedom, paid 3.03. 71
where is posthumus? 3.04. 4
where, if thou fear to strike and to make me 3.04. 29 P
where bide? 3.04.128
where then? 3.04.135
but, my gentle queen, | where is our daughter? 3.05. 30
where is she, sir? 3.05. 41
but for her, | where is she gone? 3.05. 60
villain, | where is thy lady? 3.05. 82
where is thy lady? 3.05. 84
where is she, sir? 3.05. 91
discover where thy mistress is, at once, | at 3.05. 95
such, i mean, | where they should be reliev'd. 3.06. 8
i am near to th' place where they should meet, 4.01. 1 P
displace our heads where (thanks, /ye gods!) 4.02.122
nor seek for danger | where there's no profit. 4.02.163
where? 4.02.212
say, where shall 's lay him? 4.02.233
o posthumus, alas, | where is thy head? 4.02.321
i nothing know where she remains, why gone, 4.03. 14
may drive us to a render | where we have liv'd, 4.04. 12
cam'st thou from where they made the stand? 5.03. 1
where was this lane? 5.03. 13
could not find death where i did hear him groan, 5.03. 69
hear him groan, | nor feel him where he strook. 5.03. 70
in britain where was he | that could stand up 5.04. 53
it was in rome — accurs'd | the mansion where! 5.05.155
he was too good to be | where ill men were, and 5.05.159
where i was taught | of your chaste daughter the 5.05.193
breathe not where princes are. 5.05.238
her son | is gone, we know not how, nor where. 5.05.273
where, in a frenzy, in my master's garments 5.05.282
where? 5.05.384
see where she comes, apparelled like the spring, PER 1.01. 12
where is read | nothing but curious pleasures, 1.01. 15
where now /you're both a father and a son | by 1.01.127
the tomb where grief should sleep, can breed me 1.02. 5
where, as thou know'st, against the face of 1.02. 71
intend my travel, where i'll hear from thee, 1.02.116
where each man | thinks all is writ he /speken 2.ch. 11
where when men been, there's seldom ease, | for 2.ch. 28
hark you, sir; do you know where ye are? 2.01. 96 P
it kept where i kept, i so dearly lov'd it, 2.01.130
court, | where with it it may appear a gentleman; 2.01.141
where now his /son's like a glow–worm in the 2.03. 43
where, by the loss of maidenhead, | a babe is 3.ch. 10
where, for a monument upon thy bones, | the 3.01. 61
o dear diana, | where am i? 3.02.105
where you may abide till your date expire. 3.04. 14
light into my hands, where you are like to live. 4.02. 72 P
fault | to scape his hands where i was to die. 4.02. 75
despise profit where you have most gain. 4.02.118 P
several clime | where our scenes seems to live. 4.04. 7
fortune | have plac'd me in this sty, where, 4.06. 97
where a man may serve seven years for the loss 4.06.171 P
thoughts again, | where we left him, on the sea. 5.ch. 13
where, driven before the winds, he is arriv'd 5.ch. 14
he is arriv'd | here where his daughter dwells, 5.ch. 15
where what is done in action, more, if might, 5.ch. 23
where is lord helicanus? 5.01. 1
expect even here, where is a kingly patient, 5.01. 71
where do you live? 5.01.113
where i am but a stranger. 5.01.114
where were you bred? 5.01.115
where were you born? 5.01.154
well, where were you bred? 5.01.163
where were you bred? 5.01.169
where, by her own most clear remembrance, she 5.03. 12
where shall be shown you all was found with her; 5.03. 66
where we shall find | the moi'ty of a number, TNK 1.01.213
us to an eddy | where we should turn or drown; 1.02. 11
i pity | decays where e'er i find them, but such 1.02. 32
where every evil | hath a good color; 1.02. 38
where ev'ry seeming good's | a certain evil; 1.02. 39
where not to be ev'n jump | as they are, here 1.02. 40
which is not catching | where there is faith? 1.02. 46
theseus (who where he threats appalls) hath sent 1.02. 90
execution, where nor gain | made him regard, or 1.03. 29
fought out together where death's self was 1.03. 40
commit it | to the like innocent cradle, where, 1.03. 70
where, having bound things scatter'd, we will 1.04. 48
death's the market–place, where each one meets. 1.05. 16
o cousin arcite, | where is thebes now? 2.02. 7
where is our noble country? 2.02. 7
where are our friends and kindreds? 2.02. 8
where you should never know it, and so perish 2.02. 92
misery | it is to live abroad, and every where! 2.02. 98
where sin is justice, lust and ignorance | the 2.02.106
where he himself will edify the duke | most 2.03. 52
where were you bred you know it not? 2.03. 63
place | where i may ever dwell in sight of her? 2.03. 82
i have sent him where a cedar, | higher than all 2.06. 4
and where there is a path of ground i'll venture 2.06. 33
unarm'd, and can | smell where resistance is. 3.02. 17
where am i now? 3.04. 4
laid upon ye, | and do you still cry, "where?" 3.05. 7
where be your ribands, maids? 3.05. 28
me, cousin, | where got'st thou this good armor? 3.06. 54
where this man calls me traitor, | let me say 3.06.160
but want the understanding where to use it. 3.06.216
where ever they shall travel, ever strangers 3.06.255
the place | was knee–deep where she sat; 4.01. 83
where she stay'd, | and fell, scarce to be got 4.01.101
th' wood, where palamon | lies longing for me. 4.01.144
be made the altar where the lives of lovers — 4.02. 61
which yields compassion where he conquers; 4.02.132
to spy advantages, and where he finds 'em, 4.02.133
look where she comes, you shall perceive her 4.03. 9 P
your chance to come where the blessed spirits — 4.03. 22 P
her to a place where the light may rather seem 4.03. 74 P
sails that must these vessels port even where 5.01. 29
on, where she sticks | the queen of flowers. 5.01. 44
lo where our sister is in expectation, | yet 5.03.105
o all you heavenly powers, where is /your mercy? 5.03.139
nay, any where that not adheres to england, STM II.C 129
here come and sit, where never serpent hisses, VEN 17
chin, | and where she ends, she doth anew begin. 60
bow, | who conquers where he comes in every jar, 100
love keeps his revels where there are but twain; 123
morn till night, even where i list to sport me. 154
for where they lay the shadow had forsook them, 176
feed where thou wilt, on mountain or in dale; 232
stray lower, where the pleasant fountains lie. 234
for where a heart is hard they make no batt'ry." 426
"o, where am i?" 493
his snout digs sepulchres where e'er he goes; 622
"for where love reigns, disturbing jealousy 649
and sometime where earth–delving conies keep, 687
"where did i leave?" 715
"no matter where," quoth he, | "leave me, and 715
place, | where fearfully the dogs exclaim aloud: 886
crystals, where they view'd each other's sorrow, 963
where they resign their office and their light 1039
makes more gashes where no breach should be. 1066
where lo, two lamps burnt out in darkness lies; 1128
where herself herself beheld | a thousand times, 1129
"it shall suspect where is no cause of fear, 1153
it shall not fear where it should most mistrust, 1154
perverse it shall be where it shows most toward, 1157
where their queen | means to immure herself, and 1193
where mortal stars as bright as heaven's LUC 13
where, lest between them both it should be 74
then where is truth, if there be no self–trust? 158
band | where her beloved collatinus lies. 256
who fears sinking where such treasure lies?" 280
he takes it from the rushes where it lies, | and 318
where like a virtuous monument she lies, | to be 391
where their dear governess and lady lies, | do 443
where thou with patience must my will abide — 486
pleads, in a wilderness where are no laws, | to 544
where subjects' eyes do learn, do read, do look. 616
wilt thou be the school where lust shall learn? 617
where it may find | some purer chest to close so 760
"where now i have no one to blush with me, | to 792
the adder hisses where the sweet birds sing, 871
thou sets the wolf where he the lamb may get; 878
and in thy shady cell, where none may spy him, 881
and bring him where his suit may be obtained? 898
debate where leisure serves with dull debaters; 1019
to burn the guiltless casket where it lay! 1057
seems to point her out where she sits weeping, 1087
at last she calls to mind where hangs a piece 1366
from the strond of dardan, where they fought, 1436
to find a face where all distress is stell'd. 1444
many she sees where cares have carved some, 1445
but none where all distress and dolor dwell'd, 1446
where no excuse can give the fault amending. 1614
where thou wast wont to rest thy weary head, 1621
and swear i found you where you did fulfill 1635
of that polluted prison where it breathed. 1726
where shall i live now lucrece is unlived? 1754
where all those pleasures live that art can PP 5. 6
a brook where adon us'd to cool his spleen. 6. 6
where her faith was firmly fix'd in love, 17. 7
there | where thy desert may merit praise, | by 18.15
fuel, | making a famine where abundance lies, SON 1. 7
then being ask'd where all thy beauty lies, 2. 5
where all the treasure of thy lusty days, | to 2. 6
for where is she so fair whose unear'd womb 3. 5
the lovely gaze where every eye doth dwell 5. 2
beauty o'ersnow'd and bareness every where: 5. 8
where wasteful time debateth with decay | to 15.11
to find where your true image pictur'd lies, 24. 6
love and am beloved | where i may not remove, 25.14
not show my head where thou mayst prove me. 26.14
for then my thoughts (from far where i abide) 27. 5
thou art the grave where buried love doth live, 31. 9
for still temptation follows where thou art. 41. 4
where thou art forc'd to break a twofold truth: 41.12
from limits far remote, where thou dost stay. 44. 4
as soon as think the place where he would be. 44. 8
fire, | are both with thee, where ever i abide; 45. 2
save where thou art not, though i feel thou art, 48.10
from where thou art, why should i haste me 51. 3
which parts the shore where two contracted new 56.10
with my jealous thought | where you may be, or 57.10
save where you are how happy you make those. 57.12
be where you list, your charter is so strong, 58. 9
where, alack, | shall time's best jewel from 65. 9
me untrue, | my name be buried where my body is, 72.11
/ruin'd choirs, where late the sweet birds sang. 73. 4
showing their birth and where they did proceed? 76. 8
where breath most breathes, even in the mouths 81.14
might be better us'd | where cheeks need blood, 82.14
which should example where your equal grew? 84. 4
his wit, | making his style admired every where. 84.12
and for that riches where is my deserving? 87. 6
where beauty's veil doth cover every blot, | and 95.11
what old december's bareness every where! 97. 4
from their proud lap pluck them where they grew; 98. 8
where art thou, muse, that thou forget'st so 100. 1
and make time's spoils despised every where. 100.12
the owner's tongue doth publish every where. 102. 4
where time and outward form would show it dead. 108.14
they know what beauty is, see where it lies, 137. 3
be anchor'd in the bay where all men ride, | why 137. 6
or if they have, where is my judgment fled, 148. 3
for my help lies | where cupid got new fire — 153.14
to every place at once, and no where fix'd, LC 27
lets not bounty fall | where want cries some, 42
want cries some, but where excess begs all. 42
in personal duty, following where he haunted. 130
heard where his plants in others' orchards grew, 171
be, | where neither party is nor true nor kind: 186
but yield them up where i myself must render: 221

WHEREABOUT 2 FR 0.0002 REL FR 2 V 0 P
me | whither i go, nor reason whereabout. 1H4 2.03.104
fear | the very stones prate of my whereabout, MAC 2.01. 58

WHEREAS 7 FR 0.0008 REL FR 6 V 1 P
and, whereas i was black and swart before, 1H6 1.02. 84
whereas he | from john of gaunt doth bring his 2.05. 76
whereas the contrary bringeth bliss, | and is a 5.05. 64
and whereas, before, our forefathers had no 2H6 4.07. 34 P
whereas reproof, obedient and in order, | fits PER 1.02. 42
me, | whereas no glory's got to overcome. 1.04. 70
he spying her, bounc'd in, whereas he stood; PP 6.13

WHEREAT 17 FR 0.0019 REL FR 17 V 0 P
whereat, with blade, with bloody blameful blade, MND 5.01.146

whereat the great lord of northumberland, 3H6 1.01. 4
thou hast done a deed whereat valor will weep. COR 5.06.132
the thing whereat it trembles by surmise. TIT 2.03.219
feast | whereat a villain's not a welcome guest. TIM 3.06.103
whereat griev'd, | that so his sickness, age, HAM 2.02. 65
whereat i, wretch, | made scruple of his praise, CYM 5.05.181
quoth she, whereat a sudden pale, | like lawn VEN 589
whereat th' impartial gazer late did wonder, 748
whereat amaz'd as one that unaware | hath 823
and now she beats her heart, whereat it groans, 829
whereat she starts like one that spies an adder 878
whereat her tears began to turn their tide, 979
whereat she leaps, that was but late forlorn. 1026
whereat each tributary subject quakes, | as when 1045
whereat a waxen torch forthwith he lighteth, LUC 178
whereat she smiled with so sweet a cheer | that 264

WHEREBY 13 FR 0.0014 REL FR 8 V 5 P
when you do take the means whereby i live. MV 4.01.377
for by this light whereby i see thy beauty, SHR 2.01.273
whereby we stand opposed by such means | as you 1H4 5.01. 67
prawns, whereby thou didst desire to eat some, 2H4 2.01. 96 P
whereby i told thee they were ill for a green 2.01. 97 P
when a man is being whereby 'a may be thought to 3.02. 79 P
be repeal'd | whereby my son is disinherited. 3H6 1.01.250
whereby his suit was granted | ere it was ask'd H8 1.01.186
that natural competency | whereby they live. COR 1.01.140
whereby we might express some part of our zeals, TIM 1.02. 85 P
whereby he does receive | particular addition, MAC 3.01. 98
whereby hangs a tale, sir? OTH 3.01. 9 P
whereby i see that time's the king of men, PER 2.03. 45

WHEREFORE *(also vherefore)*
/WHEREFORE 1 FR 0.0001 REL FR 1 V 0 P
/ah, /wherefore /dost /thou /urge /the /name /of TIT 3.02. 26

WHEREFORE 144 FR 0.0162 REL FR 122 V 22 P
wherefore did they not | that hour destroy us? TMP 1.02.138
wherefore this ghastly looking? 2.01.309
wherefore weep you? 3.01. 76
but wherefore waste i time to counsel thee TGV 1.01. 51
wherefore shouldst thou pity her? 4.04. 78
wherefore? 5.02. 27
wherefore shall i be content–a? WIV 1.04. 71 P
ay, sir, and wherefore; ERR 2.02. 43 P
for they say, every why hath a wherefore. 2.02. 44 P
first — for flouting me, and then wherefore — 2.02. 45
in the why and the wherefore is neither rhyme 2.02. 48
tell you when, and you'll tell me wherefore. 3.01. 39
wherefore? 3.01. 40
say, wherefore didst thou lock me forth to–day? 4.04. 95
on thee, villain, wherefore dost thou mad me? 4.04.126
be quiet, people. wherefore throng you hither? 5.01. 38
why, how now, count, wherefore are you sad? ADO 2.01.288 P
why, how now, cousin, wherefore sink you down? 4.01.110
yea, wherefore should she not? 4.01.119
wherefore? 4.01.120
little pretty, because little. wherefore apt? LLL 1.02. 22 P
and wherefore not ships? 2.01.219
wherefore was i to this keen mockery born? MND 2.02.123
wherefore speaks he this | to her he hates? 3.02.227
and wherefore doth lysander | deny your love (so 3.02.228
hate me, wherefore? 3.02.272
o, wherefore, nature, didst thou lions frame? 5.01.291
but wherefore should i go? MV 2.05. 12
wherefore do you look | upon that poor and AYL 2.01. 56
and wherefore are you gentle, strong, and 2.03. 6
foolish shepherd, wherefore do you follow her, 3.05. 49
frown, | and wherefore gaze this goodly company, SHR 3.02. 94
will be pleas'd, then wherefore should i doubt? 4.04.106
wherefore? tell true. AWW 1.03.219
with my hate to her, | and wherefore i am fled; 2.03.288
wherefore, what's the instance? 4.01. 40 P
wherefore hast thou accus'd him all this while? 5.03.288
wherefore, sweetheart? what's your metaphor? TN 1.03. 71 P
wherefore are these things hid? 1.03.125 P
wherefore have these gifts a curtain before 'em? 1.03.125 P
wherefore, gentle maiden, | do you neglect them? WT 4.04. 85
wherefore that box? 4.04.755 P
and wherefore will i do it? JN 3.04. 69
thou idle dreamer, wherefore didst thou so? 4.02.153
but wherefore do you droop? 5.01. 44
may know wherefore we took the sacrament, | and 5.02. 6
and wherefore com'st thou hither | before king R2 1.03. 31
then wherefore dost thou hope he is not shipp'd? 2.02. 45
wherefore was i born? 2.03.122
but wherefore do i tell these news to thee? 1H4 3.02.121
him, fellow, wherefore hang'st thou upon him? 2H4 2.01. 68
wherefore blush you now? 2.02. 76 P
wherefore do you so ill translate yourself | out 4.01. 47
wherefore do i this? 4.01. 53
now, cousin, wherefore stands our army still? 4.02. 98
and wherefore should these good news make me 4.04.102
but wherefore did he take away the crown? 4.05. 88
wherefore the king, most worthily, hath caus'd H5 4.07. 8 P
come, wherefore should you be so pashful? 4.08. 69 P
and causes why and wherefore in all things. 5.01. 4 P
peace to this meeting, wherefore we are met! 5.02. 1
wherefore a guard of chosen shot i had | that 1H6 1.04. 53
wherefore is charles impatient with his friend? 2.01. 54
and wherefore crave you combat? 4.01. 84
lady, wherefore talk you so? 5.03.108
but wherefore weeps warwick, my valiant son? 2H6 1.01.115
wherefore should i curse them? 3.02.309
but wherefore grieve i at an hour's poor loss, 3.02.381
wherefore, on a brick wall have i climb'd into 4.10. 6 P
or wherefore dost abuse it if thou hast it? 5.01.172
wherefore else guard we his royal tent | but to 3H6 4.03. 21
but wherefore stay we? 'tis no time to talk. 4.05. 24
brother, wherefore stand you on nice points? 4.07. 58
but wherefore dost thou come? 5.06. 29
wherefore do you come? R3 1.04.171
else wherefore breathe i in a christian land? 3.07.116
you cannot guess wherefore the welshman comes. 4.04.476
wherefore? 5.03.187
and wherefore should they, since that i myself 5.03.202
wherefore i humbly | beseech you, sir, to spare H8 2.04. 53
wherefore frowns he thus? 5.01. 87
do desire to know | wherefore i sent for you. 5.01. 90
how now, prince troilus, wherefore not a–field? TRO 1.01.105
why, how now, ajax, wherefore do ye thus? 2.01. 55
wherefore should you so? 2.03.230
approach, | with the whole quality wherefore. 4.01. 45
bite another, and wherefore should one bastard? 5.07. 19 P
that they have lov'd, they know not wherefore; COR 2.02. 10 P
wherefore? wherefore? 4.05.177 P
wherefore? wherefore? 4.05.177 P
my lovely aaron, wherefore look'st thou sad, TIT 2.03. 10
but wherefore stand'st thou with thy weapon 3.01. 48
thou not guess wherefore she plies thee thus? 4.01. 15
wherefore didst thou this? 4.02.147
why, how now, kinsman, wherefore storm you so? ROM 1.05. 60
o romeo, romeo, wherefore art thou romeo? 2.02. 33
how camest thou hither, tell me, and wherefore? 2.02. 62
but wherefore, villain, didst thou kill my 3.02.100
all this is comfort, wherefore weep i then? 3.02.107
wherefore? TIM 1.01.233 P
understand | wherefore you are not paid. 2.02. 43
you make me marvel wherefore ere this time | had 2.02.124
but wherefore art not in thy shop to–day? JC 1.01. 27
wherefore rejoice? 1.01. 32
but wherefore do you hold me here so long? 1.02. 83
but wherefore did you so much tempt the heavens? 1.03. 53
wherefore rise you now? 2.01.234
their bosoms, and i know | wherefore they do it. 5.01. 8
but wherefore could not i pronounce "amen"? MAC 2.02. 28
wherefore did you so? 2.03.107
wherefore was that cry? 5.05. 15
wherefore? HAM 1.04. 57
wherefore should you do this? 2.01. 36
i have of late — but wherefore i know not — 2.02.296 P
wherefore should i | stand in the plague of LR 1.02. 2
wherefore base? 1.02. 6
wherefore | should he sit here? 2.04.112
wherefore to dover? 3.07. 52
wherefore to dover? let him answer that. 3.07. 53
wherefore to dover? 3.07. 55
wherefore, bold peasant, | /durst thou support a 4.06.231
why? wherefore ask you this? OTH 1.01. 85
a quarrel, but nothing wherefore. 2.03.289 P
ha? wherefore? 3.04. 78
leave you? wherefore? 3.04.192
wherefore my father should revengers want, ANT 2.06. 11
wherefore is this? 3.13.122
wherefore is that? 5.01. 4
wherefore you have | commanded of me these most CYM 1.05. 7
wherefore write you not | what monsters her 3.02. 1
wherefore breaks that sigh | from th' inward of 3.04. 5
wherefore then | didst undertake it? 3.04.101
with marriage wherefore was he mock'd, | to be 5.04. 58
i know not why, wherefore, | to say "live, boy." 5.05. 95
wherefore ey'st him so? 5.05.114
wherefore she does, and swears she'll never PER 4.04. 42
and wherefore call'd marina? 5.01.155
and "wherefore?" TNK 3.05. 7
but wherefore says my love that she is young? PP 1. 9
and wherefore say not i that i am old? 1.10
but wherefore do not you a mightier way | make SON 16. 1
ah, wherefore with infection should he live, 67. 1
but wherefore says she not she is unjust? 138. 9
and wherefore say not i that i am old? 138.10

WHEREFORE'S 1 FR 0.0001 REL FR 1 V 0 P
wherefore's this noise? ANT 5.02.233

/WHEREIN 2 FR 0.0002 REL FR 2 V 0 P
/wherein /the //cub–drawn /bear /would /couch, LR 3.01. 12
up thus meanly | i' th' cave /wherein /they bow, CYM 3.03. 83

WHEREIN 142 FR 0.0160 REL FR 115 V 27 P
roots, and husks | wherein the acorn cradled. TMP 1.02.465
o'erslips me in the day | wherein i sigh not, TGV 2.02. 10
who art the table wherein all my thoughts | are 2.07. 3
that touch me near, wherein thou must be secret. 3.01. 60
you, wherein i must very much lay open mine own WIV 2.02.184 P
wherein (let no man hear me) i take pride, MM 2.04. 10
wherein if he chance to fail, he hath sentenc'd 3.02.256 P
a madman, | wherein have i so deserv'd of you, 5.01.502
wherein it doth impair the seeing sense, | it MND 3.02.179
debts | wherein my time something too prodigal MV 1.01.129
if you choose that wherein i am contain'd, 2.09. 5
wherein doth sit the dread and fear of kings; 4.01.192
thine own fair eyes, | wherein i see myself — 5.01.243
wherein i confess me much guilty to deny so fair AYL 1.02.184 P
wherein if i be foil'd, there is but one sham'd 1.02.187 P
let me see wherein | my tongue hath wrong'd him; 2.07. 83
pageants than the scene | wherein we play in. 2.07.139
wherein went he? 3.02.221 P
on the trees, wherein rosalind is so admir'd? 3.02.392 P
hand, | wherein your cunning can assist me much. SHR in.1. 92
wherein your lady and your humble wife | may in.1. 116
fit man to teach her that wherein she delights, 1.01.111 P
wherein our dearest friend | prejudicates the AWW 1.02. 7
with that malignant cause wherein the honor | of 2.01.111
wherein toward me my homely stars have fail'd 2.05. 75
wherein so curiously he had set this counterfeit 4.03. 33 P
wherein have you play'd the knave with fortune 5.02. 29 P
wherein the pregnant enemy does much. TN 2.02. 28
his way some obscure epistles of love, wherein, 2.03.156 P
not have, | wherein olivia may seem serviceable? 5.01.102
wherein our entertainment shall shame us: WT 1.01. 8 P
heart, as well | my chamber–councils, wherein, 1.02.237
wherein my hope is i shall so prevail | to force 4.04.664
wherein we step after a stranger, march | upon JN 5.02. 27
steps | esteem as foil wherein thou art to set R2 1.03.266
land, | wherein thou liest in reputation sick, 2.01. 96
wherein the king stands generally condemn'd. 2.02.132
on what condition stands it and wherein? 2.03.107
meeting, wherein it is at our pleasure to fail; 1H4 1.02.170 P
wherein you range under this subtile king! 1.03.169
yet time serves wherein you may redeem | your 1.03.180
wherein is he good, but to taste sack and drink 2.04.455 P
wherein neat and cleanly, but to carve a capon 2.04.456 P
wherein cunning, but in craft? 2.04.457 P
wherein crafty, but in villainy? 2.04.457 P
wherein villainous, but in all things? 2.04.458 P
wherein worthy, but in nothing? 2.04.459 P
wherein my youth | hath faulty wand'red and 3.02. 26
a day | wherein the fortune of ten thousand men 4.04. 9
wherein the noble youth did dress themselves: 2H4 2.03. 22
wherein have you been galled by the king? 4.01. 89
and wherein | it shall appear that your demands 4.01.141
his companions | like a strange tongue, wherein, 4.04. 69
wherein you would have sold your king to H5 2.02.170
was blessedly lost wherein such preparation was 4.01.181 P
wherein thou art less happy, being fear'd, 4.01.248
what? wherein talbot overcame, is't so? 1H6 1.01.107
wherein lord talbot was o'erthrown. 1.01.108
a tomb, wherein his corpse shall be interr'd; 2.02. 13
and safely brought to dover, wherein shipp'd, 5.01. 49
wherein am i guilty? 2H6 3.01.103
wherein have i offended most? 4.07. 97
wherein my grandsire and my father sat? 3H6 1.01.125
wherein thy counsel and consent is wanting. 2.06.102
wherein, my friends, have i offended you? R3 1.04.177
wherein thyself shalt highly be employ'd. 3.01.180
wherein my soul recorded | the history of all 3.05. 27
wherein dost thou joy? 4.04. 93
this is the day wherein i wish'd to fall | by 5.01. 16
wherein, although, | my good lord cardinal, they H8 1.02. 22
wherein? 1.02. 38
wherein he might the king his lord advertise 2.04.179
wherein he appears | as i would wish mine enemy. 3.02. 27
wherein was read | how that the cardinal did 3.02. 31
as well wherein 'tis precious of itself | as in TRO 2.02. 55
his back, | wherein he puts alms for oblivion, 3.03.146
of your speech, wherein | you told how diomed, a 4.01. 9
wherein my sword had not impressure made | /of 4.05.131
in that absence wherein he won honor than in the COR 1.03. 4 P
by all the battles wherein we have fought, | by 1.06. 56
love this painting | wherein you see me smear'd; 1.06. 69
not my blood | wherein thou seest me mask'd; 1.08. 10
wherein he gives my son the whole name of the 2.01.134 P
wherein every one of us has a single honor, in 2.03. 44 P
and revolts, wherein they show'd | most valor, 3.01.126
honor'd mould | wherein this trunk was fram'd, 5.03. 23
tell me not | wherein i seem unnatural; 5.03. 84
if you do hold the same intent wherein | you 5.06. 12
and wherein rome hath done you any scath, | let TIT 5.01. 7
wherein i had no stroke of mischief in it? 5.01.110
curse — | wherein i did not some notorious ill: 5.01.127
have we done aught amiss, show us wherein, | and 5.03.129
love, wherein thou stickest | up to the ears. ROM 1.04. 42
wherein obscurely | caesar's ambition shall be JC 1.02.319
you shall give me reasons | why, and wherein, 3.01.222
his glory not extenuated, wherein he was worthy; 3.02. 39 P
wherein hath caesar thus deserv'd your loves? 3.02.236
wherein my letters, praying on his side, 4.03. 4
the hope drunk | wherein you dress'd yourself? MAC 1.07. 36
wherein our saviour's birth is celebrated, HAM 1.01.159
wherein the spirit held his wont to walk. 1.04. 6
as in their birth, wherein they are not guilty 1.04. 25
wherein we saw thee quietly interr'd, | hath 1.04. 49
into the madness wherein now he raves, | and all 2.02.150
wherein i'll catch the conscience of the king. 2.02.605
wherein necessity, of matter beggar'd, | will 4.05. 92
hearing, for a quality | wherein, they say, you 4.07. 73
bethink yourself wherein you may have offended LR 1.02.159 P
wherein we must have use of your advice. 2.01.121
hast thou not forgot, | wherein i thee endow'd. 2.04.181
wherein the /toged consuls can propose | as OTH 1.01. 25
wherein i spoke of most disastrous chances: 1.03.134
wherein of antres vast and deserts idle, | rough 1.03.140
suit | wherein i mean to touch your love indeed, 3.03. 81
wherein none can be so determinate as the 4.02.226 P
no, i will go seek | some ditch wherein to die; ANT 4.06. 37
wherein the worship of the whole world lies. 4.14. 86
with those my former fortunes | wherein i liv'd, 4.15. 54
wherein he must be weigh'd rather by her value CYM 1.04. 15 P
trims, wherein | you made great juno angry. 3.04.164
tell him | wherein you're happy — which will 3.04.174
those employments wherein i should have cause to 3.05.110 P
wherein i am false, i am honest; 4.03. 42
wherein | our pleasure his full fortune doth 5.04.109
from the dejected state wherein he is, | he PER 2.02. 46
wherein my death might yield her any profit, 4.01. 80
have, | wherein we are not destitute for want, 5.01. 57
the peace wherein you have till now grown up STM II.C 65
wherein she fram'd thee in high heaven's despite VEN 731
their virtue lost, wherein they late excell'd, 1131
wherein i will not kiss my sweet love's flow'r." 1188
lucretia's glove, wherein her needle sticks. LUC 317
wilt thou be glass wherein it shall discern 619
balk | the prey wherein by nature they delight, 697
wherein is stamp'd the semblance of a devil. 1246
the glass fell wherein they view'd their faces 1526
by, | wherein deep policy did him disguise, 1815
my body is the frame wherein 'tis held, | and SON 24. 3
making their tomb the womb wherein they grew? 86. 4
of faults conceal'd, wherein i am attainted, 88. 7
wherein it finds a joy above the rest, | but 91. 6
all | wherein i should your great deserts repay, 117. 2

WHEREINTO 1 FR 0.0001 REL FR 1 V 0 P
as where's that palace whereinto foul things OTH 3.03.137

WHEREOF 85 FR 0.0096 REL FR 73 V 12 P
an act | whereof what's past is prologue, what TMP 2.01.253
sour ringlets make, | whereof the ewe not bites; 5.01. 38
in requital whereof, henceforth carry your TGV 1.01.145 P
tow'r, | the key whereof myself have ever kept; 3.01. 36
the least whereof would quell a lover's hope, 4.02. 13
the mirth whereof so larded with my matter, WIV 4.06. 14
for testimony whereof, one in the prison, | that MM 5.01.465
the sight whereof i think you had from me, ADO 5.04. 25
what stuff 'tis made of, whereof it is born, | i MV 1.01. 4
whereof who chooses his meaning chooses you, 1.02. 30 P
the greatness whereof i cannot enough commend, 4.01.159 P
law, | whereof you are a well–deserving pillar, 4.01.239
in lieu whereof | three thousand ducats, due 4.01.410
in sign whereof, | please ye we may contrive SHR 1.02.273
sciences, | whereof i know she is not ignorant. 2.01. 58
hath in't a bond | whereof the world takes note. AWW 1.03.189
to cure the desperate languishings whereof | the 1.03.229
in recompense whereof he hath married her. TN 5.01.364
whereof the execution did cry out | against the WT 1.02.260
whereof the least | is not this suit of mine, 1.02.401

the pretense whereof being by circumstances 3.02. 17 P
whereof i reckon | the casting forth to crows 3.02.190
in lieu whereof, i pray you bear me hence | from JN 5.04. 44
in haste whereof, most heartily i pray | your R2 1.01.150
edward's seven sons, whereof thyself art one, 1.02. 11
the revenue whereof shall furnish us | for our 1.04. 46
whereof our uncle gaunt did stand possess'd. 2.01.162
in proof whereof, there is my honor's pawn, 4.01. 70
whereof the hangman hath no lean wardrobe. 1H4 1.02. 72 P
whereof a little | more than a little is by much 3.02. 72
same grievances | whereof you did complain, 2H4 4.02.114
in aid whereof we of the spiritualty | will H5 1.02.132
whereof take you one quarter into france, | and 1.02.215
the taste whereof god of his mercy give | you 2.02.179
the enterprise whereof | shall be to you as us, 2.02.182
by the means whereof 'a faces it out, but fights 3.02. 33 P
by the means whereof 'a breaks words, and keeps 3.02. 35 P
the smell whereof shall breed a plague in france 4.03.103
in stead whereof sharp stakes pluck'd out of 1H6 1.01.117
kept | as that whereof i had the government, 2.01. 64
in sign whereof i pluck a white rose too. 2.04. 58
in sign whereof, this arm, that hath reclaim'd 3.04. 5
what is that wrong whereof you both complain? 4.01. 87
by means whereof the towns each day revolted? 2H6 3.01. 63
by means whereof his highness hath lost france. 3.01.106
whereof you cannot easily purge yourself. 3.01.135
in stead whereof let this supply the room: 3H6 2.06. 54
whereof the root was fix'd in virtue's ground, 3.03.125
whereof the king my brother was possess'd. R3 3.01.196
us | whereof i shall not have intelligence. 3.02. 24
(whereof my sovereign would have note), they are H8 1.02. 48
practices, whereof | we cannot feel too little, 1.02.127
disdain and shame whereof hath ever since kept TRO 1.02. 35 P
whereof we have record, trial did draw | bias 1.03. 14
the fever whereof all our power is sick. 1.03.139
here's "in witness whereof the parties 3.02. 58 P
in love whereof, half hector stays at home; 4.05. 84
important business, | the tide whereof is now. 5.01. 83
whereof they say | the city is well stor'd. COR 1.01.189
whereof we have ta'en good and good store — of 1.09. 32
whereof their mother daintily hath fed, | eating TIT 5.03. 61
the breath is gone whereof this praise is made. TIM 2.02.170
the want whereof doth daily make revolt | in my 4.03. 92
whereof thy proud child, arrogant man, is puff'd 4.03.180
whereof ingrateful man, with liquorish draughts 4.03.194
by means whereof this breast of mine hath buried JC 1.02. 49
sits smiling to my heart, in grace whereof, | no HAM 1.02.124
yielding of that body | whereof he is the head. 1.03. 24
good wisdom | (whereof i know you are fraught) LR 1.04.220
now, gods that we adore, whereof comes this? 1.04.290
whereof, perchance, these are but furnishings — 3.01. 29
harder than the stones whereof 'tis rais'd, 3.02. 64
from the loath'd warmth whereof deliver me, and 4.06.267 P
whereof by parcels she had something heard, OTH 1.03.154
whereof i take this that you call love to be a 1.03.331 P
the thought whereof | doth, like a poisonous 2.01.296
for joy whereof | the fam'd cassibelan, who was CYM 3.01. 29
the testimonies whereof lies bleeding in me. 3.04. 22 P
the cure whereof, my lord, | 'tis time must do. 3.05. 37
the fear whereof doth make him shake and shudder VEN 880
the spots whereof could weeping purify, | her LUC 685
the president whereof in lucrece view, 1261
my love, the loss whereof still fearing! PP 7.10
what is your substance, whereof are you made, SON 53. 1
and all those beauties whereof now he's king 63. 6

WHEREON 37 FR 0.0041 REL FR 36 V 1 P
whereon, | a treacherous army levied, one TMP 1.02.127
that | whereon this month i have been hammering. TGV 1.03. 18
be | a horse whereon the governor doth ride, MM 1.02.160
the state, whereon i studied, | is like a good 2.04. 7
and rock the ground whereon these sleepers be. MND 4.01. 86
tell me whereon the /likelihood depends. AYL 1.03. 57
on the like occasion whereon my services are now WT 1.01. 2 P
whereon he says | i shall yield up my crown, let JN 4.02.156
the grass whereon thou tread'st the presence R2 1.03.289
so looks the strond whereon the imperious flood 2H4 1.01. 62
court, | whereon this hydra son of war is born, 4.02. 38
whereon (as an offender to your father) | i gave 5.02. 81
shadow | whereon to practice your severity. 1H6 2.03. 47
and | your franchises, whereon you stood, COR 4.06. 86
we see the ground whereon these woes do lie, ROM 5.03.179
whereon hyperion's quick'ning fire doth shine: TIM 4.03.184
infected be the air whereon they ride, | and MAC 4.01.138
whereon old norway, overcome with joy, | gives HAM 2.02. 72
whereon his brains still beating puts him thus 3.01.174
whereon do you look? 3.04.124
plot | whereon the numbers cannot try the cause, 4.04. 63
a chalice for the nonce, whereon but sipping, 4.07.160
whereon, i do beseech thee, grant me this, | to OTH 3.03. 84
the watch, whereon it came | that i was cast; 5.02.326
whereon, i begg'd | his pardon for return. ANT 3.06. 59
whereon, | at three and two years old, i stole CYM 3.03.100
was a note | whereon her spirits would sojourn TNK 1.03. 77
stroke laments | the place whereon it falls, and 5.03. 5
these blue–vein'd violets whereon we lean VEN 125
"witness this primrose bank whereon i lie, 151
whereon they surfeit, yet complain on drouth: 544
within my bosom, whereon thou dost lie, | my 646
whereon with fearful eyes they long have gazed, 927
whereon the stars in secret influence comment; SON 15. 4
lie, | as the death–bed whereon it must expire, 73.11
if that be fair whereon my false eyes dote, 148. 5
whereon the thought might think sometime it saw LC 10

WHEREOUT 1 FR 0.0001 REL FR 1 V 0 P
and make distinct the very breach whereout TRO 4.05.245

/WHERE'S 1 FR 0.0001 REL FR 1 V 0 P
/done /their /mischief, /where's /thy /drum? LR 4.02. 55

WHERE'S 118 FR 0.0133 REL FR 76 V 42 P
where's the master? TMP 1.01. 9 P
where's simple, my man? can you tell, cousin? WIV 1.01.134 P
where's the cowl–staff? 3.03.146 P
where's bede? 5.05. 49
what ho, abhorson! where's abhorson, there? MM 4.02. 19 P
where's barnardine? 4.02. 65
good even. friar, where's the provost? 4.03.149 P
come, where's the chain? ERR 4.01. 58
but where's the money? 4.04. 11
now, signior, where's the count? ADO 2.01.211 P
god's my life, where's the sexton? 4.02. 70 P
where's her grace? LLL 5.02. 80
fair sir, god save you! where's the princess? 5.02.310
where's peaseblossom? MND 4.01. 5 P
where's mounsieur cobweb? 4.01. 7 P
where's mounsieur mustardseed? 4.01. 17 P
where's your master? MV 2.02.174
if you should die before him, where's her dower? SHR 2.01.389
where's the cook? 4.01. 45 P
where's my spaniel troilus? 4.01.150
now, where's my wife? 5.02. 90
where's your master? AWW 4.03. 75 P
where's malvolio? TN 3.04. 5
where's my cousin toby? 3.04. 61 P
where's antonio then? 4.03. 4
where's bohemia? speak. WT 5.01.185
where's poins, hal? 1H4 2.02. 7 P
where's bardolph? 2H4 1.02. 48 P
where's your yeoman? 2.01. 3 P
sirrah! where's snare? 2.01. 5 P
where's the roll? 3.02. 96 P
where's the roll? 3.02. 96 P
where's the roll? 3.02. 96 P
where's shadow? 3.02.124 P
where's he? 3.02.137 P
where's the prince dolphin? i have news for him. 1H6 1.02. 46
now where's the bastard's braves, and charles 3.02.123
o, where's young talbot? 4.07. 2
but where's the great alcides of the field, 4.07. 60
injurious duke, that threatest where's no cause. 2H6 1.04. 48
where's your knife? 3.02.195
where's our general? 4.02.111 P
where's dick, the butcher of ashford? 4.03. 1 P
but where's the body that i should embrace? 4.04. 6
and where's that valiant crook–back prodigy, 3H6 1.04. 75
where's captain margaret, to fence you now? 2.06. 75
where's richard gone? 5.05. 83
where's thy conscience now? R3 1.04.127 P
where's his examination? H8 1.01.116
where's gardiner? 2.02.108
where's your commission, lords? 3.02.233
where's then the saucy boat | whose weak TRO 1.03. 42
where's achilles? 2.03. 34 P
how now, where's thy master? 3.02. 1 P
where's my cousin cressid? 4.02. 24 P
where's my lord? 4.02. 80 P
diomed. calchas, i think. where's your daughter? 5.02. 3
hector, where's hector? 5.05. 47
troilus, i say, where's troilus? 5.06. 2
where's caius martius? COR 1.01.223
where's cotus? my master calls for him. cotus! 4.05. 3 P
where's that? 4.05. 41 P
leaves abroad, | and where's our lesson then? TIT 4.01.106
nurse, where's my daughter? ROM 1.03. 1
where's this girl? 1.03. 4
where's potpan, that he helps not to take away? 1.05. 1 P
ah, where's my man? 3.02. 88
o tell me, holy friar, | where's my lady's lord? 3.03. 82
where's romeo? 3.03. 82
where's romeo's man? 5.03.271
where's the fool now? TIM 2.02. 58 P
hear you, master steward, where's our master? 4.02. 1
where's publius? JC 3.01. 85
where's the thane of cawdor? MAC 1.06. 20
where's your father? HAM 3.01.129 P
now, hamlet, where's polonius? 4.03. 16 P
where's my knave? LR 1.04. 42 P
you, you, sirrah, where's my daughter? 1.04. 44 P
where's my fool? 1.04. 47 P
where's that mungrel? 1.04. 49 P
but where's my fool? 1.04. 71 P
now, edmund, where's the villain? 2.01. 37
i know you. where's the king? 3.01. 3
where's the king? 3.07. 14 P
where's my son edmund? 3.07. 85
now, where's your master? 4.02. 2
speak, edmund, where's the king? 5.03.238
and where's cordelia? 5.03.238
as where's that palace whereinto foul things OTH 3.03.137
where's satisfaction? 3.03.401
where's fulvia's process? ANT 1.01. 28
where's the soothsayer that you prais'd so to 1.02. 2 P
seek him, and bring him hither. where's alexas? 1.02. 85
or murmuring, "where's my serpent of old nile?" 1.05. 25
where's this cup i call'd for? 2.07. 54
where's antony? 3.05. 15
where's antony? 4.14.114
where's dolabella, | to second proculeius? 5.01. 69
where's seleucus? 5.02.140
where's the queen? 5.02.197
where's the queen? 5.02.320
where's thy knife? CYM 3.04. 96
where's my brother? 4.02.183
where's that? 4.02.321
where's that? 4.02.321
where's the lord governor? PER 1.04. 56
where's hourly trouble for a minute's ease. 2.04. 44
where's my lord? 3.02.105
where's arcite? TNK 2.02.244
draw up the company. where's the taborer? 3.05. 23
but i say, where's their women? 3.05. 25
where's the rest o' th' music? 3.05. 31
where's the bavian? 3.05. 33
alas, sir, where's your daughter? 4.01. 32
where's my wedding gown? 4.01.109
where's your compass? 4.01.143
where's your whistle, master? 4.01.149
where's the pilot? 4.01.150

WHERESOE'ER 10 FR 0.0011 REL FR 10 V 0 P
happy is hermia, wheresoe'er she lies, | for she MND 2.02. 90
and wheresoe'er we went, like juno's swans, AYL 1.03. 75
find out thy brother, wheresoe'er he is; 3.01. 5
i /warr'nt, good creature, wheresoe'er she is, AWW 3.05. 66
and wheresoe'er this foot of mine doth tread, JN 3.03. 62
for wheresoe'er thou art in this world's globe, 2H6 3.02.406
and wheresoe'er he is, he's surely dead. 3H6 2.06. 41
with resolution, wheresoe'er i meet thee | (as i 5.01. 95
poor naked wretches, wheresoe'er you are, | that LR 3.04. 28
gnats are unnoted wheresoe'er they fly, | but LUC 1014

WHERESOEVER 2 FR 0.0002 REL FR 0 V 2 P
but wheresoever, i wish him well. MM 3.02. 90 P
wheresoever you had it, i'll take out no work OTH 4.01.154 P

WHERESOME'ER 1 FR 0.0001 REL FR 0 V 1 P
would i were with him, wheresome'er he is, H5 2.03. 7 P

WHERE'T 1 FR 0.0001 REL FR 1 V 0 P
not born where't grows, | but worn a bait for CYM 3.04. 56

WHERETHROUGH 1 FR 0.0001 REL FR 1 V 0 P
breast, wherethrough the sun | delights to peep, SON 24.11

WHERETO 30 FR 0.0034 REL FR 29 V 1 P
good, | whereto if you'll a willing ear incline, MM 5.01.536
lysander, whereto tends all this? MND 3.02.256
hope, | whereto thy speech serves for authority, TN 1.02. 20
have you thought on | a place whereto you'll go? WT 4.04.537
whereto thy tongue a party–verdict gave. R2 1.03.234
whereto, when they shall know what men are rich, 1.04. 49
whereto my finger, like a dial's point, | is 5.05. 53
whereto we are bound, together with thy victory, COR 5.03.108
with thy victory, | whereto we are bound? 5.03.109
feast, | whereto i have invited many a guest, ROM 1.02. 21
whereto the climber–upward turns his face; JC 2.01. 23
speak | in the same pulpit whereto i am going, 3.01.250
(whereto the rather shall his day's hard journey MAC 1.07. 62
whereto serves mercy | but to confront the HAM 3.03. 46
as damn'd and black | as hell, whereto it goes. 3.03. 95
/compounded it with dust, whereto 'tis kin. 4.02. 6
and why of that loam whereto he was converted 5.01.211 P
all office | whereto our health is bound; LR 2.04.107
bent | to prove upon thy heart, whereto i speak, 5.03.141
whereto we see in all things nature tends — OTH 3.03.231
close, | whereto constrain'd by her infirmity, CYM 3.05. 47
whereto being bound, | the interim, pray you, PER 5.02. 13
whereto he'll infuse pow'r and press you forth TNK 1.01. 73
action with you | as that whereto i am going, 1.01.103
ladies, | this is a service, whereto i am going, 1.01.171
many a murther | set off whereto she's guilty. 5.03. 28
call, | whereto all bonds do tie me day by day; SON 117. 4
whereto th' inviting time our fashion calls; 124. 8
whereto the judgment of my heart is tied? 137. 8
hard, | whereto his invis'd properties did tend; LC 212

WHEREUNTIL 2 FR 0.0002 REL FR 0 V 2 P
sir, we know whereuntil it doth amount. LLL 5.02.493 P
sir, will show whereuntil it doth amount. 5.02.500 P

WHEREUNTO 2 FR 0.0002 REL FR 2 V 0 P
whereunto i never | purpose return. CYM 3.04.106
of, whereunto your levy | must be supplyant. 3.07. 13

WHEREUPON 15 FR 0.0017 REL FR 8 V 7 P
whereupon i command thee to open thy affair. WT 4.04.738 P
whereupon, after a little amazedness, we were 5.02. 5 P
we do no further ask | than whereupon our weal, JN 4.02. 65
whereupon the earl of worcester | hath broken R2 2.02. 58
and whereupon | you conjure from the breast of 1H4 4.03. 42
not in the fault, whereupon the world increases, 2H4 2.02. 26 P
now 'a said so, i can tell whereupon. 2.04. 91 P
whereupon | he is retir'd, to ripe his growing 4.01. 12
whereupon we are | now present here together: H8 2.04.202
whereupon i will show you a chamber, which bed, TRO 3.02.207 P
whereupon the grecians began to proclaim 5.04. 15 P
whereupon she grew round–womb'd, and had indeed, LR 1.01. 14 P
whereupon — | methinks i see him now — CYM 5.05.208
whereupon it made this threne | to the phoenix PHT 49
gilding the object whereupon it gazeth; SON 20. 6

WHEREVER 1 FR 0.0001 REL FR 1 V 0 P
wherever in your sightless substances | you wait MAC 1.05. 49

/WHEREWITH 1 FR 0.0001 REL FR 1 V 0 P
/the /regal /thoughts | /wherewith /i /reign'd? R2 4.01.164

WHEREWITH 10 FR 0.0011 REL FR 9 V 1 P
wherewith my brother held you in the cloister? TGV 1.03. 2
but with this i passion to say wherewith" — LLL 1.01.261 P
and all the shrouds wherewith my life should JN 5.07. 53
thoughts, | wherewith already france is overrun. 1H6 1.01.102
wherewith you now bedew king henry's hearse, | i 1.01.104
knowledge the wing wherewith we fly to heaven, 2H6 4.07. 74
thy balm wash'd off wherewith thou was anointed. 3H6 3.01. 17
against those honors deep and broad wherewith MAC 1.06. 17
friend, | whilst thou hast wherewith to spend; PP 20.34
crawls to maturity, wherewith being crown'd, SON 60. 6

WHEREWITHAL 2 FR 0.0002 REL FR 2 V 0 P
thou ladder wherewithal | the mounting R2 5.01. 55
he may, my lord, h'as wherewithal: H8 1.03. 59

WHET 11 FR 0.0012 REL FR 11 V 0 P
why dost thou whet thy knife so earnestly? MV 4.01.121
i come to whet your gentle thoughts | on his TN 3.01.105
i will whet on the king. JN 3.04.181
good queen, and whet not on these furious peers, 2H6 2.01. 33
and whet on warwick to this enterprise. 3H6 1.02. 37
and withal whet me | to be reveng'd on rivers, R3 1.03.331
he hears the king | does whet his anger to him. H8 3.02. 92
since cassius first did whet me against caesar, JC 2.01. 61
is but to whet thy almost blunted purpose. HAM 3.04.111
whet their detested knives against your throats, STM II.C 134
who did not whet his teeth at him again, | but VEN 1113

WHETHER *(also whe'er, whe'r, whither*)*

WHETHER 106 FR 0.0119 REL FR 82 V 24 P
i'll be your servant, | whether you will or no. TMP 3.01. 86
whether this be, | or be not, i'll not swear. 5.01.122
my horns are his horns, whether i wake or sleep. TGV 1.01. 79 P
whether had you rather lead mine eyes, or eye WIV 3.02. 3 P
to know, sir, whether one nym, sir, that 4.05. 32 P
whether thou art tainted or free. MM 1.02. 42 P
whether it be the fault and glimpse of newness, 1.02.158
or whether that the body public be | a horse 1.02.159
whether the tyranny be in his place, | or in his 1.02.163
whether you had not sometime in your life 2.01. 14
whether the three worthies shall come in or no. LLL 5.02.486
whether, if you yield not to your father's MND 1.01. 69
thou shalt remain here, whether thou wilt or no. 3.01.153
see me no more, whether he be dead or no. 3.02. 81
can you tell me whether one launcelot, that MV 2.02. 46 P

knows | but you, lorenzo, whether i am yours? 2.06. 31
do you hear whether antonio have had any loss at 3.01. 42 P
or whether, riding on the balls of mine, | seem 3.02.117
whether those peals of praise be his or no, | so 3.02.145
so, | as doubtful whether what i see be true, 3.02.147
to know your answer, whether you'll admit him. 4.01.146
be judge | whether bassanio had not once a love. 4.01.277
whether till the next night she had rather stay, 5.01.302
but whether wisely or no, let the forest judge. AYL 3.02.121 P
whether that thy youth and kind | will the 4.03. 59
whether i live or die, be you the sons | of AWW 2.01. 11
him, whether one captain dumaine be i' th' camp, 4.03.175 P
or whether he thinks it were not possible with 4.03.178 P
whether dost thou profess thyself — a knave or 4.05. 22 P
whether there be a scar under't or no, the 4.05. 95 P
whether i have been to blame or no, i know not. 5.03.129
whether it like me or no, i am a courtier. WT 4.04.730 P
and try whether i am not now a gentleman born. 5.02.133 P
whether hadst thou rather be a faulconbridge, JN 1.01.134
and so am i, whether i smack or no; 1.01.209
but this one word, whether thy tale be true. 3.01. 26
whether our kinsman come to see his friends. R2 1.04. 22
but whether they be ta'en or slain we hear not. 5.06. 4
i know not whether god will have it so | for 1H4 3.02. 4
whether our present five and twenty thousand 2H4 1.03. 16
and god knows whether those that /bawl out the 2.02. 23 P
and whether i shall ever see thee again or no, 2.04. 67 P
and look whether the fiery trigon, his man, be 2.04.265 P
see now whether pure fear and entire cowardice 2.04.325 P
her money, and whether she be damn'd for that, i 2.04.340 P
or whether that such cowards ought to wear 1H6 4.01. 28
brave death by speaking, whether he will or no; 4.07. 25
whether it be through force of your report, | my 5.05. 79
whether your grace be worthy, yea or no, 2H6 1.03.107
or whether he be scap'd away or no | from 3H6 2.01. 2
but whether 'twas the coldness of the king, 2.01.122
or whether 'twas report of her success, | or 2.01.125
not | to tell us whether they will come or no! R3 3.01. 23
whether ever i | did broach this business to H8 2.04.149
whether our daughter were legitimate, 2.04.180
i do not care whether you do or no. TRO 1.01. 80 P
his body | shall i destroy him — whether there, 4.05.243
but it is not known | whether for east or west. COR 1.02. 10
or whether his fall enrag'd him, or how 'twas, 1.03. 63 P
you shall perceive | whether i blush or no; 1.09. 70
neither to care whether they love or hate him 2.02. 12 P
if he did not care whether he had their love or 2.02. 16 P
i'll try whether my old wit be in request | with 3.01.250
whether to knock against the gates of rome, | or 4.05.141
whether /'twas pride, | which out of daily 4.07. 37
whether /defect of judgment, | to fail in the 4.07. 39
or whether nature, | not to be other than one 4.07. 41
but i know it is | (whether by device or no, the TIT 1.01.395
i doubt whether their legs be worth the sums TIM 1.02.232
whether caesar will come forth to-day or no; JC 2.01.194
and whether we shall meet again i know not; 5.01.114
whether yond troops are friend or enemy. 5.03. 18
whether he was combin'd | with those of norway, MAC 1.03.111
contend about them, | whether they live or die. 2.02. 8
not | whether it was his wisdom or his fear. 4.02. 5
whether in sea or fire, in earth or air, | th' HAM 1.01.153
whether aught, to us unknown, afflicts him thus, 2.02. 17
direct with me, whether you were sent for or no! 2.02.288 P
whether 'tis nobler in the mind to suffer | the 3.01. 56
whether love lead fortune, or else fortune love. 3.02.203
now whether it be | bestial oblivion, or some 4.04. 39
or whether gasted by the noise i made, | full LR 2.01. 55
tell me whether a madman be a gentleman or a 3.06. 9 P
or whether since he is advis'd by aught | to 5.01. 2
yourself | whether i in any just term am affin'd OTH 1.01. 39
whether a maid so tender, fair, and happy, | so 1.02. 66
now, whether he kill cassio, | or cassio him, or 5.01. 12
in't, | not minding whether i dislike or no! PER 2.05. 20
my /eaning time, but whether there | delivered, 3.04. 6
whether my brows may not be girt with garlands, TNK 2.03. 80
and whether, | before us that are here, can 3.06.293
stood staggering whether he should follow | his 4.01. 10
but even now had ask'd me | whether i lov'd, i 4.02. 48
and whe'er he run or fly they know not whether; VEN 304
whether it is that she reflects so bright | that LUC 376
and whether that my angel be turn'd fiend, PP 2. 9
but whether unripe years did want conceit, | or 4. 9
was this a lover, or a lecher whether? 7.17
in scorn or friendship, nill i conster whether. 14. 8
for whether beauty, birth, or wealth, or wit, SON 37. 5
whether we are mended, or whe'er better they, 59.11
they, | or whether revolution be the same. 59.12
or whether doth my mind, being crown'd with you, 114. 1
or whether shall i say mine eye saith true, 114. 3
and whether that my angel be turn'd fiend 144. 9
whether the horse by him became his deed, | or LC 111

WHET'ST 1 FR 0.0001 REL FR 1 V 0 P
fool, thou whet'st a knife to kill thyself. R3 1.03.243

WHETSTONE 4 FR 0.0004 REL FR 1 V 3 P
/and hath sent this natural for our whetstone; AYL 1.02. 54 P
of the fool is the whetstone of the wits. 1.02. 55 P
now she sharpens. well said, whetstone! TRO 5.02. 75 P
be this the whetstone of your sword, let grief MAC 4.03.228

WHETTED 2 FR 0.0002 REL FR 2 V 0 P
whom thou hast whetted on thy stony heart | to 2H4 4.05.107
till it was whetted on thy stone-hard heart | to R3 4.04.228

WHETTETH 1 FR 0.0001 REL FR 1 V 0 P
whose tushes never sheath'd he whetteth still, VEN 617

WHEW 1 FR 0.0001 REL FR 0 V 1 P
whew! 1H4 2.02. 28 P

WHEY 1 FR 0.0001 REL FR 1 V 0 P
and feed on curds and whey, and suck the goat, TIT 4.02.178

/WHEY-FACE 1 FR 0.0001 REL FR 0 V 1 P
he hath but a little /whey-face, with a little WIV 1.04. 22 P

WHEY-FACE 1 FR 0.0001 REL FR 1 V 0 P
what soldiers, whey-face? MAC 5.03. 17

/WHICH 25 FR 0.0028 REL FR 20 V 5 P
/which /tired /majesty /did /make /thee /offer: R2 4.01.178
/is /this /the /face /which /fac'd /so /many 4.01.285
/than /that /being /which /was /like /to /be? 2H4 1.01.179
/which /to /prove /fruit | /hope /gives /not /so 1.03. 39
/which /if /we /find /outweighs /ability, 1.03. 45
/in /this /great /work | (/which /is, /almost, 1.03. 49
/thick (/which /nature /made /his /blemish) 2.03. 24
/of /which /disease | /our /late /king /richard 4.01. 57
/th' /obstructions /which /begin /to /stop 4.01. 65
/we /see /which /way /the /stream /of /time 4.01. 70
/which /long /ere /this /we /offer'd /to /the 4.01. 75
/it //rouge-mount, /at /which /name /i /started, R3 4.02.105
/which in their summer beauty kiss'd each other. 4.03. 13
/which /entertain'd, /limbs /are /his TRO 1.03.354
/one, /in /which /there /are /many /confines, HAM 2.02.245 P
/which /dreams /indeed /are /ambition, /for /the 2.02.257 P
/which /they /will /make /an /obedient /father. LR 1.04.235 P
/which /the /impetuous /blasts /with /eyeless 3.01. 8
/which, /if /convenience /will /not /allow, 3.06. 99
/when /that /which /makes /me /bend /makes /the 3.06.109
/that /nature /which /contemns /it /origin 4.02. 32
/which /since /his /coming /forth /is /thought 4.03. 4 P
/of, /which /imports /to /the /kingdom /so /much 4.03. 4 P
/what /guests /were /in /her /eyes, /which, 4.03. 21
/ever /ear /received, /which /in /recounting, 5.03.216

WHICH 2535 FR 0.2865 REL FR 2137 V 398 P
which touch'd | the very virtue of compassion in TMP 1.02. 26
creature in the vessel | which thou heardst cry, 1.02. 32
which thou heardst cry, which thou saw'st sink. 1.02. 32
turn'd you to, | which is from my remembrance! 1.02. 65
was | the ivy which had hid my princely trunk, 1.02. 86
and the bettering of my mind | with that which, 1.02. 91
as my trust was, which had indeed no limit, | a 1.02. 96
which was, that he, in lieu o' th' premises, 1.02.123
to the present business | which now's upon 's; 1.02.137
without the which this story | were most 1.02.137
which rais'd in me | an undergoing stomach, to 1.02.156
necessaries, | which since have steaded much; 1.02.165
for the rest o' th' fleet | (which i dispers'd), 1.02.233
hast promis'd, | which is not yet perform'd me. 1.02.244
what thou hast been, | which thou forget'st. 1.02.263
within which rift | imprison'd, thou didst 1.02.277
within which space she died, | and left thee 1.02.279
damn'd, which sycorax | could not again undo. 1.02.290
sycorax my mother, | which thou tak'st from me. 1.02.332
that you have, | which first was mine own king; 1.02.342
which any print of goodness wilt not take, 1.02.352
had that in't which good natures | could not 1.02.359
this gallant which thou seest | was in the wrack 1.02.414
which i do last pronounce, is (o you wonder!) 1.02.427
my father's loss, the weakness which i feel, 1.02.488
this is unwonted | which now came from him. 1.02.499
which, of he or adrian, for a good wager, first 2.01. 28 P
it is — which is indeed almost beyond credit — 2.01. 59 P
at | which end o' th' beam should bow. 2.01.132
which to do, | trebles thee o'er. 2.01.220
indeed, | which throes thee much to yield. 2.01.231
'twixt which regions | there is some space. 2.01.256
if he were that which now he's like — that's 2.01.282
free thee from the tribute which thou payest, 2.01.293
(and that a strange one too) which did awake me. 2.01.318
then like hedgehogs which | lie tumbling in my 2.02. 10
here is that which will give language to you, 2.02. 83 P
upon a butt of sack which the sailors heav'd 2.02.121 P
which i made of the bark of a tree with mine own 2.02.122 P
the mistress which i serve quickens what's dead, 3.01. 6
rain grace | on that which breeds between 'em! 3.01. 76
which, when he has a house, he'll deck withal. 3.02. 97
which now we find | each putter-out of five for 3.03. 47
expos'd unto the sea (which hath requit it) 3.03. 71
for which foul deed | the pow'rs, delaying (not 3.03. 72
which here, in this most desolate isle, else 3.03. 80
of mine own life, | or that for which i live; 4.01. 4
brims, | which spungy april at thy hest betrims, 4.01. 65
which by mine art | i have from their confines 4.01.120
yea, all which it inherit, shall dissolve, | and 4.01.154
at which, like unback'd colts, they prick'd 4.01.176
and thorns, | which ent'red their frail shins. 4.01.181
your fairy, which you say is a harmless fairy, 4.01.196 P
at which my nose is in great indignation. 4.01.199 P
do that good mischief which may make this island 4.01.217
on the sixt hour, at which time, my lord, | you 5.01. 4
in the line-grove which weather-fends your cell; 5.01. 10
hast thou, which art but air, a touch, a feeling 5.01. 21
some heavenly music (which even now i do) | to 5.01. 52
amends, with which | i fear a madness held me. 5.01.115
require | my dukedom of thee, which perforce, i 5.01.133
very duke | which was thrust forth of milan, who 5.01.160
chalk'd forth the way | which brought us hither. 5.01.204
which, but three glasses since, we gave out 5.01.223
which shall be shortly, single i'll resolve you 5.01.248
resolve you | (which to you shall seem probable) 5.01.249
if these be true spies which i wear in my head, 5.01.259 P
which, part of it, i'll waste | with such 5.01.303
your life, which must | take the ear strangely. 5.01.313
i have's mine own, | which is most faint. ep 3
or else my project fails, | which was to please. ep 13
which pierces so, that it assaults | mercy ep 17
wrack, | which cannot perish having thee aboard, TGV 1.01.149
me, | in thy opinion which is worthiest love? 1.02. 6
and pray her to a fault for which i chid her. 1.02. 52
which they would have the profferer construe "ay 1.02. 56
which would be great impeachment to his age, 1.03. 15
which now shows all the beauty of the sun, | and 1.03. 86
which makes me the bolder to chide you for yours 2.01. 82 P
which i was much unwilling to proceed in, | but 2.01.106
which, like a waxen image 'gainst a fire, 2.04.201
and ev'n that pow'r which gave me first my oath 2.06. 4
lord, that which i would discover | the law of 3.01. 4
my duty pricks me on to utter that | which, else 3.01. 9
a pack of sorrows which would press you down, 3.01. 20
which to requite, command me while i live. 3.01. 23
that which thyself hast now disclos'd to me. 3.01. 32
for which the youthful lover now is gone, | and 3.01. 41
how and which way i may bestow myself | to be 3.01. 87
me for this more than for all the favors | which 3.01.162
and she hath offered to the doom | (which, 3.01.225
a sea of melting pearl, which some call tears; 3.01.226
and study help for that which thou lament'st. 3.01.244
which, being writ to me, shall be deliver'd 3.01.251
which is much in a bare christian. 3.01.273 P
which with an hour's heat | dissolves to water, 3.02. 7
which must be done by praising me as much | as 3.02. 54
of which if you should here disfurnish me, | you 4.01. 14
for that which now torments me to rehearse: 4.01. 26
which, with ourselves, all rest at thy dispose. 4.01. 74
gone to seek his dog, which to-morrow, by his 4.02. 78 P
which heaven and fortune still rewards with 4.03. 31
which since i know they virtuously are plac'd, 4.03. 38
which, if my augury deceive me not, | witness 4.04. 68
to plead for that which i would not obtain, | to 4.04.100
to carry that which i would have refus'd, | to 4.04.101
to praise his faith which i would have 4.04.102
which he will break | as easily as i do tear his 4.04.130
which served me as fit, by all men's judgments, 4.04.162
which i so lively acted with my tears | that my 4.04.169
which of you saw eglamour of late? 5.02. 32
than plural faith, which is too much by one. 5.04. 52
me to deliver a ring to madam silvia, which, out 5.04. 89 P
unrivall'd merit, | to which i thus subscribe: 5.04.145
which peradventure prings goot discretions with WIV 1.01. 44 P
page, which is daughter to master /george page, 1.01. 45 P
master /george page, which is pretty virginity. 1.01. 46 P
and ask of doctor caius' house which is the way; 1.02. 2 P
quickly, which is in the manner of his nurse — 1.02. 3 P
which of you know ford of this town? 1.03. 36 P
/in /my /head which be humors of revenge. 1.03. 89 P
mine oyster, | which i with sword will open. 2.02. 4
has been earls, nay (which is more) pensioners; 2.02. 77 P
for the which she thanks you a thousand times — 2.02. 82 P
the which hath something embold'ned me to this 2.02.167 P
which hath been on the wing of all occasions. 2.02.201 P
which now are too too strongly embattled against 2.02.250 P
for the which his wife seems to me well-favor'd. 2.02.273 P
for the which i will be thy adversary toward 2.03. 94 P
which way have you look'd for master caius, that 3.01. 3 P
which is as hateful to me as the reek of a 3.03. 78 P
i know not which pleases me better, that my 3.03.178 P
which they'll do fast enough of themselves, and 4.01. 66 P
which way should he go? 4.02. 46 P
we'll leave a proof, by that which we will do, 4.02.104
in which disguise, | while other jests are 4.06. 21
which means she to deceive, father or mother? 4.06. 46
which, at the very instant of falstaff's and our 5.03. 14 P
of money, which must be paid to master /brook. 5.05.114 P
which forced marriage would have brought upon 5.05.230
from which we would not have you warp. MM 1.01. 14
now, which of your hips has the most profound 1.02. 58 P
and, which is more, within these three days his 1.02. 68 P
me all the enrolled penalties | which have, like 1.02.167
which else would stand under grievous imposition 1.02.188 P
which for this fourteen years we have let slip, 1.03. 21
who's that which calls? 1.04. 6
for that which, if myself might be his judge, 1.04. 27
which have for long run by the hideous law, | as 1.04. 63
err'd in this point which now you censure him, 2.01. 15
which, i think, is a very ill house too. 2.01. 66 P
house, which at that very distant time stood, as 2.01. 91 P
which is the wiser here: 2.01.172 P
for which i would not plead, but that i must; 2.02. 31
for which i must not plead, but that i am | at 2.02. 32
you be | if he, which is the top of judgment, 2.02. 76
which a dismiss'd offense would after gall, 2.02.102
word, | which in the soldier is flat blasphemy. 2.02.131
which sorrow is always toward ourselves, not 2.03. 32
an idle plume, | which the air beats for vain. 2.04. 12
and so stop the air | by which he should revive; 2.04. 26
which had you rather, that the most just law 2.04. 52
which are as easy broke as they make forms. 2.04.126
in't, | which seems a little fouler than it is, 2.04.146
grossly fear'st | thy death, which is no more. 3.01. 19
for thine own bowels, which do call thee /sire, 3.01. 29
which is the least? 3.01.111
that gracious denial which he is most glad to 3.01.165 P
between which time of the contract and limit of 3.01.215 P
lamentation, which she yet wears for his sake; 3.01.228 P
picklock, which we have sent to the deputy. 3.02. 17 P
which is the way? 3.02. 50 P
merry at any thing which profess'd to make him 3.02.236 P
many deceiving promises of life, which i (by my 3.02.246 P
which from the vineyard to the garden leads; 4.01. 33
that in himself which he spurs on his pow'r | to 4.02. 82
were he meal'd with that | which he corrects, 4.02. 84
such sin | for which the pardoner himself is in. 4.02.109
for the which you are to do me both a present 4.02.161 P
pounds, of which he made five marks ready money. 4.03. 6 P
satin, which now peaches him a beggar. 4.03. 11 P
say, which you shall find | by every syllable a 4.03.125
which shall then have no power to stand against 4.04. 13 P
for that which i must speak | must either punish 5.01. 30
not impossible | that which but seems unlike; 5.01. 52
time | unfold the evil which is here wrapp'd up 5.01.117
which once thou swor'st was worth the looking on 5.01.208
this is the hand which, with a vow'd contract, 5.01.209
which was broke off, | partly for that her 5.01.218
since which time of five years | i never spake 5.01.222
villain's mouth | which here you come to accuse. 5.01.303
do you the office, friar, which consummate, 5.01.378
which i did think with slower foot came on, 5.01.395
fearing death, | than that which lives to fear. 5.01.398
which, though thou wouldst deny, denies thee 5.01.413
in that he did the thing for which he died; 5.01.449
for which i do discharge you of your office; 5.01.461
which is that barnardine? 5.01.478
the enmity and discord which of late | sprung ERR 1.01. 5
and, which was strange, the one so like the 1.01. 51
which though myself would gladly have embrac'd, 1.01. 69
rock, | which being violently borne /upon, | our 1.01.102
which princes, would they, may not disannul, 1.01.144
for which, i hope, thou felt'st i was displeas'd 2.02. 19
in debating which was best, we shall part with 3.01. 67
which doth amount to three odd ducats more 4.01. 30
but /'a's in a suit of buff which 'rested him, 4.02. 45
which he forswore most monstrously to have. 5.01. 11
deny | this chain which now you wear so openly. 5.01. 17
which of these sorrows is he subject to? 5.01. 54
the chain, | which, god he knows, i saw not; 5.01.229
for the which | he did arrest me with an officer 5.01.229
during which time he ne'er saw syracusa: 5.01.329
and so of these, which is the natural man, | and 5.01.334
is the natural man, | and which the spirit? 5.01.335
children, | which accidentally are met together. 5.01.362

stay, stand apart, i know not which is which. 5.01.365
stay, stand apart, i know not which is which. 5.01.365
which of you two did dine with me to–day? 5.01.370
that is the chain, sir, which you had of me. 5.01.378
the fine is (for the which i may go the finer), ADO 1.01.245 P
which way looks he? 1.03. 53 P
for the which blessing i am at him upon my knees 2.01. 28 P
which is one? 2.01.103 P
a comparison or two on me, which peradventure, 2.01.147 P
of hourly proof, | which i mistrusted not. 2.01.182
my dear son, which is hence a just sevennight, 2.01.359 P
undertake one of hercules' labors, which is, to 2.01.365 P
which shall bear no less likelihood than to see 2.02. 42 P
i would see, which will be merely a dumb show. 2.03.217 P
that | which simpleness and merit purchaseth. 3.01. 70
mocks, | which is as bad as die with tickling. 3.01. 80
which is the best to furnish me to–morrow. 3.01.103
for the which i hear what they say of him. 3.02. 57 P
which is now crept into a lute–string and now 3.02. 59 P
to you, which these hobby–horses must not hear. 3.02. 72 P
both which, master constable — 3.03. 17 P
partly by his oaths, which first possess'd them, 3.03.156 P
by the dark night, which did deceive them, but 3.03.157 P
which did confirm any slander that don john had 3.03.158 P
and salt too little which may season give | to 4.01.142
which was before barr'd up with ribs of iron! 4.01.151
which with experimental seal doth warrant | the 4.01.166
excuse | that which appears in proper nakedness? 4.01.175
than that which maiden modesty doth warrant, 4.01.179
which be the malefactors? 4.02. 3 P
but which are the offenders that are to be 4.02. 7 P
a wise fellow, and, which is more, an officer, 4.02. 80 P
an officer, and, which is more, a householder, 4.02. 81 P
and, which is more, as pretty a piece of flesh 4.02. 81 P
which falls into mine ears as profitless | as 5.01. 4
to that grief | which they themselves not feel, 5.01. 22
which before | would give preceptial med'cine to 5.01. 23
the which if i do not carve most curiously, say 5.01.155 P
night, which he forswore on tuesday morning. 5.01.168 P
for the which she wept heartily and said she 5.01.174 P
break jests as braggards do their blades, which, 5.01.187 P
which i had rather seal with my death than 5.01.240 P
which is the villain? 5.01.259
which of these is he? 5.01.261
sir, which indeed is not under white and black, 5.01.304 P
the which he hath us'd so long and never paid 5.01.310 P
which i beseech your worship to correct yourself 5.01.322 P
yours as blunt as the fencer's foils, which hit, 5.02. 14 P
i go, let me go with that i came, which is, with 5.02. 47 P
for which of my bad parts didst thou first fall 5.02. 60 P
which maintain'd so politic a state of evil that 5.02. 62 P
but for which of my good parts did you first 5.02. 64 P
i will never love that which my friend hates. 5.02. 70 P
her wrongs, | gives her fame which never dies. 5.03. 6
for the which, with songs of woe, | round about 5.03. 14
which i will do with confirm'd countenance. 5.04. 17
in which, good friar, i shall desire your help. 5.04. 31
which is the lady i must seize upon? 5.04. 53
soft and fair, friar. which is beatrice? 5.04. 72
which out of question thou wilt be, if my cousin 5.04.115 P
that honor which shall bate his scythe's keen LLL 1.01. 6
term, | which i hope well is not enrolled there; 1.01. 38
the which i hope is not enrolled there; 1.01. 41
which i hope well is not enrolled there. 1.01. 46
why, that to know which else we should not know. 1.01. 56
study knows that which yet it doth not know. 1.01. 68
but that most vain | which, with pain purchas'd, 1.01. 73
which is the duke's own person? 1.01.181 P
and taken following her into the park, which, 1.01.208 P
down to that nourishment which is called supper: 1.01.237 P
now for the ground which? 1.01.239 P
which, i mean, i walk'd upon: 1.01.239 P
the ebon–colored ink which here thou viewest, 1.01.243 P
"which, as i remember, hight costard" — 1.01.255 P
which with — o, with — but with this i passion 1.01.260 P
which i apprehended with the aforesaid swain, i 1.01.273 P
which each to other hath so strongly sworn. 1.01.307
to thy young days, which we may nominate tender. 1.02. 14 P
title to your old time, which we may name tough. 1.02. 17 P
which the base vulgar do call three. 1.02. 48 P
possess the same | which native she doth owe. 1.02.106
i do affect the very ground (which is base) 1.02.167 P
where her shoe (which is baser) guided by her 1.02.168 P
guided by her foot (which is basest) doth tread. 1.02.169 P
(which is a great argument of falsehood) if i 1.02.170 P
that be true love, which is falsely attempted? 1.02.171 P
which his fair tongue, conceit's expositor, 2.01. 72
in surety of the which | one part of aquitaine 2.01.134
but that one half which is unsatisfied, | we 2.01.138
which we much rather had depart withal, | and 2.01.146
of that which hath so faithfully been paid. 2.01.156
at which interview | all liberal reason i will 2.01.166
if my observation (which very seldom lies), | by 2.01.228
with that which we lovers entitle "affected." 2.01.232
speak that in words which his eye hath disclos'd 2.01.251
by adding a tongue which i know will not lie. 2.01.253
is that lead slow which is fir'd from a gun? 3.01. 62
nay, to be perjur'd, which is worst of all; 3.01.194
nothing but fair is that which you inherit. 4.01. 20
pray you, which is the head lady? 4.01. 42 P
which is the greatest lady, the highest? 4.01. 46 P
which to annothanize in the vulgar — o base and 4.01. 68 P
from which lord to which lady? 4.01.103
from which lord to which lady? 4.01.103
which we /of taste and feeling are — for those 4.02. 29
and if one should be pierc'd, which is the one? 4.02. 84 P
which is to me some praise that i thy parts 4.02.114
which, not to anger bent, is music and sweet 4.02.116
of the stranger queen's, which accidentally, or 4.02.139 P
thou, fair sun, which on my earth dost shine, 4.03. 67
is the liver–vein, which makes flesh a deity, 4.03. 72
faith infringed, which such zeal did swear? 4.03.144
which he would call "abbominable"; 5.01. 24 P
which is wit–old. 5.01. 62 P
which the rude multitude call the afternoon. 5.01. 89 P
which they'll know | by favors several which 5.02.124
know | by favors several which they did bestow. 5.02.125
rebuke me not for that which you provoke: 5.02.347
which of the vizards was it that you wore? 5.02.385
which once disclos'd, | the ladies did change 5.02.467
dies in the zeal of that which it presents. 5.02.518
that which long process could not arbitrate. 5.02.743
the holy suit which fain it would convince, 5.02.746
which parti–coated presence of loose love | put 5.02.766
which you on all estates will execute | that lie 5.02.845
please, | without the which i am not to be won, 5.02.849
which shallow laughing hearers give to fools. 5.02.860
turn'd her obedience (which is due to me) | to MND 1.01. 37
which shall be either to this gentleman, | or to 1.01. 43
than that which withering on the virgin thorn 1.01. 77
and (which is more than all these boasts can be) 1.01.103
you up | (which by no means we may extenuate) 1.01.120
which i could well | beteem them from the 1.01.130
by that which knitteth souls and prospers loves, 1.01.172
and by that fire which burn'd the carthage queen 1.01.173
of every man's name, which is thought fit, 1.02. 5 P
which, falling in the land, | hath every pelting 2.01. 90
by their increase, now knows not which is which. 2.01.114
by their increase, now knows not which is which. 2.01.114
which she with pretty and with swimming gait 2.01.130
which the ladies cannot abide. 3.01. 11 P
her eye, | which she must dote on in extremity. 3.02. 3
which now in some slight measure it will pay, 3.02. 86
which death, or absence, soon shall remedy. 3.02.244
i swear by that which i will lose for thee, | to 3.02.252
which sometime on the buds | was wont to swell 4.01. 53
which straight she gave me, and her fairy sent 4.01. 60
gaud | which in my childhood i did dote upon; 4.01.168
make choice of which your highness will see 5.01. 43
which is as brief as i have known a play; 5.01. 62
lord, it is too long, | which makes it tedious; 5.01. 64
which, when i saw rehears'd, i must confess, 5.01. 68
which never labor'd in their minds till now; 5.01. 73
that vile wall, which did these lovers sunder; 5.01.132
at the which let no man wonder. 5.01.134
this grisly beast, which lion hight by name, 5.01.139
which lion vile with bloody mouth did stain. 5.01.143
through which the lovers, pyramus and thisby, 5.01.159
through which the fearful lovers are to whisper. 5.01.164
o night, which ever art when day is not! 5.01.171
which is — no, no — which was the fairest dame 5.01.293
no — which was the fairest dame | that liv'd, 5.01.293
a mote will turn the balance, which pyramus, 5.01.318 P
which pyramus, which thisby, is the better: 5.01.319 P
will we, | which by us shall blessed be; 5.01.404
which, touching but my gentle vessel's side, MV 1.01. 32
would almost damn those ears | which, hearing 1.01. 99
that which i owe is lost, but if you please | to 1.01.147
that self way | which you did shoot the first, i 1.01.149
which makes her seat of belmont colchis' strond, 1.01.171
which is indeed to return to their home, and to 1.02.102 P
for the which, as i told you, antonio shall be 1.03. 4 P
to eat of the habitation which your prophet the 1.03. 34 P
my well–won thrift, | which he calls interest. 1.03. 51
that all the eanlings which were streak'd and 1.03. 79
and all for use of that which is mine own. 1.03.113
lichas play at dice | which is the better man, 2.01. 33
me, | miss that which one unworthier may attain, 2.01. 37
i pray you, which is the way to master jew's? 2.02. 33 P
i pray you, which is the way to master jew's? 2.02. 39 P
table, which doth offer to swear upon a book, i 2.02.159 P
this is the penthouse under which lorenzo 2.06. 1
the second, silver, which this promise carries, 2.07. 6
and for the jew's bond which he hath of me, 2.08. 41
unfold to any one | which casket 'twas i chose; 2.09. 11
which pries not to th' interior, but, like the 2.09. 28
too long a pause for that which you find there. 2.09. 53
which makes me fear th' enjoying of my love; 3.02. 29
which therein works a miracle in nature, 3.02. 90
which /make such wanton gambols with the wind 3.02. 93
the seeming truth which cunning times put on 3.02.100
which rather threaten'st than dost promise aught 3.02.105
which, to term in gross, | is an unlesson'd girl 3.02.158
which when you part from, lose, or give away, 3.02.172
which appears most strongly | in bearing thus 3.04. 3
which makes me think that this antonio, | being 3.04. 16
the which my love and some necessity | now lays 3.04. 34
to the common ferry | which trades to venice. 3.04. 54
which i denying, they fell sick and died. 3.04. 71
these bragging jacks, | which i will practice. 3.04. 78
my coach, which stays for us | at the park–gate; 3.04. 82
which is a pound of this poor merchant's flesh, 4.01. 23
seek to soften that — than which what's harder? 4.01. 79
which, like your asses, and your dogs and mules, 4.01. 91
the pound of flesh which i demand of him | is 4.01. 99
he is furnish'd with my opinion, which, better'd 4.01.157 P
which is the merchant here? 4.01.174
and which the jew? 4.01.174
which if thou follow, this strict court of 4.01.204
which here appeareth due upon the bond. 4.01.249
from which ling'ring penance | of such misery 4.01.271
a wife | which is as dear to me as life itself, 4.01.283
the party 'gainst the which he doth contrive 4.01.352
in which predicament i say thou stand'st; 4.01.357
state, | which humbleness may drive unto a fine. 4.01.372
which i did make him swear to keep for ever. 4.02. 14
not the smallest orb which thou behold'st | but 5.01. 60
which is the hot condition of their blood, | 5.01. 74
which speed, we hope, the better for our words. 5.01.115
not that, i hope, which you receiv'd of me. 5.01.185
which did refuse three thousand ducats of me, 5.01.211
and begg'd the ring, the which i did deny him, 5.01.212
and that which you did swear to keep for me, | i 5.01.225
now, by mine honor, which is yet mine own, 5.01.232
which, but for him that had your husband's ring, 5.01.250
for the which his animals on his dunghills are AYL 1.01. 15 P
spirit of my father, which i think is within me, 1.01. 23 P
i am helping you to mar that which god made, a 1.01. 33 P
which thou shalt find i will most kindly requite 1.01.138 P
kindle the boy thither, which now i'll go about. 1.01.173 P
which he will put on us, as pigeons feed their 1.02. 93 P
wrastling, which you have lost the sight of. 1.02.110 P
wrastler, which charles in a moment threw him, 1.02.126 P
which may be better supplied when i have made it 1.02.192 P
down, and that which here stands up | is but a 1.02.250
which of the two was daughter of the duke, 1.02.269
is my doom | which i have pass'd upon her; 1.03. 84
which teacheth thee that thou and i am one. 1.03. 97
which when it bites and blows upon my body 2.01. 8
which, like the toad, ugly and venomous, | wears 2.01. 13
to the which place a poor sequest'red stag, 2.01. 33
thy sum of more | to that which had too /much." 2.01. 49
which i did store to be my foster–nurse | when 2.03. 40
which is as dry as the remainder biscuit | after 2.07. 39
the which he vents | in mangled forms. 2.07. 41
in the which hope i blush, and hide my sword. 2.07.119
that every eye which in this forest looks 3.02. 7
i was an irish rat, which i can hardly remember. 3.02.177 P
which i take to be either a fool or a cipher. 3.02.290 P
in which cage of rushes i am sure you /are not 3.02.370 P
a lean cheek, which you have not; 3.02.373 P
a blue eye and sunken, which you have not; 3.02.374 P
an unquestionable spirit, which you have not; 3.02.375 P
a beard neglected, which you have not — but i 3.02.376 P
it, which i warrant she is apter to do than to 3.02.388 P
of the points in the which women still give the 3.02.390 P
at which time would i, being but a moonish youth 3.02.409 P
of love to a living humor of madness, which was, 3.02.419 P
which i have darted at thee, hurt thee not, 3.05. 25
thy company, which erst was irksome to me, | i 3.05. 95
the scholar's melancholy, which is emulation; 4.01. 11 P
nor the musician's, which is fantastical; 4.01. 11 P
nor the courtier's, which is proud; 4.01. 12 P
nor the soldier's, which is ambitious; 4.01. 13 P
nor the lawyer's, which is politic; 4.01. 14 P
nor the lady's, which is nice; 4.01. 14 P
nor the lover's, which is all these: 4.01. 15 P
in which /my often rumination wraps me in a most 4.01. 18 P
which such as you are fain to be beholding to 4.01. 59 P
which is he that kill'd the deer? 4.02. 1 P
which she did use as she was writing of it, | it 4.03. 10
a bush, under which bush's shade | a lioness, 4.03.113
in which hurtling | from miserable slumber i 4.03.131
flesh away, | which all this while had bled; 4.03.148
which he, sir? 5.01. 45 P
abandon — which is in the vulgar leave — the 5.01. 47 P
society — which in the boorish is company — of 5.01. 48 P
of this female — which in the common is woman; 5.01. 49 P
which together is, abandon the society of this 5.01. 50 P
to marriage, which they will climb incontinent, 5.02. 38 P
i do, which i tender dearly, though i say i am a 5.02. 70 P
which are the only prologues to a bad voice? 5.03. 12 P
beasts, which in all tongues are call'd fools. 5.04. 37 P
power, which were on foot | in his own conduct, 5.04.156
which in a napkin (being close convey'd) | shall SHR in.1. 127
which otherwise would grow into extremes. in.1. 138
which seem to move and wanton with her breath, in.2. 52
these, | which never were, nor no man ever saw. in.2. 96
which bars a thousand harms and lengthens life. in.2. 136
you, which is the readiest way | to the house of 1.02.219
face | which i could fancy more than any other. 2.01. 12
of that report which i so oft have heard. 2.01. 53
which i have bettered rather than decreas'd. 2.01.118
fruitful land, all which shall be her jointer. 2.01.370
to strive for that which resteth in my choice. 3.01. 17
bit and a head–stall of sheep's leather which, 3.02. 58 P
which hath two letters for her name fairly set 3.02. 61 P
which at more leisure i will so excuse | as you 3.02.108
her father's liking, which to bring to pass, 3.02.129
which once perform'd, let all the world say no, 3.02.141
which now shall die in oblivion and thou return 4.01. 82 P
knows not which way to stand, to look, to speak, 4.01.185
which hath as long lov'd me | as i have lov'd 4.02. 38
and that which spites me more than all these 4.03. 11
withal make known | which way thou travellest — 4.05. 51
a son of mine, which long i have not seen. 4.05. 57
which runs himself, and catches for his master. 5.02. 53
shall win the wager which we will propose. 5.02. 69
seeming to be most which we indeed least are. 5.02.175
in token of which duty, if he please, | my hand 5.02.178
she inherits, which makes fair gifts fairer; AWW 1.01. 41 P
mothers, which is most infallible disobedience. 1.01.137 P
which is the most inhibited sin in the canon. 1.01.145 P
make itself two, which is a goodly increase, and 1.01.148 P
brooch and the toothpick, which /wear not now. 1.01.158 P
which might be felt, that we, the poorer born, 1.01.182
must think, which never | returns us thanks. 1.01.185
in the which my instruction shall serve to 1.01.208 P
ourselves do lie, | which we ascribe to heaven. 1.01.217
what power is it which mounts my love so high, 1.01.220
youth | he had the wit which i can well observe 1.02. 32
which, followed well, would demonstrate them now 1.02. 47
come to do that for me which i am a–weary of. 1.03. 43 P
will repeat, | which men full true shall find: 1.03. 61
in ten, madam, which is a purifying a' th' song. 1.03. 82 P
which i held my duty speedily to acquaint you 1.03.118 P
which hung so tott'ring in the balance that i 1.03.124 P
which was the great'st | of his profession, that 1.03.243
which, as the dearest issue of his practice, 2.01.106
which should indeed give us a further use to be 2.03. 35 P
promis'd gift, | which but attends thy naming. 2.03. 51
which great love grant, and so i take my leave. 2.03. 85
disdain'st in her, the which | i can build up. 2.03.117
which challenges itself as honor's born, | and 2.03.134
my honor's at the stake, which to defeat, | i 2.03.149
obey our will, which travails in thy good; 2.03.158
which both thy duty owes and our power claims, 2.03.161
which late | was in my nobler thoughts most base 2.03.170
to which title age cannot bring thee. 2.03.198 P
which if — lord have mercy on thee for a hen! 2.03.212 P
which should sustain the bound and high curvet 2.03.282
to the king | that which i durst not speak. 2.03.289
title, which is within a very little of nothing. 2.04. 27 P
love, | which, as your due, time claims, he does 2.04. 42
which they distill now in the curbed time, | to 2.04. 45
which holds not color with the time, nor does 2.05. 59
ring upon my finger, which never shall come off, 3.02. 58 P
haply, | which his heart was not consenting to. 3.02. 78
and a gentleman | which i have sometime known. 3.02. 85
that too much, | which holds him much to have. 3.02. 91
that all the miseries which nature owes | were 3.02.119
her intents, | which thus she hath prevented. 3.04. 22
which of them both | is dearest to me, i have no 3.04. 38
danger known but the modesty which is so lost. 3.05. 27 P

which is the frenchman? 3.05. 77
which is he? 3.05. 84
too far in his virtue, which he hath not, he 3.06. 14 P
which you hear him so confidently undertake to 3.06. 20 P
this business, which he knows is not to be done, 3.06. 87 P
find him, which you shall see this very night. 3.06.105 P
tokens and letters which she did re-send, | and 3.06.115
for you have show'd me that which well approves 3.07. 13
which i will over-pay and pay again | when i 3.07. 16
then to-night | let us assay our plot, which, if 3.07. 44
to me, | i'll discover that which shall undo the 4.01. 73
nay, i'll speak that | which you will wonder at. 4.01. 86
which were th greatest obloquy i' th' world 4.02. 44
which were the greatest obloquy i' th' world 4.02. 48
for which live long to thank both heaven and me! 4.02. 67
which holy undertaking with most austere 4.03. 49 P
by her own letters, which makes her story true, 4.03. 56 P
which could not be her office to say is come, 4.03. 57 P
the sacrament on't, how and which way you will. 4.03.137 P
half of the which dare not shake the snow from 4.03.168 P
which gratitude | through flinty tartar's bosom 4.04. 6
to which place | we have convenient convoy. 4.04. 9
with what it loathes for that which is away — 4.04. 25
which i take to be too little for pomp to enter. 4.05. 51 P
which are their own right by the law of nature. 4.05. 61 P
which he thinks is a patent for his sauciness, 4.05. 66 P
to speak in the behalf of my daughter, which, in 4.05. 72 P
and most courteous feathers, which bow the head, 4.05.105 P
which lay nice manners by, i put you to | the 5.01. 15
for the which | i shall continue thankful. 5.01. 16
which i presume shall render you no blame, | but 5.01. 32
which warp'd the line of every other favor, 5.03. 49
which better than the first, o dear heaven, 5.03. 71
which contain'd the name | of her that threw it. 5.03. 94
to come into me, | which i would fain shut out. 5.03.115
which nothing but to close | her eyes myself 5.03.118
you give away myself, which is known mine; 5.03.172
that she which marries you must marry me, 5.03.174
and i had that which any inferior might | at 5.03.218
which on your just proceeding i'll keep off — 5.03.236
tricks he hath had in him, which gentlemen have. 5.03.240 P
and things which would derive me ill will to 5.03.264 P
which we will pay, | with strife to please you, ep 3
which she would keep fresh | and lasting in her TN 1.01. 30
the honorable lady of the house, which is she? 1.05.167 P
my name is sebastian, which i call'd rodorigo; 2.01. 17 P
her lucrece, with which she uses to seal. 2.05. 93 P
upon her, which will now be so unsuitable to her 2.05.201 P
shameful cunning | which you knew none of yours. 3.01.117
mayst move | that heart, which now abhors, to 3.01.164
which to a stranger, | unguided and unfriended, 3.03. 9
which for traffic's sake | most of our city did. 3.03. 34
for which, if i be lapsed in this place, | i 3.03. 36
which way is he, in the name of sanctity? 3.04. 84 P
at which time we will bring the device to the 3.04.139 P
may i give him that | which i have given to you? 3.04.215
that with me which with as much safety you might 3.04.249 P
which methought did promise | most venerable 3.04.362
in which thou art more puzzled than the 4.02. 43 P
with which such scathful grapple did he make 5.01. 56
which i had recommended to his use | not half an 5.01. 91
which is sebastian? 5.01.224
clad | which from the womb i did participate. 5.01.238
and jump | that i am viola — which to confirm, 5.01.253
with the which i doubt not but to do myself much 5.01.307 P
and in such forms which here were presuppos'd 5.01.350
this present hour, | which i have wond'red at. 5.01.358
bohemia the visitation which he justly owes him. WT 1.01. 6 P
affection, which cannot choose but branch now. 1.01. 24 P
which to hinder | were (in your love) a whip to 1.02. 24
which is for me less easy to commit | than you 1.02. 58
integrity, deceiv'd | in that which seems so. 1.02.241
which hoxes honesty behind, restraining | from 1.02.244
'twas a fear | which oft infects the wisest: 1.02.262
which to reiterate were sin | as deep as that. 1.02.283
would do that | which should undo more doing; 1.02.312
which draught to me were cordial. 1.02.318
of my sheets | (which to preserve is sleep, 1.02.328
is sleep, which being spotted | is goads, thorns 1.02.328
me a mirror | which shows me mine chang'd too; 1.02.382
a sickness | which puts some of us in distemper, 1.02.385
which no less adorns | our gentry than our 1.02.392
if you know aught which does behove my knowledge 1.02.395
the parts of man | which honor does acknowledge, 1.02.401
how near, | which way to be prevented, if to be; 1.02.405
which must be ev'n as swiftly followed as | i 1.02.409
that lies enclosed in this trunk which you 1.02.435
which are here | by this discovery lost. 1.02.440
which if you seek to prove, | i dare not stand 1.02.443
he is dishonor'd by a man which ever | profess'd 1.02.455
which often hath no less prevail'd than so | on 2.01. 54
form | (which on my faith deserves high speech) 2.01. 70
which i'll not call a creature of thy place, 2.01. 83
in those foundations which i build upon, | the 2.01.101
the want of which vain dew | perchance shall dry 2.01.109
that honorable grief lodg'd here which burns 2.01.111
violence, in the which three great ones suffer, 2.01.128
you — i mean, | in this which you accuse her. 2.01.133
which if you — or stupefied | or seeming so in 2.01.165
(which was as gross as ever touch'd conjecture, 2.01.176
(which never tender lady hath borne greater) 2.02. 22
which is enough, i'll warrant, | as this world 2.03. 72
that forced baseness | which he has put upon't! 2.03. 80
which is rotten | as ever oak or stone was sound 2.03. 90
which hast made it | so like to him that got it, 2.03.104
that makes the fire, | not she which burns in't. 2.03.116
which being so horrible, so bloody, must | lead 2.03.152
i'll pawn the little blood which i have left 2.03.166
proceed in justice, which shall have due course, 3.02. 6
be but that | which contradicts my accusation, 3.02. 23
which is more | than history can pattern, though 3.02. 35
royal bed, which owe | a moi'ty of the throne, a 3.02. 38
it | as i weigh grief, which i would spare; 3.02. 43
of | which comes to me in name of fault, i must 3.02. 60
which not to have done i think had been in me 3.02. 67
the level of your dreams, | which i'll lay down. 3.02. 82
which to deny concerns more than avails; 3.02. 86
(which is indeed | more criminal in thee than it 3.02. 88
the bug which you would fright me with, i seek. 3.02. 92
denied, which 'longs | to women of all fashion; 3.02.103
which i would free — if i shall be condemn'd 3.02.111
an heir, if that which is lost be not found." 3.02.135 P
which had been done, | but that the good mind of 3.02.161
quit his fortunes here | (which you knew great), 3.02.168
which i receive much better | than to be pitied 3.02.233
which thou may, if fortune please, both breed thee, 3.03. 48
which i fear the wolf will sooner find than the 3.03. 66 P
discern by that which is left of him what he is, 3.03.134 P
th' king's, which florizel | i now name to you; 4.01. 22
and what to her adheres, which follows after, 4.01. 28
so), which is another spur to my departure. 4.02. 9 P
made me businesses which none without thee can 4.02. 14 P
which if i have not enough consider'd (as too 4.02. 17 P
i have eyes under my service which look upon his 4.02. 36 P
receiv'd, which are mighty ones and millions. 4.03. 57 P
good sir, for which of his virtues it was, but 4.03. 88 P
which then will speak, that you must change this 4.04. 39
nuptial, which | we two have sworn shall come. 4.04. 50
and present yourself | that which you are, 4.04. 68
gillyvors, | which some call nature's bastards. 4.04. 83
there is an art which in their piedness shares 4.04. 87
over that art | which you say adds to nature, is 4.04. 91
this is an art | which does mend nature — 4.04. 96
and the true blood which peeps fairly through't, 4.04.148
swain is this | which dances with your daughter? 4.04.167
shall bring him that | which he not dreams of. 4.04.180
for maids, so without bawdry, which is strange; 4.04.194 P
more, which will shame you to give him again. 4.04.240 P
and they have a dance which the wenches say is a 4.04.327 P
up in my heart, which i have given already, 4.04.359
which 'tis not fit you know, i not acquaint | my 4.04.412
nor think, | nor dare to know that which i know. 4.04.452
(which i do guess | you do not purpose to him) 4.04.468
nearest to him, which is | your gracious self, 4.04.522
the which shall point you forth at every sitting 4.04.561
by which means i saw whose purse was best in 4.04.602 P
which so drew the rest of the herd to me that 4.04.608 P
and box, which none must know but the king, and 4.04.757 P
king, and which he shall know within this hour, 4.04.757 P
which though it be great pity, yet it is 4.04.775 P
which who knows how that may turn back to my 4.04.834 P
could you make | which you have not redeem'd; 5.01. 3
which was so much | that heirless it hath made 5.01. 9
which that it shall, | is all as monstrous to 5.01. 40
will bring me to consider that which may 5.01.122
which waits upon worn times, hath something 5.01.142
for which the heavens, taking angry note, | have 5.01.173
that which i shall report will bear no credit, 5.01.179
mistress, | which he counts but a trifle. 5.01.224
upon which errand | i now go toward him; 5.01.231
this news, which is call'd true, is so like an 5.02. 27 P
that which you hear you'll swear you see, there 5.02. 31 P
with it, which they know to be his character; 5.02. 34 P
of nobleness which nature shows above her 5.02. 37 P
then have you lost a sight which was to be seen, 5.02. 42 P
which stands by like a weather-bitten conduit of 5.02. 55 P
which lames report to follow it and undoes 5.02. 57 P
tale still, which will have matter to rehearse, 5.02. 61 P
has not only his innocence (which seems much) to 5.02. 65 P
all the instruments which aided to expose the 5.02. 71 P
of all, and that which angled for mine eyes 5.02. 83 P
statue, which is in the keeping of paulina — a 5.02. 95 P
grace, which never | my life may last to answer. 5.03. 7
not | that which my daughter came to look upon, 5.03. 13
which lets go by some sixteen years, and makes 5.03. 31
which has | my evils conjur'd to remembrance, 5.03. 39
on, | which sixteen winters cannot blow away, 5.03. 50
then you'll think | (which i protest against) i 5.03. 90
which sways usurpingly these several titles, JN 1.01. 13
which now the manage of two kingdoms must | with 1.01. 37
which none but heaven, and you, and i, shall 1.01. 43
the which if he can prove, 'a pops me out | at 1.01. 68
which fault lies on the hazards of all husbands 1.01.119
to dispossess that child which is not his? 1.01.131
which, though i will not practice to deceive, 1.01.214
which was so strongly urg'd past my defense. 1.01.258
that right in peace which here we urge in war, 2.01. 47
doth contain that large | which died in geffrey; 2.01.102
which owe the crown that thou o'ermasterest? 2.01.109
which heaven shall take in nature of a fee; 2.01.170
which trust accordingly, kind citizens, | and 2.01.231
then | to pay that duty which you truly owe | to 2.01.247
which here we came to spout against your town, 2.01.256
in that behalf which we have challeng'd it? 2.01.264
eye, | which, being but the shadow of your son, 2.01.499
that any thing he sees, which moves his liking, 2.01.512
gates, | let in that amity which you have made, 2.01.537
which we, god knows, have turn'd another way, 2.01.549
men, | which in the very meeting fall, and die. 3.01. 33
which harm within itself so heinous is | as it 3.01. 40
and leave those woes alone which i alone | am 3.01. 64
with a counterfeit | resembling majesty, which, 3.01.100
which only lives but by the death of faith, 3.01.212
keep in peace that hand which thou dost hold. 3.01.261
for that which thou hast sworn to do amiss | is 3.01.270
upon which better part our pray'rs come in, | if 3.01.293
name, | which till this time my tongue did ne'er 3.01.307
that which upholdeth him that thee upholds, 3.01.315
which is the side that i must go withal? 3.01.327
which else runs tickling up and down the veins, 3.03. 44
but that which ends all counsel, true redress: 3.04. 24
which cannot hear a lady's feeble voice, | which 3.04. 41
voice, | which scorns a modern invocation. 3.04. 42
lost | in this which he accounts so clearly won. 3.04.122
out of the path which shall directly lead | thy 3.04.129
and bind the boy which you shall find with me 4.01. 4
prate | he will awake my mercy, which lies dead; 4.01. 26
that mercy which fierce fire and iron extends, 4.01.119
for the which myself and them | bend their best 4.02. 50
why then your fears, which (as they say) attend 4.02. 56
which for our goods we do no further ask | than 4.02. 64
the suit which you demand is gone and dead. 4.02. 84
that blood which ow'd the breadth of all this 4.02. 99
which his nimble haste | had falsely thrust upon 4.02.197
deed, which both our tongues held vild to name. 4.02.241
which, howsoever rude exteriorly, | is yet the 4.02.257
which was embounded in this beauteous clay, 4.03.137
with that same weak wind which enkindled it. 5.02. 87
that hand which had the strength, even at your 5.02.137
and send him word by me which way you go. 5.03. 7
life, | which bleeds away even as a form of wax 5.04. 24
by the which | we will untread the steps of 5.04. 51
and your supply, which you have wish'd so long, 5.05. 12
brain | (which some suppose the soul's frail 5.07. 3
of that fell poison which assaileth him. 5.07. 9
the which he pricks and wounds | with many 5.07. 17
which, in their throng and press to that last 5.07. 19
which he hath left so shapeless and so rude. 5.07. 27
by, | which holds but till thy news be uttered, 5.07. 56
which then our leisure would not let us hear, R2 1.01. 5
which else would post until it had return'd 1.01. 56
which to maintain i would allow him odds | and 1.01. 62
which fear, not reverence, makes thee to except. 1.01. 72
which gently laid my knighthood on my shoulder, 1.01. 79
the which he hath detain'd for lewd employments, 1.01. 90
which blood, like sacrificing abel's, cries, 1.01.104
traitor, | which in myself i boldly will defend, 1.01.145
the which no balm can cure but his heart-blood 1.01.172
his heart-blood | which breath'd this poison. 1.01.173
which since we cannot do to make you friends, 1.01.197
which made the fault that we cannot correct, 1.02. 5
that which in mean men we entitle patience | is 1.02. 33
hath caus'd his death, the which if wrongfully, 1.02. 39
(which god defend a knight should violate!) 1.03. 18
farewell, my blood, which if to-day thou shed, 1.03. 57
with that dear blood which it hath fostered; 1.03.126
which in our country's cradle | draws the sweet 1.03.132
which so rous'd up with boist'rous untun'd drums 1.03.134
which i with some unwillingness pronounce: 1.03.149
which robs my tongue from breathing native 1.03.173
it so, | which finds it an enforced pilgrimage. 1.03.264
which then blew bitterly against our faces, 1.04. 7
now for the rebels which stand out in ireland, 1.04. 38
sea, | which serves it in the office of a wall, 2.01. 47
which art possess'd now to depose thyself. 2.01.108
which live like venom where no venom else | but 2.01.157
which his triumphant father's hand had won. 2.01.181
which honor and allegiance cannot think. 2.01.208
that which his noble ancestors achiev'd with 2.01.254
which shows like grief itself, but is not so; 2.02. 15
which rightly gaz'd upon | show nothing but 2.02. 18
which, look'd on as it is, is nought but shadows 2.02. 23
which for things true weeps things imaginary. 2.02. 27
life, | which false hope lingers in extremity. 2.02. 72
he was — why, so go all which way it will! 2.02. 87
i | know how or which way to order these affairs 2.02.109
which, i protest, hath very much beguil'd | the 2.03. 11
to have | the present benefit which i possess, 2.03. 14
that is not forgot | which ne'er i did remember. 2.03. 38
which elder days shall ripen and confirm | to 2.03. 43
which more enrich'd | shall be your love and 2.03. 61
which, till my infant fortune comes to years, 2.03. 66
castle, which they say is held | by bushy, bagot 2.03.164
which i have sworn to weed and pluck away. 2.03.167
which with usurping steps do trample thee. 3.02. 17
which makes the silver rivers drown their shores 3.02.107
which serves as paste and cover to our bones. 3.02.154
as if this flesh which walls about our life 3.02.167
which didst lead me forth | of that sweet way i 3.02.204
the which, how far off from the mind of 3.03. 45
knees, | which on thy royal party granted once, 3.03.115
which like unruly children make their sire 3.04. 30
the noisome weeds which without profit suck 3.04. 38
the weeds which his broad-spreading leaves did 3.04. 50
which waste of idle hours hath quite thrown down 3.04. 66
by that fair sun which shows me where thou 4.01. 35
from which awak'd, the truth of what we are 5.01. 19
which our profane hours here have thrown down. 5.01. 25
which art a lion and the king of beasts? 5.01. 34
which knowest the way | to plant unrightful 5.01. 62
which his aspiring rider seem'd to know, | with 5.02. 9
which with such gentle sorrow he shook off, 5.02. 31
which for some reasons i would not have seen. 5.02. 62
which for some reasons, sir, i mean to see. 5.02. 63
which he, young wanton and effeminate boy, 5.03. 10
which elder years | may happily bring forth. 5.03. 21
that mercy which true prayer ought to have. 5.03.110
clamorous groans, which strike upon my heart, 5.05. 56
which strike upon my heart, | which is the bell. 5.05. 57
which, like the meteors of a troubled heaven, 1H4 1.01. 10
which fourteen hundred years ago were nail'c 1.01. 26
which he in this adventure hath surpris'd | to 1.01. 93
which makes him prune himself, and bristle up 1.01. 98
to demand that truly which thou wouldest truly 1.02. 5 P
which they shall have no sooner achiev'd but 1.02.172 P
than that which hath no foil to set it off. 1.02.215
which hath been smooth as oil, soft as young 1.03. 7
which the proud soul ne'er pays but to the proud 1.03. 9
and that same greatness too which our own hands 1.03. 12
which harry percy here at holmedon took, | were, 1.03. 24
which ever and anon | he gave his nose and 1.03. 38
which many a good tall fellow had destroyed | so 1.03. 62
those mouthed wounds, which valiantly he took, 1.03. 97
your only mean | for powers in scotland, which, 1.03.262
divers reasons | which i shall send you written, 1.03.263
when time is ripe, which will be suddenly, 1.03.294
arms, | which now we hold at much uncertainty. 1.03.299
the which for sport sake are content to do the 2.01. 70 P
sweet ned — to sweeten which name of ned, i 2.04. 22 P
harry, which thou hast often heard of, and it is 2.04.411 P
both which i have had, but their date is out, 2.04.503 P
of unruly wind | within her womb, which, for 3.01. 30
which calls me pupil or hath read to me? 3.01. 45
which being sealed interchangeably | (a business 3.01. 80
the least of which haunting a nobleman | loseth 3.01.184
which thou pourest down from these swelling 3.01.199
which oft the ear of greatness needs must hear 3.02. 24
which do hold a wing | quite from the flight of 3.02. 30
which by thy younger brother is supplied, | and 3.02. 33
would say, "where, which is bullingbrook?" 3.02. 49
save mine, which hath desir'd to see thee more, 3.02. 89
which now doth that i would not have it do, 3.02. 90
foes, | which art my nearest and dearest enemy? 3.02.123
which, wash'd away, shall scour my shame with it 3.02.137

the which if he be pleas'd i shall perform, | i 3.02.154
by which account, | our business valued, some 3.02.176
to–morrow in the battle | which of us fears. 4.03. 14
forgot, | which he confesseth to be manifold, 4.03. 47
title, the which we find | too indirect for long 4.03.104
which gape and rub the elbow at the news | of 5.01. 77
of his oath–breaking, which he mended thus, | by 5.02. 37
which cannot choose but bring him quickly on. 5.02. 44
and, which became him like a prince indeed, | he 5.02. 60
give me life, which if i can save, so; 5.03. 60 P
which would have been as speedy in your end | as 5.04. 55
in the which better part i have sav'd my life. 5.04.120 P
courtesy, | which i shall give away immediately. 5.05. 33
for which of you will stop | the vent of hearing 2H4 in 1
ride, | the which in every language i pronounce, in 7
dead, | not he which says the dead is not alive. 1.01. 99
that which i would to god i had not seen, | but 1.01.106
which once in him abated, all the rest | turn'd 1.01.117
a guard too wanton for the head | which princes, 1.01.149
complices | /lean on /your health, the which, if 1.01.164
i lay aside that which grows to me? 1.02. 88 P
by yea and no, which is as much as to say, as 2.02.131 P
which was an excellent good word before it was 2.04.149 P
asia, | which cannot go but thirty mile a day, 2.04.165
able body, for the which the prince admits him. 2.04.252 P
in which doing, i have done the part of a 2.04.321 P
the law, for the which i think thou wilt howl. 2.04.345 P
his grace says that which his flesh rebels 2.04.350 P
which to his former strength may be restored 3.01. 42
but which of you was by — | you, cousin nevil, 3.01. 65
thou ladder by the which | my cousin 3.01. 70
the which observ'd, a man may prophesy, | with a 3.01. 82
which should not find a ground to root upon 3.01. 91
i beseech you, which is justice shallow? 3.02. 56 P
be accommodated — which is an excellent thing. 3.02. 80 P
sir, which i caught with ringing in the king's 3.02.181 P
's prince, and let it go which way it will, he 3.02.237 P
come, sir, which men shall i have? 3.02.241 P
four of which you please. 3.02.242 P
come, sir john, which four will you have? 3.02.246 P
with his quality, | the which he could not levy; 4.01. 12
/and either end in peace, which god so frame! 4.01.178
call the swords | which must decide it. 4.01.180
the which hath been with scorn shov'd from the 4.02. 37
for the which | i do arrest thee, traitor, of 4.02.106
grievances | whereof you did complain, which, by 4.02.114
to the which course if i be enforc'd, if you do 4.03. 49 P
the element (which show like pins' heads to her) 4.03. 53 P
which, cousin, you shall bear to comfort him, 4.03. 79
and cowards, which some of us should be too, but 4.03. 95 P
and dull and crudy vapors which environ it, 4.03. 98 P
and delectable shapes, which, deliver'd o'er to 4.03.100 P
voice, the tongue, which is the birth, becomes 4.03.101 P
is the warming of the blood, which before (cold 4.03.103 P
pale, which is the badge of pusillanimity and 4.03.105 P
which as a beacon gives warning to all the rest 4.03.108 P
both which we doubt not but your majesty | shall 4.04. 11
be look'd upon and learnt, which once attain'd, 4.04. 71
by which his grace must mete the lives of other, 4.04. 77
which ever in the haunch of winter sings | the 4.04. 92
there lies a downy feather which stirs not. 4.05. 32
which nature, love, and filial tenderness 4.05. 39
which, as immediate from thy place and blood, 4.05. 42
lo where it sits, | which god shall guard; 4.05. 44
that tyranny, which never quaff'd but blood, 4.05. 85
thou hast stol'n that which after some few hours 4.05.101
give that which gave thee life unto the worms, 4.05.116
which my most inward true and duteous spirit 4.05.147
which daily grew to quarrel and to bloodshed, 4.05.194
/my friends, which thou must make thy friends, 4.05.204
which to avoid, | i cut them off, and had a 4.05.208
be, | which i with more than with a common pain 4.05.223
which vainly i suppos'd the holy land. 4.05.238
out of six fashions, which is four terms, or two 5.01. 80 P
which cannot look more hideously upon me | than 5.02. 12
which swims against your stream of quality. 5.02. 34
for which i do commit into your hand | th' 5.02.113
in which you, father, shall have foremost hand. 5.02.140
not the ill wind which blows no man to good. 5.03. 86 P
under which king, besonian? speak, or die. 5.03.113
which i beseech you to let me have home with me. 5.05. 74 P
which if like an ill venture it come unluckily ep 11 P
which was never seen in such an assembly. ep 24 P
for the which supply, | admit me chorus to this H5 pr 31
which in th' eleventh year of the last king's 1.01. 2
which men devout | by testament have given to 1.01. 9
which is a wonder how his grace should glean it, 1.01. 53
under the veil of wildness, which (no doubt) 1.01. 64
which i have open'd to his grace at large, | as 1.01. 78
which i could with a ready guess declare, 1.01. 96
but this, which they produce from pharamond: 1.02. 37
which salique land the french unjustly gloze 1.02. 40
which salique, as i said, 'twixt /elbe and sala, 1.02. 52
say, | king pepin, which deposed childeric, 1.02. 65
blithild, which was daughter to king clothair, 1.02. 67
by the which marriage the line of charles the 1.02. 84
to which is fixed, as an aim or butt, 1.02.186
which pillage they with merry march bring home 1.02.195
in answer of which claim, the prince our master 1.02.249
which he fills | with treacherous crowns; 2.pr. 21
and, which is worse, within thy nasty mouth! 2.01. 50
by interception which they dream not of. 2.02. 7
act | for which we have in head assembled them? 2.02. 18
to which we all appeal. 2.02. 78
to the which | this knight, no less for bounty 2.02. 91
which i beseech your highness to forgive, 2.02.153
which /i in sufferance heartily will rejoice, 2.02.159
which, of a weak and niggardly projection, 2.04. 46
hear the shrill whistle which doth order give 3.pr. 9
you are worth your breeding, which i doubt not; 3.01. 28
which makes much against my manhood, if i should 3.02. 48 P
to signify to you, which is the moral of it, 3.06. 33 P
is fixed upon a spherical stone, which rolls, 3.06. 36 P
war, which they trick up with new–tun'd oaths; 3.06. 76 P
which must proportion the losses we have borne, 3.06.126 P
which in weight to re–answer, his pettiness 3.06.128 P
did they imitate that which i compos'd to my 3.07. 43 P
which is the prescript praise and perfection of 3.07. 46 P
which is both healthful and good husbandry. 4.01. 7
is not that the morning which breaks yonder? 4.01. 86 P
impieties for the which they are now visited. 4.01.176 P
that he which hath no stomach to this fight, 4.03. 35
which likes me better than to wish us one. 4.03. 77
upon the which, i trust, | shall witness live in 4.03. 96
which if they have as i will leave 'um them, 4.03.124
in which array, brave soldier, doth he lie, 4.06. 7
those waters from me which i would have stopp'd, 4.06. 29
wearing leeks in their monmouth caps, which, 4.07.100 P
i can see my glove in his cap, which he swore, 4.07.129 P
the glove which i have given him for a favor 4.07.172
has strook the glove which your majesty is take 4.08. 26 P
of the which, | five hundred were but yesterday 4.08. 85
take that praise from god | which is his only. 4.08.116
which cannot in their huge and proper life | be 5.pr. 5
which like a mighty whiffler 'fore the king 5.pr. 12
pistol, which you and yourself, and all the 5.01. 6 P
another leek in my pocket, which you shall eat. 5.01. 62 P
which hitherto have borne in them | against the 5.02. 15
which to reduce into our former favor | you are 5.02. 63
to th' imperfections | which you have cited, you 5.02. 70
to the which, as yet, | there is no answer made. 5.02. 74
which you before so urg'd, lies in his answer. 5.02. 76
downright oaths, which i never use till urg'd, 5.02.145 P
which i am sure will hang upon my tongue like a 5.02.179 P
by which honor i dare not swear thou lovest me, 5.02.221 P
which word thou shalt no sooner bless mine ear 5.02.237 P
which before would not abide looking on. 5.02.310 P
which troubles oft the bed of blessed marriage, 5.02.364
on which day, | my lord of burgundy, we'll take 5.02.370
by which the world's best garden he achieved, ep 7
which oft our stage hath shown; ep 13
which by a vision sent to her from heaven 1H6 1.02. 52
with those clear rays which she infus'd on me 1.02. 85
that beauty am i blest with which you may see. 1.02. 86
the which at touraine, in saint katherine's 1.02.100
water, | which never ceaseth to enlarge itself, 1.02.134
which caesar and his fortune bare at once. 1.02.139
which i, disdaining, scorn'd, and craved death 1.04. 32
for which i will divide my crown with her, | and 1.06. 18
then how, or which way, should they first break 2.01. 71
no further of the case, | how or which way. 2.01. 73
upon the which, that every one may read, | shall 2.02. 14
which of this princely train | call ye the 2.02. 34
with which he yoketh your rebellious necks, 2.03. 64
between two hawks, which flies the higher pitch, 2.04. 11
between two dogs, which hath the deeper mouth, 2.04. 12
two blades, which bears the better temper, 2.04. 13
between two horses, which doth bear him best, 2.04. 14
two girls, which hath the merriest eye — | i 2.04. 15
among which terms he us'd his lavish tongue 2.05. 47
which obloquy set bars before my tongue, | else 2.05. 49
of which, my lord, your honor is the last. 2.05. 93
which giveth many wounds when one will kill. 2.05.110
which somerset hath offer'd to my house, | i 2.05.125
which in the right of richard plantagenet | we 3.01.149
which in the time of henry nam'd the fift | was 3.01.195
which is so plain that exeter doth wish | his 3.01.199
through which our policy must make a breach. 3.02. 2
which, once discern'd, shows that her meaning is 3.02. 24
no way to that, for weakness, which she ent'red. 3.02. 25
which thou thyself hast given her woeful breast. 3.03. 51
which i have done, because, unworthily, | thou 4.01. 16
in which assault we lost twelve hundred men; 4.01. 24
in confutation of which rude reproach, | and in 4.01. 98
which join'd with him and made their march for 4.03. 8
of mine | which thou didst force from talbot, my 4.06. 24
antic death, which laugh'st us here to scorn, 4.07. 18
for that which we have fled | during the life, 4.07. 49
which by my lord of winchester we mean | shall 5.01. 39
in argument and proof of which contract, | bear 5.01. 46
receive | the sum of money which i promised 5.01. 52
i'll rather keep | that which i have than, 5.04.145
and, which is more, she is not so divine, | so 5.05. 16
that maine which by main force warwick did win, 2H6 1.01.210
which i will win from france, or else be slain. 1.01.213
gazing on that which seems to dim thy sight? 1.02. 6
for my part, noble lords, i care not which, | or 1.03.101
which is infallible, to england's crown. 2.02. 5
which now they hold by force and not by right; 2.02. 30
fellow, | which he had thought to have murther'd 2.03.104
which fear, if better reasons can supplant, | i 3.01. 37
which time will bring to light in smooth duke 3.01. 65
which mates him first that first intends deceit. 3.01.265
for that john mortimer, which now is dead, | in 3.01.372
and reap the harvest which that rascal sow'd. 3.01.381
which with the heart there cools and ne'er 3.02.166
the lives of those which we have lost in fight 4.01. 21
gualtier or walter, which it is, i care not. 4.01. 38
under the which is writ, "invitis nubibus." 4.01. 99
which is as much to say as, let the magistrates 4.02. 17 P
that those which fly before the battle ends 4.02.178
the lord say, which sold the towns in france; 4.07. 21 P
which makes me hope you are not void of pity. 4.07. 64
which is not amiss to cool a man's stomach this 4.10. 8 P
unto a dunghill, which shall be thy grave, | and 4.10. 81
which i will bear in triumph to the king, 4.10. 83
on which i'll toss the flow'r–de–luce of france. 5.01. 11
which dar'st not, no, nor canst not rule a 5.01. 95
us | by what we can, which can no more but fly. 5.02. 77
well, lords, we have not got that which we have: 5.03. 20
which now the house of lancaster usurps, | i vow 3H6 1.01. 23
that we are those which chas'd you from the 1.01. 90
which makes thee thus presumptuous and proud, 1.01.157
i, | or felt that pain which i did for him once, 1.01.221
had i been there, which am a silly woman, | the 1.01.243
about that which concerns your grace and us: 1.02. 8
the crown of england, father, which is yours. 1.02. 9
which held thee dearly as his soul's redemption, 2.01.102
must edward fall, which peril heaven forefend! 2.01.191
him, | which argued thee a most unloving father. 2.02. 25
which sometime they have us'd with fearful 2.02. 30
face, which promiseth | successful fortune, 2.02. 40
if that be right which warwick says is right, 2.02.131
shade, | all which secure and sweetly he enjoys, 2.05. 50
which, whiles it lasted, gave king henry light. 2.06. 2
whose soul is that which takes her heavy leave? 2.06. 42
your father's head, which clifford placed there; 2.06. 53
which in the time of death he gave our father. 2.06. 67
lands, | which we in justice cannot well deny, 3.02. 5
that love which virtue begs and virtue grants. 3.02. 63
cry "content" to that which grieves my heart, 3.02.183
which did subdue the greatest part of spain; 3.03. 82
lost | all that which henry the fift had gotten? 3.03. 90
which with her dowry shall be counterpois'd. 3.03.137
from giving aid which late i promised. 3.03.148
which are so weak of courage and in judgment 4.01. 12
which he hath giv'n for fence impregnable, | and 4.01. 44
which being shallow, you shall give me leave 4.01. 62
which if they do, yet will i keep thee safe, 4.01. 81
which, being suffer'd, rivers cannot quench. 4.08. 8
spoke, | which sounded like a cannon in a vault, 5.02. 44
give more strength to that which hath too much, 5.04. 9
which industry and courage might have sav'd? 5.04. 11
which, by the heavens' assistance and your 5.04. 68
which, traitor, thou wouldst have me answer to. 5.05. 21
which now mistrust no parcel of my fear, | and 5.06. 38
and, if the rest be true which i have heard, 5.06. 55
which plainly signified | that i should snarl, 5.06. 76
this word "love," which greybeards call divine, 5.06. 81
which says that g | of edward's heirs the R3 1.01. 39
which done, god take king edward to his mercy, 1.01.151
the which will i, not all so much for love | as 1.01.157
by marrying her which i must reach unto. 1.01.159
which this blood mad'st, revenge his death! 1.02. 62
which this blood drink'st, revenge his death! 1.02. 63
which his hell–govern'd arm hath butchered! 1.02. 67
which renders good for bad, blessings for curses 1.02. 69
the which thou once didst bend against her 1.02. 95
these eyes, which never shed remorseful tear — 1.02.155
which if thou please to hide in this true breast 1.02.175
this hand, which for thy love did kill thy love, 1.02.189
which i think proceeds | from wayward sickness 1.03. 28
from that contented hap which i enjoy'd, | i 1.03. 83
in all which time you and your husband grey 1.03.126
ay, and forswore himself — which jesu pardon! 1.03.135
which god revenge! 1.03.136
days, | which here you urge to prove us enemies, 1.03.145
in sharing that which you have pill'd from me! 1.03.158
which of you trembles not that looks on me? 1.03.159
with that sour ferryman which poets write of, 1.04. 46
him, from the which no warrant can defend me. 1.04.111 P
which of you, if you were a prince's son, 1.04.257
which i will purchase with my duteous service; 2.01. 64
which with a bounteous hand was kindly lent; 2.02. 93
which would be so much the more dangerous, | by 2.02.126
which haply by much company might be urg'd; 2.02.137
which, in his nonage, council under him, | and, 2.03. 13
of a man | than of his outward show, which, god 3.01. 10
those uncles which you want were dangerous; 3.01. 12
which, since, succeeding ages have re–edified. 3.01. 71
which by his death hath lost much majesty. 3.01.100
and being but a toy, which is no grief to give. 3.01.114
which may make you and him to rue at th' other. 3.02. 14
that they which brought me in my master's hate, 3.02. 58
which, as thou know'st, unjustly must be spilt. 3.03. 23
which i presume he'll take in gentle part. 3.04. 20
which by my presence might have been concluded. 3.04. 25
which we more hunt for than the grace of god! 3.04. 97
which now the loving haste of these our friends, 3.05. 54
which since you come too late of our intent, 3.05. 69
which by the sign thereof was termed so. 3.05. 79
which stretch'd unto their servants, daughters, 3.05. 82
which well appeared in his lineaments, | being 3.05. 91
as if the golden fee for which i plead | were 3.05. 96
which in a set hand fairly is engross'd | that 3.06. 2
which when i saw, i reprehended them, | and 3.07. 27
which pleaseth god above | and all good men of 3.07.109
which here we waken to our country's good, | the 3.07.124
which to recure, we heartily solicit | your 3.07.130
which fondly you would here impose on me. 3.07.147
which, mellow'd by the stealing hours of time, 3.07.168
which god defend that i should wring from him! 3.07.173
which we have noted in you to your kindred | and 3.07.212
which issued from my other angel husband, | and 4.01. 68
and that dear saint which then i weeping 4.01. 69
which hitherto hath held /my eyes from rest; 4.01. 81
for which your honor and your faith is pawn'd, 4.02. 89
which you have promised i shall possess. 4.02. 91
which /once," quoth forrest, "almost chang'd my 4.03. 15
from which even here i slip my /weary head, 4.04.112
which in the day of battle tire thee more | than 4.04.189
which thou supposest i have done to thee. 4.04.253
a handkercher, which, say to her, did drain 4.04.276
which after–hours gives leisure to repent. 4.04.293
which she shall purchase with still–lasting war. 4.04.344
that at her hands which the king's king forbids. 4.04.346
which now, two tender bedfellows for dust, | thy 4.04.385
this is the day which, in king edward's time, 5.01. 13
that high all–seer, which i dallied with, | hath 5.01. 20
which in his dearest need will fly from him. 5.02. 21
which they upon the adverse faction want. 5.03. 13
much | (which well i am assur'd i have not done) 5.03. 36
i, as i may — that which i would i cannot — 5.03. 91
which so long sund'red friends should dwell upon 5.03.100
which had they, what four thron'd ones could H8 1.01. 11
some life, | which action's self was tongue to. 1.01. 42
for him, which buys | a place next to the king. 1.01. 65
which is budded out, | for france hath flaw'd 1.01. 94
appliance only | which your disease requires. 1.01.125
by violent swiftness that which we run at, | and 1.01.142
now this follows | (which, as i take it, is a 1.01.175
which i do well, for i am sure the emperor 1.01.185
is on me | which makes my whit'st part black. 1.01.209
'em, which hath flaw'd the heart | of all their 1.02. 21
yea, such which breaks | the sides of loyalty, 1.02. 27
which are not wholesome | to those which would 1.02. 45
wholesome | to those which would not know them, 1.02. 46
which compels from each | the sixt part of his 1.02. 57
which neither know | my faculties nor person, 1.02. 72
fear | to cope malicious censurers, which ever, 1.02. 78
until | it forg'd him some design, which, being 1.02.181
which if granted | (as he made semblance of his 1.02.197
we shall be late else, which i would not be, 1.03. 65
for which i pay 'em | a thousand thanks, and 1.04. 73

which they would have your grace | find out, and 1.04. 83
which the duke desir'd | to him brought viva 2.01. 17
at which appear'd against him his surveyor, 2.01. 19
which he fain | would have flung from him; 2.01. 24
which makes me | a little happier than my 2.01.119
not before the king, which stopp'd our mouths, 2.02. 8 P
in which we come | to know your royal pleasure. 2.02. 69
him a foreign man still, which so griev'd him, 2.02.128
the which | to leave a thousandfold more bitter 2.03. 7
heart, which ever yet | affected eminence, 2.03. 28
which, to say sooth, are blessings; 2.03. 30
and which gifts | (saving your mincing) the 2.03. 30
to which title | a thousand pound a year, annual 2.03. 63
or which of your friends | have i not strove to 2.04. 29
my lord and me — | which god's dew quench! 2.04. 80
the which before | his highness shall speak in, 2.04.102
or | laid any scruple in your way which might 2.04.151
the region of my breast, which forc'd such way, 2.04.185
i weigh'd the danger which my realms stood in 2.04.198
conscience — which | i then did feel full sick, 2.04.204
the daring'st counsel which i had to doubt, 2.04.216
to this course | which you are running here. 2.04.218
both of his truth and him (which was too far), 3.01. 65
which of the peers | have uncontemn'd gone by 3.02. 9
to this land, which shall | in it be memoriz'd. 3.02. 51
which | have satisfied the king for his divorce, 3.02. 64
of household, which | i find at such proud rate, 3.02.126
the which | you were now running o'er. 3.02.138
to think upon the part of business which | i 3.02.145
her times of preservation, which perforce | i, 3.02.147
which went | beyond all man's endeavors. 3.02.168
which ever has and ever shall be growing, | till 3.02.178
by which power | you maim'd the jurisdiction of 3.02.311
in which you brought the king | to be your 3.02.315
which, since they are of you, and odious, | i 3.02.331
lay — to which | she was often cited by them, 4.01. 28
since which she was remov'd to kimmalton, 4.01. 34
which when the people | had the full view of, 4.01. 70
which perform'd, the choir, | with all the 4.01. 90
ye shall go my way, which | is to th' court, and 4.01.114
which he himself | foretold should be his last, 4.02. 26
were unsatisfied in getting | (which was a sin), 4.02. 56
one of which fell with him, | unwilling to 4.02. 59
which i feel | i am not worthy yet to wear. 4.02. 91
in which i have commended to his goodness | the 4.02.131
of which there is not one, i dare avow | (and 4.02.142
with which the /time will load him. 5.01. 37
with which they moved | have broken with the 5.01. 46
for i must think of that which company | would 5.01. 75
this is about that which the bishop spake. 5.01. 84
which, being consider'd, | have mov'd us and our 5.01. 99
those charges | which will require your answer, 5.01.104
will triumph o'er my person, which i weigh not, 5.01.124
out of which frailty | and want of wisdom, you, 5.02. 47
which are heresies, | and, not reform'd, may 5.02. 53
which reformation must be sudden too, | my noble 5.02. 55
mean, | which ye shall never have while i live. 5.02.182
i have a suit which you must not deny me: 5.02.195
is verified | of thee, which says thus, "do my 5.02.210
sleep | on may–day morning, which will never be. 5.03. 15
her succor, which were the hope o' th' strond, 5.03. 52 P
blessings, | which time shall bring to ripeness. 5.04. 20
which we have not done neither: ep 7
she, "which of these hairs is paris my husband?" TRO 1.02.163 P
and call them shames which are indeed nought 1.03. 19
the fineness of which metal is not found | in 1.03. 22
th' applause and approbation | the which, most 1.03. 60
which were such | as agamemnon and the hand of 1.03. 62
strong as the axle–tree | on which heaven rides, 1.03. 67
which is the ladder of all high designs, | the 1.03.102
which, slanderer, he imitation calls, | he 1.03.150
which, from the tongue of roaring typhon dropp'd 1.03.160
which with one voice | call agamemnon head and 1.03.221
which is that god in office, guiding men? 1.03.231
which is the high and mighty agamemnon? 1.03.232
what merit's in that reason which denies | the 2.02. 24
beggar the estimation which you priz'd | richer 2.02. 91
which hath our several honors all engag'd | to 2.02.124
which short–arm'd ignorance itself knows is so 2.03. 14 P
which, like a /bourn, a pale, a shore, confines 2.03.249
yet that which seems the wound to kill, | doth 3.01.122
whereupon i will show you a chamber, which bed, 3.02.208 P
which you say live to come in my behalf. 3.03. 16
and 'tis a burthen | which i am proud to bear. 3.03. 37
which his own will shall have desire to drink. 3.03. 46
which shall shake him more | than if not look'd 3.03. 53
which when they fall, as being slippery standers 3.03. 84
cannot make boast to have that which he hath, 3.03. 98
which are devour'd | as fast as they are made, 3.03.148
which hath an operation more divine | than 3.03.203
a flint, which will not show without knocking. 3.03.257 P
in a sense as strong | as that which causeth it. 4.04. 5
more bright in zeal than the devotion which 4.04. 26
(which i beseech you call a virtuous sin) 4.04. 81
all, | to which the grecians are most prompt and 4.04. 88
is the lady | which for antenor we deliver you. 4.04.110
for which we lose our heads to gild his horns! 4.05. 31
which way would hector have it? 4.05. 71
and that which looks like pride is courtesy. 4.05. 82
in which part of his body | shall i destroy him 4.05.242
which with my scimitar i'll cool to–morrow. 5.01. 2
with that which here his passion doth express? 5.02.162
spout | which shipmen do the hurricano call, 5.02.172
in you, | which better fits a lion than a man. 5.03. 38
which you do here forbid me, royal priam. 5.03. 75
and to be partly proud, which he is, even to the COR 1.01. 39 P
intend to do, which now we'll show 'em in deeds. 1.01. 59 P
which ne'er came from the lungs, but even thus 1.01.108
general food at first | which you do live upon; 1.01.132
shall find | no public benefit which you receive 1.01.152
most that | which would increase his evil. 1.01.179
in awe, which else | would feed on one another? 1.01.187
vented their complainings, which being answer'd, 1.01.209
the shadow | which he treads on at noon. 1.01.261
fame, at the which he aims, | in whom already 1.01.263
must show themselves, which in the hatching, 1.02. 21
our aim, which was | to take in many towns ere 1.02. 23
which yet seem shut, we have but pinn'd with 1.04. 18
our thoughts, | which makes me sweat with wrath. 1.04. 27
which told me they had beat you to your trenches 1.06. 40
know you on which side | they have plac'd their 1.06. 51
not outward, which of you | but is four volsces? 1.06. 77
out my command, | which men are best inclin'd. 1.06. 85
and to silence that | which, to the spire and 1.09. 24
may these same instruments, which you profane, 1.09. 41
which, without note, here's many else have done 1.09. 49
in token of the which, | my noble steed, known 1.09. 60
in which time i will make a lip at the physician 2.01.115 P
which, being advanc'd, declines, and then men 2.01.161
which i doubt not but | our rome will cast upon 2.01.201
which | that he will give them make i as little 2.01.229
teach the people — which time shall not want, 2.01.255
the people is as bad as that which he dislikes, 2.02. 22 P
which the rather | we shall be blest to do, if 2.02. 57
city, which he painted | with shunless destiny; 2.02.111
measure fit the honors | which we devise him. 2.02.124
them th' unaching scars which i should hide, 2.02.148
of the which we being members, should bring 2.03. 11 P
which way do you judge my wit would fly? 2.03. 25 P
the virtues | which our divines lose by 'em. 2.03. 58
to show you, which shall be yours in private. 2.03. 77 P
than crave the hire which first we do deserve. 2.03.114
he had wounds, which he could show in private; 2.03.166
either his gracious promise, which you might, 2.03.193
which easily endures not article | tying him to 2.03.196
which most gibingly, ungravely, he did fashion 2.03.225
'tis, their own, | which we have goaded onward. 2.03.263
lord, and that it was which caus'd | our swifter 3.01. 2
too much of that | for which the people stir. 3.01. 53
which you are out of, with a gentler spirit, 3.01. 55
which we ourselves have plough'd for, sow'd, and 3.01. 71
but that | which they have given to beggars. 3.01. 74
measles | which we disdain should tetter us, yet 3.01. 79
which they have often made against the senate, 3.01.128
which will in time | break ope the locks a' th' 3.01.137
them not lick | the sweet which is their poison. 3.01.157
state | of that integrity which should become't; 3.01.159
it would, | for th' ill which doth control't. 3.01.161
and bury all, which yet distinctly ranges, | in 3.01.205
the public power, | which he so sets at nought. 3.01.269
the which shall turn you to no further harm 3.01.282
the blood he hath lost | (which, i dare vouch, 3.01.298
put mine armor on, | which i can scarcely bear. 3.02. 35
your wars to seem | the same you are not, which, 3.02. 47
nor by th' matter which your heart prompts you, 3.02. 54
which else would put you to your fortune and 3.02. 60
which often thus correcting thy stout heart, 3.02. 78
hast not the soft way which, thou dost confess, 3.02. 82
you have put me now to such a part which never 3.02.105
which quier'd with my drum, into a pipe | small 3.02.113
and that is there which looks | with us to break 3.03. 29
which show | like graves i' th' holy churchyard. 3.03. 50
for which you are a traitor to the people. 3.03. 66
your ignorance (which finds not till it feels, 3.03.129
which doth ever cool | i' th' absence of the 4.01. 43
as i can of those mysteries which heaven | will 4.02. 35
which is his house, beseech you? 4.04. 10
and displeasure | which thou shouldst bear me. 4.05. 73
which not to cut would show thee but a fool, 4.05. 97
which friends, sir, as it were, durst not (look 4.05.206 P
the people, which before | were in wild hurry. 4.06. 3
which were inshell'd when martius stood for rome 4.06. 45
a soldier's head | which will not prove a whip. 4.06.134
to have | this true which they so seem to fear. 4.06.151
left undone | that which shall break his neck, 4.07. 25
which out of daily fortune ever taints | the 4.07. 38
of those chances | which he was lord of; 4.07. 41
he hath said | which was sometime his general, 5.01. 2
which they did refuse | and cannot now accept, 5.03. 14
doves' eyes, | which can make gods forsworn? 5.03. 28
hath an aspect of intercession which | great 5.03. 32
which by th' interpretation of full time | may 5.03. 69
else to ask but that | which you deny already. 5.03. 89
which should | make our eyes flow with joy, 5.03. 98
which is a comfort | that all but we enjoy. 5.03.105
though we had | our wish, which side should win; 5.03.113
which thou shalt thereby reap is such a name 5.03.143
that thou restrain'st from me the duty which 5.03.167
a better witness back than words, which we, | on 5.03.204
consul, which he lost | by lack of stooping — 5.06. 27
to reap the fame | which he did end all his, and 5.06. 36
for which my sinews shall be stretch'd upon him 5.06. 44
of women's rheum, which are | as cheap as lies, 5.06. 45
let him feel your sword, | which we will second. 5.06. 56
which was your shame, by this unholy braggart, 5.06.118
danger | which this man's life did owe you, 5.06.137
a one, | which to this hour bewail the injury, 5.06.152
stood, | which i have sumptuously re–edified. TIT 1.01.351
which rome reputes to be a heinous sin, | yield 1.01.448
which, cunningly effected, will beget | a very 2.03. 6
which never hopes more heaven than rests in thee 2.03. 41
which dreads not yet their lives' destruction. 2.03. 50
which, like a taper in some monument, | doth 2.03.228
which overshades the mouth of that same pit 2.03.273
harmony | which that sweet tongue hath made, 2.04. 49
and for these bitter tears which now you see 3.01. 6
for which attempt the judges have pronounc'd 3.01. 50
but that which gives my soul the greatest spurn 3.01.101
say | that to her brother which i said to thee: 3.01.145
which of your hands hath not defended rome, 3.01.167
then which way shall i find revenge's cave? 3.01.270
which made me down to throw my books, and fly — 4.01. 25
which is it, girl, of these? 4.01. 32
o, that which i would hide from heaven's eye, 4.02. 59
that which thou canst not undo. 4.02. 74
rome | which signifies what hate they bear their 5.01. 3
say on, and if it please me which thou speak'st, 5.01. 59
which i have seen thee careful to observe, 5.01. 77
and keeps the oath which by that god he swears, 5.01. 80
to that which thou shalt hear of me anon. 5.01. 90
trim sport for them which had the doing of it. 5.01. 96
revenge, which makes the foul offender quake. 5.02. 40
which i wish may prove | more stern and bloody 5.02.202
the feast is ready which the careful titus 5.03. 21
which, but their children's end, nought could ROM pr 11
the which if you with patient ears attend, pr 13
them, which is disgrace to them if they bear it. 1.01. 43 P
which, as he breath'd defiance to my ears, | he 1.01.110
which then most sought where most might not be 1.01.127
not having that which, having, makes them short. 1.01.164
which thou wilt propagate to have it press'd 1.01.187
which /on more view of many, mine, being one, 1.02. 32
which oft the angry mab with blisters plagues, 1.04. 75
drums in his ear, at which he starts and wakes, 1.04. 86
which, once untangled, much misfortune bodes. 1.04. 91
which are the children of an idle brain, | begot 1.04. 97
which is as thin of substance as the air, | and 1.04. 99
which of you all | will now deny to dance? 1.05. 18
what lady's that which doth enrich the hand | of 1.05. 41
it is my will, the which if thou respect, | show 1.05. 72
much, | which mannerly devotion shows in this; 1.05. 98
that fair for which love groan'd for and would 2.pr. 3
that which we call a rose | by any other word 2.02. 43
retain that dear perfection which he owes 2.02. 46
and for thy name, which is no part of thee, 2.02. 48
for that which thou hast heard me speak to–night 2.02. 87
love, | which the dark night hath so discovered. 2.02.106
self, | which is the god of my idolatry, | and 2.02.114
which doth cease to be | ere one can say it 2.02.119
i stretch it out for that word "broad," which, 2.04. 86 P
sir, that you do protest, which, as i take it, 2.04.178 P
which to the high top–gallant of my joy | must 2.04.190
which ten times faster glides than the sun's 2.05. 5
by the which your love | must climb a bird's 2.05. 73
fire and powder, | which as they kiss consume. 2.06. 11
which name i tender | as dearly as mine own — 3.01. 71
which too untimely here did scorn the earth. 3.01.118
which way ran he that kill'd mercutio? 3.01.137
tybalt, that murtherer, which way ran he? 3.01.138
i beg for justice, which thou, prince, must give 3.01.180
to woe, | which you, mistaking, offer up to joy. 3.02.104
which modern lamentation might have moved? 3.02.120
thee at once, which thou at once wouldst lose. 3.03.121
which, like a usurer, abound'st in all, | and 3.03.123
true use indeed | which should bedeck thy shape, 3.03.125
killing that love which thou hast vow'd to 3.03.129
bed, | which heavy sorrow makes them apt unto. 3.03.157
loss, but not the friend | which you weep for. 3.05. 76
as that the villain lives which slaughter'd him. 3.05. 79
for still thy eyes, which i may call the sea, 3.05.132
which she hath prais'd him with above compare 3.05.238
which, too much minded by herself alone, | may 4.01. 13
that is no slander, sir, which is a truth, | and 4.01. 33
that | which the commission of thy years and art 4.01. 64
which craves as desperate an execution | as that 4.01. 69
as that is desperate which we would prevent. 4.01. 70
which, well thou knowest, is cross and full of 4.03. 5
what if it be a poison which the friar 4.03. 24
which late i noted | in tatt'red weeds, with 5.01. 38
with which with sweet water nightly i will dew, | or, 5.03. 14
with which grief | it is supposed the fair 5.03. 50
which their keepers call | a lightning before 5.03. 89
this, which stains | the stony entrance of this 5.03.140
lead, boy, which way? 5.03.168
what fear is this which startles in your ears? 5.03.194
potion, which so took effect | as i intended, 5.03.244
but he which bore my letter, friar john, | was 5.03.250
strange, | which manifold record not matches? TIM 1.01. 5
that happy verse | which aptly sings the good." 1.01. 17
/gum, which /oozes | from whence 'tis nourish'd. 1.01. 21
all those which were his fellows but of late — 1.01. 78
which labor'd after him to the mountain's top 1.01. 86
to those have shut him up, which failing, 1.01. 98
well deserves a help, | which he shall have. 1.01.103
more rais'd | than one which holds a trencher. 1.01.120
into my keeping, | which is not owed to you! 1.01.151
which i do beseech | your lordship to accept. 1.01.155
'tis rated | as those which sell would give; 1.01.169
common tongue | which all men speak with him. 1.01.175
plain–dealing, which will not cast a man a doit. 1.01.211 P
here's that which is too weak to be a sinner, 1.02. 58
honest water, which ne'er left man i' th' mire. 1.02. 59
lord, which bears that office to signify their 1.02.120 P
which was not half so beautiful and kind; 1.02.148
my former sum, | which makes it five and twenty. 2.01. 3
a naked gull, | which flashes now a phoenix. 2.01. 32
of these letters, i know not which is which. 2.02. 79 P
of these letters, i know not which is which. 2.02. 79 P
whoremaster and a knave, which notwithstanding, 2.02.105 P
which craves to be rememb'red | with those five 2.02.228
an empty box, sir, which, in my lord's behalf, i 3.01. 16 P
that part of nature | which my lord paid for, be 3.01. 62
my lord, and which i hear from common rumors, 3.02. 5 P
of timon's gift, | for which i wait for money. 3.04. 20
the place which i have feasted, does it now 3.04. 82
the law, which is past depth | to those that, 3.05. 12
(/an honor in him which buys out his fault), 3.05. 17
which indeed | is valor misbegot, and came into 3.05. 28
which many my near occasions did urge me to put 3.06. 10 P
supply his life, or that which can command it. 4.02. 47
seek to thrive | by that which has undone thee; 4.03.211
which the gods grant thee t' attain to! 4.03.327 P
that which i show, heaven knows, is merely love, 4.03.515
which argues a great sickness in his judgment 5.01. 29
that nothing but himself which looks like man 5.01.118
on special dignities, which vacant lie, | for 5.01.142
which now the public body, which doth seldom 5.01.145
body, which doth seldom | play the recanter, 5.01.145
i have a tree, which grows here in my close, 5.01.205
which imported | his fellowship i' th' cause 5.02. 11
hunger for that food | which nature loathes, 5.04. 33
which in the bluster of thy wrath must fall 5.04. 41
insculpture, which | with wax i brought away, 5.04. 67
and those our droplets which | from niggard 5.04. 76
may use with a safe conscience, which is indeed, JC 1.01. 14 P
which give some soil, perhaps, to my behaviors; 1.02. 42
good friends be griev'd | (among which number, 1.02. 44
seek into myself | for that which is not in me? 1.02. 65
that of yourself which you yet know not of. 1.02. 70
which gives men stomach to digest his words 1.02.301
which did flame and burn | like twenty torches 1.03. 16
and that which would appear offense in us, | his 1.03.158
the base degrees | by which he did ascend. 2.01. 27
egg, | which, hatch'd, would as his kind grow 2.01. 33

yourself | which every noble roman bears of you. 2.01. 93
which is a great way growing on the south, 2.01.107
which to prevent, | let antony and caesar fall 2.01.160
which so appearing to the common eyes, | we 2.01.179
which busy care draws in the brains of men; 2.01.232
impatience | which seem'd too much enkindled; 2.01.249
which sometime hath his hour with every man. 2.01.251
which, by the right and virtue of my place, | i 2.01.269
vow | which did incorporate and make us one, 2.01.273
of war, | which drizzled blood upon the capitol; 2.02. 21
which, like a fountain with an hundred spouts, 2.02. 77
pipes, | in which so many smiling romans bath'd, 2.02. 86
as that same ague which hath made you lean. 2.02.113
come hither, fellow; which way hast thou been? 2.04. 21
true quality | with that which melteth fools — 3.01. 42
may be mov'd | by that which he will utter? 3.01.235
(which like dumb mouths do ope their ruby lips 3.01.260
according to the which thou shalt discourse | to 3.01.295
offenses enforc'd, for which he suffer'd death. 3.02. 40 P
in the commonwealth, as which of you shall not? 3.02. 44 P
tending to caesar's glories, which mark antony 3.02. 58
a kingly crown, | which he did thrice refuse. 3.02. 97
which, pardon me, i do not mean to read — | and 3.02.131
statue | (which all the while ran blood) great 3.02.189
i tell you that which you yourselves do know, 3.02.224
which, out of use and stal'd by other men, 4.01. 38
(which should perceive nothing but love from us) 4.02. 44
by me as the idle wind, | which i respect not. 4.03. 69
for certain sums of gold, which you denied me; 4.03. 70
gold to pay my legions, | which you denied me. 4.03. 77
when that rash humor which my mother gave me 4.03.120
from which advantage shall we cut him off | if 4.03.210
there is a tide in the affairs of men | which, 4.03.219
which we will niggard with a little rest. 4.03.228
canopy most fatal, under which | our army lies, 5.01. 87
by which i did blame cato for the death | which 5.01.101
for the death | which he did give himself — i 5.01.102
steel, | which smok'd with bloody execution, MAC 1.02. 18
which nev'r shook hands, nor bade farewell to 1.02. 21
or that indeed | which outwardly ye show? 1.03. 54
and say which grain will grow, and which will 1.03. 59
say which grain will grow, and which will not, 1.03. 59
do contend | which should be thine or his. 1.03. 93
in which addition, hail, most worthy thane, 1.03.106
bears that life | which he deserves to lose. 1.03.111
which do but what they should, by doing every 1.04. 26
which honor must | not unaccompanied invest him 1.04. 39
the rest is labor, which is not us'd for you. 1.04. 44
that is a step | on which i must fall down, or 1.04. 49
yet let that be | which the eye fears, when it 1.04. 53
made themselves air, into which they vanish'd. 1.05. 5 P
all–hail'd me 'thane of cawdor,' by which title, 1.05. 7 P
that which cries, "thus thou must do," if thou 1.05. 23
and that which rather thou dost fear to do 1.05. 24
which fate and metaphysical aid doth seem | to 1.05. 29
which shall to all our nights and days to come 1.05. 69
is our trouble, | which still we thank as love. 1.06. 12
that we but teach | bloody instructions, which, 1.07. 9
vaulting ambition, which o'erleaps itself, | and 1.07. 27
which would be worn now in their newest gloss, 1.07. 34
which thou esteem'st the ornament of life, | and 1.07. 42
defect, | which else should free have wrought. 2.01. 19
is this a dagger which i see before me, | the 2.01. 33
in form as palpable | as this which now i draw. 2.01. 41
gouts of blood, | which was not so before. 2.01. 47
it is the bloody business which informs | thus 2.01. 48
hear not my steps, which /way /they walk, for 2.01. 57
horror from the time, | which now suits with it. 2.01. 60
that which hath made them drunk hath made me 2.02. 1
bellman, | which gives the stern'st good–night. 2.02. 4
which unwip'd we found | upon their pillows. 2.03.103
is an office | which the false man does easy. 2.03.137
warrant in that theft | which steals itself, 2.03.146
within the volume of which time i have seen 2.04. 2
which puts upon them | suspicion of the deed. 2.04. 26
me, to the which my duties | are with a most 3.01. 16
(which still hath been both grave and prosperous 3.01. 21
of nature | reigns that which would be fear'd. 3.01. 50
that it was he in the times past which held you 3.01. 76
which you thought had been | our innocent self? 3.01. 77
which is now | our point of second meeting. 3.01. 84
according to the gift which bounteous nature 3.01. 97
in his life, | which in his death were perfect. 3.01.107
'tis safer to be that which we destroy | than by 3.02. 6
using those thoughts which should indeed have 3.02. 10
to pieces that great bond | which keeps me pale! 3.02. 50
which of you have done this? 3.04. 48
look on that | which might appall the devil. 3.04. 59
this is the air–drawn dagger which you said 3.04. 61
which is nothing | to those that know me. 3.04. 85
in those eyes | which thou dost glare with! 3.04. 95
almost at odds with morning, which is which. 3.04.126
almost at odds with morning, which is which. 3.04.126
which must be acted ere they may be scann'd. 3.04.139
and, which is worse, all you have done | hath 3.05. 10
your thoughts, | which can interpret farther; 3.06. 2
all which we pine for now. 3.06. 37
i conjure you, by that which you profess | (how 4.01. 50
who bears a glass | which shows me many more; 4.01.120
fell cruelty, | which is too nigh your person. 4.02. 72
that which you are, my thoughts cannot transpose 4.03. 21
which often, since my here–remain in england, 4.03.148
which i have heavily borne, there ran a rumor 4.03.182
which was to my belief witness'd the rather, 4.03.184
which shall possess them with the heaviest sound 4.03.202
that, sir, which i will not report after her. 5.01. 14 P
i have known those which have walk'd in their 5.01. 60 P
leaf, | and that which should accompany old age, 5.03. 24
which the poor heart would fain deny, and dare 5.03. 28
all is confirm'd, my lord, which was reported. 5.03. 31
perilous stuff | which weighs upon the heart? 5.03. 45
must arbitrate, | towards which advance the war. 5.04. 21
lord, | i should report that which i say i saw, 5.05. 30
if this which he avouches does appear, | there 5.05. 46
which must not yield | to one of woman born. 5.08. 12
the which no sooner had his prowess confirm'd 5.09. 7
which would be planted newly with the time, | as 5.09. 31
form | in which the majesty of buried denmark HAM 1.01. 48
in which our valiant hamlet | (for so this side 1.01. 84
all /those his lands | which he stood seiz'd of, 1.01. 89
against the which, a moi'ty competent | was 1.01. 90
which had /return'd | to the inheritance of 1.01. 91
that hath a stomach in't, which is no other, 1.01.100
which, happily, foreknowing may avoid, | o speak 1.01.134
for which, they say, your spirits oft walk in 1.01.138
which have freely gone | with this affair along. 1.02. 15
but i have that within which passes show, 1.02. 85
than that which dearest father bears his son 1.02.111
with which she followed my poor father's body, 1.02.148
which is no further | than the main voice of 1.03. 27
tenders for true pay, | which are not sterling. 1.03.107
not of that dye which their investments show, 1.03.128
which might deprive your sovereignty of reason, 1.04. 73
this must be known, which, being kept close, 2.01.115
which to him appear'd | to be a preparation 2.02. 62
sends out arrests | on fortinbras, which he, in 2.02. 68
which done, she took the fruits of my advice; 2.02.145
all which, sir, though i most powerfully and 2.02.200 P
hits on, which reason and /sanity could not so 2.02.210 P
which your modesties have not craft enough to 2.02.280 P
/lest /my extent to the players, which, i tell 2.02.373 P
and no more, | the which he loved passing well." 2.02.408
which was declining on the milky head | of 2.02.478
lines, which i would set down and insert in't, 2.02.542 P
soul | o'er which his melancholy sits on brood, 3.01.165
which for to prevent, | i have in quick 3.01.167
the censure of which one must, in your allowance 3.02. 27 P
which i have told thee of my father's death. 3.02. 77
which now, the fruit unripe, sticks on the tree, 3.02.190
things | are mortis'd and adjoin'd, which, when 3.03. 20
this fear, | which now goes too free–footed. 3.03. 26
of those effects for which i did the murther: 3.03. 54
will reword, which madness | would gambol from. 3.04.143
wind, when both contend | which is the mightier. 4.01. 8
which we do tender, as we dearly grieve | for 4.03. 41
dearly grieve | for that which thou hast done — 4.03. 42
our sovereign process, which imports at full, 4.03. 63
a thought which quarter'd hath but one part 4.04. 42
which is not tomb enough and continent | to hide 4.04. 64
which, as her winks and nods and gestures yield 4.05. 11
which bewept to the ground did not go | with 4.05. 39
without the which we are pictures, or mere 4.05. 86
that he which hath your noble father slain 4.07. 4
which may to you, perhaps, seem much unsinow'd, 4.07. 10
my virtue or my plague, be it either which — 4.07. 13
under the which he shall not choose but fall; 4.07. 65
which time she chaunted snatches of old lauds, 4.07.177
of a politician, which this ass now o'erreaches, 5.01. 78 P
or of a courtier, which could say, "good morrow, 5.01. 82 P
are sheep and calves which seek out assurance in 5.01.116 P
o, that that earth which kept the world in awe 5.01.215
dangerous, | which let thy wisdom fear. 5.01.263
which was the model of that danish seal; 5.02. 50
horses, against the which he has impawn'd, as i 5.02.148 P
which carries them through and through the most 5.02.191 P
richer than that which four successive kings 5.02.273
which have solicited — the rest is silence. 5.02.358
which now to claim my vantage doth invite me. 5.02.390
it appears not which of the dukes he values most LR 1.01. 4 P
which of you shall we say doth love us most, 1.01. 51
joys | which the most precious square of sense 1.01. 74
let pride, which she calls plainness, marry her. 1.01.129
beloved sons, be yours, which to confirm, | this 1.01.138
which we durst never yet — and with strain'd 1.01.169
which nor our nature nor our place can bear, 1.01.171
which to believe of her | must be a faith that 1.01.221
even for want of that for which i am richer — 1.01.230
nature | which often leaves the history unspoke 1.01.236
give but that portion which yourself propos'd, 1.01.242
which at this instant so rageth in him, that 1.02.162 P
that full issue | for which i raz'd my likeness. 1.04. 4
that in your countenance which i would fain call 1.04. 28 P
that which ordinary men are fit for, i am 1.04. 34 P
which i have rather blam'd as mine own jealous 1.04. 69 P
which if you should, the fault | would not scape 1.04.209
which, in the tender of a wholesome weal, 1.04.211
which else were shame, that then necessity 1.04.213
these dispositions which of late transport you 1.04.221
your age, | which know themselves and you. 1.04.252
which, like an engine, wrench'd my frame of 1.04.268
these hot tears, which break from me perforce, 1.04.298
that i'll resume the shape which thou dost think 1.04.309
thing, of a queasy question, | which i must act. 2.01. 18
that he which finds him shall deserve our thanks 2.01. 61
since i came hither | (which i can call but now) 2.01. 87
comes too short | which can pursue th' offender. 2.01. 89
which i best /thought it fit | to answer from 2.01.123
our businesses, | which craves the instant use. 2.01.128
a–twain | which are t' intrinse t' unloose; 2.02. 75
which in this plainness | harbor more craft and 2.02.101
out of my dialect, which you discommend so much. 2.02.109 P
a plain knave, which for my part i will not be, 2.02.112 P
resolve me with all modest haste which way 2.04. 25
of intermission, | which presently they read; 2.04. 34
being the very fellow which of late | display'd 2.04. 40
worth | the shame which here it suffers. 2.04. 45
that sir which serves and seeks for gain, | and 2.04. 78
which shall be needful for your entertainment. 2.04.206
in my flesh, | which i must needs call mine. 2.04.223
wear'st, | which scarcely keeps thee warm. 2.04.270
which are to france the spies and speculations 3.01. 24
or the hard rein which both of them hath borne 3.01. 27
found the king — in which your pain | that way, 3.01. 53
which even but now, demanding after you, 3.02. 65
and must draw me | that which my father loses: 3.03. 24
this is the letter which he spoke of, which 3.05. 10 P
which approves him an intelligent party to the 3.05. 11 P
a court'sy to our wrath, which men | may blame, 3.07. 26
these hairs which thou dost ravish from my chin 3.07. 38
which came from one that's of a neutral heart, 3.07. 48
fellow saw, | which made me think a man a worm. 4.01. 33
naked soul, | which i'll entreat to lead me. 4.01. 45
not feel wrongs | which tie him to an answer. 4.02. 14
you are not worth the dust which the rude wind 4.02. 30
but not without that harmful stroke which since 4.02. 77
of nature is repose, | the which he lacks; 4.04. 13
altitude | which thou hast perpendicularly fell. 4.06. 54
what thing was that | which parted from you? 4.06. 68
handy–dandy, which is the justice, which is the 4.06.153 P
which is the justice, which is the thief? 4.06.154 P
her in that kind | for which thou whip'st her. 4.06.163
general curse | which twain have brought her to. 4.06.207
one hears that, | which can distinguish sound. 4.06.211
and give the letters which thou find'st about me 4.06.248
which of them shall i take? 5.01. 57
countenance for the battle, which being done, 5.01. 63
which he intends to lear and to cordelia, | the 5.01. 66
lances in our eyes | which do command them. 5.03. 51
person, | the which immediacy may well stand up, 5.03. 65
which is that adversary? 5.03.124
which, for they yet glance by and scarcely 5.03.149
allow the compliment | which very manners urges. 5.03.235
it is a chance which does redeem all sorrows 5.03.267
the cyprus wars | (which even now stands in act) OTH 1.01.151
in which regard, | though i do hate him as i do 1.01.153
and sign of love, | which is indeed but sign. 1.01.157
by which the property of youth and maidhood 1.01.172
my services which i have done the signiory 1.02. 18
which, when i know that boasting is an honor, 1.02. 20
to leave that latest which concerns him first, 1.03. 28
which ever as she could with haste dispatch, 1.03.148
which i observing, | took once a pliant hour, 1.03.150
do give thee that with all my heart | which, but 1.03.194
which, as a grise or step, may help these lovers 1.03.200
seeing the worst, which late on hopes depended. 1.03.203
but the free comfort which from thence he hears; 1.03.213
gardens, to the which our wills are gardeners; 1.03.321 P
in the womb of time which will be deliver'd. 1.03.370 P
but does foul pranks which fair and wise ones do 2.01.142
which now again you are most apt to play the sir 2.01.173 P
beauties — all which the moor is defective in. 2.01.230 P
which the time shall more favorably minister. 2.01.269 P
without the which there were no expectation of 2.01.279 P
which thing to do, | if this poor trash of 2.01.302
with that which he hath drunk to–night already, 2.03. 49
who's that which rings the bell? 2.03.161
that | which heaven hath forbid the ottomites? 2.03.171
spare speech, which something now offends me — 2.03.199
which till to–night | i ne'er might say before. 2.03.235
indignity | which patience could not pass. 2.03.246
name | robs me of that which not enriches him, 3.03.160
it is the green–ey'd monster which doth mock 3.03.166
such vild success | which my thoughts aim'd not. 3.03.223
that which so often you did bid me steal. 3.03.309
which at the first are scarce found to distaste, 3.03.327
that sweet sleep | which thou ow'dst yesterday. 3.03.333
which lead directly to the door of truth | will 3.03.407
that which i gave you. 3.04. 53
and it was dy'd in mummy which the skillful 3.04. 74
unproper beds | which they dare swear peculiar; 4.01. 69
and here speak with me, | the which he promis'd. 4.01. 81
the fountain from the which my current runs | or 4.02. 59
which i have greater reason to believe now than 4.02.212 P
(which i will fashion to fall out between twelve 4.02.236 P
that handkerchief which i so lov'd, and gave 5.02. 48
to do | a murther, which i thought a sacrifice. 5.02. 65
and pledge of love | which i first gave her. 5.02.215
which i have /here recover'd from the moor. 5.02.240
befall'n, | which, as i think, you know not. 5.02.308
a special purpose | which wrought to his desire. 5.02.323
which in the scuffles of great fights hath burst ANT 1.01. 7
and such a twain can do't, in which i bind, 1.01. 38
property | which still should go with antony. 1.01. 59
o, that i knew this husband, which, you say, 1.02. 4 P
former fortune | than that which is to approach. 1.02. 34
death, which commits some loving act upon her, 1.02.143 P
which not to have been blest withal would have 1.02.154 P
cleopatra's, which wholly depends on your abode. 1.02.175 P
which, like the courser's hair, hath yet but 1.02.193
in time we hate that which we often fear. 1.03. 12
vows, | which break themselves in swearing! 1.03. 31
and that which most with you should safe my 1.03. 55
which are, or cease, | as you shall give th' 1.03. 67
to his love, which stands | an honorable trial. 1.03. 74
the primal state | that he which is was wish'd, 1.04. 42
which they ear and wound | with keels of every 1.04. 49
the gilded puddle | which beasts would cough at; 1.04. 63
strange flesh, | which some did die to look on; 1.04. 68
till which encounter, | it is my business too. 1.04. 79
which seem'd to tell them his remembrance lay 1.05. 57
which the wise pow'rs | deny us for our good; 2.01. 6
that which combin'd us was most great, and let 2.02. 18
i learn you take things ill which are not so — 2.02. 29
partner in the cause 'gainst which he fought, 2.02. 59
those wars | which fronted mine own peace. 2.02. 61
yours, which with a snaffle | you may pace easy, 2.02. 63
which not wanted | shrowdness of policy too — i 2.02. 68
which was as much | as to have ask'd him pardon. 2.02. 78
which you shall never | have tongue to charge me 2.02. 82
the honor is sacred which he talks on now, 2.02. 85
i requir'd them, | the which you both denied. 2.02. 89
for which myself, the ignorant motive, do | so 2.02. 96
graces speak | that which none else can utter. 2.02.130
all little jealousies, which now seem great, 2.02.131
all great fears, which now import their dangers, 2.02.132
matter of feast, which worthily deserv'd noting. 2.02.182 P
which to the tune of flutes kept stroke, and 2.02.195
the water which they beat to follow faster, | as 2.02.196
/glow the delicate cheeks which they did cool, 2.02.204
whistling to th' air, which, but for vacancy, 2.02.216
which she entreated. 2.02.222
all which time | before the gods my knee shall 2.03. 2
thy daemon, that thy spirit which keeps thee, is 2.03. 20
dress, | which will become you both, farewell. 2.04. 5
on his hook, which he | with fervency drew up. 2.05. 17
the merchandise which thou hast brought from 2.05.104
which if thou hast considered, let us know | if 2.06. 5
with which i meant | to scourge th' ingratitude 2.06. 21
which do not be entreated to, but weigh | what 2.06. 32
for a liberal thanks, | which i do owe you. 2.06. 48
which is mark antony. 2.06.125 P
that which is the strength of their amity shall 2.06.128 P
should be, which pitifully disaster the cheeks. 2.07. 16 P
it lives by that which nourisheth it, and the 2.07. 44 P

show me which way. 2.07. 69
which he achiev'd by th' minute, lost his favor. 3.01. 20
choice of loss | than gain which darkens him. 3.01. 24
that | without the which a soldier and his sword 3.01. 28
let not the piece of virtue which is set 3.02. 28
your best love draw to that point which seeks 3.04. 21
prevented | the ostentation of our love, which, 3.06. 52
which soon he granted, | being an abstract 3.06. 60
which drives | o'er your content these strong 3.06. 82
which might have well becom'd the best of men, 3.07. 26
which serve not for his vantage, he shakes off, 3.07. 33
which doth most consist | of war-mark'd footmen, 3.07. 43
quite forgo | the way which promises assurance, 3.07. 46
from which place | we may the number of the 3.09. 2
upon a course | which has no need of you. 3.11. 10
take the hint | which my despair proclaims: 3.11. 19
let /that be left | which leaves itself. 3.11. 20
which had superfluous kings for messengers | not 3.12. 5
requires to live in egypt, which not granted, 3.12. 12
for thy pains, which we | will answer as a law. 3.12. 32
from which the world should note | something 3.13. 21
a halter'd neck which does the hangman thank 3.13.130
'tis one of those odd tricks which sorrow shoots 4.02. 14
of which i do accuse myself so sorely | that i 4.06. 18
next day's fate, | which promises royal peril. 4.08. 35
which, being dried with grief, will break to 4.09. 17
which as i take't we shall, for his best force 4.11. 2
that which is now a horse, even with a thought 4.14. 9
which whilst it was mine had annex'd unto't | a 4.14. 17
than she which by her death our caesar tells, 4.14. 61
exigent should come, which now | is come indeed, 4.14. 63
shall i do that which all the parthian darts, 4.14. 70
which thou hast worn | most useful for thy 4.14. 79
for when she saw | (which never shall be found) 4.14.122
bid that welcome | which comes to punish us, and 4.14.137
must be as great | as that which makes it. 4.15. 6
which in thy absence is | no better than a sty? 4.15. 61
hand | which writ his honor in the acts it did 5.01. 22
with the courage which the heart did lend it, 5.01. 23
which shackles accidents and bolts up change, 5.02. 6
which sleeps, and never palates more the dung, 5.02. 7
which your death | will never let come forth. 5.02. 45
stuck | a sun and moon, which kept their course, 5.02. 80
which is the queen of egypt? 5.02.112
been laden with like frailties which before 5.02.123
which towards you are most gentle, you shall 5.02.127
to that destruction which i'll guard them from 5.02.132
lips than to my peril | speak that which is not. 5.02.147
command | (which my love makes religion to obey) 5.02.199
which the gods give men | to excuse their after 5.02.286
a lover's pinch, | which hurts, and is desir'd. 5.02.296
spend that kiss | which is my heaven to have. 5.02.303
to see perform'd the dreaded act which thou | so 5.02.331
no less in pity than his glory which | brought 5.02.362
for which their father, | then old and fond of CYM 1.01. 36
could make him the receiver of, which he took, 1.01. 44
liv'd in court | (which rare it is to do) most 1.01. 47
no guess in knowledge | which way they went. 1.01. 61
been the fall of an ass, which is no great hurt. 1.02. 37 P
give him that parting kiss which i had set 1.03. 34
now he is with that which makes him both without 1.04. 9 P
which else an easy battery might lay flat, for 1.04. 22 P
which i will be ever to pay and yet pay still. 1.04. 37 P
'twas a contention in public, which may, without 1.04. 55 P
which the gods have given you? 1.04. 86 P
which, by their graces, i will keep. 1.04. 87 P
which in my opinion o'ervalues it something. 1.04.109 P
that honor of hers which you imagine so reserv'd 1.04.131 P
which are the movers of a languishing death, 1.05. 9
which first, perchance, she'll prove on cats and 1.05. 38
which hath the king | five times redeem'd from 1.05. 62
i have given him that | which, if he take, shall 1.05. 79
and which she after, | except she bend her humor 1.05. 80
their honest wills, | which seasons comfort. 1.06. 9
which can distinguish 'twixt | the fiery orbs 1.06. 34
in you, which i account his, beyond all talents. 1.06. 80
which | takes prisoner the wild motion of mine 1.06.102
self exhibition | which your own coffers yield; 1.06.123
for gold | which rottenness can lend nature; 1.06.125
make your lord, | that which he is, new o'er; 1.06.165
which hath | honor'd with confirmation your 1.06.173
of a sir so rare, | which you know cannot err. 1.06.176
which i (the factor for the rest) have done | in 1.06.188
which is material | to th' tender of our present 1.06.207
in her ears, which horsehairs and calves'-guts, 2.03. 29 P
you were inspir'd to do those duties which | you 2.03. 50
'tis gold | which buys admittance (oft it doth), 2.03. 68
which makes the true man kill'd and saves the 2.03. 71
that i, which know my heart, do here pronounce 2.03.107
which i had rather | you felt than make't my 2.03.110
against | obedience, which you owe your father. 2.03.112
a second night of such sweet shortness which 2.04. 44
which i doubt not | you'll give me leave to 2.04. 64
value, which i wonder'd | could be so rarely and 2.04. 74
which you might from relation likewise reap, 2.04. 86
is it that | which i left with her? 2.04.100
they are to their virtues, which is nothing. 2.04.112
and that most venerable man which i | did call 2.05. 3
yearly three thousand pounds, which, by thee, 3.01. 9
which then they had to take from 's, to resume 3.01. 15
of your isle, which stands | as neptune's park, 3.01. 18
which swell'd so much that it did almost stretch 3.01. 49
which to shake off | becomes a warlike people, 3.01. 51
our ancestor was that mulmutius which | ordain'd 3.01. 54
who was the first of britain which did put | his 3.01. 59
honor, | which he to seek of me again, perforce, 3.01. 71
which not to read would show the britains cold. 3.01. 75
upon the love and truth and vows which i | have 3.02. 12
that it is place which lessens and sets off, 3.03. 13
name of fame and honor which dies i' th' search, 3.03. 51
which attends | in place of greater state. 3.03. 77
which to read | would be even mortal to me. 3.04. 17
in the which | i have consider'd of a course. 3.04.110
and but disguise | that which, t' appear itself, 3.04.145
which will make him know | if that his head have 3.04.174
to you | which daily she was bound to proffer. 3.05. 49
grant, heavens, that which i fear | prove false! 3.05. 52
which will then be a torment to her contempt. 3.05.139 P
and when my lust hath din'd (which, as i say, to 3.05.142 P
which i will never be | to him that is most true 3.05.158
virtue | which their own conscience seal'd them, 3.06. 84
with those legions | which i have spoke of, 3.07. 13
head, which now is growing upon thy shoulders, 4.01. 16 P
those clothes, | which, as it seems, make thee. 4.02. 83
those lines of favor | which then he wore. 4.02.105
make some stronger head, the which he hearing 4.02.139
which he did wave against my throat, i have 4.02.150
words with that | which is so serious. 4.02.231
these herblets shall, which we upon you strew. 4.02.287
yes, sir, to milford-haven, which is the way? 4.02.291
at nothing, | which the brain makes of fumes. 4.02.301
which he said was precious | and cordial to me, 4.02.326
may seem to those | which chance to find us. 4.02.332
there vanish'd in the sunbeams, which portends 4.02.350
a madness, of which her life's in danger. 4.03. 3
and so extort from 's that | which we have done, 4.04. 13
which gave advantage to an ancient soldier | (an 5.03. 15
you that | like beasts which you shun beastly, 5.03. 27
which could have turn'd | a distaff to a lance, 5.03. 33
chickens, the way which they /stoop'd eagles; 5.03. 42
which neither here i'll keep nor bear again, 5.03. 82
a stately cedar shall be lopp'd branches, which, 5.04.141 P
action of my life is like it, which | i'll keep, 5.04.149
which are often the sadness of parting, as the 5.04.159 P
you, sir, you know not which way you shall go. 5.04.176 P
upon yourself that which i am sure you do not 5.04.181 P
heir of his reward, which i will add | to you, 5.05. 13
which, being cruel to the world, concluded 5.05. 32
she had | for you a mortal mineral, which, being 5.05. 50
in which time she purpos'd, | by watching, 5.05. 52
you their captives, which ourself have granted; 5.05. 73
which i'll make bold your highness | cannot deny 5.05. 89
and the grace of it | (which is our honor), 5.05.133
torture me to leave unspoken that | which, to be 5.05.140
to utter that | which torments me to conceal. 5.05.142
and — which more may grieve thee, | as it doth 5.05.144
or at least | those which i heav'd to head! 5.05.157
of wiving, | fairness which strikes the eye — 5.05.168
picture, which by his tongue being made, | and 5.05.175
pieces of gold 'gainst this which then he wore 5.05.183
i left out one thing which the queen confess'd, 5.05.244
confess'd, | which must approve thee honest. 5.05.245
that confection | which i gave him for cordial, 5.05.247
did compound for her | a certain stuff, which, 5.05.255
if i discover'd not which way she was gone, | it 5.05.277
pocket, which directed him | to seek her on the 5.05.280
master's garments | (which he enforc'd from me), 5.05.283
punishment before | for that which i did then. 5.05.344
which for more probation | i can with ease 5.05.362
branches, which | distinction should be rich in. 5.05.383
that life, beseech you, | which i so often owe; 5.05.415
a stately cedar shall be lopp'd branches, which, 5.05.438 P
which we call mollis aer, and mollis aer | we 5.05.447
which mulier i divine | is this most constant 5.05.448
from the which | we were dissuaded by our wicked 5.05.462
the vision | which i made known to lucius, ere 5.05.468
which foreshow'd our princely eagle, | th' 5.05.473
cymbeline, | which shines here in the west. 5.05.476
which to prevent he made a law, | to keep her PER 1.ch. 35
her countless glory, which desert must gain; 1.01. 31
and which, without desert, because thine eye 1.01. 32
which read and not expounded, 'tis decreed, | as 1.01. 57
i feed | on mother's flesh which did me breed. 1.01. 65
in which labor | i found that kindness in a 1.01. 66
if this be true which makes me pale to read it? 1.01. 75
if by which time our secret be undone, | this 1.01.117
the which is good in nothing but in sight! 1.01.123
your child | (which pleasures fits a husband, 1.01.129
by flight i'll shun the danger which i fear. 1.01.142
meaning, | for which we mean to have his head. 1.01.144
and danger, which i fear'd, is at antioch, 1.02. 7
stop the course by which it might be known. 1.02. 23
which care of them, not pity of myself — | who 1.02. 29
which fence the roots they grow by and defend 1.02. 31
the thing the which is flatter'd, but a spark 1.02. 40
to which that /blast gives heat and stronger 1.02. 41
which by my knowledge found, the sinful father 1.02. 77
which fear so grew in me, i hither fled, | under 1.02. 80
which love to all, of which thyself art one, 1.02. 94
which love to all, of which thyself art one, 1.02. 94
this tharsus, o'er which i have the government, 1.04. 21
yet those which see them fall | have scarce 1.04. 48
speak out thy sorrows which /thou bring'st in 1.04. 58
to beat us down, the which are down already, 1.04. 68
the which when any shall not gratify, | or pay 1.04.101
when — the which i hope shall ne'er be seen — 1.04.105
which welcome we'll accept; 1.04.107
which if you shall refuse, when i am dead, | for 2.01. 76
which my dead father did bequeath to me, | with 2.01.124
the which the gods protect thee /from! 2.01.129
are | a model which heaven makes like to itself. 2.02. 11
which, to preserve mine honor, i'll perform. 2.02. 16
which shows that beauty hath his power and will, 2.02. 34
which can as well inflame as it can kill. 2.02. 35
last, the which the knight himself | with such a 2.02. 40
which tells /me in that glory once he was; 2.03. 38
the which hath fire in darkness, none in light: 2.03. 44
which make a sound, but kill'd are wond'red at. 2.03. 63
waste the time, which looks for other revels. 2.03. 93
for which, the most high gods not minding longer 2.04. 3
if in which time expir'd he not return, | i 2.04. 47
known, | which from her by no means can i get. 2.05. 6
/coigns | which the world together joins, | is 3.ch. 18
makes her desire — | which who shall cross? 3.ch. 41
convey, | which might not what by me is told. 3.ch. 57
these surges, | which wash both heaven and hell; 3.01. 2
through which secret art, | by turning o'er 3.02. 32
which doth give me | a more content in course of 3.02. 38
heavenly jewels | which pericles hath lost, 3.02. 99
for which the people's prayers still fall upon 3.03. 19
you in your coffer, which are | at your command. 3.04. 2
which makes /her both th' /heart and place | of 4.ch. 10
which she made more sound | by hurting it; 4.ch. 24
gets | all praises, which are paid as debts, 4.ch. 34
of my rhyme, | which never could i so convey, 4.ch. 49
'tis but a blow, which never shall be known. 4.01. 2
which is but cold in flaming, thy /lone bosom 4.01. 5
nor let pity, which | even women have cast off, 4.01. 6
which did steal | the eyes of young and old. 4.01. 40
to do that fearfully which you commit willingly, 4.02.117 P
to that with shame which is her way to go with 4.02.127 P
which, to betray, dost, with thine angel's face, 4.03. 47
a tempest, which his mortal vessel tears, | and 4.04. 30
here comes that which grows to the stalk, never 4.06. 41 P
which is not worth a breakfast in the cheapest 4.06.122 P
hold'st a place for which the pained'st fiend 4.06.163
with other virtues, which i'll keep from boast, 4.06.184
/deafen'd parts, | which now are midway stopp'd. 5.01. 48
a courtesy | which if we should deny, the most 5.01. 59
and how achiev'd you these endowments which 5.01.116
which was when i perceiv'd thee — that thou 5.01.127
save this, which is the lion's and the bear's, TNK 1.01. 53
which gives me such lamenting | as wakes my 1.01. 57
my petition was | set down in ice, which, by hot 1.01.107
the which to do | must make some work with creon 1.01.149
joy, | which breeds a deeper longing, cure their 1.01.190
about that neck | which is my fee, and which i 1.01.198
fee, and which i freely lend | to do these poor 1.01.198
celerity and nature, which | she makes it in, 1.01.202
myself to do | that which you kneel to have me. 1.01.207
feast, of which i pray you | make no abatement. 1.01.224
ingots, | which, though he won, he had not; 1.02. 18
which is not catching | where there is faith? 1.02. 45
that which rips my bosom | almost to th' heart's 1.02. 61
he | a quarter carrier of that honor which | his 1.02.108
be as for our health, which were not spent, 1.02.110
which shall be then | beyond further requiring. 1.03. 25
each side like justice, which he loves best. 1.03. 47
th' moon | (which then look'd pale at parting) 1.03. 53
this rehearsal | (which, /ev'ry innocent wots 1.03. 79
but those we will depute which shall invest 1.04. 10
'hath set a mark which nature could not reach to 1.04. 43
us, | and which is heaviest, palamon, unmarried. 2.02. 29
we shall die | (which is the curse of honor) 2.02. 54
your passion | that thus mistakes, the which, to 3.01. 49
place, which well | might justify your manhood; 3.01. 63
glass, as to | his ear which now disdains you. 3.01. 71
which will seek of me | some news from earth, 3.01. 79
so which way now? 3.02. 32
in, which being glu'd together | makes morris, 3.05.119
i am, and, which is more, dares think her his. 3.06.149
in which you swore i went beyond all women, 3.06.206
which cannot want due mercy, i beg first. 3.06.209
in this place, | in which i'll plant a pyramid; 3.06.293
means he escap'd, which was your daughter's, 4.01. 20
which you'll hear of | at better time. 4.01. 29
which shows him hardy, fearless, proud of 4.02. 80
and nimble set, | which shows an active soul; 4.02.126
which speaks him prone to labor, never fainting 4.02.129
which yields compassion where he conquers; 4.02.132
a perturb'd mind, which i cannot minister to. 4.03. 59 P
compounded odors which are grateful to the sense 4.03. 85 P
is in, which is with falsehoods to be combated. 4.03. 93 P
which doubt not will bring forth comfort. 4.03.101 P
were there aught in me which strove to show 5.01. 20
apprehension | which still is farther off it, go 5.01. 37
which if the goddess of it grant, she gives 5.01. 71
of this question, which | is true love's merit, 5.01.127
which being laid unto | mine innocent true heart 5.01.133
make a blush, | which is their order's robe: 5.01.142
which never yet | beheld thing maculate — look 5.01.144
thine ear | (which nev'r heard scurril term, 5.01.147
that which perish'd should | go to't unsentenc'd 5.01.156
'gainst the which there is | no deafing — but 5.03. 8
honor in their kind | which sometime show well, 5.03. 13
there is but envy in that light which shows 5.03. 21
darkness, which ever was | the dam of horror, 5.03. 22
an offense, | which crav'd that very time. 5.03. 64
conceives a tear, | the which it will deliver. 5.03.138
white, which some will say | weakens his price, 5.04. 51
which superstition | here finds allowance — on 5.04. 53
which the calkins | did rather tell than trample 5.04. 55
which he frets at rather | than any jot obeys; 5.04. 70
that we should things desire which do cost us 5.04.110
let us be thankful | for that which is, and with 5.04.135
which is merely to the undoing of poor prentices STM II.C 8 P
shake, which partly comes through the eating of II.C 14 P
which cannot choose but much advantage the poor II.C 70 P
which if you will mark | you shall perceive how II.C 91
sin | which oft th' apostle did forewarn us of, II.C 94
and that which we profanely term our fortunes III 2
strength of nature | which we are born /withal. III 5
which might accite thee to embrace and hug them, III 16
which bred more beauty in his angry eyes: VEN 70
which long have rain'd, making her cheeks all 83
and begg'd for that which thou unask'd shalt 102
now which way shall she turn? 253
his eye, which scornfully glisters like fire, 275
with tears which chorus-like her eyes did rain. 360
which to his speech did honey passage yield, 452
her, | which cunning love did wittily prevent: 471
which through the crystal tears gave light, 491
which purchase if thou make, for fear of slips, 515
the which, by cupid's bow she doth protest, | he 581
the warm effects which she in him finds missing 605
to which love's eyes pays tributary gazes, | nor 632
hare, | or at the fox which lives by subtilty, 675
or at the roe which no encounter dare; 676
the many musits through the which he goes | are 683
which by the rights of time thou needs must have 759
which the hot tyrant stains, and soon bereaves, 797
of those fair arms which bound him to her breast 812
which after him she darts, as one on shore 817
through which it enters to surprise her heart, 890
which madly hurries her she knows not whither: 904
which her cheek melts, as scorning it should 982
which knows no pity, but is still severe; 1000
which seen, her eyes /as murd'red with the view, 1031
which with cold terror doth men's minds confound 1048
which in round drops upon their whiteness stood. 1170
green-dropping sap, which she compares to tears. 1176
which, in pale embers hid, lurks to aspire | and LUC 5
which triumph'd in that sky of his delight; 12
made | to set forth that which is so singular? 32

that golden hap which their superiors want. 42
to quench the coal which in his liver glows. 47
which of them both should underprop her fame. 53
which virtue gave the golden age to gild | their 60
which tarquin view'd in her fair face's field, 72
which far exceeds his barren skill to show. 81
therefore that praise which collatine doth owe 82
eye, | which having all, all could not satisfy; 96
as one of which doth tarquin lie revolving | the 127
what they have not, that which they possess, 135
the things we are, for that which we expect; 149
which must be lodestar to his lustful eye; 179
with your uncleanness that which is divine; 193
which in a moment doth confound and kill | all 250
which strook her sad, and then it faster rock'd, 262
both which, as servitors to the unjust, | so 285
that eye which looks on her confounds his wits; 290
that eye which him beholds, as more divine, 291
which once corrupted takes the worser part; 294
which drives the creeping thief to some regard; 305
his hot heart, which fond desire doth scorch, 314
or as those bars which stop the hourly dial, 327
which with a yielding latch, and with no more, 339
which gives the watch–word to his hand full soon 370
his eye, which late this mutiny restrains, 426
the sight which makes supposed terror true. 455
know, | which he by dumb demeanor seeks to show; 474
which i to conquer sought with all my might; 488
which, like a falcon tow'ring in the skies, 506
which blow these pitchy vapors from their biding 550
mixed, | which to her oratory adds more grace. 564
"all which together, like a troubled ocean, 589
which in her prescience she controlled still, 727
the same disgrace which they themselves behold; 751
which underneath thy black all–hiding cloak 801
that all the faults which in thy reign are made 804
which not themselves but he that gives them 833
and suck'd the honey which thy chaste bee kept. 840
or free that soul which wretchedness hath 900
which, thronging through her lips, so vanisheth 1041
or that which from discharged cannon fumes. 1043
"o, that is gone for which i sought to live, 1051
at gaze, | wildly determining which way to fly, 1150
to live or die which of the twain were better, 1154
"my body or my soul, which was the dearer, 1163
through which i may convey this troubled soul. 1176
which by him tainted shall for him be spent, 1182
which makes the maid weep like the dewy night. 1232
not that devour'd, but that which doth devour, 1256
throng her inventions, which shall go before. 1302
from that suspicion which the world might bear 1321
before the which is drawn the power of greece, 1368
which the conceited painter drew so proud, | as 1371
which heartless peasants did so well resemble, 1392
thin winding breath, which purl'd up to the sky. 1407
which seem'd to swallow up his sound advice, 1409
which bleeding under pyrrhus' proud foot lies. 1449
which all this time hath overslipp'd her thought 1576
which when her sad–beholding husband saw, 1590
which speechless woe of his poor she attendeth, 1674
that map which deep impression bears | of hard 1712
which seems to weep upon the tainted place, 1746
abide, | blushing at that which is so putrefied. 1750
"that life was mine which thou hast here 1752
which she too early and too late hath spill'd." 1801
and that deep vow which brutus made before, | he 1847
which being done with speedy diligence, | the 1853
which is to me some praise, that i thy parts PP 5.10
which, not to anger bent, is music and sweet 5.12
which by a gift of learning did bear the maid 15.14
it be day, | that which with scorn she put away. 18.30
pleasant shade, | which a grove of myrtles made, 20. 4
thee, | which used lives th' executor to be. SON 4.14
same, | and that unfair which fairly doth excel: 5. 4
which happies those that pay the willing loan; 6. 6
why lov'st thou that which thou receiv'st not 8. 3
which to repair should be thy chief desire. 10. 8
in one of thine, from that which thou departest, 11. 2
and that fresh blood which youngly thou 11. 3
which bounteous gift thou shouldst in bounty 11.12
which erst from heat did canopy the herd, | and 12. 6
so should that beauty which you hold in lease 13. 5
which husbandry in honor might uphold | against 13.10
that life repair | which this time's pencil, or 16.10
it is but as a tomb | which hides your life, and 17. 4
which steals men's eyes and women's souls 20. 8
which in thy breast doth live, as thine in me: 22. 7
which i will keep so chary | as tender nurse her 22.11
which in my bosom's shop is hanging still, 24. 7
and all the rest forgot for which he toil'd. 25.12
which wit so poor as mine | may make seem bare, 26. 5
looking on darkness which the blind do see; 27. 8
which, like a jewel hung in ghastly night, 27.11
moan, | which i new pay as if not paid before: 30.12
hearts, | which i by lacking have supposed dead, 31. 2
and all those friends which i thought buried. 31. 4
dead, which now appear | but things remov'd that 31. 7
but those tears are pearl which thy love sheeds, 34.13
no more be griev'd at that which thou hast done: 35. 1
to that sweet thief which sourly robs from me. 35.14
which though it alter not love's sole effect, 36. 7
than those old nine which rhymers invocate, 38.10
that due to thee which thou deserv'st alone. 39. 8
which time and thoughts so sweetly dost deceive, 39.12
hide, | which heavily he answers with a groan, 50.11
the which he will not ev'ry hour survey, | for 52. 3
or as the wardrobe which the robe doth hide, 52.10
by that sweet ornament which truth doth give! 54. 2
for that sweet odor which doth in it live. 54. 4
which but to–day by feeding is allay'd, 56. 3
which parts the shore where two contracted new 56.10
as call it winter, which, being full of care, 56.13
new, but that which is | hath been before, how 59. 1
which laboring for invention bear amiss | the 59. 3
each changing place with that which goes before, 60. 3
which cannot choose | but weep to have that 64.13
but weep to have that which it fears to lose. 64.14
for i am sham'd by that which i bring forth, 72.13
upon those boughs which shake against the cold, 73. 3
which by and by black night doth take away, 73. 7
consum'd with that which it was nourish'd by. 73.12
perceiv'st, which makes thy love more strong, 73.13
love that well, which thou must leave ere long. 73.14
which for memorial still with thee shall stay. 74. 4
the earth can have but earth, which is his due, 74. 7
the worth of that is that which it contains, 74.13
the wrinkles which thy glass will truly show, 77. 5
yet be most proud of that which i compile, 78. 9
then thank him not for that which he doth say, 79.13
which eyes not yet created shall o'er–read, 81.10
o'erlook | the dedicated words which writers use 82. 3
which shall be most my glory, being dumb, | for 83.10
which can say more | than this rich praise, that 84. 1
which should example where your equal grew? 84. 4
fond on praise, which makes your praises worse. 84.14
which nightly gulls him with intelligence, | as 86.10
and other strains of woe, which now seem woe, 90.13
than that which on thy humor doth depend. 92. 8
and lovely dost thou make the shame | which, 95. 2
got | which for their habitation chose out thee, 95.10
which on thy soft cheek for complexion dwells 99. 4
to speak of that which gives thee all thy might? 100. 2
first i saw you fresh, which yet are green. 104. 8
your sweet hue, which methinks still doth stand, 104.11
for fear of which, hear this, thou age unbred: 104.13
themes in one, which wondrous scope affords. 105.12
which three till now never kept seat in one. 105.14
for we, which now behold these present days, 106.13
which hath not figur'd to thee my true spirit? 108. 2
as from my soul, which in thy breast doth lie: 109. 4
than public means which public manners breeds. 111. 4
which vulgar scandal stamp'd upon my brow, | for 112. 2
and that which governs me to go about | doth 113. 2
bird, of flow'r, or shape, which it doth /latch, 113. 6
give full growth to that which still doth grow. 115.14
love | which alters when it alteration finds, 116. 3
which should transport me farthest from your 117. 8
brought to medicine a healthful state | which, 118.12
now, | and for that sorrow which i then did feel 120. 2
the humble salve which wounded bosoms fits! 120.12
lost, which is so deemed | not by our feeling, 121. 3
which in their wills count bad what i think good 121. 8
which shall above that idle rank remain | beyond 122. 3
which works on leases of short–numb'red hours, 124.10
which die for goodness, who have liv'd for crime 124.14
which proves more short than waste or ruining? 125. 4
which is not mix'd with seconds, knows no art, 125.11
my poor lips, which should that harvest reap, 128. 7
which my heart knows the wide world's common 137.10
to follow that which flies before her face, 143. 7
so run'st thou after that which flies from thee, 143. 9
which like two spirits do suggest me still: 144. 2
for that which longer nurseth the disease, 147. 2
feeding on that which doth preserve the ill, 147. 3
desire is death, which physic did except. 147. 8
which have no correspondence with true sight, 148. 2
which borrow'd from this holy fire of love | a 153. 5
which yet men prove | against strange maladies a 153. 7
which many legions of true hearts had warm'd, 154. 6
which from love's fire took heat perpetual, 154.10
which fortified her visage from the sun, LC 9
eyne, | which on it had conceited characters, 16
jet, | which one by one she in a river threw, 38
which she perus'd, sigh'd, tore, and gave the 44
which may her suffering ecstasy assuage, | 'tis 69
set | the goodly objects which abroad they find 137
the true gouty landlord which doth owe them. 140
which remain'd the foil | of this false jewel, 153
which late her noble suit in court did shun, 234
playing the place which did no form receive, 241
the accident which brought me to her eye | upon 247
flame through water which their hue encloses. 287
"that not a heart which in his level came 309
which like a cherubin above them hover'd. 319
o, that false fire which in his cheek so glowed, 324

WHIFF 1 FR 0.0001 REL FR 1 V 0 P
but with the whiff and wind of his fell sword HAM 2.02.473

WHIFFLER 1 FR 0.0001 REL FR 1 V 0 P
which like a mighty whiffler 'fore the king H5 5.pr. 12

/WHILE 4 FR 0.0004 REL FR 3 V 1 P
/give /sorrow /leave /a /while /to /tutor /me R2 4.01.166
/o'er /this /paper /while /the /glass /doth 4.01.269
/but /rather /show /a /while /like /fearful /war 2H4 4.01. 63
/there /was /for /a /while /no /money /bid /for HAM 2.02.354 P

WHILE 339 FR 0.0383 REL FR 287 V 52 P
will guard your person while you take your rest, TMP 2.01.197
while you here do snoring lie, | open–ey'd 2.01.300
be said so again while stephano breathes at' 2.02. 62 P
sit down, | i'll bear your logs the while. 3.01. 24
such dishonor undergo, | while i sit lazy by. 3.01. 28
but, while thou liv'st, keep a good tongue in 3.02.112 P
i leave them, while i visit | young ferdinand, 3.03. 91
shall not go unrewarded while i am king of this 4.01.242 P
while other men, of slender reputation, | put TGV 1.03. 6
now the dog all this while sheds not a tear, nor 2.03. 31 P
and here he means to spend his time a while. 2.04. 80
sir thurio, give us leave, i pray, a while, | we 3.01. 1
which to requite, command me while i live. 3.01. 23
stay with me a while; 3.01. 58
while i, their king, that thither them importune 3.01.145
let's tune, and to it lustily a while. 4.02. 25
love, lend me patience to forbear a while. 5.04. 27
tarry you a little–a while. WIV 1.04. 88 P
what? while you were there? 3.05. 79 P
while i was there. 3.05. 80 P
put on the gown the while. 4.02. 83 P
while other jests are something rank on foot, 4.06. 22
while other sports are tasking of their minds, 4.06. 30
stay a little while. MM 2.02. 26
stay a while, | and you shall be conducted. 2.03. 17
yet may he live a while; 2.04. 35
but i will attend you a while. 3.01.159 P
leave me a while with the maid. 3.01.177 P
i for a while will leave you; 5.01.257
stay, sir, stay a while. 5.01.349 P
while i go to the goldsmith's house, go thou ERR 4.01. 15
and the while | his man with scissors nicks him 5.01.174
while she with harlots feasted in my house. 5.01.205
disdain should die while she hath such meet food ADO 1.01.120 P
for certainly, while she is here, a man may live 2.01.257 P
of it by your daughter, let it cool the while. 2.03.206 P
lady beatrice, have you wept all this while? 4.01.255 P
yea, and i will weep a while longer. 4.01.256 P
while truth the while | doth falsely blind the LLL 1.01. 75
while truth the while | doth falsely blind the 1.01. 75
while it doth study to have what it would, | it 1.01.143
haste, signify so much, while we attend, | like 2.01. 33
thou hast spoken no word all this while. 5.01.150 P
but while 'tis spoke each turn away /her face. 5.02.148
note, | while greasy joan doth keel the pot. 5.02.920
note, | while greasy joan doth keel the pot. 5.02.929
stay thou but here a while, | and by and by i MND 3.01. 86
and sing while thou on pressed flowers dost 3.01.159
while she was in her dull and sleeping hour, | a 3.02. 8
here therefore for a while i will remain. 3.02. 83
eye, | steal me a while from mine own company. 3.02.436
bed, | while i thy amiable cheeks do coy, | and 4.01. 2
silence a while. 4.01. 80
at large discourse, while here they do remain. 5.01.151
slumb'red here | while these visions did appear. 5.01.426
fare ye well a while, | i'll end my exhortation MV 1.01.103
but alas the while! 2.01. 31
nay more, while grace is saying, hood mine eyes 2.02.193
therefore forbear a while. 3.02. 3
let music sound while he doth make his choice; 3.02. 43
nay, let me praise you while i have a stomach. 3.05. 87
while i live i'll fear no other thing | so sore, 5.01.306
sir, be better employ'd and be naught a while. AYL 1.01. 36 P
sirs, cover the while. 2.05. 32 P
hold death a while at the arm's end. 2.06. 10 P
then forbear your food a little while, | whiles, 2.07.127
orlando, where have you been all this while? 4.01. 40 P
flesh away, | which all this while had bled; 4.03.148
while we do admire | this virtue and this moral SHR 1.01. 29
but stay a while, what company is this? 1.01. 46
but see, while idly i stood looking on, | i 1.01.150
while i make way from hence to save my life. 1.01.234
for a while i take my leave | to see my friends 1.02. 1
pray you, sir, let him go while the humor lasts. 1.02.107 P
petruchio, stand by a while. 1.02.142
you have but jested with me all this while. 2.01. 20
way, | and there i stood amazed for a while, 2.01.155
while she did call me rascal fiddler | and 2.01.157
and while i pause, serve in your harmony. 3.01. 14
you may go walk, and give me leave a while; 3.01. 59
while you, sweet dear, prove mistress of my 4.02. 10
i marvel cambio comes not all this while. 5.01. 7
while i play the good husband at home, my son 5.01. 68 P
while counterfeit supposes blear'd thine eyne. 5.01.117
while he did bear my countenance in the town, 5.01.126
while i with self–same kindness welcome thine. 5.02. 5
and while it is so, none so dry or thirsty 5.02.144
off with't while 'tis vendible; AWW 1.01.155 P
while shameful hate sleeps out the afternoon. 5.03. 66
while i was speaking, oft was fasten'd to't. 5.03. 82
wherefore hast thou accus'd him all this while? 5.03.288
seek him out, and play the tune the while. TN 2.04. 14
i frown the while, and perchance wind up my 2.05. 59 P
did she see /thee the while, old boy? 3.02. 8 P
i will meditate the while upon some horrid 3.04.199 P
years removed thing | while one would wink; 5.01. 90
for so you shall be while you are a man; 5.01.386
a great while ago the world begun, | /with hey 5.01.405
stay your thanks a while, | and pay them when WT 1.02. 9
th' other for some while a friend. 1.02.108
now, while i speak this) holds his wife by th' 1.02.193
while she lives | my heart will be a burthen to 2.03.205
woe the while! 3.02.172
my aunts, | while we lie tumbling in the hay. 4.03. 12
with any thing | that you behold the while. 4.04. 48
mark a little while. 5.03.118
james gurney, wilt thou give us leave a while? JN 1.01.230
while they weigh so even, | we hold our town for 2.01.332
urge them while their souls | are capable of 2.01.475
that i have room with rome to curse a while! 3.01.180
head lie there, | while philip breathes. 3.02. 4
all this while | you were disguis'd. 4.01.125
bad world the while! 4.02.100
face, | and bid his ears a little while be deaf, R2 1.01.112
while we return these dukes what we decree. 1.03.122
i'll not be by the while. 2.01.211
a while to work, and after holiday. 3.01. 44
who all this while hath revell'd in the night, 3.02. 48
for you have but mistook me all this while. 3.02.174
while here we march | upon the grassy carpet of 3.03. 49
while i stand fooling here, his jack of the 5.05. 60
and for this cause a while we must neglect | our 1H4 1.01.101
and will a while uphold | the unyok'd humor of 1.02.195
stay, and pause a while. 1.03.129
good cousin, give me audience for a while. 1.03.211
we'll walk afoot a while, and ease our legs. 2.02. 79 P
while i question my puny drawer to what end he 2.04. 30 P
them is fat and grows old, god help the while! 2.04.132 P
well, breathe a while, and then to it again, and 2.04.249 P
o, while you live, tell truth and shame the 3.01. 61
away, | advantage feeds him fat while men delay. 3.02.180
and that suddenly, while i am in some liking. 3.03. 5 P
made to my father, while his blood was poor, 4.03. 76
we'll withdraw a while. 4.03.107
hal, i prithee give me leave to breathe a while. 5.03. 45 P
stay and breathe a while. 5.04. 47
while covert enmity | under the smile of safety 2H4 in 9
as thou hast not done a great while, because the 2.02. 21 P
not liv'd all this while to have swaggering now. 2.04. 77 P
falstaff, where have you been all this while? 4.03. 26
while that the armed hand doth fight abroad, H5 1.02.178
in patient stillness while his rider mounts him. 3.07. 23 P
i and my bosom must debate a while, | and then i 4.01. 31
sell the lion's skin | while the beast liv'd, 4.03. 94
for many of our princes (woe the while!) 4.07. 75
upon, while that the coulter rusts | that should 5.02. 46
and while thou liv'st, dear kate, take a fellow 5.02.152 P
back, you lords, and give us leave a while. 1H6 1.02. 70
and while i live, i'll ne'er fly from a man. 1.02.103

i had | that walk'd about me every minute while; 1.04. 54
do, | let me persuade you to forbear a while. 3.01.105
let frantic talbot triumph for a while, | and 3.03. 5
i have a while given truce unto my wars, | to do 3.04. 3
that thus we die, while remiss traitors sleep. 4.03. 29
while the vulture of sedition | feeds in the 4.03. 47
while he, renowned noble gentleman, | yield up 4.04. 24
i prithee give me leave to curse a while. 5.03. 43
while these do labor for their own preferment, 2H6 1.01.181
while they do tend the profit of the land. 1.01.204
while as the silly owner of the goods | weeps 1.01.225
while all is shar'd and all is borne away, 1.01.228
while his own lands are bargain'd for and sold. 1.01.231
while gloucester bears this base and humble mind 1.02. 62
you be by her aloft, while we be busy below; 1.04. 8 P
thou shalt be waking while i shed thy blood, 3.02.227
or pick a sallet another while, which is not 4.10. 8 P
it shall ne'er be said, while england stands, 4.10. 42
but i must make fair weather yet a while, | till 5.01. 30
that i have given no answer all this while; 5.01. 33
and while 'tis mine, | it shall be stony. 5.02. 50
while we pursu'd the horsemen of the north, | he 3H6 1.01. 2
and thou shalt reign in quiet while thou liv'st. 1.01.173
while you are thus employ'd, what resteth more, 1.02. 44
i would prolong a while the traitor's life. 1.04. 52
thou smiling while he knit his angry brows: 2.02. 20
race, | i lay me down a little while to breathe; 2.03. 2
while we devise fell tortures for thy faults. 2.06. 72
for we were subjects but while you were king. 3.01. 81
that thou shouldst stand while lewis doth sit. 3.03. 3
must strike her sail and learn a while to serve 3.03. 5
my tongue, while heart is drown'd in cares. 3.03. 14
while proud ambitious edward, duke of york, 3.03. 27
while we bethink a means to break it off. 3.03. 39
for though usurpers sway the rule a while, | yet 3.03. 76
while life upholds this arm, | this arm upholds 3.03.106
while i use further conference with warwick. 3.03.111
smiles at her news, while warwick frowns at his. 3.03.168
him, | while he himself keeps in the cold field? 4.03. 14
come therefore let us fly while we may fly, | if 4.04. 34
land, | while i myself will lead a private life, 4.06. 42
while he enjoys the honor and his ease. 4.06. 52
sir john, a while, and we'll debate | by what 4.07. 51
here at the palace will i rest a while. 4.08. 33
and with thy lips keep in my soul a while. 5.02. 35
say you can swim, alas, 'tis but a while; 5.04. 29
denier, | i do mistake my person all this while! R3 1.02.252
cannot be quiet scarce a breathing while | but 1.03. 60
while great promotions | are daily given to 1.03. 79
friends suspect for traitors while thou liv'st, 1.03.222
unless it be while some tormenting dream 1.03.225
was wont to hold me but while one tells twenty. 1.04.119 P
ay, sir, it is too true, god help the while! 2.03. 8
withdraw yourself a while, i'll go with you. 3.04. 41
here's a good world the while! 3.06. 10
gone | to brecknock while my fearful head is on! 4.02.122
while we reason here, | a royal battle might be 4.04.535
my lord, | nor shall not while i have a stump. H8 1.03. 49
mean while must be an earnest motion | made to 2.04.234
have my prayers | while i shall have my life. 3.01.181
leave me a while. 3.02. 84
while her grace sate down | to rest a while, 4.01. 65
while her grace sate down | to rest a while, 4.01. 66
now, | while 'tis hot, i'll put it to the issue. 5.01.176
mean, | which ye shall never have while i live. 5.02.182
do, i know within a while | all the best men are ep 12
it now, for it has been a great while going by. TRO 1.02.168 P
a while, but ha, ha, ha! 3.01.125
what some men do, | while some men leave to do! 3.03.133
while pride is fasting in his wantonness! 3.03.137
stay a little while. 5.02. 54
us but the superfluity while it were wholesome, COR 1.01. 18 P
rapture lets her baby cry | while she chats him; 2.01.208
and give way the while | to unstable slightness. 3.01.147
tribunes, withdraw a while. 3.01.225
take good cominius | with thee a while. 4.01. 35
while i remain above the ground, you shall 4.01. 51
show duty as mistaken all this while | between 5.03. 55
while the volsces | may say, "this mercy we have 5.03.136
mean while am i possess'd of that is mine. TIT 1.01.408
mean while, sir, with the little skill i have, 2.01. 43
well could i leave our sport to sleep a while. 2.03.197
but let her rest in her unrest a while. 4.02. 31
mean while here's money for thy charges. 4.03.105
while i stand by and weep to hear him speak. 5.03. 95
but, gentle people, give me aim a while, | for 5.03.149
ay, while you live, draw your neck out of collar ROM 1.01. 4 P
me they shall feel while i am able to stand, and 1.01. 28 P
while we were interchanging thrusts and blows, 1.01.113
nurse, give leave a while, | we must talk in 1.03. 7
in bed asleep, while they do dream things true. 1.04. 52
boys, be brisk a while, and the longer liver 1.05. 15 P
then move not while my prayer's effect i take. 1.05.106
i am a-weary, give me leave a while. 2.05. 25
can you not stay a while? 2.05. 29
stay a while! 3.03. 75
muffle me, night, a while. 5.03. 21
seal up the mouth of outrage for a while, | till 5.03.216
while they have told their money, and let out TIM 3.05.106
care not, | while you have throats to answer. 5.01.179
but, woe the while, our fathers' minds are dead, JC 1.03. 82
stand close a while, for here comes one in haste 1.03.131
portia, go in a while, | and by and by thy bosom 2.01.304
statue | (which all the while ran blood) great 3.02.189
and i will seek for pindarus the while. 5.03. 79
strato, thou hast been all this while asleep; 5.05. 32
turn away thy face, | while i do run upon it. 5.05. 48
i would, while it was smiling in my face, | have MAC 1.07. 56
good repose the while! 2.01. 29
while then, god be with you! 3.01. 43
unsafe the while, that we | must lave our honors 3.02. 32
that is not often vouch'd, while 'tis a-making, 3.04. 33
a sound, | while you perform your antic round; 4.01.130
yet all this while in a most fast sleep. 5.01. 8 P
sit down a while, | and let us once again assail HAM 1.01. 30
season your admiration for a while | with an 1.02.192
while one with moderate haste might tell a 1.02.237
as to expend your time with us a while | for the 2.02. 23
i have a daughter — have while she is mine — 2.02.106
would make mouths at him while my father liv'd, 2.02.365 P
epitaph than their ill report while you live. 2.02.526 P
sweet, leave me here a while, | my spirits grow 3.02.225
for some must watch, while some must sleep, 3.02.273
sir, but "while the grass grows" — the proverb 3.02.343 P
bestow this place on us a little while. 4.01. 4
while to my shame i see | the imminent death of 4.04. 59
trade that 'a will keep out water a great while, 5.01.171 P
couch we a while and mark. 5.01.222
hold off the earth a while, | till i have caught 5.01.249
and /thus a while the fit will work on him; 5.01.285
i'll play this bout first, set it by a while. 5.02.284
thy heart, | absent thee from felicity a while, 5.02.347
perform'd | even while men's minds are wild, 5.02.394
while we | unburthen'd crawl toward death. LR 1.01. 40
repose you there, while i to this hard house 3.02. 63
he's scarce awake, let him alone a while. 4.07. 50
while i spare speech, which something now OTH 2.03.199
content thyself a while. 2.03.378
on — | myself a while to draw the moor apart, 2.03.385
she told her, while she kept it, | 'twould make 3.04. 58
i have this while with leaden thoughts been 3.04.177
do you withdraw yourself a little while, | he 4.01. 56
stand you a while apart, | confine yourself but 4.01. 74
but while i say one prayer! 5.02. 83
the while i'll place you, then the boy shall ANT 2.07.110
while he was yet in rome, | his power went out 3.07. 75
while i strook | the lean and wrinkled cassius, 3.11. 36
laugh at 's while we strut | to our confusion. 3.13.114
remain thou here, | while sense can keep it on. CYM 1.01.118
why, good fellow, | what shall i do the while? 3.04.128
had rather thou shouldst live while nature will 5.05.151
therefore, my lord, go travel for a while, PER 1.02.106
if heaven slumber while their creatures want, 1.04. 16
upon thy grave | while summer days doth last. 4.01. 17
i'll leave you, my sweet lady, for a while. 4.01. 47
pray you come hither a while. 4.02.115 P
like motes and shadows see them move a while, 4.04. 21
while our /scene must play | his daughter's woe 4.04. 48
i may depart with little, while i live; TNK 2.01. 1 P
that were a shame, sir, | while i have horses. 2.05. 54
i a while. 4.02. 70
thou art a right good man, and while i live, 5.04. 97
pray yet stay a while, | and let me look upon ye ep 3
while she takes all she can, not all she listeth VEN 564
but soundly sleeps, while now it sleeps alone. 786
bud and be blasted in a breathing while, | the 1142
while lust and murder wakes to stain and kill. LUC 168
while she, the picture of pure piety, | like a 542
and moody pluto winks while orpheus plays. 553
while in his hold-fast foot the weak mouse 555
while lust is in his pride, no exclamation | can 705
"the patient dies while the physician sleeps, 904
the orphan pines while the oppressor feeds, 905
justice is feasting while the widow weeps, 906
advice is sporting while infection breeds. 907
while thou on tereus descants better skill. 1134
a pretty while these pretty creatures stand, 1233
while others saucily | promise more speed, but 1348
that she her plaints a little while doth stay, 1364
but tarquin's shape came in her mind the while, 1536
while collatine and his consorted lords | with 1609
while with a joyless smile she turns away | the 1711
while philomela sits and sings, i sit and mark, PP 14.17
but if the while i think on thee, dear friend, SON 30.13
subject to invent | while thou dost breathe, 38. 2
while shadows like to thee do mock my sight? 61. 4
while comments of your praise, richly compil'd, 85. 2
now while the world is bent my deeds to cross, 90. 2
while he insults o'er dull and speechless tribes 107.12
counsel may stop a while what will not stay; LC 159

WHILE-ERE 1 FR 0.0001 REL FR 1 V 0 P

troll the catch | you taught me but while-ere? TMP 3.02.118

WHILES 82 FR 0.0092 REL FR 81 V 1 P

whiles you do keep from me | the rest o' th' TMP 1.02.343
wink'st | whiles thou art waking. 2.01.217
the purpose cherish | whiles thus you mock it! 2.01.225
whiles you, doing thus, | to the perpetual wink 2.01.284
whiles we stood here securing your repose, 2.01.310
whiles i | persuade this rude wretch willingly MM 4.03. 80
we prize not to the worth | whiles we enjoy it, ADO 4.01.219
would not show us | whiles it was ours. 4.01.222
i have drunk poison whiles he utter'd it. 5.01.246
she died, my lord, but whiles her slander liv'd. 5.04. 66
whiles i in this affair do thee employ, | i'll MND 3.02.374
whiles we shut the gate upon one wooer, another MV 1.02.133
whiles, like a doe, i go to find my fawn | and AYL 2.07.128
"whiles the eye of man did woo me, | that could 4.03. 47
whiles you chid me, i did love; 4.03. 54
patience once more, whiles our compact is urg'd: 5.04. 5
whiles a wedlock-hymn we sing, | feed yourselves 5.04.137
take you your instrument, play you the whiles, SHR 3.01. 22
you may be jogging whiles your boots are green. 3.02.211
whiles you beguile the time and feed your TN 3.03. 41
whiles you are willing it shall come to note, 4.03. 29
whiles other men have gates, and those gates WT 1.02.197
to your court | whiles he was hast'ning (in the 5.01.189
whiles we, god's wrathful agent, do correct JN 2.01. 87
well, whiles i am a beggar, i will rail, | and 2.01.593
whiles warm life plays in that infant's veins, 3.04.132
whiles the big year, swoll'n with some other 2H4 in 13
up | whiles england shall have generation. 4.02. 49
law, | whiles i was busy for the commonwealth, 5.02. 76
whiles his most mighty father on a hill | stood H5 1.02.108
whiles that his mountain sire, on mountain 2.04. 57
whiles yet my soldiers are in my command, 3.03. 29
whiles yet the cool and temperate wind of grace 3.03. 30
whiles the mad mothers with their howls confus'd 3.03. 39
whiles a more frosty people | sweat drops of 3.05. 24
and hold their manhoods cheap whiles any speaks 4.03. 66
this comfort, | thou shalt not die whiles — 1H6 1.04. 91
whiles thy consuming canker eats his falsehood. 2.04. 71
whiles they each other cross, | lives, honors, 4.03. 52
and whiles the honorable captain there | drops 4.04. 17
'tis well known that, whiles i was protector, 2H6 3.01.124
whiles i take order for mine own affairs. 3.01.320
whiles i in ireland nourish a mighty band, | i 3.01.348
'tis but surmis'd whiles thou art standing by, 3.02.347
wailing our losses, whiles the foe doth rage, 3H6 2.03. 26
whiles lions war and battle for their dens, 2.05. 74
which, whiles it lasted, gave king henry light. 2.06. 2
the tiger will be mild whiles she doth mourn; 3.01. 39
whiles warwick tells his title, smooths the 3.01. 48
and whiles i live, t' account this world but 3.02.169
why, i can smile, and murther whiles i smile, 3.02.182
but, whiles he thought to steal the single ten, 5.01. 43
shall, whiles thy head is warm and new cut off, 5.01. 55
whiles, in his moan, the ship splits on the rock 5.04. 10
whiles kites and buzzards /prey at liberty. R3 1.01.133
rest you, whiles i lament king henry's corse. 1.02. 32
whiles, in the mildness of your sleepy thoughts, 3.07.123
whiles here he liv'd | upon this naughty earth? H8 5.01.137
whiles others play the idiots in her eyes! TRO 3.03.135
whiles others fish with craft for great opinion, 4.04.103
whiles we have strook, | by interims and COR 1.06. 4
whiles hounds and horns and sweet melodious TIT 2.03. 27
whiles i go tell my lord the emperor | how i 5.02.138
whiles that lavinia 'tween her stumps doth hold 5.02.182
that whiles verona by that name is known, ROM 5.03.300
whiles they behold a greater than themselves, JC 1.02.209
whiles i stood rapt in the wonder of it, came MAC 1.05. 5 P
whiles i threat, he lives: 2.01. 60
whiles night's black agents to their preys do 3.02. 53
whiles i see lives, the gashes | do better upon 5.08. 2
whiles, /like a puff'd and reckless libertine, HAM 1.03. 49
whiles memory holds a seat | in this distracted 1.05. 96
whiles rank corruption, mining all within, 3.04.148
whiles i may scape | i will preserve myself, and LR 2.03. 5
for whiles this honest fool | plies desdemona to OTH 2.03.353
whiles we are suitors to their throne, decays ANT 2.01. 4
whiles yet the dew's on ground, gather those CYM 1.05. 1
thick sighs from him, whiles the jolly britain 1.06. 67
sheets, | whiles he is vaulting variable ramps, 1.06.134
thee, whiles i say | a priestly farewell to her. PER 3.01. 68
whiles they are o'er the bank of their obedience STM II.C 39
"and whiles against a thorn thou bear'st thy LUC 1135

WHILEST 11 FR 0.0012 REL FR 10 V 1 P

whilest i remember | her and her virtues, i WT 5.01. 6
purge all infection from our air whilest you 5.01.169
lo, whilest i waited on my tender lambs, | and 1H6 1.02. 76
for whilest i think i am thy married wife | and 2H6 2.04. 28
as he stood by, whilest i, his forlorn duchess, 2.04. 45
hold you his hands whilest i do set it on. 3H6 1.04. 95
and, whilest we breathe, take time to do him 1.04.108
it) his friends whilest he's in directitude. COR 4.05.208 P
hold thou my sword-hilts, whilest i run on it. JC 5.05. 28
whilest our poor malice | remains in danger of MAC 3.02. 14
whilest ours was blurted at and held a mawkin PER 4.03. 34

/WHILST 4 FR 0.0004 REL FR 4 V 0 P

/my /griefs, /whilst /you /mount /up /on /high. R2 4.01.189
/whilst /that /my /wretchedness /doth /bait 4.01.238
/whilst /thou, /a /moral /fool, /sits /still LR 4.02. 58
/whilst /i | /was /big /in /clamor, /came /there 5.03.208

WHILST 107 FR 0.0121 REL FR 101 V 6 P

i'll ne'er be drunk whilst i live again, but in WIV 1.01.181 P
but, whilst i live, forget to drink after thee. MM 1.02. 38 P
whilst my invention, hearing not my tongue, 2.04. 3
whilst i had been like heedful of the other. ERR 1.01. 82
whom whilst i labored of a love to see, | i 1.01.130
whilst i at home starve for a merry look: 2.01. 88
whilst man and master laughs my woes to scorn. 2.02.205
whilst upon me the guilty doors were shut, | and 4.04. 63
whilst to take order for the wrongs i went, 5.01.146
whilst the heavy ploughman snores, | all with MND 5.01.373
whilst the screech-owl, screeching loud, | puts 5.01.376
and, whilst thou layest in thy unhallowed dam, MV 4.01.136
but whilst this muddy vesture of decay | doth 5.01. 64
hers, | if whilst i live she will be only mine. SHR 2.01.362
thou shalt think on prating whilst thou liv'st! 4.03.113
whilst thou li'st warm at home, secure and safe; 5.02.151
a maid the better whilst i have a tooth in my AWW 2.03. 42 P
i give | me and my service, ever whilst i live, 2.03.103
whilst i can shake my sword or hear the drum. 2.05. 91
whilst i from far | his name with zealous fervor 3.04. 10
i'll call sir toby the whilst. TN 4.02. 3 P
whilst he that hears makes fearful action | with JN 4.02.191
the whilst his iron did on the anvil cool, 4.02.194
whilst others come to make him lose at home. R2 2.02. 81
whilst you have fed upon my signories, 3.01. 22
whilst bullingbrook, through our security, 3.02. 34
whilst we were wand'ring with the antipodes, 3.02. 49
his, whilst on the earth i rain | my waters — 3.03. 59
for on my heart they tread now whilst i live, 3.03.158
and spit upon him whilst i say he lies, | and 4.01. 75
and whilst all tongues cried, "god save /thee, 5.02. 11
whilst he, from the one side to the other 5.02. 18
alack, poor richard, where rode he the whilst? 5.02. 22
whilst my gross flesh sinks downward, here to 5.05.112
whilst i, by looking on the praise of him, | see 1H4 1.01. 84
hold the chamber-door | whilst /by /a slave, no H5 4.05. 15
and whilst a field should be dispatch'd and 1H6 1.01. 72
and whilst such a worthy leader, wanting aid, | unto 1.01.143
whilst any trump did sound, or drum struck up, 1.04. 80
for, whilst our pinnace anchors in the downs, 2H6 4.01. 9
and yield to mercy whilst 'tis offered you, | or 4.08. 12
were't not a shame, that whilst you live at jar, 4.08. 41
and whilst i live | to honor me as thy king and 3H6 1.01.197
whilst i propose the self-same words to thee, 5.05. 20
whilst i awhile obsequiously lament | th' R3 1.02. 3
whilst our commission from rome is read, | let H8 2.04. 1
whilst your great goodness, out of holy pity, 3.02.263
whilst i sit meditating | on that celestial 4.02. 79
slept, | whilst emulation in the army crept: TRO 2.02.212
that i could beat him, whilst he rail'd at me. 2.03. 5 P
whilst some with cunning gild their copper 4.04.105
whilst i, with those that have the spirit, will COR 1.05. 13
whilst with no softer cushion than the flint | i 5.03. 53
the people will remain uncertain whilst | 'twixt 5.06. 16
and whilst the babbling echo mocks the hounds, TIT 2.03. 17
the whilst their own birds famish in their nests 2.03.154
in dangerous wars whilst you securely slept; 3.01. 3
and never whilst i live deceive men so; 3.01.189
and lulls him whilst she playeth on her back, 4.01. 99
and whilst i at a banket hold him sure, | i'll 5.02. 76
whilst i have gold, i'll be his steward still. TIM 4.02. 50

and whilst this poor wealth lasts | to entertain 4.03.488
fly, whilst thou art blest and free. 4.03.535
whilst your purpled hands do reek and smoke, JC 3.01.158
whilst bloody treason flourish'd over us. 3.02.192
doing himself offense, whilst we, lying still, 4.03.201
whilst damned casca, like a cur, behind | strook 5.01. 43
spoil, | whilst we by antony are all enclos'd. 5.03. 8
whilst i go to meet | the noble brutus, 5.03. 73
within his truncheon's length, whilst they, HAM 1.02.204
most dear lady, whilst this machine is to him, 2.02.124 P
'a steal aught the whilst this play is playing, 3.02. 88
or, whilst i can vent clamor from my throat, LR 1.01.165
nor shall not, whilst 'tis in my custody. OTH 3.03.164
whilst you were here o'erwhelmed with your grief 4.01. 76
from syria | to lydia and to ionia, | whilst — ANT 1.02.104
make yourself my guest | whilst you abide here. 2.02.244
on him, whilst | i wore his sword philippan. 2.05. 22
whilst yet with parthian blood thy sword is warm 3.01. 6
feats, whilst they with joyful tears | wash the 4.08. 9
which whilst it was mine had annex'd unto't | a 4.14. 17
whilst the wheel'd seat | of fortunate caesar, 4.14. 75
whilst he stood up and spoke, | he was my master 5.01. 7
whilst i am bound to wonder, i am bound | to CYM 1.06. 81
on that | whilst what we have kill'd be cook'd. 3.06. 39
flowers | whilst summer lasts and i live here, 4.02.219
go fetch him, | we'll say our song whilst. 4.02.254
i died whilst in the womb he stay'd | attending 5.04. 37
whilst we dispatch | this grand act of our life, TNK 1.01.163
like lazy clouds, whilst palamon and arcite, 2.02. 14
whilst the angry swine | flies like a parthian 2.02. 49
whilst palamon is with me, let me perish | if i 2.02. 61
whilst as fickle fortune smil'd, | thou and i PP 20.27
friend, | whilst thou hast wherewith to spend; 20.34
whilst i, whom fortune of such triumph bars, SON 25. 3
whilst that this shadow doth such substance give 37.10
whilst i, my sovereign, watch the clock for you, 57. 6
thee watch i, whilst thou dost wake elsewhere, 61.13
whilst i alone did call upon thy aid, | my verse 79. 1
whilst he upon your soundless deep doth ride, 80.10
i think good thoughts whilst other write good 85. 5
whilst like a willing patient i will drink 111. 9
whilst it hath thought itself so blessed never? 119. 6
whilst my poor lips, which should that harvest 128. 7
whilst her neglected child holds her in chase, 143. 5
whilst i, thy babe, chase thee afar behind, 143.10
whilst many nymphs that vow'd chaste life to 154. 3

WHIN'D 2 FR 0.0002 REL FR 2 V 0 P
tears | he whin'd and roar'd away your victory, COR 5.06. 97
thrice, and once the hedge–pig whin'd. MAC 4.01. 2

WHINE 2 FR 0.0002 REL FR 2 V 0 P
dost /thou come here to whine? HAM 5.01.277
cringe his face, | and whine aloud for mercy. ANT 3.13.101

WHINES 1 FR 0.0001 REL FR 1 V 0 P
pig–like he whines | at the sharp rowel, which TNK 5.04. 69

/WHINID'ST 1 FR 0.0001 REL FR 0 V 1 P
speak then, thou /whinid'st leaven, speak; TRO 2.01. 14 P

WHINING 4 FR 0.0004 REL FR 3 V 1 P
this wimpled, whining, purblind, wayward boy, LLL 3.01.179
then the whining schoolboy, with his satchel AYL 2.07.145
a whining mammet, in her fortune's tender, | to ROM 3.05.184
one whom i will beat into /clamorous whining, if LR 2.02. 23 P

WHIP 37 FR 0.0041 REL FR 27 V 10 P
"whip him out," says the third. TGV 4.04. 21 P
"friend," quoth i, "you mean to whip the dog?" 4.04. 25 P
i warrant they would whip me with their fine WIV 4.05. 99 P
hoping you'll find good cause to whip them all. MM 2.01.137
whip me? 2.01.255
no, no, let carman whip his jade, | the valiant 2.01.255
sir boy, i'll whip you from your foining fence, ADO 5.01. 84
i, that have been love's whip, | a very beadle LLL 3.01.174
now step i forth to whip hypocrisy. 4.03.149
thou disputes like an infant; go whip thy gig. 5.01. 66 P
to make one, and i will whip about your infamy, 5.01. 69 P
whip to our tents, as roes /run o'er land. 5.02.309
come, thou child, | i'll whip thee with a rod. MND 3.02.410
as well a dark house and a whip as madmen do; AYL 3.02.401 P
for his presence must be the whip of the other. AWW 4.03. 36 P
to hinder | were (in your love) a whip to me; WT 1.02. 25
is well prepar'd | to whip this dwarfish war, JN 5.02.135
whip him till he leap over that same stool. 2H6 2.01.145 P
nay then whip me; he'll rather give her two. 3H6 3.02. 28
let's whip these stragglers o'er the seas again; R3 5.03.327
that was the whip of your bragg'd progeny | thou COR 1.08. 12
lest you shall chance to whip your information, 4.06. 54
go whip him 'fore the people's eyes — his 4.06. 61
a soldier's head | which will not prove a whip. 4.06.134
her whip of cricket's bone, the lash of film, ROM 1.04. 66
as phaeton would whip you to the west, | and 3.02. 3
the laws, your curb and whip, in their rough TIM 4.03.443
wilt thou whip thine own faults in other men? 5.01. 39
take heed, sirrah — the whip. LR 1.04.110 P
whip me such honest knaves. OTH 1.01. 49
and put in every honest hand a whip | to lash 4.02.142
whip me, ye devils, | from the possession of 5.02.277
take hence this jack and whip him. ANT 3.13. 93
whip him. 3.13. 96
whip him, fellows, | till like a boy you see him 3.13. 99
whom | he may at pleasure whip, or hang, or 3.13.150
marry, whip the gosling, i think i shall have PER 4.02. 86 P

WHIPPERS 1 FR 0.0001 REL FR 0 V 1 P
so ordinary that the whippers are in love too. AYL 3.02.404 P

WHIPPING 10 FR 0.0011 REL FR 1 V 9 P
and your deliverance with an unpitied whipping, MM 4.02. 13 P
is pressing to death, whipping, and hanging. 5.01.523 P
to see great hercules whipping a gig, | and LLL 4.03.165
at your whipping, and "spare not me"? AWW 2.02. 52 P
is very sequent to your whipping; 2.02. 54 P
you would answer very well to a whipping, if you 2.02. 55 P
and she shall have whipping cheer, i warrant her 2H4 5.04. 5 P
if you mean to save yourself from whipping, leap 2H6 2.01.140 P
after his desert, and who shall scape whipping? HAM 2.02.530 P
turn craver too, and so i shall scape whipping. PER 2.01. 89 P

WHIPS 7 FR 0.0008 REL FR 5 V 2 P
and goes me to the fellow that whips the dogs: TGV 4.04. 24 P
me no more ado, but whips me out of the chamber. 4.04. 28 P
impression of keen whips i'ld wear as rubies, MM 2.04.101
beadles in your town, and things call'd whips? 2H6 2.01.134
not all the whips of heaven are large enough — TIM 5.01. 61

for who would bear the whips and scorns of time, HAM 3.01. 69
whips out his rapier, cries, "a rat, a rat!" 4.01. 10

WHIP'ST 1 FR 0.0001 REL FR 1 V 0 P
her in that kind | for which thou whip'st her. LR 4.06.163

WHIPSTER 1 FR 0.0001 REL FR 1 V 0 P
but every puny whipster gets my sword. OTH 5.02.244

WHIPSTOCK 3 FR 0.0003 REL FR 2 V 1 P
for malvolio's nose is no whipstock. TN 2.03. 27 P
practic'd more the whipstock than the lance. PER 2.02. 51
he broke his whipstock and exclaim'd against TNK 1.02. 86

/WHIPT 1 FR 0.0001 REL FR 1 V 0 P
look you, i am /whipt and scourg'd with rods, 1H4 1.03.239

WHIPT 41 FR 0.0046 REL FR 14 V 27 P
play'd truant, and whipt top, i knew not what WIV 5.01. 25 P
plain–dealing, pompey, i shall have you whipt. MM 2.01.250 P
the valiant heart's not whipt out of his trade. 2.01.256
had rather it would please you i might be whipt. 5.01.506 P
whipt first, sir, and hang'd after. 5.01.507
nuptial finish'd, | let him be whipt and hang'd. 5.01.513
i whipt me behind the arras, and there heard it ADO 1.03. 60 P
bind him up a rod, as being worthy to be whipt. 2.01.220 P
to be whipt? what's his fault? 2.01.221 P
to be whipt; LLL 1.02.120 P
then shall hector be whipt for jaquenetta that 5.02.680 P
you'll be whipt for taxation one of these days. AYL 1.02. 84 P
to be whipt at the high cross every morning. SHR 1.01.132 P
you were lately whipt, sir, as i think. AWW 2.02. 50 P
and they were sons of mine, i'd have them whipt, 2.03. 87 P
would be proud, if our faults whipt them not, 4.03. 73 P
paris, from whence he was whipt for getting the 4.03.186 P
he shall be whipt through the army with this 4.03.233 P
but he was certainly whipt out of the court. WT 4.03. 89 P
there's no virtue whipt out of the court. 4.03. 92 P
came | and whipt th' offending adam out of him, H5 1.01. 29
let them be whipt through every market town, 2H6 2.01.155
for i have seen him whipt three market–days 4.02. 58 P
go see this rumorer whipt. COR 4.06. 48
whipt and tormented and — god–den, good fellow. ROM 1.02. 56
have such a fellow whipt for o'erdoing termagant HAM 3.02. 13 P
a dog must to kennel, he must be whipt out, when LR 1.04.112 P
this, let him be whipt that first finds it so. 1.04.164 P
and you lie, sirrah, we'll have you whipt. 1.04.181 P
they'll have me whipt for speaking true; 1.04.183 P
thou'lt have me whipt for lying; 1.04.184 P
and sometimes i am whipt for holding my peace. 1.04.185 P
who is whipt from tithing to tithing, and 3.04.134 P
thou shalt be whipt with wire, and stew'd in ANT 2.05. 65
you will be whipt. 3.13. 88
being whipt, | bring him again; 3.13.102
is he whipt? 3.13.131
since | thou hast been whipt for following him. 3.13.137
my messenger | he hath whipt with rods, dares me 4.01. 3
why, are /your beggars whipt then? PER 2.01. 90
for if all your beggars were whipt, i would wish 2.01. 92 P

WHIRL 3 FR 0.0003 REL FR 3 V 0 P
of both, | they whirl asunder and dismember me. JN 3.01.330
and the fift did whirl about | the other four in 4.02.183
and whirl along with thee about the globes. TIT 5.02. 49

WHIRL'D 1 FR 0.0001 REL FR 1 V 0 P
thus hath the course of justice whirl'd about, R3 4.04.105

WHIRLED 1 FR 0.0001 REL FR 1 V 0 P
my thoughts are whirled like a potter's wheel, 1H6 1.05. 19

WHIRLIGIG 1 FR 0.0001 REL FR 0 V 1 P
and thus the whirligig of time brings in his TN 5.01.376 P

WHIRLING 2 FR 0.0002 REL FR 2 V 0 P
to calm this tempest whirling in the court; TIT 4.02.160
these are but wild and whirling words, my lord. HAM 1.05.133

WHIRLPOOL 1 FR 0.0001 REL FR 0 V 1 P
and through flame, through /ford and whirlpool, LR 3.04. 53 P

WHIRLS 2 FR 0.0002 REL FR 2 V 0 P
and justice always whirls in equal measure: LLL 4.03.381
expectation whirls me round; TRO 3.02. 18

WHIRLWIND 3 FR 0.0003 REL FR 2 V 1 P
that, some whirlwind bear | unto a ragged, TGV 1.02.117
thee thither in a whirlwind. TIM 4.03.288
as i may say, whirlwind of your passion, you HAM 3.02. 6 P

WHIRLWINDS 3 FR 0.0003 REL FR 2 V 1 P
thy fame, as whirlwinds shake fair buds, | and SHR 5.02.140
bless thee from whirlwinds, star–blasting, and LR 3.04. 59 P
my sighs like whirlwinds labor hence to heave LUC 586

WHIRRING 1 FR 0.0001 REL FR 1 V 0 P
a lasting storm, | whirring me from my friends. PER 4.01. 20

WHISPER 30 FR 0.0034 REL FR 25 V 5 P
juno and ceres whisper seriously; TMP 4.01.125
to whisper and conspire against my youth? TGV 1.02. 43
whisper her ear, and tell her i and ursley ADO 3.01. 4
here, | what did you whisper in your lady's ear? LLL 5.02.436
what did the russian whisper in your ear? 5.02.443
that cranny shall pyramus and thisby whisper. MND 3.01. 71 P
poor souls, they are content | to whisper. 5.01.134
and thisby, | did whisper often, very secretly. 5.01.160
through which the fearful lovers are to whisper. 5.01.164
the blushes in my cheeks thus whisper me, | "we AWW 2.03. 69
i'll whisper with the general, and know his 4.03.296 P
we'll whisper o'er a couplet or two of most sage TN 3.04.378 P
your followers i will whisper to the business, WT 1.02.437
to his presence, whisper him in your behalfs; 4.04.797 P
mark how they whisper. JN 2.01.475
heads, | and whisper one another in the ear; 4.02.189
and lean–look'd prophets whisper fearful change, R2 2.04. 11
hand | will whisper music to my weary spirit. 2H4 4.05. 3
why whisper you, my lords, and answer not? 3H6 1.01.149
children | whisper the spirits of thine enemies R3 4.04.193
his color, but he came | to whisper wolsey), H8 1.01.179
nor i from troy come not to whisper with him. TRO 1.03.250
never admitted | a private whisper, no, not with COR 5.03. 7
some devil whisper curses in my ear, | and TIT 5.03. 11
if caesar hide himself, shall they not whisper, JC 2.02.100
at least, the whisper goes so. HAM 1.01. 80
/... | whose whisper o'er the world's diameter, 4.01. 41
ay, well said, whisper. OTH 2.01.168 P
what? did they never whisper? 4.02. 6
whistle | is as a whisper in the ears of death, PER 3.01. 9

WHISPER'D 3 FR 0.0003 REL FR 2 V 1 P
as you have whisper'd faithfully you were, | and AYL 2.07.192
of the news abroad, i mean the whisper'd ones, LR 2.01. 7 P
against | the horses of the sun, but whisper'd, TNK 1.02. 87

WHISPERING 3 FR 0.0003 REL FR 3 V 0 P
with whispering and most guilty diligence, | in MM 4.01. 38
is whispering nothing? WT 1.02.284
tell | a whispering tale in a fair lady's ear, ROM 1.05. 23

WHISPERINGS 1 FR 0.0001 REL FR 1 V 0 P
rain sacrificial whisperings in his ear, | make TIM 1.01. 81

WHISPERS 9 FR 0.0010 REL FR 9 V 0 P
so much my conscience whispers in your ear, JN 1.01. 42
the secret whispers of each other's watch. H5 4.pr. 7
and whispers to his pillow as to him | the 2H6 3.02.375
not speak | whispers the o'er–fraught heart, and MAC 4.03.210
and unwholesome in /their thoughts and whispers HAM 4.05. 82
and whispers in mine ear, "go not till he speak. PER 5.01. 96
mars's drum | and turn th' alarm to whispers; TNK 5.01. 81
knocks at my heart, and whispers in mine ear, VEN 659
cold, | she whispers in his ears a heavy tale, 1125

WHISP'RING 4 FR 0.0004 REL FR 3 V 1 P
with bated breath and whisp'ring humbleness, MV 1.03.124
they're here with me already, whisp'ring, WT 1.02.217
'tis well they are whisp'ring. 4.04.247 P
whisp'ring conspirator | with close–tongu'd LUC 769

WHISP'RINGS 1 FR 0.0001 REL FR 1 V 0 P
foul whisp'rings are abroad. MAC 5.01. 71

WHISSING 1 FR 0.0001 REL FR 0 V 1 P
dirt–rotten livers, whissing lungs, bladders TRO 5.01. 20 P

WHIST 1 FR 0.0001 REL FR 1 V 0 P
you have, and kiss'd, | the wild waves whist: TMP 1.02.378

WHISTLE 11 FR 0.0012 REL FR 7 V 4 P
tend to th' master's whistle. TMP 1.01. 7 P
to whistle /off these secrets, but you must be WT 4.04.245 P
this being done, let the law go whistle; 4.04.698 P
huswives that he heard the carmen whistle, and 2H4 3.02.318 P
hear the shrill whistle which doth order give H5 3.pr. 9
whistle then to me | as signal that thou hearest ROM 5.03. 7
time i shall sleep out, the rest i'll whistle. LR 2.02.156
i'ld whistle her off, and let her down the wind OTH 3.03.262
the seaman's whistle | is as a whisper in the PER 3.01. 8
we may go whistle; all the fat's i' th' fire. TNK 3.05. 39
where's your whistle, master? 4.01.149

WHISTLES 2 FR 0.0002 REL FR 2 V 0 P
treble, pipes | and whistles in his sound. AYL 2.07.163
the boatswain whistles, and | the master calls, PER 4.01. 63

/WHISTLING 1 FR 0.0001 REL FR 1 V 0 P
i have been worth the /whistling. LR 4.02. 29

WHISTLING 3 FR 0.0003 REL FR 3 V 0 P
to dance our ringlets to the whistling wind, MND 2.01. 86
and by his hollow whistling in the leaves 1H4 5.01. 5
whistling to th' air, which, but for vacancy, ANT 2.02.216

WHIT 19 FR 0.0021 REL FR 13 V 6 P
not a whit, when it jars so. TGV 4.02. 67 P
not a whit. WIV 1.01. 27 P
not a whit! MND 3.01. 16 P
not a whit, touchstone. AYL 3.02. 45 P
ay, sir! — ne'er a whit. SHR 1.01.235
so shall i no whit be behind in duty | to fair 1.02.174
no, not a whit, i find you passing gentle: 2.01.242
the waste is no whit lesser than thy land. R2 2.01.103
not a whit, i' faith, i lack some of thy 1H4 2.04.371 P
not a whit. 4.03. 2
woe, woe for england, not a whit for me! R3 3.04. 80
no, not a whit. TRO 5.01. 69
well, more or less, or ne'er a whit at all, TIT 4.02. 53
no, not a whit. ROM 4.04. 9
our youths and wildness shall no whit appear, JC 2.01.148
not a whit, we defy augury. HAM 5.02.219 P
not a whit, | your lady being so easy. CYM 2.04. 46
no whit less | than in his feats deserving it), 3.01. 6
yet him for this my love no whit disdaineth: SON 33.13

/WHITE 3 FR 0.0003 REL FR 1 V 2 P
i went to her in /white and cried "mum," and she WIV 5.05.197 P
might change or cease, /tears /his /white /hair, LR 3.01. 7
/in /tom's /belly /for /two /white /herring. 3.06. 31 P

WHITE 149 FR 0.0168 REL FR 109 V 40 P
sir, | the white cold virgin snow upon my heart TMP 4.01. 55
she is as white as a lily and as small as a wand TGV 2.03. 20 P
may give the dozen white luces in their coat. WIV 1.01. 16 P
the dozen white louses do become an old coat 1.01. 19 P
urchins, ouphes, and fairies, green and white, 4.04. 50
fairies, | finely attired in a robe of white. 4.04. 72
that you cannot see a white spot about her. 4.05.113 P
her father means she shall be all in white; 4.06. 35
i come to her in white, and cry "mum"; 5.02. 6 P
the white will decipher her well enough. 5.02. 9 P
fairies, black, grey, green, and white, | you 5.05. 37
em'rald tuffs, flow'rs purple, blue, and white, 5.05. 70
all the world drink brown and white bastard. MM 3.02. 3 P
which indeed is not under white and black, this ADO 5.01.305 P
my love is most immaculate white and red. LLL 1.02. 90 P
if she be made of white and red, | her faults 1.02. 99
faults are bred | and fears by pale white shown: 1.02.102
master, against the reason of white and red. 1.02.108 P
i beseech you a word. what is she in the white? 2.01.197
and to her white hand see thou do commend | this 3.01.168
to show his teeth as white as whale's bone; 5.02.332
by this white glove (how white the hand, god 5.02.411
by this white glove (how white the hand, god 5.02.411
that pure congealed white, high taurus' snow, MND 3.02.141
let me kiss | this princess of pure white, this 3.02.144
superfluity comes sooner by white hairs, but MV 1.02. 9 P
who, inward search'd, have livers white as milk, 3.02. 86
youth, by the white hand of rosalind, i am that AYL 3.02.394 P
in their new fustian, /their white stockings, SHR 4.01. 48 P
such war of white and red within her cheeks! 4.05. 30
'twas i won the wager, though you hit the white, 5.02.186
let the white death sit on thy cheek for ever, AWW 2.03. 71
whose red and white | nature's own sweet and TN 1.05.239
my lady has a white hand, and the mermidons are 2.03. 27 P
my shroud of white, stuck all with yew, | o, 2.04. 55
ere i could make thee open thy white hand | /and WT 1.02.103
in pure white robes, | like very sanctity, she 3.03. 22
the white sheet bleaching on the hedge, | with 4.03. 5
lawn as white as driven snow, | cypress black as 4.04.218
as soft as dove's down and as white as it, | or 4.04.363
by my white beard, | you offer him, if this be 4.04.404
francis, your white canvas doublet will sully. 1H4 2.04. 74 P
father's beard is turn'd white with the news. 2.04.359 P

more the pity, his white hairs do witness it, 2.04.468 P
there is not a white hair in your face but 2H4 1.02.160 P
a yellow cheek, a white beard, a decreasing leg, 1.02.181 P
with a white head and something a round belly. 1.02.188 P
bottle, i would i might never spit white again. 1.02.212 P
i perceiv'd the first white hair of my chin. 1.02.242 P
whose white investments figure innocence, | the 4.01. 45
and settled) left the liver white and pale, 4.03.104 P
how ill white hairs becomes a fool and jester! 5.05. 48
of it stands off as gross | as black and white, H5 2.02.104
by the white hand of my lady, he's a gallant 3.07. 93 P
a good soft pillow for that good white head 4.01. 14
a black beard will turn white, a curl'd pate 5.02.160 P
from off this brier pluck a white rose with me. 1H6 2.04. 30
i pluck this white rose with plantagenet. 2.04. 36
giving my verdict on the white rose side. 2.04. 48
lest, bleeding, you do paint the white rose red, 2.04. 50
in sign whereof i pluck a white rose too. 2.04. 58
shall dye your white rose in a bloody red. 2.04. 61
shall send between the red rose and the white 2.04.126
should leave me at the white hart in southwark? 2H6 4.08. 24 P
rest | until the white rose that i wear be dy'd 3H6 1.02. 33
would bring white hairs unto a quiet grave. 2.05. 40
the red rose and the white are on his face, 2.05. 97
saddle white surrey for the field to–morrow. R3 5.03. 64
we will unite the white rose and the red. 5.05. 19
came and puts me her white hand to his cloven TRO 1.02.119 P
indeed she has a marvell's white hand, i must 1.02.136 P
takes upon her to spy a white hair on his chin. 1.02.139 P
at the white hair that helen spied on troilus' 1.02.150 P
hairs on your chin — and one of them is white." 1.02.158 P
"two and fifty hairs," quoth he, "and one white. 1.02.161 P
that white hair is my father, and all the rest 1.02.161 P
with /these your white enchanting fingers 3.01.151
by this white beard, i'd fight with thee 4.05.209
dames | commit the war of white and damask in COR 2.01.216
hand, and turns up the white o' th' eye to his 4.05.196 P
this palliament of white and spotless hue, | and TIT 1.01.182
can never turn the swan's black legs to white, 4.02.102
dead, stabb'd with a white wench's black eye, ROM 2.04. 14 P
on the white wonder of dear juliet's hand, | and 3.03. 36
thus much of this will make | black white, foul TIM 4.03. 29
pity not honor'd age for his white beard, | he 4.03.112
but i shame | to wear a heart so white. MAC 2.02. 62
"in her excellent white bosom, these, etc." HAM 2.02.113 P
in the sweet heavens | to wash it white as snow? 3.03. 46
"white his shroud as the mountain snow" — 4.05. 36
"his beard was as white as snow, | /all flaxen 4.05.195
thunderbolts, | singe my white head! LR 3.02. 6
'gainst a head | so old and white as this. 3.02. 24
mildews the white wheat, and hurts the poor 3.04.118 P
be thy mouth or black or white, | tooth that 3.06. 66
so white, and such a traitor? 3.07. 37
goneril with a white beard? 4.06. 96 P
and told me i had the white hairs in my beard 4.06. 97 P
these white flakes | did challenge pity of them. 4.07. 29
an old black ram | is tupping your white ewe. OTH 1.01. 89
she'll find a white that shall her blackness 2.01.133
for the white | reprove the brown for rashness, ANT 3.11. 13
the white hand of a lady fever thee, | shake 3.13.138
white and azure lac'd | with blue of heaven's CYM 2.02. 22
so long a breeding as his white beard came to, 5.03. 17
the semblance | of their white flags display'd, PER 1.04. 72
silk | with fingers long, small, white as milk; 4.ch. 22
paphos might with the crow | vie feathers white. 4.ch. 33
blood, sir, white and red, you shall see a rose, 4.06. 34 P
as strong | as it is white, wast near to make TNK 1.01. 80
"he s' buy me a white cut, forth for to ride, 3.04. 22
and little luce with the white legs, and 3.05. 26
friend, you must eat no white bread; 3.05. 80
pure red and white, for yet no beard has blest 4.02.107
not wanton white, but such a manly color | next 4.02.124
sweet, solitary, white as chaste, and pure | as 5.01.139
owing | not a hair–worth of white, which some 5.04. 51
more white and red than doves or roses are: VEN 10
being red, she loves him best, and being white, 77
hue, | how white and red each other did destroy! 346
so white a friend engirts so white a foe: 364
so white a friend engirts so white a foe: 364
teaching the sheets a whiter hue than white, 398
was it not white? 643
whose wonted lily white | with purple tears, 1053
a purple flow'r sprung up, check'red with white, 1168
to praise the clear unmatched red and white LUC 11
virtue would stain that o'er with silver white. 56
in that white intituled | from venus' doves, 57
shame assail'd, the red should fence the white. 63
argued by beauty's red and virtue's white; 65
lay, | then white as lawn, the roses took away. 259
whose perfect white | show'd like an april daisy 394
who o'er the white sheet peers her whiter chin, 472
like a white hind under the gripe's sharp claws, 543
till with her own white fleece her voice 678
in speech it seem'd his beard, all silver white, 1405
let the priest in surplice white, | that PHT 13
and sable curls /all silver'd o'er with white; SON 12. 4
borne on the bier with white and bristly beard: 12. 8
nor did i wonder at the lily's white, | nor 98. 9
/one blushing shame, another white despair; 99. 9
a third, nor red nor white, had stol'n of both, 99.10
if snow be white, why then her breasts are dun; 130. 3
i have seen roses damask'd, red and white, | but 130. 5
in bloodless white and the encrimson'd mood, LC 201
whose white weighs down the airy scale of praise 226
there my white stole of chastity i daff'd, 297
or to turn white and sound at tragic shows; 308
WHITE–BEARDED 2 FR 0.0002 REL FR 0 V 2 P
but that the white–bearded fellow speaks it. ADO 2.03.118 P
youth, falstaff, that old white–bearded sathan. 1H4 2.04.463 P
WHITE–BEARDS 1 FR 0.0001 REL FR 1 V 0 P
white–beards have arm'd their thin and hairless R2 3.02.112
WHITE–FAC'D 1 FR 0.0001 REL FR 1 V 0 P
together with that pale, that white–fac'd shore, JN 2.01. 23
WHITE–FRIARS 1 FR 0.0001 REL FR 1 V 0 P
to white–friars, there attend my coming. R3 1.02.226
WHITE–HAIR'D 1 FR 0.0001 REL FR 1 V 0 P
he's white–hair'd, | not wanton white, but such TNK 4.02.123
WHITEHALL 1 FR 0.0001 REL FR 1 V 0 P
'tis now the king's, and call'd whitehall. H8 4.01. 97
WHITE–HANDED 1 FR 0.0001 REL FR 1 V 0 P
white–handed mistress, one sweet word with thee. LLL 5.02.230
WHITE–LIM'D 1 FR 0.0001 REL FR 1 V 0 P
ye white–lim'd walls! TIT 4.02. 98
WHITE–LIVER'D 2 FR 0.0002 REL FR 1 V 1 P
for bardolph, he is white–liver'd and red–fac'd; H5 3.02. 32 P
white–liver'd runagate, what doth he there? R3 4.04.464
WHITELY 1 FR 0.0001 REL FR 1 V 0 P
of all, | a whitely wanton with a velvet brow, LLL 3.01.196
WHITENESS 6 FR 0.0006 REL FR 5 V 1 P
whose whiteness so became them | as if but now TGV 3.01.229
cliffs, but i could find no whiteness in them. ERR 3.02.127 P
in angel whiteness beat away those blushes, ADO 4.01.161
sully | the purity and whiteness of my sheets WT 1.02.327
and the whiteness in thy cheek | is apter than 2H4 1.01. 68
which in round drops upon their whiteness stood. VEN 1170
WHITER 6 FR 0.0006 REL FR 6 V 0 P
and whiter than the paper it writ on | is the MV 2.04. 13
whiter than new snow upon a raven's back. ROM 3.02. 19
nor scar that whiter skin of hers than snow, OTH 5.02. 4
fresh lily, | and whiter than the sheets! CYM 2.02. 16
teaching the sheets a whiter hue than white, VEN 398
who o'er the white sheet peers her whiter chin, LUC 472
/WHITES 1 FR 0.0001 REL FR 1 V 0 P
/i'll /fetch /some /flax /and /whites /of /eggs LR 3.07.106
WHITES 1 FR 0.0001 REL FR 1 V 0 P
in whose comparison all whites are ink | writing TRO 1.01. 56
WHITEST 1 FR 0.0001 REL FR 1 V 0 P
calumny | the whitest virtue strikes. MM 3.02.187
WHITE–UPTURNED 1 FR 0.0001 REL FR 1 V 0 P
heaven | unto the white–upturned wond'ring eyes ROM 2.02. 29
WHITHER* *(also whe'er, whe'r, whether)*
/WHITHER* 2 FR 0.0002 REL FR 2 V 0 P
/whither? R2 4.01.314
/whither /you /will, /so /i /were /from /your 4.01.315
WHITHER* 97 FR 0.0109 REL FR 78 V 19 P
then tell me, whither were i best to send him? TGV 1.03. 24
sir valentine, whither away so fast? 3.01. 51
whither travel you? 4.01. 16
that leads toward mantua, whither they are fled. 5.02. 47
whither go you, george, hark you? WIV 2.01.149 P
well met, mistress page. whither go you? 3.02. 9 P
whither bear you this? 3.03.151 P
why, what have you to do whither they bear it? 3.03.154 P
fled | into this abbey, whither we pursu'd them, ERR 5.01.155
whither? ADO 2.01.186 P
soft, whither away so fast? LLL 4.03.184
god speed fair helena! whither away? MND 1.01.180
how now, spirit, whither wander you? 2.01. 1
whither goest thou? MV 2.04. 16
how now, wit, whither wander you? AYL 1.02. 56 P
o my poor rosalind, whither wilt thou go? 1.03. 90
whither to go, and what to bear with us, | and 1.03.101
why, whither shall we go? 1.03.106
why, whither, adam, wouldst thou have me go? 2.03. 29
no matter whither, so you come not here. 2.03. 30
such a wit, he might say, "wit, whither wilt?" 4.01.166 P
trow you whither i am going? SHR 1.02.164
sweet, | whither away, or /where is thy abode? 4.05. 38
not in heaven, whither god send her quickly! AWW 2.04. 11 P
whither are bound? 3.05. 33 P
i do beseech you, whither is he gone? 5.01. 27
i take it, to rossillion, | whither i am going. 5.01. 29
let me yet know of you whither you are bound. TN 2.01. 9 P
whither, my lord? cesario, husband, stay. 5.01.143
whither? WT 4.04.299
o, whither? 4.04.299
whither? 4.04.299
then whither goest? 4.04.308
say, whither? 4.04.308
of this escape and whither they are bound; 4.04.663
how now, rustics, whither are you bound? 4.04.715 P
whither dost thou go? JN 5.06. 3
then whither he goes, thither let me go. R2 5.01. 85
have you henceforth question me | whither i go, 1H4 2.03.104
whither i must, i must, and, to conclude, | this 2.03.105
kate, | whither i go, thither shall you go too; 2.03.115
/a fool go with thy soul, whither it goes! 5.03. 22
how now, my lord chief justice, whither away? 2H4 5.02. 1
o, whither shall we fly from this reproach? 1H6 1.01. 97
what means he now? go ask him whither he goes. 2.03. 28
whither away, sir john falstaff, in such haste? 3.02.104
whither away? 3.02.105
how now, sir william, whither were you sent? 4.04. 12
whither, my lord? 4.04. 13
hence, | i care not whither, for i beg no favor; 2H6 2.04. 92
whither goes vaux so fast? what news, i prithee? 3.02.367
ah, whither shall i fly to scape their hands? 3H6 1.03. 1
whither shall we fly? 2.03. 11
but love to go | whither the queen intends. 2.05.139
and whither fly the gnats but to the sun? 2.06. 9
but whither shall we then? 4.05. 20
good morrow, neighbor, whither away so fast? R3 2.03. 1
whither away? 2.03. 45
as much to you, good sister! whither away? 4.01. 7
wand'red away alone, | no man knows whither. 4.04.513
whither, if it please you, we may now withdraw 5.05. 11
sir thomas, | whither were you a–going? H8 1.03. 50
whither away so fast? 2.01. 1
whither so late? 5.01. 6
and whither go they? TRO 1.02. 2
lead on this preparation | whither 'tis bent. COR 1.02. 16
whither do you follow your eyes so fast? 2.01. 98 P
my first son, | whither /wilt thou go? 4.01. 34
whither wouldst thou convey | this growing image TIT 5.01. 44
whither should they come? ROM 1.02. 71
whither? to supper? 1.02. 73 P
whither art going? TIM 1.01.191 P
whither are you going? JC 3.03. 6 P
whither am i going? 3.03. 13 P
whither are they vanish'd? MAC 1.03. 80
whither should i fly? 4.02. 73
whither indeed, before /thy here–approach, | old 4.03.133
whither wilt thou lead me? HAM 1.05. 1
whither is he going? LR 2.04.296
he calls to horse, but will i know not whither. 2.04.297
or ice try whither your costard or my ballow be 4.06.241 P
whither will you that i go | to answer this your OTH 1.02. 84
sister's view, | whither straight i'll lead you. ANT 2.02.168
and the shelters whither | the routed fly; 3.01. 8
he purposeth to athens, whither, with what haste 3.01. 35
o, whither hast thou led me, egypt? 3.11. 51
whither bound? CYM 3.06. 57
and whither? 5.05.387
whither would you have me? PER 4.06.126 P
whither wilt thou have me? 4.06.153 P
but, good sir, | whither will you have me? 5.01.176
brought you to my house, | whither i invite you. 5.03. 27
pray you, whither go you? TNK 2.03. 60
whither? why, what a question's that! 2.03. 61
and whither now are you bound–a? 3.05. 64
as but to banish you, whither would you go? STM II.C 125
which madly hurries her she knows not whither: VEN 904
WHITING–TIME 1 FR 0.0001 REL FR 0 V 1 P
or — it is whiting–time — send him by your two WIV 3.03.132 P
WHITMORE 3 FR 0.0003 REL FR 3 V 0 P
the other, walter whitmore, is thy share. 2H6 4.01. 14
my name is walter whitmore. 4.01. 31
stay, whitmore, for thy prisoner is a prince, 4.01. 44
WHIT'ST 1 FR 0.0001 REL FR 1 V 0 P
is on me | which makes my whit'st part black. H8 1.01.209
WHITSTERS 1 FR 0.0001 REL FR 0 V 1 P
carry it among the whitsters in datchet–mead, WIV 3.03. 14 P
WHITSUN *(also wheeson)*
WHITSUN 2 FR 0.0002 REL FR 2 V 0 P
as i have seen them do | in whitsun pastorals. WT 4.04.134
were busied with a whitsun morris–dance; H5 2.04. 25
WHITTLE 1 FR 0.0001 REL FR 1 V 0 P
there's not a whittle in th' unruly camp | but i TIM 5.01.180
WHIZZING 1 FR 0.0001 REL FR 1 V 0 P
the exhalations whizzing in the air | give so JC 2.01. 44
/WHO 19 FR 0.0021 REL FR 15 V 4 P
best know | (/who least will seem to do so) my WT 3.02. 33
/man | /who /with /a /double /surety /binds /his 2H4 1.01.191
/who /knows /on /whom /fortune /would /then 4.01.131
/who, /when /my /heart, /all /mad /with /misery, TIT 3.02. 9
/who /maintains /'em? HAM 2.02.345 P
/peace, /who /comes /here? 5.02. 80
/into /this /scattered /kingdom, /who /already, LR 3.01. 31
/who /alone /suffers, /suffers /most /i' /th' 3.06.104
/who /since /possesses /chambermaids /and 4.01. 62 P
/do /those /villains /pity /who /are /punish'd 4.02. 54
/who /hath /he /left /behind /him /general? 4.03. 7 P
/she /was /a /queen | /over /her /passion, /who, 4.03. 14
/strove | /who /should /express /her /goodliest. 4.03. 17
/town, | /who /sometime, /in /his /better /tune, 4.03. 39
/who /is /conductor /of /his /people? 4.07. 87 P
/who, /having /seen /me /in /my /worst /estate, 5.03.210
/finding | /who /'twas /that /so /endur'd, /with 5.03.212
/but /who /was /this? 5.03.219
/who /in /disguise | /followed /his /enemy /king 5.03.220
WHO 1322 FR 0.1494 REL FR 1079 V 243 P
a brave vessel | (who had, no doubt, some noble TMP 1.02. 7
who | art ignorant of what thou art, nought 1.02. 17
how to deny them, who t' advance, and who | to 1.02. 80
t' advance, and who | to trash for overtopping, 1.02. 80
like one | who having into truth, by telling of 1.02.100
who being then appointed | master of this design 1.02.162
who was so firm, so constant, that this coil 1.02.207
who, with a charm join'd to their suff'red labor 1.02.231
who with age and envy | was grown into a hoop? 1.02.258
my slave, who never | yields us kind answer. 1.02.308
rock, | who hadst deserv'd more than a prison. 1.02.362
who with mine eyes (never since at ebb) beheld 1.02.436
who mak'st a show but dar'st not strike, thy 1.02.471
the marriage of your daughter, who is now queen. 2.01. 99 P
who is so far from italy removed | i ne'er again 2.01.111
eye, | who hath cause to wet the grief on't. 2.01.128
who are of such sensible and nimble lungs that 2.01.173 P
who, in this kind of merry fooling, am nothing 2.01.177 P
this | who shall be of as little memory | when 2.01.233
prudence, who | should not upbraid our course. 2.01.286
who with cloven tongues | do hiss me into 2.02. 13
of the isle with four legs, who hath got, as i 2.02. 66 P
they i cannot be, | who are surpris'd /withal; 3.01. 93
who am myself attach'd with weariness | to th' 3.03. 5
who, though they are of monstrous shape, yet, 3.03. 31
who would believe that there were mountaineers, 3.03. 44
who once again | i tender to thy hand. 4.01. 4
who with thy saffron wings upon my flow'rs 4.01. 78
of milan, who most strangely | upon this shore 5.01.160
say, say; who gave it thee? TGV 1.02. 37
why, sir, who bade you call her? 2.01. 9 P
who is that, servant? 2.04. 36 P
who, all enrag'd, will banish valentine; 2.06. 38
who art the table wherein all my thoughts | are 2.07. 3
wife | and turn her out to who will take her in: 3.01. 77
who then? his spirit? 3.01.195 P
who wouldst thou strike? 3.01.200 P
nor who 'tis i love; 3.01.268 P
i will try thee. tell me this: who begot thee? 3.01.293 P
ay, who art thou? 3.01.375 P
who, in my mood, i stabb'd unto the heart. 4.01. 49
who? silvia? 4.02. 23
who is silvia? 4.02. 39
who is that that spake? 4.02. 87
who calls? 4.03. 4
mine own, who is a dog as big as ten of yours, 4.04. 57 P
in love | who respects friend? 5.04. 54
who should be trusted, when one's right hand 5.04. 67
who by repentance is not satisfied | is nor of 5.04. 79
master parson, who writes himself armigero, in WIV 1.01. 9 P
page's wife, who even now gave me good eyes too, 1.03. 59 P
look who comes yonder. 2.01.157 P
who says this is improvident jealousy? 2.02.288 P
yonder is a most reverend gentleman, who, belike 3.01. 52 P
when your husband ask'd who was in the basket! 3.03.181 P
who ask'd them once or twice what they had in 3.05.101 P
ay, sir; like who more bold? 4.05. 54 P
who mutually hath answer'd my affection | (so 4.06. 10
jove, or who can blame me to piss my tallow? 5.05. 14 P
who comes here? 5.05. 15 P
this is strange. who hath got the right anne? 5.05.211 P
who, newly in the seat, that it may know | he MM 1.02.161

who i would be sorry should be thus foolishly 1.02.189 P
who may, in th' ambush of my name, strike home, 1.03. 41
peace and prosperity! who is't that calls? 1.04. 15
one who never feels | the wanton stings and 1.04. 58
sir, by my wife, who, if she had been a woman 2.01. 79 P
who is it that hath died for this offense? 2.02. 88
who, with our spleens, | would all themselves 2.02.122
the tempter, or the tempted, who sins most, ha? 2.02.163
who, falling in the flaws of her own youth, 2.03. 11
who will believe thee, isabel? 2.04.154
did i tell this, | who would believe me? 2.04.172
the great soldier who miscarried at sea? 3.01.210 P
who? 3.02.125 P
but who comes here? 3.02.189
he who the sword of heaven will bear | should be 3.02.261
the hand, | who hath a story ready for your ear. 4.01. 55
executioner, who in his office lacks a helper. 4.02. 9 P
who can do good on him? 4.02. 68
who call'd here of late? 4.02. 74
is that barnardine who is to be executed in th' 4.02.128 P
to the law than angelo who hath sentenc'd him. 4.02.158 P
who makes that noise there? 4.03. 24 P
who do prepare to meet him at the gates, | there 4.03.131
who knew of your intent and coming hither? 5.01.124
who knows that lodowick? 5.01.126
who is as free from touch or soil with her | as 5.01.141
who thinks he knows that he ne'er knew my body, 5.01.203
who should have died when claudio lost his head 5.01.488
who, wanting guilders to redeem their lives, ERR 1.01. 8
who, falling there to find his fellow forth 1.02. 37
quoth who? 2.01. 69
but soft, who wafts us yonder? 2.02.109 P
who, every word by all my wit being scann'd, 2.02.150
who, all for want of pruning, with intrusion 2.02.179
who talks within there? ho, open the door! 3.01. 38
who are those at the gate? 3.01. 48
who is that at the door that keeps all this 3.01. 61
spain, who sent whole armadoes of carrects to be 3.02.136 P
who would be jealous then of such a one? 4.02. 23
you, | by dromio here, who came in haste for it. 4.04. 84
who, but for staying on our controversy, | had 5.01. 20
who heard me to deny it or forswear it? 5.01. 25
who give their eyes the liberty of gazing? 5.01. 53
who put unluckily into this bay | against the 5.01.125
husband, | who i made lord of me and all i had, 5.01.137
then, | who parted with me to go fetch a chain, 5.01.221
who deciphers them? 5.01.335
o, my old master! who hath bound him here? 5.01.339
who is his companion now? ADO 1.01. 71 P
but i pray you, who is his companion? 1.01. 81 P
with who? 1.01.212 P
who comes here? 1.03. 40 P
who, the most exquisite claudio? 1.03. 50 P
and who, and who? 1.03. 52 P
and who, and who? 1.03. 52 P
will you not tell me who told you so? 2.01.125 P
nor will you not tell me who you are? 2.01.127 P
the flat transgression of a schoolboy, who, 2.01.223 P
and the rod he might have bestow'd on you, who, 2.01.230 P
your brother's honor, who hath made this match, 2.02. 37 P
who is thus like to be cozen'd with the 2.02. 38 P
who even now | is couched in the woodbine 3.01. 29
but who dare tell her so? 3.01. 74
nay, but i know who loves him. 3.02. 63 P
who, hero? 3.02.105 P
who think you the most desartless man to be 3.03. 9 P
much more a man who hath any honesty in him. 3.03. 64 P
who can blot that name | with any just reproach? 4.01. 80
who hath indeed, most like a liberal villain, 4.01. 92
who smirched thus and mir'd with infamy, | i 4.01.133
who lov'd her so, that, speaking of her foulness 4.01.153
who wrongs him? 5.01. 52
who have you offended, masters, that you are 5.01.226 P
who in the night overheard me confessing to this 5.01.234 P
who i believe was pack'd in all this wrong, 5.01.299
call beatrice to you, who i think hath legs. 5.02. 23 P
so much for praising myself, who, i myself will 5.02. 87 P
john is the author of all, who is fled and gone. 5.02. 99 P
who accus'd her | upon the error that you heard 5.04. 2
who dazzling so, that eye shall be his heed, LLL 1.01. 82
who devis'd this penalty? 1.01.124 P
one who the music of his own vain tongue | doth 1.01.166
who was sampson's love, my dear moth? 1.02. 75 P
consider who the king your father sends, | to 2.01. 2
who are the votaries, my loving lords, | that 2.01. 37
who are the rest? 2.01. 55
who, tend'ring their own worth from where they 2.01.244
who came? 4.01. 71 P
who overcame he? 4.01. 74 P
who gave thee this letter? 4.01.101
who is the shooter? who is the shooter? 4.01.108
who is the shooter? who is the shooter? 4.01.108
and who is your deer? 4.01.114
who now hangeth like a jewel in the ear of caelo 4.02. 4 P
who understandeth thee not, loves thee not. 4.02. 99 P
who is he comes here? 4.03. 42
who sees the heavenly rosaline, | that, like a 4.03.217
o, who can give an oath? 4.03.246
the law, | and who can sever love from charity? 4.03.362
a companion of the king's, who is intituled, 5.01. 7 P
who sent it? 5.02. 31
most meanly and in hushering | mend him who can. 5.02.329
but who comes here? MND 2.01.186
night and silence — who is here? 2.02. 70
but who is here? 2.02.100
who will not change a raven for a dove? 2.02.114
who would set his wit to so foolish a bird? 3.01.134 P
who would give a bird the lie, though he cry 3.01.135 P
who pyramus presented, in their sport, | forsook 3.02. 14
who more engilds the night | than all yon fiery 3.02.187
(who even but now did spurn me with his foot), 3.02.225
why, get you gone. who is't that hinders you? 3.02.318
who is next? 5.01.126 P
as who should say, "i am sir oracle, | and when MV 1.01. 93
i may neither choose who i would, nor refuse who 1.02. 23 P
choose who i would, nor refuse who i dislike; 1.02. 24 P
whereof who chooses his meaning chooses you, 1.02. 30 P
by any rightly but one who you shall rightly 1.02. 32 P
he doth nothing but frown, as who should say, 1.02. 46 P
but, alas, who can converse with a dumb show? 1.02. 73 P
who brings word the prince his master will be 1.02.125 P
who is he comes here? 1.03. 38 P
who then conceiving did in eaning time | fall 1.03. 87
who, if he break, thou mayst with better face 1.03.136
his wife who wins me by that means i told you, 2.01. 19
i should stay with the jew my master, who, god 2.02. 24 P
i should be rul'd by the fiend, who, saving your 2.02. 26 P
this is my true-begotten father, who, being more 2.02. 36 P
bassanio, who indeed gives rare new liveries. 2.02.109 P
see | lorenzo, who is thy new master's guest. 2.03. 6
who bids thee call? i do not bid thee call. 2.05. 7
who riseth from a feast | with that keen 2.06. 8
who are you? 2.06. 26
and my love indeed, | for who love i so much? 2.06. 30
and now who knows | but you, lorenzo, whether i 2.06. 30
this first, of gold, who this inscription bears, 2.07. 4
"who chooseth me shall gain what many men 2.07. 5
"who chooseth me shall get as much as he 2.07. 7
"who chooseth me must give and hazard all he 2.07. 9
"who chooseth me must give and hazard all he 2.07. 16
"who chooseth me shall get as much as he 2.07. 23
"who chooseth me shall gain what many men desire 2.07. 37
who went with him to search bassanio's ship. 2.08. 5
who told me, in the narrow seas that part | the 2.08. 28
"who chooseth me must give and hazard all he 2.09. 21
"who chooseth me shall gain what many men desire 2.09. 24
"who chooseth me shall get as much as he 2.09. 36
for who shall go about | to cozen fortune, and 2.09. 37
"who chooseth me shall get as much as he 2.09. 50
"who chooseth me shall have as much as he 2.09. 58
who dare scarce show his head on the rialto; 3.01. 45 P
who, inward search'd, have livers white as milk, 3.02. 86
but who comes here? 3.02.218
thy currish spirit | govern'd a wolf, who, 4.01.134
i have a wife who i protest i love; 4.01.290
who comes so fast in silence of the night? 5.01. 25
who comes with her? 5.01. 32
who calls? 5.01. 40 P
especially of my own people, who best know him, AYL 1.01.170 P
who perceiveth our natural wits too dull to 1.02. 52 P
prithee, who is't that thou mean'st? 1.02. 81 P
in mine eye, i can tell who should down. 1.02.215 P
look you, who comes here, a young man and an old 2.04. 20 P
who calls? 2.04. 67
the greenwood tree | who loves to lie with me, 2.05. 2
who doth ambition shun, | and loves to live i' 2.05. 38
who laid him down and bask'd him in the sun, 2.07. 15
who cries out on pride | that can therein tax 2.07. 70
who can come in and say that i mean her, | when 2.07. 77
but who comes here? 2.07. 87
who after me hath many a weary step | limp'd in 2.07.130
trow you who hath done this? 3.02.179 P
i prithee who? 3.02.183 P
nay, but who is it? 3.02.187 P
most petitionary vehemence, tell me who it is. 3.02.190 P
i prithee tell me who is it quickly, and speak 3.02.197 P
i'll tell you who time ambles withal, who time 3.02.309 P
who time ambles withal, who time trots withal, 3.02.310 P
who time trots withal, who time gallops withal, 3.02.310 P
gallops withal, and who he stands still withal. 3.02.311 P
i prithee, who doth he trot withal? 3.02.312 P
who ambles time withal? 3.02.318 P
who doth he gallop withal? 3.02.326 P
who stays it still withal? 3.02.330 P
me to speak, who was in his youth an inland man, 3.02.344 P
who hath promis'd to meet me in this place of 3.03. 44 P
who comes here? 3.04. 46 P
love, | who you saw sitting by me on the turf, 3.04. 49
who shut their coward gates on atomies, | should 3.05. 13
who might be your mother, | that you insult, 3.05. 35
"who ever lov'd that lov'd not at first sight?" 3.05. 82
who could be out, being before his belov'd 4.01. 81 P
look who comes here. 4.03. 5 P
who with her head nimble in threats approach'd 4.03.109
who quickly fell before him, in which hurtling 4.03.131
who gave me fresh array and entertainment, 4.03.143
love, | who led me instantly unto his cave, 4.03.145
ay, i know who 'tis; 5.01. 8 P
who is it? SHR in.1. 77
who for this seven years hath esteemed him | no in.1. 122
for who shall bear your part, | and be in padua 1.01.194
and then i know after who comes by the worst. 1.02. 14
who goes there? 1.02.140 P
but who comes here? 2.01. 38
who knows not where a wasp does wear his sting? 2.01.213
who woo'd in haste, and means to wed at leisure. 3.02. 11
who comes with him? 3.02. 64 P
who? that petruchio came? 3.02. 77 P
who is that calls so coldly? 4.01. 13 P
who knows not that? 4.01.101 P
who brought it? 4.01.160
but i, who never knew how to entreat, | nor 4.03. 7
as who should say, if i should sleep or eat, 4.03. 13
son, | who will of thy arrival be full joyous. 4.05. 70
but who is here? 5.01. 42 P
who shall begin? 5.02. 75
who comes here? AWW 1.01. 98
who ever strove | to show her merit, that did 1.01.226
who are sick | for breathing and exploit. 1.02. 16
who were below him | he us'd as creatures of 1.02. 41
who shuns thy love shuns all his love in me. 2.03. 73
base, is now | the praised of the king, who, so 2.03.172
who? god? 2.03.247 P
who was with him? 3.02. 83
unto my sick desires, | who then recovers. 4.02. 36
who had even tun'd his bounty to sing happiness 4.03. 9 P
who is a whale to virginity and devours up all 4.03.220 P
who pays before, but not when he does owe it. 4.03.230
yet who would have suspected an ambush where i 4.03.301 P
who cannot be crush'd with a plot? 4.03.325 P
who knows himself a braggart, | let him fear 4.03.334
who of herself is a good lady and would not have 5.02. 31 P
who hath for four or five removes come short 5.03.131
who by this i know | is here attending. 5.03.134
where did you buy it? or who gave it you? 5.03.271
who lent it you? 5.03.273
lord, | who hath abus'd me, as he knows himself, 5.03.298
who governs here? TN 1.02. 24
his son, her brother, | who shortly also died; 1.02. 39
who, sir andrew aguecheek? 1.03. 18 P
who are they? 1.03. 35 P
who saw cesario, ho? 1.04. 10
who of my people hold him in delay? 1.05.104 P
who was it? 2.04. 10
"jove knows i love, | but who? 2.05. 97
remember who commended thy yellow stockings, and 2.05.153 P
"thou canst not choose but know who i am. 2.05.174 P
who you are and what you would are out of my 3.01. 57 P
"remember who commended thy yellow stockings" — 3.04. 47 P
i care not who knows so much of my mettle. 3.04.272 P
who calls there? 4.02. 20 P
curate, who comes to visit malvolio the lunatic. 4.02. 21 P
"she loves another" — who calls, ha? 4.02. 79 P
who, i, sir? 4.02.100 P
who, with dagger of lath, | in his rage and his 4.02.126
who does beguile you? who does do you wrong? 5.01.140
who does beguile you? who does do you wrong? 5.01.140
who has done this, sir andrew? 5.01.179 P
who hath made this havoc with them? 5.01.202 P
who does infect her? WT 1.02.306
bohemia — who, if i | had servants true about 1.02.308
who mayst see | plainly as heaven sees earth and 1.02.314
son | (who i do think is mine and love as mine), 1.02.331
one | who, in rebellion with himself, will have 1.02.355
who have sped the better | by my regard, but 1.02.389
who taught' this? 2.01. 11
he who shall speak for her is afar off guilty 2.01.104
who is't that goes with me? 2.01.116
let him have knowledge who i am. 2.02. 2
for a worthy lady, | and one who much i honor. 2.02. 6
offer, | who but to-day hammered of this design, 2.02. 47
me, who professes | myself your loyal servant, 2.03. 53
tongue, who late hath beat her husband, | and 2.03. 92
and honor 'fore | who please to come and hear. 3.02. 42
remember you of my own lord, | who is lost too. 3.02.231
a man, who hath a daughter of most rare note. 4.02. 41 P
my father nam'd me autolycus, who being, as i am 4.03. 24 P
half a kiss to choose | who loves another best. 4.04.176
sea | with her who here i cannot hold on shore; 4.04.499
as your anchors, who | do their best office, if 4.04.570
they throng who should buy first, as if my 4.04.600 P
(who wants but something to be a reasonable man) 4.04.604 P
who have we here? 4.04.623
who, i may say, is no honest man, neither to his 4.04.700 P
he has a son, who shall be flay'd alive; 4.04.783 P
which who knows how that may turn back to my 4.04.834 P
who, on my life, | did perish with the infant. 5.01. 43
good paulina, | who hast the memory of hermione, 5.01. 50
make proselytes | of who she but bid follow. 5.01.109
who for bohemia bend, to signify | not only my 5.01.165
desires you to attach his son, who has | (his 5.01.182
who? camillo? 5.01.196
who now | has these poor men in question. 5.01.197
shepherd's son, who has not only his innocence 5.02. 64 P
who was most marble there chang'd color; 5.02. 89 P
julio romano, who, had he himself eternity and 5.02. 97 P
who would be thence that has the benefit of 5.02.109 P
be), who began to be much sea-sick, and himself 5.02.118 P
who, as you say, took pains to get this son, JN 1.01.121
who dares not stir by day must walk by night, 1.01.172
but who comes in such haste in riding-robes? 1.01.217
who was it, mother? 1.01.250
who lives and dares but say thou didst not well 1.01.271
who says it was, he lies, i say 'twas not. 1.01.276
a noble boy! who would not do thee right? 2.01. 18
who is it thou dost call usurper, france? 2.01.120
ay, who doubts that? 2.01.193
who is it that hath warn'd us to the walls? 2.01.201
who painfully with much expedient march | have 2.01.223
who by the hand of france this day hath made 2.01.302
who are at hand, triumphantly displayed, | to 2.01.309
then after fight who shall be king of it? 2.01.400
tell me, who knows. 2.01.543
who, having no external thing to lose | but the 2.01.571
the world, who of itself is peized well, | made 2.01.575
who in that sale sells pardon from himself; 3.01.167
who hath read or heard | of any kindred action 3.04. 13
look who comes here! 3.04. 17
hear'st thou the news abroad, who are arriv'd? 4.02.160
who, with his shears and measure in his hand, 4.02.196
who brought that letter from the cardinal? 4.03. 14
who speaks not truly, lies. 4.03. 92
who kill'd this prince? 4.03.103
that neptune's arms, who clippeth thee about, 5.02. 34
who else but i, | and such as to my claim are 5.02.100
who was he that said | king john did fly an hour 5.05. 16
who art thou? 5.06. 9
who thou wilt; 5.06. 9
how did he take it? who did taste to him? 5.06. 28
who didst thou leave to tend his majesty? 5.06. 32
who chaunts a doleful hymn to his own death, 5.07. 22
who half an hour since came from the dolphin, 5.07. 83
who, when they see the hour's ripe on earth, R2 1.02. 7
die, | who was the model of thy father's life. 1.02. 28
say who thou art | and why thou comest thus 1.03. 11
who hither come engaged by my oath | (which god 1.03. 17
both who he is and why he cometh hither | thus 1.03. 27
i, who ready here do stand in arms | to prove by 1.03. 36
who can hold a fire in his hand | by thinking on 1.03.294
and who abstains from meat that is not gaunt? 2.01. 76
who strongly hath set footing in this land: 2.02. 48
who shall hinder me? 2.02. 67
who gently would dissolve the bands of life, 2.02. 71
who, weak with age, cannot support myself. 2.02. 83
but who comes here? 2.03. 20
but who comes here? 2.03. 67
who all this while hath revell'd in the night, 3.02. 48
comfort, my liege, remember who you are. 3.02. 82
but who comes here? 3.02. 90
king, who lately landed | with some few private 3.03. 3
but who comes here? 3.03. 19
besides a clergyman | of holy reverence, who, i 3.03. 29
who wrought it with the king, and who perform'd 4.01. 4
and who perform'd | the bloody office of his 4.01. 4

who sets me else? 4.01. 57
who with willing soul | adopts /thee heir, and 4.01.108
and who sits here that is not richard's subject? 4.01.122
who are the violets now | that strew the green 5.02. 46
no matter then who see it. 5.02. 58
who is within there? 5.02. 74
but who comes here? 5.03. 22
he wishtly look'd on me | as who should say, "i 5.04. 8
like seely beggars | who, sitting in the stocks, 5.05. 26
who, travelling towards york, | with much ado 5.05. 73
of exton, who | lately came from the king, 5.05.100
a son who is the theme of honor's tongue, 1H4 1.01. 81
who is sweet fortune's minion and her pride, 1.01. 83
who, i rob? i a thief? not i, by my faith. 1.02.138 P
who doth permit the base contagious clouds | to 1.02.198
who therewith angry, when it next came there, 1.03. 40
who, on my soul, hath willfully betray'd | the 1.03. 81
who then, affrighted with their bloody looks, 1.03.104
who strook this heat up after i was gone? 1.03.139
who studies day and night | to answer all the 1.03.184
who bears hard | his brother's death at bristow, 1.03.270
o lord, sir, who do you mean? 2.04. 72 P
the shoulders, you care not who sees your back. 2.04.149 P
who shall say me nay? 3.01.116
have you inquir'd yet who pick'd my pocket? 3.03. 53 P
who, i? 3.03. 62 P
who leads his power? 4.01. 18
who is to bear me like a thunderbolt | against 4.01.120
suff'red his kinsman march | (who is, if every 4.03. 94
thence, | who with them was a rated sinew too, 4.04. 17
who hath it? 5.01.136 P
who, never so tame, so cherish'd and lock'd up, 5.02. 10
soft, who are you? 5.03. 32 P
but who comes here? 5.03. 38 P
the king himself, who, douglas, grieves at heart 5.04. 29
thee, | who never promiseth but he means to pay. 5.04. 43
counterfeit of a man who hath not the life of a 5.04.116 P
to see what friends are living, who are dead. 5.04.161
scroop, | who, as we hear, are busily in arms. 5.05. 38
and who but rumor, who but only i, | make 2H4 in 11
and who but rumor, who but only i, | make in 11
who in a bloody field by shrewsbury | hath in 24
who keeps the gate here ho? where is the earl? 1.01. 1
who i sent | on tuesday last to listen after 1.01. 28
who, he? 1.01. 56
it was, my lord, who lin'd himself with hope, 1.03. 27
of an house | beyond his power to build it, who, 1.03. 59
who is it like should lead his forces hither? 1.03. 81
but who is substituted against the french, | i 1.03. 84
who then persuaded you to stay at home? 2.03. 15
who knocks so loud at door? 2.04.352 P
who take the ruffian /billows by the top, 3.01. 22
soul, | who like a brother toil'd in my affairs, 3.01. 62
who in their seeds | and weak beginning lie 3.01. 84
who is next? 3.02.170 P
who hath not heard it spoken | how deep you were 4.02. 16
who shall believe | but you misuse the reverence 4.02. 22
the heart, who, great and puff'd up with this 4.03.111 P
who saw the duke of clarence? 4.05. 7
liege, | who undertook to sit and watch by you. 4.05. 52
where is the crown? who took it from my pillow? 4.05. 57
dead, | and tell him who hath sent me after him. 5.02. 41
who hath writ me down | after my seeming. 5.02.128
who, i? 5.03. 39 P
who knocks? 5.03. 71 P
who, prologue–like, your humble patience pray, H5 pr 33
who, holding in disdain the german women | for 1.02. 48
who died within the year of our redemption 1.02. 60
who usurp'd the crown | of charles the duke of 1.02. 69
who was the son | to lewis the emperor, and 1.02. 75
tenth, | who was sole heir to the usurper capet, 1.02. 78
who on the french ground play'd a tragedy, 1.02.106
who will make road upon us | with all advantages 1.02.138
who hath been still a giddy neighbor to us; 1.02.145
who, busied in his /majesty, surveys | the 1.02.197
who are the late commissioners? 2.02. 61
for who is he, whose chin is but enrich'd | with 3.pr. 22
who talks of my nation? 3.02.124 P
who came off bravely, who was shot, who 3.06. 73 P
who came off bravely, who was shot, who 3.06. 73 P
who was shot, who disgrac'd, what terms the 3.06. 74 P
who when they were in health, i tell thee, 3.06.148
bears your praises, who would trot as well, were 3.07. 76 P
who will go to hazard with me for twenty 3.07. 85 P
himself, and he said he car'd not who knew it. 3.07.108 P
who hath measur'd the ground? 3.07.127 P
who like a foul and ugly witch doth limp | so 4.pr. 21
now, who will behold | the royal captain of this 4.pr. 28
who goes there? 4.01. 90 P
who to disobey were against all proportion of 4.01.145 P
who, with a body fill'd and vacant mind, | gets 4.01.269
who twice a day their wither'd hands hold up 4.01.299
who in unnecessary action swarm | about our 4.02. 27
gold, | nor care i who doth feed upon my cost; 4.03. 25
who hath sent thee now? 4.03. 88
majesty's countryman, i care not who know it. 4.07.112 P
who, if alive and ever dare to challenge this 4.07.126 P
who serv'st thou under? 4.07.147 P
who, though i speak it before his face, if he be 5.02.241 P
who cannot see many a fair french city for one 5.02.317 P
who ever saw the like? 1H6 1.02. 22
who would e'er suppose | they had such courage 1.02. 35
who willed you? 1.03. 11
as who should say, "when i am dead and gone, 1.04. 93
here is the talbot, who would speak with him? 2.02. 37
well, well, come on, who else? 2.04. 55
who preferreth peace | more than i do, except i 3.01. 33
who should be pitiful, if you be not? 3.01.109
or who should study to prefer a peace, | if holy 3.01.110
who shall be the speaker? 3.02. 60
who craves a parley with the burgundy? 3.03. 37
who join'st thou with, but with a lordly nation 3.03. 62
ill, | who then but english henry will be lord, 3.03. 66
who in a moment even with the earth | shall lay 4.02. 12
who now is girdled with a waist of iron | and 4.03. 20
who in proud heart | doth stop my cornets, were 4.03. 24
who two hours since | i met in travel toward his 4.03. 35
who with me | set from our o'ermatch'd forces 4.04. 10
who, ring'd about with bold adversity, | cries 4.04. 14
boy, he smiles, methinks, as who should say, 4.07. 27
to know who hath obtain'd the glory of the day. 4.07. 52
who art thou? 5.03. 50
who is there? 2H6 1.03. 33 P
since thou wert king — as who is king but thou? 1.03.123
as who, my lord? 2.01. 29
by good saint albon, who said, "simon, come; 2.01. 89
who after edward the third's death reign'd as 2.02. 20
who married edmund mortimer, earl of march; 2.02. 36
king, | who kept him in captivity till he died. 2.02. 42
earl of cambridge, who was | to edmund langley, 2.02. 45
of march, who was the son | of edmund mortimer, 2.02. 48
son | of edmund mortimer, who married philippe, 2.02. 49
who cannot steal a shape that means deceit? 3.01. 79
who can accuse me? 3.01.103
wolves are gnarling who shall gnaw thee first. 3.01.192
who being accus'd a crafty murtherer, | his 3.01.254
it skills not greatly who impugns our doom. 3.01.281
who, cherish'd in your breasts, will sting your 3.01.344
and care not who they sting in his revenge. 3.02.127
who, in the conflict that it holds with death, 3.02.164
why, warwick, who should do the duke to death? 3.02.179
who finds the heifer dead and bleeding fresh, 3.02.188
who finds the partridge in the puttock's nest 3.02.191
who with their drowsy, slow, and flagging wings 4.01. 5
who in contempt shall hiss at thee again; 4.01. 78
but who can cease to weep and look on this? 4.04. 4
he nods at us, as who should say, i'll be even 4.07. 94 P
who loves the king, and will embrace his pardon, 4.08. 14
who hateth him and honors not his father, 4.08. 16
who would live turmoiled in the court | and may 4.10. 16
who would not buy thee dear? 5.01. 5
cade, | who since i heard to be discomfited. 5.01. 63
who, being suffer'd, with the bear's fell paw 5.01.153
who can be bound by any solemn vow | to do a 5.01.184
of salisbury, who can report of him, | that 5.03. 1
who in rage forgets | aged contusions and all 5.03. 2
i'll plant plantagenet, root him up who dares. 3H6 1.01. 48
who made the dolphin and the french to stoop, 1.01.108
who can be patient in such extremes? 1.01.215
who having pinch'd a few and made them cry, 2.01. 16
who crown'd the gracious duke in high despite, 2.01. 59
who look'd full gently on his warlike queen, 2.01.123
who thunders to his captives blood and death, 2.01.127
who scapes the lurking serpent's mortal sting? 2.02. 15
who hath not seen them, even with those wings 2.02. 29
who should succeed the father but the son? 2.02. 94
and i, who at his hands receiv'd my life, | have 2.05. 67
and who shines now but henry's enemies? 2.06. 10
see who it is. 2.06. 44
who, not contented that he lopp'd the branch 2.06. 47
clifford, dost thou know who speaks to thee? 2.06. 61
to who, my lord? 3.02.112
fift, | who by his prowess conquered all france: 3.03. 86
who goes there? 4.03. 26
who attended him | in secret ambush on the 4.06. 82
who should that be? belike unlook'd–for friends. 5.01. 14
confess who set thee up and pluck'd thee down, 5.01. 26
who gave his blood to lime the stones together, 5.01. 84
ah, who is nigh? 5.02. 5
and tell me who is victor, york or warwick? 5.02. 6
for who liv'd king, but i could dig his grave? 5.02. 21
and who durst smile when warwick bent his brow? 5.02. 22
that who finds edward | shall have a high reward 5.05. 9
but who comes here? R3 1.01.121
who is it that complains unto the king | that i, 1.03. 43
to who in all this presence speaks your grace? 1.03. 54
why, who knows not so? 1.03. 92
clarence, who i indeed have cast in darkness, 1.03.326
who from my cabin tempted me to walk | upon the 1.04. 12
bulk, | who almost burst to belch it in the sea. 1.04. 41
who spake aloud, "what scourge for perjury | can 1.04. 50
who sent you hither? 1.04.171
or who pronounc'd | the bitter sentence of poor 1.04.185
who made thee then a bloody minister, | when 1.04.220
who shall reward you better for my life | than 1.04.230
who knows not that the gentle duke is dead? 2.01. 80
who knows not he is dead? who knows he is? 2.01. 82
who knows not he is dead? who knows he is? 2.01. 82
who slew to–day a riotous gentleman | lately 2.01.101
who sued to me for him? 2.01.107
who (in my wrath) | kneel'd /at my feet and bid 2.01.107
who spoke of brotherhood? 2.01.109
who spoke of love? 2.01.109
who told me how the poor soul did forsake | the 2.01.110
who told me, in the field at tewksbury, | when 2.01.112
who told me, when we both lay in the field 2.01.115
you cannot guess who caus'd your father's death. 2.02. 19
who shall hinder me to wail and weep, | to chide 2.02. 34
who they shall be that straight shall post to 2.02.142
for emulation who shall now be nearest | will 2.03. 25
when the sun sets, who doth not look for night? 2.03. 34
i prithee, pretty york, who told thee this? 2.04. 31
if 'twere not she, i cannot tell who told me. 2.04. 34
who hath committed them? 2.04. 44
and those who have the wit to claim the place. 3.01. 50
who knocks? 3.02. 2
think themselves as safe | as thou and i, who 3.02. 67
who knows the lord protector's mind herein? 3.04. 7
who is most inward with the noble duke? 3.04. 8
who builds his hope in air of your good looks 3.04. 98
they smile at me who shortly shall be dead. 3.04.107
who haply may | misconster us in him and wail 3.05. 60
who is so gross | that cannot see this palpable 3.06. 10
me, | who, earnest in the service of my god, 3.07.106
who meets us here? 4.01. 1
i am their mother, who shall bar me from them? 4.01. 21
who i did suborn | to do this piece of /ruthless 4.03. 4
who comes here? 4.04. 8
ah, who hath any cause to mourn but we? 4.04. 34
who sues, and kneels, and says, "god save the 4.04. 94
who intercepts me in my expedition? 4.04.136
well then, who dost thou mean shall be her king? 4.04.265
who /should /be /else? 4.04.266
and who is england's king but great york's heir? 4.04.472
who answer'd him, they came from buckingham 4.04.525
who hath descried the number of the traitors? 5.03. 9
who prays continually for richmond's good. 5.03. 84
'zounds, who is there? 5.03.208
who saw the sun to–day? 5.03.277
and who doth lead them but a paltry fellow, 5.03.323
who (but for dreaming on this fond exploit) 5.03.330
who did guide — | i mean, who set the body and H8 1.01. 45
who set the body and the limbs | of this great 1.01. 46
i pray you, who, my lord? 1.01. 49
th' king) t' appoint | who should attend on him? 1.01. 75
a full hot horse, who being allow'd his way, 1.01.133
for worthy wolsey | (who cannot err), he did it. 1.01.174
the spinsters, carders, fullers, weavers, who, 1.02. 33
who was enroll'd 'mongst wonders, and when we, 1.02.119
who fed him every minute | with words of 1.02.149
meant to act upon | th' usurper richard, who, 1.02.196
then deputy of ireland, who remov'd, | earl 2.01. 42
nicholas vaux, | who undertakes you to your end. 2.01. 97
who first rais'd head against usurping richard, 2.01.108
who am i? 2.02. 66
who can be angry now? 2.02. 88
lo, who comes here? 2.03. 49
and who knows yet | but from this lady may 2.03. 77
this business, | who deem'd our marriage lawful; 2.04. 53
land, who are assembled | to plead your cause. 2.04. 60
yourself, who ever yet | have stood to charity, 2.04. 85
that man i' th' world who shall report he has 2.04.135
who had been hither sent on the debating | /a 2.04.174
the smile of heaven, who had | commanded nature, 2.04.188
who commands you | to render up the great seal 3.02.228
who dare cross 'em, | bearing the king's will 3.02.234
who may that be, i pray you? 4.01.108
who grieves much for your weakness, and by me 4.02.117
and who dare speak | one syllable against him? 5.01. 38
who hath so far | given ear to our complaint, of 5.01. 47
who return'd her thanks | in the great'st 5.01. 64
who waits there? 5.02. 4
who holds his state at door 'mongst pursuivants, 5.02. 24
who waits there? 5.02. 39
and hit that woman, who cried out "clubs!", 5.03. 50 P
who from the sacred ashes of her honor | shall 5.04. 45
who were those went by? TRO 1.02. 1
who comes here? 1.02. 37 P
who, troilus? 1.02. 60 P
there's laying on, take't off who will, as they 1.02.207 P
who said he came hurt home to–day? 1.02.214 P
who, as ulysses says, opinion crowns | with an 1.03.186
who in /this dull and long–continued truce | is 1.03.262
who may you else oppose | that can from hector 1.03.333
distill'd | out of our virtues, who miscarrying, 1.03.351
who broils in loud applause, and make him fall 1.03.378
who wears his wit in his belly and his guts in 2.01. 73 P
farewell. who shall answer him? 2.01.127
more ready to cry out, "who knows what follows?" 2.02. 13
who marvels then, when helenus beholds | a 2.02. 42
look you, who comes here? 2.03. 68 P
who, thersites? 2.03. 92 P
who play they to? 3.01. 21 P
who shall i command, sir? 3.01. 26 P
of paris my lord, who is there in person; 3.01. 31 P
who? my cousin cressida? 3.01. 34 P
who shall be true to us, | when we are so 3.02.124
right with right wars who shall be most right! 3.02.172
who do methinks find out | some thing not worth 3.03. 90
who, in his circumstance, expressly proves 3.03.114
who, like an arch, reverb'rate | the voice again 3.03.120
as who should say there were wit in this head, 3.03.254 P
who, i? 3.03.268 P
who most humbly desires you to invite hector to 3.03.284 P
see, ho! who is that there? 4.01. 1
who, in your thoughts, deserves fair helen best, 4.01. 54
who! 4.02. 54 P
how now? what's the matter? who was here? 4.02. 78 P
who, i? 4.04.102
who must we answer? 4.05.176
who neither looks upon the heaven nor earth, 4.05.281
who keeps the tent now? 5.01. 10 P
who calls? 5.02. 2
who should withhold me? 5.03. 51
who hath done to–day | mad and fantastic 5.05. 37
who shall tell priam so, or hecuba? 5.10. 15
soft, who comes here? COR 1.01. 50 P
o' th' state, who care for you like fathers, 1.01. 77
be restrain'd, | who is the sink a' th' body — 1.01.122
who deserves greatness | deserves your hate; 1.01.176
who desires most that | which would increase his 1.01.178
the city | you cry against the noble senate, who 1.01.186
like to rise, | who thrives, and who declines; 1.01.193
like to rise, | who thrives, and who declines; 1.01.193
enemy | (who is of rome worse hated than of you) 1.02. 13
who upon the sudden | clapp'd to their gates. 1.04. 50
who sensibly outdares his senseless sword | and, 1.04. 53
mother, | who has a charter to extol her blood, 1.09. 14
pray you, who does the wolf love? 2.01. 7 P
who, in a cheap estimation, is worth all your 2.01. 90 P
as if that whatsoever god who leads him | were 2.01.219
war, who have their provand | only for bearing 2.01.251
have flatter'd the people, who ne'er lov'd them; 2.02. 8 P
ascent is not by such easy degrees as those who, 2.02. 26 P
son, | who after great hostilius here was king; 2.03.240
who lack not virtue, no, nor power, but that 3.01. 73
and such a one as he, who puts his "shall," 3.01.105
who was wont | to call them woollen vassals, 3.02. 8
who bow'd but in my stirrup, bend like his 3.02.119
and exercise | are still together, who twin, as 4.04. 15
martius, who hath done | to thee particularly, 4.05. 65
our dastard nobles, who | have all forsook me, 4.05. 75
who now are here, taking their leaves of me, 4.05.133
me, | who am prepar'd against your territories, 4.05.134
who, my master? 4.05.164 P
blush that the world goes well, who rather had, 4.06. 5
who, hearing of our martius' banishment, 4.06. 43
and beat the messenger who bids beware | of what 4.06. 55
revolt, and who resists | are mock'd for valiant 4.06.103
who is't can blame him? 4.06.105
who shall ask it? 4.06.108
clusters, | who did hoot him out o' th' city. 4.06.123
fish, who takes it | by sovereignty of nature. 4.07. 34
who loved him | in a most dear particular. 5.01. 2

who, as i hear, mean to solicit him | for mercy 5.01. 72
who like a block hath denied my access to thee. 5.02. 78 P
who being so heighten'd, | he watered his new 5.06. 21
who wears my stripes impress'd upon him, that 5.06.107
who have we here? TIT 2.03. 55
who hath abandoned her holy groves | to see the 2.03. 58
o, tell me who it is, for ne'er till now | was i 2.03.220
who art thou that lately didst descend | into 2.03.248
who found this letter? 2.03.293
who 'twas that cut thy tongue and ravish'd thee. 2.04. 2
who is this? 2.04. 11
who, though they cannot answer my distress, 3.01. 38
but who comes with our brother marcus here? 3.01. 58
speak, gentle sister, who hath mart'red thee? 3.01. 81
o, say thou for her, who hath done this deed? 3.01. 87
who marks the waxing tide grow wave by wave, 3.01. 95
nor tongue to tell me who hath mart'red thee. 3.01.107
soft, who comes here? 4.02. 51
as who should say, "old lad, i am thine own." 4.02.121
and who should find them but the empress' 4.03. 74
as who would say, in rome no justice were. 4.04. 20
who threats, in course of this revenge, to do 4.04. 67
but who comes here, led by a lusty goth? 5.01. 19
who, when he knows thou art the empress' babe, 5.01. 35
who should i swear by? 5.01. 71
who doth molest my contemplation? 5.02. 9
who leads towards rome a band of warlike goths, 5.02.113
what, was she ravish'd? tell who did the deed. 5.03. 53
or who hath brought the fatal engine in | that 5.03. 86
who drown'd their enmity in my true tears, | and 5.03.107
who set this ancient quarrel new abroach? ROM 1.01.104
who, nothing hurt withal, hiss'd him in scorn. 1.01.112
till the prince came, who parted either part. 1.01.115
and gladly shunn'd who gladly fled from me. 1.01.130
tell me in sadness, who is that you love? 1.01.199
groan? why, no; | but sadly tell me, who? 1.01.201
where i may read who pass'd that passing fair? 1.01.236
and these, who, often drown'd, could never die, 1.02. 90
how now, who calls? 1.03. 5
lawyers' fingers, who straight dream on fees; 1.04. 73
o'er ladies' lips, who straight on kisses dream, 1.04. 74
who woos | even now the frozen bosom of the 1.04.100
who is already sick and pale with grief | that 2.02. 5
a name | i know not how to tell thee who i am. 2.02. 54
and the place death, considering who thou art, 2.02. 64
/pardon–me's, who stand so much on the new form, 2.04. 33 P
benvolio, who began this bloody fray? 3.01.151
who, all as hot, turns deadly point to point, 3.01.160
romeo, | who had but newly entertain'd revenge, 3.01.171
who now the price of his dear blood doth owe? 3.01.183
who ever would have thought it? 3.02. 42
for who is living, if those two are gone? 3.02. 68
who, even in pure and vestal modesty, | still 3.03. 38
who knocks so hard? 3.03. 78
who is't that calls? 3.05. 65
one who, to put thee from thy heaviness, | hath 3.05.108
who, raging with thy tears, and they with them, 3.05.135
who calls so loud? 5.01. 57
who bare my letter then to romeo? 5.02. 13
who is it? 5.03.129
who else? 5.03.144
dead, | who here hath lain this two days buried. 5.03.176
look who comes here; will you be chid? TIM 1.01.176
who lives that's not depraved or depraves? 1.02.140
who dies that bears not one spurn to their 1.02.141
who is not timon's? 2.02.166
who, having great and instant occasion to use 3.01. 18 P
who, the lord timon? 3.02. 1 P
who can call him | his friend that dips in the 3.02. 65
who bates mine honor shall not know my coin. 3.03. 26
who cannot keep his wealth must keep his house. 3.03. 41
who can speak broader than he that has no house 3.04. 63 P
who in hot blood | hath stepp'd into the law, 3.05. 11
who cannot condemn rashness in cold blood? 3.05. 53
but who is man that is not angry? 3.05. 57
who, stuck and spangled /with /your flatteries, 3.06. 91
who would not wish to be from wealth exempt, 4.02. 31
who would be so mock'd with glory, or to live 4.02. 33
who then dares to be half so kind again? 4.02. 40
who dares? 4.03. 13
who dares | in purity of manhood stand upright 4.03. 13
who seeks for better of thee, sauce his palate 4.03. 24
yield him who all the human sons do hate, | from 4.03.185
myself, | who had the world as my confectionary, 4.03.260
who in spite put stuff | to some she–beggar and 4.03.272
who, without those means thou talk'st of, didst 4.03.313 P
who can bring noblest minds to basest ends! 4.03.464
athens, who have thought | on special dignities, 5.01.141
who, like a boar too savage, doth root up | his 5.01.165
who once a day with his embossed froth | the 5.01.217
"timon is dead, who hath outstretch'd his span: 5.03. 3
who were the motives that you first went out; 5.04. 27
here lie i, timon, who, alive, all living men 5.04. 72
who else would soar above the view of men, | and JC 1.01. 74
ha? who calls? 1.02. 13
who is it in the press that calls on me? 1.02. 15
who offer'd him the crown? 1.02.232
for who so firm that cannot be seduc'd? 1.02.312
who glaz'd upon me, and went surly by, | without 1.03. 21
with their fear, who swore they saw | men, all 1.03. 24
who ever knew the heavens menace so? 1.03. 44
let it be who it is; 1.03. 80
this foot of mine as far | as who goes farthest. 1.03.120
at the door, | who doth desire to see you. 2.01. 71
who rated him for speaking well of pompey; 2.01.216
who did hide their faces | even from darkness. 2.01.277
soft, who comes here? a friend of antony's. 3.01.122
who else must be let blood, who else is rank; 3.01.152
who else must be let blood, who else is rank; 3.01.152
who is here so base that would be a bondman? 3.02. 29 P
who is here so rude that would not be a roman? 3.02. 30 P
who is here so vile that will not love his 3.02. 32 P
mourn'd by mark antony, who, though he had no 3.02. 41 P
wrong, | who (you all know) are honorable men. 3.02.124
live, | who is your sister's son, mark antony. 4.01. 5
and took his voice who should be prick'd to die 4.01. 16
who, much enforced, shows a hasty spark, | and 4.03.112
who comes here? 4.03.275
hands, | who to philippi here consorted us. 5.01. 82
who, having some advantage on octavius, | took 5.03. 6
who will go with me? 5.04. 2
who like a good and hardy soldier fought MAC 1.02. 4
who comes here? 1.02. 45
who neither beg nor fear | your favors nor your 1.03. 60
who was the thane lives yet, | but under heavy 1.03.109
who did report | that very frankly he confess'd 1.04. 4
the king, who all–hail'd me 'thane of cawdor,' 1.05. 7 P
who, were't so, | would have inform'd for 1.05. 32
who, almost dead for breath, had scarcely more 1.05. 36
who should against his murtherer shut the door, 1.07. 15
who dares /do more is none. 1.07. 47
who shall bear the guilt | of our great quell? 1.07. 71
who dares receive it other, | as we shall make 1.07. 77
hark! who lies i' th' second chamber? 2.02. 17
who was it that thus cried? 2.02. 41
who committed treason enough for god's sake, yet 2.03. 9 P
who can be wise, amaz'd, temp'rate, and furious, 2.03.108
who could refrain, | that had a heart to love, 2.03.116
is't known who did this more than bloody deed? 2.04. 22
who wrought with them, and all things else that 3.01. 81
who wear our health but sickly in his life, 3.01.106
but wail his fall | who i myself struck down. 3.01.122
but who did bid thee join with us? 3.03. 1
who did strike out the light? 3.03. 19
who may i rather challenge for unkindness | than 3.04. 41
son, | spiteful and wrathful, who (as others do) 3.05. 12
who cannot want the thought, how monstrous | it 3.06. 8
and hums, as who should say, "you'll rue the 3.06. 42
proud, and take no care | who chafes, who frets, 4.01. 91
and take no care | who chafes, who frets, or 4.01. 91
who can impress the forest, bid the tree | unfix 4.01. 95
who bears a glass | which shows me many more; 4.01.119
who was't came by? 4.01.140
who must hang them? 4.02. 54 P
see who comes here. 4.03.159
but who knows nothing, is once seen to smile; 4.03.167
man's knell | is there scarce ask'd for who, and 4.03.171
what need we fear who knows it, when none can 5.01. 38 P
yet who would have thought the old man to have 5.01. 39 P
walk'd in their sleep who have died holily in 5.01. 61 P
who knows if donalbain be with his brother? 5.02. 7
who then shall blame | his pester'd senses to 5.02. 22
who (as 'tis thought) by self and violent hands 5.09. 36
i think i hear them. stand ho! who is there? HAM 1.01. 14
who hath reliev'd you? 1.01. 17
who is't that can inform me? 1.01. 79
did slay this fortinbras, who, by a seal'd 1.01. 86
who, impotent and bedred, scarcely hears | of 1.02. 29
is death of fathers, and who still hath cried, 1.02.104
saw, who? 1.02.190
and how, and who, what means, and where they 2.01. 8
who in her duty and obedience, mark, | hath 2.02.107
between who? 2.02.194 P
"but who, ah woe, had seen the mobled queen" — 2.02.502
who this had seen, with tongue in venom steep'd, 2.02.510
after his desert, and who shall scape whipping? 2.02.530 P
who calls me villain, breaks my pate across, 2.02.572
who does me this? 2.02.575
for who would bear the whips and scorns of time, 3.01. 69
who would fardels bear, | to grunt and sweat 3.01. 75
who for the most part are capable of nothing but 3.02. 11 P
who, i? 3.02.123 P
none wed the second but who kill'd the first. 3.02.180
for who not needs shall never lack a friend, 3.02.207
and who in want a hollow friend doth try, 3.02.208
and how his audit stands who knows save heaven? 3.03. 82
that monster custom, who all sense doth eat, 3.04.161
for who, that's but a queen, fair, sober, wise, 3.04.189
who would do so? 3.04.191
who was in life a foolish prating knave. 3.04.215
who calls on hamlet? 4.02. 3 P
who like not in their judgment, but their eyes, 4.03. 5
who commands them, sir? 4.04. 13
who shall stay you? 4.05.137
who, dipping all his faults in their affection, 4.07. 19
from hamlet? who brought them? 4.07. 38
who builds stronger than a mason, a shipwright, 5.01. 50 P
who is to be buried in't? 5.01.134 P
who is this they follow? 5.01.218
is his mirror, and who else would trace him, his 5.02.119 P
who brings back to him that you attend him in 5.02.196 P
who does it then? 5.02.237
than this, who yet is no dearer in my account. LR 1.01. 20 P
who stirs? 1.01.126
you, who with this king | hath rivall'd for our 1.01.190
lord, who hath receiv'd you | at fortune's alms. 1.01.277
who covers faults, at last with shame derides. 1.01.281
who, in the lusty stealth of nature, take | more 1.02. 11
in the oppression of aged tyranny, who sways, 1.02. 50 P
who brought it? 1.02. 58 P
who wouldst thou serve? 1.04. 24 P
who am i, sir? 1.04. 78 P
who is it that can tell me who i am? 1.04.230
who is it that can tell me who i am? 1.04.230
who i am sure is kind and comfortable. 1.04.306
should wear a sword, | who wears no honesty. 2.02. 73
this is some fellow | who, having been prais'd 2.02. 96
king | for him attempting who was self–subdued, 2.02.122
who hath most fortunately been inform'd | of my 2.02.167
me proof and president | of bedlam beggars, who, 2.03. 14
who put my man i' th' stocks? 2.04.182
who stock'd my servant? 2.04.188
who comes here? 2.04.189
but who is with him? 3.01. 15
fool, who labors to outjest | his heart–strook 3.01. 16
who have — as who have not, that their great 3.01. 22
who have — as who have not, that their great 3.01. 22
servants, who seem no less, | which are to 3.01. 23
and she will tell you who that fellow is | that 3.01. 48
then comes the time, who lives to see't, | that 3.02. 93
who gives any thing to poor tom? 3.04. 51 P
who is whipt from tithing to tithing, and 3.04.134 P
who hath /had three suits to his back, six 3.04.135 P
who, with some other of the lord's dependants, 3.07. 18
treasons to us, | who is too good to pity thee. 3.07. 90
but who comes here? 4.01. 9
who is't can say, "i am at the worst"? 4.01. 25
who hast not in thy brows an eye discerning 4.02. 52
bending his sword | to his great master, who, 4.02. 75
who make them honors | of men's impossibilities, 4.06. 73
but who comes here? 4.06. 80
who have the power | to seal th' accuser's lips. 4.06.169
who redeems nature from the general curse 4.06.206
who, by the art of known and feeling sorrows, 4.06.222
let her who would be rid of him devise | his 5.01. 64
who with best meaning have incurr'd the worst. 5.03. 4
talk with them too — | who loses and who wins; 5.03. 15
talk with them too — | who loses and who wins; 5.03. 15
who were the opposites of this day's strife; 5.03. 42
on him, on you — who not? 5.03.100
who can arraign me for't? 5.03.160
who dead? speak, man. 5.03.226
to who, my lord? 5.03.249
who has the office? 5.03.249
who are you? 5.03.279
who hast had my purse | as if the strings were OTH 1.01. 2
others there are | who, trimm'd in forms and 1.01. 50
who would be a father! 1.01.164
to who? 1.02. 52
who e'er he be that in this foul proceeding 1.03. 65
and give us truth who 'tis that is arriv'd. 2.01. 58
who has put in? 2.01. 65
who stands so eminent in the degree of this 2.01.236 P
who let us not therefore blame. 2.03. 15 P
who began this? 2.03.178
who set it on; 2.03.210
iago, who began't? 2.03.217
who is't you mean? 3.03. 44
who has that breast so pure | /but /some 3.03.138
who steals my purse steals trash; 3.03.157
that cuckold lives in bliss | who, certain of 3.03.168
what damned minutes tells he o'er | who dotes, 3.03.170
who, he? 3.04. 30
who having, by their own importunate suit, | or 4.01. 26
in your chamber, and know not who left it there! 4.01.152 P
who, i, my lord? 4.01.251
who art so lovely fair and smell'st so sweet 4.02. 68
with who? 4.02. 99
who is thy lord? 4.02.101
who keeps her company? 4.02.137
hark, who is't that knocks? 4.03. 53 P
who would not make her husband a cuckold to make 4.03. 75 P
what is the matter ho? who is't that cried? 5.01. 74
who is't that cried? 5.01. 75
who they should be that have thus mangled you? 5.01. 79
o, who hath done this deed? 5.02.123
alas! who knows? 5.02.126
who can control his fate? 5.02.265
or who knows | if the scarce–bearded caesar have ANT 1.01. 20
common liar, who | thus speaks of him at rome; 1.01. 60
who tells me true, though in his tale lie death, 1.02. 98
great and all his dignities | upon his son, who, 1.02.189
throned gods), | who have been false to fulvia? 1.03. 29
there | a man who is th' /abstract of all faults 1.04. 9
as we rate boys who, being mature in knowledge, 1.04. 31
who neigh'd so high that what i would have spoke 1.05. 49
who at philippi the good brutus ghosted, | there 2.06. 13
we part, and let's | draw lots who shall begin. 2.06. 61
who would not have his wife so? 2.06.124 P
who seeks, and will not take when once 'tis 2.07. 83
who does i' th' wars more than his captain can 3.01. 21
who, queasy with his insolence | already, will 3.06. 20
who does he accuse? 3.06. 23
who now are levying | the kings o' th' earth for 3.06. 67
who | with half the bulk o' th' world play'd as 3.11. 63
who? 4.05. 6
serv'd, who best was worthy | best to be serv'd. 5.01. 6
who is so full of grace that it flows over | on 5.02. 24
yourself such wrong, who are in this | reliev'd, 5.02. 40
who was last with them? 5.02.338
who did join his honor | against the romans with CYM 1.01. 29
who in the wars o' th' time | died with their 1.01. 35
who to my father was a friend, to me | known but 1.01. 98
who has the note of them? 1.05. 2
who cannot be new built, nor has no friends | so 1.05. 59
boot, my son, | who shall take notice of thee. 1.05. 70
who may this be? 1.06. 9
hold, to think that man, who knows | by history, 1.06. 69
who is as far | from thy report as thou from 1.06.145
he little cares for and a daughter who | he not 1.06.154
who told you of this stranger? 2.01. 40 P
who lets go by no vantages that may | prefer you 2.03. 45
in meaner parties | (yet who than he more mean?) 2.03.117
masterless leave both | to who shall find them. 2.04. 61
or | who knows if one her women, being corrupted 2.04.116
the fam'd cassibelan, who was once at point | (o 3.01. 30
who was the first of britain which did put | his 3.01. 59
who, thy lord? 3.02. 26
pisanio, | who long'st like me to see thy lord; 3.02. 53
who long'st | (o, let me bate!) 3.02. 53
who | the king his father call'd guiderius — 3.03. 87
is not there, who was indeed | the riches of it. 3.04. 70
for when fools shall — | who is here? 3.05. 80
reckon'd, but of those | who worship dirty gods. 3.06. 55
i have a kinsman who | is bound for italy; 3.06. 60
who was made by him that made the tailor, not be 4.01. 3 P
spurn her home to her father, who may (happily) 4.01. 19 P
and a demand who is't shall die, i'ld say | "my 4.02. 23
yet who this should be | doth miracle itself, 4.02. 28
to who? 4.02. 76
thy tailor, rascal, | who is thy grandfather! 4.02. 82
who call'd me traitor, mountaineer, and swore 4.02.120
who ever yet could sound thy bottom? 4.02.204
who is this | thou mak'st thy bloody pillow? 4.02.362
or who was he | that (otherwise than noble 4.02.363
who is't? 4.02.366
who needs must know of her departure and | dost 4.03. 10
who did promise | to yield me often tidings. 4.03. 38
who find in my exile the want of breeding, | the 4.04. 26
who ne'er wore rowel | nor iron on his heel! 4.04. 39
who deserv'd | so long a breeding as his white 5.03. 16
who dares not stand his foe, i'll be his friend; 5.03. 60
who had not now been drooping here, if seconds 5.03. 90
death, who is the key | t' unbar these locks. 5.04. 7

men, | who of their broken debtors take a third, 5.04. 19
who worse than a physician | would this report 5.05. 27
err, who with wet cheeks | were present when she 5.05. 35
who is't can read a woman? 5.05. 48
who, being born your vassal, | am something 5.05.113
more resembles that sweet rosy lad | who died, 5.05.122
great king, a subject who | was call'd belarius. 5.05.316
who hath upon him still that natural stamp. 5.05.366
i divine | is this most constant wife, who, even 5.05.449
who, by belarius stol'n, | for many years 5.05.455
took a peer, | who died and left a female heir, PER 1.ch. 22
eye | i give my cause, who best can justify. 1.ch. 42
who hath taught | my frail mortality to know 1.01. 41
who tells us life's but breath, to trust it 1.01. 46
as sick men do | who know the world, see heaven, 1.01. 48
who, finger'd to make man his lawful music, 1.01. 82
who has a book of all that monarchs do, | he's 1.01. 94
and if jove stray, who dares say jove doth ill? 1.01.104
are, who though they feed | on sweetest flowers, 1.01.132
who attends us there? 1.01.150
who /am no more but as the tops of trees, 1.02. 30
who by thy wisdom makes a prince thy servant, 1.02. 64
who seem'd my good protector, and, being here, 1.02. 82
must feel war's blow, who spares not innocence: 1.02. 93
art one, | who now reprov'dst me for't — 1.02. 95
who either by public war or private treason 1.02.104
who shuns not to break one will crack /them both 1.02.121
it, | for who digs hills because they do aspire 1.04. 5
who wanteth food and will not say he wants it, 1.04. 11
these mouths who, but of late, earth, sea, and 1.04. 34
those palates who, not yet /two /summers younger 1.04. 39
those mothers who, to nousle up their babes, 1.04. 42
draw lots who first shall die to lengthen life. 1.04. 46
who makes the fairest show means most deceit. 1.04. 75
who never leave gaping till they swallow'd the 2.01. 33 P
who is the first that doth prefer himself? 2.02. 17
who is the second that presents himself? 2.02. 23
for who hates honor hates the gods above. 2.03. 22
who can be other in this royal presence? 2.03. 49
who freely give to every one that come | to 2.03. 60
who, looking for adventures in the world, | was 2.03. 83
who only by misfortune of the seas | bereft of 2.03. 88
who takes offense | at that would make me glad? 2.05. 71
who, for aught i know, | may be (nor can i think 2.05. 78
who dreamt? 3.ch. 38
who thought of such a thing?" 3.ch. 38
makes her desire — | which who shall cross? 3.ch. 41
who, if it had conceit, would die, as i | am 3.01. 16
your creatures, who by you have been restored; 3.02. 45
who finds her, give her burying, | she was the 3.02. 72
dead, | who was by good appliance recovered. 3.02. 86
who shall not be more dear to my respect | than 3.03. 33
who hath gain'd | of education all the grace, 4.ch. 8
who, monsieur verollus? 4.02.106 P
who should deny it? 4.02.133 P
who can cross it? 4.03. 16
proceeding | who ever but his approbation added, 4.03. 26
of me, who stand /i' /th' gaps to teach you, 4.04. 8
to fetch his daughter home, who first is gone. 4.04. 20
lies here, | who withered in her spring of year. 4.04. 35
your principal made known unto you who i am? 4.06. 83 P
who is my principal? 4.06. 84 P
of noble race, | who pour their bounty on her; 5.ch. 10
the governor, | who craves to come aboard. 5.01. 5
a man who for this three months hath not spoken 5.01. 24
who stood equivalent with mighty kings, | but 5.01. 91
who starves the ears she feeds, and makes them 5.01.112
of a king, | who died the minute i was born, 5.01.158
villain to attempt it, who having drawn to do't, 5.01.173
was my mother, who did end | the minute i began. 5.01.211
who is this? 5.01.218
who, hearing of your melancholy state, | did 5.01.220
who, frighted from my country, did wed | at 5.03. 3
who at fourteen years | he sought to murder, but 5.03. 8
look who kneels here! 5.03. 46
how possibly preserved, and who to thank 5.03. 57
who endured | the beaks of ravens, talents of TNK 1.01. 40
ever he had on thee, who ow'st his strength, 1.01. 88
who is a servant for | the tenor of /thy speech; 1.01. 89
who cannot feel nor see the rain, being in't, 1.01.120
who did propound | to his bold ends honor and 1.02. 16
who then shall offer | to mars's so scorn'd 1.02. 19
who only attributes | the faculties of other 1.02. 67
theseus (who where he threats appalls) hath sent 1.02. 90
who is at hand to seal | the promise of his 1.02. 92
of our fate, | who hath bounded our last minute. 1.02.103
let's to the king, who, were he | a quarter 1.02.107
who made too proud the bed, took leave o' th' 1.03. 52
who from the mounted heavens | view us their 1.04. 4
view us their mortal herd, behold who err, | and 1.04. 5
who would not? 2.02.158
not love at all! who shall deny me? 2.02.166
who knows | whether my brows may not be girt 2.03. 79
who professes | to clear his own way with the 3.01. 55
who have in them | a sense to know a man unarm'd 3.02. 15
when ye return, who wins i'll settle here; 3.06.307
who loses, yet i'll weep upon his bier. 3.06.308
but yet perceiv'd not | who made the sound, the 4.01. 61
o, who can find the bent of woman's fancy? 4.02. 33
who saw 'em? 4.02. 70
who dost pluck | with hand armipotent from forth 5.01. 53
who hast power | to call the fiercest tyrant 5.01. 77
who do bear thy yoke | as 'twere a wreath of 5.01. 95
i told them — who | a lass of fourteen brided. 5.01.108
swore it was, | and who would not believe her? 5.01.118
who to thy female knights | allow'st no more 5.01.140
horror, who does stand accurs'd | of many mortal 5.03. 23
fortune, | who, at her certain'st, reels. 5.04. 21
come! who begins? 5.04. 21
who will obey a traitor? STM II.C 116
boy, | who blush'd and pouted in a dull disdain, VEN 33
who, being look'd on, ducks as quickly in; 87
bow, | who conquers where he comes in every jar, 100
as who should say, "lo thus my strength is tried 280
the hairs, who wave like feath'red wings. 306
"who sees his true-love in her naked bed, 397
who is so faint that dares not be so bold | to 401
"who wears a garment shapeless and unfinish'd? 415
who plucks the bud before one leaf put forth? 416
for who hath she to spend the night withal, 847
who doth the world so gloriously behold | that 857
all strain court'sy who shall cope him first. 888
who, overcome by doubt and bloodless fear, 891
who when he liv'd, his breath and beauty set 935
who like sluices stopp'd | the crystal tide that 956
as striving who should best become her grief; 968
who is but drunken when she seemeth drown'd. 984
to wail his death who lives and must not die 1017
who bids them still consort with ugly night, 1041
who, like a king perplexed in his throne, | by 1043
they both would strive who first should dry his 1092
who did not whet his teeth at him again, | but 1113
who buys a minute's mirth to wail a week? LUC 213
for one sweet grape who will the vine destroy? 215
who fears a sentence or an old man's saw | shall 244
then who fears sinking where such treasure lies? 280
who, flatt'red by their leader's jocund show, 296
as who should say, "this glove to wanton tricks 320
who with a ling'ring stay his course doth let, 328
who sees the lurking serpent steps aside; 362
who, therefore angry, seems to part in sunder, 388
who like a foul usurper went about | from this 412
who, peeping forth this tumult to behold, | are 447
who, angry that the eyes fly from their lights, 461
who o'er the white sheet peers her whiter chin, 472
who seek to stain the ocean of thy blood. 655
rome, | who this accomplishment so hotly chased, 716
who in their pride do presently abuse it; 864
for who so base would such an office have | as 1000
he shall not boast who did thy stock pollute 1063
who wayward once, his mood with nought agrees. 1095
who, being stopp'd, the bounding banks o'erflows 1119
who, if it wink, shall thereon fall and die. 1139
that mother tries a merciless conclusion | who, 1161
who in a salt-wav'd ocean quench their light, 1231
body spread, | and who cannot abuse a body dead? 1267
who nothing wants to answer her but cries, | and 1459
and who she finds forlorn she doth lament. 1500
who finds his lucrece clad in mourning black, 1585
who, like a late-sack'd island, vastly stood 1740
who, mad that sorrow should his use control, 1781
weep with equal strife | who should weep most, 1792
with clamors fill'd | the dispers'd air, who, 1805
who pluck'd the knife from lucrece' side, 1807
who, wond'ring at him, did his words allow. 1845
or who is he so fond will be the tomb, | of his SON 3. 7
who confounds | in singleness the parts that 8. 7
who all in one, one pleasing note do sing: 8.12
to any, | who for thyself art so unprovident. 10. 2
who lets so fair a house fall to decay, | which 13. 9
who will believe my verse in time to come | if 17. 1
who heaven itself for ornament doth use, | and 21. 3
who with his fear is put besides his part, | or 23. 2
who plead for love and look for recompense 23.11
let those who are in favor with their stars | of 25. 1
who all their parts of me to thee did give: 31.11
by praising him here who doth hence remain! 39.14
who lead thee in their riot even there | where 41.11
who even but now come back again, assured | of 45.11
or who his spoil /of beauty can forbid? 65.12
who is it that says most, which can say more 84. 1
who, moving others, are themselves as stone, 94. 3
for what care i who calls me well or ill, | so 112. 3
die for goodness, who have liv'd for crime. 124.14
who in thy power | dost hold time's fickle glass 126. 1
who hast by waning grown, and therein show'st 126. 3
and they mourners seem | at such who, not born 127.11
who in despite of view is pleas'd to dote; 141. 4
who leaves unsway'd the likeness of a man, | thy 141.11
who like a fiend | from heaven to hell is flown 145.11
who art as black as hell, as dark as night. 147.14
who hateth thee that i do call my friend? 149. 5
who taught thee how to make me love thee more, 150. 9
yet who knows not conscience is born of love? 151. 2
who ever shunn'd by precedent | the destin'd ill LC 155
/nun, | who, disciplin'd, ay, dieted in grace, 261
who glaz'd with crystal gate the glowing roses 286
who, young and simple, would not be so lover'd? 320

WHOA 1 FR 0.0001 REL FR 0 V 1 P
whoa ho, ho! father page! WIV 5.05.177 P

WHOA-HO-HOA 1 FR 0.0001 REL FR 0 V 1 P
whoa-ho-hoa! WT 3.03. 78 P

WHOE'ER 9 FR 0.0010 REL FR 7 V 2 P
as any is in windsor, whoe'er be the other; WIV 2.02.100 P
whoe'er 'a was, 'a show'd a mounting mind. LLL 4.01. 4
whoe'er i woo, myself would be his wife. TN 1.04. 42
but mine i am sure thou art, whoe'er thou be, 1H4 5.04. 37
as good a man as he, sir, whoe'er i am. 2H4 4.03. 11 P
whoe'er helps thee, 'tis thou that must help me: 1H6 1.02.107
whoe'er he be, you may not be let in. 1.03. 7
go, some of you, whoe'er you find attach. ROM 5.03.173
whoe'er keeps me, let my heart be his guard, SON 133.11

WHOEVER 14 FR 0.0015 REL FR 14 V 0 P
whoever bound him, i will loose his bonds, | and ERR 5.01.340
and here she stands, touch her whoever dare, SHR 3.02.233
whoever shoots at him, i set him there; AWW 3.02.112
whoever charges on his forward breast, | i am 3.02.113
mine, 'twas helen's, | whoever gave it you. 5.03.105
whoever wins, on that side shall i lose; JN 3.01.335
whoever spoke it, it is true, my lord. 5.05. 19
whoever got thee, there thy mother stands, | for 3H6 2.02.133
my lord, whoever journeys to the prince, | for R3 2.02.146
noted, | and generally, whoever the king favors, H8 2.01. 47
whoever gave that counsel, to give forth | the COR 3.01.113
open, locks, | whoever knocks! MAC 4.01. 47
whoever plots the sin, thou 'point'st the season LUC 879
whoever hath her wish, thou hast thy will, | and SON 135. 1

WHOLE 129 FR 0.0145 REL FR 82 V 47 P
sure it was the roar | of a whole herd of lions. TMP 2.01.316
the whole butt, man. 2.02.134 P
no, they are both as whole as a fish. TGV 2.05. 19 P
them keep their limbs whole and hack our english WIV 3.01. 77 P
your hearts are mighty, your skins are whole, 3.01.109 P
swallow'd his vows whole, pretending in her MM 3.01.226 P
she'll burn a week longer than the whole world. ERR 3.02.100 P
spain, who sent whole armadoes of carrects to be 3.02.136 P
off, and now is the whole man govern'd with one; ADO 1.01. 67 P
man at a mark, with a whole army shooting at me. 2.01.247 P
and our whole discourse | is all of her. 3.01. 5
and there, before the whole congregation, shame 3.03.161 P
is our whole dissembly appear'd? 4.02. 1 P
to disgrace hero before the whole assembly, and 4.02. 54 P
of pandars, and a whole bookful of these quondam 5.02. 32 P
write, pen, for i am for whole volumes in folio. LLL 1.02.185 P
and the whole world again | cannot pick out five 5.02.544
and then the whole quire hold their hips and MND 2.01. 55
believe as soon | this whole earth may be bor'd, 3.02. 53
nor is my whole estate | upon the fortune of MV 1.01. 43
i'll tell thee all my whole device | when i am 3.04. 81
wilt thou show the whole wealth of thy wit in an 3.05. 56 P
he hath generally tax'd their whole sex withal. AYL 3.02.350 P
that had the whole theoric of war in the knot of AWW 4.03.142 P
all is whole, | not one word more of the 5.03. 37
i'll be reveng'd on the whole pack of you. TN 5.01.378 P
the face to sweeten | of the whole dungy earth. WT 2.01.157
the whole matter | and copy of the father — eye 2.03. 99
i had not left a purse alive in the whole army. 4.04.618 P
this might have been prevented and made whole JN 1.01. 35
john, to stop arthur's title in the whole, 2.01.562
a whole armado of convicted sail | is scattered 3.04. 2
to feast upon whole thousands of the french. 5.02.178
taking so the head, your whole head's length. R2 3.03. 14
when our sea-walled garden, the whole land, | is 3.04. 43
into) for their own credit sake make all whole. 1H4 2.01. 73 P
unsorted, and your whole plot too light for the 2.03. 13 P
i would the state of time had first been whole 4.01. 25
yet all goes well, yet all our joints are whole. 4.01. 83
what may the king's whole battle reach unto? 4.01.129
and now my whole charge consists of ancients, 4.02. 23 P
and in the neck of that, task'd the whole state; 4.03. 92
there's a whole merchant's venture of burdeaux 2H4 2.04. 63 P
what's a joint of mutton or two in a whole lent? 2.04.347 P
his back, and the whole frame stands upon pins. 3.02.144 P
i have a whole school of tongues in this belly 4.03. 18 P
and put the world's whole strength | into one 4.05. 44
should with his lion gait walk the whole world, H5 2.02.122
and his whole kingdom into desolation. 2.02.173
'a breaks words, and keeps whole weapons. 3.02. 36 P
all the whole army stood agaz'd on him. 1H6 1.01.126
i tell you, madam, were the whole frame here, 2.03. 54
alone | but all the whole inheritance i give 3.01.163
as to be call'd but viceroy of the whole? 5.04.143
that suffolk should demand a whole fifteenth 2H6 1.01.133
am but a poor petitioner of our whole township. 1.03. 24 P
you made in a day, my lord, whole towns to fly. 2.01.160
men's flesh preserv'd so whole do seldom win. 3.01.301
the mouth with a spear, and 'tis not whole yet. 4.07. 10 P
all the whole time | i was my chamber's prisoner H8 1.01. 12
consistory, | yea, the whole consistory of rome. 2.04. 93
to bring my whole cause 'fore his holiness, 2.04.120
these are the whole contents, and, good my lord, 4.02.154
state stands i' th' world, with the whole world? 5.01.127
the whole realm by your teaching and your 5.02. 51
with a general taint | of the whole state; 5.02. 64
after this, the vengeance on the whole camp! TRO 2.03. 18 P
i'll decline the whole question: 2.03. 52 P
if | the passage and whole /carriage /of /this 2.03.131
know the whole world, he is as valiant — 2.03.232
by my life, you shall make it whole again — you 3.01. 51 P
one touch of nature makes the whole world kin — 3.03.175
you told how diomed, a whole week by days, | did 4.01. 10
approach, | with the whole quality wherefore. 4.01. 45
and this whole night | hath nothing been but 5.03. 11
and affection common | of the whole body. COR 1.01.105
store-house and the shop | of the whole body. 1.01.134
he gives my son the whole name of the war. 2.01.135 P
time craves it as physic | for the whole state, 3.02. 34
by the entreaty and grant of the whole table. 4.05.200 P
what will whole months of tears thy father's TIT 2.04. 55
wits than, i am sure, i have in my whole five. ROM 2.04. 73 P
for i was come to the whole depth of my tale, 2.04. 99 P
all our whole city is much bound to him. 4.02. 32
hot ardent zeal would set whole realms on fire; TIM 3.03. 33 P
hate may grow | to the whole race of mankind, 4.01. 40
that the whole life of athens were in this! 4.03.281
gave life and influence | to their whole being! 5.01. 64
a piece of work that will make sick men whole. JC 2.01.327
but are not some whole that we must make sick? 2.01.328
whole as the marble, founded as the rock, | as MAC 3.04. 21
i drink to th' general joy o' th' whole table, 3.04. 88
for the whole space that's in the tyrant's grasp 4.03. 36
in my bosom for the dignity of the whole body. 5.01. 56 P
and our whole kingdom | to be contracted in one HAM 1.02. 3
the safety and health of this whole state, | and 1.03. 21
me, so the whole ear of denmark | is by a forged 1.05. 36
an' his whole function suiting | with forms to 2.02.556
allowance, o'erweigh a whole theatre of others. 3.02. 28 P
a whole one, i. 3.02.280 P
sir, a whole history. 3.02.298 P
bed, | go to th' creating a whole tribe of fops, LR 1.02. 14
tale deliver | of my whole course of love — OTH 1.03. 91
of my counsel | /in my whole course of wooing, 3.03.112
but, for all the whole world — /'ud's /pity, 4.03. 75 P
i would do such a wrong | for the whole world. 4.03. 79
as matter whole you have to make it with, | it ANT 2.02. 53
eight wild-boars roasted whole at a breakfast, 2.02.179 P
wilt thou be lord of the whole world? 2.07. 62
but his whole action grows | not in the power 3.07. 68
keep by land | the legions and the horse whole, 3.07. 71
but we keep whole by land. 3.07. 74
strike not by land, keep whole, provoke not 3.08. 3
and goddesses, | all the whole synod of them! 3.10. 5
wounds, and kiss | the honor'd gashes whole. 4.08. 11
wherein the worship of the whole world lies. 4.14. 86
could not stall together | in the whole world. 5.01. 40
him hence, | the whole world shall not save him. CYM 5.05.321
presumes to reach, all the whole heap must die. PER 1.01. 33
gaping till they swallow'd the whole parish, 2.01. 34 P
the god priapus, and undo a whole generation. 4.06. 4 P
under the cope, shall undo a whole household, 4.06.124 P
like lightning, | to blast whole armies, more! TNK 2.02. 25
but the whole week's not fair | if any day it 3.01. 65
grease, amongst a whole million of cutpurses, 4.03. 37 P

my heart all whole as thine, thy heart my wound! VEN 370
than they whose whole is swallowed in confusion. LUC 1159
a head | stood for the whole to be imagined. 1428
me, | he pays the whole, and yet am i not free. SON 134.14
WHOLESOME 33 FR 0.0037 REL FR 23 V 10 P
in state as wholesome as in state 'tis fit, WIV 5.05. 59
with wholesome syrups, drugs, and holy prayers, ERR 5.01.104
humor to the most wholesome physic of thy LLL 1.01.233 P
of a mutton as wholesome as the sweat of a man? AYL 3.02. 56 P
i care not what, so it be wholesome food. SHR 4.03. 16
if from me he have wholesome beverage, | account WT 1.02.346
in wholesome counsel to his unstayed youth? R2 2.01. 2
the soil's fertility from wholesome flowers. 3.04. 39
her knots disordered and her wholesome herbs 3.04. 46
and wholesome berries thrive and ripen best H5 1.01. 61
bosom up my counsel, | you'll find it wholesome. H8 1.01.113
which are not wholesome | to those which would 1.02. 45
lutheran, and not wholesome to | our cause, that 3.02. 99
us but the superfluity while it were wholesome, COR 1.01. 18 P
repeal daily any wholesome act establish'd 1.01. 82 P
you wear out a good wholesome forenoon in 2.01. 69 P
speak to 'em, i pray you, | in wholesome manner. 2.03. 60
and will he steal out of his wholesome bed | to JC 2.01.264
when shalt thou see thy wholesome days again, MAC 4.03.105
the nights are wholesome, then no planets strike HAM 1.01.162
into milk, | the thin and wholesome blood. 1.05. 70
it an honest method, as wholesome as sweet, and 2.02.444 P
property | on wholesome life usurps immediately. 3.02.260
shall please you to make me a wholesome answer, 3.02.316 P
make you a wholesome answer — my wit's diseas'd 3.02.321 P
mildewed ear, | blasting his wholesome brother. 3.04. 65
which, in the tender of a wholesome weal, LR 1.04.211
'tis on such ground and to such wholesome end 2.04.144
it seems not meet, nor wholesome to my place, OTH 1.01.145
and that in wholesome wisdom | he might not but 3.01. 46
none abroad so wholesome as that you vent. CYM 1.02. 4 P
wholesome iniquity have you, that a man may deal PER 4.06. 24 P
night, i will be here | with wholesome viands; TNK 3.01. 84
WHOLESOME-PROFITABLE 1 FR 0.0001 REL FR 1 V 0 P
is not by much so wholesome-profitable | as to LLL 5.02.750
WHOLESOM'ST 1 FR 0.0001 REL FR 1 V 0 P
the best and wholesom'st spirits of the night MM 4.02. 73
WHO'LL 1 FR 0.0001 REL FR 1 V 0 P
now, who'll take it? H8 3.02.250
WHOLLY 6 FR 0.0006 REL FR 3 V 3 P
have, master slender, i stand wholly for you; WIV 3.02. 61 P
and shape his service wholly to my device, | and LLL 5.02. 65
wholly, sir. TRO 3.01. 20 P
you shall be mistress, and command him wholly. 4.04.120
cleopatra's, which wholly depends on your abode. ANT 1.02.175 P
sleep hath seiz'd me wholly. CYM 2.02. 7
/WHOM 3 FR 0.0003 REL FR 3 V 0 P
/who /knows /on /whom /fortune /would /then 2H4 4.01.131
/whom /they /doted /on | /and /bless'd /and 4.01.136
/not /bolds /the /king, /with /others /whom, /i LR 5.01. 26
WHOM 462 FR 0.0522 REL FR 418 V 44 P
good, yet remember whom thou hast aboard. TMP 1.01. 19 P
he whom next thyself | of all the world i lov'd, 1.02. 68
whom i left cooling of the air with sighs, | in 1.02.222
he, that caliban | whom now i keep in service. 1.02.286
slave, | whom stripes may move, not kindness! 1.02.345
sure, the goddess | on whom these airs attend! 1.02.423
nor this man's threats | to whom i am subdu'd, 1.02.490
she that from whom | we all were sea-swallow'd, 2.01.250
whom i with this obedient steel, three inches of 2.01.283
he is drown'd | whom thus we stray to find, and 3.03. 9
you are three men of sin, whom destiny, | that 3.03. 53
of whom your swords are temper'd, may as well 3.03. 62
young ferdinand, whom they suppose is drown'd, 3.03. 92
bring the rabble | (o'er whom i give thee pow'r) 4.01. 38
on whom my pains, | humanely taken, all, all 4.01.189
expell'd remorse and nature, whom, with 5.01. 76
sir, whom to call brother | would even infect my 5.01.130
whom three hours since | were wrack'd upon this 5.01.136
what is this maid with whom thou wast at play? 5.01.185
milan, | of whom so often i have heard renown, 5.01.193
of whom i have | receiv'd a second life; 5.01.194
"to julia" — say, from whom? TGV 1.02. 35
for being ignorant to whom it goes, | i writ at 2.01.110
to whom? 2.01.147 P
on thurio, whom your gentle daughter hates, 3.01. 14
there is a lady in /milano here | whom i affect; 3.01. 82
by one whom she esteemeth as his friend. 3.02. 37
in breaking faith with julia whom i lov'd; 4.02. 11
yet valentine thy friend | survives, to whom, 4.02.109
marry | vain thurio, whom my very soul /abhors. 4.03. 17
from whom? 4.04.113
knave ford, on whom to-night i will be reveng'd, WIV 5.01. 28 P
of money, to whom you should have been a pander. 5.05.167 P
on whom it will, it will; MM 1.02.122
on whom it will not, so; 1.02.123
from whom we thought it meet to hide our love 1.02.152
whom i would save, had a most noble father! 2.01. 7
(whom i believe to be most strait in virtue) 2.01. 9
whom i detest before heaven and your honor — 2.01. 69 P
ay, sir; whom i thank heaven is an honest woman. 2.01. 72 P
to whom should i complain? 2.04.171
claudio, whom here you have warrant to execute, 4.02.157 P
and good fortune, by the saint whom i profess, i 4.02.179 P
by whom? 5.01. 26
whom it concerns to hear this matter forth, | do 5.01.255
himself there's one | whom he begot with child), 5.01.511
from whom my absence was not six months old ERR 1.01. 44
i, | fixing our eyes on whom our care was fix'd, 1.01. 84
and, knowing whom it was their hap to save, 1.01.113
whom whilst i labored of a love to see, | i 1.01.130
to see, | i hazarded the loss of whom i lov'd. 1.01.131
egeon, whom the fates have mark'd | to bear the 1.01.140
of whom i hope to make much benefit; 1.02. 25
she whom thou gav'st to me to be my wife; 5.01.198
whom i beseech | to give me ample satisfaction 5.01.252
brought count claudio, whom you sent me to seek. ADO 2.01.287 P
whom she hath in all outward behaviors seem'd 2.03. 96 P
's | than this for whom we rend'red up this woe. 5.03. 33
whom right and wrong | have chose as umpeer of LLL 1.01.168
to whom he sends, and what's his embassy: 2.01. 3
belonging to whom? 2.01.224
the boy, | than whom no mortal so magnificent! 3.01.178
to whom came he? 4.01. 72 P
to whom shouldst thou give it? 4.01.102
the gift is good in those /in whom it is acute, 4.02. 71 P
'gainst whom the world cannot hold argument, 4.03. 59
by whom shall i send this? — company? stay. 4.03. 75
thou for whom jove would swear | juno but an 4.03.115
or women's sake, by whom we men are men, | /let 4.03.357
and one | to whom you are but as a form in wax MND 1.01. 49
night | from perigenia, whom he ravished? 2.01. 78
whom i do love and will do till my death. 3.02.167
why should he stay, whom love doth press to go? 3.02.184
o wicked wall, through whom i see no bliss! 5.01.180
same | to whom you swore a secret pilgrimage, MV 1.01.120
sun, | to whom i am a neighbor and near bred. 2.01. 3
lord, | from whom he bringeth sensible regreets: 2.09. 89
and one in whom | the ancient roman honor more 3.02.294
but if you knew to whom you show this honor, 3.04. 5
whom i have sent for to determine this, | come 4.01.106
is antonio, | to whom i am so infinitely bound. 5.01.135
if you did know to whom i gave the ring, | if 5.01.193
if you did know for whom i gave the ring, | and 5.01.194
know you before whom, sir? AYL 1.01. 42 P
at whom so oft | your grace was wont to laugh, 2.02. 8
instead of her, from whom i took two cods and, 2.04. 52 P
to blow on whom i please, for so fools have; 2.07. 49
but myself, against whom i know most faults. 3.02.281 P
uncle, | whom he reports to be a great magician, 5.04. 33
whom should i knock? SHR 1.02. 6 P
whom would to god i had well knock'd at first, 1.02. 34
than perfume itself | to whom they go to. 1.02.153
here is a gentleman whom by chance i met, | upon 1.02.181
to whom my father is not all unknown, | and were 1.02.239
the youngest daughter, whom you hearken for, 1.02.258
to whom we all rest generally beholding. 1.02.272
i charge /thee tell | whom thou lov'st best; 2.01. 9
go, fool, and whom thou keep'st command. 2.01.257
you, | signior baptista, of whom i hear so well. 4.04. 37
happier the man whom favorable stars | allots 4.05. 40
his majesty's command, to whom i am now in ward, AWW 1.01. 5 P
thy vassal, whom i know | is free for me to ask, 2.01.199
o'er whom both sovereign power and father's 2.03. 54
to whom i promise | a counterpoise; 2.03.174
whom i serve above is my master. 2.03.246 P
me, | whom i myself embrace to set him free." 3.04. 17
whom heaven delights to hear | and loves to 3.04. 27
whom i am sure he knows not from the enemy. 3.06. 23 P
us, whom we must produce for an interpreter. 4.01. 5 P
to swear by him whom i protest to love | that i 4.02. 28
sir, of whom he hath taken a solemn leave. 4.03. 77 P
to morgan, whom he supposes to be a friar, from 4.03.108 P
i am a man whom fortune hath cruelly scratch'd. 5.02. 26 P
that she whom all men prais'd and whom myself, 5.03. 53
that she whom all men prais'd and whom myself, 5.03. 53
son, in whom my house's name | must be digested; 5.03. 73
creature, | whom sometime i have laugh'd with. 5.03.179
of messaline, whom i know you have heard of. TN 2.01. 18 P
done, that is, kill him whom you have recover'd, 2.01. 38 P
to whom should this be? 2.05. 94 P
he must observe their mood on whom he jests, 3.01. 62
brought thee to their mercies | whom thou, in 5.01. 71
but this your minion, whom i know you love, 5.01.125
and whom, by heaven i swear, i tender dearly, 5.01.126
whom the blind waves and surges have devour'd. 5.01.229
whom i from meaner form | have bench'd and WT 1.02.313
by whom, camillo? 1.02.413
whom i employ'd was pre-employ'd by him: 2.01. 49
she's an adultress, i have said with whom: 2.01. 88
dion, whom you know | of stuff'd sufficiency. 2.01.184
wife, | whom for this time we pardon. 2.03.173
for polixenes | (with whom i am accus'd), i do 3.02. 62
whom i proclaim a man of truth, of mercy; 3.02.157
from whom i have this intelligence, that he is 4.02. 36 P
quarters of a mile hence, unto whom i was going. 4.03. 81 P
breathe my life | before this ancient sir, whom, 4.04.361
divorce, young sir, | whom son i dare not call. 4.04.418
whom of force must know | the royal fool thou 4.04.423
king, my master, whom | i so much thirst to see. 4.04.512
you may | enjoy your mistress — from the whom, 4.04.528
with whom? 4.04.717 P
of your brave father, whom | (though bearing 5.01.136
whom he loves | (he bade me say so) more than 5.01.145
and son unto the king, whom heavens directing, 5.03.150
to whom am i beholding for these limbs? JN 1.01.239
from whom hast thou this great commission, 2.01.110
you are the hare of whom the proverb goes, 2.01.137
put thee down, 'gainst whom these arms we bear, 2.01.346
to whom in favor she shall give the day, | and 2.01.393
whom zeal and charity brought to the field | as 2.01.565
whom i found | with many hundreds treading on 4.02.148
to whom he sung, in rude harsh-sounding rhymes, 4.02.150
whom they say is kill'd to-night | on your 4.02.165
whom he hath us'd rather for sport than need) 5.02.175
with whom yourself, myself, and other lords, 5.07. 93
to whom with all submission, on my knee, | i do 5.07.103
against whom /com'st thou? R2 1.03. 33
than they whom youth and ease have taught to 2.01. 10
whom fair befall in heaven 'mongst happy souls, 2.01.129
of whom thy father, prince of wales, was first. 2.01.172
whom both my oath | and duty bids defend; 2.02.112
is my kinsman, whom the king hath wrong'd, 2.02.114
whom conscience and my kinred bids to right. 2.02.115
those whom you curse | have felt the worst of 3.02.138
my lord of herford here, whom you call king, 4.01.134
off | by him for whom these shames ye underwent? 1H4 1.03.179
is a virtuous man whom i have often noted in thy 2.04.417 P
whom means your grace? 2.04.461 P
from whom you now must steal and take no leave, 3.01. 92
and all the rest | to whom they are directed. 4.04. 4
but soft, whom have we here? 5.04.131
whom i have weekly sworn to marry since i 2H4 1.02.240 P
whom thou hast whetted on thy stony heart | to 4.05.107
the image of the king whom i presented, | and 5.02. 79
great-grandsire's tomb, | from whom you claim; H5 1.02.104
whom she did send to france | to fill king 1.02.161
to whom i do appeal, and in whose name | tell 1.02.290
whom he hath dull'd and cloy'd with gracious 2.02. 9
on the poor souls for whom this hungry war 2.04.104
here, | to whom expressly i bring greeting too. 2.04.112
that those whom you call'd fathers did beget you 3.01. 23
to whom the order of the siege is given, is 3.02. 65 P
the dolphin, whom of succors we entreated, 3.03. 45
on whom, as in despite, the sun looks pale, 3.05. 17
by whom this great assembly is contriv'd, | we 5.02. 6
prince, | whom like a schoolboy you may overawe. 1H6 1.01. 36
whom all france with their chief assembled 1.01.139
talbot is taken, whom we wont to fear; 1.02. 14
whom henry, our late sovereign, ne'er could 1.03. 24
whom with my bare fists i would execute, | if i 1.04. 36
'tis joan, not we, by whom the day is won; 1.06. 17
but what's that pucelle whom they term so pure? 2.01. 20
prisoner? to whom? 2.03. 34
in whom the title rested, were suppress'd. 2.05. 92
or with whom? 4.01. 84
but tell me whom thou seek'st. 4.07. 59
for whom? 5.03. 88
to whom? 5.03.132
whom i with pain have wooed and won thereto; 5.03.138
first let me tell you whom you have condemn'd: 5.04. 36
well | (there were so many) whom she may accuse. 5.04. 81
with whom i leave my curse: 5.04. 86
not whom we will, but whom his grace affects, 5.05. 57
not whom we will, but whom his grace affects, 5.05. 57
whom should we match with henry, being a king, 5.05. 66
was broke in twain (by whom i have forgot, | but 2H6 1.02. 26
whom we raise, | we will make fast within a 1.04. 21
whom we have apprehended in the fact, | raising 2.01.169
next to whom | was john of gaunt, the duke of 2.02. 13
i cannot justify whom the law condemns. 2.03. 16
through whom a thousand sighs are breath'd for 3.02.345
over whom, in time to come, i hope to reign, 4.02.130
whom have i injur'd that ye seek my death? 4.07.101
king | unto the commons, whom thou hast misled, 4.08. 8
the fearful french, whom you late vanquished, 4.08. 42
the duke of somerset, whom he terms a traitor. 4.09. 30
whom have we here? 5.01. 12
head, | the head of cade, whom i in combat slew. 5.01. 67
o'er him whom heaven created for thy ruler. 5.01.105
whom angry heavens do make their minister, 5.02. 34
whom i encount'red as the battles join'd. 3H6 1.01. 15
whom should he follow but his natural king? 1.01. 82
my son, | whom i unnaturally shall disinherit. 1.01.193
with whom the kentishmen will willingly rise; 1.02. 41
whom we have left protectors of the king, | with 1.02. 57
trull | upon their woes whom fortune captivates! 1.04.115
tell thee whence thou cam'st, of whom deriv'd, 1.04.119
to whom do lions cast their gentle looks? 2.02. 11
to whom god will, there be the victory! 2.05. 15
this man whom hand to hand i slew in fight | may 2.05. 56
whom in this conflict i, unwares, have kill'd. 2.05. 62
whom thou obey'dst thirty and six years, | and 3.03. 96
from whom i know not. 3.03.166
them sever'd | whom god hath join'd together; 4.01. 22
so your dislikes, to whom i would be pleasing, 4.01. 73
and their true sovereign whom they must obey? 4.01. 78
nay, whom they shall obey, and love thee too, 4.01. 79
to whom the heav'ns in thy nativity | adjudg'd 4.06. 33
that | of whom you seem to have so tender care? 4.06. 66
with whom /an upright zeal to right prevails 5.01. 78
her lord, whom i, some three months since, R3 1.02.240
(whom god preserve better than you would wish!) 1.03. 59
whom thou wast sworn to cherish and defend. 1.04.208
alive | with whom my soul is any jot at odds 2.01. 71
whom i will importune | with earnest prayers all 2.02. 14
this edward, whom our manners call the prince. 3.07.191
whom envy hath immur'd within your walls — 4.01. 99
know'st thou not any whom corrupting gold | will 4.02. 34
whom i will marry straight to clarence' daughter 4.02. 54
endur'd of her, for whom you bid like sorrow. 4.04.304
to whom i will retail my conquest won, | and she 4.04.335
by the false faith of him whom most i trusted; 5.01. 17
those whom we fight against | had rather have us 5.03.243
remember whom you are to cope withal — | a sort 5.03.315
whom their o'ercloyed country vomits forth | to 5.03.318
whom our fathers | have in their own land beaten 5.03.333
such | to whom as great a charge as little honor H8 1.01. 77
whom from the flow of gall i name not, but 1.01.152
to whom by oath he menac'd | revenge upon the 1.02.137
whom after under the /confession's seal | he 1.02.164
more worthy this place than myself, to whom 1.04. 79
fellows, whom to leave | is only bitter to him, 2.01. 73
whom once more i present unto your highness. 2.02. 97
from my soul | refuse you for my judge, whom, 2.04. 82
nobility, our issues | (whom, if he live, will 3.02.292
whom the king hath in secrecy long married, 3.02.403
to whom he gave these words: 4.02. 20
whom i most hated living, thou hast made me, 4.02. 73
by whom, aeneas? TRO 1.01.110
a man into whom nature hath so crowded humors 1.02. 22 P
in whom the tempers and the minds of all 1.03. 57
hive | to whom the foragers shall all repair, 1.03. 82
whom opinion crowns | the sinow and the forehand 1.03.142
of helen's needle, for whom he comes to fight. 2.01. 81 P
and for an old aunt whom the greeks held captive 2.02. 77
well may we fight for her whom, we know well, 2.02.161
whom aristotle thought | unfit to hear moral 2.02.166
whom troy hath still denied, but this antenor, 3.03. 22
(with whom relation | durst never meddle) in the 3.03.201
aims, | in whom already he's well grac'd, cannot COR 1.01.264
against whom cominius the general is gone, with 1.03. 97 P
with whom we may articulate | for their own good 1.09. 77
from whom i have receiv'd not only greetings, 2.01.197
doubt not | the commoners, for whom we stand, 2.01.227
whom | we met here both to thank and to remember 2.02. 46
whom with all praise i point at, saw him fight, 2.02. 90
on whom depending, their obedience fails | to 3.01.165
martius, | whom late you have nam'd for consul. 3.01.195
vexed, whom we see have sided | in his behalf. 4.02. 2
whom you have banish'd — does exceed you all. 4.02. 42

there is a slave, whom we have put in prison, 4.06. 38
of a state | to one whom they had punish'd. 5.01. 21
ever verified my friends | (of whom he's chief) 5.02. 18
whom with a crack'd heart i have sent to rome, 5.03. 9
thereby to destroy | the volsces whom you serve, 5.03.134
of rome, for whom we stand | a special party, TIT 1.01. 20
whom worthily you would have now succeed, | and 1.01. 40
right, | whom you pretend to honor and adore, 1.01. 42
and her to whom my thoughts are humbled all, 1.01. 51
whom your goths beheld | alive and dead, and for 1.01.122
rome, | the people will accept whom he admits. 1.01.222
surpris'd? by whom? 1.01.285
sons, | to whom i sued for my dear son's life; 1.01.453
whom thou in triumph long | hast prisoner held, 2.01. 14
would i propose to achieve her whom i love. 2.01. 80
to whom? 4.02. 62
justice lives | in saturninus' health, whom, if 4.04. 24
stands the spring whom you have stain'd with mud 5.02.170
kill'd her for whom my tears have made me blind. 5.03. 49
and she whom mighty kingdoms cur'sy to, | like a 5.03. 74
sups the fair rosaline whom thou so loves, ROM 1.02. 83
tybalt, here slain, whom romeo's hand did slay! 3.01.152
swear | it shall be romeo, whom you know i hate, 3.05.122
for whom, and not for tybalt, juliet pin'd. 5.03.236
whom this beneath world doth embrace and hug TIM 1.01. 44
whom fortune with her ivory hand wafts to her, 1.01. 70
else, | on whom i may confer what i have got. 1.01.122
of whom, even to the state's best health, i have 2.02.197
give't these fellows | to whom 'tis instant due. 2.02.230
is wealthy too, | whom he redeem'd from prison. 3.03. 4
not nature | (to whom all sores lay siege) can 4.03. 7
she, whom the spittle-house and ulcerous sores 4.03. 40
minion, whom the world | voic'd so regardfully? 4.03. 81
how dost thou pity him whom thou dost trouble? 4.03. 99
whom the oracle | hath doubtfully pronounc'd the 4.03.121
whom thy upward face | hath to the marbled 4.03.190
dost not keep a dog, | whom i would imitate. 4.03.201
and let his very breath whom thou'lt observe 4.03.212
whom fortune's tender arm | with favor never 4.03.250
whom, though in general part we were oppos'd, 5.02. 7
were not erected by their hands from whom | you 5.04. 23
whom you yourselves shall set out for reproof 5.04. 57
as we are going, | to whom it must be done. JC 2.01.331
he was a gentleman on whom i built | an absolute MAC 1.04. 13
malcolm, whom we name hereafter | the prince of 1.04. 38
o, by whom? 2.03.100
whom the vile blows and buffets of the world 3.01.108
whom we, to gain our peace, have sent to peace, 3.02. 20
and to our dear friend banquo, whom we miss; 3.04. 89
whom you may say (if't please you) fleance 3.06. 6
(from whom this tyrant holds the due of birth) 3.06. 25
in whom i know | all the particulars of vice so 4.03. 50
and let the angel whom thou still hast serv'd 5.08. 14
whom we invite to see us crown'd at scone. 5.09. 41
there is not living | to whom he more adheres. HAM 2.02. 21
to whom do you speak this? 3.04.131
whom i will trust as i will adders fang'd, 3.04.203
o'er whom his very madness, like some ore 4.01. 25
make choice of whom your wisest friends you will 4.05.205
direct me | to him from whom you brought them. 4.06. 34
orbs, | from whom we do exist and cease to be; LR 1.01.112
lear, | whom i have ever honor'd as my king, 1.01.140
way | than on a wretch whom nature is asham'd 1.01.212
she, whom even but now was your /best object, 1.01.214
so may it come, thy master, whom thou lov'st, 1.04. 6
he whom my father nam'd, your edgar? 2.01. 92
one whom i will beat into /clamorous whining, if 2.02. 23 P
whom the foul fiend hath led through fire and 3.04. 51 P
tom some charity, whom the foul fiend vexes. 3.04. 60 P
thou whom the heav'ns' plagues | have humbled to 4.01. 64
with others whom the rigor of our state | forc'd 5.01. 22
of whom his eyes had seen the proof | at rhodes, OTH 1.01. 28
is the man — this moor, whom now, it seems, 1.03. 71
of venice, whom i trace | for his quick hunting, 2.01.303
whom love hath turn'd almost the wrong side out, 2.03. 52
town, | and silence those whom this vild brawl 2.03.256
and be a member of his love | whom i, with all 3.04.113
is this the noble moor whom our full senate 4.01.264
this the nature | whom passion could not shake? 4.01.266
to whom, my lord? with whom? how am i false? 4.02. 40
to whom, my lord? with whom? how am i false? 4.02. 40
whom every thing becomes — to chide, to laugh, ANT 1.01. 49
at fifty, to whom herod of jewry may do homage. 1.02. 28 P
you shall outlive the lady whom you serve. 1.02. 31
rare indeed | whom these things cannot blemish), 1.04. 23
did famine follow, whom thou fought'st against 1.04. 59
horse, for wot'st thou whom thou mov'st? 1.05. 22
you, whom no brother | did ever love so dearly. 2.02.149
whom ne'er the word of "no" woman heard speak, 2.02.223
is gone, | through whom i might command it? 3.03. 6
sat | caesarion, whom they call my father's son, 3.06. 6
nag of egypt | (whom leprosy o'ertake!) 3.10. 11
bondman, whom | he may at pleasure whip, or hang 3.13.149
'tis the god hercules, whom antony lov'd, | now 4.03. 16
me at heels, to whom i gave | their wishes, do 4.12. 21
(whom | he purpos'd to his wive's sole son — a CYM 1.01. 4
whom | he serv'd with glory and admir'd success: 1.01. 31
to his mistress | (for whom he now is banish'd), 1.01. 51
to whom i have been often bound for no less than 1.04. 27 P
whom i commend to you as a noble friend of mine. 1.04. 31 P
whom in constancy you think stands so safe. 1.04.126 P
(on whom there is no more dependancy | but brats 2.03.118
people, whom we reckon | ourselves to be. 3.01. 52
go, | and find not her whom thou pursuest. 3.05.160
to whom being going, almost spent with hunger, 3.06. 62
the leaf of eglantine, whom not to slander, 4.02.223
even for whom my life | is every breath a death; 5.01. 26
whom best i love, i cross; 5.04.101
you whom the gods have made | preservers of my 5.05. 1
brain of britain, | by whom, i grant, she lives. 5.05. 15
whom she bore in hand to love | with such 5.05. 43
gentleman may render | of whom he had this ring. 5.05.136
'twas leonatus' jewel, | whom thou didst banish; 5.05.144
for whom my heart drops blood, and my false 5.05.148
hint, | and (not dispraising whom we prais'd; 5.05.173
am that belarius whom you sometime banish'd. 5.05.333
euriphile | (whom for the theft i wedded), stole 5.05.341
this gentleman, whom i call polydore, | most 5.05.357
whom heavens, in justice, both on her and hers, 5.05.464
with whom the father liking took, | and her to PER 1.ch. 25
for going on death's net, whom none resist. 1.01. 40
for he's no man on whom perfections wait | that, 1.01. 79
'gainst whom i am too little to contend, | since 1.02. 17
with whom each minute threatens life or death. 1.03. 24
a city on whom plenty held full hand, | for 1.04. 22
to eat those little darlings whom they lov'd. 1.04. 44
and give them life whom hunger starv'd half dead 1.04. 96
in conversation, | to whom i give my benison, 2.ch. 10
a man whom both the waters and the wind, | in 2.01. 59
child, whom nature gat | for men to see, and 2.02. 6
guest, | to whom this wreath of victory i give, 2.03. 10
whom if you find, and win unto return, | you 2.04. 52
my gentle babe marina, whom, | for she was born 3.03. 12
madam, | by bright diana, whom we honor, all 3.03. 28
whom our fast-growing scene must find | at 4.ch. 6
whom they have ravish'd must by me be slain. 4.01.102
whom thou hast pois'ned too. 4.03. 10
whom helicanus late | advanc'd in time to great 4.04. 15
on whom foul death hath made this slaughter. 4.04. 37
of this country, and a man whom i am bound to. 4.06. 54 P
forth | a maid-child call'd marina, whom, o 5.03. 6
through whom the gods have shown their power; 5.03. 60
now for the love of him whom jove hath mark'd TNK 1.01. 29
whom now, i know, hast much more power on him 1.01. 87
bid him that we, whom flaming war doth scorch, 1.01. 91
and now flurted | by peace, for whom he fought, 1.02. 19
and then to whom the birthright of this beauty 3.06. 31
he whom the gods | do of the two know best, i 5.03. 38
the stage of death, | whom i adopt my friends. 5.04.124
for whom an hour, | but one hour since, i was as 5.04.128
and whom he strikes his crooked tushes slay. VEN 624
as fearful of him, part, through whom he rushes. 630
from whom each lamp and shining star doth borrow 861
to whom she speaks, and he replies with howling. 918
the powers to whom i pray abhor this fact, | how LUC 349
she sits weeping, | to whom she sobbing speaks: 1088
for his foul act by whom thy fair wife bleeds? 1824
'gainst whom the world could not hold argument, PP 3. 2
thou for whom jove would swear | juno but an 16.15
let those whom nature hath not made for store, SON 11. 9
look whom she best endow'd she gave the more; 11.11
whilst i, whom fortune of such triumph bars, 25. 3
to whom in vassalage | thy merit hath my duty 26. 1
lascivious grace, in whom all ill well shows, 40.13
but thou, to whom my jewels trifles are, | most 48. 5
or me, to whom thou gav'st it, else mistaking, 87.10
for i must ne'er love him whom thou dost hate. 89.14
friend, | a god in love, to whom i am confin'd. 110.12
o'er whom /thy fingers walk with gentle gait, 128.11
whom thine eyes woo as mine importune thee. 142.10
on whom frown'st thou that i do fawn upon? 149. 6
and, veil'd in them, did win whom he would maim. LC 312

WHOOBUB 2 FR 0.0002 REL FR 1 V 1 P
man come in with a whoobub against his daughter WT 4.04.616 P
within this hour the whoobub | will be all o'er TNK 2.06. 35
WHOOP *(also hoop*, etc.)*
WHOOP 3 FR 0.0003 REL FR 1 V 2 P
he makes the maid to answer, "whoop, do me no WT 4.04.198 P
off, slights him, with "whoop, do me no harm, 4.04.200 P
"whoop, jug! LR 1.04.225
WHOOP'D 1 FR 0.0001 REL FR 1 V 0 P
if i whoop'd, what then? TNK 3.02. 9
WHOR'D 1 FR 0.0001 REL FR 1 V 0 P
that hath kill'd my king and whor'd my mother, HAM 5.02. 64
WHORE 46 FR 0.0052 REL FR 31 V 15 P
never name her, child, if she be a whore. WIV 4.01. 63 P
ever your fresh whore and your powder'd bawd, an MM 3.02. 59 P
your highness do not marry me to a whore. 5.01.515 P
let's beat him before his whore. 2H4 2.04.257 P
rheumatic, and talk'd of the whore of babylon. H5 2.03. 38 P
all the argument is a whore and a cuckold, a TRO 2.03. 72 P
more, | but he as he, the heavier for a whore. 4.01. 67
why, his masculine whore. 5.01. 17 P
unless she said, "my mind is now turn'd whore." 5.02.114
me any thing for the intelligence of this whore. 5.02.193 P
young troyan ass, that loves the whore there, 5.04. 6 P
hold thy whore, grecian! 5.04. 24 P
now for thy whore, troyan! 5.04. 25 P
if the son of a whore fight for a whore, he 5.07. 21 P
if the son of a whore fight for a whore, he 5.07. 21 P
'zounds, ye whore, is black so base a hue? TIT 4.02. 71
a very good whore!" ROM 2.04. 31 P
thou common whore of mankind, that puts odds TIM 4.03. 43
this fell whore of thine | hath in her more 4.03. 62
be a whore still. 4.03. 84
enough to make a whore forswear her trade, | and 4.03.134
be strong in whore, allure him, burn him up, 4.03.142
whore still, | paint till a horse may mire upon 4.03.147
more whore, more mischief first; 4.03.168
/quarrel smiling, | show'd like a rebel's whore. MAC 1.02. 15
must, like a whore, unpack my heart with words, HAM 2.02.585
leave thy drink and thy whore, | and keep in a' LR 1.04.124
fortune, that arrant whore, | ne'er turns the 2.04. 52
why dost thou lash that whore? 4.06.161
villain, be sure thou prove my love a whore; OTH 3.03.359
she gave it him, and he hath giv'n it his whore. 4.01.177 P
this is a subtile whore, | a closet lock and key 4.02. 21
most goodly book, | made to write "whore" upon? 4.02. 72
what, not a whore? 4.02. 86
i took you for that cunning whore of venice 4.02. 89
he call'd her whore. 4.02.120
to be call'd whore? 4.02.127
why should he call her whore? 4.02.137
i cannot say "whore." 4.02.161
she turn'd to folly, and she was a whore. 5.02.132
villainous whore! 5.02.229
he hath given his empire | up to a whore, who ANT 3.06. 67
triple-turn'd whore! 4.12. 13
boy my greatness | i' th' posture of a whore. 5.02.221
she hath bought the name of whore thus dearly. CYM 2.04.128
to be his whore is witless. TNK 2.04. 5
WHOREMASTER 5 FR 0.0005 REL FR 0 V 5 P
the deputy cannot abide a whoremaster. MM 3.02. 35 P
is, saving your reverence, a whoremaster, that i 1H4 2.04.469 P
we may account thee a whoremaster and a knave, TIM 2.02.105 P
what is a whoremaster, fool? 2.02.107 P
an admirable evasion of whoremaster man, to lay LR 1.02.127 P
WHOREMASTERLY 1 FR 0.0001 REL FR 0 V 1 P
that greekish whoremasterly villain with the TRO 5.04. 7 P
WHOREMONGER 1 FR 0.0001 REL FR 0 V 1 P
if he be a whoremonger, and comes before him, he MM 3.02. 36 P
/WHORE'S 1 FR 0.0001 REL FR 0 V 1 P
/health, /a /boy's /love, /or /a /whore's /oath. LR 3.06. 19 P
WHORE'S 1 FR 0.0001 REL FR 0 V 1 P
for tearing a poor whore's ruff in a bawdy-house 2H4 2.04.145 P
WHORES 8 FR 0.0009 REL FR 4 V 4 P
none, man, all idle — whores and knaves. TMP 2.01.167 P
and your whores, sir, being members of my MM 4.02. 37 P
as a monkey, and the whores call'd him mandrake. 2H4 3.02.315 P
thou that giv'st whores indulgences to sin. 1H6 1.03. 35
her trade, | and to make whores, a bawd. TIM 4.03.135
i'll trust to your conditions, be whores still. 4.03.140
field, | and bawds and whores do churches build; LR 3.02. 92
would make themselves whores but they'ld do't! ANT 1.02. 77 P
WHORESON 40 FR 0.0045 REL FR 7 V 33 P
hang, you whoreson, insolent noisemaker! TMP 1.01. 43 P
why, thou whoreson ass, thou mistak'st me. TGV 2.05. 47 P
how now, you whoreson peasant, | where have you 4.04. 43
thou whoreson, senseless villain! ERR 4.04. 24 P
ah, you whoreson loggerhead! LLL 4.03.200
you whoreson malt-horse drudge! SHR 4.01.129
you whoreson villain! 4.01.155
a whoreson, beetle-headed, flap-ear'd knave! 4.01.157
ah, whoreson caterpillars! 1H4 2.02. 84 P
why, you whoreson round man, what's the matter? 2.04.140 P
thou knotty-pated fool, thou whoreson, obscene, 2.04.228 P
why, thou whoreson, impudent, emboss'd rascal, 3.03.156 P
thou whoreson mandrake, thou art fitter to be 2H4 1.02. 14 P
a whoreson achitophel! 1.02. 35 P
the whoreson smoothy-pates do now wear nothing 1.02. 37 P
is fall'n into this same whoreson apoplexy. 1.02.108 P
of sleeping in the blood, a whoreson tingling. 1.02.113 P
away, you whoreson upright /rabbit, away! 2.02. 85 P
ah, you whoreson little valiant villain, you! 2.04.209 P
come on, you whoreson chops. 2.04.218 P
thou whoreson little tidy bartholomew boar-pig, 2.04.231 P
thou whoreson mad compound of majesty, by this 2.04.294 P
you whoreson candle-mine, you, how vildly did 2.04.300 P
a whoreson cold, sir, a cough, sir, which i 3.02.181 P
you whoreson cur! TRO 2.01. 41 P
a whoreson dog, that shall palter with us thus! 2.03.233
butt, you whoreson indistinguishable cur, no. 5.01. 28 P
a whoreson tisick, a whoreson rascally tisick so 5.03.101 P
a whoreson rascally tisick so troubles me, and 5.03.101 P
mass, and well said, a merry whoreson, ha! ROM 4.04. 20
is a sore decayer of your whoreson dead body. HAM 5.01.172 P
a whoreson mad fellow's it was. 5.01.176 P
making, and the whoreson must be acknowledg'd. LR 1.01. 24 P
you whoreson dog, you slave, you cur! 1.04. 81 P
action-taking, whoreson, glass-gazing, 2.02. 18 P
of you, you whoreson cullionly barber-monger, 2.02. 33 P
thou whoreson zed, thou unnecessary letter! 2.02. 64 P
these same whoreson devils do the gods great ANT 5.02.275 P
and then a whoreson jack-an-apes must take me up CYM 2.01. 3 P
whoreson dog! 2.01. 14 P
WHORESONS 1 FR 0.0001 REL FR 1 V 0 P
the sly whoresons | have got a speeding trick to H8 1.03. 39
WHORING 1 FR 0.0001 REL FR 1 V 0 P
this is the fruits of whoring. OTH 5.01.116
WHORISH 1 FR 0.0001 REL FR 1 V 0 P
out of whorish loins | are pleas'd to breed out TRO 4.01. 64
WHO/'S 1 FR 0.0001 REL FR 1 V 0 P
yet who/'s so bold but says he sees it not? R3 3.06. 12
WHO'S 84 FR 0.0095 REL FR 62 V 22 P
then tell me, | who's the next heir of naples? TMP 2.01.245
you cannot tell who's your friend. 2.02. 85 P
no matter who's displeas'd when you are gone: TGV 2.07. 66
who's this comes here? 5.04. 18
who's there? WIV 1.01. 74 P
who's within there, ho? 1.04.131 P
who's there, i trow? 1.04.132 P
who's at home besides yourself? 4.02. 12 P
now, sir, who's a cuckold now? 5.05.109 P
who's that, i pray thee? MM 1.02. 63 P
who's that which calls? 1.04. 6
who's there? 2.04. 17
who's there? 3.01. 45
who's here? 4.03.148
who's within? MV 2.06. 25
who's there? 2.06. 60
who's there? AYL 2.03. 1
come, where be these gallants? who's at home? SHR 3.02. 87
pray you, sir, who's his tailor? AWW 2.05. 16 P
who's that? a frenchman? 4.05. 38 P
who's there? WT 2.03. 9
speak, citizens, for england. who's your king? JN 2.01.362
who's there? 5.06. 1
who's here? 2H4 4.04. 80
look who's at door there ho! 5.03. 70 P
who's there, that knocks so imperiously? 1H6 1.03. 5
who's within there, ho? 2H6 1.04. 78
and 'twixt each groan | say, "who's a traitor, 3.01.222
who's there? 4.02. 84 P
who's this? 3H6 2.05. 61
ho, who's here? R3 1.04. 84 P
the king? who's that? 4.01. 18
and then let's dream | who's best in favor. H8 1.04.108
who's there? ha? 2.02. 63
who's there, i say? 2.02. 64
who's there? 2.02. 73
who's that that bears the sceptre? 4.01. 38
who's that? TRO 1.02.189 P
who's that? 1.02.218 P
who's there? 2.03. 23 P
who's there? 2.03. 38 P
sweet lord, who's a-field to-day? 3.01.133 P

who's that at door? 4.02. 35
who's there? 4.02. 42 P
who's there? 4.02. 45
who's like to rise, | who thrives, and who COR 1.01.192
who's yonder, | that does appear as he were 1.06. 21
who's there? ROM 3.03. 74
who's there? 5.03.122
who's here? TIM 5.03. 2
who's there? JC 1.03. 41
to find out you. who's that? metellus cimber? 1.03.134
lucius, who's that knocks? 2.01.309
who's within? 2.02. 3
to th' self-same tune and words. who's here? MAC 1.03. 88
who's there? 2.01. 10
who's there? what ho! 2.02. 8
who's there, i' th' name of belzebub? 2.03. 3 P
who's there, in th' other devil's name? 2.03. 7 P
who's there? 2.03. 12 P
who's there? 3.01. 71
who's there? HAM 1.01. 1
who's there, besides foul weather? LR 3.01. 1
who's there? 3.02. 39
give me thy hand. who's there? 3.04. 41 P
who's there? what is't you seek? 3.04.127
who's there? 3.07. 27
how now? who's there? 4.01. 24
who's in, who's out — | and take upon 's the 5.03. 15
who's in, who's out — | and take upon 's the 5.03. 15
who's that which rings the bell? OTH 2.03.161
who's there? 5.01. 48
who's there? othello? 5.02. 23
who's there? 5.02. 89
see where he is, who's with him, what he does. ANT 1.03. 2
who's born that day | when i forget to send to 1.05. 63
who's his lieutenant, hear you? 3.07. 77
who's gone this morning? 4.05. 6
who's there? my woman? helen? CYM 2.02. 1
who's there that knocks? 2.03. 77
who's here? 3.06. 22
it is great morning. come away! — who's there? 4.02. 61
who's there? 5.03. 88
for who's so dumb that cannot write to thee, SON 38. 7

/WHOSE 6 FR 0.0006 REL FR 5 V 1 P

/within /whose /strong /immures | /the /ravish'd TRO pr 8
/make /those /laugh /whose /lungs /are /tickle HAM 2.02.323 P
/whose /warp'd /looks /proclaim | /what /store LR 3.06. 53
/opinion, /whose /wrong /thoughts /defile /thee, 3.06.112
/whose /reverence /even /the //head-lugg'd /bear 4.02. 42
/whose every passion fully strives | to make ANT 1.01. 50

WHOSE 697 FR 0.0787 REL FR 652 V 45 P

to sigh | to th' winds, whose pity, sighing back TMP 1.02.150
star, whose influence | if now i court not, but 1.02.182
whose enmity he flung aside, and breasted | the 2.01.117
a space whose ev'ry cubit | seems to cry out, 2.01.257
whose throats had hanging at 'em | wallets of 3.03. 45
such men | whose heads stood in their breasts? 3.03. 47
and your ways, whose wraths to guard you from — 3.03. 79
whose shadow the dismissed bachelor loves, 4.01. 67
th' sky, | whose wat'ry arch and messenger am i, 4.01. 71
whose vows are, that no bed-right shall be paid 4.01. 96
on whose nature | nurture can never stick; 4.01.188
whose pastime | is to make midnight mushrumps, 5.01. 38
by whose aid | (weak masters though ye be) i 5.01. 40
(whose inward pinches therefore are most strong) 5.01. 77
whose honor cannot | be measur'd or confin'd. 5.01.121
of whose soft grace | for the like loss i have 5.01.142
whose high imperious thoughts have punish'd me TGV 2.04.130
her, whose worth /makes other worthies nothing: 2.04.166
whose sovereignty so oft thou hast preferr'd 2.06. 15
whose whiteness so became them | as if but now 3.01.229
whose composed rhymes | should be full-fraught 3.02. 69
whose golden touch could soften steel and stones 3.02. 78
i kill'd a man, whose death i much repent, | but 4.01. 27
upon whose grave thou vow'dst pure chastity. 4.03. 21
company, | upon whose faith and honor i repose. 4.03. 26
whose life's as tender to me as my soul! 5.04. 37
for whose dear sake thou didst then rend thy 5.04. 47
to whose falls | melodious birds sings madrigals WIV 3.01. 17
"to shallow rivers, to whose falls —" | heaven 3.01. 29
desire, | fed in heart, whose flames aspire, 5.05. 97
angelo, a man whose blood | is very snow-broth; MM 1.04. 57
under whose heavy sense your brother's life 1.04. 65
whose house, sir, was (as they say) pluck'd down 2.01. 64 P
whose father died at hallowmas. 2.01.123 P
to fine the faults whose fine stands in record, 2.02. 40
whose rate are either rich or poor | as fancy 2.02.150
from fasting maids whose minds are dedicate | to 2.02.154
that respites me a life whose very comfort | is 2.03. 41
whose credit with the judge, or own great place, 2.04. 92
for, like an ass whose back with ingots bows, 3.01. 26
whose settled visage and deliberate word | nips 3.01. 89
shame to him whose cruel striking | kills for 3.02.267
whose advice | hath often still'd my brawling 4.01. 8
whose western side is with a vineyard back'd; 4.01. 29
whose persuasion is | i come about my brother. 4.01. 46
whose contents | shall witness to him i am near 4.03. 94
and say by whose advice | thou cam'st here to 5.01.113
whose salt imagination yet hath wrong'd | your 5.01.401
whose weakness, married to thy /stronger state, ERR 2.02.175
can you tell for whose sake? 3.01. 57
/one whose hard heart is button'd up with steel; 4.02. 34
what, is he arrested? tell me at whose suit. 4.02. 43
i know not at whose suit he is arrested well; 4.02. 44
say now, whose suit is he arrested at? 4.04.131
whose beard they have sing'd off with brands of 5.01.171
against whose charms faith melteth into blood. ADO 2.01.180
whose estimation do you mightily hold up — to a 2.02. 24 P
and what have i to give you back whose worth 4.01. 27
whose spirits toil in frame of villainies. 4.01.189
but such a one whose wrongs do suit with mine. 5.01. 7
whose joy of her is overwhelm'd like mine, | and 5.01. 9
whose names yet run smoothly in the even road of 5.02. 33 P
whose edge hath power to cut, whose will still LLL 2.01. 50
whose will still wills | it should none spare 2.01. 50
pray you, sir, whose daughter? 2.01.201
on whose side? 4.01. 75 P
on whose side? 4.01. 76 P
on whose side? 4.01. 77 P

love, whose month is ever may, | spied a blossom 4.03.100
whose club kill'd cerberus, that three-headed 5.02.589
whose influence is begot of that loose grace 5.02.859
whose unwished yoke | my soul consents not to MND 1.01. 81
on whose eyes i might approve | this flower's 2.02. 68
grey, | whose note full many a man doth mark, 3.01.132
now follow, if thou dar'st, to try whose right, 3.02.336
whose liquor hath this virtuous property, | to 3.02.367
with league whose date till death shall never 3.02.373
at whose approach, ghosts, wand'ring here and 3.02.381
you, whose gentle hearts do fear | the smallest 5.01.219
why should a man, whose blood is warm within, MV 1.01. 83
there are a sort of men whose visages | do cream 1.01. 88
whose own hard dealings teaches them suspect 1.03.161
to prove whose blood is reddest, his or mine. 2.01. 7
whose ambitious head | spets in the face of 2.07. 44
within whose empty eye | there is a written 2.07. 63
whose hearts are all as false | as stairs of 3.02. 83
whose souls do bear an egall yoke of love, 3.04. 13
acceptance, whose trial shall better publish his 4.01.165 P
whose posy was | for all the world like cutler's 5.01.148
whose lands and revenues enrich the new duke; AYL 1.01.102 P
whose loves | are dearer than the natural bond 1.02.275
under an oak whose antique root peeps out | upon 2.01. 31
whose heart th' accustom'd sight of death makes 3.05. 4
whose boughs were moss'd with age | and high top 4.03.104
hand with his | whose heart within his bosom is. 5.04.115
whose sudden sight hath thrall'd my wounded eye. SHR 1.01.220
whose hap shall be to have her | will not so 1.02.267
whose tongue? 2.01.216
i complain on thee to our mistress, whose hand 4.01. 30 P
his wife, | and he whose wife is most obedient, 5.02. 67
you, whose worthiness would stir it up where it AWW 1.01. 8 P
under whose practices he hath persecuted time 1.01. 14 P
whose skill was almost as great as his honesty; 1.01. 18 P
whose baser stars do shut us up in wishes, 1.01.183
whose apprehensive senses | all but new things 1.02. 60
whose judgments are | mere fathers of their 1.02. 61
whose constancies | expire before their fashions 1.02. 62
whose aged honor cites a virtuous youth, | did 1.03.210
to her whose state is such that cannot choose 1.03.214
as notes whose faculties inclusive were | more 1.03.226
whose simple touch | is powerful to araise king 2.01. 75
hand, whose banish'd sense | thou hast repeal'd, 2.03. 48
whose ceremony | shall seem expedient on the 2.03.178
whose want, and whose delay, is strew'd with 2.04. 44
whose want, and whose delay, is strew'd with 2.04. 44
whose great decision hath much blood let forth 3.01. 3
'fore whose throne 'tis needful, | ere i can 4.04. 3
you never had a servant to whose trust | your 4.04. 15
ever a friend whose thoughts more truly labor 4.04. 17
whose villainous saffron would have made all the 4.05. 2 P
a wife | whose beauty did astonish the survey 5.03. 16
richest eyes, whose words all ears took captive, 5.03. 17
whose dear perfection hearts that scorn'd to 5.03. 18
whose age and honor | both suffer under this 5.03.162
whose high respect and rich validity | did lack 5.03.192
whose nature sickens but to speak a truth. 5.03.207
for whose dear love, | they say, she hath TN 1.02. 39
whose skull jove cram with brains! 1.05.113 P
whose red and white | nature's own sweet and 1.05.239
roses, whose fair flow'r | being once display'd, 2.04. 38
or any taint of vice whose strong corruption 3.04.356
to whose ingrate and unauspicious altars | my 5.01.113
by whose gentle help | i was preserv'd to serve 5.01.255
a part, whose issue | will hiss me to my grave: WT 1.02.188
in whose success we are gentle — i beseech you, 1.02.394
whose foundation | is pil'd upon his faith, and 1.02.429
will bring all, whose spiritual counsel had, 2.01.186
whose ignorant credulity will not | come up to 2.01.192
whose sting is sharper than the sword's, and 2.03. 87
and toward your friend, whose love had spoke, 3.02. 69
in whose easiest passage | look for no less than 3.02. 90
whose every word deserves | to taste of thy most 3.02.178
of the young prince, whose honorable thoughts 3.02.195
to whose feeling sorrows i might be some allay 4.02. 7 P
no more, whose very naming punishes me with the 4.02. 21 P
whose loss of his most precious queen and 4.02. 23 P
from whose simplicity i think it not uneasy to 4.02. 49 P
father (all whose joy is nothing else | but fair 4.04.408
whose fresh complexion and whose heart together 4.04.574
whose fresh complexion and whose heart together 4.04.574
by which means i saw whose purse was best in 4.04.603 P
in whose company | i shall re-view sicilia, for 4.04.665
for whose sight | i have a woman's longing. 4.04.666
rascals, whose miseries are to be smil'd at, 4.04.792 P
him, whose daughter | his tears proclaim'd his, 5.01.159
a graceful gentleman, against whose person | (so 5.01.171
whose honor and whose honesty till now | endur'd 5.01.194
whose honor and whose honesty till now | endur'd 5.01.194
hand, whose worth and honesty | is richly noted; 5.03.144
bear his name whose form thou bearest: JN 1.01.160
against whose fury and unmatched force | the 1.01.265
whose foot spurns back the ocean's roaring tides 2.01. 24
whose leisure i have stay'd, have given him time 2.01. 58
boy, | under whose warrant i impeach thy wrong, 2.01.116
and by whose help i mean to chastise it. 2.01.117
whose valor plucks dead lions by the beard; 2.01.138
let us hear them speak | whose title they admit, 2.01.200
let us in — your king, whose labor'd spirits, 2.01.232
whose protection | is most divinely vow'd upon 2.01.236
till you compound whose right is worthiest, | we 2.01.281
whose sons lie scattered on the bleeding ground. 2.01.304
whose equality | by our best eyes cannot be 2.01.327
whose passage, vex'd with thy impediment, 2.01.336
whose party do the townsmen yet admit? 2.01.361
whose veins bound richer blood than lady blanch? 2.01.431
whose fullness of perfection lies in him. 2.01.440
and france, whose armor conscience buckled on, 2.01.564
wrath, | a rage whose heat hath this condition, 3.01.341
whose restraint | doth move the murmuring lips 4.02. 52
under whose conduct came those pow'rs of france 4.02.129
whose private with me of the dolphin's love | is 4.03. 16
from whose obedience i forbid my soul, 4.03. 64
whose tongue soe'er speaks false, | not truly 4.03. 91
all you whose souls abhor | th' uncleanly savors 4.03.111
now happy he whose cloak and center can | hold 4.03.155

whose office is this day | to feast upon whole 5.02.177
whose black contagious breath | already smokes 5.04. 33
villain, | whose bowels suddenly burst out. 5.06. 30
at whose request the king hath pardon'd them, 5.06. 35
whose youthful spirit, in me regenerate, | doth R2 1.03. 70
as praises, of whose taste the wise are /fond, 2.01. 18
to whose venom sound | the open ear of youth 2.01. 19
whose manners still our tardy, apish nation 2.01. 22
direct not him whose way himself will choose, 2.01. 29
whose rocky shore beats back the envious siege 2.01. 62
whose hollow womb inherits nought but bones. 2.01. 83
whose compass is no bigger than thy head, | and 2.01.101
thy knee, | whose duty is deceivable and false. 2.03. 84
whose double tongue may with a mortal touch 3.02. 21
under whose colors he had fought so long. 4.01.100
to whose flint bosom my condemned lord | is 5.01. 3
to whose high will we bound our calm contents. 5.02. 38
now, | whose state and honor i for aye allow. 5.02. 40
whose soldier now, under whose blessed cross 1H4 1.01. 20
under whose blessed cross | we are impressed and 1.01. 20
whose arms were moulded in their mother's womb, 1.01. 23
over whose acres walk'd those blessed feet 1.01. 25
news, | whose worst was that the noble mortimer, 1.01. 38
upon whose dead corpse' there was such misuse, 1.01. 43
the moon, under whose countenance we steal. 1.02. 29 P
whose daughter, as we hear, that earl of march 1.03. 84
whose tongue shall ask me for one penny cost 1.03. 91
unhappy king | (whose wrongs in us god pardon!) 1.03.149
and for whose death we in the world's wide mouth 1.03.153
whose high deeds, | whose hot incursions and 3.02.107
whose hot incursions and great name in arms, 3.02.108
under whose government come they along? 4.01. 19
jack, whose fellows are these that come after? 4.02. 62 P
whose power was in the first proportion, | and 4.04. 15
whose temper i intend to stain | with the best 5.02. 93
enemies, | whose deaths are yet unreveng'd. 5.03. 43
whose swift wrath beat down | the never-daunted 2H4 1.01.109
whose spirit lent a fire | even to the dullest 1.01.112
whose well-laboring sword | had three times 1.01.127
and as the wretch whose fever-weak'ned joints, 1.01.140
your master, whose chin is not yet fledge. 1.02. 20 P
whose bosom burns | with an incensed fire of 1.03. 13
how now, whose mare's dead? what's the matter? 2.01. 43 P
honest bardolph, whose zeal burns in his nose, 2.04.329 P
shadow, whose son art thou? 3.02.126 P
whose see is by a civil peace maintain'd, 4.01. 42
whose beard the silver hand of peace hath 4.01. 43
whose learning and good letters peace hath 4.01. 44
whose white investments figure innocence, | the 4.01. 45
whose memory is written on the earth | with yet 4.01. 81
whose dangerous eyes may well be charm'd asleep 4.02. 39
as he whose brow with homely biggen bound 4.05. 27
by whose fell working i was first advanc'd, 4.05.206
and by whose power i well might lodge a fear 4.05.207
whose music, to my thinking, pleas'd the king. 5.05.108
whose high, upreared, and abutting fronts | the H5 pr 21
whose right | suits not in native colors with 1.02. 16
whose guiltless drops | are every one a woe, a 1.02. 25
'gainst him whose wrongs gives edge unto the 1.02. 27
whose hearts have left their bodies here in 1.02.128
unto whose grace our passion is as subject | as 1.02.242
and in whose name | tell you the dolphin i am 1.02.290
whose ruin you /have sought, that to her laws 2.02.176
whose chin is but enrich'd | with one appearing 3.pr. 22
whose blood is fet from fathers of war-proof! 3.01. 18
whose limbs were made in england, show us here 3.01. 26
snow | upon the valleys whose low vassal seat 3.05. 51
his followers, whose condemnation is pronounc'd. 3.06.135 P
of every fool whose sense no more can feel | but 4.01.235
whose hours the peasant best advantages. 4.01.284
perish the man whose mind is backward now! 4.03. 72
and boys, | whose shouts and claps out-voice the 5.pr. 11
whose want gives growth to th' imperfections 5.02. 69
whose tenures and particular effects | you have 5.02. 72
kate, whose face is not worth sunburning, that 5.02.147 P
whose very shores look pale | with envy of each 5.02.350
whose state so many had the managing, | that ep 11
whose bloody deeds shall make all europe quake. 1H6 1.01.156
or whose will stands but mine? 1.03. 11
lieutenant, is it you whose voice i hear? 1.03. 16
by whose approach the regions of artois, 2.01. 9
in whose conquering name | let us resolve to 2.01. 26
whose pitchy mantle over-veil'd the earth. 2.02. 2
whose glory fills the world with loud report. 2.02. 43
till you conclude that he upon whose side | the 2.04. 40
eyes, like lamps whose wasting oil is spent, 2.05. 8
are these feet, whose strengthless stay is numb 2.05. 13
reign, | before whose glory i was great in arms, 2.05. 24
during whose reign the percies of the north, 2.05. 67
o thou whose wounds become hard-favored death, 4.07. 23
whose life was england's glory, gallia's wonder. 4.07. 48
whose maiden blood, thus rigorously effus'd, 5.04. 52
whose large style | agrees not with the leanness 2H6 1.01.111
whose church-like humors fits not for a crown. 1.01.247
with whose sweet smell the air shall be perfum'd 1.01.255
whose bookish rule hath pull'd fair england down 1.01.259
god, whose name and power | thou tremblest at, 1.04. 25
whose beam stands sure, whose rightful cause 2.01.201
beam stands sure, whose rightful cause prevails. 2.01.201
clarence, from whose line | i claim the crown, 2.02. 34
death, at whose name i oft have been afeard, 2.04. 89
whose overweening arm i have pluck'd back, | by 3.01.159
whose flood begins to flow within mine eyes; 3.01.199
whose dismal tune bereft my vital pow'rs; 3.02. 41
whose fruit thou art | and never of the nevils' 3.02.214
whose conscience with injustice is corrupted. 3.02.235
with whose envenomed and fatal sting, | your 3.02.267
i swear, | whose far-unworthy deputy i am, | he 3.02.286
thy name affrights me, in whose sound is death. 4.01. 33
sink, whose filth and dirt | troubles the silver 4.01. 71
whose dreadful swords were never drawn in vain, 4.01. 92
whose hopeful colors | advance our half-fac'd 4.01. 97
and as for these whose ransom we have set, | it 4.01.139
(in whose time boys went to span-counter for 4.02.157 P
as for words, whose greatness answers words, 4.10. 53
whose smile and frown, like to achilles' spear, 5.01.100
whose warlike ears could never brook retreat, 3H6 1.01. 5
whose cowardice | hath made us by-words to our 1.01. 41

whose heir my father was, and i am his. 1.01.140
in whose cold blood no spark of honor bides. 1.01.184
comes the queen, whose looks bewray her anger. 1.01.211
whose haughty spirit, winged with desire, | will 1.01.267
within whose circuit is elysium | and all that 1.02. 30
whose father slew my father, he shall die. 1.03. 5
whose frown hath made thee faint and fly ere 1.04. 48
whose tongue more poisons than the adder's tooth 1.04.112
whose heavy looks foretell | some dreadful story 2.01. 43
whose hand is that the forest bear doth lick? 2.02. 13
whose father for his hoarding went to hell? 2.02. 48
whose father bears the title of a king | (as if 2.02.140
whose soul is that which takes her heavy leave? 2.06. 42
stifle the villain whose unstanched thirst 2.06. 83
ay, here's a deer whose skin's a keeper's fee: 3.01. 22
whose wisdom was a mirror to the wisest; 3.03. 84
call him my king by whose injurious doom | my 3.03.101
at whose hands | he hath good usage and great 4.05. 5
whose arms gave shelter to the princely eagle, 5.02. 12
under whose shade the ramping lion slept, 5.02. 13
whose top–branch overpeer'd jove's spreading 5.02. 14
whose envious gulf did swallow up his life. 5.06. 25
whose ugly and unnatural aspect | may fright the R3 1.02. 23
on me, whose all not equals edward's moi'ty? 1.02.249
spider | whose deadly web ensnareth thee about? 1.03.242
whose bright out–shining beams thy cloudy wrath 1.03.267
for whose sake did i that ill deed? 1.04.211
to those whose dealings have deserv'd the place 3.01. 49
the world, | whose unavoided eye is murtherous. 4.01. 55
whose humble means match not his haughty spirit. 4.02. 37
to stop all hopes whose growth may damage me. 4.02. 59
whose hand soever lanch'd their tender hearts, 4.04.225
the children live whose fathers thou hast 4.04.391
the parents live whose children thou hast 4.04.393
o thou whose captain i account myself, | look on 5.03.108
methought their souls whose bodies richard 5.03.230
whose puissance on either side | shall be well 5.03.299
whose grace | chalks successors their way, nor H8 1.01. 59
whose figure even this instant cloud puts on 1.01.225
master — | whose honor heaven shield from soil! 1.02. 26
discharge a horrible oath, whose tenor | was, 1.02.206
gentlemen, | whose fault is this? 1.04. 43
by whose virtue, | the court of rome commanding, 2.02.103
ever by your grace, whose hand has rais'd me. 2.02.119
whose health and royalty i pray for. 2.03. 73
spain advis'd, whose counsel | i will implore. 2.04. 55
whose bright faces | cast thousand beams upon me 4.02. 88
whose minister you are, whiles here he liv'd 5.01.137
whose honesty the devil | and his disciples only 5.02.146
into whose hand i give thy life. 5.04. 11
in whose comparison all whites are ink | writing TRO 1.01. 56
to whose soft seizure | the cygnet's down is 1.01. 57
whose height commands as subject all the vale, 1.02. 3
hector, whose patience | is as a virtue fix'd, 1.02. 4
boat | whose weak untimber'd sides but even now 1.03. 43
whose med'cinable eye | corrects the /ill 1.03. 91
(between whose endless jar justice resides) 1.03.117
player, whose conceit | lies in his hamstring, 1.03.153
a slave whose gall coins slanders like a mint, 1.03.193
whose grossness little characters sum up; 1.03.325
whose wit was mouldy ere /your grandsires had 2.01.104 P
whose youth and freshness | wrinkles apollo's, 2.02. 78
whose price hath launch'd above a thousand ships 2.02. 82
none so noble | whose life were ill bestow'd, or 2.02.159
whose present courage may beat down our foes, 2.02.201
at whose pleasure, friend? 3.01. 23 P
at whose request do these men play? 3.01. 28 P
whose glorious deeds, but in these fields of 3.03.188
on whose bright crest fame with her loud'st oyes 4.05.143
towers, whose wanton tops do buss the clouds, 4.05.220
whose was't? 5.02. 71
i will have this. whose was it? 5.02. 87
come, tell me whose it was. 5.02. 88
whose was it? 5.02. 90
and by herself, i will not tell you whose. 5.02. 92
state, whose course will on | the way it takes, COR 1.01. 69
to make him worthy whose offense subdues him, 1.01.175
whose every motion | was tim'd with dying cries. 2.02.109
people, in whose name myself | attach thee as a 3.01.173
people, in whose power | we were elected theirs, 3.01.209
whose rage doth rend | like interrupted waters, 3.01.247
whose gratitude | towards her deserving children 3.01.289
those whose great power must try him — even 3.03. 80
whose breath i hate | as reek a' th' rotten fens 3.03.120
whose loves i prize | as the dead carcasses of 3.03.121
whose double bosoms seems to wear one heart, 4.04. 13
whose hours, whose bed, whose meal and exercise 4.04. 14
whose hours, whose bed, whose meal and exercise 4.04. 14
whose meal and exercise | are still together, 4.04. 14
whose passions and whose plots have broke their 4.04. 19
whose passions and whose plots have broke their 4.04. 19
for whose old love i have | (though i show'd 5.03. 12
whose repetition will be dogg'd with curses; 5.03.144
whose chronicle thus writ: 5.03.145
whose children he hath slain, their base throats 5.06. 52
whose smoke like incense doth perfume the sky. TIT 1.01.145
whose fortunes rome's best citizens applaud! 1.01.164
whose friend in justice thou hast ever been, 1.01.180
lord saturnine, whose virtues will, i hope, 1.01.225
whose wisdom hath her fortune conquered. 1.01.336
whose fury not dissembled speaks his griefs. 1.01.438
whose mouth is covered with rude–growing briers, 2.03.199
upon whose leaves are drops of new–shed blood 2.03.200
whose circling shadows kings have sought to 2.04. 19
whose youth was spent | in dangerous wars whilst 3.01. 2
whose souls is not corrupted as 'tis thought. 3.01. 9
nay, come, agree whose hand shall go along, 3.01.174
whose loss hath pierc'd him deep and scarr'd his 4.04. 31
whose name was once our terror, now our comfort, 5.01. 10
whose high exploits and honorable deeds 5.01. 11
did not thy hue bewray whose brat thou art, 5.01. 28
whose misadventur'd piteous overthrows | doth ROM pr 7
alas that love, whose view is muffled still, 1.01.171
and like her most whose merit most shall be; 1.02. 31
persons out | whose names are written there, and 1.02. 36
find them out whose names are written here! 1.02. 38 P
to find those persons whose names are here writ, 1.02. 42 P
whose house? 1.02. 75 P
by whose direction foundst thou out this place? 2.02. 79
it back to tybalt, whose dexterity | retorts it. 3.01.163
underneath whose arm | an envious thrust from 3.01.167
for whose dear sake thou wast but lately dead: 3.03.136
nor that is not the lark whose notes do beat 3.05. 21
to whose foul mouth no healthsome air breathes 4.03. 34
now, | whose sale is present death in mantua, 5.01. 51
whose untimely death | banish'd the new–made 5.03.234
whose eyes are on this sovereign lady fix'd, TIM 1.01. 68
her, | whose present grace to present slaves and 1.01. 71
service, from whose help | i deriv'd liberty. 1.02. 7
those men | upon whose age we void it up again 1.02.138
by whose death he's stepp'd | into a great 2.02.223
whose procreation, residence, and birth | scarce 4.03. 4
whose dimpled smiles from fools exhaust their 4.03.120
whose proof nor yells of mothers, maids, nor 4.03.125
and he whose pious breath seeks to convert you, 4.03.141
whose womb unmeasurable and infinite breast 4.03.178
whose self–same mettle, | whereof thy proud 4.03.179
whose naked natures live in all the spite | of 4.03.228
of wreakful heaven, whose bare unhoused trunks, 4.03.229
whose blush doth thaw the consecrated snow 4.03.385
whose liquid surge resolves | the moon into salt 4.03.439
whose eyes do never give | but thorough lust and 4.03.484
master, in whose breast | doubt and suspect, 4.03.511
whose thankless natures (o abhorred spirits!) 5.01. 60
you, | whose star–like nobleness gave life and 5.01. 63
this, | whose fall the mark of his ambition is. 5.03. 10
whose soft impression | interprets for my poor 5.04. 68
noble timon, of whose memory | hereafter more. 5.04. 80
and that same eye whose bend doth awe the world JC 1.02.123
whose end is purpos'd by the mighty gods? 2.02. 27
of whose true–fix'd and resting quality | there 3.01. 61
whose ransoms did the general coffers fill; 3.02. 89
men | whose daggers have stabb'd caesar; 3.02.152
whose horrid image doth unfix my hair | and make MAC 1.03.135
thought, whose murther yet is but fantastical, 1.03.139
and you whose places are the nearest, know | we 1.04. 36
whose care is gone before to bid us welcome: 1.04. 57
whose howl's his watch, thus with his stealthy 2.01. 54
there is none but he | whose being i do fear; 3.01. 54
whose heavy hand hath bow'd you to the grave, 3.01. 89
bosoms, | whose execution takes your enemy off, 3.01.104
whose loves i may not drop, but wail his fall 3.01.121
whose absence is no less material to me | than 3.01.135
tyrant, whose sole name blisters our tongues, 4.03. 12
things, | whose hearts are absent too. 5.04. 14
whose arms | are hir'd to bear their staves; 5.07. 17
whose voices i desire aloud with mine: 5.09. 24
whose sore task | does not divide the sunday HAM 1.01. 75
king, | whose image even but now appear'd to us, 1.01. 81
upon whose influence neptune's empire stands 1.01.119
whose common theme | is death of fathers, and 1.02.103
i could a tale unfold whose lightest word 1.05. 15
whose love was of that dignity | that it went 1.05. 48
upon a wretch whose natural gifts were poor | to 1.05. 51
whose effect | holds such an enmity with blood 1.05. 64
love, | whose violent property fordoes itself, 2.01.100
whose judgments in such matters cried in the top 2.02.438 P
"the rugged pyrrhus, he whose sable arms, 2.02.452
upon whose property and most dear life | a 2.02.570
from whose bourn | no traveller returns, puzzles 3.01. 78
is from the purpose of playing, whose end, both 3.02. 21 P
whose blood and judgment are so well co–meddled, 3.02. 69
with the hobby–horse, whose epitaph is, "for o, 3.02.134 P
that spirit upon whose weal depends and rests 3.03. 14
to whose /huge spokes ten thousand lesser things 3.03. 19
us, whose providence | should have kept short, 4.01. 17
/... | whose whisper o'er the world's diameter, 4.01. 41
good sir, whose powers are these? 4.04. 9
whose spirit with divine ambition puff'd | makes 4.04. 49
whose worth, if praises may go back again, 4.07. 27
whose grave's this, sirrah? 5.01.117 P
whose was it? 5.01.175 P
whose do you think it was? 5.01.176 P
whose wicked deed thy most ingenious sense 5.01.248
what is he whose grief | bears such an emphasis, 5.01.254
whose phrase of sorrow | conjures the wand'ring 5.01.255
whose motive, in this case, should stir me most 5.02.245
and from his mouth whose voice will draw /on 5.02.392
to whose young love | the vines of france and LR 1.01. 83
that lord whose hand must take my plight shall 1.01.101
nor are those empty–hearted whose low sounds 1.01.153
whose nature is so far from doing harms | that 1.02.180
on whose foolish honesty | my practices ride 1.02.181
whose mind and mine, i know, in that are one, 1.03. 15
whose virtue and obedience doth this instant 2.01.113
whose life i have spar'd at suit of his grey 2.02. 62 P
whose influence, like the wreath of radiant fire 2.02.107
king, | on whose employment i was sent to you. 2.02.129
whose disposition, all the world well knows, 2.02.153
whose welcome i perceiv'd had poison'd mine — 2.04. 39
this is a slave whose easy–borrowed pride 2.04.185
old kind father, whose frank heart gave all — 3.04. 20
to whose hands you have sent the lunatic king — 3.07. 46
whose high and bending head | looks fearfully in 4.01. 73
whose power | will close the eye of anguish. 4.04. 14
whose face between her forks presages snow; 4.06.119
whose age had charms in it, whose title more, 5.03. 48
whose age had charms in it, whose title more, 5.03. 48
whose messengers are here about my side, | upon OTH 1.02. 89
rocks, /and hills whose /heads touch heaven, 1.03.141
and men whose heads | /do /grow beneath their 1.03.144
whose footing here anticipates our thoughts | a 2.01. 76
whose qualification shall come into no true 2.01.275 P
whose rude throats | th' immortal jove's dread 3.03.355
whose icy current and compulsive course | nev'r 3.03.454
why, whose is it? 3.04.187
give me the addition | whose want even kills me. 4.01.105
whose solid virtue | the shot of accident nor 4.01.266
whose noise is this that cries on murther? 5.01. 48
whose breath, indeed, these hands have newly 5.02.202
of one whose hand, | like the base /indian, 5.02.346
of one whose subdu'd eyes, | albeit unused to 5.02.348
whose better issue in the war from italy, | upon ANT 1.02. 93
whose love is never link'd to the deserver 1.02.186
whose quality, going on, | the sides o' th' 1.02.191
to such whose places under us require, | our 1.02.195
upon the present state, whose numbers threaten, 1.03. 52
at whose foot, | to mend the petty present, i 1.05. 44
whose beauty claims | no worse a husband than 2.02.127
whose virtue and whose general graces speak 2.02.129
whose virtue and whose general graces speak 2.02.129
whose wind did seem | to /glow the delicate 2.02.203
say to me, whose fortunes shall rise higher, 2.03. 16
at whose burthen | the anger'd ocean foams, with 2.06. 20
war, whose several ranges | frighted each other? 3.13. 5
whose ministers would prevail | under the 3.13. 23
whose he is, we are, and that is caesar's. 3.13. 52
whose eye beck'd forth my wars and call'd them 4.12. 26
whose bosom was my crownet, my chief end, | like 4.12. 27
whose heart i thought i had, for she had mine — 4.14. 16
to whose kindnesses i am most infinitely tied. CYM 1.06. 23 P
this hand, whose touch | (whose every touch) 1.06.100
whose touch | (whose every touch) would force 1.06.101
than some, whose tailors are as dear as yours, 2.03. 79
whose remembrance | is yet fresh in their grief. 2.04. 14
whose strength | i will confirm with oath, which 2.04. 63
(whose remembrance yet | lives in men's eyes, 3.01. 2
whose use the sword of caesar | hath too much 3.01. 55
mangled, whose repair and franchise | shall, by 3.01. 56
house with such | whose roof's as low as ours! 3.03. 2
whose top to climb | is certain falling, or so 3.03. 47
i as a tree | whose boughs did bend with fruit; 3.03. 61
whose false oaths prevail'd | before my perfect 3.03. 66
whose edge is sharper than the sword, whose 3.04. 34
whose tongue | outvenoms all the worms of nile, 3.04. 34
whose breath | rides on the posting winds and 3.04. 35
jay of italy | (whose mother was her painting) 3.04. 50
whose love–suit hath been to me | as fearful as 3.04.133
from whose so many weights of baseness cannot 3.05. 88
differs in dignity, | whose dust is both alike. 4.02. 5
whose rudeness | answer'd my steps too loud. 4.02.214
whose answer would be death | drawn on with 4.04. 13
done aught but well, | whose face i never saw? 5.04. 36
whose father then (as men report | thou orphans' 5.04. 39
you ghosts | accuse the thunderer, whose bolt, 5.04. 95
whose rags sham'd gilded arms, whose naked 5.05. 4
whose naked breast | stepp'd before targes of 5.05. 4
was as a scorpion to her sight, whose life, 5.05. 45
whose kinsmen have made suit | that their good 5.05. 71
whose containing | is so from sense in hardness, 5.05.430
whose issue | promises britain peace and plenty. 5.05.457
at whose conception, till lucina reigned, PER 1.01. 8
whose arm seems far too short to hit me here. 1.02. 8
and by whose letters i'll dispose myself. 1.02.117
thee i lay, whose wisdom's strength can bear it. 1.02.119
whose towers bore heads so high they kiss'd the 1.04. 24
whose men and dames so jetted and adorn'd, 1.04. 26
whose /delightful steps | shall make the gazer 2.01.158
in honor of whose birth these triumphs are, 2.02. 5
my commendations great, whose merit's less. 2.02. 9
whose death indeed the strongest in our censure, 2.04. 34
ship, upon whose deck | the seas–toss'd pericles 3.ch. 59
on whose grace | you may depend hereafter. 3.03. 40
and care in us | at whose expense 'tis done. 4.03. 46
her to meteline, 'gainst whose shore | riding, 5.03. 10
(whose modest scenes blush on his marriage–day, TNK pr 4
whose sovereigns fell before | the wrath of 1.01. 39
tyrant, whose successes | makes heaven unfear'd, 1.02. 63
of whose success i dare not | make any timorous 1.03. 2
for whose speed | the great bellona i'll solicit 1.03. 12
torrents whose roaring tyranny and power | i' 1.03. 38
for whose fortunes | i will now in and kneel, 1.03. 93
whose doughty dismal fame | from dis to daedalus 3.05.114
at whose great feet i offer up my penner. 3.05.124
whose servant (if there be a right in seeing 3.06.147
whose twelve strong labors crown his memory, 3.06.176
discover'd how | and by whose means he escap'd, 4.01. 20
your daughter's, | whose pardon is procur'd too; 4.01. 21
whose spirit in you | expels the seeds of fear 5.01. 35
whose havoc in vast field | unearthed skulls 5.01. 51
whose breath blows down | the teeming ceres' 5.01. 52
you whose free nobleness do make my cause | your 5.01. 73
whose youth, like wanton boys through bonfires, 5.01. 86
in mortal bosoms, whose chase is this world, 5.01.131
into whose port | ne'er ent'red wanton sound) to 5.01.147
whose lives (for this poor comfort) are laid 5.04. 14
whose title is as momentary | as to us death is 5.04. 17
in whose end | the visages of bridegrooms we'll 5.04.126
ever you can make, | whose discipline is riot. STM II.C 113
whose sinowy neck in battle ne'er did bow, | who VEN 99
whose gentle wind | shall cool the heat of this 189
whose hollow womb resounds like heaven's thunder 268
whose beams upon his hairless face are fix'd, 487
whose precious taste her thirsty lips well knew, 543
whose vultur thought doth pitch the price so 551
chiefly in love, whose leave exceeds commission: 568
whose tushes never sheath'd he whetteth still, 617
whose full perfection all the world amazes, 634
under whose sharp fangs on his back doth lie 663
whose blood upon the fresh flowers being shed 665
whose attaint | disorder breeds by heating of 741
or theirs whose desperate hands themselves do 765
under whose simple semblance he hath fed | upon 795
whose ridges with the meeting clouds contend: 820
from whose silver breast | the sun ariseth in 855
like a milch doe, whose swelling dugs do ache, 875
whose frothy mouth bepainted all with red, 901
or as the snail, whose tender horns being hit, 1033
whose wonted lily white | with purple tears, 1053
whose tongue is music now? 1077
on, | under whose brim the gaudy sun would peep; 1088
whose downward eye still looketh for a grave, 1106
by whose swift aid | their mistress mounted 1190
within whose face beauty and virtue strived LUC 52
whose inward ill no outward harm express'd. 91
not | to darken her whose light excelleth thine; 191
whose crime will bear an ever–during blame. 224
between whose hills her head entombed is; 390
whose perfect white | show'd like an april daisy 394
whose ranks of blue veins, as his hand did scale 440
whose grim aspect sets every joint a–shaking; 452
whose crooked beak threats, if he mount, he dies 508

to whose weak ruins muster troops of cares, | to 720
than they whose whole is swallowed in confusion. 1159
whose love of either to myself was nearer, 1165
by whose example thou reveng'd mayst be. 1194
whose swift obedience to her mistress hies; 1215
but they whose guilt within their bosoms lie 1342
whose waves to imitate the battle sought | with 1438
whose enchanting story | the credulous old priam 1521
whose words like wildfire burnt the shining 1523
whose deed hath made herself herself detest. 1566
whose heavenly touch | upon the lute doth ravish PP 8. 5
spenser to me, whose deep conceit is such | as, 8. 7
love, whose month was ever may, | spied a 16. 2
by whose falls | melodious birds sing madrigals. 19. 7
trumpet be, | to whose sound chaste wings obey. PHT 4
whose fresh repair if now thou not renewest, SON 3. 3
for where is she so fair whose unear'd womb 3. 5
whose speechless song, being many, seeming one, 8.13
whose strength's abundance weakens his own heart 23. 4
thou, whose shadow shadows doth make bright, 43. 5
so am i as the rich whose blessed key | can 52. 1
blessed are you, whose worthiness gives scope, 52.13
whose action is no stronger than a flower? 65. 4
whose influence is thine, and born of thee: 78.10
in whose confine immured is the store | which 84. 3
but that is in my thought, whose love to you 85.11
that love is merchandiz'd whose rich esteeming 102. 3
whose million'd accidents | creep in 'twixt vows 115. 5
whose worth's unknown, although his highth be 116. 8
upon that blessed wood whose motion sounds 128. 2
as those whose beauties proudly make them cruel; 131. 2
wilt thou, whose will is large and spacious, 135. 5
cries to catch her whose busy care is bent | to 143. 6
her "love" for whose dear love i rise and fall. 151.14
from off a hill whose concave womb reworded | a LC 1
threw, | upon whose weeping margent she was set, 39
whose bare outbragg'd the web it seem'd to wear; 95
not one whose flame my heart so much as warmed, 191
in whose fresh regard | weak sights their sickly 213
whose white weighs down the airy scale of praise 226
whose rarest havings made the blossoms dote, 235
whose sights till then were levell'd on my face, 282

WHOSO 4 FR 0.0004 REL FR 4 V 0 P

and whoso empties them | by so much fills their R2 2.02.130
law of arms is such | that whoso draws a sword, 1H6 3.04. 39
that whoso please | to stop affliction, let him TIM 5.01.209
men in awe, | that whoso ask'd her for his wife, PER 1.ch. 37

WHOSOE'ER 3 FR 0.0003 REL FR 3 V 0 P

king, | the king of naples, whosoe'er thou art. 1H6 5.03. 52
and whosoe'er gainsays king edward's right, | by 3H6 4.07. 74
to doom th' offenders, whosoe'er they be: R3 3.04. 65

WHOSOEVER 3 FR 0.0003 REL FR 2 V 1 P

if thou do pardon, whosoever pray, | more sins R2 5.03. 83
o' th' soundest judgments in troy, whosoever, TRO 1.02.192 P
for whosoever wins | loses a noble cousin for TNK 4.02.155

WHOSOMEVER 1 FR 0.0001 REL FR 0 V 1 P

for, whosomever you take him to be, he is ajax. TRO 2.01. 64 P

/WHY 16 FR 0.0018 REL FR 12 V 4 P

/why /am /i /sent /for /to /a /king | /before /i R2 4.01.162
/sometime /went /disguis'd, /and /why /not /i? 2H6 4.01. 48
/why /let /it /strike? R3 4.02.113
/why, /marcus, /no /man /should /be /mad /but /i TIT 3.02. 24
and /why such daily /cast of brazen cannon, HAM 1.01. 73
/why /then /'tis /none /to /you; 2.02.249 P
/why /then /your /ambition /makes /it /one. 2.02.252 P
/why, /he /had /none. 5.01. 34 P
/why, /man, /they /did /make /love /to /this 5.02. 57
i know not /why he comes. LR 2.01. 79
/why /she /dares /not /come /over /to /thee." 3.06. 28
/justicer, /why /hast /thou /let /her /scape? 3.06. 56
/and /cries, | "/alack, /why /does /he /so?" 4.02. 59
/why /the /king /of /france /is /so /suddenly 4.03. 1 P
/why, /good /sir? 4.03. 41
you have lost him, | /why, i have lost him too. OTH 4.02. 47

WHY 1555 FR 0.1757 REL FR 1071 V 484 P

why, that's my spirit! TMP 1.02.215
why speaks my father so ungently? 1.02.445
why, in good time. 2.01. 96 P
why | doth it not then our eyelids sink? 2.01.200
were death | that now hath seiz'd them, why, 2.01.261
why, how now, ho! 2.01.308
why are you drawn? 2.01.308
why, thou debosh'd fish thou, was there ever man 3.02. 26 P
why, i said nothing. 3.02. 50 P
why, what did i? 3.02. 72 P
why, as i told thee, 'tis a custom with him | i' 3.02. 87
sir, why stand you | in this strange stare? 3.03. 94
why hath thy queen | summon'd me hither, to this 4.01. 82
why, that's my dainty ariel! 5.01. 95
why, how now, stephano? 5.01.285 P
if lost, why then a grievous labor won; TGV 1.01. 33
why then my horns are his horns, whether i wake 1.01. 79 P
nod–ay — why, that's "noddy." 1.01.112 P
why, sir, how do you bear with me? 1.01.122 P
why? couldst thou perceive so much from her? 1.01.134 P
why not on proteus, as of all the rest? 1.02. 20
why, he, of all the rest, hath never mov'd me. 1.02. 27
why didst thou stoop then? 1.02. 70
and why not you? 1.02. 84
why, what of him? 1.03. 4
why, this it is: 1.03. 90
why then this may be yours — for this is but 2.01. 2
why, sir, who bade you call her? 2.01. 9 P
why, how know you that i am in love? 2.01. 17 P
why, sir, i know her not. 2.01. 45 P
why? 2.01. 69 P
if not, why, so. 2.01.131
why, if it please you, take it for your labor; 2.01.133
to yourself; why, she woos you by a figure. 2.01.148 P
why, she hath not writ to me? 2.01.151 P
why, do you not perceive the jest? 2.01.153 P
why, she hath given you a letter. 2.01.159 P
why muse you, sir? 2.01.169 P
why then we'll make exchange: 2.02. 6
why, my grandam, having no eyes, look you, wept 2.03. 12 P
why, there 'tis; 2.03. 28 P
why weep'st thou, man? 2.03. 35 P
why, he that's tied here, crab, my dog. 2.03. 40 P
thy service — why dost thou stop my mouth? 2.03. 44 P
why, man, if the river were dry, i am able to 2.03. 51 P
why, lady, love hath twenty pair of eyes. 2.04. 95
why, valentine, what braggadism is this? 2.04.164
why, man, she is mine own, | and i as rich in 2.04.168
why then, how stands the matter with them? 2.05. 20 P
why, stand–under and under–stand is all one. 2.05. 32 P
why, thou whoreson ass, thou mistak'st me. 2.05. 47 P
why, fool, i meant not thee, i meant thy master. 2.05. 49 P
why, i tell thee, i care not, though he burn 2.05. 52 P
why? 2.05. 56 P
why then your ladyship must cut your hair. 2.07. 44
why, ev'n what fashion thou best likes, lucetta. 2.07. 52
for why, the fools are mad, if left alone. 3.01. 99
why then i would resort to her by night. 3.01.110
why then a ladder, quaintly made of cords, | to 3.01.117
why, any cloak will serve the turn, my lord. 3.01.134
why, phaeton (for thou art merops' son), | wilt 3.01.153
and why not death, rather than living torment? 3.01.170
why, sir, i'll strike nothing. i pray you — 3.01.203 P
why, a horse can do no more; 3.01.275 P
with my /master's /ship? why, it is at sea. 3.01.282 P
why, man? how black? 3.01.287 P
why, as black as ink. 3.01.288 P
why, that word makes the faults gracious. 3.01.368 P
why then will i tell thee — that thy master 3.01.372 P
why didst not tell me sooner? 3.01.380 P
why, ne'er repent it, if it were done so. 4.01. 30
i pray you, why is it? 4.02. 27 P
why, my pretty youth? 4.02. 58 P
why dost thou cry "alas"? 4.04. 77
why do i pity him | that with his very heart 4.04. 93
why then | she's fled unto that peasant 5.02. 34
why, this it is to be a peevish girl, | that 5.02. 49
why, boy! 5.04. 86 P
why, wag! 5.04. 86 P
why, this is the ring i gave to julia. 5.04. 93
why, it is affectations. WIV 1.01.150 P
why, sir, for my part, i say the gentleman had 1.01.174 P
why, did you not lend it to alice shortcake upon 1.01.203 P
why, if it be so, i will marry her upon any 1.01.225 P
why do your dogs bark so? 1.01.286 P
why then let kibes ensue. 1.03. 32 P
"ask me no reason why i love you, for though 2.01. 4 P
why, he hath not been thrice in my company! 2.01. 26 P
why, i'll exhibit a bill in the parliament for 2.01. 28 P
why, this is the very same: 2.01. 82 P
why, look where he comes; 2.01.102 P
why, sir, my wife is not young. 2.01.112 P
how now, sweet frank, why art thou melancholy? 2.01.150 P
why then the world's mine oyster, | which i with 2.02. 3
why, thou unconfinable baseness, it is as much 2.02. 20 P
why, sir, she's a good creature. 2.02. 55 P
why, you say well. 2.02. 94 P
why, i will. 2.02.123 P
why? 3.01. 64 P
why, this boy will carry a letter twenty mile, 3.02. 32 P
why, now let me die, for i have liv'd long 3.03. 44 P
why, alas, what's the matter? 3.03.105 P
if you know yourself clear, why, i am glad of it 3.03.116 P
without cause, why then make sport at me, then 3.03.150 P
why, what have you to do whither they bear it? 3.03.154 P
make known to you why i have done this. 3.03.225 P
why, thou must be thyself. 3.04. 3
cannot attain it, why then hark you hither! 3.04. 21
why, how now? 3.04. 68
why, none but mine own people. 4.02. 14 P
why? 4.02. 20 P
why, woman, your husband is in his old lines 4.02. 21 P
why, does he talk of him? 4.02. 30 P
why then you are utterly sham'd, and he's but a 4.02. 42 P
why, this passes, master ford. 4.02.122 P
why, this is lunatics! this is mad as a mad dog! 4.02.124 P
why, man, why? 4.02.144 P
why, man, why? 4.02.144 P
why may not he be there again? 4.02.147 P
why, it is my maid's aunt of brainford. 4.02.170 P
why yet there want not many that do fear | in 4.04. 39
and ask him why, that hour of fairy revel, | in 4.04. 59
why, sir, they were nothing but about mistress 4.05. 46 P
the purpose why, is here; 4.06. 21
why, now is cupid a child of conscience, he 5.05. 28 P
why, sir john, do you think, though we would 5.05.146 P
why, this is your own folly. 5.05.194 P
why? did you take her in /green? 5.05.208 P
why went you not with master doctor, maid? 5.05.219
why then all the dukes fall upon the king. MM 1.02. 2 P
why, 'twas a commandement to command the captain 1.02. 12 P
ay, why not? 1.02. 24 P
why, here's a change indeed in the commonwealth! 1.02.104 P
fellow, why dost thou show me thus to th' world? 1.02.116
why, how now, claudio? 1.02.124
why i desire thee | to give me secret harbor, 1.03. 3
sir, | you will demand of me why i do this. 1.03. 17
why "her unhappy brother"? 1.04. 21
why dost thou not speak, elbow? 2.01. 59 P
why, very well; 2.01.109 P
why, very well then — 2.01.114 P
why, very well; 2.01.127 P
why, very well then; i hope here be truths. 2.01.133 P
why, no. 2.01.154 P
why dost thou ask again? 2.02. 9
why, every fault's condemn'd ere it be done. 2.02. 38
why, no; 2.02. 57
why, all the souls that were were forfeit once, 2.02. 73
why do you put these sayings upon me? 2.02.133
why does my blood thus muster to my heart, 2.04. 20
why, | as all comforts are: 3.01. 54
why give you me this shame? 3.01. 80
why would he for the momentary trick | be 3.01.113
why, 'tis good; 3.02. 58 P
why, 'tis not amiss, pompey. 3.02. 63 P
if imprisonment be the due of a bawd, why, 'tis 3.02. 67 P
if you take it not patiently, why, your mettle 3.02. 76 P
why, what a ruthless thing is this in him, for 3.02.114 P
wise? why, no question but he was. 3.02.138 P
why should he die, sir? 3.02.171 P
why? 3.02.172 P
and why meet him at the gates, and /redeliver 4.04. 5 P
and why should we proclaim it in an hour before 4.04. 8 P
why, you are nothing then: 5.01.177 P
why, just, my lord, and that is angelo, | who 5.01.202
why, thou unreverend and unhallowed friar, 5.01.305
foh, sir, why, you bald–pated, lying rascal, you 5.01.352 P
and you may marvel why i obscur'd myself, 5.01.390
why thou departedst from thy native home, | and ERR 1.01. 29
to me, sir? why, you gave no gold to me. 1.02. 71
why should their liberty than ours be more? 2.01. 10
why, headstrong liberty is lash'd with woe: 2.01. 15
why, mistress, sure my master is horn–mad. 2.01. 57
but i pray, sir, why am i beaten? 2.02. 39 P
shall i tell you why? 2.02. 42 P
for they say, every why hath a wherefore. 2.02. 44 P
why, first — for flouting me, and then 2.02. 45
when in the why and the wherefore is neither 2.02. 48
why is time such a niggard of hair, being, as it 2.02. 77 P
why, but there's many a man hath more hair than 2.02. 82 P
why, thou didst conclude hairy men plain dealers 2.02. 86 P
substantial, why there is no time to recover. 2.02.104 P
why prat'st thou to thyself, and answer'st not? 2.02.193
why at this time the doors are made against you. 3.01. 93
against my soul's pure truth, why labor you, 3.02. 37
why call you me love? call my sister so. 3.02. 59
why, how now, dromio, where run'st thou so fast? 3.02. 71 P
for why? 3.02.103 P
why, give it to my wife, and fetch your money. 4.01. 54
why, thou peevish sheep, | what ship of 4.01. 93
why, man, what is the matter? 4.02. 41
why, 'tis a plain case: 4.03. 23 P
why, sir, i brought you word an hour since that 4.03. 37 P
why, dromio? 4.03. 62 P
why, sir, i gave the money for the rope. 4.04. 12
and why dost thou deny the bag of gold? 4.04. 96
why, so i did. 5.01. 58
why bear you these rebukes, and answer not? 5.01. 89
why, what an intricate impeach is this! 5.01.270
why, this is strange. 5.01.281
why look you strange on me? you know me well. 5.01.296
why, here begins his morning story right: 5.01.357
why, i' faith, methinks she's too low for a high ADO 1.01.171 P
why are you thus out of measure sad? 1.03. 1 P
why then your visor should be thatch'd. 2.01. 98 P
why, he is the prince's jester, a very dull fool 2.01.137 P
why, that's spoken like an honest drovier; 2.01.194 P
why, how now, count, wherefore are you sad? 2.01.288 P
why, these are very crotchets that he speaks — 2.03. 56
why, what effects of passion shows she? 2.03.107 P
why, it must be requited. 2.03.224 P
why did you so? 3.01. 44
why, you speak truth. 3.01. 59
if black, why, nature, drawing of an antic, 3.01. 63
if speaking, why, a vane blown with all winds; 3.01. 66
if silent, why, a block moved with none. 3.01. 67
why, every day to–morrow. 3.01.101
why, what's the matter? 3.02.101 P
i see any thing to–night why i should not marry 3.02.123 P
for your favor, sir, why, give god thanks, and 3.03. 19 P
why then take no note of him, but let him go, 3.03. 28 P
why, you speak like an ancient and most quiet 3.03. 39 P
why then let them alone till they are sober. 3.03. 45 P
the less you meddle or make with them, why, the 3.03. 53 P
why then depart in peace, and let the child wake 3.03. 69 P
why, how now? do you speak in the sick tune? 3.04. 41 P
why benedictus? 3.04. 77 P
know any inward impediment why you should not be 4.01. 13 P
why then, some be of laughing, as, ah, ha, he! 4.01. 21 P
sweet prince, why speak not you? 4.01. 63
why then you are no maiden. 4.01. 87
why, how now, cousin, wherefore sink you down? 4.01.110
hero, why, hero! 4.01.114
why, doth not every earthly thing | cry shame 4.01.120
why had i one? 4.01.129
why ever wast thou lovely in my eyes? 4.01.130
why had i not with charitable hand | took up a 4.01.131
valuing of her — why, she, o, she is fall'n 4.01.139
why seek'st thou then to cover with excuse 4.01.174
lack'd and lost, | why then we rack the value; 4.01.220
why then god forgive me! 4.01.281 P
why, this is flat perjury, to call a prince's 4.02. 41 P
sixt and lastly, why they are committed; 5.01.222 P
why, shall i always keep below stairs? 5.02. 9 P
smoothly in the even road of a blank verse, why, 5.02. 34 P
why, an hour in clamor and a quarter in rheum; 5.02. 82 P
why, what's the matter, | that you have such a 5.04. 40
why then she's mine. 5.04. 55
why, no, no more than reason. 5.04. 74
why then your uncle and the prince and claudio 5.04. 75
why then my cousin, margaret, and ursula | are 5.04. 78
why, that to know which else we should not know. LLL 1.01. 56
why? 1.01. 72
why should proud summer boast | before the birds 1.01.102
why should i joy in any abortive birth? 1.01.104
sweet lord, and why? 1.01.126
what say you, lords? why, this was quite forgot. 1.01.141
why, sadness is one and the self–same thing, 1.02. 4 P
why tough signior? why tough signior? 1.02. 11 P
why tough signior? why tough signior? 1.02. 11 P
why tender juvenal? why tender juvenal? 1.02. 12 P
why tender juvenal? why tender juvenal? 1.02. 12 P
why, sir, is this such a piece of study? 1.02. 50 P
why, will shall break it, will, and nothing else 2.01.100
why, all his behaviors did make their retire 2.01.234
why, it carries it. 3.01.140 P
why, it is a fairer name than french crown! 3.01.141 P
o, why then three–farthing worth of silk. 3.01.149 P
why, villain, thou must know first. 3.01.159 P
why did he come? 4.01. 71 P
why did he see? 4.01. 72 P
why, she that bears the bow. | finely put off! 4.01.109
and why indeed "naso," but for smelling out the 4.02.123 P
why, he comes in like a perjure, wearing papers. 4.03. 46
why then incision | would let her out in saucers 4.03. 95
how now, what is in you? why dost thou tear it? 4.03.196
we cannot cross the cause why we were born; 4.03.214

why, universal plodding poisons up | the nimble 4.03.301
why, that contempt will kill the speaker's heart 5.02.149
why, that they have, and bid them so be gone. 5.02.182
why take we hands then? 5.02.220
i know the reason, lady, why you ask. 5.02.243
why, this is he | that kiss'd his hand away in 5.02.323
where? when? what vizard? why demand you this? 5.02.386
amaz'd, my lord? why looks your highness sad? 5.02.391
why look you pale? 5.02.392
why ask you? 5.02.525 P
nay, why dost thou stay? 5.02.626
why, that's the way to choke a gibing spirit, 5.02.858
why should not i then prosecute my right? MND 1.01.105
why is your cheek so pale? 1.01.128
why, what you will. 1.02. 92 P
why art thou here | come from the farthest steep 2.01. 68
why should titania cross her oberon? 2.01.119
why, then may you leave a casement of the great 3.01. 56 P
why, you must not speak that yet! 3.01. 98 P
why do they run away? 3.01.112 P
o, why rebuke you him that loves you so? 3.02. 43
why should you think that i should woo in scorn? 3.02.122
but why unkindly didst thou leave me so? 3.02.183
why should he stay, whom love doth press to go? 3.02.184
why seek'st thou me? 3.02.189
why are you grown so rude? 3.02.262
why then you left me (o, the gods forbid!) 3.02.276
why so? 3.02.289
why, get you gone. who is't that hinders you? 3.02.318
why will you suffer her to flout me thus? 3.02.327
ho, ho, ho! coward, why com'st thou not? 3.02.421
why then, we are awake. 4.01.198
why, gentle sweet, you shall see no such thing. 5.01. 87
why, all these should be in the lanthorn; 5.01.260 P
in sooth, i know not why i am so sad; MV 1.01. 1
why then you are in love. 1.01. 46
why should a man, whose blood is warm within, 1.01. 83
why, he hath a horse better than the 1.02. 58 P
why, look you how you storm! 1.03.137
why, fear not, man, i will not forfeit it. 1.03.156
why then you must. 2.02.180
but where thou art not known, why, there they 2.02.184
and rend apparel out — | why, jessica, i say! 2.05. 6
why, jessica! 2.05. 6
why, 'tis an office of discovery, love, | and i 2.06. 43
why, that's the lady. 2.07. 31
why, that's the lady, all the world desires her. 2.07. 38
why, man, i saw bassanio under sail, | with him 2.08. 1
why, all the boys in venice follow him, | crying 2.08. 23
why then to thee, thou silver treasure house! 2.09. 34
why, yet it lives there uncheck'd that antonio 3.01. 2 P
why, the end is, he hath lost a ship. 3.01. 16 P
why, i am sure, if he forfeit, thou wilt not 3.01. 51 P
why, revenge. 3.01. 71 P
why, there, there, there, there! 3.01. 83 P
why, so — and i know not what's spent in the 3.01. 91 P
why, thou loss upon loss! 3.01. 92 P
why, shall we turn to men? 3.04. 78
sir, why, let it be as humors and conceits shall 3.05. 63 P
why, if two gods should play some heavenly match 3.05. 79
you'll ask me why i rather choose to have | a 4.01. 40
be rend'red | why he cannot abide a gaping pig; 4.01. 54
why he, a harmless necessary cat; 4.01. 55
why he, a woollen bagpipe, but of force | must 4.01. 56
why he hath made the ewe bleak for the lamb; 4.01. 74
why sweat they under burthens? 4.01. 95
why dost thou whet thy knife so earnestly? 4.01.121
why, this bond is forfeit, | and lawfully by 4.01.230
why then thus it is: 4.01.244
why doth the jew pause? take thy forfeiture. 4.01.335
why then the devil give him good of it! 4.01.345
why should we go in? 5.01. 50
why, i were best to cut my left hand off, | and 5.01.177
why, this is like the mending of highways | in 5.01.263
for my soul (yet i know not why) hates nothing AYL 1.01.165 P
why, this that i speak of. 1.02.136 P
why, cousin, why, rosalind! 1.03. 1 P
why, cousin, why, rosalind! 1.03. 1 P
why should i not? doth he not deserve well? 1.03. 36 P
if she be a traitor, | why so am i. 1.03. 73
why, whither shall we go? 1.03.106
why, what make you here? 2.03. 4
why are you virtuous? 2.03. 5
why do people love you? 2.03. 5
why would you be so fond to overcome | the bonny 2.03. 7
why, what's the matter? 2.03. 16
why, whither, adam, wouldst thou have me go? 2.03. 29
why, how now, adam? 2.06. 4 P
why, how now, monsieur, what a life is this, 2.07. 9
and why, sir, must they so? 2.07. 51
the "why" is plain as way to parish church: 2.07. 52
why, who cries out on pride | that can therein 2.07. 70
why then my taxing like a wild goose flies, 2.07. 86
why, i have eat none yet. 2.07. 88
why, if thou never wast at court, thou never 3.02. 40 P
why, we are still handling our ewes, and their 3.02. 53 P
why, do not your courtier's hands sweat? 3.02. 55 P
why do you infect yourself with them? 3.02.113 P
"why should this /a desert be? 3.02.125
why, god will send more, if the man will be 3.02.209 P
and why not the swift foot of time? 3.02.306 P
and the reason why they are not so punish'd and 3.02.402 P
but why did he swear he would come this morning, 3.04. 18 P
why, now fall down, | or if thou canst not, o, 3.05. 17
and why, i pray you? 3.05. 35
why, what means this? 3.05. 41
why do you look on me? 3.05. 41
why look you so upon me? 3.05. 69 P
why, i am sorry for thee, gentle silvius. 3.05. 85
why, that were covetousness. 3.05. 91
i marvel why i answer'd not again. 3.05.132
why, 'tis good to be sad and say nothing. 4.01. 8 P
why then 'tis good to be a post. 4.01. 9 P
why, how now, orlando, where have you been all 4.01. 38 P
why, horns! 4.01. 59 P
why then, can one desire too much of a good 4.01.123 P
why now, as fast as she can marry us. 4.01.134 P
why writes she so to me? 4.03. 19

why, 'tis a boisterous and a cruel style, | a 4.03. 31
why, she defies me, | like turk to christian. 4.03. 32
"why, thy godhead laid apart, | warr'st thou 4.03. 44
and how, and why, and where | this handkercher 4.03. 96
why, how now, ganymed, sweet ganymed? 4.03.157
why, thou say'st well. 5.01. 30 P
why then to-morrow i cannot serve your turn for 5.02. 48 P
if this be so, why blame you me to love you? 5.02.103
if this be so, why blame you me to love you? 5.02.104
if this be so, why blame you me to love you? 5.02.105
why do you speak too, "why blame you me to love 5.02.106 P
you speak too, "why blame you me to love you?" 5.02.106 P
and shape be true, | why then my love adieu! 5.04.121
why, belman is as good as he, my lord; SHR in.1. 22
why, sir, you know no house nor no such maid, in.2. 91
best | put finger in the eye, and she knew why. 1.01. 79
why will you mew her up, | signior baptista, for 1.01. 87
why, and i trust i may go too, may i not? 1.01.102
and mine to endure her loud alarums, why, man, 1.01.127 P
when i am alone, why then i am tranio; 1.01.243
if thou ask me why, | sufficeth my reasons are 1.01.247
why, sir, what am i, sir, that i should knock 1.02. 9 P
why, this' a heavy chance 'twixt him and you, 1.02. 46
why, give him gold enough, and marry him to a 1.02. 78 P
why, nothing comes amiss, so money comes withal. 1.02. 81 P
why, that's nothing; 1.02.111 P
why came i hither but to that intent? 1.02.198
why, sir, i pray, are not the streets as free 1.02.231
why, how now, dame, whence grows this insolence? 2.01. 23
why dost thou wrong her that did ne'er wrong 2.01. 27
why, that is nothing; 2.01.130
how now, my friend, why dost thou look so pale? 2.01.142
why then thou canst not break her to the lute? 2.01.147
why no, for she hath broke the lute to me. 2.01.148
why then i'll tell her plain | she sings as 2.01.170
why, what's a moveable? 2.01.197
and if no gentleman, why then no arms. 2.01.223
why, here's no crab, and therefore look not sour 2.01.230
why does the world report that kate doth limp? 2.01.252
why, how now, daughter katherine, in your dumps? 2.01.284
why then the maid is mine from all the world, 2.01.384
far | to know the cause why music was ordain'd! 3.01. 10
why, gentlemen, you do me double wrong | to 3.01. 16
why, i am past my gamouth long ago. 3.01. 71
why, is it not news to /hear of petruchio's 3.02. 33 P
why, no, sir. 3.02. 36 P
why, petruchio is coming in a new hat and an old 3.02. 43 P
why, sir, he comes not. 3.02. 75 P
why, that's all one. 3.02. 81 P
why, sir, you know this is your wedding-day. 3.02. 97
curster than she? why, 'tis impossible. 3.02.154
why, he's a devil, a devil, a very fiend. 3.02.155
why, she's a devil, a devil, the devil's dam. 3.02.156
for why, he stamp'd and swore | as if the vicar 3.02.167
why, thy horn is a foot, and so long am i at the 4.01. 27 P
why, "jack, boy! 4.01. 41 P
why, therefore fire, for i have caught extreme 4.01. 44 P
why, a horse. 4.01. 71 P
why, she hath a face of her own. 4.01.100 P
why, she comes to borrow nothing of them. 4.01.105 P
why, when, i say? 4.01.143
why then the beef, and let the mustard rest. 4.03. 26
why then the mustard without the beef. 4.03. 30
why, this was moulded on a porringer — | a 4.03. 64
why, 'tis a cockle or a walnut-shell, | a knack, 4.03. 66
why, sir, i trust i may have leave to speak, 4.03. 73
why, thou say'st true, it is /a paltry cap, | a 4.03. 81
why, ay. 4.03. 86
why, what a' devil's name, tailor, call'st thou 4.03. 92
why, true, he means to make a puppet of thee. 4.03.104
why, here is the note of the fashion to testify. 4.03.129 P
why, sir, what's your conceit in that? 4.03.160
why so: this gallant will command the sun. 4.03.196
why, how now, kate, i hope thou art not mad. 4.05. 42
why, how now, gentleman? 5.01. 35 P
why, this is flat knavery, to take upon you 5.01. 36 P
why, sir, what 'cerns it you if i wear pearl and 5.01. 75 P
why, tell me, is not this my cambio? 5.01.122
why then let's home again. 5.01.147
why are our bodies soft, and weak, and smooth, 5.02.165
why, there's a wench! 5.02.180
why under mars? AWW 1.01.194 P
why think you so? 1.01.199 P
tell me thy reason why thou wilt marry. 1.03. 27 P
quoth she, | "why the grecians sacked troy? 1.03. 71
nay, a mother, | why not a mother? 1.03.140
why — that you are my daughter? 1.03.153
why, helen, thou shalt have my leave and love, 1.03.251
why, doctor she! 2.01. 79
why, what place make you special, when you put 2.02. 5 P
o lord, sir! — why, there't serves well again. 2.02. 62 P
why, 'tis the rarest argument of wonder that 2.03. 7 P
why, there 'tis, so say i too. 2.03. 15 P
why, your dolphin is not lustier. 2.03. 26 P
why, he's able to lead her a coranto. 2.03. 43 P
why then, young bertram, take her, she's thy 2.03.105
but never hope to know why i should marry her. 2.03.110
why dost thou garter up thy arms a' this fashion 2.03.249 P
why, these balls bound, there's noise in it. 2.03.297
why, i say nothing. 2.04. 22 P
why, do you not know him? 2.05. 51 P
and rather muse than ask why i entreat you, 2.05. 65
why, he will look upon his boot and sing, mend 3.02. 6 P
why should he be kill'd? 3.02. 39 P
why is he melancholy? 3.05. 85 P
why, if you have a stomach, to't, monsieur: 3.06. 64 P
why, do you think he will make no deed at all of 3.06. 94 P
why then to-night | let us assay our plot, which 3.07. 43
why does he ask him of me? 4.03.284 P
why, sir, if i cannot serve you, i can serve as 4.05. 36 P
why do you look so strange upon your wife? 5.03.168
why, so i do, the noblest that i have. TN 1.01. 17
why, let her except before excepted. 1.03. 7 P
why, he has three thousand ducats a year. 1.03. 22 P
why, i think so. 1.03. 74 P
why, would that have mended my hair? 1.03. 97 P
why dost thou not go to church in a galliard and 1.03.127 P
good madonna, why mourn'st thou? 1.05. 66 P

why, of mankind. 1.05.151 P
why, what would you? 1.05.267
why, he sent her none. 2.02. 24
why, this is the best fooling, when all is done. 2.03. 29 P
her c's, her u's, and her t's: why that? 2.05. 89 P
why, she may command me: 2.05.115 P
why, this is evident to any formal capacity, 2.05.116 P
m — malvolio; m — why, that begins my name. 2.05.125 P
why, thou hast put him in such a dream, that 2.05.193 P
why, man? 3.01. 18 P
why, sir, her name's a word, and to dally with 3.01. 19 P
why then methinks 'tis time to smile again. 3.01.126
why then build me thy fortunes upon the basis of 3.02. 33 P
why i your purse? 3.03. 43
why, what's the matter? does he rave? 3.04. 10
why, how dost thou, man? 3.04. 24 P
why dost thou smile so, and kiss thy hand so oft 3.04. 32 P
why appear you with this ridiculous boldness 3.04. 37 P
why, this is very midsummer madness. 3.04. 56 P
why, every thing adheres together, that no dram 3.04. 78 P
why, how now, my bawcock? how dost thou, chuck? 3.04.112 P
why, we shall make him mad indeed. 3.04.133 P
admire not in thy mind, why i do call thee so, 3.04.151 P
why, man, he's a very devil, i have not seen 3.04.273 P
you, sir? why, what are you? 3.04.315 P
why, there's for thee, and there, and there. 4.01. 26
why, it hath bay windows transparent as 4.02. 36 P
"alas, why is she so?" 4.02. 77
why then the worse for my friends and the better 5.01. 22 P
why, this is excellent. 5.01. 24 P
why should i not (had i the heart to do it), 5.01.117
why do you speak to me? 5.01.187
why you have given me such clear lights of favor 5.01.336
why have you suffer'd me to be imprison'd, 5.01.341
tell me why! 5.01.344
why, "some are born great, some achieve 5.01.370 P
"madam, why laugh you at such a barren rascal? 5.01.374 P
were no other excuse why they should desire to WT 1.01. 43 P
why, that was when | three crabbed months had 1.02.101
why, lo you now! 1.02.106
why, that's my bawcock. 1.02.121
why, happy man be 's dole! 1.02.163
why, that's some comfort. | what? camillo there? 1.02.208
ay, but why? 1.02.231
why then the world and all that's in't is 1.02.293
why, he that wears her like her medal hanging 1.02.307
by a man which ever | profess'd to him, why, his 1.02.456
why, my sweet lord? 2.01. 4
and why so, my lord? 2.01. 7
why, what need we | commune with you of this, 2.01.161
and why he left your court, the gods themselves 3.02. 75
why, boy, how is it? 3.03. 87 P
why, then comes in the sweet o' the year, | for 4.03. 3
why, he sings 'em over as they were gods or 4.04.207 P
why should i carry lies abroad? 4.04.271 P
why, this is a passing merry one and goes to the 4.04.288 P
why, they stay at door, sir. 4.04.342 P
why, how now, father? | speak ere thou diest. 4.04.450
why look you so upon me? 4.04.462
if they have overheard me now — why, hanging. 4.04.627 P
why shak'st thou so? 4.04.628 P
why, be so still; 4.04.631 P
why, sir? 4.04.761 P
appear soul-vex'd, | and begin, "why to me — ?" 5.01. 60
why, being younger born, | doth he lay claim to JN 1.01. 71
i know not why, except to get the land; 1.01. 73
why, what a madcap hath heaven lent us here! 1.01. 84
why then i suck my teeth, and catechize | my 1.01.192
why scorn'st thou at sir robert? 1.01.228
why stand these royal fronts amazed thus? 2.01.356
why then defy each other, and pell-mell | make 2.01.406
why answer not the double majesties | this 2.01.480
and why rail i on this commodity? 2.01.587
why dost thou look so sadly on my son? 3.01. 20
why holds thine eye that lamentable rheum, 3.01. 22
demand | why thou against the church, our holy 3.01.141
that you must use me ill, | why then you must. 4.01. 56
why then your fears, which (as they say) attend 4.02. 56
why do you bend such solemn brows on me? 4.02. 90
why seek'st thou to possess me with these fears? 4.02.203
why urgest thou so oft young arthur's death? 4.02.204
no had, my lord? why, did you not provoke me? 4.02.207
why look you sad? 5.01. 44
why should i then be false, since it is true 5.04. 28
why may not i demand | of thine affairs, as well 5.06. 4
why, here walk i in the black brow of night, 5.06. 17
why, know you not? 5.06. 33
why then i will. R2 1.02. 44
why then the champions are prepar'd, and stay 1.03. 5
and why thou comest thus knightly clad in arms, 1.03. 12
both who he is and why he cometh hither | thus 1.03. 27
why, uncle, thou hast many years to live. 1.03.225
why at our justice seem'st thou then to low'r? 1.03.235
why, cousin, wert thou regent of the world, | it 2.01.109
why, uncle, what's the matter? 2.01.186
why i should welcome such a guest as grief, 2.02. 7
why hopest thou so? 2.02. 43
why have you not proclaim'd northumberland | and 2.02. 56
he was — why, so go all which way it will! 2.02. 87
why, is he not with the queen? 2.03. 25
why have those banish'd and forbidden legs 2.03. 90
but then more "why?" 2.03. 92
why have they dar'd to march | so many miles 2.03. 92
why, foolish boy, the king is left behind, | and 2.03. 97
comfort, my liege, why looks your grace so pale? 3.02. 75
why, 'twas my care, | and what loss is it to be 3.02. 95
royally! | why, it contains no king? 3.03. 24
i live, | and buried once, why not upon my head? 3.03.159
why should we in the compass of a pale | keep 3.04. 40
why dost thou say king richard is depos'd? 3.04. 77
why, bishop, is norfolk dead? 4.01.101
why should hard-favor'd grief be lodg'd in thee, 5.01. 14
for why, the senseless brands will sympathize 5.01. 46
why, what is it, my lord? 5.02. 76
why, york, what wilt thou do? 5.02. 88
why do i rail on thee, | since thou, created to 5.05. 90
i see no reason why thou shouldst be so 1H4 1.02. 10 P
why, what a pox have i to do with my hostess of 1.02. 47 P

why, hal, 'tis my vocation, hal, 'tis no sin for 1.02.104 P
why, that's well said. 1.02.144 P
why, we will set forth before or after them and 1.02.169 P
why, yet he doth deny his prisoners, | but with 1.03. 77
why, what a wasp–stung and impatient fool | art 1.03.236
why, look you, i am /whipt and scourg'd with 1.03.239
why, what a candy deal of courtesy | this 1.03.251
why, it cannot choose but be a noble plot. 1.03.279
why, they will allow us ne'er a jordan, and then 2.01. 19 P
why is he not then? 2.03. 3 P
"the purpose you undertake is dangerous" — why, 2.03. 7 P
why, my lord of york commends the plot and the 2.03. 20 P
o my good lord, why are you thus alone? 2.03. 37
why dost thou bend thine eyes upon the earth, 2.03. 42
why hast thou lost the fresh blood in thy cheeks 2.03. 44
why, my horse, my love, my horse. 2.03. 76
why then your brown bastard is your only drink! 2.04. 73 P
why, you whoreson round man, what's the matter? 2.04.140 P
seven? why, there were but four even now. 2.04.203 P
why, thou clay–brain'd guts, thou knotty–pated 2.04.226 P
why, how couldst thou know these men in kendal 2.04.231 P
why, hear you, my masters, was it for me to kill 2.04.268 P
why, thou knowest i am as valiant as hercules; 2.04.270 P
why, he hack'd it with his dagger, and said he 2.04.305 P
why, what a rascal art thou then, to praise him 2.04.351 P
why then, it is like, if there come a hot june 2.04.361 P
why, being son to me, art thou so pointed at? 2.04.406 P
why dost thou converse with that trunk of humors 2.04.448 P
why, so it would have done | at the same season 3.01. 17
why, so can i, or so can any man, | but will 3.01. 53
why, i can teach you, cousin, to command | the 3.01. 55
why, that will i. 3.01.117
why, harry, do i tell thee of my foes, | which 3.02.122
why, my skin hangs about me like an old lady's 3.03. 3 P
why, there is it. 3.03. 13 P
why, you are so fat, sir john, that you must 3.03. 21 P
why, sir john, my face does you no harm. 3.03. 28 P
why, sir john, what do you think, sir john? 3.03. 54 P
what thing? why, a thing to thank god on. 3.03.117 P
what beast? why, an otter. 3.03.125 P
an otter, sir john, why an otter? 3.03.126 P
why? 3.03.127 P
why, hal! 3.03.145 P
and why not as the lion? 3.03.148 P
why, thou whoreson, impudent, emboss'd rascal, 3.03.156 P
letters from him! why comes he not himself? 4.01. 15
by some that know not why he is away | that 4.01. 63
why say you so? looks he not for supply? 4.03. 3
why, my good lord, you need not fear, | there is 4.04. 21
why, thou owest god a death. 5.01.126 P
why? 5.01.139 P
why didst thou tell me that thou wert a king? 5.03. 24
why then i see | a very valiant rebel of the 5.04. 61
why may not he rise as well as i? 5.04.126 P
why, percy i kill'd myself, and saw thee dead. 5.04.144
why is rumor here? 2H4 in 22
why should that gentleman that rode by travers 1.01. 55
why, he is dead. 1.01. 83
than to set me off, why then i have no judgment. 1.02. 14 P
why, sir, did i say you were an honest man? 1.02. 80 P
why, a prince should not be so loosely studied 2.02. 7 P
why, because you have been so lewd and so much 2.02. 62 P
why, this is a certificate. 2.02.121 P
why then cover and set them down, and see if 2.04. 10 P
why, that's well said; 2.04. 31 P
why then let grievous, ghastly, gaping wounds 2.04.198
why does the prince love him so then? 2.04.243 P
why, thou globe of sinful continents, what a 2.04.285 P
why rather, sleep, liest thou in smoky cribs, 3.01. 9
why li'st thou with the vile | in loathsome beds 3.01. 15
why then good morrow to you all, my lords. 3.01. 35
why not to him in part, and to us all | that 4.01. 97
why art thou not at windsor with him, thomas? 4.04. 50
why doth the crown lie there upon his pillow, 4.05. 21
why did you leave me here alone, my lords? 4.05. 50
why, davy! 5.01. 6 P
why then be sad, | but entertain no more of it, 5.02. 53
why, there spoke a king. 5.03. 69 P
why, now you have done me right. 5.03. 72 P
why then say an old man can do somewhat. 5.03. 78 P
why then lament therefore. 5.03.108
why, here it is, welcome these pleasant days! 5.03.141
and religiously unfold | why the law salique, H5 1.02. 11
why the devil should we keep knives to cut one 2.01. 91 P
thou wilt not, why then be enemies with me too. 2.01.103 P
why, how now, gentlemen? 2.02. 71
why, what read you there | that have so cowarded 2.02. 74
up, | gave thee no instance why thou shouldst do 2.02.119
why, so didst thou. 2.02.128
why, so didst thou. 2.02.129
why, so didst thou. 2.02.130
why, so didst thou. 2.02.131
if not — why, in a moment look to see | the 3.03. 33
why then rejoice therefore. 3.06. 52
why, this is an arrant counterfeit rascal, i 3.06. 61 P
why, 'tis a gull, a fool, a rogue, that now and 3.06. 67 P
why, the enemy is loud, you hear him all night. 4.01. 75 P
why do you stay so long, my lords of france? 4.02. 38
why, now thou hast unwish'd five thousand men; 4.03. 76
god, why should they mock poor fellows thus? 4.03. 92
why, all our ranks are broke. 4.05. 6
why, i pray you, is not "pig" great? 4.07. 15 P
soldier, why wear'st thou that glove in thy cap? 4.07.120 P
but why wear you your leek to–day? 5.01. 1 P
is occasions and causes why and wherefore in all 5.01. 3 P
why, here he comes, swelling like a turkey–cock. 5.01. 14 P
why that the naked, poor, and mangled peace, 5.02. 34
that i may know the let why gentle peace 5.02. 65
to dance for your sake, kate, why, you undid me: 5.02.133 P
we mourn in black, why mourn we not in blood? 1H6 1.01. 17
gloucester, why doubt'st thou of my forwardness? 1.01.100
why live we idly here? 1.02. 13
why, no, i say. 1.02.126
now beat them hence, why do you let them stay? 1.03. 54
why ring not out the bells aloud throughout the 1.06. 11
why? art not thou the man? 2.03. 48
why didst thou say, of late thou wert despis'd? 2.05. 42
why look you still so stern and tragical? 3.01.125
why, what is he? as good a man as york. 3.04. 36
why then lord talbot there shall talk with him, 4.01. 68
why speak'st thou not? what ransom must i pay? 5.03. 77
why, for my king. 5.03. 89
why, what concerns his freedom unto me? 5.03.116
why, here's a girl! 5.04. 80
why, what, i pray, is margaret more than that? 5.05. 36
why should he then protect our sovereign, | he 2H6 1.01.165
why droops my lord, like over–ripen'd corn 1.02. 1
why doth the great duke humphrey knit his brows, 1.02. 3
why are thine eyes fix'd to the sullen earth, 1.02. 5
why somerset should be preferr'd in this. 1.03.114
i'll tell thee, suffolk, why i am unmeet: 1.03.165
image of pride, why should i hold my peace? 1.03.176
why, this is just | "aio /te, aeacida, romanos 1.04. 61
why, as you, my lord, | an't like your lordly 2.01. 29
why, suffolk, england knows thine insolence. 2.01. 31
why, how now, uncle gloucester? 2.01. 48
why, that's well said. what color is my gown of? 2.01.109
why then, thou know'st what color jet is of? 2.01.111
i see no reason why a king of years | should be 2.03. 28
why, now is henry king and margaret queen, | and 2.03. 39
why, yet thy scandal were not wip'd away, | but 2.04. 65
why, madam, that is to the isle of man, | there 2.04. 94
why, 'tis well known that, whiles i was 3.01.124
why, our authority is his consent, | and what we 3.01.316
why, then from ireland come i with my strength, 3.01.380
why, that's well said. 3.02. 8
why look'st thou pale? 3.02. 27
why tremblest thou? 3.02. 27
why do you rate my lord of suffolk thus? 3.02. 56
why then dame /margaret was ne'er thy joy. 3.02. 79
why, warwick, who should do the duke to death? 3.02.179
why, how now, lords? 3.02.237
why, what tumultuous clamor have we here? 3.02.239
why only, suffolk, mourn i not for thee, | and 3.02.383
why starts thou? 4.01. 32
why com'st thou in such haste? 4.04. 26
why dost thou quiver, man? 4.07. 92 P
why, buckingham, is the traitor cade surpris'd? 4.09. 8
why, rude companion, whatsoe'er thou be, | i 4.10. 31
i know thee not, why then should i betray thee? 4.10. 32
or why thou, being a subject as i am, | against 5.01. 19
the cause why i have brought this army hither 5.01. 35
false king, why hast thou broken faith with me, 5.01. 91
why, what a brood of traitors have we here! 5.01.141
why, warwick, hath thy knee forgot to bow? 5.01.161
why art thou old, and want'st experience? 5.01.171
why dost thou pause? 5.02. 19
why faint you, lords? 3H6 1.01.129
why whisper you, my lords, and answer not? 1.01.149
why should you sigh, my lord? 1.01.191
if you be king, why should not i succeed? 1.01.227
why, how now, sons and brother, at a strife? 1.02. 4
why do we linger thus? 1.02. 32
why com'st thou in such post? 1.02. 48
why should i not now have the like success? 1.02. 75
i never did thee harm; why wilt thou slay me? 1.03. 38
why come you not? 1.04. 39
why art thou patient, man? 1.04. 89
why, now thou hast thy wish: 1.04.143
why, now thou hast thy will: 1.04.144
why is he so sad? 2.01. 8
why, therefore warwick came to seek you out, 2.01.166
amount to five and twenty thousand, | why, via! 2.01.182
why then it sorts, brave warriors. let's away. 2.01.209
why, that is spoken like a toward prince. 2.02. 66
why, that's my fortune too, therefore i'll stay. 2.02. 76
why, how now, long–tongu'd warwick, dare you 2.02.102
ah, warwick, why hast thou withdrawn thyself? 2.03. 14
why stand we like soft–hearted women here, 2.03. 25
why linger we? let us lay hands upon him. 3.01. 26
and men may talk of kings, and why not i? 3.01. 58
why, so i am — in mind, and that's enough. 3.01. 60
why? 3.01. 82
why then i will do what your grace commands. 3.02. 49
why stops my lord? shall i not hear my task? 3.02. 52
why then, thy husband's lands i freely give thee 3.02. 55
why then you mean not as i thought you did. 3.02. 65
why then thou shalt not have thy husband's lands 3.02. 71
why then mine honesty shall be my dower, | for 3.02. 72
why, 'tis a happy thing | to be the father unto 3.02.104
why, clarence, to myself. 3.02.112
why then i do but dream on sovereignty, | like 3.02.134
why, love forswore me in my mother's womb; 3.02.153
why, i can smile, and murther whiles i smile, 3.02.182
why, say, fair queen, whence springs this deep 3.03. 12
and why not queen? 3.03. 78
why, warwick, canst thou speak against thy liege 3.03. 95
why stay we now? 3.03.251
tell me some reason why the lady grey | should 4.01. 25
why, knows not montague that of itself | england 4.01. 39
why, so! 4.01.147
why then, let's on our way in silent sort. 4.02. 28
why, no; 4.03. 4
but why commands the king | that his chief 4.03. 12
why, warwick, when we parted, | thou call'dst me 4.03. 30
why, brother rivers, are you yet to learn | what 4.04. 2
leave off to wonder why i drew you hither | into 4.05. 2
why then, though loath, yet must i be content. 4.06. 48
why, and i challenge nothing but my dukedom, 4.07. 23
why, master mayor, why stand you in a doubt? 4.07. 27
why, master mayor, why stand you in a doubt? 4.07. 27
welcome, sir john! but why come you in arms? 4.07. 42
why shall we fight if you pretend no title? 4.07. 57
why, brother, wherefore stand you on nice points 4.07. 58
then why should they love edward more than me? 4.08. 47
why then 'tis mine, if but by warwick's gift. 5.01. 35
why, trowest thou, warwick, | that clarence is 5.01. 85
why ask i that? 5.02. 7
why, what is pomp, rule, reign, but earth and 5.02. 27
why then i would not fly. 5.02. 33
why, is not oxford here another anchor? 5.04. 16
why not ned and i | for once allow'd the 5.04. 19
tread on the sand, why, there you quickly sink; 5.04. 30
why, courage then! 5.04. 37
why, 'twere perpetual shame. 5.04. 51
why should she live, to fill the world with 5.05. 44
why, what a peevish fool was that of crete 5.06. 18
executing, | why then thou art an executioner. 5.06. 33
why, i, in this weak piping time of peace, R3 1.01. 24
why, this it is, when men are rul'd by women: 1.01. 62
why then he is alive. 1.02. 91
why, that was he. 1.02.142
here. why dost thou spit at me? 1.02.144
why, who knows not so? 1.03. 92
why then give way, dull clouds, to my quick 1.03.195
why, so i did, but look'd for no reply. 1.03.236
why strew'st thou sugar on that bottled spider 1.03.241
and so doth mine. i muse why she's at liberty. 1.03.304
why looks your grace so heavily to–day? 1.04. 1
why, he shall never wake until the great 1.04.103 P
why, then he'll say we stabb'd him sleeping. 1.04.105 P
why look you pale? 1.04.170
why, so he doth, when he delivers you | from 1.04.247
why, so: 2.01. 1
why, madam, have i off'red love for this, | to 2.01. 78
why do /you weep so oft, and beat your breast, 2.02. 3
why do you look on us, and shake your head, 2.02. 5
why grow the branches when the root is gone? 2.02. 41
why wither not the leaves that want their sap? 2.02. 42
why with some little train, my lord of 2.02.123
why, so hath this, both by his father and mother 2.03. 22
why, my good cousin, it is good to grow. 2.04. 9
his nurse? why, she was dead ere thou wast born. 2.04. 33
why, or for what, the nobles were committed | is 2.04. 47
why, what should you fear? 3.01.143
the cause why we are met | is to determine of 3.04. 1
alas, why would you heap this care on me? 3.07.204
why? 4.01. 65
why, buckingham, i say i would be king. 4.02. 12
why, so you are, my thrice–renowned lord. 4.02. 13
why, /there thou hast it; 4.02. 72
edward plantagenet, why art thou dead? 4.04. 19
why should calamity be full of words? 4.04.126
why then, by /god — 4.04.377
why stay'st thou here, and go'st not to the duke 4.04.446
why, what wouldst thou do there before i go? 4.04.454
why then all–souls' day is my body's doomsday. 5.01. 12
my lord of surrey, why look you so sad? 5.03. 2
why, our battalia trebles that account; 5.03. 11
great reason why — | lest i revenge. 5.03.185
why, then 'tis time to arm and give direction. 5.03.236
why, what is that to me | more than to richmond? 5.03.285
why the devil, | upon this french going out, H8 1.01. 72
why, all this business | our reverend cardinal 1.01. 99
why, we take | from every tree, lop, bark, and 1.02. 95
why, this it is! 2.03. 81
enemies, that know not | why they are so, but, 2.04.160
why should we, good lady, | upon what cause, 3.01.155
why, how now, cromwell? 3.02.372
why, well; 3.02.376
why? 5.02. 6
why are we met in council? 5.02. 37
why, my lord? 5.02.114
why, what a shame was this? 5.02.176
why should i war without the walls of troy, TRO 1.01. 2
why, paris hath color enough. 1.02. 99 P
why, he is very young, and yet will he, within 1.02.115 P
why, you know 'tis dimpled. 1.02.121 P
why, go to then. 1.02.127 P
why, he esteems her no more than i esteem an 1.02.131 P
why, this is brave now. 1.02.214 P
why, this will do helen's heart good now, ha? 1.02.215 P
why, have you any discretion? 1.02.251 P
why then, you princes, | do you with cheeks 1.03. 17
fled under shade, why then the thing of courage, 1.03. 51
why, this hath not a finger's dignity. 1.03.204
why, 'tis most meet. 1.03.333
why then we do our main opinion crush | in taint 1.03.372
why, how now, ajax, wherefore do ye thus? 2.01. 55
well! why, so i do. 2.01. 62 P
why keep we her? 2.02. 80
why, she is a pearl, | whose price hath launch'd 2.02. 81
why do you now | the issue of your proper 2.02. 88
why, brother hector, | we may not think the 2.02.118
why, there you touch'd the life of our design: 2.02.194
why, my cheese, my digestion, why hast thou not 2.03. 41 P
why hast thou not serv'd thyself in to my table 2.03. 41 P
why am i a fool? 2.03. 66 P
but why, why? 2.03. 88 P
but why, why? 2.03. 88 P
and much the reason | why we ascribe it to him; 2.03.117
why should a man be proud? 2.03.151 P
why will he not upon our fair request | untent 2.03.167
why, 'tis this naming of him does him harm. 2.03.228
why should you say cressida? 3.01. 91 P
why, this is kindly done. 3.01. 96 P
why, they are vipers. 3.01.132 P
why do you not speak to her? 3.02. 46 P
why was my cressid then so hard to win? 3.02.116
why have i blabb'd? 3.02.124
question me | why such unplausive eyes are bent, 3.03. 43
unplausive eyes are bent, why turn'd on him? 3.03. 43
why, even already | they clap the lubber ajax on 3.03.138
why, 'a stalks up and down like a peacock — a 3.03.251 P
why, he'll answer nobody; 3.03.268 P
why, but he is not in this tune, is he? 3.03.300
i was sent for to the king, but why, i know not. 4.01. 36
why sigh you so profoundly? 4.02. 80 P
why tell you me of moderation? 4.04. 2
heart, | why sigh'st thou without breaking?" 4.04. 17
hear why i speak it, love. 4.04. 75
why, beg then. 4.05. 48
why then, for venus' sake, give me a kiss | when 4.05. 49
why then will i no more. 4.05.119
why dost thou so oppress me with thine eye? 4.05.241
why, thou picture of what thou seemest, and idol 5.01. 6 P
why, thou full dish of fool, from troy. 5.01. 9 P
why, his masculine whore. 5.01. 17 P
why, thou damnable box of envy, thou, what means 5.01. 25 P
why, no, you ruinous butt, you whoreson 5.01. 28 P
why art thou then exasperate, thou idle 5.01. 30 P
guardian! why, greek! 5.02. 47
why then farewell, | thou never shalt mock 5.02. 98
why stay we then? 5.02.115

why, my negation hath no taste of madness. 5.02.127
why then fly on, i'll hunt thee for thy hide. 5.06. 31
why should our endeavor be so lov'd and the 5.10. 38 P
why stay we prating here? COR 1.01. 47 P
why, masters, my good friends, mine honest 1.01. 62
i the great toe! why the great toe? 1.01.156
why, i pray you? 1.03. 80 P
if not, why cease you till you are so? 1.06. 48
why? how are we censur'd? 2.01. 24 P
why, 'tis no great matter; 2.01. 28 P
why then you should discover a brace of 2.01. 43 P
if they love they know not why, they hate upon 2.02. 11 P
why that way? 2.03. 30 P
why in this woolvish /toge should i stand here 2.03.115
why, so he did, i am sure. 2.03.165
why either were you ignorant to see't, | or, 2.03.174
why, had your bodies | no heart among you? 2.03.203
their mouths, why rule you not their teeth? 3.01. 36
why this was known before. 3.01. 46
why then should i be consul? 3.01. 50
why, | you grave but reakless senators, have you 3.01. 91
why shall the people give | one that speaks thus 3.01.118
why did you wish me milder? 3.02. 14
why force you this? 3.02. 51
even as she speaks, why, their hearts were yours 3.02. 87
why? 4.02. 8
why stay we to be baited | with one that wants 4.02. 43
why speak'st not? 4.05. 54
why, thou mars, i tell thee, | we have a power 4.05.118
why, here's he that was wont to thwack our 4.05.178 P
why do you say, "thwack our general"? 4.05.180 P
why, he is so made on here within as if he were 4.05.191 P
why then we shall have a stirring world again. 4.05.218 P
why, so; 5.01. 15
why dost not speak? 5.03.153
why, what of that? 5.04. 3 P
why, hark you! 5.04. 48
why, noble lords, | will you be put in mind of 5.06.116
why suffer'st thou thy sons, unburied yet, | to TIT 1.01. 87
why, boy, although our mother, unadvis'd, | gave 2.01. 38
why, how now, lords? 2.01. 45
why, lords, and think you not how dangerous | it 2.01. 63
why, are ye mad? 2.01. 75
why makes thou it so strange? 2.01. 81
then why should he despair that knows to court 2.01. 91
why then it seems some certain snatch or so 2.01. 95
why, hark ye, hark ye, and are you such fools 2.01. 99
why are you sequest'red from all your train, 2.03. 75
why, i have patience to endure all this. 2.03. 88
why doth your highness look so pale and wan? 2.03. 90
why dost not comfort me and help me out | from 2.03.209
why dost not speak to me? 2.04. 21
fair philomela, why, she but lost her tongue, 2.04. 38
why, 'tis no matter, man: 3.01. 33
why, foolish lucius, dost thou not perceive 3.01. 53
why, marcus, so she is. 3.01. 63
for why my bowels cannot hide her woes, | but 3.01.230
now is a time to storm, why art thou still? 3.01.263
why dost thou laugh? it fits not with this hour. 3.01.265
why, i have not another tear to shed. 3.01.266
follows me every where, i know not why. 4.01. 2
why lifts she up her arms in sequence thus? 4.01. 37
o, why should nature build so foul a den, 4.01. 59
why do the emperor's trumpets flourish thus? 4.02. 49
why, what a caterwauling dost thou keep! 4.02. 57
why, then she is the devil's dam: 4.02. 65
why, there's the privilege your beauty bears. 4.02.116
why, so, brave lords, when we join in league | i 4.02.136
why, there it goes, god give his lordship joy! 4.03. 77
why, villain, art not thou the carrier? 4.03. 87
why, didst thou not come from heaven? 4.03. 89
why, i am going with my pigeons to the tribunal 4.03. 92 P
why, sir, that is as fit as can be to serve for 4.03. 95 P
why, lords, what wrongs are these! 4.04. 1
why, thus it shall become | high-witted tamora 4.04. 34
why should you fear? is not your city strong? 4.04. 78
why dost not speak? 5.01. 46
why, assure thee, lucius, | 'twill vex thy soul 5.01. 61
why, she was wash'd, and cut, and trimm'd, and 5.01. 95
why art thou thus attir'd, andronicus? 5.03. 30
why hast thou slain thine only daughter thus? 5.03. 55
why, there they are, both baked in this pie; 5.03. 60
ah, why should wrath be mute and fury dumb? 5.03.184
a crutch, a crutch! why call you for a sword? ROM 1.01. 76
why then, o brawling love! 1.01.176
why, such is love's transgression. 1.01.185
groan? why, no; | but sadly tell me, who? 1.01.200
why, romeo, art thou mad? 1.02. 53
such a man | as all the world — why, he's a man 1.03. 76
why, may one ask? 1.04. 49
why, how now, kinsman, wherefore storm you so? 1.05. 60
why, uncle, 'tis a shame. 1.05. 82
why then i thank you all. 1.05.123
i have forgot why i did call thee back. 2.02.170
why, that same pale hard-hearted wench, that 2.04. 4
why, what is tybalt? 2.04. 18 P
why, is not this a lamentable thing, grandsire, 2.04. 31 P
why then is my pump well flower'd. 2.04. 60 P
why, is not this better now than groaning for 2.04. 88 P
sweet nurse — o lord, why lookest thou sad? 2.05. 21
why, she is within, | where should she be? 2.05. 58
why, thou wilt quarrel with a man that hath a 3.01. 17 P
why the dev'l came you between us? 3.01.102 P
why dost thou stay? 3.01.136
ay me, what news? why dost thou wring thy hands? 3.02. 36
why followed not, when she said, "tybalt's dead, 3.02.118
why should you fall into so deep an o? 3.03. 90
why railest thou on thy birth? 3.03.119
why, how now, juliet? 3.05. 68
and why, my lady wisdom? 3.05.170
i would i knew not why it should be slowed. 4.01. 16
why, i am glad on't, this is well, stand up. 4.02. 28
why, lamb! 4.05. 2
why, lady! 4.05. 2
why, love, i say! 4.05. 3
why, bride! 4.05. 3
time, why cam'st thou now | to murther, murther 4.05. 60
why "heart's ease"? 4.05.105 P

with her silver sound" — | why "silver sound"? 4.05.129 P
why "music with her silver sound"? 4.05.129 P
why i descend into this bed of death | is partly 5.03. 28
ah, dear juliet, | why art thou yet so fair? 5.03.102
why dost thou call them knaves? TIM 1.01.181
why, apemantus? 1.01.264 P
why have you that charitable title from 1.02. 91 P
why, i have often wish'd myself poorer, that i 1.02.100 P
why then another time i'll hear thee. 1.02.178
but a beggar's dog | and give it timon, why, the 2.01. 6
horse and buy twenty moe | better than he, why, 2.01. 8
why? 2.02. 63 P
why, how now, captain, what do you in this wise 2.02. 73 P
why dost thou weep? 2.02.175
why, this hits right; 3.01. 6 P
why should it thrive and turn to nutriment 3.01. 58
why, this is the world's soul, and just of the 3.02. 64
why then preferr'd you not your sums and bills 3.04. 49
why do fond men expose themselves to battle, 3.05. 42
why then, women are more valiant | that stay at 3.05. 47
why, /i say, my lords, h'as done fair service, 3.05. 62
why, let the war receive't in valiant gore, 3.05. 83
why this? 4.03. 31
why, this | will lug your priests and servants 4.03. 31
why, fare thee well; 4.03.100
why me, timon? 4.03.106
why this spade? 4.03.204
why? 4.03.234
why dost thou seek me out? 4.03.236
why shouldst thou hate men? 4.03.269
why should you want? 4.03.417
why want? 4.03.421
why dost ask that? 4.03.473
why, how shall i requite you? 5.01. 73
why, thy verse swells with stuff so fine and 5.01. 84
why, i was writing of my epitaph; 5.01.185
why, sir, a carpenter. JC 1.01. 6 P
why, sir, cobble you. 1.01. 19 P
why dost thou lead these men about the streets? 1.01. 28
why, man, he doth bestride the narrow world 1.02.135
why should that name be sounded more than yours? 1.02.143
why, you were with him, were you not? 1.02.219 P
why, there was a crown offer'd him; 1.02.221 P
why, for that too. 1.02.225 P
why, for that too. 1.02.227 P
why, antony. 1.02.233 P
why are you breathless, and why stare you so? 1.03. 2
why are you breathless, and why stare you so? 1.03. 2
why, saw you any thing more wonderful? 1.03. 14
consider the true cause | why all these fires, 1.03. 63
all these fires, why all these gliding ghosts, 1.03. 63
why birds and beasts from quality and kind, 1.03. 64
why old men, fools, and children calculate, 1.03. 65
why all these things change from their ordinance 1.03. 66
to monstrous quality — why, you shall find 1.03. 68
and why should caesar be a tyrant then? 1.03.103
why, so i do. good portia, go to bed. 2.01.260
why you are heavy, and what men to-night | have 2.01.275
why dost thou stay? 2.04. 3
why, know'st thou any harm's intended towards 2.04. 31
why, he that cuts off twenty years of life 3.01.101
and then we will deliver you the cause | why i, 3.01.182
hope, that you shall give me reasons | why, and 3.01.222
then that friend demand why brutus rose against 3.02. 20 P
why, friends, you go to do you know not what. 3.02.235
why ask you? hear you aught of her in yours? 4.03.185
why, farewell, portia. 4.03.190
why com'st thou? 4.03.282
why, i will see thee at philippi then. 4.03.286
why did you so cry out, sirs, in your sleep? 4.03.303
why do you cross me in this exigent? 5.01. 19
why now blow wind, swell billow, and swim bark! 5.01. 67
if we do meet again, why, we shall smile; 5.01.117
if not, why then this parting was well made. 5.01.118
why then lead on. 5.01.122
why dost thou show to the apt thoughts of men 5.03. 68
why didst thou send me forth, brave cassius? 5.03. 80
why, now thou diest as bravely as titinius, 5.04. 10
why, this, volumnius: 5.05. 16
good sir, why do you start, and seem to fear MAC 1.03. 51
or why | upon this blasted heath you stop our 1.03. 76
why do you dress me | in borrowed robes? 1.03.108
ill, | why hath it given me earnest of success, 1.03.132
why do i yield to that suggestion | whose horrid 1.03.134
if chance will have me king, why, chance may 1.03.143
why have you left the chamber? 1.07. 29
why, worthy thane, | you do unbend your noble 2.02. 41
why did you bring these daggers from the place? 2.02. 45
why do we hold our tongues, | that most may 2.03.119
why, see you not? 2.04. 21
why, by the verities on thee made good, | may 3.01. 8
how now, my lord, why do you keep alone, | of 3.02. 8
shame itself, | why do you make such faces? 3.04. 66
why, what care i? 3.04. 69
why, so; 3.04.106
why, how now, hecat? you look angerly. 3.05. 1
why sinks that cauldron? 4.01.106
filthy hags, | why do you show me this? 4.01.116
but why | stands macbeth thus amazedly? 4.01.125
why should i, mother? 4.02. 36
why, i can buy me twenty at any market. 4.02. 40
why, one that swears and lies. 4.02. 47 P
why, the honest men. 4.02. 55 P
why then, alas, | do i put up that womanly 4.02. 77
why in that rawness left you wife and child, 4.03. 26
why are you silent? 4.03.137
why, well. 4.03.177
why, it stood by her. 5.01. 22 P
one — two — why then 'tis time to do't. 5.01. 36 P
why should i play the roman fool, and die | on 5.08. 1
why then, god's soldier be he! 5.09. 13
why this same strict and most observant watch HAM 1.01. 71
why such impress of shipwrights, whose sore task 1.01. 75
it be, | why seems it so particular with thee? 1.02. 75
why should we in our peevish opposition | take 1.02.100
why, 'tis a loving and a fair reply. 1.02.121
why, she should hang on him | as if increase of 1.02.143
like niobe, all tears — why, she, /even /she — 1.02.149

but tell | why thy canoniz'd bones, hearsed in 1.04. 47
why the sepulchre, | wherein we saw thee quietly 1.04. 48
say why is this? 1.04. 57
why, what should be the fear? 1.04. 64
why, right, you are in the right, | and so, 1.05.126
why day is day, night night, and time is time, 2.02. 88
i will tell you why, so shall my anticipation 2.02.293 P
majestical roof fretted with golden fire, why, 2.02.302 P
why did ye laugh then, when i said, "man 2.02.313 P
why — "one fair daughter, and no more, | the 2.02.406 P
why — "as by lot, god wot," | and then, you 2.02.415 P
why, thy face is valanc'd since i saw thee last; 2.02.423 P
why, what an ass am i! 2.02.582
get from him why he puts on this confusion, 3.01. 2
why wouldst thou be a breeder of sinners? 3.01.120 P
why should the poor be flatter'd? 3.02. 59
why, let the strooken deer go weep, | the hart 3.02.271
why then belike he likes it not, perdy. 3.02.294
why do you go about to recover the wind of me, 3.02.346 P
why, look you now, how unworthy a thing you make 3.02.363 P
why, this is /hire /and /salary, not revenge. 3.03. 79
why, how now, hamlet? 3.04. 13
why, look you there! 3.04.134
why then the polack never will defend it. 4.04. 23
and shows no cause without | why the man dies. 4.04. 29
i do not know | why yet i live to say, "this 4.04. 44
tell me, laertes, | why thou art thus incens'd. 4.05.127
why, now you speak | like a good child and a 4.05.148
me | why you /proceeded not against these feats, 4.07. 6
motive, | why to a public count i might not go, 4.07. 17
why ask you this? 4.07.109
why, 'tis found so. 5.01. 8 P
why, there thou say'st, and the more pity that 5.01. 26 P
why, e'en so, and now my lady worm's, chopless, 5.01. 88 P
why may not that be the skull of a lawyer? 5.01. 98 P
why does he suffer this mad knave now to knock 5.01.101 P
ay, marry, why was he sent into england? 5.01.149 P
why, because 'a was mad. 5.01.150 P
why? 5.01.153 P
why, here in denmark. 5.01.161 P
why he more than another? 5.01.169 P
why, sir, his hide is so tann'd with his trade 5.01.170 P
why may not imagination trace the noble dust of 5.01.203 P
and why of that loam whereto he was converted 5.01.211 P
why, i will fight with him upon this theme 5.01.266
why, even in that was heaven ordinant. 5.02. 48
why, what a king is this! 5.02. 62
why do we wrap the gentleman in our more rawer 5.02.122 P
why is this all /impawn'd, /as you call it? 5.02.163 P
why, as a woodcock to mine own springe, osric: 5.02.306
why does the drum come hither? 5.02.361
why have my sisters husbands, if they say | they LR 1.01. 99
why bastard? 1.02. 6
why brand they us | with base? 1.02. 9
why so earnestly seek you to put up that letter? 1.02. 28
why came not the slave back to me when i call'd 1.04. 52 P
why, /fool? 1.04. 98 P
why? 1.04. 99 P
why, this fellow has banish'd two on 's 1.04.102 P
why, my boy? 1.04.106 P
why, no, boy, nothing can be made out of nothing 1.04.132 P
why, after i have cut the egg i' th' middle and 1.04.158 P
thou canst tell why one's nose stands i' th' 1.05. 19 P
why, to keep one's eyes of either side 's nose, 1.05. 22 P
but i can tell why a snail has a house. 1.05. 27 P
why? 1.05. 29 P
why, to put 's head in, not to give it away to 1.05. 30 P
the reason why the seven stars are no moe than 1.05. 35 P
you know not why we came to visit you? 2.01.118
why then i care not for thee. 2.02. 8 P
why dost thou use me thus? i know thee not. 2.02. 11 P
why, what a monstrous fellow art thou, thus to 2.02. 25 P
why art thou angry? 2.02. 71
why dost thou call him knave? what is his fault? 2.02. 89
why, madam, if i were your father's dog, | you 2.02.136
why, fool? 2.04. 66 P
why, gloucester, gloucester, | i'ld speak with 2.04. 96
why not by th' hand, sir? 2.04.195
why, the hot-bloodied france, that dowerless 2.04.212
why might not you, my lord, receive attendance 2.04.243
why not, my lord? 2.04.245
why, nature needs not what thou gorgeous wear'st 2.04.269
why, he was met even now | as mad as the vex'd 4.04. 1
why should she write to edmund? 4.05. 19
why then your other senses grow imperfect | by 4.06. 5
why i do trifle thus with his despair | is done 4.06. 33
why dost thou lash that whore? 4.06.161
why, this would make a man a man of salt, | to 4.06.195
why is this reason'd? 5.01. 28
why, fare thee well, i will o'erlook thy paper. 5.01. 50
why he appears | upon this call o' th' trumpet. 5.03.118
and why you answer | this present summons? 5.03.120
alack, why thus? 5.03.240
mist or stain the stone, | why then she lives. 5.03.264
why should a dog, a horse, a rat, have life, 5.03.307
why, there's no remedy. OTH 1.01. 35
why? wherefore ask you this? 1.01. 85
why? what's the matter? 1.03. 58
practices of cunning hell | why this should be. 1.03.103
the rites for why i love him are bereft me, 1.03.257
why, go to bed and sleep. 1.03.304 P
why, thou silly gentleman? 1.03.307 P
with idleness or manur'd with industry — why, 1.03.325 P
with him? why, 'tis not possible. 2.01.220 P
why, none, why, none — a slipper and subtle 2.01.241 P
why, none, why, none — a slipper and subtle 2.01.241 P
why then let a soldier drink." 2.03. 73
why, he drinks you, with facility, your dane 2.03. 82 P
why, very well then; 2.03.118 P
why, how now ho? 2.03.169
why, but you are now well enough. 2.03.294 P
why, masters, have your instruments been in 3.01. 3 P
why, no; 3.01. 32
why, stay, and hear me speak. 3.03. 31
why, your lieutenant, cassio. 3.03. 45
why then to-morrow night, /or tuesday morn; 3.03. 60
why, this is not a boon; 3.03. 76
he did, from first to last. why dost thou ask? 3.03. 96

why of thy thought, iago? 3.03. 98
why then i think cassio's an honest man. 3.03.129
why, say they are vild and false, | as where's 3.03.136
why? 3.03.176
why is this? 3.03.176
why, go to then. 3.03.208
why did i marry? 3.03.242
why do you speak so faintly? | are you not well? 3.03.282
why, that the moor first gave to desdemona, 3.03.308
why, what is that to you? 3.03.315
why, how now, general? no more of that. 3.03.334
why, man? 3.04. 4 P
why do you speak so startingly and rash? 3.04. 79
why, so i can, /sir, but i will not now. 3.04. 86
why, whose is it? 3.04.187
why, i pray you? 3.04.195
why then 'tis hers, my lord, and, being hers, 4.01. 12
why, sweet othello? 4.01.239
why? what art thou? 4.02. 34
why do you weep? 4.02. 42
why, with my lord, madam. 4.02.100
why did he so? 4.02.122
why should he call her whore? 4.02.137
why, now i see there's mettle in thee, and even 4.02.204 P
why, then othello and desdemona return again to 4.02.222 P
why, by making him uncapable of othello's place: 4.02.229 P
why, would not you? 4.03. 65
why, the wrong is but a wrong i' th' world; 4.03. 80 P
why, we have galls; 4.03. 92
why i should fear i know not, | since guiltiness 5.02. 38
alas, why gnaw you so your nether lip? 5.02. 43
why, how should she be murd'red? 5.02.126
but why should honor outlive honesty? 5.02.245
why, any thing: 5.02.293
why he hath thus ensnar'd my soul and body? 5.02.302
why did he marry fulvia, and not love her? ANT 1.01. 41
why then we kill all our women. 1.02.133 P
why, sir, give the gods a thankful sacrifice. 1.02.161 P
why should i think you can be mine, and true 1.03. 27
why, madam? 1.05. 4
why do you send so thick? 1.05. 63
why, there's more gold. 2.05. 31
why, this it is to have a name in great men's 2.07. 11 P
why? 2.07. 89
caesar? why, he's the jupiter of men. 3.02. 9
why, enobarbus? 3.02. 53
why, methinks, by him, | this creature's no such 3.03. 40
why have you stol'n upon us thus? 3.06. 42
but why, why, why? 3.07. 2
but why, why, why? 3.07. 2
but why, why, why? 3.07. 2
us, why should not we | be there in person? 3.07. 5
why will my lord do so? 3.07. 29
why then good night indeed. 3.10. 29
do? why, what else? 3.11. 27
why should he follow? 3.13. 6
why should he not? 4.02. 2
why is my lord enrag'd against his love? 4.12. 31
do at once | the thing why thou hast drawn it. 4.14. 89
why, there then. 4.14. 94
why, how now, charmian? 4.15. 83
why, that's the way | to fool their preparation, 5.02.224
and why so? CYM 1.01. 15
why came you from your master? 1.01.169
to sadness, and oft–times | not knowing why. 1.06. 63
why do you pity me? 1.06. 89
why, so i say. 2.01. 31 P
the arras, figures, | why, such and such; 2.02. 27
why should i write this down, that's riveted, 2.02. 43
that hell knows, | why, hers, in part or all; 2.05. 28
why tribute? 3.01. 42 P
why should we pay tribute? 3.01. 42 P
a week, why may not i | glide thither in a day? 3.02. 51
why should excuse be born or e'er begot? 3.02. 65
why, one that rode to 's execution, man, | could 3.02. 70
why tender'st thou that paper to me with | a 3.04. 11
why, i must die; 3.04. 74
why hast thou abus'd | so many miles with a 3.04.102
why hast thou gone so far, | to be unbent when 3.04.107
why, good fellow, | what shall i do the while? 3.04.127
why should his mistress, who was made by him 4.01. 3 P
i know not why | i love this youth, and i have 4.02. 20
why i should yield to thee. 4.02. 80
why, worthy father, what have we to lose, | but 4.02.124
then why should we be tender | to let an 4.02.126
why, he but sleeps! 4.02.215
i nothing know where she remains, why gone, 4.03. 14
why did you suffer jachimo, | slight thing of 5.04. 63
why hast thou thus adjourn'd | the graces for 5.04. 78
that have this golden chance and know not why. 5.04.132
why so sadly | greet you our victory? 5.05. 23
i know not why, wherefore, | to say "live, boy." 5.05. 95
why stands he so perplex'd? 5.05.108
why did you throw your wedded lady /from you? 5.05.261
why, old soldier: 5.05.306
why fled you from the court? 5.05.387
why cloud they not their sights perpetually, PER 1.01. 74
it fits thee not | to ask the reason why, 1.01.157
why should this change of thoughts, | the sad 1.02. 1
if further yet you will be satisfied | why (as 1.03. 16
why, as men do a–land; 2.01. 28 P
why, man? 2.01. 38 P
why, are /your beggars whipt then? 2.01. 90
why, i'll tell you. 2.01. 99 P
why, wilt thou tourney for the lady? 2.01.144 P
why, d' ye take it, and the gods give thee good 2.01.146 P
why, sir, say if you had, who takes offense | at 2.05. 71
why do you make us love your goodly gifts | and 3.01. 23
gentlemen, | why do you stir so early? 3.02. 12
how now, marina, why do you keep alone? 4.01. 21
why will you kill me? 4.01. 70
why would she have me kill'd now? 4.01. 72
why to give over, i pray you? 4.02. 28 P
why lament you, pretty one? 4.02. 68 P
why /are you foolish? can it be undone? 4.03. 1
why, i cannot name/'t but i shall offend. 4.06. 69 P
why, the house you dwell in proclaims you to be 4.06. 77 P
why, hath your principal made known unto you who 4.06. 82 P
why, your herb–woman, she that sets seeds and 4.06. 85 P
why, i could wish him to be my master, or rather 4.06.159 P
why do you weep? 5.01.176
eftsoons i'll tell thee why. 5.01.255
why, good ladies, | this is a service, whereto i TNK 1.01.170
why am i bound | by any generous bond to follow 1.02. 49
or let me know | why mine own barber is unblest, 1.02. 53
like the elements | that know not what nor why, 1.03. 62
humm'd /one | from musical coinage, why, it was 1.03. 76
why, strong enough to laugh at misery | and bear 2.02. 2
why, madam? 2.02.125
cousin, cousin! how do you, sir? why, palamon! 2.02.131
why, what's the matter, man? 2.02.133
why, gentle madam? 2.02.136
why are you mov'd thus? 2.02.183
why then would you deal so cunningly, | so 2.02.189
why is he sent for? 2.02.225
why should a friend be treacherous? 2.02.229
why, my lord? 2.02.265
why then have with ye, boys! 2.03. 27
whither? why, what a question's that! 2.03. 61
why should i love this gentleman? 2.04. 1
why may't not be | they have made prey of him? 3.02. 12
for why, here stand i; 3.05. 12
why, timothy! 3.05. 24
why? 3.05. 78
why? 3.06.108
ask that lady | why she is fair, and why her 3.06.169
and why her eyes command me | stay here to love 3.06.169
why, as it should be: 4.01. 26
why do you ask? 4.01. 32
but why all this haste, sir? 4.01. 51
why, let it be so; farewell, coz! 5.01. 33
why, do you think she is not honest, sir? 5.02. 30
why, a day's journey, wench. 5.02. 73
why, play at stoolball: 5.02. 74
why do you rub my kiss off? 5.02. 88
why, the knights must kindle | their valor at 5.03. 29
why so, i know not; 5.03. 74
they metamorphis'd | both into one — o, why? 5.03. 85
miscarry, yet i knew not | why i did think so. 5.03.102
why even your hurly | cannot proceed but by STM II.C 113
to england, | why, you must needs be strangers; II.C 130
boy, | 'tis but a kiss i beg, why art thou coy? VEN 96
then why not lips on lips, since eyes in eyes? 120
but having no defects, why dost abhor me? 138
the earth's increase why shouldst thou feed, 169
why, there love liv'd, and there he could not 246
me my hand," saith he, "why dost thou feel it?" 373
"why, what of that?" 717
why hast thou cast into eternal sleeping | those 951
face, why then i know | he thought to kiss him, 1109
or why is collatine the publisher | of that rich LUC 33
"why hunt i then for color or excuses? 267
"why should the worm intrude the maiden bud? 848
"why hath thy servant opportunity | betray'd the 932
"why work'st thou mischief in thy pilgrimage, 960
"poor hand, why quiver'st thou at this decree? 1030
of eyes, | why pry'st thou through my window? 1089
sorrow | (for why her face wore sorrow's livery) 1222
why her two suns were cloud–eclipsed so, | nor 1224
nor why her fair cheeks over–wash'd with woe. 1225
"why should the private pleasure of some one 1478
for one's offense why should so many fall, | to 1483
priam, why art thou old, and yet not wise? 1550
why art thou thus attir'd in discontent? 1601
and why not i from this compelled stain?" 1708
"why, collatine, is woe the cure for woe? 1821
"o jove," quoth she, "why was not i a flood?" PP 6.14
for why thou lefts me nothing in thy will; 10. 8
crave, | for why i craved nothing of thee still. 10.10
for why, she sight, and bade me come to–morrow. 14.24
why dost thou spend | upon thyself thy beauty's SON 4. 1
why dost thou abuse | the bounteous largess 4. 5
why dost thou use | so great a sum of sums, yet 4. 7
music to hear, why hear'st thou music sadly? 8. 1
why lov'st thou that which thou receiv'st not 8. 3
why didst thou promise such a beauteous day, 34. 1
laws, | since why to love i can allege no cause. 49.14
where thou art, why should i haste me thence? 51. 3
why should false painting imitate his cheek, 67. 5
why should poor beauty indirectly seek | roses 67. 7
why should he live, now nature bankrout is, 67. 9
but why thy odor matcheth not thy show, | the 69.13
why is my verse so barren of new pride? 76. 1
why with the time do i not glance aside | to 76. 3
why write i still all one, ever the same, | and 76. 5
yet then my judgment knew no reason why | my 115. 3
alas, why, fearing of time's tyranny, | might i 115. 9
for why should others' false adulterate eyes 121. 5
or on my frailties why are frailer spies, 121. 7
if snow be white, why then her breasts are dun; 130. 3
why of eyes' falsehood hast thou forged hooks, 137. 7
why should my heart think that a several plot, 137. 9
why dost thou pine within and suffer dearth, 146. 3
why so large cost, having so short a lease, 146. 5
but why of two oaths' breach do i accuse thee, 152. 5
why, 'twas beautiful and hard, | whereto his LC 211

WI' *(also with)*

/WI' 3 FR 0.0003 REL FR 3 V 0 P
martius should be join'd /wi' /th' volscians — COR 4.06. 89
a thing a little soil'd /wi' /th' working, HAM 2.01. 40
/wi' leave, they're called | arcite and palamon. TNK 1.04. 22

WI' 5 FR 0.0005 REL FR 4 V 1 P
let's all sink wi' th' king. TMP 1.01. 63
wi' th' king of naples | to give him annual 1.02.112
i thank your worship, god be wi' you! LLL 3.01.150 P
that goes to bed wi' th' sun | and with him WT 4.04.105
to see it techy and fall out wi' th' dug! ROM 1.03. 32

WICK *(see week*)*

WICKED 70 FR 0.0079 REL FR 46 V 24 P
got by the devil himself | upon thy wicked dam, TMP 1.02.320
as wicked dew as e'er my mother brush'd | with 1.02.321
for you, most wicked sir, whom to call brother 5.01.130
o wicked, wicked world! WIV 2.01. 20 P
o wicked, wicked world! 2.01. 20 P
till the wicked fire of lust have melted him in 2.01. 67 P
and as wicked as his wife? 5.05.157 P
for example, thou thyself art a wicked villain, MM 1.02. 25 P
thou liest, wicked varlet! 2.01.167 P
o thou wicked hannibal! 2.01.174 P
prove this, thou wicked hannibal, or i'll have 2.01.178 P
pleasure i shall do with this wicked caitiff? 2.01.184 P
thou seest, thou wicked varlet, now, what's come 2.01.190 P
fie, sirrah, a bawd, a wicked bawd! 3.02. 19
what wicked and dissembling glass of mine | made
MND 2.02. 98
o wicked wall, through whom i see no bliss! 5.01.180
then thy manners must be wicked, and wickedness
AYL 3.02. 42 P
that same wicked bastard of venus that was begot 4.01.211 P
a most wicked sir oliver, audrey, a most vile 5.01. 5 P
madam, a wicked creature, as you and all flesh AWW 1.03. 35 P
it speed, | is wicked meaning in a lawful deed, 3.07. 45
theirs only, | that would unseen be wicked? WT 1.02.292
against) i am assisted | by wicked powers. 5.03. 91
a wicked will, | a woman's will, a cank'red JN 2.01.193
a wicked day, and not a holy day! 3.01. 83
the image of a wicked heinous fault | lives in 4.02. 71
the love of wicked men converts to fear, | that R2 5.01. 66
truly, little better than one of the wicked. 1H4 1.02. 95 P
sack and sugar be a fault, god help the wicked! 2.04.471 P
i disprais'd him before the wicked, that the 2H4 2.04.319 P
that the wicked might not fall in love with thee 2.04.320 P
is she of the wicked? 2.04.327 P
is thine hostess here of the wicked? 2.04.328 P
or is thy boy of the wicked? 2.04.329 P
whose zeal burns in his nose, of the wicked? 2.04.330 P
wicked and vile, and so her death concludes. 1H6 5.04. 16
i never had to do with wicked spirits. 5.04. 42
raising up wicked spirits from under ground, 2H6 2.01.170
o god, what mischiefs work the wicked ones, 2.01.182
by wicked means to frame our sovereign's fall. 3.01. 52
too | thou mayst be damned for that wicked deed!
R3 1.02.103
thus doth he force the swords of wicked men | to 5.01. 23
i true? how now? what wicked deem is this? TRO 4.04. 59
i'll haunt thee like a wicked conscience still, 5.10. 28
this wicked emperor may have shipp'd her hence, TIT 4.03. 23
look round about the wicked streets of rome, 5.02. 98
death, | as punishment for his most wicked life. 5.03.145
o most wicked fiend! ROM 3.05.235
what a wicked beast was i to disfurnish myself TIM 3.02. 44 P
takes virtuous copies to be wicked; 3.03. 32 P
a plague consume you, wicked caitiffs left! 5.04. 71
and wicked dreams abuse | the curtain'd sleep; MAC 2.01. 50
of my thumbs, | something wicked this way comes. 4.01. 45
o, most wicked speed! HAM 1.02.156
be thy intents wicked, or charitable, | thou 1.04. 42
o wicked wit and gifts that have the power | so 1.05. 44
and oft 'tis seen the wicked prize itself | buys 3.03. 59
go, go, you question with a wicked tongue. 3.04. 12
whose wicked deed thy most ingenious sense 5.01.248
mumbling of wicked charms, conjuring the moon LR 2.01. 39
those wicked creatures yet do look well–favor'd 2.04.256
look well–favor'd | when others are more wicked; 2.04.257
upon my soul, a lie, a wicked lie. OTH 5.02.181
which | we were dissuaded by our wicked queen, CYM 5.05.463
epitaph is for marina writ | by wicked dionyza. PER 4.04. 33
me, | till cruel cleon, with his wicked wife, 5.01.171
for wicked cleon and his wife, when fame | had 5.03. 95
such a vengeance | that, were i old and wicked, TNK 2.03. 6
and wast afeard to scratch her wicked foe, LUC 1035
but such a face should bear a wicked mind. 1540

WICKEDLY 1 FR 0.0001 REL FR 1 V 0 P
into the chamber wickedly he stalks, | and LUC 365

/WICKEDNESS 1 FR 0.0001 REL FR 1 V 0 P
/i'll /never /care /what /wickedness /i /do, LR 3.07. 99

WICKEDNESS 10 FR 0.0011 REL FR 5 V 5 P
good that children should know any wickedness. WIV 2.02.129 P
word is too good to paint out her wickedness. ADO 3.02.110 P
manners must be wicked, and wickedness is sin, AYL 3.02. 43 P
thy marriage, sooner than thy wickedness. AWW 1.03. 38 P
a very tainted fellow, and full of wickedness. 3.02. 87
i see thou art a wickedness | wherein the TN 2.02. 27
what rein can hold licentious wickedness | when H5 3.03. 22
the imputation of his wickedness, by your rule, 4.01.149 P
no, prelate, such is thy audacious wickedness, 1H6 3.01. 14
knows he the wickedness? LR 4.02. 91

WICKED'ST 1 FR 0.0001 REL FR 1 V 0 P
but one, the wicked'st caitiff on the ground, MM 5.01. 53

WIDE 60 FR 0.0067 REL FR 52 V 8 P
to be asleep | with eyes wide open — standing, TMP 2.01.214
and learning, so wide of his own respect. WIV 3.01. 58 P
lord of the wide world and wild wat'ry seas, ERR 2.01. 21
is my lord well, that he doth speak so wide? ADO 4.01. 62
that the wide sea | hath drops too few to wash 4.01.140
ha! not for the wide world. 4.01.290 P
and welcome to the wide fields too base to be LLL 2.01. 93 P
wide a' the bow–hand! 4.01.133
skin, | weed wide enough to wrap a fairy in; MND 2.01.256
of night | that the graves, all gaping wide, 5.01.380
nor is the wide world ignorant of her worth, MV 1.01.167
wilds | of wide arabia are as throughfares now 2.07. 42
he'll go along o'er the wide world with me; AYL 1.03.132
this wide and universal theatre | presents more 2.07.137
sav'd, a world too wide | for his shrunk shank, 2.07.160
not open my lips so wide as a bristle may enter, TN 1.05. 2 P
and leave the growth untried | of that wide gap, WT 4.01. 7
perform'd in this wide gap of time since first 5.03.154
and wide havoc made | for bloody power to rush JN 2.01.220
you men of angiers, open wide your gates, | and 2.01.300
the mouth of passage shall we fling wide ope, 2.01.449
and for whose death we in the world's wide mouth
1H4 1.03.153
and the villains march wide betwixt the legs, as 4.02. 40 P
of the ocean | too wide for neptune's hips; 2H4 3.01. 51
that keep'st the ports of slumber open wide | to 4.05. 24
now set the teeth and stretch the nostril wide, H5 3.01. 15
with conscience wide as hell, mowing like grass 3.03. 13
dark | fills the wide vessel of the universe. 4.pr. 3
or earth gape open wide and eat him quick, | as R3 1.02. 65
of this action | for the wide world's revenue. TRO 2.02.206
no such matter, you are wide. 3.01. 88 P
and wide unclasp the tables of their thoughts 4.05. 60
to tear with thunder the wide cheeks a' th' air, COR 5.03.151

the wide world's emperor, do i consecrate | my TIT 1.01.248
the forest walks are wide and spacious, | and 2.01.114
goose, proves thee far and wide a broad goose. ROM 2.04. 86 P
so deep as a well, nor so wide as a church–door, 3.01. 96 P
be patient, for the world is broad and wide. 3.03. 16
but moves itself | in a wide sea of wax. TIM 1.01. 47
that her wide walks encompass'd but one man? JC 1.02.155
of the mind and soul | grows wide withal. HAM 1.03. 14
pyrrhus at priam drives, in rage strikes wide, 2.02.472
to his good friends thus wide i'll ope my arms, 4.05.146
her clothes spread wide, | and, mermaid–like, 4.07.175
still, still, far wide! LR 4.07. 49
till that a capable and wide revenge | swallow OTH 3.03.459
and the wide arch | of the rang'd empire fall! ANT 1.01. 33
of your chaste daughter the wide difference CYM 5.05.194
you are wide. TNK 3.03. 45
go seek him through the world that is so wide. 3.04. 23
breast, full eye, small head, and nostril wide, VEN 296
upon the wide wound that the boar had trench'd 1052
and with his knee the door he opens wide. LUC 359
to the wide world and all her fading sweets: SON 19. 7
thee, | and keep my drooping eyelids open wide, 27. 7
but since your worth (wide as the ocean is) 80. 5
nor the prophetic soul | of the wide world, 107. 2
for nothing this wide universe i call, | save 109.13
my heart knows the wide world's common place? 137.10
eyes straight, though thy proud heart go wide. 140.14
WIDE–CHOPP'D 1 FR 0.0001 REL FR 1 V 0 P
this wide–chopp'd rascal — would thou mightst TMP 1.01. 57
WIDE–ENLARG'D 1 FR 0.0001 REL FR 1 V 0 P
be fill'd | with all graces wide–enlarg'd. AYL 3.02.143
WIDENS 1 FR 0.0001 REL FR 1 V 0 P
'tis for the followers fortune widens them, COR 1.04. 44
WIDER 4 FR 0.0004 REL FR 4 V 0 P
gape | for thee thrice wider than for other men. 2H4 5.05. 54
his arms spread wider than a dragon's wings; 1H6 1.01. 11
divides more wider than the sky and earth, | and TRO 5.02.149
without more wider and more /overt test | than OTH 1.03.107
WIDE–SKIRTED 1 FR 0.0001 REL FR 1 V 0 P
with plenteous rivers and wide–skirted meads, LR 1.01. 65
WIDE–STRETCHED 1 FR 0.0001 REL FR 1 V 0 P
and all wide–stretched honors that pertain | by H5 2.04. 82
WIDOW 62 FR 0.0070 REL FR 46 V 16 P
not since widow dido's time. TMP 2.01. 77 P
widow? 2.01. 78 P
how came that widow in? 2.01. 79 P
widow dido! 2.01. 79 P
"widow dido," said you? 2.01. 82 P
bate, i beseech you, widow dido. 2.01.101 P
o, widow dido? ay, widow dido. 2.01.102 P
o, widow dido? ay, widow dido. 2.01.102 P
a widow then? MM 5.01.175 P
neither maid, widow, nor wife? 5.01.178 P
for many of them are neither maid, widow, nor 5.01.180 P
ours, | we do enstate and widow you with all, 5.01.424
than the bell rings and the widow weeps. ADO 5.02. 80 P
i have a widow aunt, a dowager, | of great MND 1.01.157
oath, | i will be married to a wealthy widow, SHR 4.02. 37
i' faith, he'll have a lusty widow now, | that 4.02. 50
have to my widow! 4.05. 78
and thou, hortensio, with thy loving widow, 5.02. 7
now, for my life, hortensio fears his widow. 5.02. 16
my widow says, thus she conceives her tale. 5.02. 24
very well mended. kiss him for that, good widow. 5.02. 25
to her, widow! 5.02. 34
england, how may we content | this widow lady? JN 2.01.548
a widow, husbandless, subject to fears, | a 3.01. 14
a widow cries; 3.01.108
your grace, i am a poor widow of eastcheap, and 2H4 2.01. 70 P
to enforce a poor widow to so rough a course to 2.01. 82 P
so came i a widow, | and never shall have length 2.03. 57
and she a mourning widow of her nobles, | she H5 1.02.158
to wring the widow from her custom'd right, 2H6 5.01.188
widow, we will consider of your suit, | and come 3H6 3.02. 16
ay, widow? 3.02. 21
how many children hast thou, widow? tell me. 3.02. 26
the widow likes him not, she knits her brows. 3.02. 82
sweet widow, by my state i swear to thee | i 3.02. 93
you cavil, widow, i did mean my queen. 3.02. 99
thou art a widow, and thou hast some children, 3.02.102
the widow likes it not, for she looks very sad. 3.02.110
widow, go you along. 3.02.123
the jealous o'erworn widow and herself, | since R3 1.01. 81
were it to call king edward's widow sister, | i 1.01.109
prince | and made her widow to a woeful bed? 1.02.248
thou art a widow; 2.02. 55
was never widow had so dear a loss. 2.02. 77
sons, | a beauty–waning and distressed widow, 3.07.185
for making me, so young, so old a widow! 4.01. 72
for happy wife, a most distressed widow; 4.04. 98
princess dowager | and widow to prince arthur. H8 3.02. 71
the lady widow of /vitruvio; ROM 1.02. 66 P
is it | that makes the wappen'd widow wed again; TIM 4.03. 39
if, once i be a widow, ever i be a wife! HAM 3.02.223
but being widow, and my gloucester with her, LR 4.02. 84
to take the widow | exasperates, makes mad her 5.01. 59
three kings in a forenoon, and widow them all. ANT 1.02. 27 P
can from the lap of egypt's widow pluck | the 2.01. 37
madam, | she was a widow — 3.03. 27
widow? charmian, hark. 3.03. 27
sole son — a widow | that late he married), CYM 1.01. 5
o, no knees, none, widow! TNK 1.01. 74
justice is feasting while the widow weeps, LUC 906
the world will be thy widow and still weep, SON 9. 5
when every private widow well may keep, | by 9. 7
WIDOW–COMFORT 1 FR 0.0001 REL FR 1 V 0 P
my widow–comfort, and my sorrows' cure! JN 3.04.105
WIDOW–DOLOR 1 FR 0.0001 REL FR 1 V 0 P
unmoan'd, | your widow–dolor likewise be unwept! R3 2.02. 65
WIDOWED 2 FR 0.0002 REL FR 2 V 0 P
city he | hath widowed and unchilded many a one, COR 5.06.151
like widowed wombs after their lords' decease: SON 97. 8
WIDOWER 5 FR 0.0005 REL FR 3 V 2 P
what if he had said "widower aeneas" too? TMP 2.01. 80 P
now is the count rossillion a widower, his vows AWW 5.03.142 P
tell him, in hope he'll prove a widower shortly, 3H6 3.03.227
him, in hope he'll prove a widower shortly, 4.01. 99
great mark antony | is now a widower. ANT 2.02.120
WIDOWER'S 1 FR 0.0001 REL FR 1 V 0 P
stay | to see our widower's second marriage–day. AWW 5.03. 70
WIDOWHOOD 1 FR 0.0001 REL FR 1 V 0 P
i'll assure her of | her widowhood, be it that SHR 2.01.124
WIDOW–MAKER 1 FR 0.0001 REL FR 1 V 0 P
this metal from my side | to be a widow–maker! JN 5.02. 17
WIDOW'S 7 FR 0.0008 REL FR 6 V 1 P
a tapster, a poor widow's tapster. MM 2.01.198 P
o, take his mother's thanks, a widow's thanks, JN 2.01. 32
many a widow's husband grovelling lies, | coldly 2.01.305
to god, the widow's champion and defense. R2 1.02. 43
lords, give us leave. i'll try this widow's wit. 3H6 3.02. 33
and many an old man's sigh and many a widow's, 5.06. 39
is it for fear to wet a widow's eye | that thou SON 9. 1
WIDOWS' 2 FR 0.0002 REL FR 2 V 0 P
and on your head | turning the widows' tears, H5 2.04.106
widows' cries | descend again into their throats TNK 1.02. 81
WIDOWS 9 FR 0.0010 REL FR 8 V 1 P
moe widows in them of this business' making TMP 2.01.134
aleven widows and nine maids is a simple MV 2.02.162 P
mean time | will live as maids and widows. 2.01.134
for many a thousand widows | shall this his mock H5 1.02.284
had left no mourning widows for our death, | and 3H6 2.06. 19
dear, | such eyes the widows in corioles wear, COR 2.01.178
city, | 'tis i that made thy widows; 4.04. 2
each new morn | new widows howl, new orphans cry MAC 4.03. 5
take hands, | let us be widows to our woes; TNK 1.01.166
WID'ST 1 FR 0.0001 REL FR 1 V 0 P
against it, | and gape at wid'st to glut him. TMP 1.01. 60
WIELD 5 FR 0.0005 REL FR 4 V 1 P
wilt thou the spigot wield? WIV 1.03. 21 P
his hand to wield a sceptre, and himself 3H6 4.06. 73
beseeming ornaments | to wield old partisans, in ROM 1.01. 94
love you more than /words can wield the matter, LR 1.01. 55
to see their youthful sons bright weapons wield, LUC 1432
/WIFE 2 FR 0.0002 REL FR 1 V 1 P
comfort my sister, cheer her, call her /wife: ERR 3.02. 26
that attends the /general's /wife be stirring, OTH 3.01. 25 P
WIFE 476 FR 0.0538 REL FR 363 V 113 P
"farewell, my wife and children!" TMP 1.01. 61
every day some sailor's wife, | the masters of 2.01. 4
i am your wife, if you will marry me; 3.01. 83
that ne'er | dost disobey the wife of jupiter; 4.01. 77
found a wife | where he himself was lost; 5.01.210
beseeming such a wife as your fair daughter. TGV 3.01. 66
i now am full resolv'd to take a wife | and turn 3.01. 76
wife, bid these gentlemen welcome. WIV 1.01.194 P
i do mean to make love to ford's wife. 1.03. 44 P
and here another to page's wife, who even now 1.03. 59 P
sir john affects thy wife. 2.01.111
why, sir, my wife is not young. 2.01.112 P
love my wife? 2.01.116 P
he loves your wife: 2.01.132 P
my name is nym, and falstaff loves your wife. 2.01.135 P
if he should intend this voyage toward my wife, 2.01.182 P
i do not misdoubt my wife; 2.01.185 P
she's as fartuous a civil modest wife, and one 2.02. 98 P
has ford's wife and page's wife acquainted each 2.02.109 P
wife and page's wife acquainted each other how 2.02.109 P
never a wife in windsor leads a better life than 2.02.116 P
siege to the honesty of this ford's wife. 2.02.235 P
you shall, /and you will, enjoy ford's wife. 2.02.255 P
for the which his wife seems to me well–favor'd. 2.02.273 P
the peasant, and thou shalt lie with his wife. 2.02.283 P
my wife hath sent to him, the hour is fix'd, the 2.02.289 P
he will trust his wife, he will not be jealous. 2.02.301 P
my ambling gelding, than my wife with herself. 2.02.305 P
i will prevent this, detect my wife, be reveng'd 2.02.310 P
truly, sir, to see your wife. is she at home? 3.02. 11 P
is your wife at home indeed? 3.02. 26 P
and now she's going to my wife, and falstaff's 3.02. 36 P
i will take him, then torture my wife, pluck the 3.02. 41 P
but my wife, master doctor, is for you 3.02. 62 P
your wife is as honest a omans as i will desires 3.03.219 P
come, wife, come, mistress page, i pray you 3.03.226 P
what hath pass'd between me and ford's wife? 3.05. 62 P
somebody call my wife. 4.02.116 P
what, wife, i say! 4.02.119 P
the honest woman, the modest wife, the virtuous 4.02.130 P
pardon me, wife, henceforth do what thou wilt. 4.04. 6
and i will deliver his wife into your hand. 5.01. 29 P
i will never mistrust my wife again, till thou 5.05.133 P
and as wicked as his wife? 5.05.157 P
where i will desire thee to laugh at my wife, 5.05.172 P
daughter, she is, by this, doctor caius' wife. 5.05.176 P
she is fast my wife, | save that we do the MM 1.02.147
my wife, sir, whom i detest before heaven and 2.01. 69 P
how? thy wife? 2.01. 71 P
marry, sir, by my wife, who, if she had been a 2.01. 79 P
what was done to elbow's wife, that he hath 2.01.116 P
what was done to elbow's wife, once more? 2.01.139 P
you, sir, ask him what this man did to my wife. 2.01.144 P
master froth do the constable's wife any harm? 2.01.158 P
his wife is a more respected person than any of 2.01.165 P
neither maid, widow, nor wife? 5.01.178 P
many of them are neither maid, widow, nor wife. 5.01.180 P
i am affianc'd this man's wife as strongly | as 5.01.227
in 's garden–house, | he knew me as a wife. 5.01.230
look that you love your wife; 5.01.497
my wife, not meanly proud of two such boys, ERR 1.01. 58
yet the incessant weepings of my wife, | weeping 1.01. 70
my wife, more careful for the latter–born, | had 1.01. 78
the children thus dispos'd, my wife and i, 1.01. 83
your worship's wife, my mistress at the phoenix; 1.02. 88
it seems he hath great care to please his wife. 2.01. 56
quoth he, "no house, no wife, no mistress." 2.01. 71
i am not adriana, nor thy wife. 2.02.112
denied my house for his, me for his wife. 2.02.159
my wife is shrewish when i keep not hours: 3.01. 2
gold, | and that i did deny my wife and house. 3.01. 9
are you there, wife? you might have come before. 3.01. 63
your wife, sir knave! go get you from the door. 3.01. 64
of suspect | th' unviolated honor of your wife. 3.01. 88
my wife (but, i protest, without desert) | hath 3.01.112
(be it for nothing but to spite my wife) | upon 3.01.118
i know | your weeping sister is no wife of mine, 3.02. 42
thou hast no husband yet, nor i no wife. 3.02. 68
life, | so fly i from her that would be my wife. 3.02.155
husband, even my soul | doth for a wife abhor. 3.02.159
go home with it, and please your wife withal, 3.02.173
i bestow | among my wife and /her confederates, 4.01. 17
chain, and bid my wife | disburse the sum on the 4.01. 37
why, give it to my wife, and fetch your money. 4.01. 54
belike his wife, acquainted with his fits, | on 4.03. 90
and tell his wife that, being lunatic, | he 4.03. 93
my wife is in a wayward mood to–day, | and will 4.04. 4
come go along, my wife is coming yonder. 4.04. 40
she that would be your wife now ran from you. 4.04.148
holiness | to separate the husband and the wife. 5.01.111
she whom thou gav'st to me to be my wife; 5.01.198
by th' way we met | my wife, her sister, and a 5.01.236
the man | that hadst a wife once call'd aemilia, 5.01.343
she now shall be my sister, not my wife. 5.01.417
sworn the contrary, if hero would be my wife. ADO 1.01.196 P
she were an excellent wife for benedick. 2.01.351 P
and it be the right husband and the right wife; 3.04. 36 P
and when i liv'd, i was your other wife, | and 5.04. 60
thou art sad, get thee a wife, get thee a wife. 5.04.122 P
thou art sad, get thee a wife, get thee a wife. 5.04.122 P
i love, i sue, i seek a wife — | a woman, that LLL 3.01.189
a wife of such wood were felicity. 4.03.245
a wife? 5.02.824
o, shall i say, i thank you, gentle wife? 5.02.826
you of your wife, and me of my consent, | of my MND 4.01.158
of my consent that she should be your wife. 4.01.159
his wife who wins me by that means i told you, MV 2.01. 19
and i am sure margery your wife is my mother. 2.02. 90 P
become a christian and thy loving wife. 2.03. 21
take what wife you will to bed, | i will ever be 2.09. 70
with all my heart, so thou canst get a wife. 3.02.195
first go with me to church and call me wife, 3.02.303
launcelot, if you thus get my wife into corners! 3.05. 30 P
how dost thou like the lord bassanio's wife? 3.05. 72
husband | hast thou of me as she is for /a wife. 3.05. 84
commend me to your honorable wife, | tell her 4.01.273
i am married to a wife | which is as dear to me 4.01.282
but life itself, my wife, and all the world, 4.01.284
your wife would give you little thanks for that 4.01.288
i have a wife who i protest i love; 4.01.290
good sir, this ring was given me by my wife, 4.01.441
gifts, | and if your wife be not a mad woman, 4.01.445
for a light wife doth make a heavy husband, 5.01.130
you give your wife too unkind a cause of grief; 5.01.175
when i am absent, then lie with my wife. 5.01.285
that is the dowry of his wife, 'tis none of his AYL 3.03. 55 P
a good excuse for me hereafter to leave my wife. 3.03. 94 P
fortune, and prevents the slander of his wife. 4.01. 62 P
will you, orlando, have to wife this rosalind? 4.01.130 P
you must say, "i take thee, rosalind, for wife." 4.01.136 P
i take thee, rosalind, for wife. 4.01.137 P
a man that had a wife with such a wit, he might 4.01.165 P
wherein your lady and your humble wife | may SHR in.1. 116
where is my wife? in.2. 102
are you my wife and will not call me husband? in.2. 104
and husband, | i am your wife in all obedience. in.2. 107
madam wife, they say that i have dream'd | and in.2. 112
come, madam wife, sit by my side, and let the in.2. 142 P
there, there, hortensio, will you any wife? 1.01. 56
and wish thee to a shrewd ill–favor'd wife? 1.02. 60
know | one rich enough to be petruchio's wife 1.02. 67
help thee to a wife | with wealth enough, and 1.02. 85
such a life, with such a wife, were strange! 1.02.193
what dowry shall i have with her to wife? 2.01.120
myself am mov'd to woo thee for my wife. 2.01.194
hath consented | that you shall be my wife; 2.01.270
i must and will have katherine to my wife. 2.01.280
father, and wife, and gentlemen, adieu. 2.01.321
if i may have your daughter to my wife, | i'll 2.01.365
and say, "lo, there is mad petruchio's wife, 3.02. 19
hath all so long detain'd you from your wife, 3.02.103
should ask if katherine should be his wife, 3.02.159
to this most patient, sweet, and virtuous wife. 3.02.195
is my master and his wife coming, grumio? 4.01. 18 P
this is a way to kill a wife with kindness, 4.01.208
and how she's like to be lucentio's wife. 4.04. 66
the sister to my wife, this gentlewoman, | thy 4.05. 62
assurance | let's each one send unto his wife, 5.02. 66
his wife, | and he whose wife is most obedient, 5.02. 67
hound, | but twenty times so much upon my wife. 5.02. 73
pray god, sir, your wife send you not a worse. 5.02. 84
go and entreat my wife | to come to me forthwith 5.02. 86
now, where's my wife? 5.02. 90
where is your sister, and hortensio's wife? 5.02.101
he that comforts my wife is the cherisher of my AWW 1.03. 46 P
ergo, he that kisses my wife is my friend. 1.03. 49 P
then, young bertram, take her, she's thy wife. 2.03.105
my wife, my liege? 2.03.106
charge — | a poor physician's daughter my wife! 2.03.115
to the dark house and the /detested wife. 2.03.292
"till i have no wife, i have nothing in france." 3.02. 74 P
nothing in france, until he have no wife! 3.02. 79
"till i have no wife, i have nothing in france." 3.02. 99 P
nothing in france, until he has no wife! 3.02.100
rinaldo, | to this unworthy husband of his wife. 3.04. 30
'tis a hard bondage to become the wife | of a 3.05. 64
i would he lov'd his wife. 3.05. 79
duty, such, my lord, | as you owe to your wife. 4.02. 13
you have won | a wife of me, though there my 4.02. 65
shaking off so good a wife and so sweet a lady. 4.03. 7 P
his wife some two months since fled from his 4.03. 47 P
buried a wife, mourn'd for her, writ to my lady 4.03. 88 P
cozen the man of his wife and do his service. 4.05. 27 P
and i would give his wife my bauble, sir, to do 4.05. 30 P
he lost a wife | whose beauty did astonish the 5.03. 15
to marry me when his wife was dead, i blush to 5.03.140 P
why do you look so strange upon your wife? 5.03.168
this is his wife, | that ring's a thousand 5.03.198
you, that have turn'd off a first so noble wife, 5.03.220
this ring was mine, i gave it his first wife. 5.03.279
i am either maid, or else this old man's wife. 5.03.293
and at that time he got his wife with child. 5.03.301
lord, | 'tis but the shadow of a wife you see, 5.03.307
by thy honest aid | thou kept'st a wife herself, 5.03.330

whoe'er i woo, myself would be his wife. TN 1.04. 42
your wife is like to reap a proper man. 3.01.133
more, by all mores, than e'er i shall love wife. 5.01.136
on, | to think me as well a sister as a wife, 5.01.317
in those unfledg'd days was my wife a girl; WT 1.02. 78
and arms her with the boldness of a wife | to 1.02.184
while i speak this) holds his wife by th' arm, 1.02.193
man that does not think) | my wife is slippery? 1.02.273
my wife is nothing, nor nothing have these 1.02.295
i'll keep my stables where | i lodge my wife; 2.01.135
he dreads his wife. 2.03. 80
thou, traitor, hast set on thy wife to this. 2.03.131
it to the fire, | for thou set'st on thy wife. 2.03.142
death to thyself but to thy lewd–tongu'd wife, 2.03.172
the daughter of a king, our wife, and one | of 3.02. 3
thou ne'er shalt see | thy wife paulina more." 3.03. 36
married a tinker's wife within a mile where my 4.03. 97 P
daughter, when my old wife liv'd, upon | this 4.04. 55
how a usurer's wife was brought to bed of twenty 4.04.263 P
reason my son | should choose himself a wife, 4.04.407
no more such wives, therefore no wife. 5.01. 56
fear thou no wife; 5.01. 68
i'll have no wife, paulina. 5.01. 69
she is, | when once she is my wife. 5.01.209
take by my consent, | as i by thine a wife: 5.03.137
your father's wife did after wedlock bear him; JN 1.01.117
be stronger with thee than the name of wife? 3.01.314
think thou smil'st, | and buss thee as thy wife. 3.04. 35
my name is constance, i was geffrey's wife, 3.04. 46
you, in the right of lady blanch your wife, 3.04.142
thy sometimes brother's wife | with her R2 1.02. 54
me, | and then betwixt me and my married wife. 5.01. 73
my wife to france, from whence set forth in pomp 5.01. 78
wife, thou art a fool. 5.02. 68
yet no farther wise | than harry percy's wife; 1H4 2.03.108
washes his hands, and says to his wife, "fie 2.04.104 P
damn'd brawn shall play dame mortimer his wife. 2.04.110 P
as tedious | as a tired horse, a railing wife, 3.01.158
my wife can speak no english, i no welsh. 3.01.191
heart, you swear like a comfit–maker's wife: 3.01.248 P
may be the deputy's wife of the ward to thee. 3.03.115 P
i am an honest man's wife, and, setting thy 3.03.119 P
and the lightness of his wife shines through it; 2H4 1.02. 47 P
and i could get me but a wife in the stews, i 1.02. 53 P
wound, to marry me and make me my lady thy wife. 2.01. 92 P
did not goodwife keech, the butcher's wife, come 2.01. 94 P
i pray thee, loving wife, and gentle daughter, 2.03. 1
alas, sweet wife, my honor is at pawn, | and, 2.03. 7
may i ask how my lady his wife doth? 3.02. 65 P
is better /accommodated than with a wife. 3.02. 67 P
like an offensive wife | that hath enrag'd him 4.01.208
"be merry, be merry, my wife has all, | for 5.03. 32
here comes ancient pistol and his wife. H5 2.01. 26 P
be it spoken, i should quickly leap into a wife. 5.02.139 P
like a new–married wife about her husband's neck 5.02.180 P
shall kate be my wife? 5.02.324 P
as man and wife, being two, are one in love, 5.02.361
thy wife is proud, she holdeth thee in awe, 1H6 1.01. 39
fond man, remember that thou hast a wife, | then 5.03. 81
i am unworthy to be henry's wife. 5.03.122
to woo so fair a dame to be his wife | and have 5.03.124
and the protector's wife, belov'd of him? 2H6 1.02. 44
my house, and lands, and wife and all, from me. 1.03. 18 P
thy wife too? 1.03. 19 P
as that proud dame, the lord protector's wife: 1.03. 76
more like an empress than duke humphrey's wife. 1.03. 78
his wife, and't like your worship. 2.01. 78
alas, good master, my wife desired some damsons, 2.01.100
of lady eleanor, the protector's wife, | the 2.01.165
and, for my wife, i know not how it stands. 2.01.188
forth, dame eleanor cobham, gloucester's wife: 2.03. 1
for whilest i think i am thy married wife | and 2.04. 28
sometime i'll say, i am duke humphrey's wife, 2.04. 42
my wife descended of the lacies — 4.02. 44 P
come, wife, let's in, and learn to govern better 4.09. 48
how will my wife for slaughter of my son | shed 3H6 2.05.105
the french king's sister | to wife for edward. 3.01. 31
he, on his right, asking a wife for edward. 3.01. 44
that bona shall be wife to the english king. 3.03.139
should not become my wife and england's queen. 4.01. 26
is it for a wife | that thou art malecontent? 4.01. 59
nor how to be contented with one wife, | nor how 4.03. 37
my lady grey his wife, clarence, 'tis she | that R3 1.01. 64
we say that shore's wife hath a pretty foot, | a 1.01. 93
wife to thy edward, to thy slaught'red son, 1.02. 10
if ever he have wife, let her be made | more 1.02. 26
notwithstanding she's your wife | and loves not 1.03. 22
die neither mother, wife, nor england's queen! 1.03.208
o, spare my guiltless wife and my poor children! 1.04. 72
a man cannot lie with his neighbor's wife, but 1.04.137 P
wife, love lord hastings, let him kiss your hand 2.01. 21
and this is edward's wife, that monstrous witch, 3.04. 70
i mean, his conversation with shore's wife — 3.05. 31
so say we too, but not by edward's wife; 3.07.178
nor mother, wife, nor england's counted queen. 4.01. 46
and be thy wife — if any be so mad — | more 4.01. 74
rumor it abroad | that anne, my wife, is very 4.02. 51
stanley, look to your wife. 4.02. 92
and anne my wife hath bid this world good night. 4.03. 39
o harry's wife, triumph not in my woes! 4.04. 59
for happy wife, a most distressed widow; 4.04. 98
farewell, york's wife, and queen of sad 4.04.114
king, that calls your beauteous daughter wife, 4.04.315
richard, thy wife, that wretched anne thy wife, 5.03.159
richard, thy wife, that wretched anne thy wife, 5.03.159
thy adversary's wife doth pray for thee. 5.03.166
it seems the marriage with his brother's wife H8 2.02. 16
i have been to you a true and humble wife, | at 2.04. 23
that i have been your wife in this obedience 2.04. 35
world who shall report he has | a better wife, 2.04.136
the dowager, | sometimes our brother's wife. 2.04.182
seek me out, and that way i am wife in, | out 3.01. 38
since virtue finds no friends) a wife, a true 3.01.126
man living | could say, "this is my wife" there, 4.01. 80
may know | i was a chaste wife to my grave. 4.02.170
was a haberdasher's wife of small wit near him, 5.03. 47 P
of parallels, as like as vulcan and his wife; TRO 1.03.168
i take to–day a wife, and my election | is led 2.02. 61
distaste what it elected) | the wife i chose? 2.02. 67
in all humanity | than wife is to the husband? 2.02.176
if helen then be wife to sparta's king, | as it 2.02.183
your quondam wife swears still by venus' glove. 4.05.179
thy wife hath dreamt, thy mother hath had 5.03. 63
the state hath another, his wife another, and, i COR 2.01.109 P
but o, thy wife! 2.01.175
for conscience' sake to help to get thee a wife. 2.03. 33 P
i am in this | your wife, your son, these 3.02. 65
commend me to my wife. 3.02.135
to say, | if you had been the wife of hercules, 4.01. 17
farewell, my wife, my mother, | i'll do well yet 4.01. 20
come, my sweet wife, my dearest mother, and | my 4.01. 48
to corrupt a man's wife is when she's fall'n out 4.03. 32 P
his mother and his wife | hear nothing from him. 4.06. 18
his mother, wife, his child, | and this brave 5.01. 29
vain, | unless his noble mother and his wife — 5.01. 71
wife, mother, child i know not. 5.02. 82
my wife comes foremost; 5.03. 22
even he, your wife, this lady, and myself, | are 5.03. 77
making the mother, wife, and child to see | the 5.03.101
bravely shed | thy wife and children's blood. 5.03.118
his wife is in corioles, and his child | like 5.03.179
wife! 5.03.199
i say "your city," to his wife and mother, 5.06. 93
dead, if you will, but not to be his wife, TIT 1.01.297
own, | my true betrothed love, and now my wife? 1.01.406
his wife but yesternight was brought to bed; 4.02.153
"signior martino and his wife and daughters; ROM 1.02. 64 P
mine uncle capulet, his wife, and daughters; 1.02. 68 P
there stays a husband to make you a wife. 2.05. 69
when i, thy three–hours wife, have mangled it? 3.02. 99
wife, go you to her ere you go to bed, 3.04. 15
prepare her, wife, against this wedding–day. 3.04. 32
how now, wife? 3.05.137
soft, take me with you, take me with you, wife. 3.05.141
wife, we scarce thought us blest | that god had 3.05.164
happily met, my lady and my wife! 4.01. 18
that may be, sir, when i may be a wife. 4.01. 19
to live an unstain'd wife to my sweet love. 4.01. 88
all things shall be well, i warrant thee, wife; 4.02. 40
wife! 4.04. 24
thy wedding–day | hath death lain with thy wife. 4.05. 36
o my love, my wife, | death, that hath suck'd 5.03. 91
o wife, look how our daughter bleeds! 5.03.202
alas, my liege, my wife is dead to–night; 5.03.210
she, there dead, /that romeo's faithful wife. 5.03.232
more, | portia is brutus' harlot, not his wife. JC 2.01.287
you are my true and honorable wife, | as dear to 2.01.288
withal | a woman that lord brutus took to wife. 2.01.293
render me worthy of this noble wife! 2.01.303
calphurnia here, my wife, stays me at home: 2.02. 75
when caesar's wife shall meet with better dreams 2.02. 99
had you your letters from your wife, my lord? 4.03.181
a sailor's wife had chestnuts in her lap, | and MAC 1.03. 4
the hearing of my wife with your approach; 1.04. 46
this diamond he greets your wife withal, | by 2.01. 15
o, full of scorpions is my mind, dear wife! 3.02. 36
give to th' edge o' th' sword | his wife, his 4.01.152
to leave his wife, to leave his babes, | his 4.02. 6
why in that rawness left you wife and child, 4.03. 26
how does my wife? 4.03.176
your wife, and babes, | savagely slaughter'd. 4.03.204
wife, children, servants, all | that could be 4.03.211
and i must be from thence! | my wife kill'd too? 4.03.213
the thane of fife had a wife; 5.01. 42 P
my wife and children's ghosts will haunt me 5.07. 16
weighing delight and dole, | taken to wife; HAM 1.02. 14
if, once i be a widow, ever i be a wife! 3.02.223
gonzago is the duke's name, his wife, baptista. 3.02.239 P
the murtherer gets the love of gonzago's wife. 3.02.264 P
are the queen, your husband's brother's wife, 3.04. 15
father and mother is man and wife, man and wife 4.03. 52 P
is man and wife, man and wife is one flesh — so 4.03. 52 P
hop'd thou shouldst have been my hamlet's wife. 5.01.244
daughter, | our dearest regan, wife of cornwall? LR 1.01. 68
are his love, | i shall not be his wife. 1.01.249
speak with the duke of cornwall and his wife. 2.04. 97
go tell the duke, and 's wife, i'ld speak with 2.04.116
your (wife, so i would say) affectionate servant 4.06.269 P
/sister, | i bar it in the interest of my wife; 5.03. 85
he hath commission from thy wife and me | to 5.03.253
(a fellow almost damn'd in a fair wife), | that OTH 1.01. 21
state, | i crave fit disposition for my wife, 1.03.236
to his conveyance i assign my wife, | with what 1.03.285
i prithee, let thy wife attend on her, | and 1.03.296
/ear | that he is too familiar with his wife. 1.03.396
soul | till i am even'd with him, wife for wife; 2.01.299
soul | till i am even'd with him, wife for wife; 2.01.299
our general's wife is now the general — i may 2.03.315 P
my wife must move for cassio to her mistress — 2.03.383
when he may cassio find | soliciting his wife. 2.03.387
have made bold, iago, | to send in to your wife. 3.01. 34
the general and his wife are talking of it, 3.01. 43
was not that cassio parted from my wife? 3.03. 37
lik'st not that, | when cassio left my wife. 3.03.110
to make me jealous | to say my wife is fair, 3.03.184
look to your wife, observe her well with cassio, 3.03.197
set on thy wife to observe. 3.03.240
to have a foolish wife. 3.03.304
i think my wife be honest, and think she is not; 3.03.384
but if i give my wife a handkerchief — 4.01. 10
when | he hath, and is again to cope your wife. 4.01. 86
see how he prizes the foolish woman your wife! 4.01.176 P
what? strike his wife? 4.01.272
your wife, my lord; your true | and loyal wife. 4.02. 34
your wife, my lord; your true | and loyal wife. 4.02. 35
if she come in, she'll sure speak to my wife. 5.02. 96
my wife, my wife! 5.02. 97
my wife, my wife! 5.02. 97
what wife? 5.02. 97
i have no wife. 5.02. 97
he says thou toldst him that his wife was false. 5.02.173
should such a fool | do with so good a wife? 5.02.234
the woman falls; sure he hath kill'd his wife. 5.02.236
fulvia thy wife first came into the field. ANT 1.02. 88
fulvia thy wife is dead. 1.02.118
deities to take the wife of a man from him, it 1.02.162 P
his wife that's dead did trespasses to caesar; 2.01. 40
your wife and brother | made wars upon me, and 2.02. 42
as for my wife, | i would you had her spirit in 2.02. 61
you may pace easy, but not such a wife. 2.02. 64
knot, take antony | octavia to his wife; 2.02.127
true, sir, she was the wife of caius marcellus. 2.06.110 P
but she is now the wife of marcus antonius. 2.06.112 P
who would not have his wife so? 2.06.124 P
prove such a wife | as my thoughts make thee, 3.02. 25
the wife of antony | should have an army for an 3.06. 43
your wife octavia, with her modest eyes | and 4.15. 27
heart, | but keep it till you woo another wife, CYM 1.01.113
so doth my wife | the nonpareil of this. 2.05. 7
married your royalty, was wife to your place, 5.05. 39
my queen, my life, my wife! 5.05.226
mulier i divine | is this most constant wife, 5.05.449
men in awe, | that whoso ask'd her for his wife, PER 1.ch. 37
i mother, wife — and yet his child. 1.01. 69
that man and wife | draw lots who first shall 1.04. 45
rul'd by me, or i'll make you — | man and wife. 2.05. 84
that cleon's wife, with envy rare, | a present 4.ch. 37
wife, take her in, instruct her what she has to 4.02. 54 P
the loss | of a beloved daughter and a wife. 5.01. 30
my dearest wife was like this maid, and such a 5.01.107
me, | till cruel cleon, with his wicked wife, 5.01.171
reveal how thou at sea didst lose thy wife. 5.01.244
told diana's altar true, | this is your wife. 5.03. 18
for wicked cleon and his wife, when fame | had 5.03. 95
the sweet embraces of a loving wife, | loaden TNK 2.02. 30
we are one another's wife, ever begetting | new 2.02. 80
a wife might part us lawfully, or business, 2.02. 89
if that | get him a wife so noble and so fair, 2.02.230
sure | to have my wife as jealous as a turkey. 2.03. 30
i never practiced | upon man's wife, nor would 5.01.101
might have excuse to work upon his wife, | as in LUC 235
but when i fear'd, i was a loyal wife: 1048
lord | of that unworthy wife that greeteth thee, 1304
shed for the slaught'red husband by the wife; 1376
who should weep most, for daughter or for wife. 1792
"woe, woe," quoth collatine, "she was my wife, 1802
and "my wife!" 1804
and "my wife!" 1806
for his foul act by whom thy fair wife bleeds? 1824
thy wretched wife mistook the matter so, | to 1826
we will revenge the death of this true wife." 1841
the world will wail thee like a makeless wife, SON 9. 4

WIFE–LIKE 2 FR 0.0002 REL FR 2 V 0 P
thy meekness saint–like, wife–like government, H8 2.04.139
more goddess–like than wife–like, such assaults CYM 3.02. 8

WIFE'S *(also wive's)*

WIFE'S 5 FR 0.0005 REL FR 5 V 0 P
he had sworn to marry me | when his wife's dead; AWW 4.02. 72
then say | my wife's a /hobby–horse, deserves a WT 1.02.276
but my arrival, and my wife's, in safety | here, 5.01.167
see, your wife's with him. OTH 4.01.215
he's gone, but his wife's kill'd. 5.02.238

/WIGHT 1 FR 0.0001 REL FR 1 V 0 P
she was a wight (if ever such /wight were) — OTH 2.01.158

WIGHT 7 FR 0.0008 REL FR 5 V 2 P
o base hungarian wight! WIV 1.03. 20 P
i ken the wight; he is of substance good. 1.03. 37 P
armado is a most illustrious wight, | a man of LLL 1.01.177
o braggard vile and damned furious wight! H5 2.01. 60
she was a wight (if ever such /wight were) — OTH 2.01.158
he was a wight of high renown, | and thou art 2.03. 93
so for her many /a wight did die, | as yon grim PER 1.ch. 39

WIGHTS 2 FR 0.0002 REL FR 2 V 0 P
with venomous wights she stays | as tediously as TRO 4.02. 12
time | i see descriptions of the fairest wights, SON 106. 2

WILD* 95 FR 0.0107 REL FR 84 V 11 P
you have | put the wild waters in this roar, TMP 1.02. 2
you have, and kiss'd, | the wild waves whist: 1.02.378
strays | with willing sport to the wild ocean. TGV 2.07. 32
this fellow were a king for our wild faction! 4.01. 37
he kept company with the wild prince and poins; WIV 3.02. 73 P
before me, | my riots past, my wild societies, 3.04. 8
traveller, and wild half–can that stabb'd pots, MM 4.03. 17 P
lord of the wide world and wild wat'ry seas, ERR 2.01. 21
wild, and yet, too, gentle; 3.01.110
i know her spirits are as coy and wild | as ADO 3.01. 35
thee, | taming my wild heart to thy loving hand. 3.01.112
to move wild laughter in the throat of death? LLL 5.02.855
knight of his train, to trace the forests wild; MND 2.01. 25
and leave thee to the mercy of wild beasts. 2.01.228
i know a bank where the wild thyme blows, 2.01.249
as wild geese that the creeping fowler eye, | or 3.02. 20
thou art too wild, too rude, and bold of voice MV 2.02.181
spirit, lest through thy wild behavior | i be 2.02.187
turns to a wild of nothing, save of joy 3.02.182
a willow in her hand | upon the wild sea–banks, 5.01. 11
for do but note a wild and wanton herd, | or 5.01. 71
why then my taxing like a wild goose flies, AYL 2.07. 86
and to the skirts of this wild wood he came; 5.04.159
kate, | and bring you from a wild kate to a kate SHR 2.01.277
importance 'twere | most piteous to be wild), i WT 2.01.182
promising | than a wild dedication of yourselves 4.04.566
how like you this wild counsel, mighty states? JN 2.01.395
and wild amazement hurries up and down | the 5.01. 35
up, | and tame the savage spirit of wild war, 5.02. 74
these high wild hills and rough uneven ways R2 2.03. 4
against the irregular and wild glendower, | was 1H4 1.01. 40
a franklin in the wild of kent hath brought 2.01. 55 P
no more valor in that poins than in a wild duck. 2.02.101 P
subjects afore thee like a flock of wild geese, 2.04.138 P
wanton as youthful goats, wild as young bulls. 4.01.103
worse than a struck fowl or a hurt wild duck. 4.02. 20 P
up, | will have a wild trick of his ancestors. 5.02. 11
did i hear | of any prince so wild a liberty. 5.02. 71
the times are wild, contention, like a horse 2H4 1.01. 9
nature's hand | keep the wild flood confin'd! 1.01.154
and the wild dog | shall flesh his tooth on 4.05.131
together in consent, like so many wild geese. 5.01. 71 P
you, | my father is gone wild into his grave; 5.02.123
swill'd with the wild and wasteful ocean. H5 3.01. 14
our scions, put in wild and savage stock, 3.05. 7
and with wild rage | yerk out their armed heels 4.07. 79
by this unheedful, desperate, wild adventure. 1H6 4.04. 7
seen | him caper upright like a wild morisco, 2H6 3.01.365

i cut it | as wild medea young absyrtus did; 5.02. 59
frightful, desp'rate, wild, and furious, | thy R3 4.04.170
that still use of grief makes wild grief tame, 4.04.230
if i chance to talk a little wild, forgive me; H8 1.04. 26
thus hulling in | the wild sea of my conscience, 2.04.201
should the approach of this wild river break, 3.02.198
for those that tame wild horses | pace 'em not 5.02. 56
let it be call'd the wild and wand'ring flood, TRO 1.01.102
death on the wheel, or at wild horses' heels, COR 3.02. 2
more than a wild exposture to each chance | that 4.01. 36
the people, which before | were in wild hurry. 4.06. 4
thou hast more of the wild goose in one of thy ROM 2.04. 72 P
thy wild acts /denote | the unreasonable fury of 3.03.110
your looks are pale and wild, and do import 5.01. 28
and with wild looks bid me devise some mean | to 5.03.240
it almost turns my dangerous nature wild. TIM 4.03.492
drive back | of alcibiades th' approaches wild, 5.01.164
teach them to prevent wild alcibiades' wrath. 5.01.203
these | so wither'd and so wild in their attire, MAC 1.03. 40
turn'd wild in nature, broke their stalls, flung 2.04. 16
but float upon a wild and violent sea | each way 4.02. 21
these are but wild and whirling words, my lord. HAM 1.05.133
but, if't be he i mean, he's very wild, 2.01. 18
sir, such wanton, wild, and usual slips | as are 2.01. 22
perform'd | even while men's minds are wild, 5.02.394
not gone yet, if the wild geese fly that way. LR 2.04. 46 P
shut up your doors, my lord, 'tis a wild night, 2.04.308
a little fire in a wild field were like an old 3.04.111 P
maid | that paragons description and wild fame; OTH 2.01. 62
yet wild, the people's hearts brimful of fear, 2.03.214
go, you wild bedfellow, you cannot soothsay. ANT 1.02. 51 P
the wild disguise hath almost | antick'd us all. 2.07.124
of this seleucus does | even make me wild. 5.02.154
takes prisoner the wild motion of mine eye, CYM 1.06.103
with wild wood–leaves and weeds i ha' strew'd 4.02.390
i am wild in my beholding. PER 5.01.222
and clamors through the wild air flying! TNK 1.05. 6
tame tempests, | and make the wild rocks wanton. 2.03. 17
is't not mad lodging | here in the wild woods, 3.03. 23
yes, for /them | that have wild consciences. 3.03. 24
like a wild bird being tam'd with too much VEN 560
till the wild waves will have him seen no more, 819
slaughter, | to tame the unicorn and lion wild, LUC 956
continuance tames the one, the other wild, 1097
for adon's sake, a youngster proud and wild, PP 9. 4
weak and cold, | youth is wild, and age is tame. 12. 8
but that wild music burthens every bough, | and SON 102.11
WILD–BOARS 1 FR 0.0001 REL FR 0 V 1 P
eight wild–boars roasted whole at a breakfast, ANT 2.02.179 P
WILD–CAT 2 FR 0.0002 REL FR 2 V 0 P
and he sleeps by day | more than the wild–cat. MV 2.05. 48
but will you woo this wild–cat? SHR 1.02.196
WILD–CATS 1 FR 0.0001 REL FR 1 V 0 P
in your parlors, wild–cats in your kitchens, OTH 2.01.110
WILDER 3 FR 0.0003 REL FR 3 V 0 P
how he comes o'er us with our wilder days, | not H5 1.02.267
have | in them a wilder nature than the business H8 5.01. 15
wilder to him than tigers in their wildness. LUC 980
WILDERNESS 9 FR 0.0010 REL FR 8 V 1 P
and live as we do in this wilderness? TGV 4.01. 61
for such a warped slip of wilderness | ne'er MM 3.01.141
not have given it for a wilderness of monkeys. MV 3.01.122 P
or live, | i dare meet surrey in a wilderness, R2 4.01. 74
o, thou wilt be a wilderness again, | peopled 2H4 4.05.136
a wilderness is populous enough, | so suffolk 2H6 3.02.360
that rome is but a wilderness of tigers? TIT 3.01. 54
a rock, | environ'd with a wilderness of sea, 3.01. 94
pleads, in a wilderness where are no laws, | to LUC 544
WILDEST 4 FR 0.0004 REL FR 4 V 0 P
the wildest hath not such a heart as you. MND 2.01.229
when lion rough in wildest rage doth roar. 5.01.222
we marry | a gentler scion to the wildest stock, WT 4.04. 93
the wildest savagery, the vildest stroke, | that JN 4.03. 48
WILDFIRE 2 FR 0.0002 REL FR 1 V 1 P
been an ignis fatuus or a ball of wildfire, 1H4 3.03. 40 P
whose words like wildfire burnt the shining LUC 1523
WILD–FOWL 2 FR 0.0002 REL FR 0 V 2 P
is not a more fearful wild–fowl than your lion MND 3.01. 32 P
the opinion of pythagoras concerning wild–fowl? TN 4.02. 51 P
WILD–GOOSE 1 FR 0.0001 REL FR 0 V 1 P
if our wits run the wild–goose chase, i am done; ROM 2.04. 71 P
WILDLY 13 FR 0.0014 REL FR 11 V 2 P
but i prattle | something too wildly, and my TMP 3.01. 58
and blowing, and looking wildly, and would needs
WIV 3.03. 87 P
he demean'd himself rough, rude, and wildly. ERR 5.01. 88
accident is guilty | to what we wildly do, so we WT 4.04.539
and speak of something wildly | by us perform'd 5.01.129
how wildly then walks my estate in france! JN 4.02.128
cousin, that he stares and looks | so wildly? R2 5.03. 25
like prisoners wildly overgrown with hair, | put H5 5.02. 43
frame, and /start not so wildly from my affair. HAM 3.02.309 P
forth at your eyes your spirits wildly peep, 3.04.119
that wildly grows in them but yields a crop | as CYM 4.02.180
she wildly breaketh from their strict embrace, VEN 874
at gaze, | wildly determining which way to fly, LUC 1150
WILD–MARE 1 FR 0.0001 REL FR 0 V 1 P
and rides the wild–mare with the boys, and jumps
2H4 2.04.247 P
WILDNESS 10 FR 0.0011 REL FR 9 V 1 P
but prate to me of the wildness of his youth, 2H4 3.02.305 P
feign, | o, let me in my present wildness die, 4.05.152
body, | but that his wildness, mortified in him, H5 1.01. 26
his contemplation | under the veil of wildness, 1.01. 64
defective in their natures, grow to wildness. 5.02. 55
our youths and wildness shall no whit appear, JC 2.01.148
for he is given | to sports, to wildness, and 2.01.189
be the happy cause | of hamlet's wildness. HAM 3.01. 39
fear, ere wildness | vanquish my staider senses. CYM 3.04. 9
wilder to him than tigers in their wildness. LUC 980
WILDS 1 FR 0.0001 REL FR 1 V 0 P
the hyrcanian deserts and the vasty wilds | of MV 2.07. 41
WILES 3 FR 0.0003 REL FR 2 V 1 P
sure these are but imaginary wiles, | and ERR 4.03. 10
upon my wit, to defend my wiles, upon my secrecy
TRO 1.02.261 P
the wiles and guiles that women work, PP 18.37
WILL* *(also vill, woll)*

/WILL* 47 FR 0.0053 REL FR 39 V 8 P
WILL* 5259 FR 0.5944 REL FR 3642 V 1617 P
WILL'D 7 FR 0.0008 REL FR 7 V 0 P
and that he will'd me | in heedfull'st AWW 1.03.224
his body be interr'd, | for so he will'd it. JN 5.07.100
of majesty | will'd me to leave my base vocation 1H6 1.02. 80
we do no otherwise than we are will'd. 1.03. 10
they will'd me say so, madam. H8 3.01. 18
fill'd, | and wishes fall out as they're will'd. PER 5.02. 16
hath bid him rule, and will'd you to obey; STM II.C 100
WILLED 1 FR 0.0001 REL FR 1 V 0 P
who willed you? 1H6 1.03. 11
WILLETH 2 FR 0.0002 REL FR 2 V 0 P
as will the rest, so willeth winchester. 1H6 3.01.161
obey, | paying what ransom the insulter willeth; VEN 550
WILLFUL 15 FR 0.0017 REL FR 11 V 4 P
page himself for a secure and willful actaeon; WIV 3.02. 43 P
lord, when walls are so willful to hear without MND 5.01.209 P
pond, | and do a willful stillness entertain, MV 1.01. 90
i owe you much, and, like a willful youth, 1.01.146
drive you then to confess the willful abuse, and 2H4 2.04.311 P
now, we shall see willful adultery and murther H5 2.01. 37 P
stomachs be provok'd | to willful disobedience, 1H6 4.01.142
peace, willful boy, or i will charm your tongue. 3H6 5.05. 31
ask'd the mayor what meant this willful silence. R3 3.07. 28
against the willful sons | of old andronicus. TIT 4.04. 8
patience perforce with willful choler meeting ROM 1.05. 89
o sir, to willful men, | the injuries that they LR 2.04.302
this beauteous combat, willful and unwilling, VEN 365
and in his will his willful eye he tired. LUC 417
by willful taste of what thyself refusest. SON 40. 8
WILLFUL–BLAME 1 FR 0.0001 REL FR 1 V 0 P
in faith, my lord, you are too willful–blame, 1H4 3.01.175
WILLFULLY 6 FR 0.0006 REL FR 5 V 1 P
or else commit'st thy knaveries willfully. MND 3.02.346
they willfully themselves exile from light, 3.02.386
our holy mother, | so willfully dost spurn; JN 3.01.142
hath willfully betray'd | the lives of those 1H4 1.03. 81
burial when she willfully seeks her own HAM 5.01. 2 P
his) | on your broad main doth willfully appear. SON 80. 8
WILLFUL–NEGLIGENT
1 FR 0.0001 REL FR 1 V 0 P
my lord, | if ever i were willful–negligent, WT 1.02.255
WILLFULNESS 2 FR 0.0002 REL FR 2 V 0 P
nor never hydra–headed willfulness | so soon did H5 1.01. 35
book both my willfulness and errors down, | and SON 117. 9
WILLFUL–OPPOSITE 1 FR 0.0001 REL FR 1 V 0 P
the dolphin is too willful–opposite, | and will JN 5.02.124
WILLFUL–SLOW 1 FR 0.0001 REL FR 1 V 0 P
since from thee going he went willful–slow, SON 51.13
WILLIAM 40 FR 0.0045 REL FR 19 V 21 P
come hither, william; hold up your head; come. WIV 4.01. 17 P
william, how many numbers is in nouns? 4.01. 21 P
peace your tattlings! what is "fair," william? 4.01. 26 P
what is lapis, william? 4.01. 31 P
and what is "a stone," william? 4.01. 33 P
that is a good william. 4.01. 38 P
what is he, william, that does lend articles? 4.01. 39 P
what is the focative case, william? 4.01. 51 P
remember, william, focative is caret. 4.01. 53 P
what is your genitive case plural, william? 4.01. 57 P
show me now, william, some declensions of your 4.01. 74 P
god ye good ev'n, william. AYL 5.01. 14 P
a ripe age. is thy name william? 5.01. 20 P
william, sir. 5.01. 21 P
do, good william. 5.01. 58 P
i dare say my cousin william is become a good 2H4 3.02. 10 P
yea, marry, william cook, bid him come hither. 5.01. 10 P
but for william cook — are there no young 5.01. 16 P
pretty little tiny kickshaws, tell william cook. 5.01. 28 P
to countenance william visor of woncote against 5.01. 38 P
sir thomas gargrave, and sir william glansdale, 1H6 1.04. 63
away, away, good william de la pole! 2.04. 80
thee, | against proud somerset and william pole, 2.04.122
here is sir william lucy, who with me | set from 4.04. 10
how now, sir william, whither were you sent? 4.04. 12
the french king charles, and william de la pole, 2H6 1.01. 44 P
and william de la pole, first duke of suffolk. 1.02. 30
the second, william of hatfield; 2.02. 12
william of windsor was the seventh and last. 2.02. 17
but william of hatfield died without an heir. 2.02. 33
the duke of suffolk, william de la pole. 4.01. 45
now, my lord hastings and sir william stanley, 3H6 4.05. 1
to make william lord hastings of our mind | for R3 3.01.162
commend me to lord william. 3.01.181
william lord hastings had pronounc'd your part 3.04. 27
sir gilbert talbot, sir william stanley, 4.05. 13
sir william brandon, you shall bear my standard. 5.03. 22
my lord of oxford — you, sir william brandon — 5.03. 27
sir robert brakenbury, and sir william brandon. 5.05. 14
reprov'd the duke | about sir william /bulmer — H8 1.02.190
WILLIAM'S 1 FR 0.0001 REL FR 0 V 1 P
sir, do you mean to stop any of william's wages, 2H4 5.01. 24 P
/WILLING 1 FR 0.0001 REL FR 1 V 0 P
/thought /you /had /been /willing /to /resign. R2 4.01.190
WILLING 41 FR 0.0046 REL FR 34 V 7 P
ay, with a heart as willing | as bondage e'er of TMP 3.01. 88
strays | with willing sport to the wild ocean. TGV 2.07. 32
an honest, willing, kind fellow as ever servant WIV 1.04. 10 P
good, | whereto if you'll a willing ear incline, MM 5.01.536
not without the prince be willing, for indeed ADO 3.03. 80 P
worth | than you much willing to be counted wise LLL 2.01. 18
all pride is willing pride, and yours is so. 2.01. 36
i was as willing to grapple as he was to board. 2.01.218
kill'd, but one dead that is willing to be so. AYL 1.02.189 P
you say you'll marry me, if i be willing? 5.04. 11
me shall you find ready and willing | with one SHR 4.04. 34
not extort from me what i am willing to keep in; TN 2.01. 14 P
of her, she is very willing to bid you farewell. 2.03.100 P
my willing love, | the rather by these arguments 3.03. 11
whiles you are willing it shall come to note, 4.03. 29
what you will have, i'll give, and willing too, R2 3.03.206
who with willing soul | adopts /thee heir, and 4.01.108
willing you overlook this pedigree; H5 2.04. 90
send | to know what willing ransom he will give. 3.05. 63
but could be willing to march on to callice 3.06.141
i'll send them all as willing as i live. 2H6 5.01. 51
defy thee, | not willing any longer conference, 3H6 2.02.171

your standards, draw your willing swords. R3 5.03.264
the play may pass, if they be still and willing, H8 pr 11
to th' earth, | willing to leave their burthen. 4.02. 3
most willing, madam. 4.02.130
those are they | that most are willing. COR 1.06. 67
house, | willing you to demand your hostages, TIT 5.01.160
not summer more willing than we your lordship. TIM 3.06. 30 P
willing misery | outlives incertain pomp, is 4.03.242
perhaps, speak this | before a willing bondman; JC 1.03.113
i trouble thee too much, but thou art willing. 4.03.259
we have willing dames enough; MAC 4.03. 73
friending to you, | god willing, shall not lack. HAM 1.05.186
let the foils be brought, the gentleman willing, 5.02.175 P
italy, most willing spirits | that promise noble CYM 4.02.338
am going, and never yet | went i so willing way. TNK 1.01.104
a willing man dies sleeping, and all's done. 2.02. 68
their gentle sex to weep are often willing, LUC 1237
which happies those that pay the willing loan; SON 6. 6
whilst like a willing patient i will drink 111. 9
WILLINGLY 36 FR 0.0040 REL FR 28 V 8 P
when willingly i would have had her here! TGV 1.02. 61
thou know'st how willingly i would effect | the 3.02. 22
judge, but most willingly humbles himself to the MM 3.02.243 P
i | persuade this rude wretch willingly to die. 4.03. 81
that i crave death more willingly than mercy: 5.01.476
you embrace your charge too willingly. ADO 1.01.103 P
proud of employment, willingly i go. LLL 2.01. 35
and willingly could waste my time in it. AYL 2.04. 95
as willingly as e'er i came from school. SHR 3.02.150
and i, most jocund, apt, and willingly, | to do TN 5.01.132
i willingly obey your command. WT 4.02. 53 P
whole, | hath willingly departed with a part, JN 2.01.563
and well shall you perceive how willingly | i 4.02. 45
mortimer | receive so many, and all willingly. 1H4 1.03.111
marry, and shall, and very willingly. 5.02. 33
if he do not, if i come in his willingly, let 5.03. 58 P
and i accept the combat willingly. 2H6 1.03.212
as willingly do i the same resign | as ere thy 2.03. 33
and even as willingly at thy feet i leave it 2.03. 35
lord, | i'll yield myself to prison willingly, 4.09. 42
this oath i willingly take and will perform. 3H6 1.01.201
with whom the kentishmen will willingly rise; 1.02. 41
guilty | to give up willingly that noble title H8 3.01.140
most willingly; COR 2.02. 62
best, and though we willingly consented to his 4.06.144 P
i will most willingly attend your ladyship. TIT 4.01. 28
things | as willingly as one would kill a fly, 5.01.142
grow, | we would as willingly give cure as know. ROM 1.01.155
nor more willingly leaves winter, such summer TIM 3.06. 31 P
from whence though willingly i came to denmark HAM 1.02. 52
that i will not more willingly part withal — 2.02.216 P
what willingly he did confound he wail'd, ANT 3.02. 58
willingly; CYM 1.06.193
i'll willingly to him. 4.02.167
to do that fearfully which you commit willingly, PER 4.02.118 P
i | than niggard truth would willingly impart: SON 72. 8
WILLINGNESS 2 FR 0.0002 REL FR 2 V 0 P
i would expend it with all willingness. 2H6 3.01.150
will thither straight, for willingness rids way, 3H6 5.03. 21
WILLING'ST 1 FR 0.0001 REL FR 1 V 0 P
the willing'st sin i ever yet committed | may be H8 3.01. 49
WILLOUGHBY 3 FR 0.0003 REL FR 3 V 0 P
the lords of ross, beaumond, and willoughby, R2 2.02. 54
cotshall will be found | in ross and willoughby, 2.03. 10
here come the lords of ross and willoughby, 2.03. 57
WILLOW 27 FR 0.0030 REL FR 26 V 1 P
even to the next willow, about your own business ADO 2.01.187 P
a night | stood dido with a willow in her hand MV 5.01. 10
make me a willow cabin at your gate, | and call TN 1.05.268
i wear the willow garland for his sake. 3H6 3.03.228
i'll wear the willow garland for his sake." 4.01.100
there is a willow grows askaunt the brook, HAM 4.07.166
she had a song of "willow," | an old thing 'twas OTH 4.03. 28
by a sycamore tree, | sing all a green willow; 4.03. 41
head on her knee, | sing willow, willow, willow. 4.03. 43
head on her knee, | sing willow, willow, willow. 4.03. 43
head on her knee, | sing willow, willow, willow. 4.03. 43
her moans, | sing willow, willow, willow; 4.03. 45
her moans, | sing willow, willow, willow; 4.03. 45
her moans, | sing willow, willow, willow; 4.03. 45
her, and soft'ned the stones, | sing willow" — 4.03. 47
lay by these — "— willow, willow" — | prithee 4.03. 49
lay by these — "— willow, willow" — | prithee 4.03. 49
"sing all a green willow must be my garland. 4.03. 51
sing willow, willow, willow; 4.03. 56
sing willow, willow, willow; 4.03. 56
sing willow, willow, willow; 4.03. 56
"willow, willow, willow!" 5.02.248
"willow, willow, willow!" 5.02.248
"willow, willow, willow!" 5.02.248
then she sung | nothing but "willow, willow, TNK 4.01. 80
then she sung | nothing but "willow, willow, 4.01. 80
willow, willow," and between | ever was "palamon 4.01. 80
WILLOW–TREE 1 FR 0.0001 REL FR 0 V 1 P
and i off'red him my company to a willow–tree, ADO 2.01.218 P
WILL'S 1 FR 0.0001 REL FR 1 V 0 P
the sundry dangers of his will's obtaining; LUC 128
WILLS* 33 FR 0.0037 REL FR 27 V 6 P
the wills above be done! TMP 1.01. 67 P
are my mates, that make their wills their law, TGV 5.04. 14
whose will still wills | it should none spare LLL 2.01. 50
their sacred wills be done! WT 3.03. 7
be contrary, | oppose against their wills. 5.01. 46
let's choose executors and talk of wills; R2 3.02.148
form | and present execution of our wills — 2H4 4.01.172
he wills you, in the name of god almighty, H5 2.04. 77
what wills lord talbot pleaseth burgundy. 1H6 3.02.130
my lords, i thank you both for your good wills, H8 3.01. 68
of partial indulgence | to their benumbed wills, TRO 2.02.179
it shall be to him then as our good wills: COR 2.01.242
what custom wills, in all things should we do't, 2.03.118
aaron, it must, the mother wills it so. TIT 4.02. 82
juliet wills it so. ROM 3.05. 24
ladies? what are their wills? TIM 1.02.118 P
making your wills | the scope of justice; 5.04. 4
and, dying, mention it within their wills, JC 3.02.135
our wills and fates do so contrary run | that HAM 3.02.211
to quarrel with your great opposeless wills, LR 4.06. 38

gardens, to the which our wills are gardeners; OTH 1.03.321 P
corrigible authority of this lies in our wills. 1.03.326 P
these moors are changeable in their wills — 1.03.347 P
how mean soe'er, that have their honest wills, CYM 1.06. 8
you, having proceeded but | by both your wills. 2.04. 56
but imogen is your own, do your best wills, 5.01. 16
some of them too that die against their wills. 5.04.202 P
pleasures | that woo the wills of men to vanity TNK 2.02.101
but that your wills have said it must be so, 5.03.140
which in their wills count bad what i think good SON 121. 8
ay, fill it full with wills, and my will one. 136. 6
ask'd their own wills, and made their wills obey LC 133
their own wills, and made their wills obey. 133

WILL/'T 1 FR 0.0001 REL FR 0 V 1 P
but will/'t not live with the living? 1H4 5.01.138 P

WILL'T 24 FR 0.0027 REL FR 19 V 5 P
will't please you taste of what is here? TMP 3.03. 42
come, come, will't please you go? TGV 1.02.137
but tell me true, will't be a match? 2.05. 34 P
will't please your worship to come in, sir? WIV 1.01.266 P
will't please you walk aside? MM 4.01. 58
will't not off? 5.01.355 P
"will't please your lordship cool your hands?" SHR in.1. 58
will't please your /lordship drink a cup of sack in.2. 2
will't please your honor taste of these in.2. 3
will't please your mightiness to wash your hands in.2. 76
will't please you, sir, be gone? WT 4.04.446
will't not be? JN 3.01.298
my lord, will't please you to fall to? R2 5.05. 98
will't please your grace to go along with us? 2H4 4.05. 19
my lord, will't please you pass along? R3 3.01.136
will't please you eat? TIT 5.03. 54
will't please your highness feed? 5.03. 54
will't hold? will't hold? TIM 3.06. 62 P
will't hold? will't hold? 3.06. 62 P
will't please you go, my lord? HAM 4.04. 30
will't please your highness walk? LR 4.07. 82
will't please you hear me? ANT 2.05. 41
color, will't not do | rarely upon a skirt, TNK 2.02.129
will't please you arm, sir? 3.06. 35

WILT *(also wolt, woo't, wo't)*
/WILT 2 FR 0.0002 REL FR 2 V 0 P
then thou /wilt keep | my tears for glasses, and LLL 4.03. 37
my first son, | whither /wilt thou go? COR 4.01. 34

WILT 328 FR 0.0370 REL FR 235 V 93 P
which any print of goodness wilt not take, TMP 1.02.352
thou wilt anon, i know it by thy trembling. 2.02. 79 P
wilt thou go with me? 2.02.172
wilt thou tell a monstrous lie, being but half a 3.02. 28 P
lo, how he mocks me! wilt thou let him, my lord? 3.02. 30 P
wilt thou be pleas'd to hearken once again to 3.02. 38 P
wilt thou destroy him then? 3.02.114
wilt come? i'll follow stephano. 3.02.152 P
wilt thou be gone? TGV 1.01. 11
wilt thou go? 2.03. 58 P
any, | except thou wilt except against my love. 2.04.155
if thou wilt, go with me to the alehouse; 2.05. 53 P
wilt thou go? 2.05. 58 P
wilt thou aspire to guide the heavenly car, 3.01.154
wilt thou reach stars, because they shine on 3.01.156
wilt thou be of our consort? 4.01. 62
i hope thou wilt. 4.04. 43
wilt thou the spigot wield? WIV 1.03. 20 P
wilt thou revenge? 1.03. 91
wilt thou, after the expense of so much money, 2.02.140 P
pardon me, wife, henceforth do what thou wilt. 4.04. 6
wilt thou be made a man out of my vice? MM 3.01.137
thee proofs for sin, | thou wilt prove his. 3.02. 31
what, wilt thou flout me thus unto my face, ERR 1.02. 91
wilt thou still talk? 4.04. 44 P
wilt thou suffer them | to make a rescue? 4.04.110
what wilt thou do, thou peevish officer? 4.04.114
speak freely, syracusian, what thou wilt. 5.01.286
and thou wilt needs thrust thy neck into a yoke, ADO 1.01.200 P
this faith, thou wilt prove a notable argument. 1.01.256 P
in venice, thou wilt quake for this shortly. 1.01.272 P
thou wilt be like a lover presently, | and tire 1.01.306
niece, thou wilt never get thee a husband, if 2.01. 18 P
wilt thou make a trust a transgression? 2.01.225 P
come, | or, if thou wilt hold longer argument, 2.03. 53
thou wilt be condemn'd into everlasting 4.02. 56 P
wilt thou use thy wit? 5.01.124 P
which out of question thou wilt be, if my cousin 5.04.115 P
what wilt thou prove? LLL 3.01. 39 P
as thou wilt win my favor, good my knave, | do 3.01.152
o, wilt thou darkling leave me? do not so. MND 2.02. 86
thou shalt remain here, whether thou wilt or no. 3.01.153
ah, good demetrius, wilt thou give him me? 3.02. 63
that thou look'st for wars, | and wilt not come? 3.02.409
what, wilt thou hear some music, my sweet love? 4.01. 27
think what thou wilt, i am thy lover's grace; 5.01.195
wilt thou at ninny's tomb meet me straightway? 5.01.202
if thou wilt lend this money, lend it not | as MV 1.03.132
i am sorry thou wilt leave my father so. 2.03. 1
thou wilt say anon he is some kin to thee, 2.09. 97
if he forfeit, thou wilt not take his flesh. 3.01. 51 P
wilt thou show the whole wealth of thy wit in an 3.05. 55 P
thou wilt not only loose the forfeiture, | but, 4.01. 24
wilt thou lay hands on me, villain? AYL 1.01. 55 P
and what wilt thou do? 1.01. 75 P
and thou wilt show more bright and seem more 1.03. 81
o my poor rosalind, whither wilt thou go? 1.03. 90
wilt thou change fathers? 1.03. 91
wilt thou rest damn'd? 3.02. 71 P
wilt thou, silvius? 3.05.135
and wilt thou have me? 4.01.118 P
such a wit, he might say, "wit, whither wilt?" 4.01.166 P
wilt thou love such a woman? 4.03. 67 P
wilt thou have music? SHR in.2. 35
or wilt thou sleep? in.2. 37
say thou wilt walk; in.2. 40
or wilt thou ride? in.2. 41
or wilt thou hunt? in.2. 44
say thou wilt course, thy greyhounds are as in.2. 47
assist me, tranio, for i know thou wilt. 1.01.158
but wilt thou make a fire, or shall i complain 4.01. 28 P
and as much news as wilt thou. 4.01. 42 P
then both or one, or any thing thou wilt. 4.03. 29

hortensio, say thou wilt see the tailor paid. 4.03.164
so thou wilt be capable of a courtier's counsel AWW 1.01.209 P
wilt thou needs be a beggar? 1.03. 20 P
tell me thy reason why thou wilt marry. 1.03. 27 P
wilt thou ever be a foul–mouth'd and calumnious 1.03. 56 P
that wilt not know | it is in us to plant thine 2.03.155
but wilt thou faithfully? 4.01. 86
but wilt thou not speak all thou know'st? 5.03.257 P
what wilt thou do? TN 2.03.154 P
by the letters that thou wilt drop, that they 2.03.165 P
i will do every thing that thou wilt have me. 2.05.179 P
wilt thou set thy foot o' my neck? 2.05.188 P
wilt thou go to bed, malvolio? 3.04. 29 P
fool, as ever thou wilt deserve well at my hand, 4.02. 80 P
what wilt thou be | when time hath sow'd a 5.01.164
if thou wilt confess, | or else be impudently WT 1.02.273
to be hang'd, | that wilt not stay her tongue. 2.03.110
thou refuse | and wilt encounter with my wrath, 2.03.139
by this sword | thou wilt perform my bidding. 2.03.169
thou wilt amend thy life? 5.02.154 P
of thy hands and that thou wilt not be drunk; 5.02.165 P
fellow of thy hands and that thou wilt be drunk; 5.02.166 P
wilt thou forsake thy fortune, | bequeath thy JN 1.01.148
james gurney, wilt thou give us leave a while? 1.01.230
wilt thou resign them and lay down thy arms? 2.01.154
what wilt thou do, renowned faulconbridge? 4.03.101
who thou wilt; 5.06. 9
thou lack'st, and that breath wilt thou lose. R2 2.01. 30
with rage | to be o'erpow'r'd, and wilt thou, 5.01. 31
to plant unrightful kings, wilt know again, 5.01. 63
why, york, what wilt thou do? 5.02. 88
wilt thou not hide the trespass of thine own? 5.02. 89
and wilt thou pluck my fair son from mine age, 5.02. 92
woman, | wilt thou conceal this dark conspiracy? 5.02. 96
i should say, for grace thou wilt have none — 1H4 1.02. 18 P
'zounds, where thou wilt, lad, i'll make one, 1.02.100 P
hal, wilt thou make one? 1.02.137 P
and if thou wilt not tell me all things true. 2.03. 88
come, wilt thou see me ride? 2.03.100
thou wilt not utter what thou dost not know, 2.03.111
ask me when thou wilt, and thou shalt have it. 2.04. 62 P
or indeed, francis, when thou wilt. 2.04. 67 P
wilt thou rob this leathern–jerkin, 2.04. 69 P
go thy ways, old jack, die when thou wilt; 2.04.128 P
thou wilt be horribly chid to–morrow when thou 2.04.373 P
wilt thou believe me, hal, three or four bonds 3.03.101 P
not my sword, but take my pistol, if thou wilt. 5.03. 51 P
wilt thou? 2H4 2.01. 49 P
wilt thou? 2.01. 49 P
wilt thou kill god's officers and the king's? 2.01. 51 P
when wilt thou leave fighting a' days and 2.04.232 P
what stuff wilt have a kirtle of? 2.04.274 P
the law, for the which i think thou wilt howl. 2.04.345 P
that thou no more wilt weigh my eyelids down, 3.01. 7
wilt thou upon the high and giddy /mast | seal 3.01. 18
wilt thou make as many holes in an enemy's 3.02.153 P
thou wilt be as valiant as the wrathful dove or 3.02.159 P
that thou wilt needs invest thee with my honors 4.05. 95
not, | and thou wilt have me die assur'd of it. 4.05.105
what wilt thou do when riot is thy care? 4.05.135
o, thou wilt be a wilderness again, | peopled 4.05.136
if thou want'st any thing, and wilt not call, 5.03. 56 P
choose what office thou wilt in the land, 'tis 5.03.123 P
my lord shallow — be what thou wilt, i am 5.03.130 P
corporal nym, and thou wilt be friends, be H5 2.01.102 P
and thou wilt not, why then be enemies with me 2.01.103 P
if for thy ransom thou wilt now compound, 4.03. 80
the constable desires thee thou wilt mind | thy 4.03. 84
i fear thou wilt once more come again for a 4.03.128 P
to me in broken english — wilt thou have me? 5.02.246 P
maid, is't thou wilt do these wondrous feats? 1H6 1.02. 64
cain, | to slay thy brother abel, if thou wilt. 1.03. 40
thou wilt answer this before the pope. 1.03. 52
wilt thou yet leave the battle, boy, and fly, 4.06. 28
all these are sav'd if thou wilt fly away. 4.06. 41
if thou wilt fight, fight by thy father's side, 4.06. 56
we be rid of them, do with /'em what thou wilt. 4.07. 94
be what thou wilt, thou art my prisoner. 5.03. 45
wilt thou be daunted at a woman's sight? 5.03. 69
wilt thou accept of ransom, yea or no? 5.03. 80
thy head, | if thou wilt condescend to be my — 5.03.120
graceless, wilt thou deny thy parentage? 5.04. 14
fie, joan, that thou wilt be so obstacle! 5.04. 17
wilt thou not stoop? 5.04. 26
upon condition thou wilt swear | to pay him 5.04.129
and wilt thou still be hammering treachery, | to 2H6 1.02. 47
i go. come, nell, thou wilt ride with us? 1.02. 59
ask what thou wilt. that i had said, and done! 1.04. 28
him, | thou wilt but add increase unto my wrath. 3.02.292
so thou wilt let me live, and feel no pain. 3.03. 4
rate me at what thou wilt, thou shalt be paid. 4.01. 30
villain, thou wilt betray me, and get a thousand 4.10. 26 P
but thou wilt brave me with these saucy terms? 4.10. 36
wilt thou on thy death–bed play the ruffian, 5.01.164
wilt thou go dig a grave to find out war, | and 5.01.169
art thou king, and wilt be forc'd? 3H6 1.01.230
gentle son edward, thou wilt stay /with me? 1.01.259
i never did thee harm; why wilt thou slay me? 1.03. 38
now, perjur'd henry, wilt thou kneel for grace, 2.02. 81
say'st thou, henry, wilt thou yield the crown? 2.02.101
even as thou wilt, sweet warwick, let it be; 2.06. 99
what service wilt thou do me if i give them? 3.02. 44
ay, if thou wilt say ay to my request; 3.02. 79
huntsman, what say'st thou? wilt thou go along? 4.05. 25
now, warwick, wilt thou ope the city–gates, 5.01. 21
nay rather, wilt thou draw thy forces hence, 5.01. 25
thou wilt, if warwick call. 5.01. 80
perhaps thou wilt object my holy oath: 5.01. 89
warwick, wilt thou leave the town, and fight? 5.01.107
wilt thou not? 5.05. 71
what, wilt thou not? 5.05. 77
thee, | but thou wilt be aveng'd on my misdeeds, R3 1.04. 70
if thou wilt outstrip death, go cross the seas, 4.01. 41
wilt thou, o god, fly from such gentle lambs, 4.04. 22
either thou wilt die by god's just ordinance 4.04.184
and wilt thou learn of me? 4.04.270
thou wilt revolt and fly to him, i fear. 4.04.477
nice conjecture | where thou wilt hit me dead? TRO 4.05.251

god–a–mercy, that thou wilt believe me, but a 5.04. 31 P
pause, if thou wilt. 5.06. 14
wilt thou not? 5.06. 28
wilt thou not, beast, abide? 5.06. 30
their good loves, but thou wilt frame | thyself, COR 3.02. 84
that wilt revenge | thine own particular wrongs, 4.05. 85
if thou wilt have | the leading of thine own 4.05.136
store, | that thou wilt never render to me more! TIT 1.01. 95
wilt thou draw near the nature of the gods? 1.01.117
good aaron, wilt thou help to chop it off? 3.01.161
and wilt thou have a reason for this coil? 3.01.224
come, thou'lt do my message, wilt thou not? 4.01.117
wilt thou betray thy noble mistress thus? 4.02.106
i see thou wilt not trust the air | with secrets 4.02.169
if thou wilt not, befall what may befall, | i'll 5.01. 57
maidenheads, take it in what sense thou wilt. ROM 1.01. 26 P
which thou wilt propagate to have it press'd 1.01.187
thou wilt fall backward when thou hast more wit, 1.03. 42
when thou hast more wit, | wilt thou not, jule?" 1.03. 43
"wilt thou not, jule?" 1.03. 47
thou wilt fall backward when thou comest to age, 1.03. 56
when thou comest to age, | wilt thou not, jule?" 1.03. 57
and if he hear thee, thou wilt anger him. 2.01. 22
or, if thou wilt not, be but sworn my love, 2.02. 35
i know thou wilt say "ay," | and i will take thy 2.02. 90
so thou wilt woo, but else not for the world. 2.02. 97
or, if thou wilt, swear by thy gracious self, 2.02.113
o, wilt thou leave me so unsatisfied? 2.02.125
where and what time thou wilt perform the rite, 2.02.146
what wilt thou tell her, nurse? 2.04.175 P
thou wilt quarrel with a man that hath a hair 3.01. 17 P
thou wilt quarrel with a man for cracking nuts, 3.01. 19 P
and yet thou wilt tutor me from quarrelling! 3.01. 29 P
for thou wilt lie upon the wings of night, 3.02. 18
o, thou wilt speak again of banishment. 3.03. 53
romeo, arise, | thou wilt be taken. 3.03. 75
wilt thou slay thyself, | and slay thy lady that 3.03.116
wilt thou be gone? 3.05. 1
death, | i am content, so thou wilt have it so. 3.05. 18
for then i hope thou wilt not keep him long, 3.05. 63
wilt thou wash him from his grave with tears? 3.05. 70
and then i hope thou wilt be satisfied. 3.05. 92
do as thou wilt, for i have done with thee. 3.05.203
then is it likely thou wilt undertake | a thing 4.01. 73
wilt thou provoke me? then have at thee, boy! 5.03. 70
wilt dine with me, apemantus? TIM 1.01.203 P
thou wilt give away thyself in paper shortly. 1.02.241 P
thou wilt not hear me now, thou shalt not then. 1.02.247 P
if thou wilt not promise, the gods plague thee, 4.03. 74 P
if thou wilt curse, thy father (that poor rag) 4.03.271
if thou wilt, | tell them there i have gold; 4.03.288
thou wilt be throng'd to shortly. 4.03.394
wilt thou whip thine own faults in other men? 5.01. 39
what thou wilt, | thou rather shalt enforce it 5.04. 44
so thou wilt send thy gentle heart before, | to 5.04. 48
that thou wilt use the wars as thy redress | and 5.04. 51
day | where wilt thou find a cavern dark enough JC 2.01. 80
hence! wilt thou lift up olympus? 3.01. 74
art afoot, | take thou what course thou wilt! 3.02.261
is so much that thou wilt kill me straight: 5.04. 13
wilt thou, strato? 5.05. 48
fellow, wilt thou bestow thy time with me? 5.05. 61
yes, he is dead. how wilt thou do for a father? MAC 4.02. 38
but how wilt thou do for a father? 4.02. 60 P
whither wilt thou lead me? HAM 1.05. 1
or, if thou wilt needs marry, marry a fool, for 3.01.137 P
so think thou wilt no second husband wed, | but 3.02.214
what wilt thou do? 3.04. 21
thou wilt not murther me? 3.04. 21
what wilt thou do for her? 5.01.271
but wilt thou hear now how i did proceed? 5.02. 27
wilt thou know | th' effect of what i wrote? 5.02. 36
sith thus thou wilt appear, | freedom lives LR 1.01.180
wilt break my heart? 3.04. 4
thou wilt o'ertake us hence a mile or twain | i' 4.01. 42
if thou wilt weep my fortunes, take my eyes. 4.06.176
if ever thou wilt thrive, bury my body, | and 4.06.247
if thou wilt needs damn thyself, do it a more OTH 1.03.353 P
wilt thou be fast to my hopes, if i depend on 1.03.362 P
wilt thou do this? 3.01. 26 P
if for the sake of merit thou wilt hear me, ANT 2.07. 55
wilt thou be lord of all the world? 2.07. 61
wilt thou be lord of the whole world? 2.07. 62
or sky inclips, | is thine, if thou wilt ha't. 2.07. 69
thou wilt write to antony? 3.01. 29
lives he? | wilt thou not answer, man? 4.14.115
wilt lay the leaven on all proper men; CYM 3.04. 62
wilt thou serve me? 3.05.117 P
wilt thou serve me? 3.05.120 P
that thou wilt be a voluntary mute to my design. 3.05.153 P
of thy story, | so far as thou wilt speak it. 3.06. 92
wilt take thy chance with me? 4.02.382
and ask of cymbeline what boon thou wilt, 5.05. 97
my life, good lad, | and yet i know thou wilt. 5.05.102
speak, | wilt have him live? 5.05.111
wilt thou hear more, my lord? 5.05.146
wilt thou not speak to me? 5.05.266
wilt thou undo the worth thou art unpaid for, 5.05.307
as thou | wilt live, fly after, and like an PER 1.01.161
nay then thou wilt starve sure; 2.01. 68 P
why, wilt thou tourney for the lady? 2.01.144 P
storm, venomously | wilt thou spet all thyself? 3.01. 8
thou wilt not, wilt thou? 3.01. 43 P
thou wilt not, wilt thou? 3.01. 43 P
whither wilt thou have me? 4.06.153 P
lips, what wilt thou think | of rotten kings or TNK 1.01.179
thou wilt not go along? 2.03. 68
wilt thou exceed in all, or dost thou do it | to 3.06. 46
do such a justice thou thyself wilt envy. 3.06.155
if thou wilt deign this favor, for thy meed | a VEN 15
"if thou wilt chide, thy lips shall never open." 48
and one for int'rest, if thou wilt have twain. 210
feed where thou wilt, on mountain or in dale; 232
so thou wilt buy, and pay, and use good dealing, 514
wilt thou make the match?" 586
"but if thou needs wilt hunt, be rul'd by me, 673
"and wilt thou be the school where lust shall LUC 617
wilt thou be glass wherein it shall discern 619

or if thou wilt permit the sun to climb | his 775
"when wilt thou be the humble suppliant's friend 897
when wilt thou sort an hour great strifes to end 899
(if ever, love, thy lucrece thou wilt see) 1306
"thou single wilt prove none." SON 8.14
grant, if thou wilt, thou art belov'd of many, 10. 3
and do what e'er thou wilt, swift–footed time, 19. 6
and even thence thou wilt be stol'n, i fear, 48.13
these offices, so oft as thou wilt look, | shall 77.13
then hate me when thou wilt, if ever, now, | now 90. 1
if thou wilt leave me, do not leave me last, 90. 9
wilt thou not haply say, | "truth needs no color 101. 5
because he needs no praise, wilt thou be dumb? 101. 9
and yet thou wilt, for i, being pent in thee, 133.13
mine | thou wilt restore to be my comfort still: 134. 4
but thou wilt not, nor he will not be free, 134. 5
the statute of thy beauty thou wilt take, | thou 134. 9
wilt thou, whose will is large and spacious, 135. 5
when thou wilt inflame, | how coldly those LC 268

WILTSHIRE 6 FR 0.0006 REL FR 6 V 0 P
go, bushy, to the earl of wiltshire straight, R2 2.01.215
the earl of wiltshire hath the realm in farm. 2.01.256
the earl of wiltshire is already there. 2.02.136
where is the earl of wiltshire? 3.02.122
is bushy, green, and the earl of wiltshire dead? 3.02.141
i mean the earl of wiltshire, bushy, green. 3.04. 53

WILTSHIRE'S 1 FR 0.0001 REL FR 1 V 0 P
brother, here's the earl of wiltshire's blood, 3H6 1.01. 14

WIMPLED 1 FR 0.0001 REL FR 1 V 0 P
this wimpled, whining, purblind, wayward boy, LLL 3.01.179

WIN 129 FR 0.0145 REL FR 116 V 13 P
upon this island as a spy, to win it | from me, TMP 1.02.456
truly, sir, i think you'll hardly win her. TGV 1.01.133 P
cannot your grace win her to fancy him? 3.01. 67
win her with gifts, if she respect not words: 3.01. 89
man, | if with his tongue he cannot win a woman. 3.01.105
win her to consent to you; WIV 2.02.236 P
that i should win what you would enjoy? 2.02.239 P
and makes us lose the good we oft might win, MM 1.04. 78
pray heaven she win him! 2.02.125
such a man would win any woman in the world, if ADO 2.01. 16 P
win me and wear me, let him answer me. 5.01. 82
and shape to win grace though he had no wit. LLL 2.01. 60
will you win your love with a french brawl? 3.01. 8 P
as thou wilt win my favor, good my knave, | do 3.01.152
so wise | to lose an oath to win a paradise?" 4.03. 71
and win them too; 4.03.369
and therewithal to win me, if you please, 5.02.848
when 'a roars for prey, | to win /thee, lady. MV 2.01. 31
he may win, | and what is music then? 3.02. 47
no, we shall ne'er win at that sport, and stake 3.02.216 P
tell him from me, as he will win my love, | he SHR in.1. 109
and so we will, provided that he win her. 1.02.216
'tis deeds must win the prize, and he of both 2.01.342
shall win my love, and so i take my leave, | in 4.02. 42
shall win the wager which we will propose. 5.02. 69
nay, i will win my wager better yet, | and show 5.02.116
to tell him that his sword can never win | the AWW 3.02. 93
no sin | to cozen him that would unjustly win. 4.02. 76
close | her eyes myself could win me to believe, 5.03.119
i' th' world, | so soon as yours could win me. WT 1.02. 21
of their hearts | may easily win a woman's. JN 1.01.269
than e'er the coward hand of france can win. 2.01.158
win you this city without stroke or wound, 2.01.418
husband, i cannot pray that thou mayst win; 3.01.331
i have a way to win their loves again. 4.02.168
to win this easy match play'd for a crown? 5.02.106
to outlook conquest and to win renown | even in 5.02.115
i say again, if lewis do win the day, | he is 5.04. 30
if lewis by your assistance win the day. 5.04. 39
his noble hand | did win what he did spend, and R2 2.01.180
but we must win your grace to go with us | to 2.03.163
overblown, | an easy task it is to win our own. 3.02.191
our holy lives must win a new world's crown, 5.01. 24
it be, | to win thy after–love i pardon thee. 5.03. 35
and on this north side win this cape of land, 1H4 3.01.112
did he win | the hearts of all that he did angle 4.03. 83
for nothing can seem foul to those that win. 5.01. 8
art, whoe'er thou be, | and thus i win thee. 5.04. 38
that thou mightst win the more thy father's love 2H4 4.05.179
/blood and sword and fire, to win your right; H5 1.02.131
old and true, | "if that you will france win, 1.02.167
"i can never win | a soul so easy as that 2.02.124
in bloody field, | doth win immortal fame." 3.02. 11
if i could win a lady at leap–frog, or by 5.02.136 P
a base wallon, to win the dolphin's grace, 1H6 1.01.137
that henry born at monmouth should win all, 3.01.197
i'll win this lady margaret. 5.03. 88
myself did win them both. 2H6 1.01.119
that maine which by main force warwick did win, 1.01.210
which i will win from france, or else be slain. 1.01.213
men's flesh preserv'd so whole do seldom win. 3.01.301
the rebels have assay'd to win the tower. 4.05. 8
by words or blows here let us win our right. 3H6 1.01. 37
i'll win them, fear it not. 1.02. 60
and we, in them, no hope to win the day, | so 2.01.136
by this account then, margaret may win him, 3.01. 35
and yet to win her! R3 1.02.237
can from his mother win the duke of york, | anon 3.01. 38
i'll win our ancient right in france again, | or 3.01. 92
but sure i fear we shall not win him to it. 3.07. 80
this /is not the way | to win your daughter. 4.04.285
shall i go win my daughter to thy will? 4.04.426
awake and win the day! 5.03.145
had rather have us win than him they follow: 5.03.244
(the image of his maker) hope to win by it? H8 3.02.442
sir, i did never win of you before. 5.01. 58
win straying souls with modesty again, | cast 5.02. 99
and think with wagging of your tongue to win me; 5.02.162
to draw mine honor in, and let 'em win the work. 5.03. 58 P
why was my cressid then so hard to win? TRO 3.02.116
sing, | "great hector's sister did achilles win, 3.03.212
i come to lose my arm, or win my sleeve. 5.03. 96
in very spite of cunning, | bade him win all. 5.05. 42
to run, | lead'st first to win some vantage. COR 1.01.160
it will in time | win upon power, and throw 1.01.220
fought, and did | retire to win our purpose. 1.06. 50
throngs, and puff | to win a vulgar station; 2.01.215
though we had | our wish, which side should win; 5.03.113
could | but win the noble brutus to our party — JC 1.03.141
and oftentimes, to win us to our harm, | the MAC 1.03.123
win us with honest trifles, to betray 's | in 1.03.125
thou'ldst not play false, | and yet wouldst wrongly win. 1.05. 22
by many of these trains hath sought to win me 4.03.118
hold his purpose, i will win for him and i can; HAM 5.02.176 P
i shall win at the odds. 5.02.211 P
our son shall win. 5.02.287
though i should win your displeasure to entreat LR 2.02.113 P
i think this tale would win my daughter too. OTH 1.03.171
and indeed the course | to win the moor again? 2.03.339
and then for her | to win the moor, were/'t to 2.03.343
iago, | what shall i do to win my lord again? 4.02.149
his cocks do win the battle still of mine, ANT 2.03. 37
you'll win two days upon me. 2.04. 9
husband win, win brother, | prays, and destroys 3.04. 18
husband win, win brother, | prays, and destroys 3.04. 18
from antony win cleopatra, promise, | and in our 3.12. 27
so soon as i can win th' offended king, | i will CYM 1.01. 75
loss, so in our trifles | i still win of you. 1.01.121
lost to–day at bowls i'll win to–night of him. 2.01. 49 P
you are most hot and furious when you win. 2.03. 6 P
so sure | to win the king as i am bold her honor 2.04. 2
but to win time | to lose so bad employment, in 3.04.109
in suit the place of 's bed and win this ring 5.05.185
but if i cannot win you to this love, | go PER 2.04. 49
whom if you find, and win unto return, | you 2.04. 52
i durst wager, | would win some words of him. 5.01. 44
and what they win in't, boot and glory; TNK 1.02. 70
how bravely may he bear himself to win her, | if 2.02.254
i wish his weary soul that falls may win it. 3.06.100
arcite may win me, | and yet may palamon wound 5.03. 57
"what win i if i gain the thing i seek? LUC 211
to win me soon to hell, my female evil PP 2. 5
so wise | to break an oath, to win a paradise? 3.14
to win his heart she touch'd him here and there 4. 7
and the firm soil win of the wat'ry main, SON 64. 7
that thou in losing me shall win much glory. 88. 8
fears, | still losing when i saw myself to win? 119. 4
to win me soon to hell, my female evil 144. 5
and, veil'd in them, did win whom he would maim. LC 312

WINCH 2 FR 0.0002 REL FR 1 V 1 P
i will not stir, nor winch, nor speak a word, JN 4.01. 80
let the gall'd jade winch, our withers are HAM 3.02.243 P

WINCHESTER 26 FR 0.0029 REL FR 26 V 0 P
not open, | the cardinal of winchester forbids. 1H6 1.03. 19
arrogant winchester, that haughty prelate, 1.03. 23
winchester goose, i cry, "a rope! 1.03. 53
for the truce of winchester and gloucester; 2.04.118
else would i have a fling at winchester. 3.01. 64
uncles of gloucester and of winchester, | the 3.01. 65
can you, my lord of winchester, behold | my 3.01.107
yield, my lord protector, yield, winchester, 3.01.112
behold, my lord of winchester, the duke | hath 3.01.122
here, winchester, i offer thee my hand. 3.01.126
for shame, my lord of winchester, relent! 3.01.132
as will the rest, so willeth winchester. 3.01.161
what, is my lord of winchester install'd, | and 5.01. 28
which by my lord of winchester we mean | shall 5.01. 39
now winchester will not submit, i trow, | or be 5.01. 56
speak, winchester, for boiling choler chokes 5.04.120
uncle of winchester, i pray read on. 2H6 1.01. 56
thanks, uncle winchester, | gloucester, york, 1.01. 68
my lord of winchester, i know your mind. 1.01.139
/stokesly and gardiner, the one of winchester, H8 4.01.101
he of winchester | is held no great good lover 4.01.103
ah, my good lord of winchester — i thank you, 5.02. 93
my lord of winchester, y' are a little, | by 5.02.108
at sudden commendations, | bishop of winchester. 5.02.158
once more, my lord of winchester, i charge you, 5.02.204
some galled goose of winchester would hiss. TRO 5.10. 54

WINCHESTER'S 1 FR 0.0001 REL FR 1 V 0 P
to asher–house, my lord of winchester's, | till H8 3.02.231

WINCOT 1 FR 0.0001 REL FR 0 V 1 P
the fat ale–wife of wincot, if she know me not. SHR in.2. 22 P

/WIND* 2 FR 0.0002 REL FR 2 V 0 P
too slightly timber'd for so /loud /a /wind, HAM 4.07. 22
/the //to–and–fro–conflicting /wind /and /rain. LR 3.01. 11

WIND* 203 FR 0.0229 REL FR 171 V 32 P
blow till thou burst thy wind, if room enough! TMP 1.01. 7 P
deep, | to run upon the sharp wind of the north, 1.02.254
storm brewing, i hear it sing i' th' wind. 2.02. 20 P
be calm, good wind, blow not a word away | till TGV 1.02.115
if the wind were down, i could drive the boat 2.03. 53 P
a man may hear this show'r sing in the wind. WIV 3.02. 38 P
if my wind were but long enough /to /say /my 4.05.102 P
was carried with more speed before the wind, ERR 1.01.109
stop in your wind, sir; 1.02. 53
there is something in the wind, that we cannot 3.01. 69
a word with /you, sir, and words are but wind: 3.01. 75
road, | and if the wind blow any way from shore, 3.02.148
both wind and tide stays for this gentleman, 4.01. 46
her trim, the merry wind | blows fair from land: 4.01. 90
is't possible? sits the wind in that corner? ADO 2.03. 98 P
foul words is but foul wind, and foul wind is 5.02. 52 P
but foul wind, and foul wind is but foul breath, 5.02. 52 P
can brook the weather that love not the wind. LLL 4.02. 33
through the velvet leaves the wind, | all unseen 4.03.103
fleeter than arrows, bullets, wind, thought, 5.02.261
when all aloud the wind doth blow | and coughing 5.02.921
to dance our ringlets to the whistling wind, MND 2.01. 86
and grow big–bellied with the wanton wind; 2.01.129
about the wood go swifter than the wind, | and 3.02. 94
fann'd with the eastern wind, turns to a crow 3.02.142
sleep thou, and i will wind thee in my arms. 4.01. 40
plucking the grass to know where sits the wind, MV 1.01. 18
my wind cooling my broth | would blow me to an 1.01. 22
what harm a wind too great might do at sea. 1.01. 24
time | to wind about my love with circumstance, 1.01.154
bay, | hugg'd and embraced by the strumpet wind! 2.06. 16
lean, rent, and beggar'd by the strumpet wind! 2.06. 19
no masque to–night, the wind is come about, 2.06. 64
which /make such wanton gambols with the wind 3.02. 93
when the sweet wind did gently kiss the trees 5.01. 2
and churlish chiding of the winter's wind, AYL 2.01. 7
withal, as large a charter as the wind, | to 2.07. 48
blow, blow, thou winter wind, | thou art not so 2.07.174
her worth, being mounted on the wind, | through 3.02. 90
but — wind away, | be gone, i say, | i will not 3.03.103
like foggy south, puffing with wind and rain? 3.05. 50
even as the waving sedges play with wind. SHR in.2. 53
such wind as scatters young men through the 1.02. 50
though little fire grows great with little wind, 2.01.134
steely bones | looks bleak i' th' cold wind. AWW 1.01.104
by this same coxcomb that we have i' th' wind, 3.06.114
prithee allow the wind. 5.02. 9 P
in grain, sir, 'twill endure wind and weather. TN 1.05.237 P
frown the while, and perchance wind up my watch, 2.05. 60 P
tine boy, | with hey ho, the wind and the rain, 5.01.390
were they false | as o'er–dy'd blacks, as wind, WT 1.02.132
i am a feather for each wind that blows. 2.03.154
of chance, and flies | of every wind that blows. 4.04.541
no common wind, no customed event, | but they JN 3.04.155
and, like a shifted wind unto a sail, | it makes 4.02. 23
therefore thy threat'ning colors now wind up, 5.02. 73
with that same weak wind which enkindled it. 5.02. 87
faith, none for me, except the northeast wind, R2 1.04. 6
we see the wind sit sore upon our sails, | and 2.01.265
the wind sits fair for news to go for ireland, 2.02.123
corse | betwixt the wind and his nobility. 1H4 1.03. 45
the squier further afoot, i shall break my wind. 2.02. 13 P
by the imprisoning of unruly wind | within her 3.01. 29
it shall not wind with such a deep indent, | to 3.01.103
not wind? it shall, it must, you see it doth. 3.01.105
is the wind in that door, i' faith? 3.03. 88 P
that with the wind | bated like eagles having 4.01. 98
the clouds | to turn and wind a fiery pegasus, 4.01.109
the southren wind | doth play the trumpet to his 5.01. 3
drooping west | (making the wind my post–horse), 2H4 in 4
is not your voice broken, your wind short, your 1.02.183 P
we shall be winnow'd with so rough a wind | that 4.01.192
is held from falling with so weak a wind | that 4.05. 99
what wind blew you hither, pistol? 5.03. 85 P
not the ill wind which blows no man to good. 5.03. 86 P
now sits the wind fair, and we will aboard. H5 2.02. 12
borne with th' invisible and creeping wind, 3.pr. 11
whiles yet the cool and temperate wind of grace 3.03. 30
yet, by your leave, the wind was very high, 2H6 2.01. 3
if wind and fuel be brought to feed it with. 3.01.303
and twice by awkward wind from england's bank 3.02. 83
but well forewarning wind | did seem to say, 3.02. 85
turn back and fly, like ships before the wind, 3H6 1.04. 4
for raging wind blows up incessant showers, 1.04.145
for self–same wind that i should speak withal 2.01. 82
forc'd by the tide to combat with the wind; 2.05. 6
sea | forc'd to retire by fury of the wind. 2.05. 8
sometime the flood prevails, and then the wind; 2.05. 9
ill blows the wind that profits nobody. 2.05. 55
me again, | obeying with my wind when i do blow, 3.01. 86
he knows the game; how true he keeps the wind! 3.02. 14
for this is he that moves both wind and tide. 3.03. 48
it boots not to resist both wind and tide. 4.03. 59
how thou canst, have wind and tide thy friend, 5.01. 53
and kept low shrubs from winter's pow'rful wind. 5.02. 15
keep our course (though the rough wind say no) 5.04. 22
and dallies with the wind and scorns the sun. R3 1.03.264
o ill–dispersing wind of misery! 4.01. 52
but, in the wind and tempest of her frown, TRO 1.03. 26
but when the splitting wind | makes flexible the 1.03. 49
speak frankly as the wind, | it is not 1.03.253
does so blush, and fetches her wind so short, as 3.02. 32 P
false | as air, as water, wind, or sandy earth, 3.02.192
rain, to lay this wind, or my heart will be 4.04. 53 P
even in the fan and wind of your fair sword, 5.03. 41
go, wind, to wind, there turn and change 5.03.110
wind, to wind, there turn and change together. 5.03.110
one infect another | against the wind a mile! COR 1.04. 34
of my son, he should | be free as is the wind. 1.09. 89
should grind it | and throw't against the wind. 3.02.104
and to wind | yourself into a power tyrannical, 3.03. 64
the green leaves quiver with the cooling wind TIT 2.03. 14
like to a bubbling fountain stirr'd with wind, 2.04. 23
the dam will wake and if she wind ye once; 4.01. 97
the angry northen wind | will blow these sands 4.01.104
my son and i will have the wind of you; 4.02.133
you were as good to shoot against the wind. 4.03. 58
and more inconstant than the wind, who woos ROM 1.04.100
this wind you talk of blows us from ourselves: 1.04.104
body | thou counterfeits a bark, a sea, a wind: 3.05.131
and pursy insolence shall break his wind | with TIM 5.04. 12
fray, | and the wind brings it from the capitol. JC 2.04. 19
to wind, to stop, to run directly on, | his 4.01. 32
honesty | that they pass by me as the idle wind, 4.03. 68
why now blow wind, swell billow, and swim bark! 5.01. 67
i'll give thee a wind. MAC 1.03. 11
corporal melted, | as breath into the wind. 1.03. 82
in every eye, | that tears shall drown the wind. 1.07. 25
blow wind, come wrack, | at least we'll die with 5.05. 50
the wind sits in the shoulder of your sail, HAM 1.03. 56
or (not to crack the wind of the poor phrase, 1.03.108
when the wind is southerly i know a hawk from a 2.02.379 P
but with the whiff and wind of his fell sword 2.02.473
why do you go about to recover the wind of me, 3.02.346 P
mad as the sea and wind, when both contend 4.01. 7
the bark is ready, and the wind at help, | th' 4.03. 44
and for his death no wind of blame shall breathe 4.07. 66
clay, | might stop a hole to keep the wind away. 5.01.214
me, 'tis very cold, the wind is northerly. 5.02. 95 P
wind me into him, i pray you. LR 1.02. 98 P
nay, and thou canst not smile as the wind sits, 1.04.100 P
bids the wind blow the earth into the sea, | or 3.01. 5
nor rain, wind, thunder, fire are my daughters. 3.02. 15
such groans of roaring wind and rain, i never 3.02. 47
wit — | with heigh–ho, the wind and the rain — 3.02. 75
still through the hawthorn blows the cold wind. 3.04. 99 P
you are not worth the dust which the rude wind 4.02. 30
to wet me once, and the wind to make me chatter, 4.06.101 P
o, wind up | of this child–changed father! 4.07. 15
methinks the wind hath spoke aloud at land, | a OTH 2.01. 5
my boat sails freely, both with wind and stream. 2.03. 63
are these, i pray you, wind instruments? 3.01. 6 P
sir, by many a wind instrument that i know. 3.01. 10 P
and let her down the wind | to prey at fortune. 3.03.262

the bawdy wind, that kisses all it meets, | is 4.02. 78
it's the wind. 4.03. 54 P
whose wind did seem | to /glow the delicate ANT 2.02.203
the least wind i' th' world will blow them down. 2.07. 2 P
him, | and his affairs come to me on the wind. 3.06. 63
though my reason | sits in the wind against me. 3.10. 36
hear | the rain and wind beat dark december, how CYM 3.03. 37
as the rud'st wind | that by the top doth take 4.02.174
with the next benefit o' th' wind. 4.02.342
for vice repeated is like the wand'ring wind, PER 1.01. 96
seldom ease, | for now the wind begins to blow; 2.ch. 29
wind, rain, and thunder, remember earthly man 2.01. 2
a man whom both the waters and the wind, | in 2.01. 59
the sea works high, the wind is loud, and will 3.01. 48 P
by break of day, if the wind cease. 3.01. 76 P
is this wind westerly that blows? 4.01. 50
when i was born, the wind was north. 4.01. 51
never was waves nor wind more violent, | and 4.01. 59
we have, a strong wind will blow it to pieces, 4.02. 19 P
then start amongst 'em | and, as an east wind, TNK 2.02. 13
for when the west wind courts her gently, | how 2.02.138
may rude wind never hurt thee! 2.02.275
boys in athens | blow wind i' th' breech on 's, 2.03. 47
run | swifter than wind upon a field of corn, 2.03. 77
/open her before the wind! 3.04. 9
is proclaim'd | by the wind instruments. 5.03. 95
whose gentle wind | shall cool the heat of this VEN 189
to bid the wind a base he now prepares, | and 303
through his mane and tail the high wind sings, 305
glow, | even as a dying coal revives with wind, 338
even as the wind is hush'd before it raineth, 458
how he outruns the wind, and with what care | he 681
but like a stormy day, now wind, now rain, 965
as when the wind imprison'd in the ground, 1046
nor sun nor wind will ever strive to kiss you: 1082
sun doth scorn you and the wind doth hiss you. 1084
the wind would blow it off, and being gone, 1089
the wind wars with his torch to make him stay, LUC 311
puffs forth another wind that fires the torch. 315
the doors, the wind, the glove that did delay 325
abide, | and with the wind in greater fury fret. 648
and sorrow ebbs, being blown with wind of words. 1330
and falls, through wind, before the fall should PP 10. 6
through the velvet leaves the wind | all unseen 16. 5
words are easy, like the wind, | faithful 20.31
'pointing to each his thunder, rain, and wind, SON 14. 6
then should i spur though mounted on the wind, 51. 7
storming her world with sorrow's wind and rain. LC 7
and every light occasion of the wind | upon his 86

WIND–CHANGING 1 FR 0.0001 REL FR 1 V 0 P
"wind–changing warwick now can change no more." 3H6 5.01. 57

WINDED 1 FR 0.0001 REL FR 0 V 1 P
i will have a rechate winded in my forehead, or ADO 1.01.241 P

WIND–FANN'D 1 FR 0.0001 REL FR 1 V 0 P
and pure | as wind–fann'd snow, who to thy TNK 5.01.140

WINDGALLS 1 FR 0.0001 REL FR 0 V 1 P
infected with the fashions, full of windgalls, SHR 3.02. 52 P

WINDING 5 FR 0.0005 REL FR 4 V 1 P
look, he's winding up the watch of his wit, by TMP 2.01. 12 P
and so by many winding nooks he strays | with TGV 2.07. 31
winding up days with toil, and nights with sleep H5 4.01.279
fly, | or one encompass'd with a winding maze, LUC 1151
and from his lips did fly | thin winding breath, 1407

WINDING–SHEET 2 FR 0.0002 REL FR 2 V 0 P
great sorrow, | shall be my winding–sheet. 3H6 1.01.129
these arms of mine shall be thy winding–sheet; 2.05.114

WINDLASSES 1 FR 0.0001 REL FR 1 V 0 P
with windlasses and with assays of bias, | by HAM 2.01. 62

WINDMILL 2 FR 0.0002 REL FR 1 V 1 P
live | with cheese and garlic in a windmill, far 1H4 3.01.160
lay all night in the windmill in saint george's 2H4 3.02.195 P

WINDOW 29 FR 0.0032 REL FR 20 V 9 P
determin'd of — how i must climb her window, TGV 2.04.181
what lets but one may enter at her window? 3.01.113
now must we to her window, | and give some 4.02. 16
out at your window betwixt twelve and one? ADO 4.01. 84
talk with a man out at a window! 4.01.309 P
behold the window of my heart, mine eye, | what LLL 5.02.838
thou hast by moonlight at her window sung | with MND 1.01. 30
you leave a casement of the great chamber window 3.01. 57 P
mistress, look out at window, for all this — MV 2.05. 41 P
from padua and here looking out at the window. SHR 5.01. 31 P
sir — see where he looks out of the window. 5.01. 56 P
so, my good window of lettice, fare thee well! AWW 2.03.213 P
swore i leapt from the window of the citadel — 4.01. 55 P
in at the window, or else o'er the hatch. JN 1.01.171
discern no part of his face from the window. 2H4 2.02. 81 P
him th' other day into the compass'd window — TRO 1.02.111 P
peer'd forth the golden window of the east, | a ROM 1.01.119
soft, what light through yonder window breaks? 2.02. 2
then, window, let day in, and let life out. 3.05. 41
and throw this | in at his window; JC 1.03.145
searching the window for a flint, i found | this 2.01. 36
morning betime, | and i a maid at your window, HAM 4.05. 50
there the window; CYM 2.02. 25
thy crystal window ope; 5.04. 81
put but thy head out of this window more, | and, TNK 2.02.212
and fling my wanton arms | in at her window! 2.02.238
farewell, kind window. 2.02.274
eyes break each morning 'gainst thy window, 2.03. 9
of eyes, | why pry'st thou through my window? LUC 1089

WINDOW/–BARS 1 FR 0.0001 REL FR 1 V 0 P
that through the window/–bars bore at men's eyes TIM 4.03.117

WINDOW'D 2 FR 0.0002 REL FR 2 V 0 P
your /loop'd and window'd raggedness, defend you LR 3.04. 31
wouldst thou be window'd in great rome, and see ANT 4.14. 72

WINDOWS' 1 FR 0.0001 REL FR 1 V 0 P
where rude misgoverned hands from windows' tops R2 5.02. 5

WINDOWS 21 FR 0.0023 REL FR 19 V 2 P
it hath bay windows transparent as barricadoes, TN 4.02. 36 P
it would not out at windows nor at doors. JN 5.07. 29
from my own windows torn my household coat, R2 3.01. 24
you would have thought the very windows spake, 5.02. 12
our windows are broke down in every street, 1H6 3.01. 84
lo, in these windows that let forth thy life | i R3 1.02. 12
soul | ere i let fall the windows of mine eyes: 5.03.116
stalls, bulks, windows, | are smother'd up, COR 2.01.210
shuts up his windows, locks fair daylight out, ROM 1.01.139
fade | to /wanny ashes, thy eyes' windows fall, 4.01.100
to tow'rs and windows, yea, to chimney–tops, JC 1.01. 39
in several hands, in at his windows throw, | as 1.02.316
pluck down forms, windows, any thing. 3.02.259 P
downy windows, close, | and golden phoebus never ANT 5.02.316
now canopied | under these windows, white and CYM 2.02. 22
to me | the very doors and windows savor vilely. PER 4.06.110
the windows are too open. TNK 2.02.262
her two blue windows faintly she upheaveth, VEN 482
so thou through windows of thine age shalt see, SON 3.11
that hath his windows glazed with thine eyes. 24. 8
and thine for me | are windows to my breast, 24.11

WINDPIPE 1 FR 0.0001 REL FR 1 V 0 P
free, | and let not hemp his windpipe suffocate. H5 3.06. 43

WINDPIPE'S 1 FR 0.0001 REL FR 1 V 0 P
they should spy my windpipe's dangerous notes: TIM 1.02. 51

WINDRING 1 FR 0.0001 REL FR 1 V 0 P
nymphs, call'd naiades, of the windring brooks, TMP 4.01.128

WIND'S 1 FR 0.0001 REL FR 1 V 0 P
the wind's fair. TNK 4.01.147

WINDS 58 FR 0.0065 REL FR 54 V 4 P
to sigh | to th' winds, whose pity, sighing back TMP 1.02.150
thou shalt be as free | as mountain winds; 1.02.500
may as well | wound the loud winds, or with 3.03. 63
the winds did sing it to me, and the thunder, 3.03. 97
noontide sun, call'd forth the mutinous winds, 5.01. 42
to be imprison'd in the viewless winds | and MM 3.01.123
if speaking, why, a vane blown with all winds; ADO 3.01. 66
therefore the winds, piping to us in vain, | as MND 2.01. 88
for the four winds blow in from every coast MV 1.01.168
and then there is the peril of waters, winds, 1.03. 25 P
have i not heard the sea, puff'd up with winds, SHR 1.02.201
ay, to the proof, as mountains are for winds, 2.01.140
as it were, from the ends of oppos'd winds. WT 1.01. 31 P
that may blow | no sneaping winds at home, to 1.02. 13
and take | the winds of march with beauty; 4.04.120
the adverse winds, | whose leisure i have stay'd JN 2.01. 57
to make his bleak winds kiss my parched lips 5.07. 40
and the contrarious winds that held the king 1H4 5.01. 52
surge, | and in the visitation of the winds, 2H4 3.01. 21
the winds grow high, so do your stomachs, lords. 2H6 2.01. 53
against the senseless winds shall grin in vain, 4.01. 77
commotion in the winds! TRO 1.03. 98
the seas and winds, old wranglers, took a truce, 2.02. 75
then let the mutinous winds | strike the proud COR 5.03. 59
if the winds rage, doth not the sea wax mad, TIT 3.01.222
scatter'd by winds and high tempestuous gusts, 5.03. 69
he swung about his head and cut the winds, | who ROM 1.01.111
the winds, thy sighs, | who, raging with thy 3.05.134
i have seen tempests when the scolding winds JC 1.03. 5
though you untie the winds, and let them fight MAC 4.01. 52
that he might not beteem the winds of heaven HAM 1.02.141
as the winds give benefit | and convey /is 1.03. 2
the bold winds speechless, and the orb below 2.02.485
outface | the winds and persecutions of the sky. LR 2.03. 12
on, and the /bleak winds | do sorely ruffle; 2.04.300
blow, winds, and crack your cheeks! 3.02. 1
the sharp hawthorn blow the /cold winds." 3.04. 47 P
face | to be oppos'd against the /warring winds? 4.07. 31
themselves, high seas, and howling winds, | the OTH 2.01. 68
may the winds blow till they have waken'd death! 2.01.186
blow me about in winds! 5.02.279
forth weeds | when our quick winds lie still, ANT 1.02.110
we cannot call her winds and waters sighs and 1.02.148 P
that | the winds were love–sick with them; 2.02.194
and winds of all the corners kiss'd your sails, CYM 2.04. 28
rides on the posting winds and doth belie | all 3.04. 36
to commix | with winds that sailors rail at. 4.02. 56
and thou that hast | upon the winds command, PER 3.01. 3
neptune and | the gentlest winds of heaven. 3.03. 37
ships and bounteous winds have brought | this 4.04. 17
where, driven before the winds, he is arriv'd 5.ch. 14
but infects the winds | with stench of our slain TNK 1.01. 46
small winds shake him. | but what's the matter? 1.02. 88
huge rocks, high winds, strong pirates, shelves LUC 335
at last it rains, and busy winds give o'er: 1790
rough winds do shake the darling buds of may, SON 18. 3
that i have hoisted sail to all the winds 117. 7
when winds breathe sweet, unruly though they be. LC 103

WIND–SHAK'D 1 FR 0.0001 REL FR 1 V 0 P
the wind–shak'd surge, with high and monstrous OTH 2.01. 13

WIND–SHAKEN 1 FR 0.0001 REL FR 0 V 1 P
he's the rock, the oak not to be wind–shaken. COR 5.02.111 P

WINDSOR 25 FR 0.0028 REL FR 10 V 15 P
never a woman in windsor knows more of anne's WIV 1.04.128 P
tuns of oil in his belly) ashore at windsor? 2.01. 65 P
(when the court lay at windsor) could never have 2.02. 62 P
nor evening prayer, as any is in windsor, 2.02. 99 P
never a wife in windsor leads a better life than 2.02.117 P
for if there be a kind woman in windsor, she is 2.02.121 P
old windsor way, and every way but the town way. 3.01. 6 P
with all the officers in windsor, to search for 3.03.107 P
coming, with half windsor at his heels, to 3.03.114 P
in this kind for the wealth of windsor castle. 3.03.217 P
(sometime a keeper here in windsor forest) 4.04. 29
the spirit, | and mock him home to windsor. 4.04. 65
the windsor bell hath strook twelve; 5.05. 1 P
for me, i am here a windsor stag, and the 5.05. 12 P
cricket, to windsor chimneys shalt thou leap; 5.05. 43
search windsor castle, elves, within and out. 5.05. 56
now, good sir john, how like you windsor wives? 5.05.106
sir, we'll bring you to windsor, to one master 5.05.165 P
be–gar, i'll raise all windsor. 5.05.210 P
next our council we | will hold at windsor, so 1H4 1.01.104
liking his father to a singing–man of windsor, 2H4 2.01. 90 P
i think he's gone to hunt, my lord, at windsor. 4.04. 14
why art thou not at windsor with him, thomas? 4.04. 50
win all, | and henry born at windsor lose all: 1H6 3.01.198
william of windsor was the seventh and last. 2H6 2.02. 17

WIND–SWIFT 1 FR 0.0001 REL FR 1 V 0 P
and therefore hath the wind–swift cupid wings. ROM 2.05. 8

WINDY 9 FR 0.0010 REL FR 7 V 2 P
poor fool, it keeps on the windy side of care. ADO 2.01.315 P
still you keep o' th' windy side of the law; TN 3.04.164 P
zeal, now melted by the windy breath | of soft JN 2.01.477
blown with the windy tempest of my heart | upon 3H6 2.05. 86
windy attorneys to their client's woes, | aery R3 4.04.127
black, | nor windy suspiration of forc'd breath, HAM 1.02. 79
then with her windy sighs and golden hairs | to VEN 51
this windy tempest, till it blow up rain, | held LUC 1788
give not a windy night a rainy morrow, | to SON 90. 7

WINE 82 FR 0.0092 REL FR 43 V 39 P
scape being drunk, for want of wine. TMP 2.01.147
no use of metal, corn, or wine, or oil; 2.01.154
if he have never drunk wine afore, it will go 2.02. 75 P
if all the wine in my bottle will recover him, i 2.02. 92 P
in a rock by th' sea–side, where my wine is hid. 2.02.135 P
to bear this away where my hogshead of wine is, 4.01.251 P
he is drunk now. where had he wine? 5.01.278
daughter, carry the wine in, we'll drink within. WIV 1.01.188 P
terms, and in such wine and sugar of the best, 2.02. 68 P
to taverns, and sack, and wine, and metheglins, 5.05.159 P
neither disturbed with the effect of wine, | nor ERR 5.01.215
drink some wine ere you go; fare you well. ADO 3.05. 53 P
and let my liver rather heat with wine | than my MV 1.01. 81
set a deep glass of rhenish wine on the contrary 1.02. 96 P
than there is between red wine and rhenish. 3.01. 41 P
as wine comes out of a narrow–mouth'd bottle, AYL 3.02.200 P
me, | for i am falser than vows made in wine. 3.05. 73
if it be true that good wine needs no bush, 'tis ep 4 P
yet to good wine they do use good bushes; ep 5 P
after many ceremonies done, | he calls for wine. SHR 3.02.170
i am sure thy father drunk wine — but if thou AWW 2.03.100 P
a stoup of wine! TN 2.03. 14 P
a stope of wine, maria! 2.03.120 P
and that's a marvellous searching wine, and it 2H4 2.04. 27 P
by this wine, i'll thrust my knife in your 2.04.129 P
laugh, but that's no marvel, he drinks no wine. 4.03. 89 P
give master bardolph some wine, davy. 5.03. 25 P
a cup of wine, sir? 5.03. 45 P
"a cup of wine that's brisk and fine, | and 5.03. 46
it was excess of wine that set him on, | and on H5 2.02. 42
and shall our quick blood, spirited with wine, 3.05. 21
taste of your wine and see what cates you have, 1H6 2.03. 79
god, and the good wine in thy master's way. 2H6 2.03. 96 P
nothing but claret wine this first year of our 4.06. 4 P
where art thou, keeper? give me a cup of wine. R3 1.04.161
you shall have wine enough, my lord, anon. 1.04.162
fill me a bowl of wine. 5.03. 63
give me a bowl of wine. 5.03. 72
i that was wash'd to death with fulsome wine, 5.03.132
first, good company, good wine, good welcome, H8 1.04. 6
the red wine first must rise | in their fair 1.04. 43
i'll heat his blood with greekish wine to–night, TRO 5.01. 1
have we no wine here? COR 1.09. 92
that loves a cup of hot wine with not a drop of 2.01. 48 P
wine, wine, wine! 4.05. 1 P
wine, wine, wine! 4.05. 1 P
wine, wine, wine! 4.05. 1 P
of our blood | with wine and feeding, we have 5.01. 55
montagues, i pray, come and crush a cup of wine. ROM 1.02. 80 P
to see meat fill knaves, and wine heat fools. TIM 1.01.261
vaults have wept | with drunken spilth of wine, 2.02.160
fill me some wine. 3.01. 9 P
please your lordship, here is the wine. 3.01. 30 P
thy flatterers yet wear silk, drink wine, lie 4.03.206
friends, go in, and taste some wine with me, JC 2.02.126
lucius, a bowl of wine! 4.03.142
give me a bowl of wine. 4.03.158
fill, lucius, till the wine o'erswell the cup; 4.03.161
will i with wine and wassail so convince, | that MAC 1.07. 64
the wine of life is drawn, and the mere lees 2.03. 95
give me some wine, fill full. 3.04. 87
set me the stoups of wine upon that table. HAM 5.02.267
wine lov'd i /deeply, dice dearly; LR 3.04. 90 P
the wine she drinks is made of grapes. OTH 2.01.251 P
lieutenant, i have a stope of wine, and here 2.03. 30 P
some wine ho! 2.03. 68 P
some wine, boys! 2.03. 74 P
some wine ho! 2.03. 97 P
o thou invisible spirit of wine, if thou hast no 2.03.282 P
good wine is a good familiar creature, if it be 2.03.309 P
wine enough, | cleopatra's health to drink. ANT 1.02. 12
sit — and some wine! a health to lepidus! 2.07. 29 P
this wine for lepidus! 2.07. 40
that the conquering wine hath steep'd our sense 2.07.107
strong enobarb | is weaker than the wine, and 2.07.123
some wine, within there, and our viands! 3.11. 73
i'll force | the wine peep through their scars. 3.13.190
give me some wine, and let me speak a little. 4.15. 42
say we drink this standing–bowl of wine to him. PER 2.03. 65
(millions of rates) | exceed the wine of others. TNK 1.04. 30
give me more wine. 3.03. 28
she swore by wine and bread she would not break. 3.05. 47

WING 30 FR 0.0034 REL FR 25 V 5 P
which hath been on the wing of all occasions. WIV 2.02.202 P
and then there's a partridge wing sav'd, for the ADO 2.01.149 P
fear makes in you is a virtue of a good wing, AWW 1.01.204 P
ay, madam, with the swiftest wing of speed. 3.02. 73
and with what wing the /staniel checks at it! TN 2.05.113 P
will wing me to some wither'd bough and there WT 5.03.133
imp out our drooping country's broken wing, R2 2.01.292
which do hold a wing | quite from the flight of 1H4 3.02. 30
but with nimble wing | we were enforc'd, for 5.01. 64
thus with imagin'd wing our swift scene flies H5 3.pr. 1
when they stoop, they stoop with the like wing. 4.01.107 P
knowledge the wing wherewith we fly to heaven, 2H6 4.07. 74
dares stir a wing if warwick shake his bells. 3H6 1.01. 47
then fiery expedition be my wing, | jove's R3 4.03. 54
the dragon wing of night o'erspreads the earth, TRO 5.08. 17
when every feather sticks in his own wing, TIM 2.01. 30
growing feathers pluck'd from caesar's wing JC 1.01. 72
perceive | but cold demeanor in octavio's wing, 5.02. 4
that swiftest wing of recompense is slow | to MAC 1.04. 17
and the crow | makes wing to th' rooky wood; 3.02. 51
sting, | lizard's leg and howlet's wing, | for a 4.01. 17
when i had seen this hot love on the wing — HAM 2.02.132
the crows and choughs that wing the midway air LR 4.06. 13
hither | he sends so poor a pinion of his wing, ANT 3.12. 4

(the best feather of our wing) have mingled sums CYM 1.06.186
prunes the immortal wing and cloys his beak, 5.04.118
from south to west on wing soaring aloft, 5.05.471
you charg'd | upon the left wing of the enemy, TNK 3.06. 75
session interdict | every fowl of tyrant wing, PHT 10
have added feathers to the learned's wing, | and SON 78. 7
WING'D 6 FR 0.0006 REL FR 5 V 1 P
and therefore is wing'd cupid painted blind. MND 1.01.235
so do all thoughts, they are wing'd. AYL 4.01.142 P
but his evasion, wing'd thus swift with scorn, TRO 2.03.114
have never wing'd from view o' th' nest, nor CYM 3.03. 28
or, wing'd with fervor of her love, she's flown 3.05. 61
wing'd | from the spungy south to this part of 4.02.348
WINGED 14 FR 0.0015 REL FR 14 V 0 P
and the winged fowls | are their males' subjects ERR 2.01. 18
brief | with winged haste to the lord marshal, 1H4 4.04. 2
with winged heels, as english mercuries. H5 2.pr. 7
seen, | heave him away upon your winged thoughts 5.pr. 8
two talbots, winged through the lither sky, | in 1H6 4.07. 21
like lime–twigs set to catch my winged soul. 2H6 3.03. 16
whose haughty spirit, winged with desire, | will 3H6 1.01.267
died, | and that a winged mercury did bear; R3 2.01. 89
shall be well winged with our chiefest horse. 5.03.300
as is a winged messenger of heaven | unto the ROM 2.02. 28
the winged vengeance overtake such children. LR 3.07. 66
only i carried winged time | post /on the lame PER 4.ch. 47
unto the clouds bequeathed | her winged sprite, LUC 1728
wind, | in winged speed no motion shall i know. SON 51. 8
WINGFIELD 1 FR 0.0001 REL FR 1 V 0 P
lord cromwell of wingfield, lord furnival of 1H6 4.07. 66
WINGHAM 1 FR 0.0001 REL FR 0 V 1 P
there's best's son, the tanner of wingham — 2H6 4.02. 22 P
WING–LED 1 FR 0.0001 REL FR 1 V 0 P
discipline | (now wing–led with their courages) CYM 2.04. 24
WINGS' 1 FR 0.0001 REL FR 1 V 0 P
coucheth the fowl below with his wings' shade, LUC 507
/WINGS 1 FR 0.0001 REL FR 1 V 0 P
/would /he /hang /his /slender /gilded /wings TIT 3.02. 61
WINGS 61 FR 0.0069 REL FR 56 V 5 P
who with thy saffron wings upon my flow'rs TMP 4.01. 78
love, lend me wings to make my purpose swift, TGV 2.06. 42
less shall she that hath love's wings to fly, 2.07. 11
their conceits have wings | fleeter than arrows, LLL 5.02.260
wings, and no eyes, figure unheedy haste; MND 1.01.237
some war with rere–mice for their leathren wings 2.02. 4
and pluck the wings from painted butterflies, 3.01.172
with leaden legs and batty wings doth creep. 3.02.365
as they fly by them with their woven wings. MV 1.01. 14
the tailor that made the wings she flew withal. 3.01. 27 P
this haste hath wings indeed. AWW 2.01. 93
to charge in with our horse upon our own wings, 3.06. 49 P
upon me, in the name of time, | to use my wings. WT 4.01. 4
shadowing their right under your wings of war. JN 2.01. 14
o, with what wings shall his affections fly 2H4 4.04. 65
with youthful wings is flown | from this bare 4.05.228
swiftness add | more feathers to our wings; H5 1.02.307
men, they have no wings to fly from god. 4.01.168 P
his arms spread wider than a dragon's wings; 1H6 1.01. 11
another would fly swift, but wanteth wings; 1.01. 75
some light horsemen, and peruse their wings. 4.02. 43
keeping them prisoner underneath /her wings. 5.03. 57
under the wings of our protector's grace, 2H6 1.03. 38
have all lim'd bushes to betray thy wings, | and 2.04. 54
and flagging wings | cleep dead men's graves, 4.01. 5
even with those wings | which sometime they have
3H6 2.02. 29
bootless is flight, they follow us with wings, 2.03. 12
with trembling wings misdoubteth every bush; 5.06. 14
and yet, for all his wings, the fool was drown'd 5.06. 20
the sun that sear'd the wings of my sweet boy, 5.06. 23
hover about me with your aery wings | and hear R3 4.04. 13
hope is swift and flies with swallow's wings, 5.02. 23
when i should mount with wings of victory. 5.03.106
of this fair company | clapp'd wings to me. H8 1.04. 9
shade thy person | under their blessed wings! 5.01.161
do set | the very wings of reason to his heels TRO 2.02. 44
your full consent | gave wings to my propension, 2.02.133
from cupid's shoulder pluck his painted wings, 3.02. 14
show not their mealy wings but to the summer, 3.03. 79
with wings more momentary–swift than thought. 4.02. 14
he has wings, he's more than a creeping thing. COR 5.04. 13 P
knowing that with the shadow of his wings | he TIT 4.04. 85
you are a lover, borrow cupid's wings, | and ROM 1.04. 17
legs, | the cover of the wings of grasshoppers, 1.04. 63
with love's light wings did i o'erperch these 2.02. 66
and therefore hath the wind–swift cupid wings. 2.05. 8
for thou wilt lie upon the wings of night, 3.02. 18
i, with wings as swift | as meditation or the HAM 1.05. 29
save me, and hover o'er me with your wings, 3.04.103
i'll catch thine eyes | though they had wings. ANT 5.02.157
o, for a horse with wings! CYM 3.02. 48
would i had wings to follow it! 3.05.156 P
the king himself | of his wings destitute, the 5.03. 5
should clap their wings and sing | to all the TNK 4.02. 23
him, black and shining | like ravens' wings; 4.02. 84
shaking her wings, devouring all in haste, VEN 57
the hairs, who wave like feath'red wings. 306
borne by the trustless wings of false desire, LUC 2
to pluck the quills from ancient ravens' wings, 949
"the crow may bathe his coal–black wings in mire 1009
trumpet be, | to whose sound chaste wings obey. PHT 4
/WINK 2 FR 0.0002 REL FR 2 V 0 P
/like /the /sun, /did /make /beholders /wink? R2 4.01.284
/nor /wink, /nor /nod, /nor /kneel, /nor /make TIT 3.02. 43
WINK 31 FR 0.0035 REL FR 23 V 8 P
even | ambition cannot pierce a wink beyond, TMP 2.01.242
to the perpetual wink for aye might put | this 2.01.285
i see things too, although you judge | i wink. TGV 1.02.136
upon a homely object love can wink. 2.04. 98
eyes, | for i had rather wink than look on them. 5.02. 14
i'll wink and couch; WIV 5.05. 48
as good to wink, sweet love, as look on night. ERR 3.02. 58
and not be seen to wink of all the day — | when LLL 1.01. 43
now here is three studied ere ye'll thrice wink; 1.02. 51 P
wink each at other, hold the sweet jest up; MND 3.02.239
you saw my master wink and laugh upon you? SHR 4.04. 75 P
years removed thing | while one would wink; TN 5.01. 90
a cup, | to give mine enemy a lasting wink; WT 1.02.317
every wink of an eye some new grace will be born 5.02.110 P
fight, but i will wink and hold out mine iron. H5 2.01. 7 P
yet they do wink and yield, as love is blind and 5.02.300 P
i will wink on her to consent, my lord, if you 5.02.306 P
wink now; 2H6 2.01.103
wink at the duke of suffolk's insolence, | at 2.02. 70
that /th' runaway's eyes may wink, and romeo ROM 3.02. 6
good boy, wink at me, and say thou saw'st me not
TIM 3.01. 44 P
the eye wink at the hand; MAC 1.04. 52
to do this business | i have not slept one wink. CYM 3.04.100
going, but such as wink and will not use them. 5.04.186 P
pardon me, | if i were there, i'ld wink. TNK 5.03. 18
then wink again, | and i will wink, so shall the VEN 121
and i will wink, so shall the day seem night. 122
his eyes begun | to wink, being blinded with a LUC 375
who, if it wink, shall thereon fall and die. 1139
when most i wink, then do mine eyes best see, SON 43. 1
hungry eyes even till they wink with fullness, 56. 6
WINK'D 2 FR 0.0002 REL FR 1 V 1 P
i have not wink'd since i saw these sights. WT 3.03.104 P
shall not be wink'd at, how shall we stretch our H5 2.02. 55
/WINKING 1 FR 0.0001 REL FR 1 V 0 P
or given my heart a /winking, mute and dumb, HAM 2.02.137
WINKING 10 FR 0.0011 REL FR 7 V 3 P
/your city's eyes, your winking gates; JN 2.01.215
and on the winking of authority | to understand 4.02.211
death, | and, winking, leapt into destruction. 2H4 1.03. 33
that run winking into the mouth of a russian H5 3.07.143 P
my lord, teach your cousin to consent winking. 5.02.305 P
and i for winking at your discords too | have ROM 5.03.294
and winking mary–buds begin to ope their golden
CYM 2.03. 24
them) were two winking cupids | of silver, each 2.04. 89
i am sure hanging's the way of winking. 5.04.190 P
yet, winking, there appears | quick–shifting LUC 458
WINKS 4 FR 0.0004 REL FR 4 V 0 P
as her winks and nods and gestures yield them, HAM 4.05. 11
heaven stops the nose at it, and the moon winks; OTH 4.02. 77
pay, | he winks, and turns his lips another way. VEN 90
and moody pluto winks while orpheus plays. LUC 553
WINK'ST 1 FR 0.0001 REL FR 1 V 0 P
wink'st | whiles thou art waking. TMP 2.01.216
WINNER 6 FR 0.0006 REL FR 5 V 1 P
and, being a winner, god give you good night! SHR 5.02.187
the gentler gamester is the soonest winner. H5 3.06.113 P
draw both friend and foe, | winner and loser? HAM 4.05.144
i now | profess myself the winner of her honor, CYM 2.04. 53
sir, the event | is yet to name the winner. 3.05. 15
till heavens did | make hardly one the winner. TNK 5.03.130
WINNER'S 1 FR 0.0001 REL FR 1 V 0 P
about his head he wears the winner's oak, | and TNK 4.02.137
WINNERS 2 FR 0.0002 REL FR 2 V 0 P
go together, | you precious winners all; WT 5.03.131
beshrew the winners, for they play'd me false! 2H6 3.01.184
WINNING 5 FR 0.0005 REL FR 3 V 2 P
lest too light winning | make the prize light. TMP 1.02.452
and learn me how to lose a winning match, ROM 3.02. 12
would hazard the winning both of first and last. CYM 1.04. 93 P
winning will put any man into courage. 2.03. 7 P
is this winning? TNK 5.03.138
WINNOW 1 FR 0.0001 REL FR 1 V 0 P
torture shall | winnow the truth from falsehood. CYM 5.05.134
/WINNOW'D 1 FR 0.0001 REL FR 0 V 1 P
the most /profound and /winnow'd opinions, and HAM 5.02.192 P
WINNOW'D 1 FR 0.0001 REL FR 1 V 0 P
we shall be winnow'd with so rough a wind | that 2H4 4.01.192
WINNOWED 2 FR 0.0002 REL FR 2 V 0 P
good occasion | most throughly to be winnowed, H8 5.01.110
and weight | of such a winnowed purity in love! TRO 3.02.167
WINNOWS 1 FR 0.0001 REL FR 1 V 0 P
fan, | puffing at all, winnows the light away, TRO 1.03. 28
WINS 12 FR 0.0013 REL FR 9 V 3 P
his wife who wins me by that means i told you, MV 2.01. 19
whence honor but of danger wins a scar, | as oft AWW 3.02.121
this wins him, liver and all. TN 2.05. 95 P
that daily break–vow, he that wins of all, | of JN 2.01.569
whoever wins, on that side shall i lose; 3.01.335
your honor wins bad humors. H5 3.02. 26 P
and in conclusion wins the king from her | with 3H6 3.01. 50
corruption wins not more than honesty. H8 3.02.444
talk with them too — | who loses and who wins; LR 5.03. 15
so, so, so, so; they laugh that wins. OTH 4.01.122 P
when ye return, who wins i'll settle here; TNK 3.06.307
for whosoever wins | loses a noble cousin for 4.02.155
/WINTER 1 FR 0.0001 REL FR 1 V 0 P
/no /enemy | /but /winter /and /rough /weather. AYL 2.05. 45
WINTER 51 FR 0.0057 REL FR 44 V 7 P
flow'r | and make rough winter everlastingly. TGV 2.04.163
because it is an open room and good for winter. MM 2.01.132 P
the tallow in them will burn a poland winter: ERR 3.02. 99 P
this side is hiems, winter; LLL 5.02.891 P
the human mortals want their winter here; MND 2.01.101
the childing autumn, angry winter, change 2.01.112
warm'd and cool'd by the same winter and summer,
MV 3.01. 63 P
therefore my age is as a lusty winter, | frosty, AYL 2.03. 52
see | no enemy | but winter and rough weather. 2.05. 8
blow, blow, thou winter wind, | thou art not so 2.07.174
sure together, | as the winter to foul weather. 5.04.136
but thou know'st winter tames man, woman, and SHR 4.01. 23 P
a sad tale's best for winter. WT 2.01. 25
mountain, and still winter | in storm perpetual, 3.02.212
keep | seeming and savor all the winter long. 4.04. 75
well you fit our ages | with flow'rs of winter. 4.04. 79
nor on the birth | of trembling winter, the 4.04. 81
and none of you will bid the winter come | to JN 5.07. 36
as humorous as winter, and as sudden | as flaws 2H4 4.04. 34
which ever in the haunch of winter sings | the 4.04. 92
the winter coming on, and sickness growing H5 3.03. 55
after summer evermore succeeds | barren winter, 2H6 2.04. 3
that winter lion, who in rage forgets | aged 5.03. 2
that winter should cut off our spring–time so. 3H6 2.03. 47
cold biting winter mars our hop'd–for hay. 4.08. 61
now is the winter of our discontent | made R3 1.01. 1
when great leaves fall, then winter is at hand; 2.03. 33
be growing, | till death, that winter, kill it. H8 3.02.179
i'll take that winter from your lips, fair lady; TRO 4.05. 24
in winter with warm tears i'll melt the snow, TIT 3.01. 20
this goodly summer with your winter mix'd. 5.02.171
april on the heel | of limping winter treads, ROM 1.02. 28
one cloud of winter show'rs, | these flies are TIM 2.02.171
'tis deepest winter in lord timon's purse; 3.04. 14
nor more willingly leaves winter, such summer 3.06. 31 P
to teach thee there's no laboring i' th' winter. LR 2.04. 68 P
but riches fineless is as poor as winter | to OTH 3.03.173
for his bounty, | there was no winter in't; ANT 5.02. 87
tanlings and | the shrinking slaves of winter. CYM 4.04. 30
swear to th' gods that winter kills the flies, PER 4.03. 50
but dead–cold winter must inhabit here still. TNK 2.02. 45
lust's winter comes ere summer half be done; VEN 802
as winter meads when sun doth melt their snow. LUC 1218
but chide rough winter that the flow'r hath 1255
youth like summer morn, age like winter weather,
PP 12. 3
youth like summer brave, age like winter bare. 12. 4
on | to hideous winter and confounds him there, SON 5. 6
flowers distill'd, though they with winter meet, 5.13
as call it winter, which, being full of care, 56.13
how like a winter hath my absence been | from 97. 1
yet seem'd it winter still, and, you away, | as 98.13
WINTER–CRICKET 1 FR 0.0001 REL FR 1 V 0 P
thou flea, thou nit, thou winter–cricket thou! SHR 4.03.109
WINTER–GROUND 1 FR 0.0001 REL FR 1 V 0 P
are none, | to winter–ground thy corse — CYM 4.02.229
WINTERLY 1 FR 0.0001 REL FR 1 V 0 P
if winterly, thou need'st | but keep that CYM 3.04. 13
/WINTER'S 1 FR 0.0001 REL FR 1 V 0 P
should patch a wall t' expel the /winter's flaw! HAM 5.01.216
WINTER'S 21 FR 0.0023 REL FR 19 V 2 P
tears runs down his beard like winter's drops TMP 5.01. 16
hid | in sap–consuming winter's drizzled snow, ERR 5.01.313
and churlish chiding of the winter's wind, AYL 2.01. 7
a nun of winter's sisterhood kisses not more 3.04. 16 P
for the red blood reigns in the winter's pale. WT 4.03. 4
in winter's tedious nights sit by the fire R2 5.01. 40
and waste for churlish winter's tyranny. 2H4 1.03. 62
in winter's cold and summer's parching heat, 2H6 1.01. 81
well could i curse away a winter's night, 3.02.335
and kept low shrubs from winter's pow'rful wind. 3H6 5.02. 15
let aesop fable in a winter's night, | his 5.05. 25
have in our armors watch'd the winter's night, 5.07. 17
have with one winter's brush | fell from their TIM 4.03.264
both | endure the winter's cold as well as he; JC 1.02. 99
become | a woman's story at a winter's fire, MAC 3.04. 64
winter's not gone yet, if the wild geese fly LR 2.04. 46 P
quake in the present winter's state, and wish CYM 2.04. 5
o' th' sun, | nor the furious winter's rages, 4.02.259
then let not winter's ragged hand deface | in SON 6. 1
against the stormy gusts of winter's day | and 13.11
leaves look pale, dreading the winter's near. 97.14
/WINTERS 1 FR 0.0001 REL FR 1 V 0 P
/that /i /have /worn /so /many /winters /out R2 4.01.258
WINTERS 10 FR 0.0011 REL FR 10 V 0 P
till | thou hast howl'd away twelve winters. TMP 1.02.296
and six or seven winters more respect | than a MM 3.01. 75
a wither'd hermit, fivescore winters worn, LLL 4.03.238
on, | which sixteen winters cannot blow away, WT 5.03. 50
six frozen winters spent, | return with welcome R2 1.03.211
four lagging winters and four wanton springs 1.03.214
what is six winters? they are quickly gone. 1.03.260
i knew a man | of eighty winters — this i told TNK 5.01.108
when forty winters shall besiege thy brow, | and SON 2. 1
three winters cold | have from the forests shook 104. 3
WINTER–TIME 1 FR 0.0001 REL FR 1 V 0 P
doth all the winter–time, at still midnight, WIV 4.04. 30
WINT'RED 1 FR 0.0001 REL FR 1 V 0 P
wint'red garments must be lin'd, | so must AYL 3.02.105
/WIP'D 1 FR 0.0001 REL FR 1 V 0 P
shall be /wip'd out in the next parliament, 1H6 2.04.117
WIP'D 12 FR 0.0013 REL FR 11 V 1 P
feast, | if ever from your eyelids wip'd a tear, AYL 2.07.116
and wip'd our eyes | of drops that sacred pity 2.07.122
thy lips are scarce wip'd since thou drunk'st 1H4 2.04.153 P
this present grief had wip'd it from my mind. 2H4 1.01.211
why, yet thy scandal were not wip'd away, | but 2H6 2.04. 65
but with our sword we wip'd away the blot; 4.01. 40
have the soil of her fair rape | wip'd off, in TRO 2.02.149
but with his last attempt he wip'd it out, COR 5.03.146
hath from my soul | wip'd the black scruples, MAC 4.03.116
thing | from vassal actors can be wip'd away; LUC 608
and wip'd the brinish pearl from her bright eyes 1213
"how may this forced stain be wip'd from me? 1701
WIPE 27 FR 0.0030 REL FR 23 V 4 P
wipe thou thine eyes, have comfort. TMP 1.02. 25
last morning you could not see to wipe my shoes. TGV 2.01. 80 P
would from my forehead wipe a perjur'd note: LLL 4.03.123
wipe not out the rest of thy services by leaving WT 4.02. 10 P
from my succession wipe me, father, i | am heir 4.04.480
let me wipe off this honorable dew, | that JN 5.02. 45
wipe off the dust that hides our sceptre's gilt, R2 2.01.294
come let me wipe thy face. 2H4 2.04.217 P
and therefore will he wipe his tables clean 4.01.199
congeal'd with this, do make me wipe off both. 3H6 1.03. 52
child, | to bid the father wipe his eyes withal, 1.04.139
my tears shall wipe away these bloody marks; 2.05. 71
and bid her wipe her weeping eyes withal. R3 4.04.278
and to be executed ere they wipe their lips. COR 4.05.217 P
thou hast no hands to wipe away thy tears, | nor TIT 3.01.106
ah, my lavinia, i will wipe thy cheeks. 3.01.142
to heal rome's harms, and wipe away her woe! 5.03.148
to wipe out our ingratitude with loves | above TIM 5.04. 17
i'll wipe away all trivial fond records, | all HAM 1.05. 99
come, let me wipe thy face. 5.02.294
let me wipe it first, it smells of mortality. LR 4.06.133
wipe thine eyes; 5.03. 23
did i to–day | see cassio wipe his beard with. OTH 3.03.439
if we contend, | out of our question wipe him. ANT 2.02. 81
wipe thine eyes: CYM 4.02.402
worse than a slavish wipe or birth–hour's blot; LUC 537
and wipe the dim mist from thy doting eyne, 643
WIPED 1 FR 0.0001 REL FR 1 V 0 P
ne'er shall this blood be wiped from thy point, 2H6 4.10. 69
WIPES 1 FR 0.0001 REL FR 0 V 1 P
obedience to the king wipes the crime of it out H5 4.01.133 P
WIPING 1 FR 0.0001 REL FR 1 V 0 P

bloody brow | with his mail'd hand then wiping, COR 1.03. 35
WIRE 1 FR 0.0001 REL FR 1 V 0 P
thou shalt be whipt with wire, and stew'd in ANT 2.05. 65
WIRES 2 FR 0.0002 REL FR 2 V 0 P
if hairs be wires, black wires grow on her head. SON 130. 4
if hairs be wires, black wires grow on her head. 130. 4
WIRY 2 FR 0.0002 REL FR 2 V 0 P
even to that drop ten thousand wiry /friends JN 3.04. 64
the wiry concord that mine ear confounds, | do i SON 128. 4
WIS 1 FR 0.0001 REL FR 1 V 0 P
have you seen a mighty king | his child, i wis, PER 2.ch. 2
/WISDOM 1 FR 0.0001 REL FR 1 V 0 P
/wisdom /and /goodness /to /the /vild /seem LR 4.02. 38
WISDOM 99 FR 0.0112 REL FR 83 V 16 P
be it as your wisdom will. MM 2.01. 32
thus wisdom wishes to appear most bright | when 2.04. 78
upon this riddle runs the wisdom of the world. 3.02.229 P
show your wisdom, daughter, in your close 4.03.118
can, pace your wisdom | in that good path that i 4.03.132
madness, pray heaven his wisdom be not tainted! 4.04. 5 P
this — your long experience of /her wisdom, ERR 3.01. 89
wisdom and blood combating in so tender a body,
ADO 2.03.163 P
and 'tis not wisdom thus to second grief 5.01. 2
folly, in wisdom hatch'd, | hath wisdom's LLL 5.02. 70
in your rich wisdom to excuse or hide | the 5.02.732
purpose to be dress'd in an opinion | of wisdom, MV 1.01. 92
they have the wisdom by their wit to lose. 2.09. 81
have by your wisdom been this day acquitted | of 4.01.409
ay, marry, now unmuzzle your wisdom. AYL 1.02. 70 P
the wisdom of your duty, fair bianca, | hath SHR 5.02.127
see | cold wisdom waiting on superfluous folly. AWW 1.01.105
his love and wisdom, | approv'd so to your 1.02. 9
wisdom, and constancy, hath amaz'd me more 2.01. 84
youth, beauty, wisdom, courage — all | that 2.01.181
shall see you, so | i leave you to your wisdom. 2.05. 71
thus your own proper wisdom | brings in the 4.02. 49
well, god give them wisdom that have it; TN 1.05. 14 P
i think i saw your wisdom there. 3.01. 41 P
let thy fair wisdom, not thy passion, sway | in 4.01. 52
what wisdom stirs amongst you? WT 2.01. 21
with wisdom i might fear, my doricles, | you 4.04.150
do | what you in wisdom still vouchsafe to say. JN 2.01.523
didst well, for wisdom cries out in the streets, 1H4 1.02. 88 P
some that know not why he is away | that wisdom, 4.01. 64
and 'tis but wisdom to make strong against him. 4.04. 39
sweet earl, divorce not wisdom from your honor, 2H4 1.01.162
do what you will, your wisdom be your guide. 2.03. 6
though 'tis no wisdom to confess so much | unto H5 3.06.143
now is it manhood, wisdom, and defense | to give 2H6 5.02. 75
whose wisdom was a mirror to the wisest; 3H6 3.03. 84
till then, 'tis wisdom to conceal our meaning. 4.07. 60
you may, sir, 'tis a point of wisdom. R3 1.04. 98 P
your discipline in war, wisdom in peace, | your 3.07. 16
men than they can be | out of a foreign wisdom, H8 1.03. 29
your grace has given a president of wisdom 2.02. 85
and of wisdom | o'ertopping woman's pow'r. 2.04. 87
out of which frailty | and want of wisdom, you, 5.02. 48
some understanding | and wisdom of my council; 5.02.171
never | more covetous of wisdom and fair virtue 5.04. 24
count wisdom as no member of the war, TRO 1.03.198
if you'll avouch 'twas wisdom paris went — | as 2.02. 84
the amity that wisdom knits not, folly may 2.03.101 P
i will not praise thy wisdom, | which, like a 2.03.248
and since the wisdom of their choice is rather COR 2.03. 98 P
where gentry, title, wisdom, | cannot conclude 3.01.144
whose wisdom hath her fortune conquered. TIT 1.01.336
say thou hadst suck'd wisdom from thy teat. ROM 1.03. 68
and why, my lady wisdom? 3.05.170
and in his wisdom hastes our marriage, | to stop 4.01. 11
if in thy wisdom thou canst give no help, | do 4.01. 52
than the judge, | if wisdom be in suffering. TIM 3.05. 51
lord, | your wisdom is consum'd in confidence. JC 2.02. 49
i doubt not of your wisdom. 3.01.183
censure me in your wisdom, and awake your senses 3.02. 16 P
he hath a wisdom that doth guide his valor | to MAC 3.01. 52
death, and bear | his hopes 'bove wisdom, grace, 3.05. 31
t' hold what distance | his wisdom can provide. 3.06. 45
not | whether it was his wisdom or his fear. 4.02. 5
wisdom? 4.02. 6
as little is the wisdom, where the flight | so 4.02. 13
him through me, and wisdom | to offer up a weak, 4.03. 15
his power, and modest wisdom plucks me | from 4.03.119
it fits your wisdom so far to believe it | as he HAM 1.03. 25
truth, | and thus do we of wisdom and of reach, 2.01. 61
him where | your wisdom best shall think. 3.01.187
your wisdom should show itself more richer to 3.02.304 P
thought which quarter'd hath but one part wisdom 4.04. 42
greatness, wisdom, all things else | you mainly 4.07. 8
dangerous, | which let thy wisdom fear. 5.01.263
frame the business after your own wisdom. LR 1.02. 99 P
though the wisdom of nature can reason it thus 1.02.104 P
go to, have you wisdom? 1.04. 92 P
i would you would make use of your good wisdom 1.04.219
/you are much more /attax'd for want of wisdom 1.04.343
apt | to have his ear abus'd, wisdom bids fear. 2.04.307
what can man's wisdom | in the restoring his 4.04. 8
you, | i pray desire her call her wisdom to her. 4.05. 35
in wisdom i should ask thy name, | but, since 5.03.142
she that in wisdom never was so frail | to OTH 2.01.154
and that in wholesome wisdom | he might not but 3.01. 46
faults that are not), that your wisdom /then, 3.03.148
good, | nor for my manhood, honesty, and wisdom, 3.03.153
if beauty, wisdom, modesty, can settle | the ANT 2.02.240
wisdom and fortune combating together, | if that 3.13. 79
cleopatra, i approve | your wisdom in the deed. 5.02.150
with what patience | your wisdom may inform you.
CYM 1.01. 79
for wisdom sees those men | blush not in actions PER 1.01.134
who by thy wisdom makes a prince thy servant, 1.02. 64
to wisdom he's a fool that will not yield; 2.04. 54
that were a cruel wisdom! TNK 3.06.242
are you men of wisdom or what are you? STM II.C 35 P
what you will have them, but not men of wisdom. II.C 37
herein lives wisdom, beauty, and increase, SON 11. 5
WISDOM'S 4 FR 0.0004 REL FR 4 V 0 P
for wisdom's sake, a word that all men love, LLL 4.03.354
hath wisdom's warrant and the help of school, 5.02. 71
speech, | her words yclad with wisdom's majesty, 2H6 1.01. 33
thee i lay, whose wisdom's strength can bear it. PER 1.02.119
/WISDOMS 1 FR 0.0001 REL FR 1 V 0 P
argues your /wisdoms and your love to richard" R3 3.07. 40
WISDOMS 7 FR 0.0008 REL FR 6 V 1 P
honor, | and if their wisdoms be misled in this, ADO 4.01.187
what your wisdoms could not discover, these 5.01.232 P
as your wisdoms best | shall see advantageable H5 5.02. 87
my lords, what to your wisdoms seemeth best, 2H6 3.01.195
you now | the issue of your proper wisdoms rate, TRO 2.02. 89
five tribunes to defend their vulgar wisdoms, COR 1.01.215
nor have we herein barr'd | your better wisdoms, HAM 1.02. 15
/WISE* 1 FR 0.0001 REL FR 1 V 0 P
/wise /in /our /negligence, /have /secret /feet LR 3.01. 32
WISE* 175 FR 0.0197 REL FR 116 V 59 P
so rare a wond'red father and a wise | makes TMP 4.01.123
and i'll be wise hereafter, | and seek for grace 5.01.295
methinks should not be chronicled for wise. TGV 1.01. 41
wise. 2.04. 15 P
holy, fair, and wise is she; 4.02. 41
valiant, wise, remorseful, well accomplish'd: 4.03. 13
"convey," the wise it call. WIV 1.03. 29 P
he is wise, sir; 2.03. 10 P
you have show'd yourself a wise physician, and 2.03. 54 P
hath shown himself a wise and patient churchman. 2.03. 55 P
you, sir, was't not the wise woman of brainford? 4.05. 26 P
was there a wise woman with thee? 4.05. 58 P
you are wise and full of gibes and 4.05. 80 P
too, but that a wise burgher put in for them. MM 1.02.100 P
this comes off well. here's a wise officer. 2.01. 57 P
if it were damnable, he being so wise, | why 3.01.112
file of the subject held the duke to be wise. 3.02.137 P
wise? why, no question but he was. 3.02.138 P
i am sorry, one so learned and so wise | as you, 5.01.470
master, be wise, and if you give it her, | the ERR 4.03. 75
another is wise, yet i am well; ADO 2.03. 27 P
wise, or i'll none; 2.03. 31 P
and she is exceeding wise. 2.03.161 P
before god! and, in my mind, very wise. 2.03.185 P
the managing of quarrels you may say he is wise, 2.03.190 P
and wise, but for loving me; 2.03.233 P
how wise, how noble, young, how rarely featur'd, 3.01. 60
studied eight or nine wise words to speak to you 3.02. 72 P
i am a wise fellow, and, which is more, an 4.02. 80 P
"nay," said i, "the gentleman is wise." 5.01.165 P
"certain," said she, "a wise gentleman." 5.01.165 P
thou and i are too wise to woo peaceably. 5.02. 72 P
there's not one wise man among twenty that will 5.02. 74 P
therefore is it most expedient for the wise, if 5.02. 84 P
lord, how wise you are! LLL 1.02.138 P
than you much willing to be counted wise | in 2.01. 18
were my lord so, his ignorance were wise, 2.01.102
do the wise think them other? 3.01. 80
what fool is not so wise | to lose an oath to 4.03. 70
we are wise girls to mock our lovers so. 5.02. 58
not so strong a note | as fool'ry in the wise, 5.02. 76
sweet, | your wits makes wise things foolish. 5.02.374
wise things seem foolish and rich things but 5.02.378
this proves you wise and rich, for in my eye — 5.02.379
thou art as wise as thou art beautiful. MND 3.01.148
that therefore only are reputed wise | for MV 1.01. 96
i must be one of these same dumb wise men, | for 1.01.106
was | (as his wise mother wrought in his behalf) 1.03. 73
it is a wise father that knows his own child. 2.02. 76 P
for she is wise, if i can judge of her, | and 2.06. 53
and therefore, like herself, wise, fair, and 2.06. 56
had you been as wise as bold, | young in limbs, 2.07. 70
o wise young judge, how i do honor thee! 4.01.224
o wise and upright judge! 4.01.250
though yet i know no wise remedy how to avoid it
AYL 1.01. 25 P
may not speak wisely what wise men do foolishly. 1.02. 87 P
little foolery that wise men have makes a great 1.02. 90 P
that grows rank in them | that i am wise. 2.07. 47
the wise man's folly is anatomiz'd | even by the 2.07. 56
cut, | full of wise saws and modern instances; 2.07.156
learn of the wise, and perpend: 3.02. 67 P
o, but she is wise. 4.01.159 P
art thou wise? 5.01. 28 P
"the fool doth think he is wise, but the wise 5.01. 31 P
but the wise man knows himself to be a fool." 5.01. 32 P
am i not wise? SHR 2.01.265
though he be blunt, i know him passing wise; 3.02. 24
she is young, wise, fair, | in these to nature AWW 2.03.131
for two ordinaries, to be a pretty wise fellow. 2.03.202 P
am sure i lack thee, may pass for a wise man. TN 1.05. 35 P
infirmity, that decays the wise, doth ever make 1.05. 76 P
i protest i take these wise men that crow so at 1.05. 88 P
meeting, | every wise man's son doth know." 2.03. 44
this fellow is wise enough to play the fool, 3.01. 60
practice | as full of labor as a wise man's art; 3.01. 66
but wise /men, folly–fall'n, quite taint their 3.01. 68
carry his water to th' wise woman. 3.04.102 P
these wise men that give fools money get 4.01. 22 P
are to a wise man ports and happy havens. R2 1.03.276
as praises, of whose taste the wise are /fond, 2.01. 18
my lord, wise men ne'er sit and wail their woes, 3.02.178
in me it seems it will make wise men mad. 5.05. 63
i know you wise, but yet no farther wise | than 1H4 2.03.107
but yet no farther wise | than harry percy's 2.03.107
the wise may make some dram of a scruple, or 2H4 1.02.130 P
the spirits of the wise sit in the clouds and 2.02.143 P
is certain that either wise bearing or ignorant 5.01. 75 P
to your well–practic'd wise directions. 5.02.121
appear more wise and modest to the world. 5.05.101
be wise and circumspect. 2H6 1.01.157
believe me, lords, were none more wise than i — 3.01.231
if this fellow be wise, he'll never call ye jack 4.06. 9 P
for wise men say it is the wisest course. 3H6 3.01. 25
and after that wise prince, henry the fift, 3.03. 85
and now may seem as wise as virtuous | by spying 4.06. 27
a wise stout captain, and soon persuaded! 4.07. 30
lords, wise men ne'er sit and wail their loss, 5.04. 1
we say the king | is wise and virtuous, and his R3 1.01. 91
young, valiant, wise, and (no doubt) right royal 1.02.244
clouds are seen, wise men put on their cloaks; 2.03. 32
so wise so young, they say do never live long. 3.01. 79
full of wise care is this your counsel, madam; 4.01. 47
to think an english courtier may be wise | and H8 1.03. 22
that they had gather'd a wise council to them 2.04. 51
exceeding wise, fair–spoken, and persuading; 4.02. 52
i know you wise, religious, | and, let me tell 5.01. 28
not only good and wise but most religious; 5.02.151
the wise and fool, the artist and unread, | the TRO 1.03. 24
thou great, and wise, to hear ulysses speak. 1.03. 69
modest doubt is call'd | the beacon of the wise, 2.02. 16
as strong, as valiant, as wise, no less noble, 2.03.149 P
he must, he is, he cannot but be wise. 2.03.252
to angle for your thoughts, but you are wise, 3.02.155
for to be wise and love | exceeds man's might; 3.02.156
of this most wise rebellion, thou goest foremost COR 1.01.158
moe noble blows than ever thou wise words, | and 4.02. 21
and wise laertes' son | did graciously plead for TIT 1.01.380
thy life–blood out, if aaron now be wise, | then 4.04. 37
she is too fair, too wise, wisely too fair, | to ROM 1.01.221
and a good lady, and a wise and virtuous. 1.05.114
he is wise, | and, on my life, hath stol'n him 2.01. 3
how should they when that wise men have no eyes? 3.03. 62
no help, | do thou but call my resolution wise, 4.01. 53
now, captain, what do you in this wise company? TIM 2.02. 74 P
nor thou altogether a wise man; 2.02.116 P
flaminius, i have noted thee always wise. 3.01. 31 P
lord's a bountiful gentleman, but thou art wise, 3.01. 40 P
methinks thou art more honest now than wise; 4.03.502
brutus is wise, and, were he not in health, | he JC 2.01.258
brutus is noble, wise, valiant, and honest; 3.01.126
thy master is a wise and valiant roman, | i 3.01.138
they are wise and honorable, | and will no doubt 3.02.214
who can be wise, amaz'd, temp'rate, and furious, MAC 2.03.108
he is noble, wise, judicious, and best knows 4.02. 16
for wise men know well enough what monsters you
HAM 3.01.138 P
for who, that's but a queen, fair, sober, wise, 3.04.189
converse with him that is wise and says little, LR 1.04. 15 P
in a year, | for wise men are grown foppish, 1.04.167
as you are old and reverend, should be wise. 1.04.240
not have been old till thou hadst been wise. 1.05. 45 P
when a wise man gives thee better counsel, give 2.04. 75 P
the fool will stay, | and let the wise man fly. 2.04. 83
a night pities neither wise men nor fools. 3.02. 13 P
and a codpiece — that's a wise man and a fool. 3.02. 41 P
if't be your pleasure and most wise consent OTH 1.01.121
if she be fair and wise, fairness and wit, | the 2.01.129
does foul pranks which fair and wise ones do. 2.01.142
i should be wise — for honesty's a fool | and 3.03.382
nay, yet be wise; 3.03.432
o, thou art wise; 'tis certain. 4.01. 74
are you wise? 4.01.234
be wise, and get you home. 5.02.223
which the wise pow'rs | deny us for our good; ANT 2.01. 6
the wise gods seel our eyes, | in our own filth 3.13.112
to be trusted but in the keeping of wise people; 5.02.266 P
his to be more fair, virtuous, wise, chaste, CYM 1.04. 60 P
but if i were as wise as honest, then | my 3.04.118
that i reverence, those i fear — the wise: 4.02. 95
it was wise nature's end in the donation, | to 5.05.367
i perceive he was a wise fellow and had good PER 1.03. 4 P
most wise in general, tell me, if thou canst, 5.01.183
but in no wise | till he had done his sacrifice, 5.02. 11
a woman, would be master, | but you are wise. TNK 2.05. 64
i hope too wise for that, sir. 2.05. 64
be wise then | and here forget 'em; 3.06.222
is't not a wise course? 4.01.127
come hither, you are a wise man. 4.01.141
if wise nature, | with all her best endowments, 4.02. 7
how love is wise in folly, foolish witty. VEN 838
strike the wise dumb, and teach the fool to 1146
priam, why art thou old, and yet not wise? LUC 1550
what fool is not so wise | to break an oath, to PP 3.13
in howling wise, to see my doleful plight. 17.22
lest the wise world should look into your moan, SON 71.13
be wise as thou art cruel, do not press | my 140. 1
WISELIER 1 FR 0.0001 REL FR 0 V 1 P
you have taken it wiselier than i meant you TMP 2.01. 21 P
WISELY 32 FR 0.0036 REL FR 17 V 15 P
then wisely, good sir, weigh | our sorrow with TMP 2.01. 8
speak scholarly and wisely. WIV 1.03. 3 P
if i could speak so wisely under an arrest, i MM 1.02.131 P
and we must do it wisely. ADO 3.05. 60 P
the neck of my heart, says very wisely to me, MV 2.02. 14 P
that fools may not speak wisely what wise men do
AYL 1.02. 87 P
eye, | says very wisely, "it is ten a' clock. 2.07. 22
he that a fool doth very wisely hit | doth very 2.07. 53
but whether wisely or no, let the forest judge. 3.02.121 P
make your excuse wisely, you were best. TN 1.05. 30 P
for folly that he wisely shows is fit, | but 3.01. 67
very wisely, puppies! WT 4.04.706 P
and yet he talk'd very wisely, but i regarded 1H4 1.02. 86 P
i regarded him not, and yet he talk'd wisely, 1.02. 87 P
love, | pleading so wisely in excuse of it! 2H4 4.05.180
most wisely hath ulysses here discover'd | the TRO 1.03.138
know they what they speak that speak so wisely. 3.02.152
she is too fair, too wise, wisely too fair, | to ROM 1.01.221
wisely and slow, they stumble that run fast. 2.03. 94
very well took, i' faith, wisely, wisely. 2.04.126 P
very well took, i' faith, wisely, wisely. 2.04.126 P
marry, i will, and this is wisely done. 3.05.234
he's truly valiant that can wisely suffer | the TIM 3.05. 31
ay, and wisely. JC 3.03. 11 P
man directly and briefly, wisely and truly: 3.03. 16 P
wisely i say, i am a bachelor. 3.03. 16 P
and very wisely threat before you sting. 5.01. 38
ay, and wisely too; MAC 3.06. 14
you shall do marvell's wisely, good reynaldo, HAM 2.01. 3
and, as you said, and wisely was it said, | 'tis 3.03. 30
of one that lov'd not wisely but too well; OTH 5.02.344
this case of favor would | be wisely definite; CYM 1.06. 43
WISER 16 FR 0.0018 REL FR 6 V 10 P
he is the wiser man, master doctor: WIV 2.03. 38 P
which is the wiser here: MM 2.01.172 P
wrench awe from fools and tie the wiser souls 2.04. 14
albeit my wrongs might make one wiser mad. ERR 5.01.217
thus men may grow wiser every day. AYL 1.02.137 P
thou speak'st wiser than thou art ware of. 2.04. 57 P
the wiser, the waywarder. 4.01.161 P

question, hoping to be the wiser by your answer. AWW 2.02. 39 P
well, i shall be wiser. 2.03.223 P
marry, you are the wiser man; 2.04. 23 P
cut, he may be ransom'd, and we ne'er the wiser. H5 4.01.194 P
the law, | good faith, i am no wiser than a daw. 1H6 2.04. 18
he hath a lady, wiser, fairer, truer, | than TRO 1.03.275
fellow | loaden with irons wiser than the judge, TIM 3.05. 50
you are a friend, and therein the wiser. CYM 1.04.134 P
take counsel of some wiser head, | neither too PP 18. 5

WISEST 13 FR 0.0014 REL FR 11 V 2 P
his fit now, and does not talk after the wisest. TMP 2.02. 74 P
the wisest aunt, telling the saddest tale, MND 2.01. 51
cunning times put on | to entrap the wisest. MV 3.02.101
'twas a fear | which oft infects the wisest: WT 1.02.262
but the wisest beholder, that knew no more but 5.02. 16 P
for wise men say it is the wisest course. 3H6 3.01. 25
whose wisdom was a mirror to the wisest; 3.03. 84
the wisest prince that there had reign'd by many H8 2.04. 49
you wisest grecians, pardon me this brag. TRO 4.05.257
nature | that we with wisest sorrow think on him HAM 1.02. 6
we'll call up our wisest friends | and let them 4.01. 38
choice of whom your wisest friends you will, 4.05.205
name is great | in mouths of wisest censure. OTH 2.03.193

WISH 242 FR 0.0273 REL FR 208 V 34 P
i wish mine eyes | would, with themselves, shut TMP 2.01.191
i would not wish | any companion in the world 3.01. 54
we wish your peace. 4.01.163
i wish | myself were mudded in that oozy bed 5.01.150
embrace his heart | that doth not wish you joy! 5.01.215
wish me partaker in thy happiness | when thou TGV 1.01. 14
and how stand you affected to his wish? 1.03. 60
will, | and not depending on his friendly wish. 1.03. 62
my will is something sorted with his wish: 1.03. 63
you have your wish; 4.02. 93
me, | as much i wish all good befortune you. 4.03. 41
bear witness, heaven, i have my wish for ever. 5.04.119
anne is a good girl, and i wish — WIV 1.04. 35 P
now shall i sin in my wish: 3.03. 49 P
herself might be her chooser) | even to my wish. 4.06. 12
come in, the wish deserves a welcome. MM 3.01. 45
but wheresoever, i wish him well. 3.02. 90 P
and well could wish | you had not found me here 4.01. 10
in that good path that i would wish it go, | and 4.03.133
i wish you now then. 5.01. 79
i wish him joy of her. ADO 2.01.193 P
well, and i could wish he would modestly examine 2.03.207 P
benedick, | to wish him wrastle with affection, 3.01. 42
liver, | and wish he had not so accused her — 4.01.232
i wish your worship well. 5.01.324 P
than wish a snow in may's new-fangled shows; LLL 1.01.106
thy own wish wish i thee in every place. 2.01.178
thy own wish wish i thee in every place. 2.01.178
o heavens, i have my wish! 4.03. 79
o that i had my wish! 4.03. 90
dost thou not wish in heart | the chain were 5.02. 55
then wish me better, i will give you leave. 5.02.342
and i will wish thee never more to dance, | nor 5.02.400
i wish you the peace of mind, most royal 5.02.531 P
with threefold love i wish you all these three. 5.02.825
with half that wish the wisher's eyes be press'd MND 2.02. 65
or "fair ladies, i would wish you," or "i would 3.01. 39 P
now i do wish it, love it, long for it, | and 4.01.175
me, | but if you do, you'll make me wish a sin, MV 3.02. 13
i would not be ambitious in my wish | to wish 3.02.151
in my wish | to wish myself much better, yet, 3.02.152
i wish you all the joy that you can wish; 3.02.190
i wish you all the joy that you can wish; 3.02.190
for i am sure you can wish none from me; 3.02.191
i wish your ladyship all heart's content. 3.04. 42
i thank you for your wish, and am well pleas'd 3.04. 43
and am well pleas'd | to wish it back on you. 3.04. 44
and wish, for all that, that i had not kill'd 3.04. 73
the wish would make else an unquiet house. 4.01.294
i wish you well, and so i take my leave. 4.01.420
i should wish it dark | till i were couching 5.01.304
o, a good wish upon you! AYL 1.03. 24 P
and wish, for her sake more than for mine own, 2.04. 76
do you wish then that the gods had made me 3.03. 23 P
she delights, i will wish him to her father. SHR 1.01.112 P
i, faith, boy, to have the next wish after, 1.01.239
and wish thee to a shrewd ill-favor'd wife? 1.02. 60
much my friend, | and i'll not wish thee to her. 1.02. 64
regard, | to wish me wed to one half lunatic, 2.01.287
not so well apparell'd | as i wish you were. 3.02. 90
that i wish well. 'tis pity — AWW 1.01.179
i, after him, do after him wish too, | since i 1.02. 64
i wish might be found in the calendar of my past 1.03. 4 P
flame of liking | wish chastely and love dearly, 1.03.212
as one near death to those that wish him live. 2.01.131
my wish receive, | which great love grant, and 2.03. 84
nor would i wish you. 3.07. 7
my lord, and i wish it happily effected. 4.05. 79 P
i wish it might, for now i am your fool. TN 3.01.144
and i wish, my liege, | you had only in your WT 2.01.170
no more than were i painted i would wish | this 4.04.101
you do dance, i wish you | a wave o' th' sea, 4.04.140
madam, i would not wish a better father. JN 1.01.260
lo upon thy wish | our messenger chatillion is 2.01. 50
father, i may not wish the fortune thine; 3.01.333
grandam, i will not wish thy wishes thrive: 3.01.334
i had a mighty cause | to wish him dead, but 4.02.206
and wish (so please my sovereign) ere i move, R2 1.01. 45
take from my mouth the wish of happy years. 1.03. 94
then treasons make me wish myself a beggar, 5.05. 33
first, to thy sacred state wish i all happiness. 5.06. 6
though i did wish him dead, | i hate the 5.06. 39
o, i could wish this tavern were my drum! 1H4 3.03.206
as good as heart can wish: 2H4 1.01. 13
here doth he wish his person, with such powers 4.01. 10
you wish me health in very happy season, | for i 4.02. 79
and every thing lies level to our wish. 4.04. 7
thy wish was father, harry, to that thought: 4.05. 92
sword, | and i do wish your honors may increase, 5.02.104
with an inward wish | you would desire the king H5 1.01. 39
nor leave not one behind that doth not wish 2.02. 23
he could wish himself in thames up to the neck; 4.01.114 P
i think he would not wish himself any where but 4.01.119 P
you love him not so ill to wish him here alone, 4.01.124 P
god's will, i pray thee wish not one man more. 4.03. 23
no, faith, my coz, wish not a man from england. 4.03. 30
o, do not wish one more! 4.03. 33
thou dost not wish more help from england, coz? 4.03. 73
which likes me better than to wish us one. 4.03. 77
in the way for my wish shall show me the way to 5.02.328 P
the rest i wish thee gather; 1H6 2.05. 96
which is so plain that exeter doth wish | his 3.01.199
i wish some ravenous wolf had eaten thee! 5.04. 31
be as free as heart can wish or tongue can tell. 2H6 4.07.125 P
a king | as i do long and wish to be a subject. 4.09. 6
so wish i, i might thrust thy soul to hell. 4.10. 79
you shall have pay and every thing you wish. 5.01. 47
why, now thou hast thy wish: 3H6 1.04.143
so do i wish the crown, being so far off, | and 3.02.140
god forbid that i should wish them sever'd 4.01. 21
i rather wish you foes than hollow friends. 4.01.139
from those that wish the downfall of our house! 5.06. 65
the death of thee | than i can wish to wolves — R3 1.02. 19
though i wish thy death, | i will not be thy 1.02.184
(whom god preserve better than you would wish!) 1.03. 59
exceeding those that i can wish upon thee, | o, 1.03.217
the day will come that thou shalt wish for me 1.03.244
glory, | to feed my humor wish thyself no harm. 4.01. 64
i look'd on richard's face, | this was my wish: 4.01. 71
i wish the bastards dead, | and i would have it 4.02. 18
that i should wish for thee to help me curse 4.04. 80
and could wish he were | something mistaken in't H8 1.01.194
not friended by his wish, to your high person; 1.02.140
o' my conscience, | wish him ten fadom deep. 2.01. 51
that sought it i could wish more christians. 2.01. 64
ye tell me what ye wish for both — my ruin. 3.01. 98
i will not wish ye half my miseries, | i have 3.01.108
wherein he appears | as i would wish mine enemy. 3.02. 28
may you be happy in your wish, my lord, | for i 3.02. 43
speedily i wish | to hear from rome. 3.02. 89
after my death i wish no other herald, | no 4.02. 69
as you wish christian peace to souls departed, 4.02.156
stock, sir thomas, | i wish it grubb'd up now. 5.01. 23
i wish your highness | a quiet night, and my 5.01. 76
i would not wish a drop of troyan blood | spent TRO 2.02.197
fraction is more our wish than their faction. 2.03. 98 P
'tis agamemnon's wish, and great achilles | doth 4.05.152
thing but what i am, | i would wish me only he. COR 1.01.232
i will wish her speedy strength, and visit her 1.03. 78 P
i wish you much mirth. 1.03.110 P
thou wast a soldier | even to /cato's wish, not 1.04. 57
gods | lead their successes as we wish our own, 1.06. 7
though i could wish | you were conducted to a 1.06. 62
i wish no better | than have him hold that 2.01.239
to our noble consul | wish we all joy and honor. 2.02.153
i wish i had a cause to seek him there, | to 3.01. 19
long, and wish | to jump a body with a dangerous 3.01.153
why did you wish me milder? 3.02. 14
a noble wish. 3.03. 38
rais'd only that the weaker sort may wish | good 4.06. 70
yet i wish, sir | (i mean for your particular), 4.07. 12
though we had | our wish, which side should win; 5.03.113
nor wish no less, and so i take my leave. TIT 1.01.402
a charitable wish, and full of love. 4.02. 43
oft have you heard me wish for such an hour, 5.02.159
which i wish may prove | more stern and bloody 5.02.202
live to see thee married once, | i have my wish. ROM 1.03. 62
and wish his mistress were that kind of fruit 2.01. 35
and yet i wish but for the thing i have. 2.02.132
blister'd be thy tongue | for such a wish! 3.02. 91
proportion'd as one's thought would wish a man, 3.05.182
is it more sin to wish me thus forsworn, | or to 3.05.236
i could wish my best friend at such a feast. TIM 1.02. 79 P
i also wish it to you. 3.06. 2 P
who would not wish to be from wealth exempt, 4.02. 31
for thy part, i do wish thou wert a dog, | that 4.03. 55
the other, at high wish. 4.03.245
i'd exchange | for this one wish, that you had 4.03.521
neither wish i | you take much pains to mend. 5.01. 88
and every one doth wish | you had but that JC 2.01. 91
your best friends shall wish i had been further. 2.02.125
i wish your enterprise to-day may thrive. 3.01. 13
i wish we may; 3.01.144
he comes upon a wish. 3.02.266
hath given me some worthy cause to wish | things 4.02. 8
i wish your horses swift and sure of foot; MAC 3.01. 37
and wish th' estate o' th' world were now undone 5.05. 49
i would not wish them to a fairer death. 5.09. 15
i do wish | that your good beauties be the happy HAM 3.01. 37
madam, i wish it may. 3.01. 41
that he could nothing do but wish and beg | your 4.07.104
i cannot wish the fault undone, the issue of it LR 1.01. 17 P
so | will you wish on me, when the rash mood is 2.04.169
fled from her wish, and yet said, "now i may"; OTH 2.01.151
i could well wish courtesy would invent some 2.03. 34 P
as men in rage strike those that wish them best, 2.03.243
i could heartily wish this had not befall'n; 2.03.301 P
and think it no addition, nor my wish, | to have 3.04.194
ay, you did wish that i would make her turn. 4.01.252
a womb, | and /fertile every wish, a million. ANT 1.02. 39
often hurl from us, | we wish it ours again. 1.02.124
i wish, forbear. 1.03. 11
now, sirrah; you do wish yourself in egypt? 2.03. 10
and her forehead | as low as she would wish it. 3.03. 34
i wish i could be made so many men, | and all of 4.02. 16
say that i wish he never find more cause | to 4.05. 15
i wish you all joy of the worm. 5.02.260 P
yes, forsooth; i wish you joy o' th' worm. 5.02.279 P
i wish not so, unless it had been the fall of an CYM 1.02. 36 P
state, and wish | that warmer days would come. 2.04. 5
i wish ye sport. 4.02. 31
i wish my brother make good time with him, | you 4.02.108
profit, but my wish hath a preferment in't. 5.04.206 P
i know not how to wish | a pair of worthier sons 5.05.355
i life would wish, and that i might | waste it PER 1.ch. 15
of all 'say'd yet, i wish thee happiness! 1.01. 60
i would wish no better office than to be beadle. 2.01. 92 P
to my desires, i could wish to make one there. 2.01.112 P
and for his sake i wish the having of it; 2.01.139
take i your wish, i leap into the seas, 2.04. 43
sail seas in cockles, have and wish but for't, 4.04. 2
what canst thou wish thine enemy to be? 4.06.158
why, i could wish him to be my master, or rather 4.06.159 P
you wish me well. 5.01. 16
yet let me obtain my wish. 5.01. 35
i/'d wish no better choice, and think me rarely 5.01. 69
receive such pay | as thy desires can wish. 5.01. 75
and as you wish your womb may thrive with fair TNK 1.01. 27
and wish great juno would | resume her ancient 1.02. 21
yet i wish him | excess and overflow of power, 1.03. 3
a rebuke that i could wish myself a sigh to be 2.01. 43 P
garlands, | ere they have time to wish 'em ours. 2.02. 17
an offer'd opportunity | i durst not wish for. 2.03. 75
to your travel, | nor shall you lose your wish. 2.05. 31
without hypocrisy i may not wish | more than my 3.01. 95
i could wish ye | as kind a kinsman as you force 3.06. 20
and i could wish i had not said i lov'd her, 3.06. 40
i wish his weary soul that falls may win it. 3.06.100
i grant your wish, for, to say true, your cousin 3.06.180
his lineaments | are as a man would wish 'em, 4.02.114
i wish it, | but not the cause, my lord. 4.02.143
to go on, i mean, | else wish we to be snails. 5.01. 42
that remain with you could wish their office 5.03. 35
would they not wish the feast might ever last, VEN 447
sin | to wish that i their father had not been. LUC 210
the sweets we wish for turn to loathed sours 867
and wish her lays were tuned like the lark. PP 14.18
with virtuous wish would bear your living SON 16. 7
look what is best, that best i wish in thee: 37.13
this wish i have, then ten times happy me! 37.14
pity me then, and wish i were renew'd, | whilst 111. 8
whoever hath her wish, thou hast thy will, | and 135. 1

/WISH'D 1 FR 0.0001 REL FR 1 V 0 P
to death, | /wish'd himself the heavens' breath. LLL 4.03.106

WISH'D 44 FR 0.0049 REL FR 36 V 8 P
should i have wish'd a thing, it had been he. TGV 2.04. 82
if this be he you oft have wish'd to hear from. 2.04.103
i wish'd your venison better, it was ill kill'd. WIV 1.01. 82 P
no, my good lord, | nor wish'd to hold my peace. MM 5.01. 79
cover for her shame | that may be wish'd for. ADO 4.01.117
and if a merry meeting may be wish'd, god 5.01.326 P
and wish'd in silence that it were not his. MV 2.08. 32
this he wish'd. AWW 1.02. 63
late more near her than i think she wish'd me. 1.03.107 P
and wish'd to see thee ever cross-garter'd: TN 2.05.154 P
"and wish'd to see thee cross-garter'd." 3.04. 50 P
as dice are to be wish'd by one that fixes | no WT 1.02.133
i never wish'd to see you sorry, now | i trust i 2.01.123
hath something seiz'd | his wish'd ability, he 5.01.143
and your supply, which you have wish'd so long, JN 5.05. 12
but when they seldom come, they wish'd for come, 1H4 1.02.206
that wish'd him on the barren mountains starve. 1.03.159
because i wish'd this world's eternity. 2H6 2.04. 90
it, | and so i wish'd thy body might my heart. 3.02.109
and to that end we wish'd your lordship here, R3 3.05. 67
i wish'd might fall on me when i was found 5.01. 14
this is the day wherein i wish'd to fall | by 5.01. 16
have sent me such a man i would have wish'd for. H8 2.02.100
have wish'd the sleeping of this business, never 2.04.164
o cressid, how often have i wish'd me thus! TRO 3.02. 61 P
wish'd, my lord? the gods grant — o my lord! 3.02. 62 P
and yet, good faith, i wish'd myself a man, | or 3.02.127
we wish'd coriolanus | had lov'd you as we did. COR 4.06. 24
the same intent wherein | you wish'd us parties, 5.06. 13
and they have wish'd that lucius were their TIT 4.04. 77
why, i have often wish'd myself poorer, that i TIM 1.02.100 P
but yet they could have wish'd — they know not 2.02.207
when man was wish'd to love his enemies! 4.03.466
have wish'd that noble brutus had his eyes. JC 1.02. 62
he wish'd to-day our enterprise might thrive. 3.01. 16
'tis a consummation | devoutly to be wish'd. HAM 3.01. 63
she wish'd she had not heard it, yet she wish'd OTH 1.03.162
yet she wish'd | that heaven had made her such a 1.03.162
the primal state | that he which is was wish'd, ANT 1.04. 42
this | she wish'd me to make known; CYM 3.05. 50
for i wish'd | thou shouldst be color'd thus. 5.01. 1
all the good that may | be wish'd upon thy head, TNK 1.04. 3
to death, | wish'd himself the heavens' breath. PP 16. 8
makes summer's welcome thrice more wish'd, more SON 56.14

WISHED 5 FR 0.0005 REL FR 5 V 0 P
and by the benefit of his wished light | the ERR 1.01. 90
at the last | unto the wished haven of my bliss. SHR 5.01.128
work | to bring this matter to the wished end. 1H6 3.03. 28
for losing ken of albion's wished coast. 2H6 3.02.113
hath his hope, and eyes their wished sight: PP 14.22

WISHER'S 1 FR 0.0001 REL FR 1 V 0 P
half that wish the wisher's eyes be press'd! MND 2.02. 65

WISHERS 1 FR 0.0001 REL FR 1 V 0 P
wishers were ever fools — o, come, come, come, ANT 4.15. 37

WISHES' 1 FR 0.0001 REL FR 1 V 0 P
but to your wishes' height advance you both. TIT 2.01.125

WISHES 38 FR 0.0043 REL FR 32 V 6 P
thus wisdom wishes to appear most bright | when MM 2.04. 78
wishes and tears, poor fancy's followers. MND 1.01.155
that have stood by and seen our wishes prosper, MV 3.02.187
fair eyes and gentle wishes go with me to my AYL 1.02.186 P
my brother happy in having what he wishes for. 5.02. 47 P
all made of passion, and all made of wishes, 5.02. 95
madam, i desire your holy wishes. AWW 1.01. 59 P
the best wishes that can | be forg'd in your 1.01. 74
whose baser stars do shut us up in wishes, 1.01.183
twenty times above | her that so wishes, and her 2.03. 83
the unknown belov'd, this, and my good wishes": TN 2.05. 91 P
doth say, | he wishes earnestly you never may. WT 4.01. 32
grandam, i will not wish thy wishes thrive: JN 3.01.334
"if wishes would prevail with me, | my purpose H5 3.02. 15
what's he that wishes so? 4.03. 18
joy and good wishes | to our most fair and 5.02. 3
good wishes, praise, and prayers | shall suffolk 1H6 5.03.173
take it from a heart that wishes towards you H8 1.01.103
nor my wishes | more worth than empty vanities; 2.03. 68
yet prayers and wishes | are all i can return. 2.03. 69
sweet lady, does | deserve our better wishes. 5.01. 26
to see inherited my very wishes | and the COR 2.01.199
is, | being of no power to make his wishes good. TIM 1.02.196
my thoughts and wishes bend again toward france, HAM 1.02. 55
our wishes on the way | may prove effects. LR 4.02. 14

if every of your wishes had a womb, | and ANT 1.02. 38
none but your sheets are privy to your wishes. 1.02. 42 P
and he will fill thy wishes to the brim | with 3.13. 18
to whom i gave | their wishes, do discandy, melt 4.12. 22
so he wishes you all happiness, that remains CYM 3.02. 45 P
your valiant britains have their wishes in it. 3.05. 20
man sing | may to your wishes pleasure bring, PER 1.ch. 14
fill'd, | and wishes fall out as they're will'd. 5.02. 16
repeat my wishes | to our great lord, of whose TNK 1.03. 1
or entertain'st a hope to blast my wishes, 2.02.170
you outwent me, | nor could my wishes reach you. 3.06. 80
your prayers, and betwixt ye | i part my wishes. 5.01. 17
to live still, | have their good wishes; 5.04. 6

WISHEST 2 FR 0.0002 REL FR 2 V 0 P
and, in the number, thee that wishest shame! 2H6 3.01.308
dost fear to do | than wishest should be undone. MAC 1.05. 25

WISHETH 1 FR 0.0001 REL FR 1 V 0 P
with | a rising sigh he wisheth you in heaven. 1H4 3.01. 10

WISHFUL 1 FR 0.0001 REL FR 1 V 0 P
to greet mine own land with my wishful sight. 3H6 3.01. 14

WISHING 13 FR 0.0014 REL FR 12 V 1 P
wishing me with him, partner of his fortune. TGV 1.03. 59
but rather wishing a more strict restraint MM 1.04. 4
time coher'd with place, or place with wishing, 2.01. 11
i cannot be a man with wishing, therefore i will ADO 4.01.323 P
that wishing well had not a body in't, | which AWW 1.01.181
wishing clocks more swift? WT 1.02.289
wishing his foot were equal with his eye, | and 3H6 3.02.137
to me, wishing me to permit | john de la car, my H8 1.02.161
i eat do seem unsavory, | wishing him my meat. PER 2.03. 32
wishing it so much blood unto your life. 2.03. 77
wishing her cheeks were gardens full of flowers, VEN 65
them, | wishing adonis had his team to guide, 179
wishing me like to one more rich in hope, SON 29. 5

WISHTLY *(also wistly)*

WISHTLY 1 FR 0.0001 REL FR 1 V 0 P
it, he wishtly look'd on me | as who should say, R2 5.04. 7

WISP 1 FR 0.0001 REL FR 1 V 0 P
a wisp of straw were worth a thousand crowns 3H6 2.02.144

/WIST 1 FR 0.0001 REL FR 1 V 0 P
and if i /wist he did — but let it rest, 1H6 4.01.180

WISTLY *(also wishtly)*

WISTLY 3 FR 0.0003 REL FR 3 V 0 P
wistly to view | how she came stealing to the VEN 343
and, blushing with him, wistly on him gazed; LUC 1355
eye, | yet not so wistly as this queen on him. PP 6.12

WIT *(also weet)*

/WIT 3 FR 0.0003 REL FR 2 V 1 P
hector shall not have his /wit this year. TRO 1.02. 86 P
/we /shall /hear /music, /wit, /and /oracle. 1.03. 74
for i have neither /wit, nor words, nor worth, JC 3.02.221

WIT 265 FR 0.0299 REL FR 121 V 144 P
he's winding up the watch of his wit, by and by TMP 2.01. 12 P
wit shall not go unrewarded while i am king of 4.01.242 P
however — but a folly bought with wit, | or TGV 1.01. 34
with wit, | or else a wit by folly vanquished. 1.01. 35
even so by love the young and tender wit | is 1.01. 47
made wit with musing weak, heart sick with 1.01. 69
beshrew me, but you have a quick wit. 1.01.125 P
sir thurio borrows his wit from your ladyship's 2.04. 38 P
word with me, i shall make your wit bankrupt. 2.04. 42 P
and he wants wit that wants resolved will | to 2.06. 12
to learn his wit t' exchange the bad for better. 2.06. 13
as thou hast lent me wit to plot this drift. 2.06. 43
and yet i have the wit to think my master is a 3.01.264 P
she hath more hair than wit, and more faults 3.01.353 P
"item, she hath more hair than wit" — 3.01.358 P
more hair than wit? 3.01.359 P
hair that covers the wit is more than the wit, 3.01.361 P
hair that covers the wit is more than the wit, 3.01.362 P
if i had not had more wit than he, to take a 4.04. 13 P
with wit or steel? WIV 1.03. 93
that hath taught me more wit than ever i learn'd 4.05. 60 P
but that my admirable dexterity of wit, my 4.05.118 P
see now how wit may be made a jack–a–lent, when 5.05.126 P
faith, sir, few of any wit in such matters. MM 2.01.268 P
'tis wit in them, | but in the less foul 2.02.127
thousand escapes of wit | make thee the father 4.01. 62
hast thou or word, or wit, or impudence, | that 5.01.363
barren my wit? ERR 2.01. 91
or else i shall seek my wit in my shoulders. 2.02. 38 P
scanted /men in hair he hath given them in wit. 2.02. 81 P
but there's many a man hath more hair than wit. 2.02. 83 P
of those but he hath the wit to lose his hair. 2.02. 84 P
conclude hairy men plain dealers without wit. 2.02. 87 P
who, every word by all my wit being scann'd, 2.02.150
wants wit in all one word to understand. 2.02.151
meet but there's a skirmish of wit between them. ADO 1.01. 63 P
so that if he have wit enough to keep himself 1.01. 68 P
hath the fellow any wit that told you this? 1.02. 17 P
think i do not know you by your excellent wit? 2.01.122 P
and that i had my good wit out of the "hundred 2.01.130 P
is not in his wit but in his villainy, for he 2.01.140 P
despite of his quick wit and his queasy stomach, 2.01.383 P
doth indeed show some sparks that are like wit. 2.03.187 P
it is no addition to her wit, nor no great 2.03.234 P
odd quirks and remnants of wit broken on me, 2.03.236 P
and her wit | values itself so highly that to 3.01. 52
me | out of myself, press me to death with wit. 3.01. 76
having so swift and excellent a wit | as she is 3.01. 89
doth not my wit become me rarely? 3.04. 69 P
they say, "when the age is in, the wit is out." 3.05. 34 P
we will spare for no wit, i warrant you. 3.05. 61 P
wilt thou use thy wit? 5.01.124 P
dost thou wear thy wit by thy side? 5.01.126 P
so, though very many have been beside their wit. 5.01.128 P
sir, i shall meet your wit in the career, and 5.01.135 P
sir, your wit ambles well, it goes easily. 5.01.158 P
thee how beatrice prais'd thy wit the other day. 5.01.160 P
i said thou hadst a fine wit. 5.01.160 P
"no," said i, "a great wit." 5.01.162 P
"nay," said i, "a good wit." 5.01.163 P
in his doublet and hose and leaves off his wit! 5.01.200 P
thy wit is as quick as the greyhound's mouth — 5.02. 11 P
a most manly wit, margaret, it will not hurt a 5.02. 15 P
out of his right sense, so forcible is thy wit. 5.02. 56 P
he surely affected her for her wit. LLL 1.02. 88 P
it was so, sir, for she had a green wit. 1.02. 89 P
my father's wit and my mother's tongue assist me 1.02. 95 P
salomon so seduced, and he had a very good wit. 1.02.175 P
devise, wit, write, pen, for i am for whole 1.02.184 P
in spending your wit in the praise of mine. 2.01. 19
is a sharp wit match'd with too blunt a will, 2.01. 49
for he hath wit to make an ill shape good, | and 2.01. 59
and shape to win grace though he had no wit. 2.01. 60
his eye begets occasion for his wit, | for every 2.01. 69
your waist, mistress, were as slender as my wit, 4.01. 49
troth, most sweet jests, most incony vulgar wit! 4.01.142
his page a' t'other side, that handful of wit! 4.01.147
can you tell me by your wit | what was a month 4.02. 34
neither savoring of poetry, wit, nor invention. 4.02.159 P
well prov'd, wit! 4.03. 6 P
once more i'll mark how love can vary wit. 4.03. 98
how will he spend his wit! 4.03.145
a sweet touch, a quick venue of wit — snip, 5.01. 59 P
true wit! 5.01. 61 P
thou halfpenny purse of wit, thou pigeon–egg of 5.01. 74 P
well bandied both, a set of wit well played. 5.02. 29
when they are catch'd, | as wit turn'd fool; 5.02. 70
as fool'ry in the wise, when wit doth dote, 5.02. 76
power thereof it doth apply | to prove, by wit, 5.02. 78
o poverty in wit, kingly–poor flout! 5.02.269
this fellow pecks up wit as pigeons pease, | and 5.02.315
thrust thy sharp wit quite through my ignorance, 5.02.398
speak for yourselves, my wit is at an end. 5.02.430
welcome, pure wit! 5.02.484
execute | that lie within the mercy of your wit. 5.02.846
with all the fierce endeavor of your wit | to 5.02.853
who would set his wit to so foolish a bird? MND 3.01.134 P
but if i had wit enough to get out of this wood, 3.01.149 P
past the wit of man to say what dream it was. 4.01.205 P
hath simply the best wit of any handicraft man 4.02. 9 P
and hedg'd me by his wit to yield myself | his MV 2.01. 18
they have the wisdom by their wit to lose. 2.09. 81
to wit (besides commends and courteous breath), 2.09. 90
thou spend'st such high–day wit in praising him. 2.09. 98
the best grace of wit will shortly turn into 3.05. 44 P
show the whole wealth of thy wit in an instant? 3.05. 56 P
no, none that thou hast wit enough to make. 4.01.127
repair thy wit, good youth, or it will fall | to 4.01.141
nature hath given us wit to flout at fortune, AYL 1.02. 45 P
nature's natural the cutter–off of nature's wit. 1.02. 50 P
how now, wit, whither wander you? 1.02. 56 P
for since the little wit that fools have was 1.02. 89 P
as wit and fortune will. 1.02.104 P
be ware of mine own wit till i break my shins 2.04. 59 P
that hath learn'd no wit by nature nor art may 3.02. 29 P
you have too courtly a wit for me, i'll rest. 3.02. 70 P
you have a nimble wit; 3.02.276 P
nor a man's good wit seconded with the forward 3.03. 13 P
or i should think my honesty ranker than my wit. 4.01. 85 P
or else she could not have the wit to do this; 4.01.160 P
make the doors upon a woman's wit, and it will 4.01.162 P
a man that had a wife with such a wit, he might 4.01.165 P
such a wit, he might say, "wit, whither wilt?" 4.01.166 P
you met your wive's wit going to your neighbor's 4.01.168 P
and what wit could wit have to excuse that? 4.01.170 P
and what wit could wit have to excuse that? 4.01.170 P
ay, sir, i have a pretty wit. 5.01. 29 P
or, to wit, i kill thee, make thee away, 5.01. 52 P
the presentation of that he shoots his wit. 5.04.107 P
o how we joy to see your wit restor'd! SHR in.2. 77
sir, | that, hearing of her beauty and her wit, 2.01. 48
youth | he had the wit which i can well observe AWW 1.02. 32
commit, | only shape thou thy silence to my wit. TN 1.02. 61
i have no more wit than a christian or an 1.03. 84 P
of beef and i believe that does harm to my wit. 1.03. 86 P
her degree, neither in estate, years, nor wit; 1.03.110 P
wit, and't be thy will, put me into good fooling 1.05. 32 P
"better a witty fool than a foolish wit." 1.05. 36 P
have you no wit, manners, nor honesty, but to 2.03. 87 P
do not think i have wit enough to lie straight 2.03.136 P
of tartar, thou most excellent devil of wit! 2.05.206 P
sentence is but a chev'ril glove to a good wit. 3.01. 12 P
and to do that well craves a kind of wit. 3.01. 61
wise /men, folly–fall'n, quite taint their wit. 3.01. 68
and yet, when wit and youth is come to harvest, 3.01.132
pride, | nor wit nor reason can my passion hide. 3.01.152
i must have done no less with wit and safety. 5.01.211
if wit flow from't | as boldness from my bosom, WT 2.02. 50
alone shall suffer what wit can make heavy and 4.04.772 P
my head | when there is such disorder in my wit. JN 3.04.102
myself, but the cause that wit is in other men. 2H4 1.02. 10 P
and his quick wit wasted in giving reckonings; 1.02.170 P
your chin double, your wit single, and every 1.02.183 P
yea, i thank your pretty sweet wit for it. 1.02.206 P
a good wit will make use of any thing. 1.02.247 P
they say poins has a good wit. 2.04.239 P
he a good wit? 2.04.240 P
i would you had the wit, 'twere better than your 4.03. 86 P
which is the birth, becomes excellent wit. 4.03.102 P
to wit, no female | should be inheritrix in H5 1.02. 50
his jest will savor but of shallow wit, | when 1.02.295
nay, the man hath no wit that cannot, from the 3.07. 31 P
daughter, | my wit untrain'd in any kind of art. 1H6 1.02. 73
search out thy wit for secret policies, | and we 3.03. 12
such as my wit affords | and overjoy of heart 2H6 1.01. 30
and yet herein i judge mine own wit good — 3.01.232
lords, give us leave. i'll try this widow's wit. 3H6 3.02. 33
her words doth show her wit incomparable, | all 3.02. 85
away with scrupulous wit! now arms must rule. 4.07. 61
to wit, an indigested and deformed lump, | not 5.06. 51
and those who have the wit to claim the place. R3 3.01. 50
with what his valor did enrich his wit, | his 3.01. 85
wit, | his wit set down to make his valure live. 3.01. 86
with what a sharp–provided wit he reasons! 3.01.132
an excellent | and unmatch'd wit and judgment; H8 2.04. 47
(more near my life, i fear), with my weak wit, 3.01. 72
lacking wit | to make a seemly answer to such 3.01.177
was a haberdasher's wife of small wit near him, 5.03. 47 P
will not dispraise your sister cassandra's wit, TRO 1.01. 47 P
he has a shrowd wit, i can tell you, and he's 1.02.190 P
to defend my belly, upon my wit, to defend my 1.02.261 P
i shall sooner rail thee into wit and holiness, 2.01. 16 P
thou art bought and sold among those of any wit, 2.01. 47 P
lo, lo, lo, lo, what modicums of wit he utters! 2.01. 68 P
who wears his wit in his belly and his guts in 2.01. 73 P
has not so much wit — 2.01. 78 P
will you set your wit to a fool's? 2.01. 86 P
a great deal of your wit, too, lies in your 2.01. 98 P
whose wit was mouldy ere /your grandsires had 2.01.104 P
i will keep where there is wit stirring, and 2.01.119 P
less than little wit from them that they have, 2.03. 13 P
wit would be out of fashion. 2.03.216 P
where is my wit? 3.02.151
for beauty, wit, | high birth, vigor of bone, 3.03.171
as who should say there were wit in this head, 3.03.255 P
the moral of my wit | is "plain and true"; 4.04.107
should wit larded with malice and malice fac'd 5.01. 57 P
malice and malice fac'd with wit turn him to? 5.01. 58 P
which way do you judge my wit would fly? COR 2.03. 26 P
your wit will not so soon out as another man's 2.03. 27 P
i'll try whether my old wit be in request | with 3.01.250
upon her wit doth earthly honor wait, | and TIT 2.01. 10
chiron, thy years wants wit, thy wits wants edge 2.01. 26
with her sacred wit | to villainy and vengeance 2.01.120
he that had wit would think that i had none, 2.03. 1
hit | with cupid's arrow, she hath dian's wit; ROM 1.01.209
thou wilt fall backward when thou hast more wit, 1.03. 42
in going to this mask, | but 'tis no wit to go. 1.04. 49
sure wit! 2.04. 61 P
thy wit is a very bitter sweeting, it is a most 2.04. 79 P
o, here's a wit of cheverel, that stretches from 2.04. 83 P
fie, thou shamest thy shape, thy love, thy wit, 3.03.122
should bedeck thy shape, thy love, thy wit. 3.03.125
thy wit, that ornament to shape and love, 3.03.130
but much of grief shows still some want of wit. 3.05. 73
you put up your dagger, and put out your wit. 4.05.122 P
then have at you with my wit! 4.05.123 P
i will dry–beat you with an iron wit, and put up 4.05.124 P
that i had no angry wit to be a lord. TIM 1.01.234 P
foolery as i have, so much wit thou lack'st. 2.02.117 P
this rudeness is a sauce to his good wit, JC 1.02.300
thou speak'st with all thy wit, and yet, i' MAC 4.02. 42
and yet, i' faith, | with wit enough for thee. 4.02. 43
o wicked wit and gifts that have the power | so HAM 1.05. 44
my drift, | and i believe it is a fetch of wit: 2.01. 38
therefore, /since brevity is the soul of wit, 2.02. 90
gum, and that they have a plentiful lack of wit, 2.02.199 P
i like thy wit well, in good faith. 5.01. 45 P
let me, if not by birth, have lands by wit: LR 1.02.183
thou hadst little wit in thy bald crown when 1.04.162 P
thou hast par'd thy wit o' both sides, and left 1.04.187 P
be merry, thy wit shall not go slip–shod. 1.05. 11 P
having more man than wit about me, drew. 2.04. 42
"he that has and a little tine wit — | with 3.02. 74
beauty, wit, and fortunes | in an extravagant OTH 1.01.135
if she be fair and wise, fairness and wit, | the 2.01.129
if she be black, and thereto have a wit, 2.01.132
so, with no money at all and a little more wit, 2.03.368 P
thou know'st we work by wit, and not by 2.03.372
witchcraft, | and wit depends on dilatory time. 2.03.373
iago doth give up | the execution of his wit, 3.03.466
to do this is within the compass of man's wit, 3.04. 21 P
prithee bear some charity to my wit, do not 4.01.120 P
of so high and plenteous wit and invention! 4.01.190 P
that turn'd your wit the seamy side without, 4.02.146
your suspicion is not without wit and judgment. 4.02.211 P
but i have seen small reflection of her wit. CYM 1.02. 31 P
if his wit had been like him that broke it, it 2.01. 8 P
now please you wit | the epitaph is for marina PER 4.04. 31
love and beyond reason, | or wit, or safety. TNK 2.06. 12
fair fall the wit that can so well defend her! VEN 472
danger deviseth shifts, wit waits on fear. 690
could rule them both without ten women's wit." 1008
the thing we have, and all for want of wit, LUC 153
lending him wit that to bad debtors lends: 964
what wit sets down is blotted straight with will 1299
began to clothe his wit in state and pride, 1809
now set thy long–experienc'd wit to school. 1820
to hear with eyes belongs to love's fine wit. SON 23.14
ambassage | to witness duty, not to show my wit; 26. 4
which wit so poor as mine | may make seem bare, 26. 5
for whether beauty, birth, or wealth, or wit, 37. 5
and such a counterpart shall fame his wit, 84.11
if i might teach thee wit, better it were, 140. 5
with wit well blazon'd, smil'd or made some moan LC 217

/WITCH 1 FR 0.0001 REL FR 1 V 0 P
to sit and /witch me, as ascanius did | when he 2H6 3.02.116

WITCH 40 FR 0.0045 REL FR 26 V 14 P
hast thou forgot | the foul witch sycorax, who TMP 1.02.258
this damn'd witch sycorax, | for mischiefs 1.02.263
his mother was a witch, and one so strong | that 5.01.269
he swears she's a witch, forbade her my house, WIV 4.02. 86 P
let's go dress him like the witch of brainford. 4.02. 98 P
a witch, a quean, an old cozening quean! 4.02.172 P
come down, you witch, you hag you, come down, i 4.02.179 P
out of my door, you witch, you rag, you baggage, 4.02.184 P
hang her, witch! 4.02.191 P
yea and no, i think the oman is a witch indeed. 4.02.192 P
to be apprehended for the witch of brainford. 4.05.117 P
th' stocks, i' th' common stocks, for a witch. 4.05.120 P
arm, that i, amaz'd, ran from her as a witch. ERR 3.02.144 P
avaunt, thou witch! come, dromio, let us go. 4.03. 79
in my heart to stay here still, and turn witch. 4.04.156 P
for beauty is a witch | against whose charms ADO 2.01.179
a mankind witch! WT 2.03. 68
and witch the world with noble horsemanship. 1H4 4.01.110
who like a foul and ugly witch doth limp | so H5 4.pr. 21
blood will i draw on thee — thou art a witch — 1H6 1.05. 6
a witch by fear, not force, like hannibal, 1.05. 21
pucelle, that witch, that damned sorceress, 3.02. 38
see how the ugly witch doth bend her brows, | as 5.03. 34
with margery jordan, the cunning witch, | with 2H6 1.02. 75
dame eleanor gives gold to bring the witch; 1.02. 91
the witch in smithfield shall be burnt to ashes, 2.03. 7
and witch sweet ladies with my words and looks. 3H6 3.02.150
foul wrinkled witch, what mak'st thou in my R3 1.03.163
and this is edward's wife, that monstrous witch, 3.04. 70
thou stool for a witch! TRO 2.01. 42 P
beshrew the witch! 4.02. 12
you witch me in it; TIM 5.01.155
"aroint thee, witch!" MAC 1.03. 6

no fairy takes, nor witch hath power to charm, HAM 1.01.163
plight, | and aroint thee, witch, aroint thee!" LR 3.04.124
out, fool, i forgive thee for a witch. ANT 1.02. 40 P
now the witch take me, if i meant it thus! 4.02. 37
the witch shall die. 4.12. 47
such a holy witch | that he enchants societies CYM 1.06.166
one would marry a leprous witch to be rid on't, TNK 4.03. 47 P

WITCHCRAFT 17 FR 0.0019 REL FR 16 V 1 P
a witchcraft drew me hither: TN 5.01. 76
fresh piece | of excellent witchcraft, whom of WT 4.04.423
this juggling witchcraft with revenue cherish, JN 3.01.169
you have witchcraft in your lips, kate; H5 5.02.275 P
with devilish plots | of damned witchcraft, and R3 3.04. 61
that by their witchcraft thus have marked me. 3.04. 72
for he hath a witchcraft | over the king in 's H8 3.02. 18
witchcraft celebrates | pale hecat's off'rings; MAC 2.01. 51
with witchcraft of his wits, with traitorous HAM 1.05. 43
but this gallant | had witchcraft in't, he grew 4.07. 85
or lame of sense), | sans witchcraft could not. OTH 1.03. 64
this only is the witchcraft i have us'd. 1.03.169
know'st we work by wit, and not by witchcraft, 2.03.372
he thought 'twas witchcraft — but i am much to 3.03.211
let witchcraft join with beauty, lust with both, ANT 2.01. 22
nor no witchcraft charm thee! CYM 4.02.277
what a hell of witchcraft lies | in the small LC 288

WITCHCRAFT'S 1 FR 0.0001 REL FR 1 V 0 P
i do not know what witchcraft's in him, but COR 4.07. 2

WITCH'D 1 FR 0.0001 REL FR 1 V 0 P
am i not witch'd like her? 2H6 3.02.119

WITCHES 5 FR 0.0005 REL FR 5 V 0 P
soul–killing witches that deform the body, ERR 1.02.100
there's none but witches do inhabit here, | and 3.02.156
i see these witches are afraid of swords. 4.04.147
to join with witches and the help of hell! 1H6 2.01. 18
dealing with witches and with conjurers, | whom 2H6 2.01.168

WITCHING 1 FR 0.0001 REL FR 1 V 0 P
'tis now the very witching time of night, | when HAM 3.02.388

WITCH'S 1 FR 0.0001 REL FR 1 V 0 P
witch's mummy, maw and gulf | of the ravin'd MAC 4.01. 23

WIT–CRACKERS 1 FR 0.0001 REL FR 0 V 1 P
a college of wit–crackers cannot flout me out of ADO 5.04.101 P

WITH *(also wi')*
/WITH 74 FR 0.0083 REL FR 69 V 5 P
WITH 7834 FR 0.8855 REL FR 6260 V 1574 P
/WITHAL 2 FR 0.0002 REL FR 2 V 0 P
they i cannot be, | who are surpris'd /withal; TMP 3.01. 93
strength of nature | which we are born /withal. STM III 5

WITHAL 149 FR 0.0168 REL FR 106 V 43 P
which, when he has a house, he'll deck withal. TMP 3.02. 97
i fear me, he will scarce be pleas'd withal. TGV 2.07. 67
these banish'd men, that i have kept withal, 5.04.152
as ever servant shall come in house withal; WIV 1.04. 11 P
myself like one that i am not acquainted withal; 2.01. 87 P
as you would desires to be acquainted withal. 3.01. 67 P
her cause and yours | i'll perfect him withal, MM 4.03.141
such a fellow is not to be talk'd withal. 5.01.344 P
and withal so doubtfully, that i could scarce ERR 2.01. 53 P
desert) | hath oftentimes upbraided me withal: 3.01.113
go home with it, and please your wife withal, 3.02.173
soul | as this is false he burthens me withal! 5.01.209
and this is false you burthen me withal. 5.01.269
but i will acquaint my daughter withal, that she ADO 1.02. 21 P
upon a knive's point and choke a daw withal. 2.03.255 P
of truth | can cunning sin cover itself withal! 4.01. 36
mirth, | i never spent an hour's talk withal. LLL 2.01. 68
which we much rather had depart withal, | and 2.01.146
i have acquainted you withal, to the end to 5.01.116 P
and so be mock'd withal | upon the next occasion 5.02.142
and i will have you and that fault withal; 5.02.866
if you choose that, then i am yours withal. MV 2.07. 12
the tailor that made the wings she flew withal. 3.01. 27 P
to bait fish withal — if it will feed nothing 3.01. 53 P
madam, it is, so you stand pleas'd withal. 3.02.209
i could not do withal. 3.04. 72
we freely cope your courteous pains withal. 4.01.412
let his deservings and my love withal | be 4.01.450
you, i came hither to acquaint you withal, that AYL 1.01.132 P
marry, i prithee do, to make sport withal. 1.02. 26 P
i must have liberty | withal, as large a charter 2.07. 48
love have you wearied your parishioners withal, 3.02.156 P
i'll tell you who time ambles withal, who time 3.02.310 P
who time ambles withal, who time trots withal, 3.02.310 P
who time trots withal, who time gallops withal, 3.02.311 P
gallops withal, and who he stands still withal. 3.02.311 P
i prithee, who doth he trot withal? 3.02.312 P
who ambles time withal? 3.02.318 P
these time ambles withal. 3.02.325 P
who doth he gallop withal? 3.02.326 P
who stays it still withal? 3.02.330 P
he hath generally tax'd their whole sex withal. 3.02.350 P
why, nothing comes amiss, so money comes withal.
SHR 1.02. 82 P
have no more eyes to see withal than a cat. 1.02.115 P
her sister katherine welcom'd you withal? 3.01. 3
and watch withal, for, but i be deceiv'd, | our 3.01. 62
though he be merry, yet withal he's honest. 3.02. 25
that i have fondly flatter'd /her withal. 4.02. 31
and withal make known | which way thou 4.05. 50
he's within, sir, but not to be spoken withal. 5.01. 20 P
a hundred pound or two, to make merry withal? 5.01. 22 P
withal, full oft we see | cold wisdom waiting on AWW 1.01.104
i held my duty speedily to acquaint you withal, 1.03.119 P
displeasure, and, as he says, is muddied withal. 5.02. 22 P
skill, and wrath can furnish man withal. TN 3.04.233 P
and see withal | the instruments that feel. WT 2.01.153
a piece of honesty to acquaint the king withal, 4.04.681 P
philip of france, if thou be pleas'd withal, JN 2.01.531
which is the side that i must go withal? 3.01.327
pleas'd | not to be pardoned, am content withal. R2 2.01.188
adding withal, how blest this land would be | in 4.01. 18
man, | for any thing he shall be charg'd withal, 1H4 2.04.517
and withal | break with your wives of your 3.01.141
as thou art match'd withal and grafted to, 3.02. 15
can purge | myself of many i am charg'd withal; 3.02. 21
of safety, and withal to pry | into his title, 4.03.103
with the best blood that i can meet withal | in 5.02. 94
of not marking, that i am troubled withal. 2H4 1.02.122 P
peruse the men | we should have cop'd withal. 4.02. 95
and withal devise something to do thyself good. 5.03.133 P
yet | did to his predecessors part withal. H5 1.01. 81
and you withal shall make all gallia shake. 1.02.216
and withal | how terrible in constant resolution 2.04. 34
and if he be not fought withal, my lord, | let 3.05. 2
if they march along | unfought withal, but i 3.05. 12
'tis the gage of one that i should fight withal, 4.07.123 P
wanting the scythe withal, uncorrected, rank, 5.02. 50
word thou shalt no sooner bless mine ear withal, 5.02.238 P
to keep our great saint george's feast withal. 1H6 1.01.154
didst thou at first, to flatter us withal, 2.01. 51
and say withal, i think he held the right. 2.04. 38
thy praise | that i, thy enemy, due thee withal; 4.02. 34
and this withal. 5.03.184
i give thee this to dry thy cheeks withal. 3H6 1.04. 83
child, | to bid the father wipe his eyes withal, 1.04.139
for self–same wind that i should speak withal 2.01. 82
i am a subject fit to jest withal, | but far 3.02. 91
seest what's pass'd, go fear thy king withal. 3.03.226
and withal | forbear your conference with the R3 1.01.103
withal, what i have been, and what i am. 1.03.132
and withal whet me | to be reveng'd on rivers, 1.03.331
withal obdurate, do not hear him plead; 1.03.346
withal i did infer your lineaments, | being the 3.07. 12
i think the duke will not be spoke withal. 3.07. 57
if not to bless us and the land withal, | yet to 3.07.197
all — | will i withal endow a child of thine; 4.04.250
and bid her wipe her weeping eyes withal. 4.04.278
withal say that the queen hath heartily 4.05. 7
if by the way they be not fought withal. 4.05. 18
remember whom you are to cope withal — | a sort 5.03.315
have i pluck'd off to grace thy brows withal. 5.05. 6
paper in the packet, | to bless your eye withal. H8 3.02.130
confess it, say withal | if you are bound to us, 3.02.164
withal bring word if hector will to–morrow | be TRO 3.03. 34
longing, | an appetite that i am sick withal, 3.03.238
he that takes that doth take my heart withal. 5.02. 82
both divine and human, | seal what i end withal! COR 3.01.142
i was mov'd withal. 5.03.194
but hope withal | the self–same gods that arm'd TIT 1.01.135
and resolv'd withal | to do myself this reason 1.01.278
and withal | thrust those reproachful speeches 2.01. 54
will we acquaint withal what we intend, | and 2.01.122
and withal my boy | shall carry from me to the 4.01.114
a sight to vex the father's soul withal. 5.01. 52
who, nothing hurt withal, hiss'd him in scorn. ROM 1.01.112
i nurs'd her daughter that you talk'd withal; 1.05.115
i learnt even now | of one i danc'd withal. 1.05.143
that i mean to make bold withal, and, as you 3.01. 78 P
was, and urg'd withal | your high displeasure; 3.01.154
aid, hath /sense withal | of it own fall, TIM 5.01.147
but withal i am indeed, sir, a surgeon to old JC 1.01. 23 P
and withal | hoping it was but an effect of 2.01.249
but withal | a woman that lord brutus took to 2.01.292
but withal | a woman well reputed, cato's 2.01.294
and of royal hope, | that he seems rapt withal; MAC 1.03. 57
aid doth seem | to have thee crown'd withal. 1.05. 30
this diamond he greets your wife withal, | by 2.01. 15
i'll gild the faces of the grooms withal, | for 2.02. 53
i think withal | there would be hands uplifted 4.03. 41
of the mind and soul | grows wide withal. HAM 1.03. 14
than the main voice of denmark goes withal. 1.03. 28
that i will not more willingly part withal — 2.02.216 P
dear a better proposer can charge you withal, be 2.02.287 P
a man | as e'er my conversation cop'd withal. 3.02. 55
thing from death | that is but scratch'd withal. 4.07.146
as i shall find means, and acquaint you withal. LR 1.02.102 P
(for such proceeding i am charg'd withal) | i OTH 1.03. 93
the strong conception | that i do groan withal. 5.02. 56
to have been blest withal would have discredited ANT 1.02.154 P
for war, acquainted | my grieved ear withal; 3.06. 59
dignity | as we greet modern friends withal, and 5.02.167
nam'd so, here | i charge your charity withal; PER 3.03. 14
that a man may deal withal and defy the surgeon? 4.06. 25 P
e'er dull'd sleep | did mock sad fools withal. 5.01.162
here's something | to paint your pole withal. TNK 3.05.153
that she farces ev'ry business withal, fits it 4.03. 8 P
for who hath she to spend the night withal, VEN 847
beating her bulk, that his hand shakes withal. LUC 467
i, sick withal, the help of bath desired, | and SON 153.11

WITHDRAW 35 FR 0.0039 REL FR 32 V 3 P
withdraw thee, valentine: TGV 5.04. 18
let us withdraw together, | and we may soon our MM 1.01. 81
let's withdraw. 1.02.113 P
madam, withdraw, the prince, the count, signior ADO 3.04. 95 P
all, | withdraw into a chamber by yourselves, 5.04. 11
ladies, withdraw; the gallants are at hand. LLL 5.02.308
if thou say so, withdraw, and prove it too. MND 3.02.255
i pray now call her. | withdraw yourselves. WT 2.02. 15
i must withdraw and weep | upon the spot of this JN 5.02. 29
withdraw with us, and let the trumpets sound R2 1.03.121
withdraw yourselves, and leave us here alone. 5.03. 28
we'll withdraw a while. 1H4 4.03.107
harry, withdraw thyself, thou bleedest too much. 5.04. 2
let us withdraw into the other room. 2H4 4.05. 18
and i'll withdraw me and my bloody power. 1H6 4.02. 8
withdraw yourself a while, i'll go with you. R3 3.04. 41
withdraw thee, wretched margaret; 4.04. 8
withdraw, my lord, i'll help you to a horse. 5.04. 8
if it please you, we may now withdraw us. 5.05. 11
madam, to withdraw | into your private chamber, H8 3.01. 27
tribunes, withdraw a while. COR 3.01.225
that you withdraw you, and abate your strength, TIT 1.01. 43
he is not with himself, let us withdraw. 1.01.368
i will withdraw, but this intrusion shall, | now ROM 1.05. 91
wouldst thou withdraw it? 2.02.130
either withdraw unto some private place, | or 3.01. 51
i hear him coming. withdraw, my lord. HAM 3.01. 54
to withdraw with you — why do you go about to 3.02.345 P
withdraw, | i hear him coming. 3.04. 6
let us withdraw, 'twill be a storm. LR 2.04.287
i will withdraw | to furnish me with some swift OTH 3.03.477
do you withdraw yourself a little while, | he 4.01. 56
will you withdraw? 4.01. 92
let's withdraw, | and meet the time as it seeks CYM 4.03. 32
are coming, we will withdraw | into the gallery. PER 2.02. 58

WITHDRAWING 1 FR 0.0001 REL FR 0 V 1 P
i believe i know the cause of his withdrawing. MM 3.02.132 P

WITHDRAWN 2 FR 0.0002 REL FR 1 V 1 P
on hero and hath withdrawn her father to break ADO 2.01.156 P
ah, warwick, why hast thou withdrawn thyself? 3H6 2.03. 14

WITHDREW 4 FR 0.0004 REL FR 4 V 0 P
when we withdrew, my liege, we left it here. 2H4 4.05. 58
care | withdrew me from the odds of multitude. TRO 5.04. 22
and in fine withdrew | to mine own room again, HAM 5.02. 15
like stars asham'd of day, themselves withdrew. VEN 1032

/WITHER 1 FR 0.0001 REL FR 1 V 0 P
/her /material /sap, /perforce /must /wither, LR 4.02. 35

WITHER 17 FR 0.0019 REL FR 15 V 2 P
such short–liv'd wits do wither as they grow. LLL 2.01. 54
or rather do not see, | my fair rose wither; R2 5.01. 8
pate will grow bald, a fair face will wither, a H5 5.02.161 P
wear, | until it wither with me to my grave, 1H6 2.04.110
wither, garden, and be henceforth a 2H6 4.10. 63 P
wither one rose, and let the other flourish; 3H6 2.05.101
if you contend, a thousand lives must wither. 2.05.102
why wither not the leaves that want their sap? R3 2.02. 42
let two more summers wither in their pride, ROM 1.02. 10
swallow 'em, | debts wither 'em to nothing; TIM 4.03.531
it vital growth again, | it needs must wither. OTH 5.02. 15
age cannot wither her, nor custom stale | her ANT 2.02.234
and here the graces of our youths must wither TNK 2.02. 27
they wither in their prime, prove nothing worth: VEN 418
good | to wither in my breast as in his blood. 1182
but low shrubs wither at the cedar's root. LUC 665
his leaves will wither and his sap decay; 1168

WITHER'D 22 FR 0.0024 REL FR 13 V 9 P
be | the fresh–brook mussels, wither'd roots, TMP 1.02.464
a wither'd servingman a fresh tapster. WIV 1.03. 17 P
cold, wither'd, and of intolerable entrails? 5.05.153 P
a wither'd hermit, fivescore winters worn, LLL 4.03.238
yet you are wither'd. SHR 2.01.237
is like one of our french wither'd pears, it AWW 1.01.161 P
ill, it eats drily, marry, 'tis a wither'd pear; 1.01.162 P
better, marry, yet 'tis a wither'd pear. 1.01.163 P
will wing me to some wither'd bough and there WT 5.03.133
the bay–trees in our country are all wither'd, R2 2.04. 8
i am wither'd like an old apple–john. 1H4 3.03. 4 P
of these six dry, round, old, wither'd knights." 2H4 2.04. 8 P
look whe'er the wither'd elder hath not his pole 2.04.258 P
wings is flown | from this bare wither'd trunk. 4.05.229
who twice a day their wither'd hands hold up H5 4.01.299
to shrink mine arm up like a wither'd shrub, 3H6 3.02.156
arm | is like a blasted sapling, wither'd up; R3 3.04. 69
these | so wither'd and so wild in their attire, MAC 1.03. 40
and wither'd murther, | alarum'd by his sentinel 2.01. 52
but they wither'd all when my father died. HAM 4.05.185 P
o, wither'd is the garland of the war, | the ANT 4.15. 64
you were as flow'rs, now wither'd; CYM 4.02.286

WITHERED 13 FR 0.0014 REL FR 13 V 0 P
bob, | and on her withered dewlop pour the ale. MND 2.01. 50
a vengeance on your crafty withered hide! SHR 2.01.404
this is a man, old, wrinkled, faded, withered, 4.05. 43
to crop at once a too long withered flower. R2 2.01.134
arms, like to a withered vine | that droops his 1H6 2.05. 11
shall see thee withered, bloody, pale, and dead. 4.02. 38
and in my vambrace put my withered brawns, | and
TRO 1.03.297
doth that grieve thee? | o withered truth! 5.02. 46
upon a gath'red lily almost withered. TIT 3.01.113
but his present is | a withered branch, that's PER 2.02. 43
lies here, | who withered in her spring of year. 4.04. 35
no man inveigh against the withered flow'r, LUC 1254
as flowers dead lie withered on the ground, | as PP 13. 9

WITHERING 3 FR 0.0003 REL FR 3 V 0 P
long withering out a young man's revenue. MND 1.01. 6
than that which withering on the virgin thorn 1.01. 77
thy lovers withering as thy sweet self grow'st; SON 126. 4

WITHERS 2 FR 0.0002 REL FR 0 V 2 P
poor jade is wrung in the withers, out of all 1H4 2.01. 6 P
the gall'd jade winch, our withers are unwrung. HAM 3.02.243 P

WITHHELD 4 FR 0.0004 REL FR 4 V 0 P
to one his lands withheld, and to the other | a AYL 5.04.168
to enforce these rights so forcibly withheld. JN 1.01. 18
rank and bite, because he was withheld, 2H6 5.01.152
but by his mother was perforce withheld. R3 3.01. 30

WITHHOLD 10 FR 0.0011 REL FR 10 V 0 P
withhold thy speed, dreadful occasion! JN 4.02.125
withhold thine indignation, mighty heaven, | and 5.06. 37
when that my care could not withhold thy riots, 2H4 4.05.134
swearing that you withhold his levied host, 1H6 4.04. 31
withhold revenge, dear god! 3H6 2.02. 7
who should withhold me? TRO 5.03. 51
your letters did withhold our breaking forth, ANT 3.06. 79
the gods withhold me! 4.14. 69
to withhold the vengeance that they had in store PER 2.04. 4
me go, | you have no reason to withhold me so." VEN 612

WITHHOLDS 3 FR 0.0003 REL FR 3 V 0 P
but she perforce withholds the loved boy, MND 2.01. 26
and her withholds from me /and other more, SHR 1.02.121
what cause withholds you then to mourn for him?
JC 3.02.103

/WITHIN 2 FR 0.0002 REL FR 2 V 0 P
/very /true, /my /grief /lies /all /within, R2 4.01.295
/within /whose /strong /immures | /the /ravish'd TRO pr 8

WITHIN 336 FR 0.0379 REL FR 279 V 57 P
have sunk the sea within the earth or ere | it TMP 1.02. 11
swallow'd and | the fraughting souls within her. 1.02. 13
within which rift | imprison'd, thou didst 1.02.277
within which space she died, | and left thee 1.02.279
there's wood enough within. 1.02.314
i'll free thee | within two days for this. 1.02.422
within this half hour will he be asleep. 3.02.113
brains, | now useless, /boil'd within thy skull! 5.01. 60
she is not within hearing, sir. TGV 2.01. 8 P
that these follies are within you, and shine 2.01. 38 P
come not within the measure of my wrath. 5.04.127
sir, he is within; WIV 1.01. 99 P
daughter, carry the wine in, we'll drink within. 1.01.189 P
who's within there, ho? 1.04.131 P
he sent me word to stay within. 3.05. 58 P
within a quarter of an hour. 4.04. 5 P
search windsor castle, elves, within and out. 5.05. 56
within these three days his head to be chopp'd MM 1.02. 69 P
within two hours. 1.02.193
and mercy then will breathe within your lips, 2.02. 78

his filth within being cast, he would appear | a 3.01. 92
must be lock'd within the teeth and the lips. 3.02.135 P
o, what may man within him hide, | though angel 3.02.271
what ho, within! 4.01. 49
find, within these two days he will be here. 4.02.198 P
not within, sir. 4.03.150 P
would fain proclaim | favors that keep within. 5.01. 16
within this hour it will be dinner–time; ERR 1.02. 11
and then return and sleep within mine inn, | for 1.02. 14
who talks within there? ho, open the door! 3.01. 38
your cake here is warm within: 3.01. 71
and draw within the compass of suspect | th' 3.01. 87
i charge thee, sathan, hous'd within this man, 4.04. 54
more company! the fiend is strong within him. 4.04.107
some get within him, take his sword away: 5.01. 34
i never came within these abbey walls, | nor 5.01.266
within this hour i was his bondman, sir, | but 5.01.289
is philemon's roof, within the house is jove. ADO 2.01. 96 P
i like the new tire within excellently, if the 3.04. 13 P
no woman shall come within a mile of my court" LLL 1.01.120 P
to talk with a woman within the term of three 1.01.130 P
three thousand times within this three years' 1.01.150
it should none spare that come within his power. 2.01. 51
man, | within the limit of becoming mirth, | i 2.01. 67
may not come, fair princess, within my gates, 2.01.171
i, costard, running out, that was safely within, 3.01.116
you have a double tongue within your mask, | and 5.02.245
execute | that lie within the mercy of your wit. 5.02.846
and within his power | to leave the figure or MND 1.01. 50
take heed the queen come not within his sight; 2.01. 19
how long within this wood intend you stay? 2.01.138
and here am i, and wode within this wood, 2.01.192
deny your love (so rich within his soul) | and 3.02.229
astray | as one come not within another's way. 3.02.359
stood now within the pretty flouriets' eyes 4.01. 55
horns are invisible within the circumference. 5.01.243 P
why should a man, whose blood is warm within, MV 1.01. 83
within the eye of honor, be assur'd | my purse, 1.01.137
for if the devil be within, and that temptation 1.02. 97 P
within these two months, that's a month before 1.03.157
who's within? 2.06. 25
here an angel in a golden bed | lies all within. 2.07. 59
within whose empty eye | there is a written 2.07. 63
i have within my mind | a thousand raw tricks of 3.04. 76
you stand within his danger, do you not? 4.01.180
within the house, your mistress is at hand, 5.01. 52
spirit of my father, which i think is within me, AYL 1.01. 23 P
within these ten days if that thou beest found 1.03. 43
o unhappy youth, | come not within these doors! 2.03. 17
within this roof | the enemy of all your graces 2.03. 17
where you use to lie, | and you within it. 2.03. 24
him dead or living | within this twelvemonth, or 3.01. 7
rosalind, i come within an hour of my promise. 4.01. 42 P
house doth keep itself, | there's none within. 4.03. 82
left a promise to return again | within an hour, 4.03.100
hand with his | whose heart within his bosom is. 5.04.115
schoolmasters will i keep within my house, | fit SHR 1.01. 94
show myself a forward guest | within your house, 2.01. 52
holla, within! 2.01.108
my house within the city | is richly furnished 2.01.346
within rich pisa walls, as any one | old signior 2.01.367
be the jacks fair within, the gills fair without 4.01. 49 P
such war of white and red within her cheeks! 4.05. 30
they're busy within, you were best knock louder. 5.01. 14 P
is signior lucentio within, sir? 5.01. 18 P
he's within, sir, but not to be spoken withal. 5.01. 19 P
within /t' /one year it will make itself two, AWW 1.01.147 P
restrain'd yourself within the list of too cold 2.01. 51 P
within what space | hop'st thou my cure? 2.01.159
speak | his powerful sound within an organ weak; 2.01.176
title, which is within a very little of nothing. 2.04. 27 P
yonder is heavy news within between two soldiers 3.02. 33 P
within these three hours 'twill be time enough 4.01. 24 P
hadst this ring, | thou diest within this hour. 5.03.284
confine yourself within the modest limits of TN 1.03. 8 P
gate, | and call upon my soul within the house; 1.05.269
is thy lady within? 3.01. 48 P
my lady is within, sir. 3.01. 56 P
lo, how hollow the fiend speaks within him! 3.04. 91 P
love, | to spite a raven's heart within a dove. 5.01.131
reach them, nor | shall she, within my pow'r. WT 2.03. 26
within this hour bring me word 'tis done | (and 2.03.136
heat outwardly or breath within, i'll serve you 3.02.206
what's within, boy? 3.03.119 P
a tinker's wife within a mile where my land and 4.03. 97 P
if i might die within this hour, i have liv'd 4.04.461
th' earth together, | and mar the seeds within! 4.04.479
and which he shall know within this hour, if i 4.04.758 P
wrongs i have done thee stir | afresh within me, 5.01.149
of wonder is broken out within this hour that 5.02. 24 P
craves harborage within your city walls. JN 2.01.234
which harm within itself so heinous is | as it 3.01. 40
within the scorched veins of one new burn'd. 3.01.278
thou shalt rue this hour within this hour. 3.01.323
within this wall of flesh | there is a soul 3.03. 20
hot, and look thou stand | within the arras. 4.01. 2
go stand within; let me alone with him. 4.01. 84
to break within the bloody house of life, | and 4.02.210
within this bosom never ent'red yet | the 4.02.254
have i not hideous death within my view, 5.04. 22
stoop low within those bounds we have o'erlook'd 5.04. 55
within me is a hell, and there the poison | is 5.07. 46
the cardinal pandulph is within at rest, | who 5.07. 82
within my mouth you have enjail'd my tongue, R2 1.03.166
within me grief hath kept a tedious fast; 2.01. 75
a thousand flatterers sit within thy crown, 2.01.100
for within the hollow crown | that rounds the 3.02.160
lies | within the limits of yon lime and stone, 3.03. 26
fretted us a pair of graves | within the earth, 3.03.168
who is within there? 5.02. 74
my tongue cleave to my roof within my mouth, 5.03. 31
they shall not live within this world, i swear, 5.03.142
within this coffin i present | thy buried fear. 5.06. 30
i must leave you within these two hours. 1H4 2.03. 36
thy spirit within thee hath been so at war, 2.03. 56
look to the guests within. 2.04. 81 P
imprisoning of unruly wind | within her womb, 3.01. 30
and all the fertile land within that bound, | to 3.01. 76
within that space you may have drawn together 3.01. 88
be drawn, i'll away within these two hours, and 3.01.261 P
him once, and 'a come but within my /vice — 2H4 2.01. 22 P
so, i did not think thou wast within hearing. 2.04.310 P
for lo, within a ken our army lies: 4.01.149
we come within our aweful banks again, | and 4.01.174
there is a thing within my bosom tells me | that 4.01.181
that man that sits within a monarch's heart 4.02. 11
how deep you were within the books of god? 4.02. 17
how now, rain within doors, and none abroad? 4.05. 9
found no course of breath within your majesty, 4.05.150
we cram | within this wooden o the very casques H5 pr 13
suppose within the girdle of these walls | are pr 19
who died within the year of our redemption 1.02. 60
but this lies all within the will of god, | to 1.02.289
and, which is worse, within thy nasty mouth! 2.01. 50
the english lie within fifteen hundred paces of 3.07.126 P
thrice within this hour | i saw him down; 4.06. 4
within the fore–rank of our articles. 5.02. 97
as i have a saving faith within me tells me thou 5.02.204 P
i cannot be confin'd within the weak list of a 5.02.269 P
within her quarter and mine own precinct | i was 1H6 2.01. 68
within their chiefest temple i'll erect | a tomb 2.02. 12
within the temple hall we were too loud, | the 2.04. 3
my flow'ring youth | within a loathsome dungeon, 2.05. 57
lance, | and run a–tilt at death within a chair? 3.02. 51
looks, | and that within ourselves we disagree, 4.01.140
within six hours they will be at his aid. 4.04. 41
of all his wars within the realm of france? 4.07. 71
murther not then the fruit within my womb, 5.04. 63
we will make fast within a hallow'd verge. 2H6 1.04. 22
who's within there, ho? 1.04. 78
within this half hour, hath receiv'd his sight, 2.01. 62
whose flood begins to flow within mine eyes; 3.01.199
within fourteen days | at bristow i expect my 3.01.327
now art thou within point–blank of our 4.07. 26 P
arm'd as we are, let's stay within this house. 3H6 1.01. 38
within whose circuit is elysium | and all that 1.02. 30
itself | england is safe, if true within itself? 4.01. 40
are well foretold that danger lurks within. 4.07. 12
nor thou within the compass of my curse. R3 1.03.283
what sights of ugly death within /my eyes! 1.04. 23
air, | but smother'd it within my panting bulk, 1.04. 40
certain dregs of conscience are yet within me. 1.04.122 P
do, | i'll drown you in the malmsey–butt within. 1.04.270
within the guilty closure of thy walls | richard 3.03. 11
meet me within this hour at baynard's castle. 3.05.105
and yet within these five hours hastings liv'd, 3.06. 8
he is within, with two right reverend fathers, 3.07. 61
within so small a time, my woman's heart 4.01. 78
whom envy hath immur'd within your walls — 4.01. 99
another | within their alablaster innocent arms. 4.03. 11
on, | and flaky darkness breaks within the east. 5.03. 86
let us be lead within thy bosom, richard, | and 5.03.147
a thousand hearts are great within my bosom. 5.03.347
within the parish | saint lawrence poultney, did H8 1.02.152
within these forty hours surrey durst better 3.02.253
by your power legative within this kingdom 3.02.339
and i feel within me | a peace above all earthly 3.02.378
do, i know within a while | all the best men are ep 12
troy, | that find such cruel battle here within? TRO 1.01. 3
and yet will he, within three pound, lift as 1.02.116 P
within his tent, but ill dispos'd, my lord. 2.03. 77
ere the first sacrifice, within this hour, | we 4.02. 64
within my soul there doth conduce a fight | of 5.02.147
within this mile and half. COR 1.04. 8
tullus aufidius, is he within your walls? 1.04. 13
within these three hours, tullus, | alone i 1.08. 7
but then aufidius was within my view, | and 1.09. 85
alone martius did fight | within corioles gates; 2.01.163
within thine eyes sate twenty thousand deaths, 3.03. 70
in love | unseparable, shall within this hour, 4.04. 16
like a dog, but for disturbing the lords within. 4.05. 52 P
is so made on here within as if he were son and 4.05.191 P
examples of the like hath been | within my age. 4.06. 52
lives not this day within the city walls. TIT 1.01. 26
have your lath glued within your sheath, | till 2.01. 41
and hast a thing within thee called conscience, 5.01. 75
and hid the gold within that letter mentioned, 5.01.107
few come within the compass of my curse — 5.01.126
within her scope of choice | lies my consent and ROM 1.02. 18
for fair without the fair within to hide. 1.03. 90
come to thy heart as that within my breast! 2.02.124
i hear some noise within; 2.02.136
within the infant rind of this weak flower 2.03. 23
remedies | within thy help and holy physic lies. 2.03. 52
within this hour my man shall be with thee, 2.04.188
why, she is within, | where should she be? 2.05. 58
within this three hours will fair juliet wake. 5.02. 25
within there! TIM 2.02.185
th' athenians both within and out that wall! 4.01. 38
eyes, | are not within the leaf of pity writ, 4.03.118
within this mile break forth a hundred springs; 4.03.418
such | as slept within the shadow of your power 5.04. 6
you have some sick offense within your mind, JC 2.01.268
within the bond of marriage, tell me, brutus, 2.01.280
who's within? 2.02. 3
there is one within, | besides the things that 2.02. 14
they could not find a heart within the beast. 2.02. 40
bid them prepare within; 2.02.118
he lies to–night within seven leagues of rome. 3.01.286
and, dying, mention it within their wills, 3.02.135
within, a heart | dearer than pluto's mine, 4.03.101
within my tent his bones to–night shall lie, 5.05. 78
king | stands not within the prospect of belief, MAC 1.03. 74
within the volume of which time i have seen 2.04. 2
within this hour, at most, | i will advise you 3.01.127
abide within. 3.01.139
rest | that are within the note of expectation 3.03. 10
'tis better thee without than he within. 3.04. 14
within my sword's length set him; 4.03.234
his distemper'd cause | within the belt of rule. 5.02. 16
when all that is within him does condemn 5.02. 24
within this three mile may you see it coming; 5.05. 36
but i have that within which passes show, HAM 1.02. 85
by what it fed on, and yet, within a month — 1.02.145
within a month, | ere yet the salt of most 1.02.153
within his truncheon's length, whilst they, 1.02.204
sleeping within my orchard, | my custom always 1.05. 59
live | within the book and volume of my brain, 1.05.103
thus, | that, open'd, lies within our remedy. 2.02. 18
though it were hid indeed | within the centre. 2.02.159
uncurrent gold, be not crack'd within the ring. 2.02.428 P
looks, and my father died within 's two hours. 3.02.127 P
whiles rank corruption, mining all within, 3.04.148
if indeed you find him not within this month, 4.03. 36 P
there lives within the very flame of love | a 4.07.114
you do this, keep close within your chamber. 4.07.129
if aught within that little seeming substance, LR 1.01.198
him, | but yet, alas, stood i within his grace, 1.01.273
and fierce quality | than doth, within a dull, 1.02. 13
within a fortnight? 1.04.295
with the earl, sir, here within. 2.04. 59
wretch | that hast within thee undivulged crimes 3.02. 52
madam, within, but never man so chang'd. 4.02. 3
you are now within a foot | of th' extreme verge 4.06. 25
the battle done, and they within our power, 5.01. 67
man of quality or degree within the lists of the 5.03.111 P
signior, is all your family within? OTH 1.01. 84
it hard, within this hour | it will be well. 3.03.286
within these three days let me hear thee say 3.03.472
to do this is within the compass of man's wit, 3.04. 21 P
and stood within the blank of his displeasure 3.04.128
is hush'd within the hollow mine of earth | and 4.02. 79
speak within door. 4.02.144
is it within reason and compass? 4.02.218 P
good madam, keep yourself within yourself, | the ANT 2.05. 75
some wine, within there, and our viands! 3.11. 73
within our files there are, | of those that 4.01. 12
if we be not reliev'd within this hour, | we 4.09. 1
and within three days | you with your children 5.02.201
think | so fair an outward and such stuff within CYM 1.01. 23
i do extend him, sir, within himself, | crush 1.01. 25
that which makes him both without and within. 1.04. 10 P
as strongly as the conscience does within, | to 2.02. 36
put | his brows within a golden crown and call'd 3.01. 60
pisanio show'd thee, | thou wast within a ken. 3.06. 6
thy shoulders, shall within this hour be off, 4.01. 16 P
when i wake, it is | without me, as within me; 4.02.307
less without and more within. 5.01. 33
the heaviness and guilt within my bosom | takes 5.02. 1
perfections wait | that, knowing sin within, PER 1.01. 80
life, | for that's an article within our law, 1.01. 88
if i can get him within my pistol's length, 1.01.166
are like the troyan horse was stuff'd within 1.04. 93
make a fire within. 3.02. 80
would she had never come within my doors. 4.06.148 P
be buried | a second time within these arms. 5.03. 44
love of mine | will take more root within him. TNK 2.06. 28
within this hour the whoobub | will be all o'er 2.06. 35
and each within this month, accompanied | with 3.06.291
the circles of his eyes show /fire within him, 4.02. 81
within this half hour she came smiling to me 5.02. 4
i'll warrant you within these three or four days 5.02.104
arcite's body | within an inch o' th' pyramid, 5.03. 80
beauty within itself should not be wasted. VEN 130
here | within the circuit of this ivory pale, 230
"within this limit is relief enough, | sweet 235
come not within his danger by thy will, | they 639
within my bosom, whereon thou dost lie, | my 646
and says, within her bosom it shall dwell, 1173
within whose face beauty and virtue strived LUC 52
within his thought her heavenly image sits, 288
thy sea within a puddle's womb is hearsed, | and 657
within your hollow swelling feathered breasts, 1122
but they whose guilt within their bosoms lie 1342
lost, vaded, broken, dead within an hour. PP 13. 6
within thine own bud buriest thy content, | and, SON 1.11
to say within thine own deep–sunken eyes | were 2. 7
art, | within the gentle closure of my breast, 48.11
here | within the knowledge of mine own desert, 49.10
lean penury within that pen doth dwell | that to 84. 5
within his bending sickle's compass come, | love 116.10
bring me within the level of your frown, | but 117.11
distill'd from limbecks foul as hell within, 119. 2
are within my brain | full character'd with 122. 1
why dost thou pine within and suffer dearth, 146. 3
within be fed, without be rich no more: 146.12

/WITHOUT 2 FR 0.0002 REL FR 1 V 1 P
/so /we /shall /proceed | /without /suspicion. R2 4.01.157
/could /he /dig /without /arms? HAM 5.01. 37 P

WITHOUT 381 FR 0.0430 REL FR 260 V 121 P
and for the liberal arts | without a parallel; TMP 1.02. 74
without the which this story | were most 1.02.137
serv'd | without or grudge or grumblings. 1.02.249
should produce | without sweat or endeavor: 2.01.161
continue in it five weeks without changing. 2.01.184 P
now lead the way without any more talking. 2.02.173 P
for without them | he's but a sot, as i am; 3.02. 92
merciful, | i have curs'd them without cause. 5.01.179
and deal in her command without her power. 5.01.271
they are all perceiv'd without ye. TGV 2.01. 34 P
without me? they cannot. 2.01. 35 P
without you? 2.01. 36 P
for, without you were so simple, none else would 2.01. 36 P
but you are so without these follies, that these 2.01. 38 P
what, gone without a word? 2.02. 16
and not without desert so well reputed. 2.04. 57
that thus without advice begin to love her? 2.04.208
without some treachery us'd to valentine. 2.06. 32
climb it | without apparent hazard of his life. 3.01.116
without false vantage, or base treachery. 4.01. 29
common friend, that's without faith or love, 5.04. 62
i may not go in without your worship; WIV 1.01.277 P
and (without any pause or staggering) take this 3.03. 12 P
if i suspect without cause, why then make sport 3.03.149 P
i suspect without cause, mistress, do i? 4.02.132 P
can be manifested, | without the show of both. 4.06. 16
have given ourselves without scruple to hell, 5.05.148 P
first, his integrity | stands without blemish; MM 5.01.108
and strike you home without a messenger. ERR 1.02. 67
conclude hairy men plain dealers without wit. 2.02. 87 P
drop again, | without addition or diminishing, 2.02.128
a crow without feather? 3.01. 81
for a fish without a fin, there's a fowl without 3.01. 82
without a fin, there's a fowl without a feather: 3.01. 82

mean, | my wife (but, i protest, without desert) 3.01.112
a one as a man may not speak of without he say 3.02. 91 P
or else you may return without your money. 4.01. 44
and, not without some scandal to yourself, 5.01. 15
not show itself modest enough without a badge of ADO 1.01. 22 P
i can see yet without spectacles, and i see no 1.01.189 P
breeds, therefore the sadness is without limit. 1.03. 4 P
of this till you may do it without controlment. 1.03. 20 P
they will scarcely believe this without trial. 2.02. 41 P
she cannot be so much without true judgment — 3.01. 88
marry, not without the prince be willing, for 3.03. 80 P
and send her home again without a husband. 3.03.163 P
is not your lord honorable without marriage? 3.04. 31 P
that goes without a burden. 3.04. 45 P
of his heart he eats his meat without grudging; 3.04. 89 P
in language | without offense to utter them. 4.01. 98
snapp'd off with two old men without teeth. 5.01.116 P
at my hand | as honor (without breach of honor) LLL 2.01.169
but here without you shall be so receiv'd | as 2.01.172
wenches that would be betray'd without these; 3.01. 24 P
this, "by, in, and without," upon the instant: 3.01. 40 P
that soul that sees thee without wonder; 4.02.113
without the beauty of a woman's face? 4.03.297
pleasant without scurrility, witty without 5.01. 4 P
without scurrility, witty without affection, 5.01. 4 P
without affection, audacious without impudency, 5.01. 5 P
without impudency, learned without opinion, and 5.01. 5 P
without opinion, and strange without heresy. 5.01. 6 P
that we may do it still without accompt. 5.02.200
what, was your vizard made without a tongue? 5.02.242
please, | without the which i am not to be won, 5.02.849
and in the wood, a league without the town MND 1.01.165
me in the palace wood, a mile without the town, 1.02.102 P
without the peril of the athenian law — 4.01.153
'tide life, 'tide death, i come without delay. 5.01.203
walls are so willful to hear without warning. 5.01.209 P
i hope i shall make shift to go without him. MV 1.02. 91 P
and that temptation without, i know he will 1.02. 98 P
to tell me i could do nothing without bidding. 2.05. 9 P
but if you fail, without more speech, my lord, 2.09. 7
and be honorable | without the stamp of merit? 2.09. 39
without any slips of prolixity or crossing the 3.01. 11 P
here stays without | a messenger with letters 4.01.107
nothing is good, i see, without respect; 5.01. 99
ay, and i'll give them him without a fee. 5.01.290
and he that escapes me without some broken limb AYL 1.01.127 P
with reasons and the other mad without any. 1.03. 9 P
and content is without three good friends; 3.02. 25 P
and could not bear themselves without the verse, 3.02.170 P
but didst thou hear without wondering how thy 3.02.172 P
i would sing my song without a burthen; 3.02.247 P
you | than without candle may go dark to bed — 3.05. 39
say "a day," without the "ever." 4.01.146 P
you shall never take her without her answer, 4.01.172 P
answer, unless you take her without her tongue. 4.01.173 P
human as she is, and without any danger. 5.02. 67 P
without hawking or spitting or saying we are 5.03. 11 P
if without more words you will get you hence. SHR 1.02.230
the jacks fair within, the gills fair without, 4.01. 50 P
why then the mustard without the beef. 4.03. 30
for you shall hop without my custom, sir. 4.03. 99
it shall go hard if cambio go without her. 4.04.108
married my daughter without asking my good will? 5.01.134 P
and she herself, without other advantage, may AWW 1.03.102 P
knight surpris'd without rescue in the first 1.03.115 P
good alone | is good, without a name; 2.03.129
name of justice, | without all terms of pity. 2.03.166
not to be understood without bloody succeeding. 2.03.191 P
mine own direct knowledge, without any malice, 3.06. 8 P
what will you say without 'em? 4.03.121 P
i will confess what i know without constraint. 4.03.122 P
my horses be well look'd to, without any tricks. 4.05. 59 P
and both shall cease, without your remedy. 5.03.164
or four languages word for word without book, TN 1.03. 27 P
your coziers' catches without any mitigation or 2.03. 90 P
that cons state without book and utters it by 2.03.149 P
i can yield you none without words, and words 3.01. 23 P
i do not without danger walk these streets. 3.03. 25
this shall end without the perdition of souls. 3.04.289 P
have done this without thy beard and gown, he 4.02. 64 P
add | my love, without retention or restraint, 5.01. 81
you drew your sword upon me without cause, | but 5.01.188
we have left our throne | without a burthen. WT 1.02. 3
so, without | my present vengeance taken. 1.02.280
and love as mine), | without ripe moving to't? 1.02.332
judgment tried it, | without more overture. 2.01.172
that there thou leave it | (without more mercy) 2.03.178
and the king shall live without an heir, if that 3.02.135 P
which none without thee can sufficiently manage, 4.02. 14 P
i cannot do't without compters. 4.03. 36 P
love–songs for maids, so without bawdry, which 4.04.193 P
i would not prize them | without her love; 4.04.376
what an exchange had this been, without boot! 4.04.675 P
not without much content | in many singularities 5.03. 11
win you this city without stroke or wound, JN 2.01.418
but without this match, | the sea enraged is not 2.01.450
madam, | i may not go without you to the kings. 3.01. 66
without th' assistance of a mortal hand. 3.01.158
for without my wrong | there is no tongue hath 3.01.182
or if that thou couldst see me without eyes, 3.03. 48
hear me without thine ears, and make reply 3.03. 49
and make reply | without a tongue, using conceit 3.03. 50
without eyes, ears, and harmful sound of words 3.03. 51
so foul a sky clears not without a storm, | pour 4.02.108
yea, without stop, didst let thy heart consent, 4.02.239
could thought, without this object, | form such 4.03. 44
eyes, | for villainy is not without such rheum, 4.03.108
we make, | to rest without a spot for evermore. 5.07.107
let's purge this choler without letting blood. R2 1.01.153
o villains, vipers, damn'd without redemption! 3.02.129
let's march without the noise of threat'ning 3.03. 51
shall be accomplish'd without contradiction. 3.03.124
the noisome weeds which without profit suck 3.04. 38
what seal is that, that hangs without thy bosom? 5.02. 56
not be | without much shame retold or spoken of. 1H4 1.01. 46
might wear | without corrival all her dignities; 1.03.207
deliver them up without their ransom straight, 1.03.260
thou art essentially made, without seeming so. 2.04.493 P
and thou a natural coward, without instinct. 2.04.494 P
home without boots, and in foul weather too! 3.01. 67
done, | without the taste of danger and reproof. 3.01.173
if we without his help can make a head | to push 4.01. 80
shoulders like a herald's coat without sleeves; 4.02. 45 P
wales, | there without ransom to lie forfeited; 4.03. 96
we will not trust our eyes | without our ears: 5.04.137
looks upon me will take me without weighing, and 2H4 1.02.166 P
may hold up head without northumberland? 1.03. 17
but if without him we be thought too feeble, 1.03. 19
i will not undergo this sneap without reply. 2.01.122 P
that skill in the weapon is nothing without sack 4.03.114 P
be sick with joy, he'll recover without physic. 4.05. 14 P
some few hours | were thine without offense, and 4.05.102
and 'a shall laugh without intervallums. 5.01. 81 P
did contend | without much fall of blood, whose H5 1.02. 25
purpose, and be all well borne | without defeat. 1.02.213
not working with the eye without the ear, | and 2.02.135
to march on to callice | without impeachment; 3.06.142
without more help, could fight this royal battle 4.03. 75
when, without stratagem, | but in plain shock 4.08.108
a third thinks, without expense at all, | by 1H6 1.01. 76
and without all color | of base insinuating 2.04. 34
do it without invention, suddenly, | as i with 3.01. 5
they set him free without his ransom paid, | in 3.03. 72
and therefore may be broke without offense. 5.05. 35
cost and charges, without having any dowry." 2H6 1.01. 61 P
would make thee quickly hop without thy head. 1.03.137
somerset will keep me here | without discharge, 1.03.169
but william of hatfield died without an heir. 2.02. 33
for entering his fee–simple without leave. 4.10. 26 P
should raise so great a power without his leave, 5.01. 21
suppose they take offense without a cause; 3H6 4.01. 14
but such as i (without your special pardon) 4.01. 87
to trust to himself and live without it. R3 1.04.144 P
that all without desert have frown'd on me; 2.01. 68
i say, without characters fame lives long. 3.01. 81
him his fears are shallow, without instance; 3.02. 25
heart, | without control, lusted to make a prey. 3.05. 84
without her, follows to myself and thee, 4.04.407
land | have we march'd on without impediment; 5.02. 4
if without peril it be possible, | sweet blunt, 5.03. 39
be upon him | (without the privity o' th' king) H8 1.01. 74
of his substance, to be levied | without delay; 1.02. 59
things done without example, in their issue 1.02. 90
that if the king | should without issue die, 1.02.134
that wretch betray'd, | and without trial fell; 2.01.111
as i am made without him, so i'll stand, | if 2.02. 51
and that, without delay, their arguments | be 2.04. 67
a woman (i dare say without vainglory) | never 3.01.127
that, without the king's assent or knowledge, 3.02.310
that, without the knowledge | either of king or 3.02.316
without the king's will or the state's allowance 3.02.322
yes, without all doubt. 4.01.113
to have heard you | without indurance further. 5.01.121
without, my noble lords? 5.02. 40
and yet no day without a deed to crown it. 5.04. 58
why should i war without the walls of troy, TRO 1.01. 2
he is melancholy without cause, and merry 1.02. 26 P
without the rack. 1.02.138 P
con an oration without book than thou learn /a 2.01. 17 P
book than thou learn /a prayer without book. 2.01. 18 P
without some image of th' affected merit. 2.02. 60
spirit on our party | without a heart to dare, 2.02.157
without drawing their massy irons and cutting 2.03. 16 P
dispose | without observance or respect of any, 2.03.165
you must prepare to fight without achilles. 2.03.227
than blind reason stumbling without fear. 3.02. 72 P
honor for those honors | that are without him, 3.03. 82
parted, | how much in having, or without or in, 3.03. 97
a flint, which will not show without knocking. 3.03.257 P
heart, | why sigh'st thou without breaking?" 4.04. 17
a puttock, or a herring without a roe, i would 5.01. 62 P
apt, without a theme | for depravation, to 5.02.131
where reason can revolt | without perdition, and 5.02.145
and loss assume all reason | without revolt. 5.02.146
most putrefied core, so fair without, | thy 5.08. 1
which, without note, here's many else have done COR 1.09. 49
you, and not without his true purchasing. 2.01.139 P
without any further deed to have them at all 2.02. 27 P
you are never without your tricks; 2.03. 34 P
and cannot go without any honest man's voice. 2.03.132 P
cause, the other | insult without all reason; 3.01.144
physic | that's sure of death without it — at 3.01.155
bran together | he throws without distinction. 3.01.321
to some nation | that won you without blows! 3.03.133
affecting one sole throne, | without assistance. 4.06. 33
it, and rome | sits safe and still without him. 4.06. 37
size that verity | would without lapsing suffer. 5.02. 19
openly, | and basely put it up without revenge? TIT 1.01.433
without controlment, justice, or revenge? 2.01. 68
nor i no strength to climb without thy help. 2.03.242
my name, | without the help of any hand at all. 4.01. 71
should, without eyes, see pathways to his will! ROM 1.01.172
shut up in prison, kept without my food, | whipt 1.02. 55
perhaps you have learn'd it without book. 1.02. 59 P
now i'll tell you without asking. 1.02. 78 P
for fair without the fair within to hide. 1.03. 90
or shall we on without apology? 1.04. 2
perfection which he owes | without that title. 2.02. 47
without his roe, like a dried herring: 2.04. 37 P
could you not take some occasion without giving? 3.01. 43 P
there is no world without verona walls, | but 3.03. 17
without a sudden calm, will overset | thy 3.05.136
and i will do it without fear or doubt, | to 4.01. 87
woes | we cannot without circumstance descry. 5.03.181
methinks they should invite them without knives: TIM 1.02. 44
let them be receiv'd, | not without fair reward. 1.02.191
upon bare friendship without security. 3.01. 43 P
is past depth | to those that, without heed, do 3.05. 13
quietly cut their throats | without repugnancy? 3.05. 45
of twenty be without a score of villains. 3.06. 77 P
who, without those means thou talk'st of, didst 4.03.313 P
bring in thy ranks, but leave without thy rage; 5.04. 39
upon a laboring day without the sign | of your JC 1.01. 4
me, and went surly by, | without annoying me. 1.03. 22
caesar should be a beast without a heart | if he 2.02. 42
wrong, nor without cause | will he be satisfied. 3.01. 47
you all did love him once, not without cause; 3.02.102
thither sail, | and, like a rat without a tail, MAC 1.03. 9
why, chance may crown me | without my stir. 1.03.144
art not without ambition, but without | the 1.05. 19
but without | the illness should attend it. 1.05. 19
they are, my lord, without the palace gate. 3.01. 46
where our desire is got without content; 3.02. 5
things without all remedy | should be without 3.02. 11
without all remedy | should be without regard: 3.02. 12
'tis better thee without than he within. 3.04. 14
is ceremony, | meeting were bare without it. 3.04. 36
a summer's cloud, | without our special wonder? 3.04.111
a deed without a name. 4.01. 49
come in, without there! 4.01.135
strong knots of love, | without leave–taking? 4.03. 28
believe | without the sensible and true avouch HAM 1.01. 57
without more motive, into every brain | that 1.04. 76
and so, without more circumstance at all, | i 1.05.127
he seem'd to find his way without his eyes, 2.01. 95
for out a' doors he went without their helps, 2.01. 96
words without thoughts never to heaven go. 3.03. 98
eyes without feeling, feeling without sight, 3.04. 78
eyes without feeling, feeling without sight, 3.04. 78
ears without hands or eyes, smelling sans all, 3.04. 79
without, my lord, guarded, to know your pleasure 4.03. 14
and shows no cause without | why the man dies. 4.04. 28
great | is not to stir without great argument, 4.04. 54
indeed without an oath i'll make an end on't. 4.05. 57 P
without the which we are pictures, or mere 4.05. 86
where is this king? sirs, stand you all without. 4.05.113
painting of a sorrow, | a face without a heart? 4.07.109
without debatement further, more or less, | he 5.02. 45
speak, | the trumpet to the cannoneer without, 5.02.276
must be a faith that reason without miracle LR 1.01.222
without our grace, our love, our benison. 1.01.265
and that without any further delay than this 1.02. 93 P
frowning, now thou art an o without a figure. 1.04.193 P
daughters, and leave his horns without a case. 1.05. 31 P
upon his life | without the form of justice, yet 3.07. 25
but not without that harmful stroke which since 4.02. 77
chill not let go, zir, without vurther /cagion. 4.06.235 P
mere prattle, without practice, | is all his OTH 1.01. 26
i should have known it | without a prompter. 1.02. 84
without more wider and more /overt test | than 1.03.107
thy joy than to be drown'd and go without her. 1.03.361 P
without the which there were no expectation of 2.01.279 P
and here without are a brace of cyprus gallants 2.03. 30 P
oft got without merit, and lost without 2.03.269 P
got without merit, and lost without deserving. 2.03.269 P
such shadowing passion without some instruction. 4.01. 41 P
that turn'd your wit the seamy side without, 4.02.146
your suspicion is not without wit and judgment. 4.02.211 P
to come in to the cry without more help. 5.01. 44
come guard the door without; 5.02.241
should stretch | without some pleasure now. ANT 1.01. 47
you have broach'd here cannot be without you, 1.02.174 P
my greatness, nor my power | work without it. 2.02. 94
without contradiction, i have heard that. 2.07. 35 P
that | without the which a soldier and his sword 3.01. 28
better might we | have lov'd without this mean, 3.02. 32
then have look'd on him without the help of CYM 1.04. 4 P
that which makes him both without and within. 1.04. 9 P
flat, for taking a beggar without less quality. 1.04. 23 P
which may, without contradiction, suffer the 1.04. 55 P
but i beseech your grace, without offense | (my 1.05. 6
this act, and look'st | so virgin–like without? 3.02. 22
and keep their impious turbands on without 3.03. 6
heard you say, | love's reason's without reason. 4.02. 22
ne'er than answering | a slave without a knock. 4.02. 74
let their fathers lie | without a monument!), 4.02.227
when i wake, it is | without me, as within me; 4.02.307
without his top? 4.02.354
less without and more within. 5.01. 33
to himself unknown, without seeking find, and be 5.04.139 P
to himself unknown, without seeking find, and be 5.05.436 P
and which, without desert, because thine eye PER 1.01. 32
that without covering, save yon field of stars, 1.01. 37
it shall no longer grieve without reproof. 2.04. 19
and knowing this kingdom is without a head — 2.04. 35
like goodly buildings left without a roof | soon 2.04. 36
your goodness teach me to't | without your vows. 3.03. 27
pray you, without any more virginal fencing, 4.06. 57 P
petitions are not | without gifts understood, TNK 1.03. 15
could not reach to | without some imposition, 1.04. 44
without your noble hand to close mine eyes, | or 2.02. 93
your person | without hypocrisy i may not wish 3.01. 95
carry your tail without offense | or scandal to 3.05. 34
may they kill him without lets, | and the ladies 3.05.156
beauty | truly pertains (without obbraidings, 3.06. 32
without my leave and officers of arms? 3.06.135
he has felt | without doubt what he fights for, 4.02. 97
sleeps little, altogether without appetite, save 4.03. 4 P
yes, without doubt. 5.02. 93
we expire, | and not without men's pity; 5.04. 5
end without audience and are never done. VEN 846
could rule them both without ten women's wit." 1008
persuade | the eyes of men without an orator; LUC 30
without the bed her other fair hand was, | on 393
eye | receives the scroll without or yea or no, 1340
"poor instrument," quoth she, "without a sound, 1464
that soul that sees thee without wonder, | which PP 5. 9
in love, | there a nay is plac'd without remove. 17. 8
without this, folly, age, and cold decay. SON 11. 6
and make me travel forth without my cloak, | to 34. 2
without thy help, by me be borne alone. 36. 4
each check | without accusing you of injury. 58. 8
without all ornament, itself and true, | making 68.10
arrest | without all bail shall carry me away, 74. 2
and therefore mayest without attaint o'erlook 82. 2
within be fed, without be rich no more: 146.12
doubt | if best were as it was, or best without. LC 98

//WITHOUT–BOOK 1 FR 0.0001 REL FR 1 V 0 P

/nor /no //without–book /prologue, /faintly ROM 1.04. 7

WITHOUT–DOOR 1 FR 0.0001 REL FR 1 V 0 P

praise her but for this her without–door form WT 2.01. 69

WITHOUT–DOORS 1 FR 0.0001 REL FR 1 V 0 P
dinner, and will make | no wars without–doors. ANT 2.01. 13
WITH'RED 2 FR 0.0002 REL FR 2 V 0 P
have done thy charm, thou hateful with'red hag. R3 1.03.214
such with'red herbs as these | are meet for TIT 3.01.177
WITHSTAND 2 FR 0.0002 REL FR 1 V 1 P
bridge, killing all those that withstand them. 2H6 4.05. 3 P
ay, in despite of all that shall withstand you. 3H6 4.01.146
WITHSTOOD 1 FR 0.0001 REL FR 1 V 0 P
rage must be withstood, | give me his gage. R2 1.01.173
WITH'T 11 FR 0.0012 REL FR 5 V 6 P
good things will strive to dwell with't. TMP 1.02.460
i pray thee out with't, and place it for her TGV 3.01.335 P
away with't! AWW 1.01.132 P
out with't! 1.01.146 P
away with't! 1.01.149 P
off with't while 'tis vendible; 1.01.154 P
finding | myself thus alter'd with't. WT 1.02.384
away with't! 2.03.132
up with't, keep it close. 3.03.124 P
what will you do with't, that you have been so OTH 3.03.314
out with't, faith! TNK 3.03. 33
WITLESS 5 FR 0.0005 REL FR 5 V 0 P
where youth, and cost, witless bravery keeps. MM 1.03. 10
a witty mother! witless else her son. SHR 2.01.264
like witless antics, one another meet, | and all TRO 5.03. 86
fan | from me the witless chaff of such a writer TNK pr 19
to be his whore is witless. 2.04. 5
WITNESS 129 FR 0.0145 REL FR 111 V 18 P
o heaven, o earth, bear witness to this sound, TMP 3.01. 68
and silvia (witness heaven, that made her fair) TGV 2.06. 25
friend | survives, to whom, thyself art witness, 4.02.109
witness good bringing up, fortune, and truth: 4.04. 69
bear witness, heaven, i have my wish for ever. 5.04.119
i pray you bear witness that me have stay six or WIV 2.03. 35 P
heaven be my witness you do, /and if you suspect 4.02.133 P
warrant of womanhood and the witness of a good 4.02.207 P
shall witness to him i am near at home; MM 4.03. 95
is this the witness, friar? 5.01.167
this is no witness for lord angelo. 5.01.193
mouth, | and in the witness of his proper ear, 5.01.308
that the world may witness that my end | was ERR 1.01. 33
hands with me, and that my two ears can witness. 2.01. 46 P
in verity you did, my bones bears witness, 4.04. 77
and i am witness with her that she did. 4.04. 89
god and the rope–maker bear me witness | that i 4.04. 90
witness you, | that he is borne about invisible: 5.01.186
could witness it, for he was with me then, | who 5.01.220
my lord, in truth, thus far i witness with him: 5.01.255
city, | can witness with me that it is not so. 5.01.325
it is the witness still of excellency | to put a ADO 2.03. 46
'tis a truth, i can bear them witness; 2.03.231 P
as modest evidence | to witness simple virtue? 4.01. 38
as shall be prov'd upon thee by good witness. 4.02. 79 P
who, i myself will bear witness, is praiseworthy 5.02. 87 P
be witness this. LLL 5.02. 33
an evil soul producing holy witness | is like a MV 1.03. 99
and thy thoughts are witness that thou art. 2.06. 32
here | shall witness i set forth as soon as you, 5.01.271
and as mine eye doth his effigies witness | most AYL 2.07.193
hang there, my verse, in witness of my love, 3.02. 1
to make mine eye the witness | of that report SHR 2.01. 52
that love bianca more | than words can witness, 2.01.336
since mine eyes are witness of her lightness, 4.02. 24
here's packing, with a witness, to deceive us 5.01.118 P
swear not by, | but take the high'st to witness. AWW 4.02. 24
you saw one here in court could witness it. 5.03.200
i witness to | the times that brought them in; WT 4.01. 11
do, and be witness to't. 4.04.369
friends unknown, you shall bear witness to't: 4.04.384
then, good my lords, bear witness to his oath. 5.01. 72
hand and seal | witness against us to damnation! JN 4.02.218
may be a president and witness good | that thou R2 2.01.130
and you can witness with me this is true. 4.01. 63
more the pity, his white hairs do witness it, 1H4 2.04.468 P
god witness with me, when i here came in, | and 2H4 4.05.149
witness our too much memorable shame | when H5 2.04. 53
shall witness live in brass of this day's work. 4.03. 97
your majesty is pear me testimony and witness, 4.08. 36 P
witness the night, your garments, your lowliness 4.08. 51 P
your mightiness on both parts best can witness. 5.02. 28
and bear me witness all, | that here i kiss her 5.02.357
fain would mine eyes be witness with mine ears 1H6 2.03. 9
hark ye; not so; in witness, take ye that. 3.04. 37
you cannot witness for me, being slain. 4.05. 43
that can i witness, and a fouler fact | did 2H6 1.03.173
god is my witness, i am falsely accus'd by the 1.03.188 P
i have good witness of this; 1.03.201 P
for he hath witness of his servant's malice. 1.03.209
witness my tears, i cannot stay to speak. 2.04. 86
i shall not want false witness to condemn me, 3.01.168
witness the fortune he hath had in france. 3.01.292
and heavens and honor be witness that no want of 4.08. 62 P
and be a witness | that bona shall be wife to 3H6 3.03.138
witness the loving kiss i give the fruit. 5.07. 32
eyes, | the bleeding witness of my hatred by, R3 1.02.233
witness my son, now in the shade of death, 1.03.266
then be your eyes the witness of their evil. 3.04. 67
yet witness what you hear we did intend. 3.05. 70
your mother lives a witness to his vow — | and 3.07.180
a dire induction am i witness to, | and will to 4.04. 5
god witness with me, i have wept for thine. 4.04. 60
yet, heaven bear witness, | and if i have a H8 2.01. 59
heaven witness, | i have been to you a true and 2.04. 22
his noble jury and foul cause can witness. 3.02.269
bear witness, all that have not hearts of iron, 3.02.424
ever witness for him | those twins of learning 4.02. 57
or else no witness | would come against you. 5.01.107
i mean in perjur'd witness, than your master, 5.01.136
the upper germany, can dearly witness, | yet 5.02. 65
witness how dear i hold this confirmation. 5.02.207
here's "in witness whereof the parties TRO 3.02. 58 P
made, seal it, seal it, i'll be the witness. 3.02.198 P
witness the process of your speech, wherein 4.01. 9
thereto witness may | my surname, coriolanus. COR 4.05. 67
and witness of the malice and displeasure 4.05. 72
shall bear | a better witness back than words, 5.03.204
this is a witness that i am thy son. TIT 2.03.116
witness the sorrow that their sister makes. 3.01.119
great lords, be as your titles witness, 5.01. 5
well, let my deeds be witness of my worth: 5.01.103
witness this wretched stump, witness these 5.02. 22
wretched stump, witness these crimson lines, 5.02. 22
witness these trenches made by grief and care, 5.02. 23
care, | witness the tiring day and heavy night, 5.02. 24
witness all sorrow, that i know thee well | for 5.02. 25
true, 'tis true, witness my knive's sharp point. 5.03. 63
my scars can witness, dumb although they are, 5.03.114
house, | and as he is to witness, this is true. 5.03.124
i call the gods to witness, i will choose | mine TIM 1.01.137
lord timon myself, these gentlemen can witness; 3.02. 51 P
i'm weary of this charge, the gods can witness. 3.04. 25
the gods are witness, | nev'r did poor steward 4.03.479
witness the hole you made in caesar's heart, JC 5.01. 31
be thou my witness that against my will | (as 5.01. 73
and wash this filthy witness from your hand. MAC 2.02. 44
any one, having no witness to confirm my speech. 5.01. 17 P
deliver, | upon the witness of these gentlemen, HAM 1.02.194
witness this army of such mass and charge | led 4.04. 47
witness the world, that i create thee here | my LR 5.03. 77
let her witness it. OTH 1.03.170
witness, you ever–burning lights above, | you 3.03.463
witness that here iago doth give up | the 3.03.465
but now i find i had suborn'd the witness, | and 3.04.153
o, bear me witness, night — ANT 4.09. 5
be witness to me, o thou blessed moon, | when 4.09. 7
'tis mine, and this will witness outwardly, | as CYM 2.02. 35
if you will make't an action, call witness to't. 2.03.151
thy conscience witness! 3.04. 46
thou seest him, | a little witness my obedience. 3.04. 66
our cheeks and hollow eyes do witness it. PER 1.04. 51
here comes my daughter, she can witness it. 2.05. 66
"witness this primrose bank whereon i lie, VEN 151
witness the entertainment that he gave. 1108
i send this written ambassage | to witness duty, SON 26. 4
to this i witness call the fools of time, 124.13
do witness bear | thy black is fairest in my 131.11
lies, | what unapproved witness dost thou bear! LC 53
WITNESS'D 3 FR 0.0003 REL FR 3 V 0 P
shall see thy virtue witness'd every where. AYL 3.02. 8
flood | hath left a witness'd usurpation. 2H4 1.01. 63
which was to my belief witness'd the rather, MAC 4.03.184
WITNESSES 10 FR 0.0011 REL FR 7 V 3 P
all these old witnesses — i cannot err — ERR 5.01.318
her no farther till you are my witnesses. ADO 3.02.129 P
amen, say we. we will be witnesses. SHR 2.01.320
clerk, and some sufficient honest witnesses. 4.04. 95 P
feign, you witnesses above | punish my life for TN 5.01.137
it, and witnesses more than my pack will hold. WT 4.04.283 P
come on, | contract us 'fore these witnesses. 4.04.390
and if not that, i bring you witnesses, | twice JN 2.01.274
confessions | of divers witnesses, which the H8 2.01. 17
of age, | grave witnesses of true experience, TIT 5.03. 78
WITNESSETH 2 FR 0.0002 REL FR 1 V 1 P
the beggar, for so witnesseth thy lowliness. LLL 4.01. 79 P
together, | more witnesseth than fancy's images, MND 5.01. 25
WITNESSING 2 FR 0.0002 REL FR 2 V 0 P
witnessing storms to come, woe, and unrest. R2 2.04. 22
fear, as witnessing | the truth on our side. 1H6 2.04. 63
WIT–OLD 1 FR 0.0001 REL FR 0 V 1 P
which is wit–old. LLL 5.01. 63 P
WIT'S 7 FR 0.0008 REL FR 5 V 2 P
your wit's too hot, it speeds too fast, 'twill LLL 2.01.119
and wit's own grace to grace a learned fool. 5.02. 72
he is wit's pedlar, and retails his wares | at 5.02.317
where will doth mutiny with wit's regard. R2 2.01. 28
his wit's as thick as tewksbury mustard, there's 2H4 2.04.240 P
you a wholesome answer — my wit's diseas'd. HAM 3.02.321 P
when wit's more ripe, accept my rhymes, | and PER 1.ch. 12
WITS 89 FR 0.0100 REL FR 52 V 37 P
out o' your wits, and hearing too? TMP 3.02. 78 P
home–keeping youth have ever homely wits. TGV 1.01. 2
love | inhabits in the finest wits of all. 1.01. 44
here's a fellow frights english out of his wits. WIV 2.01.139 P
i will stare him out of his wits; 2.02.279 P
whip me with their fine wits till i were as 4.05.100 P
my lord, her wits, i fear me, are not firm. MM 5.01. 33
i knew he was not in his perfect wits. ERR 5.01. 42
hath scar'd thy husband from the use of wits. 5.01. 86
till i have brought him to his wits again, | or 5.01. 96
conflict four of his five wits went halting off, ADO 1.01. 66 P
sir, and his wits are not so blunt as, god help, 3.05. 10 P
make rich the ribs, but bankrout quite the wits. LLL 1.01. 27
such short–liv'd wits do wither as they grow. 2.01. 54
good wits will be jangling, but, gentles, agree: 2.01.225
this civil war of wits were much better used 2.01.226
and spend his prodigal wits in bootless rhymes, 5.02. 64
muster your wits, stand in your own defense, 5.02. 85
farewell, mad wenches, you have simple wits. 5.02.264
are these the breed of wits so wondered at? 5.02.266
well–liking wits they have — gross gross, fat 5.02.268
well, better wits have worn plain statute–caps. 5.02.281
sweet, | your wits makes wise things foolish. 5.02.374
you should fright the ladies out of their wits, MND 1.02. 80 P
our natural wits too dull to reason of such AYL 1.02. 53 P
of the fool is the whetstone of the wits. 1.02. 55 P
we that have good wits have much to answer for; 5.01. 11 P
maid, | bend thoughts and wits to achieve her. SHR 1.01.179
those wits that think they have thee do very oft TN 1.05. 33 P
he come, for sure the man is tainted in 's wits. 3.04. 13 P
of pythagoras ere i will allow of thy wits, and 4.02. 59 P
alas, sir, how fell you besides your five wits? 4.02. 86 P
i am as well in my wits, fool, as thou art. 4.02. 88 P
if you be no better in your wits than a fool. 4.02. 90 P
and do all they can to face me out of my wits. 4.02. 93 P
malvolio, thy wits the heavens restore! 4.02. 95 P
i am as well in my wits as any man in illyria. 4.02.106 P
prithee read i' thy right wits. 5.01.297 P
but to read his right wits is to read thus; 5.01.298 P
for though it have holp mad men to their wits, R2 5.05. 62
with shallow jesters, and rash bavin wits, 1H4 3.02. 61
it shall serve among wits of no higher breeding 2H4 2.02. 35 P
have you your wits? 5.05. 45
do among foaming bottles and ale–wash'd wits, is H5 3.06. 78 P
coming on, leaving their wits with their wives; 3.07.149 P
being in his right wits and his good judgments, 4.07. 47 P
that i have labor'd | with all my wits, my pains 5.02. 25
thou mayest bereave him of his wits with wonder. 1H6 5.03.195
and did my brother bedford toil his wits, | to 2H6 1.01. 83
to leave this keen encounter of our wits | and R3 1.02.115
but that our wits are so diversely color'd; COR 2.03. 20 P
i think if all our wits were to issue out of one 2.03. 21 P
we to be baited | with one that wants her wits? 4.02. 44
thy years wants wit, thy wits wants edge, | and TIT 2.01. 26
if | his sorrows have so overwhelm'd his wits? 4.04. 10
five times in that ere once in our /five wits. ROM 1.04. 47
come between us, good benvolio, my wits faints. 2.04. 67 P
nay, if our wits run the wild–goose chase, i am 2.04. 71 P
more of the wild goose in one of thy wits than, 2.04. 73 P
it strains me past the compass of my wits. 4.01. 47
for his wits | are drown'd and lost in his TIM 4.03. 89
with witchcraft of his wits, with traitorous HAM 1.05. 43
is't possible a young maid's wits | should be as 4.05.160
hadst thou thy wits and didst persuade revenge, 4.05.169
'a shall recover his wits there, or, if 'a do 5.01.151 P
faith, e'en with losing his wits. 5.01.159 P
foppish, | and know not how their wits to wear, LR 1.04.168
my wits begin to turn. 3.02. 67
bless thy five wits! 3.04. 58 P
to go, my lord, | his wits begin t' unsettle. 3.04.162
to tell thee, | the grief hath craz'd my wits. 3.04.170
all the pow'r of his wits have given way to his 3.06. 4 P
bless thy five wits! 3.06. 57 P
sir, but trouble him not — his wits are gone. 3.06. 87
poor tom hath been scar'd out of his good wits. 4.01. 57 P
'tis wonder that thy life and wits at once | had 4.07. 40
what, have you lost your wits? OTH 1.01. 92
be not too hard for my wits and all the tribe of 1.03.357 P
are his wits safe? is he not light of brain? 4.01.269
extremity, that sharpens sundry wits, | makes me TNK 1.01.118
nor would the libels read | of liberal wits. 5.01.102
being mad before, how doth she now for wits? VEN 249
call, | soothing the humor of fantastic wits? 850
that eye which looks on her confounds his wits; LUC 290
and useless barns the harvest of his wits; 859
and arm'd his long–hid wits advisedly, | to 1816
sure i am the wits of former days | to subjects SON 59.13
but my five wits nor my five senses can 141. 9
by blunting us to make our wits more keen. LC 161
WIT–SNAPPER 1 FR 0.0001 REL FR 0 V 1 P
goodly lord, what a wit–snapper are you! MV 3.05. 49 P
WITTENBERG 4 FR 0.0004 REL FR 4 V 0 P
intent | in going back to school in wittenberg, HAM 1.02.113
i pray thee stay with us, go not to wittenberg. 1.02.119
and what make you from wittenberg, horatio? 1.02.164
but what, in faith, make you from wittenberg? 1.02.168
WITTIEST 1 FR 0.0001 REL FR 0 V 1 P
it is the wittiest partition that ever i heard MND 5.01.167 P
WITTILY 2 FR 0.0002 REL FR 1 V 1 P
very wittily said to a niece of king gorboduc, TN 4.02. 13 P
her, | which cunning love did wittily prevent: VEN 471
WITTING 1 FR 0.0001 REL FR 1 V 0 P
a grave, | as witting i no other comfort have. 1H6 2.05. 16
WITTINGLY 3 FR 0.0003 REL FR 1 V 2 P
fault, | nor wittingly have i infring'd my vow. 3H6 2.02. 8
if i drown myself wittingly, it argues an act, HAM 5.01. 10 P
/argal, she drown'd herself wittingly. 5.01. 13 P
WITTOL 1 FR 0.0001 REL FR 0 V 1 P
wittol! WIV 2.02.299 P
WITTOLLY 1 FR 0.0001 REL FR 0 V 1 P
say the jealous wittolly knave hath masses of WIV 2.02.272 P
WITTY 16 FR 0.0018 REL FR 8 V 8 P
of excellent discourse, | pretty and witty; ERR 3.01.110
a marvellous witty fellow, i assure you, but i ADO 4.02. 25 P
without scurrility, witty without affection, LLL 5.01. 4 P
a witty mother! witless else her son. SHR 2.01.264
go to, thou art a witty fool, i have found thee. AWW 2.04. 32 P
thou wert as witty a piece of eve's flesh as any TN 1.05. 28 P
"better a witty fool than a foolish wit." 1.05. 36 P
it is no matter how witty, so it be eloquent and 3.02. 43 P
i am not only witty in myself, but the cause 2H4 1.02. 9 P
witty, courteous, liberal, full of spirit. 3H6 1.02. 43
the deep–revolving witty buckingham | no more R3 4.02. 42
abus'd extremely, and to cry, "that's witty!" H8 ep 6
you must be witty now: TRO 3.02. 31 P
but were our witty empress well afoot, | she TIT 4.02. 29
well prais'd! how if she be black and witty? OTH 2.01.131
how love is wise in folly, foolish witty. VEN 838
WIV'D 3 FR 0.0003 REL FR 2 V 1 P
in the stews, i were mann'd, hors'd, and wiv'd. 2H4 1.02. 54 P
but, good lieutenant, is your general wiv'd? OTH 2.01. 60
and bid me, when my fate would have me wiv'd, 3.04. 64
WIVE 4 FR 0.0004 REL FR 3 V 1 P
i had rather he should shrive me than wive me. MV 1.02.131 P
happily to wive and thrive as best i may. SHR 1.02. 56
seas, | i come to wive it wealthily in padua; 1.02. 75
but when i came, alas, to wive, | with hey ho, TN 5.01.397
WIVED 1 FR 0.0001 REL FR 1 V 0 P
that he is promis'd to be wived | to fair marina PER 5.02. 10
WIVE'S *(also wife's)*
WIVE'S 25 FR 0.0028 REL FR 15 V 10 P
and stands so firmly on his wive's frailty, yet WIV 2.01.234 P
he pieces out his wive's inclination; 3.02. 34 P
to search his house for his wive's love. 3.05. 78 P
in her invention and ford's wive's distraction, 3.05. 86 P
will you take up your wive's clothes? 4.02.142 P
search'd a hollow walnut for his wive's leman." 4.02.164 P
if he be a married man, he's his wive's head, MM 4.02. 4 P
be valued 'gainst your wive's commandement. MV 4.01.451
to part so slightly with your wive's first gift, 5.01.167
it, till you met your wive's wit going to your AYL 4.01.168 P
and i hope to have friends for my wive's sake. AWW 1.03. 40 P
were my wive's liver | infected as her life, she WT 1.02.304
philip, good old sir robert's wive's eldest son. JN 1.01.159
the ransom once again | of my wive's brother, 1H4 1.03.142
thy sumptuous buildings and thy wive's attire 2H6 1.03.130
of the lord bonville on your new wive's son, 3H6 4.01. 57
with thy embracements to my wive's allies, | and R3 2.01. 30
stanley, he is your wive's son: 4.02. 87
false to his children and his wive's allies; 5.01. 15
my dear wive's estimate, her womb's increase COR 3.03.114
spotted with strawberries in your wive's hand? OTH 3.03.435
(i am sure it was your wive's) did i to–day 3.03.438
by that handkerchief | that was my wive's? 5.02.320

(whom | he purpos'd to his wive's sole son — a CYM 1.01. 5
get, he may lawfully deal for his wive's soul. PER 2.01.115 P
WIVES' 2 FR 0.0002 REL FR 1 V 1 P
may lighten our own hearts and our wives' heels. ADO 5.04.119 P
may, even in their wives' and children's sight, 2H6 4.02.179
WIVES 58 FR 0.0065 REL FR 44 V 14 P
his intent towards our wives are a yoke of his WIV 2.01.175 P
and our revolted wives share damnation together. 3.02. 39 P
do, | wives may be merry, and yet honest too: 4.02.105
let our wives | yet once again (to make us 4.04. 12
now, good sir john, how like you windsor wives? 5.05.106
money buys lands, and wives are sold by fate. 5.05.233
do not curst wives hold that self–sovereignty LLL 4.01. 36
here's a small trifle of wives! MV 2.02.161 P
alas, fifteen wives is nothing! 2.02.162 P
you shall please to play the thieves for wives, 2.06. 23
the rest aloof are the dardanian wives, | with 3.02. 58
you not been acquainted with goldsmiths' wives, AYL 3.02.271 P
you are fain to be beholding to your wives for. 4.01. 60 P
maids, but the sky changes when they are wives. 4.01.149 P
and brings your froward wives | as prisoners to SHR 5.02.119
i wonder, sir, /sith wives are monsters to you, AWW 5.03.155
should all despair | that have revolted wives, WT 1.02.199
and five or six honest wives that were present. 4.04.270 P
no more such wives, therefore no wife. 5.01. 56
the hazards of all husbands | that marry wives. JN 1.01.120
and leave your children, wives, and you in peace 2.01.257
let wives with child | pray that their burthens 3.01. 89
some poisoned by their wives, some sleeping R2 3.02.159
shed | upon the parting of your wives and you. 1H4 3.01. 94
break with your wives of your departure hence. 3.01.142
here come our wives, and let us take our leave. 3.01.189
i have given them away to bakers' wives, they 3.03. 70 P
clouds, as did the wives of jewry | at herod's H5 3.03. 40
coming on, leaving their wits with their wives; 3.07.149 P
some upon their wives left poor behind them, 4.01.139 P
our souls, | our debts, our careful wives, | our 4.01.231
beach | pales in the flood with men, wives, and 5.pr. 10
we and our wives and children all will fight, 1H6 3.01.100
so worthless peasants bargain for their wives, 5.05. 53
large sums of gold and dowries with their wives, 2H6 1.01.129
command that their wives be as free as heart can 4.07.124 P
ravish your wives and daughters before your 4.08. 30 P
men for their sons, wives for their husbands, 3H6 5.06. 41
stretch'd unto their servants, daughters, wives, R3 3.05. 82
desire, | and his enforcement of the city wives, 3.07. 8
if you do fight in safeguard of your wives, 5.03.259
your wives shall welcome home the conquerors; 5.03.260
having lands, and blest with beauteous wives, 5.03.321
lie with our wives? 5.03.336
make wells and niobes of the maids and wives, TRO 5.10. 19
stand fast, we'll beat them to their wives, | as COR 1.04. 41
lest that thy wives with spits and boys with 4.04. 5
ourselves, our wives, and children, on our knees 4.06. 22
to see your wives dishonor'd to your noses — 4.06. 83
men, wives, and children stare, cry out, and run JC 3.01. 97
your wives, your daughters, | your matrons, and MAC 4.03. 61
the purest of their wives | is foul as slander. OTH 4.02. 18
it is their husbands' faults | if wives do fall. 4.03. 87
know | their wives have sense like them; 4.03. 94
would we had all such wives, that the men might ANT 2.02. 65 P
enter the city, clip your wives, your friends, 4.08. 8
must murther wives much better than themselves CYM 5.01. 4
be it our wives, our children, or ourselves, PER 1.04.103
WIVING 2 FR 0.0002 REL FR 2 V 0 P
no heresy, | hanging and wiving goes by destiny. MV 2.09. 83
loves woman for, besides that hook of wiving, CYM 5.05.167
WIZARD 3 FR 0.0003 REL FR 3 V 0 P
peace, doting wizard, peace! i am not mad. ERR 4.04. 58
hath made the wizard famous in his death. 2H6 5.02. 69
and says a wizard told him that by g | his issue R3 1.01. 56
WIZARDS 1 FR 0.0001 REL FR 1 V 0 P
patience, good lady, wizards know their times. 2H6 1.04. 15
WO 1 FR 0.0001 REL FR 0 V 1 P
sola, sola! wo ha, ho! sola, sola! MV 5.01. 39 P
WODE *(also wood*)*
WODE 1 FR 0.0001 REL FR 1 V 0 P
and here am i, and wode within this wood, MND 2.01.192
/WOE 1 FR 0.0001 REL FR 1 V 0 P
/thou /map /of /woe, /that /thus /dost /talk /in TIT 3.02. 12
WOE 164 FR 0.0185 REL FR 162 V 2 P
o, woe the day! TMP 1.02. 15
our hint of woe | is common: 2.01. 3
and the merchant | have just our theme of woe; 2.01. 6
i am woe for't, sir. 5.01.139
i confess | there is no woe to his correction, TGV 2.04.138
o, i have fed upon this woe already, | and now 3.01.221
them | as if but now they waxed pale for woe: 3.01.230
woe me! for what? MM 1.04. 26
pardon is still the nurse of second woe. 2.01.284
my mirth it much displeas'd, but pleas'd my woe. 4.01. 13
heaven shield your grace from woe, | as i, thus 5.01.118
with lesser weight, but not with lesser woe, ERR 1.01.108
why, headstrong liberty is lash'd with woe: 2.01. 15
converting all your sounds of woe | into hey ADO 2.03. 68
measure his woe the length and breadth of mine, 5.01. 11
knight, | for the which, with songs of woe, 5.03. 14
's | than this for whom we rend'red up this woe. 5.03. 33
alack for woe! LLL 4.01. 15
so ridest thou triumphing in my woe. 4.03. 34
never so weary, never so in woe, | bedabbled MND 3.02.442
loud, | puts the wretch that lies in woe | in 5.01.377
measures my husband's sorrow by his woe: SHR 5.02. 29
woe the while! WT 3.02.172
last — o lords, | when i have said, cry "woe!" 3.02.200
could have seen't, the woe had been universal. 5.02. 92 P
o, let us pay the time but needful woe, | since JN 5.07.110
woe doth the heavier sit | where it perceives it R2 1.03.280
though death be poor, it ends a mortal woe. 2.01.152
'tis nameless woe, i wot. 2.02. 40
so, green, thou art the midwife to my woe, | and 2.02. 62
have woe to woe, sorrow to sorrow join'd. 2.02. 66
have woe to woe, sorrow to sorrow join'd. 2.02. 66
witnessing storms to come, woe, and unrest. 2.04. 22
cry woe, destruction, ruin, and decay: 3.02.102
a king, woe's slave, shall kingly woe obey. 3.02.210
alack, alack for woe, | that any harm should 3.03. 70
woe is forerun with woe. 3.04. 28
woe is forerun with woe. 3.04. 28
meet at london london's king in woe. 3.04. 97
gard'ner, for telling me these news of woe, 3.04.100
child, child's children, cry against you "woe!" 4.01.149
so two together weeping make one woe. 5.01. 86
we make woe wanton with this fond delay, | once 5.01.101
i protest my soul is full of woe | that blood 5.06. 45
my friends, and woe to my lord chief justice! 2H4 5.03.138 P
whose guiltless drops | are every one a woe, a H5 1.02. 26
for many of our princes (woe the while!) 4.07. 75
roan | and will be partner of your weal or woe. 1H6 3.02. 92
ah, woe is me for gloucester, wretched man! 2H6 3.02. 72
be woe for me, more wretched than he is. 3.02. 73
now melt with woe | that winter should cut off 3H6 2.03. 46
for what is in this world but grief and woe? 2.05. 20
woe above woe! 2.05. 94
woe above woe! 2.05. 94
was ever king so griev'd for subjects' woe? 2.05.111
woe to that land that's govern'd by a child! R3 2.03. 11
you live that shall cry woe for this hereafter. 3.03. 7
woe, woe for england, not a whit for me! 3.04. 80
woe, woe for england, not a whit for me! 3.04. 80
compare dead happiness with living woe; 4.04.119
sad, high, and working, full of state and woe: H8 pr 3
ay, marry, | there will be woe indeed, lords; 1.03. 39
if the duke be guiltless, | 'tis full of woe; 2.01.140
woe upon ye | and all such false professors! 3.01.114
a helen and a woe! TRO 2.02.111
hope of revenge shall hide our inward woe. 5.10. 31
and they have nurs'd this woe, in feeding life; TIT 3.01. 74
o, what a sympathy of woe is this, | as far from 3.01.148
that woe is me to think upon thy woes, | more 3.01.239
now help, or woe betide thee evermore! 4.02. 56
woe to her chance, and damn'd her loathed choice 4.02. 78
to heal rome's harms, and wipe away her woe! 5.03.148
bound | i cannot bound a pitch above dull woe; ROM 1.04. 21
i have forgot that name, and that name's woe. 2.03. 46
this but begins the woe others must end. 3.01.120
brief sounds determine my weal or woe. 3.02. 51
spring, | your tributary drops belong to woe, 3.02.103
death | was woe enough if it had ended there; 3.02.115
if sour woe delights in fellowship | and needly 3.02.116
that word's death, no words can that woe sound. 3.02.126
these times of woe afford no times to woo. 3.04. 8
o woe! 4.05. 49
strew — | o woe, thy canopy is dust and stones! 5.03. 13
what further woe conspires against mine age? 5.03.212
for never was a story of more woe | than this of 5.03.309
but, woe the while, our fathers' minds are dead, JC 1.03. 82
woe to the hand that shed this costly blood! 3.01.258
woe, alas! | what, in our house? MAC 2.03. 87
mind that's honest | but in it shares some woe, 4.03.198
kingdom | to be contracted in one brow of woe, HAM 1.02. 4
these but the trappings and the suits of woe. 1.02. 86
pray you throw to earth | this unprevailing woe, 1.02.107
"but who, ah woe, had seen the mobled queen" — 2.02.502
o, woe is me, | t' have seen what i have seen, 3.01.160
but woe is me, you are so sick of late, | so far 3.02.163
one woe doth tread upon another's heel, | so 4.07.163
o, treble woe | fall ten times /treble on that 5.01.246
if aught of woe or wonder, cease your search. 5.02.363
woe, that too late repents! LR 1.04.257
his heart should make | shall of a corn cry woe, 3.02. 33
our present business | is general woe. 5.03.320
or woe upon thy life! OTH 3.03.366
alas, and woe! ANT 4.14.107
woe, woe are we, sir, you may not live to wear 4.14.133
woe, woe are we, sir, you may not live to wear 4.14.133
antony | should conquer antony, but woe 'tis so! 4.15. 17
yet the traitor | stands in worse case of woe. CYM 3.04. 87
and lucre in them | have laid this woe here. 4.02.325
i, in mine own woe charm'd, | could not find 5.03. 68
woe is my heart | that the poor soldier that so 5.05. 2
know the world, see heaven, but, feeling woe, PER 1.01. 48
omit we all their dole and woe. 3.ch. 42
thou hast a heart | that ever cracks for woe! 3.02. 77
favor's chang'd | with this unprofitable woe! 4.01. 25
this borrowed passion stands for true old woe; 4.04. 24
play | his daughter's woe and heavy well–a–day 4.04. 49
i am great with woe, and shall deliver weeping. 5.01.106
or perform my bidding, or thou livest in woe; 5.01.247
o, woe! TNK 1.01.110
despise my cruelty, and cry woe worth me, | till 3.06.249
sorrow to shepherds, woe unto the birds, | gusts VEN 455
so to so, | for love can comment upon every woe. 714
she cries, and twenty times, "woe, woe!" 833
she cries, and twenty times, "woe, woe!" 833
her heavy anthem still concludes in woe, | and 839
variable passions throng her constant woe, | as 967
thy weal and woe are both of them extremes; 987
all love's pleasure shall not match his woe. 1140
pain, | and fellowship in woe doth woe assuage, LUC 790
pain, | and fellowship in woe doth woe assuage, 790
nor why her fair cheeks over–wash'd with woe. 1225
here folds she up the tenure of her woe, | her 1310
when every part a part of woe doth bear. 1327
so woe hath wearied woe, moan tired moan, | that 1363
so woe hath wearied woe, moan tired moan, | that 1363
let guiltless souls be freed from guilty woe: 1482
a brow unbent, that seem'd to welcome woe, 1509
though woe be heavy, yet it seldom sleeps, | and 1574
ere once she can discharge one word of woe; 1605
head declin'd, and voice damm'd up with woe, 1661
which speechless woe of his poor she attendeth, 1674
my woe too sensible thy passion maketh | more 1678
let it then suffice | to drown /one woe, one 1680
"woe, woe," quoth collatine, "she was my wife, 1802
"woe, woe," quoth collatine, "she was my wife, 1802
side, | seeing such emulation in their woe, 1808
"why, collatine, is woe the cure for woe? 1821
"why, collatine, is woe the cure for woe? 1821
and weep afresh love's long since canceil'd woe, SON 30. 7
and heavily from woe to woe tell o'er | the sad 30.10
and heavily from woe to woe tell o'er | the sad 30.10
slow | but heavy tears, badges of either's woe. 44.14
the beast that bears me, tired with my woe, 50. 5
if thinking on me then should make you woe. 71. 8
come in the rearward of a conquer'd woe; 90. 6
and other strains of woe, which now seem woe, 90.13
and other strains of woe, which now seem woe, 90.13
that our night of woe might have rememb'red | my 120. 9
yet so they mourn, becoming of their woe, | that 127.13
a bliss in proof, and prov'd, /a very woe, 129.11
brine | that seasoned woe had pelleted in tears, LC 18
as often shriking undistinguish'd woe, | in 20
in brief the grounds and motives of her woe. 63
"but woe is me, too early i attended | a 78
WOE–BEGONE 1 FR 0.0001 REL FR 1 V 0 P
so dull, so dead in look, so woe–begone, | drew 2H4 1.01. 71
WOEFUL 41 FR 0.0046 REL FR 40 V 1 P
i am a woeful suitor to your honor, | please but MM 2.02. 27
shut | my woeful self up in a mourning house, LLL 5.02.808
presents more woeful pageants than the scene AYL 2.07.138
with a woeful ballad | made to his mistress' 2.07.148
comes rushing on this woeful land at once! R2 2.02. 99
a woeful pageant have we here beheld. 4.01.321
/thee tales | of woeful ages long ago betid; 5.01. 42
o lord, have mercy on me, woeful man! 1H6 1.04. 71
hand | that hath contriv'd this woeful tragedy! 1.04. 77
which thou thyself hast given her woeful breast. 3.03. 51
this place | to wash away my woeful monuments. 2H6 3.02.342
one that was a woeful looker–on | when as the 3H6 2.01. 45
how will the country for these woeful chances 2.05.107
here sits a king more woeful than you are. 2.05.124
prince | and made her widow to a woeful bed? R3 1.02.248
their kingdom's loss, my woeful banishment, 1.03.192
farewell, thou woeful welcomer of glory! 4.01. 89
'tis woeful. H8 2.01.167
a woeful cressid 'mongst the merry greeks! TRO 4.04. 56
me, as with the woeful fere | and father of that TIT 4.01. 89
welcome, dread fury, to my woeful house; 5.02. 82
i am as woeful as virginius was, | and have a 5.03. 50
o woeful sympathy! ROM 3.03. 85
o woeful time! 4.05. 30
o woeful, woeful, woeful day! 4.05. 49
o woeful, woeful, woeful day! 4.05. 49
o woeful, woeful, woeful day! 4.05. 49
lamentable day, most woeful day | that ever, 4.05. 50
o woeful day, o woeful day! 4.05. 54
o woeful day, o woeful day! 4.05. 54
o woeful day! JC 3.02.200 P
events | new hatch'd to th' woeful time. MAC 2.03. 59
if there be more, more woeful, hold it in, | for LR 5.03.203
the rough and woeful music that we have, | cause PER 3.02. 88
his woeful queen we leave at ephesus, | unto 4.ch. 3
yea, and a woeful and a piteous nullity. TNK 3.05. 55
note, | and sings extemporally a woeful ditty, VEN 836
as if they heard the woeful words she told; 1126
a woeful hostess brooks not merry guests. LUC 1125
but when she saw my woeful state, | straight in SON 145. 4
my woeful self, that did in freedom stand | and LC 143
WOEFULLEST 1 FR 0.0001 REL FR 1 V 0 P
it will the woefullest division prove | that R2 4.01.146
WOEFULL'ST 2 FR 0.0002 REL FR 2 V 0 P
lock'd into the woefull'st cask | that ever did 2H6 3.02.409
the woefull'st man that ever liv'd in rome. TIT 3.01.289
WOE'S 3 FR 0.0003 REL FR 3 V 0 P
a king, woe's slave, shall kingly woe obey. R2 3.02.210
the woe's to come; 4.01.322
woe's scene, world's shame, grave's due by life R3 4.04. 27
/WOES 3 FR 0.0003 REL FR 3 V 0 P
/tell /over /your /woes /again /by /viewing R3 4.04. 39
/will /revenge /these /bitter /woes /of /ours. TIT 3.02. 3
/we /our /betters /see /bearing /our /woes, LR 3.06.102
WOES 58 FR 0.0065 REL FR 57 V 1 P
to think upon her woes i do protest | that i TGV 4.04.144
notes | tune my distresses and record my woes. 5.04. 6
and by the doom of death end woes and all. ERR 1.01. 2
my woes end likewise with the evening sun. 1.01. 27
whilst man and master laughs my woes to scorn. 2.02.205
it shall become thee well to act my woes. TN 1.04. 26
they are heavier | than all thy woes can stir; WT 3.02.209
and leave those woes alone which i alone | am JN 3.01. 64
reason | how i may be deliver'd of these woes, 3.04. 55
what a tide of woes | comes rushing on this R2 2.02. 98
my lord, wise men ne'er sit and wail their woes, 3.02.178
or shall we play the wantons with our woes | and 3.03.164
not in words only, but in woes also. 1H4 2.04.416 P
nothing so heavy as these woes of mine. 2H6 5.02. 65
trull | upon their woes whom fortune captivates! 3H6 1.04.115
and now, to add more measure to your woes, | i 2.01.105
moan) | to overgo thy woes and drown thy cries! R3 2.02. 61
their woes are parcell'd, mine is general. 2.02. 81
o harry's wife, triumph not in my woes! 4.04. 59
these english woes shall make me smile in france 4.04.115
thy woes will make them sharp and pierce like 4.04.125
windy attorneys to their client's woes, | aery 4.04.127
man, | and here my brother, weeping at my woes; TIT 3.01.100
then into limits could i bind my woes: 3.01.220
for why my bowels cannot hide her woes, | but 3.01.230
that woe is me to think upon thy woes, | more 3.01.239
chief architect and plotter of these woes. 5.03.122
you sad andronici, have done with woes. 5.03.176
if e'er thou wast thyself and these woes thine, ROM 2.03. 77
thou and these woes were all for rosaline. 2.03. 78
these griefs, these woes, these sorrows make me 3.02. 89
light and light, more dark and dark our woes! 3.05. 36
not, and all these woes shall serve | for sweet 3.05. 52
we see the ground whereon these woes do lie, 5.03.179
but the true ground of all these piteous woes 5.03.180
and then will i be general of your woes, | and 5.03.219
and woes by wrong imaginations lose | the LR 4.06.283
our tongues and sorrows to sound deep our woes PER 1.04. 13
i'll then discourse our woes, felt several years 1.04. 18
take hands, | let us be widows to our woes; TNK 1.01.166
we convent nought else but woes: 1.05. 9
hear nothing but the clock that tells our woes; 2.02. 42
words are done, her woes the more increasing; VEN 254
base watch of woes, sin's pack–horse, virtue's LUC 928
me | to endless date of never–ending woes? 935
old woes, not infant sorrows, bear them mild; 1096
deep woes roll forward like a gentle flood, 1118
thy part | to keep thy sharp woes waking, 1136
my woes are tedious, though my words are brief." 1309
and shapes her sorrow to the beldame's woes, 1458
i'll tune thy woes with my lamenting tongue, 1465

here feelingly she weeps troy's painted woes, 1492
so mild that patience seem'd to scorn his woes. 1505
losing her woes in shows of discontent. 1580
in me moe woes than words are now depending, 1615
and ever since, as pitying lucrece' woes, 1747
and with old woes new wail my dear time's waste; SON 30. 4
to blush at speeches rank, to weep at woes, | or LC 307
WOE–WEARIED 1 FR 0.0001 REL FR 1 V 0 P
that my woe–wearied tongue is still and mute. R3 4.04. 18
WOLD *(see 'old)*
/WOLF 2 FR 0.0002 REL FR 1 V 1 P
/the /lion /and /the //belly–pinched /wolf LR 3.01. 13
/that /trusts /in /the /tameness /of /a /wolf, 3.06. 19 P
WOLF 36 FR 0.0040 REL FR 29 V 7 P
a wolf, nay worse, a fellow all in buff; ERR 4.02. 36
upon | (be it on lion, bear, or wolf, or bull, MND 2.01.180
/lion roars, | and the wolf /behowls the moon; 5.01.372
you may as well use question with the wolf | why MV 4.01. 73
thy currish spirit | govern'd a wolf, who, 4.01.134
better | to fall before the lion than the wolf! TN 3.01.129
which i fear the wolf will sooner find than the WT 3.03. 66 P
is well, keep it so, wake not a sleeping wolf. 2H4 1.02.154 P
to wake a wolf is as bad as smell a fox. 1.02.155 P
i'll chase hence, thou wolf in sheep's array. 1H6 1.03. 55
sheep run not half so treacherous from the wolf, 1.05. 30
i wish some ravenous wolf had eaten thee! 5.04. 31
for i myself will hunt this wolf to death. 3H6 2.04. 13
and yonder is the wolf that makes this spoil. 5.04. 80
so flies the reakless shepherd from the wolf; 5.06. 7
and throw them in the entrails of the wolf? R3 4.04. 23
or wolf, or both (for he is equal rav'nous | as H8 1.01.159
and appetite, an universal wolf | (so doubly TRO 1.03.121
as fox to lamb, or wolf to heifer's calf, | pard 3.02.193
pray you, who does the wolf love? COR 2.01. 7 P
deserve such pity of him as the wolf | does of 4.06.110
thou liv'dst but as a breakfast to the wolf; TIM 4.03.333 P
if thou wert the wolf, thy greediness would 4.03.334 P
poor man, i know he would not be a wolf, | but JC 1.03.104
murther, | alarum'd by his sentinel, the wolf, MAC 2.01. 53
scale of dragon, tooth of wolf, | witch's mummy, 4.01. 22
air, | to be a comrade with the wolf and owl — LR 2.04.210
fox in stealth, wolf in greediness, dog in 3.04. 93 P
like warlike as the wolf for what we eat; CYM 3.03. 41
hark, 'tis a wolf! TNK 3.02. 4
if he not answer'd, i should call a wolf, | and 3.02. 10
or as the wolf doth grin before he barketh, | or VEN 459
if he had spoke, the wolf would leave his prey, 1097
the wolf hath seiz'd his prey, the poor lamb LUC 677
thou sets the wolf where he the lamb may get; 878
how many lambs might the stern wolf betray, | if SON 96. 9
WOLL *(also vill, will*)*
WOLL 1 FR 0.0001 REL FR 0 V 1 P
these fellows woll do well, master shallow. 2H4 3.02.287 P
WOLSEY 6 FR 0.0006 REL FR 6 V 0 P
for worthy wolsey | (who cannot err), he did it. H8 1.01.173
his color, but he came | to whisper wolsey), 1.01.179
o my wolsey, | the quiet of my wounded 2.02. 73
my wolsey, see it furnish'd. 2.02.140
say wolsey, that once trod the ways of glory, 3.02.435
that the great child of honor, cardinal wolsey, 4.02. 6
WOLT *(also wilt, woo't, wo't)*
WOLT 1 FR 0.0001 REL FR 1 V 0 P
says one, "wolt out?" PER 4.01. 61
WOLVES' 1 FR 0.0001 REL FR 1 V 0 P
noise but owls' and wolves' death–boding cries; LUC 165
WOLVES 19 FR 0.0021 REL FR 17 V 2 P
thy groans | did make wolves howl, and penetrate TMP 1.02.288
the wolves have preyed, and look, the gentle day ADO 5.03. 25
the howling of irish wolves against the moon. AYL 5.02.110 P
wolves and bears, they say, | casting their WT 2.03.187
peopled with wolves, thy old inhabitants! 2H4 4.05.137
they will eat like wolves and fight like devils. H5 3.07.151 P
for he's inclin'd as is the ravenous wolves. 2H6 3.01. 78
and wolves are gnarling who shall gnaw thee 3.01.192
and now loud–howling wolves arouse the jades 4.01. 3
the trembling lamb environed with wolves. 3H6 1.01.242
or lambs pursu'd by hunger–starved wolves. 1.04. 5
of france, but worse than wolves of france, 1.04.111
the death of thee | than i can wish to wolves — R3 1.02. 19
courteous destroyers, affable wolves, meek bears TIM 3.06. 95
o thou wall | that girdles in those wolves, dive 4.01. 2
great with tigers, dragons, wolves, and bears, 4.03.189
if wolves had at thy gate howl'd that /dearn LR 3.07. 63
as salt as wolves in pride, and fools as gross OTH 3.03.404
i reak not if the wolves would jaw me, so | he TNK 3.02. 7
WOLVISH *(also woolvish)*
WOLVISH 3 FR 0.0003 REL FR 3 V 0 P
for thy desires | are wolvish, bloody, starv'd, MV 4.01.138
wolvish ravening lamb! ROM 3.02. 76
with her nails | she'll flea thy wolvish visage. LR 1.04.308
WOMAN *(also oman, omans)*
WOMAN 346 FR 0.0391 REL FR 206 V 140 P
i never saw a woman | but only sycorax my dam TMP 3.02.100
o, that she could speak now like a /wood woman! TGV 2.03. 28 P
not like a woman, for i would prevent | the 2.07. 40
a woman sometime scorns what best contents her. 3.01. 93
man, | if with his tongue he cannot win a woman. 3.01.105
and yet 'tis a woman; 3.01.268 P
but what woman, i will not tell myself; 3.01.269 P
mind, | and will not use a woman lawlessly. 5.03. 14
has brown hair, and speaks small like a woman. WIV 1.01. 48 P
never a woman in windsor knows more of anne's 1.04.128 P
how now, good woman, how dost thou? 1.04.134 P
what's the matter, woman? 2.01. 43 P
o woman — if it were not for one trifling 2.01. 44 P
hang the trifle, woman! 2.01. 46 P
you are the happier woman. 2.01.106 P
sir, here's a woman would speak with you. 2.02. 31 P
two thousand, fair woman, and i'll vouchsafe 2.02. 42 P
the sweet woman leads an ill life with him. 2.02. 89 P
woman, commend me to her, i will not fail her. 2.02. 92 P
i never knew a woman so dote upon a man; 2.02.103 P
for if there be a kind woman in windsor, she is 2.02.121 P
boy, go along with this woman. 2.02.133 P
see the hell of having a false woman! 2.02.292 P
pray you do so, she's a very tattling woman. 3.03. 92 P
your husband's coming hither, woman, with all 3.03.106 P
by gar, i see 'tis an honest woman. 3.03.222 P
as well as i love any woman in gloucestershire. 3.04. 43 P
a woman would run through fire and water for 3.04.102 P
come in, woman! 3.05. 25 P
to bring this woman to evil for your good. 3.05. 96 P
why, woman, your husband is in his old lines 4.02. 21 P
what a woman are you! 4.02. 43 P
my maid's aunt, the fat woman of brainford, has 4.02. 75 P
he cannot abide the old woman of brainford. 4.02. 85 P
mistress ford, the honest woman, the modest wife 4.02.130 P
come you and the old woman down; 4.02.167 P
old woman? what old woman's that? 4.02.169 P
gentlemen, let him /not strike the old woman. 4.02.181 P
i think you have kill'd the poor woman. 4.02.188 P
there's an old woman, a fat woman, gone up into 4.05. 11 P
there's an old woman, a fat woman, gone up into 4.05. 11 P
a fat woman? 4.05. 15 P
tarries the coming down of thy fat woman. 4.05. 21 P
mine host, an old fat woman even now with me, 4.05. 24 P
you, sir, was't not the wise woman of brainford? 4.05. 26 P
i spake with the old woman about it. 4.05. 34 P
i could have spoken with the woman herself. 4.05. 39 P
say the woman told me so. 4.05. 51 P
was there a wise woman with thee? 4.05. 58 P
my counterfeiting the action of an old woman, 4.05.118 P
from her, master /brook, like a poor old woman. 5.01. 17 P
he beat me grievously, in the shape of a woman; 5.01. 21 P
a woman. MM 1.02. 88 P
but there's a woman with maid by him. 1.02. 92 P
one that serves a bad woman; 2.01. 64 P
ay, sir; whom i thank heaven is an honest woman. 2.01. 73 P
who, if she had been a woman cardinally given, 2.01. 80 P
and his mistress is a respected woman. 2.01.164 P
that she was ever respected with man, woman, or 2.01.169 P
yes, as i love the woman that wrong'd him. 2.03. 25
be that you are, | that is, a woman; 2.04.135
images newly made woman to be had now, for 3.02. 46 P
not made by man and woman after this downright 3.02.105 P
and to set on this wretched woman here | against 5.01.132
hath this woman | most wrongfully accus'd your 5.01.139
first, for this woman, | to justify this worthy 5.01.158
know you this woman? 5.01.213
my lord, i must confess i know this woman, | and 5.01.216
thou foolish friar, and thou pernicious woman, 5.01.241
wast thou e'er contracted to this woman? 5.01.375
if any woman wrong'd by this lewd fellow | (as i 5.01.509
born, and wed | unto a woman, happy but for me, ERR 1.01. 37
a mean woman was delivered | of such a burthen 1.01. 54
this woman that i mean, | my wife (but, i 3.01.111
marry, sir, besides myself, i am due to a woman: 3.02. 82 P
the venom clamors of a jealous woman | poisons 5.01. 69
justice, sweet prince, against that woman there! 5.01.197
a grievous fault! say, woman, didst thou so? 5.01.206
o perjur'd woman! 5.01.212
this woman lock'd me out this day from dinner; 5.01.218
that a woman conceiv'd me, i thank her; ADO 1.01.238 P
such a man would win any woman in the world, if 2.01. 16 P
would it not grieve a woman to be overmaster'd 2.01. 60 P
one woman is fair, yet i am well; 2.03. 26 P
but till all graces be in one woman, one woman 2.03. 29 P
one woman, one woman shall not come in my grace. 2.03. 29 P
if he be not in love with some woman, there is 3.02. 40 P
therefore i will die a woman with grieving. 4.01.323 P
manly wit, margaret, it will not hurt a woman. 5.02. 16 P
as, not to see a woman in that term, | which i LLL 1.01. 37
that no woman shall come within a mile of my 1.01.119 P
be seen to talk with a woman within the term of 1.01.129 P
it is the manner of a man to speak to a woman; 1.01.210 P
or, for thy more sweet understanding, a woman. 1.01.265 P
a woman, master. 1.02. 77 P
years, | no woman may approach his silent court; 2.01. 24
a woman sometimes, and you saw her in the light. 2.01.198
a woman, that is like a german /clock, | still 3.01.190
are not you the chief woman? 4.01. 51
that was a woman when queen guinover of britain 4.01.123 P
a woman i forswore, but i will prove, | thou 4.03. 62
to fast, to study, and to see no woman — | flat 4.03.288
let not me play a woman; MND 1.02. 47 P
laid | will make or man or woman madly dote 2.01.171
too — | and the athenian woman by his side; 3.02. 39
this is the woman; but not this the man. 3.02. 42
she for a woman, god bless us. 5.01.320 P
well, if fortune be a woman, she's a good wench MV 2.02.166 P
my gossip report be an honest woman of her word. 3.01. 7 P
but if she be less than an honest woman, she is 3.05. 42 P
gifts, | and if your wife be not a mad woman, 4.01.445
ay, if a woman live to be a man. 5.01.160
i'll die for't but some woman had the ring! 5.01.208
no woman had it, but a civil doctor, | which did 5.01.210
the bountiful blind woman doth most mistake in AYL 1.02. 36 P
my man's apparel and to cry like a woman; 2.04. 5 P
what woman in the city do i name, | when that i 2.07. 74
do you not know i am a woman? 3.02.249 P
and i thank god i am not a woman, to be touch'd 3.02.348 P
is there none here to give the woman? 3.03. 67 P
times a properer man | than she a woman. 3.05. 52
better jointure, i think, than you make a woman. 4.01. 56 P
o, that woman that cannot make her fault her 4.01.174 P
can a woman rail thus? 4.03. 42 P
wilt thou love such a woman? 4.03. 67 P
the woman low, | and browner than her brother." 4.03. 87
i' faith, i should have been a woman by right. 4.03.176 P
he, sir, that must marry this woman. 5.01. 46 P
of this female — which in the common is woman; 5.01. 50 P
and i for no woman. 5.02. 88
and i for no woman. 5.02. 93
and so am i for no woman. 5.02.102
i will marry you, if ever i marry woman, and 5.02.113 P
and as i love no woman, i'll meet. 5.02.120 P
desire to desire to be a woman of the world. 5.03. 4 P
nor ne'er wed woman, if you be not she. 5.04.124
must accord, | or have a woman to your lord; 5.04.134
if i were a woman i would kiss as many of you as ep 18 P
beautiful | than any woman in this waning age. SHR in.2. 63
i see a woman may be made a fool, | if she had 3.02.220
but thou know'st winter tames man, woman, and 4.01. 23 P
will make the man mad, to make /a woman of him. 4.05. 36 P
a woman mov'd is like a fountain troubled, 5.02.142
even such a woman oweth to her husband; 5.02.156
world, isbel the woman and /i will do as we may. AWW 1.03. 19 P
one good woman in ten, madam, which is a 1.03. 82 P
we might have a good woman born but /or every 1.03. 86 P
of neither on the start | can woman me unto't. 3.02. 51
by him and by this woman here what know you? 5.03.237
did he love this woman? 5.03.242 P
did love her, sir, as a gentleman loves a woman. 5.03.246 P
as i am woman (now alas the day!), TN 2.02. 38
what kind of woman is't? 2.04. 26
let still the woman take | an elder than herself 2.04. 29
compare | between that love a woman can bear me 2.04.102
man, | as it might be, perhaps, were i a woman, 2.04.108
and that no woman has, nor never none | shall 3.01.159
commendation with woman than report of valor. 3.02. 38 P
carry his water to th' wise woman. 3.04.102 P
were you a woman, as the rest goes even, | i 5.01.239
thou never shouldst love woman like to me. 5.01.268
for every inch of woman in the world, | ay, WT 2.01.137
the office | becomes a woman best. 2.02. 30
have show'd too much | the rashness of a woman; 3.02.221
sir, royal sir, forgive a foolish woman. 3.02.227
he hath songs for man or woman, of all sizes; 4.04.191 P
was thought she was a woman and was turn'd into 4.04.279 P
took something good | to make a perfect woman, 5.01. 15
that she is a woman | more worth than any man; 5.01.110
to fears, | a woman, naturally born to fears; JN 3.01. 15
i am no woman, i'll not swound at it. 5.06. 22
join not with grief, fair woman, do not so, | to R2 5.01. 16
peace, foolish woman. 5.02. 80
thou fond mad woman, | wilt thou conceal this 5.02. 95
away, fond woman, were he twenty times my son, 5.02.101
make way, unruly woman! 5.02.110
a woman, and thy aunt, great king, 'tis i. 5.03. 76
thou frantic woman, what dost thou make here? 5.03. 89
been | a banish'd woman from my harry's bed? 1H4 2.03. 39
but yet a woman, and for secrecy, | no lady 2.03.109
words than a parrot, and yet the son of a woman! 2.04. 99 P
go to, you are a woman, go. 3.03. 61 P
now, as i am a true woman, holland of eight 3.03. 71 P
charge an honest woman with picking thy pocket! 3.03.156 P
he will spare neither man, woman, nor child. 2H4 2.01. 17 P
is a long one for a poor lone woman to bear, and 2.01. 33 P
unless a woman should be made an ass and a beast 2.01. 37 P
upon the easy–yielding spirit of this woman, and 2.01.115 P
of your reputation, and satisfy the poor woman. 2.01.131 P
says he, "you are an honest woman, and well 2.04. 92 P
"no woman shall succeed in salique land"; H5 1.02. 39
then come a' god's name, i fear no woman. 1H6 1.02.102
doubtless he shrives this woman to her smock, 1.02.119
woman, do what thou canst to save our honors; 1.02.147
a woman clad in armor chaseth them. 1.05. 3
she is a woman; 5.03. 79
art thou not second woman in the realm? 2H6 1.02. 43
and, being a woman, i will not be slack | to 1.02. 66
her reported to be a woman of an invincible 1.04. 6 P
what woman is this? 2.01. 77
fie, coward woman and soft–hearted wretch! 3.02.307
had i been there, which am a silly woman, | the 3H6 1.01.243
by that false woman as this king by thee. 2.02.149
no, wrangling woman, we'll no longer stay, 2.02.176
win him, | for she's a woman to be pitied much. 3.01. 36
methinks a woman of this valiant spirit | should 5.04. 39
vouchsafe, divine perfection of a woman, | of R3 1.02. 75
was ever woman in this humor woo'd? 1.02.227
was ever woman in this humor won? 1.02.228
false–boding woman, end thy frantic curse, 1.03.246
relenting fool, and shallow, changing woman! 4.04.431
that | a woman of less place might ask by law: H8 2.02.111
you, that have so fair parts of woman on you, 2.03. 27
for | i am a most poor woman, and a stranger, 2.04. 15
i am a simple woman, much too weak | t' oppose 2.04.106
be their business | with me, a poor weak woman, 3.01. 20
alas, i am a woman, friendless, hopeless! 3.01. 80
a woman lost among ye, laugh'd at, scorn'd? 3.01.107
a woman (i dare say without vainglory) | never 3.01.127
bring me a constant woman to her husband, | one 3.01.134
and to that woman (when she has done most) | yet 3.01.136
i am the most unhappy woman living. 3.01.147
you know i am a woman, lacking wit | to make a 3.01.177
in that one woman i have lost for ever. 3.02.409
(out of thy honest truth) to play the woman. 3.02.430
she is the goodliest woman | that ever lay by 4.01. 69
me, but by her woman | i sent your message, who 5.01. 63
so said her woman, and that her suff'rance made 5.01. 68
i miss'd the meteor once, and hit that woman, 5.03. 50 P
than ever i saw her look, or any woman else. TRO 1.01. 33 P
you are such a woman, a man knows not at what 1.02.258 P
o that i thought it could be in a woman — | as, 3.02.158
a woman impudent and mannish grown | is not more 3.03.217
a woman of quick sense. 4.05. 54
when he might act the woman in the scene, | he COR 2.02. 96
well said, noble woman! 3.02. 31
nay, i prithee, woman — 4.01. 12
she is a woman, therefore may be woo'd, | she is TIT 2.01. 82
she is a woman, therefore may be won, | she is 2.01. 83
what beg'st thou then? fond woman, let me go. 2.03.172
o most insatiate and luxurious woman! 5.01. 88
in sadness, cousin, i do love a woman. ROM 1.01.204
lord, lord, she will be a joyful woman. 2.04.174 P
unseemly woman in a seeming man, | and 3.03.112
always follow lover, elder brother, and woman; TIM 2.02.122 P
because thou art a woman, and disclaim'st 4.03.483
surely, this man | was born of woman. 4.03.494
i grant i am a woman; JC 2.01.292
withal | a woman that lord brutus took to wife. 2.01.293
i grant i am a woman; 2.01.294
but withal | a woman well reputed, cato's 2.01.295
how weak a thing | the heart of woman is! 2.04. 40
for none of woman born | shall harm macbeth. MAC 4.01. 80
i am yet | unknown to woman, never was forsworn, 4.03.126
o, i could play the woman with mine eyes, | and 4.03.230
was he not born of woman? 5.03. 4
no man that's born of woman | shall e'er have 5.03. 6
what's he | that was not born of woman? 5.07. 3
thou wast born of woman. 5.07. 11
brandish'd by man that's of a woman born. 5.07. 13
which must not yield | to one of woman born. 5.08. 13

and thou oppos'd, being of no woman born, | yet 5.08. 31
frailty, thy name is woman! HAM 1.02.146
o most pernicious woman! 1.05.105
when these are gone, | the woman will be out. 4.07.189
what woman then? 5.01.132 P
one that was a woman, sir, but, rest her soul, 5.01.135 P
/gain–giving, as would perhaps trouble a woman. 5.02.216 P
sir, to love a woman for singing, nor so old to LR 1.04. 37 P
was never yet fair woman but she made mouths in 3.02. 35 P
and in woman out–paramour'd the turk. 3.04. 91 P
of silks betray thy poor heart to woman. 3.04. 96 P
/shows not in the fiend | so horrid as in woman. 4.02. 61
gentle, and low, an excellent thing in woman. 5.03.274
thou bestow on a deserving woman indeed — one OTH 2.01.145 P
knave, and the woman hath found him already. 2.01.248 P
good name in man and woman, dear my lord, | is 3.03.155
go to, woman! 3.04.183
i never knew woman love man so. 4.01.110
see how he prizes the foolish woman your wife! 4.01.176 P
a fine woman! 4.01.179 P
a fair woman! 4.01.179 P
a sweet woman! 4.01.179 P
i do not think there is any such woman. 4.03. 83
o perjur'd woman, thou dost stone my heart, 5.02. 63
what needs this iterance, woman? 5.02.150
he, woman: 5.02.152
fie, | your sword upon a woman? 5.02.224
the woman falls; sure he hath kill'd his wife. 5.02.236
o, let him marry a woman that cannot go, sweet ANT 1.02. 64 P
what, says the married woman you may go? 1.03. 20
whom ne'er the word of "no" woman heard speak, 2.02.223
as well a woman with an eunuch play'd | as with 2.05. 5
a woman with an eunuch play'd | as with a woman. 2.05. 6
but there is never a fair woman has a true face. 2.06. 99 P
myself to lack | the courage of a woman — less 4.14. 60
no more but /e'en a woman, and commanded | by 4.15. 73
plac'd, and i have nothing | of woman in me; 5.02.239
no longer than yesterday, a very honest woman — 5.02.252 P
lie, as a woman should not do but in the way of 5.02.252 P
i know the devil himself will not eat a woman. 5.02.273 P
i know that a woman is a dish for the gods, if 5.02.274 P
playfellow, and he is | a man worth any woman; CYM 1.01.146
what woman is, yea, what she cannot choose | but 1.06. 71
a woman that | bears all down with her brain, 2.01. 53
who's there? my woman? helen? 2.02. 1
to dorothy my woman hie thee presently, 2.03.138
go bid my woman | search for a jewel that too 2.03.140
go, bid my woman feign a sickness, say | she'll 3.02. 74
you must forget to be a woman; 3.04.154
woman it pretty self) into a waggish courage, 3.04.157
ladies, woman, from every one | the best she 3.05. 72
were you a woman, youth, | i should woo hard, 3.06. 68
who is't can read a woman? 5.05. 48
of all the qualities that man | loves woman for, 5.05.167
suddenly, woman. PER 3.01. 69
are you a woman? 4.02. 82
what would you have me be, and i be not a woman? 4.02. 84 P
an honest woman, or not a woman. 4.02. 85
an honest woman, or not a woman. 4.02. 85
what woman i may stead that is distress'd | does TNK 1.01. 36
key — like such a woman | as any of us three; 1.01. 94
i love her as a woman, to enjoy her. 2.02.164
he has as much to please a woman in him | (if he 2.04. 9
his mother was a wondrous handsome woman, | his 2.05. 20
you have a servant | that, if i were a woman, 2.05. 63
and honor in you, | no mention of this woman. 3.03. 15
quo usque tandem? here is a woman wanting. 3.05. 38
an eel and woman, | a learned poet says, unless 3.05. 48
there's a dainty mad woman, master, | comes i' 3.05. 72
a mad woman? we are made, boys! 3.05. 76
and are you mad, good woman? 3.05. 77
yet that i will be woman, and have pity, | my 3.06.191
you are a right woman, sister, you have pity, 3.06.215
and, by the smallness of it, | a boy or woman. 4.01. 59
were here a mortal woman, and had in her | the 4.02. 10
i had one, a woman, | and women 'twere they 5.01.106
there were no woman | worth so compos'd a man! 5.03. 85
alone, | thing like a man, but of no woman bred! VEN 214
and never woman yet | could rule them both 1007
fair), | my worser spirit a woman (color'd ill). PP 2. 4
a woman i forswore; 3. 5
the joys in bed, | one woman would another wed. 18.48
and for a woman wert thou first created, | till SON 20. 9
and when a woman woos, what woman's son | will 41. 7
fair, | the worser spirit a woman color'd ill. 144. 4

WOMAN'D 1 FR 0.0001 REL FR 1 V 0 P
nor my wish, | to have him see me woman'd. OTH 3.04.195

WOMANHOOD 7 FR 0.0008 REL FR 3 V 4 P
with the warrant of womanhood and the witness of WIV 4.02.207 P
neither faith, truth, nor womanhood in me else. 1H4 3.03.110 P
in thee than in a drawn fox, and for womanhood, 3.03.114 P
setting thy womanhood aside, thou art a beast to 3.03.122 P
let it not be believ'd for womanhood! TRO 5.02.129
more | that womanhood denies my tongue to tell. TIT 2.03.174
no womanhood? 2.03.182

WOMANISH 7 FR 0.0008 REL FR 7 V 0 P
out at mine eyes in tender womanish tears. JN 4.01. 36
relent? no: 'tis cowardly and womanish. R3 1.04.261
sure he does not, | he never was so womanish. H8 2.01. 38
sorts, | for womanish it is to be from thence. TRO 1.01.107
thy tears are womanish, thy wild acts /denote ROM 3.03.110
if no inconstant toy, nor womanish fear, | abate 4.01.119
our yoke and sufferance show us womanish. JC 1.03. 84

WOMANKIND 1 FR 0.0001 REL FR 1 V 0 P
unconstant womankind! SHR 4.02. 14

WOMANLY 3 FR 0.0003 REL FR 3 V 0 P
wives | as prisoners to her womanly persuasion. SHR 5.02.120
then, alas, | do i put up that womanly defense, MAC 4.02. 78
nor the queen of ptolomy | more womanly than he; ANT 1.04. 7

WOMAN–POST 1 FR 0.0001 REL FR 1 V 0 P
what woman–post is this? JN 1.01.218

WOMAN–QUELLER 1 FR 0.0001 REL FR 0 V 1 P
a honeyseed, a man–queller, and a woman–queller. 2H4 2.01. 53 P

/WOMAN'S 1 FR 0.0001 REL FR 1 V 0 P
/a /woman's /shape /doth /shield /thee. LR 4.02. 67

WOMAN'S 87 FR 0.0098 REL FR 62 V 25 P
no woman's face remember, | save, from my glass, TMP 3.01. 49
i have no other but a woman's reason: TGV 1.02. 23
more than quick words do move a woman's mind. 3.01. 91
to be slow in words is a woman's only virtue. 3.01.334 P
our youth got me to play the woman's part, | and 4.04.160
fairest, that would have won any woman's heart; WIV 2.02. 70 P
i mine, to build upon a foolish woman's promise. 3.05. 41 P
there is no woman's gown big enough for him; 4.02. 70 P
old woman? what old woman's that? 4.02.169 P
to him (for all he was in woman's apparel) i 5.05.192 P
by the woman's means? MM 2.01. 82 P
more betray our sense | than woman's lightness? 2.02.169
head, and i can never cut off a woman's head. 4.02. 5 P
i am an ass, i am a woman's man, and besides ERR 3.02. 77 P
what woman's man, and how besides thyself? 3.02. 79 P
but nature never fram'd a woman's heart | of ADO 3.01. 49
without the beauty of a woman's face? LLL 4.03.297
now, for not looking on a woman's face, | you 4.03.305
world | teaches such beauty as a woman's eye? 4.03.309
or rather an honest woman's son, for indeed my MV 2.02. 16 P
lie there what hidden woman's fear there will — AYL 1.03.119
and certainly a woman's thought runs before her 4.01.140 P
make the doors upon a woman's wit, and it will 4.01.162 P
apart, | warr'st thou with a woman's heart?" 4.03. 45
and if the boy have not a woman's gift | to rain SHR in.1. 124
ay, the woman's maid of the house. in.2. 90
and do you tell me of a woman's tongue, | that 1.02.207
times piec'd, and a woman's crupper of velure, 3.02. 60 P
that man should be at woman's command, and yet AWW 1.03. 92 P
sir, at a woman's service, and a knave at a 4.05. 24 P
what woman's that? 5.03.157
this woman's an easy glove, my lord, she goes 5.03.277 P
sound, | and all is semblative a woman's part. TN 1.04. 34
there is no woman's sides | can bide the beating 2.04. 93
no woman's heart | so big, to hold so much; 2.04. 95
and let me see thee in thy woman's weeds. 5.01.273
ay, every dram of woman's flesh is false, | if WT 2.01.138
for whose sight | i have a woman's longing. 4.04.667
of their hearts | may easily win a woman's. JN 1.01.269
a woman's will, a cank'red grandam's will! 2.01.194
'tis not the trial of a woman's war, | the R2 1.01. 48
fool | art thou to break into this woman's mood, 1H4 1.03.237
and bring him out that is but woman's son | can 3.01. 46
neither, 'tis a woman's fault. 3.01.240 P
a woman's tailor, sir. 2H4 3.02.150 P
battle as thou hast done in a woman's petticoat? 3.02.154 P
well said, good woman's tailor! 3.02.158 P
prick the woman's tailor. 3.02.161 P
will this feeble the woman's tailor run off! 3.02.268 P
happily a woman's voice may do some good, | when H5 5.02. 93
yet hath a woman's kindness overrul'd; 1H6 2.02. 50
wilt thou be daunted at a woman's sight? 5.03. 69
if it be fond, call it a woman's fear; 2H6 3.01. 36
a woman's general: 3H6 1.02. 68
o tiger's heart wrapp'd in a woman's hide! 1.04.137
and yet be seen to wear a woman's face? 1.04.140
my woman's heart | grossly grew captive to his R3 4.01. 78
too, a woman's heart, which ever yet | affected H8 2.03. 28
and of wisdom | o'ertopping woman's pow'r. 2.04. 88
valiant, | but i am weaker than a woman's tear, TRO 1.01. 9
this woman's answer sorts, | for womanish it is 1.01.106
i have a woman's longing, | an appetite that i 3.03.237
not of a woman's tenderness to be, | requires COR 5.03.129
requires nor child nor woman's face to see. 5.03.130
o tamora, thou bearest a woman's face — TIT 2.03.136
do thou entreat her show a woman's pity. 2.03.147
lend me a fool's heart and a woman's eyes, | and TIM 5.01.157
i have a man's mind, but a woman's might. JC 2.04. 8
come to my woman's breasts, | and take my milk MAC 1.05. 47
the repetition in a woman's ear | would murther 2.03. 85
become | a woman's story at a winter's fire, 3.04. 64
as woman's love. HAM 3.02.154 P
to thee a woman's services are due, | /a fool LR 4.02. 27
o indistinguish'd space of woman's will! 4.06.271
if that the earth could teem with woman's tears, OTH 4.01.245
could i find out | the woman's part in me — for CYM 2.05. 20
in man, but i affirm | it is the woman's part: 2.05. 22
be it lying, note it, | the woman's; 2.05. 23
for 'tis said a woman's fitness comes by fits. 4.01. 6 P
speak't in a woman's key — like such a woman TNK 1.01. 94
o, who can find the bent of woman's fancy? 4.02. 33
art thou a woman's son and canst not feel | what VEN 201
if ever man were mov'd with woman's moans, | be LUC 587
full oft, | a woman's nay doth stand for nought? PP 18.42
a woman's face with nature's own hand painted SON 20. 1
a woman's gentle heart, but not acquainted 20. 3
what woman's son | will sourly leave her till 41. 7

WOMAN–TIR'D 1 FR 0.0001 REL FR 1 V 0 P
bastard, | thou dotard, thou art woman–tir'd; WT 2.03. 75

WOMB 59 FR 0.0066 REL FR 52 V 7 P
even so her plenteous womb | expresseth his full MM 1.04. 43
of memory, nourish'd in the womb of /pia /mater, LLL 4.02. 69 P
(her womb then rich with my young squire) MND 2.01.131
clad | which from the womb i did participate. TN 5.01.238
this child was prisoner to the womb and is | by WT 2.02. 57
removed from thy sin–conceiving womb. JN 2.01.182
ugly, and sland'rous to thy mother's womb, 3.01. 44
that ever spider twisted from her womb | will 4.03.128
ripping up the womb | of your dear mother 5.02.152
that bed, that womb, | that mettle, that self R2 1.02. 22
this nurse, this teeming womb of royal kings, 2.01. 51
whose hollow womb inherits nought but bones. 2.01. 83
some unborn sorrow, ripe in fortune's womb, | is 2.02. 10
whose arms were moulded in their mother's womb, 1H4 1.01. 23
imprisoning of unruly wind | within her womb, 3.01. 30
my womb, my womb, my womb undoes me. 2H4 4.03. 22 P
my womb, my womb, my womb undoes me. 4.03. 22 P
my womb, my womb, my womb undoes me. 4.03. 22 P
but i pray god the fruit of her womb miscarry. 5.04. 13 P
camp to camp, through the foul womb of night, H5 4.pr. 4
ay, rather than i'll shame my mother's womb. 1H6 4.05. 35
murther not then the fruit within my womb, 5.04. 63
why, love forswore me in my mother's womb; 3H6 3.02.153
for love of edward's offspring in my womb. 4.04. 18
thou slander of thy heavy mother's womb! R3 1.03.230
o my accursed womb, the bed of death! 4.01. 53
from forth the kennel of thy womb hath crept | a 4.04. 47
thy womb let loose to chase us to our graves. 4.04. 54
thee, | by strangling thee in her accursed womb, 4.04.138
if i have kill'd the issue of your womb, | to 4.04.296
but in your daughter's womb i bury them; 4.04.423
who had | commanded nature, that my lady's womb, H8 2.04.189
but tender–bodied and the only son of my womb; COR 1.03. 6 P
on thy mother's womb | that brought thee to this 5.03.124
i may be pluck'd into the swallowing womb | of TIT 2.03.239
and from your womb where you imprisoned were 4.02.124
what is her burying grave, that is her womb; ROM 2.03. 10
and from her womb children of divers kind | we 2.03. 11
fir'd | doth hurry from the fatal cannon's womb. 5.01. 65
thou detestable maw, thou womb of death, 5.03. 45
twinn'd brothers of one womb, | whose TIM 4.03. 3
whose womb unmeasurable and infinite breast 4.03.178
ensear thy fertile and conceptious womb, | let 4.03.187
macduff was from his mother's womb | untimely MAC 5.08. 15
life | extorted treasure in the womb of earth, HAM 1.01.137
into her womb convey sterility, | dry up in her LR 1.04.278
many events in the womb of time which will be OTH 1.03.370 P
if every of your wishes had a womb, | and ANT 1.02. 38
/smite, | till by degrees the memory of my womb, 3.13.163
i died whilst in the womb he stay'd | attending CYM 5.04. 37
all love the womb that their first being bred, PER 1.01.107
heaven can make | to herald thee from the womb. 3.01. 34
and as you wish your womb may thrive with fair TNK 1.01. 27
whose hollow womb resounds like heaven's thunder VEN 268
from earth's dark womb some gentle gust doth get LUC 549
thy sea within a puddle's womb is hearsed, | and 657
for where is she so fair whose unear'd womb SON 3. 5
making their tomb the womb wherein they grew? 86. 4
from off a hill whose concave womb reworded | a LC 1

WOMB'S 1 FR 0.0001 REL FR 1 V 0 P
her womb's increase | and treasure of my loins; COR 3.03.114

WOMBS 3 FR 0.0003 REL FR 3 V 0 P
good wombs have borne bad sons. TMP 1.02.120
or | the close earth wombs, or the profound seas WT 4.04.490
like widowed wombs after their lords' decease: SON 97. 8

WOMBY 1 FR 0.0001 REL FR 1 V 0 P
of it | that caves and womby vaultages of france H5 2.04.124

/WOMEN 2 FR 0.0002 REL FR 2 V 0 P
/of /death, | /women /will /all /turn /monsters. LR 3.07.102
but amongst honest /women. PER 4.06.194

WOMEN 169 FR 0.0191 REL FR 128 V 41 P
not | four, or five, women once that tended me? TMP 1.02. 47
and women too, but innocent and pure; 2.01.156
several virtues | have i lik'd several women, 3.01. 43
three things that women highly hold in hate. TGV 3.02. 33
no outrages | on silly women or poor passengers. 4.01. 70
how many women would do such a message? 4.04. 90
when women cannot love where they're belov'd! 5.04. 44
women to change their shapes than men their 5.04.109
you, the women have so cried and shriek'd at it, WIV 1.01.296 P
but women, indeed, cannot abide 'em, they are 1.01.298 P
of our youth in us, we are the sons of women, 2.03. 48 P
buds, that come like women in men's apparel, and 3.03. 72 P
nay, women are frail too. MM 2.04.124
women? 2.04.127
needs buy and sell men and women like beasts, we 3.02. 2 P
heard the absent duke much detected for women, 3.02.122 P
in request, for the old women were all dead. 4.03. 8 P
perceive | these poor informal women are no more 5.01.236
hath set the women on to this complaint. 5.01.251
that's the way; for women are light at midnight. 5.01.279 P
sir, did you set these women on to slander lord 5.01.288 P
is't not enough thou hast suborn'd these women 5.01.306
under | the pleasing punishment that women bear) ERR 1.01. 46
alas, poor women! 3.02. 21
a dear happiness to women, they would else have ADO 1.01.128 P
invisible baldrick, all women shall pardon me. 1.01.242 P
you look with your eyes as other women do. 3.04. 92 P
then fools you were these women to forswear, LLL 4.03.352
or for men's sake, the /authors of these women, 4.03.356
broke | (in number more than ever women spoke), MND 1.01.176
match, | and on the wager lay two earthly women, MV 3.05. 80
woman doth most mistake in her gifts to women. AYL 1.02. 36 P
and all the men and women merely players; 2.07.140
evils that he laid to the charge of women? 3.02.352 P
points in the which women still give the lie to 3.02.390 P
as boys and women are for the most part cattle 3.02.414 P
there be some women, silvius, had they mark'd 3.05.124
to conjure you, and i'll begin with the women. ep 12 P
i charge you, o women, for the love you bear to ep 12 P
for the love you bear to women (as i perceive by ep 15 P
between you and the women the play may please. ep 17 P
women are made to bear, and so are you. SHR 2.01.200
to see | how tame, when men and women are alone, 2.01.312
kindness in women, not their beauteous looks, 4.02. 41
i charge thee tell these headstrong women | what 5.02.130
i am asham'd that women are so simple | to offer 5.02.161
but a harsh hearing when women are froward. 5.02.183
a country where but women were that had receiv'd AWW 4.03.327 P
come hither, count, do you know these women? 5.03.165
for women are as roses, whose fair flow'r TN 2.04. 38
too well what love women to men may owe; 2.04.105
women say so — | that will say any thing. WT 1.02.130
become some women best, so that there be not 2.01. 9
beseech your highness | my women may be with me, 2.01.117
my women, come, you have leave. 2.01.124
is't lawful, pray you, to see her women? 2.02. 11
denied, which 'longs | to women of all fashion; 3.02.104
how? not women? 5.01.109
women will love her, that she is a woman | more 5.01.110
men, that she is | the rarest of all women. 5.01.112

women and fools, break off your conference. JN 2.01.150
sup any women with him? 2H4 2.02.151 P
for the women? 2.04.337 P
for women are shrows, both short and tall; 5.03. 33
holding in disdain the german women | for some H5 1.02. 48
as ever you come of women, come in quickly to 2.01.117 P
and of women. 2.03. 29 P
said once, the dev'l would have him about women. 2.03. 36 P
'a did in some sort, indeed, handle women; 2.03. 37 P
guarded with grandsires, babies, and old women, 3.pr. 20
and none but women left to wail the dead. 1H6 1.01. 51
these women are shrewd tempters with their 1.02.123
tush, women have been captivate ere now. 5.03.107
spirit | (more than in women commonly is seen) 5.05. 71
'tis beauty that doth oft make women proud, 3H6 1.04.128
women are soft, mild, pitiful, and flexible; 1.04.141
why stand we like soft–hearted women here, 2.03. 25
ay, edward will use women honorably. 3.02.124
women and children of so high a courage, | and 5.04. 50
the midwife wonder'd and the women cried, | "o, 5.06. 74
why, this it is, when men are rul'd by women: R3 1.01. 62
let not the heavens hear these tell–tale women 4.04.150
two women plac'd together makes cold weather. H8 1.04. 22
viscount rochford — one of her highness' women. 1.04. 93
and becoming | the action of good women. 2.03. 55
would all other women | could speak this with as 3.01. 31
more pangs and fears than wars or women have; 3.02.370
great–bellied women, | that had not half a week 4.01. 76
would have some pity | upon my wretched women, 4.02.140
i must to bed, | call in more women. 4.02.167
tool come to court, the women so besiege us? 5.03. 35 P
in | the merciful construction of good women, ep 10
there were no more comparison between the women!
TRO 1.01. 43 P
women are angels, wooing: 1.02.286
man, | or that we women had men's privilege | of 3.02.128
men be troiluses, all false women cressids, and 3.02.203 P
tell these sad women | 'tis fond to wail COR 4.01. 25
his revenges with the easy groans of old women, 5.02. 42 P
how more unfortunate than all living women | are 5.03. 97
how many women saw this child of his? TIT 4.02.135
'tis true, and therefore women, being the weaker ROM 1.01. 15 P
no less! nay, bigger: women grow by men. 1.03. 95
to bear, | making them women of good carriage. 1.04. 94
women may fall, when there's no strength in men. 2.03. 80
women are more valiant | that stay at home, if TIM 3.05. 47
if there sit twelve women at the table, let a 3.06. 78 P
women nearest, but men — men are the things 4.03.320 P
drawn | upon a heap a hundred ghastly women, JC 1.03. 23
steel with valor | the melting spirits of women, 2.01.122
how hard it is for women to keep counsel! 2.04. 9
you should be women, | and yet your beards MAC 1.03. 45
as the weird women promis'd, and i fear | thou 3.01. 2
would create soldiers, make our women fight, 4.03.187
it is the cry of women, my good lord. 5.05. 8
man delights not me — nor women neither, though
HAM 2.02.309 P
they are centaurs, | though women all above; LR 4.06.125
to be suspected — fram'd to make women false. OTH 1.03.398
if i court moe women, you'll couch with moe men. 4.03. 57
that there be women do abuse their husbands | in 4.03. 62
why then we kill all our women. ANT 1.02.133 P
under a compelling occasion, let women die. 1.02.137 P
if there were no more women but fulvia, then had 1.02.166 P
that the men might go to wars with the women! 2.02. 66 P
other women cloy | the appetites they feed, but 2.02.235
women are not | in their best fortunes strong, 3.12. 29
see, my women, | against the blown rose may they 3.13. 38
and by a gem of women, to be abus'd | by one 3.13.108
for shame, | transform us not to women. 4.02. 36
help me, my women! 4.13. 1
help me, my women — we must draw thee up. 4.15. 30
o, see, my women: 4.15. 62
how do you, women? 4.15. 82
ah, women, women! 4.15. 84
ah, women, women! 4.15. 84
ah, women, women! 4.15. 90
ah, women, women! 4.15. 90
you laugh when boys or women tell their dreams; 5.02. 74
show me, my women, like a queen; 5.02.227
very many, men and women too. 5.02.250 P
devils do the gods great harm in their women; 5.02.276 P
her bed, | and bear her women from the monument. 5.02.357
call my women. CYM 1.05. 74
i know her women are about her; 2.03. 66
i will make | one of her women lawyer to me, for 2.03. 74
the vows of women | of no more bondage be to 2.04.110
or | who knows if one her women, being corrupted 2.04.116
for men to be, but women | must be half–workers? 2.05. 1
fear and niceness | (the handmaids of all women, 3.04.156
these her women | can trip me, if i err, who 5.05. 34
heard you all this, her women? 5.05. 61
which | even women have cast off, melt thee, but PER 4.01. 7
lance, or women | that have sod their infants in TNK 1.03. 20
the poison of pure spirits, might, like women, 2.02. 75
but i say, where's their women? 3.05. 25
the powers of all women will be with us. 3.06.194
in which you swore i went beyond all women, 3.06.206
me, | till i am nothing but the scorn of women. 3.06.250
lied so lewdly | that women ought to beat me. 4.02. 36
gently they swell, like women new conceiv'd, 4.02.128
one, a woman, | and women 'twere they wrong'd. 5.01.107
a life more worthy from him than all women, | i 5.03.143
and let mild women to him lose their mildness, LUC 979
for men have marble, women waxen, minds, | and 1240
make weak–made women tenants to their shame. 1260
inconstancy | more in women than in men remain.
PP 17.12
"had women been so strong as men, | in faith, 18.35
the wiles and guiles that women work, 18.37
think women still to strive with men, | to sin 18.43
if to women he be bent, | they have at 20.43

WOMENKIND 1 FR 0.0001 REL FR 0 V 1 P
will you not go the way of womenkind? PER 4.06.150 P

WOMEN'S 25 FR 0.0028 REL FR 22 V 3 P
/prais'd women's modesty; WIV 2.01. 58 P
from women's eyes this doctrine i derive: LLL 4.03.298
from women's eyes this doctrine i derive: 4.03.347
or women's sake, by whom we men are men, | /let 4.03.357
women's gentle brain | could not drop forth such AYL 4.03. 33
in women's waxen hearts to set their forms! TN 2.02. 30
sooner lost and worn, | than women's are. 2.04. 35
i learn'd it out of women's faces. WT 2.01. 12
boys, with women's voices, | strive to speak big R2 3.02.113
these are no women's matters. 2H6 1.03.117
your virtues | with these weak women's fears. H8 3.01.169
at a few drops of women's rheum, which are | as COR 5.06. 45
both too, and women's sons. TIM 4.03.414 P
no tradesman's matters, nor women's matters; JC 1.01. 22 P
/for women's fear and love hold quantity, | in HAM 3.02.167
and let not women's weapons, water–drops, LR 2.04.277
so our leader's /led, | and we are women's men. ANT 3.07. 70
men's vows are women's traitors. CYM 3.04. 54
since men take women's gifts for impudence. PER 2.03. 69
could rule them both without ten women's wit." VEN 1008
poor women's faces are their own faults' books. LUC 1253
poor women's faults that they are so fulfill'd 1258
shifting change, as is false women's fashion; SON 20. 4
steals men's eyes and women's souls amazeth. 20. 8
since she prick'd thee out for women's pleasure, 20.13

WON *(also wan*)*

/WON 2 FR 0.0002 REL FR 1 V 1 P
/care /is /gain /of /care, /by /new /care /won; R2 4.01.197
/my /eight /shillings /i /won /from /you /at H5 2.01.105 P

WON 99 FR 0.0112 REL FR 89 V 10 P
if happ'ly won, perhaps a hapless gain; TGV 1.01. 32
if lost, why then a grievous labor won; 1.01. 33
fairest, that would have won any woman's heart; WIV 2.02. 70 P
have won his grace to come in person hither, ERR 5.01.116
once before he won it of me with false dice, ADO 2.01.280 P
i have woo'd in thy name, and fair hero is won. 2.01.299 P
small have continual plodders ever won, | save LLL 1.01. 86
'tis won as towns with fire — so won, so lost. 1.01.146
'tis won as towns with fire — so won, so lost. 1.01.146
please, | without the which i am not to be won, 5.02.849
sword, | and won thy love doing thee injuries; MND 1.01. 17
to nedar's daughter, helena, | and won her soul; 1.01.108
unless you may be won by some other sort than MV 1.02.104 P
that won three fields of sultan solyman, | i 2.01. 26
we are the jasons, we have won the fleece. 3.02.241
i would you had won the fleece that he hath lost 3.02.242
that flattering tongue of yours won me. AYL 4.01.185 P
oath, | that in a twink she won me to her love. SHR 2.01.310
petruchio, go thy ways, the field is won. 4.05. 23
the wager thou hast won, and i will add | unto 5.02.112
'twas i won the wager, though you hit the white, 5.02.186
but that your daughter, ere she seems as won, AWW 3.07. 31
you have won | a wife of me, though there my 4.02. 64
a heaven on earth i have won by wooing thee. 4.02. 66
half won is match well made; 4.03.225
his wife was dead, i blush to say it, he won me. 5.03.141 P
will you be mine now you are doubly won? 5.03.314
all is well ended, if this suit be won, | that ep 2
is he won yet? WT 1.02. 86
near or far off, well won is still well shot, JN 1.01.174
she is corrupted, chang'd, and won from thee; 3.01. 55
what he hath won, that hath he fortified. 3.04. 10
if you had won it, certainly you had. 3.04.118
lost | in this which he accounts so clearly won. 3.04.122
which his triumphant father's hand had won. R2 2.01.181
dogs, easily won to fawn on any man! 3.02.130
all's done, all's won, here breathless lies the 1H4 5.03. 16
than those proud titles thou hast won of me. 5.04. 79
let us not leave till all our own be won. 5.05. 44
so fought, so followed, and so fairly won, 2H4 1.01. 21
the sum of all | is that the king hath won, and 1.01.132
you should have won them dearer than you have. 4.03. 67
you won it, wore it, kept it, gave it me; 4.05.221
france | that can be with a nimble galliard won; H5 1.02.252
me the eight shillings i won of you at betting? 2.01. 94 P
and how the english have the suburbs won. 1H6 1.04. 2
'tis joan, not we, by whom the day is won; 1.06. 17
blois, poictiers, and tours, are won away, 4.03. 45
flight cannot stain the honor you have won, 4.05. 26
surely, by all the glory you have won, | and if 4.06. 50
therefore to be won. 5.03. 79
whom i with pain have wooed and won thereto; 5.03.138
hath won the greatest favor of the commons, 2H6 1.01.192
till france be won into the dolphin's hands. 1.03.170
by flattery hath he won the commons' hearts; 3.01. 28
but all the honor salisbury hath won | is, that 3.02.275
for they have won the bridge, killing all those 4.05. 3 P
day | is not itself, nor have we won one foot, 5.03. 6
saint albons battle won by famous york | shall 5.03. 30
many a battle have i won in france | when as the 3H6 1.02. 73
and lewis a prince soon won with moving words. 3.01. 34
warwick may lose, that now hath won the day. 4.04. 15
was ever woman in this humor won? R3 1.02.228
as it is won with blood, lost be it so! 1.03.271
that he will not be won to aught against him. 3.01.166
and be not easily won to our requests: 3.07. 50
to whom i will retail my conquest won, | and she 4.04.335
here, | a royal battle might be won and lost. 4.04.536
things won are done, joy's soul lies in the TRO 1.02.287
ere they be woo'd, they are constant being won. 3.02.111 P
hard to seem won; 3.02.117
but i was won, my lord, | with the first glance 3.02.117
in that absence wherein he won honor than in the COR 1.03. 4 P
where he hath won, | with fame, a name to 2.01.163
and end, but will | lose those he hath won. 2.01.226
to some nation | that won you without blows! 3.03.133
you have won a happy victory to rome; 5.03.186
my lord, be rul'd by me, be won at last, TIT 1.01.442
woo'd, | she is a woman, therefore may be won, 2.01. 83
mother, | as sure a card as ever won the set; 5.01.100
or if thou thinkest i am too quickly won, | i'll ROM 2.02. 95
done, | when the battle's lost and won. MAC 1.01. 4
what he hath lost, noble macbeth hath won. 1.02. 67
won to his shameful lust | the will of my most HAM 1.05. 45
i am charg'd withal) | i won his daughter. OTH 1.03. 94
caesar and antony have ever won | more in their ANT 3.01. 16
one of them rates | all that is won and lost. 3.11. 70
was mine in britain, for the ring is won. CYM 2.04. 45
and take your ring again, 'tis not yet won. 2.04.114
you have won. 2.04.150
ingots, | which, though he won, he had not; TNK 1.02. 18
the people's praises, won the garlands, | ere 2.02. 16
you have won it. 2.05. 59
all dues | fit for the honor you have won; 2.05. 61
then he has won. 5.03. 68
wear the girlond | with joy that you have won. 5.03.131
fame, | won in the fields of fruitful italy; LUC 107
and he hath won what he would lose again; 688
gentle thou art, and therefore to be won, SON 41. 5

WONCOTE 1 FR 0.0001 REL FR 0 V 1 P
william visor of woncote against clement perkes 2H4 5.01. 39 P

WONDER 131 FR 0.0148 REL FR 108 V 23 P
which i do last pronounce, is (o you wonder!) TMP 1.02.427
no wonder, sir, | but certainly a maid. 1.02.428
monster, to make a wonder of a poor drunkard! 2.02.165 P
trouble, wonder, and amazement | inhabits here. 5.01.104
at least bring forth a wonder, to content ye 5.01.170
o, wonder! 5.01.181
that you will wonder what hath fortuned. TGV 5.04.169
her | of such contents as you will wonder at; WIV 4.06. 13
for his falling, i should wonder at angelo. MM 3.01.187 P
not, | nor by what wonder you do hit of mine — ERR 3.02. 30
grace you show not | than our earth's wonder, 3.02. 32
this i wonder at, | /that he, unknown to me, 4.02. 47
i wonder much | that you would put me to this 5.01. 13
i wonder that you will still be talking, signior ADO 1.01.116 P
i wonder that thou (being, as thou say'st thou 1.03. 10 P
i do much wonder that one man, seeing how much 2.03. 7 P
wonder not till further warrant. 3.02.111 P
i wonder at it. 3.03.116 P
for my part, i am so attir'd in wonder, | i know 4.01.144
death | will quench the wonder of her infamy. 4.01.239
mean time let wonder seem familiar, | and to the 5.04. 70
navarre shall be the wonder of the world; LLL 1.01. 12
a wonder, master! 3.01. 70
that soul that sees thee without wonder; 4.02.113
by heaven, the wonder in a mortal eye! 4.03. 83
and wonder what they were, and to what end 5.02.304
i wonder if titania be awak'd; MND 3.02. 1
i wonder of their being here together. 4.01.131
gentles, perchance you wonder at this show; 5.01.127
but wonder on till truth make all things plain. 5.01.128
at the which let no man wonder. 5.01.134
i wonder if the lion be to speak. 5.01.152 P
no wonder, my lord; 5.01.153 P
i do wonder, | thou naughty jailer, that thou MV 3.03. 8
and weep, and thou must look pale and wonder. AYL 1.01.158 P
the nine days out of the wonder before you came; 3.02.174 P
that reason wonder may diminish | how thus we 5.04.139
and that's a wonder. SHR 2.01.409
make it no wonder; 3.02.191
wonder not, | nor be not grieved; 4.05. 63
here is a wonder, if you talk of a wonder. 5.02.106
here is a wonder, if you talk of a wonder. 5.02.106
and so it is; i wonder what it bodes. 5.02.107
'tis a wonder, by your leave, she will be tam'd 5.02.189
that we with thee | may spend our wonder too, or AWW 2.01. 89
rarest argument of wonder that hath shot out in 2.03. 7 P
nay, i'll speak that | which you will wonder at. 4.01. 86
i wonder, sir, /sith wives are monsters to you, 5.03.155
approach rather to wonder at you than to hear TN 1.05.198 P
with such estimable wonder overfar believe that, 2.01. 27 P
"wonder not, nor admire not in thy mind, why i 3.04.150 P
and though 'tis wonder that enwraps me thus, 4.03. 3
a boy, or a child, i wonder? WT 3.03. 71 P
can dream of yet, | enough then for your wonder. 4.04.389
earth | might thus have stood, begetting wonder, 5.01.133
a notable passion of wonder appear'd in them; 5.02. 16 P
such a deal of wonder is broken out within this 5.02. 24 P
if i do not wonder how thou dar'st venture to be 5.02.171 P
silence, it the more shows off | your wonder; 5.03. 22
a wonder, lady! JN 2.01. 50
and in her eye i find | a wonder, or a wondrous 2.01.497
yet let me wonder, harry, | at thy affections, 1H4 3.02. 29
i wonder much, | being men of such great leading 4.03. 16
and the mute wonder lurketh in men's ears | to H5 1.01. 49
which is a wonder how his grace should glean it, 1.01. 53
in | wonder to wait on treason and on murther; 2.02.110
as we his subjects have in wonder found, 2.04.135
their particular functions and wonder at him. 3.07. 39 P
"wonder of nature" — 3.07. 40 P
whose life was england's glory, gallia's wonder. 1H6 4.07. 48
thou mayest bereave him of his wits with wonder. 5.03.195
was made a wonder and a pointing–stock | to 2H6 2.04. 46
these few days' wonder will be quickly worn. 2.04. 69
i wonder how the king escap'd our hands. 3H6 1.01. 1
i wonder how our princely father scap'd; 2.01. 1
that would be ten days' wonder at the least. 3.02.113
that's a day longer than a wonder lasts. 3.02.114
by so much is the wonder in extremes. 3.02.115
leave off to wonder why i drew you hither | into 4.05. 2
i wonder he's so simple | to trust the mock'ry R3 3.02. 26
i wonder | that such a keech can with his very H8 1.01. 54
can thy spirit wonder | a great man should 3.02.374
but as when | the bird of wonder dies, the 5.04. 40
is that a wonder? TRO 3.03.195
a wonder! 3.03.242 P
i wonder now how yonder city stands | when we 4.05.211
but i do wonder | his insolence can brook to be COR 1.01.261
in congregations, to yawn, be still, and wonder, 3.02. 11
and wonder greatly that man's face can fold | in TIT 2.03.266
on the white wonder of dear juliet's hand, | and ROM 3.03. 36
i wonder at this haste, that i must wed | ere he 3.05.118
i wonder men dare trust themselves with men. TIM 1.02. 43
i wonder on't, he was wont to shine at seven. 3.04. 10
and wonder of good deeds evilly bestow'd! 4.03.461
and put on fear, and cast yourself in wonder, JC 1.03. 60
i wonder none of you have thought of him. 2.01.217
whiles i stood rapt in the wonder of it, came MAC 1.05. 6 P
a summer's cloud, | without our special wonder? 3.04.111
most like; it /harrows me with fear and wonder. HAM 1.01. 44
feeds on this wonder, keeps himself in clouds, 4.05. 89
if aught of woe or wonder, cease your search. 5.02.363
'tis wonder that thy life and wits at once | had LR 4.07. 40
the wonder is, he hath endur'd so long, | he but 5.03.317
it gives me wonder great as my content | to see OTH 2.01.183
i wonder in my soul | what you would ask me that 3.03. 68
sure, there's some wonder in this handkerchief; 3.04.101
caesar, | kneel down, kneel down, and wonder. ANT 3.02. 19

i wonder, doctor, | thou ask'st me such a CYM 1.05. 10
whilst i am bound to wonder, i am bound | to 1.06. 81
no wonder, | when rich ones scarce tell true. 3.06. 11
'tis wonder | that an invisible instinct should 4.02.176
nay, do not wonder at it; 5.03. 53
made | rather to wonder at the things you hear 5.03. 54
a sanguine star, | it was a mark of wonder. 5.05.365
her face was to mine eye beyond all wonder; PER 1.02. 75
gat | for men to see, and seeing wonder at. 2.02. 7
by jove, i wonder, that is king of thoughts, 2.03. 28
through you, increase our wonder, and sets up 3.02. 96
both th' /heart and place | of general wonder. 4.ch. 11
behold, and wonder! TNK 2.02.133
to such a well-found wonder as thy worth, | for 2.05. 27
"vouchsafe, thou wonder, to alight thy steed, VEN 13
whereat th' impartial gazer late did wonder, 748
"wonder of time," quoth she, "this is my spite, 1133
in silent wonder of still-gazing eyes. LUC 84
save sometime too much wonder of his eye, 95
that soul that sees thee without wonder, | which PP 5. 9
but in them it were a wonder. PHT 32
say | to this composed wonder of your frame, SON 59.10
nor did i wonder at the lily's white, | nor 98. 9
have eyes to wonder, but lack tongues to praise. 106.14

WONDER'D 3 FR 0.0003 REL FR 3 V 0 P
the midwife wonder'd and the women cried, | "o, 3H6 5.06. 74
to make us wonder'd at in time to come. TIT 3.01.135
value, which i wonder'd | could be so rarely and CYM 2.04. 74

WONDERED 1 FR 0.0001 REL FR 1 V 0 P
are these the breed of wits so wondered at? LLL 5.02.266

WONDERFUL 24 FR 0.0027 REL FR 10 V 14 P
her into such a canaries as 'tis wonderful. WIV 2.02. 61 P
studient from his book, and it is wonderful. 3.01. 39 P
but most wonderful that she should so dote on ADO 2.03. 95 P
o wonderful, wonderful, and most wonderful AYL 3.02.191 P
o wonderful, wonderful, and most wonderful 3.02.191 P
wonderful, and most wonderful wonderful! 3.02.191 P
wonderful, and most wonderful wonderful! 3.02.192 P
and yet again wonderful, and after that, out of 3.02.192 P
that wench is stark mad or wonderful froward. SHR 1.01. 69
i tell thee, litio, this is wonderful. 4.02. 15
nothing of that wonderful promise, to read him TN 3.04.264 P
most wonderful! 5.01.225
'tis wonderful | what may be wrought out of JN 3.04.178
it is a wonderful thing to see the semblable 2H4 5.01. 64 P
ale-wash'd wits, is wonderful to be thought on. H5 3.06. 79 P
'tis wonderful! 4.08.112
o wonderful, when devils tell the /troth! R3 1.02. 73
more wonderful, when angels are so angry. 1.02. 74
so cunning and so young is wonderful. 3.01.135
why, saw you any thing more wonderful? JC 1.03. 14
o, wonderful! HAM 1.05.118
o wonderful son, that can so stonish a mother! 3.02.328 P
had then left unseen a wonderful piece of work, ANT 1.02.153 P
after, a wonderful sweet air, with admirable CYM 2.03. 17 P

WONDERFULLY 1 FR 0.0001 REL FR 0 V 1 P
under her colors are wonderfully to extend him, CYM 1.04. 21 P

WONDERING 1 FR 0.0001 REL FR 0 V 1 P
thou hear without wondering how thy name should AYL 3.02.172 P

WONDERS 17 FR 0.0019 REL FR 13 V 4 P
that wonders | to hear thee speak of naples. TMP 1.02.433
to see the wonders of the world abroad, | than TGV 1.01. 6
at herne's oak, and you shall see wonders. WIV 5.01. 12 P
i will tell thee wonders. LLL 1.02.139 P
that nightly hoots and wonders | at our quaint MND 2.02. 6
masters, i am to discourse wonders; 4.02. 29 P
ay, and greater wonders than that. AYL 5.02. 28 P
to ambition, they do plot | unlikely wonders: R2 5.05. 19
enacted wonders with his sword and lance: 1H6 1.01.122
to compass wonders but by help of devils. 5.04. 48
he wonders to what end you have assembled | such R3 3.07. 84
the king enacts more wonders than a man, 5.04. 2
master, till the last | made former wonders its. H8 1.01. 18
who was enroll'd 'mongst wonders, and when we, 1.02.119
thou speakest wonders. 5.04. 55
of all the wonders that i yet have heard, | it JC 2.02. 34
his wonders and his praises do contend | which MAC 1.03. 92

WONDER-WOUNDED 1 FR 0.0001 REL FR 1 V 0 P
makes them stand | like wonder-wounded hearers? HAM 5.01.257

WOND'RED 11 FR 0.0012 REL FR 11 V 0 P
so rare a wond'red father and a wise | makes TMP 4.01.123
he wond'red that your lordship | would suffer TGV 1.03. 4
when men were fond, i smil'd and wond'red how. MM 2.02.186
this present hour, | which i have wond'red at. TN 5.01.358
he may be more wond'red at | by breaking through 1H4 1.02.201
not stir | but like a comet i was wond'red at, 3.02. 47
ne'er seen but wond'red at, and so my state, 3.02. 57
the contrary doth make thee wond'red at. 3H6 1.04.131
day, | if he arise, be mock'd and wond'red at. 5.04. 57
and strangers ne'er beheld but wond'red at; PER 1.04. 25
which make a sound, but kill'd are wond'red at. 2.03. 63

WOND'RING 8 FR 0.0009 REL FR 8 V 0 P
off thine | by wond'ring how thou took'st it. AWW 2.01. 90
now grown in grace | equal with wond'ring. WT 4.01. 25
makes me from wond'ring fall to weeping joys, 2H6 1.01. 34
men of heart | look'd wond'ring each at others. COR 5.06. 99
unto the white-upturned wond'ring eyes | of ROM 2.02. 29
far from home, wond'ring each other's chance. LUC 1596
who, wond'ring at him, did his words allow. 1845
not wond'ring at the present, nor the past, SON 123.10

WOND'RINGLY 1 FR 0.0001 REL FR 1 V 0 P
mortally, | yet glance full wond'ringly on us. PER 3.03. 7

/WONDROUS 1 FR 0.0001 REL FR 1 V 0 P
/and /him, /o /wondrous /him! 2H4 2.03. 32

WONDROUS 40 FR 0.0045 REL FR 36 V 4 P
thank you. wondrous heavy. TMP 2.01.198
sticks, but follow thee, | thou wondrous man. 2.02.164
match, and yet is she a wondrous fat marriage. ERR 3.02. 93 P
that is hot ice and wondrous strange snow. MND 5.01. 59
fairer than that word, | of wondrous virtues. MV 1.01.163
and with affection wondrous sensible | he wrung 2.08. 48
her wondrous qualities and mild behavior, | am SHR 2.01. 50
as if they saw some wondrous monument, | some 3.02. 95
with her but once | and found her wondrous cold, AWW 3.06.113
was like this maid, | i found you wondrous kind. 5.03.310
eye i find | a wonder, or a wondrous miracle, JN 2.01.497
now, by my life, this day grows wondrous hot; 3.02. 1
whirl about | the other four in wondrous motion. 4.02.184
and wondrous affable, and as bountiful | as 1H4 3.01.166
maid, is't thou wilt do these wondrous feats? 1H6 1.02. 64
solicit henry with her wondrous praise; 5.03.190
your wondrous rare description, noble earl, | of 5.05. 1
'tis wondrous strange, the like yet never heard 3H6 2.01. 33
and thou, brave oxford, wondrous well belov'd, 4.08. 17
must | confess yourselves wondrous malicious, COR 1.01. 88
or else your actions would grow wondrous single; 2.01. 37 P
in troth, there's wondrous things spoke of him. 2.01.137 P
wondrous! 2.01.139 P
and had you not by wondrous fortune come, | this TIT 2.03.112
o wondrous thing! 2.03.286
if thou do this, i'll show thee wondrous things, 5.01. 55
my heart is wondrous light, | since this same ROM 4.02. 46
o day and night, but this is wondrous strange! HAM 1.05.164
devil or throw him out, | with wondrous potency. 3.04.170
and to such wondrous doing brought his horse, 4.07. 86
'twas pitiful, 'twas wondrous pitiful. OTH 1.03.161
as a fair day in summer; wondrous fair. PER 2.05. 36
what e'er it be, | 'tis wondrous heavy. 3.02. 53
she is wondrous fair! TNK 2.02.147
i am wondrous merry-hearted, i could laugh now. 2.02.150
his mother was a wondrous handsome woman, | his 2.05. 20
but having thee at vantage (wondrous dread!) VEN 635
and chid the painter for his wondrous skill, LUC 1528
kind, | still constant in a wondrous excellence, SON 105. 6
themes in one, which wondrous scope affords. 105.12

WONDROUSLY 1 FR 0.0001 REL FR 0 V 1 P
my soul, my lord leans wondrously to discontent. TIM 3.04. 70 P

/WONT 1 FR 0.0001 REL FR 1 V 0 P
/wont through a secret grate of iron bars | in 1H6 1.04. 10

WONT 49 FR 0.0055 REL FR 33 V 16 P
you were wont, when you laugh'd, to crow like a TGV 2.01. 26 P
the lights they were wont to have when you chid 2.01. 72 P
my tales of love were wont to weary you; 2.04.126
cold, | and that i love him not as i was wont: 2.04.204
you were wont to be a follower, but now you are WIV 3.02. 2 P
when were you wont to use my sister thus? ERR 2.02.153
it on my shoulders, as a beggar wont her brat; 4.04. 38 P
he was wont to speak plain and to the purpose ADO 2.03. 18 P
and when was he wont to wash his face? 3.02. 56 P
when i was wont to think no harm all night, LLL 1.01. 44
i | upon faint primrose beds were wont to lie, MND 1.01.215
was wont to swell like round and orient pearls, 4.01. 54
be as thou wast wont to be; 4.01. 71
see as thou wast wont to see. 4.01. 72
your worship was wont to tell me i could do MV 2.05. 8 P
made, than they are wont | to keep obliged faith 2.06. 6
he was wont to call me usurer, let him look to 3.01. 48 P
he was wont to lend money for a christian cur'sy 3.01. 49 P
at whom so oft | your grace was wont to laugh, AYL 2.02. 9
you do, i was wont | to load my she with knacks. WT 4.04.348
that england, that was wont to conquer others, R2 2.01. 65
taste of it first, as thou art wont to do. 5.05. 99
talbot is taken, whom we were wont to fear; 1H6 1.02. 14
where i was wont to feed you with my blood, 5.03. 14
'tis not his wont to be the hindmost man, | what 2H6 3.01. 2
voice | was wont to cheer his dad in mutinies? 3H6 1.04. 77
mock thee, clifford, swear as thou wast wont. 2.06. 76
it was wont to hold me but while one tells R3 1.04.118 P
cousin, thou wast not wont to be so dull. 4.02. 17
nor cheer of mind that i was wont to have. 5.03. 74
he was wont to come home wounded. COR 2.01.119 P
who was wont | to call them woollen vassals, 3.02. 8
resume that spirit when you were wont to say, 4.01. 16
here's he that was wont to thwack our general, 4.05.178 P
there greet in silence, as the dead are wont, TIT 1.01. 90
titus, when wert thou wont to walk alone, 1.01.339
i wonder on't, he was wont to shine at seven. TIM 3.04. 10
and show of love as i was wont to have. JC 1.02. 34
wherein the spirit held his wont to walk. HAM 1.04. 6
even those you were wont to take such delight in 2.02.327 P
that were wont to set the table on a roar? 5.01.191 P
that ceremonious affection as you were wont. LR 1.04. 59 P
when were you wont to be so full of songs, 1.04.170 P
worthy montano, you were wont to be civil; OTH 2.03.190
she comes more nearer earth than she was wont, 5.02.110
sparkles this stone as it was wont, or is't not CYM 2.04. 40
where thou wast wont to rest thy weary head, LUC 1621
my curtal dog, that wont to have play'd, | plays PP 17.19
when i was wont to greet it with my lays, | as SON 102. 6

/WONTED 1 FR 0.0001 REL FR 0 V 1 P
/their /endeavor /keeps /in /the /wonted /pace; HAM 2.02.338 P

WONTED 11 FR 0.0012 REL FR 11 V 0 P
angry winter, change | their wonted liveries; MND 2.01.113
and make his eyeballs roll with wonted sight. 3.02.369
he hath intent his wonted followers | shall all 2H4 5.05. 98
or raise myself, but keep my wonted calling? 1H6 3.01. 32
entreat you to your wonted furtherance? 5.03. 21
his wonted sleep under a fresh tree's shade, 3H6 2.05. 49
knowing she will not lose her wonted greatness, H8 4.02.102
will bring him to his wonted way again, | to HAM 3.01. 40
promising | to pay our wonted tribute, from the CYM 5.05.462
whose wonted lily white | with purple tears, VEN 1053
permit the sun to climb | his wonted height, yet LUC 776

WOO 81 FR 0.0091 REL FR 64 V 17 P
yet will i woo for him, but yet so coldly | as, TGV 4.04.106
i'll woo you like a soldier, at arms' end, | and 5.04. 57
and thou shalt woo her. WIV 2.03. 88 P
good master shallow, let him woo for himself. 3.04. 50 P
till thou art able to woo her in good english. 5.05.134 P
that the prince should woo hero for himself, and ADO 1.03. 62 P
i pray thee sing, and let me woo no more. 2.03. 48
and she will die if he woo her, rather than she 2.03.176 P
planet, nor i cannot woo in festival terms. 5.02. 41 P
thou and i are too wise to woo peaceably. 5.02. 72 P
shall we resolve to woo these girls of france? LLL 4.03.368
so shall your loves | woo contrary, deceiv'd by 5.02.135
do, | if they return in their own shapes to woo? 5.02.299
nor woo in rhyme, like a blind harper's song! 5.02.405
we should be woo'd, and were not made to woo. MND 2.01.242
you do) | in such disdainful manner me to woo. 2.02.130
then will two at once woo one; 3.02.118
why should you think that i should woo in scorn? 3.02.122
to meet at ninus' tomb, there, there to woo. 5.01.138
in my life | to woo a maid in way of marriage; MV 2.09. 13
with one fool's head i came to woo, | but i go 2.09. 75
leave me alone to woo him. AYL 1.03.133
nor did not with unbashful forehead woo | the 2.03. 50
that your poor friends must woo your company? 2.07. 10
and i set him every day to woo me. 3.02.409 P
and come every day to my cote and woo me. 3.02.427 P
i had rather hear you chide than this man woo. 3.05. 65
come, woo me, woo me; 4.01. 68 P
come, woo me, woo me; 4.01. 68 P
men are april when they woo, december when they 4.01.147 P
"whiles the eye of man did woo me, | that could 4.03. 47
and loving, woo? 5.02. 3 P
begin his wooing that would thoroughly woo her, SHR 1.01.144 P
liking, | will undertake to woo curst katherine, 1.02.183
but will you woo this wild-cat? 1.02.196
will he woo her? ay — or i'll hang her. 1.02.197
i may have welcome 'mongst the rest that woo, 2.01. 96
haste, | and every day i cannot come to woo. 2.01.115
me, | for i am rough, and woo not like a babe. 2.01.137
well mayst thou woo, and happy be thy speed! 2.01.138
and woo her with some spirit when she comes. 2.01.169
myself am mov'd to woo thee for my wife. 2.01.194
he'll woo a thousand, 'point the day of marriage 3.02. 15
and here i firmly vow | never to woo her more, 4.02. 29
see that you come | not to woo honor, but to wed AWW 2.01. 15
my mother told me just how he would woo, | as if 4.02. 69
is front her, board her, woo her, assail her. TN 1.03. 57 P
i'll do my best | to woo your lady. 1.04. 41
whoe'er i woo, myself would be his wife. 1.04. 42
for that i woo, thou therefore hast no cause; 3.01.154
new woo my queen, recall the good camillo, WT 3.02.156
he hath not the gift to woo in other places; H5 5.02.155 P
that, when i come to woo ladies, i fright them. 5.02.228 P
fain would i woo her, yet i dare not speak: 1H6 5.03. 65
am | to woo so fair a dame to be his wife | and 5.03.124
since thou dost deign to woo her little worth 5.03.151
how canst thou woo her? R3 4.04.268
under what title shall i woo for thee, | that 4.04.340
leap of danger, | and woo your own destruction. H8 5.01.140
pandar, | and he's as tetchy to be woo'd to woo, TRO 1.01. 96
i must woo you | to help unarm our hector. 3.01.149
but woo her, gentle paris, get her heart, | my ROM 1.02. 16
so thou wilt woo, but else not for the world. 2.02. 97
these times of woe afford no times to woo. 3.04. 8
ere he that should be husband comes to woo. 3.05.119
and rather woo | those that would mischief me TIM 4.03.467
so did we woo | transformed timon to our city's 5.04. 18
yea, curb and woo for leave to do him good. HAM 3.04.155
how to tell my story, | and that would woo her. OTH 1.03.166
heart, | but keep it till you woo another wife, CYM 1.01.113
that our great king himself doth woo me oft 1.05. 14
i should woo hard, but be your groom in honesty: 3.06. 69
were it to woo my daughter, for it seems | you PER 5.01.262
might, like women, | woo us to wander from. TNK 2.02. 76
pleasures | that woo the wills of men to vanity 2.02.101
then take my life, i'll woo thee to't. 3.06.156
and like a bold-fac'd suitor gins to woo him. VEN 6
then woo thyself, be of thyself rejected; 159
being proud, as females are, to see him woo her, 309
by her, | under a myrtle shade began to woo him. PP 11. 2
whom thine eyes woo as mine importune thee. SON 142.10

WOO'D 29 FR 0.0032 REL FR 23 V 6 P
wealth | was the first motive that i woo'd thee, WIV 3.04. 14
music, cousin, if you be not woo'd in good time. ADO 2.01. 70 P
claudio, i have woo'd in thy name, and fair hero 2.01.298 P
and, as i woo'd for thee to obtain her, i will 3.02.126 P
but know that i have to-night woo'd margaret, 3.03.145 P
following the signs, woo'd but the sign of she. LLL 5.02.469
hippolyta, i woo'd thee with my sword, | and won MND 1.01. 16
we should be woo'd, and were not made to woo. 2.01.242
i had as lief be woo'd of a snail. AYL 4.01. 52 P
'twas where you woo'd the gentlewoman so well. SHR in.1. 85
rehears'd, | that ever katherina will be woo'd. 1.02.125
who woo'd in haste, and means to wed at leisure. 3.02. 11
yet never means to wed where he hath woo'd. 3.02. 17
now, | that shall be woo'd and wedded in a day. 4.02. 51
fear, my doricles, | you woo'd me the false way. WT 4.04.151
now it coldly stands), when first i woo'd her! 5.03. 36
when she was young, you woo'd her; 5.03.108
but for because he hath not woo'd me yet: JN 2.01.588
was ever woman in this humor woo'd? R3 1.02.227
gems, | that woo'd the slimy bottom of the deep, 1.04. 32
pandar, | and he's as tetchy to be woo'd to woo, TRO 1.01. 96
though they be long ere they be woo'd, they are 3.02.110 P
but, though i lov'd you well, i woo'd you not, 3.02.126
me clip ye | in arms as sound as when i woo'd, COR 1.06. 30
she is a woman, therefore may be woo'd, | she is TIT 2.01. 82
when and where and how | we met, we woo'd, and ROM 2.03. 62
did michael cassio, when /you woo'd my lady, OTH 3.03. 94
hath a hundred times | woo'd me to steal it; 3.03.293
/thy worth the greater, being woo'd of time, SON 70. 6

WOOD* *(also wode)*

/WOOD* 2 FR 0.0002 REL FR 1 V 1 P
o, that she could speak now like a /wood woman! TGV 2.03. 27 P
o /wood divine! LLL 4.03.244

WOOD* 63 FR 0.0071 REL FR 58 V 5 P
fetch in our wood, and serves in offices | that TMP 1.02.312
there's wood enough within. 1.02.314
and to torment me | for bringing wood in slowly. 2.02. 16
i'll bring my wood home faster. 2.02. 72 P
i'll fish for thee, and get thee wood enough. 2.02.161
go thou with her to the west end of the wood; TGV 5.03. 9
come, will this wood take fire? WIV 5.05. 88
a wife of such wood were felicity. LLL 4.03.245
and in the wood, a league without the town MND 1.01.165
and in the wood, where often you and i | upon 1.01.214
then to the wood will he to-morrow night 1.01.247
and meet me in the palace wood, a mile without 1.02.101 P
how long within this wood intend you stay? 2.01.138
thou toldst me they were stol'n unto this wood; 2.01.191
and here am i, and wode within this wood, 2.01.192
nor doth this wood lack worlds of company, | for 2.01.223
but i shall do thee mischief in the wood. 2.01.237
fair love, you faint with wand'ring in the wood; 2.02. 35
but if i had wit enough to get out of this wood, 3.01.150 P

out of this wood do not desire to go; 3.01.152
about the wood go swifter than the wind, | and 3.02. 94
i told him of your stealth unto this wood. 3.02.310
for, meeting her of late behind the wood, 4.01. 48
when in a wood of crete they bay'd the bear 4.01.113
of this their purpose hither to this wood, | and 4.01.161
upon the brook that brawls along this wood, | to AYL 2.01. 32
for here we have no temple but the wood, no 3.03. 50 P
and to the skirts of this wild wood he came; 5.04.159
and burn sweet wood to make the lodging sweet. SHR in.1. 49
or daphne roaming through a thorny wood, in.2. 57
gown, | my figur'd goblets for a dish of wood, R2 3.03.150
they shall not see — i'll tie them in the wood; 1H4 1.02.178 P
how the young whelp of talbot's, raging wood, 1H6 4.07. 35
he talks of wood; it is some carpenter. 5.03. 90
and i — like one lost in a thorny wood, | that 3H6 3.02.174
brave followers, yonder stands the thorny wood, 5.04. 67
and with our swords, upon a pile of wood, TIT 1.01.128
of me, | and stole into the covert of the wood. ROM 1.01.125
you are not wood, you are not stones, but men; JC 3.02.142
and the crow | makes wing to th' rooky wood; MAC 3.02. 51
until | great birnan wood to high dunsinane hill 4.01. 93
dead, rise never till the wood | of birnan rise, 4.01. 97
near birnan wood | shall we well meet them; 5.02. 5
till birnan wood remove to dunsinane | i cannot 5.03. 2
what wood is this before us? 5.04. 3
the wood of birnan. 5.04. 3
and anon methought | the wood began to move. 5.05. 34
not, till birnan wood | do come to dunsinane," 5.05. 43
and now a wood | comes toward dunsinane. 5.05. 44
though birnan wood be come to dunsinane, | and 5.08. 30
work like the spring that turneth wood to stone, HAM 4.07. 20
do observance | to flow'ry may, in dian's wood. TNK 2.05. 51
and out i have brought him to a little wood | a 2.06. 3
thou, o jewel | o' th' wood, o' th' world, hast 3.01. 10
when young men went a–hunting, and a wood, | and 3.03. 40
is gone to th' wood to gather mulberries. 4.01. 68
and now direct your course to th' wood, where 4.01.144
a fair wood. 4.01.151
as they were mad, unto the wood they hie them, VEN 323
life–poisoning pestilence, and frenzies wood, 740
their light blown out in some mistrustful wood, 826
upon that blessed wood whose motion sounds SON 128. 2
making dead wood more blest than living lips: 128.12

WOODBINE 3 FR 0.0003 REL FR 3 V 0 P
even now | is couched in the woodbine coverture. ADO 3.01. 30
quite over–canopied with luscious woodbine, MND 2.01.251
so doth the woodbine the sweet honeysuckle 4.01. 42

WOOD–BIRDS 1 FR 0.0001 REL FR 1 V 0 P
begin these wood–birds but to couple now? MND 4.01.140

WOODCOCK 7 FR 0.0008 REL FR 4 V 3 P
shall i not find a woodcock too? ADO 5.01.157 P
o this woodcock, what an ass it is! SHR 1.02.160
we have caught the woodcock, and will keep him AWW 4.01. 90
now is the woodcock near the gin. TN 2.05. 83 P
and fear to kill a woodcock lest thou dispossess 4.02. 59 P
ay, ay, so strives the woodcock with the gin. 3H6 1.04. 61
why, as a woodcock to mine own springe, osric: HAM 5.02.306

WOODCOCKS 2 FR 0.0002 REL FR 2 V 0 P
four woodcocks in a dish! LLL 4.03. 80
ay, springes to catch woodcocks. HAM 1.03.115

WOODEN 9 FR 0.0010 REL FR 6 V 3 P
more endure | this wooden slavery than to suffer TMP 3.01. 62
we cram | within this wooden o the very casques H5 pr 13
one may pare his nails with a wooden dagger, and 4.04. 72 P
upon a wooden coffin we attend, | and death's 1H6 1.01. 19
tush, that's a wooden thing! 5.03. 89
it rich | to hear the wooden dialogue and sound TRO 1.03.155
numb'd and mortified arms | pins, wooden pricks, LR 2.03. 16
at legs, then he wears wooden nether–stocks. 2.04. 10 P
money enough in the end to buy him a wooden one?
PER 4.06.173 P

WOODLAND 1 FR 0.0001 REL FR 0 V 1 P
i am a woodland fellow, sir, that always lov'd a AWW 4.05. 47 P

WOOD–LEAVES 1 FR 0.0001 REL FR 1 V 0 P
with wild wood–leaves and weeds i ha' strew'd CYM 4.02.390

WOODMAN 4 FR 0.0004 REL FR 2 V 2 P
am i a woodman, ha? WIV 5.05. 27 P
he's a better woodman than thou tak'st him for. MM 4.03.162 P
have prov'd best woodman and | are master of the
CYM 3.06. 28
he is no woodman that doth bend his bow | to LUC 580

WOODMONGER 1 FR 0.0001 REL FR 0 V 1 P
you shall be a woodmonger, and buy nothing of me
H5 5.01. 65 P

WOOD'S 1 FR 0.0001 REL FR 1 V 0 P
at the wood's boldness by thee blushing stand. SON 128. 8

WOODS 13 FR 0.0014 REL FR 12 V 1 P
this shadowy desert, unfrequented woods, | i TGV 5.04. 2
are not these woods | more free from peril than AYL 2.01. 3
dispark'd my parks and fell'd my forest woods, R2 3.01. 23
i hid me in these woods and durst not peep out, 2H6 4.10. 3 P
the woods are ruthless, dreadful, deaf, and dull TIT 2.01.128
the fields are fragrant and the woods are green. 2.02. 2
forc'd in the ruthless, vast, and gloomy woods? 4.01. 53
timon will to the woods, where he shall find TIM 4.01. 35
shame not these woods | by putting on the 4.03.208
be men like blasted woods, | and may diseases 4.03.531
this must be done i' th' woods. TNK 2.03. 50
he's excellent i' th' woods, | bring him to th' 2.03. 53
is't not mad lodging | here in the wild woods, 3.03. 23

WOODSTOCK 1 FR 0.0001 REL FR 1 V 0 P
the sixt was thomas of woodstock, duke of 2H6 2.02. 16

WOODSTOCK'S 1 FR 0.0001 REL FR 1 V 0 P
the part i had in woodstock's blood | doth more R2 1.02. 1

WOODVILE 2 FR 0.0002 REL FR 2 V 0 P
faint–hearted woodvile, prizest him 'fore me? 1H6 1.03. 22
anthony woodvile, her brother there, | that made R3 1.01. 67

WOOED 7 FR 0.0008 REL FR 7 V 0 P
you took occasion to be quickly wooed | to gripe 1H4 5.01. 56
and therefore to be wooed: 1H6 5.03. 78
whom i with pain have wooed and won thereto; 5.03.138
but his occasions might have wooed me first; TIM 3.03. 15
and having wooed | a villain to attempt it, who PER 5.01.172
"i have been wooed, as i entreat thee now, VEN 97
her eyes wooed still, his eyes disdain'd the 358

WOOER 8 FR 0.0009 REL FR 7 V 1 P
since many a wooer doth commence his suit | to ADO 2.03. 50
whiles we shut the gate upon one wooer, another MV 1.02.133
you brought in one night here to be her wooer. TN 1.03. 17 P
he is the bluntest wooer in christendom. 3H6 3.02. 83
crown, | to her go i, a jolly thriving wooer. R3 4.03. 43
ever young, fresh, lov'd, and delicate wooer, TIM 4.03.384
if she confess that she was half the wooer, OTH 1.03.176
a wooer | more hateful than the foul expulsion CYM 2.01. 59

WOOER'S 1 FR 0.0001 REL FR 1 V 0 P
prepare her ears to hear a wooer's tale; R3 4.04.327

WOOERS 7 FR 0.0008 REL FR 4 V 3 P
time we have confidence, and of other wooers. WIV 1.04.160 P
no means, she mocks all her wooers out of suit. ADO 2.01.349 P
i'll mark no words that smooth–fac'd wooers say. LLL 5.02.828
am glad this parcel of wooers are so reasonable, MV 1.02.108 P
execute — | to make one among these wooers. SHR 1.01.247
fair leda's daughter had a thousand wooers, 1.02.242
but thou with mildness entertain'st thy wooers, 2.01.250

WOOF 1 FR 0.0001 REL FR 1 V 0 P
as subtle | as ariachne's broken woof to enter. TRO 5.02.152

WOOING 27 FR 0.0030 REL FR 17 V 10 P
use your art of wooing; WIV 2.02.235 P
we shall have the freer wooing at master page's. 3.02. 85 P
yet, wooing thee, i found thee of more value 3.04. 15
wooing, wedding, and repenting, is as a scotch ADO 2.01. 73 P
because you talk of wooing, i will sing, | since 2.03. 49
henceforth my wooing mind shall be express'd LLL 5.02.412
our wooing doth not end like an old play: 5.02.874
for, wooing here until i sweat again, | and MV 3.02.203
and i remember the wooing of a peascod instead AYL 2.04. 51 P
and wooing, she should grant? 5.02. 3 P
the small acquaintance, my sudden wooing, nor 5.02. 7 P
padua to begin his wooing that would thoroughly SHR 1.01.143 P
(as wealth is burthen of my wooing dance), | be 1.02. 68
be contributors | and bear his charge of wooing, 1.02.215
but you will curse your wooing. 2.01. 75
but in this case of wooing, | a child shall get 2.01.410
a heaven on earth i have won by wooing thee. AWW 4.02. 66
goes to the tune of "two maids wooing a man." WT 4.04.289 P
wooing poor craftsmen with the craft of smiles R2 1.04. 28
come, come, in wooing sorrow let's be brief, 5.01. 93
kate, my wooing is fit for thy understanding. H5 5.02.122 P
women are angels, wooing: TRO 1.02.286
of my counsel | /in my whole course of wooing, OTH 3.03.112
and so stand | aloof for more serious wooing. PER 4.06. 88 P
eyes wooed still, his eyes disdain'd the wooing: VEN 358
devil, | wooing his purity with her fair pride. PP 2. 8
devil, | wooing his purity with her foul pride. SON 144. 8

WOOINGLY 1 FR 0.0001 REL FR 1 V 0 P
that the heaven's breath | smells wooingly here; MAC 1.06. 6

WOOL 3 FR 0.0003 REL FR 1 V 2 P
fifteen hundred shorn, what comes the wool to? WT 4.03. 34 P
toe of frog, | wool of bat and tongue of dog, MAC 4.01. 15
the beast no hide, the sheep no wool, the cat no LR 3.04.105 P

WOOLLEN 3 FR 0.0003 REL FR 2 V 1 P
on his face, i had rather lie in the woollen! ADO 2.01. 31 P
why he, a woollen bagpipe, but of force | must MV 4.01. 56
who was wont | to call them woollen vassals, COR 3.02. 9

WOOLLY 2 FR 0.0002 REL FR 2 V 0 P
was | between these woolly breeders in the act, MV 1.03. 83
my fleece of woolly hair that now uncurls, TIT 2.03. 34

WOOL–SACK 1 FR 0.0001 REL FR 0 V 1 P
how now, wool–sack, what mutter you? 1H4 2.04.135 P

WOOLVISH *(also wolvish)*

WOOLVISH 1 FR 0.0001 REL FR 1 V 0 P
why in this woolvish /toge should i stand here COR 2.03.115

WOOLWARD 1 FR 0.0001 REL FR 0 V 1 P
i go woolward for penance. LLL 5.02.711 P

WOOS 9 FR 0.0010 REL FR 7 V 2 P
to yourself; why, she woos you by a figure. TGV 2.01.148 P
he woos both high and low, both rich and poor, WIV 2.01.113
'tis certain so, the prince woos for himself. ADO 2.01.174
suit | to her he thinks not worthy, yet he woos, 2.03. 51
the count he woos your daughter, | lays down his AWW 3.07. 17
the count himself here hard by woos her. TN 1.03.108 P
who woos | even now the frozen bosom of the ROM 1.04.100
but then woos best when most his choice is VEN 570
and when a woman woos, what woman's son | will
SON 41. 7

WOOSEL 2 FR 0.0002 REL FR 1 V 1 P
the woosel cock so black of hue, | with MND 3.01.125
alas, a black woosel, cousin shallow! 2H4 3.02. 8 P

WOO'T *(also wilt, wolt, wo't)*

WOO'T 7 FR 0.0008 REL FR 7 V 0 P
woo't weep, woo't fight, woo't fast, woo't tear HAM 5.01.275
woo't weep, woo't fight, woo't fast, woo't tear 5.01.275
woo't fight, woo't fast, woo't tear thyself? 5.01.275
woo't fight, woo't fast, woo't tear thyself? 5.01.275
woo't drink up eisel, eat a crocadile? 5.01.276
woo't thou fight well? ANT 4.02. 7
noblest of men, woo't die? 4.15. 59

WORCESTER 15 FR 0.0017 REL FR 14 V 1 P
at worcester must his body be interr'd, | for so JN 5.07. 99
whereupon the earl of worcester | hath broken R2 2.02. 58
sent from my brother worcester, whencesoever. 2.03. 22
this is worcester, | malevolent to you in all 1H4 1.01. 96
worcester, get thee gone, for i do see | danger 1.03. 15
worcester is stol'n away to–night. 2.04.358 P
and uncle worcester — a plague upon it! 3.01. 5
i | and my good lord of worcester will set forth 3.01. 83
i learn'd in worcester, as i rode along, | he 4.01.125
and there is my lord of worcester, and a head 4.04. 25
how now, my lord of worcester? 5.01. 9
no, good worcester, no, | we love our people 5.01.103
ill–spirited worcester, did not we send grace, 5.05. 2
bear worcester to the death and vernon too. 5.05. 14
then was that noble worcester | so soon ta'en 2H4 1.01.125

WORCESTER'S 1 FR 0.0001 REL FR 1 V 0 P
your uncle worcester's horses came but to–day, 1H4 4.03. 21

WORD *(also ord, ort*, worts*)*

/WORD 8 FR 0.0009 REL FR 6 V 2 P
a /word, mounseur mock–water. WIV 2.03. 57 P
/and /if /my /word /be /sterling /yet /in R2 4.01.264
/for /that /same /word, /rebellion, /did /divide 2H4 1.01.194
/this /word, /rebellion, /it /had /froze /them 1.01.199
the /word is "pitch and pay"; H5 2.03. 49
/a /word, /my /lord. TRO 2.03. 89 P
/marcus /did /not /name /the /word /of /hands! TIT 3.02. 33
desire, | /sends /word of all that haps in tyre: PER 2.ch. 22

WORD 506 FR 0.0572 REL FR 352 V 154 P
a word, good sir, | i fear you have done TMP 1.02.443
a word. 1.02.444
soft, sir, one word more. 1.02.450
one word more: 1.02.453
one word more | shall make me chide thee, if not 1.02.476
his word is more than the miraculous harp. 2.01. 87 P
o, but one word. 2.01.296
interrupt the monster one word further, and, by 3.02. 69 P
pay thy graces | home both in word and deed. 5.01. 71
nothing but the word "noddy" for my pains. TGV 1.01.124 P
blow not a word away | till i have found each 1.02.115
'tis a word or two | of commendations sent from 1.03. 52
she gave me none, except an angry word. 2.01.158 P
what, gone without a word? 2.02. 16
should not the shoe speak a word for weeping; 2.03. 25 P
this while sheds not a tear, nor speaks a word; 2.03. 31 P
sir, if you spend word for word with me, i shall 2.04. 41 P
if you spend word for word with me, i shall make 2.04. 41 P
and, in a word (for far behind his worth | comes 2.04. 71
friend valentine, a word. 3.01.205
unless the next word that thou speak'st | have 3.01.239
mistake the word. 3.01.284 P
why, that word makes the faults gracious. 3.01.368 P
where your good word cannot advantage him, 3.02. 42
we'll have him. sirs, a word. 4.01. 38
wrong'd me, indeed he hath, at a word he hath. WIV 1.01.106 P
word of denial in thy labras here! 1.01.163
word of denial! 1.01.164
a word with you, coz; 1.01.207 P
i am at a word; 1.03. 14 P
to speak a good word to mistress anne page for 1.04. 83 P
good mine host o' th' garter, a word with you. 2.01.203 P
at a word, hang no more about me, i am no gibbet 2.02. 16 P
shall i vouchsafe your worship a word or two? 2.02. 40 P
the sword and the word? 3.01. 44 P
i pray you let–a me speak a word with your ear. 3.01. 79 P
ye, master slender would speak a word with you. 3.04. 30 P
pray you a word with you. 3.04. 35 P
and i'll be as good as my word, but speciously 3.04.108 P
i must carry her word quickly. 3.05. 47 P
he sent me word to stay within. 3.05. 58 P
he will seek there, on my word. 4.02. 60 P
on my word, it will serve him; 4.02. 77 P
to send him word they'll meet him in the park at 4.04. 17 P
to master /brook you yet shall hold your word, 5.05.244
one word, good friend. lucio, a word with you. MM 1.02.142
one word, good friend. lucio, a word with you. 1.02.142
i'll send him certain word of my success. 1.04. 89
i, that do speak a word, | may call it again. 2.02. 57
that in the captain's but a choleric word, 2.02.130
my business is a word or two with claudio. 3.01. 48
provost, a word with you. 3.01. 50 P
whose settled visage and deliberate word | nips 3.01. 89
prayers for thy death, | no word to save thee. 3.01.146
vouchsafe a word, young sister, but one word. 3.01.151
vouchsafe a word, young sister, but one word. 3.01.151
provost, a word with you. 3.01.174 P
not yet made known to mariana | a word of this. 4.01. 49
not a word. 4.03. 62 P
as any in vienna, on my word. 5.01.268 P
for the friar and you | must have a word anon. 5.01.359
hast thou or word, or wit, or impudence, | that 5.01.363
many a man would take you at your word, | and go
ERR 1.02. 17
what answer, sir? when spake i such a word? 2.02. 13
who, every word by all my wit being scann'd, 2.02.150
wants wit in all one word to understand. 2.02.151
a man may break a word with /you, sir, and words 3.01. 75
ill deeds is doubled with an evil word. 3.02. 20
i brought you word an hour since that the bark 4.03. 37 P
his word might bear my wealth at any time. 5.01. 8
wars, | and i to thee engag'd a prince's word, 5.01.162
most mighty duke, vouchsafe me speak a word: 5.01.283
at a word, i am not. ADO 2.01.114 P
at a word, i am not. 2.01.120 P
she speaks poniards, and every word stabs. 2.01.248 P
know | how much an ill word may empoison liking. 3.01. 86
the word is too good to paint out her wickedness 3.02.109 P
one word more, honest neighbors. 3.03. 91 P
one word, sir. 3.05. 45 P
i never tempted her with word too large, | but, 4.01. 52
will you not eat your word? 4.01.278 P
a word in your ear, sir. 4.02. 27 P
shall i speak a word in your ear? 5.01.143 P
hast frighted the word out of his right sense, 5.02. 55 P
first, of my word; 5.04.121 P
if i break faith, this word shall speak for me: LLL 1.01.153
not a word of costard yet. 1.01.222 P
easy it is to put "years" to the word "three," 1.02. 52 P
we arrest your word. 2.01.159
sir, i pray you a word. what lady is that same? 2.01.194
i beseech you a word. what is she in the white? 2.01.197
not a word with him but a jest. 2.01.216
and every jest but a word. 2.01.216
it was well done of you to take him at his word. 2.01.217
for l'envoy, and the word "l'envoy" for a salve? 3.01. 79 P
o, that's the latin word for three farthings: 3.01.137 P
i will never buy and sell out of this word. 3.01.142 P
thou fellow, a word. 4.01.100
a foul word. 4.03. 3 P
amen, so i had mine. is not that a good word? 4.03. 92
for wisdom's sake, a word that all men love, 4.03.354
or for love's sake, a word that loves all men, 4.03.355
thy master hath not eaten thee for a word, for 5.01. 40 P
the word is well cull'd, chose, sweet, and apt, 5.01. 93 P
thou hast spoken no word all this while. 5.01.150 P
your dark meaning, mouse, of this light word? 5.02. 19
white–handed mistress, one sweet word with thee. 5.02.230
one word in secret. 5.02.236
will you vouchsafe with me to change a word? 5.02.238
let's part the word. 5.02.249
one word in private with you ere i die. 5.02.254
not one word more, my maids, break off, break 5.02.262
the king was weeping–ripe for a good word. 5.02.274
that she vouchsafe me audience for one word. 5.02.313
they did not bless us with one happy word. 5.02.370
lord | most honorably doth uphold his word. 5.02.449

cuckoo, cuckoo" — o word of fear, | unpleasing 5.02.901
cuckoo, cuckoo" — o word of fear, | unpleasing 5.02.910
keep word, lysander; MND 1.01.222
how fit a word | is that vile name to perish on 2.02.106
no sound, no word? 2.02.152
demetrius, i will keep my word with thee. 3.02.266
i'll not trust your word. 3.02.268
not a word of me. 4.02. 34 P
for in all the play | there is not one word apt, 5.01. 65
tongue, not a word! 5.01.342
song by rote, | to each word a warbling note. 5.01.398
and, in a word, but even now worth this, | and MV 1.01. 35
and she is fair and, fairer than that word, | of 1.01.162
o me, the word choose! 1.02. 23 P
who brings word the prince his master will be 1.02.125 P
my gossip report be an honest woman of her word. 3.01. 7 P
in a word, | the seeming truth which cunning 3.02. 99
and every word in it a gaping wound | issuing 3.02.265
how every fool can play upon the word! 3.05. 43 P
that is done too, sir, only "cover" is the word. 3.05. 52 P
him, that for a tricksy word | defy the matter. 3.05. 69
i thank thee, jew, for teaching me that word. 4.01.341
and i bring word | my mistress will before the 5.01. 28
he would not have spoke such a word. AYL 1.01. 84 P
cupid have mercy, not a word? 1.03. 2 P
and in the greatness of my word, you die. 1.03. 89
answer me in one word. 3.02.224 P
'tis a word too great for any mouth of this 3.02.226 P
is it honest in deed and word? 3.03. 18 P
lover is no stronger than the word of a tapster; 3.04. 31 P
if you be a true lover, hence, and not a word; 4.03. 73 P
keep you your word, o duke, to give your 5.04. 19
keep you your word, phebe, that you'll marry me, 5.04. 21
keep your word, silvius, that you'll marry her 5.04. 23
he sent me word, if i said his beard was not cut 5.04. 71 P
if i sent him word again, it was not well cut, 5.04. 73 P
cut, he would send me word he cut it to please 5.04. 74 P
i will not eat my word, now thou art mine, | thy 5.04.149
let me have audience for a word or two. 5.04.151
but a word, i pray. SHR 1.01.113 P
a' my word, and she knew him as well as i do, 1.02.108 P
sir, a word ere you go. 1.02.227
when did she cross thee with a bitter word? 2.01. 28
and with that word she strook me on the head, 2.01.153
say she be mute, and will not speak a word, 2.01.174
whatever fortune stays him from his word. 3.02. 23
hear — | sufficeth i am come to keep my word, 3.02.106
what, not a word? 4.03. 42
for both our sakes, i would that word were true. 5.02. 15
my mistress sends you word | that she is busy, 5.02. 80
to bandy word for word and frown for frown; 5.02.172
to bandy word for word and frown for frown; 5.02.172
good sparks and lustrous, a word, good metals: AWW 2.01. 41 P
if thou proceed | as high as word, my deed shall 2.01.210
do you hear, monsieur? a word with you. 2.03.184 P
you are not worth another word, else i'd call 2.03.263 P
let every word weigh heavy of her worth, | that 3.04. 31
counsel i have spoken | is so from word to word; 3.07. 10
counsel i have spoken | is so from word to word; 3.07. 10
but with the word the time will bring on summer, 4.04. 31
i beseech your honor to hear me one single word. 5.02. 36 P
save your word. 5.02. 38 P
you beg more than "word" then. 5.02. 40 P
whole, | not one word more of the consumed time. 5.03. 38
or four languages word for word without book, TN 1.03. 27 P
or four languages word for word without book, 1.03. 27 P
he will not pass his word for twopence that you 1.05. 80 P
deliver thy indignation to him by word of mouth. 2.03.130 P
sir, her name's a word, and to dally with that 3.01. 19 P
and to dally with that word might make my sister 3.01. 20 P
i might say "element," but the word is overworn. 3.01. 58 P
i will deliver his challenge by word of mouth, 3.04.191 P
hob, nob, is his word; 3.04.240 P
that i promis'd you, i'll be as good as my word. 3.04.323 P
he has heard that word of some great man and now 4.01. 12 P
voice, and bring me word how thou find'st him. 4.02. 67 P
within this hour bring me word 'tis done | (and WT 2.03.136
whose every word deserves | to taste of thy most 3.02.178
if word nor oath | prevail not, go and see. 3.02.203
not a word, a word, we stand upon our manners. 4.04.164
not a word, a word, we stand upon our manners. 4.04.164
clamor your tongues, and not a word more. 4.04.248 P
you may know you shall not want — one word. 4.04.594
pray you a word. 4.04.661
i will tell the king all, every word, yea, and 4.04.699 P
not a word of his | but buffets better than a JN 2.01.464
no external thing to lose | but the word "maid," 2.01.572
this bawd, this broker, this all–changing word, 2.01.582
thee, for thy word | is but the vain breath of a 3.01. 7
but this one word, whether thy tale be true. 3.01. 26
come hither, little kinsman, hark, a word. 3.03. 18
and ne'er have spoke a loving word to you; 4.01. 51
i will not stir, nor winch, nor speak a word, 4.01. 80
now keep your holy word, go meet the french, 5.01. 5
and send him word by me which way you go. 5.03. 7
yet one word more! R2 1.02. 58
the hopeless word of "never to return" | breathe 1.03.152
how long a time lies in one little word! 1.03.213
winters and four wanton springs | end in a word: 1.03.215
thy word is current with him for my death, | but 1.03.231
that my tongue | should so profane the word, 1.04. 13
would the word "farewell" have length'ned hours 1.04. 16
and that word "grace" | in an ungracious mouth 2.03. 88
my liege, one word. 3.02.215
"pardon" should be the first word of thy speech. 5.03.114
i never long'd to hear a word till now, | say 5.03.115
the word is short, but not so short as sweet, 5.03.117
no word like "pardon" for kings' mouths so meet. 5.03.118
that sets the word itself against the word! 5.03.122
that sets the word itself against the word! 5.03.122
with scruples and do set the word itself 5.05. 13
and do set the word itself | against the word, 5.05. 14
but neither my good word nor princely favor. 5.06. 42
keeps, and sends me word | i shall have none but 1H4 1.01. 94
sir john stands to his word, the devil shall 1.02.117 P
thou damn'd for keeping thy word with the devil. 1.02.120 P
by how much better than my word i am, | by so 1.02.210
hear you, cousin, a word. 1.03.227

and, with a word, outfac'd you from your prize, 2.04.256 P
thou art my son i have partly thy mother's word, 2.04.403 P
so majestically, both in word and matter, hang 2.04.436 P
i will engage my word to thee | that i will by 2.04.514
and "well, go to," | but mark'd him not a word. 3.01.157
lord mortimer of scotland hath sent word | that 3.02.164
darest thou be as good as thy word now? 3.03.144 P
nay, task me to my word, approve me, lord. 4.01. 9
there is not such a word | spoke of in scotland 4.01. 84
cousin, and bring me word | what he will do. 5.01.109
a word. 5.01.134 P
what is in that word honor? 5.01.134 P
the king should keep his word in loving us. 5.02. 5
sir john falstaff, a word with you. 2H4 1.02. 92 P
no word to your master that i am yet come to 2.02.160 P
that you broke your word | when you were more 2.03. 10
bardolph hath brought word. 2.04. 18 P
will make the word as odious as the word "occupy 2.04.148 P
make the word as odious as the word "occupy," 2.04.148 P
was an excellent good word before it was ill 2.04.149 P
a' my word, captain, there's none such here. 2.04.176 P
and that same word even now cries out on us. 3.01. 94
pardon, sir, i have heard the word. 3.02. 73 P
i will maintain the word with my sword to be a 3.02. 75 P
word with my sword to be a soldier–like word, 3.02. 76 P
word, and a word of exceeding good command, by 3.02. 76 P
sir, a word with you. 3.02.243 P
go to, i have spoke at a word. god keep you! 3.02.297 P
turnbull street, and every third word a lie, 3.02.307 P
turning the word to sword and life to death. 4.02. 10
i take your princely word for these redresses. 4.02. 66
i give it you, and will maintain my word, | and 4.02. 67
the word of peace is rend'red. 4.02. 87
of them all speaks any other word but my name. 4.03. 20 P
to her), believe not the word of the noble. 4.03. 54 P
'tis needful that the most immodest word | be 4.04. 70
lord, | to see perform'd the tenure of my word. 5.05. 71
sir, i will be as good as my word. 5.05. 85 P
one word more, i beseech you. ep 26 P
before the frenchman speak a word of it. H5 1.01. 97
that is the word. 2.01. 72
and quickly bring us word of england's fall. 3.05. 68
to see it, i will never trust his word after. 4.01.196 P
you'll never trust his word after! 4.01.201 P
keep thy word; fare thee well. 4.01.221 P
kill his prisoners, | give the word through. 4.06. 38
by his blunt bearing he will keep his word, 4.07.177
in his cap, and i have been as good as my word. 4.08. 32 P
moi'ty, take the word of a king and a bachelor. 5.02.215 P
which word thou shalt no sooner bless mine ear 5.02.237 P
if thou spy'st any, run and bring me word, | and 1H6 1.04. 19
thus joan de pucelle hath perform'd her word. 1.06. 3
when gloucester says the word, king henry goes, 3.01.183
i break my warlike word; 4.03. 31
the regent hath with talbot broke his word, 4.06. 2
'tis a mere french word; 4.07. 54
say but the word, and i will be his priest. 2H6 3.01.272
the duke was dumb and could not speak a word. 3.02. 32
for every word you speak in his behalf | is 3.02.208
dread lord, the commons send you word by me, 3.02.243
had i but said, i would have kept my word; 3.02.293
it a lordship, thou shalt have it for that word. 4.07. 5 P
and i think this word "sallet" was born to do me 4.10. 10 P
and now the word "sallet" must serve me to feed 4.10. 15 P
my lord of warwick, hear but one word: 3H6 1.01.170
i will not bandy with thee word for word, | but 1.04. 49
i will not bandy with thee word for word, | but 1.04. 49
the duke of norfolk sends you word by me | the 2.01.206
for every word i speak, | ye see i drink the 5.04. 74
by heaven, brat, i'll plague ye for that word. 5.05. 27
and this word "love," which greybeards call 5.06. 81
tongue could never learn sweet smoothing word; R3 1.02.168
it again, and even with the word | this hand, 1.02.188
the urging of that word "judgment" hath bred a 1.04.107 P
iniquity, | i moralize two meanings in one word. 3.01. 83
cousin of buckingham, a word with you. 3.04. 35
color, | murther thy breath in middle of a word, 3.05. 2
lord, | the citizens are mum, say not a word. 3.07. 3
no, so god help me, they spake not a word, | but 3.07. 24
hear me a word; 4.04.181
stay, madam, i must talk a word with you. 4.04.199
conscience is but a word that cowards use, 5.03.309
our ancient word of courage, fair saint george, 5.03.349
a word with you. H8 1.02.102
spake one the least word that might | be to the 2.04.154
and with his deed did crown | his word upon you. 3.02.156
but here's yet in the word "hereafter" the TRO 1.01. 24 P
achilles shall have word of this intent, | so 1.03.306
pray you a word. 3.01. 1 P
my lord, will you vouchsafe me a word? 3.01. 59 P
your uncle's word and my firm faith. 3.02.108 P
nay, i'll give my word for her too. 3.02.109 P
withal bring word if hector will to–morrow | be 3.03. 34
neither gave to me | good word nor look. 3.03.144
lady, a word. i'll bring you to your father. 4.05. 53
not yet mature, yet matchless, firm of word, 4.05. 97
borrows of the moon when diomed keeps his word. 5.01. 94 P
now, my sweet guardian! hark, a word with you. 5.02. 7
hark a word in your ear. 5.02. 34
all hell's torments, | i will not speak a word! 5.02. 44
by jove, i will not speak a word. 5.02. 52
i will not keep my word. 5.02. 98
one cannot speak a word | but it straight starts 5.02.100
there is a word will priam turn to stone, | make 5.10. 18
cold statues of the youth, and, in a word, 5.10. 20
one word, good citizens. COR 1.01. 14 P
we have ever your good word. 1.01.166
a' my word, the father's son. 1.03. 57 P
no, at a word, madam; 1.03.109 P
bring me word thither | how the world goes, that 1.10. 31
it was his word. 2.01.237
hear me one word, | beseech you, tribunes, hear 3.01.214
beseech you, tribunes, hear me but a word. 3.01.215
i may be heard, i would crave a word or two, 3.01.281
one word more, one word: 3.01.309
one word more, one word: 3.01.309
the word is "mildly." 3.02.142
buy | their mercy at the price of one fair word, 3.03. 91

then, in a word, i also am | longer to live most 4.05. 94
each word thou hast spoke hath weeded from my 4.05.102
another word, menenius, | i will not hear thee 5.02. 91
rest on my word, and let not discontent | daunt TIT 1.01.267
what villain was it spake that word? 1.01.359
have pass'd | my word and promise to the emperor 1.01.469
sweet lords, entreat her hear me but a word. 2.03.138
let them not speak a word, the guilt is plain, 2.03.301
cousin, a word; 2.04. 12
my lord the emperor | sends thee this word — 3.01.151
no, my good lord, but pluto sends you word, | if 4.03. 38
of my word, i have written to effect, | there's 4.03. 60
not a word? 5.01. 46
no, not a word, how can i grace my talk, 5.02. 17
close their mouths, let them not speak a word. 5.02.164
gregory, on my word, we'll not carry coals. ROM 1.01. 1 P
i hate the word | as i hate hell, all montagues, 1.01. 70
three civil brawls, bred of an airy word, | by 1.01. 89
a word ill urg'd to one that is so ill! 1.01.203
tut, dun's the mouse, the constable's own word. 1.04. 40
madam, your mother craves a word with you. 1.05.111
speak to my gossip venus one fair word, | one 2.01. 11
a rose | by any other word would smell as sweet; 2.02. 44
i take thee at thy word. 2.02. 49
had i it written, i would tear the word. 2.02. 57
thou wilt say "ay," | and i will take thy word; 2.02. 91
thy purpose marriage, send me word to–morrow, 2.02.144
i stretch it out for that word "broad," which, 2.04. 85 P
pray you, sir, a word: 2.04.163 P
gentlemen, good den, a word with one of you. 3.01. 38
and but one word with one of us? 3.01. 39 P
it with something, make it a word and a blow. 3.01. 40 P
some word there was, worser than tybalt's death, 3.02.108
that "banished," that one word "banished," 3.02.113
"romeo is banished," to speak that word, | is 3.02.122
the law, | and turn'd that black word "death" to 3.03. 27
o friar, the damned use that word in hell; 3.03. 47
to mangle me with that word "banished"? 3.03. 51
i'll give thee armor to keep off that word: 3.03. 54
hear me with patience but to speak a word. 3.05.159
talk not to me, for i'll not speak a word. 3.05.202
hast thou not a word of joy? 3.05.211
what, not a word? 4.05. 4
i have one word | to say to you. TIM 1.02.167
vouchsafe me a word, it does concern you near. 1.02.177
he owes | for ev'ry word. 1.02.199
you may take my word, my lord; 1.02.214
o my good lord, the world is but a word; 2.02.152
sir, a word. 3.04. 34 P
not one word more: 4.02. 28
for each true word, a blister, and each false 5.01.132
upon the word, | accoutred as i was, i plunged JC 1.02.104
if i would not have taken him at a word, i would 1.02.267 P
send word to you he would be there to–morrow. 1.03. 38
look in the calendar, and bring me word. 2.01. 42
shall i entreat a word? 2.01.100
that have spoke the word | and will not palter? 2.01.125
if you shall send them word you will not come, 2.02. 95
yes, bring me word, boy, if thy lord look well, 2.04. 13
and bring me word what he doth say to thee. 2.04. 46
brutus, a word with you. 3.01.231
and bid me say to you by word of mouth — | o 3.01.280
but yesterday the word of caesar might | have 3.02.118
give the word ho! and stand. 4.02. 2
a word, lucilius, | how he receiv'd you; 4.02. 13
stand ho! speak the word along. 4.02. 33
ho, lucilius, hark, a word with you. 5.01. 69
o cassius, brutus gave the word too early, | who 5.03. 5
and bring us word unto octavius' tent | how 5.04. 31
slaying is the word, | it is a deed in fashion. 5.05. 4
come hither, good volumnius; list a word. 5.05. 15
cousins, a word, i pray you. MAC 1.03.127
sirrah, a word with you. 3.01. 44
but one word more — 4.01. 74
that bring you word | macduff is fled to england 4.01.141
there would have been a time for such a word. 5.05. 18
that keep the word of promise to our ear, | and 5.08. 21
form of the thing, each word made true and good, HAM 1.02.210
i could a tale unfold whose lightest word 1.05. 15
now to my word: 1.05.110
it | than is my deed to my most painted word. 3.01. 52
suit the action to the word, the word to the 3.02. 17 P
the action to the word, the word to the action, 3.02. 18 P
o, but she'll keep her word. 3.02.231 P
i'll take the ghost's word for a thousand pound. 3.02.286 P
good my lord, voutsafe me a word with you. 3.02.296 P
ay, lady, it was my word. 3.04. 30
one word more, good lady. 3.04.180
known, | the ratifiers and props of every word, 4.05.106
fine word, "legitimate"! LR 1.02. 18
no displeasure in him by word nor countenance? 1.02.157 P
not a word. 2.01. 12 P
brother, a word! 2.01. 19
i am sure on't, not a word. 2.01. 27
when priests are more in word than matter; 3.02. 81
i'll talk a word with this same learned theban. 3.04.157
let me ask you one word in private. 3.04.160
his word was still, 'fie, foh, and fum, | i 3.04.183
might not you | transport her purposes by word? 4.05. 20
give the word. 4.06. 92 P
had speech with man so poor, | hear me one word. 5.01. 39
i will but spend a word here in the house, | and OTH 1.02. 48
it does abhor me now i speak the word; 4.02.162
the voice of cassio! iago keeps his word. 5.01. 28
o, good my lord, i would speak a word with you! 5.02. 90
dost understand the word? 5.02.153
from this time forth i never will speak word. 5.02.304
a word or two before you go. 5.02.338
if they suffer our departure, death's the word. ANT 1.02.135 P
courteous lord, one word: 1.03. 86
i bring thee word | menecrates and menas, famous 1.04. 47
was theme for you — you were the word of war. 2.02. 44
whom ne'er the word of "no" woman heard speak, 2.02.223
bring me word quickly. 2.05.114
bid you alexas | bring me word how tall she is. 2.05.118
pompey, a word. 2.07. 37
thee, captain, | and hear me speak a word. 2.07. 39

that magical word of war, we have effected; 3.01. 31
i'll bring thee word | straight how 'tis like to 4.12. 2
lock yourself, and send him word you are dead. 4.13. 4
i spoke was "antony," | and word it, prithee, 4.13. 9
not be purg'd, she sent you word she was dead; 4.14.124
one word, sweet queen: 4.15. 45
hark thee, a word. CYM 1.05. 32
when thou shalt bring me word she loves my son, 1.05. 49
or i shall short my word | by length'ning my 1.06.200
in a word, or else | thou art straightway with 3.05. 82
thy mistress is, at once, | at the next word. 3.05. 96
(saving reverence of the word) for 'tis said a 4.01. 5 P
i'll weep, and word it with thee; 4.02.240
and bring me word how 'tis with her. 4.03. 1
the rest do nothing — with this word "stand, 5.03. 31
hanging is the word, sir. 5.04.153 P
pardon's the word to all. 5.05.422
i'll take thy word for faith, not ask thine oath PER 1.02.120
that will prove aweful both in deed and word. 2.ch. 4
the word: 2.02. 21
the word: 2.02. 30
the word: 2.02. 33
follow me then. lord helicane, a word. 2.04. 21
i never spake bad word, nor did ill turn | to 4.01. 75
i beseech your honor give me leave a word, and 4.06. 46 P
i could for each word give a cuff, my stomach TNK 3.01.104
but this one word: 3.01.116
i'll say never a word. 3.04. 18
hold thy word, theseus. 3.06.136
i tie you to your word now; 3.06.236
and with that word she spied the hunted boar, VEN 900
even at this word she hears a merry horn, 1025
ere once she can discharge one word of woe; LUC 1605
i should not live to speak another word; 1642
"wander," a word for shadows like myself, | as PP 14.11
that every word doth almost /tell my name, SON 76. 7
and he stole that word | from thy behavior; 79. 9

WORDLESS 1 FR 0.0001 REL FR 1 V 0 P
and wordless so greets heaven for his success. LUC 112

WORDLY *(also worldly)*

WORDLY 2 FR 0.0002 REL FR 2 V 0 P
but we wordly men | have miserable, mad, TIT 5.02. 65
hour | of love, of wordly matter and direction, OTH 1.03.299

WORD'S 5 FR 0.0005 REL FR 4 V 1 P
the mere word's a slave | debosh'd on every tomb AWW 2.03.137
shame hath spoil'd the sweet word's taste, JN 3.04.110
and at each word's deliverance | stab poniards 3H6 2.01. 97
in that word's death, no words can that woe ROM 3.02.126
obey thy parents, keep thy word's justice, swear LR 3.04. 81 P

WORDS' 2 FR 0.0002 REL FR 1 V 1 P
the folded meaning of your words' deceit. ERR 3.02. 36
than hold three words' conference with this ADO 2.01.270 P

/WORDS 2 FR 0.0002 REL FR 2 V 0 P
i love you more than /words can wield the matter LR 1.01. 55
a fury in your words, | /but /not /the /words. OTH 4.02. 33

WORDS 446 FR 0.0504 REL FR 360 V 86 P
thy purposes | with words that made them known.
TMP 1.02.358
you cram these words into mine ears against 2.01.107
of truth, their words | are natural breath; 5.01.156
o hateful hands, to tear such loving words! TGV 1.02.102
truth hath better deeds than words to grace it. 2.02. 18
a fine volley of words, gentlemen, and quickly 2.04. 33 P
you have an exchequer of words and, i think, no 2.04. 44 P
bare liveries that they live by your bare words. 2.04. 46 P
as seek to quench the fire of love with words. 2.07. 20
his words are bonds, his oaths are oracles, 2.07. 75
win her with gifts, if she respect not words: 3.01. 89
more than quick words do move a woman's mind. 3.01. 91
"item, she is slow in words." 3.01.332 P
to be slow in words is a woman's only virtue. 3.01.334 P
i weep myself to think upon thy words. 4.04.175
if the gentle spirit of moving words | can no 5.04. 55
you in your ear, i would have no words of it) my WIV 1.04.103 P
would have gone to the truth of his words; 2.01. 61 P
the very words. 2.01. 83 P
and what he gets more of her than sharp words, 2.01.183 P
you do ill to teach the child such words. 4.01. 65 P
for our offense by weight | the words of heaven: MM 1.02.122
of the law, | and you but waste your words. 2.02. 72
heaven hath my empty words, | whilst my 2.04. 2
i do arrest your words. 2.04.134
on mine honor, | my words express my purpose. 2.04.148
of the lady, and good words went with her name. 3.01.211 P
is it sad, and few words? 3.02. 51 P
go to, no more words. 3.02.206 P
for certain words he spake against your grace 5.01.129
words against me? 5.01.131
comes light from heaven, and words from breath, 5.01.225
wife as strongly | as words could make up vows; 5.01.228
yet this my comfort, when your words are done, ERR 1.01. 26
vow | that never words were music to thine ear, 2.02.114
for even her very words | didst thou deliver to 2.02.163
more common, for that's nothing but words. 3.01. 25
a word with /you, sir, and words are but wind: 3.01. 75
with words that in an honest suit might move. 4.02. 14
i am not of many words, but i thank you. ADO 1.01.157 P
and tire the hearer with a book of words. 1.01.307
no more words; the clerk is answer'd. 2.01.111 P
his words are a very fantastical banquet, just 2.03. 20 P
eight or nine wise words to speak to you, which 3.02. 72 P
the change of words with any creature, | refuse 4.01.183
when he shall hear she died upon his words, 4.01.223
and that count claudio did mean, upon his words, 4.02. 54 P
charm ache with air, and agony with words. 5.01. 26
and speak /off half a dozen dang'rous words, 5.01. 97
only foul words — and thereupon i will kiss 5.02. 50 P
foul words is but foul wind, and foul wind is 5.02. 52 P
in high–borne words, the worth of many a knight LLL 1.01.172
a man of fire–new words, fashion's own knight. 1.01.178
soever the matter, i hope in god for high words. 1.01.193 P
no words! 1.01.229 P
and study three years in two words, the dancing 1.02. 53 P
for prisoners to be too silent in their words, 1.02.164 P
delivers in such apt and gracious words | that 2.01. 73
but to speak that in words which his eye hath 2.01.251
fair payment for foul words is more than due. 4.01. 19
have liv'd long on the alms–basket of words. 5.01. 39 P
it were a fault to snatch words from my tongue. 5.02.382
sweet breath as will utter a brace of words. 5.02.523 P
honest plain words best pierce the ear of grief, 5.02.753
i'll mark no words that smooth–fac'd wooers say. 5.02.828
the words of mercury are harsh after the songs 5.02.930 P
i am amazed at your /passionate words. MND 3.02.220
no more words. 4.02. 45 P
a play there is, my lord, some ten words long, 5.01. 61
but by ten words, my lord, it is too long, 5.01. 63
his words were "farewell, mistress!" MV 2.05. 45
madam, you have bereft me of all words, | only 3.02.175
here are a few of the unpleasant'st words | that 3.02.251
waste no time in words, | but get thee gone. 3.04. 54
o dear discretion, how his words are suited! 3.05. 65
planted in his memory | an army of good words, 3.05. 67
"nearest his heart," those are the very words. 4.01.254
the words expressly are "a pound of flesh." 4.01.307
which speed, we hope, the better for our words. 5.01.115
it must appear in other ways than words, 5.01.140
thy words are too precious to be cast away upon AYL 1.03. 4 P
if their purgation did consist in words, | they 1.03. 53
he writes brave verses, speaks brave words, 3.04. 41 P
looks, i'll sauce her with bitter words. 3.05. 69 P
he talks well — | but what care i for words? 3.05.111
yet words do well | when he that speaks them 3.05.111
i cannot say the words. 4.01.128 P
such ethiop words, blacker in their effect 4.03. 35
o yes, my lord, but very idle words, | for SHR in.2. 83
spake you not these words plain, "sirrah, knock 1.02. 40 P
'twixt such friends as we | few words suffice; 1.02. 66
and perhaps with more successful words | than 1.02.157
if without more words you will get you hence. 1.02.230
hortensio, to what end are all these words? 1.02.248
but be thou arm'd for some unhappy words. 2.01.139
that love bianca more | than words can witness, 2.01.336
therefore ha' done with words; 3.02.116
even to the uttermost, as i please, in words. 4.03. 80
take no unkindness of his hasty words. 4.03.167
but your words show you a madman. 5.01. 74 P
his plausive words | he scatter'd not in ears, AWW 1.02. 53
to herself her own words to her own ears; 1.03.108 P
ah, what sharp stings are in her mildest words! 3.04. 18
i love not many words. 3.06. 84 P
your oaths | are words and poor conditions, but 4.02. 30
richest eyes, whose words all ears took captive, 5.03. 17
my words are as full of peace as matter. TN 1.05.210 P
dally nicely with words may quickly make them 3.01. 15 P
words are very rascals since bonds disgrac'd 3.01. 21 P
i can yield you none without words, and words 3.01. 24 P
without words, and words are grown so false, i 3.01. 24 P
indeed not her fool, but her corrupter of words. 3.01. 36 P
methinks his words do from such passion fly 3.04.373
maintain no words with him, good fellow. 4.02. 99 P
thee, fellow — fellow, thy words are madness. 5.01. 98
i | do come with words as medicinal as true, WT 2.03. 37
him that he use no scurrilous words in 's tunes. 4.04.213 P
mark thou my words. 4.04.431
his pettitoes till he had both tune and words, 4.04.607 P
hear me, and the words that follow'd | should be 5.01. 66
they shoot but calm words folded up in smoke, JN 2.01.229
i was never so bethump'd with words | since i 2.01.466
be these sad signs confirmers of thy words? 3.01. 24
envenom him with words, or get thee gone, | and 3.01. 63
o, that a man should speak those words to me! 3.01.130
the latest breath that gave the sound of words 3.01.230
eyes, ears, and harmful sound of words — | then 3.03. 51
puts on his pretty looks, repeats his words, 3.04. 95
his words do take possession of my bosom. 4.01. 32
face, | as bid me tell my tale in express words, 4.02.234
what e'er you think, good words, i think, were 4.03. 28
our souls religiously confirm thy words. 4.03. 73
let not my cold words here accuse my zeal. R2 1.01. 47
o, to what purpose dost thou hoard thy words, 1.03.253
that words seem'd buried in my sorrow's grave. 1.04. 15
where words are scarce, they are seldom spent in 2.01. 7
breathe truth that breathe their words in pain. 2.01. 8
these words hereafter thy tormentors be! 2.01.136
impute his words | to wayward sickliness and age 2.01.141
words, life, and all, old lancaster hath spent. 2.01.150
that speaks thy words again to do thee harm! 2.01.231
thy words are but as thoughts, therefore be bold 2.01.276
uncle, for god's sake speak comfortable words. 2.02. 76
less value is my company | than your good words. 2.03. 20
i shall not need transport my words by you, 2.03. 81
no, good my lord, let's fight with gentle words, 3.03.131
should take it off again | with words of sooth! 3.03.136
his words come from his mouth, ours from our 5.03.102
thou not mark the king, what words he spake? 5.04. 1
these were his very words. 5.04. 3
fellow should have fewer words than a parrot, 1H4 2.04. 99 P
not in words only, but in woes also. 2.04.416 P
rare words! 3.03.205
nor the throng of words that come with such more
2H4 2.01.112 P
as i am a gentleman! come, no more words of it. 2.01.138 P
no more words, let's have her. 2.01.165 P
that's to make him eat twenty of his words. 2.02.138 P
my troth, captain, these are very bitter words. 2.04.171 P
did speak these words, now prov'd a prophecy? 3.01. 69
silence, i will not use many words with you. 3.02.289 P
but /write her fair words still in foulest terms 4.04.104
so shall i live to speak my father's words: 5.02.107
by the means whereof 'a breaks words, and keeps H5 3.02. 35 P
heard that men of few words are the best men, 3.02. 37 P
but his few bad words are match'd with as few 3.02. 39 P
'a utt'red as prave words at the pridge as you 3.06. 63 P
description cannot suit itself in words | to 4.02. 53
familiar in his mouth as household words, 4.03. 52
perpend my words, o signieur dew, and mark: 4.04. 8
what are his words? 4.04. 43
upon these words i came and cheer'd him up. 4.06. 20
dare not avouch in your deeds any of your words? 5.01. 73 P
for the one i have neither words nor measure; 5.02.134 P
by guileful fair words peace may be obtain'd. 1H6 1.01. 77
believe my words, | for they are certain and 1.02. 58
and if thou vanquishest, thy words are true, 1.02. 96
i will not answer thee with words, but blows. 1.03. 69
i'll maintain my words | on any plot of ground 2.04. 88
some words there grew 'twixt somerset and me; 2.05. 46
and that my fainting words do warrant death. 2.05. 95
take heed, be wary how you place your words, 3.02. 3
o, let no words, but deeds, revenge this treason 3.02. 49
by fair persuasions, mix'd with sug'red words, 3.03. 18
speak, pucelle, and enchant him with thy words. 3.03. 40
either she hath bewitch'd me with her words, 3.03. 58
these haughty words of hers | have batt'red me 3.03. 78
thou maintain the former words thou spak'st? 3.04. 31
these words of yours draw life–blood from my 4.06. 43
words sweetly plac'd and /modestly directed. 5.03.179
strumpet, thy words condemn thy brat and thee. 5.04. 84
speech, | her words yclad with wisdom's majesty, 2H6 1.01. 33
wounds | deliver'd up again with peaceful words? 1.01.122
let not his smoothing words | bewitch your 1.01.156
seal up your lips, and give no words but mum; 1.02. 89
his words were these: 1.03.183
say, man, were these thy words? 1.03.186
my lord, hang me if ever i spake the words. 1.03.198 P
you can, | or else conclude my words effectual. 3.01. 41
and lowly words were ransom for their fault. 3.01.127
sovereign lady here | with ignominious words, 3.01.179
i thank thee, /meg, these words content me much. 3.02. 26
hide not thy poison with such sug'red words. 3.02. 45
my tongue should stumble in mine earnest words, 3.02.316
first let my words stab him, as he hath me. 4.01. 66
base slave, thy words are blunt and so art thou. 4.01. 67
thy words move rage and not remorse in me. 4.01.112
and will you credit this base drudge's words, 4.02.151
well, seeing gentle words will not prevail, 4.02.174
and such abominable words as no christian ear 4.07. 40 P
i feel remorse in myself with his words; 4.07.106 P
as for words, whose greatness answers words, 4.10. 53
as for words, whose greatness answers words, 4.10. 53
i cannot give due action to my words, | except a 5.01. 8
sons, he says, shall give their words for him. 5.01.137
ay, noble father, if our words will serve. 5.01.139
and if words will not, then our weapons shall. 5.01.140
by words or blows here let us win our right. 3H6 1.01. 37
frowns, words, and threats | shall be the war 1.01. 72
urge it no more, lest that, in stead of words, 1.01. 98
o clifford, how thy words revive my heart! 1.01.163
the passage where thy words should enter. 1.03. 22
the words would add more anguish than the wounds 2.01. 99
have done with words, my lords, and hear me 2.02.117
this meeting here | cannot be cur'd by words; 2.02.122
these words will cost ten thousand lives this 2.02.177
and no more words till they have flow'd their 2.05. 72
for (though before his face i speak the words) 2.06. 39
if so thou think'st, vex him with eager words. 2.06. 68
and lewis a prince soon won with moving words. 3.01. 34
her words doth show her wit incomparable, | all 3.02. 85
and witch sweet ladies with my words and looks. 3.02.150
those gracious words revive my drooping thoughts 3.03. 21
grant that warwick's words bewitch him not! 3.03.112
these words have turn'd my hate to love, | and i 3.03.199
my sovereign liege, no letters, and few words, 4.01. 86
tell me their words as near as thou canst guess 4.01. 90
at my depart, these were his very words: 4.01. 92
these were her words, utt'red with mild disdain: 4.01. 98
all the rest, discharg'd me with these words: 4.01.109
durst the traitor breathe out so proud words? 4.01.112
in few words, | if you'll not here proclaim 4.07. 53
speak gentle words and humbly bend thy knee, 5.01. 22
should, if a coward heard her speak these words, 5.04. 40
for my part, i'll not trouble thee with words. 5.05. 5
whilst i propose the self–same words to thee, 5.05. 20
should she live, to fill the world with words? 5.05. 44
ah, kill me with thy weapon, not with words! 5.06. 26
your grace attended to their sug'red words, R3 3.01. 13
your grace's words shall serve | as well as i 3.05. 62
heart | grossly grew captive to his honey words, 4.01. 79
my words are dull, o, quicken them with thine! 4.04.124
why should calamity be full of words? 4.04.126
and in the breath of bitter words let's smother 4.04.133
i will be mild and gentle in my words. 4.04.161
these very words | i've heard him utter to his H8 1.02.135
him every minute | with words of sovereignty. 1.02.150
'twould prove the verity of certain words 1.02.159
nor my prayers | are not words duly hallowed, 2.03. 68
where pow'rs are your retainers, and your words 2.04.113
deed to say well, | and yet words are no deeds. 3.02.154
words cannot carry | authority so weighty. 3.02.233
till i find more than will or words to do it 3.02.236
if i lov'd many words, lord, i should tell you 3.02.270
to whom he gave these words: 4.02. 20
be ever double | both in his words and meaning. 4.02. 39
to men that understand you, words and weakness. 5.02.107
and the words i utter | let none think flattery, 5.04. 15
words, vows, gifts, tears, and love's full TRO 1.02.282
nestor shall apply | thy latest words. 1.03. 33
good words, thersites. 2.01. 88 P
no more words, thersites, peace! 2.01.113 P
dear lord, you are full of fair words. 3.01. 47 P
nay, i care not for such words, no, no. 3.01. 75 P
you have bereft me of all words, lady. 3.02. 54 P
words pay no debts, give her deeds; 3.02. 55 P
few words to fair faith. 3.02. 95 P
she hath not given so many good words breath 4.01. 74
but i'll endeavor deeds to match these words, 4.05.259
and let your mind be coupled with your words. 5.02. 15
words, words, mere words, no matter from the 5.03.108
words, words, mere words, no matter from the 5.03.108
words, mere words, no matter from the heart; 5.03.108
my love with words and errors still she feeds, 5.03.111
that will give good words to thee will flatter COR 1.01.167
these are the words — i think | i have the 1.02. 7
sir, i hope | my words disbench'd you not? 2.02. 71
when blows have made me stay, i fled from words. 2.02. 72
no more words, we beseech you. 3.01. 75
coin words till their decay against those 3.01. 78
deeds express | what's like to be their words: 3.01.133
but with such words that are but roted in | your 3.02. 55
all | than to take in a town with gentle words, 3.02. 59
ask'd, as free | as words to little purpose. 3.02. 89
blows for rome | than thou hast spoken words? 4.02. 20
moe noble blows than ever thou wise words, | and 4.02. 21
behalf as you have utter'd words in your own, 5.02. 25 P

shall bear | a better witness back than words, 5.03.204
people, hoping | to purge himself with words. 5.06. 8
warrants these words in princely courtesy. TIT 1.01.272
o monstrous! what reproachful words are these? 1.01.308
these words are razors to my wounded heart. 1.01.314
these words, these looks, infuse new life in me. 1.01.461
it, | with words, fair looks, and liberality? 2.01. 92
and strike her home by force, if not by words; 2.01.118
and with a gad of steel will write these words, 4.01.103
the old andronicus | with words more sweet, and 4.04. 90
but let them hear what fearful words i utter. 5.02.168
cannot induce you to attend my words. 5.03. 79
my ears have yet not drunk a hundred words | of ROM 2.02. 58
three words, dear romeo, and good night indeed. 2.02.142
my words would bandy her to my sweet love, | and 2.05. 14
do thou but close our hands with holy words, 2.06. 6
conceit, more rich in matter than in words, 2.06. 30
that word's death, no words can that woe sound. 3.02.126
this letter doth make good the friar's words, 5.03.286
blows of fortune's | more pregnantly than words. TIM 1.01. 92
gave | good words the other day of a bay courser 1.02.211
must not be toss'd and turn'd to me in words, 2.01. 26
me so far as to use mine own words to him? 3.02. 58 P
your words have took such pains as if they 3.05. 26
'tis in few words, but spacious in effect: 3.05. 96
of this ingratitude | with any size of words. 5.01. 66
these words become your lips as they pass 5.01.195
lips, let four words go by and language end! 5.01.220
descend, and keep your words. 5.04. 64
i am glad that my weak words | have struck but JC 1.02.176
which gives men stomach to disgest his words 1.02.301
that which melteth fools — i mean sweet words, 3.01. 42
mark'd ye his words? 3.02.112
for i have neither /wit, nor words, nor worth, 3.02.221
make forth, the generals would have some words. 5.01. 25
words before blows; is it so, countrymen? 5.01. 27
not that we love words better, as you do. 5.01. 28
good words are better than bad strokes, octavius 5.01. 29
your bad strokes, brutus, you give good words; 5.01. 30
but for your words, they rob the hybla bees, 5.01. 34
peace then, no words. 5.05. 7
so well thy words become thee as thy wounds, MAC 1.02. 43
to th' self-same tune and words. who's here? 1.03. 88
would spend it in some words upon that business, 2.01. 23
words to the heat of deeds too cold breath gives 2.01. 61
i would attend his leisure | for a few words. 3.02. 4
thou marvel'st at my words, but hold thee still: 3.02. 54
for from broad words, and 'cause he fail'd | his 3.06. 21
but i have words | that would be howl'd out in 4.03.193
give sorrow words. 4.03.209
i have no words, | my voice is in my sword, thou 5.08. 6
as to give words or talk with the lord hamlet. HAM 1.03.134
these are but wild and whirling words, my lord. 1.05.133
what, have you given him any hard words of late? 2.01.104
words, words, words. 2.02.192 P
words, words, words. 2.02.192 P
words, words, words. 2.02.192 P
must, like a whore, unpack my heart with words, 2.02.585
words of so sweet breath compos'd | as made 3.01. 97
this answer, hamlet, these words are not mine. 3.02. 97 P
how in my words somever she be shent, | to give 3.02.398
my words fly up, my thoughts remain below: 3.03. 97
words without thoughts never to heaven go. 3.03. 98
and sweet religion makes | a rhapsody of words. 3.04. 48
these words like daggers enter in my ears. 3.04. 95
be thou assur'd, if words be made of breath, 3.04.197
and botch the words up fit to their own thoughts 4.05. 10
pray let's have no words of this, but when they 4.05. 46 P
i have words to speak in thine ear will make 4.06. 24 P
indeed your father's son | more than in words? 4.07.126
all 's golden words are spent. 5.02.131 P
that good effects may spring from words of love. LR 1.01.185
or worth in thee | make thy words faith'd? 2.01. 70
to bandy hasty words, to scant my sizes, | and 2.04.175
few words, but, to effect, more than all yet: 3.01. 52
swore as many oaths as i spake words, and broke 3.04. 88 P
no words, no words, hush. 3.04.181
no words, no words, hush. 3.04.181
go to, they are not men o' their words: 4.06.104 P
but words are words; OTH 1.03.218
but words are words; 1.03.218
and weigh'st thy words before thou giv'st them 3.03.119
give thy worst of thoughts | the worst of words. 3.03.133
of a sacred vow | i here engage my words. 3.03.462
it is not words that shakes me thus. 4.01. 41 P
i understand a fury in your words, | /but /not 4.02. 32
/for your words and performances are no kin 4.02.183 P
you sued staying, | then was the time for words; ANT 1.03. 34
when you hear no more words of pompey, return it 2.02.104 P
most meet | that first we come to words, and 2.06. 3
and fair words to them. 2.06. 66
what needs more words? 2.07.125
he words me, girls, he words me, that i should 5.02.191
girls, he words me, that i should not | be noble 5.02.191
with mine eyes i'll drink the words you send, CYM 1.01.100
which i had set | betwixt two charming words, 1.03. 35
rather by her value than his own, words him, i 1.04. 16 P
think on my words. 1.05. 75
think on my words. 1.05. 85
as i | have words to bid you, and shall find it 1.06. 30
sweet air, with admirable rich words to it — 2.03. 18 P
puts himself in posture | that acts my words. 3.03. 95
so tender of rebukes that words are /strokes, 3.05. 40
the words of your commission | will tie you to 3.07. 14
thy words, i grant, are bigger; 4.02. 78
and do not play in wench-like words with that 4.02.230
use like note and words, | save that euriphile 4.02.237
him in fresh cups, soft beds, | sweet words; 5.03. 72
she has here spoken holy words to the lord PER 4.06.133 P
i durst wager, | would win some words of him. 5.01. 44
all his words are worthy. TNK 2.05. 29
me down | and list'ned to the words she sung, 4.01. 63
be yet unbroken, | give me thy last words; 5.04. 89
fair, but speak fair words, or else be mute. VEN 208
her words are done, her woes the more increasing 254
free vent of words love's fire doth assuage, 334
his meaning struck her ere his words begun. 462
foul words and frowns must not repel a lover; 573
as if they heard the woeful words she told; 1126
so his unhallowed haste her words delays, | and LUC 552
"out, idle words, servants to shallow fools! 1016
this helpless smoke of words doth me no right. 1027
sometime her grief is dumb and hath no words, 1105
my woes are tedious, though my words are brief." 1309
she would not blot the letter | with words, till 1323
and sorrow ebbs, being blown with wind of words. 1330
pawn'd honest looks, but laid no words to gage. 1351
as, but for loss of nestor's golden words, | it 1420
cries, | and bitter words to ban her cruel foes; 1460
she lends them words, and she their looks doth 1498
whose words like wildfire burnt the shining 1523
with sad attention long to hear her words. 1610
"few words," quoth she, "shall fit the trespass 1613
in me moe woes than words are now depending, 1615
or keep him from heart-easing words so long, 1782
but through his lips do throng | weak words, so 1784
for sportive words and utt'ring foolish things. 1813
who, wond'ring at him, did his words allow. 1845
words are easy, like the wind, | faithful PP 20.31
may make seem bare, in wanting words to show it, SON 26. 6
so all my best is dressing old words new, 76.11
o'erlook | the dedicated words which writers use 82. 3
in true plain words by thy true-telling friend; 82.12
good thoughts whilst other write good words, 85. 5
whose love to you | (though words come hindmost) 85.12
then others for the breath of words respect, 85.13
"kind," and "true" varying to other words, | and 105.10
lest sorrow lend me words, and words express 140. 3
me words, and words express | the manner of my 140. 3
thought characters and words merely but art, LC 174

WORE *(also ware*)*

/WORE 1 FR 0.0001 REL FR 1 V 0 P
/nine, /that /wore | /their /crownets /regal, TRO pr 5

WORE 27 FR 0.0030 REL FR 20 V 7 P
my doublet as fresh as the first day i wore it? TMP 2.01.104 P
when i wore it at your daughter's marriage? 2.01.106 P
which of the vizards was it that you wore? LLL 5.02.385
he wore none but a dishclout of jaquenetta's, 5.02.713 P
and a chain, that you once wore, about his neck. AYL 3.02.181 P
thy father's father wore it, | and thy father 4.02. 15
haggish age steal on, | and wore us out of act. AWW 1.02. 30
five descents | since the first father wore it. 3.07. 25
prince florizel, and in my time wore three-pile, WT 4.03. 13 P
you won it, wore it, kept it, gave it me; 2H4 4.05.221
hangmen would | bury with those that wore them, COR 1.05. 7
with a proud heart he wore his humble weeds. 2.03.153
with what contempt he wore the humble weed, 2.03.221
these eyes are not the same i wore in rome. 5.03. 38
o yes, my lord, he wore his beaver up. HAM 1.02.230
wore gloves in my cap; LR 3.04. 86 P
on him, whilst | i wore his sword philippan. ANT 2.05. 23
and i wore my life | to spend upon his haters. 5.01. 8
the same suit he wore when he took leave of my CYM 3.05.126 P
those lines of favor | which then he wore. 4.02.105
you see, not wore him | from my remembrance. 4.04. 23
who ne'er wore rowel | nor iron on his heel! 4.04. 39
pieces of gold 'gainst this which then he wore 5.05.183
upon my right side still i wore thy picture, TNK 5.03. 73
ne'er saw the beauteous livery that he wore — VEN 1107
with modest lucrece, and wore out the night. LUC 123
sorrow | (for why her face wore sorrow's livery) 1222

WORK *(also ork)*

/WORK 4 FR 0.0004 REL FR 4 V 0 P
/much /more, /in /this /great /work | (/which 2H4 1.03. 48
/how /able /such /a /work /to /undergo, | /to 1.03. 54
/oats, | /if /it /be /man's /work, /i'll /do't. LR 5.03. 39
work on, | my medicine, /work! OTH 4.01. 45

WORK 193 FR 0.0218 REL FR 157 V 36 P
to silence, and work the peace of the present, TMP 1.01. 22 P
work you then. 1.01. 42 P
but there's more work. 1.02.238
for that vast of night that they may work, | all 1.02.327
my sweet mistress | weeps when she sees me work, 3.01. 12
alas, now pray you | work not so hard. 3.01. 16
let's follow it, and after do our work. 3.02.149 P
my high charms work, | and these, mine enemies, 3.03. 88
(like poison given to work a great time after) 3.03.105
time, my lord, | you said our work should cease. 5.01. 5
to work mine end upon their senses that | this 5.01. 53
as your worth is able, | and let them work. MM 1.01. 9
correction and instruction must both work | ere 3.02. 32
i will go darkly to work with her. 5.01.278 P
a very good piece of work, i assure you, and a MND 1.02. 13 P
you do their work, and they shall have good luck 2.01. 41
that work for bread upon athenian stalls, | were 3.02. 10
hard-handed men that work in athens here, 5.01. 72
when the work of generation was | between these MV 1.03. 82
i know you would be prouder of the work | than 3.04. 8
i have work in hand | that you yet know not of. 3.04. 57
peradventure this is not fortune's work neither, AYL 1.02. 51 P
strange effect | would they work in mild aspect? 4.03. 53
'tis a very excellent piece of work, madam lady; SHR 1.01.253 P
ay, marry, sir, now it begins to work. 3.02.218
and death should have play for lack of work. AWW 1.01. 21 P
as heaven shall work in me for thine avail, | to 1.03.184
but i shall lose the grounds i work upon. 3.07. 3
protest to love | that i will work against him; 4.02. 29
him will my revenge find notable cause to work. TN 2.03.153 P
i know my physic will work with him. 2.03.173 P
did not i say he would work it out? 2.05.127 P
nay, but say true, does it work upon him? 2.05.195 P
i'll go another way to work with him; 4.01. 34 P
but with a ling'ring dram that should not work WT 1.02.320
how would he look to see his work, so noble, 4.04. 21
sleeve-hand and the work about the square on't. 4.04.210 P
also, to smell out work for th' other senses. 4.04.673 P
session, hanging, yields a careful man work. 4.04.686 P
eternity and could put breath into his work, 5.02. 98 P
well, then to work! JN 2.01. 37
this toil of ours should be a work of thine; 2.01. 93
much work for tears in many an english mother, 2.01.303
and pell-mell | make work upon ourselves, for 2.01.407
it is a damned and a bloody work, | the 4.03. 57
hand — | if that it be the work of any hand. 4.03. 59
if that it be the work of any hand? 4.03. 60
it is the shameful work of hubert's hand, | the 4.03. 62
knew you of this fair work? 4.03.116
you look but on the outside of this work. 5.02.109
a while to work, and after holiday. R2 3.01. 44
to sport would be as tedious as to work; 1H4 1.02.205
i want work." 2.04.105 P
though it do work as strong | as aconitum or 2H4 4.04. 47
great accompt, | on your imaginary forces work. H5 pr 18
by, | all out of work and cold for action! 1.02.114
for so work the honey-bees, | creatures that by 1.02.187
to one consent, may work contrariously, | as 1.02.206
mangle the work of nature, and deface | the 2.04. 60
work, work your thoughts, and therein see a 3.pr. 25
work, work your thoughts, and therein see a 3.pr. 25
the work ish give over, the trompet sound the 3.02. 88 P
and my father's soul, the work ish ill done; 3.02. 90 P
there is not work enough for all our hands, 4.02. 19
those men in england | that do not work to-day! 4.03. 18
shall witness live in brass of this day's work. 4.03. 97
thy heart-blood i will have for this day's work. 1H6 1.03. 83
your honors shall perceive how i will work | to 3.03. 27
grace, | to work exceeding miracles on earth. 5.04. 41
i | in england work your grace's full content. 2H6 1.03. 67
and let us to our work. 1.04. 12 P
that time best fits the work we have in hand. 1.04. 20
o god, what mischiefs work the wicked ones, 2.01.182
given | to dream on evil or to work my downfall. 3.01. 73
and work in their shirt too, as myself, for 4.07. 52 P
work thou the way — and that /shall execute. 3H6 5.07. 25
come, shall we fall to work? R3 1.04.153 P
now have i done a good day's work. 2.01. 1
your honor hath no shriving work in hand. 3.02.115
come, let us to our holy work again. 3.07.246
the most replenished sweet work of nature | that 4.03. 18
or this imperious man will work us all | from H8 2.02. 46
these sad thoughts that work too much upon him. 2.02. 57
i was set at work | among my maids, full little, 3.01. 74
will this work? 3.02. 37
to your ear | much weightier than this work. 5.01. 18
to draw mine honor in, and let 'em win the work. 5.03. 58 P
of divination in our sister work | some touches TRO 2.02.114
spur them to ruthful work, rein them from ruth. 5.03. 48
on galathe his horse | and there lacks work; 5.05. 21
now is my day's work done, i'll take /good 5.08. 3
now, mars, i prithee make us quick in work, COR 1.04. 10
list what work he makes | amongst your cloven 1.04. 20
my work hath yet not warm'd me. 1.05. 17
corioles walls, | and made what work i pleas'd. 1.08. 9
if i should tell thee o'er this thy day's work, 1.09. 1
a little of that worthy work perform'd | by 2.02. 45
here's goodly work! 3.01.260
o, you have made good work! 4.06. 80
you have made fair work, i fear me. 4.06. 88
you have made good work, | you and your 4.06. 95
you have made fair work! 4.06.100
you have made | good work, you and your cry! 4.06.147
you have made good work! 5.01. 15
to make | what cannot be, slight work. 5.03. 62
out of that i'll work | myself a former fortune. 5.03.201
with him, | and work confusion on his enemies. TIT 5.02. 8
tut, i have work enough for you to do. 5.02.150
come, come with me, and we will make short work, ROM 2.06. 35
day, night, work, play, | alone, in company, 3.05.176
what if this mixture do not work at all? 4.03. 21
and bear this work of heaven with patience. 5.03.261
sir, in some work, some dedication | to the TIM 1.01. 19
i have, in this rough work, shap'd out a man 1.01. 43
i like your work, | and you shall find i like it 1.01.160
and yet he's but a filthy piece of work. 1.01.199 P
look in thy last work, where thou hast feign'd 1.01.222 P
o, may diseases only work upon't! 3.01. 60
profess'd, that you work not | in holier shapes; 4.03.426
needs | stand for a villain in thine own work? 5.01. 38
you have work for me; 5.01.113
out their shoes, to get myself into more work. JC 1.01. 30 P
what you would work me to, i have some aim. 1.02.163
/in favor's like the work we have in hand, 1.03.129
let me work; 2.01.209
and could it work so much upon your shape | as 2.01.253
a piece of work that will make sick men whole. 2.01.327
now let it work. 3.02.260
well, to our work alive. 4.03.196
must end that work the ides of march begun. 5.01.113
and question this most bloody piece of work, MAC 2.03.128
to leave no rubs nor botches in the work — 3.01.133
(with him above | to ratify the work) we may 3.06. 33
a most miraculous work in this good king, 4.03.147
in what particular thought to work i know not, HAM 1.01. 67
said, old mole, canst work i' th' earth so fast? 1.05.162
no, i went round to work, | and my young 2.02.139
what /a piece of work is a man! 2.02.303 P
will the king hear this piece of work? 3.02. 47 P
'tis a knavish piece of work, but what of that? 3.02.241 P
let it work, | for 'tis the sport to have the 3.04.205
work like the spring that turneth wood to stone, 4.07. 20
undertake it, i will work him | to an exploit, 4.07. 63
and /thus a while the fit will work on him; 5.01.285
then, venom, to thy work. 5.02.322
briefness and fortune, work! LR 2.01. 18
boy, i'll work the means | to make thee capable. 2.01. 84
kent, how shall i live and work | to match thy 4.07. 1
well, | the better shall my purpose work on him. OTH 1.03.391
you rise to play, and go to bed to work. 2.01.115
thou know'st we work by wit, and not by 2.03.372
i'll have the work ta'en out, | and give't iago. 3.03.296
in her prophetic fury sew'd the work; 3.04. 72
sweet bianca, | take me this work out. 3.04.180
i like the work well; 3.04.189
work on, | my medicine, /work! 4.01. 44
i must take out the work? 4.01.151 P
a likely piece of work, that you should find it 4.01.151 P
some minx's token, and i must take out the work? 4.01.154 P
you had it, i'll take out no work on't. 4.01.155 P
or did the letters work upon his blood | and 4.01.275
this is thy work. 5.02.364
had then left unseen a wonderful piece of work, ANT 1.02.154 P
my greatness, nor my power | work without it. 2.02. 94

caesar himself has work, and our oppression 4.07. 2
i have done my work ill, friends. 4.14.105
fearing since how it might work, hath sent | me 4.14.125
what work is here, charmian? is this well done? 5.02.325
flattering rascal, upon him | will i first work. CYM 1.05. 28
do thou work. 1.05. 48
that comes comes to decay | a day's work in him. 1.05. 57
a piece of work | so bravely done, so rich, that 2.04. 72
the heavens still must work. 4.03. 41
having work | more plentiful than tools to do't 5.03. 8
at the things you hear | than to work any. 5.03. 55
to work | her son into th' adoption of the crown 5.05. 55
no, no, alack, | there's other work in hand. 5.05.103
ear, and i am sworn | to do my work with haste. PER 4.01. 70
must take some pains to work her to your manage. 4.06. 64 P
which to do | must make some work with creon. TNK 1.01.150
and that work presents itself to th' doing: 1.01.151
fit of jealousy | to get the soldier work, that 1.02. 23
canst not thou work such flowers in silk, wench? 2.02.127
they have a noble work in hand will honor | the 5.01. 6
since her best work is ruin'd with thy rigor." VEN 954
might have excuse to work upon his wife, | as in LUC 235
if thou deny, then force must work my way, | for 513
such sweet observance in this work was had, 1385
for much imaginary work was there, | conceit 1422
the wiles and guiles that women work, PP 18.37
those hours that with gentle work did frame SON 5. 1
begins a journey in my head | to work my mind, 27. 4
and broils root out the work of masonry, | nor 55. 6

WORK-A-DAY *(see working-day, worky-day)*
/WORKING 1 FR 0.0001 REL FR 1 V 0 P
/in /no /less /working /than /are /swords /and TRO 1.03.355

WORKING 21 FR 0.0023 REL FR 17 V 4 P
that, in the working of your own affections, MM 2.01. 10
be cunning in the working this, and thy fee is a ADO 2.02. 52 P
by a familiar demonstration of the working, my LLL 1.02. 9 P
we bend to that the working of the heart; 4.01. 33
but his will hath in it a more modest working. AYL 1.02.203 P
together working with thy jealousies | (fancies WT 3.02.180
color her working with such deadly wounds, | nor 1H4 1.03.109
on ground, | confound themselves with working. 2H4 4.04. 41
by whose fell working i was first advanc'd, 4.05.206
working so grossly in /a natural cause | that H5 2.02.107
not working with the eye without the ear, | and 2.02.135
as i am sick with working of my thoughts. 1H6 5.05. 86
sad, high, and working, full of state and woe: H8 pr 3
leave working. 3.01. 2
by working wreakful vengeance on thy foes. TIT 5.02. 32
a thing a little soil'd /wi' /th' working, HAM 2.01. 40
that from her working all the visage wann'd, 2.02.554
might in their working do you that offense, LR 1.04.212
they're close dilations, working from the heart, OTH 3.03.123
more with begging than we can do with working. PER 2.01. 65 P
have you a working pulse, and are no fairy? 5.01.153

WORKING-DAY *(also worky-day)*
WORKING-DAY 2 FR 0.0002 REL FR 1 V 1 P
o, how full of briers is this working-day world! AYL 1.03. 12 P
we are but warriors for the working-day; H5 4.03.109

WORKING-DAYS 2 FR 0.0002 REL FR 1 V 1 P
unless i might have another for working-days. ADO 2.01.328 P
and plodded like a man for working-days; H5 1.02.277

WORKING-HOUSE 1 FR 0.0001 REL FR 1 V 0 P
in the quick forge and working-house of thought, H5 5.pr. 23

WORKINGS 3 FR 0.0003 REL FR 3 V 0 P
sanctities of heaven, | and our dull workings? 2H4 4.02. 22
and mock your workings in a second body? 5.02. 90
e'er thy thoughts or thy heart's workings be, SON 93.11

WORKMAN 6 FR 0.0006 REL FR 3 V 3 P
he, sir, 's a good workman, a very good tailor. AWW 2.05. 19 P
excellent workman! TIM 5.01. 31
sir, in respect of a fine workman, i am but, as JC 1.01. 10 P
occupation, thou shouldst see | a workman in't. ANT 4.04. 18
therein i must play the workman. CYM 4.01. 7 P
the well-skill'd workman this mild image drew LUC 1520

WORKMANLY 1 FR 0.0001 REL FR 1 V 0 P
so workmanly the blood and tears are drawn. SHR in.2. 60

WORKMANSHIP 3 FR 0.0003 REL FR 3 V 0 P
that it did strive | in workmanship and value, CYM 2.04. 74
his art with nature's workmanship at strife, VEN 291
to cross the curious workmanship of nature, | to 734

WORKMEN 3 FR 0.0003 REL FR 2 V 1 P
when workmen strive to do better than well, JN 4.02. 28
more, the king's council are no good workmen. 2H6 4.02. 15 P
like workmen, i'll example you with thievery: TIM 4.03.435

WORK'S 2 FR 0.0002 REL FR 2 V 0 P
what work's, my countrymen, in hand? COR 1.01. 55
to work my mind, when body's work's expired; SON 27. 4

WORKS 28 FR 0.0031 REL FR 24 V 4 P
it works. TMP 1.02.494
now prosper works upon thee. 2.02. 80 P
in some passion | that works him strongly. 4.01.144
your charm so strongly works 'em | that if you 5.01. 17
she works by charms, by spells, by th' figure, WIV 4.02.176 P
no man their works must eye. 5.05. 48
which therein works a miracle in nature, MV 3.02. 90
he that of greatest works is finisher | oft does AWW 2.01.136
and, toil'd with works of war, retir'd himself R2 4.01. 96
is throats to be cut, and works to be done, and H5 3.02.112 P
to see how god in all his creatures works! 2H6 2.01. 7
how holily he works in all his business! H8 2.02. 23
do you with cheeks abash'd behold our works, TRO 1.03. 18
graves only be men's works, and death their gain TIM 5.01.222
conceit in weakest bodies strongest works, HAM 3.04.114
that done, i will be walking on the works; OTH 3.02. 3
honesty's a fool | and loses that it works for. 3.03.383
and she did gratify his amorous works | with 5.02.213
dry and die, | but for the end it works to. CYM 3.06. 32
the sea works high, the wind is loud, and will PER 3.01. 48 P
to the pothecary, | and tell me how it works. 3.02. 10
speak of the disturbances | that nature works, 3.02. 38
blasts my bays and my fam'd works makes lighter TNK pr 20
thus treason works ere traitors be espied. LUC 361
in others' works thou dost but mend the style, SON 78.11
my nature is subdu'd | to what it works in, like 111. 7
which works on leases of short-numb'red hours, 124.10
works under you, and to your audit comes | their LC 230

WORK'ST 1 FR 0.0001 REL FR 1 V 0 P
"why work'st thou mischief in thy pilgrimage, LUC 960

WORKY-DAY *(also working-day)*
WORKY-DAY 1 FR 0.0001 REL FR 0 V 1 P
prithee tell her but a worky-day fortune. ANT 1.02. 54 P

WORLD *(also orld, varld, vorld)*
/WORLD 4 FR 0.0004 REL FR 2 V 2 P
o world, world, /world! TRO 5.10. 36 P
/then /is /the /world /one. HAM 2.02.244 P
/in /his /little /world /of /man /to /outscorn LR 3.01. 10
then, /world, thou /hast a pair of chaps — no ANT 3.05. 13

WORLD 670 FR 0.0757 REL FR 535 V 135 P
he whom next thyself | of all the world i lov'd, TMP 1.02. 69
worth | what's dearest to the world! 3.01. 39
not wish | any companion in the world but you; 3.01. 55
i, | beyond all limit of what else i' th' world, 3.01. 72
that hath to instrument this lower world | and 3.03. 54
my dearest love, | i would not for the world. 5.01.173
o brave new world | that has such people in't! 5.01.183
to see the wonders of the world abroad, | than TGV 1.01. 6
war with good counsel, set the world at nought; 1.01. 68
man, | not being tried and tutor'd in the world: 1.03. 21
not for the world. 2.04.168
how will the world repute me | for undertaking 2.07. 59
car, | and with thy daring folly burn the world? 3.01.155
then may i set the world on wheels, when she can 3.01.315 P
but count the world a stranger for thy sake. 5.04. 70
o wicked, wicked world! WIV 2.01. 21 P
discretion, as they say, and know the world. 2.02.130 P
what a world of vild ill-favor'd faults | looks 3.04. 32
my son profits nothing in the world at his book. 4.01. 15 P
i would all the world might be cozen'd, for i 4.05. 93 P
fellow, why dost thou show me thus to th' world? MM 1.02.116
profanation in the world that good christians 2.01. 55 P
but might you do't, and do the world no wrong, 2.02. 53
an outstretch'd throat i'll tell the world aloud 2.04.153
violence round about | the pendant world; 3.01.125
in death to take this poor maid from the world! 3.01.232 P
we shall have all the world drink brown and 3.02. 3 P
'twas never merry world since, of two usuries, 3.02. 5 P
is the world as it was, man? 3.02. 50 P
what news abroad i' th' world? 3.02.221 P
upon this riddle runs the wisdom of the world. 3.02.229 P
he hath releas'd him, isabel, from the world, 4.03.115
injurious world! 4.03.122
there is another comfort than this world, | that 5.01. 49
that apprehends no further than this world, 5.01.481
that the world may witness that my end | was ERR 1.01. 33
i to the world am like a drop of water, | that 1.02. 35
lord of the wide world and wild wat'ry seas, 2.01. 21
fie, brother, how the world is chang'd with you: 2.02.152
she'll burn a week longer than the whole world. 3.02.100 P
we came into the world like brother and brother; 5.01.425
the fashion of the world is to avoid cost, and ADO 1.01. 97 P
can the world buy such a jewel? 1.01.181 P
hath not the world one man but he will wear his 1.01.198 P
such a man would win any woman in the world, if 2.01. 16 P
of beatrice that puts the world into her person, 2.01.208 P
thus goes every one to the world but i, and i am 2.01.319 P
no, the world must be peopled. 2.03.242 P
god help us, it is a world to see! 3.05. 35 P
i do love nothing in the world so well as you — 4.01.267 P
ha! not for the wide world. 4.01.290 P
any purpose that the world can say against it, 5.04.106 P
navarre shall be the wonder of the world; LLL 1.01. 12
the world was very guilty of such a ballet some 1.02.111 P
when she did starve the general world beside 2.01. 11
not for the world, fair madam, by my will. 2.01. 99
well, i do nothing in the world but lie, and lie 4.03. 11 P
by the world, i would not care a pin, if the 4.03. 17 P
'gainst whom the world cannot hold argument, 4.03. 59
for where is any author in the world | teaches 4.03.308
that show, contain, and nourish all the world, 4.03.350
and i had but one penny in the world, thou 5.01. 71 P
thee it will please his grace (by the world) 5.01.102 P
by the world, i recount no fable: 5.01.105 P
a man of travel, that hath seen the world; 5.01.108 P
a world of torments though i should endure, | i 5.02.353
that more than all the world i did respect her. 5.02.437
eyesight, and did value me | above this world; 5.02.446
and the whole world again | cannot pick out five 5.02.544
"when in the world i liv'd, i was the world's 5.02.562
"when in the world i liv'd, i was the world's 5.02.568
remote from all the pleasures of the world; 5.02.796
were the world mine, demetrius being bated, MND 1.01.190
and the mazed world, | by their increase, now 2.01.113
for you in my respect are all the world. 2.01.224
when all the world is here to look on me? 2.01.226
how comes this gentle concord in the world, 4.01.143
over, | and it is nothing, nothing in the world; 5.01. 78
you have too much respect upon the world. MV 1.01. 74
i hold the world but as the world, gratiano, | a 1.01. 77
i hold the world but as the world, gratiano, | a 1.01. 77
nor is the wide world ignorant of her worth, 1.01.167
my little body is a-weary of this great world. 1.02. 2 P
why, that's the lady, all the world desires her. 2.07. 38
i think he only loves the world for him. 2.08. 50
the world is still deceiv'd with ornament. 3.02. 74
else nothing in the world | could turn so much 3.02.245
for the poor rude world | hath not her fellow. 3.05. 82
shylock, the world thinks, and i think so too, 4.01. 17
but life itself, my wife, and all the world, 4.01.284
so shines a good deed in a naughty world. 5.01. 91
was | for all the world like cutler's poetry 5.01.149
finger, for the wealth | that the world masters. 5.01.174
carelessly, as they did in the golden world. AYL 1.01.119 P
and indeed so much in the heart of the world, 1.01.169 P
fortune reigns in gifts of the world, not in the 1.02. 41 P
the world no injury, for in it i have nothing. 1.02.190 P
only in the world i fill up a place, which may 1.02.191 P
the world esteem'd thy father honorable, | but i 1.02.225
and all the world was of my father's mind. 1.02.236
hereafter, in a better world than this, | i 1.02.284
o, how full of briers is this working-day world! 1.03. 12 P
he'll go along o'er the wide world with me; 1.03.132
o, what a world is this, when what is comely 2.03. 14
the constant service of the antique world, 2.03. 57
a miserable world! 2.07. 13
thus we may see," quoth he, "how the world wags. 2.07. 23
cleanse the foul body of th' infected world, 2.07. 60
wouldst thou disgorge into the general world. 2.07. 69
sav'd, a world too wide | for his shrunk shank, 2.07.160
wind, | through all the world bears rosalind. 3.02. 91
we two will rail against our mistress the world, 3.02.278 P
will chide no breather in the world but myself, 3.02.280 P
full stream of the world and to live in a nook 3.02.420 P
you | that makes the world full of ill-favor'd 3.05. 53
though all the world could see, | none could be 3.05. 78
the poor world is almost six thousand years old, 4.01. 94 P
and show the world what the bird hath done to 4.01.203 P
he hath no interest in me in the world. 5.01. 9 P
desire to desire to be a woman of the world. 5.03. 5 P
both from his enterprise and from the world, 5.04.162
therefore paucas pallabris, let the world slide. SHR in.1. 5 P
were he the veriest antic in the world. in.1. 101
she was the fairest creature in the world, | and in.2. 66
sit by my side, and let the world slip, we shall in.2. 143 P
a merchant of great traffic through the world, 1.01. 12
there be good fellows in the world, and a man 1.01.128 P
wind as scatters young men through the world 1.02. 50
home, | and so am come abroad to see the world. 1.02. 58
now, by the world, it is a lusty wench! 2.01.160
why does the world report that kate doth limp? 2.01.252
o sland'rous world! 2.01.253
yourself and all the world, | that talk'd of her 2.01.290
'tis a world to see | how tame, when men and 2.01.311
why then the maid is mine from all the world, 2.01.384
now must the world point at poor katherine, 3.02. 18
for all the world caparison'd like the horse; 3.02. 65 P
which once perform'd, let all the world say no, 3.02.141
i'll keep mine own, despite of all the world. 3.02.142
good grumio, tell me, how goes the world? 4.01. 34 P
a cold world, curtis, in every office but thine, 4.01. 35 P
lov'd /none in the world so well as lucentio. 4.02. 13
would all the world but he had quite forsworn! 4.02. 35
he that is giddy thinks the world turns round. 5.02. 20
"he that is giddy thinks the world turns round": 5.02. 26
unapt to toil and trouble in the world, | but 5.02.166
with a world | of pretty, fond, adoptious AWW 1.01.173
your ladyship's good will to go to the world, 1.03. 18 P
may the world know them? 1.03. 34 P
would god would serve the world so all the year! 1.03. 84 P
hath in't a bond | whereof the world takes note. 1.03.189
i may truly say it is a novelty to the world. 2.03. 20 P
she's very well, and wants nothing i' th' world; 2.04. 4 P
if there be breadth enough in the world, i will 3.02. 24 P
none in the world, but return with an invention 3.06. 97 P
which were the greatest obloquy i' th' world 4.02. 44
which were the greatest obloquy i' th' world 4.02. 48
held, can serve the world for no honest use; 4.03.307 P
one of the greatest in the christian world 4.04. 2
but sure he is the prince of the world; 4.05. 49 P
all the spots a' th' world tax'd and debosh'd, 5.03.206
and might not be delivered to the world | till i TN 1.02. 42
am a fellow o' th' strangest mind i' th' world; 1.03.113 P
is it a world to hide virtues in? 1.03.131 P
is well hang'd in this world needs to fear no 1.05. 6 P
to the grave | and leave the world no copy. 1.05.243
tell her, my love, more noble than the world, 2.04. 81
'twas never merry world | since lowly feigning 3.01. 98
o world, how apt the poor are to be proud! 3.01.127
no love-broker in the world can more prevail in 3.02. 37 P
i am afraid this great lubber, the world, will 4.01. 14 P
you wrong me, and the world shall know it. 5.01.303 P
a great while ago the world begun, | /with hey 5.01.405
think there is not in the world either malice or WT 1.01. 33 P
no tongue that moves, none, none i' th' world, 1.02. 20
fear, | among the infinite doings of the world, 1.02.253
why then the world and all that's in't is 1.02.293
so, | the most replenish'd villain in the world, 2.01. 79
for every inch of woman in the world, | ay, 2.01.137
as this world goes, to pass for honest. 2.03. 73
make you, | yea, scandalous to the world. 2.03.121
if, one by one, you wedded all the world, | or, 5.01. 13
look'd as they had heard of a world ransom'd, or 5.02. 15 P
if all the world could have seen't, the woe had 5.02. 91 P
no settled senses of the world can match | the 5.03. 72
till she had kindled france, and all the world, JN 1.01. 33
he came into the world | full fourteen weeks 1.01.112
calf, bred from his cow, from all the world; 1.01.124
that thou mayst be a queen, and check the world! 2.01.123
have we ramm'd up our gates against the world. 2.01.272
holds hand with any princess of the world. 2.01.494
mad world, mad kings, mad composition! 2.01.561
commodity, | commodity, the bias of the world — 2.01.574
the world, who of itself is peized well, | made 2.01.575
day, | attended with the pleasures of the world, 3.03. 35
then with a passion would i shake the world, 3.04. 39
my life, my joy, my food, my all the world! 3.04.104
there's nothing in this world can make me joy: 3.04.107
how green you are and fresh in this old world! 3.04.145
that hubert, for the wealth of all the world, 4.01.130
bad world the while! 4.02.100
what says the world | to your proceedings? 4.02.132
never to taste the pleasures of the world, 4.03. 68
here's a good world! 4.03.116
among the thorns and dangers of this world. 4.03.141
let not the world see fear and sad distrust 5.01. 46
eyes | that never saw the giant world enrag'd, 5.02. 57
to any sovereign state throughout the world. 5.02. 82
and cull'd these fiery spirits from the world, 5.02.114
according to the fair play of the world, | let 5.02.118
what in the world should make me now deceive, 5.04. 26
what surety of the world, what hope, what stay, 5.07. 68
come the three corners of the world in arms, 5.07.116
will but remember me what a deal of world | i R2 1.03.269
where doth the world thrust forth a vanity — 2.01. 24
this happy breed of men, this little world, 2.01. 45
dear for her reputation through the world, | is 2.01. 58
why, cousin, wert thou regent of the world, | it 2.01.109
but for thy world enjoying but this land, | is 2.01.111
blood, | to show the world i am a gentleman. 3.01. 27
behind the globe, that lights the lower world, 3.02. 38
as if the world were all dissolv'd to tears, 3.02.108
'twill make me think the world is full of rubs, 3.04. 4
as i intend to thrive in this new world, 4.01. 78
they shall not live within this world, i swear, 5.03.142
this prison where i live unto the world; 5.05. 2

and for because the world is populous, | and 5.05. 3
these same thoughts people this little world, 5.05. 9
in humors like the people of this world: 5.05. 10
thorough the flinty ribs | of this hard world, 5.05. 21
is a strange brooch in this all–hating world. 5.05. 66
to smother up his beauty from the world, | that, 1H4 1.02.199
it be | that you a world of curses undergo, 1.03.164
into the good thoughts of the world again; 1.03.182
he apprehends a world of figures here, | but not 1.03.209
this is no world | to play with mammets and to 2.03. 91
a bad world, i say. 2.04.132 P
or all the racks in the world, i would not tell 2.04.237 P
could the world pick thee out three such enemies 2.04.367 P
banish plump jack, and banish all the world. 2.04.480 P
for there will be a world of water shed | upon 3.01. 93
for all the world | as thou art to this hour was 3.02. 93
brave world! 3.03.205
should go so general current through the world. 4.01. 5
that daff'd the world aside | and bid it pass? 4.01. 96
and witch the world with noble horsemanship. 4.01.110
the cankers of a calm world and a long peace, 4.02. 30 P
the prince of wales doth join with all the world 5.01. 86
are confident against the world in arms. 5.01.117
there did he pause, but let me tell the world, 5.02. 65
end | as all the poisonous potions in the world, 5.04. 56
and time, that takes survey of all the world, 5.04. 82
lord, lord, how this world is given to lying! 5.04.145 P
under the smile of safety wounds the world; 2H4 in 10
and let this world no longer be a stage | to 1.01.155
and my case so openly known to the world, let 2.01. 31 P
not in the fault, whereupon the world increases, 2.02. 26 P
a man's thought in the world keeps the road–way 2.02. 58 P
no abuse, ned, i' th' world, honest ned, none. 2.04.318 P
he was for all the world like a fork'd redish, 3.02.310 P
and never live to show th' incredulous world 4.05.153
'gainst all the world will rightfully maintain. 4.05.224
survive, | to mock the expectation of the world, 5.02.126
thee now deliver them like a man of this world. 5.03. 98 P
a foutre for the world and worldlings base! 5.03. 99
for god doth know, so shall the world perceive, 5.05. 57
look you, he must seem thus to the world. 5.05. 78 P
appear more wise and modest to the world. 5.05.101
should with his lion gait walk the whole world, H5 2.02.122
by cheshu, he is an ass, as in the world; 3.02. 70 P
as well as any military man in the world, in the 3.02. 81 P
any hurt in the world, but keeps the bridge most 3.06. 10 P
and he is a man of no estimation in the world, 3.06. 15 P
he would gladly make show to the world he is. 3.06. 84 P
tut, i have the best armor of the world. 3.07. 1 P
provided of both as any prince in the world. 3.07. 10 P
and for the world, familiar to us and unknown, 3.07. 37 P
the greatest admiration in the universal world, 4.01. 66 P
that beats upon the high shore of this world — 4.01.265
by, | from this day to the ending of the world, 4.03. 58
arrant traitor as any's in the universal world, 4.08. 10 P
it, if there is any martial law in the world. 4.08. 44 P
which you and yourself, and all the world, know 5.01. 7 P
should not in this best garden of the world, 5.02. 36
the sun with one eye vieweth all the world. 1H6 1.04. 84
whose glory fills the world with loud report. 2.02. 43
for when a world of men | could not prevail with 2.02. 48
all the talbots in the world, to save my life. 3.02.108
and we will make thee famous through the world. 3.03. 13
yield up his life unto a world of odds. 4.04. 25
his fame lives in the world, his shame in you. 4.04. 46
the world will say, he is not talbot's blood, 4.05. 16
let henry fret, and all the world repine. 5.02. 20
to fill the world with vicious qualities. 5.04. 35
face | a world of earthly blessings to my soul, 2H6 1.01. 22
brows, | as frowning at the favors of the world? 1.02. 4
enchas'd with all the honors of the world? 1.02. 8
be my last breathing in this mortal world! 1.02. 21
i have taken my last draught in this world. 2.03. 74 P
trowest thou that e'er i'll look upon the world, 2.04. 38
the world may laugh again, | and i may live to 2.04. 82
this gloucester should be quickly rid the world, 3.01.233
sits in grim majesty, to fright the world. 3.02. 50
what know i how the world may deem of me, | for 3.02. 65
the world shall not be ransom for thy life. 3.02.297
for where thou art, there is the world itself, 3.02.362
with every several pleasure in the world; 3.02.363
what is this world! 3.02.380
and i proclaim'd a coward through the world! 4.01. 43
i say, it was never merry world in england since 4.02. 8 P
man, and exhort all the world to be cowards; 4.10. 74 P
o, let the vile world end, | and the premised 5.02. 40
hard–hearted clifford, take me from the world, 3H6 1.04.167
and over–shine the earth as this the world. 2.01. 38
for this world frowns, and edward's sun is 2.03. 7
for what is in this world but grief and woe? 2.05. 20
then the world goes hard | when clifford cannot 2.06. 77
what other pleasure can the world afford? 3.02.147
whiles i live, t' account this world but hell, 3.02.169
to search the secret treasons of the world. 5.02. 18
so part we sadly in this troublous world, | to 5.05. 7
should she live, to fill the world with words? 5.05. 44
to signify thou cam'st to bite the world; 5.06. 54
i came into the world with my legs forward. 5.06. 71
laid, | for yet i am not look'd on in the world. 5.07. 22
sent before my time | into this breathing world, R3 1.01. 21
and leave the world for me to bustle in! 1.01.152
sleep | to undertake the death of all the world, 1.02.123
as all the world is cheered by the sun, | so i 1.02.129
all the world to nothing! 1.02.237
the spacious world cannot again afford. 1.02.245
the world is grown so bad | that wrens make prey 1.03. 69
i am too childish–foolish for this world. 1.03.141
thee to hell for shame, and leave this world, 1.03.142
though 'twere to buy a world of happy days — 1.04. 6
they often feel a world of restless cares; 1.04. 81
are you drawn forth among a world of men | to 1.04.181
all–seeing heaven, what a world is this! 2.01. 83
send forth plenteous tears to drown the world! 2.02. 70
i fear, i fear 'twill prove a giddy world. 2.03. 5
then, masters, look to see a troublous world. 2.03. 9
it is a reeling world indeed, my lord, | and i 3.02. 38
how goes the world with thee? 3.02. 96
t' avoid the censures of the carping world. 3.05. 68
here's a good world the while! 3.06. 10
bad is the world, and all will come to nought, 3.06. 13
will you enforce me to a world of cares? 3.07.223
a cockatrice hast thou hatch'd to the world, 4.01. 54
and anne my wife hath bid this world good night. 4.03. 39
now by the world — 4.04.375
for further life in this world i ne'er hope, H8 2.01. 69
one stroke has taken | for ever from the world. 2.01.118
i would not be a queen | for all the world. 2.03. 46
that man i' th' world who shall report he has 2.04.135
or shortly after | this world had air'd them. 2.04.194
(well worthy the best heir o' th' world) should 2.04.196
for no dislike i' th' world against the person 2.04.224
creature | that's paragon'd o' th' world. 2.04.231
(though all the world should crack their duty to 3.02.193
of all that world of wealth i have drawn 3.02.211
vain pomp and glory of this world, i hate ye! 3.02.365
he gave his honors to the world again, | his 4.02. 29
by that you love the dearest in this world, | as 4.02.155
long trouble now is passing | out of this world; 4.02.163
that all the world may know | i was a chaste 4.02.169
you not | how your state stands i' th' world, 5.01.127
state stands i' th' world, with the whole world? 5.01.127
and fair purgation to the world than malice, 5.02.187
th' ground, and all the world shall mourn her. 5.04. 62
as may be in the world, lady. TRO 1.02. 40 P
grandam, and as chaste | as may be in the world. 1.03.300
else might the world convince of levity | as 2.02.130
and never suffers matter of the world | enter 2.03.186
know the whole world, he is as valiant — 2.03.232
true swains in love shall in the world to come 3.02.173
am become | as new into the world, strange, 3.03. 12
one touch of nature makes the whole world kin — 3.03.175
with such a hell of pain and world of charge; 4.01. 58
ah, how the poor world is pest'red with such 5.01. 33 P
o world, world, /world! 5.10. 36 P
o world, world, /world! 5.10. 36 P
were half to half the world by th' ears, and he COR 1.01.233
as if the world | were feverous and did tremble. 1.04. 60
as to us, to all the world, that caius martius 1.09. 59
bring me word thither | how the world goes, that 1.10. 32
of no more soul nor fitness for the world | than 2.01.250
the man i speak of cannot in the world | be 2.02. 86
as they were | the common muck of the world. 2.02.126
his nature is too noble for the world; 3.01.254
and suffer it | a brand to th' end a' th' world. 3.01.302
there is a world elsewhere. 3.03.135
send | o'er the vast world to seek a single man, 4.01. 42
o world, thy slippery turns! 4.04. 12
of all the men i' th' world | i would have 4.05. 81
he is simply the rarest man i' th' world. 4.05.161 P
why then we shall have a stirring world again. 4.05.218 P
his friends | blush that the world goes well, 4.06. 5
thrusts forth his horns again into the world, 4.06. 44
i neither care for th' world nor your general; 5.02.102 P
and the most noble mother of the world | leave 5.03. 49
mother's womb | that brought thee to this world. 5.03.125
there's no man in the world | more bound to 's 5.03.158
age, | but not a sceptre to control the world. TIT 1.01.199
bear his betroth'd from all the world away. 1.01.286
i care not, i, knew she and all the world, | i 2.01. 71
world, | i love lavinia more than all the world. 2.01. 72
this before all the world do i prefer, | this 4.02.109
this maugre all the world will i keep safe, | or 4.02.110
my child is yet a stranger in the world, | she ROM 1.02. 8
ne'er saw her match since first the world begun. 1.02. 93
lady, such a man | as all the world — why, he's 1.03. 76
i would not for the world they saw thee here. 2.02. 74
so thou wilt woo, but else not for the world. 2.02. 97
and follow thee my lord throughout the world. 2.02.148
looks as pale as any clout in the versal world. 2.04.206 P
i am pepper'd, i warrant, for this world. 3.01. 99 P
that all the world will be in love with night, 3.02. 24
be patient, for the world is broad and wide. 3.03. 16
there is no world without verona walls, | but 3.03. 17
hence "banished" is banish'd from the world, 3.03. 19
and all the world to nothing | that he dares 3.05.213
the world is not thy friend, nor the world's law 5.01. 72
the world affords no law to make thee rich; 5.01. 73
doing more murther in this loathsome world, 5.01. 81
i have not seen you long, how goes the world? TIM 1.01. 2
whom this beneath world doth embrace and hug 1.01. 44
mine heir from forth the beggars of the world, 1.01.138
how goes the world, that i am thus encount'red 2.02. 36
o my good lord, the world is but a word; 2.02.152
is't possible the world should so much differ, 3.01. 46
and came into the world | when sects and 3.05. 29
minion, whom the world | voic'd so regardfully? 4.03. 81
the sweet degrees that this brief world affords 4.03.253
myself, | who had the world as my confectionary, 4.03.260
what things in the world canst thou nearest 4.03.318 P
what wouldst thou do with the world, apemantus, 4.03.322 P
i am sick of this false world, and will love 4.03.375
that beasts | may have the world in empire! 4.03.392
and that same eye whose bend doth awe the world JC 1.02.123
so get the start of the majestic world | and 1.02.130
man, he doth bestride the narrow world | like a 1.02.135
till then, think of the world. 1.02.307
or else the world, too saucy with the gods, 1.03. 12
if i know this, know all the world besides, 1.03. 98
are to the world in general as to caesar. 2.02. 29
so in the world: 3.01. 66
with the most noble blood of all this world. 3.01.156
o world! 3.01.207
and this indeed, o world, the heart of thee. 3.01.208
of caesar might | have stood against the world; 3.02.119
the threefold world divided, he should stand 4.01. 14
that struck the foremost man of all this world 4.03. 22
cassius, | for cassius is a–weary of the world; 4.03. 95
what, i, my lord? no, not for all the world. 5.05. 6
thou seest the world, volumnius, how it goes; 5.05. 22
might stand up | and say to all the world, "this 5.05. 75
now o'er the one half world | nature seems dead, MAC 2.01. 49
how goes the world, sir, now? 2.04. 21
whom the vile blows and buffets of the world 3.01.108
i am reckless what | i do to spite the world. 3.01.110
i remember now | i am in this earthly world — 4.02. 75
wish th' estate o' th' world were now undone. 5.05. 49
so this side of our known world esteem'd him) HAM 1.01. 85
as of a father, for, let the world take note, 1.02.108
seem to me all the uses of this world! 1.02.134
to be honest, as this world goes, is to be one 2.02.178 P
the beauty of the world! 2.02.307 P
the best actors in the world, either for tragedy 2.02.396 P
about the world have times twelve thirties been, 3.02.158
and thou shalt live in this fair world behind, 3.02.175
this world is not for aye, nor 'tis not strange 3.02.200
jest, poison in jest — no offense i' th' world. 3.02.235 P
some must sleep, | thus runs the world away. 3.02.274
itself /breathes out | contagion to this world. 3.02.390
in the corrupted currents of this world 3.03. 57
his seal | to give the world assurance of a man. 3.04. 62
says she hears | there's tricks i' th' world, 4.05. 5
lord, | and, as the world were now but to begin, 4.05.104
i do not know from what part of the world | i 4.06. 5
have count'nance in this world to drown or hang 5.01. 27 P
o, that that earth which kept the world in awe 5.01.215
no med'cine in the world can do thee good; 5.02.314
and in this harsh world draw thy breath in pain 5.02.348
and let me speak to /th' yet unknowing world 5.02.379
saucily to the world before he was sent for, yet LR 1.01. 22 P
to shield thee from disasters of the world, 1.01.174
of age makes the world bitter to the best of our 1.02. 47 P
this is the excellent foppery of the world, that 1.02.118 P
and thou must make a dullard of the world | if 2.01. 74
whose disposition, all the world well knows, 2.02.153
on you both | that all the world shall — i will 2.04.280
strike flat the thick rotundity o' th' world! 3.02. 7
world, world, o world! 4.01. 10
world, world, o world! 4.01. 10
world, world, o world! 4.01. 10
this world i do renounce, and in your sights 4.06. 35
this great world | shall so wear out to nought. 4.06.134
in a light, yet you see how this world goes. 4.06.148 P
a man may see how this world goes with no eyes. 4.06.151 P
your business of the world hath so an end, | and 5.01. 45
witness the world, that i create thee here | my 5.03. 77
what in the world /he /is | that names me 5.03. 97
that would upon the rack of this tough world 5.03.315
judge me the world, if 'tis not gross in sense, OTH 1.02. 72
and do attach thee | for an abuser of the world, 1.02. 78
and little of this great world can i speak 1.03. 86
she gave me for my pains a world of /sighs; 1.03.159
storm of fortunes | may trumpet to the world. 1.03.250
have look'd upon the world for four times seven 1.03.311 P
stillness of your youth | the world hath noted, 2.03.192
nor all the drowsy syrups of the world | shall 3.03.331
o monstrous world! 3.03.377
take note, take note, o world, | to be direct 3.03.377
by the world, | i think my wife be honest, and 3.03.383
i will catechize the world for him, that is, 3.04. 16 P
that had numb'red in the world | the sun to 3.04. 70
o, the world hath not a sweeter creature! 4.01.183 P
to lash the rascals naked through the world 4.02.143
take me from this world with treachery and 4.02.216 P
wouldst thou do such a deed for all the world? 4.03. 64
wouldst thou do such a deed for all the world? 4.03. 68
but, for all the whole world — /'ud's /pity, 4.03. 75 P
i would do such a wrong | for the whole world. 4.03. 79
why, the wrong is but a wrong i' th' world; 4.03. 80 P
and having the world for your labor, 'tis a 4.03. 81 P
'tis a wrong in your own world, and you might 4.03. 82 P
as would store the world they play'd for. 4.03. 85 P
none in the world; nor do i know the man. 5.01.103
if heaven would make me such another world | of 5.02.144
him | the triple pillar of the world transform'd ANT 1.01. 12
the world to weet | we stand up peerless. 1.01. 39
going on, | the sides o' th' world may danger. 1.02.192
or thou, the greatest soldier of the world, 1.03. 38
offended, and with you | chiefly i' th' world; 2.02. 33
the third o' th' world is yours, which with a 2.02. 63
us staunch from edge to edge | a' th' world, i 2.02.116
the world and my great office will sometimes 2.03. 1
three, | the senators alone of this great world, 2.06. 9
the least wind i' th' world will blow them down. 2.07. 2 P
wilt thou be lord of all the world? 2.07. 61
wilt thou be lord of the whole world? 2.07. 62
i am the man | will give thee all the world. 2.07. 65
'a bears the third part of the world, man; 2.07. 90 P
cup us till the world go round, | cup us till 2.07.117
go round, | cup us till the world go round! 2.07.118
twain would be | as if the world should cleave, 3.04. 31
the greater cantle of the world is lost | with 3.10. 6
i am so lated in the world, that i | have lost 3.11. 3
half the bulk o' th' world play'd as i pleas'd, 3.11. 64
when half to half the world oppos'd, he being 3.13. 9
from which the world should note | something 3.13. 21
the three–nook'd world | shall bear the olive 4.06. 5
o thou day o' th' world, | chain mine arm'd neck 4.08. 13
but let the world rank me in register | a 4.09. 21
with trees upon't that nod unto the world | and 4.14. 6
i, that with my sword | quarter'd the world, and 4.14. 58
wherein the worship of the whole world lies. 4.14. 86
darkling stand | the varying shore o' th' world! 4.15. 11
i liv'd, the greatest prince o' th' world, | the 4.15. 54
shall i abide | in this dull world, which in thy 4.15. 61
to tell them that this world did equal theirs 4.15. 77
the round world | should have shook lions into 5.01. 15
doom, in the name lay | a moi'ty of the world. 5.01. 19
could not stall together | in the whole world. 5.01. 40
let the world see | his nobleness well acted, 5.02. 44
his rear'd arm | crested the world, his voice 5.02. 83
sole sir o' th' world, | i cannot project mine 5.02.120
and may, through all the world; 5.02.134
thou tell'st the world | it is not worth 5.02.297
in this /vild world? 5.02.314
but that there is this jewel in the world | that CYM 1.01. 91
more than the world enjoys. 1.04. 79 P
durst attempt it against any lady in the world. 1.04.113 P
is his mother | should yield the world this ass! 2.01. 53
they are people such | that mend upon the world. 2.04. 26
britain's a world | by itself, and we will 3.01. 12
it did almost stretch | the sides o' th' world, 3.01. 50
o boys, this story | the world may read in me: 3.03. 56
this rock and these demesnes have been my world, 3.03. 70

winds and doth belie | all corners of the world. 3.04. 37
none in the world. you did mistake him sure. 4.02.102
yet reverence | (that angel of the world) doth 4.02.248
flow'rs are like the pleasures of the world; 4.02.296
from this most bravest vessel of the world 4.02.319
to shame the guise o' th' world, i will begin 5.01. 32
that he deserv'd the praise o' th' world, | as 5.04. 50
be not, as is our fangled world, a garment 5.04.134
which, being cruel to the world, concluded 5.05. 32
does the world go round? 5.05.232
him hence, | the whole world shall not save him. 5.05.321
two of the sweet'st companions in the world. 5.05.349
as sick men do | who know the world, see heaven, PER 1.01. 48
nor tell the world antiochus doth sin | in such 1.01.146
from all parts of the world to just and tourney 2.01.110 P
who, looking for adventures in the world, | was 2.03. 83
if in the world he live, we'll seek him out; 2.04. 29
/coigns | which the world together joins, | is 3.ch. 18
thou art the rudeliest welcome to this world 3.01. 30
doth appear, | to make the world twice rich. 3.02.102
what world is this? 3.02.105
thou canst not do a thing in the world so soon 4.01. 3
died, | this world to me is a lasting storm, 4.01. 19
you will not do't for all the world, i hope. 4.01. 84
were i chief lord of all this spacious world, 4.03. 5
and to the world and awkward casualties | bound 5.01. 93
sent hither | to make the world to laugh at me. 5.01.144
sword | that does good turns to th' world; TNK 1.01. 49
that your fame | knolls in the ear o' th' world. 1.01.134
thou still make good | the tongue o' th' world. 1.01.227
and they have all the world in their chamber. 2.01. 25 P
this is all our world: 2.02. 40
to tell the world 'tis but a gaudy shadow | that 2.02.103
this garden has a world of pleasures in't. 2.02.118
for only in thy court, of all the world, 2.05. 28
thou, o jewel | o' th' wood, o' th' world, hast 3.01. 10
night, | and darkness lord o' th' world! 3.02. 4
tell me | news from all parts o' th' world. 3.04. 13
go seek him through the world that is so wide. 3.04. 23
to delay it longer | would make the world think, 3.06. 11
then all the world will scorn us, | and say we 3.06.115
for express will, all the world must perish. 3.06.229
to all the under world the loves and fights | of 4.02. 24
dreaming of another world and a better; 4.03. 5 P
for in the next world will dido see palamon, and 4.03. 15 P
and cur'st the world | o' th' plurisy of people! 5.01. 65
in mortal bosoms, whose chase is this world, 5.01.131
how far is't now to th' end o' th' world, my 5.02. 72
his race | should show i' th' world too godlike. 5.03.118
saith that the world hath ending with thy life. VEN 12
whose full perfection all the world amazes, 634
dries up his oil to lend the world his light. 756
if so, the world will hold thee in disdain, 761
who doth the world so gloriously behold | that 857
"alas, poor world, what treasure hast thou lost! 1075
thus weary of the world, away she hies, | and 1189
are weakly fortress'd from a world of harms. LUC 28
upon the world dim darkness doth display, | and 118
when a black–fac'd cloud the world doth threat, 547
that suspicion which the world might bear her. 1321
'gainst whom the world could not hold argument, PP 3. 2
the sun look'd on the world with glorious eye, 6.11
if that the world and love were young, | and 19.17
pity the world, or else this glutton be, | to SON 1.13
thou dost beguile the world, unbless some mother 3. 4
the world will wail thee like a makeless wife, 9. 4
the world will be thy widow and still weep, 9. 5
look what an unthrift in the world doth spend 9. 9
but his place, for still the world enjoys it, 9.10
but beauty's waste hath in the world an end, 9.11
and threescore year would make the world away. 11. 8
to the wide world and all her fading sweets: 19. 7
and from the forlorn world his visage hide, 33. 7
suns of the world may stain when heaven's sun 33.14
that wear this world out to the ending doom. 55.12
that i might see what the old world could say 59. 9
bell | give warning to the world that i am fled 71. 3
the world that i am fled | from this vile world, 71. 4
lest the wise world should look into your moan, 71.13
lest the world should task you to recite | what 72. 1
better'd that the world may see my pleasure; 75. 8
though i (once gone) to all the world must die; 81. 6
when all the breathers of this world are dead; 81.12
now while the world is bent my deeds to cross, 90. 2
nor the prophetic soul | of the wide world, 107. 2
you are my all the world, and i must strive | to 112. 5
that all the world besides methinks are dead. 112.14
all this the world well knows, yet none knows 129.13
now this ill–wresting world is grown so bad, 140.11
what means the world to say it is not so? 148. 6
storming her world with sorrow's wind and rain. LC 7

WORLDLINGS 2 FR 0.0002 REL FR 2 V 0 P
he, "thou mak'st a testament | as worldlings do, AYL 2.01. 48
a foutre for the world and worldlings base! 2H4 5.03. 99

WORLDLY *(also wordly)*
WORLDLY 13 FR 0.0014 REL FR 13 V 0 P
i, thus neglecting worldly ends, all dedicated TMP 1.02. 89
else, no worldly good should draw from me. TGV 3.01. 9
the weariest and most loathed worldly life MM 3.01.128
the breath of worldly men cannot depose | the R2 3.02. 56
the worst is worldly loss thou canst unfold. 3.02. 94
thy sight | my worldly business makes a period. 2H4 4.05.230
hast thou not worldly pleasure at command 2H6 1.02. 45
for with his soul fled all my worldly solace; 3.02.151
in common worldly things 'tis call'd ungrateful R3 2.02. 91
and in no worldly suits would he be mov'd, | to 3.07. 63
rest, | secure from worldly chances and mishaps! TIT 1.01.152
but life, being weary of these worldly bars, JC 1.03. 96
rages, | thou thy worldly task hast done, | home CYM 4.02.260

WORLD'S 58 FR 0.0065 REL FR 52 V 6 P
why then the world's mine oyster, | which i with WIV 2.02. 3
/though all the world's vastidity you had, | to MM 3.01. 68
and therefore, to the world's end, will have ERR 2.02.107 P
grace command me any service to the world's end?
ADO 2.01.264 P
and the huge army of the world's desires — LLL 1.01. 10
the grosser manner of these world's delights 1.01. 29
he throws upon the gross world's baser slaves; 1.01. 30
a man in all the world's new fashion planted, 1.01.164
from tawny spain, lost in the world's debate. 1.01.173
yourself, held precious in the world's esteem, 2.01. 4
the world i liv'd, i was the world's commander; 5.02.562
world i liv'd, i was the world's commander" — 5.02.568
and the world's large tongue | proclaims you for 5.02.842
all the world's a stage, | and all the men and AYL 2.07.139
even to the world's pleasure and the increase of AWW 2.04. 36 P
save back to england, all the world's my way. R2 1.03.207
in stubborn jewry | of the world's ransom, 2.01. 56
our holy lives must win a new world's crown, 5.01. 24
and for whose death we in the world's wide mouth
1H4 1.03.153
sick in the world's regard, wretched and low, 4.03. 57
and put the world's whole strength | into one 2H4 4.05. 44
by which the world's best garden he achieved, H5 ep 7
because i wish'd this world's eternity. 2H6 2.04. 90
for wheresoe'er thou art in this world's globe, 3.02.406
on thee, the troubler of the poor world's peace! R3 1.03.220
hath not yet div'd into the world's deceit; 3.01. 8
woe's scene, world's shame, grave's due by life 4.04. 27
the world's large spaces cannot parallel. TRO 2.02.162
of this action | for the wide world's revenue. 2.02.206
be call'd to the world's end after my name; 3.02.201 P
the wide world's emperor, do i consecrate | my TIT 1.01.248
come down and welcome me to this world's light; 5.02. 33
from the world, | and world's exile is death; ROM 3.03. 20
world is not thy friend, nor the world's law, 5.01. 72
why, this is the world's soul, and just of the TIM 3.02. 64
none, my lord, but the world's grown honest. HAM 2.02.237 P
/... | whose whisper o'er the world's diameter, 4.01. 41
my will, not all the world's: 4.05.138
i think the world's asleep. LR 1.04. 48 P
bring this monstrous birth to the world's light. OTH 1.03.404
not the world's mass of vanity could make me. 4.02.164
the world's a huge thing; 4.03. 69
read not my blemishes in the world's report. ANT 2.03. 5
smiling from | the world's great snare uncaught? 4.08. 18
i' th' world's volume | our britain seems as of CYM 3.04.137
weary of this world's light, have to themselves TNK 1.01.143
this world's a city full of straying streets, 1.05. 15
take emilia, | and with her all the world's joy. 5.04. 91
"look, the world's comforter, with weary gait, VEN 529
look how the world's poor people are amazed | at 925
proving from world's minority their right: LUC 67
sell her joy, her life, her world's delight. 385
unskillful in the world's false forgeries. PP 1. 4
thou that art now the world's fresh ornament, SON 1. 9
to eat the world's due, by the grave and thee. 1.14
parts of thee that the world's eye doth view 69. 1
my heart knows the wide world's common place? 137.10
unlearned in the world's false subtilties. 138. 4

WORLDS 6 FR 0.0006 REL FR 6 V 0 P
nor doth this wood lack worlds of company, | for MND 2.01.223
of things disjoint, both the worlds suffer, MAC 3.02. 16
that both the worlds i give to negligence, | let HAM 4.05.135
i have got two worlds by't. CYM 5.05.374
blue, | a pair of maiden worlds unconquered, LUC 408
these worlds in tarquin new ambition bred, | who 411

WORLD-SHARERS 1 FR 0.0001 REL FR 1 V 0 P
these three world–sharers, these competitors, ANT 2.07. 70

WORLD-WEARIED 1 FR 0.0001 REL FR 1 V 0 P
stars | from this world–wearied flesh. ROM 5.03.112

WORLD-WITHOUT-END
2 FR 0.0002 REL FR 2 V 0 P
short | to make a world–without–end bargain in. LLL 5.02.789
nor dare i chide the world–without–end hour, SON 57. 5

WORM 33 FR 0.0037 REL FR 20 V 13 P
poor worm, thou art infected! TMP 3.01. 31
vild worm, thou wast o'erlook'd even in thy WIV 5.05. 83
fear the soft and tender fork | of a poor worm. MM 3.01. 17
where is but a humor or a worm. ADO 3.02. 27 P
is it most expedient for the wise, if don worm 5.02. 84 P
worm nor snail, do no offense. MND 2.02. 23
could not a worm, an adder, do so much? 3.02. 71
but let concealment, like a worm i' th' bud, TN 2.04.111
civil dissension is a viperous worm | that gnaws 1H6 3.01. 72
the mortal worm might make the sleep eternal. 2H6 3.02.263
the smallest worm will turn, being trodden on, 3H6 2.02. 17
the worm of conscience still begnaw thy soul! R3 1.03.221
as is the bud bit with an envious worm, | ere he ROM 1.01.151
not half so big as a round little worm | prick'd 1.04. 68
the gilded newt and eyeless venom'd worm, | with TIM 4.03.182
the worm that's fled | hath nature that in time MAC 3.04. 28
your worm is your only emperor for diet: HAM 4.03. 21 P
a man may fish with the worm that hath eat of a 4.03. 27 P
and eat of the fish that hath fed of that worm. 4.03. 28 P
thou ow'st the worm no silk, the beast no hide, LR 3.04.104 P
fellow saw, | which made me think a man a worm. 4.01. 33
hast thou the pretty worm of nilus there, | that ANT 5.02.243
truly, she makes a very good report o' th' worm; 5.02.255 P
this is most falliable, the worm's an odd worm. 5.02.258 P
i wish you all joy of the worm. 5.02.260 P
this, look you, that the worm will do his kind. 5.02.263 P
the worm is not to be trusted but in the keeping 5.02.265 P
for indeed, there is no goodness in the worm. 5.02.267 P
yes, forsooth; i wish you joy o' th' worm. 5.02.279 P
oppression, and the poor worm doth die for't. PER 1.01.102
i trod upon a worm against my will, | but i wept 4.01. 78
"grim–grinning ghost, earth's worm, what dost VEN 933
"why should the worm intrude the maiden bud? LUC 848

WORM-EATEN 3 FR 0.0003 REL FR 1 V 2 P
hercules in the smirch'd worm–eaten tapestry, ADO 3.03.136 P
concave as a cover'd goblet or a worm–eaten nut. AYL 3.04. 24 P
and this worm–eaten /hold of ragged stone, 2H4 in 35

WORM-HOLES 2 FR 0.0002 REL FR 2 V 0 P
pick'd from the worm–holes of long–vanish'd days
H5 2.04. 86
"to fill with worm–holes stately monuments, | to LUC 946

WORM'S 2 FR 0.0002 REL FR 0 V 2 P
why, e'en so, and now my lady worm's, chopless, HAM 5.01. 88 P
this is most falliable, the worm's an odd worm. ANT 5.02.258 P

WORMS' 1 FR 0.0001 REL FR 1 V 0 P
they have made worms' meat of me. ROM 3.01.107

WORMS 22 FR 0.0024 REL FR 19 V 3 P
thou thus to reprove | these worms for loving, LLL 4.03.152
gilded /tombs do worms infold. MV 2.07. 69
from time to time and worms have eaten them, but
AYL 4.01.107 P
come, come, you froward and unable worms! SHR 5.02.169
and ring these fingers with thy household worms, JN 3.04. 31
let's talk of graves, of worms, and epitaphs, R2 3.02.145
for worms, brave percy. 1H4 5.04. 87
give that which gave thee life unto the worms, 2H4 4.05.116
thy broken faith hath made the prey for worms. R3 4.04.386
when i shall dwell with worms, and my poor name
H8 4.02.126
i remain | with worms that are thy chambermaids; ROM 5.03.109
what, with worms and flies? MAC 4.02. 32
convocation of politic worms are e'en at him. HAM 4.03. 20 P
the worms were hallowed that did breed the silk, OTH 3.04. 73
whose tongue | outvenoms all the worms of nile, CYM 3.04. 35
be haunted, | and worms will not come to thee. 4.02.218
poop'd him, she made him roast–meat for worms.
PER 4.02. 25 P
lays open all the little worms that creep; LUC 1248
be death's conquest and make worms thine heir. SON 6.14
this vile world, with vildest worms to dwell: 71. 4
the prey of worms, my body being dead, | the 74.10
shall worms, inheritors of this excess, | eat up 146. 7

WORM'S-MEAT 1 FR 0.0001 REL FR 0 V 1 P
thou worm's–meat, in respect of a good piece of AYL 3.02. 65 P

WORMWOOD 5 FR 0.0005 REL FR 4 V 1 P
to weed this wormwood from your fructful brain, LLL 5.02.847
for i had then laid wormwood to my dug, ROM 1.03. 26
when it did taste the wormwood on the nipple 1.03. 30
that's wormwood! HAM 3.02.181 P
thy sug'red tongue to bitter wormwood taste; LUC 893

WORMY 1 FR 0.0001 REL FR 1 V 0 P
burial, | already to their wormy beds are gone. MND 3.02.384

/WORN 1 FR 0.0001 REL FR 1 V 0 P
/that /i /have /worn /so /many /winters /out R2 4.01.258

WORN 37 FR 0.0041 REL FR 25 V 12 P
one that is well–nigh worn to pieces with age to WIV 2.01. 21 P
you that have worn your eyes almost out in the MM 1.02.109 P
have gone round | and none of them been worn; 1.02.169
for the garland he might have worn himself, and ADO 2.01.229 P
a wither'd hermit, fivescore winters worn, LLL 4.03.238
well, better wits have worn plain statute–caps. 5.02.281
ay, and worn in the cap of a tooth–drawer. 5.02.618 P
and, for the morning now is something worn, MND 4.01.182
he should have worn the horns on his head. 5.01.240 P
the rest have worn me out | with several AWW 1.02. 73
up, and no sword worn | but one to dance with! 2.01. 32
and a half, but his right cheek is worn bare. 4.05. 98 P
th' sequent issue, | hath it been owed and worn. 5.03.198
more longing, wavering, sooner lost and worn, TN 2.04. 34
which waits upon worn times, hath something WT 5.01.142
thou art fitter to be worn in my cap than to 2H4 1.02. 15 P
sit | like a rich armor worn in heat of day, 4.05. 30
fly — | and time hath worn us into slovenry. H5 4.03.114
and worn as a memorable trophy of predeceas'd 5.01. 71 P
these few days' wonder will be quickly worn. 2H6 2.04. 69
that you might still have worn the petticoat, 3H6 5.05. 23
to't, | that sure th' have worn out christendom. H8 1.03. 15
when water–drops have worn the stones of troy, TRO 3.02.186
they are worn, lord consul, so | that we shall COR 3.01. 6
your power well on | before you had worn it out. 3.02. 18
better than he have worn vulcan's badge. TIT 2.01. 89
day | that i have worn a visor and could tell ROM 1.05. 22
this jest now, till thou hast worn out thy pump, 2.04. 62 P
when the single sole of it is worn, the jest may 2.04. 63 P
looks, | sharp misery had worn him to the bones; 5.01. 41
which would be worn now in their newest gloss, MAC 1.07. 34
successive kings | in denmark's crown have worn. HAM 5.02.274
that when old robes are worn out, there are ANT 1.02.164 P
which thou hast worn | most useful for thy 4.14. 79
or this gentleman's opinion by this worn out. CYM 1.04. 63 P
where't grows, | but worn a bait for ladies. 3.04. 57
i have worn a lighter, | but i shall make it TNK 3.06. 56

WORN-OUT 1 FR 0.0001 REL FR 1 V 0 P
even so this pattern of the worn–out age LUC 1350

WORRIED 1 FR 0.0001 REL FR 1 V 0 P
let us be worried, and our nation lose | the H5 1.02.219

WORRIES 1 FR 0.0001 REL FR 0 V 1 P
then again worries he his daughter with clipping WT 5.02. 53 P

WORRY 1 FR 0.0001 REL FR 1 V 0 P
to worry lambs and lap their gentle blood, R3 4.04. 50

WORRYING 1 FR 0.0001 REL FR 1 V 0 P
as dogs upon their masters, worrying you. H5 2.02. 83

WORSE 178 FR 0.0201 REL FR 132 V 46 P
his only heir | and princess no worse issued. TMP 1.02. 59
why, they were no worse | than now they are. 2.01.261
of you there present | are worse than devils. 3.03. 36
(worse than any death | can be at once) shall 3.03. 77
i would it were no worse. TGV 2.01.163 P
thou'dst two, | and that's far worse than none: 5.04. 51
well, heaven send anne page no worse fortune! WIV 1.04. 32 P
i shall think the worse of fat men, as long as i 2.01. 56 P
or to be worse than worst | of those that MM 3.01.125
still thus, and thus; still worse! 3.02. 53 P
spoke so of him, and much more, much worse. 5.01.338 P
this may prove worse than hanging. 5.01.360 P
ill–fac'd, worse bodied, shapeless every where; ERR 4.02. 20
unkind, | stigmatical in making, worse in mind. 4.02. 22
and yet would herein others' eyes were worse: 4.02. 26
no, he's in tartar limbo, worse than hell: 4.02. 32
a wolf, nay worse, a fellow all in buff; 4.02. 36
nay, she is worse, she is the devil's dam, and 4.03. 51 P
scratching could not make it worse, and 'twere ADO 1.01.136 P
a sport of it, and torment the poor lady worse. 2.03.157 P
i could say she were worse; 3.02.110 P
think you of a worse title, and i will fit her 3.02.111 P
they are worse fools to purchase mocking so. LLL 5.02. 59
that hid the worse and show'd the better face. 5.02.388
to have one show worse than the king's and his 5.02.513
but i should use thee worse, | for thou, i fear, MND 3.02. 45
and the worst are no worse, if imagination amend 5.01.212 P
if we imagine no worse of them than they of 5.01.215 P
he is best, he is a little worse than a man, and MV 1.02. 88 P
so rich a gem | was set in worse than gold. 2.07. 55
what, worse and worse! 3.02.247
what, worse and worse! 3.02.247
have told you | that i was worse than nothing; 3.02.260
i'll have no worse a name than jove's own page, AYL 1.03.124
are mere usurpers, tyrants, and what's worse, 2.01. 61

the more one sickens the worse at ease he is; 3.02. 24 P
worse than jove in a thatch'd house! 3.03. 10 P
to every modern censure worse than drunkards. 4.01. 7 P
and shrowd | as socrates' xantippe, or a worse, SHR 1.02. 71
alas, sir, it is worse for me than so! 4.02. 88
neither art thou the worse | for this poor 4.03.179
and if you please to like | no worse than i, 4.04. 33
pray god, sir, your wife send you not a worse. 5.02. 84
worse and worse; 5.02. 93
worse and worse; 5.02. 93
and the principal itself not much the worse. AWW 1.01.149 P
ne, worse of worst — extended | with vildest 2.01.173
i ne'er had worse luck in my life in my "o lord, 2.02. 57 P
no worse man than sir toby to look to me! TN 3.04. 64 P
you tarry longer, | i shall give worse payment. 4.01. 20
better for my foes and the worse for my friends. 5.01. 13 P
no, sir, the worse. 5.01. 15 P
why then the worse for my friends and the better 5.01. 22 P
thou shalt not be the worse for me, there's gold 5.01. 27 P
worse than the great'st infection | that e'er WT 1.02.423
here which burns | worse than tears drown. 2.01.112
to your charge, | so like you, 'tis the worse. 2.03. 98
if ever you have spent time worse ere now; 4.01. 30
one worse, | and better us'd, would make her 5.01. 56
i was, | but many a many foot of land the worse. JN 1.01.183
doth make the fault the worse by th' excuse: 4.02. 31
what i have spoke, or thou canst worse devise. R2 1.01. 77
gives but the greater feeling to the worse. 1.03.301
'tis too true, and that is worse, | the lord 2.02. 52
and all goes worse than i have power to tell. 3.02.120
three judases, each one thrice worse than judas! 3.02.132
and be slain — no worse can come to fight, 3.02.183
poor queen, so that thy state might be no worse, 3.04.102
yet a coward is worse than a cup of sack with 1H4 2.04.126 P
a railing wife, | worse than a smoky house. 3.01.159
worse than the sun in march, | this praise doth 4.01.111
report of a caliver worse than a struck fowl or 4.02. 19 P
to make that worse, suff'red his kinsman march 4.03. 93
wound my thoughts worse than thy sword my flesh. 5.04. 80
smooth comforts false, worse than true wrongs. 2H4 in 40
it is worse shame to beg than to be on the worst 1.02. 76 P
were it worse than the name of rebellion can 1.02. 77 P
god send the wench no worse fortune! 2.02.140 P
in another place, | and find me worse provided. 2.03. 50
i am the worse when one says swagger. 2.04.104 P
so much the worse, if your own rule be true. 4.02. 86
no worse than they are backbitten, sir, for they 5.01. 34 P
and, which is worse, within thy nasty mouth! H5 2.01. 50
i never saw a fellow worse bestead, | or more 2H6 2.03. 56
entreat her not the worse in that i pray | you 2.04. 81
might happily have prov'd far worse than his. 3.01.306
what, worse than nought? 3.01.307
gall, worse than gall, the daintiest that they 3.02.322
of france, but worse than wolves of france, 3H6 1.04.111
what's worse than murtherer, that i may name it? 5.05. 58
in that you brook it ill, it makes him worse; R3 1.03. 3
deserve not worse than wretched clarence did, 2.01. 94
bett'ring thy loss makes the bad causer worse; 4.04.122
sparing would show a worse sin than ill doctrine H8 1.03. 60
your fears are worse. 3.01.124
i'll startle you | worse than the sacring bell, 3.02.295
shall exceed | by showing the worse first. TRO 1.03.361
to fear the worst oft cures the worse. 3.02. 73 P
we do, and long to know each other worse. 4.01. 32
enemy | (who is of rome worse hated than of you) COR 1.02. 13
they did budge | from rascals worse than they. 1.06. 45
i do hate thee | worse than a promise–breaker. 1.08. 2
'twere a concealment | worse than a theft, no 1.09. 22
how is it less or worse | that it shall hold 3.02. 48
and love thee no worse than thy old father 5.02. 70 P
the worse to her, the better lov'd of me. TIT 2.03.167
o, keep me from their worse than killing lust, 2.03.175
by my soul, were there worse end than death, 2.03.302
for worse than philomel you us'd my daughter, 5.02.194
and worse than progne i will be reveng'd. 5.02.195
ten thousand worse than ever yet i did | would i 5.03.187
a thousand times the worse, to want thy light. ROM 2.02.155
the youngest of that name, for fault of a worse. 2.04.123 P
there is thy gold, worse poison to men's souls, 5.01. 80
and now ingratitude makes it worse than stealth. TIM 3.04. 27
i'm worse than mad. 3.05.105
i hate thee worse. 4.03.234
wretched being, | worse than the worst, content. 4.03.247
you stones, you worse than senseless things! JC 1.01. 35
for we will shake him, or worse days endure. 1.02.322
and valiant roman, | i never thought him worse. 3.01.139
i fear there will a worse come in his place. 3.02.111
he grows worse and worse, | question enrages him MAC 3.04.116
he grows worse and worse, | question enrages him 3.04.116
and, which is worse, all you have done | hath 3.05. 10
to do worse to you were fell cruelty, | which is 4.02. 71
still better, and worse. HAM 3.02.251 P
this bad begins and worse remains behind. 3.04.179
i lay | worse than the mutines in the /bilboes. 5.02. 6
worse than brutish! LR 1.02. 77 P
if i like thee no worse after dinner, i will not 1.04. 41 P
my sister may receive it much more worse | to 2.02.148
'tis worse than murther | to do upon respect 2.04. 23
between the dukes, and a worse matter than that. 3.03. 9 P
i am worse than e'er i was. 4.01. 26
and worse i may be yet: 4.01. 27
his answer was, "the worse." 4.02. 6
thou worse than any name, read thine own evil. 5.03.157
i know my price, i am worth no worse a place. OTH 1.01. 11
transported with no worse nor better guard | but 1.01.124
worse and worse. 2.01.134
worse and worse. 2.01.134
she's the worse for all this. 4.01.191 P
and let her die too, and give him a worse! ANT 1.02. 65 P
and let worse follow worse, till the worst of 1.02. 66 P
and let worse follow worse, till the worst of 1.02. 66 P
no worse a husband than the best of men; 2.02.128
he were the worse for that, were he a horse; 3.02. 52
with a fool, | frighted, and ang'red worse. CYM 2.03.140
what's worse, | must curtsy at the censure. 3.03. 54
yet the traitor | stands in worse case of woe. 3.04. 87
and falsehood | is worse in kings than beggars. 3.06. 14
ay, and that | from one bad thing to worse, not 4.02.134
for notes of sorrow out of tune are worse | than 4.02.241
to second ills with ills, each elder worse, 5.01. 14
who worse than a physician | would this report 5.05. 27
more, sir, and worse. 5.05. 49
o' th' earth amend | by being worse than they. 5.05.217
bad child, worse father, to entice his own | to PER 1.ch. 27
what being more known grows worse, to smother it 1.01.106
we offend worse. 4.02. 38 P
worse and worse, mistress, she has here spoken 4.06.132 P
worse and worse, mistress, she has here spoken 4.06.132 P
to keep us from corruption of worse men. TNK 2.02. 72
'tis worse to me than begging | to take my life 3.06.266
distemper'd | /far worse than now she shows. 4.01.120
and penn'd by no worse man than giraldo, 4.03. 12 P
what were thy lips the worse for one poor kiss? VEN 207
her, | that worse than tantalus' is her annoy, 599
a mischief worse than civil home–bred strife, 764
your treatise makes me like you worse and worse. 774
your treatise makes me like you worse and worse. 774
worse than a slavish wipe or birth–hour's blot; LUC 537
to subjects worse have given admiring praise. SON 59.14
not making worse what nature made so clear, 84.10
fond on praise, which makes your praises worse. 84.14
lilies that fester smell far worse than weeds. 94.14
and worse essays prov'd thee my best of love. 110. 8

WORSER 21 FR 0.0023 REL FR 18 V 3 P
strong'st suggestion | our worser genius can, TMP 4.01. 27
it is so, it is so — it hath the worser sole. TGV 2.03. 17 P
and the worser allow'd by order of law a furr'd MM 3.02. 6 P
what worser place can i beg in your love | (and MND 2.01.208
that were my state far worser than it is, | i SHR 1.02. 91
chang'd to a worser shape thou canst not be. 1H6 5.03. 36
iwis your grandam had a worser match. R3 1.03.101
and where the worser is predominant, | full soon ROM 2.03. 29
some word there was, worser than tybalt's death, 3.02.108
o, throw away the worser part of it, | and /live HAM 3.04.157
let not my worser spirit tempt me again | to die LR 4.06.218
these weeds are memories of those worser hours; 4.07. 7
the worser welcome; OTH 1.01. 95
the worser that you give me the addition | whose 4.01.104
our worser thoughts heavens mend! ANT 1.02. 62 P
i cannot hate thee worser than i do, | if thou 2.05. 90
urging the worser sense for vantage still; LUC 249
which once corrupted takes the worser part; 294
but she in worser taking, | from sleep disturbed 453
fair), | my worser spirit a woman (color'd ill). PP 2. 4
fair, | the worser spirit a woman color'd ill. SON 144. 4

/WORSHIP 1 FR 0.0001 REL FR 1 V 0 P
to thee be /worship, and thy saints for aye | be TIM 5.01. 52

WORSHIP 94 FR 0.0106 REL FR 30 V 64 P
for a god, | and worship this dull fool! TMP 5.01.298
your worship, sir, or else i mistook. TGV 2.01. 10 P
she that your worship loves? 2.01. 16 P
was this the idol that you worship so? 2.04.144
star, | but now i worship a celestial sun. 2.06. 10
to worship shadows and adore false shapes, 4.02.130
will't please your worship to come in, sir? WIV 1.01.266 P
i may not go in without your worship; 1.01.277 P
better that it pleases your good worship to ask. 1.04.136 P
have not your worship a wart above your eye? 1.04.146 P
and i will tell your worship more of the wart 1.04.159 P
farewell to your worship. 1.04.162 P
give your worship good morrow. 2.02. 33 P
not so, and't please your worship. 2.02. 35 P
shall i vouchsafe your worship a word or two? 2.02. 40 P
your worship says very true. 2.02. 48 P
i pray your worship come a little nearer this 2.02. 49 P
but i have another messenger to your worship. 2.02. 95 P
bade me tell your worship that her husband is 2.02.101 P
and hath sent your worship a morning's draught 2.02.146 P
he knew your worship would kill him if he came. 2.03. 10 P
give your worship good morrow. 3.05. 27 P
sir, i come to your worship from mistress ford. 3.05. 33 P
i thank your worship. 4.05. 55 P
let not your worship think me the poor duke's MM 2.01.177 P
marry, i thank your good worship for it. 2.01.182 P
marry, i thank your worship for it. 2.01.189 P
i thank your worship. 2.01.208 P
does your worship mean to geld and splay all the 2.01.230 P
if your worship will take order for the drabs 2.01.234 P
i thank your worship for your good counsel; 2.01.252 P
i hope, sir, your good worship will be my bail. 3.02. 72 P
if i should pay your worship those again, ERR 1.02. 85
it pleases your worship to say so, but we are ADO 3.05. 19 P
in my heart to bestow it all of your worship. 3.05. 22 P
exclamation on your worship as of any man in the 3.05. 26 P
them this morning examin'd before your worship. 3.05. 47 P
your worship speaks like a most thankful and 5.01.315 P
i leave an arrant knave with your worship, which 5.01.321 P
which i beseech your worship to correct yourself 5.01.322 P
god keep your worship! 5.01.323 P
i wish your worship well. 5.01.324 P
i thank your worship, god be wi' you! LLL 3.01.150 P
i will come to your worship to–morrow morning. 3.01.160 P
face, | that we (like savages) may worship it. 5.02.202
your worship was the last man in our mouths. MV 1.03. 60
god bless your worship! 2.02.120 P
of doves that i would bestow upon your worship, 2.02.136 P
as your worship shall know by this honest old 2.02.138 P
your worship was wont to tell me i could do 2.05. 8 P
calls your worship? AYL 1.01. 88 P
good morrow to your worship. 1.01. 95 P
and so god keep your worship! 1.01.162 P
that can entame my spirits to your worship. 3.05. 48
is there any man has rebus'd your worship? SHR 1.02. 7 P
to pass, | as before imparted to your worship, 3.02.130
here is the cap your worship did bespeak. 4.03. 63
she says your worship means to make a puppet of 4.03.105 P
your worship is deceiv'd, the gown is made 4.03.115
form | have bench'd and rear'd to worship, who WT 1.02.314
to th' palace, and it like your worship. 4.04.716 P
your worship had like to have given us one, if 4.04.727 P
all the faults i have committed to your worship, 5.02.150 P
ay, and it like your good worship. 5.02.155 P
gain, be my lord, for i will worship thee. JN 2.01.598
hand, | by giving it the worship of revenge. 4.03. 72
yea, even the slightest worship of his time, 1H4 3.02.151
/into smithfield to buy your worship a horse. 2H4 1.02. 51 P
your good worship is welcome. 3.02. 91 P
i grant your worship that he is a knave, sir; 5.01. 43 P
i have serv'd your worship truly, sir, this 5.01. 47 P
man, i have little credit with your worship. 5.01. 50 P
i am glad to see your worship. 5.01. 56 P
your worship! 5.03. 44 P
and't please your worship, there's one pistol 5.03. 80 P
god–den to your worship, good captain james. H5 3.02. 84 P
how may i reverently worship thee enough? 1H6 1.02.145
his wife, and't like your worship. 2H6 2.01. 78
erect his statue and worship it, | and make my 3.02. 80
agree like brothers, and worship me their lord. 4.02. 75 P
ay, but give me worship and quietness, | i like 3H6 4.03. 16
was it not she, and that good man of worship, R3 1.01. 66
and please your worship, brakenbury, | you may 1.01. 88
as i belong to worship and affect | in honor H8 1.01. 39
that all the greeks begin to worship ajax; TRO 3.03.182
this double worship, | where /one part does COR 3.01.142
your worship in that sense may call him man. ROM 3.01. 59
night, | and pay no worship to the garish sun. 3.02. 25
how? what does his cashier'd worship mutter? TIM 3.04. 60 P
wherein the worship of the whole world lies. ANT 4.14. 86
reckon'd, but of those | who worship dirty gods. CYM 3.06. 55
do — to worship her | as she is heavenly and a TNK 2.02.162
and i thank thy good worship for my brother STM II.C 59 P
when all my best doth worship thy defect, SON 149.11

WORSHIPFUL 6 FR 0.0006 REL FR 3 V 3 P
what, my old worshipful old master? SHR 5.01. 54 P
but this is worshipful society, | and fits the JN 1.01.205
o my most worshipful lord, and't please your 2H4 2.01. 69 P
accites your most worshipful thought to think so 2.02. 60 P
your very worshipful and loving friends, | and R3 3.07.138
worshipful mutiners, | your valor puts well COR 1.01.250

WORSHIPFULLY 1 FR 0.0001 REL FR 1 V 0 P
his master's child, as worshipfully he terms it, R3 3.04. 39

WORSHIPP'D 8 FR 0.0009 REL FR 6 V 2 P
thou shalt be worshipp'd, kiss'd, lov'd, and TGV 4.04.199
but god is to be worshipp'd; ADO 3.05. 39 P
lord worshipp'd might he be! MV 2.02. 93 P
call'd, | canonized and worshipp'd as a saint, JN 3.01.177
mouth, | not worshipp'd with a waxen epitaph. H5 1.02.233
shall he be worshipp'd | of that we hold an idol TRO 2.03.188
an hour before the worshipp'd sun | peer'd forth ROM 1.01.118
gold | that he is worshipp'd in a baser temple TIM 5.01. 48

WORSHIPPER 2 FR 0.0002 REL FR 2 V 0 P
adore | the sun, that looks upon his worshipper, AWW 1.03.206
devil, | little suspecteth the false worshipper: LUC 86

WORSHIPPERS 2 FR 0.0002 REL FR 2 V 0 P
more | of mortal griefs than do thy worshippers? H5 4.01.242
true worshippers of mars, whose spirit in you TNK 5.01. 35

WORSHIPPEST 1 FR 0.0001 REL FR 0 V 1 P
for i know thou worshippest saint nicholas as 1H4 2.01. 64 P

WORSHIP'S 11 FR 0.0012 REL FR 2 V 9 P
lord, lord, your worship's a wanton! WIV 2.02. 56 P
what is't your worship's pleasure i shall do MM 2.01.183 P
to your worship's house, sir? 2.01.274 P
your worship's wife, my mistress at the phoenix; ERR 1.02. 88
to–night, excepting your worship's presence, ha' ADO 3.05. 31 P
i beseech your worship's name. MND 3.01.180 P
your worship's friend and launcelot, sir. MV 2.02. 56 P
master and he (saving your worship's reverence) 2.02.130 P
is this all your worship's reason? AWW 1.03. 31 P
he and his toothpick at my worship's mess, | and JN 1.01.190
good hand, give me your worship's good hand. 2H4 3.02. 82 P

WORSHIPS' 1 FR 0.0001 REL FR 0 V 1 P
my father desires your worships' company. WIV 1.01.262 P

WORSHIPS 9 FR 0.0010 REL FR 3 V 6 P
i am glad to see your worships well. WIV 1.01. 79 P
i cry your worships mercy, heartily. MND 3.01.179 P
he worships you. AYL 5.02. 82
i /cannot say your worships have deliver'd the COR 2.01. 57 P
god–den to your worships; 2.01. 93 P
god save your good worships! 2.01.145 P
damned baseness, | to him that worships thee! TIM 3.01. 48
he desir'd their worships to think it was his JC 1.02.270 P
regard support | the worships of their name. LR 1.04.266

WOR'ST 2 FR 0.0002 REL FR 2 V 0 P
wert thou the devil, and wor'st it on thy horn, TRO 5.02. 95
thou wor'st that day the three kings fell, but TNK 3.06. 71

/WORST 4 FR 0.0004 REL FR 3 V 1 P
/things /present /worst. 2H4 1.03.108
therefore thou best of gold art /worst /of gold. 4.05.160
/dungeons, /denmark /being /one /o' /th' /worst. HAM 2.02.247 P
/who, /having /seen /me /in /my /worst /estate, LR 5.03.210

WORST 106 FR 0.0119 REL FR 84 V 22 P
all foes that a friend should be the worst! TGV 5.04. 72
his worst fault is, that he is given to prayer; WIV 1.04. 13 P
a book, his face is the worst thing about him. MM 2.01.156 P
if his face be the worst thing about him, how 2.01.157 P
or to be worse than worst | of those that 3.01.125
ay, the best for the worst. LLL 1.01.281 P
nay, to be perjur'd, which is worst of all; 3.01.194
and, among three, to love the worst of all, | a 3.01.195
the worst that may befall me in this case, | if MND 1.01. 63
and the worst are no worse, if imagination amend 5.01.212 P
a little worse than a man, and when he is worst, MV 1.02. 89 P
and the worst fall that ever fell, i hope i 1.02. 90 P
therefore for fear of the worst, i pray thee set 1.02. 95 P
the worst fault you have is to be in love. AYL 3.02.282 P
and then i know after who comes by the worst. SHR 1.02. 14
first, | then had not grumio come by the worst. 1.02. 35
a title for a maid of all titles the worst. 1.02.130
and think it not the worst of all your fortunes 4.02.105
the worst is this, that, at so slender warning, 4.04. 60
ne, worse of worst — extended | with vildest AWW 2.01.173
good, so were i | a man, the worst about you. WT 2.03. 62
word deserves | to taste of thy most worst? 3.02.179
and not the worst of the three but jumps twelve 4.04.338 P
though the pennyworth on his side be the worst, 4.04.636 P
but if you be afeard to hear the worst, | then JN 4.02.135
then let the worst unheard fall on your head. 4.02.136
we know the worst. 4.03. 27
even in condition of the worst degree, | in R2 2.03.108
the worst is worldly loss thou canst unfold. 3.02. 94
the worst is death, and death will have his day. 3.02.103
have felt the worst of death's destroying wound, 3.02.139

to lengthen out the worst that must be spoken: 3.02.199
worst in this royal presence may i speak, | yet 4.01.115
news, | whose worst was that the noble mortimer, 1H4 1.01. 38
that's the worst tidings that i hear of /yet. 4.01.127
and, to prevent the worst, sir michael, speed; 4.04. 35
worse shame to beg than to be on the worst side, 2H4 1.02. 76 P
the worst that they can say of me is that i am a 2.02. 66 P
of he, the worst of these three gentlemen! 5.02. 16
proud of destruction, | defy us to our worst; H5 3.03. 5
thou hast me, if thou hast me, at the worst; 5.02.232 P
is that the worst this letter doth contain? 1H6 4.01. 66
it is the worst, and all, my lord, he writes. 4.01. 67
the very train of her worst wearing gown | was 2H6 1.03. 85
yet am i arm'd against the worst can happen; 3H6 4.01.128
therefore, lord oxford, to prevent the worst, 4.06. 96
come, come, we fear the worst; all will be well. R3 2.03. 31
equal in lustre, were now best, now worst, | as H8 1.01. 29
what worst, as oft, | hitting a grosser quality, 1.02. 83
(i would be all) against the worst may happen. 3.01. 25
speak on, sir, | i dare your worst objections. 3.02.307
the heaviest and the worst | is your displeasure 3.02.391
you may worst | of all this table say so. 5.02.113
tent that searches | to th' bottom of the worst. TRO 2.02. 17
to fear the worst oft cures the worse. 3.02. 73 P
as what envy can say worst shall be a mock for 3.02. 96 P
thou rascal, that art worst in blood to run, COR 1.01.159
he must come, | or what is worst will follow. 3.01.334
let your general do his worst. 5.02.106 P
yea, is the worst well? ROM 2.04.125 P
faith, for the worst is filthy, and would not TIM 1.02.153 P
wisely suffer | the worst that man can breathe, 3.05. 32
when man's worst sin is, he does too much good! 4.02. 39
wretched being, | worse than the worst, content. 4.03.247
if thou hadst not been born the worst of men, 4.03.275
and let him take't at worst — for their knives 5.01.178
when thou didst hate him worst, thou lovedst him JC 4.03.106
let's reason with the worst that may befall. 5.01. 96
not i' th' worst rank of manhood, say't, | and i MAC 3.01.102
treason has done his worst; 3.02. 24
bent to know, | by the worst means, the worst. 3.04.134
bent to know, | by the worst means, the worst. 3.04.134
things at the worst will cease, or else climb 4.02. 24
not being the worst | stands in some rank of LR 2.04.257
to be worst, | the lowest and most dejected 4.01. 2
from the best, | the worst returns to laughter. 4.01. 6
the wretch that thou hast blown unto the worst 4.01. 8
who is't can say, "i am at the worst"? 4.01. 25
the worst is not | so long as we can say, "this 4.01. 27
so long as we can say, "this is the worst." 4.01. 28
no, do thy worst, blind cupid, i'll not love. 4.06.137 P
who with best meaning have incurr'd the worst. 5.03. 4
the griefs are ended | by seeing the worst, OTH 1.03.203
thou praisest the worst best. 2.01.143 P
and give thy worst of thoughts | the worst of 3.03.132
give thy worst of thoughts | the worst of words. 3.03.133
i knew | that stroke would prove the worst! 4.01.274
do thy worst! 5.02.159
till the worst of all follow him laughing to his ANT 1.02. 66 P
well, what worst? 1.02. 94
will conceive, i hope, | but the worst of me. CYM 2.03.154
i leave /you, sir, | to th' worst of discontent. 2.03.155
the worst of all her scholars, my good lord. PER 2.05. 31
fear the flaw, | it hath done to me the worst. 3.01. 40
the heavens, the gods | do like this worst. 4.03. 21
come what can come, | the worst is death: TNK 2.03. 18
have at the worst can come, then! ep 10
the worst is but denial and reproving. LUC 242
he in the worst sense consters their denial: 324
yet do thy worst, old time: SON 19.13
thrive and i be cast away, | the worst was this: 80.14
at first the very worst of fortune's might; 90.12
but do thy worst to steal thyself away, | for 92. 1
then need i not to fear the worst of wrongs, 92. 5
yet what the best is take the worst to be. 137. 4
that in my mind thy worst all best exceeds? 150. 8

WORSTED–STOCKING 1 FR 0.0001 REL FR 0 V 1 P
hundred–pound, filthy worsted–stocking knave; LR 2.02. 17 P

WORT 1 FR 0.0001 REL FR 1 V 0 P
grow so nice, | metheglin, wort, and malmsey; LLL 5.02.233

/WORTH* 1 FR 0.0001 REL FR 1 V 0 P
/on /his /fair /worth /and /single /chivalry. TRO 4.04.148

WORTH* 225 FR 0.0254 REL FR 187 V 38 P
worth | what's dearest to the world! TMP 3.01. 38
now, trust me, 'tis an office of great worth, TGV 1.02. 44
to be of worth and worthy estimation, | and not 2.04. 56
a word (for far behind his worth | comes all the 2.04. 71
welcome him then according to his worth — 2.04. 83
his worth is warrant for his welcome hither, 2.04.102
her, whose worth /makes other worthies nothing: 2.04.166
a jew, and not worth the name of a christian. 2.05. 55 P
a round hose, madam, now's not worth a pin, 2.07. 55
bounty, worth, and qualities | beseeming such a 3.01. 65
friends | unto a youthful gentleman of worth, 3.01.107
much | as you in worth dispraise sir valentine. 3.02. 55
to your sufficiency as your worth is able, | and MM 1.01. 8
if any in vienna be of worth | to undergo such 1.01. 22
carried to prison was worth five thousand of you 1.02. 61 P
once thou swor'st was worth the looking on; 5.01.208
were testimonies against his worth and credit 5.01.244
her worth worth yours. 5.01.497
her worth worth yours. 5.01.497
and owes more than he's worth to season. ERR 4.02. 58
a ring he hath of mine worth forty ducats, | and 4.03. 83
not a note of mine that's worth the noting. ADO 2.03. 55
and excellent fashion, yours is worth ten on't. 3.04. 23 P
and what have i to give you back whose worth 4.01. 27
that what we have we prize not to the worth 4.01.218
the worth of many a knight | from tawny spain, LLL 1.01.172
i am less proud to hear you tell my worth | than 2.01. 17
us, | although not valued to the money's worth. 2.01.136
tend'ring their own worth from where they were 2.01.244
o, why then three–farthing worth of silk. 3.01.149 P
apply | to prove, by wit, worth in simplicity. 5.02. 78
'tis not so much worth; 5.02.558 P
place | with the rich worth of your virginity. MND 2.01.219
and, in a word, but even now worth this, | and MV 1.01. 35
even now worth this, | and now worth nothing? 1.01. 36
your worth is very dear in my regard. 1.01. 62
you have them, they are not worth the search. 1.01.118 P
nor is the wide world ignorant of her worth, 1.01.167
a christian by, | will be worth a jewess' eye. 2.05. 43
here, catch this casket, it is worth the pains. 2.06. 33
worth seizure do we seize into our hands, | till AYL 3.01. 10
her worth, being mounted on the wind, | through 3.02. 90
is his head worth a hat? 3.02.206 P
or his chin worth a beard? 3.02.206 P
men of great worth resorted to this forest, 5.04.155
fleet, | i would esteem him worth a dozen such. SHR in.1. 27
if you accept them, then their worth is great. 2.01.101
the longer kept, the less worth. AWW 1.01.154 P
rate | worth name of life in thee hath eştimate: 2.01.180
but taking up, and that thou'rt scarce worth. 2.03.208 P
you are not worth another word, else i'd call 2.03.263 P
where death and danger dogs the heels of worth. 3.04. 15
let every word weigh heavy of her worth, | that 3.04. 31
or to the worth | of the great count himself, 3.05. 59
titled goddess, | and worth it, with addition! 4.02. 3
an eunuch to him, | it may be worth thy pains; TN 1.02. 57
that will allow me very worth his service. 1.02. 59
if it be worth stooping for, there it lies in 2.02. 14 P
she is not worth thee then. 2.04. 27
but, were my worth as is my conscience firm, 3.03. 17
he finds that now scarce to be worth talking of; 3.04.299 P
methought did promise | most venerable worth, 3.04.363
speedy, | the time is worth the use on't. WT 3.01. 14
that she is a woman | more worth than any man; 5.01.111
to greet a man not worth her pains, much less 5.01.155
your choice is not so rich in worth as beauty, 5.01.214
she was more worth such gazes | than what you 5.01.226
of this act was worth the audience of kings and 5.02. 79 P
hand, whose worth and honesty | is richly noted; 5.03.144
i am not worth this coil that's made for me. JN 2.01.165
your rage, forget | your worth, your greatness, 4.03. 86
and, by the glorious worth of my descent, | this R2 1.01.107
gaunt, | and by the worth and honor of himself, 3.03.110
and to thy worth will add right worthy gains. 5.06. 12
soft, i know a trick worth two of that, i' faith 1H4 2.01. 36 P
do so, for it is worth the list'ning to. 2.04.211 P
seal–ring of my grandfather's worth forty mark. 3.03. 82 P
a million, thy love is worth a million; 3.03.137 P
his health was never better worth than now. 4.01. 27
pray god my news be worth a welcome, lord. 4.01. 87
age shapes /them, /are not worth a gooseberry. 2H4 1.02.173 P
is worth a thousand of these bed–hangers and 2.01.146 P
a crown's worth of good interpretation. 2.02. 92 P
a good heart's worth gold. 2.04. 31 P
as hector of troy, worth five of agamemnon, and 2.04.220 P
a score of good ewes may be worth ten pounds. 3.02. 51 P
let us swear | that you are worth your breeding, H5 3.01. 28
o ceremony, show me but thy worth! 4.01.244
though all that i can do is nothing worth, 4.01.303
kate, whose face is not worth sunburning, that 5.02.147 P
england ne'er lost a king of so much worth. 1H6 1.01. 7
my worth unknown, no loss is known in me. 4.05. 23
and give them burial as beseems their worth. 4.07. 86
since thou dost deign to woo her little worth 5.03.151
marriage is a matter of more worth | than to be 5.05. 55
was better worth than all my father's lands, 2H6 1.03. 86
it is not worth th' enjoying. 3.01.334
your loving uncle, twenty times his worth, 3.02.268
cask | that ever did contain a thing of worth. 3.02.410
left me | contenteth me, and worth a monarchy. 4.10. 19
a wisp of straw were worth a thousand crowns 3H6 2.02.144
to make prescription for a kingdom's worth. 3.03. 94
scarce some two days since were worth a noble. R3 1.03. 81
crew, | and many other of great name and worth; 4.05. 16
what were't worth to know | the secret of your H8 2.03. 50
nor my wishes | more worth than empty vanities; 2.03. 69
the moon, not worth | his serious considering. 3.02.134
well worth the seeing. 4.01. 61
doth valor's show and valor's worth divide | in TRO 1.03. 46
grows dainty of his worth, and in his tent 1.03.145
the worthiness of praise distains his worth, 1.03.241
and dare avow her beauty and her worth | in 1.03.271
and not worth | the splinter of a lance. 1.03.282
his pia mater is not worth the ninth part of a 2.01. 72 P
to guard a thing not ours nor worth to us | (had 2.02. 22
weigh you the worth and honor of a king | so 2.02. 26
she is not worth what she doth cost | the 2.02. 51
is she worth keeping? 2.02. 81
imagin'd worth | holds in his blood such swoll'n 2.03.172
not for the worth that hangs upon our quarrel. 2.03.207
some thing not worth in me such rich beholding 3.03. 91
most dear in the esteem, | and poor in worth! 3.03.130
to her own worth | she shall be priz'd; 4.04.133
do deeds worth praise, and tell you them at 5.03. 93
ulysses, is not prov'd worth a blackberry. 5.04. 12 P
it is not worth the wagging of your beards, and COR 2.01. 87 P
is worth all your predecessors since deucalion, 2.01. 91 P
and to have his worth | of contradiction. 3.03. 26
that can judge as fitly of his worth | as i can 4.02. 34
some trick not worth an egg, shall grow dear 4.04. 21
worth six on him. 4.05.166 P
what is that curtsy worth? 5.03. 27
this volumnia | is worth of consuls, senators, 5.04. 53
well, let my deeds be witness of my worth: TIT 5.01.103
they are but beggars that can count their worth, ROM 2.06. 32
what dost thou think 'tis worth? TIM 1.01.213 P
not worth my thinking. how now, poet? 1.01.214 P
you have added worth unto't and lustre, | and 1.02.149
i doubt whether their legs be worth the sums 1.02.232
i'd rather than the worth of thrice the sum 3.03. 22
how cursed athens, mindless of thy worth, 4.03. 94
mind hold, and your dinner worth the eating. JC 1.02.292 P
him and his worth, and our great need of him, 1.03.161
of half that worth as those your swords, made 3.01.155
for i have neither /wit, nor words, nor worth, 3.02.221
but, i assure you, | a prize no less in worth. 5.04. 27
th' other senses, | or else worth all the rest. MAC 2.01. 45
of sorrow | must not be measur'd by his worth, 5.09. 11
he's worth more sorrow, | and that i'll spend 5.09. 16
he's worth no more; 5.09. 17
holding a weak supposal of our worth, | or HAM 1.02. 18
my thoughts be bloody, or be nothing worth! 4.04. 66
whose worth, if praises may go back again, 4.07. 27
metal as my sister, | and prize me at her worth. LR 1.01. 70
and well are worth the want that you have wanted 1.01.279
from me perforce, | should make thee worth them. 1.04.299
or worth in thee | make thy words faith'd? 2.01. 69
your son and daughter found this trespass worth 2.04. 44
i have been worth the /whistling. 4.02. 29
you are not worth the dust which the rude wind 4.02. 30
he that helps him take all my outward worth. 4.04. 10
in it a jewel | well worth a poor man's taking. 4.06. 29
i know my price, i am worth no worse a place. OTH 1.01. 11
and confine | for the sea's worth. 1.02. 28
my fortunes against any lay worth naming, this 2.03.324 P
proof, | or, by the worth of mine eternal soul, 3.03.361
ebb'd man, ne'er lov'd till ne'er worth love, ANT 1.04. 43
to, but weigh | what it is worth embrac'd. 2.06. 33
and take a queen | worth many babes and beggars! 5.02. 48
i pray you, for it is not worth the feeding. 5.02.270 P
the world | it is not worth leave–taking. 5.02.298
he had two sons (if this be worth your hearing, CYM 1.01. 57
playfellow, and he is | a man worth any woman; 1.01.146
she is not worth our debate. 1.04.160 P
creatures as | we count not worth the hanging 1.05. 20
i should have lost the worth of it in gold. 2.04. 42
but profess | had that was well worth watching), 2.04. 68
of baseness cannot | a dram of worth be drawn. 3.05. 89
not sooner | than thine own worth prefer thee. 4.02.386
strook | me, wretch, more worth your vengeance. 5.01. 11
safely, had it | been all the worth of 's car. 5.05.191
wilt thou undo the worth thou art unpaid for, 5.05.307
be | as doth befit our honor and your worth. PER 1.01.120
to beg of you, kind friends, this coat of worth, 2.01.136
deeds, | as in a title–page, your worth in arms, 2.03. 4
since every worth in show commends itself. 2.03. 6
had not a show might countervail his worth. 2.03. 56
and in your search spend your adventurous worth; 2.04. 51
lost | this queen, worth all our mundane cost. 3.02. 71
and held a mawkin | not worth the time of day. 4.03. 35
rather than twice the worth of her she had ne'er 4.06. 1 P
which is not worth a breakfast in the cheapest 4.06.122 P
there is some of worth would come aboard; 5.01. 9
the worth that learned charity aye wears. 5.03. 94
art, may yet appear | worth two hours' travail. TNK pr 29
yet what man | thirds his own worth (the case is 1.02. 96
for they were a mark | worth a god's view. 1.04. 21
concern us | much more than thebes is worth. 1.04. 33
to such a well–found wonder as thy worth, | for 2.05. 27
a chaffy lord, | nor worth the name of villain! 3.01. 42
despise my cruelty, and cry woe worth me, | till 3.06.249
there were no woman | worth so compos'd a man! 5.03. 86
they wither in their prime, prove nothing worth: VEN 418
face remains alive that's worth the viewing? 1076
will be a totter'd weed, of small worth held: SON 2. 4
neither in inward worth nor outward fair | can 16.11
take all my comfort of thy worth and truth. 37. 4
ten times more in worth | than those old nine 38. 9
o, how thy worth with manners may i sing, | when 39. 1
like stones of worth they thinly placed are, 52. 7
praising thy worth, despite his cruel hand. 60.14
and for myself mine own worth do define, | as i 62. 7
doth but approve | /thy worth the greater, being 70. 6
and so should you, to love things nothing worth. 72.14
the worth of that is that which it contains, 74.13
but since your worth (wide as the ocean is) 80. 5
hue, | finding thy worth a limit past my praise, 82. 6
speaking of worth, what worth in you doth grow. 83. 8
speaking of worth, what worth in you doth grow. 83. 8
the charter of thy worth gives thee releasing; 87. 3
thou gav'st, thy own worth then not knowing, 87. 9
the argument all bare is of more worth | than 103. 3
they had not still enough your worth to sing: 106.12
did amplify | each stone's dear nature, worth, LC 210
what are precepts worth | of stale example? 267

WORTHIED 1 FR 0.0001 REL FR 1 V 0 P
upon him such a deal of man | that worthied him, LR 2.02.121

WORTHIER 14 FR 0.0015 REL FR 12 V 2 P
twenty thousand worthier come to crave her. WIV 4.04. 90
we shall employ thee in a worthier place. MM 5.01.531
voice, | the other must be held the worthier. MND 1.01. 55
and reason says you are the worthier maid. 2.02.116
if worthier friends had not prevented me. MV 1.01. 6[illegible]
a wall'd town is more worthier than a village, AYL 3.03. 59 P
york is the worthier. 2H6 1.03.108
and worthier than himself | here tend the savage TRO 2.03.125
to the people, there was never a worthier man. COR 2.03. 39 P
my reasons, | more worthier than their voices. 3.01.120
basis /lies along | no worthier than the dust! JC 3.01.116
t' avert your liking a more worthier way | than LR 1.01.211
know not how to wish | a pair of worthier sons. CYM 5.05.356
deserves the travail of a worthier pen, | yet SON 79. 6

WORTHIES 14 FR 0.0015 REL FR 6 V 8 P
her, whose worth /makes other worthies nothing: TGV 2.04.166
where several worthies make one dignity, | where LLL 4.03.232
you shall present before her the nine worthies. 5.01.118 P
say none so fit as to present the nine worthies. 5.01.123 P
for the rest of the worthies? 5.01.142 P
or i will play | on the tabor to the worthies, 5.01.154
whether the three worthies shall come in or no. 5.02.486
art thou one of the worthies? 5.02.504 P
here is like to be a good presence of worthies: 5.02.534 P
and if these four worthies in their first show 5.02.538
but there are worthies a–coming will speak their 5.02.585 P
room for the incens'd worthies! 5.02.697 P
worthies, away! the scene begins to cloud. 5.02.721
and ten times better than the nine worthies. 2H4 2.04.221 P

WORTHIEST 16 FR 0.0018 REL FR 16 V 0 P
me, | in thy opinion which is worthiest love? TGV 1.02. 6
madam, | in that and all your worthiest affairs. AWW 3.02. 96
great alexander | left his to th' worthiest; WT 5.01. 48
till you compound whose right is worthiest, | we JN 2.01.281
we for the worthiest hold the right from both. 2.01.282
the worthiest of them tell me name by name; TRO 4.05.160
thou worthiest martius! COR 1.05. 25
you not known | the worthiest men have done't? 2.03. 49
o worthiest cousin! MAC 1.04. 14
man, and worthiest | to have command obey'd. ANT 3.13. 87
the heaviest club, | subdue my worthiest self. 4.12. 47
a lady to the worthiest sir that ever | country CYM 1.06.160
his mistress, only | for the most worthiest fit. 1.06.162

forth and levy | our worthiest instruments, TNK 1.01.163
it, | as i have serv'd her truest, worthiest, 3.06.165
honor crown the worthiest! 5.01. 17

/WORTHILY 1 FR 0.0001 REL FR 1 V 0 P
/may /deem /that /you /are /worthily /depos'd. R2 4.01.227

WORTHILY 14 FR 0.0015 REL FR 10 V 4 P
and thine own acquisition | worthily purchas'd, TMP 4.01. 14
your last service | did worthily perform; 4.01. 36
not now | worthily term'd them merciless to us! ERR 1.01. 99
or worthily, as a good subject should, | on some R2 1.01. 10
wherefore the king, most worthily, hath caus'd H5 4.07. 9 P
how may he wound, | and worthily, my falsehood! H8 2.04. 97
he hath deserv'd worthily of his country, and COR 2.02. 24 P
that's worthily | as any ear can hear. 4.01. 53
whom worthily you would have now succeed, | and TIT 1.01. 40
let the presents | be worthily entertain'd. TIM 1.02.185
worthily spoken, maecenas. ANT 2.02.102
matter of feast, which worthily deserv'd noting. 2.02.182 P
to find him so, that i may worthily note him. PER 4.06. 51 P
you have done worthily. TNK 2.05. 1

WORTHINESS 16 FR 0.0018 REL FR 14 V 2 P
bold of your worthiness, we single you | as our LLL 2.01. 28
i saw | is my report to his great worthiness. 2.01. 63
may | make tender of to thy true worthiness. 2.01.170
or half her worthiness that gave the ring, | or MV 5.01.200
you, whose worthiness would stir it up where it AWW 1.01. 9 P
even to the utmost syllable of your worthiness. 3.06. 71 P
merit, | according to the weight and worthiness. H5 2.02. 35
read them, and know i know your worthiness. 2.02. 69
and in defense of my lord's worthiness, | i 1H6 4.01. 99
the worthiness of praise distains his worth, TRO 1.03.241
as i do know the consul's worthiness, | so can i COR 3.01.276
turn | your hidden worthiness into your eye, JC 1.02. 57
will change to virtue and to worthiness. 1.03.160
and his worthiness | does challenge much respect OTH 2.01.210
o worthiness of nature! CYM 4.02. 25
blessed are you, whose worthiness gives scope, SON 52.13

WORTHLESS 18 FR 0.0020 REL FR 17 V 1 P
receiving them from such a worthless post. TGV 1.01.153
you are welcome to a worthless mistress. 2.04.113
that you are worthless. 2.04.115
and worthless valentine shall be forgot. 3.02. 10
holy, | to be corrupted with my worthless gifts. 4.02. 6
that comes to hazard for my worthless self. MV 2.09. 18
even as a flatt'ring dream or worthless fancy. SHR in.1. 44
our feet but a weak and worthless satisfaction. H5 3.06.133 P
my ransom is this frail and worthless trunk; 3.06.154
keep off aloof with worthless emulation. 1H6 4.04. 21
so worthless peasants bargain for their wives, 5.05. 53
lord | unto the daughter of a worthless king, 2H6 4.01. 81
clifford, how i scorn his worthless threats! 3H6 1.01.101
digress too much, | citing my worthless praise. TIT 5.03.117
a peevish schoolboy, worthless of such honor, JC 5.01. 61
done, some worthless slave of thine i'll slay, LUC 515
or (being wrack'd) i am a worthless boat, | he SON 80.11
spend'st thou thy fury on some worthless song, 100. 3

WORTH'S 1 FR 0.0001 REL FR 1 V 0 P
whose worth's unknown, although his highth be SON 116. 8

WORTHS 2 FR 0.0002 REL FR 2 V 0 P
disgrace to your great worths, and shame to me, TRO 2.02.151
define, | as i all other in all worths surmount. SON 62. 8

WORTHY 238 FR 0.0269 REL FR 196 V 42 P
remember i have done thee worthy service, | told TMP 1.02.247
might, | worthy sebastian, o, what might — ? 2.01.205
o worthy stephano! 4.01.222 P
worthy his youth and nobleness of birth. TGV 1.03. 33
to be of worth and worthy estimation, | and not 2.04. 56
he is as worthy for an empress' love | as meet 2.04. 76
to have a look of such a worthy mistress. 2.04.108
know, worthy prince, sir valentine, my friend, 3.01. 10
as many, worthy lady, to yourself. 4.03. 7
to pass, | i do desire thy worthy company, 4.03. 25
and think thee worthy of an empress' love. 5.04.141
withal, | are men endu'd with worthy qualities. 5.04.153
and fit for great employment, worthy lord. 5.04.157
'tis fit, | worthy the owner, and the owner it. WIV 5.05. 60
my very worthy cousin, fairly met! MM 5.01. 1
o worthy prince, dishonor not your eye | by 5.01. 22
o worthy duke, | you bid me seek redemption of 5.01. 28
this woman, | to justify this worthy nobleman, 5.01.159
these women | to accuse this worthy man, but, in 5.01.307
you love her, for the lady is very well worthy. ADO 1.01.222 P
that she is worthy, i know. 1.01.229 P
be lov'd nor know how she should be worthy, is 1.01.231 P
bind him up a rod, as being worthy to be whipt. 2.01.219 P
commence his suit | to her he thinks not worthy, 2.03. 51
record it with your high and worthy deeds. 5.01.269
will you find men worthy enough to present them? LLL 5.01.124 P
them to think me worthy of pompey the great; 5.02.505 P
i know not the degree of the worthy, but i am to 5.02.507 P
to a halfpenny, pompey proves the best worthy. 5.02.561 P
he will be the ninth worthy. 5.02.578 P
farewell, worthy lord! 5.02.736
the worthy knight of troy. 5.02.881
demetrius is a worthy gentleman. MND 1.01. 52
well, and i remember him worthy of thy praise. MV 1.02.121 P
it doth appear you are a worthy judge; 4.01.236
most worthy gentleman, i and my friend | have by 4.01.408
the ring of me to give the worthy doctor. 5.01.222
a worthy fool! AYL 2.07. 34
o worthy fool! 2.07. 36
with many things of worthy memory, which now SHR 4.01. 82 P
her dowry wealthy, and of worthy birth; 4.05. 65
or die, be you the sons | of worthy frenchmen. AWW 2.01. 12
worthy fellows, and like to prove most sinewy 2.01. 59 P
with all my heart, and thou art worthy of it. 2.03.218 P
and common speech | gives him a worthy pass. 2.05. 53
i am not worthy of the wealth i owe, | nor dare 2.05. 79
we'll strive to bear it for your worthy sake 3.03. 5
of yours | that has done worthy service. 3.05. 48
some precepts of this virgin | worthy the note. 3.05.101
of no one good quality worthy your lordship's 3.06. 11 P
i will grace the attempt for a worthy exploit. 3.06. 68 P
he has much worthy blame laid upon him for 4.03. 6 P
and not worthy to touch fortune's fingers. TN 2.05.157 P
for a worthy lady, | and one who much i honor. WT 2.02. 5
most worthy madam, | your honor and your 2.02. 40
and, lozel, thou art worthy to be hang'd, | that 2.03.109
"hermione, queen to the worthy leontes, king of 3.02. 12 P
and boasts himself | to have a worthy feeding; 4.04.169
thereof most worthy, were i the fairest youth 4.04.373
worthy enough a herdsman, yea, him too, | that 4.04.435
worthy camillo, | what color for my visitation 4.04.554
there is none worthy, | respecting her that's 5.01. 34
merits it) with you, | worthy his goodness. 5.01.176
my lord, | that all i see in you is worthy love, JN 2.01.517
or both | to worthy danger and deserved death. R2 5.01. 68
and to thy worth will add right worthy gains. 5.06. 12
wherein worthy, but in nothing? 1H4 2.04.459 P
in faith, he is a worthy gentleman, 3.01.163
he hath more worthy interest to the state | than 3.02. 98
"and was a worthy king." 2H4 2.04. 35 P
face, | most worthy brother england, fairly met! H5 5.02. 10
whilst such a worthy leader, wanting aid, | unto 1H6 1.01.143
and should (if i were worthy to be judge) | be 4.01. 42
worthy saint michael, and the golden fleece, 4.07. 69
tale | is but a preface of her worthy praise. 5.05. 11
whether your grace be worthy, yea or no, 2H6 1.03.107
that would annoy our foot | is worthy praise; 3.01. 68
that he should die is worthy policy, | but yet 3.01.235
more than mistrust, that shows him worthy death. 3.01.242
here is my hand, the deed is worthy doing. 3.01.278
that cause they have been most worthy to live. 4.07. 46 P
york | the worthy gentleman did lose his life. 3H6 3.02. 7
fair queen of england, worthy margaret, | sit 3.03. 1
from worthy edward, king of albion, | my lord 3.03. 49
hath not our brother made a worthy choice? 4.01. 3
no, warwick, thou art worthy of the sway, | to 4.06. 32
did not offend, nor were not worthy blame, | if 5.05. 54
/thanks, noble clarence, worthy brother, thanks. 5.07. 30
excused | for doing worthy vengeance on thyself, R3 1.02. 87
i have bewept a worthy husband's death, | and 2.02. 49
long live richard, england's worthy king! 3.07.240
for worthy wolsey | (who cannot err), he did it. H8 1.01.173
his person | more worthy this place than myself, 1.04. 79
(well worthy the best heir o' th' world) should 2.04.196
this same cranmer's | a worthy fellow, and hath 3.02. 72
with th' king, and truly | a worthy friend. 4.01.110
which i feel | i am not worthy yet to wear. 4.02. 92
he's worthy of it. 5.02.189
you'll confess /he brought home worthy prize — TRO 2.02. 86
but, worthy hector, | she is a theme of honor 2.02.198
o worthy satisfaction! 2.03. 3 P
this thrice worthy and right valiant lord 2.03.190
i come from the worthy achilles — 3.03.282 P
worthy all arms! 4.05.163
and, worthy warrior, welcome to our tents. 4.05.200
may worthy troilus be half attached | with that 5.02.161
worthy menenius agrippa, one that hath always COR 1.01. 51 P
to make him worthy whose offense subdues him, 1.01.175
then, worthy martius, | attend upon cominius to 1.01.236
we must follow you, | right worthy you priority. 1.01.247
worthy sir, thou bleed'st, | thy exercise hath 1.05. 14
ay, worthy menenius, and with most prosperous 2.01.103 P
my gentle martius, worthy caius, and | by 2.01.172
no more of him, he's a worthy man. 2.02. 35 P
report | a little of that worthy work perform'd 2.02. 45
worthy cominius, speak. 2.02. 66
worthy man! 2.02.122
you shall ha't, worthy sir. 2.03. 79 P
there's in all two worthy voices begg'd. 2.03. 80 P
worthy voices! 2.03.137 P
that as his worthy deeds did claim no less 2.03.186
theirs, martius is worthy | of present death. 3.01.210
put not your worthy rage into your tongue; 3.01.240
you worthy tribunes — 3.01.264
what has he done to rome that's worthy death? 3.01.296
chairs of justice | supplied with worthy men! 3.03. 35
heart the banishment of that worthy coriolanus, 4.03. 22 P
worthy martius, | had we no other quarrel else 4.05.126
caius martius was | a worthy officer i' th' war, 4.06. 30
worthy tribunes, | there is a slave, whom we 4.06. 37
yes, worthy sir, | the slave's report is 4.06. 62
the worthy fellow is our general. 5.02.110 P
but, worthy lords, have you with heed perused 5.06. 61
it doth, my worthy lord, and in this match | i TIT 1.01.244
presents well worthy rome's imperious lord: 1.01.250
my worthy lord, if ever tamora | were gracious 1.01.428
then have i kept it to a worthy end. 3.01.173
worthy andronicus, ill art thou repaid | for 3.01.234
o worthy goth, this is the incarnate devil 5.01. 40
wrought | so worthy a gentleman to be her bride? ROM 3.05.145
o, 'tis a worthy lord. TIM 1.01. 9
where thou hast feign'd him a worthy fellow. 1.01.223 P
yes, he is worthy of thee, and to pay thee for 1.01.225 P
to be flatter'd is worthy o' th' flatterer. 1.01.226 P
hail to thee, worthy timon, and to all | that of 1.02.122
noble, worthy, royal timon! 2.02.168
it is a cause worthy my spleen and fury, | that 3.05.112
my worthy friends, will you draw near? 3.06. 58 P
no, my most worthy master, in whose breast 4.03.511
hail, worthy timon! 5.01. 55
doubt it not, worthy lord. 5.01. 92
worthy timon — 5.01.134
and i'll beweep these comforts, worthy senators. 5.01.158
thoughts of great value, worthy cogitations. JC 1.02. 50
you | what hath proceeded worthy note to-day. 1.02.181
render me worthy of this noble wife! 2.01.303
in hand | any exploit worthy the name of honor. 2.01.317
good morrow, worthy caesar, | i come to fetch 2.02. 58
is there no voice more worthy than my own, | to 3.01. 49
his glory not extenuated, wherein he was worthy; 3.02. 39 P
hath given me some worthy cause to wish | things 4.02. 8
it is more worthy to leap in ourselves | than 5.05. 24
merciless macdonwald | (worthy to be a rebel, MAC 1.02. 10
o valiant cousin, worthy gentleman! 1.02. 24
the worthy thane of rosse. 1.02. 45
whence cam'st thou, worthy thane? 1.02. 48
in which addition, hail, most worthy thane, 1.03.106
worthy macbeth, we stay upon your leisure. 1.03.148
my worthy cawdor! 1.04. 47
true, worthy banquo! 1.04. 54
worthy cawdor! 1.05. 54
why, worthy thane, | you do unbend your noble 2.02. 41
is the king stirring, worthy thane? 2.03. 45
sit, worthy friends; 3.04. 57
my worthy lord, | your noble friends do lack you 3.04. 82
do not muse at me, my most worthy friends, | i 3.04. 84
a rumor | of many worthy fellows that were out, 4.03.183
you, worthy uncle, | shall with my cousin, your 5.06. 2
worthy macduff and we | shall take upon 's what 5.06. 4
a worthy pioner! HAM 1.05.163
my worthy arch and patron, comes to-night. LR 2.01. 59
worthy prince, i know't. 5.03.179
'tis true, most worthy signior; OTH 1.02. 91
i am glad on't; 'tis a worthy governor. 2.01. 30
"king stephen was and–a worthy peer, | his 2.03. 89
worthy montano, you were wont to be civil; 2.03.190
worthy othello, i am hurt to danger. 2.03.197
cassio's my worthy friend — | my lord, i see y' 3.03.223
my fears | (as worthy cause i have to fear i am) 3.03.254
and many worthy and chaste dames even thus, 4.01. 46
/god save /thee, worthy general! 4.01.216
this deed of thine is no more worthy heaven 5.02.160
more worthy heaven | than thou wast worthy her. 5.02.161
know, worthy pompey, | that what they do delay, ANT 2.01. 2
good enobarbus, 'tis a worthy deed, | and shall 2.02. 1
half the heart of caesar, worthy maecenas! 2.02.172 P
good fortune, worthy soldier, and farewell. 3.02. 22
most worthy sir, you therein throw away | the 3.07. 41
how now, worthy soldier? 3.07. 60
rebukable | and worthy shameful check it were, 4.04. 31
serv'd, who best was worthy | best to be serv'd. 5.01. 6
hold, worthy lady, hold! 5.02. 39
herself | unto a poor but worthy gentleman. CYM 1.01. 7
expected to prove so worthy as since he hath 1.04. 3 P
how worthy he is i will leave to appear 1.04. 32 P
this worthy signior, i thank him, makes no 1.04.100 P
sustain what y' are worthy of by your attempt. 1.04.116 P
the worthy leonatus is in safety | and greets 1.06. 12
you are as welcome, worthy sir, as i | have 1.06. 29
a worthy fellow, | albeit he comes on angry 2.03. 55
found their courage | worthy his frowning at. 2.04. 23
under her breast | (worthy her pressing) lies a 2.04.135
leave not the worthy lucius, good my lords, 3.05. 16
no more of "worthy lord"! 3.05. 96
not seeming | so worthy as thy birth. 4.02. 94
why, worthy father, what have we to lose, | but 4.02.124
speaks that sometime | it was a worthy building. 4.02.355
for they are worthy | to inlay heaven with stars 5.05.351
most worthy prince, as yours, is true guiderius; 5.05.358
air | how many worthy princes' bloods were shed PER 1.02. 88
judgment good | that thought you worthy of it. 4.06. 94
shall we make worthy uses of this place | that TNK 2.02. 69
what worthy blessing | can be, but our 2.02. 76
maintain | i am as worthy and as free a lover, 2.02.179
till thou art worthy, arcite, it concerns me, 2.02.201
if he dare make himself a worthy lover, | yet in 2.02.251
news continually, | thou art not worthy life. 2.02.267
all his words are worthy. 2.05. 29
a life more worthy from him than all women, | i 5.03.143
thy worthy, manly heart, be yet unbroken, | give 5.04. 88
but that which doth devour, | is worthy blame. LUC 1257
"thou worthy lord | of that unworthy wife that 1303
strike, | let reason rule things worthy blame, PP 18. 3
to show me worthy of /thy sweet respect: SON 26.12
in me | worthy perusal stand against thy sight, 38. 6
most worthy comfort, now my greatest grief, 48. 6
quite, | for you in me can nothing worthy prove; 72. 4
in me, | more worthy i to be belov'd of thee. 150.14

WORTHY'S 1 FR 0.0001 REL FR 0 V 1 P
is not quantity enough for that worthy's thumb, LLL 5.01.131 P

WORTS* *(also ord, ort*, word)*

WORTS* 2 FR 0.0002 REL FR 0 V 2 P
pauca verba; sir john, good worts. WIV 1.01.120 P
good worts? 1.01.121 P

WO'T *(also wilt, wolt, woo't)*

WO'T 4 FR 0.0004 REL FR 0 V 4 P
thou wo't, wo't thou? 2H4 2.01. 57 P
thou wo't, wo't thou? 2.01. 57 P
thou wo't, wo't ta? 2.01. 57 P
thou wo't, wo't ta? 2.01. 58 P

WOT 28 FR 0.0031 REL FR 24 V 4 P
quoth i, "'twas i did the thing you wot of." TGV 4.04. 27 P
and see the picture, she says, that you wot of. WIV 2.02. 87 P
a one were past cure of the thing you wot of, MM 2.01.111 P
anon, i wot not by what strong escape, | he ERR 5.01.148
than those that walk and wot not what they are. LLL 1.01. 91
for well i wot | thou run'st before me, shifting MND 3.02.422
my good lord, i wot not by what power | (but by 4.01.164
as blanks, benevolences, and i wot not what. R2 2.01.250
'tis nameless woe, i wot. 2.02. 40
i wot your love pursues | a banish'd traitor. 2.03. 59
forgot, | right noble is thy merit, well i wot. 5.06. 18
o, too much folly is it, well i wot, | to hazard 1H6 4.06. 32
we english warriors wot not what it means. 4.07. 55
for, well i wot, thou hast thy mother's tongue. 3H6 2.02.134
for well i wot that henry is no soldier. 4.07. 83
for well i wot ye blaze to burn them out. 5.04. 71
no, no, good friends, god wot, | for then this R3 2.03. 18
wot you what, my lord? 3.02. 90
and wot you what i found | there (on my H8 3.02.122
you wot well | my hazards still have been your COR 4.01. 27
but a greater soldier than he, you wot one. 4.05.163 P
full well i wot the ground of all this grudge. TIT 2.01. 48
brother, well i wot, | thy napkin cannot drink a 3.01.139
for well i wot the empress never wags | but 5.02. 87
romeo | to comfort you, i wot well where he is. ROM 3.02.139
why — "as by lot, god wot," | and then, you HAM 2.02.416
seely groom, god wot, it was defect | of spirit, LUC 1345
forgot, | all my lady's love is lost, god wot. PP 17. 6

WOTS 3 FR 0.0003 REL FR 3 V 0 P
but in gross brain little wots | what watch the H5 4.01.282
glideth by the mill | than wots the miller of, TIT 2.01. 86
(which, /ev'ry innocent wots well, comes in TNK 1.03. 79

WOT'ST 1 FR 0.0001 REL FR 1 V 0 P
horse, for wot'st thou whom thou mov'st? ANT 1.05. 22

WOTTING 1 FR 0.0001 REL FR 1 V 0 P
the gods themselves | (wotting no more than i) WT 3.02. 76

WOULD *(also wad)*

/WOULD 22 FR 0.0024 REL FR 21 V 1 P

/yours /would i catch, fair hermia, ere i go; MND 1.01.187
/would /it /not /shame /thee /in /so /fair /a R2 4.01.231
/would /lift /him /where /most /trade /of 2H4 1.01.174
/when /richard /liv'd, /would /have /him /die, 1.03.101
/would /turn /their /own /perfection /to /abuse 2.03. 27
/are /wrong'd /and /would /unfold /our /griefs, 4.01. 77
/on /whom /fortune /would /then /have /smil'd? 4.01.131
that /would /i learn of you, | as one being best R3 4.04.268
/for /we /would /give /much /to /use /violent TRO 5.03. 21
/how /would /he /hang /his /slender /gilded TIT 3.02. 61
/that /still /would /manage /those /authorities LR 1.03. 17
/i /would /breed /from /hence /occasions, /and 1.03. 24
/monopoly /out, /they /would /have /part /an't. 1.04.153 P
/i /would /learn /that, /for /by /the /marks /of 1.04.232
/no, /no, /they /would /not. 2.04. 19
/wherein /the //cub–drawn /bear /would /couch, 3.01. 12
/the /bedlam | /to /lead /him /where /he /would; 3.07.104
/even /the //head–lugg'd /bear /would /lick, 4.02. 42
/sorrow /would /be /a /rarity /most /beloved, 4.03. 23
/this /would /have /seem'd /a /period | /to 5.03.205
/amplify /too /much, /would /make /much /more, 5.03.207
/i /would /not there reside, | to put my father OTH 1.03.241

WOULD 2476 FR 0.2798 REL FR 1696 V 780 P

would thou mightst lie drowning | the washing of TMP 1.01. 57
now would i give a thousand furlongs of sea for 1.01. 65 P
but i would fain die a dry death. 1.01. 67 P
sky, it seems, would pour down stinking pitch, 1.02. 3
i would | have sunk the sea within the earth or 1.02. 10
your tale, sir, would cure deafness. 1.02.106
would i might | but ever see that man! 1.02.168
yards and boresprit, would i flame distinctly, 1.02.200
that this coil | would not infect his reason? 1.02.208
thing she did | they would not take her life. 1.02.267
it would control my dam's god, setebos, | and 1.02.373
pockets could speak, would it not say he lies? 2.01. 66 P
would i had never | married my daughter there! 2.01.108
that would not bless our europe with your 2.01.125
and were the king on't, what would i do? 2.01.146
i' th' commonwealth i would, by contraries, 2.01.148
for no kind of traffic | would i admit; 2.01.150
yet he would be king on't. 2.01.157
gun, or need of any engine, | would i not have; 2.01.163
i would with such perfection govern, sir, | t' 2.01.168
you would lift the moon out of her sphere, if 2.01.183 P
if she would continue in it five weeks without 2.01.183 P
we would so, and then go a–batfowling. 2.01.185 P
i wish mine eyes | would, with themselves, shut 2.01.192
like a foul bumbard that would shed his liquor. 2.02. 21 P
fool there but would give a piece of silver. 2.02. 29 P
there would this monster make a man; 2.02. 30 P
with a tang, | would cry to a sailor, 'go hang!' 2.02. 51
mean task | would be as heavy to me as odious, 3.01. 5
i would the lightning had | burnt up those logs 3.01. 16
it would become me | as well as it does you; 3.01. 28
i would not wish | any companion in the world 3.01. 54
i do think, a king | (i would, not so!), 3.01. 61
and would no more endure | this wooden slavery 3.01. 61
i would my valiant master would destroy thee. 3.02. 46
i would my valiant master would destroy thee. 3.02. 46
the clouds methought would open and show riches 3.02.141
i would i could see this taborer; 3.02.150 P
i should report this now, would they believe me? 3.03. 28
who would believe that there were mountaineers, 3.03. 44
what would my potent master? here i am. 4.01. 34
them, your affections | would become tender. 5.01. 19
mine would, sir, were i human. 5.01. 20
would here have kill'd your king, i do forgive 5.01. 78
them | that yet looks on me, or would know me! 5.01. 83
to call brother | would even infect my mouth, i 5.01.131
my dearest love, | i would not for the world. 5.01.173
should wrangle, | and i would call it fair play. 5.01.175
as you from crimes would pardon'd be, | let your ep 19
i rather would entreat thy company | to see the TGV 1.01. 5
even as i would, when i to love begin. 1.01. 10
i fear my julia would not deign my lines, 1.01.152
i would i knew his mind. 1.02. 33
he would have given it you, but i, being in the 1.02. 39
and yet i would i had o'erlook'd the letter; 1.02. 50
and would not force the letter to my view! 1.02. 54
which they would have the profferer construe "ay 1.02. 56
when willingly i would have had her here! 1.02. 61
what would your ladyship? 1.02. 66
i would it were, | that you might kill your 1.02. 67
ay; and melodious were it, would you sing it. 1.02. 83
you would be fing'ring them, to anger me. 1.02. 98
but she would be best pleas'd | to be so ang'red 1.02. 99
nay, would i were so ang'red with the same. 1.02.101
would suffer him to spend his youth at home, 1.03. 5
which would be great impeachment to his age, 1.03. 15
o, that our fathers would applaud our loves, 1.03. 48
without you were so simple, none else would: 2.01. 37 P
i would you were set,.so your affection would 2.01. 85 P
you were set, so your affection would cease. 2.01. 86 P
i would have had them writ more movingly. 2.01.128
i would it were no worse. 2.01.163 P
by my victuals, and would fain have meat. 2.01.174 P
a jew would have wept to have seen our parting; 2.03. 11 P
madam, my lord your father would speak with you. 2.04.116
for i would prevent | the loose encounters of 2.07. 40
lord, that which i would discover | the law of 3.01. 4
you, | it would be much vexation to your age. 3.01. 16
a pack of sorrows which would press you down, 3.01. 20
what would your grace have me to do in this? 3.01. 80
now therefore would i have thee to my tutor 3.01. 84
why then i would resort to her by night. 3.01.110
would serve to scale another hero's tow'r, | so 3.01.119
tow'r, | so bold leander would adventure it. 3.01.120
when would you use it? pray, sir, tell me that. 3.01.123
himself would lodge where, senseless, they are 3.01.143
thou know'st how willingly i would effect | the 3.02. 22
the least whereof would quell a lover's hope, 4.02. 13
sir, but i do; or else i would be hence. 4.02. 22
ay, i would i were deaf; 4.02. 64 P
you would have them always play but one thing? 4.02. 70 P
i would always have one play but one thing. 4.02. 72
you would quickly learn to know him by his voice 4 02. 89
'twere a substance, you would sure deceive it, 4.02.126
nor how my father would enforce me marry | vain 4.03. 16
sir eglamour, i would to valentine, | to mantua, 4.03. 22
taught him, even as one would say precisely, 4.04. 5 P
would say precisely, "thus i would teach a dog." 4.04. 6 P
i would have (as one should say) one that takes 4.04. 11 P
how many masters would do this for his servant? 4.04. 29 P
how many women would do such a message? 4.04. 90
to plead for that which i would not obtain, | to 4.04.100
to carry that which i would have refus'd, | to 4.04.101
praise his faith which i would have disprais'd. 4.04.102
as, heaven it knows, i would not have him speed. 4.04.107
what would you with her, if that i be she? 4.04.110
would better fit his chamber than this shadow. 4.04.120
and would i might be dead | if i in thought felt 4.04.171
that would have forc'd your honor and your love. 5.04. 22
i would have been a breakfast to the beast 5.04. 34
death, | would i not undergo for one calm look? 5.04. 42
and i would i could do a good office between you WIV 1.01. 99 P
or i would i might never come in mine own great 1.01.153 P
do as it shall become one that would do reason. 1.01.234 P
ay, or else i would i might be hang'd, la! 1.01.258 P
would i were young for your sake, mistress anne! 1.01.260 P
the young man, he would have been horn–mad. 1.04. 50 P
you in your ear, i would have no words of it) my 1.04.103 P
would you desire better sympathy? 2.01. 9 P
if i would but go to hell for an eternal moment 2.01. 49 P
and yet he would not swear; 2.01. 57 P
that i would have sworn his disposition would 2.01. 60 P
sworn his disposition would have gone to the 2.01. 61 P
puts into the press, when he would put us two. 2.01. 78 P
he would never have boarded me in this fury. 2.01. 88 P
it would give eternal food to his jealousy. 2.01.100 P
i do not think the knight would offer it; 2.01.174 P
toward my wife, i would turn her loose to him; 2.01.182 P
but i would be loath to turn them together. 2.01.185 P
i would have nothing lie on my head. 2.01.187 P
with my long sword i would have made you four 2.01.228 P
i do relent. what would thou more of man? 2.02. 30
sir, here's a woman would speak with you. 2.02. 31 P
fairest, that would have won any woman's heart; 2.02. 69 P
but mistress page would desire you to send her 2.02.113 P
master /brook below would fain speak with you, 2.02.145 P
and you, sir! would you speak with me? 2.02.155 P
to many to know what she would have given; 2.02.200 P
would it apply well to the vehemency of your 2.02.238 P
that i should win what you would enjoy? 2.02.239 P
i would you knew ford, sir, that you might avoid 2.02.276 P
would any man have thought this? 2.02.291 P
he knew your worship would kill him if he came. 2.03. 10 P
i had as lief you would tell me of a mess of 3.01. 63 P
a cowardly knave as you would desires to be 3.01. 67 P
if your husbands were dead, you two would marry. 3.02. 15 P
and i would not break with her for more money 3.02. 55 P
i would thy husband were dead. 3.03. 49 P
before the best lord, i would make thee my lady. 3.03. 51 P
i see how thine eye would emulate the diamond. 3.03. 55 P
firm fixture of thy foot would give an excellent 3.03. 63 P
and would needs speak with you presently. 3.03. 87 P
i would i could wash myself of the buck! 3.03.157 P
i would all of the same strain were in the same 3.03.185 P
i would not ha' your distemper in this kind for 3.03.216 P
ye, master slender would speak a word with you. 3.04. 29 P
i mean, master slender, what would you with me? 3.04. 60 P
own part, i would little or nothing with you. 3.04. 62 P
a woman would run through fire and water for 3.04.103 P
but yet i would my master had mistress anne; 3.04.104 P
or i would master slender had her; 3.04.105 P
or, in sooth, i would master fenton had her. 3.04.106 P
remorse as they would have drown'd a blind 3.05. 10 P
it, that it would yearn your heart to see it. 3.05. 43 P
as good luck would have it, comes in one 3.05. 83 P
lest the lunatic knave would have search'd it; 3.05.104 P
yet to be what i would not shall not make me 3.05.150 P
foolish christian creatures as i would desires. 4.01. 72 P
i would my husband would meet him in this shape. 4.02. 84 P
i would my husband would meet him in this shape. 4.02. 84 P
and methinks there would be no period to the 4.02.221 P
i would not have things cool. 4.02.224 P
was it, mussel–shell, what would you with her? 4.05. 28 P
i would i could have spoken with the woman 4.05. 39 P
i would all the world might be cozen'd, for i 4.05. 93 P
they would melt me out of my fat drop by drop, 4.05. 97 P
i warrant they would whip me with their fine 4.05. 99 P
enough /to /say /my /prayers, i would repent. 4.05.103 P
he would never else cross me thus. 5.05. 35 P
though we would have thrust virtue out of our 5.05.147 P
would i were hang'd la, else! 5.05.181 P
been i' th' church, i would have swing'd him, or 5.05.185 P
it had been anne page, would i might never stir! 5.05.187 P
in woman's apparel) i would not have had him. 5.05.192 P
you would have married her most shamefully, 5.05.221
which forced marriage would have brought upon 5.05.230
would seem in me t' affect speech and discourse, MM 1.01. 4
from which we would not have you warp. 1.01. 14
nay, not, as one would say, healthy; 1.02. 55 P
after all this fooling, i would not have it so. 1.02. 70 P
i would send for certain of my creditors; 1.02.132 P
what (but to speak of) would offend again. 1.02.136
which else would stand under grievous imposition 1.02.188 P
who i would be sorry should be thus foolishly 1.02.189 P
and it in you more dreadful would have seem'd 1.03. 33
i would not — though 'tis my familiar sin 1.04. 31
theirs | as they themselves would owe them. 1.04. 83
whom i would save, had a most noble father! 2.01. 7
i would know that of your honor. 2.01.158 P
i would not have you acquainted with tapsters; 2.01.204 P
truly, sir, i am a poor fellow that would live. 2.01.223 P
how would you live, pompey? 2.01.224 P
if the law would allow it, sir. 2.01.227 P
for which i would not plead, but that i must; 2.02. 31
but can you if you would? 2.02. 51
you would have slipp'd like him, but he, like 2.02. 65
he, like you, | would not have been so stern. 2.02. 66
i would to heaven i had your potency, | and you 2.02. 67
i would tell what 'twere to be a judge, | and 2.02. 69
how would you be | if he, which is the top of 2.02. 75
which a dismiss'd offense would after gall, 2.02.102
as jove himself does, jove would never be quiet, 2.02.111
officer | would use his heaven for thunder, 2.02.113
spleens, | would all themselves laugh mortal. 2.02.123
i would do more than that, if more were needful. 2.03. 9
showing we would not spare heaven as we love it, 2.03. 33
when i would pray and think, i think and pray 2.04. 1
it, would much better please me | than to demand 2.04. 32
else to let him suffer — | what would you do? 2.04. 98
to have what we would have, we speak not what we 2.04.118
did i tell this, | who would believe me? 2.04.172
lose a thing | that none but fools would keep. 3.01. 8
would bark your honor from that trunk you bear, 3.01. 71
cast, he would appear | a pond as deep as hell. 3.01. 92
claudio, | if i would yield him my virginity, 3.01. 97
yes, he would give't thee, from this rank 3.01. 99
the law by th' nose, | when he would force it? 3.01.109
why would he for the momentary trick | be 3.01.113
mercy to thee would prove itself a bawd, | 'tis 3.01.149
i would by and by have some speech with you. 3.01.154 P
the satisfaction i would require is likewise 3.01.155 P
but yet, sir, i would prove — 3.02. 29 P
that we were all, as some would seem to be, 3.02. 38
more lenity to lechery would do no harm in him. 3.02. 97 P
would the duke that is absent have done this? 3.02.116 P
ere he would have hang'd a man for the getting a 3.02.117 P
he would have paid for the nursing a thousand. 3.02.118 P
he would be drunk too, that let me inform you. 3.02.127 P
i would the duke we talk of were return'd again. 3.02.173 P
the duke yet would have dark deeds darkly 3.02.177 P
answer'd, he would never bring them to light. 3.02.177 P
would he were return'd! 3.02.178 P
say to thee again) would eat mutton on fridays. 3.02.181 P
i say to thee) he would mouth with a beggar, 3.02.183 P
this would make mercy swear and play the tyrant. 3.02.194 P
i would be glad to receive some instruction from 4.02. 17 P
give him leave to escape hence, he would not. 4.02.149 P
one would think it were mistress overdone's own 4.03. 2 P
i would desire you to clap into your prayers; 4.03. 41 P
for i would commune with you of such things 4.03.104
in that good path that i would wish it go, | and 4.03.133
one fruitful meal would set me to't. 4.03.154 P
they would else have married me to the rotten 4.03.173 P
would yet he had liv'd! 4.04. 32
nothing goes right — we would, and we would not 4.04. 34
goes right — we would, and we would not. 4.04. 34
i would say the truth, but to accuse him so, 4.06. 2
i would friar peter — 4.06. 9
that outward courtesies would fain proclaim 5.01. 15
upon a wrong'd — i would fain have said a maid! 5.01. 21
what would you say? 5.01. 68
he would not, but by gift of my chaste body | to 5.01. 97
he would have weigh'd thy brother by himself, 5.01.111
one that i would were here, friar lodowick. 5.01.125
i would he had some cause | to prattle for 5.01.181
the benefit of silence, would thou wert so too! 5.01.190 P
though they would swear down each particular 5.01.243
would he were here, my lord, for he indeed 5.01.250
isabel here once again, i would speak with her. 5.01.270 P
handled her privately, she would sooner confess; 5.01.276 P
hark how the villain would close now, after his 5.01.342 P
and would not rather | make rash remonstrance of 5.01.391
her brother's ghost his paved bed would break, 5.01.435
i would thou hadst done so by claudio. 5.01.468
but i had rather it would please you i might be 5.01.506 P
which though myself would gladly have embrac'd, ERR 1.01. 69
and would have reft the fishers of their prey, 1.01.115
which princes, would they, may not disannul, 1.01.144
many a man would take you at your word, | and go 1.02. 17
but, were you wedded, you would bear some sway. 2.01. 28
till he come home again, i would forbear. 2.01. 31
with urging helpless patience would relieve me; 2.01. 39
fair | a sunny look of his would soon repair. 2.01. 99
or else what lets it but he would be here? 2.01.105
would that alone a' love he would detain, | so 2.01.107
would that alone a' love he would detain, | so 2.01.107
so he would keep fair quarter with his bed! 2.01.108
so you would leave battering, i had rather have 2.02. 35 P
you would all this time have prov'd there is no 2.02.100 P
how dearly would it touch thee to the quick, 2.02.130
but here's a villain that would face me down 3.01. 6
your own handwriting would tell you what i think 3.01. 14
you would keep from my heels, and beware of an 3.01. 18
went in pain, master, this knave would go sore. 3.01. 65
we would fain have either. 3.01. 66
you would say so, master, if your garments were 3.01. 70
it would make a man mad as a buck to be so 3.01. 72
would you create me new? 3.02. 39
sir, such claim as you would lay to your horse, 3.02. 85 P
to your horse, and she would have me as a beast; 3.02. 86 P
i being a beast, she would have me, but that she 3.02. 87 P
as from a bear a man would run for life, | so 3.02.154
life, | so fly i from her that would be my wife. 3.02.155
that would refuse so fair an offer'd chain. 3.02.181
belike you thought our love would last too long 4.01. 25
i would not spare my brother in this case, | if 4.01. 77
who would be jealous then of such a one? 4.02. 23
and yet would herein others' eyes were worse: 4.02. 26
but she, more covetous, would have a chain. 4.03. 74
is mad, | else would he never so demean himself. 4.03. 82
i would i were senseless, sir, that i might not 4.04. 25 P
where would you had remain'd until this time, 4.04. 66
that would behold in me this shameful sport. 4.04.105
she that would be your wife now ran from you. 4.04.148
that you would put me to this shame and trouble, 5.01. 14
as roughly as my modesty would let me. 5.01. 59
to be disturb'd, would mad or man or beast: 5.01. 84
if here you hous'd him, here he would have been; 5.01.272
if he were mad, he would not plead so coldly. 5.01.273
no, and he were, i would burn my study. ADO 1.01. 80 P
she would not have his head on her shoulders for 1.01.113 P
and i would i could find in my heart that i had 1.01.126 P
women, they would else have been troubled with a 1.01.128 P
i would my horse had the speed of your tongue, 1.01.141 P
or would you have me speak after my custom, as 1.01.167 P
would you buy her, that you inquire after her? 1.01.179 P
i would scarce trust myself, though i had sworn 1.01.195 P
sworn the contrary, if hero would be my wife. 1.01.196 P
i would your grace would constrain me to tell. 1.01.206 P
i would your grace would constrain me to tell. 1.01.206 P

i would have you think so; 1.01.210 P
i would have salv'd it with a longer treatise. 1.01.315
if i had my mouth, i would bite; 1.03. 35 P
if i had my liberty, i would do my liking. 1.03. 35 P
would the cook were a' my mind! 1.03. 72 P
such a man would win any woman in the world, if 2.01. 15 P
would it not grieve a woman to be overmaster'd 2.01. 60 P
well, i would you did like me. 2.01.100 P
so would not i for your own sake, for i have 2.01.101 P
i would he had boarded me. 2.01.143 P
i too, and he swore he would marry her to–night. 2.01.169 P
you think the prince would have serv'd you thus? 2.01.196 P
one green leaf on it would have answer'd her. 2.01.240 P
near her, she would infect to the north star. 2.01.250 P
i would not marry her, though she were endow'd 2.01.250 P
she would have made hercules have turn'd spit, 2.01.253 P
i would to god some scholar would conjure her, 2.01.256 P
i would to god some scholar would conjure her, 2.01.257 P
sin upon purpose, because they would go thither; 2.01.259 P
so i would not he should do me, my lord, lest i 2.01.285 P
i would rather have one of your father's getting 2.01.322 P
a week married, they would talk themselves mad. 2.01.354 P
i would fain have it a match, and i doubt not 2.01.368 P
i know that, but i would have thee hence, and 2.03. 6 P
i have known when he would have walk'd ten mile 2.03. 15 P
have howl'd thus, they would have hang'd him, 2.03. 80 P
for to–morrow night we would have it at the lady 2.03. 86 P
never think that lady would have lov'd any man. 2.03. 93 P
me, i would have thought her spirit had been 2.03.114 P
i would have sworn it had, my lord, especially 2.03.116 P
to write to one that she knew would flout her. 2.03.142 P
he would make but a sport of it, and torment the 2.03.156 P
i would she had bestow'd this dotage on me, i 2.03.168 P
on me, i would have daff'd all other respects, 2.03.169 P
well, and i could wish he would modestly examine 2.03.207 P
that's the scene that i would see, which will be 2.03.217 P
when i said i would die a bachelor, i did not 2.03.243 P
if it had been painful, i would not have come. 2.03.252 P
featur'd, | but she would spell him backward. 3.01. 61
she would swear the gentleman should be her 3.01. 62
if i should speak, | she would mock me into air; 3.01. 75
o, she would laugh me | out of myself, press me 3.01. 75
that would be as great a soil in the new gloss 3.02. 5 P
for fancy, as you would have it appear he is. 3.02. 39 P
that would i know too. 3.02. 64 P
if your leisure serv'd, i would speak with you. 3.02. 82 P
hear, for what i would speak of concerns him. 3.02. 86 P
but it would better fit your honor to change 3.02.115 P
i knew it would be your answer. 3.03. 18 P
truly, i would not hang a dog by my will, much 3.03. 63 P
i thought there would a scab follow. 3.03.100 P
swore he would meet her as he was appointed next 3.03.160 P
i think you would have me say, "saving your 3.04. 32 P
if i would think my heart out of thinking, that 3.04. 84 P
he swore he would never marry, and yet now in 3.04. 88 P
what would you with me, honest neighbor? 3.05. 1 P
sir, i would have some confidence with you that 3.05. 2 P
as, god help, i would desire they were, but, in 3.05. 11 P
i would fain know what you have to say. 3.05. 29 P
and we would have them this morning examin'd 3.05. 46 P
would you not swear, | all you that see her, 4.01. 38
i know what you would say. 4.01. 48
myself would, on the rearward of reproaches, 4.01.126
would the two princes lie, and claudio lie, 4.01.152
the virtue that possession would not show us 4.01.221
the man deserve of me that would right her! 4.01.262 P
i would eat his heart in the market–place. 4.01.306 P
that i had any friend would be a man for my sake 4.01.318 P
before | would give preceptial med'cine to rage, 5.01. 24
with quarrelling, | some of us would lie low. 5.01. 52
being young, or what would do | were i not old. 5.01. 61
melancholy and would fain have it beaten away. 5.01.123 P
not hate him deadly, she would love him dearly. 5.01.177 P
if you would know your wronger, look on me. 5.01.262
i would bend under any heavy weight | that he'll 5.01.277
when he would play the noble beast in love. 5.04. 47
i would not deny you, but, by this good day, i 5.04. 94 P
while it doth study to have what it would, | it LLL 1.01.143
but i would see his own person in flesh and 1.01.184 P
as we would hear an oracle. 1.01.216 P
the humor of affection would deliver me from the 1.02. 60 P
thought of it, i would take desire prisoner, and 1.02. 61 P
it would neither serve for the writing nor the 1.02.113 P
nothing becomes him ill that he would well. 2.01. 46
my commendations — i would be glad to see it. 2.01.181 P
i would you heard it groan. 2.01.183
would that do it good? 2.01.187
nice wenches that would be betray'd without 3.01. 23 P
would you desire more? 3.01. 99 P
when would you have it done, sir? 3.01.154 P
not wounding, pity would not let me do't; 4.01. 27
for as it would ill become me to be vain, 4.02. 30
those pleasures live that art would comprehend. 4.02.110
light, but for her eye, i would not love her; 4.03. 10 P
by the world, i would not care a pin, if the 4.03. 18 P
i would forget her, but, a fever, she | reigns 4.03. 93
then incision | would let her out in saucers. 4.03. 96
air, would i might triumph so! 4.03.108
thou for whom jove would swear | juno but an 4.03.115
o, would the king, berowne, and longaville, 4.03.121
would from my forehead wipe a perjur'd note: 4.03.123
you would for paradise break faith and troth, 4.03.141
and jove for your love would infringe an oath. 4.03.142
see, | i would not have him know so much by me. 4.03.148
o, but for my love, day would turn to night! 4.03.229
and therefore red, that would avoid dispraise, 4.03.260
for when would you, my lord, or you, or you, 4.03.295
for when would you, my liege, or you, or you, 4.03.317
o, then his lines would ravish savage ears | and 4.03.345
which he would call "abbominable"; 5.01. 24 P
that the king would have me present the princess 5.01.110 P
as would be cramm'd up in a sheet of paper, 5.02. 7
i would you knew. 5.02. 31
ay, or i would these hands might never part. 5.02. 57
how i would make him fawn, and beg, and seek, 5.02. 62
so pair–taunt–like would i o'ersway his state 5.02. 67
a doubt | presence majestical would put him out; 5.02.102
what would these strangers? 5.02.175
know what they would. 5.02.178
what would you with the princess? 5.02.178
what would they, say they? 5.02.180
and would afford my speechless vizard half. 5.02.246
i would not yield to be your house's guest: 5.02.354
they are thirsty, fools would fain have drink. 5.02.372
that he would wed me, or else die my lover. 5.02.447
they would know | whether the three worthies 5.02.485
if your ladyship would say, "thanks, pompey," i 5.02.556
and thou wert a lion, we would do so. 5.02.624
a man so breathed, that certain he would fight, 5.02.653
the holy suit which fain it would convince, 5.02.746
if this, or more than this, i would deny, | to 5.02.813
i would my father look'd but with my eyes. MND 1.01. 56
will, | or else to wed demetrius, as he would, 1.01. 88
o that your frowns would teach my smiles such 1.01.195
would that fault were mine! 1.01.201
you would fright the duchess and the ladies, 1.02. 75 P
duchess and the ladies, that they would shrike; 1.02. 76 P
that would hang us, every mother's son. 1.02. 78 P
they would have no more discretion but to hang 1.02. 80 P
and jealous oberon would have the child | knight 2.01. 24
and here my mistress. would that he were gone! 2.01. 59
would imitate, and sail upon the land | to fetch 2.01.132
or "fair ladies, i would wish you," or "i would 3.01. 39 P
i would wish you," or "i would request you," or 3.01. 40 P
"i would request you," or "i would entreat you, 3.01. 40 P
true as truest horse, that yet would never tire, 3.01. 96
as truest horse, that yet would never tire." 3.01.102
who would set his wit to so foolish a bird? 3.01.134 P
who would give a bird the lie, though he cry 3.01.135 P
would he have stolen away | from sleeping hermia 3.02. 51
you would not do me thus much injury. 3.02.148
in show, | you would not use a gentle lady so; 3.02.152
noble sort | would so offend a virgin and extort 3.02.160
lysander's love, that would not let him bide — 3.02.186
you would not make me such an argument. 3.02.242
to break loose — take on as you would follow, 3.02.258
i would i had your bond, for i perceive | a weak 3.02.267
i would be loath to have you overflowen with a 4.01. 15 P
but, as i think — for truly would i speak, 4.01.149
they would have stol'n away, they would, 4.01.156
they would have stol'n away, they would, 4.01.156
he would have deserv'd it. 4.02. 23 P
that, if it would but apprehend some joy, | it 5.01. 19
this man is pyramus, if you would know; 5.01.129
and such a wall, as i would have you think, 5.01.157
would you desire lime and hair to speak better? 5.01.165 P
would he would change! 5.01.251 P
would he would change! 5.01.251 P
friend, would go near to make a man look sad. 5.01.289 P
garter, it would have been a fine tragedy; 5.01.359 P
the better part of my affections would | be with MV 1.01. 16
my ventures, out of doubt | would make me sad. 1.01. 22
broth | would blow me to an ague when i thought 1.01. 23
would scatter all her spices on the stream, 1.01. 33
that such a thing bechanc'd would make me sad? 1.01. 38
i would have stay'd till i had made you merry, 1.01. 60
speak, would almost damn those ears | which, 1.01. 98
hearing them, would call their brothers fools. 1.01. 99
than my faint means would grant continuance. 1.01.125
you would be, sweet madam, if your miseries were 1.02. 3 P
they would be better if well follow'd. 1.02. 11 P
i may neither choose who i would, nor refuse who 1.02. 23 P
if he would despise me, i would forgive him, for 1.02. 63 P
if he would despise me, i would forgive him, for 1.02. 64 P
and swore he would pay him again when he was 1.02. 81 P
is he yet possess'd | how much ye would? 1.03. 65
no, not take interest, not, as you would say, 1.03. 76
"shylock, we would have moneys," you say so — 1.03.116
i would be friends with you, and have your love, 1.03.138
i would not change this hue, | except to steal 2.01. 11
i would o'erstare the sternest eyes that look, 2.01. 27
or, as you would say in plain terms, gone to 2.02. 64 P
sir, but the rich jew's man, that would, sir, as 2.02.124 P
infection, sir, as one would say, to serve — 2.02.125 P
a dish of doves that i would bestow upon your 2.02.135 P
one speak for both. what would you? 2.02.141 P
i would entreat you rather to put on | your 2.02.201
i would not have my father | see me in talk with 2.03. 8
him | to one that i would have him help to waste 2.05. 50
cupid himself would blush | to see me thus 2.06. 38
bassanio told him he would make some speed | of 2.08. 37
how much low peasantry would then be gleaned 2.09. 46
here; what would my lord? 2.09. 85
i would she were as lying a gossip in that as 3.01. 8 P
i would it might prove the end of his losses. 3.01. 18 P
i would my daughter were dead at my foot, and 3.01. 88 P
would she were hears'd at my foot, and the 3.01. 89 P
i would not have given it for a wilderness of 3.01.122 P
i would not lose you, and, you know yourself, 3.02. 5
i would detain you here some month or two 3.02. 9
the other half yours — | mine own, i would say; 3.02. 17
alone | i would not be ambitious in my wish | to 3.02.151
you | i would be trebled twenty times myself, 3.02.153
i would you had won the fleece that he hath lost 3.02.242
to discharge the jew, | he would not take it. 3.02.274
that he would rather have antonio's flesh | than 3.02.286
i know you would be prouder of the work | than 3.04. 8
hates any man the thing he would not kill? 4.01. 67
i would not draw them, i would have my bond. 4.01. 87
i would not draw them, i would have my bond. 4.01. 87
i would lose all, ay, sacrifice them all | here 4.01.286
your wife would give you little thanks for that 4.01.288
i would she were in heaven, so she could 4.01.291
the wish would make else an unquiet house. 4.01.294
would any of the stock of barrabas | had been 4.01.296
she would not hold out enemy for ever | for 4.01.447
sir, i would speak with you. 4.02. 12
i would out–night you, did nobody come; 5.01. 23
would be thought | no better a musician than the 5.01.105
sleeps with endymion | and would not be awak'd. 5.01.110
if you would walk in absence of the sun. 5.01.128
would he were gelt that had it, for my part, 5.01.144
that you would wear it till your hour of death, 5.01.153
i dare be sworn for him he would not leave it, 5.01.172
and neither man nor master would take aught 5.01.183
could add a lie unto a fault, | i would deny it; 5.01.187
and would conceive for what i gave the ring, 5.01.195
when nought would be accepted but the ring, 5.01.197
you would abate the strength of your displeasure 5.01.198
you would not then have parted with the ring. 5.01.202
my honor would not let ingratitude | so much 5.01.218
i think you would have begg'd | the ring of me 5.01.221
i would not take this hand from thy throat till AYL 1.01. 59 P
he would not have spoke such a word. 1.01. 84 P
that /she would have follow'd her exile, or have 1.01.109 P
and for your love i would be loath to foil him, 1.01.129 P
mistress of, and would you yet /i were merrier? 1.02. 4 P
i would we could do so; 1.02. 34 P
i would have told you of good wrastling, which 1.02.109 P
challenger's youth i would fain dissuade him, 1.02.160 P
of your adventure would counsel you to a more 1.02.177 P
strength that i have, i would it were with you. 1.02.194 P
i would i were invisible, to catch the strong 1.02.211 P
i would thou hadst been son to some man else: 1.02.224
i would thou hadst told me of another father. 1.02.230
were i my father, coz, would i do this? 1.02.231
son — and would not change that calling | to be 1.02.233
with my fortunes, | i'll ask him what he would. 1.02.253
i would try, if i could cry "hem" and have him. 1.03. 19 P
would he not be a comfort to our travel? 1.03.131
i would not change it. 2.01. 18
why would you be so fond to overcome | the bonny 2.03. 7
go seek him, tell him i would speak with him. 2.07. 7
what, for a counter, would i do but good? 2.07. 63
what would you have? 2.07.102
that courtesy would be uncleanly if courtiers 3.02. 50 P
and would you have us kiss tar? 3.02. 63 P
of every sprite | heaven would in little show. 3.02.140
heaven would that she these gifts should have, 3.02.153
in them more feet than the verses would bear. 3.02.166 P
i would thou couldst stammer, that thou mightst 3.02.198 P
i would sing my song without a burthen; 3.02.247 P
very well. what would you? 3.02.298 P
groaning every hour would detect the lazy foot 3.02.304 P
i would give him some good counsel, for he seems 3.02.364 P
youth, i would i could make thee believe i love. 3.02.385 P
at which time would i, being but a moonish youth 3.02.409 P
would now like him, now loathe him; 3.02.415 P
i would not be cur'd, youth. 3.02.425 P
i would cure you, if you would but call me 3.02.426 P
if you would but call me rosalind and come every 3.02.426 P
truly, i would the gods had made thee poetical. 3.03. 16 P
would you not have me honest? 3.03. 28 P
i would fain see this meeting. 3.03. 46 P
as pigeons bill, so wedlock would be nibbling. 3.03. 81 P
as good cause as one would desire, therefore 3.04. 5 P
but why did he swear he would come this morning, 3.04. 18 P
i would not be thy executioner; 3.05. 8
i fly thee, for i would not injure thee. 3.05. 9
where ever sorrow is, relief would be. 3.05. 86
i would have you. 3.05. 91
would have gone near | to fall in love with him; 3.05.125
what would you say to me now, and i were your 4.01. 70 P
i would kiss before i spoke. 4.01. 72 P
say you are, because i would be talking of her. 4.01. 90 P
he would have liv'd many a fair year though hero 4.01.100 P
i would not have my right rosalind of this mind, 4.01.109 P
tell me how long you would have her after you 4.01.143 P
i knew what you would prove; 4.01.183 P
and it would do well to set the deer's horns 4.02. 4 P
patience herself would startle at this letter, 4.03. 13
strange effect | would they work in mild aspect? 4.03. 53
i would i were at home. 4.03.161
a body would think this was well counterfeited! 4.03.166 P
would open his lips when he put it into his 5.01. 34 P
i would love you if i could. 5.02.111 P
nonino, | these pretty country folks would lie, 5.03. 24
that would i, had i kingdoms to give with her. 5.04. 8
that would i, were i of all kingdoms king. 5.04. 10
cut, he would send me word he cut it to please 5.04. 74 P
not well cut, he would answer i spake not true: 5.04. 78 P
again, it was not well cut, he would say i lie: 5.04. 80 P
what you would have | i'll stay to know at your 5.04.195
if i were a woman i would kiss as many of you as ep 18 P
i would not lose the dog for twenty pound. SHR in.1. 21
fleet, | i would esteem him worth a dozen such. in.1. 27
would not the beggar then forget himself? in.1. 41
it would seem strange unto him when he wak'd. in.1. 43
which otherwise would grow into extremes. in.1. 138
what, would you make me mad? in.2. 17 P
yet would you say ye were beaten out of door, in.2. 85
and say you would present her at the leet, in.2. 87
sometimes you would call out for cicely hacket. in.2. 89
but i would be loathe to fall into my dreams in.2. 126 P
light on them, would take her with all faults, 1.01.129 P
and would i had given him the best horse in 1.01.142 P
begin his wooing that would thoroughly woo her, 1.01.143 P
the better for him, would i were so too! 1.01.238
would 'twere done! 1.01.254 P
whom would to god i had well knock'd at first, 1.02. 34
it is, | i would not wed her for a mine of gold. 1.02. 92
she would think scolding would do little good 1.02.109 P
would think scolding would do little good upon 1.02.109 P
i promis'd we would be contributors | and bear 1.02.214
i would i were as sure of a good dinner. 1.02.217
me, signior gremio, i would fain be doing. 2.01. 74
had i a glass, i would. 2.01.233
if it would please him come and marry her!" 3.02. 20
would katherine had never seen him though! 3.02. 26
for such an injury would vex a very saint, 3.02. 28
first were we sad, fearing you would not come, 3.02. 98
you would entreat me rather go than stay. 3.02.192
to marry with her though she would entreat. 4.02. 33
would all the world but he had quite forsworn! 4.02. 35
he that knocks as he would beat down the gate? 5.01. 16 P
nose, that would have sent me to the jail. 5.01.131 P
for both our sakes, i would that word were true. 5.02. 15
would say your head and butt were head and horn. 5.02. 41
i would your duty were as foolish too. 5.02.126
you, whose worthiness would stir it up where it AWW 1.01. 9 P
so far, would have made nature immortal, and 1.01. 20 P
would for the king's sake he were living! 1.01. 21 P
i think it would be the death of the king's 1.01. 22 P
i would it were not notorious. 1.01. 36 P

the hind that would be mated by the lion | must 1.01. 91
and would seem | to have us make denial. 1.02. 8
i would i had that corporal soundness now | as 1.02. 24
would demonstrate them now | but goers backward. 1.02. 47
would i were with him! 1.02. 52
he would always say — | methinks i hear him now 1.02. 52
if he were living, i would try him yet. 1.02. 72
tell my gentlewoman i would speak with her — 1.03. 68 P
would god would serve the world so all the year! 1.03. 83 P
would god would serve the world so all the year! 1.03. 83 P
god, that would not extend his might only where 1.03.113 P
that would suffer her poor knight surpris'd 1.03.115 P
would you were — | so that my lord your son 1.03.161
nor would i have him till i do deserve him, 1.03.199
tender your supposed aid, | he would receive it? 1.03.237
and, would your honor | but give me leave to try 1.03.246
i would you had kneel'd, my lord, to ask me 2.01. 64
i would i had, so i had broke thy pate, | and 2.01. 66
and what impossibility would slay | in common 2.01.177
you would answer very well to a whipping, if you 2.02. 54 P
just, you say well; so would i have said. 2.03. 19 P
that's it i would have said, the very same. 2.03. 25 P
i would have said it; 2.03. 39 P
them whipt, or i would send them to th' turk, to 2.03. 87 P
would quite confound distinction, yet stands off 2.03.120
i would it were hell–pains for thy sake, and my 2.03.232 P
no more pity of his age than i would have of — 2.03.240 P
ay, that would be known. 2.03.278
and i her money, i would she did as you say. 2.04. 21 P
well, what would you say? 2.05. 78
most fain would steal | what law does vouch mine 2.05. 81
what would you have? 2.05. 82
i would not tell you what i would, my lord. 2.05. 84
i would not tell you what i would, my lord. 2.05. 84
would in so just a business shut his bosom 3.01. 8
it hath happen'd all as i would have had it, 3.02. 1 P
not be kill'd so soon as i thought he would. 3.02. 38 P
and would you take the letter of her? 3.04. 1
might you not know she would do as she has done 3.04. 2
and yet she writes, | pursuit would be but vain. 3.04. 25
grief would have tears, and sorrow bids me speak 3.04. 42
i would he lov'd his wife. 3.05. 79
i his lady, | i would poison that vile rascal. 3.05. 84
i would i knew in what particular action to try 3.06. 17 P
performer, i would have that drum or another, or 3.06. 62 P
and would not put my reputation now | in any 3.07. 6
nor would i wish you. 3.07. 7
to buy his will, it would not seem too dear, 3.07. 27
i would the cutting of my garments would serve 4.01. 46 P
the cutting of my garments would serve the turn, 4.01. 46 P
three great oaths would scarce make that be 4.01. 59 P
i would i had any drum of the enemy's. 4.01. 61 P
i would swear i recover'd it. 4.01. 62 P
would you believe my oaths | when i did love you 4.02. 26
my mother told me just how he would woo, | as if 4.02. 69
no sin | to cozen him that would unjustly win. 4.02. 76
i would gladly have him see his company 4.03. 31 P
our virtues would be proud, if our faults whipt 4.03. 72 P
whipt them not, and our crimes would despair, if 4.03. 73 P
but to answer you as you would be understood, he 4.03.106 P
i would repent out the remainder of nature. 4.03.242 P
that you would think truth were a fool. 4.03.254 P
i would do the man what honor i can, but of this 4.03.271 P
yet who would have suspected an ambush where i 4.03.301 P
through flinty tartar's bosom would peep forth 4.04. 7
whose villainous saffron would have made all the 4.05. 2 P
i would i had not known him; 4.05. 8 P
i would cozen the man of his wife and do his 4.05. 27 P
and i would give his wife my bauble, sir, to do 4.05. 30 P
before, because i would not fall out with thee. 4.05. 57 P
majesty's ear, | if he would spend his power. 5.01. 8
and what would you have me to do? 5.02. 28 P
is a good lady and would not have knaves thrive 5.02. 31 P
help, that by this token | i would relieve her. 5.03. 86
in heavy satisfaction and would never | receive 5.03.100
that she would never put it from her finger, 5.03.109
to come into me, | which i would fain shut out. 5.03.115
than for to think that i would sink it here. 5.03.181
and things which would derive me ill will to 5.03.264 P
TN which she would keep fresh | and lasting in her 1.01. 30
among the prudent he would quickly have the gift 1.03. 32 P
i would not undertake her in this company. 1.03. 58 P
would thou mightst never draw sword again. 1.03. 61 P
i would i might never draw sword again. 1.03. 63 P
i would i had bestow'd that time in the tongues 1.03. 92 P
why, would that have mended my hair? 1.03. 97 P
i would not so much as make water but in a 1.03.130 P
whoe'er i woo, myself would be his wife. 1.04. 42
go thy way, if sir toby would leave drinking, 1.05. 27 P
one would think his mother's milk were scarce 1.05.161 P
i would be loath to cast away my speech; 1.05.172 P
what would you? 1.05.213 P
what i am, and what i would, are as secret as 1.05.216 P
life, | in your denial i would find no sense. 1.05.266
i would not understand it. 1.05.267
why, what would you? 1.05.267
he left this ring behind him, | would i or not. 1.05.302
heavens had been pleas'd, would we had so ended! 2.01. 20 P
else would i very shortly see thee there. 2.01. 46
would you have a love–song, or a song of good 2.03. 35 P
and it would please you to take leave of her, 2.03. 99 P
you would not give means for this uncivil rule. 2.03.122 P
and your horse now would make him an ass. 2.03.168 P
i would have men of such constancy put to sea, 2.04. 75 P
i would exult, man. 2.05. 7 P
i know my place as i would they should do theirs 2.05. 54 P
did not i say he would work it out? 2.05.127 P
to crush this a little, it would bow to me, for 2.05.140 P
she that would alter services with thee, the 2.05.158 P
i would therefore my sister had had no name, sir 3.01. 16 P
sir, i would it would make you invisible. 3.01. 30 P
sir, i would it would make you invisible. 3.01. 30 P
i would be sorry, sir, but the fool should be as 3.01. 39 P
though i would not have it grow on my chin. 3.01. 47 P
would not a pair of these have bred, sir? 3.01. 49 P
i would play lord pandarus of phrygia, sir, to 3.01. 51 P
you are and what you would are out of my welkin 3.01. 57 P
would they were blanks, rather than fill'd with 3.01.104

but, would you undertake another suit, | i had 3.01.108
i would you were as i would have you be! 3.01.142
i would you were as i would have you be! 3.01.142
would it be better, madam, than i am? 3.01.143
more soon | than love that would seem hid: 3.01.148
i would not by my will have troubled you, | but 3.03. 1
would you'ld pardon me. 3.03. 24
were i ta'en here, it would scarce be answer'd. 3.03. 28
i would not have him miscarry for the half of my 3.04. 63 P
my lady would not lose him for more than i'll 3.04.104 P
than ever proof itself would have earn'd him. 3.04.182 P
a little thing would make me tell them how much 3.04.303 P
i would not be in some of your coats for 4.01. 30 P
would thou'dst be rul'd by me! 4.01. 64
in't, and i would i were the first that ever 4.02. 5 P
i would we were well rid of this knavery. 4.02. 67 P
may be conveniently deliver'd, i would he were, 4.02. 69 P
but that it would be double–dealing, sir, i 5.01. 29 P
sir, i would you could make it another. 5.01. 30 P
but i would not have you to think that my desire 5.01. 46 P
years removed thing | while one would wink; 5.01. 90
what would my lord, but that he may not have, 5.01.101
my lord would speak, my duty hushes me. 5.01.107
to do you rest, a thousand deaths would die. 5.01.133
he would have tickled you othergates than he did 5.01.193 P
you would have been contracted to a maid, | nor 5.01.261
WT would they else be content to die? 1.01. 42 P
they would desire to live on crutches till he 1.01. 45 P
time as long again | would be fill'd up, my 1.02. 4
though you would seek t' unsphere the stars with 1.02. 48
at my request he would not. 1.02. 87
o, would her name were grace! 1.02. 99
in me | thoughts that would thick my blood. 1.02.171
if you would seek us, | we are yours i' th' 1.02.177
the tenth of mankind | would hang themselves. 1.02.200
he would not stay at your petitions, made | his 1.02.215
i would not be a stander–by to hear | my 1.02.279
theirs only, | that would unseen be wicked? 1.02.292
she would not live | the running of one glass. 1.02.305
they would do that | which should undo more 1.02.311
would i do this? 1.02.332
you'ld wanton with us, | if we would have you. 2.01. 19
and i'll be sworn you would believe my saying, 2.01. 63
would i knew the villain, | i would land–damn 2.01.142
i knew the villain, | i would land–damn him. 2.01.143
and more it would content me | to have her honor 2.01.159
i knew she would. 2.03. 44
and would by combat make her good, so were i | a 2.03. 61
so i would you did; 2.03. 81
it | as i weigh grief, which i would spare; 3.02. 43
the bug which you would fright me with, i seek. 3.02. 92
which i would free — if i shall be condemn'd 3.02.111
would have shed water out of fire ere done't; 3.02.193
within, i'll serve you | as i would do the gods. 3.02.207
and that | apollo would (this being indeed the 3.03. 43
i would there were no age between ten and 3.03. 59 P
or that youth would sleep out the rest; 3.03. 60 P
would any but these boil'd–brains of nineteen 3.03. 63 P
i would you did but see how it chafes, how it 3.03. 88 P
would i had been by, to have help'd the old man! 3.03.107 P
i would you had been by the ship side, to have 3.03.109 P
there your charity would have lack'd footing. 3.03.110 P
his vices, you would say; 4.03. 91 P
vices, i would say, sir. 4.03. 94 P
how would he look to see his work, so noble, 4.04. 21
what would he say? 4.04. 22
would sing her song and dance her turn; 4.04. 58
took to quench it | she would to each one sip. 4.04. 62
no more than were i painted i would wish | this 4.04.101
of january | would blow you through and through. 4.04.112
i would i had some flow'rs o' th' spring that 4.04.113
you would never dance again after a tabor and 4.04.182 P
and where some stretch–mouth'd rascal would, as 4.04.196 P
you would think a smock were a she–angel, he so 4.04.209 P
a cold fish for she would not exchange flesh 4.04.280 P
i would have ransack'd | the pedlar's silken 4.04.349
i would not prize them | without her love; 4.04.375
i told you what would come of this. 4.04.447
how often said my dignity would last | but till 4.04.475
i would your spirit were easier for advice, | or 4.04.505
that he would not stir his pettitoes till he had 4.04.606 P
i would have fil'd keys off that hung in chains. 4.04.611 P
now meet my father, | he would not call me son. 4.04.658
to acquaint the king withal, i would not do't. 4.04.681 P
to be honest, i see fortune would not suffer me: 4.04.832 P
woman, she you kill'd | would be unparallel'd. 5.01. 16
might have spoken a thousand things that would 5.01. 21
you are one of those | would have him wed again. 5.01. 24
if you would not so, | you pity not the state, 5.01. 24
would make her sainted spirit | again possess 5.01. 57
and would incense me | to murther her i married. 5.01. 61
would she begin a sect, might quench the zeal 5.01.107
would he do so, i'ld beg your precious mistress, 5.01.223
i would most gladly know the issue of it. 5.02. 8 P
embracing, as if she would pin her to her heart, 5.02. 77 P
i would fain say, bleed tears; 5.02. 88 P
his work, would beguile nature of her custom, so 5.02. 99 P
that they say one would speak to her and stand 5.02.101 P
who would be thence that has the benefit of 5.02.109 P
life in me, would preferment drop on my head. 5.02.114 P
it would not have relish'd among my other 5.02.122 P
and i would thou wouldst be a tall fellow of thy 5.02.167 P
of my poor image | would thus have wrought you 5.03. 58
would i were dead but that methinks already — 5.03. 62
see, my lord, | would you not deem it breath'd? 5.03. 64
JN now say, chatillion, what would france with us? 1.01. 1
how that ambitious constance would not cease 1.01. 32
with half that face would he have all my land — 1.01. 93
would i might never stir from off this place, 1.01.145
i would give it every foot to have this face; 1.01.146
it would not be sir nob in any case. 1.01.147
nay, i would have you go before me thither. 1.01.155
and so, ere answer knows what question would, 1.01.200
madam, i would not wish a better father. 1.01.260
a noble boy! who would not do thee right? 2.01. 18
a good grandame, boy, that would blot thee. 2.01.133
i would that i were low laid in my grave, | i am 2.01.164
i would set an ox–head to your lion's hide, 2.01.292

up | her presence would have interrupted much. 2.01.542
when his fair angels would salute my palm, | but 2.01.590
i would not care, i then would be content, | for 3.01. 48
i would not care, i then would be content, | for 3.01. 48
that faith would live again by death of need. 3.01.214
and tell me how you would bestow yourself. 3.01.225
day, | i would into thy bosom pour my thoughts. 3.03. 53
adjunct to my act, | by heaven, i would do it. 3.03. 58
then with a passion would i shake the world, 3.04. 39
i am not mad, i would to heaven i were! 3.04. 48
they would be as a call | to train ten thousand 3.04.174
young gentlemen would be as sad as night, | only 4.01. 15
and so i would be here, but that i doubt | my 4.01. 19
and i would to heaven | i were your son, so you 4.01. 23
heaven | i were your son, so you would love me, 4.01. 24
in sooth, i would you were a little sick, | that 4.01. 29
many a poor man's son would have lien still, 4.01. 50
ah, none but in this iron age would do it! 4.01. 60
near these eyes, would drink my tears, | and 4.01. 62
i would not have believ'd him — no tongue but 4.01. 70
the instrument is cold, | and would not harm me. 4.01.104
since all and every part of what we would | doth 4.02. 38
what you would have reform'd that is not well, 4.02. 44
we had a kind of light what would ensue. 4.03. 61
i would not have you, lord, forget yourself, 4.03. 83
would not my lords return to me again | after 5.01. 37
would bear thee from the knowledge of thyself, 5.02. 35
it would allay the burning quality | of that 5.07. 8
it would not out at windows nor at doors. 5.07. 29
i have a kind soul that would give thanks, | and 5.07.108
R2 which then our leisure would not let us hear, 1.01. 5
which else would post until it had return'd 1.01. 56
which to maintain i would allow him odds | and 1.01. 62
you would have bid me argue like a father. 1.03.238
had i thy youth and cause, i would not stay. 1.03.305
would the word "farewell" have length'ned hours 1.04. 16
but since it would not, he had none of me. 1.04. 19
though richard my live's counsel would not hear, 2.01. 15
ah, would the scandal vanish with my life, | how 2.01. 67
forth thy reach he would have laid thy shame, 2.01.106
grief, | or else he never would compare between. 2.01.185
who gently would dissolve the bands of life, 2.02. 71
i would to god | (so my untruth had not provok'd 2.02.100
sister — cousin, i would say — pray pardon me. 2.02.105
what would you have me do? 2.03.133
i would attach you all, and make you stoop 2.03.156
else heaven would, | and we will not. 3.02. 30
would they make peace? 3.02.133
it would beseem the lord northumberland | to say 3.03. 7
would you have been so brief with him, he would 3.03. 12
him, he would | have been so brief /with /you to 3.03. 12
would not this ill do well? 3.03.170
i could weep, madam, would it do you good. 3.04. 21
and i could sing, would weeping do me good, 3.04. 22
i would my skill were subject to thy curse. 3.04.103
how blest this land would be | in this your 4.01. 18
i would he were the best | in all this presence 4.01. 31
now, by my soul, i would it were this hour. 4.01. 42
would god that any in this noble presence | were 4.01.117
then true noblesse would | learn him forbearance 4.01.119
my lord, you told me you would tell the rest, 5.02. 1
you would have thought the very windows spake, 5.02. 12
which for some reasons i would not have seen. 5.02. 62
he twenty times my son, | i would appeach him. 5.02.102
i would to god, my lords, he might be found. 5.03. 4
his answer was, he would unto the stews, | and 5.03. 16
that | he would unhorse the lustiest challenger. 5.03. 19
he prays but faintly, and would be denied, | we 5.03.103
his weary joints would gladly rise, i know, 5.03.105
"i would thou wert the man | that would divorce 5.04. 8
that would divorce this terror from my heart" — 5.04. 9
would he not stumble? 5.05. 87
would he not fall down, | since pride must have 5.05. 87
o would the deed were good! 5.05.114
1H4 then would i have his harry and he mine. 1.01. 90
and elsewhere, so far as my coin would stretch, 1.02. 55 P
my coin would stretch, and where it would not, i 1.02. 55 P
i would to god thou and i knew where a commodity 1.02. 82 P
to sport would be as tedious as to work; 1.02.205
guns | he would himself have been a soldier. 1.03. 64
no, if a scot would save his soul, he shall not! 1.03.215
he said he would not ransom mortimer, | forbade 1.03.219
and would be glad he met with some mischance, 1.03.232
i would have him poisoned with a pot of ale. 1.03.233
to do the profession some grace, that would (if 2.01. 71 P
no, ye fat chuffs, i would your store were here! 2.02. 89 P
to london, it would be argument for a week, 2.02. 95 P
o lord, i would it had been two! 2.04. 60 P
i would i were a weaver, i could sing psalms, or 2.04.133 P
but i would give a thousand pound i could run as 2.04.147 P
all would not do. 2.04.170 P
but, as the devil would have it, three 2.04.221 P
the world, i would not tell you on compulsion. 2.04.237 P
i would give no man a reason upon compulsion, i. 2.04.240 P
of the court at door would speak with you. 2.04.288 P
and said he would swear truth out of england but 2.04.306 P
out of england but he would make you believe it 2.04.306 P
i would your grace would take me with you. 2.04.460 P
i would your grace would take me with you. 2.04.460 P
so it would have done | at the same season if 3.01. 17
and that would set my teeth nothing an edge, 3.01.131
i would i could | quit all offenses with as 3.02. 18
that men would tell their children, "this is he" 3.02. 48
others would say, "where, which is bullingbrook? 3.02. 49
which now doth that i would not have it do, 3.02. 90
on his helm | would they were multitudes, and on 3.02.143
way given to virtue, i would swear by thy face; 3.03. 34 P
thou hast drunk me would have bought me lights 3.03. 45 P
'sblood, i would my face were in your belly! 3.03. 49 P
i would cudgel him like a dog if he would say so 3.03. 86 P
would cudgel him like a dog if he would say so. 3.03. 87 P
man as he is, and said he would cudgel you. 3.03.108 P
to thank god on, i would thou shouldst know it. 3.03.118 P
call'd you jack, and said he would cudgel you. 3.03.139 P
should, how would thy guts fall about thy knees! 3.03.152 P
i would it had been of horse. 3.03.187 P
i would the state of time had first been whole 4.01. 25
but yet i would your father had been here. 4.01. 60

that you would think that i had a hundred and 4.02. 33 P
and would to god | you were of our determination 4.03. 32
i would you would accept of grace and love. 4.03.112
i would you would accept of grace and love. 4.03.112
how much they do import, you would make haste. 4.04. 5
i would 'twere bed–time, hal, and all well. 5.01.125 P
yet, i would be loath to pay him before his day. 5.01.127 P
o, would the quarrel lay upon our heads, | and 5.02. 47
which would have been as speedy in your end | as 5.04. 55
thou speak'st as if i would deny my name. 5.04. 60
and would to god | thy name in arms were now as 5.04. 69
my faith, i am afraid he would prove the better 5.04.124 P
if the man were alive and would deny it, 'zounds 5.04.152 P
i would make him eat a piece of my sword. 5.04.153 P
and would have told him half his troy was burnt; 2H4 1.01. 73
he that but fears the thing he would not know 1.01. 85
that which i would to god i had not seen, | but 1.01.106
having been well, that would have made me sick, 1.01.138
he would not take his band and yours, he lik'd 1.02. 32 P
i had as live they would put ratsbane in my 1.02. 41 P
sir, my lord would speak with you. 1.02. 91 P
you would not come when i sent for you. 1.02.105 P
you by the heels would amend the attention of 1.02.123 P
i would it were otherwise, i would my means were 1.02.142 P
i would my means were greater and my waist 1.02.142 P
say of wax, my growth would approve the truth. 1.02.159 P
bottle, i would i might never spit white again. 1.02.211 P
i would to god my name were not so terrible to 1.02.217 P
but gladly would be better satisfied | how in 1.03. 6
man of good temper would endure this tempest of 2.01. 81 P
tell me how many good young princes would do so, 2.02. 30 P
i would think thee a most princely hypocrite. 2.02. 54 P
it would be every man's thought, and thou art a 2.02. 56 P
every man would think me an hypocrite indeed. 2.02. 59 P
fain would i go to meet the archbishop, | but 2.03. 65
mistress tearsheet would fain hear some music. 2.04. 12 P
beats as extraordinarily as heart would desire, 2.04. 24 P
pistol's below, and would speak with you. 2.04. 69 P
you would bless you to hear what he said. 2.04. 95 P
more, pistol, i would not have you go off here. 2.04.136 P
they would truncheon you out for taking their 2.04.142 P
the good–year, do you think i would deny her? 2.04.177 P
pistol, i would be quiet. 2.04.185 P
'a would have made a good pantler, 'a would 'a' 2.04.237 P
a good pantler, 'a would 'a' chipp'd bread well. 2.04.238 P
would not this nave of a wheel have his ears cut 2.04.255 P
would shut the book, and sit him down and die. 3.01. 56
would of that seed grow to a greater falseness, 3.01. 90
we would, dear lords, unto the holy land. 3.01.108
and i would have done any thing indeed too, and 3.02. 18 P
'a would have clapp'd i' th' clout at twelve 3.02. 46 P
that it would have done a man's heart good to 3.02. 48 P
i would wart might have gone, sir. 3.02.163 P
i would thou wert a man's tailor, that thou 3.02.164 P
she would always say she could not abide master 3.02.202 P
men, and i would have you serv'd with the best. 3.02.255 P
fellow, and 'a would manage you his piece thus, 3.02.281 P
his piece thus, and 'a would about and about, 3.02.282 P
tah, tah," would 'a say, "bounce," would 'a say, 3.02.284 P
"bounce," would 'a say, and away again would 'a 3.02.284 P
would 'a say, and away again would 'a go, and 3.02.285 P
away again would 'a go, and again would 'a come. 3.02.285 P
'fore god, would you would. 3.02.296 P
'fore god, would you would. 3.02.296 P
would he abuse the countenance of the king, 4.02. 13
this present peace, | you would drink freely. 4.02. 75
i would be sorry, my lord, but it should be thus 4.03. 30 P
i would you had the wit, 'twere better than your 4.03. 86 P
humane principle i would teach them should be, 4.03.123 P
what would my lord and father? 4.04. 18
what would your majesty? 4.05. 49
would, by beholding him, have wash'd his knife 4.05. 86
more would i, but my lungs are wasted so | that 4.05.216
i would humor his men with the imputation of 5.01. 72 P
i would curry with master shallow that no man 5.01. 73 P
i would his majesty had call'd me with him; 5.02. 6
i am the sorrier, would 'twere otherwise! 5.02. 32
a son | that would deliver up his greatness so 5.02.111
i would not take a /knighthood for my fortune. 5.03.126 P
arrant knave, i would to god that i might die, 5.04. 1 P
i would make this a bloody day to somebody. 5.04. 12 P
i would have bestow'd the thousand pound i 5.05. 11 P
here i promis'd you i would be, and here i ep 13 P
make any possible satisfaction, and so would i. ep 22 P
that would ascend | the brightest heaven of H5 pr 1
given to the church, | would they strip from us; 1.01. 11
as much as would maintain, to the king's honor, 1.01. 12
this would drink deep. 1.01. 20
you would desire the king were made a prelate; 1.01. 40
you would say it hath been all in all his study; 1.01. 42
as i perceiv'd his grace would fain have done, 1.01. 85
we would be resolv'd, | before we hear him, of 1.02. 4
they would hold up this salique law | to bar 1.02. 91
what mightst thou do, that honor would thee do, 2.pr. 18
will you shog off? i would have you solus. 2.01. 45 P
if you would walk off, i would prick your guts a 2.01. 57 P
i would prick your guts a little in good terms, 2.01. 58 P
he is very sick, and would to bed. 2.01. 82 P
of our person, | would have him punish'd. 2.02. 60
wherein you would have sold your king to 2.02.170
would i were with him, wheresome'er he is, 2.03. 7 P
said once, the dev'l would have him about women. 2.03. 35 P
would i were in an alehouse in london, i would 3.02. 12 P
i would give all my fame for a pot of ale and 3.02. 13 P
"if wishes would prevail with me, | my purpose 3.02. 15
not fail with me, | but thither would i hie." 3.02. 17
but all they three, though they would serve me, 3.02. 30 P
that piece of service the men would carry coals. 3.02. 46 P
they would have me as familiar with men's 3.02. 47 P
the duke of gloucester would speak with you. 3.02. 55 P
i would have blowed up the town, so chrish save 3.02. 91 P
i would desire the duke to use his good pleasure 3.06. 54 P
is not the man that he would gladly make show to 3.06. 83 P
we would have all such offenders so cut off; 3.06.107 P
to re–answer, his pettiness would bow under. 3.06.129 P
we would not seek a battle as we are, | nor, as 3.06.164
would it were day! 3.07. 2 P
bears your praises, who would trot as well, were 3.07. 77 P
would i were able to load him with his desert! 3.07. 79 P
but i would it were morning, for i would fain be 3.07. 83 P
for i would fain be about the ears of the 3.07. 83 P
would it were day! 3.07.129 P
had any apprehension, they would run away. 3.07.136 P
evil, | would men observingly distill it out; 4.01. 5
a while, | and then i would no other company. 4.01. 32
if you would take the pains but to examine the 4.01. 68 P
and so i would he were, and i by him, at all 4.01.115 P
i think he would not wish himself any where but 4.01.119 P
then i would he were here alone; 4.01.121 P
and where they would be safe, they perish. 4.01.173 P
heard the king say he would not be ransom'd. 4.01.190 P
i would not lose so great an honor | as one man 4.03. 31
as one man more methinks would share from me, 4.03. 32
we would not die in that man's company | that 4.03. 38
god's will, my liege, would you and i alone, 4.03. 74
and they are both hang'd, and so would this be, 4.04. 73 P
those waters from me which i would have stopp'd, 4.06. 29
as he was a soldier, he would wear if alive, i 4.07.129 P
i would fain see the man, that hath but two legs 4.07.161 P
but i would fain see it once, and please god of 4.07.163 P
sword, | how many would the peaceful city quit, 5.pr. 33
not agree with it, i would desire you to eat it. 5.01. 26 P
if, duke of burgundy, you would the peace, 5.02. 68
marry, if you would put me to verses, or to 5.02.132 P
if thou would have such a one, take me! 5.02.165 P
to kiss before they are married, would she say? 5.02.266 P
i would have her learn, my fair cousin, how 5.02.283 P
if you would conjure in her, you must make a 5.02.292 P
which before would not abide looking on. 5.02.310 P
these news would cause him once more yield the 1H6 1.01. 67
one would have ling'ring wars with little cost; 1.01. 74
another would fly swift, but wanteth wings; 1.01. 75
these tidings would call forth her flowing tides 1.01. 83
i would ne'er have fled, | but that they left me 1.02. 23
who would e'er suppose | they had such courage 1.02. 35
the gates, here's gloucester that would enter. 1.03. 17
and would have armor here out of the tower, | to 1.03. 67
once in contempt they would have barter'd me; 1.04. 31
rather than i would be so pill'd esteem'd: 1.04. 33
whom with my bare fists i would execute, | if i 1.04. 36
for none would strike a stroke in his revenge. 1.05. 35
o, would i were to die with salisbury! 1.05. 38
here is the talbot, who would speak with him? 2.02. 37
fain would mine eyes be witness with mine ears 2.03. 9
that you on my behalf would pluck a flower. 2.04.129
i would his troubles likewise were expir'd, 2.05. 31
would some part of my young years | might but 2.05.107
else would i have a fling at winchester. 3.01. 64
i would prevail, if prayers might prevail, | to 3.01. 67
or i would see his heart out ere the priest 3.01.120
and after meet you, sooner than you would. 3.04. 45
come hither, you that would be combatants: 4.01.134
to harry king of england, | and thus he would: 4.02. 5
for fly he could not, if he would have fled; 4.04. 43
and fly would talbot never, though he might. 4.04. 44
i have what i would have, | now my old arms are 4.07. 31
doubtless he would have made a noble knight. 4.07. 44
here, | it would amaze the proudest of you all. 4.07. 84
they would but stink, and putrefy the air. 4.07. 90
as if, with circe, she would change my shape! 5.03. 35
my hand would free her, but my heart says no. 5.03. 61
fain would i woo her, yet i dare not speak: 5.03. 65
and yet i would that you would answer me. 5.03. 87
and yet i would that you would answer me. 5.03. 87
would you not suppose | your bondage happy, to 5.03.110
thee, as i would embrace | the christian prince, 5.03.171
i would the milk | thy mother gave thee, when 5.04. 27
i did imagine what would be her refuge. 5.04. 69
them) | would make a volume of enticing lines, 5.05. 14
before i would have yielded to this league. 2H6 1.01.127
and would have kept so long as breath did last! 1.01.211
i would remove these tedious stumbling–blocks, 1.02. 64
i would the college of the cardinals | would 1.03. 61
would choose him pope and carry him to rome, 1.03. 62
would make thee quickly hop without thy head. 1.03.137
did vow upon his knees he would be even with me. 1.03.200 P
i thought as much, he would be above the clouds. 2.01. 15
and would ye not think /his cunning to be great, 2.01.130
sorrow would solace, and mine age would ease. 2.03. 21
sorrow would solace, and mine age would ease. 2.03. 21
it | as others would ambitiously receive it. 2.03. 36
the fox barks not when he would steal the lamb. 3.01. 55
to mow down thorns that would annoy our foot 3.01. 67
because i would not tax the needy commons, 3.01.116
i would expend it with all willingness. 3.01.150
so that, by this, you would not have him die. 3.01.243
but i would have him dead, my lord of suffolk, 3.01.273
he never would have stay'd in france so long. 3.01.295
i rather would have lost my life betimes | than 3.01.297
i would be blind with weeping, sick with groans, 3.02. 62
yet aeolus would not be a murtherer, | but left 3.02. 92
and would not dash me with their ragged sides, 3.02. 98
did | when he to madding dido would unfold | his 3.02.117
fain would i go to chafe his paly lips | with 3.02.141
'tis like you would not feast him like a friend, 3.02.184
i would, false murd'rous coward, on thy knee 3.02.220
had i but said, i would have kept my word; 3.02.293
would curses kill, as doth the mandrake's groan, 3.02.310
i would invent as bitter searching terms, | as 3.02.311
and even now my burthen'd heart would break, 3.02.320
where biting cold would never let grass grow, 3.02.337
and such | as would (but that they dare not) 4.02.187
these kentish rebels would be soon appeas'd! 4.04. 42
yet to recover them would lose my life. 4.07. 66
how would it fare with your departed souls? 4.07.116
i thought ye would never have given out these 4.08. 25 P
who would live turmoiled in the court | and may 4.10. 16
who would not buy thee dear? 5.01. 5
set, | i would speak blasphemy ere bid you fly. 5.02. 85
would i had died a maid | and never seen thee, 3H6 1.01.216
before i would have granted to that act. 1.01.245
i would break a thousand oaths to reign one year 1.02. 17
and were i strong, i would not shun their fury. 1.04. 24
i would prolong a while the traitor's life. 1.04. 52
what would your grace have done unto him now? 1.04. 65
what, was it you that would be england's king? 1.04. 70
i would assay, proud queen, to make thee blush. 1.04.118
the hungry cannibals | would not have touch'd, 1.04.153
have touch'd, would not have stain'd with blood; 1.04.153
against the greeks that would have ent'red troy. 2.01. 52
for hand to hand he would have vanquish'd thee. 2.01. 73
ah, would she break from hence, that this my 2.01. 75
burns me up with flames that tears would quench. 2.01. 84
the words would add more anguish than the wounds 2.01. 99
not to the beast that would usurp their den. 2.02. 12
he, but a duke, would have his son a king, | and 2.02. 21
and would my father had left me no more! 2.02. 50
would thy best friends did know | how it doth 2.02. 54
i would your highness would depart the field, 2.02. 73
i would your highness would depart the field, 2.02. 73
would i were dead, if god's good will were so; 2.05. 19
would bring white hairs unto a quiet grave. 2.05. 40
o that my death would stay these ruthful deeds! 2.05. 95
o, would he did! 2.06. 64
because he would avoid such bitter taunts 2.06. 66
if this right hand would buy two hours' life 2.06. 80
so would you be again to henry, | if he were 3.01. 95
and would you not do much to do them good? 3.02. 38
to do them good i would sustain some harm. 3.02. 39
that would be ten days' wonder at the least. 3.02.113
would he were wasted, marrow, bones, and all, 3.02.125
and spies a far–off shore where he would tread, 3.02.136
alliance | would more have strength'ned this our 4.01. 37
she better would have fitted me or clarence; 4.01. 54
or else you would not have bestow'd the heir 4.01. 56
so your dislikes, to whom i would be pleasing, 4.01. 73
stands, | 'tis to be doubted he would waken him. 4.03. 19
the good old man would fain that all were well, 4.07. 31
thought, at least, he would have said the king, 5.01. 29
why then i would not fly. 5.02. 33
thy tears would wash this cold congealed blood 5.02. 37
and more he would have said, and more he spoke, 5.02. 43
if case some one of you would fly from us, 5.04. 34
had, | the thought of them would have stirr'd up 5.05. 64
didst thou not hear me swear i would not do it? 5.05. 74
i thought it would have mounted. 5.06. 62
i would i were, to be reveng'd on thee. R3 1.02.133
would it were mortal poison for thy sake! 1.02.145
would they were basilisks, to strike thee dead! 1.02.150
i would they were, that i might die at once; 1.02.151
i would i knew thy heart. 1.02.192
if he were dead, what would betide on me? 1.03. 6
would all were well! 1.03. 40
(whom god preserve better than you would wish!) 1.03. 59
i would to god my heart were flint, like 1.03.139
you well serv'd, you would be taught your duty. 1.03.249
i would not spend another such a night | though 1.04. 5
and would not let it forth | to find the empty, 1.04. 38
my soul is heavy, and i fain would sleep. 1.04. 74
i would speak with clarence, and i came hither 1.04. 86 P
he would insinuate with thee but to make thee 1.04.148 P
with sobs | that he would labor my delivery. 1.04.246
came to you, | would not entreat for life? 1.04.260
me, | as you would beg, were you in my distress. 1.04.266
would i wash my hands | of this most grievous 1.04.272
i would he knew that i had sav'd his brother! 1.04.276
i would to god all strifes were well compounded. 2.01. 75
but for my brother not a man would speak, | nor 2.01.127
yet none of you would once beg for his life. 2.01.131
and he would love me dearly as a child. 2.02. 26
which would be so much the more dangerous, | by 2.02.126
ay, mother, but i would not have it so. 2.04. 8
and since, methinks i would not grow so fast, 2.04. 14
grandam, this would have been a biting jest. 2.04. 30
would long ere this have met us on the way. 3.01. 21
would fain have come with me to meet your grace, 3.01. 29
this land | would i be guilty of so deep a sin. 3.01. 43
what, would you have my weapon, little lord? 3.01.122
i would, that i might thank you as you call me. 3.01.123
secure, | i would be so triumphant as i am? 3.02. 82
am not so well provided | as else i would be, 3.04. 45
come, dispatch, the duke would be at dinner. 3.04. 94
would you imagine, or almost believe, | were't 3.05. 35
or that we would, against the form of law, 3.05. 42
i would have had you heard | the traitor speak, 3.05. 56
citizen | only for saying he would make his son 3.05. 77
would they not speak? 3.07. 42
and in no worldly suits would he be mov'd, | to 3.07. 63
would this virtuous prince | take on his grace 3.07. 78
would it might please your grace, | on our 3.07.114
which fondly you would here impose on me. 3.07.147
that i would rather hide me from my greatness — 3.07.161
on him i lay that you would lay on me, | the 3.07.171
alas, why would you heap this care on me? 3.07.204
o, would to god that the inclusive verge | of 4.01. 58
think now what i would speak. 4.02. 10
why, buckingham, i say i would be king. 4.02. 12
dead, | and i would have it suddenly perform'd. 4.02. 19
are they that i would have thee deal upon: 4.02. 74
then would i hide my bones, not rest them here. 4.04. 33
thou didst prophesy the time would come | that i 4.04. 79
i cannot make you what amends i would, 4.04.309
her father's brother | would be her lord? 4.04.338
i, as i may — that which i would i cannot — 5.03. 91
i would these dewy tears were from the ground. 5.03.284
they would restrain the one, distain the other. 5.03.322
that would reduce these bloody days again, | and 5.05. 36
that would with treason wound this fair land's 5.05. 39
of the town, | be sad, as we would make ye. H8 pr 25
would by a good discourser lose some life, 1.01. 41
what his high hatred would effect wants not | a 1.01.107
be to yourself | as you would to your friend. 1.01.136
if with the sap of reason you would quench, | or 1.01.148
that he would please to alter the king's course, 1.01.189
that you would love yourself, and in that love 1.02. 14
wholesome | to those which would not know them, 1.02. 46
(whereof my sovereign would have note), they are 1.02. 48
i would your highness | would give it quick 1.02. 65
highness | would give it quick consideration, 1.02. 66
every day | it would infect his speech — that 1.02.133
men fear the french would prove perfidious, | to 1.02.156
i would have play'd | the part my father meant 1.02.194
his duty) would | have put his knife into him." 1.02.198
there's something more would out of thee; 1.02.202

he would outgo | his father by as much as a 1.02.207
you would swear directly | their very noses had 1.03. 8
one would take it, | that never see 'em pace 1.03. 11
now i would pray our monsieurs | to think an 1.03. 21
sparing would show a worse sin than ill doctrine 1.03. 60
we shall be late else, which i would not be, 1.03. 65
he would have all as merry | as, first, good 1.04. 5
they rested, | i think would better please 'em. 1.04. 13
i would i were, | they should find easy penance. 1.04. 16
as easy as a down–bed would afford it. 1.04. 18
but he would bite none. 1.04. 29
now, | he would kiss you twenty with a breath. 1.04. 30
i told your grace they would talk anon. 1.04. 49
with my love and duty | i would surrender it. 1.04. 81
which they would have your grace | find out, and 1.04. 83
which he fain | would have flung from him; 2.01. 25
i as free forgive you | as i would be forgiven. 2.01. 83
and when you would say something that is sad, 2.01.135
his master would be serv'd before a subject, if 2.02. 7 P
i would your grace would give us but an hour 2.02. 79
i would your grace would give us but an hour 2.02. 79
i would not be so sick though for his place. 2.02. 82
have sent me such a man i would have wish'd for. 2.02.100
and fearing he would rise (he was so virtuous), 2.02.127
was a fool — | for he would needs be virtuous. 2.02.132
would it not grieve an able man to leave | so 2.02.141
the avaunt, it is a pity | would move a monster. 2.03. 11
troth and maidenhead, | i would not be a queen. 2.03. 24
beshrew me, i would, | and venture maidenhead 2.03. 24
and so would you | for all this spice of your 2.03. 25
of your soft cheveril conscience would receive 2.03. 32
yes, troth, and troth. you would not be a queen? 2.03. 34
a threepence bow'd would hire me, | old as i am, 2.03. 36
i would not be a young count in your way | for 2.03. 41
i would not be a queen | for all the world. 2.03. 45
i myself | would for carnarvonshire, although 2.03. 48
that would not be a queen, that would she not, 2.03. 91
that would not be a queen, that would she not, 2.03. 91
would i had no being | if this salute my blood a 2.03.102
would they speak with me? 3.01. 17
me here part of a huswife | (i would be all) 3.01. 25
would all other women | could speak this with as 3.01. 31
i would your grace | would leave your griefs, 3.01. 91
i would your grace | would leave your griefs, 3.01. 92
would you have me | (if you have any justice, 3.01.115
would i had never trod this english earth, | or 3.01.143
wherein he appears | as i would wish mine enemy. 3.02. 28
would he had! 3.02. 42
i would 'twere something that would fret the 3.02.105
'twere something that would fret the string, 3.02.105
there is, betwixt that smile we would aspire to, 3.02.368
out of pity taken | a load would sink a navy — 3.02.383
he would not in mine age | have left me naked to 3.02.456
would shake the press | and make 'em reel before 4.01. 78
i' th' presence | he would say untruths, and be 4.02. 38
the king's request that i would visit you, | who 4.02.116
that his noble grace would have some pity | upon 4.02.139
that which company | would not be friendly to. 5.01. 76
or else no witness | would come against you. 5.01.108
look'd | you would have given me your petition, 5.01.118
they would shame to make me | wait else at door, 5.02. 16
would you were half so honest! 5.02.117
men's prayers then would seek you, not their 5.02.118
what other | would you expect? 5.02.129
would i were fairly out on't! 5.02.144
would try him to the utmost had ye mean, | which 5.02.181
and that i would not for a cow, god save her! 5.03. 27
what would you have me do? 5.03. 31
would i had known no more! 5.04. 59
as wedged with a sigh, would rive in twain, TRO 1.01. 35
i would not, as they term it, praise her, but i 1.01. 44 P
her, but i would somebody had heard her talk 1.01. 45 P
she would be as fair a' friday as helen is on 1.01. 76 P
better at home, if "would i might" were "may." 1.01.114
himself? alas, poor troilus, i would he were! 1.02. 72 P
would 'a were himself! 1.02. 76 P
well, i would my heart were in her body. 1.02. 78 P
idle head, you would eat chickens i' th' shell. 1.02.134 P
would i could see troilus now! 1.02.216 P
helen, to change, would give an eye to boot. 1.02.239 P
if i cannot ward what i would not have hit, i 1.02.268 P
sir, my lord would instantly speak with you. 1.02.272 P
roaring typhon dropp'd, | would seem hyperboles. 1.03.161
what would you 'fore our tent? 1.03.215
but when they would seem soldiers, they have 1.03.237
then would come some matter from him; 2.01. 8 P
i would thou didst itch from head to foot; 2.01. 27 P
i would make thee the loathsomest scab in greece 2.01. 28 P
he would pun thee into shivers with his fist, as 2.01. 39 P
i would have peace and quietness, but the fool 2.01. 83 P
would they but fat their thoughts | with this 2.02. 48
and enmity of those | this quarrel would excite? 2.02.138
it, | but i would have the soil of her fair rape 2.02.148
i would not wish a drop of troyan blood | spent 2.02.197
for i presume brave hector would not lose | so 2.02.203
would it were otherwise: 2.03. 4 P
wit would be out of fashion. 2.03.216 P
'a would have ten shares. 2.03.220 P
would he were a troyan! 2.03.234
i would fain have arm'd to–day, but my nell 3.01.136 P
arm'd to–day, but my nell would not have it so. 3.01.137 P
i would be gone. 3.02.150
what says achilles? would he aught with us? 3.03. 57
would you, my lord, aught with the general? 3.03. 58
and with his arms outstretch'd as he would fly 3.03.167
and better would it fit achilles much | to throw 3.03.207
would the fountain of your mind were clear again 3.03.310 P
would drink up | the lees and dregs of a flat 4.01. 62
our joys no longer, | i would not from thee. 4.02. 11
held off, | and then you would have tarried. 4.02. 18
would he not, a naughty man, let it sleep? 4.02. 32 P
would he were knock'd i' th' head! 4.02. 34
i would not for half troy have you seen here. 4.02. 41
i would they had broke 's neck! 4.02. 76 P
would i were as deep under the earth as i am 4.02. 82 P
would thou hadst ne'er been born! 4.02. 85 P
and would, as i shall pity, i could help! 4.03. 11
which way would hector have it? 4.05. 71
hector would have them fall upon him thus. 4.05.137
i would desire | my famous cousin to our grecian 4.05.150
as to one | that would be rid of such an enemy. 4.05.164
i would my arms could match thee in contention, 4.05.205
i would they could. 4.05.207
sir, i foretold you then what would ensue. 4.05.217
as i would buy thee, view thee limb by limb. 4.05.238
it would discredit the blest gods, proud man, 4.05.247
or a herring without a roe, i would not care; 5.01. 62 P
be menelaus, i would conspire against destiny. 5.01. 63 P
ask me /not what i would be if i were not 5.01. 64 P
in faith, i cannot. what would you have me do? 5.02. 23
what did you swear you would bestow on me? 5.02. 25
would i could meet that rogue diomed! 5.02.190 P
i would croak like a raven, i would bode, i 5.02.191 P
i would croak like a raven, i would bode, i 5.02.191 P
croak like a raven, i would bode, i would bode. 5.02.191 P
troilus, i would not have you fight to–day. 5.03. 50
i would fain see them meet, that that same young 5.04. 5 P
thou take the river styx, | i would swim after. 5.04. 20
i would laugh at that miracle — yet, in a sort, 5.04. 34 P
i would correct him. 5.06. 3
i would have been much more a fresher man, | had 5.06. 20
half–supp'd sword, that frankly would have fed, 5.08. 19
some galled goose of winchester would hiss. 5.10. 54
what authority surfeits /on would relieve us. COR 1.01. 16 P
if they would yield us but the superfluity while 1.01. 17 P
would you proceed especially against caius 1.01. 26 P
would all the rest were so! 1.01. 53 P
what would you have, you curs, | that like nor 1.01.168
most that | which would increase his evil. 1.01.179
in awe, which else | would feed on one another? 1.01.188
would the nobility lay aside their ruth | and 1.01.197
as they would hang them on the horns a' th' moon 1.01.213
thing but what i am, | i would wish me only he. 1.01.232
of his bed where he would show most love. 1.03. 5 P
considering how honor would become such a person 1.03. 10 P
i therein would have found issue. 1.03. 21 P
you would be another penelope: 1.03. 82 P
come, i would your cambric were sensible as your 1.03. 84 P
in troth, i think she would. 1.03.106 P
have you run | from slaves that apes would beat! 1.04. 36
doublets that hangmen would | bury with those 1.05. 6
top of praises vouch'd, | would seem but modest; 1.09. 25
i would i were a roman, for i cannot, | being a 1.10. 4
would i | wash my fierce hand in 's heart. 1.10. 26
as the hungry plebeians would the noble martius. 2.01. 10 P
or else your actions would grow wondrous single; 2.01. 36 P
more of your conversation would infect my brain, 2.01. 94 P
i would not have been so fidius'd for all the 2.01.130 P
never would he | appear i' th' market–place, nor 2.01.232
he would miss it rather | than carry it but by 2.01.237
that to 's power he would | have made them mules 2.01.246
would pluck reproof and rebuke from every ear 2.02. 33 P
i would you rather had been silent. 2.02. 61
he covets less | than misery itself would give, 2.02.127
to issue out of one skull, they would fly east, 2.03. 22 P
which way do you judge my wit would fly? 2.03. 26 P
the fourth would return for conscience' sake to 2.03. 32 P
if he would incline to the people, there was 2.03. 38 P
i would they would forget me, like the virtues 2.03. 57
i would they would forget me, like the virtues 2.03. 57
the dust on antique time would lie unswept, 2.03.119
and the honor go | to one that would do thus. 2.03.123
indeed i would be consul. 2.03.131
it in scorn, | "i would be consul," says he; 2.03.168
nature | would think upon you for your voices, 2.03.188
or else it would have gall'd his surly nature, 2.03.195
that he would pawn his fortunes | to hopeless 3.01. 15
was touch'd, | they would not thread the gates. 3.01.124
not having the power to do the good it would, 3.01.160
here's he that would take from you all your 3.01.181
martius would have all from you; 3.01.194
and temp'rately proceed to what you would | thus 3.01.218
i would they were barbarians, as they are, 3.01.237
he would not flatter neptune for his trident, 3.01.255
i would they were a–bed! 3.01.260
i would they were in tiber! 3.01.261
is this viper | that would depopulate the city, 3.01.263
i may be heard, i would crave a word or two, 3.01.281
would you have me | false to my nature? 3.02. 14
i would have had you put your power well on 3.02. 17
for the whole state, i would put mine armor on, 3.02. 34
which else would put you to your fortune and 3.02. 60
i would dissemble with my nature where | my 3.02. 62
i would say | "thou liest" unto thee with a 3.03. 72
i would not buy | their mercy at the price of 3.03. 90
then if i would | speak that — 3.03.115
me | with precepts that would make invincible 4.01. 10
i would i had the power | to say so to my 4.02. 15
i would my son | were in arabia, and thy tribe 4.02. 23
i would he had continued to his country | as he 4.02. 30
i would he had. 4.02. 32
"i would he had"? 4.02. 33
i would the gods had nothing else to do | but to 4.02. 45
it would unclog my heart | of what lies heavy 4.02. 47
but a small thing would make it flame again; 4.03. 21 P
what would you have, friend? 4.05. 7 P
men i' th' world | i would have 'voided thee; 4.05. 82
which not to cut would show thee but a fool, 4.05. 97
we would muster all | from twelve to seventy, 4.05.128
finger and his thumb as one would set up a top. 4.05.153 P
would i were hang'd but i thought there was more 4.05.157 P
i would not be a roman, of all nations; 4.05.175 P
the commonwealth doth stand, and so would do, 4.06. 14
these are a side that would be glad to have 4.06.150
would half my wealth | would buy this for a lie! 4.06.159
would half my wealth | would buy this for a lie! 4.06.160
than i thought he would | when first i did 4.07. 9
he would not seem to know me. 5.01. 8
coriolanus | he would not answer to; 5.01. 12
sure if you | would be your country's pleader, 5.01. 36
what he would do | he sent in writing after me; 5.01. 67
what he would not, | bound with an oath to yield 5.01. 68
size that verity | would without lapsing suffer. 5.02. 19
for i would not speak with him till after dinner 5.02. 34 P
i were here, he would use me with estimation. 5.02. 52 P
writ it for thy sake, | and would have sent it. 5.02. 91
and state of bodies would bewray what life | we 5.03. 95
this boy, that cannot tell what he would have, 5.03.174
my stead, would you have heard | a mother less? 5.03.192
that i would have spoke of: 5.06. 28
or move the people | with what he would say, let 5.06. 55
whom worthily you would have now succeed, | and TIT 1.01. 40
andronicus, would thou were shipp'd to hell, 1.01.206
hue | that i would choose were i to choose anew. 1.01.262
of mine, | my sons would never so dishonor me. 1.01.295
he that would vouch it in any place but here. 1.01.360
what, would you bury him in my despite? 1.01.361
i would not part a bachelor from the priest. 1.01.488
i would not for a million of gold | the cause 2.01. 49
nor would your noble mother for much more | be 2.01. 51
discord's ground, the music would not please. 2.01. 70
would i propose to achieve her whom i love. 2.01. 80
certain snatch or so | would serve your turns. 2.01. 96
would you had hit it too! 2.01. 97
would it offend you then | that both should 2.01.100
that what you cannot as you would achieve, | you 2.01.106
he that had wit would think that i had none, 2.03. 1
would make such fearful and confused cries, | as 2.03.102
straight they told me they would bind me here 2.03.106
and if she do, i would i were an eunuch. 2.03.128
but fierce andronicus would not relent. 2.03.165
i do dream, would all my wealth would wake me! 2.04. 13
i do dream, would all my wealth would wake me! 2.04. 13
he would not then have touch'd them for his life 2.04. 47
he would have dropp'd his knife, and fell asleep 2.04. 50
if they did hear, | they would not mark me; 3.01. 34
if they did mark, | they would not pity me; 3.01. 35
in this plight, | it would have madded me; 3.01.104
no, no, they would not do so foul a deed; 3.01.118
now would she say | that to her brother which i 3.01.144
an enemy, | and would usurp upon my wat'ry eyes, 3.01.268
o, would thou wert as thou tofore hast been! 3.01.293
somewhither would she have thee go with her. 4.01. 11
oft, | extremity of griefs would make men mad; 4.01. 19
and would not, but in fury, fright my youth, 4.01. 24
what would she find? 4.01. 46
afoot, | she would applaud andronicus' conceit, 4.02. 30
i would we had a thousand roman dames | at such 4.02. 41
and that would she for twenty thousand more. 4.02. 45
o, that which i would hide from heaven's eye, 4.02. 59
as who would say, in rome no justice were. 4.04. 20
things | as willingly as one would kill a fly, 5.01.142
if there be devils, would i were a devil, | to 5.01.147
and, would you represent our queen aright, | it 5.02. 89
but would it please thee, good andronicus, | to 5.02.111
what would you say if i should let you speak? 5.02.178
because i would be sure to have all well, | to 5.03. 31
countless and infinite, yet would i pay them! 5.03.159
ev'n with all my heart | would i were dead, so 5.03.173
i did | would i perform if i might have my will. 5.03.188
grow, | we would as willingly give cure as know. ROM 1.01.155
i would thou wert so happy by thy stay | to hear 1.01.158
i would say thou hadst suck'd wisdom from thy 1.03. 68
in a fair lady's ear, | such as would please; 1.05. 24
i would not for the wealth of all this town 1.05. 69
he that follows here, that would not dance? 1.05.132
fair for which love groan'd for and would die, 2.pr. 3
brightness of her cheek would shame those stars, 2.02. 19
would through the airy region stream so bright 2.02. 21
that birds would sing and think it were not 2.02. 22
a rose | by any other word would smell as sweet; 2.02. 44
so romeo would, were he not romeo call'd, 2.02. 45
had i it written, i would tear the word. 2.02. 57
i would not for the world they saw thee here. 2.02. 74
else would a maiden blush bepaint my cheek | for 2.02. 86
fain would i dwell on form, fain, fain deny 2.02. 88
and yet i would it were to give again. 2.02.129
else would i tear the cave where echo lies, 2.02.161
'tis almost morning, i would have thee gone — 2.02.176
i would i were thy bird. 2.02.182
sweet, so would i, | yet i should kill thee with 2.02.182
would i were sleep and peace, so sweet to rest! 2.02.187
i would have made it short, for i was come to 2.04. 98 P
one paris, that would fain lay knife aboard; 2.04.202 P
rosemary, that it would do you good to hear it. 2.04.212 P
she would be as swift in motion as a ball; 2.05. 13
my words would bandy her to my sweet love, | and 2.05. 14
i would thou hadst my bones, and i thy news. 2.05. 27
it beats as it would fall in twenty pieces. 2.05. 49
have none shortly, for one would kill the other. 3.01. 16 P
eye but such an eye would spy out such a quarrel 3.01. 21 P
as phaeton would whip you to the west, | and 3.02. 3
who ever would have thought it? 3.02. 42
that villain cousin would have kill'd my husband 3.02.101
my husband lives that tybalt would have slain, 3.02.105
tybalt's dead that would have slain my husband. 3.02.106
i would forget it fain, | but o, it presses to 3.02.109
tybalt would kill thee, | but thou slewest 3.03.137
company, | i would have been a–bed an hour ago. 3.04. 7
my lord, i would that thursday were to–morrow. 3.04. 29
o, now i would they had chang'd voices too, 3.05. 32
would none but i might venge my cousin's death! 3.05. 86
but a man | to bear a poison, i would temper it, 3.05. 97
i would the fool were married to her grave! 3.05.140
proportion'd as one's thought would wish a man, 3.05.182
i would i knew not why it should be slowed. 4.01. 16
as that is desperate which we would prevent. 4.01. 70
with music straight, | for so he said he would. 4.04. 23
here lives a caitiff wretch would sell it him." 5.01. 52
of twenty men, it would dispatch you straight. 5.01. 79
seal'd up the doors and would not let us forth, 5.02. 11
yet put it out, for i would not be seen. 5.03. 2
betroth'd and would have married her perforce 5.03.238
or in my cell there would she kill herself. 5.03.242
and she, too desperate, would not go with me, 5.03.263
would be well express'd | in our condition. TIM 1.01. 76
as 'tis extoll'd, | it would unclew me quite. 1.01.168
'tis rated | as those which sell would give; 1.01.169
i myself would have no power; 1.02. 36 P
would all those flatterers were thine enemies 1.02. 81 P
my lord, that you would once use our hearts, 1.02. 85 P
and would most resemble sweet instruments hung 1.02. 98 P
before me now | would one day stamp upon me. 1.02.144

the worst is filthy, and would not hold taking, 1.02.153 P
would i were gently put out of office | before i 1.02.201
wert not sullen), | i would be good to thee. 1.02.237
too, there would be none left to rail upon thee, 1.02.239 P
if i would sell my horse and buy twenty moe 2.01. 7
would we were all discharg'd! 2.02. 12
would we could see you at corinth! 2.02. 70 P
would i had a rod in my mouth, that i might 2.02. 76 P
ay, would they serv'd us! 2.02. 93 P
so would i — as good a trick as ever hangman 2.02. 94 P
you would not hear me; 2.02.127
you would throw them off, | and say you /found 2.02.134
if i would broach the vessels of my love, | and 2.02.177
cannot | do what they would, are sorry; 2.02.206
may catch a wrench — would all were well — 2.02.209
i would i could not think it! 2.02.232
'tis, if he would not keep so good a house. 3.01. 22 P
spend less, and yet he would embrace no counsel, 3.01. 26 P
but i would not, for the wealth of athens, i had 3.02. 51 P
me, | i would have put my wealth into donation, 3.02. 83
under hot ardent zeal would set whole realms on 3.03. 33 P
business, but he would not hear my excuse. 3.06. 14 P
what would he have borrow'd of you? 3.06. 19 P
with that spur as he would to the lip of his 3.06. 66 P
to borrow of men, men would forsake the gods. 3.06. 75 P
who would not wish to be from wealth exempt, 4.02. 31
who would be so mock'd with glory, or to live 4.02. 33
and ulcerous sores | would cast the gorge at, 4.03. 41
dost not keep a dog, | whom i would imitate. 4.03.201
thus would i eat it. 4.03.282
if not, i would it were. 4.03.286
would poison were obedient and knew my mind! 4.03.296 P
thou wert the lion, the fox would beguile thee; 4.03.328 P
if thou wert the lamb, the fox would eat thee; 4.03.329 P
thou wert the fox, the lion would suspect thee, 4.03.330 P
wert the ass, thy dullness would torment thee, 4.03.332 P
the wolf, thy greediness would afflict thee, and 4.03.334 P
pride and wrath would confound thee and make 4.03.336 P
would thou wert clean enough to spit upon! 4.03.359
i would my tongue could rot them off! 4.03.365
would thou wouldst burst! 4.03.369
would 'twere so! 4.03.392
those that would mischief me than those that do! 4.03.468
how fain would i have hated all mankind, | and 4.03.499
it is vain that you would speak with timon; 5.01.116
thank them, and would send them back the plague, 5.01.137
workman, i am but, as you would say, a cobbler. JC 1.01. 11 P
who else would soar above the view of men, | and 1.01. 74
into what dangers would you lead me, cassius, 1.02. 63
that you would have me seek into myself | for 1.02. 64
then must i think you would not have it so. 1.02. 81
i would not, cassius, yet i love him well. 1.02. 82
what is it that you would impart to me? 1.02. 84
there was a brutus once that would have brook'd 1.02.159
what you would work me to, i have some aim. 1.02.163
i would not (so with love i might entreat you) 1.02.166
would he were fatter! 1.02.198
pull'd me by the cloak, would you speak with me? 1.02.215 P
that, to my thinking, he would fain have had it. 1.02.240 P
if i would not have taken him at a word, i would 1.02.267 P
i would i might go to hell among the rogues. 1.02.267 P
their mothers, they would have done no less. 1.02.275 P
send word to you he would be there to–morrow. 1.03. 38
but if you would consider the true cause | why 1.03. 62
poor man, i know he would not be a wolf, | but 1.03.104
and that which would appear offense in us, | his 1.03.158
i would it were my fault to sleep so soundly. 2.01. 4
he would be crown'd: 2.01. 12
would run to these and these extremities; 2.01. 31
hatch'd, would as his kind grow mischievous, 2.01. 33
he would embrace the means to come by it. 2.01.259
here is a sick man that would speak with you. 2.01.310
would you were not sick! 2.01.315
they would not have you to stir forth to–day. 2.02. 38
i would have had thee there and here again | ere 2.04. 4
if i could pray to move, prayers would move me; 3.01. 59
it would become me better than to close | in 3.01.202
who is here so base that would be a bondman? 3.02. 29 P
who is here so rude that would not be a roman? 3.02. 31 P
he would not take the crown, | therefore 'tis 3.02.112
and they would go and kiss dead caesar's wounds, 3.02.132
for if you should, o, what would come of it? 3.02.146
were an antony | would ruffle up your spirits, 3.02.228
a flatterer's would not, though they do appear 4.03. 91
ill spirit, i would hold more talk with thee. 4.03.288
you said the enemy would not come down, | but 5.01. 2
they stand, and would have parley. 5.01. 21
make forth, the generals would have some words. 5.01. 25
yet would not so have been, | durst i have done 5.03. 47
night hangs upon mine eyes, my bones would rest, 5.05. 41
nor would we deign him burial of his men | till MAC 1.02. 60
would they had stay'd! 1.03. 82
would thou hadst less deserv'd, | that the 1.04. 18
so, | would have inform'd for preparation. 1.05. 33
scarcely more | than would make up his message. 1.05. 37
which would be worn now in their newest gloss, 1.07. 34
letting "i dare not" wait upon "i would," | like 1.07. 44
you were, you would | be so much more the man. 1.07. 50
did then adhere, and yet you would make both: 1.07. 52
i would, while it was smiling in my face, | have 1.07. 56
like lead upon me, | and yet i would not sleep. 2.01. 7
we would spend it in some words upon that 2.01. 23
that business, | if you would grant the time. 2.01. 24
i would thou couldst! 2.02. 71
in a woman's ear | would murther as it fell. 2.03. 86
as they would make | war with mankind. 2.04. 17
and with those | that would make good of bad, 2.04. 41
of nature | reigns that which would be fear'd. 3.01. 50
that i would set my life on any chance, | to 3.01.112
i would attend his leisure | for a few words. 3.02. 3
fear) would well become | a woman's story at a 3.04. 63
when the brains were out, the man would die, 3.04. 78
would he were here! 3.04. 90
it would be my disgrace and your discomfort. 4.02. 29
if you would not, it were a good sign that i 4.02. 62 P
all things foul would wear the brows of grace, 4.03. 23
i would not be the villain that thou think'st 4.03. 35
there would be hands uplifted in my right; 4.03. 42
all continent impediments would o'erbear | that 4.03. 64
and my more–having would be as a sauce | to make 4.03. 81
would not betray | the devil to his fellow, and 4.03.128
your eye in scotland | would create soldiers, 4.03.187
would i could answer | this comfort with the 4.03.192
that would be howl'd out in the desert air, 4.03.194
heaven look on, | and would not take their part? 4.03.224
yet who would have thought the old man to have 5.01. 39 P
i would not have such a heart in my bosom for 5.01. 55 P
would to the bleeding and the grim alarm 5.02. 4
which the poor heart would fain deny, and dare 5.03. 28
health, | i would applaud thee to the very echo, 5.03. 53
drug, | would scour these english hence? 5.03. 56
been, my senses would have cool'd | to hear a 5.05. 10
hair | would at a dismal treatise rouse and stir 5.05. 12
there would have been a time for such a word. 5.05. 18
i would the friends we miss were safe arriv'd. 5.09. 1
i would not wish them to a fairer death. 5.09. 15
which would be planted newly with the time, | as 5.09. 31
it would be spoke to. HAM 1.01. 45
o, that this too too sallied flesh would melt, 1.02.129
would have mourn'd longer — married with my 1.02.151
i would not hear your enemy say so, | nor shall 1.02.170
would i had met my dearest foe in heaven | or 1.02.182
itself to motion, like as it would speak; 1.02.217
i would i had been there. 1.02.234
it would have much amaz'd you. 1.02.235
would the night were come! 1.02.255
i would not, in plain terms, from this time 1.03.132
whose lightest word | would harrow up thy soul, 1.05. 16
say you then, would heart of man once think it? 1.05.121
or "we could, and if we would," | or "if we list 1.05.176
my lord, that would dishonor him. 2.01. 27
ay, my lord, | i would know that. 2.01. 37
your party in converse, him you would sound, 2.01. 42
such perusal of my face | as 'a would draw it. 2.01. 88
i would fain prove so. 2.02.131
been such a time — i would fain know that — 2.02.153
then i would you were so honest a man. 2.02.176 P
and those that would make mouths at him while my 2.02.364 P
fortune's state would treason have pronounc'd. 2.02.511
would have made milch the burning eyes of heaven 2.02.517
lines, which i would set down and insert in't, 2.02.542 P
what would he do, | had he the motive and /the 2.02.560
he would drown the stage with tears, | and 2.02.562
when we would bring him on to some confession 3.01. 9
for who would bear the whips and scorns of time, 3.01. 69
who would fardels bear, | to grunt and sweat 3.01. 75
i would have such a fellow whipt for o'erdoing 3.02. 12 P
meet what i would have well and it destroy! 3.02.221
and fain i would beguile | the tedious day with 3.02.226
it would cost you a groaning to take off mine 3.02.249 P
would not this, sir, and a forest of feathers — 3.02.275 P
him to his purgation would perhaps plunge him 3.02.306 P
of me, as if you would drive me into a toil? 3.02.347 P
you would play upon me, you would seem to know 3.02.364 P
play upon me, you would seem to know my stops, 3.02.364 P
you would pluck out the heart of my mystery, you 3.02.365 P
you would sound me from my lowest note to /the 3.02.366 P
my lord, the queen would speak with you, and 3.02.374 P
/business /as /the day | would quake to look on. 3.02.392
that would be scann'd: 3.03. 75
and would it were not so, you are my mother. 3.04. 16
what judgment | would step from this to this? 3.04. 71
sense | is apoplex'd, for madness would not err, 3.04. 73
what would your gracious figure? 3.04.104
preaching to stones, | would make them capable. 3.04.127
will reword, which madness | would gambol from. 3.04.144
would from a paddock, from a bat, a gib, | such 3.04.190
who would do so? 3.04.191
we would not understand what was most fit, | but 4.01. 20
if that his majesty would aught with us, | we 4.04. 5
to pay five ducats, five, i would not farm it; 4.04. 20
what would she have? 4.05. 3
indeed would make one think there might be 4.05. 12
"'so would i 'a' done, by yonder sun, | and thou 4.05. 65
but weep to think they would lay him i' th' cold 4.05. 69 P
that treason can but peep to what it would, 4.05.125
i would give you some violets, but they wither'd 4.05.184 P
what are they that would speak with me? 4.06. 1 P
/a /wind, | would have reverted to my bow again, 4.07. 23
that we would do, | we should do when we would; 4.07.118
that we would do, | we should do when we would; 4.07.119
for this "would" changes, | and hath abatements 4.07.119
what would you undertake | to show yourself 4.07.124
i have a speech a' fire that fain would blaze, 4.07.190
now o'erreaches, one that would circumvent god, 5.01. 79 P
kind of fighting | that would not let me sleep. 5.02. 5
continent of what part a gentleman would see. 5.02.111 P
him inventorially would dozy th' arithmetic of 5.02.114 P
is his mirror, and who else would trace him, his 5.02.119 P
i would you did, sir, yet, in faith, if you did, 5.02.134 P
faith, if you did, it would not much approve me. 5.02.135 P
the phrase would be more germane to the matter, 5.02.158 P
i would it /might /be hangers till then. 5.02.160 P
for nine, and it would come to immediate trial, 5.02.168 P
if your lordship would vouchsafe the answer. 5.02.169 P
/gain–giving, as would perhaps trouble a woman. 5.02.216 P
what is it you would see? 5.02.362
i would not from your love make such a stray LR 1.01.209
grace, | i would prefer him to a better place. 1.01.274
if our father would sleep till i wak'd him, you 1.02. 52 P
respect of that, i would fain think it were not. 1.02. 64 P
it would make a great gap in your own honor and 1.02. 84 P
i would unstate myself to be in a due resolution 1.02. 99 P
mischief of your person it would scarcely allay. 1.02.163 P
your countenance which i would fain call master. 1.04. 28 P
me in the roundest manner, he would not. 1.04. 55 P
he would not? 1.04. 56 P
you and tell my daughter i would speak with her. 1.04. 76 P
would i had two coxcombs and two daughters! 1.04.105 P
thy fool to lie — i would fain learn to lie. 1.04.180 P
thing than a fool, and yet i would not be thee, 1.04.186 P
the fault | would not scape censure, nor the 1.04.210
i would you would make use of your good wisdom 1.04.219
i would you would make use of your good wisdom 1.04.219
the slaughter, | if my cap would buy a halter, 1.04.320
keep me in temper, i would not be mad! 1.05. 47
some blood drawn on me would beget opinion | of 2.01. 33
if i would stand against thee, would the reposal 2.01. 68
against thee, would the reposal | of any trust, 2.01. 68
what /i /should deny | (as this i would, /ay, 2.01. 71
would he deny his letter, said he? 2.01. 78
o lady, lady, shame would have it hid! 2.01. 93
lipsbury pinfold, i would make thee care for me. 2.02. 9 P
they could not, would not do't. 2.04. 23
again, i would have none but knaves follow it, 2.04. 76 P
the king would speak with cornwall, the dear 2.04.101
the dear father | would with his daughter speak, 2.04.102
i would have all well betwixt you. 2.04.120
i would divorce me from thy /mother's tomb, 2.04.131
sister in the least | would fail her obligation. 2.04.142
her letter, | that she would soon be here. 2.04.184
leave to ponder | on things would hurt me more. 3.04. 25
he said it would be thus, poor banish'd man. 3.04.164
because i would not see thy cruel nails | pluck 3.07. 56
would have buoy'd up | and quench'd the stelled 3.07. 60
us hate thee, | life would not yield to age. 4.01. 12
would stretch thy spirits up into the air. 4.02. 23
would i could meet /him, madam! 4.05. 39
all beneath the moon | would i not leap upright. 4.06. 27
when the thunder would not peace at my bidding, 4.06.102 P
i would not take this from report; 4.06.141
why, this would make a man a man of salt, | to 4.06.195
vices of thy mistress | as badness would desire. 4.06.254
(wife, so i would say) affectionate servant, 4.06.269 P
would i were assur'd | of my condition! 4.07. 55
let her who would be rid of him devise | his 5.01. 64
when 'tis told, o, that my heart would burst! 5.03.183
that we the pain of death would hourly die 5.03.186
biting falchion | i would have made /them skip. 5.03.278
that would upon the rack of this tough world 5.03.315
by heaven, i rather would have been his hangman. OTH 1.01. 34
i would not follow him then. 1.01. 40
were i the moor, i would not be iago. 1.01. 57
i thus would play and trifle with your reverence 1.01.132
who would be a father! 1.01.164
o, would you had had her! 1.01.175
i would not my unhoused free condition | put 1.02. 26
would ever have, t' incur a general mock, | run 1.02. 69
to hear | would desdemona seriously incline; 1.03.146
still the house affairs would draw her /thence, 1.03.147
heart | that i would all my pilgrimage dilate, 1.03.153
how to tell my story, | and that would woo her. 1.03.166
i think this tale would win my daughter too. 1.03.171
with all my heart | i would keep from thee. 1.03.195
child, | for thy escape would teach me tyranny, 1.03.197
what would you, desdemona? 1.03.247
ere i would say i would drown myself for the 1.03.314 P
ere i would say i would drown myself for the 1.03.315 P
hen, i would change my humanity with a baboon. 1.03.316 P
baseness of our natures would conduct us to most 1.03.328 P
if i would time expend with such /a snipe | but 1.03.385
would she give you so much of her lips | as of 2.01.100
she oft bestows on me, | you would have enough. 2.01.102
would they were clyster–pipes for your sake! 2.01.176 P
bless'd, she would never have lov'd the moor. 2.01.252 P
cyprus gallants that would fain have a measure 2.03. 31 P
could well wish courtesy would invent some other 2.03. 35 P
and would do much | to cure him of this evil. 2.03.143
and would in action glorious i had lost | those 2.03.186
even so as one would beat his offenseless dog to 2.03.274 P
as hydra, such an answer would stop them all. 2.03.305 P
it, | that he would steal away so guilty–like, 3.03. 39
soul | what you would ask me that i should deny, 3.03. 69
those that be not, would they might seem none! 3.03.127
would take no notice, nor build yourself a 3.03.150
i would not have your free and noble nature, 3.03.199
i would i might entreat your honor | to scan 3.03.244
would i were satisfied! 3.03.390
you would be satisfied? 3.03.393
would? nay, and i will. 3.03.393
would you, the /supervisor, grossly gape on? 3.03.395
and then, sir, would he gripe and wring my hand; 3.03.421
and bid me, when my fate would have me wiv'd, 3.04. 64
then would to /god that i had never seen't! 3.04. 77
i would not be delay'd. 3.04.114
(as like enough it will) i would have it copied. 3.04.190
by heaven, i would most gladly have forgot it. 4.01. 19
nature would not invest herself in such 4.01. 40 P
i would on great occasion speak with you. 4.01. 58
would you would bear your fortune like a man! 4.01. 61
would you would bear your fortune like a man! 4.01. 61
for i would very fain speak with you. 4.01.166 P
i would have him nine years a–killing. 4.01.178 P
i would do much | t' atone them, for the love i 4.01.232
my lord, this would not be believ'd in venice, 4.01.242
each drop she falls would prove a crocodile. 4.01.246
what would you with her, sir? 4.01.250
ay, you did wish that i would make her turn. 4.01.252
he might he is not, | i would to heaven he were! 4.01.272
yet would i knew | that stroke would prove the 4.01.273
i knew | that stroke would prove the worst! 4.01.274
aches at thee, would thou hadst never been born! 4.02. 69
cheeks, | that would to cinders burn up modesty, 4.02. 75
would it not make one weep? 4.02.127
to deliver desdemona would half have corrupted a 4.02.187 P
and that you would have me to do? 4.02.231 P
i would you had never seen him! 4.03. 18
so would not i. 4.03. 19
know a lady in venice would have walk'd barefoot 4.03. 38 P
why, would not you? 4.03. 65
i would not do such a thing for a joint–ring, 4.03. 72 P
who would not make her husband a cuckold to make 4.03. 76 P
if i would do such a wrong | for the whole world 4.03. 78
to th' vantage as would store the world they 4.03. 85 P
i would not kill thy unprepared spirit, | no, 5.02. 31
i would not kill thy soul. 5.02. 32
i would not have thee linger in thy pain. 5.02. 88
o, good my lord, i would speak a word with you! 5.02. 90
if heaven would make me such another world | of 5.02.144
this sight would make him do a desperate turn, 5.02.207
caesar's, i would say — both? ANT 1.01. 28
better than i, where would you choose it? 1.02. 60 P
they would make themselves whores but they'd 1.02. 77 P

would i had never seen her! 1.02.152
been blest withal would have discredited your 1.02.155 P
would she had never given you leave to come! 1.03. 21
i would i had thy inches, thou shouldst know 1.03. 40
of rest, would purge | by any desperate change. 1.03. 53
something it is i would — | o, my oblivion is a 1.03. 89
the gilded puddle | which beasts would cough at; 1.04. 63
would stand and make his eyes grow in my brow; 1.05. 32
there would he anchor his aspect, and die | with 1.05. 33
who neigh'd so high that what i would have spoke 1.05. 49
for he would shine on those | that make their 1.05. 55
amorous surfeiter would have donn'd his helm 2.01. 33
antonio's beard, | i would not shave't to–day. 2.02. 8
i would you had her spirit in such another; 2.02. 62
would we had all such wives, that the men might 2.02. 65 P
edge to edge | a' th' world, i would pursue it. 2.02.116
import their dangers, | would then be nothing. 2.02.133
truths would be tales, | where now half tales be 2.02.133
both | would each to other and all loves to both 2.02.135
if i would say, "agrippa, be it so," | to make 2.02.141
would we had spoke together! 2.02.164
would i had never come from thence, nor you 2.03. 11 P
say to ventidius i would speak with him. 2.03. 32
o, i would thou didst; 2.05. 93
take no offense that i would not offend you; 2.05. 99
but that they would | have one man but a man? 2.06. 18
pompey, would ne'er have made this treaty. 2.06. 82 P
divine of this unity, i would not prophesy so. 2.06.117 P
who would not have his wife so? 2.06.124 P
would it were all, | that it might go on wheels! 2.07. 92
what would you more? 2.07.119
would you praise caesar, say "caesar," go no 3.02. 13
and her forehead | as low as she would wish it. 3.03. 34
wars 'twixt you twain would be | as if the world 3.04. 30
would not let him partake in the glory of the 3.05. 8 P
the mares would bear | a soldier and his horse. 3.07. 8
i little thought | you would have followed. 3.11. 56
by my affection, would | obey it on all cause. 3.11. 67
that would make his will | lord of his reason. 3.13. 3
whose ministers would prevail | under the 3.13. 23
it much would please him, | that of his fortunes 3.13. 67
but it would warm his spirits | to hear from me 3.13. 69
unto a muss, kings would start forth | and cry, 3.13. 91
would you mingle eyes | with one that ties his 3.13.156
would thou and those thy scars had once 4.05. 2
thee, would have still | followed thy heels. 4.05. 5
mine office, | or would have done't myself. 4.06. 27
to camp this host, we all would sup together, 4.08. 33
i would they'ld fight i' th' fire or i' th' air; 4.10. 3
what would my lord? 4.14. 55
i would not see't. 4.14. 77
and that your rage | would not be purg'd, she 4.14.124
lips that power, | thus would i wear them out. 4.15. 40
life in rome | would be eternal in our triumph. 5.01. 66
if your master | would have a queen his beggar, 5.02. 16
and would gladly | look him i' th' face. 5.02. 31
say, i would die. 5.02. 70
would i might never | o'ertake pursu'd success, 5.02.102
i am loath to tell you what i would you knew. 5.02.107
should we shift estates, yours would be mine. 5.02.152
but i would not be the party that should desire 5.02.245 P
as she would catch another antony | in her 5.02.347
there would be something failing | in him that CYM 1.01. 21
to live, | the loathness to depart would grow. 1.01.108
would i were | a neat–herd's daughter, and my 1.01.148
i would they were in afric both together, 1.01.167
he would not suffer me | to bring him to the 1.01.170
sir, i would advise you to shift a shirt; 1.02. 1 P
the villain would not stand me. 1.02. 14 P
i would they had not come between us. 1.02. 22 P
so would i, till you had measur'd how long a 1.02. 23 P
would there had been some hurt done! 1.02. 34 P
i would thou grew'st unto the shores o' th' 1.03. 1
i would have broke mine eye–strings, crack'd 1.03. 17
him | how i would think on him at certain hours 1.03. 27
and by such two that would by all likelihood 1.04. 50 P
as i was in france, i would abate her nothing, 1.04. 68 P
would hazard the winning both of first and last. 1.04. 93 P
would i had put my estate and my neighbor's on 1.04.123 P
what lady would you choose to assail? 1.04.125 P
of my speeches, and would undergo what's spoken, 1.04.140 P
'twixt two such shes would chatter this way, and 1.06. 40
for idiots in this case of favor would | be 1.06. 42
would force the feeler's soul | to th' oath of 1.06.101
empery | would make the great'st king double — 1.06.121
him that broke it, it would have run all out. 2.01. 9 P
would he had been one of my rank! 2.01. 15 P
bows toward her, and would under–peep her lids, 2.02. 20
ten thousand meaner moveables | would testify, 2.02. 30
it would make any man cold to lose. 2.03. 3 P
i would this music would come. 2.03. 11 P
i would this music would come. 2.03. 11 P
say i yield being silent, | i would not speak. 2.03. 95
if i would lose it for a revenue | of any king's 2.03.143
i would i were so sure | to win the king as i am 2.04. 1
state, and wish | that warmer days would come. 2.04. 6
i am sure | she would not lose it. 2.04.124
now say, what would augustus caesar with us? 3.01. 1
which not to read would show the britains cold. 3.01. 75
such assaults | as would take in some virtue. 3.02. 9
creatures, would even renew me with your eyes. 3.02. 42 P
no costlier than would fit | a franklin's 3.02. 76
thus | would be interpreted a thing perplex'd 3.04. 7
which to read | would be even mortal to me. 3.04. 18
madam, | i thought you would not back again. 3.04.116
as honest, then | my purpose would prove well. 3.04.119
my modesty, not death on't, | i would adventure. 3.04.153
would you in their serving | (and with what 3.04.170
our expectation that it would be thus | hath 3.05. 28
and truly, i would think thee an honest man. 3.05.113 P
i would these garments were come. 3.05.132 P
would i had wings to follow it! 3.05.155 P
the sweat of industry would dry and die, | but 3.06. 31
i have stol'n nought, nor would not, though i 3.06. 48
i would have left it on the board so soon | as i 3.06. 50
would it had been so, that they | had been my 3.06. 75
would i could free't! 3.06. 79
that it would fly | from so divine a temple to 4.02. 54
would, polydore, thou hadst not done't! 4.02.155
would i had done't! 4.02.156
i would revenges, | that possible strength might 4.02.159
would seek us through | and put us to our answer 4.02.160
the raddock would, | with charitable bill (o 4.02.224
whose answer would be death | drawn on with 4.04. 13
those that would die or e'er resist are grown 5.03. 50
to–day how many would have given their honors 5.03. 66
i think he would change places with his officer; 5.04.174 P
unless a man would marry a gallows and beget 5.04.198 P
i would we were all of one mind, and one mind 5.04.203 P
than a physician | would this report become? 5.05. 28
i would not | believe her lips in opening it. 5.05. 41
he, i am sure | he would have spoke to us. 5.05.126
that | which, to be spoke, would torture thee. 5.05.140
o, would | our viands had been poison'd, or at 5.05.155
and would so, had it been a carbuncle | of 5.05.189
she is serv'd | as i would serve a rat." 5.05.248
ta'en, would cease | the present pow'r of life, 5.05.255
i would not thy good deeds should from my lips 5.05.288
with language that would make me spurn the sea 5.05.294
he would have well becom'd this place, and 5.05.406
i life would wish, and that i might | waste it PER 1.ch. 15
that would be son to great antiochus. 1.01. 26
would draw heaven down, and all the gods to 1.01. 83
see clear | to stop the air would hurt them. 1.01.100
how courtesy would seem to cover sin, | when 1.01.121
and punish that before that he would punish. 1.02. 33
being bid to ask what he would of the king, 1.03. 5 P
he would depart, i'll give some light unto you. 1.03. 17
i shall not be hang'd now, although i would; 1.03. 26
would now be glad of bread and beg for it; 1.04. 41
i would have been that day in the belfry. 2.01. 37 P
i would have kept such a jangling of the bells, 2.01. 40 P
we would purge the land of these drones, that 2.01. 46 P
i would wish no better office than to be beadle. 2.01. 92 P
that's as much as you would be denied | of your 2.03.105
who takes offense | at that would make me glad? 2.05. 72
of tyrus on the head | of helicanus would set on 3.ch. 27
if it had conceit, would die, as i | am like to 3.01. 16
new sea–farer, | i would it would be quiet. 3.01. 42
new sea–farer, | i would it would be quiet. 3.01. 42
by you reliev'd, would force me to my duty; 3.03. 22
in our story, she | would ever with marina be: 4.ch. 20
or when she would with sharp needle wound | the 4.ch. 23
or when | she would with rich and constant pen 4.ch. 28
why would she have me kill'd now? 4.01. 72
what would you have me be, and i be not a woman? 4.02. 83 P
sapling, and must be bow'd as i would have you. 4.02. 88 P
to me as they would have hearken'd to their 4.02. 98 P
at it, and swore he would see her to–morrow. 4.02.109 P
none would look on her, | but cast their gazes 4.03. 32
that she would make a puritan of the devil, if 4.06. 9 P
if the peevish baggage would but give way to 4.06. 19 P
sir, if she would — but there never came her 4.06. 27 P
she would serve after a long voyage at sea. 4.06. 44 P
first, i would have you note, this is an 4.06. 49 P
would set me free from this unhallowed place, 4.06.100
doth prop it, | would sink and overwhelm you. 4.06.120
whither would you have me? 4.06.126 P
the nobleman would have dealt with her like a 4.06.138 P
would she had never come within my doors. 4.06.147 P
fiend | of hell would not in reputation change. 4.06.164
what would you have me do? 4.06.170 P
go to the wars, would you? 4.06.171 P
could he speak, | would own a name too dear. 4.06.179
gods | would safely deliver me from this place! 4.06.180
if that thy master would gain by me, | proclaim 4.06.182
there is some of worth would come aboard; 5.01. 9
this is the man that can, in aught you would, 5.01. 12
outlive the age i am, | and die as i would do. 5.01. 16
i durst wager, | would win some words of him. 5.01. 44
would allure | and make a batt'ry through his 5.01. 46
god | for every graff would send a caterpillar, 5.01. 60
my parentage, | you would not do me violence. 5.01.100
it would seem | like lies disdain'd in the 5.01.118
you said you would believe me, | but, not to be 5.01.150
she never would tell | her parentage; 5.01.187
demanded that, | she would sit still and weep. 5.01.189
grinning at the moon, | what you would do! TNK 1.01.101
i would buy you | t' instruct me 'gainst a 1.01.122
and wish great juno would | resume her ancient 1.02. 21
the flow'r that i would pluck | and put between 1.03. 66
she would long | till she had such another, and 1.03. 68
was a note | whereon her spirits would sojourn 1.03. 77
be in their dear rites, we would supply't. 1.04. 9
(sound and at liberty), i would 'em dead; 1.04. 35
i would i were really that i am deliver'd to be. 2.01. 6 P
i marvel how they would have look'd had they 2.01. 32 P
they would not make us their object. 2.01. 51 P
chances, | were we from hence, would sever us. 2.02. 95
i would hear you still. 2.02.111
honor, would be loath | to take example by her. 2.02.145
who would not? 2.02.158
why then would you deal so cunningly, | so 2.02.189
i would quickly teach thee | what 'twere to 2.02.209
once more | i would but see this fair one. 2.02.232
as her bright eyes shine on ye, would i were, 2.02.234
how i would spread, and fling my wanton arms 2.02.237
i would bring her fruit | fit for the gods to 2.02.238
i would make her | so near the gods in nature, 2.02.241
and then i am sure she would love me. 2.02.243
i would do things | of such a virtuous greatness 2.02.256
good light, | had i a sword, i would kill thee. 2.02.265
and so would any young wench, o' my conscience, 2.04. 12
would he would do so ev'ry day! 2.04. 27
would he would do so ev'ry day! 2.04. 27
know i love him, | for i would fain enjoy him? 2.04. 30
that knew me | would say it was my best piece; 2.05. 14
and greatest, | i would be thought a soldier. 2.05. 15
that, if i were a woman, would be master, | but 2.05. 63
eye, o coz, | what passion would enclose thee! 3.01. 30
my love, would make thee | a confess'd traitor! 3.01. 34
of another | you would not hear me doubted, but 3.01. 61
compell'd bears, would fly | were they not tied. 3.01. 68
no matter, would it were perpetual night, | and 3.02. 3
i reak not if the wolves would jaw me, so | he 3.02. 7
but that i would not, | should i try death by 3.02. 24
would i could find a fine frog! 3.04. 12
he would tell me | news from all parts o' th' 3.04. 12
then would i make | a carreck of a cockleshell, 3.04. 13
that gave her promise faithfully she would | be 3.05. 43
she swore by wine and bread she would not break. 3.05. 47
i would be sorry else. | give me your hand. 3.05. 77
to delay it longer | i would make the world think, 3.06. 11
would you were so in all, sir! 3.06. 20
i perceive | you would fain be at that fight. 3.06. 60
i would have nothing hurt thee but my sword, | a 3.06. 87
thee but my sword, | a bruise would be dishonor. 3.06. 88
by that you would have pity in another, | by 3.06.198
by that you would have trembled to deny | a 3.06.204
compassion to 'em both, how would you place it? 3.06.213
that you would nev'r deny me any thing | fit for 3.06.234
no, would she did! 4.01.142
yet doubtless | she would run mad for this man. 4.02. 12
would i might end first! 4.02. 57
his lineaments | are as a man would wish 'em, 4.02.114
they would show | bravely about the titles of 4.02.144
a very grievous punishment, as one would think, 4.03. 45 P
one would marry a leprous witch to be rid on't, 4.03. 46 P
and would account i had a great penn'worth on't 4.03. 66 P
i would destroy th' offender, coz, i would, 5.01. 23
i would destroy th' offender, coz, i would, 5.01. 23
place | to seat something i would confound. 5.01. 28
reveal'd secret, for i knew none — would not, 5.01. 99
nor would the libels read | of liberal wits. 5.01.101
swore it was, | and who would not believe her? 5.01.118
to those that would and cannot, a rejoicer. 5.01.121
smiling to me | and ask'd me what i would eat, 5.02. 5
me what i would eat, and when i would kiss her. 5.02. 5
she told me | she would watch with me to–night, 5.02. 9
well she knew | what hour my fit would take me. 5.02. 10
she would have me sing. 5.02. 12
and that would be a blot i' th' business. 5.02. 81
o, sir, you would fain be nibbling. 5.02. 87
for they would glance their eyes | toward my 5.03. 61
chance would have it so. 5.03. 75
i did think | good palamon would miscarry, yet i 5.03.101
surely the gods | would have him die a bachelor, 5.03.117
than all women, | i should and would die too. 5.03.144
for the horse | would make his length a mile, 5.04. 57
when neither curb would crack, girth break, nor 5.04. 74
i would now ask ye how ye like the play, | but, ep 1
you would have us upon th' hip, would you? STM II.C 18 P
you would have us upon th' hip, would you? II.C 18 P
could have topp'd the peace, as now you would, II.C 64
would shark on you, and men like ravenous fishes II.C 86
ravenous fishes | would feed on /one another. II.C 87
as but to banish you, whither would you go? II.C 125
would you be pleas'd | to find a nation of such II.C 130
would not afford you an abode on earth, | whet II.C 133
what would you think | to be thus us'd? II.C 138
backward she push'd him, as she would be thrust, VEN 41
would in thy palm dissolve, or seem to melt. 144
and now she weeps, and now she fain would speak, 221
she would, he will not in her arms be bound; 226
look when a painter would surpass the life | in 289
would thou wert as i am, and i a man, | my heart 369
for one sweet look thy help i would assure thee, 371
nothing but my body's bane would cure thee." 372
o, would thou hadst not, or i had no hearing! 428
my ears would love | that inward beauty and 433
thy outward parts would move | each part in me 435
yet would my love to thee be still as much, 442
would they not wish the feast might ever last, 447
would root these beauties as he roots the mead. 636
that on the earth would breed a scarcity | and 753
and would say after her, if she said "no." 852
"and therefore would he put his bonnet on, 1087
on, | under whose brim the gaudy sun would peep; 1088
the wind would blow it off, and being gone, 1089
then would adonis weep; 1090
they both would strive who first should dry his 1092
some hedge, because he would not fear him; 1094
the tiger would be tame and gently hear him; 1096
if he had spoke, the wolf would leave his prey, 1097
that some would sing, some other in their bills 1102
would bring him mulberries and ripe–red cherries 1103
virtue bragg'd, beauty would blush for shame; LUC 54
virtue would stain that o'er with silver white. 56
to those two armies that would let him go, 76
would with the sceptre straight be strooken down 217
and they would stand auspicious to the hour, 347
this guilt would seem death–worthy in thy 635
and he hath won what he would lose again; 688
and therefore would they still in darkness be, 752
the silver–shining queen he would distain; 786
my collatine would else have come to me | when 916
would purchase thee a thousand thousand friends, 963
for who so base would such an office have | as 1000
therefore still in night would cloist'red be. 1085
grief grieves most at that would do it good; 1117
if tears could help, mine own would do me good. 1274
she would request to know your heaviness." 1283
she would not blot the letter | with words, till 1322
and from the tow'rs of troy there would appear 1382
that one would swear he saw them quake and 1393
it seem'd they would debate with angry swords. 1421
she would have said, "can lurk in such a look"; 1535
and my laments would be drawn out too long | to 1616
here with a sigh, as if her heart would break, 1716
and would corrupt my saint to be a devil, PP 2. 7
the tender nibbler would not touch the bait, 4.11
and would not take her meaning nor her pleasure. 11.12
were i with her, the night would post too soon, 14.25
may blow, | air, would i might triumph so! 16.10
thou for whom jove would swear | juno but an 16.15
the joys in bed, | one woman would another wed. 18.48
"fie, fie, fie," now would she cry, | "tereu, 20.13
and threescore year would make the world away. SON 11. 8
with virtuous wish would bear your living 16. 7
the age to come would say, "this poet lies, 17. 7
how would thy shadow's form form happy show | to 43. 6
how would (i say) mine eyes be blessed made | by 43. 9
for then, despite of space, i would be brought, 44. 3
as soon as think the place where he would be. 44. 8

eye my heart /thy picture's sight would bar, 46. 3
with all these, from these would i be gone, 66.13
that i in your sweet thoughts would be forgot, 71. 7
unless you would devise some virtuous lie, | to 72. 5
i | than niggard truth would willingly impart: 72. 8
when others would give life and bring a tomb. 83.12
because i would not dull you with my song. 102.14
i see their antique pen would have express'd 106. 7
where time and outward form would show it dead. 108.14
which, rank of goodness, would by ill be cured. 118.12
they would change their state | and situation 128. 9
in pursuit of the thing she would have stay; 143. 4
and would corrupt my saint to be a devil, 144. 7
the boy for trial needs would touch my breast; 153.10
true to bondage, would not break from thence, LC 34
ink would have seem'd more black and damned here 54
"well could he ride, and often men would say, 106
and dialogu'd for him what he would say, | ask'd 132
and now she would the caged cloister fly: 249
not to be tempted would she be enur'd, | and now 251
and, veil'd in them, did win whom he would maim. 312
against the thing he sought he would exclaim: 313
who, young and simple, would not be so lover'd? 320
would yet again betray the fore–betray'd, | and 328

WOULDEST 5 FR 0.0005 REL FR 1 V 4 P
what a joyful father wouldest thou make me! LLL 5.01. 77 P
that truly which thou wouldest truly know. 1H4 1.02. 5 P
i knew thou wouldest be his death. TRO 4.02. 86 P
with as much speed as thou wouldest fly death. HAM 4.06. 24 P
what wouldest thou do, old man? LR 1.01.146

/WOULDST 4 FR 0.0004 REL FR 3 V 1 P
/if /thou /wouldst, | /there /shouldst /thou R2 4.01.232
/he /was /what /thou /wouldst /have /him /be! 2H4 1.03. 93
/and /now /thou /wouldst /eat /thy /dead /vomit 1.03. 99
thou /wouldst not have slipp'd out of my TRO 2.03. 26 P

WOULDST 132 FR 0.0149 REL FR 97 V 35 P
me, wouldst give me | water with berries in't, TMP 1.02.333
but wouldst gabble like | a thing most brutish, 1.02.356
wouldst thou then counsel me to fall in love? TGV 1.02. 2
and wouldst thou have me cast my love on him? 1.02. 25
thou wouldst as soon go kindle fire with snow 2.07. 19
who wouldst thou strike? 3.01.200 P
thou wouldst disprove me. 5.04. 66
thou wouldst make an absolute courtier, and the WIV 3.03. 62 P
what wouldst thou have, boor? 4.05. 1 P
in him that thou wouldst discover if thou MM 2.01.186 P
which, though thou wouldst deny, denies thee 5.01.413
when thou unurg'd wouldst vow | that never words ERR 2.02.113
wouldst thou not spit at me, and spurn at me, 2.02.134
thou wouldst have chang'd thy face for a name, 3.01. 47
should ever happen, thou wouldst be horn–mad. ADO 1.01.269 P
for, did i think thou wouldst not quickly die, 4.01.124
beatrice, wouldst thou come when i call'd thee? 5.02. 42 P
had well hop'd thou wouldst have denied beatrice 5.04.112 P
this, fellow. what wouldst? LLL 1.01.182 P
gramercy! wouldst thou aught with me? MV 2.02.121 P
wouldst thou have a serpent sting thee twice? 4.01. 69
so wouldst thou, if the truth of thy love to me AYL 1.02. 13 P
why, whither, adam, wouldst thou have me go? 2.03. 29
what, wouldst thou have me go and beg my food? 2.03. 31
fie on thee! i can tell what thou wouldst do. 2.07. 62
wouldst thou disgorge into the general world. 2.07. 69
wouldst thou not be glad to have the niggardly TN 2.05. 4 P
what wouldst thou now? 4.01. 41
thou wouldst have poison'd good camillo's honor, WT 3.02.188
and wouldst adventure | to mingle faith with him 4.04.459
and i would thou wouldst be a tall fellow of thy 5.02.167 P
do not i know thou wouldst? JN 3.03. 58
or wouldst thou drown thyself, | put but a 4.03.130
tends that thou wouldst speak to the duke of R2 2.01.232
shouldst please me better wouldst thou weep. 3.04. 20
as i have done, thou wouldst be more pitiful. 5.02.103
what wouldst thou have with me? 1H4 2.03. 95
wouldst thou have thy head broken? 3.01.237 P
and wouldst thou turn our offers contrary? 5.05. 4
this thou wouldst say, "your son did thus and 2H4 1.01. 76
what wouldst thou think of me if i should weep? 2.02. 52 P
wouldst thou have practic'd on me, for thy use H5 2.02. 99
thou wouldst find me such a plain king that thou 5.02.124 P
plain king that thou wouldst think i had sold my 5.02.125 P
lord, thou wouldst vouchsafe | to visit her poor 1H6 2.02. 40
how now, fellow? wouldst any thing with me? 2H6 1.03. 10 P
what, and wouldst climb a tree? 2.01. 96
lov'dst plums well, that wouldst venture so. 2.01. 99
wouldst have me rescue thee from this reproach? 2.04. 64
knowing that thou wouldst have me drown'd on 3.02. 95
thou wouldst not have mourn'd so much for me. 4.04. 24
wouldst have me kneel? 5.01.109
thou wouldst have left thy dearest heart–blood 3H6 1.01.223
thou wouldst be fee'd, i see, to make me sport: 1.04. 92
wouldst have me weep? 1.04.144
which, traitor, thou wouldst have me answer to. 5.05. 21
her husband, knave. wouldst thou betray me? R3 1.01.102
what wouldst thou, fellow? 1.04. 85
that thou wouldst as soon afford a grave | as 4.04. 31
if something thou wouldst swear to be believ'd, 4.04.372
why, what wouldst thou do there before i go? 4.04.454
ay, thou wouldst be gone to join with richmond; 4.04.490
what wouldst thou of us, troyan? make demand. TRO 3.03. 17
if thou wouldst not entomb thyself alive | and 3.03.186
what wouldst thou? 5.06. 2
and wouldst do so, i think, should we encounter COR 1.10. 9
wouldst thou have laugh'd had i come coffin'd 2.01.176
what wouldst thou? 4.05. 53
wouldst thou have me prove myself a bastard? TIT 2.03.148
what, wouldst thou kneel with me? 3.01.209
now, good fellow, wouldst thou speak with us? 4.04. 39
whither wouldst thou convey | this growing image 5.01. 44
thou didst know me, thou wouldst talk with me. 5.02. 20
what wouldst thou have us do, andronicus? 5.02. 92
wouldst thou withdraw it? ROM 2.02.130
thou wouldst else have made thy tale large. 2.04. 97 P
what wouldst thou have with me? 3.01. 76 P
thee at once, which thou at once wouldst lose. 3.03.121
what wouldst do then, apemantus? TIM 1.01.228 P
upon thee, and then thou wouldst sin the faster. 1.02.240 P
thou wouldst have plung'd thyself | in general 4.03.255
what wouldst thou have to athens? 4.03.287
where wouldst thou send it? 4.03.298 P
what wouldst thou do with the world, apemantus, 4.03.321 P
wouldst thou have thyself fall in the confusion 4.03.324 P
a bear, thou wouldst be kill'd by the horse; 4.03.338 P
a horse, thou wouldst be seiz'd by the leopard; 4.03.339 P
would thou wouldst burst! 4.03.369
if thou wouldst not reside | but where one 5.01.110
thou wouldst be great, | art not without MAC 1.05. 18
what thou wouldst highly, | that wouldst thou 1.05. 20
thou wouldst highly, | that wouldst thou holily; 1.05. 21
wouldst not play false, | and yet wouldst 1.05. 21
not play false, | and yet wouldst wrongly win. 1.05. 22
wouldst thou have that | which thou esteem'st 1.07. 41
what wouldst thou beg, laertes, | that shall not HAM 1.02. 45
what wouldst thou have, laertes? 1.02. 50
on lethe wharf, | wouldst thou not stir in this. 1.05. 34
why wouldst thou be a breeder of sinners? 3.01.120 P
thou wouldst not think how ill all's here about 5.02.212 P
what wouldst thou with us? LR 1.04. 11 P
what wouldst thou? 1.04. 22 P
who wouldst thou serve? 1.04. 24 P
yes indeed, thou wouldst make a good fool. 1.05. 38 P
one that wouldst be a bawd in way of good 2.02. 20 P
wouldst thou give 'em all? 3.04. 64
what wouldst write of me, if thou shouldst OTH 2.01.117
come, how wouldst thou praise me? 2.01.124
wouldst thou do such a deed for all the world? 4.03. 64
wouldst thou do such a deed for all the world? 4.03. 68
/good troth, i think thou wouldst not. 4.03. 70
antony, thou wouldst say — ANT 1.02.104
thy face, to me | thou wouldst appear most ugly. 2.05. 97
how wouldst thou have paid | my better service, 4.06. 31
what thou wouldst do | is done unto thy hand; 4.14. 28
on my command, | thou then wouldst kill me. 4.14. 67
wouldst thou be window'd in great rome, and see 4.14. 72
thou a man, | thou wouldst have mercy on me. 5.02.175
beggar, wouldst have made my throne | a seat for CYM 1.01.141
thou wouldst have told this tale for virtue, not 1.06.143
sirrah, if thou wouldst not be a villain, but do 3.05.109 P
what wouldst thou, boy? 5.05.108
i shall, | unless thou wouldst grieve quickly. 5.05.170
thy servant, | what wouldst thou have me do? PER 1.02. 65
that thou wouldst tremble to receive thyself. 1.02. 69
do the deeds of darkness, thou wouldst say. 4.06. 30 P
thou wouldst not. TNK 2.02.123
that thou toldst me thou wouldst hunt the boar. VEN 614
dread night, wouldst thou one hour come back, LUC 965
if from thyself to store thou wouldst convert; SON 14.12
o absence, what a torment wouldst thou prove, 39. 9
if thou wouldst use the strength of all thy 96.12

WOULD'T 2 FR 0.0002 REL FR 2 V 0 P
would't had been done! TMP 1.02.349
faith, holy uncle, would't were come to that! 2H6 2.01. 37

/WOUND* 2 FR 0.0002 REL FR 2 V 0 P
searching of /thy /wound, | i have by hard AYL 2.04. 44
/wound /it /with /sighing, /girl, /kill /it TIT 3.02. 15

WOUND* 85 FR 0.0096 REL FR 75 V 10 P
sometime am i | all wound with adders, who with TMP 2.02. 13
may as well | wound the loud winds, or with 3.03. 63
lodge thee till thy wound be throughly heal'd; TGV 1.02.112
the private wound is deepest: 5.04. 71
before milk–white, now purple with love's wound, MND 2.01.167
i see no blood, no wound. 2.02.101
out, sword, and wound | the pap of pyramus; 5.01.296
and every word in it a gaping wound | issuing MV 3.02.265
and if mine eyes can wound, now let them kill AYL 3.05. 16
now show the wound mine eye hath made in thee. 3.05. 20
brief, i recover'd him, bound up his wound, 4.03.150
to wound thy lord, thy king, thy governor. SHR 5.02.138
for then we wound our modesty and make foul the AWW 1.03. 5 P
if it be so, you have wound a goodly clew; 1.03.182
and wound her honor with this diffidence. JN 1.01. 65
win you this city without stroke or wound, 2.01.418
and heal the inveterate canker of one wound | by 5.02. 14
and wound our tott'ring colors clearly up, 5.05. 7
show me the very wound of this ill news; 5.06. 21
but when it first did help to wound itself. 5.07.114
shall wound my honor with such feeble wrong, R2 1.01.191
though rebels wound thee with their horses' 3.02. 7
have felt the worst of death's destroying wound, 3.02.139
/we at time of year | do wound the bark, the 3.04. 58
or take away the grief of a wound? 1H4 5.01.132 P
they wound my thoughts worse than thy sword my 5.04. 80
sirrah, with a new wound in your thigh, come you 5.04.128 P
my death, i gave him this wound in the thigh. 5.04.151 P
well, i am loath to gall a new–heal'd wound. 2H4 1.02.148 P
as i was washing thy wound, to marry me and make 2.01. 92 P
i told thee they were ill for a green wound? 2.01. 98 P
it is good for your green wound and your ploody H5 5.01. 42 P
betime, | before the wound do grow uncurable; 2H6 3.01.286
corrosive, | it is applied to a deathful wound. 3.02.404
to prick thy finger, though to wound his heart. 3H6 1.04. 55
the wound that bred this meeting here | cannot 2.02.121
this hand, fast wound about thy coal–black hair, 5.01. 54
the new–heal'd wound of malice should break out, R3 2.02.125
would with treason wound this fair land's peace! 5.05. 39
him | that i gainsay my deed, how may he wound, H8 2.04. 96
the wound of peace is /surety, | /surety secure, TRO 2.02. 14
yet that which seems the wound to kill, | doth 3.01.122
with every joint a wound, and that to–morrow! 4.01. 30
that i may give the local wound a name, | and 4.05.244
the surgeon's box, or the patient's wound. 5.01. 11 P
now to the bottom dost thou search my wound; TIT 2.03.262
deer | that hath receiv'd some unrecuring wound. 3.01. 90
ah, that this sight should make so deep a wound, 3.01.246
that wound beyond their feeling to the quick. 4.02. 28
that gives our troy, our rome, the civil wound. 5.03. 87
he jests at scars that never felt a wound. ROM 2.02. 1
i saw the wound, i saw it with mine eyes — 3.02. 52
"when griping griefs the heart doth wound, 4.05.126
giving myself a voluntary wound | here, in the JC 2.01.300
and put a tongue | in every wound of caesar, 3.02.229
peace, the charm's wound up. MAC 1.03. 37
that my keen knife see not the wound it makes, 1.05. 52
had thought you had receiv'd some bodily wound; OTH 2.03.267 P
what wound did ever heal but by degrees? 2.03.371
which they ear and wound | with keels of every ANT 1.04. 49
i had a wound here that was like a t, | but now 4.07. 7
for with a wound i must be cur'd. 4.14. 78
this is his sword, | i robb'd his wound of it; 5.01. 25
therein false strook, can take no greater wound, CYM 3.04.114
peace, | i'll give no wound to thee. 5.01. 21
heavens, how they wound | some slain before, 5.03. 46
or when she would with sharp needle wound | the PER 4.ch. 23
me, | and yet may palamon wound arcite to | the TNK 5.03. 58
spun, | a bottom great wound up, greatly undone. STM III 21
my heart all whole as thine, thy heart my wound! VEN 370
and there another licking of his wound, 915
and never wound the heart with looks again, 1042
upon the wide wound that the boar had trench'd 1052
white | with purple tears, that his wound wept, 1054
her sight dazzling makes the wound seem three, 1064
bearing away the wound that nothing healeth, LUC 731
to see the salve doth make the wound ache more, 1116
mine honor be the knife's that makes my wound, 1201
and drop sweet balm in priam's painted wound, 1466
that guides this hand to give this wound to me." 1722
burying in lucrece' wound his folly's show. 1810
such a salve can speak | that heals the wound, SON 34. 8
for that deep wound it gives my friend and me! 133. 2
wound me not with thine eye but with thy tongue, 139. 3
what need'st thou wound with cunning when thy 139. 7

WOUNDED 36 FR 0.0040 REL FR 27 V 9 P
poor wounded name: TGV 1.02.111
her, | as best befits her wounded reputation, ADO 4.01.241
lay he, stretch'd along, like a wounded knight. AYL 3.02.240 P
thy heart had been wounded with the claws of a 5.02. 22 P
wounded it is, but with the eyes of a lady. 5.02. 24 P
whose sudden sight hath thrall'd my wounded eye. SHR 1.01.220
how attentiveness wounded his daughter, till, WT 5.02. 87 P
wounded to death. JN 5.04. 9
of those physicians that first wounded thee. R2 2.01. 99
the king is almost wounded to the death, | and, 2H4 1.01. 14
over suffolk's neck | he threw his wounded arm, H5 4.06. 25
and /their wounded steeds | fret fetlock deep in 4.07. 78
shall my name with slander's tongue be wounded, 2H6 3.02. 68
and sent the ragged soldiers wounded home. 4.01. 90
is either slain or wounded dangerous; 3H6 1.01. 11
my wolsey, | the quiet of my wounded conscience, H8 2.02. 74
is he not wounded? COR 2.01.119 P
he was wont to come home wounded. 2.01.119 P
o, he is wounded, i thank the gods for't. 2.01.121 P
where is he wounded? 2.01.144 P
where is he wounded? 2.01.146 P
when most strook home, being gentle wounded, 4.01. 8
these words are razors to my wounded heart. TIT 1.01.314
with these boys mine honor thou hast wounded. 1.01.365
and he that wounded her | hath hurt me more than 3.01. 91
when as the one is wounded with the bait, | the 4.04. 92
where on a sudden one hath wounded me | that's ROM 2.03. 50
one hath wounded me | that's by me wounded; 2.03. 51
you but behold | our caesar's vesture wounded? JC 3.02.196
o god, horatio, what a wounded name, | things HAM 5.02.344
i'll yet follow | the wounded chance of antony, ANT 3.10. 35
rushes ere he waken'd | the chastity he wounded. CYM 2.02. 14
afar, | how he in peace is wounded, not in war. LUC 831
two the trusty knight was wounded with disdain: PP 15.11
the humble salve which wounded bosoms fits! SON 120.12
here what tributes wounded fancies sent me, | of LC 197

WOUNDING 10 FR 0.0011 REL FR 10 V 0 P
not wounding, pity would not let me do't; LLL 4.01. 27
if wounding, then it was to show my skill, 4.01. 28
full of comparisons and wounding flouts, | which 5.02.844
and to bloodshed, | wounding supposed peace. 2H4 4.05.195
look not upon me, for thine eyes are wounding. 2H6 3.02. 51
o caesar, what a wounding shame is this, | that ANT 5.02.159
by wounding his belief in her renown | with CYM 5.05.202
sweet music, and heart's deep sore wounding. VEN 432
a smile recures the wounding of a frown. 465
wounding itself to death, rise up and fall, LUC 466

WOUNDINGS 1 FR 0.0001 REL FR 1 V 0 P
th' untented woundings of a father's curse LR 1.04.300

WOUNDLESS 1 FR 0.0001 REL FR 1 V 0 P
may miss our name, | and hit the woundless air. HAM 4.01. 44

WOUNDS' 1 FR 0.0001 REL FR 1 V 0 P
for my wounds' sake to give their suffrage. COR 2.02.138

/WOUNDS 3 FR 0.0003 REL FR 3 V 0 P
/of /mine, | /and /made /no /deeper /wounds? R2 4.01.279
/flesh /was /capable | /of /wounds /and /scars; 2H4 1.01.173
"/these /wounds /i /had /on /crispin's /day." H5 4.03. 48

WOUNDS 84 FR 0.0095 REL FR 78 V 6 P
that wounds th' unsisting postern with these MM 4.02. 89
arrow made, | that only wounds by hearsay. ADO 3.01. 23
there's an eye | wounds like a leaden sword. LLL 5.02.481
to stop his wounds, lest he do bleed to death. MV 4.01.258
then shall you know the wounds invisible | that AYL 3.05. 30
the which he pricks and wounds | with many JN 5.07. 17
of civil wounds plough'd up with neighbors' R2 1.03.128
that wounds me with the flatteries of his tongue 3.02.216
rain'd from the wounds of slaughtered englishmen 3.03. 44
and wounds the earth, if nothing else, with rage 5.01. 30
i then, all smarting with my wounds being cold, 1H4 1.03. 49
guns, and drums, and wounds, god save the mark! 1.03. 56
no more but one tongue for all those wounds, 1.03. 96
those mouthed wounds, which valiantly he took, 1.03. 97
color her working with such deadly wounds, | nor 1.03.109
the long–grown wounds of my intemperance. 3.02.156
under the smile of safety wounds the world; 2H4 in 10
gaping wounds | untwind the sisters three! 2.04.198
side | (yoke–fellow to his honor–owing wounds) H5 4.06. 9
wounds will i lend the french in stead of eyes, 1H6 1.01. 87
but o, the treacherous falstaff wounds my heart, 1.04. 35
which giveth many wounds when one will kill. 2.05.110
behold the wounds, the most unnatural wounds, 3.03. 50
behold the wounds, the most unnatural wounds, 3.03. 50
o thou whose wounds become hard–favored death, 4.07. 23
and are the cities that i got with wounds 2H6 1.01.121

and disorder wounds | where it should guard. 5.02. 32
flies through these wounds to seek out thee. 3H6 1.04.178
words would add more anguish than the wounds. 2.01. 99
the windy tempest of my heart | upon thy wounds, 2.05. 87
are plaints, and cureless are my wounds; 2.06. 23
the air hath got into my deadly wounds, | and 2.06. 27
my pity hath been balm to heal their wounds, 4.08. 41
by the self-same hand that made these wounds! R3 1.02. 11
see dead henry's wounds | open their congeal'd 1.02. 55
bind up my wounds! 5.03.177
now civil wounds are stopp'd, peace lives again; 5.05. 40
wounds, friends, and what else dear that is TRO 2.02. 5
the /shaft /confounds | not that it wounds, 3.01.119
those wounds heal ill that men do give 3.03.229
look how thy wounds do bleed at many vents! 5.03. 82
patroclus' wounds have rous'd his drowsy blood, 5.05. 32
i have some wounds upon me, and they smart | to COR 1.09. 28
the wounds become him. 2.01.123 P
last expedition, twenty-five wounds upon him. 2.01.154 P
(as the manner is) his wounds | to th' people, 2.01.235
i had rather have my wounds to heal again | than 2.02. 69
if he show us his wounds and tell us his deeds, 2.03. 6 P
tongues into those wounds and speak for them; 2.03. 7 P
"look, sir, my wounds! 2.03. 51
i have wounds to show you, which shall be yours 2.03. 76 P
you have receiv'd many wounds for your country. 2.03.106 P
for your voices bear | of wounds two dozen odd; 2.03.128
marks of merit, wounds receiv'd for 's country. 2.03.164
he said he had wounds, which he could show in 2.03.166
think | upon the wounds his body bears, which 3.03. 50
good man, the wounds that he does bear for rome! 4.02. 28
wash they his wounds with tears? ROM 3.02.130
in the last conflict, and made plenteous wounds! TIM 3.05. 65
my wounds ache at you. 3.05. 95
usuring senate | pours into captains' wounds? 3.05.110
had i as many eyes as thou hast wounds, JC 3.01.200
over thy wounds now do i prophesy | (which like 3.01.259
and they would go and kiss dead caesar's wounds, 3.02.132
show you sweet caesar's wounds, poor, poor, dumb 3.02.225
till caesar's three and thirty wounds | be well 5.01. 53
except they meant to bathe in reeking wounds, MAC 1.02. 39
so well thy words become thee as thy wounds, 1.02. 43
each new day a gash | is added to her wounds. 4.03. 41
(it wounds thine honor that i speak it now) ANT 1.04. 69
loud, we do commit | murther in healing wounds. 2.02. 22
you misdoubt | this sword, and these my wounds? 3.07. 63
tears | wash the congealment from your wounds, 4.08. 10
fine this tyrant | can tickle where she wounds! CYM 1.01. 85
yet i may bind those wounds up, that must open TNK 4.02. 1
the bearing earth with his hard hoof he wounds, VEN 267
the knife | that wounds my body so dishonored. LUC 1185
staring on priam's wounds with her old eyes, 1448
and friend to friend gives unadvised wounds, 1488
fool," quoth she, "his wounds will not be sore." 1568
and through her wounds doth fly | live's lasting 1728
do wounds help wounds, or grief help grievous 1822
do wounds help wounds, or grief help grievous 1822
she showed hers, he saw more wounds than one, PP 9.13

WOUND'ST 1 FR 0.0001 REL FR 1 V 0 P
wrong'st his honor, wound'st his princely name. LUC 599

WOVEN *(also weav'd)*

WOVEN 4 FR 0.0004 REL FR 4 V 0 P
as they fly by them with their woven wings. MV 1.01. 14
and hath woven | a golden mesh t' entrap the 3.02.121
all were woven | so strangely in one piece. H8 4.01. 80
and now his woven girths he breaks asunder; VEN 266

WRACK 38 FR 0.0043 REL FR 36 V 2 P
the direful spectacle of the wrack, which TMP 1.02. 26
weeping again the king my father's wrack, | this 1.02.391
gallant which thou seest | was in the wrack; 1.02.415
the wrack of all my friends, nor this man's 1.02.489
go, go, be gone, to save your ship from wrack, TGV 1.01.148
hath he not lost much wealth by wrack of sea? ERR 5.01. 49
besides her urging of her wrack at sea — 5.01.360
with some of the sailors that escap'd the wrack. MV 3.01.105 P
so terrible shows in the wrack of maidenhood, AWW 3.05. 22 P
a wrack past hope he was. TN 5.01. 79
i shall have share in this most happy wrack. 5.01.266
but on this day let seamen fear no wrack; JN 3.01. 92
we see the very wrack that we must suffer, | and R2 2.01.267
now, | for suffering so the causes of our wrack. 2.01.269
sea | with sunken wrack and sumless treasuries. H5 1.02.165
hence grew the general wrack and massacre; 1H6 1.01.135
mov'd with compassion of my country's wrack, 4.01. 56
hume's knavery will be the duchess' wrack, | and 2H6 1.02.105
the commonwealth hath daily run to wrack, | the 1.03.124
as the rocks cheer them that fear their wrack: 3H6 2.02. 5
shelves and rocks that threaten us with wrack. 5.04. 23
these eyes could not endure that beauty's wrack; R3 1.02.127
found thee a way, out of his wrack, to rise in; H8 3.02.437
am not | one that rejoices in the common wrack, TIM 5.01.192
with both | he labor'd in his country's wrack, i MAC 1.03.114
blow wind, come wrack, | at least we'll die with 5.05. 50
he did but trifle | and meant to wrack thee, but HAM 2.01.110
hath seen a grievous wrack and sufferance | on OTH 2.01. 23
what wrack discern you in me | deserves your CYM 1.06. 84
what's thy interest | in this sad wrack? 4.02.366
'tis of some wrack. PER 3.02. 51
monster envy, oft the wrack | of earned praise, 4.ch. 12
that ever yet betoken'd | wrack to the seaman, VEN 454
forgetting shame's pure blush and honor's wrack. 558
"yet am i guilty of thy honor's wrack, | yet for LUC 841
i could prevent this storm, and shun thy wrack! 966
had anatomiz'd | time's ruin, beauty's wrack, 1451
if nature (sovereign mistress over wrack), | as SON 126. 5

WRACK'D 15 FR 0.0017 REL FR 11 V 4 P
supposing that they saw the king's ship wrack'd, TMP 1.02.236
at ebb) beheld | the king my father wrack'd. 1.02.437
hours since | were wrack'd upon this shore; 5.01.137
upon this shore (where you were wrack'd) was 5.01.161
her brother frederick was wrack'd at sea, having MM 3.01.216 P
ship of rich lading wrack'd on the narrow seas; MV 3.01. 3 P
wrack'd the same instant of their master's death WT 5.02. 69 P
are wrack'd three nights ago on goodwin sands; JN 5.03. 11
even as men wrack'd upon a sand, that look to be H5 4.01. 97 P
was i for this nigh wrack'd upon the sea, | and 2H6 3.02. 82
and each hour's joy wrack'd with a week of teen. R3 4.01. 96
a pair of tribunes that have wrack'd for rome COR 5.01. 16
thumb, | wrack'd as homeward he did come. MAC 1.03. 29
should house him safe is wrack'd and split, PER 2.ch. 32
or (being wrack'd) i am a worthless boat, | he SON 80.11

WRACKFUL 1 FR 0.0001 REL FR 1 V 0 P
against the wrackful siege of batt'ring days, SON 65. 6

WRACKS 1 FR 0.0001 REL FR 1 V 0 P
methoughts i saw a thousand fearful wracks; R3 1.04. 24

WRACK-THREAT'NING
1 FR 0.0001 REL FR 1 V 0 P
beat at thy rocky and wrack-threat'ning heart, LUC 590

WRANGLE 7 FR 0.0008 REL FR 5 V 2 P
yes, for a score of kingdoms you should wrangle, TMP 5.01.174
me almost ready to wrangle with mine own honesty
WIV 2.01. 85 P
you still wrangle with her, boyet, and she LLL 4.01.117
and wrangle with my reason that persuades me TN 4.03. 14
nothing but love from us) | let us not wrangle. JC 4.02. 45
men's natures wrangle with inferior things, OTH 3.04.144
you shall have time to wrangle in when you have ANT 2.02.106 P

WRANGLER 1 FR 0.0001 REL FR 1 V 0 P
him he hath made a match with such a wrangler H5 1.02.264

WRANGLERS 1 FR 0.0001 REL FR 1 V 0 P
the seas and winds, old wranglers, took a truce, TRO 2.02. 75

WRANGLING 8 FR 0.0009 REL FR 7 V 1 P
and you to wrangling, for thy loving voyage | is AYL 5.04.191
but, wrangling pedant, this is | the patroness SHR 3.01. 4
as a scolding quean to a wrangling knave, as the AWW 2.02. 26 P
or else was wrangling somerset in th' error? 1H6 2.04. 6
no, wrangling woman, we'll no longer stay, 3H6 2.02.176
hear me, you wrangling pirates, that fall out R3 1.03.157
accursed and unquiet wrangling days, | how many 2.04. 55
fie, wrangling queen! ANT 1.01. 48

/WRAP 1 FR 0.0001 REL FR 1 V 0 P
/will /in /concealment /wrap /me /up /awhile; LR 4.03. 52

WRAP 4 FR 0.0004 REL FR 3 V 1 P
skin, | weed wide enough to wrap a fairy in; MND 2.01.256
and wrap our bodies in black mourning gowns, 3H6 2.01.161
what dost thou wrap and fumble in thy arms? TIT 4.02. 58
why do we wrap the gentleman in our more rawer
HAM 5.02.122 P

WRAPP'D 10 FR 0.0011 REL FR 10 V 0 P
unfold the evil which is here wrapp'd up | in MM 5.01.117
wrapp'd in sweet clothes, rings put upon his SHR in.1. 38
wrapp'd in a paper, which contain'd the name AWW 5.03. 94
i am wrapp'd in dismal thinkings. 5.03.128
and now, instead of bullets wrapp'd in fire, JN 2.01.227
o tiger's heart wrapp'd in a woman's hide! 3H6 1.04.137
and sends them weapons wrapp'd about with lines
TIT 4.02. 27
o rash false heat, wrapp'd in repentant cold, LUC 48
wrapp'd and confounded in a thousand fears, 456
o, how are they wrapp'd in with infamies | that 636

WRAPS 1 FR 0.0001 REL FR 0 V 1 P
/my often rumination wraps me in a most humorous
AYL 4.01. 19 P

WRASTLE 8 FR 0.0009 REL FR 4 V 4 P
benedick, | to wish him wrastle with affection, ADO 3.01. 42
what, you wrastle to-morrow before the new duke?
AYL 1.01.120 P
sir, i wrastle for my credit, and he that 1.01.126 P
alone again, i'll never wrastle for prize more. 1.01.161 P
come, come, wrastle with thy affections. 1.03. 21 P
i'll wrastle with you in my strength of love. ANT 3.02. 62
he wrastle? TNK 2.03. 73
e'er you are, you run the best, and wrastle, 2.05. 3

WRASTLED *(also wrestled)*

WRASTLED 3 FR 0.0003 REL FR 1 V 2 P
the eldest of the three wrastled with charles, AYL 1.02.125 P
sir, you have wrastled well, and overthrown 1.02.254
he as freshly as he did the day he wrastled? 3.02.231 P

WRASTLER 6 FR 0.0006 REL FR 1 V 5 P
was not charles, the duke's wrastler, here to AYL 1.01. 89 P
not be so long, this wrastler shall clear all. 1.01.171 P
wrastled with charles, the duke's wrastler, 1.02.126 P
man, have you challeng'd charles the wrastler? 1.02.169 P
take the part of a better wrastler than myself! 1.03. 22 P
the parts and graces of the wrastler | that did 2.02. 13

WRASTLER'S 1 FR 0.0001 REL FR 0 V 1 P
that tripp'd up the wrastler's heels, and your AYL 3.02.213 P

WRASTLING 11 FR 0.0012 REL FR 4 V 7 P
and to-morrow the wrastling is. AYL 1.01. 94 P
i would have told you of good wrastling, which 1.02.110 P
yet tell us the manner of the wrastling. 1.02.112 P
shall we see this wrastling, cousin? 1.02.143 P
here is the place appointed for the wrastling, 1.02.145 P
are you crept hither to see the wrastling? 1.02.156 P
the duke that the wrastling might not go forward 1.02.182 P
of the duke, | that here was at the wrastling? 1.02.270
and great affections wrastling in thy bosom JN 5.02. 41
/hemm'd thee in, | like an olympian wrastling. TRO 4.05.194
wrastling and running. — 'tis a pretty fellow. TNK 2.03. 67

WRATH *(also wroth)*

WRATH 61 FR 0.0069 REL FR 55 V 6 P
my wrath shall far exceed the love | i ever bore TGV 3.01.166
come not within the measure of my wrath. 5.04.127
for oberon is passing fell and wrath, | because MND 2.01. 20
they are in the very wrath of love, and they AYL 5.02. 40 P
grant, reprieve him from the wrath | of greatest AWW 3.04. 28
skill, and wrath can furnish man withal. TN 3.04.232 P
dagger of lath, | in his rage and his wrath, 4.02.127
thou refuse | and wilt encounter with my wrath, WT 2.03.139
be thou the trumpet of our wrath, | and sullen JN 1.01. 27
the cannons have their bowels full of wrath, 2.01.210
france, i am burn'd up with inflaming wrath, | a 3.01.340
and pick strong matter of revolt and wrath | out 3.04.167
that ever wall-ey'd wrath or staring rage 4.03. 49
fell | under the wrath of noble hotspur's sword, 2H4 in 30
whose swift wrath beat down | the never-daunted 1.01.109
let my presumption not provoke thy wrath, | for 1H6 2.03. 70
him, | thou wilt but add increase unto my wrath. 2H6 3.02.292
hence, heap of wrath, foul indigested lump, | as 5.01.157
shall to my flaming wrath be oil and flax. 5.02. 55
i am too mean a subject for thy wrath, | be thou 3H6 1.03. 19
wrath makes him deaf; 1.04. 53
with fiery eyes sparkling for very wrath, | and 2.05.131
and they shall feel the vengeance of my wrath. 4.01. 82
whose bright out-shining beams thy cloudy wrath R3 1.03.267
misdeeds, | yet execute thy wrath in me alone! 1.04. 71
who (in my wrath) | kneel'd /at my feet and bid 2.01.107
all this from my remembrance brutish wrath 2.01.119
put in their hands thy bruising irons of wrath, 5.03.110
weep what it foresaw | in hector's wrath. TRO 1.02. 11
for hector in his blaze of wrath subscribes | to 4.05.105
our thoughts, | which makes me sweat with wrath.
COR 1.04. 27
within my view, | and wrath o'erwhelm'd my pity. 1.09. 86
him some way, | or wrath or craft may get him. 1.10. 16
the good gods assuage thy wrath, and turn the 5.02. 77 P
and highly mov'd to wrath | to be controll'd in TIT 1.01.419
o, do not learn her wrath — she taught it thee; 2.03.143
ah, why should wrath be mute and fury dumb? 5.03.184
pride and wrath would confound thee and make TIM 4.03.336 P
teach them to prevent wild alcibiades' wrath. 5.01.203
which in the bluster of thy wrath must fall 5.04. 41
like wrath in death and envy afterwards; JC 2.01.164
let me endure your wrath, if't be not so. MAC 5.05. 35
roasted in wrath and fire, | and thus o'er-sized HAM 2.02.461
come not between the dragon and his wrath; LR 1.01.122
our power | shall do a court'sy to our wrath, 3.07. 26
edgar, | the food of thy abused father's wrath! 4.01. 22
drunkenness to give place to the devil wrath: OTH 2.03.297 P
been born a dog | than answer my wak'd wrath! 3.03.363
the gods give men | to excuse their after wrath. ANT 5.02.287
i something fear my father's wrath, but nothing CYM 1.01. 86
your vexation, | i am senseless of your wrath; 1.01.135
let's follow him and pervert the present wrath 2.04.151
"justice, and your father's wrath, should he 3.02. 40 P
thou art unpaid for, | by tasting of our wrath? 5.05.308
ras'd, and testy wrath | could never be her mild PER 1.01. 17
the pregnant instrument of wrath | prest for 4.ch. 44
fell before | the wrath of cruel creon; TNK 1.01. 40
is at hand to seal | the promise of his wrath. 1.02. 93
wrath, envy, treason, rape, and murther's rages, LUC 909
this load of wrath that burning troy doth bear; 1474
cold modesty, hot wrath, | both fire from hence LC 293

WRATHFUL 13 FR 0.0014 REL FR 12 V 1 P
whiles we, god's wrathful agent, do correct JN 2.01. 87
bray, | and grating shock of wrathful iron arms, R2 1.03.136
wilt be as valiant as the wrathful dove or most 2H4 3.02.160 P
his sparkling eyes, replete with wrathful fire, 1H6 1.01. 12
mad ire and wrathful fury makes me weep, | that 4.03. 28
barren winter, with his wrathful nipping cold; 2H6 2.04. 3
to free us from his father's wrathful curse, | i 3.02.155
your wrathful weapons drawn | here in our 3.02.237
but angry, wrathful, and inclin'd to blood, | if 4.02.126
heart, be wrathful still: 5.02. 70
should enlarge itself | to wrathful terms. TRO 5.02. 38
son, | spiteful and wrathful, who (as others do) MAC 3.05. 12
the wrathful skies | gallow the very wanderers LR 3.02. 43

WRATHFULLY 1 FR 0.0001 REL FR 1 V 0 P
let's kill him boldly, but not wrathfully; JC 2.01.172

WRATH-KINDLED 1 FR 0.0001 REL FR 1 V 0 P
wrath-kindled /gentlemen, be rul'd by me, R2 1.01.152

WRATH'S 1 FR 0.0001 REL FR 1 V 0 P
by penitence th' eternal's wrath's appeas'd: TGV 5.04. 81

WRATHS 2 FR 0.0002 REL FR 1 V 1 P
and your ways, whose wraths to guard you from —
TMP 3.03. 79
and his furies, and his wraths, and his cholers, H5 4.07. 35 P

WREAK 4 FR 0.0004 REL FR 4 V 0 P
then if thou hast | a heart of wreak in thee, COR 4.05. 85
war | take wreak on rome for this ingratitude, TIT 4.03. 34
to send down justice for to wreak our wrongs. 4.03. 52
come to him | to wreak the love i bore my cousin ROM 3.05.101

WREAK'D 1 FR 0.0001 REL FR 1 V 0 P
be wreak'd on him, invisible commander; VEN 1004

WREAKFUL 2 FR 0.0002 REL FR 2 V 0 P
by working wreakful vengeance on thy foes. TIT 5.02. 32
live in all the spite | of wreakful heaven, TIM 4.03.229

WREAKS 1 FR 0.0001 REL FR 1 V 0 P
shall we be thus afflicted in his wreaks, | his TIT 4.04. 11

/WREATH 1 FR 0.0001 REL FR 1 V 0 P
careless tresses | a /wreath of bulrush rounded; TNK 4.01. 84

WREATH 7 FR 0.0008 REL FR 7 V 0 P
they | put on my brows this wreath of victory, JC 5.03. 82
like the wreath of radiant fire | on /flick'ring LR 2.02.107
and his device, a wreath of chivalry; PER 2.02. 29
guest, | to whom this wreath of victory i give, 2.03. 10
your wheaten wreath | was then nor thresh'd nor TNK 1.01. 64
do bear thy yoke | as 'twere a wreath of roses, 5.01. 96
his victor's wreath | even then fell off his 5.04. 79

WREATH'D 2 FR 0.0002 REL FR 2 V 0 P
a green and gilded snake had wreath'd itself, AYL 4.03.108
wreath'd up in fatal folds just in his way, VEN 879

WREATHE 1 FR 0.0001 REL FR 0 V 1 P
like sir proteus, to wreathe your arms, like a TGV 2.01. 19 P

WREATHED 2 FR 0.0002 REL FR 2 V 0 P
nor never lay his wreathed arms athwart | his LLL 4.03.133
we may, each wreathed in the other's arms | (our TIT 2.03. 25

WREATHS 3 FR 0.0003 REL FR 3 V 0 P
and we are grac'd with wreaths of victory. 3H6 5.03. 2
now are our brows bound with victorious wreaths,
R3 1.01. 5
with bruised arms and wreaths of victory. LUC 110

WRECK *(see wrack, etc.)*

WREN 7 FR 0.0008 REL FR 6 V 1 P
note so true, | the wren with little quill — MND 3.01.128
be thought | no better a musician than the wren. MV 5.01.106
look where the youngest wren of /nine comes. TN 3.02. 66 P
and thinks he that the chirping of a wren, | by 2H6 3.02. 42
for the poor wren, | the most diminutive of MAC 4.02. 9
the wren goes to't, and the small gilded fly LR 4.06.112
i had rather see a wren hawk at a fly | than TNK 5.03. 2

WRENCH 6 FR 0.0006 REL FR 6 V 0 P
wrench awe from fools and tie the wiser souls MM 2.04. 14
revenge | wrench up thy power to th' highest. COR 1.08. 11
a noble nature | may catch a wrench — would all TIM 2.02.209
wrench his sword from him. OTH 5.02.288
wrench it open straight. PER 3.02. 53
wrench it open. 3.02. 59

WRENCH'D 2 FR 0.0002 REL FR 2 V 0 P
thence to be wrench'd with an unlineal hand, MAC 3.01. 62
wrench'd my frame of nature | from the fix'd LR 1.04.268

WRENCHING* *(also wrinching)*

WRENCHING* 3 FR 0.0003 REL FR 2 V 1 P
with your manner of wrenching the true cause the

2H4 2.01.110 P
and like a glass | did break i' th' wrenching. H8 1.01.167
give me that mattock and the wrenching iron. ROM 5.03. 22
WREN'S 1 FR 0.0001 REL FR 1 V 0 P
as small a drop of pity | as a wren's eye, CYM 4.02.305
WRENS 2 FR 0.0002 REL FR 2 V 0 P
that wrens make prey where eagles dare not perch
R3 1.03. 70
the petty wrens of tharsus will fly hence | and PER 4.03. 22
/WREST 1 FR 0.0001 REL FR 1 V 0 P
/but /i, /of /these, /will /wrest /an /alphabet, TIT 3.02. 44
WREST 5 FR 0.0005 REL FR 4 V 1 P
and bad thinking do not wrest true speaking, ADO 3.04. 33 P
you | wrest once the law to your authority: MV 4.01.215
that you should fashion, wrest, or bow your H5 1.02. 14
he'll wrest the sense and hold us here all day. 2H6 3.01.186
is such a wrest in their affairs | that their TRO 3.03. 23
WRESTED 3 FR 0.0003 REL FR 3 V 0 P
beast, | the imminent decay of wrested pomp. JN 4.03.154
lavishly | wrested his meaning and authority. 2H4 4.02. 58
that doit that e'er i wrested from the king, 2H6 3.01.112
WRESTLED *(also wrastle, etc.)*
WRESTLED 1 FR 0.0001 REL FR 1 V 0 P
well i could have wrestled, | the best men TNK 2.03. 75
WRETCH 59 FR 0.0066 REL FR 58 V 1 P
o dishonest wretch! MM 3.01.136
i | persuade this rude wretch willingly to die. 4.03. 81
and you shall have your bosom on this wretch, 4.03.134
by heaven, fond wretch, thou know'st not what 5.01.105
fie on thee, wretch! ERR 5.01. 27
a needy, hollow–ey'd, sharp–looking wretch, | a 5.01.241
loud, | puts the wretch that lies in woe | in MND 5.01.377
answer | a stony adversary, an inhuman wretch, MV 4.01. 4
a meacock wretch can make the curstest shrew. SHR 2.01.313
ungracious wretch, | fit for the mountains and TN 4.01. 47
poor wretch, | that for thy mother's fault art WT 3.03. 49
o cursed wretch, | that knew'st this was the 4.04.458
thou slave, thou wretch, thou coward! JN 3.01.115
speak, thou wretch. R2 3.04. 80
and as the wretch whose fever–weak'ned joints, 2H4 1.01.140
me | are heavy orisons 'gainst this poor wretch! H5 2.02. 53
that every wretch, pining and pale before, 4.pr. 41
and, but for ceremony, such a wretch, | winding 4.01.278
laughest thou, wretch? 1H6 2.03. 44
base ignoble wretch! 5.04. 7
and binds the wretch and beats it when it strays 2H6 3.01.211
fie, coward woman and soft–hearted wretch! 3.02.307
look with a gentle eye upon this wretch! 3.03. 20
die, damned wretch, the curse of her that bare 4.10. 77
ah, timorous wretch, | thou hast undone thyself, 3H6 1.01.231
so looks the pent–up lion o'er the wretch | that 1.03. 12
that she, poor wretch, for grief can speak no 3.01. 47
more direful hap betide that hated wretch | that R3 1.02. 17
from all the slaughters, wretch, that thou hast 4.04.139
from the dead temples of this bloody wretch 5.05. 5
being distress'd, was by that wretch betray'd, H8 2.01.110
alas, poor wretch! TRO 4.02. 31 P
nose that bled, or foil'd some debile wretch — COR 1.09. 48
thou wretch, despite o'erwhelm thee! 3.01.163
sly frantic wretch, that holp'st to make me TIT 4.04. 59
die, frantic wretch, for this accursed deed! 5.03. 64
give sentence on this execrable wretch | that 5.03.177
the pretty wretch left crying and said, "ay." ROM 1.03. 44
disobedient wretch! 3.05.160
here lives a caitiff wretch would sell it him." 5.01. 52
upon a wretch whose natural gifts were poor | to HAM 1.05. 51
look where sadly the poor wretch comes reading. 2.02.168
pull'd the poor wretch from her melodious lay 4.07.182
way | than on a wretch whom nature is asham'd LR 1.01.212
thou wretch | that hast within thee undivulged 3.02. 51
the wretch that thou hast blown unto the worst 4.01. 8
a sight most pitiful in the meanest wretch, 4.06.204
what profane wretch art thou? OTH 1.01.114
excellent wretch! 3.03. 90
if any wretch have put this in your head, | let 4.02. 15
this wretch hath part confess'd his villainy. 5.02.296
come, thou mortal wretch, | with thy sharp teeth ANT 5.02.303
the contract you pretend with that base wretch, CYM 2.03.113
repent, and strook | me, wretch, more worth your 5.01. 11
whereat i, wretch, | made scruple of his praise, 5.05.181
mark the poor wretch, to overshut his troubles, VEN 680
"then shalt thou see the dew–bedabbled wretch 703
as if by some instinct the wretch did know | his SON 50. 7
thy proud heart's slave and vassal wretch to be: 141.12
WRETCHED 83 FR 0.0093 REL FR 82 V 1 P
wretched isabel! MM 4.03.121
and to set on this wretched woman here | against 5.01.132
o heaven, the vanity of wretched fools! 5.01.164
a wretched soul, bruis'd with adversity, | we ERR 2.01. 34
hast thou delight to see a wretched man | do 4.04.115
and wretched fools' secrets heedfully o'er–eye. LLL 4.03. 78
to let the wretched man outlive his wealth, | to MV 4.01.269
the wretched animal heav'd forth such groans AYL 2.01. 36
else are they very wretched. 2.04. 68
exult, and all at once, | over the wretched? 3.05. 37
a wretched ragged man, o'ergrown with hair, 4.03.106
i am, my lord, a wretched florentine, | derived AWW 5.03.158
in that thou seest thy wretched brother die, R2 1.02. 27
sick in the world's regard, wretched and low, 1H4 4.03. 57
what a wretched and peevish fellow is this king H5 3.07.132 P
can sleep so soundly as the wretched slave; 4.01.268
posterity, await for wretched years, | when at 1H6 1.01. 48
o lord, have mercy on us, wretched sinners! 1.04. 70
wretched shall france be only in my name. 1.04. 97
ah, woe is me for gloucester, wretched man! 2H6 3.02. 72
be woe for me, more wretched than he is. 3.02. 73
for yet may england curse my wretched reign. 4.09. 49
ah, wretched man, would i had died a maid | and 3H6 1.01.216
weep, wretched man; 2.05. 76
that makes us wretched by the death of thee R3 1.02. 18
outlive thy glory like my wretched self! 1.03.202
deserve not worse than wretched clarence did, 2.01. 94
is lighted on poor hastings' wretched head! 3.04. 93
thee | that ever wretched age hath look'd upon. 3.04.105
withdraw thee, wretched margaret; 4.04. 8
the wretched, bloody, and usurping boar, | that 5.02. 7
richard, thy wife, that wretched anne thy wife, 5.03.159
me | a little happier than my wretched father. H8 2.01.120
the cordial that ye bring a wretched lady, | a 3.01.106
what will become of me now, wretched lady? 3.01.146
o, how wretched | is that poor man that hangs on 3.02.366
would have some pity | upon my wretched women, 4.02.140
this way to death my wretched sons are gone, TIT 3.01. 98
see how my wretched sister sobs and weeps. 3.01.137
if any power pities wretched tears, | to that i 3.01.208
the closing up of our most wretched eyes. 3.01.262
witness this wretched stump, witness these 5.02. 22
and lively warrant | for me, most wretched, to 5.03. 45
thou wretched boy, that didst consort him here, ROM 3.01.130
man, | and then to have a wretched puling fool, 3.05.183
accurs'd, unhappy, wretched, hateful day! 4.05. 43
that man might ne'er be wretched for his mind. TIM 1.02.164
rich only to be wretched, thy great fortunes 4.02. 43
hath a distracted and most wretched being, 4.03.246
"here lies a wretched corse, of wretched soul 5.04. 70
lies a wretched corse, of wretched soul bereft; 5.04. 70
and cassius is | a wretched creature, and must JC 1.02.117
there are a crew of wretched souls | that stay MAC 4.03.141
i cannot strike at wretched kerns, whose arms 5.07. 17
and i, of ladies most deject and wretched, HAM 3.01.155
o wretched state! 3.03. 67
thou wretched, rash, intruding fool, farewell! 3.04. 31
wretched queen, adieu! 5.02.333
as full of grief as age, wretched in both. LR 2.04.273
that i am wretched | makes thee the happier; 4.01. 65
wretched though i seem, | i can produce a 5.01. 42
o wretched fool, | that lov'st to make thine OTH 3.03.375
it is my wretched fortune. 4.02.128
o wretched villain! 5.01. 41
ay me, most wretched, | that have my heart ANT 3.06. 76
and you shall find me, wretched man, a thing CYM 3.04. 19
o jove, i think | foundations fly the wretched: 3.06. 7
as you think meet. most wretched queen! PER 3.01. 54
thebes, | and therein wretched, although free. TNK 3.01. 27
if we be found, we are wretched. 3.06.109
imagine that you see the wretched strangers, STM II.C 74
to sland'rous tongues and wretched hateful days? LUC 161
such wretched hands such wretched blood should 999
wretched hands such wretched blood should spill; 999
to keep thy sharp woes waking, wretched i, | to 1136
at last she sees a wretched image bound, | that 1501
with sad set eyes, and wretched arms across, 1662
but, wretched as he is, he strives in vain, 1665
thy wretched wife mistook the matter so, | to 1826
wretched in this alone, that thou mayst take SON 91.13
take | all this away, and me most wretched make. 91.14
what wretched errors hath my heart committed, 119. 5
may time disgrace and wretched /minutes kill. 126. 8
/WRETCHEDNESS 1 FR 0.0001 REL FR 1 V 0 P
/whilst /that /my /wretchedness /doth /bait R2 4.01.238
WRETCHEDNESS 9 FR 0.0010 REL FR 9 V 0 P
i love not to see wretchedness o'ercharg'd, MND 5.01. 85
my wretchedness unto a row of /pins, | they will R2 3.04. 26
what can happen | to me above this wretchedness?
H8 3.01.123
and leave me here in wretchedness behind ye? 4.02. 84
art thou so bare and full of wretchedness, | and ROM 5.01. 68
o, the fierce wretchedness that glory brings us! TIM 4.02. 30
is wretchedness depriv'd that benefit, | to end LR 4.06. 61
tear, took pity | from most true wretchedness. CYM 3.04. 61
free that soul which wretchedness hath chained? LUC 900
WRETCHED'ST 1 FR 0.0001 REL FR 1 V 0 P
he was the wretched'st thing when he was young, R3 2.04. 18
/WRETCHES 1 FR 0.0001 REL FR 1 V 0 P
/such /as /basest /and /contemned'st /wretches LR 2.02.143
WRETCHES 13 FR 0.0014 REL FR 13 V 0 P
as wretches have o'ernight | that wait for TGV 4.02.132
and still converse | with groaning wretches; LLL 5.02.852
never saw i | wretches so quake: WT 5.01.199
as is our wretches fett'red in our prisons; H5 1.02.243
hence, | poor miserable wretches, to your death; 2.02.178
where, wretches, their poor bodies | must lie 4.03. 87
be these the wretches that we play'd at dice for 4.05. 8
and call us orphans, wretches, castaways, | if R3 2.02. 6
hark, wretches, how i mean to martyr you. TIT 5.02.180
poor naked wretches, wheresoe'er you are, | that LR 3.04. 28
expose thyself to feel what wretches feel, 3.04. 34
poor wretches that depend | on greatness' favor CYM 5.04.127
poor wretches have remorse in poor abuses, LUC 269
WRETCH'S 2 FR 0.0002 REL FR 2 V 0 P
that lays strong siege unto this wretch's soul, 2H6 3.03. 22
dead, | the coward conquest of a wretch's knife, SON 74.11
WRINCHING *(also wrenching*)*
WRINCHING 1 FR 0.0001 REL FR 1 V 0 P
wrinching our holy begging in our eyes | to make TNK 1.01.156
WRING 12 FR 0.0013 REL FR 11 V 1 P
and i wash, wring, brew, bake, scour, dress meat WIV 1.04. 96 P
not being believ'd, | or wring redress from you. MM 5.01. 32
to those that wring under the load of sorrow, ADO 5.01. 28
your overkindness doth wring tears from me. 5.01.293
rear up his body, wring him by the nose. 2H6 3.02. 34
to wring the widow from her custom'd right, 5.01.188
and wring the aweful sceptre from his fist, 3H6 2.01.154
which god defend that i should wring from him! R3 3.07.173
ay me, what news? why dost thou wring thy hands?
ROM 3.02. 36
and drop my blood for drachmaes than to wring JC 4.03. 73
and let me wring your heart, for so i shall, HAM 3.04. 35
and then, sir, would he gripe and wring my hand; OTH 3.03.421
WRINGER 1 FR 0.0001 REL FR 0 V 1 P
or his laundry — his washer and his wringer. WIV 1.02. 5 P
/WRINGING 1 FR 0.0001 REL FR 1 V 0 P
/wringing it thus) you'll tender me a fool. HAM 1.03.109
WRINGING 6 FR 0.0006 REL FR 5 V 1 P
our maid howling, our cat wringing her hands, TGV 2.03. 8 P
wringing her hands, whose whiteness so became 3.01.229
sense no more can feel | but his own wringing! H5 4.01.236
dangers, doubts, wringing of the conscience, H8 2.02. 27
leave wringing of your hands. HAM 3.04. 34
"you hurt my hand with wringing, let us part, VEN 421
WRINGS 4 FR 0.0004 REL FR 4 V 0 P
it is a hint | that wrings mine eyes to't. TMP 1.02.135
weeps over them, and wrings his hapless hands, 2H6 1.01.226
he wrings at some distress. CYM 3.06. 78
he wrings her nose, he strikes her on the cheeks VEN 475
WRINKLE 6 FR 0.0006 REL FR 6 V 0 P
hang'd in the frowning wrinkle of her brow! JN 2.01.505
age, | but stop no wrinkle in his pilgrimage; R2 1.03.230
or bend one wrinkle on my sovereign's face. 2.01.170
buried this sigh in wrinkle of a smile, | but TRO 1.01. 38
"thou canst not see one wrinkle in my brow, VEN 139
survey, | if time have any wrinkle graven there; SON 100.10
WRINKLED 15 FR 0.0017 REL FR 14 V 1 P
more grave and wrinkled than the aims and ends MM 1.03. 5
to view with hollow eye and wrinkled brow | an MV 4.01.270
this is a man, old, wrinkled, faded, withered, SHR 4.05. 43
hermione was not so much wrinkled, nothing | so WT 5.03. 28
makes fearful action | with wrinkled brows, with JN 4.02.192
war hath smooth'd his wrinkled front; R3 1.01. 9
foul wrinkled witch, what mak'st thou in my 1.03.163
virgins and boys, mid–age and wrinkled /eld, TRO 2.02.104
pluck the grave wrinkled senate from the bench, TIM 4.01. 5
that their faces are wrinkled, their eyes HAM 2.02.198 P
pinches black, | and wrinkled deep in time? ANT 1.05. 29
while i strook | the lean and wrinkled cassius, 3.11. 37
like wrinkled pebbles in a /glassy stream, | you TNK 1.01.112
"were i hard–favor'd, foul, or wrinkled old, VEN 133
respect and reason, wait on wrinkled age! LUC 275
/WRINKLES 1 FR 0.0001 REL FR 1 V 0 P
/no /deeper /wrinkles /yet? R2 4.01.277
WRINKLES 15 FR 0.0017 REL FR 13 V 2 P
with mirth and laughter let old wrinkles come, MV 1.01. 80
so that you had her wrinkles and i her money, i AWW 2.04. 20 P
the wrinkles in my brows, now fill'd with blood, 3H6 5.02. 19
whose youth and freshness | wrinkles apollo's, TRO 2.02. 79
see | filling the aged wrinkles in my cheeks, TIT 3.01. 7
a pox of wrinkles! TIM 4.03.149
let it stamp wrinkles in her brow of youth, LR 1.04.284
wrinkles forbid! ANT 1.02. 20 P
fixed | in the remorseless wrinkles of his face; LUC 562
cheeks with chops and wrinkles were disguis'd, 1452
despite of wrinkles, this thy golden time. SON 3.12
and fill'd his brow | with lines and wrinkles, 63. 4
the wrinkles which thy glass will truly show, 77. 5
writ in moods and frowns and wrinkles strange; 93. 8
of age, | nor gives to necessary wrinkles place, 108.11
WRIST 2 FR 0.0002 REL FR 2 V 0 P
he that speaks doth gripe the hearer's wrist, JN 4.02.190
he took me by the wrist, and held me hard, HAM 2.01. 84
WRISTS 1 FR 0.0001 REL FR 1 V 0 P
art fetter'd | more than my shanks and wrists. CYM 5.04. 9
WRIT *(also wrote)*
/WRIT 1 FR 0.0001 REL FR 1 V 0 P
/indeed | /where /all /my /sins /are /writ, /and R2 4.01.275
WRIT 107 FR 0.0121 REL FR 81 V 26 P
some love of yours hath writ to you in rhyme. TGV 1.02. 76
look, here is writ "kind julia." 1.02.106
and here is writ "love–wounded proteus." 1.02.110
lo, here in one line is his name twice writ, 1.02.120
are they not lamely writ? 2.01. 91 P
me, i have writ your letter | unto the secret, 2.01.104
it goes, | i writ at random, very doubtfully. 2.01.111
the lines are very quaintly writ, | but (since 2.01.122
you writ them, sir, at my request, | but i will 2.01.126
i would have had them writ more movingly. 2.01.128
and when it's writ, for my sake read it over, 2.01.130
why, she hath not writ to me? 2.01.151 P
that's the letter i writ to her friend. 2.01.160 P
"for often have you writ to her; 2.01.165
which, being writ to me, shall be deliver'd 3.01.251
she cannot, for that's writ down she is slow of; 3.01.349 P
i have writ me here a letter to her; WIV 1.03. 58 P
writ with blank space for different names (sure, 2.01. 75 P
with character too gross is writ on juliet. MM 1.02.155
but, by chance, nothing of what is writ. 4.02.203 P
every letter he hath writ hath disvouch'd other. 4.04. 1 P
her smock till she have writ a sheet of paper. ADO 2.03.133 P
o, when she had writ it, and was reading it over 2.03.136 P
for i should flout him, if he writ to me, yea, 2.03.144 P
have you writ down, that they are none? 4.02. 31 P
o that i had been writ down an ass! 4.02. 87 P
however they have writ the style of gods, | and 5.01. 37
and here's another | writ in my cousin's hand, 5.04. 89
i will have that subject newly writ o'er, that i LLL 1.02.115 P
it is writ to jaquenetta. 4.01. 58
once more i'll read the ode that i have writ. 4.03. 97
writ a' both sides the leaf, margent and all, 5.02. 8
if he that writ it had play'd pyramus and hang'd MND 5.01.358 P
and whiter than the paper it writ on | is the MV 2.04. 13
paper it writ on | is the fair hand that writ. 2.04. 14
to show the letter that i writ to you. AYL 5.02. 78
so holy writ in babes hath judgment shown, AWW 2.01.138
than these boys', | and writ as little beard. 2.03. 61
i have writ my letters, casketed my treasure, 2.05. 24
for her, writ to my lady mother i am returning, 4.03. 88 P
and writ to me this other day to turn him out a' 4.03.199 P
of the sonnet you writ to diana in behalf of the 4.03.320 P
"be not afraid of greatness": 'twas well writ. TN 3.04. 39 P
h'as here writ a letter to you; 5.01.286 P
maria writ | the letter at sir toby's great 5.01.362
you yourself | have said and writ so, but your WT 5.01. 99
is it not fair writ? JN 4.01. 37
writ in remembrance more than things long past. R2 2.01. 14
be crowing as if he had writ man ever since his 2H4 1.02. 26 P
who hath writ me down | after my seeming. 5.02.128
for in the book of numbers is it writ, | when H5 1.02. 98
i once writ a sonnet in his praise and began 3.07. 39 P
writ to your grace from th' duke of burgundy. 1H6 4.01. 12
his weapons holy saws of sacred writ, | his 2H6 1.03. 58
now pray, my lord, let's see the devil's writ. 1.04. 57
this hand of mine hath writ in thy behalf, | and 4.01. 63
under the which is writ, "invitis nubibus." 4.01. 99
kent, in the commentaries caesar writ, | is 4.07. 60
with odd old ends stol'n forth of holy writ, R3 1.03.336
let there be letters writ to every shire, | of H8 1.02.103
with all the business | i writ to 's holiness. 3.02.222
packets | you writ to th' pope against the king. 3.02.287
then, that in all you writ to rome, or else | to 3.02.313
that therefore such a writ be sued against you, 3.02.341
thee, | take this along, i writ it for thy sake, COR 5.02. 90
whose chronicle thus writ: 5.03.145
if you have writ your annals true, 'tis there 5.06.113
then all too late i bring this fatal writ, | the TIT 2.03.264
i have writ my name, | without the help of any 4.01. 70

o, do ye read, my lord, what she hath writ? 4.01. 77
to find those persons whose names are here writ, ROM 1.02. 42 P
what names the writing person hath here writ. 1.02. 44 P
and find delight writ there with beauty's pen; 1.03. 82
so many guests invite as here are writ. 4.02. 1
or, if his mind be writ, give me his letter. 5.02. 4
one writ with me in sour misfortune's book! 5.03. 82
mean time i writ to romeo, | that he should 5.03.246
eyes, | are not within the leaf of pity writ, TIM 4.03.118
nor nothing in your letters writ of her? JC 4.03.183
we have here writ | to norway, uncle of young HAM 1.02. 27
and we did think it writ down in our duty | to 1.02.222
too light, for the law of writ and the liberty: 2.02.401 P
dear father, is't writ in your revenge | that, 4.05.142
folded the writ up in the form of th' other, 5.02. 51
life for him that he hath writ this to feel my LR 1.02. 86 P
what he hath utter'd i have writ my sister; 1.04.331
what, have you writ that letter to my sister? 1.04.334
our father he hath writ, so hath our sister, 2.01.122
for my writ | is on the life of lear and on 5.03.246
confirmations strong | as proofs of holy writ; OTH 3.03.324
hand | which writ his honor in the acts it did ANT 5.01. 22
this is the tenor of the emperor's writ: CYM 3.07. 1
each man | thinks all is writ he /speken can; PER 2.ch. 12
wit | the epitaph is for marina writ | by wicked 4.04. 32
that the star–gazers, having writ on death, VEN 509
writ in the glassy margents of such books. LUC 102
how | to cipher what is writ in learned books, 811
be spent, | and as his due writ in my testament. 1183
cause craves haste, and it will soon be writ." 1295
her woe, | her certain sorrow writ uncertainly. 1311
her letter now is seal'd, and on it writ, | "at 1331
o, learn to read what silent love hath writ: SON 23.13
remember not | the hand that writ it, for i love 71. 6
let him but copy what in you is writ, | not 84. 9
is writ in moods and frowns and wrinkles strange 93. 8
those lines that i before have writ do lie, 115. 1
proved, | i never writ, nor no man ever loved. 116.14

/WRITE 1 FR 0.0001 REL FR 1 V 0 P
but /write her fair words still in foulest terms 2H4 4.04.104

WRITE 125 FR 0.0141 REL FR 90 V 35 P
she enjoin'd me to write some lines to one she TGV 2.01. 87 P
so it stead you, i will write | (please you 2.01.113
please you, i'll write your ladyship another. 2.01.129
scribe, to himself should write the letter? 2.01.140
she, when she hath made you write to yourself? 2.01.153 P
her love himself to write unto her lover." 2.01.168
write till your ink be dry, and with your tears 3.02. 74
and "honi soit qui mal y pense" write | in WIV 5.05. 69
we shall write to you, | as time and our MM 1.01. 55
let's write "good angel" on the devil's horn, 2.04. 16
now will i write letters to angelo | (the 4.03. 93
great letters as they write "here is good horse ADO 1.01.265 P
him with scorn, write to him that i love him?" 2.03.129 P
she now when she is beginning to write to him; 2.03.131 P
be so immodest to write to one that she knew 2.03.142 P
or george seacole, for they can write and read. 3.03. 12 P
fortune, but to write and read comes by nature. 3.03. 15 P
i will write against it: 4.01. 56
pray write down borachio. yours, sirrah? 4.02. 12 P
write down master gentleman conrade. 4.02. 15 P
write down, that they hope they serve god; 4.02. 18 P
and write god first, for god defend but god 4.02. 19 P
write down prince john a villain. 4.02. 41 P
let him write down the prince's officer coxcomb. 4.02. 71 P
o that he were here to write me down as ass! 4.02. 76 P
will you then write me a sonnet in praise of my 5.02. 4 P
and to the strictest decrees i'll write my name. LLL 1.01.117
so to the laws at large i write my name, | and 1.01.155
devise, wit, write, pen, for i am for whole 1.02.184 P
well, i will love, write, sigh, pray, sue, groan 3.01.204
these numbers will i tear, and write in prose! 4.03. 55
when shall you see me write a thing in rhyme, 4.03.179
never durst poet touch a pen to write | until 4.03.343
write "lord have mercy on us" on those three: 5.02.419
write me a prologue, and let the prologue seem MND 3.01. 17 P
get peter quince to write a ballet of this dream 4.01.214 P
than to live still and write mine epitaph. MV 4.01.118
every sentence end, | will i 'rosalinda' write, AYL 3.02.137
i'll write to him a very taunting letter, | and 3.05.134
i'll write it straight; 3.05.136
i know not the contents, | phebe did write it. 4.03. 22
a pen in 's hand | and write to her a love–line. AWW 2.01. 78
i must tell thee, sirrah, i write man; 2.03.198 P
write to the king | that which i durst not speak 2.03.288
but in such a 'then' i write a 'never.'" 3.02. 60 P
write, write, that from the bloody course of war 3.04. 8
write, write, that from the bloody course of war 3.04. 8
write, write, rinaldo, | to this unworthy 3.04. 29
write, write, rinaldo, | to this unworthy 3.04. 29
write loyal cantons of contemned love, | and TN 1.05.270
i'll write thee a challenge, or i'll deliver thy 2.03.129 P
i can write very like my lady your niece; 2.03.159 P
go, write it in a martial hand, be curst and 3.02. 42 P
in thy ink, though thou write with a goose–pen, 3.02. 49 P
did he write this? 5.01.312 P
write from it, if you can, in hand or phrase, 5.01.332
known betwixt us three, i'll write you down, WT 4.04.560
nor never write, regreet, nor reconcile | this R2 1.03.186
eyes | write sorrow on the bosom of the earth. 3.02.147
i must go write again | to other friends, and so 1H4 4.04. 40
any occasion to write for matter of grant, shall H5 5.02.337 P
i'll call for pen and ink, and write my mind. 1H6 5.03. 66
and so will i, and write home for it straight. 2H6 4.01. 24
he can write and read and cast accompt. 4.02. 85 P
he can make obligations, and write court–hand. 4.02. 93 P
they use to write it on the top of letters; 4.02.100 P
dost thou use to write thy name? 4.02.102 P
so well brought up that i can write my name. 4.02.106 P
and that i'll write upon thy burgonet, | might i 5.01.200
sits, | write up his title with usurping blood. 3H6 1.01.169
i'll write unto them and entreat them fair; 1.01.271
write in the dust this sentence with thy blood: 5.01. 56
with that sour ferryman which poets write of, R3 1.04. 46
eleven hours i have spent to write it over, 3.06. 5
write to me very shortly, | and you shall 4.04.428
in brass, their virtues | we write in water. H8 4.02. 46
that letter | i caus'd you write yet sent away? 4.02.128
us, we will write | to rome of our success. COR 1.09. 74
write down thy mind, bewray thy meaning so, TIT 2.04. 3
in the dust i write | my heart's deep languor, 3.01. 12
write thou, good niece, and here display at last 4.01. 73
and with a gad of steel will write these words, 4.01.103
any man that can write may answer a letter. ROM 2.04. 10 P
but i will write again to mantua, | and keep her 5.02. 28
and write in thee the figures of their love, TIM 5.01.154
mark him, and write his speeches in their books, JC 1.02.126
write them together, yours is as fair a name; 1.02.144
caesar did write for him to come to rome. 3.01.278
you wrong'd yourself to write in such a case. 4.03. 6
forth paper, fold it, write upon't, read it, MAC 5.01. 7 P
a baseness to write fair, and labor'd much | how HAM 5.02. 34
had he a hand to write this? LR 1.02. 57 P
i'll write straight to my sister | to hold my 1.03. 25
why should she write to edmund? 4.05. 19
about it, and write happy when th' hast done. 5.03. 35
write from us to him, post–post–haste. dispatch! OTH 1.03. 46
you shall not write my praise. 2.01.116
what wouldst write of me, if thou shouldst 2.01.117
most goodly book, | made to write "whore" upon? 4.02. 72
thou wilt write to antony? ANT 3.01. 29
think, speak, cast, write, sing, number, hoo! 3.02. 17
thou shalt bring him to me | where i will write. 3.03. 47
i'll write it. 3.13. 28
write to him | (i will subscribe) gentle adieus 4.05. 13
thither write, my queen, | and with mine eyes CYM 1.01. 99
if he should write | and i not have it, 'twere a 1.03. 2
i will write. 1.06.208
to note the chamber, i will write all down: 2.02. 24
why should i write this down, that's riveted, 2.02. 43
i'll write against them, | detest them, curse 2.05. 32
wherefore write you not | what monsters her 3.02. 1
i'll write to my lord she's dead. 3.05.104
to write and read | be henceforth treacherous! 4.02.316
can he write and read too? TNK 5.02. 57
her maid is gone, and she prepares to write, LUC 1296
if i could write the beauty of your eyes, | and SON 17. 5
o, let me, true in love, but truly write, | and 21. 9
for who's so dumb that cannot write to thee, 38. 7
why write i still all one, ever the same, | and 76. 5
o, know, sweet love, i always write of you, 76. 9
o, how i faint when i of you do write, | knowing 80. 1
good thoughts whilst other write good words, 85. 5
by spirits taught to write | above a mortal 86. 5
o, blame me not if i no more can write! 103. 5
he learn'd but surety–like to write for me 134. 7

WRITER 3 FR 0.0003 REL FR 2 V 1 P
only get the learned writer to set down our ADO 3.05. 63 P
i'll haste the writer, and withal | break with 1H4 3.01.141
fan | from me the witless chaff of such a writer TNK pr 19

/WRITERS 1 FR 0.0001 REL FR 0 V 1 P
/their /writers /do /them /wrong, /to /make HAM 2.02.350 P

WRITERS 6 FR 0.0006 REL FR 4 V 2 P
yet writers say: TGV 1.01. 42
and writers say: 1.01. 45
for all your writers do consent that ipse is he: AYL 5.01. 43 P
this pitch (as ancient writers do report) doth 1H4 2.04.413 P
besides, their writers say, | king pepin, which H5 1.02. 64
the dedicated words which writers use | of their SON 82. 3

WRITES 22 FR 0.0024 REL FR 15 V 7 P
lord, but that he writes | how happily he lives, TGV 1.03. 56
master parson, who writes himself armigero, in WIV 1.01. 9 P
he writes verses, he speaks holiday, he smells 3.02. 68 P
you hear the learn'd bellario, what he writes, MV 4.01.167
he writes brave verses, speaks brave words, AYL 3.04. 40 P
why writes she so to me? 4.03. 19
mark how the tyrant writes. 4.03. 39
let me see what he writes, and when he means to AWW 3.02. 10 P
and yet she writes, | pursuit would be but vain. 3.04. 24
he writes me here, that inward sickness — | and 1H4 4.01. 31
for, as he writes, there is no quailing now, 4.01. 39
he holds his place, for look you how he writes. 2H4 2.02.108 P
it is the worst, and all, my lord, he writes. 1H6 4.01. 67
hath, | writes not so tedious a style as this. 4.07. 74
a strange fellow here | writes me that man, how TRO 3.03. 96
titus lartius writes they fought together, but COR 2.01.127 P
and now he writes to heaven for his redress. TIT 4.04. 13
and here he writes that he did buy a poison | of ROM 5.03.288
from the bill | that writes them all alike: MAC 3.01.100
you, the effects he writes of succeed unhappily, LR 1.02.143 P
she writes so to you? doth she? CYM 2.04.105
but he that writes of you, if he can tell | that SON 84. 7

WRITHLED 1 FR 0.0001 REL FR 1 V 0 P
it cannot be this weak and writhled shrimp 1H6 2.03. 23

/WRITING 1 FR 0.0001 REL FR 0 V 1 P
of the party /writing to the person written unto LLL 4.02.134 P

WRITING 22 FR 0.0024 REL FR 18 V 4 P
boast of it, and for your writing and reading, ADO 3.03. 20 P
neither serve for the writing nor the tune. LLL 1.02.114 P
it is berowne's writing, and here is his name. 4.03.199
i'll read the writing. MV 2.07. 64
that took some pains in writing, he begg'd mine, 5.01.182
no more trees with writing love–songs in their AYL 3.02.259 P
which she did use as she was writing of it, | it 4.03. 10
and there it is in writing, fairly drawn. SHR 3.01. 70
alas, malvolio, this is not my writing, | though TN 5.01.345
but your writing now | is colder than that theme WT 5.01. 99
let me see the writing. R2 5.02. 57
i will be satisfied, let me see the writing. 5.02. 59
boy, let me see the writing. 5.02. 69
peruse this writing here, and thou shalt know 5.03. 49
although in writing i preferr'd | the manner of 1H6 3.01. 10
all whites are ink | writing their own reproach, TRO 1.01. 57
what he would do | he sent in writing after me; COR 5.01. 68
writing destruction on the enemy's castle? TIT 3.01.169
find what names the writing person hath here ROM 1.02. 43 P
why, i was writing of my epitaph; TIM 5.01.185
if you please | to greet your lord with writing, CYM 1.06.206
she thinks not so; peruse this writing else. PER 2.05. 41

WRITINGS 2 FR 0.0002 REL FR 2 V 0 P
writings, all tending to the great opinion JC 1.02.318
gentle i proceeded still | in all my writings. ANT 5.01. 76

WRITS 1 FR 0.0001 REL FR 1 V 0 P
let us pursue him ere the writs go forth. 2H6 5.03. 26

WRITTEN 35 FR 0.0039 REL FR 24 V 11 P
twice, or thrice, was "proteus" written down: TGV 1.02.114
there is written in your brow, provost, honesty MM 4.02.153 P
it is written, they appear to men like angels of ERR 4.03. 55 P
have written strange defeatures in my face: 5.01.300
though it be not written down, yet forget not ADO 4.02. 77 P
her, | for here's a paper written in his hand, 5.04. 86
the party /writing to the person written unto: LLL 4.02.135 P
have you the lion's part written? MND 1.02. 66 P
love's stories written in love's richest book. 2.02.122
and it shall be written in eight and six. 3.01. 24 P
let it be written in eight and eight. 3.01. 25 P
whose empty eye | there is a written scroll! MV 2.07. 64
more i'll entreat you | written to bear along. AWW 3.02. 95
that, having our fair order written down, | both JN 5.02. 4
divers reasons | which i shall send you written, 1H4 1.03.263
of youth, that are written down old with all the 2H4 1.02.179 P
whose memory is written on the earth | with yet 4.01. 81
with written pamphlets studiously devis'd? 1H6 3.01. 2
with heed perused | what i have written to you? COR 5.06. 62
i know | there is enough written upon this earth TIT 4.01. 84
a scroll, and written round about. 4.02. 18
of my word, i have written to effect, | there's 4.03. 60
and what is written shall be executed. 5.02. 15
persons out | whose names are written there, and ROM 1.02. 36
find them out whose names are written here! 1.02. 38 P
it is written that the shoemaker should meddle 1.02. 39 P
lies | find written in the margent of his eyes. 1.03. 86
had i it written, i would tear the word. 2.02. 57
raze out the written troubles of the brain, MAC 5.03. 42
is extant, and written in very choice italian. HAM 3.02.262 P
have we | our written purposes before us sent, ANT 2.06. 4
i crave our composition may be written | and 2.06. 58
though written in our flesh, we shall remember 5.02.119
stand up, | your grief is written in your cheek. TNK 1.01.110
to thee i send this written ambassage | to SON 26. 3

/WRONG 4 FR 0.0004 REL FR 3 V 1 P
/do /his /ghost /the /wrong | /to /hold /your 2H4 2.03. 39
/those /men /that /most /have /done /us /wrong. 4.01. 79
/their /writers /do /them /wrong, /to /make HAM 2.02.350 P
/opinion, /whose /wrong /thoughts /defile /thee, LR 3.06.112

WRONG 251 FR 0.0283 REL FR 210 V 41 P
sighing back again, | did us but loving wrong. TMP 1.02.151
sir, | i fear you have done yourself some wrong; 1.02.444
to wrong my friend, i shall be much forsworn. TGV 2.06. 3
now, as thou lov'st me, do him not that wrong, 2.07. 80
not asham'd | to wrong him with thy importunacy? 4.02.111
"you do him the more wrong," quoth i, "'twas i 4.04. 27 P
mine shall not do his julia so much wrong. 4.04.137
i will not do you that wrong. WIV 1.01.310 P
you do yourself wrong indeed la! 1.01.313 P
yet i wrong him to call him poor. 2.02.271 P
i shall not only receive this villainous wrong, 2.02.294 P
terms, and by him that does me this wrong. 2.02.296 P
belike having receiv'd wrong by some person, is 3.01. 53 P
i have directed you to wrong places. 3.01.108 P
you wrong yourself too much. 3.03.167 P
you do yourself mighty wrong, master ford. 3.03.207 P
you wrong me, sir, thus still to haunt my house. 3.04. 69
knowing my mind, you wrong me, master fenton. 3.04. 76
upon my life then, you took the wrong. 5.05.189 P
i think i have done myself wrong, have i not? MM 1.02. 40 P
they do you wrong to put you so oft upon't. 2.01.266 P
but might you do't, and do the world no wrong, 2.02. 53
and do him right that, answering one foul wrong, 2.02.103
hooking both right and wrong to th' appetite, 2.04.176
you do him wrong, surely. 3.02.129 P
and i should wrong it | to lock it in the wards 5.01. 9
but you are i' the wrong | to speak before your 5.01. 86
be it my wrong you are from me exempt, | but ERR 2.02.171
but wrong not that wrong with a more contempt. 2.02.172
but wrong not that wrong with a more contempt. 2.02.172
'tis double wrong, to truant with your bed, 3.02. 17
you gave me none, you wrong me much to say so. 4.01. 66
you wrong me more, sir, in denying it. 4.01. 67
you have done wrong to this my honest friend, 5.01. 19
it cannot be that she hath done thee wrong. 5.01.135
beyond imagination is the wrong | that she this 5.01.201
one day's error | have suffer'd wrong, go keep 5.01.399
i will not do them the wrong to mistrust any, i ADO 1.01.243 P
yea, but so i am apt to do myself wrong. 2.01.206 P
so turns she every man the wrong side out, | and 3.01. 68
o, do not do your cousin such a wrong. 3.01. 87
if they wrong her honor, | the proudest of them 4.01.191
marry, thou dost wrong me, thou dissembler, thou 5.01. 53
who i believe was pack'd in all this wrong, 5.01.299
whom right and wrong | have chose as umpeer of LLL 1.01.168
you do the king my father too much wrong, | and 2.01.153
wrong, | and wrong the reputation of your name, 2.01.154
as thou art, o, pardon love this wrong, | that 4.02.117
i have seen the day of wrong through the little 5.02.723 P
not seen, | newts and blind–worms, do no wrong, MND 2.02. 11
good troth, you do me wrong (good sooth, you do) 2.02.129
made senseless things begin to do them wrong, 3.02. 28
then stir demetrius up with bitter wrong; 3.02.361
and out of doubt you do me now more wrong | in MV 1.01.155
and for my love i pray you wrong me not. 1.03.170
if you choose wrong | never to speak to lady 2.01. 40
truth is that the jew, having done me wrong, 2.02.133 P
and if you wrong us, shall we not revenge? 3.01. 66 P
if a jew wrong a christian, what is his humility 3.01. 68 P
if a christian wrong a jew, what should his 3.01. 69 P
for in choosing wrong | i lose your company; 3.02. 2
substance of my praise doth wrong this shadow 3.02.127
what judgment shall i dread, doing no wrong? 4.01. 89
to do a great right, do a little wrong, | and 4.01.216
by yonder moon i swear you do me wrong; 5.01.142
portia, forgive me this enforced wrong, | and in 5.01.240
i shall do my friends no wrong, for i have none AYL 1.02.189 P
good sister, wrong me not, nor wrong yourself, SHR 2.01. 1
good sister, wrong me not, nor wrong yourself, 2.01. 1
why dost thou wrong her that did ne'er wrong 2.01. 27
dost thou wrong her that did ne'er wrong thee? 2.01. 27
you wrong me, signior gremio, give me leave. 2.01. 46
accept of him, or else you do me wrong. 2.01. 59
you do me double wrong | to strive for that 3.01. 16
the more my wrong, the more his spite appears. 4.03. 2
love all, trust a few, | do wrong to none. AWW 1.01. 65
i'll never do you wrong for your own sake. 2.03. 90
the king has done you wrong; 2.03.300

but to himself | the greatest wrong of all. 5.03. 15
he does me wrong, my lord; 5.03.189
how quickly the wrong side may be turn'd outward TN 3.01. 13 P
who does beguile you? who does do you wrong? 5.01.140
madam, you wrong me, and the world shall know it 5.01.302 P
madam, you have done me wrong, | notorious wrong 5.01.328
you have done me wrong, | notorious wrong. 5.01.329
if this be so, a wrong | something unfilial. WT 4.04.405
and so still think of | the wrong i did myself; 5.01. 9
or else it must go wrong with you and me; JN 1.01. 41
boy, | under whose warrant i impeach thy wrong, 2.01.116
for without my wrong | there is no tongue hath 3.01.182
right, | let it be lawful that law bar no wrong; 3.01.186
therefore, since law itself is perfect wrong, 3.01.189
all things that you should use to do me wrong 4.01.117
attend | the steps of wrong, should move you to 4.02. 57
hand | of stern injustice and confused wrong. 5.02. 23
shall wound my honor with such feeble wrong, R2 1.01.191
against my will to do myself this wrong. 1.03.246
long | shall tender duty make me suffer wrong? 2.01.164
to find out right with wrong — it may not be; 2.03.145
he does me double wrong | that wounds me with 3.02.215
learn him forbearance from so foul a wrong. 4.01.120
never rise | to do him wrong or any way impeach 1H4 1.03. 75
will stand to it, you will not pocket up wrong. 3.03.163 P
broke oath on oath, committed wrong on wrong, 4.03.101
broke oath on oath, committed wrong on wrong, 4.03.101
and make thee rich for doing me such wrong. 2H4 1.01. 90
this strained passion doth you wrong, my lord. 1.01.161
an ass and a beast, to bear every knave's wrong. 2.01. 38 P
you speak as having power to do wrong, but 2.01.129 P
hang'd among you, the gallows shall have wrong. 2.02. 97 P
cowardice doth not make thee wrong this virtuous 2.04.326 P
sir john, sir john, do not yourself wrong. 3.02.254 P
go to, i say, he shall have no wrong. 5.01. 52 P
and certainly she did you wrong, for you were H5 2.01. 18 P
if his cause be wrong, our obedience to the king 4.01.132 P
and yet i do thee wrong to mind thee of it, 4.03. 13
marry, for that she's in a wrong belief, | i go 1H6 2.03. 31
false, | the argument you held was wrong in you; 2.04. 57
poor gentleman, his wrong doth equal mine. 2.05. 22
thou dost then wrong me, as that slaughterer 2.05.109
crave | i may have liberty to venge this wrong, 3.04. 42
with him, my lord, for he hath done me wrong. 4.01. 85
and i with him, for he hath done me wrong. 4.01. 86
what is that wrong whereof you both complain? 4.01. 87
during the life, let us not wrong it dead. 4.07. 50
that's some wrong indeed. 2H6 1.03. 19 P
thou never didst them wrong, nor no man wrong; 3.01.209
thou never didst them wrong, nor no man wrong; 3.01.209
and have no other reason for this wrong | but 5.01.189
king henry, be thy title right or wrong, | lord 3H6 1.01.159
what wrong is this unto the prince your son! 1.01.176
think but upon the wrong he did us all, | and 1.04.173
there is no wrong, but every thing is right. 2.02.132
warwick tells his title, smooths the wrong, 3.01. 48
i will revenge his wrong to lady bona, | and 3.03.197
tell him from me that he hath done me wrong, 3.03.231
she had the wrong. 4.01.102
"tell him from me that he hath done me wrong, 4.01.110
they do me wrong, and i will not endure it! R3 1.03. 42
when done thee wrong? 1.03. 56
she hath had too much wrong, and i repent | my 1.03.306
yet you have all the vantage of her wrong. 1.03.309
i do the wrong, and first begin to brawl. 1.03.323
by false intelligence or wrong surmise | hold me 2.01. 55
wrong not her birth, she is a royal princess. 4.04.212
/god's wrong is most of all: 4.04.377
ay, if yourself's remembrance wrong yourself. 4.04.421
wrong hath but wrong, and blame the due of blame 5.01. 29
wrong hath but wrong, and blame the due of blame 5.01. 29
madam, you do me wrong, | i have no spleen H8 2.04. 88
your report, he knows | i am not of your wrong. 2.04.100
believe me, she has had much wrong. 3.01. 48
you wrong the king's love with these fears, 3.01. 81
we, good lady, | upon what cause, wrong you? 3.01.156
you wrong your virtues | with these weak women's 3.01.168
or rather, right and wrong | (between whose TRO 1.03.116
a free determination | 'twixt right and wrong; 2.02.171
persist | in doing wrong extenuates not wrong, 2.02.187
persist | in doing wrong extenuates not wrong, 2.02.187
come, you'll do him wrong ere you are ware. 4.02. 55 P
we go wrong, we go wrong. 5.01. 67
we go wrong, we go wrong. 5.01. 67
said we were i' th' wrong when we banish'd him. COR 4.06.154 P
and took some pride | to do myself this wrong; 5.06. 37
in me, | nor wrong mine age with this indignity. TIT 1.01. 8
mother's hand shall right your mother's wrong. 2.03.121
he doth me wrong to feed me with delays. 4.03. 43
show me a thousand that hath done thee wrong, 5.02. 96
they, 'twas they, that did her all this wrong. 5.03. 58
and if you leave me so, you do me wrong. ROM 1.01.196
good pilgrim, you do wrong your hand too much, 1.05. 97
you do yourselves | much wrong, you bate too TIM 1.02.206
you do yourselves but wrong to stir me up, | let 3.04. 53
will make | black white, foul fair, wrong right, 4.03. 29
now breathless wrong | shall sit and pant in 5.04. 10
know, caesar doth not wrong, nor without cause JC 3.01. 47
and pity to the general wrong of rome — | as 3.01.170
it shall advantage more than do us wrong. 3.01.242
of the matter, | caesar has had great wrong. 3.02.110
i should do brutus wrong, and cassius wrong, 3.02.123
i should do brutus wrong, and cassius wrong, 3.02.123
i will not do them wrong; 3.02.125
i rather choose | to wrong the dead, to wrong 3.02.126
to wrong the dead, to wrong myself and you, 3.02.126
and you, | than i will wrong such honorable men. 3.02.127
i fear i wrong the honorable men | whose daggers 3.02.151
most noble brother, you have done me wrong. 4.02. 37
wrong i mine enemies? 4.02. 38
and if not so, how should i wrong a brother? 4.02. 39
you wrong me every way; 4.03. 55
you wrong me, brutus: 4.03. 55
i will not do thee so much wrong to wake thee. 4.03.270
we do it wrong, being so majestical, | to offer HAM 1.01.143
th' oppressor's wrong, the proud man's contumely 3.01. 70
i have done you wrong, | but pardon't, as you 5.02.226
and when he's not himself does wrong laertes, 5.02.235
offer'd love like love, | and will not wrong it. 5.02.252
some villain hath done me wrong. LR 1.02.165 P
i did her wrong. 1.05. 24 P
and told me i had turn'd the wrong side out. 4.02. 9
and woes by wrong imaginations lose | the 4.06.283
you do me wrong to take me out o' th' grave: 4.07. 44
sisters | have (as i do remember) done me wrong: 4.07. 73
my manners tell me | we have your wrong rebuke. OTH 1.01.130
cannot but feel this wrong as 'twere their own; 1.02. 97
bade her wrong stay, and her displeasure fly; 2.01.153
whom love hath turn'd almost the wrong side out, 2.03. 52
to speak the truth | shall nothing wrong him. 2.03.224
though cassio did some little wrong to him, | as 2.03.242
if i had said i had seen him do you wrong? 4.01. 24
and light behaviors | quite in the wrong. 4.01.103
by heaven, you do me wrong. 4.02. 81
if i would do such a wrong | for the whole world 4.03. 78
why, the wrong is but a wrong i' th' world; 4.03. 80 P
why, the wrong is but a wrong i' th' world; 4.03. 80 P
for your labor, 'tis a wrong in your own world, 4.03. 81 P
hast such noble sense of thy friend's wrong! 5.01. 32
you wrong this presence, therefore speak no more ANT 2.02.109
till we perceiv'd both how you were wrong led 3.06. 80
do not yourself such wrong, who are in this 5.02. 40
i never do him wrong | but he does buy my CYM 1.01.104
and make pretense of wrong that i have done him; PER 1.02. 91
but should he wrong my liberties in my absence? 1.02.112
wrong not your prince you love. 2.04. 25
wrong not yourself then, noble helicane; 2.04. 26
thou hadst been toss'd from wrong to injury, 5.01.130
and suffer'd | your knees to wrong themselves. TNK 1.01. 56
till she for shame see what a wrong she has done 2.02. 39
'twere wrong else. 2.05. 61
he made such scruples of the wrong he did | to 2.06. 25
doctor, | methinks you are i' th' wrong still. 5.02. 27
red cheeks and fiery eyes blaze forth her wrong; VEN 219
the heart hath treble wrong | when it is barr'd 329
thy mermaid's voice hath done me double wrong: 429
he, foul creature, that hath done thee wrong, 1005
in that high task hath done her beauty wrong, LUC 80
what wrong, what shame, what sorrow i shall 499
to wrong the wronger till he render right, | to 943
i will not wrong thy true affection so, | to 1060
by that her death, to do her husband wrong. 1264
and therefore lucrece swears he did her wrong, 1462
and rail on pyrrhus that hath done him wrong, 1467
and what wrong else may be imagined | by foul 1622
with swift pursuit to venge this wrong of mine, 1691
as thou art, o, do not love that wrong: PP 5.13
despite thy wrong, | my love shall in my verse SON 19.13
to bear love's wrong than hate's known injury. 40.12
that for thy right myself will bear all wrong. 88.14
lest i (too much profane) should do it wrong, 89.11
that my steel'd sense or changes right or wrong. 112. 8
o, call not me to justify the wrong | that thy 139. 1

/WRONG'D 1 FR 0.0001 REL FR 1 V 0 P
/when /we /are /wrong'd /and /would /unfold /our 2H4 4.01. 77

WRONG'D 45 FR 0.0050 REL FR 31 V 14 P
he hath wrong'd me, master page. WIV 1.01.102 P
he hath wrong'd me, indeed he hath, at a word he 1.01.105 P
robert shallow, esquire, saith he is wrong'd. 1.01.107 P
he hath wrong'd me in some humors. 2.01.129 P
love you the man that wrong'd you? MM 2.03. 24
yes, as i love the woman that wrong'd him. 2.03. 25
do a poor wrong'd lady a merited benefit; 3.01.200 P
we shall advise this wrong'd maid to stead up 3.01.250 P
vail your regard | upon a wrong'd — i would 5.01. 21
woe, | as i, thus wrong'd, hence unbelieved go! 5.01.119
whose salt imagination yet hath wrong'd | your 5.01.401
if any woman wrong'd by this lewd fellow | (as i 5.01.509
claudio, that you wrong'd, look you restore. 5.01.525
most mighty duke, behold a man much wrong'd. ERR 5.01.331
with her told her she is much wrong'd by you. ADO 2.01.238 P
him that he hath wrong'd his honor in marrying 2.02. 23 P
surely i do believe your fair cousin is wrong'd. 4.01.260 P
sweet hero, she is wrong'd, she is sland'red, 4.01.312 P
your soul the count claudio hath wrong'd hero? 4.01.329 P
thou hast so wrong'd mine innocent child and me 5.01. 63
did ever keep your counsels, never wrong'd you; MND 3.02.308
let me see wherein | my tongue hath wrong'd him; AYL 2.07. 84
it do him right, | then he hath wrong'd himself. 2.07. 85
you may well perceive i have not wrong'd you, AWW 4.04. 1
sir topas, never was man thus wrong'd. TN 4.02. 28 P
being wrong'd as we are by this peevish town, JN 2.01.402
is my kinsman, whom the king hath wrong'd, R2 2.02.114
i will subscribe, and say i wrong'd the duke. 2H6 3.01. 38
if ever lady wrong'd her lord so much, | thy 3.02.211
and ne'er was agamemnon's brother wrong'd | by 3H6 2.02.148
then by something that thou hast not wrong'd. R3 4.04.373
hereafter time, for time past wrong'd by thee. 4.04.390
here, | is in opinion and in honor wrong'd, TIT 1.01.416
ravish'd and wrong'd as philomela was, | forc'd 4.01. 52
thou hast wrong'd caius ligarius. JC 2.03. 4 P
that you have wrong'd me doth appear in this: 4.03. 1
you wrong'd yourself to write in such a case. 4.03. 6
was't hamlet wrong'd laertes? HAM 5.02.233
be silent when i think your highness wrong'd. LR 1.04. 66 P
say you have wrong'd her. 2.04.152
if more, the more th' hast wrong'd me. 5.03.169
if thou but think'st him wrong'd, and mak'st his OTH 3.03.143
hands, heart, | to wrong'd othello's service! 3.03.467
and men's reports | give him much wrong'd. ANT 1.04. 40
one, a woman, | and women 'twere they wrong'd. TNK 5.01.107

WRONGED 10 FR 0.0011 REL FR 10 V 0 P
sir king, | the wronged duke of milan, prospero. TMP 5.01.107
that thou hast wronged in the time o'erpast; R3 4.04.388
for the wronged souls | of butchered princes 5.03.121
the wronged heirs of york do pray for thee. 5.03.137
the prayers of holy saints and wronged souls, 5.03.241
beguil'd, divorced, wronged, spited, slain! ROM 4.05. 55
so, | hamlet is of the faction that is wronged, HAM 5.02.238
no, my most wronged sister, cleopatra | hath ANT 3.06. 65
line, | how tarquin wronged me, i collatine. LUC 819
"thou wronged lord of rome," quoth he, "arise, 1818

WRONGER 4 FR 0.0004 REL FR 4 V 0 P
if you would know your wronger, look on me. ADO 5.01.262
who, certain of his fate, loves not his wronger; OTH 3.03.168
and not the wronger | of her or you, having CYM 2.04. 54
to wrong the wronger till he render right, | to LUC 943

WRONGFUL 2 FR 0.0002 REL FR 2 V 0 P
that i despise thee for thy wrongful suit, | and TGV 4.02.102
in wrongful quarrel you have slain your son. TIT 1.01.293

WRONGFULLY 8 FR 0.0009 REL FR 7 V 1 P
woman | most wrongfully accus'd your substitute, MM 5.01.140
don john for accusing the lady hero wrongfully. ADO 4.02. 49 P
hath caus'd his death, the which if wrongfully, R2 1.02. 39
if you do wrongfully seize herford's rights, 2.01.201
he had thought to have murther'd wrongfully. 2H6 2.03.104
have by my means been butchered wrongfully? TIT 4.04. 55
man, | that lucius' banishment was wrongfully, 4.04. 76
and right perfection wrongfully disgrac'd, | and SON 66. 7

WRONG–INCENSED 1 FR 0.0001 REL FR 1 V 0 P
between these swelling wrong–incensed peers. R3 2.01. 52

WRONGING 1 FR 0.0001 REL FR 0 V 1 P
wenches with child, wronging the ancientry, WT 3.03. 62 P

WRONGLY 1 FR 0.0001 REL FR 1 V 0 P
not play false, | and yet wouldst wrongly win. MAC 1.05. 22

/WRONGS 2 FR 0.0002 REL FR 2 V 0 P
/weigh'd | /what /wrongs /our /arms /may /do, 2H4 4.01. 68
/our /arms /may /do, /what /wrongs /we /suffer, 4.01. 68

WRONGS 73 FR 0.0082 REL FR 69 V 4 P
with their high wrongs i am strook to th' quick, TMP 5.01. 25
and do entreat | thou pardon me my wrongs. 5.01.119
poor gentlewoman, my master wrongs her much. TGV 4.04.141
this wrongs you. WIV 4.02.154 P
relate your wrongs. MM 5.01. 26
unfeeling fools can with such wrongs dispense: ERR 2.01.103
so it doth appear | by the wrongs i suffer, and 3.01. 16
whilst to take order for the wrongs i went, 5.01.146
albeit my wrongs might make one wiser mad. 5.01.217
but such a one whose wrongs do suit with mine. ADO 5.01. 7
who wrongs him? 5.01. 52
death, in guerdon of her wrongs, | gives her 5.03. 5
your wrongs do set a scandal on my sex. MND 2.01.240
to make some reservation of your wrongs. AWW 2.03.245 P
of what nature the wrongs are thou hast done him TN 3.04.221 P
the wrongs i have done thee stir | afresh within WT 5.01.148
his grandame's wrongs, and not his mother's JN 2.01.168
oppress'd with wrongs, and therefore full of 3.01. 13
well, ruffian, i must pocket up these wrongs, 3.01.200
and thou possessed with a thousand wrongs; 3.03. 41
o, /sit my husband's wrongs on herford's spear, R2 1.02. 47
gaunt's rebukes, nor england's private wrongs, 2.01.166
god, 'tis shame such wrongs are borne | in him, 2.01.238
look on my wrongs with an indifferent eye. 2.03.116
to rouse his wrongs and chase them to the bay. 2.03.128
i have had feeling of my cousin's wrongs, | and 2.03.141
tears drawn from her eyes by your foul wrongs; 3.01. 15
unhappy king | (whose wrongs in us god pardon!) 1H4 1.03.149
seems to weep | over his /country's wrongs, and 4.03. 82
smooth comforts false, worse than true wrongs. 2H4 in 40
'gainst him whose wrongs gives edge unto the H5 1.02. 27
for it is plain pocketing up of wrongs. 3.02. 51 P
peace, mayor, thou know'st little of my wrongs. 1H6 1.03. 59
coward of france, how much he wrongs his fame, 2.01. 16
and for those wrongs, those bitter injuries, 2.05.124
so shall his father's wrongs be recompens'd. 3.01.160
prick'd on by public wrongs sustain'd in france, 3.02. 78
herein your highness wrongs both them and me. 3H6 3.02. 75
heav'ns are just, and time suppresseth wrongs. 3.03. 77
thou drown the sad remembrance of those wrongs R3 4.04.252
'tis full of thy foul wrongs. 4.04.375
soul, | is the determin'd respite of my wrongs. 5.01. 19
awake and think our wrongs in richard's bosom 5.03.144
as you do conscience | in doing daily wrongs. H8 5.02.103
that wilt revenge | thine own particular wrongs, COR 4.05. 86
for a noble man | still to remember wrongs? 5.03.155
to quit the bloody wrongs upon her foes. TIT 1.01.141
dishonored thus and challenged of wrongs? 1.01.340
and swear unto my soul to right your wrongs. 3.01.278
if lucius live, he will requite your wrongs, 3.01.296
yet wrung with wrongs more than our backs can 4.03. 49
to send down justice for to wreak our wrongs. 4.03. 52
why, lords, what wrongs are these! 4.04. 1
despiteful and intolerable wrongs! 4.04. 50
imperious, and impatient of your wrongs, | and 5.01. 6
to join with him and right his heinous wrongs. 5.02. 4
had titus to revenge | these wrongs unspeakable, 5.03.126
can breathe, and make his wrongs | his outsides, TIM 3.05. 32
if wrongs be evils and enforce us kill, | what 3.05. 36
soldiers should brook as little wrongs as gods. 3.05.116
shall to thee blot out what wrongs were theirs, 5.01.153
and such suffering souls | that welcome wrongs; JC 2.01.131
brutus, this sober form of yours hides wrongs, 4.02. 40
wear thou thy wrongs, | the title is affeer'd! MAC 4.03. 33
by day and night he wrongs me, every hour | he LR 1.03. 3
he'll not feel wrongs | which tie him to an 4.02. 13
bear'st a cheek for blows, a head for wrongs, 4.02. 51
we then have done you bold and saucy wrongs; OTH 1.01.128
the wrongs he did me | were nothing prince–like; CYM 5.05.292
he does no wrongs, | nor takes none. TNK 4.02.134
soul that late complained | her wrongs to us, LUC 1840
those pretty wrongs that liberty commits | when SON 41. 1
then need i not to fear the worst of wrongs, 92. 5

WRONG'ST 7 FR 0.0008 REL FR 7 V 0 P
thou wrong'st thyself, if thou shouldst strive AWW 2.03.146
now, by god's will, thou wrong'st him, somerset; 1H6 2.04. 82
how much thou wrong'st me, heaven be my judge. 2H6 4.10. 76
therein thou wrong'st thy children mightily. 3H6 3.02. 74
thou wrong'st it more than tears with that ROM 4.01. 32
thou wrong'st a gentleman, who is as far | from CYM 1.06.145
thou wrong'st his honor, wound'st his princely LUC 599

WROTE *(also writ)*

WROTE 9 FR 0.0010 REL FR 7 V 2 P
i wrote the letter that thy father found, | and TIT 5.01.106
down, | devis'd a new commission, wrote it fair. HAM 5.02. 32
wilt thou know | th' effect of what i wrote? 5.02. 37

he wrote this but as an essay or taste of my LR 1.02. 45 P
i wrote to you, | when rioting in alexandria you ANT 2.02. 71
him of letters he had formerly wrote to pompey; 3.05. 11 P
my emperor hath wrote i must from hence, | and CYM 3.05. 2
lucius hath wrote already to the emperor | how 3.05. 21
my master since | i wrote him imogen was slain. 4.03. 37
WROTH *(also wrath)*
WROTH 1 FR 0.0001 REL FR 1 V 0 P
i'll keep my oath, | patiently to bear my wroth. MV 2.09. 78
/WROUGHT 2 FR 0.0002 REL FR 2 V 0 P
/poor /man, /grief /has /so /wrought /on /him, TIT 3.02. 79
/and /period /will /be /throughly /wrought, LR 4.07. 95
WROUGHT 42 FR 0.0047 REL FR 38 V 4 P
if my brother wrought by my pity, it should not MM 3.02.210 P
his friends still wrought reprieves for him; 4.02.135 P
may witness that my end | was wrought by nature, ERR 1.01. 34
was | (as his wise mother wrought in his behalf) MV 1.03. 73
love wrought these miracles. SHR 5.01.124
of my poor image | would thus have wrought you WT 5.03. 58
what may be wrought out of their discontent, JN 3.04.179
(the best i had, a princess wrought it me) | and 4.01. 43
those thy fears might have wrought fears in me. 4.02.236
who wrought it with the king, and who perform'd R2 4.01. 4
for thou hast wrought | a deed of slander with 5.06. 34
that if we wrought out life 'twas ten to one, 2H4 1.01.182
hath wrought the mure that should confine it in 4.04.119
was | that wrought upon thee so preposterously H5 2.02.112
hath the late overthrow wrought this offense? 1H6 1.02. 49
hath wrought this hellish mischief unawares, 3.02. 39
the greatest miracle that e'er ye wrought! 5.04. 66
that living wrought me such exceeding trouble. 2H6 5.01. 70
have wrought the easy-melting king like wax. 3H6 2.01.171
you wrought to be a legate, by which power | you H8 3.02.311
that hath beside well in his person wrought | to COR 2.03.246
/chance of war hath wrought this change of cheer TIT 1.01.264
that we have wrought | so worthy a gentleman to ROM 3.05.144
for it wrought on her | the form of death. 5.03.245
wrought he not well that painted it? TIM 1.01.197 P
he wrought better that made the painter, and yet 1.01.198 P
thy honorable mettle may be wrought | from that JC 1.02.309
my dull brain was wrought | with things MAC 1.03.149
defect, | which else should free have wrought. 2.01. 19
who wrought with them, and all things else that 3.01. 81
great business must be wrought ere noon: 3.05. 22
conjur'd to this effect, | he wrought upon her. OTH 1.03.106
a special purpose | which wrought to his desire. 5.02.323
of one not easily jealious, but, being wrought, 5.02.345
could be so rarely and exactly wrought, | since CYM 2.04. 75
wrought by th' hand | of his queen mother, which 5.05.361
for other ruffians, as their fancies wrought, STM II.C 84
now she unweaves the web that she hath wrought: VEN 991
so from himself impiety hath wrought, | that for LUC 341
one silly cross wrought all my loss, | o PP 17. 9
till nature, as she wrought thee, fell a-doting, SON 20.10
but that, so much of earth and water wrought, 44.11
WRUNG 5 FR 0.0005 REL FR 4 V 1 P
wondrous sensible | he wrung bassanio's hand, MV 2.08. 49
poor jade is wrung in the withers, out of all 1H4 2.01. 6 P
place is fill'd, thy sceptre wrung from thee, 3H6 3.01. 16
yet wrung with wrongs more than our backs can TIT 4.03. 49
lord, wrung from me my slow leave | by laborsome HAM 1.02. 58
WRYING 1 FR 0.0001 REL FR 1 V 0 P
than themselves | for wrying but a little! CYM 5.01. 5
WRY-NECK'D 1 FR 0.0001 REL FR 1 V 0 P
and the vile squealing of the wry-neck'd fife, MV 2.05. 30
WYE 3 FR 0.0003 REL FR 1 V 2 P
thrice from the banks of wye | and 1H4 3.01. 64
it is call'd wye at monmouth; H5 4.07. 28 P
all the water in wye cannot wash your majesty's 4.07.106 P
XANTIPPE 1 FR 0.0001 REL FR 1 V 0 P
and as curst and shrowd | as socrates' xantippe, SHR 1.02. 71
Y' *(also ye, you)*
Y' 63 FR 0.0071 REL FR 52 V 11 P
you're sham'd, y' are overthrown, y' are undone WIV 3.03. 95 P
y' are overthrown, y' are undone for ever! 3.03. 95 P
y' are as pregnant in | as art and practice hath MM 1.01. 11
y' are welcome; 2.02. 26
y' are sad, signior balthazar, pray god our ERR 3.01. 19
y' are a baggage, the slys are no rogues. SHR in.1. 3 P
y' are welcome, sir, and he, for your good sake. 2.01. 61
y' are shallow, madam — in great friends, for AWW 1.03. 42 P
y' are welcome, gentlemen. 3.02. 91
which well approves | y' are great in fortune. 3.07. 14
y' are deceiv'd, my lord, this is monsieur 4.03.140 P
go to, y' are a dry fool; TN 1.05. 41 P
y' are servant to the count orsino, youth. 3.01.100
y' are very welcome. WT 4.04.108
swear by the duty that y' owe to god | (our part R2 1.03.180
o my lord, y' are tardy; H8 1.04. 7
so now y' are fairly seated. 1.04. 31
y' are welcome, my fair guests. 1.04. 35
by all the laws of war y' are privileg'd. 1.04. 52
do not deliver | what here y' have heard to her. 2.03.107
y' are meek and humble-mouth'd, | you sign your 2.04.107
y' are excus'd; 2.04.162
y' are well met once again. 4.01. 1
thomas, y' are a gentleman | of mine own way; 5.01. 27
my lord of winchester, y' are a little, | by 5.02.108
y' have made a fine hand, fellows! 5.03. 70
y' are lazy knaves, | and here ye lie baiting of 5.03. 80
my noble gossips, y' have been too prodigal. 5.04. 12
y' are long about it. COR 1.01.127
and welcome, general, and y' are welcome all. 2.01.182
o, y' are well met. 4.02. 11
y' are goodly things, you voices! 4.06.146
can scarce think there's any, y' are so slight. 5.02.104 P
i am glad y' are well. TIM 1.01. 1
y' are a dog. 1.01.200 P
you see, my lord, how ample y' are belov'd. 1.02.130
y' are honest men; 5.01. 76
y' have heard that i have gold, | i am sure you 5.01. 76
speak truth, y' are honest men. 5.01. 77
y' have ungently, brutus, | stole from my bed; JC 2.01.237
y' are; LR 4.05. 28
y' are much deceiv'd. 4.06. 9
methinks y' are better spoken. 4.06. 10
/'zounds, sir, y' are robb'd! OTH 1.01. 86
but i do see y' are mov'd. 3.03.217
worthy friend — | my lord, i see y' are mov'd. 3.03.224
or i shall say y' are all in all in spleen, 4.01. 88
y' are caught." ANT 2.05. 15
y' have said, sir. 2.06.107 P
y' have strange serpents there? 2.07. 24 P
y' are fall'n into a princely hand, fear nothing 5.02. 22
not you sustain what y' are worthy of by your CYM 1.04.115 P
y' are like one that superstitiously | do swear PER 4.03. 49
y' are out of breath, | and this high-speeded TNK 1.03. 82
what e'er you are, y' are mine, and i shall give 2.05. 33
your virtues, | and, as your due, y' are hers. 2.05. 37
sir, y' are a noble giver. 2.05. 38
y' are mine, and somewhat better than your rank 2.05. 43
good night, good night, y' are gone. 3.04. 11
i know you, y' are a tinker. 3.05. 82
y' had best look to her, | for, if she see him 4.01.123
lord, how y' are grown! 5.02. 94
as i by yours, y' have pass'd a hell of time, SON 120. 6
Y 1 FR 0.0001 REL FR 1 V 0 P
and "honi soit qui mal y pense" write | in WIV 5.05. 69
YALLOWNESS 1 FR 0.0001 REL FR 0 V 1 P
i will possess him with yallowness, for the WIV 1.03.102 P
YARD 8 FR 0.0009 REL FR 3 V 5 P
he may not by the yard. LLL 5.02.669 P
thou yard, three-quarters, half-yard, quarter, SHR 4.03.108
or i shall so bemete thee with thy yard | as 4.03.112
you tailor's yard, you sheath, you bowcase, you 1H4 2.04.247 P
is digt himself four yard under the countermines H5 3.02. 62 P
meddle with his yard and the tailor with his ROM 1.02. 40 P
but i will delve one yard below their mines, HAM 3.04.208
draw me a clothier's yard. LR 4.06. 88 P
YARDS 5 FR 0.0005 REL FR 1 V 4 P
the yards and boresprit, would i flame TMP 1.02.200
two yards, and more. WIV 1.03. 40 P
indeed i am in the waist two yards about; 1.03. 42 P
eight yards of uneven ground is threescore and 1H4 2.02. 25 P
have sent me two and twenty yards of satin (as i 2H4 1.02. 44 P
YARE 10 FR 0.0011 REL FR 5 V 5 P
yare, yare! TMP 1.01. 6 P
yare, yare! 1.01. 6 P
yare! 1.01. 34 P
is tight and yare, and bravely rigg'd as when 5.01.224
me for your own turn, you shall find me yare; MM 4.02. 58 P
dismount thy tuck, be yare in thy preparation, TN 3.04.224 P
their ships are yare, yours heavy. ANT 3.07. 38
the hangman thank | for being yare about him. 3.13.131
yare, yare, good iras; 5.02.283
yare, yare, good iras; 5.02.283
YARELY 2 FR 0.0002 REL FR 1 V 1 P
fall to't, yarely, or we run ourselves aground. TMP 1.01. 4 P
hands, | that yarely frame the office. ANT 2.02.211
YARN 2 FR 0.0002 REL FR 0 V 2 P
the web of our life is of a mingled yarn, good AWW 4.03. 71 P
all the yarn she spun in ulysses' absence did COR 1.03. 83 P
Y'AVE 1 FR 0.0001 REL FR 1 V 0 P
y'ave seen me use my sword | against th' advice TNK 3.01. 59
YAW 1 FR 0.0001 REL FR 0 V 1 P
arithmetic of memory, and yet but yaw neither, HAM 5.02.115 P
YAWN 6 FR 0.0006 REL FR 6 V 0 P
graves, yawn and yield your dead, | till death ADO 5.03. 19
gashes | that bloodily did yawn upon his face. H5 4.06. 14
to show bare heads | in congregations, to yawn, COR 3.02. 11
when churchyards yawn and hell itself /breathes HAM 3.02.389
they yawn at it | and botch the words up fit to 4.05. 9
th' affrighted globe | did yawn at alteration. OTH 5.02.101
YAWN'D 1 FR 0.0001 REL FR 1 V 0 P
and graves have yawn'd and yielded up their dead JC 2.02. 18
YAWNING 3 FR 0.0003 REL FR 3 V 0 P
o'er to executors pale | the lazy yawning drone. H5 1.02.204
now will i dam up this thy yawning mouth | for 2H6 4.01. 73
drowsy hums | hath rung night's yawning peal, MAC 3.02. 43
YCLAD *(also clad)*
YCLAD 1 FR 0.0001 REL FR 1 V 0 P
speech, | her words yclad with wisdom's majesty, 2H6 1.01. 33
YCLIPED *(also clepes, etc., clip*, clipt*)*
YCLIPED 2 FR 0.0002 REL FR 1 V 1 P
it is ycliped thy park. LLL 1.01.240 P
"judas i am, ycliped machabeus." 5.02.598
YE *(also y')*
/YE 4 FR 0.0004 REL FR 4 V 0 P
/look /ye, /my /lord /mayor, | would you imagine R3 3.05. 34
displace our heads where (thanks, /ye gods!) CYM 4.02.122
and /ye know what wenches, ha? TNK 2.03. 39
been merry, | and have pleas'd /ye with a derry, 3.05.139
YE 342 FR 0.0386 REL FR 263 V 79 P
a south-west blow on ye, | and blister you all TMP 1.02.323
ye elves of hills, brooks, standing lakes, and 5.01. 33
and ye that on the sands with printless foot 5.01. 34
by whose aid | (weak masters though ye be) i 5.01. 41
to content ye | as much as me my dukedom. 5.01.170
yet he, of all the rest, i think best loves ye. TGV 1.02. 28
will ye be gone? 1.02. 49
they are all perceiv'd without ye. 2.01. 34 P
o, give ye good ev'n! 2.01. 98 P
know ye don antonio, your countryman? 2.04. 54
stand, sir, and throw us that you have about ye. 4.01. 3
love you 'gainst the nature of love — force ye. 5.04. 58
hark ye, master slender would speak a word with WIV 3.04. 29 P
well; you'll answer this one day. fare ye well. MM 4.03.163 P
ye light a' love with your heels! ADO 3.04. 47 P
i assure ye it was a buck of the first head. LLL 4.02. 10 P
and my familiar, i do assure ye, very good 5.01. 96 P
yet swear not, lest ye be forsworn again. 5.02.832
but fare ye well; MND 3.02.243
approach, ye furies fell! 5.01.284
fare ye well, | we leave you now with better MV 1.01. 58
fare ye well a while, | i'll end my exhortation 1.01.103
is he yet possess'd | how much ye would? 1.03. 65
i thank ye, and be blest for your good comfort! AYL 2.07.135
god ye good ev'n, william. 5.01. 14 P
yet would you say ye were beaten out of door, SHR in.2. 85
gentlemen, content ye; 1.01. 90
and other books, good ones, i warrant ye. 1.02.170
please ye we may contrive this afternoon | and 1.02.274
what will ye do? AWW 2.01. 48 P
if ye pinch me like a pasty, i can say no more. 4.03.123 P
fare ye well, sir, i am for france too. 4.03.328 P
fare ye well at once; TN 2.01. 39 P
do ye make an alehouse of my lady's house, that 2.03. 88 P
that ye squeak out your coziers' catches without 2.03. 89 P
ye lie. 2.03.113 P
get ye all three into the box-tree; 2.05. 15 P
hark ye, | the queen your mother rounds apace: WT 2.01. 15
i am a poor fellow, sir. i know ye well enough. 4.04.638 P
mistress (let my prophecy | come home to ye!), 4.04.649
and come ye now to tell me john hath made | his JN 5.02. 91
ye favorites of a king, are we not high? R2 3.02. 88
hear ye, yedward, if i tarry at home and go not, 1H4 1.02.134 P
off | by him for whom these shames ye underwent? 1.03.179
peace, ye fat-kidney'd rascal! 2.02. 5 P
peace, ye fat-guts, lie down. 2.02. 31 P
what a plague mean ye to colt me thus? 2.02. 37 P
out, ye rogue! shall i be your ostler? 2.02. 42 P
case ye, case ye, on with your vizards. 2.02. 53 P
case ye, case ye, on with your vizards. 2.02. 53 P
you lie, ye rogue, 'tis going to the king's 2.02. 56 P
hang ye, gorbellied knaves, are ye undone? 2.02. 88 P
hang ye, gorbellied knaves, are ye undone? 2.02. 88 P
no, ye fat chuffs, i would your store were here! 2.02. 89 P
what, ye knaves, young men must live! 2.02. 90 P
you are grandjurors, are ye? 2.02. 91 P
we'll jure ye, faith. 2.02. 91 P
but hark ye, what cunning match have you made 2.04. 89 P
'zounds, ye fat paunch, and ye call me coward, 2.04.144 P
ye fat paunch, and ye call me coward, by the 2.04.144 P
the lord, i knew ye as well as he that made ye. 2.04.267 P
the lord, i knew ye as well as he that made ye. 2.04.268 P
a' horseback, ye cuckoo, but afoot he will not 2.04.353 P
i grant ye, upon instinct. 2.04.356 P
nay, i'll tickle ye for a young prince, i' faith 2.04.444 P
out, ye rogue! 2.04.484 P
but in the way of bargain, mark ye me, | i'll 3.01.137
go, ye giddy goose. 3.01.228 P
lie still, ye thief, and hear the lady sing in 3.01.234 P
these two hours, and so come in when ye will. 3.01.262 P
ye lie, hostess, bardolph was shav'd and lost 3.03. 59 P
if ye will needs say i am an old man, you should 2H4 1.02.216 P
pray ye pacify yourself, sir john. 2.04. 80 P
peradventure i will with ye to the court. 3.02.295 P
but my love to ye | shall show itself more 4.02. 75
do ye yield, sir? 4.03. 12 P
look ye how they change! H5 2.02. 73
fare ye well. 5.01. 79 P
princely train | call ye the warlike talbot, for 1H6 2.02. 35
that two such noble peers as ye should jar! 3.01. 70
do what ye dare, we are as resolute. 3.01. 91
then be at peace, except ye thirst for blood. 3.01.117
good morrow, gallants, want ye corn for bread? 3.02. 41
are ye so hot, sir? 3.02. 58
dare ye come forth and meet us in the field? 3.02. 61
will ye, like soldiers, come and fight it out? 3.02. 66
hark ye; not so; in witness, take ye that. 3.04. 37
hark ye; not so; in witness, take ye that. 3.04. 37
this shall ye do, so help you righteous god! 4.01. 8
and perish ye, with your audacious prate! 4.01.124
now help, ye charming spells and periapts, | and 5.03. 2
and ye choice spirits that admonish me | and 5.03. 3
now, ye familiar spirits, that are cull'd | out 5.03. 10
and may ye both be suddenly surpris'd | by 5.03. 40
hear ye, captain? are you not at leisure? 5.03. 97
how say you, madam, are ye so content? 5.03.126
and hark ye, sirs: 5.04. 55
i am with child, ye bloody homicides! 5.04. 62
womb, | although ye hale me to a violent death. 5.04. 64
the greatest miracle that e'er ye wrought! 5.04. 66
so, now dismiss your army when ye please; 5.04.173
my lord of gloucester, now ye grow too hot: 2H6 1.01.137
but 'tis my presence that doth trouble ye; 1.01.141
pardon me, i took ye for my lord protector. 1.03. 11 P
what, minion, can ye not? 1.03.138
are ye advis'd? the east side of the grove. 2.01. 47
and would ye not think /his cunning to be great, 2.01.130
or will ye not observe | the strangeness of his 3.01. 4
what, are ye daunted now? 4.01.119
now will ye stoop? 4.01.119
come, soldiers, show what cruelty ye can, | that 4.01.132
ay, marry, will we; therefore get ye gone. 4.02.153
be wise, he'll never call ye jack cade more. 4.06. 9 P
ye shall have a hempen /caudle then, and the 4.07. 90 P
whom have i injur'd that ye seek my death? 4.07.101
away with him, and do as i command ye. 4.07.118 P
what say ye, countrymen? 4.08. 11
will ye relent | and yield to mercy whilst 'tis 4.08. 11
what, buckingham and clifford, are ye so brave? 4.08. 20 P
and you, base peasants, do ye believe him? 4.08. 21 P
i thought ye would never have given out these 4.08. 25 P
for well i wot ye blaze to burn them out. 3H6 5.04. 71
i speak, | ye see i drink the water of my eye. 5.04. 75
by heaven, brat, i'll plague ye for that word. 5.05. 27
dick, i tell ye all | i am your better, traitors 5.05. 35
ye all | i am your better, traitors as ye are, 5.05. 36
ere ye come there, be sure to hear some news. 5.05. 48
away, i say, i charge ye bear her hence. 5.05. 81
had i not reason, think ye, to make haste, | and 5.06. 72
i grant ye. R3 1.02.101
of the town, | be sad, as we would make ye. H8 pr 25
think ye see | the very persons of our noble pr 25
how have ye done | since last we saw in france? 1.01. 1
general welcome from his grace | salutes ye all; 1.04. 2
look out there, some of ye. 1.04. 50
and once more | i show'r a welcome on ye. 1.04. 63
ye have found him, cardinal. 1.04. 86
o, god save ye! 2.01. 1
fall away | like water from ye, never found 2.01.130
found again | but where they mean to sink ye. 2.01.131
i must now forsake ye. 2.01.132
ye are too bold. 2.02. 70
i'll make ye know your times of business. 2.02. 71
there ye shall meet about this weighty business. 2.02.139
ye speak like honest men (pray god ye prove so!) 3.01. 69
speak like honest men (pray god ye prove so!), 3.01. 69
but how to make ye suddenly an answer | in such 3.01. 70

for if the trial of the law o'ertake ye, 3.01. 96
ye tell me what ye wish for both — my ruin. 3.01. 98
ye tell me what ye wish for both — my ruin. 3.01. 98
out upon ye! 3.01. 99
the more shame for ye! 3.01.102
holy men i thought ye, | upon my soul, two 3.01.102
but cardinal sins and hollow hearts i fear ye. 3.01.104
the cordial that ye bring a wretched lady, | a 3.01.106
a woman lost among ye, laugh'd at, scorn'd? 3.01.107
i will not wish ye half my miseries, | i have 3.01.108
but say i warn'd ye; 3.01.109
once | the burthen of my sorrows fall upon ye. 3.01.111
ye turn me into nothing! 3.01.114
woe upon ye | and all such false professors! 3.01.114
if ye be any thing but churchmen's habits) | put 3.01.117
ye have angels' faces, but heaven knows your 3.01.145
do what ye will, my lords; 3.01.175
i feel | of what coarse metal ye are moulded, 3.02.239
how eagerly ye follow my disgraces | as if it 3.02.240
ye follow my disgraces | as if it fed ye, and 3.02.241
ye appear in every thing may bring my ruin! 3.02.242
lords, | can ye endure to hear this arrogance? 3.02.278
vain pomp and glory of this world, i hate ye! 3.02.365
gentlemen, ye shall go my way, which | is to th' 4.01.114
to th' court, and there ye shall be my guests; 4.01.115
as i walk thither, | i'll tell ye more. 4.01.117
is come to lay his weary bones among ye; 4.02. 22
spirits of peace, where are ye? 4.02. 83
are ye all gone? 4.02. 83
and leave me here in wretchedness behind ye? 4.02. 84
saw ye none enter since i slept? 4.02. 86
lay all the weight ye can upon my patience, | i 5.02.101
ye are not sound. 5.02.116
i told ye all, | when we first put this 5.02.138
only envy at, | ye blew the fire that burns ye. 5.02.148
only envy at, | ye blew the fire that burns ye. 5.02.148
now have at ye! 5.02.148
my commission | bid ye so far forget yourselves? 5.02.177
i gave ye | power as he was a councillor to try 5.02.177
there's some of ye, i see, | more out of malice 5.02.179
would try him to the utmost had ye mean, | which 5.02.181
mean, | which ye shall never have while i live. 5.02.182
as i have made ye one, lords, one remain: 5.02.214
you'll leave your noise anon, ye rascals; 5.03. 1 P
ye rude slaves, leave your gaping. 5.03. 2 P
belong to th' gallows, and be hang'd, ye rogue! 5.03. 6 P
blame me for't, i'll lay ye all | by th' heels, 5.03. 78
and here ye lie baiting of bombards, when | ye 5.03. 81
of bombards, when | ye should do service. 5.03. 82
marshalsea shall hold ye play these two months. 5.03. 86
to make parents happy | may hourly fall upon ye! 5.04. 8
i thank ye heartily; 5.04. 13
i thank ye all. 5.04. 69
your presence, | and ye shall find me thankful. 5.04. 72
ye must all see the queen, and she must thank ye 5.04. 73
must all see the queen, and she must thank ye, 5.04. 73
cooling too, or ye may chance burn your lips. TRO 1.01. 26 P
was hector arm'd and gone ere ye came to ilium? 1.02. 48 P
look ye yonder, niece; 1.02.213 P
fare ye well, good niece. 1.02.276 P
why, how now, ajax, wherefore do ye thus? 2.01. 55
if ye take not that little little less than 2.03. 12 P
fare ye well, with all my heart. 3.03.299 P
hang ye! COR 1.01.181
trust ye? 1.01.181
let me clip ye | in arms as sound as when i 1.06. 29
help, ye citizens! 3.01.179
what do ye talk? 3.01.315
you had not show'd them how ye were dispos'd 3.02. 22
draw near, ye people. 3.03. 39
fare ye well! 4.01. 44
will ye bestow them friendly on andronicus? TIT 1.01.219
ay, boy, grow ye so brave? 2.01. 45
so near the emperor's palace dare ye draw, | and 2.01. 46
why, are ye mad? 2.01. 75
or know ye not, in rome | how furious and 2.01. 75
why, hark ye, hark ye, and are you such fools 2.01. 99
hark ye, hark ye, and are you such fools | to 2.01. 99
madam, now shall ye see | our roman hunting. 2.02. 19
or be ye not henceforth call'd my children. 2.03.115
but when ye have the honey we desire, | let not 2.03.131
and if ye love me, as i think you do, | let's 3.01.286
o, do ye read, my lord, what she hath writ? 4.01. 77
the dam will wake and if she wind ye once; 4.01. 97
'zounds, ye whore, is black so base a hue? 4.02. 71
what, what, ye sanguine, shallow–hearted boys! 4.02. 97
ye white–lim'd walls! 4.02. 98
ye alehouse painted signs! 4.02. 98
hark ye, lords, you see i have given her physic, 4.02.162
look ye draw home enough, and 'tis there 4.03. 3
welcome, ye warlike goths; 5.03. 27
time | when it should move ye to attend me most, 5.03. 92
ye say honestly, rest you merry! ROM 1.02. 62 P
am i come near ye now? 1.05. 20
god ye good morrow, gentlemen. 2.04.109 P
god ye good den, fair gentlewoman. 2.04.110 P
'tis no less, i tell ye, for the bawdy hand of 2.04.112 P
but first let me tell ye, if ye should lead her 2.04.165 P
ye, if ye should lead her in a fool's paradise, 2.04.165 P
hark ye, your romeo will be here at night. 3.02.140
so will ye, i am sure, that you love me. 4.01. 26
juliet, on thursday early will i rouse ye; 4.01. 42
and weep ye now, seeing she is advanc'd | above 4.05. 73
i will be gone, sir, and not trouble ye. 5.03. 40
and rich. here is a water, look ye. TIM 1.01. 18
the gods preserve ye! 1.01.162
more welcome are ye to my fortunes | than my 1.02. 19
ye have got a humor there | does not become a 1.02. 26
what do ye ask of me, my friend? 3.04. 45
you came for gold, ye slaves. 5.01.112
ye gods, it doth amaze me | a man of such a JC 1.02.128
therein, ye gods, you make the weak most strong; 1.03. 91
therein, ye gods, you tyrants do defeat; 1.03. 92
o ye gods! 2.01.302
i do beseech ye, if you bear me hard, | now, 3.01.157
mark'd ye his words? 3.02.112
o ye gods, ye gods, must i endure all this? 4.03. 41
o ye gods, ye gods, must i endure all this? 4.03. 41
for i have seen more years, i'm sure, than ye. 4.03.132
o ye immortal gods! 4.03.157
are ye fantastical, or that indeed | which MAC 1.03. 53
or that indeed | which outwardly ye show? 1.03. 54
ay, in the catalogue ye go for men, | as hounds 3.01. 91
god buy ye, fare ye well. HAM 2.01. 66
god buy ye, fare ye well. 2.01. 66
why did ye laugh then, when i said, "man 2.02.313 P
pray ye go, there's my key. LR 1.02.169 P
beweep this cause again, i'll pluck ye out, 1.04.302
come, i'll flesh ye, come on, young master. 2.02. 46 P
plain, | i'ld drive ye cackling home to camelot. 2.02. 84
if then they chanc'd to slack ye, | we could 2.04.245
now fare ye well, good sir. 4.06. 32
keep out, che vor' ye, or ice try whither your 4.06.240 P
whip me, ye devils, | from the possession of OTH 5.02.277
to enforce no further | the griefs between ye: ANT 2.02.100
much, but i ha' prais'd ye | when you have well 2.06. 76
pray ye, sir? 2.06.113 P
if it might please ye — 5.02. 78
tempters of the night | guard me, beseech ye. CYM 2.02. 10
and am right sorry that i must report ye | my 3.05. 3
i wish ye sport. 4.02. 31
though you did love this youth, i blame ye not, 5.05.267
hark you, sir; do you know where ye are? PER 2.01. 96 P
why, d' ye take it, and the gods give thee good 2.01.146 P
madam, if this you purpose as ye speak, 3.04. 12
weep that you live as ye do makes pity in your 4.02.119 P
rarest sounds! do ye not hear? 5.01.231
ye shall. TNK 2.02.111
will ye go forward, cousin? 2.02.126
if that will lose ye, farewell, palamon! 2.02.177
ye may be. 2.02.189
still blossom | as her bright eyes shine on ye, 2.02.234
i'll shake 'em so, ye shall not sleep, | i'll 2.02.272
ye shall not sleep, | i'll make ye a new morris. 2.02.273
why then have with ye, boys! 2.03. 27
for he does all, ye know. 2.03. 41
tediosity and disensanity | is here among ye! 3.05. 3
my rudiments | been labor'd so long with ye, 3.05. 4
been labor'd so long with ye, milk'd unto ye, 3.05. 4
and marrow of my understanding laid upon ye, 3.05. 6
coarse frieze capacities, ye /jane judgments, 3.05. 8
proh deum, medius fidius, ye are all dunces! 3.05. 11
here, my mad boys, have at ye! 3.05. 24
ye have danc'd rarely, wenches. 3.05.159
i could wish ye | as kind a kinsman as you force 3.06. 20
that my embraces | might thank ye, not my blows. 3.06. 23
i thank ye. 3.06. 90
so let me be most traitor, and ye please me. 3.06.167
ye make my faith reel. 3.06.212
if ye fall in't, | think how you maim your honor 3.06.236
o all ye gods, despise me then. 3.06.258
will this content ye? 3.06.299
i embrace ye. 3.06.300
i'll give ye | now usage like to princes and to 3.06.305
when ye return, who wins i'll settle here; 3.06.307
ye are a good man | and ever bring good news. 4.01. 24
i'll warrant ye he had not so few last night 4.01.137
blow that nearness out that flames between ye, 5.01. 10
and, as the gods regard ye, fight with justice. 5.01. 15
your prayers, and betwixt ye | i part my wishes. 5.01. 16
that's all one, if ye make a noise. 5.02. 16
thank ye, doctor. 5.02. 23
he turns ye like a top. 5.02. 50
pretty soul, | how do ye? 5.02. 70
i would now ask ye how ye like the play, | but, ep 1
i would now ask ye how ye like the play, | but, ep 1
yet stay a while, | and let me look upon ye. ep 4
'tis in vain, i see, to stay ye; ep 9
now what say ye? ep 10
(for 'tis no other) any way content ye | (for to ep 13
(for to that honest purpose it was meant ye), ep 14
and ye shall have ere long, | i dare say, many a ep 15
loving offenders, thus i will excuse ye: SON 42. 5
and i assure ye | even that your pity is enough 111.13
that's to ye sworn to none was ever said, | for LC 180

/YEA 2 FR 0.0002 REL FR 2 V 0 P
/yea, /with /a /bridegroom's /fresh /alacrity TRO 4.04.145
/yea, /is't /come /to /this? LR 1.04.304

YEA 201 FR 0.0227 REL FR 135 V 66 P
waves tremble, | yea, his dread trident shake. TMP 1.02.206
yea, yea, my lord. 3.02. 60
yea, yea, my lord. 3.02. 60
have | incens'd the seas and shores — yea, all 3.03. 74
yea, all which it inherit, shall dissolve, | and 4.01.154
sir, i thank you; by yea and no, i do. WIV 1.01. 87 P
and the very yea and the no is, the french 1.04. 93 P
by yea and no, i think the oman is a witch 4.02.192 P
did not i tell thee yea? MM 2.02. 8
yea, my gravity, | wherein (let no man hear me) 2.04. 9
yea. 2.04. 38
yea, dost thou jeer and flout me in the teeth? ERR 2.02. 22
yea or no? 4.02. 3
yea, and a case to put it into. ADO 1.01.182 P
yea, but you must not make the full show of this 1.03. 19 P
yea, the same. 2.01.184 P
yea, but so i am apt to do myself wrong. 2.01.206 P
would have made hercules have turn'd spit, yea, 2.01.254 P
yea, my lord, i thank it — poor fool, it keeps 2.01.314 P
yea, my lord, but i can cross it. 2.02. 3 P
yea, my good lord. 2.03. 38
yea, marry, dost thou hear, balthasar? 2.03. 84 P
him, if he writ to me, yea, though i love him, i 2.03.144 P
yea, just so much as you may take upon a knive's 2.03.254 P
yea, or to paint himself? 3.02. 57 P
yea, or else it were pity but they should suffer 3.03. 2 P
yea, and 'twere a thousand pound more than 'tis, 3.05. 24 P
yea, wherefore should she not? 4.01.119
yea, and i will weep a while longer. 4.01.256 P
yea, as sure as i have a thought or a soul. 4.01.330 P
yea, marry, let them come before me. 4.02. 9 P
yea, sir, we hope. 4.02. 17 P
yea, marry, that's the eftest way; 4.02. 36 P
yea, by mass, that it is. 4.02. 51 P
i know them, yea, | and what they weigh, even to 5.01. 92
yea, that she did, but yet, for all that, and if 5.01.176 P
yea, and text underneath, "here dwells benedick 5.01.183 P
yea, and paid me richly for the practice of it. 5.01.248 P
yea, even i alone. 5.01.264
yea, signior, and depart when you bid me. 5.02. 44 P
by yea and nay, sir, then i swore in jest. LLL 1.01. 54
yea, he loveth. 1.02.182 P
so breathed, that certain he would fight, yea, 5.02.653
yea, and one | to whom you are but as a form in MND 1.01. 48
yea, art thou there? 3.02.411
yea, and my father. 4.01.196
yea, and the best person too; 4.02. 11 P
yea, mock the lion when 'a roars for prey, | to MV 2.01. 30
it for him in the court, | yea, twice the sum. 4.01.210
yea, a daniel! 4.01.223
yea, and of this our life, swearing that we AYL 2.01. 60
yea, providently caters for the sparrow, | be 2.03. 44
yea, brought her hither, | that thou mightst 5.04.113
yea, and perhaps with more successful words SHR 1.02.157
yea, and to marry her, if her dowry please. 1.02.184
you a suitor to the maid you talk of, yea or no? 1.02.228
yea, leave that labor to great hercules, | and 1.02.255
yea, all my raiment, to my petticoat, | or what 2.01. 5
my house, mine honor, yea, my life, be thine, AWW 4.02. 52
yea, a very trick | for them to play at will. WT 2.01. 51
make you, | yea, scandalous to the world. 2.03.121
yet for this once, yea, superstitiously, | i 3.03. 40
worthy enough a herdsman, yea, him too, | that 4.04.435
yea, | to die upon the bed my father died, | to 4.04.454
yea? 4.04.577
all, every word, yea, and his son's pranks too; 4.04.699 P
yea, faith itself to hollow falsehood change! JN 3.01. 95
yea, without stop, didst let thy heart consent, 4.02.239
yea, thrust this enterprise into my heart, | and 5.02. 90
yea, but not change his spots. R2 1.01.175
yea, at all points, and longs to enter in. 1.03. 2
yea, my lord. 3.02. 2
yea, distaff–women manage rusty bills | against 3.02.118
yea, my good lord. 3.03.209
yea, look'st thou pale? 5.02. 57
yea, there thou mak'st me sad, and mak'st me sin 1H4 1.01. 78
yea, and elsewhere, so far as my coin would 1.02. 54 P
yea, and so us'd it that, were it not here 1.02. 57 P
yea, for obtaining of suits, whereof the hangman 1.02. 72 P
yea, or the drone of a lincolnshire bagpipe. 1.02. 76 P
yea, but 'tis like that they will know us by our 1.02.174 P
yea, but i doubt they will be too hard for us. 1.02.181 P
yea, my good lord. 1.03. 22
yea, on his part i'll empty all these veins, 1.03.133
and have it, yea, and can show it you here in 2.04.257 P
yea, and to tickle our noses with speargrass to 2.04.309 P
yea, but | mark how he bears his course, and 3.01.106
yea, but a little charge will trench him here, 3.01.111
yea, even the slightest worship of his time, 3.02.151
yea, two and two, newgate fashion. 3.03. 90 P
yea, if he said my ring was copper. 3.03.142 P
yea, or to–night. 4.03. 14
both he and they and you, yea, every man | shall 5.01.107
yea, but how if honor prick me off when i come 5.01.130 P
yea, to the dead. 5.01.138 P
therefore i'll make him sure, yea, and i'll 5.04.125 P
yea, this man's brow, like to a title–leaf, 2H4 1.01. 60
yea, i thank your pretty sweet wit for it. 1.02.206 P
yea, marry, there's the point! 1.03. 18
yea, good master snare, i have ent'red him and 2.01. 9 P
yea, in truth, my lord. 2.01.117 P
thine, by yea and no, which is as much as to say 2.02.131 P
yea, my lord. 2.02.145 P
sick of a calm, yea, good faith. 2.04. 36 P
yea, joy, our chains and our jewels. 2.04. 47 P
yea, in very truth, do i, and 'twere an aspen 2.04.108 P
yea, sir. 2.04.213 P
yea, and you knew me, as you did when you ran 2.04.306 P
yea! 2.04.390 P
yea, for my sake, even to the eyes of richard 3.01. 64
by yea and no, sir. 3.02. 9 P
it is good, yea indeed is it. 3.02. 69 P
yea, marry, sir. 3.02. 98 P
yea, and't please you. 3.02.105 P
yea, marry, let me have him to sit under, he's 3.02.122 P
yea, sir. 3.02.140 P
yea, marry, let's see bullcalf. 3.02.173 P
yea, but our valuation shall be such | that 4.01.187
yea, every idle, nice, and wanton reason, 4.01.189
yea, marry, william cook, bid him come hither. 5.01. 10 P
yea, davy, i will use him well. 5.01. 30 P
yea, sir, in a pottle–pot. 5.03. 64 P
yea, marry, sir john, which i beseech you to let 5.05. 74 P
yea, at that very moment, | consideration like H5 1.01. 27
yea, strike the dolphin blind to look on us. 1.02.280
and in thy hateful lungs, yea, in thy maw, perdy 2.01. 49
wear | this ornament of knighthood, yea or no? 1H6 4.01. 29
wilt thou accept of ransom, yea or no? 5.03. 80
whether your grace be worthy, yea or no, 2H6 1.03.107
yea, i it was, proud frenchwoman. 1.03.140
yea, man and birds are fain of climbing high. 2.01. 8
yea, even my foes will shed fast–falling tears, 3H6 1.04.162
yea, is it so? 3.02. 11
yea, brother richard, are you offended too? 4.01. 19
yea, brother of clarence, art thou here too? 4.03. 41
yea, richard, when i know; R3 1.01. 52
banks | if they were his assistants, yea or no; 4.04.524
his mind and place | infecting one another, yea, H8 1.01.162
yea, such which breaks | the sides of loyalty, 1.02. 27
yea, subject to your countenance — glad, or 2.04. 26
yea, the elect o' th' land, who are assembled 2.04. 60
i utterly abhor, yea, from my soul | refuse you 2.04. 81
consistory, | yea, the whole consistory of rome. 2.04. 93
yea, as much | as you have done my truth. 2.04. 97
yea, upon mine honor, | i free you from't. 2.04.157
yea, with a spitting power, and made to tremble 2.04.184
yea, like fair fruit in an unwholesome dish, TRO 2.03.120
yea, watch | his /pettish /lines, his ebbs, /his 2.03.129
yea, what he shall receive of us in duty | gives 3.01.156
beauty than we have, | yea, overshines ourself. 3.01.158
son, | yea, let them say, to stick the heart of 3.02.195
i tell thee, yea. 4.05.251
i'll kill thee every where, yea, o'er and o'er. 4.05.256
yea, so familiar? 5.02. 8
yea, troilus? 5.06. 12

i am weary, yea, my memory is tir'd. COR 1.09. 91
cannot conclude but by the yea and no | of 3.01.145
take up a brace o' th' best of them, yea, the 3.01.243
to those that shall | say yea to thy desires. 4.05.145
yea forsooth, and your mistriship be emperial. TIT 4.04. 40 P
"yea," quoth he, "dost thou fall upon thy face? ROM 1.03. 41
"yea," quoth my husband, "fall'st upon thy face? 1.03. 55
yea, is the worst well? 2.04.125 P
yea, noise? 5.03.169
yea, from the glass–fac'd flatterer | to TIM 1.01. 58
yea, 'gainst th' authority of manners, pray'd 2.02.138
his semblable, yea, himself, timon disdains; 4.03. 22
to tow'rs and windows, yea, to chimney–tops, JC 1.01. 39
impossible, | yea, get the better of them. 2.01.326
yea, beg a hair of him for memory, | and, dying, 3.02.134
i'll use you for my mirth, yea, for my laughter, 4.03. 49
yea, from the table of my memory | i'll wipe HAM 1.05. 98
hath power | t' assume a pleasing shape, yea, 2.02.600
yea, curb and woo for leave to do him good. 3.04.155
i say yea. LR 2.04. 18
yea, or so many? 2.04.239
yea, though our proper son | stood in your OTH 1.03. 69
yea, curse his better angel from his side, | and 5.02.208
yea, like the stag, when snow the pasture sheets ANT 1.04. 65
yea, very force entangles | itself with strength 4.14. 48
yea so, | that our great king himself doth woo CYM 1.05. 13
what woman is, yea, what she cannot choose | but 1.06. 71
it doth), yea, and makes | diana's rangers false 2.03. 68
yea, happily, near | the residence of posthumus; 3.04.147
thee all this, | yea, and furr'd moss besides. 4.02.228
yea, bloody cloth, i'll keep thee, for i wish'd 5.01. 1
yea, though thou do demand a prisoner, | the 5.05. 99
yea, and she herself. 5.05.221
yea, mistress, are you so peremptory? PER 2.05. 73
yea | (we challenge too), the bank of any nymph, TNK 3.01. 7
forgive | the trespass thou hast done me, yea, 3.01. 77
yea, and a woeful and a piteous nullity. 3.05. 55
knights, kinsmen, lovers, yea, my sacrifices, 5.01. 34
hearts of lions and | the breath of tigers, yea, 5.01. 40
yea, the speed also — to go on, i mean, | else 5.01. 41
yea, him i do not love that tells close offices 5.01.122
hath outliv'd | the love o' th' people, yea, i' 5.04. 2
"yea, though i die, the scandal will survive, LUC 204
yea, the illiterate, that know not how | to 810
eye | receives the scroll without or yea or no, 1340
take all my loves, my love, yea, take them all, SON 40. 1

YEAD *(also edward, yedward)*

YEAD 1 FR 0.0001 REL FR 0 V 1 P
shilling and two pence a–piece of yead miller — WIV 1.01.157 P

YEA–FORSOOTH 1 FR 0.0001 REL FR 0 V 1 P
a /rascally yea–forsooth knave, to bear a 2H4 1.02. 36 P

YEAR* *(also ear*)*

YEAR* 98 FR 0.0110 REL FR 62 V 36 P
twelve year since, miranda, twelve year since, TMP 1.02. 53
twelve year since, miranda, twelve year since, 1.02. 53
thou did promise | to bate me a full year. 1.02.250
looks handsome in three hundred pounds a year! WIV 3.04. 33
to three thousand dolors a year. MM 1.02. 50 P
a man of fourscore pound a year; 2.01.123 P
are you of fourscore pounds a year? 2.01.195 P
that offend that way but for ten year together, 2.01.239 P
if this law hold in vienna ten year, i'll rent 2.01.241 P
seven year and a half, sir. 2.01.260 P
his child is a year and a quarter old come 3.02.201 P
compound with him by the year, and let him abide 4.02. 24 P
i buy a thousand pound a year! i buy a rope! ERR 4.01. 21
i think i told your lordship a year since, how ADO 2.02. 12 P
'a has been a vile thief this seven year; 3.03.126 P
hang me by the neck if horns that year miscarry. LLL 4.01.112
for he hath been five thousand year a boy. 5.02. 11
then, at the expiration of the year, | come 5.02.804
hold the plough for her sweet love three year. 5.02.884 P
estate | upon the fortune of this present year: MV 1.01. 44
falling out that year on ash we'nsday was four 2.05. 26 P
on ash we'nsday was four year in th' afternoon. 2.05. 27 P
so hard that it seems the length of seven year. AYL 3.02.317 P
sweet youth, i pray you chide a year together, 3.05. 64
liv'd many a fair year though hero had turn'd 4.01.101 P
i have, since i was three year old, convers'd 5.02. 60 P
and slept above some fifteen year or more. SHR in.2. 113
besides two thousand ducats by the year | of 2.01.369
two thousand ducats by the year of land! 2.01.372
within /t' /one year it will make itself two, AWW 1.01.147 P
good would serve the world so all the year! 1.03. 84 P
young" and "the next year" and "'tis too early." 2.01. 28
why, he has three thousand ducats a year. TN 1.03. 22 P
but he'll have but a year in all these ducats. 1.03. 23 P
why, then comes in the sweet o' the year, | for WT 4.03. 3
sir, the year growing ancient, | not yet on 4.04. 79
sure the gods do this year connive at us, and we 4.04.677 P
at least from fair five hundred pound a year. JN 1.01. 69
a half–fac'd groat five hundred pound a year! 1.01. 94
your face hath got five hundred pound a year, 1.01.152
/we at time of year | do wound the bark, the R2 3.04. 57
if all the year were playing holidays, | to 1H4 1.02.204
five year! 2.04. 45 P
i did that i did not this seven year before, i 2.04.312 P
of death or death's hand for this one half year. 4.01.136
whiles the big year, swoll'n with some other 2H4 in 13
for the box of the year that the prince gave you 1.02.194 P
saturn and venus this year in conjunction! 2.04.263 P
and in two year after | were they at wars. 3.01. 59
that's fifty–five year ago. 3.02.210 P
he that dies this year is quit for the next. 3.02.238 P
as the year | had found some months asleep and 4.04.123
good cheer, | and praise god for the merry year, 5.03. 18
i will lay odds that, ere this year expire, | we 5.05.105
which in th' eleventh year of the last king's H5 1.01. 2
king beside, | a thousand pounds by th' year. 1.01. 19
who died within the year of our redemption 1.02. 60
river sala, in the year | eight hundred five. 1.02. 63
and follows so the ever–running year | with 4.01.276
ne'er throughout the year to church thou go'st 1H6 1.01. 42
i myself fight not once in forty year. 1.03. 91
but claret wine this first year of our reign. 2H6 4.06. 4 P
would break a thousand oaths to reign one year. 3H6 1.02. 17
day, | how many days will finish up the year, 2.05. 28
to which title | a thousand pound a year, annual H8 2.03. 64
a thousand pounds a year for pure respect? 2.03. 95
that there had reign'd by many | a year before. 2.04. 50
hector shall not have his /wit this year. TRO 1.02. 86 P
'tis not the difference of a year or two | makes TIT 2.01. 31
now, by my maidenhead at twelve year old, | i ROM 1.03. 2
even or odd, of all days in the year, | come 1.03. 16
of all the days of the year, upon that day; 1.03. 25
i will not fail, 'tis twenty year till then. 2.02.169
with their wards | many a bounteous year, must TIM 3.03. 38
weighing the youthful season of the year. JC 2.01.108
man's memory may outlive his life half a year. HAM 3.02.132 P
of /all the days i' th' year, i came to't that 5.01.143 P
'a will last you some eight year or nine year. 5.01.167 P
'a will last you some eight year or nine year. 5.01.167 P
a tanner will last you nine year. 5.01.168 P
by order of law, some year elder than this, who LR 1.01. 20 P
"fools had ne'er less grace in a year, | for 1.04.166
for thy daughters as thou canst tell in a year. 2.04. 55 P
have been tom's food for seven long year. 3.04.139
me the story of my life | from year to year — OTH 1.03.130
me the story of my life | from year to year — 1.03.130
'tis not a year or two shows us a man: 3.04.103
to the time o' th' year between the extremes ANT 1.05. 51
that year indeed, he was troubled with a rheum; 3.02. 57
lies here, | who withered in her spring of year. PER 4.04. 35
(the prim'st of all the year) presents me with TNK 3.01. 19
maypole, and again, | ere another year run out, 3.05.146
to drive infection from the dangerous year! VEN 508
and threescore year would make the world away. SON 11. 8
since, seldom coming, in the long year set, 52. 6
speak of the spring and foison of the year, 53. 9
that time of year thou mayst in me behold | when 73. 1
from thee, the pleasure of the fleeting year! 97. 2

YEARLY 6 FR 0.0006 REL FR 6 V 0 P
yearly will i do this rite. ADO 5.03. 23
the yearly course that brings this day about JN 3.01. 81
five hundred poor i have in yearly pay, | who H5 4.01.298
will yearly on the vigil feast his neighbors, 4.03. 45
yearly three thousand pounds, which, by thee, CYM 3.01. 9
my beauty as the spring doth yearly grow, | my VEN 141

YEARN *(also earns*, ern, etc.)*

YEARN 1 FR 0.0001 REL FR 0 V 1 P
it, that it would yearn your heart to see it. WIV 3.05. 44 P

YEARNS 1 FR 0.0001 REL FR 1 V 0 P
it yearns me not if men my garments wear; H5 4.03. 26

YEAR'S 3 FR 0.0003 REL FR 1 V 2 P
it was proclaim'd a year's imprisonment to be LLL 1.01.287 P
we will eat a last year's pippin of mine own 2H4 5.03. 2 P
my youth, thou heap'st | a year's age on me. CYM 1.01.133

YEARS' 12 FR 0.0013 REL FR 9 V 3 P
a bawd of eleven years' continuance, may it MM 3.02.196 P
have sworn for three years' term to live with me LLL 1.01. 16
i am resolved, 'tis but a three years' fast: 1.01. 24
stay here in your court for three years' space. 1.01. 52
and bide the penance of each three years' day. 1.01.115
thousand times within this three years' space; 1.01.150
the element itself, till seven years' heat, TN 1.01. 25
a good report — after fourteen years' purchase. 4.01. 23 P
i saw not better sport these seven years' day; 2H6 2.01. 2
that after seven years' siege yet troy walls TRO 1.03. 12
it gives me an estate of seven years' health, in COR 2.01.115 P
since these arms of mine had seven years' pith, OTH 1.03. 83

/YEARS 1 FR 0.0001 REL FR 1 V 0 P
/send /him /many /years /of /sunshine /days! R2 4.01.221

YEARS 185 FR 0.0209 REL FR 140 V 45 P
for then thou wast not | out three years old. TMP 1.02. 41
thou didst painfully remain | a dozen years; 1.02.279
his years but young, but his experience old; TGV 2.04. 69
have done any time these three hundred years. WIV 1.01. 13 P
she is able to overtake seventeen years old. 1.01. 54 P
i have liv'd fourscore years and upward; 3.01. 56 P
which for this fourteen years we have let slip, MM 1.03. 21
you say seven years together? 2.01.262 P
and bred, one that is a prisoner nine years old. 4.02.131 P
notorious pirate, | a man of claudio's years; 4.03. 72
and five years since there was some speech of 5.01.217
since which time of five years | i never spake 5.01.222
at eighteen years became inquisitive | after his ERR 1.01.125
her sober virtue, years, and modesty, | plead on 3.01. 90
splitted my poor tongue | in seven short years, 5.01.310
but seven years since, in syracusa, boy, | thou 5.01.321
twenty years | have i been patron to antipholus, 5.01.327
thirty–three years have i but gone in travail 5.01.401
dost thou not suspect my years? ADO 4.02. 75 P
that is, to live and study here three years. LLL 1.01. 35
with a woman within the term of three years, he 1.01.130 P
and so to study three years is but short. 1.01.180
promised to study three years with the duke. 1.02. 35 P
easy it is to put "years" to the word "three," 1.02. 52 P
"three," and study three years in two words, the 1.02. 53 P
till painful study shall outwear three years, 2.01. 23
go, tenderness of years, take this key, give 3.01. 4 P
smiles his cheek in years and knows the trick 5.02.465
or else misgraffed in respect of years — MND 1.01.137
well, keep me company but two years moe, | thou MV 1.01.108
rebels it at these years? 3.01. 36 P
you let his lack of years be no impediment to 4.01.162 P
your spirits are too bold for your years. AYL 1.02.174 P
from /seventeen years till now almost fourscore 2.03. 71
at seventeen years many their fortunes seek, 2.03. 73
i'll rhyme you so eight years together, dinners 3.02. 96 P
is not very tall — yet for his years he's tall; 3.05.118
the poor world is almost six thousand years old, 4.01. 95 P
description — | such garments and such years. 4.03. 85
who for this seven years hath esteemed him | no SHR in.1. 122
these fifteen years you have been in a dream, in.2. 79
these fifteen years! in.2. 81
myself am strook in years, i must confess, | and 2.01.360
remember me | near twenty years ago in genoa, 4.04. 4
him up ever since he was three years old, and 5.01. 82 P
one that, in her sex, her years, profession, AWW 2.01. 83
her degree, neither in estate, years, nor wit; TN 1.03.110 P
for they shall yet belie thy happy years, | that 1.04. 30
of what personage and years is he? 1.05.155 P
what years, i' faith? 2.04. 27
about your years, my lord. 2.04. 28
and grew a twenty years removed thing | while 5.01. 89
from her birth | had numb'red thirteen years. 5.01.245
that day that made my sister thirteen years. 5.01.248
methoughts i did recoil | twenty–three years, WT 1.02.155
ten thousand years together, naked, fasting, 3.02.211
o'er sixteen years and leave the growth untried 4.01. 6
it is fifteen years since i saw my country; 4.02. 4 P
not at your father's house these seven years 4.04.578
a piece many years in doing and now newly 5.02. 96 P
which lets go by some sixteen years, and makes 5.03. 31
make me to think so twenty years together! 5.03. 71
no! not these twenty years. 5.03. 84
look upon the years | of lewis the dolphin and JN 2.01.424
many years of happy days befall | my gracious R2 1.01. 20
that all the treasons for these eighteen years, 1.01. 95
take from my mouth the wish of happy years. 1.03. 94
the language i have learnt these forty years, 1.03.159
a nurse, | too far in years to be a pupil now. 1.03.171
hath from the number of his banish'd years 1.03.210
me | he shortens four years of my son's exile, 1.03.217
ere the six years that he hath to spend | can 1.03.219
why, uncle, thou hast many years to live. 1.03.225
six years we banish him, and he shall go. 1.03.248
hours | and added years to his short banishment, 1.04. 17
which, till my infant fortune comes to years, 2.03. 66
elect, | anointed, crowned, planted many years, 4.01.127
which elder years | may happily bring forth. 5.03. 21
which fourteen hundred years ago were nail'd 1H4 1.01. 26
hourly any time this two and twenty years, and 2.02. 16 P
forsooth, five years, and as much as to — 2.04. 42 P
thou stolest a cup of sack eighteen years ago, 2.04.315 P
when i was about thy years, hal, i was not an 2.04.329 P
that father ruffian, that vanity in years? 2.04.454 P
and, being no more in debt to years than thou, 3.02.103
with fire any time this two and thirty years, 3.03. 48 P
desire should so many years outlive performance? 2H4 2.04.261 P
i have known thee these twenty–nine years, come 2.04.383 P
'tis not ten years gone | since richard and 3.01. 57
it is but eight years since | this percy was the 3.01. 60
you like well and bear your years very well. 3.02. 84 P
it hath been prophesied to me many years, | i 4.05.236
your worship truly, sir, this eight years; 5.01. 48 P
turning th' accomplishment of many years | into H5 pr 30
until four hundred one and twenty years | after 1.02. 57
by french fathers | had twenty years been made. 2.04. 62
posterity, await for wretched years, | when at 1H6 1.01. 48
that hast by tyranny these many years | wasted 2.03. 40
would some part of my young years | might but 2.05.107
believe me, lords, my tender years can tell, 3.01. 71
my tender years, and let us not forgo | that for 4.01.149
this seven years did not talbot see his son, 4.03. 37
alas, my years are young; 5.01. 21
i see no reason why a king of years | should be 2H6 2.03. 28
have a lease of my life for a thousand years, i 4.10. 6 P
year, | how many years a mortal man may live. 3H6 2.05. 29
so many years ere i shall shear the fleece: 2.05. 37
so minutes, hours, days, months, and years, 2.05. 38
tell a pedigree | of threescore and two years — 3.03. 93
whom thou obey'dst thirty and six years, | and 3.03. 96
even in the downfall of his mellow'd years, 3.03.104
and his noble queen | well strook in years, fair R3 1.01. 92
and, in his full and ripened years, himself, 2.03. 14
'twas full two years ere i could get a tooth. 2.04. 29
the untainted virtue of your years | hath not 3.01. 7
eighty odd years of sorrow have i seen, | and 4.01. 95
make bold her bashful years with your experience 4.04.326
can make seem pleasing to her tender years? 4.04.342
longer than i have time to tell his years; H8 2.01. 91
a jewel, has hung twenty years | about his neck, 2.02. 31
i have been begging sixteen years in court | (am 2.03. 82
wife in this obedience | upward of twenty years, 2.04. 36
lend you him i will | for half a hundred years. COR 1.04. 7
at sixteen years, | when tarquin made a head for 2.02. 87
thou hast years upon thee, and thou art too full 4.01. 45
if i could shake off but one seven years | from 4.01. 55
ten years are spent since first he undertook TIT 1.01. 31
rome, i have been thy soldier forty years, | and 1.01.193
this monument five hundreth years hath stood, 1.01.350
chiron, thy years wants wit, thy wits wants edge 2.01. 26
she hath not seen the change of fourteen years; ROM 1.02. 9
'tis since the earthquake now aleven years, 1.03. 23
and since that time it is aleven years, | for 1.03. 35
i warrant, and i should live a thousand years, 1.03. 46
i was your mother much upon these years | that 1.03. 72
by'r lady, thirty years. 1.05. 33
some five and twenty years, and then we mask'd. 1.05. 37
his son was but a ward two years ago. 1.05. 40
by this count i shall be much in years | ere i 3.05. 46
that | which the commission of thy years and art 4.01. 64
where for this many hundred years the bones | of 4.03. 40
he that cuts off twenty years of life | cuts off JC 3.01.101
life | cuts off so many years of fearing death. 3.01.102
live a thousand years, | i shall not find myself 3.01.159
for i have seen more years, i'm sure, than ye. 4.03.132
this three years i have took note of it: HAM 5.01.139 P
been sexton here, man and boy, thirty years. 5.01.162 P
lien you i' th' earth three and twenty years. 5.01.174 P
he hath been out nine years, and away he shall LR 1.01. 32 P
that infirm and choleric years bring with them. 1.01.299 P
i have years on my back forty–eight. 1.04. 39 P
though they had been but two years o' th' trade. 2.02. 60 P
your father's tenant, | these fourscore years. 4.01. 14
you shall more command with years | than with OTH 1.02. 60
of years, of country, credit, every thing, | to 1.03. 97
upon the world for four times seven years, and 1.03.312 P
loveliness in favor, sympathy in years, manners, 2.01.229 P
or for i am declin'd | into the vale of years 3.03.266
i would have him nine years a–killing. 4.01.178 P
him | report the feature of octavia, her years, ANT 2.05.112
guess at her years, i prithee. 3.03. 26
mark it), the eldest of them at three years old, CYM 1.01. 58
some twenty years. 1.01. 62
and this twenty years | this rock and these 3.03. 69
at three and two years old, i stole these babes, 3.03.101
i saw him not these many years, and yet | i know 4.02. 66
have skipp'd from sixteen years of age to sixty, 4.02.199
many years, | though cloten then but young, you 4.04. 22
which, being dead many years, shall after revive 5.04.142 P
are) these twenty years | have i train'd up; 5.05.337

which, being dead many years, shall after revive 5.05.439 P
for many years thought dead, are now reviv'd, 5.05.456
decrease not, but grow faster than the years; PER 1.02. 85
then discourse our woes, felt several years, 1.04. 18
a man may serve seven years for the loss of a 4.06.171 P
who at fourteen years | he sought to murder, but 5.03. 8
and what this fourteen years no razor touch'd, 5.03. 75
and at ten years old | they must be all gelt for TNK 4.01.132
measure my strangeness with my unripe years; VEN 524
and straight, in pity of his tender years, 1091
although i know my years be past the best, | i PP 1. 6
and age in love, loves not to have years told. 1.12
but whether unripe years did want conceit, | or 4. 9
thy beauty and thy years full well befits, | for SON 41. 3
and age in love loves not t' have years told. 138.12

YEAS 1 FR 0.0001 REL FR 1 V 0 P
in russet yeas and honest kersey noes. LLL 5.02.413

YEAST *(see yest, etc.)*

YEDWARD *(also edward, yead)*

YEDWARD 1 FR 0.0001 REL FR 0 V 1 P
hear ye, yedward, if i tarry at home and go not, 1H4 1.02.134 P

YE'LL 1 FR 0.0001 REL FR 0 V 1 P
now here is three studied ere ye'll thrice wink; LLL 1.02. 51 P

YELL 3 FR 0.0003 REL FR 3 V 0 P
the dogs did yell: LLL 4.02. 58
do, with like timorous accent and dire yell | as OTH 1.01. 75
keep, | to stop the loud pursuers in their yell, VEN 688

YELL'D 1 FR 0.0001 REL FR 1 V 0 P
and yell'd out | like syllable of dolor. MAC 4.03. 7

YELLOW 30 FR 0.0034 REL FR 19 V 11 P
come unto these yellow sands, | and then take TMP 1.02.375
her hair is auburn, mine is perfect yellow: TGV 4.04.189
a little /whey–face, with a little yellow beard, WIV 1.04. 23 P
all silver–white | and cuckoo–buds of yellow hue LLL 5.02.896
french–crown–color beard, your perfit yellow. MND 1.02. 96 P
and sat with me on neptune's yellow sands, 2.01.126
turns into yellow gold his salt green streams. 3.02.393
this cherry nose, | these yellow cowslip cheeks, 5.01.332
and with a green and yellow melancholy | she sat TN 2.04.113
remember who commended thy yellow stockings, and 2.05.153 P
she did commend my yellow stockings of late, she 2.05.166 P
stout, in yellow stockings, and cross–garter'd, 2.05.171 P
he will come to her in yellow stockings, and 2.05.199 P
he's in yellow stockings. 3.02. 73 P
not black in my mind, though yellow in my legs. 3.04. 26 P
"remember who commended thy yellow stockings" — 3.04. 47 P
thy yellow stockings? 3.04. 49 P
to put on yellow stockings and to frown | upon 5.01.338
'mongst all colors | no yelllow in't, lest she WT 2.03.107
eye, a dry hand, a yellow cheek, a white beard, 2H4 1.02.181 P
in a long motley coat guarded with yellow, H8 pr 16
with reeky shanks and yellow /chapless skulls; ROM 4.01. 83
yellow, glittering, precious gold? TIM 4.03. 26
this yellow slave | will knit and break 4.03. 34
life | is fall'n into the sear, the yellow leaf, MAC 5.03. 23
this yellow jachimo, in an hour — was't not? CYM 2.05. 14
and i'll clip my yellow locks an inch below mine TNK 3.04. 20
his head's yellow, | hard–hair'd, and curl'd, 4.02.103
thou mayst in me behold | when yellow leaves, or SON 73. 2
three beauteous springs to yellow autumn turn'd 104. 5

YELLOWED 1 FR 0.0001 REL FR 1 V 0 P
so should my papers (yellowed with their age) SON 17. 9

YELLOWING 1 FR 0.0001 REL FR 1 V 0 P
let us sit down and mark their yellowing noise; TIT 2.03. 20

YELLOWNESS *(see yallowness)*

YELLOWS 2 FR 0.0002 REL FR 1 V 1 P
sped with spavins, ray'd with the yellows, past SHR 3.02. 53 P
the yellows, blues, | the purple violets, and PER 4.01. 14

YELLS 1 FR 0.0001 REL FR 1 V 0 P
whose proof nor yells of mothers, maids, nor TIM 4.03.125

YELPING 2 FR 0.0002 REL FR 2 V 0 P
maz'd with a yelping kennel of french curs! 1H6 4.02. 47
even so the timorous yelping of the hounds VEN 881

YEMAN'S 1 FR 0.0001 REL FR 1 V 0 P
but, sir, now | it did me yeman's service. HAM 5.02. 36

YEOMAN 10 FR 0.0011 REL FR 3 V 7 P
the strachy married the yeoman of the wardrobe. TN 2.05. 40 P
where's your yeoman? 2H4 2.01. 3 P
is't a lusty yeoman? 2.01. 3 P
we grace the yeoman by conversing with him. 1H6 2.04. 81
and, till thou be restor'd, thou art a yeoman. 2.04. 95
yet not so wealthy as an english yeoman. 3H6 1.04.123
me whether a madman be a gentleman or a yeoman? LR 3.06. 10 P
he's a yeoman that has a gentleman to his son; 3.06. 12 P
for he's a mad yeoman that sees his son a 3.06. 13 P
brother arthur watchins sergeant safe's yeoman. STM II.C 43 P

YEOMEN 3 FR 0.0003 REL FR 3 V 0 P
and you, good yeomen, | whose limbs were made in H5 3.01. 25
spring crestless yeomen from so deep a root? 1H6 2.04. 85
fight, bold yeomen! R3 5.03.338

/YEOMEN'S 1 FR 0.0001 REL FR 0 V 1 P
me none but good householders, /yeomen's sons, 1H4 4.02. 15 P

YER *(also ere)*

YER 2 FR 0.0002 REL FR 2 V 0 P
be bent, | her cloudy looks will calm yer night, PP 18.26
and twice desire, yer it be day, | that which 18.29

YERK 1 FR 0.0001 REL FR 1 V 0 P
yerk out their armed heels at their dead masters H5 4.07. 80

YERK'D 1 FR 0.0001 REL FR 1 V 0 P
i had thought t' have yerk'd him here under the OTH 1.02. 5

YERWHILE *(also erewhile)*

YERWHILE 1 FR 0.0001 REL FR 1 V 0 P
thou the youth that spoke to me yerwhile? AYL 3.05.105

/YES 6 FR 0.0006 REL FR 6 V 0 P
/yes, /if /this /present /quality /of /war — 2H4 1.03. 36
/yes, /poole. 2H6 4.01. 70
/yes, /and /will /nobly /him /remunerate. TIT 1.01.398
/yes, /they /have. LR 2.04. 20
/yes, /faith; OTH 3.03. 52
/yes, presently: 5.02. 52

YES 240 FR 0.0271 REL FR 155 V 85 P
yes — caliban her son. TMP 1.02.284
yes, faith, and all his lords, the duke of milan 1.02.438
yes, for a score of kingdoms you should wrangle, 5.01.174
yes, yes; TGV 2.01.122
yes, yes; 2.01.122
yes, it is so, it is so — it hath the worser 2.03. 17 P
yes, py'r lady. WIV 1.01. 28 P
yes indeed does he. 1.04. 31 P
yes, marry, have i, what of that? 1.04.148 P
yes, and you heard what the other told me? 2.01.171 P
yes, in truth. 2.02.104 P
yes, by all means; 4.02.215 P
yes, i warrant; 4.05.110 P
yes, that thou hast; MM 1.02. 42 P
yes, truly; 1.04. 3
yes, and't please you, sir. 2.01.196 P
yes; 2.02. 49
yes, as i love the woman that wrong'd him. 2.03. 25
yes, brother, you may live; 3.01. 63
yes, thou must die: 3.01. 86
yes, he would give't thee, from this rank 3.01. 99
yes. 3.01.107
yes, faith, sir. 3.02. 62 P
yes, in good sooth, the vice is of a great 3.02.101 P
yes, your beggar of fifty; 3.02.125 P
yes, marry, did i; 4.03.172 P
yes, to pay a fine for a periwig, and recover ERR 2.02. 75 P
o, yes, if any hour meet a sergeant, 'a turns 4.02. 56
yes, that you did, sir, and forswore it too. 5.01. 24
yes, faith, it is my cousin's duty to make ADO 2.01. 52 P
yes, and his ill conditions, and, in despite of 3.02. 66 P
yes, it is apparel. 3.03.120 P
yes, the fashion is the fashion. 3.03.122 P
yes, in truth it is, sir. 3.05. 7 P
yes, i thank god i am as honest as any man 3.05. 13 P
yes, madam, fair. LLL 4.01. 16
yes, for her two eyes. 4.03. 10 P
yes, yes, he teaches boys the horn–book. 5.01. 46 P
yes, yes, he teaches boys the horn–book. 5.01. 46 P
yes, as much love in rhyme | as would be cramm'd 5.02. 6
yes, madam, and moreover | some thousand verses 5.02. 49
yes, in good faith. 5.02.280
yes; it doth shine that night. MND 3.01. 55 P
yes, sooth; and so do you. 3.02.265
yes, yes, it was bassanio — as i think, so was MV 1.02.115 P
yes, yes, it was bassanio — as i think, so was 1.02.115 P
yes, to smell pork, to eat of the habitation 1.03. 33 P
yes, shylock, i will seal unto this bond. 1.03.171
yes, other men have ill luck too. 3.01. 97 P
yes, faith, my lord. 3.02.211
yes, truly, for look you, the sins of the father 3.05. 1 P
yes, here i tender it for him in the court, 4.01.209
yes, i beseech your grace, i am not yet well AYL 1.02.217 P
o yes, into a thousand similes. 2.01. 45
o yes, i heard them all, and more, too, for some 3.02.164 P
yes, just. 3.02.264 P
yes, one, and in this manner. 3.02.407 P
yes, i think he is not a pick–purse nor a 3.04. 22 P
yes, when he is in — but i think he is not in. 3.04. 27 P
yes, i have gain'd my experience. 4.01. 26 P
yes, faith, will i, fridays and saturdays and 4.01.116 P
yes, sir. 4.02. 7 P
by my troth, yes; 5.03. 39 P
o yes, my lord, but very idle words, | for SHR in.2. 83
o yes, i saw sweet beauty in her face, | such as 1.01.167
yes, by saint anne, do i. 1.01.250 P
yes, keep you warm. 2.01.266
yes, marry, sir — see where he looks out of the 5.01. 55 P
yes, i know thee to be signior lucentio. 5.01.105 P
yes, helen, you might be my daughter–in–law. AWW 1.03.167
yes, but you will | my noble grapes, and if my 2.01. 79
yes, my good lord, | but never hope to know why 2.03.109
yes, good faith, ev'ry dram of it, and i will 2.03.221 P
yes, my lord, and of very valiant approof. 2.05. 3 P
yes, i do know him well, and common speech 2.05. 52
faith, yes: 2.05. 85
yes, so please your majesty. 5.03.258 P
yes, and shall do till the pangs of death shake TN 1.05. 75 P
yes, by saint anne, and ginger shall be hot i' 2.03.117 P
yes, being kept together and put to use. 3.01. 50 P
at your request! yes, nightingales answer daws. 3.04. 35 P
yes; WT 1.01. 43 P
yes, if you will, my lord. 1.02.127
yes, that i will; JN 3.04. 69
yes, my good lord, | it doth contain a king. R2 3.03. 24
yes, jack, upon instinct. 1H4 2.04.355 P
yes, faith, and let it be an excellent good 2H4 2.02. 33 P
yes, sir. 5.01. 18 P
yes, that 'a did, and said they were dev'ls H5 2.03. 31 P
yes. 4.01. 53 P
yes, captain; 4.08.119
yes, my conscience, he did us great good. 4.08.121 P
yes, certainly, and out of doubt and out of 5.01. 45 P
yes, verily and in truth you shall take it, or i 5.01. 61 P
yes, my lord, you see them perspectively: 5.02.320 P
yes, as an outlaw in a castle keeps | and useth 1H6 3.01. 47
yes, when his holy state is touch'd so near. 3.01. 58
yes, if it please your majesty, my liege. 3.04. 15
yes, sir, as well as you dare patronage | the 3.04. 32
yes. 4.01. 71
yes, your renowned name. shall flight abuse it? 4.05. 41
yes, there is remedy enough, my lord. 5.03.135
yes, my good lord, a pure unspotted heart, 5.03.182
yes, my lord, her father is a king, | the king 5.05. 39
yes, my good lord, i'll follow presently. 2H6 1.02. 60
yes, master, clear as day, i thank god and saint 2.01.105 P
yes, my lord, if it please your grace. 2.01.135
o yes, it doth; 3H6 2.05. 46
yes, i agree, and thank you for your motion. 3.03.244
yes, i accept her, for she well deserves it, 3.03.249
yes, warwick, edward dares, and leads the way. 5.01.112
yes, one place else, if you will hear me name it R3 1.02.110
yes, that the king is dead. 2.03. 3
yes, i am. 5.03.184
yes, heartily beseech you. H8 1.02.176
yes, if i make my play. 1.04. 46
yes, my lord. 1.04. 99
yes indeed was i. 2.01. 6
yes, truly is he, and condemn'd upon't. 2.01. 8
yes, but it held not; 2.01.149
yes, he was. 2.02.122
yes, surely. 2.02.123
yes, troth, and troth. you would not be a queen? 2.03. 34
yes, that goodness | of gleaning all the land's 3.02.283
yes, 'tis the list | of those that claim their 4.01. 14
yes. 4.01. 42
yes, without all doubt. 4.01.113
yes, madam; 4.02. 7
yes, good griffith, | i were malicious else. 4.02. 47
yes, yes, sir thomas, | there are that dare, and 5.01. 39
yes, yes, sir thomas, | there are that dare, and 5.01. 39
yes, my lord; | but yet i cannot help you. 5.02. 4
yes. 5.02. 39
yes. 5.02. 40
o yes, and 'twere a cloud in autumn. TRO 1.02.126 P
yes, he'll fight indifferent well. 1.02.223 P
yes, good sooth. to achilles, to ajax, to — 2.01.109 P
yes, lion–sick, sick of proud heart. 2.03. 86 P
remember? yes. 5.02. 13
yes, here it is: COR 1.02. 8
yes certain, there's a letter for you, i saw't. 2.01.113 P
yes, yes, yes; 2.01.133 P
yes, yes, yes; 2.01.133 P
yes, yes, yes; 2.01.133 P
yes, worthy sir, | the slave's report is 4.06. 62
yes, mercy, if you report him truly. 5.04. 25 P
yes, better, sir. ROM 1.01. 60 P
yes, madam, yet i cannot choose but laugh | to 1.03. 50
yes. TIM 1.01.183 P
yes. 1.01.218 P
yes. 1.01.221 P
yes, he is worthy of thee, and to pay thee for 1.01.225 P
yes, my lord. 1.02.159
yes, sir, i shall. 3.02. 59 P
yes, mine's three thousand crowns; what's yours? 3.04. 28
yes. 4.03. 83
yes, thou spok'st well of me. 4.03.173
yes, you are. JC 1.03.139
yes, every man of them; 2.01. 90
yes, bring me word, boy, if thy lord look well, 2.04. 13
yes, cassius, and, from henceforth, | when you 4.03.121
yes, that thou didst. didst thou see any thing? 4.03.297
o yes, and soundless too; 5.01. 36
yes, | as sparrows eagles; MAC 1.02. 34
yes, he is dead. how wilt thou do for a father? 4.02. 38
o yes, my lord, he wore his beaver up. HAM 1.02.230
yes, by heaven! 1.05.104
offend you, heartily, | yes, faith, heartily. 1.05.135
yes, by saint patrick, but there is, horatio, 1.05.136
yes, it is already garrison'd. 4.04. 24
yes, forsooth, i will hold my tongue; LR 1.04.194 P
yes, that, on every dream, | each buzz, each 1.04.324
yes indeed, thou wouldst make a good fool. 1.05. 38 P
yes, madam, he was of that consort. 2.01. 97
yes, sir, but anger hath a privilege. 2.02. 70
yes. 2.04. 16
yes, faith. 4.07. 70
half–blooded fellow, yes. 5.03. 80
yes, sir, i have indeed. OTH 1.01.174
yes, that i did; but that was but courtesy. 2.01.256 P
o yes, and went between us very oft. 3.03.100
yes, you have seen cassio and she together. 4.02. 3
yes, a dozen; 4.03. 84 P
no — yes, sure — /o /heaven, roderigo! 5.01. 90
yes. 5.02. 91
yes, gracious madam. ANT 1.05. 13
thee worser than i do, | if thou again say yes. 2.05. 91
yes, something you can deny for your own safety: 2.06. 91 P
yes, my lord, yes; 3.11. 35
yes, my lord, yes; 3.11. 35
yes, like enough! 3.13. 29
yes, forsooth; i wish you joy o' th' worm. 5.02.279 P
faith, yes, to be put to the arbiterment of CYM 1.04. 49 P
yes, i beseech; 1.06.200
yes, and a gentlewoman's son. 2.03. 78
yes; 3.06. 11
yes, sir, to milford–haven, which is the way? 4.02.291
yes indeed do i, fellow. 5.04.177 P
yes, if you love me, sir. PER 2.05. 88
yes, if't please your majesty. 2.05. 91
yes indeed shall you, and taste gentlemen of all 4.02. 78 P
yes, i pity | decays where e'er i find them, but TNK 1.02. 31
yes. 1.03. 54
yes. 2.02.122
yes. 2.02.127
yes, a matchless beauty. 2.02.154
yes, but you must not love her. 2.02.161
yes, i love her, | and if the lives of all my 2.02.174
yes, and have found me so. 2.02.183
yes. 2.02.186
yes, if he be but one. 2.02.196
yes, 'tis a question | to me that know not. 2.03. 61
yes, marry, are there; 2.03. 64
yes. 3.03. 20
yes, for /them | that have wild consciences. 3.03. 23
yes. 3.03. 38
yes, sir. 3.05. 37
yes, but all | was vainly labor'd in me; 3.06. 78
yes. 3.06.299
yes, i must, sir, | else both miscarry. 3.06.301
yes, truly, can i. 4.01.107
yes. 4.01.109
yes, wench, we know him. 4.01.117
yes, he's a fine man. 4.01.120
yes. 4.01.121
yes. 4.01.128
yes. 4.01.143
yes. 4.02. 57
yes, they are well. 4.02.121
yes, sir. 4.02.151
yes, in the way of cure. 5.02. 19
yes. 5.02. 45
yes, but you care not for me. 5.02. 83
yes, by this fair hand, will i. 5.02. 86
yes, sweet heart, | and i am glad my cousin 5.02. 90
yes, without doubt. 5.02. 93
yes. 5.02. 93
yes, marry, will we. 5.02.111
o yes, it may, thou hast no eyes to see, | but VEN 939
o yes, dear friend, i pardon crave of thee, PP 10.11

YEST 1 FR 0.0001 REL FR 0 V 1 P

and anon swallow'd with yest and froth, as WT 3.03. 93 P
YESTERDAY 25 FR 0.0028 REL FR 12 V 13 P
out of my house yesterday in this basket. WIV 4.02.146 P
went you not to her yesterday, sir, as you told 5.01. 13 P
i reason'd with a frenchman yesterday, | who MV 2.08. 27
that i made yesterday in despite of my invention AYL 2.05. 47 P
i met the duke yesterday, and had much question 3.04. 35 P
i heard my lady talk of it yesterday; TN 1.03. 15 P
child, | to him that did but yesterday suspire, JN 3.04. 80
o, call back yesterday, bid time return, | and R2 3.02. 69
exeter, | enlarge the man committed yesterday, H5 2.02. 40
for methought yesterday your mistress shrewdly 3.07. 48 P
five hundred were but yesterday dubb'd knights. 4.08. 86
and prings me pread and salt yesterday, look you 5.01. 9 P
you call'd me yesterday mountain–squire, but i 5.01. 35 P
i would somebody had heard her talk yesterday, TRO 1.01. 45 P
they say he yesterday cop'd hector in the battle 1.02. 33 P
i told you a thing yesterday, think on't. 1.02.170 P
prisoner call'd antenor, | yesterday took; 3.03. 19
and but one half of what he was yesterday; COR 4.05.198 P
and yesterday the bird of night did sit | even JC 1.03. 26
but yesterday the word of caesar might | have 3.02.118
was it not yesterday we spoke together? MAC 3.01. 73
i saw him yesterday, or th' other day, | or then HAM 2.01. 54
that sweet sleep | which thou ow'dst yesterday. OTH 3.03.333
he had one yesterday. 4.01. 51
i heard of one of them no longer than yesterday, ANT 5.02.251 P
YESTERDAYS 1 FR 0.0001 REL FR 1 V 0 P
and all our yesterdays have lighted fools | the MAC 5.05. 22
YESTERNIGHT 12 FR 0.0013 REL FR 10 V 2 P
but yesternight, my lord, she and that friar, MM 5.01.134
what man was he talk'd with you yesternight ADO 4.01. 83
or that i yesternight | maintain'd the change of 4.01.182
what yesternight our council did decree | in 1H4 1.01. 32
limits of the charge set down | but yesternight, 1.01. 36
it holds current that i told you yesternight: 2.01. 54 P
for yesternight by catesby was it sent me; R3 3.06. 6
she look'd yesternight fairer than ever i saw TRO 1.01. 32 P
his wife but yesternight was brought to bed; TIT 4.02.153
and yesternight | return'd my letter back. ROM 5.03.251
and yesternight at supper | you suddenly arose JC 2.01.238
my lord, i think i saw him yesternight. HAM 1.02.189
/YESTY 1 FR 0.0001 REL FR 0 V 1 P
habit of encounter, a kind of /yesty collection, HAM 5.02.191 P
YESTY 1 FR 0.0001 REL FR 1 V 0 P
though the yesty waves | confound and swallow MAC 4.01. 53
/YET 22 FR 0.0024 REL FR 20 V 2 P
/i /hardly /yet /have /learn'd | /to /insinuate, R2 4.01.164
/yet /i /well /remember | /the /favors /of 4.01.167
/and /yet /amen, /if /heaven /do /think /him /me 4.01.175
/the /crown, /yet /still /with /me /they /stay. 4.01.199
/yet /you /pilates | /have /here /deliver'd /me 4.01.240
/and /yet /salt /water /blinds /them /not /so 4.01.245
/great /king, /and /yet /not /greatly /good, 4.01.263
/if /my /word /be /sterling /yet /in /england, 4.01.264
/no /deeper /wrinkles /yet? 4.01.277
/yet /ask. 4.01.310
the faster it grows, /yet youth, the more it is 1H4 2.04.401 P
that's the worst tidings that i hear of /yet. 4.01.127
/yet /did /you /say, "/go /forth!" 2H4 1.01.175
/yet, /for /your /part, /it /not /appears /to 4.01.105
/the /fresh /and /yet /unbruised /greeks /do TRO pr 14
/yet, after all comparisons of truth | (as 3.02.180
/yet /i /think /we /are /not /brought /so /low, TIT 3.02. 76
you fret me, /yet you cannot play upon me. HAM 3.02.371 P
/this /rest /might /yet /have /balm'd /thy LR 3.06. 98
/and /yet /it /is /danger | /to /make /him /even 4.07. 78
/be /honest, | /i /never /yet /was /valiant. 5.01. 24
it /yet hath felt no age nor known no sorrow. OTH 3.04. 37
YET 1744 FR 0.1971 REL FR 1432 V 312 P
good, yet remember whom thou hast aboard. TMP 1.01. 19 P
yet again? 1.01. 38 P
he'll be hang'd yet, | though every drop of 1.01. 58
not yet." 1.02. 36
crown, and bend | the dukedom yet unbow'd (alas, 1.02.115
hast promis'd, | which is not yet perform'd me. 1.02.244
well, i have done. but yet — 2.01. 26
yet — 2.01. 39 P
yet — 2.01. 40 P
yet he would be king on't. 2.01.157
more — | and yet methinks i see it in thy face, 2.01.206
speaking, moving — | and yet so fast asleep. 2.01.215
spirits hear me, | and yet i needs must curse. 2.02. 4
yet a tailor might scratch her where e'er she 2.02. 53
thou dost me yet but little hurt; 2.02. 79 P
for yet ere supper–time must i perform | much 3.01. 95
lie like dogs, and yet say nothing neither. 3.02. 20 P
though they are of monstrous shape, yet, note, 3.03. 31
yet always bending | towards their project. 4.01.174
speak softly, | all's hush'd as midnight yet. 4.01.207
yet this is your harmless fairy, monster! 4.01.211 P
yet, with my nobler reason, 'gainst my fury | do 5.01. 26
not one of them | that yet looks on me, or would 5.01. 83
miss thee, | but yet thou shalt have freedom. 5.01. 96
you do yet taste | some subtleties o' th' isle, 5.01.123
no more yet of this, | for 'tis a chronicle of 5.01.162
there are yet missing of your company | some few 5.01.254
love, | and yet you never swom the hellespont. TGV 1.01. 26
yet writers say: 1.01. 42
and yet it cannot overtake your slow purse. 1.01.126 P
yet he, of all the rest, i think best loves ye. 1.02. 28
and yet i would i had o'erlook'd the letter; 1.02. 50
and yet methinks i do not like this tune. 1.02. 87
and yet i will not, sith so prettily | he 1.02.123
yet here they shall not lie, for catching cold. 1.02.133
and yet a thousand times it answers "no." 1.03. 91
and yet i was last chidden for being too slow. 2.01. 12 P
by my gazing on her, and yet know'st her not? 2.01. 47 P
and yet — 2.01.115
and yet i will not name it — and yet i care not 2.01.117
yet i will not name it — and yet i care not — 2.01.117
and yet take this again — and yet i thank you 2.01.118
yet take this again — and yet i thank you — 2.01.118
and yet you will; and yet another "yet." 2.01.120
and yet you will; and yet another "yet." 2.01.120
and yet you will; and yet another "yet." 2.01.120
yet did not this cruel–hearted cur shed one tear 2.03. 9 P
yet hath sir proteus (for that's his name) 2.04. 67
and duty never yet did want his meed. 2.04.112
if not divine, | yet let her be a principality, 2.04.152
'tis but her picture i have yet beheld, | and 2.04.209
i cannot leave to love, and yet i do; 2.06. 17
man | (a rashness that i ever yet have shunn'd), 3.01. 30
and yet i have the wit to think my master is a 3.01.263 P
that knows me to be in love, yet i am in love, 3.01.266 P
and yet 'tis a woman; 3.01.268 P
and yet 'tis a milkmaid; 3.01.269 P
yet 'tis not a maid, for she hath had gossips; 3.01.270 P
yet 'tis a maid, for she is her master's maid, 3.01.271 P
repent, | but yet i slew him manfully in fight, 4.01. 28
yet, spaniel–like, the more she spurns my love, 4.02. 14
but yet so false that he grieves my very 4.02. 61 P
yet valentine thy friend | survives, to whom, 4.02.108
vouchsafe me yet your picture for my love, | the 4.02.120
yet will i woo for him, but yet so coldly | as, 4.04.106
yet will i woo for him, but yet so coldly | as, 4.04.106
and yet the painter flatter'd her a little, 4.04.187
and yet she takes exceptions at your person. 5.02. 3
yet i have much to do | to keep them from 5.04. 16
made me drunk, yet i am not altogether an ass. WIV 1.01.172 P
yet heaven may decrease it upon better 1.01.246 P
i keep but three men and a boy yet, till my 1.01.274 P
yet i live like a poor gentleman born. 1.01.275 P
nay, it is petter yet. 1.02. 7 P
yet i say i could show you to the contrary. 2.01. 40 P
and yet he would not swear; 2.01. 57 P
yet i cannot put off my opinion so easily. 2.01.234 P
and yet you, rogue, will ensconce your rags, 2.02. 26 P
yet there has been knights, and lords, and 2.02. 63 P
of them all, and yet there has been earls, nay 2.02. 76 P
there's my purse, i am yet thy debtor. 2.02.132 P
will they yet look after thee? 2.02.140 P
yet in other places she enlargeth her mirth so 2.02.222 P
yet i wrong him to call him poor. 2.02.271 P
yet they are devils' additions, the names of 2.02.298 P
and we will yet have more tricks with falstaff. 3.03.191 P
yet, wooing thee, i found thee of more value 3.04. 15
yet seek my father's love, still seek it, sir. 3.04. 19
i ne'er made my will yet, i thank heaven. 3.04. 58 P
but yet i would my master had mistress anne; 3.04.104 P
yet to be what i would not shall not make me 3.05.149 P
that any madness i ever yet beheld seem'd but 4.02. 27 P
do, | wives may be merry, and yet honest too: 4.02.105
let our wives | yet once again (to make us 4.04. 13
why yet there want not many that do fear | in 4.04. 39
yet hear me speak. 4.06. 3
not fairies, and yet the guiltiness of my mind, 5.05.122 P
yet be cheerful, knight. 5.05.170 P
and i had appointed, and yet it was not anne, 5.05.199 P
to master /brook you yet shall hold your word, 5.05.244
yet give leave, my lord, | that we may bring you MM 1.01. 60
strength and nature | i am not yet instructed. 1.01. 80
yet still 'tis just. 1.02.123
and yet, to say the truth, i had as lief have 1.02.132 P
and yet my nature never in the fight | to do in 1.03. 42
you are yet unsworn. 1.04. 9
ay, but yet | let us be keen, and rather cut a 2.01. 4
sir, your honor cannot come to that yet. 2.01.119 P
the time is yet to come that she was ever 2.01.168 P
but yet, poor claudio! 2.01.285
yet show some pity. 2.02. 99
others, | hath yet a kind of medicine in itself, 2.02.135
yet may he live a while; 2.04. 35
yet he must die. 2.04. 36
yet hath he in him such a mind of honor | that, 2.04.179
i'll tell him yet of angelo's request, | and fit 2.04.186
to shun, | and yet run'st toward him still. 3.01. 13
oft provok'st, yet grossly fear'st | thy death, 3.01. 18
what's yet in this | that bears the name of life 3.01. 38
yet in this life | lie hid moe thousand deaths; 3.01. 39
yet death we fear | that makes these odds all 3.01. 40
/enew | as falcon doth the fowl, is yet a devil; 3.01. 91
yet, as the matter now stands, he will avoid 3.01.195 P
lamentation, which she yet wears for his sake; 3.01.228 P
forenam'd maid hath yet in her the continuance 3.01.239 P
but yet, sir, i would prove — 3.02. 29 P
the duke yet would have dark deeds darkly 3.02.177 P
he's now past it, yet (and i say to thee) he 3.02.182 P
news is old enough, yet it is every day's news. 3.02.230 P
yet had he fram'd to himself (by the instruction 3.02.244 P
i have not yet made known to mariana | a word of 4.01. 48
our corn's to reap, for yet our tithe's to sow. 4.01. 75
but yet i will be content to be a lawful hangman 4.02. 16 P
have you no countermand for claudio yet, | but 4.02. 92
yet i believe there comes | no countermand; 4.02. 96
more depends on it than we must yet deliver. 4.02.125 P
yet since i see you fearful, that neither my 4.02.188 P
yet you are amaz'd, but this shall absolutely 4.02.208 P
if yet her brother's pardon be come hither. 4.03.108
hath yet the deputy sent my brother's pardon? 4.03.114
yet reason dares her no, | for my authority 4.04. 25
would yet he had liv'd! 4.04. 32
yet i am advis'd to do it, | he says, to veil 4.06. 3
but yet most truly will i speak: 5.01. 37
on my trust, a man that never yet | did, as he 5.01.147
yet my husband | knows not that ever he knew me. 5.01.186
or impudence, | that yet can do thee office? 5.01.364
whose salt imagination yet hath wrong'd | your 5.01.401
sweet isabel, do yet but kneel by me. 5.01.437
yet did repent me, after more advice, | for 5.01.464
and yet here's one in place i cannot pardon. 5.01.499
where we'll show | what's yet behind, that/'s 5.01.539
yet this my comfort, when your words are done, ERR 1.01. 26
yet, that the world may witness that my end 1.01. 33
yet the incessant weepings of my wife, | weeping 1.01. 70
my youngest boy, and yet my eldest care, | at 1.01.124
to find, yet loath to leave unsought | or that, 1.01.135
yet will i favor thee in what i can; 1.01.149
yet the gold bides still | that others touch and 2.01.110
yet he loseth it in a kind of jollity. 2.02. 88 P
rout | against your yet ungalled estimation, 3.01.102
wild, and yet, too, gentle; 3.01.110
thou hast no husband yet, nor i no wife. 3.02. 68
match, and yet is she a wondrous fat marriage. 3.02. 92 P
and true he swore, though yet forsworn he were. 4.02. 10
and yet would herein others' eyes were worse: 4.02. 26
that runs counter, and yet draws dry–foot well; 4.02. 39
yet once again proclaim it publicly, | if any 5.01.130
but tell me yet, dost thou not know my voice? 5.01.301
up, | yet hath my night of life some memory, 5.01.315
and so do i, yet did she call me so; 5.01.373
what, my dear lady disdain! are you yet living? ADO 1.01.118 P
i can see yet without spectacles, and i see no 1.01.189 P
you strange news that you yet dreamt not of. 1.02. 4 P
but yet for all that, cousin, let him be a 2.01. 54 P
yet it had not been amiss the rod had been made, 2.01.227 P
one woman is fair, yet i am well; 2.03. 27 P
another is wise, yet i am well; 2.03. 27 P
another virtuous, yet i am well; 2.03. 28 P
suit | to her he thinks not worthy, yet he woos, 2.03. 51
yet he woos, | yet will he swear he loves. 2.03. 52
i never yet saw man, | how wise, how noble, 3.01. 59
yet tell her of it, hear what she will say. 3.01. 81
yet say i, he is in love. 3.02. 30 P
yet is this no charm for the toothache. 3.02. 70 P
if it please you — yet count claudio may hear, 3.02. 85 P
some treason, masters; yet stand close. 3.03.106 P
yet benedick was such another, and now is he 3.04. 86 P
and yet now in despite of his heart he eats his 3.04. 88 P
time hath not yet so dried this blood of mine, 4.01.193
yet, by mine honor, i will deal in this | as 4.01.247
and yet i lie not: 4.01.271 P
written down, yet forget not that i am an ass. 4.02. 77 P
with candle–wasters, bring him yet to me, | and 5.01. 18
for there was never yet philosopher | that could 5.01. 35
yet bend not all the harm upon yourself; 5.01. 39
virtues, yet at last she concluded with a sigh, 5.01.171 P
yea, that she did, but yet, for all that, and if 5.01.176 P
how to pray your patience, | yet i must speak. 5.01.272
yet sinn'd i not, | but in mistaking. 5.01.274
and yet, to satisfy this good old man, | i would 5.01.276
could not be my son–in–law, | be yet my nephew. 5.01.288
whose names yet run smoothly in the even road of 5.02. 33 P
and yet, ere i go, let me go with that i came, 5.02. 47 P
are you yet determined | to–day to marry with my 5.04. 36
study knows that which yet it doth not know. LLL 1.01. 68
yet, confident, i'll keep what i have sworn, 1.01.114
not a word of costard yet. 1.01.222 P
and yet a better love than my master. 1.02.120 P
yet was sampson so tempted, and he had an 1.02.173 P
yet was salomon so seduced, and he had a very 1.02.174 P
you back again, and "welcome" i have not yet. 2.01. 92 P
yet there remains unpaid | a hundred thousand 2.01.133
times as much more — and yet nothing at all. 3.01. 48 P
yet a kind of insinuation, as it were in via, in 4.02. 13 P
cain's birth, that's not five weeks old as yet? 4.02. 35
yet fear not thou, but speak audaciously." 5.02.104
not yet? 5.02.212
yet still she is the moon, and i the man. 5.02.215
honor, yet as pure | as the unsallied lily, i 5.02.351
yet i have a trick | of the old rage. 5.02.416
yet, since love's argument was first on foot, 5.02.747
yet swear not, lest ye be forsworn again. 5.02.832
i frown upon him; yet he loves me still. MND 1.01.194
i give him curses; yet he gives me love. 1.01.196
the rest — yet my chief humor is for a tyrant. 1.02. 28 P
yet mark'd i where the bolt of cupid fell. 2.01.165
but yet you draw not iron, for my heart | is 2.01.196
love | (and yet a place of high respect with me) 2.01.209
for my sake, my dear, | lie further off yet; 2.02. 44
yet hermia still loves you; 2.02.110
true as truest horse, that yet would never tire, 3.01. 96
why, you must not speak that yet! 3.01. 99 P
as truest horse, that yet would never tire." 3.01.102
and yet, to say the truth, reason and love keep 3.01.143 P
but hast thou yet latch'd the athenian's eyes 3.02. 36
yet you, the murtherer, look as bright, as clear 3.02. 60
seeming parted, | but yet an union in partition, 3.02.210
take on as you would follow, | but yet come not. 3.02.259
yet since night you left me: 3.02.275
i am not yet so low | but that my nails can 3.02.297
we may effect this business yet ere day. 3.02.395
yet but three? 3.02.437
but as yet, i swear, | i cannot truly say how i 4.01.147
it seems to me | that yet we sleep, we dream. 4.01.194
is he come home yet? 4.02. 2 P
out of this silence yet i pick'd a welcome; 5.01.100
but yet in courtesy, in all reason, we must stay 5.01.254 P
with the help of a surgeon he might yet recover, 5.01.310 P
he might yet recover, and yet prove an ass. 5.01.311 P
and yet, for aught i see, they are as sick that MV 1.02. 5 P
yet his means are in supposition: 1.03. 17 P
yet, to supply the ripe wants of my friend, 1.03. 63
is he yet possess'd | how much ye would? 1.03. 64
as any comer i have look'd on yet | for my 2.01. 21
say it, though old man, yet poor man, my father. 2.02.139 P
we have not spoke us yet of torch–bearers. 2.04. 5
but yet i'll go in hate, to feed upon | the 2.05. 14
and yet enough | may not extend so far as to the 2.07. 27
and yet to be afeard of my deserving | were but 2.07. 29
yet do not suddenly, for it may grieve him. 2.08. 34
yet i have not seen | so likely an embassador of 2.09. 91
yet it lives there uncheck'd that antonio hath a 3.01. 2 P
and yet a maiden hath no tongue but thought — 3.02. 8
sand, wear yet upon their chins | the beards of 3.02. 84
yet look how far | the substance of my praise 3.02.126
in my wish | to wish myself much better, yet, 3.02.152
this, she is not yet so old | but she may learn; 3.02.160
and yet, dear lady, | rating myself at nothing, 3.02.256
hear me yet, good shylock. 3.03. 3
i have work in hand | that you yet know not of. 3.04. 58
yet more quarrelling with occasion! 3.05. 55 P
what, are you answer'd yet? 4.01. 46
what, man, courage yet! 4.01.111
yet in such rule that the venetian law | cannot 4.01.178
jew, | the law hath yet another hold on you. 4.01.347
and yet, thy wealth being forfeit to the state, 4.01.365
my mind was never yet more mercenary. 4.01.418
i pray you, is my master yet return'd? 5.01. 34
and yet no matter; 5.01. 50
madam, they are not yet; 5.01.116
though not for me, yet for your vehement oaths, 5.01.155
now, by mine honor, which is yet mine own, 5.01.232
i have not yet | enter'd my house. 5.01.272

and yet i am sure you are not satisfied | of 5.01.296
though yet i know no wise remedy how to avoid it AYL 1.01. 25 P
and yet give no thousand crowns neither. 1.01. 86 P
for my soul (yet i know not why) hates nothing 1.01.165 P
yet he's gentle, never school'd and yet learned, 1.01.166 P
yet he's gentle, never school'd and yet learned, 1.01.167 P
mistress of, and would you yet /i were merrier? 1.02. 4 P
was good, and yet was not the knight forsworn. 1.02. 67 P
yet tell us the manner of the wrastling. 1.02.112 P
you may see the end, for the best is yet to do, 1.02.115 P
is there yet another dotes upon rib–breaking? 1.02.142 P
yet he looks successfully. 1.02.153 P
beseech your grace, i am not yet well breath'd. 1.02.217 P
i cannot speak to her, yet she urg'd conference. 1.02.258
yet such is now the duke's condition | that he 1.02.264
but yet indeed the /smaller is his daughter. 1.02.272
yet i hate not orlando. 1.03. 34 P
yet your mistrust cannot make me a traitor. 1.03. 56
wears yet a precious jewel in his head; 2.01. 14
and yet it irks me the poor dappled fools, 2.01. 22
no, no brother, yet the son | (yet not the son, 2.03. 19
yet the son | (yet not the son, i will not call 2.03. 20
yet this i will not do, do how i can. 2.03. 35
though i look old, yet i am strong and lusty; 2.03. 47
yet fortune cannot recompense me better | than 2.03. 75
yet i should bear no cross if i did bear you, 2.04. 12 P
yet thou liest in the bleak air. 2.06. 15 P
in good set terms, and yet a motley fool. 2.07. 17
why, i have eat none yet. 2.07. 88
yet am i inland bred | and know some nurture. 2.07. 96
as yet to question you about your fortunes. 2.07.172
bag and baggage, yet with scrip and scrippage. 3.02.161 P
and yet again wonderful, and after that, out of 3.02.192 P
but yet, for fashion sake, i thank you too for 3.02.255 P
yet i profess curing it by counsel. 3.02.404 P
am i the man yet? 3.03. 3 P
but yet have the grace to consider that tears do 3.04. 2 P
and yet it is not that i bear thee love, | but 3.05. 93
'tis but a peevish boy — yet he talks well — 3.05.110
yet words do well | when he that speaks them 3.05.111
he's proud — and yet his pride becomes him. 3.05.114
is not very tall — yet for his years he's tall; 3.05.118
his leg is but so so — and yet 'tis well; 3.05.119
and yet | have more cause to hate him than to 3.05.127
out of your apparel, and yet out of your suit. 4.01. 87 P
club, yet he did what he could to die before, 4.01. 98 P
so please you, for i never heard it yet; 4.03. 37
yet heard too much of phebe's cruelty. 4.03. 38
and yet it is not, it is but so, so. 5.01. 28 P
most profound in his art, and yet not damnable. 5.02. 61 P
in the ditty, yet the note was very untuneable. 5.03. 35 P
he's as good at any thing, and yet a fool. 5.04.105 P
yet to good wine they do use good bushes; ep 5 P
(for yet his honor never heard a play), | you SHR in.1. 96
in the world, | and yet she is inferior to none. in.2. 67
yet would you say ye were beaten out of door, in.2. 85
of you | to pardon me yet for a night or two; in.2. 119
that i should yet absent me from your bed. in.2. 123
yet, for the love i bear my sweet bianca, if i 1.01.109 P
nature of our quarrel yet never brook'd parle, 1.01.114 P
that we may yet again have access to our fair 1.01.116 P
we have not yet been seen in any house, | nor 1.01.199
and yet i'll promise thee she shall be rich, 1.02. 62
you, | did you yet ever see baptista's daughter? 1.02.250
men alive | i never yet beheld that special face 2.01. 11
yet extreme gusts will blow out fire and all; 2.01.135
sounded, | yet not so deeply as to thee belongs, 2.01.193
and yet as heavy as my weight should be. 2.01.205
yet you are wither'd. 2.01.237
in speech, yet sweet as spring–time flowers. 2.01.246
yet i have fac'd it with a card of ten. 2.01.405
pedascule, i'll watch you better yet. 3.01. 50
in time i may believe, yet i mistrust. 3.01. 51
yet read the gamouth of hortensio. 3.01. 72
yet if thy thoughts, bianca, be so humble | to 3.01. 89
and yet we hear not of our son–in–law. 3.02. 3
yet never means to wed where he hath woo'd. 3.02. 17
though he be merry, yet withal he's honest. 3.02. 25
yet oftentimes he goes but mean apparell'd. 3.02. 73
a man | is more than one, | and yet not many. 3.02. 86
and yet i come not well. 3.02. 88
and yet you halt not. 3.02. 89
but yet not stay, entreat me how you can. 3.02.203
yet, as they are, here are they come to meet you 4.01.138
are very sensible, and yet you miss my sense: 5.02. 18
nay, i will win my wager better yet, | and show 5.02.116
his sake, | and yet i know him a notorious liar, AWW 1.01.100
yet these fix'd evils sit so fit in him, | that 1.01.102
though valiant in the defense, yet is weak. 1.01.116 P
better, marry, yet 'tis a wither'd pear. 1.01.163 P
not my virginity yet /... | there shall your 1.01.165
yet, for our gentlemen that mean to see | the 1.02. 13
if he were living, i would try him yet. 1.02. 72
if one be good, | there's yet one good in ten." 1.03. 79
be at woman's command, and yet no hurt done! 1.03. 93 P
honesty be no puritan, yet it will do no hurt; 1.03. 93 P
groan, | yet i express to you a mother's care. 1.03.148
him, | yet never know how that desert should be. 1.03.200
yet in this captious and intenible sieve | i 1.03.202
and yet my heart | will not confess he owes the 2.01. 8
there's one grape yet; 2.03. 99 P
yet stands off | in differences so mighty. 2.03.120
yet the scarfs and the bannerets about thee did 2.03.203 P
yet art thou good for nothing but taking up, and 2.03.207 P
what th' import is, | i know not yet. 2.03.277
she is not well, but yet she has her health. 2.04. 2 P
she's very merry, but yet she is not well; 2.04. 3 P
but yet she is not well. 2.04. 5 P
since i cannot yet find in my heart to repent. 2.05. 12 P
and yet it is; 2.05. 80
but yet | we'll strive to bear it for your 3.03. 4
and yet she writes, | pursuit would be but vain. 3.04. 24
yet in his idle fire, | to buy his will, it 3.07. 26
where both not sin, and yet a sinful fact. 3.07. 47
yet slight ones will not carry it. 4.01. 38 P
the general is content to spare thee yet, | and, 4.01. 80
when you have conquer'd my yet maiden bed, 4.02. 57
was the greatest, but that i have not ended yet. 4.03. 92 P
yet his brother is reputed one of the best that 4.03.288 P
yet who would have suspected an ambush where i 4.03.301 P
that has a knot on't yet. 4.03.324 P
yet am i thankful. 4.03.330
under my poor instructions yet must suffer 4.04. 27
yet, i pray you: 4.04. 30
a bold charter, but i thank my god it holds yet. 4.05. 93 P
all's well that ends well yet, | though time 5.01. 25
and yet i know not: 5.03.117
her bed in florence, | where yet she never was. 5.03.127
swear them lordship, | yet you desire to marry. 5.03.157
yet for all that | he gave it to a commoner a' 5.03.193
i pray you yet | (since you lack virtue, i will 5.03.221
yet i was in that credit with them at that time 5.03.262 P
though yet he never harm'd me, here i quit him. 5.03.299
if thou beest yet a fresh uncropped flower, 5.03.327
all yet seems well, and if it end so meet, | the 5.03.333
yet of thee | i will believe thou hast a mind TN 1.02. 49
and yet i will not compare with an old man. 1.03.118 P
for they shall yet belie thy happy years, | that 1.04. 30
yet a barful strife! 1.04. 41
yet you will be hang'd for being so long absent, 1.05. 16 P
he is but mad yet, madonna, and the fool shall 1.05.137 P
not yet old enough for a man, nor young enough 1.05.156 P
and yet (by the very fangs of malice i swear) i 1.05.183 P
yet you began rudely. 1.05.212 P
yet i suppose him virtuous, know him noble, | of 1.05.258
but yet i cannot love him. 1.05.262
above my fortunes, yet my state is well: 1.05.278
"above my fortunes, yet my state is well: 1.05.290
let me yet know of you whither you are bound. 2.01. 9 P
me, was yet of many accounted beautiful; 2.01. 26 P
that, yet thus far i will boldly publish her: 2.01. 28 P
and i am yet so near the manners of my mother, 2.01. 40 P
and all the brothers too — and yet i know not. 2.04.121
silence be drawn from us with cars, yet peace. 2.05. 64 P
and yet, to crush this a little, it would bow to 2.05.140 P
here is yet a postscript. 2.05.173 P
and yet, when wit and youth is come to harvest, 3.01.132
yet come again; 3.01.163
himself possess'd him, yet i'll speak to him. 3.04. 86 P
that for his love dares yet do more | than you 3.04.316
i my brother know | yet living in my glass; 3.04.380
i dare lay any money 'twill be nothing yet. 3.04.396 P
i strook him first, yet it's no matter for that. 4.01. 36 P
and yet complainest thou of obstruction? 4.02. 38 P
that enwraps me thus, | yet 'tis not madness. 4.03. 4
yet there he was, and there i found this credit, 4.03. 6
yet doth this accident and flood of fortune | so 4.03. 11
yet, if 'twere so, | she could not sway her 4.03. 16
yet, when i saw it last, it was besmear'd | as 5.01. 52
antonio never yet was thief or pirate, | though 5.01. 74
if this be so, as yet the glass seems true, | i 5.01.265
and yet, alas, now i remember me, | they say, 5.01.279
yet have i the benefit of my senses as well as 5.01.305 P
he hath not told us of the captain yet. 5.01.381
ere he was born desire yet their life to see him WT 1.01. 40 P
and yet we should, for perpetuity, | go hence in 1.02. 5
like a cipher | (yet standing in rich place), i 1.02. 7
yet of your royal presence i'll adventure | the 1.02. 38
yet, good deed, leontes, | i love thee not a jar 1.02. 42
with oaths, | should yet say, "sir, no going." 1.02. 49
will you go yet? 1.02. 51
yet go on, | th' offenses we have made you do 1.02. 82
is he won yet? 1.02. 86
and yet the steer, the heckfer, and the calf 1.02.124
yet they say we are | almost as like as eggs; 1.02.129
yet were it true | to say this boy were like me. 1.02.134
camillo, this great sir will yet stay longer. 1.02.212
and it is caught | of you that yet are well. 1.02.387
a sickness caught of me, and yet i well? 1.02.398
yet black brows, they say, | become some women 2.01. 8
and yet partake no venom (for his knowledge | is 2.01. 41
of me, yet you | have too much blood in him. 2.01. 57
yet, for a greater confirmation | (for in an act 2.01.180
yet shall the oracle | give rest to th' minds of 2.01.190
yet that dares | less appear so, in comforting 2.03. 55
i ne'er heard yet | that any of these bolder 3.02. 54
but yet hear this — mistake me not; 3.02.109
flatness of my misery, yet with eyes | of pity, 3.02.122
and vengeance for't | not dropp'd down yet. 3.02.202
yet for this once, yea, superstitiously, | i 3.03. 40
yet i can read waiting–gentlewoman in the scape. 3.03. 72 P
up for pity — yet i'll tarry till my son come; 3.03. 76 P
the men are not yet cold under water, nor the 3.03.105 P
if never, yet that time himself doth say, | he 4.01. 31
and yet it will no more but abide. 4.03. 93 P
not yet on summer's death, nor on the birth | of 4.04. 80
yet nature is made better by no mean | but 4.04. 89
that wear upon your virgin branches yet | your 4.04.115
i shall have more than you can dream of yet, 4.04.388
yet we free thee | from the dead blow of it. 4.04.433
as hardly | will he endure your sight as yet, i 4.04.470
not any yet: 4.04.537
yet for the outside of thy poverty we must make 4.04.632 P
on his side be the worst, yet hold thee, there's 4.04.636 P
yet nature might have made me as these are, 4.04.746
though it be great pity, yet it is necessary. 4.04.776 P
bear, yet he is oft led by the nose with gold. 4.04.802 P
yet, if my lord will marry — if you will, sir, 5.01. 76
princess (she | the fairest i have yet beheld), 5.01. 87
but your petition | is yet unanswer'd. 5.01.229
excels what ever yet you look'd upon | or hand 5.03. 16
yet speak. 5.03. 22
but yet, paulina, | hermione was not so much 5.03. 27
what fine chisel | could ever yet cut breath? 5.03. 79
appears she lives, | though yet she speak not. 5.03.118
yet sell your face for five pence and 'tis dear. JN 1.01.153
yet, to avoid deceit, i mean to learn; 1.01.215
yet for both. 2.01.333
france, hast thou yet more blood to cast away? 2.01.334
whose party do the townsmen yet admit? 2.01.361
yet in some measure satisfy her so | that we 2.01.557
but for because he hath not woo'd me yet: 2.01.588
my palm, | but for my hand, as unattempted yet, 2.01.591
yet i alone, alone do me oppose | against the 3.01.170
yet indirection thereby grows direct, | and 3.01.276
good friend, thou hast no cause to say so yet, 3.03. 30
yet it shall come for me to do thee good. 3.03. 32
yet i love thee well, | and, by my troth, i 3.03. 54
courage and comfort! all shall yet go well. 3.04. 4
yet i remember, when i was in france, | young 4.01. 14
yet am i sworn, and i did purpose, boy, | with 4.01.123
stay yet, lord salisbury, i'll go with thee, 4.02. 96
of mine | is yet a maiden and an innocent hand, 4.02.252
within this bosom never ent'red yet | the 4.02.254
is yet the cover of a fairer mind | than to be 4.02.258
the wall is high, and yet will i leap down. 4.03. 1
i am afraid, and yet i'll venture it. 4.03. 5
a purity, | to the yet unbegotten sin of times; 4.03. 54
but yet i dare defend | my innocent life against 4.03. 88
yet i am none. 4.03. 91
there is not yet so ugly a fiend of hell | as 4.03.123
yet i know | our party may well meet a prouder 5.01. 78
faith | to your proceedings, yet believe me, 5.02. 11
the king | yet speaks, and peradventure may 5.06. 31
his highness yet doth speak, and holds belief 5.07. 6
we thank you both, yet one but flatters us, | as R2 1.01. 25
yet can i not of such tame patience boast | as 1.01. 52
and breathest, | yet art thou slain in him. 1.02. 25
yet one word more! 1.02. 58
lo this is all — nay, yet depart not so; 1.02. 63
my mother, and my nurse, that bears me yet! 1.03.307
though banish'd, yet a true–born englishman. 1.03.309
my death's sad tale may yet undeaf his ear. 2.01. 16
and yet, /incaged in so small a verge, | the 2.01.102
sing, | yet seek no shelter to avoid the storm; 2.01.264
and yet we strike not, but securely perish. 2.01.266
yet i know no cause | why i should welcome such 2.02. 6
yet again methinks | some unborn sorrow, ripe in 2.02. 9
but yet my inward soul | persuades me it is 2.02. 28
but what it is that is not yet known what, | i 2.02. 39
i hope the king is not yet shipp'd for ireland. 2.02. 42
and yet your fair discourse hath been as sugar, 2.03. 6
all my treasury | is yet but unfelt thanks, 2.03. 61
and yet my letters–patents give me leave. 2.03.130
may be i will go with you, but yet i'll pause, 2.03.168
and yet we hear no tidings from the king, 2.04. 3
stay yet another day, thou trusty welshman. 2.04. 5
yet, to wash your blood | from off my hands, 3.01. 5
and yet not so, for what can we bequeath | save 3.02.149
yet looks he like a king! 3.03. 68
yet know, my master, god omnipotent, | is 3.03. 85
strike | your children yet unborn and unbegot, 3.03. 88
fondly like a frantic man, | yet he is come. 3.03.186
to breathe this news, yet what i say is true: 3.04. 82
yet best beseeming me to speak the truth. 4.01.116
the children yet unborn | shall feel this day as 4.01.322
yet look up, behold, | that you in pity may 5.01. 8
and yet not so, for with a kiss 'twas made. 5.01. 75
to me, or any of my kin, | and yet i love him. 5.02.110
yet through both | i see some sparks of better 5.03. 20
not yet, i thee beseech. 5.03. 92
yet am i sick for fear, speak it again, | twice 5.03.133
yet i'll hammer it out. 5.05. 5
yet blessing on his heart that gives it me! 5.05. 64
a horse, | and yet i bear a burthen like an ass, 5.05. 93
i mark'd him not, and yet he talk'd very wisely, 1H4 1.02. 85 P
i regarded him not, and yet he talk'd wisely, 1.02. 86 P
for he was never yet a breaker of proverbs. 1.02.118 P
idleness, | yet herein will i imitate the sun, 1.02.197
and majesty might never yet endure | the moody 1.03. 18
why, yet he doth deny his prisoners, | but with 1.03. 77
yet time serves wherein you may redeem | your 1.03.180
the new chimney, and yet our horse not pack'd. 2.01. 3 P
and yet, 'zounds, i lie, for they pray 2.01. 79 P
and yet i am bewitch'd with the rogue's company. 2.02. 17 P
gaunt, your grandfather, but yet no coward, hal. 2.02. 68 P
but yet no farther wise | than harry percy's 2.03.107
but yet a woman, and for secrecy, | no lady 2.03.109
prince of wales, yet i am the king of courtesy, 2.04. 10 P
words than a parrot, and yet the son of a woman! 2.04. 99 P
i am not yet of percy's mind, the hotspur of the 2.04.101 P
yet a coward is worse than a cup of sack with 2.04.126 P
and sword on thy side, and yet thou ran'st away; 2.04.317 P
and yet there is a virtuous man whom i have 2.04.417 P
my father glendower is not ready yet, | nor 3.01. 86
yet oftentimes it doth present harsh rage, 3.01.181
yet such extenuation let me beg | as, in reproof 3.02. 22
yet let me wonder, harry, | at thy affections, 3.02. 29
have you inquir'd yet who pick'd my pocket? 3.03. 53 P
and yet you will stand to it, you will not 3.03.162 P
have thirty miles to ride yet ere dinner–time. 3.03.198
yet doth he give us bold advertisement | that 4.01. 36
lopp'd off — | and yet, in faith, it is not; 4.01. 44
but yet i would your father had been here. 4.01. 60
yet all goes well, yet all our joints are whole. 4.01. 83
yet all goes well, yet all our joints are whole. 4.01. 83
rich reprisal is so nigh, | and yet not ours. 4.01.119
of my cousin vernon's are not yet come up. 4.03. 20
but yet the king hath drawn | the special head 4.04. 27
i hope no less, yet needful 'tis to fear, | and, 4.04. 34
and yet i must remember you, my lord, | we were 5.01. 32
when yet you were in place and in account 5.01. 37
and never yet did insurrection want | such 5.01. 79
yet this before my father's majesty: 5.01. 96
'tis not due yet, i would be loath to pay him 5.01.127 P
yet once ere night | i will embrace him with a 5.02. 72
enemies, | whose deaths are yet unreveng'd. 5.03. 43
and yet, in faith, thou bearest thee like a king 5.04. 36
douglas is living, and your brother yet, | but, 2H4 1.01. 82
yet speak, morton, | tell thou an earl his 1.01. 87
yet, for all this, say not that percy's dead. 1.01. 93
yet the first bringer of unwelcome news | hath 1.01.100
one, | and yet we ventur'd for the gain propos'd 1.01.183
never so few, and never yet more need. 1.01.215
your master, whose chin is not yet fledge. 1.02. 20 P
and yet he will not stick to say his face is a 1.02. 22 P
it when he will, 'tis not a hair amiss yet. 1.02. 24 P
and yet he'll be crowing as if he had writ man 1.02. 26 P
and yet cannot he see, though he have his own 1.02. 47 P
youth, have yet some smack of an ague in you, 1.02. 97 P
and yet in some respects i grant i cannot go. 1.02.167 P
and will you yet call yourself young? 1.02.185 P
but it was alway yet the trick of our english 1.02.214 P

it never yet did hurt | to lay down likelihoods 1.03. 34
grant that our hopes (yet likely of fair birth) 1.03. 63
word to your master that i am yet come to town. 2.02.161 P
o yet, for god's sake, go not to these wars! 2.03. 9
it is but as a body yet distempered, | which to 3.01. 41
main chance of things | as yet not come to life, 3.01. 84
where i think they will talk of mad shallow yet. 3.02. 15 P
is old double of your town living yet? 3.02. 41 P
sir, as go, and yet, for mine own part, sir, i 3.02.223 P
genius of famine, yet lecherous as a monkey, and 3.02.314 P
written on the earth | with yet appearing blood, 4.01. 82
when ever yet was your appeal denied? 4.01. 88
i never knew yet but rebuke and check was the 4.03. 31 P
yet notwithstanding, being incens'd, he is flint 4.04. 33
heard he the good news yet? | tell it him. 4.05. 11
yet not so sound, and half so deeply sweet, | as 4.05. 26
yet, though thou stand'st more sure than i could 4.05.202
but yet, god forbid, sir, but a knave should 5.01. 44 P
yet be sad, good brothers, | for, by my faith, 5.02. 49
yet weep that harry's dead, and so will i, | but 5.02. 59
i will be the man yet that shall make you great. 5.05. 79 P
and yet that were but light payment, to dance ep 19 P
by night, | unseen, yet crescive in his faculty. H5 1.01. 66
than ever at one time the clergy yet | did to 1.01. 80
not yet, my cousin. 1.02. 4
yet their own authors faithfully affirm | that 1.02. 43
at home, | yet that is but a crush'd necessity, 1.02.175
and some are yet ungotten and unborn | that 1.02.287
what, are ancient pistol and you friends yet? 2.01. 4 P
patience be a tir'd /mare, yet she will plod — 2.01. 24 P
o, let us yet be merciful. 2.02. 47
so may your highness, and yet punish too. 2.02. 48
we'll yet enlarge that man, | though cambridge, 2.02. 57
to trouble himself with any such thoughts yet. 2.03. 22 P
how yet resolves the governor of the town? 3.03. 1
whiles yet my soldiers are in my command, 3.03. 29
whiles yet the cool and temperate wind of grace 3.03. 30
returns us that his powers are yet not ready 3.03. 46
yet, forgive me, god, | that i do brag thus! 3.06.150
yet, god before, tell him we will come on, 3.06.156
yet do i not use my horse for my mistress, or 3.07. 67 P
and yet my sky shall not want. 3.07. 73 P
yet sit and see, | minding true things by what 4.pr. 52
affections are higher mounted than ours, yet, 4.01.107 P
yet, in reason, no man should possess him with 4.01.110 P
and yet i determine to fight lustily for him. 4.01.189 P
and yet i do thee wrong to mind thee of it, 4.03. 13
yet all shall be forgot, | but he'll remember 4.03. 49
and my poor soldiers tell me, yet ere night, 4.03.116
we are enow yet living in the field | to smother 4.05. 19
all's not done — yet keep the french the field. 4.06. 2
no, | for yet a many of your horsemen peer | and 4.07. 85
as yet the lamentation of the french | invites 5.pr. 36
to the which, as yet, | there is no answer made. 5.02. 74
yet leave our cousin katherine here with us: 5.02. 95
measure, yet a reasonable measure in strength. 5.02.135 P
yet i love thee too. 5.02.152 P
yet my blood begins to flatter me that thou dost 5.02.222 P
being a maid yet ros'd over with the virgin 5.02.295 P
yet they do wink and yield, as love is blind and 5.02.300 P
only he hath not yet subscribed this: 5.02.335
nor yet saint philip's daughters, were like thee 1H6 1.02.143
yet tell'st thou not how thou wert entertain'd. 1.04. 38
yet liv'st thou, salisbury? 1.04. 82
talbot, farewell, thy hour is not yet come. 1.05. 13
the other yet may rise against their force. 2.01. 32
yet hath a woman's kindness overrul'd; 2.02. 50
he will be here, and yet he is not here. 2.03. 58
law, | and never yet could frame my will to it, 2.04. 8
and yet thy tongue will not confess thy error. 2.04. 67
his trespass yet lives guilty in thy blood, 2.04. 94
yet are these feet, whose strengthless stay is 2.05. 13
but yet be wary in thy studious care. 2.05. 97
but yet, methinks, my father's execution | was 2.05. 99
yet, pucelle, hold thy peace, | if talbot do but 3.02. 58
yet heavens have glory for this victory! 3.02.117
but yet before we go, let's not forget | the 3.02.131
when i was young (as yet i am not old), | i do 3.04. 17
yet never have you tasted our reward, | or been 3.04. 22
yet know, my lord, i was provok'd by him, | and 4.01.104
and so he did, but yet i like it not, | in that 4.01.176
broils, | than yet can be imagin'd or suppos'd. 4.01.186
wilt thou yet leave the battle, boy, and fly, 4.06. 28
yet call th' embassadors, and as you please, 5.01. 24
yet, if this servile usage once offend, | go, 5.03. 58
fain would i woo her, yet i dare not speak: 5.03. 65
and yet a dispensation may be had. 5.03. 86
and yet i would that you would answer me. 5.03. 87
yet so my fancy may be satisfied, | and peace 5.03. 91
duke of anjou and maine, yet is he poor, | and 5.03. 95
and yet methinks i could be well content | to be 5.03.165
were yet not taint with love, i send the king. 5.03.183
her mother liveth yet, can testify | she was the 5.04. 12
'twas neither charles nor yet the duke i nam'd, 5.04. 77
and yet, forsooth, she is a virgin pure. 5.04. 83
and yet, in substance and authority, | retain 5.04.135
forsaketh yet the lists | by reason of his 5.05. 32
my tender youth was never yet attaint | with any 5.05. 81
to us, | yet let us watch the haughty cardinal; 2H6 1.01.174
hast thou as yet conferr'd | with margery jordan 1.02. 74
yet have i gold flies from another coast — | i 1.02. 93
yet i do find it so; 1.02. 96
yet am i suffolk and the cardinal's broker. 1.02.101
yet must we join with him and with the lords, 1.03. 95
the duke yet lives that henry shall depose; 1.04. 30
"the duke yet lives that henry shall depose; 1.04. 59
yet, by your leave, the wind was very high, 2.01. 3
a subtile knave, but yet it shall not serve. 2.01.102
in my opinion yet thou seest not well. 2.01.104
and yet, i think, jet did he never see. 2.01.112
means | your lady is forthcoming yet at london. 2.01.175
it fails not yet, but flourishes in thee, | and 2.02. 57
yet so he rul'd, and such a prince he was, | as 2.04. 44
why, yet thy scandal were not wip'd away, | but 2.04. 65
yet, by reputing of his high descent, | as next 3.01. 48
a man | unsounded yet and full of deep deceit. 3.01. 57
for thousands more, that yet suspect no peril, 3.01.152
and yet, good humphrey, is the hour to come 3.01.204
and yet herein i judge mine own wit good — 3.01.232
policy, | but yet we want a color for his death. 3.01.236
and yet we have but trivial argument, | more 3.01.241
and yet be well assur'd | you put sharp weapons in a 3.01.346
yet do not go away. 3.02. 52
yet he most christian-like laments his death; 3.02. 58
yet aeolus would not be a murtherer, | but left 3.02. 92
yet, notwithstanding such a strait edict, | were 3.02.258
by them, | yet did i purpose as they do entreat; 3.02.282
o, go not yet! 3.02.353
yet now farewell, and farewell life with thee! 3.02.356
yet let not this make thee be bloody-minded; 4.01. 36
never yet did base dishonor blur our name | but 4.01. 39
if he revenge it not, yet will his friends; 4.01.146
and yet it is said, labor in thy vocation; 4.02. 16 P
the mouth with a spear, and 'tis not whole yet. 4.07. 10 P
yet to recover them would lose my life. 4.07. 66
and therefore yet relent, and save my life. 4.07.117
for yet may england curse my wretched reign. 4.09. 49
that have a sword, and yet am ready to famish! 4.10. 2 P
i have eat no meat these five days, yet, come 4.10. 39 P
but i must make fair weather yet a while, | till 5.01. 30
are old enough now, and yet methinks you lose. 3H6 1.01.113
of the realm, | and yet shalt thou be safe? 1.01.241
rise, | and yet the king not privy to my drift, 1.02. 46
arms, | yet parted but the shadow with his hand. 1.04. 69
yet not so wealthy as an english yeoman. 1.04.123
and yet be seen to wear a woman's face? 1.04.140
wondrous strange, the like yet never heard of. 2.01. 33
yet, in protection of their tender ones, | who 2.02. 28
ay, and old york, and yet not satisfied. 2.02. 99
you said so much before, and yet you fled. 2.02.106
yet know thou, since we have begun to strike, 2.02.167
yet that thy brazen gates of heaven may ope 2.03. 40
yet let us all together to our troops, | and 2.03. 49
breasts, | for yet is hope of life and victory. 2.03. 55
breast, | yet neither conqueror nor conquered; 2.05. 12
may yet, ere night, yield both my life and them 2.05. 59
yet look to have them buzz to offend thine ears. 2.06. 95
it were no less, but yet i'll make a pause. 3.02. 10
queen, | and yet too good to be your concubine. 3.02. 98
and yet, between my soul's desire and me — 3.02.128
and yet i know not how to get the crown, | for 3.02.172
yet here prince edward stands, king henry's son. 3.03. 73
yet heav'ns are just, and time suppresseth 3.03. 77
yet i confess that often ere this day, | when i 3.03.131
yet shall you have all kindness at my hand 3.03.149
yet, ere thou go, but answer me one doubt: 3.03.238
yet hasty marriage seldom proveth well. 4.01. 18
yet, to have join'd with france in such alliance 4.01. 36
and yet methinks your grace hath not done well 4.01. 51
which if they do, yet will i keep thee safe, 4.01. 81
i hear, yet say not much, but think the more. 4.01. 83
yet in marriage | i may not prove inferior to 4.01.121
yet am i arm'd against the worst can happen; 4.01.128
yet, warwick, in despite of all mischance, | of 4.03. 43
are you yet to learn | what late misfortune is 4.04. 2
yet, gracious madam, bear it as you may: 4.04. 14
yet in this one thing let me blame your grace, 4.06. 30
why then, though loath, yet must i be content. 4.06. 48
rest, | yet thus far fortune maketh us amends, 4.07. 2
yet edward, at the least, is duke of york. 4.07. 21
yet, as we may, we'll meet both thee and warwick 4.07. 86
not mutinous in peace, yet bold in war; 4.08. 10
'tis even so, yet you are warwick still. 5.01. 47
and, live we how we can, yet die we must. 5.02. 28
yet lives our pilot still. 5.04. 6
and take his thanks that yet hath nothing else. 5.04. 59
must by the roots be hewn up yet ere night. 5.04. 69
and yet, for all his wings, the fool was drown'd 5.06. 20
and yet brought forth less than a mother's hope, 5.06. 50
if any spark of life be yet remaining, | down, 5.06. 66
laid, | for yet i am not look'd on in the world. 5.07. 22
but i protest | as yet i do not. R3 1.01. 53
but yet i run before my horse to market: 1.01.160
and yet to win her! 1.02.237
and will she yet abase her eyes on me, | that 1.02.246
it is determin'd, not concluded yet; 1.03. 15
yet, derby, notwithstanding she's your wife 1.03. 22
yet that, by you depos'd, you quake like rebels? 1.03.161
yet you have all the vantage of her wrong. 1.03.309
misdeeds, | yet execute thy wrath in me alone! 1.04. 71
certain dregs of conscience are yet within me. 1.04.122 P
the deed, | o, know you yet he doth it publicly. 1.04.216
and are you yet to your own souls so blind 1.04.252
did, | and yet go current from suspicion! 2.01. 95
and yet his punishment was bitter death. 2.01.106
yet none of you would once beg for his life. 2.01.131
yet from my dugs he drew not this deceit. 2.02. 30
yet thou art a mother, | and hast the comfort of 2.02. 55
how much the estate is green and yet ungovern'd. 2.02.127
yet, since it is but green, it should be put 2.02.135
i hope he is, but yet let mothers doubt. 2.04. 22
hath not yet div'd into the world's deceit; 3.01. 8
i'll send some packing that yet think not on't. 3.02. 61
but yet you see how soon the day o'ercast. 3.02. 86
we have not yet set down this day of triumph. 3.04. 42
yet had we not determin'd he should die | until 3.05. 52
yet witness what you hear we did intend. 3.05. 70
yet touch this sparingly, as 'twere far off, 3.05. 93
and yet within these five hours hastings liv'd, 3.06. 8
yet who/'s so bold but says he sees it not? 3.06. 12
of birth, | yet so much is my poverty of spirit, 3.07.159
yet to draw forth your noble ancestry | from the 3.07.198
yet know, whe'er you accept our suit or no, 3.07.214
for never yet one hour in his bed | did i enjoy 4.01. 82
stay, yet look back with me unto the tower. 4.01. 97
that ever yet this land was guilty of. 4.03. 3
if yet your gentle souls fly in the air | and be 4.04. 11
richard yet lives, hell's black intelligencer, 4.04. 71
help nothing else, yet do they ease the heart. 4.04.131
more mild, but yet more harmful — kind in 4.04.173
yet much less spirit to curse | abides in me; 4.04.197
yet thou didst kill my children. 4.04.422
yet to beat down these rebels here at home. 4.04.530
is colder /tidings, yet they must be told. 4.04.534
yet one thing more, good captain, do for me — 5.03. 33
yet i lie, i am not. 5.03.191
'tis not yet near day. 5.03.220
time | forbids to dwell upon, yet remember this: 5.03.239
of these exactions, yet the king our master — H8 1.02. 25
and yet must | perforce be their acquaintance. 1.02. 46
yet will be | the chronicles of my doing, let me 1.02. 73
yet see, | when these so noble benefits shall 1.02.114
(nay, let 'em be unmanly), yet are follow'd. 1.03. 4
lord sands, | your colt's tooth is not cast yet? 1.03. 48
sweet partner, | i must not yet forsake you. 1.04.104
yet, heaven bear witness, | and if i have a 2.01. 59
yet let 'em look they glory not in mischief, 2.01. 66
my vows and prayers | yet are the king's; 2.01. 89
yet i am richer than my base accusers, | that 2.01.104
yet thus far we are one in fortunes: 2.01.121
yet, you that hear me, | this from a dying man 2.01.124
yet i can give you inkling | of an ensuing evil, 2.01.140
about his neck, yet never lost her lustre; 2.02. 32
yet, if that quarrel, fortune, do divorce | it 2.03. 14
heart, which ever yet | affected eminence, 2.03. 28
yet prayers and wishes | are all i can return. 2.03. 69
and who knows yet | but from this lady may 2.03. 77
years in court | (am yet a courtier beggarly) 2.03. 83
be patient yet. 2.04. 73
refuse you for my judge, whom, yet once more, 2.04. 82
yourself, who ever yet | have stood to charity, 2.04. 85
i then did feel full sick, and yet not well — 2.04.205
there's nothing i have done yet, o' my 3.01. 30
the willing'st sin i ever yet committed | may be 3.01. 49
heaven is above all yet; 3.01.100
vainglory) | never yet branded with suspicion? 3.01.128
yet will i add an honor — a great patience. 3.01.137
he has my heart yet and shall have my prayers 3.01.180
marry, this is yet but young, and may be left 3.02. 47
yet i know her for | a spleeny lutheran, and not 3.02. 98
deed to say well, | and yet words are no deeds. 3.02.154
of my desires, | yet fill'd with my abilities. 3.02.171
and | appear in forms more horrid), yet my duty, 3.02.196
yet i know | a way, if it take right, in spite 3.02.218
memory, i yet remember | some of these articles, 3.02.303
however, yet there is no great breach; 4.01.106
yet thus far, griffith, give me leave to speak 4.02. 32
me leave to speak him, | and yet with charity. 4.02. 33
(which was a sin), yet in bestowing, madam, | he 4.02. 56
the other, though unfinish'd, yet so famous, 4.02. 61
which i feel | i am not worthy yet to wear. 4.02. 92
that letter | i caus'd you write yet sent away? 4.02.128
nay, patience, | you must not leave me yet. 4.02.166
although unqueen'd, yet like | a queen, and 4.02.171
not yet, sir thomas lovell. 5.01. 10
amen, and yet my conscience says | she's a good 5.01. 24
and yet the gentleman | that was sent to me from 5.02. 1
yes, my lord; | but yet i cannot help you. 5.02. 5
'tis well there's one above 'em yet. 5.02. 27
witness, | yet freshly pitied in our memories. 5.02. 66
yet should find respect | for what they have 5.02.110
good my lords, | i have a little yet to say. 5.02.133
is, a fair young maid that yet wants baptism, 5.02.196
yet now promises | upon this land a thousand 5.04. 18
and yet no day without a deed to crown it. 5.04. 58
yet a virgin, | a most unspotted lily shall she 5.04. 60
but here's yet in the word "hereafter" the TRO 1.01. 23 P
he is very young, and yet will he, within three 1.02.115 P
yet hold i off. 1.02.286
that she was never yet that ever knew | love got 1.02.290
after seven years' siege yet troy walls stand, 1.03. 12
his experienc'd tongue, yet let it please both, 1.03. 68
troy, yet upon his bases, had been down, | and 1.03. 75
yet god achilles still cries, "excellent! 1.03.169
combat, | yet in the trial much opinion dwells; 1.03.336
yet go we under our opinion still | that we have 1.03.382
but yet you look not well upon him, for, 2.01. 63 P
yet, dread priam, | there is no lady of more 2.02. 10
yet, i protest, | were i alone to pass the 2.02.138
yet ne'er the less, | my spritely brethren, i 2.02.189
yet all his virtues, | not virtuously on his own 2.03.117
and yet he loves himself. is't not strange? 2.03.160 P
he's not yet through warm. 2.03.221 P
yet that which seems the wound to kill, | doth 3.01.122
able, and yet reserve an ability that they never 3.02. 85 P
have you not done talking yet? 3.02.101 P
and yet, good faith, i wish'd myself a man, | or 3.02.127
are grated | to dusty nothing, yet let memory, 3.02.189
and still it might, and yet it may again, | if 3.03.185
you know of him, but yet go fetch him hither, go 4.02. 57 P
but yet be true. 4.04. 74
yet is the kindness but particular, | 'twere 4.05. 20
not yet mature, yet matchless, firm of word, 4.05. 97
not yet mature, yet matchless, firm of word, 4.05. 97
yet gives he not till judgment guide his bounty, 4.05.102
i am not warm yet, let us fight again. 4.05.118
my prophecy is but half his journey yet, | for 4.05.218
there they stand yet, and modestly i think | the 4.05.222
and yet it is not; 5.02. 97
one eye yet looks on thee, | but with my heart 5.02.107
sith yet there is a credence in my heart, | an 5.02.120
and yet the spacious breadth of this division 5.02.150
and tempt not yet the brushes of the war. 5.03. 34
yet soft! 5.03. 89
i would laugh at that miracle — yet, in a sort, 5.04. 35 P
if it be so, yet bragless let it be, | great 5.09. 5
stand ho! yet are we masters of the field. 5.10. 1
stay yet. 5.10. 23
or if you cannot weep, yet give some groans, 5.10. 49
though not for me, yet for /your aching bones. 5.10. 50
they ne'er car'd for us yet. COR 1.01. 80 P
yet you must not think to fob off our disgrace 1.01. 93 P
yet i can make my audit up, that all | from me 1.01.144
discretion, | yet are they passing cowardly. 1.01.203
we never yet made doubt but rome was ready | to 1.02. 18
when yet he was but tender-bodied and the only 1.03. 5 P
yet, they say, all the yarn she spun in ulysses' 1.03. 82 P
o, good madam, there can be none yet. 1.03. 91 P
they lie in view, but have not spoke as yet. 1.04. 4
which yet seem shut, we have but pinn'd with 1.04. 18
slaves, | ere yet the fight be done, pack up. 1.05. 8
my work hath yet not warm'd me. 1.05. 17
to you, yet dare i never | deny your asking. 1.06. 64
yet cam'st thou to a morsel of this feast, 1.09. 10

men, yet they lie deadly that tell you have good 2.01. 61 P
yet you must be saying martius is proud; 2.01. 89 P
and live you yet? o my sweet lady, pardon. 2.01.180
yet, by the faith of men, | we have some old 2.01.187
yet welcome, warriors; 2.01.189
but yet my caution was more pertinent | than the 2.02. 63
yet oft, | when blows have made me stay, i fled 2.02. 71
'twas never my desire yet to trouble the poor 2.03. 69 P
he's not confirm'd, we may deny him yet. 2.03.209
us, yet sought | the very way to catch them. 3.01. 79
and bury all, which yet distinctly ranges, | in 3.01.205
of sight, yet will i still | be thus to them. 3.02. 5
but yet a brain that leads my use of anger | to 3.02. 30
yet, were there but this single plot to lose, 3.02.102
as i hear, more strong | than are upon you yet. 3.02.141
my wife, my mother, | i'll do well yet. 4.01. 21
to go rove with one | that's yet unbruis'd. 4.01. 47
i'll tell thee what — yet go! 4.02. 22
know you me yet? 4.03. 5 P
not yet thou know'st me, and, seeing me, dost 4.05. 55
prepare thy brow to frown. know'st thou me yet? 4.05. 63
yet, martius, that was much. 4.05.147
and yet my mind gave me his clothes made a false 4.05.150 P
to his banishment, yet it was against our will. 4.06.145 P
yet his nature | in that's no changeling, and i 4.07. 10
yet i wish, sir | (i mean for your particular), 4.07. 12
yet he hath left undone | that which shall break 4.07. 24
yet one time he did call me by my name. 5.01. 9
help, yet do not | upbraid 's with our distress. 5.01. 34
yet your good will | must have that thanks from 5.01. 45
yet, to bite his lip | and hum at good cominius 5.01. 48
yet, for i loved thee, | take this along, i writ 5.02. 89
yet thou behold'st! 5.02. 93
yet we will ask, | that, if you fail in our 5.03. 89
and yet to /charge thy sulphur with a bolt 5.03.152
yet here he lets me prate | like one i' th' 5.03.159
yet give us our dispatch. 5.03.180
and a butterfly, yet your butterfly was a grub. 5.04. 12 P
a merrier day did never yet greet rome, | no, 5.04. 42
the injury, | yet he shall have a noble memory. 5.06.153
TIT why suffer'st thou thy sons, unburied yet, | to 1.01. 87
which dreads not yet their lives' destruction. 2.03. 50
the trees, though summer, yet forlorn and lean, 2.03. 94
yet every mother breeds not sons alike — | do 2.03.146
yet have i heard — o, could i find it now! 2.03.150
i did, my lord, yet let me be their bail, | for 2.03.295
yet do thy cheeks look red as titan's face 2.04. 31
yet plead i must, | and bootless unto them. 3.01. 35
yet in some sort they are better than the 3.01. 39
how they are stain'd like meadows yet not dry, 3.01.125
and yet dear too, because i bought mine own. 3.01.199
but yet let reason govern thy lament. 3.01.218
and yet detested life not shrink thereat! 3.01.247
but yet so just that he will not revenge. 4.01.128
yet there's as little justice as at land. 4.03. 9
yet wrung with wrongs more than our backs can 4.03. 49
with words more sweet, and yet more dangerous, 4.04. 90
yet should both ear and heart obey my tongue. 4.04. 99
ruthful to hear, yet piteously perform'd. 5.01. 66
yet, for i know thou art religious, | and hast a 5.01. 74
and yet i think | few come within the compass of 5.01.125
this one hand yet is left to cut your throats, 5.02.181
countless and infinite, yet would i pay them! 5.03.159
ten thousand worse than ever yet i did | would i 5.03.187
ROM yet tell me not, for i have heard it all: 1.01.174
my child is yet a stranger in the world, | she 1.02. 8
and yet, to my teen be it spoken, i have but 1.03. 13
yet i cannot choose but laugh | to think it 1.03. 50
and yet i warrant it had upon it brow | a bump 1.03. 52
some consequence yet hanging in the stars 1.04.107
she speaks, yet she says nothing; 2.02. 12
my ears have yet not drunk a hundred words | of 2.02. 58
of thy tongue's uttering, yet i know the sound. 2.02. 59
i am no pilot, yet, wert thou as far | as that 2.02. 82
yet, if thou swear'st, | thou mayest prove false 2.02. 91
and yet i would it were to give again. 2.02.129
and yet i wish but for the thing i have. 2.02.132
and yet no farther than a wanton's bird, | that 2.02.177
yet i should kill thee with much cherishing. 2.02.183
none but for some, and yet all different. 2.03. 14
the sun not yet thy sighs from heaven clears, 2.03. 73
thy old groans yet ringing in mine ancient ears; 2.03. 74
sit | of an old tear that is not wash'd off yet. 2.03. 76
is /three long hours, yet she is not come. 2.05. 11
though news be sad, yet tell them merrily; 2.05. 22
than any man's, yet his leg excels all men's, 2.05. 40 P
not to be talk'd on, yet they are past compare. 2.05. 42 P
in the wanton summer air, | and yet not fall; 2.06. 20
and yet thy head hath been beaten as addle as an 3.01. 23 P
and yet thou wilt tutor me from quarrelling! 3.01. 29 P
it, and, though i am sold, | not yet enjoy'd. 3.02. 28
acquaintance at my hand, | that i yet know not? 3.03. 6
and sayest thou yet that exile is not death? 3.03. 43
yet "banished"? 3.03. 57
it is not yet near day. 3.05. 1
therefore stay yet, thou need'st not to be gone. 3.05. 16
yet let me weep for such a feeling loss. 3.05. 74
and yet no man like he doth grieve my heart. 3.05. 83
i will not marry yet, and when i do, i swear 3.05.121
and yet "not proud," mistress minion you? 3.05.151
i fear it is, and yet methinks it should not, 4.03. 28
where bloody tybalt, yet but green in earth, 4.03. 42
woeful day | that ever, ever, i did yet behold! 4.05. 51
yet nature's tears are reason's merriment. 4.05. 83
yet put it out, for i would not be seen. 5.03. 2
here in the churchyard, yet i will adventure. 5.03. 11
breath, | hath had no power yet upon thy beauty: 5.03. 93
beauty's ensign yet | is crimson in thy lips and 5.03. 94
ah, dear juliet, | why art thou yet so fair? 5.03.102
lips, | haply some poison yet doth hang on them, 5.03.165
yet most suspected, as the time and place | doth 5.03.224
TIM yet you do well | to show lord timon that mean 1.01. 92
and yet he's but a filthy piece of work. 1.01.199 P
more jewels yet? 1.02.159
thou stand'st single, th' art not on him yet. 2.02. 57 P
you hear now (too late), yet now's a time: 2.02.143
no villainous bounty yet hath pass'd my heart; 2.02.173
but yet they could have wish'd — they know not 2.02.207
spend less, and yet he would embrace no counsel, 3.01. 26 P
necessity belong'd to't, and yet was denied. 3.02. 13 P
nothing comparing to his — yet, had he mistook 3.02. 22 P
and yet — o, see the monstrousness of man 3.02. 72
yet, i protest, | for his right noble mind, 3.02. 79
is not my lord seen yet? 3.04. 9
not yet. 3.04. 9
one may reach deep enough and yet | find little. 3.04. 15
and be in debt to none — yet more to move you, 3.05. 77
and yet confusion live! 4.01. 21
yet do our hearts wear timon's livery, | that 4.02. 17
meet, for timon's sake | let's yet be fellows. 4.02. 25
th' art quick, | but yet i'll bury thee; 4.03. 46
hast thou gold yet? 4.03.130
yet may your pains six months | be quite 4.03.144
sick of man's unkindness | should yet be hungry! 4.03.177
thy flatterers yet wear silk, drink wine, lie 4.03.206
art thou proud yet? 4.03.276
yet thanks i must you con | that you are thieves 4.03.425
yet remain assur'd | that he's a made–up villain 5.01. 97
alone, | yet an arch–villain keeps him company. 5.01.108
but yet i love my country, and am not | one that 5.01.191
yet our old love made a particular force, | and 5.02. 8
yet rich conceit | taught thee to make vast 5.04. 77
JC yet if you be out, sir, i can mend you. 1.01. 17 P
bid every noise be still; peace yet again! 1.02. 14
that of yourself which you yet know not of. 1.02. 70
i would not, cassius, yet i love him well. 1.02. 82
yet if my name were liable to fear, | i do not 1.02.199
him a crown — yet 'twas not a crown neither, 1.02.237 P
there was more foolery yet, if i could remember 1.02.287 P
yet i see | thy honorable mettle may be wrought 1.02.308
yet his hand, | not sensible of fire, 1.03. 17
me, | in personal action, yet prodigious grown, 1.03. 77
come, casca, you and i will yet, ere day, | see 1.03.153
yet i fear him, | for in the ingrafted love he 2.01.183
but it is doubtful yet | whether caesar will 2.01.193
yet i insisted, yet you answer'd not, | but with 2.01.245
yet i insisted, yet you answer'd not, | but with 2.01.245
stood on ceremonies, | yet now they fright me. 2.02. 14
yet caesar shall go forth; 2.02. 28
of all the wonders that i yet have heard, | it 2.02. 34
art thou here yet? 2.04. 10
is caesar yet gone to the capitol? 2.04. 24
madam, not yet; 2.04. 25
yet in the number i do know but one | that 3.01. 68
in /states unborn and accents yet unknown! 3.01.113
but yet have i a mind | that fears him much; 3.01.144
act | you see we do, yet see you but our hands, 3.01.167
rome, | no rome of safety for octavius yet; 3.01.289
yet stay awhile, | thou shalt not back till i 3.01.290
yet brutus says he was ambitious, | and brutus 3.02. 93
yet brutus says he was ambitious, | and sure he 3.02. 98
yet hear me, countrymen, yet hear me speak. 3.02.233
yet hear me, countrymen, yet hear me speak. 3.02.233
forth of doors, | yet something leads me forth. 3.03. 4
you, | but yet my nature could not bear it so. 4.03.195
the posture of your blows are yet unknown; 5.01. 33
that make to him on the spur, | yet he spurs on. 5.03. 30
yet would not so have been, | durst i have done 5.03. 47
o julius caesar, thou art mighty yet! 5.03. 94
are yet two romans living such as these? 5.03. 98
yet ere night | we shall try fortune in a second 5.03.109
yet, countrymen! o, yet, hold up your heads! 5.04. 1
yet, countrymen! o, yet, hold up your heads! 5.04. 1
my heart doth joy that yet in all my life | i 5.05. 34
MAC be lost, | yet it shall be tempest–toss'd. 1.03. 25
inhabitants o' th' earth, | and yet are on't? 1.03. 42
and yet your beards forbid me to interpret 1.03. 46
not so happy, yet much happier. 1.03. 66
who was the thane lives yet, | but under heavy 1.03.109
home, | might yet enkindle you unto the crown, 1.03.121
thought, whose murther yet is but fantastical, 1.03.139
/are not | those in commission yet return'd? 1.04. 2
my liege, | they are not yet come back. 1.04. 3
yet let that be | which the eye fears, when it 1.04. 52
yet do i fear thy nature, | it is too full o' 1.05. 16
not play false, | and yet wouldst wrongly win. 1.05. 22
did then adhere, and yet you would make both: 1.07. 52
like lead upon me, | and yet i would not sleep. 2.01. 7
what, sir, not yet at rest? 2.01. 12
yet when we can entreat an hour to serve, | we 2.01. 22
i have thee not, and yet i see thee still. 2.01. 35
i see thee yet, in form as palpable | as this 2.01. 40
god's sake, yet could not equivocate to heaven. 2.03. 10 P
legs sometime, yet i made a shift to cast him. 2.03. 40 P
not yet. 2.03. 45
but yet 'tis one. 2.03. 49
o, yet i do repent me of my fury, | that i did 2.03.106
let's away, | our tears are not yet brew'd. 2.03.124
shaft that's shot | hath not yet lighted, and 2.03.142
and yet dark night strangles the travelling lamp 2.04. 7
yet it was said | it should not stand in thy 3.01. 3
and bid my will avouch it, yet i must not, | for 3.01.119
there's comfort yet, they are assailable. 3.02. 39
the west yet glimmers with some streaks of day; 3.03. 5
yet he's good that did the like for fleance. 3.04. 17
we are yet but young in deed. 3.04.143
but yet i'll make assurance double sure, | and 4.01. 83
yet my heart | throbs to know one thing: 4.01.100
another yet? 4.01.118
and yet the eight appears, who bears a glass 4.01.119
from what we fear, yet know not what we fear, 4.02. 20
father'd he is, and yet he's fatherless. 4.02. 27
thou speak'st with all thy wit, and yet, i' 4.02. 42
he hath not touch'd you yet. 4.03. 14
brows of grace, | yet grace must still look so. 4.03. 24
yet my poor country | shall have more vices than 4.03. 46
but fear not yet | to take upon you what is 4.03. 69
and yet seem cold, the time you may so hoodwink. 4.03. 72
yet do not fear, | scotland hath foisons to fill 4.03. 87
i am yet | unknown to woman, never was forsworn, 4.03.125
my countryman; but yet i know him not. 4.03.160
o, relation! | too nice, and yet too true. 4.03.174
the heaviest sound | that ever yet they heard. 4.03.203
yet all this while in a most fast sleep. 5.01. 8 P
yet here's a spot. 5.01. 31 P
yet who would have thought the old man to have 5.01. 39 P
yet i have known those which have walk'd in 5.01. 59 P
i tell you yet again, banquo's buried; 5.01. 63 P
'tis not needed yet. 5.03. 33
of no woman born, | yet i will try the last. 5.08. 32
and yet, by these i see, | so great a day as 5.09. 2
HAM though yet of hamlet our dear brother's death 1.02. 1
yet so far hath discretion fought with nature 1.02. 5
yet now, i must confess, that duty done, | my 1.02. 54
appetite had grown | by what it fed on, and yet, 1.02.145
ere yet the salt of most unrighteous tears | had 1.02.154
yet once methought | it lifted up it head and 1.02.215
yet here, laertes? 1.03. 55
yet he knew me not at first, 'a said i was a 2.02.188 P
yet i hold it not honesty to have it thus set 2.02.201 P
this be madness, yet there is method in't. 2.02.205 P
and yet, to me, what is this quintessence of 2.02.308 P
great baby you see there is not yet out of his 2.02.383 P
yet i, | a dull and muddy–mettled rascal, peak 2.02.566
but yet i could accuse me of such things that it 3.01.122 P
but yet do i believe | the origin and 3.01.176
die two months ago, and not forgotten yet? 3.02.131 P
yet, though i distrust, | discomfort you, my 3.02.165
for 'tis a question left us yet to prove, 3.02.202
this little organ, yet cannot you make it speak. 3.02.368 P
yet what can it, when one can not repent? 3.03. 66
nothing at all, yet all that is i see. 3.04.132
eat, | of habits devil, is angel yet in this, 3.04.162
yet must not we put the strong law on him. 4.03. 3
since yet thy cicatrice looks raw and red 4.03. 60
i do not know | why yet i live to say, "this 4.04. 44
yet the unshaped use of it doth move | the 4.05. 8
though nothing sure, yet much unhappily. 4.05. 13
yet are they much too light for the /bore of the 4.06. 25 P
much unsinow'd, | but yet to me th' are strong. 4.07. 11
yet needful too, for youth no less becomes | the 4.07. 78
but yet | it is our trick. 4.07.186
for my part, i do not lie in't, yet it is mine. 5.01.124 P
yet here she is allow'd her virgin crants, | her 5.01.232
rash, | yet have i in me something dangerous, 5.01.262
but yet methinks it is very /sultry and hot /for 5.02. 98 P
arithmetic of memory, and yet but yaw neither, 5.02.114 P
i would you did, sir, yet, in faith, if you did, 5.02.134 P
if it be not now, yet it /will come — the 5.02.222 P
i dare not drink yet, madam; by and by. 5.02.293
and yet it is almost against my conscience. 5.02.296
o, yet defend me, friends, i am but hurt. 5.02.324
here's yet some liquor left. 5.02.342
and let me speak to /th' yet unknowing world 5.02.379
LR than this, who yet is no dearer in my account. 1.01. 20 P
before he was sent for, yet was his mother fair, 1.01. 22 P
and yet not so, since i am sure my love's | more 1.01. 77
which we durst never yet — and with strain'd 1.01.169
i yet beseech your majesty — | if for i want 1.01.223
but yet, alas, stood i within his grace, | i 1.01.273
yet he hath ever but slenderly known himself. 1.01.293 P
yet nature finds itself scourg'd by the sequent 1.02.105 P
after dinner, i will not part from thee yet. 1.04. 41 P
thing than a fool, and yet i would not be thee, 1.04.186 P
yet have i left a daughter. 1.04.255
and course of yours | though i condemn not, yet, 1.04.342
like an apple, yet i can tell what i can tell. 1.05. 16 P
for they are yet but ear–/bussing arguments? 2.01. 7 P
for though it be night, yet the moon shines; 2.02. 31 P
speak yet, how grew your quarrel? 2.02. 61 P
that's something yet: 2.03. 21
winter's not gone yet, if the wild geese fly 2.04. 46 P
no, but not yet, may be he is not well: 2.04.105
will you yet hold? 2.04.198
but yet thou art my flesh, my blood, my daughter 2.04.221
i look'd not for you yet, nor am provided | for 2.04.232
those wicked creatures yet do look well–favor'd 2.04.256
thy fifty yet doth double five and twenty, | and 2.04.259
what they are yet, i know not, but they shall be 2.04.281
(although as yet the face of it is cover'd 3.01. 20
who that fellow is | that yet you do not know. 3.01. 49
few words, but, to effect, more than all yet: 3.01. 52
but yet i call you servile ministers, | that 3.02. 21
for there was never yet fair woman but she made 3.02. 35 P
part in my heart | that's sorry yet for thee. 3.02. 73
you, | yet have i ventured to come seek you out, 3.04.152
yet our power | shall do a court'sy to our wrath 3.07. 25
yet, poor old heart, he holp the heavens to rain 3.07. 62
yet better thus, and known to be contemn'd, 4.01. 1
and worse i may be yet: 4.01. 27
and yet my mind | was then scarce friends with 4.01. 34
and yet i must. 4.01. 54
and yet i know not how conceit may rob | the 4.06. 42
yet he revives. 4.06. 47
speak yet again. 4.06. 55
'twas yet some comfort, | when misery could 4.06. 62
in a light, yet you see how this world goes. 4.06.147 P
yet to be known shortens my made intent. 4.07. 9
you, and know this man, | yet i am doubtful: 4.07. 64
stay yet, hear reason. 5.03. 82
yet am i noble as the adversary | i come to cope 5.03.123
for they yet glance by and scarcely bruise, 5.03.149
yet edmund was belov'd! 5.03.240
OTH keep yet their hearts attending on themselves, 1.01. 51
joy, | yet throw such /changes of vexation on't, 1.01. 72
yet, for necessity of present life, | i must 1.01.155
yet do i hold it very stuff o' th' conscience 1.02. 2
'tis yet to know — | which, when i know that 1.02. 19
yet do they all confirm | a turkish fleet, and 1.03. 7
yet (by your gracious patience) | i will a round 1.03. 89
yet she wish'd | that heaven had made her such a 1.03.162
i never yet did hear | that the bruis'd heart 1.03.218
of most allow'd sufficiency, yet opinion, a 1.03.224 P
touching the turkish loss, yet he looks sadly, 2.01. 32
he is not yet arriv'd, nor know i aught | but 2.01. 89
she never yet was foolish that was fair, | for 2.01.136
had tongue at will, and yet was never loud, 2.01.149
never lack'd gold, and yet went never gay, 2.01.150
fled from her wish, and yet said, "now i may"; 2.01.151
yet again, your fingers to your lips? 2.01.176 P
so, yet that i put the moor | at least into a 2.01.300
but yet confus'd, | knavery's plain face is 2.01.311
that profit's yet to come 'tween me and you. 2.03. 10
'tis not yet ten o' th' clock. 2.03. 13 P

he hath not yet made wanton the night with her; 2.03. 16 P
an inviting eye; and yet methinks right modest. 2.03. 24 P
yet wild, the people's hearts brimful of fear, 2.03.214
yet, i persuade myself, to speak the truth 2.03.223
yet surely cassio, i believe, receiv'd | from 2.03.244
yet fruits that blossom first will first be ripe 2.03.377
yet i beseech you, | if you think fit, or that 3.01. 50
and yet his trespass, in our common reason 3.03. 64
nay, yet there's more in this. 3.03.130
minutes tells he o'er | who dotes, yet doubts; 3.03.170
suspects, yet /strongly loves! 3.03.170
i speak not yet of proof. 3.03.196
and yet how nature erring from itself — 3.03.227
yet, if you please to /hold him off awhile, 3.03.248
into the vale of years (yet that's not much), 3.03.266
yet 'tis the plague /of great ones, 3.03.273
but yet, i say, | if imputation and strong 3.03.405
nay, yet be wise; 3.03.432
yet we see nothing done; 3.03.432
she may be honest yet. 3.03.433
yet be content. 3.03.450
do not rise yet. 3.03.462
they that mean virtuously, and yet do so, | the 4.01. 7
that's not amiss, | but yet keep time in all. 4.01. 92
but yet the pity of it, iago! 4.01.195 P
and yet go on | and turn again; 4.01.253
yet would i knew | that stroke would prove the 4.01.273
yet she's a simple bawd | that cannot say as 4.02. 20
and yet she'll kneel and pray; 4.02. 23
yet could i bear that too, well, very well; 4.02. 56
or that i do not yet, and ever did, | and ever 4.02.156
nor am i yet persuaded to put up in peace what 4.02.179 P
but yet i protest i have dealt most directly in 4.02.208 P
he knows not yet of his honorable fortune. 4.02.234 P
we have some grace, | yet have we some revenge. 4.03. 93
and yet he hath given me satisfying reasons. 5.01. 9
yet i'll not shed her blood, | nor scar that 5.02. 3
yet she must die, else she'll betray more men. 5.02. 6
crime | unreconcil'd as yet to heaven and grace, 5.02. 27
and yet i fear you; 5.02. 37
but yet i feel i fear. 5.02. 39
but yet i hope, i hope, | they do not point on 5.02. 45
ay, but not yet to die. 5.02. 52
not yet quite dead? 5.02. 86
i that am cruel am yet merciful, | i would not 5.02. 87
but yet iago knows | that she with cassio hath 5.02.210
all, all, cry shame against me, yet i'll speak. 5.02.222
you shall be yet far fairer than you are. ANT 1.02. 17
like the courser's hair, hath yet but life, 1.02.193
yet at the first | i saw the treasons planted. 1.03. 25
you can do better yet; but this is meetly. 1.03. 81
that thou, residing here, goes yet with me; 1.03.103
yet must antony | no way excuse his foils, when 1.04. 23
yet have i fierce affections, and think | what 1.05. 17
yet, coming from him, that great med'cine hath 1.05. 36
bind up | the petty difference, we yet not know. 2.01. 49
yet if you there | did practice on my state, 2.02. 38
yet if i knew | what hoop should hold us staunch 2.02.114
yet, ere we put ourselves in arms, dispatch we 2.02.165
but yet hie you to egypt again. 2.03. 15
yet, if thou say antony lives, 'tis well, | or 2.05. 43
but yet, madam — 2.05. 49
i do not like "but yet," it does allay | the 2.05. 50
fie upon "but yet"! 2.05. 51
"but yet" is as a jailer to bring forth | some 2.05. 52
this is not yet an alexandrian feast. 2.07. 96
whilst yet with parthian blood thy sword is warm 3.01. 6
but he loves caesar best, yet he loves antony. 3.02. 15
there's nothing in her yet. 3.03. 24
i have one thing more to ask him yet, good 3.03. 45
while he was yet in rome, | his power went out 3.07. 75
i'll yet follow | the wounded chance of antony, 3.10. 34
yet now — no matter. 3.11. 40
yet he that can endure | to follow with 3.13. 43
i am | antony yet. 3.13. 93
have you done yet? 3.13.153
not know me yet? 3.13.157
there's hope in't yet. 3.13.176
we will yet do well. 3.13.187
come on, my queen, | there's sap in't yet. 3.13.191
i have yet | room for six scotches more. 4.07. 9
yet ha' we | a brain that nourishes our nerves, 4.08. 20
bad a prayer as his | was never yet for sleep. 4.09. 27
come on then, he may recover yet. 4.09. 33
yet they are not join'd. 4.12. 1
eros, thou yet behold'st me? 4.14. 1
yet cannot hold this visible shape, my knave. 4.14. 14
yet come a little — | wishers were ever fools 4.15. 36
but yet let me lament, | with tears as sovereign 5.01. 40
a poor egyptian yet; 5.01. 52
yet t' imagine | an antony were nature's piece 5.02. 98
may well be laugh'd at, | yet is it true, sir. CYM 1.01. 67
marry, yet | the fire of rage is in him, and 1.01. 76
yet i'll move him | to walk this way. 1.01.103
leave | as long a term as yet we have to live, 1.01.107
which i will be ever to pay and yet pay still. 1.04. 37 P
whiles yet the dew's on ground, gather those 1.05. 1
that satiate yet unsatisfied desire, that tub 1.06. 48
but yet heaven's bounty towards him might | be 1.06. 78
and yet of moment too, for it concerns: 1.06.182
is too new, | she hath not yet forgot him. 2.03. 42
me, for | i yet not understand the case myself. 2.03. 75
in meaner parties | (yet who than he more mean?) 2.03.117
yet you are curb'd from that enlargement by 2.03.120
whose remembrance | is yet fresh in their grief. 2.04. 15
all is well yet. 2.04. 39
i see her yet: 2.04.101
did outsell her gift, | and yet enrich'd it too. 2.04.103
and take your ring again, 'tis not yet won. 2.04.114
yet my mother seem'd | the dian of that time. 2.05. 6
yet 'tis greater skill | in a true hate, to pray 2.05. 33
(whose remembrance yet | lives in men's eyes, 3.01. 2
we have yet many among us can gripe as hard as 3.01. 40 P
content — yet not | that we two are asunder; 3.02. 31
in prison, yet | you clasp young cupid's tables. 3.02. 38
but not like me — yet long'st, | but in a 3.02. 54
yet use thee not so hardly | as prouder livers 3.03. 8
makes him fine, | yet keeps his book uncross'd. 3.03. 26
yet the traitor | stands in worse case of woe. 3.04. 86
itself, must not yet be | but by self–danger, 3.04.145
yet | report should render him hourly to your 3.04.149
sir, the event | is yet to name the winner. 3.05. 15
she can scarce be there yet. 3.05.150 P
yet famine, | ere clean it o'erthrow nature, 3.06. 19
i am weak with toil, yet strong in appetite. 3.06. 37
yet this imperceiverant thing loves him in my 4.01. 14 P
so sick i am not, yet i am not well; 4.02. 7
yet who this should be | doth miracle itself, 4.02. 28
dishonestly afflicted, but yet honest. 4.02. 40
yet said hereafter | i might know more. 4.02. 41
not these many years, and yet | i know 'tis he. 4.02. 66
yet i not doing this, the fool had borne | my 4.02.116
yet is't not probable | to come alone, either he 4.02.141
and yet as rough, | their royal blood enchaf'd, 4.02.173
yet still it's strange | what cloten's being 4.02.181
who ever yet could sound thy bottom? 4.02.204
have one dust, yet reverence | (that angel of 4.02.247
as being our foe, | yet bury him as a prince. 4.02.251
can it be six mile yet? 4.02.293
be | yet left in heaven as small a drop of pity 4.02.304
a season, but our jealousy | does yet depend. 4.03. 23
took heel to do't, | and yet died too! 5.03. 68
yet am i better | than one that's sick o' th' 5.04. 4
and though | 'tis not so dear, yet 'tis a life; 5.04. 23
deserve, | and yet are steep'd in favors; 5.04.131
yet, on my conscience, there are verier knaves 5.04.199 P
yet death | will seize the doctor too. 5.05. 29
yet, o my daughter, | that it was folly in me, 5.05. 66
my life, good lad, | and yet i know thou wilt. 5.05.102
my good master, | i will yet do you service. 5.05.404
ere the stroke | of yet this scarce–cold battle, 5.05.469
of all 'say'd yet, mayst thou prove prosperous! PER 1.01. 59
of all 'say'd yet, i wish thee happiness! 1.01. 60
yet i feed | on mother's flesh which did me 1.01. 64
i mother, wife — and yet his child. 1.01. 69
how they may be, and yet in two, | as you will 1.01. 70
and yet the end of all is bought thus dear, 1.01. 98
yet hope, succeeding from so fair a tree | as 1.01.114
on sweetest flowers, yet they poison breed. 1.01.133
yet neither pleasure's art can joy my spirits, 1.02. 9
nor yet the other's distance comfort me. 1.02. 10
if further yet you will be satisfied | why (as 1.03. 15
yet, ere you shall depart, this we desire, | as 1.03. 38
palates who, not yet /two /summers younger, 1.04. 39
yet those which see them fall | have scarce 1.04. 48
yet cease your ire, you angry stars of heaven! 2.01. 1
thanks, fortune, yet, that, after all /thy 2.01.121
i yet am unprovided | of a pair of bases. 2.01.160
he hopes by you his fortunes yet may flourish. 2.02. 47
yet pause awhile, | yon knight doth sit too 2.03. 53
and yet but justice; 2.04. 13
nor never did my actions yet commence | a deed 2.05. 53
yet for the love | of this poor infant, this 3.01. 40
and yet the fire of life kindle again | the 3.02. 83
mortally, | yet glance full wond'ringly on us. 3.03. 7
sea she lies in, yet the end | must be as 'tis. 3.03. 11
yet my good will is great, though the gift small 3.04. 18
i will do't, but yet she is a goodly creature. 4.01. 9
i will go, | but yet i have no desire to it. 4.01. 43
ay, by my faith, they shall not be chang'd yet. 4.02.136 P
yet a princess | to equal any single crown a' 4.03. 7
yet none does know but you how she came dead, 4.03. 29
yet i find | it greets me as an enterprise of 4.03. 37
we wept after her hearse, | and yet we mourn. 4.03. 42
flies, | but yet i know you'll do as i advise. 4.03. 51
mortal vessel tears, | and yet he rides it out. 4.04. 31
which grows to the stalk, never pluck'd yet, i 4.06. 42 P
my lord, she's not pac'd yet, you must take some 4.06. 63 P
any of these ways are yet better than this; 4.06.177
yet let me obtain my wish. 5.01. 35
yet nothing we'll omit | that bears recovery's 5.01. 53
yet once more | let me entreat to know at large 5.01. 61
yet i was mortally brought forth, and am | no 5.01.104
yet thou dost look | like patience gazing on 5.01.137
yet give me leave: 5.01.168
o'er, point by point, for yet he seems to dote, 5.01.225
whom, o goddess, | wears yet thy silver livery. 5.03. 7
yet there, my queen, | we'll celebrate their 5.03. 79
yet still is modesty, and still retains | more TNK pr 7
more famous yet 'twixt po and silver trent. pr 12
art, may yet appear | worth two hours' travail. pr 28
faint, | daisies smell–less, yet most quaint, 1.01. 5
am going, and never yet | went i so willing way. 1.01.103
yet i think, | did i not by th' abstaining of my 1.01.188
yet unhard'ned in | the crimes of nature — let 1.02. 2
yet be leaden–footed | till his great rage be 1.02. 84
yet what man | thirds his own worth (the case is 1.02. 95
yet to be neutral to him were dishonor; 1.02.100
yet i wish him | excess and overflow of power, 1.03. 3
yet they | must yield their tribute there. 1.03. 7
yet fate hath brought them off. 1.03. 41
yet do effect | rare issues by their operance, 1.03. 62
not | against your faith, yet i continue mine. 1.03. 97
yet they breathe | and have the name of men. 1.04. 27
it be for great ones, yet they seldom come: 2.01. 3 P
yet sometime a divided sigh, martyr'd as 'twere 2.01. 40 P
at misery | and bear the chance of war yet. 2.02. 3
yet, cousin, | even from the bottom of these 2.02. 55
we are young and yet desire the ways of honor, 2.02. 73
yet, good madam, | sometimes her modesty will 2.02.143
the cause i know not yet. 2.02.222
yet in the field to strike a battle for her; 2.02.252
not yet, sir. 2.03. 68
it so) as ever | these eyes yet look'd on. 2.04. 11
and yet he had a cousin, fair as he too; 2.04. 16
and yet his songs are sad ones. 2.04. 20
and yet they that knew me | would say it was my best 2.05. 13
food, for yet | his iron bracelets are not off. 2.06. 7
and yet he has not thank'd me | for what i have 2.06. 21
yet i hope, | when he considers more, this love 2.06. 26
yet pardon me hard language. 3.01.106
i thank thee, arcite, | thou art yet a fair foe; 3.06. 8
or, if you feel yourself not fitting yet | and 3.06. 36
yet a little | i did by imitation. 3.06. 80
yet that i will be woman, and have pity, | my 3.06.191
almost all men, and yet i yielded, theseus — 3.06.207
her, yet i'll preserve | the honor of affection, 3.06.268
eyes, and as noble | as ever fame yet spoke of. 3.06.277
and lovers yet unborn shall bless my ashes. 3.06.283
if she refuse me, yet my grave will wed me, 3.06.284
who loses, yet i'll weep upon his bier. 3.06.308
yet i might perceive, | ere i departed, a great 4.01. 5
but yet perceiv'd not | who made the sound, the 4.01. 60
yet i keep close for all this, | close as a 4.01.130
yet i may bind those wounds up, that must open 4.02. 1
yet doubtless | she would run mad for this man. 4.02. 11
yet these that we count errors may become him: 4.02. 31
what a bold gravity, and yet inviting, | has 4.02. 41
two greater and two better never yet | made 4.02. 62
stern, and yet noble, | which shows him hardy, 4.02. 79
yet a great deal short, | methinks, of him 4.02. 89
red and white, for yet no beard has blest him; 4.02.107
promises | in such a body yet i never look'd on. 4.02.119
of roses, yet is heavier | than lead itself, 5.01. 96
and vow that lover never yet made sigh | truer 5.01.125
which never yet | beheld thing maculate — look 5.01.144
yet very well, sir. 5.02. 36
yet his eye | is like an engine bent, or a sharp 5.03. 41
yet sometime 'tis not so, but alters to | the 5.03. 47
me, | and yet may palamon wound arcite to | the 5.03. 58
miscarry, yet i knew not | why i did think so. 5.03.101
is in expectation, | yet quaking and unsettled. 5.03.106
save what is bought, and yet i purchase cheaply, 5.03.113
that was thus good | encount'red yet his better. 5.03.123
glory in a life | that thou art yet to lead. 5.04. 44
yet is he living, | but such a vessel 'tis that 5.04. 82
thy worthy, manly heart, be yet unbroken, | give 5.04. 88
i am palamon, | one that yet loves thee dying. 5.04. 90
i was false, | yet never treacherous. 5.04. 93
yet in the passage | the gods have been most 5.04.114
pray yet stay a while, | and let me look upon ye ep 3
and yet mistake me not: ep 11
"and yet not cloy thy lips with loath'd satiety, VEN 19
she bathes in water, yet her fire must burn. 94
yet hath he been my captive, and my slave, | and 101
obeyed, | yet was he servile to my coy disdain. 112
though mine be not so fair, yet are they red — 116
yet mayst thou well be tasted. 128
dance on the sands, and yet no footing seen. 148
i were dumb, yet his proceedings teach thee. 406
see, | yet should i be in love by touching thee. 438
yet would my love to thee be still as much, 442
that ever yet betoken'd | wrack to the seaman, 453
whereon they surfeit, yet complain on drouth: 544
and glutton–like she feeds, yet never filleth; 548
though the rose have prickles, yet 'tis pluck'd! 574
yet love breaks through, and picks them all at 576
she's love, she loves, and yet she is not lov'd. 610
yet from mine ear the tempting tune is blown; 778
and yet she hears no tidings of her love. 867
full of respects, yet nought at all respecting, 911
yet sometimes falls an orient drop beside, 981
not to believe, and yet too credulous: 986
yet pardon me, i felt a kind of fear | when as i 998
and never woman yet | could rule them both 1007
and yet," quoth she, "behold two adons dead! 1070
thou being dead, the day should yet be light. 1134
yet their ambition makes them still to fight, LUC 68
doth yet in his fair welkin once appear, | till 116
yet ever to obtain his will resolving, | though 129
they fright him, yet he still pursues his fear. 308
stalks, | and gazeth on her yet unstained bed. 366
she dares not look, yet, winking, there appears 458
his hand, that yet remains upon her breast 463
enmity, | yet strive i to embrace mine infamy." 504
yet, foul night–waking cat, he doth but dally, 554
climb | his wonted height, yet ere he go to bed, 776
"yet am i guilty of thy honor's wrack, | yet for 841
wrack, | yet for thy honor did i entertain him; 842
yet for the self–same purpose seek a knife; 1047
"yet die i will not till my collatine | have 1177
yet with the fault i thus far can dispense: 1279
yet save that labor, for i have them here. 1290
and yet the duteous vassal scarce is gone; 1360
face, though full of cares, yet show'd content; 1503
honesty, but yet defil'd | with inward vice: 1545
priam, why art thou old, and yet not wise? 1550
though woe be heavy, yet it seldom sleeps, | and 1574
pure | doth in her poison'd closet yet endure." 1659
yet in the eddy boundeth in his pride | back to 1669
comes all too late, yet let the traitor die, 1686
but she, that yet her sad task hath not said, 1699
yet sometime "tarquin" was pronounced plain, 1786
yet neither may possess the claim they lay. 1794
fiend, | suspect i may (yet not directly tell): PP 2.10
eye, | yet not so wistly as this queen on him. 6.12
brighter than glass, and yet as glass is, 7. 3
softer than wax, and yet as iron rusty: 7. 4
yet in the mids of all her pure protestings, 7.11
fram'd the love, and yet she foil'd the framing, 7.15
she bade love last, and yet she fell a–turning. 7.16
i weep for thee, and yet no cause i have, | for 10. 7
and yet thou lefts me more than i did crave, 10. 9
yet at my parting sweetly did she smile, | in 14. 7
yet not for me, shine sun to succor flowers! 14.28
wiser head, | neither too young nor yet unwed. 18. 6
yet will she blush, here be it said, | to hear 18.53
hearts remote, yet not asunder; PHT 29
together, | to themselves yet either neither, 43
so great a sum of sums, yet canst not live? SON 4. 8
age, | yet mortal looks adore his beauty still, 7. 7
pluck, | and yet methinks i have astronomy, 14. 2
hours, | and many maiden gardens, yet unset, 16. 6
though yet, heaven knows, it is but as a tomb 17. 3
yet do thy worst, old time: 19.13
yet eyes this cunning want to grace their art, 24.13
yet in these thoughts myself almost despising, 29. 9
yet him for this my love no whit disdaineth 33.13
though thou repent, yet i have still the loss: 34.10
yet doth it steal sweet hours from love's 36. 8
but yet be blam'd, if thou this self deceivest 40. 7
and yet love knows it is a greater grief | to 40.11
kill me with spites, yet we must not be foes. 40.14
ay me, but yet thou mightst my seat forbear, 41. 9

and yet it may be said i lov'd her dearly; 42. 2
and yet to times in hope my verse shall stand, 60.13
for slander's mark was ever yet the fair; 70. 2
yet this thy praise cannot be so thy praise | to 70.11
yet be most proud of that which i compile, 78. 9
yet what of thee thy poet doth invent | he robs 79. 7
which eyes not yet created shall o'er–read, 81.10
yet when they have devis'd | what strained 82. 9
thou mayst be false, and yet i know it not. 92.14
and yet this time remov'd was summer's time, 97. 5
yet this abundant issue seem'd to me | but hope 97. 9
yet nor the lays of birds, nor the sweet smell 98. 5
yet seem'd it winter still, and, you away, | as 98.13
yet i none could see | but sweet or color it had 99.14
tomb, | and to be prais'd of ages yet to be. 101.12
first i saw you fresh, which yet are green. 104. 8
ah, yet doth beauty, like a dial hand, | steal 104. 9
can yet the lease of my true love control, 107. 3
sweet boy, but yet, like prayers divine, | i 108. 5
yet then my judgment knew no reason why | my 115. 3
yet fear her, o thou minion of her pleasure, 126. 9
yet so they mourn, becoming of their woe, | that 127.13
yet none knows well | to shun the heaven that 129.13
yet well i know | that music hath a far more 130. 9
and yet, by heaven, i think my love as rare | as 130.13
yet in good faith some say that thee behold, 131. 5
and yet thou wilt, for i, being pent in thee, 133.13
me, | he pays the whole, and yet am i not free. 134.14
the sea, all water, yet receives rain still, 135. 9
yet what the best is take the worst to be. 137. 4
yet do not so, but since i am near slain, | kill 139.13
though not to love, yet, love, to tell me so, 140. 6
fiend | suspect i may, yet not directly tell, 144.10
yet this shall i ne'er know, but live in doubt, 144.13
yet who knows not conscience is born of love? 151. 2
which yet men prove | against strange maladies a 153. 7
found yet moe letters sadly penn'd in blood, LC 47
i might as yet have been a spreading flower, 75
"small show of man was yet upon his chin, | his 92
yet showed his visage by that cost more dear, 96
yet if men mov'd him, was he such a storm | as 101
yet their purpos'd trim | piec'd not his grace, 118
"yet did i not, as some my equals did, | demand 148
and yet do question make | what i should do 321
would yet again betray the fore–betray'd, | and 328
/YEW 2 FR 0.0002 REL FR 2 V 0 P
under yond /yew trees lay thee all along, ROM 5.03. 3
as i did sleep under this /yew tree here, | i 5.03.137
YEW 4 FR 0.0004 REL FR 4 V 0 P
my shroud of white, stuck all with yew, | o, TN 2.04. 55
bows | of double–fatal yew against thy state; R2 3.02.117
bind me here | unto the body of a dismal yew, TIT 2.03.107
goat, and slips of yew | sliver'd in the moon's MAC 4.01. 27
YIELD *(also 'ield, 'ild)*
/YIELD 2 FR 0.0002 REL FR 2 V 0 P
/now, "/o /earth, /yield /us /that /king /again, 2H4 1.03.106
/means | /will /yield /to /see /his /daughter. LR 4.03. 41
YIELD 158 FR 0.0178 REL FR 144 V 14 P
indeed, | which throes thee much to yield. TMP 2.01.231
i'll yield him thee asleep, | where thou mayst 3.02. 60
kill the bees that yield it with your stings! TGV 1.02.104
i'll force thee yield to my desire. 5.04. 59
and /makes milch–kine yield blood, and shakes a WIV 4.04. 33
sick for, ere i'ld yield | my body up to shame. MM 2.04.103
on twenty bloody blocks, he'ld yield them up, 2.04.181
claudio, | if i would yield him my virginity, 3.01. 97
me your snatches, and yield me a direct answer. 4.02. 6 P
cannot but yield you forth to public thanks, 5.01. 7
confutes mine honor, | and i did yield to him; 5.01.101
transform me then, and to your pow'r i'll yield. ERR 3.02. 40
man, | to yield possession to my holy prayers, 4.04. 55
graves, yawn and yield your dead, | till death ADO 5.03. 19
by this good day, i yield upon great persuasion, 5.04. 95 P
it, i'll repay it back, | or yield up aquitaine. LLL 2.01.159
all liberal reason i will yield unto. 2.01.167
i would not yield to be your house's guest: 5.02.354
if you yield not to your father's choice, | you MND 1.01. 69
ere i will yield my virgin patent up | unto his 1.01. 80
yield | thy crazed title to my certain right. 1.01. 91
in hermia's love i yield you up my part; 3.02.165
and hedg'd me by his wit to yield myself | his MV 2.01. 18
and sigh, and yield | to christian intercessors. 3.03. 15
of force | must yield to such inevitable shame 4.01. 57
you press me far, and therefore i will yield. 4.01.425
that cannot so much as a blossom yield | in lieu AYL 2.03. 64
if this uncouth forest yield any thing savage, i 2.06. 6 P
lord, | the reasons of our state i cannot yield, AWW 3.01. 10
sir, i can yield you none without words, and TN 3.01. 23 P
you must needs yield your reason, sir andrew. 3.02. 3 P
i yield all this; WT 4.04.410
arthur of britain, yield thee to my hand, | and JN 2.01.156
whereon he says | i shall yield up my crown, let 4.02.157
ere further leisure yield them further means R2 1.04. 40
yield stinging nettles to mine enemies; 3.02. 18
the means that heavens yield must be embrac'd, 3.02. 29
what, will not this castle yield? 3.03. 20
but if he will not yield, | rebuke and dread 1H4 5.01.110
thee, | unless thou yield thee as my prisoner. 5.03. 10
do ye yield, sir? 2H4 4.03. 12 P
sir john falstaff, and in that thought yield me. 4.03. 17 P
here he is, and here i yield him, and i beseech 4.03. 45 P
he'll yield the crow a pudding one of these days H5 2.01. 87 P
will you yield, and this avoid? 3.03. 42
we yield our town and lives to thy soft mercy. 3.03. 48
england shall crouch down in fear, and yield. 4.02. 37
shall yield them little, tell the constable. 4.03.125
yield, cur! 4.04. 1 P
yet they do wink and yield, as love is blind and 5.02.300 P
be the heavens with black, yield day to night! 1H6 1.01. 1
news would cause him once more yield the ghost. 1.01. 67
i must not yield to any rites of love, | for my 1.02.113
shall yield the other in the right opinion. 2.04. 42
yield, my lord protector, yield, winchester, 3.01.112
yield, my lord protector, yield, winchester, 3.01.112
he shall submit, or i will never yield. 3.01.118
well, duke of gloucester, i will yield to thee; 3.01.134
and made me almost yield upon my knees. 3.03. 80
yield up his life unto a world of odds. 4.04. 25

speak to thy father ere thou yield thy breath! 4.07. 24
henry is youthful and will quickly yield. 5.03. 99
then yield, my lords, and here conclude with me 5.05. 77
force perforce i'll make him yield the crown, 2H6 1.01.258
let york be regent, i will yield to him. 1.03.106
and, vanquish'd as i am, i yield to thee, | or 2.01.180
therefore yield, or die. 4.02.127
and yield to mercy whilst 'tis offered you, | or 4.08. 12
is fled, my lord, and all his powers do yield, 4.09. 10
lord, | i'll yield myself to prison willingly, 4.09. 42
they seek revenge, and therefore will not yield. 3H6 1.01.190
yield to our mercy, proud plantagenet. 1.04. 30
so true men yield, with robbers so o'ermatch'd. 1.04. 64
but hercules himself must yield to odds; 2.01. 53
son, | didst yield consent to disinherit him, 2.02. 24
say'st thou, henry, wilt thou yield the crown? 2.02.101
ne'er shall dine unless thou yield the crown. 2.02.128
yield both my life and them | to some man else, 2.05. 59
and what he will, i humbly yield unto. 3.01.101
and that is more than i will yield unto. 3.02. 96
yield not thy neck | to fortune's yoke, but let 3.03. 16
it shall be eas'd if france can yield relief. 3.03. 20
that your estate requires and mine can yield. 3.03.150
and therefore i yield thee my free consent. 4.06. 36
that he consents, if warwick yield consent, 4.06. 46
for doubtless burgundy will yield him help, 4.06. 90
what, fear not, man, but yield me up the keys, 4.07. 37
shows, | that i must yield my body to the earth, 5.02. 9
first the harmless sheep doth yield his fleece, 5.06. 8
than death can yield me here by my abode. R3 1.03.168
and often did i strive | to yield the ghost; 1.04. 37
lord hastings will not yield to our complots? 3.01.192
amiss, | i cannot nor i will not yield to you. 3.07.207
a grave | as thou canst yield a melancholy seat! 4.04. 32
day, yield me not thy light, nor, night, thy 4.04.401
despairing, yield thy breath! 5.03.172
bull–bearing milo his addition yield | to sinowy TRO 2.03.247
o priam, yield not to him! 5.03. 76
if they would yield us but the superfluity while COR 1.01. 17 P
the common body | to yield what passes here. 2.02. 54
childish friendliness | to yield your voices? 2.03.176
must these have voices, that can yield them now, 3.01. 34
yield, martius, yield! 3.01.214
yield, martius, yield! 3.01.214
bound with an oath to yield to his conditions; 5.01. 69
to–morrow yield up rule, resign my life, | and TIT 1.01.191
to be a heinous sin, | yield at entreats; 1.01.449
yield to his humor, smooth and speak him fair, 5.02.140
nor will he know his purse, or yield me this, TIM 1.02.194
not that, if money and the season can yield it. 3.06. 51 P
earth, yield me roots! 4.03. 23
yield him who all the human sons do hate, | from 4.03.185
i am ashamed i did yield to them. JC 2.02.106
yield, or thou diest. 5.04. 12
only i yield to die: 5.04. 12
why do i yield to that suggestion | whose horrid MAC 1.03.134
which must not yield | to one of woman born. 5.08. 12
then yield thee, coward, | and live to be the 5.08. 23
i will not yield, | to kiss the ground before 5.08. 27
nor will it yield to norway or the pole | a HAM 4.04. 21
as her winks and nods and gestures yield them, 4.05. 11
yield! LR 2.01. 31
us hate thee, | life would not yield to age. 4.01. 12
yield up, o love, thy crown and hearted throne OTH 3.03.448
if thou so yield him, there is gold, and here ANT 2.05. 28
he'll never yield to that. 3.06. 37
then have courtesy, so she | will yield us up. 3.13. 16
i ask no more, | and the gods yield you for't! 4.02. 33
go to him, dolabella, bid him yield; 5.01. 1
if thou pleasest not, | i yield thee up my life. 5.01. 12
self exhibition | which your own coffers yield; CYM 1.06.123
is his mother | should yield the world this ass! 2.01. 53
yield up | their deer to th' stand o' th' 2.03. 69
but that you shall not say i yield being silent, 2.03. 94
yield thee, thief. 4.02. 75
why i should yield to thee. 4.02. 80
yield, rustic mountaineer. 4.02.100
who did promise | to yield me often tidings. 4.03. 39
but yield me to the veriest hind that shall 5.03. 77
man | is but a substance that must yield to you; PER 2.01. 3
to wisdom he's a fool that will not yield; 2.04. 54
therefore briefly yield 'er, for she must 3.01. 53 P
world so soon | to yield thee so much profit. 4.01. 4
wherein my death might yield her any profit, 4.01. 80
this populous city will | yield many scholars. 4.06.187
yet they | must yield their tribute there. TNK 1.03. 8
which to his speech did honey passage yield, VEN 452
soldiers when their captain once doth yield, 893
the coward captive vanquished doth yield | to LUC 75
"but if thou yield, i rest thy secret friend: 526
yield to my love, if not, enforced hate, | in 668
yield to my hand, my hand shall conquer thee: 1210
and to their hope they such odd action yield, 1433
her feeble force will yield at length, | when PP 18.33
fields, | and all the craggy mountains yield. 19. 4
the earth can yield me but a common grave, SON 81. 7
till each to raz'd oblivion yield his part | of 122. 7
but yield them up where i myself must render: LC 221
YIELDED 26 FR 0.0029 REL FR 25 V 1 P
lorded, | not only with what my revenue yielded, TMP 1.02. 98
deserve | as much as may be yielded to a man; ADO 3.01. 48
i have yielded. AWW 3.07. 36
and left them | more rich for what they yielded. WT 5.01. 55
thus have i yielded up into your hand | the JN 5.01. 1
all kent hath yielded; 5.01. 30
and shall i now give o'er the yielded set? 5.02.107
but basely yielded upon compromise | that which R2 2.01.253
and all your northern castles yielded up, | and 3.02.201
hath yielded up his body to the grave; 5.06. 21
he saw me, and yielded, that i may justly say, 2H4 4.03. 40 P
is roan yielded up? 1H6 1.01. 65
before i would have yielded to this league. 2H6 1.01.127
end, | the king hath yielded unto thy demand: 5.01. 40
and look to have it yielded with all kindness. R3 3.01.198
yielded | to bear the golden yoke of sovereignty 3.07.145
for they had so vildly | yielded the town. COR 3.01. 11
a very little | i have yielded to. 5.03. 17
graves have yawn'd and yielded up their dead; JC 2.02. 18

nor must not then be yielded to in this. ANT 3.06. 38
mine honor was not yielded, | but conquer'd 3.13. 61
my fleet hath yielded to the foe, and yonder 4.12. 11
it shall safe be kept, | and truly yielded you. CYM 1.06.210
and call'd marina | for she was yielded there. PER 5.03. 48
almost all men, and yet i yielded, theseus — TNK 3.06.207
did, | demand of him, nor being desired yielded; LC 149
YIELDER 1 FR 0.0001 REL FR 1 V 0 P
i was not born a yielder, thou proud scot, | and 1H4 5.03. 11
YIELDERS 1 FR 0.0001 REL FR 1 V 0 P
some hats, from yielders all things catch. MND 3.02. 30
YIELDER–UP 1 FR 0.0001 REL FR 1 V 0 P
treason's true bed and yielder–up of breath. 2H4 4.02.123
YIELDING 19 FR 0.0021 REL FR 17 V 2 P
brother | by yielding up thy body to my will, MM 2.04.164
and, yielding to him, humors well his frenzy. ERR 4.04. 81
how well this yielding rescues thee from shame! LLL 1.01.118
his requests so far | from reason's yielding, 2.01.150
a yielding 'gainst some reason in my breast, 2.01.151
and idle theme, | no more yielding but a dream, MND 5.01.428
i see a yielding in the looks of france; JN 2.01.474
be he the fire, i'll be the yielding water; R2 3.03. 58
therefore patiently and yielding. H5 5.02.275 P
blow, | and yielding to another when it blows, 3H6 3.01. 87
reason which denies | the yielding of her up? TRO 2.02. 25
making a treaty where | there was a yielding — COR 5.06. 68
and not impute this yielding to light love, ROM 2.02.105
unto the voice and yielding of that body HAM 1.03. 23
six kings already | show me the way of yielding. ANT 3.10. 34
make her go back, even to the yielding, had i CYM 1.04.105 P
now quick desire hath caught the yielding prey, VEN 547
which with a yielding latch, and with no more, LUC 339
kill both thyself and her for yielding so." 1036
YIELDINGS 1 FR 0.0001 REL FR 1 V 0 P
never was inclin'd | to accessary yieldings, but LUC 1658
YIELDS 18 FR 0.0020 REL FR 15 V 3 P
my slave, who never | yields us kind answer. TMP 1.02.309
or else the law of athens yields you up | (which MND 1.01.119
truly, the tree yields bad fruit. AYL 3.02.116 P
so i to her, and so she yields to me, | for i am SHR 2.01.136
tods, every tod yields pound and odd shilling; WT 4.03. 33 P
session, hanging, yields a careful man work. 4.04.686 P
that it yields nought but shame and bitterness. JN 3.04.111
and his high sceptre yields | to the possession R2 4.01.109
thy own hand yields thy death's instrument, | go 5.05.106
yields his engrossments to the ending father. 2H4 4.05. 79
thus yields the cedar to the axe's edge, | whose 3H6 5.02. 11
all places yields to him ere he sits down, | and COR 4.07. 28
upon the next encounter yields him ours. JC 1.03.156
of life, when life itself | yields to the theft. LR 4.06. 44
that wildly grows in them but yields a crop | as CYM 4.02.180
which yields compassion where he conquers; TNK 4.02.132
and yields at last to every light impression? VEN 566
as each unwilling portal yields him way, LUC 309
YOK'D 3 FR 0.0003 REL FR 3 V 0 P
be yok'd with his that did betray the best! WT 1.02.419
hath yok'd a nation strong, train'd up in arms. TIT 1.01. 30
think every bearded fellow that's but yok'd OTH 4.01. 66
YOKE 34 FR 0.0038 REL FR 30 V 4 P
our wives are a yoke of his discarded men — WIV 2.01.175 P
and thou wilt needs thrust thy neck into a yoke, ADO 1.01.201 P
"in time the savage bull doth bear the yoke." 1.01.261
whose unwished yoke | my soul consents not to MND 1.01. 81
ox hath therefore stretch'd his yoke in vain, 2.01. 93
whose souls do bear an egall yoke of love, MV 3.04. 13
if then we shall shake off our slavish yoke, R2 2.01.291
how a good yoke of bullocks at /stamford fair? 2H4 3.02. 38 P
afoot, | come underneath the yoke of government. 4.04. 10
or bring him in obedience to your yoke. 1H6 1.01.164
ah, humphrey, can i bear this shameful yoke? 2H6 2.04. 37
yield not thy neck | to fortune's yoke, but let 3H6 3.03. 17
to sunder them that yoke so well together. 4.01. 23
we'll yoke together like a double shadow | to 4.06. 49
to bear the golden yoke of sovereignty, | which R3 3.07.146
now thy proud neck bears half my burthen'd yoke, 4.04.111
bruis'd underneath the yoke of tyranny, | thus 5.02. 2
and ever may your highness yoke together | (as i H8 3.02.150
/on /their /toes, yoke you like draught–oxen, TRO 2.01.106 P
as a consul, | nor yoke with him for tribune. COR 3.01. 57
and brought to yoke, the enemies of rome. TIT 1.01. 69
return | captive to thee and to thy roman yoke; 1.01.111
for these base bondmen to the yoke of rome. 4.01.109
and shake the yoke of inauspicious stars | from ROM 5.03.111
and groaning underneath this age's yoke, | have JC 1.02. 61
our yoke and sufferance show us womanish. 1.03. 84
i think our country sinks beneath the yoke: MAC 4.03. 39
all color here | did put the yoke upon 's; CYM 3.01. 51
our subjects, sir, | will not endure his yoke; 3.05. 5
so, sir, i yoke me | in my good brother's fault. 4.02. 19
i shall with aged patience bear your yoke. PER 2.04. 48
who do bear thy yoke | as 'twere a wreath of TNK 5.01. 95
save of their lord no bearing yoke they knew, LUC 409
he, | 'unless thou yoke thy liking to my will, 1633
YOKED 2 FR 0.0002 REL FR 2 V 0 P
and he that is so yoked by a fool, | methinks TGV 1.01. 40
you are yoked with a lamb | that carries anger JC 4.03.110
YOKE–DEVILS 1 FR 0.0001 REL FR 1 V 0 P
as two yoke–devils sworn to either's purpose, H5 2.02.106
//YOKE–FELLOW 1 FR 0.0001 REL FR 1 V 0 P
/and /thou, /his //yoke–fellow /of /equity, LR 3.06. 37
YOKE–FELLOW 1 FR 0.0001 REL FR 1 V 0 P
side | (yoke–fellow to his honor–owing wounds) H5 4.06. 9
YOKE–FELLOWS 1 FR 0.0001 REL FR 1 V 0 P
yoke–fellows in arms, | let us to france, like H5 2.03. 54
YOKES 3 FR 0.0003 REL FR 3 V 0 P
do not these fair yokes | become the forest WIV 5.05.107
nobly he yokes | a smiling with a sigh, as if CYM 4.02. 51
and yokes her silver doves, by whose swift aid VEN 1190
YOKETH 1 FR 0.0001 REL FR 1 V 0 P
with which he yoketh your rebellious necks, 1H6 2.03. 64
YOKING 1 FR 0.0001 REL FR 1 V 0 P
and on his neck her yoking arms she throws. VEN 592
/YON 1 FR 0.0001 REL FR 1 V 0 P
/yon king's to me like to my father's picture, PER 2.03. 37
YON 22 FR 0.0024 REL FR 22 V 0 P
than all yon fiery oes and eyes of light. MND 3.02.188
that yon green boy shall have no sun to ripe JN 2.01.472
hubert, throw thine eye | on yon young boy. 3.03. 60

there stands the castle, by yon tuft of trees, R2 2.03. 53
lies | within the limits of yon lime and stone, 3.03. 26
bullingbrook — for yon methinks he stands — 3.03. 91
on yon proud man should take it off again | with 3.03.135
the sun begins to peer | above yon bulky hill! 1H4 5.01. 2
but first i'll turn yon fellow in his grave, R3 1.02.260
yon towers, whose wanton tops do buss the clouds TRO 4.05.220
i'll say yon grey is not the morning's eye, ROM 3.05. 19
and yon grey lines | that fret the clouds are JC 2.01.103
walks o'er the dew of yon high eastward hill. HAM 1.01.167
yon ribaudred nag of egypt | (whom leprosy ANT 3.10. 10
wight did die, | as yon grim looks do testify. PER 1.ch. 40
to taste the fruit of yon celestial tree | (or 1.01. 21
yon sometimes famous princes, like thyself, 1.01. 34
that without covering, save yon field of stars, 1.01. 37
awhile, | yon knight doth sit too melancholy, 2.03. 54
yon little tree, yon blooming apricock! TNK 2.02.236
yon little tree, yon blooming apricock! 2.02.236
hark how yon spurs to spirit do incite | the 5.03. 56
YOND 45 FR 0.0050 REL FR 35 V 10 P
eye advance | and say what thou seest yond. TMP 1.02.410
yond same black cloud, yond huge one, looks like 2.02. 20 P
yond same black cloud, yond huge one, looks like 2.02. 20 P
yond same cloud cannot choose but fall by 2.02. 23 P
for 'tis no trusting to yond foolish lout — TGV 4.04. 66
good mother, do not marry me to yond fool. WIV 3.04. 83
made his journal greeting | to yond generation, MM 4.03. 89
nerissa, cheer yond stranger, bid her welcome. MV 3.02.237
are some shrowd contents in yond same paper 3.02.243
one of you question yond man | if he for gold AYL 2.04. 64
yond young fellow swears he will speak with you. TN 1.05.139 P
get thee to yond same sovereign cruelty. 2.04. 80
yond gull malvolio is turn'd heathen, a very 3.02. 69 P
it softly, | yond crickets shall not hear it. WT 2.01. 31
do but behold yond poor and starved band, | and H5 4.02. 16
yond island carrions, desperate of their bones, 4.02. 39
ride thou unto the horsemen on yond hill. 4.07. 57
agreed. i'll to yond corner. 1H6 2.01. 33
is not yond diomed, with calchas' daughter? TRO 4.05. 13
by all diana's waiting–women yond, | and by 5.02. 91
here's a letter come from yond poor girl. 5.03. 99 P
by yond clouds, | let me deserve so ill as you, COR 3.01. 50
should from yond cloud speak divine things, 4.05.104
see you yond coign a' th' capitol, yond 5.04. 1 P
you yond coign a' th' capitol, yond cornerstone? 5.04. 1 P
come hither, nurse. what is yond gentleman? ROM 1.05.128
nightly she sings on yond pomegranate tree. 3.05. 4
yond light is not day–light, i know it, i; 3.05. 12
under yond /yew trees lay thee all along, 5.03. 3
what torch is yond, that vainly lends his light 5.03.125
furor brevis est," | but yond man is very angry. TIM 1.02. 29
is yond despis'd and ruinous man my lord? 4.03.459
yond cassius has a lean and hungry look, | he JC 1.02.194
whether yond troops are friend or enemy. 5.03. 18
when yond same star that's westward from the HAM 1.01. 36
and yond tall anchoring bark, | diminish'd to LR 4.06. 18
behold yond simp'ring dame, | whose face between 4.06.118
see how yond justice rails upon yond simple 4.06.152 P
how yond justice rails upon yond simple thief. 4.06.152 P
but look, what lights come yond? OTH 1.02. 28
now, by yond marble heaven, | in the due 3.03.460
set we our squadrons on yond side o' th' hill, ANT 3.09. 1
where yond pine does stand | i shall discover 4.12. 1
up to yond hill, | your legs are young; CYM 3.03. 10
by yond bush? 4.02.292
YONDER 70 FR 0.0079 REL FR 40 V 30 P
yonder is silvia; and silvia's mine. TGV 5.04.125
look who comes yonder. WIV 2.01.158 P
yonder he is coming, this way, sir hugh. 3.01. 27 P
yonder is a most reverend gentleman, who, belike 3.01. 52 P
he so takes on yonder with my husband; 4.02. 22 P
i came yonder at eton to marry mistress anne 5.05.183 P
there's one yonder arrested and carried to MM 1.02. 60 P
yonder man is carried to prison. 1.02. 86 P
but soft, who wafts us yonder? ERR 2.02.109 P
come go along, my wife is coming yonder. 4.04. 40
speak softly, yonder, as i think, he walks. 5.01. 9
i came yonder from a great supper. ADO 1.03. 42 P
hereby, upon the edge of yonder coppice, | a LLL 4.01. 9
as yonder venus in her glimmering sphere. MND 3.02. 61
yonder is thy dear. 3.02.176
fast, | and yonder shines aurora's harbinger, 3.02.380
yonder she comes. 5.01.187 P
yonder, sir, he walks. MV 2.02.174
by yonder moon i swear you do me wrong; 5.01.142
yonder comes my master, your brother. AYL 1.01. 26 P
yonder they lie, the poor old man, their father, 1.02.129 P
yonder sure they are coming. 1.02.147 P
is yonder the man? 1.02.151 P
o, we are spoil'd and — yonder he is. SHR 5.01.110 P
yonder is heavy news within between two soldiers AWW 3.02. 33 P
he has been yonder i' the sun practicing TN 2.05. 16 P
fabian can scarce hold him yonder. 3.04.282 P
demand of yonder champion | the cause of his R2 1.03. 7
marshal, ask yonder knight in arms, | both who 1.03. 26
yonder he comes, and that arrant malmsey–nose 2H4 2.01. 39 P
is not that the morning which breaks yonder? H5 4.01. 86 P
we see yonder the beginning of the day, but i 4.01. 89 P
call yonder fellow hither. 4.07.118
bars | in yonder tower to overpeer the city, 1H6 1.04. 11
by thrusting out a torch from yonder tower, 3.02. 23
the burning torch in yonder turret stands. 3.02. 30
brave followers, yonder stands the thorny wood, 3H6 5.04. 67
and yonder is the wolf that makes this spoil. 5.04. 80
o buckingham, take heed of yonder dog! R3 1.03.288
look you yonder, do you see? TRO 1.02.205 P
yonder comes paris, yonder comes paris. 1.02.212 P
yonder comes paris, yonder comes paris. 1.02.212 P
look ye yonder, niece; 1.02.213 P
what sneaking fellow comes yonder? 1.02.226 P
yonder? 1.02.227 P
yonder comes the troop. 4.05. 64
"lo jupiter is yonder, dealing life!" 4.05.191
i wonder now how yonder city stands | when we 4.05.211
for yonder walls, that pertly front your town, 4.05.219
no, yonder 'tis, | there where we see the lights 5.01. 67
then is he yonder, | and there the strawy greeks 5.05. 23
no, by the flame of yonder glorious heaven, | he 5.06. 23
yonder comes news: a wager they have met. COR 1.04. 1
who's yonder, | that does appear as he were 1.06. 21
empress i am, but yonder sits the emperor. TIT 4.04. 41
which doth enrich the hand | of yonder knight? ROM 1.05. 42
crows, | as yonder lady o'er her fellows shows. 1.05. 49
soft, what light through yonder window breaks? 2.02. 2
lady, by yonder blessed moon i vow, | that tips 2.02.107
do lace the severing clouds in yonder east. 3.05. 8
yonder comes a poet and a painter; TIM 4.03.351 P
this angry flood, | and swim to yonder point?" JC 1.02.104
till he have brought thee up to yonder troops 5.03. 16
lo yonder, and titinius mourning it. 5.03. 92
do you see yonder cloud that's almost in shape HAM 3.02.376 P
"'so would i 'a' done, by yonder sun, | and thou 4.05. 65
and yonder, caesar. ANT 2.02. 14
and yonder | they cast their caps up and carouse 4.12. 11
sir, yonder is your place. PER 2.03. 23
look yonder they are! TNK 2.01. 48 P
YONDER'S 6 FR 0.0006 REL FR 3 V 3 P
come to your uncle, yonder's old coil at home. ADO 5.02. 96 P
yonder's my lord your son with a patch of velvet AWW 4.05. 94 P
yonder's the head of that arch–enemy | that 3H6 2.02. 2
see, by good hap, yonder's my lord; TIM 3.02. 25 P
o, my good lord, yonder's foul murthers done! OTH 5.02.106
yonder's the sea, and there's a ship. TNK 3.04. 5
YOND'S 1 FR 0.0001 REL FR 1 V 0 P
yond's that same knave | that leads him to these AWW 3.05. 82
YORE 1 FR 0.0001 REL FR 1 V 0 P
to show false art what beauty was of yore. SON 68.14
YORICK 1 FR 0.0001 REL FR 0 V 1 P
alas, poor yorick, i knew him, horatio, a fellow HAM 5.01.184 P
YORICK'S 1 FR 0.0001 REL FR 0 V 1 P
was, sir, yorick's skull, the king's jester. HAM 5.01.181 P
/YORK 1 FR 0.0001 REL FR 1 V 0 P
/the /gentle /archbishop /of /york /is /up 2H4 1.01.189
YORK 213 FR 0.0240 REL FR 207 V 6 P
commend me to thy brother, edmund york. R2 1.02. 62
and what shall good old york there see | but 1.02. 67
be york the next that must be bankrout so! 2.01.151
york is too far gone with grief, | or else he 2.01.184
our uncle york lord governor of england; 2.01.220
here comes the duke of york. 2.02. 73
that's as york thrives to beat back bullingbrook 2.02.144
what power the duke of york had levied there, 2.03. 34
keeps good old york there with his men of war? 2.03. 52
and in it are the lords of york, berkeley, and 2.03. 55
the duke of york, to know what pricks you on 2.03. 78
i know my uncle york | hath power enough to 3.02. 89
your uncle york is join'd with bullingbrook, 3.02.200
why, york, what wilt thou do? 5.02. 88
sweet york, sweet husband, be not of that mind, 5.02.107
old, | i doubt not but to ride as fast as york. 5.02.115
sweet york, be patient. hear me, gentle liege. 5.03. 91
who, travelling towards york, | with much ado 5.05. 73
kind uncle york, the latest news we hear | is 5.06. 1
his uncle york — where i first bow'd my knee 1H4 1.03.245
of york, is it not? 1.03.269
and then the power of scotland, and of york, 1.03.280
why, my lord of york commends the plot and the 2.03. 21 P
lord edmund mortimer, my lord of york, and owen 2.03. 25 P
the archbishop's grace of york, douglas, 3.02.119
towards york shall bend you with your dearest 5.05. 36
what, to york? call him back again. 2H4 1.02. 64 P
you should have been well on your way to york. 2.01. 67
your grace of york, in god's name then set 4.01.225
my lord of york, it better show'd with you 4.02. 4
send colevile with his confederates | to york, 4.03. 74
take it, brave york. H5 4.03.132
the duke of york commends him to your majesty. 4.06. 3
suffolk first died, and york, all haggled over, 4.06. 11
edward the duke of york, the earl of suffolk, 4.08.103
and if thou be not then created york, | i will 1H6 2.04.119
from famous edmund langley, duke of york, 2.05. 85
give | that doth belong unto the house of york, 3.01.164
i girt thee with the valiant sword of york: 3.01.170
and rise created princely duke of york. 3.01.172
welcome, high prince, the mighty duke of york! 3.01.176
perish, base prince, ignoble duke of york! 3.01.177
that i wear | in honor of my noble lord of york, 3.04. 30
why, what is he? as good a man as york. 3.04. 36
law | argu'd betwixt the duke of york and him; 4.01. 96
your private grudge, my lord of york, will out, 4.01.109
good cousins both, of york and somerset, | quiet 4.01.114
i more incline to somerset than york: 4.01.154
cousin of york, we institute your grace | to be 4.01.162
my lord of york, i promise you, the king 4.01.174
to burdeaux, york! 4.03. 22
this expedition was by york and talbot | too 4.04. 2
york set him on to fight and die in shame, 4.04. 8
talbot dead, great york might bear the name. 4.04. 9
cries out for noble york and somerset | to beat 4.04. 15
york set him on, york should have sent him aid. 4.04. 29
york set him on, york should have sent him aid. 4.04. 29
and york as fast upon your grace exclaims, 4.04. 30
york lies; 4.04. 33
had york and somerset brought rescue in, | we 4.07. 33
be patient, york. 5.04.113
cousin of york, | we here discharge your grace 2H6 1.01. 65
gloucester, york, buckingham, somerset, 1.01. 69
brave york, salisbury, and victorious warwick, 1.01. 86
and, brother york, thy acts in ireland, | in 1.01.194
and so says york — for he hath greatest cause. 1.01.207
so york must sit, and fret, and bite his tongue, 1.01.230
a day will come when york shall claim his own, 1.01.239
then, york, be still awhile, till time do serve. 1.01.248
and in my standard bear the arms of york, | to 1.01.256
that the duke of york was rightful heir to the 1.03. 26 P
did the duke of york say he was rightful heir to 1.03. 28 P
somerset, buckingham, | and grumbling york; 1.03. 70
as for the duke of york, this late complaint 1.03. 97
which, | or somerset or york, all's one to me. 1.03.102
if york have ill demean'd himself in france, 1.03.103
let york be regent, i will yield to him. 1.03.106
york is the worthier. 1.03.108
york is meetest man | to be your regent in the 1.03.160
force, | that york is most unmeet of any man. 1.03.164
pray god the duke of york excuse himself! 1.03.178
doth any one accuse york for a traitor? 1.03.179
that richard duke of york | was rightful heir 1.03.183
french, | because in york this breeds suspicion; 1.03.206
your grace shall give me leave, my lord of york, 1.04. 76
sweet york, begin; 2.02. 7
the fift was edmund langley, duke of york; 2.02. 15
the fourth son, york claims it from the third; 2.02. 55
shall find their deaths, if york can prophesy. 2.02. 76
shall one day make the duke of york a king. 2.02. 79
and touching the duke of york, i will take my 2.03. 87 P
and york and impious beauford, that false priest 2.04. 53
my lord of suffolk, buckingham, and york, 3.01. 39
and dogged york, that reaches at the moon, 3.01.158
ah, york, no man alive so fain as i! 3.01.244
'tis york that hath more reason for his death. 3.01.245
if york, with all his far–fet policy, | had been 3.01.293
no more, good york; 3.01.304
thy fortune, york, hadst thou been regent there, 3.01.305
my lord of york, try what your fortune is. 3.01.309
then, noble york, take thou this task in hand. 3.01.318
a charge, lord york, that i will see perform'd. 3.01.321
i'll see it truly done, my lord of york. 3.01.330
now, york, or never, steel thy fearful thoughts, 3.01.331
how they affect the house and claim of york. 3.01.375
and now the house of york, thrust from the crown 4.01. 94
cade, the duke of york hath taught you this. 4.02.154
the duke of york is newly come from ireland, 4.09. 24
my state, 'twixt cade and york distress'd, 4.09. 31
and now is york in arms to second him. 4.09. 35
from ireland thus comes york to claim his right, 5.01. 1
york, if thou meanest well, i greet thee well. 5.01. 14
york, i commend this kind submission; 5.01. 54
doth york intend no harm to us | that thus he 5.01. 56
york doth present himself unto your highness. 5.01. 59
then, york, unloose thy long–imprisoned thoughts 5.01. 88
i arrest thee, york, | of capital treason 5.01.106
to say if that the bastard boys of york | shall 5.01.115
the sons of york, thy betters in their birth, 5.01.119
this is my king, york, i do not mistake, | but 5.01.129
then nobly, york, 'tis for a crown thou fight'st 5.02. 16
what seest thou in me, york? 5.02. 19
york not our old men spares; 5.02. 51
meet i an infant of the house of york, | into as 5.02. 57
saint albons battle won by famous york | shall 5.03. 30
and so do i, victorious prince of york. 3H6 1.01. 21
possess it, york, | for this is thine and not 1.01. 26
unless plantagenet, duke of york, be king, | and 1.01. 40
parliament | let us assail the family of york. 1.01. 65
thou factious duke of york, descend my throne, 1.01. 74
for shame, come down. he made thee duke of york. 1.01. 77
true, clifford, that's richard duke of york. 1.01. 83
/thy father was, as thou art, duke of york, 1.01.105
do right unto this princely duke of york, | or i 1.01.166
be thou a prey unto the house of york, | and die 1.01.185
now york and lancaster are reconcil'd. 1.01.204
and giv'n unto the house of york such head | as 1.01.233
disgrace, | and utter ruin of the house of york. 1.01.254
the sight of any of the house of york | is as a 1.03. 30
look, york, i stain'd this napkin with the blood 1.04. 79
alas, poor york, but that i hate thee deadly, 1.04. 84
i prithee grieve, to make me merry, york. 1.04. 86
york cannot speak unless he wear a crown. 1.04. 93
a crown for york! 1.04. 94
off with his head, and set it on york gates, 1.04.179
gates, | so york may overlook the town of york. 1.04.180
gates, | so york may overlook the town of york. 1.04.180
when as the noble duke of york was slain, | your 2.01. 46
and on the gates of york | they set the same, 2.01. 65
sweet duke of york, our prop to lean upon, | now 2.01. 68
o valiant lord, the duke of york is slain! 2.01.100
no longer earl of march, but duke of york; 2.01.192
welcome, my lord, to this brave town of york. 2.02. 1
ambitious york did level at thy crown, | thou 2.02. 19
ah, cousin york, would thy best friends did know 2.02. 54
comes warwick, backing of the duke of york, 2.02. 69
ay, and old york, and yet not satisfied. 2.02. 99
head, | for york in justice puts his armor on. 2.02.130
suppose this arm is for the duke of york, | and 2.04. 2
this is the hand that stabb'd thy father york, 2.04. 6
came on the part of york, press'd by his master; 2.05. 66
impairing henry, strength'ning misproud york. 2.06. 7
did, | giving no ground unto the house of york, 2.06. 16
come, york and richard, warwick and the rest, 2.06. 29
i mean our princely father, duke of york. 2.06. 51
from off the gates of york fetch down the head, 2.06. 52
thou didst love york, and i am son to york. 2.06. 73
thou didst love york, and i am son to york. 2.06. 73
york and young rutland could not satisfy. 2.06. 84
because in quarrel of the house of york | the 3.02. 6
while proud ambitious edward, duke of york, 3.03. 27
and i the house of york. 3.03.108
did i forget that by the house of york | my 3.03.186
king, | and come now to create you duke of york. 4.03. 34
convey'd | unto my brother, archbishop of york. 4.03. 53
now for awhile farewell, good duke of york. 4.03. 57
is new committed to the bishop of york, | fell 4.04. 11
from ravenspurgh haven before the gates of york, 4.07. 8
yet edward, at the least, is duke of york. 4.07. 21
now, for this night, let's harbor here in york; 4.07. 79
and thou shalt still remain the duke of york. 5.01. 28
have sold their lives unto the house of york, 5.01. 74
and tell me who is victor, york or warwick? 5.02. 6
speak like a subject, proud ambitious york! 5.05. 17
made glorious summer by this son of york; R3 1.01. 2
when my father york and edward wept | to hear 1.02.156
times, | during the wars of york and lancaster, 1.04. 15
when that our princely father york | blest his 1.04.235
they say my son of york | has almost overta'en 2.04. 6
how, my young york? i prithee let me hear it. 2.04. 26
i prithee, pretty york, who told thee this? 2.04. 31
i thought my mother and my brother york | would 3.01. 20
i, | the queen your mother and your brother york 3.01. 27
persuade the queen to send the duke of york 3.01. 33
can from his mother win the duke of york, | anon 3.01. 38
now in good time, here comes the duke of york. 3.01. 95
richard of york, how fares our loving brother? 3.01. 96
how fares our cousin, noble lord of york? 3.01.101

my lord of york will still be cross in talk. 3.01.126
this little prating york | was not incensed by 3.01.151
child | of that insatiate edward, noble york, 3.05. 87
how doth the prince and my young son of york? 4.01. 14
and i'll salute your grace of york as mother 4.01. 29
young york he is but boot, because both they 4.04. 65
thereon engrave | "edward" and "york"; 4.04.273
what heir of york is there alive but we? 4.04.471
the wronged heirs of york do pray for thee. 5.03.137
all this divided york and lancaster, | divided 5.05. 27
of the right reverend cardinal of york. H8 1.01. 51
my lord | cardinal of york, are join'd with me 2.02.105
my lord of york, was not one doctor pace | in 2.02.121
my lord of york, out of his noble nature, | zeal 3.01. 62
earl northumberland | arrested him at york, and 4.02. 13
YORK–PLACE 2 FR 0.0002 REL FR 2 V 0 P
full state pac'd back again | to york–place, H8 4.01. 94
you must no more call it york–place, that's past 4.01. 95
YORK'S 6 FR 0.0006 REL FR 5 V 1 P
to a dear friend of the good duke of york's R2 3.04. 70
now declare, sweet stem from york's great stock, 1H6 2.05. 41
as we were scouring my lord of york's armor. 2H6 1.03.192 P
did york's dread curse prevail so much with R3 1.03.190
farewell, york's wife, and queen of sad 4.04.114
and who is england's king but great york's heir? 4.04.472
YORKS 1 FR 0.0001 REL FR 1 V 0 P
for thousand yorks he shall not hide his head, 2H6 5.01. 85
YORKSHIRE 2 FR 0.0002 REL FR 2 V 0 P
are by the shrieve of yorkshire overthrown. 2H4 4.04. 99
'tis said, my liege, in yorkshire are in arms. R3 4.04.519
YOU *(also y')*
/YOU 106 FR 0.0119 REL FR 84 V 22 P
YOU 14326 FR 1.6194 REL FR 9705 V 4621 P
YOU'D 4 FR 0.0004 REL FR 2 V 2 P
come, come, my lord, you'd spare your spoons. H8 5.02.201
and 'twould, you'd carry half. TRO 2.03.219 P
and 'twere dark you'd close sooner. 3.02. 49 P
and that you'd guide me to your sovereign's PER 2.01.140
YOU'LD 15 FR 0.0017 REL FR 11 V 4 P
you'ld be king o' the isle, sirrah? TMP 5.01.288 P
i know you'ld fain be gone. MM 5.01.120
would you'ld pardon me. TN 3.03. 24
of these days, and then you'ld wanton with us, WT 2.01. 18
all doubt | you'ld call your children yours. 2.03. 82
froth, as you'ld thrust a cork into a hogshead. 3.03. 93 P
you'ld be so lean, that blasts of january 4.04.111
that have more in them than you'ld think, sister 4.04.216 P
you'ld think it strange if i should marry her. 3H6 3.02.111
little england | you'ld venture an emballing. H8 2.03. 47
our ends are honest, | you'ld feel more comfort. 3.01.155
six of his labors you'ld have done, and sav'd COR 4.01. 18
or, if you'ld ask, remember this before: 5.03. 79
sir, if you'ld save your life, fly to your house 5.04. 35
if he were dead, you'ld weep for him; MAC 4.02. 61 P
YOU/'LL 1 FR 0.0001 REL FR 0 V 1 P
my lord, if you/'ll give me leave, i will tread LR 2.02. 65 P
YOU'LL 165 FR 0.0186 REL FR 111 V 54 P
if you'll sit down, | i'll bear your logs the TMP 3.01. 23
but you'll lie like dogs, and yet say nothing 3.02. 19 P
so, by your circumstance, i fear you'll prove. TGV 1.01. 37
truly, sir, i think you'll hardly win her. 1.01.133 P
well — you'll still be too forward. 2.01. 11 P
ass, you'll lose the tide, if you tarry any 2.03. 35 P
you'll not confess, you'll not confess. WIV 1.01. 92 P
you'll not confess, you'll not confess. 1.01. 92 P
shallow, you'll complain of me to the king? 1.01.109 P
you'll be laugh'd at. 1.01.119 P
you'll come to dinner, george. 2.01.156 P
you'll not bear a letter for me, you rogue? 2.02. 19 P
flattering boy, now i see you'll be a courtier. 3.02. 8 P
you'll undertake her no more? 3.05.125 P
devise but how you'll use him when he comes, 4.04. 26
that you'll procure the vicar | to stay for me 4.06. 48
hoping you'll find good cause to whip them all. MM 2.01.137
you'll be glad to give out a commission for more 2.01.239 P
if you'll implore it, that will free your life, 3.01. 65
you'll forswear this again. 3.02.166 P
well; you'll answer this one day. fare ye well. 4.03.163 P
good, | whereto if you'll a willing ear incline, 5.01.536
tell you when, and you'll tell me wherefore. ERR 3.01. 39
you'll let us in, i hope? 3.01. 54
you'll cry for this, minion, if i beat the door 3.01. 59
good sir, say whe'r you'll answer me or no: 4.01. 60
that stole your meat, and you'll beat the post. ADO 2.01.199 P
you thither, my lord, if you'll vouchsafe me. 3.02. 3 P
you'll be made bring deformed forth, i warrant 3.03.172 P
enough, you'll see he shall lack no barns. 3.04. 48 P
for you'll prove perjur'd if you make me stay. LLL 2.01.113
you'll not be perjur'd, 'tis a hateful thing; 4.03.155
you'll ne'er be friends with him, 'a kill'd your 5.02. 13
you'll mar the light by taking it in snuff; 5.02. 22
armed in arguments — you'll be surpris'd. 5.02. 84
good madam, if by me you'll be advis'd, | let's 5.02.300
of usance for my moneys, and you'll not hear me. MV 1.03.141
me, | but if you do, you'll make me wish a sin, 3.02. 13
you'll ask me why i rather choose to have | a 4.01. 40
to know your answer, whether you'll admit him. 4.01.146
you'll be whipt for taxation one of these days. AYL 1.02. 84 P
for you'll be rotten ere you be half ripe, and 3.02.119 P
you say you'll marry me, if i be willing? 5.04. 11
me, | you'll give yourself to this most faithful 5.04. 14
you say that you'll have phebe, if she will? 5.04. 16
keep you your word, phebe, that you'll marry me, 5.04. 21
that you'll marry her | if she refuse me; 5.04. 23
sirrah, and you'll not knock, i'll ring it. SHR 1.02. 16
for this reason, if you'll know, | that she's 1.02.233
you'll leave his lecture when i am in tune? 3.01. 24
'tis like you'll prove a jolly surly groom, 3.02.213
you'll be gone, sir knave, and do as i command AWW 1.03. 90 P
as you'll have her. 2.05. 23 P
and out of it you'll run again, rather than 2.05. 38 P
fie, that you'll say so! TN 1.03. 25 P
you'll nothing, madam, to my lord by me? 3.01.136
but you'll not deliver't? 3.02. 57 P
you'll find it otherwise, i assure you; 3.04.229 P
you'll stay? WT 1.02. 44
you'll be found, | be you beneath the sky. 1.02.179
you'll kiss me hard and speak to me as if | i 2.01. 5
you'll leave yourself | hardly one subject. 2.03.111
several tunes faster than you'll tell money; 4.04.184 P
o, father, you'll know more of that hereafter. 4.04.343
have you thought on | a place whereto you'll go? 4.04.537
can but stay you | where you'll be loath to be. 4.04.572
and those that you'll procure from king leontes? 4.04.621
that which you hear you'll swear you see, there 5.02. 31 P
you'll mar it if you kiss it; 5.03. 82
but then you'll think | (which i protest against 5.03. 89
you'll be a fool still. 2H4 2.01.156 P
i hope you'll come to supper. 2.01.159 P
you'll pay me all together? 2.01.159 P
by the mass, you'll crack a quart together, ha, 5.03. 62 P
you'll pay me the eight shillings i won of you H5 2.01. 94 P
and, be assur'd, you'll find a difference, | as 2.04.134
you'll never trust his word after! 4.01.201 P
you'll question this gentlewoman about me; 5.02.198 P
that thus you do exclaim you'll go with him? 2H6 4.08. 35
if not in heaven, you'll surely sup in hell. 5.01.216
you'll nor fight nor fly. 5.02. 74
prove the contrary, if you'll hear me speak. 3H6 1.02. 20
closer or, good faith, you'll catch a blow. 3.02. 23
you shall have four /and you'll be rul'd by him. 3.02. 30
if you'll not here proclaim yourself our king, 4.07. 54
and ten to one you'll meet him in the tower. 5.01. 46
in weightier things you'll say a beggar nay. R3 3.01.119
bosom up my counsel, | you'll find it wholesome. H8 1.01.113
my lord, you'll bear us company? 2.02. 58
you'll find a most unfit time to disturb him. 2.02. 60
law o'ertake ye, | you'll part away disgrac'd. 3.01. 97
madam, you'll find it so. 3.01.168
cardinal, | you'll show a little honesty. 3.02.306
you'll leave your noise anon, ye rascals; 5.03. 1 P
will stand to the proof, if you'll prove it so. TRO 1.02.129 P
if you'll avouch 'twas wisdom paris went — | as 2.02. 84
if you'll confess /he brought home worthy prize 2.02. 86
you'll remember your brother's excuse? 3.01.142 P
if my lord get a boy of you, you'll give him me. 3.02.105 P
come, beshrew your heart, you'll ne'er be good, 4.02. 29
come, you'll do him wrong ere you are ware. 4.02. 54 P
you'll be so true to him, to be false to him. 4.02. 55 P
if you'll bestow a small (of what you have COR 1.01.125
you'll find | th' have not prepar'd for us. 1.02. 29
if you'll stand fast, we'll beat them to their 1.04. 41
you'll mar all. 2.03. 58
you'll sup with me? 4.02. 49
and you'll look pale | before you find it other. 4.06.101
you'll see your rome embrac'd with fire before 5.02. 7
with fire before | you'll speak with coriolanus. 5.02. 8
good sir, | what peace you'll make, advise me. 5.03.197
you, you'll rejoice | that he is thus cut off. 5.06.137
and that you'll say ere half an hour pass. TIT 3.01.191
you'll not endure him! ROM 1.05. 79
my soul, | you'll make a mutiny among my guests! 1.05. 80
you'll be the man! 1.05. 81
you'll be sick to–morrow | for this night's 4.04. 7
that with your other noble parts you'll suit TIM 2.02. 23
although i know you'll swear, terribly swear 4.03.137
you'll take it ill. 5.01. 90
you'll bear me a bang for that, i fear. JC 3.03. 18 P
napkins enow about you, here you'll sweat for't. MAC 2.03. 6 P
"you'll rue the time | that clogs me with this 3.06. 42
then you'll buy 'em to sell again. 4.02. 41
/wringing it thus) you'll tender me a fool. HAM 1.03.109
but you'll be secret? 1.05.122
knees i beg | that you'll vouchsafe me raiment, LR 2.04.156
sister, you'll go with us? 5.01. 34
/'sblood, but you'll not hear me. OTH 1.01. 4
you'll have your daughter cover'd with a barbary 1.01.111 P
horse, you'll have your nephews neigh to you; 1.01.112 P
you'll have coursers for cousins, and gennets 1.01.112 P
you'll be asham'd for ever. 2.03.163
you'll never meet a more sufficient man. 3.04. 91
/an' you'll come to supper to–night, you may; 4.01.159 P
i court moe women, you'll couch with moe men." 4.03. 57
you'll heat my blood; no more. ANT 1.03. 80
if you'll patch a quarrel, | as matter whole you 2.02. 52
you'll win two days upon me. 2.04. 9
come, you'll play with me, sir? 2.05. 6
i fear me you'll be in till then. 2.07. 32 P
to–morrow | you'll serve another master. 4.02. 28
you shall please, | if you'll employ me to him. 5.02. 70
you'll go with us? CYM 1.02. 38 P
if you'll be patient, i'll no more be mad; 2.03.103
you'll give me leave to spare when you shall 2.04. 65
if you'll back to th' court — 3.04.130
if you'll go fetch him, | we'll say our song 4.02.253
end, i think you'll never return to tell one. 5.04.183 P
you'll remember from whence you had them. PER 2.01.151 P
how? | do as i bid you, or you'll move me else. 2.03. 71
you'll lose nothing by custom. 4.02.138 P
i think you'll turn a child again. 4.03. 4
flies, | but yet i know you'll do as i advise. 4.03. 51
dare assure you | you'll find a loving mistress. TNK 2.05. 57
you'll pledge her? 3.03. 38
you'll lose all else. 3.04. 9
you'll find it. 3.06. 49
which you'll hear of | at better time. 4.01. 29
believe you'll find it so. 4.01. 47
you'll find it so. she comes. pray /humor her. 5.02. 40
you'll lose the noblest sight | that ev'r was 5.02. 99
you'll see't done now for ever. 5.04. 25
you'll put down strangers, | kill them, cut STM II.C 119
if you'll stand our friend to procure our pardon II.C 142 P
/YOUNG 2 FR 0.0002 REL FR 1 V 1 P
doting foolish /young knave's sleeve of troy TRO 5.04. 4 P
/and /go /with /me, /thy /sight /is /young, TIT 3.02. 84
YOUNG 460 FR 0.0520 REL FR 333 V 127 P
i'll get thee | young scamels from the rock. TMP 2.02.172
them, while i visit | young ferdinand, whom they 3.03. 92
bestow upon the eyes of this young couple | some 4.01. 40
how young leander cross'd the hellespont. TGV 1.01. 22
even so by love the young and tender wit | is 1.01. 47
like a young wench that had buried her grandam; 2.01. 23 P
his years but young, but his experience old; 2.04. 69
to hate young valentine and love my friend. 3.02. 65
now, my young guest, methinks you're allycholly; 4.02. 26 P
o' my life, if i were young again, the sword WIV 1.01. 40 P
i know the young gentlewoman, she has good gifts 1.01. 62 P
justice shallow, and here young master slender, 1.01. 76 P
would i were young for your sake, mistress anne! 1.01.260 P
young ravens must have food. 1.03. 35 P
run in here, good young man; 1.04. 38 P
if he had found the young man, he would have 1.04. 50 P
ay me, he'll find the young man there, and be 1.04. 65 P
the young man is an honest man. 1.04. 72 P
you are not young, no more am i; 2.01. 6 P
pieces with age to show himself a young gallant! 2.01. 22 P
why, sir, my wife is not young. 2.01.112 P
both young and old, one with another, ford. 2.01.114
what say you to young master fenton? 3.02. 66 P
i'll but bring my young man here to school. 4.01. 8 P
a young man | more fit to do another such MM 2.03. 13
vouchsafe a word, young sister, but one word. 3.01.151
first, here's young master rash, he's in for a 4.03. 4 P
then have we here young dizzy, and young master 4.03. 12 P
we here young dizzy, and young master deep–vow, 4.03. 12 P
and young drop–heir that kill'd lusty pudding, 4.03. 15 P
much honor on a young florentine call'd claudio. ADO 1.01. 10 P
is there no young squarer now that will make a 1.01. 82 P
is she not a modest young lady? 1.01.165 P
all prompting me how fair young hero is, 1.01.304
that young start–up hath all the glory of my 1.03. 66 P
grace had got the good will of this young lady, 2.01.217 P
how wise, how noble, young, how rarely featur'd, 3.01. 60
of age to brag | what i have done being young, 5.01. 61
i doubt we should have been too young for them. 5.01.119 P
to call young claudio to a reckoning for it. 5.04. 9
daughter, | and give her to young claudio. 5.04. 16
epitheton appertaining to thy young days, which LLL 1.02. 14 P
the young dumaine, a well–accomplish'd youth, 2.01. 56
young blood doth not obey an old decree. 4.03.213
your stomachs are too young, | and abstinence 4.03.290
the liker you; few taller are so young. 5.02.836
long withering out a young man's revenue. MND 1.01. 6
o spite! too old to be engag'd to young. 1.01.138
(her womb then rich with my young squire) 2.01.131
but i might see young cupid's fiery shaft 2.01.161
so i, being young, till now ripe not to reason; 2.02.118
is't not enough, is't not enough, young man, 2.02.125
"a tedious brief scene of young pyramus | and 5.01. 56
to falconbridge, the young baron of england? MV 1.02. 67 P
how like you the young german, the duke of 1.02. 84 P
pluck the young sucking cubs from the she–bear, 2.01. 29
master young man, you, i pray you, which is the 2.02. 33 P
master young gentleman, i pray you, which is the 2.02. 39 P
talk you of young master launcelot? 2.02. 48 P
talk you of young master launcelot? 2.02. 50 P
what 'a will, we talk of young master launcelot. 2.02. 55 P
beseech you, talk you of young master launcelot. 2.02. 58 P
father, for the young gentleman, according to 2.02. 61 P
i know you not, young gentleman, but i pray you 2.02. 70 P
my young master doth expect your reproach. 2.05. 19 P
young in limbs, in judgment old, | your answer 2.07. 71
is alighted at your gate | a young venetian, one 2.09. 87
than young alcides, when he did redeem | the 3.02. 55
when we are both accoutered like young men, 3.04. 63
a young and learned doctor to our court. 4.01.144
visitation was with me a young doctor of rome. 4.01.153 P
for i never knew so young a body with so old a 4.01.163 P
o wise young judge, how i do honor thee! 4.01.224
o noble judge! o excellent young man! 4.01.246
did young lorenzo swear he lov'd her well, 5.01. 18
for if i do, i'll mar the young clerk's pen. 5.01.237
come, elder brother, you are too young in this. AYL 1.01. 54 P
they say many young gentlemen flock to him every 1.01.117 P
your brother is but young and tender, and for 1.01.129 P
it is the stubbornest young fellow of france, 1.01.142 P
there is not one so young and so villainous this 1.01.154 P
he will put on us, as pigeons feed their young. 1.02. 94 P
three proper young men, of excellent growth and 1.02.121 P
alas, he is too young! 1.02.153 P
young man, have you challeng'd charles the 1.02.168 P
young gentleman, your spirits are too bold for 1.02.173 P
do, young sir, your reputation shall not 1.02.180 P
where is this young gallant that is so desirous 1.02.200 P
now hercules be thy speed, young man! 1.02.210 P
o excellent young man! 1.02.213 P
bear him away. what is thy name, young man? 1.02.221
had i before known this young man his son, | i 1.02.237
i was too young that time to value her, | but 1.03. 71
what, my young master? 2.03. 2
here, a young man and an old in solemn talk. 2.04. 20 P
here's a young maid with travel much oppressed, 2.04. 74
that young swain that you saw here but erewhile, 2.04. 89
and says, if ladies be but young and fair, 2.07. 37
here comes young master ganymed, my new 3.02. 86 P
it is young orlando, that tripp'd up the 3.02.212 P
he trots hard with a young maid between the 3.02.313 P
that abuses our young plants with carving 3.02.360 P
when last the young orlando parted from you | he 4.03. 98
truly, young gentlemen, though there was no 5.03. 34 P
welcome, young man; 5.04.166
if i achieve not this young modest girl. SHR 1.01.156
such wind as scatters young men through the 1.02. 50
with wealth enough, and young and beauteous, 1.02. 86
how the young folks lay their heads together! 1.02.139 P
fortune i have lighted well | on this young man; 1.02.168
freely give unto /you this young scholar, that 2.01. 79 P
for knowing thee to be but young and light. 2.01.203
well aim'd of such a young one. 2.01.235
now, by saint george, i am too young for you. 2.01.236
that's but a cavil; he is old, i young. 2.01.390
and may not young men die as well as old? 2.01.391
sirrah, young gamester, your father were a fool 2.01.400
young budding virgin, fair, and fresh, and sweet 4.05. 37
this young gentlewoman had a father — o, that AWW 1.01. 17 P
/rossillion, my good lord, | young bertram. 1.02. 19
i can well observe | to–day in our young lords; 1.02. 33
for young charbon the puritan and old poysam the 1.03. 51 P
even so it was with me when i was young. 1.03.128
farewell, young lords! 2.01. 1
farewell, young lords! 2.01. 10
"too young" and "the next year" and "'tis too 2.01. 28
to be young again, if we could, i will be a fool 2.02. 38 P
you are too young, too happy, and too good, | to 2.03. 96

why then, young bertram, take her, she's thy 2.03.105
she is young, wise, fair, | in these to nature 2.03.131
a young man married is a man that's marr'd; 2.03.298
i take my young lord to be a very melancholy man 3.02. 3 P
within between two soldiers and my young lady! 3.02. 34 P
he is in those suggestions for the young earl. 3.05. 17 P
this young maid might do her | a shrewd turn, if 3.05. 67
he hath perverted a young gentlewoman here in 4.03. 14 P
for i knew the young count to be a dangerous and 4.03.219 P
of that lascivious young boy the count, have i 4.03.300 P
i long to talk with the young noble soldier. 4.05.103 P
pardon — the young lord | did to his majesty, 5.03. 12
though she be, she feels her young one kick. 5.03.302
is at the gate a young gentleman much desires to TN 1.05. 99 P
'tis a fair young man, and well attended. 1.05.102 P
yond young fellow swears he will speak with you. 1.05.139 P
enough for a man, nor young enough for a boy; 1.05.156 P
my life upon't, young though thou art, thine eye 2.04. 23
the young gentleman of the count orsino's is 3.04. 57 P
the behavior of the young gentleman gives him 3.04.185 P
if this young gentleman | have done offense, i 3.04.312
come, my young soldier, put up your iron; 4.01. 39 P
when your young nephew titus lost his leg. 5.01. 63
comfort of your young prince mamillius: WT 1.01. 35 P
not cross'd the eyes | of my young playfellow. 1.02. 80
are you so fond of your young prince as we | do 1.02.164
next to thyself and my young rover, he's 1.02.176
the death | of the young prince, whose honorable 3.02.195
if young doricles | do light upon her, she shall 4.04.178
sooth, when i was young, | and handed love as 4.04.347
how prettily th' young swain seems to wash | the 4.04.366
mark your divorce, young sir, | whom son i dare 4.04.417
and leave this young man in pawn till i bring it 4.04.808 P
she shall not be so young | as was your former, 5.01. 78
their country quitted | with this young prince. 5.01.193
when she was young, you woo'd her; 5.03.108
and put the same into young arthur's hand, | thy JN 1.01. 14
of him it holds, stands young plantagenet, | son 2.01.238
to him that owes it, namely this young prince, 2.01.248
and let young arthur, duke of britain, in, | who 2.01.301
is the young dolphin every way complete: 2.01.433
what say these young ones? 2.01.521
it likes us well, young princes; 2.01.533
for we'll create young arthur duke of britain 2.01.551
of kings, of beggars, old men, young men, maids, 2.01.570
hubert, throw thine eye | on yon young boy. 3.03. 60
wife, | young arthur is my son, and he is lost. 3.04. 47
but what shall i gain by young arthur's fall? 3.04.141
may be he will not touch young arthur's life, 3.04.160
if that young arthur be not gone already, | even 3.04.163
young lad, come forth; 4.01. 8
young gentlemen would be as sad as night, | only 4.01. 15
read here, young arthur. 4.01. 33
young boy, i must. 4.01. 40
young arthur's death is common in their mouths, 4.02.187
why urgest thou so oft young arthur's death? 4.02.204
young arthur is alive. 4.02.251
again | after they heard young arthur was alive? 5.01. 38
after young arthur, claim this land for mine, 5.02. 94
but lusty, young, and cheerly drawing breath. R2 1.03. 66
for young hot colts being rag'd do rage the more 2.01. 70
than was that young and princely gentleman. 2.01.175
lord northumberland, his son young harry percy, 2.02. 53
it is my son, young harry percy, | sent from my 2.03. 21
such as it is, being tender, raw, and young, 2.03. 42
the black prince, that young mars of men, | from 2.03.101
both young and old rebel, | and all goes worse 3.02.119
cousin, i am too young to be your father, 3.03.204
go bind thou up young dangling apricocks, 3.04. 29
so many greedy looks of young and old | through 5.02. 13
which he, young wanton and effeminate boy, 5.03. 10
young harry percy, and brave archibald, | that 1H4 1.01. 53
and dishonor stain the brow | of my young harry. 1.01. 86
think you, coz, | of this young percy's pride? 1.01. 92
comparative, rascalliest, sweet young prince. 1.02. 81 P
hath been smooth as oil, soft as young down, 1.03. 7
what, ye knaves, young men must live! 2.02. 90 P
i'll tickle ye for a young prince, i' faith. 2.04.444 P
where, being but young, i framed to the harp 3.01.121
wanton as youthful goats, wild as young bulls. 4.01.103
i saw young harry with his beaver on, | his 4.01.104
more active, valiant, or more valiant, young, 5.01. 90
hath beaten down young hotspur and his troops, 2H4 in 25
young prince john | and westmerland and stafford 1.01. 17
and that young harry percy's spur was cold. 1.01. 42
said he young harry percy's spur was cold? 1.01. 49
if my young lord your son have not the day, 1.01. 52
under the conduct of young lancaster | and 1.01.134
a young knave, and begging? 1.02. 72 P
the young prince hath misled me. 1.02.145 P
you follow the young prince up and down, like 1.02.163 P
not the capacities of us that are young, you do 1.02.174 P
and will you yet call yourself young? 1.02.185 P
check'd him for it, and the young lion repents, 1.02.197 P
than 'a can part young limbs and lechery; 1.02.230 P
it was young hotspur's cause at shrewsbury. 1.03. 26
tell me how many good young princes would do so, 2.02. 30 P
a good shallow young fellow. 2.04.237 P
than i love e'er a scurvy young boy of them all. 2.04.273 P
a good-limb'd fellow, young, strong, and of good 3.02.103 P
if the young dace be a bait for the old pike, i 3.02.330 P
this same young sober-blooded boy doth not love 4.03. 87 P
for william cook — are there no young pigeons? 5.01. 17 P
indeed i think the young king loves you not. 5.02. 9
i know the young king is sick for me. 5.03.135 P
silken streamers the young phoebus /fanning. H5 3.pr. 6
as young as i am, i have observ'd these three 3.02. 28 P
and then i will proclaim young henry king. 1H6 1.01.169
to eltam will i, where the young king is, 1.01.170
i pluck this red rose with young somerset, | and 2.04. 37
was, for that (young richard thus remov'd, 2.05. 71
would some part of my young years | might but 2.05.107
for there young henry with his nobles lie, 3.02.129
when i was young (as yet i am not old), | i do 3.04. 17
and on his son young john, who two hours since 4.03. 35
to bid his young son welcome to his grave? 4.03. 40
o young john talbot, i did send for thee | to 4.05. 1
before young talbot from old talbot fly | the 4.06. 46
o, where's young talbot? 4.07. 2
young talbot's valor makes me smile at thee. 4.07. 4
now my old arms are young john talbot's grave. 4.07. 32
how the young whelp of talbot's, raging wood, 4.07. 35
"young talbot was not born | to be the pillage 4.07. 40
alas, my years are young; 5.01. 21
looking the way her harmless young one went, 2H6 3.01.215
i cut it | as wild medea young absyrtus did; 5.02. 59
in the harmless blood | of sweet young rutland, 3H6 2.01. 63
not his that spoils her young before her face. 2.02. 14
unreasonable creatures feed their young, | and 2.02. 26
'twas you that kill'd young rutland, was it not? 2.02. 98
so many days my ewes have been with young, | so 2.05. 35
york and young rutland could not satisfy. 2.06. 84
is clarence, henry, and his son young edward, 3.02.130
that if our queen and this young prince agree, 3.03.241
that young prince edward marries warwick's 4.01.117
my liege, it is young henry, earl of richmond. 4.06. 67
glad my heart with hope of this young richmond, 4.06. 93
o brave young prince! 5.04. 52
can so young a thorn begin to prick? 5.05. 13
deathsmen, you have rid this sweet young prince! 5.05. 67
in my eye | where my poor young was lim'd, was 5.06. 17
young ned, for thee, thine uncles and myself 5.07. 16
him | than i am made by my young lord and thee! R3 1.02. 28
'twas i that stabb'd young edward — | but 'twas 1.02.181
young, valiant, wise, and (no doubt) right royal 1.02.244
he is young; 1.03. 11
o that your young nobility could judge | what 1.03.256
a careful mother | of the young prince your son. 2.02. 97
forthwith from ludlow the young prince be fet 2.02.121
he was the wretched'st thing when he was young, 2.04. 18
how, my young york? i prithee let me hear it. 2.04. 26
so wise so young, they say do never live long. 3.01. 79
so cunning and so young is wonderful. 3.01.135
how doth the prince and my young son of york? 4.01. 14
i, "accurs'd | for making me, so young, so old a 4.01. 72
young edward lives: 4.02. 10
the britain richmond aims | at young elizabeth, 4.03. 41
young york he is but boot, because both they 4.04. 65
if i revolt, off goes young george's head; 4.05. 4
but tell me, is young george stanley living? 5.05. 9
you are young, sir harry guilford. H8 1.04. 9
they were young and handsome, and of the best 2.02. 3 P
i would not be a young count in your way | for 2.03. 41
marry, this is yet but young, and may be left 3.02. 47
model of our chaste loves, his young daughter — 4.02.132
she is young, and of a noble modest nature, | i 4.02.135
is, a fair young maid that yet wants baptism, 5.02.196
long | to have this young one made a christian. 5.02.213
that had a head to hit, either young or old, 5.03. 24
why, he is very young, and yet will he, within TRO 1.02.115 P
is he so young a man and so old a lifter? 1.02.117 P
i have a young conception in my brain, | be you 1.03.312
not much | unlike young men, whom aristotle 2.02.166
do you not follow the young lord paris? 3.01. 2 P
but it must grieve young pyrrhus now at home 3.03.209
the young prince will go mad. 4.02. 75 P
never did young man fancy | with so eternal and 5.02.165
how now, young man, meanest thou to fight to-day 5.03. 29
no, faith, young troilus, doff thy harness, 5.03. 31
see them meet, that that same young troyan ass, 5.04. 5 P
you that be noble, help him, young and old! COR 3.01.227
and my young boy | hath an aspect of 5.03. 31
let not young mutius then, that was thy joy, TIT 1.01.382
i do remit these young men's heinous faults. 1.01.484
young lords, beware! 2.01. 69
when did the tiger's young ones teach the dam? 2.03.142
you are a young huntsman, marcus, let alone; 4.01.101
and now, young lords, was't not a happy star 4.02. 32
here's a young lad fram'd of another leer: 4.02.119
be so bold to press to heaven in my young days. 4.03. 92 P
here's rome's young captain, let him tell the 5.03. 94
is the day so young? ROM 1.01.160
such comfort as do lusty young men feel | when 1.02. 26
a bump as big as a young cock'rel's stone — | a 1.03. 53
a man, young lady! 1.03. 75
read o'er the volume of young paris' face, | and 1.03. 81
you call'd, my young lady ask'd for, the nurse 1.03.101 P
young romeo is it? 1.05. 64
marry, that, i think, be young petruchio. 1.05.131
lie, | and young affection gapes to be his heir; 2.pr. 2
young abraham cupid, he that shot so /trim, 2.01. 13
young son, it argues a distempered head | so 2.03. 33
young men's love then lies | not truly in their 2.03. 67
but come, young waverer, come go with me, | in 2.03. 89
of you tell me where i may find the young romeo? 2.04.119 P
you, but young romeo will be older when you have 2.04.120 P
told you, my young lady bid me inquire you out; 2.04.163 P
for the gentlewoman is young; 2.04.167 P
there lies the man, slain by young romeo, | that 3.01.144
wert thou as young as i, juliet thy love, | an 3.03. 65
the gallant, young, and noble gentleman, | the 3.05.113
hang thee, young baggage! 3.05.160
i am too young, i pray you pardon me." 3.05.186
but she's best married that dies married young. 4.05. 78
she is young and apt. TIM 1.01.132
right, | base noble, old young, coward valiant. 4.03. 30
thou ever young, fresh, lov'd, and delicate 4.03.384
an ag'd interpreter, though young in days. 5.03. 8
noble and young — | when thy first griefs were 5.04. 13
that lowliness is young ambition's ladder, JC 2.01. 22
to young octavius of the state of things. 3.01.296
come, antony, and young octavius, come, 4.03. 93
and grief that young octavius with mark antony 4.03.153
letters | that young octavius and mark antony 4.03.168
i know young bloods look for a time of rest. 4.03.262
young man, thou couldst not die more honorable. 5.01. 60
and come, young cato, let us to the field. 5.03.107
o young and noble cato, art thou down? 5.04. 9
my young remembrance cannot parallel | a fellow MAC 2.03. 62
we are yet but young in deed. 3.04.143
her young ones in her nest, against the owl. 4.02. 11
what, you egg! | young fry of treachery! 4.02. 84
i am young, but something | you may discern of 4.03. 14
to kiss the ground before young malcolm's feet, 5.08. 28
now, sir, young fortinbras, | of unimproved HAM 1.01. 95
what we have seen to-night | unto young hamlet, 1.01.170
now follows that you know young fortinbras, 1.02. 17
writ | to norway, uncle of young fortinbras — 1.02. 28
believe so much in him, that he is young, | and 1.03.124
harrow up thy soul, freeze thy young blood, 1.05. 16
being of so young days brought up with him, 2.02. 11
and my young mistress thus i did bespeak: 2.02.140
what, my young lady and mistress! 2.02.424 P
and out of haunt | this mad young man. 4.01. 19
young men will do't, if they come to't, | by 4.05. 60
with more impiteous haste | than young laertes, 4.05.102
is't possible a young maid's wits | should be as 4.05.160
was that very day that young hamlet was born — 5.01.147 P
his majesty commended him to you by young osric, 5.02.196 P
give them the foils, young osric. 5.02.259
young fortinbras, with conquest come from poland 5.02.350
sir, this young fellow's mother could; LR 1.01. 13 P
to whose young love | the vines of france and 1.01. 83
so young, and so untender? 1.01.106
so young, my lord, and true. 1.01.107
not so young, sir, to love a woman for singing, 1.04. 37 P
since my young lady's going into france, sir, 1.04. 73 P
that /it had it head bit off by it young." 1.04.216
come, i'll flesh ye, come on, young master. 2.02. 46 P
strike her young bones, | you taking airs, with 2.04.163
we that are young | shall never see so much, nor 5.03.326
subdue and poison this young maid's affections? OTH 1.03.112
with heat (the young affects | in /me defunct) 1.03.263
the knave is handsome, young, and hath all those 2.01.245 P
quarrel and offense | as my young mistress' dog. 2.03. 51
she that so young could give out such a seeming 3.03.209
for here's a young and sweating devil here 3.04. 42
patience, thou young and rose-lipp'd cherubin — 4.02. 63
those that do teach young babes | do it with 4.02.111
i have rubb'd this young quat almost to the 5.01. 11
hath kill'd a young venetian | call'd roderigo. 5.02.112
i must | to the young man send humble treaties, ANT 3.11. 62
to the young roman boy she hath sold me, and i 4.12. 48
young boys and girls | are level now with men; 4.15. 65
sir, i was then a young traveller, rather CYM 1.04. 43 P
in prison, yet | you clasp young cupid's tables. 3.02. 39
up to yond hill, | your legs are young; 3.03. 11
strains his young nerves, and puts himself in 3.03. 94
no less young, more strong, not beneath him in 4.01. 10 P
all lovers young, all lovers must | consign to 4.02.274
young one, | inform us of thy fortunes, for it 4.02.360
though cloten then but young, you see, not wore 4.04. 23
would marry a gallows and beget young gibbets, i 5.04.199 P
these two young gentlemen, that call me father 5.05.328
young prince of tyre, you have at large received PER 1.01. 1
young prince of tyre, | though by the tenor of 1.01.110
here is a thing too young for such a place, 3.01. 15
which did steal | the eyes of young and old. 4.01. 41
come, you're a young foolish sapling, and must 4.02. 87 P
come, young one, i like the manner of your 4.02.133 P
did you go to't so young? 4.06. 74 P
and like young eagles teach 'em | boldly to gaze TNK 2.02. 34
we are young and yet desire the ways of honor, 2.02. 73
and call to arms | the bold young men that, when 2.02.249
and so would any young wench, o' my conscience, 2.04. 12
vow'd her maidenhead | to a young handsome man. 2.04. 14
i have not seen so young a man so noble | (if he 2.05. 18
to this lady, | this bright young virgin. 2.05. 35
was a time | when young men went a-hunting, and 3.03. 40
the straight young boughs that blush with 3.06.243
palamon," | and "palamon was a tall young man." 4.01. 82
pray did you ever hear | of one young palamon? 4.01.117
is't not a fine young gentleman? 4.01.118
all the young maids | of our town are in love 4.01.125
two such young handsome men | shall never fall 4.02. 3
and had in her | the coy denials of young maids, 4.02. 11
and quick sweetness, | has this young prince! 4.02. 14
love, and what young maid dare cross 'em? 4.02. 40
take upon you, young sir her friend, the name of 4.03. 76 P
his hoarse throat, | abuse young lays of love. 5.01. 89
this anatomy | had by his young fair fere a boy, 5.01.116
young and unwapper'd, not halting under crimes 5.04. 10
he that has | lov'd a young handsome wench then, ep 6
"ay me," quoth venus, "young, and so unkind, VEN 187
a breeding jennet, lusty, young, and proud, 260
colt that's back'd and burthen'd being young, 419
how love makes young men thrall and old men dote 837
make the young old, the old become a child. 1152
it, | and leaves it to be mast'red by his young, LUC 863
the old bees die, the young possess their hive: 1769
thus vainly thinking that she thinks me young, PP 1. 5
but wherefore says my love that she is young? 1. 9
sitting by a brook | with young adonis, lovely, 4. 2
o, my love, my love is young! 12.10
wiser head, | neither too young nor yet unwed. 18. 6
if that the world and love were young, | and 19.17
my love shall in my verse ever live young. SON 19.14
thou hast pass'd by the ambush of young days, 70. 9
thus vainly thinking that she thinks me young, 138. 5
love is too young to know what conscience is, 151. 1
he did in the general bosom reign | of young, of LC 128
who, young and simple, would not be so lover'd? 320

YOUNGER* *(also younker)*

YOUNGER* 35 FR 0.0039 REL FR 26 V 9 P

indeed he looks younger than he did, by the loss ADO 3.02. 48 P
and younger hearings are quite ravished, | so LLL 2.01. 75
how like a younger or a prodigal | the scarfed MV 2.06. 14
is banish'd by his younger brother the new duke, AYL 1.01.100 P
to understand that your younger brother, orlando 1.01.124 P
i'll do the service of a younger man | in all 2.03. 54
having in beard is a younger brother's revenue 3.02.377 P
let the world slip, we shall ne'er be younger. SHR in.2. 144 P
the younger then is free, and not before. 1.02.262
elder, set the younger free | for our access — 1.02.266
proceed in practice with my younger daughter; 2.01.164
but now, baptista, to your younger daughter — 2.01.332
a man | might be a copy to these younger times; AWW 1.02. 46
oil, to be the snuff | of younger spirits, whose 1.02. 60
if i were but two hours younger, i'd beat thee. 2.03.253 P
but i am sure the younger of our nature, | that 3.01. 17
then let thy love be younger than thyself, | or TN 2.04. 36
why, being younger born, | doth he lay claim to JN 1.01. 71
which by thy younger brother is supplied, | and 1H4 3.02. 33
servingmen, younger sons to younger brothers, 4.02. 28 P

servingmen, younger sons to younger brothers, 4.02. 28 P
troth | sworn to us in your younger enterprise. 5.01. 71
of the elder son | succeed before the younger, i 2H6 2.02. 52
clarence will have the younger. 3H6 4.01.118
thy tears are salter than a younger man's, | and COR 4.01. 22
younger than she are happy mothers made. ROM 1.02. 12
younger than you, | here in verona, ladies of 1.03. 69
as it is common for the younger sort | to lack HAM 2.01.113
conferring them on younger strengths, while we LR 1.01. 40
the younger rises when the old doth fall. 3.03. 25
do something mingle with our younger brown, yet
ANT 4.08. 20
the younger brother, cadwal, | once arviragus, CYM 3.03. 95
cadwal, arviragus, | your younger princely son. 5.05.360
palates who, not yet /two /summers younger, PER 1.04. 39
of the people, especially of the younger sort? 4.02. 97 P

YOUNGEST 25 FR 0.0028 REL FR 19 V 6 P
my youngest boy, and yet my eldest care, | at ERR 1.01.124
i am the youngest son of sir rowland de boys. AYL 1.01. 56 P
liege, the youngest son of sir rowland de boys. 1.02.222 P
his youngest son — and would not change that 1.02.233
a liking with old sir rowland's youngest son? 1.03. 28 P
not to bestow my youngest daughter | before i SHR 1.01. 50
husband we set his youngest free for a husband, 1.01.138 P
indeed had baptista's youngest daughter. 1.01.240
his youngest daughter, beautiful bianca, | and 1.02.120
the youngest daughter, whom you hearken for, 1.02.258
look where the youngest wren of /nine comes. TN 3.02. 66 P
thus eleanor's pride dies in her youngest days. 2H6 2.03. 46
brother, though i be youngest, give me leave. 3H6 1.02. 1
for then i'll marry warwick's youngest daughter. R3 1.01.153
the youngest son of priam, a true knight, | not TRO 4.05. 96
o, well fought, my youngest brother! 5.06. 12
with his own hand did slay his youngest son, TIT 1.01.418
i am the youngest of that name, for fault of a ROM 2.04.122 P
the maid is fair, a' th' youngest for a bride, TIM 1.01.123
great rivals in our youngest daughter's love, LR 1.01. 46
thy youngest daughter does not love thee least, 1.01.152
that dowerless took | our youngest born, i could 2.04.213
a sample to the youngest, to th' more mature | a CYM 1.01. 48
his youngest, sir. TNK 2.05. 8
youngest follower of thy drum, instruct this day 5.01. 57

YOUNG–EY'D 1 FR 0.0001 REL FR 1 V 0 P
still quiring to the young–ey'd cherubins; MV 5.01. 62

YOUNGLING 3 FR 0.0003 REL FR 3 V 0 P
youngling, thou canst not love so dear as i. SHR 2.01.337
youngling, learn thou to make some meaner choice
TIT 2.01. 73
she told the youngling how god mars did try her, PP 11. 3

YOUNGLINGS 1 FR 0.0001 REL FR 1 V 0 P
i tell you, younglings, not enceladus, | with TIT 4.02. 93

YOUNGLY 2 FR 0.0002 REL FR 2 V 0 P
how youngly he began to serve his country, | how COR 2.03.236
that fresh blood which youngly thou bestow'st SON 11. 3

YOUNG'S 1 FR 0.0001 REL FR 1 V 0 P
their own lives in their young's defense? 3H6 2.02. 32

YOUNG'ST 1 FR 0.0001 REL FR 1 V 0 P
as between | the young'st and oldest thing. COR 4.06. 69

YOUNGSTER 1 FR 0.0001 REL FR 1 V 0 P
for adon's sake, a youngster proud and wild, PP 9. 4

YOUNKER *(also younger*)*

YOUNKER 2 FR 0.0002 REL FR 1 V 1 P
what, will you make a younker of me? 1H4 3.03. 80 P
trimm'd like a younker prancing to his love! 3H6 2.01. 24

/YOUR 62 FR 0.0070 REL FR 51 V 11 P

YOUR 7003 FR 0.7916 REL FR 5269 V 1734 P

/YOU'RE 1 FR 0.0001 REL FR 1 V 0 P
where now /you're both a father and a son | by PER 1.01.127

YOU'RE 27 FR 0.0030 REL FR 18 V 9 P
so: you're paid! TMP 2.01. 37 P
now, my young guest, methinks you're allycholly; TGV 4.02. 26 P
you're welcome. WIV 2.02.158 P
you're sham'd, y' are overthrown, y' are undone 3.03. 95 P
if you be more, you're none; MM 2.04.135
come, come, you're mocking; SHR 5.02.132
you're loved, sir; AWW 1.02. 67
you're pow'rful at it. WT 2.01. 28
you're liars all. 2.03.146
you're a /made old man; 3.03.120 P
youth are forgiven you, you're well to live. 3.03.121 P
you're welcome, sir. 4.04. 72
you're welcome, | most learned reverend sir, H8 2.02. 75
come, come — you're drunk. OTH 2.03.155 P
for you're fatal then | when your eyes roll so. 5.02. 37
you're my prisoner, but | your jailer shall CYM 1.01. 72
thanks, good sir, | you're kindly welcome. 1.06. 14
you're very welcome. 1.06.210
madam, you're best consider. 3.02. 77
tell him | wherein you're happy — which will 3.04.174
i see you're angry. 3.06. 55
come more, for more you're ready; 4.03. 30
farewell, you're angry. 5.03. 63
to say you're welcome were superfluous. PER 2.03. 2
come, you're a young foolish sapling, and must 4.02. 87 P
i hear say you're of honorable parts, and are 4.06. 80 P
you're like something that — what 5.01.102

/YOURS 4 FR 0.0004 REL FR 4 V 0 P
/yours /would i catch, fair hermia, ere i go; MND 1.01.187
meet for rebellion /and /such /acts /as /yours. 2H4 4.02.117
i were not yours | than /yours so branchless. ANT 3.04. 24
call it by what you will, the day is /yours, PER 2.03. 13

YOURS 265 FR 0.0299 REL FR 213 V 52 P
what to come | in yours and my discharge. TMP 2.01.254
good will is to it, | and yours it is against. 3.01. 31
king, | his brother, and yours, abide all three 5.01. 12
gentle breath of yours my sails | must fill, or ep 11
some love of yours hath writ to you in rhyme. TGV 1.02. 76
why then this may be yours — for this is but 2.01. 2
makes me the bolder to chide you for yours. 2.01. 83 P
unto the secret, nameless friend of yours; 2.01.105
and how do yours? 2.04.124
that i may compass yours. 4.02. 92
own, who is a dog as big as ten of yours, and 4.04. 58 P
that done, our day of marriage shall be yours — 5.04.172
good sir john, i sue for yours — not to charge WIV 2.02.164 P
you of such things | that want no ear but yours. MM 4.03.105
her cause and yours | i'll perfect him withal, 4.03.140
her worth worth yours. 5.01.497
what's mine is yours, and what is yours is mine. 5.01.537
what's mine is yours, and what is yours is mine. 5.01.537
or i shall break that merry sconce of yours ERR 1.02. 79
i have some marks of yours upon my pate: 1.02. 82
it worse, and 'twere such a face as yours were. ADO 1.01.137 P
of my tongue is better than a beast of yours. 1.01.140 P
and say nothing, i am yours for the walk, and 2.01. 89 P
lady, as you are mine, i am yours. 2.01.308 P
troth 's but a night–gown /in respect of yours: 3.04. 19 P
and excellent fashion, yours is worth ten on't. 3.04. 23 P
it is a man's office, but not yours. 4.01.266 P
pray write down borachio. yours, sirrah? 4.02. 12 P
and yours as blunt as the fencer's foils, which 5.02. 13 P
spite it for my sake, i will spite it for yours, 5.02. 70 P
all pride is willing pride, and yours is so. LLL 2.01. 36
the roof of this court is too high to be yours, 2.01. 93 P
and yours from long living! 2.01.192
'twere good yours did; 4.03.268
and if my face were but as fair as yours, | my 5.02. 32
o, i am yours, and all that i possess! 5.02.383
'tis yours. 5.02.677 P
our love being yours, the error that love makes 5.02.771
the error that love makes | is likewise yours. 5.02.772
i mean, that my heart unto yours /is knit, | so MND 2.02. 47
my life for yours. 3.01. 42 P
and yours of helena to me bequeath, | whom i do 3.02.166
we'll make our leisures to attend on yours. MV 1.01. 68
knows | but you, lorenzo, whether i am yours? 2.06. 31
if you choose that, then i am yours withal. 2.07. 12
and if my form lie there, | then i am yours. 2.07. 62
one half of me is yours, the other half yours — 3.02. 16
one half of me is yours, the other half yours — 3.02. 16
but if mine, then yours, | and so all yours. 3.02. 17
but if mine, then yours, | and so all yours. 3.02. 18
and so, though yours, not yours. 3.02. 20
and so, though yours, not yours. 3.02. 20
spirit | commits itself to yours to be directed, 3.02.164
is mine, to you and yours | is now converted. 3.02.166
and this same myself | are yours — my lord's! 3.02.171
my eyes, my lord, can look as swift as yours: 3.02.197
let their beds | be made as soft as yours, and 4.01. 96
nor i in yours | till i again see mine! 5.01.191
a poor unworthy brother of yours, with idleness. AYL 1.01. 33 P
the condition of my estate, to rejoice in yours. 1.02. 16 P
no more do yours. 2.03. 12
that flattering tongue of yours won me. 4.01.185 P
you, yours, orlando, to receive his daughter; 5.04. 20
to you i give myself, for i am yours. 5.04.116
to you i give myself, for i am yours. 5.04.117
yours, if you talk of tales, and so farewell. SHR 2.01.217
do what you can, yours will not be entreated. 5.02. 89
katherine, that cap of yours becomes you not; 5.02.121
my mind hath been as big as one of yours, | my 5.02.170
ability enough to make such knaveries yours. AWW 1.03. 12 P
my sword and yours are kin. 2.01. 40 P
sir, i am a poor friend of yours that loves you. 2.02. 43 P
here you shall see a countryman of yours | that 3.05. 47
i am yours | upon your will to suffer. 4.04. 29
for i by vow am so embodied yours, | that she 5.03.173
she hath that ring of yours. 5.03.209
what ring was yours, i pray you? 5.03.225
this ring you say was yours? 5.03.270
if it were yours by none of all these ways, 5.03.275
it might be yours or hers, for aught i know. 5.03.280
ours be your patience then, and yours our parts; ep 5
for what is yours to bestow is not yours to TN 1.05.188 P
what is yours to bestow is not yours to reserve. 1.05.188 P
of my fate might perhaps distemper yours; 2.01. 5 P
i hope, sir, you are, and i am yours. 3.01. 73 P
and he is yours, and his must needs be yours: 3.01.101
and he is yours, and his must needs be yours: 3.01.101
shameful cunning | which you knew none of yours. 3.01.117
i' th' world, | so soon as yours could win me. WT 1.02. 21
my lord's tricks and yours when you were boys. 1.02. 61
then didst thou utter, | "i am yours for ever." 1.02.105
you would seek us, | we are yours i' th' garden. 1.02.178
will take again your queen as yours at first, 1.02.336
courts and kingdoms | known and allied to yours. 1.02.339
your evils, | than such as most seem yours. 2.03. 57
all doubt | you'ld call your children yours. 2.03. 82
it is yours: 2.03. 96
look to your babe, my lord, 'tis yours. 2.03.126
from an infant, freely, | that it was yours. 3.02. 71
might | become your time of day — and yours, 4.04.114
become your time of day — and yours, and yours, 4.04.114
come, your hand; | and, daughter, yours. 4.04.391
but began, | give me that hand of yours to kiss. 5.03. 46
my father gave me honor, yours gave land. JN 1.01.164
sir," says question, "i, sweet sir, at yours"; 1.01.199
their privilege on earth, | and so doth yours: 1.01.262
arthur of britain england's king and yours. 2.01.311
but now in arms you strengthen it with yours. 3.01.103
good reverend father, make my person yours, 3.01.224
that his compassion may | give life to yours. 4.01. 89
that there were but a mote in yours, | a grain, 4.01. 91
by heaven, i think my sword's as sharp as yours. 4.03. 82
he is forsworn if e'er those eyes of yours 5.04. 31
your own is yours, and i am yours, and all. R2 3.03.197
your own is yours, and i am yours, and all. 3.03.197
here, | in quantity equals not one of yours. 1H4 3.01. 96
not yours, in good sooth! 3.01.247 P
that salamander of yours with fire any time this 3.03. 47 P
he would not take his band and yours, he lik'd 2H4 1.02. 33 P
fathers being so sick as yours at this time is. 2.02. 31 P
and yours, most noble bardolph! 2.02. 74 P
were two honors lost, yours and your son's: 2.03. 16
for yours, the god of heaven brighten it! 2.03. 17
our battle is more full of names than yours, 4.01.152
these tardy tricks of yours will, on my life, 4.03. 28
the crown immortally | long guard it yours! 4.05.144
your royal thoughts, make the case yours: 5.02. 91
and by god's help | and yours, the noble sinews H5 1.02.223
then, richard earl of cambridge, there is yours; 2.02. 66
there yours, lord scroop of masham; 2.02. 67
grey of northumberland, this same is yours: 2.02. 68
so perhaps did yours. 3.07. 50 P
cap that day, lest he knock that about yours. 4.01. 57 P
the day is yours. 4.07. 86
when france is mine and i am yours, then yours 5.02.175 P
am yours, then yours is france and you are mine. 5.02.176 P
mouth of all find–faults, as i will do yours, 5.02.273 P
my forces and my power of men are yours. 1H6 3.03. 83
be humble to us, call my sovereign yours, | and 4.02. 6
in yours they will, in you all hopes are lost. 4.05. 25
these words of yours draw life–blood from my 4.06. 43
what's yours? 2H6 1.03. 20 P
and so much shall you give, or off goes yours. 4.01. 17
the crown of england, father, which is yours. 3H6 1.02. 9
and yours, fair queen? 3.03.171
and mine, fair lady bona, joins with yours. 3.03.217
so come to you, and yours, as to this prince! 5.05. 82
alack, my lord, that fault is none of yours; R3 1.01. 47
this sorrow that i have, by right is yours, 1.03.171
and he to yours, and all of you to god's! 1.03.302
and for your grace, and yours, my gracious lord. 1.03.320
all duteous love | doth cherish you and yours, 2.01. 34
/god, | when i am cold in love to you or yours. 2.01. 40
take hold | on me and you, and mine and yours, 2.01.133
to me | as well i tender you and all of yours! 2.04. 72
ay, brother, to our grief, as it is yours. 3.01. 98
i hold my life as dear as /you /do yours, | and 3.02. 78
he knows no more of mine than i of yours, | or i 3.04. 11
if to reprove you for this suit of yours, | so 3.07.148
no more than with my soul i mourn for yours. 4.01. 88
as i intend more good to you and yours | than 4.04.238
than ever you /or yours by me were harm'd! 4.04.239
a noble spirit | as yours was put into you, ever H8 3.01.170
wild river break, | and stand unshaken yours. 3.02.199
pray'rs | for ever and for ever shall be yours. 3.02.427
i am yours, | you valiant offspring of great TRO 2.02.206
though less than yours in /past, must o'ertop 3.03.164
less than yours in /past, must o'ertop yours; 3.03.164
had with troy | as perfectly is ours as yours, 3.03.206
is it not yours? COR 1.02. 3
my horse to yours, no. 1.04. 2
take't, 'tis yours. what is't? 1.09. 81
your hand, and yours! 2.01.194
to show you, which shall be yours in private. 2.03. 77 P
not unlike, | each way, to better yours. 3.01. 49
by the tribunes' leave, and yours, good people, 3.01.280
i have a heart as little apt as yours, | but yet 3.02. 29
as she speaks, why, their hearts were yours; 3.02. 87
sir, i have the most cause to be glad of yours. 4.03. 51 P
this is a poor epitome of yours, | which by th' 5.03. 68
and you of yours, my lord! TIT 1.01.401
enjoy | that nice–preserved honesty of yours. 2.03.135
and yours, close fighting ere i did approach. ROM 1.01.107
well, what was yours? 1.04. 51
such a case as yours constrains a man to bow in 2.04. 52 P
'tis yours, because you lik'd it. TIM 1.02.212
it is; and yours too, isidore? 2.02. 11
were it all yours to give it in a breath, | how 2.02.153
yes, mine's three thousand crowns; what's yours? 3.04. 28
what yours? 3.04. 96
and yours? 3.04. 96
an honest poor servant of yours. 4.03.475
why should that name be sounded more than yours?
JC 1.02.143
write them together, yours is as fair a name; 1.02.144
nor for yours neither. 2.01.237
now, decius brutus, yours; 3.01.187
now yours, metellus; 3.01.187
yours, cinna; 3.01.188
and, my valiant casca, yours; 3.01.188
last, not least in love, yours, good trebonius. 3.01.189
brutus, this sober form of yours hides wrongs, 4.02. 40
why ask you? hear you aught of her in yours? 4.03.185
you to the grave, | and beggar'd yours for ever? MAC 3.01. 90
fear not yet | to take upon you what is yours. 4.03. 70
war, | the day almost itself professes yours, 5.07. 27
more appear like entertainment than yours. HAM 2.02.375 P
lord, i have remembrances of yours | that i have 3.01. 92
my pulse, as yours, doth temperately keep time, 3.04.140
lie out on't, sir, and therefore 'tis not yours; 5.01.124 P
yours. 5.02.183 P
beloved sons, be yours, which to confirm, | this LR 1.01.138
your grace, | she's there, and she is yours. 1.01.201
this milky gentleness and course of yours 1.04.341
yours in the ranks of death. 4.02. 25
this speech of yours hath mov'd me, | and shall 5.03.200
so did i yours. OTH 1.03. 52
sue to him again, and he's yours. 2.03.276 P
this hand of yours requires | a sequester from 3.04. 39
o, i see that nose of yours, but not that dog i 4.01.142 P
yours, by this hand. 4.01.175 P
he that is yours, sweet lady. 4.02.101
not rather | discredit my authority with yours, ANT 2.02. 49
the third o' th' world is yours, which with a 2.02. 63
better i were not yours | than /yours so 3.04. 23
so your desires are yours. 3.04. 28
their ships are yare, yours heavy. 3.07. 38
by the rebound of yours, a grief that /smites 5.02.104
'tis yours, and we, | your scutcheons and your 5.02.134
mine will now be yours, | and, should we shift 5.02.151
should we shift estates, yours would be mine. 5.02.152
still be't yours, | bestow it at your pleasure, 5.02.181
as that diamond of yours outlustres many i have CYM 1.04. 73 P
you may wear her in title yours; 1.04. 88 P
yours, whom in constancy you think stands so 1.04.126 P
my ten thousand ducats are yours, so is your 1.04.151 P
jewel, this your jewel, and my gold are yours — 1.04.154 P
take my pow'r i' th' court for yours. 1.06.179
of his remembrance on't, | and then she's yours. 2.03. 44
than some, whose tailors are as dear as yours, 2.03. 79
tasted her in bed, my hand | and ring is yours; 2.04. 58
if you beat us out of it, it is yours; 3.01. 80 P
to him | (after long absence), such is yours. 3.06. 73
sir, my life is yours, | i humbly set it at your 4.03. 12
you rather, mine being yours; 5.04. 26
no care of yours it is, you know 'tis ours. 5.04.100
chance of war, the day | was yours by accident. 5.05. 76
upon your finger, say | how came it yours? 5.05.138
most worthy prince, as yours, is true guiderius; 5.05.358
yours, sir, | we have given order be next our PER 2.03.109
not be more dear to my respect | than yours, my 3.03. 34
be, hath endur'd a grief | might equal yours, if 5.01. 88

and this to yours. TNK 1.05. 13
yours this way. 1.05. 13
but if it did, yours is too tart, sweet cousin. 3.03. 26
will be seen, | and quickly, yours or mine. 3.06. 35
that face of yours | will bear the curses else 3.06.186
beside, i have another oath 'gainst yours, | of 3.06.230
yours to command i' th' way of honesty. 5.02. 71
i see one eye of yours conceives a tear, | the 5.03.137
no longer yours than you yourself here live: SON 13. 2
but were some child of yours alive that time, 17.13
were by my unkindness shaken | as i by yours, y' 120. 6
mine ransoms yours, and yours must ransom me. 120.14
mine ransoms yours, and yours must ransom me. 120.14
"'o, then advance of yours that phraseless hand, LC 225

/YOURSELF 1 FR 0.0001 REL FR 1 V 0 P
were | /yourself again after yourself's decease, SON 13. 7

YOURSELF 299 FR 0.0338 REL FR 233 V 66 P
and make yourself ready in your cabin for the TMP 1.01. 25 P
sir, | i fear you have done yourself some wrong; 1.02.444
sir, you may thank yourself for this great loss, 2.01.124
pray now rest yourself, | he's safe for these 3.01. 20
form a shape, | besides yourself, to like of. 3.01. 57
whereof, henceforth carry your letters yourself: TGV 1.01.146 P
what are you reasoning with yourself? 2.01.142 P
to yourself; why, she woos you by a figure. 2.01.148 P
she, when she hath made you write to yourself? 2.01.153 P
yourself, sweet lady, for you gave the fire. 2.04. 37 P
to see such lovers, thurio, as yourself: 2.04. 97
i'll die on him that says so but yourself. 2.04.114
as many, worthy lady, to yourself. 4.03. 7
there is but three skirts for yourself, in my WIV 1.01. 29 P
mistress anne, yourself shall go first. 1.01.307 P
you do yourself wrong indeed la! 1.01.313 P
sith you yourself know how easy it is to be such 2.02.188 P
you prescribe to yourself very preposterously. 2.02.240 P
shallow, you have yourself been a great fighter, 2.03. 42 P
you have show'd yourself a wise physician, and 2.03. 53 P
if you know yourself clear, why, i am glad of it 3.03.116 P
you wrong yourself too much. 3.03.167 P
you do yourself mighty wrong, master ford. 3.03.207 P
come, trouble not yourself. 3.04. 88
who's at home besides yourself? 4.02. 13 P
finding yourself desir'd of such a person, MM 2.04. 91
therefore prepare yourself to death. 3.01.167 P
only refer yourself to this advantage: 3.01.245 P
upon you anon for some advantage to yourself. 4.01. 24 P
do you persuade yourself that i respect you? 4.01. 52
well, go, prepare yourself. 4.02. 69
put not yourself into amazement how these things 4.02.204 P
reveal yourself to him. 5.01. 28
hear me yourself; 5.01. 30
and when you have | a business for yourself, 5.01. 81
the warrant's for yourself; take heed to't. 5.01. 83
and about evening come yourself alone | to know ERR 3.01. 96
what please yourself, sir; 3.02.170
then you will bring the chain to her yourself? 4.01. 40
all | but for their owner, master, and yourself. 4.01. 92
and, not without some scandal to yourself, 5.01. 15
o mistress, mistress, shift and save yourself! 5.01.168
i will send for him, and question him yourself. ADO 1.02. 19 P
but by the fair weather that you make yourself. 1.03. 24 P
take their examination yourself, and bring it me 3.05. 49 P
if you go on thus, you will kill yourself, | and 5.01. 1
wisdom thus to second grief | against yourself. 5.01. 3
yet bend not all the harm upon yourself; 5.01. 39
content yourself. 5.01. 87
choose your revenge yourself, | impose me to 5.01.272
i beseech your worship to correct yourself, for 5.01.322 P
this article, my liege, yourself must break, LLL 1.01.133
french king's daughter with yourself to speak — 1.01.135
yourself, held precious in the world's esteem, 2.01. 4
as you shall deem yourself lodg'd in my heart, 2.01.173
we choose by the horns, yourself come not near. 4.01.115
joshua, yourself; 5.01.126 P
look how you butt yourself in these sharp mocks! 5.02.251
look you arm yourself | to fit your fancies to MND 1.01.117
to leave the city and commit yourself | into the 2.01.215
do not fret yourself too much in the action, 4.01. 13 P
it, | and if it stand, as you yourself still do, MV 1.01.136
yourself, renowned prince, then stood as fair 2.01. 20
i would not lose you, and, you know yourself, 3.02. 5
with leave, bassanio, i am half yourself, | and 3.02.248
if you saw yourself with your eyes, or knew AYL 1.02.175 P
your eyes, or knew yourself with your judgment, 1.02.176 P
you, niece, provide yourself; 1.03. 87
to bear your griefs yourself, and leave me out; 1.03.103
why do you infect yourself with them? 3.02.114 P
in your accoustrements, as loving yourself, than 3.02.383 P
mistress, know yourself, down on your knees, 3.05. 57
draw a belief from you, to do yourself good, and 5.02. 58 P
me, | you'll give yourself to this most faithful 5.04. 14
i am, in all affected as yourself, | glad that SHR 1.01. 26
as firmly as yourself were still in place, | yea 1.02.156
good sister, wrong me not, nor wrong yourself, 2.01. 1
yourself and all the world, | that talk'd of her 2.01.290
wife, | and sent you hither so unlike yourself? 3.02.104
keep your hundred pounds to yourself, he shall 5.01. 23 P
'tis well, sir, that you hunted for yourself; 5.02. 55
discharg'd this honestly, keep it to yourself. AWW 1.03.123 P
but if yourself, | whose aged honor cites a 1.03.209
you have restrain'd yourself within the list of 2.01. 51 P
good, | to make yourself a son out of my blood. 2.03. 97
did you find me in yourself, sir, or were you 2.04. 33 P
is it yourself? 3.05. 43
and you shall find yourself to be well thank'd, 5.01. 36
that you are well acquainted with yourself, 5.03.106
finger, | unless she gave it to yourself in bed, 5.03.110
it is perchance that you yourself were saved. TN 1.02. 6
assure yourself, after our ship did split, 1.02. 9
but you must confine yourself within the modest 1.03. 8 P
certain, if you are she, you do usurp yourself; 1.05.188 P
me my pains, to have taken it away yourself. 2.02. 6 P
if you can separate yourself and your 2.03. 98 P
how have you made division of yourself? 5.01.222
for, to yourself, what you do know, you must, WT 1.02.379
or both yourself and me | cry lost, and so good 1.02.410
ones suffer, | yourself, your queen, your son. 2.01.129
you'll leave yourself | hardly one subject. 2.03.111
such, | so and no other, as yourself commanded; 3.02. 66
address yourself to entertain them sprightly, 4.04. 53
and present yourself | that which you are, 4.04. 67
and there present yourself and your fair 4.04.544
you must retire yourself | into some covert. 4.04.649
if you had not taken yourself with the manner. 4.04.728 P
forget your evil, | with them, forgive yourself. 5.01. 6
sir, you yourself | have said and writ so, but 5.01. 98
yourself, assisted with your honor'd friends, 5.01.113
compare our faces, and be judge yourself. JN 1.01. 79
and tell me how you would bestow yourself. 3.01.225
come, boy, prepare yourself. 4.01. 89
see else yourself, | there is no malice in this 4.01.107
i would not have you, lord, forget yourself, 4.03. 83
with whom yourself, myself, and other lords, 5.07. 93
vex not yourself, nor strive not with your R2 2.01. 3
and so your follies fight against yourself. 3.02.182
but come yourself with speed to us again, | for 1H4 1.01.105
yourself and i will not be there; 1.02.164 P
kitten'd, though yourself had never been born. 3.01. 19
in my heart's love hath no man than yourself. 4.01. 8
and pardon absolute for yourself and these 4.03. 50
as you yourself have forg'd against yourself 5.01. 68
as you yourself have forg'd against yourself 5.01. 68
and will you yet call yourself young? 2H4 1.02.185 P
hang yourself, you muddy cunger, hang yourself! 2.04. 53 P
hang yourself, you muddy cunger, hang yourself! 2.04. 54 P
pray ye pacify yourself, sir john. 2.04. 80 P
discharge yourself of our company, pistol. 2.04.137 P
sir john, sir john, do not yourself wrong. 3.02.254 P
wherefore do you so ill translate yourself | out 4.01. 47
my sovereign lord, cheer up yourself, look up. 4.04.113
behold yourself so by a son disdained; 5.02. 95
do all expect that you should rouse yourself, H5 1.02.123
that you divest yourself, and lay apart | the 2.04. 78
being as good a man as yourself, both in the 3.02.129 P
you must first go yourself to hazard, ere you 3.07. 87 P
my sovereign lord, bestow yourself with speed. 4.03. 68
your majesty came not like yourself. 4.08. 50 P
pistol, which you and yourself, and all the 5.01. 6 P
for your partaker pole, and you yourself, | i'll 1H6 2.04.100
than can yourself yourself in twain divide. 4.05. 49
than can yourself yourself in twain divide. 4.05. 49
and you yourself shall steer the happy helm. 2H6 1.03.100
protector, see to't well, protect yourself. 2.01. 52
if you mean to save yourself from whipping, leap 2.01.140 P
whereof you cannot easily purge yourself. 3.01.135
that you will clear yourself from all suspense. 3.01.140
and as for you yourself, our quondam queen, 3H6 3.03.153
in choosing for yourself, you show'd your 4.01. 61
marriage | i may not prove inferior to yourself. 4.01.122
nor how to shroud yourself from enemies? 4.03. 40
if you'll not here proclaim yourself our king, 4.07. 54
have you breath'd your curse against yourself. R3 1.03.239
come, you deceive yourself, | 'tis he that sends 1.04.242
madam, yourself is not exempt from this; 2.01. 18
withdraw yourself a while, i'll go with you. 3.04. 41
ay, i thank god, my father, and yourself. 4.04.156
ay, if yourself's remembrance wrong yourself. 4.04.421
be to yourself | as you would to your friend. H8 1.01.135
for your foe so hot | that it do singe yourself. 1.01.141
more stronger to direct you than yourself, | if 1.01.147
that you would love yourself, and in that love 1.02. 14
spread then, | even of yourself, lord cardinal. 2.02.125
make yourself mirth with your particular fancy, 2.03.101
i do profess | you speak not like yourself, who 2.04. 85
as't please | yourself pronounce their office. 2.04.115
long, be pleas'd yourself to say | how far you 2.04.211
how you may hurt yourself — ay, utterly | grow 3.01.160
hands, and to confine yourself | to asher–house, 3.02.230
you cannot with such freedom purge yourself 5.01.102
to bring together | yourself and your accusers, 5.01.120
have misdemean'd yourself, and not a little: 5.02. 49
sir, you of troy, call you yourself aeneas? TRO 1.03.245
yourself shall feast with us before you go, 1.03.308
you cannot shun yourself. 3.02.146
sweet, rouse yourself, and the weak wanton cupid 3.03.222
dear, trouble not yourself, the morn is cold. 4.02. 1
go hang yourself, you naughty mocking uncle! 4.02. 25
dead | since first i saw yourself and diomed 4.05.215
o, contain yourself; 5.02.180
or express yourself in a more comfortable sort. COR 1.03. 1 P
fie, you confine yourself most unreasonably. 1.03. 76 P
if 'gainst yourself you be incens'd, we'll put 1.09. 56
not one amongst us, save yourself, but says | he 2.03.162
'tis a sore upon us | you cannot tent yourself. 3.01.235
or defend yourself | by calmness or by absence. 3.02. 94
arm yourself | to answer mildly; 3.02.138
and to wind | yourself into a power tyrannical, 3.03. 65
of him | have borne the action of yourself, 4.07. 15
of full time | may show like all yourself. 5.03. 70
patient yourself, madam, and pardon me. TIT 1.01.121
the empress, the midwife, and yourself. 4.02.143
by having him, making yourself no less. ROM 1.03. 94
how long is't now since last yourself and i 1.05. 32
henceforward do your messages yourself. 2.05. 64
here comes your father, tell him so yourself; 3.05.124
heaven and yourself | had part in this fair maid 4.05. 66
made your minister | thus to excuse yourself. TIM 2.02.132
wealth | to requite me by making rich yourself. 4.03.522
and since you know you cannot see yourself | so JC 1.02. 67
will modestly discover to yourself | that of 1.02. 69
that of yourself which you yet know not of. 1.02. 70
and put on fear, and cast yourself in wonder, 1.03. 60
you had but that opinion of yourself | which 2.01. 92
that you unfold to me, yourself, your half, 2.01.274
am i yourself | but, as it were, in sort or 2.01.282
you wrong'd yourself to write in such a case. 4.03. 6
you yourself | are much condemn'd to have an 4.03. 9
you forget yourself | to hedge me in. 4.03. 29
abler than yourself | to make conditions. 4.03. 31
now, brutus, thank yourself; 5.01. 45
the hope drunk | wherein you dress'd yourself? MAC 1.07. 36
my dearest coz, | i pray you school yourself. 4.02. 15
nay, answer me. stand and unfold yourself. HAM 1.01. 2
truster of your own report | against yourself. 1.02.173
and you yourself shall keep the key of it. 1.03. 86
and you yourself | have of your audience been 1.03. 92
you do not understand yourself so clearly | as 1.03. 96
think yourself a baby | that you have ta'en 1.03.105
tender yourself more dearly, | or (not to crack 1.03.107
observe his inclination in yourself. 2.01. 68
honesty to have it thus set down, for yourself, 2.02.202 P
confess yourself to heaven, | repent what's past 3.04.149
to all, | to you yourself, to us, to every one. 4.01. 15
not there, seek him i' th' other place yourself. 4.03. 35 P
save yourself, my lord! 4.05. 99
to show yourself indeed your father's son | more 4.07.125
that in a dozen passes between yourself and him, 5.02.166 P
give but that portion which yourself propos'd, LR 1.01.242
do you busy yourself with that? 1.02.142 P
bethink yourself wherein you may have offended 1.02.159 P
by what yourself too late have spoke and done, 1.04.207
never afflict yourself to know more of it, | but 1.04.291
advise yourself. 2.01. 27
draw, seem to defend yourself; 2.01. 30
discerns your state | better than you yourself. 2.04.150
where have you hid yourself? 5.03.180
be judge yourself | whether i in any just term OTH 1.01. 38
straight satisfy yourself. 1.01.137
you shall yourself read in the bitter letter 1.03. 68
let me speak like yourself, and lay a sentence, 1.03.199
they were | when you yourself did part them. 2.03.239
at all, unless you repute yourself such a loser. 2.03.271 P
confess yourself freely to her; 2.03.318 P
nor build yourself a trouble | out of his 3.03.150
do you withdraw yourself a little while, | he 4.01. 56
apart, | confine yourself but in a patient list. 4.01. 75
do but encave yourself, | and mark the fleers, 4.01. 81
assure yourself i will seek satisfaction of you. 4.02.199 P
if you dare do yourself a profit and a right. 4.02.232 P
you shall think yourself bound to put it on him. 4.02.241 P
beseech you, sir, trouble yourself no further. 4.03. 1
if you bethink yourself of any crime 5.02. 26
you praise yourself | by laying defects of ANT 2.02. 54
make yourself my guest | whilst you abide here. 2.02.243
now, sirrah; you do wish yourself in egypt? 2.03. 10
good madam, keep yourself within yourself, | the 2.05. 75
good madam, keep yourself within yourself, | the 2.05. 75
you requested, | yourself shall go between 's. 3.04. 25
give up yourself merely to chance and hazard, 3.07. 47
antony, | and put yourself under his shroud, 3.13. 71
there lock yourself, and send him word you are 4.13. 4
do not yourself such wrong, who are in this 5.02. 40
my master's bounty by | th' undoing of yourself. 5.02. 44
your loss is as yourself, great; 5.02.101
if you apply yourself to our intents, | which 5.02.126
you shall bereave yourself | of my good purposes 5.02.130
dispose you as | yourself shall give us counsel. 5.02.187
were you but riding forth to air yourself, CYM 1.01.110
sir, | harm not yourself with your vexation, | i 1.01.134
and make yourself some comfort | out of your 1.01.155
frame yourself | to orderly /solicits, and be 2.03. 46
first, make yourself but like one. 3.04.167
'fore noble lucius | present yourself, desire 3.04.173
yourself | so out of thought, and thereto so 4.04. 32
or to take upon yourself that which i am sure 5.04.181 P
'twould braid yourself too near for me to tell PER 1.01. 93
let your breath cool yourself, telling your 1.01.159
such griefs as you yourself do lay upon yourself 1.02. 66
griefs as you yourself do lay upon yourself. 1.02. 66
wrong not yourself then, noble helicane; 2.04. 26
i love the king your father, and yourself, 4.01. 32
daughters, | and shortly you may keep yourself. TNK 2.06. 39
when you shall stretch yourself, and say but, 3.01. 87
or, if you feel yourself not fitting yet | and 3.06. 36
i am like to know your husband 'fore yourself 5.03. 37
give up yourself to form, obey the magistrate, STM II.C 146
o that you were yourself! SON 13. 1
no longer yours than you yourself here live: 13. 2
and fortify yourself in your decay | with means 16. 3
can make you live yourself in eyes of men: 16.12
to give away yourself keeps yourself still, 16.13
to give away yourself keeps yourself still, 16.13
so, till the judgment that yourself arise, | you 55.13
that you yourself may privilege your time | to 58.10
belong | yourself to pardon of self–doing crime. 58.12
that you yourself, being extant, well might show 83. 6

YOURSELF'S 2 FR 0.0002 REL FR 2 V 0 P
ay, if yourself's remembrance wrong yourself. R3 4.04.421
were | /yourself again after yourself's decease, SON 13. 7

/YOURSELVES 1 FR 0.0001 REL FR 0 V 1 P
you ought to consider with /yourselves, to bring MND 3.01. 29 P

YOURSELVES 75 FR 0.0084 REL FR 64 V 11 P
yourselves in order set; WIV 5.05. 77
how answer you for yourselves? ADO 4.02. 23 P
all, | withdraw into a chamber by yourselves, 5.04. 11
price you yourselves; what buys your company? LLL 5.02.224
speak for yourselves, my wit is at an end. 5.02.430
of something nearly that concerns yourselves. MND 1.01.126
masters, spread yourselves. 1.02. 15 P
we sing, | feed yourselves with questioning; AYL 5.04.138
and so i pray you all to think yourselves. SHR 2.01.113
be mad and merry, or go hang yourselves; 3.02.226
him down again, with the breach yourselves made, AWW 1.01.125 P
though you understand it not yourselves, no 4.01. 4 P
spleen, and will laugh yourselves into stitches, TN 3.02. 68 P
go hang yourselves all! 3.04.123 P
us, inform yourselves | we need no more of your WT 2.01.167
i pray now call her. | withdraw yourselves. 2.02. 15
than a wild dedication of yourselves | to 4.04.566
(our part therein we banish with yourselves) R2 1.03.181
withdraw yourselves, and leave us here alone. 5.03. 28
you have horses for yourselves. 1H4 1.02.128 P
your banish'd honors and restore yourselves 1.03.181
and, as we hear you do reform yourselves, | we 2H4 5.05. 68
that owe yourselves, your lives, and services H5 1.02. 34
therefore to our best mercy give yourselves, 3.03. 3
what is't to me, when you yourselves are cause, 3.03. 19
quiet yourselves, i pray, and be at peace. 1H6 4.01.115
mouths | to raise a mutiny betwixt yourselves. 4.01.131
you to break your necks or hang yourselves! 5.04. 91
we come to be informed by yourselves | what the 5.04.118
have you yourselves, somerset, buckingham, 2H6 1.01. 85
now show yourselves men, 'tis for liberty. 4.02.183

god should be so obdurate as yourselves, | how 4.07.115
assure yourselves, will never be unkind. 4.09. 19
disperse yourselves. 5.01. 45
if you oppose yourselves to match lord warwick. 5.01.156
heed, lest by your heat you burn yourselves. 5.01.160
fly, lords, and save yourselves, | for warwick 3H6 5.02. 48
serve me well, and teach yourselves that duty! R3 1.03.252
two such murtherers as yourselves came to you, 1.04.259
i guess, | upon the like devotion as yourselves, 4.01. 9
how dare you thrust yourselves | into my private H8 2.02. 64
my commission | bid ye so far forget yourselves? 5.02.177
not a stroke, but keep yourselves in breath, TRO 5.07. 3
honest neighbors, | will you undo yourselves? COR 1.01. 63
must | confess yourselves wondrous malicious, 1.01. 88
from them to you, | and no way from yourselves. 1.01.154
itch of your opinion | make yourselves scabs? 1.01.166
you know neither me, yourselves, nor any thing. 2.01. 67 P
your voices might | be curses to yourselves? 2.03.185
come, try upon yourselves what you have seen me. 3.01.224
beating your officers, cursing yourselves, 3.03. 78
feels, | making /not reservation of yourselves, 3.03.130
that will not suffer you to square yourselves, TIT 2.01.124
attends you, | please you to dispose yourselves. TIM 1.02.156
you do yourselves | much wrong, you bate too 1.02.205
ask me what you are, and do not know yourselves. 2.02. 65 P
you do yourselves but wrong to stir me up, | let 3.04. 53
for your own gifts, make yourselves prais'd; 3.06. 71 P
love not yourselves, away, | rob one another. 4.03.444
whom you yourselves shall set out for reproof 5.04. 57
brutus, | and, friends, disperse yourselves; JC 2.01.222
you have said, and show yourselves true romans. 2.01.223
i tell you that which you yourselves do know, 3.02.224
to walk abroad and recreate yourselves. 3.02.251
come, | revenge yourselves alone on cassius, 4.03. 94
and come yourselves, and bring messala with you 4.03.141
see, and then speak yourselves. MAC 2.03. 73
i will advise you where to plant yourselves, 3.01.128
resolve yourselves apart, | i'll come to you 3.01.137
you one face, and you make yourselves another. HAM 3.01.143 P
allow obedience, if you yourselves are old, LR 2.04.191
trouble yourselves no further; ANT 2.04. 1
lovers, | cast yourselves in a body decently, TNK 3.05. 20
even by the rule you have among yourselves, STM II.C 46
busy yourselves in skill–contending schools, LUC 1018

YOU'ST 1 FR 0.0001 REL FR 1 V 0 P
patience awhile, you'st hear the belly's answer. COR 1.01.126

/YOUTH 1 FR 0.0001 REL FR 1 V 0 P
now heavens forfend such scarcity of /youth! TRO 1.03.302

YOUTH 300 FR 0.0339 REL FR 244 V 56 P
home–keeping youth have ever homely wits. TGV 1.01. 2
wear out thy youth with shapeless idleness. 1.01. 8
to whisper and conspire against my youth? 1.02. 43
would suffer him to spend his youth at home, 1.03. 5
age, | in having known no travel in his youth. 1.03. 16
worthy his youth and nobleness of birth. 1.03. 33
forswear not thyself, sweet youth, for i am not 2.05. 3 P
to be fantastic may become a youth | of greater 2.07. 47
knowing that tender youth is soon suggested, | i 3.01. 34
such as the fury of ungovern'd youth | thrust 4.01. 43
why, my pretty youth? 4.02. 58 P
partly that i have need of such a youth | that 4.04. 64
our youth got me to play the woman's part, | and 4.04.160
she is beholding to thee, gentle youth. 4.04.173
here, youth, there is my purse; 4.04.176
we have some salt of our youth in us, we are the WIV 2.03. 48 P
he capers, he dances, he has eyes of youth; 3.02. 67 P
youth in a basket! 4.02.116 P
for in her youth | there is a prone and MM 1.02.182
than the aims and ends | of burning youth. 1.03. 6
in idle price to haunt assemblies | where youth, 1.03. 10
to geld and splay all the youth of the city? 2.01.231 P
who, falling in the flaws of her own youth, 2.03. 11
thou hast nor youth nor age, | but as it were an 3.01. 32
for all thy blessed youth | becomes as aged, and 3.01. 34
and deliberate word | nips youth i' th' head, 3.01. 90
save that his riotous youth with dangerous sense 4.04. 29
i see by you i am a sweet–fac'd youth. ERR 5.01.419
he that hath a beard is more than a youth, and ADO 2.01. 36 P
and he that is more than a youth is not for me, 2.01. 38 P
a man loves the meat in his youth that he cannot 2.03.239 P
have vanquish'd the resistance of her youth, 4.01. 46
his may of youth and bloom of lustihood. 5.01. 76
speaks like a most thankful and reverent youth, 5.01.316 P
the young dumaine, a well–accomplish'd youth, LLL 2.01. 56
vow, alack, for youth unmeet, | youth so apt to 4.03.111
youth unmeet, | youth so apt to pluck a sweet. 4.03.112
flat treason 'gainst the kingly state of youth. 4.03.289
do you not educate youth at the charge–house on 5.01. 82 P
the blood of youth burns not with such excess 5.02. 73
stir up the athenian youth to merriments, MND 1.01. 12
of strong prevailment in unhardened youth. 1.01. 35
know of your youth, examine well your blood, 1.01. 68
hath rotted ere his youth attain'd a beard. 2.01. 95
lady is in love | with a disdainful youth; 2.01.261
and the youth, mistook by me, | pleading for a 3.02.112
anon comes pyramus, sweet youth and tall, | and 5.01.144
i owe you much, and, like a willful youth, MV 1.01.146
such a hare is madness the youth, to skip o'er 1.02. 20 P
so full of unmannerly sadness in his youth. 1.02. 50 P
if that the youth of my new int'rest here | have 3.02.221
and speak of frays | like a fine bragging youth, 3.04. 69
repair thy wit, good youth, or it will fall | to 4.01.141
i pray you show my youth old shylock's house. 4.02. 11
now, by this hand, i gave it to a youth, | a 5.01.161
since the youth will not be entreated, his own AYL 1.02.149 P
of the challenger's youth i would fain dissuade 1.02.160 P
do, to try with him the strength of my youth. 1.02.172 P
but fare thee well, thou art a gallant youth. 1.02.229
gone, | that youth is surely in their company. 2.02. 16
o unhappy youth, | come not within these doors! 2.03. 16
for in my youth i never did apply | hot and 2.03. 48
though in thy youth thou wast as true a lover 2.04. 26
where dwell you, pretty youth? 3.02.334 P
me to speak, who was in his youth an inland man, 3.02.345 P
fair youth, i would i could make thee believe i 3.02.385 P
i swear to thee, youth, by the white hand of 3.02.394 P
which time would i, being but a moonish youth, 3.02.410 P
i would not be cur'd, youth. 3.02.425 P
with all my heart, good youth. 3.02.433 P
but all's brave that youth mounts and folly 3.04. 45 P
sweet youth, i pray you chide a year together, 3.05. 64
know'st thou the youth that spoke to me yerwhile 3.05.105
it is a pretty youth — not very pretty — | but 3.05.113
i prithee, pretty youth, let me /be better 4.01. 1 P
for, good youth, he went but forth to wash him 4.01.103 P
my errand is to you, fair youth, | my gentle 4.03. 6
whether that thy youth and kind | will the 4.03. 59
and to that youth he calls his rosalind | he 4.03. 92
unto the shepherd youth | that he in sport doth 4.03.155
be of good cheer, youth. 4.03.163
there is a youth here in the forest lays claim 5.01. 6 P
youth, you have done me much ungentleness, | to 5.02. 77
shepherd, tell this youth what 'tis to love. 5.02. 83
within my house, | fit to instruct her youth. SHR 1.01. 95
but youth in ladies' eyes that flourisheth. 2.01.340
youth, thou bear'st thy father's face; AWW 1.02. 19
in his youth | he had the wit which i can well 1.02. 31
doth to our rose of youth rightly belong; 1.03.130
love's strong passion is impress'd in youth. 1.03.133
whose aged honor cites a virtuous youth, | did 1.03.210
youth, beauty, wisdom, courage — all | that 2.01.181
thou be'st not an ass, i am a youth of fourteen. 2.03.101 P
and the careless lapse | of youth and ignorance; 2.03.164
if the quick fire of youth light not your mind, 4.02. 5
the unbak'd and doughy youth of a nation in his 4.05. 3 P
natural rebellion, done i' th' blade of youth, 5.03. 6
and boarded her i' th' wanton way of youth. 5.03.211
therefore, good youth, address thy gait unto her TN 1.04. 15
she will attend it better in thy youth | than in 1.04. 27
of great estate, of fresh and stainless youth; 1.05.259
if that the youth will come this way to–morrow, 1.05.305
since the youth of the count's was to–day with 2.03.132 P
y' are servant to the count orsino, youth. 3.01.100
be not afraid, good youth, i will not have you, 3.01.131
and yet, when wit and youth is come to harvest, 3.01.132
by innocence i swear, and by my youth, | i have 3.01.157
did show favor to the youth in your sight only 3.02. 18 P
you should have bang'd the youth into dumbness. 3.02. 23 P
me the count's youth to fight with him, hurt him 3.02. 34 P
and by all means stir on the youth to an answer. 3.02. 59 P
and his opposite, the youth, bears in his visage 3.02. 64 P
for youth is bought more oft than begg'd or 3.04. 3
"youth, whatsoever thou art, thou art but a 3.04.147 P
ignorant, will breed no terror in the youth; 3.04.189 P
(as i know his youth will aptly receive it) into 3.04.193 P
for your opposite hath in him what youth, 3.04.232 P
this youth that you see here | i snatch'd one 3.04.359
three months this youth hath tended upon me, 5.01. 99
hath newly pass'd between this youth and me. 5.01.155
or that youth would sleep out the rest; WT 3.03. 60 P
if the sins of your youth are forgiven you, 3.03.121 P
would wish | this youth should say 'twere well, 4.04.102
but that your youth, | and the true blood which 4.04.147
were i the fairest youth | that ever made eye 4.04.373
my liege, | your eye hath too much youth in't. 5.01.225
and deny his youth | the rich advantage of good JN 4.02. 59
i do commit his youth | to your direction. 4.02. 67
that ever fury breath'd, | the youth says well. 5.02.128
had i thy youth and cause, i would not stay. R2 1.03.305
in wholesome counsel to his unstayed youth? 2.01. 2
than they whom youth and ease have taught to 2.01. 10
the open ear of youth doth always listen; 2.01. 20
deal mildly with his youth, | for young hot 2.01. 69
were i but now lord of such hot youth | as when 2.03. 99
up | the crest of youth against your dignity. 1H4 1.01. 99
they hate us youth. 2.02. 85 P
the faster it grows, /yet youth, the more it is 2.04.401 P
that villainous abominable misleader of youth, 2.04.463 P
wherein my youth | hath faulty wand'red and 3.02. 26
that i shall make this northren youth exchange 3.02.145
it hath the excuse of youth and heat of blood, 5.02. 17
and chid his truant youth with such a grace | as 5.02. 62
o, harry, thou hast robb'd me of my youth! 5.04. 77
though not clean past your youth, have yet some 2H4 1.02. 97 P
and we that are in the vaward of our youth, i 1.02.177 P
you set down your name in the scroll of youth, 1.02.179 P
to approve my youth further, i will not. 1.02.191 P
wherein the noble youth did dress themselves: 2.03. 22
the happiest youth, viewing his progress through 3.01. 54
but prate to me of the wildness of his youth, 3.02.305 P
led on by bloody youth, guarded with rage, | and 4.01. 34
we will our youth lead on to higher fields, 4.04. 3
to weeds, | and he, the noble image of my youth, 4.04. 55
o foolish youth, | thou seek'st the greatness 4.05. 96
you shall be as a father to my youth, | my voice 5.02.118
the courses of his youth promis'd it not. H5 1.01. 24
liege | is in the very may–morn of his youth, 1.02.120
says that you savor too much of your youth, 1.02.250
now all the youth of england are on fire, | and 2.pr. 1
by a vain, giddy, shallow, humorous youth, 2.04. 28
that end, | as matching to his youth and vanity, 2.04.130
sweat drops of gallant youth in our rich fields! 3.05. 25
their bodies to the lust of english youth | to 3.05. 30
me | and hath detain'd me all my flow'ring youth 1H6 2.05. 56
and shall my youth be guilty of such blame? 4.05. 47
my death's revenge, thy youth, and england's 4.06. 39
"thou maiden youth, be vanquish'd by a maid!" 4.07. 38
for that | my tender youth was never yet attaint 5.05. 81
did my brother henry spend his youth, | his 2H6 1.01. 78
but that in all my life, when i was a youth. 2.01. 97
corrupted the youth of the realm in erecting a 4.07. 33 P
to lose thy youth in peace, and to achieve | the 5.02. 46
and, like a gallant in the brow of youth, 5.03. 4
how well resembles it the prime of youth, 3H6 2.01. 23
till youth take leave and leave you to the 3.02. 35
what youth is that | of whom you seem to have so 4.06. 65
look in his youth to have him so cut off | as, 5.05. 66
die in his youth by like untimely violence! R3 1.03.200
your children were vexation to your youth, | but 4.04.305
ungovern'd youth, to wail it /in their age; 4.04.392
think how thou stab'st me in my prime of youth 5.03.119
o admirable youth! TRO 1.02.235 P
gentleness, virtue, youth, liberality, and 1.02.254 P
his youth in flood, | i'll prove this troth with 1.03.300
whose youth and freshness | wrinkles apollo's, 2.02. 78
to keep her constancy in plight and youth, 3.02.161
one that knows the youth | even to his inches, 4.05.110
cruel way | through ranks of greekish youth, and 4.05.185
faith, young troilus, doff thy harness, youth, 5.03. 31
cold statues of the youth, and, in a word, 5.10. 20
when youth with comeliness pluck'd all gaze his COR 1.03. 7 P
hark, our drums | are bringing forth our youth. 1.04. 16
a loving nurse, a mother to his youth. TIT 1.01.332
whose youth was spent | in dangerous wars whilst 3.01. 2
my youth can better spare my blood than you, 3.01.165
and would not, but in fury, fright my youth, 4.01. 24
of his armory | to gratify your honorable youth, 4.02. 12
myself, | the vigor and the picture of my youth: 4.02.108
him | to be a virtuous and well–govern'd youth. ROM 1.05. 68
but where unbruised youth with unstuff'd brain 2.03. 37
good gentle youth, tempt not a desp'rate man. 5.03. 59
i beseech thee, youth, | put not another sin 5.03. 61
a lanthorn, slaught'red youth; 5.03. 84
than with that hand that cut thy youth in twain 5.03. 99
do instruct us | what levity's in youth. TIM 1.01.134
creep in the minds and marrows of our youth, 4.01. 26
bring down rose–cheek'd youth | to the /tub–fast 4.03. 87
melted down thy youth | in different beds of 4.03.256
flatteries | that follow youth and opulency. 5.01. 37
speaks it, | in pity of our aged and our youth, 5.01.176
is often thus, | and hath been from his youth. MAC 3.04. 53
blood, | a violet in the youth of primy nature, HAM 1.03. 7
and in the morn and liquid dew of youth 1.03. 41
youth to itself rebels, though none else near. 1.03. 44
but know, thou noble youth, | the serpent that 1.05. 38
past | that youth and observation copied there, 1.05.101
noted and most known | to youth and liberty. 2.01. 24
crimes | the youth you breathe of guilty, be 2.01. 44
and sith so neighbored to his youth and havior, 2.02. 12
and truly in my youth i suff'red much extremity 2.02.189 P
by the consonancy of our youth, by the 2.02.285 P
that unmatch'd form and stature of blown youth 3.01.159
to flaming youth let virtue be as wax | and melt 3.04. 84
a very riband in the cap of youth, | yet needful 4.07. 77
too, for youth no less becomes | the light and 4.07. 78
"in youth, when i did love, did love, 5.01. 61
that is laertes, a very noble youth. mark. 5.01.224
let it stamp wrinkles in her brow of youth, LR 1.04.284
maugre thy strength, place, youth, and eminence, 5.03.132
by which the property of youth and maidhood OTH 1.01.172
abus'd her delicate youth with drugs or minerals 1.02. 74
distressful stroke | that my youth suffer'd. 1.03.158
she must change for youth; 1.03.350 P
the gravity and stillness of your youth | the 2.03.191
blood to think on't, and flush youth revolt. ANT 1.04. 52
and carry back to sicily much tall youth | that 2.06. 7
tell him he wears the rose | of youth upon him; 3.13. 21
like the spirit of a youth | that means to be of 4.04. 26
nerves, and can | get goal for goal of youth. 4.08. 22
that shouldst repair my youth, thou heap'st | a CYM 1.01.132
my youth i spent | much under him; 3.01. 69
you can borrow | from youth of such a season) 3.04.172
money, youth? 3.06. 52
prithee, fair youth, | think us no churls; 3.06. 63
were you a woman, youth, | i should woo hard, 3.06. 68
fair youth, come in. 3.06. 89
i know not why | i love this youth, and i have 4.02. 21
die, i'ld say | "my father, not this youth." 4.02. 24
this youth, how e'er distress'd, appears he hath 4.02. 47
'lack, good youth! 4.02.374
ay, good youth, | and rather father thee than 4.02.394
thou'rt my good youth — my page; 5.05.118
though you did love this youth, i blame ye not, 5.05.267
prithee, valiant youth, | deny't again. 5.05.289
before we further | sully our gloss of youth: TNK 1.02. 5
what a wrong she has done | to youth and nature. 2.02. 40
none here, nor the seas | swallow their youth. 2.02. 88
youth and pleasure, | still as she tasted, 2.02.239
that my unspotted youth must now be soil'd 4.02. 59
whose youth, like wanton boys through bonfires, 5.01. 86
and never did he bless | my youth with his, the VEN 1120
this blur to youth, this sorrow to the sage, LUC 222
my part is youth, and beats these from the stage 278
eater of youth, false slave to false delight, 927
in youth, quick bearing and dexterity; 1389
that she might think me some untutor'd youth, PP 1. 3
"did i see a fair sweet youth | here in these 9. 9
crabbed age and youth cannot live together: 12. 1
youth is full of pleasance, age is full of care, 12. 2
youth like summer morn, age like winter weather, 12. 3
youth like summer brave, age like winter bare. 12. 4
youth is full of sport, age's breath is short, 12. 5
youth is nimble, age is lame, | youth is hot and 12. 6
youth is hot and bold, age is weak and cold, 12. 7
weak and cold, | youth is wild, and age is tame. 12. 8
age, i do abhor thee, youth, i do adore thee: 12. 9
from thy /thorn, | vow, alack, for youth unmeet, 16.13
youth unmeet, | youth, so apt to pluck a sweet. 16.14
resembling strong youth in his middle age, | yet SON 7. 6
call thine, when thou from youth convertest. 11. 4
sets you most rich in youth before my sight, 15.10
to change your day of youth to sullied night, 15.12
so long as youth and thou are of one date, | but 22. 2
to see his active child do deeds of youth, | so 37. 2
and chide thy beauty and thy straying youth, 41.10
and so of you, beauteous and lovely youth, 54.13
time doth transfix the flourish set on youth, 60. 9
fire | that on the ashes of his youth doth lie, 73.10
some say thy fault is youth, some wantonness, 96. 1
some say thy grace is youth and gentle sport; 96. 2
hath put a spirit of youth in every thing, 98. 3
these blenches gave my heart another youth, 110. 7
that she might think me some untutor'd youth, 138. 3
time had not scythed all that youth begun, | nor LC 12
nor youth all quit, but, spite of heaven's fell 13
his rudeness so with his authoriz'd youth | did 104
what with his art in youth and youth in art, 145
what with his art in youth and youth in art, 145
have of my suffering youth some feeling pity 178

YOUTHFUL 32 FR 0.0036 REL FR 30 V 2 P
how his companion, youthful valentine, | attends TGV 1.03. 26
for which the youthful lover now is gone, | and 3.01. 41
friends | unto a youthful gentleman of worth, 3.01.107
my youthful travel therein made me happy, | or 4.01. 34

and youthful still, in your doublet and hose, WIV 3.01. 46 P
love — | a sin prevailing much in youthful men, ERR 5.01. 52
herd, | or race of youthful and unhandled colts, MV 5.01. 72
and ere we have thy youthful wages spent, AYL 2.03. 67
his youthful hose, well sav'd, a world too wide 2.07.160
this youthful parcel | of noble bachelors stand AWW 2.03. 52
your mind is all as youthful as your blood. JN 3.04.125
whose youthful spirit, in me regenerate, | doth R2 1.03. 70
rouse up thy youthful blood, be valiant and live 1.03. 83
wanton as youthful goats, wild as young bulls. 1H4 4.01.103
you have misled the youthful prince. 2H4 1.02.144 P
like youthful steers unyok'd, they take their 4.02.103
with youthful wings is flown | from this bare 4.05.228
quicken'd with youthful spleen and warlike rage, 1H6 4.06. 13
henry is youthful and will quickly yield. 5.03. 99
as did the youthful paris once to greece, | with 5.05.104
it is, and lo where youthful edward comes! 3H6 5.05. 11
when she coldly eyes | the youthful phoebus. TRO 1.03.230
now, youthful troilus, do not these high strains 2.02.113
than youthful april shall with all his show'rs. TIT 3.01. 18
had she affections and warm youthful blood, ROM 2.05. 12
of fair demesnes, youthful and nobly /lien'd, 3.05.180
i met the youthful lord at lawrence' cell, | and 4.02. 25
weighing the youthful season of the year. JC 2.01.108
to see their youthful sons bright weapons wield, LUC 1432
vaunt in their youthful sap, at height decrease, SON 15. 7
when his youthful morn | hath travell'd on to 63. 4
too early i attended | a youthful suit — it was LC 79

YOUTH'S 7 FR 0.0008 REL FR 4 V 3 P
as much as to say, the sweet youth's in love. ADO 3.02. 52 P
methinks i feel this youth's perfections | with TN 1.05.296
youth's a stuff will not endure." 2.03. 52
that youth's a rare courtier — "rain odors," 3.01. 86 P
i have persuaded him the youth's a devil. 3.04.293 P
but when he saw his love, his youth's fair fee, VEN 393
thy youth's proud livery, so gaz'd on now, SON 2. 3

YOUTHS 7 FR 0.0008 REL FR 5 V 2 P
these are the youths that thunder at a playhouse H8 5.03. 60 P
the grecian youths are full of quality; TRO 4.04. 76
our youths and wildness shall no whit appear, JC 2.01.148
and many unrough youths that even now | protest MAC 5.02. 10
if in our youths we could pick up some pretty PER 4.02. 32 P
the hardy youths strive for the games of honor, TNK 2.02. 10
and here the graces of our youths must wither 2.02. 27

YRAVISHED *(also ravished)*

YRAVISHED 1 FR 0.0001 REL FR 1 V 0 P
to pentapolis, | yravished the regions round, PER 3.ch. 35

YSLACKED *(also slak'd)*

YSLACKED 1 FR 0.0001 REL FR 1 V 0 P
now sleep yslacked hath the rout, | no din but PER 3.ch. 1

ZANIES 1 FR 0.0001 REL FR 0 V 1 P
kind of fools no better than the fools' zanies. TN 1.05. 89 P

ZANY 1 FR 0.0001 REL FR 1 V 0 P
carry–tale, some please–man, some slight zany, LLL 5.02.463

ZEAL 33 FR 0.0037 REL FR 29 V 4 P
methinks my zeal to valentine is cold, | and TGV 2.04.203
me, intend a kind of zeal both to the prince and ADO 2.02. 36 P
faith infringed, which such zeal did swear? LLL 4.03.144
what zeal, what fury, hath inspir'd thee now? 4.03.225
where zeal strives to content, and the contents 5.02.517
dies in the zeal of that which it presents. 5.02.518
to have defended it | with any terms of zeal, MV 5.01.205
might quench the zeal | of all professors else, WT 5.01.107
than the constraint of hospitable zeal | in the JN 2.01.244
lest zeal, now melted by the windy breath | of 2.01.477
whom zeal and charity brought to the field | as 2.01.565
of all his people, and freeze up their zeal, 3.04.150
we swear | a voluntary zeal and an unurg'd faith 5.02. 10
let not my cold words here accuse my zeal. R2 1.01. 47
ours of true zeal and deep integrity; 5.03.108
with tears of innocency and terms of zeal, | my 1H4 4.03. 63
i should not make so dear a show of zeal; 5.04. 95
honest bardolph, whose zeal burns in his nose, 2H4 2.04.329 P
ta'en up, | under the counterfeited zeal of god, 4.02. 27
this doth infer the zeal i had to see him. 5.05. 14 P
you | with hearts create of duty and of zeal. H5 2.02. 31
'twill make them cool in zeal unto your grace. 2H6 3.01.177
with whom /an upright zeal to right prevails 3H6 5.01. 78
of thy devotion and right christian zeal. R3 3.07.103
if you refuse it — as, in love and zeal, 3.07.208
and with what zeal! H8 2.02. 24
zeal and obedience he still bore your grace, 3.01. 63
had i but serv'd my god with half the zeal | i 3.02.455
more bright in zeal than the devotion which TRO 4.04. 26
in zeal to you, and highly mov'd to wrath | to TIT 1.01.419
those that under hot ardent zeal would set whole TIM 3.03. 33 P
love, | duty, and zeal to your unmatched mind, 4.03.516
love's provocations, zeal, a mistress' task, TNK 1.04. 41

ZEALOUS 6 FR 0.0006 REL FR 6 V 0 P
with such a zealous laughter, so profound, LLL 5.02.116
far | his name with zealous fervor sanctify. AWW 3.04. 11
upon thy cheek lay i this zealous kiss | as seal JN 2.01. 19
if zealous love should go in search of virtue, 2.01.428
thence, | so sweet is zealous contemplation. R3 3.07. 94
i abide) | intend a zealous pilgrimage to thee, SON 27. 6

ZEALS 1 FR 0.0001 REL FR 0 V 1 P
whereby we might express some part of our zeals, TIM 1.02. 86 P

ZED 1 FR 0.0001 REL FR 0 V 1 P
thou whoreson zed, thou unnecessary letter! LR 2.02. 64 P

ZENELOPHON 1 FR 0.0001 REL FR 0 V 1 P
the pernicious and indubitate beggar zenelophon; LLL 4.01. 66 P

ZENITH 1 FR 0.0001 REL FR 1 V 0 P
prescience | i find my zenith doth depend upon TMP 1.02.181

ZEPHYRS 1 FR 0.0001 REL FR 1 V 0 P
as gentle | as zephyrs blowing below the violet, CYM 4.02.172

ZIR *(also sir)*

ZIR 2 FR 0.0002 REL FR 0 V 2 P
chill not let go, zir, without vurther /cagion. LR 4.06.235 P
chill pick your teeth, zir. 4.06.244 P

ZO *(also so)*

ZO 1 FR 0.0001 REL FR 0 V 1 P
life, 'twould not ha' bin zo long as 'tis by a LR 4.06.239 P

ZODIAC 1 FR 0.0001 REL FR 1 V 0 P
gallops the zodiac in his glistering coach, TIT 2.01. 7

ZODIACS 1 FR 0.0001 REL FR 1 V 0 P
so long that nineteen zodiacs have gone round MM 1.02.168

ZONE 1 FR 0.0001 REL FR 1 V 0 P
singeing his pate against the burning zone, HAM 5.01.282

'ZOUNDS *(also 'swounds)*

/'ZOUNDS 12 FR 0.0013 REL FR 7 V 5 P
/'zounds, he dies! i had forgot the reward. R3 1.04.125 P
/'zounds, 'tis even now at my elbow, persuading 1.04.145 P
/'zounds, /i'll entreat no more. 3.07.219
/'zounds, sir, y' are robb'd! OTH 1.01. 86
/'zounds, sir, you are one of those that will 1.01.108 P
/'zounds, you rogue! you rascal! 2.03.145 P
/'zounds, i bleed still, | i am hurt to th' 2.03.164
/'zounds, if i stir, | or do but lift this arm, 2.03.207
/'zounds, what dost thou mean? 3.03.154
/'zounds! 3.04. 98
/'zounds, that's fulsome! 4.01. 36 P
/'zounds, hold your peace. 5.02.219

'ZOUNDS 15 FR 0.0017 REL FR 5 V 10 P
'zounds, i was never so bethump'd with words JN 2.01.466
'zounds, where thou wilt, lad, i'll make one, 1H4 1.02.100 P
'zounds, i will speak of him, and let my soul 1.03.131
and yet, 'zounds, i lie, for they pray 2.01. 79 P
'zounds, will they not rob us? 2.02. 65 P
'zounds, and i were now by this rascal, i could 2.03. 22 P
'zounds, ye fat paunch, and ye call me coward, 2.04.144 P
'zounds, and i were at the strappado, or all the 2.04.236 P
'zounds! 4.01. 17
'zounds, i am afraid of this gunpowder percy 5.04.121 P
the man were alive and would deny it, 'zounds, i 5.04.152 P
'zounds, who is there? R3 5.03.208
'zounds, ye whore, is black so base a hue? TIT 4.02. 71
'zounds, consort! ROM 3.01. 49 P
'zounds, a dog, a rat, a mouse, a cat, to 3.01.100 P

ZWAGGER'D *(also swagger'd)*

ZWAGGER'D 1 FR 0.0001 REL FR 0 V 1 P
and chud ha' bin zwagger'd out of my life, LR 4.06.238 P

2S.2D. 1 FR 0.0001 REL FR 0 V 1 P
item, a capon ... 2s.2d. 1H4 2.04.535 P

2S.6D. 1 FR 0.0001 REL FR 0 V 1 P
item, anchoves and sack after supper ... 2s.6d. 1H4 2.04.538 P

4D. 1 FR 0.0001 REL FR 0 V 1 P
item, sauce ... 4d. 1H4 2.04.536 P

5S.8D. 1 FR 0.0001 REL FR 0 V 1 P
item, sack, two gallons ... 5s.8d. 1H4 2.04.537 P

Appendix I

Hyphenated Words 1

(ALPHABETIZED ACCORDING TO FIRST ELEMENT)

a-batfowling
a-bed
a-begging
a-billing
a-birding
a-bleeding
a-breeding
a-brewing
a-cap'ring
a-cold
a-coming
a-cursing
a-doing
a-doting
a-down
a-down-a
a-ducking
a-dying
a-feasting
a-field
a-going
a-growing
a-hanging
a-height
a-high
a-hold
a-hooting
a-hungry
a-hunting
a-killing
a-land
a-life
a-making
a-mending
a-night
a-nights
a-piece
a-pieces
a-praying
a-repairing
a-ripening
a-rolling
a-row
a-scorn
a-shaking
a-shouting
a-sleeping
a-squint
a-swearing
a-talking
a-tilt
a-turning
a-twain
a-weary
a-weeping
a-wooing
a-work
abbey-gate
acorn-cups
action-taking
adown-a
after-ages
after-debts
after-dinner's
after-eye
after-hours
after-inquiry
after-loss
after-love
after-meeting
after-nourishment
after-supper
after-times
agate-ring
aglet-baby
agot-stone
ague-proof
air-braving
air-drawn
alarum-bell
alder-liefest
ale-wash'd
ale-wife
ale-wive's
aleven-pence-farthing
all-abhorred
all-admiring
all-/binding
all-changing
all-cheering
all-disgraced
all-dreaded
all-eating
all-ending
all-fear'd
all-hail
all-hail'd
all-hallond
all-hallowmas
all-hallown
all-hating
all-hiding
all-honor'd
all-hurting
all-licens'd
all-noble
all-obeying
all-oblivious
all-praised
all-royal
all-seeing
all-seer
all-shaking
all-shunn'd
all-souls'
all-telling
all-thing
all-too-precious
all-triumphant
all-unable
all-watched
all-worthy
allons-nous
alms-basket
alms-deed
alms-drink
always-wind-obeying
amber-color'd
ames-ace
an-heires
an-hungry
and-a
angel-like
ape-bearer
appelez-vous
apple-john
apple-johns
apple-tart
apron-men
aqua-vitae
arch-enemy
arch-heretic
arch-mock
arch-one
arch-villain
arm-gaunt
arts-man
ascension-day
asher-house
ashy-pale
ass-head
attorneys-general
auger-hole
aunt-mother
ave-maries
axle-tree
baby-brow
baby-daughter
back-friend
back-return
back-trick
back-wounding
bacon-fed
baiting-place
bak'd-meats
bald-pate
bald-pated
ballad-maker's
ballad-makers
ballet-mongers
ban-dogs
barbary-a
barber-monger
bare-arm'd
bare-bon'd
bare-bone
bare-gnawn
bare-headed
bare-pick'd
bare-ribb'd
barley-break
barley-broth
barren-spirited
bartholomew-tide
base-born
base-string
base-viol
basilisco-like
basket-hilt
bate-breeding
battle-axe
bawd-born
bawdy-house
bawdy-houses
bay-trees
be-all
be-gar
bean-fed
bear-baiting
bear-baitings
bear-herd
bear-like
bear-whelp
bear-whelps
bearing-cloth
beast-eating
beauty-waning
bed-clothes
bed-hangers
bed-mate
bed-presser
bed-rid
bed-right
bed-room
bed-swerver
bed-time
bed-vow
bed-work
beef-witted
beer-barrel
beetle-headed
before-breach
before-time
beggar-fear
beggar-maid
beggar-man
beggar-woman
behind-door-work
behind-hand
bell-wether
bellows-mender
//belly-pinched
bemock'd-at
bench-holes
best-boding
best-condition'd
best-moving
best-regarded
best-temper'd
bi-fold
//bias-drawing
big-bellied
big-bon'd
big-swoll'n
bigger-look'd
bird-bolt
bird-bolts
birding-pieces
birth-child
birth-hour's
birth-strangled
bitch-wolf's
black-brow'd
black-corner'd
black-ey'd
black-fac'd
black-friars
black-hair'd
blessed-fair
blind-worm's
blind-worms
blood-bespotted
blood-bolter'd
blood-consuming
blood-drinking
blood-sacrifice
blood-shedding
blood-siz'd
blood/-stain'd
blood-stained
blood-sucker
blood-suckers
blood-sucking
blood-thirsty
//bloody-fac'd
bloody-hunting
bloody-minded
bloody-sceptred
blowers-up
blue-bottle
blue-caps
blue-ey'd
blue-vein'd
blunt-witted
bo-peep
boar-pig
boar-spear
body-curer
bohemian-tartar
boil'd-brains
boist'rous-rough
bold-beating
bold-fac'd
bolting-hutch
bond-slave
bond-slaves
bone-ache
book-mates
book-men
book-oath
boot-hose
both-sides
bottle-ale
bound-a
bow-back
bow-boy's
bow-hand
bow-string
bow-strings
bow-wow
box-tree
boy-queller
brain-pan
brain-sick
brain-sickly
brawn-buttock
brazen-fac'd
brazen-face
bread-chipper
break-neck
break-promise
break-vow
breast-deep
breed-bate
brew-house
brib'd-buck
brick-wall
bride-bed
bride-habited
bright-burning
bright-shining
brine-pit
brine-pits
bringing-up
bringings-forth
broad-fronted
broad-spreading
brokers-between
broom-groves
broom-staff
brothel-house
brother-in-law
brother-justice
brother-like
brother-love
brow-bound
buck-basket
buck-baskets
buck-washing
bugle-bracelet
bull-bearing
bull-beeves
bull-calf
bully-doctor
bully-knight
bully-monster
bully-rook
bully-stale
bum-baily
bunch-back'd
burly-bon'd
burning-glass
burthen-wise
burton-heath
burying-place
butt-end
butt-shaft
butter-woman's
butter-women's
button-hole
butt'ry-bar
by-dependances
by-drinkings
by-gone
by-past
by-paths
by-peeping
by-room
by-words
ca-caliban
caddis-garter
cain-color'd
calf-like
calve's-head
calve's-skin
calves'-guts
calves'-skins
candle-cases
candle-holder
candle-mine
candle-wasters
canker-bit
canker-blooms
canker-blossom
canker-sorrow
cannon-bullets
cannon-fire
cannon-shot
canvas-climber
cap-and-knee
cap-a-pe
captain-general
card-maker
care-craz'd
care-tun'd
carpet-mongers
carry-tale
carv'd-bone
castalion-king-urinal
castle-ditch
cat-a-mountain
cat-like
cate-log
cater-cousins

cave-keeper
cave-keeping
chair-days
chamber-councils
chamber-door
chamber-doors
chamber-hanging
chamber-lye
chamber-pot
chamber-window
charge-house
charging-staff
charing-cross
chariot-wheels
charnel-house
charnel-houses
chaw'd-grass
cheek-roses
cheese-paring
cherry-pit
cherry-stone
child-bed
child-changed
child-killer
child-like
childish-foolish
chimney-piece
chimney-sweepers
chimney-tops
choice-drawn
chop-fall'n
chorus-like
christian-like
christians-soul
church-bench
church-door
church-like
church-way
church-window
cinque-ports
cinque-spotted
cittern-head
city-gate
city-gates
city-wife
city-woman
clack-dish
//clamor-moistened
clapper-claw
clapper-clawing
clapper-de-claw
clay-brain'd
clean-timber'd
clear-shining
clear-spirited
clerk-like
climber-upward
clip-wing'd
cloak-bag
clock-setter
close-stool
close-tongu'd
closet-war
cloud-capp'd
cloud-eclipsed
cloud-kissing
clyster-pipes
//co-act
co-active
co-equal
co-heirs
co-join
co-leagued
co-mates
co-meddled
co-partners
co-supremes
coach-fellow
//coal-black
coal-black
cock-a-diddle-dow
cock-a-hoop
cock-pigeon
cock-shut
cock-sure
coffer-lids
cold-blooded
cold-hearted
cold-moving
cold-pale
colossus-wise
combinate-husband
comfit-maker's
comfort-killing
coming-in
coming-on
comings-in
common-hackney'd
common-kissing
content-a
cony-catch
cony-catch'd
cony-catching
copper-spur
copy-book
corn-field
corner-cap
coronation-day
cot-quean
council-board
council-house
counsel-keeper
counsel-keeping
count-cardinal
counter-caster
counter-gate
counter-reflect
counter-seal'd
country/-woman
country-woman
court-contempt
court-cupboard
court-gate
court-hand
court-like
court-odor
court-word
cousin-german
cow-dung
coward-like
cowl-staff
cozen-germans
crab-tree
crab-trees
crack-hemp
cradle-babe
cradle-clothes
crafty-sick
cream-fac'd
crest-wounding
crook-back
crook-knee'd
crooked-pated
crop-ear
cross-bow
cross-bows
cross-garter'd
cross-gartering
cross-row
crow-flowers
crow-keeper
cruel-hearted
crystal-button
//cub-drawn
cuckold-mad
cuckold-maker
cuckoo-birds
cuckoo-buds
cuckoo-flow'rs
cull-cold
curfew-bell
curious-good
curious-knotted
curl'd-pate
cursed-blessed
curtle-axe
custa-lorum
custard-coffin
custom-shrunk
cut-throat
cut-throats
cutter-off
dancing-rapier
dancing-schools
daring-hardy
dark-ey'd
dark-seated
dark-working
datchet-lane
datchet-mead
daughter-beamed
daughter-in-law
day-bed
day-light
day-wearied
dead-cold
dead-killing
deadly-handed
deadly-standing
dear-a
dear-belov'd
dear-bought
dear-purchas'd
dearest-valued
death-bed
death-beds
death-boding
death-counterfeiting
death/-darting
death-divining
death-like
death-mark'd
death-practic'd
death-tokens
death-worthy
death's-bed
death's-head
deed-achieving
deep-brain'd
deep-dark
deep-divorcing
//deep-drawing
deep-fet
deep-green
deep-mouth'd
deep-revolving
deep-sunken
deep-sworn
deep-vow
deep-wounded
demi-atlas
demi-cannon
demi-devil
demi-natur'd
demi-paradise
demi-puppets
demi-wolves
deuce-ace
devil-porter
devilish-holy
dew-bedabbled
dew-dropping
dew-lapp'd
dey-woman
dig-you-den
ding-dong
dining-chamber
dining-chambers
dinner-time
dire-lamenting
direction-giver
dirt-rotten
dis-horn
dis-je
dis-stain'd
distaff-women
dit-il
ditch-deliver'd
ditch-dog
dites-moi
dive-dapper
divers-color'd
dizzy-ey'd
doctor-like
dog-apes
dog-days
dog-fox
//dog-hearted
dog-hole
dog-weary
dog's-leather
dolphin-like
dooms-day
door-keeper
double-charge
double-dealer
double-dealing
double-fatal
double-henn'd
double-lock
double-meaning
double-vantage
doughty-handed
dove-cote
dove-drawn
dove-feather'd
dove-house
dove-like
down-a
down-bed
down-gyved
down-roping
down-trod
down-trodden
dragon-like
draught-oxen
//dread-bolted
drift-winds
drone-like
drop-heir
drug-damn'd
dry-beat
dry-beaten
dry-foot
dull-brain'd
dull-ey'd
dumb-discoursive
/dun-color'd
dwelling-house
dwelling-place
dwelling-places
eagle-sighted
eagle-winged
ear-/bussing
ear-deaf'ning
ear-piercing
ear-wax
earnest-gaping
earth-bound
earth-delving
earth-treading
earth-vexing
ease-dropper
easy-borrowed
easy-held
easy-melting
easy-yielding
ebon-colored
/eel-skin
eel-skin
eel-skins
/e'er-remaining
egg-shell
egg-shells
eight-penny
eight-year-old
elbow-room
elder-gun
elder-tree
eldest-born
/elf-locks
elvish-mark'd
ember-eves
empty-hearted
end-all
est-il
etes-vous
even-christen
even-handed
even-pleach'd
ever-angry
ever-blinded
ever-burning
ever-during
ever-esteemed
ever-fixed
ever-gentle
ever-harmless
ever-living
ever-preserv'd
ever-running
ever-valiant
evil-ey'd
excusez-moi
eyas-musket
eye-beams
eye-drops
eye-glance
eye-glass
eye-offending
eye-sore
eye-strings
eye-wink
fadom-line
faint-hearted
fair-betrothed
fair-ey'd
fair-fac'd
fair-play
fair-spoken
fairest-boding
fairy-like
faith-breach
falling-from
falling-off
fall'n-off
false-boding
false-derived
false-fac'd
false-heart
false-hearted
false-play'd
false-self
false-speaking
fancy-free
fancy-monger
fancy-sick
far-fet
far-off
far-unworthy
farm-house
fashion-mongers
fashion-monging
fast-closed
fast-falling
fast-growing
fast-lost
fasting-days
fat-already
fat-brain'd
fat-guts
fat-kidney'd
fat-witted
fatal-plotted
father-in-law
fault-full
fear-surprised
feast-finding
feast-won
feather-bed
fee-farm
fee-grief
fee-simple
feeling-painful
fell-lurking
fellow-fault
fellow-servant
fen-suck'd
fern-seed
fertile-fresh
fever-weak'ned
field-bed
field-dew
fiend-like
fiery-footed
fiery-pointed
fiery-red
fifty-five
fig's-end
fill-horse
filthy-mantled
finch-egg
find-faults
finder/-out
finder-out
fine-baited
finger-end
fire-brand
fire-brands
fire-drake
fire/-ey'd
fire-ey'd
fire-new
fire-rob'd
fire-shovel
firm-set
first-begotten
first-born
first-conceived
first-fruits
fish-like
fish-meals
five-and-thirty
/five-finger-tied
flame-color'd
flap-dragon
flap-dragon'd
flap-dragons
flap-ear'd
flap-jacks
flap-mouth'd
flat-long
flattering-sweet
flax-wench
fleet-foot
fleet-wing'd
flesh-fly
flint-hearted
flirt-gills
flood-gate
flood-gates
flower-de-luce
flower-de-luces
flower-soft
flow'r-de-luce
fly-bitten
fly-blowing
fly-blown
folly-fall'n
fool-begg'd
fool-born
foolish-compounded
fool's-head
foot-cloth
foot-licker
foot-path
fore-advis'd
fore-bemoaned
fore-betray'd
fore-end
fore-foot
fore-past
fore-rank
fore-recited
fore-spurrer
fore-vouch'd
forest-born
forset-seller
forth-rights
fortunate-unhappy
fortune-tell
fortune-teller
fortune-telling
forty-eight
foster-nurse
foul-fac'd
foul-mouth'd
foul-mouth'd'st
foul-spoken
four-inch'd
freckle-fac'd
free-footed
free-hearted
free-town
freestone-colored
french-crown-color
fresh-brook
frosty-spirited
fruit-dish
fruit-tree
fruit-trees
full-acorn'd
full-charg'd
full-fed
full-flowing
full-fortun'd
full-fraught
full-gorg'd
full-grown
full-hearted
full-mann'd
full-wing'd
furnace-burning
furrow-weeds
/gain-giving
gallant-springing
gallows-maker
garden-house
garlic-eaters
gentle-hearted
gentle-sleeping
gentleman-like
giant-dwarf
giant-like
giant-rude
gibbet-maker
giddy-paced
give-a
giving-back
/givings-out
glass-fac'd
glass-gazing
glow-worm
glow-worm's
glow-worms
glowing-hot
glutton-like
go-between
god-a-mercy
god-den
god-i-goden
goddess-like
goer-back
goers-between
gogs-wouns
gold-bound
good-en
good-fac'd
good-fellowship
good-jer
good-limb'd
good-night
good-nights
good-year
good-years
goose-look

goose-pen
//goose-quills
gossip-like
grand-guard
grand-jurymen
grass-green
grass-plot
grave-maker
grave-makers
grave-making
grave-stone
gravel-blind
great-bellied
great-ey'd
great-grandfather
great-grandsire
great-grandsire's
great-grown
great-siz'd
great-uncle
great-uncle's
green-a
green-dropping
green-ey'd
green-eyed
green-sickness
green-sleeves
green-sord
grey-coated
grey-ey'd
grief-shot
grim-grinning
grim-look'd
grim-visag'd
ground-piece
guest-cavalier
guest-justice
guest-wise
guilty-like
gull-catcher
gun-stones
guts-griping
hag-born
hag-seed
hair-breadth
hair-worth
half-achieved
half-blooded
half-blown
half-can
half-caps
half-cheek
half-cheek'd
half-fac'd
half-face
half-kirtles
half-moon
half-part
half-pennyworth
half-pint
half-sights
half-supp'd
half-sword
half-workers
half-yard
hand-fast
hand-in-hand
hand-saw*
handicrafts-men
handy-dandy
hang-hog
hard-a-keeping
hard-believing
hard-favor'd
hard-favored
hard-hair'd
hard-handed
hard-hearted
hard-rul'd
hardest-timber'd
hare-brain'd
hare-finder
hare-lip
/ha'rford-west
harm-doing
harsh-resounding
harsh-sounding
harvest-home
harvest-man
haste-post-haste
hasty-footed
hasty-witted
hazel-nut
hazel-nuts
hazel-twig
//head-lugg'd
head-piece
head-pieces
head-stall
heady-rash
health-giving
heart-ache
heart-blood
heart-break
heart-breaking
heart-burn'd
heart-burning
heart-burnt
heart-deep
heart-easing
heart-grief
heart-hard'ning
heart-heaviness
heart-inflaming
heart-offending
heart-pierc'd
heart-sick
heart-sore
heart-sorrowing
heart-string
heart-strings
heart-strook
heart-whole
heart-wish'd
heart's-ease
heat-oppressed
heav'd-up
heaven-bred
heaven-hu'd
/heaven-kissing
heaven-moving
heavenly-harness'd
heavy-gaited
heavy-headed
hedge-born
hedge-corner
hedge-pig
hedge-priest
hedge-sparrow
heigh-ho
heir-apparent
hell-black
hell-born
hell-broth
hell-fire
hell-govern'd
hell-hated
hell-hound
hell-hounds
hell-kite
hell-pains
helter-skelter
hence-going
herb-woman
here-approach
here-remain
hey-day
/hid-fox
high-battled
high-blown
high-born
high-borne
high/-color'd
high-day
high-engender'd
high-grown
high-judging
high-lone
high-minded
high-pitch'd
high-plac'd
high-proof
high-reaching
high-rear'd
high-repented
high-resolved
high-sighted
high-soaring
high-speeded
high-stomach'd
high-swoll'n
high-vic'd
high-witted
high-wrought
highest-peering
hinder-legs
hissing-hot
historical-pastoral
hoary-headed
/hobby-horse
hobby-horse
hobby-horses
hodge-pudding
hold-door
hold-fast
holding-anchor
holiday-time
hollow-ey'd
hollow-hearted
holy/-ales
holy-cruel
holy-day
holy-rood
holy-thistle
holy-thoughted
holy-water
home-bred
home-keeping
home-spuns
honest-hearted
honest-natur'd
honest-true
honey-bag
honey-bags
honey-bees
honey-dew
honey-drops
honey-heavy
honey-mouth'd
honey-stalks
honey-sweet
honey-tongued
honor-flaw'd
honor-giving
honor-owing
honorable-dangerous
hoodman-blind
hook-nos'd
hop'd-for
horn-beasts
horn-book
horn-mad
horn-maker
horn-ring
horse-back-breaker
horse-drench
horse-leeches
horse-piss
horse-shoe
horse-stealer
horse-tail
horse-way
hostess-ship
hot-bloodied
hot-bloods
hot-house
hour-glass
house-clogs
house-eaves
house-keeper
house-keepers
house-keeping
hovel-post
hoy-day
hugger-mugger
humble-bee
humble-bees
humble-mouth'd
humble/-visag'd
humor-letter
hundred-pound
hunger-starved
hungry-starved
hunt's-up
hurly-burly
hurly-burly's
hydra-headed
ice-brook's
idiot-worshippers
idle-headed
ill-annexed
ill-beseeming
ill-boding
ill-breeding
ill-compos'd
ill-dealing
ill-dispersing
ill-divining
ill-doing
ill-erected
ill-fac'd
//ill-favor'd
ill-favor'd
ill-favoredly
ill-headed
ill-inhabited
ill-nurtur'd
ill-resounding
ill-roasted
ill-seeming
ill-shap'd
ill-sheathed
ill-spirited
ill-starr'd
ill-ta'en
ill-temper'd
ill-tuned
ill-us'd
ill-uttering
ill-weav'd
ill-well
ill-wresting
inch-meal
inch-thick
indian-like
infant-like
iron-witted
ivy/-tods
jack-a-lent
jack-a-nape
jack-an-ape
jack-an-apes
jack-dog
jaw-bone
jewel-like
jig-maker
john-a-dreams
//join-stool
join-stools
join'd-stool
join'd-stools
joint-laborer
joint-ring
joint-servant
journey-bated
jud-as
judgment-place
juno-like
just-borne
justice-like
jutting-out
kate-hall
keen-edg'd
keeper-back
kettle-drum
key-cold
key-hole
kicky-wicky
kill-courtesy
kill-hole
kind-hearted
king-becoming
king-cardinal
king-killer
kingly-crowned
kingly-poor
kissing-comfits
knee-crooking
knee-deep
knight-arrant
knot-grass
knotty-pated
lack-beard
lack-brain
lack-linen
lack-love
lack-lustre
ladder-tackle
lady-smocks
lammas-eve
lammas-tide
land-damn
land-fish
land-rakers
land-rats
land-service
land-thieves
lank-lean
large-handed
larks'-heels
'larum-bell
lass-lorn
late-betrayed
late-deceased
late-despised
late-disturbed
late-sack'd
late-walking
latter-born
laughing-stocks
law-breaker
law-days
lay-thoughts
lay-to
layer-up
lazar-like
leaden-footed
lean-fac'd
lean-look'd
lean-witted
leap-frog
leaping-houses
leather-coats
leathern-jerkin
leave-taking
leo-natus
let-a
let-alone
letters-patents
lewd-tongu'd
liberal-conceited
lie-giver
life-blood
life-harming
life-poisoning
life-preserving
life-rend'ring
life-time
life-weary
light-foot
light-wing'd
lighter-heel'd
lily-beds
lily-liver'd
lily-tincture
lily-white
limb-meal
lime-kill
lime-kills
lime-twigs
line-grove
linsey-woolsey
lion-mettled
lion-sick
little-a
liver-vein
lock'd-up
lofty-plumed
log-man
logger-head
long-a
long-continued
long-during
long-engraff'd
long-experienc'd
long-grown
long-hid
long-imprisoned
long-lane
long-legg'd
long-liv'd
long-living
long-parted
long-staff
long-tail
long-tongu'd
long-usurped
long-vanish'd
long-winded
long'd-for
looker-on
lookers-on
//looking-glass
looking-glass
loop-holes
loose-bodied
loose-wiv'd
loud-howling
love-a
love-affairs
love-bed
love-book
love-broker
love-cause
love-day
love-devouring
love-discourse
love-feat
love-god
love-gods
love-in-idleness
love-juice
love-kindling
love-lacking
love-letters
love-line
love-monger
love-news
love-performing
love-prate
love-rhymes
love-shaft
love-shak'd
love-sick
love-song
love-songs
love-springs
love-suit
love-thoughts
love-tokens
love-wounded
loving-jealous
low-born
low-crooked
low-declined
low-laid
low-rated
low-spirited
low-voic'd
lud's-town
lurking-place
lust-breathed
lust-dieted
lust-stain'd
lute-case
lute-string
mad-brain
mad-brain'd
mad-bred
mad-headed
made-up
madly-us'd
maggot-pies
maid-child
maid-pale
maiden-hearted
maiden-tongu'd
maiden-widowed
main-course
main-top
make-a
make-peace
male-child
malmsey-butt
malmsey-nose
malt-horse
malt-worms
man-at-arms
man-child
man-engraff'd
man-ent'red
man-monster
man-of-war
man-queller
mannerly-modest
manor-house
many-color'd
many-colored
many-headed
marble-breasted
marble-constant
marble-hearted
march-chick
mark-man
market-crosses
market-days
market-maid
market-place
market-price
marriage-bed
marriage-blessing
marriage-day
marriage-dowry
marriage-feast
marrow-eating
mary-buds
master-cord
master-leaver
matter-a
may-day
may-morn
meadow-fairies
mean-born
meet-a
meeting-place
men-at-arms
men-children
merchant-like
merchant-marring
mercy-lacking
mermaid-like
merry-hearted
mete-yard
mid-age
middle-earth
milch-kine
mile-a

mile-end
milford-haven
milk-liver'd
milk-white
milking-time
mill-sixpences
mill-wheels
minute-jacks
mirth-moving
mis-sheathed
mist-like
mock-vater
mock-water
momentary-swift
money-bags
monster-like
moody-mad
moon-calf
moon-calf's
moor-ditch
more-having
morn-dew
morn-prayer
morris-dance
morris-pike
mortal-living
mortal-staring
mortar-piece
moss-grown
mother-queen
mother-wit
motley-minded
mountain-foreigner
mountain-squire
mouse-eaten
mouse-hunt
mouse-trap
mouth-filling
mouth-friends
mouth-honor
mouth-made
muddy-mettled
mumble-news
murd'ring-piece
musk-cat
musk-rose
musk-roses
mussel-shell
muster-book
muster-file
narrow-mouth'd
narrow-prying
nay-word
near-legg'd
neat-herd's
neat-herds
neat's-leather
needle-work
ne'er-changing
ne'er-cloying
/ne'er-lust-wearied
ne'er-touch'd
ne'er-yet-beaten
neighbor-stained
nestor-like
nether-stocks
nettle-seed
never-conquered
never-daunted
never-dying
never-ending
never-erring
never-heard-of
never-needed
never-quenching
never-resting
never-surfeited
never-withering
new-added
new-appearing
new-beloved
new-bleeding
new-born
new-built
new-come
new-create
new-crowned
new-dated
new-deliver'd
new-delivered
new-enkindled
new-fall'n
new-fangled
new-fir'd
new-found
new-hatch'd
new-heal'd
new-kill'd
new-made
new-married
new-planted
new-sad
new-shed
new-sprung
new-store
new-ta'en
new-transformed
new-trothed
new-tun'd
new-year's
news-cramm'd
nice-preserved
night/-bird
night-brawler
night-cap
night-caps
night-crow
night-dogs
night-flies
night-foes
night-gown
night-mare
night-oblations
night-owl
night-owl's
night-owls
night-raven
night-rest
night-rule
night-shriek
night-tapers
night-tripping
night-waking
night-walking
night-wanderers
night-wand'rers
night-wand'ring
night-watch
nimble-footed
nimble-pinion'd
nine-fold
no-bodies
no-verbs
noble-ending
noble-minded
noblest-minded
nod-ay
non-come
non-payment
non-performance
non-regardance
none-sparing
nook-shotten
noon-day
north-east
north-gate
north-north-east
north-north-west
nose-herbs
nose-painting
not-fearing
not-of-the-newest
not-pated
not-to-be-endur'd
note-book
nothing-gift
now-a-days
now-born
nurse-like
nursh-a
oak-cleaving
oath-breaking
odd-conceited
odd-even
o'er-beat
o'er-count
o'er-crows
o'er-dy'd
o'er-eaten
o'er-eye
o'er-fraught
o'er-great
o'er-green
o'er-leavens
o'er-picturing
o'er-priz'd
o'er-rank
o'er-read
o'er-sized
o'er-teemed
/o'er-wrastling
o'er-wrested
off-capp'd
office-badge
officers-at-arms
oft-subdued
oft-times
oil-dried
old-fac'd
olive-trees
olympus-high
one-trunk-inheriting
onion-ey'd
open/-arse
open-ey'd
orange-tawny
orange-wife
orchard-end
organ-pipe
out-breasted
out-burneth
out-dure
out-dwells
//out-fac'd
out-fac'd
out-frown
out-herods
out-live
out-night
out-paramour'd
out-shining
out-talk
out-tongue
out-villain'd
out-voice
out-wall
outward-sainted
over-canopied
over-careful
over-cool
over-credulous
over-daring
over-earnest
over-eyeing
over-full
//over-greedy
over-handled
/over-happy
over-long
over-measure
over-merry
over-name
over-partial
over-pay
over-proud
over-read
over-red
over-ripen'd
over-shine
over-stain'd
over-tedious
over-veil'd
over-view
over-wash'd
over-weather'd
ox-beef
ox-head
oyster-wench
pack-horse
pack-horses
pack-saddle
pair-taunt-like
pale-dead
pale-fac'd
pale-hearted
pale-visag'd
palpable-gross
paper-fac'd
paper-mill
parcel-bawd
parcel-gilt
/pardon-me's
pardonnez-moi
paring-knife
paris-ward
parish-top
park-corner
park-gate
park-ward
parrot-teacher
part-created
parti-coated
parti-color'd
//parti-ey'd
party-verdict
passy-measures
past-cure
past-proportion
past-saving
pastoral-comical
patch-breech
peace-a
peace-parted
peach-color'd
peascod-time
peevish/-fond
peg-a-ramsey
pell-mell
pent-up
penthouse-like
pepper-box
pepper-gingerbread
periwig-pated
perpetual-sober
//pers-one
pew-fellow
phoenix-like
pick-purse
pick-purses
pick-thanks
pickle-herring
pickt-hatch
picture-like
pie-corner
pig-like
pig-nuts
pigeon-egg
pigeon-liver'd
pillicock-hill
pin-buttock
pinch-spotted
pint-pot
pipe-wine
pissing-conduit
pissing-while
pistol-proof
pitch-balls
pitiful-hearted
pittie-ward
pity-pleading
pity-wanting
plague-sore
plain-dealing
plain-song
play-feres
playing-day
pleasant-spirited
please-man
plot-proof
plough-irons
plough-torn
plucker-down
plum-broth
plum-tree
plume-pluck'd
point-blank
point-device
point-devise
pointing-stock
poking-sticks
pole-clipt
poll-axe
poor-john
pork-eaters
post-haste
post-horse
post-horses
post-post-haste
pottle-deep
pottle-pot
pottle-pot's
pouncet-box
powd'ring-tub
prayer-book
prayer-books
pre-contract
pre-eminence
pre-employ'd
precious-dear
precious-juiced
precious-princely
present-absent
press-money
prick-ear'd
prick-song
priest-like
prince-like
prison-house
privy-kitchen
process-server
procure-a
prologue-like
promise-breach
promise-breaker
promise-cramm'd
promise-keeping
proper-false
prophet-like
proud-hearted
proud-minded
proud-pied
puke-stocking
puller-down
pullet-sperm
pupil-like
puppy-dog
puppy-dogs
puppy-headed
purple-color'd
purple-hu'd
purple-in-grain
purpose-changer
purse-bearer
purse-taking
pursuivant-at-arms
push-pin
putter-on
putter-out
putting-by
putting-on
qu'ai-je
quatch-buttock
queen-mother
quick-answer'd
quick-conceiving
quick-ey'd
quick-raised
quick-shifting
quick-witted
rabbit-sucker
rain-water
ram-tender
rank-scented
rascal-like
rash-embrac'd
rash-levied
rat-catcher
rato-lorum
raven-colored
raw-bon'd
re-answer
re-edified
re-salute
re-send
re-survey
re-united
re-view
//rebel-like
red-ey'd
red-fac'd
red-hipp'd
red-hot
red-lattice
red-look'd
red-nose
red-plague
red-tail'd
rere-mice
rib-breaking
rich-built
rich-jewell'd
rich-left
riddle-like
riding-robes
riding-rods
riding-suit
right-hand
ring-carrier
ripe-red
rival-hating
road-way
roast-meat
robin-redbreast
rocky-hard
rope-maker
rope-tricks
rose-cheek'd
rose-lipp'd
rose-water
//rouge-mount
rough-cast
rough-grown
rough-hew
round-fac'd
round-hoof'd
round-womb'd
rowel-head
ruby-color'd
rude-growing
rug-headed
rump-fed
rush-candle
russet-pated
rut-time
rye-straw
sable-colored
sad-beholding
sad-ey'd
sad-fac'd
sad-hearted
sad-tun'd
saddle-bow
safe-conduct
safe-conducting
saint-like
saint-seducing
sale-work
salt-butter
salt-fish
salt-sea
salt-water
salt-wav'd
sand-blind
sandy-bottom'd
sap-consuming
savage-wild
scarce-bearded
scarce-cold
scent-snuffing
school-days
school-doing
school-maids
screech-owl
screech-owls
scritch-owl
scythe-tusk'd
sea-bank
sea-banks
//sea-boy
sea-cap
sea-change
sea-coal
sea-farer
sea-faring
sea-fight
sea-gown
sea-like
sea-maid
sea-maid's
sea-marge
sea-mark
sea-monster
sea-nymphs
sea-room
//sea-salt
sea-sick
sea-side
sea-sorrow
sea-storm
sea-swallow'd
sea-walled
sea-water
sea-wing
seal-ring
seal'd-up
sealing-day
seas-toss'd
secret-false
seld-shown
self-abuse
self-admission
self-affairs
self-affected
self-affrighted
self-applied
self-assumption
self-born
self-borne
self-bounty
self-breath
self-charity
self-comparisons
//self-cover'd
self-danger
self-doing
self-drawing
self-endeared
self-example
self-explication
self-figur'd
self-glorious
self-gracious
self-harming
self-kill'd
self-love
self-loving

self-mettle
self-misus'd
self-neglecting
self-offenses
self-reproving
self-same
/self-slaughter
self-slaughter
self-slaught'red
self-sovereignty
self-subdued
self-substantial
self-trust
self-unable
self-will
self/-will'd
self-will'd
self-wrong
senate-house
send-a
senior/-junior
senseless-obstinate
serpent-like
servant-monster
serving-creature
serving-creature's
setter-up
seventy-five
shag-ear'd
shag-hair'd
shallow-hearted
shallow-rooted
shame-fac'd
shame-proof
shard-borne
sharp-ground
sharp-looking
sharp-pointed
sharp-provided
sharp-quill'd
sharp-tooth'd
she-angel
she-bear
she-beggar
//she-foxes
she-lamb
she-mercury
she-wolf
sheep-biter
sheep-biting
sheep-cote
sheep-cotes
sheep-hook
sheep-shearing
sheep-skins
sheep-whistling
sherris-sack
ship-boy's
ship-boys
ship-tire
shoe-tie
shoeing-horn
short-arm'd
short-grass'd
short-jointed
short-legg'd
short-liv'd
short-numb'red
short-winded
shot-free
shoulder-blade
shoulder-bone
shoulder-clapper
shoulder-piece
shoulder-shotten
shove-groat
shovel-boards
show-place
shrill-gorg'd
shrill-shriking
shrill-sounding
shrill-tongu'd
shrill/-voic'd
shrove-tide
sick-fall'n
sick-thoughted
side-piercing
side-stitches
sight-holes
sight-outrunning
silk-man
silken-coated
silly-ducking
silver-bright
silver-shedding
silver-shining
silver-sweet
silver-voic'd
silver-white
simple-answer'd
sin-absolver
sin-concealing
sin-conceiving
singing-man
single-sol'd
sink-a-pace
sinking-ripe
/sir-reverence
sir-reverence
//six-gated
six-or-seven-times-honor'd
skains-mates
skill-contending
skim-milk
skimble-skamble
skin-coat
sky-aspiring
sky-planted
slaughter-house
slaughter-man
slaughter-men
slave-like
sleave-silk
sleek-headed
sleeping-hours
sleeve-hand
slip-shod
slow-gaited
slow-wing'd
slug-a-bed
small-knowing
smell-less
smooth-fac'd
smooth-tongue
smoothy-pates
snail-pac'd
snail-slow
snapper-up
sneak-up
snipt-taffata
snow-broth
snow-white
so-forth
so-seeming
sober-blooded
sober-sad
sober-suited
sodden-witted
soft-conscienc'd
soft-hearted
softly-sprighted
soldier-breeder
soldier-like
something-settled
son-in-law
son-in-law's
son-in-laws
song-men
soon-believing
soon-speeding
//sorrow-wreathen
soul-confirming
soul-curer
soul-fearing
soul-killing
soul-vex'd
sound-a
sour-ey'd
sour-fac'd
sourest-natur'd
south-fog
south-sea
south-west
south-wind
sow-skin
span-counter
spaniel-like
spanish-pouch
speak-a
spell-stopp'd
spider-like
spirit-stirring
spittle-house
spoon-meat
sporting-place
spring-time
spring-time's
squire-like
stair-work
stalking-horse
stand-under
stander-by
standers-by
standing-bed
standing-bowl
star-blasting
star-cross'd
star-gazers
star-like
stark-nak'd
start-up
starting-hole
starve-lackey
state-statues
statute-caps
steadfast-gazing
steep-down
steep-up
step-dame
stickler-like
//stiff-borne
stile-a
still-born
still-breeding
still-closing
still-discordant
still-gazing
still-lasting
still-peering
still-pining
still-slaughtered
still-soliciting
still-stand
still-vex'd
still-waking
stock-fish
stock-fishes
/stock-punish'd
stomach-qualm'd
stone-bow
stone-cutter
stone-hard
stone-still
stony-hearted
stony-stratford
store-house
store-houses
storm-beaten
stout-hearted
straight-pight
strange-achieved
strange-disposed
strangely-visited
straw-color
stretch-mouth'd
stretch'd-out
strong-barr'd
strong-bas'd
strong-besieged
strong-bonded
strong-fram'd
strong-hearted
strong-jointed
strong-knit
strong-neck'd
strong-ribb'd
strong-temper'd
strong-wing'd
stubble-land
stubborn-chaste
stubborn-hard
stumbling-blocks
sub-contracted
subtile-witted
such-a-one
such-a-one's
such-like
su'd-for
sugar-candy
suivez-vous
summer-seeming
summer-swelling
sun-beamed
sun-bright
sun-expelling
sun-rise
sunday-citizens
super-dainty
super-subtle
supper-time
sur-addition
sur-rein'd
surety-like
surfeit-swell'd
surfeit-taking
swaddling-clouts
swag-bellied
swan-like
swart-complexion'd
sweet-complaining
sweet-fac'd
sweet-savor'd
sweet-season'd
sweet-smelling
sweet-suggesting
swift-footed
swift-winged
swine-drunk
swine-herds
swine-keeping
sword-and-buckler
sword-hilts
table-book
table-sport
table-talk
tag-rag
take-a
taking-off
tale-porter
tallow-catch
tallow-face
taming-school
tap-house
taper-light
tardy-gaited
tassel-gentle
tavern-bills
tavern-reckonings
tawdry-lace
tawny-coats
tawny/-finn'd
tear-distained
tear-falling
tear-stain'd
tell-a
tell-tale
tell-tales
tempest-toss'd
tempest-tossed
temple-haunting
ten-times-barr'd-up
tender-bodied
tender-dying
tender-feeling
tender-hearted
tender-hefted
tender-minded
tender-smelling
tennis-balls
tennis-court
tennis-court-keeper
tent-royal
thick-coming
thick-ey'd
thick-grown
thick-lipp'd
thick-lips
thick-pleach'd
thick-ribbed
thick-sighted
thick-skin
thief-stol'n
thin/-bellied
thin-fac'd
thirty-one
thirty-three
thorn-bush
thought-executing
thought-sick
three-a
three-and-twenty
three-farthing
three-farthings
three-foot
three-headed
three-hoop'd
three-hours
three-inch
three-legg'd
three-man
three-nook'd
three-pil'd
three-pile
three-quarters
three-suited
thrice-blessed
thrice-crowned
thrice-double
thrice-driven
thrice-fair
thrice-famed
thrice-gentle
thrice-gorgeous
thrice-gracious
thrice-noble
thrice-nobler
thrice-puissant
thrice-renowned
thrice-repured
thrice-valiant
thrice-victorious
thrice-worthy
thrower-out
thumb-ring
thunder-bearer
thunder-claps
thunder-darter
thunder-like
thunder-master
thunder-stone
thunder-stroke
tick-tack
tied-up
tiger-footed
tilly-fally
tilly-vally
tilt-yard
time-beguiling
time-bettering
time-bewasted
time-honored
time-pleaser
time-pleasers
timely-parted
tinder-like
tire-valiant
tiring-house
tirra-lyra
tithe-pig's
tithe-woman
title-leaf
title-page
tittle-tattling
//to-and-fro-conflicting
to-be-pitied
//to-day
to-day
to-morrow
to-morrow's
to-morrow't
//to-night
/to-night
to-night
toad-spotted
toasting-iron
toasts-and-butter
tongue-tied
too-timely
tooth-drawer
top-branch
top-gallant
top-proud
topsy-turvy
torch-bearer
torch-bearers
torch-staves
toss-pots
tower-hill
town-crier
trade-fall'n
//tragical-comical-historical-pastoral
//tragical-historical
trans-shape
travel-tainted
tray-trip
treble-dated
treble-sinew'd
trencher-friends
trencher-knight
trial-fire
tripe-visag'd
triple-turn'd
troll-my-dames
troth-plight
trotting-horse
truckle-bed
true-anointed
true-begotten
true-born
true-bred
true-derived
true-devoted
true-disposing
true-divining
true-fix'd
true-hearted
true-love
true-love's
true-meant
true-telling
truer-hearted
trumpet-clangor
trumpet-tongu'd
trundle-tail
trunk-work
tu-whit
tu-who
/tub-fast
tumbling-trick
tun-dish
turkey-cock
turkey-cocks
turtle-doves
twenty-five
twenty-nine
twenty-one
twenty-seven
twenty-six
twenty-three
twice-told
twin-born
twin-brother
two-and-twenty
two-hand
two-headed
two-legg'd
uncle-father
under-foot
under-hangman
under-honest
under-peep
under-skinker
under-stand
under-wrought
unlook'd-for
unpaid-for
unthought-of
unthought-on
up-cast
up-fill
up-locked
up-prick'd
up-rous'd
up-spring
up-staring
up-till
urchin-shows
urchin-snouted
valley-fountain
vapor-vow
vaunt-couriers
velvet-guards
venom'd-mouth'd
victor-sword
vile-concluded
vile-drawing
villain-like
villain-slave
viol-de-gamboys
virgin-knot
virgin-like
virgin-violator
vizard-like
vlouting-stocks
vlouting-stog
vow-fellows
wafer-cakes
waggon-spokes
waggon-wheel
wain-ropes
waiting-gentlewoman
//waiting-women
waiting-women
walking-staff
wall-ey'd
wall-newt
walnut-shell
wand-like
want-wit
war-like
war-man
war-mark'd
war-proof
war-thoughts
war-wearied
war-worn
ware-a
warming-pan
wasp-stung
waspish-headed
watch-case
watch-dogs
watch-ords
watch-word

water-colors
//water-drops
water-drops
water-flies
water-flowers
water-flowing
water-fly
water-galls
water-pots
water-rats
water-rugs
water-spaniel
water-standing
water-thieves
water-walled
wave-worn
wax-red
weak-built
weak-hearted
weak-hing'd
weak-made
weal-balanc'd
wear-a
weather-beaten
weather-bitten
weather-fends
//weav'd-up
wedding-bed
wedding-day
wedding-dow'r
wedding-ring
wedding-sheets
wedlock-hymn
weeder-out
weeping-ripe
well-accomplish'd
well-acquainted
well-a-day
well-advis'd
well-advised
well-a-near
well-apparell'd
//well-appointed
well-appointed
well-armed
well-behav'd
well-belov'd
well-beloved
well-beseeming
well-born
well-breath'd
well-chosen
well-contented
well-dealing
well-defended
well-derived
well-deserved
well-deserving
well-disposed
well-divided
well-doing
well-educated
well-ent'red
well-experienc'd
well-fam'd
well-favor'd
well-favored
well-foughten
well-found
well-govern'd
well-graced
well-hallow'd
well-knit
well-known
well-laboring
well-learned
well-liking
well-lost
well-meaning
well-meant
well-minded
well-nigh
well-noted
well-order'd
well-paid
well-painted
well-practic'd
well-proportion'd
well-proportioned
well-refined
//well-rememb'red
well-reputed
well-respected
well-sailing
well/-seeming
well-seeming
well-skill'd
well-spoken
well-steel'd
well-took
well-tun'd
well-tuned
well-warranted
well-weighing
well-willer
well-willers
well-wish'd
well-won
wench-like
westward-ho
what-do-ye-call
what-ye-call't
/whey-face
whey-face
while-ere
white-bearded
white-beards
white-fac'd
white-friars
white-hair'd
white-handed
white-lim'd
white-liver'd
white-upturned
whiting-time
whoa-ho-hoa
wholesome-profitable
wide-chopp'd
wide-enlarg'd
wide-skirted
wide-stretched
widow-comfort
widow-dolor
widow-maker
wife-like
wild-boars
wild-cat
wild-cats
wild-fowl
wild-goose
wild-mare
willful-blame
willful-negligent
willful-opposite
willful-slow
willow-tree
wind-changing
wind-fann'd
wind-shak'd
wind-shaken
wind-swift
winding-sheet
window/-bars
wing-led
winter-cricket
winter-ground
winter-time
wit-crackers
wit-old
wit-snapper
//without-book
without-door
without-doors
woe-begone
woe-wearied
woman-post
woman-queller
woman-tir'd
wonder-wounded
wood-birds
wood-leaves
wool-sack
working-day
working-days
working-house
worky-day
world-sharers
world-wearied
world-without-end
worm-eaten
worm-holes
worm's-meat
worn-out
worsted-stocking
wrack-threat'ning
wrath-kindled
wrong-incensed
wry-neck'd
yea-forsooth
yielder-up
yoke-devils
//yoke-fellow
yoke-fellow
yoke-fellows
york-place
young-ey'd

Hyphenated Words 2

(ALPHABETIZED ACCORDING TO SECOND ELEMENT)

adown-a
and-a
barbary-a
bound-a
cap-a-pe
cat-a-mountain
cock-a-diddle-dow
cock-a-hoop
content-a
dear-a
down-a
give-a
god-a-mercy
green-a
hard-a-keeping
jack-a-lent
jack-a-nape
john-a-dreams
let-a
little-a
long-a
love-a
make-a
matter-a
meet-a
mile-a
now-a-days
nursh-a
peace-a
peg-a-ramsey
procure-a
send-a
sink-a-pace
slug-a-bed
sound-a
speak-a
stile-a
such-a-one
such-a-one's
take-a
tell-a
three-a
ware-a
wear-a
well-a-day
well-a-near
all-abhorred
present-absent
sin-absolver
self-abuse
well-accomplish'd
ames-ace
deuce-ace
bone-ache
heart-ache
half-achieved
strange-achieved
deed-achieving
full-acorn'd
well-acquainted
//co-act
co-active
new-added
sur-addition
all-admiring
self-admission
fore-advis'd
well-advis'd
well-advised
love-affairs
self-affairs
self-affected
self-affrighted
mid-age
after-ages
bottle-ale
holy/-ales

be-all
end-all
let-alone
fat-already
jack-an-ape
jack-an-apes
holding-anchor
cap-and-knee
five-and-thirty
sword-and-buckler
three-and-twenty
//to-and-fro-conflicting
toasts-and-butter
two-and-twenty
she-angel
ever-angry
ill-annexed
true-anointed
re-answer
quick-answer'd
simple-answer'd
dog-apes
well-apparell'd
heir-apparent
new-appearing
self-applied
//well-appointed
well-appointed
here-approach
bare-arm'd
short-arm'd
well-armed
knight-arrant
open/-arse
jud-as
sky-aspiring
self-assumption
bemock'd-at
man-at-arms
men-at-arms
officers-at-arms
pursuivant-at-arms
demi-atlas
battle-axe
curtle-axe
poll-axe
nod-ay
cradle-babe
aglet-baby
bow-back
crook-back
giving-back
goer-back
horse-back-breaker
keeper-back
bunch-back'd
office-badge
cloak-bag
honey-bag
honey-bags
money-bags
bum-baily
fine-baited
bear-baiting
bear-baitings
weal-balanc'd
pitch-balls
tennis-balls
sea-bank
sea-banks
butt'ry-bar
strong-barr'd
beer-barrel
window/-bars
strong-bas'd
alms-basket
buck-basket

buck-baskets
breed-bate
journey-bated
a-batfowling
high-battled
parcel-bawd
to-be-pitied
daughter-beamed
sun-beamed
eye-beams
she-bear
lack-beard
scarce-bearded
white-bearded
white-beards
ape-bearer
purse-bearer
thunder-bearer
torch-bearer
torch-bearers
bull-bearing
horn-beasts
dry-beat
o'er-beat
dry-beaten
storm-beaten
weather-beaten
bold-beating
king-becoming
a-bed
bride-bed
child-bed
day-bed
death-bed
death's-bed
down-bed
feather-bed
field-bed
love-bed
marriage-bed
standing-bed
truckle-bed
wedding-bed
dew-bedabbled
death-beds
lily-beds
humble-bee
ox-beef
honey-bees
humble-bees
bull-beeves
she-beggar
fool-begg'd
a-begging
woe-begone
first-begotten
true-begotten
time-beguiling
well-behav'd
sad-beholding
hard-believing
soon-believing
alarum-bell
curfew-bell
'larum-bell
big-bellied
great-bellied
swag-bellied
thin/-bellied
dear-belov'd
well-belov'd
new-beloved
well-beloved
fore-bemoaned
church-bench
ill-beseeming
well-beseeming

strong-besieged
blood-bespotted
fore-betray'd
late-betrayed
fair-betrothed
time-bettering
brokers-between
go-between
goers-between
time-bewasted
a-billing
tavern-bills
all-/binding
night/-bird
a-birding
cuckoo-birds
wood-birds
canker-bit
sheep-biter
sheep-biting
fly-bitten
weather-bitten
//coal-black
coal-black
hell-black
shoulder-blade
willful-blame
point-blank
star-blasting
a-bleeding
new-bleeding
cursed-blessed
thrice-blessed
marriage-blessing
gravel-blind
hoodman-blind
sand-blind
ever-blinded
stumbling-blocks
heart-blood
life-blood
cold-blooded
half-blooded
sober-blooded
hot-bloodied
hot-bloods
canker-blooms
canker-blossom
fly-blowing
fly-blown
half-blown
high-blown
council-board
shovel-boards
wild-boars
loose-bodied
tender-bodied
no-bodies
best-boding
death-boding
fairest-boding
false-boding
ill-boding
bird-bolt
//dread-bolted
blood-bolter'd
bird-bolts
bare-bon'd
big-bon'd
burly-bon'd
raw-bon'd
strong-bonded
bare-bone
carv'd-bone
jaw-bone
shoulder-bone
copy-book

horn-book
love-book
muster-book
note-book
prayer-book
table-book
//without-book
prayer-books
base-born
bawd-born
eldest-born
first-born
fool-born
forest-born
hag-born
hedge-born
hell-born
high-born
latter-born
low-born
mean-born
new-born
now-born
self-born
still-born
true-born
twin-born
well-born
high-borne
just-borne
self-borne
shard-borne
//stiff-borne
easy-borrowed
blue-bottle
sandy-bottom'd
dear-bought
brow-bound
earth-bound
gold-bound
self-bounty
cross-bow
saddle-bow
stone-bow
standing-bowl
cross-bows
pepper-box
pouncet-box
//sea-boy
bow-boy's
ship-boy's
ship-boys
bugle-bracelet
lack-brain
mad-brain
clay-brain'd
deep-brain'd
dull-brain'd
fat-brain'd
hare-brain'd
mad-brain'd
boil'd-brains
top-branch
fire-brand
fire-brands
air-braving
night-brawler
before-breach
faith-breach
promise-breach
hair-breadth
barley-break
heart-break
law-breaker
promise-breaker
heart-breaking
oath-breaking

rib-breaking
marble-breasted
out-breasted
self-breath
well-breath'd
lust-breathed
heaven-bred
home-bred
mad-bred
true-bred
patch-breech
soldier-breeder
a-breeding
bate-breeding
ill-breeding
still-breeding
a-brewing
silver-bright
sun-bright
love-broker
fresh-brook
ice-brook's
barley-broth
hell-broth
plum-broth
snow-broth
twin-brother
baby-brow
black-brow'd
brib'd-buck
cuckoo-buds
mary-buds
new-built
rich-built
weak-built
cannon-bullets
hurly-burly
hurly-burly's
heart-burn'd
out-burneth
bright-burning
ever-burning
furnace-burning
heart-burning
heart-burnt
thorn-bush
ear-/bussing
malmsey-butt
salt-butter
brawn-buttock
pin-buttock
quatch-buttock
crystal-button
putting-by
stander-by
standers-by
wafer-cakes
bull-calf
moon-calf
moon-calf's
ca-caliban
half-can
rush-candle
sugar-candy
demi-cannon
over-canopied
corner-cap
night-cap
sea-cap
cloud-capp'd
off-capp'd
a-cap'ring
blue-caps
half-caps
night-caps
statute-caps
count-cardinal

king-cardinal
over-careful
ring-carrier
lute-case
watch-case
candle-cases
rough-cast
up-cast
counter-caster
musk-cat
wild-cat
cony-catch
tallow-catch
cony-catch'd
gull-catcher
rat-catcher
cony-catching
wild-cats
love-cause
guest-cavalier
dining-chamber
dining-chambers
sea-change
child-changed
purpose-changer
all-changing
ne'er-changing
wind-changing
full-charg'd
double-charge
self-charity
stubborn-chaste
half-cheek
half-cheek'd
rose-cheek'd
all-cheering
march-chick
birth-child
maid-child
male-child
man-child
men-children
bread-chipper
wide-chopp'd
well-chosen
even-christen
sunday-citizens
trumpet-clangor
shoulder-clapper
thunder-claps
clapper-claw
clapper-clawing
oak-cleaving
canvas-climber
pole-clipt
house-clogs
fast-closed
still-closing
bearing-cloth
foot-cloth
bed-clothes
cradle-clothes
swaddling-clouts
ne'er-cloying
sea-coal
skin-coat
grey-coated
parti-coated
silken-coated
leather-coats
tawny-coats
turkey-cock
turkey-cocks
custard-coffin
a-cold
cull-cold
dead-cold
key-cold
scarce-cold
straw-color
amber-color'd
cain-color'd
divers-color'd
/dun-color'd
flame-color'd
high/-color'd
many-color'd
parti-color'd
peach-color'd
purple-color'd
ruby-color'd
ebon-colored
freestone-colored
many-colored
raven-colored
sable-colored

water-colors
new-come
non-come
kissing-comfits
widow-comfort
pastoral-comical
//tragical-comical-
historical-pastoral
a-coming
thick-coming
self-comparisons
sweet-complaining
swart-complexion'd
ill-compos'd
foolish-compounded
sin-concealing
liberal-conceited
odd-conceited
first-conceived
quick-conceiving
sin-conceiving
vile-concluded
best-condition'd
safe-conduct
safe-conducting
pissing-conduit
soul-confirming
never-conquered
soft-conscienc'd
marble-constant
blood-consuming
sap-consuming
court-contempt
skill-contending
well-contented
long-continued
pre-contract
sub-contracted
over-cool
master-cord
hedge-corner
park-corner
pie-corner
black-corner'd
dove-cote
sheep-cote
sheep-cotes
chamber-councils
o'er-count
span-counter
death-counterfeiting
vaunt-couriers
main-course
tennis-court
tennis-court-keeper
kill-courtesy
cater-cousins
//self-cover'd
wit-crackers
news-cramm'd
promise-cramm'd
care-craz'd
new-create
part-created
serving-creature
serving-creature's
over-credulous
winter-cricket
town-crier
low-crooked
knee-crooking
charing-cross
star-cross'd
market-crosses
night-crow
french-crown-color
kingly-crowned
new-crowned
thrice-crowned
o'er-crows
holy-cruel
court-cupboard
acorn-cups
past-cure
body-curer
soul-curer
a-cursing
stone-cutter
super-dainty
step-dame
land-damn
drug-damn'd
morris-dance
handy-dandy
self-danger
honorable-dangerous

dive-dapper
over-daring
deep-dark
thunder-darter
death/-darting
new-dated
treble-dated
baby-daughter
never-daunted
ascension-day
coronation-day
dooms-day
hey-day
high-day
holy-day
hoy-day
love-day
marriage-day
may-day
noon-day
playing-day
sealing-day
//to-day
to-day
wedding-day
working-day
worky-day
chair-days
dog-days
fasting-days
law-days
market-days
school-days
working-days
clapper-de-claw
flower-de-luce
flower-de-luces
flow'r-de-luce
viol-de-gamboys
pale-dead
ear-deaf'ning
double-dealer
double-dealing
ill-dealing
plain-dealing
well-dealing
precious-dear
after-debts
late-deceased
low-declined
alms-deed
breast-deep
heart-deep
knee-deep
pottle-deep
well-defended
ditch-deliver'd
new-deliver'd
new-delivered
earth-delving
god-den
by-dependances
false-derived
true-derived
well-derived
well-deserved
well-deserving
late-despised
point-device
demi-devil
yoke-devils
point-devise
true-devoted
love-devouring
field-dew
honey-dew
morn-dew
lust-dieted
after-dinner's
still-discordant
love-discourse
dumb-discoursive
all-disgraced
clack-dish
fruit-dish
tun-dish
ill-dispersing
strange-disposed
well-disposed
true-disposing
tear-distained
late-disturbed
castle-ditch
moor-ditch
well-divided
death-divining

ill-divining
true-divining
deep-divorcing
what-do-ye-call
bully-doctor
ditch-dog
jack-dog
puppy-dog
ban-dogs
night-dogs
puppy-dogs
watch-dogs
a-doing
harm-doing
ill-doing
school-doing
self-doing
well-doing
widow-dolor
ding-dong
behind-door-work
chamber-door
church-door
hold-door
without-door
chamber-doors
without-doors
a-doting
thrice-double
turtle-doves
a-down
a-down-a
plucker-down
puller-down
steep-down
wedding-dow'r
marriage-dowry
flap-dragon
flap-dragon'd
flap-dragons
fire-drake
tooth-drawer
//bias-drawing
//deep-drawing
self-drawing
vile-drawing
air-drawn
choice-drawn
//cub-drawn
dove-drawn
all-dreaded
horse-drench
oil-dried
alms-drink
blood-drinking
by-drinkings
thrice-driven
ease-dropper
dew-dropping
green-dropping
eye-drops
honey-drops
//water-drops
water-drops
kettle-drum
swine-drunk
a-ducking
silly-ducking
cow-dung
out-dure
ever-during
long-during
giant-dwarf
out-dwells
o'er-dy'd
a-dying
never-dying
tender-dying
crop-ear
flap-ear'd
prick-ear'd
shag-ear'd
over-earnest
middle-earth
heart's-ease
heart-easing
north-east
mouse-eaten
o'er-eaten
worm-eaten
garlic-eaters
pork-eaters
all-eating
beast-eating
marrow-eating
house-eaves

cloud-eclipsed
keen-edg'd
re-edified
well-educated
finch-egg
pigeon-egg
forty-eight
rash-embrac'd
pre-eminence
pre-employ'd
good-en
butt-end
fig's-end
finger-end
fore-end
mile-end
orchard-end
self-endeared
all-ending
never-ending
noble-ending
arch-enemy
high-engender'd
long-engraff'd
new-enkindled
wide-enlarg'd
man-ent'red
well-ent'red
co-equal
while-ere
ill-erected
never-erring
ever-esteemed
lammas-eve
odd-even
ember-eves
self-example
thought-executing
sun-expelling
long-experienc'd
well-experienc'd
self-explication
black-ey'd
blue-ey'd
dark-ey'd
dizzy-ey'd
dull-ey'd
evil-ey'd
fair-ey'd
fire/-ey'd
fire-ey'd
great-ey'd
green-ey'd
grey-ey'd
hollow-ey'd
onion-ey'd
open-ey'd
//parti-ey'd
quick-ey'd
red-ey'd
sad-ey'd
sour-ey'd
thick-ey'd
wall-ey'd
young-ey'd
after-eye
o'er-eye
green-eyed
over-eyeing
black-fac'd
//bloody-fac'd
bold-fac'd
brazen-fac'd
cream-fac'd
fair-fac'd
false-fac'd
foul-fac'd
freckle-fac'd
glass-fac'd
good-fac'd
half-fac'd
ill-fac'd
lean-fac'd
old-fac'd
//out-fac'd
out-fac'd
pale-fac'd
paper-fac'd
red-fac'd
round-fac'd
sad-fac'd
shame-fac'd
smooth-fac'd
sour-fac'd
sweet-fac'd
thin-fac'd

white-fac'd
brazen-face
half-face
tallow-face
/whey-face
whey-face
blessed-fair
thrice-fair
meadow-fairies
fast-falling
tear-falling
chop-fall'n
folly-fall'n
new-fall'n
sick-fall'n
trade-fall'n
tilly-fally
proper-false
secret-false
well-fam'd
thrice-famed
new-fangled
wind-fann'd
sea-farer
sea-faring
fee-farm
three-farthing
three-farthings
hand-fast
hold-fast
/tub-fast
double-fatal
uncle-father
fellow-fault
find-faults
hard-favor'd
//ill-favor'd
ill-favor'd
well-favor'd
hard-favored
well-favored
ill-favoredly
beggar-fear
all-fear'd
not-fearing
soul-fearing
marriage-feast
a-feasting
love-feat
dove-feather'd
bacon-fed
bean-fed
full-fed
rump-fed
tender-feeling
coach-fellow
pew-fellow
//yoke-fellow
yoke-fellow
vow-fellows
yoke-fellows
good-fellowship
weather-fends
play-feres
deep-fet
far-fet
a-field
corn-field
sea-fight
self-figur'd
muster-file
up-fill
mouth-filling
hare-finder
feast-finding
/five-finger-tied
tawny/-finn'd
new-fir'd
cannon-fire
hell-fire
trial-fire
land-fish
salt-fish
stock-fish
stock-fishes
fifty-five
seventy-five
twenty-five
true-fix'd
ever-fixed
honor-flaw'd
night-flies
water-flies
crow-flowers
water-flowers
full-flowing

water-flowing
cuckoo-flow'rs
flesh-fly
water-fly
night-foes
south-fog
bi-fold
nine-fold
peevish/-fond
childish-foolish
dry-foot
fleet-foot
fore-foot
light-foot
three-foot
under-foot
fiery-footed
free-footed
hasty-footed
leaden-footed
nimble-footed
swift-footed
tiger-footed
hop'd-for
long'd-for
su'd-for
unlook'd-for
unpaid-for
mountain-foreigner
yea-forsooth
bringings-forth
so-forth
full-fortun'd
well-foughten
new-found
well-found
valley-fountain
wild-fowl
dog-fox
/hid-fox
//she-foxes
strong-fram'd
full-fraught
o'er-fraught
fancy-free
shot-free
fertile-fresh
black-friars
white-friars
back-friend
mouth-friends
trencher-friends
leap-frog
falling-from
broad-fronted
out-frown
first-fruits
fault-full
over-full
heavy-gaited
slow-gaited
tardy-gaited
top-gallant
water-galls
earnest-gaping
be-gar
caddis-garter
cross-garter'd
cross-gartering
abbey-gate
city-gate
counter-gate
court-gate
flood-gate
north-gate
park-gate
//six-gated
city-gates
flood-gates
arm-gaunt
star-gazers
glass-gazing
steadfast-gazing
still-gazing
attorneys-general
captain-general
ever-gentle
tassel-gentle
thrice-gentle
waiting-gentlewoman
cousin-german
cozen-germans
nothing-gift
flirt-gills
parcel-gilt
pepper-gingerbread

direction-giver
lie-giver
/gain-giving
health-giving
honor-giving
eye-glance
burning-glass
eye-glass
hour-glass
//looking-glass
looking-glass
self-glorious
bare-gnawn
love-god
love-gods
a-going
hence-going
by-gone
curious-good
wild-goose
full-gorg'd
shrill-gorg'd
thrice-gorgeous
hell-govern'd
well-govern'd
night-gown
sea-gown
well-graced
self-gracious
thrice-gracious
great-grandfather
great-grandsire
great-grandsire's
chaw'd-grass
knot-grass
short-grass'd
o'er-great
//over-greedy
deep-green
grass-green
o'er-green
fee-grief
heart-grief
grim-grinning
guts-griping
shove-groat
palpable-gross
sharp-ground
winter-ground
line-grove
broom-groves
a-growing
fast-growing
rude-growing
full-grown
great-grown
high-grown
long-grown
moss-grown
rough-grown
thick-grown
grand-guard
velvet-guards
elder-gun
calves'-guts
fat-guts
down-gyved
bride-habited
common-hackney'd
all-hail
all-hail'd
black-hair'd
hard-hair'd
shag-hair'd
white-hair'd
kate-hall
all-hallond
well-hallow'd
all-hallowmas
all-hallown
behind-hand
bow-hand
court-hand
right-hand
sleeve-hand
two-hand
deadly-handed
doughty-handed
even-handed
hard-handed
large-handed
white-handed
over-handled
bed-hangers
a-hanging
chamber-hanging

under-hangman
/over-happy
rocky-hard
stone-hard
stubborn-hard
heart-hard'ning
daring-hardy
life-harming
self-harming
ever-harmless
heavenly-harness'd
post-haste
pickt-hatch
new-hatch'd
hell-hated
all-hating
rival-hating
temple-haunting
milford-haven
more-having
ass-head
calve's-head
cittern-head
death's-head
fool's-head
logger-head
ox-head
rowel-head
bare-headed
beetle-headed
heavy-headed
hoary-headed
hydra-headed
idle-headed
ill-headed
mad-headed
many-headed
puppy-headed
rug-headed
sleek-headed
three-headed
two-headed
waspish-headed
new-heal'd
never-heard-of
false-heart
cold-hearted
cruel-hearted
//dog-hearted
empty-hearted
faint-hearted
false-hearted
flint-hearted
free-hearted
full-hearted
gentle-hearted
hard-hearted
hollow-hearted
honest-hearted
kind-hearted
maiden-hearted
marble-hearted
merry-hearted
pale-hearted
pitiful-hearted
proud-hearted
sad-hearted
shallow-hearted
soft-hearted
stony-hearted
stout-hearted
strong-hearted
tender-hearted
true-hearted
truer-hearted
weak-hearted
burton-heath
heart-heaviness
honey-heavy
lighter-heel'd
larks'-heels
tender-hefted
a-height
drop-heir
an-heires
co-heirs
easy-held
crack-hemp
double-henn'd
nose-herbs
bear-herd
neat-herd's
neat-herds
swine-herds
arch-heretic
out-herods

pickle-herring
rough-hew
long-hid
all-hiding
a-high
olympus-high
pillicock-hill
tower-hill
basket-hilt
sword-hilts
weak-hing'd
red-hipp'd
//tragical-historical
heigh-ho
westward-ho
whoa-ho-hoa
hang-hog
a-hold
candle-holder
auger-hole
button-hole
dog-hole
key-hole
kill-hole
starting-hole
bench-holes
loop-holes
sight-holes
worm-holes
devilish-holy
harvest-home
under-honest
mouth-honor
all-honor'd
time-honored
round-hoof'd
sheep-hook
three-hoop'd
a-hooting
dis-horn
shoeing-horn
fill-horse
/hobby-horse
hobby-horse
malt-horse
pack-horse
post-horse
stalking-horse
trotting-horse
hobby-horses
pack-horses
post-horses
boot-hose
glowing-hot
hissing-hot
red-hot
hell-hound
hell-hounds
birth-hour's
after-hours
sleeping-hours
three-hours
asher-house
bawdy-house
brew-house
brothel-house
charge-house
charnel-house
council-house
dove-house
dwelling-house
farm-house
garden-house
hot-house
manor-house
prison-house
senate-house
slaughter-house
spittle-house
store-house
tap-house
tiring-house
working-house
bawdy-houses
charnel-houses
leaping-houses
store-houses
loud-howling
heaven-hu'd
purple-hu'd
a-hungry
an-hungry
mouse-hunt
a-hunting
bloody-hunting
all-hurting

combinate-husband
bolting-hutch
wedlock-hymn
god-i-goden
dit-il
est-il
long-imprisoned
brother-in-law
coming-in
comings-in
daughter-in-law
father-in-law
hand-in-hand
love-in-idleness
purple-in-grain
son-in-law
son-in-law's
son-in-laws
wrong-incensed
three-inch
four-inch'd
heart-inflaming
ill-inhabited
after-inquiry
toasting-iron
plough-irons
flap-jacks
minute-jacks
dis-je
qu'ai-je
loving-jealous
good-jer
leathern-jerkin
rich-jewell'd
apple-john
poor-john
apple-johns
co-join
short-jointed
strong-jointed
high-judging
love-juice
precious-juiced
senior/-junior
grand-jurymen
brother-justice
guest-justice
cave-keeper
counsel-keeper
crow-keeper
door-keeper
house-keeper
house-keepers
cave-keeping
counsel-keeping
home-keeping
house-keeping
promise-keeping
swine-keeping
fat-kidney'd
lime-kill
new-kill'd
self-kill'd
child-killer
king-killer
a-killing
comfort-killing
dead-killing
soul-killing
lime-kills
wrath-kindled
love-kindling
milch-kine
castalion-king-urinal
half-kirtles
cloud-kissing
common-kissing
/heaven-kissing
privy-kitchen
hell-kite
crook-knee'd
paring-knife
bully-knight
trencher-knight
strong-knit
well-knit
virgin-knot
curious-knotted
small-knowing
well-known
joint-laborer
well-laboring
tawdry-lace
starve-lackey
love-lacking
mercy-lacking

low-laid
she-lamb
dire-lamenting
a-land
stubble-land
datchet-lane
long-lane
dew-lapp'd
still-lasting
red-lattice
title-leaf
co-leagued
lank-lean
well-learned
dog's-leather
neat's-leather
o'er-leavens
master-leaver
wood-leaves
wing-led
horse-leeches
rich-left
long-legg'd
near-legg'd
short-legg'd
three-legg'd
two-legg'd
hinder-legs
smell-less
humor-letter
love-letters
rash-levied
all-licens'd
foot-licker
coffer-lids
alder-liefest
a-life
day-light
taper-light
angel-like
basilisco-like
bear-like
brother-like
calf-like
cat-like
child-like
chorus-like
christian-like
church-like
clerk-like
court-like
coward-like
death-like
doctor-like
dolphin-like
dove-like
dragon-like
drone-like
fairy-like
fiend-like
fish-like
gentleman-like
giant-like
glutton-like
goddess-like
gossip-like
guilty-like
indian-like
infant-like
jewel-like
juno-like
justice-like
lazar-like
merchant-like
mermaid-like
mist-like
monster-like
nestor-like
nurse-like
penthouse-like
phoenix-like
picture-like
pig-like
priest-like
prince-like
prologue-like
prophet-like
pupil-like
rascal-like
//rebel-like
riddle-like
saint-like
sea-like
serpent-like
slave-like
soldier-like

spaniel-like
spider-like
squire-like
star-like
stickler-like
such-like
surety-like
swan-like
thunder-like
tinder-like
villain-like
virgin-like
vizard-like
wand-like
war-like
wench-like
wife-like
well-liking
good-limb'd
white-lim'd
fadom-line
love-line
lack-linen
hare-lip
rose-lipp'd
thick-lipp'd
thick-lips
long-liv'd
short-liv'd
out-live
lily-liver'd
milk-liver'd
pigeon-liver'd
white-liver'd
ever-living
long-living
mortal-living
double-lock
up-locked
/elf-locks
cate-log
high-lone
flat-long
over-long
goose-look
bigger-look'd
grim-look'd
lean-look'd
red-look'd
sharp-looking
lass-lorn
custa-lorum
rato-lorum
after-loss
fast-lost
well-lost
after-love
brother-love
lack-love
self-love
true-love
true-love's
self-loving
//head-lugg'd
fell-lurking
/ne'er-lust-wearied
lack-lustre
chamber-lye
tirra-lyra
cuckold-mad
horn-mad
moody-mad
mouth-made
new-made
weak-made
beggar-maid
market-maid
sea-maid
sea-maid's
school-maids
card-maker
cuckold-maker
gallows-maker
gibbet-maker
grave-maker
horn-maker
jig-maker
rope-maker
widow-maker
ballad-maker's
comfit-maker's
ballad-makers
grave-makers
a-making
grave-making
arts-man
beggar-man
harvest-man
log-man
mark-man
please-man
silk-man
singing-man
slaughter-man
three-man
war-man
full-mann'd
filthy-mantled
night-mare
wild-mare
sea-marge
ave-maries
sea-mark
death-mark'd
elvish-mark'd
war-mark'd
new-married
merchant-marring
thunder-master
bed-mate
book-mates
co-mates
skains-mates
datchet-mead
inch-meal
limb-meal
fish-meals
double-meaning
well-meaning
true-meant
well-meant
over-measure
passy-measures
roast-meat
spoon-meat
worm's-meat
bak'd-meats
co-meddled
after-meeting
pell-mell
easy-melting
apron-men
book-men
handicrafts-men
slaughter-men
song-men
bellows-mender
a-mending
she-mercury
over-merry
/pardon-me's
self-mettle
lion-mettled
muddy-mettled
rere-mice
skim-milk
paper-mill
bloody-minded
high-minded
motley-minded
noble-minded
noblest-minded
proud-minded
tender-minded
well-minded
candle-mine
self-misus'd
arch-mock
mannerly-modest
dites-moi
excusez-moi
pardonnez-moi
//clamor-moistened
press-money
barber-monger
fancy-monger
love-monger
ballet-mongers
carpet-mongers
fashion-mongers
fashion-monging
bully-monster
man-monster
sea-monster
servant-monster
half-moon
may-morn
to-morrow
to-morrow's
to-morrow't
aunt-mother
queen-mother
//rouge-mount
deep-mouth'd
flap-mouth'd
foul-mouth'd
honey-mouth'd
humble-mouth'd
narrow-mouth'd
stretch-mouth'd
venom'd-mouth'd
foul-mouth'd'st
best-moving
cold-moving
heaven-moving
mirth-moving
hugger-mugger
eyas-musket
troll-my-dames
stark-nak'd
over-name
demi-natur'd
honest-natur'd
sourest-natur'd
leo-natus
break-neck
strong-neck'd
wry-neck'd
never-needed
self-neglecting
willful-negligent
fire-new
love-news
mumble-news
wall-newt
well-nigh
a-night
good-night
out-night
//to-night
/to-night
to-night
a-nights
good-nights
twenty-nine
all-noble
thrice-noble
thrice-nobler
three-nook'd
north-north-east
north-north-west
hook-nos'd
malmsey-nose
red-nose
well-noted
after-nourishment
allons-nous
short-numb'red
foster-nurse
ill-nurtur'd
hazel-nut
hazel-nuts
pig-nuts
sea-nymphs
book-oath
all-obeying
night-oblations
all-oblivious
senseless-obstinate
court-odor
man-of-war
not-of-the-newest
unthought-of
cutter-off
falling-off
fall'n-off
far-off
taking-off
eye-offending
heart-offending
self-offenses
wit-old
coming-on
looker-on
lookers-on
putter-on
putting-on
unthought-on
arch-one
//pers-one
thirty-one
twenty-one
willful-opposite
heat-oppressed
six-or-seven-times-honor'd
well-order'd
watch-ords
finder/-out
finder-out
/givings-out
jutting-out
putter-out
stretch'd-out
thrower-out
weeder-out
worn-out
sight-outrunning
honor-owing
night-owl
screech-owl
scritch-owl
night-owl's
night-owls
screech-owls
draught-oxen
snail-pac'd
giddy-paced
title-page
well-paid
feeling-painful
hell-pains
well-painted
nose-painting
ashy-pale
cold-pale
maid-pale
brain-pan
warming-pan
demi-paradise
out-paramour'd
cheese-paring
half-part
long-parted
peace-parted
timely-parted
over-partial
co-partners
by-past
fore-past
historical-pastoral
bald-pate
curl'd-pate
bald-pated
crooked-pated
knotty-pated
not-pated
periwig-pated
russet-pated
letters-patents
smoothy-pates
foot-path
by-paths
over-pay
non-payment
make-peace
bo-peep
under-peep
by-peeping
highest-peering
still-peering
goose-pen
aleven-pence-farthing
eight-penny
half-pennyworth
non-performance
love-performing
bare-pick'd
o'er-picturing
a-piece
chimney-piece
ground-piece
head-piece
mortar-piece
murd'ring-piece
shoulder-piece
a-pieces
birding-pieces
head-pieces
proud-pied
heart-pierc'd
ear-piercing
side-piercing
maggot-pies
boar-pig
hedge-pig
cock-pigeon
straight-pight
tithe-pig's
morris-pike
three-pil'd
three-pile
push-pin
//belly-pinched
still-pining
nimble-pinion'd
half-pint
organ-pipe
clyster-pipes
horse-piss
brine-pit
cherry-pit
high-pitch'd
brine-pits
high-plac'd
baiting-place
burying-place
dwelling-place
judgment-place
lurking-place
market-place
meeting-place
show-place
sporting-place
york-place
dwelling-places
red-plague
new-planted
sky-planted
fair-play
false-play'd
even-pleach'd
thick-pleach'd
pity-pleading
time-pleaser
time-pleasers
troth-plight
grass-plot
fatal-plotted
plume-pluck'd
lofty-plumed
fiery-pointed
sharp-pointed
life-poisoning
kingly-poor
devil-porter
tale-porter
cinque-ports
haste-post-haste
hovel-post
post-post-haste
woman-post
chamber-pot
pint-pot
pottle-pot
pottle-pot's
toss-pots
water-pots
spanish-pouch
hundred-pound
death-practic'd
well-practic'd
all-praised
love-prate
morn-prayer
a-praying
ever-preserv'd
nice-preserved
life-preserving
bed-presser
market-price
up-prick'd
hedge-priest
precious-princely
o'er-priz'd
wholesome-profitable
break-promise
ague-proof
high-proof
pistol-proof
plot-proof
shame-proof
war-proof
past-proportion
well-proportion'd
well-proportioned
over-proud
top-proud
sharp-provided
narrow-prying
hodge-pudding
thrice-puissant
/stock-punish'd
demi-puppets
dear-purchas'd
pick-purse
pick-purses
stomach-qualm'd
three-quarters
cot-quean
mother-queen
boy-queller
man-queller
woman-queller
never-quenching
sharp-quill'd
//goose-quills
tag-rag
quick-raised
land-rakers
fore-rank
o'er-rank
dancing-rapier
heady-rash
low-rated
land-rats
water-rats
night-raven
high-reaching
o'er-read
over-read
high-rear'd
fore-recited
tavern-reckonings
fiery-red
over-red
ripe-red
wax-red
robin-redbreast
well-refined
counter-reflect
non-regardance
best-regarded
sur-rein'd
here-remain
/e'er-remaining
//well-rememb'red
life-rend'ring
thrice-renowned
a-repairing
high-repented
self-reproving
thrice-repured
well-reputed
high-resolved
harsh-resounding
ill-resounding
well-respected
night-rest
never-resting
back-return
/sir-reverence
sir-reverence
deep-revolving
love-rhymes
bare-ribb'd
strong-ribb'd
thick-ribbed
bed-rid
bed-right
forth-rights
agate-ring
horn-ring
joint-ring
seal-ring
thumb-ring
wedding-ring
sinking-ripe
weeping-ripe
over-ripen'd
a-ripening
sun-rise
ill-roasted
fire-rob'd
riding-robes
riding-rods
a-rolling
holy-rood
bully-rook
bed-room
by-room
elbow-room
sea-room
shallow-rooted
wain-ropes
down-roping
musk-rose
cheek-roses
musk-roses
dirt-rotten
boist'rous-rough
up-rous'd
a-row
cross-row
all-royal
tent-royal

giant-rude
water-rugs
hard-rul'd
night-rule
ever-running
sherris-sack
wool-sack
late-sack'd
blood-sacrifice
new-sad
sober-sad
pack-saddle
well-sailing
outward-sainted
//sea-salt
re-salute
self-same
past-saving
sweet-savor'd
hand-saw*
rank-scented
bloody-sceptred
taming-school
dancing-schools
a-scorn
salt-sea
south-sea
counter-seal'd
sweet-season'd
dark-seated
saint-seducing
fern-seed
hag-seed
nettle-seed
all-seeing
ill-seeming
so-seeming
summer-seeming
well/-seeming
well-seeming
all-seer
false-self
forset-seller
re-send
fellow-servant
joint-servant
process-server
land-service
firm-set
clock-setter
something-settled
twenty-seven
butt-shaft
love-shaft
love-shak'd
wind-shak'd
wind-shaken
a-shaking
all-shaking
ill-shap'd
trans-shape
world-sharers
sheep-shearing
ill-sheathed
mis-sheathed
new-shed
blood-shedding
silver-shedding
winding-sheet
wedding-sheets
egg-shell
mussel-shell
walnut-shell
egg-shells
quick-shifting
over-shine
bright-shining
clear-shining
out-shining
silver-shining
hostess-ship
slip-shod
horse-shoe
cannon-shot
grief-shot
nook-shotten
shoulder-shotten
a-shouting
fire-shovel
seld-shown
urchin-shows
night-shriek
shrill-shriking
custom-shrunk
all-shunn'd
cock-shut

brain-sick
crafty-sick
fancy-sick
heart-sick
lion-sick
love-sick
sea-sick
thought-sick
brain-sickly
green-sickness
sea-side
both-sides
eagle-sighted
high-sighted
thick-sighted
half-sights
sleave-silk
fee-simple
treble-sinew'd
twenty-six
mill-sixpences
blood-siz'd
great-siz'd
o'er-sized
skimble-skamble
helter-skelter
well-skill'd
calve's-skin
/eel-skin
eel-skin
sow-skin
thick-skin
under-skinker
calves'-skins
eel-skins
sheep-skins
wide-skirted
/self-slaughter
self-slaughter
still-slaughtered
self-slaught'red
bond-slave
villain-slave
bond-slaves
a-sleeping
gentle-sleeping
green-sleeves
snail-slow
willful-slow
sweet-smelling
tender-smelling
lady-smocks
wit-snapper
urchin-snouted
scent-snuffing
high-soaring
perpetual-sober
flower-soft
single-sol'd
still-soliciting
love-song
plain-song
prick-song
love-songs
green-sord
eye-sore
heart-sore
plague-sore
canker-sorrow
sea-sorrow
heart-sorrowing
christians-soul
all-souls'
harsh-sounding
shrill-sounding
self-sovereignty
water-spaniel
none-sparing
hedge-sparrow
false-speaking
boar-spear
high-speeded
soon-speeding
pullet-sperm
barren-spirited
clear-spirited
frosty-spirited
ill-spirited
low-spirited
pleasant-spirited
fair-spoken
foul-spoken
well-spoken
waggon-spokes
table-sport
cinque-spotted

pinch-spotted
toad-spotted
broad-spreading
softly-sprighted
up-spring
gallant-springing
love-springs
new-sprung
home-spuns
copper-spur
fore-spurrer
a-squint
mountain-squire
broom-staff
charging-staff
cowl-staff
long-staff
walking-staff
blood/-stain'd
dis-stain'd
lust-stain'd
over-stain'd
tear-stain'd
blood-stained
neighbor-stained
bully-stale
honey-stalks
head-stall
still-stand
under-stand
deadly-standing
water-standing
mortal-staring
up-staring
ill-starr'd
hunger-starved
hungry-starved
state-statues
torch-staves
horse-stealer
well-steel'd
poking-sticks
stone-still
spirit-stirring
side-stitches
pointing-stock
puke-stocking
worsted-stocking
laughing-stocks
nether-stocks
vlouting-stocks
vlouting-stog
thief-stol'n
high-stomach'd
agot-stone
cherry-stone
grave-stone
thunder-stone
gun-stones
close-stool
//join-stool
join'd-stool
join-stools
join'd-stools
spell-stopp'd
new-store
sea-storm
birth-strangled
stony-stratford
rye-straw
wide-stretched
base-string
bow-string
heart-string
lute-string
bow-strings
eye-strings
heart-strings
thunder-stroke
heart-strook
wasp-stung
oft-subdued
self-subdued
self-substantial
super-subtle
fen-suck'd
blood-sucker
rabbit-sucker
blood-suckers
blood-sucking
sweet-suggesting
love-suit
riding-suit
sober-suited
three-suited
deep-sunken

half-supp'd
after-supper
co-supremes
cock-sure
never-surfeited
fear-surprised
re-survey
sea-swallow'd
a-swearing
chimney-sweepers
flattering-sweet
honey-sweet
silver-sweet
surfeit-swell'd
summer-swelling
bed-swerver
momentary-swift
wind-swift
big-swoll'n
high-swoll'n
half-sword
victor-sword
deep-sworn
tick-tack
ladder-tackle
ill-ta'en
new-ta'en
snipt-taffata
horse-tail
long-tail
trundle-tail
red-tail'd
travel-tainted
action-taking
leave-taking
purse-taking
surfeit-taking
carry-tale
tell-tale
tell-tales
out-talk
table-talk
a-talking
night-tapers
apple-tart
bohemian-tartar
tittle-tattling
pair-taunt-like
orange-tawny
parrot-teacher
over-tedious
o'er-teemed
fortune-tell
fortune-teller
all-telling
fortune-telling
true-telling
best-temper'd
ill-temper'd
strong-temper'd
ram-tender
pick-thanks
inch-thick
land-thieves
water-thieves
all-thing
blood-thirsty
holy-thistle
holy-thoughted
sick-thoughted
lay-thoughts
love-thoughts
war-thoughts
wrack-threat'ning
thirty-three
twenty-three
cut-throat
cut-throats
bartholomew-tide
lammas-tide
shrove-tide
shoe-tie
tongue-tied
up-till
a-tilt
clean-timber'd
hardest-timber'd
bed-time
before-time
dinner-time
holiday-time
life-time
milking-time
peascod-time
rut-time
spring-time

supper-time
whiting-time
winter-time
too-timely
spring-time's
after-times
oft-times
ten-times-barr'd-up
lily-tincture
woman-tir'd
ship-tire
lay-to
not-to-be-endur'd
ivy/-tods
death-tokens
love-tokens
twice-told
close-tongu'd
lewd-tongu'd
long-tongu'd
maiden-tongu'd
shrill-tongu'd
trumpet-tongu'd
out-tongue
smooth-tongue
honey-tongued
all-too-precious
well-took
sharp-tooth'd
main-top
parish-top
chimney-tops
plough-torn
seas-toss'd
tempest-toss'd
tempest-tossed
ne'er-touch'd
free-town
lud's-town
new-transformed
mouse-trap
earth-treading
axle-tree
box-tree
crab-tree
elder-tree
fruit-tree
plum-tree
willow-tree
bay-trees
crab-trees
fruit-trees
olive-trees
back-trick
tumbling-trick
rope-tricks
tray-trip
night-tripping
all-triumphant
down-trod
down-trodden
new-trothed
honest-true
one-trunk-inheriting
self-trust
powd'ring-tub
care-tun'd
new-tun'd
sad-tun'd
well-tun'd
ill-tuned
well-tuned
triple-turn'd
a-turning
topsy-turvy
scythe-tusk'd
a-twain
hazel-twig
lime-twigs
all-unable
self-unable
great-uncle
great-uncle's
stand-under
fortunate-unhappy
re-united
far-unworthy
blowers-up
bringing-up
heav'd-up
hunt's-up
layer-up
lock'd-up
made-up
pent-up
seal'd-up

setter-up
snapper-up
sneak-up
start-up
steep-up
tied-up
//weav'd-up
yielder-up
white-upturned
climber-upward
ill-us'd
madly-us'd
long-usurped
ill-uttering
ever-valiant
thrice-valiant
tire-valiant
tilly-vally
dearest-valued
long-vanish'd
double-vantage
mock-vater
over-veil'd
liver-vein
blue-vein'd
no-verbs
party-verdict
soul-vex'd
still-vex'd
earth-vexing
high-vic'd
thrice-victorious
over-view
re-view
arch-villain
out-villain'd
base-viol
virgin-violator
grim-visag'd
humble/-visag'd
pale-visag'd
tripe-visag'd
strangely-visited
aqua-vitae
low-voic'd
shrill/-voic'd
silver-voic'd
out-voice
fore-vouch'd
appelez-vous
etes-vous
suivez-vous
bed-vow
break-vow
deep-vow
vapor-vow
night-waking
still-waking
late-walking
night-walking
brick-wall
out-wall
sea-walled
water-walled
night-wanderers
night-wand'rers
night-wand'ring
beauty-waning
pity-wanting
closet-war
paris-ward
park-ward
pittie-ward
well-warranted
ale-wash'd
over-wash'd
buck-washing
candle-wasters
night-watch
all-watched
holy-water
mock-water
rain-water
rose-water
salt-water
sea-water
salt-wav'd
ear-wax
church-way
horse-way
road-way
fever-weak'ned
day-wearied
war-wearied
woe-wearied
world-wearied

a-weary
dog-weary
life-weary
over-weather'd
ill-weav'd
furrow-weeds
a-weeping
well-weighing
ill-well
flax-wench
oyster-wench
/ha'rford-west
south-west
bell-wether
waggon-wheel
chariot-wheels
mill-wheels
bear-whelp
bear-whelps
pissing-while
sheep-whistling
tu-whit
lily-white
milk-white
silver-white
snow-white
tu-who
heart-whole
kicky-wicky
maiden-widowed
ale-wife
city-wife
orange-wife
savage-wild
self-will
self/-will'd
self-will'd
well-willer
well-willers
always-wind-obeying
south-wind
long-winded
short-winded
chamber-window
church-window
drift-winds
pipe-wine
sea-wing
clip-wing'd
fleet-wing'd
full-wing'd
light-wing'd
slow-wing'd
strong-wing'd
eagle-winged
swift-winged
eye-wink
burthen-wise
colossus-wise
guest-wise
heart-wish'd
well-wish'd
mother-wit
want-wit
never-withering
world-without-end
beef-witted
blunt-witted
fat-witted
hasty-witted
high-witted
iron-witted
lean-witted
quick-witted
sodden-witted
subtile-witted
loose-wiv'd
ale-wive's
she-wolf
bitch-wolf's
demi-wolves
beggar-woman
city-woman
country/-woman
country-woman
dey-woman
herb-woman
tithe-woman
butter-woman's
round-womb'd
distaff-women
//waiting-women
waiting-women
butter-women's
feast-won
well-won
a-wooing
linsey-woolsey
court-word
nay-word
watch-word
by-words
a-work
bed-work
needle-work
sale-work
stair-work
trunk-work
half-workers
dark-working
glow-worm
blind-worm's
glow-worm's
blind-worms
glow-worms
malt-worms
war-worn
wave-worn
idiot-worshippers
hair-worth
all-worthy
death-worthy
thrice-worthy
deep-wounded
love-wounded
wonder-wounded
back-wounding
crest-wounding
gogs-wouns
bow-wow
/o'er-wrastling
//sorrow-wreathen
o'er-wrested
ill-wresting
self-wrong
high-wrought
under-wrought
half-yard
mete-yard
tilt-yard
what-ye-call't
eight-year-old
good-year
new-year's
good-years
ne'er-yet-beaten
easy-yielding
dig-you-den

Hyphenated Words 3

(ALPHABETIZED ACCORDING TO THIRD ELEMENT)

a-down-a
jack-an-ape
jack-an-apes
man-at-arms
men-at-arms
officers-at-arms
pursuivant-at-arms
ten-times-barr'd-up
not-to-be-endur'd
ne'er-yet-beaten
slug-a-bed
horse-back-breaker
sword-and-buckler
toasts-and-butter

what-ye-call't
clapper-de-claw
french-crown-color
troll-my-dames
well-a-day
now-a-days
dig-you-den
cock-a-diddle-dow
john-a-dreams
north-north-east
world-without-end
aleven-pence-farthing
//to-and-fro-conflicting
viol-de-gamboys

god-i-goden
purple-in-grain
hand-in-hand
haste-post-haste
post-post-haste
//tragical-comical-historical-pastoral
whoa-ho-hoa
cock-a-hoop
love-in-idleness
one-trunk-inheriting
tennis-court-keeper
hard-a-keeping

cap-and-knee
brother-in-law
daughter-in-law
father-in-law
son-in-law
son-in-law's
son-in-laws
jack-a-lent
pair-taunt-like
flower-de-luce
flow'r-de-luce
flower-de-luces
god-a-mercy

cat-a-mountain
jack-a-nape
well-a-near
always-wind-obeying
never-heard-of
eight-year-old
such-a-one
such-a-one's
sink-a-pace
cap-a-pe
to-be-pitied
all-too-precious
peg-a-ramsey

six-or-seven-times-honor'd
not-of-the-newest
five-and-thirty
/five-finger-tied
three-and-twenty
two-and-twenty
castalion-king-urinal
man-of-war
/ne'er-lust-wearied
north-north-west
behind-door-work
what-do-ye-call

Appendix II

Homographs

A'	at; in; of; on
A	*indef. art.;* note in music; *Fr. prep.; interj.,* ah
ABIDE	remain, endure; aby
ABLE	strong, capable; warrant
ABRAM	Abraham; auburn
AERY	nest; airy
AFFECTION	emotion, disposition; affectation
AN	*indef. art.;* on
ANCIENT	old; ensign
ANGLE	corner; fish
AN'T	if't; on't
ARCH	curve; prime
ARM	limb; weapon
ARM'D	furnished with weapons; limbed
ARMS	see ARM
ARRANT	downright; errand
ART	*vb.;* skill, learning
AS	*adv., conj., prep.; Fr. vb.*
ATTORNEY	deputy; commission
AY	yes; *interj.*
BAND	tie; company; bond
BANDS	see BAND
BAR	shut off; name
BARBARY	place; Barbara
BARE	naked; *p.,* bear
BARK	ship; rind; cry of dog
BARKS	see BARK
BARNES	name; bairns
BASE	fundament, low; game; bass *(mus.)*
BASES	fundaments, pleated skirt; basses *(mus.)*
BASTING	moistening meat; beating
BAT	mammal; club
BATE	reduce; flap wings
BATED	see BATE
BATES	reduces; name
BATH	ablution; both
BATS	see BAT
BAWD	procurer; hare
BAY	bark; body of water; color; opening *(architecture)*
BE	*vb.;* by
BEAR	carry; animal
BEARS	see BEAR
BEETLE	insect; heavy mallet
BEETLES	insects; overhangs
BEHOLDING	seeing; beholden
BESEECH'D	implored; besieged
BID	order, offer; *p.,* bide
BILL	written paper; beak; weapon
BILLS	see BILL
BIT	*pp.,* bite; part of bridle; small piece
BITS	parts of bridles; small pieces
BLAZE	flame; proclaim
BLEAK	cold; bleat
BLOW	stir air; stroke; bloom
BLOWING	stirring air; blooming
BLOWN	see BLOWING
BLOWS	see BLOW
BLUNT	dull, rude; name
BLUNTS	dulls; name
BOB	buffet; cheat
BOBB'D	see BOB
BONA	name; *Lat. adj.*
BONE	hard tissue; *Lat. adv.*
BOOT	profit; shoe
BOOTS	see BOOT
BORE	drill; *p.,* bear
BOTTLE	container; bundle of hay
BOTTLES	see BOTTLE
BOUND	*p., pp.,* bind; leap; limit; ready, destined
BOUNDING	leaping; limiting
BOUNDS	see BOUNDING
BOURN	boundary; brook
BOW	incline, stoop; curved thing
BOWL	vessel; game
BOWLING	game; bowline
BOWLS	see BOWL
BOWS	see BOW
BOX	blow; container
BOYS	male children; name
BRAID	upbraid; deceitful
BRAKE	*p.,* break; thicket
BRAKES	thickets; cage (?), engine of torture (?)
BRAWL	quarrel; Fr. dance
BREEZE	gadfly; wind
BRIEF	letter; short
BRITAIN	Great Britain; Brittany; Briton; Breton
BRITAINS	Briton; Breton
BRITTANY	Bretagne; Britain
BROILS	quarrels; cooks
BROOK	endure; stream
BROOKS	see BROOK
BRUSHES	rubs, smoothes; forcible rushes
BRUTE	bestial; *Lat. voc.*
BUCK	animal; lye
BUGLE	horn; shiny, black
BULK	mass; projecting part of building
BURY	inter; place
BUTT	strike; cask; mark; bottom
BUTTS	strikes; name
BUY	purchase; be with
BUZZ	hum, whisper; *interj.*
BUZZARD	bird; buzzing insect
CADE	small barrel; name
CAIUS	Roman name; name of doctor
CALF	animal; part of leg
CALM	quiet; qualm
CAN	*vb.;* container; gan
CANDY	confection; name
CAPE	garment; headland
CAPER	leap; flower used for pickling
CAPILET	name; name of horse
CAR	vehicle; name; *Fr. conj.*
CARP	cavil; fish
CASE	enclose; condition
CASES	see CASE
CENTURY	hundred; sentry
CESS	assessment; cease
CHAPS	jaws; cracks in skin
CHE	I; *Ital. pron.*
CHILL	cold; I will
CHOPS	see CHAPS
CLAMOR	shout; silence
CLEAVE	split; cling
CLEAVING	see CLEAVE
CLIFF	steep rock; clef
CLIP	embrace; cut; call
CLIPT	see CLIP
COCK	bird; God; cockboat
COCKLE	shell; weed
COCK'S	bird's; God's
COMMENT	discourse; *Fr. pron.*
COMPACT	join; convenant, plot
CON	learn by heart; *Ital. prep.*
CONSORT	escort; company of musicians
CONTENT	satisfy; matter contained
CONTENTS	see CONTENT
CONTRIVE	devise; pass time
COPE	encounter; exchange; firmament
CORE	center; *Ital. n.*
CORN	grain; horny thickening of skin
CORPORAL	military rank; physical
COTE	cottage; quote
COTED	passed by; quoted
COUNT	number; title; gown
COUNTER	metal token; in opposite direction
COUNTS	numbers; titles
COUPLE	pair; *Fr. coupe* (?)
CRAB	apple; shellfish
CREW	*p.,* crow; band
CROW	cry; bird, crowbar
CUFFS	strikes; parts of sleeves
CUTS	pierces, splits; lots
CYPRESS	tree; cloth
D'	the; do
DAM	stop up; female parent
DANK	moist; thank
DARE	challenge; daze
DATE	time; fruit
DATES	see DATE
DE	the; do; *Fr., Sp. prep.;* exclamation
DEAR	precious; dire
DEAREST	see DEAR
DEN	cave; evening; then
DESERT	merit; barren waste
DESERTS	see DESERT
DEW	moisture; name
DIE	expire, cease; cube
DIES	expires, ceases; *Lat. n.*
DIRE	dreadful; *Fr. vb.*
DISTEMP'RING	disordering; diluting
DIVES	plunges; Lat. name
DO	perform; exclamation
DOLE	share; sorrow
DOLPHIN	mammal; Dauphin
DOLPHIN'S	see DOLPHIN
DON	put on; title
DOUT	put out; doubt
DOWN	opposite of up; feathers; land
DRONE	male bee; humming sound
DRUGS	medicines; drudges
DUCK	dive; bird
DUCKS	see DUCK
DUE	debt; endow
DUN	color; Don
EAR	organ of hearing; plow; spike of cereal plant
EARNEST	pledge; serious
EARNS	deserves; yearns
EARS	see EAR
EKE	increase; also
ELDER	tree; older
EMBOSS'D	driven to extremity; swollen
END	finish; harvest
ERRANT	wandering; errand
EVE	name; evening
EVEN	level; evening
EVILS	wickedness; privies (?)
EV'N	see EVEN
EXACT	require; precise

EXCREMENT	outgrowth; waste matter
FAIR	market; pleasing
FAIRS	see FAIR
FALL	drop; fault
FALLOW	uncultivated land; color
FAR	distant; name
FASHIONS	kinds, makes; farcins
FAST	abstain from food; firm, swift
FAT	flesh, grease; vat
FAWN	act servilely; young deer
FELL	*p.,* fall; hew; skin; fierce
FELLS	hews; skins
FELT	*p., pp.,* feel; fabric
FETCHES	brings, tricks; vetches
FIFE	musical instrument; place
FIG	fruit; gesture of contempt
FIL'D	smoothed; defiled
FILE	smooth; order, line
FILES	see FILE
FILLS	makes full; thills
FIN	organ of fish; *Fr. n.*
FINE	excellent, refine; end, sum required
FIT	suit; paroxysm
FITS	suits; paroxysms; cantos
FITTED	see FIT
FLAG	banner; plant
FLAW	sudden gust; fragment
FLAWS	see FLAW
FLEA	insect; flay
FLED	*p., pp.,* flee; *p., pp.,* fly
FLEET	naval force, flit; London prison; swift
FLIES	moves through air; flees; insects
FLIGHT	flying; fleeing
FLIGHTS	see FLIGHT
FLOCKS	groups; wool
FLOWN	*pp.,* fly; *pp.,* flow
FLY	see FLIES
FLYING	see FLIGHT
FOIL	defeat; setting off; fencing weapon
FOLD	double, enclose; sheep pen; suffix
FOOL	simpleton, etc.; kind of food
FORCE	constrain, strength; farce
FORT	fortified place; *Fr. adv.*
FOUNDER	fail; originator
FRANK	sty; open, generous; name
FRET	vex; adorn
FRETS	vexes; parts of mus. instruments
FRETTED	see FRET
FRIEZE	cloth; part of entablature *(architecture)*
FRY	cook; offspring
GALL	chafe; bile
GALLS	see GALL
GAUNT	lean; name
GERMANS	natives of Germany; kin
GILLS	respiratory organs; liquid measures; girls
GIN	begin; snare
GINS	see GIN
GLAZ'D	covered; glared
GLIB	smooth; castrate
GOD'S	*poss.,* God; God save
GORE	pierce; blood
GOT	*p., pp.,* get; God
GRAINED	dyed; lined; forked
GRATE	rub; frame of bars
GRAV'D	carved; buried
GRAVE	entomb, tomb; carve; serious
GRAZE	feed; touch lightly
GREECE	place; name of hamlet
GREY	color; name
GROUND	*pp.,* grind; base, soil
GULL	dupe; unfledged bird
GUMS	part of mouth; tree sap
GUST	taste; wind
HACK	chop; grow common (?)
HAG	ugly old woman; *Lat. haec*
HAIL	greeting; ice pellets
HAIL'D	see HAIL
HALLOW	make holy; shout
HALLOW'D	see HALLOW
HAND-SAW	tool; hernshaw
HANG	suspend; *Lat. hanc*
HATCH	bring forth; door
HATCH'D	*p., pp.,* hatch; closed with door; engraved
HAWK	bird; tool
HAWKING	falconry; clearing throat
HAY	fodder; dance; fencing term
HE	*masc. pron.;* exclamation
HELM	helmet; rudder
HELMS	see HELM
HEM	clear throat; border
HEMS	see HEM
HER	*fem. pron.;* their
HIDE	conceal; skin
HIDES	see HIDE
HIND	animal; menial; back
HINDS	animals; menials
HOB	name; hab
HOG	animal; *Lat. hoc*
HOLD	grasp; part of ship
HOLLOW	shout; cavity
HOOD	head covering; name
HOOP	circle; shout
HOST	one who entertains; army
HOSTS	see HOST
HUE	color; outcry
HUM	sound; *interj.*
HUMS	see HUM
HUNG	*p., pp.,* hang; *Lat. hunc*
I	*pron.;* vowel
ICE	frozen water; I shall
ILLUSTRIOUS	glorious; not lustrous
IMP	offspring; engraft feathers
IMPRESS	levy; pressure
IMPRESS'D	see IMPRESS
IMPRESSED	see IMPRESS
INCENSE	inflame; fragrance
INCH	measure of length; isle
INCONTINENT	at once; lacking restraint
INGENIOUS	skillful; ingenuous
JACKS	fellows; drinking vessels
JANE	name; cloth
JET	strut; black mineral
JORDAN	chamber pot; name
JOWL	strike; part of jaw
JUST	fair, exactly; joust
KEEL	part of ship; cool
KENNEL	doghouse; gutter
KINDLED	ignited; brought forth
KNAPP'D	bit; rapped
L	letter of alphabet; Roman numeral
LA	*interj.; Fr. art.; Fr. adv.;* tone in music
LAP	lick up; wrap, seat formed by sitting person
LAPS	see LAP
LAST	continue, endure; shoe mold; hindmost
LAW	rules; la
LAY	place; *p.,* lie; song; of the laity
LAYS	places; songs
LEAD	guide; metal
LEADS	see LEAD
LEAGUE	alliance; measure of distance
LEAGUES	see LEAGUE
LEAN	bend; meager
LEAVE	depart; permission
LEAVES	departs; *pl.,* leaf; permission
LEER	glance; complexion
LEFT	*p., pp.,* leave; opposite of right
LENT	*p., pp.,* lend; fasting period
LET	allow; hinder
LETS	see LET
LIE	recline; untruth
LIES	see LIE
LIEST	see LIE
LIGHT	opposite of dark; not heavy; alight
LIGHTED	gave light; alighted
LIGHTEN	illuminate; make less heavy
LIGHTENS	see LIGHTEN
LIGHTNESS	levity; brightness
LIGHTS	see LIGHTED
LIK'D	pleased, felt affection; compared
LIKE	please, feel affection; similar
LIKES	see LIKE
LIKING	see LIK'D
LIN'D	covered on inside; drawn
LINE	cover on inside; cord, row; lime
LINK	chain; torch
LINKS	see LINK
LI'ST	see LIE
LIST	listen; desire; boundary; catalogue
LISTS	desires; boundaries; catalogues
LIVE	have life, life; lief
LIVER	organ; one who lives
LIVERS	see LIVER
LOCK	fasten; hair
LOCKS	see LOCK
LONG	yearn; not short; owing to
LOOP	metal ring; loophole
LOW	not high; moo
LOW'RING	louring; lowering
LUCE	name; fish
LYING	see LIE
MACE	club; spice
MAIDENHEAD	virginity; place
MAIL	armor; bag
MAIN	principal, broad expanse; *Fr. n.;* betting term
MAKE	bring into being; mate
MAN	human being; place
MANES	hair; *Lat. n.*
MANNER	mode; act
MARCH	move; month; name
MARCHES	moves; borders
MARE	horse; nightmare
MARK	sign; coin; name
MARKS	signs; coins
MARRY	wed; *interj.*
MARS	spoils; Roman god
MASS	church service; quantity
MAST	part of ship; acorns
MATED	paired; checkmated
MATES	companions; checkmates
MAY	*vb.;* month
MEAL	repast; flour
MEAN	intend; low; middle
MEANEST	intend; lowest
MEANLY	lowly; moderately
MEANS	intends; resources; commoners; moans
MEAN'ST	see MEANEST
MEET	encounter; fitting
MEET'ST	see MEET
MESS	food, group; mass
MEW	confine; cat sound
MEW'D	see MEW
MI	tone in music; *Ital. pron.*
MIGHT	*vb.;* power
MINE	*poss. pron.;* excavation
MINT	place of coining; plant
MISPRIS'D	despised; mistaken
MISPRISION	see MISPRIS'D
MOLE	spot; animal
MOLES	see MOLE
MOOD	state of mind; mode
MOODS	see MOOD
MOOR	African; heath
MORE	greater in amount; name
MORRIS	dance; game
MOTH	insect; name
MOULD	form; clay
MOUNT	ascend; mountain
MOW	cut down; grimace
MOWING	see MOW
MUSE	ponder; goddess
MYSTERIES	secrets; skills
MYSTERY	see MYSTERIES
NAP	sleep; cloth surface
NAVE	hub of wheel; navel
NE	nor; *Lat. adv.;* neigh
NEAT	trim; cattle
NICK	notch; name; neck
NINNY'S	ninny is; Ninus
NOB	name; nab
NON	*Lat., Fr. adv.;* word of refrain
NOUNS	class of words; wounds
O'	of; on; one
O	*interj.;* letter of alphabet; cipher
'OD'S	God's; God save
OR	*conj.;* before
ORT	scrap; word
OUGHT	*vb.;* owed
OUNCE	unit of weight; animal
OW'D	indebted; owned
OWE	see OW'D
OWED	see OW'D
OWES	see OW'D
OWEST	see OW'D
OWING	see OW'D
OW'ST	see OW'D
PACE	step; name
PACK	bundle; conspire
PACK'D	see PACK
PACKING	see PACK
PALE	not colorful; fence

PALL	wane; cover
PALM	part of hand; tree
PAR	*Fr. prep.;* nonce word
PARIS	place; son of Priam; name
PARISH	district; Paris
PASH	strike; head
PATCH	mend; dolt
PATCHES	see PATCH
PEAR	fruit; bear
PEAT	pet; beat
PECK	strike with beak; unit of measure; pitch
PEEP	look; pip
PEER	appear; nobleman
PEERS	see PEER
PELTING	beating; paltry
PEN	write; enclose
PENS	see PEN
PIBBLE	pebble; bibble
PICK	pierce, select; pitch
PIE	baked dish; magpie, oath
PIED	dappled; *Fr. n.*
PIERCE	penetrate; name
PIES	baked dishes; magpies
PIG	animal; big
PIKE	weapon; fish
PIL'D	heaped; having nap; peeled
PILE	heap; nap
PINE	languish, starve; tree
PINES	see PINE
PINK	flower; winking
PITCH	throw, height; tar
PLAIN	clear, level, explain; complain
PLANTS	sets in, young trees; soles
PLIGHT	pledge; condition
PLIGHTED	pledged; platted
POINT	aim, location; *Fr. adv.*
POLE	shaft; end of axis; native of Poland; name; poll
PORT	harbor; bearing; gate
PORTAGE	port-hole; port fees (?)
PORTER	doorkeeper; bearer
PORTERS	see PORTER
PORTS	harbors; gates
POST	go speedily, messenger; pillar
POSTS	see POST
POUND	enclose; unit of weight
POUR	emit steadily; *Fr. prep.*
PREGNANT	apt; significant
PRESENT	show, immediate; gift
PRESENTS	see PRESENT
PRESIDENT	head; precedent
PRESS	urge, burden; conscript
PRESS'D	see PRESS
PRIZE	value; reward; booty; contest
PROSPER	thrive; Prospero
PRUNE	trim, preen; fruit
PRUNES	see PRUNE
PUSH	thrust; *interj.*
QUILL	feather; in a body
QUIVER	tremble; arrow case; nimble
RACE	lineage; course; root
RACK	stretch; cloud mass
RAIL	scold; horizontal bar
RANK	order; gross
RASE	raze; pluck off
RASED	see RASE
RASH	hasty; strike
RATE	estimate; chide
RATED	see RATE
RATES	see RATE
REAR	raise; back part
RECORDER	mus. instrument; magistrate
RECOVER	get back; cover again
REINS	bridles; kidneys
RELISH	taste; sing
RENT	least; *inf., pp.,* rend
RENTS	see RENT
REPAIR	betake; restore
REST	repose; remain, remainder
RESTETH	see REST
RESTING	see REST
RESTS	see REST
RICE	food; name
RID	clear; *pp.,* ride
RING	circle; sound
RINGS	see RING
ROAN	color; Rouen
ROAR	cry; tumult
ROCK	sway; stone
ROE	deer; spawn
ROOT	plant; dig up
ROOTS	see ROOT
ROSE	*p.,* rise; flower; name
ROUND	circle; whisper
ROUNDED	see ROUND
ROUNDER	*comp.,* round; rondure
ROUSE	stir; drinking
ROUT	defeat; crowd, brawl
ROUTS	see ROUT
RUE	regret; plant
RUFFLE	stir up; snatch rudely
RUSH	move swiftly; plant
RUSHES	see RUSH
'S	as; is; his; us; this; she is
S'	shall; so
SACK	pillage; wine; bag
SALLET	salad; headpiece
SALLIES	sorties; sullies
SALT	seasoning; lascivious
SALVE	palliate; greeting
SANDAL	shoe; name
SATE	*p., pp.,* sit; surfeit
SAVE	preserve; except
SAVING	see SAVE
SAW	*p.,* see; tool, cut; saying
SAY	speak; name; silk; touch
SCAL'D	weighed; covered with scales
SCALD	burn; scurvy
SCALE	climb; balance; body covering
SCALES	balances; steps; name
SCALING	weighing; climbing
SCONCE	head; fortification
SCORCH	burn; score
SCORCH'D	see SCORCH
SCOT	native of Scotland; payment
SCOUR	rub; run quickly
SCOURING	see SCOUR
SCOUT	lookout; deride
SCRIP	writing; bag
SEASON	time; spice
SEASONS	see SEASON
SEE	perceive; official seat
SERE	withered; catch in gunlock
SET	place, contest; collection
SHARDS	fragments; wing-cases
SHIVERING	shattering; trembling
SHORE	land; *p., pp.,* shear
SHORES	land; sewers
SIDE	bounding surface; long
SIGHT	vision; sighed
SIN	trespass; chin
SIT	be seated; *Lat. vb.*
SLIP	move smoothly; cutting; counterfeit coin
SLIPPER	shoe; slippery
SLIPS	see SLIP
SLOUGH	snakeskin; mire
SMACK	taste; kiss
SOIL	stain; earth; solution
SOL	tone in music; sun
SOLE	bottom of shoe; only
SON	male child; *Fr. n.; Fr. pron.*
SORE	pain; buck
SORES	see SORE
SORT	order; lot
SOUND	noise; fathom; healthy; swoon
SOUNDED	made noise; fathomed; swooned
SOUNDING	see SOUNDED
SOUNDLESS	noiseless; unfathomable
SOUNDS	noises; inlets; swoons
SOW	seed; animal
SPELL	magic formula; read letters
SPIT	eject; prong
SPITS	see SPIT
SPITTING	see SPIT
STABLE	building; steady
STAKE	wager; post
STAKES	see STAKE
STALE	not fresh; decoy; urine
STALK	move; stem
STAY	remain; support
STAYS	see STAY
STEEP	immerse; sharply rising
STEER	guide; animal
STEERS	see STEER
STEM	stalk; prow; check
STERN	severe; part of ship
STICK	pierce, fix; wood
STICKS	see STICK
STOCK	trunk, stocking, lineage; sword thrust
STOLE	*p., pp.,* steal; garment
STRAIN	exert; lineage
STRAINS	see STRAIN
STROKE	blow; rub gently
STROKES	see STROKE
STUCK	*p., pp.,* stick; stoccado
SUP	eat; drink
SUUM	*Lat. pron.;* exclamation
SWALLOW	devour; bird
SWALLOWS	see SWALLOW
SWATH	path of scythe; swaddling band
T'	the; to; too
TALENT	ability, money; talon
TALENTS	see TALENT
TAM	*Lat. adv.;* dam
TANG	sound; point
TAP	broach; light blow
TARTAR	native of Tartary; Tartarus
TAURUS'	constellation; mountains
TEAR	pull apart; drop of water
TEARS	see TEAR
TEMPLE	building; part of head
TEMPLES	see TEMPLE
TEND	incline; attend
TENDER	have regard for, delicate; offer
TENDING	see TEND
TEND'RING	having regard for; offering
TENDS	see TEND
TENT	shelter; probe
TENURES	holdings; tenors
TH'	the; they; thou; thy
THOU'ST	thouest; thou hast
TINE	tiny; thyme
TIRE	fatigue; attire; tear
TIRED	see TIRE
TIRES	see TIRE
TIRING	see TIRE
TOIL	labor; net
TOILS	see TOIL
TOLL	tax; sound
TOLLING	see TOLL
TON	unit of weight; *Fr. pron.*
TOP	surpass, crop, uppermost part; toy; nautical term
TOTTERS	shakes; tatters
TOTT'RING	see TOTTERS
TRACE	track; strap
TRAINS	retinues; plots
TRASH	worthless matter; leash
TREE	woody plant; three
TRIM	fit out, dress up; fine
TROT	move; old woman; troth
TROY	place; weight
UNDONE	ruined; not done
UNFOLDING	releasing; disclosing
UNHATCH'D	not ripe; unhacked
UNION	alliance; pearl
UNMANN'D	without manly qualities; not trained
UTTER	speak; complete
UTTERANCE	statement; uttermost
VAILS	lowers; gratuities
VARY	change; very
VAULTED	leaped; arched
VAUNT	boast; beginning
VEAL	calf; *viel* (?)
VER	Spring; for
VERE	name; where
VICE	screw; defect
VIE	compete; *Fr. n.*
VOW	promise; assert
WAFT	convey; beckon
WAIN	wagon; wean
WAN	pale; *p.,* win
WARDER	keeper; staff
WARE	beware, aware; *p.,* wear; place
WASHING	cleansing; swashing
WAT	hare; what
WAX	grow; plastic substance
WAXEN	see WAX
WEED	plant, root out; garment
WEEDS	see WEED
WEEK	period of time; wick
WELL	good, etc.; spring
WHITHER	where; whether
WILD	not tame; weald
WILL	*vb.;* intention; name
WILLS	orders; intentions
WIND	blow; turn
WISE	judicious; manner
WOOD	trees; mad
WORTH	value; befall
WORTS	cabbage; words
WOUND	injure; *p., pp.,* wind
WRENCHING	pulling; rinsing
YEAR	period of time; ear
YOUNGER	*comp.,* young; younker

Appendix III

A Conversion Table To Through Line Numbering

EXPLANATORY NOTE

For every twenty lines, and beginning anew at the head of every act and scene, of the text upon which this concordance is based (hereafter called Evans), a corresponding Through Line Numbering reference (hereafter called TLN) is given. Since TLN, based on the lineation of the First Folio, numbers all typographical lines of a play successively, whereas Evans uses the more customary system, the following conventions have been employed when there is no simple line to line correspondence between the two texts: a full line in Evans and a relevant portion of a line in the Folio are considered corresponding; lines in Evans which occupy two or more corresponding lines in the Folio are recorded individually in TLN; split lines, counted as one line in Evans, are recorded individually in TLN; stage directions and scene headings, not counted in Evans, are recorded individually in TLN; when lines in Evans do not appear in the Folio the number of the last line in the Folio before the missing material is given, followed by a plus sign and the appropriate intermediate line number (beginning with +1) according to the Evans lineation. The TLN for *Pericles* and *The Two Noble Kinsmen*, both not in the Folio, is based on a "through numbering" of the quartos; the *Sir Thomas More* fragments and the poems are not included in the conversion table.

The "Through Line Numbers" as established by Charlton Hinman in *The Norton Facsimile: The First Folio of Shakespeare* and in the forthcoming *Norton Shakespeare* are Copyright © 1968 by W.W. Norton & Company, Inc., and used with their permission.

TMP	
1.1.1	5
1.1.20	28
1.1.40	49
1.1.60	70–1
1.2.1	82
1.2.20	104
1.2.40	128
1.2.60	153
1.2.80	176
1.2.100	197
1.2.120	220–1
1.2.140	245
1.2.160	268
1.2.180	291
1.2.200	312
1.2.220	337
1.2.240	361
1.2.260	386–7
1.2.280	407
1.2.300	432
1.2.320	458
1.2.340	479
1.2.360	501
1.2.380	524–5
1.2.400	542
1.2.420	564–5
1.2.440	591
1.2.460	614–5
1.2.480	642
1.2.500	668
2.1.1	675
2.1.20	695
2.1.40	715
2.1.60	733–4
2.1.80	753
2.1.100	770
2.1.120	791
2.1.140	814–5
2.1.160	837
2.1.180	857
2.1.200	879–80
2.1.220	905
2.1.240	932
2.1.260	956
2.1.280	979
2.1.300	1004
2.1.320	1027
2.2.1	1040
2.2.20	1059
2.2.40	1078–9
2.2.60	1101–2
2.2.80	1121–2
2.2.100	1143
2.2.120	1163–4
2.2.140	1184
2.2.160	1205–6
2.2.180	1226
3.1.1	1236
3.1.20	1256
3.1.40	1284
3.1.60	1306
3.1.80	1330
3.2.1	1352
3.2.20	1369–70
3.2.40	1390–1
3.2.60	1412
3.2.80	1432–3
3.2.100	1454
3.2.120	1476
3.2.140	1497
3.3.1	1516
3.3.20	1542
3.3.40	1567–8
3.3.60	1593
3.3.80	1613
3.3.100	1637
4.1.1	1652
4.1.20	1672
4.1.40	1694
4.1.60	1718
4.1.80	1738
4.1.100	1760
4.1.120	1781–2
4.1.140	1810
4.1.160	1831
4.1.180	1853
4.1.200	1875
4.1.220	1895–6
4.1.240	1914
4.1.260	1937
5.1.1	1947
5.1.20	1969–70
5.1.40	1991
5.1.60	2016
5.1.80	2036
5.1.100	2057
5.1.120	2079–80
5.1.140	2106
5.1.160	2129
5.1.180	2155
5.1.200	2180–1
5.1.220	2206–7
5.1.240	2229
5.1.260	2252–3
5.1.280	2277
5.1.300	2297
EP.1	2322
EP.20	2341

TGV	
1.1.1	4
1.1.20	23
1.1.40	44
1.1.60	64
1.1.80	83–4
1.1.100	104
1.1.120	123
1.1.140	139–40
1.2.1	154
1.2.20	173
1.2.40	193
1.2.60	214
1.2.80	240
1.2.100	263
1.2.120	283
1.3.1	302
1.3.20	322
1.3.40	342
1.3.60	362
1.3.80	382
2.1.1	397–8
2.1.20	414–5
2.1.40	433–4
2.1.60	453–4
2.1.80	472–3
2.1.100	492
2.1.120	510
2.1.140	531–2
2.1.160	551
2.2.1	568
2.2.20	589
2.3.1	593
2.3.20	611–2
2.3.40	633
2.4.1	655
2.4.20	674
2.4.40	689
2.4.60	710
2.4.80	730
2.4.100	750
2.4.120	771
2.4.140	792
2.4.160	814
2.4.180	835
2.4.200	855
2.5.1	873
2.5.20	891
2.5.40	907–8
2.6.1	930
2.6.20	949
2.6.40	969
2.7.1	976
2.7.20	995
2.7.40	1015
2.7.60	1035
2.7.80	1055
3.1.1	1070
3.1.20	1089
3.1.40	1109
3.1.60	1129
3.1.80	1149
3.1.100	1169
3.1.120	1189
3.1.140	1210
3.1.160	1229
3.1.180	1249
3.1.200	1269
3.1.220	1287
3.1.240	1307
3.1.260	1327
3.1.280	1346
3.1.300	1362
3.1.320	1381–2
3.1.340	1401
3.1.360	1419–20
3.1.380	1439
3.2.1	1446
3.2.20	1465
3.2.40	1485
3.2.60	1505
3.2.80	1525
4.1.1	1545
4.1.20	1564
4.1.40	1586
4.1.60	1606
4.2.1	1623
4.2.20	1642
4.2.40	1662
4.2.60	1681
4.2.80	1698–9
4.2.100	1722
4.2.120	1743
4.2.140	1764
4.3.1	1767
4.3.20	1788
4.3.40	1808
4.4.1	1820
4.4.20	1838–9
4.4.40	1857
4.4.60	1877
4.4.80	1899
4.4.100	1919
4.4.120	1939
4.4.140	1959
4.4.160	1979
4.4.180	1998
4.4.200	2018
5.1.1	2026
5.2.1	2040
5.2.20	2059
5.2.40	2082
5.3.1	2101
5.4.1	2120
5.4.20	2139
5.4.40	2159
5.4.60	2182
5.4.80	2204
5.4.100	2224
5.4.120	2244
5.4.140	2265
5.4.160	2285

WIV	
1.1.1	6
1.1.20	22
1.1.40	41
1.1.60	60
1.1.80	77
1.1.100	96
1.1.120	116
1.1.140	131–2
1.1.160	148
1.1.180	166
1.1.200	184–5
1.1.220	203
1.1.240	220
1.1.260	237–8
1.1.280	254–5
1.1.300	273
1.2.1	288
1.3.1	301
1.3.20	319
1.3.40	334
1.3.60	350–1
1.3.80	371
1.3.100	391
1.4.1	400
1.4.20	417
1.4.40	434–5
1.4.60	452–3
1.4.80	471
1.4.100	490
1.4.120	508
1.4.140	524–5
1.4.160	544–5
2.1.1	554
2.1.20	568
2.1.40	586
2.1.60	604–5
2.1.80	623–4
2.1.100	641–2
2.1.120	662
2.1.140	679
2.1.160	696
2.1.180	713
2.1.200	733
2.1.220	749

2.1.240 768
2.2.1 771 +1
2.2.20 790–1
2.2.40 810
2.2.60 829–30
2.2.80 848
2.2.100 866–7
2.2.120 883–4
2.2.140 901–2
2.2.160 920
2.2.180 940
2.2.200 959–60
2.2.220 979
2.2.240 996–7
2.2.260 1014
2.2.280 1032–3
2.2.300 1050–1
2.3.1 1067
2.3.20 1085
2.3.40 1102–3
2.3.60 1121
2.3.80 1139
3.1.1 1160
3.1.20 1176
3.1.40 1191
3.1.60 1210
3.1.80 1227–8
3.1.100 1245
3.1.120 1263–4
3.2.1 1271
3.2.20 1285–6
3.2.40 1302
3.2.60 1322
3.2.80 1338–9
3.3.1 1353
3.3.20 1368
3.3.40 1384
3.3.60 1403
3.3.80 1422
3.3.100 1437–8
3.3.120 1456
3.3.140 1472–3
3.3.160 1491
3.3.180 1509
3.3.200 1528–9
3.3.220 1545–6
3.3.240 1561–2
3.4.1 1569
3.4.20 1590
3.4.40 1607–8
3.4.60 1628
3.4.80 1648
3.4.100 1668
3.5.1 1680
3.5.20 1697
3.5.40 1713–4
3.5.60 1732
3.5.80 1749
3.5.100 1766–7
3.5.120 1786–7
3.5.140 1808
4.1.1 1823
4.1.20 1838–9
4.1.40 1858
4.1.60 1875
4.1.80 1894
4.2.1 1901
4.2.20 1916
4.2.40 1934
4.2.60 1951
4.2.80 1970
4.2.100 1989
4.2.120 2008–9
4.2.140 2025
4.2.160 2044
4.2.180 2063
4.2.200 2082
4.2.220 2102
4.3.1 2109
4.4.1 2123
4.4.20 2142
4.4.40 2162
4.4.60 2182
4.4.80 2206–7
4.5.1 2220
4.5.20 2238
4.5.40 2257–8
4.5.60 2276–7
4.5.80 2296–7
4.5.100 2315–6
4.5.120 2334–5
4.6.1 2345
4.6.20 2364
4.6.40 2383
5.1.1 2402
5.1.20 2419–20
5.2.1 2432
5.3.1 2448
5.3.20 2467
5.4.1 2474
5.5.1 2482
5.5.20 2501–2
5.5.40 2522
5.5.60 2542
5.5.80 2562
5.5.100 2582
5.5.120 2603–4
5.5.140 2625
5.5.160 2645
5.5.180 2665
5.5.200 2685
5.5.220 2702
5.5.240 2723

MM

1.1.1 4
1.1.20 23
1.1.40 46
1.1.60 68–9
1.1.80 90
1.2.1 97
1.2.20 116
1.2.40 135
1.2.60 153
1.2.80 170
1.2.100 188–9
1.2.120 211
1.2.140 231
1.2.160 253
1.2.180 273
1.3.1 290
1.3.20 310
1.3.40 332
1.4.1 349
1.4.20 370
1.4.40 390
1.4.60 412
1.4.80 436
2.1.1 451
2.1.20 471
2.1.40 494
2.1.60 515
2.1.80 533–4
2.1.100 553–4
2.1.120 572
2.1.140 592
2.1.160 611
2.1.180 630
2.1.200 648
2.1.220 666–7
2.1.240 686
2.1.260 704
2.1.280 723
2.2.1 733
2.2.20 760
2.2.40 786
2.2.60 810
2.2.80 833
2.2.100 856
2.2.120 877
2.2.140 898
2.2.160 922–3
2.2.180 944
2.3.1 953
2.3.20 974
2.3.40 997
2.4.1 1003
2.4.20 1023
2.4.40 1044
2.4.60 1066
2.4.80 1088
2.4.100 1108
2.4.120 1130
2.4.140 1152
2.4.160 1174
2.4.180 1194
3.1.1 1204
3.1.20 1223
3.1.40 1243
3.1.60 1269–70
3.1.80 1294–5
3.1.100 1317
3.1.120 1340
3.1.140 1362
3.1.160 1382
3.1.180 1401
3.1.200 1421
3.1.220 1440–1
3.1.240 1460–1
3.1.260 1480–1
3.2.1 1491
3.2.20 1509
3.2.40 1530
3.2.60 1548–9
3.2.80 1569
3.2.100 1588
3.2.120 1608
3.2.140 1627
3.2.160 1646
3.2.180 1665–6
3.2.200 1686–7
3.2.220 1706
3.2.240 1726
3.2.260 1745
3.2.280 1765
4.1.1 1770
4.1.20 1790
4.1.40 1811–2
4.1.60 1835
4.2.1 1857
4.2.20 1873
4.2.40 1892–3
4.2.60 1914
4.2.80 1940
4.2.100 1962
4.2.120 1986
4.2.140 2006
4.2.160 2025–6
4.2.180 2045–6
4.2.200 2066
4.3.1 2078
4.3.20 2097
4.3.40 2118
4.3.60 2138–9
4.3.80 2162
4.3.100 2183
4.3.120 2210
4.3.140 2231
4.3.160 2253
4.4.1 2273
4.4.20 2291
4.5.1 2308
4.6.1 2325
5.1.1 2348
5.1.20 2370
5.1.40 2394
5.1.60 2417
5.1.80 2444
5.1.100 2467
5.1.120 2489
5.1.140 2510
5.1.160 2531
5.1.180 2553
5.1.200 2571–2
5.1.220 2594
5.1.240 2617
5.1.260 2638–9
5.1.280 2658–9
5.1.300 2679
5.1.320 2700
5.1.340 2720–1
5.1.360 2741
5.1.380 2763
5.1.400 2788
5.1.420 2809
5.1.440 2832
5.1.460 2854
5.1.480 2879
5.1.500 2899
5.1.520 2919

ERR

1.1.1 5
1.1.20 24
1.1.40 44
1.1.60 64
1.1.80 83
1.1.100 103
1.1.120 123
1.1.140 143
1.2.1 163
1.2.20 183
1.2.40 204
1.2.60 225
1.2.80 245
1.2.100 266
2.1.1 275
2.1.20 294
2.1.40 314
2.1.60 337
2.1.80 356
2.1.100 376
2.2.1 395
2.2.20 415
2.2.40 435
2.2.60 454
2.2.80 474
2.2.100 494
2.2.120 515
2.2.140 535
2.2.160 554
2.2.180 574
2.2.200 596
3.1.1 619
3.1.20 639
3.1.40 665–6
3.1.60 704–5
3.1.80 741
3.1.100 761
3.1.120 781
3.2.1 787
3.2.20 806
3.2.40 827
3.2.60 848–50
3.2.80 870–1
3.2.100 890–1
3.2.120 911
3.2.140 928–9
3.2.160 950
3.2.180 974
4.1.1 982
4.1.20 1002
4.1.40 1023–4
4.1.60 1046
4.1.80 1068
4.1.100 1089
4.2.1 1104
4.2.20 1126
4.2.40 1149
4.2.60 1175
4.3.1 1184
4.3.20 1202–3
4.3.40 1221–2
4.3.60 1243
4.3.80 1262–3
4.4.1 1281
4.4.20 1301–2
4.4.40 1323–4
4.4.60 1344
4.4.80 1367
4.4.100 1388
4.4.120 1412
4.4.140 1436
5.1.1 1464
5.1.20 1484
5.1.40 1507
5.1.60 1528–9
5.1.80 1549
5.1.100 1569
5.1.120 1589
5.1.140 1612
5.1.160 1632
5.1.180 1653
5.1.200 1676
5.1.220 1697
5.1.240 1716
5.1.260 1736
5.1.280 1757
5.1.300 1780
5.1.320 1800
5.1.340 1825
5.1.360 1835
5.1.380 1868
5.1.400 1889
5.1.420 1911

ADO

1.1.1 5
1.1.20 23
1.1.40 39–40
1.1.60 57
1.1.80 75
1.1.100 96–7
1.1.120 117
1.1.140 136–7
1.1.160 156
1.1.180 175
1.1.200 193–4
1.1.220 212–3
1.1.240 232–3
1.1.260 251
1.1.280 269–70
1.1.300 291
1.1.320 310
1.2.1 320
1.2.20 337
1.3.1 345
1.3.20 361–2
1.3.40 380
1.3.60 398–9
2.1.1 417
2.1.20 434
2.1.40 451–2
2.1.60 469–70
2.1.80 487
2.1.100 508
2.1.120 527
2.1.140 546–7
2.1.160 565–6
2.1.180 586
2.1.200 605
2.1.220 624
2.1.240 642–3
2.1.260 661
2.1.280 680–1
2.1.300 698–9
2.1.320 717–8
2.1.340 736
2.1.360 755
2.1.380 773–4
2.2.1 782
2.2.20 798–9
2.2.40 817–8
2.3.1 835
2.3.20 852–3
2.3.40 872
2.3.60 895–6
2.3.80 916–7
2.3.100 935
2.3.120 954
2.3.140 972
2.3.160 989–90
2.3.180 1008–9
2.3.200 1026
2.3.220 1044
2.3.240 1061–2
2.3.260 1081–2
3.1.1 1088
3.1.20 1107
3.1.40 1129
3.1.60 1150
3.1.80 1170
3.1.100 1190
3.2.1 1209
3.2.20 1226–7
3.2.40 1243
3.2.60 1260–1
3.2.80 1279
3.2.100 1296
3.2.120 1314–5
3.3.1 1331
3.3.20 1349–50
3.3.40 1369–70
3.3.60 1388
3.3.80 1406–7
3.3.100 1427–8
3.3.120 1446
3.3.140 1464–5
3.3.160 1482–3
3.3.180 1500–1
3.4.1 1503
3.4.20 1520–1
3.4.40 1540
3.4.60 1557
3.4.80 1575–6
3.5.1 1596–7
3.5.20 1614–5
3.5.40 1634
3.5.60 1651
4.1.1 1659
4.1.20 1676–7
4.1.40 1697
4.1.60 1717
4.1.80 1739
4.1.100 1760
4.1.120 1783
4.1.140 1803
4.1.160 1822
4.1.180 1843
4.1.200 1863–4
4.1.220 1884
4.1.240 1904
4.1.260 1924
4.1.280 1942–3
4.1.300 1963
4.1.320 1981–2
4.2.1 1999
4.2.20 2013
4.2.40 2031–2
4.2.60 2052
4.2.80 2069–70
5.1.1 2079
5.1.20 2099
5.1.40 2119
5.1.60 2144
5.1.80 2166
5.1.100 2187–8
5.1.120 2210
5.1.140 2229
5.1.160 2247–8
5.1.180 2264–5
5.1.200 2284–5
5.1.220 2303
5.1.240 2321–2
5.1.260 2343
5.1.280 2365
5.1.300 2386–7
5.1.320 2406
5.2.1 2424
5.2.20 2443
5.2.40 2459–60
5.2.60 2478–9
5.2.80 2496–7
5.2.100 2516
5.3.1 2522
5.3.20 2541
5.4.1 2555
5.4.20 2574
5.4.40 2595
5.4.60 2616
5.4.80 2639
5.4.100 2659
5.4.120 2677

LLL

1.1.1 5
1.1.20 24
1.1.40 44
1.1.60 65
1.1.80 85
1.1.100 109
1.1.120 128–30
1.1.140 150
1.1.160 171
1.1.180 191
1.1.200 211–2
1.1.220 231–2
1.1.240 249–50
1.1.260 260–1
1.1.280 275–6
1.1.300 295
1.2.1 312
1.2.20 330–1
1.2.40 349
1.2.60 365–6
1.2.80 385–6
1.2.100 404
1.2.120 424
1.2.140 443
1.2.160 462–3
1.2.180 482–3
2.1.1 492
2.1.20 511
2.1.40 532
2.1.60 552
2.1.80 572–4
2.1.100 595
2.1.120 616
2.1.140 636
2.1.160 657
2.1.180 677
2.1.200 698–9
2.1.220 722
2.1.240 744
3.1.1 772
3.1.20 788–9
3.1.40 809
3.1.60 828
3.1.80 853–4
3.1.100 863–4
3.1.120 886
3.1.140 905–6
3.1.160 926
3.1.180 946
3.1.200 966
4.1.1 975
4.1.20 995
4.1.40 1015
4.1.60 1041
4.1.80 1059–60
4.1.100 1081–2
4.1.120 1108–9
4.1.140 1137
4.2.1 1151
4.2.20 1170
4.2.40 1198
4.2.60 1223–4
4.2.80 1243

4.2.100	1261–2
4.2.120	1284–5
4.2.140	1305–6
4.2.160	1324–5
4.3.1	1334–5
4.3.20	1352
4.3.40	1373
4.3.60	1395
4.3.80	1416
4.3.100	1439
4.3.120	1459
4.3.140	1479
4.3.160	1499
4.3.180	1520
4.3.200	1548–9
4.3.220	1573
4.3.240	1593
4.3.260	1613
4.3.280	1633
4.3.300	1654
4.3.320	1674
4.3.340	1694
4.3.360	1714
4.3.380	1734
5.1.1	1740
5.1.20	1759–60
5.1.40	1779–80
5.1.60	1796–7
5.1.80	1814
5.1.100	1833–4
5.1.120	1852–3
5.1.140	1871–2
5.2.1	1888
5.2.20	1907
5.2.40	1928
5.2.60	1950
5.2.80	1971
5.2.100	1992
5.2.120	2012
5.2.140	2032
5.2.160	2055
5.2.180	2078
5.2.200	2099
5.2.220	2122–3
5.2.240	2151–2
5.2.260	2176
5.2.280	2200–1
5.2.300	2223
5.2.320	2245
5.2.340	2266
5.2.360	2286
5.2.380	2307
5.2.400	2332
5.2.420	2353
5.2.440	2378
5.2.460	2399
5.2.480	2419
5.2.500	2442–3
5.2.520	2464
5.2.540	2483
5.2.560	2509
5.2.580	2533
5.2.600	2553
5.2.620	2572
5.2.640	2596
5.2.660	2617
5.2.680	2636
5.2.700	2656
5.2.720	2677–8
5.2.740	2698
5.2.760	2718
5.2.780	2738
5.2.800	2760
5.2.820	2780
5.2.840	2801
5.2.860	2821
5.2.880	2843
5.2.900	2866
5.2.920	2887

MND

1.1.1	4
1.1.20	26
1.1.40	48
1.1.60	69
1.1.80	89
1.1.100	109
1.1.120	129
1.1.140	150
1.1.160	170
1.1.180	192
1.1.200	213
1.1.220	233
1.1.240	254
1.2.1	269
1.2.20	288
1.2.40	301–2
1.2.60	322
1.2.80	342–3
1.2.100	360–1
2.1.1	375
2.1.20	390
2.1.40	410
2.1.60	434–5
2.1.80	455
2.1.100	475
2.1.120	495
2.1.140	516
2.1.160	537
2.1.180	558
2.1.200	579
2.1.220	599
2.1.240	619
2.1.260	641
2.2.1	651
2.2.20	670
2.2.40	692
2.2.60	712
2.2.80	733
2.2.100	755
2.2.120	775
2.2.140	795
3.1.1	814
3.1.20	831–2
3.1.40	850–1
3.1.60	870–1
3.1.80	893
3.1.100	912–3
3.1.120	937
3.1.140	958
3.1.160	977
3.1.180	996–7
3.1.200	1019
3.2.1	1022
3.2.20	1042
3.2.40	1062
3.2.60	1083
3.2.80	1103
3.2.100	1123
3.2.120	1144
3.2.140	1165
3.2.160	1185
3.2.180	1207
3.2.200	1227
3.2.220	1247
3.2.240	1267
3.2.260	1290
3.2.280	1313
3.2.300	1334
3.2.320	1355–6
3.2.340	1380–1
3.2.360	1401
3.2.380	1421
3.2.400	1439
3.2.420	1464
3.2.440	1488
3.2.460	1503
4.1.1	1511
4.1.20	1530
4.1.40	1553
4.1.60	1575
4.1.80	1596
4.1.100	1618
4.1.120	1641
4.1.140	1664
4.1.160	1685
4.1.180	1705
4.1.200	1728
4.2.1	1747
4.2.20	1766–7
4.2.40	1784–5
5.1.1	1793
5.1.20	1811
5.1.40	1837
5.1.60	1856–7
5.1.80	1877
5.1.100	1897
5.1.120	1917–8
5.1.140	1939
5.1.160	1961
5.1.180	1982
5.1.200	2003
5.1.220	2023
5.1.240	2041
5.1.260	2060
5.1.280	2080
5.1.300	2096
5.1.320	2113 +1
5.1.340	2126
5.1.360	2142–3
5.1.380	2163
5.1.400	2183
5.1.420	2203

MV

1.1.1	4
1.1.20	23
1.1.40	44
1.1.60	67
1.1.80	89
1.1.100	109
1.1.120	129
1.1.140	149
1.1.160	169
1.1.180	189
1.2.1	196
1.2.20	214–5
1.2.40	233
1.2.60	251–2
1.2.80	270
1.2.100	290
1.2.120	311
1.3.1	326
1.3.20	344–5
1.3.40	364
1.3.60	385
1.3.80	407
1.3.100	428
1.3.120	448
1.3.140	468
1.3.160	489
1.3.180	510
2.1.1	518
2.1.20	537
2.1.40	559
2.2.1	568
2.2.20	584
2.2.40	602–3
2.2.60	623
2.2.80	641–2
2.2.100	661–2
2.2.120	681
2.2.140	699–700
2.2.160	719–20
2.2.180	742
2.2.200	763–4
2.3.1	772
2.3.20	791
2.4.1	794
2.4.20	814
2.5.1	836
2.5.20	857
2.5.40	876–7
2.6.1	896
2.6.20	917–8
2.6.40	941
2.6.60	963
2.7.1	973
2.7.20	993
2.7.40	1013
2.7.60	1033
2.8.1	1056
2.8.20	1075
2.8.40	1096
2.9.1	1112
2.9.20	1132
2.9.40	1152
2.9.60	1172
2.9.80	1193
2.9.100	1215
3.1.1	1219
3.1.20	1236–7
3.1.40	1252–3
3.1.60	1270–1
3.1.80	1292–3
3.1.100	1312
3.1.120	1331
3.2.1	1342
3.2.20	1361
3.2.40	1383
3.2.60	1403
3.2.80	1426
3.2.100	1446
3.2.120	1467
3.2.140	1487
3.2.160	1507
3.2.180	1527
3.2.200	1547
3.2.220	1570
3.2.240	1593
3.2.260	1616
3.2.280	1637
3.2.300	1658
3.2.320	1676–7
3.3.1	1686
3.3.20	1707
3.4.1	1727
3.4.20	1746
3.4.40	1767
3.4.60	1787
3.4.80	1808
3.5.1	1814
3.5.20	1830–1
3.5.40	1851
3.5.60	1868
3.5.80	1888
4.1.1	1904
4.1.20	1925
4.1.40	1945
4.1.60	1965
4.1.80	1986
4.1.100	2006
4.1.120	2028–9
4.1.140	2049
4.1.160	2068
4.1.180	2089
4.1.200	2111
4.1.220	2131
4.1.240	2152
4.1.260	2175
4.1.280	2195
4.1.300	2215
4.1.320	2238
4.1.340	2257
4.1.360	2278
4.1.380	2298
4.1.400	2320
4.1.420	2341
4.1.440	2361
4.2.1	2380
5.1.1	2404
5.1.20	2429–30
5.1.40	2453
5.1.60	2472
5.1.80	2493
5.1.100	2514
5.1.120	2539
5.1.140	2562
5.1.160	2582
5.1.180	2602
5.1.200	2624
5.1.220	2644
5.1.240	2665
5.1.260	2687
5.1.280	2708
5.1.300	2730

AYL

1.1.1	4
1.1.20	22
1.1.40	43
1.1.60	60–1
1.1.80	79–80
1.1.100	101–2
1.1.120	120
1.1.140	137–8
1.1.160	155–6
1.2.1	171
1.2.20	188–9
1.2.40	209
1.2.60	228
1.2.80	245
1.2.100	265
1.2.120	283
1.2.140	302
1.2.160	322–3
1.2.180	343
1.2.200	361
1.2.220	381
1.2.240	404
1.2.260	428
1.2.280	448
1.3.1	460
1.3.20	478
1.3.40	497
1.3.60	521
1.3.80	541
1.3.100	564
1.3.120	585
2.1.1	607
2.1.20	626
2.1.40	647
2.1.60	668
2.2.1	681
2.2.20	700
2.3.1	704
2.3.20	724
2.3.40	744
2.3.60	764
2.4.1	784
2.4.20	802–3
2.4.40	822
2.4.60	841
2.4.80	865
2.4.100	887
2.5.1	891
2.5.20	908
2.5.40	929
2.5.60	944–5
2.6.1	951
2.7.1	973
2.7.20	993
2.7.40	1013
2.7.60	1034
2.7.80	1054
2.7.100	1076
2.7.120	1097
2.7.140	1119
2.7.160	1139
2.7.180	1160
2.7.200	1178
3.1.1	1181
3.2.1	1201
3.2.20	1219–20
3.2.40	1238
3.2.60	1257
3.2.80	1276–7
3.2.100	1298
3.2.120	1317–8
3.2.140	1338
3.2.160	1358
3.2.180	1376
3.2.200	1395–6
3.2.220	1413–4
3.2.240	1434
3.2.260	1455
3.2.280	1472
3.2.300	1491
3.2.320	1508–9
3.2.340	1528
3.2.360	1545–6
3.2.380	1564–5
3.2.400	1580
3.2.420	1597–8
3.3.1	1615
3.3.20	1630–1
3.3.40	1649
3.3.60	1667–8
3.3.80	1686–7
3.3.100	1703–4
3.4.1	1710
3.4.20	1730
3.4.40	1747
3.5.1	1771
3.5.20	1791
3.5.40	1813
3.5.60	1833
3.5.80	1852
3.5.100	1874
3.5.120	1894
4.1.1	1917
4.1.20	1935
4.1.40	1954–5
4.1.60	1973–4
4.1.80	1992–3
4.1.100	2011–2
4.1.120	2029
4.1.140	2048–9
4.1.160	2069
4.1.180	2086
4.1.200	2105–6
4.2.1	2127
4.3.1	2148
4.3.20	2168
4.3.40	2189
4.3.60	2209
4.3.80	2230
4.3.100	2251
4.3.120	2271
4.3.140	2294
4.3.160	2314
4.3.180	2335
5.1.1	2341
5.1.20	2361
5.1.40	2382
5.1.60	2403
5.2.1	2409
5.2.20	2429–30
5.2.40	2448–9
5.2.60	2468–9
5.2.80	2487
5.2.100	2507
5.2.120	2524–5
5.3.1	2532
5.3.20	2551
5.3.40	2569–70
5.4.1	2575
5.4.20	2596
5.4.40	2617
5.4.60	2636–7
5.4.80	2654–5
5.4.100	2673–4
5.4.120	2695
5.4.140	2714
5.4.160	2736
5.4.180	2757
EP.1	2776
EP.20	2793–4

SHR

IN.1.1	4
IN.1.20	23
IN.1.40	44
IN.1.60	64
IN.1.80	89
IN.1.100	110
IN.1.120	131
IN.2.1	153
IN.2.20	172–3
IN.2.40	192
IN.2.60	212
IN.2.80	233
IN.2.100	254
IN.2.120	274
IN.2.140	294
1.1.1	300
1.1.20	319
1.1.40	339
1.1.60	363
1.1.80	383
1.1.100	404
1.1.120	424
1.1.140	442–3
1.1.160	463
1.1.180	483
1.1.200	506
1.1.220	526
1.1.240	548–9
1.2.1	566
1.2.20	588
1.2.40	606–7
1.2.60	626
1.2.80	645–6
1.2.100	666
1.2.120	685
1.2.140	706
1.2.160	726
1.2.180	746
1.2.200	767
1.2.220	789
1.2.240	814
1.2.260	834
1.2.280	854
2.1.1	856
2.1.20	875
2.1.40	901
2.1.60	921
2.1.80	942–3
2.1.100	963
2.1.120	985
2.1.140	1005
2.1.160	1028
2.1.180	1049
2.1.200	1074
2.1.220	1097
2.1.240	1119
2.1.260	1139
2.1.280	1160
2.1.300	1180
2.1.320	1200
2.1.340	1222
2.1.360	1242
2.1.380	1262
2.1.400	1282
3.1.1	1296
3.1.20	1315
3.1.40	1333
3.1.60	1353
3.1.80	1373
3.2.1	1389
3.2.20	1408
3.2.40	1429
3.2.60	1446–7
3.2.80	1464
3.2.100	1483
3.2.120	1503
3.2.140	1523

3.2.160	1544
3.2.180	1561
3.2.200	1583–4
3.2.220	1606
3.2.240	1626
4.1.1	1640
4.1.20	1657–8
4.1.40	1675–6
4.1.60	1693
4.1.80	1710–1
4.1.100	1728
4.1.120	1747
4.1.140	1767
4.1.160	1789–92
4.1.180	1813
4.1.200	1834
4.2.1	1847
4.2.20	1868
4.2.40	1888
4.2.60	1912
4.2.80	1936
4.2.100	1956
4.2.120	1975
4.3.1	1979
4.3.20	1998
4.3.40	2021
4.3.60	2042
4.3.80	2065
4.3.100	2085
4.3.120	2106
4.3.140	2123
4.3.160	2143
4.3.180	2163
4.4.1	2181
4.4.20	2203
4.4.40	2222
4.4.60	2242
4.4.80	2265–6
4.4.100	2284–5
4.5.1	2295–6
4.5.20	2317
4.5.40	2338
4.5.60	2359
5.1.1	2381
5.1.20	2401
5.1.40	2418
5.1.60	2437
5.1.80	2457–8
5.1.100	2477–8
5.1.120	2500
5.1.140	2520
5.2.1	2538
5.2.20	2558
5.2.40	2582
5.2.60	2603
5.2.80	2628–9
5.2.100	2655
5.2.120	2676
5.2.140	2698
5.2.160	2718
5.2.180	2738–9

AWW

1.1.1	5
1.1.20	23–4
1.1.40	41–2
1.1.60	62
1.1.80	84
1.1.100	105
1.1.120	125
1.1.140	144–5
1.1.160	164–5
1.1.180	184
1.1.200	206
1.1.220	227
1.2.1	240
1.2.20	266
1.2.40	286
1.2.60	307
1.3.1	329
1.3.20	349
1.3.40	369
1.3.60	387
1.3.80	402
1.3.100	420–1
1.3.120	441
1.3.140	463–4
1.3.160	486–7
1.3.180	507
1.3.200	531
1.3.220	553
1.3.240	574
2.1.1	597
2.1.20	617
2.1.40	640
2.1.60	659–60
2.1.80	683
2.1.100	707
2.1.120	729
2.1.140	749
2.1.160	769–70
2.1.180	791
2.1.200	812
2.2.1	825
2.2.20	843
2.2.40	864
2.2.60	880
2.3.1	893
2.3.20	912
2.3.40	931–2
2.3.60	953
2.3.80	977
2.3.100	998
2.3.120	1022
2.3.140	1042
2.3.160	1063
2.3.180	1085
2.3.200	1107
2.3.220	1125
2.3.240	1144–5
2.3.260	1165–6
2.3.280	1188
2.3.300	1208
2.4.1	1210
2.4.20	1229
2.4.40	1250
2.5.1	1270
2.5.20	1290
2.5.40	1311
2.5.60	1333
2.5.80	1357
3.1.1	1374
3.1.20	1397
3.2.1	1402
3.2.20	1421–2
3.2.40	1441
3.2.60	1462–3
3.2.80	1487
3.2.100	1509
3.2.120	1529
3.3.1	1541
3.4.1	1556
3.4.20	1576
3.4.40	1598
3.5.1	1606–7
3.5.20	1629–30
3.5.40	1651
3.5.60	1677
3.5.80	1705
3.5.100	1727
3.6.1	1732
3.6.20	1752–3
3.6.40	1771
3.6.60	1792
3.6.80	1812
3.6.100	1833–4
3.7.1	1856
3.7.20	1879
3.7.40	1900
4.1.1	1913
4.1.20	1931–2
4.1.40	1952–3
4.1.60	1971–2
4.1.80	1995
4.2.1	2019
4.2.20	2043–4
4.2.40	2065
4.2.60	2089
4.3.1	2108
4.3.20	2125–6
4.3.40	2146
4.3.60	2166
4.3.80	2187
4.3.100	2208
4.3.120	2228
4.3.140	2247
4.3.160	2266
4.3.180	2285–6
4.3.200	2304
4.3.220	2322–3
4.3.240	2343–4
4.3.260	2362–3
4.3.280	2380–1
4.3.300	2398–9
4.3.320	2417–8
4.3.340	2438
4.4.1	2440–1
4.4.20	2462
4.5.1	2482
4.5.20	2501
4.5.40	2520–1
4.5.60	2541
4.5.80	2561
4.5.100	2582–3
5.1.1	2595
5.1.20	2616
5.2.1	2641
5.2.20	2661
5.2.40	2681
5.3.1	2697
5.3.20	2720
5.3.40	2746
5.3.60	2767
5.3.80	2787–8
5.3.100	2811
5.3.120	2833
5.3.140	2856–7
5.3.160	2879
5.3.180	2901
5.3.200	2925
5.3.220	2948
5.3.240	2971
5.3.260	2989–90
5.3.280	3012
5.3.300	3034
5.3.320	3058
EP.1	3073

TN

1.1.1	5
1.1.20	26
1.1.40	47
1.2.1	51
1.2.20	70
1.2.40	90
1.2.60	112
1.3.1	119
1.3.20	137
1.3.40	155–6
1.3.60	175
1.3.80	194
1.3.100	212
1.3.120	228
1.3.140	247
1.4.1	251
1.4.20	270
1.4.40	291–2
1.5.1	297
1.5.20	314–5
1.5.40	332
1.5.60	352
1.5.80	371–2
1.5.100	393
1.5.120	413
1.5.140	434
1.5.160	453–4
1.5.180	473–4
1.5.200	493–4
1.5.220	512
1.5.240	531
1.5.260	552
1.5.280	575
1.5.300	597
2.1.1	612
2.1.20	628–9
2.1.40	646–7
2.2.1	657
2.2.20	676
2.2.40	696
2.3.1	700
2.3.20	719–20
2.3.40	740
2.3.60	760
2.3.80	778
2.3.100	796–7
2.3.120	814–5
2.3.140	833
2.3.160	851–2
2.3.180	870–1
2.4.1	884
2.4.20	904
2.4.40	928
2.4.60	948
2.4.80	966
2.4.100	987
2.4.120	1009
2.5.1	1017
2.5.20	1035–6
2.5.40	1054–5
2.5.60	1075
2.5.80	1094
2.5.100	1110–1
2.5.120	1128–9
2.5.140	1145–6
2.5.160	1163–4
2.5.180	1182
2.5.200	1202–3
3.1.1	1214
3.1.20	1232
3.1.40	1251–2
3.1.60	1271
3.1.80	1291–2
3.1.100	1311
3.1.120	1333
3.1.140	1355
3.1.160	1375
3.2.1	1382
3.2.20	1399–1400
3.2.40	1420
3.2.60	1439–40
3.2.80	1458–9
3.3.1	1467
3.3.20	1487
3.3.40	1509
3.4.1	1522
3.4.20	1541–2
3.4.40	1562
3.4.60	1582–3
3.4.80	1602
3.4.100	1623–4
3.4.120	1642
3.4.140	1661–2
3.4.160	1679–80
3.4.180	1696–7
3.4.200	1716–7
3.4.220	1739
3.4.240	1757–8
3.4.260	1778
3.4.280	1798
3.4.300	1816–7
3.4.320	1838
3.4.340	1857
3.4.360	1880
3.4.380	1901
4.1.1	1919
4.1.20	1936–7
4.1.40	1955–6
4.1.60	1977
4.2.1	1986
4.2.20	2006
4.2.40	2026
4.2.60	2044–5
4.2.80	2065
4.2.100	2085
4.2.120	2105
4.3.1	2115
4.3.20	2134
5.1.1	2154
5.1.20	2172–3
5.1.40	2190
5.1.60	2211
5.1.80	2232
5.1.100	2255
5.1.120	2276
5.1.140	2297
5.1.160	2322
5.1.180	2343
5.1.200	2363
5.1.220	2384
5.1.240	2406
5.1.260	2426
5.1.280	2447
5.1.300	2467
5.1.320	2486
5.1.340	2510
5.1.360	2531
5.1.380,	2550
5.1.400	2571

WT

1.1.1	4
1.1.20	23
1.1.40	41–2
1.2.1	50
1.2.20	75
1.2.40	97
1.2.60	121
1.2.80	145–6
1.2.100	170
1.2.120	193–5
1.2.140	216
1.2.160	239
1.2.180	262
1.2.200	282
1.2.220	305–6
1.2.240	329
1.2.260	351
1.2.280	372
1.2.300	396
1.2.320	418
1.2.340	441
1.2.360	463
1.2.380	486
1.2.400	509
1.2.420	534
1.2.440	556
1.2.460	577
2.1.1	586
2.1.20	612
2.1.40	637
2.1.60	660
2.1.80	683
2.1.100	705–6
2.1.120	728
2.1.140	752
2.1.160	775
2.1.180	798
2.2.1	821
2.2.20	846
2.2.40	868–9
2.2.60	892
2.3.1	900
2.3.20	921
2.3.40	946
2.3.60	971–2
2.3.80	997–8
2.3.100	1022
2.3.120	1047
2.3.140	1068
2.3.160	1090
2.3.180	1112
2.3.200	1136
3.1.1	1146
3.1.20	1171
3.2.1	1176
3.2.20	1193–4
3.2.40	1214
3.2.60	1237
3.2.80	1257
3.2.100	1279
3.2.120	1300
3.2.140	1321
3.2.160	1345
3.2.180	1367
3.2.200	1387
3.2.220	1411
3.2.240	1432
3.3.1	1439
3.3.20	1462
3.3.40	1482
3.3.60	1502
3.3.80	1522
3.3.100	1541–2
3.3.120	1559
4.1.1	1580
4.1.20	1599
4.2.1	1614
4.2.20	1632–3
4.2.40	1653
4.3.1	1669
4.3.20	1688
4.3.40	1709
4.3.60	1728
4.3.80	1747–8
4.3.100	1767–8
4.3.120	1787–8
4.4.1	1798
4.4.20	1820
4.4.40	1842–3
4.4.60	1865
4.4.80	1888
4.4.100	1913
4.4.120	1934
4.4.140	1956
4.4.160	1980
4.4.180	2005
4.4.200	2024–5
4.4.220	2046
4.4.240	2063–4
4.4.260	2082
4.4.280	2101–2
4.4.300	2123
4.4.320	2142
4.4.340	2161
4.4.360	2183
4.4.380	2208–9
4.4.400	2235
4.4.420	2263
4.4.440	2284
4.4.460	2307
4.4.480	2332
4.4.500	2354
4.4.520	2380–1
4.4.540	2404
4.4.560	2427
4.4.580	2452
4.4.600	2476–7
4.4.620	2497
4.4.640	2518
4.4.660	2542
4.4.680	2562–3
4.4.700	2582–3
4.4.720	2602
4.4.740	2622
4.4.760	2642
4.4.780	2661–2
4.4.800	2681
4.4.820	2700–1
4.4.840	2720–1
5.1.1	2727
5.1.20	2749–50
5.1.40	2773
5.1.60	2796–7
5.1.80	2823
5.1.100	2850
5.1.120	2874
5.1.140	2896
5.1.160	2920
5.1.180	2943
5.1.200	2967
5.1.220	2992
5.2.1	3011
5.2.20	3030
5.2.40	3050
5.2.60	3068–9
5.2.80	3088–9
5.2.100	3107–8
5.2.120	3127–8
5.2.140	3147–8
5.2.160	3168
5.3.1	3186
5.3.20	3208
5.3.40	3231
5.3.60	3256
5.3.80	3281–2
5.3.100	3308
5.3.120	3331
5.3.140	3354

JN

1.1.1	5
1.1.20	25
1.1.40	46
1.1.60	68
1.1.80	88
1.1.100	108
1.1.120	128
1.1.140	148
1.1.160	168–9
1.1.180	189
1.1.200	210
1.1.220	230
1.1.240	253
1.1.260	273
2.1.1	294
2.1.20	313
2.1.40	333
2.1.60	354
2.1.80	375
2.1.100	397
2.1.120	417
2.1.140	440
2.1.160	461
2.1.180	482
2.1.200	503
2.1.220	526
2.1.240	546
2.1.260	566
2.1.280	587
2.1.300	610
2.1.320	631
2.1.340	654
2.1.360	674
2.1.380	694
2.1.400	714
2.1.420	735
2.1.440	755
2.1.460	776
2.1.480	796
2.1.500	816
2.1.520	838
2.1.540	860
2.1.560	881
2.1.580	901
3.1.1	922
3.1.20	941
3.1.40	961
3.1.60	981

3.1.80	1005
3.1.100	1025
3.1.120	1046
3.1.140	1067
3.1.160	1087
3.1.180	1108
3.1.200	1128
3.1.220	1151
3.1.240	1171
3.1.260	1191
3.1.280	1211
3.1.300	1232–3
3.1.320	1253
3.1.340	1273
3.2.1	1285
3.3.1	1299
3.3.20	1319
3.3.40	1339
3.3.60	1360
3.4.1	1383
3.4.20	1403
3.4.40	1424
3.4.60	1444
3.4.80	1465
3.4.100	1485
3.4.120	1505
3.4.140	1525
3.4.160	1545
3.4.180	1565
4.1.1	1571
4.1.20	1593
4.1.40	1613–5
4.1.60	1637
4.1.80	1657
4.1.100	1679
4.1.120	1700
4.2.1	1718
4.2.20	1737
4.2.40	1757
4.2.60	1777
4.2.80	1798
4.2.100	1818
4.2.120	1839
4.2.140	1861
4.2.160	1881
4.2.180	1902–3
4.2.200	1925
4.2.220	1945
4.2.240	1965
4.2.260	1985
4.3.1	1997
4.3.20	2017
4.3.40	2039
4.3.60	2059
4.3.80	2080
4.3.100	2102
4.3.120	2123
4.3.140	2145
5.1.1	2167
5.1.20	2187
5.1.40	2208
5.1.60	2228
5.2.1	2252
5.2.20	2271
5.2.40	2291
5.2.60	2311
5.2.80	2333
5.2.100	2353
5.2.120	2374
5.2.140	2394
5.2.160	2414
5.2.180	2436
5.3.1	2440
5.4.1	2460
5.4.20	2481
5.4.40	2501
5.4.60	2521
5.5.1	2525
5.5.20	2546
5.6.1	2551–2
5.6.20	2577
5.6.40	2598
5.7.1	2605
5.7.20	2626
5.7.40	2648
5.7.60	2670
5.7.80	2690
5.7.100	2710–1

R2

1.1.1	5
1.1.20	25
1.1.40	45
1.1.60	65
1.1.80	85
1.1.100	105
1.1.120	125
1.1.140	145
1.1.160	165
1.1.180	188
1.1.200	210
1.2.1	218
1.2.20	237
1.2.40	257
1.2.60	277
1.3.1	294
1.3.20	316
1.3.40	337
1.3.60	357
1.3.80	377
1.3.100	397
1.3.120	417
1.3.140	433
1.3.160	453
1.3.180	473
1.3.200	493
1.3.220	513
1.3.240	531 + 2
1.3.260	550
1.3.280	557 + 13
1.3.300	564
1.4.1	576
1.4.20	594
1.4.40	614
1.4.60	635
2.1.1	642
2.1.20	661
2.1.40	681
2.1.60	701
2.1.80	723
2.1.100	743
2.1.120	764
2.1.140	784
2.1.160	807
2.1.180	827
2.1.200	848
2.1.220	868
2.1.240	890
2.1.260	910
2.1.280	929 + 1
2.1.300	949
2.2.1	953
2.2.20	972
2.2.40	992
2.2.60	1014
2.2.80	1034
2.2.100	1055
2.2.120	1074
2.2.140	1092
2.3.1	1106
2.3.20	1125
2.3.40	1148–9
2.3.60	1170
2.3.80	1191
2.3.100	1211
2.3.120	1231
2.3.140	1251
2.3.160	1271
2.4.1	1285
2.4.20	1304
3.1.1	1313
3.1.20	1332
3.1.40	1352
3.2.1	1361
3.2.20	1380
3.2.40	1396
3.2.60	1415
3.2.80	1437
3.2.100	1458
3.2.120	1478
3.2.140	1499
3.2.160	1520
3.2.180	1540
3.2.200	1559
3.3.1	1584
3.3.20	1605
3.3.40	1624
3.3.60	1644
3.3.80	1667
3.3.100	1687
3.3.120	1707
3.3.140	1727
3.3.160	1748
3.3.180	1768
3.3.200	1792–3
3.4.1	1808
3.4.20	1829
3.4.40	1850
3.4.60	1872
3.4.80	1892
3.4.100	1912
4.1.1	1924
4.1.20	1943
4.1.40	1963
4.1.60	1975–6
4.1.80	1999
4.1.100	2019
4.1.120	2040
4.1.140	2060
4.1.160	2081
4.1.180	2102
4.1.200	2121
4.1.220	2141
4.1.240	2162
4.1.260	2182
4.1.280	2203
4.1.300	2224
4.1.320	2245
5.1.1	2261
5.1.20	2281
5.1.40	2301
5.1.60	2322
5.1.80	2342
5.1.100	2362
5.2.1	2367
5.2.20	2387
5.2.40	2407
5.2.60	2430
5.2.80	2452
5.2.100	2475
5.3.1	2497
5.3.20	2516
5.3.40	2537
5.3.60	2559
5.3.80	2580
5.3.100	2601
5.3.120	2622
5.3.140	2644
5.4.1	2653–4
5.5.1	2668
5.5.20	2686
5.5.40	2706
5.5.60	2726
5.5.80	2748
5.5.100	2770–1
5.6.1	2794
5.6.20	2816
5.6.40	2837

1H4

1.1.1	5
1.1.20	24
1.1.40	44
1.1.60	64
1.1.80	83
1.1.100	103
1.2.1	115
1.2.20	134
1.2.40	153–4
1.2.60	170–1
1.2.80	190–1
1.2.100	208
1.2.120	227
1.2.140	244–5
1.2.160	263
1.2.180	281–2
1.2.200	301
1.3.1	322
1.3.20	341
1.3.40	362
1.3.60	382
1.3.80	402
1.3.100	422
1.3.120	441
1.3.140	462
1.3.160	483
1.3.180	503
1.3.200	524
1.3.220	549
1.3.240	568
1.3.260	588
1.3.280	609
1.3.300	630
2.1.1	635
2.1.20	655
2.1.40	675
2.1.60	695–6
2.1.80	715–6
2.2.1	736
2.2.20	755–6
2.2.40	774
2.2.60	793
2.2.80	813–4
2.2.100	834–5
2.3.1	850
2.3.20	867–8
2.3.40	888
2.3.60	908
2.3.80	927–8
2.3.100	945
2.4.1	966
2.4.20	983
2.4.40	1003
2.4.60	1022
2.4.80	1044
2.4.100	1063–4
2.4.120	1082
2.4.140	1100
2.4.160	1119
2.4.180	1139
2.4.200	1159
2.4.220	1178
2.4.240	1197–8
2.4.260	1216–7
2.4.280	1235
2.4.300	1255–6
2.4.320	1276
2.4.340	1297
2.4.360	1317
2.4.380	1337
2.4.400	1358–9
2.4.420	1378
2.4.440	1398
2.4.460	1418
2.4.480	1437–8
2.4.500	1462–3
2.4.520	1485
2.4.540	1508
3.1.1	1522
3.1.20	1543
3.1.40	1566
3.1.60	1586
3.1.80	1609
3.1.100	1629
3.1.120	1651
3.1.140	1670–1
3.1.160	1693
3.1.180	1714
3.1.200	1740
3.1.220	1763
3.1.240	1785
3.1.260	1805–6
3.2.1	1816–7
3.2.20	1838
3.2.40	1859
3.2.60	1879
3.2.80	1899
3.2.100	1920
3.2.120	1940
3.2.140	1960
3.2.160	1980
3.2.180	2001
3.3.1	2004
3.3.20	2022–3
3.3.40	2042–3
3.3.60	2062
3.3.80	2084
3.3.100	2108
3.3.120	2127–8
3.3.140	2147
3.3.160	2166–7
3.3.180	2190
3.3.200	2209
4.1.1	2221
4.1.20	2244
4.1.40	2264
4.1.60	2285
4.1.80	2306
4.1.100	2331
4.1.120	2352
4.2.1	2376
4.2.20	2395
4.2.40	2414–5
4.2.60	2435
4.2.80	2455
4.3.1	2460–1
4.3.20	2485
4.3.40	2507
4.3.60	2529
4.3.80	2549
4.3.100	2570
4.4.1	2588
4.4.20	2608
4.4.40	2629
5.1.1	2635
5.1.20	2657
5.1.40	2677
5.1.60	2697
5.1.80	2717
5.1.100	2737
5.1.120	2758
5.1.140	2777–8
5.2.1	2782
5.2.20	2802
5.2.40	2825
5.2.60	2846
5.2.80	2867
5.2.100	2888
5.3.1	2892
5.3.20	2912
5.3.40	2934
5.3.60	2953–4
5.4.1	2960
5.4.20	2978
5.4.40	3000
5.4.60	3022
5.4.80	3045
5.4.100	3065
5.4.120	3085–6
5.4.140	3105–6
5.4.160	3126
5.5.1	3137
5.5.20	3157
5.5.40	3176

2H4

IN.1	4
IN.20	23
IN.40	43–4
1.1.1	47–8
1.1.20	72
1.1.40	94
1.1.60	118
1.1.80	139
1.1.100	160
1.1.120	180
1.1.140	200
1.1.160	220
1.1.180	239
1.1.200	259
1.2.1	277
1.2.20	294–5
1.2.40	313–4
1.2.60	334
1.2.80	352
1.2.100	371
1.2.120	389
1.2.140	405
1.2.160	421
1.2.180	439–40
1.2.200	456
1.2.220	469 + 6
1.2.240	489
1.3.1	501
1.3.20	521
1.3.40	541
1.3.60	561
1.3.80	582
1.3.100	603
2.1.1	616
2.1.20	632
2.1.40	649–50
2.1.60	664–5
2.1.80	683
2.1.100	701–2
2.1.120	718–9
2.1.140	736
2.1.160	753–4
2.1.180	773
2.2.1	792
2.2.20	810–1
2.2.40	824–5
2.2.60	841–2
2.2.80	862–3
2.2.100	881
2.2.120	900–1
2.2.140	918
2.2.160	939
2.3.1	959
2.3.20	978
2.3.40	998
2.3.60	1020
2.4.1	1031
2.4.20	1047–8
2.4.40	1067–8
2.4.60	1086
2.4.80	1108
2.4.100	1127–8
2.4.120	1147
2.4.140	1164–5
2.4.160	1182
2.4.180	1200–1
2.4.200	1221
2.4.220	1240–1
2.4.240	1264
2.4.260	1285
2.4.280	1305–6
2.4.300	1326
2.4.320	1345–6
2.4.340	1365–6
2.4.360	1387
2.4.380	1408–9
3.1.1	1422
3.1.20	1441
3.1.40	1462
3.1.60	1478
3.1.80	1498
3.1.100	1520
3.2.1	1534
3.2.20	1552–3
3.2.40	1573
3.2.60	1594–5
3.2.80	1613–4
3.2.100	1634–5
3.2.120	1655
3.2.140	1675
3.2.160	1696–7
3.2.180	1716
3.2.200	1735
3.2.220	1755
3.2.240	1774
3.2.260	1792–3
3.2.280	1811
3.2.300	1830–1
3.2.320	1846–7
4.1.1	1863
4.1.20	1886
4.1.40	1908
4.1.60	1928
4.1.80	1948
4.1.100	1968
4.1.120	1988
4.1.140	2008
4.1.160	2028
4.1.180	2048–9
4.1.200	2069
4.1.220	2090
4.2.1	2101
4.2.20	2120
4.2.40	2141
4.2.60	2163
4.2.80	2186
4.2.100	2210
4.2.120	2231
4.3.1	2236
4.3.20	2255
4.3.40	2275–6
4.3.60	2295
4.3.80	2317
4.3.100	2337–8
4.3.120	2356–7
4.4.1	2371
4.4.20	2394
4.4.40	2414
4.4.60	2438
4.4.80	2458–60
4.4.100	2482
4.4.120	2506
4.5.1	2520
4.5.20	2543
4.5.40	2563
4.5.60	2591
4.5.80	2612
4.5.100	2633
4.5.120	2653
4.5.140	2674
4.5.160	2694
4.5.180	2715
4.5.200	2736
4.5.220	2757
4.5.240	2784
5.1.1	2788
5.1.20	2807
5.1.40	2829
5.1.60	2850
5.1.80	2869–70
5.2.1	2881–2
5.2.20	2905
5.2.40	2925
5.2.60	2946
5.2.80	2965
5.2.100	2985
5.2.120	3005
5.2.140	3025
5.3.1	3034
5.3.20	3050–1
5.3.40	3068–9
5.3.60	3086
5.3.80	3101
5.3.100	3121

5.3.120	3145
5.3.140	3166
5.4.1	3171
5.4.20	3192
5.5.1	3207
5.5.20	3227–8
5.5.40	3245–6
5.5.60	3272
5.5.80	3291
5.5.100	3312
EP.1	3325–6
EP.20	3339–40

H5

PR.1	2
PR.20	21
1.1.1	39
1.1.20	58–9
1.1.40	81
1.1.60	101
1.1.80	123
1.2.1	145
1.2.20	167
1.2.40	187
1.2.60	207
1.2.80	227
1.2.100	247
1.2.120	267
1.2.140	287
1.2.160	307
1.2.180	326
1.2.200	347
1.2.220	367
1.2.240	388
1.2.260	410
1.2.280	430
1.2.300	451
2.PR.1	463
2.PR.20	482
2.PR.40	502
2.1.1	506
2.1.20	524
2.1.40	543–4
2.1.60	562
2.1.80	579
2.1.100	600
2.1.120	617–8
2.2.1	628
2.2.20	649
2.2.40	669
2.2.60	688
2.2.80	709
2.2.100	729
2.2.120	749
2.2.140	769
2.2.160	789
2.2.180	809
2.3.1	824
2.3.20	842
2.3.40	861
2.3.60	880
2.4.1	888
2.4.20	908
2.4.40	929
2.4.60	950
2.4.80	974
2.4.100	994
2.4.120	1015
2.4.140	1035
3.PR.1	1045
3.PR.20	1064
3.1.1	1083–4
3.1.20	1103
3.2.1	1120
3.2.20	1137
3.2.40	1156–7
3.2.60	1178
3.2.80	1198–9
3.2.100	1217–8
3.2.120	1237–8
3.2.140	1257–8
3.3.1	1260
3.3.20	1279
3.3.40	1299
3.4.1	1321
3.4.20	1338
3.4.40	1357
3.4.60	1375
3.5.1	1380
3.5.20	1399
3.5.40	1419
3.5.60	1440
3.6.1	1451
3.6.20	1470
3.6.40	1489
3.6.60	1507
3.6.80	1526–7
3.6.100	1548
3.6.120	1570
3.6.140	1590
3.6.160	1610
3.7.1	1626
3.7.20	1645–6
3.7.40	1666
3.7.60	1687
3.7.80	1706–7
3.7.100	1726
3.7.120	1747
3.7.140	1768
4.PR.1	1790
4.PR.20	1809
4.PR.40	1829
4.1.1	1845
4.1.20	1865
4.1.40	1888
4.1.60	1907
4.1.80	1929
4.1.100	1951
4.1.120	1968–9
4.1.140	1987–8
4.1.160	2007–8
4.1.180	2027–8
4.1.200	2047–8
4.1.220	2069
4.1.240	2090
4.1.260	2110
4.1.280	2130
4.1.300	2152–3
4.2.1	2167–8
4.2.20	2191
4.2.40	2212
4.2.60	2233–4
4.3.1	2240
4.3.20	2264
4.3.40	2284
4.3.60	2303
4.3.80	2326
4.3.100	2347
4.3.120	2367
4.4.1	2386
4.4.20	2402
4.4.40	2422
4.4.60	2440–1
4.5.1	2459
4.5.20	2479
4.6.1	2485
4.6.20	2504
4.7.1	2526
4.7.20	2545
4.7.40	2564
4.7.60	2585
4.7.80	2608
4.7.100	2629–30
4.7.120	2651
4.7.140	2670–1
4.7.160	2689
4.7.180	2709
4.8.1	2714
4.8.20	2736
4.8.40	2757
4.8.60	2777
4.8.80	2799
4.8.100	2819
4.8.120	2841
5.PR.1	2851
5.PR.20	2870
5.PR.40	2890
5.1.1	2898
5.1.20	2918
5.1.40	2937
5.1.60	2956
5.1.80	2975
5.2.1	2988
5.2.20	3007
5.2.40	3027
5.2.60	3047
5.2.80	3068
5.2.100	3090
5.2.120	3109–10
5.2.140	3129–30
5.2.160	3149
5.2.180	3168–9
5.2.200	3187–8
5.2.220	3208
5.2.240	3227–8
5.2.260	3248
5.2.280	3267–8
5.2.300	3290
5.2.320	3310
5.2.340	3330–1
5.2.360	3351
EP.1	3368

1H6

1.1.1	9
1.1.20	28
1.1.40	49
1.1.60	70
1.1.80	90
1.1.100	111
1.1.120	132
1.1.140	152
1.1.160	172
1.2.1	195
1.2.20	214
1.2.40	238
1.2.60	260
1.2.80	282
1.2.100	302
1.2.120	325
1.2.140	347
1.3.1	360
1.3.20	382
1.3.40	406
1.3.60	431
1.3.80	450
1.4.1	465
1.4.20	484
1.4.40	507
1.4.60	528
1.4.80	551
1.4.100	573
1.5.1	591
1.5.20	615
1.6.1	641
1.6.20	661
2.1.1	676
2.1.20	698
2.1.40	724
2.1.60	745
2.1.80	769
2.2.1	772
2.2.20	791
2.2.40	812
2.2.60	833
2.3.1	836
2.3.20	856
2.3.40	879
2.3.60	901
2.3.80	923
2.4.1	928–9
2.4.20	949
2.4.40	969
2.4.60	989
2.4.80	1011
2.4.100	1031
2.4.120	1053
2.5.1	1071
2.5.20	1090
2.5.40	1111
2.5.60	1131
2.5.80	1151
2.5.100	1171
2.5.120	1191
3.1.1	1205
3.1.20	1224
3.1.40	1244
3.1.60	1267
3.1.80	1292
3.1.100	1314
3.1.120	1336
3.1.140	1356
3.1.160	1378
3.1.180	1398
3.1.200	1420
3.2.1	1424
3.2.20	1445
3.2.40	1468
3.2.60	1496
3.2.80	1516
3.2.100	1537
3.2.120	1566
3.3.1	1586
3.3.20	1605
3.3.40	1631–2
3.3.60	1652
3.3.80	1673
3.4.1	1693
3.4.20	1712
3.4.40	1736
4.1.1	1746
4.1.20	1766
4.1.40	1786
4.1.60	1807
4.1.80	1829
4.1.100	1849
4.1.120	1870
4.1.140	1891
4.1.160	1911
4.1.180	1932
4.2.1	1950
4.2.20	1970
4.2.40	1991
4.3.1	2010
4.3.20	2030
4.3.40	2050
4.4.1	2065
4.4.20	2084
4.4.40	2105
4.5.1	2114
4.5.20	2133
4.5.40	2153
4.6.1	2172
4.6.20	2191
4.6.40	2211
4.7.1	2231
4.7.20	2251
4.7.40	2273
4.7.60	2294
4.7.80	2314
5.1.1	2335
5.1.20	2354
5.1.40	2375
5.1.60	2395
5.2.1	2401–2
5.2.20	2422
5.3.1	2426
5.3.20	2449
5.3.40	2472
5.3.60	2497
5.3.80	2517
5.3.100	2537
5.3.120	2558–9
5.3.140	2582
5.3.160	2604
5.3.180	2624
5.4.1	2641
5.4.20	2660
5.4.40	2680
5.4.60	2700
5.4.80	2720
5.4.100	2741
5.4.120	2762
5.4.140	2782
5.4.160	2802
5.5.1	2822
5.5.20	2841
5.5.40	2862
5.5.60	2882
5.5.80	2902
5.5.100	2922

2H6

1.1.1	8
1.1.20	27
1.1.40	47
1.1.60	65–6
1.1.80	87
1.1.100	107
1.1.120	127
1.1.140	147
1.1.160	167
1.1.180	188
1.1.200	208
1.1.220	232
1.1.240	252
1.2.1	274
1.2.20	293
1.2.40	314
1.2.60	335
1.2.80	355
1.2.100	376
1.3.1	386
1.3.20	405
1.3.40	426
1.3.60	446
1.3.80	466
1.3.100	486
1.3.120	510
1.3.140	532
1.3.160	555
1.3.180	576–7
1.3.200	596–7
1.3.220	617
1.4.1	620
1.4.20	640
1.4.40	667
1.4.60	690
1.4.80	713
2.1.1	717
2.1.20	737
2.1.40	760
2.1.60	788–9
2.1.80	812
2.1.100	842–3
2.1.120	867
2.1.140	890–1
2.1.160	915
2.1.180	936
2.1.200	956
2.2.1	960
2.2.20	979
2.2.40	1001
2.2.60	1024
2.2.80	1047
2.3.1	1053–4
2.3.20	1074
2.3.40	1096
2.3.60	1121
2.3.80	1141
2.3.100	1162
2.4.1	1171
2.4.20	1196
2.4.40	1216
2.4.60	1236
2.4.80	1257–8
2.4.100	1280
3.1.1	1295
3.1.20	1314
3.1.40	1334
3.1.60	1354
3.1.80	1374
3.1.100	1398
3.1.120	1420
3.1.140	1440
3.1.160	1460
3.1.180	1480
3.1.200	1501
3.1.220	1521
3.1.240	1542
3.1.260	1562
3.1.280	1582
3.1.300	1603
3.1.320	1625
3.1.340	1646
3.1.360	1666
3.1.380	1686
3.2.1	1692
3.2.20	1714
3.2.40	1740
3.2.60	1760
3.2.80	1780
3.2.100	1800
3.2.120	1820
3.2.140	1842
3.2.160	1864
3.2.180	1884
3.2.200	1904
3.2.220	1925
3.2.240	1950
3.2.260	1972
3.2.280	1994
3.2.300	2014
3.2.320	2035
3.2.340	2055
3.2.360	2075
3.2.380	2097
3.2.400	2117
3.3.1	2134–5
3.3.20	2154
4.1.1	2170
4.1.20	2189
4.1.40	2209
4.1.60	2228
4.1.80	2248
4.1.100	2268
4.1.120	2288
4.1.140	2309
4.2.1	2320
4.2.20	2338–9
4.2.40	2360
4.2.60	2378
4.2.80	2396–7
4.2.100	2417
4.2.120	2438–9
4.2.140	2460
4.2.160	2480
4.2.180	2500
4.3.1	2513
4.4.1	2533
4.4.20	2553
4.4.40	2576
4.4.60	2597
4.5.1	2600
4.6.1	2615–6
4.7.1	2635
4.7.20	2653
4.7.40	2673–4
4.7.60	2694
4.7.80	2713
4.7.100	2733
4.7.120	2752–3
4.8.1	2775
4.8.20	2796
4.8.40	2817
4.8.60	2836–7
4.9.1	2850
4.9.20	2872
4.9.40	2894
4.10.1	2906
4.10.20	2925
4.10.40	2943–4
4.10.60	2965
4.10.80	2985
5.1.1	2992
5.1.20	3012
5.1.40	3032
5.1.60	3053
5.1.80	3074
5.1.100	3095
5.1.120	3115
5.1.140	3137
5.1.160	3159–60
5.1.180	3180
5.1.200	3200
5.2.1	3219
5.2.20	3241
5.2.40	3262
5.2.60	3282
5.2.80	3307
5.3.1	3321
5.3.20	3342

3H6

1.1.1	6
1.1.20	25
1.1.40	46
1.1.60	69
1.1.80	92
1.1.100	113
1.1.120	137–8
1.1.140	158
1.1.160	179
1.1.180	202
1.1.200	225
1.1.220	251
1.1.240	271
1.1.260	292
1.2.1	309–10
1.2.20	332–3
1.2.40	353
1.2.60	377
1.3.1	400
1.3.20	421
1.3.40	444
1.4.1	458
1.4.20	477
1.4.40	500
1.4.60	520
1.4.80	543
1.4.100	563
1.4.120	585–6
1.4.140	606
1.4.160	627
1.4.180	649
2.1.1	653
2.1.20	672
2.1.40	693
2.1.60	716
2.1.80	736
2.1.100	759
2.1.120	778
2.1.140	798
2.1.160	818
2.1.180	838
2.1.200	858
2.2.1	873
2.2.20	892
2.2.40	912
2.2.60	932
2.2.80	953
2.2.100	975
2.2.120	997
2.2.140	1017
2.2.160	1037
2.3.1	1057
2.3.20	1080
2.3.40	1100

2.4.1	1120
2.5.1	1135
2.5.20	1154
2.5.40	1174
2.5.60	1197
2.5.80	1218
2.5.100	1238
2.5.120	1258
2.6.1	1282
2.6.20	1300
2.6.40	1322
2.6.60	1343
2.6.80	1365
2.6.100	1385
3.1.1	1398
3.1.20	1418
3.1.40	1438
3.1.60	1458
3.1.80	1478
3.1.100	1498
3.2.1	1501
3.2.20	1521
3.2.40	1547–8
3.2.60	1572
3.2.80	1593
3.2.100	1615–6
3.2.120	1642
3.2.140	1664
3.2.160	1684
3.2.180	1704
3.3.1	1725
3.3.20	1746
3.3.40	1768–9
3.3.60	1794
3.3.80	1815
3.3.100	1835
3.3.120	1858
3.3.140	1880
3.3.160	1900
3.3.180	1926
3.3.200	1947
3.3.220	1967
3.3.240	1988
3.3.260	2010
4.1.1	2018
4.1.20	2044
4.1.40	2066
4.1.60	2086
4.1.80	2107
4.1.100	2129
4.1.120	2152
4.1.140	2174
4.2.1	2188
4.2.20	2208
4.3.1	2221
4.3.20	2242–3
4.3.40	2275
4.3.60	2298
4.4.1	2304
4.4.20	2324
4.5.1	2343
4.5.20	2366–7
4.6.1	2382
4.6.20	2401
4.6.40	2421
4.6.60	2442
4.6.80	2467
4.6.100	2488
4.7.1	2493
4.7.20	2517
4.7.40	2543
4.7.60	2568
4.7.80	2591
4.8.1	2602
4.8.20	2621
4.8.40	2642
4.8.60	2666
5.1.1	2674
5.1.20	2696
5.1.40	2717
5.1.60	2740
5.1.80	2763
5.1.100	2783
5.2.1	2801
5.2.20	2821
5.2.40	2842
5.3.1	2857
5.3.20	2876
5.4.1	2884
5.4.20	2903
5.4.40	2923
5.4.60	2945
5.4.80	2967
5.5.1	2973
5.5.20	2994
5.5.40	3017
5.5.60	3040
5.5.80	3060
5.6.1	3074–5
5.6.20	3094
5.6.40	3114
5.6.60	3135
5.6.80	3156
5.7.1	3172
5.7.20	3191
5.7.40	3211

R3

1.1.1	3
1.1.20	22
1.1.40	42
1.1.60	64
1.1.80	84
1.1.100	105
1.1.120	127
1.1.140	148
1.1.160	169
1.2.1	175
1.2.20	194
1.2.40	216
1.2.60	237
1.2.80	257
1.2.100	281
1.2.120	306
1.2.140	327
1.2.160	351
1.2.180	373
1.2.200	395
1.2.220	414
1.2.240	437
1.2.260	457
1.3.1	464
1.3.20	485
1.3.40	505
1.3.60	526
1.3.80	546
1.3.100	566
1.3.120	588–9
1.3.140	610
1.3.160	630
1.3.180	650
1.3.200	670
1.3.220	690
1.3.240	712
1.3.260	732–3
1.3.280	753
1.3.300	774
1.3.320	796
1.3.340	818
1.4.1	837
1.4.20	856
1.4.40	876
1.4.60	896
1.4.80	917
1.4.100	939
1.4.120	956
1.4.140	973–4
1.4.160	992
1.4.180	1012
1.4.200	1031
1.4.220	1051
1.4.240	1072
1.4.260	1094
1.4.280	1115
2.1.1	1124
2.1.20	1143
2.1.40	1164
2.1.60	1184
2.1.80	1205
2.1.100	1227
2.1.120	1247
2.1.140	1268
2.2.1	1273
2.2.20	1292
2.2.40	1314
2.2.60	1334
2.2.80	1354
2.2.100	1373
2.2.120	1395
2.2.140	1416
2.3.1	1434–5
2.3.20	1457
2.3.40	1477
2.4.1	1488
2.4.20	1507
2.4.40	1529–30
2.4.60	1552
3.1.1	1572–3
3.1.20	1596
3.1.40	1619
3.1.60	1639
3.1.80	1659
3.1.100	1682
3.1.120	1703
3.1.140	1724
3.1.160	1746
3.1.180	1768
3.1.200	1791
3.2.1	1795
3.2.20	1816
3.2.40	1838
3.2.60	1860
3.2.80	1880
3.2.100	1903
3.2.120	1927
3.3.1	1931 + 1
3.3.20	1955
3.4.1	1967
3.4.20	1987
3.4.40	2009
3.4.60	2031
3.4.80	2053
3.4.100	2073
3.5.1	2084–5
3.5.20	2105
3.5.40	2126
3.5.60	2146
3.5.80	2167
3.5.100	2187
3.6.1	2199
3.7.1	2214
3.7.20	2233
3.7.40	2253
3.7.60	2276
3.7.80	2296
3.7.100	2320
3.7.120	2341
3.7.140	2361
3.7.160	2381
3.7.180	2401
3.7.200	2421
3.7.220	2440 + 1
3.7.240	2462
4.1.1	2473–4
4.1.20	2496
4.1.40	2520
4.1.60	2540
4.1.80	2560
4.1.100	2582
4.2.1	2590
4.2.20	2611
4.2.40	2631–2
4.2.60	2654
4.2.80	2677
4.2.100	2697 + 2
4.2.120	2701
4.3.1	2705
4.3.20	2724
4.3.40	2748
4.4.1	2771
4.4.20	2791
4.4.40	2810
4.4.60	2831
4.4.80	2851
4.4.100	2871
4.4.120	2891
4.4.140	2913
4.4.160	2935–6
4.4.180	2957–8
4.4.200	2979
4.4.220	2999
4.4.240	3019
4.4.260	3040
4.4.280	3064
4.4.300	3085
4.4.320	3105
4.4.340	3125
4.4.360	3145
4.4.380	3170
4.4.400	3191
4.4.420	3211
4.4.440	3232
4.4.460	3257
4.4.480	3278
4.4.500	3302
4.4.520	3327
4.5.1	3349
4.5.20	3368
5.1.1	3373
5.1.20	3392
5.2.1	3406
5.2.20	3425
5.3.1	3433
5.3.20	3456
5.3.40	3476
5.3.60	3501
5.3.80	3522
5.3.100	3542
5.3.120	3565
5.3.140	3589
5.3.160	3617
5.3.180	3642
5.3.200	3662
5.3.220	3681
5.3.240	3706
5.3.260	3726
5.3.280	3748
5.3.300	3769
5.3.320	3790
5.3.340	3811
5.4.1	3825–6
5.5.1	3845–6
5.5.20	3866
5.5.40	3886

H8

PR.1	2
PR.20	21
1.1.1	39
1.1.20	64
1.1.40	85
1.1.60	109
1.1.80	131–2
1.1.100	159–60
1.1.120	188
1.1.140	213
1.1.160	235
1.1.180	256
1.1.200	281
1.1.220	307
1.2.1	321
1.2.20	347
1.2.40	369–70
1.2.60	393
1.2.80	415
1.2.100	436
1.2.120	459
1.2.140	481
1.2.160	506
1.2.180	528
1.2.200	552
1.3.1	571
1.3.20	596
1.3.40	620
1.3.60	649
1.4.1	666–7
1.4.20	691
1.4.40	717–8
1.4.60	748
1.4.80	779
1.4.100	808
2.1.1	821–2
2.1.20	847
2.1.40	871–2
2.1.60	901
2.1.80	923
2.1.100	945–6
2.1.120	966
2.1.140	988
2.1.160	1013
2.2.1	1028
2.2.20	1052
2.2.40	1073
2.2.60	1097
2.2.80	1124–5
2.2.100	1148
2.2.120	1170
2.2.140	1196
2.3.1	1202
2.3.20	1225
2.3.40	1250
2.3.60	1275
2.3.80	1297–9
2.3.100	1321–2
2.4.1	1350
2.4.20	1373
2.4.40	1393
2.4.60	1414
2.4.80	1437
2.4.100	1458
2.4.120	1479
2.4.140	1502
2.4.160	1524
2.4.180	1545
2.4.200	1565
2.4.220	1588
2.4.240	1610
3.1.1	1616–7
3.1.20	1640
3.1.40	1663
3.1.60	1683
3.1.80	1705
3.1.100	1730
3.1.120	1751
3.1.140	1774
3.1.160	1796
3.1.180	1818
3.2.1	1826
3.2.20	1849
3.2.40	1876
3.2.60	1903
3.2.80	1933
3.2.100	1957
3.2.120	1982
3.2.140	2008
3.2.160	2031–2
3.2.180	2054
3.2.200	2076
3.2.220	2099
3.2.240	2124
3.2.260	2147
3.2.280	2170
3.2.300	2192–3
3.2.320	2217
3.2.340	2239
3.2.360	2260
3.2.380	2285
3.2.400	2310–1
3.2.420	2333
3.2.440	2354
4.1.1	2378–9
4.1.20	2401
4.1.40	2450
4.1.60	2477–9
4.1.80	2500
4.1.100	2524
4.2.1	2251–2
4.2.20	2574
4.2.40	2595
4.2.60	2618
4.2.80	2638
4.2.100	2681–2
4.2.120	2708
4.2.140	2732
4.2.160	2753
5.1.1	2771–2
5.1.20	2794–5
5.1.40	2819
5.1.60	2841
5.1.80	2867
5.1.100	2897
5.1.120	2919
5.1.140	2941–2
5.1.160	2965
5.2.1	2989
5.2.20	3016–7
5.2.40	3049–51
5.2.60	3073
5.2.80	3093
5.2.100	3114
5.2.120	3139–40
5.2.140	3169–70
5.2.160	3194
5.2.180	3215
5.2.200	3237
5.3.1	3259
5.3.20	3277
5.3.40	3299
5.3.60	3318
5.3.80	3341
5.4.1	3364–5
5.4.20	3390
5.4.40	3411
5.4.60	3432
EP.1	3450

TRO

PR.1	2
PR.20	21
1.1.1	36
1.1.20	53
1.1.40	75
1.1.60	94
1.1.80	114
1.1.100	134
1.2.1	156–7
1.2.20	178–9
1.2.40	198
1.2.60	218–9
1.2.80	236
1.2.100	256
1.2.120	275
1.2.140	294–5
1.2.160	315
1.2.180	334
1.2.200	354–5
1.2.220	375–6
1.2.240	398
1.2.260	417
1.2.280	438
1.3.1	456
1.3.20	475
1.3.40	496
1.3.60	519
1.3.80	539
1.3.100	559
1.3.120	579
1.3.140	600
1.3.160	620
1.3.180	640
1.3.200	660
1.3.220	680
1.3.240	700
1.3.260	724
1.3.280	744
1.3.300	764
1.3.320	786–7
1.3.340	807
1.3.360	828
1.3.380	848
2.1.1	860
2.1.20	878
2.1.40	894–5
2.1.60	915
2.1.80	935
2.1.100	954–5
2.1.120	973
2.2.1	985
2.2.20	1003
2.2.40	1024
2.2.60	1045
2.2.80	1065
2.2.100	1088
2.2.120	1109
2.2.140	1129
2.2.160	1150
2.2.180	1170
2.2.200	1190
2.3.1	1206
2.3.20	1223–4
2.3.40	1243
2.3.60	1261
2.3.80	1283
2.3.100	1304
2.3.120	1325
2.3.140	1345
2.3.160	1367
2.3.180	1388
2.3.200	1407
2.3.220	1427–8
2.3.240	1448
2.3.260	1470
3.1.1	1479
3.1.20	1497
3.1.40	1516–7
3.1.60	1536
3.1.80	1555
3.1.100	1573–4
3.1.120	1592
3.1.140	1611–2
3.2.1	1633
3.2.20	1652
3.2.40	1673–4
3.2.60	1692
3.2.80	1710
3.2.100	1731
3.2.120	1751
3.2.140	1771
3.2.160	1792
3.2.180	1813
3.2.200	1833–4
3.3.1	1849
3.3.20	1869
3.3.40	1891
3.3.60	1911
3.3.80	1932
3.3.100	1953
3.3.120	1972
3.3.140	1992
3.3.160	2013
3.3.180	2032
3.3.200	2055
3.3.220	2075
3.3.240	2097
3.3.260	2116–7
3.3.280	2135
3.3.300	2154
4.1.1	2171
4.1.20	2192
4.1.40	2212

4.1.60	2235
4.1.80	2255
4.2.1	2257
4.2.20	2280
4.2.40	2300
4.2.60	2321
4.2.80	2342
4.2.100	2362
4.3.1	2375
4.4.1	2389
4.4.20	2404–5
4.4.40	2426
4.4.60	2447
4.4.80	2470
4.4.100	2492
4.4.120	2514
4.4.140	2536–7
4.5.1	2549
4.5.20	2572
4.5.40	2593
4.5.60	2617
4.5.80	2641
4.5.100	2662
4.5.120	2684
4.5.140	2705
4.5.160	2727
4.5.180	2748
4.5.200	2768
4.5.220	2787
4.5.240	2811
4.5.260	2832–3
4.5.280	2855
5.1.1	2871
5.1.20	2889 + 1
5.1.40	2907
5.1.60	2926–7
5.1.80	2952
5.2.1	2974
5.2.20	2996
5.2.40	3016–7
5.2.60	3042
5.2.80	3066
5.2.100	3090
5.2.120	3114
5.2.140	3137
5.2.160	3157
5.2.180	3177–8
5.3.1	3198
5.3.20	3219
5.3.40	3242
5.3.60	3266
5.3.80	3291–2
5.3.100	3314
5.4.1	3333
5.4.20	3352–3
5.5.1	3372
5.5.20	3393
5.5.40	3414
5.6.1	3426
5.6.20	3454
5.7.1	3470
5.7.20	3491–2
5.8.1	3497
5.8.20	3517
5.9.1	3523
5.10.1	3535
5.10.20	3556
5.10.40	3576–7

COR

1.1.1	5
1.1.20	21–2
1.1.40	40–1
1.1.60	61–2
1.1.80	80–1
1.1.100	102
1.1.120	123–4
1.1.140	147
1.1.160	168
1.1.180	191
1.1.200	212
1.1.220	234
1.1.240	263
1.1.260	289–90
1.2.1	314
1.2.20	336
1.3.1	362
1.3.20	381
1.3.40	402
1.3.60	422–3
1.3.80	444
1.3.100	463–4
1.4.1	482–3
1.4.20	510
1.4.40	535
1.4.60	562
1.5.1	570
1.5.20	592–3
1.6.1	604
1.6.20	626
1.6.40	652
1.6.60	677
1.6.80	701
1.7.1	714
1.8.1	724
1.9.1	748
1.9.20	770–1
1.9.40	793
1.9.60	816
1.9.80	838–9
1.10.1	859
1.10.20	879
2.1.1	898
2.1.20	917
2.1.40	935–6
2.1.60	955–6
2.1.80	975
2.1.100	997
2.1.120	1017
2.1.140	1036
2.1.160	1057
2.1.180	1087
2.1.200	1113–4
2.1.220	1139
2.1.240	1165–6
2.1.260	1190–1
2.2.1	1205
2.2.20	1222–3
2.2.40	1247
2.2.60	1268–9
2.2.80	1294
2.2.100	1314
2.2.120	1333–4
2.2.140	1360–1
2.2.160	1386
2.3.1	1388
2.3.20	1405–6
2.3.40	1428–9
2.3.60	1451–3
2.3.80	1471
2.3.100	1490–1
2.3.120	1511
2.3.140	1533–4
2.3.160	1558
2.3.180	1581
2.3.200	1603
2.3.220	1623
2.3.240	1643
2.3.260	1666–7
3.1.1	1674
3.1.20	1698
3.1.40	1723
3.1.60	1748
3.1.80	1772–3
3.1.100	1794
3.1.120	1817
3.1.140	1838–9
3.1.160	1859
3.1.180	1887
3.1.200	1911
3.1.220	1937
3.1.240	1965
3.1.260	1989–90
3.1.280	2016–7
3.1.300	2039
3.1.320	2064
3.2.1	2084
3.2.20	2107
3.2.40	2135
3.2.60	2159
3.2.80	2181
3.2.100	2206
3.2.120	2228
3.2.140	2251
3.3.1	2259
3.3.20	2283
3.3.40	2311–2
3.3.60	2338
3.3.80	2362–3
3.3.100	2385
3.3.120	2408
3.3.140	2430
4.1.1	2437
4.1.20	2458
4.1.40	2480
4.2.1	2503
4.2.20	2528–9
4.2.40	2552
4.3.1	2571
4.3.20	2589
4.3.40	2609
4.4.1	2623
4.4.20	2646
4.5.1	2654
4.5.20	2675
4.5.40	2694
4.5.60	2717
4.5.80	2737
4.5.100	2757
4.5.120	2778
4.5.140	2799
4.5.160	2820
4.5.180	2840
4.5.200	2859–60
4.5.220	2877–8
4.6.1	2893
4.6.20	2915–6
4.6.40	2942
4.6.60	2966–7
4.6.80	2994–5
4.6.100	3017–8
4.6.120	3041–2
4.6.140	3067
4.6.160	3088–9
4.7.1	3091
4.7.20	3111
4.7.40	3131
5.1.1	3152
5.1.20	3173
5.1.40	3196
5.1.60	3218–9
5.2.1	3236–7
5.2.20	3258
5.2.40	3276–7
5.2.60	3297
5.2.80	3315
5.2.100	3336
5.3.1	3347
5.3.20	3367
5.3.40	3389–90
5.3.60	3411
5.3.80	3435
5.3.100	3455
5.3.120	3475
5.3.140	3497
5.3.160	3517
5.3.180	3537
5.3.200	3559
5.4.1	3571
5.4.20	3588–9
5.4.40	3611
5.4.60	3635–6
5.5.1	3641
5.6.1	3650
5.6.20	3673
5.6.40	3694–5
5.6.60	3721–2
5.6.80	3746
5.6.100	3770–1
5.6.120	3793
5.6.140	3820

TIT

1.1.1	7
1.1.20	28
1.1.40	48
1.1.60	71
1.1.80	101
1.1.100	122
1.1.120	142
1.1.140	163
1.1.160	187
1.1.180	209
1.1.200	229
1.1.220	250
1.1.240	271
1.1.260	291
1.1.280	312
1.1.300	336
1.1.320	356
1.1.340	378
1.1.360	401
1.1.380	422
1.1.400	449
1.1.420	469
1.1.440	490
1.1.460	511–2
1.1.480	536
2.1.1	555
2.1.20	574
2.1.40	595
2.1.60	618
2.1.80	639–40
2.1.100	663
2.1.120	683
2.2.1	701
2.2.20	725–6
2.3.1	734
2.3.20	755
2.3.40	776
2.3.60	799
2.3.80	819
2.3.100	841
2.3.120	862
2.3.140	883
2.3.160	905
2.3.180	926
2.3.200	951
2.3.220	974
2.3.240	994
2.3.260	1016
2.3.280	1038
2.3.300	1060
2.4.1	1070
2.4.20	1093
2.4.40	1113
3.1.1	1135
3.1.20	1155
3.1.40	1175
3.1.60	1197
3.1.80	1219
3.1.100	1242
3.1.120	1263
3.1.140	1284
3.1.160	1305
3.1.180	1326
3.1.200	1348
3.1.220	1368
3.1.240	1389
3.1.260	1409
3.1.280	1429
3.1.300	1450
3.2.1	1453
3.2.20	1472
3.2.40	1492
3.2.60	1513
3.2.80	1534
4.1.1	1544
4.1.20	1563
4.1.40	1584
4.1.60	1604
4.1.80	1628
4.1.100	1648
4.1.120	1668
4.2.1	1681
4.2.20	1699
4.2.40	1719
4.2.60	1742
4.2.80	1763
4.2.100	1783
4.2.120	1803
4.2.140	1823
4.2.160	1844
4.2.180	1864
4.3.1	1868
4.3.20	1886
4.3.40	1905
4.3.60	1926
4.3.80	1947
4.3.100	1967
4.3.120	1987
4.4.1	1993–4
4.4.20	2013
4.4.40	2034
4.4.60	2054
4.4.80	2075
4.4.100	2095
5.1.1	2111
5.1.20	2132
5.1.40	2152
5.1.60	2172
5.1.80	2194
5.1.100	2216
5.1.120	2236
5.1.140	2256
5.1.160	2277
5.2.1	2284
5.2.20	2304–5
5.2.40	2326
5.2.60	2346
5.2.80	2366
5.2.100	2386
5.2.120	2406
5.2.140	2427
5.2.160	2448
5.2.180	2469
5.2.200	2489
5.3.1	2497
5.3.20	2518
5.3.40	2542
5.3.60	2563
5.3.80	2584
5.3.100	2604
5.3.120	2624
5.3.140	2644
5.3.160	2664
5.3.180	2684
5.3.200	2704

ROM

PR.1	+1
1.1.1	5
1.1.20	23
1.1.40	42
1.1.60	57
1.1.80	81
1.1.100	102
1.1.120	122
1.1.140	142
1.1.160	163–4
1.1.180	185
1.1.200	208–9
1.1.220	218
1.2.1	248
1.2.20	267
1.2.40	286–7
1.2.60	309
1.2.80	328–9
1.2.100	349
1.3.1	352
1.3.20	374
1.3.40	389–90
1.3.60	407
1.3.80	426
1.3.100	447
1.4.1	456
1.4.20	473
1.4.40	493
1.4.60	521
1.4.80	530–1
1.4.100	551
1.5.1	569
1.5.20	590
1.5.40	613
1.5.60	633–4
1.5.80	656
1.5.100	678
1.5.120	702
1.5.140	723
2.PR.1	733
2.1.1	748
2.1.20	770
2.1.40	790
2.2.1	794
2.2.20	812
2.2.40	834
2.2.60	856
2.2.80	878
2.2.100	898
2.2.120	920
2.2.140	942
2.2.160	966
2.2.180	989
2.3.1	1006
2.3.20	1025
2.3.40	1047
2.3.60	1067
2.3.80	1087
2.4.1	1106
2.4.20	1124–5
2.4.40	1144–5
2.4.60	1164
2.4.80	1183
2.4.100	1198–9
2.4.120	1220
2.4.140	1237
2.4.160	1256–7
2.4.180	1275
2.4.200	1293–4
2.5.1	1311
2.5.20	1331
2.5.40	1351–2
2.5.60	1372
2.6.1	1393
2.6.20	1413
3.1.1	1432
3.1.20	1450–1
3.1.40	1470–1
3.1.60	1492
3.1.80	1511–2
3.1.100	1533–4
3.1.120	1555
3.1.140	1582
3.1.160	1604
3.1.180	1624
3.2.1	1645
3.2.20	1664
3.2.40	1687–8
3.2.60	1710
3.2.80	1732
3.2.100	1754
3.2.120	1774
3.2.140	1794
3.3.1	1800–1
3.3.20	1823
3.3.40	1845
3.3.60	1862
3.3.80	1894–5
3.3.100	1916
3.3.120	1937
3.3.140	1957
3.3.160	1977
3.4.1	1995
3.4.20	2015
3.5.1	2033
3.5.20	2052
3.5.40	2073
3.5.60	2093
3.5.80	2117–8
3.5.100	2138
3.5.120	2158
3.5.140	2180
3.5.160	2202
3.5.180	2227
3.5.200	2247
3.5.220	2269
3.5.240	2290
4.1.1	2294
4.1.20	2314
4.1.40	2335
4.1.60	2355
4.1.80	2375
4.1.100	2395
4.1.120	2415
4.2.1	2425
4.2.20	2446
4.2.40	2469
4.3.1	2479
4.3.20	2501
4.3.40	2520
4.4.1	2540–1
4.4.20	2565
4.5.1	2576
4.5.20	2597
4.5.40	2620
4.5.60	2640
4.5.80	2660
4.5.100	2679
4.5.120	2698
4.5.140	2715
5.1.1	2723
5.1.20	2743
5.1.40	2767
5.1.60	2789
5.1.80	2815
5.2.1	2819
5.2.20	2839
5.3.1	2852
5.3.20	2872
5.3.40	2893
5.3.60	2913
5.3.80	2933
5.3.100	2953
5.3.120	2977
5.3.140	3003
5.3.160	3023
5.3.180	3047
5.3.200	3073
5.3.220	3095
5.3.240	3115
5.3.260	3135
5.3.280	3154
5.3.300	3175

TIM

1.1.1	5–6
1.1.20	31–2
1.1.40	56
1.1.60	77
1.1.80	101
1.1.100	127
1.1.120	149–50
1.1.140	174
1.1.160	199
1.1.180	224
1.1.200	243
1.1.220	265
1.1.240	287

1.1.260	311
1.1.280	332–3
1.2.1	342
1.2.20	362
1.2.40	382
1.2.60	402
1.2.80	422
1.2.100	440–1
1.2.120	462–3
1.2.140	484
1.2.160	511
1.2.180	535
1.2.200	558–9
1.2.220	581
1.2.240	604–5
2.1.1	616
2.1.20	637
2.2.1	657
2.2.20	682
2.2.40	707
2.2.60	725–6
2.2.80	747
2.2.100	767
2.2.120	788
2.2.140	812
2.2.160	834
2.2.180	856–7
2.2.200	879
2.2.220	901
3.1.1	918
3.1.20	936–7
3.1.40	956–7
3.1.60	976
3.2.1	981
3.2.20	998–9
3.2.40	1021
3.2.60	1041
3.2.80	1063
3.3.1	1073–4
3.3.20	1095
3.3.40	1115
3.4.1	1120
3.4.20	1146
3.4.40	1168
3.4.60	1189
3.4.80	1212
3.4.100	1235
3.5.1	1257–8
3.5.20	1276
3.5.40	1298
3.5.60	1319
3.5.80	1340–1
3.5.100	1364
3.6.1	1384
3.6.20	1402–3
3.6.40	1423
3.6.60	1442
3.6.80	1460–1
3.6.100	1480
3.6.120	1501
4.1.1	1504
4.1.20	1523
4.1.40	1543
4.2.1	1546
4.2.20	1568
4.2.40	1590
4.3.1	1603
4.3.20	1622
4.3.40	1642
4.3.60	1666
4.3.80	1688
4.3.100	1709–10
4.3.120	1733
4.3.140	1754
4.3.160	1776
4.3.180	1800
4.3.200	1821
4.3.220	1841
4.3.240	1867
4.3.260	1887
4.3.280	1909
4.3.300	1931
4.3.320	1949
4.3.340	1968–9
4.3.360	1995–6
4.3.380	2020
4.3.400	2046–7
4.3.420	2070
4.3.440	2090
4.3.460	2111
4.3.480	2133
4.3.500	2154
4.3.520	2174
5.1.1	2193
5.1.20	2221–2
5.1.40	2246–7
5.1.60	2269
5.1.80	2296
5.1.100	2323–4
5.1.120	2347
5.1.140	2375
5.1.160	2397
5.1.180	2419
5.1.200	2444
5.1.220	2465
5.2.1	2477
5.3.1	2497
5.4.1	2509
5.4.20	2532
5.4.40	2555
5.4.60	2579
5.4.80	2602

JC

1.1.1	5
1.1.20	26
1.1.40	47
1.1.60	67
1.2.1	87–9
1.2.20	110
1.2.40	132
1.2.60	154
1.2.80	176–8
1.2.100	198
1.2.120	218
1.2.140	239
1.2.160	259
1.2.180	282
1.2.200	302
1.2.220	323
1.2.240	343–4
1.2.260	364
1.2.280	384
1.2.300	405
1.2.320	427
1.3.1	433
1.3.20	452
1.3.40	472–3
1.3.60	498–9
1.3.80	520
1.3.100	540–1
1.3.120	561–2
1.3.140	586–7
1.3.160	608
2.1.1	616
2.1.20	636
2.1.40	658
2.1.60	681
2.1.80	705
2.1.100	730
2.1.120	751
2.1.140	771
2.1.160	793
2.1.180	813
2.1.200	837
2.1.220	857
2.1.240	881
2.1.260	901
2.1.280	922
2.1.300	942
2.1.320	965
2.2.1	985–6
2.2.20	1007
2.2.40	1030
2.2.60	1052
2.2.80	1073
2.2.100	1093
2.2.120	1119
2.3.1	1130
2.4.1	1145
2.4.20	1167
2.4.40	1192
3.1.1	1204
3.1.20	1225
3.1.40	1247
3.1.60	1268
3.1.80	1291
3.1.100	1315
3.1.120	1337
3.1.140	1358
3.1.160	1381
3.1.180	1401
3.1.200	1422
3.1.220	1443
3.1.240	1466
3.1.260	1488
3.1.280	1509
3.2.1	1530
3.2.20	1549–50
3.2.40	1568–9
3.2.60	1594
3.2.80	1617
3.2.100	1637
3.2.120	1657
3.2.140	1677
3.2.160	1697
3.2.180	1717
3.2.200	1737
3.2.220	1757
3.2.240	1778
3.2.260	1799
3.3.1	1814
3.3.20	1833
4.1.1	1854
4.1.20	1875
4.1.40	1896
4.2.1	1910
4.2.20	1931
4.2.40	1954
4.3.1	1970
4.3.20	1990
4.3.40	2013
4.3.60	2036
4.3.80	2057
4.3.100	2079
4.3.120	2103
4.3.140	2126
4.3.160	2151
4.3.180	2174
4.3.200	2198
4.3.220	2219
4.3.240	2247–8
4.3.260	2271
4.3.280	2293
4.3.300	2314–5
5.1.1	2329
5.1.20	2350
5.1.40	2373
5.1.60	2394
5.1.80	2420
5.1.100	2442
5.1.120	2464
5.2.1	2471
5.3.1	2479
5.3.20	2500
5.3.40	2521
5.3.60	2545
5.3.80	2566
5.3.100	2590
5.4.1	2603
5.4.20	2625
5.5.1	2640–1
5.5.20	2663–4
5.5.40	2685
5.5.60	2709
5.5.80	2729

MAC

1.1.1	3
1.2.1	18
1.2.20	39
1.2.40	61
1.2.60	87
1.3.1	98
1.3.20	118
1.3.40	139
1.3.60	160
1.3.80	181
1.3.100	204–5
1.3.120	229–30
1.3.140	251–2
1.4.1	280–1
1.4.20	303
1.4.40	327
1.5.1	349
1.5.20	366
1.5.40	391
1.5.60	414–5
1.6.1	434–5
1.6.20	456–7
1.7.1	475
1.7.20	494
1.7.40	517
1.7.60	541
1.7.80	564
2.1.1	571
2.1.20	596
2.1.40	620
2.1.60	640
2.2.1	648
2.2.20	677–8
2.2.40	700
2.2.60	724
2.3.1	744
2.3.20	762
2.3.40	782
2.3.60	809–10
2.3.80	835
2.3.100	863–4
2.3.120	887
2.3.140	914–5
2.4.1	925
2.4.20	948–50
2.4.40	977
3.1.1	982
3.1.20	1006
3.1.40	1028
3.1.60	1051
3.1.80	1076–7
3.1.100	1101
3.1.120	1124
3.1.140	1148
3.2.1	1152
3.2.20	1175
3.2.40	1198
3.3.1	1218–9
3.3.20	1248–9
3.4.1	1256–7
3.4.20	1279–80
3.4.40	1305
3.4.60	1330
3.4.80	1353
3.4.100	1378
3.4.120	1401–2
3.4.140	1424
3.5.1	1431
3.5.20	1450
3.6.1	1472–3
3.6.20	1492
3.6.40	1514
4.1.1	1528
4.1.20	1547
4.1.40	1568
4.1.60	1590
4.1.80	1621
4.1.100	1644
4.1.120	1667
4.1.140	1692
4.2.1	1712
4.2.20	1734
4.2.40	1760
4.2.60	1779
4.2.80	1803
4.3.1	1814
4.3.20	1836
4.3.40	1860
4.3.60	1883
4.3.80	1905
4.3.100	1926–7
4.3.120	1948
4.3.140	1969–70
4.3.160	1994
4.3.180	2020
4.3.200	2045
4.3.220	2069–70
4.3.240	2091
5.1.1	2095
5.1.20	2112–3
5.1.40	2131–2
5.1.60	2150–1
5.2.1	2176
5.2.20	2198
5.3.1	2215
5.3.20	2237
5.3.40	2262
5.3.60	2284
5.4.1	2291
5.4.20	2316
5.5.1	2321
5.5.20	2341
5.5.40	2365
5.6.1	2381–2
5.7.1	2396
5.7.20	2422
5.8.1	2436
5.8.20	2460
5.9.1	2480
5.9.20	2505–6
5.9.40	2527

HAM

1.1.1	4
1.1.20	29
1.1.40	51–2
1.1.60	76
1.1.80	97
1.1.100	117
1.1.120	124 + 13
1.1.140	137
1.1.160	159
1.2.1	179
1.2.20	198
1.2.40	219
1.2.60	240 + 2
1.2.80	261
1.2.100	282
1.2.120	302–3
1.2.140	324
1.2.160	345–6
1.2.180	368
1.2.200	391
1.2.220	413–4
1.2.240	440
1.3.1	462
1.3.20	483
1.3.40	503
1.3.60	525
1.3.80	545
1.3.100	566
1.3.120	586
1.4.1	604
1.4.20	621 + 4
1.4.40	625
1.4.60	646–7
1.4.80	665–6
1.5.1	682
1.5.20	705
1.5.40	727–8
1.5.60	745
1.5.80	765
1.5.100	785
1.5.120	809–10
1.5.140	833
1.5.160	856
1.5.180	876
2.1.1	890
2.1.20	911
2.1.40	933
2.1.60	955
2.1.80	979
2.1.100	1000
2.2.1	1021
2.2.20	1039
2.2.40	1064
2.2.60	1085
2.2.80	1105–6
2.2.100	1128
2.2.120	1148
2.2.140	1169
2.2.160	1192–3
2.2.180	1217
2.2.200	1238
2.2.220	1263–4
2.2.240	1285–6
2.2.260	1306
2.2.280	1327–8
2.2.300	1346–7
2.2.320	1366–7
2.2.340	1387–8
2.2.360	1407
2.2.380	1428
2.2.400	1448
2.2.420	1464–5
2.2.440	1484–5
2.2.460	1502
2.2.480	1521
2.2.500	1539–40
2.2.520	1561
2.2.540	1580
2.2.560	1600
2.2.580	1620
2.2.600	1640
3.1.1	1648
3.1.20	1668
3.1.40	1691
3.1.60	1715
3.1.80	1735
3.1.100	1756
3.1.120	1776
3.1.140	1795–6
3.1.160	1816
3.1.180	1837
3.2.1	1849
3.2.20	1868
3.2.40	1888
3.2.60	1911
3.2.80	1931
3.2.100	1955
3.2.120	1973
3.2.140	2006–7
3.2.160	2029
3.2.180	2048
3.2.200	2068
3.2.220	2086
3.2.240	2107–8
3.2.260	2130
3.2.280	2152
3.2.300	2171
3.2.320	2191
3.2.340	2210
3.2.360	2231
3.2.380	2251
3.3.1	2272
3.3.20	2293
3.3.40	2316
3.3.60	2336
3.3.80	2356
3.4.1	2375–6
3.4.20	2400
3.4.40	2422–3
3.4.60	2444
3.4.80	2456 + 3
3.4.100	2479
3.4.120	2501
3.4.140	2523
3.4.160	2544
3.4.180	2556
3.4.200	2576–7
4.1.1	2587–8
4.1.20	2607
4.1.40	2628
4.2.1	2631
4.2.20	2649–50
4.3.1	2662
4.3.20	2685–6
4.3.40	2701
4.3.60	2725
4.4.1	2735
4.4.20	2743 + 12
4.4.40	2743 + 32
4.4.60	2743 + 52
4.5.1	2745
4.5.20	2765
4.5.40	2782
4.5.60	2798
4.5.80	2817
4.5.100	2839
4.5.120	2863
4.5.140	2887–8
4.5.160	2912
4.5.180	2932
4.5.200	2949–50
4.5.220	2971
4.6.1	2973
4.6.20	2992
4.7.1	3007
4.7.20	3028
4.7.40	3051
4.7.60	3070
4.7.80	3078 + 12
4.7.100	3099
4.7.120	3112 + 7
4.7.140	3131
4.7.160	3151
4.7.180	3172
5.1.1	3190
5.1.20	3209
5.1.40	3229
5.1.60	3249–50
5.1.80	3271
5.1.100	3291
5.1.120	3311
5.1.140	3331
5.1.160	3350
5.1.180	3367–8
5.1.200	3388
5.1.220	3409
5.1.240	3431
5.1.260	3456
5.1.280	3477
5.2.1	3500
5.2.20	3520
5.2.40	3542
5.2.60	3563
5.2.80	3584–5
5.2.100	3605
5.2.120	3610 + 15
5.2.140	3610 + 35
5.2.160	3625–6
5.2.180	3644
5.2.200	3657 + 6
5.2.220	3669
5.2.240	3692
5.2.260	3716–7
5.2.280	3741–5
5.2.300	3774
5.2.320	3801
5.2.340	3824–5
5.2.360	3850
5.2.380	3875

5.2.400	3901

LR

1.1.1	4
1.1.20	23
1.1.40	45
1.1.60	65
1.1.80	86
1.1.100	107
1.1.120	127–8
1.1.140	149
1.1.160	172–3
1.1.180	194
1.1.200	218
1.1.220	241
1.1.240	263
1.1.260	285
1.1.280	306
1.1.300	325
1.2.1	335
1.2.20	354
1.2.40	375
1.2.60	395
1.2.80	413–4
1.2.100	430
1.2.120	448–9
1.2.140	469
1.2.160	481–2
1.2.180	500
1.3.1	507–8
1.3.20	522 + 5
1.4.1	531
1.4.20	550–1
1.4.40	571
1.4.60	589
1.4.80	610
1.4.100	629–30
1.4.120	650
1.4.140	669 + 1
1.4.160	674–5
1.4.180	693
1.4.200	711
1.4.220	732
1.4.240	749
1.4.260	772
1.4.280	794
1.4.300	819
1.4.320	840
1.4.340	864
1.5.1	875
1.5.20	893–4
1.5.40	912
2.1.1	928
2.1.20	950
2.1.40	974–5
2.1.60	997
2.2.80	1018
2.1.100	1039
2.1.120	1063
2.2.1	1076
2.2.20	1093
2.2.40	1113
2.2.60	1132 -3
2.2.80	1153
2.2.100	1175
2.2.120	1196
2.2.140	1220
2.2.160	1237
2.3.1	1252
2.3.20	1271
2.4.1	1274
2.4.20	1294 + 2
2.4.40	1316
2.4.60	1332
2.4.80	1352
2.4.100	1375
2.4.120	1396
2.4.140	1418–9
2.4.160	1442
2.4.180	1464
2.4.200	1492–3
2.4.220	1514
2.4.240	1536
2.4.260	1558–9
2.4.280	1580
2.4.300	1603
3.1.1	1616
3.1.20	1629
3.1.40	1638 + 11
3.2.1	1656
3.2.20	1675
3.2.40	1692
3.2.60	1713–4
3.2.80	1735
3.3.1	1753
3.3.20	1770
3.4.1	1778
3.4.20	1800
3.4.40	1820–1
3.4.60	1840–1
3.4.80	1860
3.4.100	1880
3.4.120	1900
3.4.140	1919
3.4.160	1939
3.4.180	1964
3.5.1	1971
3.5.20	1990
3.6.1	1998
3.6.20	2014 + 4
3.6.40	2014 + 24
3.6.60	2018
3.6.80	2036–7
3.6.100	2056 + 3
3.7.1	2060
3.7.20	2079–80
3.7.40	2106
3.7.60	2132
3.7.80	2154
3.7.100	2176 + 2
4.1.1	2179
4.1.20	2201
4.1.40	2226–7
4.1.60	2248 + 2
4.2.1	2268
4.2.20	2288
4.2.40	2303 + 9
4.2.60	2309
4.2.80	2325
4.3.1	2347 + 1
4.3.20	2347 + 20
4.3.40	2347 + 40
4.4.1	2351
4.4.20	2371–3
4.5.1	2384–5
4.5.20	2406
4.5.40	2427–8
4.6.1	2431
4.6.20	2455
4.6.40	2479
4.6.60	2502
4.6.80	2525–7
4.6.100	2546–7
4.6.120	2564–5
4.6.140	2584
4.6.160	2603–4
4.6.180	2622
4.6.200	2642
4.6.220	2667
4.6.240	2693
4.6.260	2713
4.6.280	2734
4.7.1	2745–6
4.7.20	2772
4.7.40	2789
4.7.60	2815–6
4.7.80	2838–9
5.1.1	2847
5.1.20	2865
5.1.40	2884
5.1.60	2907
5.2.1	2921
5.3.1	2940
5.3.20	2961
5.3.40	2983
5.3.60	2999
5.3.80	3024–5
5.3.100	3048
5.3.120	3071
5.3.140	3094
5.3.160	3117–8
5.3.180	3142
5.3.200	3162–3
5.3.220	3168 + 15
5.3.240	3195–6
5.3.260	3219
5.3.280	3244
5.3.300	3271
5.3.320	3294

OTH

1.1.1	4
1.1.20	22
1.1.40	43–4
1.1.60	66
1.1.80	87
1.1.100	110
1.1.120	133
1.1.140	153–4
1.1.160	176
1.1.180	198
1.2.1	204
1.2.20	224
1.2.40	249
1.2.60	277–8
1.2.80	298
1.3.1	325
1.3.20	350
1.3.40	371
1.3.60	397
1.3.80	419
1.3.100	441
1.3.120	463–4
1.3.140	485
1.3.160	505
1.3.180	526–7
1.3.200	549
1.3.220	568
1.3.240	588–9
1.3.260	610
1.3.280	631
1.3.300	653
1.3.320	673
1.3.340	692–3
1.3.360	711–2
1.3.380	727 + 4
1.3.400	746
2.1.1	753
2.1.20	774
2.1.40	796–7
2.1.60	820
2.1.80	844
2.1.100	869
2.1.120	893–4
2.1.140	915
2.1.160	935
2.1.180	955
2.1.200	981–2
2.1.220	1003
2.1.240	1022–3
2.1.260	1042
2.1.280	1061–2
2.1.300	1083
2.2.1	1098–9
2.3.1	1111
2.3.20	1132
2.3.40	1151
2.3.60	1173
2.3.80	1192
2.3.100	1212
2.3.120	1231–2
2.3.140	1255
2.3.160	1277
2.3.180	1299
2.3.200	1319
2.3.220	1340–1
2.3.240	1361
2.3.260	1384
2.3.280	1404
2.3.300	1423
2.3.320	1443–4
2.3.340	1466
2.3.360	1486
2.3.380	1508
3.1.1	1519
3.1.20	1538
3.1.40	1559–60
3.2.1	1581
3.3.1	1590
3.3.20	1612
3.3.40	1634–5
3.3.60	1659
3.3.80	1680
3.3.100	1704
3.3.120	1728
3.3.140	1751
3.3.160	1774
3.3.180	1796
3.3.200	1816
3.3.220	1843
3.3.240	1869–70
3.3.260	1891
3.3.280	1913
3.3.300	1936
3.3.320	1960
3.3.340	1983
3.3.360	2003
3.3.380	2025
3.3.400	2048
3.3.420	2067
3.3.440	2090
3.3.460	2110
3.3.480	2135
3.4.1	2138
3.4.20	2157
3.4.40	2183
3.4.60	2208
3.4.80	2230
3.4.100	2252
3.4.120	2275
3.4.140	2297
3.4.160	2317
3.4.180	2340–1
3.4.200	2366
4.1.1	2371–3
4.1.20	2392
4.1.40	2416–7
4.1.60	2439–40
4.1.80	2462
4.1.100	2485
4.1.120	2506–8
4.1.140	2525
4.1.160	2545–6
4.1.180	2565
4.1.200	2586
4.1.220	2609
4.1.240	2634
4.1.260	2658
4.1.280	2683
4.2.1	2688
4.2.20	2709
4.2.40	2733–4
4.2.60	2755
4.2.80	2776
4.2.100	2801
4.2.120	2827
4.2.140	2852
4.2.160	2874
4.2.180	2896–7
4.2.200	2917
4.2.220	2938
4.2.240	2959
4.3.1	2968
4.3.20	2989
4.3.40	3011
4.3.60	3030
4.3.80	3053
4.3.100	3073
5.1.1	3082–3
5.1.20	3102
5.1.40	3130
5.1.60	3157
5.1.80	3181
5.1.100	3205
5.1.120	3226
5.2.1	3240
5.2.20	3260
5.2.40	3286–7
5.2.60	3312
5.2.80	3337
5.2.100	3363
5.2.120	3388
5.2.140	3411
5.2.160	3436
5.2.180	3460
5.2.200	3487–8
5.2.220	3510
5.2.240	3537
5.2.260	3560
5.2.280	3580
5.2.300	3604
5.2.320	3628–9
5.2.340	3650
5.2.360	3672

ANT

1.1.1	4
1.1.20	30
1.1.40	51–2
1.1.60	74–5
1.2.1	80
1.2.20	99
1.2.40	118
1.2.60	136–7
1.2.80	159–61
1.2.100	187–8
1.2.120	215–6
1.2.140	238–9
1.2.160	259
1.2.180	280
1.3.1	299–300
1.3.20	325
1.3.40	351
1.3.60	372
1.3.80	396–7
1.3.100	421
1.4.1	430
1.4.20	450
1.4.40	472–3
1.4.60	496
1.4.80	518
1.5.1	524
1.5.20	547
1.5.40	569
1.5.60	591
2.1.1	616
2.1.20	640
2.1.40	664
2.2.1	679
2.2.20	704
2.2.40	729–30
2.2.60	751
2.2.80	771
2.2.100	794
2.2.120	817–8
2.2.140	839–40
2.2.160	866
2.2.180	891
2.2.200	912
2.2.220	934
2.2.240	957
2.3.1	964–5
2.3.20	984
2.3.40	1006
2.4.1	1012–3
2.5.1	1025
2.5.20	1048
2.5.40	1073
2.5.60	1100
2.5.80	1126
2.5.100	1153
2.6.1	1178
2.6.20	1199
2.6.40	1225–6
2.6.60	1251
2.6.80	1276
2.6.100	1298
2.6.120	1316–7
2.7.1	1335
2.7.20	1357
2.7.40	1379
2.7.60	1401
2.7.80	1426
2.7.100	1449–50
2.7.120	1474
3.1.1	1496
3.1.20	1517
3.2.1	1539
3.2.20	1561
3.2.40	1584
3.2.60	1609
3.3.1	1621–2
3.3.20	1647
3.3.40	1673
3.4.1	1685
3.4.20	1705–6
3.5.1	1727
3.5.20	1746
3.6.1	1752
3.6.20	1771–2
3.6.40	1794
3.6.60	1815–6
3.6.80	1838
3.7.1	1859
3.7.20	1882–3
3.7.40	1907–8
3.7.60	1930–2
3.7.80	1958–9
3.8.1	1961
3.9.1	1969
3.10.1	1977
3.10.20	2001
3.11.1	2024
3.11.20	2044
3.11.40	2065
3.11.60	2088
3.12.1	2108
3.12.20	2132
3.13.1	2153–4
3.13.20	2176
3.13.40	2198
3.13.60	2223–5
3.13.80	2248
3.13.100	2274
3.13.120	2297
3.13.140	2320
3.13.160	2343
3.13.180	2365
3.13.200	2388
4.1.1	2391
4.2.1	2411–2
4.2.20	2437
4.2.40	2461
4.3.1	2468
4.3.20	2498
4.4.1	2503–4
4.4.20	2529
4.5.1	2553
4.6.1	2577
4.6.20	2601
4.7.1	2623
4.8.1	2649–50
4.8.20	2673
4.9.1	2695
4.9.20	2717
4.10.1	2737
4.11.1	2748
4.12.1	2754–5
4.12.20	2776
4.12.40	2799
4.13.1	2810
4.14.1	2824–5
4.14.20	2847
4.14.40	2873
4.14.60	2895
4.14.80	2917–8
4.14.100	2942
4.14.120	2973
4.14.140	2995
4.15.1	2998
4.15.20	3024
4.15.40	3048–9
4.15.60	3072
4.15.80	3095
5.1.1	3110
5.1.20	3133
5.1.40	3157
5.1.60	3179–80
5.2.1	3201
5.2.20	3223
5.2.40	3247
5.2.60	3269
5.2.80	3297
5.2.100	3320–1
5.2.120	3346–7
5.2.140	3368
5.2.160	3390
5.2.180	3412
5.2.200	3440
5.2.220	3463
5.2.240	3490
5.2.260	3511
5.2.280	3531
5.2.300	3551–2
5.2.320	3575–6
5.2.340	3605–7
5.2.360	3630

CYM

1.1.1	4–5
1.1.20	27
1.1.40	49
1.1.60	69
1.1.80	95–6
1.1.100	117
1.1.120	141
1.1.140	170
1.1.160	199–200
1.2.1	227
1.2.20	242
1.2.40	260
1.3.1	264
1.3.20	288
1.3.40	311–2
1.4.1	316
1.4.20	333–4
1.4.40	354
1.4.60	373–4
1.4.80	394
1.4.100	415
1.4.120	435
1.4.140	456
1.4.160	474–5
1.5.1	490–1
1.5.20	512
1.5.40	537
1.5.60	560
1.5.80	580
1.6.1	593
1.6.20	615
1.6.40	637
1.6.60	661
1.6.80	686
1.6.100	712
1.6.120	735
1.6.140	758
1.6.160	778
1.6.180	800

1.6.200	824
2.1.1	840
2.1.20	857–8
2.1.40	877
2.1.60	896
2.2.1	904–5
2.2.20	927
2.2.40	947
2.3.1	962
2.3.20	982
2.3.40	1001–2
2.3.60	1025
2.3.80	1050
2.3.100	1074
2.3.120	1096
2.3.140	1120
2.4.1	1144
2.4.20	1165
2.4.40	1192
2.4.60	1217
2.4.80	1243–4
2.4.100	1269–70
2.4.120	1294
2.4.140	1318
2.5.1	1338
2.5.20	1358
3.1.1	1377
3.1.20	1399
3.1.40	1418
3.1.60	1438
3.1.80	1460–1
3.2.1	1469
3.2.20	1488
3.2.40	1509
3.2.60	1528
3.2.80	1550
3.3.1	1555
3.3.20	1576
3.3.40	1597
3.3.60	1618
3.3.80	1640
3.3.100	1661
3.4.1	1671
3.4.20	1691
3.4.40	1711
3.4.60	1732
3.4.80	1754
3.4.100	1775–6
3.4.120	1802
3.4.140	1827–8
3.4.160	1850
3.4.180	1873
3.5.1	1891–2
3.5.20	1916
3.5.40	1938
3.5.60	1964
3.5.80	1988
3.5.100	2013–4
3.5.120	2035–6
3.5.140	2056–7
3.5.160	2077
3.6.1	2082
3.6.20	2101
3.6.40	2125
3.6.60	2150
3.6.80	2176–7
3.7.1	2198
4.1.1	2219
4.1.20	2237–8
4.2.1	2246
4.2.20	2269
4.2.40	2294
4.2.60	2323

4.2.80	2348–9
4.2.100	2378
4.2.120	2404
4.2.140	2426
4.2.160	2451
4.2.180	2474
4.2.200	2503
4.2.220	2530
4.2.240	2553
4.2.260	2579
4.2.280	2599
4.2.300	2622
4.2.320	2642
4.2.340	2664
4.2.360	2688
4.2.380	2712
4.2.400	2732
4.3.1	2738
4.3.20	2759
4.3.40	2783
4.4.1	2792–3
4.4.20	2816
4.4.40	2839
5.1.1	2858
5.1.20	2877
5.2.1	2898
5.3.1	2926
5.3.20	2948
5.3.40	2968
5.3.60	2990
5.3.80	3011
5.4.1	3034–5
5.4.20	3055
5.4.40	3081
5.4.60	3101
5.4.80	3115
5.4.100	3136
5.4.120	3157
5.4.140	3177–8
5.4.160	3198–9
5.4.180	3218–9
5.4.200	3239–40
5.5.1	3250
5.5.20	3274
5.5.40	3298–9
5.5.60	3320
5.5.80	3344
5.5.100	3365–6
5.5.120	3392–3
5.5.140	3417–8
5.5.160	3439
5.5.180	3461
5.5.200	3481
5.5.220	3502
5.5.240	3527
5.5.260	3550–1
5.5.280	3577
5.5.300	3600–1
5.5.320	3628–9
5.5.340	3652
5.5.360	3674
5.5.380	3700
5.5.400	3721
5.5.420	3746–7
5.5.440	3770
5.5.460	3792
5.5.480	3813

PER

1.CH.1	2
1.CH.20	21
1.CH.40	41
1.1.1	45
1.1.20	65
1.1.40	85
1.1.60	105
1.1.80	126
1.1.100	146
1.1.120	166
1.1.140	187
1.1.160	213–4
1.2.1	224
1.2.20	243
1.2.40	264
1.2.60	284
1.2.80	305
1.2.100	326
1.2.120	344
1.3.1	350
1.3.20	372
1.4.1	391
1.4.20	411
1.4.40	431
1.4.60	451–2
1.4.80	470–1
1.4.100	491
2.CH.1	501
2.CH.20	526
2.CH.40	546
2.1.1	548
2.1.20	568
2.1.40	590–1
2.1.60	609
2.1.80	627–8
2.1.100	644
2.1.120	663
2.1.140	683
2.1.160	702
2.2.1	709
2.2.20	729
2.2.40	749–50
2.3.1	770
2.3.20	788
2.3.40	810
2.3.60	831
2.3.80	849
2.3.100	869
2.4.1	887
2.4.20	908
2.4.40	929
2.5.1	950
2.5.20	968
2.5.40	990
2.5.60	1011
2.5.80	1031
3.CH.1	1046
3.CH.20	1071
3.CH.40	1091
3.CH.60	1111
3.1.1	1113
3.1.20	1133
3.1.40	1156
3.1.60	1176
3.1.80	1196
3.2.1	1199
3.2.20	1219–20
3.2.40	1238
3.2.60	1261
3.2.80	1281–2
3.2.100	1300–1
3.3.1	1314
3.3.20	1331–2
3.3.40	1351–2
3.4.1	1355
4.CH.1	1371
4.CH.20	1390
4.CH.40	1410
4.1.1	1424
4.1.20	1442
4.1.40	1460
4.1.60	1481
4.1.80	1498–9
4.1.100	1517–8
4.2.1	1523
4.2.20	1540
4.2.40	1562
4.2.60	1578–9
4.2.80	1597–8
4.2.100	1616–7
4.2.120	1635–6
4.2.140	1655–6
4.3.1	1669
4.3.20	1685–6
4.3.40	1705
4.4.1	1717
4.4.20	1739
4.4.40	1763
4.5.1	1777
4.6.1	1787
4.6.20	1804
4.6.40	1821
4.6.60	1839
4.6.80	1857
4.6.100	1876
4.6.120	1894–5
4.6.140	1913–4
4.6.160	1930–1
4.6.180	1946–7
4.6.200	1963–4
5.CH.1	1966
5.CH.20	1985
5.1.1	1991
5.1.20	2010
5.1.40	2024–5
5.1.60	2041
5.1.80	2063–4
5.1.100	2081
5.1.120	2101–2
5.1.140	2118–9
5.1.160	2140–1
5.1.180	2159
5.1.200	2178
5.1.220	2194–5
5.1.240	2213–4
5.1.260	2229
5.2.1	2236
5.2.20	2255
5.3.1	2256
5.3.20	2275–6
5.3.40	2295–6
5.3.60	2315–6
5.3.80	2334
5.3.100	2356

TNK

PR.1	2
PR.20	21
1.1.1	47
1.1.20	66
1.1.40	93
1.1.60	114
1.1.80	136
1.1.100	155
1.1.120	180
1.1.140	201–2
1.1.160	227
1.1.180	251
1.1.200	273–4
1.1.220	295–6
1.2.1	314
1.2.20	334
1.2.40	357
1.2.60	378
1.2.80	402
1.2.100	425
1.3.1	447
1.3.20	470
1.3.40	493
1.3.60	516
1.3.80	536
1.4.1	561–2
1.4.20	583
1.4.40	606
1.5.1	619
2.1.1	638
2.1.20	660
2.1.40	679–80
2.2.1	699–700
2.2.20	721
2.2.40	742
2.2.60	763
2.2.80	785
2.2.100	806
2.2.120	832
2.2.140	865
2.2.160	896–8
2.2.180	922
2.2.200	949–51
2.2.220	975–6
2.2.240	999
2.2.260	1023–4
2.3.1	1051
2.3.20	1070
2.3.40	1094
2.3.60	1117–8
2.3.80	1146
2.4.1	1150
2.4.20	1169
2.5.1	1185
2.5.20	1213
2.5.40	1238
2.5.60	1263
2.6.1	1270
2.6.20	1289
3.1.1	1311
3.1.20	1330
3.1.40	1353
3.1.60	1376
3.1.80	1399
3.1.100	1424–5
3.1.120	1452
3.2.1	1457
3.2.20	1476
3.3.1	1496
3.3.20	1521–3
3.3.40	1549
3.4.1	1569
3.4.20	1588
3.5.1	1597
3.5.20	1610–1
3.5.40	1636–7
3.5.60	1659–60
3.5.80	1680
3.5.100	1705
3.5.120	1725
3.5.140	1745
3.6.1	1767
3.6.20	1789
3.6.40	1811
3.6.60	1842–3
3.6.80	1871
3.6.100	1897
3.6.120	1922
3.6.140	1948
3.6.160	1971
3.6.180	1991
3.6.200	2015
3.6.220	2039
3.6.240	2061
3.6.260	2082
3.6.280	2105–6
3.6.300	2130–1
4.1.1	2145
4.1.20	2168
4.1.40	2198
4.1.60	2224
4.1.80	2246
4.1.100	2267
4.1.120	2295–6
4.1.140	2320–1
4.2.1	2345
4.2.20	2364
4.2.40	2384
4.2.60	2408
4.2.80	2437
4.2.100	2459
4.2.120	2481–2
4.2.140	2504
4.3.1	2526
4.3.20	2544–5
4.3.40	2563
4.3.60	2580
4.3.80	2600–1
4.3.100	2620–1
5.1.1	2625
5.1.20	2649
5.1.40	2674
5.1.60	2694
5.1.80	2719
5.1.100	2739
5.1.120	2759
5.1.140	2788
5.1.160	2808
5.2.1	2829
5.2.20	2856–7
5.2.40	2883
5.2.60	2910
5.2.80	2938
5.2.100	2968–70
5.3.1	2996–7
5.3.20	3020–1
5.3.40	3046
5.3.60	3068
5.3.80	3093
5.3.100	3119
5.3.120	3143
5.3.140	3164
5.4.1	3175
5.4.20	3196
5.4.40	3226
5.4.60	3250
5.4.80	3270
5.4.100	3294
5.4.120	3316
EP.1	3335

Corrigenda

The following changes—in the main, slight stylistic modifications—were received too late for inclusion.

AN* *for* AN'	AWW 1.3.249
ARM'S *for* ARMS'	TGV 5.4.57
BE'ST *for* BEEST	TMP 2.2.103; 5.1.111
	AYL 3.2.83
BROTHERS' *for* BROTHER'S	HAM 5.2.253
add BUT	AYL 2.7.127
BUT *for* /NOT	COR 3.3.130
COUNCILLOR *for* COUNSELLOR	TMP 1.1.21
ENNEMIE *for* ENEMY	H5 5.2.169
ENTITULED *for* INTITULED	LUC 57
HATH *for* 'HATH	TNK 1.4.43
add I*	AYL 3.5.100
INTITLED *for* ENTITLED	SON 37.7
LEGEND *for* /LEGION	WIV 1.3.53
LONG-INGRAFF'D *for* LONG-ENGRAFF'D	LR 1.1.297
MAJESTEE *for* MAJESTY	H5 5.2.264
MARY *for* MARRY*	H5 3.2.104, 118
/OFF *for* OFF	ERR 2.2.136
delete ON	COR 5.3.125
QUEST *for* /QUESTS	MM 4.1.61
SATE* *for* SAT	MND 2.2.150; AYL 2.7.115
	AWW 4.3.101; TN 2.4.114
	2H6 1.2.36
SCATHE *for* SCATH	R3 1.3.316
/SIR *for* SIR	AYL 5.1.37
STRIFE *for* /SUIT	ROM 2.2.152
TEACHY *for* TETCHY	TRO 1.1.96
TEACHY *for* TECHY	ROM 1.3.32
/TERRESTIAL *for* /TERRESTRIAL	WIV 3.1.106
TH'* *for* THE	H5 3.2.116
THIS' *for* THIS	WT 5.3.149
TO *for* AND	ROM 4.2.21
WE'N'SDAY *for* WE'NSDAY	Throughout
YES *for* NO	3H6 1.1.93
YOU *for* /THEE	OTH 4.1.216
YOU/'RE *for* /YOU'RE	PER 1.1.127